THE
SOURCEBOOK

To Public Record Information

*The Comprehensive Guide to County, State, & Federal
Public Records Sources*

Third Edition

BRB Publications, Inc.
www.brbpub.com

Dedicated to the Searching & Understanding of Public Records

Public Record Research Library

THE
SOURCEBOOK

To Public Record Information - Third Edition

Edited by: Pam Crittenden, Annette Talley, Peter J. Weber, and Michael Sankey

©2002 By BRB Publications, Inc.
1971 East Fifth Street, Suite 101
Tempe, AZ 85281
800-929-3811   Fax 800-929-4981

www.brbpub.com

ISBN 1-879792-64-8

The sourcebook to public record information : the
 comprehensive guide to county, state, & federal public
 records sources / [edited by Michael L. Sankey, Peter J.
 Weber, Pamela J. Crittenden]. – 3rd ed.
  p. cm.
  ISBN: 1-879792-64-8

 1. Public records--United States--States--Information
Services--Directories. 2. Courts--United States--States
--Directories. 3. Public records--United States--States
--Computer network resources.   I. Sankey, Michael L.,
1949- II. Weber, Peter J. (Peter Julius), 1952-
III. Crittenden, Pamela J.

JK468.P76S68 2001   352.3'87
                 QBI01-201153

Contents

Section II: Public Records by State   63

Introduction

Complex and Mysterious?

The access to and use of current public records is one of the fundamental pillars of our democratic society.

Yet, the words "Public Records" often convey a complex, almost mysterious source of information that is perceived as difficult to access, hard to decipher, and likely to be of interest only to private investigators and reporters.

This view could not be further from the truth!

Your Access to Over 20,000 Government Agencies

Herein, we will examine these paper trails that begin or are maintained at the federal, state, county, and in certain instances, the city and town level. This *Sourcebook* is especially useful for these applications:

    Legal Research

    Background Investigation

    Pre-Employment and Tenant Screening

    Locating People

    Locating Assets

    Skiptracing

    Genealogy

This *Sourcebook* reveals where records are kept, outlines the access requirements and gives searching hints, tells which agencies are online. Over 20,000 government agencies are profiled so you can explore the depths of the public record industry.

Public records are meant to be used for the benefit of society. As a member of the public, you or someone in authority is entitled to review the public records held by government agencies. Whether you are a business owner, a reporter, an investigator, or even a father trying to check on your daughter's first date, you can access public records to meet your needs.

Equipped with the information contained in these pages, you can find the facts, gain access to the information you need, and even track your own "information trail!"

Special Note From the Editors

The Third Edition *of The Sourcebook to Public Record Information* represents thousands of hours of research right up to the day of printing. We have compiled what we feel is the most up-to-date and unique compendium of its kind.

This year's edition contains an enormous amount of new information in the *Recording Offices* section of each state chapter. This additional information includes:

- statement regarding searching real estate record records

- statement regarding searching Uniform Commercial Code (UCC) records

- statement regarding searching state and federal tax lien records

- 5,501 additional agency phone numbers (assessor, treasurer, elections, etc.)

For those of you who need to know more or need to have this information constantly updated, we recommend two expanded versions of this product. *The Public Records Research System* (PRRS) is available on CD-ROM with semi-annual updates or as a subscription service on the Internet at www.publicrecordsources.com.

BRB Publications is 100% devoted to the understanding of public records. We hope you find the *Sourcebook* a valuable asset for your business or use.

The editorial staff at BRB Publications—

Pam Crittenden

Annette Talley

Peter J. Weber

Michael Sankey

How This Book is Organized

General Layout

The Sourcebook is organized into two Sections--

1. Public Record Primer
2. 51 Individual State Chapters

The Public Record Primer

The purpose of *The Public Record Primer* section is to assist the reader in knowing *where categories of records can be found* and *how to search.* An important segment of this section is the discussion of privacy issues including public information vs. personal information and how records enter the public domain.

The Primer contains many searching hints and is an excellent overall source of information that will especially help those not familiar with searching government records.

The **Finding Federal Records Online** chapter contains an excellent article contributed by Alan Schlein, author of *Find it Online!* (Facts on Demand Press). Mr. Schlein presents a unique dissertation about the best federal government Internet sites for finding usual information quickly and efficiently.

Another important chapter is **Using a Vendor to Obtain Public Records.** This chapter contains a wealth of information about commercial public record vendors, especially those who offer online access to records.

The State Chapters

The individual state chapters in the *Sourcebook* have been compiled into an easy to use format.

Six sub-chapters or sections are presented in this order:

1. State Public Record Agencies
2. State Licensing and Regulatory Boards
3. Federal Courts (US District and Bankruptcy)
4. County Courts
5. County Recorder Offices
6. County Locator

Information Found in the Agency Profiles

The depth of knowledge presented about each government agency is what separates this *Sourcebook* from a typical address and phone listing reference book. The beginning of each state and/or county sub-chapter has an overall discussion of the public records policies, with important characteristics and searching hints.

The following details are have been researched and presented (when applicable) within each profile:

- **Agency Facts**: office hours; time zone; web sites.

- **Searching Facts**: methods of access; indexing; search requirements; if records are available online; when free public access terminals are at the counter; turnaround times, how far back (years) records are kept.

- **Privacy Facts**: restrictions that the agencies impose on searchers or types of searchers; when signed releases or notarized statements are required.

- **Fees**: access fees, copy fees; certification fees; expedited fees, if credit cards accepted; what types of checks accepted; to whom to make the check payable to.

- **Misc:** how to purchase databases or customized lists; if the more than one agency must be visited in the county to get all records; if results will or will not be returned by fax, etc.

Using The County Locator

The County Locator portion of each state chapter is extremely useful when it is unclear which county to perform a localized record search. This section contains two cross reference indices. The City/County Cross Reference will indicate what county(s) in which a "place" (city or town) is located. There are over 40,000 places referenced. The ZIP Code/City Cross Reference assists those people who have an address with ZIP Code, but are unsure in which county the ZIP in located.

Section I
Public Record Primer

Public Records Unveiled

Definition of Public Records

The strict **definition** of **public records** is—

> *"Those records maintained by government agencies*
> *that are open without restriction to public inspection,*
> *either by statute or by tradition."*

If access to a record that is held by a government agency is restricted in some way, then it is not a public record.

Accessibility Paradox

Adding to the mystique of government records is the accessibility paradox. For example, in some states a specific category of records is severely restricted, and therefore those records are not "public," while the very same category of records may be 100% open in other states. Among these categories are criminal histories, vehicle ownership records and worker's compensation records.

At times, you will see the following box printed on pages throughout the *Sourcebook*. We are not trying to fill up space. As your public record searching takes you from state-to-state, this is the one important adage to keep in mind.

> "Just because records are maintained in a certain way in
> your state or county, do not assume that any other county or
> state does things the same way you are used to."

Public vs. Private vs. Personal

Before reading further, let's define types of records held by government or by private industry. Of course, not all information about a company or individual is public. The boundaries between public and private information are not well understood, and continually undergo intense scrutiny. The following is an introduction to the subject from a viewpoint of a professional record searcher.

Public Record

Public records are records of **incidents** or **actions** filed or recorded with a government agency for the purpose of notifying others about the matter—the "public." The **deed** to your house recorded at the county recorder's office is a public record—it is a legal requirement that you record with the county recorder. Anyone requiring details about your property may review or copy the documents.

Public Information

Your **telephone listing** in the phone book is public information; that is, you freely furnished the information to ease the flow of commercial and private communications.

Personal Information

Any information about a person or business that the person or business might consider private and confidential in nature, such as your **Social Security Number**, is personal information. Such information will remain private to a limited extent unless it is disclosed to some outside entity that could make it public. **Personal information may be found in either public records or in public information.**

How Personal Information Enters the Public Domain

Many people confuse the three categories above, lump them into one and wonder how "big brother" accumulated so much information about them. Therefore, these distinctions are important. The reality is that **much of this information is given willingly**.

Actually, there are two ways that personal information can enter the public domain—statutory and voluntary. In a **voluntary** transaction, you **share** personal information of your own free will. In a **statutory** transaction, you **disclose** personal information because the law requires you to.

The confusion of terms used today feeds the increasing conflict between privacy advocates and commercial interests. This, in turn, is driving legislation towards more and more **restrictions** on the **dissemination of personal information**—the same personal information that, in fact, is willingly shared by most people and companies in order to participate in our market economy.

Where Public Records are Held

There are two places you can find public records—

1. at a government agency
2. within the database of a private company

Government agencies maintain records in a variety of ways. While many state agencies and highly populated county agencies are computerized, many others use microfiche, microfilm, and paper to store files and indexes. Agencies that have converted to computer will not necessarily place complete file records on their system; they are more apt to include only an index, pointer or summary data to the files.

Private enterprises develop their databases in one of two ways: they buy the records in bulk from government agencies; or they send personnel to the agencies and compile this information by using a copy machine or keying information into a laptop computer. The database is then available for internal use or for resale purposes. An example of such a company is *Superior Information* (800 848-0489). Superior maintains a very comprehensive database of civil judgments, tax liens, Uniform Commercial Code filings and bankruptcy data gathered from the Mid-Atlantic States.

The Common Methods Used to Access Public Records

The following is a look at the various methods available to access public records.

Visit in Person

This is easy if you live close by. Many courthouses and recorders offices have free access terminals open to the public. Certain records, such as corporate or UCC records generally found at the Secretary of State, can be viewed or pulled for free, but will incur a fee for copies. A signed release is a common requirement for accessing motor vehicle and criminal records.

Mail, Fax, or Telephone

Although some agencies permit phone or fax requests, the majority of agencies prefer mail requests. Some agencies consider fax requesting an expedited service that incurs higher fees. Agencies that permit telephone requests may merely answer "Yes" or "No" to questions such as "Does John Doe have a civil court case in his name?" We have indicated when telephone and fax requesting is available, as well as the extent of the service.

Online and the Internet

The Internet may be a free means to certain agency records or may be the conduit to a subscription or commercial site. This commercial online access method of public records is much more prevalent at the state level compared to the county level. Many agencies, such as DMVs, make the information available to pre-approved, high volume, ongoing accounts. Typically, this access involves fees and a specified, minimum amount of usage.

However, there is a definite trend of certain agencies posting public record data on the Internet for free. Two examples are Secretary of State offices (whose records include corporation, UCC and tax liens) and county/city tax assessor offices (whose records reveal property ownership). Usually this information is limited to name indexes and summary data, rather than document images. In addition, a growing number of state licensing boards are posting their membership lists on the net (although addresses and phone numbers of the licensed individuals typically are not listed).

Also, the Internet is a good place to find *general* information about government agencies. Many web sites enable one to download, read and/or print current forms, policies and regulations.

Hire Someone Else

As mentioned above, one method to access public records is from a vendor. These companies must comply with state and federal laws, thus if the government agency will not a release a record, chances are a vendor company will not either. There are a variety of types of companies that can be hired to perform record searches. An excellent, quick source to find the right vendor for a particular need is www.publicrecordsources.com or *The National Directory of Public Record Vendors*.

Bulk or Database Purchases

Many agencies offer programs to purchase all or parts of their database for statistical or commercial purposes. The restrictions vary widely from state to state, even within the same record type or category. Typically, records are available (to those who qualify) in the following media types; magnetic tapes, cartridges, paper printouts, labels, disks, CDs, microfiche and/or microfilm. Throughout the individual state chapters, we have indicated where these bulk purchases are available, to whom, and for what purposes as well as the costs involved.

Using the Freedom of Information Act and Other Acts

The Federal Freedom of Information Act has no bearing on state, county or local government agencies because these agencies are subject to that state's individual act. Further, the government agencies profiled in this book generally already have systems in place to release information and the act is not needed. However, if you are trying to obtain records from agencies beyond the scope of this book, there are many useful Internet sites that will give you the information you need to complete such a request. We can recommend these sites:

www.epic.org/open_gov/rights.html

http://spj.org/foia

Public Record & Public Information Categories

The following descriptions of the record categories fall into our definitions of either "public records" or "public information."

In considering these definitions, keep the following points in mind:

♦ Very little government record information is truly open to the public. Even presumably harmless information is subject to restrictions somewhere in the US. Likewise items that you believe should be highly confidential are probably considered "public information" in one or more states.

♦ Just because your state or county has certain rules, regulations and practices regarding the accessibility and content of public records does not mean that any other state or county follows the same rules.

Business Records

Corporation Records (found at the state level)

Checking to see if a corporation is incorporated is considered a **"status check."** The information that results from a status check typically includes the date of incorporation, status, type, registered agent and, sometimes, officers or directors. This is a good way to find the start of a paper trail and/or to find affiliates of the subject of your search. Some states permit status checks over the telephone.

If available, articles of incorporation (or amendments to them) as well as copies of annual reports may also provide useful information about a business or business owner. However, corporate records may *not* be a good source for a business address because most states allow corporations to use a registered agent as their address for service of process.

Partnership Records (found at the state level)

Some state statutes require registration of certain kinds of partnerships at the state level. Sometimes, these partner names and addresses may be available from the same office that handles corporation records. Some states have a department created specifically to administer limited partnerships and the records associated with them. These filings provide a wealth of information about other partners. Such information can be used to uncover other businesses that may be registered as well.

Limited Liability Companies (found at state level)

A newer form of business entity, similar to a corporation but has the favorable tax characteristics of a partnership, is known as the Limited Liability Company (LLC). An LLC is legal in most every state. An offspring of this, which many states now permit, is the Limited Liability Partnership (LLP).

Trademark & Trade Name (found at state or county levels)

"Trade names" and "trademarks" are relative terms. A trademark may be known as a "service mark." Trade names may be referred to as "fictitious names," "assumed names," or "DBAs." States (or counties) will not let two entities register and use the same (or close to the same) name or trademark

Typically, the agency that oversees corporation records usually maintains the files for trademarks and/or trade names. Most states will allow verbal status checks of names or worded marks. Some states will administer "fictitious names" at the state level while county agencies administer "trade names," or vice versa.

Sales Tax Registrations (found at state level)

Any individual or firm that sells applicable goods or services to an end-user, is required to register with the appropriate state agency. Such registration is necessary to collect applicable sales tax on the goods and services, and to ensure remittance of those taxes to the state.

45 states collect some sort of sales tax on a variety of goods and services. Of these, 38 will at the very least confirm that a tax permit exists. Each sales tax registrant is given a special state tax permit number, which may be called by various names, including tax ID number or seller's permit number. These numbers are not to be confused with the federal employer identification number.

SEC & Other Financial Data

The Federal Securities and Exchange Commission (SEC) is the public repository for information about publicly held companies. These companies are required to share their material facts with existing and prospective stockholders. See page 33 for information about the SEC database EDGAR.

Private companies, on the other hand, are not subject to public scrutiny. Their financial information is public information only to the extent that the company itself decides to disclose information.

Lien and Security Interest Records

Uniform Commercial Code (found at state and county or city levels)

All 50 states and the District of Columbia have passed a version of the model Uniform Commercial Code (UCC). UCC filings are used to record liens in financing transactions such as equipment loans, leases, inventory loans, and accounts receivable financing. Revised Article 9 (see pages 49-51) of the Code covers security interests in personal property. The Code allows potential lenders to be notified that certain assets of a debtor are already used to secure a loan or lease. *Therefore, examining UCC filings is an excellent way to find bank accounts, security interests, financiers, and assets.*

Prior to July 2001, of the 7.5 million new UCC financing statements filed annually, 2.5 million were filed at the state level; 5 million were filed at the local level. Although there are significant variations among state statutes, the state level is usually a good starting place to uncover liens filed against an individual or business.

Tax Liens (found at state and county or city levels)

The federal government and every state have some sort of taxes, such as those associated with sales, income, withholding, unemployment, and/or personal property. When these taxes go unpaid, the appropriate state agency can file a lien on the real or personal property of the subject. *Normally, the state agency that maintains UCC records also maintains tax liens.*

Individuals vs. Businesses

Tax liens filed against individuals are frequently maintained at separate locations from those liens filed against businesses. For example, a large number of states require liens filed against businesses to be filed at a central state location (i.e., Secretary of State's office) and liens against individuals to be filed at the county level (i.e., Recorder, Register of Deeds, Clerk of Court, etc.).

State vs. Federal Liens

Liens on a company may not all be filed in the same location. A federal tax lien will not necessarily be filed (recorded) at the same location/jurisdiction as a lien filed by the state. This holds true for both individual liens and as well as business liens filed against personal property. Typically, state tax liens on personal property will be found where UCCs are filed. *Tax liens on real property will be found where real property deeds are recorded,* with few exceptions. Unsatisfied state and federal tax liens may be renewed if prescribed by individual state statutes. However, once satisfied, the time the record will remain in the repository before removal varies by jurisdiction.

Real Estate and Tax Assessor (found at county and local levels)

Traditionally, real estate records are public so that everyone can know who owns what property. Liens on real estate must be public so a buyer knows all the facts. The county (or parish) recorder's office is the record source. However, many private companies purchase entire county record databases and create their own database for commercial purposes.

This category of public record is perhaps the fastest growing in regards to freely accessible over the Internet. We have indicated all the recorder offices that offer web **name queries;** many more offer location searches (using maps and parcel numbers to locate an address).

Bankruptcies (found at federal court level)

This entails case information about people and businesses that have filed for protection under the bankruptcy laws of the United States. Only federal courts handle bankruptcy cases. Some private companies compile databases with names and dates. Many types of financial records maintained by government agencies are considered public records; bankruptcy records, unlike some other court records, are in this class of fully open court records.

Important Individual Records

Criminal Records (found at state level, county courts, and federal courts)

Every state has a central repository of major misdemeanor, felony arrest records and convictions. States submit criminal record activity to the National Crime Information Center (which is not open to the public). *Not all states open their criminal records to the public*. Of those states that *will* release records to the public, many require fingerprints or signed release forms. The information that *could be* disclosed on the report includes the arrest record, criminal charges, fines, sentencing and incarceration information.

In states where records are not released, the best places to search for criminal record activity is at the city or county level with the county or district court clerk. Many of these searches can be done with a phone call. For detailed information about criminal records, see *The Criminal Guide*.

Litigation & Civil Judgments (found at county, local, and federal courts)

Actions under federal laws are found at US District Courts. Actions under state laws are found within the state court system at the county level. Municipalities also have courts. Records of civil litigation case and records about judgments are often collected by commercial database vendors. For more information, please refer to the **County Court Records** chapter.

Motor Vehicle Records (found at state level, but, on occasion, accessible at county level)

The retrieval industry often refers to driving records as "MVRs." Typical information on an MVR might include full name, address, Social Security Number, physical description and date of birth along with the conviction and accident history. Also, the license type, restrictions and/or endorsements can provide background data on an individual.

In recent years there have been major changes regarding the release of motor vehicle data to the public. This is the result of the Driver's Privacy Protection Act (DPPA). States differentiate between *permissible users* (14 are designated in DPPA) and *casual requesters* to determine who may receive a record and/or how much personal information is reported on the record. Effective June 2000, (see below), if a state DMV chooses to sell a record to a "casual requester," the record can contain personal information (address, etc.) only with the consent of the subject.

Ironically, as states are moving towards making data readily available electronically, they are also closing the door to many users. Pay particular attention to the restriction requirements mentioned in this category throughout this publication. Also, we strongly urge those interested in further information about either driver or vehicle records to obtain BRB Publication's *The MVR Book*.

Vehicle & Vessel Ownership, Registration, VINs, Titles, & Liens (found at state and, on occasion, at county level)

State repositories of vehicle/vessel registration and ownership records hold a wide range of information. Generally, record requesters submit a name to uncover vehicle(s) owned or submit vehicle information to obtain an owner's name and address. However, this category of record information is also subject to the DPPA as described above.

The original language of DPPA required the states to offer an "opt out" option to drivers and vehicle owners, if they (the states) sold marketing lists or individual records to casual requesters (those requesters not specifically mentioned in DPPA). Public Law 106-69 reversed this. Effective June 1, 2000, states automatically opt out all individuals, unless the individual specifically asks to be included. While nearly all states have this "opt in" procedure in place, very few individuals request to be placed on marketing lists and such.

Passage of Public Law 106-69 was dramatic since it essentially did away with sales of:

- marketing lists;
- records (with addresses and other personal information) to "casual" requesters;
- record databases to information vendors and database compilers.

Accident Reports (found at state level or local level)

The State Police or Department of Public Safety usually maintains accident reports. For the purposes of this publication, "accident records" are designated as those prepared by the investigating officer. Copies of a *citizen's* accident report are not usually available to the public and are not mentioned here. Typical information found on a state accident report includes drivers' addresses and license numbers as well as a description of the incident. Accidents investigated by local officials or minor accidents where the damage does not exceed a reporting limit (such as $1,000), are not available from state agencies. Most state DMVs adhere to DPPA guidelines with regards to record requests.

Occupational Licensing & Business Registration (found at state boards)

Occupational licenses and business registrations contain a plethora of information readily available from various state agencies. A common reason to call these agencies is to corroborate professional or industry credentials. Often, a telephone call to the agency may secure an address and phone number.

GED Records (found at state level)

By contacting the state offices that oversee GED Records, one can verify whether someone truly received a GED certificate for the high school education equivalency. These records are useful for pre-employment screening or background checking purposes. Most state agencies will verify over the phone the existence of a GED certificate. Many even offer copies of transcripts free-of-charge. When doing a record search, you must know the name of the student at the time of the test and a general idea of the year and test location. GED Records are *not* useful when trying to locate an individual.

Hunting & Fishing Licenses (found at state, county & local levels)

We have singled out one type of state license that merits a closer look. When trying to locate an individual, state hunting and fishing license information can be very informative. Currently 37 states maintain a central repository of fishing and/or hunting license records that may be accessed in some capacity by the public. Although some of these record repositories are literally "in boxes in the basement," more and more are becoming computerized.

Effects of Cooperative State-Federal Program on Hunting/Fishing License Databases

In 1992, the US Fish and Wildlife Service implemented a Migratory Bird Harvest Information Program that changed state hunting licensing procedures. Under this cooperative program, that helps biologists better manage the Nation's migratory bird populations, hunters provide their names and addresses when buying state licenses to hunt migratory birds. The states then must provide the name and address information to the US Fish and Wildlife Service on a timely basis. As of today, all states except Hawaii participate. Each state has several options for how they provide the US Fish and Wildlife Service with the names and address of their hunters.

The policy of the US Service is to use the names and addresses only for conducting hunter surveys. All records of hunters' names and addresses are after the surveys, and no permanent records are maintained.

However, since the states collect these names and addresses under state authority, the state may decide not to delete the information. Therefore, as states began or continue to maintain new automated record repositories, the release of these records for investigative or search purposes depends upon individual "state sunshine laws." For more information about the federal program, contact the Office of Migratory Bird Management in Laurel, MD at 301-497-5980.

Workers' Compensation Records (found at state level)

Research at state workers' compensation boards is generally limited to determining if an employee has filed a claim and/or obtaining copies of the claim records themselves. With the passage of the Americans with Disabilities Act (ADA) in the early 1990s, using information from workers' compensation boards for pre-employment screening was virtually eliminated. However, *a review of workers' compensation histories may be conducted after a conditional job offer has been made* and when medical information is reviewed. The legality of performing this review is subject to individual state statutes, which vary widely.

Voter Registration (found at state & county levels)

Every state has a central election agency or commission, and most have a central repository of voter information. The degree or level of accessibility to these records varies widely from state to state. Over half of the states will sell portions of the registered voter database, but only ten states permit individual searching by name. Most states only allow access for political purposes such as "Get Out the Vote" campaigns or compilation of campaign contribution lists.

Voting Registration Records are a good place to find addresses and voting history. Nearly every state blocks the release of Social Security Numbers and telephone numbers found on these records. However, the records can generally be viewed at the local level.

Vital Records: Birth, Death, Marriage, & Divorce Records (found at state & county levels)

Copies of vital record certificates are needed for a variety of reasons—social security, jobs, passports, family history, litigation, lost heir searching, proof of identity, etc. Most states understand the urgency of these requests, and many offer an expedited service. *A number of states will even take requests over the phone if you use a credit card.* Searchers must also be aware that in many instances certain vital records are *not* kept at the state level. The searcher must then turn to city and county record repositories to find the information needed.

Most states offer expedited fax ordering, requiring the use of a credit card, through the services of an outside vendor known as VitalChek. This independent company maintains individual fax lines at each state office they service. Whether it is behind the scenes or not, ordering vital records by fax typically involves VitalChek in some manner. Go to www.vitalchek.com for more information.

Older vital records are usually found in the state archives. Another source of historical vital record information is the Family History Library of the Church of Jesus Christ of Latter Day Saints (located at 35 North West Temple, Salt Lake City 84150). They have millions of microfilmed records from church and civil registers from all over the world.

Credit Information and Social Security Numbers

Social Security Numbers

The Social Security Number is the subject of a persistent struggle between privacy rights groups and various business interests. The truth is that many individuals gave up the privacy of their number by writing it on a voter registration form, product registration form, or any of a myriad of other voluntary disclosures made over the years. It is probable that a good researcher can legally find the Social Security Number of anyone (along with at least an approximate birth date) with some ease.

Credit Information

Credit data is derived from financial transactions of people or businesses. **Private companies maintain this information; government only regulates access.** Certain credit information about individuals is restricted by law, such as the Fair Credit Reporting Act, at the federal level and by even more restrictive laws in many states. Recently, "credit header" information (see below) have been closed to most business entities. Credit information about businesses is not restricted by law and is fully open to anyone who requests (pays for) it.

Credit Header Ban Went Into Effect July 1st, 2001

July 1st was an important date for skiptracers, fraud investigators, and other businesses that rely on "credit headers." A credit header is essentially the upper portion of a credit report containing the Social Security Number, age, phone number, last several addresses, and any AKAs. This information has always been available without the consent of the individual (subject). Per a federal court ruling, beginning July 1st 2001, access to credit header information was treated in the same manner as access to credit reports—there has to be permission granted by the individual.

The basis of this ban is traced to the Gramm-Leach-Bliley Act. Section 502 of this act prohibits a financial institution from disclosing nonpublic personal information about a consumer to non-affiliated third parties, unless a consumer has elected not to opt out from disclosure. Trans Union and other members of the Individual References Services Group (IRSG), among others, filed suit in an effort to keep this information open for "appropriate commercial purposes." The ruling, dated April 30th, denied this argument. The sale of credit headers seemed to be on borrowed time anyway—originally, the ban was to begin November 2000. However, due to the lawsuits and action involving the FTC, a provision changed the start of the ban until July 1st, 2001.

Impact of Changes

The impact of the ruling (and an FTC opinion) was far ranging. The ruling restricted credit bureaus from selling the above-mentioned data to information vendors who compile their own proprietary databases. But there are some alternatives to those business entities that rely on this type of public record information. The data is grandfathered. Provider companies that purchased files from the credit bureaus can continue to sell the data to their customers. Although data will never be updated from the credit bureaus, the existing data can still be used without the restrictions imposed by the ruling.

According to our friends at Merlin Information Services, one of the credit bureaus is now in the process of creating a compliant "Super File" that will replace the credit header file. This new file is being creating from a "…public record databases, telephone listing files and postal change of address records."

The Gramm-Leach-Bliley Act did not deny access to public record sources or databases that may contain age, SSN, phone, prior addresses, and AKAs. The Act only forbid financial institutions from disclosing this data. Therefore, those businesses that were shut-off from credit headers, had to investigate alternative sources of public records. For example, there are over 150 private companies in the US that maintain a proprietary database of public records, see BRB Publication's *National Directory of Public Record Vendors.*

Additional Record Sources Worth Reviewing

State Legislation & Regulations

Telephone numbers, costs and procedures for obtaining copies of passed and pending bills are listed under the heading "Legislation." Most state legislative bodies offer free Internet access to bill text and status, some even offer subject queries. Notwithstanding federal guidelines, the state legislatures and legislators control the policies and provisions for the release of state held information. Every year there is a multitude of bills introduced in state legislatures that would, if passed, create major changes in the access and retrieval of records and personal information.

Education & Employment

Information about an employee's or prospective employee's schooling, training, education, and jobs is important to any employer. Learning institutions maintain their own records of attendance, completion and degree/certification granted. Also, employers will confirm certain information about former employees. This is an example of private information that becomes public by voluntary disclosure. As part of your credit record, this information would be considered restricted. If, however, you disclose this information to Who's Who, or to a credit card company, it becomes public information.

Environmental

Information about hazards to the environment is critical. There is little tradition and less law regarding how open or restricted information is at the state and local (recorder's office) levels. Most information on hazardous materials, soil composition, even OSHA inspection reports is public record.

Medical

Medical record Information about an individual's medical status and history are summarized in various repositories that are accessible only to authorized insurance and other private company employees. Medical information is neither public information nor closed record. Like credit information, it is not meant to be shared with anyone, unless you give authorization.

Military

Each branch maintains its own records. Much of this, such as years of service and rank, is open public record. However, some details in the file of an individual may be subject to restrictions on access—approval by the subject may be required.

Addresses & Phone Numbers

This basic locator information about a person or organization is a category of information that may be obtained from both government and private sources. Even though you have an unlisted telephone number, anyone can still find you if you have listed your number on, for example, a voter registration card or magazine subscription form. As one the most elementary of public information categories, addresses and telephone number data is considered unrestricted information by many people.

More About Searching State Agency Records

The previous chapter includes a wealth of knowledge about the various types of public records found at the state level. This chapter in the Primer explains how to use the State Agencies Sections found in each state chapter in the body of this *Sourcebook*.

Additional State Offices

Each state chapter begins with a list of four important state offices that may be helpful to your record searching needs. This is followed by several helpful web sites.

Governor's Office

The office of the Governor is a good place to start if you are looking for an obscure agency, phone number or address. We have found that typically the person who answers the phone will point you in the right direction if he or she cannot answer your question.

Attorney General's Office

This is another excellent starting point. For example, if you are looking for a non-profit organization, the Attorney General's Office may be able to help you out.

State Archives

The state archives contain an abundance of historical documents and records, especially useful to those interested in genealogy.

State Court Administrator

The court administrator oversees the state court system, which is also known as the county court system. This office can inform you of the structure of that system (i.e. the courts of general and limited jurisdiction and the types of cases they handle). The state judicial web site is a good place to find opinions from the state supreme court and for appeals court opinions.

In some states, the state court administration office oversees a statewide online access system to court records. Some of these systems are commercial fee-based. Other systems offer free access, but are usually very limited in comparison.

Understanding the State Agency Profiles

Each state agency profile is broken into distinct segments that create a total picture of record searching including access methods and privacy restrictions.

Indexing & Storage

This segment examines the following—

- How many years of records are accessible

- How long before new records are available

- How records are indexed and in what format are they maintained.

Searching

This segment looks in depth at the searching requirements and when privacy restrictions are in place. For example, here you learn what the agencies requirements are for doing a search, such as if a signed release is needed from the subject, or if a certain state form must be used.

Access Methods

The following access methods are both listed and described in a detailed paragraph—

- Mail

- Phone

- In person

- Fax

- Online

Here you will learn the turnaround time for mail requests, or if there is free Internet access, or if the agency will release any information over the phone. In addition, there is a section describing expedited services or bulk database purchases, when applicable.

Fee & Payments

Fee coverage includes search fees, copy fees, certification fees, and expedite fees. Also covered if credit cards are accepted, if personal checks (many agencies only accept business checks) are accepted and who to make the check payable to.

Special Situations

We won't waste your time reading about agencies if the record data is truly unavailable. The following special situations are noted—

- If the state agency does not release any information period, except to government personnel.

- If the records are not maintained by a state level agency…and where to find these records if they are held at the local level.

Searching State Occupational Licensing Boards

The Privacy Question

While some agencies consider this information private and confidential, most agencies freely release at least some basic data over the phone or by mail.

Our research indicates that many agencies appear to make their own judgments regarding what specifically is private and confidential in their files. For example, although most agencies will not release an SSN, 8% do. On the other side, approximately 45% of the agencies indicate that they will disclose adverse information about a registrant, and many others will only disclose selected portions of the information.

In any event, the basic rule to follow when you contact a licensing agency is to **ask for the specific kinds of information available.**

What Information May Be Available

An agency may be willing to release part or all of the following—

- Field of Certification
- Status of License/Certificate
- Date License/Certificate Issued
- Date License/Certificate Expires
- Current or Most Recent Employer
- Social Security Number
- Address of Subject
- Complaints, Violations or Disciplinary Actions

Using the State Licenses Section

Each *State Licenses* section is separated into three parts—

1. Licenses Searchable Online
2. Licensing Quick Finder
3. Licensing Agency Information

A "Key Number" ties the sections together.

The License Searchable Online List

This is a list of boards and their corresponding URLs that offer **free Internet access** to their records. This means that you can do a name search or query from this web site.

Using the Quick Finder

The place to start a verification search is in the **Licensing Quick Finder.** Here you will find, licenses, registrations or occupations listed in alphabetical order.

Although we reflect the official name used in a state for most items, names of some of the major license types have been standardized to make them easier to locate. For example, some states use the word "Physician" rather than "Medical Doctor." We have chosen to use the latter.

Agency Information

This section gives the address and telephone number of the agency or board where the records are maintained.

Use the "Key Number"

The **Key Number** is the *identifying number* for the agency that maintains information about this license. By matching the Key Number found in the Quick Finder to the profile in the Agency Information, you will have the address and other details about how this agency operates. The key number follows the "#" sign in the Quick Finder Section.

An Example of How to Use the Sections

Let's say the following appears in the *Quick Finder Section*:

Beautician #03   216-123-4536

As stated above, the Key Number, which follows the # sign, leads you to the Agency Information Section, where you will find the Agency or Board's address and phone number. For example, "#3" refers to the following:

(3) Department of Health & Social Services, Division of Public Health, 123 Sesame Street, Mapletown, OH 44414, 216-123-4536

Search Fees

Several trends are observed when verifying search fees of the various licensing agencies. They are—

1. There is no charge to verify if a particular person is licensed; this can usually be done by phone.

2. The fee for copies or faxes ranges from $.25 to $2.00.

3. A fee of $5 to $20 usually applies to written requests. This is due to the fact that written certifications give more information than verbal inquiries, i.e. disciplinary action, exam scores.

4. A fee that is $25 or more is typically for a list of licensed professionals. For example, a hospital might need a roster of registered nurses in a certain geographic area.

Searching Tip—Distinguish the Type of Agency

Within the agency category listings, it is important to note that there are five general types of agencies. When you are verifying credentials, you should be aware of what distinguishes each type, which in turn could alter the questions you ask.

Private Certification

Private Licensing and Certification—requires a proven level of minimum competence before license is granted. These professional licenses separate the true "professions" from the third category below. In many of these professions, the certification body, such as the American Institute of Certified Public Accountants, is a private association whereas the licensing body, such as the New York State Education Department, is the licensing agency. Also, many professions may provide additional certifications in specialty areas.

State Certification

State Licensing & Certification—requires certification through an *examination* and/or other *requirements supervised* directly *by the state* rather than by a private association.

By Individual

Individual Registration—required if an individual intends to offer specified products or services in the designated area, but does not require certification that the person has met minimum requirements. An everyday example would be registering a handgun in a state that does not require passing a gun safety course.

By Business

Business Registration—required if a business intends to do business or offer specified products or services in a designated area, such as registering a liquor license. Some business license agencies require testing or a background check. Others merely charge a fee after a cursory review of the application.

Special Permits

Permits—give the grantee specific permission to do something, whether it is to sell hot-dogs on the corner or to put up a three story sign. Permits are usually granted at the local level rather than the state level of government.

Other Forms of Licensing & Registration

Although the state level is where much of the licensing and registration occurs, you should be aware of other places you may want to search.

Local Government Agencies

Local government agencies at both the **county** and **municipal levels** require a myriad of business registrations and permits in order to do business (construction, signage, etc.) within their borders. Even where you think a business or person, such as a remodeling contractor, should have local registrations you want to check out, it is still best to start at the state level.

County Recording Office and City Hall

If you decide to check on local registrations and permits, call the offices at both the county—try the **county recording office**—and municipal level—try **city hall**—to find out what type of registrations may be required for the person or business you are checking out.

Like the state level, you should expect that receiving basic information will only involve a phone call and that you will not be charged for obtaining a status summary.

Professional Associations

As mentioned above, many professional licenses are based on completion of the requirements of professional associations. In addition, there are *many professional designations* from such associations that *are not recognized as official licenses by government*. Other designations are basic certifications in fields that are so specialized that they are not of interest to the states, but rather only to the professionals within an industry. For example, if your company needs to hire an investigator to check out a potential fraud against you, you might want to hire a CFE—Certified Fraud Examiner— who has met the minimum requirements for that title from the Association of Certified Fraud Examiners.

Other Information Available

Mail Lists & Databases

Many agencies make their lists available in reprinted or computer form, and a few maintain online access to their files. If you are interested in the availability of licensing agency information in bulk (e.g. mailing lists, magnetic tapes, disks) or online, call the agency and ask about formats that are available.

Online Searching & CD-ROMS

A number of private vendors also compile lists from these agencies and make them available online or on CD-ROM. We do not suggest these databases for credential searching because they may not be complete, may not be up to date and may not contain all the information you can obtain directly from the licensing agency. However, these databases are extremely valuable as a general source of background information on an individual or company that you wish to do business with.

Searching Federal Court Records

First published in May 1993, the BRB Publication The Sourcebook of Federal Courts *provided the first truly complete coverage of where and how to search for case records in the United States Federal Courts. Now, this book has been fully revised and integrated into* The Sourcebook.

In addition to detailing how to obtain Federal Court information, another objective of this publication is to show searchers how the Federal Court system has evolved during the past few years. One problem searchers encounter is that older records may be in a different form or in a different location from newer records. For example, a searcher can go astray trying to find bankruptcy cases in Ohio unless they know about changes in Dayton.

One development that continues to change the fundamental nature of Federal Courts case record access is, of course, computerization. Now, every Federal Court in the United States has converted to a computerized index.

Federal Court Structure

The Federal Court system includes three levels of courts, plus some special courts, described as follows—

Supreme Court of the United States

The Supreme Court of the United States is the court of last resort in the United States. It is located in Washington, DC, where it hears appeals from the United States Courts of Appeals and from the highest courts of each state.

United States Court of Appeals

The United States Court of Appeals consists of thirteen appellate courts that hear appeals of verdicts from the courts of general jurisdiction. They are designated as follows:

The Federal Circuit Court of Appeals hears appeals from the US Claims Court and the US Court of International Trade. It is located in Washington, DC.

The District of Columbia Circuit Court of Appeals hears appeals from the district courts in Washington, DC as well as from the Tax Court.

Eleven geographic **Courts of Appeals**—each of these appeal scourts covers a designated number of states and territories. The chart on the pages 30-31 lists the circuit numbers (1 through 11) and location of the Court of Appeals for each state.

United States District Courts

The United States District Courts are the courts of general jurisdiction, or trial courts, and are subdivided into two categories—

The District Courts are courts of general jurisdiction, or trial courts, for federal matters, excluding bankruptcy. Essentially, this means they hear cases involving federal law and cases where there is diversity of citizenship. Both **civil** and **criminal** cases come before these courts.

The Bankruptcy Courts generally follow the same geographic boundaries as the US District Courts. There is at least one bankruptcy court for each state; within a state there may be one or more judicial districts and within a judicial district there may be more than one location (division) where the courts hear cases. While civil lawsuits may be filed in either state or federal courts depending upon the applicable law, all bankruptcy actions are filed with the US Bankruptcy Courts.

Special Courts/Separate Courts

The Special Courts/Separate Courts have been created to hear cases or appeals for certain areas of litigation demanding special expertise. Examples include the US Tax Court, the Court of International Trade and the US Claims Court.

How Federal Trial Courts are Organized

At the federal level, all cases involve federal or US constitutional law or interstate commerce. The task of locating the right court is seemingly simplified by the nature of the federal system—

- All court locations are based upon the plaintiff's county of domicile.

- All civil and criminal cases go to the US District Courts.

- All bankruptcy cases go to the US Bankruptcy Courts.

However, a plaintiff or defendant may have cases in any of the 500 court locations, so it is really not all that simple to find them.

There is at least one District and one Bankruptcy Court in each state. In many states there is more than one court, often divided further into judicial districts—e.g., the State of New York consists of four judicial districts, the Northern, Southern, Eastern and Western. Further, many judicial districts contain more than one court location (usually called a division).

The Bankruptcy Courts generally use the same hearing locations as the District Courts. If court locations differ, the usual variance is to have fewer Bankruptcy Court locations.

Case Numbering

When a case is filed with a federal court, a case number is assigned. This is the primary indexing method. Therefore, in searching for case records, you will need to know or find the applicable case number. If you have the number in good form already, your search should be fast and reasonably inexpensive.

You should be aware that case numbering procedures are not consistent throughout the Federal Court system: one judicial district may assign numbers by district while another may assign numbers by location (division) within the judicial district or by judge. Remember that case numbers appearing in legal text citations may not be adequate for searching unless they appear in the proper form for the particular court.

All the basic civil case information that is entered onto docket sheets, and into computerized systems like PACER (see below), starts with standard form JS-44, the Civil Cover Sheet, or the equivalent.

Docket Sheet

As in the state court system, information from cover sheets, and from documents filed as a case goes forward, is recorded on the **docket sheet**, which then contains the case history from initial filing to its current status. While docket sheets differ somewhat in format, the basic information contained on a docket sheet is consistent from court to court. As noted earlier in the state court section, all docket sheets contain:

- Name of court, including location (division) and the judge assigned;
- Case number and case name;
- Names of all plaintiffs and defendants/debtors;
- Names and addresses of attorneys for the plaintiff or debtor;
- Nature and cause (e.g., US civil statute) of action;
- Listing of documents filed in the case, including docket entry number, the date and a short description (e.g., 12-2-92, #1, Complaint).

Assignment of Cases and Computerization

Traditionally, cases were assigned within a district by county. Although this is still true in most states, the introduction of computer systems to track dockets has led to a more flexible approach to case assignment, as is the case in Minnesota and Connecticut. Rather than blindly assigning all cases from a county to one judge, their districts are using random numbers and other logical methods to balance caseloads among their judges.

This trend may appear to confuse the case search process. Actually, the only problem that the searcher may face is to figure out where the case records themselves are located. Finding cases has become significantly easier with the wide availability of PACER from remote access and on-site terminals in each court location with the same district-wide information base.

Computerized Indexes are Available

Computerized courts generally index each case record by the names of some or all the parties to the case—the plaintiffs and defendants (debtors and creditors in Bankruptcy Court) as well as by case number. Therefore, when you search by name you will first receive a listing of all cases in which the name appears, both as plaintiff and defendant.

Electronic Access to Federal Courts

Numerous programs have been developed for electronic access to Federal Court records. In recent years the Administrative Office of the United States Courts in Washington, DC has developed three innovative public access programs: VCIS, PACER, and the Case Management/ Electronic Case Files (CM/ECF) project. The most useful program for online searching is PACER.

PACER

PACER, the acronym for **P**ublic **A**ccess to **E**lectronic **C**ourt **R**ecords, provides docket information online for open cases at **all US Bankruptcy courts** and **most US District courts**. Access is via either a commercial dial-up system (user fee of $.60 a minute) or through the Internet (user fee is $.07 per page). Cases for the US Court of Federal Claims are also available.

Each court controls its own computer system and case information database; therefore, there are some variations among jurisdictions as to the information offered.

Sign-up and technical support is handled at the PACER Service Center in San Antonio, Texas (800) 676-6856. You can sign up for all or multiple districts at once. In many judicial districts, when you sign up for PACER access, you will receive a PACER Primer that has been customized for each district. The primer contains a summary of how to access PACER, how to select cases, how to read case numbers and docket sheets, some searching tips, who to call for problem resolution, and district specific program variations.

A continuing problem with PACER is that each court determines when records will be purged and how records will be indexed, leaving you to guess how a name is spelled or abbreviated and how much information about closed cases your search will uncover. A PACER search for anything but open cases **cannot** take the place of a full seven-year search of the federal court records available by written request from the court itself or through a local document retrieval company. Many districts report that they have closed records back a number of years, but at the same time indicate they purge docket items every six months.

Before Accessing PACER, Search the "National" US Party/Case Index

It is no longer necessary to call each court in every state and district to determine where a debtor has filed bankruptcy, or if someone is a defendant in Federal litigation. National and regional searches of district and bankruptcy filings can be made with one call (via modem) to the US Party/Case Index.

The **US Party/Case Index** is a national index for U.S. district, bankruptcy, and appellate courts. This index allows searches to determine whether or not a party is involved in federal litigation almost anywhere in the nation.

The US Party/Case Index provides the capability to perform national or regional searches on party name and Social Security Number in the bankruptcy index, party name and nature of suit in the civil index, and party name in the criminal and appellate indices.

The search will provide a list of case numbers, filing locations and filing dates for those cases matching the search criteria. If you need more information about the case, you must obtain it from the court directly or through that court's individual PACER system.

You may access the US Party/Case Index by dialup connection or via the Internet. The Internet site for the US Party/Case Index is http://pacer.uspci.uscourts.gov. The toll-free dial-up number for the US Party/Case Index is 800-974-8896. For more information, call the PACER service center at 800-676-6856.

In accordance with Judicial Conference policy, most courts charge a $.60 per minute access fee for the traditional dial-up service or $.07 per page for Internet service.

RACER

RACER stands for Remote Access to Court Electronic Records. Accessed through the Internet, RACER offers access to the same records as PACER. At present, searching RACER is free in a few courts, but normally the fee structure is $.07 per page. There are plans to make it a fee-based system.

Miscellaneous Online Systems

Many courts have developed their own online systems. The Bankruptcy Courts for the Eastern District of Virginia have an elaborate system accessible for free and available on their web site. In addition to RACER, Idaho's Bankruptcy and District Courts have other searching options available on their web site. Likewise, the Southern District Court of New York offers CourtWeb, which provides information to the public on selected recent rulings of those judges who have elected to make information available in electronic form.

Case Management/Electronic Case Files (CM/ECF)

Electronic Case Files (ECF) is a prototype system for the filing of cases electronically. This service, initially introduced in January 1996, enables participating attorneys and litigants to electronically submit pleadings and corresponding docket entries to the court via the Internet thereby eliminating substantial paper handling and processing time. ECF permits any interested parties to instantaneously access the entire official case docket and documents on the Internet of selective civil and bankruptcy cases within these jurisdictions.

The federal judiciary's *Case management/Electronic Case Files (CM/ECF)* project is designed to replace the aging electronic docketing and case management systems in more than 200 bankruptcy, district and appellate courts by 2005. CM/ECF will provide the capability for courts to have case file documents in electronic format and to accept filings over the Internet. Eighteen federal courts are currently operational as we go to press, and another thirty-nine courts are in the process of implementing CM/ECF.

It is important to note that when you search ECF, you are ONLY searching cases that have been filed electronically. A case may not have been filed electronically through CM-ECF, so you must still conduct a search using PACER if you want to know if a case exists.

For further information about CM/ECF visit http://pacer.psc.uscourts.gov/cmecf.

VCIS

Another important system is **VCIS** (Voice Case Information System). Nearly all of the US Bankruptcy Court judicial districts provide **VCIS**, a means of accessing information regarding open bankruptcy cases by merely using a touch-tone telephone. There is no charge. Individual names are entered last name first with as much of the first name as you wish to include. For example, Carl R. Ernst could be entered as ERNSTC or ERNSTCARL. Do not enter the middle initial. Business names are entered as they are written, without blanks.

The VCIS System, like the PACER System, has become pervasive and now covers open cases for all but a few US Bankruptcy Court locations. Each Bankruptcy Court profile includes that court's VCIS phone number.

Federal Courts Searching Hints

- VCIS should *only* be used to locate information about open cases. Do not attempt to use VCIS as a substitute for a PACER search.

- Since this publication includes the counties of jurisdiction for each court, the list of counties in each Court's profile is a good starting point for determining where case records may or may not be found.

- Before performing a general PACER search to determine whether cases exist under a particular plaintiff, debtor, or defendant name, first be certain to review that Court's profile, which will show the earliest dates of case records available on the PACER. Also, searchers need to be sure that the Court's case index includes all cases, open and closed, for that particular period. Be aware that some courts purge older, closed cases after a period of time, making such a PACER search incomplete. (Wherever known, this publication indicates within the court profiles the purge timeframe for PACER records. Times vary from court to court and state to state.)

- Experience shows that court personnel are typically not aware of — nor concerned about — the types of searches performed by readers of this publication. Court personnel often focus on only open cases, whereas a searcher may want to know as much about closed cases as open ones. Thus, court personnel are sometimes fuzzy in answering questions about how far back case records go on PACER, and whether closed cases have been purged. If you are looking for cases older than a year or two, there is no substitute for a real, on-site search performed by the court itself or by a local search expert (if the court allows full access to its indexes).

- Some courts may be more willing than others to give out information by telephone. This is because most courts have converted from the old card index system to fully computerized indexes, which are easily accessible, while on the phone.

Federal Records Centers and the National Archives

After a federal case is closed, the documents are held by Federal Courts themselves for a number of years, then stored at a designated Federal Records Center (FRC). After 20 to 30 years, the records are then transferred from the FRC to the regional archives offices of the National Archives and Records Administration (NARA). The length of time between a case being closed and its being moved to an FRC varies widely by district. Each court has its own transfer cycle and determines access procedures to its case records, even after they have been sent to the FRC.

When case records are sent to an FRC, the boxes of records are assigned accession, location and box numbers. These numbers, which are called case locator information, **must be obtained from the originating court in order to retrieve documents from the FRC.** Some courts will provide such information over the telephone, but others require a written request. This information is now available on PACER in certain judicial districts. The Federal Records Center for each state is listed as follows:

State	Circuit	Appeals Court	Federal Records Center
AK	9	San Francisco, CA	Anchorage (Some records are in temporary storage in Seattle)
AL	11	Atlanta, GA	Atlanta
AR	8	St. Louis, MO	Fort Worth
AZ	9	San Francisco, CA	Los Angeles
CA	9	San Francisco, CA	Los Angeles (Central & Southern CA) San Francisco (Eastern & Northern CA)
CO	10	Denver, CO	Denver
CT	2	New York, NY	Boston
DC		Washington, DC	Washington, DC
DE	3	Philadelphia, PA	Philadelphia
FL	11	Atlanta, GA	Atlanta
GA	11	Atlanta, GA	Atlanta
GU	9	San Francisco, CA	San Francisco
HI	9	San Francisco, CA	San Francisco
IA	8	St. Louis, MO	Kansas City, MO
ID	9	San Francisco, CA	Seattle
IL	7	Chicago, IL	Chicago
IN	7	Chicago, IL	Chicago
KS	10	Denver, CO	Kansas City, MO
KY	6	Cincinnati, OH	Atlanta
LA	5	New Orleans, LA	Fort Worth
MA	1	Boston, MA	Boston
MD	4	Richmond, VA	Philadelphia

State	Circuit	Appeals Court	Federal Records Center
ME	1	Boston, MA	Boston
MI	6	Cincinnati, OH	Chicago
MN	8	St. Louis, MO	Chicago
MO	8	St. Louis, MO	Kansas City, MO
MS	5	New Orleans, LA	Atlanta
MT	9	San Francisco, CA	Denver
NC	4	Richmond, VA	Atlanta
ND	8	St. Louis, MO	Denver
NE	8	St. Louis, MO	Kansas City, MO
NH	1	Boston, MA	Boston
NJ	3	Philadelphia, PA	New York
NM	10	Denver, CO	Denver
NV	9	San Francisco, CA	Los Angeles (Clark County, NV) San Francisco (Other NV counties)
NY	2	New York, NY	New York
OH	6	Cincinnati, OH	Chicago; Dayton has some bankruptcy
OK	10	Denver, CO	Fort Worth
OR	9	San Francisco, CA	Seattle
PA	3	Philadelphia, PA	Philadelphia
PR	1	Boston, MA	New York
RI	1	Boston, MA	Boston
SC	4	Richmond, VA	Atlanta
SD	8	St. Louis, MO	Denver
TN	6	Cincinnati, OH	Atlanta
TX	5	New Orleans, LA	Fort Worth
UT	10	Denver, CO	Denver
VA	4	Richmond, VA	Philadelphia
VI	3	Philadelphia, PA	New York
VT	2	New York, NY	Boston
WA	9	San Francisco, CA	Seattle
WI	7	Chicago, IL	Chicago
WV	4	Richmond, VA	Philadelphia
WY	10	Denver, CO	Denver

Notes to the Chart:

GU is Guam, PR is Puerto Rico, and VI is the Virgin Islands.

According to some odd logic, the following Federal Records Centers are not located in the city named above, but are actually somewhere else. Below are the exceptions:

Atlanta—in East Point, GA;   Boston—in Waltham, MA;   Los Angeles—in Laguna Niguel, CA; New York—in Bayonne, NJ;   San Francisco—in San Bruno, CA

Searching Other Federal Records Online

EDGAR

EDGAR, the Electronic Data Gathering Analysis, and Retrieval system was established by the Securities and Exchange Commission (SEC) to allow companies to make required filing to the SEC by direct transmission. As of May 6, 1996, all public domestic companies are required to make their filings on EDGAR, except for filings made to the Commission's regional offices and those filings made on paper due to a hardship exemption.

EDGAR is an extensive repository of US corporation information and it is available online.

What Information is Available on EDGAR?

Companies must file the following reports with the SEC:

- 10-K, an annual financial report, which includes audited year-end financial statements.

- 10-Q, a quarterly report, unaudited.

- 8K - a report detailing significant or unscheduled corporate changes or events.

- Securities offering and trading registrations and the final prospectus.

The list above is not conclusive. There are other miscellaneous reports filed, including those dealing with security holdings by institutions and insiders. Access to these documents provides a wealth on information.

How to Access EDGAR Online

EDGAR is searchable online at: www.sec.gov/edgarhp.htm. LEXIS/NEXIS acts as the data wholesaler or distributor on behalf of the government. LEXIS/NEXIS sells data to information retailers, including it's own NEXIS service.

Aviation Records

The Federal Aviation Association (FAA) is the US government agency with the responsibility of all matters related to the safety of civil aviation. The FAA, among other functions, provides the system that registers aircraft, and documents showing title or interest in aircraft. Their web site, at www.faa.gov, is the ultimate source of aviation records, airports and facilities, safety regulations, and civil research and engineering.

The Aircraft Owners and Pilots Association is the largest organization of its kind with a 340,000 members. Their web site is www.aopa.org and is an excellent source of information regarding the aviation industry.

Another excellent source of aircraft information is *Jane's World Airlines* at www.janes.com .

Military Records

This topic is so broad that there can be a book written about it, and in fact there is! *The Armed Forces Locator Directory* from MIE Publishing (800-937-2133) is an excellent source. The book, now in its 8th edition, covers every conceivable topic regarding military records. Their web site www.militaryusa.com offers free access to some useful databases.

The Privacy Act of 1974 (5 U.S.C. 552a) and the Department of Defense directives require a written request, signed and dated, to access military personnel records. For further details, visit the NPRC site listed below.

Military Internet Sources

There are a number of great Internet sites that provide valuable information on obtaining military and military personnel records as follows:

www.nara.gov/regional/mpr.html This is the National Personnel Records Center (NPRC), maintained by the National Archives and Records Administration. This site is full of useful information and links.

www.army.mil	The official site of the US Army
www.af.mil	The official site of the US Air Force
www.navy.mil	The official site of the US Navy
www.usmc.mil	The official site of the US Marine Corps
www.ngb.dtic.mil	The official site of the National Guard
www.uscg.mil	The official site of the US Coast Guard

Online Sources Used by the Experts

The remainder of this Chapter was written and contributed by online pioneer and award winning journalist Alan M. Schlein, author of Find It Online.

We sincerely thank Alan for permitting the use of his material in this Sourcebook. Alan can be reached at his www.deadlineonline.com. Check out his web site—it is a great source with lots of useful links!

Almost every federal government agency is online. There's a nationwide network of depository libraries, including the enormous resources of the National Archives (www.nara.gov), the twelve presidential libraries, and four national libraries (the Library of Congress, the National Agricultural Library, the National Library of Education and the National Library of Medicine). A 1997 government survey counted 4,300 web sites and 215 computer bulletin boards at 42 departments and agencies, and those numbers keep growing. State and city government web sites are mushrooming, too. While the material is easily accessible, finding it sometimes requires professional researching skills. In response, the government has been developing government resource gateways and finding aids. Many of them are quite good. Among them:

Fedstats

www.fedstats.gov

A terrific collection of statistical sites from the federal government.

Healthfinder

www.healthfinder.gov

This is a great starting point for health-related government information

Best Gateways to Government Records

In addition, there are hundreds of web sites, called government gateways, that organize and link government sites. Some are simply collections of links. Others provide access to bulletin boards of specific government agencies so that you find and contact employees with specific knowledge. Guides are becoming increasingly important in light of the growing number of reports and publications that aren't printed any more, but simply posted online.

Here are some of the best government gateway sites:

Documents Center

www.lib.umich.edu/libhome/Documents.center/index.html

Documents Center is a clearinghouse for local, state, federal, foreign, and international government information. It is one of the more comprehensive online searching aids for all kinds of government information on the Internet. It's especially useful as a meta-site of meta-sites.

FedLaw

http://fedlaw.gsa.gov

FedLaw is an extremely broad resource for federal legal and regulatory research containing 1600+ links to law-related information. It has very good topical and title indexes that group web links into hundreds of subjects. It is operated by the General Services Administration (GSA).

FedWorld Information Network

www.fedworld.gov

FedWorld is a massive collection of 14,000 files and databases of government sites, including bulletin boards that can help you identify government employees with expertise in a broad range of subjects. A surprising number of these experts will take the time to discuss questions from the general public.

US Federal Government Agencies Directory

www.lib.lsu.edu/gov/fedgov.html

This directory of federal agencies is maintained by Louisiana State University and links to hundreds of federal government Internet sites. It's divided by branch and agency and is very thorough, but focus on your target because it's easy to lose your way or become overwhelmed en route.

US Government Information

www-libraries.colorado.edu/ps/gov/us/federal.htm

This is a gem of a site and a good starting point. From the University of Colorado, it's not as thorough as the LSU site above, but still very valuable.

INFOMINE: Scholarly Internet Resource Collections

http://lib-www.ucr.edu

INFOMINE provides collections of scholarly Internet resources, best for academics. Its government portion — Government INFOMINE — is easily searchable by subject. It has detailed headings and its resource listings are very specific. Since it's run by a university, some of its references are to limited to student use only.

YAHOO! Government

www.yahoo.com/Government

Yahoo is one of the best-known and most frequently-used general Internet engines. Its' subject approach is especially good for subjects like government. It is substantial, frequently updated, broad in scope and has sections for all levels of government.

Federal Web Locator

http://www.infoctr.edu/fwl

This web locator is really two sites in one: a federal government web site and a separate site that tracks federal courts – (http://vls.law.vil.edu/compass) both of which are browsable by category or by keywords. Together they provide links to thousands of government agencies and departments. In addition, this site has an excellent **State Web Locator** at www.infoctr.edu/swl.

Best Online Government Resources

Your tax dollars are put to good and visible use here. A few of the government's web pages are excellent. Some can be used in lieu of commercial tools, but only if you have the time to invest.

A few of the top government sites – the Census and the Securities and Exchange Commission – are models of content and presentation. They are very deep, very thorough and easy to use. If only the rest of the federal government would follow suit. Unfortunately, the best of the federal government is just that: *the best*. Not all agencies maintain such detailed and relevant resources.

Following are the crown jewels of the government's collection, in ranked order:

US Census Bureau

www.census.gov

Without question, this is the US government's top site. It's saturated with information and census publications – at times overwhelmingly so – but worth every minute of your time. A few hours spent here is a worthwhile investment for almost anyone seeking to background a community, learn about business or find any kind of demographic information. You can search several ways: alphabetically by subject, by word, by location, and by geographic map. The only problem is the sheer volume of data.

One feature, the **Thematic Mapping System**, allows users to extract data from Census CD-ROMs and display them in maps by state or county. You can create maps on all kinds of subjects – for example, tracking violent crime to farm income by region.

The site also features the **Statistical Abstract of the US** in full text, with a searchable version at http://www.census.gov/statab/www

The potential uses of census data are infinite. Marketers use it to find community information. Reporters search out trends by block, neighborhood or region. Educators conduct research. Businesses evaluate new business prospects. Genealogists trace family trees though full census data. You can even use it to identify ideal communities in which to raise a family. The *San Jose Mercury News'* Jennifer LaFleur used it to find eligible bachelors in specific areas of San Jose for an article on which she was working.

US Securities & Exchange Commission (SEC)

www.sec.gov

This SEC site, which is first-rate and surpassed only by the Census site, is a must-stop place for information shopping on US companies. Its **EDGAR** database search site www.sec.gov/edaux/searches.htm is easy to use and provides access to documents that companies and corporations are required to file under regulatory laws.

The SEC site is a great starting point for information about specific companies and industry trends. The SEC requires all publicly held corporations and some large privately held corporations to disclose detailed financial information about their activities, plans, holdings, executives' salaries and stakes, legal problems and so forth. For more details, see the Chapter 9.

Library of Congress (LOC)

An extraordinary collection of documents. **Thomas**, the Library's Congressional online center site (http://thomas.loc.gov/home/thomas2.html) provides an exhaustive collection of congressional documents, including bill summaries, voting records and the full Congressional Record, which is the official record of Congressional action. This LOC site also links to many international, federal, state and local government sites. You can also access the library's 4.8 million records online, some versions in full-text and some in abstract form. Though the Library's entire 27 million-item collection is not yet available online, the amount increases daily. In addition to books and papers, it includes an extensive images collection ranging from Frank Lloyd Wright's designs to the Dead Sea Scrolls to the world's largest online collection of baseball cards.

Superintendent of Documents Home Page (GPO)

www.access.gpo.gov/su_docs

The GPO is the federal government's primary information printer and distributor. All federally funded information from every agency is sent here, which makes the GPO's holdings priceless. Luckily, the GPO site is well-constructed and easy to use. For example, it has the full-text of the Federal Register, which lists all federal regulations and proposals, and full-text access to the Congressional Record. The GPO also produces an online version of the Congressional Directory, providing details on every congressional district, profiles of members, staff profiles, maps of every district and historical documents about Congress. With EFOIA requiring all federal government resources to be computerized and available online by the end of 1999, this site will expand exponentially over the next few years, as the number of materials go out of print and online.

National Technical Information Service (NTIS)

www.ntis.gov

The best place to find federal government reports related to technology and science. NTIS is the nation's clearinghouse for unclassified technical reports of government-sponsored research. NTIS collects, indexes, abstracts and sells US and foreign research – mostly in science and technology – as well as behavioral and social science data.

IGnet: Internet. . . . for the Federal IG Community

www.ignet.gov

This is a truly marvelous collection of reports and information from the Inspector Generals of about sixty federal agency departments. Well worth checking when starting research on government-related matters.

White House

www.whitehouse.gov

This site wouldn't make this list if not for two features. One, a terrific list of federal government links called **Commonly Requested Federal Services** and two, a transcript of every official action the US President takes. Unfortunately, as with many government sites, its primary focus is in promoting itself.

Defense LINK – US Department of Defense (DOD)

www.defenselink.mil

This is the brand-name site for Pentagon-related information. There's a tremendous amount of data here, categorized by branch of service – including US troop deployments worldwide. But the really valuable information is on the DTIC site below.

Defense Technical Information Center (DTIC)

www.dtic.mil

The DTIC site is loaded with links and defense information – everything from contractors to weapon systems. It even includes recently de-classified information about the Gulf War. It is the best place to start for defense information. You can even find a list of all military-related contracts, including beneficiary communities and the kinds of contracts awarded.

Bureau of Transportation Statistics

www.bts.gov

The US Department of Transportation's enormous collection of information about every facet of transportation. There's a lot of valuable material here including the Transportation Statistics Annual Report. It also holds financial data for airlines and searchable databases containing information about fatal accidents and on-time statistics for airlines, which can be narrowed to your local airport.

National Archives & Records Administration

www.nara.gov

A breathtaking collection of research online. The National Archives has descriptions of more than 170,000 documents related to the Kennedy assassination, for example. It also contains a world-class database holding descriptions of more than 95,000 records held by the Still Picture and Motion Picture, Sound and Video Branches. This site also links to the twelve Presidential Archives with their records of every person ever mentioned in Executive Branch correspondence. You can view an image of the original document.

State & Regional Resources

The federal government isn't the only government entity with valuable information online. Each of the fifty state governments and the US territories have a web presence. Some are top quality, like Texas and Florida. Others aren't as good. Here are some of the better regional compilation sites:

NASCIO - National Association of State Information Resource Executives

https://www.nascio.org

This site provides state-specific information on state-government innovations and is a companion to the NASCIO (formerly NASIRE) State Search site mentioned by Greg Notess in book *Government Information on the Internet*.

Government Information Sharing Project

http://govinfo.kerr.orst.edu

This site, from the Oregon State University Library, is a great collection of online databases about everything from economics to demographics. It's particularly valuable because it has regional information on the economy and demographic breakdowns all the way down to the county level. Its content is sometimes outdated. Still, it's worthwhile for finding how federal money trickles down to localities and where state and local agencies spend tax dollars.

USADATA

www.usadata.com

This is an innovative site for finding information about a particular region or part of the country. Data is not only sorted by region, but also by twenty subjects within each region. Click on "Data-To-Go."

Global Computing

www.globalcomputing.com/states.html

A solid collection of links on a variety of topics. This site is especially strong on state and local government topics.

Searching County Court Records

The County Court Records Sections

The purpose of the County Court Records Sections is to provide quick yet detailed access information on the more than 6,400 major courts that have jurisdiction over significant criminal and civil cases under state law.

Included in *The Sourcebook* are all state felony courts, larger claim civil courts, and probate courts in the United States. Since most courts have jurisdiction over a number of categories of cases, we also include many of the courts that hear misdemeanor, eviction, and small claims court cases. In addition, each County Court Records Section begins with an introduction that summarizes where other major categories of court cases—DUI, preliminary hearings, and juvenile cases—can be found.

The term "County Courts," as used in this publication, refers to those courts of original jurisdiction (trial courts) within each state's court system that handle...

- **Felonies** -- Generally defined as crimes punishable by one year or more of jail time
- **Civil Actions** -- For money damages usually greater than $3,000
- **Probate** -- Estate matters
- **Misdemeanors** -- Generally defined as minor infractions with a fine or minimal jail time
- **Evictions** -- Landlord/tenant actions
- **Small Claims** -- Actions for minor money damages, generally under $3,000

Useful Applications

The County Court Record Sections are especially useful for four kinds of applications—

General litigation searching/background searching... Combined with the *Federal Court section*, you have complete coverage of all the important courts in the United States.

Employment background checking... Included is full coverage of local criminal courts at the felony level, and many misdemeanor courts as well.

Tenant background checking... Courts where landlord/tenant cases are filed are indicated in the state introduction charts, and most of the courts handling such cases are profiled.

Asset searching... The probate courts have records of wills sand estate matters that can be used to determine assets, related parties, and useful addresses.

Reading the State Court Charts

On the first page of each County Court Records Section are three charts. Together, they present that state's court structure.

When searching for case records, keep in mind that many of the higher level courts also handle appeals from lower courts.

The First Chart

The chart at the top of the page summarizes the structure of the court system, listing the court of general jurisdiction, followed underneath by the courts of limited, municipal, and special jurisdiction. Court types with an asterisk (*) after their names are profiled in *The Sourcebook*.

The number of case record locations is indicated for each court. Where two classifications of courts are combined into one location and only one entry appears in the profiles, the number of combined courts is noted. The number of locations for courts not profiled in *The Sourcebook* are estimates.

Where useful, the number and type of organization of each of the classifications of court are indicated under the "How Organized" column.

The Civil and Criminal Charts

The other two charts consolidate information about what types of cases each court hears, i.e. the "jurisdiction" of the type of court.

Where more than one court has jurisdiction for a particular kind of civil case, the minimum and maximum claim fields clarify whether there is overlapping jurisdiction in the state. In most states, the lower and upper court civil claim limits dovetail nicely between the court levels, so you can readily tell which court has the type of civil case you are concerned about.

Although these charts oversimplify complex sets of state statues, their purpose is to provide you with a practical starting point to help you decide where to search for case records.

Beyond the Charts

When you cannot make a determination to your satisfaction where to search, we suggest you contact that state's administrator of courts by telephone or visit their Internet site.

The address, telephone number, and Internet address of the administrative office in each state are listed under the heading "Administration."

Reading the Court Profiles

Basic Information

The 3,139 US counties (and where applicable—parishes, towns, cities, etc.) are listed in alphabetical order, within each state. When a county has more than one court profiled, the courts appear in order beginning with the court of general jurisdiction, then proceeding down to more limited jurisdictions. Each profile specifically lists the types of cases handled by that court. If a level of court has divisions, civil courts are listed before criminal courts. Where more than one court of the same type is located in a county, they are listed in alphabetical order by the name of the city where they are located.

All city/ZIP Code combinations have been verified against our latest version of *The County Locator* database for accuracy. In addition to the address and telephone number, the time zone is indicated (see below for an explanation of the abbreviations used). Fax numbers are given for most courts.

Watch for Name Variations From State to State

Do not assume that the structure of the court system in another state is anything like your own. In one state, the Circuit Court may be the highest trial court whereas in another it is a limited jurisdiction court. Examples are: (1) New York, where the Supreme Court is not very "supreme," and the downstate court structure varies from upstate; and (2) Tennessee, where circuit courts are in districts.

Access and Searching Details

Each court profile indicates acceptable searching methods including phone, fax mail, in person, and online. The profiles also indicate all fees (including search, copy and certification) and acceptable payment methods. For example, some courts accept credit cards, some do not accept personal checks, and some may bill for copies.

Here are some searching hints to keep in mind:

- When a county has multiple courts of the same level, general information is provided to help determine which office to search in, depending upon the subject's address.

- In many instances two types of courts within a county (e.g., circuit and district) are combined. When phoning or writing these courts, we recommend that your request specifically state in your request that you want both courts included in the search.

- Be aware that the number of courts that no longer conduct name searches has risen. For these courts, you must hire a local retriever, directly or through a search company, to search for you. It should be noted that usually these courts still take specific document copy requests by mail. Because of long mail turnaround times and court fees, local retrievers are frequently used even when the court will honor a request by mail. A court's entry indicates if it is one of the many to offer a public access terminal, free of charge, to view case documents or indexes.

Index & Record Systems

Most profiles of the civil courts indicate whether the plaintiffs as well as the defendants are indexed. A plaintiff search is useful, for example, to determine if someone is especially litigious.

During the past decade, thousands of courts have installed computerized indexing systems. The year when computer indexing started in each of these courts is indicated in the profile of most of the automated courts. Computerized systems are considerably faster and easier to search, allowing for more indexing capability than the microfilm and card indexes that preceded them.

Search Requirements

There is a strong tendency for courts to overstate their search requirements. For civil cases, the usual reasonable requirement is a defendant (or plaintiff) name—full name if it is a common name—and the time frame to search—e.g., 1987-1996. For criminal cases, the court may require more identification, such as date of birth (DOB), to ascertain the correct individual. Other information "required" by courts— such as Social Security Number (SSN)—is often just "helpful" to narrow the search on a common name. Further, we have indicated when certain pieces of information may be helpful but are not required.

Restricted Records

Most courts have a number of types of case records, such as juvenile and adoptions, which are not released without a court order. These types are indicated in each profile.

Fees & Other Requirements

As mentioned above, search, copy, and certification fees are given for most courts, as well as fax fees if known. Where specified, we indicate whether the court requires a self-addressed stamped envelope (SASE) to accompany a written search request. Even where it is not indicated, we recommend including a SASE to make sure the results are returned to you.

Some Court Basics

Before trudging into a courthouse and demanding to view a document, you should first be aware of some basic court procedures. Whether the case is filed in a state, municipal, or federal court, each case follows a similar process.

A **civil case** usually commences when a plaintiff files a complaint with a court against defendants. The defendants respond to the complaint with an answer. After this initial round, there may be literally hundreds of activities before the court issues a judgment. These activities can include revised complaints and their answers, motions of various kinds, discovery proceedings (including depositions) to establish the documentation and facts involved in the case. All of these activities are listed on a **docket sheet**, which may be a piece of paper or a computerized index.

Once the court issues a judgment, either party may appeal the ruling to an appellate division or court. In the case of a money judgment, the winning side can usually file it as a judgment lien with the county recorder. Appellate divisions usually deal only with legal issues and not the facts of the case.

In a **criminal case**, the plaintiff is a government jurisdiction. The Government brings the action against the defendant for violation of one or more of its statutes.

In a **bankruptcy case,** which can be heard only in federal courts, there is neither defendant nor plaintiff. Instead, the debtor files voluntarily for bankruptcy protection against creditors, or the creditors file against the debtor in order to force the debtor into involuntary bankruptcy.

Types of Litigation in Trial Courts

Criminal

Criminal cases are categorized as *felonies* or *misdemeanors*. A general rule, a felony involves a jail term of one year or more, whereas a misdemeanor may only involve a monetary *fine*.

Civil

Civil cases are categorized as *tort*, *contract*, and *real property* rights. Torts can include *automobile accidents*, *medical malpractice*, and *product liability* cases. Actions for small money damages, typically under $3,000, are known as *small claims*.

Other

Other types of cases that frequently are handled by separate courts or specialized divisions of courts include *juvenile*, *probate* (wills and estates), and *domestic relations*.

State Court Structure

The secret to determining where a state court case is located is to understand how the court system is structured in that particular state. The general structure of all state court systems has four parts:

Appellate courts

Intermediate appellate courts

Limited jurisdiction trial courts

General jurisdiction trial courts

The two highest levels, appellate and intermediate appellate courts, only hear cases on appeal from the trial courts. Opinions of these appellate courts are of interest primarily to attorneys seeking legal precedents for new cases.

General jurisdiction trial courts usually handle a full range of civil and criminal litigation. These courts usually handle felonies and larger civil cases.

Limited jurisdiction trial courts come in two varieties. First, many limited jurisdiction courts handle smaller civil claims (usually $10,000 or less), misdemeanors, and pretrial hearing for felonies. Second, some of these courts, sometimes called special jurisdiction courts, are limited to one type of litigation, for example the Court of Claims in New York, which only handles liability cases against the state.

Some states, for instance Iowa, have consolidated their general and limited jurisdiction court structure into one combined court system. In other states there may be a further distinction between state-supported courts and municipal courts. In New York, for example, nearly 1,300 Justice Courts handle local ordinance and traffic violations, including DWI.

Generalizations should not be made about where specific types of cases are handled in the various states. Misdemeanors, probate, landlord/tenant (eviction), domestic relations, and juvenile cases may be handled in either or both the general and limited jurisdiction courts. To help you locate the correct court to perform your search in, this publication specifically lists the types of cases handled by each court.

How Courts Maintain Records

Case Numbering

When a case is filed, it is assigned a case number. This is the primary indexing method in every court. Therefore, in searching for case records, you will need to know—or find—the applicable case number. If you have the number in good form already, your search should be fast and reasonably inexpensive.

You should be aware that case numbering procedures are not consistent throughout a state court system. One district may assign numbers by district while another may assign numbers by location (division) within the district, or by judge. Remember: case numbers appearing in legal text citations may not be adequate for searching unless they appear in the proper form for the particular court in which you are searching.

All basic civil case information is entered onto docket sheets.

Docket Sheet

Information from cover sheets and from documents filed as a case goes forward is recorded on the docket sheet. The docket sheet then contains an outline of the case history from initial filing to its current status. While docket sheets differ somewhat in format, the basic information contained on a docket sheet is consistent from court to court. All docket sheets contain:

- Name of court, including location (division) and the judge assigned;
- Case number and case name;
- Names of all plaintiffs and defendants/debtors;
- Names and addresses of attorneys for the plaintiff or debtor;
- Nature and cause (e.g., statute) of action.

Computerization

Most courts are computerized, which means that the docket sheet data is entered into a computer system. Within a state or judicial district, the courts *may* be linked together via a single computer system.

Docket sheets from cases closed before the advent of computerization may not be in the computer system. For pre-computer cases, most courts keep summary case information on microfilm, microfiche, or index cards.

Case documents are not generally available on computer because courts are still experimenting with and developing electronic filing and imaging of court documents. Generally, documents are only available to be copied by contacting the court where the case records are located.

Searching Recording Office Records

Combined, the Recording Offices section for each state section contains 4,265 local recording offices where Uniform Commercial Code and real estate records are maintained.

The Lowdown on Recorded Documents

Documents filed and record at local county, parish, city or town offices represent some of the best opportunities to gain access to open public records. If you are lucky enough to live in close proximity, you can visit your local office and, for free, view records. Recorded documents are also one of the most available types of public records that can be viewed or obtain via online and through the Internet.

Real Estate

As mentioned previously, real estate records are public so that everyone can know who owns what property. Liens on real estate must be public so a buyer knows all the facts. The county (or parish or city) recorder's office is the source. Also, access is also available from many private companies that purchase entire county record databases and create their own database for commercial purposes.

Uniform Commercial Code (UCC)

UCC filings are to personal property what mortgages are to real estate property. UCCs are in the category of financial records that must be fully open to public scrutiny so that other potential lenders are on notice about which assets of the borrower have been pledged as collateral.

As with tax liens, UCC recordings are filed, according to state law, either at the state or local (county, town, parish) level. Until June 30, 2001, liens on certain types of companies required dual filing (must file at BOTH locations, thus records can be searched at BOTH locations). As of July 1, 2001, UCC filings other than those that go into real estate records are no longer filed at the local filing offices in most states, but older filings can still be located there until 2008. As with real estate records, there are a number of private companies who have created their own databases for commercial resale.

A Great Source of Information

Although recorded documents are a necessity to making an informed business-related decision, they are also a virtual treasure trove of data. UCC filing documents will you the names and addresses of creditors and debtors, describe the asset offered for collateral, the date of the filing, and whether or note the loan has been satisfied. This information contained on the statements can lead an experience investigator to other roads done the information trail. For example, if the collateral is a plane or a vessel, this will lead to registration records or if the debtor is a business, other names on the filing may lead to other traceable business partners or ventures.

EDITOR'S NOTE: An excellent book that gives great insight on how to use these and other public records to find information about any person or business in Dennis King's *Get the Facts on Anyone* published by Peterson's.

How the Recording Offices Section is Organized

General Organization

The mailing address, telephone, time zone and fax number are listed for each office. If online access is available from the agencies, a detailed profile is provided. Included are other categories of information offered online from this or a related agency, such as tax assessor information and vital records, licenses, etc. Searching fees are listed. Other important phone numbers in the county are listed to the extent that we have researched and verified these numbers. Examples are telephone numbers for the assessor, treasure, vital records and elections offices.

An introduction to each state Recording Offices section contains a summary of the facts about where and how real estate records are maintained, as well as indicating information about Uniform Commercial Code and tax lien filings. It mentions any unusual conditions pertaining to real estate, tax lien and UCC searching in that state. A list of some of the other liens that are filed at the local level is also included.

Recording Office Searching Rules

The general rules for background searching of UCC records are as follows:

- *Except in local filing states, a search at the state level is adequate to locate all UCC records on a subject.*

- *Mortgage record searches will include any real estate related UCC filings.*

See the sections below for discussions of special collateral rules.

Due diligence searching, however, usually demands searching the local records in dual filing states as well.

Special Categories of Collateral

Real Estate Related UCC Collateral

A specific purpose of lien statutes under both the UCC and real estate laws is to put a buyer or potential secured creditor on notice that someone has a prior security interest in real or personal property. UCC financing statements are to personal property what mortgages or deeds of trust are to real property.

One problem addressed by the UCC is that certain types of property have the characteristics of both real and personal property. In those instances, it is necessary to have a way to provide lien notice to two different categories of interested parties: those who deal with the real estate aspect of the property and those who deal with the "personal" aspect of the property.

In general, our definition of real estate related UCC collateral is any property that in one form is attached to land, but that in another form is not attached. For the sake of simplicity, we can define the characteristics of two broad types of property that meet this definition:

> *Property that is initially attached to real property, but then is separated.* Three specific types of collateral have this characteristic: *minerals* (including oil and gas), *timber*, and *crops*. These things are grown on or extracted from land. While they are on or in the ground they are thought of as real property, but once they are harvested or extracted they become personal property. Some states have a separate central filing system for crops.

> *Property that is initially personal property, but then is attached to land, generally called **fixtures**.* Equipment such as telephone systems or heavy industrial equipment permanently affixed to a building are examples of fixtures. It is important to realize that what is a fixture, like beauty, is in the eye of the beholder, since it is a vague concept at best.

UCC financing statements applicable to real estate related collateral must be filed where the real estate and mortgage records are kept, which is generally at the county level—except in Connecticut, Rhode Island and Vermont, where the Town/City Clerk maintains these records. The chart gives the titles of the local official who maintains these records.

Consumer Goods

Among the state-to-state variations, some states required filing where real estate is filed for certain consumer goods. However, as of July 1, 2001 all non-realty related UCC filings in most states, including consumer goods, now go only to the central filing office in the state.

Equipment Used in Farming Operations

33 states required only local filing for equipment used in farming operations. However as of July 1, 2001, only Arkansas and Indiana (until June 30, 2002) still require local filing. All non-realty-related UCC filing has been centralized in all other states.

Searching Note

If you are looking for information on subjects that might have these types of filings against them, a search of county records may still be revealing even if you would normally search only at the state level.

The Importance of Revised Article 9

Revised Article 9

On July 1, 2001, Revised Article 9 became law in 46 states and the District of Columbia. It will be the law in the other four states shortly. They are Alabama (January 1, 2002), Connecticut (October 1, 2001), Florida (January 1, 2002) and Mississippi (January 1, 2002). Under this new law, most UCC filings will go to the state where a business is organized, not where the collateral or chief executive offices are located. Thus, you will find new filings against IBM only in Delaware (IBM and many other public companies are Delaware corporations), and not in New York or in any other states where it has branch offices. Therefore, you will need to know where a company is organized in order to know where to find new UCC filings against it.

The place to file against individuals is the state where the person resides.

However, the new law does not apply to federal tax liens, which are still generally filed where the chief executive office is located. IBM's chief executive offices, for example, may still be in New York State.

As stated above, realty-related UCC filings continue to go to land recording offices where the property is located.

Old Article 9

Under old Article 9, Uniform Commercial Code financing statements and changes to them might be filed at two or three government agencies in each state, depending upon the type of collateral involved in the transaction. Each state's UCC statute contained variations on a nationally recommended Model Act. Each variation is explained below. The charts appear at the end of this chapter.

You will still need to know about where UCC filings are located under old Article 9 because the transition period to Revised Article 9 is five years long. UCC filings on record before July 1, 2001 remain effective until they lapse, which is generally five years from initial filing date.

A lot of UCC filings against IBM, for example, made before July 1, 2001 will still be on record in New York's central filing office, and may also be found in county filing offices since New York was a dual filing state, as explained below.

Under old Article 9, 33 states were central filing states. Central filing states are those where most types of personal property collateral require filing of a UCC financing statement only at a central filing location within that state.

Under old Article 9, five states had statewide UCC database systems. Some of these systems are still in effect under Revised Article 9. Minnesota and **Wisconsin** were central filing states with a difference: UCC financing statements filed at the county level are also entered into a statewide database. In **North Dakota** UCC financing statements may be filed at either the state or county level, and all filings are entered into a statewide database. In **Louisiana**, **Nebraska**, and **Georgia**, UCC financing statements may be filed with **any** county (parish). Under Revised Article 9, Minnesota has established a county/state system like North Dakota in all but six county offices, and Nebraska is now a central filing state. In each of these six states the records are entered into a central, statewide database that is available for searching in each county, as well as at the state agency (no state agency in Louisiana or Georgia).

Under old Article 9, eight states required dual filing of certain types of UCC financing statements. The usual definition of a dual filing state is one in which financing statements containing collateral such as inventory, equipment or receivables *must* be filed in *both* a central filing office, usually with the Secretary of State, and in a local (county) office where the collateral or business is located. The three states below were also dual filing states, with a difference. Under Revised Article 9, no dual filing is required within a state

Under old Article 9, the filing systems in three states, MA, NH, and PA, can be described as triple filing because the real estate portion of the filings goes to an office separate from the UCC filing offices. In Massachusetts and New Hampshire, UCC filings were submitted to the town/city while real estate filings go to the county. In Pennsylvania, county government was separated into the Prothonotary for UCC filings and the Recorder for real estate filings. The local filing offices for non-realty-related UCC filings no longer take filings under Revised Article 9, but they will continue to perform searches of the old records.

Some counties in other states do have separate addresses for real estate recording, but this is usually just a matter of local departmentalization.

Under old Article 9, Kentucky and Wyoming were the only *local filing only* states. In both these states a few filings were also found at the state level because filings for out of state debtors went to the Secretary of State, and in Wyoming, filings for Wyoming debtor accounts receivable and farm products require dual filing. Under Revised Article 9, all filings have been centralized.

The Old Article 9 UCC Locator Chart

This handy chart will tell you at a glance where UCC and real estate records are filed under old Article 9 on a state-by-state basis. Under Revised Article 9, effective July 1, 2001 except as noted above for Alabama, Connecticut, Florida and Mississippi, all new personal property filings go to the central filing office.

| State | Most Personal Property | | All Real Property |
	Central Filing Office	Local Filing Office	Filing Office
AK	Department of Natural Resources		District Recorder
AL	Secretary of State		Judge of Probate
AR	Secretary of State	and Circuit Clerk	Circuit Clerk
AZ	Secretary of State		County Recorder
CA	Secretary of State		County Recorder
CO	Secretary of State	or any County Recorder (as of July 1, 1996)	County Clerk & Recorder
CT	Secretary of State		Town/City Clerk
DC	County Recorder		County Recorder
DE	Secretary of State		County Recorder
FL	Secretary of State		Clerk of Circuit Court
GA	None	Clerk Superior Court	Clerk of Superior Court
HI	Bureau of Conveyances		Bureau of Conveyances
IA	Secretary of State		County Recorder
ID	Secretary of State		County Recorder
IL	Secretary of State		County Recorder
IN	Secretary of State		County Recorder
KS	Secretary of State		Register
KY	Secretary of State (Out of state only)	County Clerk	County Clerk
LA	None	Clerk of Court	Clerk of Court
MA	Secretary of the Commonwealth	and Town/City Clerk	Register of Deeds
MD	Department of Assessments & Taxation	and Clerk of Circuit Court (until 7/1/95)	Clerk of Circuit Court
ME	Secretary of State		County Register
MI	Secretary of State		County Register
MN	Secretary of State or Recorder		County Recorder
MO	Secretary of State	and County Recorder	County Recorder
MS	Secretary of State	and Chancery Clerk	Chancery Clerk

| State | Most Personal Property | | All Real Property |
	Central Filing Office	Local Filing Office	Filing Office
MT	Secretary of State		Clerk & Recorder
NC	Secretary of State	and Register of Deeds	Register of Deeds
ND	Secretary of State or County Register		County Register
NE	Secretary of State (Out of state only)	County Clerk	County Register
NH	Secretary of State	and Town/City Clerk	County Register
NJ	Secretary of State		County Clerk/Register
NM	Secretary of State		County Clerk
NV	Secretary of State		County Recorder
NY	Secretary of State	and County Clerk (Register)	County Clerk (Register)
OH	Secretary of State	and County Recorder	County Recorder
OK	Oklahoma County Clerk		County Clerk
OR	Secretary of State		County Clerk
PA	Department of State	and Prothonotary	County Recorder
RI	Secretary of State		County Clerk & Recorder
SC	Secretary of State		County Register/Clerk
SD	Secretary of State		County Register
TN	Secretary of State		County Register
TX	Secretary of State		County Clerk
UT	Division of Corporations & Commercial Code		County Recorder
VA	Corporation Commission	and Clerk of Circuit Court	Clerk of Circuit Court
VT	Secretary of State	and Town/City Clerk (until 7/1/95)	Town/City Clerk
WA	Department of Licensing		County Auditor
WI	Dept. of Financial Institutions		County Register
WV	Secretary of State		County Clerk
WY	Secretary of State (Out of state and A/R only)	County Clerk	County Clerk

Using the County Locator Section

A list at the end of each state section cross references place names to counties. Comprised of every official US Postal Service place name, the city/county cross references contain more that 40,000 entries. This information is summarized from the BRB publication The County Locator.

The cross references contain a special feature that identifies ZIP Codes that cross county lines.

Using ZIP Codes When Searching For Public Records

A place name (capitalized type) may be listed more than once in the city/county cross references. For example,

> LOS GATOS (95030) Santa Clara (88), Santa Cruz (12)
> LOS GATOS Santa Clara

This duplicate listing indicates that the bulk of LOS GATOS addresses is in Santa Clara county, but those addresses with the ZIP Code 95030 may be in Santa Cruz county. Specifically, ZIP Code 95030 is approximately 88% in Santa Clara and 12% in Santa Cruz.

Note: county names are listed in upper and lower case type, and place names are always capitalized.

10,000 Problems Pointed Out

Multiple county ZIP Codes always appear, as in the above example, before the main entry for a place name. The percentages may not always add up to 100% because of rounding off. Counties that represent less than 1% of the addresses in a ZIP Code have also been eliminated. In all, there are almost 10,000 ZIP Codes shown in this *Sourcebook* that cross county lines.

Using Multiple County Information

The special multiple county entries put you on notice that addresses within a ZIP Code may not be in the county usually associated with that place name. This information can be crucial to finding public records, including court cases that are filed based on the location of property or residence. Remember, if you search in the wrong county, then you may get a false "no hit" response.

Non-Geographic Zip Codes

When trying to locate public records based upon place names and ZIP Codes, be aware that 10,000 ZIP Codes are useless in determining county of residence because they are assigned exclusively to post office boxes or rural routes. Anyone can have a post office box in any county. Never use an address containing one of these non-geographic ZIP Codes to determine where to search.

For More Extensive Information

BRB's publication *The County Locator* contains an additional 40,000 place names, as well as information about the characteristics of each ZIP Code. For example, the book indicates whether the ZIP Code only contains post office boxes, high rise building, or general delivery.

A Few More Hints About Public Record Searching

How you search depends on what information you have, what you are looking for, and the time frame you are dealing with. Whichever access method you decide to use, before you begin, you must gather as much of the required, essential information as you can, and be prepared to be as specific as possible in your search request.

Ways to Obtain Records

Here are five ways you can access information from government agencies and courts.

Telephone

While the amount of information agencies and courts will release over the telephone varies, this is an inexpensive way to begin a search. Today's widespread computerization of records allows agency/court personnel nearly immediate access to more readily available data. This book contains the phone numbers for every court profiled. However, the trend is that fewer courts are providing information via telephone.

Mail

Many courts and state agencies will conduct a search based upon a written request. Generally, you can call first to see if the agency has the record you are seeking and what the fee will be. Always be sure to be specific in your written request, and include a self-addressed stamped envelope for quicker service.

In Person

If you are near the court or agency where you want to search, you can visit the location yourself. Personnel are usually available to assist you. Many courts now have *public access computer terminals* for viewing case information within their districts. We recommend that you take the opportunity to visit the nearest court or recorder's office for another reason: by seeing how the office is physically organized and by chatting with personnel, you will get "a feel" for what is involved in searching a similar agency elsewhere.

Online

You will find online access is more readily available at the federal court level, certain state agencies, and county recorder or assessor offices than can be found at the county court level. The trend to access information on the Internet is slowing coming to the state court systems. Internet site addresses are indicated for those courts that have a site with some substance. We have indicated in the introductions to each state's court section when online access is available statewide. In the court profiles, we indicate if online access is available for that particular court. Keep in mind, many are primarily commercial fee-based systems.

Provider or Retriever Firm

If you cannot access records yourself and cannot wait for mail service, then you must hire a public record vendor. Hiring a service company that knows the local court(s) in its area is frequently the only way to access remote locations effectively. Among these are national companies that cover all courts, and local companies that cover courts in their geographic vicinity. See the next chapter for more information about hiring a public record vendor.

Fees, Charges, and Usage

Public records are not necessarily free of charge, certainly not if they are maintained by private industry. Remember that **public records are records of incidents or transactions**. These incidents can be civil or criminal court actions, recordings, filings or occurrences such as speeding tickets or accidents. **It costs money** (time, salaries, supplies, etc.) **to record and track these events**. Common charges found at the government level include copy fees (to make copies of the document), search fees (for clerical personnel to search for the record), and certification fees (to certify that a document as being accurate and coming from the particular agency). Fees can vary from $.10 per page for copies to a $25.00 search fee for government personnel to do the actual look-up. Some government agencies will allow you to walk in and view records at no charge. Fewer will release information over the phone for no fee.

If a private enterprise is in the business of maintaining a public records database, it generally does so to offer these records for resale. Typical clients include financial institutions, the legal industry, the insurance industry, and pre-employment screening firms among others. Usually, records are sold via online access or on a CD-ROM.

Also, there are a number of public record search firms—companies that will do a name search—for a fee. These companies do not warehouse the records, but search on demand for a specific name.

Private companies usually offer different price levels based on volume of usage, while government agencies have one price per category, regardless of the amount of requests.

The Myth of Searching Public Records Online

No, you will not find an abundance of public records on the Internet. The availability of online public records is not as widespread as one might think. According to studies conducted by the *Public Record Research Library*, only *20% of public records can be found online*. Nonetheless, more than 200 private companies offer online access to proprietary database(s) of public record information.

A key to purchasing public records online direct from a government agency is the frequency of usage. Many agencies require a minimum amount of requests per month or per session. Certainly, it does not make economic sense to spend a lot of money for programming and set-up fees if you will be ordering fewer than five records a month. You would be better off to do the search by more conventional methods—in-person, via mail, fax, or by hiring a vendor. Going online direct to the source is not always the least expensive way to go!

Using a Public Record Vendor

Hiring Someone to Obtain the Record

There are five main categories of public record professionals: distributors and gateways; search firms; local document retrievers; investigative firms; and information brokers.

Distributors and Gateways (Proprietary Database Vendors)

Distributors are automated public record firms who combine public sources of bulk data and/or online access to develop their own database product(s). Primary Distributors include companies that collect or buy public record information from its original source and reformat the information in some useful way. They tend to focus on one or a limited number of types of information, although a few firms have branched into multiple information categories.

Gateways are companies that either compile data from or provide an automated gateway to Primary Distributors. Gateways thus provide "one-stop shopping" for multiple geographic areas and/or categories of information.

Companies can be both Primary Distributors and Gateways. For example, a number of online database companies are both primary distributors of corporate information and also gateways to real estate information from other Primary Distributors

Search Firms

Search firms are companies that furnish public record search and document retrieval services through outside online services and/or through a network of specialists, including their own employees or correspondents (see Retrievers below). There are three types of Search Firms.

Search Generalists offer a full range of search capabilities in many public record categories over a wide geographic region. They may rely on gateways, primary distributors and/or networks of retrievers. They combine online proficiency with document retrieval expertise.

Search Specialists focus either on one geographic region—like Ohio—or on one specific type of public record information—like driver/vehicle records.

Application Specialists focus on one or two types of services geared to specific needs. In this category are pre-employment screening firms and tenant screening firms. Like investigators, they search many of the public record categories in order to prepare an overall report about a person or business.

Local Document Retrievers

Local document retrievers use their own personnel to search specific requested categories of public records usually in order to obtain documentation for legal compliance (e.g., incorporations), for lending, and for litigation. They do not usually review or interpret the results or issue reports in the sense that investigators do, but rather return documents with the results of searches. They tend to be localized, but there are companies that offer a national network of retrievers and/or correspondents. The retriever or his/her personnel goes directly to the agency to look up the information. A retriever may be relied upon for strong knowledge in a local area, whereas a search generalist has a breadth of knowledge and experience in a wider geographic range.

The 725+ members of the **Public Record Retriever Network (PRRN)** can be found, by state and counties served, at http://www.brbpub.com/PRRN. This organization has set industry standards for the retrieval of public record documents and operates under a Code of Professional Conduct. Using one of these record retrievers is an excellent way to access records in those jurisdictions that do not offer online access.

Private Investigation Firms

Investigators use public records as tools rather than as ends in themselves, in order to create an overall, comprehensive "picture" of an individual or company for a particular purpose. They interpret the information they have gathered in order to identify further investigation tracks. They summarize their results in a report compiled from all the sources used.

Many investigators also act as Search Firms, especially as tenant or pre-employment screeners, but this is a different role from the role of Investigator per se, and screening firms act very much like investigators in their approach to a project. In addition, an investigator may be licensed, and may perform the types of services traditionally thought of as detective work, such as surveillance.

Information Brokers

There is one additional type of firm that occasionally utilizes public records. **Information Brokers** (IB) gather information that will help their clients make informed business decisions. Their work is usually done on a custom basis with each project being unique. IBs are extremely knowledgeable in online research of full text databases and most specialize in a particular subject area, such as patent searching or competitive intelligence. The Association of Independent Information Professionals (AIIP), at www.aiip.org, has over 750 experienced professional information specialist members from 21 countries.

Which Type of Vendor is Right for You?

With all the variations of vendors and the categories of information, the obvious question is; "How do I find the right vendor to go to for the public record information I need?" Before you start calling every interesting online vendor that catches your eye, you need to narrow your search to the **type** of vendor for your needs. To do this, ask yourself the following questions—

What is the Frequency of Usage?

If you have on-going, recurring requests for a particular type of information, it is probably best to choose a different vendor then if you have infrequent requests. Setting up an account with a primary distributor, such as Metronet, will give you an inexpensive per search fee, but the monthly minimum requirements will be prohibitive to the casual requester, who would be better off finding a vendor who accesses or is a gateway to Metronet. **EDITOR'S NOTE**: Check out Metronet and similar vendors in the *National Directory of Public Record Vendors*.

What is the Complexity of the Search?

The importance of hiring a vendor who understands and can interpret the information in the final format increases with the complexity of the search. Pulling a corporation record in Maryland is not difficult, but doing an online criminal record search in Maryland, when only a portion of the felony records are online, is not so easy.

Thus, part of the answer to determining which vendor or type of vendor to use is to become conversant with what is (and is not) available from government agencies. Without knowing what is available (and what restrictions apply), you cannot guide the search process effectively. Once you are comfortable knowing the kinds of information available in the public record, you are in a position to find the best method to access needed information.

What are the Geographic Boundaries of the Search?

A search of local records close to you may require little assistance, but a search of records nationally or in a state 2,000 miles away will require seeking a vendor who covers the area you need to search. Many national primary distributors and gateways combine various local and state databases into one large comprehensive system available for searching. However, if your record searching is narrowed by a region or locality, then an online source that specializes in a specific geographic region (like Superior Information Services in NJ) may be an alternative to a national vendor. Keep in mind that many national firms allow you to order a search online, even though results cannot be delivered immediately and some hands-on local searching is required.

Of course, you may want to use the government agency online system if available for the kind of information you need.

10 Questions to Ask a Public Records Vendor

(Or a Vendor Who Uses Online Sources)

The following discussion focuses specifically on automated sources of information because many valuable types of public records have been entered into a computer and, therefore, require a computer search to obtain reliable results. The original version of the text to follow was written by **Mr. Leroy Cook.** Mr. Cook is the founder and Director of ION and The Investigators Anywhere Resource Line (800-338-3463, http://ioninc.com). Mr. Cook has graciously allowed us to edit the article and reprint it for our readers.

1. Where does he or she get the information?

You may feel awkward asking a vendor where he or she obtained the information you are purchasing. The fake Rolex watch is a reminder that even buying physical things based on looks alone—without knowing where they come from—is dangerous.

Reliable information vendors *will* provide verification material such as the name of the database or service accessed, when it was last updated, and how complete it is.

It is important that you know the gathering process in order to better judge the reliability of the information being purchased. There *are* certain investigative sources that a vendor will not be willing to disclose to you. However, that type of source should not be confused with the information that is being sold item by item. Information technology has changed so rapidly that some information vendors may still confuse "items of information" with "investigative reports." Items of information sold as units are *not* investigative reports. The professional reputation of an information vendor is a guarantee of sorts. Still, because information as a commodity is so new, there is little in the way of an implied warranty of fitness.

2. How long does it take for the new information or changes to get into the system?

Any answer *except* a clear, concise date and time or the vendor's personal knowledge of an ongoing system's methods of maintaining information currency is a reason to keep probing. In view of the preceding question, this one might seem repetitive, but it *really* is a different issue. Microfiche or a database of records may have been updated last week at a courthouse or a DMV, but the department's computer section may also be working with a three-month backlog. In this case, a critical incident occurring one month ago would *not* show up in the information updated last week. The importance of timeliness is a variable to be determined by you, but to be truly informed you need to know how "fresh" the information is. Ideally, the mechanism by which you purchase items of information *should* include an update or statement of accuracy—as a part of the reply—*without* having to ask.

3. What are the searchable fields? Which fields are mandatory?

If your knowledge of "fields" and "records" is limited to the places where cattle graze and those flat, round things that play music, you *could* have a problem telling a good database from a bad one. An MVR vendor, for example, should be able to tell you that a subject's middle initial is critical when pulling an Arizona driving record. You don't have to become a programmer to use a computer and you needn't know a database management language to benefit from databases, *but* it is very helpful to understand how databases are constructed and (*at the least*) what fields, records, and indexing procedures are used.

As a general rule, the computerized, public-record information world is not standardized from county to county or from state to state; in the same way, there is little standardization within or between information vendors. Look at the system documentation from the vendor. The manual should include this sort of information.

4. How much latitude is there for error (misspellings or inappropriate punctuation) in a data request?

If the vendor's requirements for search data appear to be concise and meticulous, then you're probably on the right track. Some computer systems will tell (or "flag") an operator when they make a mistake such as omitting important punctuation or using an unnecessary comma. Other systems allow you to make inquiries by whatever means or in whatever format you like—and then tell you the requested information has *not* been found. In this instance, the desired information may *actually* be there, but the computer didn't understand the question because of the way in which it was asked. It is easy to misinterpret "no record found" as "there is no record." Please take note that the meanings of these two phrases are quite different.

5. What method is used to place the information in the repository and what error control or edit process is used?

In some databases, information may be scanned in or may be entered by a single operator as it is received and, in others, information may be entered *twice* to allow the computer to catch input errors by searching for non-duplicate entries. You don't have to know *everything* about all the options, but the vendor selling information in quantity *should*.

6. How many different databases or sources does the vendor access *and* how often?

The chance of obtaining an accurate search of a database increases with the frequency of access and the vendor's/searcher's level of knowledge. If he or she only makes inquiries once a month—and the results are important—you may need to find someone who sells data at higher volume. The point here is that it is better to find someone who specializes in the type of information you are seeking than it is to utilize a vendor who *can* get the information, but actually specializes in another type of data.

7. Does the price include assistance in interpreting the data received?

A report that includes coding and ambiguous abbreviations may look impressive in your file, but may not be too meaningful. For all reports, except those you deal with regularly, interpretation assistance can be *very* important. Some information vendors offer searches for information they really don't know much about through sources that they only use occasionally. Professional pride sometimes prohibits them from disclosing their limitations—until *you* ask the right questions.

8. Do vendors "keep track" of requesters and the information they seek (usage records)?

This may not seem like a serious concern when you are requesting information you're legally entitled to; however, there *is* a possibility that your usage records could be made available to a competitor. Most probably, the information itself is *already* being (or will be) sold to someone else, but you may not necessarily want *everyone* to know what you are requesting and how often. If the vendor keeps records of who-asks-what, the confidentiality of that information should be addressed in your agreement with the vendor.

9. Will the subject of the inquiry be notified of the request?

If your inquiry is sub rosa or if the subject's discovery of the search could lead to embarrassment, double check! There are laws that mandate the notification of subjects when certain types of inquires are made into their files. If notification is required, the way it is accomplished could be critical.

10. Is the turnaround time and cost of the search made clear at the outset?

You should be crystal clear about what you expect and/or need; the vendor should be succinct when conveying exactly what will be provided and how much it will cost. Failure to address these issues can lead to disputes and hard feelings.

These are excellent questions and concepts to keep in mind when searching for the right public record vendor to meet your needs.

Section II

Public Records by State

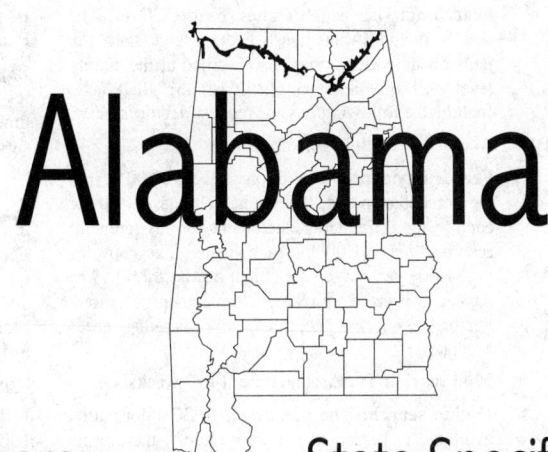

Alabama

General Help Numbers:

Governor's Office
600 Dexter Ave, #N-104   334-242-7100
Montgomery, AL 36130   Fax 334-242-0937
http://www.governor.state.al.us   8AM-5PM

Attorney General's Office
State House   334-242-7300
11 S. Union Street, 3rd Fl   Fax 334-242-7458
Montgomery, AL 36130   8AM-5PM
http://www.ago.state.al.us

State Court Administrator
300 Dexter Ave   334-242-0300
Montgomery, AL 36104-3741   Fax 334-242-2099
http://www.alacourt.org   8AM-5PM

State Archives
Archives & History Department   334-242-4435
Reference Room, PO Box 300100   Fax 334-240-3433
Montgomery, AL 36130-0100   8AM-5PM T-F,
http://www.archives.state.al.us   9AM-5PM SA

State Specifics:

Capital:
Montgomery
Montgomery County

Time Zone:
CST

Number of Counties:
67

Population:
4,447,100

Web Site:
www.state.al.us/2k1

State Agencies

Criminal Records

Alabama Department of Public Safety, A.B.I., Identification Unit, PO Box 1511, Montgomery, AL 36102-1511 (Courier: 2720 A Gunter PK Dr W, Montgomery, AL 36109); 334-395-4340, 334-395-4350 (Fax), 8AM-5PM.

http://www.dps.state.al.us

Note: Sex offender data is available online at www.gsiweb.net/so_doc/so_index_new.html.

Indexing & Storage: Records are available from 1942 on.

Searching: Must have notarized release from subject. The request must be on a state form (call to have copy sent). They will release records of arrests without dispositions. Include the following in your request-date of birth, Social Security Number, full name, race, sex. The following data is not released: juvenile records.

Access by: mail, in person, online.

Fee & Payment: The fee is $25.00 per name. Prepayment required. Fee payee: Alabama Bureau of Investigation. Cashier checks and money orders

accepted. No personal checks accepted. No credit cards accepted.

Mail search: Turnaround time: 7 days. No self addressed stamped envelope is required.

In person search: You may bring in the required release and request form.

Online search: The State Court Administration provides records over its State Judicial Online System (SJIS) at www.alacourt.org. The SJIS contains criminal records from all county courthouses. Access to this statewide system, which is used by the courts as well as the public, requires a $150 setup fee plus a $50 per month for unlimited access. The system is open 24 hours daily. Call Cheryl Lenoir at 334-242-0300 for more information.

Corporation Records
Limited Partnership Records
Limited Liability Company Records
Limited Liability Partnerships
Trade Names
Trademarks/Servicemarks

Secretary of State, Corporations Division, PO Box 5616, Montgomery, AL 36103-5616 (Courier: 11 S Union St, Ste 207, Montgomery, AL 36104); 334-242-5324, 334-242-5325 (Trademarks), 334-240-3138 (Fax), 8AM-5PM.

http://www.sos.state.al.us

Note: The office for trademarks, servicemarks, and trade names is located in Room 208.

Indexing & Storage: Records are available for all corporations, active or inactive. All information here on file is considered public information. Formal registration of trademarks and service marks was codified in 1981, and trade name registration in 1989. It takes 1 month before new records are available for inquiry. Records are indexed on microfiche, inhouse computer.

Searching: Include the following in your request-full name of business. In addition to the articles of incorporation, corporation records include the following information: Annual Reports, Officers, Directors, Prior (Merged) names, Inactive and Reserved names.

Access by: mail, phone, in person, online.

Fee & Payment: There is no search fee, but copies are $1.00 per page. Prepayment is required. Fee payee: Secretary of State. The agency will invoice members of the AL state bar. Personal checks accepted. No credit cards accepted.

Mail search: Turnaround time: 1 week. A self addressed stamped envelope is requested.

Phone search: There is a limit of 3 inquiries per call.

In person search: Call first for page amount before going to their office.

Online search: Two systems are available. The commercial online system is called STARPAS. It functions 24 hours a day, 7 days a week. The initial set-up fee is $36 and access costs $.30 per minute. Call 602-542-0685 for a sign-up package. The web site has free searches of corporate and UCC records. Search individual files for Active Names at http://arc-sos.state.al.us/CGI/SOSCRP01.MBR/INPUT.

Expedited service: Expedited service is available for mail and phone searches, call for fees. Turnaround time: 24 to 48 hours. Expedited service ends at 2PM each day.

Uniform Commercial Code
Federal Tax Liens
State Tax Liens

UCC Division, Secretary of State, PO Box 5616, Montgomery, AL 36103-5616 (Courier: 11 South Union St, Suite 207, Montgomery, AL 36104); 334-242-5231, 8AM-5PM.

http://www.sos.state.al.us/sosinfo/inquiry.cfm

Indexing & Storage: Records are indexed on inhouse computer.

Searching: Use search request form UCC-11. The search includes tax liens. Federal and state tax liens on individuals may also be filed at the county level. All tax liens on businesses are filed here. Include the following in your request-debtor name.

Access by: mail, in person, online.

Fee & Payment: In addition to the $20.00 search fee per debter name, this agency charges $1.00 for each page (financing statement or assignment) searched plus $1.00 for each listing. The copy fee is $1.00 per page. Certification is $5.00. Fee payee: Secretary of State. Prepayment required. Personal checks accepted. No credit cards accepted.

Mail search: Turnaround time: 1 to 2 weeks.

Online search: The agency has UCC information available to search at the web address, there is no fee. Corporation data is also available. You can search by name or file number.

Expedited service: This service is available for an additional $100.00, usually same day service.

Sales Tax Registrations
Access to Records is Restricted

Alabama Department of Revenue, Sales, Use and Business Tax Division, 4303 Gordon Persons Bldg, 50 N Ripley St, Montgomery, AL 36104; 334-242-1490, 334-242-8916 (Fax), 8AM-5PM.

http://www.ador.state.al.us

Note: According to state law 40-2A-10, Code of Alabama 1975, this agency is unable to release any information about tax registrations.

Birth Certificates

Center for Health Statistics, Record Services Division, PO Box 5625, Montgomery, AL 36103-5625 (Courier: RSA Tower Suite 1150, 201 Monroe St, Montgomery, AL 36104); 334-206-5418, 334-262-9563 (Fax), 8AM-5PM.

http://www.alapubhealth.org

Note: Certificates can, also, be delivered in any County Health Department for any vital record event occurring in AL. Delivery time is usually 15-30 minutes.

Indexing & Storage: Records are available from 1908 to present. New records are available for inquiry immediately. Records are indexed on microfiche, inhouse computer.

Searching: Requester must be immediate family for birth records less than 125 years old. Include the following in your request-full name, names of parents, mother's maiden name, date of birth, county, reason for information request. Include a daytime phone number and a signature.

Access by: mail, phone, fax, in person.

Fee & Payment: Fee is $12.00, add $4.00 per name for each additional copy. Additional expedite fee is $10.00, use of credit card is $5.00. Fee payee: State Board of Health Prepayment required. Credit cards accepted for phone, fax and expedited requests only. Personal checks accepted. Credit cards accepted: MasterCard, Visa, AmEx, Discover.

Mail search: Turnaround time: 2 to 3 weeks. No self addressed stamped envelope is required.

Phone search: Telephone requests allowed using a credit card, see expedited service.

Fax search: Same criteria as phone searching.

In person search: Also, go to the nearest County Health Department.

Expedited service: Expedited service is available for mail, phone and fax searches. Turnaround time: 1 day. Include the expedite fee and credit card fee, and overnight shipping if desired.

Death Records

Center for Health Statistics, Record Services Division, PO Box 5625, Montgomery, AL 36103-5625 (Courier: RSA Tower Suite 1150, 201 Monroe St, Montgomery, AL 36104); 334-206-5418, 334-262-9563 (Fax), 8AM-5PM.

http://www.alapubhealth.org

Indexing & Storage: Records are available from 1908 on. New records are available for inquiry immediately. Records are indexed on microfiche, inhouse computer.

Searching: Must be immediate family for ordering death records less than 25 years old. Include the following in your request-full name, date of death, names of parents, county, reason for information request, and signature of requester. Include a daytime phone number.

Access by: mail, phone, fax, in person.

Fee & Payment: Fee is $12.00, add $4.00 per copy for each additional copy. Additional expedite fee is $10.00, use of credit card is $5.00. Fee payee: State Board of Health Prepayment required. Personal checks accepted. Credit cards accepted: MasterCard, Visa, AmEx, Discover.

Mail search: Turnaround time: 2 to 3 weeks. No self addressed stamped envelope is required.

Phone search: Telephone requests allowed using a credit card, see expedited service.

Fax search: Same criteria as phone searching.

In person search: Also, you can go to the nearest County Health Department.

Other access: Records are available on microfilm for $40.00 per roll. There are 6 rolls of records for 1908 through 1959.

Expedited service: Expedited service is available for mail, phone and fax searches. Include the expedite fee and credit card fee, and overnight shipping if desired.

Marriage Certificates

Center for Health Statistics, Record Services Division, PO Box 5625, Montgomery, AL 36103-5625 (Courier: RSA Tower Suite 1150, 201 Monroe St, Montgomery, AL 36104); 334-206-5418, 334-262-9563 (Fax), 8AM-5PM.

http://www.alapubhealth.org

Indexing & Storage: Records are available from 1936 to present. New records are available for inquiry immediately. Records are indexed on microfiche, inhouse computer.

Searching: Include the following in your request-names of husband and wife, date of marriage, county of license issue. Include a daytime phone number and signature of requester.

Access by: mail, phone, fax, in person.

Fee & Payment: Fee is $12.00, add $4.00 per copy for additional copies. Additional expedite fee is $10.00, the credit card fee is $5.00. Fee payee:

State Board of Health Prepayment required. Personal checks accepted. Credit cards accepted: MasterCard, Visa, AmEx, Discover.

Mail search: Turnaround time: 2 to 3 weeks. No self addressed stamped envelope is required.

Phone search: Telephone requests allowed using a credit card, see expedited service.

Fax search: Same criteria as phone searches.

In person search: Also, you can go to the nearest County Health Department.

Other access: Microfilm rolls are available for purchase at $40.00 each. There are 11 rolls available which includes records from 1936 to 1969.

Expedited service: Expedited service is available for mail, phone and fax searches. Turnaround time: 1 to 2 days. Include the expedite fee and credit card fee, and overnight shipping if desired.

Divorce Records

Center for Health Statistics, Record Services Division, PO Box 5625, Montgomery, AL 36103-5625 (Courier: RSA Tower Suite 1150, 201 Monroe St, Montgomery, AL 36104); 334-206-5418, 334-206-2659 (Fax), 8AM-5PM.

http://www.alapubhealth.org

Indexing & Storage: Records are available from 1950 to present. New records are available for inquiry immediately. Records are indexed on inhouse computer, microfiche.

Searching: Include the following in your request-names of husband and wife, date of divorce, county. Include a daytime phone number, all requests must have signature of the requester.

Access by: mail, phone, fax, in person.

Fee & Payment: Fee is $12.00, add $4.00 per copy for additional copies. Additional expedite fee is $10.00, the credit card fee is $5.00. Fee payee: State Board of Health Prepayment required. Personal checks accepted. Credit cards accepted: MasterCard, Visa, AmEx, Discover.

Mail search: Turnaround time: 2 to 3 weeks. No self addressed stamped envelope is required.

Phone search: Telephone requests allowed using a credit card, see expedited service.

Fax search: Same criteria as phone searches.

In person search: Also, you can go to the nearest County Health Department.

Other access: There is one microfilm roll of records for 1950-59 available for $40.00

Expedited service: Expedited service is available for mail, phone and fax searches. Turnaround time: 1 to 2 days. Include the expedite fee and credit card fee, and overnight shipping if desired.

Workers' Compensation Records

Department of Industrial Relations, Disclosure Unit, 649 Monroe Street, Rm. 276, Montgomery, AL 36131; 334-242-8980, 334-261-2304 (Fax), 8AM-4:30PM.

http://www.dir.state.al.us/uc.htm

Indexing & Storage: Records are available from 1986 on computer (index). Actual file copies are placed on microfilm after 6 months. Older records (pre 1986) are on microfiche and must be searched by SSN.

Searching: Must have a written, notarized release from claimant. Include the following in your request-claimant name, Social Security Number.

Access by: mail, in person.

Fee & Payment: The fee is $8.00 per record. Fee payee: Department of Industrial Relations, Workers Compensation. Prepayment required. Personal checks accepted. No credit cards accepted.

Mail search: Turnaround time: 1 week. No self addressed stamped envelope is required.

In person search: A notarized release form is required.

Driver Records

Department of Public Safety, Driver Records-License Division, PO Box 1471, Montgomery, AL 36102-1471 (Courier: 502 Dexter Ave, Montgomery, AL 36104); 334-242-4400, 334-242-4639 (Fax), 8AM-5PM.

http://www.ador.state.al.us/motorvehicle/MVD_MAIN.html

Note: Ticket information must be secured at the local level.

Indexing & Storage: Records are available for convictions in last five years for moving violations, surrendered licenses, DWI and suspensions. It takes 2 weeks before new records are available for inquiry.

Searching: Some juvenile records are considered confidential and are not released. The driver's address and personal information is not included, even if the requester is a DPPA permissible user. Need full name, DOB and license number to obtain a record. Use Form MV-DPPA1 if you are a permissible user.

Access by: mail, in person, online.

Fee & Payment: The fee is $5.75 per record for all access modes. Fee payee: Alabama DPS, Drivers License Division. Prepayment required. No credit cards accepted.

Mail search: Turnaround time: 3 to 5 days. Providing a self-addressed return envelope usually means quicker service.

In person search: Walk-in requesters are not charged for a no record found report.

Online search: Alabama offers real time batch processing access via the AAMVAnet 3270 Terminal Connection. There is a minimum order requirement of 500 requests per month. Fee is $5.75 per record. Requesters must provide their own connection device and terminal emulation software. Generally, requests are available 30 minutes after request transmission.

Vehicle Ownership
Vehicle Identification

Motor Vehicle Division, Title Section, PO Box 327640, Montgomery, AL 36132-7640 (Courier: 50 North Ripley St, 1202 Gordon Persons Bldg, Montgomery, AL 36140); 334-242-9000, 334-242-9102 (Title Inquiry), 334-242-0312 (Fax), 8AM-5PM.

http://www.ador.state.al.us/motorvehicle/MVD_MAIN.html

Indexing & Storage: Records are available from 1975 for title records and 10 years for registration records. It takes 2 weeks before new records are available for inquiry.

Searching: The restrictions specified under the DPPA (Driver's Privacy Protection Act) apply. Access is restricted to permissible users who must use Form MV-DPPA1. Non-permissible users must have notarized release of subject. The address of the title or registration holder must be included as part of the request. The following data is not released: bulk information or lists for commercial purposes.

Access by: mail.

Fee & Payment: Fees are $3.00 per record per year for registration records and $15.00 for title searches (includes lien data). Fee payee: Alabama Department of Revenue. Prepayment required. Only certified funds are accepted. No credit cards accepted.

Mail search: Turnaround time: 3 to 4 weeks. No self addressed stamped envelope is required.

Accident Reports

Alabama Department of Public Safety, Accident Records, PO Box 1471, Montgomery, AL 36102-1471 (Courier: 502 Washington Ave, Montgomery, AL 36104); 334-242-4241, 8AM-5PM.

Indexing & Storage: Records are available for a minimum of 10 years. After 2 years, they put reports on microfiche. It takes 2 weeks before new records are available for inquiry.

Searching: Include the following in your request-date of accident, location of accident, county. Also, submit names of drivers.

Access by: mail, phone, in person.

Fee & Payment: Prepayment required. Fee payee: Alabama DPS, Accident Reports. Only certified funds or cash is accepted. No credit cards accepted.

Mail search: Turnaround time: within 2 weeks. A self addressed stamped envelope is requested. Search costs $5.00 per record.

Phone search: No fee for telephone request. They will search to see if a report exists, but will not give any information over the phone.

In person search: Search costs $5.00 per record. Turnaround time is while you wait.

Vessel Ownership
Vessel Registration

Dept of Conservation & Natural Resources, Marine Police Div. Boat Reg. Records, PO Box 301451, Montgomery, AL 36130 (Courier: 64 N Union St, Montgomery, AL 36104); 334-242-3673, 334-242-0336 (Fax), 8AM-5PM.

http://www.dcnr.state.al.us

Indexing & Storage: Records are available from 1985 to the present. Records are indexed on computer. All mechanically propelled, sail or rental boats must be registered. It takes 2 months before new records are available for inquiry.

Searching: Vessels that have been commercially documented by the Coast Guard are not required to register with Alabama. Liens are not recorded here, but at the central state locations for UCC filings. To search, at least one of the following is required: owner's name, hull id #, current decal #, or registration #. For purged records, the registration # is required to search.

Access by: mail, phone, fax, in person.

Fee & Payment: There is no search fee, except for bulk searches (see below) or lengthy lists ($1.00 per record). Fee payee: Department of Conservation. Prepayment required. No credit cards accepted.

Mail search: Turnaround time: 1 to 2 days. No self addressed stamped envelope is required.

Phone search: Records are available by phone.

Fax search: Turnaround time is within 1 day.

Other access: The state accepts e-mail requests for records at rthornell@dcnr.state.al.us. The state will sell all or parts of its database. Fees start at $100.00 for the first 2,500 records.

Legislation Records

Alabama Legislature, State House, 11 S Union St, Montgomery, AL 36130-4600; 334-242-7826 (Senate), 334-242-7637 (House), 334-242-8819 (Fax), 8:30AM-4:30PM.

http://www.legislature.state.al.us

Note: Use Room 716 for the Senate, Room 512 for the House.

Indexing & Storage: Records are available from 1995 to present on computer and from 1819 in journal books. Records are indexed on inhouse computer, books (volumes).

Searching: Include the following in your request-bill number. You may also request bills by subject or sponsor.

Access by: mail, phone, fax, in person, online.

Fee & Payment: The search fee is $1.00 per page with a $25.00 maximum. Computer printouts are $1.00 per page. The state will charge postage for large print runs. Fee payee: Either to the Senate or the House. Prepayment required. Personal checks accepted. No credit cards accepted.

Mail search: Turnaround time: 1 day. No self addressed stamped envelope is required.

Phone search: Records are available by phone.

Fax search: The fax fee is $5.00.

In person search: You may make copies at $.25 per page. This is the preferred request method.

Online search: There is a free service on the Internet for bill text and status. The commercial access system is called "ALIS" and provides state code, bill text, bill status, voting history, statutory retrieval, and boards/commission information. The initial fee is $400 plus $100 per month. You must sign up for 12 months. The fees entitle you to unlimited usage 24 hours a day, 7 days a week. For details, call Angela Sayers at 334-242-7482.

Voter Registration
Access to Records is Restricted

Alabama State House, Voter Registration, 11 S Union, Rm 236, Montgomery, AL 36130; 334-242-4337, 334-242-2940 (Fax), 8AM-5PM.

Note: Individual name requests must be done at the county level, there are no restrictions. The SSN is not released. Bulk requests can be ordered from this office for data from 61 of 67 counties. Call for fees and breakdowns of customized requests.

GED Certificates

State Dept of Education, GED Testing Office, PO Box 302101, Montgomery, AL 36130-2101 (Courier: Gordon Persons Bldg Rm 5345, 50 N Ripley St, Montgomery, AL 36104); 334-242-8181 (Main Number), 334-242-2236 (Fax), 8AM-5PM.

http://www.alsbe.edu

Searching: Only the name is needed to verify. All of the following is required for a transcript: a signed release, name, year of test, date of birth, Social Security Number, and city of testing.

Access by: mail, phone, fax, in person.

Fee & Payment: There is no search fee, but there is a $5.00 certification fee. If transcript is needed, fee is $5.00 plus $5.00 for certification. Fee payee: GED Testing. Only cashier's checks and money orders are accepted. No credit cards accepted.

Mail search: Turnaround time is 1-2 days.No self addressed stamped envelope is required.

Phone search: Verification only.

Fax search: Turnaround time is same day. Results will be called or faxed.

In person search: No fee for request. Turnaround time is a few minutes.

Hunting License Information
Fishing License Information
Access to Records is Restricted

Conservation & Natural Resources Department, Division of Wildlife & Freshwater Fisheries, 64 N Union Street, Room 559, Montgomery, AL 36130-1456; 334-242-3829, 334-353-5239, 334-242-3032 (Fax), 8AM-5PM.

Note: They do not have a central computerized database. Records must be hand searched and are grouped by issuing agent. This makes searching very time consuming and thus it is discouraged.

Alabama State Licensing Agencies

Licenses Searchable Online

Abortion/Reproductive Health Center #31.............www.alapubhealth.org/ProviderServices/ProvDir.htm
Ambulatory Surgery Center #31..........................www.alapubhealth.org/ProviderServices/ProvDir.htm
Architect #08...www.alarchbd.state.al.us/rostersearch/rostersearch.asp
Assisted Living Facility/Unit #31.........................www.alapubhealth.org/ProviderServices/ProvDir.htm
Attorney #03...www.alabar.org/Database_search/dirSearch.cfm
Birthing Center #31...www.alapubhealth.org/ProviderServices/ProvDir.htm
Cerebral Palsy Center #31..................................www.alapubhealth.org/ProviderServices/ProvDir.htm
Forester #26...http://home.earthlink.net/~pbsears/foresters.html
Home Health Agency #31....................................www.alapubhealth.org/ProviderServices/ProvDir.htm
Home Inspector #42..www.sos.state.al.us/sosinfo/inquiry.cfm
Hospice #31..www.alapubhealth.org/ProviderServices/ProvDir.htm
Hospital #31..www.alapubhealth.org/ProviderServices/ProvDir.htm
Hospital, Rural Primary Care #31........................www.alapubhealth.org/ProviderServices/ProvDir.htm
Independent Clinical/Physiological Lab #31..........www.alapubhealth.org/ProviderServices/ProvDir.htm
Insurance Agent #39...www.aldoi.org/Agents/dirSearch.cfm
Insurance Company #39.......................................www.aldoi.org/examiners/dirSearch.cfm
Medical Doctor #19...www.albme.org/verification.htm
Mental Health Center #31....................................www.alapubhealth.org/ProviderServices/ProvDir.htm
Notary Public #42...www.sos.state.al.us/sosinfo/inquiry.cfm
Nursing Home #31...www.alapubhealth.org/ProviderServices/ProvDir.htm
Nursing Home Administrator #22.........................www.alboenha.state.al.us/logon.html
Optometrist #20..www.odfinder.org/LicSearch.asp
Public Accountant-CPA #25.................................www.asbpa.state.al.us
Real Estate Broker #02..www.arec.state.al.us/search/search.asp
Real Estate Salesperson/Agent #02....................www.arec.state.al.us/search/search.asp
Rehabilitation Center #31....................................www.alapubhealth.org/ProviderServices/ProvDir.htm
Renal Disease (End Stage) Treatment Ctr. #31....www.alapubhealth.org/ProviderServices/ProvDir.htm
Sleep Disorder Center #31...................................www.alapubhealth.org/ProviderServices/ProvDir.htm
Social Worker #58...www.abswe.state.al.us/Lic_Search/search.asp
X-ray (Portable) Supplier #31..............................www.alapubhealth.org/ProviderServices/ProvDir.htm

Licensing Quick Finder

Abortion/Reproductive Health Ctr. #31 ..334-206-5175
Aircraft Personnel #51 205-731-1557
Ambulatory Surgery Center #31.............334-206-5175
Anesthesiologist Assistant #19 334-242-4116
Architect #08...334-242-4179
Assisted Living Facility/Unit #31............334-206-5175
Attorney #03 334-269-1515
Auctioneer #09......................................334-269-9990
Bank #05 334-242-3452
Beauty Shop/Booth Rental #11..............334-242-1918
Beauty Shop/Salon #11.........................334-242-1918
Birthing Center #31 334-206-5175
Boxer #52 334-242-1380
Broker/Dealer Agent #48.......................334-242-2984
Cerebral Palsy Center #31 334-206-5175
Chiropractor #10 205-755-8000
Clinical Nurse Specialist #21 334-242-0767
Consumer Finance Company #05..........334-242-3452
Contractor, General #07........................334-242-2839
Cosmetic Studio #11 334-242-1918
Cosmetologist /Cosmetology Instructor #11 ....
....334-242-1918
Cosmetology/Esthetician/Manicurist Instructor #11.....
....334-242-1918
Cosmetologist Mgr. Pending Exam #11 334-242-1918
Cosmetologist Student/Apprentice #11 .334-242-1918

Cosmetologist, Restricted Mgr.#11 334-242-1918
Cosmetologist/Esthetician/Manicurist Manager #11 ....
....334-242-1918
Cosmetologist/Esthetician/Manicurist Master #11 ....
....334-242-1918
Cosmetologist/Pending Exam #11 334-242-1918
Cosmetology School #11.......................334-242-1918
Counselor #15.......................................205-458-8716
Dental Hygienist #12 256-533-4638
Dental Scholarship Award #13..............205-934-4384
Dentist #12..256-533-4638
Dietitian/Nutritionist #33.......................334-242-4505
Education Administrator #49..................334-242-9977
Electrical Contractor #14 334-269-9990
Embalmer #17 334-242-4049
Emergency Medical Technician #50......334-206-5383
Engineer/Engineer in Training #27........334-242-5568
Esthetician School/Salon #11 334-242-1918
Esthetician, Pending Exam #11 334-242-1918
Esthetician/Esthetician Apprentice #11 .334-242-1918
Esthetician/Manicurist Student #11 334-242-1918
Explosives Handler #22.........................907-269-4925
Firefighter #36.......................................205-391-3776
Forester #26 334-240-9368
Funeral Director #17..............................334-242-4049
Gas Fitter #46..205-945-4857

Geologist #37...334-264-0730
Hearing Instrument Dealer #35..............334-242-1925
Heating & Air Condition Contractor #38.334-242-5550
Home Builder #53 334-242-2230
Home Health Agency #31......................334-206-5175
Home Inspector #42...............................334-242-7205
Hospice #31...334-206-5175
Hospital #31...334-206-5175
Hospital, Rural Primary Care #31..........334-206-5175
Independent Clinical/Physiological Lab #31...............
....334-206-5175
Insurance Adjuster #39..........................334-241-4126
Insurance Agent #39 334-241-4126
Insurance Broker #39 334-241-4126
Insurance Company #39 334-241-4126
Insurance Corporation/Partnership #39.334-241-4126
Interior Designer #54.............................205-669-0542
Investment Advisor #48.........................334-242-2984
Investment Advisor Rep. #48.................334-242-2984
Journeyman Electrician #14...................334-269-9990
Landscape Architect #18 334-262-1351
Landscape Planter #55..........................334-240-7171
Law Enforcement Personnel #44 334-242-4047
Legal/Dental Service Rep. #39 334-241-4126
Livestock Market Operator #30 334-240-7208
LPG-Liquified Petroleum Broker #40.....334-242-5649

Manicurist Salon/School #11 334-242-1918
Manicurist/Manicurist Apprentice/Pending Exam #11
....334-242-1918
Massage Therapist #56 334-263-3407
Medical Doctor #19 334-242-4116
Medical Gas #46 205-945-4857
Mental Health Center #31...................334-206-5175
Midwife Nurse #21 334-242-0767
Mine Personnel #34 205-254-1275
Mine Safety and Inspection #32...........205-254-1275
Mobile Home Manufacturer #41...........334-242-4036
Mobile Home Set-up/Installer #41 334-242-4036
Motor Club Representative #39 334-241-4126
Notary Public #42..............................334-242-7205
Nurse #21 334-242-0767
Nurse Anesthetist #21 334-242-0767
Nurse-LPN #21 334-242-0767
Nurse-RN #21 334-242-0767
Nursing Home #31 334-206-5175
Nursing Home Administrator #22 334-271-6214
Occupational Therapist #57 334-353-4466
Occupational Therapist Assistant #57 ...334-353-4466
Optometrist #20 256-538-9903

Osteopathic Physician #19 334-242-4116
Pawn Shop #05...................................334-242-3452
Pest Control #30 334-240-7239
Pesticide Applicator/Dealer #30 334-240-7239
Pharmacist #23..................................205-967-0130
Physical Therapist #24 334-242-4064
Physical Therapist Assistant #24 334-242-4064
Physician Assistant #19......................334-242-4116
Pilot/Bar Pilot #45..............................334-479-9247
Plumber #46 205-945-4857
Podiatrist #04....................................205-995-8537
Polygraph Examiner #47 334-260-1182
Psychological Technician #16...............334-242-4127
Psychologist #16...............................334-242-4127
Public Accountant-CPA #25.................334-242-5700
Real Estate Appraiser #43...................334-242-8747
Real Estate Broker #02.......................334-242-5544
Real Estate Salesperson/Agent #02......334-242-5544
Rehabilitation Center #31 334-206-5175
Reinsurance Intermediary #39..............334-241-4126
Renal Disease (End Stage) Treatment Center #31.....
....334-206-5175
School Bus Driver #49.........................334-242-9730

School Counselor #49 334-242-9977
Securities Broker/Dealer #48 334-242-2984
Shampoo Assistant #11.......................334-242-1918
Sleep Disorder Center #31 334-206-5175
Social Worker #58 334-242-5860
Soil Classifier #01 334-242-2620
Speech Pathologist/Audiologist #28......334-269-1434
Subcontractor #07..............................334-242-2839
Surface Mining #32 334-242-8265
Surplus Line Broker #39 334-241-4126
Surveyor #27 334-242-5568
Teacher #49......................................334-242-9977
Teacher, Elementary School #49...........334-242-9977
Timeshare Real Estate Seller #43........334-242-8747
Timeshare Seller #02 334-242-5544
Tree Surgeon #55 334-240-7171
Veterinarian #29................................256-353-3544
Veterinary Premise Permit #29 256-353-3544
Veterinary Technician #29 256-353-3544
Water Transportation Personnel #45.....334-479-9247
Wrestler #52 334-242-1380
X-ray (Portable) Supplier #31 334-206-5175

Licensing Agency Information

#01 Soil and Water Conservation Committee, 100 N Union St #334, Montgomery, AL 36104-3702; 334-242-2620, Fax: 334-242-0551.

#02 Real Estate Commission, 1201 Carmichael Way, Montgomery, AL 36106; 334-242-2620, Fax: 334-242-0551.
www.arec.state.al.us/
Direct web site URL to search for licensees: www.arec.state.al.us/search/search.asp. You can search online using license #, company or last name

#03 Alabama State Bar Association, 415 Dexter Ave (36104), Montgomery, AL 36106; 334-269-1515, Fax: 334-261-6310.
www.alabar.org
Direct web site URL to search for licensees: www.alabar.org/Database_search/dirSearch.cfm. You can search online using name, city, firm, and law school.

#04 Board of Podiatry, 13 Innisbrook Ln, Birmingham, AL 35242; 205-995-8537, Fax: 205-995-8537.
www.alabamapodiatryboard.org

#05 Banking Department, 401 Adams St, #680, Montgomery, AL 36130; 334-242-3452, Fax: 334-353-5961.

#06 Bear Creek Development Authority, PO Box 670, Russelville, AL 35653; 256-332-4392, Fax: 256-332-4372.
www.getaway.net/bcda

#07 Board for General Contractors, 2525 Fairlane Drive, Montgomery, AL 36116; 334-272-5030, Fax: 334-395-5336.
http://agencies.state.al.us/gencontrbd/2k-welcome

#08 Board for Registration of Architects, 770 Washington Ave, Montgomery, AL 36130-4450; 334-242-4179, Fax: 334-242-4531.
www.alarchbd.state.al.us
Direct web site URL to search for licensees: www.alarchbd.state.al.us/rostersearch/rostersearch.asp. You can search online using name, firm name, registration number, city, and ZIP Code.

#09 Board of Auctioneers, 610 S McDonough St, Montgomery, AL 36104-5612; 334-269-9990, Fax: 334-263-6115.

#10 Board of Chiropractic Examiners, 737 Logan Road, Clanton, AL 35056; 205-755-8000, Fax: 205-755-0081.
http://chiro.state.al.us

#11 Board of Cosmetology, PO Box 301750, RSA Union Bldg #320, Montgomery, AL 36130-1750; 334-242-1918, Fax: 334-242-1926.
www.aboc.state.al.us

#12 Board of Dental Examiners, 2327-B Pansy St, Huntsville, AL 35801; 256-533-4638, Fax: 256-533-4690.

#13 Board of Dental Scholarship Awards, 1600 University, Volker P115, Birmingham, AL 35294; 205-934-4384, Fax: 205-975-6066.
www.uab.edu/uasom

#14 Board of Electrical Contractors, 660 Adams Ave #301, Montgomery, AL 36104; 334-269-9990, Fax: 334-263-6115.
www.aecb@state.al.us

#15 Board of Examiners in Counseling, 950 22nd St N. #670, Birmingham, AL 35203; 205-458-8716, Fax: 205-458-8718.

#16 Board of Examiners in Psychology, 660 Adams Ave, #360, Mongomery, AL 36104; 334-242-4127.
www.psychology.state.al.us

#17 Board of Funeral Service, 11 South Union #219, Montgomery, AL 36130; 334-242-4049, Fax: 334-353-7988.

#18 Board of Landscape Architects, 908 S Hull St, Montgomery, AL 36104; 334-262-1351, Fax: 334-262-1351.

#19 Board of Medical Examiners, 848 Washington Ave, Montgomery, AL 36104; 334-242-4116, Fax: 334-242-4155.
www.albme.org You cannot actually search online. However, you can download ASCII and

dbf files of currently licensed physicians for offline viewing.

#20 Board of Optometry, PO Box 448, Attalla, AL 35954; 256-538-9903, Fax: 256-538-9904.
www.al-optometry.com
Direct web site URL to search for licensees: www.odfinder.org/LicSearch.asp. You can search online using national database by name, city or state.

#21 Board of Nursing, PO Box 303900, Montgomery, AL 36130-3900; 334-242-4060, Fax: 334-242-4360.
www.abn.state.al.us

#22 Board of Nursing Home Administrators, 4156 Carmichael Road, Montgomery, AL 36130; 334-271-6214, Fax: 334-244-6509.
www.alboenha.state.al.us
Direct web site URL to search for licensees: www.alboenha.state.al.us/logon.html. You can search online using first, last and middle names are all required along with the license number.

#23 Board of Pharmacy, 1 Perimeter Park S, #425, Birmingham, AL 35243; 205-967-0130, Fax: 205-967-1009.
www.albop.com

#24 Board of Physical Therapy, 100 N Union St, #627, Montgomery, AL 36130-5040; 334-242-4064, Fax: 334-240-3288.

#25 Board of Public Accountancy, PO Box 300375 (770 Washington Ave, #236), Montgomery, AL 36130-0375; 334-242-5700, Fax: 334-240-2711.
www.asbpa.state.al.us
Direct web site URL to search for licensees: www.asbpa.state.al.us. You can search online using licensee or firm name.

#26 Board of Registration for Foresters, 513 Madison Ave, Montgomery, AL 36130; 334-353-3640, Fax: 334-353-3641.
http://home.earthlink.net/~pbsears/
Direct web site URL to search for licensees: http://home.earthlink.net/~pbsears/foresters.html. You can search online using new forester list only

#27 Board of Registration for Professional Engineers & Land Surveyors, PO Box 304451, Montgomery, AL 36130-4451; 334-242-5568, Fax: 334-242-5105.

#28 Board of Examiners for Speech-Language Pathology & Audiology, PO Box 304760 (400 S Union St #225), Montgomery, AL 36130-4760; 334-269-1434, Fax: 334-269-6379.
www.mindspring.net/~abespa

#29 Board of Veterinary Medical Examiners, PO Box 1968, Decatur, AL 35602; 256-353-3544, Fax: 256-350-5629.

#30 Department of Agriculture & Industries, PO Box 3336 (1445 Federal Dr), Montgomery, AL 36109; 334-240-7282, Fax: 334-240-7168.
www.agi.state.al.us

#31 Department of Health, 434 Monroe St, Montgomery, AL 36130-3017; 334-206-5175, Fax: 334-206-5219.
www.alapubhealth.org
Direct web site URL to search for licensees: www.alapubhealth.org/ProviderServices/ProvDir.htm

#32 Department of Industrial Relations, 649 Monroe St, Rm 2211, Montgomery, AL 36131-5200; 334-242-8265, Fax: 334-242-8403.
http://dir.state.al.us/sp.htm

#33 Dietetic/Nutrition Examiners Board, 400 S Union St #445, Montgomery, AL 36104; 334-242-4505, Fax: 334-834-6398.

#34 Examiners of Mine Personnel, PO Box 10444, Birmingham, AL 35202; 205-254-1275, Fax: 205-254-1278.

#35 Hearing Aid Dealers, 400 S Union St, #445, Montgomery, AL 36130-3010; 334-242-1925, Fax: 334-834-6389.

#36 Fire College & Personnel Standards Commission, 2501 Phoenix Dr, Tuscaloosa, AL 35405; 205-391-3776, Fax: 205-391-3747.
www.alabamafirecollege.cc.al.us

#37 Geological Survey, PO Box 175, Montgomery, AL 36104; 334-264-0730, Fax: 334-263-6115.
www.algeobd.com

#38 Heating & Air Conditioning Contractors Board, 100 N Union St, #630, Montgomery, AL 36130; 334-242-5550, Fax: 334-353-7050.
www.hvacboard.state.al.us

#39 Department of Insurance, 201 Monroe St #1700, Mongomery, AL 36130-3351; 334-241-4126, Fax: 334-240-3282.
www.aldoi.org

#40 Liquefied Petroleum Gas Board, 818 S Perry St, Montgomery, AL 36104; 334-242-5649, Fax: 334-240-3255.

#41 Manufactured Housing Commission, 350 S Decator St, Montgomery, AL 36104; 334-242-4036, Fax: 334-240-3178.
www.amac.state.al.us

#42 Office of the Secretary of State, PO Box 5616, Montgomery, AL 36104; 334-242-7205, Fax: 334-242-4993.
www.sos.state.al.us
Direct web site URL to search for licensees: www.sos.state.al.us/sosinfo/inquiry.cfm

#43 Office of the Secretary of State, 100 North Union Street #370, RSA Bldg, Montgomery, AL 36103-5616; 334-242-8747, Fax: 334-242-8749.
http://agencies.state.al.us/reab

#44 Peace Officers Standards & Training Commission, 100 Union St, RSA Union Bldg, #600, Montgomery, AL 36130-0075; 334-242-4045, Fax: 334-242-4633.
www.apostc.state.al.us

#45 Pilotage Commission, PO Box 273, Mobile, AL 36601; 334-432-2639, Fax: 334-432-9964.

#46 Plumbers & Gas Fitters Examining Board, 11 W Oxmoor, #104, Birmingham, AL 35209; 205-945-4857, Fax: 205-945-9915.
www.pgfb.state.al.us

#47 Polygraph Examiners Board, 2720-A W Gunter Park Dr, Montgomery, AL 36109; 344-260-1182, Fax: 344-260-8788.

#48 Securities Division, 770 Washington Ave, #570, Montgomery, AL 36130; 334-260-2984, Fax: 334-242-0240.

#49 Department of Education, 50 N Ripley St, Montgomery, AL 36104; 334-242-9977, Fax: 334-242-2818.
www.alsde.edu

#50 Department of Health, PO Box 303017, Birmingham, AL 36130-3017; 334-206-5383, Fax: 334-206-5260.
www.alapubhealth.org/ems/

#51 Department of Transportation, 1500 Urban Center Dr #250, Vestavia Hills, AL 35242; 205-731-1557, Fax: 205-731-0939.
www.faa.gov/fsdo/bhm/

#52 Department of Revenue, 50 N Ripley St Rm 4131, Montgomery, AL 36132; 334-242-1380.

#53 Home Builders Licensure Board, 400 S Union St #195, Montgomery, AL 36130; 334-242-2230.

#54 Board of Registration for Interior Designers, PO Box 11026 (65 Bagby Dr #3B), Birmingham, AL 53202; 205-942-6487.

#55 Department of Agriculture & Industries, PO Box 3336 - Beard Building, Montgomery, AL 36109-0336; 334-240-7171.

#56 Board of Massage Therapy, PO Box 56, Montgomery, AL 36101-0056; 334-263-3407.

#57 Board of Occupational Therapy, 64 N Union St #734, PO Box 304510, Montgomery, AL 36130-4510; 334-353-4466, Fax: 334-353-4465.

#58 Board of Social Work Examiners, 64 N Union St #129, Montgomery, AL 36130; 334-242-5860, Fax: 334-242-0280.
www.abswe.state.al.us

Alabama Federal Courts

The following list indicates the district and division name for each county in the state. If the bankruptcy court location is different from the district court, then the location of the bankruptcy court appears in parentheses.

County/Court Cross Reference

County	District	Location
Autauga	Middle	Montgomery
Baldwin	Southern	Mobile
Barbour	Middle	Montgomery
Bibb	Northern	Birmingham (Tuscaloosa)
Blount	Northern	Birmingham
Bullock	Middle	Montgomery
Butler	Middle	Montgomery
Calhoun	Northern	Birmingham (Anniston)
Chambers	Middle	Opelika (Montgomery)
Cherokee	Northern	Gadsden (Anniston)
Chilton	Middle	Montgomery
Choctaw	Southern	Mobile
Clarke	Southern	Mobile
Clay	Northern	Birmingham (Anniston)
Cleburne	Northern	Birmingham (Anniston)
Coffee	Middle	Dothan (Montgomery)
Colbert	Northern	Florence (Decatur)
Conecuh	Southern	Mobile
Coosa	Middle	Montgomery
Covington	Middle	Montgomery
Crenshaw	Middle	Montgomery
Cullman	Northern	Huntsville (Decatur)
Dale	Middle	Dothan (Montgomery)
Dallas	Southern	Selma (Mobile)
De Kalb	Northern	Gadsden (Anniston)
Elmore	Middle	Montgomery
Escambia	Southern	Mobile
Etowah	Northern	Gadsden (Anniston)
Fayette	Northern	Jasper (Tuscaloosa)
Franklin	Northern	Florence (Decatur)
Geneva	Middle	Dothan (Montgomery)
Greene	Northern	Birmingham (Tuscaloosa)
Hale	Southern	Selma (Mobile)
Henry	Middle	Dothan (Montgomery)
Houston	Middle	Dothan (Montgomery)
Jackson	Northern	Huntsville (Decatur)
Jefferson	Northern	Birmingham
Lamar	Northern	Jasper (Tuscaloosa)
Lauderdale	Northern	Florence (Decatur)
Lawrence	Northern	Huntsville (Decatur)
Lee	Middle	Opelika (Montgomery)
Limestone	Northern	Huntsville (Decatur)
Lowndes	Middle	Montgomery
Macon	Middle	Opelika (Montgomery)
Madison	Northern	Huntsville (Decatur)
Marengo	Southern	Selma (Mobile)
Marion	Northern	Jasper (Tuscaloosa)
Marshall	Northern	Gadsden (Anniston)
Mobile	Southern	Mobile
Monroe	Southern	Mobile
Montgomery	Middle	Montgomery
Morgan	Northern	Huntsville (Decatur)
Perry	Southern	Selma (Mobile)
Pickens	Northern	Birmingham (Tuscaloosa)
Pike	Middle	Montgomery
Randolph	Middle	Opelika (Montgomery)
Russell	Middle	Opelika (Montgomery)
Shelby	Northern	Birmingham
St. Clair	Northern	Gadsden (Anniston)
Sumter	Northern	Birmingham (Tuscaloosa)
Talladega	Northern	Birmingham (Anniston)
Tallapoosa	Middle	Opelika (Montgomery)
Tuscaloosa	Northern	Birmingham (Tuscaloosa)
Walker	Northern	Jasper (Tuscaloosa)
Washington	Southern	Mobile
Wilcox	Southern	Selma (Mobile)
Winston	Northern	Jasper (Tuscaloosa)

US District Court

Middle District of Alabama

Dothan Division c/o Montgomery Division, PO Box 711, Montgomery, AL 36101 (Courier Address: 15 Lee St, Montgomery, AL 36104), 334-223-7308.

http://www.almd.uscourts.gov

Counties: Coffee, Dale, Geneva, Henry, Houston.

Indexing/Storage: Cases are indexed by defendant and plaintiff as well as by case number. New cases are available in the index immediately after filing date. A computer index is maintained. Open records are located at the Division.

Fee & Payment: The fee is $20.00 per item (one party name or case number). Payment may be made by money order, cashier check. Business checks are not accepted. Personal checks are not accepted. Certification fee: $7.00 per document. Copy fee: $.50 per page.

Phone Search: An automated voice case information service (VCIS) is not available.

Mail Search: Always enclose a stamped self addressed envelope.

In Person: In person searching is available.

PACER: Sign-up number is 800-676-6856. Access fee is $.60 per minute. Local access: 334-223-7023. Case records are available back to 1994. New records are available online after 1 day.

Montgomery Division Records Search, PO Box 711, Montgomery, AL 36101-0711 (Courier Address: 15 Lee St, Montgomery, AL 36104), 334-223-7308.

http://www.almd.uscourts.gov

Counties: Autauga, Barbour, Bullock, Butler, Chilton, Coosa, Covington, Crenshaw, Elmore, Lowndes, Montgomery, Pike.

Indexing/Storage: Cases are indexed by defendant and plaintiff as well as by case number. New cases are available in the index immediately after filing date. Both computer and card indexes are maintained. Records are also indexed on microfiche. Open records are located at this court.

Fee & Payment: The fee is $20.00 per item (one party name or case number). Payment may be made by money order, cashier check, business check. Personal checks are not accepted. Prepayment is required. Payee: Clerk, US District Court. Certification fee: $7.00 per document. Copy fee: $.50 per page.

Phone Search: Searching is not available by phone.

Mail Search: Always enclose a stamped self addressed envelope.

In Person: In person searching is available.

PACER: Sign-up number is 800-676-6856. Access fee is $.60 per minute. Local access: 334-223-7023. Case records are available back to 1994. New records are available online after 1 day.

Opelika Division c/o Montgomery Division, PO Box 711, Montgomery, AL 36101 (Courier

Address: 15 Lee St, Montgomery, AL 36104), 334-223-7308.

http://www.almd.uscourts.gov

Counties: Chambers, Lee, Macon, Randolph, Russell, Tallapoosa.

Indexing/Storage: Cases are indexed by defendant and plaintiff as well as by case number. New cases are available in the index immediately after filing date. A computer index is maintained. Open records are located at the Division.

Fee & Payment: The fee is $20.00 per item (one party name or case number). Payment may be made by money order, cashier check. Business checks are not accepted. Personal checks are not accepted. Certification fee: $7.00 per document. Copy fee: $.50 per page.

Phone Search: An automated voice case information service (VCIS) is not available.

Mail Search: Always enclose a stamped self addressed envelope.

In Person: In person searching is available.

PACER: Sign-up number is 800-676-6856. Access fee is $.60 per minute. Local access: 334-223-7023. Case records are available back to 1994. New records are available online after 1 day.

US Bankruptcy Court

Middle District of Alabama

Montgomery Division PO Box 1248, Montgomery, AL 36102-1248 (Courier Address: Suite 127, 1 Court Square, Montgomery, AL 36104), 334-206-6300, Fax: 334-206-6374.

http://www.almb.uscourts.gov

Counties: Autauga, Barbour, Bullock, Butler, Chambers, Chilton, Coffee, Coosa, Covington, Crenshaw, Dale, Elmore, Geneva, Henry, Houston, Lee, Lowndes, Macon, Montgomery, Pike, Randolph, Russell, Tallapoosa.

Indexing/Storage: Cases are indexed by debtor as well as by case number. New cases are available in the index 3 days after filing date. A computer index is maintained. Open records are located at this court.

Fee & Payment: The fee is $20.00 per item (one party name or case number). Payment may be made by money order, cashier check, business check. Personal checks are not accepted. Court may bill on request. Payee: Clerk of Court. Certification fee: $7.00 per document. Copy fee: $.50 per page.

Phone Search: Docket information is available by phone. An automated voice case information service (VCIS) is available.

Fax Search: The fee is $1.50 per page to fax back.

Mail Search: Always enclose a stamped self addressed envelope.

In Person: In person searching is available.

PACER: Sign-up number is 800-676-6856. Access fee is $.60 per minute. Toll-free access: 888-247-9272. Local access: 334-223-7486. NIBS court. Use of PC Anywhere V4.0 recommended. Case records are available back to case 89-02000. Records are purged every 6 months. New civil records are available online after 2-3 days.

US District Court

Northern District of Alabama

Birmingham Division Room 104, US Courthouse, 1729 5th Ave N, Birmingham, AL 35203 (Courier Address: Use mail address for courier delivery), 205-278-1700.

http://www.alnd.uscourts.gov

Counties: Bibb, Blount, Calhoun, Clay, Cleburne, Greene, Jefferson, Pickens, Shelby, Sumter, Talladega, Tuscaloosa.

Indexing/Storage: Cases are indexed by defendant and plaintiff as well as by case number. New cases are available in the index 2-3 days after filing date. A computer index is maintained. Records are also indexed on microfiche. Open records are located at this court.

Fee & Payment: The fee is $20.00 per item (one party name or case number). Payment may be made by money order, cashier check, personal check. Prepayment is required. Payee: Clerk of Court. Certification fee: $7.00 per document. Copy fee: $.50 per page. You are allowed to make your own copies. These copies cost Not Applicable per page.

Phone Search: All public information will be released over the phone. An automated voice case information service (VCIS) is not available.

Mail Search: Always enclose a stamped self addressed envelope.

In Person: In person searching is available.

PACER: Sign-up number is 800-676-6856. Access fee is $.60 per minute. Local access: 205-278-3502. Case records are available back to 1994. Records are purged every 18 months. New records are available online after 1 day. PACER is available online at http://pacer.alnd.uscourts.gov.

Florence Division PO Box 776, Florence, AL 35630 (Courier Address: 210 Court St, Florence, AL 35631), 205-760-5815, Fax: 205-760-5727.

http://www.alnd.uscourts.gov

Counties: Colbert, Franklin, Lauderdale.

Indexing/Storage: Cases are indexed by defendant and plaintiff as well as by case number. New cases are available in the index 2-3 days after filing date. A computer index is maintained. Records are also indexed on microfiche. Open records are located at this court. Some case files may be held in Birmingham if a Birmingham judge is assigned.

Fee & Payment: The fee is $20.00 per item (one party name or case number). Payment may be made by money order, cashier check, personal check. Prepayment is required. Payee: US District Court. Certification fee: $7.00 per document. Copy fee: $.50 per page.

Phone Search: Only docket information is available by phone. An automated voice case information service (VCIS) is not available.

Mail Search: A stamped self addressed envelope is not required.

In Person: In person searching is available.

PACER: Sign-up number is 800-676-6856. Access fee is $.60 per minute. Local access: 205-278-3502. Case records are available back to 1994. Records are purged every 18 months. New records are available online after 1 day. PACER is available online at http://pacer.alnd.uscourts.gov.

Gadsden Division c/o Birmingham Division, Room 140, US Courthouse, 1729 5th Ave N, Birmingham, AL 35203 (Courier Address: Use mail address for courier delivery), 205-278-1700.

http://www.alnd.uscourts.gov

Counties: Cherokee, De Kalb, Etowah, Marshall, St. Clair.

Indexing/Storage: Cases are indexed by defendant and plaintiff as well as by case number. New cases are available in the index 2-3 days after filing date. A computer index is maintained. Open records are located at the Division.

Fee & Payment: The fee is $20.00 per item (one party name or case number). Payment may be made by money order, cashier check. Business checks are not accepted. Personal checks are not accepted. Certification fee: $7.00 per document. Copy fee: $.50 per page.

Phone Search: An automated voice case information service (VCIS) is not available.

Mail Search: Always enclose a stamped self addressed envelope.

In Person: In person searching is available.

PACER: Sign-up number is 800-676-6856. Access fee is $.60 per minute. Local access: 205-278-3502. Case records are available back to 1994. Records are purged every 18 months. New records are available online after 1 day. PACER is available online at http://pacer.alnd.uscourts.gov.

Huntsville Division Clerk's Office, US Post Office & Courthouse, 101 Holmes Ave NE, Huntsville, AL 35801 (Courier Address: Use mail address for courier delivery), 205-534-6495.

http://www.alnd.uscourts.gov

Counties: Cullman, Jackson, Lawrence, Limestone, Madison, Morgan.

Indexing/Storage: Cases are indexed by defendant and plaintiff as well as by case number. New cases are available in the index 2 days after filing date. A computer index is maintained. Records are also indexed on microfiche. Open records are located at this court.

Fee & Payment: The fee is $20.00 per item (one party name or case number). Payment may be made by money order, cashier check, personal check. Prepayment is required. Payee: US District Court Clerk. Certification fee: $7.00 per document. Copy fee: $.50 per page.

Phone Search: All public information will be released over the phone. An automated voice case information service (VCIS) is not available.

Mail Search: All requests for criminal searches will be sent to Birmingham. Always enclose a stamped self addressed envelope.

In Person: In person searching is available.

PACER: Sign-up number is 800-676-6856. Access fee is $.60 per minute. Local access: 205-278-3502. Case records are available back to 1994. Records are purged every 18 months. New records are available online after 1 day. PACER is available online at http://pacer.alnd.uscourts.gov.

Jasper Division c/o Birmingham Division, Room 140, US Courthouse, 1729 5th Ave N, Birmingham, AL 35203 (Courier Address: Use mail address for courier delivery), 205-278-1700.

http://www.alnd.uscourts.gov

Counties: Fayette, Lamar, Marion, Walker, Winston.

Indexing/Storage: Cases are indexed by defendant and plaintiff as well as by case number. New cases are available in the index 2-3 days after filing date. A computer index is maintained. Open records are located at the Division. Some case records may be held in Florence, depending upon the judge assigned.

Fee & Payment: The fee is $20.00 per item (one party name or case number). Payment may be made by money order, cashier check. Business checks are not accepted. Personal checks are not accepted. Certification fee: $7.00 per document. Copy fee: $.50 per page.

Phone Search: An automated voice case information service (VCIS) is not available.

Mail Search: Always enclose a stamped self addressed envelope.

In Person: In person searching is available.

PACER: Sign-up number is 800-676-6856. Access fee is $.60 per minute. Local access: 205-278-3502. Case records are available back to 1994. Records are purged every 18 months. New records are available online after 1 day. PACER is available online at http://pacer.alnd.uscourts.gov.

US Bankruptcy Court

Northern District of Alabama

Anniston Division 914 Noble St, Anniston, AL 36201 (Courier Address: Use mail address for courier delivery), 256-741-1500, Fax: 256-741-1503.

http://www.alnb.uscourts.gov

Counties: Calhoun, Cherokee, Clay, Cleburne, De Kalb, Etowah, Marshall, St. Clair, Talladega.

Indexing/Storage: Cases are indexed by debtor as well as by case number. New cases are available in the index immediately after filing date. A computer index is maintained. Open records are located at this court.

Fee & Payment: The fee is $20.00 per item (one party name or case number). Payment may be made by money order, cashier check, personal check. Prepayment is required. Payee: Clerk, US Bankruptcy Court, Northern District. Certification fee: $7.00 per document. Copy fee: $.50 per page.

Phone Search: An automated voice case information service (VCIS) is available.

Mail Search: Always enclose a stamped self addressed envelope.

In Person: In person searching is available.

PACER: Sign-up number is 800-676-6856. Access fee is $.60 per minute. Toll-free access: 800-689-7645. Local access: 256-238-0456. Use of PC Anywhere v4.0 suggested. Case records are available back to October 31, 1976. New civil records are available online after 1 day. PACER is available online at http://pacer.alnb.uscourts.gov.

Birmingham Division Room 120, 1800 5th Ave N, Birmingham, AL 35203 (Courier Address: Use mail address for courier delivery), 205-714-4000.

http://www.alnb.uscourts.gov

Counties: Blount, Jefferson, Shelby.

Indexing/Storage: Cases are indexed by debtor as well as by case number. New cases are available in the index immediately after filing date. Along with the debtor's name and the case number, the searcher must provide the year the case was closed

and the location where the case was filed. A computer index is maintained. Open records are located at this court.

Fee & Payment: The fee is $20.00 per item (one party name or case number). Payment may be made by money order, cashier check, personal check. Prepayment is required. Payee: Clerk, US Bankruptcy Court. Certification fee: $7.00 per document. Copy fee: $.50 per page.

Phone Search: Only docket information is available by phone. An automated voice case information service (VCIS) is available.

Mail Search: Always enclose a stamped self addressed envelope.

In Person: In person searching is available.

PACER: Sign-up number is 800-676-6856. Access fee is $.60 per minute. Toll-free access: 800-689-7621. Local access: 205-731-3746, 205-731-3749, 205-731-3750. Use of PC Anywhere v4.0 suggested. Case records are available back to 1992. Records are purged every six months. New civil records are available online after 1 day. PACER is available online at http://pacer.alnb.uscourts.gov.

Decatur Division PO Box 1289, Decatur, AL 35602 (Courier Address: Room 220, 400 Well St, Decatur, AL 35601), 256-353-2817, Fax: 256-350-7334.

http://www.alnb.uscourts.gov

Counties: Colbert, Cullman, Franklin, Jackson, Lauderdale, Lawrence, Limestone, Madison, Morgan. The part of Winston County North of Double Springs is handled by this division.

Indexing/Storage: Cases are indexed by debtor as well as by case number. New cases are available in the index immediately after filing date. Along with the debtor's name and the case number, the searcher must provide the year the case was closed and the location where the case was filed. A computer index is maintained. Open records are located at this court.

Fee & Payment: The fee is $20.00 per item (one party name or case number). Payment may be made by money order, cashier check, personal check. Prepayment is required. Payee: Clerk, US Bankruptcy Court. Certification fee: $7.00 per document. Copy fee: $.50 per page.

Phone Search: If a searcher calls, the court will indicate charges but not release information. An automated voice case information service (VCIS) is available.

Mail Search: Always enclose a stamped self addressed envelope.

In Person: In person searching is available.

PACER: Sign-up number is 800-676-6856. Access fee is $.60 per minute. Toll-free access: 800-362-9279. Local access: 256-355-2349. Use of PC Anywhere v4.0 suggested. Case records are available back to 1992. Records are purged every six months. New civil records are available online after 1 day. PACER is available online at http://pacer.alnb.uscourts.gov.

Tuscaloosa Division PO Box 3226, Tuscaloosa, AL 35403 (Courier Address: 1118 Greensboro Ave, Tuscaloosa, AL 35401), 205-752-0426, Fax: 205-752-6468.

http://www.alnb.uscourts.gov

Counties: Bibb, Fayette, Greene, Lamar, Marion, Pickens, Sumter, Tuscaloosa, Walker, Winston.

The part of Winston County North of Double Springs is handled by Decatur Division.

Indexing/Storage: Cases are indexed by debtor as well as by case number. New cases are available in the index 2 days after filing date. Both computer and card indexes are maintained. Card indexes are maintained on cases filed prior to October 1, 1979. Computer indexes only on cases filed commencing October 1, 1979. Open records are located at this court.

Fee & Payment: The fee is $20.00 per item (one party name or case number). Payment may be made by money order, cashier check, business check. Personal checks are not accepted. Prepayment is required. Payee: Clerk, US Bankruptcy Court. Certification fee: $7.00 per document. Copy fee: $.50 per page.

Phone Search: An automated voice case information service (VCIS) is available.

Mail Search: Always enclose a stamped self addressed envelope.

In Person: In person searching is available.

PACER: Sign-up number is 800-676-6856. Access fee is $.60 per minute. Toll-free access: 800-686-5824. Local access: 205-758-1309. Use of PC Anywhere v4.0 suggested. Case records are available back to 1990. Records are never purged. New civil records are available online after 1 day. PACER is available online at http://pacer.alnb.uscourts.gov.

US District Court

Southern District of Alabama

Mobile Division Clerk, 113 St Joseph St, Mobile, AL 36602 (Courier Address: Use mail address for courier delivery), 334-690-2371.

http://www.als.uscourts.gov

Counties: Baldwin, Choctaw, Clarke, Conecuh, Escambia, Mobile, Monroe, Washington.

Indexing/Storage: Cases are indexed by defendant and plaintiff as well as by case number. New cases are available in the index immediately after filing date. A computer index is maintained. Open records are located at this court.

Fee & Payment: The fee is $20.00 per item (one party name or case number). Payment may be made by money order, cashier check, personal check. Prepayment is required. Payee: Clerk, US District Court. Certification fee: $7.00 per document. Copy fee: $.50 per page. You are allowed to make your own copies. These copies cost $.25 per page.

Phone Search: Will only check docket information for a case number over the phone. An automated voice case information service (VCIS) is not available.

Mail Search: Always enclose a stamped self addressed envelope.

In Person: In person searching is available.

PACER: Sign-up number is 800-676-6856. Access fee is $.60 per minute. Toll-free access: 800-622-9392. Local access: 334-694-4672. Case records are available back to 1993. New records are available online after 1 day. PACER is available online at http://pacer.alsd.uscourts.gov.

Other Online Access: Search records on the Internet using RACER at http://racer.alsd.uscourts.gov/perl/bkplog.html. Acess fee is 7 cents per page.

Selma Division c/o Mobile Division, 113 St Joseph St, Mobile, AL 36602 (Courier Address: Use mail address for courier delivery), 334-690-2371.

http://www.als.uscourts.gov

Counties: Dallas, Hale, Marengo, Perry, Wilcox.

Indexing/Storage: Cases are indexed by defendant and plaintiff as well as by case number. New cases are available in the index immediately after filing date. A computer index is maintained. Open records are located at the Division.

Fee & Payment: The fee is $20.00 per item (one party name or case number). Payment may be made by money order, cashier check. Business checks are not accepted. Personal checks are not accepted. Certification fee: $7.00 per document. Copy fee: $.50 per page.

Phone Search: An automated voice case information service (VCIS) is not available.

Mail Search: Always enclose a stamped self addressed envelope.

In Person: In person searching is available.

PACER: Sign-up number is 800-676-6856. Access fee is $.60 per minute. Toll-free access: 800-622-9392. Local access: 334-694-4672. Case records are available back to 1993. New records are available online after 1 day. PACER is available online at http://pacer.alsd.uscourts.gov.

Other Online Access: Search records on the Internet using RACER at http://racer.alsd.uscourts.gov/perl/bkplog.html. Acess fee is 7 cents per page.

US Bankruptcy Court

Southern District of Alabama

Mobile Division Clerk, 201 St. Louis St, Mobile, AL 36602 (Courier Address: Use mail address for courier delivery), 334-441-5391, Fax: 334-441-6286.

http://www.alsb.uscourts.gov

Counties: Baldwin, Choctaw, Clarke, Conecuh, Dallas, Escambia, Hale, Marengo, Mobile, Monroe, Perry, Washington, Wilcox.

Indexing/Storage: Cases are indexed by debtor as well as by case number. New cases are available in the index immediately after filing date. Both computer and card indexes are maintained. Open records are located at this court. District wide computer searches are available for information from 1985 for this court.

Fee & Payment: The fee is $20.00 per item (one party name or case number). Payment may be made by money order, cashier check, business check. Personal checks are not accepted. Prepayment is required. Payee: Clerk, US Bankruptcy Court. Certification fee: $7.00 per document. Copy fee: $.50 per page. You are allowed to make your own copies. These copies cost $.25 per page.

Phone Search: Only the name and case number is released over the phone. An automated voice case information service (VCIS) is available.

Mail Search: A stamped self addressed envelope is not required.

In Person: In person searching is available.

PACER: Sign-up number is 800-676-6856. Access fee is $.60 per minute. Toll-free access: 800-622-9392. Local access: 334-441-5638, 334-441-5639. Case records are available back to 1993. New civil records are available online after 1 day.

Alabama County Courts

Court	Jurisdiction	No. of Courts	How Organized
Circuit Courts*	General	17	40 Circuits
District Courts*	Limited	15	67 Districts
Combined Courts*		61	
Municipal Courts	Municipal	253	
Probate Courts*	Probate	68	

* Profiled in this Sourcebook.

Court	CIVIL								
	Tort	Contract	Real Estate	Min. Claim	Max. Claim	Small Claims	Estate	Eviction	Domestic Relations
Circuit Courts*	X	X	X	$3000	No Max				X
District Courts*	X	X	X	$3000	$10,000	$3000		X	
Municipal Courts									
Probate Courts*							X		

Court	CRIMINAL				
	Felony	Misdemeanor	DWI/DUI	Preliminary Hearing	Juvenile
Circuit Courts*	X				
District Courts*		X	X	X	X
Municipal Courts		X	X		
Probate Courts*					

ADMINISTRATION   Director of Courts, 300 Dexter Ave, Montgomery, AL, 36104; 334-242-0300, Fax: 334-242-2099. www.alacourt.org

COURT STRUCTURE   Circuit Courts are the courts of general jurisdiction; District Courts have limited jurisdiction in civil matters. These courts are combined in all but eight larger counties. Barbour, Coffee, Jefferson, St. Clair, Talladega, and Tallapoosa Counties have two court locations within the county.

Jefferson County (Birmingham), Madison (Huntsville), Marshall, and Tuscaloosa Counties have separate criminal divisions for Circuit and/or District Courts. Misdemeanors committed with felonies are tried with the felony. The Circuit Courts are appeals courts for misdemeanors.

District Courts can receive guilty pleas in felony cases.

ONLINE ACCESS   A commercial online system is available over the Internet or through the Remote Access system of the State Judicial Information System (SJIS). Access is designed to provide "off-site" users with a means to retrieve basic case information and to allow a user access to any criminal, civil, or traffic record in the state. The system is available 24 hours per day. There is a $150 setup fee, and the monthly charge is $50 for unlimited access Call Cheryl Lenoir at 334-242-0300 for add'l information. The Alabama legal information web site offers commercial access to appellate opinions. For more information, go to http://alacourt.org. Also, a private firm offers access to these records; visit their web site at www.alacourt.com.

ADDITIONAL INFORMATION   Although in most counties Circuit and District courts are combined, each index may be separate. Therefore, when you request a search of both courts, be sure to state that the search is to cover "both the Circuit and District Court records." Several offices do not perform searches. Some offices do not have public access computer terminals.

📖📖📖📖📖📖

Autauga County

Circuit & District Court 134 N Court St, #114, Prattville, AL 36067-3049; 334-361-3737. Hours: 8AM-5PM (CST). *Felony, Misdemeanor, Civil, Eviction, Small Claims.*

Civil Records: Access: Mail, online, in person. Both court and visitors may perform in person searches. No search fee. Required to search: name, years to search.

Civil cases indexed by defendant, plaintiff. Civil records on computer since 1977 and in books from 1950. Online access available through SJIS. See state introduction.

Criminal Records: Access: Mail, online, in person. Both court and visitors may perform in person searches. No search fee. Required to search: name, years to search; also helpful: DOB, SSN. Criminal records on computer since 1977 and in books from 1950. Online access available through SJIS. See state introduction.

General Information: Public Access terminal is available. No sealed, adoptions, youthful offenders or juvenile records released. Turnaround time 1-2 weeks. Copy fee: $.25 per page. Certification fee: $2.25. Fee payee: Circuit Court. Only cashiers checks and money orders accepted. Prepayment is required.

Probate Court 176 W 5th, Prattville, AL 36067; 334-361-3725; Fax: 334-361-3740. Hours: 8:30AM-5PM (CST). *Probate.*

Baldwin County

Circuit & District Court PO Box 1149, Bay Minette, AL 36507; 334-937-0370; Civil phone: 334-937-0277; Criminal phone: 334-937-0280. Hours: 8AM-4:30PM (CST). *Felony, Misdemeanor, Civil, Eviction, Small Claims.*

Civil Records: Access: Online, in person. Visitors must perform in person searches for themselves. No search fee. Required to search: name, years to search. Civil cases indexed by defendant, plaintiff. Civil records indexed on computer from 1977, index books by case # to early 1900s. Online access available through SJIS. See state introduction.

Criminal Records: Access: Online, in person. Visitors must perform in person searches for themselves. No search fee. Required to search: name, years to search, DOB. Criminal records indexed on computer from 1977, index books by case # to early 1900s. Online access available through SJIS. See state introduction.

General Information: Public Access terminal is available. No sealed, adoptions, youthful offenders or juvenile records released. Certification fee: $1.00. Fee payee: Circuit Court Clerk. Only cashiers checks and money orders accepted. Prepayment is required.

Probate Court PO Box 459, Bay Minette, AL 36507; 251-937-9561. Hours: 8AM-4:30PM (CST). *Probate.*

Barbour County

Circuit & District Court - Clayton Division

PO Box 219, Clayton, AL 36016; 334-775-8366; Probate phone: 334-775-8371; Fax: 334-775-1125. Hours: 8AM-5PM (CST). *Felony, Misdemeanor, Civil, Eviction, Small Claims, Probate.*

Note: Probate court is separate from this court, and can be contacted at the telephone number above.

Civil Records: Access: Phone, mail, online, in person. Both court and visitors may perform in person searches. Search fee: $5.00 per name. Fee is per division. Required to search: name, years to search. Civil cases indexed by defendant. Civil records on computer back to 1993; books from 1977; archives back to 1920. Online access available through SJIS. See state introduction.

Criminal Records: Access: Mail, online, in person. Both court and visitors may perform in person searches. Search fee: $5.00 per name. $5.00 per division. Required to search: name, years to search, DOB; also helpful: SSN. Criminal records on computer back to 1993, books from 1977; archives back to 1920. Online access available through SJIS. See state introduction.

General Information: Public Access terminal is available. No sealed, adoptions, youthful offenders records released. SASE required. Turnaround time 2-3 days. Fax notes: Fee to fax results is $.50 per page. Copy fee: $.50 per page. Certification fee: $1.50. Fee payee: David S Nix. Business checks accepted.

Circuit & District Court - Eufaula Division

303 E Broad St, Rm 201, Eufaula, AL 36027; 334-687-1513/1516; Probate phone: 334-687-1530; Fax: 334-687-1599. Hours: 8AM-4:30PM (CST). *Misdemeanor, Civil, Eviction, Small Claims, Probate.*

Note: Probate court is separate from this court, and can be contacted at the telephone number above.

Civil Records: Access: Online, in person. Visitors must perform in person searches for themselves. No search fee. Required to search: name, years to search. Civil cases indexed by defendant, plaintiff. Civil records on computer from 1993. Index from 1977 to present, records are easily searched, prior to 1977 more difficult

to search. Online access available through SJIS. See state introduction.

Criminal Records: Access: Online, in person. Visitors must perform in person searches for themselves. No search fee. Required to search: name, years to search; also helpful: DOB, SSN. Criminal records on computer from 1993. Index from 1977 to present, records are easily searched, prior to 1977 more difficult to search. Online access available through SJIS. See state introduction.

General Information: Public Access terminal is available. No sealed, adoptions, youthful offenders or juvenile records released. Copy fee: $.25 per page. Certification fee: $3.00. Fee payee: Clerk of Courts. Personal checks accepted. Prepayment is required.

Bibb County

Circuit & District Court Bibb County Courthouse, PO Box 185, Centreville, AL 35042; 205-926-3103 Civil (Circuit); Civil phone: 205-926-3100 (Dist); Criminal phone: 205-926-3107; Probate phone: 205-926-3108; Fax: 205-926-3132. Hours: 8AM-5PM (CST). *Felony, Misdemeanor, Civil, Eviction, Small Claims, Probate.*

Note: Probate court is separate from this court, and can be contacted at the telephone number above.

Civil Records: Access: Mail, online, in person. Both court and visitors may perform in person searches. No search fee. Required to search: name, years to search. Civil cases indexed by defendant. Civil records on index book back to 1940s. Online access available through SJIS. See state introduction.

Criminal Records: Access: Mail, online, in person. Both court and visitors may perform in person searches. No search fee. Required to search: name, years to search, DOB; also helpful: SSN. Criminal records on computer from 1988, on index books back to 1940s. Online access available through SJIS. See state introduction.

General Information: Public Access terminal is available. No sealed, adoptions, youthful offenders or juvenile records released. SASE required. Turnaround time 3-4 days. Copy fee: $.25 per page. Certification fee: $1.00 plus $.25 per page. Fee payee: John H Stacy, Clerk. Business checks accepted. Prepayment required.

Blount County

Circuit & District Court 220 2nd Ave East Room 208, Oneonta, AL 35121; 205-625-4153. Hours: 8AM-5PM (CST). *Felony, Misdemeanor, Civil, Eviction, Small Claims.*

Civil Records: Access: Mail, online, in person. Both court and visitors may perform in person searches. Search fee: $10.00 per name. Required to search: name, years to search. Civil cases indexed by defendant, plaintiff. Civil records on computer from March 1994, on index books from 1977. Online access available through SJIS. See state introduction.

Criminal Records: Access: Mail, online, in person. Both court and visitors may perform in person searches. Search fee: $10.00 per name. Required to search: name, years to search, DOB; also helpful: SSN. Criminal records on computer from March 1994, on index books from 1977. Online access available through SJIS. See state introduction.

General Information: Public Access terminal is available. No sealed, adoptions, youthful offenders or juvenile records released. SASE required. Turnaround time up to 1 month. Copy fee: $.25 per page. Certification fee: $1.25. Fee payee: Mike Chriswell. No personal checks accepted. Prepayment is required.

Probate Court 220 2nd Ave E, Oneonta, AL 35121; 205-625-4191; Fax: 205-625-4206. Hours: 8AM-4PM M,T,W,F 8AM-Noon Th,Sat (CST). *Probate.*

Bullock County

Circuit & District Court PO Box 230, Union Springs, AL 36089; 334-738-2280; Probate phone: 334-738-2250; Fax: 334-738-2282. Hours: 8AM-4:30PM (CST). *Felony, Misdemeanor, Civil, Eviction, Small Claims, Probate.*

Note: Probate court is separate from this court, and can be contacted at the telephone number above.

Civil Records: Access: Phone, fax, mail, online, in person. Both court and visitors may perform in person searches. No search fee. Required to search: name, years to search. Civil cases indexed by defendant, plaintiff. Civil records on index books back to 1930s; on computer back to 1996. Online access available through SJIS. See state introduction.

Criminal Records: Access: Phone, fax, mail, online, in person. Both court and visitors may perform in person searches. No search fee. Required to search: name, years to search, DOB; also helpful: SSN, signed release. Criminal records on index books back to 1930s; on computer back to 1996. Online access available through SJIS. See state introduction.

General Information: No sealed, adoptions, youthful offenders or juvenile records released. SASE required. Turnaround time depends on clerk availability. Fax notes: No fee to fax results.

Butler County

Circuit & District Court PO Box 236, Greenville, AL 36037; 334-382-3521; Probate phone: 334-382-3512. Hours: 8AM-4PM (CST). *Felony, Misdemeanor, Civil, Eviction, Small Claims, Probate.*

Note: Probate court is separate from this court, and can be contacted at the telephone number above.

Civil Records: Access: Mail, online, in person. Both court and visitors may perform in person searches. Search fee: $5.00 per name. Fee is for first 2-3 years. Required to search: name, years to search. Civil cases indexed by defendant, plaintiff. Civil records on computer from 1992, books to 1979. Online access available through SJIS. See state introduction.

Criminal Records: Access: Mail, online, in person. Both court and visitors may perform in person searches. Search fee: $5.00 per name. Fee for first 2-3 years. Required to search: name, years to search, DOB; also helpful: SSN. Criminal records on computer from 1992, books to 1979. Online access available through SJIS. See state introduction.

General Information: No sealed, adoptions, youthful offenders or juvenile records released. SASE requested. Turnaround time 1-2 weeks. Copy fee: $.50 per page. Certification fee: $1.50 per page. Fee payee: Butler County District Court. Business checks accepted. Prepayment is required.

Calhoun County

Circuit Court 25 W 11th St, Suite 300, Anniston, AL 36201; 256-231-1750; Fax: 256-231-1826. Hours: 8AM-4:30PM (CST). *Felony, Civil Actions Over $10,000.*

Civil Records: Access: Online, in person. Visitors must perform in person searches for themselves. No search fee. Required to search: name, years to search. Civil cases indexed by defendant, plaintiff. Civil records indexed on computer from 1970s, prior in books. Online access available through SJIS. See state introduction.

Criminal Records: Access: Online, in person. Visitors must perform in person searches for themselves. No search fee. Required to search: name, years to search, DOB; also helpful: SSN. Criminal records indexed on computer from 1970s, prior on books. Online access available through SJIS. See state introduction.

General Information: Public Access terminal is available. No sealed, adoptions, youthful offenders or juvenile records released. Copy fee: $.25 per page. Certification fee: $1.00. Personal checks accepted. Prepayment is required.

District Court 25 W 11th St, Box 9, Anniston, AL 36201; 256-231-1850; Fax: 256-231-1826. Hours: 8AM-4:30PM (CST). *Misdemeanor, Civil Actions Under $10,000, Eviction, Small Claims.*

Civil Records: Access: Online, in person. Visitors must perform in person searches for themselves. No search fee. Required to search: name, years to search. Civil cases indexed by defendant, plaintiff. Civil records on computer from 1989, books from 1977 to 1989. Online access available through SJIS. See state introduction.

Criminal Records: Access: Online, in person. Visitors must perform in person searches for themselves. No search fee. Required to search: name, years to search; also helpful: SSN. Criminal records on computer from 1989, books from 1977 to 1989. Online access available through SJIS. See state introduction.

General Information: Public Access terminal is available. No sealed, adoptions, youthful offenders or juvenile records released. Copy fee: $.25 per page. Certification fee: $1.25. Fee payee: District Court. Personal checks accepted. Prepayment is required.

Probate Court 1702 Noble St, #102, Anniston, AL 36201; 256-241-2825. *Probate.*

Chambers County

Circuit & District Court Chambers County Courthouse, Lafayette, AL 36862; 334-864-4348; Probate phone: 334-864-4372. Hours: 8AM-4:30PM (CST). *Felony, Misdemeanor, Civil, Eviction, Small Claims, Probate.*

Note: Probate court is separate from this court, and can be contacted at the telephone number above.

Civil Records: Access: Mail, online, in person. Both court and visitors may perform in person searches. No search fee. Required to search: name, years to search. Civil cases indexed by defendant, plaintiff. Civil records on computer from 4/93, on index books to early 1900s. Online access available through SJIS. See state introduction.

Criminal Records: Access: Mail, online, in person. Both court and visitors may perform in person searches. No search fee. Required to search: name, years to search; also helpful: DOB, SSN. Criminal records are computerized since 1993. Online access available through SJIS. See state introduction.

General Information: No sealed, adoptions, youthful offenders or juvenile records released. Turnaround time 1 week. Copy fee: $.25 per page. Certification fee: $1.00. Business checks accepted.

Cherokee County

Circuit & District Court 100 Main St, Rm 203, Centre, AL 35960-1532; 256-927-3340. Hours: 8AM-4:30PM (CST). *Felony, Misdemeanor, Civil, Eviction, Small Claims.*

Civil Records: Access: Mail, online, in person. Both court and visitors may perform in person searches. No search fee. Required to search: name, years to search. Civil cases indexed by defendant, plaintiff. Civil records on books from 1977. Online access available through SJIS. See state introduction.

Criminal Records: Access: Mail, online, in person. Both court and visitors may perform in person searches. No search fee. Required to search: name, years to search; also helpful: DOB, SSN. Criminal records on books from 1977. Online access available through SJIS. See state introduction.

General Information: Public Access terminal is available. No sealed, adoptions, youthful offenders or juvenile records released. Turnaround time up to 2 wks. Copy fee: $.25 per page. Certification fee: $1.00. Fee

payee: Circuit Clerk. Business checks accepted. Prepayment is required.

Probate Court 100 Main St, Rm 204, Centre, AL 35960; 256-927-3363; Fax: 256-927-6949. Hours: 8AM-4PM M-F, 8AM-Noon Sat (CST). *Probate.*

Chilton County

Circuit & District Court PO Box 1946, Clanton, AL 35046; 205-755-4275; Probate phone: 205-755-1555. Hours: 8AM-5PM (CST). *Felony, Misdemeanor, Civil, Eviction, Small Claims, Probate.*

Note: Probate court is separate from this court, and can be contacted at the telephone number above.

Civil Records: Access: Online, in person. Visitors must perform in person searches for themselves. No search fee. Required to search: name, years to search. Civil cases indexed by defendant, plaintiff. Civil records on computer from 9/93, on books from 1950s. Online access available through SJIS. See state introduction.

Criminal Records: Access: Online, in person. Visitors must perform in person searches for themselves. No search fee. Required to search: name, years to search; also helpful: DOB, SSN. Criminal records on computer since 1977. Online access available through SJIS. See state introduction.

General Information: Public Access terminal is available. No sealed, adoptions, youthful offenders or juvenile records released. Copy fee: $.25 per page. Certification fee: $1.00. Fee payee: Clerk. Business checks accepted. Prepayment is required.

Choctaw County

Circuit & District Court Choctaw County Courthouse, Ste 10, Butler, AL 36904; 205-459-2155; Probate phone: 205-459-2417. Hours: 8AM-4:30PM (CST). *Felony, Misdemeanor, Civil, Eviction, Small Claims, Probate.*

Note: Probate court is separate from this court, and can be contacted at the telephone number above.

Civil Records: Access: Mail, online, in person. Both court and visitors may perform in person searches. No search fee. Required to search: name, years to search. Civil cases indexed by defendant, plaintiff. Civil records on index books from 1940. Putting records on computer starting September 1994. Online access available through SJIS. See state introduction.

Criminal Records: Access: Mail, online, in person. Both court and visitors may perform in person searches. No search fee. Required to search: name, years to search; also helpful: DOB, SSN. Criminal records on index books from 1940. Putting records on computer starting September 1994. Online access available through SJIS. See state introduction.

General Information: Public Access terminal is available. No sealed, adoptions, youthful offenders or juvenile records released. Copy fee: $.25 per page. Certification fee: $1.00. Fee payee: Circuit Clerk. Business checks accepted. Prepayment is required.

Clarke County

Circuit & District Court PO Box 921, Grove Hill, AL 36451; 334-275-3363; Probate phone: 334-275-3251. Hours: 8AM-5PM (CST). *Felony, Misdemeanor, Civil, Eviction, Small Claims, Probate.*

Note: Probate court is separate from this court, and can be contacted at the telephone number above.

Civil Records: Access: Mail, online, in person. Both court and visitors may perform in person searches. Search fee: $5.00 per name. Required to search: name, years to search. Civil cases indexed by defendant, plaintiff. Civil records on index cards from 1977. Online access available through SJIS. See state introduction.

Criminal Records: Access: Mail, online, in person. Both court and visitors may perform in person searches. Search fee: $5.00 per name. Required to search: name, years to search; also helpful: DOB, SSN. Criminal records on index cards from 1977. Online access available through SJIS. See state introduction.

General Information: No sealed, adoptions, youthful offenders or juvenile records released. Turnaround time 1 week. Copy fee: $.40 per page. Certification fee: $2.50. Fee payee: Circuit Clerk. Business checks accepted.

Clay County

Circuit & District Court PO Box 816, Ashland, AL 36251; 256-354-7926; Probate phone: 256-354-2198. Hours: 8AM-4:30PM (CST). *Felony, Misdemeanor, Civil, Eviction, Small Claims, Probate.*

Note: Probate court is separate from this court, and can be reached at the telephone number given above.

Civil Records: Access: Mail, online, in person. Visitors must perform in person searches for themselves. No search fee. Required to search: name, years to search. Civil cases indexed by defendant, plaintiff. Overall records go back to 1977; computerized records go back to 1994. Online access available through SJIS. See state introduction.

Criminal Records: Access: Mail, online, in person. Visitors must perform in person searches for themselves. No search fee. Required to search: name, years to search; also helpful: SSN, DOB, signed release. Overall records go back to 1977; computerized records go back to 1994. Online access available through SJIS. See state introduction.

General Information: Public Access terminal is available. No sealed, adoptions, youthful offenders or juvenile records released. Fax notes: Fee to fax results is $1.00 per page. Copy fee: $.25 per page. Certification fee: $1.25. Fee payee: Circuit Clerk. Business checks accepted.

Cleburne County

Circuit & District Court 120 Vickery St Room 202, Heflin, AL 36264; 256-463-2651; Probate phone: 256-463-5655; Fax: 256-463-2257. Hours: 8AM-4:30PM (CST). *Felony, Misdemeanor, Civil, Eviction, Small Claims, Probate.*

Note: Probate court is separate from this court, and can be contacted at the telephone number above.

Civil Records: Access: Phone, mail, online, in person. Both court and visitors may perform in person searches. No search fee. Required to search: name, years to search. Civil cases indexed by defendant, plaintiff. Civil records on computer from 1993, on books and cards from 1900. Online access available through SJIS. See state introduction.

Criminal Records: Access: Phone, mail, online, in person. Both court and visitors may perform in person searches. No search fee. Required to search: name, years to search, DOB; also helpful: SSN. Criminal records on computer from 1993, on books and cards from 1900. Online access available through SJIS. See state introduction.

General Information: Public Access terminal is available. No sealed, adoptions, youthful offenders or juvenile records released. SASE required. Turnaround time 1-2 days. Copy fee: $.25 per page. Certification fee: $1.00. Fee payee: Clerk. Only cashiers checks and money orders accepted.

Coffee County

Circuit & District Court - Elba Division 230
M Court Ave, Elba, AL 36323; 334-897-2954. Hours: 8AM-noon, 1-5PM (CST). *Felony, Misdemeanor, Civil, Eviction, Small Claims, Probate.*

Civil Records: Access: Mail, online, in person. Both court and visitors may perform in person searches. No search fee. Required to search: name, years to search. Civil cases indexed by defendant. Civil records on computer back to 8/1993. Online access available through SJIS. See state introduction.

Criminal Records: Access: Mail, online, in person. Both court and visitors may perform in person searches. No search fee. Required to search: name, years to search; also helpful: DOB. Criminal records on computer back to 8/1993. Online access available through SJIS. See state introduction.

General Information: Public Access terminal is available. No sealed, adoptions, youthful offenders or juvenile records released. SASE required. Turnaround time 3-4 days. Copy fee: $.25 per page. Certification fee: $1.25. Fee payee: Circuit Clerk. Business checks accepted.

Circuit & District Court - Enterprise Division PO Box 1294, Enterprise, AL 36331; 334-347-2519. Hours: 8AM-5PM (CST). *Felony, Misdemeanor, Civil, Eviction, Small Claims.*

Civil Records: Access: Mail, fax, online, in person. Both court and visitors may perform in person searches. No search fee. Required to search: name, years to search. Civil cases indexed by defendant, plaintiff. Civil records on computer since 8/1993. Online access available through SJIS. See state introduction.

Criminal Records: Access: Mail, fax, online, in person. Both court and visitors may perform in person searches. No search fee. Required to search: name, years to search, DOB; also helpful: SSN. Criminal records on computer since 8/1993. Online access available through SJIS. See state introduction.

General Information: No sealed, adoptions, youthful offenders or juvenile records released. Turnaround time up to 1 week. Copy fee: $.25 per page. Certification fee: $1.25. Fee payee: Clerk of Courts. Only cashiers checks and money orders accepted. Prepayment is required.

Probate Court - Enterprise Division PO Box 311247, Enterprise, AL 36331; 334-347-2688; Fax: 334-347-2095. Hours: 8AM-4:30PM (CST). *Probate.*

Colbert County

Circuit Court Colbert County Courthouse, 201 N main Street, Tuscumbia, AL 35674; 256-386-8512; Probate phone: 256-386-8542. Hours: 8AM-4:30PM (CST). *Felony, Civil Actions Over $10,000, Probate.*

Note: Probate court is separate from this court, and can be contacted at the telephone number above.

Civil Records: Access: Online, in person. Visitors must perform in person searches for themselves. No search fee. Required to search: name, years to search. Civil cases indexed by defendant, plaintiff. Civil records on computer from 1993, books from 1959. Online access available through SJIS. See state introduction.

Criminal Records: Access: Online, in person. Visitors must perform in person searches for themselves. No search fee. Required to search: name, years to search; also helpful: DOB, SSN. Criminal records on computer from 1993, books prior. Online access available through SJIS. See state introduction.

General Information: No sealed, youthful offenders or juvenile records released. Copy fee: $.25 per page. Certification fee: $1.00. Fee payee: Circuit Court Clerk. Business checks accepted. Prepayment is required.

District Court Colbert County Courthouse, 201 N Main Street, Tuscumbia, AL 35674; 256-386-8518. Hours: 7:30AM-4:30PM (CST). *Misdemeanor, Civil Actions Under $10,000, Eviction, Small Claims.*

Civil Records: Access: Online, in person. Visitors must perform in person searches for themselves. No search fee. Required to search: name, years to search. Civil cases indexed by defendant, plaintiff. Civil records on computer from 1993, prior on books. Online access available through SJIS. See state introduction.

Criminal Records: Access: Online, in person. Visitors must perform in person searches for themselves. No search fee. Required to search: name, years to search; also helpful: SSN. Criminal records on computer from 1993, prior on books. Online access available through SJIS. See state introduction.

General Information: Public Access terminal is available. No sealed, adoptions, youthful offenders or juvenile records released. Copy fee: $.25 per page. Certification fee: $1.00. Fee payee: Circuit Clerk. Only cashiers checks and money orders accepted. Prepayment is required.

Conecuh County

Circuit & District Court PO Box 107, Evergreen, AL 36401; 334-578-2066; Probate phone: 334-578-1221. Hours: 8AM-4:30PM (CST). *Felony, Misdemeanor, Civil, Eviction, Small Claims, Probate.*

Note: Probate court is separate from this court, and can be contacted at the telephone number above.

Civil Records: Access: Mail, online, in person. Both court and visitors may perform in person searches. No search fee. Required to search: name, years to search. Civil cases indexed by defendant, plaintiff. Civil records on index cards from 1977, on computer back to 12/1994. Online access available through SJIS. See state introduction.

Criminal Records: Access: Mail, online, in person. Both court and visitors may perform in person searches. No search fee. Required to search: name, years to search, DOB; also helpful: SSN. Criminal records on index cards from 1977, on computer back to 1994. Online access available through SJIS. See state introduction.

General Information: Public Access terminal is available. No sealed, adoptions, youthful offenders or juvenile records released. Turnaround time 1 week. Fax notes: Fee to fax results is $1.00 per page. Copy fee: $.50 per page. Certification fee: $2.50. Fee payee: Circuit Clerk, George Hendrix. Business checks accepted. Prepayment is required.

Coosa County

Circuit & District Court PO Box 98, Rockford, AL 35136; 256-377-4988; Probate phone: 256-377-4919. Hours: 8AM-4:30PM (CST). *Felony, Misdemeanor, Civil, Eviction, Small Claims, Probate.*

Note: Probate court is separate from this court, and can be contacted at the telephone number above.

Civil Records: Access: Online, in person. Visitors must perform in person searches for themselves. No search fee. Required to search: name, years to search. Civil cases indexed by plaintiff. Civil records on books from the late 1800s, computerized records go back to July 1994. Online access available through SJIS. See state introduction.

Criminal Records: Access: Online, in person. Visitors must perform in person searches for themselves. No search fee. Required to search: name, years to search; also helpful: DOB, SSN. Criminal records on books from the late 1800s, computerized records go back to July 1994. Online access available through SJIS. See state introduction.

General Information: No sealed, adoptions, youthful offenders or juvenile records released. Copy fee: $.25

per page. Certification fee: $1.00. Fee payee: Clerk of Court. Business checks accepted.

Covington County

Circuit & District Court Covington County Courthouse, Andalusia, AL 36420; 334-428-2520; Probate phone: 334-428-2510. Hours: 8AM-5PM (CST). *Felony, Misdemeanor, Civil, Eviction, Small Claims, Probate.*

Note: Probate court is separate from this court, and can be contacted at the telephone number above.

Civil Records: Access: Online, in person. Only the court performs in person searches; visitors may not. No search fee. Required to search: name, years to search. Civil cases indexed by defendant, plaintiff. Civil records on computer from 3/94; prior on books to 1920. Online access available through SJIS. See state introduction. Also, online access to probate records is available by subscription at www.recordsusa.com/Alabama/CovingtonCnAl.htm. Credit card, username and password is required; choose either monthly or per-use plan. Visit the web site or call Lisa at 601-264-7701 for information.

Criminal Records: Access: Online, in person. Only the court performs in person searches; visitors may not. No search fee. Required to search: name, years to search, DOB; also helpful: SSN. Criminal records on computer from 3/94; prior on books to 1920. Online access available through SJIS. See state introduction.

General Information: Public Access terminal is available. No sealed, adoptions, youthful offenders or juvenile records released. Copy fee: $.25 per page. Certification fee: $1.00. Fee payee: Circuit Clerk. Business checks accepted.

Crenshaw County

Circuit & District Court PO Box 167, Luverne, AL 36049; 334-335-6575; Probate phone: 334-335-6568; Fax: 334-335-2076. Hours: 8AM-4:30PM (CST). *Felony, Misdemeanor, Civil, Eviction, Small Claims, Probate.*

Note: Probate court is separate from this court, and can be contacted at the telephone number above.

Civil Records: Access: Mail, online, in person. Both court and visitors may perform in person searches. No search fee. Required to search: name, years to search. Civil cases indexed by defendant, plaintiff. Civil records on computer from 1993, on book from 1977. Online access available through SJIS. See state introduction.

Criminal Records: Access: Mail, online, in person. Both court and visitors may perform in person searches. No search fee. Required to search: name, years to search, DOB; also helpful: SSN. Criminal records on computer from 1993, on book from 1977. Online access available through SJIS. See state introduction.

General Information: Public Access terminal is available. No sealed, adoptions, youthful offenders or juvenile records released. SASE requested. Turnaround time 2-3 days. Copy fee: $.50 per page. Certification fee: No cert fee. Only cashiers checks and money orders accepted.

Cullman County

Circuit Court Cullman County Courthouse, Rm 303, 500 2nd Ave SW, Cullman, AL 35055; 256-775-4654; Probate phone: 256-775-4652. Hours: 8AM-4:30PM (CST). *Felony, Civil Actions Over $10,000, Probate.*

Civil Records: Access: Mail, online, in person. Both court and visitors may perform in person searches. No search fee. Required to search: name, years to search. Civil cases indexed by defendant, plaintiff. Civil records on computer back to 1993, books from 1900. Online access available through SJIS. See state introduction.

Criminal Records: Access: Mail, online, in person. Both court and visitors may perform in person searches. No search fee. Required to search: name, DOB; also helpful: years to search, SSN. Criminal records on computer back to 1993; prior in books. Online access available through SJIS. See state introduction.

General Information: Public Access terminal is available. No sealed, adoptions, youthful offenders or juvenile records released. SASE not required. Turnaround time 10 days. Copy fee: $.25 per page. Add postage costs if by mail. Certification fee: $1.00. Fee payee: Robert Bates, Circuit Clerk. Business checks accepted. Prepayment is required.

District Court 500 2nd Ave SW, Courthouse Rm 211, Cullman, AL 35055-4197; 256-775-4660. Hours: 8AM-4:30PM (CST). *Misdemeanor, Civil Actions Under $10,000, Eviction, Small Claims.*

Civil Records: Access: Mail, online, in person. Visitors must perform in person searches for themselves. No search fee. Required to search: name, years to search. Civil cases indexed by defendant. Civil records on computer from 11/92, on books 10 yrs back. Online access available through SJIS. See state introduction.

Criminal Records: Access: Mail, online, in person. Visitors must perform in person searches for themselves. No search fee. Required to search: name, years to search, DOB; also helpful: SSN. Criminal records on computer from 11/92, on books 10 yrs back. Online access available through SJIS. See state introduction.

General Information: Public Access terminal is available. No sealed, adoptions, youthful offenders or juvenile records released. SASE required. Turnaround time 1 week. Copy fee: $.25 per page. Certification fee: $1.25. Fee payee: District Clerk. Only cashiers checks and money orders accepted. Prepayment is required.

Dale County

Circuit & District Court PO Box 1350, Ozark, AL 36361; 334-774-5003; Probate phone: 334-774-2754. Hours: 8AM-4:30PM (CST). *Felony, Misdemeanor, Civil, Eviction, Small Claims, Probate.*

Note: Probate court is separate from this court, and can be contacted at the telephone number above.

Civil Records: Access: Online, in person. Visitors must perform in person searches for themselves. No search fee. Required to search: name, years to search. Civil cases indexed by defendant, plaintiff. Civil records on computer from 8/92, on books and index cards from the 1920s. Online access available through SJIS. See state introduction.

Criminal Records: Access: Online, in person. Visitors must perform in person searches for themselves. No search fee. Required to search: name, years to search, DOB; also helpful: SSN. Criminal records on computer from 8/92, on books and index cards from the 1920s. Online access available through SJIS. See state introduction.

General Information: Public Access terminal is available. No sealed, adoptions, youthful offenders or juvenile records released. Copy fee: $.25 per page. Certification fee: $1.00. Fee payee: Dale County Circuit Clerk. Only cashiers checks and money orders accepted.

Dallas County

Circuit Court PO Box 1148, Selma, AL 36702; 334-874-2523; Probate phone: 334-874-2597. Hours: 8AM-5PM (CST). *Felony, Civil Actions Over $10,000, Probate.*

Note: Probate court is separate from this court, and can be contacted at the telephone number above.

Civil Records: Access: Mail, online, in person. Both court and visitors may perform in person searches. No search fee. Required to search: name, years to search.

Civil cases indexed by defendant, plaintiff. Civil records on computer from 1980, on microfiche from the late 1800s, index books prior. Online access available through SJIS. See state introduction.

Criminal Records: Access: Phone, mail, online, in person. Both court and visitors may perform in person searches. No search fee. Required to search: name, years to search, DOB; also helpful: SSN. Criminal records on computer from 1980, on microfiche from the late 1800s, index books prior. Online access available through SJIS. See state introduction.

General Information: Public Access terminal is available. No sealed, adoptions, youthful offenders or juvenile records released. SASE required. Turnaround time less than 1 week for civil cases. Copy fee: $.25 per page. Certification fee: $1.00. Fee payee: Dallas County Circuit Court. Personal checks accepted. Prepayment is required.

District Court PO Box 1148, Selma, AL 36702; 334-874-2526. Hours: 8AM-5PM (CST). *Misdemeanor, Civil Actions Under $10,000, Eviction, Small Claims.*

Civil Records: Access: Phone, mail, online, in person. Visitors must perform in person searches for themselves. No search fee. Required to search: name, years to search. Civil cases indexed by defendant. Civil records on books from 1967, on computer since 1993. Online access available through SJIS. See state introduction.

Criminal Records: Access: Mail, online, in person. Visitors must perform in person searches for themselves. No search fee. Required to search: name, years to search; also helpful: DOB, SSN. Criminal records on books from 1967, on computer since 1993. Online access available through SJIS. See state introduction.

General Information: Public Access terminal is available. No sealed, adoptions, youthful offenders or juvenile records released. Copy fee: $.25 per page. Certification fee: $1.00. Fee payee: District Clerk. Personal checks accepted. Prepayment is required.

De Kalb County

Circuit & District Court PO Box 681149, Fort Payne, AL 35968; 256-845-8525; Probate phone: 256-845-8510. Hours: 8AM-4PM (CST). *Felony, Misdemeanor, Civil, Eviction, Small Claims, Probate.*

Note: Probate court is separate from this court, and can be contacted at the telephone number above.

Civil Records: Access: Mail, online, in person. Both court and visitors may perform in person searches. No search fee. Required to search: name, years to search. Civil cases indexed by defendant. Civil records on computer from August 1991, on books from 1959. Online access available through SJIS. See state introduction.

Criminal Records: Access: Mail, online, in person. Both court and visitors may perform in person searches. No search fee. Required to search: name, years to search; also helpful: DOB, SSN. Criminal records on computer from August 1991, on books from 1959. Online access available through SJIS. See state introduction.

General Information: Public Access terminal is available. No sealed, adoptions, youthful offenders or juvenile records released. Turnaround time 1 week. Copy fee: $.25 per page. Certification fee: $1.25. Business checks accepted.

Elmore County

Circuit & District Court - Civil Division PO Box 310, Wetumpka, AL 36092; 334-567-1123; Probate phone: 334-567-1139; Fax: 334-567-5957. Hours: 8AM-4:30PM (CST). *Civil, Probate.*

Note: Probate court is separate from this court, and can be contacted at the telephone number above.

Civil Records: Access: Online, in person. Visitors must perform in person searches for themselves. No search fee. Required to search: name, years to search. Civil cases indexed by defendant, plaintiff. Civil records on computer from 1983, books from 1930. Online access available through SJIS. See state introduction. **General Information:** Public Access terminal is available. No sealed, adoptions, youthful offenders or juvenile records released. Copy fee: $.25 per page. Certification fee: $1.25. Fee payee: Circuit Court Clerk. Business checks accepted. Prepayment is required.

Circuit Court - Criminal Division PO Box 310, 8935 US Hwy 23, Wetumpka, AL 36092; 334-567-1123; Fax: 334-567-5957. Hours: 8AM-4:30PM (CST). *Felony, Misdemeanor.*

Criminal Records: Access: Online, in person. Visitors must perform in person searches for themselves. No search fee. Required to search: name, years to search, DOB, SSN. Criminal records on computer from mid 1991, books from 1960-1992. Online access available through SJIS. See state introduction.

General Information: Public Access terminal is available. No sealed, adoptions, youthful offenders or juvenile records released. Copy fee: $.25 per page. Certification fee: $1.25. Fee payee: Circuit Court Clerk. Only cashiers checks and money orders accepted. Prepayment is required.

Escambia, County

Circuit & District Court PO Box 856, Brewton, AL 36427; 334-867-0305; Probate phone: 334-867-0201; Fax: 334-867-0365. Hours: 8AM-4:30PM (CST). *Felony, Misdemeanor, Civil, Eviction, Small Claims, Probate.*

Note: Probate court is separate from this court, and can be contacted at the telephone number above.

Civil Records: Access: Mail, fax, online, in person. Both court and visitors may perform in person searches. No search fee. Required to search: name, years to search. Civil cases indexed by defendant, plaintiff. Civil records on computer from 10/93, books and cards back 5 years. Online access available through SJIS. See state introduction.

Criminal Records: Access: Mail, fax, online, in person. Both court and visitors may perform in person searches. No search fee. Required to search: name, years to search, DOB. Criminal records on computer from 10/93, books and cards back 5 years. Online access available through SJIS. See state introduction.

General Information: No sealed, adoptions, youthful offenders or juvenile records released. SASE required. Turnaround time 2-3 days. Fax notes: Fee to fax results is $1.00 per document and $.25 per page. Copy fee: $.25 per page. Certification fee: $1.00. Business checks accepted.

Etowah County

Circuit & District Court PO Box 798 (801 Forrest Ave #202), Gadsden, AL 35902; 256-549-5437/5430; Probate phone: 256-549-8135. Hours: 8AM-5PM (CST). *Felony, Misdemeanor, Civil, Eviction, Small Claims.*

Note: Probate court is separate from this court.

Civil Records: Access: Mail, online, in person. Both court and visitors may perform in person searches. No search fee. Required to search: name, years to search. Civil cases indexed by defendant, plaintiff. Civil records on computer from 1984, index on computer since 1977, books prior to 1977. Online access available through SJIS. See state introduction.

Criminal Records: Access: Mail, online, in person. Both court and visitors may perform in person searches. No search fee. Required to search: name, years to search; also helpful: DOB, SSN. Criminal records on computer from 1984, index on computer since 1977, books prior to 1977. Online access available through SJIS. See state introduction.

General Information: Public Access terminal is available. No sealed, adoptions, youthful offenders or juvenile records released. SASE requested. Turnaround time 4-6 weeks. Copy fee: $.25 per page. Certification fee: $1.25. Fee payee: Clerk of Court. Only cashiers checks and money orders accepted.

Probate Court PO Box 187, Gadsden, AL 35901; 256-549-2150. *Probate.*

Fayette County

Circuit & District Court PO Box 206, Fayette, AL 35555; 205-932-4617; Probate phone: 205-932-4519. Hours: 8AM-4:30PM (CST). *Felony, Misdemeanor, Civil, Eviction, Small Claims, Probate.*

Note: Probate court is separate from this court, and can be contacted at the telephone number above.

Civil Records: Access: Online, mail, fax, in person. Visitors must perform in person searches for themselves. No search fee. Required to search: name, years to search. Civil cases indexed by defendant. Civil records on computer from 3/94, on books and cards from 1977. Online access available through SJIS. See state introduction.

Criminal Records: Access: Online, mail, fax, in person. Visitors must perform in person searches for themselves. No search fee. Required to search: name, years to search, DOB; also helpful: SSN. Criminal records on computer from 3/94, on books and cards from 1977. Online access available through SJIS. See state introduction.

General Information: Public Access terminal is available. No sealed, adoptions, youthful offenders or juvenile records released. Copy fee: $.25 per page. Certification fee: $1.00. Fee payee: Circuit Clerk. Business checks accepted.

Franklin County

Circuit & District Court PO Box 160, Russellville, AL 35653; 256-332-8861; Probate phone: 256-332-8801. Hours: 8AM-4:30PM (CST). *Felony, Misdemeanor, Civil, Eviction, Small Claims, Probate.*

Note: Note: Probate court is separate from this court, and can be contacted at the telephone number above or PO Box 70.

Civil Records: Access: Mail, online, in person. Both court and visitors may perform in person searches. Search fee: $5.00 per five years searched per name. Required to search: name, years to search; also helpful: address. Civil cases indexed by defendant, plaintiff. Civil records on computer from 1993, on index books prior. SSN and DOB helpful, but records are not indexed by SSN. Online access available through SJIS. See state introduction.

Criminal Records: Access: Mail, online, in person. Both court and visitors may perform in person searches. Search fee: $5.00 per five years searched per name. Required to search: name, years to search, DOB; also helpful: SSN. Criminal records on computer from 1993, on index books prior. SSN and DOB helpful, but records are not indexed by SSN. Online access available through SJIS. See state introduction.

General Information: Public Access terminal is available. No sealed, youthful offenders or juvenile released. SASE required. Turnaround time 3-4 days. Copy fee: $.25 per page. Certification fee: $1.00. Fee

payee: Circuit Court Clerk. Business checks accepted. Prepayment is required.

Geneva County

Circuit & District Court PO Box 86, Geneva, AL 36340; 334-684-5620; Probate phone: 334-684-2276; Fax: 334-684-5605. Hours: 8AM-5PM (CST). *Felony, Misdemeanor, Civil, Eviction, Small Claims, Probate.*

Note: Probate court is separate from this court, and can be contacted at the telephone number above.

Civil Records: Access: Mail, online, in person. Both court and visitors may perform in person searches. Search fee: $5.00 per name. Required to search: name, years to search; also helpful: address. Civil cases indexed by defendant, plaintiff. Civil records on computer from 1992, index cards from the 1950s. Online access available through SJIS. See state introduction.

Criminal Records: Access: Mail, online, in person. Both court and visitors may perform in person searches. Search fee: $5.00 per name. Required to search: name, years to search, DOB; also helpful: SSN. Criminal records on computer from 1992, index cards from the 1950s. Online access available through SJIS. See state introduction.

General Information: Public Access terminal is available. No sealed, adoptions, youthful offenders or juvenile records released. Turnaround time 1 week. Copy fee: $.25 per page. Certification fee: $1.50. Fee payee: Circuit Clerk Valerie Thomley. Business checks accepted. Out of state personal checks not accepted. Prepayment is required.

Greene County

Circuit & District Court PO Box 307, Eutaw, AL 35462; 205-372-3598; Probate phone: 205-372-3340. Hours: 8AM-4PM (CST). *Felony, Misdemeanor, Civil, Eviction, Small Claims, Probate.*

Note: Probate court is separate from this court, and can be contacted at the telephone number above.

Civil Records: Access: Mail, online, in person. Both court and visitors may perform in person searches. No search fee. Required to search: name, years to search; also helpful: DOB, SSN and signed release. Civil cases indexed by defendant, plaintiff. Civil records on books from 1984. Online access available through SJIS. See state introduction.

Criminal Records: Access: Mail, online, in person. Both court and visitors may perform in person searches. No search fee. Required to search: name, years to search; also helpful: DOB, SSN and signed release. Criminal records on books from 1984. Online access available through SJIS. See state introduction.

General Information: Public Access terminal is available. No sealed, adoptions, youthful offenders or juvenile records released. SASE required. Turnaround time 1 week. Copy fee: $.25 per page. Certification fee: $1.25. Fee payee: Circuit Clerk. Business checks accepted. Prepayment is required.

Hale County

Circuit & District Court Hale County Courthouse, Rm 8, PO Drawer 99, Greensboro, AL 36744; 334-624-4334; Probate phone: 334-624-7391. Hours: 8AM-5PM (CST). *Felony, Misdemeanor, Civil, Eviction, Small Claims, Probate.*

Note: Probate court is separate from this court, and can be contacted at the telephone number above.

Civil Records: Access: Mail, online, in person. Both court and visitors may perform in person searches. No search fee. Required to search: name, years to search. Civil cases indexed by defendant, plaintiff. Civil records on books from 1985. Online access available through SJIS. See state introduction.

Criminal Records: Access: Mail, online, in person. Both court and visitors may perform in person searches. No search fee. Required to search: name, years to search; also helpful: DOB, SSN. Criminal records on books from 1985. Online access available through SJIS. See state introduction.

General Information: Public Access terminal is available. No sealed, adoptions, youthful offenders or juvenile records released. Turnaround time 1 week. Copy fee: $.25 per page. Certification fee: $1.00. Fee payee: Clerk of the Court. Business checks accepted. In state personal checks accepted. Prepayment is required.

Henry County

Circuit & District Court 101 W Court St, Suite J, Abbeville, AL 36310-2135; 334-585-2753; Probate phone: 334-585-3257; Fax: 334-585-5006. Hours: 8AM-4:30PM (CST). *Felony, Misdemeanor, Civil, Eviction, Small Claims, Probate.*

Note: Probate court is separate from this court, and can be contacted at the telephone number above.

Civil Records: Access: Mail, online, in person. Both court and visitors may perform in person searches. Search fee: $3.00 per name. Required to search: name, years to search. Civil cases indexed by defendant. Civil records on computer from 1994, index cards 10 yrs back. Online access available through SJIS. See state introduction.

Criminal Records: Access: Mail, online, in person. Both court and visitors may perform in person searches. Search fee: $3.00 per name. Required to search: name, years to search, DOB; also helpful: SSN. Criminal records on computer from 5/93, index cards 10 yrs back. Online access available through SJIS. See state introduction.

General Information: No sealed, adoptions, youthful offenders or juvenile records released. SASE required. Turnaround time 2-3 day. Copy fee: $.25 per page. Certification fee: $1.00. Fee payee: Circuit Clerk. Personal checks accepted. Prepayment is required.

Houston County

Circuit & District Court PO Drawer 6406, Dothan, AL 36302; 334-677-4800/4872; Probate phone: 334-677-4719. Hours: 7:30AM-4:30PM (CST). *Felony, Misdemeanor, Civil, Eviction, Small Claims, Probate.*

Note: Probate court is separate from this court, and can be contacted at the telephone number above.

Civil Records: Access: Mail, online, in person. Both court and visitors may perform in person searches. No search fee. Required to search: name, years to search. Civil cases indexed by defendant. Civil records on computer from 1977, index books from 1950s. Online access available through SJIS. See state introduction.

Criminal Records: Access: Mail, online, in person. Both court and visitors may perform in person searches. No search fee. Required to search: name, years to search; also helpful: DOB, SSN. Criminal records on computer from 1977, index books from 1950s. Online access available through SJIS. See state introduction.

General Information: Public Access terminal is available. No sealed, adoptions, youthful offenders or juvenile records released. Turnaround time 1 week. Copy fee: $.25 per page. Certification fee: $1.00. Fee payee: Judy Byrd. Business checks accepted. Prepayment is required.

Jackson County

Circuit & District Court PO Box 397, Scottsboro, AL 35768; Civil phone: 256-574-9320; Criminal phone: 256-574-9323; Probate phone: 256-574-9290; Fax: 256-259-9981. Hours: 8AM-4:30PM (CST). *Felony, Misdemeanor, Civil, Eviction, Small Claims, Probate.*

Note: Probate court is separate from this court, and can be contacted at the telephone number above.

Civil Records: Access: Mail, fax, online, in person. Both court and visitors may perform in person searches. No search fee. Required to search: name, years to search. Civil cases indexed by defendant. Civil records on computer from 5/1993, on cards from 1977. Online access available through SJIS. See state introduction.

Criminal Records: Access: Mail, fax, online, in person. Both court and visitors may perform in person searches. No search fee. Required to search: name, years to search, DOB; also helpful: SSN. Criminal records on computer from 5/1993, on cards from 1977. Online access available through SJIS. See state introduction.

General Information: Public Access terminal is available. No sealed, adoptions, youthful offenders or juvenile records released. SASE required. Turnaround time 1-2 days. Copy fee: $.25 per page. Certification fee: $2.00. Fee payee: Circuit Court Clerk. Only cashiers checks and money orders accepted. Prepayment is required.

Jefferson County

Circuit Court - Bessemer Division Rm 606, Courthouse Annex, Bessemer, AL 35020; 205-481-4165. Hours: 8AM-5PM (CST). *Felony, Civil Actions Over $10,000.*

Civil Records: Access: Online, in person. Visitors must perform in person searches for themselves. No search fee. Required to search: name, years to search. Civil cases indexed by defendant, plaintiff. Civil records on computer from 1988, on index books from 1930s to 1977. Online access available through SJIS. See state introduction.

Criminal Records: Access: Online, in person. Visitors must perform in person searches for themselves. No search fee. Required to search: name, years to search, DOB; also helpful: SSN. Criminal records on computer from 1988, on index books from 1930s to 1977. Online access available through SJIS. See state introduction.

General Information: Public Access terminal is available. No sealed, adoptions, youthful offenders or juvenile records released. Copy fee: $.25 per page. Certification fee: $1.25. Fee payee: Clerk of Circuit Court. Business checks accepted. Prepayment is required.

District Court - Bessemer Division Rm 506, Courthouse Annex, Bessemer, AL 35020; 205-481-4187. Hours: 8AM-5PM (CST). *Misdemeanor, Civil Actions Under $10,000, Eviction, Small Claims.*

Civil Records: Access: Online, in person. Visitors must perform in person searches for themselves. No search fee. Required to search: name, years to search. Civil cases indexed by defendant, plaintiff. Civil records on computer from 1986, on index cards from 1977, prior on docket books. Online access available through SJIS. See state introduction.

Criminal Records: Access: Online, in person. Visitors must perform in person searches for themselves. No search fee. Required to search: name, years to search, DOB; also helpful: SSN. Criminal records on computer from 1986, on index cards from 1977, prior on docket books. Online access available through SJIS. See state introduction.

General Information: Public Access terminal is available. No sealed, adoptions, youthful offenders or

juvenile records released. Copy fee: $.25 per page. Certification fee: $1.25. Fee payee: Bessemer District Court. Business checks accepted. Prepayment is required.

Circuit Court - Birmingham Civil Division 716 N 21st St, Rm 400, Birmingham, AL 35263; 205-325-5355. Hours: 8AM-5PM (CST). *Civil Actions Over $10,000 (Over $5,000 if jury trial).*

Civil Records: Access: Phone, mail, online, in person. Both court and visitors may perform in person searches. No search fee. Required to search: name, years to search. Civil cases indexed by defendant, plaintiff. Civil records on computer from 1976, on index books from 1976 to 1986, prior to 1976 archived. Online access available through SJIS. See state introduction. **General Information:** Public Access terminal is available. No sealed, adoptions, youthful offenders or juvenile records released. Turnaround time 1-2 weeks. Copy fee: $.25 per page. Certification fee: $1.25. Fee payee: Clerk of Circuit Court. Business checks accepted. Prepayment is required. Under $10.00 need not prepay.

Circuit Court - Birmingham Criminal Division 801 N 21st St, Rm 506, Birmingham, AL 35263; 205-325-5285. Hours: 8AM-4:55PM (CST). *Felony.*

Criminal Records: Access: Online, in person. Visitors must perform in person searches for themselves. No search fee. Required to search: name, years to search, DOB, signed release; also helpful: address, SSN. Criminal records on computer from 1960s, index books prior. Online access available through SJIS. See state introduction.

General Information: Public Access terminal is available. No sealed, adoptions, youthful offenders, sex offender cases or juvenile records released. Copy fee: $.25 per page. Certification fee: $1.00. Fee payee: Clerk of Court. Only cashiers checks and money orders accepted. Prepayment is required.

District Court - Birmingham Civil Division 716 Richard Arrington BLVD N, Birmingham, AL 35203; 205-325-5331. Hours: 8AM-5PM (CST). *Civil Actions Under $10,000, Eviction, Small Claims.*

Civil Records: Access: Phone, mail, online, in person. Both court and visitors may perform in person searches. No search fee. Required to search: name, years to search. Civil cases indexed by defendant, plaintiff. Civil records on computer from 1977, index books stored in warehouse. Online access available through SJIS. See state introduction. **General Information:** Public Access terminal is available. No sealed, adoptions, youthful offenders or juvenile records released. SASE required. Turnaround time 1-2 days. Copy fee: $.25 per page. Certification fee: $1.00. Fee payee: District Court. Only cashiers checks and money orders accepted. Prepayment is required.

District Court - Birmingham Criminal Division 801 Richard Arrington Blvd N, Rm 207, Birmingham, AL 35203; 205-325-5309. Hours: 8AM-5PM (CST). *Misdemeanor.*

Criminal Records: Access: Mail, online, in person. Both court and visitors may perform in person searches. Search fee: $1.25. Required to search: name, DOB; also helpful: years to search, SSN, sex, date of arrest. Criminal records on computer from 1986. To search for records prior to 1987, require arrest date. Online access available through SJIS. See state introduction.

General Information: Public Access terminal is available. No sealed, sexual abuse, adoptions, youthful offenders or juvenile records released. Turnaround time 5-10 days. Copy fee: $.25 per page. Certification fee: $1.25. Fee payee: District Court. Only cashiers checks and money orders accepted. Prepayment is required.

Probate Court 716 Richard Arrington Jr Blvd N., Birmingham, AL 35203; 205-325-5420 x350; Fax: 205-325-4885. Hours: 8AM-4:45PM (CST). *Probate.*

Lamar County

Circuit & District Court PO Box 434, Vernon, AL 35592; 205-695-7193; Probate phone: 205-695-9119; Fax: 205-695-1871. Hours: 8AM-4:30PM (CST). *Felony, Misdemeanor, Civil, Eviction, Small Claims, Probate.*

Note: Probate court is separate from this court, and can be contacted at the telephone number above.

Civil Records: Access: Mail, online, in person. Both court and visitors may perform in person searches. No search fee. Required to search: name, years to search; also helpful: address. Civil cases indexed by defendant, plaintiff. Civil records on books from 1900; computerized records go back to 1995. Online access available through SJIS. See state introduction.

Criminal Records: Access: Mail, fax, online, in person. Both court and visitors may perform in person searches. No search fee. Required to search: name, years to search, DOB, signed release; also helpful: SSN. Criminal records on books from 1900; computerized records go back to 1995. Online access available through SJIS. See state introduction.

General Information: Public Access terminal is available. No sealed, adoptions, youthful offenders or juvenile records released. SASE required. Turnaround time 1-2 days. Copy fee: $.25 per page. Certification fee: $2.25. Fee payee: Circuit Clerk. Only cashiers checks and money orders accepted. Will bill copy fees.

Lauderdale County

Circuit Court PO Box 795, Florence, AL 35631; 256-760-5710; Probate phone: 256-760-5800. Hours: 8AM-Noon, 1-5PM (CST). *Felony, Civil Actions Over $10,000, Probate.*

Note: Probate court is separate from this court, and can be contacted at the telephone number above.

Civil Records: Access: Online, in person. Visitors must perform in person searches for themselves. No search fee. Required to search: name, years to search. Civil cases indexed by defendant, plaintiff. Civil records on computer from 1977, index books from the 1930s. Online access available through SJIS. See state introduction.

Criminal Records: Access: Online, in person. Visitors must perform in person searches for themselves. No search fee. Required to search: name, years to search, DOB; also helpful: SSN. Criminal records on computer from 1977, index books from the 1930s. Online access available through SJIS. See state introduction.

General Information: Public Access terminal is available. No sealed, adoptions, youthful offenders or juvenile records released. Copy fee: $.25 per page. Certification fee: $1.00. Fee payee: Circuit Court Clerk. Personal checks accepted. Prepayment is required.

District Court PO Box 776, Florence, AL 35631; 256-760-5726; Fax: 256-760-5727. Hours: 8AM-Noon, 1-5PM (CST). *Misdemeanor, Civil Actions Under $10,000, Eviction, Small Claims.*

Civil Records: Access: Mail, online, in person. Both court and visitors may perform in person searches. No search fee. Required to search: name, years to search. Civil cases indexed by defendant, plaintiff. Civil records on computer from 1986, books from the 1930s. Online access available through SJIS. See state introduction.

Criminal Records: Access: Mail, online, in person. Both court and visitors may perform in person searches. No search fee. Required to search: name, years to search, DOB; also helpful: SSN. Criminal records on computer from 1986, books from the 1930s. Online access available through SJIS. See state introduction.

General Information: Public Access terminal is available. No sealed, adoptions, youthful offenders or juvenile records released. Turnaround time 1 week. Copy fee: $.25 per page. Certification fee: $1.00. Fee payee: Circuit Clerk. Personal checks accepted. Prepayment is required.

Lawrence County

Circuit & District Court PO Box 249, Moulton, AL 35650; 256-974-2432; Probate phone: 256-974-2439. Hours: 8AM-5PM (CST). *Felony, Misdemeanor, Civil, Eviction, Small Claims, Probate.*

Note: Probate court is separate from this court, and can be contacted at the telephone number above.

Civil Records: Access: Online, in person. Visitors must perform in person searches for themselves. No search fee. Required to search: name, years to search. Civil cases indexed by defendant. Civil records on computer from mid-1994, on books and index cards from 1920s. Online access available through SJIS. See state introduction.

Criminal Records: Access: Online, in person. Visitors must perform in person searches for themselves. No search fee. Required to search: name, years to search; also helpful: DOB, SSN. Criminal records on computer from mid-1994, on books and index cards from 1920s. Online access available through SJIS. See state introduction.

General Information: Public Access terminal is available. No sealed, adoption, youthful offender, juvenile records released. Copy fee: $.25 per page. Certification fee: $1.00. Fee payee: Clerk. Business checks accepted. Prepayment is required.

Lee County

Circuit & District Court 2311 Gateway Dr, Rm 104, Opelika, AL 36801; 334-749-7141 X244; Fax: 334-749-5886. Hours: 8:30AM-4:30PM (CST). *Felony, Misdemeanor, Civil, Eviction, Small Claims.*

Note: Probate court is separate from this court, and can be contacted at 334-745-9761 or at Lee County Courthouse, 215 S 9 St, Opelika, AL 36801.

Civil Records: Access: Phone, mail, online, in person. Only the court performs in person searches; visitors may not. No search fee. Required to search: name, years to search. Civil cases indexed by defendant, plaintiff. Civil records on computer from 1980s, on index cards from 1988. Online access available through SJIS. See state introduction.

Criminal Records: Access: Phone, mail, online, in person. Only the court performs in person searches; visitors may not. No search fee. Required to search: name, years to search; also helpful: DOB, SSN. Criminal records on computer from 1980s, on index cards from 1988. Online access available through SJIS. See state introduction.

General Information: No sealed, adoptions, youthful offenders or juvenile records released. Turnaround time 1 week. Copy fee: $.50 per page. Certification fee: $1.00. Fee payee: Clerk's Office. Business checks accepted.

Limestone County

Circuit & District Court 200 Washington St West, Athens, AL 35611; 256-233-6406; Probate phone: 256-233-6427. Hours: 8AM-4:30PM (CST). *Felony, Misdemeanor, Civil, Eviction, Small Claims, Probate.*

Note: Probate court is separate from this court, and can be contacted at the telephone number above.

Civil Records: Access: Mail, online, in person. Both court and visitors may perform in person searches. No search fee. Required to search: name, years to search. Civil cases indexed by defendant, plaintiff. Civil records

on computer since 1992; prior in docket books. Online access available through SJIS. See state introduction.

Criminal Records: Access: Mail, online, in person. Both court and visitors may perform in person searches. No search fee. Required to search: name, years to search, DOB; also helpful: SSN, sex. Criminal records on computer since 1992, prior in docket books. Online access available through SJIS. See state introduction.

General Information: Public Access terminal is available. No juvenile, youthful offender records released. SASE required. Turnaround time 2 weeks. Copy fee: $.25 per page. Certification fee: $1.00. Fee payee: Clerk of Court. Personal checks accepted.

Lowndes County

Circuit & District Court PO Box 876, Hayneville, AL 36040; 334-548-2252; Probate phone: 334-548-2365. Hours: 8AM-4:30PM (CST). *Felony, Misdemeanor, Civil, Eviction, Small Claims, Probate.*

Note: Probate court is separate from this court, and can be contacted at the telephone number above.

Civil Records: Access: Mail, online, in person. Both court and visitors may perform in person searches. Search fee: $10.00 per name. Required to search: name, years to search. Civil cases indexed by defendant, plaintiff. Civil records on index cards from 1977. Online access available through SJIS. See state introduction.

Criminal Records: Access: Mail, online, in person. Both court and visitors may perform in person searches. Search fee: $10.00 per name. Required to search: name, years to search; also helpful: DOB, SSN. Criminal records on index cards from 1977. Online access available through SJIS. See state introduction.

General Information: No sealed, adoptions, youthful offenders or juvenile records released. SASE required. Turnaround time up to 1 week. Copy fee: $.25 per page. Certification fee: $1.00. Fee payee: District Court Clerk. Business checks accepted.

Macon County

Circuit & District Court PO Box 830723, Tuskegee, AL 36083; 334-724-2614; Probate phone: 334-724-2611. Hours: 8AM-4:30PM (CST). *Felony, Misdemeanor, Civil, Eviction, Small Claims, Probate.*

Note: Probate court is separate from this court, and can be contacted at the telephone number above.

Civil Records: Access: Mail, online, in person. Both court and visitors may perform in person searches. Search fee: $10.00 per name. Required to search: name, years to search. Civil cases indexed by defendant, plaintiff. Civil records on index books from 1950s, on computer since beginning of 1994. Online access available through SJIS. See state introduction.

Criminal Records: Access: Mail, online, in person. Both court and visitors may perform in person searches. Search fee: $10.00 per name. Required to search: name, years to search; also helpful: DOB, SSN. Criminal records computerized starting in 1994. Online access available through SJIS. See state introduction.

General Information: No sealed, adoption, youthful offender, juvenile records released. SASE not required. Turnaround time 1-2 days. Copy fee: $.25 per page. Certification fee: $2.50. Fee payee: Office of Circuit Clerk. Business checks accepted.

Madison County

Circuit Court- Civil 100 N Side Square, Courthouse, Huntsville, AL 35801; 256-532-3381; Probate phone: 256-532-3330. Hours: 8AM-5PM (CST). *Civil Actions Over $10,000, Probate.*

Note: Probate court is separate from this court, and can be contacted at the telephone number above

Civil Records: Access: Online, in person. Visitors must perform in person searches for themselves. No search

fee. Required to search: name, years to search; also helpful: address. Civil cases indexed by defendant, plaintiff. Civil records on computer from 1977, index books from 1937. Online access available through SJIS. See state introduction. **General Information:** Public Access terminal is available. No sealed, adoptions, youthful offenders or juvenile records released. Copy fee: $.25 per page. Certification fee: $1.00. Personal checks accepted. Prepayment is required. Cost bill will be sent for search and copies.

Circuit Court - Criminal 100 N Side Square, Courthouse, Huntsville, AL 35801-4820; 256-532-3389. Hours: 8AM-5PM (CST). *Felony.*

Criminal Records: Access: Online, in person. Visitors must perform in person searches for themselves. No search fee. Required to search: name, years to search; also helpful: DOB, SSN. Criminal records on computer from 1977, books from 1937. Online access available through SJIS. See state introduction.

General Information: Public Access terminal is available. No sealed, adoptions, youthful offenders or juvenile records released. Copy fee: $.25 per page. Certification fee: $1.25. Fee payee: Circuit Court Clerk. Personal checks accepted. Prepayment is required.

District Court 100 N Side Square, Rm 822 Courthouse, Huntsville, AL 35801; Civil phone: 256-532-3622; Criminal phone: 256-532-3373; Fax: 256-532-6972. Hours: 8AM-5PM (CST). *Misdemeanor, Civil Actions Under $10,000, Eviction, Small Claims.*

Civil Records: Access: Online, in person. Visitors must perform in person searches for themselves. No search fee. Required to search: name, years to search. Civil cases indexed by defendant, plaintiff. Civil records on computer from 1982, index books prior. Online access available through SJIS. See state introduction.

Criminal Records: Access: Online, in person. Visitors must perform in person searches for themselves. No search fee. Required to search: name, years to search; also helpful: DOB, SSN. Criminal records on computer from 1982, index books prior since 1979. Online access available through SJIS. See state introduction.

General Information: Public Access terminal is available. No sealed, adoptions, youthful offenders or juvenile records released. Copy fee: $.25 per page. Certification fee: $1.25. Fee payee: District Court. Business checks accepted. Prepayment is required.

Marengo County

Circuit & District Court PO Box 480566, Linden, AL 36748; 334-295-2223. Hours: 8AM-4:30PM (CST). *Felony, Misdemeanor, Civil, Eviction, Small Claims, Probate.*

Civil Records: Access: Mail, online, in person. Both court and visitors may perform in person searches. No search fee. Required to search: name, years to search. Civil cases indexed by defendant, plaintiff. Civil records on computer from 6/94, on books and index cards from 1965. Online access available through SJIS. See state introduction.

Criminal Records: Access: Mail, online, in person. Both court and visitors may perform in person searches. No search fee. Required to search: name, years to search; also helpful: DOB, SSN. Criminal records on computer from 6/94, on books and index cards from 1965. Online access available through SJIS. See state introduction.

General Information: Public Access terminal is available. No sealed, adoptions, youthful offenders or juvenile records released. Turnaround time 1 week. Copy fee: $.25 per page. Certification fee: $1.00. Fee payee: Circuit Clerk. Business checks accepted. Prepayment is required.

Marion County

Circuit & District Court PO Box 1595, Hamilton, AL 35570; 205-921-7451; Probate phone: 205-921-2471. Hours: 8AM-5PM (CST). *Felony, Misdemeanor, Civil, Eviction, Small Claims, Probate.*

Note: Probate court is separate from this court, and can be contacted at the telephone number above.

Civil Records: Access: Mail, online, in person. Both court and visitors may perform in person searches. No search fee. Required to search: name, years to search. Civil cases indexed by defendant, plaintiff. Civil records on computer from 5/94, on books from 1950s. Online access available through SJIS. See state introduction.

Criminal Records: Access: Mail, online, in person. Both court and visitors may perform in person searches. No search fee. Required to search: name, years to search; also helpful: DOB, SSN. Criminal records on computer from 5/94, on books from 1950s. Online access available through SJIS. See state introduction.

General Information: Public Access terminal is available. No sealed, adoptions, youthful offenders or juvenile records released. SASE required. Turnaround time 2 days. Copy fee: $.50 per page. Certification fee: $1.50. Fee payee: Circuit Clerk. Only cashiers checks and money orders accepted.

Marshall County

Circuit & District Court - Albertville Division 200 W Main, Albertville, AL 35950; 256-878-4522/4521/4515. Hours: 8AM-4:30PM (CST). *Felony, Misdemeanor, Civil, Eviction, Small Claims.*

Civil Records: Access: Mail, online, in person. Both court and visitors may perform in person searches. No search fee. Required to search: name, years to search. Civil cases indexed by defendant. Civil records on computer from 8/92, on index books from 1974. Online access available through SJIS. See state introduction.

Criminal Records: Access: Mail, online, in person. Both court and visitors may perform in person searches. No search fee. Required to search: name, years to search, DOB; also helpful: SSN. Criminal records on computer from 8/92, on index books from 1974. Online access available through SJIS. See state introduction.

General Information: Public Access terminal is available. No sealed, adoptions, youthful offenders or juvenile records released. SASE required. Turnaround time 2-3 days for criminal, 1-2 weeks civil. Copy fee: $.25 per page. Certification fee: $1.25. Fee payee: Clerk of Courts. Business checks accepted. Prepayment is required.

Circuit Court - Guntersville Civil Division

PO Box 248, Guntersville, AL 35976; 256-571-7788; Probate phone: 256-571-7764. Hours: 8AM-4:30PM (CST). *Civil Actions Over $10,000, Small Claims, Probate.*

Note: Probate court is separate from this court, and can be contacted at the telephone number above

Civil Records: Access: Online, in person. Visitors must perform in person searches for themselves. No search fee. Required to search: name, years to search. Civil cases indexed by defendant, plaintiff. Civil records on computer for past 3 years, on index books early 1900s. Online access available through SJIS. See state introduction. **General Information:** Public Access terminal is available. No sealed, adoptions, youthful offenders or juvenile records released. SASE required. Copy fee: $.25 per page. Certification fee: $1.00. Fee payee: Circuit Clerk. Business checks accepted. Prepayment is required.

Circuit Court - Guntersville Criminal Division

425 Gunter Ave, PO Box 248, Guntersville, AL 35976; 256-571-7791. Hours: 8AM-4:30PM (CST). *Felony, Misdemeanor.*

Criminal Records: Access: Online, mail, in person. Visitors must perform in person searches for themselves. No search fee. Required to search: name, years to search; also helpful: DOB, SSN. Criminal records on computer from 1992, on index books from 1984, prior back to 1930s. Online access available through SJIS. See state introduction.

General Information: Public Access terminal is available. No sealed, adoptions, youthful offenders or juvenile records released. SASE required. Turnaround time 2 or more weeks. Copy fee: $.25 per page. Certification fee: $1.00. Fee payee: Circuit Clerk. Business checks accepted. Prepayment is required.

Mobile County

Circuit Court 205 Government St #C-913, Mobile, AL 36644-2913; 334-574-8786. Hours: 8AM-5PM (CST). *Felony, Civil Actions Over $10,000.*

Civil Records: Access: Online, in person. Visitors must perform in person searches for themselves. No search fee. Required to search: name, years to search. Civil cases indexed by defendant. Civil records on computer from 1977, microfiche from early 1900s. Online access available through SJIS. See state introduction.

Criminal Records: Access: Online, in person. Visitors must perform in person searches for themselves. No search fee. Required to search: name, years to search; also helpful: DOB, SSN. Criminal records on computer from 1977, microfiche from early 1900s. Online access available through SJIS. See state introduction.

General Information: Public Access terminal is available. No sealed, adoptions, youthful offenders or juvenile records released. Copy fee: $.25 per page. Certification fee: $1.00. Fee payee: Susan F Wilson, Circuit Clerk. Only cashiers checks and money orders accepted. Prepayment is required. Exact change for payments is required.

District Court 205 Government St, Mobile, AL 36644; 334-574-8520, 334-690-8525 (small claims); Civil phone: 334-574-8526; Criminal phone: 334-574-8511; Probate phone: 334-574-8502; Fax: 334-574-4840. Hours: 8AM-5PM (CST). *Misdemeanor, Civil Actions Under $10,000, Eviction, Small Claims, Probate.*

Note: Probate court is a separate court, and can be reached at the telephone number given above.

Civil Records: Access: Phone, fax, mail, online, in person. Both court and visitors may perform in person searches. No search fee. Required to search: name, years to search. Civil cases indexed by defendant, plaintiff. Civil records on computer from 1977, index books from 1950s. Online access available through SJIS. See state introduction.

Criminal Records: Access: Phone, fax, mail, online, in person. Both court and visitors may perform in person searches. No search fee. Required to search: name, years to search, DOB; also helpful: SSN. Criminal records on computer from 1977, index books from 1950s. Online access available through SJIS. See state introduction.

General Information: Public Access terminal is available. No sealed, youthful offenders, protected files or juvenile records released. Turnaround time 2-3 days. Copy fee: $.25 per page. Certification fee: $1.25. Fee payee: Clerk, District Court. Business checks accepted. Business checks must be approved. Prepayment is required.

Monroe County

Circuit & District Court County Courthouse, 65 North Alabama Ave, Monroeville, AL 36460; 334-743-2283; Probate phone: 334-743-4107. Hours: 8AM-5PM (CST). *Felony, Misdemeanor, Civil, Eviction, Small Claims, Probate.*

Note: Probate court is separate from this court, and can be contacted at the telephone number above.

Civil Records: Access: Mail, online, in person. Both court and visitors may perform in person searches. No search fee. Required to search: name, years to search. Civil cases indexed by defendant. Civil records on index cards from 1977 and on computer since July 1994. Online access available through SJIS. See state introduction.

Criminal Records: Access: Mail, online, in person. Both court and visitors may perform in person searches. No search fee. Required to search: name, years to search; also helpful: DOB, SSN, Criminal records on index cards from 1977 and on computer since July 1994. Online access available through SJIS. See state introduction.

General Information: Public Access terminal is available. No sealed, adoptions, youthful offenders or juvenile records released. SASE required. Turnaround time 1 wk. Copy fee: $.25 per page. Certification fee: $1.25 per page. Fee payee: John Sawyer, Circuit Clerk. Business checks accepted. Prepayment is required.

Montgomery County

Circuit Court PO Box 1667, Montgomery, AL 36102-1667; 334-832-1260; Probate phone: 334-832-1237. Hours: 8AM-5PM (CST). *Felony, Civil Actions Over $10,000, Probate.*

Note: Probate court is separate from this court, and can be contacted at the telephone number above.

Civil Records: Access: Mail, online, in person. Both court and visitors may perform in person searches. No search fee. Required to search: name, years to search. Civil cases indexed by defendant, plaintiff. Civil records on computer from 1982, microfiche from 1976. Online access available through SJIS. See state introduction.

Criminal Records: Access: Mail, online, in person. Both court and visitors may perform in person searches. No search fee. Required to search: name, years to search; also helpful: DOB, SSN. Criminal records on computer from 1982, microfiche from 1976. Online access available through SJIS. See state introduction.

General Information: Public Access terminal is available. No sealed, youthful offenders or juvenile records released. SASE required. Turnaround time 3-4 days. Copy fee: $.25 per page. Certification fee: $1.00. Fee payee: Circuit Clerk. Business checks accepted. Prepayment is required.

District Court PO Box 1667, Montgomery, AL 36102; 334-832-4950. Hours: 8AM-5PM (CST). *Misdemeanor, Civil Actions Under $10,000, Eviction, Small Claims.*

Civil Records: Access: Mail, online, in person. Both court and visitors may perform in person searches. No search fee. Required to search: name, years to search. Civil cases indexed by defendant. Civil records on computer from the 1980s, index books from 1977. Online access available through SJIS. See state introduction.

Criminal Records: Access: Mail, online, in person. Both court and visitors may perform in person searches. No search fee. Required to search: name, years to search; also helpful: DOB, SSN. Criminal records on computer from the 1980s, index books from 1977. Online access available through SJIS. See state introduction.

General Information: Public Access terminal is available. No sealed, youthful offender, juvenile records released. SASE required. Turnaround time 3-4 days. Copy fee: $.25 per page. Certification fee: $1.00. Fee payee: District Court. Only cashiers checks and money orders accepted.

Morgan County

Circuit Court PO Box 668, Decatur, AL 35602; 256-351-4790; Probate phone: 256-351-4675. Hours: 8AM-4:30PM (CST). *Felony, Civil Actions Over $10,000, Probate.*

Note: Probate court is separate from this court, and can be contacted at the telephone number above.

Civil Records: Access: Online, in person. Visitors must perform in person searches for themselves. No search fee. Required to search: name, years to search. Civil cases indexed by defendant, plaintiff. Civil records on computer from 1994, on microfiche from 1950s, books from 1965. Online access available through SJIS. See state introduction.

Criminal Records: Access: Online, in person. Visitors must perform in person searches for themselves. No search fee. Required to search: name, years to search; also helpful: DOB, SSN. Criminal records on computer from 1992. Online access available through SJIS. See state introduction.

General Information: Public Access terminal is available. No sealed, adoption, youthful offender, juvenile records released. Copy fee: $.25 per page. Certification fee: $1.25 per page. Fee payee: John Pat Orr, Circuit Clerk. Personal checks accepted. Prepayment is required.

District Court PO Box 668, Decatur, AL 35602; 256-351-4640. Hours: 8:30AM-4:30PM (CST). *Misdemeanor, Civil Actions Under $10,000, Eviction, Small Claims.*

Civil Records: Access: Online, in person. Visitors must perform in person searches for themselves. No search fee. Required to search: name, years to search. Civil cases indexed by defendant. Civil records on computer from 1987, books from 1979. Online access available through SJIS. See state introduction.

Criminal Records: Access: Online, in person. Visitors must perform in person searches for themselves. No search fee. Required to search: name, years to search; also helpful: DOB, SSN. Criminal records on computer from 1987, books from 1979. Online access available through SJIS. See state introduction.

General Information: Public Access terminal is available. No sealed, adoption, youthful offender, juvenile records released. Copy fee: $.25 per page. Certification fee: $1.00. Fee payee: District Court. Business checks accepted. Prepayment is required.

Perry County

Circuit & District Court PO Box 505, Marion, AL 36756; 334-683-6106; Probate phone: 334-683-2210. Hours: 8AM-4:30PM (CST). *Felony, Misdemeanor, Civil, Eviction, Small Claims, Probate.*

Note: Probate court is separate from this court, and can be contacted at the telephone number above.

Civil Records: Access: Mail, online, in person. Both court and visitors may perform in person searches. No search fee. Required to search: name, years to search. Civil cases indexed by defendant, plaintiff. Civil records on books from 1977, on computer starting January 1995. Online access available through SJIS. See state introduction.

Criminal Records: Access: Mail, online, in person. Both court and visitors may perform in person searches. No search fee. Required to search: name, years to search; also helpful: DOB, SSN. Criminal records on index cards. Online access available through SJIS. See state introduction.

General Information: No sealed, adoption, youthful offender, juvenile records released. SASE required.

Turnaround time 2-3 days. Copy fee: $.25 per page. Certification fee: $1.00. Fee payee: District Court Clerk. Business checks accepted. Prepayment is required.

Pickens County

Circuit & District Court PO Box 418, Carrollton, AL 35447; 205-367-2050; Probate phone: 205-367-2010. Hours: 8AM-4:30PM (CST). *Felony, Misdemeanor, Civil, Eviction, Small Claims, Probate.*

Civil Records: Access: Mail, online, in person. Both court and visitors may perform in person searches. No search fee. Required to search: name, years to search. Civil cases indexed by defendant, plaintiff. Civil records on computer from 10/93, on books and index cards from 1840s. Online access available through SJIS. See state introduction.

Criminal Records: Access: Mail, online, in person. Both court and visitors may perform in person searches. No search fee. Required to search: name, years to search; also helpful: DOB, SSN. Criminal records on computer, on books and index cards from 1840s. Online access available through SJIS. See state introduction.

General Information: Public Access terminal is available. No sealed, adoption, youthful offender, juvenile records released. SASE required. Turnaround time 1-2 weeks. Copy fee: $.25 per page. Certification fee: $1.00. Fee payee: District Court. Business checks accepted. Prepayment is required.

Pike County

Circuit & District Court PO Box 948, Troy, AL 36081; 334-566-4622; Probate phone: 334-566-1246. Hours: 8AM-5PM (CST). *Felony, Misdemeanor, Civil, Eviction, Small Claims, Probate.*

Note: Probate court is separate from this court, and can be contacted at the telephone number above.

Civil Records: Access: Mail, online, in person. Both court and visitors may perform in person searches. Search fee: $5.00 per name. Required to search: name, years to search. Civil cases indexed by defendant, plaintiff. Civil records on computer from 1977, on books from 1938. Online access available through SJIS. See state introduction.

Criminal Records: Access: Mail, online, in person. Both court and visitors may perform in person searches. Search fee: $5.00 per name. Required to search: name, years to search, DOB, SSN. Criminal records on computer from 1977, on books from 1938. Online access available through SJIS. See state introduction.

General Information: Public Access terminal is available. No sealed, adoption, youthful offender, juvenile records released. SASE required. Turnaround time same day. Copy fee: $.25 per page. Certification fee: $1.00. Fee payee: Pike County Circuit/District Court. Only cashiers checks and money orders accepted. Prepayment is required.

Randolph County

Circuit & District Court PO Box 328, Wedowee, AL 36278; 256-357-4551; Probate phone: 256-357-4933. Hours: 8AM-Noon, 1-5PM (CST). *Felony, Misdemeanor, Civil, Eviction, Small Claims, Probate.*

Note: Probate court is separate from this court, and can be contacted at the telephone number above.

Civil Records: Access: Online, in person. Visitors must perform in person searches for themselves. No search fee. Required to search: name, years to search. Civil cases indexed by defendant, plaintiff. Civil records on computer from 1994. Online access available through SJIS. See state introduction.

Criminal Records: Access: Online, in person. Visitors must perform in person searches for themselves. No search fee. Required to search: name, years to search; also helpful: DOB, SSN. Criminal records on computer

from 1994. Online access available through SJIS. See state introduction.

General Information: Public Access terminal is available. No sealed, adoption, youthful offender, juvenile records released. Copy fee: $.25 per page. Certification fee: $1.50. Fee payee: Kim S Benefield. Business checks accepted. Prepayment is required.

Russell County

Circuit & District Court PO Box 518, Phenix City, AL 36868; 334-298-0516; Fax: 334-297-6250. Hours: 8:30AM-4:30PM (EST). *Felony, Misdemeanor, Civil, Eviction, Small Claims, Probate.*

Note: Probate court is separate from this court, and can be contacted at the telephone number above.

Civil Records: Access: Mail, online, in person. Both court and visitors may perform in person searches. No search fee. Required to search: name, years to search. Civil cases indexed by defendant, plaintiff. Civil records on computer from 1988, books from 1800s (prior to 1940 extremely difficult to find). Online access available through SJIS. See state introduction.

Criminal Records: Access: Mail, online, in person. Both court and visitors may perform in person searches. No search fee. Required to search: name, years to search; also helpful: DOB, SSN. Criminal records on computer from 1988, books from 1800s (prior to 1940 extremely difficult to find). Online access available through SJIS. See state introduction.

General Information: Public Access terminal is available. No sealed, adoption, youthful offender, juvenile records released. Turnaround time 2 days. Copy fee: $.25 per page. Certification fee: $1.00. Fee payee: Clerk of Circuit Court. Business checks accepted.

Shelby County

Circuit & District Court PO Box 1810, Columbiana, AL 35051; 205-669-3760; Probate phone: 205-669-3711. Hours: 8AM-4:30PM (CST). *Felony, Misdemeanor, Civil, Eviction, Small Claims, Probate.*

Note: Probate court is separate from this court, and can be contacted at the telephone number above.

Civil Records: Access: Mail, fax, online, in person. Visitors must perform in person searches for themselves. No search fee. Required to search: name, years to search. Civil cases indexed by defendant, plaintiff. Civil records on computer from 1993, on index books from 1820s. Online access available through SJIS. See state introduction.

Criminal Records: Access: Mail, fax, online, in person. Visitors must perform in person searches for themselves. No search fee. Required to search: name, years to search, DOB; also helpful: SSN. Criminal records on computer from 1993, on index books from 1820s. Online access available through SJIS. See state introduction.

General Information: Public Access terminal is available. No sealed, adoption, youthful offender, juvenile records released. Copy fee: $.25 per page. Certification fee: $1.00. Fee payee: Mary Harris, Circuit Clerk. Only cashiers checks and money orders accepted.

St. Clair County

Circuit & District Court - Ashville Division PO Box 1569, Ashville, AL 35953; 205-594-2184; Probate phone: 205-594-2120. Hours: 8AM-5PM (CST). *Felony, Misdemeanor, Civil, Eviction, Small Claims, Probate.*

Note: Probate court is separate from this court and can be contacted at the telephone number above.

Civil Records: Access: Mail, online, in person. Both court and visitors may perform in person searches. No search fee. Required to search: name, years to search.

Civil cases indexed by defendant, plaintiff. Civil records on computer from 1/94, in books from 1800s, no index before 1940. Online access available through SJIS. See state introduction. Also, online access to probate records is available by subscription at www.recordsusa.com/Alabama/StClairCnAl.htm. Credit card, username and password is required; choose either monthly or per-use plan. Visit the web site or call Lisa at 601-264-7701 for information.

Criminal Records: Access: Mail, online, in person. Both court and visitors may perform in person searches. No search fee. Required to search: name, years to search, DOB; also helpful: SSN. Criminal records on computer from 1/94, in books from 1800s, no index before 1940. Online access available through SJIS. See state introduction.

General Information: Public Access terminal is available. No sealed, adoption, youthful offender, juvenile records released. SASE required. Turnaround time 10 days. Copy fee: $.25 per page. Certification fee: $1.25. Fee payee: Jean Browning Circuit Clerk. Business checks accepted.

Circuit & District Court - Pell City Division

1815 Cogswell Ave, #217, Pell City, AL 35125; 205-338-2511; Circuit: 205-338-7224 District; Probate phone: 205-338-9449. Hours: 8AM-5PM (CST). *Felony, Misdemeanor, Civil, Eviction, Small Claims, Probate.*

Note: Probate court is separate from this court, and can be contacted at the telephone number above.

Civil Records: Access: Mail, online, in person. Both court and visitors may perform in person searches. No search fee. Required to search: name, years to search. Civil cases indexed by defendant, plaintiff. Civil records on computer from 11/93, on books from early 1940s. Online access available through SJIS. See state introduction. Also, online access to probate records is available by subscription at www.recordsusa.com/Alabama/StClairCnAl.htm. Credit card, username and password is required; choose either monthly or per-use plan. Visit the web site or call Lisa at 601-264-7701 for information.

Criminal Records: Access: Mail, online, in person. Both court and visitors may perform in person searches. No search fee. Required to search: name, years to search, DOB; also helpful: SSN. Criminal records on computer from 11/93, on books from early 1940s. Online access available through SJIS. See state introduction.

General Information: Public Access terminal is available. No sealed, adoption, youthful offender, juvenile records released. SASE required. Turnaround time 7-14 days. Copy fee: $.25 per page. Certification fee: $1.25. Fee payee: Clerk of Courts. Business checks accepted. Prepayment is required.

Sumter County

Circuit & District Court PO Box 936, Livingston, AL 35470; 205-652-2291; Probate phone: 205-652-7281. Hours: 8AM-4:30PM (CST). *Felony, Misdemeanor, Civil, Eviction, Small Claims.*

Civil Records: Access: Mail, online, in person. Both court and visitors may perform in person searches. No search fee. Required to search: name, years to search. Civil cases indexed by defendant, plaintiff. Civil records on computer from early 1995, on index books from 1962. Online access available through SJIS. See state introduction.

Criminal Records: Access: Mail, online, in person. Both court and visitors may perform in person searches. No search fee. Required to search: name, years to search; also helpful: DOB, SSN. Criminal records on computer from early 1995, on index books from 1962. Online access available through SJIS. See state introduction.

General Information: Public Access terminal is available. No sealed, adoption, youthful offender, juvenile records released. SASE required. Turnaround time 2 wks. Copy fee: $.50 per page. Certification fee: $1.50. Fee payee: Circuit Court Clerk. Business checks accepted. Prepayment is required.

Probate Court PO Box 1040, Livingston, AL 35470; 205-652-7281; Fax: 205-652-2606. Hours: 8AM-4PM (CST). *Probate.*

Talladega County

Circuit & District Court - Northern Division

PO 6137, Talladega, AL 35161; 256-761-2102. Hours: 8AM-5PM (CST). *Felony, Misdemeanor, Civil, Eviction, Small Claims.*

Civil Records: Access: Online, in person. Visitors must perform in person searches for themselves. No search fee. Required to search: name, years to search. Civil cases indexed by defendant, plaintiff. Civil records on computer from 1989, index books from 1970s. Online access available through SJIS. See state introduction.

Criminal Records: Access: Online, in person. Visitors must perform in person searches for themselves. No search fee. Required to search: name, years to search; also helpful: DOB, SSN. Criminal records on computer from 1989, index books from 1970s. Online access available through SJIS. See state introduction.

General Information: Public Access terminal is available. No sealed, adoption, youthful offender, juvenile records released. Copy fee: $.25 per page. Certification fee: $1.25. Fee payee: Circuit Court Clerk. Business checks accepted.

District Court - Southern Division

PO Box 183, Sylacauga, AL 35150; 256-245-4352. Hours: 7:30AM-4:30AM (CST). *Misdemeanor, Civil Actions Under $10,000, Eviction, Small Claims.*

Civil Records: Access: Mail, online, in person. Both court and visitors may perform in person searches. No search fee. Required to search: name, years to search. Civil cases indexed by defendant. Civil records on computer from 1977, on index books and cards prior to 1982 at the Northern Division District Court. Online access available through SJIS. See state introduction.

Criminal Records: Access: Mail, online, in person. Both court and visitors may perform in person searches. No search fee. Required to search: name, years to search; also helpful: DOB, SSN. Criminal records on computer from 1977, on index books and cards prior to 1982 at the Northern Division District Court. Online access available through SJIS. See state introduction.

General Information: No juvenile, youthful offender records released. SASE required. Turnaround time up to 7-10 days. Copy fee: $.25 per page. Certification fee: $1.25. Fee payee: Clerk of District Court. Business checks accepted. Prepayment is required.

Probate Court PO Box 737, Talladega, AL 35161; 256-362-4175. *Probate.*

Tallapoosa County

Circuit & District Court - Eastern Division

Tallapoosa County Courthouse, Dadeville, AL 36853; 256-825-1098; Probate phone: 256-825-4266. Hours: 8AM-5PM (CST). *Felony, Misdemeanor, Civil, Eviction, Small Claims, Probate.*

Note: Probate court is separate from this court, and can be contacted at the telephone number above.

Civil Records: Access: Mail, online, in person. Only the court performs in person searches; visitors may not. Search fee: $3.00 per name. Required to search: name, years to search. Civil cases indexed by defendant, plaintiff. Civil records on computer from 1993, on index books from 1977. Online access available through SJIS. See state introduction.

Criminal Records: Access: Mail, online, in person. Only the court performs in person searches; visitors may not. Search fee: $3.00 per name. Required to search: name, years to search, DOB; also helpful: SSN. Criminal records on computer from 1993, on index books from 1977. Online access available through SJIS. See state introduction.

General Information: No sealed, adoption, youthful offender, juvenile records released. SASE required. Turnaround time 1-2 weeks. Copy fee: $.50 per page. Certification fee: $1.00. Fee payee: Circuit Clerk. Business checks accepted. Prepayment is required.

Circuit & District Court - Western Division

PO Box 189, Alexander City, AL 35011; 256-329-8123/234-4361. Hours: 8AM-5PM (CST). *Felony, Misdemeanor, Civil, Eviction, Small Claims.*

Civil Records: Access: Mail, online, in person. Both court and visitors may perform in person searches. Search fee: $3.00 per name. Required to search: name, years to search. Civil cases indexed by defendant, plaintiff. Civil records on index books from 1977, prior in docket books; on computer back to 1994. Online access available through SJIS. See state introduction.

Criminal Records: Access: Mail, online, in person. Both court and visitors may perform in person searches. Search fee: $3.00 per name. Required to search: name, years to search, DOB; also helpful: SSN, signed release. Criminal records on index books from 1977, prior in docket books; on computer back to 1994. Online access available through SJIS. See state introduction.

General Information: No sealed, adoption, youthful offender, juvenile records released. SASE requested. Turnaround time up to 2 weeks. Copy fee: $.50 per page. Certification fee: $1.00. Fee payee: Clerk of Courts. Business checks accepted. Prepayment is required.

Tuscaloosa County

Circuit & District Courts - Civil

714 Greensboro Ave, Tuscaloosa, AL 35401; 205-349-3870 X267; Probate phone: 205-349-3870 X203. Hours: 8:30AM-5PM (CST). *Civil, Probate.*

Note: The District Court civil records are concurrent with the District Court Probate court is separate from this court, and can be contacted at the telephone number above

Civil Records: Access: Online, in person. Visitors must perform in person searches for themselves. No search fee. Required to search: name, years to search. Civil cases indexed by defendant, plaintiff. Civil records on computer from 1977, index books early 1900s. Online access available through SJIS. See state introduction. Also, online access to probate records is available by subscription at www.recordsusa.com/Alabama/TuscaloosaCnAl.htm. Credit card, username and password is required; choose either monthly or per-use plan. Visit the web site or call Lisa at 601-264-7701 for information. **General Information:** Public Access terminal is available. No sealed, adoption, youthful offender, juvenile records released. Copy fee: $.25 per page. Certification fee: $1.00. Fee payee: Doris Turner, Circuit Clerk. Business checks accepted. Prepayment is required.

Circuit Court - Criminal

714 Greensboro Ave, Tuscaloosa, AL 35401; 205-349-3870 X326. Hours: 8AM-5PM (CST). *Felony.*

Criminal Records: Access: Mail, online, in person. Both court and visitors may perform in person searches. No search fee. Required to search: name, years to search, DOB; also helpful: SSN. Criminal records on computer and index books back to 1977. Online access available through SJIS. See state introduction.

General Information: Public Access terminal is available. No sealed, adoption, youthful offender, juvenile records released. SASE required. Turnaround time 1-2 days. Fax notes: Will not fax results. Copy fee: $.25 per page. Certification fee: $1.00. Fee payee: Circuit Clerk. Business checks accepted. Prepayment is required.

District Court - Criminal Division

PO Box 1687, Tuscaloosa, AL 35403; 205-349-3870 X357. Hours: 8:30AM-5PM (CST). *Misdemeanor.*

Criminal Records: Access: Phone, mail, online, in person. Both court and visitors may perform in person searches. No search fee. Required to search: name, years to search, signed release; also helpful: DOB, SSN. Criminal records on computer from 1985, books in storage from early 1965. Online access available through SJIS. See state introduction.

General Information: Public Access terminal is available. No sealed, youthful offender records released. SASE preferred. Turnaround time 5 days. Copy fee: $.25 per page. Certification fee: $1.25. Business checks accepted. Prepayment is required.

Walker County

Circuit & District Court

PO Box 749, Jasper, AL 35502; 205-384-7268; Fax: 205-384-7271. Hours: 8AM-4:30PM (CST). *Felony, Misdemeanor, Civil, Eviction, Small Claims, Probate.*

Note: Probate court is separate from this court, and can be contacted at PO Box 502 or at 205-384-7281.

Civil Records: Access: Online, in person. Visitors must perform in person searches for themselves. No search fee. Required to search: name, years to search. Civil cases indexed by defendant, plaintiff. Civil records on computer from 3/93, on index books from 1920s. Online access available through SJIS. See state introduction.

Criminal Records: Access: Online, in person. Visitors must perform in person searches for themselves. No search fee. Required to search: name, years to search. Criminal records on computer from 3/93, on index books from 1920s. Online access available through SJIS. See state introduction.

General Information: Public Access terminal is available. No sealed, adoption, youthful offender, juvenile records released. Copy fee: $.25 per page. Certification fee: $1.00. Fee payee: Vinita Thomspon,

Circuit Clerk. Only cashiers checks and money orders accepted. Prepayment is required.

Washington County

Circuit & District Court

PO Box 548, Chatom, AL 36518; 334-847-2239. Hours: 8AM-4:30PM (CST). *Felony, Misdemeanor, Civil, Eviction, Small Claims, Probate.*

www.millry.net/~spgrimes

Civil Records: Access: Online, in person. Visitors must perform in person searches for themselves. No search fee. Required to search: name, years to search. Civil cases indexed by defendant. Civil records on computer since September 1994; prior 7 years on index cards. Online access available through SJIS. See state introduction. Also, online access to probate records is available by subscription at www.recordsusa.com/Alabama/WashingtonCnAl.htm. Credit card, username and password is required; choose either monthly or per-use plan. Visit the web site or call Lisa at 601-264-7701 for information.

Criminal Records: Access: Online, in person. Visitors must perform in person searches for themselves. No search fee. Required to search: name, years to search, DOB; also helpful: SSN. Criminal records on computer since September 1994; prior 7 years on index cards. Online access available through SJIS. See state introduction.

General Information: Public Access terminal is available. No sealed, adoption, youthful offender, juvenile records released. Copy fee: $.25 per page. Certification fee: $1.00. Fee payee: Circuit Clerk. Only cashiers checks and money orders accepted. Prepayment is required.

Wilcox County

Circuit & District Court

PO Box 656, Camden, AL 36726; 334-682-4126; Probate phone: 334-682-4883. Hours: 8AM-Noon, 1-5PM (CST). *Felony, Misdemeanor, Civil, Eviction, Small Claims, Probate.*

Note: Probate court is separate from this court, and can be contacted at the telephone number above.

Civil Records: Access: Online, in person. Visitors must perform in person searches for themselves. No search

fee. Required to search: name, years to search, address. Civil cases indexed by defendant, plaintiff. Civil records on computer since 1995; prior records on index books from 1970s, prior to 1970s in vault. Online access available through SJIS. See state introduction.

Criminal Records: Access: Online, in person. Visitors must perform in person searches for themselves. No search fee. Required to search: name, years to search; also helpful: DOB. Criminal records on computer since 1995; prior records on index books from 1970s, prior to 1970s in vault. Online access available through SJIS. See state introduction.

General Information: No sealed, adoption, youthful offender, juvenile records released. Copy fee: $.25 per page. Certification fee: $1.50. Fee payee: Circuit Clerk. Business checks accepted.

Winston County

Circuit & District Court

PO Box 309, Double Springs, AL 35553; 205-489-5533; Probate phone: 205-489-5219. Hours: 8AM-4:30PM (CST). *Felony, Misdemeanor, Civil, Eviction, Small Claims, Probate.*

Note: Probate court is separate from this court, and can be contacted at the telephone number above.

Civil Records: Access: Online, in person. Visitors must perform in person searches for themselves. No search fee. Required to search: name, years to search. Civil cases indexed by defendant, plaintiff. Civil records on index books from 1977, on computer since June 1994 including pending cases. Online access available through SJIS. See state introduction.

Criminal Records: Access: Online, in person. Visitors must perform in person searches for themselves. No search fee. Required to search: name, years to search, DOB; also helpful: SSN. Criminal records on index books from 1977, on computer since June 1994 including pending cases. Online access available through SJIS. See state introduction.

General Information: Public Access terminal is available. No sealed, adoption, youthful offender, juvenile records released. Copy fee: $.25 per page. Certification fee: $1.00. Fee payee: Circuit Clerk. Business checks accepted. Prepayment is required.

Alabama Recording Offices

ORGANIZATION   67 counties, 71 recording offices. The recording officer is Judge of Probate. Four counties have two recording offices-Barbour, Coffee, Jefferson, and St. Clair. See the notes under each county regarding how to determine which office is appropriate to search. The entire state is in the Central Time Zone (CST).

REAL ESTATE RECORDS   Most counties do not perform real estate searches. Copy fees vary. Certification fees vary. Tax records are located at the Assessor's Office.

UCC RECORDS   Alabama has adopted Revised Article 9 effective 01/01/2002. Financing statements are filed at the state level; real estate related collateral with the County Judge of Probate. Prior to 01/01/2002, consumer goods and farm collateral were filed with the county Judge of Probate. AfterOnly one-third of counties will perform UCC searches. Use search request form UCC-11. Search fees vary from $5.00 to $12.00 per debtor name. Copies usually cost $1.00 per page.

TAX LIEN RECORDS   Federal and state tax liens on personal property of businesses are filed with the Secretary of State. Other federal and state tax liens are filed with the county Judge of Probate. Counties do not perform separate tax lien searches although the liens are usually filed in the same index with UCC financing statements.

OTHER LIENS   Mechanics, judgment, lis pendens, hospital, vendor.

Autauga County

County Judge of Probate, 176 W. 5th St., Prattville, AL 36067-3041. 334-361-3731 R/E Recording: 334-361-3732 UCC Recording: 334-361-3732; Fax 334-361-3740.
Will not search UCC records. This agency will not do a tax lien search. Will not search real estate records. **Other Phone Numbers:** Elections 334-361-3728.

Baldwin County

County Judge of Probate, P.O. Box 459, Bay Minette, AL 36507. 334-937-0230; Fax 334-580-2563.
Will search UCC records. This agency will not do a tax lien search. Will not search real estate records. **Other Phone Numbers:** Assessor 334-937-0301; Treasurer 334-937-0282.

Barbour County (Clayton Division)

County Judge of Probate, P.O. Box 158, Clayton, AL 36016. 334-775-8371; Fax 334-775-1126.
File and search here for addresses in Clayton. File and search for Eufaula addresses there. For other addresses in the county, call for where to file. Will search UCC records. Tax liens not included in UCC search. RE owner, mortgage, and property transfer searches available. **Other Phone Numbers:** Assessor 334-775-1110; Treasurer 334-775-3203.

Barbour County (Eufaula Division)

County Judge of Probate, P.O. Box 758, Eufaula, AL 36072. 334-687-1530; Fax 334-687-0921.
File and search for Eufaula addresses here. File and search for Clayton addresses there. For other addresses in the county, call for where to file. Will search UCC records. This agency will not do a tax lien search. Will not search real estate records. **Other Phone Numbers:** Assessor 334-687-1575.

Bibb County

County Judge of Probate, 8 Court Square W, #A, 455 Walnut St, Centerville, AL 35042. 205-926-3104; Fax 205-926-1131.
Will not search UCC records. This agency will not do a tax lien search. Will not search real estate records. **Other Phone Numbers:** Assessor 205-926-3105; Treasurer 205-926-3114.

Blount County

County Judge of Probate, 220 2nd Avenue East, Oneonta, AL 35121. 205-625-4180.
Will search UCC records. This agency will not do a tax lien search. Will not search real estate records. **Other**

Phone Numbers: Assessor 205-625-4117; Treasurer 205-625-4117.

Bullock County

County Judge of Probate, P.O. Box 71, Union Springs, AL 36089. 334-738-2250; Fax 334-738-3839.
Will search UCC records. This agency will not do a tax lien search. Will not search real estate records. **Other Phone Numbers:** Assessor 334-738-2888.

Butler County

County Judge of Probate, P.O. Box 756, Greenville, AL 36037. 334-382-3512; Fax 334-382-5489.
Will search UCC records. This agency will not do a tax lien search. Will not search real estate records. **Other Phone Numbers:** Assessor 334-382-3221.

Calhoun County

County Judge of Probate, 1702 Noble Street, Suite 102, Anniston, AL 36201. 256-241-2834 R/E Recording: 256-241-2825; Fax 256-231-1728.
Will not search UCC records. This agency will not do a tax lien search. Will help look for a specific property. **Other Phone Numbers:** Assessor 256-241-2855.

Chambers County

County Judge of Probate, Courthouse, Lafayette, AL 36862. 334-864-4384 R/E Recording: 334-864-4397 UCC Recording: 334-864-4393; Fax 334-864-4394.
Will search UCC records. This agency will not do a tax lien search. Will not search real estate records. **Other Phone Numbers:** Assessor 334-864-4389; Appraiser/Auditor 334-864-4379; Elections 334-864-4380; Vital Records 334-864-4393.

Cherokee County

County Judge of Probate, Main Street, Centre, AL 35960. 256-927-3363; Fax 256-927-6949.
Will search UCC records. This agency will not do a tax lien search. Will not search real estate records. **Other Phone Numbers:** Assessor 256-927-5527.

Chilton County

County Judge of Probate, P.O. Box 270, Clanton, AL 35046. County Judge of Probate, R/E and UCC Recording 205-755-1555; Fax 205-280-7204.
Will not search UCC records. This agency will not do a tax lien search. Will not search real estate records. **Other Phone Numbers:** Assessor 205-755-0155; Appraiser/Auditor 205-755-0160.

Choctaw County

County Judge of Probate, 117 South Mulberry, Courthouse, Butler, AL 36904. 205-459-2417; Fax 205-459-4666.
Will search UCC records. This agency will not do a tax lien search. Will not search real estate records. **Other Phone Numbers:** Assessor 205-459-2412; Treasurer 205-459-2411.

Clarke County

County Judge of Probate, P.O. Box 10, Grove Hill, AL 36451. County Judge of Probate, R/E and UCC Recording 334-275-3251; Fax 334-275-8517.
Will search UCC records. This agency will not do a tax lien search. Will not search real estate records. **Other Phone Numbers:** Assessor 334-275-3376; Treasurer 334-275-3507; Appraiser/Auditor 334-275-3010; Elections 334-275-3251; Vital Records 334-275-3251.

Clay County

County Judge of Probate, P.O. Box 1120, Ashland, AL 36251. 256-354-3006; Fax 256-354-2197.
Will search UCC records. This agency will not do a tax lien search. Will not search real estate records. **Other Phone Numbers:** Assessor 256-354-2454.

Cleburne County

County Judge of Probate, 120 Vickery Street, Room 101, Heflin, AL 36264. 256-463-5655; Fax 256-463-2257.
Will search UCC records. This agency will not do a tax lien search. Will not search real estate records. **Other Phone Numbers:** Assessor 256-463-5419; Treasurer 205-463-2873.

Coffee County (Elba Division)

County Judge of Probate, 230-P North Court Avenue, Elba, AL 36323. 334-897-2211; Fax 334-897-2028.
Will search UCC records. This agency will not do a tax lien search. Will not search real estate records.

Coffee County (Enterprise Division)

County Judge of Probate, P.O. Box 311247, Enterprise, AL 36331. 334-347-2688; Fax 334-347-2095.
Will search UCC records. This agency will not do a tax lien search. Will not search real estate records. **Other Phone Numbers:** Assessor 334-347-8734.

Colbert County

County Judge of Probate, P.O. Box 47, Tuscumbia, AL 35674. 256-386-8546; Fax 256-386-8547.
Will search UCC records. This agency will not do a tax lien search. Will not search real estate records. **Other Phone Numbers:** Assessor 256-386-8530.

Conecuh County

County Judge of Probate, P.O. Box 149, Evergreen, AL 36401. 334-578-1221; Fax 334-578-7021.
Will not search real estate records. **Other Phone Numbers:** Assessor 334-578-7019.

Coosa County

County Judge of Probate, P.O. Box 218, Rockford, AL 35136. 256-377-4919; Fax 256-377-1549.
Will search UCC records. This agency will not do a tax lien search. Will look up specific book and page number. **Other Phone Numbers:** Assessor 256-377-4919; Appraiser/Auditor 256-377-2684.

Covington County

County Judge of Probate, P.O. Box 789, Andalusia, AL 36420-0789. 334-428-2510 R/E Recording: 334-428-2518 UCC Recording: 334-428-2519; Fax 334-428-2536.
Will not search UCC records. This agency will not do a tax lien search. Will not search real estate records. **Other Phone Numbers:** Assessor 334-428-2540.

Crenshaw County

County Judge of Probate, P.O. Box 328, Luverne, AL 36049-0328. 334-335-6568 R/E Recording: 334-335-6568 x227 UCC Recording: 334-335-6568 x227; Fax 334-335-3616.
Will not search UCC records. This agency will not do a tax lien search. Will not search real estate records. **Other Phone Numbers:** Assessor 334-335-6568 x115; Treasurer 334-335-6568 x222; Appraiser/Auditor 334-335-6568 x236; Elections 334-335-6568 x254; Vital Records 334-335-2471.

Cullman County

County Judge of Probate, P.O. Box 970, Cullman, AL 35055. County Judge of Probate, R/E and UCC Recording 256-775-4807; Fax 256-775-4813.
Will search UCC records. This agency will not do a tax lien search. Will not search real estate records. **Other Phone Numbers:** Assessor 256-775-4844; Appraiser/Auditor 256-775-4825; Elections 256-775-4815.

Dale County

County Judge of Probate, P.O. Box 580, Ozark, AL 36361-0580. 334-774-2754; Fax 334-774-0468.
Will search UCC records. This agency will not do a tax lien search. Will not search real estate records. **Other Phone Numbers:** Assessor 334-774-8100.

Dallas County

County Judge of Probate, P.O. Box 987, Selma, AL 36702-0997. 334-874-2516.
Will search UCC records. UCC search includes tax liens if requested. Will not search real estate records. **Other Phone Numbers:** Assessor 334-874-2520; Tax Collector 334-874-2519.

De Kalb County

County Judge of Probate, 300 Grand South West, Courthouse, Suite 100, Fort Payne, AL 35967. 256-845-8510; Fax 256-845-8514.
Will search UCC records. This agency will not do a tax lien search. Will not search real estate records. **Other Phone Numbers:** Assessor 256-845-8515; Treasurer 256-845-8520.

Elmore County

County Judge of Probate, P.O. Box 280, Wetumpka, AL 36092. County Judge of Probate, R/E and UCC Recording 334-567-1143 UCC Recording: 334-567-1143 or 1145; Fax 334-567-1144.
Will not search UCC records. This agency will not do a tax lien search. Will not search real estate records. **Other Phone Numbers:** Assessor 334-567-1118; Treasurer 334-567-1156; Appraiser/Auditor 334-567-1117; Vital Records 334-567-1145.

Escambia County

County Judge of Probate, P.O. Box 557, Brewton, AL 36427. 334-867-0206; Fax 334-867-0284. http://www.clerk.co.escambia.fl.us
Will search UCC records. This agency will not do a tax lien search. Will not search real estate records. **Other Phone Numbers:** Assessor 334-867-0214; Appraiser/Auditor 334-867-9168.

Etowah County

County Judge of Probate, P.O. Box 187, Gadsden, AL 35902. 256-549-5341; Fax 256-546-1149.
Will search UCC records. This agency will not do a tax lien search. Will not search real estate records. **Other Phone Numbers:** Assessor 256-549-5341 x121.

Fayette County

County Judge of Probate, P.O. Box 509, Fayette, AL 35555. 205-932-4519; Fax 205-932-7600.
Will not search UCC records. This agency will not do a tax lien search. Will not search real estate records. **Other Phone Numbers:** Assessor 205-932-6081.

Franklin County

County Judge of Probate, P.O. Box 70, Russellville, AL 35653. 256-332-8801; Fax 256-332-8855.
Will not search UCC records. This agency will not do a tax lien search. Will not search real estate records. **Other Phone Numbers:** Assessor 256-332-8831; Treasurer 256-332-8850.

Geneva County

County Judge of Probate, P.O. Box 430, Geneva, AL 36340-0430. 334-684-5647; Fax 334-684-5602.
Will search UCC records. This agency will not do a tax lien search. Will not search real estate records. **Other Phone Numbers:** Assessor 334-684-3119.

Greene County

County Judge of Probate, P.O. Box 790, Eutaw, AL 35462-0790. 205-372-3340; Fax 205-372-0499.
Will search UCC records. This agency will not do a tax lien search. Will not search real estate records. **Other Phone Numbers:** Assessor 205-372-3202.

Hale County

County Judge of Probate, 1001 Main Street, Courthouse, Greensboro, AL 36744. 334-624-8740; Fax 334-624-8725.
Will search UCC records. Tax liens not included in UCC search. Will not search real estate records. **Other Phone Numbers:** Assessor 334-624-3854; Treasurer 334-624-4257.

Henry County

County Judge of Probate, 101 Court Square, Ste A, 101 West Court Square, Abbeville, AL 36310. County Judge of Probate, R/E and UCC Recording 334-585-3257; Fax 334-585-3610.
Will search UCC records. This agency will not do a tax lien search. Will not search real estate records. **Other Phone Numbers:** Assessor 334-585-3043.

Houston County

County Judge of Probate, P.O. Drawer 6406, Dothan, AL 36302. County Judge of Probate, R/E and UCC Recording 334-677-4723; Fax 334-677-4733.
Will search UCC records. This agency will not do a tax lien search. Will not search real estate records. **Other Phone Numbers:** Assessor 334-677-4714.

Jackson County

County Judge of Probate, P.O. Box 128, Scottsboro, AL 35768. 256-574-9292; Fax 256-574-9318.
Will search UCC records. This agency will not do a tax lien search. Will not search real estate records. **Other Phone Numbers:** Assessor 256-574-9270.

Jefferson County (Bessemer Division)

County Judge of Probate, 1801 3rd Ave., Bessemer, AL 35020. 205-481-4100.
Will search UCC records. This agency will not do a tax lien search. Will not search real estate records. **Other Phone Numbers:** Assessor 205-481-4125.

Jefferson County (Birmingham Division)

County Judge of Probate, 716 North 21st Street, Courthouse, Birmingham, AL 35203. 205-325-5112; Fax 205-325-1437.
Will search UCC records. This agency will not do a tax lien search. Will not search real estate records. **Other Phone Numbers:** Assessor 205-325-5505; Treasurer 205-325-5372.

Lamar County

County Judge of Probate, P.O. Box 338, Vernon, AL 35592. 205-695-9119; Fax 205-695-9253.
Will search UCC records. This agency will not do a tax lien search. Will not search real estate records. **Other Phone Numbers:** Assessor 205-695-9139; Treasurer 205-695-7151.

Lauderdale County

County Judge of Probate, P.O. Box 1059, Florence, AL 35631-1059. 256-760-5800.
Will search UCC records. This agency will not do a tax lien search. Will not search real estate records. **Other Phone Numbers:** Assessor 256-760-5785.

Lawrence County

County Judge of Probate, P.O. Box 310, Moulton, AL 35650. County Judge of Probate, R/E and UCC Recording 256-974-2440; Fax 256-974-3188.
Will not search UCC records. This agency will not do a tax lien search. Will not search real estate records. **Other Phone Numbers:** Assessor 256-974-2476; Appraiser/Auditor 256-974-2546.

Lee County

County Judge of Probate, P.O. Drawer 2266, Opelika, AL 36803. 334-745-9761.
Will search UCC records. This agency will not do a tax lien search. Will not search real estate records.

Limestone County

County Judge of Probate, PO Box 1145, Athens, AL 35612. 256-233-6427; Fax 256-233-6474.
Will not search UCC records. This agency will not do a tax lien search. Will not search real estate records. **Other Phone Numbers:** Assessor 256-233-6435; Appraiser/Auditor 256-233-6437.

Lowndes County

County Judge of Probate, P.O. Box 5, Hayneville, AL 36040-0005. 334-548-2365; Fax 334-548-5398.

Will search UCC records. UCC search includes tax liens if requested. RE owner, mortgage, and property transfer searches available. **Other Phone Numbers:** Assessor 334-548-2271.

Macon County

County Judge of Probate, 101 E. Northside St., Suite 101, Tuskegee, AL 36083-1731. 334-724-2611 R/E Recording: 334-724-2508 UCC Recording: 334-724-2508; Fax 334-724-2512.
Will search UCC records. This agency will not do a tax lien search. Will send RE document requested by mail with fee. **Other Phone Numbers:** Assessor 334-724-2603; Treasurer 334-724-5120; Appraiser/Auditor 334-724-2607; Elections 334-724-2611; Vital Records 334-724-2611.

Madison County

County Judge of Probate, 100 Northside Square, Room 101, Huntsville, AL 35801-4820. 256-532-3341; Fax 256-532-6977.
Will search UCC records. This agency will not do a tax lien search. Will not search real estate records. **Other Phone Numbers:** Assessor 256-532-3350.

Marengo County

County Judge of Probate, P.O. Box 480668, Linden, AL 36748. 334-295-2210; Fax 334-295-2254.
Will search UCC records. UCC search includes tax liens if requested. Will not search real estate records. **Other Phone Numbers:** Assessor 334-295-2215.

Marion County

County Judge of Probate, P.O. Box 1687, Hamilton, AL 35570. 205-921-2471; Fax 205-921-5109.
Will search UCC records. This agency will not do a tax lien search. Will not search real estate records. **Other Phone Numbers:** Assessor 205-921-2606; Treasurer 205-921-3561.

Marshall County

County Judge of Probate, 425 Gunter Avenue, Guntersville, AL 35976. 256-571-7767 R/E Recording: 256-571-7764 x208 UCC Recording: 256-571-7764 x208; Fax 256-571-7732.
Will search UCC records. This agency will not do a tax lien search. Will not search real estate records. **Other Phone Numbers:** Assessor 256-571-5733; Treasurer 256-571-7758; Elections 256-571-7764 x202.

Mobile County

County Judge of Probate, P.O. Box 7, Mobile, AL 36601. 334-574-8497 R/E Recording: 334-690-8497 UCC Recording: 334-690-8497; Fax 334-690-4939.
http://mobile-county.net/probate
Will search UCC records. This agency will not do a tax lien search. Will not search real estate records. **Other Phone Numbers:** Assessor 334-574-8530; Treasurer 334-690-8585; Appraiser/Auditor 334-690-8531; Elections 334-574-8480.

Monroe County

County Judge of Probate, P.O. Box 665, Monroeville, AL 36461-0665. 334-743-4107 R/E Recording: 334-743-4107 x121 UCC Recording: 334-743-4107 x121; Fax 334-575-7934.
Will not search UCC records. This agency will not do a tax lien search. Will not search real estate records. **Other Phone Numbers:** Assessor 334-743-4107 x124; Appraiser/Auditor 334-743-4107 x124; Elections 334-743-4107 x120; Vital Records 334-743-4107 x121.

Montgomery County

County Judge of Probate, P.O. Box 223, Montgomery, AL 36195. 334-832-1237.

Will search UCC records. This agency will not do a tax lien search. Will not search real estate records. **Other Phone Numbers:** Assessor 334-832-4950.

Morgan County

County Judge of Probate, P.O. Box 848, Decatur, AL 35602-0848. County Judge of Probate, R/E and UCC Recording 256-351-4680.
Will search UCC records. This agency will not do a tax lien search. Will not search real estate records. **Other Phone Numbers:** Assessor 256-351-4690.

Perry County

County Judge of Probate, P.O. Box 478, Marion, AL 36756. County Judge of Probate, R/E and UCC Recording 334-683-2210; Fax 334-683-2201.
Will search UCC records. This agency will not do a tax lien search. Will not search real estate records. **Other Phone Numbers:** Assessor 334-683-2219; Appraiser/Auditor 334-683-2221; Elections 334-683-2210; Collector 334-683-2220.

Pickens County

County Judge of Probate, P.O. Box 370, Carrollton, AL 35447. 205-367-2010; Fax 205-367-2011.
Will search UCC records. This agency will not do a tax lien search. Will not search real estate records. **Other Phone Numbers:** Assessor 205-367-2041.

Pike County

County Judge of Probate, P.O. Drawer 1008, Troy, AL 36081. 334-566-1246; Fax 334-566-8585.
Will search UCC records. This agency will not do a tax lien search. Will not search real estate records.

Randolph County

County Judge of Probate, P.O. Box 249, Wedowee, AL 36278. 256-357-4933; Fax 256-357-9053.
Will search UCC records. This agency will not do a tax lien search. Will not search real estate records. **Other Phone Numbers:** Assessor 256-357-4343.

Russell County

County Judge of Probate, P.O. Box 700, Phenix City, AL 36868-0700. 334-298-7979; Fax 334-298-7979.
Will search UCC records. This agency will not do a tax lien search. Will not search real estate records.

Shelby County

County Judge of Probate, P.O. Box 825, Columbiana, AL 35051. 205-669-3720; Fax 205-669-3714.
Will search UCC records. This agency will not do a tax lien search. Will not search real estate records. **Other Phone Numbers:** Assessor 205-669-3902; Appraiser/Auditor 205-669-3902.

St. Clair County (Northern Congressional District)

County Judge of Probate, P.O. Box 220, Ashville, AL 35953. 205-594-2124; Fax 205-594-2110.
Will search UCC records. This agency will not do a tax lien search. Will not search real estate records.

St. Clair County (Southern Congressional District)

County Judge of Probate, 1815 Cogswell Ave, Suite 212, 1815 Cogswell Ave., Pell City, AL 35125. County Judge of Probate, R/E and UCC Recording 205-338-9449; Fax 205-884-1182.
Will search UCC records. This agency will not do a tax lien search. Will not search real estate records. **Other Phone Numbers:** Assessor 205-884-2395; Appraiser/Auditor 205-884-2395.

Sumter County

County Judge of Probate, P.O. Box 1040, Livingston, AL 35470-1040. 205-652-7281; Fax 205-652-6206.
Will search UCC records. This agency will not do a tax lien search. Will not search real estate records. **Other Phone Numbers:** Assessor 205-652-2424; Treasurer 205-652-2731.

Talladega County

County Judge of Probate, P.O. Box 737, Talladega, AL 35161. 256-362-4175; Fax 256-761-2128.
Will search UCC records. This agency will not do a tax lien search. Will not search real estate records. **Other Phone Numbers:** Assessor 256-761-2123.

Tallapoosa County

County Judge of Probate, Courthouse, Room 126, 125 N. Broadnax St., Dadeville, AL 36853. 256-825-1090; Fax 256-825-1604.
Will search UCC records. This agency will not do a tax lien search. Will not search real estate records. **Other Phone Numbers:** Assessor 256-825-7831.

Tuscaloosa County

County Judge of Probate, P.O. Box 20067, Tuscaloosa, AL 35402-0067. 205-349-3870 x205/6; http://www.tuscco.com/
Will search UCC records. This agency will not do a tax lien search. Will search RE names if slack time. **Online Access:** Real Estate, Liens, UCC, Grantor/Grantee, Probate, Marriage. Online access to the records database is available free at www.tuscco.com/RecordsRoom/Records.htm. Also included are searches for mortgages, incorporations, bonds, discharges, exemptions. **Other Phone Numbers:** Assessor 205-349-3870 x370.

Walker County

County Judge of Probate, P.O. Box 502, Jasper, AL 35502-0502. 205-384-7282; Fax 205-384-7005.
Will search UCC records. This agency will not do a tax lien search. Will not search real estate records. **Other Phone Numbers:** Assessor 205-384-7265; Treasurer 205-384-7276.

Washington County

County Judge of Probate, P.O. Box 549, Chatom, AL 36518. County Judge of Probate, R/E and UCC Recording 334-847-2201; Fax 334-847-3677. www.recordsusa.com
Will search UCC records. This agency will not do a tax lien search. Will not search real estate records. **Other Phone Numbers:** Assessor 334-847-2780; Treasurer 334-847-2208.

Wilcox County

County Judge of Probate, P.O. Box 668, Camden, AL 36726. 334-682-4883; Fax 334-682-9484.
Will search UCC records. This agency will not do a tax lien search. Will not search real estate records. **Other Phone Numbers:** Assessor 334-682-4625; Treasurer 334-682-9112.

Winston County

County Judge of Probate, P.O. Box 27, Double Springs, AL 35553. County Judge of Probate, R/E and UCC Recording 205-489-5219; Fax 205-489-5135.
Will not search UCC records. This agency will not do a tax lien search. Will not search real estate records. **Other Phone Numbers:** Assessor 205-489-5166; Appraiser/Auditor 205-489-5166; Vital Records 205-489-5219 (marriages).

Alabama County Locator

You will usually be able to find the city name in the City/County Cross Reference below. In that case, it is a simple matter to determine the county from the cross reference. However, only the official US Postal Service city names are included in this index. There are an additional 40,000 place names that people use in their addresses. Therefore, we have also included a ZIP/City Cross Reference immediately following the City/County Cross Reference.

If you know the ZIP Code but the city name does not appear in the City/County Cross Reference index, look up the ZIP Code in the ZIP/City Cross Reference, find the city name, then look up the city name in the City/County Cross Reference. For example, you want to know the county for an address of Menands, NY 12204. There is no "Menands" in the City/County Cross Reference. The ZIP/City Cross Reference shows that ZIP Codes 12201-12288 are for the city of Albany. Looking back in the City/County Cross Reference, Albany is in Albany County.

City/County Cross Reference

ABBEVILLE Henry
ABERNANT Tuscaloosa
ADAMSVILLE Jefferson
ADDISON (35540) Winston(93), Cullman(7)
ADGER (35006) Jefferson(91), Walker(6), Tuscaloosa(3)
AKRON Hale
ALABASTER Shelby
ALBERTA Wilcox
ALBERTVILLE (35951) De Kalb(82), Marshall(18)
ALBERTVILLE Marshall
ALEXANDER CITY (35010) Tallapoosa(96), Elmore(3), Coosa(1)
ALEXANDER CITY Tallapoosa
ALEXANDRIA Calhoun
ALICEVILLE (35442) Pickens(95), Sumter(5)
ALLEN Clarke
ALLGOOD Blount
ALMA Clarke
ALPINE Talladega
ALTON Jefferson
ALTOONA (35952) Etowah(62), Blount(38)
ANDALUSIA (36420) Covington(96), Escambia(3), Conecuh(1)
ANDERSON (35610) Lauderdale(75), Limestone(25)
ANNEMANIE Wilcox
ANNISTON (36203) Calhoun(80), Talladega(20)
ANNISTON Calhoun
ARAB (35016) Marshall(97), Cullman(2)
ARDMORE (35739) Limestone(80), Madison(21)
ARITON (36311) Dale(50), Barbour(44), Coffee(6)
ARLEY (35541) Winston(95), Cullman(6)
ARLINGTON (36722) Wilcox(96), Marengo(4)
ASHFORD Houston
ASHLAND Clay
ASHVILLE St. Clair
ATHENS Limestone
ATMORE (36502) Escambia(93), Monroe(4), Baldwin(3)
ATMORE Escambia
ATTALLA Etowah
AUBURN (36830) Lee(88), Macon(12)
AUBURN Lee
AUBURN UNIVERSITY Lee
AUTAUGAVILLE Autauga
AXIS Mobile
BAILEYTON (35019) Cullman(72), Morgan(28)
BANKS (36005) Pike(68), Bullock(31), Barbour(1)
BANKSTON Fayette
BAY MINETTE Baldwin
BAYOU LA BATRE Mobile
BEAR CREEK Marion
BEATRICE Monroe
BEAVERTON Lamar

BELK Fayette
BELLAMY Sumter
BELLE MINA Limestone
BELLWOOD Geneva
BERRY (35546) Fayette(63), Tuscaloosa(33), Walker(4)
BESSEMER (35022) Jefferson(96), Shelby(4)
BESSEMER Jefferson
BIGBEE Washington
BILLINGSLEY (36006) Autauga(60), Chilton(40)
BIRMINGHAM (35242) Shelby(91), Jefferson(9)
BIRMINGHAM (35244) Shelby(53), Jefferson(47)
BIRMINGHAM Jefferson
BLACK Geneva
BLOUNTSVILLE Blount
BOAZ (35957) Marshall(79), De Kalb(18), Blount(3)
BOAZ Etowah
BOLIGEE Greene
BOLINGER Choctaw
BON AIR Talladega
BON SECOUR Baldwin
BOOTH Autauga
BOYKIN Wilcox
BRANTLEY (36009) Crenshaw(94), Coffee(6)
BREMEN (35033) Cullman(90), Walker(10)
BRENT (35034) Bibb(97), Perry(3)
BREWTON Escambia
BRIDGEPORT Jackson
BRIERFIELD Bibb
BRILLIANT Marion
BROOKLYN Conecuh
BROOKSIDE Jefferson
BROOKWOOD (35444) Tuscaloosa(90), Jefferson(10)
BROWNSBORO Madison
BRUNDIDGE Pike
BRYANT Jackson
BUCKS Mobile
BUHL Tuscaloosa
BURNT CORN Monroe
BURNWELL Walker
BUTLER Choctaw
BYNUM Calhoun
CALERA (35040) Shelby(76), Chilton(24)
CALVERT Washington
CAMDEN Wilcox
CAMP HILL (36850) Tallapoosa(76), Chambers(21), Lee(3)
CAMPBELL Clarke
CAPSHAW Limestone
CARBON HILL (35549) Walker(80), Fayette(20)
CARDIFF Jefferson
CARLTON Clarke
CARROLLTON Pickens
CASTLEBERRY (36432) Conecuh(65), Escambia(35)

CATHERINE Wilcox
CECIL (36013) Montgomery(94), Macon(6)
CEDAR BLUFF Cherokee
CENTRE Cherokee
CENTREVILLE (35042) Bibb(96), Perry(4)
CHANCELLOR (36316) Geneva(56), Coffee(44)
CHAPMAN Butler
CHATOM Washington
CHELSEA Shelby
CHEROKEE Colbert
CHILDERSBURG Talladega
CHOCCOLOCCO Calhoun
CHUNCHULA Mobile
CITRONELLE (36522) Mobile(96), Washington(4)
CLANTON (35046) Chilton(99), Coosa(2)
CLANTON Chilton
CLAY Jefferson
CLAYTON Barbour
CLEVELAND Blount
CLINTON Greene
CLIO Barbour
CLOPTON (36317) Henry(76), Barbour(13), Dale(11)
CLOVERDALE Lauderdale
COALING Tuscaloosa
CODEN Mobile
COFFEE SPRINGS (36318) Geneva(74), Coffee(27)
COFFEEVILLE Clarke
COKER Tuscaloosa
COLLINSVILLE (35961) De Kalb(73), Cherokee(16), Etowah(10)
COLUMBIA (36319) Houston(62), Henry(38)
COLUMBIANA Shelby
COOK SPRINGS St. Clair
COOSADA Elmore
CORDOVA Walker
COTTONDALE Tuscaloosa
COTTONTON Russell
COTTONWOOD Houston
COURTLAND Lawrence
COWARTS Houston
COY Wilcox
CRAGFORD (36255) Clay(96), Tallapoosa(3)
CRANE HILL (35053) Cullman(98), Winston(3)
CREOLA Mobile
CROMWELL Choctaw
CROPWELL St. Clair
CROSSVILLE (35962) De Kalb(94), Marshall(7)
CUBA Sumter
CULLMAN Cullman
CUSSETA (36852) Lee(73), Chambers(27)
DADEVILLE Tallapoosa
DALEVILLE Dale
DANVILLE (35619) Morgan(53), Lawrence(47)
DAPHNE Baldwin

DAUPHIN ISLAND Mobile
DAVISTON (36256) Tallapoosa(94), Clay(6)
DAWSON De Kalb
DAYTON Marengo
DE ARMANVILLE Calhoun
DEATSVILLE (36022) Elmore(81), Autauga(19)
DECATUR (35603) Morgan(99), Lawrence(1)
DECATUR Morgan
DEER PARK Washington
DELMAR Winston
DELTA (36258) Clay(54), Cleburne(32), Randolph(14)
DEMOPOLIS Marengo
DETROIT (35552) Marion(60), Lamar(41)
DICKINSON Clarke
DIXONS MILLS Marengo
DOCENA Jefferson
DOLOMITE Jefferson
DORA (35062) Jefferson(75), Walker(25)
DOTHAN (36303) Houston(96), Dale(4)
DOTHAN (36305) Houston(93), Geneva(7)
DOTHAN Houston
DOUBLE SPRINGS Winston
DOUGLAS Marshall
DOZIER (36028) Covington(64), Crenshaw(36)
DUNCANVILLE (35456) Tuscaloosa(99), Bibb(1)
DUTTON Jackson
EAST TALLASSEE Tallapoosa
EASTABOGA (36260) Calhoun(66), Talladega(34)
ECHOLA Tuscaloosa
ECLECTIC Elmore
EDWARDSVILLE Cleburne
EIGHT MILE Mobile
ELBA Coffee
ELBERTA Baldwin
ELDRIDGE (35554) Fayette(68), Walker(28), Marion(4)
ELKMONT Limestone
ELMORE Elmore
ELROD Tuscaloosa
EMELLE Sumter
EMPIRE (35063) Walker(70), Blount(21), Jefferson(10)
ENTERPRISE (36330) Coffee(92), Dale(8)
ENTERPRISE Coffee
EPES Sumter
EQUALITY (36026) Elmore(61), Coosa(39)
ESTILLFORK Jackson
ETHELSVILLE (35461) Lamar(54), Pickens(46)
EUFAULA Autauga
EUFAULA Barbour
EUTAW Greene
EVA (35621) Morgan(90), Cullman(10)
EVERGREEN Conecuh
EXCEL Monroe
FACKLER Jackson

FAIRFIELD Jefferson
FAIRHOPE Baldwin
FALKVILLE (35622) Morgan(85), Cullman(15)
FAUNSDALE Marengo
FAYETTE (35555) Fayette(93), Tuscaloosa(5), Lamar(2)
FITZPATRICK (36029) Bullock(75), Macon(19), Montgomery(6)
FIVE POINTS Chambers
FLAT ROCK (35966) Jackson(65), De Kalb(35)
FLOMATON Escambia
FLORALA Covington
FLORENCE Lauderdale
FOLEY Baldwin
FOREST HOME (36030) Butler(95), Wilcox(5)
FORKLAND Greene
FORT DAVIS Macon
FORT DEPOSIT (36032) Lowndes(82), Butler(19)
FORT MITCHELL Russell
FORT PAYNE (35967) De Kalb(96), Cherokee(4)
FORT PAYNE De Kalb
FORT RUCKER Dale
FOSTERS Tuscaloosa
FRANKLIN Monroe
FRANKVILLE Washington
FRISCO CITY Monroe
FRUITDALE Washington
FRUITHURST Cleburne
FULTON Clarke
FULTONDALE Jefferson
FURMAN Wilcox
FYFFE De Kalb
GADSDEN (35905) Etowah(62), Calhoun(38)
GADSDEN (35907) Etowah(99), Calhoun(2)
GADSDEN Etowah
GAINESTOWN Clarke
GAINESVILLE (35464) Sumter(94), Greene(6)
GALLANT (35972) Etowah(75), St. Clair(25)
GALLION (36742) Marengo(96), Hale(4)
GANTT Covington
GARDEN CITY Cullman
GARDENDALE Jefferson
GAYLESVILLE Cherokee
GENEVA Geneva
GEORGIANA (36033) Butler(93), Conecuh(5), Monroe(2)
GERALDINE De Kalb
GILBERTOWN Choctaw
GLEN ALLEN Fayette
GLENWOOD (36034) Pike(95), Crenshaw(5)
GOODSPRINGS Walker
GOODWATER (35072) Clay(52), Coosa(26), Tallapoosa(22)
GOODWAY Monroe
GORDO (35466) Pickens(79), Tuscaloosa(21)
GORDON Houston
GOSHEN (36035) Pike(76), Crenshaw(24)
GRADY (36036) Montgomery(69), Crenshaw(31)
GRAHAM Randolph
GRAND BAY Mobile
GRANT Marshall
GRAYSVILLE Jefferson
GREEN POND Bibb
GREENSBORO Hale
GREENVILLE (36037) Butler(96), Bullock(3)
GROVE HILL Clarke
GROVEOAK (35975) De Kalb(93), Marshall(7)

GUIN (35563) Marion(92), Fayette(5), Lamar(4)
GULF SHORES Baldwin
GUNTERSVILLE (35976) Marshall(96), Blount(4)
GURLEY (35748) Madison(95), Jackson(5)
HACKLEBURG Marion
HALEYVILLE (35565) Winston(51), Marion(43), Franklin(6)
HAMILTON Marion
HANCEVILLE Cullman
HARDAWAY Macon
HARPERSVILLE Shelby
HARTFORD Geneva
HARTSELLE Morgan
HARVEST (35749) Madison(73), Limestone(27)
HATCHECHUBBEE Russell
HAYDEN Blount
HAYNEVILLE Lowndes
HAZEL GREEN Madison
HEADLAND (36345) Henry(76), Houston(21), Dale(3)
HEFLIN (36264) Cleburne(93), Randolph(7)
HELENA Shelby
HENAGAR (35978) De Kalb(82), Jackson(18)
HIGDON (35979) De Kalb(68), Jackson(32)
HIGHLAND HOME (36041) Crenshaw(98), Montgomery(2)
HILLSBORO Lawrence
HODGES (35571) Franklin(73), Marion(27)
HOLLINS Clay
HOLLY POND Cullman
HOLLYTREE Jackson
HOLLYWOOD Jackson
HOLY TRINITY Russell
HONORAVILLE (36042) Crenshaw(56), Butler(44)
HOPE HULL (36043) Montgomery(84), Lowndes(16)
HORTON (35980) Marshall(65), Blount(35)
HOUSTON Winston
HUNTSVILLE Madison
HURTSBORO (36860) Russell(87), Bullock(8), Macon(5)
HUXFORD Escambia
IDER De Kalb
IRVINGTON Mobile
JACHIN Choctaw
JACK Coffee
JACKSON Clarke
JACKSONS GAP Tallapoosa
JACKSONVILLE Calhoun
JASPER (35503) Walker(96), Winston(4)
JASPER Walker
JEFFERSON Marengo
JEMISON Chilton
JONES (36749) Dallas(54), Autauga(46)
JOPPA (35087) Cullman(48), Morgan(39), Marshall(12)
KANSAS Walker
KELLERMAN Tuscaloosa
KELLYTON (35089) Tallapoosa(62), Coosa(38)
KENNEDY (35574) Lamar(78), Fayette(15), Pickens(7)
KENT Elmore
KILLEN Lauderdale
KIMBERLY Jefferson
KINSTON (36453) Coffee(56), Geneva(41), Covington(3)
KNOXVILLE (35469) Tuscaloosa(59), Greene(41)
LACEYS SPRING (35754) Morgan(98), Marshall(2)
LAFAYETTE Chambers
LAMISON Wilcox
LANETT Chambers
LANGSTON (35755) Marshall(58), Jackson(42)

LAPINE (36046) Crenshaw(53), Montgomery(47)
LAVACA Choctaw
LAWLEY (36793) Chilton(53), Bibb(32), Perry(15)
LEEDS (35094) Jefferson(71), Shelby(18), St. Clair(11)
LEESBURG Cherokee
LEIGHTON Colbert
LENOX Conecuh
LEROY Washington
LESTER Limestone
LETOHATCHEE (36047) Lowndes(68), Montgomery(32)
LEXINGTON Lauderdale
LILLIAN Baldwin
LINCOLN (35096) Talladega(90), Calhoun(10)
LINDEN Marengo
LINEVILLE (36266) Clay(84), Randolph(16)
LISMAN (36912) Choctaw(95), Sumter(5)
LITTLE RIVER Baldwin
LIVINGSTON Sumter
LOACHAPOKA Lee
LOCKHART Covington
LOCUST FORK Blount
LOGAN (35098) Cullman(99), Winston(1)
LOUISVILLE Barbour
LOWER PEACH TREE (36751) Wilcox(54), Monroe(29), Clarke(16)
LOWNDESBORO Lowndes
LOXLEY Baldwin
LUVERNE Crenshaw
LYNN (35575) Winston(98), Russell(2)
MADISON (35756) Limestone(80), Madison(20)
MADISON (35757) Madison(91), Limestone(10)
MADISON Madison
MAGNOLIA Marengo
MAGNOLIA SPRINGS Baldwin
MALCOLM Washington
MALVERN Geneva
MAPLESVILLE (36750) Chilton(99), Bibb(1)
MARBURY (36051) Autauga(43), Elmore(31), Chilton(26)
MARGARET St. Clair
MARION Perry
MARION JUNCTION (36759) Dallas(96), Perry(4)
MATHEWS Montgomery
MAYLENE Shelby
MC CALLA (35111) Tuscaloosa(62), Jefferson(37), Bibb(1)
MC INTOSH Washington
MC KENZIE (36456) Butler(57), Conecuh(35), Covington(8)
MC SHAN Pickens
MC WILLIAMS Wilcox
MEGARGEL Monroe
MELVIN Choctaw
MENTONE (35984) De Kalb(80), Cherokee(21)
MERIDIANVILLE Madison
MEXIA Monroe
MIDLAND CITY (36350) Dale(90), Houston(10)
MIDWAY (36053) Barbour(59), Bullock(41)
MILLBROOK Elmore
MILLERS FERRY Wilcox
MILLERVILLE Clay
MILLPORT (35576) Lamar(89), Pickens(11)
MILLRY (36558) Washington(92), Choctaw(8)
MINTER (36761) Dallas(91), Lowndes(9)
MOBILE Mobile
MONROEVILLE Monroe
MONTEVALLO (35115) Shelby(82), Chilton(18)
MONTGOMERY Montgomery

MONTROSE Baldwin
MOODY St. Clair
MOORESVILLE Limestone
MORRIS Jefferson
MORVIN (36762) Clarke(93), Marengo(7)
MOULTON Lawrence
MOUNDVILLE (35474) Hale(88), Tuscaloosa(12)
MOUNT HOPE Lawrence
MOUNT MEIGS Montgomery
MOUNT OLIVE Jefferson
MOUNT VERNON Mobile
MULGA Jefferson
MUNFORD Talladega
MUSCADINE Cleburne
MUSCLE SHOALS Colbert
MYRTLEWOOD Marengo
NANAFALIA Marengo
NATURAL BRIDGE Winston
NAUVOO (35578) Walker(95), Winston(5)
NEEDHAM Choctaw
NEW BROCKTON Coffee
NEW CASTLE Jefferson
NEW HOPE (35760) Madison(89), Marshall(11)
NEW MARKET Madison
NEWBERN (36765) Hale(84), Perry(16)
NEWELL Randolph
NEWTON (36352) Houston(71), Dale(28), Geneva(1)
NEWVILLE (36353) Henry(68), Dale(32)
NORMAL Madison
NORTHPORT Tuscaloosa
NOTASULGA (36866) Macon(74), Tallapoosa(21), Lee(5)
OAK HILL Wilcox
OAKMAN (35579) Walker(98), Tuscaloosa(2)
ODENVILLE St. Clair
OHATCHEE Calhoun
ONEONTA (35121) Blount(99), St. Clair(1)
OPELIKA (36801) Lee(99), Chambers(1)
OPELIKA (36804) Lee(97), Macon(2), Russell(2)
OPELIKA Lee
OPP Covington
ORANGE BEACH Baldwin
ORRVILLE Dallas
OWENS CROSS ROADS Madison
OZARK Dale
PAINT ROCK Jackson
PALMERDALE Jefferson
PANOLA Sumter
PANSEY Houston
PARRISH Walker
PELHAM Shelby
PELL CITY St. Clair
PENNINGTON Choctaw
PERDIDO (36562) Baldwin(91), Escambia(9)
PERDUE HILL Monroe
PEROTE (36061) Crenshaw(88), Bullock(13)
PETERMAN (36471) Monroe(97), Conecuh(3)
PETERSON Tuscaloosa
PETREY Crenshaw
PHENIX CITY (36867) Russell(90), Lee(10)
PHENIX CITY (36870) Lee(71), Russell(29)
PHENIX CITY Russell
PHIL CAMPBELL (35581) Franklin(88), Marion(12)
PIEDMONT (36272) Calhoun(62), Cherokee(27), Etowah(9), Cleburne(3)
PIKE ROAD Montgomery
PINCKARD Dale
PINE APPLE Wilcox
PINE HILL Wilcox
PINE LEVEL Montgomery
PINSON (35126) Jefferson(96), Blount(5)
PISGAH (35765) Jackson(94), De Kalb(6)
PITTSVIEW Russell

PLANTERSVILLE (36758) Dallas(87), Autauga(11), Chilton(2)
PLEASANT GROVE Jefferson
POINT CLEAR Baldwin
PRAIRIE Wilcox
PRATTVILLE (36066) Autauga(95), Elmore(5)
PRATTVILLE Autauga
PRINCETON Jackson
QUINTON (35130) Walker(59), Jefferson(41)
RAGLAND St. Clair
RAINBOW CITY Etowah
RAINSVILLE De Kalb
RALPH (35480) Tuscaloosa(98), Greene(2)
RAMER (36069) Montgomery(97), Pike(3)
RANBURNE Cleburne
RANDOLPH (36792) Chilton(64), Bibb(36)
RANGE Conecuh
RED BAY Franklin
RED LEVEL (36474) Covington(94), Conecuh(6)
REFORM Pickens
REMLAP (35133) Blount(95), St. Clair(5)
REPTON (36475) Conecuh(73), Monroe(27)
RIVER FALLS Covington
RIVERSIDE St. Clair
ROANOKE (36274) Randolph(87), Chambers(13)
ROBERTSDALE Baldwin
ROCKFORD Coosa
ROGERSVILLE Lauderdale
RUSSELLVILLE (35653) Franklin(96), Colbert(3)
RUSSELLVILLE (35654) Franklin(90), Colbert(7), Lawrence(4)
RUTLEDGE (36071) Crenshaw(94), Butler(7)
RYLAND Madison
SAFFORD (36773) Dallas(90), Marengo(10)
SAGINAW Shelby
SAINT ELMO Mobile
SAINT STEPHENS Washington
SALEM (36874) Lee(96), Russell(4)
SALITPA Clarke
SAMANTHA Tuscaloosa

SAMSON (36477) Geneva(94), Coffee(6)
SARALAND Mobile
SARDIS (36775) Dallas(97), Lowndes(4)
SATSUMA Mobile
SAWYERVILLE Hale
SAYRE Jefferson
SCOTTSBORO (35769) Jackson(70), Marshall(30)
SCOTTSBORO Jackson
SEALE Russell
SECTION (35771) Jackson(97), De Kalb(3)
SELMA (36701) Dallas(99), Perry(1)
SELMA (36703) Dallas(97), Autauga(3)
SELMA Dallas
SEMINOLE Baldwin
SEMMES Mobile
SHANNON Jefferson
SHEFFIELD Colbert
SHELBY Shelby
SHORTER Macon
SHORTERVILLE Henry
SILAS (36919) Choctaw(98), Washington(2)
SILURIA Shelby
SILVERHILL Baldwin
SIPSEY Walker
SKIPPERVILLE (36374) Dale(72), Barbour(28)
SLOCOMB (36375) Geneva(71), Houston(29)
SMITHS Lee
SNOW HILL Wilcox
SOMERVILLE Morgan
SPANISH FORT Baldwin
SPRING GARDEN Cherokee
SPRINGVILLE (35146) St. Clair(80), Blount(18), Jefferson(2)
SPROTT Perry
SPRUCE PINE Franklin
STANTON Chilton
STAPLETON Baldwin
STEELE St. Clair
STERRETT Shelby
STEVENSON Jackson
STOCKTON Baldwin
SULLIGENT Lamar
SUMITON Walker
SUMMERDALE Baldwin

SUNFLOWER Washington
SWEET WATER Marengo
SYCAMORE Talladega
SYLACAUGA (35150) Talladega(99), Coosa(2)
SYLACAUGA (35151) Talladega(68), Coosa(32)
SYLVANIA De Kalb
TALLADEGA (35160) Talladega(97), Clay(3)
TALLADEGA Talladega
TALLASSEE (36078) Elmore(77), Tallapoosa(23)
TANNER Limestone
THEODORE Mobile
THOMASTON Marengo
THOMASVILLE (36784) Clarke(97), Marengo(3)
THORSBY Chilton
TIBBIE Washington
TITUS (36080) Elmore(99), Coosa(1)
TONEY (35773) Madison(72), Limestone(28)
TOWN CREEK (35672) Lawrence(95), Colbert(5)
TOWNLEY Walker
TOXEY Choctaw
TRAFFORD (35172) Blount(84), Jefferson(16)
TRENTON Jackson
TRINITY (35673) Lawrence(80), Morgan(20)
TROY (36081) Pike(98), Bullock(2)
TROY Pike
TRUSSVILLE (35173) Jefferson(85), St. Clair(15)
TUSCALOOSA Tuscaloosa
TUSCUMBIA Colbert
TUSKEGEE Macon
TUSKEGEE INSTITUTE Macon
TYLER (36785) Dallas(71), Lowndes(30)
UNION GROVE (35175) Marshall(90), Morgan(10)
UNION SPRINGS Bullock
UNIONTOWN (36786) Perry(90), Hale(5), Marengo(5)
URIAH Monroe
VALHERMOSO SPRINGS Morgan

VALLEY (36854) Chambers(72), Lee(28)
VALLEY Lee
VALLEY HEAD De Kalb
VANCE Tuscaloosa
VANDIVER Shelby
VERBENA (36091) Chilton(95), Autauga(4)
VERNON Lamar
VINA (35593) Franklin(87), Marion(13)
VINCENT (35178) Shelby(71), St. Clair(29)
VINEGAR BEND Washington
VINEMONT (35179) Cullman(97), Morgan(3)
VREDENBURGH Monroe
WADLEY (36276) Randolph(66), Chambers(17), Clay(12), Tallapoosa(5)
WAGARVILLE Washington
WALKER SPRINGS Clarke
WALNUT GROVE Etowah
WARD (36922) Choctaw(64), Sumter(36)
WARRIOR (35180) Jefferson(52), Blount(48)
WATERLOO Lauderdale
WATSON Jefferson
WATTSVILLE St. Clair
WAVERLY (36879) Lee(51), Chambers(49)
WEAVER Calhoun
WEBB Houston
WEDOWEE Randolph
WELLINGTON Calhoun
WEOGUFKA Coosa
WEST BLOCTON (35184) Bibb(95), Tuscaloosa(6)
WEST GREENE Greene
WESTOVER Shelby
WETUMPKA Elmore
WHATLEY (36482) Clarke(99), Monroe(2)
WILMER Mobile
WILSONVILLE Shelby
WILTON Shelby
WINFIELD (35594) Fayette(57), Marion(43)
WING (36483) Escambia(65), Covington(35)
WOODLAND Randolph
WOODSTOCK (35188) Bibb(90), Tuscaloosa(10)
WOODVILLE (35776) Jackson(77), Marshall(21), Madison(2)
YORK Sumter

ZIP/City Cross Reference

35004-35004	MOODY	35055-35058	CULLMAN	35116-35116	MORRIS	35173-35173	TRUSSVILLE
35005-35005	ADAMSVILLE	35060-35060	DOCENA	35117-35117	MOUNT OLIVE	35175-35175	UNION GROVE
35006-35006	ADGER	35061-35061	DOLOMITE	35118-35118	MULGA	35176-35176	VANDIVER
35007-35007	ALABASTER	35062-35062	DORA	35119-35119	NEW CASTLE	35178-35178	VINCENT
35010-35011	ALEXANDER CITY	35063-35063	EMPIRE	35120-35120	ODENVILLE	35179-35179	VINEMONT
35013-35013	ALLGOOD	35064-35064	FAIRFIELD	35121-35121	ONEONTA	35180-35180	WARRIOR
35014-35014	ALPINE	35068-35068	FULTONDALE	35123-35123	PALMERDALE	35181-35181	WATSON
35015-35015	ALTON	35070-35070	GARDEN CITY	35124-35124	PELHAM	35182-35182	WATTSVILLE
35016-35016	ARAB	35071-35071	GARDENDALE	35125-35125	PELL CITY	35183-35183	WEOGUFKA
35019-35019	BAILEYTON	35072-35072	GOODWATER	35126-35126	PINSON	35184-35184	WEST BLOCTON
35020-35023	BESSEMER	35073-35073	GRAYSVILLE	35127-35127	PLEASANT GROVE	35185-35185	WESTOVER
35031-35031	BLOUNTSVILLE	35074-35074	GREEN POND	35128-35128	PELL CITY	35186-35186	WILSONVILLE
35032-35032	BON AIR	35077-35077	HANCEVILLE	35130-35130	QUINTON	35187-35187	WILTON
35033-35033	BREMEN	35078-35078	HARPERSVILLE	35131-35131	RAGLAND	35188-35188	WOODSTOCK
35034-35034	BRENT	35079-35079	HAYDEN	35133-35133	REMLAP	35201-35299	BIRMINGHAM
35035-35035	BRIERFIELD	35080-35080	HELENA	35135-35135	RIVERSIDE	35401-35407	TUSCALOOSA
35036-35036	BROOKSIDE	35082-35082	HOLLINS	35136-35136	ROCKFORD	35440-35440	ABERNANT
35038-35038	BURNWELL	35083-35083	HOLLY POND	35137-35137	SAGINAW	35441-35441	AKRON
35040-35040	CALERA	35085-35085	JEMISON	35139-35139	SAYRE	35442-35442	ALICEVILLE
35041-35041	CARDIFF	35087-35087	JOPPA	35142-35142	SHANNON	35443-35443	BOLIGEE
35042-35042	CENTREVILLE	35089-35089	KELLYTON	35143-35143	SHELBY	35444-35444	BROOKWOOD
35043-35043	CHELSEA	35091-35091	KIMBERLY	35144-35144	SILURIA	35446-35446	BUHL
35044-35044	CHILDERSBURG	35094-35094	LEEDS	35146-35146	SPRINGVILLE	35447-35447	CARROLLTON
35045-35045	CLANTON	35096-35096	LINCOLN	35147-35147	STERRETT	35448-35448	CLINTON
35048-35048	CLAY	35097-35097	LOCUST FORK	35148-35148	SUMITON	35449-35449	COALING
35049-35049	CLEVELAND	35098-35098	LOGAN	35149-35149	SYCAMORE	35452-35452	COKER
35051-35051	COLUMBIANA	35111-35111	MC CALLA	35150-35151	SYLACAUGA	35453-35453	COTTONDALE
35052-35052	COOK SPRINGS	35112-35112	MARGARET	35160-35161	TALLADEGA	35456-35456	DUNCANVILLE
35053-35053	CRANE HILL	35114-35114	MAYLENE	35171-35171	THORSBY	35457-35457	ECHOLA
35054-35054	CROPWELL	35115-35115	MONTEVALLO	35172-35172	TRAFFORD	35458-35458	ELROD

ZIP	City	ZIP	City	ZIP	City	ZIP	City
35459-35459	EMELLE	35650-35650	MOULTON	36005-36005	BANKS	36272-36272	PIEDMONT
35460-35460	EPES	35651-35651	MOUNT HOPE	36006-36006	BILLINGSLEY	36273-36273	RANBURNE
35461-35461	ETHELSVILLE	35652-35652	ROGERSVILLE	36008-36008	BOOTH	36274-36274	ROANOKE
35462-35462	EUTAW	35653-35654	RUSSELLVILLE	36009-36009	BRANTLEY	36275-36275	SPRING GARDEN
35463-35463	FOSTERS	35660-35660	SHEFFIELD	36010-36010	BRUNDIDGE	36276-36276	WADLEY
35464-35464	GAINESVILLE	35661-35662	MUSCLE SHOALS	36013-36013	CECIL	36277-36277	WEAVER
35466-35466	GORDO	35670-35670	SOMERVILLE	36015-36015	CHAPMAN	36278-36278	WEDOWEE
35468-35468	KELLERMAN	35671-35671	TANNER	36016-36016	CLAYTON	36279-36279	WELLINGTON
35469-35469	KNOXVILLE	35672-35672	TOWN CREEK	36017-36017	CLIO	36280-36280	WOODLAND
35470-35470	LIVINGSTON	35673-35673	TRINITY	36020-36020	COOSADA	36301-36305	DOTHAN
35471-35471	MC SHAN	35674-35674	TUSCUMBIA	36022-36022	DEATSVILLE	36310-36310	ABBEVILLE
35473-35473	NORTHPORT	35677-35677	WATERLOO	36023-36023	EAST TALLASSEE	36311-36311	ARITON
35474-35474	MOUNDVILLE	35699-35699	DECATUR	36024-36024	ECLECTIC	36312-36312	ASHFORD
35475-35476	NORTHPORT	35739-35739	ARDMORE	36025-36025	ELMORE	36313-36313	BELLWOOD
35477-35477	PANOLA	35740-35740	BRIDGEPORT	36026-36026	EQUALITY	36314-36314	BLACK
35478-35478	PETERSON	35741-35741	BROWNSBORO	36027-36027	EUFAULA	36316-36316	CHANCELLOR
35480-35480	RALPH	35742-35742	CAPSHAW	36028-36028	DOZIER	36317-36317	CLOPTON
35481-35481	REFORM	35744-35744	DUTTON	36029-36029	FITZPATRICK	36318-36318	COFFEE SPRINGS
35482-35482	SAMANTHA	35745-35745	ESTILLFORK	36030-36030	FOREST HOME	36319-36319	COLUMBIA
35485-35487	TUSCALOOSA	35746-35746	FACKLER	36031-36031	FORT DAVIS	36320-36320	COTTONWOOD
35490-35490	VANCE	35747-35747	GRANT	36032-36032	FORT DEPOSIT	36321-36321	COWARTS
35491-35491	WEST GREENE	35748-35748	GURLEY	36033-36033	GEORGIANA	36322-36322	DALEVILLE
35501-35504	JASPER	35749-35749	HARVEST	36034-36034	GLENWOOD	36323-36323	ELBA
35540-35540	ADDISON	35750-35750	HAZEL GREEN	36035-36035	GOSHEN	36330-36331	ENTERPRISE
35541-35541	ARLEY	35751-35751	HOLLYTREE	36036-36036	GRADY	36340-36340	GENEVA
35542-35542	BANKSTON	35752-35752	HOLLYWOOD	36037-36037	GREENVILLE	36343-36343	GORDON
35543-35543	BEAR CREEK	35754-35754	LACEYS SPRING	36038-36038	GANTT	36344-36344	HARTFORD
35544-35544	BEAVERTON	35755-35755	LANGSTON	36039-36039	HARDAWAY	36345-36345	HEADLAND
35545-35545	BELK	35756-35758	MADISON	36040-36040	HAYNEVILLE	36346-36346	JACK
35546-35546	BERRY	35759-35759	MERIDIANVILLE	36041-36041	HIGHLAND HOME	36349-36349	MALVERN
35548-35548	BRILLIANT	35760-35760	NEW HOPE	36042-36042	HONORAVILLE	36350-36350	MIDLAND CITY
35549-35549	CARBON HILL	35761-35761	NEW MARKET	36043-36043	HOPE HULL	36351-36351	NEW BROCKTON
35550-35550	CORDOVA	35762-35762	NORMAL	36045-36045	KENT	36352-36352	NEWTON
35551-35551	DELMAR	35763-35763	OWENS CROSS ROADS	36046-36046	LAPINE	36353-36353	NEWVILLE
35552-35552	DETROIT	35764-35764	PAINT ROCK	36047-36047	LETOHATCHEE	36360-36361	OZARK
35553-35553	DOUBLE SPRINGS	35765-35765	PISGAH	36048-36048	LOUISVILLE	36362-36362	FORT RUCKER
35554-35554	ELDRIDGE	35766-35766	PRINCETON	36049-36049	LUVERNE	36370-36370	PANSEY
35555-35555	FAYETTE	35767-35767	RYLAND	36051-36051	MARBURY	36371-36371	PINCKARD
35559-35559	GLEN ALLEN	35768-35769	SCOTTSBORO	36052-36052	MATHEWS	36373-36373	SHORTERVILLE
35560-35560	GOODSPRINGS	35771-35771	SECTION	36053-36053	MIDWAY	36374-36374	SKIPPERVILLE
35563-35563	GUIN	35772-35772	STEVENSON	36054-36054	MILLBROOK	36375-36375	SLOCOMB
35564-35564	HACKLEBURG	35773-35773	TONEY	36057-36057	MOUNT MEIGS	36376-36376	WEBB
35565-35565	HALEYVILLE	35774-35774	TRENTON	36061-36061	PEROTE	36401-36401	EVERGREEN
35570-35570	HAMILTON	35775-35775	VALHERMOSO SPRINGS	36062-36062	PETREY	36419-36419	ALLEN
35571-35571	HODGES	35776-35776	WOODVILLE	36064-36064	PIKE ROAD	36420-36420	ANDALUSIA
35572-35572	HOUSTON	35801-35899	HUNTSVILLE	36065-36065	PINE LEVEL	36425-36425	BEATRICE
35573-35573	KANSAS	35901-35905	GADSDEN	36066-36068	PRATTVILLE	36426-36427	BREWTON
35574-35574	KENNEDY	35906-35906	RAINBOW CITY	36069-36069	RAMER	36429-36429	BROOKLYN
35575-35575	LYNN	35907-35907	GADSDEN	36071-36071	RUTLEDGE	36431-36431	BURNT CORN
35576-35576	MILLPORT	35950-35951	ALBERTVILLE	36072-36072	EUFAULA	36432-36432	CASTLEBERRY
35577-35577	NATURAL BRIDGE	35952-35952	ALTOONA	36075-36075	SHORTER	36435-36435	COY
35578-35578	NAUVOO	35953-35953	ASHVILLE	36078-36078	TALLASSEE	36436-36436	DICKINSON
35579-35579	OAKMAN	35954-35954	ATTALLA	36079-36079	TROY	36439-36439	EXCEL
35580-35580	PARRISH	35956-35957	BOAZ	36080-36080	TITUS	36441-36441	FLOMATON
35581-35581	PHIL CAMPBELL	35958-35958	BRYANT	36081-36082	TROY	36442-36442	FLORALA
35582-35582	RED BAY	35959-35959	CEDAR BLUFF	36083-36083	TUSKEGEE	36444-36444	FRANKLIN
35584-35584	SIPSEY	35960-35960	CENTRE	36087-36088	TUSKEGEE INSTITUTE	36445-36445	FRISCO CITY
35585-35585	SPRUCE PINE	35961-35961	COLLINSVILLE	36089-36089	UNION SPRINGS	36446-36446	FULTON
35586-35586	SULLIGENT	35962-35962	CROSSVILLE	36091-36091	VERBENA	36449-36449	GOODWAY
35587-35587	TOWNLEY	35963-35963	DAWSON	36092-36093	WETUMPKA	36451-36451	GROVE HILL
35592-35592	VERNON	35964-35964	DOUGLAS	36101-36191	MONTGOMERY	36453-36453	KINSTON
35593-35593	VINA	35966-35966	FLAT ROCK	36201-36207	ANNISTON	36454-36454	LENOX
35594-35594	WINFIELD	35967-35968	FORT PAYNE	36250-36250	ALEXANDRIA	36455-36455	LOCKHART
35601-35609	DECATUR	35971-35971	FYFFE	36251-36251	ASHLAND	36456-36456	MC KENZIE
35610-35610	ANDERSON	35972-35972	GALLANT	36253-36253	BYNUM	36457-36457	MEGARGEL
35611-35614	ATHENS	35973-35973	GAYLESVILLE	36254-36254	CHOCCOLOCCO	36458-36458	MEXIA
35615-35615	BELLE MINA	35974-35974	GERALDINE	36255-36255	CRAGFORD	36460-36462	MONROEVILLE
35616-35616	CHEROKEE	35975-35975	GROVEOAK	36256-36256	DAVISTON	36467-36467	OPP
35617-35617	CLOVERDALE	35976-35976	GUNTERSVILLE	36257-36257	DE ARMANVILLE	36470-36470	PERDUE HILL
35618-35618	COURTLAND	35978-35978	HENAGAR	36258-36258	DELTA	36471-36471	PETERMAN
35619-35619	DANVILLE	35979-35979	HIGDON	36260-36260	EASTABOGA	36473-36473	RANGE
35620-35620	ELKMONT	35980-35980	HORTON	36261-36261	EDWARDSVILLE	36474-36474	RED LEVEL
35621-35621	EVA	35981-35981	IDER	36262-36262	FRUITHURST	36475-36475	REPTON
35622-35622	FALKVILLE	35983-35983	LEESBURG	36263-36263	GRAHAM	36476-36476	RIVER FALLS
35630-35634	FLORENCE	35984-35984	MENTONE	36264-36264	HEFLIN	36477-36477	SAMSON
35640-35640	HARTSELLE	35986-35986	RAINSVILLE	36265-36265	JACKSONVILLE	36480-36480	URIAH
35643-35643	HILLSBORO	35987-35987	STEELE	36266-36266	LINEVILLE	36481-36481	VREDENBURGH
35645-35645	KILLEN	35988-35988	SYLVANIA	36267-36267	MILLERVILLE	36482-36482	WHATLEY
35646-35646	LEIGHTON	35989-35989	VALLEY HEAD	36268-36268	MUNFORD	36483-36483	WING
35647-35647	LESTER	35990-35990	WALNUT GROVE	36269-36269	MUSCADINE	36501-36501	ALMA
35648-35648	LEXINGTON	35999-35999	GADSDEN	36270-36270	NEWELL	36502-36504	ATMORE
35649-35649	MOORESVILLE	36003-36003	AUTAUGAVILLE	36271-36271	OHATCHEE	36505-36505	AXIS

ZIP	City	ZIP	City	ZIP	City	ZIP	City
36507-36507	BAY MINETTE	36564-36564	POINT CLEAR	36744-36744	GREENSBORO	36852-36852	CUSSETA
36509-36509	BAYOU LA BATRE	36567-36567	ROBERTSDALE	36745-36745	JEFFERSON	36853-36853	DADEVILLE
36511-36511	BON SECOUR	36568-36568	SAINT ELMO	36748-36748	LINDEN	36854-36854	VALLEY
36512-36512	BUCKS	36569-36569	SAINT STEPHENS	36749-36749	JONES	36855-36855	FIVE POINTS
36513-36513	CALVERT	36570-36570	SALITPA	36750-36750	MAPLESVILLE	36856-36856	FORT MITCHELL
36515-36515	CARLTON	36571-36571	SARALAND	36751-36751	LOWER PEACH TREE	36858-36858	HATCHECHUBBEE
36518-36518	CHATOM	36572-36572	SATSUMA	36752-36752	LOWNDESBORO	36859-36859	HOLY TRINITY
36521-36521	CHUNCHULA	36574-36574	SEMINOLE	36753-36753	MC WILLIAMS	36860-36860	HURTSBORO
36522-36522	CITRONELLE	36575-36575	SEMMES	36754-36754	MAGNOLIA	36861-36861	JACKSONS GAP
36523-36523	CODEN	36576-36576	SILVERHILL	36756-36756	MARION	36862-36862	LAFAYETTE
36524-36524	COFFEEVILLE	36577-36577	SPANISH FORT	36758-36758	PLANTERSVILLE	36863-36863	LANETT
36525-36525	CREOLA	36578-36578	STAPLETON	36759-36759	MARION JUNCTION	36865-36865	LOACHAPOKA
36526-36526	DAPHNE	36579-36579	STOCKTON	36760-36760	MILLERS FERRY	36866-36866	NOTASULGA
36527-36527	SPANISH FORT	36580-36580	SUMMERDALE	36761-36761	MINTER	36867-36870	PHENIX CITY
36528-36528	DAUPHIN ISLAND	36581-36581	SUNFLOWER	36762-36762	MORVIN	36871-36871	PITTSVIEW
36529-36529	DEER PARK	36582-36582	THEODORE	36763-36763	MYRTLEWOOD	36872-36872	VALLEY
36530-36530	ELBERTA	36583-36583	TIBBIE	36764-36764	NANAFALIA	36874-36874	SALEM
36532-36533	FAIRHOPE	36584-36584	VINEGAR BEND	36765-36765	NEWBERN	36875-36875	SEALE
36535-36536	FOLEY	36585-36585	WAGARVILLE	36766-36766	OAK HILL	36877-36877	SMITHS
36538-36538	FRANKVILLE	36586-36586	WALKER SPRINGS	36767-36767	ORRVILLE	36879-36879	WAVERLY
36539-36539	FRUITDALE	36587-36587	WILMER	36768-36768	PINE APPLE	36901-36901	BELLAMY
36540-36540	GAINESTOWN	36590-36590	THEODORE	36769-36769	PINE HILL	36904-36904	BUTLER
36541-36541	GRAND BAY	36601-36612	MOBILE	36773-36773	SAFFORD	36906-36906	CROMWELL
36542-36542	GULF SHORES	36613-36613	EIGHT MILE	36775-36775	SARDIS	36907-36907	CUBA
36543-36543	HUXFORD	36614-36695	MOBILE	36776-36776	SAWYERVILLE	36908-36908	GILBERTOWN
36544-36544	IRVINGTON	36701-36703	SELMA	36778-36778	SNOW HILL	36910-36910	JACHIN
36545-36545	JACKSON	36720-36720	ALBERTA	36779-36779	SPROTT	36912-36912	LISMAN
36547-36547	GULF SHORES	36721-36721	ANNEMANIE	36782-36782	SWEET WATER	36913-36913	MELVIN
36548-36548	LEROY	36722-36722	ARLINGTON	36783-36783	THOMASTON	36915-36915	NEEDHAM
36549-36549	LILLIAN	36723-36723	BOYKIN	36784-36784	THOMASVILLE	36916-36916	PENNINGTON
36550-36550	LITTLE RIVER	36726-36726	CAMDEN	36785-36785	TYLER	36919-36919	SILAS
36551-36551	LOXLEY	36727-36727	CAMPBELL	36786-36786	UNIONTOWN	36921-36921	TOXEY
36553-36553	MC INTOSH	36728-36728	CATHERINE	36790-36790	STANTON	36922-36922	WARD
36555-36555	MAGNOLIA SPRINGS	36731-36731	DAYTON	36792-36792	RANDOLPH	36925-36925	YORK
36556-36556	MALCOLM	36732-36732	DEMOPOLIS	36793-36793	LAWLEY		
36558-36558	MILLRY	36736-36736	DIXONS MILLS	36801-36804	OPELIKA		
36559-36559	MONTROSE	36738-36738	FAUNSDALE	36830-36832	AUBURN		
36560-36560	MOUNT VERNON	36740-36740	FORKLAND	36849-36849	AUBURN UNIVERSITY		
36561-36561	ORANGE BEACH	36741-36741	FURMAN	36850-36850	CAMP HILL		
36562-36562	PERDIDO	36742-36742	GALLION	36851-36851	COTTONTON		

General Help Numbers:

Governor's Office
PO Box 110001
Juneau, AK 99811-0001
http://www.gov.state.ak.us

907-465-3500
Fax 907-465-3532
8AM-5PM

Attorney General's Office
Law Department
PO Box 110300
Juneau, AK 99811-0300
http://www.law.state.ak.us

907-465-3600
Fax 907-465-2075
8AM-4:30PM

State Court Administrator
303 K St
Anchorage, AK 99501
http://www.alaska.net/~akctlib/
homepage.htm

907-264-0547
Fax 907-264-0881
8AM-4:30PM

State Archives
Alaska State Archives
141 Willoughby Ave
Juneau, AK 99801-1720
http://www.archives.state.ak.us

907-465-2270
Fax 907-465-2465
9AM-5PM

State Specifics:

Capital:

Juneau
Juneau Borough

Time Zone: AK (Alaska Standard Time)*
* Alaska's Aleutian Islands are HT (Hawaii Standard Time)

Number of Counties: 23

Population: 629,932

Web Site: www.state.ak.us

State Agencies

Criminal Records

Department of Public Safety, Records and Identification, 5700 E Tudor Rd, Anchorage, AK 99507; 907-269-5765, 907-269-5091 (Fax), 8AM-4:30PM.

http://www.dps.state.ak.us

Note: If authorized, a requester may also request a national check by the FBI for an additional $24.00. Sex offender data is available online at www.dps.state.ak.us/Sorcr/search.asp.

Indexing & Storage: Records are available for 10 years from the unconditional discharge date of the incident.

Searching: "Interested Party" reports are processed for employment purposes. "Any Person" reports can be processed for those who have a proper letter of explanation (and fingerprints). "Full Criminal History Report" is only available for criminal justice agencies. Include the following in your request-set of fingerprints, full name. Requester must provide verification of status as an "interested party." Interested party is defined a

person who employs, appoints or permits the subject with or without compensation with supervisory power over others. The following data is not released: sealed records.

Access by: mail, in person.

Fee & Payment: The fee is $35.00 per search. Fee payee: State of Alaska. Prepayment required. No credit cards accepted.

Mail search: Results of search are also sent to the subject.

In person search: Results are usually mailed.

Corporation Records
Trademarks/Servicemarks
Fictitious Name
Assumed Name
Limited Partnership Records
Limited Liability Company Records
Limited Liability Partnership Records

Corporation Section, Department of Community & Econ Dev, PO Box 110808, Juneau, AK 99811-0808 (Courier: 150 Third Street Rm 217, Juneau, AK 99801); 907-465-2530, 907-465-3257 (Fax), 8AM-5PM.

http://www.dced.state.ak.us/bsc/corps.htm

Indexing & Storage: Records are available from early 1900's on. Prior to 1960, the records are kept at the State Archives. You must go through this office in order to get records. New records are available for inquiry immediately. Records are indexed on microfiche, inhouse computer.

Searching: All information contained is considered public record. Include the following in your request-full name of business. In addition to the articles of incorporation, corporation records include the following information: Annual Reports, Officers, Directors, DBAs, Prior (Merged) names, Inactive and Reserved names.

Access by: mail, phone, fax, in person, online.

Fee & Payment: Fees are $10.00 for articles and amendments and $30.00 for everything on file. The fee is $5.00 to certify a document and $10.00 for a good standing. A copy of a one page document is $1.00 and a print of a computer screen is $1.00. Fee payee: State of Alaska. Prepayment required. Personal checks accepted. Credit cards accepted: MasterCard, Visa.

Mail search: Turnaround time: 2 weeks.

Phone search: You can make a search request only if you are local and you plan to pick-up.

Fax search: Typical fax searches involve use of a credit card.

In person search: All results are mailed unless request is being processed using expedited service. The agency will call the requester when his/her request has been processed and is ready for pick-up, if it is a local call.

Online search: At the web site, one can access status information on corps, LLCs, LLP, LP (all both foreign and domestic), registered and reserved names, as well as trademark information. There is no fee.

Other access: For bulk purchase, the requester must use a third party. Call 907-465-2530 for more information.

Expedited service: Expedited service is available for mail, phone and in person searches. Turnaround time: 48 hours. Add $35.00 per business name. It is an additional $150.00 to expedite a filing.

Uniform Commercial Code

UCC Central File Systems Office, State Recorder's Office, 550 West 7th Ave #1200A, Anchorage, AK 99501-3564; 907-269-8873, 8AM-3:30PM.

http://www.dnr.state.ak.us/ssd/ucc/index.cfm

Note: There are 14 recording offices and 34 recording districts in the state.

Indexing & Storage: Records are available from 1961 when the UCC system was established. Records are computerized since October 20, 1986 or earlier if with continuations. Records are kept on microfiche since 1981 or prior if continuations filed.

Searching: Use search request form UCC-11. Search results include all filings up to one year after lapse. All tax liens are filed at the local District Recorder offices. Include the following in your request-debtor name. All requests must be in writing.

Access by: mail, in person, online.

Fee & Payment: Fee to search by name is $5.00 per debtor name. For information and copies, fee is $15.00 per debtor name. Certification costs an additional $5.00. Single page copies are $2.00 each. Fee payee: Alaska Department of Revenue. Prepayment required. Personal checks accepted. Credit cards accepted: MasterCard, Visa.

Mail search: Turnaround time: 1 to 2 days. No self addressed stamped envelope is required.

In person search: A public access terminal is available. State UCC personnel will not perform official record searches for in-person requests.

Online search: One can search by granter-grantee name, date, or dcoument number at http://www.dnr.state.ak.us/ucc/search. There is no fee.

Other access: Bulk file tapes of the entire UCC database can be purchased from the State Recorder's Office (907-269-8881). Also, a private vendor offers online service. Call Motznik Computer Services at 907-344-6254 for more information.

Federal Tax Liens
State Tax Liens
Records not maintained by a state level agency.

Note: All tax liens are filed at local District Recorder Offices.

Sales Tax Registrations
State does not impose sales tax.

Birth Certificates

Department of Health & Social Services, Bureau of Vital Statistics, PO Box 110675, Juneau, AK 99811-0675 (Courier: 350 Main, Room 114, Juneau, AK 99811); 907-465-3392, 907-465-3618 (Fax), 8AM-4:30PM.

http://www.hss.state.ak.us/dph/bvs/bvs_home.htm

Indexing & Storage: Records are available from 1913 to present. New records are available for inquiry immediately. Records are indexed on microfiche, inhouse computer.

Searching: Person requesting must be a parent or guardian or give a justifying reason for request. No adoption information will be given except according to statute. Records are public after 100 years. Include the following in your request-full name, names of parents, mother's maiden name, date of birth, place of birth, reason for information request, relationship to person of record. Also, include a day time phone number.

Access by: mail, phone, fax, in person.

Fee & Payment: The $15.00 search fee includes a 3 year search; add $1.00 per year for each additional year searched. Fee payee: Bureau of Vital Statistics. Prepayment required. Personal checks accepted. Credit cards accepted: MasterCard, Visa, AmEx, Discover.

Mail search: Turnaround time: 2 weeks. No self addressed stamped envelope is required.

Phone search: Credit card requests require an additional $10.00.

Fax search: Same criteria as phone searching.

In person search: Turnaround time 10 minutes.

Expedited service: Expedited service is available for mail, phone and fax searches. Turnaround time: 2 days. Add $10.00 if using a credit card and $15.50 for Fed Ex or $11.75 for Express Mail.

Death Records

Department of Health & Social Services, Bureau of Vital Statistics, PO Box 110675, Juneau, AK 99811-0675 (Courier: 350 Main, Room 114, Juneau, AK 99811); 907-465-3392, 907-465-3618 (Fax), 8AM-4:30PM.

http://www.hss.state.ak.us/dph/bvs/bvs_home.htm

Indexing & Storage: Records are available from 1913 to present. New records are available for inquiry immediately. Records are indexed on microfiche, inhouse computer.

Searching: You must be next of kin or have a notarized release statement from immediate family. Records are public after 50 years. Include the following in your request-full name, date of death, place of death, names of parents, reason for information request, relationship to person of record. Also, include a daytime phone number.

Access by: mail, phone, fax, in person.

Fee & Payment: The $15.00 search fee includes a 3 year search. Add $1.00 per year searched for each year over 3 years. Fee payee: Bureau of Vital Statistics. Prepayment required. Personal checks accepted. Credit cards accepted: MasterCard, Visa, AmEx, Discover.

Mail search: Turnaround time: 2 weeks.

Phone search: Add $10.00 for using a credit card.

Fax search: Same criteria as phone searching.

In person search: Turnaround time 10 minutes.

Expedited service: Expedited service is available for mail, phone and fax searches. Turnaround time: 2 days. Add $10.00 if using a credit card and add $15.50 for Fed Ex or $11.75 for Express Mail.

Marriage Certificates

Department of Health & Social Services, Bureau of Vital Statistics, PO Box 110675, Juneau, AK 99811-0675 (Courier: 350 Main, Room 114, Juneau, AK 99811); 907-465-3392, 907-465-3618 (Fax), 8AM-4:30PM.

http://www.hss.state.ak.us/dph/bvs/bvs_home.htm

Indexing & Storage: Records are available from 1913 to present. New records are available for inquiry immediately. Records are indexed on microfiche, inhouse computer.

Searching: Person requesting must be one of the registrants or an attorney representing one of them. Records are public after 50 years. Include the following in your request-names of husband and wife, date of marriage, place or county of marriage. Include wife's maiden name and a daytime phone number.

Access by: mail, phone, fax, in person.

Fee & Payment: The $15.00 search fee includes a 3 year search. Add $1.00 per year searched for each year over 3 years. Fee payee: Bureau of Vital Statistics. Prepayment required. Personal checks accepted. Credit cards accepted: MasterCard, Visa.

Mail search: Turnaround time: 2 weeks.

Phone search: Add $10.00 for using a credit card.

Fax search: Same criteria as phone searches.

In person search: Turnaround time 10 minutes.

Expedited service: Expedited service is available for mail, phone and fax searches. Turnaround time: 2 days. Add $10.00 if using a credit card and add $15.50 for Fed Ex or $11.75 for Express Mail.

Divorce Records

Department of Health & Social Services, Bureau of Vital Statistics, PO Box 110675, Juneau, AK 99811-0675 (Courier: 350 Main, Room 114, Juneau, AK 99811); 907-465-3392, 907-465-3618 (Fax), 8AM-4:30PM.

http://www.hss.state.ak.us/dph/bvs/bvs_home.htm

Indexing & Storage: Records are available from 1950 to present. New records are available for inquiry immediately. Records are indexed on microfiche, inhouse computer.

Searching: Person requesting must be one of the registrants or an attorney representing a registrant. Records are public after 50 years. Include the following in your request-names of husband and wife, date of divorce, place of divorce. Also, include a daytime phone number.

Access by: mail, phone, fax, in person.

Fee & Payment: The $15.00 search fee includes a 3 year search. Add $1.00 per year searched for each year over 3 years. Fee payee: Bureau of Vital Statistics. Prepayment required. Personal checks accepted. Credit cards accepted: MasterCard, Visa, AmEx, Discover.

Mail search: Turnaround time: 2 weeks. No self addressed stamped envelope is required.

Phone search: Add $10.00 for use of a credit card.

Fax search: Same criteria as phone searches.

In person search: Turnaround time 10 minutes.

Expedited service: Expedited service is available for mail, phone and fax searches. Turnaround time: 2 days. Add $10.00 if using a credit card and add $15.50 for Fed Ex or $11.75 for Express Mail.

Workers' Compensation Records

Workers' Compensation, PO Box 25512, Juneau, AK 99802 (Courier: 1111 W Eighth St, Room 307, Juneau, AK 99802); 907-465-2790, 907-465-2797 (Fax), 8AM-4:30PM.

http://www.labor.state.ak.us/wc/wc.htm

Indexing & Storage: Records are available from 1982 on the computer and prior to 1982 the records are on microfilm and/or microfiche to the 1960s. New records are available for inquiry immediately.

Searching: All requests must be in writing. To receive a copy of a file, a signed medical release from claimant is required. Include the following in your request-claimant name, Social Security Number, date of accident.

Access by: mail, fax, in person.

Fee & Payment: Copies cost $.35 per page for active files and $.75 per page for microfilmed files. A computer printout costs $.50 per screen. There is no search fee. Fee payee: State of Alaska. Large orders require prepayment. Personal checks accepted. No credit cards accepted.

Mail search: Turnaround time: 2 to 3 weeks. No self addressed stamped envelope is required.

Fax search: Fax searching available.

Driver Records

Division of Motor Vehicles, Driver's Records, 2760 Sherwood Lane #B, Juneau, AK 99801; 907-465-4361 (Motor Vehicle Reports Desk), 907-465-4363 (Licensing), 907-465-5509 (Fax), 8AM-5PM.

http://www.state.ak.us/dmv

Note: Copies of tickets are only released, in writing, to the participant, legal representative, or insurance representative.

Indexing & Storage: Records are available for minor moving violations and suspensions for three years, major moving violations for five years. Convictions are automatically purged from public record by conviction date. Accidents are reported only if action is taken.

Searching: Records are considered confidential. Any private company or individual requester must have a signed release from the licensee or a subpoena. High volume requesters may maintain these forms rather than send in with requests. Include the following in your request-name, driver's license number, date of birth. Driver's residence and mailing address are included as part of the search report.

Access by: mail, in person, online.

Fee & Payment: Prepayment required. Fee payee: State of Alaska. Personal checks accepted. No credit cards accepted.

Mail search: Turnaround time: 3 to 4 working days. No self addressed stamped envelope is required. Search costs $5.00 per record.

In person search: Search costs $5.00 per record. Turnaround time is while you wait.

Online search: Online access costs $5.00 per record. Inquiries may be made at any time, 24 hours a day. Batch inquiries may call back within thirty minutes for responses. Search by the first four letters of driver's name, license number and date of birth. At present, there is only one phone line available for users; you may experience a busy signal.

Vehicle Ownership
Vehicle Identification
Vessel Registration

Division of Motor Vehicles, Research, 2150 E Dowling Rd, Anchorage, AK 99507; 907-269-5551, 8AM-5PM.

http://www.state.ak.us/dmv

Indexing & Storage: Records are available for 7 years to present.

Searching: Record requests are honored for employment, insurance, court or impound purposes. Otherwise, a signed release is required, signed by requester, attesting to purpose of request. Service is generally slower in the summer months.

Access by: mail, in person.

Fee & Payment: The fee is $5.00 per record. There is no fee to do a vessel search. Fee payee: State of Alaska. Prepayment required. No credit cards accepted.

Mail search: Turnaround time: 2 to 3 weeks. No self addressed stamped envelope is required.

In person search: Turnaround time depends on workload and complexity of request. Typically, requests are processed within 5 to 10 days, but can extend to 5 weeks or more.

Other access: The entire master tape file of registration information is available at a cost of approximately $50 per 1,000 records. Call the Director's Office (907-269-5551) for more information.

Accident Reports

Department of Public Safety, Driver Services, 2760 Sherwood Lane #B, Juneau, AK 99801; 907-465-4361, 907-463-5509 (Fax), 8AM-5PM.

http://www.state.ak.us/dmv

Indexing & Storage: Records are available from seven years.

Searching: Only legal representatives and insurance agents of the participants, or the participant him/herself may obtain copies. The lawyer or legal representative must have a notarized request, an insurance agent a signed request with reason. Items required for search include names, date of incident, city, physical location of the accident.

Access by: mail, in person.

Fee & Payment: The cost of obtaining an accident report is $1.00 for the first page and $.25 for each additional page. Fee payee: State of Alaska, Department of Public Safety. Prepayment required. Personal checks accepted. No credit cards accepted.

Mail search: Turnaround time: 1 to 2 weeks. No self addressed stamped envelope is required.

In person search: Turnaround time is while you wait.

Vessel Ownership
Records not maintained by a state level agency.

Note: Alaska is not a title state. Until Jan. 1, 2000 all boat registrations were done through the US Coast Guard (970-463-2294). As of Jan. 1 2000 they are at the DMV. Liens are filed with the Department of Natural Resources at 907-269-8882.

Legislation Records

Alaska State Legislative Affairs Agency, Legislative Information Office, 120 4th St #111-State Capitol, Juneau, AK 99801-1182; 907-465-4648, 907-465-2864 (Fax), 8AM-5PM.

http://www.legis.state.ak.us

Indexing & Storage: Records are available from 1982 to present. Records are indexed on inhouse computer.

Searching: Include the following in your request-bill number, year.

Access by: mail, phone, in person, online.

Fee & Payment: There is no search fee nor is there a fee for one copy of a bill. Copy fees vary; therefore, call for fees, if you need more than one copy. Fee payee: State of Alaska. Prepayment required. Personal checks accepted. No credit cards accepted.

Mail search: Turnaround time: 1 day. No self addressed stamped envelope is required.

Phone search: You may call for copies.

In person search: Turnaround time is while you wait.

Online search: All information, including statutes, is available on the Internet. At the main web site, click on "Bills."

Voter Registration

Division of Elections, PO Box 110017, Juneau, AK 99811-0017 (Courier: Court Plaza Building, 4th Floor, 240 Main Street, Juneau, AK 99801); 907-465-4611, 8AM-4:30PM.

http://www.elections.state.ak.us

Note: There are four regional Elections Offices, each has access to the election records database.

Indexing & Storage: Records are available from 1983. It takes 1 day before new records are available for inquiry.

Searching: Searching by name is permitted. The following data is not released: Social Security Numbers or date of birth.

Access by: mail, phone, fax, in person.

Fee & Payment: There is no fee.

Mail search: Turnaround time: 1 day.

Phone search: Records are available by phone.

Fax search: Fax searching available.

In person search: Turnaround time is immediate unless extensive lists or requests for older records are presented.

Other access: The agency offers the complete record database on CD-ROM for $178. Individual districts (there are 40) can be purchased on disk for $20.00 each.

GED Certificates

Department of Labor, Employment Security Division, PO Box 25509, Juneau, AK 99802-5509 (Courier: 111 8th Street #210, Juneau, AK 99802); 907-465-4685, 907-465-8753 (Fax), 8:30AM-5PM.

http://www.eed.state.ak.us

Searching: Include the full name, DOB, SSN, year of test and city of test. Fax requesters must include a signed release.

Access by: mail, fax, in person.

Fee & Payment: There is no fee for a verification or a transcript copy. There is a $10.00 fee for a copy of a diploma.

Mail search: Turnaround time: 1 to 2 weeks. No self addressed stamped envelope is required.

Fax search: A written release form is required.

Hunting License Information
Fishing License Information

Department of Fish & Game, Licensing Section, PO Box 25525, Juneau, AK 99802-5525 (Courier: 1255 W 8th St, Juneau, AK 99802); 907-465-2376, 907-465-2440 (Fax), 8AM-5PM.

http://www.state.ak.us/local/akpages/FISH.GAME/adfghome.htm

Indexing & Storage: Records are available from 10 years to present. Records since 1994 are computerized, older records are on microfiche. It takes 4 weeks before new records are available for inquiry.

Searching: Information used to search includes SSN, DOB, address, driver's license number, or year license issued. The following data is not released: Social Security Numbers or telephone numbers.

Access by: mail, phone, fax, in person.

Fee & Payment: No fee unless you request a large list. For certified copies the turnaround time is 6 weeks. Fee payee: State of Alaska. Prepayment required. Personal checks accepted. Credit cards accepted.

Mail search: Turnaround time: within 3 weeks. No self addressed stamped envelope is required.

Phone search: Limited number of requests given over the phone.

Fax search: Same criteria as phone searches.

In person search: Large lists will not be processed immediately.

Other access: The vendor file is available for $25 on paper or disk. The entire license file is available for $350 on CD-ROM.

Alaska State Licensing Agencies

Licenses Searchable Online

Acupuncturist #20..www.dced.state.ak.us/occ/search3.htm
Anesthetist (Dental), General/Permit #20 ....www.dced.state.ak.us/occ/search3.htm
Architect #20 ....www.dced.state.ak.us/occ/search3.htm
Athletic Promoter #20 ....www.dced.state.ak.us/occ/search3.htm
Athletic Trainer #20..www.dced.state.ak.us/occ/search3.htm
Attorney #11 ....www.alaskabar.org/422.cfm
Audiologist/Hearing Aid Dealer #20............................www.dced.state.ak.us/occ/search3.htm
Bail Bondsman #13 ....www.dced.state.ak.us/ins/apps/InsLicStart.cfm
Barber #20...www.dced.state.ak.us/occ/search3.htm
Barber Shop Owner/School/Instructor #20 ....www.dced.state.ak.us/occ/search3.htm
Big Game Guide/Assistant/Transporter #20 ....www.dced.state.ak.us/occ/search3.htm
Boxer #20 ....www.dced.state.ak.us/occ/search3.htm
Boxing Physician #20..www.dced.state.ak.us/occ/search3.htm
Boxing/Wrestling Personnel #20 ....www.dced.state.ak.us/occ/search3.htm
Chiropractor #20...www.dced.state.ak.us/occ/search3.htm
Collection Agency/Operator #20................................www.dced.state.ak.us/occ/search3.htm
Concert Promoter #20..www.dced.state.ak.us/occ/search3.htm
Construction Contractor #20 ....www.dced.state.ak.us/occ/search3.htm
Contractor - Civil/Elect./Mech./Mining/Petrol. #20.........www.dced.state.ak.us/occ/search3.htm
Cosmetologist/Hairdresser #20 ....www.dced.state.ak.us/occ/search3.htm
Cosmetology Shop Owner/School/Instructor #20 ....www.dced.state.ak.us/occ/search3.htm
Counselor, Professional #20 ....www.dced.state.ak.us/occ/OccStart.cfm
Dental Hygienist #20..www.dced.state.ak.us/occ/search3.htm
Dentist/Dental Examiner #20...................................www.dced.state.ak.us/occ/search3.htm
Dietitian/Nutritionist #20..www.dced.state.ak.us/occ/OccStart.cfm
Drug Distributor/Drug Room #20...............................www.dced.state.ak.us/occ/search3.htm
Electrical Administrator #20.....................................www.dced.state.ak.us/occ/search3.htm
Employment Agency Operator/Agency Permit #05 ....www.dced.state.ak.us/occ/search3.htm
Engineer #20 ....www.dced.state.ak.us/occ/search3.htm
Esthetician #20...www.dced.state.ak.us/occ/search3.htm
Funeral Director/Establishment #20 ....www.dced.state.ak.us/occ/search3.htm
Geologist #20 ....www.dced.state.ak.us/occ/search3.htm
Guide Outfitter, Hunting #20 ....www.dced.state.ak.us/occ/search3.htm
Hearing Aid Dealer #20...www.dced.state.ak.us/occ/search3.htm
Independent Adjuster #13 ....www.dced.state.ak.us/ins/apps/InsLicStart.cfm
Insurance Agent, Managing General #13....................www.dced.state.ak.us/ins/apps/InsLicStart.cfm
Insurance Occupation #13 ....www.dced.state.ak.us/ins/apps/InsLicStart.cfm
Insurance Producer #13...www.dced.state.ak.us/ins/apps/InsLicStart.cfm
Lobbyist #09..www.state.ak.us/local/akpages/ADMIN/apoc/lobcov.htm
Marine Pilot #20..www.dced.state.ak.us/occ/search3.htm
Marriage & Family Therapist #20 ....www.dced.state.ak.us/occ/OccStart.cfm
Mechanical Administrator #20..................................www.dced.state.ak.us/occ/search3.htm
Medical Doctor/Surgeon #20...................................www.dced.state.ak.us/occ/search3.htm
Midwife #20 ....www.dced.state.ak.us/occ/OccStart.cfm
Mortician/Embalmer #20..www.dced.state.ak.us/occ/search3.htm
Naturopathic Physician #20 ....www.dced.state.ak.us/occ/search3.htm
Nurse (names (A-K) #20 ....www.dced.state.ak.us/occ/search3.htm
Nurse (names (L-Z) #20...www.dced.state.ak.us/occ/search3.htm
Nurse Anesthetist #20...www.dced.state.ak.us/occ/search3.htm
Nurse-RN-LPN #20...www.dced.state.ak.us/occ/search3.htm
Nurses' Aide #20...www.dced.state.ak.us/occ/search3.htm
Nursing Home Administrator #20 ....www.dced.state.ak.us/occ/search3.htm
Occupational Therapist/Assistant #20 ....www.dced.state.ak.us/occ/search3.htm

Optician, Dispensing #20 ....www.dced.state.ak.us/occ/search3.htm
Optometrist #20 ....www.dced.state.ak.us/occ/search3.htm
Osteopathic Physician #20 ....www.dced.state.ak.us/occ/search3.htm
Paramedic #20 ....www.dced.state.ak.us/occ/search3.htm
Parenteral Sedation (Dental) #20 ....www.dced.state.ak.us/occ/search3.htm
Pharmacist/Pharmacy/Pharmacist Intern #20 ....www.dced.state.ak.us/occ/search3.htm
Physical Therapist/Assistant #20 ....www.dced.state.ak.us/occ/search3.htm
Physician Assistant #20 ....www.dced.state.ak.us/occ/search3.htm
Podiatrist #20 ....www.dced.state.ak.us/occ/search3.htm
Psychologist/Psychological Assistant #20 ....www.dced.state.ak.us/occ/search3.htm
Public Accountant-CPA #20 ....www.dced.state.ak.us/occ/OccStart.cfm
Real Estate Agent/Broker/Associate #20 ....www.dced.state.ak.us/occ/search3.htm
Real Estate Appraiser #20 ....www.dced.state.ak.us/occ/search3.htm
Referee #20 ....www.dced.state.ak.us/occ/OccStart.cfm
Reinsurance Intermediary Broker/Manager #13 ....www.dced.state.ak.us/ins/apps/InsLicStart.cfm
Residential Contractor #20 ....www.dced.state.ak.us/occ/search3.htm
Social Worker #20 ....www.dced.state.ak.us/occ/OccStart.cfm
Social Worker, Clinical #20 ....www.dced.state.ak.us/occ/OccStart.cfm
Surplus Line Broker #13 ....www.dced.state.ak.us/ins/apps/InsLicStart.cfm
Surveyor #20 ....www.dced.state.ak.us/occ/search3.htm
Underground Storage Tank Worker/Contractor#20 ....www.dced.state.ak.us/occ/search3.htm
Vessel Agent #20 ....www.dced.state.ak.us/occ/search3.htm
Veterinarian/Veterinary Technician #20 ....www.dced.state.ak.us/occ/search3.htm
Wrestler #20 ....www.dced.state.ak.us/occ/OccStart.cfm

Licensing Quick Finder

Acupuncturist #20 907-465-2695
Aircraft Related Occupation #18 907-271-2000
Alcohol Server #21 907-269-0350
Anesthetist (Dental), General #20 907-465-2542
Architect #20 907-465-2540
Asbestos Removal Worker #07 907-269-4925
Athletic Promoter #20 907-465-2695
Athletic Trainer #20 907-465-2695
Attorney #11 907-272-7469
Audiologist/Hearing Aid Dealer #20 907-465-2695
Bail Bondsman #13 907-465-2515
Barber #20 907-465-2547
Barber Shop Owner/School/Instructor #20 ....
....907-465-2547
Big Game Guide/Assistant/Transporter #20 ....
....907-465-2543
Boiler Operator #07 907-269-4925
Boxer #20 907-465-2695
Boxing Physician #20 907-465-2695
Boxing/Wrestling Personnel #20 907-465-2695
Broker/Dealer #12 907-465-2521
Child Care Provider (Home/enter) #16 ..907-465-3207
Chiropractor #20 907-465-2589
Collection Agency/Operator #20 907-465-2695
Concert Promoter #20 907-465-2534
Construction Contractor #20 907-465-2546
Contractor - Civil/Elect./Mech./Mining/Petrol. #20 ....
....907-465-2546
Cosmetologist/Hairdresser #20 907-465-2547
Cosmetology Shop Owner/School/Instructor #20 ....
....907-465-2547
Counselor, Professional #20 907-465-2551
Crewmember (Fishing Boat) #04 907-465-2376
Defibillator Technician #17 907-465-3029
Dental Hygienist #20 907-465-2542
Dentist/Dental Examiner #20 907-465-2542
Dietitian/Nutritionist #20 907-465-2534
Drug Distributor/Drug Room #20 907-465-2589

Electrical Administrator #20 907-465-2589
Electrician #07 907-269-4925
Emergency Medical Technician #17 907-465-3029
Employment Agency Operator/Agency Permit #05 .....
....907-269-8160
Engineer #20 907-465-2540
Esthetician #20 907-465-2547
Explosives Handler #07 907-269-4925
Fishing Operation #08 907-260-4882
Funeral Director/Establishment #20 607-465-2695
Geologist #20 907-465-2695
Guide. Sport Fishing #08 907-260-4882
Guide Outfitter, Hunting #20 907-465-2543
Hearing Aid Dealer #20 907-465-2695
Hunting Guide #20 907-465-2543
Independent Adjuster #13 907-465-2515
Insurance Agent, Mgr.General #13 907-465-2515
Insurance Occupation #13 907-465-2515
Insurance Producer #13 907-465-2515
Investment Advisor #12 907-465-2521
Investment Broker/Dealer/Related Occupation #12 ....
....907-465-2521
Lobbyist #09 907-465-4864
Marine Pilot #20 907-465-2548
Marriage & Family Therapist #20 907-465-2551
Mechanical Administrator #20 907-465-2589
Medical Doctor/Surgeon #20 907-465-2541
Midwife #20 907-465-2580
Mobile Home Dealer #20 907-465-2547
Mortician/Embalmer #20 607-465-2695
Naturopathic Physician #20 907-465-2695
Notary Public #19 907-465-3509
Nurse (names (A-K) #20 907-465-2544
Nurse (names (L-Z) #20 907-465-2648
Nurse Anesthetist #20 907-465-2544
Nurse-RN-LPN #20 907-465-2544
Nurses' Aide #20 907-269-8169
Nursing Home Administrator #20 907-465-2695

Occupational Therapist/Assistant #20 ...907-465-2580
Optician, Dispensing #20 907-465-5470
Optometrist #20 907-465-2580
Osteopathic Physician #20 907-465-2541
Painter #07 907-269-4925
Paramedic #20 907-465-2541
Parenteral Sedation (Dental) #20 907-465-2542
Pesticide Applicator #02 907-745-3236
Pharmacist/Pharmacy/Pharmacist Intern #20
....907-465-2589
Physical Therapist/Assistant #20 907-465-2580
Physician Assistant #20 907-269-8163
Plumber #07 907-269-4925
Podiatrist #20 907-465-2541
Process Server #10 907-269-0392
Psychologist/Psychological Assist. #20 .907-465-3811
Public Accountant-CPA #20 907-465-3817
Real Estate Agent/Broker/Assoc. #20 ...907-269-8162
Real Estate Appraiser #20 907-465-2542
Referee #20 907-465-2695
Reinsurance Intermediary Broker/Manager #13 ....
....907-465-2515
Residential Contractor #20 907-465-2546
Securities Agent #12 907-465-2521
Security Guard #10 907-269-0393
Social Worker #20 907-465-2551
Social Worker, Clinical #20 907-465-2551
Surplus Line Broker #13 907-465-2515
Surveyor #20 907-465-2540
Taxidermist #04 907-465-2376
Teacher #01 907-465-2831
Underground Storage Tank Worker/Contractor #20
....907-465-5470
Vessel Agent #20 907-465-2548
Veterinarian/Veterinary Technician #20 .907-465-5470
Waste Water System Operator #03 907-465-5140
Wrestler #20 907-465-2695

Licensing Agency Information

#01 Department of Education & Early Development, 801 W 10th St, #200, Juneau, AK 99801-1894; 907-465-2831, Fax: 907-465-2441. www.eed.state.ak.us

#02 Department of Environmental Conservation, 500 S Alaska St, Palmer, AK 99645; 907-745-3236, Fax: 907-745-8125. www.state.ak.us/dec/

#03 Department of Environmental Conservation, 410 Willoughby Ave, Juneau, AK 99801-1795; 907-465-5140, Fax: 907-465-5177. www.state.ak.us/local/akpages/ENV.CONSERV/home.htm

#04 Department of Fish & Game, PO Box 25525, Juneau, AK 99802-5525; 907-465-2376, Fax: 907-265-2440. www.state.ak.us/local/akpages/FISH.GAME/admin/license/crew.htm

#05 Department of Labor, Department of Commerce, 13601 C St, #722, Anchorage, AK 99503; 907-269-8160, Fax: 907-261-8156. www.dced.state.ak.us/occ
Direct web site URL to search for licensees: www.dced.state.ak.us/occ/search3.htm

#07 Department of Labor, Labor Standards & Safety, PO Box 107020, Anchorage, AK 99510; 907-269-4925, Fax: 907-269-4932.

#08 Department of Natural Resources, 514 Funny River Rd, Soldotna, AK 99669; 907-260-4882, Fax: 907-260-5992.

#09 Public Offices Commission, PO Box 110222, Juneau, AK 99811-0222; 907-465-4864, Fax: 907-465-4832.
www.state.ak.us/local/akpages/ADMIN/apoc/lobcov.htm
Direct web site URL to search for licensees: www.state.ak.us/local/akpages/ADMIN/apoc/lobcov.htm   By visiting the web site, you can download directories of licensed lobbyists. There is no actual searching online; however, once you've downloaded the file for the appropriate year, you can begin your search.

#10 Alaska State Troopers, 5700 E Tudor Rd, Anchorage, AK 99507-1225; 907-269-0391, Fax: 907-269-0394.
www.dps.state.ak.us

#11 Alaska Bar Association, PO Box 100279, Anchorage, AK 99510-0279; 907-272-7469, Fax: 907-272-2932.
www.alaskabar.org
Direct web site URL to search for licensees: www.alaskabar.org/422.cfm.   You can search online using last name or member number.

#12 Department of Commerce & Economic Development, PO Box 110807, Juneau, AK 99811-0807; 907-465-2521, Fax: 907-465-1230.
www.dced.state.ak.us/bsc/secur.htm

#13 Department of Community & Economic Development, PO Box 110805, Juneau, AK 99811-0805; 907-465-2816, Fax: 907-465-3422.
www.dced.state.ak.us/insurance/

#16 Department of Health & Social Services, 3025 Clinton Dr, 2nd Fl, Juneau, AK 99801; 907-465-3207, Fax: 907-465-3397.
www.hss.state.ak.us/dfys

#17 Department of Health & Social Services, PO Box 110616, Juneau, AK 99811-0616; 907-465-3027, Fax: 907-465-4101.
www.chems.alaska.gov
Direct web site URL to search for licensees: http://chems.alaska.gov/emsdata/. You can search online using Last name, SSN, Certificate #.

#18 Federal Aviation Administration, 222 W 7th Ave, AAL 200, #14, Anchorage, AK 99513-7587; 907-271-5514, Fax: 907-271-1665.

#19 Office of Lieutenant Governor, PO Box 110015, State Capitol, Juneau, AK 99811-0015; 907-465-3520, Fax: 907-465-5400.
http:www.gov.state.ak.us/ltgov

#20 Department of Community & Economic Development, PO Box 110806, Juneau, AK 99811-0806; 907-465-2534, Fax: 907-465-2974.
www.dced.state.ak.us/occ
Direct web site URL to search for licensees: www.dced.state.ak.us/occ/search3.htm

#21 Department of Revenue, 550 W 7th Ave #350, Anchorage, AK 99501-3510; 907-269-0350.

Alaska Federal Courts

The following list indicates the district and division name for each county in the state. If the bankruptcy court location is different from the district court, then the location of the bankruptcy court appears in parentheses.

County/Court Cross Reference

Aleutian Islands, East	Anchorage
Aleutian Islands, West	Anchorage
Anchorage Borough Borough	Anchorage
Bethel	Fairbanks (Anchorage)
Bristol Bay Borough Borough	Anchorage
Fairbanks North Star Borough Borough	Fairbanks (Anchorage)
Haines. Borough Borough	Juneau (Anchorage)
Juneau Borough Borough	Juneau (Anchorage)
Kenai Peninsula Borough Borough	Anchorage
Ketchikan Gateway Borough Borough	Ketchikan (Anchorage)
Kodiak Island Borough Borough	Anchorage
Matanuska-Susitna Borough Borough	Anchorage
Nome	Nome (Anchorage)
North Slope Borough Borough	Fairbanks (Anchorage)
Northwest Arctic Borough	Fairbanks (Anchorage)
Prince of Wales-Outer Ketchikan	Juneau (Anchorage)
Sitka Borough Borough	Juneau (Anchorage)
Southeast Fairbanks	Fairbanks (Anchorage)
Valdez-Cordova	Anchorage
Wade Hampton	Fairbanks (Anchorage)
Wrangell-Petersburg	Juneau (Anchorage)
Yakutat	Juneau (Anchorage)
Yukon-Koyukuk	Fairbanks (Anchorage)

US District Court

District of Alaska

Anchorage Division Box 4, 222 W 7th Ave, Anchorage, AK 99513-7564 (Courier Address: Use mail address for courier delivery), 907-677-6100.

http://www.akd.uscourts.gov

Counties: Aleutian Islands-East, Aleutian Islands-West, Anchorage Borough, Bristol Bay Borough, Kenai Peninsula Borough, Kodiak Island Borough, Matanuska-Susitna Borough, Valdez-Cordova.

Indexing/Storage: Cases are indexed by defendant and plaintiff as well as by case number. New cases are available in the index immediately after filing date. Both computer and card indexes are maintained. An index card system was used to index files prior to May 1987. Records after May 1987 are on computer. Open records are located at this court. If a case was tried, the file will be sent to the Anchorage Federal Records Center. If the case did not go to trial, the file will be sent to the Seattle Federal Records Center. Case records are sent to a Center after the case is closed.

Fee & Payment: The fee is $20.00 per item (one party name or case number). Payment may be made by money order, cashier check, personal check. Prepayment is required. Payee: Clerk, US District Court. Certification fee: $7.00 per document. Copy fee: $.50 per page. You are allowed to make your own copies. These copies cost $.50 per page.

Phone Search: Only docket information is available by phone.

Mail Search: Always enclose a stamped self addressed envelope.

In Person: In person searching is available.

PACER: Sign-up number is 800-676-6856. Access fee is $.60 per minute. Toll-free access: 888-271-6212. Local access: 907-271-6212. Case records are available back to 1987. Records are purged every 6 months. New records are available online after 1 day.

Fairbanks Division Box 1, 101 12th Ave, Fairbanks, AK 99701 (Courier Address: Use mail address for courier delivery), 907-451-5791.

http://www.akd.uscourts.gov

Counties: Bethel, Fairbanks North Star Borough, North Slope Borough, Northwest Arctic Borough, Southeast Fairbanks, Wade Hampton, Yukon-Koyukuk.

Indexing/Storage: Cases are indexed by defendant and plaintiff as well as by case number. New cases are available in the index 1-2 days after filing date. A computer index is maintained. Open records are located at this court.

Fee & Payment: The fee is $20.00 per item (one party name or case number). Payment may be made by money order, cashier check, personal check. Prepayment is required unless other arrangements have been made. Payee: US District Court. Certification fee: $7.00 per document. Copy fee: $.50 per page.

Phone Search: Only docket information is available by phone.

Mail Search: Always enclose a stamped self addressed envelope.

In Person: In person searching is available.

PACER: Sign-up number is 800-676-6856. Access fee is $.60 per minute. Toll-free access: 888-271-6212. Local access: 907-677-6178. Case records are available back to 1987. Records are purged every 6 months. New records are available online after 1 day.

Juneau Division PO Box 020349, Juneau, AK 99802-0349 (Courier Address: Room 979, Federal Bldg-US Courthouse, 709 W 9th, Juneau, AK 99802), 907-586-7458.

http://www.akd.uscourts.gov

Counties: Haines Borough, Juneau Borough, Prince of Wales-Outer Ketchikan, Sitka Borough, Skagway-Hoonah-Angoon, Wrangell-Petersburg.

Indexing/Storage: Cases are indexed by defendant and plaintiff as well as by case number. New cases are available in the index immediately after filing date. A computer index is maintained. Case files are indexed on computer and then stored in file cabinets. Open records are located at this court. If the case was tried, the file will be sent to

the divison where it was filed. If the case did not go to trial, it will be sent to the Seattle Federal Records Center some time after the case is closed.

Fee & Payment: The fee is $20.00 per item (one party name or case number). Payment may be made by money order, cashier check, personal check. Payee: Clerk, US District Court. Certification fee: $7.00 per document. Copy fee: $.50 per page.

Phone Search: Only docket information is available by phone.

Mail Search: Always enclose a stamped self addressed envelope.

In Person: In person searching is available.

PACER: Sign-up number is 800-676-6856. Access fee is $.60 per minute. Toll-free access: 888-271-6212. Local access: 907-677-6178. Case records are available back to 1987. Records are purged every 6 months. New records are available online after 1 day.

Ketchikan Division 648 Mission St, Room 507, Ketchikan, AK 99901 (Courier Address: Use mail address for courier delivery), 907-247-7576.

http://www.akd.uscourts.gov

Counties: Ketchikan Gateway Borough.

Indexing/Storage: Cases are indexed by defendant and plaintiff as well as by case number. New cases are available in the index immediately after filing date. A computer index is maintained. Case files are indexed on computer and then stored in file cabinets. Open records are located at this court. If the case was tried, the file will be sent to the Anchorage Division. If the case did not go to trial, it will be sent to the Seattle Federal Records Center. Case records are sent to a Center after the case is closed.

Fee & Payment: The fee is $20.00 per item (one party name or case number). Payment may be made by money order, cashier check, business check. Personal checks are not accepted. Prepayment is required. Payee: Clerk, US District Court. Certification fee: $7.00 per document. Copy fee: $.50 per page.

Phone Search: Only docket information is available by phone.

Mail Search: Always enclose a stamped self addressed envelope.

In Person: In person searching is available.

PACER: Sign-up number is 800-676-6856. Access fee is $.60 per minute. Toll-free access: 888-271-6212. Local access: 907-677-6178. Case records are available back to 1987. Records are purged every 6 months. New records are available online after 1 day.

Nome Division PO Box 130, Nome, AK 99762 (Courier Address: 2nd Floor, Federal Bldg, Front St, Nome, AK 99762), 907-443-5216, Fax: 907-443-2192.

http://www.akd.uscourts.gov

Counties: Nome.

Indexing/Storage: Cases are indexed by defendant and plaintiff as well as by case number. New cases are available in the index immediately after filing date. A card index is maintained. Open records are located at this court. Records have been retained at this court since 1960. No records have been sent to the repository.

Fee & Payment: The fee is $20.00 per item (one party name or case number). Payment may be made by money order, cashier check, personal check. Prepayment is not required, but is preferred. For copies, make checks payable to Alaska Court System. For searches and certified copies, make checks payable to US District Court. Certification fee: $7.00 per document. Copy fee: $.25 per page. The fee for copies made by court personnel is $.50 per page.

Phone Search: Only docket information is available by phone. The court prefers that requests be submitted in writing.

Fax Search: Will bill for fax search like a mail search. Fax requests should be sent AFTER hours. Prefer not to fax results, but will in expedited cases at cost of fax, search and copies. Fax copies cannot be certified.

Mail Search: A stamped self addressed envelope is not required.

In Person: In person searching is available.

PACER: Sign-up number is 800-676-6856. Access fee is $.60 per minute. Toll-free access: 888-271-6212. Local access: 907-677-6178. Case records are available back to 1987. Records are purged every 6 months. New records are available online after 1 day.

US Bankruptcy Court

District of Alaska

Anchorage Division Historic Courthouse, Suite 138, 605 W 4th Ave, Anchorage, AK 99501-2296 (Courier Address: Use mail address for courier delivery), 907-271-2655.

http://www.akb.uscourts.gov

Counties: All boroughs and districts in Alaska.

Indexing/Storage: Cases are indexed by debtor as well as by case number. New cases are available in the index 1-2 days after filing date. To insure accuracy, the court advises including a social security number or tax ID number. A computer index is maintained. Open records are located at this court. If the case was tried, it will be sent to Anchorage Federal Records Center. If the case did not go to trial, it will be sent to Seattle Federal Records Center. Case records are sent to a Center 60 days after the case is closed.

Fee & Payment: The fee is $20.00 per item (one party name or case number). Payment may be made by money order, cashier check, personal check. Prepayment is required. Payee: Clerk, US Bankruptcy Court. Certification fee: $7.00 per document. Copy fee: $.50 per page. You are allowed to make your own copies. These copies cost $.15 per page. The copy machine works on a debit card system. The cards may be purchased through the State Law Library. The card costs $.50 and can be credited with $1.00, $5.00, $10.00 or $20.00 amounts.

Phone Search: Accession numbers will be released over the phone if a case number is provided. If the case number is unknown, the information must be requested in writing with the $15.00 search fee. An automated voice case information service (VCIS) is available. Call VCIS at 888-878-3110 or 907-271-2658.

Mail Search: Always enclose a stamped self addressed envelope.

In Person: In person searching is available.

PACER: Sign-up number is 800-676-6856. Access fee is $.60 per minute. Toll-free access: 888-878-3110. Local access: 907-271-2695, 907-271-2696, 907-271-2697, 907-271-2698, 907-271-2699. Case records are available back to July 1991. Records are purged 6 months. New civil records are available online after 2 days. PACER is available online at http://pacer.akb.uscourts.gov.

Other Online Access: Search records on the Internet using RACER at https://racer.akb.uscourts.gov/perl/bkplog.html. Access fee is 7 cents per page.

Alaska Local Courts

Court	Jurisdiction	No. of Courts	How Organized
Superior Courts*	General		4 Districts
District Courts*	Limited	3	4 Districts
Combined Courts*		15	
Magistrate Courts*	Limited	32	4 Districts

* Profiled in this Sourcebook

Court	CIVIL								
	Tort	Contract	Real Estate	Min. Claim	Max. Claim	Small Claims	Estate	Eviction	Domestic Relations
Superior Courts*	X	X	X	$0	No Max		X	X	X
District Courts*	X	X		$0	$50,000	$7500		X	X
Magistrate Courts*	X	X	X	$0	$7500	$7500			

Court	CRIMINAL				
	Felony	Misdemeanor	DWI/DUI	Preliminary Hearing	Juvenile
Superior Courts*	X				X
District Courts*		X	X	X	X
Magistrate Courts*		X	X	X	

ADMINISTRATION Office of the Administrative Director, 303 K St, Anchorage, AK, 99501; 907-264-0547, Fax: 907-264-0881. www.alaska.net/~akctlib/homepage.htm

COURT STRUCTURE Alaska is not organized into counties, but rather into 15 boroughs (3 unified home rule municipalities that are combination borough and city, and 12 boroughs) and 12 home rule cities, which do not directly coincide with the 4 Judicial Districts into which the judicial system is divided, that is, judicial boundaries cross borough boundaries. We have listed the courts by their borough or home rule city in keeping with the format of this book. You should search through the city court location names to determine the correct court for your search. Probate is handled by the Superior Courts.

The First District encompasses all of S.E. Alaska. Magistrates act as judicial officers. This 1st District has five trial courts: Ketchikan, Wrangell, Petersburg, Sitka and Juneau. District Magistrate Courts are Haines, Skagway, Yakutat, Angoon, Kake, Hoona, Craig.

ONLINE ACCESS There is no internal or external online statewide judicial computer system available.

ADDITIONAL INFORMATION Documents may not be filed by fax in any Alaska court location without prior authorization of a judge.

The fees established by court rules for Alaska courts are: search fee - $15.00 per hour or fraction thereof; certification fee - $5.00 per document and $2.00 per additional copy of the document; copy fee - $.25 per page.

Magistrate Courts vary widely in how records are maintained and in the hours of operation (some are open only a few hours per week)

Aleutian Islands

Unalaska District Court (3rd District) PO Box 245, Unalaska, AK 99685-0245; 907-581-1266; Fax: 907-581-2809. Hours: 8:30AM-4:30PM (HT). *Felony, Misdemeanor, Civil Actions Under $7,500, Small Claims.*

Civil Records: Access: In person, mail. Only the court performs in person searches; visitors may not. Search fee: $15.00 per hour. Civil records on computer back to 1992.

Criminal Records: Access: In person, mail. Only the court performs in person searches; visitors may not.

Search fee: $15.00 per hour. Required to search: name, years to search, DOB. Criminal records on computer back to 1992.

General Information: Turnaround time 1-2 weeks. Certification fee: $15.00. Fee payee: State of Alaska. Prepayment is required.

Sand Point Magistrate Court (3rd District) c/o Cordova Court, PO Box 898, Seward, AK 99574; 907-424-3378; Fax: 907-424-7581. *Felony, Misdemeanor, Civil Actions Under $7,500, Small Claims.*

Note: Court closed; records at Cordova Court, address and phone here.

St Paul Island Magistrate Court (3rd District) c/o Seward Magistrate Court, PO Box 1929, Valdez, AK 99664; 907-224-3075; Fax: 907-227-7192. *Misdemeanor, Civil Actions Under $7,500, Small Claims.*

Note: Court closed. See Seward Magistrate Court, address and phone here.

Anchorage Borough

Superior & District Court (3rd District) 825 West 4th, Anchorage, AK 99501-2004; 907-264-0444; Probate phone: 907-264-0435; Fax: 907-264-0873. Hours: 8AM-4:30PM (AK). *Felony, Misdemeanor, Civil, Eviction, Small Claims, Probate.*

Civil Records: Access: Phone, fax, mail, in person. Both court and visitors may perform in person searches. Search fee: $15.00 per hour. Required to search: name, years to search; also helpful: address. Civil cases indexed by defendant, plaintiff. Civil records on computer from 1990, on microfiche and archived from 1977 to 1989, on roll index from 1940s.

Criminal Records: Access: Phone, fax, mail, in person. Both court and visitors may perform in person searches. Search fee: $15.00 per hour. Required to search: name, years to search; also helpful: address, DOB, SSN. Criminal records on computer from 1990, on microfiche and archived from 1977 to 1989, on roll index from 1940s.

General Information: Public Access terminal is available. No adoption, juvenile, sealed or mental records released. SASE required. Turnaround time 1-3 days. Fax notes: No fee to fax results. Local fax only. Copy fee: $.25 per page. Certification fee: $5.00. Fee payee: Alaska Court System. Personal checks accepted. Prepayment is required.

Bethel Borough

Superior & District Court (4th District) PO Box 130, Bethel, AK 99559-0130; 907-543-2298; Fax: 907-543-4419. Hours: 8AM-4:30PM (AK). *Felony, Misdemeanor, Civil, Eviction, Small Claims, Probate.*

Civil Records: Access: Fax, mail, in person. Both court and visitors may perform in person searches. Search fee: $15.00 per name. Required to search: name, years to search. Civil cases indexed by defendant, plaintiff. Civil records on computer back to 1983, on microfiche, archived and on index from 1977.

Criminal Records: Access: Fax, mail, in person. Both court and visitors may perform in person searches. Search fee: $15.00 per name. Required to search: name, years to search, DOB. Criminal records on computer back to 1983, on microfiche, archived and on index from 1977.

General Information: Public Access terminal is available. No adoption, juvenile, guardianship or mental records released. SASE required. Turnaround time 2 weeks. Fax notes: Fee to fax results is $.25 per page. Copy fee: $.25 per page. Certification fee: $5.00 plus $2.00 per page after first. Fee payee: Clerk of Court. Personal checks accepted. Prepayment is required.

Aniak District Court (4th District) PO Box 147, Aniak, AK 99557-0147; 907-675-4325; Fax: 907-675-4278. Hours: 8AM-4:30PM (AK). *Misdemeanor, Civil Actions Under $7,500, Small Claims.*

Civil Records: Access: Phone, mail, fax, in person. Both court and visitors may perform in person searches. Search fee: $15.00 per search. Civil records go back to 1960; on computer back to 1998.

Criminal Records: Access: Phone, mail, fax, in person. Both court and visitors may perform in person searches. Search fee: $15.00 per search. Required to search: name, years to search, DOB. Civil records go back to 1960; on computer back to 1998.

General Information: Turnaround time 1-2 weeks. Certification fee: $15.00. Fee payee: Aniak District Court. Prepayment is required.

Quinhagak Magistrate Court (Bethel Area) c/o Bethel Clerk, PO Box 130, Bethel, AK 99559-0130; 907-543-1105. *Misdemeanor, Civil Actions Under $7,500, Small Claims.*

Note: Court closed; records at Bethel Clerk of Courts at address and phone here.

Bristol Bay Borough

Naknek Magistrate Court (3rd District) PO Box 229, Naknek, AK 99633-0229; 907-246-6151; Fax: 907-246-7418. Hours: 8:30AM-4PM (AK). *Misdemeanor, Civil Actions Under $7,500, Small Claims.*

Note: Call Dillingham Superior Court for felony case location.

Civil Records: Access: Mail, in person. Only the court performs in person searches; visitors may not. Search fee: $15.00 per hour. Records go back to 1970's; computerized from 1993.

Criminal Records: Access: Mail, in person. Only the court performs in person searches; visitors may not. Search fee: $15.00 per hour. Required to search: name, years to search. Records go back to 1970's; computerized from 1993.

General Information: Turnaround time same day. Certification fee: $10.00. Fee payee: Alaska Court System. Prepayment is required.

Denali Borough

Healy Magistrate Court (4th District) PO Box 298, Healy, AK 99743-0298; 907-683-2213; Fax: 907-683-1383. Hours: 8AM-4:30PM *Misdemeanor, Civil Actions Under $7,500, Small Claims.*

Note: Felony cases are at Fairbanks Superior & District Court.

Civil Records: Access: Phone, mail, fax, in person. Only the court performs in person searches; visitors may not. No search fee. Required to search: name, years to search, DOB. Records on computer back to 1972.

Criminal Records: Access: Phone, mail, fax, in person. Only the court performs in person searches; visitors may not. Search fee: $15.00 per hour. Required to search: name, years to search, DOB. Records on computer back to 1972.

General Information: Public Access terminal is available. Turnaround time 1-2 weeks. Fax notes: Will only fax to a toll-free when no record is found. Certification fee: $5.00. Fee payee: State of Alaska. Prepayment is required.

Dillingham Borough

Dillingham Superior Court (3rd District) PO Box 909, Dillingham, AK 99576-0909; 907-842-5215; Fax: 907-842-5746. Hours: 8AM-4:30PM (AK). *Felony, Misdemeanor, Civil, Small Claims.*

Civil Records: Access: In person, mail. Only the court performs in person searches; visitors may not. Search fee: $15.00.

Criminal Records: Access: In person, mail. Only the court performs in person searches; visitors may not. Search fee: $15.00 per hour. Required to search: name, years to search, DOB.

General Information: Turnaround time 1-2 weeks. Fee payee: State of Alaska. Prepayment is required.

Fairbanks North Star Borough

Superior & District Court (4th District) 101 Lacey St, Fairbanks, AK 99701; 907-452-9277; Fax: 907-452-9392. Hours: 8AM-4:30PM (AK). *Felony, Misdemeanor, Civil, Eviction, Small Claims, Probate.*

www.alaska.net/~akctlib/courtdir.htm#fairbanks

Civil Records: Access: In person only. Visitors must perform in person searches for themselves. No search fee. Required to search: name, years to search. Civil cases indexed by defendant, plaintiff. Civil records on computer from 1988, on microfiche, archived and on index from 1900s.

Criminal Records: Access: In person only. Visitors must perform in person searches for themselves. No search fee. Required to search: name, years to search,

DOB. Criminal records on computer from 1988, on microfiche, archived and on index from 1900s.

General Information: Public Access terminal is available. No adoption, juvenile, guardianship or mental records released. Copy fee: $.25 per page. Certification fee: $5.00 plus $2.00 per copy after first. Fee payee: Clerk of Court. Personal checks accepted. In person only. Prepayment is required.

Haines Borough

District Court (1st District) PO Box 169, Haines, AK 99827-0169; 907-766-2801; Fax: 907-766-3148. Hours: 8AM-N, 1-4:30PM (AK). *Misdemeanor, Civil Actions Under $50,000, Small Claims.*

Note: Felony cases are at Juneau Superior & District Court.

Civil Records: Access: Phone, fax, mail, in person. Only the court performs in person searches; visitors may not. Search fee: $15.00 per hour. Required to search: name, years to search; also helpful: address. Civil cases indexed by defendant, plaintiff. Civil records on computer since 1993, index from 1960s. Limited information is available by phone.

Criminal Records: Access: Phone, fax, mail, in person. Only the court performs in person searches; visitors may not. Search fee: $15.00 per hour. Required to search: name, years to search; also helpful: address, DOB, SSN. Criminal records on computer since 1993, index from 1960s.

General Information: No juvenile records released. SASE required. Turnaround time 1-2 days. Copy fee: $.25 per page. Certification fee: $5.00 plus $2.00 per each additional document requested at same time. Fee payee: Alaska Court System. Personal checks accepted. Prepayment is required.

Juneau Borough

Superior & District Court (1st District) Dimond Courthouse, PO Box 114100, Juneau, AK 99811-4100; 907-463-4700; Fax: 907-463-3788. Hours: 8AM-4:30PM (AK). *Felony, Misdemeanor, Civil, Eviction, Small Claims, Probate.*

www.alaska.net/~akctlib/courtdir.htm#juneau

Civil Records: Access: Fax, mail, in person. Both court and visitors may perform in person searches. Search fee: $15.00 per hour. Required to search: name, years to search. Civil cases indexed by defendant. Civil records on computer back to 1987, on microfiche from 1960 to 1986, on index from 1959 to 1987.

Criminal Records: Access: Fax, mail, in person. Both court and visitors may perform in person searches. Search fee: $15.00 per hour. Required to search: name, years to search. Criminal records on computer back to 1987, on microfiche from 1960 to 1986, on index from 1959 to 1987.

General Information: Public Access terminal is available. No adoption, juvenile, guardianship or mental records released. SASE required. Turnaround time 2-5 days. Copy fee: $.25 per page. Certification fee: $5.00 plus $2.00 per page after first. Fee payee: Juneau Trial Court. Personal checks accepted. Prepayment is required.

Kenai Peninsula

Superior & District Court (3rd District) 125 Trading Bay Dr, Ste 100, Kenai, AK 99611; 907-283-3110; Fax: 907-283-8535. Hours: 8AM-4:30PM (AK). *Felony, Misdemeanor, Civil, Eviction, Small Claims, Probate.*

www.alaska.net/~akctlib/index.htm#kenai

Civil Records: Access: Mail, in person. Both court and visitors may perform in person searches. Search fee: $15.00 per hour. Required to search: name, years to search. Civil cases indexed by defendant, plaintiff. Civil records on computer from 1983, on microfiche, archived and on index from 1959.

Criminal Records: Access: Mail, in person. Both court and visitors may perform in person searches. Search fee: $15.00 per hour. Required to search: name, years to search, DOB. Criminal records on computer from 1983, on microfiche, archived and on index from 1959.

General Information: Public Access terminal is available. No adoption, guardianship, children's, conservatorship or coroner records released. SASE required. Turnaround time 1 week. Copy fee: $.25 per page. Certification fee: $5.00 plus $2.00 per page after first. Fee payee: Clerk of Court. Personal checks accepted. Prepayment is required.

District Court (3rd District) 3670 Lake St, Ste 400, Homer, AK 99603-9647; 907-235-8171; Fax: 907-235-4257. Hours: 8AM-4:30PM (AK). *Misdemeanor, Civil Actions Under $50,000, Small Claims.*

www.alaska.net/~akctlib/index.htm

Civil Records: Access: Phone, fax, mail, in person. Both the court and visitors may perform in person searches. Search fee: $15.00 per hour. Required to search: name, years to search. Civil cases indexed by defendant, plaintiff. Civil records on computer back to 1984. Phone access limited to name searches.

Criminal Records: Access: Phone, fax, mail, in person. Only the court performs in person searches; visitors may not. Search fee: $15.00 per hour. Required to search: name, years to search. Criminal records on computer back to 1984.

General Information: No confidential or sealed records released. SASE required. Turnaround time 5 days. Copy fee: $.25 per page. Certification fee: $5.00. Fee payee: Alaska Court System. Personal checks accepted. Prepayment is required.

Seward Magistrate Court (3rd District) PO Box 1929, Seward, AK 99664-1929; 907-224-3075; Fax: 907-227-7192. Hours: 8AM-4:30PM (AK). *Misdemeanor, Civil Actions Under $7,500, Small Claims.*

Civil Records: Access: In person, mail. Both court and visitors may perform in person searches. No search fee.

Criminal Records: Access: In person, mail. Both court and visitors may perform in person searches. Search fee: $15.00 per hour. Required to search: name, years to search, DOB.

General Information: Turnaround time 1-2 weeks. Fee payee: State of Alaska. Prepayment is required.

Ketchikan Gateway

Superior & District Court (1st District) 415 Main, Rm 400, Ketchikan, AK 99901-6399; 907-225-3195; Fax: 907-225-7849. Hours: 8AM-4:30PM M-Th, 9AM-4:30PM Fridays (AK). *Felony, Misdemeanor, Civil, Eviction, Small Claims, Probate.*

Civil Records: Access: Fax, mail, in person. Both court and visitors may perform in person searches. Search fee: $15.00 per hour. Required to search: name, years to search. Civil cases indexed by defendant, plaintiff. Civil records on computer from 1983, on microfiche from 1972 to 1989, index from 1972.

Criminal Records: Access: Fax, mail, in person. Both court and visitors may perform in person searches. Search fee: $15.00 per hour. Required to search: name, years to search, DOB. Criminal records on computer from 1983, on microfiche from 1972 to 1989, index from 1972.

General Information: Public Access terminal is available. No confidential probate or children's records released. SASE required. Turnaround time 2 weeks. Fax notes: No fee to fax results. Copy fee: $.25 per page. Certification fee: $5.00. Fee payee: Alaska Court System. Personal checks accepted. Prepayment is required.

Kodiak Island

Superior & District Court (3rd District) 204 Mission Road, Rm 10, Kodiak, AK 99615-7312; 907-486-1600; Fax: 907-486-1660. Hours: 8AM-4:30PM M,T,Th,F; 9AM-4:30PM W (AK). *Felony, Misdemeanor, Civil, Eviction, Small Claims, Probate.*

Civil Records: Access: Mail, fax, in person. Both court and visitors may perform in person searches. Search fee: $15.00 per hour. Required to search: name, years to search; also helpful: address. Civil cases indexed by defendant, plaintiff. Civil records on computer from 1982, on microfiche, index and archived from 1959.

Criminal Records: Access: Mail, fax, in person. Both court and visitors may perform in person searches. Search fee: $15.00 per hour. Required to search: name, years to search; also helpful: address, DOB, SSN. Criminal records on computer from 1982, on microfiche, index and archived from 1959.

General Information: Public Access terminal is available. No adoption, juvenile, guardianship or mental records released. SASE required. Turnaround time 1-3 weeks. Copy fee: $.25 per page. Certification fee: $5.00 plus $2.00 per add'l copy. Fee payee: Clerk of Court. Personal checks accepted. Prepayment is required.

Matanuska-Susitna

Superior & District Court (3rd District) 435 S Denali, Palmer, AK 99645-6437; Civil phone: 907-746-8108; Criminal phone: 907-746-8104; Fax: 907-746-4151. Hours: 8AM-4:30PM (AK). *Felony, Misdemeanor, Civil, Eviction, Small Claims, Probate.*

Civil Records: Access: Mail, in person. Both court and visitors may perform in person searches. Search fee: $15.00 per hour. Required to search: name, years to search; also helpful: address. Civil cases indexed by defendant, plaintiff. Civil records on computer from 1988, on microfiche, archived and index from 1974.

Criminal Records: Access: Mail, in person. Both court and visitors may perform in person searches. Search fee: $15.00 per hour. Required to search: name, years to search; also helpful: address, DOB, SSN. Criminal records on computer from 1988, on microfiche, archived and index from 1974.

General Information: Public Access terminal is available. No adoption, juvenile, guardianship or mental records released. SASE required. Turnaround time 1-3 weeks. Copy fee: $.25 per page. Certification fee: $5.00. A second copy is $2.00 per document. Fee payee: State of Alaska. Personal checks accepted. Prepayment is required.

Nome Borough

Superior & District Court (2nd District) PO Box 1110, Nome, AK 99762-1110; 907-443-5216; Fax: 907-443-2192. Hours: 8AM-4:30PM *Felony, Misdemeanor, Civil, Eviction, Small Claims, Probate.*

www.alaska.net/~akctlib/index.htm#nome

Civil Records: Access: Fax, mail, in person. Both court and visitors may perform in person searches. Search fee: $15.00 per hour or fraction of. Required to search: name, years to search; also helpful: DOB. Civil cases indexed by defendant, plaintiff. Civil records on computer from 1983, on microfiche from 1960 to 1983, on index and archived from 1960.

Criminal Records: Access: Fax, mail, in person. Both court and visitors may perform in person searches. Search fee: $15.00 per hour or fraction of. Required to search: name, years to search; also helpful: DOB, SSN. Criminal records on computer from 1983, on microfiche from 1960 to 1983, on index and archived from 1960.

General Information: Public Access terminal is available. No adoption, juvenile, guardianship or mental records released. SASE required. Turnaround time 5 days. Fax notes: Will fax results to toll-free numbers

only. Copy fee: $.25 per page. Certification fee: $5.00 plus $2.00 per copy after first. Fee payee: Nome Trial Courts. Personal checks accepted. Prepayment is required.

Gambell Magistrate Court (2nd District) PO Box 1110, Nome, AK 99702-1110; 907-443-5216. *Misdemeanor, Civil Actions Under $7,500, Small Claims.*

Note: Court is vacant; records at Superior Court in Nome at address and phone here.

Unalakleet Magistrate Court (2nd District) PO Box 250, Unalakleet, AK 99684-0250; 907-624-3015; Fax: 907-624-3118. Hours: 8AM-1:30PM (AK). *Misdemeanor, Civil Actions Under $7,500, Small Claims.*

Civil Records: Access: In person, mail. Only the court performs in person searches; visitors may not. Search fee: $15.00 per hour. Required to search: name, years to search.

Criminal Records: Access: In person, mail. Only the court performs in person searches; visitors may not. Search fee: $15.00 per hour. Required to search: name, years to search.

General Information: Turnaround time 1-2 weeks. Fee payee: Magistrate Court. Prepayment is required.

North Slope

Superior & District Court (2nd District) PO Box 270, Barrow, AK 99723-0270; 907-852-4800 X80; Fax: 907-852-4804. Hours: 8AM-4:30PM (AK). *Felony, Misdemeanor, Civil, Eviction, Small Claims, Probate.*

Civil Records: Access: Fax, mail, in person. Only the court performs in person searches; visitors may not. Search fee: $15.00 per hour. Required to search: name, years to search; also helpful: address. Civil cases indexed by defendant, plaintiff. Civil records on computer from 1983, prior on microfiche.

Criminal Records: Access: Fax, mail, in person. Only the court performs in person searches; visitors may not. Search fee: $15.00 per hour. Required to search: name, years to search; also helpful: address, DOB, SSN. Criminal records on computer from 1983, prior on microfiche.

General Information: No confidential records released. SASE required. Turnaround time 1-2 weeks. Fax notes: No fee to fax results. Copy fee: $.25 per page. Certification fee: $5.00 plus $2.00 per page after first. Fee payee: Alaska Court System. Personal checks accepted. Prepayment is required.

Northwest Arctic

Superior & District Court (2nd District) PO Box 317, Kotzebue, AK 99752-0317; 907-442-3208; Fax: 907-442-3974. Hours: 8AM-4:30PM *Felony, Misdemeanor, Civil, Eviction, Small Claims, Probate.*

Civil Records: Access: Fax, mail, in person. Both court and visitors may perform in person searches. Search fee: $15.00. Required to search: name, years to search. Civil cases indexed by defendant. Civil records on computer from 1983, prior records on microfilm, archived and index from 1966. Copy of check required for fax access.

Criminal Records: Access: Mail, in person. Both court and visitors may perform in person searches. Search fee: $15.00. Required to search: name, years to search, DOB; also helpful: SSN. Criminal records on computer from 1983, prior records on microfilm, archived and index from 1966.

General Information: Public Access terminal is available. No adoption, juvenile, guardianship or mental records released. Turnaround time 2-3 days. Copy fee: $1.00 for first page, $.25 each add'l. Certification fee: $5.00 plus $2.00 per page after first. Certified Judgment

$3.00 notary fee. Fee payee: Alaska Court System. Personal checks accepted. Prepayment is required.

Ambler Magistrate Court (2nd District) PO
Box 317, Kotzebue, AK 99752; 907-442-3208; Fax: 907-442-3974. Hours: 9AM-2PM *Misdemeanor, Civil Actions Under $7,500, Small Claims.*

Note: Court is closed; for records, contact Kotzebue Court at the phone number and address here.

Kiana Magistrate Court (2nd District) PO
Box 317, Kotzebue, AK 99749-0170; 907-442-3208. Hours: 10AM-3PM M,W,F (AK). *Misdemeanor, Civil Actions Under $7,500, Small Claims.*

Note: Court is temporarily vacant; for records, contact Kotzebue Court at address and phone here.

Prince of Wales-Outer Ketchikan

Craig Magistrate Court (1st District) PO
Box 646, Craig, AK 99921-0646; 907-826-3316/3306; Fax: 907-826-3904. 8AM-4:30PM *Misdemeanor, Civil Actions Under $7,500, Small Claims.*

Note: Felony cases are at Ketchican Superior & District Court.

Civil Records: Access: In person, mail. Only the court performs in person searches; visitors may not. Search fee: $15.00 per hour. Required to search: name, years to search; also helpful: DOB.
Criminal Records: Access: In person, mail. Only the court performs in person searches; visitors may not. Search fee: $15.00 per hour. Required to search: name, years to search; also helpful: DOB.
General Information: Turnaround time 2 weeks. Fee payee: Alaska Court System. Prepayment is required.

Sitka Borough

Superior & District Court (1st District) 304
Lake St, Rm 203, Sitka, AK 99835-7759; 907-747-3291; Fax: 907-747-6690. Hours: 8AM-4:30PM (AK). *Felony, Misdemeanor, Civil, Eviction, Small Claims, Probate.*

Civil Records: Access: Phone, fax, mail, in person. Both court and visitors may perform in person searches. Search fee: $15.00 per hour. Required to search: name. Civil cases indexed by defendant, plaintiff. Civil records on computer from 1983, on microfilm and archived from 1970 to 1987, on index from 1960.
Criminal Records: Access: Phone, fax, mail, in person. Both court and visitors may perform in person searches. Search fee: $15.00 per hour. Required to search: name. Criminal records on computer from 1983, on microfilm and archived from 1970 to 1987, on index from 1960.
General Information: Public Access terminal is available. No adoption, juvenile, guardianship or mental records released. SASE required. Turnaround time 1 week. Fax notes: No fee to fax results. Will fax collect. Copy fee: $.25 per page. Certification fee: $5.00. Fee payee: Alaska Court System. Personal checks accepted. Prepayment is required.

Skagway-Yakutat-Angoon

Hoonah District Court (1st District) PO Box
430, Hoonah, AK 99829-0430; 907-945-3668; Fax: 907-945-3637. Hours: 8AM-Noon, 1-4:30PM (AK). *Misdemeanor, Civil Actions Under $50,000, Small Claims.*

www.alaska.net/~akctlib/homepage.htm
Note: Felony cases are at Juneau Superior & District Court.

Civil Records: Access: Mail, in person. Only the court performs in person searches; visitors may not. No search fee. Required to search: name, years to search. Civil cases indexed by defendant, plaintiff. Civil records on index from 1971 to present.

Criminal Records: Access: Mail, in person. Only the court performs in person searches; visitors may not. No search fee. Required to search: name, years to search; also helpful: DOB. Criminal records on index from 1971 to present.

General Information: No confidential, juvenile or sex related records released. SASE not required. Turnaround time 2-3 days. Copy fee: $.25 per page. Certification fee: $5.00 plus $2.00 per page after first. Fee payee: Alaska Court System. Personal checks accepted. Prepayment is required.

Angoon Magistrate Court (1st District) PO
Box 250, Angoon, AK 99820-0123; 907-788-3229; Fax: 907-788-3108. 11AM-2PM (AK). *Misdemeanor, Civil Actions Under $7,500, Small Claims.*

Note: Felony cases are at Juneau Superior & District Court.

Civil Records: Access: In person, mail. Only the court performs in person searches; visitors may not. Search fee: $15.00 per hour. Required to search: name, years to search.
Criminal Records: Access: In person, mail. Only the court performs in person searches; visitors may not. Search fee: $15.00 per hour. Required to search: name, years to search.
General Information: Turnaround time 1-2 weeks. Fee payee: Alaska Court System. Prepayment is required.

Pelican Magistrate Court (1st District) 304
Lake St #203, Sitka, AK 99835; 907-747-6271. *Misdemeanor, Civil Actions Under $7,500, Small Claims.*

Note: This court closed permanently on 12/31/99. All records are at Sitka court, address & phone given here.

Skagway Magistrate Court (1st District)
PO Box 495, Skagway, AK 99840-0495; 907-983-2368; Fax: 907-983-3801. Hours: 9AM-4:30PM T-Th (AK). *Misdemeanor, Civil Actions Under $7,500, Small Claims.*

Note: Hours will vary from Summer to Winter. Felony cases are at Juneau Superior & District Court.

Civil Records: Access: Phone, mail, fax, in person. No search fee. Civil records go back to 1970; on computer back to 1998.
Criminal Records: Access: In person, mail. Only the court performs in person searches; visitors may not. Search fee: $15.00 per hour. Required to search: name, years to search, DOB. Criminal records go back to 1970; on computer back to 1998. No charge for a simple name search.
General Information: Turnaround time 1-2 weeks. Fax notes: Will fax back to toll-free numbers no charge. Certification fee: $3.00 per document. Fee payee: Magistrate Court. Prepayment is required.

Yakutat Magistrate Court (1st District) PO
Box 426, Yakutat, AK 99689-0426; 907-784-3274; Fax: 907-784-3257. Hours: 9AM-4:30PM (AK). *Misdemeanor, Civil Actions Under $7,500, Small Claims.*

Note: Felony cases are at Juneau Superior & District Court.

Civil Records: Access: Phone, mail, fax, in person, email. Only the court performs in person searches; visitors may not. Search fee: $15.00 per hour or a fraction of. Required to search: name. Civil records go back to 1976; on computer back to 1976.
Criminal Records: Access: Mail, fax, in person, email. Only the court performs in person searches; visitors may not. Search fee: $15.00 per hour or a fraction of. Required to search: name, DOB. Criminal records go back to 1976; on computer back to 1976.
General Information: Certification fee: $5.00. Fee payee: Alaska Court System. Prepayment is required.

Southeast Fairbanks

Delta Junction Magistrate Court (4th District) PO Box 401, Delta Junction, AK 99737-0401; 907-895-4211; Fax: 907-895-4204. Hours: 8AM-Noon, 1-4:30PM (AK). *Misdemeanor, Civil Actions Under $7,500, Small Claims.*

Note: Felony cases are at Fairbanks Superior & District Court.

Civil Records: Access: In person, mail. Only the court performs in person searches; visitors may not. No search fee.
Criminal Records: Access: phone, mail, fax, in person. Only the court performs in person searches; visitors may not. Search fee: $15.00 per hour. Required to search: name, years to search. Criminal records computerized go back to 1980; prior records go back to mid-70's.
General Information: Turnaround time 1 week. Certification fee: $5.00. Fee payee: District Court. Prepayment is required.

Tok Magistrate Court (4th District) PO Box
187, Tok, AK 99780-0187; 907-883-5171; Fax: 907-883-4367. Hours: 8AM-4:30PM (AK). *Misdemeanor, Civil Actions Under $7,500, Small Claims.*

Note: Felony cases are at Fairbanks Superior & District Court.

Civil Records: Access: In person, mail. Only the court performs in person searches; visitors may not. No search fee.
Criminal Records: Access: In person, mail. Only the court performs in person searches; visitors may not. No search fee. Required to search: name, years to search, DOB.
General Information: Turnaround time 5 days.

Valdez-Cordova

Superior & District Court (3rd District) PO
Box 127, Valdez, AK 99686-0127; 907-835-2266; Fax: 907-835-3764. Hours: 8AM-4:30PM (AK). *Felony, Misdemeanor, Civil, Eviction, Small Claims, Probate.*

Civil Records: Access: Fax, mail, in person. Both court and visitors may perform in person searches. Search fee: $15.00 per hour. Required to search: name, years to search; also helpful: address. Civil cases indexed by defendant, plaintiff. Civil records on computer from 1984, on microfiche, archived and index from 1960.
Criminal Records: Access: Fax, mail, in person. Both court and visitors may perform in person searches. Search fee: $15.00 per hour. Required to search: name, years to search; also helpful: address, DOB, SSN. Criminal records on computer from 1984, on microfiche, archived and index from 1960.
General Information: No adoption, juvenile, guardianship or mental records released. SASE required. Turnaround time 1-3 weeks. Copy fee: $.25 per page. Certification fee: $5.00. Fee payee: Valdez Trial Court of Alaska. Personal checks accepted. Prepayment is required.

Cordova Court (3rd District) PO Box 898,
Cordova, AK 99574-0898; 907-424-3378; Fax: 907-424-7581. Hours: 8AM-4:30PM (AK). *Felony, Misdemeanor, Civil, Small Claims, Probate.*

Civil Records: Access: Phone, mail, fax, in person. Both court and visitors may perform in person searches. No search fee. Civil records on computer back to 1993; other records back to 1975. Access by phone if time allows.
Criminal Records: Access: Phone, mail, fax, in person. Both court and visitors may perform in person searches. Search fee: $15.00 per hour. Required to search: name, years to search, DOB. Criminal records on computer back to 1993; other records back to 1975. Will take phone requests if time allows.

General Information: Public Access terminal is available. Turnaround time 1 week. Certification fee: $5.00. Fee payee: State of Alaska. Prepayment required.

Glennallen District Court (3rd District) PO

Box 86, Glennallen, AK 99588-0086; 907-822-3405; Fax: 907-822-3601. 8AM-4:30PM *Misdemeanor, Civil Actions Under $10,000, Small Claims.*

Civil Records: Access: In person, mail. Both court and visitors may perform in person searches. No search fee.

Criminal Records: Access: In person, mail. Both court and visitors may perform in person searches. Search fee: $15.00 per hour. Required to search: name, years to search; also helpful: DOB.

General Information: Turnaround time 1-2 weeks. Fee payee: Alaska Court System. Prepayment is required.

Whittier Magistrate Court (3rd District) c/o

Karla Utter, 825 W 4th Ave, Anchorage, AK 99501-2004; 907-264-0456. *Misdemeanor, Civil Actions Under $7,500, Small Claims.*

Note: Court closed; records available at the address and phone here.

Wade Hampton

Chevak Magistrate Court (Bethel Area)

PO Box 238, Chevak, AK 99563-0238; 907-858-7231; Fax: 907-858-7232. 9AM-3:30PM *Misdemeanor, Civil Actions Under $7,500, Small Claims.*

Note: Felony cases are at Bethel Superior & District Court.

Civil Records: Access: Mail, fax, in person. Only the court performs in person searches; visitors may not. No search fee. Required to search: name, years to search. Civil records go back to 1993; on computer to 1997.

Criminal Records: Access: Mail, fax, in person. Both court and visitors may perform in person searches. Search fee: $15.00 per hour. Required to search: name, years to search, address, DOB, SSN, signed release. Criminal records go back to 1993; on computer back to 1997.

General Information: Public Access terminal is available. Turnaround time 1-2 weeks. Certification fee: $3.00. Fee payee: Magistrate Court. Prepayment is required.

Emmonak Magistrate Court (Bethel Area)

PO Box 176, Emmonak, AK 99581-0176; 907-949-1748; Fax: 907-949-1535. Hours: 8AM-4:30PM (AK). *Misdemeanor, Civil Actions Under $7,500, Small Claims.*

Note: Felony cases are at Bethel Superior & District Court.

Civil Records: Access: In person, mail. Only the court performs in person searches; visitors may not. No search fee.

Criminal Records: Access: In person, mail. Only the court performs in person searches; visitors may not. Search fee: $15.00 per hour. Required to search: name, years to search, address, DOB, signed release; also helpful: SSN.

General Information: Turnaround time 1-2 weeks. Fee payee: Magistrate Court. Prepayment is required.

St Mary's Magistrate Court (Bethel Area)

PO Box 183, St Mary's, AK 99658-0183; 907-438-2912; Fax: 907-438-2819. Hours: 8AM-4:30PM (AK). *Misdemeanor, Civil Actions Under $7,500, Small Claims.*

Note: Felony cases are at Bethel Superior & District Court.

Civil Records: Access: In person, mail. Only the court performs in person searches; visitors may not. No search fee.

Criminal Records: Access: In person, mail. Only the court performs in person searches; visitors may not. No search fee. Required to search: name, years to search; also helpful: DOB.

General Information: Turnaround time 3 weeks.

Wrangell-Petersburg

Petersburg Superior & District Court (1st District) PO Box 1009, Petersburg, AK 99833-1009;

907-772-3824; Fax: 907-772-3018. Hours: 8AM-4:30PM (AK). *Felony, Misdemeanor, Civil, Eviction, Small Claims, Probate.*

Civil Records: Access: Phone, fax, mail, in person. Both court and visitors may perform in person searches. No search fee. Required to search: name, years to search; also helpful: address. Civil cases indexed by defendant, plaintiff. Civil records on computer from 1988, on microfiche and index from 1960s, archived from 1920s.

Criminal Records: Access: Phone, fax, mail, in person. Both court and visitors may perform in person searches. No search fee. Required to search: name, years to search; also helpful: address, DOB, SSN. Criminal records on computer from 1988, on microfiche and index from 1960s, archived from 1920s.

General Information: No adoption, juvenile, guardianship or mental records released. SASE required. Turnaround time 1 week. Fax notes: Outgoing fax limited to 10 pages; call for fee. Copy fee: $.25 per page. Certification fee: $5.00. Fee payee: Alaska Court System. Personal checks accepted. Prepayment is required.

Wrangell Superior & District Court (1st District) PO Box 869, Wrangell, AK 99929-0869;

907-874-2311; Fax: 907-874-3509. Hours: 8AM-4:30PM (AK). *Felony, Misdemeanor, Civil, Eviction, Small Claims, Probate.*

Civil Records: Access: Phone, fax, mail, in person. Only the court performs in person searches; visitors may not. Search fee: $15.00 per hour. Search fee is charged for all written requests. Required to search: name, years to search. Civil cases indexed by defendant, plaintiff. Civil records on computer from 1988, on microfiche and card files to 1959, archived from 1900s.

Criminal Records: Access: Phone, fax, mail, in person. Only the court performs in person searches; visitors may not. Search fee: $15.00 per hour. Required to search: name, years to search, DOB. Criminal records on computer from 1988, on microfiche and card files from 1959, archived from 1900s.

General Information: No adoption, juvenile, guardianship or mental records released. SASE required. Turnaround time 3 days. Fax notes: Fee to fax results is $15.00 per document. Copy fee: $.25 per page. Certification fee: $5.00 plus $2.00 per copy after first. Fee payee: Alaska Court System or State of Alaska. Personal checks accepted. Prepayment is required.

Kake Magistrate Court (1st District) PO

Box 100, Kake, AK 99830-0100; 907-785-3651; Fax: 907-785-3152. Hours: 8AM-Noon *Misdemeanor, Civil Actions Under $7,500, Small Claims.*

Civil Records: Access: In person, mail. Only the court performs in person searches; visitors may not. No search fee.

Criminal Records: Access: In person, mail. Only the court performs in person searches; visitors may not. Search fee: $15.00 per hour. Required to search: name, years to search, DOB, SSN, signed release.

General Information: Turnaround time 1-2 weeks. Fee payee: Alaska Court System. Prepayment is required.

Yukon-Koyukuk

Fort Yukon Magistrate Court (4th District) PO Box 211, Fort Yukon, AK 99740-0211;

907-662-2336; Fax: 907-662-2824. Hours: 9:30AM-3PM (AK). *Misdemeanor, Civil Actions Under $7,500, Small Claims.*

Note: Felony cases are at Fairbanks Superior & District Court.

Civil Records: Access: Fax, mail, in person. Only the court performs in person searches; visitors may not. No search fee. Required to search: name, DOB. Records go back to 1960s.

Criminal Records: Access: Fax, mail, in person. Only the court performs in person searches; visitors may not. Search fee: $15.00 per hour. Required to search: name, years to search, DOB. Records go back to 1960s.

General Information: Turnaround time 1-2 weeks. Fee payee: District Court. Prepayment is required.

Galena Magistrate Court (4th District) PO

Box 167, Galena, AK 99741-0167; 907-656-1322; Fax: 907-656-1546. 8AM-4:30PM (AK). *Misdemeanor, Civil Actions Under $7,500, Small Claims.*

Note: Felony cases are at Fairbanks Superior & District Court.

Civil Records: Access: In person, mail. Only the court performs in person searches; visitors may not. No search fee.

Criminal Records: Access: In person, mail. Only the court performs in person searches; visitors may not. Search fee: $15.00 per hour. Required to search: name, years to search.

General Information: Turnaround time 1-2 weeks. Fee payee: Magistrate Court. Prepayment is required.

McGrath Magistrate Court (4th District)

PO Box 167, Galena, AK 99741-0167; 907-656-1322; Fax: 907-656-1546. Hours: 8:30AM-4:30PM (AK). *Misdemeanor, Civil Actions Under $7,500, Small Claims.*

Note: McGrath Court is vacant. Court records at Galena Magistrate Court, address and phone here.

Nenana Magistrate Court (4th District) PO

Box 449, Nenana, AK 99760-0449; 907-832-5430; Fax: 907-832-5841. 8:30AM-4PM *Misdemeanor, Civil Actions Under $7,500, Small Claims.*

Note: Felony cases are at Fairbanks Superior & District Court.

Civil Records: Access: In person, mail. Only the court performs in person searches; visitors may not. No search fee.

Criminal Records: Access: In person, mail. Only the court performs in person searches; visitors may not. No search fee. Required to search: name, years to search.

General Information: Turnaround time 2 weeks.

Tanana Magistrate Court (4th District) PO

Box 449, Nenana, AK 99777; 907-366-7243; Fax: 907-832-5841. Hours: Th-F 2nd full week each month (AK). *Misdemeanor, Civil Actions Under $7,500, Small Claims.*

Note: Magistrate may also be contacted by phone at 907-832-5430. Felony cases are at Fairbanks Superior & District Court.

Civil Records: Access: In person, mail. Only the court performs in person searches; visitors may not. No search fee.

Criminal Records: Access: In person, mail. Only the court performs in person searches; visitors may not. Search fee: $15.00 per hour. Required to search: name, years to search, DOB, signed release.

General Information: Turnaround time 1-2 weeks. Fee payee: Magistrate Court. Prepayment is required.

Alaska Recording Offices

ORGANIZATION   The 23 Alaskan counties are called boroughs. However, real estate recording is done under a system that was established at the time of the Gold Rush (whenever that was) of 34 Recording Districts. Some of the Districts are identical in geography to boroughs, such as the Aleutian Islands, but other boroughs and districts overlap. Therefore, you need to know which recording district any given town or city is located in. The entire state except the Aleutian Islands is in the Alaska Time Zone (AK).

REAL ESTATE RECORDS   Districts do not perform real estate searches. Certification fees are usually $5.00 per document. Copies usually cost $1.25 for the first page, $.25 per additional page.

UCC RECORDS   Financing statements are filed at the state level, except for real estate related collateral, which are filed with the District Recorder. However, prior to 07/2001, consumer goods and farm collateral were filed at the District Recorder and can be searched there. All districts will perform UCC searches at $5.00 per debtor name for information and $15.00 with copies. Use search request form UCC-11. Copies ordered separately usually cost $2.00 per financing statement.

TAX LIEN RECORDS   All state and federal tax liens are filed with the District Recorder. Districts do not perform separate tax lien searches.

Aleutian Islands District

District Recorder, 550 W 7th Ave, #1200, Suite 1140, Anchorage, AK 99501. 907-269-8899 R/E Recording: 907-762-2444.
Will search UCC records. This agency will not do a tax lien search. Will not search real estate records. **Other Phone Numbers:** Assessor 907-343-6770.

Anchorage District

District Recorder, 550 W 7th Ave, #1200, Suite 1140, Anchorage, AK 99501. 907-269-8899 R/E Recording: 907-762-2443.
Will search UCC records. This agency will not do a tax lien search. Will not search real estate records. **Other Phone Numbers:** Assessor 907-343-6770.

Barrow District

District Recorder, 1648 S Cushman St. #201, Fairbanks, AK 99701-6206. 907-452-3521.
Will search UCC records. This agency will not do a tax lien search. Will not search real estate records.

Bethel District

District Recorder, P.O. Box 426, Bethel, AK 99559. 907-543-3391.
Will search UCC records. This agency will not do a tax lien search. Will not search real estate records. **Other Phone Numbers:** Assessor 907-543-2296; Treasurer 907-543-2298.

Bristol Bay District

District Recorder, 550 W 7th Ave, #1200, Suite 1140, Anchorage, AK 99501. 907-269-8899 R/E Recording: 907-762-2443.
Will search UCC records. This agency will not do a tax lien search. Will not search real estate records. **Other Phone Numbers:** Assessor 907-343-6770.

Cape Nome District

District Recorder, Box 431, Nome, AK 99762. 907-443-5178.
Will search UCC records. This agency will not do a tax lien search. Will not search real estate records.

Chitina District

District Recorder, Box 86, Glennallen, AK 99588. 907-822-3726 R/E Recording: 907-745-9683.
Will search UCC records. This agency will not do a tax lien search. Will not search real estate records.

Cordova District

District Recorder, 550 W 7th Ave, #1200, Suite 1140, Anchorage, AK 99501. 907-269-8899 R/E Recording: 907-762-2443.
Will search UCC records. This agency will not do a tax lien search. Will not search real estate records. **Other Phone Numbers:** Assessor 907-343-6770.

Fairbanks District

District Recorder, 1648 S Cushman St. #201, Fairbanks, AK 99701-6206. 907-452-3521; http://www.co.fairbanks.ak.us
Will search UCC records. This agency will not do a tax lien search. Will not search real estate records. **Online Access:** Real Estate. Access to the City of Fairbanks Property database is available for free online at www.co.fairbanks.ak.us/database/aurora/default.asp. **Other Phone Numbers:** Assessor 907-459-1000.

Fort Gibbon District

District Recorder, 1648 S Cushman St. #201, Fairbanks, AK 99701-6206. 907-452-3521.
Will search UCC records. This agency will not do a tax lien search. Will not search real estate records.

Haines District

District Recorder, 400 Willoughby, 3rd Floor, Juneau, AK 99801. 907-465-3449.
Will search UCC records. This agency will not do a tax lien search. Will not search real estate records.

Homer District

District Recorder, 195 E. Bunnell Ave., Suite A, Homer, AK 99603. 907-235-8136.
Will search UCC records. This agency will not do a tax lien search. Will not search real estate records.

Iliamna District

District Recorder, 550 W 7th Ave, #1200, Suite 1140, Anchorage, AK 99501. 907-269-8899 R/E Recording: 907-762-2443.
Will search UCC records. This agency will not do a tax lien search. Will not search real estate records. **Other Phone Numbers:** Assessor 907-343-6770.

Juneau District

District Recorder, 400 Willoughby, 3rd Floor, Juneau, AK 99801. 907-465-3449; http://www.juneau.org/cbj/main.htm
Will search UCC records. This agency will not do a tax lien search. Will not search real estate records. **Online Access:** Real Estate. Access to City of Juneau Property Records database is available free online at http://www.juneau.lib.ak.us/assessordata/assessor.asp. Also includes link access to Juneau rentals data and the Records home page. **Other Phone Numbers:** Assessor 907-586-5220.

Kenai District

District Recorder, 120 Trading Bay Road #230, Suite 230, Kenai, AK 99611. 907-283-3118 R/E Recording: 907-225-3142;
www.dnr.state.ak.us/ssd/recoff/default.htm
Will search UCC records. This agency will not do a tax lien search. Will not search real estate records. **Online Access:** Assessor. Access to Kenai Peninsula Borough Assessing Department Public Information Search Page is available free at www.borough.kenai.ak.us/assessingdept/Parcel/SEARCH.HTM. **Other Phone Numbers:** Assessor 907-343-6770.

Ketchikan District

District Recorder, 415 Main Street, Room 320, Ketchikan, AK 99901. 907-225-3142.
Will search UCC records. This agency will not do a tax lien search. Will not search real estate records. **Other Phone Numbers:** Assessor 907-225-0277.

Kodiak District

District Recorder, 204 Mission Road, Room 16, Kodiak, AK 99615. 907-486-9432.
Will search UCC records. This agency will not do a tax lien search. Will not search real estate records. **Other Phone Numbers:** Assessor 907-486-9353.

Kotzebue District

District Recorder, 1648 S. Cushman St. #201, Fairbanks, AK 99701-6206. 907-452-3521.
Will search UCC records. This agency will not do a tax lien search. Will not search real estate records.

Kuskokwim District

District Recorder, P.O. Box 426, Bethel, AK 99559. 907-543-3391.
Will search UCC records. This agency will not do a tax lien search. Will not search real estate records.

Kvichak District

District Recorder, 550 W 7th Ave, #1200, Suite 1140, Anchorage, AK 99501. 907-269-8899 R/E Recording: 907-762-2443.
Will search UCC records. This agency will not do a tax lien search. Will not search real estate records. **Other Phone Numbers:** Assessor 907-343-6770.

Manley Hot Springs District

District Recorder, 1648 S Cushman St. #201, Fairbanks, AK 99701-6206. 907-452-3521.
Will search UCC records. This agency will not do a tax lien search. Will not search real estate records.

Mount McKinley District

District Recorder, 1648 S Cushman St. #201, Fairbanks, AK 99701-6206. 907-452-3521.
Will search UCC records. This agency will not do a tax lien search. Will not search real estate records.

Nenana District

District Recorder, 1648 S Cushman St. #201, Fairbanks, AK 99701-6206. 907-452-3521.
Will search UCC records. This agency will not do a tax lien search. Will not search real estate records.

Nulato District

District Recorder, 1648 S Cushman St. #201, Fairbanks, AK 99701-6206. 907-452-3521.
Will search UCC records. This agency will not do a tax lien search. Will not search real estate records.

Palmer District

District Recorder, 1800 Glenn Hwy #7, Palmer, AK 99645. 907-745-3080.
Will search UCC records. This agency will not do a tax lien search. Will not search real estate records.

Petersburg District

District Recorder, 415 Main Street, Room 320, Ketchikan, AK 99901. 907-225-3142.
Will search UCC records. This agency will not do a tax lien search. Will not search real estate records.

Rampart District

District Recorder, 1648 S. Cushman St. #201, Fairbanks, AK 99701-6206. 907-452-3521.
Will search UCC records. This agency will not do a tax lien search. Will not search real estate records.

Seldovia District

District Recorder, 195 E. Bunnell Ave., Suite A, Homer, AK 99603. 907-235-8136.
Will search UCC records. This agency will not do a tax lien search. Will not search real estate records.

Seward District

District Recorder, Box 1929, Seward, AK 99664. 907-224-3075.
Will search UCC records. This agency will not do a tax lien search. Will not search real estate records.

Sitka District

District Recorder, 210C Lake Street, Sitka, AK 99835. 907-747-3275.
Will search UCC records. This agency will not do a tax lien search. Will not search real estate records.

Skagway District

District Recorder, 400 Willoughby, 3rd Floor, Juneau, AK 99801. 907-269-8899 R/E Recording: 907-465-3449.
Will search UCC records. This agency will not do a tax lien search. Will not search real estate records.

Talkeetna District

District Recorder, 1800 Glenn Hwy #7, Palmer, AK 99645. 907-745-3080.
Will search UCC records. This agency will not do a tax lien search. Will not search real estate records.

Valdez District

District Recorder, Box 127, Valdez, AK 99686. 907-835-2266.
Will search UCC records. This agency will not do a tax lien search. Will not search real estate records.

Wrangell District

District Recorder, 415 Main Street, Room 320, Ketchikan, AK 99901. 907-225-3142.
Will search UCC records. This agency will not do a tax lien search. Will not search real estate records.

Alaska County Locator

You will usually be able to find the city name in the City/County Cross Reference below. In that case, it is a simple matter to determine the county from the cross reference. However, only the official US Postal Service city names are included in this index. There are an additional 40,000 place names that people use in their addresses. Therefore, we have also included a ZIP/City Cross Reference immediately following the City/County Cross Reference.

If you know the ZIP Code but the city name does not appear in the City/County Cross Reference index, look up the ZIP Code in the ZIP/City Cross Reference, find the city name, then look up the city name in the City/County Cross Reference. For example, you want to know the county for an address of Menands, NY 12204. There is no "Menands" in the City/County Cross Reference. The ZIP/City Cross Reference shows that ZIP Codes 12201-12288 are for the city of Albany. Looking back in the City/County Cross Reference, Albany is in Albany County.

City/County Cross Reference

AKIACHAK Bethel
AKIAK Bethel
AKUTAN Aleutian Islands, East
ALAKANUK Wade Hampton
ALEKNAGIK Dillingham
ALLAKAKET Yukon-Koyukuk
AMBLER Northwest Arctic
ANAKTUVUK PASS North Slope Borough
ANCHOR POINT Kenai Peninsula Borough
ANCHORAGE Anchorage Borough
ANDERSON Denali
ANGOON Skagway-Yakutat-Angoon
ANIAK Bethel
ANVIK Yukon-Koyukuk
ARCTIC VILLAGE Yukon-Koyukuk
ATKA Aleutian Islands, West
ATQASUK North Slope Borough
AUKE BAY Juneau Borough
BARROW North Slope Borough
BEAVER Yukon-Koyukuk
BETHEL Bethel
BETTLES FIELD Yukon-Koyukuk
BIG LAKE Matanuska-Susitna Borough
BREVIG MISSION Nome
BUCKLAND Northwest Arctic
CANTWELL Denali
CENTRAL Yukon-Koyukuk
CHALKYITSIK Yukon-Koyukuk
CHEFORNAK Bethel
CHEVAK Wade Hampton
CHICKEN Southeast Fairbanks
CHIGNIK Lake & Peninsula
CHIGNIK LAGOON Lake & Peninsula
CHIGNIK LAKE Lake & Peninsula
CHITINA Valdez-Cordova
CHUGIAK Anchorage Borough
CIRCLE Yukon-Koyukuk
CLAM GULCH Kenai Peninsula Borough
CLARKS POINT Dillingham
CLEAR Denali
COFFMAN COVE Prince of Wales-Outer
   Ketchikan
COLD BAY Aleutian Islands, East
COOPER LANDING Kenai Peninsula
   Borough
COPPER CENTER Valdez-Cordova
CORDOVA Valdez-Cordova
CRAIG Prince of Wales-Outer Ketchikan
CROOKED CREEK Bethel
DEERING Northwest Arctic
DELTA JUNCTION Southeast Fairbanks
DENALI NATIONAL PARK Denali
DILLINGHAM Dillingham
DOUGLAS Juneau Borough
DUTCH HARBOR Aleutian Islands, West
EAGLE Southeast Fairbanks
EAGLE RIVER Anchorage Borough
EEK Bethel
EGEGIK Lake & Peninsula
EIELSON AFB Fairbanks North Star
   Borough
EKWOK Dillingham

ELFIN COVE Skagway-Yakutat-Angoon
ELIM Nome
ELMENDORF AFB Anchorage Borough
EMMONAK Wade Hampton
ESTER Fairbanks North Star Borough
FAIRBANKS Fairbanks North Star Borough
FALSE PASS Aleutian Islands, East
FLAT Yukon-Koyukuk
FORT RICHARDSON Anchorage Borough
FORT WAINWRIGHT Fairbanks North Star
   Borough
FORT YUKON Yukon-Koyukuk
GAKONA Valdez-Cordova
GALENA Yukon-Koyukuk
GAMBELL Nome
GIRDWOOD Anchorage Borough
GLENNALLEN Valdez-Cordova
GOODNEWS BAY Bethel
GRAYLING Yukon-Koyukuk
GUSTAVUS Skagway-Yakutat-Angoon
HAINES (99827) Haines. Borough(98),
   Yakutat(2)
HEALY Denali
HOLY CROSS Yukon-Koyukuk
HOMER Kenai Peninsula Borough
HOONAH Skagway-Yakutat-Angoon
HOOPER BAY Wade Hampton
HOPE Kenai Peninsula Borough
HOUSTON Matanuska-Susitna Borough
HUGHES Yukon-Koyukuk
HUSLIA Yukon-Koyukuk
HYDABURG Prince of Wales-Outer
   Ketchikan
HYDER Prince of Wales-Outer Ketchikan
ILIAMNA Lake & Peninsula
INDIAN Anchorage Borough
JUNEAU Juneau Borough
KAKE Wrangell-Petersburg
KAKTOVIK North Slope Borough
KALSKAG Bethel
KALTAG Yukon-Koyukuk
KARLUK Kodiak Island Borough
KASIGLUK Bethel
KASILOF Kenai Peninsula Borough
KENAI Kenai Peninsula Borough
KETCHIKAN Ketchikan Gateway Borough
KIANA Northwest Arctic
KING COVE Aleutian Islands, East
KING SALMON Bristol Bay Borough
KIPNUK Bethel
KIVALINA Northwest Arctic
KLAWOCK Prince of Wales-Outer
   Ketchikan
KOBUK Northwest Arctic
KODIAK Kodiak Island Borough
KOTLIK Wade Hampton
KOTZEBUE Northwest Arctic
KOYUK Nome
KOYUKUK Yukon-Koyukuk
KWETHLUK Bethel
KWIGILLINGOK Bethel
LAKE MINCHUMINA Yukon-Koyukuk

LARSEN BAY Kodiak Island Borough
LEVELOCK Lake & Peninsula
LOWER KALSKAG Bethel
MANLEY HOT SPRINGS Yukon-Koyukuk
MANOKOTAK Dillingham
MARSHALL Wade Hampton
MC GRATH Yukon-Koyukuk
MEKORYUK Bethel
METLAKATLA Prince of Wales-Outer
   Ketchikan
MEYERS CHUCK Prince of Wales-Outer
   Ketchikan
MINTO Yukon-Koyukuk
MOOSE PASS Kenai Peninsula Borough
MOUNTAIN VILLAGE Wade Hampton
NAKNEK Bristol Bay Borough
NAPAKIAK Bethel
NENANA Yukon-Koyukuk
NEW STUYAHOK Dillingham
NIGHTMUTE Bethel
NIKISKI Kenai Peninsula Borough
NIKOLAI Yukon-Koyukuk
NIKOLSKI Aleutian Islands, West
NINILCHIK Kenai Peninsula Borough
NOATAK Northwest Arctic
NOME Nome
NONDALTON Lake & Peninsula
NOORVIK Northwest Arctic
NORTH POLE Fairbanks North Star
   Borough
NORTHWAY Southeast Fairbanks
NUIQSUT North Slope Borough
NULATO Yukon-Koyukuk
NUNAPITCHUK Bethel
OLD HARBOR Kodiak Island Borough
OUZINKIE Kodiak Island Borough
PALMER Matanuska-Susitna Borough
PEDRO BAY Lake & Peninsula
PELICAN Skagway-Yakutat-Angoon
PERRYVILLE Lake & Peninsula
PETERSBURG Wrangell-Petersburg
PILOT POINT Lake & Peninsula
PILOT STATION Wade Hampton
PLATINUM Bethel
POINT BAKER Prince of Wales-Outer
   Ketchikan
POINT HOPE North Slope Borough
POINT LAY North Slope Borough
PORT ALEXANDER Wrangell-Petersburg
PORT ALSWORTH Lake & Peninsula
PORT HEIDEN Lake & Peninsula
PORT LIONS Kodiak Island Borough
PRUDHOE BAY North Slope Borough
QUINHAGAK Bethel
RAMPART Yukon-Koyukuk
RED DEVIL Bethel
RUBY Yukon-Koyukuk
RUSSIAN MISSION Wade Hampton
SAINT GEORGE ISLAND Aleutian Islands,
   West
SAINT MARYS Wade Hampton
SAINT MICHAEL Nome

SAINT PAUL ISLAND Aleutian Islands,
   West
SALCHA Fairbanks North Star Borough
SAND POINT Aleutian Islands, East
SAVOONGA Nome
SCAMMON BAY Wade Hampton
SELAWIK Northwest Arctic
SELDOVIA Kenai Peninsula Borough
SEWARD Kenai Peninsula Borough
SHAGELUK Yukon-Koyukuk
SHAKTOOLIK Nome
SHELDON POINT Wade Hampton
SHISHMAREF Nome
SHUNGNAK Northwest Arctic
SITKA Sitka Borough
SKAGWAY Skagway-Yakutat-Angoon
SKWENTNA Matanuska-Susitna Borough
SLEETMUTE Bethel
SOLDOTNA Kenai Peninsula Borough
SOUTH NAKNEK Bristol Bay Borough
STEBBINS Nome
STERLING Kenai Peninsula Borough
STEVENS VILLAGE Yukon-Koyukuk
SUTTON Matanuska-Susitna Borough
TAKOTNA Yukon-Koyukuk
TALKEETNA Matanuska-Susitna Borough
TANACROSS Southeast Fairbanks
TANANA Yukon-Koyukuk
TATITLEK Valdez-Cordova
TELLER Nome
TENAKEE SPRINGS Skagway-Yakutat-
   Angoon
TETLIN Southeast Fairbanks
THORNE BAY Prince of Wales-Outer
   Ketchikan
TOGIAK Dillingham
TOK Southeast Fairbanks
TOKSOOK BAY Bethel
TRAPPER CREEK Matanuska-Susitna
   Borough
TULUKSAK Bethel
TUNTUTULIAK Bethel
TUNUNAK Bethel
TWO RIVERS Fairbanks North Star
   Borough
TYONEK Kenai Peninsula Borough
UNALAKLEET Nome
UNALASKA Aleutian Islands, West
VALDEZ Valdez-Cordova
VENETIE Yukon-Koyukuk
WAINWRIGHT North Slope Borough
WALES Nome
WARD COVE Ketchikan Gateway Borough
WASILLA Matanuska-Susitna Borough
WHITE MOUNTAIN Nome
WHITTIER Valdez-Cordova
WILLOW Matanuska-Susitna Borough
WRANGELL Wrangell-Petersburg
YAKUTAT Skagway-Yakutat-Angoon

ZIP/City Cross Reference

ZIP	City	ZIP	City	ZIP	City	ZIP	City
99501-99504	ANCHORAGE	99615-99619	KODIAK	99684-99684	UNALAKLEET	99762-99762	NOME
99505-99505	FORT RICHARDSON	99620-99620	KOTLIK	99685-99685	UNALASKA	99763-99763	NOORVIK
99506-99506	ELMENDORF AFB	99621-99621	KWETHLUK	99686-99686	VALDEZ	99764-99764	NORTHWAY
99507-99524	ANCHORAGE	99622-99622	KWIGILLINGOK	99687-99687	WASILLA	99765-99765	NULATO
99540-99540	INDIAN	99624-99624	LARSEN BAY	99688-99688	WILLOW	99766-99766	POINT HOPE
99547-99547	ATKA	99625-99625	LEVELOCK	99689-99689	YAKUTAT	99767-99767	RAMPART
99548-99548	CHIGNIK LAKE	99626-99626	LOWER KALSKAG	99690-99690	NIGHTMUTE	99768-99768	RUBY
99549-99549	PORT HEIDEN	99627-99627	MC GRATH	99691-99691	NIKOLAI	99769-99769	SAVOONGA
99550-99550	PORT LIONS	99628-99628	MANOKOTAK	99692-99692	DUTCH HARBOR	99770-99770	SELAWIK
99551-99551	AKIACHAK	99630-99630	MEKORYUK	99693-99693	WHITTIER	99771-99771	SHAKTOOLIK
99552-99552	AKIAK	99631-99631	MOOSE PASS	99694-99694	HOUSTON	99772-99772	SHISHMAREF
99553-99553	AKUTAN	99632-99632	MOUNTAIN VILLAGE	99695-99695	ANCHORAGE	99773-99773	SHUNGNAK
99554-99554	ALAKANUK	99633-99633	NAKNEK	99697-99697	KODIAK	99774-99774	STEVENS VILLAGE
99555-99555	ALEKNAGIK	99634-99634	NAPAKIAK	99701-99701	FAIRBANKS	99775-99775	FAIRBANKS
99556-99556	ANCHOR POINT	99635-99635	NIKISKI	99702-99702	EIELSON AFB	99776-99776	TANACROSS
99557-99557	ANIAK	99636-99636	NEW STUYAHOK	99703-99703	FORT WAINWRIGHT	99777-99777	TANANA
99558-99558	ANVIK	99637-99637	TOKSOOK BAY	99704-99704	CLEAR	99778-99778	TELLER
99559-99559	BETHEL	99638-99638	NIKOLSKI	99705-99705	NORTH POLE	99779-99779	TETLIN
99561-99561	CHEFORNAK	99639-99639	NINILCHIK	99706-99712	FAIRBANKS	99780-99780	TOK
99563-99563	CHEVAK	99640-99640	NONDALTON	99714-99714	SALCHA	99781-99781	VENETIE
99564-99564	CHIGNIK	99641-99641	NUNAPITCHUK	99716-99716	TWO RIVERS	99782-99782	WAINWRIGHT
99565-99565	CHIGNIK LAGOON	99643-99643	OLD HARBOR	99720-99720	ALLAKAKET	99783-99783	WALES
99566-99566	CHITINA	99644-99644	OUZINKIE	99721-99721	ANAKTUVUK PASS	99784-99784	WHITE MOUNTAIN
99567-99567	CHUGIAK	99645-99645	PALMER	99722-99722	ARCTIC VILLAGE	99785-99785	BREVIG MISSION
99568-99568	CLAM GULCH	99647-99647	PEDRO BAY	99723-99723	BARROW	99786-99786	AMBLER
99569-99569	CLARKS POINT	99648-99648	PERRYVILLE	99724-99724	BEAVER	99788-99788	CHALKYITSIK
99571-99571	COLD BAY	99649-99649	PILOT POINT	99725-99725	ESTER	99789-99789	NUIQSUT
99572-99572	COOPER LANDING	99650-99650	PILOT STATION	99726-99726	BETTLES FIELD	99790-99790	FAIRBANKS
99573-99573	COPPER CENTER	99651-99651	PLATINUM	99727-99727	BUCKLAND	99791-99791	ATQASUK
99574-99574	CORDOVA	99652-99652	BIG LAKE	99729-99729	CANTWELL	99801-99811	JUNEAU
99575-99575	CROOKED CREEK	99653-99653	PORT ALSWORTH	99730-99730	CENTRAL	99820-99820	ANGOON
99576-99576	DILLINGHAM	99654-99654	WASILLA	99732-99732	CHICKEN	99821-99821	AUKE BAY
99577-99577	EAGLE RIVER	99655-99655	QUINHAGAK	99733-99733	CIRCLE	99824-99824	DOUGLAS
99578-99578	EEK	99656-99656	RED DEVIL	99734-99734	PRUDHOE BAY	99825-99825	ELFIN COVE
99579-99579	EGEGIK	99657-99657	RUSSIAN MISSION	99736-99736	DEERING	99826-99826	GUSTAVUS
99580-99580	EKWOK	99658-99658	SAINT MARYS	99737-99737	DELTA JUNCTION	99827-99827	HAINES
99581-99581	EMMONAK	99659-99659	SAINT MICHAEL	99738-99738	EAGLE	99829-99829	HOONAH
99583-99583	FALSE PASS	99660-99660	SAINT PAUL ISLAND	99739-99739	ELIM	99830-99830	KAKE
99584-99584	FLAT	99661-99661	SAND POINT	99740-99740	FORT YUKON	99832-99832	PELICAN
99585-99585	MARSHALL	99662-99662	SCAMMON BAY	99741-99741	GALENA	99833-99833	PETERSBURG
99586-99586	GAKONA	99663-99663	SELDOVIA	99742-99742	GAMBELL	99835-99835	SITKA
99587-99587	GIRDWOOD	99664-99664	SEWARD	99743-99743	HEALY	99836-99836	PORT ALEXANDER
99588-99588	GLENNALLEN	99665-99665	SHAGELUK	99744-99744	ANDERSON	99840-99840	SKAGWAY
99589-99589	GOODNEWS BAY	99666-99666	SHELDON POINT	99745-99745	HUGHES	99841-99841	TENAKEE SPRINGS
99590-99590	GRAYLING	99667-99667	SKWENTNA	99746-99746	HUSLIA	99850-99850	JUNEAU
99591-99591	SAINT GEORGE ISLAND	99668-99668	SLEETMUTE	99747-99747	KAKTOVIK	99901-99901	KETCHIKAN
99599-99599	ANCHORAGE	99669-99669	SOLDOTNA	99748-99748	KALTAG	99903-99903	MEYERS CHUCK
99602-99602	HOLY CROSS	99670-99670	SOUTH NAKNEK	99749-99749	KIANA	99918-99918	COFFMAN COVE
99603-99603	HOMER	99671-99671	STEBBINS	99750-99750	KIVALINA	99919-99919	THORNE BAY
99604-99604	HOOPER BAY	99672-99672	STERLING	99751-99751	KOBUK	99921-99921	CRAIG
99605-99605	HOPE	99674-99674	SUTTON	99752-99752	KOTZEBUE	99922-99922	HYDABURG
99606-99606	ILIAMNA	99675-99675	TAKOTNA	99753-99753	KOYUK	99923-99923	HYDER
99607-99607	KALSKAG	99676-99676	TALKEETNA	99754-99754	KOYUKUK	99925-99925	KLAWOCK
99608-99608	KARLUK	99677-99677	TATITLEK	99755-99755	DENALI NATIONAL PARK	99926-99926	METLAKATLA
99609-99609	KASIGLUK	99678-99678	TOGIAK	99756-99756	MANLEY HOT SPRINGS	99927-99927	POINT BAKER
99610-99610	KASILOF	99679-99679	TULUKSAK	99757-99757	LAKE MINCHUMINA	99928-99928	WARD COVE
99611-99611	KENAI	99680-99680	TUNTUTULIAK	99758-99758	MINTO	99929-99929	WRANGELL
99612-99612	KING COVE	99681-99681	TUNUNAK	99759-99759	POINT LAY	99950-99950	KETCHIKAN
99613-99613	KING SALMON	99682-99682	TYONEK	99760-99760	NENANA		
99614-99614	KIPNUK	99683-99683	TRAPPER CREEK	99761-99761	NOATAK		

Arizona

General Help Numbers:

Governor's Office
State Capitol, 1700 W Washington   602-542-4331
Phoenix, AZ 85007   Fax 602-542-1381
http://www.governor.state.az.us   8AM-5PM

Attorney General's Office
1275 W Washington   602-542-5025
Phoenix, AZ 85007   Fax 602-542-4085
http://www.attorney_general.state.az.us   8AM-5PM

State Court Administrator
Arizona Supreme Court Bldg   602-542-9301
1501 W Washington   Fax 602-542-9484
Phoenix, AZ 85007-3231   8AM-5PM
http://www.supreme.state.az.us/aoc

State Archives
1700 W Washington, Room 342   602-542-4159
Phoenix, AZ 85007   Fax 602-542-4402
http://www.dlapr.lib.az.us/archives   8AM-5PM

State Specifics:

Capital: Phoenix
                                   Maricopa County

Time Zone: MST

Number of Counties: 15

Population: 5,130,632

Web Site: http://azportal.clearlake.ibm.com/webapp/portal

State Agencies

Criminal Records

Department of Public Safety, Applicant Team One, PO Box 18430//Mail Code 2250, Phoenix, AZ 85005-8430 (Courier: 2320 N 20th Ave, Phoenix, AZ 85005); 602-223-2223, 8AM-5PM.

http://www.dps.state.az.us

Note: Address requests to Applicant Team One. Sex offender data is available online at www.azsexoffender.com.

Indexing & Storage: Records are available from 1988.

Searching: Record access is limited to agencies that have specific authorization by law including

employers or pre-employment search firms located in AZ. Fingerprints are needed for a search. Include the following in your request-full set of fingerprints plus demographic information on the applicant.

Access by: mail.

Fee & Payment: The fee is $6.00 per name. Fee payee: Department of Public Safety. Only cashier's checks and money orders accepted. No credit cards accepted.

Mail search: Turnaround time: 2 to 3 days. Arizona employers may call 602-223-2223 to

request fingerprint cards and forms.No self addressed stamped envelope is required.

Corporation Records
Limited Liability Company Records

Corporation Commission, 1300 W Washington, Phoenix, AZ 85007; 602-542-3026 (Status), 602-542-3285 (Annual Reports), 602-542-3414 (Fax), 8AM-5PM.

http://www.cc.state.az.us

Note: Fictitious Name & Assumed Name records are found at the county level.

Indexing & Storage: Records are available from 1809 on. You must go through this office for records. If copies are needed for historical records, it can take as long as 4 to 6 weeks due to the filming process. It takes after 2-3 months before new records are available for inquiry. Records are indexed on microfiche, inhouse computer, microfilm.

Searching: Include the following in your request-full name of business, specific records that you need copies of. In addition to the articles of incorporation, corporation records include the following information: Annual Reports, Officers, Directors, Prior (Merged) Names, Inactive and Reserved Names.

Access by: mail, phone, fax, in person, online.

Fee & Payment: There is no charge for a search. Copies cost $.50 per page. Fee payee: Arizona Corporation Commission. Prepayment required. Phone and fax orders require deposit accounts. Personal checks accepted. No credit cards accepted.

Mail search: Turnaround time: 3 to 5 days. Enclose a check marked "Not to exceed $20."A self addressed stamped envelope is requested.

Phone search: Phone requests are limited to 3 inquiries per call.

Fax search: Established accounts may fax multiple requests per day. There is an additional charge of $.50 per page.

In person search: Turnaround time is while you wait for up to 5 corporate names.

Online search: The web site provides free access to all corporation information.

Expedited service: Expedited service is available for mail, phone and in person searches. Turnaround time: 24 hours. Add $35.00 per request. The fee applies to large orders that must be completed within 24 hours. Generally, smaller orders or single document orders do not require this fee.

Fictitious Name
Assumed Name
Records not maintained by a state level agency.

Note: Records are found at the county level.

Trademarks/Servicemarks
Trade Names
Limited Partnership Records

Secretary of State, Trademarks/Tradenames/ Limited Partnership Division, 1700 W Washington, 7th Floor, Phoenix, AZ 85007; 602-542-6187, 602-542-7386 (Fax), 8AM-5PM.

http://www.sosaz.com

Indexing & Storage: Records are available from 1984 to present on computer. It takes 1 to 3 days before new records are available for inquiry.

Searching: Provide the entity name, owner name or file number to search.

Access by: mail, phone, in person.

Fee & Payment: There is no search fee, but certification is $3.00 plus the copy fee of $.10 per page. Fee payee: Secretary of State. Prepayment

required. Personal checks accepted. No credit cards accepted.

Mail search: Turnaround time: 1 to 3 days. Trademarks may take longer.A self addressed stamped envelope is requested.

Phone search: They will give general information at no charge over the phone for up to 3 searches, such as owner's name, date of application, mailing address & expiration date.

In person search: If there are more than 5 pages of copy, service is overnight. You may view microfiche at no charge.

Other access: Bulk purchase is available on microfiche.

Expedited service: Expedited service is available for mail, phone and in person searches. Add $25.00 per filing.

Uniform Commercial Code
Federal Tax Liens
State Tax Liens

UCC Division, Secretary of State, State Capitol, West Wing, 7th Floor, Phoenix, AZ 85007; 602-542-6178, 602-542-7386 (Fax), 8AM - 5PM.

http://www.sosaz.com

Indexing & Storage: Records are available from 3/80 to present on microfiche and from 06/95 to present on the Internet.

Searching: Use search request form UCC-3. The search includes tax liens recorded here. Please note that tax liens recorded on individuals may be filed at the county level and not here. Include the following in your request-debtor name.

Access by: mail, phone, fax, in person, online.

Fee & Payment: The search fee is $6.00 per debtor name, except via the web which is no charge. Copies are $.10 each. Fee payee: Secretary of State. Prepayment required. Personal checks accepted. No credit cards accepted.

Mail search: Turnaround time: 5 days.

Phone search: Records are available by phone.

Fax search: Records are available by fax.

Online search: UCC records can be searched for free over the web site. Searching can be done by debtor, secured party name, or file number. From this site you can also pull down a weekly microfiche file of filings (about 10 megabytes).

Other access: E-mail requests are accepted. Microfilm of filings is available for purchase.

Expedited service: Expedited service is available for mail and phone searches. Turnaround time: same day if possible. Add $25.00 per package.

Sales Tax Registrations

Revenue Department, Taxpayer Assistance, 1600 W Monroe, Phoenix, AZ 85007; 602-542-4656, 602-542-4772 (Fax), 8AM-5PM.

http://www.state.az.us/dor

Indexing & Storage: Records are available from 1980.

Searching: This agency will only confirm that a business is registered and whether it is active. It will provide no other information without a power of attorney. Include the following in your request-business name. The tax permit number is very helpful.

Access by: mail, phone, in person.

Mail search: A self addressed stamped envelope is requested. No fee for mail request.

Phone search: No fee for telephone request.

In person search: No fee for request.

Birth Certificates

Department of Health Services, Vital Records Section, PO Box 3887, Phoenix, AZ 85030 (Courier: 2727 W Glendale Ave, Phoenix, AZ 85051); 602-255-3260, 602-364-1300 (Recording), 602-249-3040 (Fax), 8AM-5PM.

http://www.hs.state.az.us/vitalrcd/index.htm

Indexing & Storage: Records are available from late 1800's to present. Records are computerized from 1950 to present. Records are indexed on file folders.

Searching: Must by 18 years of age or older to request a record and be the person named or that person's parent or legal guardian. Records 75 years or older available to the public for a $2.00 fee. Include the following in your request-full name, names of parents, mother's maiden name, date of birth, place of birth, relationship to person of record, reason for information request. A certificate of birth resulting in stillbirth is available as of 08/09/2001.

Access by: mail, fax, in person.

Fee & Payment: Bring a government issued picture ID (or send a copy) with signature. For birth records prior to 1950, the fee for a certified photo copy is $9.00. For birth records after 1950, the fee for a certified computerized copy is $6.00. Fee payee: Vital Records Section. Prepayment required. Credit cards accepted: MasterCard, Visa, AmEx, Discover.

Mail search: Turnaround time: 2 weeks. No self addressed stamped envelope is required.

Fax search: Include the following additional information on the request: copy of government ID with your signature, return address, phone #, credit card #, and expiration date. Fee is $5.00 plus cost of copy. Turnaround time is 2 days.

In person search: Turnaround time is usually less than 1 hour.

Expedited service: Expedited service is available for mail and phone searches. Turnaround time: 1 day. The agency will not accept expedited requests over the phone. They must be sent by fax. There is $17.50 fee to have the results returned by Federal Express. Use of credit card required.

Death Records

Department of Health Services, Vital Records Section, PO Box 3887, Phoenix, AZ 85030 (Courier: 2727 W Glendale Ave, Phoenix, AZ 85051); 602-255-3260, 602-364-1300 (Recording), 602-249-3040 (Fax), 8AM-5PM.

http://www.hs.state.az.us/vitalrcd/index.htm

Indexing & Storage: Records are available from late 1800's to present. New records are available for inquiry immediately. Records are indexed on file folders.

Searching: Must have notarized release from immediate family. Only immediate family, attorney or funeral director acting for immediate family can get records. Records 50 years or older are available to the public for a $2.00 fee. Include the following in your request-full name, date of death, place of death, relationship to person of record, reason for information request. Send a copy of your ID or your signature must be notarized.

Access by: mail, fax, in person.

Fee & Payment: There is no search fee, but there is a certification fee of $6.00. Fee payee: Vital Records Section. Prepayment required. Personal checks accepted. Credit cards accepted: MasterCard, Visa, AmEx, Discover.

Mail search: Turnaround time: 2 weeks. A self addressed stamped envelope is requested.

Fax search: Include the following additional information on the request: copy of government ID with signature, return address, phone #, credit card #, and expiration date. Fee is $5.00 for processing/handling. Certification fee is $6.00.

In person search: Turnaround time is usually 30-50 minutes.

Expedited service: Expedited service is available for fax searches. Include your Fed Ex number. Expedited service is by fax only (must use credit card), the agency will not accept phone requests. Use of credit card required.

Marriage Certificates
Divorce Records
Records not maintained by a state level agency.

Note: These records are not available from the state.

they must be requested from the county or court of issue.

Workers' Compensation Records

State Compensation Fund, 3031 N Second St, Phoenix, AZ 85012; 602-631-2000, 602-631-2213 (Fax), 8AM-5PM.

http://www.statefund.com

Indexing & Storage: Records are available from 1926 on. New records are available for inquiry immediately. Records are indexed on microfilm, inhouse computer.

Searching: Records that are closed or inactive are stored on microfilm. All active records are on the in-house computer. Claim and policy records are confidential, but you can get claim records with release form from claimant. Most other records are public. Include the following in your request-claimant name, Social Security Number, claim number. Requester must have signed release from claimant or policyholder prior to obtaining confidential records. Copies of legal, claims, and policy working files are not released otherwise.

Access by: mail, in person.

Fee & Payment: Copies are $.25 per page. There is no search fee. Fee payee: State Compensation Fund. Requesters will be billed. Personal checks accepted. No credit cards accepted.

Mail search: Turnaround time: 1 to 2 weeks. No self addressed stamped envelope is required.

Driver Records

Motor Vehicle Division, Record Services Section, PO Box 2100, Mail Drop 539M, Phoenix, AZ 85001-2100 (Courier: Customer Records Services, 1801 W Jefferson, Rm 111, Phoenix, AZ 85007); 602-255-0072, 8AM-5PM.

http://www.dot.state.az.us/MVD/mvd.htm

Note: Arizona will suspend the license for unpaid out-of-state tickets.

Indexing & Storage: Records are available for either a thirty-nine month record or for a five-year record. CDL records may be available for ten years. It takes 2 weeks before new records are available for inquiry.

Searching: Any person requesting a motor vehicle record shall identify himself and state the reason for the request. ID may be required. Certain requesters, identified by law, are labeled as "exempt" (generally, in line with DPPA requirements). Include the following in your request-full name, date of birth, driver's license number. Exempt requesters need only supply 2 out of the 3 items required to search. The driver's mailing address is provided as part of the record to exempt requesters.

Access by: mail, in person, online.

Fee & Payment: The current fees are $3 for 39 month records and $5 for certified 5 year records. Insurers may only receive the 39 month record. All non-exempt requests must be signed and notarized. Fee payee: Motor Vehicle Division, Record Services. Prepayment required. Personal checks accepted. No credit cards accepted.

Mail search: Turnaround time: 1 week to 10 days. If express mail is requested, then envelope must be pre-paid. If mail requester is not DPPA permissible, the requester's signature must be notarized. No self addressed stamped envelope is required.

In person search: There is a limit of 4 requests for immediate service.

Online search: Arizona's online system is interactive and open 24 hours daily. Fee is $3.00 per record. This system is primarily for those requesters who are exempt. For more information call 602-712-7235.

Other access: Overnight magnetic tape-to-tape ordering is available.

Vehicle Ownership
Vehicle Identification

Motor Vehicle Division, Record Services Section, PO Box 2100, Mail Drop 504M, Phoenix, AZ 85001-2100 (Courier: Customer Records Services, 1801 W Jefferson, Rm 111, Phoenix, AZ 85007); 602-255-0072, 8AM-5PM.

http://www.dot.state.az.us/MVD/mvd.htm

Indexing & Storage: Records are available for 5 years to present. It takes 2 weeks before new records are available for inquiry.

Searching: The record searcher must state the reason for the request and have his/her signature notarized. Records are not given by merely giving a plate license number or a name for ownership searches. The vehicle's owner, VIN, and plate number must be submitted to receive a vehicle history.

Access by: mail, fax, in person, online.

Fee & Payment: The fee is $3.00, $2.00 if walk-in is willing to pick up the next day, and $5.00 if the record is certified. Fee payee: Motor Vehicle Division. Prepayment required. Money orders and checks are accepted through the mail. Walk-ins may pay with cash. Personal checks accepted. No credit cards accepted.

Mail search: Turnaround time: 1 week to 10 days. A self addressed stamped envelope is requested.

Fax search: Ongoing, permissible users may have requests returned by fax, usually next day service, for an additional fee of $2.00 per record.

In person search: You may request information in person.

Online search: Online access is offered to permissible users. Fee is $3.00 per record. The system is open 24 hours a day, seven days a week. For more information, call 602-712-7235.

Accident Reports

Department of Public Safety, Accident Reports, PO Box 6638, Phoenix, AZ 85005 (Courier: 2102 W Encanto, 1st Floor, Phoenix, AZ 85005-6638), 602-223-2230, 8AM-5PM.

Indexing & Storage: It takes 2 weeks before new records are available for inquiry. Records are indexed on inhouse computer.

Searching: A written request is required and the requester must state his/her connection to the incident. Include the following in your request-relationship to person of record, date of accident, location of accident, full name, report number.

Access by: mail, in person.

Fee & Payment: The fee is $9.00 per record. Fee payee: Department of Public Safety. Prepayment required; business check or money order. No credit cards or personal checks accepted.

Mail search: Turnaround time: 1 week to 14 days. A self addressed stamped envelope is requested. No fee for mail request.

In person search: Turnaround time is while you wait.

Vessel Ownership
Vessel Registration

Game & Fish Dept, 2222 W Greenway Rd, Phoenix, AZ 85023-4399; 602-942-3000, 602-789-3729 (Fax), 8AM-5PM M-F.

http://www.azgf.com

Note: Lien information is recorded at the county level. Maricopa County has some liens from other counties.

Indexing & Storage: Records are available from 1977 to present. Records are indexed on computer for the last 5 years. No titles are issued. All watercraft must be registered unless they are non-motorized.

Searching: To search, the following information is required: Arizona #, hull ID, owner's name, and a picture ID.

Access by: mail, phone, fax, in person.

Fee & Payment: There is no search fee.

Mail search: Turnaround time is within 30 days. No self addressed stamped envelope is required.

Phone search: Only lawyers, private investigators, boat owners, and government representatives can search by phone or fax.

Fax search: Same criteria as phone searching.

In person search: Turnaround time is normally immediate.

Legislation Records

Arizona Legislature, State Senate - Room 203, 1700 W Washington, Phoenix, AZ 85007 (Courier: Senate Wing or, House Wing, Phoenix, AZ 85007); 602-542-3559 (Senate Information), 602-542-4221 (House Information), 602-542-3429 (Senate Fax), 602-542-3550 (Senate Resource Ctr), 602-542-4099 (Fax), 8AM-5PM.

http://www.azleg.state.az.us

Note: The phone number provides information on current session bills and on some previous bills.

Indexing & Storage: Records are available from 1969 to 1989 on microfilm for bill files. Committee minutes are available from 1967 to present on hard copy.

Searching: Include the following in your request- bill number, year.

Access by: mail, fax, in person, online.

Fee & Payment: Copies are $.10 per page. Fee payee: State Senate or House of Representatives. Prepayment is requested for large photocopying projects. Personal checks accepted. No credit cards accepted.

Mail search: Turnaround time: 1 day. All research requests are processed ASAP, determined by the demands of the legislative sessions on the staff.No self addressed stamped envelope is required. No fee for mail request.

Fax search: Fee is $.10 per page, with a turnaround time of 1 day or sooner.

In person search: No fee for request. A desk is provided for reviewing files, reading minutes, etc. Staff will assist if time and workload permits.

Online search: Most information, beginning with 1997, is available through the Internet (i.e. bill text, committee minutes, committee assignments, member bios, etc.). There is no fee.

Other access: Name, address, and office # lists are available at no charge. Roll call vote histories of individuals per year are available at $.10 per page.

Voter Registration
Access to Records is Restricted

Secretary of State, Election Division, 1700 W Washington, 7th Floor, Phoenix, AZ 85007.

http://www.sosaz.com

Note: Records are maintained at the county recorder offices. Records are permitted to be sold in bulk only for political related purposes. Go to the county level to can confirm names on a single inquiry basis.

GED Certificates

Department of Education, GED Testing, 1535 W Jefferson, Phoenix, AZ 85007; 602-542-5802, 602-542-1161 (Fax), 8AM-5PM.

http://www.ade.az.gov/adult-ed

Indexing & Storage: Records are available from 1945 to present. It takes 3 to 4 weeks before new records are available for inquiry.

Searching: Include the following in your request- date of birth, Social Security Number, signed release, year of test and test site. All requests must be in writing, all require student signature.

Access by: mail, fax, in person.

Fee & Payment: There is no fee for either a verification or a copy of transcript.

Mail search: Turnaround time: 5 to 7 days. No self addressed stamped envelope is required. No fee for mail request.

Fax search: Same criteria as mail searching.

In person search: No fee for request.

Hunting License Information
Fishing License Information

Game & Fish Department, Information & Licensing Division, 2221 W Greenway Rd, Phoenix, AZ 85023-4399; 602-942-3000, 602-789-3924 (Fax), 8AM-5PM.

http://www.azgfd.com

Note: This agency will also release watercraft registration information within specific legal constraints.

Indexing & Storage: Records are available for past 3 years.

Searching: Records are not available to the public except as a mailing list. They will release certain data to attorneys for pending litigation.

Access by: mail.

Fee & Payment: Prepayment required. Fee payee: Arizona Game & Fish. Personal checks accepted. Credit cards accepted: MasterCard, Visa.

Mail search: Turnaround time: variable. Must complete a request form.No self addressed stamped envelope is required.

Other access: There is a program to purchase the database or portions of. You can get 3 years of approximately 160,000 to 190,000 names for $.05 per name, which includes addresses. This is available for commercial purposes only. Lists are completed within 30 days.

Arizona State Licensing Agencies

Licenses Searchable Online

Advance Fee Loan Broker #05 ....www.azbanking.com/ListsofLicensees.htm
Architect #29 ....www.btr.state.az.us
Assayer #29 ....www.btr.state.az.us
Attorney #30 ....www.azbar.org/MemberFinder
Bank #05 ....www.azbanking.com/ListsofLicensees.htm
Bank #00 ....www.azbanking.com/Lists/BA_List.HTML
Behavioral Health Emerg./Residential Svc #47..www.hs.state.az.us/als/databases/index.html
Behavioral Outpatient Clinic #47 ....www.hs.state.az.us/als/databases/index.html
Behavioral Outpatient Rehab Center #47 ....www.hs.state.az.us/als/databases/index.html
Charity #71 ....www.sosaz.com/scripts/Charity_Search_engine.cgi
Collection Agency #05 ....www.azbanking.com/ListsofLicensees.htm
Consumer Lender #05 ....www.azbanking.com/ListsofLicensees.htm
Contractor #70...www.rc.state.az.us/AZROCLicenseQuery
Counselor, Professional #10 ....http://aspin.asu.edu/~azbbhe/directory/listing.html
Court Reporter #00 ....www.supreme.state.az.us/cr/CRcertlist2001.htm
Credit Union #05...www.azbanking.com/ListsofLicensees.htm
Day Care Establishment #45...........................www.hs.state.az.us/als/databases/index.html
Debt Management #05 ....www.azbanking.com/ListsofLicensees.htm
Engineer #29 ....www.btr.state.az.us
Escrow Agent #05..www.azbanking.com/ListsofLicensees.htm
Funeral Pre-Need Trust Company #05 ....www.azbanking.com/ListsofLicensees.htm
Geologist #29 ....www.btr.state.az.us
Hearing Aid Dispenser #49 ....www.hs.state.az.us/als/databases/index.html
Home Inspector #29 ....www.btr.state.az.us
Landscape Architect #29.................................www.btr.state.az.us
Liquor Producer/Wholesaler #52......................www.azll.com/query.htm
Liquor Retail Co-Operative/Agent/Manager #52www.azll.com/query.htm
Lobbyist #71...www.sosaz.com/scripts/lobbyist_engine.cgi
Marriage & Family Therapist #10 ....http://aspin.asu.edu/~azbbhe/directory/listing.html
Medical Doctor #17...www.docboard.org/az/df/azsearch.htm
Money Transmitter #05 ....www.azbanking.com/ListsofLicensees.htm
Mortgage Banker, Commercial #05 ....www.azbanking.com/ListsofLicensees.htm
Mortgage Banker/Broker #05 ....www.azbanking.com/ListsofLicensees.htm
Motor Vehicle Dealer/Sales Finance #05 ....www.azbanking.com/ListsofLicensees.htm
Notary Public #71 ....www.sosaz.com/scripts/Notary_Search_engine.cgi
Optometrist #22..www.odfinder.org/LicSearch.asp
Pawn Shop #00 ....www.azbanking.com/Lists/DPC_List.HTML
Pesticide Company #72 ....www.sb.state.az.us/pdf/codir.pdf
Physician Assistant #18...................................www.docboard.org/az/df/azsearch.htm
Premium Finance Company #05.......................www.azbanking.com/ListsofLicensees.htm
Property Tax Agent #08 ....www.appraisal.state.az.us/Directory/taxagent.html
Psychologist #27 ....www.goodnet.com/~azbpe/dir.html
Public Accountant-CPA #07 ....www.accountancy.state.az.us/Aug%2000%20CPA%20LIST.htm
Public Accounting Firm-CPA/PA #07 ....www.accountancy.state.az.us
Real Estate Appraiser #08 ....www.appraisal.state.az.us/Directory/appr1.html
Real Estate Broker/Salesperson #55 ....www.re.state.az.us/db.html
Real Estate Firm #55 ....www.re.state.az.us/db.html
Sales Finance Company #05 ....www.azbanking.com/ListsofLicensees.htm
Social Worker #10 ....http://aspin.asu.edu/~azbbhe/directory/listing.html
Substance Abuse Counselor #10 ....http://aspin.asu.edu/~azbbhe/directory/listing.html
Surveyor #29 ....www.btr.state.az.us
Telemarketing Firm #71 ....www.sosaz.com/scripts/TS_Search_engine.cgi
Trust Company #05 ....www.azbanking.com/ListsofLicensees.htm
Trust Division (of Chartered Fin. Institution) #05www.azbanking.com/ListsofLicensees.htm

Licensing Quick Finder

Acupuncturist #11 602-255-1444
Adult Care Home Manager #68 602-542-3095
Advance Fee Loan Broker #05 602-255-4421
Aesthetician #12 480-784-4539
Aesthetics Instructor #12 480-784-4539
Agricultural Aircraft Pilot #33......602-542-0904
Agricultural Grower Permit #33......602-542-0904
Agricultural Grower/Seller #33 602-542-0904
Agricultural Pest Control Advisor #33....602-542-0904
Agricultural Seller Permit #33 602-542-0904
Air Pollution Source #39......602-207-2338
Air Quality Permit #65 602-506-6970
Aircraft Dealer for Wreckers or Salvage #57...... 602-294-9144
Aircraft Dealer/Retail #57......602-294-9144
Aircraft Manufacturer/Importer/Dist./Transporter #57 602-294-9144
Aircraft Owner #57 602-294-9144
Aircraft Pilot Trainer School/Instructor #57 602-294-9144
Aircraft Use Fuel Dealer/Mfg. #56......602-542-4565
Ambulance Service #48......602-861-0809
Ambulatory Surgical Center #43 602-674-9750
Amusement Park #56......602-542-4565
Amusement Printing & Advertising #56 .602-542-4565
Appraiser, Real/Personal Property #56 .602-542-4565
Aquifer Protection Permit #41 602-207-4743
Architect #29......602-255-4053
Assayer #29......602-255-4053
Assisted Living Facility #49......602-674-4340
Attorney #30 602-252-4804
Audiologist #49 602-674-4340
Bank #05 602-255-4421
Barber School/Instruction #09......602-542-4498
Barber/Barber Shop #09......602-542-4498
Bathing Place #65......602-506-6970
Bedding/Furniture Manufacturer #65......602-506-6970
Behavioral Health Emergency/Residential Service #47 602-674-4300
Behavioral Outpatient Clinic #47......602-674-4300
Behavioral Outpatient Rehab Ctr #47....602-674-4300
Bingo Operation #56......602-542-4565
Bondsman (Insurance) #51 602-912-8470
Bone Densitometer Operator #66 602-255-4845 x242
Bottled Water Processor #65......602-506-6970
Boxer #03......602-542-1417
Boxing Professional #03......602-542-1417
Campground Membership Broker/Salesman #55 602-468-1414
Cannabis & Controlled Substance Dealer #56...... 602-542-4565
Cemetery Broker/Salesman #55......602-468-1414
Charity #71 602-542-6670
Child Adoption Agency #37 602-542-2287
Child Foster Home #37......602-542-2287
Child Placing Agency #37......602-542-2375
Child Residential & Shelter Care #37 602-542-2287
Chiropractor #11 602-255-1444
Citrus Fruit Broker/Dealer/Packer/Shipper #35 602-542-0943
Clinical Laboratory #44......602-255-3454
Collection Agency #05......602-255-4421
Commercial Leasing #56......602-542-4565
Consumer Lender #05......602-255-4421
Contractor #70......602-542-1525
Cosmetologist #12 480-784-4539
Cosmetology Instructor #12......480-784-4539
Cosmetology or Nail Technology Salon or School #12 480-784-4539
Counselor, Professional #10......602-542-1851
Credit Union #05 602-255-4421
Day Care Establishment #45 602-674-4220
Debt Management #05......602-255-4421
Degree Program #06......602-542-5709
Dental Assistant #13 602-242-1492
Dental Hygienist #13......602-242-1492
Dentist #13 602-242-1492
Denturist #13 602-242-1492
Detoxification Service #47......602-674-4300
Developmentally Disabled Group Home #49 602-674-4340
Dog Racing Kennel #54......602-277-1704
Drug Manufacturer #24......602-255-5125
Drug Wholesaler #24......602-255-5125
Dry Well Registration #41......602-207-4696
DUI Education Agency #47......602-674-4300
DUI Screening/Treatment Agency #47 ..602-674-4300
Elementary & Special Education Teacher #38...... 602-542-4368
Embalmer #15 602-542-3095
Emergency Medical Technician #48......602-861-1188
Emergency Medical Technician Instructor #48 602-861-1188
Emergency Response Div. #66.... 602-255-4845 x239
Engineer #29 602-255-4053
Environmental Laboratory #44......602-255-3454
Escrow Agent #05......602-255-4421
Falconer #59......602-942-3000
Family Day Care Home #37......602-542-2287
Feed & Fertilizer #33......602-542-0904
Feed Distribution, Commercial #34 602-242-0814
Feed, Wholesale #56 602-542-4565
Fertilizer Distribution, Commercial #34..602-253-0949
Field Trial License #59 602-942-3000
Food Establishment #65......602-506-6970
Food Packer/Grower/Shipper, Contract #35...... 602-542-0943
Foster Care Home #49......602-674-4340
Fruit/Vegetable Broker/Dealer #35......602-542-0943
Funeral Director #15......602-542-3095
Funeral Pre-Need Trust Company #05..602-255-4421
Fur Dealer #59......602-942-3000
Game Farm, Private #59 602-942-3000
Game Resident Guide #59 602-942-3000
Geologist #29......602-255-4053
Groom #54......602-277-1704
Guidance Counselor #38......602-542-4368
Hazardous Waste Facility #40 602-207-4197
Headstart Facility #45......602-674-4220
Hearing Aid Dispenser #49......602-674-4340
Home Health Agency #43......602-674-9750
Home Inspector #29......602-255-4053
Homeopathic Physician #16 602-542-3095
Horse or Greyhound Racing #54......602-277-1704
Horse Owner #54 602-277-1704
Horse Trainer #54 602-277-1704
Hospice #43......602-674-9750
Hospital #43......602-674-9750
Hotel/Motel/Tourist Court #65 602-506-6970
Hunting & Fishing License Dealer #59 ..602-942-3000
Industrial Laser #66...... 602-255-4845 x237
Infirmary #43......602-674-9750
Insurance Agent #51 602-912-8470
Insurance Broker P&C only #51......602-912-8470
Intern & Resident #17......480-551-2700
Investment Advisor Rep. #32......602-542-0678
Investment Advisors #32 602-542-0678
Jockey #54 602-277-1704
Landscape Architect #29 602-255-4053
Laser Light Show #56......602-255-4845
Laser, Medical #66...... 602-255-4845 x237
Lay Midwife #50......602-364-1400
Liquor Producer #52......602-542-5141
Liquor Retail Co-Operative/Agent/Manager (Retail) #52 602-542-5141
Liquor Wholesaler #52......602-542-5141
Lobbyist #71 602-542-0229
Long-Term Care Facilities #49......602-674-4340
Lottery Retailer #04......480-921-4400
Marriage & Family Therapist #10 602-542-1851
Medical Doctor #17 480-551-2700
Medical Facility #49......602-674-4340
Mental Health Screening/Evaluation/Treatment #47 602-674-4300
Mining #56......602-542-4565
Mining Elevator/Diesel #67 602-542-5971
Mining Operator/Start-up #67 602-542-5971
Minnow Dealer #59 602-942-3000
Mobile Home Dealer/Broker/Salesperson #36 ...... 602-255-4072 x251
Mobile Home Installer/Mfg. #36 ... 602-255-4072 x251
Money Transmitter #05......602-255-4421
Mortgage Banker, Commercial #05......602-255-4421
Mortgage Banker/Broker #05......602-255-4421
Motor Vehicle Dealer/Sales Finance #05...... 602-255-4421
MRI License #66...... 602-255-4845 x237
Nail Technician #12......480-784-4539
Nail Technology Instructor #12 480-784-4539
Naturopathic Physician #19......602-542-8242
Notary Public #71......602-542-4086
Nuclear Medicine Tech. #66...... 602-255-4845 x242
Nurse-LPN #20 602-331-8111
Nurse-RN #20......602-331-8111
Nurses' Aide #20......602-331-8111
Nursing Care Institution Administrator #68 602-255-3095
Occupational Therapist/Assistant #21 ...602-589-8352
Oil & Gas Production #56 602-542-4565
Optical Establishment #14......602-542-3095
Optician #14......602-542-3095
Optometrist #22 602-542-3095
Osteopathic Physician #23 ...... 480-657-7703 x21
Out-Patient Surgical Center/Out-Patient Treatment Clinic #43......602-674-9750
P & C Broker #51 602-912-8470
P & C Managing Agent, & Life/Dis #51..602-912-8470
Pesticide Applicator #33 602-542-0904
Pesticide Applicator/Supervisor/Advisor #72 602-255-3664
Pesticide Company #72......602-255-3664
Pesticide Distribution #34......602-253-0949
Pesticide Qualifying Party #72......602-255-3664
Pharmacist #24......602-255-5125
Pharmacy Intern #24......602-255-5125
Physical Therapist #25......602-542-3095
Physical Therapist Assistant #25 602-542-3095
Physician Assistant #18......602-255-3751 x7103
Physician Assistant #17......480-551-2700
Physiotherapist #11......602-255-1444
Pipeline #56......602-542-4565
Plant Operator #41......602-207-4643
Podiatrist #26......602-542-3095
Pollutant Discharge Permit #41......602-207-4665
Post-Secondary Vocational Program, Private #06 602-542-5709
Premium Finance Company #05......602-255-4421
Preschool #45......602-674-4220
Private Car, Rail & Aircraft #56......602-542-4565
Private Investigator #53......602-223-2361
Property Broker #51......602-912-8470
Property Tax Agent #08......602-542-1539
Psychiatric Unit #47......602-674-4300
Psychologist #27......602-542-8162
Public Accountant-CPA #07......602-255-3648
Public Accounting Firm-CPA/PA #07 602-255-3648
Publishing #56 602-542-4565
Radiation Machine Possession Facility #66...... 602-255-4845 x231
Radiation Therapy Tech #66...... 602-255-4845 x242
Radioactive Mat. Possessor #66.. 602-255-4845 x227
Radioactive Materials Lab #66..... 602-255-4845 x246
Radiologic Technologist #66...... 602-255-4845 x242
Radiology Practical Tech. #66 ..... 602-255-4845 x242
Radon Mitigation Specialist #66... 602-255-4845 x244

Real Estate Appraiser #08 602-542-1539
Real Estate Broker/Salesperson #55 602-468-1414
Real Estate Division #62 602-542-1704
Real Estate Firm #55............................602-468-1414
Real Estate School/Instructor/Course #55.................
....602-468-1414
Rehabilitation Agency #43 602-674-9750
Rehabilitation Unit #47 602-674-4300
Renal Disease Facility #43 602-674-9750
Rental of Personal Property #56 602-542-4565
Respiratory Therapist #28 602-542-5995
Restaurant/Bar #56................................602-542-4565
Retail Sales Outlet #56...........................602-542-4565
Risk Management Company #51 602-912-8470
Sales Finance Company #05...................602-255-4421
Sanitarian #46..602-230-5911
School Bus Driver #01............................602-223-2646
School Bus Driver Instructor #01............602-223-2646
School Librarian #38 602-542-4368
School Psychologist/Psychometrist #38 602-542-4368
School Superintendent #38 602-542-4368
School Supervisor #38 602-542-4368
Scientific Collector #59 602-942-3000
Securities Dealer #32.............................602-542-0678
Securities Salesperson #32....................602-542-0678
Security Guard #53 602-223-2361
Self Insured Employer #60 602-542-1836
Sewage, Sludge & Septic Pumping Vehicle #40 ....
....602-207-4123

Shooting Preserve License #59 602-942-3000
Social Worker #10..................................602-542-1851
Solid Waste Facility #40 602-207-4123
Speech-Language Pathologist #49 602-674-4340
Spray Process Applicator/Sterilizer/Renovator #65
....602-506-6970
Subdivision Public Report #55 602-468-1414
Substance Abuse Counselor #10...........602-542-1851
Substance Abuse Treatment Svc. #47 ..602-674-4300
Surety #51 602-912-8470
Surplus Line Broker #51 602-912-8470
Surveyor #29 602-255-4053
Tanning Facility #66 .... 602-255-4845 x237
Taxidermist #59 602-942-3000
Teacher, Community College #31 602-255-5582
Telemarketing Firm #71..........................602-542-6670
Timbering #56...602-542-4565
Timeshare Public Report #55 602-468-1414
Tobacco Products Distributor #56 602-542-4565
Trailer Coach Park #65...........................602-506-6970
Transporting & Towing Company #56 ...602-542-4565
Travel Agent, Limited #51......................602-912-8470
Trust Company #05.................................602-255-4421
Trust Division (of Chartered Financial Institution) #05
....602-255-4421
Vehicle Emission-Fleet Inspection Station #42 ....
....602-207-7011
Vehicle Emission-Fleet Inspector #42 ...602-207-7011
Vendor/Concession on State Park Land #69 ....

....602-542-2155
Veterinary Medicine & Surgery #73.......602-542-3095
Veterinary Premise (Hospital) #73 602-542-3095
Veterinary Technician #73 602-542-3095
Vocational Rehabilitation #61 602-542-3294
Waste Water Collection, Treatment, Construction #41
....602-207-4692
Waste Water Facility Operator #41 602-207-4625
Waste Water Reuse #41 602-207-4464
Water Distribution System Operator #41 ....
....602-207-4643
Water Quality Certification #41 602-207-4625
Water Rights Assignment #58 602-417-2405
Water Transporter (out of state) #58 602-417-2405
Watercraft Registration Agent #59 602-942-3000
Weighmaster, Public #02........................602-255-5211
Weights & Measures Rep./Service Agency #02..........
....602-255-5211
Well Drilling Firm #58 ....602-417-2470 x 7141
Well Registration/Construction #58 602-417-2405
White Amor Stocking License #59 602-942-3000
Wildlife Hobby License #59 602-942-3000
Wildlife Holding Permit #59....................602-942-3000
Wildlife Rehab/Service License #59 602-942-3000
X-ray Supplier #66 .... 602-255-4845 x231
Zoo #59 602-942-3000

Licensing Agency Information

#01 Department of Public Safety, PO Box 6638 - Mail Drop 1250, Phoenix, AZ 85005-6638; 602-223-2646, Fax: 602-223-2923.
www.dps.state.az.us

#02 Department of Weights & Measures, 4425 W Olive Av #134, Glendale, AZ 85302-3844; 602-255-5211, Fax: 602-255-1950.

#03 Boxing Commission, 1400 W Washington, #210, Phoenix, AZ 85007; 602-542-1417, Fax: 602-542-1458.

#04 Arizona State Lottery, 4740 E University Dr, Phoenix, AZ 85034; 800-921-4400, Fax: 480-921-4512.
www.arizonalottery.com

#05 Banking Department, 2910 N 44th St, #310, Phoenix, AZ 85018; 602-255-4421, Fax: 602-381-1225.
www.azbanking.com
Direct web site URL to search for licensees: www.azbanking.com/ListsofLicensees.htm. You can search online using name.

#06 Board for Private Postsecondary Education, 1400 W Washington, Rm 260, Phoenix, AZ 85007; 602-542-5709, Fax: 602-542-1253.

#07 Board of Accountancy, 3877 N Seventh St, #106, Phoenix, AZ 85014; 602-255-3648, Fax: 602-255-1283.
www.accountancy.state.az.us
Direct web site URL to search for licensees: www.accountancy.state.az.us. You can search online using roster button, then search by name.

#08 Board of Appraisal, 1400 W Washington, #360, Phoenix, AZ 85007; 602-542-1539, Fax: 602-542-1598.
www.appraisal.state.az.us
Direct web site URL to search for licensees: www.appraisal.state.az.us/Directory/directory.html

#09 Board of Barbers, 1400 W Washington, Rm 220, Phoenix, AZ 85007; 602-542-4498.

#10 Board of Behavioral Health Examiners, 1400 E Washington St #320, Phoenix, AZ 85007; 602-542-1882, Fax: 602-542-1830.
www.aspin.asu/~azbbhe
Direct web site URL to search for licensees: http://aspin.asu.edu/~azbbhe/directory/listing.html. You can search online using name.

#11 Board of Chiropractic Examiners, 5060 N 19th Ave #416, Phoenix, AZ 85015; 602-255-1444, Fax: 602-255-4289.
www.goodnet.com/~board/ Accupuncture and physiotherapy are certifications under a Chiropractic license.

#12 Information Services, 1721 E Broadway Rd, Tempe, AZ 85282; 480-784-4539, Fax: 480-255-3680.

#13 Board of Dental Examiners, 5060 N 19th Ave, #406, Phoenix, AZ 85015; 602-242-1492, Fax: 602-242-1445.

#14 Board of Dispensing Opticians, 1400 W Washington, Rm 230, Phoenix, AZ 85007; 602-542-3095, Fax: 602-542-3093.

#15 Board of Funeral Directors & Embalmers, 1400 W Washington, Room 230, Phoenix, AZ 85007; 602-542-3095, Fax: 602-542-3093.

#16 Board of Homeopathic Medical Examiners, 1400 W Washington, Rm 230, Phoenix, AZ 85007; 602-542-3095, Fax: 602-542-3093.
www.goodnet.com/~bhme/

#17 Board of Medical Examiners, 9545 E Doubletree Ranch Dr, Scottsdale, AZ 85258-5514; 480-551-2700, Fax: 480-551-2704.
www.bomex.org
Direct web site URL to search for licensees: www.docboard.org/az/df/azsearch.htm. You can search online using name or license number.

#19 Board of Naturopathic Physicians Examiners, 1400 W Washington, Rm 230, Phoenix, AZ 85007; 602-542-8242, Fax: 602-542-3093.

#20 Board of Nursing, 1651 E Morton, #210, Phoenix, AZ 85020-7605; 602-331-8111, Fax: 602-906-9365.
www.azboardofnursing.org

#21 Board of Occupational Therapy Examiners, 5060 N 19th Av #209, Phoenix, AZ 85015-3212; 602-589-8352, Fax: 602-589-8354.
www.primenet.com/~abote/index.html

#22 Board of Optometry, 1400 W Washington, Rm 230, Phoenix, AZ 85007; 602-542-3095, Fax: 602-542-3093.
Direct web site URL to search for licensees: www.odfinder.org/LicSearch.asp

#23 Board of Osteopathic Medicine & Surgery Examiners, 9535 E Doubletree Ranch Rd, Scottsdale, AZ 85258-5539; 480-657-7703 x21, Fax: 480-657-7715.
www.azosteoboard.org

#24 Board of Pharmacy, 4425 W Olive #140, Glendale, AZ 85302-3844; 623-463-2727, Fax: 623-934-0583.
www.pharmacy.state.az.us

#25 Board of Physical Therapy, 1400 W Washington, Rm 230, Phoenix, AZ 85007; 602-542-3095, Fax: 602-542-3093.

#26 Board of Podiatry Examiners, 1400 W Washington, Rm 230, Phoenix, AZ 85007; 602-542-3095, Fax: 602-542-3093.

#27 Board of Psychologist Examiners, 1400 W Washington St, Rm 235, Phoenix, AZ 85007; 602-542-8162, Fax: 602-542-8279.
www.goodnet.com/~azbpe/
Direct web site URL to search for licensees: www.goodnet.com/~azbpe/dir.html. You can search online using name.

#28 Board of Respiratory Care Examiners, 1400 W Washington, #200, Phoenix, AZ 85007; 602-542-5995, Fax: 602-542-5900.

#29 Board of Technical Registration, 1990 W Camelback, #400, Phoenix, AZ 85015-7465; 602-255-4053, Fax: 602-255-4051.
www.btr.state.az.us
Direct web site URL to search for licensees: www.btr.state.az.us

#30 State Bar of Arizona, 111 W Monroe, #1800, Phoenix, AZ 85003-1742; 602-252-4804, Fax: 602-271-4930.
www.azbar.org
Direct web site URL to search for licensees: www.azbar.org/MemberFinder. You can search online using name, firm, practice area, area of specialization, city, and county.

#31 Community College Board of Directors, 2020 N Central Ave. #570, Phoenix, AZ 85004-4578; 602-255-5582, Fax: 602-279-3464.
www.stbd.cc.az.us

#32 Registration Department, Securities Division, 1300 W Washington, 3rd Fl, Phoenix, AZ 85007; 602-542-4242, Fax: 602-594-7470.
www.ccsd.cc.state.az.us/licensing_and_registration/index.asp

#33 Department of Agriculture, 1688 W Adams St, Phoenix, AZ 85007; 602-542-0904, Fax: 602-542-5420; 602-542-0466.
www.agriculture.state.az.us

#34 Department of Agriculture, 1688 W Adams St, 1st Fl, Phoenix, AZ 85007; 602-542-3579, Fax: 602-542-0466.
www.agriculture.state.az.us

#35 Department of Agriculture, Plant Services, 1688 W Adams, Phoenix, AZ 85007; 602-542-0947, Fax: 602-542-0898.
www.agriculture.state.az.us

#36 Department of Building & Fire Safety, 99 E Virginia, Wildlife & Parks Bldg, #100, Phoenix, AZ 85004; 602-255-4072, Fax: 602-255-4962.

#37 Department of Economic Security, Child Care Administration, 1789 W Jefferson, Site Code 940A, 3rd Fl, Phoenix, AZ 85007; 602-542-2287, Fax: 602-542-3330.

#38 Department of Education, PO Box 6490 (1535 W Jefferson St, Bin 34), Phoenix, AZ 85005; 602-542-4367, Fax: 602-542-5388.
www.ade.state.az.us

#39 Department of Environmental Quality, 3033 N Central T5109B, Phoenix, AZ 85012; 602-207-2338, Fax: 602-207-2366.
www.adeq.state.az.us

#40 Department of Environmental Quality, 3033 N Central Ave, 6th Fl, Phoenix, AZ 85012; 602-207-2300, Fax: 602-207-4138.
www.adeq.state.az.us

#41 Department of Environmental Quality, 3033 N Central, 2nd Fl, Phoenix, AZ 85012; 602-207-2300, Fax: 602-207-4674.
www.adeq.state.az.us

#42 Department of Environmental Quality, 600 N 40th St, Phoenix, AZ 85008; 602-207-7000, Fax: 602-207-7020.
www.adeq.state.us

#43 Department of Health Services, 1647 E Morten, #160, Phoenix, AZ 85020; 602-674-9750, Fax: 602-395-8913.

www.hs.state.az.us

#44 Department of Health Services, 1740 W Adams St, Phoenix, AZ 85007; 602-255-3454, Fax: 602-255-3462.
www.hs.state.az.us

#45 Department of Health Services, 1647 E Morten, #230, Phoenix, AZ 85020; 602-674-4220, Fax: 602-861-0674.
www.hs.state.az.us

#46 Department of Health Services, 3815 N Black Canyon Hwy, Phoenix, AZ 85015; 602-230-5911, Fax: 602-230-5817.
www.hs.state.az.us

#47 Department of Health Services, 1647 E Morten, #240, Phoenix, AZ 85020; 602-674-4300, Fax: 602-861-0643.
www.hs.state.az.us
Direct web site URL to search for licensees: www.hs.state.az.us/als/databases/index.html. You can search online using self extracting files, then by name.

#48 Department of Health Services, 1651 E Morten, #120, Phoenix, AZ 85020; 602-861-0708, Fax: 602-861-9812.
www.hs.state.az.us

#49 Department of Health Services, 1647 E Morten Ave, #110, Phoenix, AZ 85020; 602-674-4340, Fax: 602-861-0463.
www.hs.state.az.us

#50 Department of Health Services, 2927 N 35th Ave, Phoenix, AZ 85017-5253; 602-364-1400, Fax: 602-364-1496.
www.hs.state.az.us

#51 Department of Insurance, 2910 N 44th St, #210, Phoenix, AZ 85018-7256; 602-912-8470, Fax: 602-912-8453.
www.state.az.us/id

#52 Department of Liquor License & Control, 800 W Washington, 5th Fl, Phoenix, AZ 85007; 602-542-5141, Fax: 602-542-5707.
www.azll.com
Direct web site URL to search for licensees: www.azll.com/query.htm. You can search online using license number, business name, and location address. By visiting the web site, you can also search recently issued, expired, closed, suspended and inactive licenses.

#53 Department of Public Safety, 2102 W Encanto Blvd (85009), Phoenix, AZ 85005-6328; 602-223-2361, Fax: 602-223-2938.
www.dps.state.az.us/mq/dpsmqpi.htm

#54 Department of Racing, 3877 N 7th St, #201, Phoenix, AZ 85014; 602-277-1704, Fax: 602-277-1165.
www.raccom.state.az.us

#55 Dept. of Real Estate, 2910 N 44th St, Phoenix, AZ 85018; 602-468-1414, Fax: 602-468-0562.
www.re.state.az.us
Direct web site URL to search for licensees: www.re.state.az.us/db.html

#56 Department of Revenue, PO Box 29002, Phoenix, AZ 85038-9069; 602-542-4565.
www.revenue.state.az.us

#57 Department of Transportation, 255 E Osborn #101, Phoenix, AZ 85012; 602-294-9144, Fax: 602-294-9141.
www.dot.state.az.us/ABOUT/aero/index.htm

#58 Department of Water Resources, 500 N 3rd St, Phoenix, AZ 85004-3903; 602-417-2400, Fax: 602-417-2421.
www.adwr.state.az.us

#59 Game & Fish Department, 2222 W Greenway Rd, Phoenix, AZ 85023; 602-942-3000, Fax: 602-789-3921.
www.gf.state.az.us

#60 Division of Administration, 800 W Washington, 3rd Fl, Phoenix, AZ 85007; 602-542-4653, Fax: 602-542-3070.
www.ica.state.az.us

#61 Special Fund Division, 800 W Washington, 4th Fl, Rm 401, Phoenix, AZ 85007; 602-542-3294, Fax: 602-542-3696.

#65 Maricopa Environmental Services, 1001 N Central, #550, Phoenix, AZ 85004; 602-506-6970, Fax: 602-506-5141.
www.maricopa.gov/envsvc/default.asp

#66 Medical Radiologic Technology Board of Examiners, 4814 S 40th St, Phoenix, AZ 85040-2940; 602-255-4845, Fax: 602-437-0705.

#67 Mine Inspector, 1700 W Washington, #400, Phoenix, AZ 85007-2805; 602-542-5971, Fax: 602-542-5335.
www.asmi.state.az.us

#68 Nursing Care Board, 1400 W Washington, #230, Phoenix, AZ 85007; 602-542-3095, Fax: 602-542-3093.

#69 Parks Board, 1300 W Washington, #221, Phoenix, AZ 85007; 602-542-2155, Fax: 602-542-4180.

#70 Registrar of Contractors, 800 W Washington, 6th Fl, Phoenix, AZ 85007; 602-542-1525, Fax: 602-542-1599.
www.rc.state.az.us
Direct web site URL to search for licensees: www.rc.state.az.us/AZROCLicenseQuery. You can search online using license number and name. Results of online searches are sent via fax.

#71 Secretary of State, 1700 W Washington St, Exec Towers, 7th Fl, Phoenix, AZ 85007; 602-542-4285, Fax: 602-542-6172.
www.sosaz.com
Direct web site URL to search for licensees: www.sosaz.com/ Online searching is only available for lobbyists and notaries. You can search lobbyists using the public body's name, the lobbyist's name or the lobbyist's employee's name. You can search notaries using name, ZIP Code and/or a range of dates.

#72 Structural Pest Control Commission, 9535 E Doubletree Ranch Rd, Scottsdale, AZ 85258-5514; 602-255-3664.
www.sb.state.az.us

#73 Veterinary Medical Examining Board, 1400 W Washington, #230, Phoenix, AZ 85007; 602-542-3095, Fax: 602-542-3093.

Arizona Federal Courts

The following list indicates the district and division name for each county in the state. If the bankruptcy court location is different from the district court, then the location of the bankruptcy court appears in parentheses.

County/Court Cross Reference

Apache	Prescott (Phoenix)	Mohave	Prescott (Yuma)
Cochise	Tucson	Navajo	Prescott (Phoenix)
Coconino	Prescott (Phoenix)	Pima	Tucson
Gila	Phoenix (Tucson)	Pinal	Phoenix (Tucson)
Graham	Tucson	Santa Cruz	Tucson
Greenlee	Tucson	Yavapai	Prescott (Phoenix)
La Paz	Phoenix (Yuma)	Yuma	Phoenix (Yuma)
Maricopa	Phoenix		

US District Court

District of Arizona

Phoenix Division Room 1400, 230 N 1st Ave, Phoenix, AZ 85025-0093 (Courier Address: Use mail address for courier delivery), 602-514-7101.

http://www.azd.uscourts.gov

Counties: Gila, La Paz, Maricopa, Pinal, Yuma. Some Yuma cases handled by San Diego Division of the Southern District of California.

Indexing/Storage: Cases are indexed by defendant and plaintiff as well as by case number. New cases are available in the index 2-3 weeks after filing date. A computer index is maintained. Records are also indexed on microfiche. Open records are located at this court.

Fee & Payment: The fee is $20.00 per item (one party name or case number). Payment may be made by money order, cashier check, business check, Mastercard. In state personal checks are also accepted. Prepayment is required. Payee: Clerk, US District Court. Certification fee: $7.00 per document. Copy fee: $.50 per page.

Phone Search: Searching is not available by phone. If case number is known by the caller, basic information will be released over the phone.

Mail Search: All information is public unless the file is sealed. Always enclose a stamped self addressed envelope.

In Person: In person searching is available.

PACER: Sign-up number is 800-676-6856. Access fee is $.60 per minute. Toll-free access: 888-372-5707. Local access: 602-322-7194. Case records are available back to 1992. Records are purged every 12 months. New records are available online after 1-3 days. PACER is available online at http://pacer.azd.uscourts.gov.

Prescott Division c/o Phoenix Division, Room 1400, 230 N 1st Ave, Phoenix, AZ 85025-0093 (Courier Address: Use mail address for courier delivery), 602-514-7101.

http://www.azd.uscourts.gov

Counties: Apache, Coconino, Mohave, Navajo, Yavapai.

Indexing/Storage: Cases are indexed by as well as by case number. New cases are available in the index after filing date. Open records are located at the Division.

Fee & Payment: The fee is $20.00 per item (one party name or case number). Payment may be made by money order, cashier check. Business checks are not accepted. Personal checks are not accepted.

Phone Search: Searching not available by phone.

Mail Search: Always enclose a stamped self addressed envelope.

In Person: In person searching is available.

PACER: Sign-up number is 800-676-6856. Access fee is $.60 per minute. Toll-free access: 888-372-5707. Local access: 602-322-7194. Case records are available back to 1992. Records are purged every 12 months. New records are available online after 1-3 days. PACER is available online at http://pacer.azd.uscourts.gov.

Tucson Division 405 W. Congress, Tucson, AZ 85701-1711 (Courier Address: Use mail address for courier delivery), 520-205-4200, Fax: 520-205-4209.

http://www.azd.uscourts.gov

Counties: Cochise, Graham, Greelee, Pima, Santa Cruz. The Globe Division was closed effective January 1994, and all case records for that division are now found here.

Indexing/Storage: Cases are indexed by defendant and plaintiff as well as by case number. New cases are available in the index immediately after filing date. A computer index is maintained. Open records are located at this court.

Fee & Payment: The fee is $20.00 per item (one party name or case number). Payment may be made by money order, cashier check, business check. In state personal checks are also accepted. A copy service at a much lower rate (currently $.07 per page) may be used in lieu of court staff. The copy service has a one day turnaround time. Prepayment is required. Payee: Clerk, US District Court. Certification fee: $7.00 per document. Copy fee: $.50 per page.

Phone Search: Only docket information is available by phone.

Mail Search: A stamped self addressed envelope is not required.

In Person: In person searching is available.

PACER: Sign-up number is 800-676-6856. Access fee is $.60 per minute. Toll-free access: 888-372-5707. Local access: 602-322-7194. Case records are available back to 1992. Records are purged every 12 months. New records are available online after 1-3 days. PACER is available online at http://pacer.azd.uscourts.gov.

US Bankruptcy Court

District of Arizona

Phoenix Division PO Box 34151, Phoenix, AZ 85067-4151 (Courier Address: Use mail address for courier delivery), 602-640-5800.

http://www.azb.uscourts.gov

Counties: Apache, Coconino, Maricopa, Navajo, Yavapai.

Indexing/Storage: Cases are indexed by debtor as well as by case number. New cases are available in the index immediately after filing date. Creditors are also indexed from case # 95-1668 forward. A computer index is maintained. Case files are stored alphabetically. Open records are located at this court. Individuals cannot request files from the Federal Records Center themselves.

Fee & Payment: The fee is $20.00 per item (one party name or case number). Payment may be made by money order, cashier check, business check. Personal checks are not accepted. Prepayment is required. Payee: Clerk, US Bankruptcy Court. Certification fee: $7.00 per document. Copy fee: $.50 per page.

Phone Search: Only docket information is available by phone. An automated voice case information service (VCIS) is available.

Mail Search: Always enclose a stamped self addressed envelope.

In Person: In person searching is available.

PACER: Sign-up number is 800-676-6856. Access fee is $.60 per minute. Toll-free access: 800-556-9230. Local access: 602-640-5832. Use of PC Anywhere v4.0 suggested. Case records are available back to 1986. Records are purged every six months. New civil records are available online after 1 week. PACER is available online at http://pacer.azb.uscourts.gov.

Electronic Filing: Searching of electronically filed cases requires registration and password. Electronic filing information is available online at http://pacer.psc.uscourts.gov/bk/azbh.html

Tucson Division Suite 8112, 110 S Church Ave, Tucson, AZ 85701-1608 (Courier Address: Use mail address for courier delivery), 520-620-7500.

http://www.azb.uscourts.gov

Counties: Cochise, Gila, Graham, Greenlee, Pima, Pinal, Santa Cruz.

Indexing/Storage: Cases are indexed by debtor as well as by case number. New cases are available in the index immediately after filing date. Records are also indexed by adversary case number if applicable. A master list of creditors is available for each case from 1995 on. A computer index is maintained. Open records are located at this court.

Fee & Payment: The fee is $20.00 per item (one party name or case number). Payment may be made by money order, cashier check, business check. Personal checks are not accepted. Prepayment is required. Payee: Clerk, US Bankruptcy Court. Certification fee: $7.00 per document. Copy fee: $.50 per page.

Phone Search: Only docket and cover sheet information will be released over the phone. An automated voice case information service (VCIS) is available.

Mail Search: Always enclose a stamped self addressed envelope.

In Person: In person searching is available.

PACER: Sign-up number is 800-676-6856. Access fee is $.60 per minute. Toll-free access: 800-556-9224. Local access: 520-620-7470. Use of PC Anywhere v4.0 suggested. Case records are available back to 1914. Records are purged every six months. New civil records are available online after 1 week. PACER is available online at http://pacer.azb.uscourts.gov.

Electronic Filing: Searching of electronically filed cases requires registration and password. Electronic filing information is available online at http://pacer.psc.uscourts.gov/bk/azbh.html

Yuma Division Suite D, 325 W 19th St, Yuma, AZ 85364 (Courier Address: Use mail address for courier delivery), 520-783-2288.

http://www.azb.uscourts.gov

Counties: La Paz, Mohave, Yuma.

Indexing/Storage: Cases are indexed by debtor as well as by case number. New cases are available in the index immediately after filing date. A computer index is maintained. Open records are located at this court.

Fee & Payment: The fee is $20.00 per item (one party name or case number). Payment may be made by money order, cashier check, business check. Personal checks are not accepted. Prepayment is required. Payee: Clerk, US Bankruptcy Court. Certification fee: $7.00 per document. Copy fee: $.50 per page.

Phone Search: Docket information is available by phone. An automated voice case information service (VCIS) is available.

Mail Search: Always enclose a stamped self addressed envelope.

In Person: In person searching is available.

PACER: Sign-up number is 800-676-6856. Access fee is $.60 per minute. Toll-free access: 800-556-9227. Local access: 520-783-9535. Use of PC Anywhere v4.0 suggested. Case records are available back to the mid 1980's. Records are purged every six months. New civil records are available online after 1 day. PACER is available online at http://pacer.azb.uscourts.gov.

Electronic Filing: Searching of electronically filed cases requires registration and password. Electronic filing information is available online at http://pacer.psc.uscourts.gov/bk/azbh.html

Arizona County Courts

Court	Jurisdiction	No. of Courts	How Organized
Superior Courts*	General	15	15 Counties
Justice of the Peace Courts*	Limited	79	79 Precincts
Municipal Courts	Municipal	85	

* Profiled in this Sourcebook.

					CIVIL				
Court	Tort	Contract	Real Estate	Min. Claim	Max. Claim	Small Claims	Estate	Eviction	Domestic Relations
Superior Courts*	X	X	X	$5000	No Max			X	
Justice of the Peace Courts*	X	X	X	$0	$5000	$2500		X	X
Municipal Courts									X

			CRIMINAL		
Court	Felony	Misdemeanor	DWI/DUI	Preliminary Hearing	Juvenile
Superior Courts*	X	X			X
Justice of the Peace Courts*		X	X	X	
Municipal Courts		X	X		

ADMINISTRATION Administrative Office of the Courts, Arizona Supreme Court Bldg, 1501 W Washington, Phoenix, AZ, 85007; 602-542-9301, Fax: 602-542-9484.

www.supreme.state.az.us/aoc

COURT STRUCTURE The Superior is the court of general jurisdiction. Justice, and Municipal courts generally have separate jurisdiction over case types as indicated in the text. Most courts will search their records by plaintiff or defendant. Estate cases are handled by Superior Court. Fees are the same as for civil and criminal case searching.

ONLINE ACCESS A system called ACAP (Arizona Court Automation Project) is implemented in over 100 courts. Mohave County is not a part of ACAP. ACAP is, fundamentally, a case and cash management information processing system. When fully implemented ACAP will provide all participating courts access to all records on the system. Plans call for public availability over the Internet sometime in the near future. For more information, call Tim Lawler at 602-542-9614.

The Maricopa and Pima county courts maintain their own systems, but will also, under current planning, be part of ACAP. These two counties provide ever-increasing online access to the public.

ADDITIONAL INFORMATION Public access to all Maricopa County court case indexes is available at a central location - 1 W Madison Ave in Phoenix. Copies, however, must be obtained from the court where the case is heard.

Many offices do not perform searches due to personnel and/or budget constraints. As computerization of record offices increases across the state, more record offices are providing public access computer terminals.

Fees across all jurisdictions, as established by the Arizona Supreme Court and State Legislature, are as follows as of August 9, 2001: search - Superior Court: $18.00 per name; lower courts: $17.00 per name; certification - Superior Court: $18.00 per document; lower courts: $17.00 per document; copies - $.50 per page. Courts may choose to charge no fees.

Apache County

Superior Court PO Box 365, St John's, AZ 85936; 928-337-7550; Fax: 928-337-2771. Hours: 8AM-5PM (MST). *Felony, Civil Actions Over $5,000, Probate.*

Civil Records: Access: Mail, in person. Both court and visitors may perform in person searches. Search fee: $18.00 per name. Required to search: name, years to search; also helpful: address. Civil cases indexed by defendant, plaintiff. Civil records on computer and docket books.

Criminal Records: Access: Mail, in person. Both court and visitors may perform in person searches. Search fee: $18.00 per name. Required to search: name, years to search, DOB; also helpful: address, SSN. Criminal records on computer and docket books.

General Information: Public Access terminal is available. No juvenile dependencies, mental health, victims, sealed or adoption records released. SASE required. Copy fee: $.50 per page. Certification fee: $18.00. Fee payee: Clerk of the Courts. Business checks accepted. Prepayment is required.

Chinle Justice Court PO Box 888, Chinle, AZ 86503; 928-674-5922; Fax: 928-674-5926. Hours: 8AM-5PM (MST). *Misdemeanor, Civil Actions Under $5,000, Eviction, Small Claims.*

Civil Records: Access: Fax, mail, in person. Only the court performs in person searches; visitors may not. Search fee: $17.00 per name. Required to search: name, years to search; also helpful: address. Civil cases indexed by defendant. Civil records on docket books from 1977, computerized back to 2000.

Criminal Records: Access: Fax, mail, in person. Only the court performs in person searches; visitors may not. Search fee: $17.00 per name. Required to search: name, years to search; also helpful: address, DOB, SSN. Criminal records on docket books from 1977, computerized back to 2000. Phone access is discouraged.

General Information: No juvenile, mental health, victims, sealed or adoption records released. SASE required. Turnaround time 1-2 days. Fax notes: Fee to fax results is $1.25 per page. Copy fee: $1.25 per page. Certification fee: $17.00. Fee payee: Chinle Justice Court. Business checks accepted. Prepayment is required.

Puerco Justice Court PO Box 610, Sanders, AZ 86512; 928-688-2954. Hours: 8AM-Noon, 1-5PM (MST). *Misdemeanor, Civil Actions Under $5,000, Eviction, Small Claims.*

Civil Records: Access: Mail, in person. Only the court performs in person searches; visitors may not. Search fee: $17.00 per name. Required to search: name, years to search; also helpful: address. Civil cases indexed by defendant. Civil records on docket books.

Criminal Records: Access: Mail, in person. Only the court performs in person searches; visitors may not. Search fee: $18.00 per name. Required to search: name, years to search, DOB; also helpful: address, SSN. Criminal records on docket books.

General Information: No juvenile, mental health, victims, sealed or adoption records released. SASE required. Turnaround time as soon as possible. Copy fee: $.50 per page. Certification fee: $17.00. Fee payee: Sanders Justice Court. Only cashiers checks and money orders accepted. Prepayment is required.

Round Valley Justice Court PO Box 1356, Springerville, AZ 85938; 928-333-4613; Fax: 928-333-4205. Hours: 8AM-Noon, 1-5PM (MST). *Misdemeanor, Civil Actions Under $5,000, Eviction, Small Claims.*

Civil Records: Access: Phone, fax, mail, in person. Both court and visitors may perform in person searches. Search fee: $17.00 per name. Required to search: name, years to search; also helpful: address. Civil cases indexed by defendant, plaintiff. Civil records on docket books, computerized since 02/96.

Criminal Records: Access: Phone, fax, mail, in person. Both court and visitors may perform in person searches. Search fee: $17.00 per name. Required to search: name, years to search; also helpful: address, DOB, SSN. Criminal records on docket books, computerized since 02/96.

General Information: No juvenile, mental health, victims, sealed or adoption records released. SASE required. Turnaround time 5 working days. Copy fee: $.50 per page. Certification fee: $17.00. Fee payee: Round Valley Justice Court. Only cashiers checks and money orders accepted. Prepayment is required.

St John's Justice Court PO Box 308, St John's, AZ 85936; 928-337-7558; Fax: 928-337-2683. Hours: 8AM-5PM (MST). *Misdemeanor, Civil Actions Under $5,000, Eviction, Small Claims.*

Civil Records: Access: Mail, in person. Both court and visitors may perform in person searches. Search fee: $17.00 per name. Required to search: name, years to search; also helpful: address. Civil cases indexed by defendant. Civil records on docket books since 1972; on computer since 1996.

Criminal Records: Access: Mail, in person. Both court and visitors may perform in person searches. Search fee: $17.00 per name. Required to search: name, years to search, DOB; also helpful: address, SSN. Criminal records on docket books since 1972; on computer since 1996.

General Information: No juvenile, mental health, victims, sealed or adoption records released. SASE required. Turnaround time 48 hours. Copy fee: $.50 per page. Certification fee: $17.00. Fee payee: St John's Justice Court. Only cashiers checks and money orders accepted. Prepayment is required.

Cochise County

Cochise County Superior Court PO Box CK, Bisbee, AZ 85603; 520-432-9364; Fax: 520-432-4850. Hours: 8AM-5PM (MST). *Felony, Civil Actions Over $5,000, Probate.*

www.co.cochise.az.us/Court/ClrkOfSC.htm

Civil Records: Access: Fax, mail, in person, email. Both court and visitors may perform in person searches. Search fee: $18.00 per name per year. Required to search: name, years to search. Civil cases indexed by defendant, plaintiff. Civil records on computer since 1996 and on index books from 1881 to present.

Criminal Records: Access: Fax, mail, in person, email. Both court and visitors may perform in person searches. Search fee: $18.00 per name. Per every 5 years. Required to search: name, years to search; also helpful: DOB, SSN. Criminal records on computer since 1996; prior records on index books.

General Information: Public Access terminal is available. (Records after 1/1/96 are available.) No juvenile, mental health, victims, sealed or adoption records released. SASE required. Turnaround time 7-14 days. Fax notes: Fee to fax results is $.50 per page. Copy fee: $.50 per page. Certification fee: $18.00. Fee payee: Clerk of Superior Court. Only cashiers checks and money orders accepted. Prepayment is required.

Benson Justice Court PO Box 2167, Benson, AZ 85602; 520-586-2247; Fax: 520-586-9647. Hours: 8AM-5PM (MST). *Misdemeanor, Civil Actions Under $5,000, Eviction, Small Claims.*

Civil Records: Access: Fax, mail, in person. Only the court performs in person searches; visitors may not. Search fee: $17.00 per name. Required to search: name, years to search; also helpful: address. Civil cases indexed by defendant.

Criminal Records: Access: Fax, mail, in person. Only the court performs in person searches; visitors may not. Search fee: $17.00 per name. Required to search: name, years to search; also helpful: address, DOB, SSN.

General Information: No juvenile, mental health, victims, sealed records released. SASE required. Turnaround time 1-3 days. Fax notes: No fee to fax results. Copy fee: $.50 per page. Certification fee: $17.00. Fee payee: Benson Justice Court. Only cashiers checks and money orders accepted. Prepayment is required.

Bisbee Justice Court 207 N Judd Dr, Bisbee, AZ 85603; 520-432-9542; Fax: 520-432-9594. Hours: 8AM-5PM (MST). *Misdemeanor, Civil Actions Under $5,000, Eviction, Small Claims.*

Civil Records: Access: Fax, mail, in person. Only the court performs in person searches; visitors may not. No search fee. Required to search: name, years to search; also helpful: address. Civil cases indexed by defendant, plaintiff. Civil records on computer from 7/85. Some records on dockets.

Criminal Records: Access: Fax, mail, in person. Only the court performs in person searches; visitors may not. No search fee. Required to search: name, years to search; also helpful: address, DOB, SSN. Criminal records on computer from 7/85. Some records on dockets.

General Information: No juvenile, mental health, victims, sealed or adoption records released. SASE required. Turnaround time 1-7 days. Fax notes: No fee to fax results. Copy fee: $.50 per page. Certification fee: $17.00. Fee payee: Bisbee Justice Court #1. Personal checks accepted. Prepayment is required.

Bowie Justice Court PO Box 317, Bowie, AZ 85605; 520-847-2303; Fax: 520-847-2242. Hours: 8AM-5PM (MST). *Misdemeanor, Civil Actions Under $5,000, Eviction, Small Claims.*

Civil Records: Access: Phone, fax, mail, in person. Only the court performs in person searches; visitors may not. Search fee: $17.00 per name. Required to search: name, years to search; also helpful: address. Civil cases indexed by defendant. Civil records on computer from 7/85. Some records on dockets.

Criminal Records: Access: Phone, fax, mail, in person. Only the court performs in person searches; visitors may not. Search fee: $17.00 per name. Required to search: name, years to search, DOB; also helpful: address, SSN. Criminal records on computer from 1996. Some records on dockets.

General Information: No juvenile, mental health, victims, sealed or adoption records released. SASE required. Turnaround time 1-3 days. Fax notes: $2.00 per page. Copy fee: $1.25 per page. Certification fee: $17.00. Fee payee: Bowie Justice Court. Only cashiers checks and money orders accepted. Credit cards accepted: Visa, MasterCard. Prepayment is required.

Douglas Justice Court 661 G Ave, Douglas, AZ 85607; 520-364-3561; Fax: 520-364-3684. Hours: 8AM-5PM (MST). *Misdemeanor, Civil Actions Under $5,000, Eviction, Small Claims.*

Civil Records: Access: Fax, mail, in person. Only the court performs in person searches; visitors may not. No search fee. Required to search: name, years to search; also helpful: address. Civil cases indexed by defendant, plaintiff. Civil records on computer from 1990. Some records on dockets.

Criminal Records: Access: Fax, mail, in person. Only the court performs in person searches; visitors may not. No search fee. Required to search: name, years to search, DOB; also helpful: address, SSN. Criminal records on computer from 1990. Some records on dockets.

General Information: No juvenile, mental health, victims, sealed or adoption records released. SASE required. Turnaround time 1-3 days. Fax notes: Fee to fax certified search information is $.50 per page. Copy fee: $.50 per page. Certification fee: $17.00. Fee payee: Douglas Justice Court. Personal checks accepted. Prepayment is required.

Sierra Vista Justice Court 4001 E Foothills Dr, Sierra Vista, AZ 85635; 520-452-4980; Fax: 520-452-4986. Hours: 8AM-5PM (MST). *Misdemeanor, Civil Actions Under $5,000, Eviction, Small Claims.*

Civil Records: Access: Fax, mail, in person. Only the court performs in person searches; visitors may not. Search fee: $17.00 per name. Required to search: name, years to search; also helpful: address. Civil cases indexed by plaintiff. Civil records on computer since 08/96. In person access requires a written request.

Criminal Records: Access: Fax, mail, in person. Only the court performs in person searches; visitors may not. Search fee: $17.00 per name. Required to search: name, years to search; also helpful: address, DOB, SSN. Criminal records by case number, traffic alphabetically; on computer back to 8/1996. In person access requires a written request.

General Information: Public Access terminal is available. No juvenile, mental health, victims, sealed, financial, or adoption records released. SASE required. Turnaround time 3-7 days. Copy fee: $.50 per page. Certification fee: $17.00. Fee payee: Cochise County Treasurer. Personal checks accepted. Credit cards accepted: Visa, MasterCard. Not accepted by phone. Prepayment is required.

Willcox Justice Court 450 S Haskell, Willcox, AZ 85643; 520-384-2105; Fax: 520-384-4305. Hours: 8AM-5PM (MST). *Misdemeanor, Civil Actions Under $5,000, Eviction, Small Claims.*

Civil Records: Access: Phone, fax, mail, in person. Only the court performs in person searches; visitors may not. Search fee: $17.00. Required to search: name; also helpful: years to search, address. Civil cases indexed by defendant, plaintiff. Civil records on computer from 1996. Some records on dockets.

Criminal Records: Access: Phone, fax, mail, in person. Only the court performs in person searches; visitors may not. Search fee: $17.00. Required to search: name, DOB; also helpful: years to search, address, SSN. Criminal records on computer from 1996. Some records on dockets.

General Information: No juvenile, mental health, victims, sealed or adoption records released. SASE required. Turnaround time usually 1-3 days. Fax notes: No fee to fax results. Copy fee: $.50 per page. Certification fee: $17.00. Fee payee: Willcox Justice Court. Only cashiers checks and money orders accepted. Prepayment is required.

Coconino County

Superior Court 100 E Birch St, Flagstaff, AZ 86001; 928-779-6535. Hours: 8AM-5PM (MST). *Felony, Civil Actions Over $5,000, Probate.*

Civil Records: Access: Mail, in person. Both court and visitors may perform in person searches. Search fee: $18.00 per name per year. Required to search: name, years to search; also helpful: address. Civil cases indexed by defendant. Civil records on handwritten ledger from 1890. Some records on microfiche and dockets; computer from 1994.

Criminal Records: Access: Mail, in person. Both court and visitors may perform in person searches. Search fee: $18.00 per name per year. Required to search: name, years to search, DOB; also helpful: address, SSN. Criminal records on handwritten ledger books from 1890. Some records on microfiche and dockets; computer from 1994.

General Information: No mental health, victims, sealed or adoption records released. SASE required. Turnaround time 2 weeks. Copy fee: $.50 per page. Certification fee: $18.00. Fee payee: Clerk of Superior

Court. Business checks accepted. Prepayment is required.

Flagstaff Justice Court 100 E Birch Ave, Flagstaff, AZ 86001; 928-779-6806. Hours: 8AM-5PM (MST). *Misdemeanor, Civil Actions Under $5,000, Eviction, Small Claims.*

Civil Records: Access: Mail, in person. Only the court performs in person searches; visitors may not. Search fee: $17.00 per name. Required to search: name, years to search; also helpful: address. Civil records on docket books. Will only maintain records for 5 years.

Criminal Records: Access: Mail, in person. Only the court performs in person searches; visitors may not. Search fee: $17.00 per name per year. Required to search: name, years to search, DOB; also helpful: address, SSN. Criminal records on computer since 1987. Will only maintain records for 5 years.

General Information: No juvenile, mental health, victims, sealed or adoption records released. SASE required. Turnaround time 10 days. Copy fee: $.50 per page. Certification fee: $17.00. Fee payee: Flagstaff Justice Court. Only cashiers checks and money orders accepted. Prepayment is required.

Fredonia Justice Court PO Box 559, 100 N Main, Fredonia, AZ 86022; 928-643-7472; Fax: 928-643-7491. Hours: 8AM-5PM (MST). *Misdemeanor, Civil Actions Under $5,000, Eviction, Small Claims.*

Civil Records: Access: Mail, in person. Only the court performs in person searches; visitors may not. Search fee: $17.00 per name. Required to search: name, years to search; also helpful: address. Civil cases indexed by number. Civil records on docket books. Will only maintain records for 5 years.

Criminal Records: Access: Mail, in person. Only the court performs in person searches; visitors may not. Search fee: $17.00 per name. Required to search: name, years to search, DOB; also helpful: address, SSN. Criminal records for misdemeanors on computer from 1992, all others on docket books.

General Information: No juvenile, mental health, victims, sealed or adoption records released. SASE required. Turnaround time 5 days from date request/receive. Copy fee: $.50 per page. Certification fee: $17.00. Fee payee: Justice Court. Only cashiers checks and money orders accepted.

Page Justice Court PO Box 1565, Page, AZ 86040; 928-645-8871; Fax: 928-645-1869. Hours: 8AM-5PM (MST). *Misdemeanor, Civil Actions Under $5,000, Eviction, Small Claims.*

Civil Records: Access: Mail, in person. Only the court performs in person searches; visitors may not. Search fee: $17.00 per name. Required to search: name, years to search; also helpful: address. Civil cases indexed by defendant. Civil records on computer since 9/96; prior on docket books. Will only maintain records for 5 years.

Criminal Records: Access: Mail, in person. Only the court performs in person searches; visitors may not. Search fee: $17.00 per name. Required to search: name, years to search, DOB; also helpful: address, SSN. Criminal records for misdemeanors on computer from 1987, felony since 1991, all others on docket books.

General Information: No juvenile, mental health, victims, sealed or adoption records released. SASE required. Turnaround time 5 days. Copy fee: $.50 per page. Certification fee: $17.00. Fee payee: Page Justice Court. Only cashiers checks and money orders accepted. Credit cards accepted: Visa, MasterCard. Prepayment is required.

Williams Justice Court 117 W Route 66 #180, Williams, AZ 86046; 928-635-2691. Hours: 8AM-5PM (MST). *Misdemeanor, Civil Actions Under $5,000, Eviction, Small Claims.*

Civil Records: Access: Mail, in person. Both court and visitors may perform in person searches. Search fee:

$17.00 per name. Required to search: name, years to search; also helpful: address. Civil cases indexed by defendant, plaintiff. Civil records on docket books. Will only maintain records for 5 years.

Criminal Records: Access: Mail, in person. Both court and visitors may perform in person searches. Search fee: $17.00 per name. Required to search: name, years to search, DOB; also helpful: address, SSN. Criminal records on docket books.

General Information: No juvenile, mental health, victims, sealed or adoption records released. SASE required. Turnaround time 2-3 weeks. Copy fee: $1.25 per page. Certification fee: $17.00. Fee payee: Williams Justice Court. Only cashiers checks and money orders accepted. Prepayment is required.

Gila County

Superior Court 1400 E Ash, Globe, AZ 85501; 928-425-3231 X241. Hours: 8AM-5PM (MST). *Felony, Civil Actions Over $5,000, Probate.*

Civil Records: Access: Mail, in person. Both court and visitors may perform in person searches. Search fee: $18.00 per name per year. Required to search: name, years to search; also helpful: address. Civil cases indexed by defendant, plaintiff. Civil records indexed on computer from 1982. On microfiche from 1913 to 1982. Some records on docket books and index cards.

Criminal Records: Access: Mail, in person. Both court and visitors may perform in person searches. Search fee: $18.00 per name. Required to search: name, years to search, DOB; also helpful: address, SSN. Criminal records on computer from 1913.

General Information: No juvenile prior to June 1996, mental health, victims, sealed or adoption records released. SASE Required. Turnaround time 10 days to 2 weeks. Copy fee: $.50 per page. Certification fee: $18.00. Fee payee: Clerk of Superior Court. Personal checks accepted. Prepayment is required.

Globe Regional Justice Court 1400 E Ash, Globe, AZ 85501; 928-425-3231; Fax: 928-425-4773. Hours: 8AM-5PM (MST). *Misdemeanor, Civil Actions Under $5,000, Eviction, Small Claims.*

Note: This courts holds the records for the Justice Court formally located in Miami.

Civil Records: Access: Mail, fax, in person. Only the court performs in person searches; visitors may not. Search fee: $17.00 per name. Required to search: name, years to search. Civil cases indexed by defendant, plaintiff. Civil records on computer from 1995. Some records on dockets. Will retain criminal and civil for 5 years.

Criminal Records: Access: Mail, fax, in person. Only the court performs in person searches; visitors may not. Search fee: $17.00 per name. Required to search: name, years to search; also helpful: SSN, DOB, signed release. Criminal records on computer from 1995. Some records on dockets. Will retain criminal and civil for 5 years.

General Information: No juvenile, mental health, victims, sealed or adoption records released. SASE required. Turnaround time 2-4 days. Copy fee: $.50 per page. Certification fee: $17.00. Fee payee: Globe Justice Court. Business checks accepted. Prepayment is required.

Payson Justice Court 714 S Beeline Hwy #103, Payson, AZ 85541; 928-474-5267; Fax: 928-474-6214. Hours: 8AM-5PM (MST). *Misdemeanor, Civil Actions Under $5,000, Eviction, Small Claims.*

Note: This court holds the records for the Pine Justice Court which is closed.

Civil Records: Access: Fax, mail, in person. Only the court performs in person searches; visitors may not. Search fee: $17.00 per name. Required to search: name, years to search; also helpful: address. Civil cases indexed by defendant. Civil records on computer since

1990. Records on dockets. Will retain criminal and civil for 5 years.
Criminal Records: Access: Phone, fax, mail, in person. Only the court performs in person searches; visitors may not. Search fee: $17.00 per name. Required to search: name, years to search, DOB; also helpful: address, SSN. Criminal records on computer since 1990. Records on dockets. Will retain criminal and civil for 5 years.
General Information: No juvenile, mental health, victims, sealed or adoption records released. SASE required. Turnaround time 10 days. Copy fee: $.25 per page. Certification fee: $17.00. Fee payee: Payson Justice Court. No personal checks accepted. Prepayment is required.

Winkleman Justice Court 1400 E Ash St, Globe, AZ 85501-1414. *Misdemeanor, Civil Actions Under $5,000, Eviction, Small Claims.*

Note: Now part of the Globe Regional Justice Court.

Graham County

Superior Court 800 Main St, Safford, AZ 85546-3803; 928-428-3100; Fax: 928-428-0061. Hours: 8AM-5PM (MST). *Felony, Civil Actions Over $5,000, Probate.*
Civil Records: Access: Fax, mail, in person. Both court and visitors may perform in person searches. Search fee: $18.00 per name. Required to search: name, years to search. Civil cases indexed by defendant, plaintiff. Civil records on dockets.
Criminal Records: Access: Phone, fax, mail, in person. Both court and visitors may perform in person searches. Search fee: $18.00 per name per year. Required to search: name, years to search. Criminal records on dockets.
General Information: No mental health, victims, sealed or adoption records released. SASE required. Turnaround time 3 days minimum. Copy fee: $.50 per page. Certification fee: $18.00. Fee payee: Clerk of Superior Court. Personal checks accepted. Prepayment is required.

Justice Court Precinct #1 800 W Main St, Safford, AZ 85546; 928-428-1210; Fax: 928-428-3523. Hours: 8AM-5PM (MST). *Misdemeanor, Civil Actions Under $5,000, Eviction.*
Civil Records: Access: Mail, in person. Both court and visitors may perform in person searches. Search fee: $17.00 per name. Required to search: name, years to search; also helpful: address. Civil cases indexed by case number. Civil records on computer from 1995, on dockets prior.
Criminal Records: Access: Mail, in person. Both court and visitors may perform in person searches. Search fee: $17.00 per name. Required to search: name, years to search, DOB; also helpful: address, SSN. Criminal records on computer from 1995, on dockets prior.
General Information: No juvenile, mental health, victims, sealed or adoption records released. SASE required. Turnaround time 2 days. Copy fee: $.50 per page. Certification fee: $17.00. Fee payee: Safford Justice Court. Only cashiers checks and money orders accepted. Prepayment is required.

Pima Justice Court Precinct #2 PO Box 1159, 136 W Center St, Pima, AZ 85543; 928-485-2771; Fax: 928-485-9961. Hours: 8AM-5PM (MST). *Misdemeanor, Civil Actions Under $5,000, Eviction, Small Claims.*
Civil Records: Access: Fax, mail, in person. Both court and visitors may perform in person searches. Search fee: $17.00 per name. Required to search: name, years to search; also helpful: address. Civil cases indexed by defendant. Civil records on dockets back to 1985; on computer back to 1995. Retained for 5 years.

Criminal Records: Access: Fax, mail, in person. Both court and visitors may perform in person searches. Search fee: $17.00 per name. Required to search: name, years to search, DOB; also helpful: address, SSN. Criminal records on dockets back to 1985; on computer back to 1995. Retained for 5 years.
General Information: No juvenile, mental health, victims, sealed or adoption records released. SASE required. Turnaround time 2 weeks. Fax notes: $17.00 per document. Copy fee: $5.00 per document. Certification fee: $17.00. Fee payee: Graham Justice Court. Only cashiers checks and money orders accepted. Prepayment is required.

Greenlee County

Superior Court PO Box 1027, Clifton, AZ 85533; 928-865-4242; Fax: 928-865-5358. Hours: 8AM-5PM (MST). *Felony, Civil Actions Over $5,000, Probate.*
Civil Records: Access: Mail, in person. Both court and visitors may perform in person searches. Search fee: $18.00 per name per year. Required to search: name, years to search. Civil cases indexed by defendant, plaintiff. Civil records in docket books from 1911; on computer from 12/97.
Criminal Records: Access: Mail, in person. Both court and visitors may perform in person searches. Search fee: $18.00 per name per year. Required to search: name, years to search. Criminal records on computer since 12/97; on books from 1911.
General Information: No juvenile or adoptions released. SASE required. Turnaround time 7 days. Copy fee: $.50 per page. Certification fee: $18.00. Fee payee: Clerk of Superior Court. Personal checks accepted. Prepayment is required.

Justice Court Precinct #1 PO Box 517, Clifton, AZ 85533; 928-865-4312; Fax: 928-865-4417. Hours: 9AM-5PM (MST). *Misdemeanor, Civil Actions Under $5,000, Eviction, Small Claims.*
Civil Records: Access: Mail, in person. Only the court performs in person searches; visitors may not. Search fee: $17.00 per name. Required to search: name, years to search. Civil cases indexed by defendant, plaintiff. Civil records in docket books.
Criminal Records: Access: Mail, in person. Only the court performs in person searches; visitors may not. Search fee: $17.00 per name. Required to search: name, years to search; also helpful: DOB, SSN. Criminal records in docket books.
General Information: No juvenile, sealed, victims, mental health or adoption records released. SASE not required. Turnaround time 1 week. No copy fee. Certification fee: $17.00. Fee payee: Justice of the Peace. Only cashiers checks and money orders accepted.

Justice Court Precinct #2 PO Box 208, Duncan, AZ 85534; 928-359-2536; Fax: 928-359-2079. Hours: 9AM-5PM (MST). *Misdemeanor, Civil Actions Under $5,000, Eviction, Small Claims.*
Civil Records: Access: Mail, in person. Both court and visitors may perform in person searches. Search fee: $17.00 per name. Required to search: name, years to search. Civil cases indexed by defendant, plaintiff. Civil records on computer since 1996. Documents retained for 5 years.
Criminal Records: Access: Mail, in person. Both court and visitors may perform in person searches. Search fee: $17.00 per name. Required to search: name, years to search. Criminal Records computerized since 1996.
General Information: No juvenile, victims, sealed, mental health or adoption records released. Turnaround time 2 days. Copy fee: $.50 per page. Certification fee: $17.00. Fee payee: Justice Court. Personal checks accepted. Prepayment is required.

La Paz County

Superior Court 1316 Kofa Ave, Suite 607, Parker, AZ 85344; 928-669-6131; Fax: 928-669-2186. Hours: 8AM-5PM (MST). *Felony, Civil Actions Over $5,000, Probate.*
www.la-paz.co.org
Civil Records: Access: Mail, in person. Both court and visitors may perform in person searches. Search fee: $18.00 per name per year. Required to search: name, years to search; also helpful: address. Civil cases indexed by defendant, plaintiff. Civil records on docket books. For records prior to 1983, check with Yuma County Superior Court.
Criminal Records: Access: Mail, in person. Both court and visitors may perform in person searches. Search fee: $18.00 per name per year. Required to search: name, years to search; also helpful: address, DOB, SSN. Criminal records on docket books. For records prior to 1983, check with Yuma County Superior Court.
General Information: No dependency or adoption records released. SASE required. Turnaround time 2-3 days. Copy fee: $.50 per page. Certification fee: $18.00. Fee payee: Clerk of Superior Court. Business checks accepted. Prepayment is required.

Parker Justice Court 1105 Arizona Ave, Parker, AZ 85344; 928-669-2504; Fax: 928-669-2915. Hours: 8AM-5PM (MST). *Misdemeanor, Civil Actions Under $5,000, Eviction, Small Claims.*
Civil Records: Access: Mail, in person. Visitors must perform in person searches for themselves. No search fee. Required to search: name, years to search; also helpful: address. Civil cases indexed by defendant. Civil records on dockets back to 1800s, computerized since 1996.
Criminal Records: Access: Mail, in person. Visitors must perform in person searches for themselves. No search fee. Required to search: name, years to search, DOB; also helpful: address, SSN. Criminal records on dockets back to 1800s, computerized since 1996.
General Information: No juvenile, mental health, victims or sealed records released. SASE required. Turnaround time 2-3 weeks. Copy fee: $1.25 per page. Certification fee: $17.50. Fee payee: Clerk of Justice Court. Only cashiers checks and money orders accepted.

Quartzsite Justice Court PO Box 580, Quartzsite, AZ 85346; 928-927-6313; Fax: 928-927-4842. Hours: 8AM-5PM (MST). *Misdemeanor, Civil Actions Under $5,000, Eviction, Small Claims.*
Civil Records: Access: Fax, mail, in person. Both court and visitors may perform in person searches. Search fee: $17.00 per name/year. Required to search: name, years to search. Civil cases indexed by defendant, plaintiff. Civil records on dockets and computer. Retained for 5 yrs after final disposition.
Criminal Records: Access: Fax, mail, in person. Both court and visitors may perform in person searches. Search fee: $17.00 per name per year. Required to search: name, years to search, date of offense; also helpful: DOB, SSN, offense. Criminal records on dockets and computer. Retained for 5 yrs after final disposition.
General Information: No juvenile, mental health, victims, sealed or adoption records released. SASE required. Turnaround time within 3 weeks. Copy fee: $.50 per page. Certification fee: $17.00. Fee payee: Quartsite Justice Court. Only cashiers checks and money orders accepted. Prepayment is required.

Salome Justice Court PO Box 661, Salome, AZ 85348; 928-859-3871; Fax: 928-859-3709. Hours: 8AM-5PM (MST). *Misdemeanor, Civil Actions Under $5,000, Eviction, Small Claims.*

Civil Records: Access: Mail, in person. Only the court performs in person searches; visitors may not. No search fee. Required to search: name, years to search; also helpful: address. Civil cases indexed by defendant. Civil records on dockets from mid-1960s. Records destroyed after 5 years. Computerized back to 1996.
Criminal Records: Access: Mail, in person. Only the court performs in person searches; visitors may not. No search fee. Required to search: name, years to search, DOB; also helpful: address, SSN. Criminal records on dockets from mid-1960s. Records destroyed after 5 years. Computerized back to 1996.
General Information: No juvenile, mental health, victims, sealed or adoption records released. SASE not required. Turnaround time 2-3 days. Copy fee: $.50 per page. Certification fee: $17.00. Fee payee: Salome Justice Court. Only cashiers checks and money orders accepted. Prepayment is required.

Maricopa County

Superior Court 601 W. Jackson St., Phoenix, AZ 85003; 602-506-3360; Fax: 602-506-7619. Hours: 8AM-5PM (MST). *Felony, Civil Actions Over $5,000, Probate.*

www.superiorcourt.maricopa.gov
Note: Address for in person searches is 601 W Jackson St, Phoenix, AZ 85003.

Civil Records: Access: Fax, mail, online, in person. Both court and visitors may perform in person searches. Search fee: $18.00 per name. Required to search: name, years to search. Civil cases indexed by defendant, plaintiff. Civil records on computer from 7/87, on microfiche from 1969 to present. Some records on docket books. Online access is available free at www.superiorcourt.maricopa.gov/docket/public_new.html. Case file can be printed.
Criminal Records: Access: Fax, mail, online, in person. Both court and visitors may perform in person searches. Search fee: $18.00 per name. Required to search: name, years to search; also helpful: DOB. Criminal records on computer from 7/87, on microfiche from 1969 to present. Some records on docket books. Online access to criminal records is the same as civil.
General Information: No mental health, victims, sealed or adoption records released. Turnaround time 4 weeks. Fax notes: $18.50 for first page, $.50 each add'l. Copy fee: $.50 per page. Certification fee: $18.00. Fee payee: Clerk of Superior Court. Personal checks accepted.

Buckeye Justice Court 100 N Apache Rd, Buckeye, AZ 85326; 623-386-4289; Fax: 623-386-5796. Hours: 8AM-5PM (MST). *Misdemeanor, Civil Actions Under $5,000, Eviction, Small Claims.*

www.maricopa.gov/justicecourts/jc_buckeye.asp
Civil Records: Access: Mail, in person. Only the court performs in person searches; visitors may not. Search fee: $17.00 per name. Required to search: name, years to search. Civil cases indexed by defendant, plaintiff. Civil records on dockets by number.
Criminal Records: Access: Mail, in person. Only the court performs in person searches; visitors may not. Search fee: $17.00 per name. Required to search: name, years to search, DOB. Criminal records on dockets by number.
General Information: Public Access terminal is available. (Available in Justice Court.) No juvenile, mental health, victims, sealed or adoption records released. SASE required. Turnaround time 1-2 weeks. Copy fee: $.50 per page. Certification fee: $17.00. Fee

payee: Buckeye Justice Court. Personal checks accepted. Credit cards accepted: Visa, MasterCard.

Central Phoenix Justice Court 1 W Madison St, Phoenix, AZ 85003; 602-254-1488; Fax: 602-254-1496. Hours: 8AM-5PM (MST). *Misdemeanor, Civil Actions Under $5,000, Eviction, Small Claims.*

www.maricopa.gov/justicecourts/jc_central_phoenix.asp
Civil Records: Access: Mail, in person. Only the court performs in person searches; visitors may not. Search fee: $17.00 per name. Required to search: name, years to search. Civil cases indexed by defendant, plaintiff. Civil records on computer since 1985.
Criminal Records: Access: Mail, in person. Only the court performs in person searches; visitors may not. Search fee: $17.00 per name. Required to search: name, years to search, DOB, SSN. Criminal records on computer since 1985.
General Information: Public Access terminal is available. No juvenile, mental health, victims, sealed or adoption records released. SASE required. Turnaround time 1-2 weeks. Copy fee: $.50 per page. Certification fee: $17.00. Fee payee: Central Phoenix Justice Court. Personal checks accepted. Personal checks accepted with DL. Credit cards accepted: Visa, MasterCard. Visa, MC.

Chandler Justice Court 2051 W Warner Rd, Chandler, AZ 85224; 480-963-6691; Fax: 480-786-6210. Hours: 8AM-5PM (MST). *Misdemeanor, Civil Actions Under $5,000, Eviction, Small Claims.*

www.maricopa.gov/justicecourts/jc_chandler.asp
Civil Records: Access: Mail, in person. Only the court performs in person searches; visitors may not. Search fee: $17.00 per name. Required to search: name, years to search; also helpful: address. Civil records on dockets by number; records go back 5 years.
Criminal Records: Access: Mail, in person. Only the court performs in person searches; visitors may not. Search fee: $17.00 per name. Required to search: name, years to search, DOB; also helpful: address, SSN. Criminal records on dockets by number; records go back 5 years.
General Information: No juvenile, mental health, victims, sealed or adoption records released. SASE required. Turnaround time 1-2 weeks. Copy fee: $.50 per page. Certification fee: $17.00. Fee payee: Clerk of Justice Court. Personal checks accepted. Credit cards accepted: Visa, MasterCard. Prepayment is required.

East Mesa Justice Court 4811 E Julep #128, Mesa, AZ 85205; 480-985-0188; Fax: 480-396-6327. Hours: 7AM-5PM (MST). *Misdemeanor, Civil Actions Under $5,000, Eviction, Small Claims.*

www.maricopa.gov/justicecourts/jc_east_mesa.asp
Civil Records: Access: Mail, in person. Only the court performs in person searches; visitors may not. Search fee: $17.00 per name. Required to search: name, years to search; also helpful: address. Civil cases indexed by defendant, plaintiff. Civil records on computer since 1990. Prior records in docket books by number.
Criminal Records: Access: Mail, in person. Only the court performs in person searches; visitors may not. Search fee: $17.00 per name. Required to search: name, years to search, DOB; also helpful: address, SSN. Criminal records on computer since 1990. Prior records in docket books by number.
General Information: No juvenile, mental health, victims, sealed or adoption records released. SASE required. Turnaround time 1-2 weeks. Copy fee: $.50 per page. Certification fee: $17.00. Fee payee: East Mesa Justice Court. Personal checks accepted. Credit cards accepted: Visa, MasterCard. Prepayment is required.

East Phoenix Justice Court #1 1 W Madison St #1, Phoenix, AZ 85003; 602-254-1599; Fax: 602-254-1603. Hours: 8AM-5PM (MST). *Misdemeanor, Civil Actions Under $5,000, Eviction, Small Claims.*

www.maricopa.gov/justicecourts/jc_east_phoenix1.asp
Civil Records: Access: Phone, mail, in person. Only the court performs in person searches; visitors may not. Search fee: $17.00 per name. Required to search: name, years to search. Civil cases indexed by defendant, plaintiff. Civil records on dockets by number.
Criminal Records: Access: Phone, mail, in person. Only the court performs in person searches; visitors may not. Search fee: $17.00 per name. Required to search: name, years to search, DOB. Criminal records on dockets by number.
General Information: Public Access terminal is available. No mental health, victims or sealed records released. SASE required. Turnaround time 1-2 weeks. Copy fee: $.50 per page. Certification fee: $17.00. Fee payee: East Phoenix #1 Justice Court. Personal checks accepted. Credit cards accepted: Visa, MasterCard. Credit cards only if paid in person.

East Phoenix Justice Court #2 4109 N 12th St, Phoenix, AZ 85014; 602-266-3741; Fax: 602-277-9442. Hours: 8AM-4:30PM (MST). *Misdemeanor, Civil Actions Under $5,000, Eviction, Small Claims.*

www.maricopa.gov/justicecourts/jc_east_phoenix2.asp
Civil Records: Access: Mail, in person. Both court and visitors may perform in person searches. Search fee: $17.00 per name. Required to search: name, years to search. Civil cases indexed by defendant, plaintiff. Civil records on computer since 1981.
Criminal Records: Access: Mail, in person. Both court and visitors may perform in person searches. Search fee: $17.00 per name. Required to search: name, years to search, DOB. Criminal records computerized since 1991.
General Information: No juvenile, mental health, victims, sealed or adoption records released. SASE required. Turnaround time immediate. Copy fee: $.50 per page. Certification fee: $17.00. Fee payee: East Phoenix #2 Justice Court. Personal checks accepted. Credit cards accepted: Visa, MasterCard. Prepayment is required.

East Tempe Justice Court 1845 E Broadway #8, Tempe, AZ 85282; 480-967-8856; Fax: 480-921-7413. Hours: 8AM-5PM (MST). *Misdemeanor, Civil Actions Under $5,000, Eviction, Small Claims.*

www.maricopa.gov/justicecourts/jc_east_tempe.asp
Civil Records: Access: Mail, in person. Only the court performs in person searches; visitors may not. No search fee. Required to search: name, years to search. Civil cases indexed by defendant, plaintiff. Civil records on computer by case number.
Criminal Records: Access: Mail, in person. Only the court performs in person searches; visitors may not. No search fee. Required to search: name, years to search, DOB. Criminal records on computer by case number.
General Information: No juvenile, mental health, victims, sealed records released. SASE required. Copy fee: $.50 per page. Certification fee: $17.00. Fee payee: Tempe Justice Court. Personal checks accepted. Credit cards accepted: Visa, MasterCard. Prepayment is required.

Gila Bend Justice Court PO Box 648 (209 E. Pima Street), Gila Bend, AZ 85337; 928-683-2651; Fax: 928-683-6412. Hours: 8AM-5PM (MST). *Misdemeanor, Civil Actions Under $5,000, Eviction, Small Claims.*

www.maricopa.gov/justicecourts/jc_gila_bend.asp
Civil Records: Access: Mail, in person. Only the court performs in person searches; visitors may not. Search fee: $17.00 per name. Required to search: name, years

to search. Civil cases indexed by defendant, plaintiff. Civil records on computer since 1987. Public access terminal available only in main Phoenix court.

Criminal Records: Access: Mail, in person. Only the court performs in person searches; visitors may not. Search fee: $17.00 per name. Required to search: name, years to search; also helpful: DOB. Criminal records on computer since 1987. Public terminal access in main Phoenix court only.

General Information: No juvenile, mental health, victims, sealed or adoption records released. SASE required. Turnaround time 1-2 weeks. Copy fee: $.50 per page. Certification fee: Included in search fee. Fee payee: Gila Bend Justice Court. Personal checks accepted. Credit cards accepted: Visa, MasterCard. Prepayment is required.

Glendale Justice Court 5222 W Glendale, Glendale, AZ 85301; 623-939-9477; Fax: 623-842-2260. Hours: 8AM-5PM (MST). *Misdemeanor, Civil Actions Under $5,000, Eviction, Small Claims.*

www.maricopa.gov/justicecourts/jc_glendale.asp

Civil Records: Access: Mail, in person. Only the court performs in person searches; visitors may not. Search fee: $17.00 per name. Required to search: name, years to search. Civil records on dockets by case number.

Criminal Records: Access: Mail, in person. Only the court performs in person searches; visitors may not. Search fee: $17.00 per name. Required to search: name, years to search, DOB; also helpful: SSN. Criminal records on dockets by case number.

General Information: No juvenile, mental health, victims, sealed or adoption records released. SASE required. Turnaround time 1-2 weeks. Copy fee: $1.25 per page. Certification fee: $17.00. Fee payee: Glendale Justice Court. Personal checks accepted. Credit cards accepted: Visa, MasterCard. Prepayment is required.

Maryvale Justice Court 4622 W Indian School Rd Bldg D, Phoenix, AZ 85031; 623-245-0432; Fax: 623-245-1216. Hours: 8AM-5PM (MST). *Misdemeanor, Civil Actions Under $5,000, Eviction, Small Claims.*

www.maricopa.gov/justicecourts/jc_maryvale.asp

Civil Records: Access: Mail, in person. Only the court performs in person searches; visitors may not. Search fee: $17.00 per name. Required to search: name, years to search, address. Civil records on dockets by number.

Criminal Records: Access: Mail, in person. Only the court performs in person searches; visitors may not. Search fee: $17.00 per name. Required to search: name, years to search, address, DOB; also helpful: SSN, aliases. Criminal records on dockets by number.

General Information: No juvenile, mental health, victims, sealed or adoption records released. SASE required. Turnaround time 2-4 weeks. Copy fee: $.50 per page. Certification fee: $17.00. Fee payee: Maryvale Justice Court. Personal checks accepted. Credit cards accepted: Visa, MasterCard. Prepayment is required.

North Mesa Justice Court 1837 S Mesa Dr #A-201, Mesa, AZ 85210; 480-926-9731; Fax: 480-926-7763. Hours: 8AM-5PM (MST). *Misdemeanor, Civil Actions Under $5,000, Eviction, Small Claims.*

www.maricopa.gov/justicecourts/jc_maryvale.asp

Civil Records: Access: Fax, mail, in person. Visitors must perform in person searches for themselves. No search fee. Required to search: name, years to search. Civil cases indexed by defendant, plaintiff. Civil records on computer by case number. Public access terminal available only in main Phoenix court.

Criminal Records: Access: Fax, mail, in person. Visitors must perform in person searches for themselves. No search fee. Required to search: name, years to search, offense; also helpful: DOB. Criminal records on computer by case number. Public access terminal available only in main Phoenix court.

General Information: Public Access terminal is available. No juvenile, mental health, victims or sealed records released. SASE required. Turnaround time 1-2 weeks. Fax notes: No fee to fax results. Copy fee: $.50 per page. Certification fee: $17.00. Fee payee: North Mesa Justice Court. Personal checks accepted. Credit cards accepted: Visa, MasterCard. Prepayment is required.

North Valley Justice Court 5222 W Glendale, Glendale, AZ 85301; 623-915-2877; Fax: 623-463-0670. Hours: 8AM-5PM (MST). *Misdemeanor, Civil Actions Under $5,000, Eviction, Small Claims.*

www.maricopa.gov/justicecourts

Civil Records: Access: Mail, in person. Only the court performs in person searches; visitors may not. Search fee: $17.00 per name. Required to search: name, years to search. Civil records on dockets by case number; on computer back to 1999.

Criminal Records: Access: Mail, in person. Only the court performs in person searches; visitors may not. Search fee: $17.00 per name. Required to search: name, years to search, DOB; also helpful: SSN. Criminal records on dockets by case number; on computer back to 1999.

General Information: No juvenile, mental health, victims, sealed or adoption records released. SASE required. Turnaround time 1-2 weeks. Copy fee: $.50 per page. Certification fee: $17.00. Fee payee: North Valley Justice Court. Personal checks accepted. Credit cards accepted: Visa, MasterCard. Prepayment is required.

Northeast Phoenix Justice Court 10255 N 32nd St, Phoenix, AZ 85028; 602-494-0620; Fax: 602-952-2315. Hours: 8AM-5PM (MST). *Misdemeanor, Civil Actions Under $5,000, Eviction, Small Claims.*

www.maricopa.gov/justicecourts/jc_northeast_phoenix. asp

Civil Records: Access: Mail, in person. Only the court performs in person searches; visitors may not. Search fee: $17.00 per name; no fee if records are on-site. Required to search: name, years to search; also helpful: address. Civil cases indexed by defendant, plaintiff. Civil records on computer since 1993. Records on dockets by name and case number.

Criminal Records: Access: Mail, in person. Only the court performs in person searches; visitors may not. Search fee: $17.00 per name; no fee if records are on-site. Required to search: name, years to search, DOB; also helpful: address, SSN. Criminal records on dockets by name and case number.

General Information: No juvenile, mental health, victims, sealed or adoption records released. SASE required. Turnaround time 1-2 weeks. Copy fee: $.50 per page. Certification fee: $17.00. Fee payee: Clerk of Justice Court-Northeast. Personal checks accepted. Checks accepted for civil filings, for traffic-cashier's check or MO only. Credit cards accepted: Visa, MasterCard.

Northwest Phoenix Justice Court 11601 N 19th Ave, Phoenix, AZ 85029; 602-395-0293; Fax: 602-678-4508. Hours: 8AM-5PM (MST). *Misdemeanor, Civil Actions Under $5,000, Eviction, Small Claims.*

www.maricopa.gov/justicecourts/jc_northwest_phoenix .asp

Civil Records: Access: Mail, in person. Both court and visitors may perform in person searches. Search fee: $17.00 per name. Required to search: name, years to search. Civil cases indexed by defendant, plaintiff. Civil records on dockets. Will retain criminal and civil for 5 years.

Criminal Records: Access: Mail, in person. Both court and visitors may perform in person searches. Search fee: $17.00 per name. Required to search: name, years to search. Criminal records on dockets. Will retain criminal and civil for 5 years.

General Information: SASE required. Turnaround time 1 week. Copy fee: $.50 per page. Certification fee: $17.00. Fee payee: Northwest Phoenix Justice Court. Personal checks accepted. Credit cards accepted: Visa, MasterCard.

Peoria Justice Court 7420 W Cactus Rd, Peoria, AZ 85381; 623-979-3234; Fax: 623-979-1194. Hours: 8AM-5PM (MST). *Misdemeanor, Civil Actions Under $5,000, Eviction, Small Claims.*

www.maricopa.gov/justicecourts/jc_peoria.asp

Civil Records: Access: Phone, fax, mail, in person. Both court and visitors may perform in person searches. Search fee: $17.00 per name. Required to search: name, years to search. Civil cases indexed by defendant, plaintiff. Civil records on computer by case number.

Criminal Records: Access: Phone, fax, mail, in person. Both court and visitors may perform in person searches. Search fee: $17.00 per name. Required to search: name, years to search; also helpful: DOB. Criminal records on computer by case number.

General Information: No juvenile, mental health, victims, sealed or adoption records released. SASE required. Turnaround time 1-2 weeks. Fax notes: $1.25 per page. Will only fax to 602 area code. Copy fee: $.50 per page. Certification fee: $17.00. Fee payee: Peoria Justice Court. Personal checks accepted. Credit cards accepted: Visa, MasterCard.

Scottsdale Justice Court 8250 E Butherus Dr, Scottsdale, AZ 85260; 480-443-6600; Fax: 480-443-5980. Hours: 8AM-5PM (MST). *Misdemeanor, Civil Actions Under $5,000, Eviction, Small Claims.*

www.maricopa.gov/justicecourts/jc_scottsdale.asp

Civil Records: Access: Phone, mail, in person. Only the court performs in person searches; visitors may not. Search fee: $17.00 per name. Required to search: name, years to search. Civil cases indexed by defendant, plaintiff. Civil records on computer since 1985. Records kept for 5 years on closed cases.

Criminal Records: Access: Phone, mail, in person. Only the court performs in person searches; visitors may not. Search fee: $17.00 per name. Required to search: name, years to search. Criminal records on computer since 1985. Records kept for 5 years on closed cases.

General Information: No juvenile, mental health, victims, sealed or adoption records released. SASE required. Turnaround time 2-3 weeks. Copy fee: $.50 per page. Certification fee: $17.00. Fee payee: Scottsdale Justice Court. Personal checks accepted. Credit cards accepted: Visa, MasterCard. Prepayment is required.

South Mesa/Gilbert Justice Court 1837 S Mesa Dr #B103, Mesa, AZ 85210; 480-926-3051; Fax: 480-545-1638. Hours: 8AM-5PM (MST). *Misdemeanor, Civil Actions Under $5,000, Eviction, Small Claims.*

www.maricopa.gov/justicecourts/jc_south_mesa.asp

Civil Records: Access: Mail, in person. Only the court performs in person searches; visitors may not. Search fee: $17.00 per name. Required to search: name, years to search, DOB, SSN, signed release. Civil cases indexed by defendant, plaintiff. Civil records on computer by case number back to 1994.

Criminal Records: Access: Mail, in person. Only the court performs in person searches; visitors may not. Search fee: $17.00 per name. Required to search: name, years to search, DOB, SSN, signed release. Criminal records on computer by case number; computerized back to 1994.

General Information: No juvenile, mental health, victims, sealed or adoption records released. SASE required. Turnaround time 1-2 weeks. Copy fee: $.50

per page. Certification fee: $17.00. Fee payee: South Mesa/Gilbert Justice Court. Only cashiers checks and money orders accepted. Prepayment is required.

South Phoenix Justice Court 217 E Olympic
Dr, Phoenix, AZ 85040; 602-243-0318; Fax: 602-243-6389. Hours: 8AM-5PM (MST). *Misdemeanor, Civil Actions Under $5,000, Eviction, Small Claims.*

www.maricopa.gov/justicecourts/jc_south_phoenix.asp

Civil Records: Access: In person only. Only the court performs in person searches; visitors may not. No search fee. Required to search: name, years to search; also helpful: address. Civil cases indexed by defendant, plaintiff. Civil records on computer since 1990, on dockets by number.
Criminal Records: Access: In person only. Only the court performs in person searches; visitors may not. No search fee. Required to search: name, years to search; also helpful: DOB. Criminal records on dockets by number.
General Information: No juvenile, mental health, victims, sealed or adoption records released. Copy fee: $.50 per page. Certification fee: $17.00. Fee payee: South Phoenix Justice Court. Personal checks accepted. Credit cards accepted: Visa, MasterCard.

Tolleson Justice Court 9550 W Van Buren #6,
Tolleson, AZ 85353; 623-936-1449; Fax: 623-936-4859. Hours: 8AM-5PM (MST). *Misdemeanor, Civil Actions Under $5,000, Eviction, Small Claims.*

www.maricopa.gov/justicecourts/jc_tolleson.asp

Civil Records: Access: Mail, in person. No search fee. Required to search: name, years to search; also helpful: address. Civil cases indexed by defendant, plaintiff. Civil records in docket books by number prior to 1992, on computer since 1993.
Criminal Records: Access: Mail, in person. Only the court performs in person searches; visitors may not. No search fee. Required to search: name, years to search, DOB; also helpful: address, SSN. Criminal records in docket books by number prior to 1992, on computer since 1993.
General Information: No juvenile, mental health, victims, sealed or adoption records released. SASE required. Turnaround time 1-2 weeks. Copy fee: $.50 per page. Certification fee: $17.00. Fee payee: Tolleson Justice Court. Personal checks accepted. Credit cards accepted: Visa, MasterCard.

West Mesa Justice Court 2050 W University
Dr, Mesa, AZ 85201; 480-964-2958; Fax: 480-969-1098. Hours: 8AM-5PM (MST). *Misdemeanor, Civil Actions Under $5,000, Eviction, Small Claims.*

www.maricopa.gov/justicecourts/jc_west_mesa.asp

Civil Records: Access: In person only. Visitors must perform in person searches for themselves. No search fee. Required to search: name, years to search. Civil cases indexed by defendant, plaintiff. Civil records on computer since 1990 by case number.
Criminal Records: Access: In person only. Visitors must perform in person searches for themselves. No search fee. Required to search: name, years to search, DOB; also helpful: SSN. Criminal records on computer since 1990 by case number.
General Information: No juvenile, mental health, victims, sealed or adoption records released. Copy fee: $.50 per page. Certification fee: $17.00. Fee payee: West Mesa Justice Court. Personal checks accepted. Credit cards accepted: Visa, MasterCard. Prepayment is required.

West Phoenix Justice Court 1 W Madison St,
Phoenix, AZ 85003; 602-256-0292; Fax: 602-256-7959. Hours: 8AM-5PM (MST). *Misdemeanor, Civil Actions Under $5,000, Eviction, Small Claims.*

www.maricopa.gov/justicecourts/jc_west_phoenix.asp

Civil Records: Access: Mail, in person. Both court and visitors may perform in person searches. Search fee: $17.00 per name. Required to search: name, years to search. Civil cases indexed by defendant, plaintiff. Civil records on computer since 1993.
Criminal Records: Access: In person only. Both court and visitors may perform in person searches. Search fee: $17.00 per name. Required to search: name, years to search, DOB. Criminal records on computer by case number.
General Information: Public Access terminal is available. No juvenile, mental health, victims, sealed or adoption records released. SASE required. Turnaround time is 1-2 days. Copy fee: $.50 per page. Certification fee: $17.00. Fee payee: West Phoenix Justice Court. Personal checks accepted. Credit cards accepted: Visa, MasterCard.

West Tempe Justice Court 1845 E Broadway
#109, Tempe, AZ 85282; 480-350-9442; Fax: 480-968-6510. Hours: 8AM-5PM (MST). *Misdemeanor, Civil Actions Under $5,000, Eviction, Small Claims.*

www.maricopa.gov/justicecourts/jc_west_tempe.asp

Civil Records: Access: Mail, in person. Only the court performs in person searches; visitors may not. No search fee. Required to search: name, years to search. Civil cases indexed by defendant, plaintiff. Civil records on computer by case number.
Criminal Records: Access: Mail, in person. Only the court performs in person searches; visitors may not. No search fee. Required to search: name, years to search, DOB. Criminal records on computer by case number.
General Information: No juvenile, mental health, victims, sealed records released. SASE required. Copy fee: $.50 per page. Certification fee: $17.00. Fee payee: Tempe Justice Court. Personal checks accepted. Credit cards accepted: Visa, MasterCard. Prepayment is required.

Wickenburg Justice Court 155 N Tegner,
Suite D, Wickenburg, AZ 85390; 928-506-1554; Fax: 928-684-9639. Hours: 8AM-5PM (MST). *Misdemeanor, Civil Actions Under $5,000, Eviction, Small Claims.*

www.maricopa.gov/justicecourts/jc_wickenburg.asp

Civil Records: Access: Mail, in person. Both court and visitors may perform in person searches. Search fee: $17.00 per name. Required to search: name, years to search; also helpful: address. Civil cases indexed by defendant, plaintiff. Civil records on computer since 1994.
Criminal Records: Access: Mail, in person. Both court and visitors may perform in person searches. Search fee: $17.00 per name. Required to search: name, years to search, DOB; also helpful: SSN. Criminal records on computer by name and case number.
General Information: No juvenile, mental health, victims, sealed records released. SASE required. Turnaround time 1-2 weeks. Copy fee: $.50 per page. Certification fee: $17.00. Fee payee: Wickenburg Justice Court. Personal checks accepted. Credit cards accepted: Visa, MasterCard. Prepayment is required.

Mohave County

Superior Court PO Box 7000, Kingman, AZ
86402-7000; 928-753-0713; Fax: 928-753-0781. Hours: 8AM-5PM (MST). *Felony, Civil Actions Over $5,000, Probate.*

www.mohavecourts.com

Civil Records: Access: Phone, fax, mail, in person. Both court and visitors may perform in person searches. Search fee: $18.00 per name. Fee is per source. Required to search: name, years to search. Civil cases indexed by defendant, plaintiff. Civil records on computer since 11/95; prior records on microfiche and index books.

Criminal Records: Access: Phone, fax, mail, in person. Both court and visitors may perform in person searches. Search fee: $18.00 per name. Fee is per source. Required to search: name, years to search; also helpful: DOB, SSN. Criminal records on computer since 11/95; prior records on microfiche and index books.
General Information: No juvenile, mental health, victims, sealed or adoption records released. SASE required. Turnaround time 3 days. Fax notes: $.50. Copy fee: $.50 per page. Certification fee: $18.00. Fee payee: Clerk of Superior Court. Business checks accepted. Prepayment is required.

Bullhead City Justice Court 2225 Trane Rd,
Bullhead City, AZ 86442; 928-758-0709; Fax: 928-758-2644. Hours: 8AM-5PM (MST). *Misdemeanor, Civil Actions Under $5,000, Eviction, Small Claims.*

Civil Records: Access: Phone, mail, in person. Only the court performs in person searches; visitors may not. No search fee. Required to search: name, years to search. Civil cases indexed by defendant, plaintiff. Civil records on computer from 1988. Some records on docket books. Records retained for 5 years. Will only search back to 1988 unless w/docket number.
Criminal Records: Access: Phone, mail, in person. Only the court performs in person searches; visitors may not. No search fee. Required to search: name, years to search; also helpful: DOB, SSN. Criminal records on computer from 1988. Some records on docket books. Records retained for 5 years. Will only search back to 1988 unless w/docket number.
General Information: No juvenile, mental health, victims, sealed or adoption records released. SASE required. Turnaround time 2-3 days. Copy fee: $.50 per page. Certification fee: $17.00. Fee payee: Bullhead City Justice Court. Personal checks accepted. Prepayment is required.

Kingman/Cerbat Justice Court 524 W Beale
St, PO Box 29, Kingman, AZ 86401-0029; 928-753-0710; Fax: 928-753-7840. Hours: 8AM-5PM (MST). *Misdemeanor, Civil Actions Under $5,000, Eviction, Small Claims.*

Civil Records: Access: Phone, fax, mail, in person. Only the court performs in person searches; visitors may not. Search fee: $17.00 per name. Required to search: name, years to search. Civil cases indexed by defendant, plaintiff. Civil records on computer from 1988. Some records on docket books. Records retained for 5 years.
Criminal Records: Access: Phone, fax, mail, in person. Only the court performs in person searches; visitors may not. Search fee: $17.00 per name. Required to search: name, years to search; also helpful: DOB, SSN. Criminal records on computer from 1988. Some records on docket books. Records retained for 5 years.
General Information: No juvenile, mental health, victims, sealed or adoption records released. SASE required. Turnaround time 2-3 days. Fax notes: $.50 per page. Copy fee: $.50 per page. Certification fee: $17.00. Fee payee: Kingman/Cerbat Justice Court. Personal checks accepted. Credit cards accepted: Visa, MasterCard. Prepayment is required.

Lake Havasu City Justice Court 2001
College Dr Suite 148, Lake Havasu City, AZ 86403; 928-453-0705; Fax: 928-680-0193. Hours: 8AM-5PM (MST). *Misdemeanor, Civil Actions Under $5,000, Eviction, Small Claims.*

Civil Records: Access: Mail, in person. Only the court performs in person searches; visitors may not. Search fee: $17.00 per name. Required to search: name, years to search. Civil cases indexed by defendant, plaintiff. Civil records on computer from 1988. Some records on docket books. Records retained for 5 years.
Criminal Records: Access: Fax, mail, in person. Only the court performs in person searches; visitors may not.

Search fee: $17.00 per name. Required to search: name, years to search; also helpful: DOB. Criminal records on computer from 1988. Some records on docket books. Records retained for 5 years.

General Information: No juvenile, mental health, victims, sealed or adoption records released. SASE required. Turnaround time 2-3 days. Copy fee: $.50 per page. Certification fee: $17.00. Fee payee: Lake Havasu City Justice Court. Personal checks accepted. Prepayment is required.

Moccasin Justice Court PO Box 90, Moccasin, AZ 86022; 928-643-7104; Fax: 928-643-6206. Hours: 8AM-5PM (MST). *Misdemeanor, Civil Actions Under $5,000, Eviction, Small Claims.*

Civil Records: Access: Mail, in person. Only the court performs in person searches; visitors may not. Search fee: $17.00 per name. Required to search: name, years to search. Civil cases indexed by defendant, plaintiff. Civil records on docket books. Records retained for 5 years.

Criminal Records: Access: Mail, in person. Only the court performs in person searches; visitors may not. Search fee: $17.00 per name. Required to search: name, years to search. Criminal records on docket books. Records retained for 5 years.

General Information: No juvenile, mental health, victims, sealed or adoption records released. SASE required. Turnaround time 2-3 days. Copy fee: $.50 per page. Certification fee: $17.00. Fee payee: Moccasin Justice Court. Personal checks accepted. Prepayment is required.

Navajo County

Superior Court PO Box 668, Holbrook, AZ 86025; 928-524-4188; Fax: 928-524-4261. Hours: 8AM-5PM (MST). *Felony, Civil Actions Over $5,000, Probate.*

Civil Records: Access: Phone, fax, mail, in person. Both court and visitors may perform in person searches. Search fee: $18.00 per document. Required to search: name, years to search. Civil cases indexed by defendant, plaintiff. Civil records on docket books, index cards and microfiche back to 1890; computerized back to 1994.

Criminal Records: Access: Phone, fax, mail, in person. Only the court performs in person searches; visitors may not. Search fee: $18.00 per document. Required to search: name, years to search; also helpful: DOB, SSN. Criminal records on docket books, index cards and microfiche back to 1890; computerized back to 1994.

General Information: No juvenile, mental health, victims, sealed or adoption records released. SASE required. Turnaround time 3 days. Fax notes: Fee to fax is $18.00. Copy fee: $.50 per page. Certification fee: $18.00. Fee payee: Clerk of Superior Court. Only cashiers checks and money orders accepted. Prepayment is required.

Holbrook Justice Court PO Box 366, Holbrook, AZ 86025; 928-524-4720; Fax: 928-524-4725. Hours: 8AM-5PM (MST). *Misdemeanor, Civil Actions Under $5,000, Eviction, Small Claims.*

Civil Records: Access: Mail, in person. Search fee: $17.00 per name. Required to search: name, years to search. Civil cases indexed by defendant, plaintiff. Civil records on computer since 1994. Records on dockets and index cards back for 3 years.

Criminal Records: Access: Mail, in person. Only the court performs in person searches; visitors may not. Search fee: $17.00 per name. Required to search: name, years to search. Criminal records on computer since 1992. Records on dockets and stat books back for 3 years.

General Information: Public Access terminal is available. No victim names or sealed records released. SASE required. Turnaround time 1 week. Copy fee:

$.50 per page. Certification fee: $17.00. Fee payee: Holbrook Justice Court. Business checks accepted. Prepayment is required.

Kayenta Justice Court Box 38, Kayenta, AZ 86033; 928-697-3522; Fax: 928-697-3528. Hours: 8AM-Noon,1-5PM (MST). *Misdemeanor, Civil Actions Under $5,000, Eviction, Small Claims.*

Note: If planning to make an in-person search, call to make an appointment.

Civil Records: Access: Mail, in person. Only the court performs in person searches; visitors may not. Search fee: $17.00 per name. Required to search: name, years to search, address. Civil cases indexed by defendant, plaintiff. Civil records on docket books and index cards; on computer back to 1994.

Criminal Records: Access: Mail, in person. Only the court performs in person searches; visitors may not. Search fee: $17.00 per name. Required to search: name, years to search, address, DOB, SSN, signed release. Criminal records on docket books and index cards; on computer back to 1994.

General Information: No victim's names released. SASE required. Turnaround time 1 week. Copy fee: $.50 per page. Certification fee: $17.00. Fee payee: Kayenta Justice Court. Only cashiers checks and money orders accepted. Prepayment is required.

Pinetop-Lakeside Justice Court Box 2020, Lakeside, AZ 85929; 928-368-6200; Fax: 928-368-8674. Hours: 8AM-5PM (MST). *Misdemeanor, Civil Actions Under $5,000, Eviction, Small Claims.*

Civil Records: Access: Fax, mail, in person. Only the court performs in person searches; visitors may not. Search fee: $17.00 per name. Required to search: name, years to search. Civil cases indexed by defendant, plaintiff. Civil records on electronic dockets by case number and case files by alpha.

Criminal Records: Access: Fax, mail, in person. Only the court performs in person searches; visitors may not. Search fee: $17.00 per name. Required to search: name, years to search. Criminal records on electronic dockets by case number and case files by alpha back to 1970. Computerized back to 1996.

General Information: Public Access terminal is available. No victim's names released. SASE required. Turnaround time 1 week. Fax notes: No fee to fax results. Copy fee: $.50 per page. Certification fee: $17.00. Fee payee: Pinetop-Lakeside Justice Court. Personal checks accepted. Prepayment is required.

Show Low Justice Court PO Box 3085, Show Low, AZ 85902-3085; 928-532-6030; Fax: 928-532-6035. Hours: 8AM-5PM (MST). *Misdemeanor, Civil Actions Under $5,000, Eviction, Small Claims.*

Civil Records: Access: Fax, mail, in person. Only the court performs in person searches; visitors may not. Search fee: $17.00 per name. Required to search: name, years to search. Civil cases indexed by defendant, plaintiff. Civil records on computer. In person access requires a written request.

Criminal Records: Access: Fax, mail, in person. Only the court performs in person searches; visitors may not. Search fee: $17.00 per name per year. Required to search: name, years to search; also helpful: DOB, SSN. Criminal records on computer. In person access requires a written request.

General Information: No victim's names released. SASE required. Turnaround time 1 week. Copy fee: $.50 per page. Certification fee: $17.00. Fee payee: Show Low Justice Court. Personal checks accepted. Prepayment is required.

Snowflake Justice Court 73 West First South St, Snowflake, AZ 85937; 928-536-4141; Fax: 928-536-3511. Hours: 8AM-5PM (MST). *Misdemeanor, Civil Actions Under $5,000, Eviction, Small Claims.*

Civil Records: Access: Phone, fax, mail, in person. Only the court performs in person searches; visitors may not. Search fee: $17.00 per name per year. No charge if search is for two years or less. Required to search: name, years to search. Civil cases indexed by defendant, plaintiff. Civil records on computer back to 6/96, prior on docket books and index cards. Misdemeanors, DUI's and traffic records kept for 3 years, others held for 5 years.

Criminal Records: Access: Fax, mail, in person. Only the court performs in person searches; visitors may not. Search fee: $17.00 per name per year. No charge if search is for two years or less. Required to search: name, years to search; also helpful: DOB, SSN. Criminal records on computer back to 6/96, prior on docket books and index cards. Misdemeanors, DUI's and traffic records kept for 3 years, others held for 5 years.

General Information: No victim's names or search warrants released, no juvenile records released. SASE required. Turnaround time 2 weeks. Copy fee: $1.25 per page. Certification fee: $17.00. Fee payee: Snowflake Justice Court. Only cashiers checks and money orders accepted. Prepayment is required.

Winslow Justice Court Box 808, Winslow, AZ 86047; 928-289-6840; Fax: 928-289-2197. Hours: 8AM-5PM (MST). *Misdemeanor, Civil Actions Under $5,000, Eviction, Small Claims.*

Civil Records: Access: Fax, mail, in person. Only the court performs in person searches; visitors may not. No search fee. Required to search: name, years to search. Civil cases indexed by defendant, plaintiff. Civil records on docket books; on computer since.

Criminal Records: Access: Fax, mail, in person. Only the court performs in person searches; visitors may not. No search fee. Required to search: name, years to search; also helpful: DOB, SSN. Criminal records on docket books; on computer since.

General Information: No victim's names released. SASE required. Turnaround time 1 week. Copy fee: $.50 per page. Certification fee: $18.00. Fee payee: Winslow Justice Court. Personal checks accepted. Prepayment is required.

Pima County

Superior Court 110 W Congress, Tucson, AZ 85701; 520-740-3240; Fax: 520-798-3531. Hours: 8AM-5PM (MST). *Felony, Civil Actions Over $5,000, Probate.*

www.sc.co.pima.az.us

Note: Address correspondence to attention of civil or criminal section.

Civil Records: Access: Mail, in person. Both court and visitors may perform in person searches. Search fee: $18.00 per name. Required to search: name, years to search. Civil cases indexed by defendant, plaintiff. Civil records on computer since 1980s, on microfilm since late 1800s.

Criminal Records: Access: Mail, in person. Both court and visitors may perform in person searches. Search fee: $18.00 per name. Add $5.00 for postage and handling. Required to search: name, years to search. Criminal records on computer since 1980s, on microfilm since late 1800s.

General Information: No juvenile, mental health, adoption, victims or sealed records released. SASE required. Turnaround time 2 days. Plus $5.00 mailing fee. Fax notes: Fee to fax results is $5.00 plus $.50 per page. Copy fee: $.50 per page. Certification fee: $18.00. Fee payee: Clerk of Superior Court. Only cashiers checks and money orders accepted. Credit cards accepted: Visa, MasterCard. In person only. Prepayment is required.

Ajo Justice Court 111 La Mina, Ajo, AZ 85321; 520-387-7684. Hours: 8AM-5PM (MST). *Misdemeanor, Civil Actions Under $5,000, Eviction, Small Claims.*

Civil Records: Access: Mail, in person. Only the court performs in person searches; visitors may not. No search fee. Required to search: name, years to search. Civil cases indexed by defendant, plaintiff. Civil records on computer since 1987, prior in docket books.

Criminal Records: Access: Mail, in person. Only the court performs in person searches; visitors may not. No search fee. Required to search: name, years to search. Criminal records on computer since 1987, prior in docket books.

General Information: No juvenile, sealed, victim records released. Turnaround time 1 week. Copy fee: $.50 per page. Certification fee: $17.00. Fee payee: Ajo Justice Court. Personal checks accepted. Prepayment is required.

Green Valley Justice Court 601 N LaCanada, Green Valley, AZ 85614; 520-648-0658; Fax: 520-648-2235. Hours: 8AM-5PM (MST). *Misdemeanor, Civil Actions Under $5,000, Eviction, Small Claims.*

Civil Records: Access: Mail, in person. Only the court performs in person searches; visitors may not. Search fee: $17.00 per name. Required to search: name, years to search. Civil cases indexed by defendant, plaintiff. Civil records on computer back to 1996; card files prior. Clerk will only search computerized records.

Criminal Records: Access: Mail, in person. Only the court performs in person searches; visitors may not. Search fee: $17.00 per name. Required to search: name, years to search, DOB. Criminal records on computer back to 1996; card files prior. Clerk will only search computerized records.

General Information: No juvenile, mental health, victims, sealed or adoption records released. SASE required. Turnaround time 5 days. Copy fee: $.50 per page. Certification fee: $17.00. Fee payee: Green Valley Justice Court. Personal checks accepted. Prepayment is required.

Pima County Consolidated Justice Court 115 N Church Ave, Tucson, AZ 85701; 520-740-3171; Fax: 520-884-0346. Hours: 8AM-5PM (MST). *Misdemeanor, Civil Actions Under $5,000, Eviction, Small Claims.*

http://jp.co.pima.az.us

Civil Records: Access: Fax, mail, online, in person. Both court and visitors may perform in person searches. Search fee: $10.00 per name. Required to search: name, years to search. Civil cases indexed by defendant, plaintiff. Civil records on computer since 1988, on docket books prior. Online access is free through the Internet site. You can search docket information for civil, criminal or traffic cases by name, docket or citation number.

Criminal Records: Access: Fax, mail, online, in person. Both court and visitors may perform in person searches. Search fee: $10.00 per name. Required to search: name, years to search, DOB, SSN. Criminal records on computer since 1988, on docket books prior. Online access to criminal records is the same as civil.

General Information: Public Access terminal is available. No information about set-aside judgments, unserved search warrants or felony warrants released. SASE required. Turnaround time 10 days. Copy fee: $1.25 per page. Certification fee: $17.00. Fee is per page. Fee payee: Pima County Justice Court. Personal checks accepted. Credit cards accepted: Visa, MasterCard. Visa, MC. Prepayment is required.

Pinal County

Superior Court PO Box 2730, Florence, AZ 85232-2730; 520-868-6296; Fax: 520-868-6252. Hours: 8AM-5PM (MST). *Felony, Civil Actions Over $5,000, Probate.*

Civil Records: Access: Phone, mail, in person. Both court and visitors may perform in person searches. Search fee: $18.00 per name. Required to search: name, years to search. Civil cases indexed by defendant, plaintiff. Civil records on computer from 1987. Some records on docket books back to 1775.

Criminal Records: Access: Phone, mail, in person. Both court and visitors may perform in person searches. Search fee: $18.00 per name. Required to search: name, years to search. Criminal records on computer from 1987. Some records on docket books back to 1775.

General Information: Public Access terminal is available. No victim names, adoption records released. SASE required. Turnaround time 2 days. Fax notes: Fee to fax results is $.50 per page. Copy fee: $.50 per page. Certification fee: $18.00. Fee payee: Clerk of Superior Court. Business checks accepted. Prepayment is required.

Apache Junction Justice Court 575 N Idaho, Suite 200, Apache Junction, AZ 85219; 480-982-2921; Fax: 480-982-9472. Hours: 8AM-Noon, 1-5PM (MST). *Misdemeanor, Civil Actions Under $5,000, Eviction, Small Claims.*

Civil Records: Access: Fax, mail, in person. Both court and visitors may perform in person searches. Search fee: $17.00. Required to search: name, years to search. Civil cases indexed by defendant, plaintiff. Civil records on computer since 1993. Records retained for 5 years.

Criminal Records: Access: Fax, mail, in person. Only the court performs in person searches; visitors may not. Search fee: $17.00. Required to search: name, years to search. Criminal records on computer since 1993. Records retained for 7 years.

General Information: Turnaround time varies. Fax notes: $1.25 per page. Copy fee: $.50 per page. Certification fee: $17.00. Fee payee: Apache Junction Justice Court. Personal checks accepted. Prepayment is required.

Casa Grande Justice Court - Precinct #2 820 E Cottonwood Lane, Bldg B, Casa Grande, AZ 85222; 520-836-5471; Fax: 520-868-7404. Hours: 8AM-5PM (MST). *Misdemeanor, Civil Actions Under $5,000, Eviction, Small Claims.*

Civil Records: Access: Mail, in person. Only the court performs in person searches; visitors may not. No search fee. Required to search: name, years to search. Civil cases indexed by defendant, plaintiff. Civil records on computer since 1992.

Criminal Records: Access: Mail, in person. Only the court performs in person searches; visitors may not. No search fee. Required to search: name, years to search, DOB; also helpful: SSN. Criminal records on computer since 1992.

General Information: No juvenile, mental health, victims, sealed or adoption records released. SASE required. Turnaround time 1 day. Copy fee: $.50. Certification fee: $17.00. Fee payee: Casa Grande Justice Court. Business checks accepted. Credit cards accepted: Visa, MasterCard. Prepayment is required.

Eloy Justice Court PO Box 586, Eloy, AZ 85231; 520-466-9221; Fax: 520-466-4473. Hours: 8AM-Noon, 1-5PM (MST). *Misdemeanor, Civil Actions Under $5,000, Eviction, Small Claims.*

Civil Records: Access: Fax, mail, in person. Only the court performs in person searches; visitors may not. No search fee. Required to search: name, years to search. Civil cases indexed by defendant, plaintiff. Civil records

on computer since 8/92. On docket books and index cards from 1981.

Criminal Records: Access: Fax, mail, in person. Only the court performs in person searches; visitors may not. No search fee. Required to search: name, years to search. Criminal records on computer since 8/92. On docket books and index cards from 1981.

General Information: No juvenile, mental health, victims, sealed or adoption records released. SASE required. Turnaround time 1-2 weeks. Copy fee: $.50 per page. Certification fee: $17.00. Fee payee: Eloy Justice Court. Business checks accepted. Prepayment is required.

Florence Justice Court PO Box 1818, Florence, AZ 85232; 520-868-7194; Fax: 520-868-7190. Hours: 8AM-5PM (MST). *Misdemeanor, Civil Actions Under $5,000, Eviction, Small Claims.*

Civil Records: Access: Mail, in person. Only the court performs in person searches; visitors may not. Search fee: $17.00 per name. Required to search: name, years to search. Civil cases indexed by defendant, plaintiff. Civil records are on computer since January 1999.

Criminal Records: Access: Mail, in person. Only the court performs in person searches; visitors may not. Search fee: $17.00 per name. Required to search: name, years to search. Criminal records are on computer since January 1999.

General Information: No juvenile, mental health, victims, sealed or adoption records released. SASE required. Turnaround time 1 week. Copy fee: $.50 per page. Certification fee: $17.00. Fee payee: Florence Justice Court. Only cashiers checks and money orders accepted. Prepayment is required.

Mammoth Justice Court PO Box 777, Mammoth, AZ 85618; 520-487-2262; Fax: 520-487-2585. Hours: 8AM-5PM (MST). *Misdemeanor, Civil Actions Under $5,000, Eviction, Small Claims.*

Civil Records: Access: Mail, in person. Both court and visitors may perform in person searches. Search fee: $17.00 per name. Required to search: name, years to search. Civil cases indexed by defendant, plaintiff. Civil records on docket books. Misdemeanor and civil records retained for 7 years.

Criminal Records: Access: Mail, in person. Both court and visitors may perform in person searches. Search fee: $17.00 per name. Required to search: name, years to search. Criminal records on docket books. Misdemeanor and civil records retained for 7 years.

General Information: No juvenile, mental health, victims, sealed or adoption records released. SASE required. Turnaround time 2 days. Copy fee: $.50 per page. Certification fee: $17.00. Fee payee: Mammoth Justice Court. Personal checks accepted. Prepayment is required.

Maricopa Justice Court PO Box 201, Maricopa, AZ 85239; 520-568-2451; Fax: 520-568-2924. Hours: 8AM-4PM (MST). *Misdemeanor, Civil Actions Under $5,000, Eviction, Small Claims.*

Civil Records: Access: Fax, mail, in person. Only the court performs in person searches; visitors may not. Search fee: $17.00 per name. Required to search: name, years to search. Civil cases indexed by defendant. Civil records on computer since 1992.

Criminal Records: Access: Mail, in person. Only the court performs in person searches; visitors may not. Search fee: $17.00 per name. Required to search: name, years to search. Criminal records on computer since 1992. Records on dockets.

General Information: No juvenile, mental health, victims, sealed or adoption records released. SASE required. Turnaround time 2 days. Copy fee: $.50 per page. Certification fee: $17.00. Fee payee: Maricopa Justice Court. Personal checks accepted. Prepayment is required.

Oracle Justice Court PO Box 3924, Oracle, AZ 85623; 520-896-9250; Fax: 520-868-7812. Hours: 8AM-5PM (MST). *Misdemeanor, Civil Actions Under $5,000, Eviction, Small Claims.*

Civil Records: Access: Mail, in person. Both court and visitors may perform in person searches. Search fee: $17.00 per name. Required to search: name, years to search; also helpful: address. Civil cases indexed by defendant. Civil records on docket books and computer back to 1991.

Criminal Records: Access: Mail, in person. Both court and visitors may perform in person searches. Search fee: $17.00 per name. Required to search: name, years to search, DOB; also helpful: address, SSN. Criminal records on docket books and computer back to 1991.

General Information: Public Access terminal is available. No juvenile, mental health, victims, sealed, adoption records released. SASE required. Fax notes: Fee to fax results is $1.00 per page. Copy fee: $1.50 per page. Certification fee: $17.00. Fee payee: Oracle Justice Court. Personal checks accepted. Prepayment is required.

Superior/Kearny Justice Court 60 E Main St, Superior, AZ 85273; 520-689-5871; Fax: 520-689-2369. Hours: 8AM-Noon, 1-5PM (MST). *Misdemeanor, Civil Actions Under $5,000, Eviction, Small Claims.*

Civil Records: Access: Fax, mail, in person. Only the court performs in person searches; visitors may not. Search fee: $5.00 per name. Required to search: name, years to search. Civil cases indexed by defendant, plaintiff. Civil records on computer since 1993, on docket books from 1985.

Criminal Records: Access: Fax, mail, in person. Only the court performs in person searches; visitors may not. Search fee: $5.00 per name. Required to search: name, years to search, DOB; also helpful: SSN. Criminal records on computer since 1993, on docket books from 1985.

General Information: No juvenile, mental health, victims, sealed or adoption records released. SASE required. Turnaround time 3 days. Fax notes: No fee to fax results. Copy fee: $1.25 per page. Certification fee: $17.00. Fee payee: Superior/Kearny Justice Court. Personal checks accepted. Prepayment is required.

Santa Cruz County

Superior Court PO Box 1265, Nogales, AZ 85628; 520-761-7808; Fax: 520-761-7857. Hours: 8AM-5PM (MST). *Felony, Civil Actions Over $5,000, Probate.*

http://sccazcourts.org

Civil Records: Access: Mail, fax, in person. Both court and visitors may perform in person searches. Search fee: $18.00 per year/source. Required to search: name, years to search. Civil cases indexed by defendant, plaintiff. Civil records on microfiche from 1898 to 1950. Records on docket books from 1950 to 1996; on computer after 1996.

Criminal Records: Access: Mail, fax, in person. Both court and visitors may perform in person searches. Search fee: $18.00 per year/source. Required to search: name, years to search, DOB; also helpful: SSN. Criminal records on microfiche from 1898 to 1989. Records on docket books from 1977 to 1996; on computer after 1996.

General Information: No mental health, victims, sealed or adoption records released. SASE required. Turnaround time 1 1/2 weeks. Fax notes: Fee to fax results is $.50 per page. Copy fee: $.50 per page. Certification fee: $18.00. Fee payee: Clerk of Superior Court. Personal checks accepted. Prepayment is required.

East Santa Cruz County Justice Court - Precinct #2 PO Box 100, Patagonia, AZ 85624; 520-455-5796; Fax: 520-455-5517 (Attn: Justice Court). Hours: 8:30AM-4:30PM (MST). *Misdemeanor, Civil Actions Under $5,000, Eviction, Small Claims.*

Civil Records: Access: Mail, in person. Only the court performs in person searches; visitors may not. Search fee: $17.00 per name. Required to search: name, years to search; also helpful: address. Civil cases indexed by plaintiff. Civil records on docket books.

Criminal Records: Access: Mail, in person. Only the court performs in person searches; visitors may not. Search fee: $17.00 per name. Required to search: name, years to search, DOB, SSN, signed release; also helpful: address. Criminal records on docket books.

General Information: No juvenile, mental health, victims, sealed or adoption records released. SASE not required. Turnaround time 3-5 days. Copy fee: $.50 per page. Certification fee: $17.00. Fee payee: East Santa Cruz County Justice Court. Personal checks accepted. Prepayment is required.

Santa Cruz Justice Court PO Box 1150, Nogales, AZ 85628; 520-761-7853; Fax: 520-761-7929. Hours: 8AM-5PM (MST). *Misdemeanor, Civil Actions Under $5,000, Eviction, Small Claims.*

Civil Records: Access: Fax, mail, in person. Both court and visitors may perform in person searches. Search fee: $17.00 per name. Required to search: name, years to search; also helpful: address. Civil cases indexed by defendant, plaintiff. Civil records on computer since 2/96.

Criminal Records: Access: Fax, mail, in person. Both court and visitors may perform in person searches. Search fee: $17.00 per name. Required to search: name, years to search, DOB; also helpful: address, SSN. Criminal records on computer since 2/96.

General Information: No juvenile, mental health, victims, sealed or adoption records released. SASE required. Turnaround time 1-3 weeks. Copy fee: $.50 per page. Certification fee: $17.00. Fee payee: Santa Cruz Justice Court. Personal checks accepted.

Yavapai County

Superior Court Yavapai County Courthouse, Prescott, AZ 86301; 928-771-3313; Fax: 928-771-3111. Hours: 8AM-5PM (MST). *Felony, Civil Actions Over $5,000, Probate.*

Civil Records: Access: Fax, mail, in person. Both court and visitors may perform in person searches. Search fee: $18.00 per name. Required to search: name, years to search. Civil cases indexed by defendant, plaintiff. Civil records archived from 1900s. Some records on handwritten index book.

Criminal Records: Access: Fax, mail, in person. Both court and visitors may perform in person searches. Search fee: $18.00 per name per year. Required to search: name, years to search, offense. Criminal records archived from 1900s. Some records on handwritten index book.

General Information: Public Access terminal is available. No juvenile, mental health, victims, sealed or adoption records released. SASE required. Turnaround time 10 days. Fax notes: $.50 per page. Copy fee: $.50 per page. Certification fee: $18.00. Fee payee: Clerk of Superior Court. Personal checks accepted. Prepayment is required.

Bagdad Justice Court PO Box 243, Bagdad, AZ 86321; 928-633-2141; Fax: 928-633-4451. Hours: 8AM-5PM M-Th (MST). *Misdemeanor, Civil Actions Under $5,000, Eviction, Small Claims.*

Civil Records: Access: Mail, in person. Only the court performs in person searches; visitors may not. Search fee: $17.00 per name. Required to search: name, years

to search; also helpful: address. Civil records on computer since 3/94. Records on docket books and index cards. Records purged after 10 years.

Criminal Records: Access: Mail, in person. Only the court performs in person searches; visitors may not. Search fee: $17.00 per name. Required to search: name, years to search, DOB; also helpful: address, SSN. Criminal records on computer since 3/94. Records on docket books and index cards. Records purged after 10 years.

General Information: No juvenile, mental health, victims, sealed or adoption records released. SASE required. Turnaround time 2 days. Copy fee: $.50 per page. Certification fee: $17.00. Fee payee: Bagdad Justice Court. Only cashiers checks and money orders accepted.

Bagdad-Yarnell Justice Court PO Box 65, Yarnell, AZ 85362; 928-427-3318; Fax: 928-771-3362. Hours: 8AM-5PM (MST). *Misdemeanor, Civil Actions Under $5,000, Eviction, Small Claims.*

Civil Records: Access: Mail, in person. Only the court performs in person searches; visitors may not. Search fee: $17.00 per name. Required to search: name, years to search. Civil cases indexed by defendant, plaintiff. Civil records on computer from 1989. Prior records on docket books. Records purged after 10 years.

Criminal Records: Access: Mail, in person. Only the court performs in person searches; visitors may not. Search fee: $17.00 per name. Required to search: name, years to search. Criminal records on computer from 1989. prior on docket books. Records purged after 5 years.

General Information: No juvenile, mental health, victims, sealed or adoption records released. SASE required. Turnaround time 5 days. Copy fee: $.50 per page. Certification fee: $17.00. Fee payee: Yarnell Justice Court. Only cashiers checks and money orders accepted. Prepayment is required.

Mayer Justice Court PO Box 245, Mayer, AZ 86333; 928-771-3355. Hours: 8AM-5PM (MST). *Misdemeanor, Civil Actions Under $5,000, Eviction, Small Claims.*

Civil Records: Access: Mail, in person. Only the court performs in person searches; visitors may not. No search fee. Required to search: name, years to search. Civil cases indexed by defendant, plaintiff. Civil records on computer from 1989. Records purged after 5 years.

Criminal Records: Access: Mail, in person. Only the court performs in person searches; visitors may not. No search fee. Required to search: name, years to search; also helpful: DOB. Criminal records on computer from 1989. Records purged after 5 years.

General Information: No juvenile, mental health, victims, sealed or adoption records released. SASE required. Turnaround time 4 days. Copy fee: $.50 per page. Certification fee: $17.00. Fee payee: Mayer Justice Court. Only cashiers checks and money orders accepted. Prepayment is required.

Prescott Justice Court Yavapai County Courthouse, Room 103, Prescott, AZ 86301; 928-771-3300; Fax: 928-771-3302. Hours: 8AM-5PM (MST). *Misdemeanor, Civil Actions Under $5,000, Eviction, Small Claims.*

Civil Records: Access: Fax, mail, in person. Both court and visitors may perform in person searches. No search fee. Required to search: name, years to search; also helpful: address. Civil cases indexed by defendant, plaintiff. Civil records are indexed on computer then purged after 5 years. Searches only available for past 5 years.

Criminal Records: Access: Fax, mail, in person. Both court and visitors may perform in person searches. No search fee. Required to search: name, years to search, DOB; also helpful: address, SSN. Criminal records are indexed on computer then purged after 5 years. Searches only available for past 5 years.

General Information: Public Access terminal is available. No juvenile, victims or sealed records released. SASE required. Turnaround time 2 days. Fax notes: $17.00 per document. Copy fee: $.50 per page. Certification fee: $17.00. Fee payee: City of Prescott. Personal checks accepted. No two party checks. Credit cards accepted: Visa, MasterCard. Prepayment is required.

Seligman Justice Court PO Box 56, Seligman, AZ 86337-0056; 928-422-3281; Fax: 928-422-3282. Hours: 8AM-5PM (MST). *Misdemeanor, Civil Actions Under $5,000, Eviction, Small Claims.*

Civil Records: Access: Phone, fax, mail, in person. Both court and visitors may perform in person searches. No search fee. Required to search: name, years to search; also helpful: address. Civil cases indexed by defendant, plaintiff. Civil records on computer. Records purged after 5 years.

Criminal Records: Access: Phone, fax, mail, in person. Both court and visitors may perform in person searches. No search fee. Required to search: name, years to search, DOB; also helpful: address, SSN. Criminal records on computer. Records purged after 5 years.

General Information: No juvenile or victims records released. SASE required. Turnaround time 2 days. Fax notes: No fee to fax results. Copy fee: $1.25 per page. Certification fee: $17.00. Fee payee: Seligman Justice Court. Business checks accepted.

Verde Valley Justice Court 10 S 6th St, Cottonwood, AZ 86326; 928-639-5820; Fax: 928-639-5828. Hours: 8AM-5PM (MST). *Misdemeanor, Civil Actions Under $5,000, Eviction, Small Claims.*

Civil Records: Access: Mail, in person. Both court and visitors may perform in person searches. Search fee: $17.00. Required to search: name, years to search; also helpful: address. Civil cases indexed by defendant, plaintiff. Civil records on computer from 1994. Records purged after 5 years.

Criminal Records: Access: Mail, in person. Both court and visitors may perform in person searches. Search fee: $17.00. Required to search: name, years to search, DOB; also helpful: address, SSN. Criminal records on

docket books and index cards. Records purged after 5 years.

General Information: No juvenile, mental health, victims, sealed or adoption records released. SASE required. Turnaround time 2 days. Copy fee: $.50 per page. Certification fee: $17.00. Fee payee: Verde Valley Justice Court.

Yuma County

Superior Court 168 S 2nd Ave, Yuma, AZ 85364; 928-329-2164; Fax: 928-329-2007. Hours: 8AM-5PM (MST). *Felony, Civil Actions Over $5,000, Probate.*

Civil Records: Access: Fax, mail, in person. Both court and visitors may perform in person searches. Search fee: $18.00 per name. Required to search: name, years to search. Civil cases indexed by defendant. Civil records on docket books from 1900s, new and pending cases from November 1994 on computer.

Criminal Records: Access: Fax, mail, in person. Both court and visitors may perform in person searches. Search fee: $18.00 per name. Required to search: name, years to search. Criminal records on docket books from 1900s, new and pending cases from November 1994 on computer.

General Information: No adoption, mental health records released. SASE required. Turnaround time 1 week. Fax notes: $18.00 per document. Copy fee: $.50 per page. Certification fee: $18.00. Fee payee: Clerk of Superior Court. Business checks accepted. Credit cards accepted: Visa, MasterCard. Prepayment is required.

Somerton Justice Court PO Box 458, Somerton, AZ 85350; 928-627-2722; Fax: 928-627-1076. Hours: 8AM-5PM (MST). *Misdemeanor, Civil Actions Under $5,000, Eviction, Small Claims.*

Civil Records: Access: Phone, fax, mail, in person. Both court and visitors may perform in person searches. No search fee. Required to search: name, years to search. Civil cases indexed by defendant. Civil records on computer.

Criminal Records: Access: Phone, fax, mail, in person. Only the court performs in person searches; visitors may not. No search fee. Required to search: name, years to search, DOB, SSN, offense, date of offense. Criminal records on computer.

General Information: No set aside judgment records released. SASE required. Turnaround time 2-4 days. Fax notes: $1.25 per page. Copy fee: $1.25 per page.

Certification fee: $17.00. Fee payee: Somerton Justice Court. Business checks accepted. Prepayment is required.

Wellton Justice Court PO Box 384, Wellton, AZ 85356; 928-785-3321; Fax: 928-785-4933. Hours: 8AM-5PM (MST). *Misdemeanor, Civil Actions Under $5,000, Eviction, Small Claims.*

Civil Records: Access: Phone, fax, mail, in person. Only the court performs in person searches; visitors may not. No search fee. Required to search: name, years to search. Civil cases indexed by defendant, plaintiff. Civil records on computer.

Criminal Records: Access: Phone, fax, mail, in person. Only the court performs in person searches; visitors may not. No search fee. Required to search: name, years to search, offense, date of offense. Criminal records on computer.

General Information: No set aside judgment records released. SASE not required. Turnaround time same day. Copy fee: $.50 per page. Certification fee: No cert fee. Fee payee: Wellton Justice Court. Personal checks accepted. Credit cards accepted: Visa, MasterCard, Discover, American Express.

Yuma Justice Court 168 S 2nd Ave, Yuma, AZ 85364; 928-329-2180; Fax: 928-329-2005. Hours: 8AM-5PM (MST). *Misdemeanor, Civil Actions Under $5,000, Eviction, Small Claims.*

Civil Records: Access: Mail, in person. Both court and visitors may perform in person searches. Search fee: $17.00 per name. Required to search: name, years to search. Civil cases indexed by defendant. Civil records on computer. Purged after 5 years. Info available only for cases after 09/01/94.

Criminal Records: Access: Mail, in person. Only the court performs in person searches; visitors may not. Search fee: $17.00 per name. Required to search: name, years to search. Criminal records on computer. Purged after 5 years. Info available only for cases after 09/01/94.

General Information: Public Access terminal is available. Will not release victim's names. SASE required. Turnaround time 2-4 days. Copy fee: $.50 per page. Certification fee: $17.00. Fee payee: Justice Court #1. Personal checks accepted. Credit cards accepted: Visa, MasterCard. Visa, MC. Prepayment is required.

Arizona Recording Offices

ORGANIZATION   15 counties, 16 recording offices. The Navajo Nation is profiled here. The recording officer is County Recorder. Recordings are usually placed in a Grantor/Grantee index. The entire state is in the Mountain Time Zone (MST), and does not change to daylight savings time.

REAL ESTATE RECORDS   Counties do not perform real estate searches. Copy fees are usually $1.00 per page. Certification fees are usually $3.00 per document.

UCC RECORDS   Financing statements are filed at the state level, except for real estate related collateral, which are filed with the County Recorder. However, prior to 07/2001, consumer goods and farm collateral were filed at the County Recorder and these older records can be searched there. All counties will perform UCC searches. Use search request form UCC-3. Search fees are generally $10.00 per debtor name. Copies usually cost $1.00 per page.

TAX LIEN RECORDS   Federal and state tax liens on personal property of businesses are filed with the Secretary of State. Other federal and state tax liens are filed with the County Recorder. Several counties will do a separate tax lien search.

OTHER LIENS   Executions, judgments, labor.

Apache County

County Recorder, P.O. Box 425, St. Johns, AZ 85936. 928-337-4364 R/E Recording: 928-337-7515 UCC Recording: 928-337-7515; Fax 928-337-2003. http://www.co.apache.az.us/Recorder/index.htm Will search UCC records. UCC search does not include tax liens. Separate combined tax lien search-$20.00 first name, $10.00 each additional name Will not search real estate records. **Online Access:** Real Estate, Recording. Online access to the Apache County Recorder Query Index are available free at www.co.apache.az.us/ Recorder/index/query.asp. **Other Phone Numbers:** Assessor 928-337-7521; Treasurer 928-337-7515; Elections 928-337-7515.

Cochise County

County Recorder, P.O. Box 184, Bisbee, AZ 85603. County Recorder, R/E and UCC Recording 520-432-9270; Fax 520-432-9274. www.co.cochise.az.us Will search UCC records. This agency will not do a tax lien search. Will not search real estate records. **Other Phone Numbers:** Assessor 520-432-9329; Treasurer 520-432-9222; Elections 520-432-9236.

Coconino County

County Recorder, 100 E. Birch, Flagstaff, AZ 86001. 928-779-6585; Fax 928-779-6739. Will search UCC records. Tax liens included in UCC search if requested with extra $2.00 fee. Also charge $1.00 per finding. RE record owner searches available. **Other Phone Numbers:** Assessor 928-779-6502.

Gila County

County Recorder, 1400 East Ash Street, Globe, AZ 85501. 928-425-3231 R/E Recording: 928-425-3231 x238 UCC Recording: 928-425-3231 x238; Fax 928-425-9270. Will search UCC records. This agency will do a federal or state tax lien search for $10.00 per search. Will search real estate records. Fee is $10.00 per hour for searches 1983 to present; $15 per hour if prior to 1983. **Other Phone Numbers:** Assessor 928-425-3231 x238; Treasurer 928-425-3231 x201; Elections 928-425-3231 x441.

Graham County

County Recorder, 921 Thatcher Blvd., Safford, AZ 85546. County Recorder, R/E and UCC Recording 928-428-3560; Fax 928-428-5951. www.graham.az.gov Will search UCC records. UCC search includes tax liens if requested. Will not search real estate records.

Other Phone Numbers: Assessor 928-428-2828; Treasurer 928-428-3440; Elections 928-428-3930.

Greenlee County

County Recorder, P.O. Box 1625, Clifton, AZ 85533-1625. 928-865-2632; Fax 928-865-4417. Will search UCC records. This agency will not do a tax lien search. Will not search real estate records. **Other Phone Numbers:** Assessor 928-865-5302.

La Paz County

County Recorder, Suite 201, 1112 Joshua Ave., Parker, AZ 85344. 928-669-6136; Fax 928-669-5638. http://www.co.la-paz.az.us/recorder.htm Will search UCC records. This agency will not do a tax lien search. Will not search real estate records. **Other Phone Numbers:** Assessor 928-669-6165; Treasurer 928-669-6145.

Maricopa County

County Recorder, 111 South 3rd Avenue, Phoenix, AZ 85003. 602-506-3535; Fax 602-506-3069. http://recorder.maricopa.gov Will search UCC records. This agency will not do a tax lien search. Will not search real estate records. **Online Access:** Real Estate, Liens. Access is available by direct dial-up or on the Internet. Dial-up access requires one-time set-up fee of $300 plus $.06 per minute. Dial-up hours are 8am-10pm M-F, 8-5 S-S. Records date back to 1983. For additional information, contact Linda Kinchloe at 602-506-3637. Also, access to the County Recorder's database is available free at http://recorder.maricopa.gov/recdocdata. Records go back to 1983. Also, access to the Assessor database is available free at www.maricopa.gov/ assessor/default.asp. Residential data is available. Also, perform name/parcel/property tax lookups free on the SBOE site at www.sboe.state.az.us/cgi-bin/name_lookup.pl. **Other Phone Numbers:** Assessor 602-506-3406.

Mohave County

County Recorder, P.O. Box 70, Kingman, AZ 86402-0070. County Recorder, R/E and UCC Recording 928-753-0701; Fax 928-753-0727. http://www. co.mohave.az.us Will search UCC records. This agency will not do a tax lien search. Will not search real estate records. **Online Access:** Real Estate, Grantor/Grantee, Liens, Assessor. Online access to the Recorder's System is available free at http://216.173.151.223/splash.jsp. Registration and password is required. Also, online access to the Assessor's property database is available free (no registration) at www.co.mohave.az.us/1moweb/

depts_files/assessor_files/assessdata.asp. A sales history database is also here. Also, the treasurer's tax sale parcel search is available at www.co.mohave.az.us/ 1moweb/depts_files/treasure_files/about_treasure.htm. **Other Phone Numbers:** Assessor 928-753-0703; Treasurer 928-753-0737; Appraiser/Auditor 928-753-0703; Elections 928-753-0733.

Navajo County

County Recorder, P.O. Box 668, Holbrook, AZ 86025-0668. 928-524-4194; Fax 928-524-4308. Will search UCC records. UCC search includes tax liens if requested. Will not search real estate records. **Other Phone Numbers:** Assessor 928-524-6161 x230.

Navajo Nation

County Recorder, P.O. Box 663, Window Rock, AZ 86515. 928-871-7365; Fax 928-871-7381. Will search UCC records. This agency will not do a tax lien search. Will not search real estate records.

Pima County

County Recorder, 115 North Church Avenue, Tucson, AZ 85701. 520-740-4350; Fax 520-623-1785. http://www.recorder.co.pima.az.us Will search UCC records. Tax liens not included in UCC search. Will not search real estate records. **Online Access:** Assessor, Real Estate, Lien, Recording. Online access to the recorder's Research Records database is available free at www.recorder.co.pima. az.us/research.html. Click "Enter Here" and use the word "public" for user name and password. Also, records on the Pima County Tax Assessor database are available free online at www.asr.co.pima.az.us/apiq/index.html. Also, a name/parcel/property tax lookup may be performed free on the SBOE site at www.sboe.state.az.us/cgi-bin/name_lookup.pl. Also, search by parcel number on the Treasurer's tax inquiry database at www.to.co.pima.az.us/inquiry.html. **Other Phone Numbers:** Assessor 520-740-8630.

Pinal County

County Recorder, P.O. Box 848, Florence, AZ 85232-0848. 520-868-7100; Fax 520-868-7170. Will search UCC records. RE record owner searches available. The Recorder's office does inquiries by grantor/grantee name. **Other Phone Numbers:** Assessor 520-868-6361.

Santa Cruz County

County Recorder, 2150 N. Congress, County Complex, Nogales, AZ 85621. 520-761-7800 x3037; Fax 520-761-7938.

Will search UCC records. This agency will not do a tax lien search. Will not search real estate records. **Other Phone Numbers:** Assessor 520-761-7938 x3008.

Yavapai County

County Recorder, 1015 Fair St, Room 228, Prescott, AZ 86305. 928-771-3244; Fax 928-771-3258. http://www.co.yavapai.az.us/departments/recorder/RecorderMain.asp

A second office is located at 10 S 6th St, Cottonwood AZ 86326, phone 928-639-5807, fax: 928-639-5812.

Will search UCC records. Will not perform "open-ended" real estate records searches. Call or visit the website for search information and criteria. **Online Access:** Assessor, Real Estate, Recordings. Online access to the recording office iCRIS database is available free at http://icris.co.yavapai.az.us/splash.jsp. Records from 1976 to present; images from 1986 to present. Also, assessor and land records on the County Geographic Information Systems (GIS) database are available free online at www.co.yavapai.az.us/departments/gis/gisOnlineApps.asp. To search, choose a "session" in the "Locate Property Information" box. **Other Phone Numbers:** Assessor 520-771-3220; Treasurer 928-771-3233; Elections 928-771-3250; Voter Registration 928-771-3248

Yuma County

County Recorder, 410 S Maiden Lane, Yuma, AZ 85364-2311. 928-373-6020 R/E Recording: 928-373-6029 UCC Recording: 928-373-6028; Fax 928-373-6024.

Will search UCC records. This agency will not do a tax lien search. Will not search real estate records. **Other Phone Numbers:** Assessor 928-373-6040; Treasurer 928-539-7781; Elections 928-329-2119; Vital Records 928-317-4530.

Arizona County Locator

You will usually be able to find the city name in the City/County Cross Reference below. In that case, it is a simple matter to determine the county from the cross reference. However, only the official US Postal Service city names are included in this index. There are an additional 40,000 place names that people use in their addresses. Therefore, we have also included a ZIP/City Cross Reference immediately following the City/County Cross Reference.

If you know the ZIP Code but the city name does not appear in the City/County Cross Reference index, look up the ZIP Code in the ZIP/City Cross Reference, find the city name, then look up the city name in the City/County Cross Reference. For example, you want to know the county for an address of Menands, NY 12204. There is no "Menands" in the City/County Cross Reference. The ZIP/City Cross Reference shows that ZIP Codes 12201-12288 are for the city of Albany. Looking back in the City/County Cross Reference, Albany is in Albany County.

City/County Cross Reference

AGUILA Maricopa
AJO Pima
ALPINE Apache
AMADO (85645) Pima(83), Santa Cruz(17)
APACHE JUNCTION (85220) Pinal(79), Maricopa(21)
APACHE JUNCTION Pinal
ARIVACA Pima
ARIZONA CITY Pinal
ARLINGTON Maricopa
ASH FORK Yavapai
AVONDALE Maricopa
BAGDAD Yavapai
BAPCHULE Pinal
BELLEMONT Coconino
BENSON (85602) Cochise(92), Pima(8)
BISBEE Cochise
BLACK CANYON CITY Yavapai
BLUE Greenlee
BLUE GAP Navajo
BOUSE La Paz
BOWIE Cochise
BUCKEYE Maricopa
BULLHEAD CITY Mohave
BYLAS Graham
CAMERON Coconino
CAMP VERDE Yavapai
CAREFREE Maricopa
CASA GRANDE Pinal
CASHION Maricopa
CATALINA Pima
CAVE CREEK Maricopa
CENTRAL Graham
CHAMBERS Apache
CHANDLER (85248) Maricopa(99), Pinal(1)
CHANDLER Maricopa
CHANDLER HEIGHTS Maricopa
CHINLE Apache
CHINO VALLEY Yavapai
CHLORIDE Mohave
CIBICUE Navajo
CIBOLA La Paz
CLARKDALE Yavapai
CLAY SPRINGS Navajo
CLAYPOOL Gila
CLIFTON Greenlee
COCHISE Cochise
COLORADO CITY Mohave
CONCHO Apache
CONGRESS Yavapai
COOLIDGE Pinal
CORNVILLE Yavapai
CORTARO Pima
COTTONWOOD Yavapai
CROWN KING Yavapai
DATELAND Yuma
DENNEHOTSO Apache
DEWEY Yavapai
DOLAN SPRINGS Mohave
DOUGLAS Cochise
DRAGOON Cochise
DUNCAN Greenlee

EAGAR Apache
EDEN Graham
EHRENBERG La Paz
EL MIRAGE Maricopa
ELFRIDA Cochise
ELGIN Santa Cruz
ELOY Pinal
FLAGSTAFF Coconino
FLORENCE Pinal
FOREST LAKES Coconino
FORT APACHE Navajo
FORT DEFIANCE Apache
FORT HUACHUCA Cochise
FORT MCDOWELL Maricopa
FORT MOHAVE Mohave
FORT THOMAS Graham
FOUNTAIN HILLS Maricopa
FREDONIA Coconino
GADSDEN Yuma
GANADO Apache
GILA BEND Maricopa
GILBERT Maricopa
GLENDALE Maricopa
GLOBE Gila
GOLDEN VALLEY Mohave
GOODYEAR Maricopa
GRAND CANYON Coconino
GRAY MOUNTAIN Coconino
GREEN VALLEY Pima
GREER Apache
HACKBERRY Mohave
HAPPY JACK Coconino
HAYDEN Gila
HEBER Navajo
HEREFORD Cochise
HIGLEY Maricopa
HOLBROOK Navajo
HOTEVILLA Navajo
HOUCK Apache
HUACHUCA CITY Cochise
HUALAPAI Mohave
HUMBOLDT Yavapai
INDIAN WELLS Navajo
IRON SPRINGS Yavapai
JEROME Yavapai
JOSEPH CITY Navajo
KAIBITO Coconino
KAYENTA Navajo
KEAMS CANYON Navajo
KEARNY Pinal
KINGMAN Mohave
KIRKLAND Yavapai
KYKOTSMOVI VILLAGE Navajo
LAKE HAVASU CITY Mohave
LAKE MONTEZUMA Yavapai
LAKESIDE Navajo
LAVEEN Maricopa
LEUPP Coconino
LITCHFIELD PARK Maricopa
LITTLEFIELD Mohave
LUKACHUKAI Apache
LUKE AFB Maricopa

LUKEVILLE Pima
LUPTON Apache
MAMMOTH (85618) Pinal(96), Pima(4)
MANY FARMS Apache
MARANA (85653) Pima(89), Pinal(11)
MARBLE CANYON Coconino
MARICOPA Pinal
MAYER Yavapai
MC NARY Apache
MC NEAL Cochise
MEADVIEW Mohave
MESA Maricopa
MIAMI (85539) Gila(97), Pinal(3)
MOHAVE VALLEY Mohave
MORENCI Greenlee
MORMON LAKE Coconino
MORRISTOWN Maricopa
MOUNT LEMMON Pima
MUNDS PARK Coconino
NACO Cochise
NAZLINI Apache
NOGALES Santa Cruz
NORTH RIM Coconino
NUTRIOSO Apache
OATMAN Mohave
ORACLE Pinal
OVERGAARD Navajo
PAGE Coconino
PALO VERDE Maricopa
PARADISE VALLEY Maricopa
PARKER La Paz
PARKS Coconino
PATAGONIA Santa Cruz
PAULDEN Yavapai
PAYSON Gila
PEACH SPRINGS Mohave
PEARCE Cochise
PEORIA Maricopa
PERIDOT Gila
PETRIFIED FOREST NATL PK Apache
PHOENIX Maricopa
PICACHO Pinal
PIMA Graham
PINE Gila
PINEDALE Navajo
PINETOP Navajo
PINON Navajo
PIRTLEVILLE Cochise
POLACCA Navajo
POMERENE Cochise
POSTON La Paz
PRESCOTT Yavapai
PRESCOTT VALLEY Yavapai
QUARTZSITE La Paz
QUEEN CREEK (85242) Pinal(61), Maricopa(39)
RED ROCK Pinal
RED VALLEY Apache
RILLITO Pima
RIMROCK Yavapai
RIO RICO Santa Cruz
RIO VERDE Maricopa

ROCK POINT Apache
ROLL Yuma
ROOSEVELT Gila
ROUND ROCK Apache
SACATON Pinal
SAFFORD Graham
SAHUARITA Pima
SAINT DAVID Cochise
SAINT JOHNS Apache
SAINT MICHAELS Apache
SALOME La Paz
SAN CARLOS Gila
SAN LUIS Yuma
SAN MANUEL Pinal
SAN SIMON Cochise
SANDERS Apache
SASABE Pima
SAWMILL Apache
SCOTTSDALE Maricopa
SECOND MESA Navajo
SEDONA (86336) Yavapai(56), Coconino(44)
SEDONA (86351) Yavapai(97), Coconino(3)
SEDONA Coconino
SEDONA Yavapai
SELIGMAN Yavapai
SELLS Pima
SHONTO Navajo
SHOW LOW Navajo
SIERRA VISTA Cochise
SKULL VALLEY Yavapai
SNOWFLAKE Navajo
SOLOMON Graham
SOMERTON Yuma
SONOITA (85637) Santa Cruz(80), Pima(20)
SPRINGERVILLE Apache
STANFIELD Pinal
SUN CITY Maricopa
SUN CITY WEST Maricopa
SUN VALLEY Navajo
SUPAI Coconino
SUPERIOR Pinal
SURPRISE Maricopa
TACNA Maricopa
TAYLOR Navajo
TEEC NOS POS Apache
TEMPE Maricopa
TEMPLE BAR MARINA Mohave
THATCHER Graham
TOLLESON Maricopa
TOMBSTONE Cochise
TONALEA Coconino
TONOPAH Maricopa
TONTO BASIN Gila
TOPAWA Pima
TOPOCK Mohave
TORTILLA FLAT Maricopa
TSAILE Apache
TUBA CITY Coconino
TUBAC Santa Cruz

TUCSON (85739) Pima(55), Pinal(45)
TUCSON Pima
TUMACACORI Santa Cruz
VAIL Pima
VALENTINE Mohave
VALLEY FARMS Pinal
VERNON Apache

WADDELL Maricopa
WELLTON Yuma
WENDEN La Paz
WHITE MOUNTAIN LAKE Navajo
WHITERIVER Navajo
WICKENBURG Maricopa
WIKIEUP Mohave

WILLCOX (85643) Cochise(94), Graham(6)
WILLCOX Cochise
WILLIAMS Coconino
WILLOW BEACH Mohave
WINDOW ROCK Apache
WINKELMAN (85292) Pinal(50), Gila(50)
WINSLOW Navajo

WITTMANN Maricopa
WOODRUFF Navajo
YARNELL Yavapai
YOUNG Gila
YOUNGTOWN Maricopa
YUCCA Mohave
YUMA Yuma

ZIP/City Cross Reference

85001-85099	PHOENIX	85346-85346	QUARTZSITE	85625-85625	PEARCE	86032-86032	JOSEPH CITY
85201-85216	MESA	85347-85347	ROLL	85626-85626	PIRTLEVILLE	86033-86033	KAYENTA
85217-85220	APACHE JUNCTION	85348-85348	SALOME	85627-85627	POMERENE	86034-86034	KEAMS CANYON
85221-85221	BAPCHULE	85349-85349	SAN LUIS	85628-85628	NOGALES	86035-86035	LEUPP
85222-85222	CASA GRANDE	85350-85350	SOMERTON	85629-85629	SAHUARITA	86036-86036	MARBLE CANYON
85223-85223	ARIZONA CITY	85351-85351	SUN CITY	85630-85630	SAINT DAVID	86038-86038	MORMON LAKE
85224-85226	CHANDLER	85352-85352	TACNA	85631-85631	SAN MANUEL	86039-86039	KYKOTSMOVI VILLAGE
85227-85227	CHANDLER HEIGHTS	85353-85353	TOLLESON	85632-85632	SAN SIMON	86040-86040	PAGE
85228-85228	COOLIDGE	85354-85354	TONOPAH	85633-85633	SASABE	86042-86042	POLACCA
85230-85230	CASA GRANDE	85355-85355	WADDELL	85634-85634	SELLS	86043-86043	SECOND MESA
85231-85231	ELOY	85356-85356	WELLTON	85635-85636	SIERRA VISTA	86044-86044	TONALEA
85232-85232	FLORENCE	85357-85357	WENDEN	85637-85637	SONOITA	86045-86045	TUBA CITY
85233-85234	GILBERT	85358-85358	WICKENBURG	85638-85638	TOMBSTONE	86046-86046	WILLIAMS
85235-85235	HAYDEN	85359-85359	QUARTZSITE	85639-85639	TOPAWA	86047-86047	WINSLOW
85236-85236	HIGLEY	85360-85360	WIKIEUP	85640-85640	TUMACACORI	86052-86052	NORTH RIM
85237-85237	KEARNY	85361-85361	WITTMANN	85641-85641	VAIL	86053-86053	KAIBITO
85239-85239	MARICOPA	85362-85362	YARNELL	85643-85644	WILLCOX	86054-86054	SHONTO
85240-85240	MESA	85363-85363	YOUNGTOWN	85645-85645	AMADO	86301-86304	PRESCOTT
85241-85241	PICACHO	85364-85369	YUMA	85646-85646	TUBAC	86312-86312	PRESCOTT VALLEY
85242-85242	QUEEN CREEK	85371-85371	POSTON	85648-85648	RIO RICO	86313-86313	PRESCOTT
85244-85244	CHANDLER	85372-85373	SUN CITY	85652-85652	CORTARO	86314-86314	PRESCOTT VALLEY
85245-85245	RED ROCK	85374-85374	SURPRISE	85653-85653	MARANA	86320-86320	ASH FORK
85246-85246	CHANDLER	85375-85376	SUN CITY WEST	85654-85654	RILLITO	86321-86321	BAGDAD
85247-85247	SACATON	85377-85377	CAREFREE	85655-85655	DOUGLAS	86322-86322	CAMP VERDE
85248-85249	CHANDLER	85378-85378	SURPRISE	85662-85662	NOGALES	86323-86323	CHINO VALLEY
85250-85252	SCOTTSDALE	85380-85382	PEORIA	85670-85670	FORT HUACHUCA	86324-86324	CLARKDALE
85253-85253	PARADISE VALLEY	85390-85390	WICKENBURG	85671-85671	SIERRA VISTA	86325-86325	CORNVILLE
85254-85262	SCOTTSDALE	85501-85502	GLOBE	85701-85737	TUCSON	86326-86326	COTTONWOOD
85263-85263	RIO VERDE	85530-85530	BYLAS	85738-85738	CATALINA	86327-86327	DEWEY
85264-85264	FORT MCDOWELL	85531-85531	CENTRAL	85739-85777	TUCSON	86329-86329	HUMBOLDT
85266-85267	SCOTTSDALE	85532-85532	CLAYPOOL	85901-85902	SHOW LOW	86330-86330	IRON SPRINGS
85268-85269	FOUNTAIN HILLS	85533-85533	CLIFTON	85911-85911	CIBICUE	86331-86331	JEROME
85271-85271	SCOTTSDALE	85534-85534	DUNCAN	85912-85912	WHITE MOUNTAIN LAKE	86332-86332	KIRKLAND
85272-85272	STANFIELD	85535-85535	EDEN	85920-85920	ALPINE	86333-86333	MAYER
85273-85273	SUPERIOR	85536-85536	FORT THOMAS	85922-85922	BLUE	86334-86334	PAULDEN
85274-85277	MESA	85539-85539	MIAMI	85923-85923	CLAY SPRINGS	86335-86335	RIMROCK
85278-85278	APACHE JUNCTION	85540-85540	MORENCI	85924-85924	CONCHO	86336-86336	SEDONA
85279-85279	FLORENCE	85541-85541	PAYSON	85925-85925	EAGAR	86337-86337	SELIGMAN
85280-85289	TEMPE	85542-85542	PERIDOT	85926-85926	FORT APACHE	86338-86338	SKULL VALLEY
85290-85290	TORTILLA FLAT	85543-85543	PIMA	85927-85927	GREER	86339-86341	SEDONA
85291-85291	VALLEY FARMS	85544-85544	PINE	85928-85928	HEBER	86342-86342	LAKE MONTEZUMA
85292-85292	WINKELMAN	85545-85545	ROOSEVELT	85929-85929	LAKESIDE	86343-86343	CROWN KING
85296-85299	GILBERT	85546-85546	SAFFORD	85930-85930	MC NARY	86351-86351	SEDONA
85301-85308	GLENDALE	85547-85547	PAYSON	85931-85931	FOREST LAKES	86401-86402	KINGMAN
85309-85309	LUKE AFB	85548-85548	SAFFORD	85932-85932	NUTRIOSO	86403-86406	LAKE HAVASU CITY
85310-85318	GLENDALE	85550-85550	SAN CARLOS	85933-85933	OVERGAARD	86411-86411	HACKBERRY
85320-85320	AGUILA	85551-85551	SOLOMON	85934-85934	PINEDALE	86412-86412	HUALAPAI
85321-85321	AJO	85552-85552	THATCHER	85935-85935	PINETOP	86413-86413	GOLDEN VALLEY
85322-85322	ARLINGTON	85553-85553	TONTO BASIN	85936-85936	SAINT JOHNS	86426-86427	FORT MOHAVE
85323-85323	AVONDALE	85554-85554	YOUNG	85937-85937	SNOWFLAKE	86429-86430	BULLHEAD CITY
85324-85324	BLACK CANYON CITY	85601-85601	ARIVACA	85938-85938	SPRINGERVILLE	86431-86431	CHLORIDE
85325-85325	BOUSE	85602-85602	BENSON	85939-85939	TAYLOR	86432-86432	LITTLEFIELD
85326-85326	BUCKEYE	85603-85603	BISBEE	85940-85940	VERNON	86433-86433	OATMAN
85327-85327	CAVE CREEK	85605-85605	BOWIE	85941-85941	WHITERIVER	86434-86434	PEACH SPRINGS
85328-85328	CIBOLA	85606-85606	COCHISE	85942-85942	WOODRUFF	86435-86435	SUPAI
85329-85329	CASHION	85607-85608	DOUGLAS	86001-86011	FLAGSTAFF	86436-86436	TOPOCK
85331-85331	CAVE CREEK	85609-85609	DRAGOON	86015-86015	BELLEMONT	86437-86437	VALENTINE
85332-85332	CONGRESS	85610-85610	ELFRIDA	86016-86016	GRAY MOUNTAIN	86438-86438	YUCCA
85333-85333	DATELAND	85611-85611	ELGIN	86017-86017	MUNDS PARK	86439-86439	BULLHEAD CITY
85334-85334	EHRENBERG	85613-85613	FORT HUACHUCA	86018-86018	PARKS	86440-86440	MOHAVE VALLEY
85335-85335	EL MIRAGE	85614-85614	GREEN VALLEY	86020-86020	CAMERON	86441-86441	DOLAN SPRINGS
85336-85336	GADSDEN	85615-85615	HEREFORD	86021-86021	COLORADO CITY	86442-86442	BULLHEAD CITY
85337-85337	GILA BEND	85616-85616	HUACHUCA CITY	86022-86022	FREDONIA	86443-86443	TEMPLE BAR MARINA
85338-85338	GOODYEAR	85617-85617	MC NEAL	86023-86023	GRAND CANYON	86444-86444	MEADVIEW
85339-85339	LAVEEN	85618-85618	MAMMOTH	86024-86024	HAPPY JACK	86445-86445	WILLOW BEACH
85340-85340	LITCHFIELD PARK	85619-85619	MOUNT LEMMON	86025-86025	HOLBROOK	86446-86446	MOHAVE VALLEY
85341-85341	LUKEVILLE	85620-85620	NACO	86028-86028	PETRIFIED FOREST	86502-86502	CHAMBERS
85342-85342	MORRISTOWN	85621-85621	NOGALES		NATL PK	86503-86503	CHINLE
85343-85343	PALO VERDE	85622-85622	GREEN VALLEY	86029-86029	SUN VALLEY	86504-86504	FORT DEFIANCE
85344-85344	PARKER	85623-85623	ORACLE	86030-86030	HOTEVILLA	86505-86505	GANADO
85345-85345	PEORIA	85624-85624	PATAGONIA	86031-86031	INDIAN WELLS	86506-86506	HOUCK

86507-86507	LUKACHUKAI	86512-86512	SANDERS	86535-86535	DENNEHOTSO	86545-86545	ROCK POINT
86508-86508	LUPTON	86514-86514	TEEC NOS POS	86538-86538	MANY FARMS	86547-86547	ROUND ROCK
86510-86510	PINON	86515-86515	WINDOW ROCK	86540-86540	NAZLINI	86549-86549	SAWMILL
86511-86511	SAINT MICHAELS	86520-86520	BLUE GAP	86544-86544	RED VALLEY	86556-86556	TSAILE

Arkansas

General Help Numbers:

Governor's Office
State Capitol   501-682-2345
Little Rock, AR 72201   Fax 501-682-3597
http://www.accessarkansas.org/governor   8AM-5PM

Attorney General's Office
323 Center St #200   501-682-2007
Little Rock, AR 72201   Fax 501-682-8084
http://www.ag.state.ar.us   8AM-5PM

State Court Administrator
625 Marshall Street, 1100 Justice Bldg   501-682-9400
Little Rock, AR 72201-1078   Fax 501-682-9410
http://courts.state.ar.us/courts/aoc.html   8AM-5PM

State Archives
State Archives   501-682-6900
One Capitol Mall
Little Rock, AR 72201   8AM-4:30PM M-SA
http://www.state.ar.us/ahc

State Specifics:

Capital: Little Rock
                                      Pulaski County

Time Zone: CST

Number of Counties: 75

Population: 2,673,400

Web Site: www.state.ar.us

State Agencies

Criminal Records

Arkansas State Police, Identification Bureau, #1 State Police Plaza Dr, Little Rock, AR 72209; 501-618-8500, 501-618-8404 (Fax), 8AM-5PM.

http://www.asp.state.ar.us

Indexing & Storage: Records are available for the past 25 years. Older records are located in the off-site State Archives. It takes 2-3 weeks before new records are available for inquiry. Records are indexed on fingerprint cards.

Searching: Must have signed and notarized release from person of record. You must use the Bureau's form. Include the following in your request-name, date of birth, sex, Social Security Number, driver's license number.

Access by: mail, in person.

Fee & Payment: The fee is $15.00 per record. Fee payee: Arkansas State Police. Prepayment required. Personal checks accepted. No credit cards accepted.

Mail search: Turnaround time: 3 to 4 weeks. A self addressed stamped envelope is requested.

In person search: Bring in signed release. If applicant is subject, record is released immediately, otherwise it is mailed back.

Corporation Records
Fictitious Name
Limited Liability Company Records
Limited Partnerships

Secretary of State, Corporation Department-Aegon Bldg, 501 Woodlane, Rm 310, Little Rock, AR 72201-1094; 501-682-3409, 888-233-0325, 501-682-3437 (Fax), 8AM-5PM.

http://www.sosweb.state.ar.us/corps

Indexing & Storage: Records are available from late 1800's on. Corporation records are on computer from 1987 on. Prior records, such as dissolved corporations, may be in paper files. New records are available for inquiry immediately. Records are indexed on inhouse computer, file folders.

Searching: Franchise tax information is not released except for names and addressees of parties involved and certain information about the shares of stock. Include the following in your request-full name of business. In addition to the articles of incorporation, corporation records include the following information: Prior (Merged) names, Reserved names, Good standing. Officers listed on franchise tax form is now public information.

Access by: mail, phone, in person, online.

Fee & Payment: There are no search fees. Certification of records costs $5.00. Fee payee: Secretary of State. Prepayment required. Personal checks accepted. No credit cards accepted.

Mail search: Turnaround time: same day if possible. Call first for copy fees. Records prior to 1988 will take longer to search.No self addressed stamped envelope is required. Copies cost $.50 per page.

Phone search: They will give incorporation dates, history, agent name, and status over the phone.

In person search: Copies cost $.50 per page.

Online search: The Internet site permits free searching of corporation records. You can search by name, registered agent, or filing number.

Other access: Bulk release of records is available for $.50 per page. Contact David Morrow at 501-682-3409 for details.

Trademarks/Servicemarks

Secretary of State, Trademarks Section-Aegon Bldg, 501 Woodlane, #310, Little Rock, AR 72201; 501-682-3409, 888-233-0325, 501-682-3437 (Fax), 8AM-5PM.

http://www.sosweb.state.ar.us/corps/trademk

Indexing & Storage: Records are available from the 1950s. It takes 2 to 3 days before new records are available for inquiry. Records are indexed on inhouse computer.

Searching: Include the following in your request-name.

Access by: mail, phone, in person, online.

Fee & Payment: There is no search fee, copy fees are $.50 per copy. Fee payee: Secretary of State. Prepayment required. Personal checks accepted. No credit cards accepted.

Mail search: Turnaround time: 3 to 4 working days. No self addressed stamped envelope is required.

Phone search: They will give information over the phone.

In person search: Turnaround time is within a few minutes, there is an in-house terminal available to the public.

Online search: Searching is available at no fee over the Internet site. Search by name, owner, city, or filing number. You can also search via e-mail at corprequest@sosmail.state.as.us.

Other access: Records can be provided in bulk for $.50 per page. Contact David Morrow at 501-682-3409 for details.

Uniform Commercial Code Federal Tax Liens

UCC Division, Secretary of State-Aegon Bldg, 501 Woodlane, Rm 310, Little Rock, AR 72201-1094; 501-682-5078, 501-682-3500 (Fax), 8AM-5PM.

http://www.sosweb.state.ar.us/ucc.htm

Indexing & Storage: Records are available from 1962. Records are indexed on cards. You can make requests by fax, but they will be returned by mail. Records are not searched by phone, but they will inform if there is anything on file.

Searching: Use search request form UCC-11. A search includes tax liens on businesses, via a lien search certificate. Federal tax liens on individuals and all state tax liens (AKA municipal judgments before 1978) are filed at the county. Include the following in your request-debtor name.

Access by: mail, fax, in person.

Fee & Payment: A lien search certificate is $10.00. Photostat copies of financing statements are $10.00 for the first page, $.50 each additional, maximum $100.00. The fee for certification of a copy of a filed financing statement is $1.00. Fee payee: Secretary of State. Prepayment required. Personal checks accepted. No credit cards accepted.

Mail search: Turnaround time: 1 to 2 days. No self addressed stamped envelope is required.

Fax search: There is an additional fee of $5.00 plus $.50 per page.

In person search: Walk-in customers may view the index cards for no charge.

State Tax Liens
Records not maintained by a state level agency.

Note: Records are at the county level.

Sales Tax Registrations

Finance & Administration Department, Sales & Use Tax Office, PO Box 1272, Little Rock, AR 72203; 501-682-7104, 501-682-7900 (Fax), 8AM-4:30PM.

http://www.state.ar.us/salestax

Indexing & Storage: Records are available from the 1940s.

Searching: This agency will only confirm that a business is registered. They will provide no other information. All searches are based upon tax permit number

Access by: mail, phone, fax, in person.

Mail search: Turnaround time: 3 to 5 days. A self addressed stamped envelope is requested. No fee for mail request.

Phone search: No fee for telephone request. This is the recommended search request method.

Fax search: Fax searching available.

In person search: No fee for request.

Birth Certificates

Arkansas Department of Health, Division of Vital Records, 4815 W Markham St, Slot 44, Little Rock, AR 72205; 501-661-2174, 501-661-2336 (Message Number), 506-661-2726 (Credit Card Line), 800-637-9314 (Toll Free), 501-663-2832 (Fax), 8AM-4:30PM.

http://www.healthyarkansas.com

Note: Thre types of records are available; certification copy, actual copy, and wallet size copy.

Indexing & Storage: Records are available from 1914 on. New records are available for inquiry immediately. Records are indexed on microfiche, inhouse computer.

Searching: Must have a signed release from person of record if requester is not a member of parents, grandparents or spouse. Include your name, address and signature on the request. Include the following in your request-full name, names of parents, mother's maiden name, date of birth, place of birth, relationship to person of record, reason for information request. Also include your phone number.

Access by: mail, phone, fax, in person.

Fee & Payment: The fee is $8.00 for the first copy and $5.00 for each add'l of same record. Add $5.00 if you use a credit card. Fee payee: Division of Vital Records. Prepayment required. Personal checks accepted. Credit cards accepted: MasterCard, Visa, AmEx, Discover.

Mail search: Turnaround time: 3 weeks. No self addressed stamped envelope is required.

Phone search: You must use a credit card. Turnaround time is 1 week.

Fax search: Fax requests require the use of a credit card or prepayment. No certificates may be faxed back. Turnaround time is 1 week.

In person search: Search costs $5.00 for each name in request. Turnaround time: While you wait.

Other access: Research projects require the approval of the director.

Expedited service: Expedited service is available for mail, phone and fax searches. Turnaround time: next day. Add $21.25 for use of credit card and for express delivery. Overnight express is available.

Death Records

Arkansas Department of Health, Division of Vital Records, 4815 W Markham St, Slot 44, Little Rock, AR 72205; 501-661-2174, 501-661-2336 (Message number), 501-661-2726 (Credit Card Line), 501-663-2832 (Fax), 8AM-4:30PM.

http://www.healthyarkansas.com

Note: This agency does not hold the actual records, but does have an index of all deaths since 1914 and some death index records for Fort Smith and Little Rock prior to 1914.

Indexing & Storage: Records are available from 1914 on. New records are available for inquiry immediately. Records are indexed on microfiche, inhouse computer.

Searching: Must have a signed release from immediate family member if requester is not a member of family. Include the following in your request-full name, date of death, place of death, relationship to person of record, reason for information request, wife's maiden name. Include requester's signature and phone number.

Access by: mail, phone, fax, in person.

Fee & Payment: The fee is $8.00 for the first copy and $3.00 for each add'l of same record. Add $5.00 if you use a credit card. Fee payee: Division of Vital Records. Prepayment required. Personal checks accepted. Credit cards accepted: MasterCard, Visa, AmEx, Discover.

Mail search: Turnaround time: 3 weeks. Turnaround time with a credit card is 1 week.No self addressed stamped envelope is required.

Phone search: You must use a credit card.

Fax search: You must use a credit card or prepay before record is sent.

In person search: Turnaround time is usually 1 to 2 hours.

Expedited service: Expedited service is available for mail, phone and fax searches. Turnaround time: overnight delivery. Add $21.25 for delivery and use of credit card.

Marriage Certificates

Arkansas Department of Health, Division of Vital Records, 4815 W Markham St, Slot 44, Little Rock, AR 72205; 501-661-2174, 501-661-2336 (Message Number), 501-661-2726 (Credit Card Line), 501-663-2832 (Fax), 8AM-4:30PM.

http://www.healthyarkansas.com

Indexing & Storage: Records are available from 1917 on. New records are available for inquiry immediately. Records are indexed on microfiche, inhouse computer.

Searching: Must have a signed release from person of record if requester is not a member of immediate family. Include the following in your request-full names of husband and wife, registration number, date of marriage, place or county of marriage, wife's maiden name. Requester must sign request and provide phone number.

Access by: mail, phone, fax, in person.

Fee & Payment: The fee is $8.00 for the first copy and $5.00 for each add'l of same record. Add $5.00 if you use a credit card. Fee payee: Division of Vital Records. Prepayment required. Personal checks accepted. Credit cards accepted: MasterCard, Visa, AmEx, Discover.

Mail search: Turnaround time: 3 weeks. Turnaround time with a credit card is 1 week.No self addressed stamped envelope is required.

Phone search: You may call in your request, but you must use a credit card. Turnaround time is 1 week.

Fax search: A credit card is required or must prepay before records sent.

In person search: Turnaround time is 30 minutes to an hour.

Expedited service: Expedited service is available for mail, phone and fax searches. Turnaround time: overnight delivery. Add $21.25 for use of credit card and express delivery.

Divorce Records

Arkansas Department of Health, Department of Vital Records, 4815 W Markham St, Slot 44, Little Rock, AR 72205; 501-661-2174, 501-661-2336 (Message Number), 501-661-2726 (Credit Card Line), 800-637-9314, 501-663-2832 (Fax), 8AM-4:30PM.

http://www.healthyarkansas.com

Indexing & Storage: Records are available from 1914 to present. New records are available for inquiry immediately.

Searching: Must have a signed release from person of record if requester is not a member of the immediate family. Include the following in your request-names of husband and wife, date of divorce, place of divorce. Signature of requester required.

Access by: mail, phone, fax, in person.

Fee & Payment: The fee is $8.00 for the first copy and $5.00 for each add'l of same record. Add $5.00 if you use a credit card. Fee payee: Division of Public Records. Prepayment required. Personal checks accepted. Credit cards accepted: MasterCard, Visa, AmEx, Discover.

Mail search: Turnaround time: 3 weeks. Turnaround time with a credit card is 1 week.No self addressed stamped envelope is required.

Phone search: You must use a credit card. Turnaround time is 1 week.

Fax search: A credit card or prepayment is required.

In person search: Turnaround time is within 1 hour.

Expedited service: Expedited service is available for mail, phone and fax searches. Turnaround time: overnight delivery. The fee of $21.25 includes the $5.00 credit card fee and express delivery.

Workers' Compensation Records

Workers Compensation Department, 324 Spring Street, PO Box 950, Little Rock, AR 72203-0950; 501-682-3930, 800-622-4472, 501-682-6761 (Fax), 8AM-4:30PM M-F.

http://www.awcc.state.ar.us

Indexing & Storage: Records are available from 1940's on. New records are available for inquiry immediately. Records are indexed on microfilm, index cards, inhouse computer.

Searching: Only written requests are accepted. You may fax a request, but it is returned by mail. Include the following in your request-claimant name, Social Security Number, place of employment at time of accident, file number (if known). The following data is not released: Social Security Numbers or medical information.

Access by: mail, phone, fax, in person, online.

Fee & Payment: The fee is $5.00 per name searched and $.50 per page for copies. Fee payee: Workers' Compensation Commission. An invoice is mailed with the results of the request. Personal checks accepted. No credit cards accepted.

Mail search: Turnaround time: 10 days. No self addressed stamped envelope is required.

Phone search: Records are available by phone.

Fax search: Same criteria as mail searching.

In person search: You may make copies at $.25 per page. You are allowed to look through the files without charge.

Online search: To perform an online claim search, one must be a subscriber to the Information Network of Arkansas (INA). Fee is $3.50 per claim per search. If 20 searches are reached in a month then fee goes to $2.50 per search. Records are from May 1, 1997 forward. There is an annual $50 subscriber fee to INA. For more information, visit the web site at www.state.ar.us/ina.html.

Driver Records

Department of Driver Services, Driving Records Division, PO Box 1272, Room 1130, Little Rock, AR 72203 (Courier: 1900 W 7th, #1130, Little Rock, AR 72201); 501-682-7207, 501-682-7908, 501-682-2075 (Fax), 8AM-4:30PM.

http://www.accessarkansas.org/dfa/driverservices

Note: Copies of tickets must be requested from the local jurisdiction where the ticket was issued.

Indexing & Storage: Records are available for 3 years for moving violations, 3 years for employment or insurance purposes and are retained indefinitely for departmental purposes. DWI and suspensions show until all requirements are met. Records are indexed on inhouse computer.

Searching: Arkansas requires signed authorization by the driver to obtain a driving record. Volume requesters must have these authorizations on file. Violations on an interstate highway not exceeding 75 mph won't show on records requested for insurance purposes. Include the following in your request-full name, driver's license number, date of birth. Driver's address is included as part of the search report.

Access by: mail, in person, online.

Fee & Payment: Fees are $7.00 for insurance record and $10.00 for CDLs. There is a full charge for a "no record found." Fee payee: State of Arkansas, Driver Services. Prepayment required. Personal checks accepted. No credit cards accepted.

Mail search: Turnaround time: 24 hours. Requester must enclose written release, full name, DOB, driver's license number, and proper fees.No self addressed stamped envelope is required.

In person search: The state will process up to 5 requests while you wait.

Online search: Access is available through the Information Network of Arkansas (INA). The system offers both batch and interactive service. The system is only available to INA subscribers who have statutory rights to the data. The record fee is $8.00, or $11.00 for commercial drivers. Visit www.state.ar.us/ina.html.

Other access: High volume requesters use magnetic tape-to-tape for overnight access.

Vehicle Ownership
Vehicle Identification

Office of Motor Vehicles, MV Title Records, PO Box 1272, Room 1100, Little Rock, AR 72203 (Courier: 7th & Battery Sts, Ragland Bldg, Room 1100, Little Rock, AR 72201); 501-682-4692, 800-662-8247, 8AM-4:30PM.

http://www.state.ar.us/dfa

Note: The state has plans to offer online access to permissible users soon. This will be through the Information Network of Arkansas.

Indexing & Storage: Records are available from 1950 for titles; license plate records from 1968 on microfilm; plate number and name from 1981 on microfiche. It takes 4 to 6 weeks before new records are available for inquiry.

Searching: Vehicle registration information cannot be sold or used for solicitation purposes. Requesters that do not have DPPA approved purpose, cannot receive records with personal information, unless consent of subject is given.

The following data is not released: Social Security Numbers or date of birth.

Access by: mail, phone, in person.

Fee & Payment: The fee for vehicle and/or ownership searches is $1.00 per copy and $1.00 per search. Fee payee: Department of Finance and Administration. Prepayment required. If mailing a check to open a new account, place "Attn: Search Account" on the request. If mailing an information request, place "Attn: Correspondence Desk" on the request. Personal checks accepted. No credit cards accepted.

Mail search: Turnaround time: 24 hours. No self addressed stamped envelope is required.

Phone search: Searching by phone is available for established accounts. A $25.00 deposit is required.

In person search: Turnaround time: while you wait.

Other access: The bulk purchase of records, except for recall or statistical purposes, is prohibited.

Accident Reports

Arkansas State Police, Accident Records Section, 1 State Police Plaza Drive, Little Rock, AR 72209; 501-618-8130, 501-618-8131 (Fax), 8AM-5PM.

http://www.asp.state.ar.us/ar/ar.html

Indexing & Storage: Records are available from 1958 to present. Records are on microfilm from 1958 to 1982, off-line storage 1982-1994, and on computer 1994 to present. It takes 5 to 10 days before new records are available for inquiry.

Searching: Include the following in your request-date of accident, location, name of at least on driver.

Access by: mail, phone, fax, in person.

Fee & Payment: The fee is $10.00 per record. There is no charge for a "no record found." Payment will be refunded. Fee payee: Arkansas State Police, Accident Records. Prepayment required. Personal checks accepted. No credit cards accepted.

Mail search: Turnaround time: 1 to 2 weeks. A self addressed stamped envelope is requested.

Phone search: Limited information is available.

Fax search: Records are available by fax.

In person search: Turnaround time is while you wait if 1994 or newer, otherwise 1-2 weeks.

Vessel Ownership
Vessel Registration

Office of Motor Vehicles, Boat Registration, PO Box 1272, Little Rock, AR 72203; 501-682-4692, 8AM-4:30PM.

Note: Lien information may be filed at the Secretary of State or at this agency.

Indexing & Storage: Records are available from 1980. All sail boats and all motorized boats must be registered. Vessels are not titled in this state.

Searching: Casual (non-DPPA) requesters cannot obtain records with personal information unless subject has given consent. Search by name or registration number or hull number.

Access by: mail, in person.

Fee & Payment: The search fee is $1.00 per search and $1.00 per copy of a record. Fee payee: Office of Motor Vehicles. Prepayment required. No credit cards accepted.

Mail search: Turnaround time: 2 weeks. No self addressed stamped envelope is required.

In person search: Records are usually obtained at once, unless they require extensive research.

Legislation Records

Elections Department, State Capitol, Room 026, Little Rock, AR 72201; 501-682-5070, 501-682-3408 (Fax), 8AM-5PM.

http://www.arkleg.state.ar.us

Note: This agency will not do any research; they will only respond to requests by act number.

Indexing & Storage: Records are available from 1909 to present.

Access by: mail, fax, in person, online.

Fee & Payment: You can purchase copies of bills for $.25 per page. They will return copies by Federal Express if you give your billing number. Fee payee: Secretary of State. Prepayment required. Personal checks accepted. No credit cards accepted.

Mail search: No self addressed stamped envelope is required.

Fax search: Fax searching available.

Online search: Probably the best way to search is through the Internet site listed above. You may also search by subject matter.

Voter Registration
Access to Records is Restricted

Secretary of State, Voter Services, State Capitol, Room 026, Little Rock, AR 72201; 501-682-3526, 501-682-3548 (Fax), 8AM-5PM.

http://www.sosweb.state.ar.us/elect.html

Note: The state will sell the voter database for voting or election purposes. All individual search requests must be at the local County Clerk's office. The SSN will not be released.

GED Certificates

GED Testing, Dept of Workforce Education, 409 Shall St, Little Rock, AR 72202; 501-682-1978 (Main Number), 501-682-1982 (Fax).

http://www.work-ed.state.ar.us

Searching: For verification or for a copy of a transcript, all of the following is required: a signed release, name, year of test, date of birth, and Social Security Number.

Access by: mail, fax.

Fee & Payment: There is no fee.

Mail search: Turnaround time is next day.No self addressed stamped envelope is required.

Fax search: Turnaround time is next day, but results returned by mail.

Hunting License Information
Fishing License Information

Game & Fish Commission, Two Natural Resources Dr, Little Rock, AR 72205; 501-223-6300, 501-223-6425 (Fax), 8AM-4:30PM.

http://www.agfc.com

Note: Lists maintained here include fish farmers, put & take pay lakes, shell buyers, commercial game breeders, commercial shooting resorts, fur dealers, and bull frog permits.

Indexing & Storage: Records are available for 2 to 3 years then purged. It takes 4 days before new records are available for inquiry. Records are indexed on inhouse computer.

Searching: Must mention request is under the Freedom of Information Act. Include the following in your request-full name. Addresses are given and telephone numbers, if available.

Access by: mail, in person.

Fee & Payment: The search and copy fee is $2.00. Fee payee: Game & Fish Commission. Personal checks accepted. No credit cards accepted.

Mail search: Turnaround time: 1 to 2 days. No self addressed stamped envelope is required.

In person search: Some searches require 1 to 2 days to process.

Arkansas State Licensing Agencies

Licenses Searchable Online

Architect #06 .... www.state.ar.us/arch/search.html

Attorney #43 .... http://courts.state.ar.us/attylist/new/

Bank #38 .... www.sosweb.state.ar.us/corps/bkin

Cemetery, Perpetual Care #39 .... www.ark.org/arsec/database/dbsearch.cgi?dbname=7&LIMIT=20&LISTALL=ON

Child Care Provider #26 .... www.state.ar.us/childcare/search.html

Chiropractor #09 .... www.accessarkansas.org/asbce

Contractor #23 .... www.state.ar.us/clb/search.html

Cosmetologist #49 .... www.accessarkansas.org/cos/search.php

Cosmetology Instructor #49 .... www.accessarkansas.org/cos/search.php

Counselor #51 .... www.state.ar.us/abec/search.php

Dental Hygienist #11 .... www.asbde.org/RDH-Web-10-2000.PDF

Dentist #11 .... www.asbde.org/DDS-Web-10-2000.PDF

Electrologist #49 .... www.accessarkansas.org/cos/search.php

Electrolysis Instructor #49 .... www.accessarkansas.org/cos/search.php

Embalmer/Embalmer Apprentice #12 .... www.accessarkansas.org/fdemb/

Engineer/Engineer in Training #19 .... www.state.ar.us/pels/search.html

Funeral Director/Apprentice #12 .... www.accessarkansas.org/fdemb/

Funeral Home/Crematory #12 .... www.accessarkansas.org/fdemb/

Home Inspector #38 .... www.sosweb.state.ar.us/corps/homeinsp

Homebuilder #38 .... www.sosweb.state.ar.us/corps/homebldr

Insurance Agency #38 .... www.sosweb.state.ar.us/corps/bkin

Insurance Sales Agent #02 .... www.accessarkansas.org/insurance/license/search.php

Investment Advisor #39 .... www.ark.org/arsec/database/dbsearch.cgi?dbname=2&LIMIT=20&LISTALL=ON

Landscape Architect #06 .... www.state.ar.us/arch/search.html

Lobbyist #38 .... www.sosweb.state.ar.us/elect.html

Manicurist #49 .... www.accessarkansas.org/cos/search.php

Marriage & Family Therapist #51 .... www.state.ar.us/abec/search.php

Midwife Nurse #15 .... www.accessarkansas.org/nurse/registry/index.html

Mortgage Loan Broker/Company #39 .... www.ark.org/arsec/database/dbsearch.cgi?dbname=7&LIMIT=20&LISTALL=ON

Notary Public #38 .... www.sosweb.state.ar.us/corps/notary

Nurse #15 .... www.accessarkansas.org/nurse/registry/index.html

Nurse Anesthetist #15 .... www.accessarkansas.org/nurse/registry/index.html

Nurse-LPN #15 .... www.accessarkansas.org/nurse/registry/index.html

Optometrist #16 .... www.odfinder.org/LicSearch.asp

Public Accountant-CPA #18 .... www.accessarkansas.org/asbpa

Real Estate Broker #37 .... www.accessarkansas.org/arec/db/

Real Estate Sales Agent #37 .... www.accessarkansas.org/arec/db/

Securities Agent #39 .... www.ark.org/arsec/database/dbsearch.cgi?dbname=7&LIMIT=20&LISTALL=ON

Securities Broker/Dealer #39 .... www.ark.org/arsec/database/dbsearch.cgi?dbname=7&LIMIT=20&LISTALL=ON

Social Worker #40 .... www.state.ar.us/swlb/search/index.html

Surveyor #19 .... www.state.ar.us/pels/search.html

Surveyor-in-Training #19 .... www.state.ar.us/pels/search.html

Teacher #32 .... www.as-is.org/directory/search_lic.html

Licensing Quick Finder

Abstractor #48	870-942-8064
Acupuncturist #46	501-668-8851
Agricultural Consultant #33	501-225-1598
Agriculture Education #32	501-682-4695
Anesthetician #15	501-686-2200
Announcer, Athletic Event (Ring) #04	501-666-5544
Architect #06	501-682-3171
Armored Car Guard #42	501-618-8600
Asbestos Abatement Inspector #28	501-682-0718
Asbestos Abatement Management Planner #28	501-682-0718
Asbestos Abate. Training Provider #28	501-682-0718
Asbestos Removal Worker #28	501-682-0718
Athletic Manager #04	501-666-5544
Athletic Promoter/Matchmaker #04	501-666-5544
Attorney #43	501-682-6849
Auctioneer #05	501-682-1156
Audiologist #41	501-320-4319
Bail Bondsman #02	501-686-9050
Bank #38	501-682-3409
Barber Instructor #07	501-682-4035
Barber/Barber Technician #07	501-682-4035
Boiler Inspector/Installer/Repairer #27	501-682-4513
Boiler Operator #27	501-682-4513
Boxer #04	501-666-5544
Boxing/Wrestling Referee #04	501-666-5544
Burglar Alarm Systems Agent/Mgr. #42	501-618-8600
Business Education Teacher #32	501-682-4695
Career Education Coordinator #32	501-682-4695
Career Orientation Teacher #32	501-682-4695
Cemetery, Perpetual Care #39	501-324-9260
Chauffeur #24	501-371-1741
Check Casher #10	501-244-9194
Child Care Provider #26	501-682-9699
Chiropractor #09	501-682-9015
Claims Adjuster #02	501-371-2750
Collection Agency #10	501-376-9814
Collection Agency Collector/Mgr. #10	501-376-9814
Combination Welder #35	501-812-2254
Contractor #23	501-372-4661
Cosmetologist #49	501-682-2168
Cosmetology Instructor #49	501-682-2168
Counselor #51	870-235-4131
Court Reporter #08	501-682-6850
Dental Assistant #11	501-682-2085
Dental Hygienist #11	501-682-2085
Dentist #11	501-682-2085
Dietitian #29	501-374-8212
Egg Grader #53	501-907-2400
Electrical Contractor #27	501-682-4549
Electrologist #49	501-682-2168
Electrolysis Instructor #49	501-682-2168
Elevator/Lifting Device Inspector #27	501-682-4531
Embalmer/Embalmer Apprentice #12	501-682-0574
Emergency Medical Technician #25	501-661-2262
Emergency Medical Technician-Paramedic #25	501-661-2262
Employment Agency Manager #27	501-682-4505
Employment Agent/Counselor #27	501-682-4505
Engineer/Engineer in Training #19	501-682-2824
Exterminator #33	501-225-1598
Fire Equipment Inspector #56	501-661-7903
Fire Extinguisher Repairer #56	501-661-7903
Fire Extinguisher Sprinkler Inspect. #56	501-661-7903
Forester #20	501-296-1998
Funeral Director/Apprentice #12	501-682-0574
Funeral Home/Crematory #12	501-682-0574
Gas Fitter/Trainee #25	501-661-2000
Geologist #21	501-296-1877
Grain Warehouseman #33	501-225-1598
Greyhound Racing #36	501-682-1467
Hearing Instrument Dispenser #14	501-663-5869
Home Inspector #38	501-682-3409
Homebuilder #38	501-682-3409
Horse Racing #36	501-682-1467
Hospital Maintenance Plumber #25	501-661-2262
Industrial Maintenance Electrician #27	501-682-4549
Insurance Agency #38	501-682-3409
Insurance Sales Agent #02	501-371-2750
Investment Advisor #39	501-324-9260
Landscape Architect #06	501-682-3393
Liquor Distributor #01	501-682-1105
Livestock Brand #53	501-907-2400
Livestock Dealer #53	501-907-2400
Lobbyist #38	501-682-1010
Manicurist #49	501-682-2168
Manufactured Home Dealer #54	501-324-9032
Manufactured Home Installer #54	501-324-9032
Manufactured Home Manufacturer #54	501-324-9032
Marriage & Family Therapist #51	870-235-4131
Martial Arts #04	501-666-5544
Massage Therapy Technician (Masseur/Masseuse) #22	501-534-4734
Medical Doctor/Surgeon #31	501-296-1802
Midwife Nurse #15	501-686-2200
Mortgage Loan Broker/Company #39	501-324-9260
Motor Vehicle Dealer/Salesperson, New #55	501-682-1428
Motor Vehicle Dealer/Salesperson, Used #42	501-618-8600
Notary Public #38	501-682-3409
Nurse #15	501-686-2200
Nurse Anesthetist #15	501-686-2200
Nurse-LPN #15	501-686-2200
Nurseryman #33	501-225-1598
Nursing Home Administrator #52	501-682-1001
Occupational Therapist/Assistant #31	501-296-1802
Optician #50	870-572-2847
Optometrist #16	501-268-4351
Osteopathic Physician #31	501-296-1802
Permanent Cosmetic/Tattoo Artist #25	501-661-2000
Pesticide Applicator #33	501-225-1598
Petroleum Dealer #30	501-324-9228
Pharmacist #17	501-682-0190
Pharmacist Intern #17	501-682-0190
Physical Therapist #03	501-228-7100
Podiatrist #34	501-664-3668
Polygraph Examiner #42	501-618-8600
Private Investigator #42	501-618-8600
Psychological Examiner #13	501-682-6167
Psychologist #13	501-682-6167
Public Accountant-CPA #18	501-682-1520
Pump Installer #45	501-682-1025
Real Estate Appraiser #37	501-683-8010
Real Estate Broker #37	501-683-8010
Real Estate Sales Agent #37	501-683-8010
Respiratory Care Practitioner #31	501-296-1802
Safety Supervisor #30	501-324-9228
School Counselor #32	501-682-4344
School Principal/Administrator/Superintendent #32	501-682-4344
Securities Agent #39	501-324-9260
Securities Broker/Dealer #39	501-324-9260
Security Guard #42	501-618-8600
Seed Dealer #33	501-225-1598
Septic Tank Cleaner #25	501-661-2000
Social Worker #40	501-372-5071
Solid Waste Facility Operator #28	501-682-0585
Speech Pathologist #41	501-320-4319
State Trooper #42	501-618-8600
Surveyor #19	501-682-2824
Surveyor-in-Training #19	501-682-2824
Teacher #32	501-682-4695
Veterinarian #44	501-224-2836
Veterinary Technician #44	501-224-2836
Waste Water Treatment Plant Operator #28	501-682-0998
Water Supply Operator #25	501-661-2000
Water Well Driller #45	501-682-1025
Wrestler #04	501-666-5544

Licensing Agency Information

#01 Alcoholic Beverage Control Division, 100 Main St, #503, Little Rock, AR 72201; 501-682-1105, Fax: 501-682-2221.

#02 Department of Insurance, 1200 W 3rd St, Little Rock, AR 72201; 800-282-9134, Fax: 501-371-2618.
www.accessarkansas.org/insurance/index.html
Direct web site URL to search for licensees: www.accessarkansas.org/insurance/license/search.php. You can search online using name and city.

#03 Board of Physical Therapy, 9 Shackelford Plaza, #3, Little Rock, AR 72211; 501-228-7100, Fax: 501-228-5535.

#04 Athletic Commission, 809 N Palm St, Little Rock, AR 72205-1946; 501-666-5544, Fax: 501-666-5546.

#05 Auctioneers Licensing Board, 101 E Capital, #112B, Little Rock, AR 72201; 501-682-1156, Fax: 501-682-1158.
http://aalb.org

#06 Board of Architecture, 101 E Capitol, #208, Little Rock, AR 72201; 501-682-3171, Fax: 501-682-3172.
www.accessarkansas.org/arch
Direct web site URL to search for licensees: www.state.ar.us/arch/search.html. You can search online using name, city, and organization name.

#07 Board of Barber Examiners, 103 E 7th St Rm 212, Little Rock, AR 72201-4512; 501-682-4035, Fax: 501-682-2806.

#08 Board of Certified Court Reporter Examiners, 625 Marshall St, Justice Bldg, Little Rock, AR 72201; 501-682-6850, Fax: 501-682-6877 c/o Renee.

#09 Board of Chiropractic Examiners, 101 E Capital, #209, Little Rock, AR 72201; 501-682-9015, Fax: 501-682-9016.
www.accessarkansas.org/asbce/
Direct web site URL to search for licensees: www.state.ar.us/asbce/search.html. You can search online using last name or city.

#10 Board of Collection Agencies, 523 S Louisiana St, #460, Little Rock, AR 72201; 501-376-9814, Fax: 501-372-5383.

#11 Board of Dental Examiners, 101 E Capitol Ave, #111, Little Rock, AR 72201; 501-682-2085, Fax: 501-682-3543.
www.asbde.org

Direct web site URL to search for licensees: www.asbde.org/Licensee-Stats%20home.htm

#12 Board of Embalmers & Funeral Directors, 101 E Capitol Ave, #113, Little Rock, AR 72201; 501-682-0574, Fax: 501-682-0575. www.accessarkansas.org/fdemb
Direct web site URL to search for licensees: www.accessarkansas.org/fdemb

#13 Board of Examiners in Psychology, 101 E Capitol Ave, #415, Little Rock, AR 72201; 501-682-6167, Fax: 501-682-6165. www.accessarkansas.org/abep/

#14 Board of Hearing Instrument Dispensers, 305 N Monroe, Little Rock, AR 72205; 501-663-5869, Fax: 501-663-6359.

#15 Board of Nursing, 1123 S University, University Tower Bldg, #800, Little Rock, AR 72204-1619; 501-686-2700, Fax: 501-686-2714. www.accessarkansas.org/nurse/
Direct web site URL to search for licensees: www.accessarkansas.org/nurse/registry/index.html
Search online using name and license number.

#16 Board of Optometry, 410 W Race St, Searcy, AR 72143; 501-268-4351, Fax: 501-268-5631. www.state.ar.us/opt/arkopt.html
Direct web site URL to search for licensees: www.odfinder.org/LicSearch.asp. You can search online using national database by name, city, or state.

#17 Board of Pharmacy, 101 E Capitol, #218, Little Rock, AR 72201; 501-682-0190, Fax: 501-682-0195. www.accessarkansas.org/asbp/

#18 Board of Public Accountancy, 101 E Capitol, #430, Little Rock, AR 72201; 501-682-1520, Fax: 501-682-5538. www.accessarkansas.org/asbpa/

#19 Board of Registration for Engineers/Land Surveyors, PO Box 3750, Little Rock, AR 72203; 501-682-2824, Fax: 501-682-2827. www.state.ar.us/pels/
Direct web site URL to search for licensees: www.state.ar.us/pels/search.html. You can search online using name, company, city, company or license #

#20 Board of Registration for Foresters, PO Box 7424, Little Rock, AR 72217; 501-296-1998, Fax: 501-296-1949.

#21 Board of Registration for Professional Geologists, 3815 W Roosevelt Rd, Little Rock, AR 72204; 501-296-1877, Fax: 501-663-7360. www.state.ar.us/agc/BOR.htm

#22 Board of Massage Therapy, 103 Airways (PO Box 20739), Hot Springs, AR 71903-0739; 501-623-0444, Fax: 501-623-4130.

#23 Contractors Licensing Board, 621 E Capitol, Little Rock, AR 72202; 501-372-4661, Fax: 501-372-2247. www.accessarkansas.org/clb/
Direct web site URL to search for licensees: www.state.ar.us/clb/search.html. Search online using name, city, class/description, and specialty.

#24 Department of Finance & Administration, Ledbetter Bldg, 7th & Wolfe Streets #215, Little Rock, AR 72203; 501-324-9057, Fax: 501-682-7075.

#25 Department of Health, 4815 W Markham, Slot 38, Little Rock, AR 72205-3867; 501-661-2262, Fax: 501-280-4901.

#26 Department of Human Services, 101 E Capitol, #106, Little Rock, AR 72201; 501-682-4891, Fax: 501-682-4897. www.accessarkansas.org/childcare/
Direct web site URL to search for licensees: www.state.ar.us/childcare/search.html. You can search online using name or company name, city, and ZIP Code.

#27 Department of Labor, 10421 W Markham, Little Rock, AR 72205; 501-682-4500, Fax: 501-682-4535. www.accessarkansas.org/labor/

#28 Department of Environmental Quality, PO Box 8913, Little Rock, AR 72219-8913; 501-682-0744, Fax: 501-682-0798.
www.adeq.state.ar.us The Wastewater division may put liceensees online at www.adeq.state.ar.us/custsvs/wwlicpro.htm.

#29 Dietetics Licensing Board, PO Box 1016, Little Rock, AR 72115; 501-221-0566, Fax: 501-843-0878.

#30 Liquefied Petroleum Gas Board, 1421 W 6th St, Little Rock, AR 72201; 501-324-9228, Fax: 501-324-9230.

#31 Medical Board, 2100 Riverside, Little Rock, AR 72202-1435; 501-296-1802, Fax: 501-296-1805.
www.armedicalboard.org They offer online verification using a modem system. To obtain more information on the program, fax a request including a contact name to the fax number listed above.

#32 Department of Education, State Education Bldg, Rm 106, Capitol Mall #4, Little Rock, AR 72201; 501-682-4695, Fax: 501-682-4898. http://arkedu.state.ar.us/teacher.htm

#33 Plant Board, PO Box 1069 (One Natural Resources Dr), Little Rock, AR 72203; 501-225-1598, Fax: 501-225-3590. www.plantboard.org

#34 Board of Podiatrical Medicine, 2001 Georgia Ave, Little Rock, AR 72207-5014; 501-664-3668, Fax: 501-666-3338.

#35 Pulaski Technical College, 3000 W Scenic Dr, North Little Rock, AR 72118; 501-812-2254, Fax: 501-812-2316. www.ptc.tec.ar.us

#36 Racing Commission, PO Box 3076, Little Rock, AR 72203-3076; 501-682-1467, Fax: 501-682-5273.

#37 Real Estate Commission, 612 Summit St, Little Rock, AR 72201; 501-683-8010, Fax: 501-682-2729. www.state.ar.us/arec/frmain.htm
Direct web site URL to search for licensees: www.accessarkansas.org/arec/db/. You can search online using name, city, and firm name.

#38 Secretary of State, 256 State Capitol, Little Rock, AR 72201; 501-682-3409, Fax: 501-682-3437.
Direct web site URL to search for licensees: www.sosweb.state.ar.us. You can search online using name

#39 Securities Department, 201 W Markham, Heritage West Bldg, 3rd Fl, Little Rock, AR 72201; 501-324-9260, Fax: 501-324-9268. www.accessarkansas.org/arsec/
Direct web site URL to search for licensees: www.state.ar.us/arsec. You can search online using alphabetical lists

#40 Social Work Licensing Board, 2020 W 3rd St #503, POB 2560381, Little Rock, AR 72225; 501-372-5071, Fax: 501-372-6301. www.accessarkansas.org/swlb/
Direct web site URL to search for licensees: www.state.ar.us/swlb/search/index.html. You can search online using last name and city

#41 Speech Pathology & Audiology, Arkansas Children's Hospital, 800 Marshall St., Little Rock, AR 72202; 501-320-4319, Fax: 501-320-6881. www.archildrens.org

#42 Wes Adams, #1 State Police Plaza Drive, Little Rock, AR 72209; 501-618-8608.

#43 Supreme Court, 625 Marshall, Justice Bldg, Little Rock, AR 72201; 501-682-6849, Fax: 501-682-6877. http://courts.state.ar.us
Direct web site URL to search for licensees: http://courts.state.ar.us/attylist/new/

#44 Veterinary Medical Examining Board, PO Box 8505, Little Rock, AR 72215; 501-224-2836, Fax: 501-224-1100.

#45 Waterwell Construction Commission, 101 E Capitol #350, Little Rock, AR 72201; 501-682-1025, Fax: 501-682-3991. www.accessarkansas.org/aswcc

#46 Acupuncture Board, 5110 Kavanaugh Blvd, Little Rock, AR 72207; 501-668-8851, Fax: 501-688-8807.

#48 Abstractor's Board of Examiners, 71 Pinecrest Cir, Sheridan, AR 72150; 870-942-8064.

#49 Board of Cosmetology, 101 E Capitol #108, Little Rock, AR 72201; 501-682-2168. www.accessarkansas.org/cos

#50 Board of Dispensing Opticians, Box 627, Helena, AR 72342; 870-572-2847.

#51 Board of Examiners for Counselors & Marriage/Family Therapists, 124 South Jackson #312 (PO Box 90), Magnolia, AR 71753; 870-901-7055, Fax: 870-234-1842. www.accessarkansas.org/abec/
Direct web site URL to search for licensees: www.state.ar.us/abec/search.php. You can search online using name, city, license number

#52 Department of Human Services, 7th & Main Streets, Little Rock, AR 72203; 501-682-1001.

#53 Livestock & Poultry Commission, 1 Natural Resources Dr, PO Box 8505, Little Rock, AR 72215; 501-907-2400, Fax: 501-907-2425.

#54 Manufactured Home Commission, 523 S Louisiana #500, Little Rock, AR 72201; 501-324-9032.

#55 Motor Vehicle Commission, 101 E Capitol #210, Little Rock, AR 72201; 501-682-1428.

#56 Fire Protection Licensing Board, 7509 Cantrell Rd #103-A, Little Rock, AR 72207; 501-661-7903.

Arkansas Federal Courts

The following list indicates the district and division name for each county in the state. If the bankruptcy court location is different from the district court, then the location of the bankruptcy court appears in parentheses.

County/Court Cross Reference

County	District	Division
Arkansas	Eastern	Pine Bluff (Little Rock)
Ashley	Western (Eastern)	El Dorado (Little Rock)
Baxter	Western	Harrison (Fayetteville)
Benton	Western	Fayetteville
Boone	Western	Harrison (Fayetteville)
Bradley	Western (Eastern)	El Dorado (Little Rock)
Calhoun	Western (Eastern)	El Dorado (Little Rock)
Carroll	Western	Harrison (Fayetteville)
Chicot	Eastern	Pine Bluff (Little Rock)
Clark	Western (Eastern)	Hot Springs (Little Rock)
Clay	Eastern	Jonesboro (Little Rock)
Cleburne	Eastern	Batesville (Little Rock)
Cleveland	Eastern	Pine Bluff (Little Rock)
Columbia	Western (Eastern)	El Dorado (Little Rock)
Conway	Eastern	Little Rock
Craighead	Eastern	Jonesboro (Little Rock)
Crawford	Western	Fort Smith (Fayetteville)
Crittenden	Eastern	Jonesboro (Little Rock)
Cross	Eastern	Helena (Little Rock)
Dallas	Eastern	Pine Bluff (Little Rock)
Desha	Eastern	Pine Bluff (Little Rock)
Drew	Eastern	Pine Bluff (Little Rock)
Faulkner	Eastern	Little Rock
Franklin	Western	Fort Smith (Fayetteville)
Fulton	Eastern	Batesville (Little Rock)
Garland	Western (Eastern)	Hot Springs (Little Rock)
Grant	Eastern	Pine Bluff (Little Rock)
Greene	Eastern	Jonesboro (Little Rock)
Hempstead	Western (Eastern)	Texarkana (Little Rock)
Hot Spring	Western (Eastern)	Hot Springs (Little Rock)
Howard	Western (Eastern)	Texarkana (Little Rock)
Independence	Eastern	Batesville (Little Rock)
Izard	Eastern	Batesville (Little Rock)
Jackson	Eastern	Batesville (Little Rock)
Jefferson	Eastern	Pine Bluff (Little Rock)
Johnson	Western	Fort Smith (Fayetteville)
Lafayette	Western (Eastern)	Texarkana (Little Rock)
Lawrence	Eastern	Jonesboro (Little Rock)
Lee	Eastern	Helena (Little Rock)
Lincoln	Eastern	Pine Bluff (Little Rock)
Little River	Western (Eastern)	Texarkana (Little Rock)
Logan	Western	Fort Smith (Fayetteville)
Lonoke	Eastern	Little Rock
Madison	Western	Fayetteville
Marion	Western	Harrison (Fayetteville)
Miller	Western (Eastern)	Texarkana (Little Rock)
Mississippi	Eastern	Jonesboro (Little Rock)
Monroe	Eastern	Helena (Little Rock)
Montgomery	Western (Eastern)	Hot Springs (Little Rock)
Nevada	Western (Eastern)	Texarkana (Little Rock)
Newton	Western	Harrison (Fayetteville)
Ouachita	Western (Eastern)	El Dorado (Little Rock)
Perry	Eastern	Little Rock
Phillips	Eastern	Helena (Little Rock)
Pike	Western (Eastern)	Hot Springs (Little Rock)
Poinsett	Eastern	Jonesboro (Little Rock)
Polk	Western	Fort Smith (Fayetteville)
Pope	Eastern	Little Rock
Prairie	Eastern	Little Rock
Pulaski	Eastern	Little Rock
Randolph	Eastern	Jonesboro (Little Rock)
Saline	Eastern	Little Rock
Scott	Western	Fort Smith (Fayetteville)
Searcy	Western	Harrison (Fayetteville)
Sebastian	Western	Fort Smith (Fayetteville)
Sevier	Western (Eastern)	Texarkana (Little Rock)
Sharp	Eastern	Batesville (Little Rock)
St. Francis	Eastern	Helena (Little Rock)
Stone	Eastern	Batesville (Little Rock)
Union	Western (Eastern)	El Dorado (Little Rock)
Van Buren	Eastern	Little Rock
Washington	Western	Fayetteville
White	Eastern	Little Rock
Woodruff	Eastern	Helena (Little Rock)
Yell	Eastern	Little Rock

US District Court

Eastern District of Arkansas

Batesville Division c/o Little Rock Division, PO Box 869, Little Rock, AR 72201-3325 (Courier Address: 600 W Capital, Room 402, Little Rock, AR 72201), 501-604-5351.

http://www.are.uscourts.gov

Counties: Cleburne, Fulton, Independence, Izard, Jackson, Sharp, Stone.

Indexing/Storage: Cases are indexed by as well as by case number. New cases are available in the index after filing date. Open records are located at the Division.

Fee & Payment: The fee is $20.00 per item (one party name or case number). Payment may be made by money order, cashier check. Business checks are not accepted. Personal checks are not accepted. Certification fee: $7.00 per document. Copy fee: $.50 per page.

Phone Search: Will search name.

Mail Search: Always enclose a stamped self addressed envelope.

In Person: In person searching is available.

PACER: Sign-up number is 800-676-6856. Access fee is $.60 per minute. Toll-free access: 800-371-8842. Local access: 501-324-6190. Case records are available back to 1987-89. Records are purged every five years. New records are available online after 1 day.

Other Online Access: Search records on the Internet using RACER at www.are.uscourts.gov/perl/bkplog.html. Access fee is 7 cents per page.

Helena Division c/o Little Rock Division, 600 W Capital Rm 402, Little Rock, AR 72201-3325 (Courier Address: 600 W Capital, Room 402, Little Rock, AR 72201), 501-604-5351.

http://www.are.uscourts.gov

Counties: Cross, Lee, Monroe, Phillips, St. Francis, Woodruff.

Indexing/Storage: Cases are indexed by as well as by case number. New cases are available in the index after filing date. Open records are located at the Division.

Fee & Payment: The fee is no charge per item (one party name or case number). Payment may be made by money order, cashier check. Business checks are not accepted. Personal checks are not accepted.

Phone Search: Will search name.

In Person: In person searching is available.

PACER: Sign-up number is 800-676-6856. Access fee is $.60 per minute. Toll-free access: 800-371-8842. Local access: 501-324-6190. Case records are available back to 1987-89. Records are purged every five years. New records are available online after 1 day.

Other Online Access: Search records on the Internet using RACER at www.are.uscourts.gov/perl/bkplog.html. Access fee is 7 cents per page.

Jonesboro Division PO Box 7080, Jonesboro, AR 72403 (Courier Address: Federal Office Bldg, Room 312, 615 S Main St, Jonesboro, AR 72401), 870-972-4610, Fax: 870-972-4612.

http://www.are.uscourts.gov

Counties: Clay, Craighead, Crittenden, Greene, Lawrence, Mississippi, Poinsett, Randolph.

Indexing/Storage: Cases are indexed by defendant and plaintiff as well as by case number. New cases are available in the index immediately after filing date. A computer index is maintained. Open records are located at this court.

Fee & Payment: The fee is $20.00 per item (one party name or case number). Payment may be made by money order, cashier check, personal check. Prepayment is required. Payee: Clerk, US District Court. Certification fee: $7.00 per document. Copy fee: $.50 per page.

Phone Search: Docket information available by phone.

Fax Search: Fax requests accepted on same basis as mail requests.

Mail Search: A stamped self addressed envelope is not required.

In Person: In person searching is available.

PACER: Sign-up number is 800-676-6856. Access fee is $.60 per minute. Toll-free access: 800-371-8842. Local access: 501-324-6190. Case records are available back to 1987-89. Records are purged every five years. New records are available online after 1 day.

Other Online Access: Search records on the Internet using RACER at www.are.uscourts.gov/perl/bkplog.html. Access fee is 7 cents per page.

Little Rock Division Room 402, 600 W Capitol, Little Rock, AR 72201 (Courier Address: Use mail address for courier delivery), 501-324-5351.

http://www.are.uscourts.gov

Counties: Conway, Faulkner, Lonoke, Perry, Pope, Prairie, Pulaski, Saline, Van Buren, White, Yell.

Indexing/Storage: Cases are indexed by defendant and plaintiff as well as by case number. New cases are available in the index immediately after filing date. Both computer and card indexes are maintained. Records are also indexed on microfiche. Open records are located at this court.

Fee & Payment: The fee is $20.00 per item (one party name or case number). Payment may be made by money order, cashier check, personal

check, Visa, Mastercard. Prepayment is required. Payee: Clerk, US District Court. Certification fee: $7.00 per document. Copy fee: $.50 per page.

Phone Search: Docket information available by phone.

Mail Search: Always enclose a stamped self addressed envelope.

In Person: In person searching is available.

PACER: Sign-up number is 800-676-6856. Access fee is $.60 per minute. Toll-free access: 800-371-8842. Local access: 501-324-6190. Case records are available back to 1987-89. Records are purged every five years. New records are available online after 1 day.

Other Online Access: Search records on the Internet using RACER at www.are.uscourts.gov/perl/bkplog.html. Access fee is 7 cents per page.

Pine Bluff Division PO Box 8307, Pine Bluff, AR 71611-8307 (Courier Address: US Post Office & Courthouse, 100 E 8th St, Room 3103, Pine Bluff, AR 71601), 870-536-1190, Fax: 870-536-6330.

http://www.are.uscourts.gov

Counties: Arkansas, Chicot, Cleveland, Dallas, Desha, Drew, Grant, Jefferson, Lincoln.

Indexing/Storage: Cases are indexed by defendant and plaintiff as well as by case number. New cases are available in the index immediately after filing date. A computer index is maintained. Records are on the computer from 1989. Records are also indexed on microfiche. Open records are located at this court.

Fee & Payment: The fee is $20.00 per item (one party name or case number). Payment may be made by money order, cashier check, personal check. Prepayment is required for copies and certification. Payee: US District Clerk. Certification fee: $7.00 per document. Copy fee: $.50 per page.

Phone Search: Will search name.

Mail Search: Always enclose a stamped self addressed envelope.

In Person: In person searching is available.

PACER: Sign-up number is 800-676-6856. Access fee is $.60 per minute. Toll-free access: 800-371-8842. Local access: 501-324-6190. Case records are available back to 1987-89. Records are purged every five years. New records are available online after 1 day.

Other Online Access: Search records on the Internet using RACER at www.are.uscourts.gov/perl/bkplog.html. Access fee is 7 cents per page.

US Bankruptcy Court

Eastern District of Arkansas

Little Rock Division PO Drawer 3777, Little Rock, AR 72203 (Courier Address: Room 101, 600 W Capitol, Little Rock, AR 72201), 501-918-5500, Fax: 501-918-5520.

http://www.areb.uscourts.gov

Counties: Same counties as included in Eastern District of Arkansas, plus the counties included in the Western District divisions of El Dorado, Hot Springs and Texarkana. All bankruptcy cases in Arkansas prior to mid-1993 were heard here.

Indexing/Storage: Cases are indexed by debtor and creditors as well as by case number. New cases are available in the index immediately after filing date. Both computer and card indexes are maintained. Records are also indexed on microfiche. Open records are located at this court.

Fee & Payment: The fee is $20.00 per item (one party name or case number). Payment may be made by money order, cashier check, personal check, Visa or Mastercard. Prepayment is required. Debtor's checks are not accepted. Payee: Clerk, US Bankruptcy Court. Certification fee: $7.00 per document. Copy fee: $.50 per page.

Phone Search: Only the basic information not provided on the VCIS will be released over the phone. This includes the case number, chapter, judge, attorney, trustee, date if case closed, etc. An automated voice case information service (VCIS) is available. Call VCIS at 800-891-6741 or 501-918-5555.

Mail Search: Always enclose a stamped self addressed envelope.

In Person: In person searching is available.

PACER: Sign-up number is 800-676-6856. Access fee is $.60 per minute. Toll-free access: 800-891-6572. Local access: 501-918-5565. Case records are available back to May 1989. Records are purged every six months. New civil records are available online after 1 day. PACER is available online at http://pacer.areb.uscourts.gov.

US District Court

Western District of Arkansas

El Dorado Division PO Box 1566, El Dorado, AR 71731 (Courier Address: Room 205, 101 S Jackson, El Dorado, AR 71731), 870-862-1202.

http://www.arwd.uscourts.gov

Counties: Ashley, Bradley, Calhoun, Columbia, Ouachita, Union.

Indexing/Storage: Cases are indexed by defendant and plaintiff as well as by case number. New cases are available in the index immediately after filing date. A computer index is maintained. Files are maintained numerically by year. Open records are located at this court.

Fee & Payment: The fee is $20.00 per item (one party name or case number). Payment may be made by money order, cashier check, personal check, Visa, Mastercard. Prepayment is required for out of state searchers. Payee: Clerk, US District Court. Certification fee: $7.00 per document. Copy fee: $.50 per page.

Phone Search: Only docket information is available by phone.

Fax Search: Will accept fax request usually at no cost as long as results do not have to be in writing. Call for more information.

Mail Search: Always enclose a stamped self addressed envelope.

In Person: In person searching is available.

PACER: Sign-up number is 501-783-6833. Access fee is $.60 per minute. Local access: 501-783-3538. Case records are available back to September 1990. Records are purged every five years. New records are available online after 1 day.

Other Online Access: PACER via E-mail offers case information directly to your e-mailbox. Visit www.arwd.uscourts.gov/mailform.html and input the information you are looking for; the system will automatically send the results to you by e-mail.

Fayetteville Division PO Box 6420, Fayetteville, AR 72702 (Courier Address: Room 510, 35 E Mountain, Fayetteville, AR 72701), 501-521-6980, Fax: 501-575-0774.

http://www.arwd.uscourts.gov

Counties: Benton, Madison, Washington.

Indexing/Storage: Cases are indexed by defendant and plaintiff as well as by case number. New cases are available in the index immediately after filing date. A computer index is maintained. Files are maintained numerically by year. Open records are located at this court.

Fee & Payment: The fee is $20.00 per item (one party name or case number). Payment may be made by money order, cashier check, personal check, Visa, Mastercard. Prepayment is required for out of state searchers. Payee: Clerk, Western District of Arkansas. Certification fee: $7.00 per document. Copy fee: $.50 per page. You are allowed to make your own copies. These copies cost $.50 per page. Searches can be done in person at no charge to the searcher if no written record is furnished.

Phone Search: Only docket information is available by phone.

Fax Search: Will accept fax request on same basis as mail request. Call for information regarding fax results.

Mail Search: A stamped self addressed envelope is not required.

In Person: In person searching is available.

PACER: Sign-up number is 501-783-6833. Access fee is $.60 per minute. Local access: 501-783-3538. Case records are available back to September 1990. Records are purged every five years. New records are available online after 1 day.

Other Online Access: PACER via E-mail offers case information directly to your e-mailbox. Visit www.arwd.uscourts.gov/mailform.html and input the information you are looking for, and the system will automatically send the results to you by e-mail.

Fort Smith Division PO Box 1547, Fort Smith, AR 72902 (Courier Address: Judge Isaac C. Parker Federal Bldg #1038, 6th & Rogers Ave, Fort Smith, AR 72901), 501-783-6833, Fax: 501-783-6308.

http://www.arwd.uscourts.gov

Counties: Crawford, Franklin, Johnson, Logan, Polk, Scott, Sebastian.

Indexing/Storage: Cases are indexed by defendant and plaintiff as well as by case number. New cases are available in the index immediately after filing date. A computer index is maintained. Files are maintained numerically by year. Open records are located at this court.

Fee & Payment: The fee is $20.00 per item (one party name or case number). Payment may be made by money order, cashier check, personal check, Visa, Mastercard. Prepayment is required for out of state searchers. Payee: Clerk of Court. Certification fee: $7.00 per document. Copy fee: $.50 per page. You are allowed to make your own copies. These copies cost $.50 per page.

Phone Search: Only docket information is available by phone.

Mail Search: A stamped self addressed envelope is not required.

In Person: In person searching is available.

PACER: Sign-up number is 501-783-6833. Access fee is $.60 per minute. Local access: 501-783-3538. Case records are available back to September 1990. Records are purged every five years. New records are available online after 1 day.

Other Online Access: PACER via E-mail offers case information directly to your e-mailbox. Visit www.arwd.uscourts.gov/mailform.html and input the information you are looking for; the system will automatically send the results to you by e-mail.

Hot Springs Division PO Drawer I, Hot Springs, AR 71902 (Courier Address: Federal Bldg Room 347, 100 Reserve, Hot Springs, AR 71901), 501-623-6411.

http://www.arwd.uscourts.gov

Counties: Clark, Garland, Hot Springs, Montgomery, Pike.

Indexing/Storage: Cases are indexed by defendant and plaintiff as well as by case number. New cases are available in the index immediately after filing date. A computer index is maintained. Files are maintained numerically by year. Open records are located at this court.

Fee & Payment: The fee is $20.00 per item (one party name or case number). Payment may be made by money order, cashier check, personal check, Visa, Mastercard. Prepayment is required for out of state searchers. Payee: Clerk, Western District of Arkansas. Certification fee: $7.00 per document. Copy fee: $.50 per page.

Phone Search: Searching is not available by phone.

Mail Search: Always enclose a stamped self addressed envelope.

In Person: In person searching is available.

PACER: Sign-up number is 501-783-6833. Access fee is $.60 per minute. Local access: 501-783-3538. Case records are available back to September 1990. Records are purged every five years. New records are available online after 1 day.

Other Online Access: PACER via E-mail offers case information directly to your e-mailbox. Visit www.arwd.uscourts.gov/mailform.html and input the information you are looking for, and the system will automatically send the results to you by e-mail.

Texarkana Division PO Box 2746, Texarkana, AR 75504-2746 (Courier Address: 500 State Line Ave, Texarkana, AR 71854), 870-773-3381.

http://www.arwd.uscourts.gov

Counties: Hempstead, Howard, Lafayette, Little River, Miller, Nevada, Sevier.

Indexing/Storage: Cases are indexed by defendant and plaintiff as well as by case number. New cases are available in the index immediately after filing date. A computer index is maintained. Files are maintained numerically by year. Records are also indexed by microfiche. Open records are located at this court.

Fee & Payment: The fee is $20.00 per item (one party name or case number). Payment may be

made by money order, cashier check, personal check, Visa, Mastercard. Prepayment is required for out of state searchers. Payee: Clerk of the Court. Certification fee: $7.00 per document. Copy fee: $.50 per page. You are allowed to make your own copies. These copies cost $.50 per page.

Phone Search: Case numbers are released by phone. Anything else will depend on workload of deputy clerk.

Mail Search: A stamped self addressed envelope is not required.

In Person: In person searching is available.

PACER: Sign-up number is 501-783-6833. Access fee is $.60 per minute. Local access: 501-783-3538. Case records are available back to September 1990. Records are purged every five years. New records are available online after 1 day.

Other Online Access: PACER via E-mail offers case information directly to your e-mailbox. Visit www.arwd.uscourts.gov/mailform.html and input the information you are looking for; the system will automatically send the results to you by e-mail.

US Bankruptcy Court

Western District of Arkansas

Fayetteville Division PO Box 3097, Fayetteville, AR 72702-3097 (Courier Address: 35 E Mountain, Room 316, Fayetteville, AR 72701), 501-582-9800, Fax: 501-582-9825.

http://www.arb.uscourts.gov

Counties: Same counties as included in the Western District of Arkansas except that counties included in the divisions of El Dorado and Texarkana are heard in Little Rock.

Indexing/Storage: Cases are indexed by debtor and creditors as well as by case number. New cases are available in the index immediately after filing date. A computer index is maintained. Open records are located at this court.

Fee & Payment: The fee is $20.00 per item (one party name or case number). Payment may be made by money order, cashier check, personal check, Visa. Prepayment is required. Personal checks are not accepted from debtors. Licensed attorneys may be invoiced for copywork. Payee: Clerk, US Bankruptcy Court. Certification fee: $7.00 per document. Copy fee: $.50 per page.

Phone Search: Only the basic information not provided on the VCIS will be released over the phone. This includes the case number, chapter, judge, attorney, and trustee. An automated voice case information service (VCIS) is available. Call VCIS at 800-891-6741 or 501-918-5555.

Mail Search: Always enclose a stamped self addressed envelope.

In Person: In person searching is available.

PACER: Sign-up number is 800-676-6856. Access fee is $.60 per minute. Toll-free access: 800-891-6572. Local access: 501-918-5565. Case records are available back to May 1989. Records are purged every six months. New civil records are available online after 1 day.

Arkansas County Courts

Court	Jurisdiction	No. of Courts	How Organized
Circuit Courts*	General	28	28 Circuits
County Courts*	Limited	0	
Combined Courts*		47	
Chancery and Probate Courts*	Limited	29	28 Circuits
Combined Circuit/Chancery*		53	
District (Municipal) Courts*	Limited	126	
City Courts	Limited	1084	
Court of Common Pleas	Limited	4	
Justice of the Peace Courts	Limited	55	
Police Courts	Limited	5	

* Profiled in this Sourcebook.

Court	CIVIL								
	Tort	Contract	Real Estate	Min. Claim	Max. Claim	Small Claims	Estate	Eviction	Domestic Relations
Circuit Courts*	X	X	X	$5000	No Max				
County Courts*			X						
Chancery and Probate Courts*	X	X	X				X		X
District (Munici-pal) Courts*		X	X	$0	$5000	$5000		X	
City Courts		X	X	$0	$300				
Court of Common Pleas		X		$500	$1000				
Justice of the Peace Courts						$300			
Police Courts		X	X	$0	$300				

Court	CRIMINAL				
	Felony	Misdemeanor	DWI/DUI	Preliminary Hearing	Juvenile
Circuit Courts*	X				
County Courts*					
Chancery and Probate Courts*					X
District (Munici-pal) Courts*		X	X	X	
City Courts		X	X	X	
Court of Common Pleas					
Justice of the Peace Courts		X			
Police Courts		X	X		

ADMINISTRATION   Administrative Office of Courts, 625 Marshall St, Justice Bldg, Little Rock, AR, 72201; 501-682-9400, Fax: 501-682-9410. http://courts.state.ar.us

COURT STRUCTURE   Circuit Courts are the courts of general jurisdiction and are arranged in 25 circuits. County Courts are, fundamentally, administrative courts dealing with county fiscal issues. Circuit and County courts can be combined. Chancery and Circuit courts may be combined under the same judge. As of 8/2/97, the civil limit raised to $5000 in limited jurisidiction District Courts. As of 7/1/2001, Municipal Courts are known as District Courts.

ONLINE ACCESS   There is a very limited internal online computer system at the Administrative Office of Courts.

ADDITIONAL INFORMATION   Most courts that allow written search requests require an SASE. Fees vary widely across jurisdictions as do prepayment requirements.

Arkansas County

Circuit & Chancery Courts - Northern District PO Box 719, Stuttgart, AR 72160; 870-673-2056; Fax: 870-673-3869. Hours: 8AM-5PM (CST). *Felony, Civil Actions, Probate.*

Note: The court is not bonded to search Civil or Chancery records.

Civil Records: Access: In person only. Visitors must perform in person searches for themselves. No search fee. Required to search: name, years to search. Civil cases indexed by defendant, plaintiff. Civil records in files from 1923, prior to 1923 records located in DeWitt (946-4219).

Criminal Records: Access: In person only. Visitors must perform in person searches for themselves. No search fee. Required to search: name, years to search, DOB. Criminal records in files from 1923, prior to 1923 records located in DeWitt (946-4219).

General Information: No juvenile records released. Fax notes: Fee to fax results is $1.00 per page. Copy fee: $.50 per page. Certification fee: $4.00. Personal checks accepted. Prepayment is required.

Circuit & Chancery Courts - Southern District 101 Courthouse Sq, De Witt, AR 72042; 870-946-4219; Fax: 870-946-1394. Hours: 8AM-5PM (CST). *Felony, Civil Actions Over $5,000.*

Civil Records: Access: Fax, mail, in person. Both court and visitors may perform in person searches. Search fee: $6.00 per name. Required to search: name, years to search. Civil cases indexed by defendant, plaintiff. Civil records in files from 1923, prior records (the two other courts in this county also) located at this court.

Criminal Records: Access: Fax, mail, in person. Both court and visitors may perform in person searches. Search fee: $6.00 per name. Required to search: name, years to search, DOB; also helpful: SSN. Criminal records in files from 1923, prior records (the two other courts in this county also) located at this court. Search request must be in writing.

General Information: No juvenile, expunged records released. SASE requested. Turnaround time 1-2 days. Fax notes: Fax fee $1.00 per copy; $6.00 per search. Copy fee: $.50 per page. Certification fee: $4.00. Fee payee: Arkansas County Circuit Clerk. Personal checks accepted. Prepayment is required.

Stuttgart District Court PO Box 819, Stuttgart, AR 72160; 870-673-7951; Fax: 870-673-6522. Hours: 8AM-5PM (CST). *Misdemeanor, Civil Actions Under $5,000, Eviction, Small Claims.*

Civil Records: Access: In person, mail. Both court and visitors may perform in person searches. No search fee.

Criminal Records: Access: In person, mail. Both court and visitors may perform in person searches. No search fee. Required to search: name, years to search; also helpful: DOB, SSN.

General Information: Turnaround time 3 days.

Ashley County

Circuit & Chancery Courts Ashley County Courthouse, 205 E Jefferson, Hamburg, AR 71646; 870-853-2030; Fax: 870-853-2034. Hours: 8AM-4:30PM (CST). *Felony, Civil Actions Over $5,000, Probate.*

Civil Records: Access: Mail, in person. Visitors must perform in person searches for themselves. No search fee. Required to search: name, years to search. Civil cases indexed by defendant, plaintiff. Civil records on files and index cards from 1950s. Mail requests must have case numbers.

Criminal Records: Access: Mail, in person. Visitors must perform in person searches for themselves. No search fee. Required to search: name, years to search; also helpful: DOB, SSN. Criminal records on files and index cards from 1950s. No name searches by mail, must have case numbers.

General Information: No juvenile records released. SASE required. Fax notes: Fee to fax results is $1.00 per page. Copy fee: $.50 per page. Certification fee: $2.50. Fee payee: Circuit Clerk's Office. Personal checks accepted. Prepayment is required.

Hamburg District Court PO Box 558, City Hall, Hamburg, AR 71646; 870-853-8326; Fax: 870-853-8600. Hours: 8AM-4:30PM (CST). *Misdemeanor, Civil Actions Under $5,000, Eviction, Small Claims.*

Civil Records: Access: Mail, in person. Both court and visitors may perform in person searches. Search fee: $5.00. Civil records go back to 1976; on computer back to 1989.

Criminal Records: Access: Mail, in person. Both court and visitors may perform in person searches. Search fee: $5.00. Required to search: name, years to search, DOB. Criminal records go back to 1976; on computer back to 1989.

General Information: Turnaround time 1-2 days. Certification fee: $10.00. Fee payee: District Court.

Baxter County

Circuit & Chancery Courts 1 E 7th St Courthouse Square, Mountain Home, AR 72653; 870-425-3475; Fax: 870-424-5105. Hours: 8AM-4:30PM (CST). *Felony, Civil Actions Over $5,000, Probate.*

Civil Records: Access: Fax, mail, in person. Both court and visitors may perform in person searches. Search fee: $6.00 per name. Required to search: name, years to search. Civil cases indexed by defendant, plaintiff. Civil records on computer from 1982, on criminal fee book from early 1900s.

Criminal Records: Access: Mail, in person. Both court and visitors may perform in person searches. Search fee: $6.00 per name. Required to search: name, years to search, SSN. Criminal records on computer from 1982, on criminal fee book from early 1900s.

General Information: Public Access terminal is available. No adoption or juvenile records released. SASE required. Turnaround time 1-2 days. Copy fee: $.25 per page. Certification fee: $3.00. Fee payee: Baxter County Clerk. Personal checks accepted. Prepayment is required. Fee to fax results is $5.00 per page.

District Court 720 S Hickory, Mountain Home, AR 72653; 870-425-3140; Fax: 870-425-9290. Hours: 8AM-4:30PM (CST). *Misdemeanor, Civil Actions Under $5,000, Eviction, Small Claims.*

Civil Records: Access: In person, mail. Only the court performs in person searches; visitors may not. No search fee.

Criminal Records: Access: In person, mail. Only the court performs in person searches; visitors may not. No search fee. Required to search: name, years to search, DOB, SSN.

General Information: Turnaround time 1-2 days.

Benton County

Circuit & Chancery Courts 102 NE "A" St, Bentonville, AR 72712; 501-271-1015; Fax: 501-271-5719. Hours: 8AM-4:30PM (CST). *Felony, Civil Actions Over $5,000, Probate.*

www.co.benton.ar.us

Civil Records: Access: Online, in person. Visitors must perform in person searches for themselves. No search fee. Required to search: name, years to search. Civil cases indexed by defendant, plaintiff. Civil records on computer from 1991, on dockets from 1880s. Court dockets and judgments from the circuit clerk's web site are available free at http://64.217.42.130:5061.

Criminal Records: Access: Online, in person. Visitors must perform in person searches for themselves. No search fee. Required to search: name, years to search. Criminal records on computer from 1991, on dockets from 1880s. Online access to criminal records is the same as civil.

General Information: Public Access terminal is available. No juvenile records released. Copy fee: $.50 per page. Certification fee: $2.00. Fee payee: Benton County Circuit Clerk. Personal checks accepted. Prepayment is required.

District Court 117 W Central, Bentonville, AR 72712; 501-271-3120; Fax: 501-271-3134. Hours: 8AM-4:30PM (CST). *Misdemeanor, Civil Actions Under $5,000, Small Claims.*

Civil Records: Access: In person, mail. Both court and visitors may perform in person searches. No search fee. Civil records on computer back to 1992; other records go back to 1982.

Criminal Records: Access: In person, mail. Both court and visitors may perform in person searches. No search fee. Required to search: name, years to search, DOB. Civil records on computer back to 1992; other records go back to 1982.

General Information: Public Access terminal is available. Turnaround time 5 days. Copy fee: $.25 per page. Fee payee: Bentonville District Court. Prepayment is required.

Boone County

Circuit & Chancery Courts 100 N Main St #200, Harrison, AR 72601; 870-741-5560; Fax: 870-741-4335. Hours: 8AM-4:30PM (CST). *Felony, Civil Actions Over $5,000.*

Note: Probate records are in the County Clerk's office, 870-741-8428.

Civil Records: Access: Mail, in person. Visitors must perform in person searches for themselves. No search fee. Required to search: name, years to search. Civil cases indexed by defendant, plaintiff. Civil records archived from 1940, index from 1977, computerized from 1990.

Criminal Records: Access: Mail, in person. Visitors must perform in person searches for themselves. No search fee. Required to search: name, years to search. Criminal records archived from 1940, index from 1977, computerized from 1990.

General Information: Public Access terminal is available. No indictments or juvenile records released. SASE required. Turnaround time 1 day. Fax notes: Fee to fax results is $5.00 per document. Copy fee: $.25 per page. Certification fee: $5.00. Fee payee: Circuit Clerk. Personal checks accepted. Prepayment is required.

District Court PO Box 968, Harrison, AR 72602; 870-741-2788; Fax: 870-741-4329. Hours: 8:30AM-4PM (CST). *Misdemeanor, Civil Actions Under $5,000, Eviction, Small Claims.*

Civil Records: Access: In person, mail. Both court and visitors may perform in person searches. No search fee.

Criminal Records: Access: In person, mail. Both court and visitors may perform in person searches. No search fee. Required to search: name, years to search; also helpful: DOB.

General Information: Turnaround time 2 weeks.

Bradley County

Circuit & Chancery Courts Bradley County Courthouse - Records, 101 E Cedar, Warren, AR 71671; 870-226-2272; Probate phone: 870-226-3464; Fax: 870-226-8401. Hours: 8AM-4:30PM (CST). *Felony, Civil Actions Over $5,000, Probate.*

Civil Records: Access: In person only. Visitors must perform in person searches for themselves. No search fee. Required to search: name, years to search. Civil cases indexed by defendant, plaintiff. Civil records (active cases) on dockets, retired cases on indexes from 1850, no computerization.

Criminal Records: Access: Mail, in person. Both court and visitors may perform in person searches. Search fee: $6.00. Required to search: name, years to search; also helpful: DOB, SSN. Criminal records (active cases) on dockets, retired cases on indexes from 1850, no computerization.

General Information: No juvenile released. SASE required. Turnaround time 1 week. Copy fee: $.25 per page. Certification fee: $3.00. Fee payee: Circuit Court. Personal checks accepted. Prepayment is required.

District Court PO Box 352, Warren, AR 71671; 870-226-2567; Fax: 870-226-2567. Hours: 8AM-5PM (CST). *Misdemeanor, Civil Actions Under $5,000, Eviction, Small Claims.*

Civil Records: Access: In person, mail. Only the court performs in person searches; visitors may not. No search fee.

Criminal Records: Access: In person, mail. Only the court performs in person searches; visitors may not. Search fee: $5.00 per name. Required to search: name, years to search, SSN.

General Information: Turnaround time 1 week. Fee payee: District Court.

Calhoun County

Circuit & County Courts PO Box 1175, Hampton, AR 71744; 870-798-2517. Hours: 8:30AM-4:30PM (CST). *Felony, Civil Actions Over $5,000, Probate.*

Civil Records: Access: Mail, in person. Both court and visitors may perform in person searches. No search fee. Required to search: name, years to search. Civil cases indexed by defendant, plaintiff. Civil records on dockets from 1851.

Criminal Records: Access: Mail, in person. Visitors must perform in person searches for themselves. No search fee. Required to search: name, years to search, DOB; also helpful: SSN. Criminal records on dockets from 1851.

General Information: No juvenile or adoption released. SASE required. Turnaround time 1-3 days. Copy fee: $.25 per page. Certification fee: $3.50. Fee payee: Calhoun County Clerk. Personal checks accepted. Prepayment is required.

District Court PO Box 783, Hampton, AR 71744; 870-798-2753; Fax: 870-798-3665. Hours: 8AM-4:30PM (CST). *Misdemeanor, Civil Actions Under $5,000, Eviction, Small Claims.*

Civil Records: Access: In person, mail. Both court and visitors may perform in person searches. No search fee.

Criminal Records: Access: In person, mail. Both court and visitors may perform in person searches. No search fee. Required to search: name, years to search, SSN.

General Information: Turnaround time 2 days.

Carroll County

Berryville Circuit & Chancery Courts - Eastern District Carroll County Circuit Court, PO Box 71, Berryville, AR 72616; 870-423-2422; Fax: 870-423-4796. Hours: 8:30AM-4:30PM (CST). *Felony, Civil Actions Over $5,000, Eviction, Probate.*

Civil Records: Access: Fax, mail, in person. Both court and visitors may perform in person searches. Search fee: $6.00 per name. Required to search: name, years to search. Civil cases indexed by defendant, plaintiff. Civil records on computer; on index books since 1869.

Criminal Records: Access: Fax, mail, in person. Both court and visitors may perform in person searches. Search fee: $6.00 per name. Required to search: name, years to search; also helpful: DOB, SSN. Criminal records on computer; on index books since 1869.

General Information: Public Access terminal is available. No juvenile records released. SASE required. Turnaround time 1-2 days. Fax notes: Fee to fax results is $1.00 per page. Copy fee: $.25 per page. Certification fee: $2.00. Fee payee: Circuit Clerk of Carroll County. Personal checks accepted. Prepayment is required.

Eureka Springs Circuit, County & Chancery Courts - Western District 44 S Main, PO Box 109, Eureka Springs, AR 72632; 501-253-8646. Hours: 8:30AM-4:30PM (CST). *Felony, Civil Actions Over $5,000, Eviction, Probate.*

Civil Records: Access: In person only. Visitors must perform in person searches for themselves. No search fee. Required to search: name, years to search. Civil cases indexed by defendant, plaintiff. Civil records on indexes from 1883.

Criminal Records: Access: Phone, mail, in person. Both court and visitors may perform in person searches. Search fee: $6.00 per name. Required to search: name, years to search; also helpful: DOB. Criminal records on indexes from 1883.

General Information: No expunged criminal records released. SASE required. Turnaround time varies. Fax notes: Fee to fax results is $1.00 per page. Copy fee: $.50 by mail or $.25 in person. Certification fee: $2.00; $3.00 for Probate records. Fee payee: Circuit Clerk of

Carroll County or County Clerk. Personal checks accepted. Prepayment is required.

Berryville District Court 103 S Springs, Berryville, AR 72616; 870-423-6247; Fax: 870-423-7069. Hours: 8AM-4:30PM (CST). *Misdemeanor, Civil Actions Under $5,000, Small Claims.*

Civil Records: Both court and visitors may perform in person searches. No search fee.

Criminal Records: Access: In person, mail. Both court and visitors may perform in person searches. No search fee. Required to search: name, years to search; also helpful: DOB.

General Information: Turnaround time 1-2 days.

Eureka Springs District Court Courthouse, 44 S Main, Eureka Springs, AR 72632; 501-253-8574; Fax: 501-253-6887. Hours: 8AM-5PM (CST). *Misdemeanor, Civil Actions Under $5,000, Small Claims.*

www.cityofeureka.springs.org

Civil Records: Access: In person, mail. Both court and visitors may perform in person searches. No search fee.

Criminal Records: Access: In person, mail. Both court and visitors may perform in person searches. No search fee. Required to search: name, years to search.

General Information: Turnaround time 1 week.

Chicot County

Circuit & Chancery Courts 108 Main St, County Courthouse, Lake Village, AR 71653; 870-265-8010; Fax: 870-265-5102. Hours: 8AM-4:30PM (CST). *Felony, Civil Actions Over $5,000, Probate.*

Civil Records: Access: Mail, in person. Both court and visitors may perform in person searches. Search fee: $6.00 per name. Required to search: name, years to search. Civil cases indexed by defendant, plaintiff. Civil records on dockets and files from 1900s.

Criminal Records: Access: Mail, in person. Both court and visitors may perform in person searches. Search fee: $6.00 per name. Required to search: name, years to search. Criminal records on dockets and files from 1900s.

General Information: No juvenile records released. SASE required. Turnaround time 1-2 days. Copy fee: $.50 per page. Certification fee: $2.00. Fee payee: Circuit Clerk. Personal checks accepted. Prepayment is required.

Lake Village District Court PO Box 832, Lake Village, AR 71653; 870-265-3283. Hours: 9AM-5PM (CST). *Misdemeanor, Civil Actions Under $5,000, Eviction, Small Claims.*

Civil Records: Access: Phone, mail, fax, in person. Both court and visitors may perform in person searches. Search fee: $5.00 per name. Civil records on computer go back to 8/2000; other records go back to 1977.

Criminal Records: Access: Phone, mail, fax, in person. Both court and visitors may perform in person searches. Search fee: $5.00 per name. Required to search: name, years to search; also helpful: DOB, SSN. Criminal records on computer go back to 8/2000; other records go back to 1977.

General Information: Turnaround time ASAP. Fee payee: Lake Village District Court.

Clark County

Circuit & Chancery Courts PO Box 576, Arkadelphia, AR 71923; 870-246-4281. Hours: 8:30AM-4:30PM (CST). *Felony, Civil Actions Over $5,000, Probate.*

Civil Records: Access: Mail, in person. Both court and visitors may perform in person searches. Search fee: $5.00 per name. Required to search: name, years to search. Civil cases indexed by defendant, plaintiff. Civil records on computer since 1985.

Criminal Records: Access: Mail, in person. Both court and visitors may perform in person searches. Search fee: $5.00 per name. Required to search: name, years to search. Criminal records on computer since 1980.

General Information: No juvenile records released. SASE required. Turnaround time 1-2 days. Copy fee: $.50 per page. Certification fee: $5.00. Fee payee: Pamela King Circuit Clerk. Personal checks accepted. Prepayment is required.

District Court PO Box 449, Arkadelphia, AR 71923; 870-246-9552. Hours: 8:30AM-4:30PM (CST). *Misdemeanor, Civil Actions Under $5,000, Eviction, Small Claims.*

Civil Records: Access: Phone, mail, fax, in person. Both court and visitors may perform in person searches. No search fee. Records go back to 1980; on computer since 1990.

Criminal Records: Access: Phone, mail, fax, in person. Both court and visitors may perform in person searches. No search fee. Required to search: name, years to search; also helpful: DOB. Records go back to 1980; on computer since 1990.

General Information: Turnaround time same day.

Clay County

Corning Circuit & County Courts PO Box 176, Corning, AR 72422; 870-857-3271; Fax: 870-857-9201. Hours: 8AM-4:30PM (CST). *Felony, Civil Actions Over $5,000, Probate.*

Civil Records: Access: Mail, in person. Both court and visitors may perform in person searches. Search fee: $6.00 per name. Required to search: name, years to search. Civil cases indexed by defendant, plaintiff. Civil records on books from 1893.

Criminal Records: Access: Mail, in person. Both court and visitors may perform in person searches. Search fee: $6.00 per name. Required to search: name, years to search; also helpful: DOB, SSN. Criminal records on books from 1893.

General Information: No juvenile records released. Turnaround time 1-2 days. Copy fee: $1.00 per page. Certification fee: $5.00. Fee payee: Circuit Clerk. Personal checks accepted. Prepayment is required.

Piggott Circuit & County Courts PO Box 29, Piggott, AR 72454; 870-598-2524; Fax: 870-598-2524. Hours: 8AM-4:30PM (CST). *Felony, Civil Actions Over $5,000.*

Civil Records: Access: Mail, in person. No search fee. Required to search: name, years to search. Civil cases indexed by defendant, plaintiff. Civil records on books from 1893.

Criminal Records: Access: Mail, in person. Visitors must perform in person searches for themselves. No search fee. Required to search: name, years to search. Criminal records on books from 1893.

General Information: Public Access terminal is available. No expunged criminal records released. SASE required. Turnaround time 1-2 days. Fax notes: $5.00 per document. Copy fee: $1.00 per page. Certification fee: $5.00 per page. Fee payee: Circuit Clerk. Personal checks accepted. Prepayment is required.

Clay County District Court 121 W Main St, Piggott, AR 72454; 870-598-2265. Hours: 8AM-4:30PM (CST). *Misdemeanor, Civil Actions Under $5,000, Eviction, Small Claims.*

Note: Office is open 20 hours per week only.

Civil Records: Access: Mail, in person. Both court and visitors may perform in person searches. Search fee: $8.00. Records on computer back to 1998.

Criminal Records: Access: Mail, in person. Both court and visitors may perform in person searches. No search fee. Required to search: name, years to search, SSN; also helpful: DOB. Records on computer back to 1998.

General Information: Turnaround time 3-4 days. Fee payee: District Court. Prepayment is required.

Cleburne County

Circuit & County Courts PO Box 543, Heber Springs, AR 72543; 501-362-8149; Fax: 501-362-4650. Hours: 8:30AM-4:30PM (CST). *Felony, Civil Actions Over $5,000, Probate, Eviction.*

Civil Records: Access: Phone, mail, in person. Both court and visitors may perform in person searches. Search fee: $6.00 per name. Required to search: name, years to search. Civil cases indexed by defendant, plaintiff. Civil records on dockets from 1883; computerized records from 1994.

Criminal Records: Access: Phone, mail, in person. Both court and visitors may perform in person searches. Search fee: $6.00 per name. Required to search: name, years to search. Criminal records on dockets from 1883; computerized records from 1994.

General Information: No juvenile records released. SASE required. Turnaround time 1-2 days. Copy fee: $.25 per page. Certification fee: $1.00. Fee payee: Circuit Clerk. Personal checks accepted. Prepayment is required.

District Court 102 E Main, Heber Springs, AR 72543; 501-362-6585; Fax: 501-362-4661. Hours: 8:30AM-4:30PM (CST). *Misdemeanor, Civil Actions Under $5,000, Small Claims.*

Civil Records: Access: Phone, mail, fax, in person. Both court and visitors may perform in person searches. No search fee. Civil records on computer back to 1989.

Criminal Records: Access: Phone, mail, fax, in person. Both court and visitors may perform in person searches. No search fee. Required to search: name, years to search, offense, DOB. Criminal records on computer back to 1989.

General Information: Public Access terminal is available. Turnaround time 10 working days.

Cleveland County

Circuit & County Courts PO Box 368, Rison, AR 71665; 870-325-6521; Fax: 870-325-6144. Hours: 8AM-4:30PM (CST). *Felony, Civil Actions Over $5,000, Probate.*

Civil Records: Access: Mail, in person. Visitors must perform in person searches for themselves. Search fee: $6.00. Required to search: name, years to search. Civil cases indexed by defendant, plaintiff. Civil records from 1980.

Criminal Records: Access: Mail, in person. Both court and visitors may perform in person searches. Search fee: $6.00. Required to search: name, years to search, DOB. Criminal records from 1980.

General Information: No juvenile or adoption records released. Fax notes: Fee to fax results is $1.00 per document. Copy fee: $.25 per page. Certification fee: $3.00. Fee payee: Clerk of Circuit Court. Personal checks accepted. Prepayment is required.

District Court PO Box 405, City Hall, Rison, AR 71665; 870-325-7382; Fax: 870-325-6152. Hours: 8AM-4PM (CST). *Misdemeanor, Civil Actions Under $5,000, Eviction, Small Claims.*

Civil Records: Access: In person only. Both court and visitors may perform in person searches. No search fee.

Criminal Records: Access: In person only. Both court and visitors may perform in person searches. No search fee. Required to search: name, years to search, SSN.

Columbia County

Circuit & County Courts 1 Court Square Ste 6, Magnolia, AR 71753-3595; 870-235-3700; Fax: 870-235-3786. Hours: 8AM-4:30PM (CST). *Felony, Civil Actions Over $5,000, Probate.*

Civil Records: Access: Mail, in person. Both court and visitors may perform in person searches. Search fee: $10.00 per name. Required to search: name, years to search. Civil cases indexed by defendant, plaintiff. Civil records on dockets and index cards.

Criminal Records: Access: Mail, in person. Both court and visitors may perform in person searches. Search fee: $10.00 per name. Required to search: name, years to search, DOB, SSN. Criminal records on dockets and index cards.

General Information: No juvenile or adoption. SASE required. Turnaround time 2-4 days. Copy fee: $1.00 per page. Certification fee: $3.00. Fee payee: Circuit Clerk. Personal checks accepted. Prepayment is required.

Magnolia District Court PO Box 1126, Magnolia, AR 71753; 870-234-7312. Hours: 8AM-5PM (CST). *Misdemeanor, Civil Actions Under $5,000, Eviction, Small Claims.*

Civil Records: Access: Mail, in person. Both court and visitors may perform in person searches. No search fee.

Criminal Records: Access: Mail, in person. Only the court performs in person searches; visitors may not. Search fee: $1.00 per name. Required to search: name, years to search; also helpful: address.

General Information: SASE is required. Turnaround time 3 days. Copy fee: $1.00 per page. Fee payee: District Court Clerk. Prepayment is required.

Conway County

Circuit & Chancery Courts Conway County Courthouse, Rm 206, Morrilton, AR 72110; 501-354-9617; Probate phone: 501-354-9621; Fax: 501-354-9612. Hours: 8AM-5PM (CST). *Felony, Civil Actions Over $5,000, Probate.*

Civil Records: Access: Phone, fax, mail, in person. Both court and visitors may perform in person searches. Search fee: $8.00 per name. Required to search: name, years to search. Civil cases indexed by defendant, plaintiff. Civil records (child support) on computer. All others on dockets from 1930s.

Criminal Records: Access: Phone, mail, in person. Both court and visitors may perform in person searches. Search fee: $8.00 per name. Required to search: name, years to search, DOB; also helpful: sex, SSN. Criminal records indexed in books, on computer since.

General Information: No juvenile records released. SASE required. Turnaround time 1-2 days. Fax notes: Fee to fax results is $1.00 per page. Copy fee: $1.00 per page. Certification fee: $5.00. Fee payee: Circuit Clerk. Personal checks accepted. Prepayment is required.

District Court Conway County Courthouse, PO Box 127, Morrilton, AR 72110; 501-354-9615; Fax: 501-354-9633. Hours: 8AM-4:30PM (CST). *Misdemeanor, Civil Actions Under $5,000, Eviction, Small Claims.*

Civil Records: Access: In person, mail. Both court and visitors may perform in person searches. No search fee.

Criminal Records: Access: In person, mail. Only the court performs in person searches; visitors may not. Search fee: $5.00 per name. Required to search: name, years to search; also helpful: DOB.

General Information: Turnaround time 1-2 days. Fee payee: District Court Clerk. Prepayment is required.

Craighead County

Jonesboro Circuit & Chancery Courts PO Box 120, Jonesboro, AR 72403; 870-933-4530; Fax: 870-933-4534. Hours: 8AM-5PM (CST). *Felony, Civil Actions Over $5,000, Probate.*

Civil Records: Access: Fax, mail, in person. Both court and visitors may perform in person searches. Search fee: $6.00 per name. Required to search: name, years to search. Civil cases indexed by defendant, plaintiff. Civil records on computer from 1972, on microfiche from 1800s.
Criminal Records: Access: Fax, mail, in person. Both court and visitors may perform in person searches. Search fee: $6.00 per name. Required to search: name, years to search, DOB; also helpful: address, SSN. Criminal records on computer from 1972, on microfiche from 1800s.
General Information: Public Access terminal is available. No juvenile records released. SASE required. Turnaround time 1-2 days. Fax notes: $1.00 per page. Copy fee: $.50 per page. Certification fee: $3.00. Fee payee: Circuit Clerk. Personal checks accepted. Prepayment is required.

Lake City Circuit & County Courts PO Box 537, Lake City, AR 72437; 870-237-4342; Fax: 870-237-8174. Hours: 8AM-5PM (CST). *Felony, Civil Actions Over $5,000, Probate.*

Civil Records: Access: Mail, fax, in person. Both court and visitors may perform in person searches. Search fee: $6.00 per name. Required to search: name, years to search, address. Civil cases indexed by defendant, plaintiff. Civil records on computer from 1972, on microfiche from 1800s.
Criminal Records: Access: Mail, fax, in person. Both court and visitors may perform in person searches. Search fee: $6.00 per name. Required to search: name, years to search, address, DOB; also helpful: SSN. Criminal records on computer from 1972, on microfiche from 1800s.
General Information: Public Access terminal is available. No adoption records released. SASE required. Turnaround time 1-2 days. Copy fee: $.50 per page. Certification fee: $3.00 per page. Fee payee: Circuit Clerk. Business checks accepted. Prepayment is required.

Craighead County District Court 410 W Washington, Jonesboro, AR 72401; 870-933-4508; Fax: 870-933-4582. Hours: 8AM-5PM (CST). *Misdemeanor, Civil Actions Under $5,000, Eviction, Small Claims.*

Civil Records: Access: In person, mail. Both court and visitors may perform in person searches. No search fee.
Criminal Records: Access: In person, mail. Both court and visitors may perform in person searches. No search fee. Required to search: name, years to search, SSN.
General Information: Turnaround time 1-2 days.

Crawford County

Circuit & Chancery Courts County Courthouse, 300 Main St, Rm 22, Van Buren, AR 72956; 501-474-1821; Fax: 501-471-0622. Hours: 8AM-5PM (CST). *Felony, Civil Actions Over $5,000, Probate.*

Civil Records: Access: Mail, in person. Both court and visitors may perform in person searches. Search fee: $6.00 per name. Required to search: name, years to search. Civil cases indexed by defendant, plaintiff. Civil records on computer from 1993, on dockets from 1877.
Criminal Records: Access: In person only. Both court and visitors may perform in person searches. Search fee: $6.00 per name. Required to search: name, years to search. Criminal records on computer from 1993, on dockets from 1877.

General Information: Public Access terminal is available. No juvenile records released. SASE required. Turnaround time 1-2 days. Copy fee: $1.00 per page. Certification fee: $2.00. Fee payee: Circuit Clerk. Personal checks accepted. Prepayment is required.

District Court 1003 Broadway, Van Buren, AR 72956; 501-474-1671; Fax: 501-471-5010. Hours: 8AM-5PM (CST). *Misdemeanor, Civil Actions Under $5,000, Eviction, Small Claims.*

Civil Records: Access: In person, mail. Both court and visitors may perform in person searches. No search fee.
Criminal Records: Access: In person, mail. Both court and visitors may perform in person searches. Search fee: $10.00 per name. Required to search: name, years to search; also helpful: DOB, SSN.
General Information: Public Access terminal is available. Turnaround time 2-3 days. Fee payee: Van Buren District Court. Prepayment is required.

Crittenden County

Circuit & Chancery Courts 100 Court St, Marion, AR 72364; 870-739-3248. Hours: 8AM-4:30PM (CST). *Felony, Civil Actions Over $5,000, Probate.*

Civil Records: Access: Mail, in person. Both court and visitors may perform in person searches. Search fee: $6.00 per name. Required to search: name, years to search. Civil cases indexed by plaintiff. Civil records on dockets or microfiche from 1930s.
Criminal Records: Access: Mail, in person. Both court and visitors may perform in person searches. Search fee: $6.00 per name. Required to search: name, years to search, DOB. Criminal records on dockets or microfiche from 1930s.
General Information: Public Access terminal is available. No juvenile records released. SASE not required. Turnaround time 1-2 days. Fax notes: Fee to fax results is $4.50 per document. Copy fee: $.25 per page. Certification fee: $2.00. Fee payee: Circuit Court. Personal checks accepted. Prepayment is required.

District Court PO Box 766, West Memphis, AR 72301; 870-732-7560; Fax: 870-732-7538. Hours: 8AM-5PM (CST). *Misdemeanor, Civil Actions Under $5,000, Eviction, Small Claims.*

Civil Records: Access: Phone, mail, in person. Both court and visitors may perform in person searches. No search fee. Civil records on computer back to 1989; other records go back to 1945.
Criminal Records: Access: Phone, mail, in person. Both court and visitors may perform in person searches. No search fee. Required to search: name, years to search; also helpful: SSN, race, sex, DOB. Criminal records on computer back to 1989; other records go back to 1945.
General Information: Public Access terminal is available. Turnaround time 2-3 days. Fax notes: No fee to fax results.

Cross County

Circuit & County Courts County Courthouse, 705 E Union, Rm 9, Wynne, AR 72396; 870-238-5720. Hours: 8AM-4PM (CST). *Felony, Civil Actions Over $5,000, Probate.*

Civil Records: Access: Mail, in person. Search fee: $6.00 per name. Required to search: name, years to search. Civil cases indexed by defendant. Civil records (child support) on computer. All on dockets from 1800s.
Criminal Records: Access: Mail, in person. Both court and visitors may perform in person searches. Search fee: $6.00 per name. Required to search: name, years to search; also helpful: SSN. Criminal records (child support) on computer. All on dockets from 1800s.
General Information: No juvenile records released. SASE required. Turnaround time same day. Copy fee:

$.25 per page. Certification fee: $3.00. Fee payee: Cross County Circuit Court. Personal checks accepted. Prepayment is required.

District Court 205 Mississippi St, Wynne, AR 72396; 870-238-9171; Fax: 870-238-3930. Hours: 8AM-4PM (CST). *Misdemeanor, Civil Actions Under $5,000, Eviction, Small Claims.*

Civil Records: Access: Mail, in person. Both court and visitors may perform in person searches. Search fee: $2.00. Required to search: name, years to search. Records on computer back to 1986.
Criminal Records: Access: Mail, in person. Both court and visitors may perform in person searches. Search fee: $2.00. Required to search: name, years to search, signed release; also helpful: SSN. Records on computer back to 1986.
General Information: Public Access terminal is available. Turnaround time 1-2 days. Fax notes: Fee to fax results is $2.00 per document. Certification fee: $2.00. Fee payee: Wynne District Court. Prepayment is required.

Dallas County

Circuit & County Courts Dallas County Courthouse, Fordyce, AR 71742; 870-352-2307; Fax: 870-352-7179. Hours: 8:30AM-4:30PM (CST). *Felony, Civil Actions Over $5,000, Probate.*

Civil Records: Access: Phone, fax, mail, in person. Both court and visitors may perform in person searches. No search fee. Required to search: name, years to search. Civil cases indexed by defendant, plaintiff. Civil records go back to 1863; on computer back to 8/1997.
Criminal Records: Access: In person only. Visitors must perform in person searches for themselves. No search fee. Required to search: name, years to search, DOB; also helpful: SSN. Criminal records go back to 1863; on computer back to 8/1997.
General Information: Public Access terminal is available. No juvenile records released. SASE required. Turnaround time 1-2 days. Fax notes: $2.00 fax fee plus $.25 per page. Copy fee: $.50 per page. Certification fee: $3.00. Fee payee: Circuit Clerk. Business checks accepted. Law firm accounts, money orders and cashier checks allowed. Prepayment is required.

District Court 202 W 3rd St, Fordyce, AR 71742; 870-352-2332; Fax: 870-352-3414. Hours: 8AM-4PM (CST). *Misdemeanor, Civil Actions Under $5,000, Eviction, Small Claims.*

Civil Records: Access: In person, mail. Only the court performs in person searches; visitors may not. No search fee.
Criminal Records: Access: In person, mail. Only the court performs in person searches; visitors may not. No search fee. Required to search: name, years to search, SSN; also helpful: DOB.
General Information: Turnaround time 1-2 days.

Desha County

Circuit & Chancery Courts PO Box 309, Arkansas City, AR 71630; 870-877-2411; Fax: 870-877-3407. Hours: 8AM-4PM (CST). *Felony, Civil Actions Over $5,000, Probate.*

Civil Records: Access: Fax, mail, in person. Both court and visitors may perform in person searches. Search fee: $5.00 per name. Required to search: name, years to search. Civil cases indexed by defendant, plaintiff. Civil records on dockets from 1920s.
Criminal Records: Access: Fax, mail, in person. Both court and visitors may perform in person searches. Search fee: $5.00 per name. Required to search: name, years to search, SSN. Criminal records on dockets from 1920s.
General Information: No juvenile records released. SASE required. Turnaround time 1-2 days. Fax notes: No fee to fax results. Copy fee: $.50 per page.

Certification fee: $3.00. Fee payee: Skippy Leek, Circuit Court Clerk. Personal checks accepted. Prepayment is required.

District Court PO Box 157, Dumas, AR 71639-2226; 870-382-6972; Fax: 870-382-1106. Hours: 8AM-4:30PM (CST). *Misdemeanor, Civil Actions Under $5,000, Eviction, Small Claims.*

Civil Records: Access: In person, mail. Only the court performs in person searches; visitors may not. Search fee: $5.00 per name. Required to search: name, years to search, signed release; also helpful: address.

Criminal Records: Access: In person, mail. Only the court performs in person searches; visitors may not. Search fee: $5.00 per name. Required to search: name, years to search, signed release; also helpful: address.

General Information: Turnaround time 1-2 days. Fee payee: Dumas District Court. Prepayment is required.

Drew County

Circuit & County Courts 210 S Main, Monticello, AR 71655; 870-460-6250; Fax: 870-460-6246. Hours: 8AM-4:30PM (CST). *Felony, Civil Actions Over $5,000, Probate.*

Civil Records: Access: Phone, fax, mail, in person. Both court and visitors may perform in person searches. No search fee. Required to search: name, years to search. Civil cases indexed by defendant, plaintiff. Civil records on dockets from 1846; on computer back to 1992 approx.

Criminal Records: Access: In person only. Visitors must perform in person searches for themselves. No search fee. Required to search: name, years to search. Criminal records on dockets from 1846; on computer back to 1992 approx.

General Information: No juvenile or expunged records released. SASE required. Turnaround time 1-2 days. Fax notes: $1.25 for first page, $1.00 each add'l. Copy fee: $.50 per page. Certification fee: $2.00. Fee payee: Drew County Circuit Clerk. Personal checks accepted. Prepayment is required.

District Court PO Box 505, Monticello, AR 71655; 870-367-4420; Fax: 870-460-9056. Hours: 8:30AM-5PM (CST). *Misdemeanor, Civil Actions Under $5,000, Eviction, Small Claims.*

Civil Records: Access: Mail, fax, in person. Only the court performs in person searches; visitors may not. Search fee: No search fee. Required to search: name, years to search, DOB or SSN. Records go back 10 years.

Criminal Records: Access: Mail, fax, in person. Only the court performs in person searches; visitors may not. No search fee. Required to search: name, years to search, DOB; also helpful: sex. Records go back 10 years.

General Information: Turnaround time 1-2 days.

Faulkner County

Circuit & Chancery Courts PO Box 9, Conway, AR 72033; 501-450-4911; Fax: 501-450-4948. Hours: 8AM-4:30PM (CST). *Felony, Civil Actions Over $5,000, Probate.*

Civil Records: Access: Fax, mail, in person. Both court and visitors may perform in person searches. No search fee. Required to search: name, years to search. Civil cases indexed by defendant, plaintiff. Civil records on computer since June 1989, on docket from 1800s.

Criminal Records: Access: In person only. Visitors must perform in person searches for themselves. No search fee. Required to search: name, years to search. Criminal records on computer since June 1989, on docket from 1800s.

General Information: Public Access terminal is available. No juvenile records released. SASE required. Turnaround time 1-2 days. Fax notes: $1.00 if local, $3.50 plus $.25 per page if long distance. Copy fee:

$.25 per page. Certification fee: $3.00. Fee payee: Faulkner County Circuit Clerk. Personal checks accepted. Prepayment is required.

District Court 810 Parkway, Conway, AR 72032; 501-450-6112; Fax: 501-450-6184. Hours: 8AM-4:30PM (CST). *Misdemeanor, Civil Actions Under $5,000, Eviction, Small Claims.*

Civil Records: Access: Mail, fax, in person, online. Both court and visitors may perform in person searches. Search fee: $10.00 for 3 years; $20.00 more than 3 years. Required to search: name, years to search, DOB, signed release; also helpful: address, SSN. Computerized records go back to 1993.

Criminal Records: Access: Mail, fax, in person, online. Both court and visitors may perform in person searches. Search fee: $10.00 for 3 years; $20.00 more than 3 years. Required to search: name, years to search, DOB, signed release; also helpful: address, SSN. Computerized records go back to 1993.

General Information: Public Access terminal is available. Turnaround time 2 days. Certification fee: $5.00. Fee payee: Conway District Court.

Franklin County

Charleston Circuit & Chancery Courts PO Box 387, Charleston, AR 72933; 501-965-7332. Hours: 8AM-4:30PM (CST). *Felony, Civil Actions Over $5,000, Probate.*

Civil Records: Access: Mail, in person. Both court and visitors may perform in person searches. Search fee: $6.00 per name. Required to search: name, years to search, DOB. Civil cases indexed by defendant, plaintiff. Civil records on dockets from 1900s.

Criminal Records: Access: Mail, in person. Both court and visitors may perform in person searches. Search fee: $6.00 per name. Required to search: name, years to search, DOB. Criminal records on dockets from 1900s.

General Information: No juvenile records released. SASE required. Turnaround time 1-2 days. Fax notes: $1.00 per page to fax back. Copy fee: $.25 per page. Certification fee: $2.00. Fee payee: Franklin County. Personal checks accepted. Prepayment is required.

Ozark Circuit & Chancery Courts PO Box 1112, 211 W Commercial, Ozark, AR 72949; 501-667-3818; Probate phone: 501-667-3607; Fax: 501-667-5174. Hours: 8AM-4:30PM (CST). *Felony, Civil Actions Over $5,000, Probate.*

Note: Probate is maintained at the County Clerk's Office.

Civil Records: Access: Fax, mail, in person. Both court and visitors may perform in person searches. Search fee: $6.00 per name. Required to search: name, years to search. Civil cases indexed by plaintiff. Civil records on dockets from 1900s.

Criminal Records: Access: Fax, mail, in person. Both court and visitors may perform in person searches. Search fee: $6.00 per name. Required to search: name, years to search. Criminal records on dockets from 1900s.

General Information: No juvenile records released. SASE required. Turnaround time 1-2 days. Fax notes: $1.00 per page. Copy fee: $.25 per page. Certification fee: $2.00. Fee payee: Circuit Clerk. Personal checks accepted. Prepayment is required.

District Court PO Box 426, Charleston, AR 72933; 501-965-7455; Fax: 501-965-2231. Hours: 8AM-5PM (CST). *Misdemeanor, Civil Actions Under $5,000, Small Claims.*

Civil Records: Access: Mail, fax, in person. Both court and visitors may perform in person searches. No search fee. Civil records on computer back to 1/2000.

Criminal Records: Access: Mail, fax, in person. Both court and visitors may perform in person searches. No search fee. Required to search: name, years to search,

DOB; also helpful-SSN, signed release. Criminal records on computer back to 1/2000.

General Information: Turnaround time 1-2 days.

Fulton County

Circuit & Chancery Courts PO Box 485, Salem, AR 72576; 870-895-3310; Fax: 870-865-3362. Hours: 8AM-4:30PM (CST). *Felony, Civil Actions Over $5,000, Probate.*

Civil Records: Access: Phone, mail, in person. Both court and visitors may perform in person searches. Search fee: $6.00 per name. Required to search: name, years to search. Civil cases indexed by defendant, plaintiff. Civil records on dockets from 1900s.

Criminal Records: Access: Phone, mail, in person. Both court and visitors may perform in person searches. Search fee: $6.00 per name. Required to search: name, years to search. Criminal records on dockets from 1900s.

General Information: No juvenile records released. SASE required. Turnaround time 1-2 days. Copy fee: $.20 per page. Certification fee: No cert fee. Fee payee: Fulton County Clerks. Personal checks accepted. Prepayment is required.

District Court PO Box 928, Salem, AR 72576; 870-895-4136; Fax: 870-895-4114. Hours: 8AM-4:30PM (CST). *Misdemeanor, Civil Actions Under $5,000, Eviction, Small Claims.*

Civil Records: Access: In person, mail. Both court and visitors may perform in person searches. No search fee.

Criminal Records: Access: In person, mail. Both court and visitors may perform in person searches. No search fee. Required to search: name, years to search, DOB.

General Information: Turnaround time 1 week.

Garland County

Circuit & Chancery Courts Garland County Courthouse, 501 Ouachita Ave, Room 207, Hot Springs, AR 71901; Civil phone: 501-622-3630; Criminal phone: 501-622-3640; Probate phone: 501-622-3610; Fax: 501-609-9043. Hours: 8AM-5PM (CST). *Felony, Civil Actions Over $5,000, Probate.*

Civil Records: Access: In person only. Visitors must perform in person searches for themselves. No search fee. Required to search: name; also helpful: years to search. Civil cases indexed by defendant, plaintiff. Civil records on microfiche and docket from 1900s; on computer back to 1989.

Criminal Records: Access: Fax, mail, in person. Both court and visitors may perform in person searches. No search fee. Required to search: name, years to search; also helpful: DOB, SSN, maiden name, race, aliases, sex. Criminal records on microfiche and docket from 1900s; on computer back to 1989.

General Information: Public Access terminal is available. No expunged, sealed records released. SASE required. Turnaround time 1-2 days. Fax notes: Fee to fax results is $2.00 plus $.25 per page. Copy fee: $.25 per page. Certification fee: $.50. Fee payee: Garland County Circuit Clerk. Personal checks accepted. Prepayment is required.

District Court PO Box 700, Hot Springs, AR 71902; 501-321-6765; Fax: 501-321-6764. Hours: 8AM-5PM (CST). *Misdemeanor, Civil Actions Under $5,000, Eviction, Small Claims.*

Civil Records: Access: In person, mail. Both court and visitors may perform in person searches. No search fee. Computerized records go back to 1990.

Criminal Records: Access: In person, mail. Both court and visitors may perform in person searches. No search fee. Required to search: name, years to search, offense.

General Information: Turnaround time 1-2 days. Certification fee: $5.00.

Grant County

Circuit & County Courts Grant County Courthouse, 101 W Center, Rm 106, Sheridan, AR 72150; 870-942-2631; Fax: 870-942-3564. Hours: 8AM-4:30PM (CST). *Felony, Civil Actions Over $5,000, Probate.*

Civil Records: Access: In person only. Visitors must perform in person searches for themselves. No search fee. Required to search: name, years to search. Civil cases indexed by defendant, plaintiff. Civil records on dockets and index from 1982.

Criminal Records: Access: In person only. Visitors must perform in person searches for themselves. No search fee. Required to search: name, years to search. Criminal records on dockets and index from 1982.

General Information: No juvenile, probate or adoption records released. Copy fee: $.25 per page. Certification fee: $3.00. Fee payee: Circuit Clerk. Personal checks accepted. Prepayment is required.

District Court PO Box 603, Sheridan, AR 72150; 870-942-3464; Fax: 870-942-8885. Hours: 8AM-4:30PM (CST). *Misdemeanor, Civil Actions Under $5,000, Eviction, Small Claims.*

Civil Records: Access: In person, mail. Both court and visitors may perform in person searches. No search fee.

Criminal Records: Access: In person, mail. Both court and visitors may perform in person searches. No search fee. Required to search: name, years to search.

General Information: Turnaround time 1-2 days.

Greene County

Circuit & County Courts 320 W Court #124, Paragould, AR 72450; 870-239-6330; Fax: 870-239-3550. Hours: 8AM-4:30PM (CST). *Felony, Civil Actions Over $5,000, Probate.*

Civil Records: Access: Fax, mail, in person. Both court and visitors may perform in person searches. Search fee: $6.00 per name. Required to search: name, years to search. Civil cases indexed by plaintiff. Civil records on computer from 1986, on index from 1930s.

Criminal Records: Access: Fax, mail, in person. Both court and visitors may perform in person searches. Search fee: $6.00 per name. Required to search: name, years to search; also helpful: DOB, SSN. Criminal records computerized since 1990.

General Information: No juvenile records released. SASE required. Turnaround time 1-2 days. Fax notes: For fax back, $1.00 for first 3 pages then $.25 per page. Copy fee: $.50 per page. Certification fee: $3.00. Fee payee: Green County Circuit Clerk. Personal checks accepted. Prepayment is required.

District Court 320 W Court, Rm 227, Paragould, AR 72450; 870-239-7507; Fax: 870-239-7506. Hours: 8AM-4:30PM (CST). *Misdemeanor, Civil Actions Under $5,000, Eviction, Small Claims.*

Civil Records: Access: In person, mail. Only the court performs in person searches; visitors may not. No search fee. Required to search: name, years to search, DOB or SSN. Records on computer back to 1989.

Criminal Records: Access: In person, mail. Only the court performs in person searches; visitors may not. Search fee: $5.00 per name. Required to search: name, years to search, DOB or SSN. Records on computer back to 1989.

General Information: Turnaround time 2 days. Fee payee: District Clerk. Prepayment is required.

Hempstead County

Circuit & Chancery Courts PO Box 1420, Hope, AR 71802; 870-777-2384; Probate phone: 870-777-2241; Fax: 870-777-7827. Hours: 8AM-4PM (CST). *Felony, Civil Actions Over $5,000, Probate.*

Note: Probate is handled by the County Clerk at same address.

Civil Records: Access: Phone, fax, mail, in person. Both court and visitors may perform in person searches. Search fee: $6.00 per name. Required to search: name, years to search. Civil cases indexed by defendant, plaintiff. Civil records on dockets from 1910.

Criminal Records: Access: Phone, fax, mail, in person. Both court and visitors may perform in person searches. Search fee: $6.00 per name. Required to search: name, years to search, DOB, SSN. Criminal records on dockets from 1910.

General Information: Public Access terminal is available. No juvenile records released. SASE required. Turnaround time 1-2 days. Copy fee: $.50 per page. Certification fee: $5.00. Fee payee: Circuit Clerk. Personal checks accepted. Prepayment is required.

District Court PO Box 1420, Hope, AR 71802-1420; 870-777-2525; Fax: 870-777-7830. Hours: 8AM-4PM (CST). *Misdemeanor, Civil Actions Under $5,000, Eviction, Small Claims.*

Civil Records: Access: Mail, fax, in person. Both court and visitors may perform in person searches. No search fee. Required to search: name, years to search. Civil records on computer back to 1987.

Criminal Records: Access: Mail, fax, in person. Both court and visitors may perform in person searches. Search fee: $5.00 per name. Required to search: name, years to search, SSN, DOB. Criminal records on computer back to 1987.

General Information: Turnaround time less than 1 week. Fee payee: District Court. Prepayment is required.

Hot Spring County

Circuit & Chancery Court 200 Locust St, PO Box 1200, Malvern, AR 72104; 501-332-2281. Hours: 8:00AM-4:30PM (CST). *Felony, Civil Actions Over $5,000, Probate.*

Civil Records: Access: Mail, in person. Both court and visitors may perform in person searches. Search fee: $5.00 per name. Required to search: name, years to search. Civil cases indexed by plaintiff. Civil records on dockets from 1800s.

Criminal Records: Access: Mail, in person. Both court and visitors may perform in person searches. Search fee: $5.00 per name. Required to search: name, years to search, DOB or SSN. Criminal records on dockets from 1800s.

General Information: No juvenile records released. SASE required. Turnaround time 1-2 days. Copy fee: $.50 per page. Certification fee: $5.00. Fee payee: Circuit Clerk. Personal checks accepted. Prepayment is required.

Malvern District Court 305 Locust St, Rm 201, Malvern, AR 72104; 501-332-7604; Fax: 501-332-3144. Hours: 8AM-4:30PM (CST). *Misdemeanor, Civil Actions Under $5,000, Eviction, Small Claims.*

Note: Formerly known as Malvern Municipal Court before 7/1/01.

Civil Records: Access: Mail, fax, in person. Visitors must perform in person searches for themselves. No search fee. Required to search: name, years to search and DOB or SSN. Records computerized back to 1994.

Criminal Records: Access: mail, fax, in person. Visitors must perform in person searches for themselves. No search fee. Required to search: name, years to search, DOB; also helpful: address, SSN. Records computerized back to 1994.

General Information: Turnaround time 3 days.

Howard County

Circuit & County Courts 421 N Main, Rm 7, Nashville, AR 71852; 870-845-7506; Probate phone: 870-845-7503. Hours: 8AM-4:30PM (CST). *Felony, Civil Actions Over $5,000, Probate.*

Note: Probate is handled by the County Clerk at this address.

Civil Records: Access: Phone, mail, in person. Both court and visitors may perform in person searches. No search fee. Required to search: name, years to search. Civil cases indexed by defendant, plaintiff. Civil records on dockets from 1873.

Criminal Records: Access: In person only. Visitors must perform in person searches for themselves. No search fee. Required to search: name, years to search, DOB. Criminal records on dockets from 1873.

General Information: No juvenile or sealed records released. SASE required. Turnaround time 1 week. Copy fee: $.25 per page. Certification fee: $2.00. Fee payee: Circuit Clerk. Personal checks accepted. Prepayment is required.

District Court 426 N Main, Suite #7, Nashville, AR 71852-2009; 870-845-7522; Fax: 870-845-3705. Hours: 8AM-4:30PM (CST). *Misdemeanor, Civil Actions Under $5,000, Eviction, Small Claims.*

Civil Records: Access: In person, mail. Visitors must perform in person searches for themselves. No search fee.

Criminal Records: Access: In person, mail. Both court and visitors may perform in person searches. No search fee. Required to search: name, years to search, DOB; also helpful: address, SSN.

General Information: Turnaround time 1-3 days.

Independence County

Circuit & County Courts Main and Broad St, Batesville, AR 72501; 870-793-8833; Fax: 870-793-8888. Hours: 8AM-4:30PM (CST). *Felony, Civil Actions Over $5,000.*

Civil Records: Access: In person only. Visitors must perform in person searches for themselves. Search fee: $6.00 per name. Required to search: name, years to search; also helpful: address. Civil cases indexed by defendant, plaintiff. Civil judgments on computer from 1980, all others on index books from 1970s.

Criminal Records: Access: Mail, in person. Both court and visitors may perform in person searches. Search fee: $6.00 per name. Required to search: name, years to search, DOB; also helpful: address. Criminal records on index books from 1970s.

General Information: No juvenile records released. SASE required. Turnaround time varies, but usually same day. Copy fee: $.50 per page. Certification fee: No cert fee. Fee payee: Circuit Clerk. Personal checks accepted. Prepayment is required.

District Court 368 E Main, Rm 205, Batesville, AR 72501; 870-793-8817; Fax: 870-793-8875. Hours: 8AM-4:30PM (CST). *Misdemeanor, Civil Actions Under $5,000, Eviction, Small Claims.*

Civil Records: Access: In person, mail. Both court and visitors may perform in person searches. No search fee.

Criminal Records: Access: In person, mail. Both court and visitors may perform in person searches. No search fee. Required to search: name, years to search.

General Information: Turnaround time 1-2 days.

Izard County

Circuit & County Courts PO Box 95, Melbourne, AR 72556; 870-368-4316; Fax: 870-368-4748. Hours: 8:30AM-4:30PM (CST). *Felony, Civil Actions Over $5,000, Probate.*

Civil Records: Access: Fax, mail, in person. Both court and visitors may perform in person searches. Search fee: $6.00 per name. Required to search: name, years to search, address. Civil cases indexed by plaintiff. Civil records on judgment books from 1889.

Criminal Records: Access: Fax, mail, in person. Both court and visitors may perform in person searches. Search fee: $6.00 per name. Required to search: name, years to search, DOB; also helpful: address. Criminal records on judgment books from 1889.

General Information: No juvenile records released. SASE required. Turnaround time 2 weeks. Fax notes: No fee to fax results. Copy fee: $.20 per page. Certification fee: $3.00. Fee payee: Izard County and Circuit Clerk. Personal checks accepted. Prepayment is required.

District Court PO Box 337, Melbourne, AR 72556; 870-368-4390; Fax: 870-368-5042. Hours: 8:30AM-4:30PM (CST). *Misdemeanor, Civil Actions Under $5,000, Eviction, Small Claims.*

Civil Records: Access: Mail, fax, in person. Both court and visitors may perform in person searches. No search fee. Civil records go back to 1977; on computer back to 1993.

Criminal Records: Access: Mail, fax, in person. Both court and visitors may perform in person searches. No search fee. Required to search: name, years to search, DOB. Criminal records go back to 1977; on computer back to 1993.

General Information: Turnaround time varies.

Jackson County

Circuit & Chancery Courts Jackson County Courthouse, 208 Main St, Newport, AR 72112; 870-523-7423; Fax: 870-523-7404. Hours: 8AM-4:30PM (CST). *Felony, Civil Actions Over $5,000, Probate.*

Civil Records: Access: In person only. Visitors must perform in person searches for themselves. No search fee. Required to search: name, years to search. Civil cases indexed by defendant, plaintiff. Civil records on dockets from 1800s.

Criminal Records: Access: In person only. Visitors must perform in person searches for themselves. No search fee. Required to search: name, years to search. Criminal records on dockets from 1800s.

General Information: No juvenile records released. Copy fee: $.25 per page. Certification fee: $3.00. Fee payee: Circuit Clerk. Personal checks accepted. Prepayment is required.

District Court 615 3rd St, Newport, AR 72112; 870-523-9555; Fax: 870-523-4365. Hours: 8AM-4:30PM (CST). *Misdemeanor, Civil Actions Under $5,000, Eviction, Small Claims.*

Civil Records: Access: Phone, mail, fax, in person. Both court and visitors may perform in person searches. Search fee: No search fee. Civil records go back to 1987.

Criminal Records: Access: Mail, fax, in person. Both court and visitors may perform in person searches. No search fee. Required to search: name, years to search, DOB. Criminal records go back to 1987 on computer.

General Information: Turnaround time 5-7 days. Certification fee: $3.00. Fee payee: Newport District Court. Prepayment is required.

Jefferson County

Circuit & Chancery Courts PO Box 7433, Pine Bluff, AR 71611; Civil phone: 870-541-5307; Criminal phone: 870-541-5306. Hours: 8:30PM-5PM (CST). *Felony, Civil Actions Over $5,000, Probate.*

Civil Records: Access: In person only. Visitors must perform in person searches for themselves. No search fee. Required to search: name, years to search. Civil cases indexed by defendant, plaintiff. Civil records on dockets from 1950.

Criminal Records: Access: In person only. Visitors must perform in person searches for themselves. No search fee. Required to search: name, years to search, DOB. Criminal records on dockets from 1950.

General Information: Public Access terminal is available. No juvenile records released. Copy fee: $.50 per page. Certification fee: $2.00. Fee payee: Circuit Clerk. Personal checks accepted. Prepayment is required.

District Court 200 E 8th Ave, Pine Bluff, AR 71601; 870-543-1860; Fax: 870-543-1889. Hours: 8AM-5PM (CST). *Misdemeanor, Civil Actions Under $5,000, Eviction, Small Claims.*

Civil Records: Access: In person, mail. Both court and visitors may perform in person searches. No search fee.

Criminal Records: Access: In person, mail. Both court and visitors may perform in person searches. No search fee. Required to search: name, years to search; also helpful: DOB, SSN.

General Information: Turnaround time 1-2 days.

Johnson County

Circuit Court PO Box 217, Clarksville, AR 72830; 501-754-2977; Probate phone: 501-754-3967. Hours: 8AM-4:30PM (CST). *Felony, Civil Actions Over $5,000, Probate.*

Note: Probate is handled by County Clerk, PO Box 57.

Civil Records: Access: Fax, mail, in person. Both court and visitors may perform in person searches. Search fee: $6.00 per name. Required to search: name, years to search. Civil cases indexed by defendant, plaintiff. Civil records on index from 1900s. Fax access limited to 800#'s.

Criminal Records: Access: Fax, mail, in person. Both court and visitors may perform in person searches. Search fee: $6.00. Required to search: name, years to search, DOB; also helpful: SSN. Criminal records on index from 1900s. Fax access limited to 800#'s.

General Information: No juvenile records released. SASE required. Turnaround time 1-2 days. Fax notes: No fee to fax results. Will fax to 800 numbers only. Copy fee: $.50 per page. Certification fee: $1.00. Fee payee: Circuit. Personal checks accepted. Draft or two party checks not allowed.

District Court PO Box 581, Clarksville, AR 72830; 501-754-8533; Fax: 501-754-6014. Hours: 8AM-4PM (CST). *Misdemeanor, Civil Actions Under $5,000, Eviction, Small Claims.*

Civil Records: Access: In person, mail. Both court and visitors may perform in person searches. No search fee.

Criminal Records: Access: In person, mail. Both court and visitors may perform in person searches. No search fee. Required to search: name, years to search; also helpful: DOB, SSN.

General Information: Turnaround time 1-2 days.

Lafayette County

Circuit & Chancery Courts #3 Courthouse Square, Lewisville, AR 71845; 870-921-4878; Probate phone: 870-921-4633; Fax: 870-921-4505. Hours: 8AM-4:30PM (CST). *Felony, Civil Actions Over $5,000, Probate.*

Civil Records: Access: Phone, mail, in person. Both court and visitors may perform in person searches. Search fee: $6.00 per name. Required to search: name, years to search. Civil cases indexed by defendant, plaintiff. Civil records on dockets from 1950s.

Criminal Records: Access: Mail, in person. Both court and visitors may perform in person searches. Search fee: $6.00 per name. Required to search: name, years to search. Criminal records on dockets from 1950s.

General Information: No juvenile records released without written order form the judge. SASE required. Turnaround time 2 days. Copy fee: $.50 per page. Certification fee: $3.00. Fee payee: Circuit Clerk. Personal checks accepted. Prepayment is required.

District Court 23 Courthouse Square, Lewisville, AR 71845; 870-921-5555; Fax: 870-921-4256. Hours: 8AM-4:30PM (CST). *Misdemeanor, Civil Actions Under $5,000, Eviction, Small Claims.*

Civil Records: Access: In person only. Both court and visitors may perform in person searches. No search fee.

Criminal Records: Access: In person only. Both court and visitors may perform in person searches. No search fee. Required to search: name, years to search, DOB, SSN.

Lawrence County

Circuit & Chancery Courts PO Box 581 (W. Main St.), Walnut Ridge, AR 72476; 870-886-1112; Fax: 870-886-1128. Hours: 8AM-4:30PM (CST). *Felony, Civil Actions Over $5,000, Probate.*

Civil Records: Access: Phone, fax, mail, in person. Visitors must perform in person searches for themselves. No search fee. Required to search: name, years to search. Civil cases indexed by defendant, plaintiff. Civil records on index from 1981, on docket sheets from 1960s.

Criminal Records: Access: Phone, fax, mail, in person. Visitors must perform in person searches for themselves. No search fee. Required to search: name, years to search. Criminal records on index from 1981, on docket sheets from 1960s.

General Information: No juvenile records released. SASE required. Turnaround time 1 day. Fax notes: $1.00 per page. Copy fee: $.25 per page. Certification fee: $3.00. Fee payee: Circuit Clerk. Personal checks accepted. Prepayment is required.

Walnut Ridge District Court 201 SW 2nd St, Walnut Ridge, AR 72476; 870-886-3905. Hours: 8AM-4:30PM (CST). *Misdemeanor, Civil Actions Under $5,000, Eviction, Small Claims.*

Civil Records: Access: In person, mail. Both court and visitors may perform in person searches. No search fee.

Criminal Records: Access: In person, mail. Both court and visitors may perform in person searches. No search fee. Required to search: name, years to search, offense.

General Information: Turnaround time 2-3 days.

Lee County

Circuit & Chancery Courts 15 E Chestnut, Marianna, AR 72360; 870-295-7710; Fax: 870-295-7766. Hours: 8:30AM-4:30PM (CST). *Felony, Civil Actions Over $5,000, Probate.*

Civil Records: Access: In person only. Visitors must perform in person searches for themselves. No search fee. Required to search: name, years to search. Civil

cases indexed by defendant, plaintiff. Civil records on index books from 1873.

Criminal Records: Access: In person only. Only the court performs in person searches; visitors may not. No search fee. Required to search: name, years to search, DOB. Criminal records on index books from 1873.

General Information: No juvenile records released. Copy fee: $.25 per page. Certification fee: $2.50. Fee payee: Circuit Court. Personal checks accepted. Prepayment is required.

District Court 45 W Mississippi, Marianna, AR 72360; 870-295-3813; Fax: 870-295-5726. Hours: 8AM-Noon; 1-5PM (CST). *Misdemeanor, Civil Actions Under $5,000, Eviction, Small Claims.*

Civil Records: Access: In person, mail. Only the court performs in person searches; visitors may not. No search fee.

Criminal Records: Access: In person, mail. Only the court performs in person searches; visitors may not. No search fee. Required to search: name, years to search.

General Information: Turnaround time 5 days.

Lincoln County

Circuit & County Courts Courthouse, 300 S Drew, Star City, AR 71667; 870-628-3154; Probate phone: 870-628-5114; Fax: 870-628-5546. Hours: 8AM-5PM (CST). *Felony, Civil Actions Over $5,000, Probate.*

Civil Records: Access: Mail, in person. Both court and visitors may perform in person searches. No search fee. Required to search: name, years to search. Civil cases indexed by defendant, plaintiff. Civil records on index from 1920, archived from 1920.

Criminal Records: Access: In person only. Visitors must perform in person searches for themselves. No search fee. Criminal records on index from 1920, archived from 1920.

General Information: No sealed records released. SASE required. Turnaround time 8 hours. Fax notes: Fee to fax results is $1.00 per page. Copy fee: $.50 per page. Certification fee: $3.00. Fee payee: Lincoln County Circuit Court. Personal checks accepted. Prepayment is required.

Lincoln County District Court 300 S Drew St, Star City, AR 71667; 870-628-4904. Hours: 8AM-4:30PM (CST). *Misdemeanor, Civil Actions Under $5,000, Eviction, Small Claims.*

Civil Records: Access: Mail, in person. Both court and visitors may perform in person searches. Search fee: $6.00 per name. Required to search: name, years to search, DOB. Civil records go back to 1980; on computer back to 1991.

Criminal Records: Access: Mail, in person. Both court and visitors may perform in person searches. Search fee: $6.00 per name. Required to search: name, years to search, DOB, signed release; also helpful: address, SSN, DL#. Criminal records go back to 1980; on computer back to 1991.

General Information: Turnaround time 3-5 days. Fax notes: No fee to fax back 5 pages or less; if 6 or more, $.50 per page. Certification fee: $25.00. Fee payee: District Court of Star City. Prepayment is required.

Little River County

Circuit & County Courts PO Box 575, Ashdown, AR 71822; 870-898-7211; Fax: 870-898-7207. Hours: 8:30AM-4:30PM (CST). *Felony, Civil Actions Over $5,000, Probate.*

Civil Records: Access: Phone, mail, in person. Both court and visitors may perform in person searches. Search fee: $6.00 per name. Required to search: name, years to search. Civil cases indexed by plaintiff. Civil records docket books from early 1900s.

Criminal Records: Access: Phone, mail, in person. Both court and visitors may perform in person searches.

Search fee: $6.00 per name. Required to search: name, years to search, address, DOB, signed release. Criminal records on docket books back to 1868.

General Information: No juvenile records released. SASE required. Turnaround time 1 day. Copy fee: $.50 per page. Certification fee: $5.00. Fee payee: Circuit Clerk. Personal checks accepted. Prepayment is required.

District Court 351 N 2nd St, #8, Ashdown, AR 71822; 870-898-7230; Fax: 870-898-7262. Hours: 8:30AM-4:30PM (CST). *Misdemeanor, Civil Actions Under $5,000, Eviction, Small Claims.*

Civil Records: Access: In person, mail. Both court and visitors may perform in person searches. No search fee.

Criminal Records: Access: In person, mail. Both court and visitors may perform in person searches. No search fee. Required to search: name, years to search; also helpful: DOB, SSN.

General Information: Turnaround time 1 week.

Logan County

Circuit & Chancery Courts Courthouse, 25 W Walnut, Paris, AR 72855; 501-963-2164; Fax: 501-963-3304. Hours: 8AM-4:30PM (CST). *Felony, Civil Actions Over $5,000, Probate.*

Civil Records: Access: Fax, mail, in person. Both court and visitors may perform in person searches. Search fee: $6.00 per name. Required to search: name, years to search. Civil cases indexed by defendant, plaintiff. Civil records on criminal index from 1901.

Criminal Records: Access: Fax, mail, in person. Both court and visitors may perform in person searches. Search fee: $6.00 per name. Required to search: name, years to search. Criminal records on criminal index from 1901.

General Information: No adoption or probate records released. SASE required. Turnaround time 1 days. Fax notes: $1.00 per page. Copy fee: $.50 per page. Certification fee: $5.00. Fee payee: Circuit Clerk. Personal checks accepted. Prepayment is required.

Paris District Court Paris Courthouse, Paris, AR 72855; 501-963-3792; Fax: 501-963-2590. Hours: 8:30AM-4:30PM (CST). *Misdemeanor, Civil Actions Under $5,000, Eviction, Small Claims.*

Civil Records: Access: In person, mail. Both court and visitors may perform in person searches. No search fee.

Criminal Records: Access: In person, mail. Both court and visitors may perform in person searches. No search fee. Required to search: name, years to search; also helpful: DOB.

General Information: Public Access terminal is available. Turnaround time 1-2 days.

Lonoke County

Circuit & Chancery Courts PO Box 218 Attn: Circuit Clerk, Lonoke, AR 72086; 501-676-2316. Hours: 8AM-4:30PM (CST). *Felony, Civil Actions Over $5,000, Probate.*

Civil Records: Access: Mail, in person. Both court and visitors may perform in person searches. Search fee: $6.00 per name. Required to search: name, years to search. Civil cases indexed by defendant. Civil records on computer from 1989, on dockets from 1918's (not for public use).

Criminal Records: Access: Mail, in person. Both court and visitors may perform in person searches. Search fee: $6.00 per name. Required to search: name, years to search, SSN. Criminal records on computer from 1989, on dockets from 1918's (not for public use).

General Information: No juvenile records released. SASE required. Turnaround time 1-2 days. Copy fee: $.25 per page. Certification fee: $6.00. Fee payee: Circuit Clerk. Personal checks accepted. Prepayment is required.

Lonoke District Court 107 W 2nd St, Lonoke, AR 72086-2701; 501-676-3585; Fax: 501-676-2500. Hours: 8AM-4:30PM (CST). *Misdemeanor, Civil Actions Under $5,000, Eviction, Small Claims.*

Civil Records: Access: In person only. Both court and visitors may perform in person searches. No search fee.

Criminal Records: Access: In person only. Both court and visitors may perform in person searches. Search fee: $6.00 per name. Required to search: name, years to search.

General Information: Fee payee: District Court. Prepayment is required.

Madison County

Circuit & Chancery Courts PO Box 416, Huntsville, AR 72740; 501-738-2215; Fax: 501-738-1544. Hours: 8AM-4:30PM (CST). *Felony, Civil Actions Over $5,000, Probate.*

Note: Probate is in the County Clerk's office.

Civil Records: Access: In person only. Visitors must perform in person searches for themselves. No search fee. Required to search: name, years to search; also helpful: address. Civil cases indexed by defendant, plaintiff. Civil records on dockets back to 1906.

Criminal Records: Access: In person only. Visitors must perform in person searches for themselves. No search fee. Required to search: name, years to search; also helpful: address, DOB, SSN. Criminal records on dockets back to 1906.

General Information: Public Access terminal is available. No juvenile records released. Copy fee: $.25 per page. Certification fee: $5.00. Fee payee: Circuit Clerk. Personal checks accepted. Prepayment is required.

District Court PO Box 549, Huntsville, AR 72740; 501-738-2911; Fax: 501-738-6846. Hours: 8AM-4:30PM (CST). *Misdemeanor, Civil Actions Under $5,000, Eviction, Small Claims.*

Civil Records: Access: In person, mail. Both court and visitors may perform in person searches. No search fee.

Criminal Records: Access: In person, mail. Both court and visitors may perform in person searches. No search fee. Required to search: name, years to search, DOB, SSN.

General Information: Turnaround time 1 week.

Marion County

Circuit & County Courts PO Box 385, Yellville, AR 72687; 870-449-6226; Fax: 870-449-5143. Hours: 8AM-5PM (CST). *Felony, Civil Actions Over $5,000, Eviction, Probate.*

Civil Records: Access: In person only. Visitors must perform in person searches for themselves. No search fee. Required to search: name, years to search. Civil cases indexed by plaintiff. Civil records on dockets from 1956, records are not computerized.

Criminal Records: Access: Mail, in person. Both court and visitors may perform in person searches. Search fee: $6.00 per name. Required to search: name, years to search. Criminal records on dockets from 1956, records are not computerized.

General Information: Public Access terminal is available. No juvenile or adoption records released. SASE required. Turnaround time 1 day. Copy fee: $.50 per page. Certification fee: $3.00. Fee payee: Marion County Circuit Clerk. Personal checks accepted. Prepayment is required.

District Court PO Box 301, Yellville, AR 72687; 870-449-6030. Hours: 8AM-4:30PM (CST). *Misdemeanor, Civil Actions Under $5,000, Small Claims.*

Civil Records: Access: Mail, in person. Both court and visitors may perform in person searches. No search fee.

Civil records go back to 1985; on computer back to 1996.

Criminal Records: Access: Mail, in person. Both court and visitors may perform in person searches. No search fee. Required to search: name, years to search, DOB. Criminal records go back to 1985; on computer back to 1996.

Miller County

Circuit & County Courts 412 Laurel St Rm 109, Texarkana, AR 71854; 870-774-4501; Fax: 870-772-5293. Hours: 8AM-4:30PM (CST). *Felony, Civil Actions Over $5,000, Probate.*

Note: Probate is at the County Clerk's office.

Civil Records: Access: Phone, mail, in person. Both court and visitors may perform in person searches. Search fee: $6.00 per name. Required to search: name, years to search. Civil cases indexed by defendant, plaintiff. Civil records on index from 1850s.

Criminal Records: Access: Phone, mail, in person. Both court and visitors may perform in person searches. Search fee: $6.00 per name. Required to search: name, years to search. Criminal records on index from 1850s.

General Information: No expunged records released. SASE required. Turnaround time 1-2 days. Copy fee: $1.00 per page. Certification fee: $3.50. Fee payee: Miller County Circuit Clerk. Personal checks accepted. Prepayment is required.

District Court 400 Laurel Suite 101, Texarkana, AR 71854; 870-772-2780; Fax: 870-773-3595. Hours: 8AM-4:30PM (CST). *Misdemeanor, Civil Actions Under $5,000, Eviction, Small Claims.*

Civil Records: Access: Mail, in person. Both court and visitors may perform in person searches. Search fee: $25.00 per search. Civil records on computer back to 1997.

Criminal Records: Access: In person, mail. Both court and visitors may perform in person searches. Search fee: $25.00 per search. Required to search: name, years to search, DOB. Criminal records on computer back to 1997.

General Information: Turnaround time 2 days. Fee payee: Miller County Court. Prepayment is required.

Mississippi County

Blytheville Circuit & Chancery Courts PO Box 1498, Blytheville, AR 72316; 870-762-2332; Fax: 870-763-0150. Hours: 9AM-4:30PM (CST). *Felony, Civil Actions Over $5,000, Probate.*

Civil Records: Access: In person only. Visitors must perform in person searches for themselves. No search fee. Required to search: name, years to search. Civil cases indexed by plaintiff. Civil records on computer since 1990, prior on index from 1940.

Criminal Records: Access: Phone, fax, mail, in person. Both court and visitors may perform in person searches. Search fee: $6.00 per name. Required to search: name, years to search, DOB, SSN. Criminal records on computer since 1990, prior on index from 1940. Will search 7 years.

General Information: No juvenile records released. SASE required. Turnaround time 1-2 days. Fax notes: $5.00 per document. Copy fee: $.25 per page. Certification fee: $3.00. Fee payee: Circuit Clerk. Personal checks accepted. Prepayment is required.

Osceola Circuit & Chancery Courts County Courthouse, PO Box 466 (200 W Hale), Osceola, AR 72370; 870-563-6471. Hours: 9AM-4:30PM (CST). *Felony, Civil Actions Over $5,000, Probate.*

Civil Records: Access: Mail, in person. Visitors must perform in person searches for themselves. No search fee. Required to search: name, years to search. Civil cases indexed by defendant, plaintiff. Civil records computerized since 1992, on index from 1940.

Criminal Records: Access: Mail, in person. Visitors must perform in person searches for themselves. No search fee. Required to search: name, years to search, DOB, SSN. Criminal records on computer (not for public use) since 1992.

General Information: Public Access terminal is available. No juvenile records released. SASE required. Turnaround time 1-2 days. Copy fee: $.50 per page. Certification fee: $3.00. Fee payee: Circuit Clerk. Personal checks accepted. Prepayment is required.

Blytheville District Court 121 N 2nd St, #104, Blytheville, AR 72315; 870-763-7513; Fax: 870-762-0443. Hours: 8AM-5PM (CST). *Misdemeanor, Civil Actions Under $5,000, Small Claims.*

Civil Records: Access: Mail, fax, in person. Both court and visitors may perform in person searches. Search fee: $4.00 per name. Civil records go back to 1960; on computer back to 1987.

Criminal Records: Access: Mail, fax, in person. Both court and visitors may perform in person searches. Search fee: $4.00 per name. Required to search: name, years to search; also helpful: DOB, SSN. Criminal records go back to 1960; on computer back to 1987.

General Information: Turnaround time 1-2 days. Certification fee: $2.50. Fee payee: City of Blythville.

Osceola District Court 397 W Keiser, Osceola, AR 72370; 870-563-1303; Fax: 870-563-5657. Hours: 8AM-4PM (CST). *Misdemeanor, Civil Actions Under $5,000, Eviction, Small Claims.*

Civil Records: Access: Mail, in person. Visitors must perform in person searches for themselves. No search fee.

Criminal Records: Access: Mail, in person. Visitors must perform in person searches for themselves. No search fee. Required to search: name, years to search; also helpful: address, DOB, SSN.

General Information: Turnaround time 1-2 days.

Monroe County

Circuit & Chancery Courts 123 Madison St, Courthouse, Clarendon, AR 72029; 870-747-3615; Fax: 870-747-3710. Hours: 8AM-4:30PM (CST). *Felony, Civil Actions Over $5,000, Probate.*

Civil Records: Access: Fax, mail, in person. Both court and visitors may perform in person searches. No search fee. Required to search: name, years to search. Civil cases indexed by defendant, plaintiff. Civil records on index books from 1900.

Criminal Records: Access: In person only. Visitors must perform in person searches for themselves. No search fee. Required to search: name, years to search. Criminal records on index books from 1900.

General Information: No juvenile records released. SASE required. Turnaround time 1-2 days. Fax notes: $2.50 per document. Additional fee of $.50 if more than 10 pages. Copy fee: $.50 per page. Certification fee: $2.50. Fee payee: Monroe County Circuit Clerk. Personal checks accepted. Prepayment is required.

District Court City Hall, 270 Madison St, Clarendon, AR 72029; 870-747-5200; Fax: 870-747-9969. Hours: 8AM-5PM (CST). *Misdemeanor, Civil Actions Under $5,000, Eviction, Small Claims.*

Civil Records: Access: In person only. Both court and visitors may perform in person searches. No search fee. Required to search: name, years to search, DOB. Records go back to 1988, on computer since 1994.

Criminal Records: Access: In person only. Both court and visitors may perform in person searches. No search fee. Required to search: name, years to search, DOB, SSN. Records go back to 1988, on computer since 1994.

General Information: Certification fee: $1.00. Fee payee: Clarendon District Court.

Montgomery County

Circuit & County Courts PO Box 369, Courthouse, Mount Ida, AR 71957; 870-867-3521; Fax: 870-867-2177. Hours: 8AM-4:30PM (CST). *Felony, Civil Actions Over $5,000, Probate.*

Civil Records: Access: Phone, fax, mail, in person. Both court and visitors may perform in person searches. No search fee. Required to search: name, years to search; also helpful: address. Civil cases indexed by defendant, plaintiff. Civil records on card files from 1960s.

Criminal Records: Access: In person only. Visitors must perform in person searches for themselves. No search fee. Required to search: name, years to search; also helpful: address, DOB, SSN. Criminal records on card files from 1960s.

General Information: No juvenile or adoption records released. SASE required. Turnaround time 1 day. Copy fee: $.50 per page. Certification fee: $3.00. Fee payee: Circuit Clerk. Personal checks accepted. Prepayment is required.

District Court PO Box 548, Mount Ida, AR 71957; 870-867-2221. Hours: 8AM-4:30PM M-Th, other days hours may vary (CST). *Misdemeanor, Civil Actions Under $5,000, Eviction, Small Claims.*

Civil Records: Access: In person, mail. Both court and visitors may perform in person searches. No search fee. Required to search: name, years to search, DOB, SSN. Records go back to 1973; computerized records go back to 1993.

Criminal Records: Access: In person, mail. Both court and visitors may perform in person searches. No search fee. Required to search: name, years to search, DOB, SSN. Records go back to 1973; computerized records go back to 1993.

General Information: Turnaround time 1-2 days. Fax notes: No fee to fax results.

Nevada County

Circuit & Chancery Courts PO Box 204, Prescott, AR 71857; 870-887-2511; Fax: 870-887-5795. Hours: 8AM-5PM (CST). *Felony, Civil Actions Over $5,000, Probate.*

Civil Records: Access: Phone, fax, mail, in person. Both court and visitors may perform in person searches. Search fee: $6.00 per name. Required to search: name, years to search. Civil cases indexed by defendant, plaintiff. Civil records on index since 1850.

Criminal Records: Access: Phone, fax, mail, in person. Both court and visitors may perform in person searches. Search fee: $6.00 per name. Required to search: name, years to search, DOB. Criminal records on index since 1850.

General Information: No juvenile records released. SASE required. Turnaround time 1-2 days. Fax notes: $.25 per page. Copy fee: $.25 per page. Certification fee: $2.00. Fee payee: Nevada County Circuit Clerk. Personal checks accepted. Prepayment is required.

District Court PO Box 22, Prescott, AR 71857; 870-887-6016; Fax: 870-887-5795. Hours: 8AM-5PM (CST). *Misdemeanor, Civil Actions Under $5,000, Eviction, Small Claims.*

Civil Records: Access: In person, mail. Both court and visitors may perform in person searches. No search fee.

Criminal Records: Access: In person, mail. Both court and visitors may perform in person searches. No search fee. Required to search: name, years to search, DOB, SSN.

General Information: Turnaround time 2-5 days.

Newton County

Circuit & Chancery Courts PO Box 410, Jasper, AR 72641; 870-446-5125; Fax: 870-446-5155. Hours: 8AM-4:30PM (CST). *Felony, Civil Actions Over $5,000, Probate.*

Civil Records: Access: Fax, mail, in person. Both court and visitors may perform in person searches. Search fee: $5.00 per name. Required to search: name, years to search. Civil cases indexed by defendant, plaintiff. Civil records on dockets.

Criminal Records: Access: Fax, mail, in person. Both court and visitors may perform in person searches. Search fee: $5.00 per name. Required to search: name, years to search, DOB. Criminal records on dockets.

General Information: No juvenile records released. SASE required. Turnaround time varies. Fax notes: $2.50 for first page, $.50 each add'l. Copy fee: $.25 per page. Certification fee: $5.00. Fee payee: Circuit Clerk. Personal checks accepted. Prepayment is required.

District Court PO Box 550, Jasper, AR 72641; 870-446-5335; Fax: 870-446-2234. Hours: 8AM-4:30PM (CST). *Misdemeanor, Civil Actions Under $5,000, Eviction, Small Claims.*

Civil Records: Access: Phone, mail, fax, in person. Both court and visitors may perform in person searches. No search fee. Required to search: name plus years to search, and DOB or SSN. Records go back to 1972, on computer back to 1993.

Criminal Records: Access: Phone, mail, fax, in person. Both court and visitors may perform in person searches. No search fee. Required to search: name plus years to search, and DOB or SSN. Records go back to 1972, on computer back to 1993.

General Information: Certification fee: $10.00. Fee payee: District Court.

Ouachita County

Circuit & Chancery Courts PO Box 667, Camden, AR 71701; 870-837-2230 (Circuit); Probate phone: 870-837-2220; Fax: 870-837-2252. Hours: 8AM-4:30PM (CST). *Felony, Civil Actions Over $5,000, Probate.*

Civil Records: Access: In person only. Visitors must perform in person searches for themselves. No search fee. Required to search: name, years to search. Civil cases indexed by defendant, plaintiff. Civil records archived from 1950s; on computer back to 3/1999.

Criminal Records: Access: In person only. Visitors must perform in person searches for themselves. No search fee. Required to search: name, years to search; also helpful: DOB, SSN. Criminal records archived from 1950s; on computer back to 3/1999.

General Information: Public Access terminal is available. No juvenile records released. Copy fee: $1.00 per page. Certification fee: $2.50. Fee payee: Circuit Clerk of Ouachita County. Personal checks accepted. Prepayment is required.

Ouachita County District Court 213 Madison St, Camden, AR 71701; 870-836-0331; Fax: 870-837-5530. Hours: 8AM-4:30PM (CST). *Misdemeanor, Civil Actions Under $5,000, Eviction, Small Claims.*

Civil Records: Access: Mail, fax, in person. Both court and visitors may perform in person searches. Search fee: $5.00 per name. Required to search: name, years to search. Records go back to 1950; computerized since 1987.

Criminal Records: Access: Mail, fax, in person. Both court and visitors may perform in person searches. Search fee: $5.00 per name. Required to search: name, years to search, DOB; also helpful: SSN. Records go back to 1950; computerized since 1987.

General Information: Turnaround time 1-2 days. Certification fee: $5.00. Fee payee: District Court. Prepayment is required.

Perry County

Circuit & Chancery Courts PO Box 358, Perryville, AR 72126; 501-889-5126; Fax: 501-889-5759. Hours: 8AM-4:30PM (CST). *Felony, Civil Actions Over $5,000, Probate.*

Civil Records: Access: In person only. Visitors must perform in person searches for themselves. No search fee. Required to search: name, years to search. Civil cases indexed by defendant, plaintiff. Civil records on computer from 1991, on dockets from 1974.

Criminal Records: Access: In person only. Visitors must perform in person searches for themselves. No search fee. Required to search: name, years to search, DOB. Criminal records on computer from 1991, on dockets from 1974.

General Information: Public Access terminal is available. No juvenile or adoption records released. Copy fee: $.50 for first page, $.25 each add'l. Certification fee: $5.00. Fee payee: Circuit Clerk. Personal checks accepted. Prepayment is required.

District Court PO Box 186, Perryville, AR 72126; 501-889-5296; Fax: 501-889-5835. Hours: 8AM-4:30PM (CST). *Misdemeanor, Civil Actions Under $5,000, Eviction, Small Claims.*

Civil Records: Access: In person, mail. Both court and visitors may perform in person searches. Search fee: $2.00.

Criminal Records: Access: In person, mail. Both court and visitors may perform in person searches. Search fee: $2.00. Required to search: name, years to search, DOB, SSN.

General Information: Turnaround time 3-5 days. Fee payee: District Court. Prepayment is required.

Phillips County

Circuit & Chancery Courts Courthouse, 620 Cherry St Suite 206, Helena, AR 72342; 870-338-5515; Probate phone: 870-338-5505; Fax: 870-338-5513. Hours: 8AM-4:30PM (CST). *Felony, Civil Actions Over $5,000, Probate.*

Civil Records: Access: In person only. Visitors must perform in person searches for themselves. No search fee. Required to search: name, years to search. Civil cases indexed by plaintiff. Civil records on fee books from 1970; on computer back to 1998.

Criminal Records: Access: In person only. Visitors must perform in person searches for themselves. No search fee. Required to search: name, years to search. Criminal records on fee books from 1970; on computer back to 1998.

General Information: No juvenile records released. Fax notes: Fee to fax results is $2.00 per document. Copy fee: $.25 per page. Certification fee: $3.00. Fee payee: Circuit Clerk. Personal checks accepted. Prepayment is required.

District Court 226 Perry ST, City Hall, Helena, AR 72342; 870-338-9831; Fax: 870-338-9832. Hours: 8AM-4:30PM (CST). *Misdemeanor, Civil Actions Under $5,000, Eviction, Small Claims.*

Civil Records: Access: In person, mail. Both court and visitors may perform in person searches. No search fee.

Criminal Records: Access: In person, mail. Both court and visitors may perform in person searches. Search fee: $5.00 per name. Required to search: name, years to search, address, DOB, SSN.

General Information: Turnaround time 3 days. Fee payee: City of Helena District Court. Prepayment is required.

Pike County

Circuit & Chancery Courts PO Box 219, Murfreesboro, AR 71958; 870-285-2231; Fax: 870-285-3281. Hours: 8AM-4:30PM (CST). *Felony, Civil Actions Over $5,000, Probate.*

Civil Records: Access: Fax, mail, in person. Both court and visitors may perform in person searches. Search fee: $6.00 per name. Required to search: name, years to search. Civil cases indexed by defendant. Civil records archived from 1895. Some records on dockets, fee books and computer.

Criminal Records: Access: Fax, mail, in person. Both court and visitors may perform in person searches. Search fee: $6.00 per name. Required to search: name, years to search, DOB. Criminal records archived from 1895. Some records on dockets, fee books and computer.

General Information: No juvenile or adoption records released. Turnaround time 1 week. Fax notes: Fax fee $1.50 1st 3 pages, $.50 each additional page. Copy fee: $.50 per page. Certification fee: $3.00. Fee payee: Pike County Clerk. Prepayment is required.

District Court PO Box 197, Murfreesboro, AR 71958; 870-285-3865; Fax: 870-285-2660. Hours: 8AM-4:30PM (CST). *Misdemeanor, Civil Actions Under $5,000, Eviction, Small Claims.*

Civil Records: Access: In person, mail. Both court and visitors may perform in person searches. No search fee.

Criminal Records: Access: In person, mail. Both court and visitors may perform in person searches. Search fee: $6.00 per name. Required to search: name, years to search, offense.

General Information: Turnaround time 2-3 days. Fee payee: Pike County District Court. Prepayment is required.

Poinsett County

Circuit & Chancery Courts PO Box 46, Harrisburg, AR 72432; 870-578-4420; Fax: 870-578-2441. Hours: 8:30AM-4:30PM (CST). *Felony, Civil Actions Over $5,000, Probate.*

Civil Records: Access: Mail, in person. Both court and visitors may perform in person searches. Search fee: $6.00 per name. Required to search: name, years to search. Civil cases indexed by defendant, plaintiff. Civil records on computer from 1985. Some records on dockets.

Criminal Records: Access: Mail, in person. Both court and visitors may perform in person searches. Search fee: $6.00 per name. Required to search: name, years to search, DOB. Criminal records on computer from 1985. Some records on dockets.

General Information: Public Access terminal is available. No juvenile records released. SASE required. Turnaround time 1-2 days. Copy fee: $.25 per page. Certification fee: $2.00. Fee payee: Circuit Clerk. Personal checks accepted. Prepayment is required.

Harrisburg District Court 202 N East St, Harrisburg, AR 72432; 870-578-4110; Fax: 870-578-4123. Hours: 8AM-4:30PM (CST). *Misdemeanor, Civil Actions Under $5,000, Eviction, Small Claims.*

Civil Records: Access: In person only. Both court and visitors may perform in person searches. Search fee: $2.00. Civil records go back to 1987.

Criminal Records: Access: In person only. Both court and visitors may perform in person searches. No search fee. Required to search: name, years to search; also helpful: DOB, SSN. Criminal records on computer back to 1987. Court does not allow public access to computer index.

General Information: Certification fee: $5.00. Fee payee: Harrisburg District Court. Prepayment is required.

Polk County

Circuit & Chancery Courts 507 Church St, Mena, AR 71953; 501-394-8100; Probate phone: 501-394-8123. Hours: 8AM-4:30PM (CST). *Felony, Civil Actions Over $5,000, Probate.*

Note: Probate is handled separately from the court.

Civil Records: Access: Mail, in person. Both court and visitors may perform in person searches. Search fee: $6.00 per name. Required to search: name, years to search. Civil cases indexed by defendant, plaintiff. Civil records on dockets and index from late 1800s.

Criminal Records: Access: Mail, in person. Both court and visitors may perform in person searches. Search fee: $6.00 per name. Required to search: name, years to search, DOB. Criminal records on dockets and index from late 1800s.

General Information: No juvenile records released. SASE required. Turnaround time 1-2 days. Copy fee: $.25 per page. $.50 for legal size copies. Certification fee: $2.00. Fee payee: Circuit Clerk. Personal checks accepted. Prepayment is required.

District Court Courthouse, 507 Church St, Mena, AR 71953; 501-394-8140; Fax: 501-394-6199. Hours: 8AM-4:30PM (CST). *Misdemeanor, Civil Actions Under $5,000, Eviction, Small Claims.*

Civil Records: Access: In person, mail. Visitors must perform in person searches for themselves. No search fee.

Criminal Records: Access: In person, mail. Visitors must perform in person searches for themselves. No search fee. Required to search: name, years to search, DOB; also helpful: SSN.

General Information: Turnaround time 1-2 days.

Pope County

Circuit & Chancery Courts 100 W Main, Russellville, AR 72801; 501-968-7499. Hours: 8AM-5PM (CST). *Felony, Civil Actions Over $5,000, Probate.*

Note: This court will not do record searches; a local retriever must be hired.

Civil Records: Access: In person only. Visitors must perform in person searches for themselves. No search fee. Required to search: name, years to search. Civil cases indexed by defendant, plaintiff. Civil records on dockets from early 1900s; on computer back to 1998.

Criminal Records: Access: In person only. Visitors must perform in person searches for themselves. No search fee. Required to search: name, years to search, DOB; also helpful: SSN. Criminal records on dockets from early 1900s; on computer back to 1998.

General Information: Public Access terminal is available. No juvenile records released. Copy fee: If the court makes the copy, the fee is $1.00 per page, otherwise $.15. Certification fee: $3.00. Fee payee: Pope County. Personal checks accepted.

District Court 205 W Second, Russellville, AR 72801; 501-968-1393; Fax: 501-968-4166. Hours: 8:30AM-5PM (CST). *Misdemeanor, Civil Actions Under $5,000, Eviction, Small Claims.*

Civil Records: Access: Phone, fax, mail, in person. Both court and visitors may perform in person searches. No search fee. Civil records go back to 1970s; on computer back to 1991.

Criminal Records: Access: Phone, fax, mail, in person. Both court and visitors may perform in person searches. No search fee. Required to search: name, years to search; also helpful: DOB. Criminal records go back to 1970s; on computer back to 1991.

General Information: Turnaround time 2-3 days. Certification fee: $5.00. Fee payee: District Court. Prepayment is required.

Prairie County

Circuit & Chancery Courts - Southern District PO Box 283, De Valls Bluff, AR 72041; 870-998-2314; Fax: 870-998-2314. Hours: 8AM-4:30PM (CST). *Felony, Civil Actions Over $5,000, Probate.*

Civil Records: Access: Phone, fax, mail, in person. Both court and visitors may perform in person searches. No search fee. Required to search: name, years to search. Civil cases indexed by defendant, plaintiff. Civil records on dockets from 1800s.

Criminal Records: Access: Phone, fax, mail, in person. Both court and visitors may perform in person searches. No search fee. Required to search: name, years to search, DOB, SSN. Criminal records on dockets from 1800s.

General Information: No juvenile or adoption records released. SASE required. Turnaround time 1 day. Fax notes: $1.00 per page. Copy fee: $.25 per page. Certification fee: $6.00. Fee payee: Circuit Clerk. Personal checks accepted. Prepayment is required.

Circuit & County Courts - Northern District PO Box 1011, Des Arc, AR 72040; 870-256-4434; Fax: 870-256-4434. Hours: 8AM-4:30PM (CST). *Felony, Civil Actions Over $5,000, Probate.*

Civil Records: Access: Mail, in person. Both court and visitors may perform in person searches. Search fee: $6.00 per name. Required to search: name, years to search. Civil cases indexed by defendant, plaintiff. Civil records on dockets from 1800s; limited records on computer.

Criminal Records: Access: Mail, in person. Both court and visitors may perform in person searches. Search fee: $6.00 per name. Required to search: name, years to search. Criminal records on dockets from 1800s; limited records on computer.

General Information: No juvenile, adoption records released. SASE required. Turnaround time 1 day. Fax notes: Fee to fax results is $.25 per page. Copy fee: $.25 per page. Certification fee: $6.00. Fee payee: Circuit Clerk. Personal checks accepted. Prepayment is required.

Des Arc District Court PO Box 389, Des Arc, AR 72040; 870-256-3011; Fax: 870-256-4612. Hours: 8AM-5PM (CST). *Misdemeanor, Civil Actions Under $5,000, Eviction, Small Claims.*

Civil Records: Access: In person, mail. Both court and visitors may perform in person searches. No search fee.

Criminal Records: Access: In person, mail. Both court and visitors may perform in person searches. No search fee. Required to search: name, years to search.

General Information: Turnaround time 1-2 days.

Pulaski County

Circuit & Chancery Courts Courthouse, Rm 102, 401 W Markham St, Ste 102, Little Rock, AR 72201; 501-340-8431; Probate phone: 501-340-8411; Fax: 501-340-8420. Hours: 8:30AM-4:30PM (CST). *Felony, Civil Actions Over $5,000, Probate.*

Note: Probate is handled by the Chancery Court #120 until July 1, 2001.

Civil Records: Access: In person only. Visitors must perform in person searches for themselves. No search fee. Required to search: name, years to search. Civil cases indexed by defendant, plaintiff. Civil records on computer from 1982, on microfiche from 1974 to 1982, archived from 1900.

Criminal Records: Access: In person only. Visitors must perform in person searches for themselves. No search fee. Required to search: name, years to search, DOB, SSN. Criminal records on computer from 1982, on microfiche from 1974 to 1982, archived from 1900.

General Information: Public Access terminal is available. No expunged records released. Copy fee: $.25 per page. Certification fee: $2.50. Fee payee: Circuit Clerk. Personal checks accepted. Prepayment is required.

Pulaski County District Court 3001 W Roosevelt, Little Rock, AR 72204; 501-340-6824; Fax: 501-340-6899. Hours: 8AM-4:30PM (CST). *Misdemeanor, Civil Actions Under $5,000, Eviction, Small Claims.*

Civil Records: Access: In person, mail. Both court and visitors may perform in person searches. No search fee.

Criminal Records: Access: In person, mail. Both court and visitors may perform in person searches. No search fee. Required to search: name, years to search; also helpful: SSN.

General Information: Turnaround time 2-3 days.

Randolph County

Circuit & Chancery Courts 107 West Broadway, Pocahontas, AR 72455; 870-892-5522; Fax: 870-892-8794. Hours: 8AM-4:30PM (CST). *Felony, Civil Actions Over $5,000, Probate.*

Civil Records: Access: Mail, in person. Both court and visitors may perform in person searches. Search fee: $6.00 per name. Required to search: name, years to search. Civil cases indexed by defendant, plaintiff. Civil records on criminal index from 1836.

Criminal Records: Access: Mail, in person. Both court and visitors may perform in person searches. Search fee: $6.00 per name. Required to search: name, years to search, DOB. Criminal records on criminal index from 1836.

General Information: No juvenile records released. SASE required. Turnaround time same day. Copy fee: $.25 per page. Certification fee: $2.00. Fee payee: Circuit Clerk. Personal checks accepted.

District Court 1510 Pace Rd, Pocahontas, AR 72455; 870-892-4033; Fax: 870-892-4392. Hours: 8:00AM-4:30PM (CST). *Misdemeanor, Civil Actions Under $5,000, Eviction, Small Claims.*

Civil Records: Access: In person, mail. Both court and visitors may perform in person searches. Search fee: $6.00. Required to search: name, years to search, DOB, SSN.

Criminal Records: Access: In person, mail. Both court and visitors may perform in person searches. Search fee: $6.00. Required to search: name, years to search, DOB, SSN.

General Information: Turnaround time 1 day. Fee payee: District Court. Prepayment is required.

Saline County

Circuit & Chancery Courts 200 North Main St, Benton, AR 72018; 501-303-5615; Fax: 501-303-5675. Hours: 8AM-4:30PM (CST). *Felony, Civil Actions Over $5,000, Probate.*

www.salinecounty.org

Civil Records: Access: In person only. Visitors must perform in person searches for themselves. No search fee. Required to search: name, years to search. Civil cases indexed by defendant, plaintiff. Civil records on computer since 9/94, prior on docket books.

Criminal Records: Access: In person only. Visitors must perform in person searches for themselves. No search fee. Required to search: name, years to search, DOB, SSN. Criminal records on computer since 9/94, prior on docket books.

General Information: No juvenile records released. Copy fee: $.25 per page. Certification fee: $3.00. Fee payee: Circuit Court. Personal checks accepted. Prepayment is required.

Benton District Court 1605 Edison Ave, Benton, AR 72015; 501-303-5670/1 & 5975; Fax: 501-776-5696. Hours: 8AM-4:30PM (CST). *Misdemeanor, Civil Actions Under $5,000, Eviction, Small Claims.*

Civil Records: Access: In person, mail. Both court and visitors may perform in person searches. No search fee.
Criminal Records: Access: In person, mail. Both court and visitors may perform in person searches. No search fee. Required to search: name, years to search; also helpful: DOB, SSN.
General Information: Turnaround time 1 day.

Scott County

Circuit & Chancery Courts PO Box 2165, Waldron, AR 72958; 870-637-2642. Hours: 8AM-4:30PM *Felony, Civil Actions Over $5,000, Probate.*

Civil Records: Access: Phone, mail, fax, in person. Both court and visitors may perform in person searches. No search fee. Required to search: name, years to search. Civil cases indexed by defendant, plaintiff. Civil records on index books from 1882.
Criminal Records: Access: Phone, mail, fax, in person. Both court and visitors may perform in person searches. No search fee. Required to search: name, years to search, DOB, SSN. Criminal records on index books from 1882.
General Information: No juvenile or adoption records released. SASE required. Turnaround time 1 week. Copy fee: $.25 per page. Certification fee: $3.00. Fee payee: Scott County. Personal checks accepted. Prepayment is required.

District Court 100 W 1st St, Box 15, Waldron, AR 72958; 501-637-4694; Fax: 501-437-4199. Hours: 8AM-4:30PM (CST). *Misdemeanor, Civil Actions Under $5,000, Eviction, Small Claims.*

Civil Records: Access: In person, mail. Both court and visitors may perform in person searches. No search fee.
Criminal Records: Access: In person, mail. Both court and visitors may perform in person searches. No search fee. Required to search: name, years to search.
General Information: Turnaround time 1-2 days.

Searcy County

Circuit & Chancery Courts PO Box 998, Marshall, AR 72650; 870-448-3807. Hours: 8AM-4:30PM (CST). *Felony, Civil Actions Over $5,000, Probate.*

Civil Records: Access: Mail, in person. Both court and visitors may perform in person searches. No search fee. Required to search: name, years to search. Civil cases indexed by defendant, plaintiff. Civil records archived from 1881. Some records on dockets.
Criminal Records: Access: In person only. Visitors must perform in person searches for themselves. No search fee. Required to search: name, years to search, offense; also helpful: DOB, SSN. Criminal records archived from 1881. Some records on dockets.
General Information: No juvenile or adoption records released. SASE required. Turnaround time 1-2 days. Copy fee: $.25 per page. Fee is for civil division only. Certification fee: $3.00. Fee payee: Searcy County Clerk. Personal checks accepted. Prepayment is required.

District Court PO Box 837, Marshall, AR 72650; 870-448-5411; Fax: 870-448-5692. Hours: 9AM-5PM (CST). *Misdemeanor, Civil Actions Under $5,000, Eviction, Small Claims.*

Civil Records: Access: In person, mail. Both court and visitors may perform in person searches. No search fee.
Criminal Records: Access: In person, mail. Both court and visitors may perform in person searches. No search fee. Required to search: name, years to search, DOB, SSN.
General Information: Turnaround time 1 week.

Sebastian County

Circuit Court - Greenwood Division PO Box 310, County Courthouse, Greenwood, AR 72936; 501-996-4175; Fax: 501-996-6885. Hours: 8AM-5PM (CST). *Felony, Civil Actions Over $5,000, Probate.*

Civil Records: Access: Mail, in person. Both court and visitors may perform in person searches. Search fee: $6.00 per name. Required to search: name, years to search. Civil cases indexed by defendant, plaintiff. Civil records on computer from 10/87, on dockets from 1900.
Criminal Records: Access: Mail, in person. Both court and visitors may perform in person searches. Search fee: $6.00 per name. Required to search: name, years to search; also helpful: SSN. Criminal records on computer from 10/87, on dockets from 1900.
General Information: Public Access terminal is available. No juvenile records released. SASE required. Turnaround time 1-2 weeks. Fax notes: $1.00 per page. Copy fee: $1.00 per page. Certification fee: $2.50. Fee payee: Circuit Clerk. Personal checks accepted. Prepayment is required.

Circuit Court - Fort Smith 35 S 6th St, PO Box 1179, Fort Smith, AR 72902; 501-782-1046. Hours: 8AM-5PM (CST). *Felony, Civil Actions Over $5,000, Probate.*

Civil Records: Access: Fax, mail, in person. Both court and visitors may perform in person searches. Search fee: $6.00 per name. Required to search: name, years to search; also helpful: address. Civil cases indexed by defendant, plaintiff. Civil records on computer from 1988, on dockets from 1900.
Criminal Records: Access: Fax, mail, in person. Both court and visitors may perform in person searches. Search fee: $6.00 per name. Required to search: name, years to search; also helpful: address, DOB, SSN. Criminal records on computer from 1988, on dockets from 1900. Court will only perform searches for criminal justice purposes.
General Information: Public Access terminal is available. No juvenile records released. SASE required. Turnaround time 1-2 weeks. Fax notes: $1.00 per page. Copy fee: $1.00 per page. The fee is $.50 if in person, $1.00 for mail requesters. Certification fee: $2.50. Fee payee: Circuit Clerk. Personal checks accepted. Prepayment is required.

Fort Smith District Court Courthouse, 35 S 6th St, Fort Smith, AR 72901; 501-784-2420; Fax: 501-784-2438. Hours: 8:30AM-5PM (CST). *Misdemeanor, Civil Actions Under $5,000, Eviction, Small Claims.*

Civil Records: Access: In person, mail. Both court and visitors may perform in person searches. No search fee.
Criminal Records: Access: In person, mail. Both court and visitors may perform in person searches. No search fee. Required to search: name, years to search, DOB; also helpful: SSN.
General Information: Public Access terminal is available. Turnaround time 1-2 days.

Sevier County

Circuit Court 115 N 3rd, Courthouse, De Queen, AR 71832; 870-584-3055; Probate phone: 870-642-2852; Fax: 870-642-9638. Hours: 8AM-4:30PM (CST). *Felony, Civil Actions Over $5,000, Probate.*

Note: Probate court is located in the same building; probate phone is above.

Civil Records: Access: In person only. Visitors must perform in person searches for themselves. No search fee. Required to search: name, years to search. Civil cases indexed by defendant, plaintiff. Civil records archived from 1900.
Criminal Records: Access: Mail, fax, in person. Both court and visitors may perform in person searches. Search fee: $6.00 per name. Required to search: name,

years to search, DOB. Criminal records on record and index books.
General Information: No juvenile records released. SASE required. Turnaround time 3 days. Fax notes: Fee to fax is $5.00 per document; free if to a toll-free number. Copy fee: $.50 per page. Certification fee: $3.00. Fee payee: Circuit Clerk. Personal checks accepted. Prepayment is required.

District Court 115 N 3rd St, Rm 215, De Queen, AR 71832; 870-584-7311; Fax: 870-642-6651. Hours: 8AM-4:30PM (CST). *Misdemeanor, Civil Actions Under $5,000, Eviction, Small Claims.*

Civil Records: Access: In person, mail. Both court and visitors may perform in person searches. Search fee: $6.00.
Criminal Records: Access: In person, mail. Both court and visitors may perform in person searches. Search fee: $6.00. Required to search: name, years to search, DOB.
General Information: Turnaround time 1-2 weeks. Fee payee: District Court.

Sharp County

Circuit & County Courts PO Box 307, Ash Flat, AR 72513; 870-994-7361; Fax: 870-994-7712. Hours: 8AM-4PM (CST). *Felony, Civil Actions Over $5,000, Probate.*

Civil Records: Access: Fax, mail, in person. Both court and visitors may perform in person searches. Search fee: $6.00 per name. Required to search: name, years to search. Civil cases indexed by defendant, plaintiff. Civil records on card files from 1970s. Some records on dockets.
Criminal Records: Access: Fax, mail, in person. Both court and visitors may perform in person searches. Search fee: $6.00 per name. Required to search: name, years to search; also helpful: DOB, SSN. Criminal records on card files from 1970s. Some records on dockets.
General Information: No juvenile or expunged records released. SASE required. Turnaround time 1 day. Fax notes: No fee to fax results. Will only fax to 800 numbers. Copy fee: $.15 per page. Certification fee: $3.00. Fee payee: Sharp County Clerk. Personal checks accepted. Prepayment is required.

District Court PO Box 2, Ash Flat, AR 72513; 870-994-2745; Fax: 870-994-7901. Hours: 8AM-4PM (CST). *Misdemeanor, Civil Actions Under $5,000, Eviction, Small Claims.*

Civil Records: Access: In person, mail. Both court and visitors may perform in person searches. No search fee.
Criminal Records: Access: In person, mail. Both court and visitors may perform in person searches. No search fee. Required to search: name, years to search; also helpful: DOB, SSN.
General Information: Turnaround time 1 day.

St. Francis County

Circuit & County Courts PO Box 1775, Forrest City, AR 72335; 870-261-1715; Fax: 870-261-1723. Hours: 8AM-4:30PM (CST). *Felony, Civil Actions Over $5,000, Probate.*

Civil Records: Access: Fax, mail, in person. Both court and visitors may perform in person searches. Search fee: $5.00 per name. Required to search: name, years to search. Civil cases indexed by defendant, plaintiff. Civil records on index from 1982, archived from 1920s.
Criminal Records: Access: Fax, mail, in person. Both court and visitors may perform in person searches. Search fee: $5.00 per name. Required to search: name, years to search, DOB, SSN. Criminal records on index from 1982, archived from 1920s.
General Information: No juvenile records released. SASE required. Turnaround time 2-3 days. Fax notes: No fee to fax results. Local or toll free calls only. Copy

fee: $.50 per page. Certification fee: $3.00. Fee payee: Circuit Clerk. Personal checks accepted.

District Court 615 East Cross, Forrest City, AR 72335; 870-261-1410; Fax: 870-261-1411. Hours: 8AM-4:30PM (CST). *Misdemeanor, Civil Actions Under $5,000, Eviction, Small Claims.*

Civil Records: Access: In person, mail. Only the court performs in person searches; visitors may not. No search fee.

Criminal Records: Access: In person, mail. Only the court performs in person searches; visitors may not. Search fee: $5.00 per name. Required to search: name, years to search.

General Information: Turnaround time 5 days. Fee payee: District Court. Prepayment is required.

Stone County

Circuit & Chancery Courts HC71 Box 1, Mountain View, AR 72560; 870-269-3271; Fax: 870-269-2303. Hours: 8AM-4:30PM (CST). *Felony, Civil Actions Over $5,000, Probate.*

Civil Records: Access: In person only. Visitors must perform in person searches for themselves. No search fee. Required to search: name, years to search. Civil cases indexed by defendant, plaintiff. Civil records on dockets from 1960s. Mountain View Abstract Corp does searches by mail. Call 870-269-8410.

Criminal Records: Access: In person only. Visitors must perform in person searches for themselves. No search fee. Required to search: name, years to search, DOB; also helpful: SSN. Criminal records on dockets from 1960s.

General Information: No juvenile or adoption records released. Copy fee: $.25 per page. Certification fee: $3.00. Fee payee: Stone County Clerk. Personal checks accepted. Prepayment is required.

District Court HC 71 Box 4, Mountain View, AR 72560; 870-269-3465. Hours: 8AM-4:30PM (CST). *Misdemeanor, Civil Actions Under $5,000, Eviction, Small Claims.*

Civil Records: Access: Phone, fax, mail, in person. Both court and visitors may perform in person searches. No search fee. Required to search: names, years to search. Records on computer since 1990.

Criminal Records: Access: Phone, fax, mail, in person. Both court and visitors may perform in person searches. No search fee. Required to search: name, years to search; also helpful: DOB, SSN. Records on computer since 1990.

General Information: Turnaround time varies. Certification fee: $3.00. Fee payee: District Court.

Union County

Circuit & Chancery Courts PO Box 1626, El Dorado, AR 71730; 870-864-1940. Hours: 8:30AM-5PM (CST). *Felony, Civil Actions Over $5,000, Probate.*

www.recordsusa.com/Arkansas/UnionCnAr.htm

Civil Records: Access: Mail, in person, online. Both court and visitors may perform in person searches. Search fee: $6.00 per name. Required to search: name, years to search. Civil cases indexed by defendant, plaintiff. Civil records on computer back to 1980, on dockets from 1800s. Online access to circuit court dockets is available by subscription through RecordsUSA.com. Credit card, username and password is required; choose either monthly or per-use plan. Visit the web site for sign-up or call Lisa at 601-264-7701 for information.

Criminal Records: Access: Mail, in person, online. Both court and visitors may perform in person searches. Search fee: $6.00 per name. Required to search: name, years to search, DOB; also helpful: SSN. Criminal records on computer back to 1980, on dockets from

1800s. Online access to criminal dockets is the same as civil.

General Information: Public Access terminal is available. No juvenile records released. SASE required. Turnaround time 2 days. Fax notes: Fee to fax results is $1.00 per page. Copy fee: $.50 per page. Certification fee: $3.00. Fee payee: Circuit Clerk. Personal checks accepted. Prepayment is required.

District Court 101 N Washington, Suite 203, El Dorado, AR 71730; 870-864-1950; Fax: 870-864-1955. Hours: 8:30AM-5PM (CST). *Misdemeanor, Civil Actions Under $5,000, Eviction, Small Claims.*

Civil Records: Access: In person, mail. Both court and visitors may perform in person searches. No search fee.

Criminal Records: Access: In person, mail. Both court and visitors may perform in person searches. No search fee. Required to search: name, years to search, DOB; also helpful: SSN.

General Information: Turnaround time 1-2 days.

Van Buren County

Circuit & County Courts Route 6 Box 254-9, Clinton, AR 72031; 501-745-4140. Hours: 8AM-5PM (CST). *Felony, Civil Actions Over $5,000, Probate.*

Civil Records: Access: Mail, in person. Visitors must perform in person searches for themselves. No search fee. Required to search: name, years to search; also helpful: address. Civil cases indexed by defendant, plaintiff. Civil records on computer from 1987, archived from 1900s.

Criminal Records: Access: Mail, in person. Both court and visitors may perform in person searches. Search fee: $6.00 per name. Required to search: name, years to search; also helpful: address, DOB, SSN. Criminal records on computer from 1987, archived from 1900s.

General Information: No juvenile or adoption records released. SASE required. Turnaround time 7-10 days. Copy fee: $.25 per page. $.50 for microfilm copies. Certification fee: $3.00. Fee payee: Van Buren County Clerk's Office. Personal checks accepted. Prepayment is required.

District Court PO Box 181, Clinton, AR 72031; 501-745-8894; Fax: 501-745-5810. Hours: 8:30AM-4:30PM (CST). *Misdemeanor, Civil Actions Under $5,000, Eviction, Small Claims.*

Civil Records: Access: Phone, mail, fax, in person. Visitors must perform in person searches for themselves. No search fee. Civil records on computer back to 1988; in books back to 1993.

Criminal Records: Access: Phone, mail, fax, in person. Both court and visitors may perform in person searches. Search fee: $5.00 per name. Required to search: name, years to search, DOB, SSN; also helpful-docket or ticket number. Criminal records on computer back to 1988; in books back to 1993.

General Information: Certification fee: $5.00. Fee payee: Clinton District Court. Prepayment is required.

Washington County

Circuit & Chancery Courts 280 N College, Fayetteville, AR 72701; 501-444-1542; Fax: 501-444-1537. Hours: 8AM-4:30PM (CST). *Felony, Civil Actions Over $5,000, Probate.*

Civil Records: Access: Fax, mail, in person. Both court and visitors may perform in person searches. Search fee: $6.00. Required to search: name, years to search. Civil cases indexed by defendant, plaintiff. Civil records on computer from 1992, on index from 1950.

Criminal Records: Access: Fax, mail, in person. Both court and visitors may perform in person searches. Search fee: $6.00. Required to search: name, years to search; also helpful: address, DOB, SSN. Criminal records on computer from 1992, on index from 1950.

General Information: Public Access terminal is available. No juvenile records released. Turnaround

time 1-2 days. Fax notes: $5.00 per document. Copy fee: $.25 per page. Certification fee: $2.00. Fee payee: Circuit Clerk. Personal checks accepted. Prepayment is required.

Fayetteville District Court 100 B West Rock, Fayetteville, AR 72701; 501-587-3596; Fax: 501-444-3480. Hours: 8AM-5PM (CST). *Misdemeanor, Civil Actions Under $5,000, Small Claims.*

Civil Records: Access: In person, mail. Both court and visitors may perform in person searches. No search fee.

Criminal Records: Access: In person, mail. Both court and visitors may perform in person searches. Search fee: $5.00 per name. Required to search: name, years to search, address, DOB, SSN.

General Information: Turnaround time 1 week. Fee payee: City of Fayetteville. Prepayment is required.

White County

Circuit & Chancery Courts 301 W Arch, Searcy, AR 72143; 501-279-6223; Probate phone: 501-279-6204; Fax: 501-279-6218. Hours: 8AM-4:30PM (CST). *Felony, Civil Actions Over $5,000, Probate.*

Civil Records: Access: Phone, mail, in person. Both court and visitors may perform in person searches. Search fee: $6.00 per name. Required to search: name, years to search; also helpful: address. Civil cases indexed by plaintiff. Civil records on dockets from 1982.

Criminal Records: Access: Phone, mail, in person. Both court and visitors may perform in person searches. Search fee: $6.00 per name. Required to search: name, years to search, DOB, SSN; also helpful: address. Criminal records on dockets from 1982.

General Information: Public Access terminal is available. No juvenile records released. SASE required. Turnaround time 1 day. Fax notes: $1.00 per page to fax results. Copy fee: $.50 per page. Certification fee: $2.50. Fee payee: Chancery Clerk. Personal checks accepted. Prepayment is required.

Searcy District Court 311 N Gum, Searcy, AR 72143; 501-268-7622. Hours: 8:30AM-4:30PM (CST). *Misdemeanor, Civil Actions Under $5,000, Small Claims.*

Civil Records: Access: Mail, in person. Both court and visitors may perform in person searches. Search fee: $6.00. Records go back 7 years; on computer since 6/1995.

Criminal Records: Access: In person, mail. Only the court performs in person searches; visitors may not. Search fee: $6.00 if after 6/1995; $10.00 if before and $15.00 is record found. Required to search: name, years to search, DOB, SSN. Records go back 7 years; on computer since 6/1995.

General Information: Turnaround time 5 days. Copy fee: $.50 per page. Certification fee: No cert fee. Fee payee: Searcy District Court.

Woodruff County

Circuit & County Courts PO Box 492, Augusta, AR 72006; 870-347-2391; Probate phone: 870-347-2871; Fax: 870-347-2915. Hours: 8AM-4PM (CST). *Felony, Civil Actions Over $5,000.*

Note: Probate is handled by the County Clerk.

Civil Records: Access: Phone, mail, in person. Both court and visitors may perform in person searches. No search fee. Required to search: name, years to search. Civil cases indexed by defendant, plaintiff. Civil records on dockets from 1982.

Criminal Records: Access: Phone, mail, in person. Both court and visitors may perform in person searches. No search fee. Required to search: name, years to search, DOB. Criminal records on dockets from 1982.

General Information: No juvenile records released. SASE required. Turnaround time 1-2 days. Copy fee:

$.50 per page. Certification fee: $3.00. Fee payee: Circuit Clerk. Personal checks accepted. Prepayment is required.

District Court PO Box 381, Augusta, AR 72006; 870-347-2790; Fax: 870-347-2436. Hours: 8:30AM-5PM (CST). *Misdemeanor, Civil Actions Under $5,000, Eviction, Small Claims.*

Civil Records: Access: In person, mail. Both court and visitors may perform in person searches. No search fee. Computerized records go back to 1995.

Criminal Records: Access: In person, mail. Both court and visitors may perform in person searches. Search fee: $5.00 per name. Required to search: name, years to search, DOB, signed release. Computerized records go back to 1995.

General Information: Turnaround time 10 days. Fax notes: No fee to fax results. Fee payee: Augusta District Court. Prepayment is required.

Yell County

Danville Circuit & County Courts PO Box 219, Danville, AR 72833; 501-495-4850; Fax: 501-495-4875. Hours: 8AM-4PM (CST). *Felony, Civil Actions Over $5,000, Probate.*

Civil Records: Access: Mail, fax, in person. Both court and visitors may perform in person searches. Search fee: $6.00 per name. Required to search: name, years to search; also helpful: address. Civil cases indexed by defendant. Civil records on dockets from 1800s.

Criminal Records: Access: Mail, fax, in person. Both court and visitors may perform in person searches. Search fee: $6.00 per name. Required to search: name, years to search, DOB; also helpful: address. Criminal records on dockets from 1800s.

General Information: No juvenile or adoption records released. SASE required. Turnaround time 1 day. Copy fee: $.25 per page. Certification fee: $3.00. Fee payee: Circuit Clerk of Yell County. Personal checks accepted. Prepayment is required.

Dardanelle Circuit & County Courts County Courthouse, PO Box 457, Dardanelle, AR 72834; 501-229-4404. Hours: 8AM-4PM (CST). *Felony, Civil Actions Over $5,000, Probate.*

Civil Records: Access: Mail, in person. Both court and visitors may perform in person searches. Search fee: $6.00 per name. Required to search: name, years to search. Civil cases indexed by defendant. Civil records on computer from 1989, on dockets from 1800s.

Criminal Records: Access: Mail, in person. Both court and visitors may perform in person searches. Search fee: $6.00 per name. Required to search: name, years to search; also helpful: DOB. Criminal records on computer from 1989, on dockets from 1800s.

General Information: No adoption or juvenile records released. SASE required. Turnaround time 1 day. Copy fee: $.25 per page. Certification fee: $3.00. Fee payee: Circuit Clerk of Yell County. Personal checks accepted. Prepayment is required.

District Court County Courthouse, Dardanelle, AR 72834; 501-229-1389. Hours: 8AM-4PM (CST). *Misdemeanor, Civil Actions Under $5,000, Eviction, Small Claims.*

Civil Records: Access: In person, mail. Both court and visitors may perform in person searches. No search fee.

Criminal Records: Access: In person, mail. Both court and visitors may perform in person searches. Search fee: $3.00 per name. Required to search: name, years to search; also helpful: address, DOB, SSN.

General Information: Turnaround time 2-4 days. Fee payee: District Court. Prepayment is required.

Arkansas Recording Offices

ORGANIZATION   75 counties, 85 recording offices. The recording officer is the Clerk of Circuit Court, who is Ex Officio Recorder. Ten counties have two recording offices - Arkansas, Carroll, Clay, Craighead, Franklin, Logan, Mississippi, Prairie, Sebastian, and Yell. See the notes under each county for how to determine which office is appropriate to search. The entire state is in the Central Time Zone (CST).

REAL ESTATE RECORDS   Most counties do not perform real estate searches. Copy fees and certification fees vary.

UCC RECORDS   Prior to 07/01 this was a dual filing state. Financing statements were filed at the state level and with the Circuit Clerk, except for consumer goods, farm and real estate related collateral, which were filed only with the Circuit Clerk. Now all financing statements are filed at the state level, except for real estate related collateral, which is still filed with the Circuit Clerk. Most counties will perform UCC searches. Use search request form UCC-11. Search fees are usually $10.00 per debtor name. Copy fees vary.

TAX LIEN RECORDS   Federal tax liens on personal property of businesses are filed with the Secretary of State. Other federal and all state tax liens are filed with the Circuit Clerk. Many counties will perform separate tax lien searches. Search fees are usually $6.00 per name.

OTHER LIENS   Mechanics, lis pendens, judgments, hospital, child support, materialman.

Arkansas County (Northern District)

County Circuit Clerk, P.O. Box 719, Stuttgart, AR 72160. County Circuit Clerk, R/E and UCC Recording 870-673-2056; Fax 870-673-3869.
Will search UCC records. This agency will not do a tax lien search. Will not search real estate records. **Other Phone Numbers:** Assessor 870-673-6586.

Arkansas County (Southern District)

County Circuit Clerk, 101 Court Square, De Witt, AR 72042. 870-946-4219; Fax 870-946-1394.
Will search UCC records. This agency will not do a tax lien search. Will not search real estate records. **Other Phone Numbers:** Assessor 870-946-1795; Tax Collector 870-946-4210.

Ashley County

County Circuit Clerk, Jefferson Street, Courthouse, Hamburg, AR 71646. 870-853-2030 R/E Recording: 870-853-5113; Fax 870-853-2005.
Will search UCC records. This agency will not do a tax lien search. Will not search real estate records. **Other Phone Numbers:** Assessor 870-853-2060; Tax Collector 870-853-2010.

Baxter County

County Circuit Clerk, Courthouse Square, 1 East 7th Street, Mountain Home, AR 72653. 870-425-3475; Fax 870-425-5105.
Will search UCC records. UCC search includes tax liens. Property transfer searches available. **Online Access:** Assessor, Real Estate. Assessor/property records are available trough Arcountydata.com at www.arcountydata.com. Registration required; setup fee is $200 with a $.10 per minute charge. **Other Phone Numbers:** Assessor 870-425-3453; Tax Collector 870-425-3444.

Benton County

County Circuit Clerk, 215 East Central Street, Suite 6, Bentonville, AR 72712. County Circuit Clerk, R/E and UCC Recording 501-271-1017; Fax 501-271-5719. http://www.co.benton.ar.us
Will not search UCC records. This agency will not do a tax lien search. Will not search real estate records. **Online Access:** Real Estate, Liens, Property Tax. Benton County Assessor, tax collector, and circuit court information is available free online at

http://64.217.42.130:5061. Also, assessor/property records are available trough Arcountydata.com at www.arcountydata.com. Registration required; setup fee is $200 with a $.10 per minute charge. Also, online access to property records is available by subscription at www.recordsusa.com. Credit card, username and password is required; choose either monthly or per-use plan. Visit the web site or call Lisa at 601-264-7701 for information. **Other Phone Numbers:** Assessor 501-271-1037; Elections 501-271-1013; Tax Collector 501-271-1037.

Boone County

County Circuit Clerk, Courthouse, Suite 200, 100 N. Main, Harrison, AR 72601. County Circuit Clerk, R/E and UCC Recording 870-741-5560; Fax 870-741-4335.
Will search UCC records. This agency will not do a tax lien search. Will not search real estate records. **Other Phone Numbers:** Assessor 870-741-3783; Elections 870-741-8428; Tax Collector 870-741-6646; Marriages 870-741-8428;

Bradley County

County Circuit Clerk, 101 E. Cedar Street, Courthouse, Warren, AR 71671. County Circuit Clerk, R/E and UCC Recording 870-226-2272; Fax 870-226-8401.
Will search UCC records. This agency will not do a tax lien search. Will not search real estate records. **Other Phone Numbers:** Assessor 870-226-2211; Treasurer 870-226-8402; Elections 870-226-3464.

Calhoun County

County Circuit Clerk, P.O. Box 626, Hampton, AR 71744. 870-798-2517 R/E Recording: 870-423-2422; Fax 870-798-2428.
Will search UCC records. This agency will not do a tax lien search. Will not search real estate records. **Other Phone Numbers:** Assessor 870-798-2740; Tax Collector 870-798-2827.

Carroll County (Eastern District)

County Circuit Clerk, P.O. Box 71, Berryville, AR 72616. County Circuit Clerk, R/E and UCC Recording 870-423-2422; Fax 870-423-4796.
Will search UCC records. UCC search includes tax liens if requested. Will not search real estate records. **Other Phone Numbers:** Assessor 870-423-2388; Tax Collector 870-423-3189.

Carroll County (Western District)

County Circuit Clerk, P.O. Box 109, Eureka Springs, AR 72632. 870-253-8646 R/E Recording: 870-423-2422.
Will search UCC records. UCC search includes tax liens if requested. Will not search real estate records. **Other Phone Numbers:** Assessor 870-423-2388.

Chicot County

County Circuit Clerk, Courthouse, 108 Main St., Lake Village, AR 71653. 870-265-8010 R/E Recording: 870-265-236; Fax 870-265-8012.
Will search UCC records. This agency will not do a tax lien search. Will not search real estate records. **Other Phone Numbers:** Assessor 870-265-8025; Tax Collector 870-265-8040.

Clark County

County Circuit Clerk, P.O. Box 576, Arkadelphia, AR 71923. 870-246-4281.
Will search UCC records. This agency will not do a tax lien search. Will not search real estate records. **Other Phone Numbers:** Assessor 870-246-4431; Tax Collector 870-246-2211.

Clay County (Eastern District)

County Circuit Clerk, P.O. Box 29, Piggott, AR 72454. 870-598-2524; Fax 870-598-2524.
Will search UCC records. UCC search includes tax liens. Will not search real estate records. **Other Phone Numbers:** Assessor 870-598-3870.

Clay County (Western District)

County Circuit Clerk, P.O. Box 176, Corning, AR 72422. 870-857-3271; Fax 870-857-9201.
Will search UCC records. UCC search includes tax liens. Will not search real estate records. **Other Phone Numbers:** Assessor 870-857-3133; Tax Collector 870-855-3011.

Cleburne County

County Circuit Clerk, P.O. Box 543, Heber Springs, AR 72543. County Circuit Clerk, R/E and UCC Recording 501-362-8149; Fax 501-362-4650.
Will search UCC records. UCC search includes tax liens if requested. Will not search real estate records. **Other Phone Numbers:** Assessor 501-362-8147; Tax Collector 501-362-8124.

Cleveland County

County Circuit Clerk, P.O. Box 368, Rison, AR 71665. County Circuit Clerk, R/E and UCC Recording 870-325-6521; Fax 870-325-6144.

Will search UCC records. This agency will not do a tax lien search. Will not search real estate records. **Other Phone Numbers:** Assessor 870-325-6695; Tax Collector 870-325-6681.

Columbia County

County Circuit Clerk, P.O. Box 327, Magnolia, AR 71753. County Circuit Clerk, R/E and UCC Recording 870-235-3700; Fax 870-235-3778.

Will search UCC records. This agency will not do a tax lien search. Will search real estate records. **Other Phone Numbers:** Assessor 870-235-4380; Appraiser/Auditor 870-235-4380; Elections 870-235-3774; Tax Collector 870-235-3704.

Conway County

County Circuit Clerk, 115 S. Moose Street, County Courthouse - Room 206, Morrilton, AR 72110. 501-354-9617; Fax 501-354-9612.

Will search UCC records. This agency will not do a tax lien search. Will not search real estate records. **Other Phone Numbers:** Assessor 501-354-9622; Tax Collector 501-354-9623.

Craighead County (Eastern District)

County Circuit Clerk, P.O. Box 537, Lake City, AR 72437. 870-237-4342; Fax 870-237-8174.

Will search UCC records. This agency will not do a tax lien search. Will not search real estate records.

Craighead County (Western District)

County Circuit Clerk, P.O. Box 120, Jonesboro, AR 72401. 870-933-4530; Fax 870-933-4534.

Will search UCC records. This agency will not do a tax lien search. Will not search real estate records. **Other Phone Numbers:** Assessor 870-933-4570; Tax Collector 870-933-4540.

Crawford County

County Circuit Clerk, 300 Main, Courthouse Room 22, Van Buren, AR 72956-5799. County Circuit Clerk, R/E and UCC Recording 501-474-1821.

Will search UCC records. This agency will not do a tax lien search. Will not search real estate records. **Other Phone Numbers:** Assessor 501-471-1751; Tax Collector 501-474-6641.

Crittenden County

County Circuit Clerk, 100 Court St., Marion, AR 72364. 870-739-3248 R/E Recording: 501-739-3248; Fax 870-739-3072.

Will search UCC records. Will not search real estate records.

Cross County

County Circuit Clerk, 705 East Union, Room 9, Wynne, AR 72396. 870-238-5720 R/E Recording: 870-238-5735; Fax 870-238-5739.

Will search UCC records. UCC search includes tax liens if requested. Will not search real estate records. **Other Phone Numbers:** Assessor 870-238-5720; Tax Collector 870-238-5720.

Dallas County

County Circuit Clerk, Courthouse, 206 West 3rd St, Fordyce, AR 71742-3299. County Circuit Clerk, R/E and UCC Recording 870-352-2307; Fax 870-352-7179.

Will search UCC records. UCC search includes tax liens. Will not search real estate records. **Other Phone Numbers:** Assessor 870-352-2232; Tax Collector 870-352-7983.

Desha County

County Circuit Clerk, P.O. Box 309, Arkansas City, AR 71630. 870-877-2411; Fax 870-877-3407.

Will search UCC records. Will not search real estate records. **Online Access:** Real Estate, Recording. Online access to county recorder records is available by subscription at www.recordsusa.com. Credit card, username and password is required; choose either monthly or per-use plan. Visit the web site or call Lisa at 601-264-7701 for information. **Other Phone Numbers:** Assessor 870-877-2431; Tax Collector 870-877-2353.

Drew County

County Circuit Clerk, 210 South Main, Monticello, AR 71655. 870-460-6250 R/E Recording: 870-367-2446; Fax 870-460-6246.

Will search UCC records. RE owner, mortgage, and property transfer searches available. **Online Access:** UCC, Land Records. Also, online access to UCC and Land Records is available by subscription at www.recordsusa.com. Credit card, username and password is required; choose either monthly or per-use plan. Visit the web site or call Lisa at 601-264-7701 for information. **Other Phone Numbers:** Assessor 870-460-6240; Tax Collector 870-460-6225.

Faulkner County

Faulkner County Circuit Clerk, P.O. Box 9, Conway, AR 72033. Faulkner County Circuit Clerk, R/E and UCC Recording 501-450-4911; Fax 501-450-4948.

Will search UCC records. This agency will not do a tax lien search. Will not search real estate records. **Other Phone Numbers:** Assessor 501-450-4905; Tax Collector 501-450-4902.

Franklin County (Charleston District)

County Circuit Clerk, P.O. Box 387, Charleston, AR 72933. County Circuit Clerk, R/E and UCC Recording 501-965-7332; Fax 501-965-9322.

Will search UCC records. UCC search includes tax liens if requested. Will not search real estate records. **Other Phone Numbers:** Assessor 501-965-7797.

Franklin County (Ozark District)

County Circuit Clerk, P.O. Box 1112, Ozark, AR 72949. 501-667-3818; Fax 501-667-5174.

Will search UCC records. Tax liens not included in UCC search. Will not search real estate records. **Other Phone Numbers:** Assessor 501-667-2415.

Fulton County

County Circuit Clerk, P.O. Box 485, Salem, AR 72576-0485. 870-895-3310; Fax 870-895-3362.

Will search UCC records. UCC search includes tax liens. Will not search real estate records. **Other Phone Numbers:** Assessor 870-895-3592; Tax Collector 870-895-3522.

Garland County

County Circuit Clerk, Courthouse - Room 207, Quachita and Hawthorn Streets, Hot Springs, AR 71901. County Circuit Clerk, R/E and UCC Recording 501-622-3630.

Will search UCC records. This agency will not do a tax lien search. Will not search real estate records. **Other Phone Numbers:** Assessor 501-622-3730; Elections 501-622-3610; Tax Collector 501-622-3710.

Grant County

County Circuit Clerk, Courthouse, 101 W. Center, Room 106, Sheridan, AR 72150. 870-942-2631; Fax 870-942-3564.

Will search UCC records. UCC search includes tax liens if requested. RE owner, mortgage, and property transfer searches available. **Other Phone Numbers:** Assessor 870-942-3711; Tax Collector 870-942-4315.

Greene County

County Circuit Clerk, 320 W. Court St., Room 124, Paragould, AR 72450. 870-239-6330; Fax 870-239-3550.

Will search UCC records. Tax liens not included in UCC search. **Other Phone Numbers:** Assessor 870-239-6303.

Hempstead County

County Circuit Clerk, P.O. Box 1420, Hope, AR 71802. County Circuit Clerk, R/E and UCC Recording 870-777-2384; Fax 870-777-7827.

Will search UCC records. This agency will not do a tax lien search. Will not search real estate records. **Other Phone Numbers:** Assessor 870-777-6190; Tax Collector 870-777-4103.

Hot Spring County

County Circuit Clerk, P.O. Box 1200, Malvern, AR 72104. 501-332-2281.

Will search UCC records. This agency will not do a tax lien search. Will not search real estate records. **Other Phone Numbers:** Assessor 501-332-2461; Tax Collector 501-332-7211.

Howard County

County Circuit Clerk, 421 North Main St, Rm 7, Room 7, Nashville, AR 71852. 870-845-7506.

Will search UCC records. UCC search includes tax liens if requested. Will not search real estate records. **Other Phone Numbers:** Assessor 870-845-7511.

Independence County

County Circuit Clerk, P.O. Box 2155, Batesville, AR 72503. 870-793-8865 R/E Recording: 870-793-8833; Fax 870-793-8888.

Will search UCC records. UCC search includes tax liens if requested. Will not search real estate records. **Other Phone Numbers:** Assessor 870-793-8842.

Izard County

County Circuit Clerk, P.O. Box 95, Melbourne, AR 72556. 870-368-4316; Fax 870-368-4748.

Will search UCC records. UCC search includes tax liens. Will not search real estate records. **Other Phone Numbers:** Assessor 870-368-7810; Tax Collector 870-368-4394.

Jackson County

County Circuit Clerk, Courthouse, Main Street, Newport, AR 72112. 870-523-7423 R/E Recording: 870-523-3826.

Will search UCC records. Will not search real estate records. **Other Phone Numbers:** Assessor 870-523-7410; Tax Collector 870-523-7401.

Jefferson County

County Circuit Clerk, P.O. Box 7433, Pine Bluff, AR 71611. 870-541-5309 R/E Recording: 870-541-5360.

Will search UCC records. Will not search real estate records. **Other Phone Numbers:** Assessor 870-541-5338; Tax Collector 870-541-5302.

Johnson County

County Circuit Clerk, P.O. Box 217, Clarksville, AR 72830. County Circuit Clerk, R/E and UCC Recording 501-754-2977; Fax 501-754-4235.
Will not search UCC records. Will not search real estate records. **Other Phone Numbers:** Assessor 501-754-8839; Appraiser/Auditor 501-754-8839; Tax Collector 501-754-3056.

Lafayette County

County Circuit Clerk, 3 Courthouse Square, Third & Spruce, Lewisville, AR 71845. 870-921-4878.
Will search UCC records. This agency will not do a tax lien search. Will not search real estate records. **Other Phone Numbers:** Assessor 870-921-4808; Tax Collector 870-921-4755.

Lawrence County

County Circuit Clerk, P.O. Box 581, Walnut Ridge, AR 72476. 870-886-1112 R/E Recording: 870-886-3421; Fax 870-886-1128.
Will search UCC records. This agency will not do a tax lien search. Will search for deed with a date or book and page. **Other Phone Numbers:** Assessor 870-886-1113; Tax Collector 870-886-1116.

Lee County

County Circuit Clerk, 15 East Chestnut Street, Courthouse, Marianna, AR 72360. 870-295-7710; Fax 870-295-7766. http://www.leeclerk.org/wb_or1
Will search UCC records. Will not search real estate records. **Online Access:** Real Estate, Recordings. Online access to the clerk of circuit court official records/land records database is available free at the web site. **Other Phone Numbers:** Assessor 870-295-7750; Tax Collector 870-295-5296.

Lincoln County

County Circuit Clerk, 300 South Drew St, Star City, AR 71667. County Circuit Clerk, R/E and UCC Recording 870-628-3154; Fax 870-628-5546.
Will search UCC records. UCC search includes tax liens. Will not search real estate records. **Other Phone Numbers:** Assessor 870-628-4401; Tax Collector 870-628-4816.

Little River County

County Circuit Clerk, P.O. Box 575, Ashdown, AR 71822-0575. 870-898-7211; Fax 870-898-7207.
Will search UCC records. UCC search includes tax liens if requested. Will not search real estate records. **Other Phone Numbers:** Assessor 870-898-7204.

Logan County (Northern District)

County Circuit Clerk, Courthouse, Paris, AR 72855. 501-963-2164 R/E Recording: 501-963-2618; Fax 501-963-3304.
Will search UCC records. Will not search real estate records. **Other Phone Numbers:** Assessor 501-963-2716; Tax Collector 501-963-2038.

Logan County (Southern District)

County Circuit Clerk, Courthouse, 366 N Broadway #2, Booneville, AR 72927. 501-675-2894; Fax 501-675-0577.
Will search UCC records. Will not search real estate records. **Other Phone Numbers:** Assessor 501-675-3942; Tax Collector 501-675-5131.

Lonoke County

County Circuit Clerk, P.O. Box 219, Lonoke, AR 72086-0219. County Circuit Clerk, R/E and UCC Recording 501-676-2316.
Will search UCC records. This agency will not do a tax lien search. Will not search real estate records. **Other Phone Numbers:** Assessor 501-676-6938.

Madison County

County Circuit Clerk, P.O. Box 416, Huntsville, AR 72740. 501-738-2215 R/E Recording: 501-738-2747; Fax 501-738-1544.
Will search UCC records. This agency will not do a tax lien search. Will not search real estate records. **Other Phone Numbers:** Assessor 501-738-2325; Tax Collector 501-738-6514.

Marion County

County Circuit Clerk, P.O. Box 385, Yellville, AR 72687. 870-449-6226; Fax 870-449-4979.
Will search UCC records. This agency will not do a tax lien search. Will not search real estate records. **Other Phone Numbers:** Assessor 870-449-4113; Tax Collector 870-449-6253.

Miller County

County Circuit Clerk, County Courthouse-Suite 109, 412 Laurel St., Texarkana, AR 71854. 870-774-4501; Fax 870-772-5293.
Will search UCC records. Tax liens not included in UCC search. Mortgage searches available. **Other Phone Numbers:** Assessor 870-772-1502; Tax Collector 870-772-0003.

Mississippi County (Chickasawba District)

County Circuit Clerk, P.O. Box 1498, Blytheville, AR 72316-1498. 870-762-2332; Fax 870-762-8148.
Will search UCC records. This agency will not do a tax lien search. Will not search real estate records. **Other Phone Numbers:** Assessor 870-763-6860; Tax Collector 870-762-2152.

Mississippi County (Osceola District)

County Circuit Clerk, P.O. Box 466, Osceola, AR 72370. 870-563-6471; Fax 870-563-2543.
Will search UCC records. Will not search real estate records. **Other Phone Numbers:** Assessor 870-563-2682; Tax Collector 870-762-2152.

Monroe County

County Circuit Clerk, 123 Madison Street, Clarendon, AR 72029. 870-747-3615; Fax 870-747-3710.
Will search UCC records. This agency will not do a tax lien search. Will not search real estate records. **Other Phone Numbers:** Assessor 870-747-3847; Tax Collector 870-747-3722.

Montgomery County

County Circuit Clerk, P.O. Box 369, Mount Ida, AR 71957-0369. 870-867-3521; Fax 870-867-2177.
Will search UCC records. UCC search includes tax liens. Will not search real estate records. **Other Phone Numbers:** Assessor 870-867-3271; Tax Collector 870-867-3411.

Nevada County

County Circuit Clerk, PO Box 204, Prescott, AR 71857. 870-887-2511; Fax 870-887-5795.
Will search UCC records. UCC search includes tax liens if requested. RE record owner and mortgage searches available. **Other Phone Numbers:** Assessor 870-887-3410; Tax Collector 870-887-2811.

Newton County

County Circuit Clerk, P.O. Box 410, Jasper, AR 72641. 870-446-5125.
Will search UCC records. This agency will not do a tax lien search. Will not search real estate records. **Other Phone Numbers:** Assessor 870-446-2937; Treasurer 870-446-2936; Tax Collector 870-446-2936.

Ouachita County

County Circuit Clerk, P.O. Box 667, Camden, AR 71701. County Circuit Clerk, R/E and UCC Recording 870-837-2230; Fax 870-837-2252.
Will search UCC records. This agency will not do a tax lien search. Will not search real estate records. **Other Phone Numbers:** Assessor 870-837-2240; Treasurer 870-837-2250; Appraiser/Auditor 870-837-2240; Elections 870-837-2220; Vital Records 501-661-2336.

Perry County

County Circuit Clerk, P.O. Box 358, Perryville, AR 72126. 501-889-5126; Fax 501-889-5759.
Will search UCC records. This agency will not do a tax lien search. Will not search real estate records. **Other Phone Numbers:** Assessor 501-889-2865; Treasurer 501-889-2710; Tax Collector 501-889-2710.

Phillips County

County Circuit Clerk, Courthouse, Suite 206, 620 Cherry St., Helena, AR 72342. County Circuit Clerk, R/E and UCC Recording 870-338-5515; Fax 870-338-5513.
Will search UCC records. This agency will not do a tax lien search. Will not search real estate records. **Other Phone Numbers:** Assessor 870-338-5535; Treasurer 870-338-5510; Tax Collector 870-338-5510.

Pike County

County Circuit Clerk, P.O. Box 219, Murfreesboro, AR 71958. 870-285-2231; Fax 870-285-3281.
Will search UCC records. Will not search real estate records. **Other Phone Numbers:** Assessor 870-285-3316; Treasurer 870-285-2422; Tax Collector 870-285-2422.

Poinsett County

County Circuit Clerk, P.O. Box 46, Harrisburg, AR 72432-0046. 870-578-4420 R/E Recording: 870-578-2244; Fax 870-578-2441.
Will search UCC records. This agency will not do a tax lien search. Will not search real estate records. **Other Phone Numbers:** Assessor 870-578-4430; Treasurer 870-578-4405; Tax Collector 870-578-4405.

Polk County

County Circuit Clerk, 507 Church, Courthouse, Mena, AR 71953. County Circuit Clerk, R/E and UCC Recording 501-394-8100.
Will search UCC records. Tax liens not included in UCC search. Will not search real estate records. **Other Phone Numbers:** Assessor 501-394-8121; Treasurer 501-394-8150; Tax Collector 501-394-8150.

Pope County

County Circuit Clerk, 100 West Main, 3rd Floor, County Courthouse, Russellville, AR 72801. 501-968-7499.
Will search UCC records. This agency will not do a tax lien search. Will not search real estate records. **Other Phone Numbers:** Assessor 501-968-7418; Treasurer 501-968-7016; Tax Collector 501-968-7016.

Prairie County (Northern District)

County Circuit Clerk, P.O. Box 1011, Des Arc, AR 72040. 870-256-4434; Fax 870-256-4434.
Will search UCC records. Tax liens not included in UCC search. Will not search real estate records. **Other Phone Numbers:** Assessor 870-256-4692; Treasurer 870-256-4137; Tax Collector 870-256-4137.

Prairie County (Southern District)

County Circuit Clerk, P.O. Box 283, De Valls Bluff, AR 72041-0283. County Circuit Clerk, R/E and UCC Recording 870-998-2314; Fax 870-998-2314.

Will search UCC records. UCC search includes tax liens. Will not search real estate records. **Other Phone Numbers:** Assessor 870-256-4692; Treasurer 870-998-4786; Tax Collector 870-998-4786.

Pulaski County

County Circuit Clerk, Room S216, 401 W. Markham St., Little Rock, AR 72201. 501-340-8433 R/E Recording: 501-372-8433; Fax 501-340-8420.

Will search UCC records. Tax liens not included in UCC search. Will not search real estate records. **Online Access:** Assessor, Real Estate. Assessor/property records are available trough Arcountydata.com at www.arcountydata.com. Registration required; setup fee is $200 with a $.10 per minute charge. **Other Phone Numbers:** Assessor 501-340-6170; Treasurer 501-340-8345; Tax Collector 501-340-8345.

Randolph County

County Circuit Clerk, 107 W. Broadway, Pocahontas, AR 72455. 870-892-5522 R/E Recording: 870-372-8433; Fax 870-892-8794.

Will search UCC records. Tax liens not included in UCC search. Will not search real estate records. **Other Phone Numbers:** Assessor 870-892-3200; Treasurer 870-892-5238; Tax Collector 870-892-5238.

Saline County

County Circuit Clerk, P.O. Box 1560, Benton, AR 72018. 501-303-5615 R/E Recording: 501-776-5615; Fax 501-303-5675.

Will search UCC records. Will not search real estate records. **Other Phone Numbers:** Assessor 501-776-5622; Treasurer 501-776-5633; Tax Collector 501-776-5633.

Scott County

County Circuit Clerk, P.O. Box 2165, Waldron, AR 72958. County Circuit Clerk, R/E and UCC Recording 501-637-2642; Fax 501-637-0124.

Will search UCC records. Will not search real estate records. **Other Phone Numbers:** Assessor 501-637-2666; Treasurer 501-637-2780; Tax Collector 501-637-2780.

Searcy County

County Circuit Clerk, P.O. Box 935, Marshall, AR 72650. 870-448-3807 R/E Recording: 870-448-3809. Will search UCC records. This agency will not do a tax lien search. Will not search real estate records. **Other Phone Numbers:** Assessor 870-448-2464; Tax Collector 870-448-5050.

Sebastian County (Fort Smith District)

County Clerk and Recorder, P.O. Box 1089, Fort Smith, AR 72902-1089. 501-782-5065 R/E Recording:

501-782-1046 UCC Recording: 501-782-1546; Fax 501-784-1567.

Will search UCC records. This agency will not do a tax lien search. Will not search real estate records. **Other Phone Numbers:** Assessor 501-783-8948; Elections 501-782-5065.

Sebastian County (Southern District)

County Clerk, P.O. Box 428, Greenwood, AR 72936. 501-996-4195 R/E Recording: 501-996-4175; Fax 501-996-4165.

Will search UCC records. This agency will not do a tax lien search. Will not search real estate records. **Other Phone Numbers:** Assessor 501-996-6591.

Sevier County

County Circuit Clerk, 115 North 3rd Street, De Queen, AR 71832. 870-584-3055; Fax 870-642-9638.

Will search UCC records. This agency will not do a tax lien search. Will not search real estate records. **Other Phone Numbers:** Assessor 870-584-3182; Treasurer 870-642-2358; Tax Collector 870-642-2358.

Sharp County

County Circuit Clerk, P.O. Box 307, Ash Flat, AR 72513. 870-994-7361 R/E Recording: 501-994-7361; Fax 870-994-7712.

Will search UCC records. Will not search real estate records. **Other Phone Numbers:** Assessor 501-994-7328; Treasurer 501-994-7347; Tax Collector 501-994-7347.

St. Francis County

County Circuit Clerk, P.O. Box 1775, Forrest City, AR 72336-1775. 870-261-1715 R/E Recording: 870-633-8640; Fax 870-261-1725.

Will search UCC records. Will not search real estate records. **Other Phone Numbers:** Assessor 870-261-1710; Treasurer 870-261-1705; Tax Collector 870-261-1705.

Stone County

County Circuit Clerk, Courthouse, HC 71 Box 1, Mountain View, AR 72560. 870-269-3271; Fax 870-269-2303.

Will search UCC records. UCC search includes tax liens if requested. Will not search real estate records. **Other Phone Numbers:** Assessor 870-269-3524; Treasurer 870-269-8426; Tax Collector 870-269-8426.

Union County

County Circuit Clerk, P.O. Box 1626, El Dorado, AR 71731-1626. 870-864-1940.

Will search UCC records. UCC search includes tax liens if requested. Will not search real estate records. **Other Phone Numbers:** Assessor 870-864-1920; Treasurer 870-864-1928; Tax Collector 870-864-1928.

Van Buren County

County Circuit Clerk, RR6 Box 254-9, Clinton, AR 72031-9806. County Circuit Clerk, R/E and UCC Recording 501-745-4140; Fax 501-745-7400.

Will search UCC records. UCC search includes tax liens. RE owner, mortgage, and property transfer searches available. **Other Phone Numbers:** Assessor 501-745-2464; Treasurer 501-745-2400; Appraiser/Auditor 501-745-2474; Elections 501-745-4140.

Washington County

County Circuit Clerk, Courthouse, 280 N. College, Suite 302, Fayetteville, AR 72701. 501-444-1538; Fax 501-444-1537.

Will search UCC records. Will not search real estate records. **Other Phone Numbers:** Assessor 501-444-1520; Treasurer 501-444-1526; Tax Collector 501-444-1526.

White County

County Circuit Clerk, White County Courthouse, Spring St./East Entrance/Courthouse Sq., Searcy, AR 72143. 501-279-6203; Fax 501-279-6233.

Will search UCC records. Will not search real estate records. **Online Access:** Assessor, Real Estate. Assessor/property records are available trough Arcountydata.com at www.arcountydata.com. Registration required; setup fee is $200 with a $.10 per minute charge. **Other Phone Numbers:** Assessor 501-279-6205; Treasurer 501-279-6206; Tax Collector 501-279-6206.

Woodruff County

County Circuit Clerk, P.O. Box 492, Augusta, AR 72006. 870-347-2391.

Will search UCC records. Tax liens not included in UCC search. Will not search real estate records. **Other Phone Numbers:** Assessor 870-347-5151; Treasurer 870-347-5416; Tax Collector 870-347-5416.

Yell County (Danville District)

County Circuit Clerk, P.O. Box 219, Danville, AR 72833. County Circuit Clerk, R/E and UCC Recording 501-495-4850; Fax 501-495-4875.

Will search UCC records. Tax liens not included in UCC search. Will not search real estate records. **Other Phone Numbers:** Assessor 501-495-2940; Treasurer 501-495-2933; Elections 501-495-4850; Vital Records 501-495-4850.

Yell County (Dardanelle District)

County Circuit Clerk, P.O. Box 457, Dardanelle, AR 72834. 501-229-4404; Fax 501-229-1130.

Will search UCC records. Tax liens not included in UCC search. Will not search real estate records. **Other Phone Numbers:** Assessor 501-229-2693.

Arkansas County Locator

You will usually be able to find the city name in the City/County Cross Reference below. In that case, it is a simple matter to determine the county from the cross reference. However, only the official US Postal Service city names are included in this index. There are an additional 40,000 place names that people use in their addresses. Therefore, we have also included a ZIP/City Cross Reference immediately following the City/County Cross Reference.

If you know the ZIP Code but the city name does not appear in the City/County Cross Reference index, look up the ZIP Code in the ZIP/City Cross Reference, find the city name, then look up the city name in the City/County Cross Reference. For example, you want to know the county for an address of Menands, NY 12204. There is no "Menands" in the City/County Cross Reference. The ZIP/City Cross Reference shows that ZIP Codes 12201-12288 are for the city of Albany. Looking back in the City/County Cross Reference, Albany is in Albany County.

City/County Cross Reference

ADONA (72001) Perry(77), Conway(23)
ALCO (72610) Stone(88), Searcy(13)
ALEXANDER (72002) Saline(88), Pulaski(12)
ALICIA Lawrence
ALIX Franklin
ALLEENE Little River
ALMA Crawford
ALMYRA Arkansas
ALPENA (72611) Boone(76), Carroll(24)
ALPINE Clark
ALTHEIMER (72004) Jackson(88), Jefferson(12)
ALTUS (72821) Franklin(80), Johnson(19)
AMAGON Jackson
AMITY Clark
ANTOINE Pike
ARKADELPHIA (71923) Clark(97), Hot Spring(3)
ARKADELPHIA Clark
ARKANSAS CITY Desha
ARMOREL Mississippi
ASH FLAT (72513) Sharp(59), Fulton(30), Izard(12)
ASHDOWN Little River
ATKINS (72823) Pope(95), Conway(5)
ATKINS Pope
AUBREY Lee
AUGUSTA Woodruff
AUSTIN Lonoke
AVOCA Benton
BALCH Jackson
BALD KNOB White
BANKS Bradley
BARLING Sebastian
BARTON Phillips
BASS Newton
BASSETT Mississippi
BATES Scott
BATESVILLE Independence
BAUXITE Saline
BAY Craighead
BEARDEN (71720) Ouachita(85), Dallas(11), Calhoun(4)
BEAVER Carroll
BEE BRANCH Van Buren
BEEBE White
BEECH GROVE Greene
BEEDEVILLE Jackson
BEIRNE Clark
BELLA VISTA Benton
BELLEVILLE Yell
BEN LOMOND Sevier
BENTON Saline
BENTONVILLE Benton
BERGMAN Boone
BERRYVILLE Carroll
BEXAR Fulton
BIG FLAT (72617) Stone(75), Baxter(25)
BIGELOW (72016) Pulaski(56), Perry(44)
BIGGERS Randolph
BIRDEYE Cross

BISCOE Prairie
BISMARCK Hot Spring
BLACK OAK Craighead
BLACK ROCK Lawrence
BLAKELY Garland
BLEVINS Hempstead
BLUE MOUNTAIN Logan
BLUFF CITY Nevada
BLUFFTON (72827) Yell(96), Scott(4)
BLYTHEVILLE Mississippi
BOARD CAMP Polk
BOLES Scott
BONNERDALE (71933) Garland(69), Hot Spring(25), Montgomery(7)
BONO (72416) Craighead(77), Greene(23)
BOONEVILLE (72927) Logan(90), Sebastian(8), Scott(2)
BOSWELL Izard
BRADFORD (72020) Jackson(50), White(37), Independence(13)
BRADLEY Lafayette
BRANCH (72928) Franklin(96), Logan(4)
BRICKEYS Lee
BRIGGSVILLE Yell
BRINKLEY Monroe
BROCKWELL Izard
BROOKLAND Craighead
BRUNO Marion
BRYANT Saline
BUCKNER Lafayette
BULL SHOALS Marion
BURDETTE Mississippi
CABOT (72023) Lonoke(74), Pulaski(26)
CADDO GAP Montgomery
CALDWELL St. Francis
CALE Nevada
CALICO ROCK (72519) Baxter(79), Izard(19), Stone(2)
CALION Union
CAMDEN (71701) Ouachita(98), Calhoun(2)
CAMDEN Ouachita
CAMP Fulton
CANEHILL Washington
CARAWAY Craighead
CARLISLE (72024) Lonoke(97), Prairie(3)
CARTHAGE Dallas
CASA (72025) Perry(95), Conway(5)
CASH Craighead
CASSCOE Arkansas
CAVE CITY (72521) Sharp(64), Independence(36)
CAVE SPRINGS Benton
CECIL (72930) Sebastian(56), Franklin(44)
CEDARVILLE Crawford
CENTER RIDGE Conway
CENTERTON Benton
CENTERVILLE Yell
CHARLESTON (72933) Franklin(54), Sebastian(45)
CHARLOTTE Independence
CHATFIELD Crittenden

CHEROKEE VILLAGE Sharp
CHERRY VALLEY Cross
CHESTER Crawford
CHIDESTER Ouachita
CHOCTAW Van Buren
CLARENDON Monroe
CLARKEDALE Crittenden
CLARKRIDGE Baxter
CLARKSVILLE Johnson
CLEVELAND (72030) Conway(84), Van Buren(16)
CLINTON (72031) Van Buren(94), Conway(3), Stone(3)
COAL HILL Johnson
COLLEGE STATION Pulaski
COLLINS Drew
COLT St. Francis
COLUMBUS Hempstead
COMBS (72721) Madison(90), Franklin(10)
COMPTON (72624) Newton(84), Carroll(16)
CONCORD (72523) Cleburne(86), Independence(14)
CONWAY Faulkner
CORD Independence
CORNING Clay
COTTER Baxter
COTTON PLANT Woodruff
COVE Polk
COY Lonoke
CRAWFORDSVILLE Crittenden
CROCKETTS BLUFF Arkansas
CROSSETT Ashley
CRUMROD Phillips
CURTIS Clark
CUSHMAN Independence
DAMASCUS (72039) Faulkner(54), Van Buren(46)
DANVILLE Yell
DARDANELLE Yell
DATTO Clay
DE QUEEN Sevier
DE VALLS BLUFF Prairie
DE WITT Arkansas
DECATUR Benton
DEER Newton
DELAPLAINE Greene
DELAWARE Logan
DELIGHT Pike
DELL Mississippi
DENNARD (72629) Van Buren(96), Searcy(4)
DERMOTT (71638) Chicot(91), Drew(7), Desha(2)
DES ARC Prairie
DESHA Independence
DIAMOND CITY Boone
DIAZ Jackson
DIERKS Howard
DODDRIDGE Miller
DOLPH Izard
DONALDSON Hot Spring

DOVER Pope
DRASCO (72530) Cleburne(89), Stone(11)
DRIVER Mississippi
DUMAS (71639) Desha(97), Lincoln(3)
DYER Crawford
DYESS Mississippi
EARLE (72331) Crittenden(71), Cross(28)
EDGEMONT (72044) Cleburne(60), Stone(40)
EDMONDSON Crittenden
EGYPT Craighead
EL DORADO Union
EL PASO White
ELAINE Phillips
ELIZABETH (72531) Baxter(78), Fulton(22)
ELKINS (72727) Washington(90), Madison(10)
ELM SPRINGS Washington
EMERSON (71740) Columbia(69), Scott(31)
EMMET (71835) Nevada(62), Hempstead(38)
ENGLAND (72046) Lonoke(70), Jefferson(17), Pulaski(12)
ENOLA Faulkner
ETHEL Arkansas
ETOWAH Mississippi
EUDORA Chicot
EUREKA SPRINGS (72631) Carroll(77), Benton(23)
EUREKA SPRINGS Carroll
EVANSVILLE Washington
EVENING SHADE Sharp
EVERTON (72633) Marion(71), Boone(23), Searcy(6)
FAIRFIELD BAY (72088) Van Buren(92), Cleburne(8)
FARMINGTON Washington
FAYETTEVILLE Washington
FERNDALE Pulaski
FIFTY SIX Stone
FISHER Poinsett
FLIPPIN Marion
FLORAL (72534) Independence(87), Cleburne(13)
FORDYCE Dallas
FOREMAN Little River
FORREST CITY St. Francis
FORT SMITH Sebastian
FOUKE Miller
FOUNTAIN HILL (71642) Ashley(71), Drew(29)
FOX Stone
FRANKLIN Izard
FRENCHMANS BAYOU Mississippi
FRIENDSHIP Hot Spring
FULTON Hempstead
GAMALIEL Baxter
GARFIELD Benton
GARLAND CITY (71839) Miller(79), Lafayette(21)
GARNER White

GASSVILLE Baxter
GATEWAY Benton
GENOA Miller
GENTRY Benton
GEPP (72538) Fulton(63), Baxter(38)
GILBERT Searcy
GILLETT Arkansas
GILLHAM (71841) Sevier(90), Polk(10)
GILMORE Crittenden
GLENCOE Fulton
GLENWOOD Pike
GOODWIN St. Francis
GOSHEN Washington
GOSNELL Mississippi
GOULD Lincoln
GRADY (71644) Jefferson(68), Lincoln(32)
GRANNIS Polk
GRAPEVINE Grant
GRAVELLY (72838) Yell(75), Scott(25)
GRAVETTE Benton
GREEN FOREST Carroll
GREENBRIER Faulkner
GREENLAND Washington
GREENWAY Clay
GREENWOOD Sebastian
GREGORY Woodruff
GRIFFITHVILLE (72060) White(81), Prairie(19)
GRUBBS Jackson
GUION Izard
GURDON Clark
GUY Faulkner
HACKETT Sebastian
HAGARVILLE (72839) Johnson(95), Pope(5)
HAMBURG Ashley
HAMPTON Calhoun
HARDY (72542) Sharp(89), Fulton(11)
HARRELL Calhoun
HARRIET Searcy
HARRISBURG Poinsett
HARRISON Boone
HARTFORD Sebastian
HARTMAN Johnson
HARVEY (72841) Scott(84), Yell(16)
HASTY Newton
HATFIELD Polk
HATTIEVILLE (72063) Conway(95), Pope(5)
HATTON Polk
HAVANA Yell
HAYNES Lee
HAZEN Prairie
HEBER SPRINGS Cleburne
HECTOR Pope
HELENA Phillips
HENDERSON Baxter
HENSLEY (72065) Saline(83), Pulaski(13), Grant(4)
HERMITAGE Bradley
HETH (72346) St. Francis(94), Cross(6)
HICKORY PLAINS Prairie
HICKORY RIDGE (72347) Cross(86), Jackson(14)
HIGDEN (72067) Cleburne(97), Van Buren(3)
HIGGINSON White
HINDSVILLE (72738) Washington(45), Madison(44), Benton(12)
HIWASSE Benton
HOLLY GROVE Monroe
HOPE Hempstead
HORATIO Sevier
HORSESHOE BEND Izard
HOT SPRINGS NATIONAL PARK Garland
HOT SPRINGS VILLAGE (71909) Garland(77), Saline(24)
HOT SPRINGS VILLAGE Garland
HOUSTON Perry
HOWELL Woodruff
HOXIE Lawrence

HUGHES (72348) St. Francis(79), Crittenden(17), Lee(4)
HUMNOKE (72072) Jefferson(96), Lonoke(4)
HUMPHREY (72073) Arkansas(85), Jefferson(16)
HUNT Johnson
HUNTER Woodruff
HUNTINGTON Sebastian
HUNTSVILLE (72740) Madison(96), Carroll(4)
HUTTIG Union
IDA Cleburne
IMBODEN (72434) Randolph(91), Lawrence(9)
IVAN Dallas
JACKSONPORT Jackson
JACKSONVILLE (72076) Pulaski(95), Lonoke(4)
JACKSONVILLE Pulaski
JASPER Newton
JEFFERSON (72079) Jefferson(94), Grant(6)
JENNIE Chicot
JEROME Drew
JERSEY Bradley
JERUSALEM (72080) Van Buren(55), Conway(32), Pope(14)
JESSIEVILLE Garland
JOHNSON Washington
JOINER Mississippi
JONES MILLS Hot Spring
JONESBORO (72401) Craighead(95), Greene(6)
JONESBORO Craighead
JUDSONIA White
JUNCTION CITY Union
KEISER Mississippi
KENSETT White
KEO Lonoke
KINGSLAND Cleveland
KINGSTON (72742) Madison(73), Newton(27)
KIRBY Pike
KNOBEL (72435) Greene(96), Clay(4)
KNOXVILLE Johnson
LA GRANGE Lee
LAFE Greene
LAKE CITY Craighead
LAKE VILLAGE Chicot
LAKEVIEW Baxter
LAMAR (72846) Johnson(98), Pope(2)
LAMBROOK Phillips
LANEBURG Nevada
LANGLEY Pike
LAVACA Sebastian
LAWSON Union
LEACHVILLE Mississippi
LEAD HILL Boone
LEOLA (72084) Grant(77), Dallas(21), Hot Spring(3)
LEPANTO (72354) Poinsett(75), Mississippi(25)
LESLIE (72645) Searcy(71), Van Buren(22), Stone(6)
LETONA White
LEWISVILLE Lafayette
LEXA (72355) Phillips(94), Lee(6)
LIGHT Greene
LINCOLN Washington
LITTLE ROCK (72206) Pulaski(95), Saline(5)
LITTLE ROCK (72210) Pulaski(91), Saline(10)
LITTLE ROCK Pulaski
LITTLE ROCK AIR FORCE BASE Pulaski
LOCKESBURG Sevier
LOCUST GROVE (72550) Independence(66), Cleburne(34)
LONDON (72847) Pope(90), Johnson(10)
LONOKE Lonoke

LONSDALE (72087) Saline(55), Garland(45)
LOUANN Ouachita
LOWELL Benton
LUXORA Mississippi
LYNN Lawrence
MABELVALE (72103) Saline(79), Pulaski(21)
MADISON St. Francis
MAGAZINE Logan
MAGNESS Independence
MAGNOLIA (71753) Columbia(98), Union(2)
MAGNOLIA Columbia
MALVERN (72104) Hot Spring(96), Saline(4)
MAMMOTH SPRING (72554) Fulton(91), Sharp(9)
MANILA Mississippi
MANSFIELD (72944) Sebastian(60), Scott(40)
MARBLE FALLS Newton
MARCELLA Stone
MARIANNA Lee
MARION Crittenden
MARKED TREE Poinsett
MARMADUKE Greene
MARSHALL (72650) Searcy(96), Stone(4)
MARVELL (72366) Phillips(97), Lee(3)
MAUMELLE Pulaski
MAYFLOWER Faulkner
MAYNARD Randolph
MAYSVILLE Benton
MC CASKILL Hempstead
MC CRORY (72101) Woodruff(69), Jackson(16), White(15)
MC CRORY Woodruff
MC DOUGAL Clay
MC GEHEE Desha
MC NEIL (71752) Columbia(98), Nevada(2)
MC RAE White
MELBOURNE Izard
MELLWOOD Phillips
MENA Polk
MENIFEE Conway
MIDLAND Sebastian
MIDWAY Baxter
MINERAL SPRINGS Howard
MINTURN Lawrence
MOKO Fulton
MONETTE Craighead
MONROE Monroe
MONTICELLO Drew
MONTROSE Ashley
MORO Lee
MORRILTON Conway
MORROW Washington
MOSCOW Jefferson
MOUNT HOLLY Union
MOUNT IDA Montgomery
MOUNT JUDEA Newton
MOUNT PLEASANT Izard
MOUNT VERNON (72111) Faulkner(70), White(30)
MOUNTAIN HOME Baxter
MOUNTAIN PINE Garland
MOUNTAIN VIEW Stone
MOUNTAINBURG Crawford
MULBERRY (72947) Crawford(87), Franklin(13)
MURFREESBORO Pike
NASHVILLE (71852) Howard(91), Hempstead(6), Pike(3)
NATURAL DAM Crawford
NEW BLAINE Logan
NEW EDINBURG (71660) Cleveland(90), Bradley(10)
NEWARK Independence
NEWHOPE (71959) Howard(62), Pike(38)
NEWPORT Jackson
NORFORK Baxter
NORMAN Montgomery

NORPHLET Union
NORTH LITTLE ROCK (72116) Pulaski(97), Faulkner(3)
NORTH LITTLE ROCK Pulaski
O KEAN Randolph
OAK GROVE (72660) Baxter(60), Carroll(40)
OAKLAND Marion
OARK (72852) Newton(50), Johnson(46), Madison(4)
ODEN Montgomery
OGDEN Little River
OIL TROUGH Independence
OKOLONA Clark
OLA (72853) Yell(97), Perry(3)
OMAHA Boone
ONEIDA Phillips
ONIA Stone
OSCEOLA Mississippi
OXFORD Izard
OZAN Hempstead
OZARK (72949) Franklin(98), Johnson(2)
OZONE (72854) Johnson(74), Newton(26)
PALESTINE St. Francis
PANGBURN White
PARAGOULD Greene
PARIS Logan
PARKDALE (71661) Ashley(87), Chicot(14)
PARKIN Cross
PARKS Scott
PARON (72122) Saline(67), Pulaski(33)
PARTHENON Newton
PATTERSON Woodruff
PEA RIDGE Benton
PEACH ORCHARD (72453) Greene(91), Clay(9)
PEARCY (71964) Garland(90), Hot Spring(10)
PEEL Marion
PELSOR (72856) Pope(57), Newton(43)
PENCIL BLUFF Montgomery
PERRY (72125) Conway(52), Perry(48)
PERRYVILLE (72126) Perry(86), Pulaski(14)
PETTIGREW (72752) Madison(87), Johnson(10), Newton(3)
PICKENS (71662) Lincoln(62), Desha(39)
PIGGOTT Clay
PINDALL Searcy
PINE BLUFF (71602) Jefferson(98), Grant(2)
PINE BLUFF Jefferson
PINEVILLE Izard
PLAINVIEW (72857) Yell(64), Perry(37)
PLEASANT GROVE Stone
PLEASANT PLAINS Independence
PLUMERVILLE Conway
POCAHONTAS Randolph
POLLARD Clay
PONCA Newton
POPLAR GROVE Phillips
PORTIA Lawrence
PORTLAND (71663) Ashley(91), Chicot(9)
POTTSVILLE Pope
POUGHKEEPSIE Sharp
POWHATAN Lawrence
POYEN (72128) Grant(99), Hot Spring(1)
PRAIRIE GROVE Washington
PRATTSVILLE Grant
PRESCOTT Nevada
PRIM Cleburne
PROCTOR Crittenden
PYATT Marion
QUITMAN (72131) Cleburne(65), Faulkner(29), Van Buren(5)
RATCLIFF (72951) Logan(85), Franklin(15)
RAVENDEN Lawrence
RAVENDEN SPRINGS Randolph
RECTOR (72461) Clay(90), Greene(10)
REDFIELD (72132) Jefferson(92), Grant(8)
REYDELL Jefferson
REYNO Randolph

RISON Cleveland
RIVERVALE Poinsett
ROE Monroe
ROGERS Benton
ROLAND Pulaski
ROMANCE White
ROSE BUD (72137) White(57), Cleburne(43)
ROSIE Independence
ROSSTON Nevada
ROUND POND St. Francis
ROVER Yell
ROYAL Garland
RUDY Crawford
RUSSELL White
RUSSELLVILLE Pope
SAFFELL (72572) Lawrence(65), Independence(35)
SAGE Izard
SAINT CHARLES Arkansas
SAINT FRANCIS Clay
SAINT JOE (72675) Searcy(79), Marion(21)
SAINT PAUL Madison
SALADO Independence
SALEM (72576) Fulton(99), Izard(1)
SARATOGA Howard
SCOTLAND Van Buren
SCOTT (72142) Pulaski(95), Lonoke(5)
SCRANTON Logan
SEARCY White
SEDGWICK Lawrence
SHERIDAN (72150) Grant(99), Jefferson(1)
SHERRILL Jefferson
SHERWOOD (72120) Pulaski(97), Faulkner(3)
SHIRLEY (72153) Van Buren(93), Cleburne(4), Stone(3)
SIDNEY (72577) Sharp(52), Izard(48)
SILOAM SPRINGS Benton
SIMS Montgomery

SMACKOVER (71762) Union(97), Ouachita(3)
SMITHVILLE Lawrence
SNOW LAKE Desha
SOLGOHACHIA Conway
SPARKMAN (71763) Dallas(72), Ouachita(27), Clark(1)
SPRINGDALE (72762) Washington(95), Benton(5)
SPRINGDALE (72764) Washington(97), Benton(3)
SPRINGDALE Washington
SPRINGFIELD Conway
SPRINGTOWN Benton
STAMPS (71860) Lafayette(90), Columbia(10)
STAR CITY (71667) Lincoln(98), Cleveland(2)
STATE UNIVERSITY Craighead
STEPHENS (71764) Ouachita(56), Columbia(40), Nevada(2), Union(2)
STEPROCK White
STORY Montgomery
STRAWBERRY (72469) Lawrence(97), Sharp(3)
STRONG Union
STURKIE Fulton
STUTTGART Arkansas
SUBIACO Logan
SUCCESS Clay
SULPHUR ROCK Independence
SULPHUR SPRINGS Benton
SUMMERS Washington
SUMMIT Marion
SWEET HOME Pulaski
SWIFTON Jackson
TAYLOR Columbia
TEXARKANA Miller
THIDA Independence
THORNTON Calhoun
TICHNOR Arkansas
TILLAR (71670) Drew(69), Desha(31)

TILLY (72679) Pope(82), Van Buren(15), Searcy(4)
TIMBO Stone
TOMATO Mississippi
TONTITOWN Washington
TRASKWOOD (72167) Saline(89), Hot Spring(7), Grant(5)
TRUMANN Poinsett
TUCKER Jefferson
TUCKERMAN Jackson
TUMBLING SHOALS Cleburne
TUPELO Jackson
TURNER Phillips
TURRELL Crittenden
TWIST Cross
TYRONZA (72386) Poinsett(43), Mississippi(36), Crittenden(22)
ULM Prairie
UMPIRE (71971) Howard(99), Pike(1)
UNIONTOWN Crawford
URBANA Union
VALLEY SPRINGS Boone
VAN BUREN Crawford
VANDERVOORT Polk
VANNDALE Cross
VENDOR Newton
VILLAGE Columbia
VILONIA Faulkner
VIOLA Fulton
VIOLET HILL Izard
WABASH Phillips
WABBASEKA Jefferson
WALCOTT Greene
WALDENBURG Poinsett
WALDO Columbia
WALDRON Scott
WALNUT RIDGE (72476) Lawrence(88), Greene(10), Craighead(3)
WARD (72176) Lonoke(97), Prairie(3)
WARM SPRINGS Randolph
WARREN (71671) Bradley(99), Cleveland(1)

WASHINGTON Hempstead
WATSON Desha
WAVELAND Yell
WEINER (72479) Poinsett(89), Jackson(12)
WESLEY (72773) Madison(94), Washington(7)
WEST FORK Washington
WEST HELENA Phillips
WEST MEMPHIS Crittenden
WEST POINT White
WEST RIDGE Mississippi
WESTERN GROVE (72685) Newton(88), Searcy(8), Boone(4)
WHEATLEY St. Francis
WHEELER Washington
WHELEN SPRINGS Clark
WICKES Polk
WIDEMAN Izard
WIDENER St. Francis
WILBURN Cleburne
WILLIFORD Sharp
WILLISVILLE Nevada
WILMAR (71675) Bradley(64), Drew(33), Lincoln(3)
WILMOT (71676) Ashley(98), Chicot(2)
WILSON Mississippi
WILTON Little River
WINCHESTER Drew
WINSLOW Washington
WINTHROP Little River
WISEMAN Izard
WITTER Madison
WITTS SPRINGS (72686) Searcy(87), Pope(13)
WOODSON Pulaski
WOOSTER Faulkner
WRIGHT Jefferson
WRIGHTSVILLE Pulaski
WYNNE Cross
YELLVILLE Marion
YORKTOWN Lincoln

ZIP/City Cross Reference

71601-71613	PINE BLUFF	71720-71720	BEARDEN	71825-71825	BLEVINS	71909-71910	HOT SPRINGS VILLAGE
71630-71630	ARKANSAS CITY	71721-71721	BEIRNE	71826-71826	BRADLEY	71913-71914	HOT SPRINGS NATIONAL PARK
71631-71631	BANKS	71722-71722	BLUFF CITY	71827-71827	BUCKNER		
71635-71635	CROSSETT	71724-71724	CALION	71828-71828	CALE	71920-71920	ALPINE
71638-71638	DERMOTT	71725-71725	CARTHAGE	71831-71831	COLUMBUS	71921-71921	AMITY
71639-71639	DUMAS	71726-71726	CHIDESTER	71832-71832	DE QUEEN	71922-71922	ANTOINE
71640-71640	EUDORA	71728-71728	CURTIS	71833-71833	DIERKS	71923-71923	ARKADELPHIA
71642-71642	FOUNTAIN HILL	71730-71731	EL DORADO	71834-71834	DODDRIDGE	71929-71929	BISMARCK
71643-71643	GOULD	71740-71740	EMERSON	71835-71835	EMMET	71931-71931	BLAKELY
71644-71644	GRADY	71742-71742	FORDYCE	71836-71836	FOREMAN	71932-71932	BOARD CAMP
71646-71646	HAMBURG	71743-71743	GURDON	71837-71837	FOUKE	71933-71933	BONNERDALE
71647-71647	HERMITAGE	71744-71744	HAMPTON	71838-71838	FULTON	71935-71935	CADDO GAP
71649-71649	JENNIE	71745-71745	HARRELL	71839-71839	GARLAND CITY	71937-71937	COVE
71650-71650	JEROME	71747-71747	HUTTIG	71840-71840	GENOA	71940-71940	DELIGHT
71651-71651	JERSEY	71748-71748	IVAN	71841-71841	GILLHAM	71941-71941	DONALDSON
71652-71652	KINGSLAND	71749-71749	JUNCTION CITY	71842-71842	HORATIO	71942-71942	FRIENDSHIP
71653-71653	LAKE VILLAGE	71750-71750	LAWSON	71844-71844	LANEBURG	71943-71943	GLENWOOD
71654-71654	MC GEHEE	71751-71751	LOUANN	71845-71845	LEWISVILLE	71944-71944	GRANNIS
71655-71657	MONTICELLO	71752-71752	MC NEIL	71846-71846	LOCKESBURG	71945-71945	HATFIELD
71658-71658	MONTROSE	71753-71754	MAGNOLIA	71847-71847	MC CASKILL	71946-71946	HATTON
71659-71659	MOSCOW	71758-71758	MOUNT HOLLY	71851-71851	MINERAL SPRINGS	71949-71949	JESSIEVILLE
71660-71660	NEW EDINBURG	71759-71759	NORPHLET	71852-71852	NASHVILLE	71950-71950	KIRBY
71661-71661	PARKDALE	71762-71762	SMACKOVER	71853-71853	OGDEN	71951-71951	HOT SPRINGS NATIONAL PARK
71662-71662	PICKENS	71763-71763	SPARKMAN	71854-71854	TEXARKANA		
71663-71663	PORTLAND	71764-71764	STEPHENS	71855-71855	OZAN	71952-71952	LANGLEY
71665-71665	RISON	71765-71765	STRONG	71857-71857	PRESCOTT	71953-71953	MENA
71666-71666	MC GEHEE	71766-71766	THORNTON	71858-71858	ROSSTON	71956-71956	MOUNTAIN PINE
71667-71667	STAR CITY	71767-71767	HAMPTON	71859-71859	SARATOGA	71957-71957	MOUNT IDA
71670-71670	TILLAR	71768-71768	URBANA	71860-71860	STAMPS	71958-71958	MURFREESBORO
71671-71671	WARREN	71769-71769	VILLAGE	71861-71861	TAYLOR	71959-71959	NEWHOPE
71674-71674	WATSON	71770-71770	WALDO	71862-71862	WASHINGTON	71960-71960	NORMAN
71675-71675	WILMAR	71772-71772	WHELEN SPRINGS	71864-71864	WILLISVILLE	71961-71961	ODEN
71676-71676	WILMOT	71801-71802	HOPE	71865-71865	WILTON	71962-71962	OKOLONA
71677-71677	WINCHESTER	71820-71820	ALLEENE	71866-71866	WINTHROP	71964-71964	PEARCY
71678-71678	YORKTOWN	71822-71822	ASHDOWN	71901-71903	HOT SPRINGS NATIONAL PARK	71965-71965	PENCIL BLUFF
71701-71711	CAMDEN	71823-71823	BEN LOMOND			71966-71966	ODEN

Zip	Place	Zip	Place	Zip	Place	Zip	Place
71968-71968	ROYAL	72088-72088	FAIRFIELD BAY	72326-72326	COLT	72442-72442	MANILA
71969-71969	SIMS	72089-72089	BRYANT	72327-72327	CRAWFORDSVILLE	72443-72443	MARMADUKE
71970-71970	STORY	72099-72099	LITTLE ROCK AIR	72328-72328	CRUMROD	72444-72444	MAYNARD
71971-71971	UMPIRE		FORCE BASE	72329-72329	DRIVER	72445-72445	MINTURN
71972-71972	VANDERVOORT	72101-72101	MC CRORY	72330-72330	DYESS	72447-72447	MONETTE
71973-71973	WICKES	72102-72102	MC RAE	72331-72331	EARLE	72449-72449	O KEAN
71998-71999	ARKADELPHIA	72103-72103	MABELVALE	72332-72332	EDMONDSON	72450-72451	PARAGOULD
72001-72001	ADONA	72104-72104	MALVERN	72333-72333	ELAINE	72453-72453	PEACH ORCHARD
72002-72002	ALEXANDER	72105-72105	JONES MILLS	72335-72336	FORREST CITY	72454-72454	PIGGOTT
72003-72003	ALMYRA	72106-72106	MAYFLOWER	72338-72338	FRENCHMANS BAYOU	72455-72455	POCAHONTAS
72004-72004	ALTHEIMER	72107-72107	MENIFEE	72339-72339	GILMORE	72456-72456	POLLARD
72005-72005	AMAGON	72108-72108	MONROE	72340-72340	GOODWIN	72457-72457	PORTIA
72006-72006	AUGUSTA	72110-72110	MORRILTON	72341-72341	HAYNES	72458-72458	POWHATAN
72007-72007	AUSTIN	72111-72111	MOUNT VERNON	72342-72342	HELENA	72459-72459	RAVENDEN
72009-72009	BALCH	72112-72112	NEWPORT	72346-72346	HETH	72460-72460	RAVENDEN SPRINGS
72010-72010	BALD KNOB	72113-72113	MAUMELLE	72347-72347	HICKORY RIDGE	72461-72461	RECTOR
72011-72011	BAUXITE	72114-72119	NORTH LITTLE ROCK	72348-72348	HUGHES	72462-72462	REYNO
72012-72012	BEEBE	72120-72120	SHERWOOD	72350-72350	JOINER	72464-72464	SAINT FRANCIS
72013-72013	BEE BRANCH	72121-72121	PANGBURN	72351-72351	KEISER	72465-72465	SEDGWICK
72014-72014	BEEDEVILLE	72122-72122	PARON	72352-72352	LA GRANGE	72466-72466	SMITHVILLE
72015-72015	BENTON	72123-72123	PATTERSON	72353-72353	LAMBROOK	72467-72467	STATE UNIVERSITY
72016-72016	BIGELOW	72124-72124	NORTH LITTLE ROCK	72354-72354	LEPANTO	72469-72469	STRAWBERRY
72017-72017	BISCOE	72125-72125	PERRY	72355-72355	LEXA	72470-72470	SUCCESS
72018-72018	BENTON	72126-72126	PERRYVILLE	72358-72358	LUXORA	72471-72471	SWIFTON
72020-72020	BRADFORD	72127-72127	PLUMERVILLE	72359-72359	MADISON	72472-72472	TRUMANN
72021-72021	BRINKLEY	72128-72128	POYEN	72360-72360	MARIANNA	72473-72473	TUCKERMAN
72022-72022	BRYANT	72129-72129	PRATTSVILLE	72364-72364	MARION	72474-72474	WALCOTT
72023-72023	CABOT	72130-72130	PRIM	72365-72365	MARKED TREE	72475-72475	WALDENBURG
72024-72024	CARLISLE	72131-72131	QUITMAN	72366-72366	MARVELL	72476-72476	WALNUT RIDGE
72025-72025	CASA	72132-72132	REDFIELD	72367-72367	MELLWOOD	72478-72478	WARM SPRINGS
72026-72026	CASSCOE	72133-72133	REYDELL	72368-72368	MORO	72479-72479	WEINER
72027-72027	CENTER RIDGE	72134-72134	ROE	72369-72369	ONEIDA	72482-72482	WILLIFORD
72028-72028	CHOCTAW	72135-72135	ROLAND	72370-72370	OSCEOLA	72501-72503	BATESVILLE
72029-72029	CLARENDON	72136-72136	ROMANCE	72372-72372	PALESTINE	72512-72512	HORSESHOE BEND
72030-72030	CLEVELAND	72137-72137	ROSE BUD	72373-72373	PARKIN	72513-72513	ASH FLAT
72031-72031	CLINTON	72139-72139	RUSSELL	72374-72374	POPLAR GROVE	72515-72515	BEXAR
72032-72035	CONWAY	72140-72140	SAINT CHARLES	72376-72376	PROCTOR	72516-72516	BOSWELL
72036-72036	COTTON PLANT	72141-72141	SCOTLAND	72377-72377	RIVERVALE	72517-72517	BROCKWELL
72037-72037	COY	72142-72142	SCOTT	72379-72379	SNOW LAKE	72519-72519	CALICO ROCK
72038-72038	CROCKETTS BLUFF	72143-72149	SEARCY	72381-72381	TOMATO	72520-72520	CAMP
72039-72039	DAMASCUS	72150-72150	SHERIDAN	72383-72383	TURNER	72521-72521	CAVE CITY
72040-72040	DES ARC	72152-72152	SHERRILL	72384-72384	TURRELL	72522-72522	CHARLOTTE
72041-72041	DE VALLS BLUFF	72153-72153	SHIRLEY	72385-72385	TWIST	72523-72523	CONCORD
72042-72042	DE WITT	72156-72156	SOLGOHACHIA	72386-72386	TYRONZA	72524-72524	CORD
72043-72043	DIAZ	72157-72157	SPRINGFIELD	72387-72387	VANNDALE	72525-72525	CHEROKEE VILLAGE
72044-72044	EDGEMONT	72158-72158	BENTON	72389-72389	WABASH	72526-72526	CUSHMAN
72045-72045	EL PASO	72159-72159	STEPROCK	72390-72390	WEST HELENA	72527-72527	DESHA
72046-72046	ENGLAND	72160-72160	STUTTGART	72391-72391	WEST RIDGE	72528-72528	DOLPH
72047-72047	ENOLA	72164-72164	SWEET HOME	72392-72392	WHEATLEY	72529-72529	CHEROKEE VILLAGE
72048-72048	ETHEL	72165-72165	THIDA	72394-72394	WIDENER	72530-72530	DRASCO
72051-72051	FOX	72166-72166	TICHNOR	72395-72395	WILSON	72531-72531	ELIZABETH
72052-72052	GARNER	72167-72167	TRASKWOOD	72396-72397	WYNNE	72532-72532	EVENING SHADE
72053-72053	COLLEGE STATION	72168-72168	TUCKER	72401-72404	JONESBORO	72533-72533	FIFTY SIX
72055-72055	GILLETT	72169-72169	TUPELO	72410-72410	ALICIA	72534-72534	FLORAL
72057-72057	GRAPEVINE	72170-72170	ULM	72411-72411	BAY	72536-72536	FRANKLIN
72058-72058	GREENBRIER	72173-72173	VILONIA	72412-72412	BEECH GROVE	72537-72537	GAMALIEL
72059-72059	GREGORY	72175-72175	WABBASEKA	72413-72413	BIGGERS	72538-72538	GEPP
72060-72060	GRIFFITHVILLE	72176-72176	WARD	72414-72414	BLACK OAK	72539-72539	GLENCOE
72061-72061	GUY	72178-72178	WEST POINT	72415-72415	BLACK ROCK	72540-72540	GUION
72063-72063	HATTIEVILLE	72179-72179	WILBURN	72416-72416	BONO	72542-72542	HARDY
72064-72064	HAZEN	72180-72180	WOODSON	72417-72417	BROOKLAND	72543-72543	HEBER SPRINGS
72065-72065	HENSLEY	72181-72181	WOOSTER	72419-72419	CARAWAY	72544-72544	HENDERSON
72066-72066	HICKORY PLAINS	72182-72182	WRIGHT	72421-72421	CASH	72545-72545	HEBER SPRINGS
72067-72067	HIGDEN	72183-72183	WRIGHTSVILLE	72422-72422	CORNING	72546-72546	IDA
72068-72068	HIGGINSON	72189-72189	MC CRORY	72424-72424	DATTO	72550-72550	LOCUST GROVE
72069-72069	HOLLY GROVE	72190-72199	NORTH LITTLE ROCK	72425-72425	DELAPLAINE	72553-72553	MAGNESS
72070-72070	HOUSTON	72201-72207	LITTLE ROCK	72426-72426	DELL	72554-72554	MAMMOTH SPRING
72071-72071	HOWELL	72208-72208	FERNDALE	72427-72427	EGYPT	72555-72555	MARCELLA
72072-72072	HUMNOKE	72209-72295	LITTLE ROCK	72428-72428	ETOWAH	72556-72556	MELBOURNE
72073-72073	HUMPHREY	72301-72303	WEST MEMPHIS	72429-72429	FISHER	72557-72557	MOKO
72074-72074	HUNTER	72310-72310	ARMOREL	72430-72430	GREENWAY	72560-72560	MOUNTAIN VIEW
72075-72075	JACKSONPORT	72311-72311	AUBREY	72431-72431	GRUBBS	72561-72561	MOUNT PLEASANT
72076-72078	JACKSONVILLE	72312-72312	BARTON	72432-72432	HARRISBURG	72562-72562	NEWARK
72079-72079	JEFFERSON	72313-72313	BASSETT	72433-72433	HOXIE	72564-72564	OIL TROUGH
72080-72080	JERUSALEM	72314-72314	BIRDEYE	72434-72434	IMBODEN	72565-72565	OXFORD
72081-72081	JUDSONIA	72315-72316	BLYTHEVILLE	72435-72435	KNOBEL	72566-72566	PINEVILLE
72082-72082	KENSETT	72319-72319	GOSNELL	72436-72436	LAFE	72567-72567	PLEASANT GROVE
72083-72083	KEO	72320-72320	BRICKEYS	72437-72437	LAKE CITY	72568-72568	PLEASANT PLAINS
72084-72084	LEOLA	72321-72321	BURDETTE	72438-72438	LEACHVILLE	72569-72569	POUGHKEEPSIE
72085-72085	LETONA	72322-72322	CALDWELL	72439-72439	LIGHT	72571-72571	ROSIE
72086-72086	LONOKE	72324-72324	CHERRY VALLEY	72440-72440	LYNN	72572-72572	SAFFELL
72087-72087	LONSDALE	72325-72325	CLARKEDALE	72441-72441	MC DOUGAL	72573-72573	SAGE

72575-72575	SALADO	72660-72660	OAK GROVE	72745-72745	LOWELL	72853-72853	OLA
72576-72576	SALEM	72661-72661	OAKLAND	72747-72747	MAYSVILLE	72854-72854	OZONE
72577-72577	SIDNEY	72662-72662	OMAHA	72749-72749	MORROW	72855-72855	PARIS
72578-72578	STURKIE	72663-72663	ONIA	72751-72751	PEA RIDGE	72856-72856	PELSOR
72579-72579	SULPHUR ROCK	72666-72666	PARTHENON	72752-72752	PETTIGREW	72857-72857	PLAINVIEW
72581-72581	TUMBLING SHOALS	72668-72668	PEEL	72753-72753	PRAIRIE GROVE	72858-72858	POTTSVILLE
72583-72583	VIOLA	72669-72669	PINDALL	72756-72758	ROGERS	72860-72860	ROVER
72584-72584	VIOLET HILL	72670-72670	PONCA	72760-72760	SAINT PAUL	72863-72863	SCRANTON
72585-72585	WIDEMAN	72672-72672	PYATT	72761-72761	SILOAM SPRINGS	72865-72865	SUBIACO
72587-72587	WISEMAN	72675-72675	SAINT JOE	72762-72766	SPRINGDALE	72867-72867	WAVELAND
72601-72602	HARRISON	72677-72677	SUMMIT	72767-72767	SPRINGTOWN	72901-72919	FORT SMITH
72610-72610	ALCO	72679-72679	TILLY	72768-72768	SULPHUR SPRINGS	72921-72921	ALMA
72611-72611	ALPENA	72680-72680	TIMBO	72769-72769	SUMMERS	72923-72923	BARLING
72612-72612	BASS	72682-72682	VALLEY SPRINGS	72770-72770	TONTITOWN	72924-72924	BATES
72613-72613	BEAVER	72683-72683	VENDOR	72773-72773	WESLEY	72926-72926	BOLES
72615-72615	BERGMAN	72685-72685	WESTERN GROVE	72774-72774	WEST FORK	72927-72927	BOONEVILLE
72616-72616	BERRYVILLE	72686-72686	WITTS SPRINGS	72776-72776	WITTER	72928-72928	BRANCH
72617-72617	BIG FLAT	72687-72687	YELLVILLE	72801-72812	RUSSELLVILLE	72930-72930	CECIL
72619-72619	BULL SHOALS	72701-72704	FAYETTEVILLE	72820-72820	ALIX	72932-72932	CEDARVILLE
72623-72623	CLARKRIDGE	72711-72711	AVOCA	72821-72821	ALTUS	72933-72933	CHARLESTON
72624-72624	COMPTON	72712-72712	BENTONVILLE	72822-72823	ATKINS	72934-72934	CHESTER
72626-72626	COTTER	72714-72715	BELLA VISTA	72824-72824	BELLEVILLE	72935-72935	DYER
72628-72628	DEER	72716-72716	BENTONVILLE	72826-72826	BLUE MOUNTAIN	72936-72936	GREENWOOD
72629-72629	DENNARD	72717-72717	CANEHILL	72827-72827	BLUFFTON	72937-72937	HACKETT
72630-72630	DIAMOND CITY	72718-72718	CAVE SPRINGS	72828-72828	BRIGGSVILLE	72938-72938	HARTFORD
72631-72632	EUREKA SPRINGS	72719-72719	CENTERTON	72829-72829	CENTERVILLE	72940-72940	HUNTINGTON
72633-72633	EVERTON	72721-72721	COMBS	72830-72830	CLARKSVILLE	72941-72941	LAVACA
72634-72634	FLIPPIN	72722-72722	DECATUR	72832-72832	COAL HILL	72943-72943	MAGAZINE
72635-72635	GASSVILLE	72727-72727	ELKINS	72833-72833	DANVILLE	72944-72944	MANSFIELD
72636-72636	GILBERT	72728-72728	ELM SPRINGS	72834-72834	DARDANELLE	72945-72945	MIDLAND
72638-72638	GREEN FOREST	72729-72729	EVANSVILLE	72835-72835	DELAWARE	72946-72946	MOUNTAINBURG
72639-72639	HARRIET	72730-72730	FARMINGTON	72837-72837	DOVER	72947-72947	MULBERRY
72640-72640	HASTY	72732-72732	GARFIELD	72838-72838	GRAVELLY	72948-72948	NATURAL DAM
72641-72641	JASPER	72733-72733	GATEWAY	72839-72839	HAGARVILLE	72949-72949	OZARK
72642-72642	LAKEVIEW	72734-72734	GENTRY	72840-72840	HARTMAN	72950-72950	PARKS
72644-72644	LEAD HILL	72735-72735	GOSHEN	72841-72841	HARVEY	72951-72951	RATCLIFF
72645-72645	LESLIE	72736-72736	GRAVETTE	72842-72842	HAVANA	72952-72952	RUDY
72648-72648	MARBLE FALLS	72737-72737	GREENLAND	72843-72843	HECTOR	72955-72955	UNIONTOWN
72650-72650	MARSHALL	72738-72738	HINDSVILLE	72844-72844	HUNT	72956-72957	VAN BUREN
72651-72651	MIDWAY	72739-72739	HIWASSE	72845-72845	KNOXVILLE	72958-72958	WALDRON
72653-72654	MOUNTAIN HOME	72740-72740	HUNTSVILLE	72846-72846	LAMAR	72959-72959	WINSLOW
72655-72655	MOUNT JUDEA	72741-72741	JOHNSON	72847-72847	LONDON		
72657-72657	TIMBO	72742-72742	KINGSTON	72851-72851	NEW BLAINE		
72658-72659	NORFORK	72744-72744	LINCOLN	72852-72852	OARK		

California

General Help Numbers:

Governor's Office
State Capitol, 1st Floor
Sacramento, CA 95814
http://www.governor.ca.gov/state
/govsite/gov_homepage.jsp

916-445-2841
Fax 916-445-4633
8:30AM-5PM

Attorney General's Office
Justice Department
PO Box 944255
Sacramento, CA 94244-2550
http://caag.state.ca.us

916-445-9555
Fax 916-324-5205
8AM-5PM

State Court Administrator
455 Golden Gate Ave
San Francisco, CA 94102-3660
http://www.courtinfo.ca.gov

415-865-4200
Fax 415-865-4205
8AM-5PM

State Archives
1020 "O" St
Sacramento, CA 95814
http://www.ss.ca.gov/archives/
archives.htm

916-653-7715
Fax 916-653-7363
9:30AM-4PM

State Specifics:

Capital: Sacramento
                              Sacramento County

Time Zone: PST

Number of Counties: 58

Population: 33,871,648

Web Site: http://www.state.ca.us/state/
                    portal/myca_homepage.jsp

State Agencies

Criminal Records
Access to Records is Restricted
Department of Justice, PO Box 903417, Sacramento, CA 94203-4170 (Courier: 4949 Broadway, Sacramento, CA 95820); 916-227-3460, 916-227-3849 (General Information), 916-227-3812 (Sealing & Dismissal), 916-227-3315 (Criminal record purges), 8AM-5PM.

http://www.caag.state.ca.us

Note: Penal Code section 11105 prohibits person who are not the subject of the report, or who are not law enforcement officers acting in their capacity, to obtain copies of criminal history records. The person of record can get his/her own information. Certain other authorized persons may include county agencies, adoption agencies, public schools.

Corporation Records
Limited Liability Company Records
Limited Partnerships
Limited Liability Partnerships,
Secretary of State, Information Retrieval/ Certification Unit, 1500 11th Street, 3rd Fl, Sacramento, CA 95814; 916-657-5448 (Corps), 916-653-3794 (LLCs), 916-653-3365 (Partnerships), 8AM-4:30PM.

http://www.ss.ca.gov

Indexing & Storage: New records are available for inquiry immediately. Records are indexed on microfiche, inhouse computer.

Searching: Include the following in your request-full name of business. In addition to the articles of incorporation, corporation records include the following information: Statement of Officers, (up to 2), Prior (merged) or amended names, Inactive names and Reserved names.

Access by: mail, phone, fax, in person, online.

Fee & Payment: Statement of Officers is $5.00 uncertified, $10.00 certified; status report $4.00; articles of incorporation and amendments $1.00 for the first page and $.50 for each additional page, plus $5.00 for certification. Add $5.00 to have copies faxed. Fee payee: Secretary of State. Prepayment required. Personal checks accepted. No credit cards accepted.

Mail search: Turnaround time: 2 to 3 weeks. A self addressed stamped envelope is requested.

Phone search: Only pre-approved accounts have telephone access to corporate status and name availability/reservation.

Fax search: Return of documents and/or status information is $5.00 per name.

In person search: Turnaround time is while you wait if search not extensive.

Online search: The web site offers access to more than 2 million records including corporation, LLC, LP and LLP. Information available includes status, file number, date of filing and agent for service of process. Please note the file is updated weekly (not daily).

Assumed Name
Fictitious Name
Records not maintained by a state level agency.

Note: Records are found at the county level.

Trademarks/Servicemarks
Limited Partnership Records

Secretary of State, Trademark Unit, 1500 11th Street, Rm 345, Sacramento, CA 95814; 916-653-4984 (Trademark/Servicemarks), 916-653-3365 (Partnership Information), 8AM-5PM.

http://www.ss.ca.gov

Indexing & Storage: Records are available for active and expired records. Records are indexed on index cards.

Searching: Include the following in your request-trademark/servicemark name. Information returned includes name of trademark, name of owner and address, and date of filing.

Access by: mail, phone, in person.

Fee & Payment: Copies are $1.00 per page, certification is $5.00 per document. Fee payee: Secretary of State. Prepayment required. Personal checks accepted. No credit cards accepted.

Mail search: Turnaround time: 2 to 3 weeks. A self addressed stamped envelope is requested. No fee for mail request.

Phone search: No fee for telephone request. There is a limit of 2 searches per call.

In person search: There is a special handling fee of $6.00. You can wait for results. If lists are presented, then the results are returned by mail.

Other access: Annual contracts are available to purchase the entire database. The price is $3,000.

Uniform Commercial Code
Federal Tax Liens
State Tax Liens

UCC Division, Secretary of State, PO Box 942835, Sacramento, CA 94235-0001 (Courier: 1500 11th St, 2nd Fl, Sacramento, CA 95814); 916-653-3516, 8AM-5PM.

http://www.ss.ca.gov

Note: This office does not currently offer fax service, but may make it available in the near future.

Indexing & Storage: Records are available for current records and expired records up to 1 year after lapse. There is an index on computer dating back to 1965. Records are indexed on inhouse computer.

Searching: Use search request form UCC-11; one form per debtor name. The search includes federal and some state tax liens on businesses. Federal tax liens on individuals are filed at the county level, state tax liens are filed at either location. Include the following in your request-debtor name.

Access by: mail, in person, online.

Fee & Payment: The search fee is $10.00 per debtor name. The copy fee is $1.00 for the first page of the document and $.50 each additional page. Fee payee: Secretary of State. Prepayment required. Credit cards are only for over-the-counter services. Those conducting business frequently with this office may utilize a prepaid account option. Personal checks accepted. Credit cards accepted: MasterCard, Visa.

Mail search: Records are available by mail.

In person search: There is an additional $6.00 special handling fee for each document received over the counter.

Online search: Direct Access provides dial-up searching via PC and modem. Fees range from $1-3 dollars, depending on type of search. Each page scroll is $.25. Requesters operate from a prepaid account.

Sales Tax Registrations

Board of Equalization, Sales and Use Tax Department, PO Box 942879, Sacramento, CA 94279-0001; 916-445-6362, 800-400-7115 (In California Only), 916-324-4433 (Fax), 8AM-5PM.

http://www.boe.ca.gov

Note: District Offices include: Oakland, 510-286-0347; Sacramento, 916-255-3350; San Diego, 619-525-4526; San Jose, 408-277-1231; Orange County, 714-558-4059; Van Nuys, 818-904-2300; Norwalk, 562-466-1694; Torrance, 310-516-4300; Riverside, 909-680-6400.

Searching: This Board will provide owners' name, firm name, business address, account number, starting date, whether account is active or closed and, if closed, the closing date. The responsibility of assisting taxpayers in verifying the validity of resale certificates is primarily at the District level, but this office will provide search services. Requesters must provide the name of the business, its location, and the permit #.

Access by: mail, phone, fax.

Fee & Payment: No charge is required for verification of resale certificates and permits.

However, a fee for other requests, such as those received from attorneys and collection agencies, is $3.00 per name searched. Fee payee: Board of Equalization. Prepayment required. Monthly billing is available for ongoing requesters. Personal checks accepted. No credit cards accepted.

Mail search: Turnaround time: 2 weeks. A self addressed stamped envelope is requested.

Phone search: No fee for telephone request. Phone service is offered to verify a seller's permit is valid. Calls are limited to three requests.

Fax search: Generally, turnaround time is 2 weeks.

Other access: Lists are available for a fee sorted in a number of ways, including CA Industry Code. For further information and fees, call the Technical Services Division at 916-323-1088.

Birth Certificates

State Department of Health Svcs, Office of Vital Records, PO Box 730241, Sacramento, CA 94244-0241 (Courier: 304 S Street, Sacramento, CA 95814); 916-445-2684 (Recording), 916-445-1719 (Attendant), 800-858-5553 (Fax), 8AM-4:30PM.

http://www.dhs.ca.gov/chs

Indexing & Storage: Records are available from July 1905 on. It takes 1 to 3 months before new records are available for inquiry. Records are indexed on microfiche, inhouse computer.

Searching: Include the following in your request-full name, mother's full maiden name, date of birth, place of birth, father's full name is optional. If you do not use their form, the search can take up to 7 weeks.

Access by: mail, fax, in person, online.

Fee & Payment: The fee for a certified copy is $12.00, if the birth date is not known, a fee of $12.00 is charged for each decade searched. Fee payee: Office of Vital Records. Prepayment required. Personal checks accepted. Credit cards accepted: MasterCard, Visa, AmEx, Discover.

Mail search: Turnaround time: within 1 month. Always include your daytime phone number.No self addressed stamped envelope is required.

Fax search: There is an additional $7.00 fee for faxing and use of a credit card. Turnaround time is about 3 weeks.

In person search: Turnaround time is 3 weeks.

Online search: Birth records from 1905-1995 can be accessed at http://userdb.rootsweb.com/ca/birth/search.cgi. The site is maintained by a private entity, but the data is provided by this agency.

Expedited service: Expedited service is available for mail, phone and fax searches. Turnaround time: 1 day. Add $11.25 per package. You may send request by special mail (express, registered, etc.) and mark "urgent."

Death Records

State Department of Health Svcs, Office of Vital Records, PO Box 730241, Sacramento, CA 94244-0241 (Courier: 304 S Street, Sacramento, CA 95814); 916-445-2684, 916-445-1719 (Attendant), 800-858-5553 (Fax), 8AM-4:30PM.

http://www.dhs.ca.gov/chs

Indexing & Storage: Records are available from July 1905 to present. It takes 1 to 2 months before new records are available for inquiry. Records are indexed on microfiche, inhouse computer.

Searching: Include the following in your request- full name, date of death, date of birth, place of death, Social Security Number. There will be a 2-3 week delay if you do not use their form.

Access by: mail, fax, in person.

Fee & Payment: Search fee is $8.00 per name for each decade searched. Fee payee: Office of Vital Records. Prepayment required. Personal checks accepted. Credit cards accepted: MasterCard, Visa, AmEx, Discover.

Mail search: Turnaround time: within 1 month.

Fax search: There is an extra $7.00 fee, a credit card must be used. Turnaround time is 3 weeks.

In person search: Turnaround time is 3 weeks.

Expedited service: Expedited service is available for mail, phone and fax searches. Turnaround time: 1 day. Add $11.25 per package. Send request by special mail (express, registered, etc.) and mark "urgent."

Marriage Certificates

State Department of Health Svcs, Office of Vital Records, PO Box 730241, Sacramento, CA 94244-0241 (Courier: 304 S Street, Sacramento, CA 95814); 916-445-2684, 916-445-1719 (Attendant), 800-858-5553 (Fax), 8AM-4:30PM.

http://www.dhs.ca.gov/chs

Note: Records between 1986 and 1997 must be searched at the county level (state does not have access to these records).

Indexing & Storage: Records are available from July 1905 to March 1986 and 1998 forward. Records are indexed on microfiche.

Searching: Include the following in your request- names of husband and wife, date of marriage, place or county of marriage.

Access by: mail, fax, in person.

Fee & Payment: Search fee is $12.00 per name for each decade searched. Fee payee: Office of Vital Records. Prepayment required. Personal checks accepted. Credit cards accepted: MasterCard, Visa, AmEx, Discover.

Mail search: Turnaround time: within 1 month. No self addressed stamped envelope is required.

Fax search: There is an extra fee of $7.00 for use of fax and credit card.

In person search: Turnaround time 3 weeks.

Expedited service: Expedited service is available for mail, phone and fax searches. Turnaround time: 1 day. Add $11.25 per package. Send request by special mail (express, registered, etc.) and mark "urgent."

Divorce Records

State Department of Health Svcs, Office of Vital Records, PO Box 730241, Sacramento, CA 94244-0241 (Courier: 304 S Street, Sacramento, CA 95814); 916-445-2684, 916-445-1719 (Attendant), 800-858-5553 (Fax), 8AM-4:30PM.

http://www.dhs.ca.gov/chs

Indexing & Storage: Records are available from 1962 to 1984 for certificate of record only. All divorce records are found at the country court issuing the decree. Records are indexed on microfiche.

Searching: Include the following in your request- names of husband and wife, place of divorce, date of divorce.

Access by: mail, fax, in person.

Fee & Payment: Search fee is $12.00 per name for decade searched. Fee payee: Office of Vital Records. Prepayment required. Personal checks accepted. Credit cards accepted: MasterCard, Visa, AmEx, Discover.

Mail search: Turnaround time: within 1 month. No self addressed stamped envelope is required.

Fax search: There is an additional $7.00 fee for faxing and using a credit card.

Expedited service: Expedited service is available for mail, phone and fax searches. Turnaround time: 1 day. Add $11.25 per package. Send request by special mail (express, registered, etc.) and mark "urgent."

Workers' Compensation Records

Division of Workers' Compensation, Headquarters, PO Box 420603, San Francisco, CA 94142 (Courier: 455 Golden Gate Ave, 9th Fl, San Francisco, CA 94102); 415-703-4600, 415-703-4717 (Fax), 8AM-5PM.

http://www.dir.ca.gov/dwc/dwc_home_page.htm

Note: Per law, no addresses of any injured workers are given out.

Indexing & Storage: Records are available for varying periods depending on injury.

Searching: Using the proper forms, one can either view a file or ask if records exist. This authorization process does not require the signature or approval of the claimant. Forms may be faxed. All forms must be obtained from this agency and require approval before a searcher can present a request at the district office.

Access by: mail, fax, in person.

Fee & Payment: There is no search fee.

Mail search: Turnaround time: variable. You must use "Request for WCAB Case # Search Form" and the agency will let you know if there is a record. The state suggests that out-of-state requesters use a local CA retriever who already has the necessary authorization to search.No self addressed stamped envelope is required.

Fax search: Turnaround is usually 1 week.

In person search: Requester must be authorized first (by this office) with either the "Request to View a WCAB Case File" or "Request for DWC Authorization # for Access to Index Cards." Then, with a case number, requester can visit any of the 25 district offices.

Driver Records

Department of Motor Vehicles, Information Services, PO Box 944247, Mail Station G199, Sacramento, CA 94244-2470; 916-657-8098, 916-657-6525 (Driver Licensing), 8AM-5PM.

http://www.dmv.ca.gov

Note: Non-commercial requesters are known as "casual requesters." These requests are held for 10 days while the state notifies the licensee who can then deny the release. If released, address is shielded. Copies of tickets are not available at the state level.

Indexing & Storage: Records are available for 3 years for accidents and minor moving violations, 4

years for fatal accidents and major violations, and 10 years for DWIs. It takes 10 days or more before new records are available for inquiry. Records are normally destroyed after the Director determines they are no longer necessary to retain.

Searching: Commercial requesters/users who meet certain criteria must maintain a Commercial Requester Account, which may require a $50,000 bond if confidential address information is released. For more information about a Requester Account call (916) 657-5564. Include the following in your request-driver's license number, full name, date of birth. The following data is not released: mental health records, medical records, pending records, residence addresses and Social Security Numbers.

Access by: mail, phone, in person, online.

Fee & Payment: Searches-driver record by name and license #, full name and DOB-$5.00; Driver record by magnetic tape-name and license #-$2.00; full name and DOB-$4.00; guarantor's signature-$20.00; license status only $1.00. Fee payee: California Department of Motor Vehicles. Prepayment required. Personal checks accepted. No credit cards accepted.

Mail search: Turnaround time: 2 to 3 days. Individuals mailing any request forms may be subject to a 10 day delay due to a notice to subject(s) of the record request.

Phone search: However, records are only released to the subject. Call 916-657-6525.

In person search: Commercial Requester Account Holders receive same-day service on up to 8 items, next day service for 9 or more items.

Online search: The department offers online access, but a $10,000 one-time setup fee is required. The system is open 24 hours, 7 days a week. For more information call (916) 657-5582.

Other access: Access by magnetic tape is available for high volume requesters.

Vehicle Ownership
Vehicle Identification
Vessel Ownership
Vessel Registration

Department of Motor Vehicle, Public Contact Unit, PO Box 944247, MS-G199, Sacramento, CA 94244-2470; 916-657-8098 (Walk-in/Mail-in Phone), 916-657-7914 (Commercial Accounts), 916-657-6739 (Vessel Registration), 916-657-5583 (Fax), 8AM-5PM.

http://www.dmv.ca.gov

Indexing & Storage: Records are available for three years. Beyond that, a subpoena is required. Hardcopy and microfilmed records date back to 1976. All watercraft must be registered if over 8 ft (except rowboats).

Searching: It is suggested to use departmental forms, which can be obtained from the Forms Management Unit, PO Box 932382, Sacramento, 94232-3820 or fax request to 916-657-7243. There are two types of requesters: "casual requesters" and "requester account holders." For those businesses and entities who need to access on a regular basis, call 916-657-5564.

Access by: mail, phone, in person, online.

Fee & Payment: Current record by license, VIN or CR#, by registration owner name and address-$5.00; magnetic tape inquiry-$2.00; owner as of data by license, VIN or CR#-$5.00; current automated history data-$5.00; photocopies-$20.00. Fee payee: California Department of Motor Vehicles. Prepayment required. Personal checks accepted. No credit cards accepted.

Mail search: Turnaround time: 1 to 3 days. A self addressed stamped envelope is requested.

Phone search: Phone requesters must be pre-approved and are limited to 7 verbal responses. Hours of operation are 7 AM to 6 PM. The phone number is (916) 657-7914.

In person search: Same day service is available for up to 15 items requested. Same day service is not extended to photo history or ANI edit lists.

Online search: Online access is limited to certain Authorized Vendors. Hours are 6 AM to midnight. Requesters are may not use the data for direct marketing, solicitation, nor resell for those purposes. A bond is required and very high fees are involved. For more information, call Sue Jefferson at 916-657-5582.

Other access: California offers delivery of registration information on magnetic tape, disk or paper within special parameters. Release of information is denied for commercial marketing purposes.

Accident Reports

Department of Motor Vehicles, Accident Reports, PO Box 942884, Sacramento, CA 9.

http://www.dmv.ca.gov

Note: Most accident reports are held by the California Highway Patrol or local law enforcement agency that filed the report. There are 115 area offices of the California Highway Patrol. Fees vary.

Access by:.

Fee & Payment: Copies of SR-1 accident reports are provided to limited requesters by the Department of Motor Vehicles, PO Box 942884,

Sacramento 94284-0001. The fee is $20. Records are available by mail.

Legislation Records

California State Legislature, State Capitol, Room B-32 (Legislative Bill Room), Sacramento, CA 95814, 916-445-2323 (Current/Pending Bills), 916-653-7715 (State Archives), 8AM-5PM.

http://www.leginfo.ca.gov

Note: This office carries only latest amended versions (last 2 years). The agency recommends that any California law library would have complete copies of all bills for other years and may be easier to search.

Indexing & Storage: Records are available from 1997 to present here and from 1976 in the Archives.

Searching: Include the following in your request-bill number, year.

Access by: mail, phone, in person, online.

Fee & Payment: There is no charge for up to 5 bills. They will compute copy charges, if needed. Fee payee: Legislative Bill Room. Personal checks accepted. No credit cards accepted.

Mail search: Turnaround time: 5 to 7 days. You must first know what the copies will be prior to ordering.

Phone search: You may call for bill copies.

In person search: You may request copies in person.

Online search: The Internet site has all legislative information back to 1993. The site also gives access to state laws.

Voter Registration

Access to Records is Restricted

Secretary of State, Elections Division, 1500 11th Street, Sacramento, CA 95814; 916-657-2166, 916-653-3214 (Fax), 8AM-5PM.

Note: Records are not open and cannot be viewed at this agency. Individual verification must be done at the local level. The state will sell all or portions of the statewide database for political or pre-approved purposes. Call 916-653-6224 for details.

GED Certificates

Dept of Education, State GED Office, PO Box 710273, Sacramento, CA 94244-0273; 916-651-6623, 800-331-6316.

http://cde.ca.gov/ged

Searching: To verify or to obtain a copy of a transcript, all of the following is required: a signed release, name, date of birth, date/year of test, Social Security Number, and city of test.

Access by: mail.

Fee & Payment: There is no fee for verifications or transcripts.

Mail search: Turnaround time is 7-10 working days or 2-3 weeks if the information is older than 1990. No self addressed stamped envelope is required.

Hunting License Information
Fishing License Information

Access to Records is Restricted

Department of Fish & Game, License & Revenue Branch, 3211 "S" St, Sacramento, CA 95816; 916-227-2245, 916-227-2261 (Fax), 8AM-5PM.

http://www.dfg.ca.gov

Note: Records are not available to the public.

California State Licensing Agencies

Licenses Searchable Online

Air Conditioning Contractor #28 .... www.cslb.ca.gov/license+request.html
Alarm Company #22 .... www.dca.ca.gov/bsis/lookup.htm
Alarm Company Employee/Manager #22 .... www.dca.ca.gov/bsis/lookup.htm
Animal Health Technician #40 .... www.vmb.ca.gov/2licensg/lic1list.htm
Architect #07 .... www.cab.ca.gov/Templates/querysearch.cfm
Athletic Event Manager/Promoter/Matchmaker #03 .. www.dca.ca.gov/csac/directories.htm
Attorney #23 .... www.calsb.org/MM/SBMBRSHP.HTM
Automobile Dealer/Repair #19 .... www.smogcheck.ca.gov/stdhome.asp
Bank #11 .... www.sbd.ca.gov/directry/db.asp
Baton Training Facility/Instructor #22 .... www.dca.ca.gov/bsis/lookup.htm
Boiler, Hot Water & Steam Fitting #28 .... www.cslb.ca.gov/license+request.html
Boxer #03 .... www.dca.ca.gov/csac/directories.htm
Brake & Lamp Adjuster #19 .... www.smogcheck.ca.gov/stdhome.asp
Brake Station #19 .... www.smogcheck.ca.gov/stdhome.asp
Building Contractor, General-Class B #28 .... www.cslb.ca.gov/license+request.html
Building Moving/Demolition #28 .... www.cslb.ca.gov/license+request.html
Cabinet & Millwork #28 .... www.cslb.ca.gov/license+request.html
Cemetery, Cemetery Broker/Sales Agent #25 .... www.dca.ca.gov/cemetery/lookup.htm
Clinic Pharmaceutical Permit #13 .... www.pharmacy.ca.gov/license_lookup.htm
Concrete Contractor/Company #28 .... www.cslb.ca.gov/license+request.html
Continuing Education Providers #08 .... www.bbs.ca.gov/weblokup.htm
Contractor #46 .... www.cslb.ca.gov
Court Reporter (Certified Shorthand Reporter) #29 ... www.courtreportersboard.ca.gov
Credit Union #11 .... www.sbd.ca.gov/directry/cu.asp
Cremated Remains Disposer #25 .... www.dca.ca.gov/cemetery/lookup.htm
Crematory #25 .... www.dca.ca.gov/cemetery/lookup.htm
Dental Assistant/ Extended Function Assistant #27 .. www.dbc.ca.gov/License.html
Dental Hygienist #27 .... www.dbc.ca.gov/License.html
Dentist #09 .... www.dbc.ca.gov/License.html
Drug Wholesaler/Drug Room #13 .... www.pharmacy.ca.gov/license_lookup.htm
Drywall #28 .... www.cslb.ca.gov/license+request.html
Earthwork & Paving #28 .... www.cslb.ca.gov/license+request.html
Educational Psychologist #08 .... www.bbs.ca.gov/weblokup.htm
Electrical (General) & Electrical Sign #28 .... www.cslb.ca.gov/license+request.html
Electronics & Appliance Repairs #20 .... http://appserv1.dca.ca.gov:80/wllpub/plsql/wllquery$.startup
Elevator Installation #28 .... www.cslb.ca.gov/license+request.html
Embalmer/Embalmer Apprentice #25 .... www.dca.ca.gov/cemetery/lookup.htm
Engineer (Various) #10 .... www.dca.ca.gov/pels/l_lookup.htm
Fencing #28 .... www.cslb.ca.gov/license+request.html
Fire Protection #28 .... www.cslb.ca.gov/license+request.html
Firearm Permit #22 .... www.dca.ca.gov/bsis/lookup.htm
Firearm Training Facility/Instructor #22 .... www.dca.ca.gov/bsis/lookup.htm
Flooring & Floor Covering #28 .... www.cslb.ca.gov/license+request.html
Fumigation #44 .... www.dca.ca.gov/pestboard/lookup.htm
Funeral Director/Establishment #25 .... www.dca.ca.gov/cemetery/lookup.htm
Funerary Training Establishment/Apprentice #25 ..... www.dca.ca.gov/cemetery/lookup.htm
Geologist #18 .... www.dca.ca.gov/geology/lookup/
Geologist, Engineering #18 .... www.dca.ca.gov/geology/lookup/
Geophysicist #18 .... www.dca.ca.gov/geology/lookup/
Glazier #28 .... www.cslb.ca.gov/license+request.html
Heating & Warm-Air Ventilating #28 .... www.cslb.ca.gov/license+request.html
Horse Racing #24 .... www.chrb.ca.gov/license.htm
Hospital Exemptees #13 .... www.pharmacy.ca.gov/license_lookup.htm
Hydrogeologist #18 .... www.dca.ca.gov/geology/lookup/
Hypodermic Needle & Syringe Distributor #13 .... www.pharmacy.ca.gov/license_lookup.htm
Industrial Loan Company, Premium #11 .... www.sbd.ca.gov/directry/pf.asp
Insulation & Accoustical Contractor #28 .... www.cslb.ca.gov/license+request.html
Insurance Adjuster #32 .... www.insurance.ca.gov/LIC/Licensestatus.htm
Insurance Agent/Broker #32 .... www.insurance.ca.gov/LIC/Licensestatus.htm
Insurance Broker #32 .... www.insurance.ca.gov/LIC/Licensestatus.htm

Insurance Company #32	www.insurance.ca.gov/docs/FS-CompanyProfiles.htm
Lamp Station #19	www.smogcheck.ca.gov/stdhome.asp
Landscaping #28	www.cslb.ca.gov/license+request.html
Lathing #28	www.cslb.ca.gov/license+request.html
Lobbyist/Lobbyist Firm/Lobbyist Employer #47	www.ss.ca.gov/prd/ld/contents.htm
Locksmith/Locksmith Company #22	www.dca.ca.gov/bsis/lookup.htm
Manufactured Housing #28	www.cslb.ca.gov/license+request.html
Marriage & Family Therapist #08	www.bbs.ca.gov/weblokup.htm
Masonry #28	www.cslb.ca.gov/license+request.html
Medical Doctor/Surgeon #36	www.docboard.org/ca/df/casearch.htm
Money Orders/Payment Instruments Issuer #11	www.sbd.ca.gov/directry/pi.asp
Optometrist #12	www.optometry.ca.gov/search.asp
Optometry Branch Office #12	www.optometry.ca.gov/search.asp
Optometry Fictitious Name Practice #12	www.optometry.ca.gov/search.asp
Ornamental Metal #28	www.cslb.ca.gov/license+request.html
Painting & Decorating #28	www.cslb.ca.gov/license+request.html
Parking & Highway Improvement #28	www.cslb.ca.gov/license+request.html
Patrol Operator, Private #22	www.dca.ca.gov/bsis/lookup.htm
Pest Control Professional #44	www.dca.ca.gov/pestboard/lookup.htm
Pesticide Applicator #44	www.dca.ca.gov/pestboard/lookup.htm
Pharmacist/Pharmacist Intern #13	www.pharmacy.ca.gov/license_lookup.htm
Pharmacy #13	www.pharmacy.ca.gov/license_lookup.htm
Pharmacy Technician #13	www.pharmacy.ca.gov/license_lookup.htm
Physician Assistant #39	www.docboard.org/ca/df/casearch.htm
Pipeline #28	www.cslb.ca.gov/license+request.html
Plastering #28	www.cslb.ca.gov/license+request.html
Plumber #28	www.cslb.ca.gov/license+request.html
Podiatrist #14	www.docboard.org/ca/df/casearch.htm
Polygraph Examiner #48	www.wordnet.net/cape/docs/camemb.htm
Polygraph Examiner of Sex Offenders #48	www.wordnet.net/cape/docs/certified.htm
Private Investigator #22	www.dca.ca.gov/bsis/lookup.htm
Psychiatric Technician #17	www.bvnpt.ca.gov/licverif.htm
Psychological Assistant #15	www.psychboard.ca.gov
Psychologist #15	www.psychboard.ca.gov
Real Estate Broker/Corporation #33	www.dre.ca.gov/licstats.htm
Real Estate Sales Agent #33	www.dre.ca.gov/licstats.htm
Refrigeration #28	www.cslb.ca.gov/license+request.html
Repossessor Agency/Manager/Employee #22	www.dca.ca.gov/bsis/lookup.htm
Roofing #28	www.cslb.ca.gov/license+request.html
Sanitation System #28	www.cslb.ca.gov/license+request.html
Savings & Loan Association #11	www.sbd.ca.gov/directry/sl.asp
Security Guard/Armored Car Guard #22	www.dca.ca.gov/bsis/lookup.htm
Sheet Metal #28	www.cslb.ca.gov/license+request.html
Smog Check Station #19	www.smogcheck.ca.gov/stdhome.asp
Smog Check Technician #19	www.smogcheck.ca.gov/stdhome.asp
Social Worker, Clinical #08	www.bbs.ca.gov/weblokup.htm
Social Worker, Clinical Associate #08	www.bbs.ca.gov/weblokup.htm
Solar Energy #28	www.cslb.ca.gov/license+request.html
Specialty Contractor-Class C #28	www.cslb.ca.gov/license+request.html
Specialty Sublicenses (Limited) #28	www.cslb.ca.gov/license+request.html
Steel, Reinforcing & Structural #28	www.cslb.ca.gov/license+request.html
Supervising Physician #39	www.docboard.org/ca/df/casearch.htm
Surveyor #10	www.dca.ca.gov/pels/l_lookup.htm
Swimming Pool #28	www.cslb.ca.gov/license+request.html
Tax Education Provider #45	www.ctec.org/html/approved_education_providers_.html
Termite Control #44	www.dca.ca.gov/pestboard/lookup.htm
Thrift & Loan Company #11	www.sbd.ca.gov/directry/tl.asp
Tile (Ceramic & Mosaic) #28	www.cslb.ca.gov/license+request.html
Travelers Checks Issuer #11	www.sbd.ca.gov/directry/tc.asp
Trust Company #11	www.sbd.ca.gov/directry/trust.asp
Veterinarian #40	www.vmb.ca.gov/2licensg/lic1list.htm
Veterinary Food-Animal Drug Retailer #13	www.pharmacy.ca.gov/license_lookup.htm
Veterinary Hospital #40	www.vmb.ca.gov/2licensg/lic1list.htm
Vocational Nurse #17	www.bvnpt.ca.gov/licverif.htm
Water Well Driller #28	www.cslb.ca.gov/license+request.html

Licensing Quick Finder

- Acupuncturist #01 ... 916-263-2680
- Agricultural Engineer #10 ... 916-263-2222
- Air Conditioning Contractor #28 ... 916-255-3985
- Alarm Company #22 ... 800-952-5210
- Alarm Company Employee/Manager #22 ... 800-952-5210
- Animal Health Technician #40 ... 916-263-2613
- Announcer, Athletic Event (Ring) #03 ... 916-263-2195
- Architect #07 ... 916-445-3393
- Athletic Event Box Office Employee/Ticket Seller #03 ... 916-263-2195
- Athletic Event Manager/Promoter/Matchmaker #03 ... 916-263-2195
- Athletic Event Referee/Judge/Timekeeper/Doorperson #03 ... 916-263-2195
- Athletic Gym #03 ... 916-263-2195
- Athletic Trainer/Second #03 ... 916-263-2195
- Attorney #23 ... 415-538-2303
- Audiologist #42 ... 916-263-2666
- Automobile Dealer/Repair #19 ... 916-322-4010
- Automobile Manufacturer Arbitration Program #02 ... 916-323-3406
- Bank #11 ... 800-622-0620
- Barber Instructor/School #04 ... 916-445-7061
- Barber Shop/Barber/Barber Apprentice #04 ... 916-445-7061
- Baton Training Facility/Instructor #22 ... 800-952-5210
- Bedding Manufacturer/Renovator/Retailer/Wholesaler #21 ... 800-952-5210
- Boiler, Hot Water & Steam Fitting #28 ... 916-255-3985
- Boxer #03 ... 916-263-2195
- Boxing Second #03 ... 916-263-2195
- Brake & Lamp Adjuster #19 ... 916-322-4010
- Brake Station #19 ... 916-322-4010
- Building Contractor, General-Class B #28 ... 916-255-3985
- Building Moving/Demolition #28 ... 916-255-3985
- Cabinet & Millwork #28 ... 916-255-3985
- Cemetery, Cemetery Broker/Agent #25 ... 916-322-7737
- Clinic Pharmaceutical Permit #13 ... 916-445-5014
- Clinical Nurse Specialist #16 ... 800-838-6828
- Collection Agency Manager/Collector/Bookkeeper #22 ... 800-952-5210
- Concrete Contractor/Company #28 ... 916-255-3985
- Continuing Education Providers #08 ... 916-445-4933
- Contractor #46 ... 800-321-2752
- Cosmetician/Cosmetologist #04 ... 916-445-7061
- Cosmetology Establishment/Instructor/School #04 ... 916-445-7061
- Court Reporter (Shorthand Reporter) #29 ... 916-263-3660
- CPA #06 ... 916-263-3680
- Credit Union #11 ... 800-622-0620
- Cremated Remains Disposer #25 ... 916-322-7737
- Crematory #25 ... 916-322-7737
- Dental Assistant #27 ... 916-263-2595
- Dental Assist.-Extended Function #27 ... 916-263-2595
- Dental Hygienist #27 ... 916-263-2595
- Dentist #09 ... 916-263-2300
- Diagnostic Pharmaceutical #12 ... 916-323-8720
- Drug Wholesaler/Drug Room #13 ... 916-445-5014
- Dry Cleaning Plant #21 ... 916-574-0280
- Drywall #28 ... 916-255-3985
- Earthwork & Paving #28 ... 916-255-3985
- Educational Psychologist #08 ... 916-445-4933
- Electrical (General) & Electric Sign #28 ... 916-255-3985
- Electrologist #04 ... 916-445-7061
- Electrology Establishment/Instructor/School #04 ... 916-445-7061
- Electroneuromyographer #38 ... 916-263-2550
- Electronics & Appliance Repairs #20 ... 916-574-2067
- Elevator Installation #28 ... 916-255-3985
- Embalmer/Embalmer Apprentice #25 ... 916-322-7737
- Engineer (Various) #10 ... 916-263-2222
- Esthetician #04 ... 916-445-7061
- Fencing #28 ... 916-255-3985
- Fire Protection #28 ... 916-255-3985
- Firearm Permit #22 ... 800-952-5210
- Firearm Training Facility/Instructor #22 ... 800-952-5210
- Flooring & Floor Covering #28 ... 916-255-3985
- Fumigation #44 ... 916-263-2540
- Fund Raiser to Establish Training School #43 ... 916-263-8956 (Guide Dogs for Blind)
- Funeral Director/Establishment #25 ... 916-322-7737
- Funerary Training Establishment/Apprentice #25 ... 916-322-7737
- Furniture & Bedding Retailer #21 ... 916-574-0280
- Furniture Manufacturer/Retailer/Wholesaler #21 ... 916-574-0280
- Geologist #18 ... 916-263-2113
- Geologist, Engineering #18 ... 916-263-2113
- Geophysicist #18 ... 916-263-2113
- Glazier #28 ... 916-255-3985
- Guard Dog Instructor #43 ... 916-263-8956
- Guard Dog Training School #43 ... 916-263-8956
- Guard/Protection Dog Operator/Employee #22 ... 800-952-5210
- Healing Art Supervisor #31 ... 916-445-6430
- Hearing Aid Dispenser #34 ... 916-263-2288
- Heating & Warm-Air Ventilating #28 ... 916-255-3985
- Home Furnishings/Thermal Insulation Importer/ Headquarters/Supply Dealer #21 ... 916-574-0280
- Horse Racing #24 ... 916-263-6000
- Hospital Exemptees #13 ... 916-445-5014
- Hydrogeologist #18 ... 916-263-2113
- Hygienist #09 ... 916-263-2300
- Hypodermic Needle & Syringe Dist. #13 ... 916-445-5014
- Industrial Loan Company, Premium #11 ... 800-622-0620
- Insulation & Accoustical Contractor #28 ... 916-255-3985
- Insurance Adjuster #32 ... 916-322-3555
- Insurance Agent #32 ... 916-322-3555
- Insurance Broker #32 ... 916-322-3555
- Insurance Company #32 ... 916-322-3555
- Investment Advisors #30 ... 916-445-3062
- Kickboxer, Amateur #03 ... 916-263-2195
- Kickboxer/Full Contact Karate #03 ... 916-263-2195
- Kinesiological Electromyographer #38 ... 916-263-2550
- Lamp Station #19 ... 916-322-4010
- Landscape Architect #35 ... 916-445-4954
- Landscaping #28 ... 916-255-3985
- Lathing #28 ... 916-255-3985
- Lobbyist/Lobbyist Firm/ Employer #47 ... 916-653-6224
- Locksmith/Locksmith Company #22 ... 800-952-5210
- Mamagraphic Facility Accrdt. #31 ... 916-323-2772
- Manicurist #04 ... 916-445-7061
- Manufactured Housing #28 ... 916-255-3985
- Marriage & Family Therapist #08 ... 916-445-4933
- Masonry #28 ... 916-255-3985
- Medical Doctor/Surgeon #36 ... 916-263-2635
- Medical Provider Consultant #22 ... 800-952-5210
- Midwife #36 ... 916-263-2393
- Midwife Nurse #16 ... 800-838-6828
- Money Orders/Payment Instruments Issuer #11 ... 800-622-0620
- Notary Public #37 ... 916-653-3595
- Nuclear Medicine Technologist #31 ... 916-445-8820
- Nurse #16 ... 800-838-6828
- Nurse Anesthetist #16 ... 800-838-6828
- Nursing Home Administrator #05 ... 916-323-6838
- Optician, Dispensing #36 ... 916-263-2634
- Optometric Corporation #12 ... 916-323-8720
- Optometrist #12 ... 916-323-8720
- Optometry Branch Office #12 ... 916-323-8720
- Optometry Fictitious Name Practice #12 ... 916-323-8720
- Ornamental Metal #28 ... 916-255-3985
- Painting & Decorating #28 ... 916-255-3985
- Parking & Highway Improvement #28 ... 916-255-3985
- Patrol Operator, Private #22 ... 800-952-5210
- Pest Control Field Representative #44 ... 916-263-2540
- Pest Control Operator/Professional #44 ... 916-263-2540
- Pesticide Applicator #44 ... 916-263-2540
- Pharmaceutical Dist., Out-of-State #13 ... 916-445-5014
- Pharmaceutical Wholesaler/Exemptee #13 ... 916-445-5014
- Pharmacist/Pharmacist Intern #13 ... 916-445-5014
- Pharmacy #13 ... 916-445-5014
- Pharmacy Continuing Education Provider #13 ... 916-445-5014
- Pharmacy Technician #13 ... 916-445-5014
- Pharmacy, Non-resident #13 ... 916-445-5014
- Photogrammetrist #10 ... 916-263-2222
- Physical Therapist/Assistant #38 ... 916-263-2550
- Physician Assistant #39 ... 916-263-2323
- Pipeline #28 ... 916-255-3985
- Plastering #28 ... 916-255-3985
- Plumber #28 ... 916-255-3985
- Podiatrist #14 ... 916-263-2382
- Polygraph Examiner #48 ... 800-593-8598
- Private Investigator #22 ... 800-952-5210
- Psychiatric Mental Health Nurse #16 ... 800-838-6828
- Psychiatric Technician #17 ... 916-263-7800
- Psychological Assistant #15 ... 916-263-2699
- Psychologist #15 ... 916-263-2699
- Public Accountant-CPA #06 ... 916-263-3680
- Public Health Nurse #16 ... 800-838-6828
- Radioactive Material License #31 ... 916-445-0931
- Radiologic Technologist #31 ... 916-445-8820
- Real Estate Broker/Corporation #33 ... 916-227-0931
- Real Estate Sales Agent #33 ... 916-227-0931
- Refrigeration #28 ... 916-255-3985
- Repossessor Agency/Mgr./Person #22 ... 800-952-5210
- Research Psychoanalyst #36 ... 916-263-2370
- Respiratory Care Practitioner #41 ... 916-263-2626
- Roofing #28 ... 916-255-3985
- Sanitation System #28 ... 916-255-3985
- Sanitizer of Home Furnishing Products #21 ... 916-574-0280
- Savings & Loan Association #11 ... 800-622-0620
- School Administrator #26 ... 916-445-7254
- School Library Media Specialist #26 ... 916-445-7254
- Securities Broker/Dealer #30 ... 916-445-3062
- Security Guard/Armored Car Guard #22 ... 800-952-5210
- Sheet Metal #28 ... 916-255-3985
- Smog Check Station #19 ... 916-322-4010
- Smog Check Technician #19 ... 916-322-4010
- Social Worker, Clinical #08 ... 916-445-4933
- Social Worker, Clinical Associate #08 ... 916-445-4933
- Solar Energy #28 ... 916-255-3985
- Sparring Permit #03 ... 916-263-2195
- Specialty Contractor-Class C #28 ... 916-255-3985
- Specialty Sublicenses (Limited) #28 ... 916-255-3985
- Speech Pathologist/AudiologyAide #42 ... 916-263-2666
- Speech-Language Pathologist #42 ... 916-263-2666
- Steel, Reinforcing & Structural #28 ... 916-255-3985
- Supervising Physician #39 ... 916-263-2323
- Surgical Clinic, Nonprofit #13 ... 916-445-5014
- Surveyor #10 ... 916-263-2222
- Surveyor-in-Training #10 ... 916-263-2222
- Swimming Pool #28 ... 916-255-3985
- Tax Education Provider #45 ... 916-492-0457
- Tax Interviewer #45 ... 916-492-0457
- Tax Preparer #45 ... 916-492-0457
- Teacher #26 ... 916-445-7254
- Termite Control #44 ... 916-263-2540
- Thermal Insulation Manufacturer #21 ... 916-574-0280
- Thrift & Loan Company #11 ... 800-622-0620
- Tile (Ceramic & Mosaic) #28 ... 916-255-3985
- Travelers Checks Issuer #11 ... 800-622-0620
- Trust Company #11 ... 800-622-0620
- Upholsterer, Custom #21 ... 800-952-5210
- Veterinarian #40 ... 916-263-2610
- Veterinary Food-Animal Drug Retailer #13 ... 916-445-5014
- Veterinary Hospital #40 ... 916-263-2610
- Vocational Nurse #17 ... 916-263-7800
- Water Well Driller #28 ... 916-255-3985
- X-ray Machine Reg./Technician #31 ... 916-445-0931

Licensing Agency Information

#01 Acupuncture Committee, 1424 Howe Ave, #37, Sacramento, CA 95825-3233; 916-263-2680, Fax: 916-263-2654.
www.dca.ca.gov/acup/

#02 Arbitration Review Program, 401 S St #201, Sacramento, CA 95814; 916-323-3406, Fax: 916-323-3968.
www.dca.ca.gov/acp/acp_resp.htm

#03 Athletic Commission, 1424 Howe Ave, #33, Sacramento, CA 95825; 916-263-2195, Fax: 916-263-2197.
www.dca.ca.gov/csac/
Direct web site URL to search for licensees: www.dca.ca.gov/csac/directories.htm. You can search online using search directory lists.

#04 Barber & Cosmetology Program, 400 R St, #5100, Sacramento, CA 95814-6200; 916-445-1254, Fax: 916-445-8893.
www.dca.ca.gov/barber

#05 Nursing Home Administrator Program, PO Box 942732 (1800 3rd St #162), Sacramento, CA 95234-7320; 916-323-6838, Fax: 916-323-6845.
www.dca.ca.gov/r_r/nurseho1.htm

#06 Board of Accountancy, 2000 Evergreen St, #250, Sacramento, CA 95815-3832; 916-263-7777, Fax: 916-263-3675.
www.dca.ca.gov/cba/

#07 Architects Board, 400 R St, #4000, Sacramento, CA 95814-6238; 916-445-3393, Fax: 916-445-8524.
www.cab.ca.gov
Direct web site URL to search for licensees: www.cab.ca.gov/Templates/querysearch.cfm. You can search online using license number, name, address, or city.

#08 Board of Behavioral Sciences, 400 R St, #3150, Sacramento, CA 95814-6200; 916-445-4933, Fax: 916-323-0707.
www.bbs.ca.gov
Direct web site URL to search for licensees: www.bbs.ca.gov/weblokup.htm. You can search online using first and/or last name, or license number

#09 Dental Board, 1432 Howe Ave, #85, Sacramento, CA 95825-3241; 916-263-2300, Fax: 916-263-2140.
www.dca.ca.gov/r_r/dentalbd.htm

#10 Board of Professional Engineers & Land Surveyors, PO Box 349002, (2535 Capitol Oaks Dr, #300), Sacramento, CA 95834-9002; 916-263-2222, Fax: 916-263-2246.
www.dca.ca.gov/pels
Direct web site URL to search for licensees: www.dca.ca.gov/pels/l_lookup.htm. You can search online using name, license #, city, state, country Member lists may be downloaded. Engineers include: civil, fire protection, electrical, mechanical, geotechnical, structural, traffic, oil, nuclear, control system, chemical, industrial, manufacturing, metallurgical, petroleum, corrosion, quality, safety

#11 Department of Financial Institutions, 801 Street #2124, Sacramento, CA 95814; 916-322-5966.
www.sbd.ca.gov
Direct web site URL to search for licensees: www.sbd.ca.gov/directry/directry.asp. You can search online using alphabetical lists

#12 Board of Optometry, 400 R St, #4090, Sacramento, CA 95814-6200; 916-323-8720, Fax: 916-445-8711.
www.optometry.ca.gov
Direct web site URL to search for licensees: www.odfinder.org/LicSearch.asp. You can search online using national database by name, city, or state.

#13 Board of Pharmacy, 400 R St, #4070, Sacramento, CA 95814-6200; 916-445-5014, Fax: 916-327-6308.
www.pharmacy.ca.gov
Direct web site URL to search for licensees: www.pharmacy.ca.gov/license_lookup.htm

#14 Board of Podiatric Medicine, 1420 Howe Ave, #8, Sacramento, CA 95825-3229; 916-263-2647, Fax: 916-263-2651.
www.dca.ca.gov/bpm
Direct web site URL to search for licensees: www.docboard.org/ca/df/casearch.htm. You can search online using name and license number.

#15 Board of Psychology, 1422 Howe Ave, #22, Sacramento, CA 95825-3200; 916-263-2699.
www.psychboard.ca.gov
Direct web site URL to search for licensees: www.psychboard.ca.gov

#16 Board of Registered Nursing, 400 R St, #4030, Sacramento, CA 95814-6200; 916-322-3350, Fax: 916-327-4402.
www.rn.ca.gov

#17 Board of Vocational Nursing & Psychiatric Treatment, 2535 Capitol Oaks Dr, #205, Sacramento, CA 95833; 916-263-7800, Fax: 916-263-7859.
www.bvnpt.ca.gov
Direct web site URL to search for licensees: www.bvnpt.ca.gov/licverif.htm

#18 Board of Registration for Geologists & Geophysicists, 2535 Capitol Oaks Dr, #300A, Sacramento, CA 95833; 916-263-2113, Fax: 916-263-2099.
www.dca.ca.gov/geology
Direct web site URL to search for licensees: www.dca.ca.gov/geology/lookup/. You can search online using license number, name, and location.

#19 Bureau of Automotive Repair, PO Box 989001, West Sacramento, CA 95798-9001; 916-322-4000, Fax: 916-322-4274.
www.smogcheck.ca.gov/stdhome.asp Click on "Verify a License" to open the search page.

#20 Department of Consumer Affairs, 400 R St, #3080, Sacramento, CA 95814; 916-574-2067, Fax: 916-574-2043.
www.dca.ca.gov/r_r/electron.htm

#21 Department of Consumer Affairs, 3485 Orange Grove Ave, North Highlands, CA 95660; 916-574-0280, Fax: 916-574-2449.
www.dca.ca.gov/bhfti/

#22 Bureau of Security & Investigative Services, 400 R St, #3080, Sacramento, CA 95814; 800-952-5210, Fax: 916-445-1694.
www.dca.ca.gov/bsis
Direct web site URL to search for licensees: www.dca.ca.gov/bsis/lookup.htm. You can search online using name, license number, and county.

#23 State Bar of California, 180 Howard St, San Francisco, CA 94105; 415-538-2577, Fax: 415-538-2361.
www.calbar.org
Direct web site URL to search for licensees: www.calsb.org/MM/SBMBRSHP.HTM. You can search online using member number or name. The member records online database does not include judges or deceased former members.

#24 Horse Racing Board, 1010 Hurley Way, #300, Sacramento, CA 95825; 916-263-6000, Fax: 916-263-6042.
www.chrb.ca.gov
Direct web site URL to search for licensees: www.chrb.ca.gov/license.htm. You can search online using name, license number, and organization.

#25 Cemetery and Funeral Bureau, 400 R St, #3040, Sacramento, CA 95814; 916-322-7737, Fax: 916-323-1890.
www.dca.ca.gov/cemetery/
Direct web site URL to search for licensees: www.dca.ca.gov/cemetery/lookup.htp. You can search online using name, city, license number.

#26 Commission on Teacher Credentialing, 1900 Capitol Ave (95814-4213), Sacramento, CA 95814-7000; 916-445-7254, Fax: 916-445-7255.
www.ctc.ca.gov

#27 Committee on Dental Auxiliaries, 1428 Howe Ave, #58, Sacramento, CA 95825-3235; 916-263-2595, Fax: 916-263-2709.
www.comda.ca.gov/licensestatus.html
Direct web site URL to search for licensees: www2.dca.ca.gov:8001/wllpub/plsql/wllquery$.startup. You can search online using name, license number, city, or county

#28 Contractors License Board, PO Box 26000, Sacramento, CA 95826; 916-255-3900, Fax: 916-361-7497 or 800-321-2752.
www.cslb.ca.gov
Direct web site URL to search for licensees: www.cslb.ca.gov/license+request.html. You can search online using license number.

#29 Court Reporters Board of California, 2535 Capitol Oaks Dr, #230, Sacramento, CA 95833; 916-263-3660, Fax: 916-263-3664.
www.courtreportersboard.ca.gov
Direct web site URL to search for licensees: www.courtreportersboard.ca.gov To search, click on red "License Verification" button.

#30 Department of Corporations, 1515 K St, Sacramento, CA 95814; 916-445-7205.
www.corp.ca.gov old address: 980 9th St #500. Stated that they are moving later this year. Did not give a time. Putting the new address at top.

#31 Department of Health Services, 601 N 7th ST, Mail Stop #178, Sacramento, CA 95814; 916-445-6695, Fax: 916-324-3610.

#32 Department of Insurance, 320 Capitol Mall, Sacramento, CA 95814; 916-322-3555, Fax: 916327-6907.
www.insurance.ca.gov
Direct web site URL to search for licensees: www.insurance.ca.gov/LIC/Licensestatus.htm. Search online using name and license number.

#33 Department of Real Estate, 2201 Broadway, Sacramento, CA 95826; 916-227-0931, Fax: 916-227-0925.
www.dre.ca.gov
Direct web site URL to search for licensees: www.dre.ca.gov/licstats.htm. You can search online using name, city, and license number.

#34 Hearing Aid Dispensers Examining Committee, 1422 Howe Ave #5, Sacramento, CA 95825-3204; 916-263-2288, Fax: 916-263-2290.
www.dca.ca.gov/hearingaid/

#35 Landscape Architects Technical Committee, 400 R St, #4000, Sacramento, CA 95814-6200; 916-445-4954, Fax: 916-324-2333.
www.latc.dca.ca.gov
Direct web site URL to search for licensees: www.latc.dca.ca.gov/geninfo/querylic.htm. You can search online using name, license # or city Online searching available Sept. 1, 2000

#36 Medical Board of California, 1426 Howe Ave, #54, Sacramento, CA 95825-3236; 916-263-2382, Fax: 916-263-2567.
www.medbd.ca.gov

#37 Office of the Secretary of State, 1500 11th St, 2nd Fl, Sacramento, CA 95814; 916-653-3595, Fax: 916-653-9580.

www.ss.ca.gov/business/notary/notary.htm
Direct web site URL to search for licensees: www.ss.ca.gov/prd/ld/contents.htm. You can search online using lobbyist name, firm, or employer, also nature or interest categories.

#38 Physical Therapy Examining Committee, 1418 Howe Ave #16, Sacramento, CA 95825-3204; 916-263-2550, Fax: 916-263-2560.
www.ptb.ca.gov/

#39 Department of Consumer Affairs, 1424 Howe Ave, #35, Sacramento, CA 95825-3237; 916-263-2323, Fax: 916-263-2671.
www.medbd.ca.gov
Direct web site URL to search for licensees: www.docboard.org/ca/df/casearch.htm. You can search online using name or license #

#40 Veterinary Medical Board, 1420 Howe Ave, #6, Sacramento, CA 95825-3228; 916-263-2610, Fax: 916-263-2621.
www.vmb.ca.gov
Direct web site URL to search for licensees: www.vmb.ca.gov/2licensg/lic1list.htm

#41 Respiratory Care Examining Committee, 1426 Howe Ave, #48, Sacramento, CA 95825-3234; 916-263-2626, Fax: 916-263-2630.

#42 Speech Language Pathology & Audiology Board, 1434 Howe Ave, #86, Sacramento, CA 95825-3240; 916-263-2666, Fax: 916-263-2668.
www.dca.ca.gov/slpab

#43 Board of Guide Dogs, 2000 Evergreen, Sacramento, CA 95815; 916-263-8956, Fax: 916-263-7479.

#44 Structural Pest Control Board, 1418 Howe Ave #18, Sacramento, CA 95825-3280; 916-263-2540 or 916-263-2533 complaints, Fax: 916-263-2469.
www.dca.ca.gov/pestboard/
Direct web site URL to search for licensees: www.dca.ca.gov/pestboard/lookup.htm. You can search online using business name, employee name, city or license number.

#45 Tax Preparer Program, CA Tax Education Council, PO Box 2890, Sacramento, CA 95812-2840; 916-492-0457.
www.ctec.org

#46 Contractors State License Board, 9821 Business Park Drive, Sacramento, CA 95826; 800-321-2752, Fax: 916-366-9130.
www.cslb.ca.gov

#47 Secretary of State, P.O. Box 1467 (1500 11th Street, Room 495), Sacramento, CA 95812-1467; 916-653-6224, Fax: 916-653-5045.
http://cal-access.ss.ca.gov/lobbycategory.asp
Direct web site URL to search for licensees: www.ss.ca.gov/prd/ld/contents.htm. You can search online using lobbyist name, firm, or employer, also nature or interest categories.

#48 Association of Polygraph Examiners, 969-G Edgewater Blvd #330, Foster City, CA 94404; 800-593-8598.
www.wordnet.net/cape/
Direct web site URL to search for licensees: www.wordnet.net/cape/

California Federal Courts

The following list indicates the district and division name for each county in the state. If the bankruptcy court location is different from the district court, then the location of the bankruptcy court appears in parentheses.

County/Court Cross Reference

County	District	Division
Alameda	Northern	San Jose (Oakland)
Alpine	Eastern	Sacramento
Amador	Eastern	Sacramento
Butte	Eastern	Sacramento
Calaveras	Eastern	Sacramento (Modesto)
Colusa	Eastern	Sacramento
Contra Costa	Northern	San Jose (Oakland)
Del Norte	Northern	San Jose (Santa Rosa)
El Dorado	Eastern	Sacramento
Fresno	Eastern	Fresno
Glenn	Eastern	Sacramento
Humboldt	Northern	San Jose (Santa Rosa)
Imperial	Southern	San Diego
Inyo	Eastern	Fresno
Kern	Eastern	Fresno
Kings	Eastern	Fresno
Lake	Northern	San Jose (Santa Rosa)
Lassen	Eastern	Sacramento
Los Angeles	Central	Los Angeles (Western)
Madera	Eastern	Fresno
Marin	Northern	San Jose (Santa Rosa)
Mariposa	Eastern	Fresno
Mendocino	Northern	San Jose (Santa Rosa)
Merced	Eastern	Fresno
Modoc	Eastern	Sacramento
Mono	Eastern	Sacramento
Monterey	Northern	San Jose
Napa	Northern	San Jose (Santa Rosa)
Nevada	Eastern	Sacramento
Orange	Central	Santa Ana (Southern)
Placer	Eastern	Sacramento
Plumas	Eastern	Sacramento
Riverside	Central	Riverside (Eastern)
Sacramento	Eastern	Sacramento
San Benito	Northern	San Jose
San Bernardino	Central	Riverside (Eastern)
San Diego	Southern	San Diego
San Francisco	Northern	San Jose (San Francisco)
San Joaquin	Eastern	Sacramento (Modesto)
San Luis Obispo	Central	Los Angeles (Western)
San Mateo	Northern	San Jose (San Francisco)
Santa Barbara	Central	Los Angeles (Western)
Santa Clara	Northern	San Jose
Santa Cruz	Northern	San Jose
Shasta	Eastern	Sacramento
Sierra	Eastern	Sacramento
Siskiyou	Eastern	Sacramento
Solano	Eastern	Sacramento
Sonoma	Northern	San Jose (Santa Rosa)
Stanislaus	Eastern	Fresno (Modesto)
Sutter	Eastern	Sacramento
Tehama	Eastern	Sacramento
Trinity	Eastern	Sacramento
Tulare	Eastern	Fresno
Tuolumne	Eastern	Fresno (Modesto)
Ventura	Central	Los Angeles (Western)
Yolo	Eastern	Sacramento
Yuba	Eastern	Sacramento

US District Court

Central District of California

Los Angeles (Western) Division US Courthouse, Attn: Correspondence, 312 N Spring St, Room G-8, Los Angeles, CA 90012 (Courier Address: Use mail address for courier delivery), 213-894-5261.

http://www.cacd.uscourts.gov

Counties: Los Angeles, San Luis Obispo, Santa Barbara, Ventura.

Indexing/Storage: Cases are indexed by defendant and plaintiff as well as by case number. New cases are available in the index 3 days after filing date. Both computer and card indexes are maintained. Open records are located at this court. In general, criminal case records from 1989 back and civil cases from 1992 back have been sent to the Federal Records Center.

Fee & Payment: The fee is $20.00 per item (one party name or case number). Payment may be made by money order, cashier check, business check. Personal checks are not accepted. Prepayment is required. Payee: Clerk, US District Court. Certification fee: $7.00 per document. Copy fee: $.50 per page.

Phone Search: Searching is not available by phone.

Fax Search: Fax search allowed for the urgent matters of attorneys with approval of Supervisor. An account must be established first. Call 213-894-3649.

Mail Search: Always enclose a stamped self addressed envelope.

In Person: In person searching is available.

PACER: Sign-up number is 800-676-6856. Access fee is. Case records are available back to 1993. New records are available online after 2 days. PACER is available online at http://pacer.cacd.uscourts.gov.

Opinions Online: Court opinions are available online at http://www.cacd.uscourts.gov

Riverside (Eastern) Division US District Court, PO Box 13000, Riverside, CA 92502-3000 (Courier Address: 3470 12th St., Riverside, CA 92501), 909-328-4450.

http://www.cacd.uscourts.gov

Counties: Riverside, San Bernardino.

Indexing/Storage: Cases are indexed by defendant and plaintiff as well as by case number. New cases are available in the index 3 days after filing date. Both computer and card indexes are maintained. Open records are located at this court.

Fee & Payment: The fee is $20.00 per item (one party name or case number). Payment may be made by money order, cashier check, business check. Personal checks are not accepted. Prepayment is required. Payee: Clerk, US District Court. Certification fee: $7.00 per document. Copy fee: $.50 per page.

Phone Search: Searching is not available by phone.

Mail Search: Always enclose a stamped self addressed envelope.

In Person: In person searching is available.

PACER: Sign-up number is 800-676-6856. Access fee is. Case records are available back to 1993. New records are available online after 2 days. PACER is available online at http://pacer.cacd.uscourts.gov.

Opinions Online: Court opinions are available online at http://www.cacd.uscourts.gov

Santa Ana (Southern) Division 411 W 4th St Rm 1053, Santa Ana, CA 92701-4516 (Courier Address: Use mail address for courier delivery), 714-338-4750.

http://www.cacd.uscourts.gov

Counties: Orange.

Indexing/Storage: Cases are indexed by defendant and plaintiff as well as by case number.

New cases are available in the index 3 days after filing date. Both computer and card indexes are maintained. Open records are located at this court.

Fee & Payment: The fee is $20.00 per item (one party name or case number). Payment may be made by money order, cashier check, business check. Personal checks are not accepted. Prepayment is required unless a deposit account is set up with the court. Payee: Clerk, US District Court. Certification fee: $7.00 per document. Copy fee: $.50 per page.

Phone Search: Only docket information is available by phone.

Mail Search: Always enclose a stamped self addressed envelope.

In Person: In person searching is available.

PACER: Sign-up number is 800-676-6856. Access fee is. Case records are available back to 1993. New records are available online after 2 days. PACER is available online at http://pacer.cacd.uscourts.gov.

Opinions Online: Court opinions are available online at http://www.cacd.uscourts.gov

US Bankruptcy Court

Central District of California

Los Angeles Division 255 E Temple St, Los Angeles, CA 90012 (Courier Address: Use mail address for courier delivery), 213-894-3118, Fax: 213-894-1261.

http://www.cacb.uscourts.gov

Counties: Los Angeles (certain Los Angeles ZIP Codes are shared with San Fernando Valley Division.).

Indexing/Storage: Cases are indexed by debtor as well as by case number. New cases are available in the index immediately after filing date. A card index is maintained. Records are indexed on microfiche. Open records are located at this court.

Fee & Payment: The fee is $20.00 per item (one party name or case number). Payment may be made by money order, cashier check. Business checks are not accepted. Personal checks are not accepted. Prepayment is required. Payee: Clerk, US Bankruptcy Court. Certification fee: $7.00 per document. Copy fee: $.50 per page.

Phone Search: An automated voice case information service (VCIS) is available.

Fax Search: Handled like mail searches.

Mail Search: Always enclose a stamped self addressed envelope.

In Person: In person searching is available.

PACER: Sign-up number is 800-676-6856. Access fee is $.60 per minute. Toll-free access: 800-257-3887. Local access: 213-620-0031. Case records are available back to 1992. Records are purged once a year. New civil records are available online after 1 day. PACER is available online at https://pacerla.cacb.uscourts.gov/cgi-bin/bkplog.html. WebPACER Dial-up Networking is available at IP address of 156.131.137.252.

Riverside (East) Division 3420 12th St #125, Riverside, CA 92501-3819 (Courier Address: Use mail address for courier delivery), 909-774-1000.

http://www.cacb.uscourts.gov

Counties: Riverside, San Bernardino.

Indexing/Storage: Cases are indexed by debtor as well as by case number. New cases are available in the index immediately after filing date. A computer index is maintained. Files are stored in numerical sequence. Open records are located at this court. The time that records are kept at the

Riverside court is varied. There is no set time limit before they are sent to the Los Angeles Federal Records Center.

Fee & Payment: The fee is $20.00 per item (one party name or case number). Payment may be made by money order, cashier check. Business checks are not accepted, Visa or Mastercard. Personal checks are not accepted. Prepayment is required. Payee: US Bankruptcy Court. Certification fee: $7.00 per document. Copy fee: $.50 per page.

Phone Search: Only docket information is available by phone. An automated voice case information service (VCIS) is available. Call VCIS at 888-457-0604 or 909-774-1150.

Mail Search: Include the case number, document title, document number (if available), your phone number, and any applicable fees. Always enclose a stamped self addressed envelope.

In Person: In person searching is available.

PACER: Sign-up number is 800-676-6856. Access fee is $.60 per minute. Toll-free access: 888-819-0233. Local access: 909-276-2914. Case records are available back to 1992. Records are purged once a year. New civil records are available online after 1 day. PACER is available online at https://pacerrs.cacb.uscourts.gov/cgi-bin/bkplog.html. WebPACER Dial-up Networking is available at IP address 156.131.39.252.

San Fernando Valley Division 21041 Burbank Blvd, Woodland Hills, CA 91367 (Courier Address: Use mail address for courier delivery), 818-587-2900.

http://www.cacb.uscourts.gov

Counties: Los Angeles (certain Los Angeles ZIP Codes are shared with Los Angeles Division), Ventura.

Indexing/Storage: Cases are indexed by debtor as well as by case number. New cases are available in the index immediately after filing date. Open records at court. A card index is maintained. Open records are located at this court.

Fee & Payment: The fee is $20.00 per item (one party name or case number). Payment may be made by money order, cashier check. Business checks are not accepted. Personal checks are not accepted. Prepayment is required. Payee: Clerk, US Bankruptcy Court. Certification fee: $7.00 per document. Copy fee: $.50 per page.

Phone Search: An automated voice case information service (VCIS) is available. Call VCIS at 818-587-2936 or.

Fax Search: Handled like mail searches.

Mail Search: Include SASE.

In Person: In person searching is available.

PACER: Sign-up number is 800-676-6856. Access fee is $.60 per minute. Toll-free access: 800-838-2479. Local access: 818-587-2802. Case records are available back to 1992. Records are purged once a year. New civil records are available online after 1 day. PACER is available online at https://pacersv.cacb.uscourts.gov/cgi-bin/bkplog.html. WebPACER Dial-up Networking is available at IP address 156.131.45.56.

Santa Ana Division Ronald Reagan Federal Bldg & US Courthouse, 411 W 4th St #2030, Santa Ana, CA 92701-4593 (Courier Address: Use mail address for courier delivery), 714-836-2993.

http://www.cacb.uscourts.gov

Counties: Orange.

Indexing/Storage: Cases are indexed by debtor and creditors as well as by case number. New cases are available in the index 24-48 hours after filing date. A computer index is maintained. Open records are located at this court.

Fee & Payment: The fee is $20.00 per item (one party name or case number). Payment may be made by money order, cashier check, business check. Personal checks are not accepted. Prepayment is required unless prior arrangements have been made. Payee: US Bankruptcy Court. Certification fee: $7.00 per document. Copy fee: $.50 per page.

Phone Search: Docket information available by phone. An automated voice case information service (VCIS) is available.

Mail Search: Always enclose a stamped self addressed envelope.

In Person: In person searching is available.

PACER: Sign-up number is 800-676-6856. Access fee is $.60 per minute. Local access: 714-338-5406. Case records are available back to June 3, 1991. New civil records are available online after 1 day. PACER is available online at https://pacersa.cacb.uscourts.gov/cgi-bin/bkplog.html. WebPACER Dial-up Networking is available at IP address 156.131.41.252.

Santa Barbara (Northern) Division 1415 State St, Santa Barbara, CA 93101 (Courier Address: Use mail address for courier delivery), 805-884-4800.

http://www.cacb.uscourts.gov

Counties: San Luis Obispo, Santa Barbara, Ventura. Certain Ventura ZIP Codes are assigned to the new office in San Fernando Valley.

Indexing/Storage: Cases are indexed by debtor as well as by case number. New cases are available in the index immediately after filing date. A computer index is maintained. Open records are located at this court. There is no set time for sending records to the repository.

Fee & Payment: The fee is $20.00 per item (one party name or case number). Payment may be made by money order, cashier check. Business checks are not accepted. Personal checks are not accepted. Prepayment is required. Payee: US Bankruptcy Court. Certification fee: $7.00 per document. Copy fee: $.50 per page.

Phone Search: An automated voice case information service (VCIS) is available.

Mail Search: Include case number, document title, document number (if available), your phone number and applicable fees. Always enclose a stamped self addressed envelope.

In Person: In person searching is available.

PACER: Sign-up number is 800-676-6856. Access fee is $.60 per minute. Toll-free access: 888-819-0231. Case records are available back to June 1992. New civil records are available online after 1 day. PACER is available online at https://pacernd.cacb.uscourts.gov/cgi-bin/bkplog.html. WebPACER Dial-up Networking is available at IP address 156.131.453.252.

US District Court

Eastern District of California

Fresno Division US Courthouse, Room 5000, 1130 "O" St, Fresno, CA 93721-2201 (Courier Address: Use mail address for courier delivery), 559-498-7483.

http://www.caed.uscourts.gov

Counties: Fresno, Inyo, Kern, Kings, Madera, Mariposa, Merced, Stanislaus, Tulare, Tuolumne.

Indexing/Storage: Cases are indexed by defendant and plaintiff as well as by case number. New cases are available in the index 24 hours after filing date. A computer index is maintained. Records are stored by case type and case number. Open records are located at this court.

Fee & Payment: The fee is $20.00 per item (one party name or case number). Payment may be made by money order, cashier check, personal check. Prepayment is required. Payee: Clerk, US District Court. Certification fee: $7.00 per document. Copy fee: $.50 per page.
Phone Search: Only docket information is available by phone.
Mail Search: A stamped self addressed envelope is not required.
In Person: In person searching is available.
PACER: Sign-up number is 800-676-6856. Access fee is $.60 per minute. Toll-free access: 800-530-7682. Local access: 916-498-6567. Case records are available back to 1990 (some earlier). Records are purged at varying intervals. New records are available online after 1 day. PACER is available online at http://pacer.caed.uscourts.gov.
Opinions Online: Court opinions are available online at http://www.caed.uscourts.gov
Other Online Access: Search records on the Internet using RACER at https://racer.caed.uscourts.gov/Perl/bkplog.html. Access fee is 7 cents per page.

Sacramento Division 501 I St, Sacramento, CA 95814 (Courier Address: Use mail address for courier delivery), 916-930-4000, Fax: 916-930-4015.
http://www.caed.uscourts.gov
Counties: Alpine, Amador, Butte, Calaveras, Colusa, El Dorado, Glenn, Lassen, Modoc, Mono, Nevada, Placer, Plumas, Sacramento, San Joaquin, Shasta, Sierra, Siskiyou, Solano, Sutter, Tehama, Trinity, Yolo, Yuba.
Indexing/Storage: Cases are indexed by defendant and plaintiff as well as by case number. New cases are available in the index immediately after filing date. Archived records are stored by case number. A case number can be researched by the plaintiff's or defendant's name. A computer index is maintained. Archived case records are indexed on microfiche. Open records are located at this court.
Fee & Payment: The fee is $20.00 per item (one party name or case number). Payment may be made by money order, cashier check, business check. Personal checks are not accepted. Prepayment is required. Payee: Clerk, US District Court. Certification fee: $7.00 per document. Copy fee: $.50 per page. You are allowed to make your own copies. These copies cost $.15 per page. For copy service, call 916-448-8875. A 24-hour drop box is located on the premises.
Phone Search: Only docket information is available by phone.
Mail Search: Always enclose a stamped self addressed envelope.
In Person: In person searching is available.
PACER: Sign-up number is 800-676-6856. Access fee is $.60 per minute. Toll-free access: 800-530-7682. Local access: 916-498-6567. Case records are available back to 1990 (some earlier). Records are purged at varying intervals. New records are available online after 1 day. PACER is available online at http://pacer.caed.uscourts.gov.
Opinions Online: Court opinions are available online at http://www.caed.uscourts.gov
Other Online Access: Search records on the Internet using RACER at https://racer.caed.uscourts.gov/Perl/bkplog.html. Access fee is 7 cents per page.

US Bankruptcy Court
Eastern District of California

Fresno Division Room 2656, 1130 O Street, Fresno, CA 93721 (Courier Address: Use mail address for courier delivery), 559-498-7217.
http://www.caeb.uscourts.gov
Counties: Fresno, Inyo, Kern, Kings, Madera, Mariposa, Merced, Tulare. Three Kern ZIP Codes, 93243 and 93523-24, are handled by San Fernando Valley in the Central District.
Indexing/Storage: Cases are indexed by debtor as well as by case number. New cases are available in the index immediately after filing date. A computer index is maintained. Open records are located at this court.
Fee & Payment: The fee is $20.00 per item (one party name or case number). Payment may be made by money order, cashier check, business check. Personal checks are not accepted. Prepayment is required. Payee: Clerk, US Bankruptcy Court. Certification fee: $7.00 per document. Copy fee: $.50 per page. You are allowed to make your own copies. These copies cost $.15 per page.
Phone Search: Only docket information is available by phone. An automated voice case information service (VCIS) is available. Call VCIS at 800-736-0158 or 916-551-2989.
Mail Search: Always enclose a stamped self addressed envelope.
In Person: In person searching is available.
PACER: Sign-up number is 800-676-6856. Access fee is. Case records are available back to August 1990. Records are purged every six months. New civil records are available online after 1 day. PACER is available online at http://pacer.caeb.uscourts.gov/pacerhome.html.

Modesto Division PO Box 5276, Modesto, CA 95352 (Courier Address: Suite C, 1130 12th St, Modesto, CA 95354), 209-521-5160.
http://www.caeb.uscourts.gov
Counties: Calaveras, San Joaquin, Stanislaus, Tuolumne. The following ZIP Codes in San Joaquin County are handled by the Sacramento Division: 95220, 95227, 95234, 95237, 95240-95242, 95253, 95258, and 95686.Mariposa and Merced counties were transferred to the Fresno Division as of January 1, 1995.
Indexing/Storage: Cases are indexed by debtor as well as by case number. New cases are available in the index 1 day after filing date. Case numbers can be researched by using the debtor's name. A computer index is maintained. Open records are located at this court.
Fee & Payment: The fee is $20.00 per item (one party name or case number). Payment may be made by money order, cashier check, personal check. Prepayment is required. Payee: Clerk, US Bankruptcy Court. Certification fee: $7.00 per document. Copy fee: $.50 per page. You are allowed to make your own copies. These copies cost $.25 per page.
Phone Search: Only docket information is available by phone. An automated voice case information service (VCIS) is available. Call VCIS at 800-736-0158 or 916-551-2989.
Mail Search: A stamped self addressed envelope is not required.
In Person: In person searching is available.
PACER: Sign-up number is 800-676-6856. Access fee is $.60 per minute. Case records are available back to August 1990. Records are purged every six months. New civil records are available

online after 1 day. PACER is available online at http://pacer.caeb.uscourts.gov/pacerhome.html.

Sacramento Division US Courthouse, 501 I St, Rm 3-200, Sacramento, CA 95814 (Courier Address: Use mail address for courier delivery), 916-930-4400.
http://www.caeb.uscourts.gov
Counties: Alpine, Amador, Butte, Colusa, El Dorado, Glenn, Lassen, Modoc, Mono, Nevada, Placer, Plumas, Sacramento, Shasta, Sierra, Siskiyou, Solano, Sutter, Tehama, Trinity, Yolo, Yuba. This court also handles the following ZIP Codes in San Joaquin County:95220, 95227, 95234, 95237, 95240-95242, 95253, 95258 and 95686.
Indexing/Storage: Cases are indexed by debtor as well as by case number. New cases are available in the index immediately after filing date. A computer index is maintained. Open records are located at this court.
Fee & Payment: The fee is $20.00 per item (one party name or case number). Payment may be made by money order, cashier check, business check. Personal checks are not accepted. Prepayment is required. Payee: Clerk, US Bankruptcy Court. Certification fee: $7.00 per document. Copy fee: $.50 per page. You are allowed to make your own copies. These copies cost $.15 per page. You must make an appointment in order to conduct a search yourself.
Phone Search: Only docket information is available by phone. An automated voice case information service (VCIS) is available. Call VCIS at 800-736-0158 or 916-551-2989.
Mail Search: Always enclose a stamped self addressed envelope.
In Person: In person searching is available.
PACER: Sign-up number is 800-676-6856. Access fee is $.60 per minute. Case records are available back to August 1990. Records are purged every six months. New civil records are available online after 1 day. PACER is available online at http://pacer.caeb.uscourts.gov/pacerhome.html.

US District Court
Northern District of California

Oakland Division 1301 Clay St, Ste 400S, Oakland, CA 94612-5212 (Courier Address: Use mail address for courier delivery), 510-637-3530.
http://www.cand.uscourts.gov
Counties: Alameda, Contra Costa.
Indexing/Storage: Cases are indexed by defendant and plaintiff as well as by case number. New cases are available in the index immediately after filing date. Records are stored by case number, however, a case number can be researched by using the plaintiff's or the defendant's name. Records on computer since 1994. Records are also indexed on microfiche. Open records are located at this court.
Fee & Payment: The fee is $20.00 per item (one party name or case number). Payment may be made by money order, cashier check, personal check. Prepayment is required. Payee: Clerk, US District Court. Certification fee: $7.00 per document. Copy fee: $.50 per page. You are allowed to make your own copies. These copies cost Not Applicable per page. Use public pay copier for copies.
Phone Search: Only docket information is available by phone.
Mail Search: Always enclose a stamped self addressed envelope.
In Person: In person searching is available.

PACER: Sign-up number is 800-676-6856. Access fee is $.60 per minute. Toll-free access: 888-877-5883. Local access: 415-522-2144. Case records are available back to 1984. Records are purged every six months. New records are available online after 1 day. PACER is available online at http://pacer.cand.uscourts.gov.

Electronic Filing: Electronic filing information is available online at https://ecf.cand.uscourts.gov

San Francisco Division 450 Golden Gate Ave, 16th Fl, San Francisco, CA 94102 (Courier Address: Use mail address for courier delivery), 415-522-2000.

http://www.cand.uscourts.gov

Counties: Del Norte, Humboldt, Lake, Marin, Mendocino, Napa, San Francisco, San Mateo, Sonoma.

Indexing/Storage: Cases are indexed by defendant and plaintiff as well as by case number. New cases are available in the index immediately after filing date. Records are stored by case number, however, a case number can be researched by using the plaintiff's or the defendant's name. Records on computer since 1994. Records are also indexed on microfiche. Open records are located at this court.

Fee & Payment: The fee is $20.00 per item (one party name or case number). Payment may be made by money order, cashier check, personal check. Prepayment is required. Payee: Clerk, US District Court. Certification fee: $7.00 per document. Copy fee: $.50 per page. You are allowed to make your own copies. These copies cost Not Applicable per page. Use public pay copier for copies.

Phone Search: Only docket information is available by phone.

Mail Search: Always enclose a stamped self addressed envelope.

In Person: In person searching is available.

PACER: Sign-up number is 800-676-6856. Access fee is $.60 per minute. Toll-free access: 888-877-5883. Local access: 415-522-2144. Case records are available back to 1984. Records are purged every six months. New records are available online after 1 day. PACER is available online at http://pacer.cand.uscourts.gov.

Electronic Filing: Electronic filing information is available online at https://ecf.cand.uscourts.gov

San Jose Division Room 2112, 280 S 1st St, San Jose, CA 95113 (Courier Address: Use mail address for courier delivery), 408-535-5364.

http://www.cand.uscourts.gov

Counties: Monterey, San Benito, Santa Clara, Santa Cruz.

Indexing/Storage: Cases are indexed by defendant and plaintiff as well as by case number. New cases are available in the index immediately after filing date. Records are stored by case number, however, a case number can be researched by using the plaintiff's or the defendant's name. A computer index is maintained. Records are also indexed on microfiche. Open records are located at this court.

Fee & Payment: The fee is $20.00 per item (one party name or case number). Payment may be made by money order, cashier check, personal check. Prepayment is required. Payee: Clerk, US District Court. Certification fee: $7.00 per document. Copy fee: $.50 per page. You are allowed to make your own copies. These copies cost Not Applicable per page. Use public pay copier for copies.

Phone Search: Only docket information is available by phone.

Mail Search: Always enclose a stamped self addressed envelope.

In Person: In person searching is available.

PACER: Sign-up number is 800-676-6856. Access fee is $.60 per minute. Toll-free access: 888-877-5883. Local access: 415-522-2144. Case records are available back to 1984. Records are purged every six months. New records are available online after 1 day. PACER is available online at http://pacer.cand.uscourts.gov.

Electronic Filing: Electronic filing information is available online at https://ecf.cand.uscourts.gov

US Bankruptcy Court

Northern District of California

Oakland Division PO Box 2070, Oakland, CA 94604 (Courier Address: Suite 300, 1300 Clay St, Oakland, CA 94612), 510-879-3600.

http://www.canb.uscourts.gov

Counties: Alameda, Contra Costa.

Indexing/Storage: Cases are indexed by debtor as well as by case number. New cases are available in the index 2 days after filing date. Both computer and card indexes are maintained. Open records are located at this court.

Fee & Payment: The fee is $20.00 per item (one party name or case number). Payment may be made by money order, cashier check, business check. Personal checks are not accepted. Prepayment is required. Payee: Clerk, US Bankruptcy Court. Certification fee: $7.00 per document. Copy fee: $.50 per page. You are allowed to make your own copies. These copies cost $.25 per page.

Phone Search: An automated voice case information service (VCIS) is available. Call VCIS at 800-570-9819 or 415-705-3160.

Mail Search: Always enclose a stamped self addressed envelope.

In Person: In person searching is available.

PACER: Sign-up number is 800-676-6856. Access fee is $.60 per minute. Toll-free access: 888-773-8548. Local access: 415-268-4832. Case records are available back to 1993. Records are purged every six months to one year. New civil records are available online after 1 day. PACER is available online at http://pacer.canb.uscourts.gov.

San Francisco Division PO Box 7341, San Francisco, CA 94120-7341 (Courier Address: 235 Pine St, San Francisco, CA 94104), 415-268-2300.

http://www.canb.uscourts.gov

Counties: San Francisco, San Mateo.

Indexing/Storage: Cases are indexed by debtor as well as by case number. New cases are available in the index 3-4 working days after filing date. All searches are conducted by a copy service. To reach them, call 415-781-4910. A computer index is maintained. Records are also indexed on microfiche. Open records are located at this court.

Fee & Payment: The fee is $20.00 per item (one party name or case number). Payment may be made by money order, cashier check, business check. Personal checks are not accepted. Prepayment is required. Payee: Clerk of the Court. Certification fee: $7.00 per document. Copy fee: $.50 per page. You are allowed to make your own copies. These copies cost $.25 per page.

Phone Search: Only information available from dockets of open cases is released over the phone. An automated voice case information service (VCIS) is available. Call VCIS at 800-570-9819 or 415-705-3160.

Mail Search: A stamped self addressed envelope is not required.

In Person: In person searching is available.

PACER: Sign-up number is 800-676-6856. Access fee is $.60 per minute. Toll-free access: 888-773-8548. Local access: 415-268-4832. Case records are available back to 1993. Records are purged every six months to one year. New civil records are available online after 1 day. PACER is available online at http://pacer.canb.uscourts.gov.

San Jose Division Room 3035, 280 S 1st St, San Jose, CA 95113-3099 (Courier Address: Use mail address for courier delivery), 408-535-5118.

http://www.canb.uscourts.gov

Counties: Monterey, San Benito, Santa Clara, Santa Cruz.

Indexing/Storage: Cases are indexed by debtor as well as by case number. New cases are available in the index 1-2 days after filing date. A computer index is maintained. Open records are located at this court.

Fee & Payment: The fee is $20.00 per item (one party name or case number). Payment may be made by money order, cashier check, business check. Personal checks are not accepted. Prepayment is required. Payee: Clerk, US Bankruptcy Court. Certification fee: $7.00 per document. Copy fee: $1.00 per page. The fee for copies made by court personnel is $.50 per page.

Phone Search: Only basic information, such as date of filing is released over the phone. An automated voice case information service (VCIS) is available. Call VCIS at 800-570-9819 or 415-705-3160.

Mail Search: Always enclose a stamped self addressed envelope.

In Person: In person searching is available.

PACER: Sign-up number is 800-676-6856. Access fee is $.60 per minute. Toll-free access: 888-773-8548. Local access: 415-268-4832. Case records are available back to 1993. Records are purged every six months to one year. New civil records are available online after 1 day. PACER is available online at http://pacer.canb.uscourts.gov.

Santa Rosa Division 99 South E St, Santa Rosa, CA 95404 (Courier Address: Use mail address for courier delivery), 369-525-8539, Fax: 369-579-0374.

http://www.canb.uscourts.gov

Counties: Del Norte, Humboldt, Lake, Marin, Mendocino, Napa, Sonoma.

Indexing/Storage: Cases are indexed by debtor as well as by case number. New cases are available in the index immediately after filing date. A computer index is maintained. Open records are located at this court.

Fee & Payment: The fee is $20.00 per item (one party name or case number). Payment may be made by money order, cashier check, business check. Personal checks are not accepted. Prepayment is required. This court will not bill. Payee: Clerk - US Bankruptcy Court. Certification fee: $7.00 per document. Copy fee: $.50 per page. You are allowed to make your own copies. These copies cost $.20 per page. This court urges use of their contracted copy service, Attorney's Diversified (707-545-5455).

Phone Search: Names and accession numbers will be released over the phone. An automated voice case information service (VCIS) is available. Call VCIS at 800-570-9819 or 415-705-3160.

Mail Search: Always enclose a stamped self addressed envelope.

In Person: In person searching is available.

PACER: Sign-up number is 800-676-6856. Access fee is $.60 per minute. Toll-free access:

888-773-8548. Local access: 415-268-4832. Case records are available back to 1993. Records are purged every six months to one year. New civil records are available online after 1 day. PACER is available online at http://pacer.canb.uscourts.gov.

US District Court

Southern District of California

San Diego Division Room 4290, 880 Front St, San Diego, CA 92101-8900 (Courier Address: Use mail address for courier delivery), 619-557-5600, Fax: 619-557-6684.
http://www.casd.uscourts.gov
Counties: Imperial, San Diego. Court also handles some cases from Yuma County, AZ.
Indexing/Storage: Cases are indexed by defendant and plaintiff as well as by case number. New cases are available in the index 24 hours after filing date. A computer index is maintained. Open records are located at this court.
Fee & Payment: The fee is $20.00 per item (one party name or case number). Payment may be made by money order, cashier check, personal check. Contract copy service makes copies at $.24 per page. Prepayment is required. Payee: US District Court. Certification fee: $7.00 per document. Copy fee: $.50 per page.

Phone Search: Searching is not available by phone.
Mail Search: A stamped self addressed envelope is not required.
In Person: In person searching is available.
PACER: Sign-up number is 800-676-6856. Access fee is $.60 per minute. Toll-free access: 888-241-9760. Local access: 619-557-7138. Case records are available back to 1990. New records are available online after 1 day. PACER is available online at http://pacer.casd.uscourts.gov.
Other Online Access: A computer bulletin board is accessible at 619-557-6779.

US Bankruptcy Court

Southern District of California

San Diego Division Office of the clerk, US Courthouse, 325 West "F" St., San Diego, CA 92101 (Courier Address: Use mail address for courier delivery), 619-557-5620.
http://www.casb.uscourts.gov
Counties: Imperial, San Diego.
Indexing/Storage: Cases are indexed by debtor as well as by case number. New cases are available in the index 3 days after filing date. A computer index is maintained. Open records are located at this court.

Fee & Payment: The fee is $20.00 per item (one party name or case number). Payment may be made by money order, cashier check, personal check. Prepayment is required. Payee: Clerk, US Bankruptcy Court. Certification fee: $7.00 per document. Copy fee: $.50 per page.
Phone Search: Only docket information is available by phone. An automated voice case information service (VCIS) is available.
Fax Search: The court has contracted Court Copy Ltd to handle copies and fax requests. To make arrangements for a fax transaction, call Court Copy Ltd at 619-234-4425. They will accept credit cards.
Mail Search: A stamped self addressed envelope is not required.
In Person: In person searching is available.
PACER: Sign-up number is 800-676-6856. Access fee is $.60 per minute. Toll-free access: 800-870-9972. Local access: 619-557-6875. Case records are available back to 1989. Records are purged every six months. New civil records are available online after 3 days. PACER is available online at http://pacer.casb.uscourts.gov.
Electronic Filing: Electronic filing information is available online at http://ecf.casb.uscourts.gov

California County Courts

Court	Jurisdiction	No. of Courts	How Organized
Superior Courts*	General	29	
Limited Superior Courts*	Limited	122	
Combined Superior Courts*	Limited & General	58	

* Profiled in this Sourcebook.

Court	CIVIL								
	Tort	Contract	Real Estate	Min. Claim	Max. Claim	Small Claims	Estate	Eviction	Domestic Relations
General Jurisdiction	X	X	X	$25,000	No Max		X		X
Limited Jurisdiction	X	X	X	$0	$25,000	$5000		X	

Court	CRIMINAL				
	Felony	Misdemeanor	DWI/DUI	Preliminary Hearing	Juvenile
General Jurisdiction*	X	X	X		X
Limited Jurisdiction*		X	X	X	

ADMINISTRATION

Administrative Office of Courts, 455 Golden Gate Ave, San Francisco, CA, 94102; 415-865-4200, Fax: 415-865-4205. www.courtinfo.ca.gov

COURT STRUCTURE

In July, 1998, the judges in individual counties were given the opportunity to vote on unification of superior and municipal courts within their respective counties. By late 2000, all counties had voted to unify these courts. Courts that were formally Municipal Courts are now known as Limited Jurisdiction Superior Courts. In some counties, superior and municipal courts were combined into one superior court. Civil under $25,000 is a Limited Civil Court, over $25,000 is an Unlimited Civil Court, and if both are over and under, then the court is a Combined Civil Court.

It is important to note that Limited or Municipal Courts may try minor felonies not included under our felony definition.

Due to its large number of courts - 38 - the Los Angeles County section is arranged uniquely in this book. Each Branch or Division of the Los Angeles Superior Court is given by name, which usually indicates a court's general jurisdictional and geographic boundary (the actual jurisdiction area is noted in the text). The court name is followed by the District it is located in - South Central, West, Northeast, Central, etc. Also, a court name may mention whether its jurisdiction is "Civil" only or "Criminal" only.

ONLINE ACCESS

There is no statewide online computer access available, internal or external. However, a number of counties have developed their own online access sytems and provide Internet access at no fee. Also, www.courtinfo.ca.gov contains very useful information about the state court system.

ADDITIONAL INFORMATION

If there is more than one court of a type within a county, where the case is tried and where the record is held depends on how a citation is written, where the infraction occurred, or where the filer chose to file the case.

Some courts now require signed releases from the subject in order to perform criminal searches and will no longer allow the public to conduct such searches.

Personal checks are acceptable by state law.

Although fees are set by statute, courts interpret them differently. For example, the search fee is supposed to be $5.00 per name per year searched, but many courts charge only $5.00 per name. Generally, certification is $6.00 per document and copies are $.50 per page, in some counties $.75 each, and in Los Angeles county, $.57 each.

Alameda County

Superior Court - Criminal 1225 Fallon St Rm 107, Oakland, CA 94612; 510-272-6777; Fax: 510-835-4850. Hours: 8:30AM-4:30PM (PST). *Felony.*

www.co.alameda.ca.us/courts/index.shtml

Note: Located at the Rene C Davidson Alameda County Courthouse.

Criminal Records: Access: Mail, in person. Both court and visitors may perform in person searches. Search fee: $5.00 per name per year. There is no fee if you do the search. Required to search: name, years to search; also helpful: DOB, SSN. Criminal records on computer from 1975, on microfiche from 1940, archived and indexed from 1880.

General Information: No probation, medical, adoption, juvenile or sealed records released. SASE required. Turnaround time 1 week. Copy fee: $.75 per page. Certification fee: $6.00. Fee payee: Clerk of Superior Court. Personal checks accepted. Prepayment is required.

Superior Court North Branch - Civil 1225 Fallon St Rm 109, Oakland, CA 94612; 510-272-6799. Hours: 8:30AM-4:30PM (PST). *Civil Actions Over $25,000, Probate.*

www.co.alameda.ca.us/courts/index.shtml

Note: Located at the Rene C Davidson Alameda County Courthouse.

Civil Records: Access: Mail, in person, online. Both court and visitors may perform in person searches. Search fee: $5.00 per name per year. Additional $5.00 fee for years prior to 1974. Required to search: name, years to search. Civil cases indexed by defendant, plaintiff. Civil records on computer from 1974, on microfiche and archived from 1900s. Online access to calendars, limited civil case summaries and complex litigations are available free from the Register of Actions/Domain Web at the web site. Search limited cases by number; litigations by case name or number.

General Information: Public Access terminal is available. No sealed records nor adoption records released unless court ordered. SASE required. Turnaround time 2 weeks. Copy fee: $.75 per page. Certification fee: $6.00. Fee payee: Superior Court. Personal checks accepted. Prepayment is required.

Superior Court Pleasanton Branch - Civil 5672 Stoneridge Dr 1st Fl, Pleasanton, CA 94588; 925-803-7123. Hours: 8:30AM-4:30PM (PST). *Civil Actions Over $25,000, Probate.*

www.co.alameda.ca.us/courts/index.shtml

Note: Located at the Schenone Hall of Justice.

Civil Records: Access: Mail, in person, online. Both court and visitors may perform in person searches. Search fee: $5.00 per name per year. Required to search: name, years to search. Civil cases indexed by defendant, plaintiff. Civil records on computer from 1976, on microfiche and archived from 1900s. Online access to calendars, limited civil case summaries and complex litigations are available free from the Register of Actions/Domain Web at the web site. Search limited cases by number; litigations by case name or number.

General Information: Public Access terminal is available. No sealed or confidential records released. SASE required. Turnaround time 2 weeks. Copy fee: $.75 per page. Certification fee: $6.00. Fee payee: Alameda County Superior Court. Personal checks accepted. Prepayment is required.

Superior Court South Branch/Hayward - Civil 24405 Amador St Rm 108, Hayward, CA 94544; 510-670-5060; Fax: 510-783-9456. Hours: 8:30AM-4:30PM (PST). *Civil Actions Over $25,000, Probate.*

www.co.alameda.ca.us/courts/index.shtml

Note: Located at the Hayward Hall of Justice.

Civil Records: Access: Mail, in person, online. Both court and visitors may perform in person searches. Search fee: $5.00 per name. Required to search: name, years to search. Civil cases indexed by defendant, plaintiff. Civil records on computer from 1976, on microfiche and archived from 1900s. Online access to calendars, limited civil case summaries and complex litigations are available free from the Register of Actions/Domain Web at the web site. Search limited cases by number; litigations by case name or number.

General Information: No sealed files, paternity or adoption records released. SASE required. Turnaround time 4-6 weeks. Copy fee: $.75 per page. Certification fee: $6.00. Fee payee: Clerk of Superior Court. Personal checks accepted. Prepayment is required.

Alameda Branch Superior Court 2233 Shoreline Dr, Alameda, CA 94501; 510-268-4208; Civil phone: 510-268-7484; Criminal phone: 510-268-4293; Fax: 510-523-7964. Hours: 8:30AM-4:30PM (PST). *Misdemeanor, Civil Actions Under $25,000, Eviction, Small Claims.*

www.co.alameda.ca.us/courts/index.shtml

Note: Co-extensive with the city limits of Alameda only. Located at the George E McDonald Hall of Justice.

Civil Records: Access: Mail, in person, online. Both court and visitors may perform in person searches. Search fee: $5.00 per name. Required to search: name, years to search. Civil cases indexed by defendant, plaintiff. Civil records on computer since 1987. Online access to calendars, limited civil case summaries and complex litigations are available free from the Register of Actions/Domain Web at the web site. Search limited cases by number; litigations by case name or number.

Criminal Records: Access: Mail, in person. Both court and visitors may perform in person searches. Search fee: $5.00 per name. Required to search: name, years to search, DOB, signed release; also helpful: SSN. Criminal records on computer 7 years back. Only seven year search available.

General Information: No confidential records released. SASE required. Turnaround time 1 week. Copy fee: $.75 per page. Certification fee: $6.00. Fee payee: Alameda Superior Court. Personal checks accepted. Credit cards accepted. Accepted in person only. Prepayment is required.

Berkeley/Albany Superior Court - Civil 2000 Center St, Room 202, Berkeley, CA 94704; 510-644-6423. Hours: 8:30AM-4:30PM (PST). *Civil Actions Under $25,000, Eviction, Small Claims.*

www.co.alameda.ca.us/courts/index.shtml

Note: Co-extensive with the city limits of Berkeley and Albany.

Civil Records: Access: Mail, in person, online. Both court and visitors may perform in person searches. Search fee: $5.00 per name. Required to search: name, years to search. Civil cases indexed by defendant, plaintiff. Civil records on computer from 1986. Online access to calendars, limited civil case summaries and complex litigations are available free from the Register of Actions/Domain Web at the web site. Search limited cases by number; litigations by case name or number.

General Information: Public Access terminal is available. No sealed, judge's notes or confidential records released. SASE required. Turnaround time 1 week. Copy fee: $.75 per page. Certification fee: $6.00.

Fee payee: Berkeley Superior Court. Personal checks accepted. Prepayment is required.

Berkeley/Albany Superior Court - Criminal 2120 Martin Luther King Jr Way, Berkeley, CA 94704; 510-644-6917; Fax: 510-848-6916. Hours: 8:30AM-4:30PM (PST). *Misdemeanor.*

www.co.alameda.ca.us/courts/index.shtml

Note: Co-extensive with the city limits of Berkeley and Albany. Located at the Berkeley Courthouse.

Criminal Records: Access: Mail, in person. Only the court performs in person searches; visitors may not. Search fee: $5.00 per name. Required to search: name, signed release, years to search (within 3-7 years), DOB; also helpful: SSN. Criminal records on computer from 1984.

General Information: No sealed or confidential records released. SASE required. Turnaround time 1 week. Copy fee: $.75 per page. Certification fee: $6.00 per document. Fee payee: Superior Court. Personal checks accepted. Prepayment is required.

Fremont/Newark/Union City Superior Court 39439 Paseo Padre Pky, Fremont, CA 94538; Civil phone: 510-795-2345; Criminal phone: 510-795-2300; Fax: 510-795-2349. Hours: 8:30AM-5PM (PST). *Misdemeanor, Civil Actions Under $25,000, Eviction, Small Claims.*

www.co.alameda.ca.us/courts/index.shtml

Note: Jurisdiction includes Fremont, Newark and Union City. Located at the Fremont Hall of Justice.

Civil Records: Access: Fax, mail, in person, online. Both court and visitors may perform in person searches. Search fee: $5.00 per name. Required to search: name, years to search. Civil cases indexed by defendant, plaintiff. Civil records on computer from 1990. Online access to calendars, limited civil case summaries and complex litigations are available free from the Register of Actions/Domain Web at the web site. Search limited cases by number; litigations by case name or number.

Criminal Records: Access: Fax, mail, in person. Both court and visitors may perform in person searches. Search fee: $5.00 per name. Required to search: name, years to search, DOB, signed release. Criminal records on computer only go back 7 years.

General Information: Public Access terminal is available. (Public access terminal for civil only.) No sealed or confidential records released. SASE required. Turnaround time 1 week. Fax notes: Will fax civil results only, $1.00 per page. Copy fee: $.75 per page. Certification fee: $6.75. Fee payee: Fremont Superior Court. Personal checks accepted. Prepayment is required.

Hayward Superior Court 24405 Amador St, Hayward, CA 94544; Civil phone: 510-670-6432; Criminal phone: 510-670-6434; Fax: 510-670-5522. Hours: 8:30AM-4:30PM (PST). *Misdemeanor, Civil Actions Under $25,000, Eviction, Small Claims.*

www.co.alameda.ca.us/courts/index.shtml

Note: Formerly San Leandro/Hayward Superior Ct. Includes the cities of San Leandro, Hayward and adjoining unincorporated areas of Castro Valley and San Lorenzo. Located at the Hayward Hall of Justice.

Civil Records: Access: Fax, mail, in person, online. Both court and visitors may perform in person searches. Search fee: $5.00 per name. Required to search: name, years to search. Civil cases indexed by defendant, plaintiff. Civil records on computer back 20 years; also on paper index. Online access to calendars, limited civil case summaries and complex litigations are available free from the Register of Actions/Domain Web at the web site. Search limited cases by number; litigations by case name or number.

Criminal Records: Access: Fax, mail, in person. Both court and visitors may perform in person searches. Search fee: $5.00 per name. Fee is per case. Required to search: name, years to search, DOB, signed release; also helpful: SSN. Criminal records on computer back 20 years; also on paper index.

General Information: Public Access terminal is available. No sealed or confidential records released. SASE required. Turnaround time 2 weeks. Fax notes: No fee to fax results. Copy fee: $.75 per page. Certification fee: $6.00. Fee payee: Clerk of the Court. Personal checks accepted. Credit cards accepted: Visa, MasterCard. ATM card accepted. Prepayment is required.

Livermore/Pleasanton/Dublin Superior Court

5672 Stoneridge Dr, Pleasanton, CA 94588; 925-803-7123; Fax: 925-803-7979 (civ) 803-7989 (crim). Hours: 8:30AM-4:30PM (PST). *Misdemeanor, Civil Actions Under $25,000, Eviction, Small Claims.*

www.co.alameda.ca.us/courts/index.shtml

Note: Includes the cities of Livermore, Dublin, Sunol and Pleasanton and all areas east to San Joaquin County line, north of Highway 580 to Contra Costa line. Located at the Gale/Schenone Hall of Justice.

Civil Records: Access: Mail, in person, online. Both court and visitors may perform in person searches. Search fee: $5.00 per name. Required to search: name, years to search. Civil cases indexed by defendant, plaintiff. Civil records on computer from 1990. Online access to calendars, limited civil case summaries and complex litigations are available free from the Register of Actions/Domain Web at the web site. Search limited cases by number; litigations by case name or number.

Criminal Records: Access: Mail, in person. Both court and visitors may perform in person searches. Search fee: $5.00 per name. Required to search: name, years to search; also helpful: address, DOB. Criminal records on computer from 1990.

General Information: No records older than 10 years are released. SASE required. Turnaround time 1 week. Copy fee: $.75 per page. Certification fee: $6.00. Fee payee: Livermore Superior Court. Personal checks accepted. Credit cards accepted: Visa, MasterCard. Prepayment is required.

Oakland/Piedmont/Emeryville Superior Court - Civil

600 Washington St, 4th Floor, Oakland, CA 94607; 510-268-7724; Fax: 510-268-7807. Hours: 8:30AM-4:30PM (PST). *Civil Actions Under $25,000, Eviction, Small Claims.*

www.co.alameda.ca.us/courts/index.shtml

Note: Comprises the cities of Oakland, Piedmont and Emeryville. Located at the Allen E Broussard Justice Center.

Civil Records: Access: Mail, in person, online. Both court and visitors may perform in person searches. Search fee: $5.00 per name. Required to search: name, years to search. Civil cases indexed by defendant, plaintiff. Civil records on computer from 1990. Online access to calendars, limited civil case summaries and complex litigations are available free from the Register of Actions/Domain Web at the web site. Search limited cases by number; litigations by case name or number.

General Information: No sealed or confidential records released. SASE required. Turnaround time 1 week. Copy fee: $.75 per page. Certification fee: $6.00. Fee payee: Oakland Superior Court. Personal checks accepted. Prepayment is required.

Oakland/Piedmont/Emeryville Superior Court - Criminal

661 Washington St, 2nd Floor, Oakland, CA 94607; 510-268-7700; Fax: 510-268-7705. Hours: 8:30AM-4:30PM (PST). *Misdemeanor.*

www.co.alameda.ca.us/courts/index.shtml

Note: Comprises the cities of Oakland, Piedmont and Emeryville. Located at the Wiley W Manuel Courthouse.

Criminal Records: Access: Mail, in person. Both court and visitors may perform in person searches. Search fee: $5.00 per name. Required to search: name, years to search. Criminal records on computer from 1990.

General Information: No sealed or confidential records released. SASE required. Turnaround time 1 week. Copy fee: $.75 per page. Certification fee: $6.00. Fee payee: Oakland Superior Court. Personal checks accepted. Prepayment is required.

Alpine County

Superior Court PO Box 518, Markleeville, CA 96120; 530-694-2113; Fax: 530-694-2119. Hours: 8AM-Noon, 1-5PM (PST). *Felony, Misdemeanor, Civil, Eviction, Small Claims, Probate.*

www.alpine.courts.ca.gov

Civil Records: Access: Mail, in person. Both court and visitors may perform in person searches. Search fee: $5.00 per name per year. Required to search: name, years to search. Civil cases indexed by defendant, plaintiff. Civil records on index file from 1981, archived from 1800s. Computer records go back 10 years.

Criminal Records: Access: Mail, in person. Both court and visitors may perform in person searches. Search fee: $5.00 per name per year. Required to search: name, years to search; also helpful-SSN. Criminal records on index file from 1981, archived from 1800s. Computer records go back 10 years.

General Information: No juvenile, paternity, adoption or sealed released. SASE required. Turnaround time 2 days. Fax notes: Fee to fax results is $1.00 per page. Copy fee: $.50 per page. Certification fee: $6.00 per page. Fee payee: Alpine County Court Services. Personal checks accepted. Prepayment is required.

Amador County

Superior Court 108 Court St, Jackson, CA 95642; 209-223-6463. Hours: 8AM-4PM (PST). *Felony, Misdemeanor, Civil, Eviction, Small Claims, Probate.*

Civil Records: Access: Mail, in person. Both court and visitors may perform in person searches. Search fee: $5.00 per name. Required to search: name, years to search. Civil cases indexed by defendant, plaintiff. Civil records on computer from 1989, archived and indexed from 1800s.

Criminal Records: Access: Phone, fax, mail, in person. Only the court performs in person searches; visitors may not. Search fee: $5.00 per name. $5.00 for search by case number. Required to search: name, years to search. Criminal records on computer from 1989, archived and indexed from 1800s. Phone & fax access limited to short searches.

General Information: No adoption, juvenile or paternity records released. SASE required. Turnaround time 7-14 days. Fax notes: Will fax results to 800 numbers only. Copy fee: $1.00 for first page, $.20 each add'l. Certification fee: $6.00. Fee payee: Superior Court Clerk. Personal checks accepted. Prepayment is required.

Butte County

Superior Court One Court St, Oroville, CA 95965; 530-538-7551; Fax: 530-538-2112. Hours: 8:30AM-4PM (PST). *Felony, Misdemeanor, Civil, Probate.*

www.courtinfo.ca.gov/trialcourts/butte

Note: This courthouse physically holds most court files for the county; however, one can search the countywide computer index at any court. Closed Probate cases are archived in the court's basement; Active case records are at Chico court, 530-891-2988.

Civil Records: Access: Fax, mail, in person. Both court and visitors may perform in person searches. Search

fee: $5.00 per name. Required to search: name, years to search; also helpful: address. Civil cases indexed by defendant, plaintiff. Civil records on computer from 1988, on microfiche from 1983 thru 1988, archives at University, in index file from 1925.

Criminal Records: Access: Mail, in person. Both court and visitors may perform in person searches. Search fee: $5.00 per name. Required to search: name, years to search; also helpful: DOB. Criminal records on computer from 1988, on microfiche from 1983 thru 1988, archives at University, in index file from 1925.

General Information: Public Access terminal is available. No juvenile, paternity or adoption records released. SASE required. Turnaround time 1 week. Fax notes: $5.00 for first page, $1.00 each add'l. Copy fee: $.50 per page. $1.00 minimum. Certification fee: $6.00. Fee payee: Butte County Superior Court. Personal checks accepted. Credit cards accepted: Visa, MasterCard. Prepayment is required.

Chico Branch - Superior Court

655 Oleander Ave, Chico, CA 95926; 530-891-2716 (Traffic); Civil phone: 530-891-2702; Criminal phone: 530-891-2703. Hours: 8:30AM-4PM (PST). *Misdemeanor, Civil Actions Under $25,000, Eviction, Small Claims, Probate.*

Note: Active county Probate case records are located here; closed cases are archived in the basement at the main Superior Court in Oroville.

Civil Records: Access: Mail, in person. Only the court performs in person searches; visitors may not. Search fee: $5.00 per name. Required to search: name, years to search. Civil cases indexed by defendant, plaintiff. Civil records in index files. Records destroyed after 10 years.

Criminal Records: Access: Mail, in person. Only the court performs in person searches; visitors may not. Search fee: $5.00 per name. Required to search: name, years to search; also helpful: DOB. Criminal records in index files. Records destroyed after 10 years.

General Information: No sealed records released. SASE required. Turnaround time 2-3 days. Copy fee: $1.00 for first page, $.50 each add'l. Certification fee: $6.00. Fee payee: Superior Court. Personal checks accepted. Prepayment is required.

Gridley Branch - Superior Court

1931 Arlin Rhine Dr., Oroville, CA 95965; 530-846-5701. Hours: 8AM-1PM 2 days a month (PST). *Misdemeanor, Eviction, Small Claims.*

Note: Open the first "full week" Thursday and 3rd Thursday. The court's physical address is 239 Sycamore, Gridley, CA.

Criminal Records: Access: In person, mail. Only the court performs in person searches; visitors may not. Search fee: $5.00 per name. Required to search: name, years to search.

General Information: Turnaround time 2 days. Fee payee: Butte County Superior Court. Prepayment is required.

Paradise Branch - Superior Court

747 Elliott Rd, Paradise, CA 95969; 530-872-6347. Hours: 8AM-1PM M-W & F; 8AM-Noon, 1-5PM Th; Phone Hours: 9AM-Noon M-F (PST). *Misdemeanor, Eviction, Small Claims.*

Civil Records: Access: Mail, in person. Only the court performs in person searches; visitors may not. Search fee: $5.00 per name. Required to search: name; also helpful: years to search. Civil cases indexed by defendant, plaintiff. Civil records are located in North Butte County Municipal Court. Records go back to 1980; on computer back to 1997.

Criminal Records: Access: Mail, in person. Only the court performs in person searches; visitors may not. Search fee: $5.00 per name. Required to search: name, years to search. Criminal records are located in North

Butte County Municipal Court. Records go back to 1980; on computer back to 1997.

General Information: No sealed records released. SASE required. Turnaround time 2-3 days. Copy fee: $1.00 for first page, $.50 each add'l. Certification fee: $6.00. Fee payee: Superior Court. Personal checks accepted. Prepayment is required.

Calaveras County

Superior Court 891 Mt Ranch Rd, San Andreas, CA 95249; 209-754-6310/6311/6338; Fax: 209-754-6689. Hours: 8AM-4PM (PST). *Misdemeanor, Civil, Small Claims, Probate.*

www.co.calaveras.ca.us/departments/courts.html

Civil Records: Access: Phone, mail, in person. Both court and visitors may perform in person searches. Search fee: $5.00 per name. Fee is for each 15 year period. Required to search: name, years to search. Civil cases indexed by defendant, plaintiff. Civil records on computer since 6/96; in index books and microfiche from 1975.

Criminal Records: Access: Mail, in person. Both court and visitors may perform in person searches. Search fee: $5.00 per name. Fee is for each 15 year period. Required to search: name, years to search, DOB; also helpful: aliases. Criminal records on computer since 6/96; in index books and microfiche from 1975.

General Information: No juvenile or confidential records released. SASE required. Turnaround time 2-3 weeks. Copy fee: $.50 per page. Certification fee: $6.00. Fee payee: Calaveras Superior Court. Personal checks accepted. Prepayment is required.

Colusa County

Superior Court 547 Market St - Dept. 1, Colusa, CA 95932; 530-458-0507; Fax: 530-458-2230. Hours: 8:30AM-5PM (PST). *Felony, Civil Actions Over $25,000, Probate.*

Note: Since 1995, the records have been combined for both courts in this county; prior records must be searched at the individual courts. Mailing address is 532 Oak St.

Civil Records: Access: Mail, in person. Both court and visitors may perform in person searches. Search fee: $5.00 per name. Required to search: name, years to search. Civil cases indexed by defendant, plaintiff. Civil records on computer from 1986, in index files from 1800s.

Criminal Records: Access: Mail, in person. Both court and visitors may perform in person searches. Search fee: $5.00 per name. Required to search: name, years to search. Criminal records on computer from 1986, in index files from 1800s.

General Information: Public Access terminal is available. No juvenile, paternity (except Judgment) or adoption records released. SASE required. Turnaround time 2 days. Copy fee: $.50 per page. Certification fee: $6.00. Fee payee: Colusa County Superior Court. Personal checks accepted. Prepayment is required.

Colusa Superior Court 532 Oak St, Dept 2, Colusa, CA 95932; 530-458-5149; Fax: 530-458-2230. Hours: 8:30AM-5PM (PST). *Misdemeanor, Civil Actions Under $25,000, Eviction, Small Claims.*

Note: Since 1995, records from both courts in this county have been combined; prior records must be searched at the individual courts.

Civil Records: Access: Mail, in person. Both court and visitors may perform in person searches. Search fee: $5.00 per name per year. Required to search: name, years to search. Civil cases indexed by defendant, plaintiff. Civil records on computer from 1994, index books prior.

Criminal Records: Access: Mail, in person. Both court and visitors may perform in person searches. Search fee: $5.00 per name per year. Required to search: name,

years to search, DOB. Criminal records on computer from 1994, index books prior.

General Information: Public Access terminal is available. No sealed records released. SASE required. Turnaround time 1-2 days. Copy fee: $.50 per page. Certification fee: $6.00. Fee payee: Colusa Superior Court. Personal checks accepted. Prepayment is required.

Contra Costa County

Superior Court 725 Court St Rm 103, Martinez, CA 94553; 925-646-2950; Civil phone: 925-646-2951; Criminal phone: 925-646-2440. Hours: 8AM-4PM (PST). *Felony, Civil Actions Over $25,000, Probate.*

www.co.contra-costa.ca.us

Civil Records: Access: Mail, online, in person. Both court and visitors may perform in person searches. Search fee: $5.00 per name. Required to search: name, years to search. Civil cases indexed by defendant, plaintiff. Civil records on computer from 1987, on microfiche from 1900s. There is a free remote dial-up system for civil, probate and county law records. Call 925-646-2479 for details.

Criminal Records: Access: Mail, in person. Both court and visitors may perform in person searches. Search fee: $5.00 per name. Required to search: name, years to search; also helpful: DOB. Criminal records on computer from 1987, on microfiche from 1900s.

General Information: No adoption, juvenile or sealed records released. SASE required. Turnaround time 1 week. Copy fee: $1.00 per page. Certification fee: $6.00. Fee payee: Clerk of the Superior Court. Business checks accepted. Prepayment is required.

Walnut Creek Branch - Superior Court 640 Ygnacio Valley Rd (PO Box 5128), Walnut Creek, CA 94596-1128; 925-646-6578; Civil phone: 925-646-6579; Criminal phone: 925-646-6572. Hours: 8:30AM-4:30PM (PST). *Felony, Misdemeanor, Civil Actions Under $25,000, Eviction, Small Claims.*

www.co.contra-costa.ca.us

Note: Includes Alamo, Canyon, Danville, Lafayette, Moraga, Orinda, Rheem, San Ramon, St Mary's College, Walnut Creek and Ygnacio Valley. Effective 01/01/99, this court has all civil records formally at the municipal court in Concord.

Civil Records: Access: Phone, mail, online, in person. Both court and visitors may perform in person searches. Search fee: $5.00 per name. Add $5.00 archive retrieval fee for older cases. In person searching of microfiche is free. Required to search: name; also helpful: years to search. Civil cases indexed by defendant, plaintiff. Civil records on computer from 1991. Records are destroyed after 10 years. There is a free remote dial-up system for civil, probate and family law records. Call 925-646-2479 for sign-up.

Criminal Records: Access: Mail, in person. Both court and visitors may perform in person searches. Search fee: $5.00 per name. Add $5.00 archive retrieval fee for older cases. Required to search: name, years to search, DOB.

General Information: No probation reports or sealed case records released. SASE required. Turnaround time 2 days. Copy fee: $1.00 per page. Certification fee: $6.00. Fee payee: Walnut Creek Superior Court. Personal checks accepted. Credit cards accepted. Prepayment is required.

Pittsburg Branch - Superior Court 45 Civic Ave, Pittsburg, CA 94565-0431; Civil phone: 925-427-8159; Criminal phone: 925-427-8173. Hours: 8AM-4PM; 8AM-5PM Tues. (PST). *Misdemeanor, Civil Actions Under $25,000, Eviction, Small Claims.*

www.co.contra-costa.ca.us

Note: Includes Antioch, Bay Pt., Bradford Island, Brentwood, Byron, Discovery Bay, Knightsen, Oakley, Pittsburg.

Civil Records: Access: Mail, online, in person. Both court and visitors may perform in person searches. Search fee: $5.00 per name. Required to search: name, years to search. Civil cases indexed by defendant, plaintiff. Civil records on computer from 1991. Records are destroyed after 10 years. There is a free remote dial-up system for civil, probate and family law records. Call 925-646-2479 for sign-up.

Criminal Records: Access: Mail, in person. Both court and visitors may perform in person searches. Search fee: $5.00 per name. Required to search: name, years to search, DOB. Criminal records on computer from 1991, index files for 10 years. Records are destroyed after 10 years. Visitor may search microfiche only.

General Information: No probation reports released. SASE required. Turnaround time 2 days. Copy fee: $1.00 per page. Certification fee: $6.00. Fee payee: Superior Court. Personal checks accepted. Prepayment is required.

Richmond Superior Court 100 37th St Rm 185, Richmond, CA 94805; Civil phone: 510-374-3137; Criminal phone: 510-374-3158. Hours: 8AM-4PM (PST). *Misdemeanor, Civil Actions Under $25,000, Eviction, Small Claims.*

www.co.contra-costa.ca.us

Note: Includes Crockett, El Cerrito, El Sobrante, Hercules, Kensington, North Richmond, Pinole, Point Richmond, Port Costa, Richmond, Rodeo, Rollingwood and San Pablo.

Civil Records: Access: Mail, in person. Both court and visitors may perform in person searches. Search fee: $5.00 per name. Required to search: name. Civil cases indexed by defendant, plaintiff. Civil records on computer from 1991. Records are destroyed after 10 years. There is a free remote dial-up service for civil, probate and family law records. Call 925-646-2479 for sign-up and fee information.

Criminal Records: Access: Mail, in person. Only the court performs in person searches; visitors may not. Search fee: $5.00 per name. There is an additional fee for retrieval of archive files. Required to search: name, years to search; also helpful: address, DOB, SSN. Criminal records on computer from 1991, index files from 1983. Records are destroyed after 10 years.

General Information: No probation reports released. SASE required. Turnaround time 5 days. Copy fee: $1.00 per page. Certification fee: $6.00. Fee payee: Richmond Superior Court. Personal checks accepted. Prepayment is required.

Del Norte County

Superior Court 450 "H" St Rm 182, Crescent City, CA 95531; 707-464-7205; Fax: 707-465-4005. Hours: 8AM-Noon,1-5PM (PST). *Felony, Misdemeanor, Civil, Eviction, Small Claims, Probate.*

Civil Records: Access: Phone, fax, mail, in person. Both court and visitors may perform in person searches. Search fee: $5.00 per name per year. Required to search: name, years to search. Civil cases indexed by defendant, plaintiff. Civil records archived and in index file from 1970s.

Criminal Records: Access: Mail, fax, in person. Both court and visitors may perform in person searches. Search fee: $5.00 per name per year. Required to search: name, years to search, DOB, middle name; also helpful-SSN. Criminal records archived and in index file from 1970s, index books prior in handwritten records.

General Information: No adoption, juvenile, probate, LPS conservatorship released. SASE required. Turnaround time 1-2 days. Copy fee: $.50 per page. Certification fee: $6.00. Plus $.50 per page. Fee payee:

Superior Court. Personal checks accepted. Prepayment is required.

El Dorado County

Placerville Branch - Superior Court 495 Main St, Placerville, CA 95667; 530-621-6426; Fax: 530-622-9774. Hours: 8AM-4PM (PST). *Felony, Civil, Probate.*

http://co.el-dorado.ca.us/superiorcourts

Civil Records: Access: Mail, in person. Both court and visitors may perform in person searches. Search fee: $5.00 per name. Required to search: name, years to search. Civil cases indexed by defendant, plaintiff. Civil records on computer from 1989, in hardbound books from 1979 to 1989, prior archived in Placerville.
Criminal Records: Access: Mail, fax, in person. Both court and visitors may perform in person searches. Search fee: $5.00 per name. Required to search: name, years to search. Criminal records on computer from 1989, in hardbound books from 1979 to 1989, prior archived in Placerville.
General Information: No adoption, juvenile, mental or confidential released. SASE required. Turnaround time 2 weeks. Copy fee: $.50 per page. Certification fee: $6.00. Fee payee: Clerk of Court. Personal checks accepted. Prepayment is required.

South Lake Tahoe Branch - Superior Court - Civil 1354 Johnson Blvd #2, South Lake Tahoe, CA 96150; 530-573-3075/3069; Fax: 530-544-6532. Hours: 8AM-4PM (PST). *Civil, Eviction, Probate.*

Civil Records: Access: Phone, mail, in person. Both court and visitors may perform in person searches. Search fee: $5.00 per name. Required to search: name, years to search. Civil cases indexed by defendant, plaintiff. Civil records on computer from 1989, in hardbound books from 1979 to 1989, prior archived in Placerville. **General Information:** No adoption, juvenile, mental or confidential released. SASE required. Turnaround time 2 weeks. Copy fee: $.50 per page. Certification fee: $6.00. Fee payee: Superior Court. Personal checks accepted. Prepayment is required.

South Lake Tahoe Branch - Superior Court - Criminal 1354 Johnson Blvd #1, South Lake Tahoe, CA 96150; 530-573-3047; Fax: 530-542-9102. Hours: 8AM-4PM (PST). *Felony, Misdemeanor.*

www.co.el-dorado.ca.us/superiorcourts

Criminal Records: Access: Mail, in person. Both court and visitors may perform in person searches. Search fee: $5.00 per name. Required to search: name, years to search; also helpful: DOB, SSN. Criminal records on computer from 1991, index files from 1983. Records are destroyed after 10 years.
General Information: No probation reports released. SASE required. Turnaround time 2 days. Copy fee: $.50 per page. Certification fee: $6.00. Fee payee: El Dorado Superior Court. Personal checks accepted. Prepayment is required.

Cameron Park Branch - Superior Court 3321 Cameron Park Dr, Cameron Park, CA 95682; 530-621-5867; Fax: 530-672-2413. Hours: 8AM-4PM (PST). *Misdemeanor.*

www.co.el-dorado.ca.us/superiorcourts/index.html

Note: This is a trial court only. Only records prior to 1995 are housed here. Records from 1995 and after are available at the Placerville Branch Superior Court. Civil cases are handled in Placerville.

Criminal Records: Access: Mail, in person. Both court and visitors may perform in person searches. Search fee: $5.00 per name. Required to search: name, years to search; also helpful: address, DOB. Criminal records on

computer from 1991, index files from 1983. Records are destroyed after 10 years.
General Information: No probation reports released. SASE required. Turnaround time 1 week. Copy fee: $.50 per page. Certification fee: $6.00. Fee payee: Superior Court. Personal checks accepted. Prepayment is required.

Fairlane Branch Superior Court 2850 Fairlane Ct, Placerville, CA 95667; Civil phone: 530-621-6460; Criminal phone: 530-621-7464. Hours: 8AM-4PM (PST). *Misdemeanor, Small Claims, Traffic.*

Civil Records: Access: Mail, in person. Both court and visitors may perform in person searches. Search fee: $1.75 per name per year. Required to search: name, years to search. Civil cases indexed by defendant, plaintiff. Civil records on computer from 1991. Actual records after 1996 are kept at the main Superior Court in Placerville. Address to Dept. 8.
Criminal Records: Access: Mail, in person. Both court and visitors may perform in person searches. Search fee: $5.00 per name. Required to search: name, years to search; also helpful: DOB. Criminal records on computer from 1994, prior on index books, index files from 1983. Records are destroyed after 10 years. Address to Dept 7.
General Information: No probation reports released. SASE required. Turnaround time 2 weeks. Copy fee: $.50 per page. Certification fee: $6.00. Fee payee: El Dorado County Superior Courts. Personal checks accepted. Prepayment is required.

Fresno County

Superior Court 1100 Van Ness Ave, #401, Fresno, CA 93724; Civil phone: 559-448-3352; Criminal phone: 559-488-3142; Probate phone: 559-488-3618; Fax: 559-488-1976. Hours: 8AM-4PM (PST). *Felony, Misdemeanor, Civil, Small Claims, Probate.*

www.fresno.ca.gov/2810/index.htm

Note: The telephone number for the Limited Civil clerk is 599-488-3453.

Civil Records: Access: Phone, fax, mail, in person. Both court and visitors may perform in person searches. Search fee: $5.00 per name. Required to search: name, years to search. Civil cases indexed by defendant, plaintiff. Civil records on computer back to 1976, on microfiche, index files and archived from 1800s.
Criminal Records: Access: Phone, fax, mail, in person. Both court and visitors may perform in person searches. Search fee: $5.00 per name. Required to search: name, years to search. Criminal records on computer back to 1976, microfiche, index files and archived from 1800s.
General Information: Public Access terminal is available. No confidential, adoption or juvenile records released. SASE required. Turnaround time 3-5 days. Copy fee: $.50 per page. Certification fee: $6.00. Fee payee: Superior Court Clerk's Office. Personal checks accepted. Prepayment is required.

Kingsburg Division - Superior Court 1600 California St, Kingsburg, CA 93631; 559-897-2241; Fax: 559-897-1419. Hours: 8AM-Noon, 1-4PM (PST). *Felony, Misdemeanor, Civil Actions Under $25,000, Eviction, Small Claims.*

www.fresno.ca.gov/2810/kingsburg.htm

Note: This court includes records from the branch court closed in Riverdale.

Civil Records: Access: Mail, in person. Only the court performs in person searches; visitors may not. Search fee: $5.00 per name. Required to search: name, years to search.
Criminal Records: Access: Mail, in person. Only the court performs in person searches; visitors may not.

Search fee: $5.00 per name. Required to search: name, years to search, DOB. Criminal records on computer from April, 1994, index cards prior.
General Information: No confidential records released. SASE required. Turnaround time 1 week. Copy fee: $.50 per page. Certification fee: $6.00. Fee payee: Superior Court. Personal checks accepted. Prepayment is required.

Clovis Division - Superior Court 1011 5th St, Clovis, CA 93612; 559-299-4964; Fax: 559-299-2595. Hours: 8AM-4PM (PST). *Misdemeanor, Civil Actions Under $25,000, Eviction, Small Claims.*

www.fresno.ca.gov/2810/clovis.htm

Note: Includes the city of Clovis and surrounding area.

Civil Records: Access: Mail, in person. Only the court performs in person searches; visitors may not. Search fee: $5.00. Required to search: name, years to search. Civil cases indexed by defendant, plaintiff. Civil records on computer and index files from 1983. Records destroyed after 10 years.
Criminal Records: Access: Mail, in person. Only the court performs in person searches; visitors may not. Search fee: $5.00. Required to search: name, years to search, DOB. Criminal records on computer and index files from 1983. Records destroyed after 10 years.
General Information: No probation reports released. SASE required. Turnaround time 1 week. Copy fee: $.50 per page. Certification fee: $6.00. Fee payee: Clovis Superior Court. Personal checks accepted. Prepayment is required.

Coalinga Division - Superior Court 160 West Elm St, Coalinga, CA 93210; 559-935-2017/2018; Fax: 559-935-5324. Hours: 8AM-Noon, 1-4PM (PST). *Misdemeanor, Civil Actions Under $25,000, Eviction, Small Claims.*

www.fresno.ca.gov/2810/coalinga

Civil Records: Access: Mail, in person. Only the court performs in person searches; visitors may not. No search fee. Required to search: name, years to search; also helpful: address. Civil cases indexed by defendant, plaintiff. Civil records on index cards and are computerized since 1990. Will only search back 10 years.
Criminal Records: Access: Mail, in person. Only the court performs in person searches; visitors may not. No search fee. Required to search: name, years to search, DOB; also helpful: address, SSN. Criminal records on computer from 1990, on index cards prior. Will only search back 10 years, Traffic 10 years.
General Information: No confidential records or cases not finished released. SASE required. Turnaround time 1 week. Copy fee: $.50 per page. Certification fee: $6.00. Fee payee: Superior Court. Personal checks accepted. Prepayment is required.

Firebaugh Division - Superior Court 1325 "O" St, Firebaugh, CA 93622; 559-659-2011/2012; Fax: 559-659-6228. Hours: 8AM-4:30 M; 8AM-4PM T-F (PST). *Misdemeanor, Civil Actions Under $25,000, Eviction, Small Claims.*

www.fresno.ca.gov/2810/firebaugh

Civil Records: Access: Phone, fax, mail, in person. Only the court performs in person searches; visitors may not. Search fee: $5.00 per name. Required to search: name, years to search. Civil cases indexed by defendant, plaintiff. Civil records on computer from 1990, index cards prior. Will only search back 7 years.
Criminal Records: Access: Phone, fax, mail, in person. Only the court performs in person searches; visitors may not. Search fee: $5.00 per name. Required to search: name, years to search, DOB. Criminal records on computer from 1990, index cards prior. Will only search back 7 years.

General Information: No confidential records released. SASE required. Turnaround time 1 week. Copy fee: $.50 per page. Certification fee: $6.00. Fee payee: Firebaugh Superior Court. Personal checks accepted. Prepayment is required.

Fowler Division - Superior Court PO Box
400, Fowler, CA 93625; 559-834-3215; Fax: 559-834-1645. Hours: 8AM-4PM (PST). *Misdemeanor, Civil Actions Under $25,000, Eviction, Small Claims.*

www.fresno.ca.gov/2810/fowler.htm

Note: This court holds the records for the closed courts in Caruthers and Parlier.

Civil Records: Access: Mail, in person. Only the court performs in person searches; visitors may not. Search fee: $5.00 per name. Required to search: name, years to search. Civil cases indexed by defendant, plaintiff. Civil records on index cards. Will only search back 7 years.
Criminal Records: Access: Mail, in person. Only the court performs in person searches; visitors may not. Search fee: $5.00 per name. Required to search: name, years to search; also helpful: DOB, SSN. Criminal records on computer from 1990, index cards prior. Will only search back 7 years.
General Information: No confidential records released. SASE required. Turnaround time 1 week. Copy fee: $.50 per page. Certification fee: $6.00. Fee payee: Fowler Superior Court. Personal checks accepted. Prepayment is required.

Kerman Division - Superior Court 719 S
Madera Ave, Kerman, CA 93630; 559-846-7371/7372; Fax: 559-846-5751. Hours: 8AM-4PM (2-4 for phone calls) (PST). *Misdemeanor, Civil Actions Under $25,000, Eviction, Small Claims.*

www.fresno.ca.gov/2810/default.htm

Note: The court holds preliminary hearings for felonies.

Civil Records: Access: Phone, mail, in person. Both court and visitors may perform in person searches. No search fee. Required to search: name, years to search. Civil cases indexed by defendant, plaintiff. Civil records on index cards. Will only search back 7 years.
Criminal Records: Access: Phone, mail, in person. Both court and visitors may perform in person searches. No search fee. Required to search: name, years to search. Criminal records on computer from 1990, index cards prior. Will only search back 7 years.
General Information: No confidential records released. SASE required. Turnaround time 1 week. Copy fee: $.50 per page. Certification fee: $6.00. Fee payee: Superior Court. Personal checks accepted. Prepayment is required.

Reedley Division - Superior Court 815 "G"
St, Reedley, CA 93654; 559-638-3114; Fax: 559-637-1534. Hours: 8AM-Noon, 1-4PM (1-4 for phone calls) (PST). *Felony, Misdemeanor, Civil Actions Under $25,000, Eviction, Small Claims.*

www.fresno.ca.gov/2810/reedley.htm

Civil Records: Access: Mail, in person. Both court and visitors may perform in person searches. Search fee: $5.00 per name. Required to search: name, years to search. Civil cases indexed by defendant, plaintiff. Civil records on computer back 10 years, index cards prior. Will only search back 7 years.
Criminal Records: Access: Mail, in person. Both court and visitors may perform in person searches. Search fee: $5.00 per name. Required to search: name, years to search, DOB. Criminal records on computer back 10 years, index cards prior. Will only search back 7 years.
General Information: No confidential records released. SASE required. Turnaround time 1 week. Copy fee: $.50 per page. Certification fee: $6.00. Fee payee: Reedley Superior Court. Personal checks accepted. Prepayment is required.

Sanger Division - Superior Court 619 "N"
St, Sanger, CA 93657; 559-875-7158/7159; Fax: 559-875-0002. Hours: 8AM-Noon, 1-4PM (PST). *Misdemeanor, Civil Actions Under $25,000, Eviction, Small Claims.*

www.fresno.ca.gov/2810/sanger.htm

Note: The clerk's office answers telephone calls from 1-4pm.

Civil Records: Access: Mail, in person. Only the court performs in person searches; visitors may not. Search fee: $5.00 per name. Required to search: name, years to search. Civil cases indexed by defendant, plaintiff. Will only search back 10 years.
Criminal Records: Access: Mail, in person. Only the court performs in person searches; visitors may not. Search fee: $5.00 per name. Required to search: name, years to search, DOB. Criminal records on computer from 1990, index cards prior. Will only search back 10 years.
General Information: No confidential records released. SASE required. Turnaround time 1 week. Copy fee: $.50 per page. Certification fee: $6.00. Fee payee: Superior Court. Personal checks accepted.

Selma Division - Superior Court 2117 Selma
St, Selma, CA 93662; 559-896-2123; Fax: 559-896-4465. Hours: 8AM-Noon, 1-4PM (PST). *Misdemeanor, Civil Actions Under $25,000, Eviction, Small Claims.*

www.fresno.ca.gov/2810/selma.htm

Civil Records: Access: Mail, in person. Only the court performs in person searches; visitors may not. No search fee. Required to search: name, years to search. Civil cases indexed by defendant, plaintiff. Civil records on index cards. Will only search back 7 years.
Criminal Records: Access: Mail, in person. Only the court performs in person searches; visitors may not. No search fee. Required to search: name, years to search, DOB. Criminal records on computer from 1985, index cards prior. Will only search back 7 years.
General Information: No confidential records released. SASE required. Turnaround time 1 week. Copy fee: $.50 per page. Certification fee: $6.00. Fee payee: Selma Superior Court. Personal checks accepted. Prepayment is required.

Glenn County

Superior Court 526 W Sycamore, Willows, CA 95988; 530-934-6446; Fax: 530-934-6406. Hours: 8AM-5PM (PST). *Felony, Misdemeanor, Civil, Small Claims, Probate.*

Note: Records from the municipal court were combined with this court when the courts were consolidated.

Civil Records: Access: Mail, in person. Both court and visitors may perform in person searches. Search fee: $5.00 per search. Required to search: name, years to search. Civil cases indexed by defendant, plaintiff. Civil records on computer from 1996, on microfiche, archived and in index file from 1894.
Criminal Records: Access: Mail, in person. Both court and visitors may perform in person searches. Search fee: $5.00 per search. Required to search: name, years to search; also helpful: DOB. Criminal records on computer from 1996, on microfiche, archived and in index file from 1894.
General Information: No adoption, juvenile or paternity released. SASE required. Turnaround time 1 day. Copy fee: $.50 per page. Certification fee: $6.00. Fee payee: Superior Court. Personal checks accepted. Prepayment is required.

Humboldt County

Superior Court 825 5th Street, Eureka, CA 95501; 707-445-7256. Hours: 8:30AM-Noon, 1-4PM (PST). *Felony, Civil, Probate.*

Note: Countywide searching can be done from this court, records computerized for 10 years. The former Eureka, Eel River, and North Humboldt Municipal Court Divisions have been combined with this court. Physical address is at 421 I Street.

Civil Records: Access: Mail, in person. Both court and visitors may perform in person searches. Search fee: $5.00 per name. Required to search: name, years to search. Civil cases indexed by defendant, plaintiff. Civil records on computer back to 1985; on microfiche and archived from 1964.
Criminal Records: Access: Mail, in person. Both court and visitors may perform in person searches. Search fee: $5.00 per name. Required to search: name, years to search; also helpful: DOB. Criminal records on computer back to 1985; on microfiche and archived from 1964.
General Information: No probation, medical, adoption, juvenile or sealed records released. SASE required. Turnaround time 3 weeks. Copy fee: $1.00 per page. Certification fee: $6.00. Fee payee: Humboldt Superior Court. Personal checks accepted. Prepayment is required.

Garberville Branch - Superior Court 483
Conger St, Garberville, CA 95542; 707-923-2141; Fax: 707-923-3133. Hours: 8:30AM-Noon, 1-4PM (PST). *Misdemeanor, Civil Actions Under $25,000, Eviction, Small Claims.*

Note: Court no longer opens new civil cases.

Civil Records: Access: Mail, in person. Both court and visitors may perform in person searches. Search fee: $5.00 per name. Required to search: name, years to search. Civil cases indexed by defendant, plaintiff. Civil records on index cards. Will only search back 10 years.
Criminal Records: Access: Mail, in person. Both court and visitors may perform in person searches. Search fee: $5.00 per name. Required to search: name, years to search, DOB. Criminal records on computer from 1990, index cards prior. Will only search back 10 years.
General Information: No juvenile or adoption records released. SASE not required. Turnaround time 1 day to 1 week. Copy fee: $1.00 per page. Certification fee: $6.00. Fee payee: Humboldt Courts. Personal checks accepted. Prepayment is required.

Klamath/Trinity Branch - Superior Court
825 5th St, Eureka, CA 95501; 707-445-7256. Hours: 8:30AM-Noon, 1-5PM (PST). *Misdemeanor, Civil Actions Under $25,000, Eviction, Small Claims.*

Note: Records for this branch are housed at the main court in Eureka.

Civil Records: Access: Mail, in person. Both court and visitors may perform in person searches. Search fee: $5.00 per name. Required to search: name, years to search. Civil cases indexed by defendant, plaintiff. Civil records in index files from 1983. Records destroyed after 10 yrs.
Criminal Records: Access: Mail, in person. Both court and visitors may perform in person searches. Search fee: $5.00 per name. Required to search: name, years to search. Criminal records on computer from 1987, index and dockets kept for 10 years, files kept for 5 years.
General Information: No probation reports released. SASE required. Turnaround time 2 days. Copy fee: $1.00 per page. Certification fee: $6.00. Fee payee: Humboldt Superior Court. Personal checks accepted. Prepayment is required.

Imperial County

Imperial Branch - Superior Court
939 W Main St, El Centro, CA 92243; Civil phone: 760-339-4217; Criminal phone: 760-339-4259; Fax: 760-352-3184. Hours: 8AM-4PM (PST). *Felony, Misdemeanor, Civil, Eviction, Small Claims, Probate.*

Note: All record searching for Imperial county must be done at each location.

Civil Records: Access: Mail, in person. Both court and visitors may perform in person searches. Search fee: $5.00 per name. Required to search: name, years to search. Civil cases indexed by defendant, plaintiff. Civil records on microfiche from 1972, in index file from 1917.

Criminal Records: Access: Mail, in person. Both court and visitors may perform in person searches. Search fee: $5.00 per name. Required to search: name, years to search. Criminal records on microfiche from 1972, index file from 1917.

General Information: No adoptions, juvenile, medical, probation or sealed records released. SASE required. Turnaround time 2 weeks. Copy fee: $1.00 for first page, $.50 each add'l. Certification fee: $6.00. Fee payee: Imperial County Superior Court. Personal checks accepted. Prepayment is required.

Brawley Branch - Superior Court
383 Main St, Brawley, CA 92227; 760-344-0710; Fax: 760-344-9231. Hours: 8AM-4PM (PST). *Misdemeanor, Civil Actions Under $25,000, Eviction, Small Claims.*

Note: There is no countywide database in this county.

Civil Records: Access: Phone, fax, mail, in person. Both court and visitors may perform in person searches. Search fee: $5.00 per name. Required to search: name, years to search. Civil cases indexed by defendant, plaintiff. Civil records on computer back 2 years (traffic from 1991), in index files from 1983. Records destroyed after 10 years.

Criminal Records: Access: Phone, fax, mail, in person. Only the court performs in person searches; visitors may not. Search fee: $5.00 per name. Required to search: name, years to search, DOB. Criminal records on computer back 2 years (traffic only from 1991), in index files from 1983. Records destroyed after 10 years.

General Information: No probation reports released. SASE required. Turnaround time 1 week. Copy fee: $1.00 for first page, $.50 each add'l. Certification fee: $6.00. Fee payee: Brawley Superior Court. Personal checks accepted. Prepayment is required.

Calexico Branch - Superior Court
415 4th St, Calexico, CA 92231; 760-357-3726; Fax: 760-357-6571. Hours: 8AM-4PM (PST). *Misdemeanor, Civil Actions Under $25,000, Eviction, Small Claims.*

Note: There is no countywide database in this county.

Civil Records: Access: Fax, mail, in person. Both court and visitors may perform in person searches. Search fee: $5.00 per name. Required to search: name, years to search. Civil cases indexed by defendant, plaintiff. Civil records on computer from 1991, index files from 1983. Records destroyed after 10 years.

Criminal Records: Access: Fax, mail, in person. Only the court performs in person searches; visitors may not. Search fee: $5.00 per name. Required to search: name, years to search. Criminal records on computer from 1991, index files from 1983. Records destroyed after 10 years.

General Information: No probation reports released. SASE required. Turnaround time within 2 weeks. Copy fee: $.50 per page. Certification fee: $6.00. Fee payee: Superior Court. Personal checks accepted. Write case # on check. Prepayment is required.

Winterhaven Branch - Superior Court
PO Box 1087, Winterhaven, CA 92283-1087; 760-572-0354; Fax: 760-572-2683. Hours: 8AM-Noon, 1-4PM (PST). *Eviction, Small Claims.*

Note: Misdemeanor and civil records have been moved to the Calexico Branch. Only small claims and traffic records remain here

Civil Records: Access: Phone, fax, mail, in person. Both court and visitors may perform in person searches. Search fee: $5.00 per name. Required to search: name, years to search. Civil cases indexed by defendant, plaintiff. Civil records on computer from 1991, index files from 1983. Records destroyed after 10 years.

General Information: SASE required. Turnaround time 2-3 days. Copy fee: $1.00 for first page, $.50 each add'l. Certification fee: $6.00. Fee payee: Superior-Winterhaven. Personal checks accepted. Prepayment is required.

Inyo County

Superior Court
168 N Edwards St (PO Drawer 4), Independence, CA 93526; 760-878-0218. Hours: 9AM-5PM (PST). *Felony, Civil Actions Over $25,000, Probate.*

Note: There is no central record database, each court in the county has its own records.

Civil Records: Access: Mail, in person. Both court and visitors may perform in person searches. Search fee: $5.00 per name. Required to search: name, years to search. Civil cases indexed by defendant, plaintiff. Civil records on computer to mid-1999, on microfiche and in index files from 1800s.

Criminal Records: Access: Mail, in person. Both court and visitors may perform in person searches. Search fee: $5.00 per name. Required to search: name, years to search. Criminal records on computer back to 1992, on microfiche and in index files from 1800s.

General Information: No adoptions, juvenile, medical, probation or sealed records released. SASE required. Turnaround time 2-3 business days. Copy fee: $1.00 per page. Certification fee: $6.00. Fee payee: Inyo Superior Court. Personal checks accepted. Prepayment is required.

Bishop Branch - Superior Court
301 W Line St, Bishop, CA 93514; 760-872-4971. Hours: 9AM-Noon, 1-5PM; Phone: 2-5PM (PST). *Misdemeanor, Civil Actions Under $25,000, Eviction, Small Claims.*

Note: There is no countywide database, each court must be searched.

Civil Records: Access: Mail, in person. Only the court performs in person searches; visitors may not. Search fee: $5.00 per name. Required to search: name, years to search. Civil cases indexed by defendant, plaintiff. Civil records on index cards. Will only search back 7 years.

Criminal Records: Access: Mail, in person. Only the court performs in person searches; visitors may not. Search fee: $5.00 per name. Required to search: name, years to search. Criminal records on computer from 1993, index cards prior. Will only search back 7 years.

General Information: No confidential records released. SASE required. Turnaround time 1 week. Copy fee: $1.00 per page. Certification fee: $6.00. Fee payee: Superior Court. Personal checks accepted. Prepayment is required.

Independence Limited Branch - Superior Court
168 N Edwards St (PO Box 518), Independence, CA 93526; 760-878-0319; Fax: 760-872-1060. Hours: 9AM-Noon, 1-5PM (PST). *Misdemeanor, Civil Actions Under $25,000, Eviction, Small Claims.*

Note: There is no countywide database, each court must be searched.

Civil Records: Access: Mail, in person. Both court and visitors may perform in person searches. Search fee: $5.00 per name. Required to search: name, years to search. Civil cases indexed by defendant, plaintiff. Civil records on computer back to 1999, in index books and index cards. Will only search back 7 years.

Criminal Records: Access: Mail, in person. Both court and visitors may perform in person searches. Search fee: $5.00 per name. Required to search: name, years to search, DOB. Criminal records on computer from 2/1993, index books and index cards prior. Will only search back 7 years.

General Information: No confidential records released. SASE required. Turnaround time 1 week. Fax notes: Fee to fax results is $1.00 per page. Copy fee: $1.00 per page. Certification fee: $7.00. Fee payee: Inyo County Court. Personal checks accepted. Prepayment is required.

Kern County

Superior Court
1415 Truxtun Ave, Bakersfield, CA 93301; 661-868-5393. Hours: 8AM-5PM (PST). *Felony, Civil Actions Over $25,000, Probate.*

www.co.kern.ca.us

Civil Records: Access: Mail, in person. Visitors must perform in person searches for themselves. No search fee. Required to search: name, years to search. Civil cases indexed by defendant, plaintiff. Civil records on microfiche from 1964, archived and in index file from 1800s.

Criminal Records: Access: Mail, in person. Visitors must perform in person searches for themselves. No search fee. Required to search: name, years to search, DOB. Criminal records on computer from 1989, on microfiche, archived, and in index files.

General Information: No adoptions, juvenile, medical, probation or sealed records released. SASE required. Turnaround time 1 day to 1 week. Copy fee: $.75 per page. Certification fee: $6.00. Fee payee: Kern County Superior Court. Personal checks accepted. Prepayment is required.

Delano/McFarland Branch Superior Court - North Division
1122 Jefferson St, Delano, CA 93215; 661-720-5800; Fax: 661-721-1237. Hours: 8AM-Noon, 1-4:30PM (PST). *Misdemeanor, Civil Actions Under $25,000, Eviction, Small Claims.*

www.co.kern.ca.us

Civil Records: Access: Phone, fax, mail, in person. Both court and visitors may perform in person searches. Search fee: $5.00 per name per year. Required to search: name, years to search. Civil cases indexed by defendant, plaintiff. Civil records in index files from 1983. Records destroyed after 10 years.

Criminal Records: Access: Phone, fax, mail, in person. Both court and visitors may perform in person searches. Search fee: $5.00 per name per year. Required to search: name, years to search; also helpful: DOB. Criminal records on computer from 1988, in index files from 1983. Records destroyed after 10 years.

General Information: Public Access terminal is available. No probation reports released. SASE required. Turnaround time 2 days. Copy fee: $.75 per page. Certification fee: $6.00. Fee payee: Superior Court Kern County-Delano/McFarland Branch. Personal checks accepted. Prepayment is required.

Kern River Branch Superior Court - East Division
7046 Lake Isabella Blvd, Lake Isabella, CA 93240; 760-379-3635; Fax: 760-379-4544. Hours: 8AM-4PM M-Th 8AM-5PM F (PST). *Misdemeanor, Civil Actions Under $25,000, Eviction, Small Claims.*

Civil Records: Access: Phone, fax, mail, in person. Only the court performs in person searches; visitors may not. No search fee. Required to search: name, years to search. Civil cases indexed by defendant, plaintiff. Civil records on computer from 1991, in index files from 1983. Records destroyed after 10 years.

Criminal Records: Access: Phone, mail, in person. Only the court performs in person searches; visitors may not. No search fee. Required to search: name, years to search. Criminal records on computer from 1991, in index files from 1983. Records destroyed after 10 years.

General Information: No probation reports released. SASE required. Turnaround time 2 days. Copy fee: $.75 per page. Certification fee: $6.00. Fee payee: East Kern Superior Court. Personal checks accepted. Credit cards accepted: Visa, AmEx. Prepayment is required.

Lamont/Arvin Branch Superior Court - South Division
12022 Main St, Lamont, CA 93241; 661-845-3741 or 868-5700; Fax: 661-845-9142. Hours: 8AM-4PM (PST). *Misdemeanor, Civil Actions Under $25,000, Eviction, Small Claims.*

Civil Records: Access: Fax, mail, in person. Only the court performs in person searches; visitors may not. Search fee: $5.00 per name. Required to search: name, years to search. Civil cases indexed by defendant, plaintiff. Civil records on computer from 1989. Records destroyed after 10 years. Current court calendars are available free online at www.co.kern.ca.us/apps/courtcal/courtcalendar.asp.

Criminal Records: Access: Fax, mail, in person. Only the court performs in person searches; visitors may not. Search fee: $5.00 per name. Required to search: name, years to search, DOB; also helpful CA DL#, SSN, signed release. Criminal records on computer from 1989. Records destroyed after 10 years. Current court calendars are available free online at www.co.kern.ca.us/apps/courtcal/courtcalendar.asp.

General Information: No probation reports released. SASE required. Turnaround time 2 days. Fax notes: No fee to fax results. Copy fee: $.75 per page. Certification fee: $6.00. Fee payee: Superior Court Lamont Branch. Personal checks accepted. Credit cards accepted: Visa, AmEx. Prepayment is required.

Mojave Branch Superior Court - East Division
1773 Hwy 58, Mojave, CA 93501; 661-824-2436. Hours: 8AM-5PM (PST). *Misdemeanor, Civil Actions Under $25,000, Eviction, Small Claims.*

Civil Records: Access: Mail, in person. Only the court performs in person searches; visitors may not. Search fee: $5.00 per name. Required to search: name, years to search. Civil cases indexed by defendant, plaintiff. Civil records on computer from 1991, in index files from 1983. Records destroyed after 10 years.

Criminal Records: Access: Mail, in person. Only the court performs in person searches; visitors may not. Search fee: $5.00. Required to search: name, years to search; also helpful: DOB. Criminal records on computer from 1991, in index files from 1983.

General Information: No probation reports released. SASE required. Turnaround time up to 1 week. Copy fee: $.75 per page. Certification fee: $6.00. Fee payee: East Kern Superior Court. Personal checks accepted. Credit cards accepted: Visa, AmEx. Additional fee charged for use of credit card. Prepayment is required.

Ridgecrest Branch Superior Court - East Division
132 E Coso St, Ridgecrest, CA 93555; 760-375-1397; Fax: 760-375-2112. Hours: 8AM-4PM M-T, 8AM-5PM F (PST). *Misdemeanor, Civil Actions Under $25,000, Eviction, Small Claims.*

Note: Includes Eastern Kern County, including Edwards Air Force Base, Lake Isabella, Kernville, China Lake NWC, California City, Ridgecrest, Mojave and Tehachapi.

Civil Records: Access: Mail, in person. Both court and visitors may perform in person searches. Search fee: $5.00 per name. Required to search: name, years to search. Civil cases indexed by defendant, plaintiff. Civil records on computer from 1990, in index files from 1983. Records destroyed after 10 years.

Criminal Records: Access: Mail, in person. Both court and visitors may perform in person searches. Search fee: $5.00 per name. Required to search: name, years to search; also helpful: DOB, SSN. Criminal records on computer from 1990, in index files from 1983. Records destroyed after 10 years.

General Information: No probation reports released. SASE required. Turnaround time 2 days. Copy fee: $.75 per page. Certification fee: $6.00. Fee payee: Kern County Superior Court. Personal checks accepted. Credit cards accepted: Visa, AmEx. Prepayment is required.

Shafter/Wasco Branch Superior Court - North Division
325 Central Valley Hwy, Shafter, CA 93263; 661-746-7500; Fax: 661-746-0545. Hours: 8AM-4:30PM (PST). *Misdemeanor, Civil Actions Under $25,000, Eviction, Small Claims.*

Civil Records: Access: Phone, fax, mail, in person. Only the court performs in person searches; visitors may not. Search fee: $5.00 per name per year. Required to search: name, years to search; also helpful: address. Civil cases indexed by defendant, plaintiff.

Criminal Records: Access: Phone, fax, mail, in person. Only the court performs in person searches; visitors may not. Search fee: $5.00 per name per year. Required to search: name, years to search, DOB; also helpful: address, SSN. Criminal records on computer since 1988, traffic since 1991.

General Information: No probation reports released. SASE required. Turnaround time 2 days. Fax notes: No fee to fax results. Copy fee: $.75 per page. Certification fee: $6.00. Fee payee: Superior Court North Division. Personal checks accepted. Prepayment is required.

Superior Court Metropolitan Division
1215 Truxtun Ave, Bakersfield, CA 93301; Civil phone: 661-868-2456; Criminal phone: 661-868-2482; Fax: 800-487-45675 (civ); 661-868-2695 (crim). Hours: 8AM-5PM (PST). *Misdemeanor, Civil Actions Under $25,000, Eviction, Small Claims.*

www.co.kern.ca.us/courts

Note: Formerly Bakersfield Municipal Court. Includes Bakersfield, Oildale, Edison, Glenville, Woody.

Civil Records: Access: Fax, in person. Both court and visitors may perform in person searches. Search fee: $5.00 per name per year. Required to search: name, years to search. Civil cases indexed by defendant, plaintiff. Civil records on index files from 1977 on microfilm. Records destroyed after 10 years.

Criminal Records: Access: Fax, in person. Both court and visitors may perform in person searches. Search fee: $5.00 per name per year. Required to search: name, years to search. Criminal records on computer since 1988, microfilm since 1952.

General Information: Public Access terminal is available. No probation reports, rap sheets, medical or financial released. Mail requests not accepted. Fax notes: No fee to fax results. Fax fee varies by quantity. Copy fee: $.75 per page. Certification fee: $6.00. Fee payee: Superior Court of California. Personal checks accepted. Prepayment is required.

Taft/Maricopa Branch Superior Court - South Division
311 N Lincoln St, Taft, CA 93268; 661-763-2401/861-2885; Fax: 661-763-2439. Hours: 8AM-Noon,1-4PM (PST). *Misdemeanor, Civil Actions Under $25,000, Eviction, Small Claims.*

Civil Records: Access: Phone, mail, in person. Only the court performs in person searches; visitors may not. Search fee: $5.00 per name. Required to search: name, years to search; also helpful: address. Civil cases indexed by defendant, plaintiff. Civil records on computer from 1988, in index files from 1983. Records destroyed after 10 years.

Criminal Records: Access: Phone, mail, in person. Only the court performs in person searches; visitors

may not. Search fee: $5.00 per name. Purchase of complaint and docket required. Required to search: name, years to search, DOB; also helpful: address, SSN. Criminal records on computer from 1988, in index files from 1983. Records destroyed after 10 years.

General Information: No probation reports released. SASE required. Turnaround time 2 days. Copy fee: $.75 per page. Certification fee: $6.00. Fee payee: South Taft Court. Personal checks accepted. Credit cards accepted: Visa, Discover. Prepayment is required.

Kings County

Superior Court
1400 W Lacey Blvd, Hanford, CA 93230; 559-582-3211 X2430; Fax: 559-584-0319. Hours: 8AM-5PM (PST). *Felony, Misdemeanor, Civil Actions Over $25,000, Probate.*

Civil Records: Access: Mail, in person. Both court and visitors may perform in person searches. Search fee: $5.00 per name. Required to search: name, years to search. Civil cases indexed by defendant, plaintiff. Civil records on computer from 1989, on microfiche and archived from 1970s, in index file from 1914.

Criminal Records: Access: Mail, in person. Both court and visitors may perform in person searches. Search fee: $5.00 per name. Required to search: name, years to search. Criminal records on computer from 1989, on microfiche and archived from 1970s, in index file from 1914.

General Information: Public Access terminal is available. No adoptions, juvenile, medical, probation or sealed records released. SASE required. Turnaround time 1 week. Copy fee: $.50 per page. Certification fee: $6.00. Fee payee: Kings County Superior Court. Business checks accepted. Checks accepted with proper identification. Prepayment is required.

Avenal Division Superior Court
501 E Kings St, Avenal, CA 93204; 559-386-5225; Fax: 559-386-9452. Hours: 8AM-5PM (PST). *Misdemeanor, Civil Actions Under $25,000, Eviction, Small Claims.*

Civil Records: Access: Phone, fax, mail, in person. Both court and visitors may perform in person searches. No search fee. Required to search: name, years to search. Civil records on index cards. Will only search back to 1993.

Criminal Records: Access: Phone, fax, mail, in person. Both court and visitors may perform in person searches. No search fee. Required to search: name, years to search, DOB. Criminal records on computer from 1990, index cards prior. Will only search back 3 years.

General Information: Public Access terminal is available. No juvenile or adoption records released. SASE required. Turnaround time 1 week. Copy fee: $.50 per page. Certification fee: $1.50. Fee payee: Avenal Superior Court. Personal checks accepted. Prepayment is required.

Corcoran Division Superior Court
1000 Chittenden Ave, Corcoran, CA 93212; 559-992-5193/5194; Fax: 559-992-5933. Hours: 8AM-5PM (PST). *Misdemeanor, Civil Actions Under $25,000, Eviction, Small Claims.*

Civil Records: Access: Fax, mail, in person. Only the court performs in person searches; visitors may not. Search fee: $1.75 per name per year. Required to search: name, years to search; also helpful: address. Civil cases indexed by defendant, plaintiff. Civil records on computer from 1990, index cards to 1974. Will only search back 7 years.

Criminal Records: Access: Mail, in person. Only the court performs in person searches; visitors may not. Search fee: $1.75 per name per year. Required to search: name, years to search, DOB; also helpful: address, aka's. Criminal records on computer from 1990, index cards to 1974. Will only search back 7 years.

General Information: No juvenile or adoption records released. SASE required. Turnaround time 1 week. Fax notes: No fee to fax results. Copy fee: $.50 per page. Certification fee: $6.00. Fee payee: Kings County Superior Court. Personal checks accepted. Prepayment is required.

Hanford Division Superior Court 1400 W
Lacey Blvd, Hanford, CA 93230; Civil phone: 559-582-4379; Criminal phone: 559-582-4370; Fax: 559-584-7054. Hours: 8AM-5PM (PST). *Misdemeanor, Civil Actions Under $25,000, Eviction, Small Claims.*

Civil Records: Access: Fax, mail, in person. Both court and visitors may perform in person searches. Search fee: $1.75 per name per year. Required to search: name, years to search. Civil cases indexed by defendant, plaintiff. Civil records on computer from 1991, in index files from 1983. Records destroyed after 10 years.

Criminal Records: Access: Mail, in person. Both court and visitors may perform in person searches. Search fee: $1.75 per name per year. Required to search: name, years to search, DOB. Criminal records on computer from 1991, in index files from 1983. Records destroyed after 10 years.

General Information: Public Access terminal is available. No probation or police reports released. SASE required. Turnaround time 1 week. Fax notes: $1.00 per page. Copy fee: $.50 per page. Certification fee: $6.00. Fee payee: Kings County Superior Court. Personal checks accepted. Prepayment is required.

Lemoore Division Superior Court 449 "C"
St, Lemoore, CA 93245; 559-924-7757; Fax: 559-925-0319. Hours: 8AM-5PM (PST). *Misdemeanor, Civil Actions Under $25,000, Eviction, Small Claims.*

Civil Records: Access: Mail, in person. Both court and visitors may perform in person searches. Search fee: $5.00 per name. Required to search: name, years to search. Civil cases indexed by defendant, plaintiff. Civil records computerized since 1991, older records on index cards. In person access limited.

Criminal Records: Access: Mail, in person. Both court and visitors may perform in person searches. Search fee: $5.00 per name. Required to search: name, years to search. Criminal records on computer since 1991, index cards prior.

General Information: Public Access terminal is available. SASE required. Turnaround time 10 days. Copy fee: $.50 per page. Certification fee: $6.00. Fee payee: Clerk of Courts. Personal checks accepted. Prepayment is required.

Lake County

Superior Court 255 N Forbes St, Lakeport, CA
95453; 707-263-2374; Fax: 707-262-1327. Hours: 8AM-5PM (PST). *Felony, Misdemeanor, Civil, Eviction, Small Claims, Probate.*

www.courtinfo.ca.gov/courts/trial/lake/lakeport.htm

Note: This court holds the records for the former Northlake Municipal Court.

Civil Records: Access: Mail, in person. Only the court performs in person searches; visitors may not. Search fee: $5.00 per name. Required to search: name, years to search. Civil cases indexed by defendant, plaintiff. Civil records on computer from 1991, on microfiche, archived, and in index files from 1800s.

Criminal Records: Access: Mail, in person. Only the court performs in person searches; visitors may not. Search fee: $5.00 per name. Required to search: name, years to search, DOB. Criminal records on computer from 1991, on microfiche, archived, and in index files from 1800s.

General Information: Public Access terminal is available. No adoptions, juvenile, medical, probation or sealed records released. SASE required. Turnaround time 1-3 weeks. Copy fee: $.25 per page. Certification

fee: $6.00. Fee payee: Lake County Superior Court. Personal checks accepted. Prepayment is required.

South Lake Division - Superior Court 7000
S Center Dr, Clearlake, CA 95422; 707-994-4859; Civil phone: 707-994-8262; Criminal phone: 707-994-6598; Fax: 707-994-1625. Hours: 8AM-4:30PM; Phone hours 8:30AM-12:30PM (PST). *Misdemeanor, Civil Actions Under $25,000, Eviction, Small Claims.*

www.co.lake.ca.us

Civil Records: Access: Mail, in person. Visitors must perform in person searches for themselves. Search fee: $5.00 per name. Required to search: name, years to search. Civil cases indexed by defendant, plaintiff. Civil records on index books.

Criminal Records: Access: Mail, in person. Only the court performs in person searches; visitors may not. Search fee: $5.00 per name. Required to search: name, years to search, DOB. Criminal records on computer from 1990, index books prior.

General Information: No police reports or sealed records released. SASE required. Turnaround time 1 week (civil) or 30 days (criminal). Copy fee: $.25 per page. Certification fee: $6.00. Fee payee: Lake County Superior Court. Personal checks accepted. Prepayment is required.

Lassen County

Superior Court 220 S Lassen St, #6, Susanville,
CA 96130; 530-251-8189 (dept 1);251-8205 (dept 2). Hours: 8AM-5PM (PST). *Felony, Misdemeanor, Civil, Eviction, Small Claims, Probate.*

www.lassencourt.org

Civil Records: Access: Phone, mail, in person. Both court and visitors may perform in person searches. Search fee: $5.00 per name. Required to search: name, years to search. Civil cases indexed by defendant, plaintiff. Civil records on computer from 11/89, archived and in index files from 1900s.

Criminal Records: Access: Phone, mail, in person. Both court and visitors may perform in person searches. Search fee: $5.00 per name. Required to search: name, years to search. Criminal records on computer from 11/89, archived and in index files from 1900s.

General Information: No adoptions, juvenile, medical, probation or sealed records released. SASE required. Turnaround time 1-5 days. Copy fee: $1.50 for first page, $.50 each add'l. Certification fee: $6.00. Fee payee: Lassen County Superior Court. Business checks accepted. Prepayment is required.

Los Angeles County

Los Angeles Superior Court - Central
District - Civil 110 N Grand Ave, Rm 426, Los Angeles, CA 90012; 213-974-6135 (974-5171 if over $25,000); Fax: 213-621-2701. Hours: 8:30AM-4:30PM (PST). *Civil Actions, Eviction, Small Claims.*

www.lasuperiorcourt.org

Note: This court handles civil cases over and under $25,000. Cases here under $25,000 are co-extensive with the city limits of Los Angeles and includes the City of San Fernando and sections designated as San Pedro, West Los Angeles, Van Nuys, Venice and the unincorporated area of the county known as Florence. Cases over $25,000 are county-wide.

Civil Records: Access: Phone, mail, online, in person. Both court and visitors may perform in person searches. Search fee: $5.00 per name. Required to search: name, years to search. Civil cases indexed by defendant, plaintiff. Civil records on computer from 1991, index files from 1983. Records destroyed after 10 years. Online access available at www.lasuperiorcourt.org/CivilRegister. Court location, case number, and last name are all required to search. Available for civil,

small claims, and unlawful detainer records. Also, online access to Probate Notes is available free, with case number, at www.lasuperiorcourt.org/ProbateNotes. Three other Courts in Los Angeles County handle civil cases over $25,000; they are Norwalk, Palmdale, and Van Nuys. **General Information:** Public Access terminal is available. No probation reports released. SASE required. Turnaround time 24 hours, more if busy. Copy fee: $.57 per page. Certification fee: $6.00. Fee payee: Los Angeles Superior Court. Personal checks accepted. Credit cards accepted: Visa, MasterCard. Prepayment is required.

Los Angeles Superior Court - Probate
Department 111 N. Hill St, Rm 112, Los Angeles, CA 90012; 213-974-5471. Hours: 8AM-4PM (PST). *Probate.*

www.lasuperiorcourt.org/probate

Note: Probate Notes Online are available for cases being heard in Central District, Burbank, Compton, Glendale, Lancaster, Long Beach, Pasadena, Pomona, San Fernando, Santa Monica and Torrance District Courts only. Search by case prefix, number and suffix.

Los Angeles Superior Court - Central
District - Felony 210 W Temple St Rm M-6, Los Angeles, CA 90012; 213-974-5259; Fax: 213-617-1224. Hours: 8:30AM-4:30PM (PST). *Felony.*

www.lasuperiorcourt.org

Criminal Records: Access: Mail, in person. Only the court performs in person searches; visitors may not. Search fee: $5.00 per name. Required to search: name, years to search, DOB, sex. Criminal records on microfiche and index files since 1956, computerized misdemeanors since 1988; felonies since 1996. Court suggests to include full spelling of middle name.

General Information: No adoptions, juvenile, medical, probation or sealed records released. SASE required. Turnaround time 24 hours; up to 3 weeks if busy. Copy fee: $.57 per page. Certification fee: $6.00. Fee payee: Los Angeles Superior Court. Personal checks accepted. Prepayment is required.

Airport Superior Court - West District
11701 S La Cienega Blvd, Los Angeles, CA 90045; 310-727-6020; Criminal phone: 310-727-6100. Hours: 8:30AM-4:30PM (PST). *Felony, Misdemeanor.*

www.lasuperiorcourt.org/Locations/LAX.htm

Note: New Court in 2000, includes the areas of Palms, Mar Vista, Rancho Park, Marina del Rey, Venice, Playa del Rey and Sawtelle. Holds records for the former Robertson branch.

Criminal Records: Access: Mail, in person. Only the court performs in person searches; visitors may not. Search fee: $5.00 per name. Required to search: name, years to search; also helpful: DOB, address. Criminal records index goes back to.

General Information: No probation reports released. SASE required. Turnaround time 3-5 days. Copy fee: $.57 per page. Certification fee: $6.00. Fee payee: Los Angeles Superior Court. Personal checks accepted. Prepayment is required.

Alhambra Superior Court - Northeast
District 150 W Commonwealth Ave, Alhambra, CA 91801; 626-308-5521. Hours: 8AM-4:30PM (PST). *Misdemeanor, Civil Actions Under $25,000, Eviction, Small Claims.*

www.lasuperiorcourt.org

Note: Includes cities of Alhambra, Monterey Park, San Gabriel, Temple City and the unincorporated County area known as South San Gabriel. Address the specific division (criminal, civil, small claims) in correspondence.

Los Angeles County - Con't

Civil Records: Access: Mail, online, in person. Only the court performs in person searches; visitors may not. Search fee: $5.00 per name. Required to search: name, years to search. Civil cases indexed by defendant, plaintiff. Civil records on computer from 1991, index files from 1983. Records destroyed after 10 years. Online access available at www.lasuperiorcourt.org/CivilRegister/. Court location, case number, and last name are all required to search. Available for civil, small claims, and unlawful detainer records.

Criminal Records: Access: Mail, in person. Only the court performs in person searches; visitors may not. Search fee: $5.00 per name. Required to search: name, years to search; also helpful: DOB, SSN. Criminal records on computer from 1987, index files from 1983. Records destroyed after 10 years.

General Information: No probation records released. SASE required. Turnaround time 2 days. Copy fee: $.57 per page. Certification fee: $6.00. Fee payee: Los Angeles Superior Court. Personal checks accepted. Prepayment is required.

Beverly Hills Superior Court - West District

9355 Burton Way, Beverly Hills, CA 90210; 310-860-0070. Hours: 8:30AM-4:30PM (PST). *Misdemeanor, Civil Actions Under $25,000, Eviction, Small Claims.*

www.lasuperiorcourt.org

Note: Includes cities of Beverly Hills and West Hollywood

Criminal Records: Access: Phone, mail, in person. Only the court performs in person searches; visitors may not. Search fee: $5.00 per name. Fee is per data bank per year. Required to search: name, years to search, DOB; also helpful: address, SSN, sex, signed release. Criminal records on computer from 1991, index files from 1983. Records destroyed after 10 years.

General Information: No probation, arrest records released. SASE required. Turnaround time 3 days. Copy fee: $.57 per page. Certification fee: $6.00. Court location, case number, and last name are all required to search. Available for civil, small claims, and unlawful detainer records. Fee payee: Los Angeles Superior Court. Personal checks accepted. Credit cards accepted: Visa, MasterCard, Discover. Visa, Dicover plus user fees. Prepayment is required.

Burbank Superior Court - North Central District

300 E Olive, PO Box 750, Burbank, CA 91503; Civil phone: 818-557-3461; Criminal phone: 818-557-3466. Hours: 8AM-4:30PM (PST). *Misdemeanor, Civil Actions Under $25,000, Eviction, Small Claims.*

www.lasuperiorcourt.org

Note: Co-extensive with the city limits of Burbank.

Civil Records: Access: Mail, online, in person. Both court and visitors may perform in person searches. Search fee: $5.00 per name. Required to search: name, years to search. Civil cases indexed by defendant, plaintiff. Civil records on computer from 1991, index files from 1983. Records destroyed after 10 years. Online access available at www.lasuperiorcourt.org/CivilRegister/. Court location, case number, and last name are all required to search. Available for civil, small claims, and unlawful detainer records.

Criminal Records: Access: Mail, in person. Only the court performs in person searches; visitors may not. Search fee: $5.00 per name. Required to search: name, years to search. Criminal records on computer from 1991, index files from 1983. Records destroyed after 10 years.

General Information: No probation reports released. SASE required. Turnaround time 3-5 days. Copy fee: $.57 per page. Certification fee: $6.00. Fee payee: Los

Angeles Superior Court. Personal checks accepted. Prepayment is required.

Citrus Superior Court - East District

1427 W Covina Pky, West Covina, CA 91790; Civil phone: 626-813-3236; Criminal phone: 626-813-3239; Fax: 626-338-7364. Hours: 8AM-4:30PM (PST). *Misdemeanor, Civil Actions Under $25,000, Eviction, Small Claims.*

www.lasuperiorcourt.org

Note: Includes cities of Azusa, Baldwin Park, Covina, Glendora, Industry, Irwindale, Valinda, West Covina and surrounding unincorporated County area.

Civil Records: Access: Mail, online, in person. Both court and visitors may perform in person searches. Search fee: $5.00 per name. Required to search: name, years to search. Civil cases indexed by defendant, plaintiff. Civil records on computer from 1991, index files from 1983. Records destroyed after 10 years. Online access available at www.lasuperiorcourt.org/CivilRegister/. Court location, case number, and last name are all required to search. Available for civil, small claims, and unlawful detainer records.

Criminal Records: Access: Mail, in person. Both court and visitors may perform in person searches. Search fee: $5.00 per name. Required to search: name, years to search. Criminal records on computer from 1991, index files from 1983. Records destroyed after 10 years. Court may choose not to run lists of names.

General Information: Public Access terminal is available. No probation reports released. SASE required. Turnaround time 1 week. Copy fee: $.57 per page. Certification fee: $6.00. Fee payee: Los Angeles Superior Court. Personal checks accepted. Prepayment is required.

Compton Superior Court - South Central District

200 W Compton Blvd, Compton, CA 90220; Civil phone: 310-603-8251; Criminal phone: 310-603-7112; Fax: 310-763-4984. Hours: 8AM-4:30PM (PST). *Misdemeanor, Civil Actions Under $25,000, Eviction, Small Claims.*

www.lasuperiorcourt.org

Note: Includes cities of Carson, Compton, Lynwood and Paramount and the unincorporated portions of county that surround them. There is a branch in Lynwood (323-357-5200) that handles pretrials only.

Civil Records: Access: Mail, online, in person. Both court and visitors may perform in person searches. Search fee: $5.00 per name. Fee is per year prior to 1991. Required to search: name, years to search. Civil cases indexed by defendant, plaintiff. Civil records on computer from 1991, index files from 1983. Records destroyed after 10 years. Online access available at www.lasuperiorcourt.org/CivilRegister/. Court location, case number, and last name are all required to search. Available for civil, small claims, and unlawful detainer records. Also, online access to Probate Notes is available free, with case number, at www.lasuperiorcourt.org/ProbateNotes.

Criminal Records: Access: Mail, in person. Only the court performs in person searches; visitors may not. Search fee: $5.00 per name. Required to search: name, years to search, DOB. Criminal records maintained per G.C. 68152(E).

General Information: No complaint records released. SASE required. Turnaround time 2 days. Copy fee: $.57 per page. Certification fee: $6.00. Fee payee: Los Angeles Superior Court-Compton. Personal checks accepted. Credit cards accepted: Visa, MasterCard, Discover. Prepayment is required.

Culver City Superior Court - West District

4130 Overland Ave, Culver City, CA 90230; 310-202-3181; Civil phone: 310-202-3160; Criminal phone: 310-202-3158; Fax: 310-836-8345. Hours: 8:30AM-4:30PM (PST). *Misdemeanor, Civil Actions Under $25,000, Eviction, Small Claims.*

www.lasuperiorcourt.org

Note: Includes Culver City and surrounding unincorporated areas including Angelus Vista, portions of Marina del Rey, View Park and Windsor Hills, all surrounded by the City of Los Angeles, on south bounded by Inglewood.

Civil Records: Access: Mail, online, in person. Only the court performs in person searches; visitors may not. Search fee: $5.00 per name. Required to search: name, years to search. Civil cases indexed by defendant, plaintiff. Civil records on computer from 1987, index files from 1983. Records destroyed after 10 years. Online access available at www.lasuperiorcourt.org/CivilRegister/. Court location, case number, and last name are all required to search. Available for civil, small claims, and unlawful detainer records.

Criminal Records: Access: Mail, in person. Only the court performs in person searches; visitors may not. Search fee: $5.00 per name. Required to search: name, years to search. Criminal records computerized since 1987. Closed cases over 10 years old are destroyed. Court may choose not to run lists of names.

General Information: No probation reports released. SASE required. Turnaround time 2 days. Copy fee: $.57 per page. Certification fee: $6.00. Fee payee: Los Angeles Superior Court. Personal checks accepted. Prepayment is required.

Downey Superior Court - Southeast District

7500 E Imperial Hwy, Downey, CA 90242; Civil phone: 562-803-7052; Criminal phone: 562-803-7049. Hours: 8:30AM-4:30PM T-F; 8:30AM-6PM M (PST). *Misdemeanor, Civil Actions Under $25,000, Eviction, Small Claims.*

www.lasuperiorcourt.org

Note: Comprises the cities of Downey, Norwalk and La Mirada.

Civil Records: Access: Mail, online, in person. Both court and visitors may perform in person searches. Search fee: $5.00 per name. Required to search: name, years to search. Civil cases indexed by defendant, plaintiff. Civil records on microfiche from 1964, archived and index file from 1800s. Online access available at www.lasuperiorcourt.org/CivilRegister/. Court location, case number, and last name are all required to search. Available for civil, small claims, and unlawful detainer records.

Criminal Records: Access: Mail, in person. Only the court performs in person searches; visitors may not. Search fee: $5.00 per name. Required to search: name, years to search; also helpful: DOB. Criminal records on computer from 1989, on microfiche, archived, and index files. Court may choose not to run lists of names.

General Information: No adoptions, juvenile, medical, probation or sealed records released. SASE required. Turnaround time 5 days. Copy fee: $.57 per page. Certification fee: $6.00. Fee payee: Los Angeles Superior Court. Personal checks accepted. Credit cards accepted: Discover. Prepayment is required.

East Los Angeles Superior Court - Central District

214 S Fetterly Ave, Los Angeles, CA 90022; Civil phone: 323-780-2017; Criminal phone: 323-780-2025. Hours: 8AM-4:30PM (PST). *Misdemeanor, Civil Actions Under $25,000, Eviction, Small Claims.*

www.lasuperiorcourt.org

Note: Includes cities of Montebello and Commerce and adjacent unincorporated territory bordering Monterey Park on the north and Los Angeles on the west.

Los Angeles County - Con't

Civil Records: Access: Mail, online, in person. Only the court performs in person searches; visitors may not. Search fee: $5.00 per name. Required to search: name, years to search. Civil cases indexed by defendant, plaintiff. Civil records on computer from 1991, index files from 1983. Records destroyed after 10 years. Online access available at www.lasuperiorcourt.org/ CivilRegister/. Court location, case number, and last name are all required to search. Available for civil, small claims, and unlawful detainer records.

Criminal Records: Access: Mail, in person. Only the court performs in person searches; visitors may not. Search fee: $5.00 per name. Required to search: name, years to search, DOB; also helpful: SSN. Criminal records on computer from 1991, index files from 1983. Records destroyed after 10 years.

General Information: No probation reports released. SASE required. Turnaround time 2 days. Copy fee: $.57 per page. Certification fee: $6.00. Fee payee: Superior Court of East Los Angeles. Personal checks accepted. Credit cards accepted: Discover. Prepayment is required.

Glendale Superior Court - NorthCentral

District Los Angeles Superior Court, 600 E Broadway, Glendale, CA 91206; 818-500-5840; Civil phone: 818-500-3538; Criminal phone: 818-500-3541; Fax: 818-548-0486 Civ; 0236 Crim. Hours: 8:30AM-4:30PM (PST). *Misdemeanor, Civil Actions Under $25,000, Eviction, Small Claims.*

www.lasuperiorcourt.org

Note: Includes cities of Glendale, LaCanada-Flintridge and unincorporated county are known as Montrose, La Crescenta, Verdugo City, Highway Highlands, and Kogel Canyon.

Civil Records: Access: Mail, online, in person. Only the court performs in person searches; visitors may not. Search fee: $5.00 per name. Required to search: name, years to search. Civil cases indexed by defendant, plaintiff. Civil records on computer from 1990, small claims from 07/92, index files from 1983. Records destroyed after 10 years. Online access available at www.lasuperiorcourt.org/CivilRegister/. Court location, case number, and last name are all required to search. Available for civil, small claims, and unlawful detainer records. Also, online access to Probate Notes is available free, with case number, at www.lasuperiorcourt.org/ProbateNotes.

Criminal Records: Access: Mail, in person. Only the court performs in person searches; visitors may not. Search fee: $5.00 per name. Required to search: name, years to search. Criminal records on computer from 1990, microfilm past 10 years.

General Information: No probation reports, police reports, CII records released. SASE required. Turnaround time 2 days. Copy fee: $.57 per page. Certification fee: $6.00. Fee payee: Los Angeles Superior Court. Personal checks accepted. Credit cards accepted: Visa, MasterCard. Prepayment is required.

Hollywood Superior Court - Central

District 5925 Hollywood Blvd, Los Angeles, CA 90028; 323-856-5747. Hours: 8AM-4:30PM (PST). *Misdemeanor.*

www.lasuperiorcourt.org

Note: High-grade and low-grade Misdemeanors for the Hollywood area.

Criminal Records: Access: Mail, in person. Only the court performs in person searches; visitors may not. Search fee: $5.00 per name. Required to search: name, years to search, DOB. Criminal records on computer from 1991, prior on books.

General Information: No probation, driver's license, medical, arrest report or confidential reports released.

SASE required. Turnaround time 2-3 days. Copy fee: $.57 per page. Certification fee: $6.00. Fee payee: Los Angeles Superior Court. Personal checks accepted. Credit cards accepted. Prepayment is required.

Huntington Park Superior Court - Southeast District

6548 Miles Ave, Huntington Park, CA 90255; Civil phone: 323-586-6365; Criminal phone: 323-586-6363; Fax: 323-589-6769. Hours: 8AM-4PM (PST). *Misdemeanor, Civil Actions Under $25,000, Eviction, Small Claims.*

www.lasuperiorcourt.org

Note: Includes cities of Bell, Bell Gardens, Cudahy, Huntington Park, Maywood and Vernon.

Civil Records: Access: Mail, online, in person. Only the court performs in person searches; visitors may not. Search fee: $5.00 per name. Required to search: name, years to search. Civil cases indexed by defendant, plaintiff. Civil records on computer from 1991, index files from 1983. Records destroyed after 10 years. Online access available at www.lasuperiorcourt.org/CivilRegister/. Court location, case number, and last name are all required to search. Available for civil, small claims, and unlawful detainer records.

Criminal Records: Access: Phone, mail, in person. Only the court performs in person searches; visitors may not. Search fee: $5.00 per name. Required to search: name, years to search; also helpful: DOB. Criminal records on computer from 1991, index files from 1983. Records destroyed after 10 years.

General Information: No probation reports released. SASE required. Turnaround time 2 days. Copy fee: $.57 per page. Certification fee: $6.00. Fee payee: Los Angeles Superior Court. Personal checks accepted. Credit cards accepted: Visa, MasterCard, Discover. Prepayment is required.

Inglewood Superior Court - Southwest

District 1 Regent St, Inglewood, CA 90301; 310-419-5132; Civil phone: 310-419-5125; Criminal phone: 310-419-5128; Fax: 310-674-4862. Hours: 8AM-4:30PM (PST). *Misdemeanor, Civil Actions Under $25,000, Eviction, Small Claims.*

www.lasuperiorcourt.org

Note: Includes cities of Inglewood, Hawthorne, El Segundo, Lennox and adjoining unincorporated area.

Civil Records: Access: Mail, online, in person. Only the court performs in person searches; visitors may not. Search fee: $5.00 per name. Required to search: name, years to search. Civil cases indexed by defendant, plaintiff. Civil records on computer from 1991, index files from 1983. Records destroyed after 10 years. Online access available at www.lasuperiorcourt.org/CivilRegister/. Court location, case number, and last name are all required to search. Available for civil, small claims, and unlawful detainer records.

Criminal Records: Access: Mail, in person. Only the court performs in person searches; visitors may not. Search fee: $5.00 per name. Required to search: name, years to search; also helpful: DOB. Criminal records on computer from 1991, index files from 1983. Records destroyed after 10 years.

General Information: No probation reports released. SASE required. Turnaround time 2 days. Copy fee: $.57 per page. Certification fee: $6.00. Fee payee: Los Angeles Superior Court. Personal checks accepted. Credit cards accepted: Visa, MasterCard, Discover, AmEx, Visa, Discover. Prepayment is required.

Lancaster Superior Court - North District

1040 W Ave J, #107, Lancaster, CA 93534; 661-945-6355. Hours: 8AM-4:30PM (PST). *Felony, Misdemeanor.*

www.lasuperiorcourt.org

Note: Formerly Antelope; includes Lancaster, City of Palmdale, and unincorporated County territory including Acton, Agua Dulce, Fairmont, Lake Hughes, Llano, Leona Valley, Littlerock, Pearblossom, Quartz Hill, Roosevelt, Green Valley Big Pines, Lake Elizabeth

Criminal Records: Access: Mail, in person. Only the court performs in person searches; visitors may not. Search fee: $5.00 per name. Required to search: name, years to search; also helpful: case number. Criminal records on computer since 1989, index books since 1983. Records destroyed after 10 years. Court may choose not to run lists of names.

General Information: No probation reports released. SASE required. Turnaround time 2 days. Copy fee: $.57 per page. Certification fee: $6.00. Fee payee: Los Angeles Superior Court. Personal checks accepted. Checks accepted (must be pre-imprinted). Prepayment is required.

Long Beach Superior Court - South

District 415 W Ocean Blvd, Long Beach, CA 90801; 562-491-6201; Civil phone: 562-491-6234; Criminal phone: 562-491-6226; Fax: 562-437-0147 (Criminal). Hours: 8:30AM-4:30PM (PST). *Misdemeanor, Civil Actions Under $25,000, Eviction, Small Claims.*

www.lasuperiorcourt.org

Note: Includes cities of Long Beach and Signal Hill and adjoining unincorporated area. Address requests to civil or criminal division.

Civil Records: Access: Mail, online, in person. Both court and visitors may perform in person searches. Search fee: $5.00 per name. Required to search: name, years to search. Civil cases indexed by defendant, plaintiff. Civil records on computer from 1991, index files from 1983. Records destroyed after 10 years. Online access available at www.lasuperiorcourt.org/ CivilRegister/. Court location, case number, and last name are all required to search. Available for civil, small claims, and unlawful detainer records. Also, online access to Probate Notes is available free, with case number, at www.lasuperiorcourt.org/ProbateNotes.

Criminal Records: Access: Mail, in person. Both court and visitors may perform in person searches. Search fee: $5.00 per name. Required to search: name, years to search, DOB. Criminal records on computer from 1991, index files from 1983. Records destroyed after 10 years.

General Information: No probation reports released. SASE required. Turnaround time 2 days. Copy fee: $.57 per page. Certification fee: $6.00. Fee payee: Los Angeles Superior Court. Personal checks accepted. Credit cards accepted: Discover. Accepted in person only. Prepayment is required.

Los Angeles Superior Court - Central

District - Misdemeanor 210 W Temple St Rm 5-305, Los Angeles, CA 90012; 213-974-6151. Hours: 8:30AM-4:30PM (PST). *Misdemeanor.*

www.lasuperiorcourt.org

Note: Includes incorporated City of Los Angeles excluding communities of San Pedro, West Los Angeles, Hollywood and San Fernando Valley

Criminal Records: Access: Phone, mail, in person. Only the court performs in person searches; visitors may not. Search fee: $5.00 per name. Required to search: name, years to search; also helpful: address, DOB. Criminal records are kept back to 1985. Search request phone: 213-974-6141.

General Information: No probation reports released. SASE required. Turnaround time 24 hours to 1 week. Copy fee: $.57 per page. Certification fee: $6.00. Fee payee: Los Angeles Superior Court. Personal checks accepted. Credit cards accepted: Visa, MasterCard. Accepted in person only. Prepayment is required.

Los Angeles County - Con't

Los Cerritos Superior Court - Southeast District
10025 E Flower St, Bellflower, CA 90706; 562-804-8025; Civil phone: 562-804-8009; Criminal phone: 562-804-8018. Hours: 8AM-4:30PM (PST). *Misdemeanor, Civil Actions Under $25,000, Eviction, Small Claims.*

www.lasuperiorcourt.org/Locations/LosCerritos.htm

Note: Includes Artesia, Bellflower, Hawaiian Gardens, Lakewood and Cerritos. Specify civil or criminal search request.

Civil Records: Access: Mail, online, in person. Only the court performs in person searches; visitors may not. Search fee: $5.00 per name. Required to search: name, years to search. Civil cases indexed by defendant, plaintiff. Civil records on computer from 1991, index files from 1983. Records destroyed after 10 years. Online access available at www.lasuperiorcourt.org/CivilRegister/. Court location, case number, and last name are all required to search. Available for civil, small claims, and unlawful detainer records.

Criminal Records: Access: Mail, in person. Only the court performs in person searches; visitors may not. Search fee: $5.00 per name. Required to search: name, years to search, DOB; also helpful: SSN, sex. Criminal records on computer from 1991, index files from 1983. Records destroyed after 10 years.

General Information: No probation reports released. SASE required. Turnaround time 2-3 days. Copy fee: $.57 per page. Certification fee: $6.00. Fee payee: Los Angeles Superior Court. Personal checks accepted. Credit cards accepted: Visa, MasterCard, Discover. Prepayment is required.

Malibu Superior Court - West District
23525 W Civic Center Way, Malibu, CA 90265; 310-317-1312; Fax: 310-456-7415. Hours: 8AM-4:30PM (PST). *Misdemeanor, Civil Actions Under $25,000, Eviction, Small Claims.*

www.lasuperiorcourt.org

Note: Includes Malibu, Agoura Hills, Calabasas, Westlake Village, Hidden Hills and unincorporated areas known as Topanga and Chatsworth Lake, bounded by Ventura County on the west and north, Pacific Ocean on the south and City of Los Angeles on the east.

Civil Records: Access: Mail, online, in person. Only the court performs in person searches; visitors may not. Search fee: $5.00 per name. Required to search: name, years to search. Civil cases indexed by defendant, plaintiff. Civil records on computer from 1991, index files from 1983. Records destroyed after 10 years. Online access available at www.lasuperiorcourt.org/CivilRegister/. Court location, case number, and last name are all required to search. Available for civil, small claims, and unlawful detainer records.

Criminal Records: Access: Mail, in person. Only the court performs in person searches; visitors may not. Search fee: $5.00 per name. Required to search: name, years to search; also helpful: DOB. Criminal records on computer from 1991, index files from 1983. Records destroyed after 10 years.

General Information: No probation reports released. SASE required. Turnaround time 1-5 days. Copy fee: $.57 per page. Certification fee: $6.00. Court location, case number, and last name are all required to search. Available for civil, small claims, and unlawful detainer records. Fee payee: Los Angeles Superior Court. Personal checks accepted. Prepayment is required.

Metropolitan Los Angeles Superior Court - Central District
1945 S Hill St Rm 200, Los Angeles, CA 90007; 213-744-1884; Fax: 213-744-1879. Hours: 8AM-4:30PM (PST). *Misdemeanor.*

www.lasuperiorcourt.org

Note: Vehicle Code misdemeanor and traffic citations for the incorporated City of Los Angeles excluding the areas known as San Pedro, West Los Angeles and communities of San Fernando Valley and the unincorporated County area more commonly known as Florence

Criminal Records: Access: Phone, mail, in person. Only the court performs in person searches; visitors may not. Search fee: $5.00 per name. Required to search: name, years to search, DOB. Criminal records on computer from 1991, index files from 1983. Records destroyed after 10 years.

General Information: No probation, driver's license, medical, arrest report or confidential reports released. SASE required. Turnaround time 2-3 days. Copy fee: $.57 per page. Certification fee: $6.00. Fee payee: Los Angeles Superior Court. Personal checks accepted. Credit cards accepted. Prepayment is required.

Norwalk Superior Court - Southeast District
12720 Norwalk Blvd, Norwalk, CA 90650; 562-807-7340. Hours: 8:30AM-4PM (PST). *Felony, Civil Actions Over $25,000, Probate.*

www.lasuperiorcourt.org

Civil Records: Access: Mail, online, in person. Only the court performs in person searches; visitors may only use public access to find case numbers. Search fee: $5.00 per name. Required to search: name, years to search. Civil cases indexed by defendant, plaintiff. Civil records on computer from 1991, index files from 1983. Online access available at www.lasuperiorcourt.org/CivilRegister/. Court location, case number, and last name are all required to search. Available for civil, small claims, and unlawful detainer records.

Criminal Records: Access: Mail, in person. Only the court performs in person searches; visitors may only use public access to find case numbers. Search fee: $5.00 per name. Required to search: name, years to search, DOB; also helpful: SSN, sex. Criminal records on computer from 1991, index files from 1983.

General Information: Public Access terminal is available. (Public access terminal to find case number only.) No probation reports released. SASE required. Turnaround time 2-10 days. Copy fee: $.57 per page. Certification fee: $6.00. Fee payee: Los Angeles Superior Court. Personal checks accepted. Credit cards accepted. Prepayment is required.

Palmdale Superior Court - North District
38256 Sierra Highway, Palmdale, CA 93550; 661-537-2714. Hours: 8AM-4:30PM (PST). *Civil Actions, Eviction, Small Claims, Probate.*

www.lasuperiorcourt.org

Note: Includes City of Lancaster, City of Palmdale, and unincorporated County territory including Acton, Agua Dulce, Fairmont, Lake Hughes, Llano, Leona Valley, Littlerock, Pearblossom, Quartz Hill, Roosevelt, Green Valley Big Pines, Lake Elizabeth

Civil Records: Access: Phone, mail, online, in person. Only the court performs in person searches; visitors may not. Search fee: $5.00 per name. Required to search: name, years to search. Civil cases indexed by defendant, plaintiff. Civil records on computer since 1989, index books since 1983. Records destroyed after 10 years. Online access available at www.lasuperiorcourt.org/CivilRegister/. Court location, case number, and last name are all required to search. Available for civil, small claims, and unlawful detainer records. Also, online access to Probate Notes is available free, with case number, at

www.lasuperiorcourt.org/ProbateNotes. **General Information:** No probation reports released. SASE required. Turnaround time 2-10 days. Copy fee: $.57 per page. Certification fee: $6.00. Fee payee: Los Angeles Superior Court. Personal checks accepted. Prepayment is required.

Pasadena Superior Court - Northeast District
300 E Walnut, Pasadena, CA 91101; Civil phone: 626-356-5695; Criminal phone: 626-356-5254; Fax: 626-568-3903. Hours: 8:30AM-4:30PM (PST). *Misdemeanor, Civil Actions Under $25,000, Eviction, Small Claims.*

www.lasuperiorcourt.org

Note: Includes cities of Pasadena, South Pasadena, San Marino, Sierra Madre and area of Altadena and East Pasadena.

Civil Records: Access: Mail, online, in person. Both court and visitors may perform in person searches. Search fee: $5.00 per name. Required to search: name, years to search. Civil cases indexed by defendant, plaintiff. Civil records on computer from 1991, index files from 1983. Records destroyed after 10 years. Online access available at www.lasuperiorcourt.org/CivilRegister/. Court location, case number, and last name are all required to search. Available for civil, small claims, and unlawful detainer records. Also, online access to Probate Notes is available free, with case number, at www.lasuperiorcourt.org/ProbateNotes.

Criminal Records: Access: Mail, in person. Only the court performs in person searches; visitors may not. Search fee: $5.00 per name. Required to search: name, years to search. Criminal records on computer from 1991, index files from 1983. Records destroyed:10 years.

General Information: No probation reports released. SASE required. Turnaround time 2 days. Copy fee: $.57 per page. Certification fee: $6.00. Fee payee: Los Angeles Superior Court. Personal checks accepted. Prepayment is required.

Pomona Superior Court - East District
350 W Mission Blvd, Pomona, CA 91766; 909-620-3201; Civil phone: 909-620-3213; Criminal phone: 909-620-3219; Fax: 909-622-2305/865-6767. Hours: 8AM-4:30PM; Phone Hours: 8AM-Noon, 2-4PM (PST). *Misdemeanor, Civil Actions Under $25,000, Eviction, Small Claims.*

www.lasuperiorcourt.org

Note: Includes cities of Pomona, Claremont, La Verne, Walnut, San Dimas and unincorporated area including Diamond Bar.

Civil Records: Access: Fax, mail, online, in person. Both court and visitors may perform in person searches. Search fee: $5.00 per name. Required to search: name, years to search. Civil cases indexed by defendant, plaintiff. Civil records on computer from 1990, index files from 1983. Records destroyed after 10 years. Online access available at www.lasuperiorcourt.org/CivilRegister/. Court location, case number, and last name are all required to search. Available for civil, small claims, and unlawful detainer records. Also, online access to Probate Notes is available free, with case number, at www.lasuperiorcourt.org/ProbateNotes.

Criminal Records: Access: Mail, in person. Only the court performs in person searches; visitors may not. Search fee: $5.00 per name. Required to search: name, years to search, DOB. Criminal records on computer from 1990, index files from 1983. Records destroyed after 10 years. Drop box available.

General Information: No probation, mental health or police reports released. SASE required. Turnaround time 2-4 days. Copy fee: $.57 per page. Certification fee: $6.00. Court location, case number, and last name are all required to search. Available for civil, small claims, and unlawful detainer records. Fee payee: Los …

Los Angeles County - Con't

Angeles Superior Court. Personal checks accepted. Prepayment is required.

Redondo Beach Superior Court - Southwest District
117 W Torrance Blvd, Redondo Beach, CA 90277-3638; 310-798-6875; Fax: 310-376-4051. Hours: 8:15AM-4:30PM (PST). *Civil Actions Under $25,000, Eviction, Small Claims.*

www.lasuperiorcourt.org

Note: Also known as the Southwest District South Bay Court - Beach Cities Branch

Civil Records: Access: Mail, online, in person. Only the court performs in person searches; visitors may not. Search fee: $5.00 per name. Required to search: name, years to search. Civil cases indexed by defendant, plaintiff. Civil records on computer from 1991, index files from 1983. Records destroyed after 10 years. Online access available at www.lasuperiorcourt.org/CivilRegister/. Court location, case number, and last name are all required to search. Available for civil, small claims, and unlawful detainer records. **General Information:** Unlawful detainers held for 60 days. SASE required. Turnaround time 3-4 days. Copy fee: $.57 for first page, $.20 each add'l. Certification fee: $6.00. Fee payee: Los Angeles Superior Court. Personal checks accepted. Prepayment is required.

Rio Hondo Superior Court - East District
11234 E Valley Blvd, El Monte, CA 91731; Civil phone: 626-575-4117; Criminal phone: 626-575-4121; Fax: 626-444-9029. Hours: 8AM-4:30PM (PST). *Misdemeanor, Civil Actions Under $25,000, Eviction, Small Claims.*

www.lasuperiorcourt.org

Note: Includes cities of El Monte, South El Monte, La Puente, Rosemead and adjacent unincorporated county area.

Civil Records: Access: Mail, online, in person. Only the court performs in person searches; visitors may not. No search fee. Required to search: name, years to search. Civil cases indexed by defendant, plaintiff. Civil records on computer since 1989, microfiche since 1980. Records destroyed after 10 years. Online access available at www.lasuperiorcourt.org/CivilRegister/. Court location, case number, and last name are all required to search. Available for civil, small claims, and unlawful detainer records.
Criminal Records: Access: Phone, mail, in person. Only the court performs in person searches; visitors may not. Search fee: $5.00 per name. Required to search: name, years to search; also helpful: DOB. Criminal records on computer since 1985, microfiche since 1980.
General Information: Will not release unlawful detainer for 60 days. No probation reports, medical records, search warrants, rap sheet, CLETS report, transcripts or sealed records released. SASE required. Turnaround time 5 days. Copy fee: $.57 per page. Certification fee: $6.00. Fee payee: Los Angeles Superior Court. Personal checks accepted. Two-party checks not accepted. Write "not to exceed $x.xx" on check.

San Fernando Superior Court - North Valley District
900 Third St, #1137, San Fernando, CA 91340; 818-898-2401. Hours: 8AM-4:30PM (PST). *Misdemeanor, Small Claims.*

http://lasuperiorcourt.org

Note: Includes Granada Hills, Northridge, Chatsworth, Sunland, Tujunga, Pacoima, Mission Hills, Sylmar, Arleta, Lake View Terrace, Sun Valley and City of San Fernando. They merged with the Newhall Court to from the North Valley District Court

Criminal Records: Access: Mail, online, in person. Only the court performs in person searches; visitors may not. Search fee: $5.00 per name. Required to search: name, years to search; also helpful: DOB. Criminal records on computer from 1988. Records destroyed after 10 years. Limited criminal records are available online.
General Information: Public Access terminal is available. No probation reports or arrest reports released. SASE required. Turnaround time 2 days. Copy fee: $.57 per page. Certification fee: $6.00. Fee payee: Los Angeles Superior Court. Personal checks accepted. Checks accepted (no 3 party checks). Credit cards accepted. Prepayment is required.

San Pedro Superior Court - South District
505 S Centre St Rm 202, San Pedro, CA 90731; 310-519-6014 Sm Claims; 519-6016 Traffic; Civil phone: 310-519-6015; Criminal phone: 310-519-6018. Hours: 8:30AM-4:30PM (civ, sm claims & criminal); 8AM-4:30PM (traffic) (PST). *Misdemeanor, Civil Actions Under $25,000, Eviction, Small Claims.*

www.lasuperiorcourt.org

Note: Includes San Pedro, Wilmington and a county strip in Torrance extending up to Western Avenue. Holds records for Catalina Branch.

Civil Records: Access: Mail, online, in person. Only the court performs in person searches; visitors may not. Search fee: $5.00 per name. Required to search: name, years to search. Civil cases indexed by defendant, plaintiff. Civil records on computer from 1991, index files from 1984. Records destroyed after 10 years. Online access available at www.lasuperiorcourt.org/CivilRegister/. Court location, case number, and last name are all required to search. Available for civil, small claims, and unlawful detainer records.
Criminal Records: Access: Mail, in person. Only the court performs in person searches; visitors may not. Search fee: $5.00 per name. Required to search: name, years to search, DOB. Criminal records on computer from 1991, index files from 1984. Records destroyed after 10 years.
General Information: No probation, arrest, records released. SASE required. Turnaround time 2 days. Copy fee: $.57 per page. Certification fee: $6.00. Fee payee: Los Angeles Superior Court. Personal checks accepted. Credit cards accepted: Visa. Visa-additional 6% fee charged. Prepayment is required.

Santa Anita Superior Court - Northeast District
300 W Maple Ave, Monrovia, CA 91016; 626-301-4056; Civil phone: 626-301-4050; Criminal phone: 626-301-4051; Fax: 626-357-7825. Hours: 8AM-4:30PM (PST). *Misdemeanor, Civil Actions Under $25,000, Eviction, Small Claims.*

www.lasuperiorcourt.org

Note: Includes cities of Monrovia, Arcadia, Duarte, Bradbury and unincorporated county territory in surrounding area.

Civil Records: Access: Mail, online, in person. Only the court performs in person searches; visitors may not. Search fee: $5.00 per name. Required to search: name, years to search. Civil cases indexed by defendant, plaintiff. Civil records on computer from 1991, index files from 1983. Records destroyed after 10 years. Online access available at www.lasuperiorcourt.org/CivilRegister/. Court location, case number, and last name are all required to search. Available for civil, small claims, and unlawful detainer records.
Criminal Records: Access: Mail, in person. Only the court performs in person searches; visitors may not. Search fee: $5.00 per name. Required to search: name, years to search; also helpful: DOB. Criminal records on computer from 1991, index files from 1983. Records destroyed after 10 years.

General Information: Will not release unlawful detainers less than 60 days old. No sealed, criminal history information, arrest reports or any documents containing witness information records released. SASE required. Turnaround time 2 days. Copy fee: $.57 per page. Certification fee: $6.00. Fee payee: Los Angeles Superior Court. Personal checks accepted. Credit cards accepted: Visa, MasterCard, Discover. Prepayment is required.

Santa Clarita Superior Court - North Valley District
23747 W Valencia Blvd, Valencia, CA 91355; 661-253-7316; Civil phone: 661-253-7313; Criminal phone: 661-253-7384; Fax: 661-254-4107. Hours: 8:30AM-4:30PM (PST). *Misdemeanor, Civil Actions Under $25,000, Eviction, Small Claims.*

www.lasuperiorcourt.org

Note: Formerly known as Newhall Sup. Court, it includes Saugus, Valencia, Santa Clarita and unincorporated area bound by Ventura County line (west), Kern County line (north), Agua Dulce on the east, and Glendale and Los Angeles city limits (South).

Civil Records: Access: Mail, online, in person. Only the court performs in person searches; visitors may not. Search fee: $5.00 per name. There is no fee to view records on microfiche or for first 3 records searched in person. Required to search: name, years to search. Civil cases indexed by defendant, plaintiff. Civil records on computer from 1991, index files from 1983. Records destroyed after 10 years, many records on microfiche. Call first for fax access. Online access available at www.lasuperiorcourt.org/CivilRegister/. Court location, case number, and last name are all required to search. Available for civil, small claims, and unlawful detainer records.
Criminal Records: Access: Mail, in person. Only the court performs in person searches; visitors may not. Search fee: $5.00 per name. Required to search: name, years to search; also helpful: DOB, SSN. Criminal records on computer from 1991, index files from 1983. Records destroyed after 10 years, many records on microfiche.
General Information: No probation, or police reports w/out court approval released. SASE required. Turnaround time 7-10 days. Copy fee: $.57 per page. Certification fee: $6.00. Court location, case number, and last name are all required to search. Available for civil, small claims, and unlawful detainer records. Fee payee: Los Angeles Superior Court. Personal checks accepted. Prepayment is required.

Santa Monica Superior Court - West District
1725 Main St Rm 224, Santa Monica, CA 90401; Civil phone: 310-260-3706; Criminal phone: 310-260-3518. Hours: 8:30AM-4:30PM (PST). *Misdemeanor, Civil Actions Under $25,000, Eviction, Small Claims.*

www.lasuperiorcourt.org

Note: Includes City of Santa Monica and the unincorporated territory of the Veteran's Administration facilities located at West Los Angeles.

Civil Records: Access: Mail, online, in person. Both court and visitors may perform in person searches. Search fee: $5.00 per name per year. Required to search: name, years to search. Civil cases indexed by defendant, plaintiff. Civil records on computer from 1991, index files from 1983. Records destroyed after 10 years. Online access available at www.lasuperiorcourt.org/CivilRegister/. Court location, case number, and last name are all required to search. Available for civil, small claims, and unlawful detainer records. Also, online access to Probate Notes is available free, with case number, at www.lasuperiorcourt.org/ProbateNotes.

Los Angeles County - Con't

Criminal Records: Access: Mail, in person. Only the court performs in person searches; visitors may not. Search fee: $5.00 per name per year. Required to search: name, years to search. Criminal records on computer from 1991, index files from 1983. Records destroyed after 10 years.

General Information: No probation reports or unlawful detainer records released. SASE required. Turnaround time 1-2 days. Copy fee: $.57 per page. Certification fee: $6.00. Fee payee: Los Angeles Superior Court. Personal checks accepted. Prepayment is required.

South Gate Superior Court - Southeast District

8640 California Ave, South Gate, CA 90280; Civil phone: 323-563-4037; Criminal phone: 323-563-4012; Fax: 323-569-4840. Hours: 8AM-4PM T-F; 8AM-7PM M traffic (PST). *Misdemeanor, Civil Actions Under $25,000, Eviction, Small Claims.*

www.lasuperiorcourt.org

Note: Includes city of South Gate, Hollydale and unincorporated area of Walnut Park.

Civil Records: Access: Mail, online, in person. Only the court performs in person searches; visitors may not. Search fee: $5.00 per name. Required to search: name, years to search. Civil cases indexed by defendant, plaintiff. Civil records on computer from 1991, index files from 1983. Records destroyed after 10 years. Online access available at www.lasuperiorcourt.org/CivilRegister/. Court location, case number, and last name are all required to search. Available for civil, small claims, and unlawful detainer records.

Criminal Records: Access: Mail, in person. Only the court performs in person searches; visitors may not. Search fee: $5.00 per name. Required to search: name, years to search. Criminal records on computer from 1991, index files from 1983. Records destroyed after 10 years.

General Information: No probation reports released. SASE required. Turnaround time 2 days. Copy fee: $.57 per page. Certification fee: $6.00. Fee payee: Los Angeles Superior Court. Personal checks accepted. Credit cards accepted: Visa, MasterCard, Discover. Prepayment is required.

Torrance Superior Court - Southwest District

825 Maple Ave, Torrance, CA 90503-5058; 310-222-6501; Civil phone: 310-222-6400; Criminal phone: 310-222-6505; Fax: 310-222-7277. Hours: 8:30AM-4PM (PST). *Misdemeanor, Traffic, Eviction, Small Claims.*

www.lasuperiorcourt.org

Note: Includes cities of Torrance, Gardena, Rolling Hills, Rolling Hills Estates, Manhattan Beach, Lomita, Redondo Beach, Hermosa Beach, Palos Verdes Estates, Rancho Palos Verdes and Lawndale.

Civil Records: Access: Mail, online, in person. Only the court performs in person searches; visitors may not. Search fee: $5.00 per name. Required to search: name, years to search. Civil cases indexed by defendant, plaintiff. Civil records on computer from 1991, index files from 1983. Records destroyed after 10 years. Online access available at www.lasuperiorcourt.org/CivilRegister/. Court location, case number, and last name are all required to search. Available for civil, small claims, and unlawful detainer records. Also, online access to Probate Notes is available free, with case number, at www.lasuperiorcourt.org/ProbateNotes.

Criminal Records: Access: Mail, in person. Only the court performs in person searches; visitors may not. Search fee: $5.00 per name. Required to search: name, years to search, DOB. Criminal records on computer from 1991, index files from 1983. Records destroyed after 10 years.

General Information: No probation reports, medical or psychiatric reports, criminal history rap sheets released. SASE required. Turnaround time 5 days. Copy fee: $.57 per page. Certification fee: $6.00. Fee payee: Los Angeles Superior Court. Personal checks accepted. Prepayment is required.

Van Nuys Superior Court - Northwest District - Civil

6230 Sylmar St, Van Nuys, CA 91401; 818-374-3060. Hours: 8:30AM-4:30PM (PST). *Civil Actions, Eviction, Small Claims.*

www.lasuperiorcourt.org

Note: Small Claims and Civil for that part of city known as Sherman Oaks, Van Nuys, Reseda, North Hollywood, Woodland Hills, Canoga Park, Tarzana, Proter Ranch, Winnetka and Panorama City

Civil Records: Access: Mail, online, in person. Both court and visitors may perform in person searches. Search fee: $5.00 per name. Required to search: name, years to search. Civil cases indexed by defendant, plaintiff. Civil records on computer from 1991, index files from 1983. Records destroyed after 10 years. Online access available at www.lasuperiorcourt.org/CivilRegister/. Court location, case number, and last name are all required to search. Available for civil, small claims, and unlawful detainer records. **General Information:** No probation reports or arrest reports released. SASE required. Turnaround time 2-3 days. Copy fee: $.57 per page. Certification fee: $6.00. Fee payee: Los Angeles Superior Court or LASC. Personal checks accepted. Credit cards accepted for limited jurisdiction records. Prepayment is required.

Van Nuys Superior Court - Northwest District - Criminal

14400 Erwin St Mall 2nd Fl, Van Nuys, CA 91401; 818-374-2628. Hours: 8:30AM-4:30PM (PST). *Misdemeanor.*

www.lasuperiorcourt.org

Note: Misdemeanors for that part of city known as Sherman Oaks, Van Nuys, Reseda, North Hollywood, Woodland Hills, Canoga Park, Tarzana, Proter Ranch, Winnetka and Panorama City

Criminal Records: Access: Phone, mail, in person. Only the court performs in person searches; visitors may not. Search fee: $5.00 per name. Required to search: name, years to search, sex; also helpful: DOB. Criminal records on computer from 1991, index files from 1983. Records destroyed after 10 years.

General Information: No probation reports or arrest reports released. SASE required. Turnaround time 2-3 days. Copy fee: $.57 per page. Certification fee: $6.00. Fee payee: Los Angeles Superior Court. Personal checks accepted. Prepayment is required.

West Los Angeles Superior Court - West District

1633 Purdue Ave, Los Angeles, CA 90025; 310-914-7477; Fax: 310-312-2902. Hours: 8:30AM-4:30PM (PST). *Civil Actions Under $25,000, Eviction, Small Claims.*

www.lasuperiorcourt.org

Note: Includes the areas of Palms, Mar Vista, Rancho Park, Marina del Rey, Venice, Playa del Rey and Sawtelle. Holds records for the former Robertson branch. Criminal felony and misdemeanors are at the new Airport Court.

Civil Records: Access: Phone, mail, online, in person. Only the court performs in person searches; visitors may not. Search fee: $5.00 per name. Required to search: name, years to search. Civil cases indexed by defendant, plaintiff. Online access available at www.lasuperiorcourt.org/CivilRegister/. Court location, case number, and last name are all required to search. Available for civil, small claims, and unlawful detainer records.

Criminal Records: Access: Mail, in person. Search fee: $5.00 per name. Required to search: name, years to search; also helpful: DOB. Felony and misdemeanor records have been moved to the Airport Court.

General Information: SASE required. Turnaround time 1-5 days. Copy fee: $.57 per page. Certification fee: $6.00. Fee payee: Los Angeles Superior Court. Personal checks accepted. Prepayment is required.

Whittier Superior Court - Southeast District

7339 S Painter Ave, Whittier, CA 90602; Civil phone: 562-907-3127; Criminal phone: 562-907-3113. Hours: 8AM-4:30PM (PST). *Misdemeanor, Civil Actions Under $25,000, Eviction, Small Claims.*

www.lasuperiorcourt.org

Note: Includes cities of Whittier, Santa Fe Springs, Pico Rivera, La Habra Heights plus unincorporated territory in the Whittier area including areas designated as Los Nietos and South Whittier.

Civil Records: Access: Mail, online, in person. Both court and visitors may perform in person searches. No search fee. Required to search: name, years to search. Civil cases indexed by defendant, plaintiff. Civil records on computer from 1991, index files from 1983. Records destroyed after 10 years. Online access available at www.lasuperiorcourt.org/CivilRegister/. Court location, case number, and last name are all required to search. Available for civil, small claims, and unlawful detainer records.

Criminal Records: Access: Mail, in person. Only the court performs in person searches; visitors may not. Search fee: $5.00 per name. Required to search: name, years to search; also helpful: DOB. Criminal records computerized since 1987.

General Information: No probation reports released. SASE required. Turnaround time 2 days. Copy fee: $.57 per page. Certification fee: $6.00. Fee payee: Los Angeles Superior Court. Personal checks accepted. Credit cards accepted: Visa, MasterCard, Discover. Prepayment is required.

Madera County

Superior Court 209 W Yosemite Ave, Madera, CA 93637; 559-675-7995; Civil phone: 559-675-7996; Criminal phone: 559-675-7334; Fax: 559-675-0701. Hours: 8AM-5PM (PST). *Felony, Civil, Probate, Eviction.*

Note: The Superior and Municipal courts located in the city of Madera have combined into a consolidated court. There is no countywide database of records; each court must be searched.

Civil Records: Access: Mail, fax, in person. Both court and visitors may perform in person searches. Search fee: $5.00 per name. There is no fee if searcher comes to court and does search. Required to search: name, years to search. Civil cases indexed by defendant, plaintiff. Civil records on microfiche, archived and index file from 1893.

Criminal Records: Access: Mail, fax, in person. Both court and visitors may perform in person searches. Search fee: $5.00 per name. There is no fee if searcher comes to court and does search. Required to search: name, years to search; also helpful: DOB, signed release. Criminal records on microfiche, archived and index file from 1893.

General Information: No adoptions, juvenile, medical, probation or sealed records released. SASE required. Turnaround time 2 days. Copy fee: $.50 per page. Certification fee: $6.00. Fee payee: Madera Superior Court. Personal checks accepted. Prepayment is required.

Borden Division - Superior Court 14241 Road 28, Madera, CA 93638; 559-675-7930; Fax: 559-673-0542. Hours: 8AM-5PM (PST). *Small Claims.*

Civil Records: Access: Mail, in person. Only the court performs in person searches; visitors may not. Search fee: $15.00 plus $1.00 per name per year. Required to search: name, years to search. Cases indexed by defendant, plaintiff. Records on index cards since 1986, on computer back to 10/98. Will only search back 7 years. **General Information:** SASE required. Turnaround time 1 week. Copy fee: $.50 per page. Certification fee: $6.00. Fee payee: Madera Superior Court. Personal checks accepted. Prepayment is required.

Sierra Division - Superior Court 40601 Road 274, Bass Lake, CA 93604; 559-642-3235; Fax: 559-642-3445. Hours: 8AM-5PM (PST). *Misdemeanor, Civil Actions Under $25,000, Eviction, Small Claims.*

Civil Records: Access: Mail, in person. Only the court performs in person searches; visitors may not. Search fee: $5.00 per name. Required to search: name, years to search. Civil cases indexed by defendant, plaintiff. Civil records on index cards. Will only search back 7 years.
Criminal Records: Access: Mail, in person. Only the court performs in person searches; visitors may not. Search fee: $5.00 per name. Required to search: name, years to search; also helpful: DOB. Criminal records on computer (traffic only), index cards for criminal.
General Information: No adoptions, juvenile, medical, probation or sealed records released. SASE required. Turnaround time 1-2 weeks. Copy fee: $.50 per page. Certification fee: $6.00. Fee payee: Madera Superior Court. Personal checks accepted. Prepayment is required.

Marin County

Superior Court PO Box 4988, San Rafael, CA 94913-4988; 415-499-6244; Civil phone: 415-499-6407; Criminal phone: 415-499-6225. Hours: 8:30AM-4PM (PST). *Felony, Misdemeanor, Civil, Eviction, Small Claims, Probate.*

www.co.marin.ca.us/courts

Civil Records: Access: Phone, mail, in person, online. Both court and visitors may perform in person searches. Search fee: $5.00 per name per year. Required to search: name, years to search. Civil cases indexed by defendant, plaintiff. Civil records on computer from 1986, on microfiche from 1973 to 1985, archived from 1900 to 1972, on reel from 1900. Online access to the current court calendar is available free at www.co.marin.ca.us/depts/MC/main/courtcal/name.cfm. Phone requests are limited to one name.
Criminal Records: Access: Phone, mail, in person, online. Both court and visitors may perform in person searches. Search fee: $5.00 per name per year. Required to search: name, years to search. Criminal records on computer from 1986, on microfiche from 1973 to 1985, archived from 1900 to 1972, on reel from 1900. Online Access to the active criminal calendar is the same as civil. Phone requests are limited to one name.
General Information: Public Access terminal is available. No adoptions, juvenile, medical, probation or sealed records released. SASE required. Turnaround time 3 weeks. Copy fee: $1.00 per page. Certification fee: $6.00. Fee payee: Marin County Superior Court. Personal checks accepted. Out-of-state checks not accepted. Write "not to exceed $x.xx" on check. Call first. Prepayment is required.

Mariposa County

Superior Court 5088 Bullion St (PO Box 28), Mariposa, CA 95338; Civil phone: 209-966-6599; Criminal phone: 209-966-2005; Probate phone: 209-966-6599; Fax: 209-742-6860. Hours: 8AM-5PM (PST). *Felony, Misdemeanor, Civil, Small Claims, Eviction, Probate.*

www.mariposacourts.org

Note: This former municipal court is now known as Department 2.

Civil Records: Access: Phone, fax, mail, in person. Only the court performs in person searches; visitors may not. Search fee: $5.00 per name. Fee applies to years prior to 1990. No fee for computer records search. Required to search: name, years to search. Civil records on computer from 1989, on microfiche and index files from 1800s. Phone access limited to short searches.
Criminal Records: Access: Phone, fax, mail, in person. Only the court performs in person searches; visitors may not. Search fee: $5.00 per name per year. Required to search: name, years to search. Criminal records on computer from 1989, on microfiche and index files from 1800s.
General Information: No adoptions, juvenile, medical, probation or sealed records released. SASE required. Turnaround time 2-3 days. Copy fee: $.50 per page. Certification fee: $6.00. Fee payee: Mariposa Superior Court. Personal checks accepted. Prepayment is required.

Mendocino County

Superior Court State & Perkins Sts (PO Box 996), Ukiah, CA 95482; Civil phone: 707-463-4481; Criminal phone: 707-463-4486; Fax: 707-468-3459. Hours: 8AM-4PM (PST). *Felony, Civil Actions Over $25,000, Probate.*

Civil Records: Access: Mail, in person. Both court and visitors may perform in person searches. Search fee: $5.00 per name. Fee for mail search only. Required to search: name, years to search. Civil cases indexed by defendant, plaintiff. Civil records on computer from 1990s, on microfilm from 1800 to 1940.
Criminal Records: Access: Mail, in person. Both court and visitors may perform in person searches. Search fee: $5.00 per name. Required to search: name, years to search. Criminal records on computer from 1990s, on microfilm from 1800 to 1940.
General Information: No adoptions, juvenile, medical, probation or sealed records released. SASE required. Turnaround time 1 week. Copy fee: $1.00 for first page, $.50 each add'l. Certification fee: $6.00. Fee payee: Mendocino Superior Court. Personal checks accepted. Prepayment is required.

Anderson Branch - Superior Court 14400 Hwy 128 Veteran Bldg, PO Box 336, Boonville, CA 95415; 707-895-3329; Fax: 707-895-2349. Hours: 9AM-Noon, 1-5PM (PST). *Misdemeanor, Civil Actions Under $25,000, Eviction, Small Claims.*

www.mendocino.ca.us

Civil Records: Access: Phone, fax, mail, in person. Only the court performs in person searches; visitors may not. Search fee: $5.00 per name. Required to search: name, years to search. Civil cases indexed by defendant, plaintiff. Civil records on computer back to 1996; prior on index cards. Will only search back 7 years.
Criminal Records: Access: Phone, fax, mail, in person. Both court and visitors may perform in person searches. Search fee: $5.00 per name. Required to search: name, years to search, DOB. Criminal records on computer back to 1996, index books prior.
General Information: No juvenile records released. SASE required. Turnaround time 1-2 weeks. Fax notes: Fax Fee: Local $1.00 per pg; Long Distance or out of

county $1.50 per pg. Copy fee: $1.00 for first page, $.50 each add'l. Certification fee: $6.00. Fee payee: Superior Court. Personal checks accepted. Prepayment is required.

Arena Branch - Superior Court 24000 S Hwy 1 (PO Box 153), Point Arena, CA 95468; 707-882-2116. Hours: 9AM-Noon, 1-4PM (PST). *Misdemeanor, Civil Actions Under $25,000, Eviction, Small Claims.*

Civil Records: Access: Mail, in person. Both court and visitors may perform in person searches. Search fee: $5.00 per name. Required to search: name, years to search. Civil cases indexed by defendant, plaintiff. Civil records on index cards, computerized since 07/98. Will search back 10 years.
Criminal Records: Access: Mail, in person. Only the court performs in person searches; visitors may not. Search fee: $5.00 per name. Required to search: name, years to search. Criminal records indexed on cards, computerized since 07/98.
General Information: No juvenile records released. SASE required. Turnaround time 1 week. Copy fee: $1.00 for first page, $.50 each add'l. $2.00 minimum. Certification fee: $6.00. Fee payee: Arena Court. Personal checks accepted. Prepayment is required.

Long Valley Branch - Superior Court PO Box 157, Leggett, CA 95585; 707-925-6460; Fax: 707-925-6225. Hours: 8AM-4PM (PST). *Misdemeanor, Civil Actions Under $25,000, Eviction, Small Claims.*

Civil Records: Access: Mail, fax, in person. Both court and visitors may perform in person searches. Search fee: $5.00 per name. Required to search: name, years to search. Civil cases indexed by defendant, plaintiff. Civil records on computer (DMV only) back 2 to 3 years, index cards back 7 years. Will only search back 7 years.
Criminal Records: Access: Mail, fax, in person. Both court and visitors may perform in person searches. Search fee: $5.00 per name. Required to search: name, years to search. Criminal records on index cards back 7 years. Will only search back 7 years. Computer records go back 5 years.
General Information: No probation records released. SASE required. Turnaround time 1 week. Copy fee: $1.00 per page. Certification fee: $6.00. Fee payee: Mendocino Superior Court. Personal checks accepted. Prepayment is required.

Round Valley Branch - Superior Court 76091 Covelo Rd (PO Box 25), Covelo, CA 95428; 707-983-6446; Fax: 707-983-6996. Hours: 8:30AM-5PM M-Th (PST). *Misdemeanor, Civil Actions Under $25,000, Eviction, Small Claims.*

Civil Records: Access: Mail, in person. Both court and visitors may perform in person searches. Search fee: $5.00 per name. Required to search: name, years to search. Civil cases indexed by defendant, plaintiff. Civil records on index cards. Will only search back 7 years.
Criminal Records: Access: Mail, in person. Both court and visitors may perform in person searches. Search fee: $5.00 per name. Required to search: name, years to search, DOB. Criminal records on computer from 1990, index cards prior. Will only search back 7 years.
General Information: No juvenile or probation records released. SASE required. Turnaround time 1 week. Copy fee: $1.00 per page. Certification fee: $7.00. Fee payee: Superior Court. Personal checks accepted. Prepayment is required.

Ten Mile Branch - Superior Court 700 S Franklin St, Fort Bragg, CA 95437; 707-964-3192; Fax: 707-961-2611. Hours: 8AM-4PM (PST). *Misdemeanor, Civil Actions Under $25,000, Eviction, Small Claims.*

Civil Records: Access: Fax, mail, in person. Only the court performs in person searches; visitors may not. Search fee: $5.00 per name. Required to search: name, years to search. Civil cases indexed by defendant, plaintiff. Civil records on index cards. Will only search back 7 years.

Criminal Records: Access: Fax, mail, in person. Only the court performs in person searches; visitors may not. Search fee: $5.00 per name. Required to search: name, years to search, DOB. Criminal records on computer since 1995; prior records in archives.

General Information: No juvenile or probation records released. SASE required. Turnaround time 2 weeks. Copy fee: $1.00 for first page, $.50 each add'l. Certification fee: $6.00. Fee payee: Superior Court. Personal checks accepted. Prepayment is required.

Willits Branch - Superior Court 125 E Commercial St Rm 100, Willits, CA 95490; 707-459-7800; Fax: 707-459-7818. Hours: 8AM-4PM (PST). *Misdemeanor, Civil Actions Under $25,000, Eviction, Small Claims.*

Civil Records: Access: Mail, in person. Both court and visitors may perform in person searches. Search fee: $5.00 per name. Required to search: name, years to search. Civil cases indexed by defendant, plaintiff. Civil records on computer since 1992, index files prior.

Criminal Records: Access: Mail, in person. Both court and visitors may perform in person searches. Search fee: $5.00 per name. Required to search: name, years to search, DOB. Criminal records on computer since 1992, index files prior.

General Information: No probation reports released. SASE required. Turnaround time 1 week. Copy fee: $1.00 per page. Certification fee: $6.00. Fee payee: MCSC. Personal checks accepted. Prepayment is required.

Merced County

Superior Court 2222 "M" St, Merced, CA 95340; 209-385-7531; Fax: 209-725-9223. Hours: 8AM-4PM (PST). *Felony, Civil Actions Over $25,000, Probate.*

Note: Courier address is 627 West 21st St.

Civil Records: Access: Mail, in person. Both court and visitors may perform in person searches. Search fee: $5.00 per name. Required to search: name, years to search. Civil cases indexed by defendant, plaintiff. Civil records in index files from 1900s, computer from 1979, on microfiche from 1900s.

Criminal Records: Access: Mail, in person. Both court and visitors may perform in person searches. Search fee: $5.00 per name. Required to search: name, years to search. Criminal records in index files from 1900s, computer from 1979, on microfiche from 1900s.

General Information: Public Access terminal is available. No juvenile nor adoption records released. SASE required. Turnaround time 1 week. Copy fee: $.50 per page. Certification fee: $6.00. Fee payee: Merced County Superior Court. Business checks accepted. Prepayment is required.

4, 5, 7 & 8 Divisions - Merced Limited Superior Court 670 W 22nd St, Merced, CA 95340; Civil phone: 209-385-7337; Criminal phone: 209-385-7335; Fax: 209-725-0323. Hours: 8AM-4PM M-F (civil); Noon-4PM M-F (civ only) (PST). *Misdemeanor, Civil Actions Under $25,000, Eviction, Small Claims.*

Civil Records: Access: Mail, in person. Search fee: $5.00 per name. Required to search: name, years to search. Civil cases indexed by defendant, plaintiff. Civil records on computer from 1990, index cards prior. Will only search back 7 years.

Criminal Records: Access: Mail, in person. Both court and visitors may perform in person searches. Search fee: $5.00 per name. Required to search: name, years to search. Criminal records on computer from 1990, index cards prior. Will only search back 7 years.

General Information: No juvenile or probation records released. SASE required. Turnaround time 2-5

days. Copy fee: $.50 per page. Certification fee: $6.00. Fee payee: Merced County Superior Court. Personal checks accepted. Prepayment is required.

Los Banos Branch - Superior Court 445 "I" St, Los Banos, CA 93635; 209-826-6500; Fax: 209-826-8108. Hours: 8AM-4PM (PST). *Misdemeanor, Civil Actions Under $25,000, Eviction, Small Claims.*

Note: This court was combined with the old Dos Palos and Gustine Municipal Courts.

Civil Records: Access: Mail, in person. Both court and visitors may perform in person searches. Search fee: $5.00 per name. Required to search: name, years to search. Civil cases indexed by defendant, plaintiff. Civil records on microfiche.

Criminal Records: Access: Mail, in person. Both court and visitors may perform in person searches. Search fee: $5.00 per name. Required to search: name, years to search; also helpful: DOB. Criminal records on microfiche.

General Information: No juvenile or probation records released. SASE required. Turnaround time 2-3 days. Copy fee: $.50 per page. Certification fee: $6.00. Fee payee: Merced Superior Court. Personal checks accepted. Prepayment is required.

Modoc County

Superior Court 205 S East St, Alturas, CA 96101; 530-233-6515/6; Fax: 530-233-6500. Hours: 8:30AM-5PM (PST). *Felony, Misdemeanor, Civil, Small Claims, Eviction, Probate.*

Civil Records: Access: Mail, in person. Only the court performs in person searches; visitors may not. Search fee: $5.00 per name. Required to search: name, years to search. Civil cases indexed by plaintiff. Civil records in index file from 1874, computerized since 07/25/95.

Criminal Records: Access: Fax, mail, in person. Only the court performs in person searches; visitors may not. Search fee: $5.00 per name. Required to search: name, years to search; also helpful: DOB. Criminal records computerized since 1991.

General Information: No adoptions, juvenile, medical, probation or sealed records released. SASE required. Turnaround time 1-2 weeks. Copy fee: $.50 per page. Certification fee: $7.00. Fee payee: Modoc County Superior Courts. Personal checks accepted. Prepayment is required.

Mono County

Superior Court - Bridgeport Branch PO Box 537, Bridgeport, CA 93517; 760-932-5239. Hours: 8:30AM-5PM (PST). *Felony, Civil, Probate.*

Civil Records: Access: Mail, in person. Both court and visitors may perform in person searches. Search fee: $5.00 per name. Required to search: name, years to search. Civil cases indexed by defendant, plaintiff. Civil records in index files from 1873.

Criminal Records: Access: Mail, in person. Both court and visitors may perform in person searches. Search fee: $5.00 per name. Required to search: name, years to search. Criminal records in index files from 1873.

General Information: No adoptions, juvenile, medical, probation or sealed records released. SASE required. Turnaround time 1-3 weeks. Copy fee: $.50 per page. Certification fee: $6.00 first page and $1.00 each additional. Fee payee: Mono County Superior Court. Personal checks accepted. Prepayment is required.

Mammoth Lakes Division - Superior Court PO Box 1037, Mammoth Lakes, CA 93546; 760-924-5444; Fax: 760-924-5419. Hours: 9AM-5PM (PST). *Felony, Misdemeanor, Civil, Eviction, Small Claims.*

Civil Records: Access: Mail, in person. Only the court performs in person searches; visitors may not. Search fee: $5.00 per name. Required to search: name, years to

search. Civil cases indexed by defendant, plaintiff. Civil records on index cards. Will only search back 10 years.

Criminal Records: Access: Mail, in person. Only the court performs in person searches; visitors may not. Search fee: $5.00 per name. Required to search: name, years to search. Criminal records on computer from 1989, index cards prior. Will only search back 7 years.

General Information: No juvenile or probation records released. SASE required. Turnaround time 1 week. Copy fee: $.50 per page. Certification fee: $6.00 plus $1.00 per page. Fee payee: Mono Superior Court. Personal checks accepted. Prepayment is required.

Monterey County

Superior Court - Monterey Branch 1200 Aguajito Rd, First Floor, Monterey, CA 93940; 831-647-7730. Hours: 8AM-4PM (PST). *Civil, Probate, Eviction.*

www.co.monterey.ca.us/court

Note: This court holds the civil records from the city of Salinas. Criminal records for Monterey are held in Salinas.

Civil Records: Access: Mail, in person, online. Both court and visitors may perform in person searches. Search fee: $5.00 per name per year. Required to search: name, years to search. Civil cases indexed by defendant, plaintiff. Civil records computerized since 09/90, on microfiche from 1973, index books prior. Online access to calendars and current cases is available free online at www.co.monterey.ca.us/court/calendar.asp. **General Information:** No juvenile or probation records released. SASE required. Turnaround time 1 week. Copy fee: $.75 per page. Certification fee: $6.00 general; $10.00 if for final re dissolution. Fee payee: Superior Court. Personal checks accepted. Prepayment is required.

Superior Court - Salinas Division 240 Church St Rm 318 PO Box 1819, Salinas, CA 93902; 831-755-5052. Hours: 8AM-4PM (PST). *Felony, Misdemeanor.*

www.co.monterey.ca.us/court

Note: All criminal records from the city of Monterey are found here. Salinas sends all civil records to Monterey.

Criminal Records: Access: Mail, in person, online. Both court and visitors may perform in person searches. Search fee: $5.00 per name. Required to search: name, years to search; also helpful: DOB. Felony records computerized since 1998, on microfiche to 1940s. Misdemeanor records computerized since 1992, on microfiche since 1986. Online access to calendars and current cases is available free online at www.co.monterey.ca.us/court/calendar.asp.

General Information: No adoptions, juvenile, medical, probation or sealed records released. SASE required. Turnaround time 1 week. Copy fee: $.75 per page. Certification fee: $6.00. Fee payee: Clerk of Court. Personal checks accepted. Prepayment is required.

King City Division - Consolidated Trial Court 250 Franciscan Way (PO Box 647), King City, CA 93930; Civil phone: 831-385-8339; Criminal phone: 831-385-8338. Hours: 8AM-5PM; Public Hours: 8AM-4PM (PST). *Felony, Misdemeanor, Civil Actions Under $25,000, Eviction, Small Claims.*

www.co.monterey.ca.us/court

Note: Encompasses the cities of King City, Greenfield, Soledad, areas south of King City to the San Luis Obispo County line.

Civil Records: Access: Mail, in person, online. Both court and visitors may perform in person searches. Search fee: $5.00 per name. Required to search: name, years to search. Civil cases indexed by defendant,

plaintiff. Civil records on computer from 1992, index files from 1983. Records destroyed after 10 years. Online access to calendars and current cases is available free online at www.co.monterey.ca.us/court/calendar.asp.
Criminal Records: Access: Mail, in person, online. Both court and visitors may perform in person searches. Search fee: $5.00 per name. Required to search: name, years to search; also helpful: DOB. Criminal records on computer from 1992, index files from 1983. Records destroyed after 10 years. Online access to criminal records is the same as civil.
General Information: No probation reports released. SASE required. Turnaround time 1 week. Copy fee: $.75 per page. Certification fee: $6.00. Fee payee: Monterey County Courts. Personal checks accepted. Credit cards accepted: Visa, AmEx. Additional fee charged. Prepayment is required.

Marina Extension 3180 Del Monte Blvd, Marina, CA 93933; 831-884-1953; Fax: 831-884-1951. Hours: 8AM-3PM (PST). *Small Claims, Traffic.*

www.co.monterey.ca.us/court

Civil Records: Access: Online, in person. Both court and visitors may perform in person searches. Search fee: $5.00 per name. Required to search: name, years to search. Online access to calendars and current cases is available free online at www.co.monterey.ca.us/court/calendar.asp. **General Information:** Copy fee: $.75 per page. Certification fee: $6.00. Fee payee: Monterey County Courts. Prepayment is required.

Napa County

Superior Court 825 Brown St, PO Box 880, Napa, CA 94559; Civil phone: 707-253-4481; Criminal phone: 707-253-4573; Fax: 707-253-4229, 707-253-4673 (Criminal). Hours: 8AM-5PM (PST). *Felony, Misdemeanor, Civil, Eviction, Small Claims, Probate.*

www.napa.courts.ca.gov

Civil Records: Access: Mail, in person. Both court and visitors may perform in person searches. Search fee: $5.00 per name per year. Required to search: name, years to search. Civil cases indexed by defendant, plaintiff. Civil records on computer since 1989; prior records on index books or microfilm back to 1800s.
Criminal Records: Access: Mail, in person. Both court and visitors may perform in person searches. Search fee: $5.00 per name per year. Required to search: name, years to search, DOB; also helpful: address, SSN. Misdemeanor records on computer since 1986 and felonies since 1989.
General Information: Public Access terminal is available. No adoptions, juvenile, medical, probation or sealed records released. SASE required. Turnaround time 2-3 weeks. Copy fee: $1.00 per page. Certification fee: $6.00. Fee payee: Napa Superior Court. Personal checks accepted. Prepayment is required.

Nevada County

Superior Court 201 Church St Suite 7, Nevada City, CA 95959; 530-265-1311; Fax: 530-265-1779. Hours: 8AM-5PM (PST). *Felony, Misdemeanor, Small Claims, Eviction, Probate.*

www.co.nevada.ca.us/courts

Criminal Records: Access: Phone, mail, in person. Only the court performs in person searches; visitors may not. Search fee: No fee unless extensive research required. Required to search: name, years to search; also helpful: DOB. Criminal Records on computer from 1977, prior in books back to 1800s.
General Information: No adoptions, paternity, juvenile, medical, probation or sealed records released. SASE not required. Turnaround time 2 weeks. Copy fee: $1.00 per page. Certification fee: $6.00. Fee payee:

Nevada County Courts. Personal checks accepted. Prepayment is required.

Superior Court - Civil Division 201 Church St, Suite 5, Nevada City, CA 95959; 530-265-1294; Fax: 530-265-1606. Hours: 8AM-5PM (PST). *Civil, Eviction, Small Claims.*

www.co.nevada.ca.us/court

Note: The phone number for Family Law, Probate and Juvenile is 530-265-1293. The phone number for Evictions and Small Claims is 530-265-1294.

Civil Records: Access: Phone, mail, in person. Both court and visitors may perform in person searches. Search fee: $5.00 per name. Required to search: name, years to search. Civil cases indexed by defendant, plaintiff. Civil records on computer back to 1983. Cases with previous disposition are available on microfilm in most cases. Some of the Limited Civil, Small Claims and Unlawful Detainer cases have been destroyed.
General Information: Public Access terminal is available. No probation reports released. SASE required. Turnaround time 2 days. Fax notes: Will not fax results. Copy fee: $.50 per page. Certification fee: $6.00. Plus copy fees. Fee payee: Superior Court. Personal checks accepted. Prepayment is required.

Truckee Branch - Superior Court 10075 Levon Ave #301, Truckee, CA 96161; Civil phone: 530-582-7837; Criminal phone: 530-582-7836; Fax: 530-582-7875. Hours: 8AM-5PM (PST). *Misdemeanor, Civil, Eviction, Small Claims.*

www.co.nevada.ca.us/court

Civil Records: Access: Mail, in person. Both court and visitors may perform in person searches. Search fee: $5.00 per name. Required to search: name, years to search. Civil cases indexed by defendant, plaintiff. Civil records on computer from 1991, index files from 1983. Records destroyed after 10 years.
Criminal Records: Access: Mail, in person. Both court and visitors may perform in person searches. Search fee: $5.00 per name. Required to search: name, years to search. Criminal records on computer from 1991, index files from 1983. Records destroyed after 10 years.
General Information: Public Access terminal is available. No probation reports released. SASE required. Turnaround time 1 week. Copy fee: $1.00 per page. Certification fee: $6.00. Fee payee: Superior Court. Personal checks accepted. Prepayment is required.

Orange County

Superior Court - Civil 700 Civic Center Dr W, Santa Ana, CA 92701; 714-834-2208. Hours: 9AM-5PM (PST). *Civil Actions Over $25,000.*

www.oc.ca.gov/superior/civil.htm

Note: There is no countywide database, all searches must be conducted within each court

Civil Records: Access: Mail, in person. Only the court performs in person searches; visitors may not. Search fee: $5.00 per name. Required to search: name, years to search. Civil cases indexed by defendant, plaintiff. Civil records on computer from mid 1980s, partial prior to 1986, microfiche and index file from 1900s. **General Information:** No adoptions, juvenile, medical, probation or sealed records released. SASE required. Turnaround time 1-2 weeks. Copy fee: $.80 per page. Certification fee: $6.00. Fee payee: Clerk of the Court. Personal checks accepted. Prepayment is required.

Superior Court - Criminal Operations 700 Civic Center Dr W, Santa Ana, CA 92701; 714-834-2266. Hours: 8AM-5PM (PST). *Felony.*

www.oc.ca.gov/superior

Criminal Records: Access: Mail, in person. Both court and visitors may perform in person searches. Search

fee: $5.00 per name. Required to search: name, years to search, DOB. Criminal records on computer from 1988, on microfiche and archived from 1966, index files from 1918.
General Information: No adoptions, juvenile, medical, probation or sealed records released. SASE required. Turnaround time 1-2 weeks. Copy fee: $.80 per page. Certification fee: $6.00. Fee payee: Clerk of the Court. Personal checks accepted. Prepayment is required.

Central Orange County Superior Court - Limited Jurisdiction 700 Civic Ctr Dr W (PO Box 1138, 92702), Santa Ana, CA 92701; Civil phone: 714-834-3580; Criminal phone: 714-834-3575; Fax: 714-953-9032. Hours: 7:30AM-5PM (PST). *Misdemeanor, Civil Actions Under $25,000, Eviction, Small Claims.*

www.oc.ca.gov/superior

Note: Includes cities of Santa Ana, Orange, Tustin and surrounding unincorporated territories including Cowan Heights, El Modena, Tustin Marine Air Base, Lemon Heights, Modjeska, Orange Park Acres, Silverado Canyon and Villa Park.

Civil Records: Access: Mail, in person. Only the court performs in person searches; visitors may not. Search fee: $5.00 per name per year. Required to search: name, years to search. Civil cases indexed by defendant, plaintiff. Civil records on index files from 1985. Records destroyed after 10 years.
Criminal Records: Access: Mail, in person. Only the court performs in person searches; visitors may not. Search fee: $5.00 per name per year. Required to search: name, years to search, DOB. Criminal records on index files from 1979; on computer since 1988 (in some cases longer). Records destroyed after 10 years.
General Information: Public Access terminal is available. No probation reports released. SASE required. Turnaround time 2-4 days. Copy fee: $.80 per page. Certification fee: $6.00. Fee payee: Clerk of Court. Personal checks accepted. Credit cards accepted: Visa, MasterCard. Prepayment is required.

Harbor - Laguna Hills Superior Court - Civil Division 23141 Moulton Pkwy, Laguna Hills, CA 92653; 949-472-6964. Hours: 8AM-5PM (PST). *Civil Actions Under $25,000, Eviction, Small Claims.*

www.oc.ca.gov/southcourt

Note: Formerly known as South Orange, this includes Aliso Viejo, Capistrano Bch, Coto De Caza, Dana Pt, Laguna (various), Lake Forest, Mission Viejo, Rancho St. Margarita, San Clemente, San Juan Capistrano, Trabuco Canyon.

Civil Records: Access: Mail, in person. Both court and visitors may perform in person searches. Search fee: $5.00 per name per year. Fee only applies if court does search and case number is required. Required to search: name, years to search. Civil cases indexed by defendant, plaintiff. Civil records in index files and on microfiche back 10+ years; on computer back to 2000. **General Information:** Public Access terminal is available. No unlawful detainer records released for 60 days. SASE required. Turnaround time 2-3 days. Copy fee: $.80 per page. Certification fee: $6.00. Fee payee: Clerk of Courtnex. Personal checks accepted. Credit cards accepted: Visa, MasterCard, Discover. Prepayment is required.

Harbor - Laguna Niguel Superior Court - Criminal Division 30143 Crown Valley Parkway, Justice Center, Laguna Niguel, CA 92677; 949-249-5113. Hours: 8AM-5PM (PST). *Misdemeanor.*

www.oc.ca.gov/superior

Note: Also known as South Orange County Superior Court. Includes Capistrano Bch, Coto De Caza, Dana Pt, Laguna Hills, Laguna Niguel, Mission Viejo,

Rancho St. Margarita, San Clemente, San Juan Capistrano, Trabuco Canyon.

Criminal Records: Access: Mail, in person. Both court and visitors may perform in person searches. Search fee: $5.00 per name per year. $1.75 to pull a case file. Required to search: name, years to search, DOB; also helpful: SSN. Criminal records on computer since 1987; prior records on books.

General Information: No probation report, unlawful detainer records released. SASE required. Turnaround time 2-3 days. Copy fee: $.80 per page. Certification fee: $6.00. Fee payee: Clerk of Court. Personal checks accepted. Credit cards accepted: Visa, MasterCard, Discover. Prepayment is required.

Harbor - Newport Beach Superior Court

4601 Jamboree Road #104, Newport Beach, CA 92660-2595; 949-476-4765; Civil phone: 949-476-4699. Hours: 8AM-5PM (PST). *Misdemeanor, Civil Actions Under $25,000, Eviction, Small Claims.*

www.oc.ca.gov/superior

Note: Includes Balboa Island, Corona Del Mar, Costa Mesa, Newport Beach, Irvine, Santa Ana Heights, John Wayne/Orange Co Airport, Lido Isle and surrounding unincorporated areas.

Civil Records: Access: Mail, in person. Both court and visitors may perform in person searches. Search fee: $5.00 per name. Required to search: name, years to search. Civil cases indexed by defendant, plaintiff. Civil records are indexed on microfiche.

Criminal Records: Access: Mail, in person. Only the court performs in person searches; visitors may not. Search fee: $5.00 per name. Required to search: name, years to search; also helpful: DOB. Criminal records are on microfiche, felonies kept 75 years, misd 5 years.

General Information: No probation reports nor police reports released. SASE required. Turnaround time 2-5 days. Copy fee: $1.00 for first page, $.80 each add'l. Certification fee: $6.00. Fee payee: Clerk of Court. Personal checks accepted. Checks accepted (must be in-state and be imprinted with name and address). Credit cards accepted: Visa, MasterCard, Discover. Prepayment is required.

North Orange County Superior Court

1275 N Berkeley Ave, PO Box 5000, Fullerton, CA 92838-0500; 714-773-4555; 773-4667 (small claims); Civil phone: 714-773-4664; Criminal phone: 714-773-4661. Hours: 7:30AM-4:30PM (PST). *Misdemeanor, Civil Actions Under $25,000, Eviction, Small Claims.*

www.oc.ca.gov/superior

Note: Includes the cities of Anaheim, Brea, Buena Park, Fullerton, La Habra, La Palma, Placentia, Yorba Linda and surrounding unincorporated area including Anaheim Hills.

Civil Records: Access: Mail, in person. Both court and visitors may perform in person searches. Search fee: $5.00 per name per year. Fee also applies to requests by case number. Required to search: name, years to search. Civil cases indexed by defendant, plaintiff. Civil records on computer from 1991, index files from 1983. Records destroyed after 10 years.

Criminal Records: Access: Mail, in person. Both court and visitors may perform in person searches. Search fee: $5.00 per name per year. Required to search: name, years to search. Criminal records on computer from 1991, index files from 1983. Records destroyed after 10 years.

General Information: No probation reports or UD's for 60 days released. SASE required. Turnaround time 5 days. Copy fee: $.80 per page. Certification fee: $6.00. Fee payee: Clerk of Court. Personal checks accepted. Personal checks accepted with proper ID. Credit cards accepted: Visa, MasterCard, Discover. Prepayment is required.

West Orange County Superior Court

8141 13th St, Westminster, CA 92683; 714-896-7181; Civil phone: 714-896-7191; Criminal phone: 714-896-7351; Fax: 714-896-7404. Hours: 8AM-4:30PM (PST). *Misdemeanor, Civil Actions Under $25,000, Eviction, Small Claims.*

www.oc.ca.gov/superior

Note: Includes the cities of Cypress, Fountain Valley, Garden Grove, Huntington Beach, Los Alamitos, Rossmore, Seal Beach, Stanton, Sunset Beach, Surfside, Westminster and adjoining and unincorporated territory.

Civil Records: Access: Mail, in person. Both court and visitors may perform in person searches. Search fee: $5.00 per name per year. Required to search: name, years to search. Civil cases indexed by defendant, plaintiff. Civil records on computer from 1991, microfiche from 1983. Records destroyed after 10 years.

Criminal Records: Access: Mail, in person. Both court and visitors may perform in person searches. Search fee: $5.00 per name per year. Required to search: name, years to search; also helpful: DOB. Criminal records on computer from 1991, microfiche from 1983. Records destroyed after 10 years.

General Information: No probation reports, unlawful detainer (under 60 days old) records released. SASE required. Turnaround time 2 days. Copy fee: $.80 per page. Certification fee: $6.00. Fee payee: Clerk of Court. Personal checks accepted. Credit cards accepted: Visa, MasterCard. Prepayment is required.

Orange County Probate Court

341 The City Dr, Orange, CA 92868; 714-935-8043. Hours: 8AM-5PM (PST). *Probate.*

www.oc.ca.gov/superior

Note: Jurisdiction includes juvenile, family law, and mental health filings.

Placer County

Superior Court

101 Maple St, Auburn, CA 95603; Civil phone: 530-889-6550; Criminal phone: 530-886-1200. Hours: 8AM-3PM (PST). *Felony, Civil, Eviction, Probate.*

www.placer.ca.gov/courts

Note: This court holds the records for the Foresthill Division Court which has closed.

Civil Records: Access: Phone, mail, in person. Both court and visitors may perform in person searches. Search fee: $5.00 per year for records prior to 1974; 1975 and forward are $5.00 per name. Required to search: name, years to search. Civil cases indexed by defendant, plaintiff. Civil records on computer from 1992, on microfiche from 1974, archived and index file from 1800s.

Criminal Records: Access: Phone, mail, in person. Both court and visitors may perform in person searches. Search fee: Same fees as civil. Required to search: name, years to search. Criminal records on computer from 1992, on microfiche from 1974, archived and index file from 1800s.

General Information: Public Access terminal is available. No adoptions, juvenile, medical, paternity, probation or sealed records released. SASE required. Turnaround time 2 weeks. Copy fee: $.50 for first page, $.25 each add'l. Certification fee: $6.00. Fee payee: Clerk of the Court. Personal checks accepted. Prepayment is required.

Auburn Branch - Superior Court

11532 "B" Ave, Auburn, CA 95603; 530-886-1200; Fax: 530-886-1209. Hours: 8AM-4PM Office (8AM-3PM phone hours) (PST). *Felony, Misdemeanor.*

www.placer.ca.gov/courts

Note: Includes Auburn, Penryn, Newcastle, Bowman, Colfax, Weimar, Alta, Dutch Flat, Loomis. Also includes criminal for Roseville, Rocklin, Lincoln criminal as of 12/8/97

Criminal Records: Access: Mail, in person. Both court and visitors may perform in person searches. Search fee: $5.00 per name per year. Required to search: name, years to search, DOB. Criminal Records indexed on computer back to 1992; records go back 10 years.

General Information: Public Access terminal is available. No probation reports or copies of warrants released. SASE required. Turnaround time 2 weeks. Copy fee: $.50 per page. Certification fee: $6.00. Fee payee: Superior Court. Personal checks accepted. Prepayment is required.

Tahoe Division - Superior Court

PO Box 5669, Tahoe City, CA 96145; 530-581-6340; Fax: 530-581-6344. Hours: 8AM-4PM (PST). *Misdemeanor, Civil Actions Under $25,000, Eviction, Small Claims.*

www.placer.ca.gov/courts

Civil Records: Access: Mail, in person. Both court and visitors may perform in person searches. Search fee: $5.00 per name. Required to search: name, years to search. Civil cases indexed by defendant, plaintiff. Civil records computerized for 2 years, previous on index cards.

Criminal Records: Access: Mail, in person. Both court and visitors may perform in person searches. Search fee: $5.00 per name. Required to search: name, years to search. Criminal records on index cards. Will only search back 7 years.

General Information: No probation reports released. SASE required. Turnaround time 1 week. Copy fee: $.50 per page. Certification fee: $6.00. Fee payee: Clerk of Court. Personal checks accepted. Write "not to exceed $x.xx" on check. Prepayment is required.

Lincoln Division - Superior Court

C/O Roseville Court, 300 Taylor St, Roseville, CA 95678-2628; 916-645-8955; Fax: 916-783-1690. Hours: 8AM-Noon, 12:30-4PM F (PST). *Small Claims.*

www.placer.ca.gov/courts

Note: The mailing address is in Roseville, the location is 453 G Street, Lincoln 95648

Civil Records: Access: Mail, in person. Both court and visitors may perform in person searches. Search fee: $5.00 per name/record. Required to search: name, years to search. Civil cases indexed by defendant, plaintiff. Civil records on index cards. Will only search back 7 years. **General Information:** No probation reports released. SASE required. Turnaround time 1 week. Copy fee: $.50 per page. Certification fee: $6.00. Fee payee: Superior Court. Personal checks accepted. Prepayment is required.

Roseville Division - Superior Court

300 Taylor St, Roseville, CA 95678; 916-783-1600; Fax: 916-783-1690. Hours: 8AM-4PM (PST). *Small Claims, Traffic.*

www.placer.ca.gov/courts

Note: This court holds the records for the Foresthill Division Court which has closed.

Civil Records: Access: Mail, in person. Both court and visitors may perform in person searches. Search fee: $5.00 per name. Required to search: name, years to search. Civil cases indexed by defendant, plaintiff. Traffic on computer, index cards for civil. Records destroyed after 10 years. **General Information:** SASE required. Turnaround time 2 weeks. Copy fee: $.50 for first page, $.25 each add'l. Certification fee: $6.00. Fee payee: Superior Court. Personal checks accepted. Prepayment is required.

Plumas County

Superior Court - Civil Division 520 Main St, Rm 104, Quincy, CA 95971; 530-283-6305; Fax: 530-283-6415. Hours: 8AM-5PM (PST). *Civil, Small Claims, Probate.*

Civil Records: Access: Phone, fax, mail, in person. Both court and visitors may perform in person searches. Search fee: $1.75 per name per year. Required to search: name, years to search. Civil cases indexed by defendant, plaintiff. Civil records on computer from 1993, archived from 1980, index file from 1850. **General Information:** No adoptions, juvenile, confidential, medical, probation or sealed records released. SASE required. Turnaround time 1 week. Fax notes: $5.00 per document. Copy fee: $1.00 per page. Certification fee: $6.00. Fee payee: Plumas County Courts. Personal checks accepted. Prepayment is required.

Superior Court - Criminal Division 520 Main St, Rm 104, Quincy, CA 95971; 530-283-6232; Fax: 530-283-6293. Hours: 8AM-5PM (PST). *Felony, Misdemeanor.*

Criminal Records: Access: Mail, in person. Only the court performs in person searches; visitors may not. Search fee: $5.00 per name. Required to search: name, years to search. Criminal records indexed on computer since 1993. **General Information:** No probation reports, financial statements or juvenile released. SASE required. Turnaround time 1-2 days. Copy fee: $1.00 per page. Certification fee: $6.00. Fee payee: Superior Court. Personal checks accepted. Prepayment is required.

Chester Branch - Superior Court 1st & Willow Way (PO Box 722), Chester, CA 96020; 530-258-2646; Fax: 530-258-2652. Hours: 8AM-3PM (PST). *Civil Actions Under $25,000, Eviction, Small Claims.*

www.psln.com/pccourt

Civil Records: Access: Phone, mail, in person. Only the court performs in person searches; visitors may not. Search fee: $5.00 per name per year. Required to search: name, years to search. Civil cases indexed by defendant, plaintiff. Traffic on computer, index cards for civil records. Will only search back 7 years. Records on computer go back 13 years. **General Information:** No probation reports released. SASE required. Turnaround time 1-2 days. Fax notes: Fee to fax results is $6.00 per document. Copy fee: $1.00 per page. Certification fee: $6.00 to $10.00. Fee payee: Superior Court. Personal checks accepted. Prepayment is required.

Portola Branch - Superior Court 161 Nevada St (PO Box 1054), Portola, CA 96122; 530-832-4286; Fax: 530-832-4286. Hours: 8AM-4PM (PST). *Misdemeanor, Civil Actions Under $25,000, Eviction, Small Claims.*

Civil Records: Access: Phone, fax, mail, in person. Only the court performs in person searches; visitors may not. Search fee: $1.75 per name. Required to search: name, years to search. Civil cases indexed by defendant, plaintiff. Traffic on computer, index cards for civil records. Will only search back 7 years.

Criminal Records: Access: Phone, mail, in person. Only the court performs in person searches; visitors may not. Search fee: $1.75 per name. Required to search: name, years to search. Traffic on computer, index cards for criminal records. Will only search back 7 years.

General Information: No probation reports released. SASE required. Turnaround time as soon as possible. Copy fee: $1.00 per page. Certification fee: $6.00. Fee payee: Superior Court. Personal checks accepted. Prepayment is required.

Greenville Branch - Superior Court 115 Hwy 89 (PO Box 706), Greenville, CA 95947; 530-284-7213. Hours: 8AM-5PM (PST). *Small Claims.*

Civil Records: Access: Phone, mail, in person. Only the court performs in person searches; visitors may not. Search fee: $1.75 per name per year. Required to search: name, years to search. Civil cases indexed by defendant. **General Information:** No sealed records released. SASE required. Turnaround time 1-2 days. Copy fee: $1.00 per page. Certification fee: $6.00. Fee payee: Superior Court. Personal checks accepted. Prepayment is required.

Riverside County

Superior Court - Civil Division 4050 Main St, Riverside, CA 92501; 909-955-1960; Fax: 909-955-1751. Hours: 8AM-5PM (PST). *Civil Actions Over $25,000, Probate.*

www.co.riverside.ca.us/depts/courts

Civil Records: Access: Phone, fax, mail, online, in person. Both court and visitors may perform in person searches. Search fee: $5.00 per name. Required to search: name, years to search. Civil cases indexed by defendant, plaintiff. Civil records on computer and microfiche from 1970, index file from 1956, archived from 1900s. The Automated Case Management System is the pay system for Riverside County Superior Courts; there is a one-time fee of $225 for Internet access. Records date back to 1984 and include civil, criminal, family law, probate & traffic case information for all Riverside and Indio Courts. For further information, call 909-955-5945. **General Information:** Public Access terminal is available. No adoptions, juvenile, medical, probation, unlawful detainers for 60 days or sealed records released. SASE required. Turnaround time 3 days. Fax notes: $1.00 per page. Copy fee: $.50 per page. Certification fee: $6.00. Fee payee: Riverside County Superior Court. Personal checks accepted. Credit cards accepted: Visa, MasterCard, Discover. Prepayment is required.

Superior Court - Criminal Division 4100 Main St, Riverside, CA 92501; 909-955-2300; Fax: 909-955-4007. Hours: 7:30AM-5PM (PST). *Felony, Misdemeanor.*

www.co.riverside.ca.us/depts/courts

Criminal Records: Access: Phone, fax, mail, online, in person. Both court and visitors may perform in person searches. Search fee: $5.00 per name per year. Required to search: name, years to search; also helpful: DOB, SSN. Criminal Records on microfiche and computer since 1970, index file from 1956. The Automated Case Management System is the pay system for Riverside County Superior Courts; there is a one-time fee of $225 for Internet access. Records date back to 1984 and include civil, criminal, family law, probate & traffic case information for all Riverside and Indio Courts. For further information, call 909-955-5945. **General Information:** Public Access terminal is available. No adoptions, juvenile, medical, probation, unlawful detainers for 60 days or sealed records released. SASE required. Turnaround time 1 day to 1 week. Fax notes: $1.00 for first page, $.50 each add'l. Must pay fax fee by credit card. Copy fee: $.50 per page. Certification fee: $6.00. Fee payee: Clerk of Circuit Court. Personal checks accepted. Credit cards accepted: Visa, MasterCard, Discover. Prepayment is required.

Banning Division - Superior Court 155 E Hays St, Banning, CA 92220; Civil phone: 909-922-7155; Criminal phone: 909-922-7145; Fax: 909-922-7150; Fax: 909-922-7160. Hours: 7:30AM-5PM (PST). *Misdemeanor, Civil Actions Under $25,000, Eviction, Small Claims.*

www.co.riverside.ca.us/depts/courts

Note: Includes Banning, Cabazon, Highland Springs, Poppet Flatt, Silent Valley, Beaumont, Calimesa, Cherry Valley and Whitewater.

Civil Records: Access: Phone, fax, mail, online, in person. Only the court performs in person searches; visitors may not. No search fee. Required to search: name, years to search; also helpful-case number. Civil cases indexed by defendant, plaintiff. Civil records on computer from 1991, index files from 1983. Records destroyed after 10 years. See Riverside Division location for online information. Phone and fax access limited to short searches.

Criminal Records: Access: Phone, fax, mail, online, in person. Only the court performs in person searches; visitors may not. No search fee. Required to search: name, years to search; also helpful-case number. Criminal records on computer back to 1992, index files from 1983. Records destroyed after 10 years. See Riverside Division for online information.

General Information: No probation reports released. SASE required. Turnaround time 2 days. Fax notes: Fee to fax results is $.50 per page. Copy fee: $.50 per page. Certification fee: $6.00. Fee payee: Clerk of the Court. Personal checks accepted. Credit cards accepted: Visa, MasterCard, Discover. Prepayment is required.

Blythe Division - Superior Court 265 N Broadway, Blythe, CA 92225; 760-921-7828; Civil phone: 760-921-7981; Fax: 760-921-7941. Hours: 7:30AM-5PM (PST). *Felony, Misdemeanor, Civil Actions Under $25,000, Eviction, Small Claims.*

www.co.riverside.ca.us/depts/courts

Note: Includes Blythe, Ripley. Phone for Family Law is 760-921-7982.

Civil Records: Access: Phone, fax, mail, online, in person. Both court and visitors may perform in person searches. Search fee: $5.00 per name per year. Required to search: name, years to search. Civil cases indexed by defendant, plaintiff. Civil records on computer from 1991, index files from 1983. Records destroyed after 10 years. See the Riverside Division location for online information.

Criminal Records: Access: Phone, fax, mail, online, in person. Both court and visitors may perform in person searches. Search fee: $5.00 per name per year. Required to search: name, years to search; also helpful: DOB, sex. Criminal records on computer from 1991, index files from 1983. Records destroyed after 10 years. See Riverside Division for online information.

General Information: Public Access terminal is available. No probation reports released. SASE required. Turnaround time 2 days. Fax notes: $1.00 per page. Copy fee: $.50 per page. Certification fee: $6.00. Fee payee: Clerk of the Court. Personal checks accepted. Credit cards accepted: Visa, MasterCard, Discover. Prepayment is required.

Corona Branch - Superior Court 505 S Buena Vista Rm 201, Corona, CA 91720; Civil phone: 909-272-5620; Criminal phone: 909-272-5630; Fax: 909-272-5651 (Civil) 272-5691 (Criminal). Hours: 7:30AM-5PM (PST). *Misdemeanor, Civil Actions Under $25,000, Eviction, Small Claims.*

www.co.riverside.ca.us/depts/courts

Note: Includes Corona, El Cerrito, Home Gardens, Norco, Santa Ana Canyon.

Civil Records: Access: Fax, mail, online, in person. Both court and visitors may perform in person searches. Search fee: $5.00 per name per year. Required to search: name, years to search. Civil cases indexed by defendant, plaintiff. Civil records on computer from 1991, index files from 1983, microfiche since 1978. Records destroyed after 10 years. Judicial council fax cover required. See Riverside Branch location for online information.

Criminal Records: Access: Fax, mail, online, in person. Both court and visitors may perform in person searches. Search fee: $5.00 per name per year. Required to search: name, years to search, DOB. Criminal records on computer from 1991, index files from 1983, microfiche since 1978. Records destroyed after 10 years. See Riverside Division for online information. **General Information:** No probation reports released. SASE required. Turnaround time 2 days. Fax notes: $1.00 per page. Copy fee: $.50 per page. Certification fee: $6.00. Fee payee: Clerk of Court. Personal checks accepted. Credit cards accepted: Visa, MasterCard, Discover. Prepayment is required.

Hemet Division - Superior Court 880 N State
St, Hemet, CA 92543; 909-766-2321; Criminal phone: 909-766-2310; Fax: 909-766-2317. Hours: 7:30AM-4:30PM; Criminal, Civil/SC 8AM-Noon; (PST). *Misdemeanor, Civil Actions Under $25,000, Eviction, Small Claims.*

www.co.riverside.ca.us/depts/courts

Note: Includes Aguanga, Anza, Gilman Hot Springs, Hemet, Idylwild, Mountain Center, Pine Cove, Redec, Sage, San Jacinto, Sobba Hot Spring, Valle Vista and Winchester.

Civil Records: Access: Fax, mail, online, in person. Both court and visitors may perform in person searches. Search fee: $5.00 per name. If not on computer, is $5.00 per year. Required to search: name, years to search. Civil cases indexed by defendant, plaintiff. Civil records on computer from 1991, index files from 1983. Records destroyed after 10 years. See Riverside Division location for online information.

Criminal Records: Access: Mail, online, in person. Only the court performs in person searches; visitors may not. Search fee: $5.00 per name. If not on computer, is $5.00 per year. Required to search: name, years to search. Criminal records on computer from 1991, index files from 1983. Records destroyed after 10 years. See Riverside Division for online information. **General Information:** No probation reports released. SASE required. Fax notes: No fee to fax results. Copy fee: $.50 per page. Certification fee: $6.00. Fee payee: Clerk of the Court. Personal checks accepted. Credit cards accepted: Visa, MasterCard, Discover. Prepayment is required.

Indio Division - Superior Court 46200 Oasis
St, Indio, CA 92201; Civil phone: 760-863-8208; Criminal phone: 760-863-8206; Fax: 760-863-8707. Hours: 7:30AM-5PM (PST). *Misdemeanor, Civil Actions Under $25,000, Eviction, Small Claims.*

www.co.riverside.ca.us/depts/courts

Note: Includes Desert Center, Eagle Mountain, Indio, La Quinta, Coachella, Bermuda Dunes, Mecca, North Shore, Pinyon Pines, Palm Springs, Salton Sea, Oasis, Thermal. Most Palm Springs records are here.

Civil Records: Access: Phone, fax, mail, online, in person. Only the court performs in person searches; visitors may not. Search fee: $5.00 per name. Required to search: name, years to search. Civil cases indexed by defendant, plaintiff. Civil records on computer from 1990, index files from 1983. Records destroyed after 10 years. Phone & fax access limited to short searches. See Riverside Division for online information.

Criminal Records: Access: Phone, fax, mail, online, in person. Only the court performs in person searches; visitors may not. Search fee: $5.00 per name. Required to search: name, years to search, signed release. Criminal records on computer from 1990, index files from 1983. Records destroyed after 10 years. See Riverside Division for online information.

General Information: No probation reports released. SASE required. Turnaround time 2 days. Fax notes: $1.00 per page. Copy fee: $.50 per page. Certification fee: $6.00. Fee payee: Clerk of Court. Personal

checks accepted. Credit cards accepted: Visa, MasterCard, Discover. Prepayment is required.

Lake Elsinore Division - Superior Court
117 S Langstaff, Lake Elsinore, CA 92530; 909-245-3370; Fax: 909-245-3366. Hours: 7:30AM-5PM (PST). *Civil Actions Under $25,000, Eviction, Small Claims.*

www.co.riverside.ca.us/depts/courts

Civil Records: Access: Phone, fax, mail, online, in person. Both court and visitors may perform in person searches. No search fee. Required to search: name, years to search; also helpful: case number. Civil cases indexed by defendant, plaintiff. Civil records on computer since 1991, on index books until 08/91. Holds civil records from 3/1/95-3/1/97. See Riverside Branch Location for online information. **General Information:** No confidential records released. SASE required. Turnaround time 2 days. Fax notes: $1.00 per page. Copy fee: $.50 per page. Certification fee: $6.00. Fee payee: Superior Court. Personal checks accepted. Credit cards accepted: Visa, MasterCard, Discover. Prepayment is required.

Palm Springs Division - Superior Court
3255 Tahkuits Canyon Way, Palm Springs, CA 92262; 760-320-9764; Fax: 760-778-2269. Hours: 7:30AM-5PM (PST). *Misdemeanor, Traffic.*

www.co.riverside.ca.us/depts/courts

Note: Includes Cathedral City, Palm Springs, Rancho Mirage, Thousand Palms, Indian Wells, Palm Desert, Desert Hot Springs. See also Indio Court. Call to determine which court to search

Criminal Records: Access: Fax, mail, online, in person. Both court and visitors may perform in person searches. Search fee: $5.00 per name. Required to search: name, years to search. Criminal records on computer from 1991, index files from 1983. Records destroyed after 10 years. See Riverside Division for online information.

General Information: No probation reports released. SASE required. Turnaround time 2-4 days. Fax notes: $1.00 per page. Copy fee: $.50 per page. Certification fee: $6.00. Fee payee: Clerk of the Court. Personal checks accepted. Credit cards accepted: Visa, MasterCard, Discover. Prepayment is required.

Perris Branch - Superior Court 227 N "D"
St., Perris, CA 92370; 909-940-6820; 940-6830 (Traffic); Civil phone: 909-940-6840; Criminal phone: 909-940-6840; Fax: 909-940-6810. Hours: 7:30AM-5PM (PST). *Felony, Misdemeanor, Small Claims.*

www.co.riverside.ca.us/depts/courts

Note: Holds all records for the former Three Lakes District including Lake Elsinore, Moreno Valley, Temecula. Records are for past 10 years.

Civil Records: Access: Mail, fax, online, in person. Both court and visitors may perform in person searches. No search fee. Required to search: name, years to search. Civil cases indexed by defendant, plaintiff. Civil records on computer since 1991, on index books from 08/91. See Riverside Division location for online information.

Criminal Records: Access: Mail, online, in person. Both court and visitors may perform in person searches. No search fee. Required to search: name, years to search; also helpful: DOB. Criminal records on computer since 1991, on index books from 08/91. See Riverside Division for online information.

General Information: Mental health, police reports, items marked confidential not released. SASE required. Turnaround time 2 days. Copy fee: $.50 per page. Certification fee: $6.00. Fee payee: Clerk of the Court. Personal checks accepted. Credit cards accepted: Visa, MasterCard, Discover. Prepayment is required.

Temecula Branch - Superior Court 41002
County Center Dr, Temecula, CA 92591; 909-600-6430; Fax: 909-600-6423. Hours: 7:30AM-5PM (PST). *Civil Actions Under $25,000, Eviction, Small Claims.*

www.co.riverside.ca.us/depts/courts

Civil Records: Access: Phone, fax, mail, online, in person. Both court and visitors may perform in person searches. No search fee. Required to search: name, years to search. Civil cases indexed by defendant, plaintiff. Civil records on computer since 1991, on index books until 08/91. See Riverside Division location for online information. **General Information:** Public Access terminal is available. No confidential, adoption or sealed records released. Unlawful detainers not released for 60 days. SASE required. Turnaround time 3days. Copy fee: $.50 per page. Certification fee: $6.00. Fee payee: Clerk of the Court. Personal checks accepted. Credit cards accepted: Visa, MasterCard, Discover. Prepayment is required.

Moreno Valley Branch - Superior Court
13800 Heacock Ave Ste D201, Moreno Valley, CA 92553-3338; 909-955-1960; Fax: 909-341-8876. Hours: 7:30AM-5PM (PST). *Small Claims, Traffic.*

www.co.riverside.ca.us/depts/courts

Civil Records: Access: Phone, fax, mail, online, in person. Both court and visitors may perform in person searches. No search fee. Required to search: name, years to search. Civil cases indexed by defendant, plaintiff. Civil records on computer. See Riverside Division location for online information. **General Information:** No adoptions, juvenile, medical, probation or sealed records released. SASE required. Turnaround time 1 week. Fax notes: $1.00 per page. Copy fee: $.50 per page. Certification fee: $6.00. Fee payee: Clerk of the Court. Personal checks accepted. Credit cards accepted: Visa, MasterCard, Discover. Prepayment is required.

Sacramento County

Superior Court 720 9th St Rm 102, Sacramento, CA 95814; 916-874-5522; Criminal phone: 916-874-6936; Probate phone: 916-874-5621; Fax: 916-874-5620. Hours: 8:30AM-4:30PM (PST). *Felony, Misdemeanor, Civil, Eviction, Small Claims, Probate.*

www.saccourt.com

Note: Probate is located at 3342 Power Inn Rd, Sacramento 95826.

Civil Records: Access: Phone, fax, mail, online, in person. Both court and visitors may perform in person searches. Search fee: $5.00 per name per year. Also charge $9.00 per hour for court. Required to search: name, years to search; also helpful: address. Civil cases indexed by defendant, plaintiff. Civil records on microfiche and archived from 1937, index books from 1800s. All civil records for Sacramento County are available free on the Internet at www.saccourt.com.

Criminal Records: Access: Phone, mail, online, in person. Both court and visitors may perform in person searches. Search fee: $5.00 per name per year. Required to search: name, years to search; also helpful: address, DOB, SSN. Criminal records on computer since 1993 (Superior) 1995 (Municipal), on microfiche and archived from 1962. All criminal records for Sacramento County are available free on the Internet at www.saccourt.com.

General Information: No adoptions, juvenile, medical, probation or sealed records released. SASE required. Turnaround time 1-3 weeks. Copy fee: $.50 per page. Certification fee: $6.00. Fee payee: Superior Court. Personal checks accepted. Prepayment is required.

Galt Division - Superior Court

380 Civic Dr, Galt, CA 95632; 209-745-1577; Fax: 209-745-6176. Hours: 8:30AM-4:30PM (PST). *Misdemeanor, Small Claims.*

www.saccourt.com

Civil Records: Access: Mail, online, in person. Only the court performs in person searches; visitors may not. Search fee: $5.00. is per case. Required to search: name, years to search. Civil cases indexed by defendant, plaintiff. Civil records in index files from 1984. Records destroyed after 10 years. All civil records for Sacramento County are available free on the Internet at www.saccourt.com.

Criminal Records: Access: Mail, online, in person. Only the court performs in person searches; visitors may not. Search fee: $5.00 per case. Required to search: name, years to search, DOB, signed release. Criminal records in index files from 1984. Records destroyed after 10 years. All criminal records for Sacramento County are available free on the Internet at www.saccourt.com.

General Information: No adoptions, juvenile, medical, probation or sealed records released. SASE required. Turnaround time 2-4 weeks. Copy fee: $1.00 per page. Certification fee: $6.00. Final Judgment certificate $7.00. Fee payee: Superior Court. Personal checks accepted. Prepayment is required.

South Sacramento Superior Court - Elk Grove Branch

8978 Elk Grove Blvd, Elk Grove, CA 95624-1994; 916-685-9825; Fax: 916-685-4689. Hours: 8:30AM-4:30PM (PST). *Misdemeanor, Civil Actions Under $25,000, Eviction, Small Claims.*

www.saccourt.com

Note: Includes southern portion of county with two other branches. This court holds all case records for South Sacramento branches.

Civil Records: Access: Mail, online, in person. Both court and visitors may perform in person searches. Search fee: $5.00 per name per year. Required to search: name, years to search. Civil cases indexed by defendant, plaintiff. Civil records in index files from 1984. Records destroyed after 10 years. All civil records for Sacramento County are available free on the Internet at www.saccourt.com.

Criminal Records: Access: Mail, online, in person. Both court and visitors may perform in person searches. Search fee: $5.00 per name per year. Required to search: name, years to search, DOB. Criminal records in index files from 1984. Records destroyed after 10 years. Online access for criminal records is the same as civil.

General Information: No adoptions, juvenile, medical, probation or sealed records released. SASE required. Turnaround time 2-4 days. Copy fee: $.50 per page. Certification fee: $6.00. Final Judgment certificate $7.00. Fee payee: South Sacramento Superior Court. Personal checks accepted. Prepayment is required.

Walnut Grove Branch - Superior Court

14177 Market St, PO Box 371, Walnut Grove, CA 95690; 916-776-1416; Fax: 916-776-1624. Hours: 8AM-Noon, 1-4:30PM (PST). *Misdemeanor, Eviction, Small Claims.*

www.saccourt.com

Civil Records: Access: Fax, mail, online, person. Both court and visitors may perform in person searches. Search fee: $6.00 per name per year. Required to search: name, years to search. Civil cases indexed by defendant, plaintiff. Civil records in index files from 1984. Records destroyed after 10 years. All civil records for Sacramento County are available free on the Internet at www.saccourt.com.

Criminal Records: Access: Fax, mail, online, in person. Both court and visitors may perform in person searches. Search fee: $6.00 per name per year. Required to search: name, years to search, DOB. Criminal records

in index files from 1984. Records destroyed after 10 years. All criminal records for Sacramento County are available free on the Internet at www.saccourt.com.

General Information: No adoptions, juvenile, medical, probation or sealed records released. SASE required. Turnaround time 3-4 days. Copy fee: $.50 per page. $5.00 maximum. Certification fee: $6.00. Final Judgment certificate $7.00. Fee payee: Superior Court. Personal checks accepted. Prepayment is required.

San Benito County

Superior Court

Courthouse, 440 5th St-Rm 205, Hollister, CA 95023; 831-636-4057; Fax: 831-636-2046. Hours: 8AM-4PM (PST). *Felony, Misdemeanor, Civil, Small Claims, Eviction, Probate.*

www.superior-court.co.san-benito.ca.us

Note: As of 11/2000, Small Claims, Family Law, and Eviction records are located at the Limited Jurisdiction Court, 390 5th St, Hollister. Phone: 831-630-5115. Fax: 831-636-4117. Same search requirements as stated below.

Civil Records: Access: Mail, in person. Both court and visitors may perform in person searches. Search fee: $5.00 per name. If visitor does search, no fee. Required to search: name, years to search. Civil cases indexed by defendant, plaintiff. Civil records on computer for last 9 years, index books and archived from 1900.

Criminal Records: Access: Mail, in person. Both court and visitors may perform in person searches. Search fee: $5.00 per name. If visitor does search, no fee. Required to search: name, years to search. Criminal records on computer for last 9 years, index books and archived from 1900.

General Information: No adoptions, juvenile, medical, probation or sealed records released. SASE required. Turnaround time 1-2 weeks. Copy fee: $.50 per page. Certification fee: $7.00. Fee payee: Superior Court. Personal checks accepted. Prepayment is required.

San Bernardino County

Barstow District - Superior Court

235 E Mountain View, Barstow, CA 92311; Civil phone: 760-256-4907; Criminal phone: 760-256-4785. Hours: 8AM-4PM (PST). *Felony, Misdemeanor, Civil, Eviction, Small Claims.*

www.co.san-bernardino.ca.us/Courts

Note: Includes the City of Barstow and the unincorporated areas of Yermo, Lenwood, Daggett, Hinkley and Baker.

Civil Records: Access: Mail, in person. Both court and visitors may perform in person searches. Search fee: $5.00 per name. Required to search: name, years to search. Civil cases indexed by defendant, plaintiff. Civil records on computer from 1991, index books and microfilm. Microfilm is 3 to 4 weeks current. Records destroyed after 10 years.

Criminal Records: Access: Mail, in person. Both court and visitors may perform in person searches. Search fee: $5.00 per name. Required to search: name, years to search. Criminal records on computer from 1991, index books and microfilm. Microfilm is 3 to 4 weeks current. Records destroyed after 10 years.

General Information: No probation or confidential reports released. SASE required. Turnaround time 2-5 days. Copy fee: $.50 per page. Certification fee: $6.00. Fee payee: Clerk of the Court. Only cashiers checks and money orders accepted. Credit cards accepted: Visa, MasterCard. Accepted for filings only. Prepayment is required.

Central District - Superior Court

351 N Arrowhead Ave, San Bernardino, CA 92415; Civil phone: 909-387-3922; Criminal phone: 909-384-1888; Fax: 909-387-4428 (387-4993 criminal). Hours: 8AM-4PM (PST). *Felony, Misdemeanor, Civil, Eviction, Small Claims, Probate.*

www.co.san-bernardino.ca.us/courts

Civil Records: Access: Mail, in person. Both court and visitors may perform in person searches. Search fee: $5.00 per name. Required to search: name, years to search. Civil cases indexed by defendant, plaintiff. Civil records on computer from 04/99, microfiche from 1972, archived and index file from 1856. Address mail search access requests to Research Dept.

Criminal Records: Access: Mail, in person. Both court and visitors may perform in person searches. Search fee: $5.00 per name. Required to search: name, years to search; also helpful: DOB. Criminal records on computer from 04/99, microfiche from 1972, archived and index file from 1856.

General Information: Public Access terminal is available. No adoptions, juvenile, medical, probation or sealed records released. SASE required. Turnaround time 1-2 weeks. Copy fee: $.50 per page. Certification fee: $6.00. Fee payee: Clerk of the Court. Business checks accepted. Credit cards accepted: Visa, Discover. Prepayment is required.

Joshua Tree Division - Superior Court

6527 White Feather Rd (PO Box 6602), Joshua Tree, CA 92252; 760-366-4100; Fax: 760-366-4156. Hours: 8AM-4PM (PST). *Felony, Misdemeanor, Civil, Eviction, Small Claims.*

www.co.san-bernardino.ca.us/courts

Note: Includes the incorporated area of City of Twenty-Nine Palms, Town of Yucca Valley and Morongo Valley.

Civil Records: Access: Mail, in person. Only the court performs in person searches; visitors may not. Search fee: $5.00 per name per year. Required to search: name, years to search. Civil cases indexed by defendant, plaintiff. Civil records on computer from 1991, index books from 1983. Records destroyed after 10 years.

Criminal Records: Access: Mail, in person. Only the court performs in person searches; visitors may not. Search fee: $5.00 per name per year. Required to search: name, years to search, DOB. Criminal records on computer from 1991, index books from 1983. Records destroyed after 10 years.

General Information: No probation reports, confidential records released. SASE required. Turnaround time 1 week. Copy fee: $.50 per page. Certification fee: $6.00. Fee payee: Joshua Tree Superior Court. Personal checks accepted. Prepayment is required.

Rancho Cucamonga District - Superior Court

8303 N. Haven Ave, Rancho Cucamonga, CA 91730; Civil phone: 909-945-4131; Criminal phone: 909-350-9764; Fax: 909-945-4154. Hours: 8AM-4PM (PST). *Felony, Misdemeanor, Civil, Eviction, Small Claims, Probate.*

www.co.san-bernardino.ca.us/courts

Note: Formerly West District Superior Ct. Includes cities of Montclair, Ontario, Upland, Rancho Cucamonga, alta Loma, Etiwanda, Guasti and surrounding unincorporated area of Mt Baldy.

Civil Records: Access: Phone, fax, mail, in person. Both court and visitors may perform in person searches. Search fee: $5.00 per name. Required to search: name, years to search. Civil cases indexed by defendant, plaintiff. Civil records on computer since April 1994, index cards prior. Records destroyed after 10 years.

Criminal Records: Access: Phone, fax, mail, in person. Only the court performs in person searches;

visitors may not. Search fee: $5.00 per name. Required to search: name, years to search; also helpful: DOB. Criminal records computerized since 1994, also on index cards and microfiche.

General Information: No probation reports released. SASE required. Turnaround time 2-4 days. Copy fee: $.50 per page. Certification fee: $6.00. Fee payee: Superior Court. Personal checks accepted. Checks over $10.00 accepted. Credit cards accepted: Visa, AmEx. Prepayment is required.

Victorville District - Superior Court 14455
Civic Dr, Victorville, CA 92392; Civil phone: 760-243-8672; Criminal phone: 760-243-8631; Fax: 760-243-8790 (civil); 8794 (criminal). Hours: 8AM-4PM (PST). *Felony, Misdemeanor, Civil, Eviction, Small Claims.*

www.co.san-bernardino.ca.us/Courts

Note: Includes the Cities of Victorville, Adelanto Hesperia and the unincorporated area of Apple Valley, El Mirage, Helendale, Lucerne Valley, Oro Grande, Phelan, Pinon Hill and Wrightwood.

Civil Records: Access: Mail, in person. Both court and visitors may perform in person searches. Search fee: $5.00 per name. Required to search: name, years to search. Civil cases indexed by defendant, plaintiff. Civil records on microfiche from 1982 to July 1999, on computer from 1989 to present, index books prior. Records destroyed after 10 years.

Criminal Records: Access: Mail, in person. Only the court performs in person searches; visitors may not. Search fee: $5.00 per name. Required to search: name, years to search; also helpful: DOB, date of offense. Criminal index books by defendant 1986 - present. Only court allowed to search computer index.

General Information: No probation reports released. SASE required. Turnaround time within 1 week. Copy fee: $.50 per page. Certification fee: $6.00. Fee payee: Superior Court. Personal checks accepted. $5.00 minimum. Prepayment is required.

Big Bear Lake District - Superior Court
PO Box 2806 (477 summit Blvd.), Big Bear Lake, CA 92315; 909-866-0150; Fax: 909-866-0160. Hours: 8AM-4PM (PST). *Misdemeanor, Civil Actions Under $25,000, Eviction, Small Claims.*

www.co.san-bernardino.ca.us/courts

Civil Records: Access: Mail, in person. Both court and visitors may perform in person searches. Search fee: $5.00 per name per year. Required to search: name, years to search. Civil cases indexed by defendant, plaintiff. Civil records on computer since 9/1/96; prior on index books. Will only search back 7 years.

Criminal Records: Access: Mail, in person. Both court and visitors may perform in person searches. Search fee: $5.00 per name per year. Required to search: name, years to search, DOB; also helpful: SSN. Criminal records on index books. Will only search back 7 years.

General Information: No probation reports released. SASE required. Turnaround time 1 week. Copy fee: $.50 per page. Certification fee: $6.00. Fee payee: Superior Court. Personal checks accepted. Prepayment is required.

Central Division Branch - Superior Court
351 N Arrowhead, San Bernardino, CA 92415; Civil phone: 909-885-0139; Probate phone: 909-387-3952; Fax: 909-387-4428. Hours: 8AM-4PM (PST). *Misdemeanor, Civil Actions, Eviction, Small Claims, Probate.*

www.co.san-bernardino.ca.us/courts

Note: Includes the City of Bernardino, cities of Grand Terrace, Loma Linda, Colton and Highland and the unincorporated area of Del Rosa, Devore, Miscoy, Patton, Verdemont.

Civil Records: Access: Phone, mail, fax, in person. Both court and visitors may perform in person searches.

Search fee: $5.00 per name. Required to search: name, years to search. Civil cases indexed by defendant, plaintiff. Civil records on computer from 1991, index files from 1983, microfiche from 1972. Specify which city you are searching in.

Criminal Records: Access: Mail, in person. Both court and visitors may perform in person searches. Search fee: $5.00 per name. Required to search: name, years to search; also helpful: DOB. Criminal records on computer from 1991, index files from 1983, microfiche from 1972. Specify which city you are searching in.

General Information: Public Access terminal is available. No probation reports released. SASE required. Turnaround time 2 days. Fax notes: Fee to fax results is $1.00 per page. Copy fee: $.50 per page. Certification fee: $6.00. Fee payee: San Bernardino Superior Court. Personal checks accepted. Prepayment is required.

Chino Division - Superior Court 13260
Central Ave, Chino, CA 91710; Civil phone: 909-465-5266; Criminal phone: 909-465-5260; Fax: 909-465-5221. Hours: 8AM-4PM (PST). *Misdemeanor, Eviction, Small Claims.*

www.co.san-bernardino.ca.us/courts

Note: Includes City of Chino and surrounding unincorporated area. Rancho Cucamonga Courts handles all civil cases since 01/01/99.

Civil Records: Access: Fax, mail, in person. Only the court performs in person searches; visitors may not. Search fee: $5.00 per name. Required to search: name, years to search; also helpful: address. Civil cases indexed by defendant, plaintiff. Civil records on computer from 1991, index books from 1983. Records destroyed after 10 years.

Criminal Records: Access: Mail, in person. Only the court performs in person searches; visitors may not. Search fee: $5.00 per name. Required to search: name, years to search, DOB; also helpful: address. Criminal records on computer from 1991, index books from 1983. Records destroyed after 10 years.

General Information: No probation reports released. SASE required. Turnaround time 2 days. Copy fee: $.50 per page. Certification fee: $6.00. Fee payee: Chino Superior Court. Personal checks accepted. Prepayment is required.

Fontana Division - Superior Court 17780
Arrow Blvd, Fontana, CA 92335; 909-350-9322. Hours: 8AM-4PM (PST). *Felony, Misdemeanor, Civil Actions Under $25,000, Traffic.*

www.co.san-bernadino.ca.us/courts

Note: Includes the Cities of Fontana, Rialto, Crestmore and the unincorporated areas of Lytle Creek Canyon and Bloomington.

Civil Records: Access: Mail, in person. Only the court performs in person searches; visitors may not. Search fee: $5.00 per name. Required to search: name, years to search; also helpful: address. Civil cases indexed by defendant, plaintiff. Civil records on computer from 1987, microfilm prior. Records destroyed after 10 years.

Criminal Records: Access: Mail, in person. Both court and visitors may perform in person searches. Search fee: $5.00 per name. Required to search: name, years to search; also helpful: DOB. Criminal records on computer from 1987, microfilm prior. Records destroyed after 10 years.

General Information: No probation reports or police records released. SASE required. Turnaround time 2-5 days. Copy fee: $.50 per page. Certification fee: $6.00. Fee payee: Fontana Courts. Personal checks accepted. Prepayment is required.

Needles Division - Superior Court 1111
Bailey Ave, Needles, CA 92363; 760-326-9245; Fax: 760-326-9254. Hours: 8AM-4PM (PST). *Misdemeanor, Civil Actions Under $25,000, Eviction, Small Claims.*

www.co.san-bernardino.ca.us/courts

Civil Records: Access: Mail, in person. Only the court performs in person searches; visitors may not. Search fee: $5.00 per name. Required to search: name, years to search. Civil cases indexed by plaintiff. Civil records in index books. Will only search back 7 years.

Criminal Records: Access: Mail, in person. Only the court performs in person searches; visitors may not. Search fee: $5.00 per name. Required to search: name, years to search. Criminal records on computer from 1990, index books prior. Will only search back 7 years.

General Information: No probation reports released. SASE required. Turnaround time 1-2 weeks. Copy fee: $.50 per page. Certification fee: $6.00. Fee payee: Superior Court. Personal checks accepted. Prepayment is required.

Redlands District - Superior Court 216
Brookside Ave, Redlands, CA 92373; Civil phone: 909-888-4260; Criminal phone: 909-888-4770; Fax: 909-798-8588. Hours: 8AM-4PM (PST). *Felony, Misdemeanor, Eviction, Small Claims.*

www.co.san-bernardino.ca.us/Courts

Note: Includes Cities of Redlands, Yucaipa and the unincorporated areas of Angeles Oaks, Barton Flats, Forest Home and Mentone.

Civil Records: Access: Mail, in person. Only the court performs in person searches; visitors may not. No search fee. Required to search: name, years to search. Civil cases indexed by defendant, plaintiff. Civil records on computer from 1991, index books prior. Records destroyed after 10 years.

Criminal Records: Access: Mail, in person. Only the court performs in person searches; visitors may not. No search fee. Required to search: name, years to search, DOB. Criminal records on computer from 1998, index books prior. Records destroyed after 10 years.

General Information: No probation reports released. SASE required. Turnaround time 2 days. Copy fee: $.50 per page. Certification fee: $6.00. Fee payee: Superior Court. Prepayment is required.

Twin Peaks District - Superior Court 26010
State Hwy 189 (PO Box 394), Twin Peaks, CA 92391; 909-336-0620; Fax: 909-336-0683. Hours: 8AM-4PM (PST). *Felony, Misdemeanor, Civil under $25,000, Eviction, Small Claims.*

www.co.san-bernardino.ca.us/courts

Civil Records: Access: Mail, in person. Only the court performs in person searches; visitors may not. Search fee: $5.00 per name per year. Required to search: name, years to search. Civil cases indexed by defendant, plaintiff. Civil records on index cards. Will only search back 7 years.

Criminal Records: Access: Mail, in person. Only the court performs in person searches; visitors may not. Search fee: $5.00 per name per year. Required to search: name, years to search, DOB. Criminal records on computer from 1990, index cards prior. Will only search back 7 years.

General Information: No probation or arrest reports released. SASE required. Turnaround time 1 week. Copy fee: $.50 per page. Certification fee: $6.00. Fee payee: Superior Court. No checks accepted.

San Diego County

Superior Court - Civil

Hall of Justice, PO Box 10128 (330 W Broadway), San Diego, CA 92112; Civil phone: 619-531-3151; Probate phone: 619-687-2292. Hours: 8:30AM-4:30PM (PST). *Civil, Probate, Eviction, Small Claims, Probate.*

www.sandiego.courts.ca.gov/superior

Note: Now has Central Division Limited Jurisdiction civil cases. For any San Diego County requests, always specify which division - Central, East, North or South. Central Div. Probate is located at the Madge Bradley Bldg, 1409 Fourth Avenue, 92101.

Civil Records: Access: Mail, in person. Both court and visitors may perform in person searches. Search fee: $5.00 per name. Required to search: name, years to search. Civil cases indexed by defendant, plaintiff. Civil records index on computer from 06/74. The court offers for sale a CD-ROM of civil, domestic, mental health, and probate indices. **General Information:** Public Access terminal is available. No probation reports released. SASE required. Turnaround time 1 day. Copy fee: $.50 per page. Certification fee: $6.00. Fee payee: Clerk of Superior Court. Personal checks accepted. Prepayment is required.

Superior Court - Criminal

PO Box 120128 (220 W Broadway), San Diego, CA 92112-0128; 619-531-3040 Misdemeanor; Criminal phone: 619-685-6220. Hours: 8:30AM-4:30PM (PST). *Felony, Misdemeanor.*

www.sandiego.courts.ca.gov/superior/

Note: Both General and Limited Criminal records are located here.

Criminal Records: Access: Mail, in person. Both court and visitors may perform in person searches. Search fee: $5.00 per name. Fee is per index. Required to search: name, years to search, DOB. Criminal records on computer from 1974 to present, paper ledgers from 1860s. The court offers for a sale a CD-ROM of criminal records; felonies back to 6/1974; misdemeanors back 10 years. **General Information:** Public Access terminal is available. No adoptions, juvenile, medical, probation or sealed records released. SASE required. Turnaround time 1 week. Copy fee: $.50 per page. Certification fee: $6.00. Fee payee: San Diego Superior Court. Personal checks accepted. No out of state personal checks. Prepayment is required.

East County Division - Superior Court

250 E Main St, El Cajon, CA 92020; 619-441-4622. Hours: 8AM-4:30PM (PST). *Felony, Misdemeanor, Civil, Small Claims, Eviction.*

www.sandiego.courts.ca.gov

Note: This court now houses the former municipal court records.

Civil Records: Access: Mail, in person. Both court and visitors may perform in person searches. Search fee: $5.00 per name. Required to search: name, years to search. Civil cases indexed by defendant, plaintiff. Civil records on computer since 1974; microfilm prior.
Criminal Records: Access: Mail, in person. Both court and visitors may perform in person searches. Search fee: $5.00 per name. Required to search: name, years to search; also helpful: DOB. Criminal records on computer since 1974; microfilm prior.
General Information: Public Access terminal is available. No confidential or sealed records released. SASE required. Turnaround time 3-5 days. Copy fee: $.50 per page. Certification fee: $6.00. Fee payee: Clerk of Superior Court. Personal checks accepted. California checks with preprinted name and address only. Law firm business checks accepted. Prepayment is required.

North County Branch - Superior Court

325 S Melrose Dr, Suite 120, Vista, CA 92083-6627; 760-940-9595; Probate phone: 760-806-6150. Hours: 8:30AM-4:30PM (PST). *Felony, Misdemeanor, Civil Actions, Eviction, Small Claims, Probate.*

www.sandiego.courts.ca.gov

Note: Includes Cities of Oceanside, Del Mar, Carlsbad, Solana Beach, Encinitas, Escondido, San Marcos, Vista and unincorporated towns of Del Dios, Olivehain, San Luis Rey, San Pasqual, Rancho Santa Fe, Valley Center, Bonsall, Palomar Mountain, etc.

Civil Records: Access: Mail, in person. Both court and visitors may perform in person searches. Search fee: $5.00 per name. Required to search: name, years to search. Civil cases indexed by defendant, plaintiff. Civil records on computer back to 1993; prior on microfiche and index books.
Criminal Records: Access: Mail, in person. Both court and visitors may perform in person searches. Search fee: $5.00 per name. Required to search: name, years to search. Criminal records on computer back to 1993; prior on microfiche and index books.
General Information: Public Access terminal is available. No sealed or confidential documents released. SASE required. Turnaround time 2-3 days. Copy fee: $.50 per page. Certification fee: $6.00. Fee payee: Clerk of the Superior Court. Personal checks accepted. Out of state checks not accepted. Prepayment is required.

South County Branch - Superior Court

500-C 3rd Ave, Chula Vista, CA 91910; Civil phone: 619-691-4439; Criminal phone: 619-691-4728; Fax: 619-691-4969 (Civil). Hours: 8:30AM-4:30PM (PST). *Felony, Misdemeanor, Civil Actions, Probate, Eviction, Small Claims.*

www.sandiego.courts.ca.gov

Note: Includes National City, Chula Vista, Coronado, Imperial Beach and that portion of the City of San Diego lying south of the City of Chula Vista and contiguous unincorporated areas.

Civil Records: Access: Fax, mail, in person. Both court and visitors may perform in person searches. Search fee: $5.00 per name per year. Required to search: name, years to search. Civil cases indexed by defendant, plaintiff. Civil records on computer; for case files prior to 1991, contact Superior Court's Main Records Division, Downtown.
Criminal Records: Access: Phone, fax, mail, in person. Both court and visitors may perform in person searches. Search fee: $5.00 per name. Required to search: name, years to search, DOB. Criminal records on computer, cases files in or before 1986 on microfiche.
General Information: Public Access terminal is available. No juvenile, medical, probation reports or pronouncement of judgment records released. SASE required. Turnaround time up to 1 week (civil)-Turnaround time depends on availability of clerk (criminal). Copy fee: $.60 per page. Certification fee: $6.00. Fee payee: Superior Court (Civil)-Clerk of the Court (Criminal). Personal checks accepted. Prepayment is required.

Kearny Mesa Branch - Central Division

8950 Clairemont Mesa Blvd, San Diego, CA 92123; 858-694-2066 Small Claims. Hours: 8AM-4PM (PST). *Small Claims, Traffic.*

www.sandiego.courts.ca.gov/superior/index.html

Civil Records: Access: Mail, in person. Search fee: $5.00 per name. Required to search: Name, years to search. **General Information:** Public Access terminal is available. No confidential or sealed records released. SASE required. Copy fee: $.50 per copy. Certification fee: $6.00. Fee payee: Clerk of the Court.

Ramona Branch - East Division

1428 Montecito Rd, Ramona, CA 92065; 760-738-2435. Hours: 8AM-4:30PM (PST). *Misdemeanor, Civil Actions Under $25,000, Eviction, Small Claims.*

www.sandiego.courts.ca.gov

Note: Jurisdiction over the northeast area of the county.

Civil Records: Access: Fax, mail, in person. Both court and visitors may perform in person searches. Search fee: $5.00 per name. Required to search: name, years to search. Civil cases indexed by defendant, plaintiff. Civil records on computer from 1991, index files since 1983. Files destroyed after 10 years.
Criminal Records: Access: Fax, mail, in person. Both court and visitors may perform in person searches. Search fee: $5.00 per name. Required to search: name, years to search, SSN; also helpful: DOB. Criminal records on computer from 1991, index files since 1983. Files destroyed after 10 years.
General Information: No probation reports or DMV records released. SASE required. Turnaround time 2-3 days. Fax notes: No fee to fax results. Copy fee: $.50 per page. Certification fee: $6.00. Fee payee: Clerk of the Court. Personal checks accepted. Credit cards accepted: Visa, MasterCard. Prepayment is required.

San Marcos Branch - North Division

338 Via Vera Cruz, San Marcos, CA 92069-2693; 760-940-2888; Fax: 760-940-2802. Hours: 8:30AM-4PM (PST). *Misdemeanor, Traffic.*

www.sandiego.courts.ca.gov

Civil Records: Access: Mail, in person. Both court and visitors may perform in person searches. Search fee: $5.00 per name. Required to search: name, years to search; also helpful: address. Civil records on computer since 1994.
Criminal Records: Access: Mail, in person. Both court and visitors may perform in person searches. Search fee: $5.00 per name. Required to search: name, years to search; also helpful: address. Criminal records on computer since 1994.
General Information: Juvenile and adoption records are not released. Turnaround time 3 days. Copy fee: $.50 per page. Certification fee: $6.00. Fee payee: Clerk of the Court. Personal checks accepted. Prepayment is required.

San Francisco County

Superior Court - Criminal Division

850 Bryant St #306, San Francisco, CA 94107/94103; 415-553-1159. Hours: 8AM-4:30PM (PST). *Felony.*

www.ci.sf.ca.us/courts

Criminal Records: Access: Fax, mail, in person. Both court and visitors may perform in person searches. Search fee: $4.00 per name per year. Add warehouse retrieval fee of $5.00. Required to search: name, years to search, DOB. If searching by mail, direct your letter to Catherine Hill, Prior Convictions.
General Information: No medical, probation or sealed records released. SASE required. Turnaround time 1 week. Fax notes: No fee to fax results. Copy fee: $1.00 per page. Certification fee: $6.00. Fee payee: Clerk of the Superior Court. Personal checks accepted. Cashier checks and personal checks with ID only. Prepayment is required.

Superior Court - Civil Division

400 McAllister St, Rm 103, San Francisco, CA 94102; 415-551-3802; Probate phone: 415-551-3892. Hours: 8AM-4PM (PST). *Civil, Probate.*

www.ci.sf.ca.us/courts

Civil Records: Access: Mail, in person. Both court and visitors may perform in person searches. Search fee: $5.00 per name per year. Required to search: name, years to search. Civil cases indexed by defendant, plaintiff. Civil records on computer since 1987; prior records on microfilm and microfiche. **General Information:** Public Access terminal is available. No medical, probation or sealed records released. SASE required. Turnaround time 2 weeks. Copy fee: $1.00 per page. Certification fee: $6.00 plus $1.00 per page. Fee payee: Clerk of the Superior Court. Personal checks accepted. Credit cards accepted: Visa, MasterCard. Prepayment is required.

Limited Superior - Civil Division 400
McAllister St, Rm 103, San Francisco, CA 94107; 415-551-4032 (Records Section); Civil phone: 415-551-4047; Fax: 415-551-4041. Hours: 8AM-4:30PM (PST). *Civil Actions Under $25,000, Eviction, Small Claims.*

www.ci.sf.ca.us/courts

Note: Includes all of San Francisco County, including former municipal court on Folsom St

Civil Records: Access: Mail, in person. Both court and visitors may perform in person searches. Search fee: $5.00 per name per year. No charge if easily pulled from computer. Required to search: name, years to search. Civil cases indexed by defendant, plaintiff. Civil records on computer from 1991, index files from 1983. Records destroyed after 10 years. **General Information:** Public Access terminal is available. No sealed records released. SASE required. Turnaround time 2 days. Copy fee: $.75 per page. Certification fee: $6.00 plus $1.00 per page & copy fee. Fee payee: Superior Court. Personal checks accepted. Prepayment is required.

Superior Court - Misdemeanor Division
850 Bryant St Rm 201, San Francisco, CA 94103; 415-553-1665 (Records Dept); Criminal phone: 415-553-9395. Hours: 8AM-4:30PM (PST). *Misdemeanor.*

www.ci.sf.ca.us/courts

Note: Includes all of San Francisco County

Criminal Records: Access: Mail, in person. Both court and visitors may perform in person searches. Search fee: $5.00 per name per year. Required to search: name, years to search; also helpful: DOB. Criminal records (pending) on computer from 1991, index files from 1983. Records are destroyed after 10 years. **General Information:** No probation reports released. SASE required. Turnaround time 3-4 weeks. Copy fee: $1.00 per page. Microfilm copies $1.50 per page. Certification fee: $1.75. Fee payee: Superior Court. Personal checks accepted. Prepayment is required.

San Joaquin County

Superior Court - Civil 222 E Weber Ave, Rm
303, Stockton, CA 95202-2709; 209-468-2355; Fax: 209-468-0539. Hours: 7:30AM-5 M-F (office); 8AM-5PM M-F (phones) (PST). *Civil Actions, Eviction, Small Claims, Probate.*

www.stocktoncourt.org

Note: Includes City of Stockton and suburban area, Farmington and Linden, Delta area and surrounding unincorporated areas

Civil Records: Access: Mail, in person. Both court and visitors may perform in person searches. Search fee: $5.00 per name. No fee if search is done by customer. Required to search: name, years to search. Civil cases indexed by defendant, plaintiff. Civil records on computer from 1996; indices/books from 1850-1973; Microfiche 1973-1996. Records destroyed after 10 years. **General Information:** Public Access terminal is available. No probation, confidential records released. SASE required. Turnaround time 5-7 days. Copy fee: $.50 per page. Certification fee: $6.00. Fee payee: Superior Court. Personal checks accepted. Prepayment is required.

Superior Court - Criminal Division 222 E
Weber St Rm 101, Stockton, CA 95202; 209-468-2935. Hours: 7:30AM-5PM (PST). *Felony, Misdemeanor.*

www.stocktoncourt.org/courts

Criminal Records: Access: Mail, in person. Both court and visitors may perform in person searches. Search fee: $5.00 per name. Required to search: name, years to search, signed release; also helpful: DOB, SSN. Criminal Records on computer since 1992, on microfiche since 1972, older records archived to 1800s. Mail access only available to authorized agencies. **General Information:** Public Access terminal is available. No juvenile, medical, probation, sealed records released. SASE required. Turnaround time 1 week. Copy fee: $.50 per page. Certification fee: $6.00. Fee payee: San Joaquin Superior Court. Personal checks accepted. Cash only for forms and kits. Prepayment is required.

Lodi Division - Superior Court 315 W Elm St
(Civil), 230 W Elm St (Criminal), Lodi, CA 95240; Civil phone: 209-331-2101; Criminal phone: 209-331-2121; Fax: 209-331-2135. Hours: 8AM-5PM (PST). *Misdemeanor, Civil Actions Under $25,000, Eviction, Small Claims.*

www.stocktoncourt.org/courts

Note: Includes eight mile road to Sacramento County line, towns of Acampo, Clements, Lockeford, Terminous, Thornton, Woodbridge.

Civil Records: Access: Phone, mail, fax, in person. Only the court performs in person searches; visitors may not. Search fee: $6.00 per name. Required to search: name, years to search. Civil cases indexed by defendant, plaintiff. Civil records on computer from 1991, index files from 1983. Records destroyed after 10 years.

Criminal Records: Access: Phone, mail, fax, in person. Only the court performs in person searches; visitors may not. Search fee: $6.00 per name. Required to search: name, years to search, DOB; also helpful: address, SSN, sex. Criminal records on computer from 1991, index files from 1983. Records destroyed after 10 years.

General Information: Public Access terminal is available. No probation reports released. SASE required. Turnaround time 5 days. Copy fee: $.50 per page. Certification fee: $6.00. Fee payee: Superior Court. Personal checks accepted. Prepayment is required.

Manteca Branch - Superior Court 315 E
Center St, Manteca, CA 95336; Civil phone: 209-239-9188; Criminal phone: 209-239-1316. Hours: 8AM-4PM (PST). *Felony, Misdemeanor, Civil Actions Under $25,000, Eviction, Small Claims.*

www.stocktoncourt.org/courts

Note: Includes Cities of Manteca, Ripon, Escalon, French Camp, Lathrop and surrounding unincorporated areas.

Civil Records: Access: Mail, in person. Only the court performs in person searches; visitors may not. Search fee: $5.00 per name. Fee is for cases more than 3 years old. Required to search: name, years to search. Civil cases indexed by defendant, plaintiff. Civil records on computer from 1991, microfiche since 1986, index files from 1983. Records destroyed after 10 years.

Criminal Records: Access: Mail, in person. Only the court performs in person searches; visitors may not. Search fee: $5.00 per name. Fee is for cases prior to 1990. Required to search: name, years to search; also helpful: DOB. Criminal records on computer since 1990, microfiche since 1986, index files from 1983. Records destroyed after 10 years. Special request form required to view files.

General Information: No judge's notes, probation or police reports released. SASE required. Turnaround time 1-2 days. Copy fee: $.50 per page. Certification fee: $6.00. Fee payee: Superior Court. Personal checks accepted. Prepayment is required.

Tracy Branch - Superior Court 475 E 10th St,
Tracy, CA 95376; Civil phone: 209-831-5902; Criminal phone: 209-831-5900; Fax: 209-831-5919. Hours: 8AM-4PM (PST). *Felony, Misdemeanor, Civil Actions Under $25,000, Eviction, Small Claims.*

www.stocktoncourt.org/courts

Note: Includes Cities of Tracy, Banta, portion of Vernalis and surrounding unincorporated area.

Civil Records: Access: Phone, mail, in person. Only the court performs in person searches; visitors may not. Search fee: $5.00 per name. If on computer, no charge. Required to search: name, years to search. Civil cases indexed by defendant, plaintiff. Civil records on computer since 03/95; on index files from 1983. Records destroyed after 10 years.

Criminal Records: Access: Mail, in person. Only the court performs in person searches; visitors may not. Search fee: $5.00 per name. Required to search: name, years to search, DOB. Criminal records on computer from 1991; on index files from 1983. Records destroyed after 10 years.

General Information: No probation reports, DMV history and criminal history records released. SASE required. Turnaround time 5-10 days. Copy fee: $.50 per page. Certification fee: $6.00. Fee payee: Tracy Superior Court. Personal checks accepted. Prepayment is required.

San Luis Obispo County

Superior Court - Civil Division 1035 Palm
Street, Room 385, Government Center, San Luis Obispo, CA 93408; 805-781-5243. Hours: 9AM-4PM (PST). *Civil Actions, Small Claims, Eviction, Probate.*

www.slocourts.net/civil_division.htm

Note: This Court has jurisdiction over all of San Luis Obispo County, San Luis Obispo, Morro Bay, Avila Beach areas for Civil actions over $25,000, and also the current and former "limited jurisdiction" (under $25,000) civil cases in the immediate area.

Civil Records: Access: Mail, in person. Both court and visitors may perform in person searches. No search fee. Required to search: name, years to search. Civil cases indexed by defendant, plaintiff. Civil records on computer from 1991, index files from 1983. Records destroyed after 10 years. **General Information:** Public Access terminal is available. No probation reports released. SASE required. Turnaround time 2-5 days. Copy fee: $.50 per page. Certification fee: $6.00. Fee payee: Superior Court. Personal checks accepted. Prepayment is required.

Superior Court - Criminal Division
Government Center, Rm 220, 1035 Palm Street, San Luis Obispo, CA 93408; Criminal phone: 805-781-5670. Hours: 8:30AM-4PM (PST). *Felony, Misdemeanor.*

www.slocourts.net/

Note: Due to re-organization of the courts in this city, this court now handles misdemeanor cases which were formerly handled by the limited jurisdiction court. The civil cases are now located at the new Superior Court - Civil Division.

Criminal Records: Access: Mail, in person. Both court and visitors may perform in person searches. Search fee: $5.00 per name. Required to search: name, years to search. Criminal records on computer and microfiche from 1975, archived and index file from late 1800s.

General Information: Public Access terminal is available. No adoptions, juvenile, medical, probation or sealed records released. SASE required. Turnaround time 2-5 days. Copy fee: $.50 per page. Certification fee: $6.00. Fee payee: Superior Court Criminal Court Operations. Personal checks accepted. Prepayment is required.

Grover Beach Branch - Superior Court

214 S 16th St, Grover Beach, CA 93433-2299; Civil phone: 805-473-7077; Criminal phone: 805-473-7072. Hours: 8:30AM-4PM (PST). *Misdemeanor, Civil Actions Under $25,000, Eviction, Small Claims.*

www.slocourts.net

Note: Includes Nipomo, Grover Beach, Arroyo Grande, Pismo Beach, Ociano, South Coast unincorporated areas.

Civil Records: Access: Phone, mail, in person. Only the court performs in person searches; visitors may not. Search fee: First name is free, then $5.00 per name. Required to search: name, years to search. Civil cases indexed by defendant, plaintiff. Civil records on index cards to 1976; on computer back to 1986. Records destroyed after 10 years.

Criminal Records: Access: Phone, mail, in person. Only the court performs in person searches; visitors may not. Search fee: First name is free, then $5.00 per name. Required to search: name, years to search. Criminal records on index cards to 1976; on computer back to 1986. Records destroyed after 10 years.

General Information: No probation reports released. SASE required. Turnaround 2-3 weeks civil; 1 week criminal. Copy fee: $.50 per page. Certification fee: $6.00. Fee payee: Superior Court. Personal checks accepted. Prepayment is required.

Paso Robles Branch - Superior Court

549 10th St, Paso Robles, CA 93446-2593; Civil phone: 805-237-3079; Criminal phone: 805-237-3080. Hours: 8:30AM-4PM (PST). *Misdemeanor, Civil Actions Under $25,000, Eviction, Small Claims.*

www.slocourts.net/

Note: Includes Atascadero, Templeton, Paso Robles, San Miguel, Shandon, Cholame, areas north and east of the Cuesta Grade.

Civil Records: Access: Phone, mail, in person. Only the court performs in person searches; visitors may not. Search fee: $5.00 per name. Search is free if only one name. Required to search: name, years to search. Civil cases indexed by defendant, plaintiff. Civil records on computer from 1975, index files from 1983. Records destroyed after 10 years. Mail requests limited to 5 at a time.

Criminal Records: Access: Phone, mail, in person. Only the court performs in person searches; visitors may not. Search fee: $5.00. Search is free for only one name. Required to search: name, years to search; also helpful: DOB. Criminal records on computer from 1975, index files from 1983. Records destroyed after 10 years. Mail requests limited to 5 at a time.

General Information: Public Access terminal is available. No driving histories, rap sheets, sealed or probation reports released. SASE required. Turnaround time 1-2 days. Copy fee: $.50 per page. Certification fee: $6.00. Fee payee: Superior Court. Personal checks accepted. Prepayment is required.

San Mateo County

Superior Court 400 County Center, Redwood City, CA 94063; Civil phone: 650-363-4711; Criminal phone: 650-363-4302; Fax: 650-363-4914. 8AM-4PM *Felony, Civil Actions Over $25,000, Probate.*

www.sanmateocourt.org

Civil Records: Access: Mail, in person. Both court and visitors may perform in person searches. Search fee: $5.00 per name. Required to search: name, years to search. Civil cases indexed by defendant, plaintiff. Civil records on computer from 1978; index books prior.

Criminal Records: Access: Mail, in person. Both court and visitors may perform in person searches. Search fee: $5.00 per name. Required to search: name, years to search; also helpful: address, DOB, SSN. Criminal records on computer since 1964; prior on books.

General Information: Public Access terminal is available. No confidential jackets on conservatorships & guardianships, adoptions, juvenile, medical, probation or sealed records released. SASE required. Turnaround time 1 week. Copy fee: $.75 per page. Certification fee: $6.00. Fee payee: Superior Court. Personal checks accepted. Prepayment is required.

Northern Branch - Superior Court

1050 Mission Rd, South San Francisco, CA 94080; 650-877-5773; Civil phone: 877-5778 (Sm Claims). Hours: 8AM-4PM *Misdemeanor, Small Claims, Traffic.*

www.sanmateocourt.org

Note: Includes Brisbane, Daly City (including Westlake), Pacifica, San Bruno, South San Francisco, the northern coastal towns and all unincorporated areas in the county north including Colma and Broadmoor.

Criminal Records: Access: Mail, in person. Both court and visitors may perform in person searches. Search fee: $5.00 per name. Required to search: name, years to search; also helpful: DOB. Criminal records on computer from 1991, index files from 1983. Records destroyed after 10 years.

General Information: Public Access terminal is available. No probation reports or confidential information records released. SASE required. Turnaround time 2 days-2 weeks. Copy fee: $.75 per page. Certification fee: $6.00. Fee payee: Superior Court. Personal checks accepted. Prepayment required.

San Mateo Combined Superior Court

400 County Center, Redwood City, CA 94063; 650-363-4302. Hours: 8AM-4PM (PST). *Misdemeanor, Civil, Eviction, Small Claims.*

www.sanmateocourt.org

Note: Includes Atherton, Menlo Park, Portola Valley, Redwood City, San Carlos, Woodside, East Palo Alto and all unincorporated areas including La Honda and the southern coastal area south of Tunitas Creek Road which includes Pescadara and San Gregorio.

Civil Records: Access: Mail, in person. Both court and visitors may perform in person searches. Search fee: $5.00 per name. Required to search: name, years to search. Civil cases indexed by defendant, plaintiff. Civil Records on computer since 1991.

Criminal Records: Access: Mail, in person. Both court and visitors may perform in person searches. Search fee: $5.00 per name. Required to search: name, years to search. Criminal records on computer from 1991, index files from 1983. Records destroyed after 10 years.

General Information: Public Access terminal is available. No probation reports or confidential information records released. SASE required. Turnaround time 2 weeks. Copy fee: $.75 per page. Certification fee: $6.00. Fee payee: Superior Court. Personal checks accepted. Write "not to exceed $x.xx" on check. Credit cards accepted: Visa, MasterCard. Credit card accepted in person only. Prepayment is required.

Santa Barbara County

Superior Court Box 21107, Santa Barbara, CA 93121; 805-568-2237; Fax: 805-568-2219. Hours: 8AM-4:45PM (PST). *Felony, Civil Actions Over $25,000, Probate.*

www.sbcourts.org/index.htm

Note: Also known as the Anacapa Division.

Civil Records: Access: Phone, fax, mail, in person. Both court and visitors may perform in person searches. No search fee. Required to search: name, years to search. Civil cases indexed by defendant, plaintiff. Civil records on computer and microfiche from 1975, archived and index file from 1920.

Criminal Records: Access: Phone, fax, mail, in person. Both court and visitors may perform in person searches. Search fee: $5.00 per name. Required to search: name, years to search, DOB. Criminal records on computer and microfiche from 1975, archived and index file from 1920.

General Information: No adoptions, juvenile, medical, probation or sealed records released. SASE required. Turnaround time 1 week. Copy fee: $.75 per page. Certification fee: $6.00. Fee payee: Superior Court. Personal checks accepted. Credit cards accepted: Visa, MasterCard. Prepayment is required.

Figueroa Division - Santa Barbara Superior Court

118 E Figueroa St, Santa Barbara, CA 93101; 805-568-2735; Civil phone: 805-568-2741; Criminal phone: 805-568-2752; Fax: 805-568-3208. Hours: 7:45AM-4PM (PST). *Felony, Misdemeanor, Civil Actions Under $25,000, Eviction, Small Claims.*

www.sbcourts.org/index.htm

Note: Includes the City of Santa Barbara, Goleta and adjacent unincorporated areas, Carpenteria, Montecito. For civil cases prior to 09/01/98, call 805-568-2200.

Civil Records: Access: Mail, in person. Both court and visitors may perform in person searches. Search fee: $5.00 per name. Required to search: name, years to search. Civil cases indexed by defendant, plaintiff. Civil records on computer from 1991, index files from 1983, microfiche from 1975. Records destroyed after 10 years. Civil records can be obtained from 1100 Anacapa St, Santa Barbara, CA 93101.

Criminal Records: Access: Mail, in person. Both court and visitors may perform in person searches. Search fee: $5.00 per name. Required to search: name, years to search; also helpful: DOB. Criminal records on computer from 1991, index files from 1983, microfiche from 1975. Records destroyed after 10 years. Will accept fax requests from gov't agencies only.

General Information: No probation reports released. SASE required. Turnaround time 2 days. Copy fee: $.75 per page. Certification fee: $6.00. Fee payee: Clerk of the Court. Personal checks accepted. Prepayment is required.

Lompoc Division - Superior Court

115 Civic Center Plz, Lompoc, CA 93436; Civil phone: 805-737-7796; Criminal phone: 805-737-7790; Fax: 805-737-7786. Hours: 8:30AM-4:55PM (PST). *Misdemeanor, Civil Actions Under $25,000, Eviction, Small Claims.*

www.sbcourts.org/index.htm

Note: Includes Lompoc and adjacent unincorporated areas, including sections of Vandenburg Air Force Base.

Civil Records: Access: Phone, mail, in person. Both court and visitors may perform in person searches. No search fee. Required to search: name, years to search. Civil cases indexed by defendant, plaintiff. Civil records on computer from 1991, index files from 1983. Records destroyed after 10 years. Phone searches only for computerized records.

Criminal Records: Access: Phone, mail, in person. Both court and visitors may perform in person searches. No search fee. Required to search: name, years to search, DOB; also helpful: address. Criminal records on computer from 1991, index files from 1983. Records destroyed after 10 years. Phone searches only for computerized records. Includes Solvang jurisdiction filings from 1997 to present.
General Information: Public Access terminal is available. No probation reports released. SASE required. Turnaround time 2 days. Copy fee: $.75 per page. Certification fee: $6.00. Fee payee: Clerk of the Superior Court. Personal checks accepted. Prepayment is required.

Santa Maria Cook Division - Superior Court
312-C East Cook St (PO Box 5369), Santa Maria, CA 93454-5369; 805-346-7414; Civil phone: 805-346-7405; Fax: 805-346-7616. Hours: 7:30AM-4:30PM (PST). *Civil Actions Under $25,000, Probate, Eviction, Small Claims.*

www.sbcourts.org/general_info/index.htm

Note: This Cook Division handles Civil; its sister court (Miller Division) handles Criminal. Includes Betteravia, Casmalia, Cuyama, Guadalupe, Gary, Los Alamos, New Cuyama, Orcutt, Santa Maria, Sisquoc, Tepusquet and sections of the Vandenburg Air Force Base

Civil Records: Access: Mail, in person. Both court and visitors may perform in person searches. Search fee: $5.00 per name. Required to search: name, years to search. Civil cases indexed by defendant, plaintiff. Civil records in index files from 1983. Records destroyed after 10 years. **General Information:** Public Access terminal is available. No probation reports, financial, judges notes, confidential or sealed records released. SASE required. Turnaround time 2 days. Fax notes: Will fax results. Copy fee: $.75 per page. Certification fee: $6.00. Fee payee: Clerk of Court. Personal checks accepted. Credit cards accepted: Visa, MasterCard. Prepayment is required.

Santa Maria Miller Division - Superior Court
312-C East Cook St, Bldg E, Santa Maria, CA 93454-5165; 805-346-7590; Criminal phone: 805-346-7565; Fax: 805-346-7591. Hours: 7:30AM-4:30PM (PST). *Misdemeanor, Traffic.*

www.sbcourts.org/general_info/index.htm

Note: The Miller is in the same building complex as the Cook Division, which handles civil, small claims, family cases. Miller includes the same jurisdictional area as Cook Division.

Criminal Records: Access: Mail, fax, in person. Both court and visitors may perform in person searches. Search fee: $5.00 per name. Required to search: name, years to search, DOB. Criminal records in index files from 1983. Records destroyed after 10 years.
General Information: Public Access terminal is available. No probation reports, financial, judges notes, confidential or sealed records released. SASE required. Turnaround time 2 days. Copy fee: $.75 per page. Certification fee: $6.00. Fee payee: Clerk of Court. Personal checks accepted. Credit cards accepted: Visa, MasterCard. Prepayment is required.

Solvang Division - Superior Court
1745 Mission Dr, #C, Solvang, CA 93463; 805-686-5040; Fax: 805-686-5079. Hours: 8AM-4PM (PST). *Misdemeanor, Small Claims, Traffic.*

www.sbcourts.org/general_info/index.htm

Civil Records: Access: Phone, mail, in person. Both court and visitors may perform in person searches. No search fee. Required to search: name, years to search. Civil cases indexed by defendant, plaintiff. Civil records on computer from 1990, index cards prior. Will only search back 7 years.

Criminal Records: Access: Mail, in person. Both court and visitors may perform in person searches. No search fee. Required to search: name, years to search, DOB. Criminal records on computer from 1988, index cards prior.
General Information: Public Access terminal is available. No sealed or confidential records released. SASE required. Turnaround time 1 week. Copy fee: $.75 per page. Certification fee: $7.00. Fee payee: Superior Court. Personal checks accepted. Credit cards accepted: Visa, MasterCard. Credit cards are only accepted at the counter, not by mail. Prepayment is required.

Santa Clara County

Superior Court - Civil 191 N 1st Street, San Jose, CA 95113; 408-299-2966; Civil phone: 408-299-2964. Hours: 8:30AM-4PM (PST). *Civil, Eviction, Probate.*

www.sccsuperiorcourt.org

Note: Handles cases for San Jose, Milpitas, Santa Clara, Los Gatos and Campbell areas

Civil Records: Access: Mail, in person. Both court and visitors may perform in person searches. Search fee: $5.00 per name per year. Required to search: name, years to search. Civil records on computer 1993 to present; prior on books to 1800s. **General Information:** Public Access terminal is available. No probation reports or confidential records released. SASE required. Turnaround time 2 weeks. Copy fee: $1.00 per page. Certification fee: $6.00. Fee payee: Superior Court. Personal checks accepted. Prepayment is required.

Superior Court - Criminal 190 W Hedding St, San Jose, CA 95110-1774; 408-299-2230; Criminal phone: 408-299-2281. Hours: 8:30AM-4PM (PST). *Felony, Misdemeanor.*

www.sccsuperiorcourt.org

Criminal Records: Access: Mail, in person. Both court and visitors may perform in person searches. Search fee: $5.00 per name per year. Required to search: name, years to search, DOB. Criminal records on microfiche from 1975-2000. Old files are kept in archives or on microfilm.
General Information: No probation, confidential or sealed records released. SASE required. Turnaround time 3-7 days. Copy fee: $1.00 per page. Postage also charged based on number of pages copied. Certification fee: $6.00. Fee payee: Santa Clara Superior Court. Personal checks accepted. Prepayment is required.

South County Facility - Superior Court 12425 Monterey Rd, San Martin, CA 95046-9590; Civil phone: 408-686-3520; Criminal phone: 408-686-3510. Hours: 8:30AM-4PM (PST). *Felony, Misdemeanor, Civil Actions Under $25,000, Eviction, Small Claims.*

http://sccsuperiorcourt.org

Note: Small Claims phone is 408-686-3521. Jurisdiction includes the Cities of Gilroy, Morgan Hill, San Martin and surrounding unincorporated areas.

Civil Records: Access: Mail, in person. Both court and visitors may perform in person searches. Search fee: $5.00 per name per year. Required to search: name, years to search. Civil records on microfiche.
Criminal Records: Access: Mail, in person. Both court and visitors may perform in person searches. Search fee: $5.00 per name per year. Required to search: name, years to search; also helpful: DOB. Same record keeping as civil.
General Information: No adoptions, juvenile, medical, probation or sealed records released. SASE required. Turnaround time 1 week. Copy fee: $1.00 per page. Certification fee: $6.00. Fee payee: Superior Court. Personal checks accepted. Prepayment is required.

Palo Alto Facility - Superior Court 270 Grant Ave, Palo Alto, CA 94306; 650-324-0373. Hours: 8:30AM-4PM (PST). *Felony, Misdemeanor, Small Claims.*

www.sccsuperiorcourt.org

Note: Includes Palo Alto, Mountain View, Los Altos, Los Altos Hills, Stanford University and the surrounding unincorporated areas.

Civil Records: Access: Mail, in person. Both court and visitors may perform in person searches. Search fee: $5.00 per name per year. Required to search: name, years to search.
Criminal Records: Access: Mail, in person. Both court and visitors may perform in person searches. Search fee: $5.00 per name per year. Required to search: name, years to search; also helpful: DOB. Criminal Records on microfiche.
General Information: No probation, doctor report, pretrial report records released. SASE required. Turnaround time 1 week. Copy fee: $1.00 per page. Certification fee: $6.00. Fee payee: Superior Court. Personal checks accepted. Prepayment is required.

Sunnyvale Facility - Superior Court 605 W El Camino Real, Sunnyvale, CA 94087; 408-739-1503. Hours: 8:30AM-4PM (PST). *Felony, Misdemeanor.*

www.sccsuperiorcourt.org

Note: Includes the cities of Sunnyvale and Cupertino. All traffic and small claims are filed at the Palo Alto Facility.

Criminal Records: Access: Mail, in person. Both court and visitors may perform in person searches. Search fee: $5.00 per name per year. Required to search: name, years to search, DOB.
General Information: No probation reports, confidential or sealed records released. SASE required. Turnaround time 2-4 days. Copy fee: $1.00 per page. Certification fee: $6.00. Fee payee: Clerk of Court. Personal checks accepted. Prepayment is required.

Los Gatos Facility - Superior Court 14205 Capri Dr, Los Gatos, CA 95032; 408-866-8331. Hours: 8:30AM-4PM (PST). *Small Claims.*

http://sccsuperiorcourt.org

Note: Includes the towns of Los Gatos and Monte Sereno and the cities of Campbell, Saratoga, and surrounding unincorporated areas as well as San Jose, Milpitas and Santa Clara

Civil Records: Access: Phone, mail, in person. Both court and visitors may perform in person searches. Search fee: $5.00 per name per year. Required to search: name, years to search. Civil cases indexed by defendant, plaintiff. Civil record index on microfiche.
General Information: Copy fee: $1.00 per page. Certification fee: $6.00. Fee payee: Superior Court. Personal checks accepted. Prepayment is required.

Santa Cruz County

Superior Court - Civil 701 Ocean St Rm 110, Santa Cruz, CA 95060; 831-454-2020; Fax: 831-454-2215. Hours: 8AM-4PM (PST). *Civil, Probate.*

www.co.santa-cruz.ca.us/crt/courts.htm

Civil Records: Access: Phone, mail, in person. Both court and visitors may perform in person searches. No search fee. Required to search: name, years to search. Civil cases indexed by defendant, plaintiff. Civil records on computer back to 6/1985; microfiche, archived and index books from 1820. **General Information:** Public Access terminal is available. No adoptions, juvenile, medical, probation or sealed records released. SASE required. Turnaround time 5-10 days. Copy fee: $.50 per page. Certification fee: $6.00 plus $1.00 per page. Fee payee: Clerk of Court. Personal checks accepted. Prepayment is required.

Superior Court - Criminal 701 Ocean St Rm 120, Santa Cruz, CA 95060; 831-454-2230; Fax: 831-454-2215. Hours: 8AM-4PM (PST). *Felony, Misdemeanor.*

www.co.santa-cruz.ca.us/crt/courts.htm

Criminal Records: Access: Fax, mail, in person. Both court and visitors may perform in person searches. Search fee: $5.00 per name. Required to search: name; also helpful: years to search, DOB. Criminal records on computer since 1985; also on microfiche index by party name back; other records go back to 1880's.
General Information: Public Access terminal is available. No juvenile, probation or sealed records released. SASE required. Turnaround time 1-2 weeks. Copy fee: $.50 per page. Certification fee: $6.00 plus $1.00 per page. Fee payee: Clerk of Court. Personal checks accepted. Prepayment is required.

Watsonville Division - Superior Court 1430 Freedom Blvd, Watsonville, CA 95076; 831-763-8060. Hours: 8AM-4PM (PST). *Misdemeanor, Civil Actions Under $25,000, Eviction, Small Claims.*

www.co.santa-cruz.ca.us/crt/courts.htm

Note: Includes all of Santa Cruz County.
Civil Records: Access: Mail, in person. Search fee: $5.00 per name. Required to search: name, years to search. Civil cases indexed by defendant, plaintiff. Civil records on computer from 1992, index books prior. Records destroyed after 10 years.
Criminal Records: Access: Mail, in person. Both court and visitors may perform in person searches. Search fee: $5.00 per name. Required to search: name, years to search; also helpful: DOB. Criminal records on computer from 1992, index books prior. Records destroyed after 10 years.
General Information: No probation or juvenile records released. SASE required. Turnaround time 2-5 days. Copy fee: $.50 per page. Certification fee: $6.00. Fee payee: Superior Court. Personal checks accepted. Prepayment is required.

Shasta County

Superior Court 1500 Court St, Redding, CA 96001; 530-245-6789; Fax: 530-225-5564 Civil; 245-6483 Criminal. Hours: 8:30AM-4:30PM (PST). *Felony, Misdemeanor, Civil, Small Claims, Eviction, Probate.*

www.shastacourts.com

Note: Address Room 319 for civil division and Room 219 for criminal division.
Civil Records: Access: Mail, in person. Both court and visitors may perform in person searches. Search fee: $5.00 per name per year. Required to search: name, years to search. Civil cases indexed by defendant, plaintiff. Civil records on computer from 1993, index books prior.
Criminal Records: Access: Mail, in person. Both court and visitors may perform in person searches. Search fee: $5.00 per name per year. Required to search: name, years to search. Criminal records on computer from 1993, index books prior.
General Information: No probation or confidential records released. SASE required. Turnaround time 2-7 days. Copy fee: $.50 per page. Certification fee: $6.00. Fee payee: Superior Courts. Personal checks accepted. Prepayment is required.

Burney Branch - Superior Court 20509 Shasta St, Burney, CA 96013; 530-335-3571; Fax: 530-225-5684. Hours: 8AM-Noon, 1-4:30PM (PST). *Misdemeanor, Civil, Eviction, Small Claims.*

www.shastacourts.com/burney.shtml

Note: Civil actions handled by Redding Branch since 1992. Prior civil limited jurisdiction records maintained here.
Civil Records: Access: Mail, in person. Only the court performs in person searches; visitors may not. Search fee: $5.00 per name per year. Required to search: name, years to search. Civil cases indexed by defendant, plaintiff. Civil records on computer from 1993, index books prior.
Criminal Records: Access: Mail, in person. Only the court performs in person searches; visitors may not. Search fee: $5.00 per name. Required to search: name, years to search, DOB. Criminal records on computer from 1993, index books prior.
General Information: No probation, juvenile, or DMV reports released. SASE required. Turnaround time 2-14 days. Copy fee: $1.00 1st page; $.50 each add'l. Certification fee: $6.00. Fee payee: Superior Court. Personal checks accepted. Prepayment is required.

Sierra County

Superior Court PO Box 476 Courthouse Square, Downieville, CA 95936; 530-289-3698; Fax: 530-289-0205. Hours: 8AM-Noon, 1-5PM (PST). *Felony, Misdemeanor, Civil, Eviction, Small Claims, Probate.*

Civil Records: Access: Phone, fax, mail, in person. Both court and visitors may perform in person searches. Search fee: $1.75 per name per year. Required to search: name, years to search. Civil cases indexed by defendant, plaintiff. Civil records on computer from 1985, index books from 1852.
Criminal Records: Access: Phone, fax, mail, in person. Both court and visitors may perform in person searches. Search fee: $1.75 per name per year. Required to search: name, years to search. Criminal records on computer from 1985, index books from 1852.
General Information: No adoptions, juvenile, medical, probation or sealed records released. SASE required. Turnaround time 2-4 days. Fax notes: $1.00 per page. Copy fee: $1.00 per page. Certification fee: $6.00 per document. Fee payee: Superior Court. Personal checks accepted. Prepayment is required.

Siskiyou County

Superior Court 311 4th St PO Box 1026, Yreka, CA 96097; Civil phone: 530-842-8196; Criminal phone: 530-842-8182; Fax: 530-842-0164(Civ); 530-842-8178(Crim). Hours: 8AM-5PM (PST). *Felony, Misdemeanor, Civil, Probate.*

Civil Records: Access: Phone, mail, in person. Both court and visitors may perform in person searches. Search fee: $5.00 per name. Fee is per 10 years searched. Required to search: name, years to search. Civil cases indexed by defendant, plaintiff. Civil records on computer since 1991, archived and index book from 1900.
Criminal Records: Access: Phone, mail, in person. Both court and visitors may perform in person searches. Search fee: $5.00 per name. Fee is per 10 years searched. Required to search: name, years to search. Criminal records on computer since 1991, archived and index book from 1900.
General Information: No adoptions, juvenile, medical, probation or sealed records released. SASE required. Turnaround time 1 week. Copy fee: $.50 per page. Certification fee: $6.00. Fee payee: Siskiyou Superior Court. Personal checks accepted. Prepayment is required.

Superior Court 550 Main St, Weed, CA 96094; 530-938-2483; Civil phone: 530-938-3897; Fax: 530-842-0109. Hours: 8AM-5PM (PST). *Misdemeanor, Civil Actions Under $25,000, Eviction, Small Claims.*

Note: This court holds misdemeanor records for Dorris/Tulelake branch.

Civil Records: Access: Mail, in person. Only the court performs in person searches; visitors may not. Search fee: $5.00 per name per 10 years. Required to search: full name, years to search. Civil cases indexed by defendant, plaintiff. Civil records go back to 1980; on computer since 1995. Will only search back 7 years.
Criminal Records: Access: Mail, in person. Only the court performs in person searches; visitors may not. Search fee: $5.00 per name per 10 years. Required to search: full name, years to search, DOB, SSN. Criminal records on computer since 1995, index books prior. Will only search back 7 years.
General Information: No probation reports released. SASE required. Turnaround time 10 days. Fax notes: Fee to fax results is $1.00 per page. Copy fee: $.50 per page. Certification fee: $6.00 or $10 for a judgment. Fee payee: Siskiyou Superior Court. Personal checks accepted. Prepayment is required.

Dorris Branch - Superior Court PO Box 828, Dorris, CA 96023; 530-397-3161; Fax: 530-397-3169. Hours: 8AM-Noon, 1-4PM (PST). *Civil Actions Under $25,000, Eviction, Small Claims.*

Note: All new misdemeanor cases are referred to Southeastern branch in Weed, CA. Only maintains a few criminal records for a year
Civil Records: Access: Phone, mail, in person. Only the court performs in person searches; visitors may not. Search fee: $5.00 per name. Required to search: name, years to search. **General Information:** No probation reports released. SASE required. Turnaround time 1 week. Copy fee: $.50 per page. Certification fee: $6.00. Fee payee: Siskiyou Superior Court. Personal checks accepted. Prepayment is required.

Solano County

Superior Court - Civil 600 Union Ave, Fairfield, CA 94533; 707-421-6053; Probate phone: 707-421-6471; Fax: 707-435-2950. Hours: 8AM-4PM (PST). *Civil, Eviction, Probate.*

www.solanocourts.com

Note: The Northern Solano Municipal Court has been combined with the Superior Court
Civil Records: Access: Phone, mail, online, in person. Both court and visitors may perform in person searches. Search fee: $5.00 per name. Required to search: name, years to search. Civil cases indexed by defendant, plaintiff. Civil records on computer since 1992, microfiche since 1971, archived and index files since 1800s. Online access to civil records is available free at the web site; click on "Court Connect.". Phone access limited to short searches. **General Information:** Public Access terminal is available. No sealed records released. SASE required. Turnaround time 2-3 days. Copy fee: $1.00 per page. Certification fee: $6.00. Fee payee: Solano County Courts. Personal checks accepted. Prepayment is required.

Superior Court - Criminal 530 Union Ave #200, Fairfield, CA 94533; 707-421-7440; 421-7834 Sup Court Records; Fax: 707-421-7439. Hours: 8AM-4PM (PST). *Felony, Misdemeanor.*

www.co.solano.ca.us/courts

Note: The Northern Solano Municipal Court has been combined with the Superior Court
Criminal Records: Access: Mail, in person, online. Both court and visitors may perform in person searches. Search fee: $5.00 per name. Required to search: name, years to search; also helpful: DOB, SSN. Superior Court records on computer since 1992, microfiche since 1971; Municipal Court records on computer for past 10 years. Online access to criminal records is available free at the web site; click on "Court Connect."
General Information: No probation reports released. SASE required. Turnaround time 1-3 weeks. Copy fee:

$5.00 for first page. Certification fee: $6.00. Fee payee: Solano Superior Court. Personal checks accepted. Prepayment is required.

Vallejo Branch - Superior Court 321 Tuolumne St, Vallejo, CA 94590; Civil phone: 707-553-5346; Criminal phone: 707-553-5341; Fax: 707-553-5661. Hours: 8AM-4PM (PST). *Misdemeanor, Civil, Eviction, Small Claims.*

www.co.solano.ca.us/courts

Note: Includes Cities of Vallejo and Benicia and the unincorporated area adjacent thereto.

Civil Records: Access: Mail, in person, online. Both court and visitors may perform in person searches. Search fee: $5.00 per name. Required to search: name, years to search. Civil cases indexed by defendant, plaintiff. Civil records on computer from 1991, index files from 1983. Records destroyed after 10 years. Online access to civil records is available free at the web site; click on "Court Connect.".

Criminal Records: Access: Mail, in person, online. Only the court performs in person searches; visitors may not. Search fee: $5.00 per name. Required to search: name, years to search. Criminal records on computer from 1991, index files from 1983. Records destroyed after 10 years. Online access to criminal records is the same as civil.

General Information: No probation reports released. SASE required. Turnaround time 2 days. Copy fee: $1.00 per page. Certification fee: $6.00. Fee payee: Superior Court. Personal checks accepted. Credit cards accepted: Visa, AmEx. Prepayment is required.

Sonoma County

Superior Court - Criminal 600 Administration Dr, Room 105J, Santa Rosa, CA 95403-0281; 707-565-1100. Hours: 8AM-4PM (PST). *Felony, Misdemeanor, Probate.*

www.sonomasuperiorcourt.com

Civil Records: Access: Phone, mail, in person. Both court and visitors may perform in person searches. Search fee: $15.00 per hour. Required to search: name, years to search. Civil cases indexed by defendant, plaintiff. Civil records on computer from 1985, microfiche and index books from 1850 to 1984. Phone access limited to 2 names or cases per call.

Criminal Records: Access: Phone, mail, in person. Both court and visitors may perform in person searches. Search fee: $15.00 per hour. Required to search: name, years to search, DOB. Criminal Records on computer back to 1985, microfiche and index books 1850 to 1984. Misdemeanor records destroyed after 10 years.

General Information: Public Access terminal is available. No adoptions, juvenile, medical, probation or sealed records released. SASE required. Turnaround time 2-3 weeks. Copy fee: $1.00 per page. 10 page limit. If more than 10 pages must wait 3-5 days. Certification fee: $6.00 plus $1.00 per page. Fee payee: Superior Court. Personal checks accepted. No out of state personal checks accepted. Prepayment is required.

Superior Court - Civil Division 600 Administration Dr, Rm 107J, Santa Rosa, CA 95403; 707-565-1100. Hours: 8AM-4PM (PST). *Civil, Eviction, Small Claims.*

www.sonomasuperiorcourt.com

Civil Records: Access: Mail, in person. Both court and visitors may perform in person searches. No search fee. Required to search: name, years to search. Civil cases indexed by defendant, plaintiff. Civil records on computer to 10/84, index files prior. Records destroyed after 10 years. **General Information:** Public Access terminal is available. No probation reports or sealed records released. SASE required. Turnaround time 2 days - 2 weeks. Copy fee: $1.00 per page. Certification

fee: $6.00. Fee payee: Superior Court. Personal checks accepted. Prepayment is required.

Stanislaus County

Superior Court - Criminal 800 11 Street, Rm 140, PO Box 1098, Modesto, CA 95353; 209-558-6000. Hours: 8AM-Noon, 1-4PM (PST). *Felony, Misdemeanor.*

www.co.stanislaus.ca.us/courts

Note: Physical address Zip Code is 95354

Criminal Records: Access: Mail, in person. Both court and visitors may perform in person searches. Search fee: $5.00 per name per year. Required to search: name, years to search. Criminal Records on microfiche since 1974, archived back to 1800s.

General Information: No adoptions, juvenile, medical, probation or sealed records released. SASE required. Turnaround time 1-2 weeks. Copy fee: $.50 per page. Certification fee: $6.00. Fee payee: Superior Court Clerk. Personal checks accepted. Prepayment is required.

Superior Court - Civil 1100 "I" St PO Box 828, Modesto, CA 95353; 209-558-6000; Fax: 209-525-4348 (civil). Hours: 8AM-4PM (PST). *Civil, Eviction, Small Claims, Probate.*

www.co.stanislaus.ca.us/courts

Note: Ceres Branch has been closed and records transferred here

Civil Records: Access: Mail, fax, in person. Both court and visitors may perform in person searches. Search fee: $5.00 per name. Required to search: name, years to search. Civil cases indexed by defendant, plaintiff. Civil records on computer from 1991, in index files from 1983. Records destroyed after 10 years. **General Information:** Public Access terminal is available. No probation or juvenile records released. SASE required. Turnaround time 2-5 days. Copy fee: $.50 per page. Certification fee: $6.00. Fee payee: Superior Court. Personal checks accepted. Prepayment is required.

Turlock Division - Superior Court 300 Starr Ave, Turlock, CA 95380; 209-558-6000; Fax: 209-664-8009. Hours: 8AM-Noon, 12:30-4PM (PST). *Small Claims.*

www.co.stanislaus.ca.us/courts

Civil Records: Access: In person, mail. Only the court performs in person searches; visitors may not. Search fee: $5.00. Required to search: name, years to search, DOB. Civil records on computer; older records on microfiche. **General Information:** Turnaround time 3 days. Fax notes: Fee to fax results is $1 per page. Fee payee: Superior Court. Accepted thru automated phone service 209-558-6000. Prepayment is required.

Sutter County

Superior Court - Civil Division 463 2nd St, Rm 211, Courthouse East, 2nd Floor, Yuba City, CA 95991; 530-822-7352; Fax: 530-822-7192. Hours: 8AM-5PM (PST). *Civil, Eviction, Small Claims, Probate.*

www.suttercourts.com

Civil Records: Access: Mail, in person. Both court and visitors may perform in person searches. Search fee: $5.00 per name. Required to search: name, years to search. Civil cases indexed by defendant, plaintiff. Civil records in index books and archived from 1800s, on computer back to 1/95. **General Information:** Public Access terminal is available. No adoptions, juvenile, medical, probation or sealed records released. SASE required. Turnaround time 2 days if records on site. Fax notes: Will not fax results. Copy fee: $.50 per page. Certification fee: $6.00. Fee payee: Superior Court. Personal checks accepted. Prepayment is required.

Superior Court - Criminal Division 446 2nd St, Yuba City, CA 95991; 530-822-7360; Fax: 530-822-7159. Hours: 8AM-5PM (PST). *Felony, Misdemeanor.*

Criminal Records: Access: Fax, mail, in person. Both court and visitors may perform in person searches. Search fee: $5.00 per name. Required to search: name, years to search. Criminal records in index books and archived from 1800s, computerized since 1995.

General Information: Public Access terminal is available. No police reports or probation records released. Turnaround time 1 week. Copy fee: $.50 per page. Certification fee: $6.00. Fee payee: Sutter County Superior Court. Personal checks accepted. Prepayment is required.

Tehama County

Superior Court PO Box 310, Red Bluff, CA 96080; 530-527-6441. Hours: 9AM-4PM (PST). *Civil, Small Claims, Eviction, Probate.*

Civil Records: Access: Mail, in person. Both court and visitors may perform in person searches. Search fee: $2.50 per name. Fee is $5.00 if years before 1991 are requested. Required to search: name, years to search. Civil cases indexed by defendant, plaintiff. Civil records on computer back to 1992, archived and index books from 1900s. **General Information:** No adoptions, juvenile, mental, probation or sealed records released. SASE required. Turnaround time same day. Copy fee: $.50 per page. Certification fee: $6.00. Fee payee: Tehama County Superior Court Clerk. Personal checks accepted. Prepayment is required.

Superior Court - Criminal Division 445 Pine St PO Box 1170, Red Bluff, CA 96080; 530-527-3563; Criminal phone: 530-527-7314; Fax: 530-527-0956. Hours: 8AM-5PM (PST). *Felony, Misdemeanor.*

Criminal Records: Access: Mail, in person. Both court and visitors may perform in person searches. Search fee: $5.00 per name. Required to search: name, years to search; also helpful: DOB. Criminal records on computer from 1991, index cards prior. Will only search back 7 years.

General Information: No probation reports released. SASE required. Turnaround time within 1 week. Copy fee: $.50 per page. Certification fee: $6.00. Fee payee: Superior Court. Personal checks accepted. Prepayment is required.

Corning Branch - Superior Court 720 Hoag St, Corning, CA 96021; 530-824-4601; Fax: 530-824-6457. Hours: 8AM-4PM (PST). *Misdemeanor, Civil Actions Under $25,000, Eviction, Small Claims.*

Civil Records: Access: Mail, in person. Search fee: $5.00 per name. Required to search: name, years to search. Civil cases indexed by defendant, plaintiff. Civil records on index cards. Will only search back 7 years.

Criminal Records: Access: Mail, in person. Both court and visitors may perform in person searches. Search fee: $5.00 per name. Required to search: name, years to search; also helpful: DOB. Criminal records on computer from 1990, index cards prior. Will only search back 7 years.

General Information: No probation reports released. SASE required. Turnaround time 1 week. Copy fee: $.50 per page. Certification fee: $6.00. Fee payee: Tehama Superior Court. Personal checks accepted. Prepayment is required.

Trinity County

Superior Court 101 Court St PO Box 1258, Weaverville, CA 96093; 530-623-1208; Fax: 530-623-3762. Hours: 9AM-4PM (PST). *Felony, Misdemeanor, Civil, Eviction, Small Claims, Probate.*

Civil Records: Access: Mail, in person. Both court and visitors may perform in person searches. Search fee:

$5.00 per name per year. Required to search: name, years to search. Civil cases indexed by defendant, plaintiff. Civil records on microfiche, archived and index files from 1900s.

Criminal Records: Access: Mail, in person. Both court and visitors may perform in person searches. Search fee: $5.00 per name per year. Required to search: name, years to search. Criminal records on microfiche, archived and index files from 1900s.

General Information: No adoptions, juvenile, medical, probation or sealed records released. SASE required. Turnaround time 1 week. Copy fee: $.50 per page. Certification fee: $6.00. Fee payee: Superior Court. Personal checks accepted. Prepayment is required.

Tulare County

Superior Court Courthouse, 221 S Mooney, Visalia, CA 93291; Civil phone: 559-733-6454; Criminal phone: 559-733-6830; Fax: 559-737-4547. Hours: 8AM-5PM (PST). *Felony, Civil, Eviction, Small Claims, Probate.*

www.tularesuperiorcourt.ca.gov

Note: This court has records from Exeter, Woodlake, Farmersville, Goshen and Three Rivers. Address criminal record requests to Room 124 and civil to Room 201.

Civil Records: Access: Mail, in person. Both court and visitors may perform in person searches. Search fee: $5.00 per name. Required to search: name, years to search. Civil cases indexed by defendant, plaintiff. Civil records on computer back to 2/1986; microfiche and index books from 1800s.

Criminal Records: Access: Mail, in person. Both court and visitors may perform in person searches. Search fee: $5.00 per name. Required to search: name, years to search, DOB or SSN. Criminal records on computer back to 2/1986; microfiche and index books from 1800s.

General Information: Public Access terminal is available. No adoptions, juvenile, mental, probation reports or sealed records released. SASE required. Turnaround time 1 week. Copy fee: $.50 per page. Certification fee: $6.00. Fee payee: Tulare County Superior Court. Personal checks accepted. Prepayment is required.

Dinuba Division - Superior Court 640 S Alta Dinuba, Dinuba, CA 93618; 559-591-5815. Hours: 8AM-4PM (PST). *Felony, Misdemeanor, Civil Actions Under $25,000, Eviction, Small Claims.*

Note: Includes Dinuba, Cutler, Orosi, Seville, Traver, London, Delf, Orange Cove.

Civil Records: Access: Mail, in person. Only the court performs in person searches; visitors may not. Search fee: $5.00 per name. Required to search: name, years to search. Civil cases indexed by defendant, plaintiff. Civil records on computer from 1993, index files from 1983. Records destroyed after 10 years.

Criminal Records: Access: Mail, in person. Only the court performs in person searches; visitors may not. Search fee: $5.00 per name. Required to search: name, years to search, DOB. Criminal records on computer from 1993, index files from 1983. Records destroyed after 10 years.

General Information: No probation reports released. SASE required. Turnaround time 2-3 days. Copy fee: $.50 per page. Certification fee: $6.00. Fee payee: Dinuba Superior Court. In-state checks accepted. Prepayment is required.

Porterville Division - Superior Court 87 E Morton Ave, Porterville, CA 93257; 559-782-4710; Fax: 559-782-4805. Hours: 8AM-4PM (PST). *Misdemeanor, Civil Actions Under $25,000, Eviction, Small Claims.*

Note: Includes Porterville, Springville, Camp Nelson, Johnsondale, Terra Bella, Ducor, Richgrove, Poplar, Lindsey, Strathmore and surrounding areas.

Civil Records: Access: Mail, in person. Both court and visitors may perform in person searches. Search fee: $5.00 per name. also is per case. Required to search: name, years to search. Civil cases indexed by defendant, plaintiff. Civil records on computer from February, 1994, index book prior. Records destroyed after 10 years.

Criminal Records: Access: Mail, in person. Both court and visitors may perform in person searches. Search fee: $5.00 per name. Also is per case. Required to search: name, years to search; also helpful: DOB, SSN. Criminal records on computer from February, 1994, index book prior. Records destroyed after 10 years.

General Information: Public Access terminal is available. No probation reports released. SASE required. Turnaround time 2 days. Copy fee: $.50 per page. Certification fee: $6.00. Fee payee: Porterville Superior Court. Personal checks accepted. Prepayment is required.

Tulare/Pixley Division - Superior Court 425 E Kern St (PO Box 1136), Tulare, CA 93275; 559-685-2556; Fax: 559-685-2663. Hours: 8AM-4PM (PST). *Misdemeanor, Civil Actions Under $25,000, Eviction, Small Claims.*

Note: Includes Tulare, Pixley, Tipton, Earlimart, Alpaugh, Allensworth, Woodville, Waukena and surrounding areas.

Civil Records: Access: Mail, fax, in person. Both court and visitors may perform in person searches. Search fee: $5.00 per name. Required to search: name, years to search. Civil cases indexed by defendant, plaintiff. Civil records in index books. Records destroyed after 10 years; on computer back to 1992.

Criminal Records: Access: Mail, fax, in person. Both court and visitors may perform in person searches. Search fee: $5.00 per name. Required to search: name, years to search, DOB; also helpful: address, SSN. Criminal records in index books. Records destroyed after 10 years; on computer back to 1992.

General Information: Public Access terminal is available. No probation reports released. SASE required. Turnaround time 2 days. Copy fee: $.50 per page. Certification fee: $6.00. Fee payee: Superior Court. Personal checks accepted. Prepayment is required.

Tuolumne County

Superior Court - Civil 41 W Yaney, Sonora, CA 95370; 209-533-5555; Fax: 209-533-5618. Hours: 8AM-5PM (PST). *Civil, Eviction, Small Claims, Probate.*

www.courtinfo.ca.gov/courts/trial/tuolumne

Civil Records: Access: Mail, in person. Both court and visitors may perform in person searches. Search fee: $5.00 per name. Fee is per record. Required to search: name, years to search. Civil cases indexed by defendant, plaintiff. Civil records on computer back to 1994, microfiche and archived from 1900s, index files from 1800s. **General Information:** Public Access terminal is available. No adoptions, juvenile, medical, probation or sealed records released. SASE required. Turnaround time 1 week. Copy fee: $.50 per page. Certification fee: $6.00. Fee payee: Superior Court. Personal checks accepted. Out of state checks not accepted. Prepayment is required.

Superior Court - Criminal 60 N Washington St, Sonora, CA 95370; 209-533-5671; Fax: 209-533-5581. Hours: 8AM-4PM (PST). *Felony, Misdemeanor, Traffic.*

www.courtinfo.ca.gov/courts/trial/tuolumne

Criminal Records: Access: Mail, in person. Both court and visitors may perform in person searches. Search fee: $5.00 per name. Required to search: name, years to search, DOB. Felony records on computer from 1993; misdemeanors from 1999; index files prior. Will only search back 7 years.

General Information: Public Access terminal is available. No sealed records released. Most records are public. SASE required. Turnaround time 1 week. Fax notes: Will only fax to public agencies. Copy fee: $.50 per page. Certification fee: $6.00. Fee payee: Tuolomne County Superior Court. Personal checks accepted. Prepayment is required.

Ventura County

Ventura Superior Court 800 S Victoria Ave PO Box 6489, Ventura, CA 93006-6489; Civil phone: 805-654-2609; Criminal phone: 805-654-2611; Fax: 805-650-4032. Hours: 8AM-5PM (PST). *Felony, Misdemeanor, Civil, Eviction, Small Claims, Probate.*

http://courts.countyofventura.org

Civil Records: Access: Phone, fax, mail, online, in person, email. Both court and visitors may perform in person searches. Search fee: $5.00 per name. Required to search: name, years to search. Civil cases indexed by defendant, plaintiff. Civil records on computer 5 years back, microfiche prior. Access to civil court records 10/93 to present is available free online at http://courts.countyofventura.org/case_inquir.htm. Search by defendant or plaintiff name, case number, or date.

Criminal Records: Access: Phone, fax, mail, online, in person, email. Both court and visitors may perform in person searches. Search fee: $5.00 per name. Required to search: name, years to search, DOB. Criminal records on computer back to 1989. Access to criminal court records is available free online at http://courts.countyofventura.org/criminalindex.htm. There are two indices to search: Music (older cases) or Vision (newer). Search by name & DOB, or code and citation number.

General Information: Public Access terminal is available. No adoptions, mental health, paternity actions, juvenile, medical, probation or sealed records released. SASE required. Turnaround time 5-10 days. Copy fee: $.50 per page. Certification fee: $6.00. Fee payee: Superior Court. Personal checks accepted. Credit cards accepted: Visa, AmEx. Additional fee charged. Prepayment is required.

East County Superior Court PO Box 1200, Simi Valley, CA 93062-1200; 805-582-8080. Hours: 8AM-5PM (PST). *Felony, Misdemeanor, Civil, Eviction, Small Claims, Probate.*

http://courts.countyofventura.org

Civil Records: Access: Phone, mail, online, in person. Both court and visitors may perform in person searches. Search fee: $5.00 per name. Fee is per court. Required to search: name, years to search. Access to civil court records 10/93 to present is available free online at http://courts.countyofventura.org/case_inquir.htm. Search by defendant or plaintiff name, case number, or date.

Criminal Records: Access: Phone, mail, in person, online. Both court and visitors may perform in person searches. Search fee: $5.00 per name. Fee is per court. Required to search: name, years to search, DOB. Same record keeping as civil. Access to criminal court records is available free online at http://courts.countyofventura.org/criminalindex.htm. There are two indices to search:

Music (older cases) or Vision (newer). Search by name & DOB, or code and citation number.

General Information: Public Access terminal is available. No adoptions, mental health, paternity actions, juvenile, medical, probation or sealed records released. SASE required. Turnaround time 5 days. Copy fee: $.50 per page. Certification fee: $6.00. Fee payee: Ventura County Superior Courts. Personal checks accepted. Credit cards accepted: Visa, MasterCard, Discover, AmEx. Additional fee charged. Prepayment is required.

Yolo County

Superior Court 725 Court St, Rm 308, Woodland, CA 95695; 530-666-8598; Civil phone: 530-666-8170; Criminal phone: 530-666-8050; Fax: 530-666-8576. Hours: 8AM-4PM (PST). *Felony, Misdemeanor, Civil, Eviction, Small Claims, Probate.*

www.yolocourts.com

Note: Address civil requests to Room 103 and criminal to Room 111. Small claims phone is 530-666-8060.

Civil Records: Access: Phone, mail, in person. Both court and visitors may perform in person searches. Search fee: $5.00 per name. Required to search: name, years to search. Civil cases indexed by defendant, plaintiff. Civil records on computer from 1995, microfiche, archived and index files from 1800s.

Criminal Records: Access: Phone, mail, in person. Both court and visitors may perform in person searches. Search fee: $5.00 per name. Required to search: name, years to search; also helpful: DOB. Criminal records on computer from 1995, microfiche, archived and index files from 1800s.

General Information: No adoptions, juvenile, medical, probation or sealed records released. SASE required. Turnaround time 2 weeks. Copy fee: $1.00 per page. Certification fee: $6.00. Fee payee: Yolo Superior Court. Personal checks accepted. Prepayment is required.

Yuba County

Superior Court 215 5th St, Marysville, CA 95901; 530-749-7600; Fax: 530-749-7351. Hours: 8:30AM-4:30PM (PST). *Felony, Misdemeanor, Civil, Small Claims, Probate.*

Civil Records: Access: Mail, in person. Both court and visitors may perform in person searches. Search fee: $5.00 per name. Required to search: name, years to search. Civil cases indexed by defendant, plaintiff. Civil records on computer from 1992, index books through 1962, archives and index files from 1854.

Criminal Records: Access: Mail, in person. Both court and visitors may perform in person searches. Search fee: $5.00 per name. Required to search: name, years to search. Criminal records on computer from 1992, index books through 1962, archives and index files from 1854.

General Information: Public Access terminal is available. No adoptions, paternity, juvenile, medical, probation or sealed records released. SASE required. Turnaround time 1-4 weeks. Copy fee: $1.00 per page. Certification fee: $6.00. Fee payee: Yuba County Superior Court. Personal checks accepted. Prepayment is required.

Marysville Civil Limited Superior Court 215 5th St, Marysville, CA 95901; 530-749-7600; Fax: 530-749-7354. Hours: 8:30AM-4:30PM (PST). *Civil Actions Under $25,000, Eviction, Small Claims.*

Civil Records: Access: Fax, mail, in person. Only the court performs in person searches; visitors may not. Search fee: $5.00 per name. Required to search: name, years to search, DOB. Civil cases indexed by defendant, plaintiff. Civil records on computer through 1992, index books prior. Records destroyed after 10 years. **General Information:** Public Access terminal is available. No labor commissioner judgment, juvenile, or judge's records released. SASE required. Turnaround time 2 days. Fax notes: $20.00 per document and $1.00 per page. Copy fee: $1.00 per page. Certification fee: $6.00. Fee payee: Yuba County Superior Court. Personal checks accepted. Prepayment is required.

California Recording Offices

ORGANIZATION   58 counties, 58 recording offices. The recording officer is County Recorder. Recordings are usually located in a Grantor/Grantee or General index. The entire state is in the Pacific Time Zone (PST).

REAL ESTATE RECORDS   Most counties do not perform real estate name searches. Copy fees and certification fees vary.

UCC RECORDS   Financing statements are filed at the state level, except for real estate related collateral, which are filed with the County Recorder. However, prior to 07/2001, consumer goods and farm collateral were also filed at the County Recorder and these older records can be searched there. All counties will perform UCC searches. Use search request form UCC-11. Search fees are usually $15.00 per debtor name. Copy costs vary.

TAX LIEN RECORDS   Federal and state tax liens on personal property of businesses are filed with the Secretary of State. Other federal and state tax liens are filed with the County Recorder. Some counties will perform separate tax lien searches. Fees vary for this type of search.

OTHER LIENS   Judgment (Note - Many judgments are also filed with the Secretary of State), child support, mechanics.

STATEWIDE ONLINE INFO: A number of counties offer aonline access to assessor and real estate information. The system in Los Angeles is a commercial subscription system.

Alameda County

County Recorder, 1225 Fallon Street, Courthouse, Room 100, Oakland, CA 94612. 510-272-6363; Fax 510-272-6382. http://www.co.alameda.ca.us
Will search UCC records. Tax liens not included in UCC search. Will not search real estate records. **Online Access:** Assessor. Access to the Property Value and Tax Information database is available free online at www.co.alameda.ca.us/aswpinq. **Other Phone Numbers:** Assessor 510-272-3755; Treasurer 510-272-6800.

Alpine County

County Recorder, P.O. Box 217, Markleeville, CA 96120. 530-694-2286; Fax 530-694-2491.
Will search UCC records. This agency will not do a tax lien search. Will not search real estate records. **Other Phone Numbers:** Assessor 530-694-2283; Treasurer 530-694-2286.

Amador County

County Recorder, 500 Argonaut Lane, Jackson, CA 95642. County Recorder, R/E and UCC Recording 209-223-6468; Fax 209-223-6204.
Will search UCC records. This agency will not do a tax lien search. Will not search real estate records. **Online Access:** Recordings, Fictitious Names, Birth, Death, Marriage. Online access to the county clerk database is available free at www.criis.com/amador/official.htm. **Other Phone Numbers:** Assessor 209-223-6351 x209; Treasurer 209-223-6364; Appraiser/Auditor 209-223-6351; Elections 209-223-6465; Vital Records 209-223-6468.

Butte County

County Recorder, 25 County Center Drive, Oroville, CA 95965-3375. County Recorder, R/E and UCC Recording 530-538-7691; Fax 530-538-7975. http://www.buttecounty.net
Will search UCC records. Will not search real estate records. **Online Access:** Real Estate, Fictitious Names, Marriage, Birth, Death, Recording. Online access to the County Recorder's database of official documents is free at http://clerk-recorder.buttecounty.net/election/index.html. Records go back to 1988. **Other Phone Numbers:** Assessor 530-538-7721; Treasurer 530-538-7576; Appraiser/ Auditor 530-538-7721; Elections 530-538-7761; Vital Records 530-538-7690.

Calaveras County

County Recorder, Government Center, 891 Mountain Ranch Rd, San Andreas, CA 95249. 209-754-6372.
Will search UCC records. This agency will not do a tax lien search. Will not search real estate records. **Online Access:** Contact Calaveras County Tech Services at 209-754-6366 for online information. **Other Phone Numbers:** Assessor 209-754-6356; Treasurer 209-754-6350; Appraiser/Auditor 209-754-6356; Elections 209-754-6376; Vital Records 209-754-6372.

Colusa County

County Recorder, 546 Jay Street, Colusa, CA 95932. 530-458-0500; Fax 530-458-0512. http://www.colusanet.com/colusaclerk
Will search UCC records. This agency will not do a tax lien search. Will search for a specific deed at $.50 per year. **Other Phone Numbers:** Assessor 530-458-0450; Treasurer 530-458-0440.

Contra Costa County

County Recorder, P.O. Box 350, Martinez, CA 94553. 925-646-2360; http://www.co.contra-costa.ca.us/depart/elect/Rindex.html
Will search UCC records. This agency will not do a tax lien search. Will not search real estate records. **Online Access:** Recordings, Fictitious Business Names, Marriage, Death, Birth. Recorder Office records back to 1996 are available free at www.criis.com/contracosta/srecord_current.shtml. County Birth records are at www.criis.com/contracosta/sbirth.htm. County Death records are at www.criis.com/contracosta/sdeath.htm. Fictitious Business names are at www.criis.com/contracosta/sfictitious.htm. Marriage records are at www.criis.com/contracosta/smarriage.htm. **Other Phone Numbers:** Assessor 925-313-7400.

Del Norte County

County Recorder, 981 H St #160, Crescent City, CA 95531. 707-464-7216.
Will search UCC records. Tax liens not included in UCC search. RE owner, mortgage, and property transfer searches available. **Other Phone Numbers:** Assessor 707-464-7200; Treasurer 707-464-7283.

El Dorado County

County Recorder, 360 Fair Lane, Placerville, CA 95667-4197. County Recorder, R/E and UCC Recording 530-621-5490; Fax 530-621-2147. http://www.co.el-dorado.ca.us/countyclerk/
Will search UCC records. UCC search includes tax liens if requested. Will not search real estate records. **Online Access:** Real Estate, Personal Property, Vital Statistics, Fictitious Names. Online access to the Recorder's index is available free on the Internet at http://main.co.el-dorado.ca.us/CGI/WWB012/WWM501/R. Records go back to 1949. Official records on the County Recorder database are available free on the Internet at http://main.co.el-dorado.ca.us/CGI/WWB012/WWM501/C. Search by date range and name or document number. County vital statistics - births, deaths, non-confidential marriages, and fictitious names - are available free on the Internet at http://main.co.el-dorado.ca.us/CGI/WWB012/WWM500/C. **Other Phone Numbers:** Assessor 530-621-5719; Treasurer 530-621-5800; Vital Records 530-621-5490.

Fresno County

County Recorder, P.O. Box 766, Fresno, CA 93712. 559-488-3471; Fax 559-488-6774. http://www.fresno.ca.gov/0420/recorders_web/index.htm
Husband and wife count as one search, if so indicated. Will search UCC records. Will not search real estate records. **Online Access:** Assessor, Birth, Death, Marriage, Fictitious Names. Recording office records on the county recorder database are available free at http://assessor.fresno.ca.gov/fresno/srecord.shtml. County Birth Records are at http://assessor.fresno.ca.gov/fresno/sbirth.htm. County death records are at http://assessor.fresno.ca.gov/fresno/sdeath.htm. Marriage records are at http://assessor.fresno.ca.gov/fresno/smarriage.htm. Search fictitious names at http://assessor.fresno.ca.gov/fresno/sfictitious.htm. **Other Phone Numbers:** Assessor 559-488-3514; Treasurer 559-488-3486.

Glenn County

County Recorder, 526 West Sycamore Street, Willows, CA 95988. County Recorder, R/E and UCC Recording 530-934-6412; Fax 530-934-6305.
Will search UCC records. Will not search real estate records. **Other Phone Numbers:** Assessor 530-934-6402; Treasurer 530-934-6410; Elections 530-934-6414; Vital Records 530-934-6412.

Humboldt County

County Recorder, 825 Fifth Street, Room 108, Eureka, CA 95501. 707-445-7593; Fax 707-445-7324.

Will search UCC records. This agency will not do a tax lien search. Will not search real estate records. **Other Phone Numbers:** Assessor 707-445-7276; Treasurer 707-445-7331.

Imperial County

County Recorder, 940 Main Street, Room 202, El Centro, CA 92243-2865. 760-339-4272.
Will search UCC records. Tax liens not included in UCC search. Will not search real estate records. **Other Phone Numbers:** Assessor 760-339-4244; Treasurer 760-339-6281.

Inyo County

County Recorder, P.O. Box F, Independence, CA 93526. County Recorder, R/E and UCC Recording 760-878-0222; Fax 760-878-1805.
Will search UCC records. This agency will not do a tax lien search. Will not search real estate records. **Online Access:** Recordings, Fictitious Names, Birth, Death, Marriage. Online access to the county clerk database is available free online at www.criis.com/inyo/official.htm. **Other Phone Numbers:** Assessor 760-878-0302; Treasurer 760-878-0333; Appraiser/Auditor 760-878-0302; Elections 760-878-0223; Vital Records 760-878-0410.

Kern County

County Recorder, 1655 Chester Avenue, Hall of Records, Bakersfield, CA 93301. County Recorder, R/E and UCC Recording 661-868-6400; Fax 661-868-6401.
http://www.co.kern.ca.us/recorder
Will search UCC records. Tax liens not included in UCC search. Mortgage searches available. **Online Access:** Assessor. Records on the County of Kern Online Assessor database are available free online at www.co.kern.ca.us/assessor/search.htm. Birth, Death, Marriage records may be purchased through vitalchek at www.vitalchek.com. **Other Phone Numbers:** Assessor 661-868-3485; Treasurer 661-868-3490; Appraiser/Auditor 661-868-3485; Elections 661-868-3590; Vital Records 661-868-6449.

Kings County

County Recorder, 1400 West Lacey Blvd., Hanford, CA 93230. 559-582-3211 x2475 R/E Recording: 559-582-3211 x2470 UCC Recording: 559-582-3211 x2470; Fax 559-582-6639. www.countyofkings.com
Will search UCC records. This agency will not do a tax lien search. Will not search real estate records. **Other Phone Numbers:** Assessor 559-582-3211 x2486; Treasurer 559-582-3211 x2477; Elections 559-582-3211 x2439; Vital Records 559-582-3211 x2470.

Lake County

County Recorder, 255 North Forbes, Room 223, Lakeport, CA 95453. County Recorder, R/E and UCC Recording 707-263-2293; Fax 707-263-3703.
Will search UCC records. This agency will not do a tax lien search. Will not search real estate records. **Other Phone Numbers:** Assessor 707-263-2302; Treasurer 707-263-2236; Elections 707-263-2372; Vital Records 707-263-2293.

Lassen County

County Recorder, 220 S. Lassen Street, Suite 5, Susanville, CA 96130. County Recorder, R/E and UCC Recording 530-251-8234; Fax 530-257-3480.
http://clerk.lassencounty.org
Will search UCC records. This agency will not do a tax lien search. Will not search real estate records. **Online Access:** Real Estate, Recordings. Online access to the county recorder database is available free at http://icris.lassencounty.org. Registration is required. Recorded documents go back to 7/1985. Vital statistics back to 7/12/1999. **Other Phone Numbers:** Assessor

530-251-8242; Treasurer 530-251-8220; Elections 530-251-8217; Vital Records 530-251-8234.

Los Angeles County

County Recorder, P.O. Box 53115, Los Angeles, CA 90053-0115. 562-462-2125.
Will search UCC records. Tax liens not included in UCC search. Will not search real estate records. **Online Access:** Assessor, Fictitious Business Names. The PDB Inquiry System is a dial-up service with a $100.00 monthly fee plus $1.00 per inquiry, also a $75 sign-up fee for 3-year dial-up. Usage fee is $6.50 per hour or 11 cents per minute. Contract must be approved. Send registration request letter, stating reason for request, to: Data Systems Supervisor II Tech Admin, LA County Assessor's, 500 W Temple St Rm 293, LA, CA 90012-2770. Further info: 213-974-3237 or visit http://assessor.co.la.ca.us/html/online.htm. Also, property and assessor information (no name searching) is available free online at http://assessor.co.la.ca.us/html/pais.cfm. Search the map or by address. Search for county Fictitious Names free online at http://regrec.co.la.ca.us/fbn/FBN.cfm. **Other Phone Numbers:** Assessor 562-974-3211; Treasurer 562-974-2101.

Madera County

County Recorder, 209 West Yosemite, Madera, CA 93637. County Recorder, R/E and UCC Recording 559-675-7724; Fax 559-675-7870.
Will search UCC records. Will not search real estate records. **Other Phone Numbers:** Assessor 559-675-7710; Treasurer 559-675-7713; Elections 559-675-7720; Vital Records 559-675-7724.

Marin County

County Recorder, 3501 Civic Center Dr., Room 234, San Rafael, CA 94903. 415-499-6092; Fax 415-499-7893.
Will search UCC records. UCC search includes tax liens if requested. Will not search real estate records. **Other Phone Numbers:** Assessor 415-499-7215; Treasurer 415-499-6145.

Mariposa County

County Recorder, P.O. Box 35, Mariposa, CA 95338. 209-966-5719.
Will search UCC records. This agency will not do a tax lien search. Will not search real estate records. **Other Phone Numbers:** Assessor 209-966-2332; Treasurer 209-966-2621.

Mendocino County

County Recorder, 501 Low Gap Rd. Room 1020, Ukiah, CA 95482. County Recorder, R/E and UCC Recording 707-463-4376; Fax 707-463-4257. www.@co.mendocino.ca.us
Will search UCC records. This agency will not do a tax lien search. RE record owner searches available. **Other Phone Numbers:** Assessor 707-463-4311; Treasurer 707-463-4388; Appraiser/Auditor 707-463-4311; Elections 707-463-4374; Vital Records 707-463-4371.

Merced County

County Recorder, 2222 M Street, Merced, CA 95340. 209-385-7627.
Will search UCC records. Tax liens not included in UCC search. Will not search real estate records. **Other Phone Numbers:** Assessor 209-385-7631; Treasurer 209-385-7307.

Modoc County

County Recorder, 204 Court Street, Alturas, CA 96101. County Recorder, R/E and UCC Recording 530-233-6205; Fax 530-233-6666.

Will search UCC records. This agency will not do a tax lien search. Will not search real estate records. **Online Access:** Recordings, Fictitious Names, Birth, Death, Marriage. Online access to the county clerk database is available free at www.criis.com/modoc/official.htm. **Other Phone Numbers:** Assessor 530-233-6217; Treasurer 530-233-6223; Appraiser/Auditor 530-233-6221; Elections 530-233-6201; Vital Records 530-233-6205.

Mono County

County Recorder, P.O. Box 237, Bridgeport, CA 93517. County Recorder, R/E and UCC Recording 760-932-5240; Fax 760-932-7145.
Will search UCC records. UCC search does not include tax liens RE record owner searches available. **Other Phone Numbers:** Assessor 760-932-5204; Treasurer 760-932-5265; Elections 760-932-5240; Vital Records 760-932-5240.

Monterey County

County Recorder, P.O. Box 29, Salinas, CA 93902. 831-755-5041; Fax 831-755-5064.
Will search UCC records. This agency will not do a tax lien search. Will not search real estate records. **Other Phone Numbers:** Assessor 831-755-5035; Treasurer 831-755-5015.

Napa County

County Recorder, P.O. Box 298, Napa, CA 94559-0298. 707-253-4246; Fax 707-259-8149.
Will search UCC records, generally $.50 per name per year. RE record owner searches available. **Other Phone Numbers:** Assessor 707-253-4466; Treasurer 707-253-4311; Elections 707-253-4321.

Nevada County

County Recorder, 950 Maidu Avenue, Nevada City, CA 95959. 530-265-1221; Fax 530-265-1497.
http://recorder.co.nevada.ca.us/
Will search UCC records. This agency will not do a tax lien search. Will not search real estate records. **Online Access:** Recording, Fictious Names, Birth, Death, Marriage. Online access to the county clerk database is available free at www.criis.com/nevada/official.htm. **Other Phone Numbers:** Assessor 530-265-1232; Treasurer 530-265-1285.

Orange County

County Recorder, P.O. Box 238, Santa Ana, CA 92702-0238. 714-834-2500; Fax 714-834-2675.
Will search UCC records. UCC search includes tax liens if requested. Will not search real estate records. **Online Access:** Grantor/Grantee. Orange County Grantor/Grantee records are available free online at http://cr.ocgov.com/grantorgrantee/index.asp. **Other Phone Numbers:** Assessor 714-834-2727; Treasurer 714-834-2682.

Placer County

County Recorder, 2954 Richardson Dr., Auburn, CA 95603. 530-886-5600; Fax 530-886-5687.
http://www.placer.ca.gov/clerk/clerk.htm
Will search UCC records. This agency will not do a tax lien search. Will not search real estate records. **Online Access:** Recordings, Fictitious Names, Birth, Death, Marriage. Recorder office records are available free at the web site. County Birth records are at www.criis.com/placer/sbirth.htm. County Death records are at www.criis.com/placer/sdeath.htm. County Marriage records are at www.criis.com/placer/smarriage.htm. County Fictitious Business Names are at www.criis.com/placer/sfictitious.htm. **Other Phone Numbers:** Assessor 530-889-4300.

Plumas County

County Recorder, 520 Main Street, Room 102, Quincy, CA 95971. 530-283-6218; Fax 530-283-6415.
Will search UCC records. UCC search includes tax liens if requested. Will not search real estate records. **Other Phone Numbers:** Assessor 530-283-6380; Treasurer 530-283-6260.

Riverside County

County Recorder, P.O. Box 751, Riverside, CA 92502-0751. 909-486-7000; Fax 909-486-7007. https://riverside.ca.ezgov.com/ezproperty
Will search UCC records. This agency will not do a tax lien search. Will not search real estate records. **Online Access:** Assessor, Property Records. Property tax information from the County Treasurer database is available free from EZproperty.com on the internet at https://riverside.ca.ezgov.com/ezproperty/review_searc h.jsp. **Other Phone Numbers:** Assessor 909-275-6250; Treasurer 909-275-3900.

Sacramento County

County Clerk & Recorder, P.O. Box 839, Sacramento, CA 95812-0839. County Clerk & Recorder, R/E and UCC Recording 916-874-6334; http://www. saccounty.net/index.html
Will search UCC records. This agency will not do a tax lien search. Will not search real estate records. **Online Access:** Recordings, Fictitious Names, Birth, Death, Marriage. Online access to the county clerk database is available free at www.criis.com/sacramento/ official.htm. **Other Phone Numbers:** Assessor 916-874-5231; Treasurer 916-874-6725; Appraiser/Auditor 916-874-5231; Elections 916-874-6451; Vital Records 916-874-6334.

San Benito County

County Recorder, 440 Fifth Street, Room 206, Hollister, CA 95023. 831-636-4046; Fax 831-636-2939.
Will search UCC records. This agency will not do a tax lien search. Will not search real estate records. **Other Phone Numbers:** Assessor 831-636-4030.

San Bernardino County

County Recorder, 222 W. Hospitality Ln., 1st Floor, San Bernardino, CA 92415-0022. 909-387-8306; Fax 909-386-8940. http://www.co.san-bernardino.ca.us
Will search UCC records. This agency will not do a tax lien search. Will not search real estate records. **Online Access:** Recorder, Assessor, Fictitious Names. Records on the County Assessor database are available free on the Internet at www.co.san-bernardino.ca.us/tax/ trsearch.asp. For automated call distribution, call 909-387-8306; for fictitious names information, call 909-386-8970. Fictitious business names are also available online at www.co.san-bernardino.ca.us/ACR/ RecSearch.htm. **Other Phone Numbers:** Assessor 909-386-8307.

San Diego County

County Recorder, P.O. Box 121750, San Diego, CA 92112. 6192388158; Fax 619-557-4155. http://www.co.san-diego.ca.us
Will search UCC records. Tax liens not included in UCC search. RE owner, mortgage, and property transfer searches available. **Online Access:** Assessor, Fictitious Names. Records on the County Assessor/Recorder/County Clerk Online Services site are available free online at www.co.san-diego.ca.us/cnty/cntydepts/general/assessor/online.html including fictitious business names, indexes, maps, property information. Grantee/grantor index search by name for individual record data is free at http://arcc.co.san-diego.ca.us/services/grantorgrantee. Bulk data downloads are also available but require pre-

payment or credit card payment. **Other Phone Numbers:** Assessor 619-238-8158; Treasurer 619-236-3121.

San Francisco County

County Recorder, City Hall, Room 190, 1 Dr. Carlton E. Goodlet Pl., San Francisco, CA 94102. 415-554-4176; Fax 415-554-4179.
Will search UCC records. This agency will not do a tax lien search. Will not search real estate records. **Online Access:** Property Tax, Recordings, Fictitious Names, Birth, Death, Marriage. Online access to the City Property Tax database is available free at https://cityservices.sfgov.org/serv/ttx_pt. No name searching; and address or Block/lot # is required. Also, online access recording, birth, death, marriage and fictitious name records on the county clerk database is available free at www.criis.com/sanfrancisco/ official.htm. **Other Phone Numbers:** Assessor 415-554-5507.

San Joaquin County

County Recorder, PO Box 1968, Stockton, CA 95201. 209-468-3939; Fax 209-468-8040.
Will search UCC records. This agency will not do a tax lien search. Will not search real estate records. **Other Phone Numbers:** Assessor 209-468-2630; Treasurer 209-468-2133.

San Luis Obispo County

County Recorder, 1144 Monterey St., Suite C, San Luis Obispo, CA 93408. County Recorder, R/E and UCC Recording 805-781-5080; www.slonet.org/~clerkrec
Will search UCC records. This agency will not do a tax lien search. Will not search real estate records. **Other Phone Numbers:** Assessor 805-781-5643; Treasurer 805-781-5842; Elections 805-781-5228; Vital Records 805-781-5080.

San Mateo County

County Recorder, 555 County Center, 1st Fl, Redwood City, CA 94063. County Recorder, R/E and UCC Recording 650-363-4713; Fax 650-363-4843. http://www.care.co.sanmateo.ca.us
Will search UCC records. This agency will not do a tax lien search. Will not search real estate records. **Online Access:** Property Tax, Fictitious Name. Records on the county Property Taxes database are available free online at www.co.sanmateo.ca.us/taxcollector/online/index.htm. Search by address, city or parcel ID#. Also, records on the Fictitious Business Name Center are available free online at www.care.co.sanmateo.ca.us/frames/ our_office/ceo_d.htm. **Other Phone Numbers:** Assessor 650-363-4500; Treasurer 650-363-4840; Appraiser/Auditor 650-363-4500; Elections 650-312-5222; Vital Records 650-363-4500.

Santa Barbara County

County Recorder, P.O. Box 159, Santa Barbara, CA 93102-0159. 805-568-2250; Fax 805-568-2266. http://www.sb-democracy.com
County also has a branch office in Santa Maria. Will search UCC records. Tax liens not included in UCC search. Will not search real estate records. **Online Access:** Assessor. Online access to assessor online property info system (OPIS) in available free at the web site with parcel #. Records go back 10 years. Database is free to view but only subscribers will be able to download. Full access requires registration. Contact Larry Herrera for an account. herrera@co.santa-barbara.ca.us. **Other Phone Numbers:** Assessor 805-586-2550; Treasurer 805-568-2490.

Santa Clara County

County Recorder, County Government Center, East Wing, 70 West Hedding St., San Jose, CA 95110. 408-299-2481; Fax 408-280-1768.
Will search UCC records. Tax liens not included in UCC search. Search by RE document type in index. **Other Phone Numbers:** Assessor 408-299-3227.

Santa Cruz County

County Recorder, 701 Ocean Street, Rm 230, Room 230, Santa Cruz, CA 95060. 831-454-2800; Fax 831-454-3169. http://www.co.santa-cruz.ca.us/rcd/
Will search UCC records. This agency will not do a tax lien search. Will not search real estate records. **Other Phone Numbers:** Assessor 831-454-2002; Elections 831-454-2060.

Shasta County

County Recorder, 1500 Court St., Room 102, Redding, CA 96001. 530-225-5671; Fax 530-225-5673. http://www.ci.redding.ca.us
Will search UCC records. This agency will not do a tax lien search. Will not search real estate records. **Online Access:** Assessor. Records on the City of Redding Parcel Search By Parcel Number Server are available free online. At the main site, look under "Online Services" to find "Property Lookup". **Other Phone Numbers:** Assessor 530-225-5501.

Sierra County

County Recorder, Drawer D, Downieville, CA 95936. County Recorder, R/E and UCC Recording 530-289-3295; Fax 530-289-3300.
Will search UCC records. This agency will not do a tax lien search. RE record owner searches available. **Other Phone Numbers:** Assessor 530-289-3283; Treasurer 530-289-3286; Appraiser/Auditor 530-289-3283; Elections 530-289-3295; Vital Records 530-289-3295.

Siskiyou County

County Recorder, P.O. Box 8, Yreka, CA 96097. 530-842-8065; Fax 530-842-8077.
Will search UCC records. This agency will not do a tax lien search. Will not search real estate records. **Other Phone Numbers:** Assessor 530-842-8036.

Solano County

County Recorder, Old Courthouse, 580 Texas St., 1st Floor, Fairfield, CA 94533. County Recorder, R/E and UCC Recording 707-421-6290; http://www. solanocounty.com
Will search UCC records. Tax liens not included in UCC search. Searches only performed back to 1974. RE owner, mortgage, and property transfer searches available. Searches only performed to 1974 and only if searcher is purchasing copies **Online Access:** Property Tax. Online access to the Treasurer/Tax Collector/county Clerk property database is available free at www.solanocounty.com/treasurer/propquery.asp. **Other Phone Numbers:** Assessor 707-421-6200; Appraiser/Auditor 707-421-6210; Vital Records 707-421-6294.

Sonoma County

County Recorder, P.O. Box 1709, Santa Rosa, CA 95406-1709. 707-565-2651; Fax 707-565-3905.
Will search UCC records. Tax liens not included in UCC search. Will not search real estate records. **Other Phone Numbers:** Assessor 707-565-1888.

Stanislaus County

County Recorder, P.O. Box 1008, Modesto, CA 95353. 209-525-5260; Fax 209-525-5207. http://criis.com/ stanislaus/official.htm

Will search UCC records. This agency will not do a tax lien search. Will not search real estate records. **Online Access:** Recordings, Fictitious Names, Birth, Death, Marriage. Recorder office records are available free at www.criis.com/stanislaus/srecord_current.shtml.
County Birth records are at www.criis.com/stanislaus/sbirth.htm. Death records are at www.criis.com/stanislaus/sdeath.htm. Marriage records are at www.criis.com/stanislaus/smarriage.htm. County Fictitious Business Name records are at www.criis.com/stanislaus/sfictitious.htm. **Other Phone Numbers:** Assessor 209-525-6361.

Sutter County

County Recorder, P.O. Box 1555, Yuba City, CA 95992-1555. County Recorder, R/E and UCC Recording 530-822-7134; Fax 530-822-7214.
Will search UCC records. This agency will not do a tax lien search. Will not search real estate records. **Other Phone Numbers:** Assessor 530-822-7160; Treasurer 530-822-7117; Appraiser/Auditor 530-822-7160; Elections 530-822-7120; Vital Records 530-822-7134.

Tehama County

County Recorder, P.O. Box 250, Red Bluff, CA 96080. County Recorder, R/E and UCC Recording 530-527-3350; Fax 530-527-1140.
Will search UCC records. This agency will not do a tax lien search. Will not search real estate records. **Other Phone Numbers:** Assessor 530-527-5931; Treasurer 530-527-4535; Appraiser/Auditor 530-527-5931; Elections 530-527-8190; Vital Records 530-527-3350.

Trinity County

County Recorder, P.O. Box 1258, Weaverville, CA 96093-1258. 530-623-1215; Fax 530-623-8398. http://www.trinitycounty.org/index.html
Will search UCC records. UCC search includes tax liens if requested. Will not search real estate records. **Online Access:** Vital Statistics, Fictitious Names. Online access to the Recorder's vital statisctics database is available free at http://halfile.trinitycounty.org. For user name, enter "vital"; leave password field empty. **Other Phone Numbers:** Assessor 530-623-1257; Treasurer 530-623-1251; Elections 530-623-1220; Vital Records 530-623-1215.

Tulare County

County Recorder, County Civic Center, Room 103, 221 S. Mooney Blvd., Visalia, CA 93291-4593. 559-733-6377.
Will search UCC records. This agency will not do a tax lien search. Will not search real estate records. **Other Phone Numbers:** Assessor 559-733-6361.

Tuolumne County

County Recorder, 2 South Green Street, County Administration Center, Sonora, CA 95370. 209-533-5531; Fax 209-533-6543.
Will search UCC records. This agency will not do a tax lien search. Will not search real estate records. **Other Phone Numbers:** Assessor 209-533-5535; Treasurer 209-533-5544; Elections 209-533-5570.

Ventura County

County Recorder, 800 South Victoria Avenue, Ventura, CA 93009. 805-654-2292; Fax 805-654-2392. http://www.ventura.org/assessor/index.html
Will search UCC records. This agency will not do a tax lien search. Will not search real estate records. **Online Access:** Recordings, Fictitious Names, Births, Deaths, Marriage. Online access to the county clerks database is available free at www.criis.com/ventura/official.htm. **Other Phone Numbers:** Assessor 805-654-2181; Treasurer 805-654-3735.

Yolo County

County Recorder, P.O. Box 1130, Woodland, CA 95776-1130. 530-666-8130; Fax 530-666-8109. http://www.yolocounty.org/org/Recorder
Will search UCC records. Tax liens not included in UCC search. Will not search real estate records. **Online Access:** Assessor, Birth, Death, Marriage, Fictitious Business Names. Online access to recordings on the county clerk database are available free at www.criis.com/yolo/srecord_current.shtml. County Birth records are at www.criis.com/yolo/sbirth.htm. County Death records are at www.criis.com/yolo/sdeath.htm. Marriage records are at www.criis.com/yolo/smarriage.htm. County Fictitious Business Name records are at www.criis.com/yolo/sfictitious.htm. **Other Phone Numbers:** Assessor 530-666-8135; Treasurer 530-666-8625.

Yuba County

County Recorder, 935 14th Street, Marysville, CA 95901. 530-741-6547; Fax 530-741-6285.
Will search UCC records. This agency will not do a tax lien search. Will not search real estate records. **Other Phone Numbers:** Assessor 530-741-6222.

California County Locator

You will usually be able to find the city name in the City/County Cross Reference below. In that case, it is a simple matter to determine the county from the cross reference. However, only the official US Postal Service city names are included in this index. There are an additional 40,000 place names that people use in their addresses. Therefore, we have also included a ZIP/City Cross Reference immediately following the City/County Cross Reference.

If you know the ZIP Code but the city name does not appear in the City/County Cross Reference index, look up the ZIP Code in the ZIP/City Cross Reference, find the city name, then look up the city name in the City/County Cross Reference. For example, you want to know the county for an address of Menands, NY 12204. There is no "Menands" in the City/County Cross Reference. The ZIP/City Cross Reference shows that ZIP Codes 12201-12288 are for the city of Albany. Looking back in the City/County Cross Reference, Albany is in Albany County.

City/County Cross Reference

ACAMPO San Joaquin
ACTON Los Angeles
ADELANTO San Bernardino
ADIN (96006) Modoc(67), Lassen(33)
AGOURA HILLS (91301) Los Angeles(69), Ventura(31)
AGOURA HILLS Los Angeles
AGUANGA Riverside
AHWAHNEE (93601) Madera(93), Mariposa(7)
ALAMEDA Alameda
ALAMO Contra Costa
ALBANY Alameda
ALBION Mendocino
ALDERPOINT Humboldt
ALHAMBRA Los Angeles
ALISO VIEJO Orange
ALLEGHANY Sierra
ALPAUGH Tulare
ALPINE San Diego
ALTA Placer
ALTA LOMA San Bernardino
ALTADENA Los Angeles
ALTAVILLE Calaveras
ALTURAS Modoc
ALVISO Santa Clara
AMADOR CITY Amador
AMBOY San Bernardino
ANAHEIM Orange
ANDERSON Shasta
ANGELS CAMP Calaveras
ANGELUS OAKS San Bernardino
ANGWIN Napa
ANNAPOLIS Sonoma
ANTELOPE Sacramento
ANTIOCH Contra Costa
ANZA Riverside
APPLE VALLEY San Bernardino
APPLEGATE Placer
APTOS Santa Cruz
ARBUCKLE (95912) Colusa(98), Yolo(2)
ARCADIA Los Angeles
ARCATA Humboldt
ARMONA Kings
ARNOLD Calaveras
AROMAS (95004) San Benito(66), Monterey(34)
ARROYO GRANDE San Luis Obispo
ARTESIA Los Angeles
ARTOIS Glenn
ARVIN Kern
ATASCADERO San Luis Obispo
ATHERTON San Mateo
ATWATER Merced
ATWOOD Orange
AUBERRY Fresno
AUBURN Placer
AVALON Los Angeles
AVENAL Kings
AVERY Calaveras
AVILA BEACH San Luis Obispo
AZUSA Los Angeles
BADGER Tulare

BAKER San Bernardino
BAKERSFIELD Kern
BALDWIN PARK Los Angeles
BALLICO Merced
BANGOR (95914) Butte(90), Yuba(10)
BANNING Riverside
BANTA San Joaquin
BARD Imperial
BARSTOW San Bernardino
BASS LAKE Madera
BAYSIDE Humboldt
BEALE AFB Yuba
BEAUMONT Riverside
BECKWOURTH Plumas
BELDEN Plumas
BELL Los Angeles
BELL GARDENS Los Angeles
BELLA VISTA Shasta
BELLFLOWER Los Angeles
BELMONT San Mateo
BELVEDERE TIBURON Marin
BEN LOMOND Santa Cruz
BENICIA Solano
BENTON Mono
BERKELEY (94707) Alameda(73), Contra Costa(27)
BERKELEY (94708) Alameda(84), Contra Costa(16)
BERKELEY Alameda
BERRY CREEK Butte
BETHEL ISLAND Contra Costa
BEVERLY HILLS Los Angeles
BIEBER Lassen
BIG BAR Trinity
BIG BEAR CITY San Bernardino
BIG BEAR LAKE San Bernardino
BIG BEND Shasta
BIG CREEK Fresno
BIG OAK FLAT Tuolumne
BIG PINE (93513) Inyo(96), Kern(4)
BIG SUR Monterey
BIGGS Butte
BIOLA Fresno
BIRDS LANDING Solano
BISHOP (93514) Inyo(93), Mono(7)
BISHOP Inyo
BLAIRSDEN-GRAEAGLE Plumas
BLOCKSBURG Humboldt
BLOOMINGTON San Bernardino
BLUE JAY San Bernardino
BLUE LAKE Humboldt
BLYTHE Riverside
BODEGA Sonoma
BODEGA BAY Sonoma
BODFISH Kern
BOLINAS Marin
BONITA San Diego
BONSALL San Diego
BOONVILLE Mendocino
BORON (93516) Kern(95), San Bernardino(5)
BORON Kern

BORREGO SPRINGS (92004) San Diego(95), Imperial(5)
BOULDER CREEK Santa Cruz
BOULEVARD San Diego
BOYES HOT SPRINGS Sonoma
BRADLEY (93426) Monterey(99), San Luis Obispo(1)
BRANDEIS Ventura
BRANSCOMB Mendocino
BRAWLEY Imperial
BREA Orange
BRENTWOOD Contra Costa
BRIDGEPORT Mono
BRIDGEVILLE (95526) Humboldt(89), Trinity(12)
BRISBANE San Mateo
BROOKDALE Santa Cruz
BROOKS Yolo
BROWNS VALLEY Yuba
BROWNSVILLE (95919) Yuba(88), Butte(12)
BRYN MAWR San Bernardino
BUELLTON Santa Barbara
BUENA PARK Orange
BURBANK Los Angeles
BURLINGAME San Mateo
BURNEY Shasta
BURNT RANCH Trinity
BURREL Fresno
BURSON Calaveras
BUTTE CITY Glenn
BUTTONWILLOW Kern
BYRON (94514) Contra Costa(91), Alameda(8), San Joaquin(1)
CABAZON Riverside
CADIZ San Bernardino
CALABASAS Los Angeles
CALEXICO Imperial
CALIENTE Kern
CALIFORNIA CITY Kern
CALIFORNIA HOT SPRINGS Tulare
CALIMESA Riverside
CALIPATRIA Imperial
CALISTOGA (94515) Napa(90), Sonoma(10)
CALLAHAN Siskiyou
CALPELLA Mendocino
CALPINE Sierra
CAMARILLO Ventura
CAMBRIA San Luis Obispo
CAMINO El Dorado
CAMP MEEKER Sonoma
CAMP NELSON Tulare
CAMP PENDLETON San Diego
CAMPBELL Santa Clara
CAMPO San Diego
CAMPO SECO Calaveras
CAMPTONVILLE (95922) Yuba(95), Sierra(5)
CANBY Modoc
CANOGA PARK (91304) Los Angeles(99), Ventura(1)
CANOGA PARK Los Angeles

CANTIL Kern
CANTUA CREEK Fresno
CANYON Contra Costa
CANYON COUNTRY Los Angeles
CANYONDAM Plumas
CAPAY Yolo
CAPISTRANO BEACH Orange
CAPITOLA Santa Cruz
CARDIFF BY THE SEA San Diego
CARLOTTA Humboldt
CARLSBAD San Diego
CARMEL Monterey
CARMEL VALLEY Monterey
CARMICHAEL Sacramento
CARNELIAN BAY Placer
CARPINTERIA Santa Barbara
CARSON Los Angeles
CARUTHERS Fresno
CASMALIA Santa Barbara
CASPAR Mendocino
CASSEL Shasta
CASTAIC Los Angeles
CASTELLA Shasta
CASTRO VALLEY Alameda
CASTROVILLE Monterey
CATHEDRAL CITY Riverside
CATHEYS VALLEY Mariposa
CAYUCOS San Luis Obispo
CAZADERO Sonoma
CEDAR GLEN San Bernardino
CEDAR RIDGE Nevada
CEDARPINES PARK San Bernardino
CEDARVILLE Modoc
CERES Stanislaus
CERRITOS Los Angeles
CHALLENGE (95925) Yuba(58), Butte(42)
CHATSWORTH (99999) Los Angeles(99), Ventura(1)
CHESTER Plumas
CHICAGO PARK Nevada
CHICO Butte
CHILCOOT Plumas
CHINESE CAMP Tuolumne
CHINO San Bernardino
CHINO HILLS San Bernardino
CHOLAME San Luis Obispo
CHOWCHILLA (93610) Madera(98), Merced(2)
CHUALAR Monterey
CHULA VISTA San Diego
CIMA San Bernardino
CITRUS HEIGHTS Sacramento
CITY OF INDUSTRY Los Angeles
CLAREMONT Los Angeles
CLARKSBURG Yolo
CLAYTON Contra Costa
CLEARLAKE Lake
CLEARLAKE OAKS Lake
CLEARLAKE PARK Lake
CLEMENTS San Joaquin
CLIO Plumas
CLIPPER MILLS Butte
CLOVERDALE Sonoma

CLOVIS Fresno
COACHELLA Riverside
COALINGA Fresno
COARSEGOLD Madera
COBB Lake
COLEVILLE Mono
COLFAX Placer
COLLEGE CITY Colusa
COLOMA El Dorado
COLTON (92324) San Bernardino(96),
   Riverside(4)
COLUMBIA Tuolumne
COLUSA Colusa
COMPTCHE Mendocino
COMPTON Los Angeles
CONCORD Contra Costa
COOL El Dorado
COPPEROPOLIS Calaveras
CORCORAN (93212) Tulare(99), Kings(2)
CORNING Tehama
CORONA Riverside
CORONA DEL MAR Orange
CORONADO San Diego
CORTE MADERA Marin
COSTA MESA Orange
COTATI Sonoma
COTTONWOOD (96022) Tehama(51),
   Shasta(49)
COULTERVILLE (95311) Mariposa(94),
   Tuolumne(7)
COURTLAND Sacramento
COVELO Mendocino
COVINA Los Angeles
COYOTE Santa Clara
CRESCENT CITY Del Norte
CRESCENT MILLS Plumas
CRESSEY Merced
CREST PARK San Bernardino
CRESTLINE San Bernardino
CRESTON San Luis Obispo
CROCKER NAT BANK San Francisco
CROCKETT Contra Costa
CROWS LANDING Stanislaus
CULVER CITY Los Angeles
CUPERTINO Santa Clara
CUTLER Tulare
CUTTEN Humboldt
CUYAMA Santa Barbara
CYPRESS Orange
DAGGETT San Bernardino
DALY CITY San Mateo
DANA POINT Orange
DANVILLE Contra Costa
DARDANELLE Tuolumne
DARWIN Inyo
DAVENPORT Santa Cruz
DAVIS Yolo
DAVIS CREEK Modoc
DEATH VALLEY Inyo
DEER PARK Napa
DEL MAR San Diego
DEL REY Fresno
DELANO Kern
DELHI Merced
DENAIR Stanislaus
DESCANSO San Diego
DESERT CENTER Riverside
DESERT HOT SPRINGS Riverside
DI GIORGIO Kern
DIABLO Contra Costa
DIAMOND BAR Los Angeles
DIAMOND SPRINGS El Dorado
DILLON BEACH Marin
DINUBA (93618) Tulare(99), Fresno(1)
DIXON Solano
DOBBINS Yuba
DORRIS Siskiyou
DOS PALOS (93620) Merced(88),
   Fresno(12)
DOS RIOS Mendocino
DOUGLAS CITY Trinity
DOUGLAS FLAT Calaveras

DOWNEY Los Angeles
DOWNIEVILLE Sierra
DOYLE Lassen
DRYTOWN Amador
DUARTE Los Angeles
DUBLIN Alameda
DUCOR Tulare
DULZURA San Diego
DUNCANS MILLS Sonoma
DUNLAP Fresno
DUNNIGAN Yolo
DUNSMUIR (96025) Siskiyou(94),
   Shasta(6)
DURHAM Butte
DUTCH FLAT Placer
EAGLEVILLE Modoc
EARLIMART Tulare
EARP San Bernardino
EAST IRVINE Orange
ECHO LAKE El Dorado
EDISON Kern
EDWARDS Kern
EL CAJON San Diego
EL CENTRO Imperial
EL CERRITO Contra Costa
EL DORADO El Dorado
EL DORADO HILLS El Dorado
EL GRANADA San Mateo
EL MACERO Yolo
EL MONTE Los Angeles
EL NIDO Merced
EL PORTAL Mariposa
EL SEGUNDO Los Angeles
EL SOBRANTE Contra Costa
EL VERANO Sonoma
ELDRIDGE Sonoma
ELK Mendocino
ELK CREEK Glenn
ELK GROVE Sacramento
ELMIRA Solano
ELVERTA Sacramento
EMERYVILLE Alameda
EMIGRANT GAP Placer
EMPIRE Stanislaus
ENCINITAS San Diego
ENCINO Los Angeles
ESCALON San Joaquin
ESCONDIDO San Diego
ESPARTO Yolo
ESSEX San Bernardino
ETNA Siskiyou
EUREKA Humboldt
EXETER Tulare
FAIR OAKS Sacramento
FAIRFAX Marin
FAIRFIELD Solano
FALL RIVER MILLS Shasta
FALLBROOK San Diego
FARMERSVILLE Tulare
FARMINGTON (95230) Stanislaus(40),
   San Joaquin(35), Calaveras(22),
   Tuolumne(3)
FAWNSKIN San Bernardino
FEATHER FALLS Butte
FELLOWS Kern
FELTON Santa Cruz
FERNDALE Humboldt
FIDDLETOWN (95629) El Dorado(72),
   Amador(28)
FIELDS LANDING Humboldt
FILLMORE Ventura
FINLEY Lake
FIREBAUGH (93622) Madera(88),
   Fresno(11), Merced(1)
FISH CAMP (93623) Mariposa(80),
   Madera(20)
FIVE POINTS Fresno
FLORISTON Nevada
FLOURNOY Tehama
FOLSOM Sacramento
FONTANA San Bernardino
FOOTHILL RANCH Orange

FORBESTOWN (95941) Butte(83),
   Yuba(17)
FOREST FALLS San Bernardino
FOREST KNOLLS Marin
FOREST RANCH Butte
FORESTHILL Placer
FORESTVILLE Sonoma
FORKS OF SALMON Siskiyou
FORT BIDWELL Modoc
FORT BRAGG Mendocino
FORT DICK Del Norte
FORT IRWIN San Bernardino
FORT JONES Siskiyou
FORTUNA Humboldt
FOUNTAIN VALLEY Orange
FOWLER Fresno
FPO
FRAZIER PARK Kern
FREEDOM Santa Cruz
FREMONT Alameda
FRENCH CAMP San Joaquin
FRENCH GULCH Shasta
FRESNO Fresno
FRIANT (93626) Fresno(62), Madera(38)
FT ORD Monterey
FULLERTON Orange
FULTON Sonoma
GALT (95632) Sacramento(96), San
   Joaquin(4)
GARBERVILLE Humboldt
GARDEN GROVE Orange
GARDEN VALLEY El Dorado
GARDENA Los Angeles
GASQUET (95543) Del Norte(97), Trinity(3)
GAZELLE Siskiyou
GEORGETOWN El Dorado
GERBER Tehama
GEYSERVILLE Sonoma
GILROY Santa Clara
GLEN ELLEN Sonoma
GLENCOE Calaveras
GLENDALE Los Angeles
GLENDORA Los Angeles
GLENHAVEN Lake
GLENN Glenn
GLENNVILLE Kern
GOLD RUN Placer
GOLETA Santa Barbara
GONZALES Monterey
GOODYEARS BAR Sierra
GOSHEN Tulare
GRANADA HILLS Los Angeles
GRAND TERRACE San Bernardino
GRANITE BAY Placer
GRASS VALLEY Nevada
GRATON Sonoma
GREEN VALLEY LAKE San Bernardino
GREENBRAE Marin
GREENFIELD Monterey
GREENVIEW Siskiyou
GREENVILLE Plumas
GREENWOOD El Dorado
GRENADA Siskiyou
GRIDLEY Butte
GRIMES Colusa
GRIZZLY FLATS El Dorado
GROVELAND (95321) Tuolumne(99),
   Mariposa(1)
GROVER BEACH San Luis Obispo
GUADALUPE Santa Barbara
GUALALA (95445) Mendocino(99), Lake(1)
GUASTI San Bernardino
GUATAY San Diego
GUERNEVILLE Sonoma
GUINDA Yolo
GUSTINE Merced
HACIENDA HEIGHTS Los Angeles
HALF MOON BAY San Mateo
HAMILTON CITY Glenn
HANFORD Kings
HAPPY CAMP Siskiyou
HARBOR CITY Los Angeles

HARMONY San Luis Obispo
HAT CREEK Shasta
HATHAWAY PINES Calaveras
HAWAIIAN GARDENS Los Angeles
HAWTHORNE Los Angeles
HAYFORK Trinity
HAYWARD Alameda
HEALDSBURG Sonoma
HEBER Imperial
HELENDALE San Bernardino
HELM Fresno
HEMET Riverside
HERALD Sacramento
HERCULES Contra Costa
HERLONG Lassen
HERMOSA BEACH Los Angeles
HESPERIA San Bernardino
HICKMAN Stanislaus
HIGHLAND San Bernardino
HILMAR Merced
HINKLEY San Bernardino
HOLLISTER San Benito
HOLT San Joaquin
HOLTVILLE Imperial
HOLY CITY Santa Clara
HOMELAND Riverside
HOMEWOOD (96141) Placer(92), Yolo(8)
HONEYDEW Humboldt
HOOD Sacramento
HOOPA Humboldt
HOPLAND Mendocino
HORNBROOK Siskiyou
HORNITOS Mariposa
HORSE CREEK Siskiyou
HUGHSON Stanislaus
HUME Fresno
HUNTINGTON BEACH Orange
HUNTINGTON LAKE Fresno
HUNTINGTON PARK Los Angeles
HURON Fresno
HYAMPOM Trinity
HYDESVILLE Humboldt
IDYLLWILD Riverside
IGO Shasta
IMPERIAL Imperial
IMPERIAL BEACH San Diego
INDEPENDENCE Inyo
INDIAN WELLS Riverside
INDIO Riverside
INGLEWOOD Los Angeles
INVERNESS Marin
INYOKERN (93527) Kern(94), Inyo(3),
   Tulare(3)
IONE Amador
IRVINE Orange
ISLETON Sacramento
IVANHOE Tulare
JACKSON Amador
JACUMBA San Diego
JAMESTOWN Tuolumne
JAMUL San Diego
JANESVILLE Lassen
JENNER Sonoma
JOHANNESBURG Kern
JOLON Monterey
JOSHUA TREE San Bernardino
JULIAN San Diego
JUNCTION CITY Trinity
JUNE LAKE Mono
KAWEAH Tulare
KEELER Inyo
KEENE Kern
KELSEYVILLE Lake
KENTFIELD Marin
KENWOOD Sonoma
KERMAN Fresno
KERNVILLE (93238) Kern(91), Tulare(9)
KETTLEMAN CITY Kings
KEYES Stanislaus
KING CITY Monterey
KINGS BEACH Placer
KINGS CANYON NATIONAL PK Tulare

KINGSBURG (93631) Fresno(83), Tulare(12), Kings(5)
KIRKWOOD Alpine
KIT CARSON Amador
KLAMATH Del Norte
KLAMATH RIVER Siskiyou
KNEELAND Humboldt
KNIGHTS LANDING (95645) Sutter(85), Yolo(15)
KNIGHTSEN Contra Costa
KORBEL Humboldt
KYBURZ El Dorado
LA CANADA FLINTRIDGE Los Angeles
LA COUNTY TAX COLLECTOR Los Angeles
LA CRESCENTA Los Angeles
LA GRANGE (95329) Tuolumne(57), Mariposa(36), Stanislaus(8)
LA HABRA (90631) Orange(87), Los Angeles(13)
LA HABRA Orange
LA HONDA San Mateo
LA JOLLA San Diego
LA MESA San Diego
LA MIRADA Los Angeles
LA PALMA Orange
LA PUENTE Los Angeles
LA QUINTA Riverside
LA VERNE Los Angeles
LAFAYETTE Contra Costa
LAGUNA BEACH Orange
LAGUNA HILLS Orange
LAGUNA NIGUEL Orange
LAGUNITAS Marin
LAKE ARROWHEAD San Bernardino
LAKE CITY Modoc
LAKE ELSINORE Riverside
LAKE FOREST Orange
LAKE HUGHES Los Angeles
LAKE ISABELLA Kern
LAKEHEAD Shasta
LAKEPORT Lake
LAKESHORE Fresno
LAKESIDE San Diego
LAKEVIEW Riverside
LAKEWOOD Los Angeles
LAMONT Kern
LANCASTER Los Angeles
LANDERS San Bernardino
LARKSPUR Marin
LATHROP San Joaquin
LATON (93242) Fresno(88), Kings(12)
LAWNDALE Los Angeles
LAYTONVILLE Mendocino
LE GRAND Merced
LEBEC (93243) Kern(82), Los Angeles(18)
LEE VINING Mono
LEGGETT Mendocino
LEMON COVE Tulare
LEMON GROVE San Diego
LEMOORE Kings
LEWISTON Trinity
LIKELY Modoc
LINCOLN Placer
LINCOLN ACRES San Diego
LINDEN San Joaquin
LINDSAY Tulare
LITCHFIELD Lassen
LITTLE LAKE Inyo
LITTLERIVER Mendocino
LITTLEROCK Los Angeles
LIVE OAK Sutter
LIVERMORE (94550) Alameda(98), Contra Costa(2)
LIVERMORE Alameda
LIVINGSTON Merced
LLANO Los Angeles
LOCKEFORD San Joaquin
LOCKWOOD Monterey
LODI San Joaquin
LOLETA Humboldt
LOMA LINDA San Bernardino

LOMA MAR San Mateo
LOMITA Los Angeles
LOMPOC Santa Barbara
LONE PINE Inyo
LONG BARN Tuolumne
LONG BEACH Los Angeles
LOOKOUT Modoc
LOOMIS Placer
LOS ALAMITOS Orange
LOS ALAMOS Santa Barbara
LOS ALTOS Santa Clara
LOS ANGELES Los Angeles
LOS BANOS Merced
LOS GATOS (95033) Santa Cruz(65), Santa Clara(35)
LOS GATOS Santa Clara
LOS MOLINOS Tehama
LOS OLIVOS Santa Barbara
LOS OSOS San Luis Obispo
LOST HILLS Kern
LOTUS El Dorado
LOWER LAKE Lake
LOYALTON Sierra
LUCERNE Lake
LUCERNE VALLEY San Bernardino
LUDLOW San Bernardino
LYNWOOD Los Angeles
LYTLE CREEK San Bernardino
MACDOEL Siskiyou
MAD RIVER Trinity
MADELINE Lassen
MADERA Madera
MADISON Yolo
MAGALIA Butte
MALIBU (90265) Los Angeles(95), Ventura(5)
MALIBU Los Angeles
MAMMOTH LAKES Mono
MANCHESTER Mendocino
MANHATTAN BEACH Los Angeles
MANTECA San Joaquin
MANTON (96059) Tehama(69), Shasta(31)
MARCH AIR FORCE BASE Riverside
MARICOPA (93252) Kern(62), Santa Barbara(21), Ventura(13), San Luis Obispo(4)
MARINA Monterey
MARINA DEL REY Los Angeles
MARIPOSA Mariposa
MARKLEEVILLE Alpine
MARSHALL Marin
MARTELL Amador
MARTINEZ Contra Costa
MARYSVILLE Yuba
MATHER Sacramento
MAXWELL Colusa
MAYWOOD Los Angeles
MC FARLAND Kern
MC KITTRICK Kern
MCARTHUR (96056) Lassen(47), Shasta(35), Modoc(18)
MCARTHUR Lassen
MCCLELLAN AFB Sacramento
MCCLOUD Siskiyou
MCKINLEYVILLE Humboldt
MEADOW VALLEY Plumas
MEADOW VISTA Placer
MECCA Riverside
MENDOCINO Mendocino
MENDOTA Fresno
MENIFEE Riverside
MENLO PARK San Mateo
MENTONE San Bernardino
MERCED Merced
MERIDIAN Sutter
MI WUK VILLAGE Tuolumne
MIDDLETOWN Lake
MIDPINES Mariposa
MIDWAY CITY Orange
MILFORD Lassen
MILL CREEK Tehama
MILL VALLEY Marin

MILLBRAE San Mateo
MILLVILLE Shasta
MILPITAS Santa Clara
MINERAL Tehama
MIRA LOMA Riverside
MIRAMONTE (93641) Fresno(76), Tulare(25)
MIRANDA Humboldt
MISSION HILLS Los Angeles
MISSION VIEJO Orange
MOBIL OIL CREDIT CORPORATION Contra Costa
MOCCASIN Tuolumne
MODESTO Stanislaus
MOJAVE Kern
MOKELUMNE HILL Calaveras
MONO HOT SPRINGS Fresno
MONROVIA Los Angeles
MONTAGUE Siskiyou
MONTARA San Mateo
MONTCLAIR San Bernardino
MONTE RIO Sonoma
MONTEBELLO Los Angeles
MONTEREY Monterey
MONTEREY PARK Los Angeles
MONTGOMERY CREEK Shasta
MONTGOMERY WARD Contra Costa
MONTROSE Los Angeles
MOORPARK Ventura
MORAGA Contra Costa
MORENO VALLEY Riverside
MORGAN HILL Santa Clara
MORONGO VALLEY San Bernardino
MORRO BAY San Luis Obispo
MOSS BEACH San Mateo
MOSS LANDING Monterey
MOUNT AUKUM El Dorado
MOUNT HAMILTON Santa Clara
MOUNT HERMON Santa Cruz
MOUNT LAGUNA San Diego
MOUNT SHASTA Siskiyou
MOUNT WILSON Los Angeles
MOUNTAIN CENTER Riverside
MOUNTAIN PASS San Bernardino
MOUNTAIN RANCH Calaveras
MOUNTAIN VIEW Santa Clara
MT BALDY Los Angeles
MURPHYS Calaveras
MURRIETA Riverside
MYERS FLAT Humboldt
NAPA Napa
NATIONAL CITY San Diego
NAVARRO Mendocino
NEEDLES San Bernardino
NELSON Butte
NESTOR San Diego
NEVADA CITY Nevada
NEW ALMADEN Santa Clara
NEW CUYAMA Santa Barbara
NEWARK Alameda
NEWBERRY SPRINGS San Bernardino
NEWBURY PARK Ventura
NEWCASTLE Placer
NEWHALL Los Angeles
NEWMAN Stanislaus
NEWPORT BEACH Orange
NEWPORT COAST Orange
NICASIO Marin
NICE Lake
NICOLAUS Sutter
NILAND Imperial
NIPOMO San Luis Obispo
NIPTON San Bernardino
NORCO Riverside
NORDEN Nevada
NORTH FORK Madera
NORTH HIGHLANDS Sacramento
NORTH HILLS Los Angeles
NORTH HOLLYWOOD Los Angeles
NORTH PALM SPRINGS Riverside
NORTH SAN JUAN (95960) Nevada(54), Sierra(39), Yuba(7)

NORTHRIDGE Los Angeles
NORWALK Los Angeles
NOVATO Marin
NUBIEBER Lassen
NUEVO Riverside
O NEALS Madera
OAK RUN Shasta
OAK VIEW Ventura
OAKDALE Stanislaus
OAKHURST Madera
OAKLAND Alameda
OAKLEY Contra Costa
OAKVILLE Napa
OBRIEN Shasta
OCCIDENTAL Sonoma
OCEANO San Luis Obispo
OCEANSIDE San Diego
OCOTILLO Imperial
OJAI Ventura
OLANCHA Inyo
OLD STATION Shasta
OLEMA Marin
OLIVEHURST Yuba
OLYMPIC VALLEY Placer
ONTARIO San Bernardino
ONYX Kern
ORANGE Orange
ORANGE COVE (93646) Fresno(91), Tulare(9)
ORANGEVALE Sacramento
OREGON HOUSE Yuba
ORICK Humboldt
ORINDA Contra Costa
ORLAND Glenn
ORLEANS Humboldt
ORO GRANDE San Bernardino
OROSI Tulare
OROVILLE Butte
OXNARD Ventura
PACIFIC GROVE Monterey
PACIFIC PALISADES Los Angeles
PACIFICA San Mateo
PACOIMA Los Angeles
PAICINES San Benito
PALA San Diego
PALERMO Butte
PALM DESERT Riverside
PALM SPRINGS Riverside
PALMDALE Los Angeles
PALO ALTO (94303) Santa Clara(54), San Mateo(46)
PALO ALTO San Mateo
PALO ALTO Santa Clara
PALO CEDRO Shasta
PALO VERDE Imperial
PALOMAR MOUNTAIN San Diego
PALOS VERDES PENINSULA Los Angeles
PANORAMA CITY Los Angeles
PARADISE Butte
PARAMOUNT Los Angeles
PARKER DAM San Bernardino
PARLIER Fresno
PASADENA Los Angeles
PASKENTA Tehama
PASO ROBLES San Luis Obispo
PATTERSON Stanislaus
PATTON San Bernardino
PAUMA VALLEY San Diego
PAYNES CREEK Tehama
PEARBLOSSOM Los Angeles
PEBBLE BEACH Monterey
PENN VALLEY Nevada
PENNGROVE Sonoma
PENRYN Placer
PERRIS Riverside
PESCADERO San Mateo
PETALUMA Sonoma
PETROLIA Humboldt
PHELAN San Bernardino
PHILLIPSVILLE Humboldt
PHILO Mendocino

PICO RIVERA Los Angeles
PIEDMONT Alameda
PIEDRA Fresno
PIERCY Mendocino
PILOT HILL El Dorado
PINE GROVE Amador
PINE VALLEY San Diego
PINECREST Tuolumne
PINOLE Contra Costa
PINON HILLS San Bernardino
PIONEER Amador
PIONEERTOWN San Bernardino
PIRU Ventura
PISMO BEACH San Luis Obispo
PITTSBURG Contra Costa
PIXLEY Tulare
PLACENTIA Orange
PLACERVILLE El Dorado
PLANADA Merced
PLATINA (96076) Shasta(50), Trinity(29),
   Tehama(21)
PLAYA DEL REY Los Angeles
PLEASANT GROVE (95668) Sutter(75),
   Placer(25)
PLEASANT HILL Contra Costa
PLEASANTON Alameda
PLYMOUTH Amador
POINT ARENA Mendocino
POINT MUGU NAWC Ventura
POINT REYES STATION Marin
POLLOCK PINES El Dorado
POMONA (91766) Los Angeles(95), San
   Bernardino(5)
POMONA Los Angeles
POPE VALLEY Napa
PORT COSTA Contra Costa
PORT HUENEME Ventura
PORT HUENEME CBC BASE Ventura
PORTERVILLE Tulare
PORTOLA Plumas
PORTOLA VALLEY San Mateo
POSEY Tulare
POTRERO San Diego
POTTER VALLEY Mendocino
POWAY San Diego
PRATHER Fresno
PRINCETON (95970) Glenn(77),
   Colusa(23)
PROBERTA Tehama
QUINCY Plumas
RACKERBY Yuba
RAIL ROAD FLAT Calaveras
RAISIN Fresno
RAMONA San Diego
RANCHITA San Diego
RANCHO CORDOVA Sacramento
RANCHO CUCAMONGA San Bernardino
RANCHO MIRAGE Riverside
RANCHO PALOS VERDES Los Angeles
RANCHO SANTA FE San Diego
RANCHO SANTA MARGARITA Orange
RANDSBURG Kern
RAVENDALE Lassen
RAYMOND (93653) Madera(90),
   Mariposa(10)
RED BLUFF Tehama
RED MOUNTAIN Kern
REDCREST Humboldt
REDDING Shasta
REDLANDS (92373) San Bernardino(97),
   Riverside(3)
REDLANDS San Bernardino
REDONDO BEACH Los Angeles
REDWAY Humboldt
REDWOOD CITY San Mateo
REDWOOD ESTATES Santa Clara
REDWOOD VALLEY Mendocino
REEDLEY (93654) Fresno(98), Tulare(2)
REPRESA Sacramento
RESCUE El Dorado
RESEDA Los Angeles
RIALTO San Bernardino

RICHGROVE Tulare
RICHMOND Contra Costa
RICHVALE Butte
RIDGECREST (93555) Kern(98), San
   Bernardino(2)
RIDGECREST Kern
RIMFOREST San Bernardino
RIO DELL Humboldt
RIO LINDA Sacramento
RIO NIDO Sonoma
RIO OSO Sutter
RIO VISTA (94571) Solano(96),
   Sacramento(4)
RIPLEY (92272) Riverside(98), San
   Diego(2)
RIPON San Joaquin
RIVER PINES Amador
RIVERBANK Stanislaus
RIVERDALE (93656) Fresno(88), Kings(12)
RIVERSIDE Riverside
ROBBINS Sutter
ROCKLIN Placer
RODEO Contra Costa
ROHNERT PARK Sonoma
ROSAMOND (93560) Kern(98), Los
   Angeles(2)
ROSEMEAD Los Angeles
ROSEVILLE Placer
ROSS Marin
ROUGH AND READY Nevada
ROUND MOUNTAIN Shasta
ROWLAND HEIGHTS Los Angeles
RUMSEY (95679) Yolo(67),
   Sacramento(33)
RUNNING SPRINGS San Bernardino
RUTHERFORD Napa
RYDE Sacramento
SACRAMENTO Sacramento
SAINT HELENA Napa
SALIDA Stanislaus
SALINAS Monterey
SALTON CITY Imperial
SALYER Trinity
SAMOA Humboldt
SAN ANDREAS Calaveras
SAN ANSELMO Marin
SAN ARDO Monterey
SAN BERNARDINO San Bernardino
SAN BRUNO San Mateo
SAN CARLOS San Mateo
SAN CLEMENTE Orange
SAN DIEGO San Diego
SAN DIMAS Los Angeles
SAN FERNANDO Los Angeles
SAN FRANCISCO San Francisco
SAN FRANCISCO San Mateo
SAN GABRIEL Los Angeles
SAN GERONIMO Marin
SAN GREGORIO San Mateo
SAN JACINTO Riverside
SAN JOAQUIN Fresno
SAN JOSE Santa Clara
SAN JUAN BAUTISTA San Benito
SAN JUAN CAPISTRANO Orange
SAN LEANDRO Alameda
SAN LORENZO Alameda
SAN LUCAS Monterey
SAN LUIS OBISPO San Luis Obispo
SAN LUIS REY San Diego
SAN MARCOS San Diego
SAN MARINO Los Angeles
SAN MARTIN Santa Clara
SAN MATEO San Mateo
SAN MIGUEL (93451) San Luis
   Obispo(56), Monterey(44)
SAN PABLO Contra Costa
SAN PEDRO Los Angeles
SAN QUENTIN Marin
SAN RAFAEL Marin
SAN RAMON Contra Costa
SAN SIMEON San Luis Obispo
SAN YSIDRO San Diego

SANGER Fresno
SANTA ANA Orange
SANTA BARBARA Santa Barbara
SANTA CLARA Santa Clara
SANTA CLARITA Los Angeles
SANTA CRUZ Santa Cruz
SANTA FE SPRINGS Los Angeles
SANTA MARGARITA San Luis Obispo
SANTA MARIA (93454) Santa Barbara(98),
   San Luis Obispo(2)
SANTA MARIA Santa Barbara
SANTA MONICA Los Angeles
SANTA PAULA Ventura
SANTA RITA PARK Merced
SANTA ROSA Sonoma
SANTA YNEZ Santa Barbara
SANTA YSABEL San Diego
SANTEE San Diego
SARATOGA Santa Clara
SAUSALITO Marin
SCOTIA Humboldt
SCOTT BAR Siskiyou
SCOTTS VALLEY Santa Cruz
SEAL BEACH Orange
SEASIDE Monterey
SEBASTOPOL Sonoma
SEELEY Imperial
SEIAD VALLEY Siskiyou
SELMA Fresno
SEQUOIA NATIONAL PARK Tulare
SHAFTER Kern
SHANDON San Luis Obispo
SHASTA Shasta
SHASTA LAKE Shasta
SHAVER LAKE Fresno
SHEEP RANCH Calaveras
SHERIDAN Placer
SHERMAN OAKS Los Angeles
SHINGLE SPRINGS El Dorado
SHINGLETOWN Shasta
SHOSHONE Inyo
SIERRA CITY Sierra
SIERRA MADRE Los Angeles
SIERRAVILLE Sierra
SILVERADO Orange
SIMI VALLEY Ventura
SKYFOREST San Bernardino
SLOUGHHOUSE Sacramento
SMARTVILLE (95977) Nevada(66),
   Yuba(34)
SMITH RIVER Del Norte
SNELLING Merced
SODA SPRINGS Nevada
SOLANA BEACH San Diego
SOLEDAD Monterey
SOLVANG Santa Barbara
SOMERSET El Dorado
SOMES BAR Siskiyou
SOMIS Ventura
SONOMA Sonoma
SONORA Tuolumne
SOQUEL Santa Cruz
SOULSBYVILLE Tuolumne
SOUTH DOS PALOS Merced
SOUTH EL MONTE Los Angeles
SOUTH GATE Los Angeles
SOUTH LAKE TAHOE El Dorado
SOUTH PASADENA Los Angeles
SOUTH SAN FRANCISCO San Mateo
SPRECKELS Monterey
SPRING VALLEY San Diego
SPRINGVILLE Tulare
SQUAW VALLEY Fresno
STANDARD Tuolumne
STANDISH Lassen
STANTON Orange
STEVENSON RANCH Los Angeles
STEVINSON Merced
STEWARTS POINT Sonoma
STINSON BEACH Marin
STIRLING CITY Butte
STOCKTON San Joaquin

STONYFORD Colusa
STORRIE Plumas
STRATFORD Kings
STRATHMORE Tulare
STRAWBERRY Tuolumne
STRAWBERRY VALLEY Yuba
STUDIO CITY Los Angeles
SUGARLOAF San Bernardino
SUISUN CITY Solano
SULTANA Tulare
SUMMERLAND Santa Barbara
SUN CITY Riverside
SUN VALLEY Los Angeles
SUNLAND Los Angeles
SUNNYVALE Santa Clara
SUNOL Alameda
SUNSET BEACH Orange
SURFSIDE Orange
SUSANVILLE Lassen
SUTTER Sutter
SUTTER CREEK Amador
SYLMAR Los Angeles
TAFT Kern
TAHOE CITY Placer
TAHOE VISTA Placer
TAHOMA (96142) Placer(92), El Dorado(8)
TALMAGE Mendocino
TARZANA Los Angeles
TAYLORSVILLE Plumas
TECATE San Diego
TECOPA Inyo
TEHACHAPI Kern
TEHAMA Tehama
TEMECULA Riverside
TEMPLE CITY Los Angeles
TEMPLETON San Luis Obispo
TERMO Lassen
TERRA BELLA Tulare
THE SEA RANCH Sonoma
THERMAL (92274) Riverside(63),
   Imperial(37)
THORNTON San Joaquin
THOUSAND OAKS (91362) Ventura(93),
   Los Angeles(7)
THOUSAND OAKS Ventura
THOUSAND PALMS Riverside
THREE RIVERS Tulare
TIPTON Tulare
TOLLHOUSE Fresno
TOLUCA LAKE Los Angeles
TOMALES Marin
TOPANGA Los Angeles
TOPAZ Mono
TORRANCE Los Angeles
TRABUCO CANYON Orange
TRACY San Joaquin
TRANQUILLITY Fresno
TRAVER Tulare
TRAVIS AFB Solano
TRES PINOS San Benito
TRINIDAD Humboldt
TRINITY CENTER (96091) Siskiyou(66),
   Trinity(34)
TRONA San Bernardino
TRUCKEE (96161) Nevada(89), Placer(11)
TRUCKEE Nevada
TUJUNGA Los Angeles
TULARE Tulare
TULELAKE (96134) Modoc(69),
   Siskiyou(31)
TUOLUMNE Tuolumne
TUPMAN Kern
TURLOCK Stanislaus
TUSTIN Orange
TWAIN Plumas
TWAIN HARTE Tuolumne
TWENTYNINE PALMS San Bernardino
TWIN BRIDGES El Dorado
TWIN PEAKS San Bernardino
UKIAH Mendocino
UNION CITY Alameda
UNIVERSAL CITY Los Angeles

UPLAND San Bernardino
UPPER LAKE Lake
VACAVILLE Solano
VALENCIA Los Angeles
VALLECITO Calaveras
VALLEJO (94589) Solano(73), Napa(28)
VALLEJO Solano
VALLEY CENTER San Diego
VALLEY FORD Sonoma
VALLEY HOME Stanislaus
VALLEY SPRINGS Calaveras
VALLEY VILLAGE Los Angeles
VALYERMO Los Angeles
VAN NUYS Los Angeles
VAN NUYS Ventura
VENICE Los Angeles
VENTURA Ventura
VERDUGO CITY Los Angeles
VERNALIS San Joaquin
VICTOR San Joaquin
VICTORVILLE San Bernardino
VIDAL San Bernardino
VILLA GRANDE Sonoma
VII I A PARK Orange
VINA Tehama
VINEBURG Sonoma
VINTON Plumas
VISALIA Tulare

VISTA San Diego
VOLCANO Amador
WALLACE Calaveras
WALNUT (91795) Los Angeles(50), Orange(50)
WALNUT Los Angeles
WALNUT CREEK Contra Costa
WALNUT GROVE (95690) San Joaquin(87), Sacramento(13)
WARNER SPRINGS San Diego
WASCO Kern
WASHINGTON Nevada
WATERFORD Stanislaus
WATSONVILLE (95076) Santa Cruz(84), Monterey(15)
WATSONVILLE Santa Cruz
WAUKENA Tulare
WEAVERVILLE Trinity
WEED Siskiyou
WEIMAR Placer
WELDON Kern
WENDEL Lassen
WEOTT Humboldt
WEST COVINA Los Angeles
WEST HILLS (91307) Los Angeles(94), Ventura(6)
WEST HILLS Los Angeles
WEST HOLLYWOOD Los Angeles

WEST POINT Calaveras
WEST SACRAMENTO Yolo
WESTLAKE VILLAGE (91361) Ventura(72), Los Angeles(28)
WESTLAKE VILLAGE Los Angeles
WESTLAKE VILLAGE Ventura
WESTLEY Stanislaus
WESTMINSTER Orange
WESTMORLAND Imperial
WESTPORT Mendocino
WESTWOOD (96137) Plumas(55), Lassen(45)
WHEATLAND Yuba
WHISKEYTOWN Shasta
WHITE WATER Riverside
WHITETHORN (95589) Humboldt(98), Mendocino(2)
WHITMORE Shasta
WHITTIER Los Angeles
WILDOMAR Riverside
WILLIAMS Colusa
WILLITS Mendocino
WILLOW CREEK Humboldt
WILLOWS Glenn
WILMINGTON Los Angeles
WILSEYVILLE Calaveras
WILTON Sacramento
WINCHESTER Riverside

WINDSOR Sonoma
WINNETKA Los Angeles
WINTERHAVEN Imperial
WINTERS Yolo
WINTON Merced
WISHON Madera
WITTER SPRINGS Lake
WOFFORD HEIGHTS Kern
WOODACRE Marin
WOODBRIDGE San Joaquin
WOODLAKE Tulare
WOODLAND Yolo
WOODLAND HILLS Los Angeles
WOODY Kern
WRIGHTWOOD San Bernardino
YERMO San Bernardino
YETTEM Tulare
YOLO Yolo
YORBA LINDA Orange
YORKVILLE Mendocino
YOSEMITE NATIONAL PARK Mariposa
YOUNTVILLE Napa
YREKA Siskiyou
YUBA CITY Sutter
YUCAIPA San Bernardino
YUCCA VALLEY San Bernardino
ZAMORA Yolo
ZENIA Trinity

ZIP/City Cross Reference

90001-90068 LOS ANGELES	90704-90704 AVALON	91319-91320 NEWBURY PARK	91601-91603 NORTH HOLLYWOOD
90069-90069 WEST HOLLYWOOD	90706-90707 BELLFLOWER	91321-91322 NEWHALL	91604-91604 STUDIO CITY
90070-90185 LOS ANGELES	90710-90710 HARBOR CITY	91324-91330 NORTHRIDGE	91605-91606 NORTH HOLLYWOOD
90201-90201 BELL	90711-90715 LAKEWOOD	91331-91334 PACOIMA	91607-91607 VALLEY VILLAGE
90202-90202 BELL GARDENS	90716-90716 HAWAIIAN GARDENS	91335-91337 RESEDA	91608-91608 UNIVERSAL CITY
90209-90213 BEVERLY HILLS	90717-90717 LOMITA	91340-91341 SAN FERNANDO	91609-91609 NORTH HOLLYWOOD
90220-90224 COMPTON	90720-90721 LOS ALAMITOS	91342-91342 SYLMAR	91610-91610 TOLUCA LAKE
90230-90233 CULVER CITY	90723-90723 PARAMOUNT	91343-91343 NORTH HILLS	91611-91612 NORTH HOLLYWOOD
90239-90242 DOWNEY	90731-90734 SAN PEDRO	91344-91344 GRANADA HILLS	91614-91614 STUDIO CITY
90245-90245 EL SEGUNDO	90740-90740 SEAL BEACH	91345-91346 MISSION HILLS	91615-91616 NORTH HOLLYWOOD
90247-90249 GARDENA	90742-90742 SUNSET BEACH	91350-91350 SANTA CLARITA	91617-91617 VALLEY VILLAGE
90250-90251 HAWTHORNE	90743-90743 SURFSIDE	91351-91351 CANYON COUNTRY	91618-91618 UNIVERSAL CITY
90254-90254 HERMOSA BEACH	90744-90744 WILMINGTON	91352-91353 SUN VALLEY	91701-91701 ALTA LOMA
90255-90255 HUNTINGTON PARK	90745-90747 CARSON	91354-91355 VALENCIA	91702-91702 AZUSA
90260-90261 LAWNDALE	90748-90748 WILMINGTON	91356-91357 TARZANA	91706-91706 BALDWIN PARK
90262-90262 LYNWOOD	90749-90749 CARSON	91358-91358 THOUSAND OAKS	91708-91708 CHINO
90263-90265 MALIBU	90801-90888 LONG BEACH	91359-91359 WESTLAKE VILLAGE	91709-91709 CHINO HILLS
90266-90267 MANHATTAN BEACH	91001-91003 ALTADENA	91360-91360 THOUSAND OAKS	91710-91710 CHINO
90270-90270 MAYWOOD	91006-91007 ARCADIA	91361-91361 WESTLAKE VILLAGE	91711-91711 CLAREMONT
90272-90272 PACIFIC PALISADES	91009-91010 DUARTE	91362-91362 THOUSAND OAKS	91714-91716 CITY OF INDUSTRY
90274-90274 PALOS VERDES PENINSULA	91011-91012 LA CANADA FLINTRIDGE	91363-91363 WESTLAKE VILLAGE	91718-91720 CORONA
	91016-91017 MONROVIA	91364-91371 WOODLAND HILLS	91722-91724 COVINA
90275-90275 RANCHO PALOS VERDES	91020-91021 MONTROSE	91372-91372 CALABASAS	91729-91730 RANCHO CUCAMONGA
	91023-91023 MOUNT WILSON	91376-91376 AGOURA HILLS	91731-91732 EL MONTE
90277-90278 REDONDO BEACH	91024-91025 SIERRA MADRE	91380-91380 SANTA CLARITA	91733-91733 SOUTH EL MONTE
90280-90280 SOUTH GATE	91030-91031 SOUTH PASADENA	91381-91381 STEVENSON RANCH	91734-91735 EL MONTE
90290-90290 TOPANGA	91040-91041 SUNLAND	91382-91383 SANTA CLARITA	91737-91737 ALTA LOMA
90291-90291 VENICE	91042-91043 TUJUNGA	91384-91384 CASTAIC	91739-91739 RANCHO CUCAMONGA
90292-90292 MARINA DEL REY	91046-91046 VERDUGO CITY	91385-91385 VALENCIA	91740-91741 GLENDORA
90293-90293 PLAYA DEL REY	91050-91051 PASADENA	91386-91386 CANYON COUNTRY	91743-91743 GUASTI
90294-90294 VENICE	91066-91077 ARCADIA	91388-91388 VAN NUYS	91744-91744 LA PUENTE
90295-90295 MARINA DEL REY	91101-91107 PASADENA	91392-91392 SYLMAR	91745-91745 HACIENDA HEIGHTS
90296-90296 PLAYA DEL REY	91108-91108 SAN MARINO	91393-91393 NORTH HILLS	91746-91747 LA PUENTE
90301-90398 INGLEWOOD	91109-91117 PASADENA	91394-91394 GRANADA HILLS	91748-91748 ROWLAND HEIGHTS
90401-90411 SANTA MONICA	91118-91118 SAN MARINO	91395-91395 MISSION HILLS	91749-91749 LA PUENTE
90501-90510 TORRANCE	91121-91191 PASADENA	91396-91396 WINNETKA	91750-91750 LA VERNE
90601-90612 WHITTIER	91201-91210 GLENDALE	91399-91399 WOODLAND HILLS	91752-91752 MIRA LOMA
90620-90622 BUENA PARK	91214-91214 LA CRESCENTA	91401-91401 VAN NUYS	91754-91756 MONTEREY PARK
90623-90623 LA PALMA	91221-91222 GLENDALE	91402-91402 PANORAMA CITY	91758-91758 ONTARIO
90624-90624 BUENA PARK	91224-91224 LA CRESCENTA	91403-91403 SHERMAN OAKS	91759-91759 MT BALDY
90630-90630 CYPRESS	91225-91226 GLENDALE	91404-91411 VAN NUYS	91760-91760 NORCO
90631-90633 LA HABRA	91301-91301 AGOURA HILLS	91412-91412 PANORAMA CITY	91761-91762 ONTARIO
90637-90639 LA MIRADA	91302-91302 CALABASAS	91413-91413 SHERMAN OAKS	91763-91763 MONTCLAIR
90640-90640 MONTEBELLO	91303-91305 CANOGA PARK	91416-91416 ENCINO	91764-91764 ONTARIO
90650-90659 NORWALK	91306-91306 WINNETKA	91423-91423 SHERMAN OAKS	91765-91765 DIAMOND BAR
90660-90665 PICO RIVERA	91307-91308 WEST HILLS	91426-91436 ENCINO	91766-91769 POMONA
90670-90671 SANTA FE SPRINGS	91309-91309 CANOGA PARK	91470-91482 VAN NUYS	91770-91772 ROSEMEAD
90680-90680 STANTON	91310-91310 CASTAIC	91495-91495 SHERMAN OAKS	91773-91773 SAN DIMAS
90701-90702 ARTESIA	91311-91313 CHATSWORTH	91496-91499 VAN NUYS	91775-91778 SAN GABRIEL
90703-90703 CERRITOS	91316-91316 ENCINO	91501-91526 BURBANK	91780-91780 TEMPLE CITY

Zip Range	City	Zip Range	City	Zip Range	City	Zip Range	City
91784-91786	UPLAND	92210-92210	INDIAN WELLS	92352-92352	LAKE ARROWHEAD	92701-92707	SANTA ANA
91788-91789	WALNUT	92211-92211	PALM DESERT	92354-92354	LOMA LINDA	92708-92708	FOUNTAIN VALLEY
91790-91793	WEST COVINA	92220-92220	BANNING	92356-92356	LUCERNE VALLEY	92709-92710	IRVINE
91795-91795	WALNUT	92222-92222	BARD	92357-92357	LOMA LINDA	92711-92712	SANTA ANA
91797-91797	BALDWIN PARK	92223-92223	BEAUMONT	92358-92358	LYTLE CREEK	92728-92728	FOUNTAIN VALLEY
91798-91798	ONTARIO	92225-92226	BLYTHE	92359-92359	MENTONE	92735-92735	SANTA ANA
91799-91799	POMONA	92227-92227	BRAWLEY	92363-92363	NEEDLES	92780-92782	TUSTIN
91801-91899	ALHAMBRA	92230-92230	CABAZON	92364-92364	NIPTON	92799-92799	SANTA ANA
91901-91901	ALPINE	92231-92232	CALEXICO	92365-92365	NEWBERRY SPRINGS	92801-92808	ANAHEIM
91902-91902	BONITA	92233-92233	CALIPATRIA	92366-92366	MOUNTAIN PASS	92811-92811	ATWOOD
91903-91903	ALPINE	92234-92235	CATHEDRAL CITY	92368-92368	ORO GRANDE	92812-92817	ANAHEIM
91905-91905	BOULEVARD	92236-92236	COACHELLA	92369-92369	PATTON	92821-92823	BREA
91906-91906	CAMPO	92239-92239	DESERT CENTER	92371-92371	PHELAN	92825-92825	ANAHEIM
91908-91908	BONITA	92240-92241	DESERT HOT SPRINGS	92372-92372	PINON HILLS	92831-92838	FULLERTON
91909-91915	CHULA VISTA	92242-92242	EARP	92373-92375	REDLANDS	92840-92846	GARDEN GROVE
91916-91916	DESCANSO	92243-92244	EL CENTRO	92376-92377	RIALTO	92850-92850	ANAHEIM
91917-91917	DULZURA	92249-92249	HEBER	92378-92378	RIMFOREST	92856-92859	ORANGE
91921-91921	CHULA VISTA	92250-92250	HOLTVILLE	92382-92382	RUNNING SPRINGS	92861-92861	VILLA PARK
91931-91931	GUATAY	92251-92251	IMPERIAL	92384-92384	SHOSHONE	92862-92869	ORANGE
91932-91933	IMPERIAL BEACH	92252-92252	JOSHUA TREE	92385-92385	SKYFOREST	92870-92871	PLACENTIA
91934-91934	JACUMBA	92253-92253	LA QUINTA	92386-92386	SUGARLOAF	92885-92887	YORBA LINDA
91935-91935	JAMUL	92254-92254	MECCA	92389-92389	TECOPA	92899-92899	ANAHEIM
91941-91944	LA MESA	92255-92255	PALM DESERT	92391-92391	TWIN PEAKS	93001-93009	VENTURA
91945-91946	LEMON GROVE	92256-92256	MORONGO VALLEY	92392-92394	VICTORVILLE	93010-93012	CAMARILLO
91947-91947	LINCOLN ACRES	92257-92257	NILAND	92397-92397	WRIGHTWOOD	93013-93014	CARPINTERIA
91948-91948	MOUNT LAGUNA	92258-92258	NORTH PALM SPRINGS	92398-92398	YERMO	93015-93016	FILLMORE
91950-91951	NATIONAL CITY	92259-92259	OCOTILLO	92399-92399	YUCAIPA	93020-93021	MOORPARK
91962-91962	PINE VALLEY	92260-92261	PALM DESERT	92401-92427	SAN BERNARDINO	93022-93022	OAK VIEW
91963-91963	POTRERO	92262-92264	PALM SPRINGS	92501-92517	RIVERSIDE	93023-93024	OJAI
91976-91979	SPRING VALLEY	92266-92266	PALO VERDE	92518-92518	MARCH AIR FORCE	93030-93035	OXNARD
91980-91987	TECATE	92267-92267	PARKER DAM		BASE	93040-93040	PIRU
91990-91990	POTRERO	92268-92268	PIONEERTOWN	92519-92522	RIVERSIDE	93041-93041	PORT HUENEME
92003-92003	BONSALL	92270-92270	RANCHO MIRAGE	92530-92532	LAKE ELSINORE	93042-93042	POINT MUGU NAWC
92004-92004	BORREGO SPRINGS	92273-92273	SEELEY	92536-92536	AGUANGA	93043-93043	PORT HUENEME CBC
92007-92007	CARDIFF BY THE SEA	92274-92274	THERMAL	92539-92539	ANZA		BASE
92008-92009	CARLSBAD	92275-92275	SALTON CITY	92543-92546	HEMET	93044-93044	PORT HUENEME
92014-92014	DEL MAR	92276-92276	THOUSAND PALMS	92548-92548	HOMELAND	93060-93061	SANTA PAULA
92018-92018	CARLSBAD	92277-92278	TWENTYNINE PALMS	92549-92549	IDYLLWILD	93062-93063	SIMI VALLEY
92019-92022	EL CAJON	92280-92280	VIDAL	92551-92557	MORENO VALLEY	93064-93064	BRANDEIS
92023-92024	ENCINITAS	92281-92281	WESTMORLAND	92561-92561	MOUNTAIN CENTER	93065-93065	SIMI VALLEY
92025-92027	ESCONDIDO	92282-92282	WHITE WATER	92562-92564	MURRIETA	93066-93066	SOMIS
92028-92028	FALLBROOK	92283-92283	WINTERHAVEN	92567-92567	NUEVO	93067-93067	SUMMERLAND
92029-92033	ESCONDIDO	92284-92284	YUCCA VALLEY	92570-92572	PERRIS	93093-93099	SIMI VALLEY
92036-92036	JULIAN	92285-92285	LANDERS	92581-92583	SAN JACINTO	93101-93111	SANTA BARBARA
92037-92039	LA JOLLA	92286-92286	YUCCA VALLEY	92584-92584	MENIFEE	93116-93118	GOLETA
92040-92040	LAKESIDE	92292-92292	PALM SPRINGS	92585-92587	SUN CITY	93120-93190	SANTA BARBARA
92046-92046	ESCONDIDO	92301-92301	ADELANTO	92589-92593	TEMECULA	93199-93199	GOLETA
92049-92054	OCEANSIDE	92304-92304	AMBOY	92595-92595	WILDOMAR	93201-93201	ALPAUGH
92055-92055	CAMP PENDLETON	92305-92305	ANGELUS OAKS	92596-92596	WINCHESTER	93202-93202	ARMONA
92056-92058	OCEANSIDE	92307-92308	APPLE VALLEY	92599-92599	PERRIS	93203-93203	ARVIN
92059-92059	PALA	92309-92309	BAKER	92602-92604	IRVINE	93204-93204	AVENAL
92060-92060	PALOMAR MOUNTAIN	92310-92310	FORT IRWIN	92605-92605	HUNTINGTON BEACH	93205-93205	BODFISH
92061-92061	PAUMA VALLEY	92311-92312	BARSTOW	92606-92606	IRVINE	93206-93206	BUTTONWILLOW
92064-92064	POWAY	92313-92313	GRAND TERRACE	92607-92607	LAGUNA NIGUEL	93207-93207	CALIFORNIA HOT
92065-92065	RAMONA	92314-92314	BIG BEAR CITY	92610-92610	FOOTHILL RANCH		SPRINGS
92066-92066	RANCHITA	92315-92315	BIG BEAR LAKE	92612-92614	IRVINE	93208-93208	CAMP NELSON
92067-92067	RANCHO SANTA FE	92316-92316	BLOOMINGTON	92615-92615	HUNTINGTON BEACH	93210-93210	COALINGA
92068-92068	SAN LUIS REY	92317-92317	BLUE JAY	92616-92623	IRVINE	93212-93212	CORCORAN
92069-92069	SAN MARCOS	92318-92318	BRYN MAWR	92624-92624	CAPISTRANO BEACH	93215-93216	DELANO
92070-92070	SANTA YSABEL	92319-92319	CADIZ	92625-92625	CORONA DEL MAR	93218-93218	DUCOR
92071-92072	SANTEE	92320-92320	CALIMESA	92626-92628	COSTA MESA	93219-93219	EARLIMART
92074-92074	POWAY	92321-92321	CEDAR GLEN	92629-92629	DANA POINT	93220-93220	EDISON
92075-92075	SOLANA BEACH	92322-92322	CEDARPINES PARK	92630-92630	LAKE FOREST	93221-93221	EXETER
92079-92079	SAN MARCOS	92323-92323	CIMA	92646-92649	HUNTINGTON BEACH	93222-93222	FRAZIER PARK
92082-92082	VALLEY CENTER	92324-92324	COLTON	92650-92650	EAST IRVINE	93223-93223	FARMERSVILLE
92083-92085	VISTA	92325-92325	CRESTLINE	92651-92652	LAGUNA BEACH	93224-93224	FELLOWS
92086-92086	WARNER SPRINGS	92326-92326	CREST PARK	92653-92654	LAGUNA HILLS	93225-93225	FRAZIER PARK
92088-92088	FALLBROOK	92327-92327	DAGGETT	92655-92655	MIDWAY CITY	93226-93226	GLENNVILLE
92090-92090	EL CAJON	92328-92328	DEATH VALLEY	92656-92656	ALISO VIEJO	93227-93227	GOSHEN
92091-92091	RANCHO SANTA FE	92329-92329	PHELAN	92657-92657	NEWPORT COAST	93230-93232	HANFORD
92092-92093	LA JOLLA	92332-92332	ESSEX	92658-92663	NEWPORT BEACH	93234-93234	HURON
92096-92096	SAN MARCOS	92333-92333	FAWNSKIN	92672-92674	SAN CLEMENTE	93235-93235	IVANHOE
92101-92117	SAN DIEGO	92334-92337	FONTANA	92675-92675	SAN JUAN CAPISTRANO	93237-93237	KAWEAH
92118-92118	CORONADO	92338-92338	LUDLOW	92676-92676	SILVERADO	93238-93238	KERNVILLE
92119-92142	SAN DIEGO	92339-92339	FOREST FALLS	92677-92677	LAGUNA NIGUEL	93239-93239	KETTLEMAN CITY
92143-92143	SAN YSIDRO	92340-92340	HESPERIA	92678-92679	TRABUCO CANYON	93240-93240	LAKE ISABELLA
92145-92172	SAN DIEGO	92341-92341	GREEN VALLEY LAKE	92683-92685	WESTMINSTER	93241-93241	LAMONT
92173-92173	SAN YSIDRO	92342-92342	HELENDALE	92688-92688	RANCHO SANTA	93242-93242	LATON
92174-92177	SAN DIEGO	92345-92345	HESPERIA		MARGARITA	93243-93243	LEBEC
92178-92178	CORONADO	92346-92346	HIGHLAND	92690-92692	MISSION VIEJO	93244-93244	LEMON COVE
92179-92199	SAN DIEGO	92347-92347	HINKLEY	92693-92693	SAN JUAN CAPISTRANO	93245-93246	LEMOORE
92201-92203	INDIO	92350-92350	LOMA LINDA	92697-92698	IRVINE	93247-93247	LINDSAY

Zip	City	Zip	City	Zip	City	Zip	City
93249-93249	LOST HILLS	93531-93531	KEENE	93669-93669	WISHON	94540-94545	HAYWARD
93250-93250	MC FARLAND	93532-93532	LAKE HUGHES	93670-93670	YETTEM	94546-94546	CASTRO VALLEY
93251-93251	MC KITTRICK	93534-93539	LANCASTER	93673-93673	TRAVER	94547-94547	HERCULES
93252-93252	MARICOPA	93541-93541	LEE VINING	93675-93675	SQUAW VALLEY	94548-94548	KNIGHTSEN
93254-93254	NEW CUYAMA	93542-93542	LITTLE LAKE	93701-93888	FRESNO	94549-94549	LAFAYETTE
93255-93255	ONYX	93543-93543	LITTLEROCK	93901-93915	SALINAS	94550-94551	LIVERMORE
93256-93256	PIXLEY	93544-93544	LLANO	93920-93920	BIG SUR	94552-94552	CASTRO VALLEY
93257-93258	PORTERVILLE	93545-93545	LONE PINE	93921-93923	CARMEL	94553-94553	MARTINEZ
93260-93260	POSEY	93546-93546	MAMMOTH LAKES	93924-93924	CARMEL VALLEY	94555-94555	FREMONT
93261-93261	RICHGROVE	93549-93549	OLANCHA	93925-93925	CHUALAR	94556-94556	MORAGA
93262-93262	SEQUOIA NATIONAL PARK	93550-93552	PALMDALE	93926-93926	GONZALES	94557-94557	HAYWARD
93263-93263	SHAFTER	93553-93553	PEARBLOSSOM	93927-93927	GREENFIELD	94558-94559	NAPA
93265-93265	SPRINGVILLE	93554-93554	RANDSBURG	93928-93928	JOLON	94560-94560	NEWARK
93266-93266	STRATFORD	93555-93556	RIDGECREST	93930-93930	KING CITY	94561-94561	OAKLEY
93267-93267	STRATHMORE	93558-93558	RED MOUNTAIN	93932-93932	LOCKWOOD	94562-94562	OAKVILLE
93268-93268	TAFT	93560-93560	ROSAMOND	93933-93933	MARINA	94563-94563	ORINDA
93270-93270	TERRA BELLA	93561-93561	TEHACHAPI	93940-93944	MONTEREY	94564-94564	PINOLE
93271-93271	THREE RIVERS	93562-93562	TRONA	93950-93950	PACIFIC GROVE	94565-94565	PITTSBURG
93272-93272	TIPTON	93563-93563	VALYERMO	93953-93953	PEBBLE BEACH	94566-94566	PLEASANTON
93274-93275	TULARE	93581-93582	TEHACHAPI	93954-93954	SAN LUCAS	94567-94567	POPE VALLEY
93276-93276	TUPMAN	93584-93586	LANCASTER	93955-93955	SEASIDE	94568-94568	DUBLIN
93277-93279	VISALIA	93590-93591	PALMDALE	93960-93960	SOLEDAD	94569-94569	PORT COSTA
93280-93280	WASCO	93592-93592	TRONA	93962-93962	SPRECKELS	94570-94570	MORAGA
93282-93282	WAUKENA	93596-93596	BORON	94002-94003	BELMONT	94571-94571	RIO VISTA
93283-93283	WELDON	93599-93599	PALMDALE	94005-94005	BRISBANE	94572-94572	RODEO
93285-93285	WOFFORD HEIGHTS	93601-93601	AHWAHNEE	94010-94012	BURLINGAME	94573-94573	RUTHERFORD
93286-93286	WOODLAKE	93602-93602	AUBERRY	94014-94017	DALY CITY	94574-94574	SAINT HELENA
93287-93287	WOODY	93603-93603	BADGER	94018-94018	EL GRANADA	94575-94575	MORAGA
93291-93292	VISALIA	93604-93604	BASS LAKE	94019-94019	HALF MOON BAY	94576-94576	DEER PARK
93301-93399	BAKERSFIELD	93605-93605	BIG CREEK	94020-94020	LA HONDA	94577-94579	SAN LEANDRO
93401-93401	SAN LUIS OBISPO	93606-93606	BIOLA	94021-94021	LOMA MAR	94580-94580	SAN LORENZO
93402-93402	LOS OSOS	93607-93607	BURREL	94022-94024	LOS ALTOS	94581-94581	NAPA
93403-93410	SAN LUIS OBISPO	93608-93608	CANTUA CREEK	94025-94026	MENLO PARK	94582-94582	PLEASANTON
93412-93412	LOS OSOS	93609-93609	CARUTHERS	94027-94027	ATHERTON	94583-94583	SAN RAMON
93420-93421	ARROYO GRANDE	93610-93610	CHOWCHILLA	94028-94028	PORTOLA VALLEY	94585-94585	SUISUN CITY
93422-93423	ATASCADERO	93611-93613	CLOVIS	94029-94029	MENLO PARK	94586-94586	SUNOL
93424-93424	AVILA BEACH	93614-93614	COARSEGOLD	94030-94031	MILLBRAE	94587-94587	UNION CITY
93426-93426	BRADLEY	93615-93615	CUTLER	94035-94035	MOUNTAIN VIEW	94588-94588	PLEASANTON
93427-93427	BUELLTON	93616-93616	DEL REY	94037-94037	MONTARA	94589-94592	VALLEJO
93428-93428	CAMBRIA	93618-93618	DINUBA	94038-94038	MOSS BEACH	94595-94598	WALNUT CREEK
93429-93429	CASMALIA	93620-93620	DOS PALOS	94039-94043	MOUNTAIN VIEW	94599-94599	YOUNTVILLE
93430-93430	CAYUCOS	93621-93621	DUNLAP	94044-94045	PACIFICA	94601-94607	OAKLAND
93432-93432	CRESTON	93622-93622	FIREBAUGH	94059-94059	REDWOOD CITY	94608-94608	EMERYVILLE
93433-93433	GROVER BEACH	93623-93623	FISH CAMP	94060-94060	PESCADERO	94609-94619	OAKLAND
93434-93434	GUADALUPE	93624-93624	FIVE POINTS	94061-94065	REDWOOD CITY	94620-94620	PIEDMONT
93435-93435	HARMONY	93625-93625	FOWLER	94066-94067	SAN BRUNO	94621-94661	OAKLAND
93436-93438	LOMPOC	93626-93626	FRIANT	94070-94071	SAN CARLOS	94662-94662	EMERYVILLE
93440-93440	LOS ALAMOS	93627-93627	HELM	94074-94074	SAN GREGORIO	94666-94666	OAKLAND
93441-93441	LOS OLIVOS	93628-93628	HUME	94080-94083	SOUTH SAN FRANCISCO	94701-94705	BERKELEY
93442-93443	MORRO BAY	93629-93629	HUNTINGTON LAKE	94086-94091	SUNNYVALE	94706-94706	ALBANY
93444-93444	NIPOMO	93630-93630	KERMAN	94096-94098	SAN BRUNO	94707-94720	BERKELEY
93445-93445	OCEANO	93631-93631	KINGSBURG	94099-94099	SOUTH SAN FRANCISCO	94801-94802	RICHMOND
93446-93447	PASO ROBLES	93633-93633	KINGS CANYON NATIONAL PK	94101-94188	SAN FRANCISCO	94803-94803	EL SOBRANTE
93448-93449	PISMO BEACH	93634-93634	LAKESHORE	94203-94299	SACRAMENTO	94804-94805	RICHMOND
93450-93450	SAN ARDO	93635-93635	LOS BANOS	94301-94310	PALO ALTO	94806-94806	SAN PABLO
93451-93451	SAN MIGUEL	93637-93639	MADERA	94401-94497	SAN MATEO	94807-94808	RICHMOND
93452-93452	SAN SIMEON	93640-93640	MENDOTA	94501-94502	ALAMEDA	94820-94820	EL SOBRANTE
93453-93453	SANTA MARGARITA	93641-93641	MIRAMONTE	94506-94506	DANVILLE	94850-94850	RICHMOND
93454-93458	SANTA MARIA	93642-93642	MONO HOT SPRINGS	94507-94507	ALAMO	94901-94903	SAN RAFAEL
93460-93460	SANTA YNEZ	93643-93643	NORTH FORK	94508-94508	ANGWIN	94904-94904	GREENBRAE
93461-93461	SHANDON	93644-93644	OAKHURST	94509-94509	ANTIOCH	94912-94913	SAN RAFAEL
93463-93464	SOLVANG	93645-93645	O NEALS	94510-94510	BENICIA	94914-94914	KENTFIELD
93465-93465	TEMPLETON	93646-93646	ORANGE COVE	94511-94511	BETHEL ISLAND	94915-94915	SAN RAFAEL
93483-93483	GROVER BEACH	93647-93647	OROSI	94512-94512	BIRDS LANDING	94920-94920	BELVEDERE TIBURON
93501-93502	MOJAVE	93648-93648	PARLIER	94513-94513	BRENTWOOD	94922-94922	BODEGA
93504-93505	CALIFORNIA CITY	93649-93649	PIEDRA	94514-94514	BYRON	94923-94923	BODEGA BAY
93510-93510	ACTON	93650-93650	FRESNO	94515-94515	CALISTOGA	94924-94924	BOLINAS
93512-93512	BENTON	93651-93651	PRATHER	94516-94516	CANYON	94925-94925	CORTE MADERA
93513-93513	BIG PINE	93652-93652	RAISIN	94517-94517	CLAYTON	94926-94926	COTATI
93514-93515	BISHOP	93653-93653	RAYMOND	94518-94522	CONCORD	94927-94928	ROHNERT PARK
93516-93516	BORON	93654-93654	REEDLEY	94523-94523	PLEASANT HILL	94929-94929	DILLON BEACH
93517-93517	BRIDGEPORT	93656-93656	RIVERDALE	94524-94524	CONCORD	94930-94930	FAIRFAX
93518-93518	CALIENTE	93657-93657	SANGER	94525-94525	CROCKETT	94931-94931	COTATI
93519-93519	CANTIL	93660-93660	SAN JOAQUIN	94526-94526	DANVILLE	94933-94933	FOREST KNOLLS
93522-93522	DARWIN	93661-93661	SANTA RITA PARK	94527-94527	CONCORD	94937-94937	INVERNESS
93523-93524	EDWARDS	93662-93662	SELMA	94528-94528	DIABLO	94938-94938	LAGUNITAS
93526-93526	INDEPENDENCE	93664-93664	SHAVER LAKE	94529-94529	CONCORD	94939-94939	LARKSPUR
93527-93527	INYOKERN	93665-93665	SOUTH DOS PALOS	94530-94530	EL CERRITO	94940-94940	MARSHALL
93528-93528	JOHANNESBURG	93666-93666	SULTANA	94531-94531	ANTIOCH	94941-94942	MILL VALLEY
93529-93529	JUNE LAKE	93667-93667	TOLLHOUSE	94533-94533	FAIRFIELD	94945-94945	NOVATO
93530-93530	KEELER	93668-93668	TRANQUILLITY	94535-94535	TRAVIS AFB	94946-94946	NICASIO
				94536-94539	FREMONT	94947-94949	NOVATO

ZIP Range	City	ZIP Range	City	ZIP Range	City	ZIP Range	City
94950-94950	OLEMA	95248-95248	RAIL ROAD FLAT	95416-95416	BOYES HOT SPRINGS	95543-95543	GASQUET
94951-94951	PENNGROVE	95249-95249	SAN ANDREAS	95417-95417	BRANSCOMB	95545-95545	HONEYDEW
94952-94955	PETALUMA	95250-95250	SHEEP RANCH	95418-95418	CALPELLA	95546-95546	HOOPA
94956-94956	POINT REYES STATION	95251-95251	VALLECITO	95419-95419	CAMP MEEKER	95547-95547	HYDESVILLE
94957-94957	ROSS	95252-95252	VALLEY SPRINGS	95420-95420	CASPAR	95548-95548	KLAMATH
94960-94960	SAN ANSELMO	95253-95253	VICTOR	95421-95421	CAZADERO	95549-95549	KNEELAND
94963-94963	SAN GERONIMO	95254-95254	WALLACE	95422-95422	CLEARLAKE	95550-95550	KORBEL
94964-94964	SAN QUENTIN	95255-95255	WEST POINT	95423-95423	CLEARLAKE OAKS	95551-95551	LOLETA
94965-94966	SAUSALITO	95257-95257	WILSEYVILLE	95424-95424	CLEARLAKE PARK	95552-95552	MAD RIVER
94970-94970	STINSON BEACH	95258-95258	WOODBRIDGE	95425-95425	CLOVERDALE	95553-95553	MIRANDA
94971-94971	TOMALES	95267-95298	STOCKTON	95426-95426	COBB	95554-95554	MYERS FLAT
94972-94972	VALLEY FORD	95301-95301	ATWATER	95427-95427	COMPTCHE	95555-95555	ORICK
94973-94973	WOODACRE	95303-95303	BALLICO	95428-95428	COVELO	95556-95556	ORLEANS
94974-94974	SAN QUENTIN	95304-95304	BANTA	95429-95429	DOS RIOS	95558-95558	PETROLIA
94975-94975	PETALUMA	95305-95305	BIG OAK FLAT	95430-95430	DUNCANS MILLS	95559-95559	PHILLIPSVILLE
94976-94976	CORTE MADERA	95306-95306	CATHEYS VALLEY	95431-95431	ELDRIDGE	95560-95560	REDWAY
94977-94977	LARKSPUR	95307-95307	CERES	95432-95432	ELK	95562-95562	RIO DELL
94978-94978	FAIRFAX	95309-95309	CHINESE CAMP	95433-95433	EL VERANO	95563-95563	SALYER
94979-94979	SAN ANSELMO	95310-95310	COLUMBIA	95435-95435	FINLEY	95564-95564	SAMOA
94998-94998	NOVATO	95311-95311	COULTERVILLE	95436-95436	FORESTVILLE	95565-95565	SCOTIA
94999-94999	PETALUMA	95312-95312	CRESSEY	95437-95437	FORT BRAGG	95567-95567	SMITH RIVER
95001-95001	APTOS	95313-95313	CROWS LANDING	95439-95439	FULTON	95568-95568	SOMES BAR
95002-95002	ALVISO	95314-95314	DARDANELLE	95441-95441	GEYSERVILLE	95569-95569	REDCREST
95003-95003	APTOS	95315-95315	DELHI	95442-95442	GLEN ELLEN	95570-95570	TRINIDAD
95004-95004	AROMAS	95316-95316	DENAIR	95443-95443	GLENHAVEN	95571-95571	WEOTT
95005-95005	BEN LOMOND	95317-95317	EL NIDO	95444-95444	GRATON	95573-95573	WILLOW CREEK
95006-95006	BOULDER CREEK	95318-95318	EL PORTAL	95445-95445	GUALALA	95585-95585	LEGGETT
95007-95007	BROOKDALE	95319-95319	EMPIRE	95446-95446	GUERNEVILLE	95587-95587	PIERCY
95008-95009	CAMPBELL	95320-95320	ESCALON	95448-95448	HEALDSBURG	95589-95589	WHITETHORN
95010-95010	CAPITOLA	95321-95321	GROVELAND	95449-95449	HOPLAND	95595-95595	ZENIA
95011-95011	CAMPBELL	95322-95322	GUSTINE	95450-95450	JENNER	95601-95601	AMADOR CITY
95012-95012	CASTROVILLE	95323-95323	HICKMAN	95451-95451	KELSEYVILLE	95602-95602	AUBURN
95013-95013	COYOTE	95324-95324	HILMAR	95452-95452	KENWOOD	95605-95605	WEST SACRAMENTO
95014-95016	CUPERTINO	95325-95325	HORNITOS	95453-95453	LAKEPORT	95606-95606	BROOKS
95017-95017	DAVENPORT	95326-95326	HUGHSON	95454-95454	LAYTONVILLE	95607-95607	CAPAY
95018-95018	FELTON	95327-95327	JAMESTOWN	95456-95456	LITTLERIVER	95608-95609	CARMICHAEL
95019-95019	FREEDOM	95328-95328	KEYES	95457-95457	LOWER LAKE	95610-95611	CITRUS HEIGHTS
95020-95021	GILROY	95329-95329	LA GRANGE	95458-95458	LUCERNE	95612-95612	CLARKSBURG
95023-95024	HOLLISTER	95330-95330	LATHROP	95459-95459	MANCHESTER	95613-95613	COLOMA
95026-95026	HOLY CITY	95333-95333	LE GRAND	95460-95460	MENDOCINO	95614-95614	COOL
95030-95033	LOS GATOS	95334-95334	LIVINGSTON	95461-95461	MIDDLETOWN	95615-95615	COURTLAND
95035-95036	MILPITAS	95335-95335	LONG BARN	95462-95462	MONTE RIO	95616-95617	DAVIS
95037-95038	MORGAN HILL	95336-95337	MANTECA	95463-95463	NAVARRO	95618-95618	EL MACERO
95039-95039	MOSS LANDING	95338-95338	MARIPOSA	95464-95464	NICE	95619-95619	DIAMOND SPRINGS
95041-95041	MOUNT HERMON	95340-95341	MERCED	95465-95465	OCCIDENTAL	95620-95620	DIXON
95042-95042	NEW ALMADEN	95342-95342	ATWATER	95466-95466	PHILO	95621-95621	CITRUS HEIGHTS
95043-95043	PAICINES	95343-95344	MERCED	95468-95468	POINT ARENA	95623-95623	EL DORADO
95044-95044	REDWOOD ESTATES	95345-95345	MIDPINES	95469-95469	POTTER VALLEY	95624-95624	ELK GROVE
95045-95045	SAN JUAN BAUTISTA	95346-95346	MI WUK VILLAGE	95470-95470	REDWOOD VALLEY	95625-95625	ELMIRA
95046-95046	SAN MARTIN	95347-95347	MOCCASIN	95471-95471	RIO NIDO	95626-95626	ELVERTA
95050-95056	SANTA CLARA	95348-95348	MERCED	95472-95473	SEBASTOPOL	95627-95627	ESPARTO
95060-95065	SANTA CRUZ	95350-95358	MODESTO	95476-95476	SONOMA	95628-95628	FAIR OAKS
95066-95067	SCOTTS VALLEY	95360-95360	NEWMAN	95480-95480	STEWARTS POINT	95629-95629	FIDDLETOWN
95070-95071	SARATOGA	95361-95361	OAKDALE	95481-95481	TALMAGE	95630-95630	FOLSOM
95073-95073	SOQUEL	95363-95363	PATTERSON	95482-95482	UKIAH	95631-95631	FORESTHILL
95075-95075	TRES PINOS	95364-95364	PINECREST	95485-95485	UPPER LAKE	95632-95632	GALT
95076-95077	WATSONVILLE	95365-95365	PLANADA	95486-95486	VILLA GRANDE	95633-95633	GARDEN VALLEY
95101-95139	SAN JOSE	95366-95366	RIPON	95487-95487	VINEBURG	95634-95634	GEORGETOWN
95140-95140	MOUNT HAMILTON	95367-95367	RIVERBANK	95488-95488	WESTPORT	95635-95635	GREENWOOD
95141-95196	SAN JOSE	95368-95368	SALIDA	95490-95490	WILLITS	95636-95636	GRIZZLY FLATS
95201-95219	STOCKTON	95369-95369	SNELLING	95492-95492	WINDSOR	95637-95637	GUINDA
95220-95220	ACAMPO	95370-95370	SONORA	95493-95493	WITTER SPRINGS	95638-95638	HERALD
95221-95221	ALTAVILLE	95372-95372	SOULSBYVILLE	95494-95494	YORKVILLE	95639-95639	HOOD
95222-95222	ANGELS CAMP	95373-95373	STANDARD	95497-95497	THE SEA RANCH	95640-95640	IONE
95223-95223	ARNOLD	95374-95374	STEVINSON	95501-95503	EUREKA	95641-95641	ISLETON
95224-95224	AVERY	95375-95375	STRAWBERRY	95511-95511	ALDERPOINT	95642-95642	JACKSON
95225-95225	BURSON	95376-95378	TRACY	95514-95514	BLOCKSBURG	95644-95644	KIT CARSON
95226-95226	CAMPO SECO	95379-95379	TUOLUMNE	95518-95518	ARCATA	95645-95645	KNIGHTS LANDING
95227-95227	CLEMENTS	95380-95382	TURLOCK	95519-95519	MCKINLEYVILLE	95646-95646	KIRKWOOD
95228-95228	COPPEROPOLIS	95383-95383	TWAIN HARTE	95521-95521	ARCATA	95648-95648	LINCOLN
95229-95229	DOUGLAS FLAT	95385-95385	VERNALIS	95524-95524	BAYSIDE	95650-95650	LOOMIS
95230-95230	FARMINGTON	95386-95386	WATERFORD	95525-95525	BLUE LAKE	95651-95651	LOTUS
95231-95231	FRENCH CAMP	95387-95387	WESTLEY	95526-95526	BRIDGEVILLE	95652-95652	MCCLELLAN AFB
95232-95232	GLENCOE	95388-95388	WINTON	95527-95527	BURNT RANCH	95653-95653	MADISON
95233-95233	HATHAWAY PINES	95389-95389	YOSEMITE NATIONAL PARK	95528-95528	CARLOTTA	95654-95654	MARTELL
95234-95234	HOLT			95531-95532	CRESCENT CITY	95655-95655	MATHER
95236-95236	LINDEN	95390-95390	RIVERBANK	95534-95534	CUTTEN	95656-95656	MOUNT AUKUM
95237-95237	LOCKEFORD	95397-95397	MODESTO	95536-95536	FERNDALE	95658-95658	NEWCASTLE
95240-95242	LODI	95401-95409	SANTA ROSA	95537-95537	FIELDS LANDING	95659-95659	NICOLAUS
95245-95245	MOKELUMNE HILL	95410-95410	ALBION	95538-95538	FORT DICK	95660-95660	NORTH HIGHLANDS
95246-95246	MOUNTAIN RANCH	95412-95412	ANNAPOLIS	95540-95540	FORTUNA	95661-95661	ROSEVILLE
95247-95247	MURPHYS	95415-95415	BOONVILLE	95542-95542	GARBERVILLE	95662-95662	ORANGEVALE

Code	Name	Code	Name	Code	Name	Code	Name
95663-95663	PENRYN	95931-95931	COLLEGE CITY	96038-96038	GRENADA	96135-96135	VINTON
95664-95664	PILOT HILL	95932-95932	COLUSA	96039-96039	HAPPY CAMP	96136-96136	WENDEL
95665-95665	PINE GROVE	95934-95934	CRESCENT MILLS	96040-96040	HAT CREEK	96137-96137	WESTWOOD
95666-95666	PIONEER	95935-95935	DOBBINS	96041-96041	HAYFORK	96140-96140	CARNELIAN BAY
95667-95667	PLACERVILLE	95936-95936	DOWNIEVILLE	96044-96044	HORNBROOK	96141-96141	HOMEWOOD
95668-95668	PLEASANT GROVE	95937-95937	DUNNIGAN	96046-96046	HYAMPOM	96142-96142	TAHOMA
95669-95669	PLYMOUTH	95938-95938	DURHAM	96047-96047	IGO	96143-96143	KINGS BEACH
95670-95670	RANCHO CORDOVA	95939-95939	ELK CREEK	96048-96048	JUNCTION CITY	96145-96145	TAHOE CITY
95671-95671	REPRESA	95940-95940	FEATHER FALLS	96049-96049	REDDING	96146-96146	OLYMPIC VALLEY
95672-95672	RESCUE	95941-95941	FORBESTOWN	96050-96050	KLAMATH RIVER	96148-96148	TAHOE VISTA
95673-95673	RIO LINDA	95942-95942	FOREST RANCH	96051-96051	LAKEHEAD	96150-96158	SOUTH LAKE TAHOE
95674-95674	RIO OSO	95943-95943	GLENN	96052-96052	LEWISTON	96160-96162	TRUCKEE
95675-95675	RIVER PINES	95944-95944	GOODYEARS BAR	96053-96053	MCARTHUR		
95676-95676	ROBBINS	95945-95945	GRASS VALLEY	96054-96054	LOOKOUT		
95677-95677	ROCKLIN	95946-95946	PENN VALLEY	96055-96055	LOS MOLINOS		
95678-95678	ROSEVILLE	95947-95947	GREENVILLE	96056-96056	MCARTHUR		
95679-95679	RUMSEY	95948-95948	GRIDLEY	96057-96057	MCCLOUD		
95680-95680	RYDE	95949-95949	GRASS VALLEY	96058-96058	MACDOEL		
95681-95681	SHERIDAN	95950-95950	GRIMES	96059-96059	MANTON		
95682-95682	SHINGLE SPRINGS	95951-95951	HAMILTON CITY	96061-96061	MILL CREEK		
95683-95683	SLOUGHHOUSE	95953-95953	LIVE OAK	96062-96062	MILLVILLE		
95684-95684	SOMERSET	95954-95954	MAGALIA	96063-96063	MINERAL		
95685-95685	SUTTER CREEK	95955-95955	MAXWELL	96064-96064	MONTAGUE		
95686-95686	THORNTON	95956-95956	MEADOW VALLEY	96065-96065	MONTGOMERY CREEK		
95687-95688	VACAVILLE	95957-95957	MERIDIAN	96067-96067	MOUNT SHASTA		
95689-95689	VOLCANO	95958-95958	NELSON	96068-96068	NUBIEBER		
95690-95690	WALNUT GROVE	95959-95959	NEVADA CITY	96069-96069	OAK RUN		
95691-95691	WEST SACRAMENTO	95960-95960	NORTH SAN JUAN	96070-96070	OBRIEN		
95692-95692	WHEATLAND	95961-95961	OLIVEHURST	96071-96071	OLD STATION		
95693-95693	WILTON	95962-95962	OREGON HOUSE	96073-96073	PALO CEDRO		
95694-95694	WINTERS	95963-95963	ORLAND	96074-96074	PASKENTA		
95695-95695	WOODLAND	95965-95966	OROVILLE	96075-96075	PAYNES CREEK		
95696-95696	VACAVILLE	95967-95967	PARADISE	96076-96076	PLATINA		
95697-95697	YOLO	95968-95968	PALERMO	96078-96078	PROBERTA		
95698-95698	ZAMORA	95969-95969	PARADISE	96079-96079	SHASTA LAKE		
95699-95699	DRYTOWN	95970-95970	PRINCETON	96080-96080	RED BLUFF		
95701-95701	ALTA	95971-95971	QUINCY	96084-96084	ROUND MOUNTAIN		
95703-95703	APPLEGATE	95972-95972	RACKERBY	96085-96085	SCOTT BAR		
95709-95709	CAMINO	95973-95973	CHICO	96086-96086	SEIAD VALLEY		
95712-95712	CHICAGO PARK	95974-95974	RICHVALE	96087-96087	SHASTA		
95713-95713	COLFAX	95975-95975	ROUGH AND READY	96088-96088	SHINGLETOWN		
95714-95714	DUTCH FLAT	95976-95976	CHICO	96089-96089	SHASTA LAKE		
95715-95715	EMIGRANT GAP	95977-95977	SMARTVILLE	96090-96090	TEHAMA		
95717-95717	GOLD RUN	95978-95978	STIRLING CITY	96091-96091	TRINITY CENTER		
95720-95720	KYBURZ	95979-95979	STONYFORD	96092-96092	VINA		
95721-95721	ECHO LAKE	95980-95980	STORRIE	96093-96093	WEAVERVILLE		
95722-95722	MEADOW VISTA	95981-95981	STRAWBERRY VALLEY	96094-96094	WEED		
95724-95724	NORDEN	95982-95982	SUTTER	96095-96095	WHISKEYTOWN		
95726-95726	POLLOCK PINES	95983-95983	TAYLORSVILLE	96096-96096	WHITMORE		
95728-95728	SODA SPRINGS	95984-95984	TWAIN	96097-96097	YREKA		
95735-95735	TWIN BRIDGES	95986-95986	WASHINGTON	96099-96099	REDDING		
95736-95736	WEIMAR	95987-95987	WILLIAMS	96101-96101	ALTURAS		
95741-95743	RANCHO CORDOVA	95988-95988	WILLOWS	96103-96103	BLAIRSDEN-GRAEAGLE		
95746-95746	GRANITE BAY	95991-95993	YUBA CITY	96104-96104	CEDARVILLE		
95747-95747	ROSEVILLE	96001-96003	REDDING	96105-96105	CHILCOOT		
95758-95759	ELK GROVE	96006-96006	ADIN	96106-96106	CLIO		
95762-95762	EL DORADO HILLS	96007-96007	ANDERSON	96107-96107	COLEVILLE		
95763-95763	FOLSOM	96008-96008	BELLA VISTA	96108-96108	DAVIS CREEK		
95765-95765	ROCKLIN	96009-96009	BIEBER	96109-96109	DOYLE		
95776-95776	WOODLAND	96010-96010	BIG BAR	96110-96110	EAGLEVILLE		
95798-95799	WEST SACRAMENTO	96011-96011	BIG BEND	96111-96111	FLORISTON		
95812-95842	SACRAMENTO	96013-96013	BURNEY	96112-96112	FORT BIDWELL		
95843-95843	ANTELOPE	96014-96014	CALLAHAN	96113-96113	HERLONG		
95851-95899	SACRAMENTO	96015-96015	CANBY	96114-96114	JANESVILLE		
95901-95901	MARYSVILLE	96016-96016	CASSEL	96115-96115	LAKE CITY		
95903-95903	BEALE AFB	96017-96017	CASTELLA	96116-96116	LIKELY		
95910-95910	ALLEGHANY	96019-96019	SHASTA LAKE	96117-96117	LITCHFIELD		
95912-95912	ARBUCKLE	96020-96020	CHESTER	96118-96118	LOYALTON		
95913-95913	ARTOIS	96021-96021	CORNING	96119-96119	MADELINE		
95914-95914	BANGOR	96022-96022	COTTONWOOD	96120-96120	MARKLEEVILLE		
95915-95915	BELDEN	96023-96023	DORRIS	96121-96121	MILFORD		
95916-95916	BERRY CREEK	96024-96024	DOUGLAS CITY	96122-96122	PORTOLA		
95917-95917	BIGGS	96025-96025	DUNSMUIR	96123-96123	RAVENDALE		
95918-95918	BROWNS VALLEY	96027-96027	ETNA	96124-96124	CALPINE		
95919-95919	BROWNSVILLE	96028-96028	FALL RIVER MILLS	96125-96125	SIERRA CITY		
95920-95920	BUTTE CITY	96029-96029	FLOURNOY	96126-96126	SIERRAVILLE		
95922-95922	CAMPTONVILLE	96031-96031	FORKS OF SALMON	96128-96128	STANDISH		
95923-95923	CANYONDAM	96032-96032	FORT JONES	96129-96129	BECKWOURTH		
95924-95924	CEDAR RIDGE	96033-96033	FRENCH GULCH	96130-96130	SUSANVILLE		
95925-95925	CHALLENGE	96034-96034	GAZELLE	96132-96132	TERMO		
95926-95929	CHICO	96035-96035	GERBER	96133-96133	TOPAZ		
95930-95930	CLIPPER MILLS	96037-96037	GREENVIEW	96134-96134	TULELAKE		

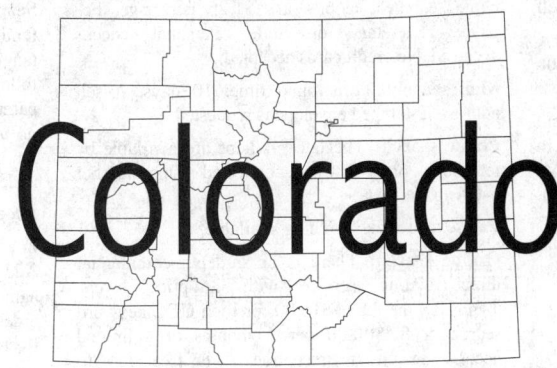

Colorado

General Help Numbers:

Governor's Office

136 State Capitol Bldg
Denver, CO 80203-1792
http://www.state.co.us/gov_dir/
governor_office.html

303-866-2471
Fax 303-866-2003
8AM-5PM

Attorney General's Office

Department of Law
1525 Sherman St, 5th Floor
Denver, CO 80203
http://www.ago.state.co.us

303-866-4500
Fax 303-866-5691
8AM-5PM

State Court Administrator

1301 Pennsylvania St, Suite 300
Denver, CO 80203
http://www.courts.state.co.us

303-861-1111
Fax 303-837-2340
8AM-5PM

State Archives

Archives & Public Records
1313 Sherman St, Room 1B-20
Denver, CO 80203
http://www.archives.state.co.us

303-866-2055
Fax 303-866-2257
9AM-4:30PM

State Specifics:

Capital:	Denver Denver County
Time Zone:	MST
Number of Counties:	63
Population:	4,301,261
Web Site:	www.state.co.us

State Agencies

Criminal Records

Bureau of Investigation, State Repository, Identification Unit, 690 Kipling St, Suite 3000, Denver, CO 80215; 303-239-4208, 303-239-0865 (Fax), 8AM-4:30PM.

http://cbi.state.co.us

Indexing & Storage: Records are available from 1967 on. Records prior to 1967 are in on-site computer archives. Records are indexed on inhouse computer, fingerprint cards.

Searching: Must have a request disclaimer stating "This record shall not be used for the direct solicitation of business or pecuniary gain" signed by requester. Include the following in your request-full name, date of birth, sex, race. The SSN is optional, but suggested. The following data is not released: sealed records or juvenile records.

Access by: mail, in person, online.

Fee & Payment: Name check-$10.00 per name; fingerprint search-$13.00 per fingerprint; fingerprint search plus notification of subsequent arrest in CO-$14.00; nationwide fingerprint search-$22.00. Possible fee changes take place in July each year. Fee payee: Colorado Bureau of Investigations (CBI). Prepayment required. No personal checks accepted. Credit cards accepted: MasterCard, Visa.

Mail search: Turnaround time: 3 days. No self addressed stamped envelope is required.

In person search: You may request information in person.

Online search: There is a remote access system available called the Electronic Clearance System (ECS). This is an overnight batch system, open M-F from 7AM to 4PM. The fee is $5.50 per record. There is no set-up fee, but requesters must register. Billing is monthly. For more information, call (303) 239-4230.

Corporation Records
Trademarks/Servicemarks
Fictitious Name
Limited Liability Company Records
Assumed Name

Secretary of State, Business Division, 1560 Broadway, Suite 200, Denver, CO 80202; 303-894-2251 (Corporations), 900-555-1717 (Status-Name), 303-894-2242 (Fax), 7:30AM-5PM.

http://www.sos.state.co.us

Indexing & Storage: Records are available for all active companies. Inactive company records are archived. New records are available for inquiry immediately. Records are indexed on microfilm, inhouse computer.

Searching: Include the following in your request-full name of business.

Access by: mail, phone, fax, in person, online.

Fee & Payment: There is no fee for searching active companies; there is a $5.00 per business name searched fee for archived records. The copy fee is $.50 per page. Fee payee: Secretary of State. Prepayment required. Personal checks accepted. No credit cards accepted.

Mail search: Turnaround time: 2 to 3 days.

Phone search: The 900 number service is available for $1.50 per minute.

Fax search: Orders requested by fax are $3.00 and returned by fax for $2.50 per page.

Online search: The Sec. of State's Business Record Search page offers free searching of corporate names and associate information at www.sos.state.co.us/pubs/business/main.htm.

Expedited service: Expedited service is available for mail, phone and fax searches. Turnaround time: 1 day. Add $15.00 per business name.

Uniform Commercial Code
Federal Tax Liens
State Tax Liens

Secretary of State, UCC Division, 1560 Broadway, Suite 200, Denver, CO 80202; 303-894-2200, 303-894-2242 (Fax), 7:30AM-5PM.

http://ww.sos.state.co.us

Indexing & Storage: Records are available from 1966. Records are indexed on computer from 1979, and on microfiche from 1987 to 1997.

Searching: Use search request form UCC-11. The search includes tax liens. Include the following in your request-debtor name.

Access by: mail, phone, fax, in person, online.

Fee & Payment: The search fee is $13.00 per name searched. Copies are $1.25 per page. Fee payee: Secretary of State. Personal checks accepted. No credit cards accepted.

Mail search: Turnaround time: 10 days. A self addressed stamped envelope is requested.

Phone search: The latest 4 liens are available by telephone, press 3 when connected using number listed above.

Fax search: Fax searching available.

Online search: There is an in-depth commercial direct dial-up service with 3 price levels. Typically, the fee is $15.00 for each UCC keyword search or $2,500.00 per 6 months of unlimited access. Search by reception # is free. Go to www.cocis.com. There is no fee to search notice of farm product liens, the sales tax by address locator, or trade names. The commercial system has filings from the state and the counties and lien records from the DMV. Registrants may also file UCCs electronically for $5.00 each.

Expedited service: Expedited service is available for mail, phone and in person searches. Turnaround time: 1 day. There is a $15.00 fee per debtor name.

Sales Tax Registrations

Revenue Department, Taxpayers Services Office, 1375 Sherman St, Denver, CO 80261 (Courier: 1625 Broadway, Ste 805, Denver, CO 80261); 303-232-2416, 303-866-3211 (Fax), 8AM-4:30PM.

http://www.revenue.state.co.us

Indexing & Storage: Records are available from 1988 and are computerized. Records are indexed on computer.

Searching: This agency will confirm that a business is registered and, if the business is in the Trade Name Information file, they will, also, provide the business name, status, if liens, filing date, and address. Include the following in your request-business name. They will also search by tax permit number.

Access by: mail, phone, in person.

Fee & Payment: There is no search fee.

Mail search: A self addressed stamped envelope is requested.

Phone search: No fee for telephone request. They will only search by trade name.

In person search: They will release the owner's name if petitioned in writing.

Other access: Tradename lists are available on diskette, tape or paper.

Birth Certificates

Department of Public Health & Environment, Vital Records Section HSVR-A1, 4300 Cherry Creek Dr S, Denver, CO 80246-1530; 303-756-4464 (Recorded Message), 303-692-2224 (Credit Card Ordering), 303-692-2234, 800-423-1108 (Fax), 8:30AM-4:30PM.

http://www.cdphe.state.co.us/hs/certs.asp

Note: Certified copies for birth years 1924 to present can also be ordered at most county health departments.

Indexing & Storage: Records are available from 1910 to present. New records are available for

inquiry immediately. Records are indexed on microfiche, inhouse computer.

Searching: Records are released to immediate family members or to those with a direct and tangible interest in the record. Include the following in your request-full name, names of parents, mother's maiden name, date of birth, place of birth, relationship to person of record, reason for information request. Birth Certificates are filed under person of record's last name.

Access by: mail, phone, fax, in person.

Fee & Payment: Search fee is $15.00 per name. Add $5.00 if you use a credit card. Add $6.00 per name requested for additional copies. You can order by fax using a credit card. Fee payee: Vital Records. Prepayment required. Personal checks accepted. Credit cards accepted: MasterCard, Visa, AmEx, Discover.

Mail search: Turnaround time: 2 weeks. Include a daytime telephone number.No self addressed stamped envelope is required.

Phone search: You must use a credit card for an additional $5.00 fee. Turnaround time is 5 working days.

Fax search: Turnaround time 1 day, credit card required.

In person search: Turnaround time is 30-45 minutes.

Expedited service: Expedited service is available for fax searches. Turnaround time: next day. Add credit card fee ($5.00) and express delivery fee.

Death Records

Department of Public Health & Environment, Vital Records Section HSVR-A1, 4300 Cherry Creek Dr S, Denver, CO 80246-1530; 303-756-4464 (Recorded Message), 303-692-2224 (Credit Card Ordering), 303-692-2234, 800-423-1108 (Fax), 8:30AM-4:30PM.

http://www.cdphe.state.co.us/hs/certs.asp

Indexing & Storage: Records are available from 1900 to present. It takes within 4 weeks before new records are available for inquiry. Records are indexed on microfiche, inhouse computer.

Searching: Records are released to immediate family or to those with a direct and tangible interest in the records. Include the following in your request-full name, date of death, place of death, names of parents, relationship to person of record, reason for information request. Death certificates are indexed by decedent's last name and the year of death. Include date of birth or age at death.

Access by: mail, phone, fax, in person.

Fee & Payment: Search fee is $15.00 per name. Add $5.00 if you use a credit card. Add $6.00 per name requested for an additional copy. Fee payee: Vital Records. Prepayment required. Personal checks accepted. Credit cards accepted: MasterCard, Visa, AmEx, Discover.

Mail search: Turnaround time: 3 weeks. Also include a day time phone number.

Phone search: You must use a credit card. Turnaround time is 5 working days.

Fax search: Same criteria as phone searching, but turnaround time is next day.

In person search: You may request records in person for same day service. Turnaround time 30-45 minutes.

Expedited service: Expedited service is available for fax searches. Turnaround time: next day. Add use of credit card fee ($5.00) and express delivery fee.

Marriage Certificates

Department of Public Health & Environment, Vital Records Section, 4300 Cherry Creek Dr S, Denver, CO 80246-1530; 303-756-4464 (Recorded Message), 303-692-2224 (Credit Card Ordering), 303-692-2234, 800-423-1108 (Fax), 8:30AM-4:30PM.

http://www.cdphe.state.co.us/hs/certs.asp

Note: Actual marriage records are found at county where license was purchased. Records from 1900-1939 are available at no charge at the Denver Public Library and Colorado State Archives.

Indexing & Storage: Records are available for years other than listed must be searched at the county. It takes 6 months before new records are available for inquiry.

Searching: Records are open to the public. Include the following in your request-date of marriage, county of license issue. The index for records from 1900 to 1939 is by groom only.

Access by: mail, phone, fax, in person, online.

Fee & Payment: The state fee for a marriage verification is $15.00. If the year is not known and the entire index is searched, there is an additional $5.00. Fee payee: Vital Records. Prepayment required. Credit card use is only for fax, phone, and Internet searches. Personal checks accepted. Credit cards accepted: MasterCard, Visa, AmEx, Discover.

Mail search: Turnaround time: 2 weeks.

Phone search: Turnaround time is 5 days. There is an additional $5.00 fee for use of a credit card.

Fax search: Use of credit card (extra $5.00) required, turnaround time 1 day.

In person search: Turnaround time is 30 to 45 minutes. These indexes can also be searched, for no fee, at many public libraries throughout the state.

Online search: Marriages from 1975-to present can be searched at no charge on the web at www.quickinfo.net/madi/comadi.html. Only index information (names and date) is available. You may order a certified verification for $15.00 at www.cdphe.state.co.us/hs/certs.asp. Index information only. We advise customers to order record from county where license was purchased.

Expedited service: Expedited service is available. Use of credit card is required (extra $5.00 fee). Total fee depends on delivery service requested.

Divorce Records

Department of Public Health & Environment, Vital Records Section, 4300 Cherry Creek Dr S, Denver, CO 80246-1530; 303-756-4464 (Recorded Message), 303-692-2224 (Credit Card Ordering), 303-692-2234, 800-423-1108 (Fax), 8:30AM-4:30PM.

http://www.cdphe.state.co.us/hs/certs.asp

Note: This office only houses records from 1968 to current; 1900 to 1939 are found at the Denver Public Library and State Archives, as well as State Office. Searches must be performed at the county level for all other years.

Indexing & Storage: Records are available 1968 to current within this office. Records are available

1900-1939 at State Office. It takes 6 months before new records are available for inquiry.

Searching: Records are open to the public. Include the following in your request-date of divorce, county. The state only has an INDEX of the records and will provide a certified verification. Actual copies of the dissolution must be obtained from the county of issue.

Access by: mail, phone, fax, in person, online.

Fee & Payment: The state fee for a divorce verification is $15.00. If the year is not known and the entire index is searched, there is an additional $5.00. Fee payee: Vital Records. Prepayment required. Personal checks accepted. Credit cards accepted: MasterCard, Visa, AmEx, Discover.

Mail search: Turnaround time: 2 weeks. A self addressed stamped envelope is requested.

Phone search: A credit card is required with an additional fee of $5.00. Turnaround time is 5 business days.

Fax search: Same criteria as phone searching, but turnaround time is next business day.

In person search: Records can be obtained across the counter within 30 to 45 minutes.

Online search: Divorces from 1968-to present can be searched at no charge on the web at www.quickinfo.net/madi/comadi.html. Only index information (names and dates) is available. You may order a certified verification for $15.00 at www.cdphe.state.co.us/hs/certs.asp.

Expedited service: Expedited service is available for fax searches. Turnaround time: 1 day. Use of credit card is required (extra $5.00 fee). Total fee depends on delivery service requested.

Workers' Compensation Records

Division of Workers' Compensation, Customer Service, 1515 Arapahoe St, Tower 2, Ste 500, Denver, CO 80202-2117; 303-575-8700, 303-575-8882 (Fax), 8AM-5PM.

http://workerscomp.cdle.state.co.us

Indexing & Storage: Records are available from as far back 1979. If the physical records have been destroyed, the wage information is still on computer. New records are available for inquiry immediately. Records are indexed on inhouse computer.

Searching: If you are not a party to the claim, you must have a notarized release from claimant not older than 90 days. Judges notes, transcripts and depositions are not released. Older purged files will get a screen print only. Include the following in your request-claimant name, Social Security Number.

Access by: mail, phone, fax, in person.

Fee & Payment: There is no search fee, copies are $.25 per page, rush copies are $.50 per page, the fee to return via fax is $1.00 per page. Fee payee: Division of Workers' Compensation. Prepayment required. Approved accounts are billed monthly. Personal checks accepted. No credit cards accepted.

Mail search: Turnaround time: 1 to 2 days. A self addressed stamped envelope is requested.

Phone search: Limited information is given over the phone only if caller is a party to the case.

Fax search: Turnaround time is 1-2 days, unless otherwise requested.

In person search: You should call first so that they can locate records. Bring ID and notarized statement.

Other access: Lists and/or labels of carriers, adjusting companies, and attorneys are available upon request. Fees range from $3.00 to $7.00 (for list, not per name) plus postage.

Accident Reports

Department of Motor Vehicles, Driver Services, Driver Services, Denver, CO 80261-0016 (Courier: 1881 Pierce Street, Lakewood, CO 80261); 303-205-5613, 8AM-5PM.

Indexing & Storage: Records are available for 6 years from date of the accident. It takes 30 to 60 days before new records are available for inquiry.

Searching: Use of "Requestor Release and Information Request" form is required. Include the following in your request-full name, date of accident, location of accident.

Access by: mail, in person.

Fee & Payment: The fee is $2.20 per record for walk-in or mail-in searches. Fee payee: Department of Revenue. Prepayment required. Personal checks accepted. No credit cards accepted.

Mail search: Turnaround time: variable. No self addressed stamped envelope is required.

In person search: Turnaround time depends on availability of report.

Driver Records

Motor Vehicle Division, Driver Services, Denver, CO 80261-0016 (Courier: 1881 Pierce Street, Lakewood, CO 80214); 303-205-5613, 303-205-5990 (Fax), 8AM-5PM.

http://www.state.co.us/gov_dir/revenue_dir/MV_dir/mv.html

Note: Copies of tickets may be obtained this address for a fee of $2.20 per record. All requests must be submitted in writing and include the driver's name, DOB, and the specific ticket number.

Indexing & Storage: Records are available for up to 7 years. The "worse" the record, the farther back the record will be kept. It takes 3 to 12 days before new records are available for inquiry.

Searching: Address and personal data is given to certain pre-approved, permissible requesters. Otherwise the "Requester Release and Information Request" form must be signed by requester. Include the following in your request-name, date of birth, driver's license number.

Access by: mail, in person.

Fee & Payment: The fee is $2.20 per record, $2.70 if certified. Fee payee: Department of Revenue. Prepayment required. Personal checks accepted. No credit cards accepted.

Mail search: Turnaround time: 24 hours. No self addressed stamped envelope is required.

In person search: Turnaround time is immediate. Up to 50 records will be processed while you wait.

Other access: Colorado offers magnetic tape retrieval for high volume users, call 303-205-5762. Records are restricted to a one time use and cannot be stored and resold.

Vehicle Ownership
Vehicle Identification

Department of Motor Vehicles, Driver Services, Denver, CO 80261-0016 (Courier: 1881 Pierce Street, Lakewood, CO 80214); 303-205-5600, 303-205-5990 (Fax), 8AM-5PM.

http://www.state.co.us/gov_dir/revenue_dir/MV_dir/mv.htm

Indexing & Storage: Records are available 6 years back plus the current year.

Searching: Handicap and disabled vet plate data are not released. To obtain vehicle or ownership information, or for title and lien records, the requester's driver license number, and the Requestor Release and Information Request Form are required.

Access by: mail, in person.

Fee & Payment: The fee for searches is $2.20 per record. Fee payee: Department of Revenue. Prepayment required. Personal checks accepted. No credit cards accepted.

Mail search: Turnaround time: 24 hours. A self addressed stamped envelope is requested.

In person search: Turnaround time is while you wait.

Other access: Bulk requests of vehicle information on magnetic tape, computer paper, and on microfiche are available. Direct inquires to the Data Services Section, Motor Vehicle Extractions, at the address listed above.

Vessel Ownership
Vessel Registration

Colorado State Parks, Registration, 13787 S Highway 85, Littleton, CO 80125; 303-791-1920, 303-470-0782 (Fax), 8AM-5PM.

http://www.dnr.state.co.us/parks

Note: Liens must be searched at the Secretary of State.

Indexing & Storage: Records are available for the past 5 years. Older records are available on microfiche. All sail and motorized vessels must be registered.

Searching: To search, submit the registration # or serial #, DOB and a Release of Registration Records Form must be completed and signed. The following data is not released: residence addresses.

Access by: mail, fax, in person.

Fee & Payment: There is a $2.00 charge per page. Fee payee: Colorado State Parks. Prepayment

required. Personal checks accepted. No credit cards accepted.

Mail search: Turnaround time: 1 week. No self addressed stamped envelope is required.

Fax search: Turnaround time varies. Results are faxed or mailed back.

Other access: Lists are available without addresses. The fee is $10.00 plus $.05 per record. It can take as long as 2 months to process.

Legislation Records

Colorado General Assembly, State Capitol, 200 E Colfax Ave, Denver, CO 80203-1776; 303-866-2316 (Senate), 303-866-3055 (Bill Data (if in session)), 303-866-2390 (Archives), 303-866-2904 (House), 8AM-5PM.

http://www.state.co.us/gov_dir/stateleg.html

Note: The House is room 271, the Senate room 274. The legislative Council Library can be reached at 303-866-4011.

Indexing & Storage: Records are available from 1998 to present on computer, older records are on microfiche and CD-Rom. Records are indexed on inhouse computer, microfiche, CD.

Searching: Include the following in your request-bill number, year.

Access by: mail, phone, in person, online.

Fee & Payment: There is no fee for searching the current year. Prior years or voluminous requests will require a fee determined on extent of request. Fee payee: State of Colorado. Personal checks accepted. No credit cards accepted.

Mail search: Turnaround time: same day if possible. Mail searches are done only if in-depth research is not required.No self addressed stamped envelope is required. No fee for mail request.

Phone search: No fee for telephone request. Only general information is provided over the phone. There is no fee.

In person search: No fee for request.

Online search: The web site gives access to bills, status, journals from the last two sessions, and much more.

Voter Registration

Department of State, Elections Department, 1560 Broadway #200, Denver, CO 80202; 303-894-2680, 303-894-7732 (Fax), 8:30AM-5PM.

http://www.state.co.us/gov_dir/sos

Indexing & Storage: Records are available for the current year only.

Searching: Voters may request not to have their information released. Provide name and address or DOB to search. The following data is not released: Social Security Numbers.

Access by: mail, fax, in person.

Fee & Payment: The fee is $.50 per name. Fee payee: Department of State. Prepayment required. No credit cards accepted.

Mail search: Turnaround time: 2 to 3 days. A self addressed stamped envelope is requested.

Fax search: Same criteria as mail searching.

Other access: The entire database is available on tape or CD-ROM. The cost is $500. No customization is available.

GED Certificates

Colorado Dept of Education, GED Testing, 201 E Colfax Ave Rm 100, Denver, CO 80203; 303-866-6613.

http://www.colosys.net/click/ONLINE.html

Searching: All written requests must have a yes or no answer to the following question in the upper right hand corner of the request: Did the person who received the GED ever attend a Colorado public school (as in elementary or high school)? All of the following are required to search: a signed release, name, date/year of test, date of birth, Social Security Number, and location of testing.

Access by: mail, in person.

Fee & Payment: The search fee $2.00 per transcript. Fee payee: GED Testing. Prepayment required. Personal checks accepted. No credit cards accepted.

Mail search: Turnaround time: 7 days. No self addressed stamped envelope is required.

In person search: Turnaround time is 24 hours.

Hunting License Information
Fishing License Information
Access to Records is Restricted

Department of Natural Resources, Wildlife Division, 6060 Broadway, Denver, CO 80216; 303-297-1192, 303-294-0874 (Fax), 8AM-5PM.

http://www.wildlife.state.co.us

Note: The state attorney general has decided that no information on holders of individual hunting and fishing licenses can be given to the public. It is only available to law enforcement officials or to the licensed individual.

Colorado State Licensing Agencies

Licenses Searchable Online

Acupuncturist #14 .... www.dora.state.co.us/pls/real/ARMS_Search.Set_Up
Architect #15 .... www.dora.state.co.us/pls/real/ARMS_Search.Set_Up
Architectural Firm #15 .... www.dora.state.co.us/pls/real/ARMS_Search.Set_Up
Audiologist #14 .... www.dora.state.co.us/pls/real/ARMS_Search.Set_Up
Barber #16 .... www.dora.state.co.us/pls/real/ARMS_Search.Disclaimer_Page
Chiropractor #17 .... www.dora.state.co.us/pls/real/ARMS_Search.Disclaimer_Page
Cosmetician #16 .... www.dora.state.co.us/pls/real/ARMS_Search.Disclaimer_Page
Cosmetologist #16 .... www.dora.state.co.us/pls/real/ARMS_Search.Disclaimer_Page
Counselor, Professional #20 .... www.dora.state.co.us/pls/real/ARMS_Search.Disclaimer_Page
Credit Union #09 .... www.dora.state.co.us/Financial-Services/homeregu.html#credit
Dental Hygienist #18 .... www.dora.state.co.us/pls/real/ARMS_Search.Disclaimer_Page
Dentist #18 .... www.dora.state.co.us/pls/real/ARMS_Search.Disclaimer_Page
Electrical Contractor #41 .... www.dora.state.co.us/pls/real/ARMS_Search.Disclaimer_Page
Electrician Journeyman/Master #41 .... www.dora.state.co.us/pls/real/ARMS_Search.Disclaimer_Page
Engineer/Engineer in Training #19 .... www.dora.state.co.us/pls/real/ARMS_Search.Disclaimer_Page
Family Therapist #20 .... www.dora.state.co.us/pls/real/ARMS_Search.Disclaimer_Page
Hearing Aid Dealer #14 .... www.dora.state.co.us/pls/real/ARMS_Search.Set_Up
Land Surveyor/ Land Surveyor Intern #19 .... www.dora.state.co.us/pls/real/ARMS_Search.Disclaimer_Page
Lobbyist #37 .... www.sos.state.co.us/pubs/bingo_raffles/new2001lobbyist_dir.htm
Manicurist #16 .... www.dora.state.co.us/pls/real/ARMS_Search.Disclaimer_Page
Manufactured Housing Dealer #22 .... www.dola.state.co.us/doh/dealers.htm
Marriage Therapist #20 .... www.dora.state.co.us/pls/real/ARMS_Search.Disclaimer_Page
Medical Doctor #21 .... www.dora.state.co.us/pls/real/ARMS_Search.Disclaimer_Page
Midwife #28 .... www.dora.state.co.us/pls/real/ARMS_Search.Disclaimer_Page
Nurse #01 .... www.dora.state.co.us/pls/real/ARMS_Search.Disclaimer_Page
Nurses' Aide #01 .... www.dora.state.co.us/pls/real/ARMS_Search.Disclaimer_Page
Nursing Care Facility #23 .... www.dora.state.co.us/pls/real/ARMS_Search.Set_Up
Nursing Home Administrator #23 .... www.dora.state.co.us/pls/real/ARMS_Search.Set_Up
Optometrist #33 .... www.dora.state.co.us/pls/real/ARMS_Search.Disclaimer_Page
Outfitter #24 .... www.dora.state.co.us/pls/real/ARMS_Search.Disclaimer_Page
Pharmacist/Pharmacy/Intern #26 .... www.dora.state.co.us/pls/real/ARMS_Search.Disclaimer_Page
Physical Therapist #32 .... www.dora.state.co.us/pls/real/ARMS_Search.Disclaimer_Page
Physician Assistant #21 .... www.dora.state.co.us/pls/real/ARMS_Search.Disclaimer_Page
Plumber Journeyman/Master/Residential #35 ..... www.dora.state.co.us/pls/real/ARMS_Search.Disclaimer_Page
Podiatrist #27 .... www.dora.state.co.us/pls/real/ARMS_Search.Disclaimer_Page
Psychologist #20 .... www.dora.state.co.us/pls/real/ARMS_Search.Disclaimer_Page
Public Accountant-CPA #13 .... www.dora.state.co.us/pls/real/ARMS_Search.Disclaimer_Page
Real Estate Appraiser #12 .... www.dora.state.co.us/pls/real/re_estate_home
Real Estate Broker/Salesperson #12 .... www.dora.state.co.us/pls/real/re_estate_home
River Outfitter #38 .... www.dora.state.co.us/pls/real/ARMS_Search.Disclaimer_Page
Savings & Loan Association #09 .... www.dora.state.co.us/Financial-Services/homeregu.html#savings
Securities Broker #34 .... http://pdpi.nasdr.com/pdpi/disclaimer_frame.htm
Securities Dealer #34 .... http://pdpi.nasdr.com/pdpi/disclaimer_frame.htm
Social Worker #20 .... www.dora.state.co.us/pls/real/ARMS_Search.Disclaimer_Page
Stock Broker #34 .... http://pdpi.nasdr.com/pdpi/disclaimer_frame.htm
Veterinarian #31 .... www.dora.state.co.us/pls/real/ARMS_Search.Disclaimer_Page
Veterinary Student #31 .... www.dora.state.co.us/pls/real/ARMS_Search.Disclaimer_Page

Licensing Quick Finder

Acupuncturist #14	303-894-2464
Architect #15	303-894-7441
Architectural Firm #15	303-894-7441
Artificial Inseminator #31	303-894-7755
Asbestos Building Inspector #05	303-692-3158
Asbestos Inspector/Management Planner #05	303-692-3158
Asbestos Project Designer #05	303-692-3158
Asbestos Supervisor #05	303-692-3158
Asbestos Worker #05	303-692-3158
Attorney #04	303-893-8096
Audiologist #14	303-894-2464
Bail Bond Agent #10	303-894-7583
Bank, Commercial/Industrial #08	303-894-7575
Barber #16	303-894-7772
Bulk Milk Hauler #06	303-692-3643
Child Care Facility #29	800-799-5876
Chiropractor #17	303-894-7762
Collection Agency #03	303-866-5706
Commercial Driving School #07	303-205-5841
Cosmetician #16	303-894-7772
Cosmetologist #16	303-894-7772
Counselor, Professional #20	303-894-7766
Court Reporter #36	303-837-3695
Credit Union #09	303-894-2336
Dairy Farm #06	303-692-3643
Dairy Plant #06	303-692-3643
Debt Management Company #08	303-894-7575
Dental Hygienist #18	303-894-7758
Dentist #18	303-894-7758
Egg Seller #02	303-239-4140
Electrical Contractor #41	303-894-2300
Electrician Journeyman/Master #41	303-894-2300
Engineer/Engineer in Training #19	303-894-7788
Family Care Home #29	303-866-5958
Family Therapist #20	303-894-7766

Food Plant Operator #02	303-239-4140
Greyhound Racing #11	303-205-2990
Hearing Aid Dealer #14	303-894-2464
Horse Racing #11	303-205-2990
Insurance Agency #10	303-894-2419
Insurance Producer #10	303-894-2419
Investment Advisors #34	303-894-2320
Kennel #02	303-239-4166
Land Surveyor #19	303-894-7788
Land Surveyor Intern #19	303-894-7788
Life Care Institution #09	303-894-2336
Liquor Control #39	303-205-2300
Lobbyist #37	303-894-2200
Manicurist #16	303-894-7772
Manufactured Housing Dealer #22	303-866-4616
Manufacturer Housing Installer #22	303-866-4616
Marriage Therapist #20	303-894-7766
Medical Doctor #21	303-894-7690
Midwife #28	303-894-2464
Milk & Cream Sampler #06	303-692-3643
Milk & Cream Tester #06	303-692-3643
Money Order Company #08	303-894-7575
Motor Vehicle Buyer #42	303-205-5604
Motor Vehicle Dealer, Franchised #42	303-205-5604
Motor Vehicle Dealer, Used #42	303-205-5604
Motor Vehicle Mfg. Representative #42	303-205-5604
Motor Vehicle Salesperson #42	303-205-5604
Motor Vehicle Wholesaler #42	303-205-5604
Notary Public #37	303-894-2680
Nurse #01	303-894-2430
Nursery #02	303-239-4140
Nurses' Aide #01	303-894-2816
Nursing Care Facility #23	303-894-7800
Nursing Home Administrator #23	303-894-7760
Optometrist #33	303-894-7750
Outfitter #24	303-894-7778

Pesticide Applicator #02	303-239-4140
Pet Animal/Bird Dealer #02	303-239-4166
Pharmacist/Pharmacy/Intern #26	303-894-7750
Physical Therapist #32	303-894-2440
Physician Assistant #21	303-894-7690
Physiotherapist #32	303-894-2440
Plumber Journeyman/Master/Residential #35	303-894-2300 x110
Podiatrist #27	303-894-2464
Psychiatric Technician #01	303-894-2430
Psychologist #20	303-894-7766
Public Accountant-CPA #13	303-894-7441
Public Adjuster #10	303-894-7499
Real Estate Appraiser #12	303-894-2166
Real Estate Broker/Salesperson #12	303-894-2166
River Outfitter #38	303-894-7772
Savings & Loan Association #09	303-894-2336
School Administrator/Principal #40	303-866-6628
School Special Service Associate #40	303-866-6628
Securities Broker #34	303-894-2320
Securities Dealer #34	303-894-2320
Securities Sales Promoter #34	303-894-2320
Ski Lift #25	303-894-7785
Small Business Dev. Credit Corp. #09	303-894-2336
Social Worker #20	303-894-7766
Solicitor/Telemarketer #03	303-866-5079
Stock Broker #34	303-894-2320
Substitute Teacher #40	303-866-6968
Teacher #40	303-866-6628
Tramway #25	303-894-7785
Trust Company #08	303-894-7575
Veterinarian #31	303-894-7755
Veterinary Student #31	303-894-7755
Vocational Education Teacher #40	303-866-6628
Wireman, Residential #41	303-894-2300

Licensing Agency Information

#01 Board of Nursing, 1560 Broadway, #880, Denver, CO 80202; 303-894-2430, Fax: 303-894-2821.
www.dora.state.co.us/Nursing
Direct web site URL to search for licensees: www.dora.state.co.us/pls/real/ARMS_Search.Disc laimer_Page. You can search online using license number, name, and city.

#02 Agriculture Department, 700 Kipling St, #4000, Lakewood, CO 80215-5894; 303-239-4100, Fax: 303-239-4125.
www.ag.state.co.us

#03 Attorney General's Office, 1525 Sherman St, 5th Fl, Denver, CO 80203; 303-866-4500, Fax: 303-866-5691.
www.ago.state.co.us

#04 Board of Law Examiners, 600 17th St, Dominion Plaza Bldg, #910S, Denver, CO 80202; 303-534-7841, Fax: 303-534-3643.
www.courts.state.co.us/ble/ble.htm

#05 Department of Public Health & Environment, 4300 Cherry Creek Dr S, Denver, CO 80246; 303-692-3150, Fax: 303-782-0278.
www.cdphe.state.co.us/ap/asbeshom.asp

#06 Consumer Protection Division, 4300 Cherry Creek Dr S, Denver, CO 80222-1530; 303-692-3622, Fax: 303-753-6809.
www.cdphe2.state.co.us/cp/dairy.asp

#07 Department of Revenue, 1375 Sherman St, Denver, CO 80261; 303-866-3091, Fax: 303-205-5634.

#08 Division of Banking, 1560 Broadway, #1175, Denver, CO 80202; 303-894-7575, Fax: 303-894-7570.
www.dora.state.co.us/Banking

#09 Division of Financial Services, 1560 Broadway, #1520, Denver, CO 80202; 303-894-2336, Fax: 303-894-7886.
www.dora.state.co.us/Financial-Services

#10 Division of Insurance, 1560 Broadway, #850, Denver, CO 80202; 303-894-7499, Fax: 303-894-7455.
www.dora.state.co.us/Insurance

#11 Division of Racing Events, 1881 Pierce St, #108, Lakewood, CO 80214; 303-205-2990, Fax: 303-205-2950.
www.state.co.us/gov_dir/revenue_dir/racing_dir/c oracing.html

#12 Division of Real Estate, 1900 Grant St, #600, Denver, CO 80203; 303-894-2166, Fax: 303-894-2683.
www.dora.state.co.us/Real-Estate
Direct web site URL to search for licensees: www.dora.state.co.us/pls/real/re_estate_home.
You can search online using company or individual name.

#13 Division of Registrations, 1560 Broadway, #1340, Denver, CO 80202; 303-894-7800, Fax: 303-894-7802.
www.dora.state.co.us/Accountants
Direct web site URL to search for licensees: www.dora.state.co.us/pls/real/ARMS_Search.Disc laimer_Page. You can search online using license

number, name, and city. Click on "Locate Colo. CPAs & Firms Online."

#14 Division of Registrations, 1560 Broadway, #680, Denver, CO 80202; 303-894-2464, Fax: 303-894-7885.
www.dora.state.co.us
Direct web site URL to search for licensees: www.dora.state.co.us/pls/real/ARMS_Search.Set Up. You can search online using license number, name, and city.

#15 Division of Registrations, 1560 Broadway, #1340, Denver, CO 80202; 303-894-7801, Fax: 303-894-7802.
www.dora.state.co.us/Architects/
Direct web site URL to search for licensees: www.dora.state.co.us/pls/real/ARMS_Search.Disc laimer_Page. You can search online using license number, name, and city. Click on "Locate Colorado Architects."

#16 Division of Registrations, 1560 Broadway, #1340, Denver, CO 80202; 303-894-7772.
www.dora.state.co.us/Barbers_Cosmetologists
Direct web site URL to search for licensees: www.dora.state.co.us/pls/real/ARMS_Search.Disc laimer_Page. You can search online using license number, name, and city.

#17 Division of Registrations, 1560 Broadway, #1310, Denver, CO 80202; 303-894-7800.
www.dora.state.co.us/chiropratic
Direct web site URL to search for licensees: www.dora.state.co.us/pls/real/ARMS_Search.Disc

laimer_Page. You can search online using license number, name, and city.

#18 Division of Registrations, 1560 Broadway, #1310, Denver, CO 80202; 303-894-7758, Fax: 303-894-7764.
www.dora.state.co.us/Dental
Direct web site URL to search for licensees: www.dora.state.co.us/pls/real/ARMS_Search.Disc laimer_Page. You can search online using license number, name, and city.

#19 Division of Registrations, 1560 Broadway, #1370, Denver, CO 80202; 303-894-7788, Fax: 303-894-7790.
www.dora.state.co.us/Engineers_Surveyors/
Direct web site URL to search for licensees: www.dora.state.co.us/pls/real/ARMS_Search.Disc laimer_Page. You can search online using license number, name, and city.

#20 Division of Registrations, 1560 Broadway, #1340, Denver, CO 80202; 303-894-7766.
www.dora.state.co.us/Mental-Health
Direct web site URL to search for licensees: www.dora.state.co.us/pls/real/ARMS_Search.Disc laimer_Page. You can search online using license number, name, and city.

#21 Div of Registrations, Dept of Regulatory Agencies, 1560 Broadway, #1300, Denver, CO 80202-5140; 303-894-7690, Fax: 303-894-7692.
www.dora.state.co.us/Medical/
Direct web site URL to search for licensees: www.dora.state.co.us/pls/real/ARMS_Search.Disc laimer_Page

#22 Division of Housing, 1313 Sherman St, Denver, CO 80203; 303-866-4656, Fax: 303-866-4077.
www.dola.state.co.us/doh/doh.htm

#23 Division of Registrations, 1560 Broadway, #1310, Denver, CO 80202; 303-894-7800, Fax: 303-894-7764.
Direct web site URL to search for licensees: www.dora.state.co.us/pls/real/ARMS_Search.Set_ Up. You can search online using license number, name, and city.

#24 Division of Registrations, 1560 Broadway, #1340, Denver, CO 80202; 303-894-7778.
www.dora.state.co.us/Outfitters
Direct web site URL to search for licensees: www.dora.state.co.us/pls/real/ARMS_Search.Disc laimer_Page. You can search online using license number, name, and city.

#25 Division of Registrations, 1560 Broadway, #1370, Denver, CO 80202; 303-894-7785, Fax: 303-894-7790.
www.dora.state.co.us/Tramway

#26 Division of Registrations, 1560 Broadway, #1310, Denver, CO 80202-5146; 303-894-7750, Fax: 303-894-7764.
www.dora.state.co.us/Pharmacy
Direct web site URL to search for licensees: www.dora.state.co.us/pls/real/ARMS_Search.Disc laimer_Page. You can search online using license number, name, and city.

#27 Division of Registrations, 1560 Broadway, #680, Denver, CO 80202; 303-894-2464, Fax: 303-894-2821.
www.dora.state.co.us/Podiatrists
Direct web site URL to search for licensees: www.dora.state.co.us/pls/real/ARMS_Search.Disc laimer_Page. You can search online using license number, name, or city.

#28 Division of Registrations, 1560 Broadway, #1545, Denver, CO 80202; 303-894-2464, Fax: 303-894-7885.
www.dora.state.co.us/Midwives
Direct web site URL to search for licensees: www.dora.state.co.us/pls/real/ARMS_Search.Disc laimer_Page. You can search online using license number, name, and city.

#29 Department of Human Services, 1575 Sherman St, Denver, CO 80202; 800-799-5958, Fax: 303-866-4453.
www.cdhs.state.co.us/cyf/ccare/index.html

#31 Division of Registrations, 1560 Broadway, #1310, Denver, CO 80202-5146; 303-894-7755, Fax: 303-894-7764.
www.dora.state.co.us/Veterinarians
Direct web site URL to search for licensees: www.dora.state.co.us/pls/real/ARMS_Search.Disc laimer_Page. You can search online using license number, name, and city.

#32 Division of Registrations, 1560 Broadway, #680, Denver, CO 80202; 303-894-7800, Fax: 303-894-2821.
www.dora.state.co.us/Physical-Therapy
Direct web site URL to search for licensees: www.dora.state.co.us/pls/real/ARMS_Search.Disc laimer_Page. You can search online using license number, name, and city.

#33 Division of Registrations, 1560 Broadway, #1310, Denver, CO 80202-5146; 303-894-7800, Fax: 303-894-7764.
www.dora.state.co.us/Optometry
Direct web site URL to search for licensees: www.dora.state.co.us/pls/real/ARMS_Search.Disc laimer_Page. You can search online using license number or last name, first name and city.

#34 Department of Regulatory Agencies, 1580 Lincoln, #420, Denver, CO 80203-1506; 303-894-2320, Fax: 303-861-2126.

www.dora.state.co.us/Securities/brokers.htm
Direct web site URL to search for licensees: http://pdpi.nasdr.com/pdpi/disclaimer_frame.htm.
You can search online using NASD database and procedures

#35 Examining Board of Plumbers, 1580 Logan St, #550, Denver, CO 80203-1941; 303-894-2300, Fax: 303-894-2310.
www.dora.state.co.us/Plumbing
Direct web site URL to search for licensees: www.dora.state.co.us/pls/real/ARMS_Search.Disc laimer_Page. You can search online using license number, name, and city.

#36 Judicial Department, 1301 Pennsylvania St, #300, Denver, CO 80203; 303-837-3695, Fax: 303-837-2340.
www.courts.state.co.us

#37 Office of Secretary of State, 1560 Broadway, #200, Denver, CO 80202; 303-894-2200, Fax: 303-894-2242.
www.sos.state.co.us/pubs/business/main.htm
Direct web site URL to search for licensees: www.sos.state.co.us/pubs/bingo_raffles/main.htm

#38 Division of Registrations, 1560 Broadway, #1340, Denver, CO 80202; 303-894-7778, Fax: 303-470-0782.
www.dora.state.co.us/Outfitters
Direct web site URL to search for licensees: www.dora.state.co.us/pls/real/ARMS_Search.Disc laimer_Page

#39 Revenue Department, 1881 Pierce, #108A, Lakewood, CO 80214; 303-205-2300, Fax: 303-205-2341.
www.state.co.us/gov_dir/revenue_dir/liquor_dir/li c&permit.htm

#40 Department of Education, 201 E Colifax, Denver, CO 80203; 303-866-6628, Fax: 303-866-6968.
www.cde.state.co.us/index_license.htm

#41 Electrical Board, 1580 Logan St, #550, Denver, CO 80203-1939; 303-894-2300, Fax: 303-894-2310.
www.dora.state.co.us/Electrical
Direct web site URL to search for licensees: www.dora.state.co.us/pls/real/ARMS_Search.Disc laimer_Page. You can search online using license number, name, and city.

#42 Motor Vehicle Dealer Board, 1881 Pierce St Rm 142, Lakewood, CO 80215; 303-205-5604, Fax: 303-205-5977.
www.mv.state.co.us

Colorado Federal Courts

The following list indicates the district and division name for each county in the state.

County/Court Cross Reference

County	District	County	District
Adams	Denver	La Plata	Denver
Alamosa	Denver	Lake	Denver
Arapahoe	Denver	Larimer	Denver
Archuleta	Denver	Las Animas	Denver
Baca	Denver	Lincoln	Denver
Bent	Denver	Logan	Denver
Boulder	Denver	Mesa	Denver
Chaffee	Denver	Mineral	Denver
Cheyenne	Denver	Moffat	Denver
Clear Creek	Denver	Montezuma	Denver
Conejos	Denver	Montrose	Denver
Costilla	Denver	Morgan	Denver
Crowley	Denver	Otero	Denver
Custer	Denver	Ouray	Denver
Delta	Denver	Park	Denver
Denver	Denver	Phillips	Denver
Dolores	Denver	Pitkin	Denver
Douglas	Denver	Prowers	Denver
Eagle	Denver	Pueblo	Denver
El Paso	Denver	Rio Blanco	Denver
Elbert	Denver	Rio Grande	Denver
Fremont	Denver	Routt	Denver
Garfield	Denver	Saguache	Denver
Gilpin	Denver	San Juan	Denver
Grand	Denver	San Miguel	Denver
Gunnison	Denver	Sedgwick	Denver
Hinsdale	Denver	Summit	Denver
Huerfano	Denver	Teller	Denver
Jackson	Denver	Washington	Denver
Jefferson	Denver	Weld	Denver
Kiowa	Denver	Yuma	Denver
Kit Carson	Denver		

US District Court

Denver Division US Courthouse, Room C-145, 1929 Stout St, Denver, CO 80294-3589 (Courier Address: Use mail address for courier delivery), 303-844-3433.

http://www.co.uscourts.gov

Counties: All counties in Colorado.

Indexing/Storage: Cases are indexed by defendant and plaintiff as well as by case number. New cases are available in the index immediately after filing date. A computer index is maintained. Open records are located at this court.

Fee & Payment: The fee is $20.00 per item (one party name or case number). Payment may be made by money order, cashier check, personal check, Visa, Mastercard. There is no prepayment required for any copies unless the bill is over $100.00. Payee: Clerk, US District Court. Certification fee: $7.00 per document. Copy fee: $.50 per page.

Phone Search: Over the phone, the court will release anything of public record, although they will not read long excerpts over the phone.

Mail Search: Always enclose a stamped self addressed envelope.

In Person: In person searching is available.

PACER: Sign-up number is 800-676-6856. Access fee is $.60 per minute. Local access: 303-335-2335, 303-335-2370. Case records are available back to 1990. Records are purged on a varying schedule. New records are available online after 1 day. PACER is available online at http://pacer.cod.uscourts.gov.

US Bankruptcy Court

Denver Division US Custom House, Room 114, 721 19th St, Denver, CO 80202-2508 (Courier Address: Use mail address for courier delivery), 303-844-4045.

http://www.co.uscourts.gov

Counties: All counties in Colorado.

Indexing/Storage: Cases are indexed by debtor as well as by case number. New cases are available in the index 24-48 hours after filing date. A computer index is maintained. Records are also on microfilm of all cases prior to June 1990. Open records are located at this court.

Fee & Payment: The fee is $20.00 per item (one party name or case number). Payment may be made by money order, cashier check, personal check. Prepayment is required. Personal checks are not accepted from debtors. Payee: Clerk, US Bankruptcy Court. Certification fee: $7.00 per document. Copy fee: $.50 per page. You are allowed to make your own copies. These copies cost $.10 per page. Records are available for viewing from 8:00 a.m. to 4:45 p.m., Monday through Friday in Room 114.

Phone Search: An automated voice case information service (VCIS) is available.

Mail Search: A stamped self addressed envelope is not required.

In Person: In person searching is available.

PACER: Sign-up number is 800-676-6856. Access fee is $.60 per minute. Toll-free access: 888-213-4715. Local access: 303-844-0263. Case records are available back to July 1981. New civil records are available online after 1 day. PACER is available online at http://pacer.cob.uscourts.gov.

Colorado County Courts

Court	Jurisdiction	No. of Courts	How Organized
District Courts*	General	14	22 Districts
County Courts*	Limited	17	63 Counties
Combined Courts*		49	
Denver Probate Courts*	Probate	1	
Municipal Courts	Municipal	206	
Denver Juvenile Courts	Special	1	
Water Courts	Special	7	7 Districts

* Profiled in this Sourcebook.

Court	CIVIL								
	Tort	Contract	Real Estate	Min. Claim	Max. Claim	Small Claims	Estate	Eviction	Domestic Relations
District Courts*	X	X	X	$0	No Max		X		X
County Courts*	X	X	X	$0	$15,000	$7500		X	
Denver Probate Courts*							X		
Denver Juvenile Courts									
Water Courts			X	$0	No Max				

Court	CRIMINAL				
	Felony	Misdemeanor	DWI/DUI	Preliminary Hearing	Juvenile
District Courts*	X				X
County Courts*		X	X	X	
Denver Probate Courts*					
Denver Juvenile Courts					X
Water Courts					

ADMINISTRATION   State Court Administrator, 1301 Pennsylvania St, Suite 300, Denver, CO, 80203; 303-861-1111, Fax: 303-837-2340. www.courts.state.co.us

COURT STRUCTURE   As of 9/1/2001, the maximum civil claim in County Courts was increased to $15,000. The District and County Courts have overlapping jurisdiction over civil cases involving less than $15,000 ($10,000 prior to 9/1/2001). Fortunately, District and County Courts are combined in most counties. Combined courts usually search both civil or criminal indexes for a single fee, except as indicated in the profiles.

Municipal courts only have jurisdiction over traffic, parking, and ordinance violations.

ONLINE ACCESS   There is no official governmentsystems, but we can mention a unique commercial system. All district courts and all county courts except Denver County Court are available on the Internet at www.cocourts.com as of 9/2001. Real-time records include civil, civil water, small claims, domestic, felony, misdemeanor, and traffic cases and can be accessed by name or case number. Court records go as far back as 1995. There is a fee for this subscription Internet access, generally $5.00 per search and there are discounts for volume users. Contact Jeff Mueller, Major Accounts, by telephone at 866-COCOURT, or by e-mail at Jeffm@cocourts.com. Note: Denver County Court civil records are available free online.

ADDITIONAL INFORMATION

All state agencies require a self-addressed, stamped envelope (SASE) for return of information.

Co-located with seven district courts are divisions known as Water Courts. The Water Courts are located in Weld, Pueblo, Alamosa, Montrose, Garfield, Routt, and La Platta counties; see the District Court discussion for those counties to determine the jurisdictional area for the Water Court. Water Court records are maintained by the Water Clerk and fees are similar to those for other court records. To retrieve a Water Court record, one must furnish the Case Number or the Legal Description (section, township, and range) or the Full Name of the respondent (note that the case number or legal description are preferred).

PROBATE COURTS

Denver is the only county where Probate Court is separate from the District Court.

📖 📖 📖 📖 📖 📖

Adams County

17th District Court 1100 Judicial Center Drive, Brighton, CO 80601; 303-659-1161; Fax: 303-654-3216. Hours: 8AM-5PM (MST). *Felony, Civil Actions Over $10,000, Probate.*

www.17thjudicialdistrict.com

Note: The District and County courts have combined, but records are searched separately unless requester asks to search both courts (at no extra fee).

Civil Records: Access: Mail, in person, online. Both court and visitors may perform in person searches. Search fee: $5.00 per name. Fee is $10.00 for cases before 1976. There is no fee if search done by visitor. Required to search: name, years to search. Civil cases indexed by defendant, plaintiff. Civil records on computer from Jan 1976, index books back to early 1900s. Online access to statewide court records is available at www.cocourts.com.

Criminal Records: Access: Mail, in person, online. Both court and visitors may perform in person searches. Search fee: $5.00 per name. Fee is $8.00 for cases before 1976. Required to search: name, years to search, DOB. Criminal records on computer from Jan 1976, index books back to early 1900s. Online access to criminal records is the same as civil.

General Information: No adoptions, sealed, juvenile, mental health or expunged cases released. SASE required. Turnaround time 2 days. Copy fee: $.75 per page. Certification fee: $5.00. Fee payee: Clerk of the District Court. Personal checks accepted. Credit cards accepted. Accepted in person only. Prepayment is required.

County Court 1100 Judicial Center Drive, Brighton, CO 80601; 303-659-1161. Hours: 8AM-5PM (MST). *Misdemeanor, Civil Actions Under $15,000, Eviction, Small Claims.*

Note: The District and County courts have combined, but records are searched separately unless specifically asked to search both courts for no additional fee.

Civil Records: Access: Mail, in person, online. Both court and visitors may perform in person searches. Search fee: $5.00 per name. $8.00 per name for pre-computer records. Required to search: name, years to search. Civil cases indexed by defendant, plaintiff. Civil records on computer from Jan 1990, index books back to 1965. Online access to statewide court records is available at www.cocourts.com.

Criminal Records: Access: Mail, in person, online. Both court and visitors may perform in person searches. Search fee: $5.00 per name. $8.00 per name for pre-computer records. Required to search: name, years to search, DOB. Criminal records on computer from Jan 1990, index books back to 1965. Online access to criminal records is the same as civil.

General Information: No adoptions, sealed, juvenile, mental health or expunged cases released. SASE required. Turnaround time 2 working days. Copy fee: $.75 per page. Certification fee: $5.00. Fee payee:

Adams County Combined Court. Personal checks accepted. Credit cards accepted: Visa, MasterCard. In person only. Prepayment is required.

Alamosa County

Alamosa Combined Court 702 4th St, Alamosa, CO 81101; 719-589-4996; Fax: 719-589-4998. Hours: 8AM-noon, 1-4:30PM (MST). *Felony, Civil, Eviction, Small Claims, Probate.*

Civil Records: Access: Mail, in person, online. Only the court performs in person searches; visitors may not. Search fee: $5.00 per name. Required to search: name, years to search. Civil cases indexed by defendant. Civil records on computer from May 1978, index books back to 1913. Online access to statewide court records is available at www.cocourts.com.

Criminal Records: Access: Mail, in person, online. Only the court performs in person searches; visitors may not. Search fee: $5.00 per name. Required to search: name, years to search, DOB. Criminal records on computer from May 1978, index books to 1913. Online access to criminal records is the same as civil.

General Information: Public Access terminal is available. No adoptions, sealed, juvenile, mental health or expunged cases released. SASE required. Turnaround time 10 days. Fax notes: Fee to fax results is $10.00 minimum plus $1.00 per page after 1st 10. Copy fee: $.75 per page. Certification fee: $5.00. Fee payee: Clerk, Combined Court. Personal checks accepted. Prepayment is required.

Arapahoe County

18th District Court 7325 S Potomac, Englewood, CO 80112; 303-649-6355. Hours: 8AM-5PM (MST). *Felony, Civil Actions Over $10,000, Probate.*

Civil Records: Access: Phone, mail, in person, online. Both court and visitors may perform in person searches. Search fee: $5.00 per name. Required to search: name, years to search. Civil cases indexed by defendant, plaintiff. Civil records on computer from 1985, microfiche back to 1903. Online access to statewide court records is available at www.cocourts.com.

Criminal Records: Access: Phone, mail, in person, online. Both court and visitors may perform in person searches. Search fee: $5.00 per name. Required to search: name, years to search, DOB. Criminal records on computer from 1985, microfiche back to 1903. Online access to criminal records is the same as civil.

General Information: No adoptions, sealed, juvenile, mental health or expunged cases released. SASE required. Turnaround time 1-2 days. Fax notes: No fee to fax results. Copy fee: $.75 per page. Certification fee: $5.00. Fee payee: Clerk of District Court. Personal checks accepted. Prepayment is required.

Arapahoe County Court Division B 15400 E 14th Pl, Aurora, CO 80011; 303-214-4000. Hours: 8AM-5PM (MST). *Misdemeanor, Civil Actions Under $15,000, Eviction, Small Claims.*

Civil Records: Access: Phone, mail, in person, online. Both court and visitors may perform in person searches.

Search fee: $5.00 per name. Required to search: name, years to search. Civil cases indexed by defendant, plaintiff. Civil records on computer from April 1986, microfiche from 1980-1983, index cards from 1980. Online access to statewide court records is available at www.cocourts.com.

Criminal Records: Access: Phone, mail, in person, online. Both court and visitors may perform in person searches. Search fee: $5.00 per name. Required to search: name, years to search, DOB. Criminal records on computer from April 1986, microfiche from 1980-1983, index cards from 1980. Online access to criminal records is the same as civil.

General Information: No adoptions, sealed, juvenile, mental health or expunged cases released. SASE required. Turnaround time 2 days. Copy fee: $.75 per page. Certification fee: $5.00. Fee payee: Clerk of County Court. Personal checks accepted. Credit cards accepted: Visa, MasterCard. Prepayment is required.

Littleton County Court Division A 1790 W Littleton Blvd, Littleton, CO 80120-2060; 303-798-4591. Hours: 8AM-5PM (MST). *Misdemeanor, Civil Actions Under $15,000, Eviction, Small Claims.*

Civil Records: Access: Phone, mail, fax, in person, online. Both court and visitors may perform in person searches. Search fee: $5.00 per name. Required to search: name, years to search. Civil cases indexed by defendant, plaintiff. Civil records on computer from 1986, index cards from 1965, microfiche from 1861 in District Court. Only court performs searches prior to March 1986. Online access to statewide court records is available at www.cocourts.com. Registration required; transaction fee.

Criminal Records: Access: Mail, fax, in person, online. Both court and visitors may perform in person searches. Search fee: $5.00 per name. Required to search: name, years to search, DOB. Criminal records on computer from 1986, index cards from 1965, microfiche from 1861 in District Court. Online access to criminal records is the same as civil. Only court performs searches prior to March 1986.

General Information: No adoptions, sealed, juvenile, mental health or expunged cases released. SASE required. Turnaround time 2 weeks. Copy fee: $.75 per page. Certification fee: $5.00. Fee payee: Clerk of County Court. Personal checks accepted. Credit cards accepted: Visa, MasterCard, Discover. Prepayment is required.

Archuleta County

6th District & County Courts PO Box 148, Pagosa Springs, CO 81147; 970-264-2400; Fax: 970-264-2407. Hours: 8AM-5PM (MST). *Felony, Misdemeanor, Civil, Eviction, Small Claims, Probate.*

Civil Records: Access: Mail, in person, online. Only the court performs in person searches; visitors may not. Search fee: $5.00 per name. Specific case information is $2.00 per file. Required to search: name, years to search. Civil cases indexed by defendant, plaintiff. Civil records on index cards from 1976, index books back to

1885. Online access to statewide court records is available at www.cocourts.com.

Criminal Records: Access: Mail, in person, online. Only the court performs in person searches; visitors may not. Search fee: $5.00 per name. Specific case information $2.00 per file. Required to search: name, years to search, DOB. Criminal records on index cards from 1976, index books back to 1885. Online access to criminal records is the same as civil.

General Information: No adoptions, sealed, juvenile, mental health or expunged cases released. SASE required. Turnaround time 5 days. Copy fee: $.75 per page. Certification fee: $5.00. Fee payee: Archuleta Combined Court. Personal checks accepted. Prepayment is required.

Baca County

Baca County District & County Courts 741 Main St, Springfield, CO 81073; 719-523-4555. Hours: 8AM-5PM (MST). *Felony, Misdemeanor, Civil, Eviction, Small Claims, Probate.*

Civil Records: Access: Mail, in person, online. Only the court performs in person searches; visitors may not. Search fee: $5.00 per name. Required to search: name, years to search. Civil cases indexed by defendant, plaintiff. Civil records on index cards from 1945, index books back to 1910. Online access to statewide court records is available at www.cocourts.com.

Criminal Records: Access: Mail, in person, online. Only the court performs in person searches; visitors may not. Search fee: $5.00 per name. Required to search: name, years to search, DOB. Criminal records on index cards from 1945, index books back to 1910. Online access to criminal records is the same as civil.

General Information: No adoptions, sealed, juvenile, mental health or expunged cases released. SASE required. Turnaround time 1-2 days. Copy fee: $.75 per page. Certification fee: $5.00. Fee payee: Baca County Courts. Personal checks accepted. Prepayment is required.

Bent County

16th District Court Bent County Courthouse, 725 Bent, Las Animas, CO 81054; 719-456-1353; Fax: 719-456-0040. Hours: 8AM-12, 1-5PM (MST). *Felony, Misdemeanor, Civil, Eviction, Small Claims, Probate.*

www.courts.state.co.us/district/16th/dist-16.htm

Civil Records: Access: Mail, in person, online. Both court and visitors may perform in person searches. Search fee: $5.00 per name. Required to search: name, years to search. Civil cases indexed by defendant, plaintiff. Civil records on index cards from 1975, prior to 1975 some on microfilm, on computer from 11/95 forward- all indexes available at this office. Online access to statewide court records is available at www.cocourts.com.

Criminal Records: Access: Mail, in person, online. Both court and visitors may perform in person searches. Search fee: $5.00 per name. Required to search: name, years to search, DOB, signed release. Criminal records on index cards from 1975, prior to 1975 some on microfilm, on computer from 11/95 forward- all indexes available at this office. Online access to criminal records is the same as civil.

General Information: Public Access terminal is available. No adoptions, sealed, juvenile, mental health or expunged cases released. SASE required. Turnaround time 4-5 days. Copy fee: $.75 per page. Certification fee: $5.00. Fee payee: Clerk of Combined Court. Personal checks accepted. Prepayment is required.

Boulder County

20th District & County Courts 6th & Canyon, 1777 6th St, Boulder, CO 80306; 303-441-3750. Hours: 8AM-5PM (MST). *Felony, Misdemeanor, Civil, Eviction, Small Claims, Probate.*

Civil Records: Access: Mail, in person, online. Both court and visitors may perform in person searches. Search fee: $5.00 per name. Required to search: name, years to search. Civil cases indexed by defendant, plaintiff. Civil records on computer from 1983, microfiche prior from 1977, all prior records in books. Online access to statewide court records is available at www.cocourts.com.

Criminal Records: Access: Mail, in person, online. Both court and visitors may perform in person searches. Search fee: $5.00 per name. Required to search: name, years to search, DOB, signed release. Criminal records on computer from 1983, microfiche prior from 1977, all prior records in books. Online access to criminal records is the same as civil.

General Information: No adoptions, sealed, juvenile, mental health or expunged cases released. SASE required. Turnaround time 5 days. Copy fee: $.75 per page. Certification fee: $5.00. Fee payee: 20th Judicial District. Business checks accepted. Attorney checks accepted. Credit cards accepted: Visa, MasterCard.

Chaffee County

11th District Court PO Box 279, Salida, CO 81201; 719-539-2561; Fax: 719-539-6281. Hours: 8AM-5PM (MST). *Felony, Civil Actions Over $10,000, Probate.*

Civil Records: Access: Fax, mail, in person, online. Only the court performs in person searches; visitors may not. Search fee: $5.00 per name. Fee applies if 3 or more files involved. Required to search: name, years to search. Civil cases indexed by defendant, plaintiff. Civil records on computer back to 1995; index cards from April 1976, index books back to late 1800s. Online access to statewide court records is available at www.cocourts.com.

Criminal Records: Access: Fax, mail, in person, online. Only the court performs in person searches; visitors may not. Search fee: $5.00 per name. Fee applies if 3 or more files involved. Required to search: name, years to search, DOB. Criminal records on computer back to 1995; index cards back to April 1976, index books back to late 1800s. Online access to criminal records is the same as civil.

General Information: No adoptions, sealed, juvenile, mental health or expunged cases released. SASE required. Turnaround time 2-3 days. Fax notes: Fee to fax results is $.50 per page. Copy fee: $.75 per page. Certification fee: $5.00. Fee payee: Clerk of District Court. Personal checks accepted. Prepayment is required.

County Court PO Box 279, Salida, CO 81201; 719-539-6031; Fax: 719-539-6281. Hours: 8AM-5PM (MST). *Misdemeanor, Civil Actions Under $15,000, Eviction, Small Claims.*

Civil Records: Access: Phone, fax, mail, in person, online. Both court and visitors may perform in person searches. No search fee. Required to search: name. Civil cases indexed by defendant, plaintiff. Civil records on computer since 1995; prior on index cards from 1970s. Online access to statewide court records is available at www.cocourts.com.

Criminal Records: Access: Phone, fax, mail, in person, online. Both court and visitors may perform in person searches. No search fee. Required to search: name, years to search, DOB, aliases. Criminal records on computer since 1995; prior on index cards from 1970s. Online access to criminal records is the same as civil.

General Information: No adoptions, sealed, juvenile, mental health or expunged cases released. SASE required. Turnaround time 3-4 days. Fax notes: $1.00 per page. Copy fee: $.75 per page. Certification fee: $5.00. Fee payee: Clerk of County Court. Personal checks accepted. Prepayment is required.

Cheyenne County

15th District & County Courts PO Box 696, Cheyenne Wells, CO 80810; 719-767-5649. Hours: 8AM-4:30PM (MST). *Felony, Misdemeanor, Civil, Eviction, Small Claims, Probate.*

Civil Records: Access: Mail, in person, online. Only the court performs in person searches; visitors may not. Search fee: $5.00 per name. Required to search: name, years to search. Civil cases indexed by defendant, plaintiff. Civil records on computer since 11/1/95, index cards from 1960, index books back to early 1900s. Online access to statewide court records is available at www.cocourts.com.

Criminal Records: Access: Mail, in person, online. Only the court performs in person searches; visitors may not. Search fee: $5.00 per name. Required to search: name, years to search, DOB. Criminal records on computer since 11/1/95, index cards from 1960, index books back to early 1900s. Online access to criminal records is the same as civil.

General Information: No adoptions, sealed, juvenile, mental health or expunged cases released. SASE required. Turnaround time 5-7 days. Fax notes: Fee to fax results is $1.00 per page. Copy fee: $.75 per page. Certification fee: $5.00. Fee payee: Cheyenne County Combined Court. Business checks accepted. Will bill attorneys only.

Clear Creek County

5th District & County Courts PO Box 367, Georgetown, CO 80444; 303-569-3273; Fax: 303-569-3274. Hours: 8AM-5PM (MST). *Felony, Misdemeanor, Civil, Eviction, Small Claims, Probate.*

Civil Records: Access: Mail, in person, online. Both court and visitors may perform in person searches. Search fee: $5.00 per name. Required to search: name, years to search. Civil cases indexed by defendant, plaintiff. Civil records on index cards from 1976, ledger books back to late 1800. Online access to statewide court records is available at www.cocourts.com. No searches done on records prior to 1976.

Criminal Records: Access: Mail, in person, online. Both court and visitors may perform in person searches. Search fee: $5.00 per name. Required to search: name, years to search, DOB. Criminal records on index cards from 1976, ledger books back to late 1800. Online access to criminal records is the same as civil.

General Information: No adoptions, sealed, juvenile, mental health or expunged cases released. SASE required. Turnaround time 1 week. Copy fee: $.75 per page. Certification fee: $5.00 per page. Fee payee: Clerk of Combined Court. Personal checks accepted. Prepayment is required.

Conejos County

12th District & County Courts 6683 County Road 13, Conejos, CO 81129; 719-376-5466; Fax: 719-376-5465. Hours: 8AM-4PM (MST). *Felony, Misdemeanor, Civil, Eviction, Small Claims, Probate.*

Civil Records: Access: Mail, in person, online. Only the court performs in person searches; visitors may not. Search fee: $10.00 per name. Required to search: name, years to search. Civil cases indexed by defendant, plaintiff. Civil records on computer since 6/94, on index cards from 1980. Online access to statewide court records is available at www.cocourts.com.

Criminal Records: Access: Mail, in person, online. Only the court performs in person searches; visitors may not. Search fee: $10.00 per name. Required to search: name, years to search, DOB. Criminal records on computer since 6/94, on index cards from 1980. Online access to criminal records is the same as civil.

General Information: No adoptions, sealed, juvenile, mental health or expunged cases released. SASE required. Turnaround time 1 week. Copy fee: $.75 per page. Certification fee: $5.00. Fee payee: Conejos Combined Court. Personal checks accepted. Prepayment is required.

Costilla County

12th District & County Courts PO Box 301, San Luis, CO 81152; 719-672-3681; Fax: 719-672-3681. Hours: 8AM-Noon, 1-4PM (MST). *Felony, Misdemeanor, Civil, Eviction, Small Claims, Probate.*

www.courts.state.co.us/district/12th/dist-12.shtml

Civil Records: Access: Fax, mail, in person, online. Both court and visitors may perform in person searches. Search fee: $5.00 per name. There is no fee if the visitor performs the search. Required to search: name, years to search; also helpful: address. Civil cases indexed by defendant, plaintiff. Civil records on index cards from 1970, index books back to 1900s, indexed on computer since 1994. Archived prior to 1970. Online access to statewide court records is available at www.cocourts.com.

Criminal Records: Access: Fax, mail, in person, online. Only the court performs in person searches; visitors may not. Search fee: $5.00 per name. Required to search: name, years to search; also helpful: address, DOB, SSN. Criminal records on index cards from 1970, index books back to 1900s, indexed on computer since 1994. Archived prior to 1970. Online access to criminal records is the same as civil.

General Information: No adoptions, sealed, juvenile, mental health, certain criminal cases or expunged cases released. SASE required. Turnaround time 1-2 weeks. Fax notes: Fee to fax results is $10.00 per document. Copy fee: $.75 per page. Certification fee: $5.00 per document. Fee payee: Costilla Combined Courts. Personal checks accepted. Prepayment is required.

Crowley County

16th District & County Courts 110 E 6th St, #303, Ordway, CO 81063; 719-267-4468; Fax: 719-267-3753. Hours: 8AM-4:30PM (MST). *Felony, Misdemeanor, Civil, Eviction, Small Claims, Probate.*

www.courts.state.co.us/district/16th/dist-16.htm

Civil Records: Access: Mail, fax, in person, online. Only the court performs in person searches; visitors may not. Search fee: $5.00 per name. Required to search: name, years to search. Civil cases indexed by defendant, plaintiff. Civil records on computer back to 1993, fiche since 1980'2, index books back to 1915. Online access to statewide court records is available at www.cocourts.com.

Criminal Records: Access: Mail, fax, in person, online. Only the court performs in person searches; visitors may not. Search fee: $5.00 per name. Required to search: name, years to search, DOB, SSN. Criminal records on computer back to 1993, fiche since 1980'2, index books back to 1915. Online access to criminal records is the same as civil.

General Information: No adoptions, sealed, juvenile, mental health or expunged cases released. SASE required. Turnaround time 3-5 days. Fax notes: Fee to fax results is $1.00 per page. Copy fee: $.75 per page. Certification fee: $5.00. Fee payee: Crowley Combined Court. Personal checks accepted. Prepayment is required.

Custer County

11th District & County Courts PO Box 60, Westcliffe, CO 81252; 719-783-2274; Fax: 719-783-2995. Hours: 8AM-2PM (MST). *Felony, Misdemeanor, Civil, Eviction, Small Claims, Probate.*

Civil Records: Access: Mail, in person, online. Both court and visitors may perform in person searches. Search fee: $5.00 per name. Required to search: name, years to search. Civil cases indexed by defendant, plaintiff. Civil records on index cards from 1973, ledger books back to 1965, archived from 1879-1965. Online access to statewide court records is available at www.cocourts.com.

Criminal Records: Access: Mail, in person, online. Both court and visitors may perform in person searches. Search fee: $5.00 per name. Required to search: name, years to search, DOB. Criminal records on index cards from 1973, ledger books back to 1965, archived from 1879-1965. Online access to criminal records is the same as civil.

General Information: No adoptions, sealed, juvenile, mental health or expunged cases released. SASE required. Turnaround time 1-2 weeks. Copy fee: $.75 per page. Certification fee: $5.00. Fee payee: Custer Combined Court. Personal checks accepted. Prepayment is required.

Delta County

District & County Courts - Delta County 501 Palmer St Rm 338, Delta, CO 81416; 970-874-4416. Hours: 8:30AM-4:30PM (MST). *Felony, Misdemeanor, Civil, Eviction, Small Claims, Probate.*

www.7thjudicialdistrictco.org/delta.html

Civil Records: Access: Mail, in person, online. Only the court performs in person searches; visitors may not. Search fee: $5.00 per name. Required to search: name, years to search. Civil cases indexed by defendant, plaintiff. Civil records on computer back to 10/1994, index cards from 1972, index books back to 1900. Online access to statewide court records is available at www.cocourts.com.

Criminal Records: Access: Mail, in person, online. Only the court performs in person searches; visitors may not. Search fee: $5.00 per name. Required to search: name, years to search, DOB, signed release. Criminal records on computer back to 10/1994, index cards from 1972, index books back to 1900. Online access to criminal records is the same as civil.

General Information: No adoptions, sealed, juvenile, mental health or expunged cases released. SASE required. Turnaround time 3 days. Copy fee: $.75 per page. Certification fee: $5.00. Fee payee: Clerk of Court. Only cashiers checks and money orders accepted. Prepayment is required.

Denver County

2nd District Court 1437 Bannock, Office of the Court Clerk, Denver, CO 80202; Civil phone: 720-865-8301; Criminal phone: 720-865-9060. Hours: 8AM-5PM (MST). *Felony, Civil Actions Over $10,000.*

www.courts.state.co.us/district/02nd/dcadmn02.htm

Civil Records: Access: Mail, in person. Both court and visitors may perform in person searches. No search fee. Required to search: name, years to search. Civil cases indexed by defendant, plaintiff. Civil records on computer from 1974, index books back to the late 1800s if convicted of criminal charges.

Criminal Records: Access: Mail, in person. Both court and visitors may perform in person searches. No search fee. Required to search: name, years to search, DOB. Criminal records on computer from 1974, index books back to the late 1800s if convicted of criminal charges.

General Information: No adoptions, sealed, juvenile, mental health or expunged cases released. SASE required. Turnaround time 1 week. Copy fee: $.75 per

page. Certification fee: $5.00. Fee payee: Denver District Court. Personal checks accepted. Prepayment is required.

County Court - Civil Division 1515 Cleveland Pl 4th Floor, Denver, CO 80202; 303-640-5161; Fax: 303-640-4730. Hours: 8AM-5PM (MST). *Civil Actions Under $15,000, Eviction, Small Claims.*

www.courts.state.co.us/district/02nd/dcadmn02.htm

Civil Records: Access: Mail, in person, online. Both court and visitors may perform in person searches. No search fee. Required to search: name, years to search. Civil cases indexed by defendant, plaintiff. Civil records on computer from 1987, microfiche since 1965. Online searching of the Denver County Civil Division court cases is available at www.denvergov.org/civilcourts.asp. Search by name, business name, or case number. **General Information:** No adoptions, sealed, juvenile, mental health or expunged cases released. SASE required. Turnaround time 1 week. Copy fee: $1.00 per page. Certification fee: $5.00. Fee payee: Denver County Court. Personal checks accepted. Prepayment is required.

County Court - Criminal Division 1437 Bannock St Room 111A, Denver, CO 80202; 303-640-5911. Hours: 8AM-5PM (MST). *Misdemeanor.*

www.courts.state.co.us/district/02nd/dcadmn02.htm

Criminal Records: Access: Mail, in person. Both court and visitors may perform in person searches. No search fee. Required to search: name, years to search, DOB; also helpful: address. Criminal records computerized since 1985.

General Information: No adoptions, sealed, juvenile, mental health or expunged cases released. SASE required. Turnaround time 1 week. Copy fee: $.75 per page. Certification fee: $5.00. Fee payee: Denver County Court. Personal checks accepted. Prepayment is required.

Probate Court 1437 Bannock, Rm 230, Denver, CO 80202; 720-865-8310; Fax: 720-865-8576. Hours: 8AM-5PM (MST). *Probate.*

www.cobar.org/probate.ct/index.htm

Dolores County

22nd District & County Courts PO Box 511, Dove Creek, CO 81324; 970-677-2258. Hours: 8AM-5PM M & T; 8AM-Noon W (MST). *Felony, Misdemeanor, Civil, Eviction, Small Claims, Probate.*

Civil Records: Access: Phone, mail, in person, online. Only the court performs in person searches; visitors may not. No search fee. Required to search: name, years to search. Civil cases indexed by defendant, plaintiff. Civil records on index cards from 1972, index books back to 1895, on computer from 06/95 to present. Online access to statewide court records is available at www.cocourts.com.

Criminal Records: Access: Phone, mail, in person, online. Only the court performs in person searches; visitors may not. No search fee. Required to search: name, years to search, DOB. Criminal records on index cards from 1972, index books back to 1895, on computer from 06/95 to present. Online access to criminal records is the same as civil.

General Information: No adoptions, sealed, juvenile, mental health or expunged cases released. SASE required. Turnaround time 1 week. Copy fee: $.75 per page. Certification fee: $5.00. Fee payee: Dolores County Combined. Only cashiers checks and money orders accepted. Prepayment is required.

Douglas County

Douglas County Combined Court 4000 Justice Way #2009, Castle Rock, CO 80104; 303-663-7200. Hours: 8AM-5PM (MST). *Felony, Misdemeanor, Civil, Eviction, Small Claims, Probate.*

Civil Records: Access: Mail, in person, online. Both court and visitors may perform in person searches. Search fee: $5.00 per name. $20.00 per hour for extensive search. Required to search: name, years to search. Civil cases indexed by defendant, plaintiff. Civil records on computer since 1/1988, index cards from 1975, index books to 1880s. Online access to statewide court records is available at www.cocourts.com.

Criminal Records: Access: Mail, in person, online. Both court and visitors may perform in person searches. Search fee: $5.00 per name. $20.00 per hour for extensive search. Required to search: name, years to search, DOB. Criminal records on computer since 1/1988, index cards from 1975, index books to 1880s. Online access to criminal records is the same as civil.

General Information: No adoptions, sealed, juvenile, mental health or expunged cases released. SASE required. Turnaround time 1 week. Copy fee: $.75 per page. Certification fee: $5.00. Fee payee: Clerk of Combined Courts. Only cashiers checks and money orders accepted. Prepayment is required.

Eagle County

Eagle Combined Court PO Box 597, Eagle, CO 81631; 970-328-6373; Fax: 970-328-6328. Hours: 8AM-5PM (MST). *Felony, Misdemeanor, Civil, Eviction, Small Claims, Probate.*

Civil Records: Access: Fax, mail, in person, online. Visitors must perform in person searches for themselves. No search fee. Required to search: name, years to search. Civil cases indexed by defendant, plaintiff. Civil records on computer since 09/95; prior on fiche to 1970, books to 1930. Online access to statewide court records is available at www.cocourts.com.

Criminal Records: Access: Fax, mail, in person, online. Visitors must perform in person searches for themselves. No search fee. Required to search: name, years to search, DOB. Criminal records on computer since 09/95; prior on fiche to 1970, books to 1930. Online access to criminal records is the same as civil.

General Information: Public Access terminal is available. No adoptions, sealed, juvenile, mental health or expunged cases released. SASE required. Turnaround time 5-7 days. Fax notes: $1.00 per page. Fax fee must be paid with credit card. Copy fee: $.75 per page. Certification fee: $5.00. Fee payee: Eagle Combined Courts. Personal checks accepted. Credit cards accepted: Visa, MasterCard. Prepayment is required.

El Paso County

El Paso Combined Court 20 E Vermijo Rm 105, Colorado Springs, CO 80903; 719-448-7650; Fax: 719-448-7685. Hours: 8AM-5PM (MST). *Felony, Misdemeanor, Civil Actions, Probate.*

www.gofourth.org

Note: Records for the County and District Courts are combined.

Civil Records: Access: Fax, mail, in person, online. Both court and visitors may perform in person searches. Search fee: $5.00 per name. Required to search: name, years to search. Civil cases indexed by defendant, plaintiff. Civil records on computer from Jan, 1975, index cards to 1975, index books to 1861. Online access to statewide court records is available at www.cocourts.com.

Criminal Records: Access: Fax, mail, in person, online. Both court and visitors may perform in person

searches. Search fee: $5.00 per name; if pre-1975, fee is $20.00 per hour. Required to search: name, years to search, DOB; also helpful: SSN. Criminal records on computer from Jan, 1975, index cards to 1975, index books to 1861. Online access to criminal records is the same as civil.

General Information: No adoptions, sealed, juvenile, mental health, expunged cases or other access restricted cases released. SASE required. Turnaround time 5-7 days. Fax notes: Fee is $.75 per page plus $1.50 if long distance. Copy fee: $.75 per page. Certification fee: $5.00. Fee payee: Clerk of District Court. Personal checks accepted. Credit cards accepted: Visa, MasterCard, Discover. Prepayment is required.

Elbert County

Elbert District & County Courts PO Box 232, Kiowa, CO 80117; 303-621-2131. Hours: 8AM-5PM (MST). *Felony, Misdemeanor, Civil, Eviction, Small Claims, Probate.*

Civil Records: Access: Phone, mail, in person, online. Only the court performs in person searches; visitors may not. Search fee: $5.00 per name. Required to search: name, years to search. Civil cases indexed by defendant, plaintiff. Civil records on index cards from 1978, index books from 1920s, archived prior to 1920. Online access to statewide court records is available at www.cocourts.com.

Criminal Records: Access: Phone, mail, in person, online. Only the court performs in person searches; visitors may not. Search fee: $5.00 per name. Required to search: name, years to search, DOB. Criminal records on index cards from 1978, index books from 1920s, archived prior to 1920. Online access to criminal records is the same as civil.

General Information: No adoptions, sealed, juvenile, mental health or expunged cases released. SASE required. Turnaround time 1-2 weeks. Copy fee: $.75 per page. Certification fee: $5.00. Fee payee: Elbert Combined Courts. Business checks accepted. Prepayment is required.

Fremont County

District & County Courts 136 Justice Center Rd, Rm 103, Canon City, CO 81212; 719-269-0100; Fax: 719-269-0134. Hours: 8AM-5PM (MST). *Felony, Misdemeanor, Civil, Eviction, Small Claims, Probate.*

www.courts.state.co.us

Civil Records: Access: Mail, fax, in person, online. Only the court performs in person searches; visitors may not. Search fee: $5.00 per name. Required to search: name, years to search; also helpful: address. Civil cases indexed by defendant, plaintiff. Civil records on index cards from 1978, index books in Denver (except criminal) back to 1861. Online access to statewide court records is available at www.cocourts.com.

Criminal Records: Access: Mail, fax, in person, online. Only the court performs in person searches; visitors may not. Search fee: $5.00 per name. Required to search: name, years to search; also helpful: address, DOB. Criminal records on index cards from 1978, index books in Denver (except criminal) back to 1861. Online access to criminal records is the same as civil.

General Information: Public Access terminal is available. No adoptions, sealed, juvenile, mental health or expunged cases released. SASE required. Turnaround time 10 working days. Copy fee: $.75 per page. Certification fee: $5.00. Fee payee: Clerk of the Combined Courts. Personal checks accepted. Prepayment is required.

Garfield County

9th District & County Courts 109 8th St #104, Glenwood Springs, CO 81601; 970-945-5075; Fax: 970-945-8756. Hours: 8AM-5PM (MST). *Felony, Misdemeanor, Civil, Eviction, Small Claims, Probate.*

Note: This court handles cases in the county for the area east of New Castle.

Civil Records: Access: Mail, in person, online. Only the court performs in person searches; visitors may not. Search fee: $5.00 per name. Required to search: name, years to search. Civil cases indexed by defendant, plaintiff. Civil records on computer from 1992, on fiche from 1970, index books back to late 1800s. Online access to statewide court records is available at www.cocourts.com.

Criminal Records: Access: Mail, in person, online. Only the court performs in person searches; visitors may not. Search fee: $5.00 per name. Required to search: name, years to search. Criminal records on computer from 1992, on fiche from 1970, index books back to late 1800s. Online access to criminal records is the same as civil.

General Information: Public Access terminal is available. (Records available since 09/98.) No adoptions, sealed, juvenile, mental health or expunged cases released. SASE required. Turnaround time 1-2 weeks. Copy fee: $.75 per page. Certification fee: $5.00. Fee payee: Garfield Combined Courts. Personal checks accepted. Credit cards accepted: Visa, MasterCard. Prepayment is required.

County Court - Rifle 110 E 18th St, Rifle, CO 81650; 970-625-5100; Fax: 970-625-1125. Hours: 8AM-5PM (MST). *Misdemeanor, Civil Actions Under $15,000, Eviction, Small Claims.*

Note: This court handles cases in the county for the area from New Castle to the west.

Civil Records: Access: Phone, fax, mail, in person, online. Only the court performs in person searches; visitors may not. No search fee. Required to search: name, years to search. Civil cases indexed by defendant, plaintiff. Civil records on index cards from 1965, computerized since 1994. Online access to statewide court records is available at www.cocourts.com.

Criminal Records: Access: Phone, fax, mail, in person, online. Only the court performs in person searches; visitors may not. No search fee. Required to search: name, years to search, DOB. Criminal records on index cards from 1965, computerized since 1994. Online access to criminal records is the same as civil.

General Information: No adoptions, sealed, juvenile, mental health or expunged cases released. SASE required. Turnaround time 1 week. Fax notes: $1.00 per page to send or receive a fax. Copy fee: $.75 per page. Certification fee: $5.00 per page. Fee payee: Associate County Court. Personal checks accepted. Credit cards accepted: MasterCard, Visa. Prepayment is required.

Gilpin County

1st District & County Courts 2960 Dory Hill Rd #200, Golden, CO 80403-8768; 303-582-5323; Fax: 303-582-3112. Hours: 8AM-5PM (MST). *Felony, Misdemeanor, Civil, Eviction, Small Claims, Probate.*

Civil Records: Access: Mail, in person, online. Only the court performs in person searches; visitors may not. Search fee: $5.00 per name. Fee is for past 7 years. Required to search: name, years to search. Civil cases indexed by defendant, plaintiff. Civil records on computer (County-1993, District-1994), on index cards from 1970s, index books from 1950s. Online access to statewide court records is available at www.cocourts.com.

Criminal Records: Access: Mail, in person, online. Only the court performs in person searches; visitors may not. Search fee: $10.00 per name. Fee is for past 7 years. Required to search: name, years to search, DOB. Criminal records on computer (County-1993, District-1994), on index cards to 1970s, index books to 1950s. Online access to criminal records is the same as civil.

General Information: No adoptions, sealed, juvenile, mental health or expunged cases released. SASE required. Turnaround time 5 days. Copy fee: $.75 per page. Certification fee: $5.00. Fee payee: Clerk of the Combined Courts. Personal checks accepted. Prepayment is required.

Grand County

14th District & County Courts PO Box 192, Hot Sulphur Springs, CO 80451; 970-725-3357. Hours: 8AM-5PM (MST). *Felony, Misdemeanor, Civil, Eviction, Small Claims, Probate.*

Civil Records: Access: Phone, mail, in person, online. Only the court performs in person searches; visitors may not. Search fee: $5.00 per name if 1976-1991. $20.00 if pre-1976. No fee 1992-present. Required to search: name, years to search. Civil cases indexed by defendant, plaintiff. Civil records on computer from July, 1991, fiche from 1970, index books from 1900. Online access to statewide court records is available at www.cocourts.com. Phone requests accepted only if no fees involved.

Criminal Records: Access: Phone, mail, in person, online. Only the court performs in person searches; visitors may not. Search fee: $5.00 per name if 1976-1991. $20.00 if pre-1976. No fee 1992-present. Required to search: name, years to search, DOB. Criminal records on computer from July, 1991, fiche from 1970, index books from 1900. Online access to criminal records is the same as civil. Phone requests accepted only if no fees involved.

General Information: No adoptions, sealed, juvenile, mental health or expunged cases released. SASE required. Turnaround time 1 week. Copy fee: $.75 per page. Certification fee: $5.00. Fee payee: Grand County Combined Court. Personal checks accepted. Prepayment is required.

Gunnison County

7th District & County Courts 200 E Virginia Ave, Gunnison, CO 81230; 970-641-3500; Fax: 970-641-6876. Hours: 8:30AM-4:30PM (MST). *Felony, Misdemeanor, Civil, Eviction, Small Claims, Probate.*

Civil Records: Access: Mail, in person, online. Only the court performs in person searches; visitors may not. Search fee: $5.00 per name. Required to search: name, years to search. Civil cases indexed by defendant. Civil records on computer from 1994, index cards from 1977, index books back to 1877. Online access to statewide court records is available at www.cocourts.com.

Criminal Records: Access: Mail, in person, online. Only the court performs in person searches; visitors may not. Search fee: $5.00 per name. Required to search: name, years to search, DOB. Criminal records on computer from 1994, index cards from 1977, index books back to 1877. Online access to criminal records is the same as civil.

General Information: No adoptions, sealed, juvenile, mental health or expunged cases released. SASE required. Turnaround time 1-2 days. Copy fee: $.75 per page. Certification fee: $5.00. Fee payee: Gunnison Combined Courts. Personal checks accepted. Prepayment is required.

Hinsdale County

7th District & County Courts PO Box 245, Lake City, CO 81235; 970-944-2227; Fax: 970-944-2289. Hours: 8:30-Noon MWF (Jun-Aug) 8:30-12:00 TF (Sept-May) (MST). *Felony, Misdemeanor, Civil, Eviction, Small Claims, Probate.*

Civil Records: Access: Phone, fax, mail, in person, online. Only the court performs in person searches;

visitors may not. No search fee. Required to search: name, years to search. Civil cases indexed by defendant, plaintiff. Civil records on index cards from 1975, index books back to 1900. Online access to statewide court records is available at www.cocourts.com.

Criminal Records: Access: Phone, fax, mail, in person, online. Only the court performs in person searches; visitors may not. Search fee: Fee depends on time required for search. Required to search: name, years to search, DOB. Criminal records on index cards from 1975, index books back to 1900. Online access to criminal records is the same as civil.

General Information: No adoptions, sealed, juvenile, mental health or expunged cases released. SASE required. Turnaround time 2-4 weeks. Fax notes: $.75 per page. 1-10 pgs $2.00, 11-20 pgs $5.00, 21-30 pgs $10.00. Copy fee: $.75 per page. Certification fee: $5.00. Fee payee: Clerk of the Combined Courts. Personal checks accepted. Prepayment is required.

Huerfano County

3rd District & County Courts 401 Main St, Suite 304, Walsenburg, CO 81089; 719-738-1040; Fax: 719-738-1267. Hours: 8AM-4PM (MST). *Felony, Misdemeanor, Civil, Eviction, Small Claims, Probate.*

Civil Records: Access: Mail, in person, online. Only the court performs in person searches; visitors may not. Search fee: $5.00 per name. Required to search: name, years to search. Civil cases indexed by defendant, plaintiff. Civil records on computer from 1995 (county court only), index cards from 1978, index books from 1861. Online access to statewide court records is available at www.cocourts.com.

Criminal Records: Access: Mail, in person, online. Only the court performs in person searches; visitors may not. Search fee: $5.00 per name. Required to search: name, years to search, DOB. Criminal records on computer from 1995 (county court only), index cards from 1978, index books from 1861. Online access to criminal records is the same as civil.

General Information: No adoptions, sealed, juvenile, mental health or expunged cases released. SASE required. Turnaround time 2 weeks. Copy fee: $.75 per page. Certification fee: $5.00. Fee payee: Huerfano County Combined Courts. Personal checks accepted. Prepayment is required.

Jackson County

8th District & County Courts PO Box 308, Walden, CO 80480; 970-723-4363. Hours: 9AM-1PM (MST). *Felony, Misdemeanor, Civil, Eviction, Small Claims, Probate.*

Civil Records: Access: Mail, in person, online. Only the court performs in person searches; visitors may not. No search fee. Required to search: name, years to search. Civil cases indexed by defendant, plaintiff. Civil records on computer since 1994;prior on index cards from 1974, index books from the 1900s. Online access to statewide court records is available at www.cocourts.com.

Criminal Records: Access: Mail, in person, online. Only the court performs in person searches; visitors may not. No search fee. Required to search: name, years to search, DOB. Criminal records on computer since 1994; prior on index cards from 1974, index books from the 1900s. Online access to criminal records is the same as civil.

General Information: No adoptions, sealed, juvenile, mental health or expunged cases released. SASE required. Turnaround time 1 week. Copy fee: $.75 per page. Will bill in excess of 10 pages. Certification fee: $5.00. Fee payee: Clerk of the Combined Courts. Personal checks accepted. If a file has been pulled, information found and it is in excess of 10 pages, will bill the requesting party providing the request is honorable.

Jefferson County

1st District & County Courts 100 Jefferson County Parkway, Golden, CO 80401-6002; 303-271-6267; Fax: 303-271-6188. Hours: 8AM-5PM (MST). *Felony, Misdemeanor, Civil, Eviction, Small Claims, Probate.*

Civil Records: Access: Mail, in person, online. Both court and visitors may perform in person searches. Search fee: $5.00 per name. Fee is per case. Required to search: name, years to search; also helpful: address. Civil cases indexed by defendant, plaintiff. Civil records on computer from 1985, microfiche from 1975, index books from 1963-1974, archived prior to 1963. Online access to statewide court records is available at www.cocourts.com.

Criminal Records: Access: Mail, in person, online. Both court and visitors may perform in person searches. Search fee: $5.00 per name. Fee varies depending on # of years searched. Required to search: name, years to search, DOB; also helpful: address. Criminal records on computer from 1985, microfiche from 1975, index books from 1963-1974, archived prior to 1963. Online access to criminal records is the same as civil.

General Information: No adoptions, sealed, juvenile, mental health or expunged cases released. SASE required. Turnaround time 1 week. Copy fee: $.75 per page. Certification fee: $5.00. Fee payee: Clerk of Combined Courts. Personal checks accepted. Prepayment is required.

Kiowa County

15th District & County Courts PO Box 353, Eads, CO 81036; 719-438-5558; Fax: 719-438-5300. Hours: 8AM-5PM (MST). *Felony, Misdemeanor, Civil, Eviction, Small Claims, Probate.*

www.courts.state.co.us/district/15th/dist-15.shtml

Civil Records: Access: Phone, fax, mail, in person, online. Only the court performs in person searches; visitors may not. Search fee: $5.00 per name. Required to search: name, years to search. Civil cases indexed by defendant, plaintiff. Civil records on index cards from the 1960s, index books from 1889. Recent records are computerized. Online access to statewide court records is available at www.cocourts.com.

Criminal Records: Access: Phone, fax, mail, in person, online. Only the court performs in person searches; visitors may not. Search fee: $5.00 per name. Required to search: name, years to search, DOB. Criminal records on index cards from the 1960s, index books from 1889. Recent records are computerized. Online access to criminal records is the same as civil.

General Information: No adoptions, sealed, juvenile, mental health or expunged cases released. SASE required. Turnaround time 1 week. Fax notes: $1.00 per document. Copy fee: $.75 per page. Certification fee: $5.00. Fee payee: Kiowa County Court. Business checks accepted.

Kit Carson County

13th District & County Courts PO Box 547, Burlington, CO 80807; 719-346-5524. Hours: 8AM-4PM (MST). *Felony, Misdemeanor, Civil, Eviction, Small Claims, Probate.*

Civil Records: Access: Mail, in person, online. Only the court performs in person searches; visitors may not. Search fee: $5.00 per name. Required to search: name, years to search. Civil cases indexed by defendant, plaintiff. Civil records on index cards from 1910, index books from 1889. Online access to statewide court records is available at www.cocourts.com.

Criminal Records: Access: Mail, in person, online. Only the court performs in person searches; visitors may not. No search fee. Required to search: name, years to search, DOB. Criminal records on index cards from

1910, index books from 1889. Online access to criminal records is the same as civil.

General Information: No adoptions, sealed, juvenile, mental health or expunged cases released. SASE required. Turnaround time 1 week. Fax notes: $5.00 fee per document to fax. Copy fee: $.75 per page. Certification fee: $5.00. Fee payee: Combined Courts. No personal checks accepted. Prepayment is required.

La Plata County

6th District Court PO Box 3340, Durango, CO 81302-3340; 970-247-2304; Fax: 970-247-4348. Hours: 8AM-5PM (MST). *Felony, Civil Actions Over $10,000, Probate.*

Civil Records: Access: Mail, in person, online. Only the court performs in person searches; visitors may not. Search fee: $5.00 per name. Fee is per case. Required to search: name, years to search. Civil cases indexed by defendant, plaintiff. Civil records on computer from 1990, index cards from 1976, index books from 1874. Online access to statewide court records is available at www.cocourts.com.

Criminal Records: Access: Mail, in person, online. Only the court performs in person searches; visitors may not. Search fee: $5.00 per name. Required to search: name, years to search, DOB. Criminal records on computer from 1990, index cards from 1976, index books from 1874. Online access to criminal records is the same as civil.

General Information: No adoptions, sealed, juvenile, mental health or expunged cases released. SASE required. Turnaround time 3-7 days. Fax notes: Fee to fax results is $3.00 per document. Copy fee: $.75 per page. Certification fee: $5.00. Fee payee: Clerk of the Combined Courts. Personal checks accepted. Prepayment is required.

County Court PO Box 759, Durango, CO 81302; 970-247-2004; Fax: 970-247-4348. Hours: 8AM-5PM (MST). *Misdemeanor, Civil Actions Under $15,000, Eviction, Small Claims.*

www.courts.state.co.us/counties.htm

Civil Records: Access: Mail, in person, online. Only the court performs in person searches; visitors may not. Search fee: $5.00 per name. Fee is per case. Required to search: name, years to search. Civil cases indexed by defendant, plaintiff. Civil records on computer from February, 1990, index cards from 1965, index books in Denver prior to 1965. $5.00 per name; $5.00 per case. Online access to statewide court records is available at www.cocourts.com.

Criminal Records: Access: Mail, in person, online. Only the court performs in person searches; visitors may not. Search fee: $5.00 per name. Required to search: name, years to search, DOB. Criminal records on computer from February, 1990, index cards from 1965, index books in Denver prior to 1965. Online access to criminal records is the same as civil.

General Information: No adoptions, sealed, juvenile, mental health or expunged cases released. SASE required. Turnaround time 7-10 days. Copy fee: $.75 per page. Certification fee: $5.00. Fee payee: Clerk of the Combined Courts. Personal checks accepted. Prepayment is required.

Lake County

Lake County Combined Courts PO Box 55, Leadville, CO 80461; 719-486-0535. Hours: 8AM-Noon, 1-5PM (MST). *Felony, Misdemeanor, Civil, Eviction, Small Claims, Probate.*

Civil Records: Access: Mail, in person, online. Only the court performs in person searches; visitors may not. Search fee: $10.00 per name. Required to search: name, years to search. Civil cases indexed by defendant, plaintiff. Civil records on index cards from 1988 (District), 1970 (County), index books from 1865.

Online access to statewide court records is available at www.cocourts.com.

Criminal Records: Access: Mail, in person, online. Only the court performs in person searches; visitors may not. Search fee: $10.00 per name. Required to search: name, years to search, DOB. Criminal records on index cards from 1988 (District), 1970 (County), index books from 1865. Online access to criminal records is the same as civil.

General Information: No adoptions, sealed, juvenile, mental health or expunged cases released. SASE required. Turnaround time 30 days. Copy fee: $.75 per page. Certification fee: $5.00. Fee payee: Lake County Court. Business checks accepted. Prepayment is required.

Larimer County

8th District Court 201 La Porte Ave #100, Ft Collins, CO 80521; 970-498-6100; Fax: 970-498-6110. Hours: 8AM-5PM (MST). *Felony, Civil Actions Over $10,000, Probate.*

Civil Records: Access: Phone, mail, in person, online. Both court and visitors may perform in person searches. Search fee: $5.00 per name. Required to search: name; also helpful: years to search. Civil cases indexed by defendant, plaintiff. Civil records on computer from 1976, index books back to 1861. Online access to statewide court records is available at www.cocourts.com.

Criminal Records: Access: Mail, in person, online. Only the court performs in person searches; visitors may not. Search fee: $5.00 per name. Required to search: name; also helpful: years to search, DOB, SSN. Criminal records on computer from 1976, index books back to 1861. Online access to criminal records is the same as civil.

General Information: No adoptions, sealed, juvenile, mental health or expunged cases released. SASE required. Turnaround time 7-10 days. Copy fee: $.75 per page. Certification fee: $5.00. Fee payee: Clerk of District Court. Personal checks accepted. Prepayment is required.

County Court 201 La Porte Ave #100, Ft Collins, CO 80521; 970-498-7550; Fax: 970-498-7569. Hours: 8AM-5PM (MST). *Misdemeanor, Civil Actions Under $15,000, Eviction, Small Claims.*

Civil Records: Access: Fax, mail, in person, online. Only the court performs in person searches; visitors may not. Search fee: $5.00 per name. Required to search: name, years to search; also helpful: address. Civil cases indexed by defendant, plaintiff. Some records on computer from 1986, index cards from 1965. Online access to statewide court records is available at www.cocourts.com.

Criminal Records: Access: Fax, mail, in person, online. Only the court performs in person searches; visitors may not. Search fee: $5.00 per name. Required to search: name, years to search, DOB, signed release, offense; also helpful: address. Some records on computer from 1986, index cards from 1965. Online access to criminal records is the same as civil.

General Information: No sealed cases released. SASE required. Turnaround time 7-10 days. Copy fee: $.75 per page. Certification fee: $5.00. Fee payee: Larimer County Court Clerk. Personal checks accepted. Prepayment is required.

Las Animas County

3rd District Court 200 E 1st St Rm 304, Trinidad, CO 81082; 719-846-3316/2221; Fax: 719-846-9367. Hours: 8AM-5PM (MST). *Felony, Misdemeanor, Civil, Eviction, Small Claims, Probate.*

Civil Records: Access: Mail, in person, online. Only the court performs in person searches; visitors may not. Search fee: $5.00 per name. Required to search: name,

years to search. Civil cases indexed by defendant, plaintiff. Civil records on index cards from 1976, index books to 1950. Online access to statewide court records is available at www.cocourts.com.

Criminal Records: Access: Mail, in person, online. Only the court performs in person searches; visitors may not. Search fee: $5.00 per name. Required to search: name, years to search, DOB; also helpful: SSN. Criminal records on index cards from 1976, index books to 1950. Online access to criminal records is the same as civil.

General Information: No adoptions, sealed, juvenile, mental health or expunged cases released. SASE required. Turnaround time 1 week. Fax notes: Fee to fax results is $2.00 per page. Copy fee: $.75 per page. Certification fee: $5.00. Fee payee: Combined courts. Only cashiers checks and money orders accepted. Prepayment is required.

Lincoln County

18th District & County Courts PO Box 128, Hugo, CO 80821; 719-743-2455. Hours: 8AM-5PM (MST). *Felony, Misdemeanor, Civil, Eviction, Small Claims, Probate.*

Civil Records: Access: Phone, mail, in person, online. Only the court performs in person searches; visitors may not. Search fee: $5.00. Required to search: name, years to search. Civil cases indexed by defendant, plaintiff. Civil records on computer since 12/94, index cards from 1977, index books back to 1889, archived 10 years back. Online access to statewide court records is available at www.cocourts.com.

Criminal Records: Access: Phone, mail, in person, online. Only the court performs in person searches; visitors may not. Search fee: $5.00. Required to search: name, years to search, DOB. Criminal records on computer since 12/94, index cards from 1977, index books back to 1889, archived 10 years back. Online access to criminal records is the same as civil.

General Information: No adoptions, sealed, juvenile, mental health or expunged cases released. SASE required. Turnaround time within 10 days. Copy fee: $.75 per page. Certification fee: $5.00. Fee payee: Lincoln County Combined Courts. Personal checks accepted. Prepayment is required.

Logan County

13th District Court PO Box 71, Sterling, CO 80751; 970-522-6565; Fax: 970-522-6566. Hours: 8AM-4PM (MST). *Felony, Civil Actions Over $10,000, Probate.*

Civil Records: Access: Mail, in person, online. Only the court performs in person searches; visitors may not. Search fee: $5.00 per name. Required to search: name, years to search. Civil cases indexed by defendant, plaintiff. Civil records computerized since 08/95, on index cards from 1973, index books back to 1887. Online access to statewide court records is available at www.cocourts.com.

Criminal Records: Access: Mail, in person, online. Only the court performs in person searches; visitors may not. Search fee: $5.00 per name. Required to search: name, years to search, DOB. Criminal records computerized since 08/95, on index cards from 1973, index books back to 1887. Online access to criminal records is the same as civil.

General Information: No adoptions, sealed, juvenile, mental health or expunged cases released. SASE required. Turnaround time 1-2 weeks. Fax notes: Fee to fax results is $1.00 per page local; $2.00 per page long distance. Copy fee: $.75 per page. Certification fee: $5.00. Fee payee: Logan District Court. Personal checks accepted. Prepayment is required.

County Court PO Box 1907, Sterling, CO 80751; 970-522-1572; Fax: 970-522-2875. Hours: 8AM-4PM (MST). *Misdemeanor, Civil Actions Under $15,000, Eviction, Small Claims.*

Civil Records: Access: Phone, mail, in person, online. Both court and visitors may perform in person searches. Search fee: $5.00 per name. Required to search: name, years to search. Civil cases indexed by defendant, plaintiff. Civil records on computer since 08/95; prior on index cards from 1972 and index books from 1965. Online access to statewide court records is available at www.cocourts.com.

Criminal Records: Access: Phone, mail, in person, online. Both court and visitors may perform in person searches. Search fee: $5.00 per name. Required to search: name, years to search, DOB. Criminal records on computer since 08/95; prior on index cards from 1972 and index books from 1965. Online access to criminal records is the same as civil.

General Information: No adoptions, sealed, juvenile, mental health or expunged cases released. SASE required. Turnaround time 1-2 weeks. Fax notes: Fee to fax results is $2.00 per document. Copy fee: $.75 per page. Certification fee: $5.00. Fee payee: Logan County Court. Business checks accepted.

Mesa County

21st District Court Mesa County District Court, PO Box 20000, Grand Junction, CO 81502; 970-257-3625; Fax: 970-257-8776. Hours: 8AM-5PM (MST). *Felony, Civil Actions Over $10,000, Probate.*

Civil Records: Access: Phone, mail, in person, online. Both court and visitors may perform in person searches. Search fee: $5.00 per name. Required to search: name, years to search. Civil cases indexed by defendant, plaintiff. Civil records on computer since 1994, on microfiche to 1976, books from late 1800s. Online access to statewide court records is available at www.cocourts.com.

Criminal Records: Access: Mail, in person, online. Only the court performs in person searches; visitors may not. Search fee: $5.00 per name. Required to search: name, years to search, DOB. Criminal records on computer since 1994, on microfiche to 1976, books from late 1800s. Online access to criminal records is the same as civil.

General Information: No adoptions, sealed, juvenile, mental health or expunged cases released. SASE required. Turnaround time 5-7 days. Copy fee: $.75 per page. Certification fee: $5.00. Fee payee: Mesa County Combined Court. Business checks accepted. Credit cards accepted: Visa, MasterCard. Prepayment is required.

County Court PO Box 20000, Grand Junction, CO 81502-5032; 970-257-3640. Hours: 8AM-5PM (MST). *Misdemeanor, Civil Actions Under $15,000, Eviction, Small Claims.*

Civil Records: Access: Mail, in person, online. Only the court performs in person searches; visitors may not. Search fee: $5.00 per name. Required to search: name, years to search. Civil cases indexed by defendant, plaintiff. Civil records on computer from 10/89. Online access to statewide court records is available at www.cocourts.com.

Criminal Records: Access: Mail, in person, online. Only the court performs in person searches; visitors may not. Search fee: $5.00 per name. Required to search: name, years to search, DOB. Criminal records on computer from 10/89. Online access to criminal records is the same as civil.

General Information: No adoptions, sealed, juvenile, mental health or expunged cases released. SASE required. Turnaround time immediate if case is on computer. Copy fee: $.75 per page. Certification fee: $5.00. Fee payee: Mesa County Court. Personal checks

accepted. Credit cards accepted: Visa, MasterCard. Accepted in person only. Prepayment is required.

Mineral County

12th District & County Courts PO Box 337, Creede, CO 81130; 719-658-2575; Fax: 719-658-2575. Hours: 10AM-3PM (MST). *Felony, Misdemeanor, Civil, Eviction, Small Claims, Probate.*

Civil Records: Access: Mail, in person, online. Only the court performs in person searches; visitors may not. Search fee: $5.00 per name. Required to search: name, years to search. Civil cases indexed by defendant, plaintiff. Civil records on computer since July 1993, on index cards from 1977, index books back to 1893. Online access to statewide court records is available at www.cocourts.com.

Criminal Records: Access: Mail, in person, online. Only the court performs in person searches; visitors may not. Search fee: $5.00 per name. Required to search: name, years to search, DOB. Criminal records on computer since July 1993, on index cards from 1977, index books back to 1893. Online access to criminal records is the same as civil.

General Information: No adoptions, sealed, juvenile, mental health or expunged cases released. SASE required. Turnaround time 2-3 days. Copy fee: $.75 per page. Certification fee: $5.00. Fee payee: Mineral Combined Courts. Personal checks accepted. Prepayment is required.

Moffat County

Moffat County Combined Court 221 W Victory Wy, Craig, CO 81625; 970-824-8254. Hours: 8AM-5PM (MST). *Felony, Misdemeanor, Civil, Eviction, Small Claims, Probate.*

Civil Records: Access: Phone, mail, in person, online. Only the court performs in person searches; visitors may not. Search fee: $5.00 for records 1976-91; $20.00 prior to 1976. Required to search: name, years to search. Civil cases indexed by defendant, plaintiff. Civil records on computer from 1992, index cards from 1976, either microfilmed or archived back to 1911. Online access to statewide court records is available at www.cocourts.com.

Criminal Records: Access: Mail, in person, online. Only the court performs in person searches; visitors may not. Search fee: $5.00 1976-1991; $20.00 prior to 1976. Required to search: name, years to search, DOB. Criminal records on computer from 1992, index cards from 1976, either microfilmed or archived back to 1911. Online access to criminal records is the same as civil.

General Information: No adoptions, sealed, juvenile, mental health or expunged cases released. SASE required. Turnaround time 1-2 weeks. Copy fee: $.75 per page. Certification fee: $5.00. Fee payee: Moffat County Combined Courts. Personal checks accepted. Prepayment is required.

Montezuma County

22nd District Court 109 W Main St, #210, Cortez, CO 81321; 970-565-1111. Hours: 8AM-4:30PM (MST). *Felony, Civil Actions Over $10,000, Probate.*

Civil Records: Access: Phone, mail, in person, online. Only the court performs in person searches; visitors may not. Search fee: $5.00 per name or case number, or $20.00 per hour to search. Required to search: name, years to search. Civil cases indexed by defendant, plaintiff. Civil records on computer back to 6/95, microfiche up to 1988, index cards from 1975, index books back to late 1890s. Online access to statewide court records is available at www.cocourts.com.

Criminal Records: Access: Mail, in person, online. Only the court performs in person searches; visitors may not. Search fee: $5.00 per name or case number, or

$20.00 per hour to search. Required to search: name, years to search, DOB. Criminal records on computer back to 6/95, microfiche up to 1988, index cards from 1975, index books back to late 1890s. Online access to criminal records is the same as civil.

General Information: No adoptions, sealed, juvenile, mental health or expunged cases released. SASE required. Turnaround time 1-2 weeks. Copy fee: $.75 per page. Certification fee: $5.00. Fee payee: Montezuma District Court. Personal checks accepted. Will bill mailing and copy costs.

County Court 601 N Mildred Rd, Cortez, CO 81321; 970-565-7580; Fax: 970-565-8798. Hours: 8AM-4:30PM (MST). *Misdemeanor, Civil Actions Under $15,000, Eviction, Small Claims.*

Civil Records: Access: Mail, in person, online. Only the court performs in person searches; visitors may not. Search fee: $5.00. Required to search: name, years to search. Civil cases indexed by defendant, plaintiff. Civil records on computer since 1993. Online access to statewide court records is available at www.cocourts.com.

Criminal Records: Access: Mail, in person, online. Only the court performs in person searches; visitors may not. Search fee: $5.00. Required to search: name, years to search, DOB. Criminal records on index cards from 1975, index books prior. Online access to criminal records is the same as civil.

General Information: No adoptions, sealed, juvenile, mental health or expunged cases released. SASE required. Turnaround time 5-7 days. Copy fee: $.75 per page. Certification fee: $5.00. Fee payee: Montezuma County Court. Personal checks accepted. Prepayment is required.

Montrose County

7th District & County Courts 1200 N Grand Ave #A, Montrose, CO 81401-3164; 970-252-4300; 242-4309; Fax: 970-252-4345. Hours: 8:30AM-4:30PM (MST). *Felony, Misdemeanor, Civil, Eviction, Small Claims, Probate.*

www.courts.state.co.us

Civil Records: Access: Mail, in person, online. Search fee: $5.00 per name. Required to search: name, years to search. Civil cases indexed by defendant, plaintiff. Civil records on index cards from 1975, index books back to 1890. Online access to statewide court records is available at www.cocourts.com.

Criminal Records: Access: Mail, in person, online. Only the court performs in person searches; visitors may not. Search fee: $5.00 per name. Required to search: name, years to search, DOB. Criminal records on index cards from 1975, index books back to 1890. Online access to criminal records is the same as civil.

General Information: No adoptions, sealed, juvenile, mental health or expunged cases released. SASE required. Turnaround time 1 week. Copy fee: $.75 per page. Certification fee: $5.00. Fee payee: Montrose Combined Courts. Personal checks accepted. Prepayment is required.

Morgan County

13th District Court PO Box 130, Ft Morgan, CO 80701; 970-542-3435; Fax: 970-542-3436. Hours: 8AM-4PM (MST). *Felony, Civil Actions Over $10,000, Probate.*

Civil Records: Access: Fax, mail, in person, online. Only the court performs in person searches; visitors may not. No search fee. Required to search: name, years to search. Civil cases indexed by defendant, plaintiff. Civil records on index cards from 1967, index books back to 1906; recent on computer. Online access to statewide court records is available at www.cocourts.com.

Criminal Records: Access: Fax, mail, in person, online. Only the court performs in person searches; visitors may not. No search fee. Required to search: name, years to search, DOB, SSN; also helpful: signed release, sex. Criminal records on index cards from 1967, index books back to 1906, recent on computer. Online access to criminal records is the same as civil.

General Information: No adoptions, sealed, juvenile, mental health or expunged cases released. SASE required. Turnaround time 2-3 days. Copy fee: $.75 per page. Certification fee: $5.00. Fee payee: Morgan District Court. Personal checks accepted. Will bill copy fees to attorneys.

County Court PO Box 695, Ft Morgan, CO 80701; 970-542-3414; Fax: 970-542-3416. Hours: 8AM-4PM (MST). *Misdemeanor, Civil Actions Under $15,000, Eviction, Small Claims.*

Civil Records: Access: Mail, in person, online. Only the court performs in person searches; visitors may not. Search fee: $5.00. Required to search: name, years to search. Civil cases indexed by defendant, plaintiff. Civil records on computer since 08/95; prior on index cards from 1980. Online access to statewide court records is available at www.cocourts.com.

Criminal Records: Access: Mail, in person, online. Only the court performs in person searches; visitors may not. Search fee: $5.00. Required to search: name, years to search, DOB. Criminal records on computer since 08/95; prior on index cards from 1980. Online access to criminal records is the same as civil.

General Information: Public Access terminal is available. No adoptions, sealed, juvenile, mental health or expunged cases released. Copy fee: $.75 per page. Certification fee: $5.00. Fee payee: Morgan County Court. Personal checks accepted. Prepayment is required.

Otero County

16th District Court Courthouse Rm 207, 13 W 3rd St, La Junta, CO 81050; 719-384-4951; Fax: 719-384-4991. Hours: 8AM-5PM (MST). *Felony, Civil, Probate.*

www.courts.state.co.us/district/16th/dist-16.htm

Civil Records: Access: Mail, in person, online. Only the court performs in person searches; visitors may not. Search fee: $5.00 per name. Required to search: name, years to search. Civil cases indexed by defendant, plaintiff. Civil records on index cards from 1978, index books back to 1889, microfiche from 1889-1992. Online access to statewide court records is available at www.cocourts.com.

Criminal Records: Access: Mail, in person, online. Only the court performs in person searches; visitors may not. Search fee: $5.00 per name. Required to search: name, years to search, DOB. Criminal records on index cards from 1978, index books back to 1889, microfiche from 1889-1992. Online access to criminal records is the same as civil.

General Information: No adoptions, sealed, juvenile, mental health or expunged cases released. SASE required. Turnaround time 1 week. Copy fee: $.75 per page. Certification fee: $5.00. Fee payee: Otero County Combined Courts. Personal checks accepted. Prepayment is required.

County Court Courthouse Rm 105, 13 W 3rd St, La Junta, CO 81050; 719-384-4721; Fax: 384-4772. Hours: 8AM-Noon, 1-5PM (MST). *Misdemeanor, Civil Actions Under $15,000, Eviction, Small Claims.*

Civil Records: Access: Mail, fax, in person, online. Only the court performs in person searches; visitors may not. Search fee: $5.00 per name. Required to search: name, years to search. Civil cases indexed by defendant, plaintiff. Civil records on microfilm prior to 1991, index cards back to 1950s; on computer back 6

years. Online access to statewide court records is available at www.cocourts.com.

Criminal Records: Access: Mail, fax, in person, online. Only the court performs in person searches; visitors may not. Search fee: $5.00 per name. Required to search: name; also helpful: years to search. Criminal records on microfilm prior to 1991, index cards back to 1950s; on computer back 6 years. Online access to criminal records is the same as civil.

General Information: Public Access terminal is available. No adoptions, sealed, juvenile, sexual abuse, assault, mental health or expunged cases released. SASE required. Turnaround time 5 days. Fax notes: Fee to fax results is $1.00 per page. Copy fee: $.75 per page. Certification fee: $5.00. Fee payee: Otero County Courts. Personal checks accepted. Prepayment is required.

Ouray County

7th District & County Courts PO Box 643, Ouray, CO 81427; 970-325-4405; Fax: 970-325-7364. Hours: 8:30AM-Noon, 1-4PM (MST). *Felony, Misdemeanor, Civil, Eviction, Small Claims, Probate.*

Civil Records: Access: Mail, in person, online. Only the court performs in person searches; visitors may not. Search fee: $5.00 per name. Required to search: name, years to search. Civil cases indexed by defendant, plaintiff. Civil records on computer since 1994, index cards from 1976, index books back to 1886, archived prior to 1925. Online access to statewide court records is available at www.cocourts.com.

Criminal Records: Access: Mail, in person, online. Only the court performs in person searches; visitors may not. Search fee: $5.00 per name. Required to search: name, years to search, DOB. Criminal records on computer since 1994, index cards from 1976, index books back to 1886, archived prior to 1925. Online access to criminal records is the same as civil.

General Information: No adoptions, sealed, juvenile, financial, drug/alcohol evaluations, mental health or expunged cases released. SASE requested. Turnaround time 1 week. Fax notes: Fee to fax results is $.75 per page. Copy fee: $.75 per page. Certification fee: $5.00. Fee payee: Ouray Combined Courts. Personal checks accepted. Prepayment is required.

Park County

Park County Combined Courts PO Box 190, Fairplay, CO 80440; 719-836-2940 x226; Fax: 719-836-2892. Hours: 8AM-5PM (MST). *Felony, Misdemeanor, Civil, Eviction, Small Claims, Probate.*

Civil Records: Access: Mail, in person, online. Only the court performs in person searches; visitors may not. Search fee: $5.00 per name. Required to search: name, years to search. Civil cases indexed by defendant, plaintiff. Civil records computerized since 1995, on index cards from 1978, index books back to 1950, archived prior to 1950. Online access to statewide court records is available at www.cocourts.com.

Criminal Records: Access: Mail, in person, online. Only the court performs in person searches; visitors may not. Search fee: $5.00 per name. Required to search: name, years to search, DOB, signed release. Criminal records computerized since 1995, on index cards from 1978, index books back to 1950, archived prior to 1950. Online access to criminal records is the same as civil.

General Information: No adoptions, sealed, juvenile, mental health or expunged cases released. SASE required. Turnaround time within 1 week. Fax notes: Fee to fax results is $1.00 per page. Copy fee: $.50 per page. Certification fee: $5.00. Fee payee: Park County Combined Court. Personal checks accepted. Prepayment is required.

Phillips County

13th District & County Courts 221 S Interocean, Holyoke, CO 80734; 970-854-3279; Fax: 970-854-3179. Hours: 8AM-Noon, 1-4PM (MST). *Felony, Misdemeanor, Civil, Eviction, Small Claims, Probate.*

Civil Records: Access: Phone, fax, mail, in person, online. Only the court performs in person searches; visitors may not. No search fee. Required to search: name, years to search. Civil cases indexed by defendant, plaintiff. Civil records on computer since 08/85; prior on index cards from 1970, index books back to 1889. Online access to statewide court records is available at www.cocourts.com.

Criminal Records: Access: Phone, fax, mail, in person, online. Only the court performs in person searches; visitors may not. No search fee. Required to search: name, years to search, DOB. Criminal records on computer since 08/85; prior on index cards from 1970, index books back to 1889. Online access to criminal records is the same as civil.

General Information: No adoptions, sealed, juvenile, mental health or expunged cases released. SASE required. Turnaround time 1-3 days. Copy fee: $.75 per page. Certification fee: $5.00. Fee payee: Phillips County Combined Court. Personal checks accepted. Prepayment is required.

Pitkin County

9th District & County Courts 506 E Main St, Ste 300, Aspen, CO 81611; 970-925-7635; Fax: 970-925-6349. Hours: 8AM-Noon, 1-5PM (MST). *Felony, Misdemeanor, Civil, Eviction, Small Claims, Probate.*

Civil Records: Access: Phone, mail, fax, in person, online. Both court and visitors may perform in person searches. Search fee: No fee for computer search. Required to search: name, years to search. Civil cases indexed by defendant. Civil records on computer back to 1990, microfiche from 1940-1970, index cards from 1975. Online access to statewide court records is available at www.cocourts.com.

Criminal Records: Access: Mail, fax, in person, online. Both court and visitors may perform in person searches. Search fee: There is no fee for searching computer, otherwise rate determined by time and volume. Required to search: name, years to search, DOB, signed release. Criminal records on computer back to 1990, microfiche from 1940-1970, index cards from 1975. Online access to criminal records is the same as civil.

General Information: No adoptions, sealed, juvenile, mental health or expunged cases released. Turnaround time 1 week. Fax notes: Fee to fax results is $5.00 per page. Copy fee: $.75 per page. Certification fee: $5.00. Fee payee: Pitkin County Combined Court. Only cashiers checks and money orders accepted. Credit cards accepted: Visa, MasterCard. Prepayment is required.

Prowers County

15th District Court 301 S Main St #300, Lamar, CO 81052-2834; 719-336-7424; Fax: 719-336-9757. Hours: 8AM-5PM (MST). *Felony, Civil Actions Over $10,000, Probate.*

Civil Records: Access: Fax, mail, in person, online. Only the court performs in person searches; visitors may not. No search fee. Required to search: name, years to search. Civil cases indexed by defendant, plaintiff. Civil records computerized since 1995, on microfiche from 1920, index books from the late 1800s. Online access to statewide court records is available at www.cocourts.com.

Criminal Records: Access: Fax, mail, in person, online. Only the court performs in person searches; visitors may not. No search fee. Required to search:

name, years to search, DOB. Criminal records computerized since 1995, on microfiche from 1920, index books from the late 1800s. Online access to criminal records is the same as civil.

General Information: No adoptions, sealed, juvenile, mental health or expunged cases released. SASE required. Turnaround time 1 week. Fax notes: $1.00 per page. Copy fee: $.75 per page. Certification fee: $5.00. Fee payee: Clerk of District Court. Only cashiers checks and money orders accepted. Prepayment is required.

County Court 301 S Main St #100, Lamar, CO 81052-2634; 719-336-7416; Fax: 719-336-4145. Hours: 8AM-5PM (MST). *Misdemeanor, Civil Actions Under $15,000, Eviction, Small Claims.*

Civil Records: Access: Mail, phone, in person, online. Both court and visitors may perform in person searches. No search fee. Required to search: name, years to search. Civil cases indexed by defendant, plaintiff. Civil records on computer since 10/95, prior on books. Online access to statewide court records is available at www.cocourts.com.

Criminal Records: Access: Mail, phone, in person, online. Both court and visitors may perform in person searches. No search fee. Required to search: name, years to search; also helpful: DOB. Criminal records on computer since 10/95, prior on books. Online access to criminal records is the same as civil.

General Information: No adoptions, sealed, juvenile, mental health or expunged cases released. SASE required. Turnaround time 2-3 days. Copy fee: $.75 per page. Certification fee: $5.00. Fee payee: Prowers County Court. Personal checks accepted. Prepayment is required.

Pueblo County

Combined Courts 320 West 10th St, Pueblo, CO 81003; 719-583-7125; Fax: 719-583-7126. Hours: 8AM-5PM (MST). *Felony, Misdemeanor, Civil, Eviction, Small Claims, Probate.*

Civil Records: Access: Mail, in person, online. Only the court performs in person searches; visitors may not. Search fee: $5.00 per name. Required to search: name, years to search; also helpful: address. Civil cases indexed by defendant, plaintiff. Civil records on computer from 1976, index books back to the 1890s. Online access to statewide court records is available at www.cocourts.com.

Criminal Records: Access: Mail, in person, online. Only the court performs in person searches; visitors may not. Search fee: $5.00 per name. Required to search: name, years to search, DOB; also helpful: address, SSN. Criminal records on computer from 1976, index books back to the 1890s. Online access to criminal records is the same as civil.

General Information: No adoptions, sealed, juvenile, mental health or expunged cases released. SASE required. Turnaround time 3-5 days. Copy fee: $.75 per page. Certification fee: $5.00. Fee payee: Clerk of Court. Personal checks accepted. Prepayment required.

Rio Blanco County

9th District & County Courts 555 Main St Rm 303, PO Box 1150, Meeker, CO 81641; 970-878-5622; Fax: 970-878-4295. Hours: 8AM-Noon, 1-5PM (MST). *Felony, Misdemeanor, Civil, Eviction, Small Claims, Probate.*

Civil Records: Access: Phone, fax, mail, in person. Only the court performs in person searches; visitors may not. Search fee: $5.00 per name. May charge for lengthy in-person search request. Required to search: name; also helpful: years to search. Civil cases indexed by defendant, plaintiff. Civil records on computer since 8/1984, on index cards from April 1976, index books back to 1889. Online access to statewide court records is available at www.cocourts.com.

Criminal Records: Access: Phone, fax, mail, in person, online. Only the court performs in person searches; visitors may not. Search fee: $5.00 per name. May charge for lengthy in-person search request. Required to search: name, years to search; also helpful: DOB. Criminal records on computer since 8/1984, on index cards from April 1976, index books back to 1889. Online access to criminal records is the same as civil.

General Information: No adoptions, sealed, juvenile, mental health or expunged cases released. SASE required. Turnaround time 2 days. Fax notes: Fee to fax results is $1.00 per page. Copy fee: $.75 per page. Certification fee: $5.00. Fee payee: Clerk of the Combined Courts. Business checks accepted. Prepayment is required.

Rio Grande County

12th District & County Courts 6th & Cherry, PO Box 427, Del Norte, CO 81132; 719-657-3394. Hours: 8AM-Noon, 1-4PM (MST). *Felony, Misdemeanor, Civil, Eviction, Small Claims, Probate.*

Civil Records: Access: Mail, in person, online. Only the court performs in person searches; visitors may not. Search fee: $5.00 per name. Required to search: name, years to search. Civil cases indexed by defendant, plaintiff. Civil records on computer from 5/95, County on index cards from 1950s, District from 1977. All on index books from the 1800s. Online access to statewide court records 1995 to present is available at www.cocourts.com.

Criminal Records: Access: Mail, in person, online. Only the court performs in person searches; visitors may not. Search fee: $5.00 per name. Required to search: name, DOB; also helpful: years to search. Criminal records on computer from 5/95, County on index cards from 1950s, District from 1977. All on index books from the 1800s. Online access to criminal records is the same as civil.

General Information: No adoptions, sealed, juvenile, mental health or expunged cases released. SASE required. Turnaround time 2-4 days. Fax notes: Fee to fax results is $10.00 for 10 pg document. Copy fee: $.75 per page. Certification fee: $5.00. Fee payee: Rio Grande Combined Court. Personal checks accepted. In-state personal & business checks accepted. Prepayment is required.

Routt County

Routt Combined Courts PO Box 773117, Steamboat Springs, CO 80477; 970-879-5020; Fax: 970-879-3531. Hours: 8AM-5PM (MST). *Felony, Misdemeanor, Civil, Eviction, Small Claims, Probate.*

Civil Records: Access: Mail, in person, online. Both court and visitors may perform in person searches. Search fee: $5.00 for 1976-1991; prior to 1976 $20.00. There is no fee to search computer records. Required to search: name, years to search. Civil cases indexed by defendant. Civil records on computer since 1992, on index cards from 1977, microfiche from January 1977 to December 1990, archived from 1877. Online access to statewide court records is available at www.cocourts.com.

Criminal Records: Access: Mail, in person, online. Both court and visitors may perform in person searches. Search fee: Same fees as civil. Required to search: name, years to search, DOB, maiden name, aliases. Criminal records on computer since 1992, on index cards from 1977, microfiche from January 1977 to December 1990, archived from 1877. Online access to criminal records is the same as civil.

General Information: No adoptions, sealed, juvenile, mental health or expunged cases released. SASE required. Turnaround time is as time permits. Copy fee: $.75 per page. Certification fee: $5.00. Fee payee: Routt Combined Court. Personal checks accepted. Prepayment is required.

Saguache County

12th District & County Courts PO Box 164, Saguache, CO 81149; 719-655-2522; Fax: 719-655-2522. Hours: 8AM-Noon, 1-5PM (MST). *Felony, Misdemeanor, Civil, Eviction, Small Claims, Probate.*

Civil Records: Access: Mail, in person, online. Only the court performs in person searches; visitors may not. Search fee: $5.00 per name. Required to search: name, years to search. Civil cases indexed by defendant, plaintiff. Civil records on computer since 06/94, on index cards from 1980s, index books back to 1866. Online access to statewide court records is available at www.cocourts.com.

Criminal Records: Access: Mail, in person, online. Only the court performs in person searches; visitors may not. Search fee: $5.00 per name. Required to search: name, years to search, DOB. Criminal records on computer since 06/94, on index cards from 1980s, index books back to 1866. Online access to criminal records is the same as civil.

General Information: No adoptions, sealed, juvenile, mental health or expunged cases released. SASE required. Turnaround time within 10-12 days. Copy fee: $.75 per page. Certification fee: $5.00. Fee payee: Saguache Combined Courts. Personal checks accepted. Prepayment is required.

San Juan County

6th District & County Courts PO Box 900, Silverton, CO 81433; 970-387-5790. Hours: 8AM-4PM T & TH, 8AM-Noon W (MST). *Felony, Misdemeanor, Civil, Eviction, Small Claims, Probate.*

Civil Records: Access: Mail, in person, online. Both court and visitors may perform in person searches. Search fee: $20.00 per hour. Fee is for lengthy search. Required to search: name, years to search. Civil cases indexed by defendant, plaintiff. Civil records on computer since 1995; prior on index cards from 1975, index books back to 1876. Online access to statewide court records is available at www.cocourts.com.

Criminal Records: Access: Mail, in person, online. Both court and visitors may perform in person searches. Search fee: $8.00 per name. Required to search: name, years to search; also helpful: DOB. Criminal records on computer since 1995; prior on index cards from 1975, index books back to 1876. Online access to criminal records is the same as civil.

General Information: No adoptions, sealed, juvenile, mental health, open domestic, probate or expunged cases released. SASE required. Turnaround time 1 week. Copy fee: $.75 per page. Certification fee: $5.00. Fee payee: San Juan County Court. Business checks accepted. Prepayment is required.

San Miguel County

7th District & County Courts PO Box 919, Telluride, CO 81435; 970-728-3891; Fax: 970-728-6216. Hours: 9AM-Noon, 1PM-4:30PM (MST). *Felony, Misdemeanor, Civil, Eviction, Small Claims, Probate.*

Civil Records: Access: Phone, mail, in person, online. Only the court performs in person searches; visitors may not. Search fee: $5.00 per name if after 1994. Required to search: name, years to search. Civil cases indexed by defendant, plaintiff. Civil records on index cards from 1970, index books back to 1861, archived back to 1880; on computer back to 1994. Online access to statewide court records is available at www.cocourts.com. Will do very limited phone searches back to 1994.

Criminal Records: Access: Phone, mail, in person, online. Only the court performs in person searches; visitors may not. Search fee: $5.00 per name if after 1994. Required to search: name, years to search, DOB. Criminal records on index cards from 1970, index books back to 1861, archived back to 1880; on computer back to 1994. Online access to criminal records is the same as civil. Will do very limited phone searches back to 1994.

General Information: No adoptions, sealed, juvenile, mental health or expunged cases released. SASE required. Turnaround time 30 days. Copy fee: $.75 per page. Certification fee: $5.00. Fee payee: Combined Courts. Personal checks accepted. Prepayment is required.

Sedgwick County

13th District & County Courts Third & Pine, Julesburg, CO 80737; 970-474-3627; Fax: 970-474-2026. Hours: 8AM-1PM (MST). *Felony, Misdemeanor, Civil, Eviction, Small Claims, Probate.*

Civil Records: Access: Fax, mail, in person, online. Both court and visitors may perform in person searches. No search fee. Required to search: name; also helpful: years to search. Civil cases indexed by defendant, plaintiff. Civil records on index cards from early 1970s, index books back to 1889; on computer back to 8/1995. Online access to statewide court records is available at www.cocourts.com.

Criminal Records: Access: Fax, mail, in person, online. Both court and visitors may perform in person searches. Search fee: The court reserves the right to charge if an extensive search is required. Required to search: name, DOB; also helpful: years to search. Criminal records on index cards from early 1970s, index books back to 1889; on computer back to 8/1995. Online access to criminal records is the same as civil.

General Information: No adoptions, sealed, juvenile, mental health or expunged cases released. SASE required. Turnaround time 1-2 days. Fax notes: Fee to fax results is $5.00 per document. Copy fee: $.75 per page. Certification fee: $5.00. Fee payee: Sedgwick County Combined Court. Personal checks accepted. Prepayment is required.

Summit County

5th District & County Courts PO Box 185, Breckenridge, CO 80424; 970-453-2241. Hours: 8AM-5PM (MST). *Felony, Misdemeanor, Civil, Eviction, Small Claims, Probate.*

www.courts.state.co.us

Note: District Court uses PO Box 269.

Civil Records: Access: In person, online. Visitors must perform in person searches for themselves. No search fee. Required to search: name. Civil cases indexed by defendant, plaintiff. Civil records on index cards from the early 1970s, index books back to 1861, archived from 1980 and prior. Online access to statewide court records is available at www.cocourts.com.

Criminal Records: Access: In person, online. Visitors must perform in person searches for themselves. No search fee. Required to search: name, DOB, signed release. Criminal records name index on computer as of 09/95. Online access to criminal records is the same as civil.

General Information: No adoptions, sealed, juvenile, mental health or expunged cases released. Copy fee: $.75 per page. Certification fee: $5.00. Only cashiers checks and money orders accepted. Cash accepted in person. Prepayment is required.

Teller County

4th District & County Courts PO Box 997, Cripple Creek, CO 80813; 719-689-2543. Hours: 8:30AM-4PM (MST). *Felony, Misdemeanor, Civil, Eviction, Small Claims, Probate.*

www.gofourth.org

Civil Records: Access: Mail, in person, online. Only the court performs in person searches; visitors may not. Search fee: $5.00 per name. If not on computer, fee is $20.00 per hour. Required to search: name, years to search. Civil cases indexed by defendant, plaintiff. Civil records computerized since 1988, on index cards from 1960, index books back to 1899. Online access to statewide court records is available at www.cocourts.com.

Criminal Records: Access: Mail, in person, online. Only the court performs in person searches; visitors may not. Search fee: $5.00 per name. If records not on computer, fee is $20.00 per hour. Required to search: name, years to search, DOB; also helpful: address, SSN. Criminal records computerized since 1988, on index cards from 1960, index books back to 1899. Online access to criminal records is the same as civil.

General Information: No adoptions, sealed, juvenile, mental health or expunged cases released. SASE required. Turnaround time 3-5 days, 4-6 weeks if not computerized. Copy fee: $.75 per page. Certification fee: $5.00. Fee payee: Teller County Combined Courts. Only cashiers checks and money orders accepted. Prepayment is required.

Washington County

Washington County Combined Court PO Box 455, Akron, CO 80720; 970-345-2756; Fax: 970-345-2829. Hours: 8AM-Noon, 1-5PM (MST). *Felony, Misdemeanor, Civil, Eviction, Small Claims, Probate.*

Civil Records: Access: Phone, mail, in person, online. Both court and visitors may perform in person searches. No search fee. Required to search: name, years to search. Civil cases indexed by defendant. Civil records on index cards from 1970, index books back to 1887. Online access to statewide court records is available at www.cocourts.com.

Criminal Records: Access: Phone, mail, in person, online. Only the court performs in person searches; visitors may not. No search fee. Required to search: name, years to search, DOB. Criminal records on index cards from 1970, index books back to 1887. Online access to criminal records is the same as civil.

General Information: No adoptions, sealed, juvenile, mental health or expunged cases released. SASE

required. Turnaround time 2-3 days. Copy fee: $.75 per page. Certification fee: $5.00. Fee payee: Washington County Combined Court. Personal checks accepted. Prepayment is required.

Weld County

19th District & County Courts PO Box 2038, Greeley, CO 80632; 970-351-7300; Fax: 970-356-4356. Hours: 8AM-5PM (MST). *Felony, Misdemeanor, Civil, Eviction, Small Claims, Probate.*

Civil Records: Access: Mail, in person, online. Only the court performs in person searches; visitors may not. Search fee: $5.00 per name. Required to search: name, years to search. Civil cases indexed by defendant, plaintiff. Civil records on computer from 1975 (District), 1990 (County), index cards from 1958, index books back to 1876. Online access to statewide court records is available at www.cocourts.com.

Criminal Records: Access: Mail, in person, online. Only the court performs in person searches; visitors may not. Search fee: $5.00 per name. Required to search: name, years to search; also helpful: DOB. Criminal records on computer from 1975 (District), 1990 (County), index cards from 1958, index books back to 1876. Online access to criminal records is the same as civil.

General Information: No adoptions, sealed, juvenile, mental health or expunged cases released. SASE required. Turnaround time 3 days. Copy fee: $.75 per page. Certification fee: $5.00. Fee payee: Clerk of Court. Personal checks accepted. Prepayment is required.

Yuma County

13th District & County Courts PO Box 347, Wray, CO 80758; 970-332-4118; Fax: 970-332-4119. Hours: 8AM-4PM (MST). *Felony, Misdemeanor, Civil, Eviction, Small Claims, Probate.*

Civil Records: Access: Mail, in person, online. Only the court performs in person searches; visitors may not. Search fee: $5.00 per name. Required to search: name, years to search. Civil cases indexed by defendant. Civil records on index cards from 1982, index books back to 1889. Online access to statewide court records is available at www.cocourts.com.

Criminal Records: Access: Mail, in person, online. Only the court performs in person searches; visitors may not. Search fee: $5.00 per name. Required to search: name. Criminal records on index cards from 1982, index books back to 1889. Online access to criminal records is the same as civil.

General Information: No adoptions, sealed, juvenile, mental health or expunged cases released. SASE required. Turnaround time 2-5 days. Copy fee: $.75 per page. Certification fee: $5.00. Fee payee: Yuma County Combined Court. Personal checks accepted. Prepayment is required.

Colorado Recording Offices

ORGANIZATION   63 counties, 63 recording offices. The recording officer is County Clerk and Recorder. The entire state is in the Mountain Time Zone (MST).

REAL ESTATE RECORDS   Counties do not perform real estate searches. Copy fees are usually $1.25 per page and certification fees are usually $1.00 per document. Tax records are located in the Assessor's Office.

UCC RECORDS   Financing statements are filed at the state level, except for real estate related collateral, which are filed with the County Clerk & Recorder. However, prior to 07/2001, consumer goods and farm collateral were also filed at the County Clerk & Recorder and these older records can be searched there. Nearly all counties will perform UCC searches. Use search request form UCC-11. Search fees are usually $5.00 per debtor name for the first year and $2.00 for each additional year searched (or $13.00 for a five year search). Copies usually cost $1.25 per page.

TAX LIEN RECORDS   Federal and some state tax liens on personal property are filed with the Secretary of State. Other federal and state tax liens are filed with the County Clerk and Recorder. Many counties will perform tax lien searches, usually at the same fees as UCC searches. Copies usually cost $1.25 per page

OTHER LIENS   Judgments, motor vehicle, mechanics.

STATEWIDE ONLINE INFO: To date, over 15 Colorado Counties offer free access to property assessor records.

There is an excellent commercial service at at www.cocis.com. You can search for an EFS or UCC filing by the name of the debtor, the reception ID number assigned the filing by a county clerk or a Secretary of State, or by the name of the lender. Registration and password is required; registration is now free but there is a $15.00 fee for a name search. Searches by reception number are free. Fee to print UCC images is $1.00 each. Lender searches are $15.00.

Adams County

County Clerk & Recorder, 450 South 4th Avenue, Administrative Building, Brighton, CO 80601-3197. County Clerk & Recorder, R/E and UCC Recording 303-654-6020; Fax 303-654-6009.
Will search UCC records. UCC search includes tax liens. Will not search real estate records. **Online Access:** Assessor. Records from the Adams County Assessor database are available free online at www.co.adams.co.us/AssessorSearch/asrsearch.htm. **Other Phone Numbers:** Assessor 303-654-6038; Treasurer 303-654-6160; Elections 303-654-6030.

Alamosa County

County Clerk & Recorder, P.O. Box 630, Alamosa, CO 81101. 719-589-6681; Fax 719-589-6118.
Will search UCC records. Tax liens not included in UCC search. Separate tax lien search-$5.00 per name for the first year, $2.00 each add'l year. Will not search real estate records. **Other Phone Numbers:** Assessor 719-589-6365; Treasurer 719-589-3626.

Arapahoe County

County Clerk & Recorder, 5334 South Prince Street, Littleton, CO 80166-0060. County Clerk & Recorder, R/E and UCC Recording 303-795-4520; Fax 303-794-4625. http://www.co.arapahoe.co.us
Will search UCC records. Tax Lien search fee-$5.00 1st year; $2.00 thereafter. Will not search real estate records. **Online Access:** Assessor. Records on the Arapahoe County Assessor database are available free online at www.co.arapahoe.co.us/as/ResForm.htm. **Other Phone Numbers:** Assessor 303-795-4600; Treasurer 303-795-4550; Appraiser/Auditor 303-795-4611; Elections 303-795-4511; Vital Records 303-756-4464.

Archuleta County

County Clerk & Recorder, P.O. Box 2589, Pagosa Springs, CO 81147-2589. 970-264-5633; Fax 970-264-6423.
Will search UCC records. This agency will not do a tax lien search. Will not search real estate records. **Other Phone Numbers:** Assessor 970-264-4896; Treasurer 970-264-2152.

Baca County

County Clerk & Recorder, 741 Main Street, Courthouse, Springfield, CO 81073. County Clerk & Recorder, R/E and UCC Recording 719-523-4372; Fax 719-523-4881.
Will search UCC records. UCC search includes tax liens. Separate search costs same as UCC search Will not search real estate records. **Other Phone Numbers:** Assessor 719-523-4332; Treasurer 719-523-4262; Appraiser/Auditor 719-523-4332; Elections 719-523-4372; Vital Records 719-523-6665.

Bent County

County Clerk & Recorder, P.O. Box 350, Las Animas, CO 81054. 719-456-2009; Fax 719-456-0375.
Will search UCC records. This agency will not do a tax lien search. Will not search real estate records. **Other Phone Numbers:** Assessor 719-456-2010; Treasurer 719-456-2211.

Boulder County

County Clerk & Recorder, 1750 33rd St #201, Boulder, CO 80301. 303-413-7770; http://www.co.boulder.co.us/departments/Default.htm
Will search UCC records. UCC search includes tax liens. Separate tax lien search costs same as UCC search Will not search real estate records. **Online Access:** Assessor. Online access to the assessor's property database is available free at www.co.boulder.co.us/assessor/disclaimer.htm. Also, the county treasurer has data available electronically and on microfiche; Alpha index by owner name is $25.00 per set. **Other Phone Numbers:** Assessor 303-441-3530; Treasurer 303-441-3520; Elections 303-413-7740.

Chaffee County

County Clerk & Recorder, P.O. Box 699, Salida, CO 81201. 719-539-6913 R/E Recording: 719-539-4004; Fax 719-539-8588.
Will not search UCC records. UCC search includes tax liens. RE owner, mortgage, and property transfer searches available. **Other Phone Numbers:** Assessor 719-539-4016; Treasurer 719-539-6808; Elections 719-539-6913.

Cheyenne County

County Clerk & Recorder, P.O. Box 567, Cheyenne Wells, CO 80810. County Clerk & Recorder, R/E and UCC Recording 719-767-5685; Fax 719-767-5540.
Will search UCC records. This agency will not do a tax lien search. Will not search real estate records. **Other Phone Numbers:** Assessor 719-767-5664; Treasurer 719-767-5657; Elections 719-767-5685; Vital Records 719-767-5661.

Clear Creek County

County Clerk & Recorder, P.O. Box 2000, Georgetown, CO 80444-2000. County Clerk & Recorder, R/E and UCC Recording 303-679-2339; Fax 303-679-2441. http://www.co.clear-creek.co.us/Depts/depts.htm
Will not search UCC records. Will not search real estate records. **Other Phone Numbers:** Assessor 303-679-2322; Treasurer 303-679-2353; Appraiser/Auditor 303-679-2322; Elections 303-679-2339; Vital Records 303-679-2357.

Conejos County

County Clerk & Recorder, P.O. Box 127, Conejos, CO 81129-0127. 719-376-5422; Fax 719-376-5661.
Will search UCC records. UCC search includes tax liens if requested. Separate tax liens search costs the same as UCC search RE owner, mortgage, and property transfer searches available. **Other Phone Numbers:** Assessor 719-376-5585; 303-894-2202.

Costilla County

County Clerk & Recorder, P.O. Box 308, San Luis, CO 81152. 719-672-3301; Fax 719-672-3962.
Will search UCC records. This agency will not do a tax lien search. Will not search real estate records. **Other Phone Numbers:** Assessor 719-672-3642.

Crowley County

County Clerk & Recorder, 110 W. 6th St., Ordway, CO 81063-1092. 719-267-4643 x3; Fax 719-267-4608.
Will not search UCC records. Will not search real estate records. **Other Phone Numbers:** Assessor 719-267-4421 x5; Treasurer 719-267-4624 x4.

Custer County

County Clerk & Recorder, P.O. Box 150, Westcliffe, CO 81252. County Clerk & Recorder, R/E and UCC Recording 719-783-2441; Fax 719-783-2885.
Will search UCC records. UCC search includes tax liens if requested. Will not search real estate records. **Other Phone Numbers:** Assessor 719-783-2218; Treasurer 719-783-2341; Appraiser/Auditor 719-783-2218; Elections 719-783-2441; Vital Records 719-783-2441.

Delta County

County Clerk & Recorder, 501 Palmer Street, Suite 211, Delta, CO 81416. County Clerk & Recorder, R/E and UCC Recording 970-874-2150; Fax 970-874-2161. Will search UCC records. This agency will not do a tax lien search. Will not search real estate records. **Other Phone Numbers:** Assessor 970-874-2120; Treasurer 970-874-2135; Appraiser/Auditor 970-874-2120; Elections 970-874-2150; Vital Records 970-874-2150.

Denver County

County Clerk & Recorder, 1437 Bannock Street #200, Denver, CO 80202. 303-640-7290; Fax 303-640-3628. http://www.denvergov.org
Will search UCC records. Tax liens not included in UCC search. Separate tax lien searches performed at same cost as UCC searches Will not search real estate records. **Online Access:** Assessor. Records on the Denver City and Denver County Assessor database are available free online at www.denvergov. org/realproperty.asp. **Other Phone Numbers:** Assessor 303-640-5555; Treasurer 303-640-5555.

Dolores County

County Clerk & Recorder, P.O. Box 58, Dove Creek, CO 81324-0058. County Clerk & Recorder, R/E and UCC Recording 970-677-2381; Fax 970-677-2815.
Will search UCC records. UCC search includes tax liens if requested. Separate tax lien search costs the same as a UCC search Will not search real estate records. **Other Phone Numbers:** Assessor 970-677-2385; Treasurer 970-677-2386; Appraiser/Auditor 970-677-2385; Elections 970-677-2381; Vital Records 970-677-2381.

Douglas County

County Clerk & Recorder, P.O. Box 1360, Castle Rock, CO 80104. 303-660-7446; Fax 303-688-3060. http://www.douglas.co.us/assessor
Will search UCC records. This agency will not do a tax lien search. Will not search real estate records. **Online Access:** Assessor, Property. Records on the county assessor database are available free on the Internet at the web site. **Other Phone Numbers:** Assessor 303-660-7450.

Eagle County

County Clerk & Recorder, P.O. Box 537, Eagle, CO 81631. 970-328-8710 R/E Recording: 970-328-8723 UCC Recording: 970-328-8723; Fax 970-328-8716. http://www.eagle-county.com/frames/gov.htm
Will search UCC records. UCC search includes tax liens. Will not search real estate records. **Online Access:** Assessor. Records on the County Assessor Database are available free online at www.eagle-county.com/frames/tax.htm. **Other Phone Numbers:** Assessor 970-328-8640; Treasurer 970-328-8860; Elections 970-328-8715.

El Paso County

County Clerk & Recorder, P.O. Box 2007, Colorado Springs, CO 80901-2007. 719-520-6200; Fax 719-520-6230. http://www.co.el-paso.co.us

Will search UCC records. UCC search includes federal tax liens Will not search real estate records. **Online Access:** Assessor. Records on the county Assessor database are available free online at www.co.el-paso.co.us/assessor/asr_location/srch.htm. **Other Phone Numbers:** Assessor 719-520-6600.

Elbert County

County Clerk & Recorder, P.O. Box 37, Kiowa, CO 80117. 303-621-3116; Fax 303-621-3168.
Will search UCC records. Tax liens not included in UCC search. Separate tax lien searches performed at same cost as UCC searches. Will not search real estate records. **Other Phone Numbers:** Assessor 303-621-2341; Treasurer 303-621-2341.

Fremont County

County Clerk & Recorder, 615 Macon Avenue, Room 100, Canon City, CO 81212-3311. 719-275-1522; Fax 719-275-1594.
Will search UCC records. UCC search includes tax liens if requested. Separate tax lien search costs same as UCC search Will not search real estate records. **Other Phone Numbers:** Assessor 719-275-1627.

Garfield County

County Clerk & Recorder, 109 8th Street, Suite 200, Glenwood Springs, CO 81601. 970-945-2377; Fax 970-945-7785.
Will search UCC records. Tax liens not included in UCC search. Separate tax lien searches performed at same cost as UCC searches. Will not search real estate records. **Other Phone Numbers:** Assessor 970-945-1377.

Gilpin County

County Clerk & Recorder, P.O. Box 429, Central City, CO 80427. 303-582-5321; Fax 303-582-3086.
Will search UCC records. This agency will not do a tax lien search. Will not search real estate records. **Other Phone Numbers:** Assessor 303-582-5451; Treasurer 303-582-5322; Appraiser/Auditor 303-582-5451; Elections 303-582-5321.

Grand County

County Clerk & Recorder, P.O. Box 120, Hot Sulphur Springs, CO 80451. 970-725-3347 x273; Fax 970-725-0100.
Will search UCC records. This agency will not do a tax lien search. Will not search real estate records. **Other Phone Numbers:** Assessor 970-725-3347 x219.

Gunnison County

County Clerk & Recorder, 200 East Virginia Avenue, Courthouse, Gunnison, CO 81230. 970-641-1516; Fax 970-641-7690.
Will search UCC records. UCC search includes state tax liens. Separate tax lien searches performed at same cost as UCC searches Will not search real estate records.

Hinsdale County

County Clerk & Recorder, P.O. Box 9, Lake City, CO 81235. 970-944-2228; Fax 970-944-2202.
Will search UCC records. Tax liens not included in UCC search. Separate tax lien searches performed at same cost as UCC searches. Will not search real estate records.

Huerfano County

County Clerk & Recorder, Courthouse, Suite 204, 410 Main St., Walsenburg, CO 81089. 719-738-2380; Fax 719-738-2364.
Will search UCC records. UCC search includes tax liens. Separate tax lien search costs same as UCC search

Will not search real estate records. **Other Phone Numbers:** Assessor 719-738-1280; Treasurer 719-782-1191.

Jackson County

County Clerk & Recorder, P.O. Box 337, Walden, CO 80480-0337. 970-723-4334.
Will search UCC records. UCC search includes tax liens. Separate tax lien search costs same as UCC search Will not search real estate records. **Other Phone Numbers:** Treasurer 970-723-4220.

Jefferson County

County Clerk & Recorder, 100 Jefferson County Parkway, #2530, Golden, CO 80419-2530. 303-271-8188; Fax 303-271-8180. http://buffy.co.jefferson.co.us
Will search UCC records. This agency will not do a tax lien search. RE record owner and mortgage searches available. **Online Access:** Assessor. Records on the county Assessor database are available free online at http://buffy.co.jefferson.co.us/cgi-bin/mis/ats/assr. **Other Phone Numbers:** Assessor 303-271-8666.

Kiowa County

County Clerk & Recorder, P.O. Box 37, Eads, CO 81036-0037. 719-438-5421; Fax 719-438-5327.
Will search UCC records. This agency will not do a tax lien search. Will not search real estate records. **Other Phone Numbers:** Assessor 719-438-5521.

Kit Carson County

County Clerk & Recorder, P.O. Box 249, Burlington, CO 80807-0249. 719-346-8638; Fax 719-346-7242.
Will search UCC records. Tax liens not included in UCC search. Separate tax lien searches performed at $13.00 per name for five years, then $2.00 per year. Will not search real estate records. **Other Phone Numbers:** Assessor 719-346-8946; Treasurer 719-346-8434; Elections 719-346-8638; Vital Records 719-346-8133.

La Plata County

County Clerk & Recorder, P.O. Box 519, Durango, CO 81302-0519. 970-382-6281; Fax 970-382-6299. http://www.laplatainfo.com
Will search UCC records. UCC search includes tax liens if requested. Separate tax lien search costs $13.00 for five year search Will not search real estate records. **Online Access:** Assessor. Records on the county Assessor database are available free online at www.laplatainfo.com/search2.html. **Other Phone Numbers:** Treasurer 970-382-6245.

Lake County

County Clerk & Recorder, P.O. Box 917, Leadville, CO 80461. County Clerk & Recorder, R/E and UCC Recording 719-486-4131 UCC Recording: 719-894-2200; Fax 719-486-3972.
Will not search UCC records. This agency will not do a tax lien search. Will not search real estate records. **Other Phone Numbers:** Assessor 719-486-0413; Treasurer 719-486-0530; Elections 719-486-1410; Vital Records 719-486-0708.

Larimer County

County Clerk & Recorder, P.O. Box 1280, Fort Collins, CO 80522-1280. 970-498-7860; http://www.larimer.co.us assessor/query/search.cfm
Will search UCC records. UCC search includes tax liens. Separate tax lien search costs the same as UCC search Will not search real estate records. **Online Access:** Property Tax, Assessor, Treasurer, Voter Records. Assessor records on the Larimer County Property Records database are available free at the web site. Search for County Treasurer Property Tax Records

at www.co.larimer.co.us/depts/treasu/query/search.cfm. Search the County Clerk Recorder records for years 1971 to 1989 at www.co.larimer.co.us/depts/clerkr/query/arch_search.htm. Search the County Clerk Recorder records for years 1990 to present at www.co.larimer.co.us/depts/clerkr/query/search.htm. Search for County Voter records at www.co.larimer.co.us/depts/clerkr/elections/voter_inquiry.cfm. **Other Phone Numbers:** Assessor 970-498-7050.

Las Animas County

County Clerk & Recorder, P.O. Box 115, Trinidad, CO 81082. 719-846-3314; Fax 719-846-0333.
Will search UCC records. UCC search includes tax liens if requested. Separate tax lien search costs the same as UCC search Will not search real estate records. **Other Phone Numbers:** Assessor 719-846-2981; Treasurer 719-846-2295.

Lincoln County

County Clerk & Recorder, P.O. Box 67, Hugo, CO 80821-0067. 719-743-2444; Fax 719-743-2838.
Will search UCC records. Tax liens not included in UCC search. Separate tax lien searches performed at same fees as UCC searches. Will not search real estate records. **Other Phone Numbers:** Assessor 719-742-2358; Treasurer 719-742-2633; Vital Records 719-743-2796.

Logan County

County Clerk & Recorder, 315 Main Street, Logan County Courthouse, Sterling, CO 80751. County Clerk & Recorder, R/E and UCC Recording 970-522-1544; Fax 970-522-2063. http://www.loganco.gov/departments.htm
Will search UCC records prior to 1/2001. UCC search includes tax liens if requested. Separate tax lien search costs same as UCC search Will not search real estate records. **Online Access:** Assessor, Real Estate. Online access to the Assessor's Property Search database is available free at www.loganco-assessor.org/search.asp?. **Other Phone Numbers:** Assessor 970-522-2797; Treasurer 970-522-2462; Elections 970-522-1544.

Mesa County

County Clerk & Recorder, P.O. Box 20000-5007, Grand Junction, CO 81502-5007. County Clerk & Recorder, R/E and UCC Recording 970-244-1679; Fax 970-256-1588. http://www.co.mesa.co.us
Will search UCC records. UCC search includes federal tax liens only Will not search real estate records. **Online Access:** Assessor, Real Estate, Property Tax. Records on the county Assessor database are available free online at http://205.169.141.11/Assessor/Database/netsearch.html. Any search is by address or parcel #. You may also do parcel searches at http://mcweb.co.mesa.co.us/imd/gis/autoFrame.htm. There is also a GIS-mapping search page for property information at http://198.204.117.70/maps/index.htm. Also, an interactive Voice Response System lets callers access real property information at 970-256-1563. Fax back service is available. Also, search the Treasurer's Tax Status Information database at http://205.169.141.11/Treasurer/Database/NETSearch.HTML#Top. **Other Phone Numbers:** Assessor 970-244-1610; Treasurer 970-244-1824; Elections 970-244-1662; Vital Records 970-248-6900 (birth/death); Marriage Records 970-244-1679.

Mineral County

County Clerk & Recorder, P.O. Box 70, Creede, CO 81130. County Clerk & Recorder, R/E and UCC Recording 719-658-2440; Fax 719-658-2931.
Will search UCC records. UCC search includes tax liens if requested. Separate tax lien search costs $5.00 for first year, then $2.00 per year Will not search real estate records. **Other Phone Numbers:** Assessor 719-658-2669; Treasurer 719-658-2325; Elections 719-658-2440; Vital Records 719-658-2497.

Moffat County

County Clerk & Recorder, 221 West Victory Way, Craig, CO 81625-2716. County Clerk & Recorder, R/E and UCC Recording 970-824-9104; Fax 970-824-4975.
Will search UCC records. UCC search includes tax liens if requested. Will not search real estate records. **Other Phone Numbers:** Assessor 970-824-9102; Treasurer 970-824-9111; Elections 970-824-9104; Vital Records 970-824-9233.

Montezuma County

County Clerk & Recorder, 109 West Main Street, Room 108, Cortez, CO 81321. 970-565-3728 R/E Recording: 970-565-3728 x3 UCC Recording: 303-894-2200; Fax 970-564-0215. www.montezumainfo.com
Will not search real estate records. **Other Phone Numbers:** Assessor 970-565-3428; Treasurer 970-565-7550; Elections 970-565-3728 x4; Vital Records 970-565-3728 x3.

Montrose County

County Clerk & Recorder, P.O. Box 1289, Montrose, CO 81402. 970-249-3362; Fax 970-249-0757.
Will not search UCC records. This agency will not do a tax lien search. Will not search real estate records. **Other Phone Numbers:** Assessor 970-249-3753; Treasurer 970-249-3565.

Morgan County

County Clerk & Recorder, P.O. Box 1399, Fort Morgan, CO 80701. County Clerk & Recorder, R/E and UCC Recording 970-542-3521; Fax 970-542-3520.
Will search UCC records. This agency will not do a tax lien search. Will not search real estate records. **Other Phone Numbers:** Assessor 970-542-3512; Treasurer 970-542-3518; Appraiser/Auditor 970-542-3512; Elections 970-542-3521; Vital Records 970-867-4918.

Otero County

County Clerk & Recorder, P.O. Box 511, La Junta, CO 81050-0511. 719-383-3020; Fax 719-383-3090.
Will not search UCC records. Will not search real estate records. **Other Phone Numbers:** Assessor 719-383-3010; Treasurer 719-383-3030; Elections 719-383-3024; Vital Records 719-383-3040.

Ouray County

County Clerk & Recorder, P.O. Bin C, Ouray, CO 81427. County Clerk & Recorder, R/E and UCC Recording 970-325-4961 UCC Recording: 970-894-2200; Fax 970-325-0452. http://co.ouray.co.us
Will search UCC records. This agency will not do a tax lien search. Will not search real estate records. **Other Phone Numbers:** Assessor 970-325-4371; Treasurer 970-325-4487; Elections 970-325-4961; Vital Records 970-325-4487.

Park County

County Clerk & Recorder, P.O. Box 220, Fairplay, CO 80440. County Clerk & Recorder, R/E and UCC Recording 719-836-4333; Fax 719-836-4348. http://www.parkco.org
Will search UCC records. Separate tax lien search costs same as UCC search. Will not search real estate records. **Online Access:** Assessor. Records on the county Assessor database are available free online at www.parkco.org/Search2.asp? including tax information, owner, address, building characteristics, legal and deed information. **Other Phone Numbers:**

Assessor 719-836-2771 x186; Treasurer 719-836-2771 x242; Elections 719-836-4223; Vital Records 719-836-4227.

Phillips County

County Clerk & Recorder, 221 South Interocean, Holyoke, CO 80734. 970-854-3131; Fax 970-664-3811.
Will search UCC records. This agency will not do a tax lien search. Will not search real estate records. **Other Phone Numbers:** Assessor 970-854-3151; Treasurer 970-852-2822.

Pitkin County

County Clerk & Recorder, 530 East Main St., #101, Aspen, CO 81611. 970-920-5180; Fax 970-920-5196. http://aimwebdomain.aspen.com
Will search UCC records. UCC search includes tax liens. Separate tax lien search costs same as UCC search Will not search real estate records. **Online Access:** Assessor. Records on the county Assessor database are available free online at http://aimwebdomain.aspen.com/db/pca/pcareg1.asp. **Other Phone Numbers:** Assessor 970-920-5160.

Prowers County

County Clerk & Recorder, 301 South Main Street #210, Lamar, CO 81052. County Clerk & Recorder, R/E and UCC Recording 719-336-8011; Fax 719-336-5306.
Will search UCC records. This agency will not do a tax lien search. Will not search real estate records. **Other Phone Numbers:** Assessor 719-336-8000; Treasurer 719-336-8081; Appraiser/Auditor 719-336-8000; Elections 719-336-8011; Vital Records 719-336-2606.

Pueblo County

County Clerk & Recorder, P.O. Box 878, Pueblo, CO 81002-0878. 719-583-6625 R/E Recording: 719-583-6629; Fax 719-583-6549. http://www.co.pueblo.co.us/index2.htm
Will search UCC records. This agency will not do a tax lien search. Will not search real estate records. **Online Access:** Assessor, Real Estate. Online access to the county assessor database is available free at http://pueblocountyassessor.org/FrontPage.html. **Other Phone Numbers:** Assessor 719-583-6564; Treasurer 719-583-6015; Appraiser/Auditor 719-583-6596; Elections 719-583-6620; Vital Records 719-583-4555; Main switchboard 719-583-6000.

Rio Blanco County

County Clerk & Recorder, P.O. Box 1067, Meeker, CO 81641. 970-878-5068.
Will not search UCC records, requesters sent to state level. Tax lien records filed with real property records. Will not search real estate records. **Other Phone Numbers:** Assessor 970-878-5686; Treasurer 970-878-3614.

Rio Grande County

County Clerk & Recorder, P.O. Box 160, Del Norte, CO 81132. 719-657-3334; Fax 719-657-2621.
Will search UCC records. This agency will not do a tax lien search. Will not search real estate records.

Routt County

County Clerk & Recorder, P.O. Box 773598, Steamboat Springs, CO 80477. 970-870-5556; Fax 970-870-1329. http://www.co.routt.co.us/clerk
Will search UCC records. UCC search includes tax liens. Will not search real estate records. **Online Access:** Real Estate, Assessor, Treasurer. Records on the county Assessor/Treasurer Property Search database are available free online at http://pioneer.yampa.com/asp/assessor/search.asp?.

Records on the Routt County Clerk and Recorder Reception Search database are available free online at http://pioneer.yampa.com/asp/clerk/search.asp?. **Other Phone Numbers:** Assessor 970-879-2756.

Saguache County

County Clerk & Recorder, P.O. Box 176, Saguache, CO 81149-0176. 719-655-2512; Fax 719-655-2635. Will search UCC records. UCC search includes tax liens. Separate tax lien search costs same as UCC search Will not search real estate records. **Other Phone Numbers:** Assessor 719-655-2521; Treasurer 719-655-2656.

San Juan County

County Clerk & Recorder, P.O. Box 466, Silverton, CO 81433-0466. County Clerk & Recorder, R/E and UCC Recording 970-387-5671; Fax 970-387-5671. Will search UCC records. UCC search includes tax liens if requested. Will not search real estate records. **Other Phone Numbers:** Assessor 970-387-5632; Treasurer 970-389-5488; Elections 970-387-5671; Vital Records 970-387-5488.

San Miguel County

County Clerk & Recorder, P.O. Box 548, Telluride, CO 81435-0548. 970-728-3954; Fax 970-728-4808. Will search UCC records. This agency will not do a tax lien search. Will not search real estate records. **Other Phone Numbers:** Assessor 970-728-3174; Treasurer 970-728-4451.

Sedgwick County

County Clerk & Recorder, P.O. Box 50, Julesburg, CO 80737. County Clerk & Recorder, R/E and UCC Recording 970-474-3346; Fax 970-474-0954. Will not search or retrieve UCC records unless provided the book and page number. Will not search real estate records. **Other Phone Numbers:** Assessor 970-474-2531; Treasurer 970-474-3473; Elections 970-474-3346; Vital Records 970-474-3473.

Summit County

County Clerk & Recorder, P.O. Box 1538, Breckenridge, CO 80424. County Clerk & Recorder, R/E and UCC Recording 970-453-3475; Fax 970-453-3540. http://www.co.summit.co.us/ Will search UCC records. UCC search includes tax liens. Will not search real estate records. **Other Phone Numbers:** Assessor 970-453-3480; Treasurer 970-453-3440; Appraiser/Auditor 970-453-3480; Elections 970-453-3479; Vital Records 970-453-3472.

Teller County

County Clerk & Recorder, P.O. Box 1010, Cripple Creek, CO 80813-1010. 719-689-2951; Fax 719-689-3524. Will search UCC records. Separate tax lien search costs same as UCC search. Will not search real estate records. **Other Phone Numbers:** Assessor 719-689-2941; Treasurer 719-689-2985.

Washington County

County Clerk & Recorder, P.O. Box L, Akron, CO 80720-0380. 970-345-6565; Fax 970-345-6607. Will search UCC records. This agency will not do a tax lien search. Will not search real estate records.

Weld County

County Clerk & Recorder, P.O. Box 459, Greeley, CO 80632-0459. 970-353-3065 x3065 R/E Recording: 970-304-6530 x3065 UCC Recording: 970-304-6530 x3065; Fax 970-353-1964. http://www.co.weld.co.us Will not search UCC records. Separate tax lien search costs $5.00 for first year, $2.00 each add'l year. Will not search real estate records. **Online Access:** Real Estate. Online access to property information on the map server database is available at the web site. Click on the "Property Information and mapping" button then search by name. **Other Phone Numbers:** Assessor 970-304-3845 x3650; Treasurer 970-304-3845 x3290; Elections 970-304-6525 x3070.

Yuma County

County Clerk & Recorder, P.O. Box 426, Wray, CO 80758-0426. County Clerk & Recorder, R/E and UCC Recording 970-332-5809.

Will search UCC records. UCC search includes tax liens. Will not search real estate records. **Other Phone Numbers:** Assessor 970-332-5032; Treasurer 970-332-4965; Appraiser/Auditor 970-332-5032; Elections 970-332-5809; Vital Records 970-332-5809.

Colorado County Locator

You will usually be able to find the city name in the City/County Cross Reference below. In that case, it is a simple matter to determine the county from the cross reference. However, only the official US Postal Service city names are included in this index. There are an additional 40,000 place names that people use in their addresses. Therefore, we have also included a ZIP/City Cross Reference immediately following the City/County Cross Reference.

If you know the ZIP Code but the city name does not appear in the City/County Cross Reference index, look up the ZIP Code in the ZIP/City Cross Reference, find the city name, then look up the city name in the City/County Cross Reference. For example, you want to know the county for an address of Menands, NY 12204. There is no "Menands" in the City/County Cross Reference. The ZIP/City Cross Reference shows that ZIP Codes 12201-12288 are for the city of Albany. Looking back in the City/County Cross Reference, Albany is in Albany County.

City/County Cross Reference

AGATE Elbert
AGUILAR Las Animas
AKRON Washington
ALAMOSA (81101) Alamosa(99), Conejos(2)
ALAMOSA Alamosa
ALLENSPARK Boulder
ALMA Park
ALMONT Gunnison
AMHERST Phillips
ANTON Washington
ANTONITO Conejos
ARAPAHOE Cheyenne
ARBOLES Archuleta
ARLINGTON (81021) Kiowa(81), Lincoln(19)
ARRIBA Lincoln
ARVADA (80002) Jefferson(97), Adams(3)
ARVADA (80003) Jefferson(86), Adams(14)
ARVADA Jefferson
ASPEN Pitkin
ATWOOD Logan
AULT Weld
AURORA (80010) Adams(50), Arapahoe(50)
AURORA (80011) Arapahoe(58), Adams(42)
AURORA (80014) Arapahoe(96), Denver(4)
AURORA Adams
AURORA Arapahoe
AUSTIN Delta
AVON Eagle
AVONDALE Pueblo
BAILEY Park
BASALT (81621) Eagle(67), Pitkin(33)
BATTLEMENT MESA Garfield
BAYFIELD La Plata
BEDROCK Montrose
BELLVUE Larimer
BENNETT (80102) Adams(58), Arapahoe(37), Elbert(5)
BERTHOUD (80513) Larimer(90), Weld(10)
BETHUNE Kit Carson
BEULAH (81023) Pueblo(99), Custer(1)
BLACK HAWK Gilpin
BLANCA Costilla
BONCARBO Las Animas
BOND Eagle
BOONE Pueblo
BOULDER Boulder
BOYERO Lincoln
BRANSON Las Animas
BRECKENRIDGE Summit
BRIGGSDALE Weld
BRIGHTON (80601) Adams(88), Weld(12)
BRISTOL Prowers
BROOMFIELD (80020) Boulder(47), Adams(33), Jefferson(19)
BROOMFIELD (80021) Jefferson(96), Boulder(4)
BROOMFIELD Boulder

BRUSH (80723) Morgan(99), Washington(1)
BUENA VISTA Chaffee
BUFFALO CREEK Jefferson
BURLINGTON (80807) Kit Carson(98), Yuma(2)
BURNS Eagle
BYERS (80103) Arapahoe(83), Adams(17)
CAHONE Dolores
CALHAN (80808) El Paso(95), Elbert(5)
CAMPO Baca
CANON CITY Fremont
CAPULIN Conejos
CARBONDALE (81623) Garfield(62), Eagle(15), Gunnison(13), Pitkin(10)
CARR Weld
CASCADE El Paso
CASTLE ROCK Douglas
CEDAREDGE Delta
CENTER (81125) Saguache(66), Rio Grande(31), Alamosa(3)
CENTRAL CITY Gilpin
CHAMA Costilla
CHERAW Otero
CHEYENNE WELLS Cheyenne
CHIMNEY ROCK Archuleta
CHROMO Archuleta
CIMARRON (81220) Gunnison(91), Montrose(9)
CLARK Routt
CLIFTON Mesa
CLIMAX Lake
COAL CREEK Fremont
COALDALE Fremont
COALMONT Jackson
COKEDALE Las Animas
COLLBRAN Mesa
COLORADO CITY Pueblo
COLORADO SPRINGS (80926) El Paso(97), Fremont(3)
COLORADO SPRINGS El Paso
COMMERCE CITY Adams
COMO Park
CONEJOS Conejos
CONIFER Jefferson
COPE (80812) Washington(98), Yuma(3)
CORTEZ Montezuma
CORY Delta
COTOPAXI Fremont
COWDREY Jackson
CRAIG Moffat
CRAWFORD (81415) Delta(78), Montrose(22)
CREEDE Mineral
CRESTED BUTTE Gunnison
CRESTONE Saguache
CRIPPLE CREEK Teller
CROOK Logan
CROWLEY Crowley
DACONO Weld
DE BEQUE (81630) Garfield(61), Mesa(39)
DEER TRAIL (80105) Arapahoe(59), Elbert(30), Adams(11)

DEL NORTE (81132) Rio Grande(93), Saguache(7)
DELTA (81416) Delta(96), Montrose(4)
DENVER (80212) Denver(78), Jefferson(19), Adams(3)
DENVER (80214) Jefferson(99), Denver(1)
DENVER (80216) Denver(83), Adams(17)
DENVER (80221) Adams(92), Denver(8)
DENVER (80222) Denver(94), Arapahoe(6)
DENVER (80227) Jefferson(74), Denver(26)
DENVER (80231) Denver(75), Arapahoe(25)
DENVER (80235) Jefferson(58), Denver(42)
DENVER (80236) Denver(88), Arapahoe(12)
DENVER (80246) Denver(67), Arapahoe(34)
DENVER (80249) Denver(88), Adams(12)
DENVER Adams
DENVER Denver
DENVER Jefferson
DILLON Summit
DINOSAUR Moffat
DIVIDE Teller
DOLORES Montezuma
DOVE CREEK (81324) Dolores(97), San Miguel(3)
DRAKE Larimer
DUMONT Clear Creek
DUPONT Adams
DURANGO La Plata
EADS Kiowa
EAGLE Eagle
EASTLAKE Adams
EATON Weld
ECKERT Delta
ECKLEY Yuma
EDWARDS Eagle
EGNAR (81325) Dolores(63), San Miguel(38)
EL JEBEL Eagle
ELBERT (80106) El Paso(58), Elbert(40), Douglas(2)
ELDORADO SPRINGS Boulder
ELIZABETH Elbert
EMPIRE Clear Creek
ENGLEWOOD (80112) Arapahoe(97), Douglas(2)
ENGLEWOOD Arapahoe
ERIE (80516) Weld(79), Boulder(21)
ESTES PARK Larimer
EVANS Weld
EVERGREEN (80439) Jefferson(85), Clear Creek(15)
EVERGREEN Jefferson
FAIRPLAY (80440) Park(96), Adams(4)
FIRESTONE Weld
FLAGLER (80815) Kit Carson(87), Washington(13)
FLEMING Logan
FLORENCE Fremont

FLORISSANT (80816) Teller(79), Park(21)
FORT COLLINS (80525) Larimer(99), Boulder(1)
FORT COLLINS Larimer
FORT GARLAND Costilla
FORT LUPTON Weld
FORT LYON Bent
FORT MORGAN (80701) Morgan(93), Adams(7)
FOUNTAIN El Paso
FOWLER (81039) Otero(93), Pueblo(5), Crowley(1)
FOXTON Jefferson
FRANKTOWN Douglas
FRASER Grand
FREDERICK Weld
FRISCO Summit
FRUITA Mesa
GALETON Weld
GARCIA Costilla
GARDNER Huerfano
GATEWAY Mesa
GENOA (80818) Lincoln(79), Washington(21)
GEORGETOWN Clear Creek
GILCREST Weld
GILL Weld
GLADE PARK Mesa
GLEN HAVEN Larimer
GLENWOOD SPRINGS Garfield
GOLDEN (80403) Jefferson(67), Gilpin(28), Boulder(5)
GOLDEN Jefferson
GRANADA (81041) Prowers(92), Baca(8)
GRANBY Grand
GRAND JUNCTION Mesa
GRAND LAKE Grand
GRANITE (81228) Chaffee(75), Lake(25)
GRANT Park
GREELEY Weld
GREEN MOUNTAIN FALLS El Paso
GROVER Weld
GUFFEY Park
GULNARE Las Animas
GUNNISON Chaffee
GUNNISON Gunnison
GYPSUM (81637) Eagle(91), Garfield(9)
HAMILTON (81638) Moffat(59), Routt(32), Rio Blanco(9)
HARTMAN Prowers
HARTSEL Park
HASTY Bent
HASWELL (81045) Kiowa(71), Lincoln(17), Cheyenne(13)
HAXTUN (80731) Yuma(63), Logan(27), Phillips(10)
HAYDEN Routt
HENDERSON Adams
HEREFORD Weld
HESPERUS La Plata
HILLROSE Morgan
HILLSIDE Fremont
HOEHNE Las Animas

HOLLY (81047) Prowers(95), Kiowa(3), Baca(2)
HOLYOKE (80734) Phillips(95), Yuma(5)
HOMELAKE Rio Grande
HOOPER (81136) Alamosa(96), Saguache(4)
HOT SULPHUR SPRINGS Grand
HOTCHKISS Delta
HOWARD Fremont
HUDSON Weld
HUGO Lincoln
HYGIENE Boulder
IDAHO SPRINGS Clear Creek
IDALIA (80735) Yuma(80), Weld(21)
IDLEDALE Jefferson
IGNACIO La Plata
ILIFF Logan
INDIAN HILLS Jefferson
JAMESTOWN Boulder
JAROSO Costilla
JEFFERSON Park
JOES Yuma
JOHNSTOWN Weld
JULESBURG Sedgwick
KARVAL Lincoln
KEENESBURG Weld
KERSEY Weld
KIM Las Animas
KIOWA Elbert
KIRK (80824) Yuma(99), Kit Carson(1)
KIT CARSON Cheyenne
KITTREDGE Jefferson
KREMMLING (80459) Grand(99), Summit(1)
LA JARA Conejos
LA JUNTA Otero
LA SALLE Weld
LA VETA Huerfano
LAFAYETTE Boulder
LAKE CITY Hinsdale
LAKE GEORGE (80827) Teller(70), Park(30)
LAKEWOOD (80226) Jefferson(99), Denver(1)
LAKEWOOD Jefferson
LAMAR (81052) Prowers(99), Bent(1)
LAPORTE Larimer
LARKSPUR Douglas
LAS ANIMAS Bent
LAZEAR Delta
LEADVILLE Lake
LEWIS Montezuma
LIMON (80828) Lincoln(71), Elbert(29)
LIMON Lincoln
LINDON Washington
LITTLETON (80120) Arapahoe(98), Douglas(2)
LITTLETON (80123) Jefferson(53), Arapahoe(31), Denver(15)
LITTLETON (80124) Douglas(98), Arapahoe(2)
LITTLETON (80128) Jefferson(97), Arapahoe(3)
LITTLETON Arapahoe
LITTLETON Douglas
LITTLETON Jefferson
LIVERMORE Larimer
LOG LANE VILLAGE Morgan
LOMA Mesa
LONGMONT (80504) Weld(96), Boulder(4)

LONGMONT Boulder
LOUISVILLE Boulder
LOUVIERS Douglas
LOVELAND (80537) Larimer(99), Weld(2)
LOVELAND Larimer
LUCERNE Weld
LYONS (80540) Larimer(55), Boulder(45)
MACK Mesa
MAHER Delta
MANASSA Conejos
MANCOS (81328) Montezuma(96), La Plata(4)
MANITOU SPRINGS El Paso
MANZANOLA (81058) Otero(80), Crowley(20)
MARVEL La Plata
MASONVILLE Larimer
MATHESON Elbert
MAYBELL Moffat
MC CLAVE Bent
MC COY (80463) Eagle(75), Routt(25)
MEAD Weld
MEEKER (81641) Rio Blanco(94), Moffat(5), Garfield(2)
MEREDITH Pitkin
MERINO (80741) Logan(92), Washington(6), Morgan(2)
MESA Mesa
MESA VERDE NATIONAL PARK Montezuma
MILLIKEN Weld
MINTURN Eagle
MODEL (81059) Las Animas(76), Otero(24)
MOFFAT Saguache
MOLINA Mesa
MONARCH Chaffee
MONTE VISTA (81144) Rio Grande(97), Alamosa(4)
MONTROSE (81401) Montrose(97), Ouray(3)
MONTROSE Montrose
MONUMENT El Paso
MORRISON Jefferson
MOSCA Alamosa
NATHROP Chaffee
NATURITA Montrose
NEDERLAND Boulder
NEW CASTLE Garfield
NEW RAYMER (80742) Weld(89), Morgan(12)
NIWOT Boulder
NORWOOD San Miguel
NUCLA Montrose
NUNN Weld
OAK CREEK Routt
OHIO CITY (81237) Gunnison(75), Washington(25)
OLATHE Montrose
OLNEY SPRINGS (81062) Crowley(96), Pueblo(4)
OPHIR San Miguel
ORCHARD (80649) Morgan(57), Weld(43)
ORDWAY (81063) Crowley(96), Lincoln(4)
OTIS (80743) Washington(97), Logan(3)
OURAY Ouray
OVID Sedgwick
PADRONI Logan
PAGOSA SPRINGS Archuleta
PALISADE Mesa

PALMER LAKE (80133) El Paso(84), Douglas(16)
PAOLI Phillips
PAONIA Delta
PARACHUTE Garfield
PARADOX Montrose
PARKER (80134) Douglas(98), Elbert(2)
PARKER (80138) Douglas(74), Elbert(26)
PARLIN Gunnison
PARSHALL Grand
PEETZ Logan
PENROSE Fremont
PEYTON El Paso
PHIPPSBURG Routt
PIERCE Weld
PINE (80470) Jefferson(66), Park(34)
PINECLIFFE Boulder
PITKIN Gunnison
PLACERVILLE San Miguel
PLATTEVILLE Weld
PLEASANT VIEW Montezuma
PONCHA SPRINGS Chaffee
POWDERHORN Gunnison
PRITCHETT (81064) Baca(75), Las Animas(25)
PRYOR Huerfano
PUEBLO (81008) Pueblo(98), El Paso(2)
PUEBLO Pueblo
RAMAH (80832) Elbert(57), El Paso(39), Lincoln(5)
RAND Jackson
RANGELY Rio Blanco
RED CLIFF Eagle
RED FEATHER LAKES Larimer
RED WING Huerfano
REDVALE Montrose
RICO Dolores
RIDGWAY Ouray
RIFLE (81650) Garfield(95), Rio Blanco(5)
ROCKVALE Fremont
ROCKY FORD Otero
ROGGEN Weld
ROLLINSVILLE Gilpin
ROMEO Conejos
RUSH (80833) Lincoln(48), El Paso(43), Elbert(10)
RYE Pueblo
SAGUACHE Saguache
SALIDA Chaffee
SAN ACACIO Costilla
SAN LUIS Costilla
SAN PABLO Costilla
SANFORD (81151) Conejos(89), Costilla(9), Rio Grande(2)
SARGENTS Saguache
SEDALIA Douglas
SEDGWICK Sedgwick
SEGUNDO Las Animas
SEIBERT (80834) Kit Carson(89), Washington(11)
SEVERANCE Weld
SHAWNEE Park
SHERIDAN LAKE Kiowa
SILT Garfield
SILVER CLIFF Custer
SILVER PLUME Clear Creek
SILVERTHORNE Summit
SILVERTON San Juan
SIMLA (80835) Elbert(89), El Paso(11)
SLATER Moffat

SLICK ROCK San Miguel
SNOWMASS Pitkin
SNOWMASS VILLAGE Pitkin
SNYDER Morgan
SOMERSET (81434) Gunnison(93), Delta(8)
SOUTH FORK Rio Grande
SPRINGFIELD Baca
STARKVILLE Las Animas
STEAMBOAT SPRINGS Routt
STERLING Logan
STONEHAM Weld
STONINGTON Baca
STRASBURG (80136) Adams(70), Arapahoe(30)
STRATTON (80836) Kit Carson(99), Yuma(1)
SUGAR CITY (81076) Crowley(96), Kiowa(2), Lincoln(2)
SWINK Otero
TABERNASH Grand
TELLURIDE San Miguel
TIMNATH Larimer
TOPONAS Routt
TOWAOC Montezuma
TRINCHERA Las Animas
TRINIDAD Las Animas
TWIN LAKES Lake
TWO BUTTES (81084) Baca(90), Prowers(10)
U S A F ACADEMY El Paso
VAIL Eagle
VERNON Yuma
VICTOR Teller
VILAS Baca
VILLA GROVE Saguache
VONA Kit Carson
WALDEN Jackson
WALSENBURG Huerfano
WALSH Baca
WARD Boulder
WATKINS (80137) Arapahoe(60), Adams(40)
WELDONA Morgan
WELLINGTON (80549) Larimer(97), Weld(3)
WESTCLIFFE Custer
WESTMINSTER (80030) Adams(93), Jefferson(7)
WESTMINSTER Jefferson
WESTON Las Animas
WETMORE (81253) Custer(63), Fremont(30), Pueblo(7)
WHEAT RIDGE Jefferson
WHITEWATER Mesa
WIGGINS (80654) Morgan(98), Adams(3)
WILD HORSE Cheyenne
WILEY (81092) Prowers(60), Bent(38), Kiowa(2)
WINDSOR Weld
WINTER PARK Grand
WOLCOTT Eagle
WOODLAND PARK Teller
WOODROW Washington
WOODY CREEK Pitkin
WRAY Yuma
YAMPA Routt
YELLOW JACKET Montezuma
YODER El Paso
YUMA Yuma

ZIP/City Cross Reference

ZIP Range	City	ZIP Range	City	ZIP Range	City	ZIP Range	City
80001-80007	ARVADA	80033-80034	WHEAT RIDGE	80105-80105	DEER TRAIL	80132-80132	MONUMENT
80010-80019	AURORA	80035-80036	WESTMINSTER	80106-80106	ELBERT	80133-80133	PALMER LAKE
80020-80021	BROOMFIELD	80037-80037	COMMERCE CITY	80107-80107	ELIZABETH	80134-80134	PARKER
80022-80022	COMMERCE CITY	80038-80038	BROOMFIELD	80110-80112	ENGLEWOOD	80135-80135	SEDALIA
80024-80024	DUPONT	80040-80047	AURORA	80116-80116	FRANKTOWN	80136-80136	STRASBURG
80025-80025	ELDORADO SPRINGS	80101-80101	AGATE	80117-80117	KIOWA	80137-80137	WATKINS
80026-80026	LAFAYETTE	80102-80102	BENNETT	80118-80118	LARKSPUR	80138-80138	PARKER
80027-80028	LOUISVILLE	80103-80103	BYERS	80120-80128	LITTLETON	80150-80155	ENGLEWOOD
80030-80031	WESTMINSTER	80104-80104	CASTLE ROCK	80131-80131	LOUVIERS	80160-80166	LITTLETON

80201-80214	DENVER	80534-80534	JOHNSTOWN	80813-80813	CRIPPLE CREEK	81092-81092	WILEY
80215-80215	LAKEWOOD	80535-80535	LAPORTE	80814-80814	DIVIDE	81101-81102	ALAMOSA
80216-80225	DENVER	80536-80536	LIVERMORE	80815-80815	FLAGLER	81120-81120	ANTONITO
80226-80226	LAKEWOOD	80537-80539	LOVELAND	80816-80816	FLORISSANT	81121-81121	ARBOLES
80227-80227	DENVER	80540-80540	LYONS	80817-80817	FOUNTAIN	81122-81122	BAYFIELD
80228-80228	LAKEWOOD	80541-80541	MASONVILLE	80818-80818	GENOA	81123-81123	BLANCA
80229-80231	DENVER	80542-80542	MEAD	80819-80819	GREEN MOUNTAIN	81124-81124	CAPULIN
80232-80232	LAKEWOOD	80543-80543	MILLIKEN		FALLS	81125-81125	CENTER
80233-80299	DENVER	80544-80544	NIWOT	80820-80820	GUFFEY	81126-81126	CHAMA
80301-80329	BOULDER	80545-80545	RED FEATHER LAKES	80821-80821	HUGO	81127-81127	CHIMNEY ROCK
80401-80419	GOLDEN	80546-80546	SEVERANCE	80822-80822	JOES	81128-81128	CHROMO
80420-80420	ALMA	80547-80547	TIMNATH	80823-80823	KARVAL	81129-81129	CONEJOS
80421-80421	BAILEY	80549-80549	WELLINGTON	80824-80824	KIRK	81130-81130	CREEDE
80422-80422	BLACK HAWK	80550-80551	WINDSOR	80825-80825	KIT CARSON	81131-81131	CRESTONE
80423-80423	BOND	80553-80553	FORT COLLINS	80826-80826	LIMON	81132-81132	DEL NORTE
80424-80424	BRECKENRIDGE	80601-80601	BRIGHTON	80827-80827	LAKE GEORGE	81133-81133	FORT GARLAND
80425-80425	BUFFALO CREEK	80610-80610	AULT	80828-80828	LIMON	81134-81134	GARCIA
80426-80426	BURNS	80611-80611	BRIGGSDALE	80829-80829	MANITOU SPRINGS	81135-81135	HOMELAKE
80427-80427	CENTRAL CITY	80612-80612	CARR	80830-80830	MATHESON	81136-81136	HOOPER
80428-80428	CLARK	80614-80614	EASTLAKE	80831-80831	PEYTON	81137-81137	IGNACIO
80429-80429	CLIMAX	80615-80615	EATON	80832-80832	RAMAH	81138-81138	JAROSO
80430-80430	COALMONT	80620-80620	EVANS	80833-80833	RUSH	81140-81140	LA JARA
80432-80432	COMO	80621-80621	FORT LUPTON	80834-80834	SEIBERT	81141-81141	MANASSA
80433-80433	CONIFER	80622-80622	GALETON	80835-80835	SIMLA	81143-81143	MOFFAT
80434-80434	COWDREY	80623-80623	GILCREST	80836-80836	STRATTON	81144-81144	MONTE VISTA
80435-80435	DILLON	80624-80624	GILL	80840-80841	U S A F ACADEMY	81146-81146	MOSCA
80436-80436	DUMONT	80631-80639	GREELEY	80860-80860	VICTOR	81147-81147	PAGOSA SPRINGS
80437-80437	EVERGREEN	80640-80640	HENDERSON	80861-80861	VONA	81148-81148	ROMEO
80438-80438	EMPIRE	80642-80642	HUDSON	80862-80862	WILD HORSE	81149-81149	SAGUACHE
80439-80439	EVERGREEN	80643-80643	KEENESBURG	80863-80863	WOODLAND PARK	81151-81151	SANFORD
80440-80440	FAIRPLAY	80644-80644	KERSEY	80864-80864	YODER	81152-81152	SAN LUIS
80442-80442	FRASER	80645-80645	LA SALLE	80866-80866	WOODLAND PARK	81153-81153	SAN PABLO
80443-80443	FRISCO	80646-80646	LUCERNE	80901-80997	COLORADO SPRINGS	81154-81154	SOUTH FORK
80444-80444	GEORGETOWN	80648-80648	NUNN	81001-81015	PUEBLO	81155-81155	VILLA GROVE
80446-80446	GRANBY	80649-80649	ORCHARD	81019-81019	COLORADO CITY	81157-81157	PAGOSA SPRINGS
80447-80447	GRAND LAKE	80650-80650	PIERCE	81020-81020	AGUILAR	81201-81201	SALIDA
80448-80448	GRANT	80651-80651	PLATTEVILLE	81021-81021	ARLINGTON	81210-81210	ALMONT
80449-80449	HARTSEL	80652-80652	ROGGEN	81022-81022	AVONDALE	81211-81211	BUENA VISTA
80451-80451	HOT SULPHUR SPRINGS	80653-80653	WELDONA	81023-81023	BEULAH	81212-81215	CANON CITY
80452-80452	IDAHO SPRINGS	80654-80654	WIGGINS	81024-81024	BONCARBO	81220-81220	CIMARRON
80453-80453	IDLEDALE	80701-80701	FORT MORGAN	81025-81025	BOONE	81221-81221	COAL CREEK
80454-80454	INDIAN HILLS	80705-80705	LOG LANE VILLAGE	81027-81027	BRANSON	81222-81222	COALDALE
80455-80455	JAMESTOWN	80720-80720	AKRON	81029-81029	CAMPO	81223-81223	COTOPAXI
80456-80456	JEFFERSON	80721-80721	AMHERST	81030-81030	CHERAW	81224-81225	CRESTED BUTTE
80457-80457	KITTREDGE	80722-80722	ATWOOD	81033-81034	CROWLEY	81226-81226	FLORENCE
80459-80459	KREMMLING	80723-80723	BRUSH	81036-81036	EADS	81227-81227	MONARCH
80461-80461	LEADVILLE	80726-80726	CROOK	81038-81038	FORT LYON	81228-81228	GRANITE
80463-80463	MC COY	80727-80727	ECKLEY	81039-81039	FOWLER	81230-81231	GUNNISON
80465-80465	MORRISON	80728-80728	FLEMING	81040-81040	GARDNER	81232-81232	HILLSIDE
80466-80466	NEDERLAND	80729-80729	GROVER	81041-81041	GRANADA	81233-81233	HOWARD
80467-80467	OAK CREEK	80731-80731	HAXTUN	81042-81042	GULNARE	81235-81235	LAKE CITY
80468-80468	PARSHALL	80732-80732	HEREFORD	81043-81043	HARTMAN	81236-81236	NATHROP
80469-80469	PHIPPSBURG	80733-80733	HILLROSE	81044-81044	HASTY	81237-81237	OHIO CITY
80470-80470	PINE	80734-80734	HOLYOKE	81045-81045	HASWELL	81239-81239	PARLIN
80471-80471	PINECLIFFE	80735-80735	IDALIA	81046-81046	HOEHNE	81240-81240	PENROSE
80473-80473	RAND	80736-80736	ILIFF	81047-81047	HOLLY	81241-81241	PITKIN
80474-80474	ROLLINSVILLE	80737-80737	JULESBURG	81049-81049	KIM	81242-81242	PONCHA SPRINGS
80475-80475	SHAWNEE	80740-80740	LINDON	81050-81050	LA JUNTA	81243-81243	POWDERHORN
80476-80476	SILVER PLUME	80741-80741	MERINO	81052-81052	LAMAR	81244-81244	ROCKVALE
80477-80477	STEAMBOAT SPRINGS	80742-80742	NEW RAYMER	81054-81054	LAS ANIMAS	81246-81246	CANON CITY
80478-80478	TABERNASH	80743-80743	OTIS	81055-81055	LA VETA	81247-81247	GUNNISON
80479-80479	TOPONAS	80744-80744	OVID	81057-81057	MC CLAVE	81248-81248	SARGENTS
80480-80480	WALDEN	80745-80745	PADRONI	81058-81058	MANZANOLA	81251-81251	TWIN LAKES
80481-80481	WARD	80746-80746	PAOLI	81059-81059	MODEL	81252-81252	WESTCLIFFE
80482-80482	WINTER PARK	80747-80747	PEETZ	81062-81062	OLNEY SPRINGS	81253-81253	WETMORE
80483-80483	YAMPA	80749-80749	SEDGWICK	81063-81063	ORDWAY	81290-81290	FLORENCE
80487-80488	STEAMBOAT SPRINGS	80750-80750	SNYDER	81064-81064	PRITCHETT	81301-81302	DURANGO
80498-80498	SILVERTHORNE	80751-80751	STERLING	81066-81066	RED WING	81320-81320	CAHONE
80501-80504	LONGMONT	80754-80754	STONEHAM	81067-81067	ROCKY FORD	81321-81321	CORTEZ
80510-80510	ALLENSPARK	80755-80755	VERNON	81069-81069	RYE	81323-81323	DOLORES
80511-80511	ESTES PARK	80757-80757	WOODROW	81071-81071	SHERIDAN LAKE	81324-81324	DOVE CREEK
80512-80512	BELLVUE	80758-80758	WRAY	81073-81073	SPRINGFIELD	81325-81325	EGNAR
80513-80513	BERTHOUD	80759-80759	YUMA	81074-81074	STARKVILLE	81326-81326	HESPERUS
80514-80514	DACONO	80801-80801	ANTON	81076-81076	SUGAR CITY	81327-81327	LEWIS
80515-80515	DRAKE	80802-80802	ARAPAHOE	81077-81077	SWINK	81328-81328	MANCOS
80516-80516	ERIE	80804-80804	ARRIBA	81081-81081	TRINCHERA	81329-81329	MARVEL
80517-80517	ESTES PARK	80805-80805	BETHUNE	81082-81082	TRINIDAD	81330-81330	MESA VERDE NATIONAL
80520-80520	FIRESTONE	80807-80807	BURLINGTON	81084-81084	TWO BUTTES		PARK
80521-80528	FORT COLLINS	80808-80808	CALHAN	81087-81087	VILAS	81331-81331	PLEASANT VIEW
80530-80530	FREDERICK	80809-80809	CASCADE	81089-81089	WALSENBURG	81332-81332	RICO
80532-80532	GLEN HAVEN	80810-80810	CHEYENNE WELLS	81090-81090	WALSH	81333-81333	SLICK ROCK
80533-80533	HYGIENE	80812-80812	COPE	81091-81091	WESTON	81334-81334	TOWAOC

81335-81335	YELLOW JACKET	81428-81428	PAONIA	81610-81610	DINOSAUR	81640-81640	MAYBELL
81401-81402	MONTROSE	81429-81429	PARADOX	81611-81612	ASPEN	81641-81641	MEEKER
81410-81410	AUSTIN	81430-81430	PLACERVILLE	81615-81615	SNOWMASS VILLAGE	81642-81642	MEREDITH
81411-81411	BEDROCK	81431-81431	REDVALE	81620-81620	AVON	81643-81643	MESA
81413-81413	CEDAREDGE	81432-81432	RIDGWAY	81621-81621	BASALT	81645-81645	MINTURN
81414-81414	CORY	81433-81433	SILVERTON	81623-81623	CARBONDALE	81646-81646	MOLINA
81415-81415	CRAWFORD	81434-81434	SOMERSET	81624-81624	COLLBRAN	81647-81647	NEW CASTLE
81416-81416	DELTA	81435-81435	TELLURIDE	81625-81626	CRAIG	81648-81648	RANGELY
81418-81418	ECKERT	81501-81506	GRAND JUNCTION	81628-81628	EL JEBEL	81649-81649	RED CLIFF
81419-81419	HOTCHKISS	81520-81520	CLIFTON	81630-81630	DE BEQUE	81650-81650	RIFLE
81420-81420	LAZEAR	81521-81521	FRUITA	81631-81631	EAGLE	81652-81652	SILT
81421-81421	MAHER	81522-81522	GATEWAY	81632-81632	EDWARDS	81653-81653	SLATER
81422-81422	NATURITA	81523-81523	GLADE PARK	81633-81633	DINOSAUR	81654-81654	SNOWMASS
81423-81423	NORWOOD	81524-81524	LOMA	81635-81635	PARACHUTE	81655-81655	WOLCOTT
81424-81424	NUCLA	81525-81525	MACK	81636-81636	BATTLEMENT MESA	81656-81656	WOODY CREEK
81425-81425	OLATHE	81526-81526	PALISADE	81637-81637	GYPSUM	81657-81658	VAIL
81426-81426	OPHIR	81527-81527	WHITEWATER	81638-81638	HAMILTON		
81427-81427	OURAY	81601-81602	GLENWOOD SPRINGS	81639-81639	HAYDEN		

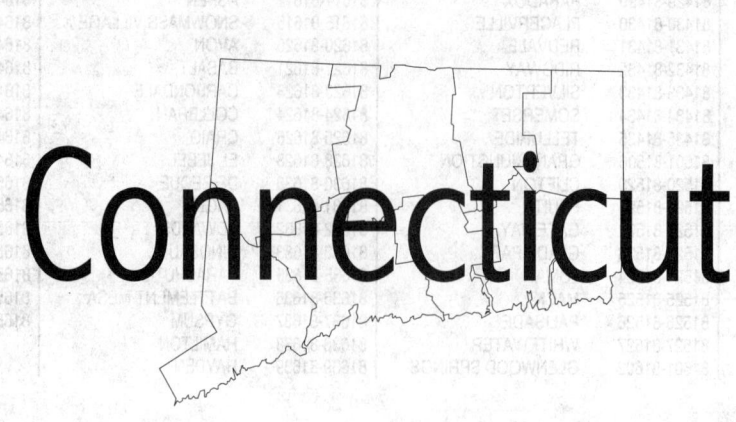

Connecticut

General Help Numbers:

Governor's Office

State Capitol, 210 Capitol Ave   860-566-4840
Hartford, CT 06106   Fax 860-566-4677
http://www.state.ct.us/governor   8AM-5PM

Attorney General's Office

PO Box 120   860-808-5318
Hartford, CT 06141-0120   Fax 860-808-5387
http://www.cslib.org/attygenl   8:30AM-4:30PM

State Court Administrator

231 Capitol Ave   860-757-2100
Hartford, CT 06106   Fax 860-757-2130
http://www.jud.state.ct.us   9AM-5PM

State Archives

History & Genealogy Unit   860-757-6580
231 Capitol Ave   Fax 860-757-6503
Hartford, CT 06106   9AM-5PM M-F
http://www.cslib.org

State Specifics:

Capital: Hartford
                                        Hartford County

Time Zone: EST

Number of Counties: 8

Population: 3,405,565

Web Site: www.state.ct.us

State Agencies

Criminal Records

Department of Public Safety, Bureau of Identification, PO Box 2794, Middletown, CT 06757-9294 (Courier: 1111 Country Club Rd, Middleton, CT 06457); 860-685-8480, 860-685-8361 (Fax), 8:30AM-4:30PM.

http://www.state.ct.us/dps

Note: There is a State Record Center that receives criminal records from the courts. Records are sent from 3 months to 5 years after disposition. The

Center can be reached at 860-741-3714. Sex offender data is online at www.state.ct.us/dps/Sor.htm.

Indexing & Storage: Records are available from the 1950's on. Records were first computerized in 1983.

Searching: Records are open to the public. Forms can be mailed or downloaded from the web site. The only information released to the public is conviction only criminal records. Include the following in your request-date of birth. Request

forms may be downloaded from the web site. The following data is not released: pending cases, dismissals or juvenile records.

Access by: mail.

Fee & Payment: The fee is $25.00 per request. The copy fee is $.25 per page. Fee payee: Commissioner of Public Safety. Prepayment required. Personal checks accepted. No credit cards accepted.

Mail search: Turnaround time: 2 weeks. Records can only be requested by mail. If you come in-person, the results are still mailed.

Corporation Records
Limited Partnership Records
Trademarks/Servicemarks
Limited Liability Company Records

Secretary of State, Commercial Recording Division, 30 Trinity St, Hartford, CT 06106; 860-509-6001, 860-509-6068 (Fax), 8:30AM-4:30PM.

http://www.sots.state.ct.us

Note: Assumed names are found at the town level.

Indexing & Storage: New records are available for inquiry immediately. Records are indexed on microfilm, inhouse computer.

Searching: Include the following in your request-full name of business, specific records that you need copies of. In addition to the articles of incorporation, corporation records include the following information: Annual Reports, Officers, Directors, Prior (merged) names, Inactive and Reserved names.

Access by: mail, phone, in person, online.

Fee & Payment: The search fee is $25.00 per business name for UCC searches performed by the office personnel. Fee payee: Secretary of State. Prepayment required. Personal checks accepted. Credit cards accepted: MasterCard, Visa.

Mail search: Turnaround time: 2 to 3 days. No self addressed stamped envelope is required.

Phone search: Only limited, basic information is available by phone.

In person search: Certain, limited information is available at no charge.

Online search: Click on the CONCORD option at the web site for free access to corporation and UCC records. The system is open from 7AM to 11PM. You can search by business name only.

Expedited service: Expedited service is available on limited filings for an add'l $25.00. Turnaround time: 24 hours. Add $25.00 per business name. The fee is per transaction requested; review is one transaction, copy is another, etc.

Uniform Commercial Code
Federal Tax Liens
State Tax Liens

UCC Division, Secretary of State, PO Box 150470, Hartford, CT 06115-0470 (Courier: 30 Trinity St, Hartford, CT 06106); 860-509-6004, 860-509-6068 (Fax), 8:30AM-4PM.

http://www.sots.state.ct.us

Indexing & Storage: Records are available from 8/94 on computer, earlier records are on microfilm from 10/80.

Searching: Use search request form UCC-11. The search includes tax liens. Include the following in your request-debtor name.

Access by: mail, in person, online.

Fee & Payment: UCC searches include tax liens and are free if requested in person, $25.00 per name by mail. Financing statements copies are $5.00 including 2 pages of attachments. Additional pages of attachments cost $5.00 each. Fee payee: Secretary of State. Prepayment required. Credit cards are accepted for in-person searching only. Personal checks accepted. Credit cards accepted: MasterCard, Visa.

Mail search: Turnaround time: 3 to 5 days. A self addressed stamped envelope is requested.

Online search: Records may be accessed at no charge on the Internet. Click on the CONCORD option. The system is open 7AM to 11PM.

Sales Tax Registrations

Department of Revenue Services, Taxpayer Services Division, 25 Sigourney St, Hartford, CT 06106; 860-297-4885, 860-297-5714 (Fax), 8AM-5PM.

http://www.drs.state.ct.us

Searching: This agency will only confirm that the business is registered and active. They will provide no other information. Include the following in your request-business name. They will also search by tax permit number.

Access by: mail, phone, fax, in person.

Fee & Payment: There is no search fee

Mail search: Turnaround time: 1 day.

Phone search: Records are available by phone.

Fax search: Same criteria as mail searches.

Birth Certificates
Death Records
Marriage Certificates
Divorce Records
Access to Records is Restricted

Department of Public Health, Vital Records Section MS# 11VRS, PO Box 340308, Hartford, CT 06134-0308 (Courier: 410 Capitol Ave, Hartford, CT 06134); 860-509-7897, 860-509-7964 (Fax), 8:30AM-4:30PM M-F.

http://www.state.ct.us/dph/OPPE/hpvital.htm

Note: The state is in the process of microfilming all records. You must contact the town/city clerk of occurrence to obtain copies of records. The web site has a great list of towns and phone numbers. Records are $5.00 each.

Workers' Compensation Records

Workers Compensation Commission, 21 Oak Street, Hartford, CT 06106; 860-493-1500, 860-247-1361 (Fax), 7:45AM-4:30PM.

http://wcc.state.ct.us

Note: All files are kept at one of the eight district offices. This agency will forward the request to the proper district office.

Indexing & Storage: Records are available on microfilm from 1914 thru 1985 and computerized from 1985 forward, for insurance coverage files. The case files since 1995 are indexed on computer. It takes 1 month before new records are available for inquiry.

Searching: Claims information is not released without a signed release from the employee. Include the following in your request-claimant name, Social Security Number (if available), date of injury, name and address of employer. Include as much information as possible. The following data is not released: medical records.

Access by: mail, phone, fax, in person.

Fee & Payment: Fees vary depending upon the nature of the request and are determined at that time. Fee payee: Workers Compensation Commission. Personal checks accepted. No credit cards accepted.

Mail search: Turnaround time: variable. A self addressed stamped envelope is requested.

Phone search: You may call for information.

Fax search: A mail request must follow.

In person search: You may request information in person.

Other access: The agency will sell self-insured lists for $5.00.

Driver Records

Department of Motor Vehicles, Copy Records Unit, 60 State St., Wethersfield, CT 06161-1896; 860-263-5154, 8:30AM-4:30PM T,W,F; 8:30AM-7:30PM TH; 8:30AM-12:30 S.

http://dmvct.org

Note: Copies of tickets may be obtained from the Superior Court Records Center, 111 Phoenix Ave, Enfield, 06082, 860-741-3714 for a fee of $1.00, or $3.00 for certified. Written requests must include name, DOB, date of disposition, document # and court.

Indexing & Storage: Records are available for 3/5/10 years to present, dependent upon the type of violation. It takes 5 to 7 days before new records are available for inquiry. Records are normally destroyed after 5 years at the discretion of the commissioner. The state does not report accidents on the driving record.

Searching: Mail and in person requesters must complete From J-23. Casual requests must include evidence of the individual's consent. The form can be ordered from the web site at http://dmvct.org/formsrec.htm or by calling 860-263-5700. The driver's license number, name and address are needed when searching, the DOB is optional. A DWI first offense violation will not appear if the offender attends an "Accelerated Alcohol Class."

Access by: mail, in person, online.

Fee & Payment: The fee for walk-in or mail-in driving records is $10.00 per record. The fee for ordering online or on a tape-to-tape system is $5.00. The fee for a license status check is $5.50. Fee payee: Department of Motor Vehicles. Prepayment required. Personal checks accepted. No credit cards accepted.

Mail search: Turnaround time: 2 weeks. A self addressed stamped envelope is requested.

In person search: The state will process up to three requests for walk-in requesters who have a permissible use as stipulated in C.G.S.#14-10. Please note the office is closed on Mondays.

Online search: Online access is provided to approved businesses that enter into written contract. The contract requires a prepayment with minimum hits annually. Fee is $5.00 per record. The address is part of the record. For more information, call 203-263-5348.

Other access: Magnetic tape ordering is available for approved users. The state will process tapes on Mondays. Input time is 11:00 AM, so service is essentially 2 days. Also, the state will sell its driver license file on a contract basis to permitted users only.

Vehicle Ownership
Vehicle Identification

Department of Motor Vehicles, Copy Record Unit, 60 State St, Wethersfield, CT 06161-1896; 860-263-5154, 8:AM-4:30PM T,W,TH,F.

http://dmvct.org

Note: With the passage of Public Act 97-266, the release of records adheres to the DPPA guidelines.

Indexing & Storage: Records are available for 3 years to present. Any records prior to this period may be destroyed at the discretion of the commissioner. It takes six weeks before new records are available for inquiry. Records are normally destroyed after http://dmvct.org/formsrec.htm.

Searching: Only acceptable requesters are listed on back of Form J-23. This form can be ordered from the web site at http://dmvct.org/formsrec.htm or by calling 860-263-5700. Casual requests must include evidence of the individual's consent; businesses may only use to confirm the accuracy of personal information submitted by an individual to them.

Access by: mail, in person, online.

Fee & Payment: Title searches-$17.50 per search; current owner searches-$7.00 per search; registration information-$70.00. There is a full charge for a "no record found." Fee payee: Department of Motor Vehicles. Prepayment required. Personal checks accepted. No credit cards accepted.

Mail search: Turnaround time: 3 to 4 working days. The agency requests that you use their Form J-23.A self addressed stamped envelope is requested.

In person search: The office is closed on Mondays.

Online search: The Department has started a pilot program for online access that is not yet open to the general business public. This program, when available to all, will have the same restrictions and criteria as described in the Driving Records Section.

Other access: The state will sell the entire vehicle record database, upon approval of purpose, but the records cannot be resold.

Accident Reports

Department of Public Safety, Reports and Records Unit, PO Box 2794, Middletown, CT 06457-9294; 860-685-8250, 8:30AM-4:30PM.

Indexing & Storage: Records are available from 10 years to present. Searching by name only goes back 5 years.

Searching: The request should include data and location of incident, names of operators, and the 9 digit case number (if known). The following data is not released: pending cases or sealed records.

Access by: mail.

Fee & Payment: Prepayment of the $8.00 fee per record is required. Fee payee: Commissioner of Public Safety. Personal checks accepted. No credit cards accepted.

Mail search: Turnaround time: 2 to 4 weeks. A self addressed stamped envelope is requested.

Vessel Ownership
Vessel Registration

Department of Motor Vehicles, Marine Vessel Section, 60 State Street, Wethersfield, CT 06161-3032; 860-263-5151, 860-263-5555 (Fax), 8AM-5PM M-F.

http://dmvct.org/BOATING.HTM

Note: Lien information is found at the Secretary of State.

Indexing & Storage: Records are available from 1981, records are maintained on computer for 4 years then placed on microfiche. All motorized boats and all vessels over 19.5 ft must be registered.

Searching: All requests must be in writing. Requests follow requirements of DPPA. Either the name, CT registration number or hull number is needed to do a search.

Access by: mail, in person.

Fee & Payment: The fee is $4.50 for a current owner search, $7.00 for a copy of the registration and $17.50 for a complete boat history. Fee payee: Department of Motor Vehicles. Prepayment required. No credit cards accepted.

Mail search: Turnaround time: 1 to 2 weeks. No self addressed stamped envelope is required.

In person search: Results are returned by mail. The agency is closed to the public on Mondays.

Other access: Bulk list information is available by contract. The fee depends on data requested. Call 860-263-5241 for ordering procedures.

Legislation Records

Connecticut General Assembly, State Library, Bill Room at State Library, 231 Capitol Ave, Bill Room, Hartford, CT 06106; 860-757-6550, 860-757-6594 (Fax), 9AM-5PM.

http://www.cga.state.ct.us/default.asp

Indexing & Storage: Records are available for the current session only. Records are indexed on inhouse computer.

Searching: Include the following in your request-bill number. You may also ask for bills by subject or statute number. Past bills are located in another office (call 860-757-6590).

Access by: mail, phone, fax, in person, online.

Fee & Payment: Fees: No charge for current bills; $.25 per page if you request a large document or a bill that has not been printed. They will compute the charge. Fee payee: Connecticut State Library. Personal checks accepted. No credit cards accepted.

Mail search: Turnaround time: 4 to 7 days. No self addressed stamped envelope is required.

Phone search: You may call for information.

Fax search: Copies of bills totaling 30 pages or less can be returned by fax if local or toll free.

In person search: You may request information in person.

Online search: From the web site you can track bills, find update or status, and print copies of bills. Also, you can request via e-mail at billroom@cslib.org.

Voter Registration
Records not maintained by a state level agency.

Note: Records are open at the town level. There are 169 towns.

GED Certificates

Department of Education, GED Records, 25 Industrial Park Rd, Middletown, CT 06457; 860-807-2110, 860-807-2112 (Fax), 8AM-5PM.

http://www.state.ct.us/sde

Searching: Include the following in your request-signed release, Social Security Number, date of birth. The year of the test is helpful. For records prior to 1982, the location of the test is needed.

Access by: mail, fax, in person.

Fee & Payment: There is no search fee.

Mail search: Turnaround time: 2 to 3 days. No self addressed stamped envelope is required.

Fax search: There is no fee to fax back to a local phone number.

In person search: Photo ID is required.

Hunting License Information
Fishing License Information

Department of Environmental Protection, License Division, 79 Elm St, Hartford, CT 06106; 860-424-3105, 860-424-4072 (Fax), 9AM-4PM.

http://www.dep.state.ct.us

Indexing & Storage: Records are available for 1 year back. Records are indexed on inhouse computer.

Searching: Only deer tag information is released. Include the following in your request-full name, Social Security Number. Records are indexed by Social Security Number. All requests must be in writing.

Access by: mail, in person.

Fee & Payment: There is no search fee. Copies are $.50 per page. Fee payee: Department of Environmental Protection. Prepayment required. Personal checks accepted. No credit cards accepted.

Mail search: Turnaround time: 1 to 3 days. No self addressed stamped envelope is required.

In person search: Must have the request in writing.

Connecticut State Licensing Agencies
Licenses Searchable Online

Acupuncturist #11 .... www.state.ct.us/dph/scripts/hlthprof.asp
Alcohol/Drug Counselor #11 .... www.state.ct.us/dph/scripts/hlthprof.asp
Antenna Service Dealer/Technician #05 .... www.dcp.state.ct.us
Appraiser (MVR) #02 .... www.state.ct.us/cid/license/licweb1.asp
Appraiser, MVPD #02 .... www.state.ct.us/cid/license/licweb1.asp
Arborist #07 .... www.dcp.state.ct.us
Architect #03 .... www.dcp.state.ct.us/Default.asp
Architectural Firm #03 .... www.dcp.state.ct.us/Default.asp
Asbestos Professional #11 .... www.state.ct.us/dph/scripts/hlthprof.asp
Athletic Promoter #07 .... www.dcp.state.ct.us
Audiologist #11 .... www.state.ct.us/dph/scripts/hlthprof.asp
Automobile Insurance Adjuster #02 .... www.state.ct.us/cid/license/licweb1.asp
Bail Bond Agent #02 .... www.state.ct.us/cid/license/licweb1.asp
Bank #06 .... www.state.ct.us/dob/pages/banklist.htm
Bank & Trust Company #06 .... www.state.ct.us/dob/pages/bcharter.htm
Bank Branch #06 .... www.state.ct.us/dob/pages/branch1.htm
Barber #11 .... www.state.ct.us/dph/scripts/hlthprof.asp
Boxer #07 .... www.dcp.state.ct.us
Building Contractor #07 .... www.dcp.state.ct.us
Casualty Adjuster #02 .... www.state.ct.us/cid/license/licweb1.asp
Check Cashing Service #06 .... www.state.ct.us/dob/pages/chckcash.htm
Chiropractor #11 .... www.state.ct.us/dph/scripts/hlthprof.asp
Collection Agency #06 .... www.state.ct.us/dob/pages/collect.htm
Collection Agency, Consumer #06 .... www.state.ct.us/dob/pages/collect.htm
Cosmetologist #11 .... www.state.ct.us/dph/scripts/hlthprof.asp
Counselor, Professional #11 .... www.state.ct.us/dph/scripts/hlthprof.asp
Credit Union #06 .... www.state.ct.us/dob/pages/culist.htm
Debt Adjuster #06 .... www.state.ct.us/dob/pages/debtadj.htm
Dental Anes/Conscious Sedation Permittee #11 ... www.state.ct.us/dph/scripts/hlthprof.asp
Dentist/Dental Hygienist #11 .... www.state.ct.us/dph/scripts/hlthprof.asp
Dietician/Nutritionist #11 .... www.state.ct.us/dph/scripts/hlthprof.asp
Electrical Contractor/Inspector #07 .... www.dcp.state.ct.us
Electrical Journeyman/Apprentice #04 .... www.dcp.state.ct.us/default.asp
Electrical Sign Installer #07 .... www.dcp.state.ct.us
Electrician #07 .... www.dcp.state.ct.us
Electrologist/Hypertricologist #11 .... www.state.ct.us/dph/scripts/hlthprof.asp
Electronics Service Dealer/Technician #05 .... www.dcp.state.ct.us
Elevator Inspector/Mechanic #04 .... www.dcp.state.ct.us/default.asp
Embalmer #11 .... www.state.ct.us/dph/scripts/hlthprof.asp
Emergency Medical Service Professional #11 .... www.state.ct.us/dph/scripts/hlthprof.asp
Emergency Medical Technician #11 .... www.state.ct.us/dph/scripts/hlthprof.asp
Engineer #04 .... www.dcp.state.ct.us/default.asp
Fire Protection Inspector/Contractor #04 .... www.dcp.state.ct.us/default.asp
Funeral Director #11 .... www.state.ct.us/dph/scripts/hlthprof.asp
Funeral Home #11 .... www.state.ct.us/dph/scripts/hlthprof.asp
Hairdresser #11 .... www.state.ct.us/dph/scripts/hlthprof.asp
Hearing Instrument Specialist #11 .... www.state.ct.us/dph/scripts/hlthprof.asp
Heating, Piping, Cooling Contr./Journeyman #04 . www.dcp.state.ct.us/default.asp
Homeopathic Physician #11 .... www.state.ct.us/dph/scripts/hlthprof.asp
Hypertrichologist #11 .... www.state.ct.us/dph/scripts/hlthprof.asp
Insurance Adjuster/Public Adjuster #02 .... www.state.ct.us/cid/license/licweb1.asp
Insurance Agent, Fraternal #02 .... www.state.ct.us/cid/license/licweb1.asp
Insurance Agent/Broker #02 .... www.state.ct.us/cid/license/licweb1.asp

Insurance Appraiser #02 .... www.state.ct.us/cid/license/licweb1.asp
Insurance Company/Producer/Consultant #02 ..... www.state.ct.us/cid/license/licweb1.asp
Interior Designer #07 .... www.dcp.state.ct.us
Land Surveyor Firm #03 .... www.dcp.state.ct.us/Default.asp
Lead Planner/Project Designer #11 .... www.state.ct.us/dph/scripts/hlthprof.asp
Lead Professional #11 .... www.state.ct.us/dph/scripts/hlthprof.asp
Loan Company, Small #06 .... www.state.ct.us/dob/pages/smalloan.htm
Lobbyist #18 .... www.lobbyist.net/Connecti/CONLOB.htm
LPN #11 .... www.state.ct.us/dph/scripts/hlthprof.asp
Marriage & Family Therapist #11 .... www.state.ct.us/dph/scripts/hlthprof.asp
Massage Therapist #11 .... www.state.ct.us/dph/scripts/hlthprof.asp
Medical Doctor #11 .... www.state.ct.us/dph/scripts/hlthprof.asp
Medical Response Technician #11 .... www.state.ct.us/dph/scripts/hlthprof.asp
Midwife #11 .... www.state.ct.us/dph/scripts/hlthprof.asp
Mobile Home Park/Seller #17 .... www.dcp.state.ct.us/Default.asp
Money Forwarder #06 .... www.state.ct.us/dob/pages/$forward.htm
Mortgage Broker/Lender; First #06 .... www.state.ct.us/dob/pages/1stmtg.htm
Mortgage Broker/Lender; Secondary #06 .... www.state.ct.us/dob/pages/2ndmtg.htm
Naturopathic Physician #11 .... www.state.ct.us/dph/scripts/hlthprof.asp
Nurse #11 .... www.state.ct.us/dph/scripts/hlthprof.asp
Nurse, Advance Registered Practice #11 .... www.state.ct.us/dph/scripts/hlthprof.asp
Nurse-LPN #11 .... www.state.ct.us/dph/scripts/hlthprof.asp
Nursing Home Administrator #11 .... www.state.ct.us/dph/scripts/hlthprof.asp
Occupational Therapist/Assistant #11 .... www.state.ct.us/dph/scripts/hlthprof.asp
Optical Shop #11 .... www.state.ct.us/dph/scripts/hlthprof.asp
Optician #11 .... www.state.ct.us/dph/scripts/hlthprof.asp
Optometrist #11 .... www.state.ct.us/dph/scripts/hlthprof.asp
Osteopathic Physician #11 .... www.state.ct.us/dph/scripts/hlthprof.asp
Paramedic #11 .... www.state.ct.us/dph/scripts/hlthprof.asp
Pharmacist/Pharmacy/Intern #04 .... www.dcp.state.ct.us/default.asp
Physical Therapist/Assistant #11 .... www.state.ct.us/dph/scripts/hlthprof.asp
Physician Assistant #11 .... www.state.ct.us/dph/scripts/hlthprof.asp
Pipefitter #07 .... www.dcp.state.ct.us
Plumber #04 .... www.dcp.state.ct.us/default.asp
Podiatrist #11 .... www.state.ct.us/dph/scripts/hlthprof.asp
Psychologist #11 .... www.state.ct.us/dph/scripts/hlthprof.asp
Public Service Technician #04 .... www.dcp.state.ct.us/default.asp
Radiographer #11 .... www.state.ct.us/dph/scripts/hlthprof.asp
Real Estate Appraiser #17 .... www.dcp.state.ct.us/Default.asp
Real Estate Broker/Salesperson #17 .... www.dcp.state.ct.us/Default.asp
Reinsurance Intermediary #02 .... www.state.ct.us/cid/license/licweb1.asp
Respiratory Care Practitioner #11 .... www.state.ct.us/dph/scripts/hlthprof.asp
Sales Finance Company #06 .... www.state.ct.us/dob/pages/salefinc.htm
Sanitarian #11 .... www.state.ct.us/dph/scripts/hlthprof.asp
Savings & Loan Association Bank #06 .... www.state.ct.us/dob/pages/bcharter.htm
Savings Bank #06 .... www.state.ct.us/dob/pages/bcharter.htm
Social Worker #11 .... www.state.ct.us/dph/scripts/hlthprof.asp
Solar Energy Contractor/Journeyman #04 .... www.dcp.state.ct.us/default.asp
Speech Pathologist #11 .... www.state.ct.us/dph/scripts/hlthprof.asp
Sprinkler Layout Technician #04 .... www.dcp.state.ct.us/default.asp
Subsurface Sewage Cleaner/Installer #11 .... www.state.ct.us/dph/scripts/hlthprof.asp
Surplus Line Broker #02 .... www.state.ct.us/cid/license/licweb1.asp
Surveyor #03 .... www.dcp.state.ct.us/Default.asp
Tree Surgeon #07 .... www.dcp.state.ct.us
Veterinarian #11 .... www.state.ct.us/dph/scripts/hlthprof.asp
Well Driller #07 .... www.dcp.state.ct.us
Wrestler/Wrestling Manager #07 .... www.dcp.state.ct.us

Licensing Quick Finder

Acupuncturist #11 860-509-7603
Alcohol/Drug Counselor #11 860-509-7603
Antenna Service Dealer/Technician #05860-566-3275
Appraiser (MVR) #02............860-297-3845
Appraiser, MVPD #02............860-297-3845
Arborist #07 860-566-3290
Architect #03 860-566-2093
Architectural Firm #03 860-566-2093
Asbestos Professional #11 860-509-7603
Athletic Promoter #07............860-566-6980
Attorney #01 860-756-7900
Audiologist #11 860-509-7603
Automobile Dealer #23 860-566-2796
Automobile Insurance Adjuster #02........860-297-3845
Bail Bond Agent #02.............860-297-3845
Bait Seller (Live Bait) #10 860-424-3474
Bank #06 860-240-8299
Bank & Trust Company #06.............860-240-8299
Bank Branch #06 860-240-8299
Banking Office, Non-depository #06......860-240-8299
Barber #11.............860-509-7603
Boxer #07 860-566-6980
Broker/Dealer Agent #06 860-240-8299
Building Contractor #07 860-566-2825
Bus Driver #23.............860-566-2796
Business Opportunity Offering #06.......860-240-8299
Casino #12 860-594-0567
Casualty Adjuster #02 860-297-3845
Cattle Dealer #22 860-566-4845
Chauffeur/Driver #24.............860-594-2865
Check Cashing Service #06...........860-240-8299
Chiropractor #11 860-509-7603
Collection Agency #06.............860-240-8299
Collection Agency, Consumer #06 860-240-8299
Cosmetologist #11 860-509-7603
Counselor, Professional #11...............860-509-7603
Credit Union #06 860-240-8299
Dairy Laboratory Analyst #22...............860-566-4845
Dairy Sample Collector #22 860-566-4845
Dairy Transporter #22.............860-566-4845
Day Care Provider #11 860-509-8000
Debt Adjuster #06 860-240-8299
Dental Anes/Conscious Sedation Permittee #11.........
.............860-509-7603
Dentist/Dental Hygienist #11.............860-509-7603
Dietician/Nutritionist #11.............860-509-7603
Digger of Shellfish #20 203-874-0696
Dog Racing #12 860-594-0567
Driving Instructor #23 860-566-2796
Electrical Contractor/Inspector #07.......860-566-2825
Electrical Journeyman/Apprentice #04..860-566-3290
Electrical Sign Installer #07 860-566-2825
Electrician #07 860-566-2825
Electrologist/Hypertricologist #11 860-509-7603
Electronics Service Dealer/Technician #05...............
.............860-566-3275
Elevator Inspector/Mechanic #04 860-566-3290
Embalmer #11 860-509-7603
Emergency Medical Service Professional #11860-509-7603
Emergency Medical Technician #11......860-509-7603
Engineer #04 860-566-3290

Fire Protection Inspector/Contractor #04860-566-3290
Fisher #10.............860-424-3105
Funeral Director #11.............860-509-7603
Funeral Home #11 860-509-7603
Fur Breeder #22 860-566-4845
Game Breeder #10.............860-424-3011
Guard #19.............860-685-8290
Hairdresser #11 860-509-7603
Hearing Instrument Specialist #11 860-509-7603
Heating, Piping & Cooling Contractor/Journeyman #04
.............860-566-3290
Hoisting Equipment Operator #19 860-685-8290
Homeopathic Physician #11 860-509-7603
Hypertrichologist #11.............860-509-7603
Insurance Adjuster/Public Adjuster #02.860-297-3845
Insurance Agent, Fraternal #02............860-297-3845
Insurance Agent/Broker #02............860-297-3845
Insurance Appraiser #02 860-297-3845
Insurance Company/Producer #02........860-297-3817
Insurance Consultant #02.............860-297-3845
Interior Designer #07 860-566-2825
Investment Advisor/Agent #06 860-240-8299
Issuer Agent (Financial) #06 860-240-8299
Jai Alai #12 860-594-0567
Land Surveyor Firm #03 860-566-3290
Lead Planner/Project Designer #11.......860-509-7603
Lead Professional #11.............860-509-7603
Liquor License #15.............860-713-6200
Livestock Dealer #22.............860-566-4845
Loan Company, Small #06.............860-240-8299
Lobbyist #18 860-566-4472
Lobster Seller #10.............860-424-6043
Lottery #12.............860-594-0567
LPN #11 860-509-7603
Marriage & Family Therapist #11 860-609-7603
Massage Therapist #11 860-509-7603
Medical Doctor #11 860-509-7603
Medical Response Technician #11 860-509-7603
Midwife #11 860-509-7603
Milk Dealer #22 860-566-4845
Mobile Home Park/Seller #17 860-713-6150
Money Forwarder #06 860-240-8299
Mortgage Broker/Lender; First #06 ...860-240-8299
Mortgage Broker/Lender; Secondary #06860-240-8299
Motion Picture Operator #25.............860-685-8470
Naturopathic Physician #11 860-509-7603
Notary Public #16.............860-509-6200
Nurse #11.............860-509-7603
Nurse, Advance Reg. Practice #11 860-509-7603
Nurse-LPN #11 860-509-7603
Nurses' Aide #11.............860-509-7603
Nursing Home Administrator #11 860-509-7603
Occupational Therapist/Assistant #11 ...860-509-7603
Off-Track Betting #12 860-594-0567
Optical Shop #11 860-509-7603
Optician #11.............860-509-7603
Optometrist #11 860-509-7603
Osteopathic Physician #11 860-509-7603
Paramedic #11.............860-509-7603
Pawnbroker #21.............860-297-5962
Pesticide Dealer/Applicator #14 860-424-3369
Pet Store Operator #22 860-566-4845

Pharmacist/Pharmacy/Intern #04 860-566-3290
Physical Therapist/Assistant #11 860-509-7603
Physician Assistant #11.............860-509-7603
Pipefitter #07.............860-566-2825
Plumber #04 860-566-3290
Podiatrist #11 860-509-7603
Premium Finance Company #02.............860-297-3845
Private Investigator #13.............860-685-8000
Psychologist #11.............860-509-7603
Public Accountant-CPA #16..............860-509-6179
Public Service Technician #04 860-566-3290
Radiographer #11 860-509-7603
Real Estate Appraiser #17............860-713-6150
Real Estate Broker/Salesperson #17 860-713-6150
Reinsurance Intermediary #02............860-297-3845
Rental Car Company #02.............860-297-3953
Respiratory Care Practitioner #11 860-509-7603
Sales Finance Company #06.............860-240-8299
Sanitarian #11 860-509-7603
Savings & Loan Association Bank #06..860-240-8299
Savings Bank #06 860-240-8299
School Administrator/Supervisor #09 ..860-566-5201
School Bus Driver #23.............860-566-2796
School Guidance Counselor #09 860-566-5201
School Library Media Associate #09 860-566-5201
School Principal/Superintendent #09 860-566-5201
Securities Agent #06 860-240-8299
Securities Broker/Dealer #06 860-240-8299
Septic Tank Cleaner #11.............860-509-8000
Sewage Disposal System Installer #11 .860-509-8000
Social Worker #11.............860-509-7603
Solar Energy Contr./Journeyman #04 ...860-566-3290
Solid Waste Facility Operator #10.........860-424-4051
Speech Pathologist #11.............860-509-7603
Sprinkler Layout Technician #04 860-566-3290
Subsurface Sewage Cleaner/Installer #11...............
.............860-509-7603
Surplus Line Broker #02.............860-297-3845
Surveyor #03.............860-566-3290
Tattoo Artist #11.............860-509-8000
Taxi Driver #24.............860-594-2865
Taxidermist #10 860-424-3105
Teacher #09.............860-566-5201
Ticket Broker #12.............860-667-5073
Trapper #10 860-424-3105
Tree Surgeon #07.............860-566-2825
Truck Driver #23.............860-566-2796
Utilitization Review Company #02.........860-297-3862
Veterinarian #11.............860-509-7603
Viatical Settlement Broker/Provider #02 860-297-3845
Water Dist. System Operator #11 860-509-8000
Water Treatment Plant Operator #11 860-509-8000
Weigher #08 860-713-6160
Weights & Measures Dealer/Repairer/Regulator #08
.............860-713-6160
Well Driller #07.............860-566-2825
Wildlife Control Operator (Nuisance Wildlife) #10 ....
.............860-424-3011
Wildlife Rehabilitator #10 860-424-3011
Wrestler/Wrestling Manager #07..........860-566-2825

Licensing Agency Information

#01 Bar Examining Committee, 80 Washington St, Hartford, CT 06106-4424; 860-568-7900.
www.jud.state.ct.us/colp/Barexam.html

#02 Department of Insurance, 153 Market St, Hartford, CT 06142-0816; 860-297-3845, Fax: 860-297-3872.
www.state.ct.us/cid/
Direct web site URL to search for licensees: www.state.ct.us/cid/license/licweb1.asp

#03 Consumer Protection Department, 165 Capitol Ave, #110, Hartford, CT 06106; 860-713-6135, Fax: 860-713-7239.
Direct web site URL to search for licensees: www.dcp.state.ct.us/Default.asp

#04 Consumer Protection Department, 165 Capitol Ave, Hartford, CT 06106; 860-713-7239.
Direct web site URL to search for licensees: www.dcp.state.ct.us/Default.asp

#05 Consumer Protection Dept/Occupational Licensing, 165 Capitol Ave, Hartford, CT 06106; 860-713-6135, Fax: 860-713-7239.
www.state.ct.us/dcp/
Direct web site URL to search for licensees: www.dcp.state.ct.us

#06 Department of Banking, 260 Constitution Plaza, Hartford, CT 06106-1800; 860-240-8299, Fax: 860-240-8178.
www.state.ct.us/dob
Direct web site URL to search for licensees: www.state.ct.us/dob. You can search online using alphabetical lists

#07 Department of Consumer Protection, 165 Capitol Ave, Hartford, CT 06106; 860-713-6300, Fax: 860-713-7239.
www.state.ct.us/dcp/
Direct web site URL to search for licensees: www.dcp.state.ct.us

#08 Department of Consumer Protection, 165 Capitol Ave, State Office Bldg, Hartford, CT 06106-1630; 860-713-6160, Fax: 860-713-7244.
www.state.ct.us/dcp/

#09 Department of Education, PO Box 150471, Rm 243, Hartford, CT 06115-0471; 860-566-5201, Fax: 860-566-8929.
www.state.ct.us/sde/

#10 Department of Environmental Protection, 79 Elm St, Hartford, CT 06106; 860-424-3372, Fax: 860-424-4051.
http://dep.state.ct.us/pao/index.htm

#11 Department of Public Health & Addiction Services, 410 Capital Ave, Mail Stop 12MQA, Hartford, CT 06134-0308; 860-509-7603, Fax: 860-509-7607.
www.state.ct.us/dph
Direct web site URL to search for licensees: www.state.ct.us/dph/scripts/hlthprof.asp. You can search online using license number, first and last name.

#12 Division of Special Revenue, PO Box 11424 (555 Russell Rd), Newington, CT 06111; 860-594-0656, Fax: 860-594-0649.
www.state.ct.us/dosr

#13 Division of State Police, 1111 Country Club Rd, Middletown, CT 06457; 860-685-8046, Fax: 860-685-8496.
www.state.ct.us/dps

#14 Environmental Protection Department, 79 Elm St, Hartford, CT 06134; 860-424-3372, Fax: 860-509-8457.

#15 Liquor Control Department, 165 Capitol Ave, Hartford, CT 06106; 860-713-6200, Fax: 860-713-7235.
www.dosr.state.ct.us/

#16 Office of the Secretary of the State, PO Box 150470 (30 Trinity St), Hartford, CT 06115; 860-509-6200, Fax: 860-509-6230.
www.sots.state.ct.us

#17 Consumer Protection Department, 165 Capitol Ave, Rm 110, Hartford, CT 06106; 860-713-6150, Fax: 860-713-7239.
www.dcp.state.ct.us/licensing
Direct web site URL to search for licensees: www.dcp.state.ct.us/Default.asp

#18 Ethics Commission, 20 Trinity St, Hartford, CT 06106; 860-566-4472, Fax: 860-566-3806.
www.ethics.state.ct.us
Direct web site URL to search for licensees: www.lobbyist.net/Connecti/CONLOB.htm

#19 Department of Public Safety, 1111 Country Club Rd, Middletown, CT 06457-9294; 860-685-8290.

#20 Department of Agriculture, 190 Rogers Ave, Milford, CT 06460; 203-874-0696.

#21 Department of Revenue Svcs, 25 Sigourney St, Hartford, CT 06106; 860-297-5962.

#22 Department of Agriculture, 765 Asylum Av, Hartford, CT 06105; 860-566-4845, Fax: 860-713-2515.
www.state.ct.us/doag

#23 Department of Motor Vehicles, 60 State St, Wethersfield, CT 06109; 860-566-2796.

#24 Department of Transportation, 2800 Berlin Turnpike, PO Box 317546, Newington, CT 06131-7546; 860-594-2865.

#25 Department of Public Safety, 1111 Country Club Rd, Middletown, CT 06457-9294; 860-685-8470.

Connecticut Federal Courts

The following list indicates the district and division name for each county in the state. If the bankruptcy court location is different from the district court, then the location of the bankruptcy court appears in parentheses.

County/Court Cross Reference

Fairfield	Bridgeport	New Haven	New Haven
Hartford	Hartford	New London	New Haven
Litchfield	New Haven (Hartford)	Tolland	Hartford
Middlesex	New Haven (Hartford)	Windham	Hartford

US District Court

District of Connecticut

Bridgeport Division Office of the clerk, Room 400, 915 Lafayette Blvd, Bridgeport, CT 06604 (Courier Address: Use mail address for courier delivery), 203-579-5861.
http://www.ctd.uscourts.gov
Counties: Fairfield (prior to 1993). Since January 1993, cases from any county may be assigned to any of the divisions in the district.
Indexing/Storage: Cases are indexed by defendant and plaintiff as well as by case number. New cases are available in the index immediately after filing date. A computer index is maintained. Records are stored by docket number, accession number and box number. Open records are located at this court.
Fee & Payment: The fee is $20.00 per item (one party name or case number). Payment may be made by money order, cashier check. Business checks are not accepted. Personal checks are not accepted. Prepayment is required. Payee: Clerk, US District Court. Certification fee: $7.00 per document. Copy fee: $.50 per page. You are allowed to make your own copies. These copies cost $.25 per page.
Phone Search: Only docket information is available by phone.
Mail Search: A stamped self addressed envelope is not required.
In Person: In person searching is available.
PACER: Sign-up number is 800-676-6856. Access fee is $.60 per minute. Toll-free access: 800-292-0658. Local access: 203-773-2451. Case records are available back to November 1, 1991. New records are available online after 1 day. PACER is available online at http://pacer.ctd.uscourts.gov.

Hartford Division 450 Main St, Hartford, CT 06103 (Courier Address: Use mail address for courier delivery), 860-240-3200.
http://www.ctd.uscourts.gov
Counties: Hartford, Tolland, Windham (prior to 1993). Since 1993, cases from any of the divisions in the district.
Indexing/Storage: Cases are indexed by defendant and plaintiff as well as by case number. New cases are available in the index immediately after filing date. A computer index is maintained. Records are kept where the assigned judge sits, and are stored by a federal record number system. Open records are located at this court.

Fee & Payment: The fee is $20.00 per item (one party name or case number). Payment may be made by money order, cashier check, personal check. Prepayment is required. Payee: Clerk, US District Court. Certification fee: $7.00 per document. Copy fee: $.50 per page. You are allowed to make your own copies. These copies cost $.25 per page.
Phone Search: Only docket information is available by phone.
Mail Search: Always enclose a stamped self addressed envelope.
In Person: In person searching is available.
PACER: Sign-up number is 800-676-6856. Access fee is $.60 per minute. Toll-free access: 800-292-0658. Local access: 203-773-2451. Case records are available back to November 1, 1991. New records are available online after 1 day. PACER is available online at http://pacer.ctd.uscourts.gov.

New Haven Division 141 Church St, New Haven, CT 06510 (Courier Address: Use mail address for courier delivery), 203-773-2140.
http://www.ctd.uscourts.gov
Counties: Litchfield, Middlesex, New Haven, New London (prior to 1993). Since 1993, cases from any county may be assigned to any of the divisions in the district.
Indexing/Storage: Cases are indexed by defendant and plaintiff as well as by case number. New cases are available in the index immediately after filing date. A computer index is maintained. Older records are indexed on microfiche. Open records are located at this court. District wide searches are available for information from 1982 to the present from this court.
Fee & Payment: The fee is no charge per item (one party name or case number). Payment may be made by money order, cashier check, business check. Personal checks are not accepted. There is a $15.00 search fee charged for each additional name after the first. Payee: District Court Clerk. Certification fee: $7.00 per document. Copy fee: $.50 per page. You are allowed to make your own copies. These copies cost $.25 per page.
Phone Search: Only docket information is available by phone.
Mail Search: Always enclose a stamped self addressed envelope.
In Person: In person searching is available.
PACER: Sign-up number is 800-676-6856. Access fee is $.60 per minute. Toll-free access: 800-292-0658. Local access: 203-773-2451. Case records are available back to November 1, 1991. New records are available online after 1 day.

PACER is available online at http://pacer.ctd.uscourts.gov.

US Bankruptcy Court

District of Connecticut

Bridgeport Division 915 Lafayette Blvd, Bridgeport, CT 06604 (Courier Address: Use mail address for courier delivery), 203-579-5808.
http://www.ctb.uscourts.gov
Counties: Fairfield.
Indexing/Storage: Cases are indexed by debtor as well as by case number. New cases are available in the index immediately after filing date. A computer index is maintained. Open records are located at this court. District wide searches are available from this division.
Fee & Payment: The fee is $20.00 per item (one party name or case number). Payment may be made by money order, cashier check, business check. Personal checks are not accepted. Prepayment is required. Payee: Clerk, US Bankruptcy Court. Certification fee: $7.00 per document. Copy fee: $.50 per page. You are allowed to make your own copies. These copies cost $.25 per page.
Phone Search: An automated voice case information service (VCIS) is available. Call VCIS at 800-800-5113 or 860-240-3345.
Mail Search: Always enclose a stamped self addressed envelope.
In Person: In person searching is available.
PACER: Sign-up number is 800-676-6856. Access fee is $.60 per minute. Local access: 860-240-3570, 860-240-3571, 860-240-3572. Case records are available back to 1979. Records are purged every 6 months. New civil records are available online after 1 day. PACER is available online at http://pacer.ctb.uscourts.gov.

Hartford Division 450 Main St, Hartford, CT 06103 (Courier Address: Use mail address for courier delivery), 860-240-3675.
http://www.ctb.uscourts.gov
Counties: Hartford, Litchfield, Middlesex, Tolland, Windham.
Indexing/Storage: Cases are indexed by debtor as well as by case number. New cases are available in the index 1 week after filing date. A computer index is maintained. Open records are located at this court.
Fee & Payment: The fee is $20.00 per item (one party name or case number). Payment may be made by money order, cashier check, personal

check. Prepayment is required. Payee: Clerk, US Bankruptcy Court. Certification fee: $7.00 per document. Copy fee: $.50 per page. You are allowed to make your own copies. These copies cost $.25 per page.

Phone Search: Only docket information is available by phone. An automated voice case information service (VCIS) is available. Call VCIS at 800-800-5113 or 860-240-3345.

Mail Search: Always enclose a stamped self addressed envelope.

In Person: In person searching is available.

PACER: Sign-up number is 800-676-6856. Access fee is $.60 per minute. Local access: 860-240-3570, 860-240-3571, 860-240-3572. Case records are available back to 1979. Records are purged every 6 months. New civil records are available online after 1 day. PACER is available online at http://pacer.ctb.uscourts.gov.

New Haven Division The Connecticut Financial Center, 157 Church St, 18th Floor, New Haven, CT 06510 (Courier Address: Use mail address for courier delivery), 203-773-2009. http://www.ctb.uscourts.gov

Counties: New Haven, New London.

Indexing/Storage: Cases are indexed by debtor as well as by case number. New cases are available in the index 1 week after filing date. A computer index is maintained. Open records are located at this court.

Fee & Payment: The fee is $20.00 per item (one party name or case number). Payment may be made by money order, cashier check, personal check. Prepayment is required. Payee: Clerk, US Bankruptcy Court. Certification fee: $7.00 per document. Copy fee: $.50 per page. You are allowed to make your own copies. These copies cost $.25 per page.

Phone Search: Only docket information is available by phone. An automated voice case information service (VCIS) is available. Call VCIS at 800-800-5113 or 860-240-3345.

Mail Search: Always enclose a stamped self addressed envelope.

In Person: In person searching is available.

PACER: Sign-up number is 800-676-6856. Access fee is $.60 per minute. Local access: 860-240-3570, 860-240-3571, 860-240-3572. Case records are available back to 1979. Records are purged every 6 months. New civil records are available online after 1 day. PACER is available online at http://pacer.ctb.uscourts.gov.

Connecticut County Courts

Court	Jurisdiction	No. of Courts	How Organized
Judicial District Courts*	General	13	13 Geographic Areas
Geographic Area Courts*	Limited	22	22 Geographic Areas
Probate Courts*	Probate	129	

* Profiled in this Sourcebook.

Court	CIVIL								
	Tort	Contract	Real Estate	Min. Claim	Max. Claim	Small Claims	Estate	Eviction	Domestic Relations
Judicial District Courts*	X	X	X	No Min	No Max				X
Geographic Area Courts*						$2500		X	
Probate Courts*							X		

Court	CRIMINAL				
	Felony	Misdemeanor	DWI/DUI	Preliminary Hearing	Juvenile
Judicial District Courts*	X				X
Geographic Area Courts*		X	X	X	
Probate Courts*					

ADMINISTRATION

Chief Court Administrator, 231 Capitol Av, Hartford, CT, 06106; 860-757-2100, Fax: 860-757-2130. www.jud.state.ct.us

COURT STRUCTURE

The Superior Court is the sole court of original jurisdiction for all causes of action, except for matters over which the probate courts have jurisdiction as provided by statute. The state is divided into 13 Judicial Districts, 22 Geographic Area Courts, and 14 Juvenile Districts. The Superior Court - comprised primarily of the Judicial District Courts and the Geographical Area Courts - has five divisions: Criminal, Civil, Family, Juvenile, and Administrative Appeals. When not combined, the Judicial District Courts handle felony and civil cases while the Geographic Area Courts handle misdemeanors and small claims.

ONLINE ACCESS

The Judicial Branch provides access to civil and family records via the Internet, located online at www.jud2.state.ct.us/Civil_Inquiry. It contains assignment lists and calendars. Also, questions about the fuller commercial system available through Judicial Information Systems should be directed to the CT JIS Office at 860-282-6500. There is currently no online access to criminal records; however, criminal and motor vehicle data is available for purchase in database format.

Probate is handled by city Probate Courts, which we have listed, and are not part of the state court system. Information request requirements are consistent across the state; requesters must provide full name of decedent, year and place of death, and SASE. Written or in person searches are allowed, prepayment is required; there is no search fee; the certification fee is $5.00 for 1st 2 pages and $2.00 for each additional page; and, the copy fee is $1.00 per page.

ADDITIONAL INFORMATION

Mail requests to perform criminal searches should be made to the Department of Public Safety, 1111 Country Club Rd, PO Box 2794, Middletown, CT 06457, 860-685-8480. The search fee is $25.00.

The State Record Center in Enfield, CT is the repository for criminal and some civil records; open 9AM-5PM M-F. Case records are sent to the Record Center from 3 months to 5 years after disposition by the courts. These records are then maintained 10 years for misdemeanors and 20+ years for felonies. If a requester is certain that the record is at the Record Center, it is quicker to direct the request there rather than to the original court of record. Only written requests are accepted. Search requirements: full defendant name, docket number, disposition date, and court action. Fee is $5.00 for each docket. Fee payee is Treasurer-State of Connecticut. Direct Requests to: Connecticut Record Ctr., 111 Phoenix Avenue, Enfield CT 06082, 860-741-3714.

Personal checks must have name and address printed on the check; if requesting in person, check must have same address as drivers' license.

Fairfield County

Bridgeport Judicial District Court 1061 Main St Attn: criminal or civil, Bridgeport, CT 06604; 203-579-6527. Hours: 9AM-5PM (EST). *Felony, Civil Actions.*

Civil Records: Access: Mail, online, in person. Only the court performs in person searches; visitors may not. No search fee. Required to search: name, years to search; also helpful: address. Civil cases indexed by defendant, plaintiff. Civil records on computer for 2 years, on microfiche from 1975 to 1990, prior on index cards. After 5 years sent to Records Center at Enfield, CT. Access to civil case records is available free on the Internet at www.jud2.state.ct.us/.
Criminal Records: Access: Mail, in person. Only the court performs in person searches; visitors may not. No search fee. Required to search: name, years to search, DOB. Criminal records on computer since 1997, on microfiche from 1975 to 1996.
General Information: No sealed, adoption records released. SASE required. Turnaround time 2-3 weeks for civil, 4 weeks for criminal. Copy fee: $1.00 per page. Certification fee: $2.00. Fee payee: Chief Clerk Superior Court. Personal checks accepted. Prepayment is required.

Danbury Judicial District Court 146 White St, Danbury, CT 06810; 203-207-8600. Hours: 9AM-5PM (EST). *Felony, Civil Actions.*

Civil Records: Access: Mail, online, in person. Only the court performs in person searches; visitors may not. No search fee. Required to search: name, years to search. Civil cases indexed by plaintiff and defendant. Civil records on microfilm from 11-87, prior on index cards. See state introduction for online access information. Free access to civil case records is available on the Internet at www.jud2.state.ct.us.
Criminal Records: Access: Mail, in person. Only the court performs in person searches; visitors may not. No search fee. Required to search: name, years to search, DOB. Criminal records on microfilm from 11-87, prior on index cards but only list docket number and disposal date.
General Information: No sealed records released. Turnaround time 2-4 days for civil and family, 3-4 days for motor vehicle and criminal. Fax notes: Will not fax results. Copy fee: $1.00 per page. Certification fee: $2.00 and $1.00 per page. Fee payee: Clerk of Superior Court. Personal checks accepted. Require ID with personal check. Prepayment is required.

Stamford-Norwalk Judicial District Court 123 Hoyt St, Stamford, CT 06905; Civil phone: 203-965-5307; Criminal phone: 203-965-5208. Hours: 9AM-Noon, 1:30PM-4PM (EST). *Felony, Civil Actions.*

Civil Records: Access: Mail, online, in person. Both court and visitors may perform in person searches. No search fee. Required to search: name, years to search. Civil cases indexed by defendant, plaintiff. Only pending civil cases on computer, on microfiche from 1970s, on index cards from 1958. Access to civil case records is available free on the Internet at www.jud2.state.ct.us/.
Criminal Records: Access: Phone, mail, in person. Only the court performs in person searches; visitors may not. No search fee. Required to search: name, years to search. Only pending cases on computer, on microfiche from 1970s, on index cards from 1958.
General Information: No sealed records released. Copy fee: $1.00 per page. Certification fee: $2.00. Fee payee: Clerk of Superior Court. Personal checks accepted.

Geographical Area Court #2 172 Golden Hill St, Bridgeport, CT 06604; 203-579-6560. Hours: 9AM-4PM (EST). *Misdemeanor, Eviction, Small Claims.*

Civil Records: Access: Phone, mail, online, in person. Both court and visitors may perform in person searches. No search fee. Required to search: name, years to search. Civil cases indexed by defendant. Civil records pending and from 1990 on computer, on microfiche from 1982 to 1990, prior on index cards. After microfilmed and entered on index cards, sent to Records Center at Enfield, CT. Access to civil case records is available free on the Internet at www.jud2.state.ct.us/.
Criminal Records: Access: In person only. Visitors must perform in person searches for themselves. No search fee. Required to search: name, years to search. Criminal records pending and from 1990 on computer, on microfiche from 1982. Mail requests are referred the state criminal records agency.
General Information: No sealed records released. Turnaround time up to 4 weeks. Copy fee: $1.00 per page. Certification fee: $3.00. Fee payee: Clerk of Superior Court. Personal checks accepted. Prepayment is required.

Geographical Area Court #20 17 Belden Ave, Norwalk, CT 06850; 203-846-3237. Hours: 9AM-5PM (EST). *Misdemeanor, Eviction, Small Claims.*

Civil Records: Access: Online, in person. Visitors must perform in person searches for themselves. No search fee. Required to search: name, years to search. Civil cases indexed by defendant, plaintiff. Civil records on computer from 1986. Access to civil case records is available free on the Internet at www.jud2.state.ct.us/.
Criminal Records: Access: In person only. Visitors must perform in person searches for themselves. No search fee. Required to search: name, years to search; also helpful: DOB. Criminal records on computer from 1986, prior records on index cards.
General Information: Copy fee: $1.00 per page. Certification fee: $2.00. Fee payee: Superior Court GA #20. Only cashiers checks and money orders accepted. Prepayment is required.

Geographical Area Court #3 146 White St, Danbury, CT 06810; 203-207-8600. Hours: 9AM-5PM (EST). *Misdemeanor, Eviction, Small Claims.*

Civil Records: Access: Mail, online, in person. Only the court performs in person searches; visitors may not. No search fee. Required to search: name, years to search. Civil cases indexed by defendant. Civil records on microfilm from 11-87, prior on index cards, but only list docket number and disposal date, then referred to Records Center at Enfield, CT. In person searches returned by mail. Access to civil case records is available free on the Internet at www.jud2.state.ct.us/.
Criminal Records: Access: Phone, mail, in person. Visitors must perform in person searches for themselves. No search fee. Required to search: name, years to search; also helpful: DOB. Criminal records on computer from 11/9/87. The court refers all requests to one of the 2 statewide agencies.
General Information: No youthful offender or dispositions by dismissal after 20 days from date of judgment records released. SASE required. Turnaround time up to 1 week. Copy fee: $1.00 per page. Certification fee: $2.00. Fee payee: Clerk of Superior Court. Personal checks accepted. Prepayment is required.

Bethel Probate Court 1 School St, PO Box 144, Bethel, CT 06801; 203-794-8508; Fax: 203-794-8564. Hours: 9AM-1:00PM (EST). *Probate.*

Bridgeport Probate District 202 State St, McLevy Hall, 3rd Floor, Bridgeport, CT 06604; 203-576-3945; Fax: 203-576-7898. Hours: 9AM-5PM M-Th; 9AM-4PM F (EST). *Probate.*

Brookfield Probate Court 100 Pocono Rd, PO Box 5192, Brookfield, CT 06804; 203-775-3700; Fax: 203-740-9008. Hours: 9AM-2PM (and by app't) (EST). *Probate.*

Danbury Probate Court 155 Deer Hill Ave, Danbury, CT 06810; 203-797-4521; Fax: 203-796-1526. Hours: 8:30AM-4:30PM (EST). *Probate.*

Darien Probate Court Town Hall, 2 Renshaw Rd, Darien, CT 06820; 203-656-7342; Fax: 203-656-0774. Hours: 9AM-12:30PM, 1:30-4:30PM; 9AM-12:30PM Fri July-Labor Day (EST). *Probate.*

Fairfield Probate Court Independence Hall, 725 Old Post Rd, Fairfield, CT 06430; 203-256-3041; Fax: 203-256-3044. Hours: 9AM-5PM, 9AM-4:30PM (July-Aug) (EST). *Probate.*

Greenwich Probate Court 101 Field Point Rd, PO Box 2540, Greenwich, CT 06836; 203-622-3766; Fax: 203-622-6451. Hours: 8AM-4PM, 8AM-Noon Fri July-Aug (EST). *Probate.*

New Canaan Probate Court PO Box 326, 77 Main St, New Canaan, CT 06840; 203-972-7500; Fax: 203-966-5555. Hours: 8:30AM-1PM 2-4:30PM; (8:30AM-1PM Fri July-Aug) (EST). *Probate.*

New Fairfield Probate Court 4 Brush Hill Rd, New Fairfield, CT 06812; 203-312-5627; Fax: 203-312-5612. Hours: 9AM-Noon W-Th (and by app't) (EST). *Probate.*

Newtown Probate Court Edmond Town Hall, 45 Main St, Newtown, CT 06470; 203-270-4280; Fax: 203-270-4205. Hours: 8:30AM-Noon,1-4:30PM (EST). *Probate.*

Norwalk Probate Court 125 East Ave, PO Box 2009, Norwalk, CT 06852-2009; 203-854-7737; Fax: 203-854-7825. Hours: 9AM-4:30PM (EST). *Probate.*

Note: District includes Town of Wilton

Redding Probate Court Town Hall, Lonetown Rd, PO Box 1125, Redding, CT 06875-1125; 203-938-2326; Fax: 203-938-8816. Hours: 9AM-1PM (EST). *Probate.*

Ridgefield Probate Court Town Hall, 400 Main St, Ridgefield, CT 06877; 203-431-2776; Fax: 203-431-2772. Hours: 8:30AM-4:30PM (EST). *Probate.*

Shelton Probate Court 40 White St, PO Box 127, Shelton, CT 06484; 203-924-8462; Fax: 203-924-8943. Hours: 9AM-Noon, 1-4:30PM (EST). *Probate.*

Sherman Probate Court Mallory Town Hall, Rt. 39 Center, PO Box 39, Sherman, CT 06784; 860-355-1821; Fax: 860-350-5041. Hours: 9AM-Noon Tu (and by app't) (EST). *Probate.*

Stamford Probate Court 888 Washington Blvd, 8th Floor, PO Box 10152, Stamford, CT 06904-2152; 203-323-2149; Fax: 203-964-1830. Hours: 9AM-4PM (EST). *Probate.*

Stratford Probate Court 2725 Main St, Town Hall, Stratford, CT 06615; 203-385-4023; Fax: 203-375-6253. Hours: 9:30AM-4:30PM (EST). *Probate.*

Trumbull Probate Court Town Hall, 5866 Main St, Trumbull, CT 06611-5416; 203-452-5068; Fax: 203-452-5092. Hours: 9AM-4:30PM (EST). *Probate.*

Note: District includes Town of Easton

Westport Probate Court Town Hall, 110 Myrtle Ave, Westport, CT 06880; 203-341-1100; Fax: 203-341-1153. Hours: 9AM-4:30PM (EST). *Probate.*

Note: District includes Town of Weston

Hartford County

Hartford Judicial District Court - Civil
95 Washington St, Hartford, CT 06106; 860-548-2700; Fax: 860-548-2711. Hours: 9AM-5PM (EST). *Civil Actions.*

www.jud.state.ct.us

Civil Records: Access: Mail, online, in person. Both court and visitors may perform in person searches. No search fee. Required to search: name, years to search. Civil cases indexed by defendant, plaintiff. Civil records on computer if active, otherwise on microfiche, older records at Enfield Records Center. Access to active civil case records is available free on the Internet at www.jud2.state.ct.us. **General Information:** Public Access terminal is available. No paternity, support agreement, sealed files, acknowledgments (filed before 10/01/95) records released. SASE required. Turnaround time 7-10 days. Copy fee: $1.00 per page. Certification fee: $2.00. Fee payee: Clerk of Superior Court. Personal checks accepted. Credit cards accepted: Visa, MasterCard. Accepted in person only. $10.00 minimum. Prepayment is required.

Hartford Judicial District Court - Criminal
101 LaFayette St, Hartford, CT 06106; 860-566-1634. Hours: 9AM-5PM (EST). *Felony.*

Criminal Records: Access: Mail, in person. Only the court performs in person searches; visitors may not. No search fee. Required to search: name, years to search; also helpful: DOB. Criminal records on computer from 1989.
General Information: No youthful offender records or dismissals released. SASE required. Turnaround time 7-10 days. Copy fee: $1.00 per page. Certification fee: $2.00. Fee payee: Clerk of Superior Court. Personal checks accepted. Prepayment is required.

New Britain Judicial District Court
20 Franklin Square, New Britain, CT 06051; Civil phone: 860-515-5180; Criminal phone: 860-515-5080. Hours: 9AM-5PM (EST). *Felony, Civil Actions, Small Claims.*

Civil Records: Access: Phone, mail, online, in person. Both court and visitors may perform in person searches. No search fee. Required to search: name, years to search. Civil cases indexed by plaintiff. Civil records on computer up to one year after closing, index cards back to 1989, prior in Hartford. Access to civil case records is available free on the Internet at www.jud2.state.ct.us/.
Criminal Records: Access: Phone, mail, in person. Both court and visitors may perform in person searches. No search fee. Required to search: name, years to search. Criminal records on computer for 2 years, then purged when cases sent to State Record Center.
General Information: Public Access terminal is available. No paternity, family case studies or sealed records released. SASE required. Turnaround time 3 days. Copy fee: $1.00 per page. Certification fee: $2.00. Fee payee: Clerk of Superior Court. Prepayment is required.

Geographical Area Court #12
410 Center St, Manchester, CT 06040; 860-647-1091. Hours: 9AM-5PM; Phone Hours: 9AM-4PM (EST). *Misdemeanor, Eviction, Small Claims.*

Note: Evictions are handled by a special Housing Court, 18 Trinity, Hartford, CT, 860-566-8550.

Civil Records: Access: Mail, online, in person. Both court and visitors may perform in person searches. No search fee. Required to search: name, years to search. Civil cases indexed by defendant. Civil records on computer for 3 years. Access to civil case records is available free on the Internet at www.jud2.state.ct.us/.
Criminal Records: Access: Mail, in person. Only the court performs in person searches; visitors may not. No search fee. Required to search: name, years to search,

DOB. Criminal records on computer for 3 years. In person search results returned by mail only.
General Information: No non disclosable records released. SASE required. Turnaround time 1-2 weeks. Copy fee: $1.00 per page. Certification fee: $2.00. Fee payee: Clerk of Superior Court.

Geographical Area Court #13
111 Phoenix, Enfield, CT 06082; 860-741-3727. Hours: 9AM-1PM, 2:30-4PM (EST). *Misdemeanor, Eviction.*

Civil Records: Access: Online, in person. Visitors must perform in person searches for themselves. No search fee. Required to search: name, years to search. Civil cases indexed by defendant. Civil records on computer for 1 year, microfiche by year, archived at Record Center at Enfield, CT. Access to civil case records is available free on the Internet at www.jud2.state.ct.us/.
Criminal Records: Access: In person only. Visitors must perform in person searches for themselves. No search fee. Required to search: name, years to search, DOB. Criminal records on computer for 1 year, microfiche by year, archived at Record Center at Enfield, CT.
General Information: No copy fee. Certification fee: None; Certification available from State Record Center. Fee payee: Clerk of Superior Court. Personal checks accepted. Prepayment is required.

Geographical Area Court #15
20 Franklin Square, New Britain, CT 06051; Civil phone: 860-515-5180; Criminal phone: 860-515-5080. Hours: 8:15AM-5PM (EST). *Misdemeanor, Eviction, Small Claims.*

Civil Records: Access: Mail, online, in person. Only the court performs in person searches; visitors may not. No search fee. Required to search: name, years to search. Civil cases indexed by defendant, plaintiff. Civil records on computer for 3 years, then on microfiche. All info in archives at Record Center at Enfield, CT. Access to civil case records is available free on the Internet at www.jud2.state.ct.us/.
Criminal Records: Access: Mail, in person. Only the court performs in person searches; visitors may not. No search fee. Required to search: name, years to search, DOB. Criminal records on computer from 1985, then on microfiche. All info in archives at Record Center @ Enfield, CT. Data is purged every two years.
General Information: No sealed records released. SASE required. Turnaround time 1 month. Copy fee: $1.00 per page. Certification fee: $2.00. Certification fee is for criminal division. Civil fee varies. Fee payee: Clerk of Superior Court. Business checks accepted. Prepayment is required.

Geographical Area Court #17
131 N Main St, Bristol, CT 06010; 860-582-8111. Hours: 9AM-5PM (EST). *Misdemeanor, Eviction, Small Claims.*

www.jud2.state.ct.us

Criminal Records: Access: Phone, mail, in person. Only the court performs in person searches; visitors may not. No search fee. Required to search: name, years to search, DOB. Criminal records on computer from 1986, on microfiche from 1982, prior on index cards from 1979-1992, microfiche 1988-1992 and docket books.
General Information: No dismissals, not guilty, youthful offender or NOLLE records released. SASE required. Turnaround time 1-2 days. Copy fee: $1.00 per page. Certification fee: No cert fee. Fee payee: Clerk of Superior Court. Personal checks accepted. Prepayment is required.

Geographical Area Court #14
101 LaFayette St, Hartford, CT 06106; 860-566-1630. Hours: 1PM-2:30PM (EST). *Misdemeanor.*

Criminal Records: Access: Phone, mail, in person. Only the court performs in person searches; visitors may not. No search fee. Required to search: name, years to search.

General Information: SASE required. Turnaround time 1 week. Copy fee: $1.00 per page. Certification fee: $2.00. Fee payee: Clerk of Superior Court. Personal checks accepted. Prepayment is required.

Geographical Area Court #16
105 Raymond Rd, West Hartford, CT 06107; 860-236-4551; Fax: 860-236-9311. Hours: 9AM-5PM (EST). *Misdemeanor.*

Criminal Records: Access: Mail, in person. Only the court performs in person searches; visitors may not. No search fee. Required to search: name, years to search, DOB, signed release.
General Information: No dismissal, Nolles, YO records released. SASE required. Turnaround time 3-5 days. Copy fee: $1.00 per page. Certification fee: $3.00. Fee payee: Clerk of Superior Court. Personal checks accepted. Credit cards accepted: Visa, MasterCard. Accepted in person only. Prepayment is required.

Avon Probate Court
60 W Main St, Avon, CT 06001-0578; 860-409-4348; Fax: 860-409-4368. Hours: 9AM-Noon (EST). *Probate.*

Berlin Probate Court
177 Columbus Blvd, PO Box 400, New Britain, CT 06050-0400; 860-826-2696; Fax: 860-826-2695. Hours: 9AM-4PM (EST). *Probate.*

Note: District includes Town of New Britain

Bloomfield Probate Court
Town Hall, 800 Bloomfield Ave, Bloomfield, CT 06002; 860-769-3548; Fax: 860-769-3598. Hours: 9AM-1PM, 2AM-4:30PM (EST). *Probate.*

Bristol Probate Court
111 N Main St, City Hall, Bristol, CT 06010; 860-584-7650; Fax: 860-584-3818. Hours: 9AM-5PM (EST). *Probate.*

Burlington Probate Court
200 Spielman Highway, Burlington, CT 06013; 860-673-2108; Fax: 860-675-9312. Hours: 9AM-1PM Fri (and by app't) (EST). *Probate.*

Canton Probate Court
Town Hall, 4 Market St, PO Box 175, Collinsville, CT 06022; 860-693-7851; Fax: 860-693-7889. Hours: 8:30AM-1PM Tu-Th (and by app't) (EST). *Probate.*

East Granby Probate Court
PO Box 542, 9 Center St, East Granby, CT 06026-0542; 860-653-3434; Fax: 860-653-7085. Hours: 10AM-1PM Tu; 9AM-Noon W-Th (and by app't) (EST). *Probate.*

East Hartford Probate Court
Town Hall, 740 Main St, East Hartford, CT 06108; 860-291-7278; Fax: 860-289-0831. Hours: 9AM-4PM (EST). *Probate.*

East Windsor Probate Court
Town Hall, 1540 Sullivan Ave, South Windsor, CT 06074; 860-644-2511 X271; Fax: 860-648-5047. Hours: 8AM-2PM (EST). *Probate.*

Note: District includes Town of South Windsor

Enfield Probate Court
820 Enfield St, Enfield, CT 06082; 860-253-6305; Fax: 860-253-6388. Hours: 9AM-4:30PM (till 6:30PM 1st Monday) (EST). *Probate.*

Farmington Probate Court
One Monteith Dr, Farmington, CT 06032; 860-673-2360; Fax: 860-673-8262. Hours: 9AM-4PM (EST). *Probate.*

Glastonbury Probate Court
PO Box 6523, 2155 Main St, Glastonbury, CT 06033-6523; 860-652-7629; Fax: 860-652-7590. Hours: 9:30AM-4:30PM (EST). *Probate.*

Granby Probate Court
15 N Granby Rd, Town Hall, PO Box 240, Granby, CT 06035-0240; 860-653-

8944; Fax: 860-653-4769. Hours: 9AM-Noon T,W,F (EST). *Probate.*

Hartford Probate Court 10 Prospect St, 4th Fl, Hartford, CT 06103; 860-522-1813; Fax: 860-724-1503. Hours: 9AM-4PM (4-6:30PM Mon. by app't) (EST). *Probate.*

Hartland Probate Court PO Box 158, West Hartland, CT 06027; 860-653-9710, 203-379-8625 (After hours); Fax: 860-738-1003. Hours: 10AM-1PM (and by app't) (EST). *Probate.*

Manchester Probate Court 66 Center St, Manchester, CT 06040; 860-647-3227; Fax: 860-647-3236. Hours: 8:30AM-Noon, 1-4:30PM (EST). *Probate.*

Marlborough Probate Court 26 N Main St, PO Box 29, Marlborough, CT 06447; 860-295-6239; Fax: 860-295-0317. Hours: 9AM-4:30PM M; 2:30-7PM T; 2PM-4:30 Th (and by app't) (EST). *Probate.*

Note: Hours are 9AM-4:30PM on Mon, 2:30PM-7PM on Tues, and 2PM-4:30PM on Thurs

Newington Probate Court 66 Cedar Street, Rear, Newington, CT 06111; 860-665-1285; Fax: 860-665-1331. Hours: 9AM-4PM M-W, F; 9AM-7PM Th (EST). *Probate.*

Note: District includes towns of Rocky Hill, Wethersfield

Plainville Probate Court 1 Central Square, Plainville, CT 06062; 860-793-0221 x250; Fax: 860-793-2424. Hours: 9AM-3PM M-Th; 9AM-1PM F (EST). *Probate.*

Simsbury Probate Court 933 Hopmeadow St, PO Box 495, Simsbury, CT 06070; 860-658-3277; Fax: 860-658-3206. Hours: 9AM-1PM, 2-4:30PM (and by app't) (EST). *Probate.*

Southington Probate Court Town Hall, 75 Main St, PO Box 165, Southington, CT 06489; 860-276-6253; Fax: 860-276-6255. Hours: 8:30AM-4:30PM M-W, F; 8:30AM-7PM Th (EST). *Probate.*

Suffield Probate Court 83 Mountain Rd, Town Hall, PO Box 234, Suffield, CT 06078; 860-668-3835; Fax: 860-668-3029. Hours: 9AM-1PM (and by app't) (EST). *Probate.*

West Hartford Probate Court 50 S Main St, West Hartford, CT 06107; 860-523-3174; Fax: 860-236-8352. Hours: 8:30AM-4:30PM (EST). *Probate.*

Windsor Locks Probate Court Town Office Bldg, 50 Church St, Windsor Locks, CT 06096; 860-627-1450; Fax: 860-627-1451. Hours: 9AM-2PM M-Th (EST). *Probate.*

Windsor Probate Court 275 Broad St, PO Box 342, Windsor, CT 06095; 860-285-1976; Fax: 860-285-1909. Hours: 8:30AM-4:30PM M-Th; 8:30AM-Noon Fri (EST). *Probate.*

Litchfield County

Litchfield Judicial District Court PO Box 247, Litchfield, CT 06759; 860-567-0885; Fax: 860-567-4779. Hours: 9AM-5PM (EST). *Felony, Civil Actions.*

Civil Records: Access: Fax, mail, online, in person. Only the court performs in person searches; visitors may not. No search fee. Required to search: name, years to search. Civil cases indexed by defendant, plaintiff. Pending cases only on computer, on index cards from 1972. Access to civil case records is available free on the Internet at www.jud2.state.ct.us/.
Criminal Records: Access: Fax, mail, in person. Only the court performs in person searches; visitors may not. No search fee. Required to search: name, years to search; also helpful: DOB. Pending cases only on computer, on index cards from 1972.
General Information: No sealed files released. SASE required. Turnaround time 3-4 weeks. Fax notes: No fee to fax results. Copy fee: $1.00 per page. Certification fee: $2.00. Fee payee: Clerk of Superior Court. Personal checks accepted. Prepayment is required.

Geographical Area Court #18 80 Doyle Rd (PO Box 667), Bantam, CT 06750; 860-567-3942. Hours: 9AM-5PM (EST). *Misdemeanor, Eviction, Small Claims.*

Civil Records: Access: Mail, online, in person. Both court and visitors may perform in person searches. No search fee. Required to search: name, years to search. Civil cases indexed by defendant. Civil records on computer for 2 years, on microfiche from 1986. Access to civil case records is available free on the Internet at www.jud2.state.ct.us/.
Criminal Records: Access: Mail, in person. Only the court performs in person searches; visitors may not. No search fee. Required to search: name, years to search, DOB; also helpful: address. Criminal records on computer for 1 year, microfiche from 1986, on index cards for 40 years. Archived at Records Center at Enfield, CT.
General Information: No youthful offender or non-discloseable records released. SASE required. Turnaround time 1 week. Copy fee: $1.00 per page. Certification fee: $2.00. Fee payee: Clerk of Superior Court. Personal checks accepted.

Barkhamsted Probate Court 67 Ripley Rd, PO Box 185, Pleasant Valley, CT 06063-0185; 860-379-8665; Fax: 860-379-9284. Hours: 10AM-1PM M-W (and by app't) (EST). *Probate.*

Canaan Probate Court Town Hall, 100 Pease St, PO Box 905, Canaan, CT 06018-0905; 860-824-7114; Fax: 860-824-3139. Hours: 9AM-1PM (and by app't) (EST). *Probate.*

Cornwall Probate Court PO Box 157, Town Office Bldg, Cornwall, CT 06753-0157; 860-672-2677; Fax: 860-672-2677. Hours: 9AM-4PM M-Th (EST). *Probate.*

Harwinton Probate Court Town Hall, 100 Bentley Dr, Harwinton, CT 06791; 860-485-1403; Fax: 860-485-0051. Hours: 9AM-1PM Tu-W (and by app't) (EST). *Probate.*

Kent Probate Court Town Hall, 41 Kent Green Blvd, PO Box 185, Kent, CT 06757-0185; 860-927-3729; Fax: 860-927-1313. Hours: 9AM-Noon Tu & Th (and by app't) (EST). *Probate.*

Litchfield Probate Court 74 West St, PO Box 505, Litchfield, CT 06759; 860-567-8065; Fax: 860-567-2538. Hours: 9AM-1PM (and by app't) (EST). *Probate.*

Note: District includes towns of Morris, Warren, and Litchfield

New Hartford Probate Court Town Hall, 530 Main St, PO Box 308, New Hartford, CT 06057; 860-379-3254; Fax: 860-379-8560. Hours: 9AM-Noon M,W (and by app't) (EST). *Probate.*

New Milford Probate Court 10 Main St, New Milford, CT 06776; 860-355-6029; Fax: 860-355-6002. Hours: 9AM-Noon, 1-5PM M-Th, 9AM-Noon Fri (EST). *Probate.*

Note: District includes Town of Bridgewater

Norfolk Probate Court 19 Maple Ave, PO Box 648, Norfolk, CT 06058; 860-542-5134; Fax: 860-542-5876. Hours: 9AM-Noon Tu & Th (and by app't) (EST). *Probate.*

Plymouth Probate Court 80 Main St, Terryville, CT 06786; 860-585-4014. Hours: 9AM-2PM Tu & Th (and by app't) (EST). *Probate.*

Roxbury Probate Court Town Hall, 29 North St, PO Box 203, Roxbury, CT 06783; 860-354-1184; Fax: 860-354-0560. Hours: 9AM-3PM Tu-Th (and by app't) (EST). *Probate.*

Salisbury Probate Court Town Hall, 27 Main St, PO Box 525, Salisbury, CT 06068; 860-435-5183; Fax: 860-435-5172. Hours: 9AM-Noon (and by app't) (EST). *Probate.*

Sharon Probate Court 63 Main St, PO Box 1177, Sharon, CT 06069; 860-364-5514; Fax: 860-364-5789. Hours: 2-4PM M-W & F (and by app't) (EST). *Probate.*

Thomaston Probate Court 158 Main St, Town Hall Bldg, PO Box 136, Thomaston, CT 06787; 860-283-4874; Fax: 860-283-1013 (police dept). Hours: 3-6PM M-W (and by app't) (EST). *Probate.*

Torrington Probate Court Municipal Bldg, 140 Main St, Torrington, CT 06790; 860-489-2215; Fax: 860-496-5910. Hours: 9AM-4:30PM (EST). *Probate.*

Note: District includes Town of Goshen

Washington Probate Court Town Hall, 3 Bryan Mem. Plaza, PO Box 295, Washington Depot, CT 06794; 860-868-7974; Fax: 860-868-0512. Hours: 9AM-Noon, 1-3PM M,W,F (and by app't) (EST). *Probate.*

Watertown Probate Court 37 DeForest St, Town Hall, Watertown, CT 06795; 860-945-5237; Fax: 860-945-4741. Hours: 9AM-Noon, 1-3PM (EST). *Probate.*

Winchester Probate Court 338 Main St, PO Box 625, Winsted, CT 06098; 860-379-5576; Fax: 860-738-7053. Hours: 9AM-12,1-4PM M-W, 9Am-2PM, 3-7PM Th, til noon Fri (EST). *Probate.*

Note: District includes towns of Colebrook, Winsted

Woodbury Probate Court 281 Main St, South, PO Box 84, Woodbury, CT 06798; 203-263-2417; Fax: 203-263-2748. Hours: 9AM-4PM Tu,Th (and by app't) (EST). *Probate.*

Note: District includes Town of Bethlehem

Middlesex County

Middlesex District Court - Criminal & GA Court #9
1 Court St, 1st Flr, Middletown, CT 06457-3348; 860-343-6445. Hours: 9AM-5PM (EST). *Felony, Misdemeanor.*

Criminal Records: Access: Mail, in person. Only the court performs in person searches; visitors may not. No search fee. Required to search: name, years to search, DOB, signed release; also helpful: address, SSN. Criminal records on computer for 1 year from disposition or sentence, on microfiche 1985 to present, prior on index cards.
General Information: No youthful offender records or dismissals released. Turnaround time 3-4 days. Copy fee: $1.00 per page. Certification fee: $2.50. Fee payee: Clerk, Superior Court. Personal checks accepted. Prepayment is required.

Middlesex Judicial District Court
1 Court St, 2nd Floor, Middletown, CT 06457-3374; 860-343-6400; Fax: 860-343-6423. Hours: 9AM-5PM (EST). *Civil Actions.*

www.jud.state.ct.us/directory/direcetory/location/middlesex.htm
Civil Records: Access: Mail, online, in person. Only the court performs in person searches; visitors may not. No search fee. Required to search: name, years to search; also helpful: type of case. Civil cases indexed by defendant, plaintiff. Civil records on computer 1 year post-judgment; on index card back 15 years, prior on docket books, microfiche. Access to civil case records is available free on the Internet at www.jud2.state.ct.us/.
General Information: Public Access terminal is available. No sealed records released. SASE required. Turnaround time 1 week. Copy fee: $1.00 per page. Certification fee: $2.00. Fee payee: Clerk, Superior Court. Personal checks accepted. Name & address must be pre-printed on check. Prepayment is required.

Clinton Probate Court
50 E Main St, PO Box 130, Clinton, CT 06413-0130; 860-669-6447; Fax: 860-669-6447 (call first). Hours: 10AM-3PM M-Th (Fri. by app't) (EST). *Probate.*

Deep River Probate Court
Town Hall, 174 Main St, PO Box 391, Deep River, CT 06417; 860-526-6026; Fax: 860-526-6094 (call first). Hours: 9AM-Noon, 1PM-4PM Tu,Th (and by app't) (EST). *Probate.*

East Haddam Probate Court
PO Box 217, 7 Main St, East Haddam, CT 06423; 860-873-5028; Fax: 860-873-5025. Hours: 10AM-2PM (and by app't) (EST). *Probate.*

East Hampton Probate Court
20 East High St, Annex, East Hampton, CT 06424; 860-267-9262; Fax: 860-267-6453. Hours: 9AM-2PM T-Th (EST). *Probate.*

Essex Probate Court
Town Hall, 29 West Ave, Essex, CT 06426; 860-767-4347; Fax: 860-767-8509. Hours: 9AM-1PM (and by app't) (EST). *Probate.*

Haddam Probate Court
30 Field Park Dr, Haddam, CT 06438; 860-345-8531; Fax: 860-345-3730. Hours: 10AM-2PM T-Th (and by app't) (EST). *Probate.*

Killingworth Probate Court
323 Route 81, Killingworth, CT 06419; 860-663-2304; Fax: 860-663-3305. Hours: 9AM-Noon M,W,F (and by app't) (EST). *Probate.*

Middletown Probate Court
94 Court St, Middletown, CT 06457; 860-347-7424; Fax: 860-346-1520. Hours: 8:30AM-4:30PM (EST). *Probate.*

Note: District includes towns of Cornwall, Durham, Middlefield

Old Saybrook Probate Court
263 Main St, #105, Old Saybrook, CT 06475; 860-395-3128; Fax: 860-395-3125. Hours: 9AM-1PM M,T,TH,F (Wed. eves by app't) (EST). *Probate.*

Note: Court is open on Wed. evenings, also

Portland Probate Court
33 E Main St, PO Box 71, Portland, CT 06480; 860-342-6739; Fax: 860-342-0001. Hours: 9AM-Noon (and by app't) (EST). *Probate.*

Saybrook Probate Court
65 Main St, PO Box 628, Chester, CT 06412; 860-526-0007; Fax: 860-526-0004. Hours: 9:30AM-12:30PM T,Th (and by app't) (EST). *Probate.*

Note: District includes Town of Chester

Westbrook Probate Court
1163 Boston Post Rd, PO Box 676, Westbrook, CT 06498; 860-399-5661; Fax: 860-399-9568. Hours: 1-4:30PM (EST). *Probate.*

New Haven County

Ansonia-Milford Judicial District Court
14 W River St (PO Box 210), Milford, CT 06460; 203-877-4293. Hours: 9AM-4PM (EST). *Felony, Civil Actions.*

Civil Records: Access: Mail, fax, online, in person. Only the court performs in person searches; visitors may not. No search fee. Required to search: name, years to search. Civil cases indexed by defendant, plaintiff. Civil records on computer back to 1993, on index cards from 1978. Purged computer records are on microfilm. Maintain 75 yrs at Records Center at Enfield, CT. Access to civil case records is available free on the Internet at www.jud2.state.ct.us/.
Criminal Records: Access: Mail, in person. Only the court performs in person searches; visitors may not. No search fee. Required to search: name, years to search, DOB; also helpful-SSN. Criminal records on computer back to 1993, on index cards from 1978. Purged computer records are on microfilm. Maintain 75 yrs at Records Center at Enfield, CT.
General Information: Public Access terminal is available. SASE required. Turnaround time 1-2 weeks. Fax notes: Will fax back results only to toll-free or local numbers. Copy fee: $1.00 per page. Fee payee: Clerk of Superior Court. Personal checks accepted. Prepayment is required.

Meriden Judicial District Court
54 W Main St, Meriden, CT 06451; 203-238-6666. Hours: 9AM-4PM (EST). *Civil Actions.*

Civil Records: Access: Mail, online, in person. Only the court performs in person searches; visitors may not. No search fee. Required to search: name, years to search. Civil cases indexed by defendant, plaintiff. Pending and 1 yr after disposed cases on computer, on microfiche from 1984, prior on index cards. Access to civil case records is available free on the Internet at www.jud2.state.ct.us/.   **General Information:** No acknowledgments of paternity, agreements to support prior to 10/01/95 records released. SASE required. Turnaround time 1-2 days. Copy fee: $1.00 per page. Certification fee: $2.00. Fee payee: Clerk of Superior Court. Personal checks accepted. In state personal checks accepted. Prepayment is required.

New Haven Judicial District Court
235 Church St, New Haven, CT 06510; 203-503-6800; Fax: 203-789-6424. Hours: 9AM-5PM (EST). *Felony, Civil Actions.*

www.jud.state.ct.us/directory/directory/location/newhaven.htm
Civil Records: Access: Phone, mail, online, in person. Only the court performs in person searches; visitors

may not. No search fee. Required to search: name, years to search. Civil cases indexed by defendant, plaintiff. Pending cases on computer, disposed cases deleted after 1 year, on microfiche from 1972, prior on index cards. Access to civil case records is available free on the Internet at www.jud2.state.ct.us/.
Criminal Records: Access: Mail, in person. Only the court performs in person searches; visitors may not. No search fee. Required to search: name, years to search, DOB. Pending criminal cases on computer, disposed deleted after 1 year, prior on index cards.
General Information: Public Access terminal is available. (Live civil cases only.) No sealed records released. SASE required. Turnaround time 2-5 weeks. Copy fee: $1.00 per page. Certification fee: $2.00. Fee payee: Clerk of Superior Court. Personal checks accepted. CT personal checks accepted if address on check matches address on drivers license. Prepayment is required.

Waterbury Judicial District Court
300 Grand St, Waterbury, CT 06702; 203-596-4023; Civil phone: Small claims: 203-596-4050; Fax: 203-596-4032. Hours: 9AM-5PM (EST). *Civil Actions, Small Claims.*

Note: Address mail requests for Misdemeanor criminal searches to 400 Grand St. (Geographical Area Court #4)

Civil Records: Access: Phone, fax, mail, online, in person. Only the court performs in person searches; visitors may not. No search fee. Required to search: name, years to search. Civil cases indexed by defendant. Civil records on computer back to 1990; none-computer records go back to 1900. Phone access limited to one search. Access to civil case records is available free on the Internet at www.jud2.state.ct.us/.   **General Information:** SASE required. Turnaround time 1-2 weeks. Copy fee: $1.00 per page. Certification fee: $2.00. Fee payee: Clerk of Superior Court. Personal checks accepted. Prepayment is required.

Geographical Area Court #22
14 W River St, Milford, CT 06460; 203-874-0674 (Small Claims); Civil phone: 203-877-4293; Criminal phone: 203-874-1116. Hours: 1-2:30PM, 4-5PM (EST). *Misdemeanor, Eviction, Small Claims.*

Civil Records: Access: Mail, online, in person. Only the court performs in person searches; visitors may not. No search fee. Required to search: name, years to search. Civil cases indexed by defendant, plaintiff. Civil records on computer for 6 months, after disposal, on microfiche from 1986, prior on index cards and docket books. Access to civil case records is available free on the Internet at www.jud2.state.ct.us/.
Criminal Records: Access: Mail, in person. Only the court performs in person searches; visitors may not. No search fee. Required to search: name, years to search; also helpful: DOB. Criminal records on computer for 6 months, after disposal, on microfiche from 1986, prior on index cards and docket books.
General Information: SASE required. Turnaround time 1 week. Copy fee: $1.00 per page. Certification fee: $2.00. Fee payee: Clerk of Superior Court. Personal checks accepted. Prepayment is required.

Geographical Area Court #4
400 Grand St, Waterbury, CT 06702; 203-236-8100; Fax: 203-236-8099. Hours: 9AM-5PM (EST). *Felony, Misdemeanor, Traffic.*

www.jud.state.ct.us
Criminal Records: Access: Phone, mail, in person. Only the court performs in person searches; visitors may not. No search fee. Required to search: name, years to search; also helpful: DOB. Criminal records on computer since 1985.
General Information: No youthful offenders records or dismissals released. SASE required. Turnaround time 1-2 weeks. Copy fee: $1.00 per page. Certification fee:

$2.00. Fee payee: Clerk of Superior Court. Personal checks accepted. Prepayment is required.

Geographical Area Court #5 106 Elizabeth St, Derby, CT 06418; 203-735-7438. Hours: 9AM-4PM (EST). *Misdemeanor, Eviction, Small Claims.*

Civil Records: Access: Mail, online, in person. Only the court performs in person searches; visitors may not. No search fee. Required to search: name, years to search. Civil cases indexed by defendant, plaintiff. Pending and records for 1 yr after disposal on computer, on microfiche from 1986, prior on index cards. In person search results are mailed back. Access to civil case records is available free on the Internet at www.jud2.state.ct.us/.

Criminal Records: Access: Mail, in person. Only the court performs in person searches; visitors may not. No search fee. Required to search: name, years to search, DOB. Pending and records for 1 yr after disposal on computer, on microfiche from 1986, prior on index cards. In person search results returned by mail only.

General Information: No sealed records released. SASE required. Turnaround time 1-2 weeks. Copy fee: $1.00 per page. Certification fee: $2.00. Fee payee: Clerk of Superior Court. Personal checks accepted. Prepayment is required.

Geographical Area Court #6 121 Elm St, New Haven, CT 06510; 203-789-7461; Fax: 203-789-6455. Hours: 9AM-5PM (EST). *Misdemeanor, Eviction, Small Claims.*

Civil Records: Access: Mail, online, in person. Only the court performs in person searches; visitors may not. No search fee. Required to search: name, years to search. Civil records on log book for small claims. Access to civil case records is available free on the Internet at www.jud2.state.ct.us/.

Criminal Records: Access: Mail, in person. Only the court performs in person searches; visitors may not. No search fee. Required to search: name, years to search, DOB. Criminal records on computer back 13 months, microfiche from 1986, prior archived for criminal and motor vehicle. In person search results mailed back.

General Information: No dismissals, juvenile records released. SASE required. Turnaround time 2-3 weeks. Copy fee: $1.00 per page. Certification fee: $2.00. Fee payee: Superior Court. Personal checks accepted. Prepayment is required.

Geographical Area Court #7 54 W Main St, Meriden, CT 06451; Criminal phone: 203-238-6130; Fax: 203-238-6322. Hours: 9AM-5PM (EST). *Misdemeanor, Small Claims.*

Civil Records: Access: Mail, online, in person. Only the court performs in person searches; visitors may not. No search fee. Required to search: name, years to search. Civil cases indexed by defendant, plaintiff. Pending and 1 yr after disposed cases on computer, on microfiche from 1985, prior on index cards. All manual records by docket number. Access to civil case records is available free on the Internet at www.jud2.state.ct.us/.

Criminal Records: Access: Phone, mail, in person. Only the court performs in person searches; visitors may not. No search fee. Required to search: name, years to search, DOB. Criminal records on computer since 1986, purged every 6 months & maintained in Enfield, CT.

General Information: No sealed records released. SASE required. Turnaround time 1-2 days. Copy fee: $1.00 per page. Certification fee: $10.00. Fee payee: Clerk of Superior Court. Personal checks accepted. Prepayment is required.

Bethany Probate Court Town Hall, 40 Peck Rd, Bethany, CT 06524; 203-393-3744; Fax: 203-393-0821. Hours: 9AM-Noon T,TH (EST). *Probate.*

Branford Probate Court PO Box 638, 1019 Main St, Branford, CT 06405-0638; 203-488-0318; Fax: 203-315-4715. Hours: 9AM-Noon, 1-4:30PM (till Noon, Fridays in Summer) (EST). *Probate.*

Cheshire Probate Court 84 S Main St, Cheshire, CT 06410; 203-271-6608; Fax: 203-271-6628. Hours: 8:30AM-12:30PM, 1:30PM-4PM M-Th; 8:30AM-12:30PM Fri (EST). *Probate.*

Note: District includes town of Prospect. On Fridays, they close at 12:30

Derby Probate Court 253 Main St, 2nd Fl, Ansonia, CT 06401; 203-734-1277; Fax: 203-734-0922. Hours: 9AM-5:30PM M-W; 8:30-6:30 PM Th (EST). *Probate.*

Note: District includes towns of Ansonia, Seymour

East Haven Probate Court 250 Main St, Town Hall, East Haven, CT 06512; 203-468-3895. Hours: 9AM-3:30PM, except 1PM on Fri (EST). *Probate.*

Guilford Probate Court Town Hall, 31 Park St, Guilford, CT 06437; 203-453-8006; Fax: 203-453-8017. Hours: 9AM-Noon,1-4PM M,T,Th,F; 9AM-Noon W (EST). *Probate.*

Hamden Probate Court 2372 Whitney Ave, Memorial Town Hall, Hamden, CT 06518; 203-287-2570; Fax: 203-287-2571. Hours: 8:30AM-4:30PM (EST). *Probate.*

Madison Probate Court 8 Campus Dr, PO Box 205, Madison, CT 06443; 203-245-5661; Fax: 203-245-5653. Hours: 9AM-3PM (and by app't) (EST). *Probate.*

Meriden Probate Court City Hall, E Main St, Rm 113, Meriden, CT 06450; 203-630-4150; Fax: 203-630-4043. Hours: 8:30AM-7PM M; 8:30-4:30 T-F (EST). *Probate.*

Milford Probate Court Parsons Office Complex, 70 W River St, PO Box 414, Milford, CT 06460; 203-783-3205; Fax: 203-783-3364. Hours: 9AM-5PM (EST). *Probate.*

Naugatuck Probate Court Town Hall, 229 Church St, Naugatuck, CT 06770; 203-720-7046; Fax: 203-729-9452. Hours: 9AM-4PM M-Th; 9AM-3PM F (EST). *Probate.*

Note: District includes Town of Beacon Falls

New Haven Probate Court 200 Orange St, 1st Floor, PO Box 905, New Haven, CT 06504; 203-946-4880; Fax: 203-946-5962. Hours: 9AM-4PM (EST). *Probate.*

North Branford Probate Court 1599 Foxon Rd, PO Box 214, North Branford, CT 06471; 203-315-6007; Fax: 203-315-6025. Hours: 8:45AM-12:45PM (EST). *Probate.*

North Haven Probate Court 18 Church St, PO Box 175, North Haven, CT 06473-0175; 203-239-5321 X775; Fax: 203-239-1874. Hours: 8:30AM-4:30PM M-Th (and by app't) (EST). *Probate.*

Orange Probate Court 525 Orange Center Rd, Orange, CT 06477; 203-891-2160; Fax: 203-891-2161. Hours: 9AM-Noon (EST). *Probate.*

Oxford Probate Court Town Hall, Rt. 67, Oxford, CT 06478; 203-888-2543 x3014; Fax: 203-888-2136. Hours: 7-9PM Mon, 1-5PM Tu-W, 9AM-5PM, 7-9PM Th (EST). *Probate.*

Southbury Probate Court Townhall Annex, 421 Main St South, PO Box 674, Southbury, CT

06488; 203-262-0641; Fax: 203-264-9310. Hours: 9AM-4:30PM (and by app't) (EST). *Probate.*

Wallingford Probate Court Town Hall, 45 S Main St, Rm 114, Wallingford, CT 06492; 203-294-2100; Fax: 203-294-2109. Hours: 9AM-5PM (EST). *Probate.*

Waterbury Probate Court 236 Grand St, Waterbury, CT 06702; 203-755-1127; Fax: 203-597-0824. Hours: 9AM-4:45PM MTWF; 9AM-6PM Th; 9AM-Noon Sat (EST). *Probate.*

Note: District includes towns of Middlebury, Wolcott

West Haven Probate Court 355 Main St, PO Box 127, West Haven, CT 06516; 203-937-3552; Fax: 203-937-3556. Hours: 9AM-4PM (EST). *Probate.*

Woodbridge Probate Court Town Hall, 11 Meetinghouse Ln, Woodbridge, CT 06525; 203-389-3410; Fax: 203-389-3480. Hours: 3-7PM M, 9AM-1PM W (EST). *Probate.*

New London County

New London Judicial District Court 70 Huntington St, New London, CT 06320; 860-443-5363. Hours: 9AM-5PM (EST). *Felony, Civil Actions.*

Civil Records: Access: Mail, online, in person. No search fee. Required to search: name, years to search. Civil cases indexed by defendant, plaintiff. Civil records pending and 1 yr after disposed on computer, on microfiche from mid-70s. In person access limited to five names. Access to civil case records is available free on the Internet at www.jud2.state.ct.us/.

Criminal Records: Access: Mail, in person. Only the court performs in person searches; visitors may not. No search fee. Required to search: name, years to search; also helpful: DOB. Criminal records on computer from 1991, prior on index cards.

General Information: No sealed or youthful offender records released. SASE required. Turnaround time 2 weeks. Copy fee: $1.00 per page. Certification fee: $2.00. Fee payee: Clerk of Superior Court. Personal checks accepted. Prepayment is required.

Norwich Judicial District Court 1 Courthouse Square, Norwich, CT 06360; 860-887-3515; Fax: 860-887-8643. Hours: 9AM-5PM (EST). *Civil Actions.*

www.jud.state.ct.us

Civil Records: Access: Phone, mail, fax, online, in person. Only the court performs in person searches; visitors may not. No search fee. Required to search: name, years to search. Civil cases indexed by defendant, plaintiff. Pending and disposed cases on computer from 1992, on microfiche from 1975, prior on index cards. Access to civil case records is available free at the web site. **General Information:** No criminal search warrant, acknowledgment of paternity prior to 1995, sealed records released. SASE required. Turnaround time up to a month. Copy fee: $1.00 per page. Judgment copies $10.00. Certification fee: $2.00. Certified copy of Judgment $15.00. Fee payee: Clerk of Superior Court. Personal checks accepted. Checks must have imprinted name and address and match valid CT driver license. Prepayment is required.

Geographical Area Court #10 112 Broad St, New London, CT 06320; 860-443-8343. Hours: 9AM-5PM (EST). *Misdemeanor, Eviction, Small Claims.*

www.jud.state.ct.us

Civil Records: Access: Mail, online, in person. Both court and visitors may perform in person searches. No search fee. Required to search: name, years to search. Civil cases indexed by defendant. Civil records on microfiche from early '85, prior on index cards and docket books. Access to civil case records is available free on the Internet at www.jud2.state.ct.us/.

Criminal Records: Access: Mail, in person. Only the court performs in person searches; visitors may not. No search fee. Required to search: name, years to search; also helpful: DOB, SSN. Criminal records on computer for 2 years; prior records on microfiche.

General Information: No sealed, dismissed, youth or program records released. SASE required. Turnaround time up to 1 month. Copy fee: $1.00 per page. Certification fee: None; Certification available from State Record Center. Fee payee: Clerk, Superior Court. Personal checks accepted.

Geographical Area Court #21 1 Courthouse Sq, Norwich, CT 06360; Civil phone: 860-887-3515; Criminal phone: 860-889-7338. Hours: 1-2:30PM, 4-5PM (EST). *Misdemeanor, Eviction, Small Claims.*

www.jud.state.ct.us

Civil Records: Access: Mail, online, in person. No search fee. Required to search: name, years to search. Civil cases indexed by defendant. Pending and 2-4 years history of disposed on computer, on microfiche from 1986, prior on index cards and docket books. Small claims, evictions not on computer. Access to civil case records is available free on the Internet at www.jud2.state.ct.us/.

Criminal Records: Access: In person only. Visitors must perform in person searches for themselves. No search fee. Required to search: name, years to search, DOB. Pending and 2-4 years history of disposed on computer, on microfiche from 1986, prior on index cards and docket books. Small claims, evictions not on computer. Mail requests are referred to the Judicial Records Center in Enfield.

General Information: No youthful offender or dismissed/erased records released. SASE required. Turnaround time 1-2 weeks. Copy fee: $1.00 per page. Certification fee: $2.00. Certified copy of Judgment $15.00. Fee payee: Superior Court GA #21. Personal checks accepted. Prepayment is required.

Bozrah Probate Court Town Hall, 2nd FL, One River Rd, Bozrah, CT 06334; 860-889-2958; Fax: 860-887-7571. Hours: 10AM-1PM M,W (and by app't) (EST). *Probate.*

Colchester Probate Court Town Hall, 127 Norwich Ave, Colchester, CT 06415; 860-537-7290; Fax: 860-537-0547. Hours: 12:30PM-4:30PM M,T,Th,F; 9AM-1PM Wed (EST). *Probate.*

East Lyme Probate Court PO Box 519, 108 Pennsylvania Ave, Niantic, CT 06357; 860-739-6931; Fax: 860-739-6930. Hours: 8:30AM-12:30PM (EST). *Probate.*

Griswold Probate Court Town Hall, 32 School St, PO Box 369, Jewett City, CT 06351; 860-376-0216; Fax: 860-376-0216. Hours: 5PM-8PM M; 1PM-5PM T-F (EST). *Probate.*

Lebanon Probate Court Town Hall, 579 Exeter Rd, Lebanon, CT 06249; 860-642-7429; Fax: 860-642-7716. Hours: 10AM-Noon, 1:30-4PM T; 4-6PM Th; 10AM-Noon F (and by appt.) (EST). *Probate.*

Ledyard Probate Court 741 Colonel Ledyard Hwy, Route 17, Ledyard, CT 06339; 860-464-3219; Fax: 860-464-8531. Hours: 9:30AM-1PM M,T; 9AM-4PM W; 9-11AM Th-F (and by app't) (EST). *Probate.*

Lyme Probate Court Town Hall, 480 Hamburg Rd, Lyme, CT 06371; 860-434-7733; Fax: 860-434-2989. Hours: 9AM-Noon (and by app't) (EST). *Probate.*

Montville Probate Court 310 Norwich-New London Turnpike, Uncasville, CT 06382; 860-848-9847; Fax: 860-848-4534. Hours: 9AM-1PM M,T,Th,F; 9AM-4:30PM W (EST). *Probate.*

New London Probate Court 181 Captain's Walk, Municipal Bldg, PO Box 148, New London, CT 06320; 860-443-7121; Fax: 860-437-8155. Hours: 9AM-4PM (EST). *Probate.*

Note: District includes Town of Waterford

North Stonington Probate Court 391 Norwich Westerly Rd #2, PO Box 204, North Stonington, CT 06359; 860-535-8441; Fax: 860-535-8441 (call first). Hours: 9AM-Noon M & W; 1-4PM T, F; 4-7PM Th (EST). *Probate.*

Norwich Probate Court 100 Broadway, Rm 101, PO Box 38, Norwich, CT 06360; 860-887-2160; Fax: 860-887-2401. Hours: 9AM-4:30PM *Probate.*

Note: District includes Towns of Franklin, Lisbon, Preston, Sprague, Voluntown

Old Lyme Probate Court 52 Lyme St, Memorial Town Hall, Old Lyme, CT 06371; 860-434-1406 X222; Fax: 860-434-9283. Hours: 9AM-Noon, 1-4PM (EST). *Probate.*

Salem Probate Court 270 Hartford Rd, Salem, CT 06420; 860-859-3873, 203-859-3036 (After hours); Fax: 860-537-0547. Hours: By app't (EST). *Probate.*

Stonington Probate Court 152 Elm St, PO Box 312, Stonington, CT 06378; 860-535-5090; Fax: 860-535-0520. Hours: 9AM-Noon, 1-4PM *Probate.*

Note: District includes Town of Mystic

Tolland County

Tolland Judicial District Court - Civil 69 Brooklyn St, Rockville, CT 06066; 860-875-6294. Hours: 9AM-5PM (EST). *Civil Actions.*

Civil Records: Access: Mail, online, in person. Only the court performs in person searches; visitors may not. No search fee. Required to search: name, years to search. Civil cases indexed by defendant, plaintiff. Civil records on computer from 1990, on microfiche from 1980, all prior on index cards. Access to civil case records is available free on the Internet at www.jud2.state.ct.us/. **General Information:** No youthful offender, dismissed or not guilty verdict records released. SASE required. Turnaround time 1-2 weeks. Fax notes: Will not fax results. Copy fee: $1.00 per page. Certification fee: $2.00. Fee payee: Clerk of Superior Court. Personal checks accepted. Prepayment is required.

Tolland Judicial District Court - Criminal 20 Park St, Vernon, CT 06066; 860-870-3200. Hours: 9AM-5PM (EST). *Felony.*

Note: The address can use either Rockville or Vernon, but the US Postal Service will sometimes return mail addressed to Rockville.

Criminal Records: Access: Mail, in person. Only the court performs in person searches; visitors may not. No search fee. Required to search: name, years to search; also helpful: DOB. Criminal records are for active cases only. Completed cases must be searched in Enfield through DPS.

General Information: No youthful offender, dismissed or not guilty verdict records released. SASE required. Turnaround time 1 week. Copy fee: $1.00 per page. Certification fee: $2.00. Fee payee: Clerk of Superior Court. Personal checks accepted. Prepayment required.

Geographical Area Court #19 20 Park St, PO Box 980, Rockville, CT 06066-0980; 860-870-3200. Hours: 9AM-4PM (EST). *Misdemeanor.*

www.jud2.state.ct.us

Criminal Records: Access: Mail, in person. Only the court performs in person searches; visitors may not. No search fee. Required to search: name, years to search,

DOB. Criminal records on computer approx. 2 yrs from disposition, on microfiche from 1985, prior on index cards.

General Information: No youthful offender records released. SASE required. Turnaround time 1-7 days. Copy fee: $1.00 per page. Certification fee: $2.00. Fee payee: Clerk of Superior Court. Personal checks accepted. Prepayment is required.

Andover Probate Court 222 Bolton Center Rd, Bolton, CT 06043; 860-647-7979; Fax: 860-649-3187. 9AM-4PM M & W; 9AM-3PM F (EST). *Probate.*

Note: District includes towns of Andover, Bolton and Columbia

Ashford Probate Court 20 Pompey Hollow Rd, PO Box 61, Ashford, CT 06278; 860-429-4986. Hours: 1AM-3:30PM Th (and by app't) (EST). *Probate.*

Ellington Probate Court PO Box 268, 14 Park Place, Rockville, CT 06066; 860-872-0519; Fax: 860-870-5140. Hours: 8:30-4:30 M-W; 8:30-7PM TH; 8:30-1PM F (EST). *Probate.*

Note: District includes Town of Vernon

Hebron Probate Court 15 Gilead Rd, Hebron, CT 06248; 860-228-5971; Fax: 860-228-4859. Hours: 8AM-4PM Tu; 4-6PM Th (and by app't) (EST). *Probate.*

Mansfield Probate Court 4 South Eagleville Rd, Storrs, CT 06268; 860-429-3313; Fax: 860-429-6863. Hours: 9AM-5PM T; 2-5PM W; 2-6:30PM Th; 9AM-Noon F (EST). *Probate.*

Somers Probate Court, CT. *Probate.*

Note: The Sommers Probate Court merged with the Stafford Probate Court on 1-6-99

Stafford Probate Court Town Hall, 1 Main St, PO Box 63, Stafford Springs, CT 06076; 860-684-3423; Fax: 860-684-7173. 9AM-Noon, 1-4:30PM M; 9AM-Noon Tu-F (and by app't) (EST). *Probate.*

Note: District includes towns of Union and Somers

Tolland Probate Court 21 Tolland Green, Tolland, CT 06084; 860-871-3640; Fax: 860-871-3641. Hours: 9AM-12:30 M-W; 5:30-8:30PM Th (and by app't) (EST). *Probate.*

Note: District includes Town of Willington

Windham County

Windham Judicial District Court 155 Church St, Putnam, CT 06260; 860-928-7749; Fax: 860-928-7076. Hours: 9AM-5PM (EST). *Civil Actions.*

Civil Records: Access: Phone, mail, online, in person. Only the court performs in person searches; visitors may not. No search fee. Required to search: name, years to search. Civil cases indexed by defendant, plaintiff. Civil records on computer for 1 year, prior on index cards, prior to 70s archived. Access to civil case records is available free on the Internet at www.jud2.state.ct.us/. **General Information:** No sealed, dismissed criminal, not guilty verdict records released. SASE required. Turnaround time 1-2 days. Copy fee: $1.00 per page. Certification fee: $2.00. Fee payee: Clerk of Superior Court. Personal checks accepted. Prepayment required.

Geographical Area Court #11 120 School St #110, Danielson, CT 06239-3024; 860-779-8480; Fax: 860-779-8488. Hours: 9AM-5PM (EST). *Felony, Misdemeanor, Eviction, Small Claims.*

Civil Records: Access: Phone, mail, online, in person. Only the court performs in person searches; visitors may not. No search fee. Required to search: name, years to search. Civil cases indexed by defendant. Small claims records on computer since 08/96; all other records on index cards. Access to civil case records is available free on the Internet at www.jud2.state.ct.us/.

Criminal Records: Access: Phone, mail, in person. Only the court performs in person searches; visitors may not. No search fee. Required to search: name, years to search, DOB. Pending criminal and 1 year after disposed on computer, on microfiche from 1986, prior on index cards.

General Information: No sealed records released. SASE required. Turnaround time 1-2 weeks. Copy fee: $1.00 per page. Certification fee: $2.00. Fee payee: Clerk of Superior Court. Personal checks accepted.

Brooklyn Probate Court Town Hall, 4 Wolf Den Rd, PO Box 356, Brooklyn, CT 06234-0356; 860-774-5973; Fax: 860-779-3744. Hours: 10AM-4:30PM T (and by app't) (EST). *Probate.*

Canterbury Probate Court 43 Maple Lane, Canterbury, CT 06331; 860-546-9605; Fax: 860-546-7805. Hours: 9AM-4:00PM Wed (and by app't) (EST). *Probate.*

Chaplin Probate Court c/o Eastford Probate District, PO Box 61, Ashford, CT 06278-0061; 860-974-1885; Fax: 860-974-0624. *Probate.*

Eastford Probate Court PO Box 207, 16 Westford Rd, Eastford, CT 06242-0207; 860-974-3024; Fax: 860-974-0624. Hours: 2-4PM Tu (and by app't) (EST). *Probate.*

Hampton Probate Court Town Hall, 164 Main St, PO Box 84, Hampton, CT 06247; 860-455-9132/0201; Fax: 860-455-0517. Hours: 10AM-Noon Th (and by app't) (EST). *Probate.*

Killingly Probate Court 172 Main St, Danielson, CT 06239; 860-779-5319; Fax: 860-779-5394. Hours: 8:30AM-Noon, 1-4PM (EST). *Probate.*

Plainfield Probate Court Town Hall, 8 Community Ave, Plainfield, CT 06374; 860-230-3031; Fax: 860-230-3033. Hours: 8:30-3:30PM M-Th; 8:30AM-Noon Fri (EST). *Probate.*

Pomfret Probate Court 5 Haven Rd, Rt. 44, Pomfret Center, CT 06259; 860-974-0186; Fax: 860-974-3950. Hours: 10AM-4PM Tu-Th (and by app't) (EST). *Probate.*

Putnam Probate Court Town Hall, 126 Church St, Putnam, CT 06260; 860-963-6868; Fax: 860-963-6814. Hours: 9AM-Noon M-Th (and by app't) (EST). *Probate.*

Sterling Probate Court 1114 Plainfield Pike, PO Box 157, Oneco, CT 06373; 860-564-8488; Fax: 860-564-1660. Hours: 8:30AM-Noon M,W (and by app't) (EST). *Probate.*

Thompson Probate Court 815 Riverside Dr, Town Hall, PO Box 74, North Grosvenordale, CT 06255; 860-923-2203; Fax: 860-923-3836. Hours: 9AM-Noon (and by app't) (EST). *Probate.*

Windham Probate Court 979 Main St, PO Box 34, Willimantic, CT 06226; 860-465-3049; Fax: 860-465-3012. Hours: 9AM-1PM M,Tu,Th; 9AM-1PM Fri (EST). *Probate.*

Note: District includes Town of Scottland

Woodstock Probate Court 415 Route 169, Woodstock, CT 06281; 860-928-2223; Fax: 860-963-7557. Hours: 3PM-6PM W, 1:30PM-4:30PM Th (and by app't) (EST). *Probate.*

Connecticut Recording Offices

ORGANIZATION   8 counties and 170 towns/cities. There is no county recording in this state. The recording officer is Town/City Clerk. Be careful not to confuse searching in the following towns/cities as equivalent to a county-wide search: Fairfield, Hartford, Litchfield, New Haven, New London, Tolland, and Windham. The entire state is in the Eastern Time Zone (EST).

REAL ESTATE RECORDS   Many towns do not perform real estate searches. Copy fees are usually $1.00 per page. Certification fees are usually $1.00 per document or per page.

UCC RECORDS   Connecticut adopted Revised Article 9 on October 1, 2001. Financing statements are filed at the state level, except for real estate related collateral, which are filed only with the Town/City Clerk. Some towns will perform UCC searches. Copies usually cost $1.00 per page.

TAX LIEN RECORDS   All federal and state tax liens on personal property are filed with the Secretary of State. Federal and state tax liens on real property are filed with the Town/City Clerk. Towns will not perform tax lien searches.

OTHER LIENS   Mechanics, judgments, lis pendens, municipal, welfare, carpenter, sewer & water, city/town.

STATEWIDE ONLINE INFO: The State's Municipal Public Access Initiative has produced a website of Town and Municipality information at www.munic.state.ct.us.

Andover Town
Town Clerk, PO Box 328, Andover, CT 06232-0328. Town Clerk, R/E and UCC Recording 860-742-0188; Fax 860-742-7535.
Will search UCC records. This agency will not do a tax lien search. Will not search real estate records. **Other Phone Numbers:** Assessor 860-742-7305; Tax Collector 860-742-4035.

Ansonia City
City Clerk, 253 Main Street, City Hall, Ansonia, CT 06401. 203-736-5980.
Will search UCC records. This agency will not do a tax lien search. Will not search real estate records. **Other Phone Numbers:** Assessor 203-734-5950; Treasurer 203-734-5920.

Ashford Town
Town Clerk, 25 Pompey Hollow Road, Ashford, CT 06278. 860-429-7044 R/E Recording: 203-429-7044; Fax 860-487-2025.
Will search UCC records. This agency will not do a tax lien search. Will not search real estate records. **Other Phone Numbers:** Assessor 860-429-8583.

Avon Town
Town Clerk, 60 West Main Street, Avon, CT 06001. 860-409-4310; Fax 860-677-8428.
Will not search UCC records. This agency will not do a tax lien search. Will not search real estate records. **Other Phone Numbers:** Assessor 860-409-4335; Elections 860-409-4350; Vital Records 860-409-4310.

Barkhamsted Town
Town Clerk, 67 Ripley Hill Rd., Pleasant Valley, CT 06063. Town Clerk, R/E and UCC Recording 860-379-8665; Fax 860-379-9284.
Will not search UCC records. This agency will not do a tax lien search. Will not search real estate records. **Other Phone Numbers:** Assessor 860-379-3600; Treasurer 860-379-8665; Elections 860-379-8665; Vital Records 860-379-8665.

Beacon Falls Town
Town Clerk, 10 Maple Avenue, Beacon Falls, CT 06403. Town Clerk, R/E and UCC Recording 203-729-8254; Fax 203-720-1078.

Will not search UCC records. This agency will not do a tax lien search. Will not search real estate records. **Other Phone Numbers:** Assessor 203-723-5253; Vital Records 203-729-8254.

Berlin Town
Town Clerk, P.O. Box 1, Kensington, CT 06037. Town Clerk, R/E and UCC Recording 860-828-7075; Fax 860-828-7180. http://www.town.berlin.ct.us/town.htm
Will search UCC records. This agency will not do a tax lien search. Will not search real estate records. **Other Phone Numbers:** Assessor 860-828-7039; Treasurer 860-828-7023; Elections 860-828-7075; Vital Records 860-828-7075.

Bethany Town
Town Clerk, 40 Peck Road, Bethany, CT 06524-3338. 203-393-2100 x104, x105 R/E Recording: 203-393-0820; Fax 203-393-0821.
Will not search UCC records. This agency will not do a tax lien search. Will not search real estate records. **Other Phone Numbers:** Assessor 203-393-1977; Treasurer 203-393-2100 x100.

Bethel Town
Town Clerk, 1 School St., Bethel, CT 06801. Town Clerk, R/E and UCC Recording 203-794-8505; Fax 203-794-8588.
Will not search UCC records. This agency will not do a tax lien search. Will not search real estate records. **Other Phone Numbers:** Assessor 203-794-8507.

Bethlehem Town
Town Clerk, P.O. Box 160, Bethlehem, CT 06751. Town Clerk, R/E and UCC Recording 203-266-7510; Fax 203-266-7670. http://www.ci.bethlehem.ct.us
Will search UCC records. This agency will not do a tax lien search. Will not search real estate records. **Other Phone Numbers:** Assessor 203-266-5479; Treasurer 203-266-7677; Elections 203-266-7961; Vital Records 203-266-7510.

Bloomfield Town
Town Clerk, P.O. Box 337, Bloomfield, CT 06002. 860-769-3506 R/E Recording: 860-769-3507; Fax 860-769-3597.
Will search UCC records. This agency will not do a tax lien search. Will not search real estate records. **Other Phone Numbers:** Assessor 860-769-3530; Elections 860-769-3507; Vital Records 860-769-3507.

Bolton Town
Town Clerk, 222 Bolton Center Road, Bolton, CT 06043-7698. 860-649-8066 R/E Recording: 860-649-8066 x106 UCC Recording: 860-649-8066 x107; Fax 860-643-0021.
Will not search UCC records. This agency will not do a tax lien search. Will not search real estate records. **Other Phone Numbers:** Assessor 860-649-8066 x100; Treasurer 860-649-7780; Elections 860-649-8066 x116; Vital Records 860-649-8066 x106.

Bozrah Town
Town Clerk, P.O. Box 158, Bozrah, CT 06334. 860-889-2689 R/E Recording: 203-889-2689; Fax 860-887-5449.
Will search UCC records. This agency will not do a tax lien search. Will not search real estate records. **Other Phone Numbers:** Assessor 860-889-2689.

Branford Town
Town Clerk, P.O. Box 150, Branford, CT 06405. 203-488-6305; Fax 203-481-5561.
Will not search UCC records. This agency will not do a tax lien search. Will not search real estate records. **Other Phone Numbers:** Assessor 203-488-2039 x144.

Bridgeport Town
City Clerk, 45 Lyon Terrace, City Hall, Room 124, Bridgeport, CT 06604. 203-576-7207.
Will search UCC records. This agency will not do a tax lien search. Will not search real estate records. **Other Phone Numbers:** Assessor 203-576-7077.

Bridgewater Town
Town Clerk, P.O. Box 216, Bridgewater, CT 06752-0216. Town Clerk, R/E and UCC Recording 860-354-5102; Fax 860-350-5944.
Will search UCC records. This agency will not do a tax lien search. Will not search real estate records. **Other Phone Numbers:** Assessor 860-355-9379; Treasurer 860-354-2683; Elections 860-354-5102; Vital Records 860-354-5102.

Bristol City
City Clerk, P.O. Box 114, Bristol, CT 06010-0114. City Clerk, R/E and UCC Recording 860-584-7656.
Will search UCC records. This agency will not do a tax lien search. Will not search real estate records. **Other**

Phone Numbers: Assessor 860-584-7651; Treasurer 860-584-7618; Elections 860-584-7656; Vital Records 860-584-7656.

Brookfield Town

Town Clerk, P.O. Box 5106, Brookfield, CT 06804-5106. 203-775-7313 R/E Recording: 203-775-3087. Will search UCC records. This agency will not do a tax lien search. Will not search real estate records. **Other Phone Numbers:** Assessor 203-775-7302.

Brooklyn Town

Town Clerk, P.O. Box 356, Brooklyn, CT 06234. Town Clerk, R/E and UCC Recording 860-774-9543; Fax 860-779-3744. Will search UCC records. This agency will not do a tax lien search. Will not search real estate records. **Other Phone Numbers:** Assessor 860-774-5611; Treasurer 860-774-9543; Elections 860-774-9543; Vital Records 860-774-9543.

Burlington Town

Town Clerk, 200 Spielman Highway, Burlington, CT 06013. 860-673-2108 R/E Recording: 203-673-2108; Fax 860-675-9312. Will search UCC records. This agency will not do a tax lien search. Will not search real estate records. **Other Phone Numbers:** Assessor 860-673-3901.

Canaan Town

Town Clerk, P.O. Box 47, Falls Village, CT 06031. 860-824-0707; Fax 860-824-4506. Will search UCC records. This agency will not do a tax lien search. Will not search real estate records. **Other Phone Numbers:** Assessor 860-824-0707.

Canterbury Town

Town Clerk, P.O. Box 27, Canterbury, CT 06331-0027. 860-546-9377 R/E Recording: 203-546-9377; Fax 860-546-7805. Will search UCC records. This agency will not do a tax lien search. Will not search real estate records. **Online Access:** Assessor. Property tax records on the Assessor's database are available online at http://data.visionappraisal.com/canterburyct/. Registration is required for full access; registration is free. **Other Phone Numbers:** Assessor 860-546-6035.

Canton Town

Town Clerk, P.O. Box 168, Collinsville, CT 06022. Town Clerk, R/E and UCC Recording 860-693-7870; Fax 860-693-7840. Will not search UCC records. This agency will not do a tax lien search. Will not search real estate records. **Other Phone Numbers:** Assessor 860-693-7842; Treasurer 860-693-7852; Elections 860-693-7870; Vital Records 860-693-7870.

Chaplin Town

Town Clerk, P.O. Box 286, Chaplin, CT 06235. Town Clerk, R/E and UCC Recording 860-455-9455; Fax 860-455-0027. Will not search UCC records. This agency will not do a tax lien search. Will not search real estate records. **Other Phone Numbers:** Assessor 860-455-9333; Treasurer 860-455-9455; Elections 860-455-9455; Vital Records 860-455-9455.

Cheshire Town

Town Clerk, 84 South Main Street, Town Hall, Cheshire, CT 06410. 203-271-6601. Will search UCC records. This agency will not do a tax lien search. Will not search real estate records. **Other Phone Numbers:** Assessor 203-271-6620.

Chester Town

Town Clerk, P.O. Box 328, Chester, CT 06412-0328. Town Clerk, R/E and UCC Recording 860-526-0006; Fax 860-526-0004. Will search UCC records. This agency will not do a tax lien search. Will not search real estate records. **Online Access:** Assessor. Property records on the Assessor's Taxpayer Information System database are available free online at http://140.239.211.227/chesterct. Registration is required for full access; registration is free. **Other Phone Numbers:** Assessor 860-526-0012; Treasurer 860-526-0010; Elections 860-526-0005; Vital Records 860-526-0006.

Clinton Town

Town Clerk, 54 East Main Street, Clinton, CT 06413. Town Clerk, R/E and UCC Recording 860-669-9101. Will search UCC records. This agency will not do a tax lien search. Will not search real estate records. **Other Phone Numbers:** Assessor 860-669-9269; Treasurer 860-669-9465; Elections 860-669-9101; Vital Records 860-669-9101.

Colchester Town

Town Clerk, 127 Norwich Avenue, Colchester, CT 06415. Town Clerk, R/E and UCC Recording 860-537-7215; Fax 860-537-0547. Will not search UCC records. This agency will not do a tax lien search. Will not search real estate records. **Other Phone Numbers:** Assessor 860-537-7205; Treasurer 860-537-7225; Elections 860-537-7204; Vital Records 860-537-7215.

Colebrook Town

Town Clerk, P.O. Box 5, Colebrook, CT 06021. 860-379-3359 R/E Recording: 203-379-3359; Fax 860-379-7215. Will search UCC records. This agency will not do a tax lien search. Will not search real estate records. **Other Phone Numbers:** Assessor 203-379-3738.

Columbia Town

Town Clerk, 323 Jonathan Trumbull Hwy, Columbia, CT 06237. 860-228-3284 R/E Recording: 203-228-3283; Fax 860-228-1952. Will search UCC records. This agency will not do a tax lien search. Will not search real estate records. **Other Phone Numbers:** Assessor 203-228-9555.

Cornwall Town

Town Clerk, P.O. Box 97, Cornwall, CT 06753-0097. Town Clerk, R/E and UCC Recording 860-672-2709. Will search UCC records. This agency will not do a tax lien search. Will not search real estate records. **Other Phone Numbers:** Assessor 860-672-2703; Treasurer 860-672-2707; Vital Records 860-672-2709.

Coventry Town

Town Clerk, 1712 Main Street, Coventry, CT 06238. Town Clerk, R/E and UCC Recording 860-742-7966; Fax 860-742-8911. Will not search UCC records. This agency will not do a tax lien search. Will not search real estate records. **Other Phone Numbers:** Assessor 860-742-4067; Treasurer 860-742-7966; Elections 860-742-4061; Vital Records 860-742-7966.

Cromwell Town

Town Clerk, 41 West Street, Cromwell, CT 06416-2100. 860-632-3440; Fax 860-632-7048. http://www.cromwellct.com Will not search UCC records. This agency will not do a tax lien search. Will not search real estate records. **Other Phone Numbers:** Assessor 860-632-3442.

Danbury City

Town Clerk, 155 Deer Hill Avenue, City Hall, Danbury, CT 06810. 203-797-4531. Will search UCC records. This agency will not do a tax lien search. Will not search real estate records. **Other Phone Numbers:** Assessor 203-797-4554; Treasurer 203-797-4650.

Darien Town

Town Clerk, 2 Renshaw Road, Darien, CT 06820-5397. 203-656-7307. Will search UCC records. This agency will not do a tax lien search. Will not search real estate records. **Other Phone Numbers:** Assessor 203-656-7310; Treasurer 203-656-7334.

Deep River Town

Town Clerk, 174 Main Street, Town Hall, Deep River, CT 06417. Town Clerk, R/E and UCC Recording 860-526-6024; Fax 860-526-6023. Will search UCC records. This agency will not do a tax lien search. Will not search real estate records. **Other Phone Numbers:** Assessor 860-526-6029; Elections 860-526-6024; Vital Records 860-526-6024.

Derby City

City Clerk, 35 Fifth Street, Derby, CT 06418-1897. City Clerk, R/E and UCC Recording 203-736-1462; Fax 203-736-1458. Will search UCC records. This agency will not do a tax lien search. Will not search real estate records. **Other Phone Numbers:** Assessor 203-736-1455; Treasurer 203-736-1452; Appraiser/Auditor 203-736-1452; Elections 203-736-1462; Vital Records 203-736-1462.

Durham Town

Town Clerk, P.O. Box 428, Durham, CT 06422. Town Clerk, R/E and UCC Recording 860-349-3452; Fax 860-349-0547. Will search UCC records. This agency will not do a tax lien search. Will not search real estate records. **Other Phone Numbers:** Assessor 860-349-3453; Treasurer 860-349-3625; Elections 860-349-3452; Vital Records 860-349-3452.

East Granby Town

Town Clerk, P.O. Box TC, East Granby, CT 06026-0459. Town Clerk, R/E and UCC Recording 860-653-6528; Fax 860-653-4017. Will not search UCC records. This agency will not do a tax lien search. Will not search real estate records. **Other Phone Numbers:** Assessor 860-653-2852; Treasurer 860-653-0096; Elections 860-653-0097; Vital Records 860-653-6528; Selectmen 860-653-2576.

East Haddam Town

Town Clerk, PO Box K, Town Office Bldg, Town Office Building. PO Box K, East Haddam, CT 06423. 860-873-5027 R/E Recording: 203-873-8279. Will search UCC records. This agency will not do a tax lien search. Will not search real estate records. **Other Phone Numbers:** Assessor 203-873-5026.

East Hampton Town

Town Clerk, 20 East High Street, Town Hall, East Hampton, CT 06424. 860-267-2519 R/E Recording: 203-267-2519; Fax 860-267-1027. Will search UCC records. This agency will not do a tax lien search. Will not search real estate records. **Other Phone Numbers:** Assessor 203-267-2510.

East Hartford Town

Town Clerk, 740 Main Street, East Hartford, CT 06108-3126. 860-291-7230; Fax 860-289-0831. http://www.ci.east-hartford.ct.us/

Will search UCC records. This agency will not do a tax lien search. Will not search real estate records. **Other Phone Numbers:** Assessor 860-291-7260 x268; Vital Records 860-291-7230.

East Haven Town

Town Clerk, 250 Main Street, East Haven, CT 06512-3034. 203-468-3201; Fax 203-468-3372.
Will search UCC records. This agency will not do a tax lien search. Will not search real estate records. **Other Phone Numbers:** Assessor 203-468-3233.

East Lyme Town

Town Clerk, P.O. Box 519, Niantic, CT 06357. Town Clerk, R/E and UCC Recording 860-739-6931; Fax 860-739-6930.
Will search UCC records. This agency will not do a tax lien search. Will not search real estate records. **Other Phone Numbers:** Assessor 860-739-6931; Treasurer 860-739-6931; Vital Records 860-739-6931.

East Windsor Town

Town Clerk, P.O. Box 213, Broad Brook, CT 06016-0213. 860-623-9467 R/E Recording: 860-292-8255; Fax 860-623-4798.
Will search UCC records. This agency will not do a tax lien search. Will not search real estate records. **Other Phone Numbers:** Assessor 860-623-8878; Treasurer 860-292-5909; Elections 860-292-5915; Vital Records 860-292-8255.

Eastford

Town Clerk, P.O. Box 273, Eastford, CT 06242. 860-974-1885 R/E Recording: 203-974-1885; Fax 860-974-0624.
Will not search UCC records. This agency will not do a tax lien search. Will not search real estate records. **Other Phone Numbers:** Assessor 203-974-1291.

Easton Town

Town Clerk, 225 Center Road, Easton, CT 06612. 203-268-6291; Fax 203-261-6080.
Will search UCC records. This agency will not do a tax lien search. Will not search real estate records. **Other Phone Numbers:** Assessor 203-268-6291; Treasurer 203-268-6291; Appraiser/Auditor 203-268-6291; Elections 203-268-6291; Vital Records 203-268-6291.

Ellington Town

Town Clerk, P.O. Box 187, Ellington, CT 06029-0187. 860-875-3190 R/E Recording: 860-875-3105 UCC Recording: 860-875-3105; Fax 860-875-0788.
Will search UCC records. This agency will not do a tax lien search. Will not search real estate records. **Other Phone Numbers:** Assessor 860-870-3109; Treasurer 860-875-3115; Elections 860-875-3107; Vital Records 860-875-3105.

Enfield Town

Town Clerk, 820 Enfield Street, Enfield, CT 06082-2997. 860-253-6440 R/E Recording: 860-253-6435 UCC Recording: 860-253-6435; Fax 860-253-6310.
Will not search UCC records. This agency will not do a tax lien search. Will not search real estate records. **Online Access:** Tax Sales. Online access to the town's tax sale list is available free at http://www.enfield.org/Link_Tax.HTM. Use Control+F and search for name. **Other Phone Numbers:** Assessor 860-253-6339; Treasurer 860-253-6330; Elections 860-253-6320; Vital Records 860-253-6440.

Essex Town

Town Clerk, P.O. Box 98, Essex, CT 06426. 860-767-4344 R/E Recording: 860-767-4344 x129 UCC Recording: 860-767-4344 x129.

Will search UCC records. This agency will not do a tax lien search. Will not search real estate records. **Other Phone Numbers:** Assessor 860-767-4340 x124; Treasurer 860-767-4340 x122; Elections 860-767-4344 x129; Vital Records 860-767-4344 x129.

Fairfield Town

Town Clerk, 611 Old Post Road, Fairfield, CT 06430-6690. Town Clerk, R/E and UCC Recording 203-256-3090.
Will search UCC records. This agency will not do a tax lien search. Will not search real estate records. **Other Phone Numbers:** Assessor 203-256-3110; Elections 203-256-3090; Vital Records 203-256-3090.

Farmington Town

Town Clerk, 1 Monteith Drive, Farmington, CT 06032-1053. 860-673-8247 R/E Recording: 203-673-8247; Fax 860-675-7140.
Will search UCC records. This agency will not do a tax lien search. Will provide information on a simple RE search **Other Phone Numbers:** Assessor 203-673-8245.

Franklin Town

Town Clerk, 7 Meeting House Hill Road, Town Hall, Franklin, CT 06254. 860-642-7352 R/E Recording: 203-642-7352; Fax 860-642-6606.
Will not search UCC records. This agency will not do a tax lien search. Will not search real estate records. **Other Phone Numbers:** Assessor 203-642-6475; Treasurer 860-642-7352.

Glastonbury Town

Town Clerk, 2155 Main Street, Glastonbury, CT 06033. Town Clerk, R/E and UCC Recording 860-652-7616; Fax 860-652-7639. http://www.glasct.org
Will not search UCC records. This agency will not do a tax lien search. Will not search real estate records. **Online Access:** Property. Online access to town property information is available free on the GIS Interactive Mapping site at http://www.glasct.org/isa/intermaps.html. Click on "Property Information (Parcels)." **Other Phone Numbers:** Assessor 860-652-7604; Elections 860-652-7616; Vital Records 860-652-7616.

Goshen Town

Town Clerk, P.O. Box 54, Goshen, CT 06756-0054. Town Clerk, R/E and UCC Recording 860-491-3647.
Will not search UCC records. This agency will not do a tax lien search. Will not search real estate records. **Other Phone Numbers:** Assessor 860-491-2115; Elections 860-491-2398 x236; Vital Records 860-491-3275.

Granby Town

Town Clerk, 15 North Granby Road, Granby, CT 06035. 860-653-8949 R/E Recording: 203-653-4817.
Will search UCC records. This agency will not do a tax lien search. Will not search real estate records. **Online Access:** Assessor. Property tax records on the Assessor's database are available online at http://140.239.211.227/granbyct. Registration is required for full access; registration is free. **Other Phone Numbers:** Assessor 203-653-8952.

Greenwich Town

Town Clerk, P.O. Box 2540, Greenwich, CT 06836. 203-622-7897.
Will search UCC records. This agency will not do a tax lien search. Will not search real estate records. **Other Phone Numbers:** Assessor 203-622-7885.

Griswold Town

Town Clerk, P.O. Box 369, Jewett City, CT 06351. Town Clerk, R/E and UCC Recording 860-376-7064; Fax 860-376-7070.
Will search UCC records. This agency will not do a tax lien search. Will not search real estate records. **Other Phone Numbers:** Assessor 860-376-7072; Treasurer 860-376-7075; Appraiser/Auditor 860-376-7072; Elections 860-376-7062; Vital Records 860-376-7063.

Groton Town

Town Clerk, 45 Fort Hill Road, Groton, CT 06340. Town Clerk, R/E and UCC Recording 860-441-6642.
Will not search UCC records. This agency will not do a tax lien search. Will not search real estate records. **Other Phone Numbers:** Assessor 860-441-6660; Treasurer 860-441-6609; Elections 860-441-6640; Vital Records 860-441-6640.

Guilford Town

Town Clerk, 31 Park Street, Town Hall, Guilford, CT 06437. 203-453-8001; http://www.ci.guilford.ct.us/
This agency will not search UCC records. This agency will not do a tax lien search. Will not search real estate records. **Other Phone Numbers:** Assessor 203-453-8010; Treasurer 203-453-8022.

Haddam Town

Town Clerk, P.O. Box 87, Haddam, CT 06438. 860-345-8531 R/E Recording: 203-345-8531; Fax 860-345-3730.
Will search UCC records. This agency will not do a tax lien search. Will not search real estate records. **Other Phone Numbers:** Assessor 203-345-8531 x213.

Hamden Town

Town Clerk, 2372 Whitney Avenue, Memorial Town Hall, Hamden, CT 06518. 203-287-2510 R/E Recording: 203-287-2500; Fax 203-287-2518.
Will search UCC records. Will search real estate records **Online Access:** Assessor. Property records on the Assessor's database are available free online at http://data.visionappraisal.com/hamdenct. Registration is required for full access; registration is free. **Other Phone Numbers:** Assessor 203-287-2529; Treasurer 203-387-2530.

Hampton Town

Town Clerk, P.O. Box 143, Hampton, CT 06247-0143. 860-455-9132 R/E Recording: 860-455-9132 x1 UCC Recording: 860-455-9132 x1; Fax 860-455-0517.
Will search UCC records; no search fee. This agency will not do a tax lien search. Will not search real estate records. **Other Phone Numbers:** Assessor 860-455-9132 x5; Treasurer 860-455-9132 x4; Elections 860-455-9132 x1; Vital Records 860-455-9132 x1.

Hartford City

City Clerk, 550 Main Street, Hartford, CT 06103-2992. 860-543-8580 R/E Recording: 203-722-8040; Fax 860-722-8041.
Will search UCC records. This agency will not do a tax lien search. Will not search real estate records. **Other Phone Numbers:** Assessor 203-543-8540; Treasurer 860-543-8530.

Hartland Town

Town Clerk, Town Office Building, 22 South Road, East Hartland, CT 06027. 860-653-3542; Fax 860-653-7919.
Will search UCC records. This agency will not do a tax lien search. Will not search real estate records. **Other Phone Numbers:** Assessor 860-653-9687; Selectmen 860-653-6800.

Harwinton Town

Town Clerk, 100 Bentley Drive, Town Hall, Harwinton, CT 06791. Town Clerk, R/E and UCC Recording 860-485-9613; Fax 860-485-0051.
Will not search UCC records. This agency will not do a tax lien search. Will not search real estate records. **Other Phone Numbers:** Assessor 860-485-0898; Treasurer 860-485-9051; Elections 860-485-9613; Vital Records 860-485-9613.

Hebron Town

Town Clerk, P.O. Box 156, Hebron, CT 06248. 860-228-5971 x124 R/E Recording: 860-228-5971 UCC Recording: 860-228-5971; Fax 860-228-4859.
Will not search UCC records. This agency will not do a tax lien search. Will not search real estate records. **Other Phone Numbers:** Assessor 860-228-5971; Treasurer 860-228-5971; Appraiser/Auditor 860-228-5971; Elections 860-228-5971; Vital Records 860-228-5971.

Kent Town

Town Clerk, P.O. Box 678, Kent, CT 06757-0678. 860-927-3433 R/E Recording: 203-927-3433.
Will search UCC records. This agency will not do a tax lien search. Will not search real estate records. **Other Phone Numbers:** Assessor 203-927-3160.

Killingly Town

Town Clerk, P.O. Box 6000, Danielson, CT 06239. 860-779-5307 R/E Recording: 203-774-8601; Fax 860-779-5394.
Will not search UCC records. This agency will not do a tax lien search. Will not search real estate records. **Other Phone Numbers:** Assessor 203-779-5323; Treasurer 203-779-5337; Elections 203-779-5302; Vital Records 860-779-5307.

Killingworth Town

Town Clerk, 323 Route 81, Killingworth, CT 06419-1298. 860-663-1616 R/E Recording: 203-63-1765; Fax 860-663-3305.
Will search UCC records. This agency will not do a tax lien search. Will not search real estate records. **Other Phone Numbers:** Assessor 203-663-2002.

Lebanon Town

Town Clerk, 579 Exeter Road, Town Hall, Lebanon, CT 06249. 860-642-7319 R/E Recording: 203-642-7319.
Will search UCC records. This agency will not do a tax lien search. Will not search real estate records. **Online Access:** Assessor. Property Tax records on the Assessor's Database are available free online at http://140.239.211.227/lebanonct. Registration is required for full access; registration is free. **Other Phone Numbers:** Assessor 203-642-6141.

Ledyard Town

Town Clerk, 741 Col. Ledyard Highway, Ledyard, CT 06339. 860-464-8740 x230 R/E Recording: 203-464-8740; Fax 860-464-1126.
Will search UCC records. This agency will not do a tax lien search. Will not search real estate records. **Other Phone Numbers:** Assessor 203-464-8740 x237; Treasurer 860-464-8740 x228.

Lisbon Town

Town Clerk, 1 Newent Road, RD 2 Town Hall, Lisbon, CT 06351-9802. 860-376-2708; Fax 860-376-6545.
Will not search UCC records. This agency will not do a tax lien search. Will not search real estate records. **Other Phone Numbers:** Assessor 860-376-5115; Treasurer 860-376-3400.

Litchfield Town

Town Clerk, P.O. Box 488, Litchfield, CT 06759-0488. Town Clerk, R/E and UCC Recording 860-567-7561.
Will not search UCC records. This agency will not do a tax lien search. Will not search real estate records. **Other Phone Numbers:** Assessor 860-567-7559; Treasurer 860-567-7554; Vital Records 860-567-7561; Registrar 860-567-7558.

Lyme Town

Town Clerk, 480 Hamburg Rd., Town Hall, Lyme, CT 06371. Town Clerk, R/E and UCC Recording 860-434-7733; Fax 860-434-2989.
Will search UCC records. This agency will not do a tax lien search. Will not search real estate records. **Other Phone Numbers:** Assessor 860-434-8094; Treasurer 860-434-7733; Appraiser/Auditor 860-434-8094; Elections 860-434-7733; Vital Records 860-434-7733.

Madison Town

Town Clerk, 8 Campus Dr., Madison, CT 06443-2538. Town Clerk, R/E and UCC Recording 203-245-5672; Fax 203-245-5613. http://140.239.211.227/MadisonCT
Will search UCC records. This agency will not do a tax lien search. Will not search real estate records. **Online Access:** Assessor. Property records on the Town assessor database are available free online at http://140.239.211.227/MadisonCT. Registration is required for full access; registration is free. **Other Phone Numbers:** Assessor 203-245-5652; Elections 203-245-5671; Vital Records 203-245-5672.

Manchester Town

Town Clerk, P.O. Box 191, Manchester, CT 06045-0191. 860-647-3037 R/E Recording: 203-647-3037; Fax 860-647-3029. http://140.239.211.227/manchesterCT
Will search UCC records. This agency will not do a tax lien search. Will not search real estate records. **Online Access:** Assessor. Property records on the Town assessor database are available free online at http://140.239.211.227/manchesterCT. Registration is required for full access; registration is free. **Other Phone Numbers:** Assessor 203-647-3016; Treasurer 860-647-3023.

Mansfield Town

Town Clerk, 4 South Eagleville Road, Mansfield, CT 06268. 860-429-3302 R/E Recording: 203-429-3302.
Will not search UCC records. This agency will not do a tax lien search. Will not search real estate records. **Other Phone Numbers:** Assessor 203-429-3327; Elections 860-429-3369.

Marlborough Town

Town Clerk, P.O. Box 29, Marlborough, CT 06447. 860-295-6206 R/E Recording: 203-295-0713; Fax 860-295-0317.
Will search UCC records. This agency will not do a tax lien search. Will not search real estate records. **Other Phone Numbers:** Assessor 203-295-6201.

Meriden City

City Clerk, 142 East Main Street, Meriden, CT 06450-8022. City Clerk, R/E and UCC Recording 203-630-4030; Fax 203-630-4059. http://www.cityofmeriden.org/government/
Will search UCC records. This agency will not do a tax lien search. Will not search real estate records. **Other Phone Numbers:** Assessor 203-630-4071; Elections 203-630-4075; Vital Records 203-630-4030.

Middlebury Town

Town Clerk, P.O. Box 392, Middlebury, CT 06762-0392. Town Clerk, R/E and UCC Recording 203-758-2557.
Will search UCC records. This agency will not do a tax lien search. Will not search real estate records. **Other Phone Numbers:** Assessor 203-758-1447; Elections 203-758-2557; Vital Records 203-758-2557.

Middlefield Town

Town Clerk, P.O. Box 179, Middlefield, CT 06455. Town Clerk, R/E and UCC Recording 860-349-7116; Fax 860-349-7115. http://www.munic.state.ct.us/MIDDLEFIELD/contents.htm
Will search UCC records. This agency will not do a tax lien search. Will not search real estate records. **Other Phone Numbers:** Assessor 860-349-7111; Treasurer 860-349-7114; Elections 860-349-7119; Vital Records 860-349-7116.

Middletown City

City Clerk, P.O. Box 1300, Middletown, CT 06457. City Clerk, R/E and UCC Recording 860-344-3459; Fax 860-344-3591. http://www.cityofmiddletown.com/Departments.htm
Will search UCC records. This agency will not do a tax lien search. Will not search real estate records. **Other Phone Numbers:** Assessor 860-344-3454; Treasurer 860-344-3438; Elections 860-344-3459; Vital Records 860-344-3474.

Milford City

City Clerk, 70 West River Street, Milford, CT 06460-3364. 203-783-3210.
Will search UCC records. This agency will not do a tax lien search. Will not search real estate records. **Online Access:** Assessor. Online access to the Assessor's database for Milford is available free online at http://data.visionappraisal.com/milfordct/. User ID is required; registration is free. **Other Phone Numbers:** Assessor 203-788-3215; Vital Records 203-783-3210.

Monroe Town

Town Clerk, 7 Fan Hill Road, Monroe, CT 06468-1800. 203-452-5417 R/E Recording: 203-452-5427 UCC Recording: 203-452-5427; Fax 203-261-6197.
Will search UCC records. This agency will not do a tax lien search. Will not search real estate records. **Other Phone Numbers:** Assessor 203-452-5469; Treasurer 203-452-5433; Elections 203-452-5417; Vital Records 203-452-5427.

Montville Town

Town Clerk, 310 Norwich-New London Tpke., Town Hall, Uncasville, CT 06382. 860-848-1349 R/E Recording: 203-848-1349; Fax 860-848-1521.
Will search UCC records. This agency will not do a tax lien search. Will not search real estate records. **Other Phone Numbers:** Assessor 203-848-8221; Treasurer 860-848-0139.

Morris Town

Town Clerk, P.O. Box 66, Morris, CT 06763-0066. 860-567-7433; Fax 860-567-7432.
Will not search UCC records. This agency will not do a tax lien search. Will not search real estate records. **Other Phone Numbers:** Assessor 860-567-7435; Treasurer 860-567-7435; Elections 860-567-7433; Vital Records 860-567-7433.

Naugatuck Town

Town Clerk, Town Hall, 229 Church Street, Naugatuck, CT 06770. 203-720-7055 R/E Recording: 203-729-4571; Fax 203-720-7099.

Will search UCC records. This agency will not do a tax lien search. Will not search real estate records. **Other Phone Numbers:** Assessor 203-729-4571; Treasurer 203-729-4571.

New Britain Town

Town Clerk, 27 W. Main Street, New Britain, CT 06051. 860-826-3344 R/E Recording: 203-826-3344; Fax 860-826-3348.
Will not search UCC records. This agency will not do a tax lien search. Will not search real estate records. **Other Phone Numbers:** Assessor 203-826-3323.

New Canaan Town

Town Clerk, 77 Main Street, Town Hall, New Canaan, CT 06840. 203-972-2323; Fax 203-966-2387.
Will not search UCC records. This agency will not do a tax lien search. Will not search real estate records. **Other Phone Numbers:** Assessor 203-927-2335; Treasurer 203-927-2340; Elections 203-972-8877; Vital Records 203-972-2323.

New Fairfield Town

Town Clerk, Route 39, Town Hall, New Fairfield, CT 06812. 203-312-5616 R/E Recording: 203-746-8110.
Will search UCC records. This agency will not do a tax lien search. Will not search real estate records. **Other Phone Numbers:** Assessor 203-312-5624.

New Hartford Town

Town Clerk, P.O. Box 426, New Hartford, CT 06057. Town Clerk, R/E and UCC Recording 860-379-5037; Fax 860-379-0940.
Will not search UCC records. This agency will not do a tax lien search. Will not search real estate records. **Other Phone Numbers:** Assessor 860-379-5235; Treasurer 860-379-3389; Elections 860-738-9721; Vital Records 860-379-5037.

New Haven City

City Clerk, 200 Orange Street, Room 202, New Haven, CT 06510. 203-946-8339 R/E Recording: 203-946-8344 UCC Recording: 203-946-8344; Fax 203-946-6974.
Will search UCC records. This agency will not do a tax lien search. Will not search real estate records. **Other Phone Numbers:** Assessor 203-787-8066; Treasurer 203-946-8300; Elections 203-946-8346; Vital Records 203-946-8084.

New London City

City Clerk, 181 State Street, New London, CT 06320. 860-447-5205 R/E Recording: 203-447-5205; Fax 860-447-1644.
File here only for the city of New London, not for the county. There is no county filing in Connecticut. Will search UCC records. This agency will not do a tax lien search. Will not search real estate records. **Online Access:** Assessor. Property tax records on the Assessor's database are available free online at http://140.239.211.227/newlondonct. Registration is required for full access; registration is free. **Other Phone Numbers:** Assessor 203-447-5216; Treasurer 860-447-5209/5321.

New Milford Town

Town Clerk, P.O. Box 360, New Milford, CT 06776. 860-355-6020 R/E Recording: 203-355-6020; Fax 860-355-6002.
http://www.newmilford.org/agencies/home.htm
Will search UCC records. This agency will not do a tax lien search. Will not search real estate records. **Other Phone Numbers:** Assessor 203-355-6070.

Newington Town

Town Clerk, 131 Cedar Street, Newington, CT 06111-2696. Town Clerk, R/E and UCC Recording 860-665-8545; http://www.ci.newington.ct.us
Will not search UCC records. This agency will not do a tax lien search. Will not search real estate records. **Other Phone Numbers:** Assessor 860-665-8530; Elections 860-665-8516; Vital Records 860-665-8545.

Newtown Town

Town Clerk, 45 Main Street, Newtown, CT 06470. 203-270-4210.
Will not search UCC records. This agency will not do a tax lien search. Will not search real estate records. **Other Phone Numbers:** Assessor 203-270-4240; Treasurer 203-270-4221; Elections 203-270-4250; Vital Records 203-270-4210.

Norfolk Town

Town Clerk, P.O. Box 552, Norfolk, CT 06058-0552. 860-542-5679.
Will not search UCC records. This agency will not do a tax lien search. Will not search real estate records. **Other Phone Numbers:** Assessor 860-542-5287; Treasurer 860-542-5679; Elections 860-542-5679; Vital Records 860-542-5679.

North Branford Town

Town Clerk, P.O. Box 287, North Branford, CT 06471-0287. 203-315-6015.
Will not search UCC records. This agency will not do a tax lien search. Will not search real estate records. **Other Phone Numbers:** Assessor 203-315-6013; Treasurer 203-315-6002; Vital Records 203-315-6015.

North Canaan Town

Town Clerk, P.O. Box 338, North Canaan, CT 06018. 860-824-3138 R/E Recording: 203-824-7246; Fax 860-824-3139.
Will search UCC records. This agency will not do a tax lien search. Will not search real estate records. **Other Phone Numbers:** Assessor 203-824-3137.

North Haven Town

Town Clerk, 18 Church Street, Town Hall, North Haven, CT 06473. 203-239-5321 x541 R/E Recording: 203-239-5321.
Will search UCC records. This agency will not do a tax lien search. Will not search real estate records. **Other Phone Numbers:** Assessor 203-239-5321 x700.

North Stonington Town

Town Clerk, 40 Main Street, North Stonington, CT 06359. 860-535-2877 x21; Fax 860-535-4554.
Will search UCC records. This agency will not do a tax lien search. Will not search real estate records. **Online Access:** Assessor. Online access to the town assessor database is available free at http://data.vision appraisal.com/NorthStoningtonCT. **Other Phone Numbers:** Assessor 860-535-2877 x23; Treasurer 860-535-2877 x10.

Norwalk City

Town Clerk, P.O. Box 5125, Norwalk, CT 06856-5125. 203-854-7746 R/E Recording: 203-854-7748.
Will search UCC records. This agency will not do a tax lien search. Will not search real estate records. **Other Phone Numbers:** Assessor 203-854-7887.

Norwich City

City Clerk, 100 Broadway, City Hall, Room 214, Norwich, CT 06360. 860-823-3732 R/E Recording: 203-886-2381; Fax 860-823-3790.

Will not search UCC records. This agency will not do a tax lien search. Will not search real estate records. **Other Phone Numbers:** Assessor 860-886-2381 x222.

Old Lyme Town

Town Clerk, 52 Lyme Street, Old Lyme, CT 06371. 860-434-1605 x221 R/E Recording: 203-434-1605 x221; Fax 860-434-9283.
Will search UCC records. This agency will not do a tax lien search. Will not search real estate records. **Online Access:** Assessor. Property tax records on the Assessor's database are available online at http://140.239.211.227/oldlymect. Registration is required for full access; registration is free. **Other Phone Numbers:** Assessor 203-434-1605 x218; Treasurer 203-434-1605 x232; Appraiser/Auditor 203-434-1605 x218; Elections 203-434-1605 x230; Vital Records 860-434-1605 x221.

Old Saybrook Town

Town Clerk, 302 Main Street, Old Saybrook, CT 06475. Town Clerk, R/E and UCC Recording 860-395-3135 UCC Recording: 860-395-3137; Fax 860-395-5014. http://www.oldsaybrookct.com
Will not search real estate records. **Online Access:** Assessor. Property tax records on the Assessor's database are available free online at http://oldsaybrookct. Registration is required for full access; registration is free. **Other Phone Numbers:** Assessor 860-395-3137; Treasurer 860-395-3132; Elections 860-395-3135; Vital Records 860-395-3135.

Orange Town

Town Clerk, Town Hall, 617 Orange Center Rd., Orange, CT 06477. 203-891-2122 R/E Recording: 203-795-0751; Fax 203-891-2185.
Will search UCC records. This agency will not do a tax lien search. Will not search real estate records. **Other Phone Numbers:** Assessor 203-891-2122 x722.

Oxford Town

Town Clerk, 486 Oxford Road, Oxford, CT 06478. 203-888-2543.
Will not search UCC records. This agency will not do a tax lien search. Will not search real estate records. **Other Phone Numbers:** Assessor 203-888-2543; Treasurer 203-888-2543; Elections 203-888-2543; Vital Records 203-888-2543.

Plainfield Town

Town Clerk, 8 Community Avenue, Town Hall, Plainfield, CT 06374. 860-564-4075 R/E Recording: 860-230-3009 UCC Recording: 860-230-3009.
Will not search UCC records. This agency will not do a tax lien search. Will not search real estate records. **Other Phone Numbers:** Assessor 860-230-3006; Treasurer 860-230-3003; Elections 860-230-3024; Vital Records 860-230-3009.

Plainville Town

Town Clerk, 1 Central Square, Municipal Center, Plainville, CT 06062. 860-793-0221 R/E Recording: 203-793-0221.
Will not search UCC records. This agency will not do a tax lien search. Will not search real estate records. **Other Phone Numbers:** Assessor 203-793-0221 x242.

Plymouth Town

Town Clerk, 80 Main Street, Town Hall, Terryville, CT 06786. 860-585-4039; Fax 860-585-4015.
Will search UCC records. This agency will not do a tax lien search. Will not search real estate records. **Other Phone Numbers:** Assessor 860-585-4006; Treasurer 860-585-4009; Elections 860-585-4033; Vital Records 860-585-4039.

Pomfret Town

Town Clerk, 5 Haven Road, Pomfret Center, CT 06259. Town Clerk, R/E and UCC Recording 860-974-0343; Fax 860-974-3950.
Will search UCC records. This agency will not do a tax lien search. Will not search real estate records. **Online Access:** Assessor. Property records on the Assessor's database are available free online at http://data.visionappraisal.com/pomfretct. Registration is required for full access; registration is free. **Other Phone Numbers:** Assessor 860-974-1674; Vital Records 860-974-0343.

Portland Town

Town Clerk, P.O. Box 71, Portland, CT 06480. Town Clerk, R/E and UCC Recording 860-342-6743; Fax 860-342-0001.
Will search UCC records. This agency will not do a tax lien search. Will not search real estate records. **Other Phone Numbers:** Assessor 860-342-6744; Treasurer 860-342-6726; Elections 860-342-6743; Vital Records 860-342-6743.

Preston Town

Town Clerk, 389 Route 2, Town Hall, Preston, CT 06365-8830. 860-887-9821 R/E Recording: 203-887-9821; Fax 860-885-1905.
Will search UCC records. This agency will not do a tax lien search. Will not search real estate records. **Other Phone Numbers:** Assessor 203-889-2529.

Prospect Town

Town Clerk, 36 Center Street, Prospect, CT 06712-1699. 203-758-4461; Fax 203-758-4466.
Will search UCC records. This agency will not do a tax lien search. Will not search real estate records. **Other Phone Numbers:** Assessor 203-758-4461; Vital Records 203-758-4461.

Putnam Town

Town Clerk, 126 Church Street, Putnam, CT 06260. Town Clerk, R/E and UCC Recording 860-963-6807; Fax 860-963-2001.
Will search UCC records. This agency will not do a tax lien search. Will not search real estate records. **Other Phone Numbers:** Assessor 860-963-6802; Treasurer 860-963-6809.

Redding Town

Town Clerk, P.O. Box 1028, Redding, CT 06875-1028. Town Clerk, R/E and UCC Recording 203-938-2377; Fax 203-938-8816.
Will not search UCC records. This agency will not do a tax lien search. Will not search real estate records. **Other Phone Numbers:** Assessor 203-938-2626.

Ridgefield Town

Town Clerk, 400 Main Street, Ridgefield, CT 06877. 203-431-2783 R/E Recording: 203-438-7301; Fax 203-431-2722.
http://www.ridgefieldct.org/townhall/assessor.htm
Will search UCC records. This agency will not do a tax lien search. Will not search real estate records. **Other Phone Numbers:** Assessor 203-431-2706.

Rocky Hill Town

Town Clerk, P.O. Box 657, Rocky Hill, CT 06067. 860-258-2705.
Will search UCC records. This agency will not do a tax lien search. Will not search real estate records. **Other Phone Numbers:** Assessor 860-258-2774.

Roxbury Town

Town Clerk, 29 North St., Roxbury, CT 06783-1405. 860-354-3328 R/E Recording: 203-354-3328; Fax 860-354-0560.
Will search UCC records. This agency will not do a tax lien search. Will not search real estate records. **Other Phone Numbers:** Assessor 203-354-2634.

Salem Town

Town Clerk, Town Office Building, 270 Hartford Road, Salem, CT 06420. 860-859-3873 x170 R/E Recording: 203-859-3873; Fax 860-859-1184.
Will search UCC records. This agency will not do a tax lien search. Will not search real estate records. **Other Phone Numbers:** Assessor 203-859-3873.

Salisbury Town

Town Clerk, P.O. Box 548, Salisbury, CT 06068. 860-435-5182 R/E Recording: 203-435-9511; Fax 860-435-5172.
Will search UCC records. This agency will not do a tax lien search. Will not search real estate records. **Other Phone Numbers:** Assessor 203-435-9570; Treasurer 860-435-9140.

Scotland Town

Town Clerk, P.O. Box 122, Scotland, CT 06264. 860-423-9634 R/E Recording: 203-423-9634; Fax 860-423-3666.
Will search UCC records. This agency will not do a tax lien search. Will not search real estate records. **Other Phone Numbers:** Assessor 203-423-9634; Treasurer 203-423-9634.

Seymour Town

Town Clerk, 1 First Street, Town Hall, Seymour, CT 06483-2817. 203-888-0519.
Will search UCC records. This agency will not do a tax lien search. Will not search real estate records. **Other Phone Numbers:** Assessor 203-888-9508; Treasurer 203-888-0581.

Sharon Town

Town Clerk, P.O. Box 224, Sharon, CT 06069-0224. 860-364-5224 R/E Recording: 203-364-5224; Fax 860-364-5789.
Will search UCC records. This agency will not do a tax lien search. Will not search real estate records. **Other Phone Numbers:** Assessor 203-364-0205.

Shelton City

City Clerk, P.O. Box 364, Shelton, CT 06484-0364. 203-924-1555 R/E Recording: 203-924-1562; Fax 203-924-1721.
Will search UCC records. This agency will not do a tax lien search. Will not search real estate records. **Other Phone Numbers:** Assessor 203-924-1555 x335.

Sherman Town

Town Clerk, P.O. Box 39, Sherman, CT 06784-0039. Town Clerk, R/E and UCC Recording 860-354-5281; Fax 860-350-5041.
Will not search UCC records. This agency will not do a tax lien search. Will not search real estate records. **Other Phone Numbers:** Assessor 860-355-0376; Treasurer 860-354-5281; Vital Records 860-354-5281.

Simsbury Town

Town Clerk, P.O. Box 495, Simsbury, CT 06070. 860-658-3243 R/E Recording: 203-651-3751; Fax 860-658-3206.
Will search UCC records. This agency will not do a tax lien search. Will not search real estate records. **Other Phone Numbers:** Assessor 203-651-3751.

Somers Town

Town Clerk, P.O. Box 308, Somers, CT 06071. 860-763-8206; Fax 860-763-8228.
Will search UCC records. This agency will not do a tax lien search. Will not search real estate records. **Other Phone Numbers:** Assessor 860-763-8203; Treasurer 860-763-8204; Vital Records 860-763-8206.

South Windsor Town

Town Clerk, 1540 Sullivan Avenue, South Windsor, CT 06074. 860-644-2511 x225 R/E Recording: 203-644-2511; Fax 860-644-3781. www.southwindsor.org
Will not search UCC records. This agency will not do a tax lien search. Will not search real estate records. **Other Phone Numbers:** Assessor 203-644-2511 x213; Treasurer 860-644-2511 x261.

Southbury Town

Town Clerk, 501 Main Street South, Southbury, CT 06488-2295. Town Clerk, R/E and UCC Recording 203-262-0657; Fax 203-264-9762.
Will not search UCC records. This agency will not do a tax lien search. Will not search real estate records. **Other Phone Numbers:** Assessor 203-262-0647; Treasurer 203-262-0663; Elections 203-262-0657; Vital Records 203-262-0657.

Southington Town

Town Clerk, P.O. Box 152, Southington, CT 06489. 860-276-6211 R/E Recording: 203-276-6211; Fax 860-628-8669.
Will search UCC records. This agency will not do a tax lien search. Will not search real estate records. **Other Phone Numbers:** Assessor 203-276-6205.

Sprague Town

Town Clerk, P.O. Box 162, Baltic, CT 06330. 860-822-3001 R/E Recording: 203-822-6223; Fax 860-822-3013.
Will not search UCC records. This agency will not do a tax lien search. Will not search real estate records. **Other Phone Numbers:** Assessor 203-822-3002; Treasurer 203-822-3004.

Stafford Town

Town Clerk, P.O. Box 11, Stafford Springs, CT 06076. 860-684-1765 R/E Recording: 203-684-2532; Fax 860-684-1765.
Will not search UCC records. This agency will not do a tax lien search. Will not search real estate records. **Other Phone Numbers:** Assessor 203-684-1786.

Stamford City

City Clerk, PO Box 10152, Stamford, CT 06904. City Clerk, R/E and UCC Recording 203-977-4054 UCC Recording: 203-977-4707; Fax 203-977-4943.
http://www.cityofstamford.org/Welcome.htm
Will search UCC records. This agency will not do a tax lien search. Will not search real estate records. **Online Access:** Assessor, Real Estate, Personal Property. Online access to the city tax assessor database is available free online at www.cityofstamford.org/Tax/main.htm. A land records index should be online in Fall, 2001. **Other Phone Numbers:** Assessor 203-977-4019; Treasurer 203-977-4185; Elections 203-977-4011; Vital Records 203-977-4055.

Sterling Town

Town Clerk, P.O. Box 157, Oneco, CT 06373-0157. Town Clerk, R/E and UCC Recording 860-564-2657; Fax 860-564-1660.
Will search UCC records. This agency will not do a tax lien search. Will not search real estate records. **Other Phone Numbers:** Assessor 860-564-3030; Treasurer

860-564-2904; Elections 860-564-2657; Vital Records 860-564-2657.

Stonington Town

Town Clerk, P.O. Box 352, Stonington, CT 06378. 860-535-5060 R/E Recording: 203-535-4721; Fax 860-535-5062.
Will not search UCC records. This agency will not do a tax lien search. Will not search real estate records. **Other Phone Numbers:** Assessor 203-535-5098; Elections 203-535-5047.

Stratford Town

Town Clerk, 2725 Main Street, Room 101, Stratford, CT 06615. 203-385-4020; Fax 203-385-4108.
Will search UCC records. This agency will not do a tax lien search. Will not search real estate records. **Other Phone Numbers:** Assessor 203-385-4025; Elections 203-385-4028.

Suffield Town

Town Clerk, 83 Mountain Road, Town Hall, Suffield, CT 06078. 860-668-3880 R/E Recording: 203-668-7391; Fax 860-668-3898.
Will search UCC records. This agency will not do a tax lien search. Will not search real estate records. **Online Access:** Assessor. Property tax records on the Assessor's database are available free online at http://140.239.211.227/suffieldct. Registration is required for full access; registration is free. **Other Phone Numbers:** Assessor 203-668-3866.

Thomaston Town

Town Clerk, 158 Main Street, Thomaston, CT 06787. 860-283-4141 R/E Recording: 203-283-4141; Fax 860-283-1013.
Will not search UCC records. This agency will not do a tax lien search. Will not search real estate records. **Other Phone Numbers:** Assessor 203-283-0305; Treasurer 203-283-9678.

Thompson Town

Town Clerk, P.O. Box 899, No. Grosvenor Dale, CT 06255. 860-923-9900 R/E Recording: 203-923-9900; Fax 860-923-3836.
Will search UCC records. This agency will not do a tax lien search. Will not search real estate records. **Other Phone Numbers:** Assessor 203-923-2259.

Tolland Town

Town Clerk, Hicks Memorial Municipal Center, 21 Tolland Green, Tolland, CT 06084. 860-871-3630 R/E Recording: 203-871-3630; Fax 860-871-3663.
Do not confuse this town with the County of Tolland. Only Town of Tolland filings go here. Will not search UCC records. This agency will not do a tax lien search. Will not search real estate records. **Other Phone Numbers:** Assessor 203-871-3650; Treasurer 203-871-3658; Elections 203-871-3634; Vital Records 860-871-3630.

Torrington City

Town Clerk, 140 Main Street, City Hall, Torrington, CT 06790. 860-489-2236 R/E Recording: 860-489-2241; Fax 860-489-2548. http://www.torrington-ct.org
Will search UCC records. This agency will not do a tax lien search. Will not search real estate records. **Other Phone Numbers:** Assessor 860-489-2222; Treasurer 860-489-2334; Elections 860-489-2236; Vital Records 860-489-2236.

Trumbull Town

Town Clerk, 5866 Main Street, Trumbull, CT 06611. 203-452-5035; Fax 203-452-5094.

Will search UCC records. This agency will not do a tax lien search. Will not search real estate records. **Other Phone Numbers:** Assessor 203-452-5016; Treasurer 203-452-5014; Elections 203-452-5058; Vital Records 203-452-5035.

Union Town

Town Clerk, 1043 Buckley Highway, Route 171, Union, CT 06076-9520. 860-684-3770 R/E Recording: 203-684-3770; Fax 860-684-8830.
Will search UCC records. This agency will not do a tax lien search. Will not search real estate records. **Other Phone Numbers:** Assessor 203-684-5705.

Vernon Town

Town Clerk, 14 Park Place, Rockville, CT 06066. Town Clerk, R/E and UCC Recording 860-870-3662; Fax 860-870-3683. http://www.munic.state.ct.us/vernon/vernon.htm
Will not search UCC records. This agency will not do a tax lien search. Will not search real estate records. **Other Phone Numbers:** Assessor 860-870-3625; Treasurer 860-870-3660.

Voluntown Town

Town Clerk, P.O. Box 96, Voluntown, CT 06384-0096. Town Clerk, R/E and UCC Recording 860-376-4089; Fax 860-376-3295. http://www.voluntown.gov
Will search UCC records. This agency will not do a tax lien search. Will not search real estate records. **Other Phone Numbers:** Assessor 860-376-3927; Treasurer 860-376-3927.

Wallingford Town

Town Clerk, P.O. Box 427, Wallingford, CT 06492. Town Clerk, R/E and UCC Recording 203-294-2145; Fax 203-294-2150.
Will not search UCC records. This agency will not do a tax lien search. Will not search real estate records. **Other Phone Numbers:** Assessor 203-294-2001; Treasurer 203-294-2042; Appraiser/Auditor 203-294-2001; Elections 203-294-2125; Vital Records 203-294-2145.

Warren Town

Town Clerk, 7 Sackett Hill Road, Town Hall, Warren, CT 06754. 860-868-0090 R/E Recording: 203-868-0090; Fax 860-868-0090.
Will search UCC records. This agency will not do a tax lien search. Will not search real estate records. **Other Phone Numbers:** Assessor 203-868-7887.

Washington Town

Town Clerk, P.O. Box 383, Washington Depot, CT 06794. 860-868-2786 R/E Recording: 203-868-2786; Fax 860-868-3103.
Will search UCC records. This agency will not do a tax lien search. Will not search real estate records. **Other Phone Numbers:** Assessor 203-868-0398.

Waterbury City

Town Clerk, 235 Grand Street, City Hall, Waterbury, CT 06702. Town Clerk, R/E and UCC Recording 203-574-6806; Fax 203-574-6887.
Will search UCC records. This agency will not do a tax lien search. Will not search real estate records. **Other Phone Numbers:** Assessor 203-574-6821; Elections 203-574-6751; Vital Records 203-574-6801.

Waterford Town

Town Clerk, 15 Rope Ferry Road, Waterford, CT 06385. Town Clerk, R/E and UCC Recording 860-444-5831; Fax 860-437-0352.
Will search UCC records. This agency will not do a tax lien search. Will not search real estate records. **Other**

Phone Numbers: Assessor 860-444-5820; Vital Records 860-444-5831.

Watertown Town

Town Clerk, 37 DeForest Street, Watertown, CT 06795. Town Clerk, R/E and UCC Recording 860-945-5230.
Will not search UCC records. This agency will not do a tax lien search. Will not search real estate records. **Other Phone Numbers:** Assessor 860-945-5235; Treasurer 860-945-5261; Elections 860-945-5230; Vital Records 860-945-5230.

West Hartford Town

Town Clerk, 50 South Main Street, Room 313 Town Hall Common, West Hartford, CT 06107-2431. 860-523-3148 R/E Recording: 860-523-3100; Fax 860-523-3522.
Will not search UCC records. This agency will not do a tax lien search. Will not search real estate records. **Other Phone Numbers:** Assessor 860-523-3119; Treasurer 860-523-3188; Appraiser/Auditor 860-523-3119; Elections 860-523-3181; Vital Records 860-523-3151.

West Haven City

City Clerk, P.O. Box 526, West Haven, CT 06516. 203-937-3534 R/E Recording: 203-937-3535; Fax 203-937-3706.
Will search UCC records. This agency will not do a tax lien search. Will not search real estate records. **Other Phone Numbers:** Assessor 203-937-3513.

Westbrook Town

Town Clerk, P.O. Box G, Westbrook, CT 06498-0676. 860-399-3044 R/E Recording: 860-399-9723; Fax 860-399-9568.
Will search UCC records. This agency will not do a tax lien search. Will not search real estate records. **Other Phone Numbers:** Assessor 860-399-3045.

Weston Town

Town Clerk, P.O. Box 1007, Weston, CT 06883. 203-222-2616 R/E Recording: 203-222-2682; Fax 203-222-8871. http://www.weston-ct.com
Will search UCC records. This agency will not do a tax lien search. Will not search real estate records. **Other Phone Numbers:** Assessor 203-222-2606.

Westport Town

Town Clerk, P.O. Box 549, Westport, CT 06881. 203-341-1110 R/E Recording: 203-226-8311; Fax 203-341-1112. http://www.ci.westport.ct.us/govt/services
Will search UCC records. This agency will not do a tax lien search. Will not search real estate records. **Online Access:** Assessor. Online access to the 2000 assessments database is available free at www.ci.westport.ct.us/govt/services/finance/assessor/default.asp. **Other Phone Numbers:** Assessor 203-226-8311 x103.

Wethersfield Town

Town Clerk, 505 Silas Deane Highway, Wethersfield, CT 06109. Town Clerk, R/E and UCC Recording 860-721-2880; Fax 860-721-2994.
Will search UCC records. This agency will not do a tax lien search. Will not search real estate records. **Online Access:** Assessor. **Other Phone Numbers:** Assessor 860-721-2810; Treasurer 860-721-2861; Elections 860-721-2819; Vital Records 860-721-2880.

Willington Town

Town Clerk, 40 Old Farms Road, Willington, CT 06279. Town Clerk, R/E and UCC Recording 860-429-9965; Fax 860-429-8415. www.willingtonct.org

Will not search UCC records. This agency will not do a tax lien search. Will not search real estate records. **Online Access:** Property Records. Records on the Town of Willington Property Records database are available free online at http://univers.akanda.com/ProcessSearch.asp?cmd=Willington. **Other Phone Numbers:** Assessor 860-429-3400; Treasurer 860-429-8496; Elections 860-429-4942; Vital Records 860-429-9965.

Wilton Town

Town Clerk, 238 Danbury Road, Wilton, CT 06897. Town Clerk, R/E and UCC Recording 203-563-0106; Fax 203-563-0299. http://www.munic.state.ct.us/WILTON/wilton.htm

Will search UCC records. This agency will not do a tax lien search. Will not search real estate records. **Other Phone Numbers:** Assessor 203-563-0121; Treasurer 203-563-0114; Elections 203-563-0112; Vital Records 203-563-0106.

Winchester Town

Town Clerk, 338 Main Street, Town Hall, Winsted, CT 06098-1697. Town Clerk, R/E and UCC Recording 860-738-6963; Fax 860-738-6595. http://townofwinchester.org

Will search UCC records. This agency will not do a tax lien search. Will not search real estate records. **Other Phone Numbers:** Assessor 860-379-5461; Treasurer 860-738-6961; Appraiser/Auditor 860-379-5461; Elections 860-738-6963 x355; Vital Records 860-738-6963.

Windham Town

Town Clerk, P.O. Box 94, Willimantic, CT 06226. 860-465-3013 R/E Recording: 860-456-3593; Fax 860-465-3012. http://www.windhamct.com

Will not search UCC records. This agency will not do a tax lien search. Will not search real estate records. **Other Phone Numbers:** Assessor 860-465-3025; Treasurer 860-465-3060.

Windsor Locks Town

Town Clerk, 50 Church Street, Town Office Building, Windsor Locks, CT 06096. Town Clerk, R/E and UCC Recording 860-627-1441.

Will not search UCC records. This agency will not do a tax lien search. Will not search real estate records. **Other Phone Numbers:** Assessor 860-627-1448; Treasurer 860-627-1449; Elections 860-654-1619; Vital Records 860-627-1441.

Windsor Town

Town Clerk, P.O. Box 472, Windsor, CT 06095-0472. Town Clerk, R/E and UCC Recording 860-285-1902; Fax 860-285-1909. http://www.townofwindsorct.com

Will not search UCC records. This agency will not do a tax lien search. Will not search real estate records. **Online Access:** Assessor, Real Estate. Online access to the Town Clerk's Recording database is available free at www.townofwindsorct.com/records.htm. Records go back to 1991; plan is to go back to 1970. Also, records on the Assessor's Taxpayer Information System database are available free online at http://140.239.211.227/windsorct. Registration is required for full access; registration is free. **Other Phone Numbers:** Assessor 860-285-1817; Treasurer 860-285-1890; Elections 860-285-1902; Vital Records 860-285-1902.

Wolcott Town

Town Clerk, 10 Kenea Avenue, Town Hall, Wolcott, CT 06716. 203-879-8100 R/E Recording: 203-879-4666; Fax 203-879-8105.

Will search UCC records. This agency will not do a tax lien search. Will not search real estate records. **Other Phone Numbers:** Assessor 203-879-8100; Treasurer 203-879-8100; Elections 203-879-8100; Vital Records 203-879-8100.

Woodbridge Town

Town Clerk, 11 Meetinghouse Lane, Woodbridge, CT 06525. Town Clerk, R/E and UCC Recording 203-389-3422; Fax 203-389-3473. http://www.munic.state.ct.us/woodbridge/townclerk.html

Will search UCC records. This agency will not do a tax lien search. Will not search real estate records. **Online Access:** Assessor. Online access to the Assessor's database for Woodbridge is available free online at http://data.visionappraisal.com/woodbridgeCT. User ID is required; registration is free. **Other Phone Numbers:** Assessor 203-389-3416; Treasurer 203-389-3414; Appraiser/Auditor 203-389-3414; Elections 203-389-3408; Vital Records 203-389-3424.

Woodbury Town

Town Clerk, P.O. Box 369, Woodbury, CT 06798-3407. 203-263-2144; Fax 203-263-4755.

Will search UCC records. This agency will not do a tax lien search. Will not search real estate records. **Other Phone Numbers:** Assessor 203-263-2435.

Woodstock Town

Town Clerk, Town Office Building, 415 Route 169, Woodstock, CT 06281. 860-928-6595 R/E Recording: 203-928-6595; Fax 860-963-7557.

Will search UCC records. This agency will not do a tax lien search. Will not search real estate records. **Other Phone Numbers:** Assessor 203-928-6929.

Connecticut County Locator

You will usually be able to find the city name in the City/County Cross Reference below. In that case, it is a simple matter to determine the county from the cross reference. However, only the official US Postal Service city names are included in this index. There are an additional 40,000 place names that people use in their addresses. Therefore, we have also included a ZIP/City Cross Reference immediately following the City/County Cross Reference.

If you know the ZIP Code but the city name does not appear in the City/County Cross Reference index, look up the ZIP Code in the ZIP/City Cross Reference, find the city name, then look up the city name in the City/County Cross Reference. For example, you want to know the county for an address of Menands, NY 12204. There is no "Menands" in the City/County Cross Reference. The ZIP/City Cross Reference shows that ZIP Codes 12201-12288 are for the city of Albany. Looking back in the City/County Cross Reference, Albany is in Albany County.

City/County Cross Reference

ABINGTON Windham
AMSTON Tolland
ANDOVER Tolland
ANSONIA New Haven
ASHFORD Windham
AVON Hartford
BALLOUVILLE Windham
BALTIC (06330) New London(94), Windham(6)
BANTAM Litchfield
BEACON FALLS New Haven
BETHANY New Haven
BETHEL Fairfield
BETHLEHEM Litchfield
BLOOMFIELD Hartford
BOLTON Tolland
BOTSFORD Fairfield
BOZRAH New London
BRANFORD New Haven
BRIDGEPORT Fairfield
BRIDGEWATER Litchfield
BRISTOL Hartford
BROAD BROOK Hartford
BROOKFIELD Fairfield
BROOKLYN Windham
BURLINGTON Hartford
CANAAN Litchfield
CANTERBURY (06331) Windham(99), New London(1)
CANTON Hartford
CANTON CENTER Hartford
CENTERBROOK Middlesex
CENTRAL VILLAGE Windham
CHAPLIN Windham
CHESHIRE New Haven
CHESTER Middlesex
CLINTON Middlesex
COBALT Middlesex
COLCHESTER (06415) New London(90), Middlesex(10)
COLEBROOK Litchfield
COLLINSVILLE (06022) Hartford(92), Litchfield(8)
COLUMBIA Tolland
CORNWALL Litchfield
CORNWALL BRIDGE Litchfield
COS COB Fairfield
COVENTRY Tolland
CROMWELL Middlesex
DANBURY Fairfield
DANIELSON Windham
DARIEN Fairfield
DAYVILLE Windham
DEEP RIVER Middlesex
DERBY New Haven
DURHAM Middlesex
EAST BERLIN Hartford
EAST CANAAN Litchfield
EAST GLASTONBURY Hartford
EAST GRANBY Hartford
EAST HADDAM Middlesex
EAST HAMPTON Middlesex
EAST HARTFORD Hartford
EAST HARTLAND Hartford
EAST HAVEN New Haven
EAST KILLINGLY Windham
EAST LYME New London

EAST WINDSOR Hartford
EAST WINDSOR HILL Hartford
EAST WOODSTOCK Windham
EASTFORD (06242) Windham(97), Tolland(3)
EASTON Fairfield
ELLINGTON Tolland
ENFIELD Hartford
ESSEX Middlesex
FABYAN Windham
FAIRFIELD Fairfield
FALLS VILLAGE Litchfield
FARMINGTON Hartford
GALES FERRY New London
GAYLORDSVILLE Litchfield
GEORGETOWN Fairfield
GILMAN New London
GLASGO New London
GLASTONBURY Hartford
GOSHEN Litchfield
GRANBY Hartford
GREENS FARMS Fairfield
GREENWICH Fairfield
GROSVENOR DALE Windham
GROTON New London
GUILFORD New Haven
HADDAM Middlesex
HADLYME New London
HAMDEN New Haven
HAMPTON Windham
HANOVER New London
HARTFORD Hartford
HARWINTON Litchfield
HAWLEYVILLE Fairfield
HEBRON Tolland
HIGGANUM Middlesex
IVORYTON Middlesex
JEWETT CITY New London
KENSINGTON Hartford
KENT Litchfield
KILLINGWORTH Middlesex
LAKESIDE Litchfield
LAKEVILLE Litchfield
LEBANON New London
LEDYARD New London
LITCHFIELD Litchfield
MADISON New Haven
MANCHESTER (06040) Hartford(98), Tolland(2)
MANCHESTER Hartford
MANSFIELD CENTER (06250) Tolland(95), Windham(5)
MANSFIELD DEPOT Tolland
MARION Hartford
MARLBOROUGH Hartford
MELROSE Hartford
MERIDEN New Haven
MIDDLE HADDAM Middlesex
MIDDLEBURY New Haven
MIDDLEFIELD Middlesex
MIDDLETOWN Middlesex
MILFORD New Haven
MILLDALE Hartford
MONROE Fairfield
MONTVILLE New London
MOODUS Middlesex
MOOSUP Windham

MORRIS Litchfield
MYSTIC New London
NAUGATUCK New Haven
NEW BRITAIN Hartford
NEW CANAAN Fairfield
NEW FAIRFIELD Fairfield
NEW HARTFORD Litchfield
NEW HAVEN New Haven
NEW LONDON New London
NEW MILFORD Litchfield
NEW PRESTON MARBLE DALE Litchfield
NEWINGTON Hartford
NEWTOWN Fairfield
NIANTIC New London
NORFOLK Litchfield
NORTH BRANFORD New Haven
NORTH CANTON (06059) Litchfield(64), Hartford(36)
NORTH FRANKLIN New London
NORTH GRANBY Hartford
NORTH GROSVENORDALE Windham
NORTH HAVEN New Haven
NORTH STONINGTON New London
NORTH WESTCHESTER New London
NORTH WINDHAM Windham
NORTHFIELD Litchfield
NORTHFORD New Haven
NORWALK Fairfield
NORWICH New London
OAKDALE New London
OAKVILLE Litchfield
OLD GREENWICH Fairfield
OLD LYME New London
OLD MYSTIC New London
OLD SAYBROOK Middlesex
ONECO Windham
ORANGE New Haven
OXFORD New Haven
PAWCATUCK New London
PEQUABUCK Litchfield
PINE MEADOW Litchfield
PLAINFIELD Windham
PLAINVILLE Hartford
PLANTSVILLE Hartford
PLEASANT VALLEY Litchfield
PLYMOUTH Litchfield
POMFRET Windham
POMFRET CENTER Windham
POQUONOCK Hartford
PORTLAND Middlesex
PRESTON New London
PROSPECT New Haven
PUTNAM Windham
QUAKER HILL New London
QUINEBAUG Windham
REDDING Fairfield
REDDING CENTER Fairfield
REDDING RIDGE Fairfield
RIDGEFIELD Fairfield
RIVERSIDE Fairfield
RIVERTON Litchfield
ROCKFALL Middlesex
ROCKY HILL Hartford
ROGERS Windham
ROXBURY Litchfield
SALEM New London
SALISBURY Litchfield

SANDY HOOK Fairfield
SCOTLAND Windham
SEYMOUR New Haven
SHARON Litchfield
SHELTON Fairfield
SHERMAN (06784) Fairfield(99), Litchfield(1)
SIMSBURY Hartford
SOMERS Tolland
SOMERSVILLE Tolland
SOUTH BRITAIN New Haven
SOUTH GLASTONBURY Hartford
SOUTH KENT Litchfield
SOUTH LYME New London
SOUTH WILLINGTON Tolland
SOUTH WINDHAM Windham
SOUTH WINDSOR Hartford
SOUTH WOODSTOCK Windham
SOUTHBURY New Haven
SOUTHINGTON Hartford
SOUTHPORT Fairfield
STAFFORD Tolland
STAFFORD SPRINGS (06076) Tolland(92), Windham(8)
STAFFORDVILLE Tolland
STAMFORD Fairfield
STERLING Windham
STEVENSON Fairfield
STONINGTON New London
STORRS MANSFIELD Tolland
STRATFORD Fairfield
SUFFIELD Hartford
TACONIC Litchfield
TAFTVILLE New London
TARIFFVILLE Hartford
TERRYVILLE Litchfield
THOMASTON Litchfield
THOMPSON Windham
TOLLAND Tolland
TORRINGTON Litchfield
TRUMBULL Fairfield
UNCASVILLE New London
UNIONVILLE Hartford
VERNON ROCKVILLE Tolland
VERSAILLES New London
VOLUNTOWN (06384) New London(99), Windham(1)
W HARTFORD Hartford
WALLINGFORD New Haven
WASHINGTON DEPOT Litchfield
WATERBURY New Haven
WATERFORD New London
WATERTOWN Litchfield
WAUREGAN Windham
WEATOGUE Hartford
WEST CORNWALL Litchfield
WEST GRANBY Hartford
WEST HARTLAND Hartford
WEST HAVEN New Haven
WEST MYSTIC New London
WEST SIMSBURY Hartford
WEST SUFFIELD Hartford
WESTBROOK Middlesex
WESTON Fairfield
WESTPORT Fairfield
WETHERSFIELD Hartford

WILLIMANTIC (06226) Windham(99), Tolland(1)
WILLINGTON Tolland
WILTON Fairfield

WINCHESTER CENTER Litchfield
WINDHAM Windham
WINDSOR Hartford
WINDSOR LOCKS Hartford

WINSTED Litchfield
WOLCOTT New Haven
WOODBRIDGE New Haven
WOODBURY Litchfield

WOODSTOCK Windham
WOODSTOCK VALLEY Windham
YANTIC New London

ZIP/City Cross Reference

ZIP	City	ZIP	City	ZIP	City	ZIP	City
06001-06001	AVON	06117-06117	W HARTFORD	06371-06371	OLD LYME	06492-06494	WALLINGFORD
06002-06002	BLOOMFIELD	06118-06118	EAST HARTFORD	06372-06372	OLD MYSTIC	06497-06497	STRATFORD
06006-06006	WINDSOR	06119-06119	W HARTFORD	06373-06373	ONECO	06498-06498	WESTBROOK
06010-06011	BRISTOL	06120-06126	HARTFORD	06374-06374	PLAINFIELD	06501-06511	NEW HAVEN
06013-06013	BURLINGTON	06127-06127	W HARTFORD	06375-06375	QUAKER HILL	06512-06512	EAST HAVEN
06016-06016	BROAD BROOK	06128-06128	EAST HARTFORD	06376-06376	SOUTH LYME	06513-06513	NEW HAVEN
06018-06018	CANAAN	06129-06129	WETHERSFIELD	06377-06377	STERLING	06514-06514	HAMDEN
06019-06019	CANTON	06131-06131	NEWINGTON	06378-06378	STONINGTON	06515-06515	NEW HAVEN
06020-06020	CANTON CENTER	06132-06132	HARTFORD	06379-06379	PAWCATUCK	06516-06516	WEST HAVEN
06021-06021	COLEBROOK	06133-06133	W HARTFORD	06380-06380	TAFTVILLE	06517-06518	HAMDEN
06022-06022	COLLINSVILLE	06134-06134	HARTFORD	06382-06382	UNCASVILLE	06519-06521	NEW HAVEN
06023-06023	EAST BERLIN	06137-06137	W HARTFORD	06383-06383	VERSAILLES	06524-06524	BETHANY
06024-06024	EAST CANAAN	06138-06138	EAST HARTFORD	06384-06384	VOLUNTOWN	06525-06525	WOODBRIDGE
06025-06025	EAST GLASTONBURY	06140-06199	HARTFORD	06385-06386	WATERFORD	06530-06540	NEW HAVEN
06026-06026	EAST GRANBY	06226-06226	WILLIMANTIC	06387-06387	WAUREGAN	06601-06610	BRIDGEPORT
06027-06027	EAST HARTLAND	06230-06230	ABINGTON	06388-06388	WEST MYSTIC	06611-06611	TRUMBULL
06028-06028	EAST WINDSOR HILL	06231-06231	AMSTON	06389-06389	YANTIC	06612-06612	EASTON
06029-06029	ELLINGTON	06232-06232	ANDOVER	06401-06401	ANSONIA	06650-06699	BRIDGEPORT
06030-06030	FARMINGTON	06233-06233	BALLOUVILLE	06403-06403	BEACON FALLS	06701-06710	WATERBURY
06031-06031	FALLS VILLAGE	06234-06234	BROOKLYN	06404-06404	BOTSFORD	06712-06712	PROSPECT
06032-06032	FARMINGTON	06235-06235	CHAPLIN	06405-06405	BRANFORD	06716-06716	WOLCOTT
06033-06033	GLASTONBURY	06237-06237	COLUMBIA	06409-06409	CENTERBROOK	06720-06749	WATERBURY
06034-06034	FARMINGTON	06238-06238	COVENTRY	06410-06411	CHESHIRE	06750-06750	BANTAM
06035-06035	GRANBY	06239-06239	DANIELSON	06412-06412	CHESTER	06751-06751	BETHLEHEM
06037-06037	KENSINGTON	06241-06241	DAYVILLE	06413-06413	CLINTON	06752-06752	BRIDGEWATER
06039-06039	LAKEVILLE	06242-06242	EASTFORD	06414-06414	COBALT	06753-06753	CORNWALL
06040-06041	MANCHESTER	06243-06243	EAST KILLINGLY	06415-06415	COLCHESTER	06754-06754	CORNWALL BRIDGE
06043-06043	BOLTON	06244-06244	EAST WOODSTOCK	06416-06416	CROMWELL	06755-06755	GAYLORDSVILLE
06045-06045	MANCHESTER	06245-06245	FABYAN	06417-06417	DEEP RIVER	06756-06756	GOSHEN
06049-06049	MELROSE	06246-06246	GROSVENOR DALE	06418-06418	DERBY	06757-06757	KENT
06050-06053	NEW BRITAIN	06247-06247	HAMPTON	06419-06419	KILLINGWORTH	06758-06758	LAKESIDE
06057-06057	NEW HARTFORD	06248-06248	HEBRON	06420-06420	SALEM	06759-06759	LITCHFIELD
06058-06058	NORFOLK	06249-06249	LEBANON	06422-06422	DURHAM	06762-06762	MIDDLEBURY
06059-06059	NORTH CANTON	06250-06250	MANSFIELD CENTER	06423-06423	EAST HADDAM	06763-06763	MORRIS
06060-06060	NORTH GRANBY	06251-06251	MANSFIELD DEPOT	06424-06424	EAST HAMPTON	06770-06770	NAUGATUCK
06061-06061	PINE MEADOW	06254-06254	NORTH FRANKLIN	06426-06426	ESSEX	06776-06776	NEW MILFORD
06062-06062	PLAINVILLE	06255-06255	NORTH GROSVENORDALE	06430-06432	FAIRFIELD	06777-06777	NEW PRESTON MARBLE DALE
06063-06063	PLEASANT VALLEY			06436-06436	GREENS FARMS		
06064-06064	POQUONOCK	06256-06256	NORTH WINDHAM	06437-06437	GUILFORD	06778-06778	NORTHFIELD
06065-06065	RIVERTON	06258-06258	POMFRET	06438-06438	HADDAM	06779-06779	OAKVILLE
06066-06066	VERNON ROCKVILLE	06259-06259	POMFRET CENTER	06439-06439	HADLYME	06781-06781	PEQUABUCK
06067-06067	ROCKY HILL	06260-06260	PUTNAM	06440-06440	HAWLEYVILLE	06782-06782	PLYMOUTH
06068-06068	SALISBURY	06262-06262	QUINEBAUG	06441-06441	HIGGANUM	06783-06783	ROXBURY
06069-06069	SHARON	06263-06263	ROGERS	06442-06442	IVORYTON	06784-06784	SHERMAN
06070-06070	SIMSBURY	06264-06264	SCOTLAND	06443-06443	MADISON	06785-06785	SOUTH KENT
06071-06071	SOMERS	06265-06265	SOUTH WILLINGTON	06444-06444	MARION	06786-06786	TERRYVILLE
06072-06072	SOMERSVILLE	06266-06266	SOUTH WINDHAM	06447-06447	MARLBOROUGH	06787-06787	THOMASTON
06073-06073	SOUTH GLASTONBURY	06267-06267	SOUTH WOODSTOCK	06450-06454	MERIDEN	06790-06790	TORRINGTON
06074-06074	SOUTH WINDSOR	06268-06269	STORRS MANSFIELD	06455-06455	MIDDLEFIELD	06791-06791	HARWINTON
06075-06075	STAFFORD	06277-06277	THOMPSON	06456-06456	MIDDLE HADDAM	06793-06794	WASHINGTON DEPOT
06076-06076	STAFFORD SPRINGS	06278-06278	ASHFORD	06457-06459	MIDDLETOWN	06795-06795	WATERTOWN
06077-06077	STAFFORDVILLE	06279-06279	WILLINGTON	06460-06460	MILFORD	06796-06796	WEST CORNWALL
06078-06078	SUFFIELD	06280-06280	WINDHAM	06461-06461	BRIDGEPORT	06798-06798	WOODBURY
06079-06079	TACONIC	06281-06281	WOODSTOCK	06466-06466	MILFORD	06801-06801	BETHEL
06080-06080	SUFFIELD	06282-06282	WOODSTOCK VALLEY	06467-06467	MILLDALE	06804-06804	BROOKFIELD
06081-06081	TARIFFVILLE	06320-06320	NEW LONDON	06468-06468	MONROE	06807-06807	COS COB
06082-06083	ENFIELD	06330-06330	BALTIC	06469-06469	MOODUS	06810-06811	DANBURY
06084-06084	TOLLAND	06331-06331	CANTERBURY	06470-06470	NEWTOWN	06812-06812	NEW FAIRFIELD
06085-06087	UNIONVILLE	06332-06332	CENTRAL VILLAGE	06471-06471	NORTH BRANFORD	06813-06817	DANBURY
06088-06088	EAST WINDSOR	06333-06333	EAST LYME	06472-06472	NORTHFORD	06820-06820	DARIEN
06089-06089	WEATOGUE	06334-06334	BOZRAH	06473-06473	NORTH HAVEN	06829-06829	GEORGETOWN
06090-06090	WEST GRANBY	06335-06335	GALES FERRY	06474-06474	NORTH WESTCHESTER	06830-06836	GREENWICH
06091-06091	WEST HARTLAND	06336-06336	GILMAN	06475-06475	OLD SAYBROOK	06840-06842	NEW CANAAN
06092-06092	WEST SIMSBURY	06337-06337	GLASGO	06477-06477	ORANGE	06850-06860	NORWALK
06093-06093	WEST SUFFIELD	06339-06339	LEDYARD	06478-06478	OXFORD	06870-06870	OLD GREENWICH
06094-06094	WINCHESTER CENTER	06340-06349	GROTON	06479-06479	PLANTSVILLE	06875-06875	REDDING CENTER
06095-06095	WINDSOR	06350-06350	HANOVER	06480-06480	PORTLAND	06876-06876	REDDING RIDGE
06096-06096	WINDSOR LOCKS	06351-06351	JEWETT CITY	06481-06481	ROCKFALL	06877-06877	RIDGEFIELD
06098-06098	WINSTED	06353-06353	MONTVILLE	06482-06482	SANDY HOOK	06878-06878	RIVERSIDE
06101-06106	HARTFORD	06354-06354	MOOSUP	06483-06483	SEYMOUR	06879-06879	RIDGEFIELD
06107-06107	W HARTFORD	06355-06355	MYSTIC	06484-06484	SHELTON	06880-06881	WESTPORT
06108-06108	EAST HARTFORD	06357-06357	NIANTIC	06487-06487	SOUTH BRITAIN	06883-06883	WESTON
06109-06109	WETHERSFIELD	06359-06359	NORTH STONINGTON	06488-06488	SOUTHBURY	06888-06889	WESTPORT
06110-06110	W HARTFORD	06360-06360	NORWICH	06489-06489	SOUTHINGTON	06896-06896	REDDING
06111-06111	NEWINGTON	06365-06365	PRESTON	06490-06490	SOUTHPORT	06897-06897	WILTON
06112-06115	HARTFORD	06370-06370	OAKDALE	06491-06491	STEVENSON	06901-06928	STAMFORD

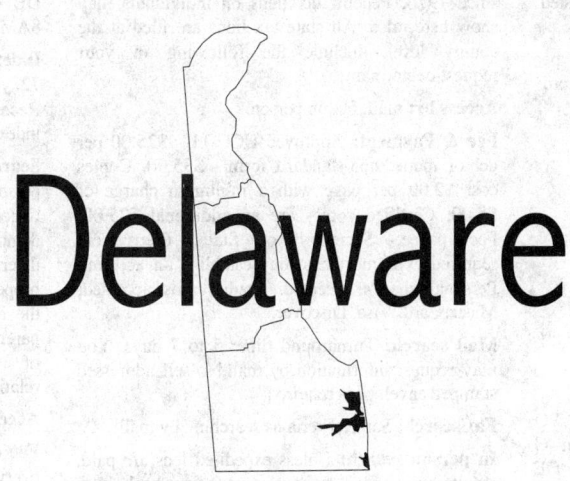

Delaware

General Help Numbers:

Governor's Office

820 N. French St, Carvel State Bldg   302-577-3210
Wilmington, DE 19801   Fax 302-577-3118
http://www.state.de.us/governor/index.htm   8AM-5:30PM

Attorney General's Office

Carvel State Office Bldg   302-577-8400
820 N French St   Fax 302-577-6630
Wilmington, DE 19801   8:30AM-4:30PM
http://www.state.de.us/attgen

State Court Administrator

Supreme Court of Delaware   302-577-2480
820 N French, 11th Fl   Fax 302-577-3139
Wilmington, DE 19   8:30AM-5PM
http://courts.state.de.us/supreme/index.htm

State Archives

121 Duke of York St   302-739-5318
Dover, DE 19901   Fax 302-739-2578
http://www.archives.lib.de.us   8:30AM-4:15PM M-F

State Specifics:

Capital:	Dover
	Kent County
Time Zone:	EST
Number of Counties:	3
Population:	783,600
Web Site:	www.state.de.us

State Agencies

Criminal Records

Delaware State Police Headquarters, Criminal Records Section, PO Box 430, Dover, DE 19903-0430 (Courier: 1407 N Dupont Highway, Dover, DE 19930); 302-739-5880, 302-739-5888 (Fax), 8AM-4PM.

http://www.state.de.us/dsp

Note: This agency will only release records with dispositions for pre-employment requesters. Sex offender data is available online at www.state.de.us/dsp/sexoff/search.htm.

Indexing & Storage: Records are available from 1935. New records are available for inquiry immediately.

Searching: You do not need to use the state's forms. Must have a signed release form for the fingerprint search and release of information. Include name and fingerprints in your request. The following data is not released: traffic ticket information.

Access by: mail, in person.

Fee & Payment: Prepayment required. Fee payee: Delaware State Police. Funds must be certified or money order. No credit cards accepted.

Mail search: Turnaround time: 14 days. Must have a signed release and full set of fingerprints.A self addressed stamped envelope is requested. Search costs $25.00 per request.

In person search: Search costs $25.00 per request. It can take up to 14 days before records are ready for pickup.

Corporation Records
Partnerships
Limited Partnership Records
Trademarks/Servicemarks
Limited Liability Company Records
Limited Liability Partnerships

Secretary of State, Division of Corporations, PO Box 898, Dover, DE 19903 (Courier: John G Townsend Bldg, 401 Federal Street #4, Dover, DE 19901); 302-739-3073, 302-739-3812 (Fax), 8AM-4:30PM.

http://www.state.de.us/corp

Note: There is no online access to the public; however, there is a system available to only registered agents.

Indexing & Storage: Records are available from the formation of the Division. Indexes are maintained on imaging system and in-house computer. Delaware Registered Agents have online access. New records are available for inquiry immediately.

Searching: Include the following in your request-full name of business. In addition to the articles of incorporation, corporation records include the following information: Annual Reports, Officers, Directors, Prior (merged) names, Inactive and Reserved names.

Access by: mail, phone, fax, in person.

Fee & Payment: Fees are $20.00 for a status of an entity; $20.00 for certified plus $1.00 per page; plain copies are $5.00 for the first page and $1.00 each additional. Fee payee: Delaware Secretary of State. Prepayment required. Personal checks accepted. Credit cards accepted: MasterCard, Visa, Discover.

Mail search: Turnaround time: 3 days. No self addressed stamped envelope is required.

Phone search: There is no fee for general information given over the phone.

Fax search: Fax requests can be received by fax, but are not returned by fax.

In person search: Requests are returned by regular mail unless expedite fee is paid.

Expedited service: Expedited service available for mail, fax, phone, and in person. Fees are up to $100.00 for 24 hour; up to $200.00 for same day; $500.00 for 2 hour.

Uniform Commercial Code
Federal Tax Liens

UCC Division, Secretary of State, PO Box 793, Dover, DE 19903 (Courier: Townsend Bldg, 401 Federal Street, Dover, DE 19901); 302-739-3077, 302-739-3813 (Fax), 8:30AM-4:30PM.

http://www.state.de.us/corp/ucc.htm

Indexing & Storage: Records are available from 1967. Records are computerized since 1992. Records are indexed on inhouse computer.

Searching: Use search request form UCC-11. The search includes federal tax liens on businesses

since 1976. Federal tax liens on individuals may show here, also. All state tax liens are filed at the county level. Include the following in your request-debtor name.

Access by: mail, fax, in person.

Fee & Payment: Approved UCC-11 - $25.00 per debtor name; non-standard form - $35.00. Copies cost $2.00 per page with a minimum charge of $5.00. Certified copies are an additional $25.00. Fee payee: Secretary of State. Prepayment required. Volume users may establish an account. Personal checks accepted. Credit cards accepted: MasterCard, Visa, Discover.

Mail search: Turnaround time: 5 to 7 days. You may request information by mail.No self addressed stamped envelope is required.

Fax search: Same criteria as searching by mail.

In person search: Unless expedited fees are paid, results are mailed or you must come back in 5 days.

Other access: Bulk purchase of paper copies is $2.00 per page.

Expedited service: Expedited service is available for mail and phone searches. Three levels of expedited service are available at extra fees as follows: 24 hrs-$25.00; same day-$50.00; 2 hrs-$75.00.

State Tax Liens
Records not maintained by a state level agency.

Note: Records are at the county level.

Sales Tax Registrations

Finance Department, Revenue Division, PO Box 8911, Wilmington, DE 19899-8911 (Courier: Carvel State Office Bldg, 820 N French St, 8th Fl, Wilmington, DE 19801); 302-577-8450, 302-577-8662 (Fax), 8AM-4:30PM.

http://www.state.de.us/revenue

Note: This state has a gross receipts tax, not a sales tax per se. They will release the information found on the face of the certificate issued to the business.

Indexing & Storage: Records are available back to 1998 on computer and from 1992-2001 on optical readers.

Searching: This state will do an alpha search for a business name and will provide the business name, address and business license number, type of business, and amount of license fee paid. They will not release business owner or officer names. Include the following in your request-business name. The federal tax ID can also be used.

Access by: mail, phone, fax, in person.

Mail search: Turnaround time: 1 week. A self addressed stamped envelope is requested. No fee for mail request.

Phone search: No fee for telephone request. There is a limit of 3 searches per phone call.

Fax search: There is no fee for fax searches. Turnaround time is 2 days.

In person search: No fee for request.

Birth Certificates

Department of Health, Office of Vital Statistics, PO Box 637, Dover, DE 19903 (Courier: William Penn & Federal Sts, Jesse Cooper Bldg, Dover,

DE 19901); 302-739-4721, 302-736-1862 (Fax), 8AM-4:30PM (Counter closes at 4:20 PM).

Indexing & Storage: Records are available from 72 years. Prior records are at the State Archives. Records are indexed on microfilm, microfiche, and index cards.

Searching: Must have a signed release from person of record or immediate family member. Others may only obtain records if they demonstrate the record is needed for the determination or protection of their personal property rights or for genealogical uses. Include the following in your request-full name, names of parents, mother's maiden name, date of birth, place of birth, reason for information request, relationship to person of record.

Access by: mail, fax, in person, online.

Fee & Payment: Search fee is $6.00 per name for every 5 years searched. Add $5.00 if you use a credit card. Add $4.00 for each additional copy of the same record. Fee payee: Office of Vital Statistics. Prepayment required. Personal checks accepted. Credit cards accepted: MasterCard, Visa, AmEx, Discover.

Mail search: Turnaround time: 1 day to 1 week. No self addressed stamped envelope is required.

Fax search: Available from VitalChek. Use of credit card and photo ID required.

In person search: Turnaround time is generally 10 minutes or less.

Online search: Access available at vitalchek.com.

Expedited service: Expedited service is available for mail, fax and in person searches. Turnaround time: overnight delivery. Add $15.00 per package.

Death Records

Department of Health, Office of Vital Statistics, PO Box 637, Dover, DE 19903 (Courier: William Penn & Federal Sts, Jesse Cooper Bldg, Dover, DE 19901); 302-739-4721, 302-736-1862 (Fax), 8AM-4:30PM.

Indexing & Storage: Records are available for the past 40 years. Prior records are at the State Archives. It takes 3 days before new records are available for inquiry. Records are indexed on microfilm, microfiche, and index cards.

Searching: Must have a signed release from immediate family member. Include the following in your request-full name, date of death, place of death, names of parents, reason for information request, relationship to person of record.

Access by: mail, fax, in person, online.

Fee & Payment: The search fee is $6.00 per name for every 5 years searched. Add $5.00 if you use a credit card. Add $4.00 for each additional copy. Fee payee: Office of Vital Statistics. Prepayment required. Personal checks accepted. Credit cards accepted: MasterCard, Visa, AmEx, Discover.

Mail search: Turnaround time: 1 day. No self addressed stamped envelope is required.

Fax search: Records are available form VitalChek. Use of credit card and photo ID required.

In person search: Turnaround time is 10 to 15 minutes.

Online search: Access available at vitalchek.com.

Expedited service: Expedited service is available for mail, fax and in person searches. Turnaround time: overnight delivery. Add $15.00 per package.

Marriage Certificates

Department of Health, Office of Vital Statistics, PO Box 637, Dover, DE 19903 (Courier: William Penn & Federal Sts, Jesse Cooper Bldg, Dover, DE 19901); 302-739-4721, 302-739-1862 (Fax), 8AM-4:30PM.

Indexing & Storage: Records are available for 40 years. Prior records are in the State Public Archives. It takes 5 days before new records are available for inquiry. Records are indexed on microfilm, microfiche, and index cards.

Searching: Must have a signed release from person or persons of record or immediate family member. Include the following in your request- names of husband and wife, date of marriage, place or county of marriage, relationship to person of record, reason for information request, wife's maiden name.

Access by: mail, fax, in person, online.

Fee & Payment: The search fee is $6.00 per name for every 5 years searched. Add $5.00 if you use a credit card. Add $4.00 for each additional copy. Fee payee: Office of Vital Statistics. Prepayment required. Personal checks accepted. Credit cards accepted: MasterCard, Visa, AmEx, Discover.

Mail search: Turnaround time: 1 day. No self addressed stamped envelope is required.

Fax search: This is available through VitalChek. Credit card and photo ID are required.

In person search: Turnaround time is 10 to 15 minutes.

Online search: Access is available via VitalChek.com.

Expedited service: Expedited service is available for mail, fax and in person searches. Turnaround time: overnight delivery. Add $15.00 per package.

Divorce Records

Records not maintained by a state level agency.

Note: This agency will verify whether a divorce occurred after 1935 but will issue no copies of the record. For records 1976 to present go to the Family Court at the county; prior to 1976 go to the Prothonotary at the county level.

Workers' Compensation Records

Labor Department, Industrial Accident Board, 4425 N Market Street, Wilmington, DE 19802; 302-761-8200, 302-761-6601 (Fax), 8AM-4:30PM.

http://delawareworks.com

Note: Case records must have been adjudicated to be considered public. First reports of injury only (non-adjudicated) are not covered under FOIA.

Indexing & Storage: Records are available from 1985. New records are available for inquiry immediately.

Searching: Must have signed authorization from injured party in letter form or a court subpoena. They will not honor out-of-state requests. Information required includes claimant name, SSN, and date of accident.

Access by: mail.

Fee & Payment: There is no fee. Copies are $.25 each. Fee payee: DOL/IA. Prepayment required. Payment is for copies only. Personal checks accepted. No credit cards accepted.

Mail search: Turnaround time: 2 to 5 days. A self addressed stamped envelope is requested.

Driver Records

Division of Motor Vehicles, Driver Services, PO Box 698, Dover, DE 19903 (Courier: 303 Transportation Circle, Dover, DE 19901); 302-744-2506, 302-739-2602 (Fax), 8AM-4:30PM M-T-TH-F; 12:00PM-8PM W.

http://www.delaware.gov/yahoo/DMV

Note: For tickets: Delaware does not keep copies of tickets in a central repository for request purposes and suggests you go to the appropriate local jurisdiction.

Indexing & Storage: Records are available for 3 years to present for public record purposes. It takes 2 to 3 weeks before new records are available for inquiry.

Searching: Casual requesters can obtain records only with MV703 Form with notarized signature of subject. Include the following in your request- full name, driver's license number, date of birth. Authorized account holders must have an application and contract on file. The following data is not released: Social Security Numbers or medical information.

Access by: mail, in person, online.

Fee & Payment: The fee for all search modes is $4.00 per request. Fee payee: Division of Motor Vehicles. Prepayment required. Personal checks accepted. No credit cards accepted.

Mail search: Turnaround time: 3 to 5 days. A self addressed stamped envelope is requested.

In person search: Walk-in requesters may obtain records from centers in Wilmington, New Castle, Dover, and Georgetown.

Online search: Online searching is single inquiry only, no batch request mode is offered. Searching is done by driver's license number or name and DOB. A signed contract application and valid "business license" is required. Hours of operation are 8 AM to 4:30 PM. Access is provided through a 900 number at a fee of $1.00 per minute, plus the $4.00 per record fee. For more information, call 302-744-2606.

Other access: Tape-to-tape is offered for high volume, batch requesters. Also, the state will release data from the driver license file on tapes or cartridges, but this cannot be resold.

Vehicle Ownership

Vehicle Identification

Division of Motor Vehicles, Correspondence Section, PO Box 698, Dover, DE 19903 (Courier: 303 Transportation Circle, Dover, DE 19901); 302-744-2500, 302-739-2042 (Fax), 8:30AM-4:30PM M-T-TH-F; 12-8PM W.

http://www.delaware.gov/yahoo/DMV

Indexing & Storage: Records are available for 3 years to present. It takes 2 to 3 weeks before new records are available for inquiry.

Searching: Casual requesters can only obtain records with notarized consent. Those routinely seeking information must complete an Application and Contract for Direct Access to become an account holder. Casual requesters must use Form MV703 which requires notarized signature of subject.

Access by: mail, in person, online.

Fee & Payment: The fee for ownership, plate, and registration searches is $4.00 per record. Fee payee: Division of Motor Vehicles. Prepayment required. Personal checks accepted. No credit cards accepted.

Mail search: Turnaround time: 3 to 5 days. A self addressed stamped envelope is requested.

In person search: Turnaround time is while you wait.

Online search: There is an additional $1.00 per minute fee for using the on-line "900 number" system. Records are $4.00 each. The system is single inquiry mode and open from 8 AM to 4:30 PM, except on Wed. from noon to 8PM. For more information, call 302-744-2606.

Other access: Bulk information can be obtained on a customized basis in tape, cartridge or paper format. However, the purpose of the request is carefully screened and information cannot be resold.

Accident Reports

Delaware State Police, Traffic Records, PO Box 430, Dover, DE 19903 (Courier: 1441 N Dupont Hwy, Dover, DE 19901); 302-739-5931, 302-739-5982 (Fax), 8AM-4PM.

Indexing & Storage: Records are available for 3 years as public record. It takes 2 to 3 weeks before new records are available for inquiry.

Searching: Include the following in your request- full name, date of accident, location of accident.

Access by: mail, phone.

Fee & Payment: The fee is $18.50 per report, $60.00 if fatal accident report. Fee payee: Delaware State Police. Prepayment required. Personal checks accepted. No credit cards accepted.

Mail search: Turnaround time: 3 to 5 days. A self addressed stamped envelope is requested.

Phone search: You cannot search by phone, but you can verify by phone if a report exists.

Vessel Ownership

Vessel Registration

Dept of Natural Resources & Environmental Control, Delaware Boat Registration Office, 89 Kings Highway, Dover, DE 19901; 302-739-3498, 302-739-6157 (Fax), 8AM-4:30PM.

http://www.dnrec.state.de.us

Note: Liens are filed with UCC filings, not at this location.

Indexing & Storage: Records are available from 1978 to present. Records are registration only, no titles, and are indexed on microfiche from 1978 to 1989. Records are computer indexed from 1990 to the present. All motorized craft are registered. There are no titles. It takes one month or less before new records are available for inquiry.

Searching: No searching of records is allowed. However, they will verify information over the phone using "yes" and "no" only. Liens are not filed here, they are filed with UCCs. Either the owner's name, hull ID# or registration number must be submitted for a verification.

Access by: mail, phone, fax, in person.

Fee & Payment: There is no fee.

Mail search: Records are available by mail.

Phone search: They will verify information over the phone using "yes" and "no" only.

Fax search: If DPPA approved.

In person search: Verification only.

Legislation Records

Legislative Hall, Division of Research, PO Box 1401, Dover, DE 19903; 302-744-4114, 302-739-5318 (Archives for old bills), 800-282-8545 (In-state), 8AM-4:30PM.

http://www.legis.state.de.us

Indexing & Storage: Records are available for current and 1 prior session only. Records are indexed on microfiche.

Searching: Include the following in your request-bill number.

Access by: mail, phone, in person, online.

Fee & Payment: There is no charge unless you want many copies or a copy of a large document. They will compute the charges. Fee payee: State of Delaware. Personal checks accepted. No credit cards accepted.

Mail search: Turnaround time: variable. No self addressed stamped envelope is required.

Phone search: You may call for copies.

In person search: You may request copies in person.

Online search: Access information at the Internet site, no fee.

Voter Registration

Commissioner of Elections, 32 W Lockerman, M-101, Dover, DE 19904; 302-739-4277, 8AM-4:30PM.

http://www.state.de.us/election

Indexing & Storage: Records are available for both active and inactive records.

Searching: There is no individual record searching permitted, except in person. The following data is not released: Social Security Numbers or telephone numbers.

Access by: in person.

Fee & Payment: There is no search fee, the copy fee is $.25 per copy. Fee payee: State of Delaware. Prepayment required. No credit cards accepted. Records are available by mail.

Other access: The entire state database is available on tape for $250. Individual districts (378) are available on disk for $2.00 per district or $.025 per name on labels. Also, there are several different types of printed lists available.

GED Certificates

Department of Education, GED Testing, PO Box 1402, Dover, DE 19903; 302-739-3743, 302-739-2770 (Fax).

http://www.doe.state.de.us

Searching: Include the following in your request-signed release, date of birth, Social Security Number. The year of the test is very helpful.

Access by: mail, fax, in person.

Fee & Payment: There is no fee.

Mail search: Turnaround time: 1 to 2 days. No self addressed stamped envelope is required.

Fax search: Same criteria as mail searching.

In person search: Requester must present a photo ID.

Hunting License Information
Fishing License Information
Access to Records is Restricted

Natural Resources & Environmental Control Dept, Division of Fish & Wildlife, 89 Kings Hwy, Dover, DE 19901; 302-739-5296, 302-739-6157 (Fax), 8AM-4:30PM.

http://www.dnrec.state.de.us/fw/fwwel.htm

Note: Records are not on a computerized database, but kept in paper and filed alphabetically. They will release name, address, driver license number, and physical characteristics.

Delaware State Licensing Agencies

Licenses Searchable Online

Engineering Firm #12 .... www.dape.org/CofAuths.html
Lobbyist #09 .... www.lobbyist.net/Delaware/DELLOB.htm
Optometrist #11 .... www.odfinder.org/LicSearch.asp
School Administrative Supervisor/Assistant #04 ... www.doe.state.de.us/EduDir/EduDirStart.asp
School Counselor #04 .... www.doe.state.de.us/EduDir/EduDirStart.asp
School Principal/Superintendent #04 .... www.doe.state.de.us/EduDir/EduDirStart.asp
Teacher #04 .... www.doe.state.de.us/EduDir/EduDirStart.asp

Licensing Quick Finder

Adult Entertainment #11 .... 302-739-4522 x207
Aesthetician #11 302-739-4522
Alarm Company/Employee #03 302-739-5991
Alcoholic Beverage Establishment #01 .302-577-5222
Ambulance Attendant #18 302-739-4773
Architect #11 .... 302-739-4522 x218
Armored Car Agencies/Employees #03.302-739-5991
Asbestos Abatement Worker #15..........302-739-3930
Athletic Trainer #11 .... 302-739-4522 x205
Attorney #02 302-651-3113
Audiologist #11 302-739-4522
Barber #11 .... 302-739-4522 x204
Boiler Inspector #14 302-739-5889
Chiropractor #11 .... 302-739-4522 x204
Constable #03...............................302-739-5991
Contractor, General #05 302-577-8778
Cosmetologist #11 .... 302-739-4522 x204
Counselor, Professional #11....... 302-739-4522 x220
Deadly Weapons Dealer #11 .... 302-739-4522 x209
Dental Hygienist #11 302-739-4522
Dental Radiographer #16....................302-739-3787
Dentist #11 .... 302-739-4522 x220
Dietician/Nutritionist #11 302-739-4522
Electrician #11 .... 302-739-4522 x203
Electrologist #11 302-739-4522
Emergency Medical Technician-Paramedic #07 ....
....302-739-6637
Engineer #12 302-577-6500
Engineering Firm #12 302-577-6500

Funeral Director #11.................... 302-739-4522 x206
Gaming Control #11 .... 302-739-4522 x202
Geologist #11 .... 302-739-4522 x207
Harness Racing #06...........................302-739-4811
Hearing Aid Dealer/Fitter #11 ...... 302-739-4522 x204
Horse Racing (Thorobred) #06 302-739-4811
Human Relations Specialist (Education) #13.............
....888-759-9133
Insurance Adjuster #08......................302-739-4254
Insurance Advisor #08.......................302-739-4254
Insurance Agent/Consultant #08...........302-739-4254
Insurance Broker #08 302-739-4254
Land Surveyor #11 .... 302-739-4522 x218
Landscape Architect #11 .... 302-739-4522 x218
Library Media Specialist #13................888-759-9133
Lobbyist #09 302-739-2397
Massage #11 .... 302-739-4522 x203
Medical Doctor/Surgeon #11 .... 302-739-4522 x211
Mental Health Counselor #11 302-739-4522
Midwife Nurse #11 302-739-4522
Nail Technician #11...........................302-739-4522
Notary Public #09.............................302-739-3073
Nuclear Medicine Technologist #16 302-739-3787
Nurse #11 .... 302-739-4522 x216
Nursing Home Administrator #11 . 302-739-4522 x207
Occupational Therapist/Assistant #11 ....
.... 302-739-4522 x207
Optometrist #11 .... 302-739-4522 x206
Osteopathic Physician #11 .... 302-739-4522 x211

Pesticide Applicator #10 302-739-4811
Pharmacist #11 .... 302-739-4522 x215
Pharmacist #07...............................302-739-4798
Physical Therapist/Assistant #11 . 302-739-4522 x206
Plumber #11 302-739-4522
Podiatrist #11............................ 302-739-4522 x207
Private Investigative Agency/Employee #03..............
....302-739-5991
Private Security Agency/Employee #03.302-739-5991
Psychological Assistant #11 302-739-4522
Psychologist #11 .... 302-739-4522 x218
Public Accountant-CPA #11........... 302-739-4522 x218
Radiation Therapist #16 302-739-3787
Real Estate Appraiser #11 .... 302-739-4522 x211
Real Estate Broker/Agent #11 ..... 302-739-4522 x219
River Pilot #11 .... 302-739-4522 x204
School Admin. Supervisor/Assist. #04...302-739-4601
School Counselor #04 302-739-4601
School Principal/Superintendent #04 302-739-4601
Securities Agent #08 302-739-4254
Securities Broker/Dealer #08 302-739-4254
Social Worker #11 .... 302-739-4522 x220
Speech Pathologist/Audiologist #11302-739-4522 x204
Teacher #04...................................302-739-4601
Veterinarian #11........................ 302-739-4522 x206
Waste Water Operator #17.................302-739-4860
Water Supply Operator #07 302-739-5410
X-ray Technician #07 302-739-3787

Licensing Agency Information

#01 Alcoholic Beverage Control Division, 820 N French St, Carvel State Office Bldg, Wilmington, DE 19801; 302-577-5222, Fax: 302-577-3204.

#02 Board of Bar Examiners, 200 W 9th St, #300B, Wilmington, DE 19801; 302-577-7038, Fax: 302-658-4605.
http://courts.state.de.us/bbe

#03 State Police, PO Box 430, Dover, DE 19903; 302-739-5991, Fax: 302-739-5888.
www.state.de.us/DSP

#04 Department of Education, PO Box 1402 (401 Federal St), Dover, DE 19903; 302-739-4601, Fax: 302-739-3092.
www.doe.state.de.us
Direct web site URL to search for licensees: www.doe.state.de.us/EduDir/EduDirStart.asp

#05 Division of Revenue, 820 N French St, Carvel State Office Bldg, Wilmington, DE 19801; 302-577-3363, Fax: 302-577-8203.
www.state.de.us/revenue/index.htm

#06 Harness Racing Commission, 2320 S DuPont Hwy, Dover, DE 19901; 302-739-4811, Fax: 302-697-4748.
www.state.de.us/deptagri

#07 Health & Social Services Department, Division of Public Health, PO Box 637, Dover, DE 19903-.

#08 Insurance Department, 841 Silver Lake Blvd, Dover, DE 19904; 302-739-4254, Fax: 302-739-5280.
www.state.de.us/inscom

#09 Notary Division, PO Box 898, Dover, DE 19903; 302-739-3073, Fax: 302-739-3812.

#10 Department of Agriculture, 2320 S DuPont Hwy, Dover, DE 19901; 302-739-4811, Fax: 302-697-6287.
www.state.de.us/deptagri/index.htm

#11 Division of Professional Regulations, 861 Silver Lake Blvd, Cannon Bldg #203, Dover, DE 19903; 302-739-4522, Fax: 302-739-2711.

#12 Assoc. of Professional Engineers, 56 W Main St #208, Wilmington, DE 19702-1500; 302-577-6500, Fax: 302-577-6502.
www.dape.org

#13 Department of Public Instruction, Townsend Bldg, PO Box 1402, Dover, DE 19903; 888-759-9133.
www.doe.state.de.us

#14 Division of Boiler Safety, PO Box 674, Dover, DE 19903-0674; 302-739-5889.

#15 Division of Facilities Mgmt, O'Neill Bldg, PO Box 1401, Dover, DE 19903; 302-739-3930.

#16 Division of Public Health, PO Box 637, Dover, DE 19903; 302-739-3787.

#17 Department of Natural Resources & Environmental Control, 89 Kings Hwy, Dover, DE 19901; 302-739-4860.

#18 Fire Prevention Commission, 1461 Chestnut Grove Rd, Dover, DE 19904; 302-739-4773.

Delaware Federal Courts

The following list indicates the district and division name for each county in the state.

County/Court Cross Reference

Kent... Wilmington
New Castle.. Wilmington
Sussex... Wilmington

US District Court

District of Delaware

Wilmington Division US Courthouse, Lock Box 18, 844 N King St, Wilmington, DE 19801 (Courier Address: US Courthouse, 844 N King St, Clerk's Office, 4th Floor, Room 4209, Wilmington, DE 19801), 302-573-6170.

http://www.ded.uscourts.gov

Counties: All counties in Delaware.

Indexing/Storage: Cases are indexed by defendant and plaintiff as well as by case number. New cases are available in the index 1 day after filing date. A computer index is maintained. Open records are located at this court.

Fee & Payment: The fee is $20.00 per item (one party name or case number). Payment may be made by money order, cashier check, personal check. Prepayment is required. A copy vendor is used for civil court documents. Parcels Incorporated, 1-800-343-1742 -- orders may be placed with them directly. Payee: Clerk, US District Court. Certification fee: $7.00 per document. Copy fee: $.50 per page.

Phone Search: They will search civil and criminal cases from 1982 to the present over the phone. The only information released over the phone is whether a case was found and, if so, its case number.

Mail Search: Search can include all computer, microfiche and judgment indexes. A stamped self addressed envelope is not required.

In Person: In person searching is available.

PACER: Sign-up number is 800-676-6856. Access fee is $.60 per minute. Toll-free access: 888-793-9488. Local access: 302-573-6651. Case records are available back to January 1991. Records are purged every few years (not since 1/91). New records are available online after 2 days. PACER is available online at http://pacer.ded.uscourts.gov.

Opinions Online: Court opinions are available online at http://www.lawlib.widener.edu/pages/deopind.htm

US Bankruptcy Court

District of Delaware

Wilmington Division 824 Market St, 5th Floor, Marine Midland Plaza, Wilmington, DE 19801 (Courier Address: Use mail address for courier delivery), 302-573-6174.

http://www.deb.uscourts.gov

Counties: All counties in Delaware.

Indexing/Storage: Cases are indexed by debtor as well as by case number. New cases are available in the index 1 day after filing date. A computer index is maintained. Open records are located at this court.

Fee & Payment: The fee is $20.00 per item (one party name or case number). Payment may be made by money order, cashier check, personal check. Prepayment is required. Payee: Clerk, US Bankruptcy Court. Certification fee: $7.00 per document. Copy fee: $.50 per page. You are allowed to make your own copies. These copies cost $.50 per page. There is an in-house private copy service that you must use.

Phone Search: The only information that is released over the telephone is whether the search is positive or negative. If positive they will release the case number. An automated voice case information service (VCIS) is available. Call VCIS at 888-667-5530 or 302-573-6233.

Mail Search: Always enclose a stamped self addressed envelope.

In Person: In person searching is available.

PACER: Sign-up number is 800-676-6856. Access fee is $.60 per minute. Toll-free access: 800-249-9857. Local access: 302-573-6243. Case records are available back to 1991. Records are purged every four years. New civil records are available online after 1 day. WebPACER Dial-up Networking is available at IP address 156.122.36.150.

Electronic Filing: Electronic filing information is available online at https://ecf.deb.uscourts.gov/

Delaware County Courts

Court	Jurisdiction	No. of Courts	How Organized
Superior Courts*	General	3	
Chancery Courts*	General	3	
Court of Common Pleas*	Limited	3	
Justice of the Peace Courts*	Municipal	19	
Alderman's Courts	Municipal	9	
Family Courts	Special	3	

* Profiled in this Sourcebook.

Court	CIVIL								
	Tort	Contract	Real Estate	Min. Claim	Max. Claim	Small Claims	Estate	Eviction	Domestic Relations
Superior Courts*	X	X	X	$50000	No Max				
Chancery Courts*	X	X	X	$0	No Max		X		
Court of Common Pleas*	X	X	X	$0	$50000				
Justice of the Peace Courts*			X	$0	$15000	$5000		X	
Alderman's Courts						$2500			
Family Courts									X

Court	CRIMINAL				
	Felony	Misdemeanor	DWI/DUI	Preliminary Hearing	Juvenile
Superior Courts*	X	X			
Chancery Courts*					
Court of Common Pleas*		X		X	
Justice of the Peace Courts*		X	X		
Alderman's Courts		X	X		
Family Courts		X			X

ADMINISTRATION Administrative Office of the Courts, PO Box 8911, Wilmington, DE, 19899; 302-577-2480, Fax: 302-577-3139. http://courts.state.de.us/supreme/index.htm

COURT STRUCTURE Superior Courts have jurisdiction over felonies and all drug offenses, the Court of Common Pleas has jurisdiction over all misdemeanors. Court of Chancery handles corporation and equity matters, as well as probate and estates. Guardianships are handled by the Register of Wills, corporate matters such as equity disputes and injunctions are handled by the Clerk of Chancery. The Municipal Court of Wilmington merged with the Court of Common Pleas in New Castle in May 1998.

ONLINE ACCESS Only Supreme Court Final Orders and Opinions are available at http://courts.state.de.us/supreme/opinions.htm.

An online system called CLAD, developed by Mead Data Central and the New Castle Superior Court, is currently available in Delaware. CLAD contains only toxic waste, asbestos, and class action cases; however, based on CLAD's success, Delaware may pursue development of online availability of other public records by working in conjunction with private information resource enterprises.

ADDITIONAL INFORMATION Effective 1/15/95, the civil case limit of the Justice of the Peace Courts increased from $5,000 to $15,000; the Courts of Common Pleas' limit went from $15,000 to $50,000.

Criminal histories are available with a signed release from the offender at the Delaware State Police Headquarters, Criminal Records Section in Dover DE. For information on criminal history retrieval requirements, call 302-739-5880.

Kent County

Chancery Court 38 The Green, Dover, DE 19901; 302-736-2242; Probate phone: 302-744-2330; Fax: 302-736-2240. Hours: 8:30AM-4:30PM (EST). *Civil, Probate.*

http://courts.state.de.us/chancery

Civil Records: Access: In person only. Visitors must perform in person searches for themselves. No search fee. Required to search: name, years to search. Civil cases indexed by defendant, plaintiff. Civil records on index books. The Court of Chancery oversees corporate and equity matters and guardianship. The Register of Wills oversees estate, and probate matters. **General Information:** No juvenile, sealed or mental health records released. Turnaround time 24 hrs. Fax notes: Fee to fax results is $1.00 per document. Copy fee: $1.00 per page. Certification fee: $5.00 plus $1.00 per page. Fee payee: Register in Chancery (Register of Wills for Probate). Personal checks accepted. May bill law firms and businesses.

Superior Court Office of Prothonotary, 38 The Green, Dover, DE 19901; 302-739-3184; Fax: 302-739-6717. Hours: 8AM-5PM (EST). *Felony, Misdemeanor, Civil Actions Over $50,000.*

http://courts.state.de.us/superior

Civil Records: Access: Mail, in person. Only the court performs in person searches; visitors may not. No search fee. Required to search: name, years to search. Civil cases indexed by defendant, plaintiff. Judgments on computer from 1996, on microfiche from 1918.
Criminal Records: Access: In person only. Visitors must perform in person searches for themselves. No search fee. Required to search: name, years to search, DOB; also helpful: race. Judgments on computer from 1996, on microfiche from 1918. Contact Dept of Records for search assistance.
General Information: No sealed or psychological evaluation records released. SASE required. Copy fee: $1.00 per page. Certification fee: $6.00 fee for 3 pages and $1.00 each add'l page. Fee payee: Prothonotary. Personal checks accepted. Prepayment is required.

Court of Common Pleas 38 The Green, Dover, DE 19901; 302-739-4618; Fax: 302-739-4501. Hours: 8:30AM-4:30PM (EST). *Misdemeanor, Civil Actions Under $50,000.*

http://courts.state.de.us/commonpleas

Civil Records: Access: Mail, in person. Both court and visitors may perform in person searches. No search fee. Required to search: name, years to search. Civil cases indexed by defendant, plaintiff. Civil records on computer from 1992, on microfiche from 10/85, archived prior.
Criminal Records: Access: Mail, in person. Visitors must perform in person searches for themselves. No search fee. Required to search: name, years to search, DOB, offense, date of offense. Criminal records on computer from 1/94, on microfiche from 10/85, archived prior.
General Information: No sealed records released. SASE required. Turnaround time 1-3 days. Copy fee: $1.00 per page. Certification fee: $5.00. Fee payee: Court of Common Pleas. Personal checks accepted. Prepayment is required.

Dover Justice of the Peace #16 480 Bank Lane, Dover, DE 19904; 302-739-4316; Fax: 302-739-6797. Hours: 8AM-4PM (EST). *Civil Actions Under $15,000, Eviction, Small Claims.*

http://courts.state.de.us/jpcourt

Civil Records: Access: Mail, in person. Both court and visitors may perform in person searches. No search fee. Required to search: name, years to search. Civil cases indexed by defendant, plaintiff. Civil records

computerized since 10/98. **General Information:** Copy fee: $.25 per page. Certification fee: $10.00. Fee payee: JCP Court 16. Personal checks accepted. Prepayment is required.

Dover Justice of the Peace #7 480 Bank Lane, Dover, DE 19903; 302-739-4554; Fax: 302-739-6797. Hours: Open 24 hours (EST). *Misdemeanor.*

http://courts.state.de.us/jpcourt

Criminal Records: Only the court performs in person searches; visitors may not. Search fee: $7.00 per name. Fee is per charge. Required to search: name, years to search, DOB, signed release; also helpful: address, offense, date of offense.
General Information: Fee payee: State of Delaware. Prepayment is required.

Harrington Justice of the Peace #6 17111 South DuPont Hwy, Harrington, DE 19952; 302-398-8247; Fax: 302-397-4237. Hours: 8AM-4PM (EST). *Misdemeanor.*

http://courts.state.de.us/jpcourt

Criminal Records: Access: In person, mail. Only the court performs in person searches; visitors may not. No search fee. Required to search: name, years to search, DOB. Court form required for all searches.
General Information: Turnaround time 2-3 days. Fee payee: State of Delaware. Prepayment is required.

Smyrna Justice of the Peace #8 100 Monrovia Ave, Smyrna, DE 19977; 302-653-7083; Fax: 302-653-2888. Hours: 8AM-4PM *Misdemeanor.*

http://courts.state.de.us/jpcourt

Criminal Records: Only the court performs in person searches; visitors may not. No search fee. Required to search: name, years to search; also helpful: DOB.
General Information: Fee payee: State of Delaware. Prepayment is required.

New Castle County

Chancery Court 1020 N King St, Wilmington, DE 19801; 302-571-7540; Probate phone: 302-571-7545; Fax: 302-571-7751. Hours: 8:30AM-5PM (EST). *Civil, Probate.*

http://courts.state.de.us/chancery

Civil Records: Access: Phone, fax, mail, in person. Both court and visitors may perform in person searches. No search fee. Required to search: name; also helpful: years to search. Civil cases indexed by defendant, plaintiff. Civil records indexed on computer since 1963, in books prior to 1963. The civil records for the Court of Chancery deal with corporate and equity matters, there is no money jurisdiction. The Register of Wills oversees estates, guardianships and probate. **General Information:** Public Access terminal is available. No guardianship records released. SASE requested. Turnaround time 2 days. Fax notes: $5.00 for first page, $2.00 each add'l. Copy fee: $1.00 per page. $2.00 if from microfilm. Certification fee: $5.00. Fee payee: Register in Chancery (Register of Wills for Probate). Personal checks accepted. Will bill fax requests.

Superior Court Office of the Prothonotary, 1020 N King Street, Wilmington, DE 19801; 302-577-2400; Fax: 302-577-6487/577-6212. Hours: 8:30AM-5PM (EST). *Felony, Misdemeanor, Civil Actions Over $50,000.*

http://courts.state.de.us/superior

Civil Records: Access: In person only. Visitors must perform in person searches for themselves. No search fee. Required to search: name, years to search. Civil cases indexed by defendant, plaintiff. Civil records on computer from 4/80, prior on microfiche.
Criminal Records: Access: In person only. Visitors must perform in person searches for themselves. No

search fee. Required to search: name, DOB; also helpful: years to search. Criminal records on computer from 4/80, prior on microfiche.
General Information: Public Access terminal is available. (Civil only.) No psychological evaluation, sealed records released. Copy fee: $1.00 per page. Certification fee: $6.00. Fee payee: Prothonotary's Office. Personal checks accepted. Prepayment required.

Court of Common Pleas 1000 N King St, Wilmington, DE 19801-3348; 302-577-2430; Fax: 302-577-2193. Hours: 8:30AM-4:30PM (EST). *Misdemeanor, Civil Actions Under $50,000.*

http://courts.state.de.us/commonpleas

Note: Fax for civil is 302-577-2431.

Civil Records: Access: Phone, fax, mail, in person. Both court and visitors may perform in person searches. No search fee. Required to search: name, years to search. Civil cases indexed by defendant, plaintiff. Civil records on computer from 1993; prior records on docket books.
Criminal Records: Access: Phone, fax, mail, in person. Both court and visitors may perform in person searches. No search fee. Required to search: name, years to search; also helpful: DOB. Criminal records on computer from 1993; prior records on docket books.
General Information: No closed records released. SASE required. Turnaround time up to a week. Fax notes: $1.00 per page. Copy fee: $1.00 per page. Certification fee: $5.00. Fee payee: Court of Common Pleas. Personal checks accepted. Prepayment is required.

Middletown Justice of the Peace #9 757 N Broad St, Middletown, DE 19709; 302-378-5221. Hours: 8AM-4PM (EST). *Civil Under$15,000, Misdemeanor, Eviction, Small Claims.*

http://courts.state.de.us/jpcourt

Note: Due to a court fire, criminal cases 7/24/2000 to 5/1/2001 are heard at New Castle JP Court 11, 323-4450. Civil cases are heard at Prices Corner (Wilmington) JP Court 12, 995-8646.

Civil Records: Access: In person only. Both court and visitors may perform in person searches. No search fee. Required to search: name, years to search. Civil cases indexed by defendant. Due to fire, records on computer only back to mid-1990s. The court will not do name searches, but will search if a civil action # is presented.
Criminal Records: Access: In person only. Visitors must perform in person searches for themselves. No search fee. Required to search: name, years to search, DOB. Due to fire, records on computer only back to mid-1990s.
General Information: Copy fee: $.25 per page. Certification fee: Civil record certification is $7.00, criminal is $10.00.

Prices Corner Justice of the Peace #12 212 Greenbank Rd, Wilmington, DE 19808; 302-995-8646; Fax: 302-995-8642. Hours: 8:30AM-4:30PM (EST). *Civil Actions Under $15,000, Eviction, Small Claims.*

http://courts.state.de.us/jpcourt

Civil Records: Access: In person only. Visitors must perform in person searches for themselves. No search fee. Required to search: name, years to search. **General Information:** No sealed, juvenile, adoption or mental health records released. Certification fee: $10.00. Fee payee: Justice of the Peace Court 12. Personal checks accepted. Prepayment is required.

Wilmington Justice of the Peace #13 1010 Concord Ave, Concord Professional Center, Wilmington, DE 19802; 302-577-2550; Fax: 302-577-2526. Hours: 8AM-4PM (EST). *Civil Actions Under $15,000, Eviction, Small Claims.*

http://courts.state.de.us/jpcourt

Civil Records: Access: In person only. Visitors must perform in person searches for themselves. No search fee. Required to search: name, years to search. Civil cases indexed by defendant, plaintiff. Civil records are computerized since 09/01/99. The court will pull specific case data if CA# given, if and when time permitting. **General Information:** No sealed, juvenile, adoption or mental health records released. Copy fee: $.25 per page. Certification fee: $10.00. Fee payee: Justice of the Peace Court #13. Personal checks accepted. Prepayment is required.

New Castle Justice of the Peace #11 61
Christiana Rd, New Castle, DE 19720; 302-323-4450; Fax: 302-323-4452. Hours: Open 24 hours (EST). *Misdemeanor.*

http://courts.state.de.us/jpcourt

Criminal Records: Access: In person, mail. Visitors must perform in person searches for themselves. No search fee. Required to search: name, years to search. **General Information:** Turnaround time 2-3 days. Fee payee: State of Delaware. Prepayment is required.

Prices Corner Justice of the Peace #10
210 Greenbank Rd, Wilmington, DE 19808; 302-995-8640; Fax: 302-995-8642. Hours: 8AM-11PM (EST). *Misdemeanor.*

http://courts.state.de.us/jpcourt

Criminal Records: Access: In person, mail. Only the court performs in person searches; visitors may not. Search fee: $7.00 per name. Required to search: name, years to search, DOB. **General Information:** Turnaround time 2 weeks. Fee payee: Justice of the Peace Court 10. Prepayment is required.

Wilmington Justice of the Peace #15 130
Hickman Rd #13, Claymont, DE 19703; 302-798-5327; Fax: 302-798-4508. Hours: 8AM-4PM M; 8AM-Midnight T-F; 8AM-4PM Sat (EST). *Misdemeanor.*

http://courts.state.de.us/jpcourt

Note: Effective 06/01/99, the court assumed DUI and truancy cases. This court was formally located at 716 Philadelphia Pike in Wilmington

Criminal Records: Access: In person, mail. Only the court performs in person searches; visitors may not. Search fee: $7.00 per name. Fee is per case & includes certification & copy fees. Required to search: name, years to search, DOB; also helpful: offense. **General Information:** Turnaround time 2-4 weeks. Fee payee: State of Delaware. Prepayment is required.

Wilmington Justice of the Peace #18 1301
E 12th St, PO Box 9279, Wilmington, DE 19809; 302-429-7740; Fax: 302-577-6140. Hours: 8:30AM-Midnight (EST). *Misdemeanor.*

http://courts.state.de.us/jpcourt

Criminal Records: Access: In person, mail. Only the court performs in person searches; visitors may not. Search fee: $7.50 per name. Required to search: name, years to search, DOB. **General Information:** Turnaround time varies.

Wilmington Justice of the Peace #20
Public Safety Building, 300 N Walnut Street, Wilmington, DE 19801; 302-577-7234; Fax: 302-577-7237. Hours: 8AM-midnight (EST). *Misdemeanor.*

http://courts.state.de.us/jpcourt

Criminal Records: Visitors must perform in person searches for themselves. No search fee. Required to search: name, years to search. **General Information:** Fee payee: Justice of the Peace Court #13.

Sussex County

Chancery Court PO Box 424 (The Circle),
Georgetown, DE 19947; 302-855-7842; Probate phone: 302-855-7875. Hours: 8:30AM-4:30PM (EST). *Civil, Probate.*   http://courts.state.de.us/chancery

Civil Records: Access: Phone, mail, in person. Both court and visitors may perform in person searches. No search fee. Required to search: name, years to search. Civil cases indexed by defendant, plaintiff. Civil records on index books. **General Information:** All records public. Turnaround time 1-3 days. Copy fee: $1.00 per page. Certification fee: $5.00 plus $1.00 per page. Fee payee: Register in Chancery (Register of Wills for Probate). Personal checks okay. Prepayment required.

Superior Court PO Box 756 (The Circle),
Georgetown, DE 19947; 302-856-5740; Fax: 302-856-5739. Hours: 8AM-4:30PM (EST). *Felony, Misdemeanor, Civil Actions.*

http://courts.state.de.us/superior

Civil Records: Access: In person only. Visitors must perform in person searches for themselves. No search fee. Required to search: name, years to search. Civil cases indexed by defendant, plaintiff. Civil records on computer from 6/91 or form 1980 if case was pending in 1991, microfiche prior.

Criminal Records: Access: In person only. Visitors must perform in person searches for themselves. No search fee. Required to search: name, years to search. Criminal records on manual index.

General Information: Public Access terminal is available. No divorce, victim info, sealed records, expungments, or CCDW permit records released. Copy fee: $.30 per page. Certification fee: $6.00 plus $1.00 per page after the first three. Fee payee: Prothonotary. Personal checks accepted. Prepayment is required.

Court of Common Pleas PO Box 426,
Georgetown, DE 19947; 302-856-5333; Fax: 302-856-5056. Hours: 8:30AM-4:30PM (EST). *Misdemeanor, Civil Actions Under $50,000.*

http://courts.state.de.us/commonpleas

Civil Records: Access: Phone, fax, mail, in person. Only the court performs in person searches; visitors may not. Search fee: $10.00 per name. Required to search: name, years to search. Civil cases indexed by defendant. Civil records on computer from 1993, on microfiche from 10/85, archives prior.

Criminal Records: Access: Phone, fax, mail, in person. Only the court performs in person searches; visitors may not. Search fee: $10.00 per name. Required to search: name, years to search, DOB, offense, date of offense. Criminal records on computer from 1994, on microfiche from 10/85, archives prior.

General Information: Public Access terminal is available. No closed case records released. SASE required. Turnaround time 1-2 weeks. Fax notes: No fee to fax results. Copy fee: $1.00 per page. Certification fee: $1.00. Fee payee: Court of Common Pleas. Personal checks accepted. Prepayment is required.

Georgetown Justice of the Peace #17 17
Shortly Rd, Georgetown, DE 19947; 302-856-1447; Fax: 302-856-5923. Hours: 8AM-4PM (EST). *Civil Actions Under $15,000, Eviction, Small Claims.*

http://courts.state.de.us/jpcourt

Civil Records: Access: Mail, in person. Both court and visitors may perform in person searches. No search fee. Required to search: name, years to search. Civil cases indexed by defendant, plaintiff. Civil records on index books from 1966 to present. **General Information:** SASE requested. Turnaround time 1-2 days. Copy fee: $10.00 per page. Certification fee: $10.00. Fee payee: State of Delaware. Personal checks accepted. Prepayment is required.

Seaford Justice of the Peace #19 408 Stein
Highway, Seaford, DE 19973; 302-629-5433; Fax: 302-628-2049. Hours: 8AM-4PM (EST). *Civil Actions Under $15,000, Eviction, Small Claims.*

http://courts.state.de.us/jpcourt

Civil Records: Access: In person only. Visitors must perform in person searches for themselves. No search fee. Required to search: name, years to search. Civil cases indexed by defendant, plaintiff. In person access requires identification. **General Information:** Copy fee: $1.00 per page. Certification fee: $10.00. Fee payee: State of Delaware. Personal checks accepted. Prepayment is required.

Milford Justice of the Peace #5 715 S
DuPont Highway, Milford, DE 19963; 302-422-5922. Hours: 8AM-4PM (EST). *Misdemeanor.*

http://courts.state.de.us/jpcourt

Note: Some old civil cases also located here

Criminal Records: Access: In person only. Visitors must perform in person searches for themselves. No search fee. Required to search: name, years to search, DOB. Court refers written requests to State Bureau of Investigation in Dover at 302-739-5882. **General Information:** No juvenile records released. Copy fee: $1.00 per page. Certification fee: $7.00. Fee payee: State of Delaware. Personal checks accepted. Credit cards accepted: Visa, MasterCard, Discover. Prepayment is required.

Georgetown Justice of the Peace #3 17
Shortly Rd, Georgetown, DE 19947; 302-856-1445; Fax: 302-856-5844. Hours: 24 hours daily (EST). *Misdemeanor.*

http://courts.state.de.us/jpcourt

Criminal Records: Only the court performs in person searches; visitors may not. Search fee: $7.00 per name. Search fee includes certification. Also must be recent case. Required to search: name, years to search, DOB; also helpful: SSN. **General Information:** Fee payee: State of Delaware. Prepayment is required.

Millsboro Justice of the Peace #1 553 E
DuPont Hwy, Millsboro, DE 19966; 302-934-7268; Fax: 302-934-1414. Hours: 8AM-4PM *Misdemeanor.*
http://courts.state.de.us/jpcourt

Criminal Records: Access: In person, mail. Only the court performs in person searches; visitors may not. No search fee. Required to search: name, years to search, DOB. **General Information:** Turnaround time same day. Prepayment is required.

Rehoboth Beach Justice of the Peace #2
31 Route 24, Rehoboth Beach, DE 19971-9738; 302-645-6163; Fax: 302-645-8842. Hours: 8AM-4PM M & Sat; 8AM-Noon T-F (EST). *Misdemeanor.*

http://courts.state.de.us/jpcourt

Criminal Records: Both court and visitors may perform in person searches. No search fee. Required to search: name, years to search, DOB. **General Information:** Fee payee: State of Delaware. Prepayment is required.

Seaford Justice of the Peace #4 408 Stein
Highway, Seaford, DE 19973; 302-628-2036; Fax: 302-528-2049. Hours: 8AM-4PM M & Sat; 8AM-Noon T-F (EST). *Misdemeanor.*

http://courts.state.de.us/jpcourt

Criminal Records: Visitors must perform in person searches for themselves. No search fee. Required to search: name, years to search.

Delaware Recording Offices

ORGANIZATION   Delaware has 3 counties and 3 recording offices. The recording officer is County Recorder in both jurisdictions. Delaware is in the Eastern Time Zone (EST).

REAL ESTATE RECORDS   Counties do not perform real estate searches, but will provide copies.

UCC RECORDS   Financing statements are filed at the state level, except for real estate related collateral, which are filed only with the County Recorder. All counties perform UCC searches. Copy and certification fees vary.

TAX LIEN RECORDS   Federal tax liens on personal property of businesses are filed with the Secretary of State. Other federal and all state tax liens on personal property are filed with the County Recorder. Copy and certification fees vary.

Kent County

County Recorder of Deeds, County Administration Bldg., Room 218, 414 Federal St., Dover, DE 19901. 302-744-2314; Fax 302-736-2035.
Will search UCC records. Will not search real estate records. **Other Phone Numbers:** Assessor 302-744-2401; Treasurer 302-744-2341.

New Castle County

County Recorder of Deeds, 800 French Street, 4th Floor, Wilmington, DE 19801. County Recorder of Deeds, R/E and UCC Recording 302-571-7550; Fax 302-571-7708.
www.co.new-castle.de.us/recdeeds1.htm
Will search UCC records. This agency will not do a tax lien search. Will not search real estate records. **Online Access:** Real Estate. Records on the City of New Castle Geographic Information System database are available free online at www.2isystems.com/newcastle/Search2.CFM. **Other Phone Numbers:** Assessor 302-395-5400; Treasurer 302-395-5177; Appraiser/Auditor 302-395-5400; Elections 302-577-3464.

Sussex County

County Recorder of Deeds, P.O. Box 827, Georgetown, DE 19947-0827. 302-855-7785; Fax 302-855-7787.
Will search UCC records. This agency will not do a tax lien search. Will not search real estate records. **Other Phone Numbers:** Assessor 302-855-7824; Treasurer 302-855-7763.

Delaware County Locator

You will usually be able to find the city name in the City/County Cross Reference below. In that case, it is a simple matter to determine the county from the cross reference. However, only the official US Postal Service city names are included in this index. There are an additional 40,000 place names that people use in their addresses. Therefore, we have also included a ZIP/City Cross Reference immediately following the City/County Cross Reference.

If you know the ZIP Code but the city name does not appear in the City/County Cross Reference index, look up the ZIP Code in the ZIP/City Cross Reference, find the city name, then look up the city name in the City/County Cross Reference. For example, you want to know the county for an address of Menands, NY 12204. There is no "Menands" in the City/County Cross Reference. The ZIP/City Cross Reference shows that ZIP Codes 12201-12288 are for the city of Albany. Looking back in the City/County Cross Reference, Albany is in Albany County.

City/County Cross Reference

BEAR New Castle
BETHANY BEACH Sussex
BETHEL Sussex
BRIDGEVILLE Sussex
CAMDEN WYOMING Kent
CHESWOLD Kent
CLAYMONT New Castle
CLAYTON (19938) Kent(86), New Castle(14)
DAGSBORO Sussex
DELAWARE CITY New Castle
DELMAR Sussex
DOVER Kent
DOVER AFB Kent
ELLENDALE Sussex
FARMINGTON Kent

FELTON Kent
FENWICK ISLAND Sussex
FRANKFORD Sussex
FREDERICA Kent
GEORGETOWN Sussex
GREENWOOD (19950) Kent(61), Sussex(39)
HARBESON (19951) Sussex(99), Kent(1)
HARRINGTON Kent
HARTLY Kent
HOCKESSIN New Castle
HOUSTON Kent
KENTON Kent
KIRKWOOD New Castle
LAUREL Sussex
LEWES Sussex

LINCOLN Sussex
LITTLE CREEK Kent
MAGNOLIA Kent
MARYDEL Kent
MIDDLETOWN New Castle
MILFORD (19963) Sussex(52), Kent(48)
MILLSBORO Sussex
MILLVILLE Sussex
MILTON Sussex
MONTCHANIN New Castle
NASSAU Sussex
NEW CASTLE New Castle
NEWARK New Castle
OCEAN VIEW Sussex
ODESSA New Castle
PORT PENN New Castle

REHOBOTH BEACH Sussex
ROCKLAND New Castle
SAINT GEORGES New Castle
SEAFORD Sussex
SELBYVILLE Sussex
SMYRNA (19977) Kent(88), New Castle(12)
TOWNSEND New Castle
VIOLA Kent
WILMINGTON New Castle
WINTERTHUR New Castle
WOODSIDE Kent
YORKLYN New Castle

ZIP/City Cross Reference

ZIP	City	ZIP	City	ZIP	City	ZIP	City
19701-19701	BEAR	19735-19735	WINTERTHUR	19943-19943	FELTON	19963-19963	MILFORD
19702-19702	NEWARK	19736-19736	YORKLYN	19944-19944	FENWICK ISLAND	19964-19964	MARYDEL
19703-19703	CLAYMONT	19801-19899	WILMINGTON	19945-19945	FRANKFORD	19966-19966	MILLSBORO
19706-19706	DELAWARE CITY	19901-19901	DOVER	19946-19946	FREDERICA	19967-19967	MILLVILLE
19707-19707	HOCKESSIN	19902-19902	DOVER AFB	19947-19947	GEORGETOWN	19968-19968	MILTON
19708-19708	KIRKWOOD	19903-19905	DOVER	19950-19950	GREENWOOD	19969-19969	NASSAU
19709-19709	MIDDLETOWN	19930-19930	BETHANY BEACH	19951-19951	HARBESON	19970-19970	OCEAN VIEW
19710-19710	MONTCHANIN	19931-19931	BETHEL	19952-19952	HARRINGTON	19971-19971	REHOBOTH BEACH
19711-19718	NEWARK	19933-19933	BRIDGEVILLE	19953-19953	HARTLY	19973-19973	SEAFORD
19720-19721	NEW CASTLE	19934-19934	CAMDEN WYOMING	19954-19954	HOUSTON	19975-19975	SELBYVILLE
19725-19726	NEWARK	19936-19936	CHESWOLD	19955-19955	KENTON	19977-19977	SMYRNA
19730-19730	ODESSA	19938-19938	CLAYTON	19956-19956	LAUREL	19979-19979	VIOLA
19731-19731	PORT PENN	19939-19939	DAGSBORO	19958-19958	LEWES	19980-19980	WOODSIDE
19732-19732	ROCKLAND	19940-19940	DELMAR	19960-19960	LINCOLN		
19733-19733	SAINT GEORGES	19941-19941	ELLENDALE	19961-19961	LITTLE CREEK		
19734-19734	TOWNSEND	19942-19942	FARMINGTON	19962-19962	MAGNOLIA		

District of Columbia

General Help Numbers:

Governor's Office

One Judiciary Square, 441 4th St NW #1100 202-727-2980
Washington, DC 20001   Fax 202-727-0505
http://www.washingtondc.gov   8:30AM-5:30PM
mayor/index.htm

State Court Administrator

500 Indiana Ave NW, Room 1500   202-879-1700
Washington, DC 20001   Fax 202-879-4829
http://www.dcsc.gov   8:30AM-5PM

State Archives

Office of Archives/Public Records   202-671-1105
1300 Naylor Ct NW   Fax 202-727-6076
Washington, DC 20001-4225 9AM-3:30PM research hours

District Specifics:

Time Zone: EST

Population: 572,059

Web Site: www.washingtondc.gov

District Agencies

Criminal Records

Metropolitan Police Department, Identification and Records Section, 300 Indiana Ave NW, Rm 3055, Washington, DC 20001; 202-727-4302 (Police), 202-879-1373 (Superior Court), 8AM-5PM.

http://mpdc.dc.gov/main.shtm

Note: The Superior Court, Criminal Division, is located at 500 Indiana NW, same zip. They do not charge a fee for a search and they will indicate over the phone if there is an existing record. The Sex Offender Registry can be searched at http://mpdc.dc.gov/serv/sor/sor.shtm.

Indexing & Storage: Records are available for 10 years. Records at the Superior Court are indexed in microfilm from 1974 on, index cards from 1970 on, in house computer from 1978 on and District

Archives from 1962 on. New records are available for inquiry immediately.

Searching: Must have release form from person of record. Neither location will supply records without dispositions. Include the following in your request-full name, date of birth, year. The SSN and case number, if known, are helpful. The following data is not released: pending cases.

Access by: mail, in person.

Fee & Payment: Prepayment required. Fee payee: Metropolitan Police. Personal checks accepted. No credit cards accepted.

Mail search: Turnaround time: 2 to 4 weeks. Search costs $5.00 per page.

In person search: Search costs $5.00 per page. Records are returned by mail.

Corporation Records
Limited Partnership Records
Limited Liability Company Records

Department of Consumer & Regulatory Affairs, 941 N Capitol St NE, Washington, DC 20002-4259; 202-442-4434, 9AM-3PM.

http://www.dcra.org

Indexing & Storage: Records are available from the 1850s. There is no trademark or servicemark statute. Records are indexed on inhouse computer.

Searching: Include the following in your request-full name of business. The web site provides download capability of forms.

Access by: mail, phone, in person.

Fee & Payment: Fees: $25.00 per legal document in folder. A document can be 1-100 pages. A Good Standing is $10.00, $20.00 if a not-for-profit. Fee payee: DC Treasury. Prepayment required. Personal checks accepted. Credit cards accepted: MasterCard, Visa, Discover.

Mail search: Turnaround time: 5 to 10 days.

Phone search: They will release agent's name and address, date of incorporation, and status over the phone at no fee. Names and addresses of Officers and Directors will not be released over the phone.

In person search: You may request information in person. There is no fee unless copies of documents are needed.

Other access: For information concerning lists and bulk file purchases, contact the office of Information Services.

Uniform Commercial Code
Federal Tax Liens
State Tax Liens

UCC Recorder, District of Columbia Recorder of Deeds, 515 D Street NW, Washington, DC 20001; 202-727-7116, 8:15AM-4:45PM.

http://www.dccfo.com

Note: Records from 1983 forward are located in Room 101, prior records are in Room 304. This agency will not perform name searches (you must do yourself or hire someone), but will provide certificates for a fee.

Indexing & Storage: Records are available from the 1900's. Records are indexed on microfiche.

Searching: Use search request form UCC-11. Local tax liens are called district tax liens. Include the following in your request-debtor name. Searches prior to 1973 need a book and page number. To search records after 1973, you must have an instrument number.

Access by: mail, in person.

Fee & Payment: There is no search fee; however, a certificate of search can be provided for $30.00. Copies cost $2.25 per page. Fee payee: DC Treasurer. Prepayment required. Personal checks accepted. No credit cards accepted.

Mail search: Turnaround time: 2 weeks. No name searches.

In person search: There is a public access terminal available to look up names to find instrument numbers.

Sales Tax Registrations

Office of Tax and Revenue, Audit Division, 941 N. Capitol Street NE, Washington, DC 20002; 202-727-4829, 202-442-6550 (Fax), 8:15AM-4:30PM.

http://www.dccfo.com/main.shtm

Indexing & Storage: Records are available from the 1980's. Records are computerized since 1990, otherwise are hard copies.

Searching: This agency will only confirm that the business is registered. They will provide no other information. Include the following in your request-business name, federal employer identification number, address. They will also search by tax permit number.

Access by: mail, phone, fax.

Mail search: Turnaround time: 3 to 5 days. A self addressed stamped envelope is requested. No fee for mail request.

Phone search: No fee for telephone request.

Fax search: Same criteria as mail searches.

Birth Certificates

Department of Health, Vital Records Division, 825 North Capitol St NE, 2st Fl, Washington, DC 20002; 202-442-9009, 800-255-2414, 8:30AM-3:30PM.

http://www.dchealth.com

Indexing & Storage: Records are available from 1874 to present. New records are available for inquiry immediately. Records are indexed on microfiche, inhouse computer.

Searching: Records less than 100 years old are only released to person of record or immediate family members or to legal representative of family. Requester should include a copy of photo ID and daytime phone number. Include the following in your request-full name, date of birth, place of birth, names of parents, name of the hospital.

Access by: mail, phone, fax, in person.

Fee & Payment: The $12.00 fee is for the short form of birth certificate for every consecutive 3 years searched. The archival long form costs $18.00. All copies are certified. Fee payee: DC Treasurer. Prepayment required. Credit cards are only accepted for expedited services. Personal checks accepted. Credit cards accepted: MasterCard, Visa, AmEx, Discover.

Mail search: Turnaround time: 2 weeks. All genealogical searches must be done by mail and cannot be expedited.No self addressed stamped envelope is required.

Phone search: Phone requests are considered expedited and extra fees are involved.

Fax search: See expedited services.

Expedited service: Expedited service is available for fax searches. Expedited service is available from VitalChek and requires a credit card and additional $8.95 fee for regular mail or $23.95 for overnight delivery after processing.

Death Records

Department of Health, Vital Records Division, 825 North Capitol St NE, 1st Fl, Washington, DC 20002; 202-442-9009, 800-255-2414 (Vital Chek), 8:30AM-3:30PM.

www.dchealth.com

Indexing & Storage: Records are available from August 1874 on. New records are available for inquiry immediately. Records are indexed on microfiche, inhouse computer.

Searching: Records up to 50 years old are only released to immediate family members of person of record or to legal representative of family. Requester should include copy of a photo ID and daytime phone number. Include the following in your request-full name, date of death, Social Security Number.

Access by: mail, phone, fax, in person.

Fee & Payment: All copies are certified. Fee payee: DC Treasurer. Prepayment required. Credit cards are only accepted for expedited services. Personal checks accepted. Credit cards accepted: MasterCard, Visa, AmEx, Discover.

Mail search: Turnaround time: 2 weeks. Genealogical searches must be in writing and cannot be expedited.No self addressed stamped envelope is required. Search costs $12.00 for each name in request.

Phone search: See expedited services.

Fax search: See expedited services.

In person search: Search costs $12.00 for each name in request. Turnaround time is 1/2 hour unless extensive search required.

Expedited service: Expedited service is available for fax searches. Expedited service is available from VitalChek, credit card required. Fee is an additional $8.95 or $23.95 if overnight delivery is required.

Marriage Certificates

Superior Court House, Marriage Bureau, 500 Indiana Ave, NW, Room 4485, Washington, DC 20001; 202-879-4840, 202-879-1280 (Fax), 9AM-4PM.

http://www.dcbar.org/dcsc/fam.html

Indexing & Storage: Records are available from 1811 on. New records are available for inquiry immediately. Records are indexed on microfilm, books (volumes).

Searching: Include the following in your request-both names, wife's maiden name, date of marriage.

Access by: mail, in person.

Fee & Payment: Search fee is $10.00. Extra copies are $.50 per page. Fee payee: Clerk of the Superior Court. Prepayment required. Only money orders are accepted unless requester is an attorney or a minister/priest/rabbi. No credit cards accepted.

Mail search: Turnaround time: 1 to 2 weeks. A self addressed stamped envelope is requested.

In person search: Search costs $10.00 per request. Turnaround time is within the same day.

Divorce Records

Superior Court House, Divorce Records, 500 Indiana Ave, NW, Room 4230, Washington, DC 20001; 202-879-1261, 202-879-1572 (Fax), 9AM-4PM.

http://www.dcbar.org/dcsc/fam.html

Indexing & Storage: Records are available from 1956 on. Records prior to 1956 are located at the US District Court at 202-273-0520. New records are available for inquiry immediately. Records are indexed on microfilm, books (volumes).

Searching: Include the following in your request-names of husband and wife, date of divorce, year divorce case began, case number (if known). The following data is not released: sealed records.

Access by: mail, fax, in person.

Fee & Payment: Search fee is $10.00. Certification is $5.00. Copy fee is $.50 per page. Fee payee: Clerk of the Superior Court. Prepayment required. Use either a money order or a cashier's check if ordering by mail. No credit cards accepted.

Mail search: Turnaround time: 3 weeks. Written requests must include requester's phone number so the court can call back with the charge.A self addressed stamped envelope is requested.

Fax search: Requesters must prepay before records are returned.

In person search: Turnaround time is same day for record after 1988. Prior records are kept off site and will take longer to retrieve.

Workers' Compensation Records

Office of Workers' Compensation, PO Box 56098 3rd Floor, Washington, DC 20011 (Courier: 1200 Upshur St NW, Washington, DC 20011); 202-576-6265, 202-541-3595 (Fax), 8:30AM-5PM.

http://does.ci.washington.dc.us

Indexing & Storage: Records are available from June 1982 on. Records are archived after a year and will take longer to locate. Records are only from private employers. New records are available for inquiry immediately. Records are indexed on inhouse computer.

Searching: Only claimant or parties to claim can access records. All others must have signed release from claimant. Include the following in your request-claimant name, Social Security Number, date of accident, employer.

Access by: mail, phone, fax, in person.

Fee & Payment: There is no search fee, copies are $.20 per page. Fee payee: DC Treasurer. Prepayment required. Personal checks accepted. No credit cards accepted.

Mail search: Turnaround time: 2 to 3 days. A self addressed stamped envelope is requested.

Phone search: There will only confirm if a person is a claimant.

Fax search: Limit 2 pages, turnaround time is 2-3 days.

In person search: Limited to interested parties or with signed release from claimant.

Driver Records

Department of Motor Vehicles, Driver Records Division, 301 "C" St, NW, Washington, DC 20001; 202-727-6761, 202-727-5000 (General), 8:15AM-4PM M-T-TH-F; 8:15AM-7:00PM W.

http://www.dmv.washingtondc.gov/main.htm

Note: Copies of tickets are available from the Bureau of Traffic Adjudication, Correspondence Unit, 65 "K" Street, NE, Washington 20002. The fee is $1.00 per ticket.

Indexing & Storage: Records are available for 3 years for moving violations, suspensions/revocations for 7 years, and DWIs for an indefinite period. Accidents are listed on the record if there is a conviction, but fault is not indicated.

Searching: Requests are classified as either Authorized or General. General records are actually permissible users under DPPA, but personal information is suppressed unless authority is granted by subject. Mail requesters must submit name and DL number; DOB is optional. Online requesters must submit DL, name and DOB; the sex and middle initial is optional.

Access by: mail, in person, online.

Fee & Payment: The cost for a driving record by any method is $5.00. Fee payee: DC Treasurer. Prepayment required. Personal checks accepted. No credit cards accepted.

Mail search: Turnaround time: 3 days. No self addressed stamped envelope is required.

In person search: Walk-in requesters may obtain up to 5 records at once. The rest are available overnight.

Online search: Online requests are taken throughout the day and are available in batch the next morning after 8:15 am. There is no minimum order requirement. Fee is $5.00 per record. Billing is a "bank" system which draws from pre-paid account. Requesters are restricted to high volume, ongoing users. Each requester must be approved and sign a contract. For more information, call (202) 727-5692.

Vehicle Ownership
Vehicle Identification

Department of Motor Vehicles, Vehicle Control Division, 301 "C" St, NW, Room 1063, Washington, DC 20001; 202-727-4768, 8:15AM-4PM M-T-TH-F; 8:15AM-7PM W.

http://www.dmv.washingtondc.gov/main.htm

Searching: Records are classified as either "Authorized" or "General." General records suppress personal information. Casual requesters must have permission of the subject. The following data is not released: Social Security Numbers or financial information.

Access by: mail, in person.

Fee & Payment: The current fee is $5.00 per request for VIN, registration or lien information. Fee payee: DC Treasurer. Prepayment required. Cash is accepted for in person transactions. Personal checks accepted. No credit cards accepted.

Mail search: Turnaround time: 10 days. No self addressed stamped envelope is required.

In person search: You may request information in person.

Other access: Bulk requests can be obtained for commercial purposes upon approval by the Chief of the Bureau of Motor Vehicles if it is determined that the requested use "is for the public interest." Commercial purposes are not permitted.

Accident Reports

Criminal Justice Information Div, Accident Report Section, 300 Indiana Ave NW, Room 3055, Washington, DC 20001; 202-727-4245, 202-727-4357, 7AM-4PM (8PM on Wed).

http://www.dmv.washingtondc.gov

Note: This office holds the officer investigated accident reports known as PD-10s "Citizen reports" can be secured for $2.00 each at the Insurance Operations Branch at 202-727-4601.

Searching: Include the following in your request-date of accident, location of accident, full name. The six-digit identifying number is helpful if known.

Access by: mail, in person.

Fee & Payment: The fee is $2.00 per report for walk-in or mail-in requests. Fee payee: DC Treasurer. Prepayment required. Personal checks accepted. No credit cards accepted.

Mail search: Turnaround time: 3 days. A self addressed stamped envelope is requested.

In person search: You may request information in person.

Vessel Ownership
Vessel Registration
Access to Records is Restricted

Metropolitan Police Dept, Harbor Patrol, 550 Water St SW, Washington, DC 20024; 202-727-4582, 202-727-3663 (Fax).

www.mpdc.org

Note: All vessels regardless of size must be titled and registered. Information is not open to the public. Any emergency requests must be in writing and the agency will use some discretion in release of data for lawful purposes.

Legislation Records

Council of the District of Columbia, 441 4th Street, Rm 714, Washington, DC 20004; 202-724-8050, 202-347-3070 (Fax), 9AM-5:30PM.

http://www.dccouncil.washington.dc.us

Indexing & Storage: Records are available from 1975 to present. Records are indexed on microfilm.

Searching: Include the following in your request-bill number.

Access by: mail, phone, fax, in person, online.

Fee & Payment: 1993-2000 bills are considered current and are on paper. 1975 through 1988 are on microfilm, and you must do your own copying at $.10 per page. 1989-1992 are stored offsite at archives. Fee payee: DC Treasurer. Prepayment required. Personal checks accepted. No credit cards accepted.

Mail search: Turnaround time: 1 to 4 days. No self addressed stamped envelope is required.

Phone search: No fee for telephone request. Bill status is given over the phone.

Fax search: Same criteria as phone searching.

In person search: You may request copies in person.

Online search: Bill text and status may be reviewed at the Internet site.

Voter Registration

DC Board of Elections and Ethics, 441 4th St NW, #250 North, Washington, DC 20001; 202-727-2525, 8:30AM-4:45PM.

http://www.dcboee.org

Indexing & Storage: Records are available for active records. The database is updated every four months.

Searching: Records are open to the public. The following data is not released: Social Security Numbers or date of birth.

Access by: mail, phone, fax, in person.

Fee & Payment: There is no fee for a search, but there is a $.10 copy fee. Fee payee: DC Treasurer. Prepayment required. If purchasing the database, certified funds are required. No credit cards accepted.

Mail search: Turnaround time: 7 to 10 days.

Phone search: For verification purposes only.

Fax search: Fax searching available.

In person search: Information is available immediately.

Other access: Records can be purchased on tape, labels, and printed lists from the SHARE Program. A variety of data is available from party registration to voter history. Minimum fee is $50 plus supplies. Call Karen Jordan at 202-727-6783 for details.

GED Certificates

GED Testing Center, 4200 Connecticut Ave. NW, MB1005, Washington, DC 20008; 202-576-6308, 202-576-7899 (Fax), 8AM-5PM.

Searching: To search, all of the following are required: a signed release, name, date/year test, Social Security Number, and city of test.

Access by: mail, fax, in person.

Fee & Payment: There is no fee for verification. Copies of transcripts are $3.00 per copy. Fee payee: DC Public Schools. Money orders are accepted. No credit cards accepted.

Mail search: Turnaround time: 10-14 days. No self addressed stamped envelope is required.

Fax search: Same criteria as phone searching.

In person search: Results are still mailed within two weeks.

Fishing License Information
Access to Records is Restricted

Environmental Health Regulation, Fisheries & Wildlife Division, 51 N Street NE - 5th Fl, Washington, DC 20002-3323; 202-535-2266, 202-535-1359 (Fax), 8AM-5PM.

Note: Hunting of any kind is prohibited within the District of Columbia. Records are not available to the public, they are only released as a Freedom of Information Act request. Certain data may be released to attorneys for pending litigation or statistical use with a written request.

District of Columbia State Licensing Agencies

Licenses Searchable Online

Attorney #03 .... www.dcbar.org/memberlookup/searchform.cfm
Lobbyist #09 .... www.lobbyist.net/Federal/FEDLOB.htm
Optometrist #05 .... www.odfinder.org/LicSearch.asp

Licensing Quick Finder

Acupuncturist #02 202-442-4776
Air Conditioning/Refrigeration #05 202-727-7480
Alcohol Mfg./Vendor/Distributor #01......202-442-4423
Architect #05 202-727-7480
Athletic Trainer/Coach #08 202-442-5377
Attorney #03 202-626-3475
Auctioneer #05 202-727-7480
Automobile Repossessor #05 202-727-7480
Bank #10 202-727-1563
Barber #06 202-727-7505
Bingo Operation #13 202-645-8041
Boxing/Wrestling Event/Professional #6 202-727-7505
Chiropractor #06 202-727-7505
Contractor #05 202-727-7480
Cosmetologist #06 202-727-7505
Counselor, Professional #05 202-727-7480
Credit Union #10 202-727-1563
Dental Hygienist #05 202-727-7480
Dentist #06 202-727-7505
Dietitian/Nutritionist #06 202-727-7505
Electrician #05 202-727-7480
Emergency Medical Technician #11......202-442-9111
Engineer #05 202-727-7480
Firearms Instructor #14 410-799-0191
Firearms Permit #14 410-799-0191
Funeral Director #05 202-727-7480
Gas Fitter #05 202-727-7480

Hearing Aid Dispenser #05 202-727-7480
Insurance Broker/Agent #12 202-727-7425
Interior Designer #05 202-727-7480
Investment Advisor #07 202-442-7853
Investment Advisor Representative #07 202-442-7853
K-9 Units #14 410-799-0191
Lobbyist #09 202-939-8717
Lottery Retailer #13 202-645-8042
Mechanic, Master #05 202-727-7480
Medical Doctor #02 202-442-4776
Midwife Nurse #05 202-727-7480
Mortgage Broker/Lender #10 202-727-1563
Motor Vehicle Dealer/Salesperson #05 .202-727-7480
Notary Public #15 202-727-3117
Nurse #06 202-727-7505
Nursing Home Administrator #06 202-727-7505
Occupational Therapist #05 202-727-7480
Optometrist #05 202-727-7480
Osteopathic Physician #02 202-442-4776
Parking Lot Attendant #05 202-727-7480
Pesticide Applicator #04 202-442-4307
Pesticide Dealer #04 202-442-4307
Pesticide Employee/Operator #04..........202-442-4307
Pharmacist #06 202-727-7505
Physical Therapist #05 202-727-7480
Physician Assistant #06 202-727-7505
Plumber #05 202-727-7170

Podiatrist #05 202-727-7480
Private Investigator #14 410-799-0191
Property Manager #05 202-727-7480
Psychologist #06 202-727-7505
Psychometrist/School Psychologist #08 202-442-5377
Public Accountant #06 202-727-7505
Real Estate Appraiser #05 202-727-7480
Real Estate Broker/Salesperson #05 202-727-7480
Savings & Loan Company #10...............202-727-1563
School Attendance Officer/Worker #08 .202-442-5377
School Counselor #08 202-442-5377
School Librarian/Media Specialist #08...202-442-5377
School Social Worker #08 202-442-5377
Securities Agent #07 202-442-7826
Securities Broker/Dealer #07 202-442-7826
Security Agency #14 410-799-0191
Security Alarm Dealer/Agent #05 202-727-7480
Security Guard #14 410-799-0191
Social Worker #06 202-727-7505
Solicitor #05 202-727-7480
Solid Waste Collector #05 202-727-7480
Speech Language Pathologist/Audiologist #08...........
....202-442-5377
Teacher/Teacher Trainer #08 202-442-5377
Tour Guide #05 202-727-7480
Veterinarian #06 202-727-7505

Licensing Agency Information

#01 Dept. of Consumer Regulatory Affairs, 941 N Capitol St NE, Washington, DC 20002-4259; 202-442-4445.
http://dcra.dc.gov/services/abra/index.shtm

#02 Health Care Licensing, 825 N Capitol St NE 2nd Fl, Washington, DC 20002-4210; 202-442-9200, Fax: 202-442-9431.
www.dchealth.com

#03 District of Columbia Bar Association, 1250 H St NW, 6th Fl, Washington, DC 20005; 202-737-4700, Fax: 202-626-3471.
www.dcbar.org
Direct web site URL to search for licensees:
www.dcbar.org/memberlookup/searchform.cfm

#04 Department of Consumer & Regulatory Affairs, 941 N Capitol St NE, Room 100, Washington, DC 20002; 202-535-2299.

#05 Department of Consumer & Regulatory Affairs, 941 N Capitol St NE, Washington, DC 20002-4259.

#06 Department of Consumer & Regulatory Affairs, 941 N Capitol St NE, Washington, DC 20002-4259; 202-727-7480, Fax: 202-727-7662.

#07 Department of Insurance & Securities Regulation - Securities Bureau, 810 1st St NE #602, Washington, DC 20002-4227; 202-727-8000, Fax: 202-535-1199.
http://disr.washingtondc.gov/main.htm

#08 Public Schools, Licensure & Credentials, 825 N Capitol St NE #9026, Washington, DC 20002; 202-442-5377, Fax: 202-442-5311.
www.k12.dc.us/dcps/home.html

#09 Director of Campaign Finance, 2000 14th St NW, #420, Washington, DC 20009; 202-671-0550, Fax: 202-671-0658.
www.dcocf.org
Direct web site URL to search for licensees:
www.dcocf.org/ocfpdf/registrantsfilers2001JanPUB.PDF

#10 Economic Development, 1400 L St NW #400, Washington, DC 20005; 202-727-1563, Fax: 202-727-1588. www.dbfi.dc.gov

#11 Emergency, Health & Medical Svcs. Office, 825 N Capitol St NE, Washington, DC 20002; 202-442-9111, Fax: 202-442-4812.
www.dchealth.com

#12 Dept of Insurance & Securities Regulation, 810 1st St NE #701, Washington, DC 20002; 202-727-8000.
www.disr.washingtondc.gov

#13 Lottery & Charitable Games Control Board, 2101 Martin Luther King Jr Ave SE, Washington, DC 20020; 202-645-8041, Fax: 202-645-0006.

#14 Metropolitian Police Department, 7751 Washington Blvd, Jessup, MD 20794; 410-799-0191, Fax: 410-799-5934.

#15 Notary Commissions & Authentications Section, Office of the Secretary, 441 4th St NW #810A South, Washington, DC 20001; 202-727-3117, Fax: 202-727-8457.

District of Columbia Federal Courts

US District Court

District of Columbia

Washington DC Division US Courthouse, Clerk's Office, Room 1225, 333 Constitution Ave NW, Washington, DC 20001 (Courier Address: Use mail address for courier delivery), 202-727-2947, Fax: 202-354-3524.

www.dcd.uscourts.gov

Indexing/Storage: Cases are indexed by defendant and plaintiff as well as by case number. New cases are available in the index 48 hours after filing date. Both computer and card indexes are maintained. Civil records are indexed on computer since 1987 with an archive program available of some older cases, microfiche from 1932 to mid-1991. Criminal records are indexed on computer since mid-1991, microfiche from 1932 to mid-1991. District wide searches are available from this court. Archived records are not available over the phone; the court must be contacted in writing and will be made available through a copy service. Turnaround time: 3-5 days.

Fee & Payment: The fee is $20.00 per item (one party name or case number). Payment may be made by. Payment must be received before copies will be released. Payee: Clerk, US District Court. Certification fee: $7.00 per document. Copy fee: $.50 per page.

Phone Search: Searchers calling locally will not be given information over the phone. Out of state calls will be given the 3 most current docket entries only.

Mail Search: Always enclose a stamped self addressed envelope.

In Person: In person searching is available.

PACER: Sign-up number is 800-676-6856. Access fee is. Toll-free access: 888-253-6878. Local access: 202-273-0606. New records are available online after. PACER is available online at http://pacer.dcd.uscourts.gov.

Electronic Filing: Electronic filing information is available online at https://ecf.dcd.uscourts.gov

Opinions Online: Court opinions are available online at http://www.dcd.uscourts.gov

US Bankruptcy Court

District of Columbia

Washington DC Division E Barrett Prettyman Courthouse, Room 4400, 333 Constitution Ave NW, Washington, DC 20001 (Courier Address: Use mail address for courier delivery), 202-273-0042.

http://www.dcb.uscourts.gov

Indexing/Storage: Cases are indexed by debtor and creditors as well as by case number. New cases are available in the index 24 hours after filing date. Both computer and card indexes are maintained. Records are indexed on computer from 1990 to present. For records prior to 1990, a card index is maintained. Open records are located at this court.

Fee & Payment: The fee is $20.00 per item (one party name or case number). Payment may be made by money order, cashier check, business check. Personal checks are not accepted. Prepayment is required. Cash accepted in person. Payee: Clerk, US Bankruptcy Court. Certification fee: $7.00 per document. Copy fee: $.50 per page.

Phone Search: An automated voice case information service (VCIS) is available. Call VCIS at 888-667-5530 or 202-273-0048.

Mail Search: Always enclose a stamped self addressed envelope.

In Person: In person searching is available.

PACER: Sign-up number is 800-676-6856. Access fee is $.60 per minute. Toll-free access: 888-289-2414. Local access: 202-273-0630. Case records are available back to 1991. Records are purged every six months. New civil records are available online after 2 days. PACER is available online at http://pacer.dcb.uscourts.gov.

District of Columbia Courts

Court	Jurisdiction	No. of Courts	How Organized
Superior Courts*	General	3	
Probate/Tax Court*	Special	1	

* Profiled in this Sourcebook.

Court	CIVIL								
	Tort	Contract	Real Estate	Min. Claim	Max. Claim	Small Claims	Estate	Eviction	Domestic Relations
Superior Courts*	X	X	X	$5000	No Max	$5000		X	X
Probate/Tax Courts*							X		

Court	CRIMINAL				
	Felony	Misdemeanor	DWI/DUI	Preliminary Hearing	Juvenile
Superior Courts*	X	X	X	X	X
Probate/Tax Courts*					

ADMINISTRATION   Executive Office, 500 Indiana Av NW, Room 1500, Washington, DC, 20001; 202-879-1700, Fax: 202-879-4829. www.dcsc.gov

COURT STRUCTURE   The Superior Court in DC is divided into 17 divisions, 4 of which are shown in this book: Criminal, Civil, Family, and Tax-Probate. The Tax-Probate Division of the Superior Court handles probate. Eviction is part of the court's Landlord and Tenant Branch (202-879-4879).

ONLINE ACCESS   The Court of Appeals maintains a bulletin board system for various court notices, and can be dialed from computer at 202-626-8863. Additionally, opinions from 1/1997 to 5/2001 are listed, also memorandum opinions and judgments from 9/1999 to 5/2001. The Court of Appeals has their own web site at www.dcca.state.state.dc.us. The Superior Court at www.dcsc.gov lists Administrative Orders from 1/16/2001 to 5/25/2001.

📖 📖 📖 📖 📖 📖 📖

Superior Court - Criminal Division 500 Indiana Ave NW Room 4001, Washington, DC 20001; 202-879-1373; Fax: 202-638-5352. Hours: 8:30AM-4PM (EST). *Felony, Misdemeanor.*

www.dcsc.gov

Criminal Records: Access: Phone, mail, in person. Both court and visitors may perform in person searches. No search fee. Required to search: name, years to search, DOB. Criminal records on computer from 1978, on microfiche from 1974, on index from 1970, archived from 1962.
General Information: No sealed records released. Turnaround time depends on case involved. No copy fee. Certification fee: No cert fee.

Superior Court - Civil Division 500 Indiana Ave NW JM 170, Washington, DC 20001; 202-879-1133; Fax: 202-737-0827. Hours: 8:30AM-4PM M-F; 9AM-Noon Sat (EST). *Civil Actions, Small Claims.*

www.dcsc.gov

Civil Records: Access: Phone, mail, in person. Both court and visitors may perform in person searches. Search fee: $10.00 per name. Required to search: name. Civil cases indexed by defendant, plaintiff. Civil records on computer from 1983, on microfiche, archived and on index from 1976. Only out-of-District inquires are taken by phone. **General Information:** Public Access terminal is available. No sealed records released. SASE required. Turnaround time depends on case involved. Copy fee: $.50 per page. Certification fee: $5.00. Fee payee: Clerk-Superior Court of DC. Only cashiers checks and money orders accepted. Prepayment is required.

DC Superior Court - Landlord & Tenant Branch 500 Indiana Ave NW Room JM 255, Washington, DC 20001; 202-879-4879. Hours: 8:30AM-4PM M-F; 9AM-Noon Sat (EST). *Eviction.*

www.dcsc.gov

Civil Records: Access: In person, mail. Both court and visitors may perform in person searches. No search fee. Only out-of-District inquires are taken by phone. **General Information:** Public Access terminal is available. Turnaround time depends on case involved. Copy fee: $.25 each. Fee payee: Clerk-Superior Court of DC. Prepayment is required.

Superior Court - Probate Division 500 Indiana Ave NW, Washington, DC 20001; 202-879-4800; Fax: 202-393-5849/879-1452(auditing). Hours: 9AM-4PM (EST). *Probate.*

District of Columbia Recording Offices

ORGANIZATION District of Columbia is in the Eastern Time Zone (EST).

REAL ESTATE RECORDS The District does not perform real estate searches.

UCC RECORDS Financing statements are filed with the Recorder, including real estate related collateral. UCC searches performed for $30.00 per debtor name. Copies cost $2.25 per page.

TAX LIEN RECORDS Federal tax liens on personal property of businesses are filed with the Secretary of State. Other federal and all state tax liens on personal property are filed with the Recorder.

District of Columbia

Recorder of Deeds, 515 D Street NW, Room 203, Washington, DC 20001. 202-727-7110.

Will search UCC records. UCC search includes tax liens if requested. Will not search real estate records. **Other Phone Numbers:** Assessor 202-727-6447; Treasurer 202-727-6055.

District of Columbia County Locator

You will usually be able to find the city name in the City/County Cross Reference below. In that case, it is a simple matter to determine the county from the cross reference. However, only the official US Postal Service city names are included in this index. There are an additional 40,000 place names that people use in their addresses. Therefore, we have also included a ZIP/City Cross Reference immediately following the City/County Cross Reference.

If you know the ZIP Code but the city name does not appear in the City/County Cross Reference index, look up the ZIP Code in the ZIP/City Cross Reference, find the city name, then look up the city name in the City/County Cross Reference. For example, you want to know the county for an address of Menands, NY 12204. There is no "Menands" in the City/County Cross Reference. The ZIP/City Cross Reference shows that ZIP Codes 12201-12288 are for the city of Albany. Looking back in the City/County Cross Reference, Albany is in Albany County.

City/County Cross Reference

WASHINGTON District of Columbia

ZIP/City Cross Reference

20001-20599   WASHINGTON

Florida

General Help Numbers:

Governor's Office
The Capitol 850-488-4441
Tallahassee, FL 32399-0001 Fax 850-487-0801
http://www.myflorida.com/myflorida/governorsoffice/inde
x.html 8AM-5PM

Attorney General's Office
Legal Affairs Department 850-414-3300
The Capitol, PL-01 Fax 850-488-4872
Tallahassee, FL 32399-1050 8AM-5PM
http://legal.firn.edu

State Court Administrator
Supreme Court Bldg, 500 S Duval 850-922-5082
Tallahassee, FL 32399-1900 Fax 850-488-0156
http://www.flcourts.org 8AM-5PM

State Archives
Archives & Records 850-245-6700
R A Gray Bldg, 500 S Bronough Fax 850-488-4894
Tallahassee, FL 32399-0250 8AM-5PM M-F;
http://dlis.dos.state.fl.us 9AM-3PM SA

State Specifics:

Capital: Tallahassee
Leon County

Time Zone: EST*
* Florida's ten western-most counties are CST:
They are: Bay, Calhoun, Escambia, Gulf, Holmes,
Jackson, Okaloosa, Santa Rosa, Walton, Washington.

Number of Counties: 67

Population: 15,982,378

Web Site: www.state.fl.us

State Agencies

Criminal Records

Florida Department of Law Enforcement, User Services Bureau, PO Box 1489, Tallahassee, FL 32302 (Courier: 2331 Phillip Rd, Tallahassee, FL 32308); 850-410-8109, 850-410-8107, 8AM-5PM.

http://www.fdle.state.fl.us/index.asp

Note: Sex offender data is available online at www.fdle.state.fl.us/sexual_predators.

Indexing & Storage: Records are available from the early 1930's. New records are available for inquiry immediately. Records are indexed on microfilm, NIST Archive inhouse computer.

Searching: Include the following in your request-date of birth, race, sex, name. You can submit fingerprints, for the same fee, but it is not required. The following data is not released: sealed, juvenile or expunged records.

Access by: mail, in person, online.

Fee & Payment: The fee is $15.00 per individual. With a pre-paid account you can get better turnaround time, which is normally two working days Fee payee: Department of Law Enforcement. Prepayment required. Personal checks accepted. Credit cards accepted only for online requests.

Mail search: Turnaround time: 5 working days. No self addressed stamped envelope is required.

Online search: Criminal history information from 1967 forward may be ordered over the Department Program Internet site at www.fdle.state.fl.us. Click on "Background Checks." A $15.00 fee applies. Juvenile records from 10/1994 forward are also available. Credit card ordering will return records to your screen or via e-mail.

Expedited service: Expedited service is available for mail and phone searches. Turnaround time: overnight delivery.

Corporation Records
Limited Partnership Records
Limited Liability Company Records
Trademarks/Servicemarks
Fictitious Names

Division of Corporations, Department of State, PO Box 6327, Tallahassee, FL 32314 (Courier: 409 E Gaines St, Tallahassee, FL 32399); 850-488-9000 (Telephone Inquires), 850-487-6053 (Copy Requests), 850-487-6056 (Annual Reports), 8AM-5PM.

http://www.sunbiz.org

Note: This agency recommends accessing the Internet site.

Indexing & Storage: Records are available from the late 1800's. New records are available for inquiry immediately. Records are indexed on inhouse computer, on-line.

Searching: Addresses of judges and police are not released. Include the following in your request-full name of business. In addition to the articles of incorporation, corporation records include the following information: Annual Reports (date of filing and updates), Officers, Directors, Prior (merged) names, Inactive names, and US Tax ID number.

Access by: mail, phone, in person, online.

Fee & Payment: Copies of documents on microfilm or by image are $1.00 per page. Certification for corporate documents is $8.75, $52.50 for limited partnership records, and $30.00 for Limited Liability Company records. Fee payee: Secretary of State. Prepayment required. Personal checks accepted. Accepts credit cards for online filing of annuals, only.

Mail search: Turnaround time: 2 to 3 days.

Phone search: The agency will not release name availability over the phone.

In person search: Fees: $1.00 per non-certified page or $10.00 for a complete copy on file regardless of number of pages.

Online search: The state's excellent Internet site gives detailed information on all corporate, trademark, limited liability company and limited partnerships (from 01/96): fictitious names (from 01/97); and UCC records (from 01/97).

Other access: The state offers record purchases on microfiche sets and on CD disks.

Uniform Commercial Code
Federal Tax Liens

UCC Division, Secretary of State, PO Box 5588, Tallahassee, FL 32314 (Courier: 409 E Gaines St, Tallahassee, FL 32399); 850-487-6055, 850-487-6013 (Fax), 8AM-5PM.

http://www.sunbiz.org

Indexing & Storage: Records are available from 1966, if active. Records are on computer and microfiche. Records filed by electronic process are available in image format. New records are available for inquiry immediately.

Searching: Federal tax liens on businesses are filed here; state tax liens are not. It is suggested to search state tax liens at the county level. Effective 10/1/2001 judgment liens will be filed on the state level. Include the following in your request-debtor name. The state will not do a search. You must hire an outside firm, come in-person, or use the division's web page.

Access by: in person, online.

Fee & Payment: Fees are $1.00 per page for non-certified and $10.00 per document certified. Copies are $1.00 per page. Fee payee: Secretary of State. Prepayment required. Personal checks accepted. No credit cards accepted. No self addressed stamped envelope is required. No searching by mail.

In person search: Front counter debit accounts are available for local filers.

Online search: The state Internet site allows access for no charge. The state also has a document image delivery system on the web site. This includes all UCC filings since 01/97 and all documents that were filed electronically since 03/95.

Other access: Microfilm reels and CD's of images are available for bulk purchase requesters. Call 850-488-1486 for information.

State Tax Liens
Records not maintained by a state level agency.

Note: These records are filed and found at the county level.

Sales Tax Registrations

Florida Department of Revenue, 168 Blountstown Highway #C, Tallahassee, FL 32304-3702; 850-488-9925, 850-922-5936 (Fax), 8AM-5PM.

http://www.state.fl.us/dor

Indexing & Storage: Records are available for 5 years, then they are purged.

Searching: This agency will confirm that a business is registered and has filed returns with the department. The following are required to search; business name, tax ID number, and business location. They can also search by the owner's name.

Access by: mail, fax, in person.

Fee & Payment: There is no fee.

Mail search: The turnaround time is 7-10 days.

Fax search: Same criteria as mail searching.

In person search: Records are still returned by mail.

Birth Certificates

Department of Health, Office of Vital Statistics, PO Box 210, Jacksonville, FL 32231-0042 (Courier: 1217 Pearl St, Jacksonville, FL 32202); 904-359-6900, 904-359-6993 (Fax), 8AM-5PM.

http://www.doh.state.fl.us

Note: The web site includes general information and ordering instructions.

Indexing & Storage: Records are available from 1865 to present, however few records where filed prior to 1917. It takes 4 weeks after birth before new records are available for inquiry. Records are indexed on microfiche, inhouse computer.

Searching: Records released only to individual named, if of legal age, or to parents or legal guardians. If deceased, proof of death required for same if a certification of birth needed. Include the following in your request-full name, names of parents, mother's maiden name, date of birth, county.

Access by: mail, phone, fax, in person.

Fee & Payment: Fee is $9.00 plus $5.00 if ordered by credit card. $4.00 per copy when ordering additional same name at the same time. If the specific year is not known, additional years may be searched for a fee of $2.00 per year with a maximum fee of $55.00. Fee payee: Office of Vital Statistics. Prepayment required. Credit cards accepted through VitalChek Corporation (800-255-2414). A $5.00 fee is added for all credit card transactions. Personal checks accepted. Credit cards accepted: MasterCard, Visa, AmEx, Discover.

Mail search: Turnaround time: 15 to 20 days. No self addressed stamped envelope is required.

Phone search: See expedited services.

Fax search: See expedited services.

In person search: Turnaround time is same day.

Other access: Commemorative birth certificates in large size, signed by the governor, and suitable for framing are available. The fee is $34.00 or $25.00 when ordered in conjunction with other certified copies of the same record. Allow 4 to 6 weeks for delivery.

Expedited service: Expedited service is available for mail, phone and fax searches. Cost is $24.00 and if you wish to use Federal Express, an additional fee of $13.00 is charged. Turnaround time is 2 days plus delivery time.

Death Records

Department of Health, Office of Vital Statistics, PO Box 210, Jacksonville, FL 32231-0042 (Courier: 1217 Pearl St, Jacksonville, FL 32202); 904-359-6900, 904-359-6993 (Fax), 8AM-5PM.

http://www.doh.state.fl.us

Note: The web site contains general information, ordering instructions, and forms.

Indexing & Storage: Records are available from 1877 to present. It takes 4 weeks after death before new records are available for inquiry. Records are indexed on microfiche, inhouse computer.

Searching: The death certificate minus cause of death is public information. Cause is released 50 years after death to public. Otherwise, requester must be family member or demonstrate legal interest in the estate. Include the following in your request-full name, date of death, county. The following data is not released: cause of death.

Access by: mail, phone, fax, in person.

Fee & Payment: Fee is $5.00 for the first year searched. If the specific year is not known, additional years may be searched for $2.00 per year with a maximum fee of $55.00. Add $4.00 per copy when ordering additional copies at the same time. Fee payee: Office of Vital Statistics. Prepayment required. Credit cards are accepted through VitalChek Corporation (800-255-2414).

Personal checks accepted. Credit cards accepted: MasterCard, Visa, AmEx, Discover.

Mail search: Turnaround time: 15 to 20 days. No self addressed stamped envelope is required.

Phone search: See expedited service.

Fax search: See expedited service.

In person search: Turnaround time is same day.

Expedited service: Expedited service is available for mail, phone and fax searches. Include $5.00 credit card fee. Cost is $20.00 and if you wish to use Federal Express, an additional fee of $13.00 is charged. Turnaround time is 2 days plus delivery time.

Marriage Certificates

Department of Health, Office of Vital Statistics, PO Box 210, Jacksonville, FL 32231-0042 (Courier: 1217 Pearl St, Jacksonville, FL 32202); 904-359-6900, 904-359-6993 (Fax), 8AM-5PM.

http://www.doh.state.fl.us

Note: The web site contains general information, ordering instructions and order forms to download.

Indexing & Storage: Records are available from 1927 to present on microfiche, from 1970 to present on computer.

Searching: Records are indexed by husband's name and/or by wife's maiden name. Include date of marriage and county of marriage in request. The following data is not released: Social Security Numbers.

Access by: mail, phone, fax, in person.

Fee & Payment: The fee is $5.00 per name for the first year searched. Additional years may be searched for $2.00 per year with a maximum fee of $55.00. Add $4.00 per copy when ordering additional copies at the same time. Credit card fee is $4.50. Fee payee: Office of Vital Statistics. Prepayment required. Credit cards are accepted through VitalChek Corporation (800 255-2414). Personal checks accepted. Credit cards accepted: MasterCard, Visa, AmEx, Discover.

Mail search: Turnaround time: 15 to 20 days. No self addressed stamped envelope is required.

Phone search: See expedited service.

Fax search: See expedited service.

In person search: Turnaround time is same day.

Other access: A large size, commemorative marriage certificate signed by the governor is available for $30.00 or $25.00 when ordered in conjunction with other certified copies of the same record. Allow 4 to 6 weeks for delivery.

Expedited service: Expedited service is available for mail, phone and fax searches. Include use of credit card. Total cost is $19.50 and if you wish to use Federal Express, an additional fee of $12.50 is charged. Turnaround time is 2 days plus delivery time.

Divorce Records

Department of Health, Office of Vital Statistics, PO Box 210, Jacksonville, FL 32231-0042 (Courier: 1217 Pearl St, Jacksonville, FL 32202); 904-359-6900, 904-359-6993 (Fax), 8AM-5PM.

http://www.doh.state.fl.us

Note: The web site provides general information and ordering instructions.

Indexing & Storage: Records are available from 1927 to present. It takes 6-8 weeks after divorce before new records are available for inquiry.

Searching: Records are indexed by husband's name only. Include county of divorce in request. In each of the last 5 years in Florida, there have been 140,000 marriages and 80,000 divorces per year. (This is over 1025 per court day.)

Access by: mail, phone, fax, in person.

Fee & Payment: Fees are $5.00 per request for the first year and $2.00 per year for each additional search year, with a maximum search fee of $55.00. Add $4.00 per copy per name when ordering additional copies at the same time. Fee payee: Office of Vital Statistics. Prepayment required. Credit cards are accepted through VitalChek Corporation (800-255-2414). A $5.00 fee is added for credit cards. Personal checks accepted. Credit cards accepted: MasterCard, Visa, AmEx, Discover.

Mail search: Turnaround time: 15 to 20 days. No self addressed stamped envelope is required.

Phone search: See expedited service.

Fax search: See expedited service.

In person search: The fee is nonrefundable. Turnaround time is same day.

Expedited service: Expedited service is available for mail, phone and fax searches. Turnaround time: 2 days. The fee of $20.00 includes the credit card surcharge. If you wish to use Federal Express, an additional fee of $13.00 is charged.

Workers' Compensation Records

Workers Compensation Division, Information Management Unit, Forrest Bldg, 2728 Centerview Dr, Ste 202, Tallahassee, FL 32399; 850-488-3030, 850-921-0305 (Fax), 7:30AM-5PM.

http://www.fdles.state.fl.us/wc

Indexing & Storage: Records are available from 1985 on microfilm. Indexes are also on microfiche (older) and on an image process (recent). It takes 3 days (imaged) before new records are available for inquiry. Records are indexed on microfilm, microfiche.

Searching: To get medical records you must have a signed release of subject, except for legal representatives or an involved insurance company. Include the following in your request-claimant name, Social Security Number, date of accident.

Access by: mail, fax, in person.

Fee & Payment: There is no search fee, but copies are $.15 per page. Fee payee: Workers Compensation Trust Fund. Prepayment required. Personal checks accepted. No credit cards accepted.

Mail search: Turnaround time: 2 weeks. They will send an invoice, and will send you the copies after they receive the check.No self addressed stamped envelope is required.

Fax search: Same criteria as mail searching.

In person search: Requests are still returned by mail, unless you have a subpoena.

Driver Records

Department of Highway Safety & Motor Vehicles, Division of Drivers Licenses, PO Box 5775, Tallahassee, FL 32314-5775 (Courier: 2900 Apalachee Pky, Rm B-133, Neil Kirkman Bldg,

Tallahassee, FL 32399); 850-488-0250, 850-487-7080 (Fax), 8AM-5PM.

http://www.hsmv.state.fl.us

Note: Copies of tickets may be obtained from the same address listed above. The fee is $.50 each or $1.00 for certified copies.

Indexing & Storage: Records are available for a 3 year record or for a 7 year record. Accidents will appear only if a citation is issued, but the record will not show fault.

Searching: Driving records are deemed public information and no restrictions to requests or usage are maintained, as long as the usage is of a legal nature. Casual requesters cannot obtain personal information without consent. Either the driver license number or the name, DOB and sex are required for ordering.

Access by: mail, in person, online.

Fee & Payment: The fee is $3.10 for a certified three or seven year record. Online is $2.10, and these records not considered certified. There is a full charge for a "no record found." Fee payee: Division of Drivers Licenses. Prepayment required. Personal checks accepted. No credit cards accepted.

Mail search: Turnaround time: 10 days. No self addressed stamped envelope is required.

In person search: Normally, up to 50 requests can be processed for walk-in requests, while you wait. Some Clerks of Courts will also process driving records.

Online search: Online requests an on interactive basis. The state differentiates between high and low volume users. Requesters with 5,000 or more records per month are considered Network Providers. Call 850-488-6264 to become a Provider. Requesters with less than 5,000 requests per month (called Individual Users) are directed to a Provider. A list of providers is found at the web site.

Other access: The state will process magnetic tape requests. Also, they will provide customized database searches of the license information. Call 850-487-4467 for more details.

Vehicle Ownership
Vehicle Identification

Division of Motor Vehicles, Information Research Section, Neil Kirkman Bldg, A-126, Tallahassee, FL 32399; 850-488-5665, 850-488-8983 (Fax), 8AM-4:30PM.

http://www.hsmv.state.fl.us

Indexing & Storage: Records are available for 12 years.

Searching: Florida expects to adopt legislation in 2001 to become fully compliant with DPPA. FL imposes no access restrictions as long as the request is of a legal nature. However, casual requesters cannot obtain personal information without consent of subject. Please submit the city (residence) and DOB if doing a name search.

Access by: mail, in person, online.

Fee & Payment: The fee for a computer printout of information is $.50, $1.00 per page copy fee, and $3.00 if certification is needed. The current license plate registration is $2.00. A complete microfilm title history can be $15.00 or more. Fee payee: Division of Motor Vehicles. Prepayment required. Personal checks accepted. No credit cards accepted.

308   *The Sourcebook to Public Record Information*   State Agencies - Florida

Mail search: Turnaround time: 2 to 3 weeks. If records are on microfiche, the wait may be as long as 4 weeks.No self addressed stamped envelope is required.

In person search: In cases when the information is not readily available the wait is 2 to 3 days.

Online search: Florida has contracted to release vehicle information through approved Network Providers. Accounts must be approved by the state first. For each record accessed, the charge is $.50 plus the subscriber fee. Users must work from an estimated 2 1/2 month pre-paid bank. New subscribers must complete an application with the Department 850-488-6264.

Other access: A user may obtain ownership information by county or statewide vehicle class code basis. For more information, call the Motor Vehicle Data Listing Information Services at 850-488-4280.

Accident Reports

DHSMV- MS-28, Crash Records-Room A325, Neil Kirkman Bldg, 2900 Apalachee Prky, Tallahassee, FL 32399-0538; 850-488-5017, 850-922-0488 (Fax), 8AM-4:45PM.

http://www.hsmv.state.fl.us

Indexing & Storage: Records are available from 1941 to the present. Records are stored on microfilm from 1983 forward. It takes 12 weeks before new records are available for inquiry. Records are indexed on microfilm and computer.

Searching: Records sealed by court order and juvenile information cannot be accessed. Homicide reports less than 5 years old should be requested from the local law enforcement agency that wrote the report. Include the following in your request-the full name of driver, exact date of crash (after 1983), county and city, local agency that investigated. For reports prior to 1983 the exact date, county, location and if crash involved a fatality must be supplied with request.

Access by: mail, in person.

Fee & Payment: The cost is $2.00 per report, $25.00 if a homicide. You cannot search by phone; however, you can call to determine if report is available. Fee payee: Department of Highway Safety and Motor Vehicles. Prepayment required. Personal checks accepted. No credit cards accepted.

Mail search: Turnaround time: 2 to 4 weeks. A self addressed stamped envelope is requested.

In person search: You may request information in person at the customer service counter on 1st floor (Room B-133).

Other access: List or bulk purchase is available by special request.

Vessel Ownership
Vessel Registration

Dept of Highway Safety, Vessel Records, Bureau of Titles & Registrations, 2900 Apalachee Parkway, MS 68, Tallahassee, FL 32399; 850-922-9000, 850-921-1935 (Fax).

http://www.hsmv.state.fl.us

Indexing & Storage: Records are available for 12 years to present. Records are indexed on computer. Motorized vessels must be titled and registered. Non-powered vessels are not required to be registered; however, non-powered vessels 16 ft and over must be titled. Liens show on records. It takes 6 weeks before new records are available for inquiry.

Searching: A written request is required for all searches. To search one of the following is required: Florida registration #, title #, hull id #, or the exact name.

Access by: mail, fax, in person.

Fee & Payment: $.50 per page for computer print-out. $1.00 per photocopy of record. Additional $3.00 for each item to be certified. Fee payee: Dept of Highway Safety. Personal checks accepted. No credit cards accepted.

Mail search: Turnaround time: 1 week. No self addressed stamped envelope is required.

Fax search: Records are available by fax.

Other access: A bulk purchase program is available for magnetic tape, labels or printed list. There is a $50.00 deposit required and a fee of $.01 per record.

Legislation Records

Office of Legislative Services, Legislative Information Services Division, 111 W Madison St, Pepper Bldg, Rm 704, Tallahassee, FL 32399-1400; 850-488-4371, 850-487-5915 (Senate Bills), 850-488-7475 (House Bills), 850-488-8427 (Session Laws), 850-921-5334 (Fax), 8AM-5PM.

http://www.leg.state.fl.us

Indexing & Storage: Records are available from 1965 to present in book format, from 1972 to present on microfiche, and current and prior year on computer.

Searching: Include the following in your request-bill number. You may search by subject also.

Access by: mail, phone, fax, in person, online.

Fee & Payment: They will let you know the fee. Requests will be referred to House or Senate documents department. Fee payee: Florida Legislature. Prepayment required. Personal checks accepted. No credit cards accepted.

Mail search: Turnaround time: 3 days. No self addressed stamped envelope is required.

Phone search: You may call for copies. There is an in-state toll-free line, 800-342-1827, for bill information.

Fax search: Fax requesting is permitted, but the state asks to call first to make arrangements.

In person search: You may request copies in person.

Online search: Their Internet site contains full text of bills and a bill history session outlining actions taken on bills. The site is updated every day at 11 PM. Records go back to 1995. There is a more extensive online information service available. This system also includes information on lobbyists. Fees are involved.

Voter Registration
Access to Records is Restricted

Department of State, Division of Elections, Room 1801, The Capitol, Tallahassee, FL 32399-0250; 850-488-7690, 850-488-1768 (Fax), 8AM-5PM.

http://election.dos.state.fl.us

Note: All individual searching must be done at the county level. However, the state maintains a central voter file for data and statistical purposes.

GED Certificates

GED Testing Office, 325 W Gaines St Rm 634, Tallahassee, FL 32399; 850-487-1619, 8AM-5PM.

Searching: To verify, the following is required: name, date of birth, year of test, Social Security Number, and county/city of test. If known, the GED Diploma number is helpful. A signed release is needed to get a copy of a transcript or diploma.

Access by: mail, phone, in person.

Fee & Payment: The fee is $4.00 per copy of transcript or diploma. There is no fee for verification. Money orders and cashiers' checks are required. Personal checks are not accepted. No credit cards accepted.

Mail search: Turnaround time 7-10 working days.A self addressed stamped envelope is requested.

Phone search: You must leave a message then call back in three days to get the results.

Hunting License Information
Fishing License Information

Fish & Wildlife Cons. Comm, Licensing & Permit Board, 2590 Executive Center Circle, #200, Tallahassee, FL 32301; 850-488-3641, 850-414-8212 (Fax), 8AM-5PM.

http://fcn.state.fl.us/fwc

Indexing & Storage: Records are available from 2/97 forward.

Searching: Requests must be in writing. The agency will release address, telephone number, and type of license. Include the following in your request-date of birth, address.

Access by: mail, in person.

Fee & Payment: There is no search fee.

Mail search: Turnaround time: 2 to 4 days.

Florida State Licensing Agencies

Licenses Searchable Online

Acupuncturist #01 .... www.doh.state.fl.us/irm00praes/praslist.asp

Air Conditioning Contractor #16 .... www.state.fl.us/oraweb/owa/www_dbpr2.qry_lic_menu

Alcoholic Beverage Permit #06 .... www.state.fl.us/oraweb/owa/www_dbpr2.qry_lic_menu

Asbestos Remover/Contractor #16 .... www.state.fl.us/oraweb/owa/www_dbpr2.qry_lic_menu

Asbestos Surveyor Consultant #16 .... www.state.fl.us/oraweb/owa/www_dbpr2.qry_lic_menu

Assisted Living Facility #26 .... www.floridahealthstat.com/qs/owa/facilitylocator.facllocator

Athletic Agent #06 .... www.state.fl.us/oraweb/owa/www_dbpr2.qry_lic_menu

Athletic Trainer #01 .... www.doh.state.fl.us/irm00praes/praslist.asp

Attorney #23 .... www.flabar.org/newflabar/findlawyer.html

Auction Company #22 .... www.state.fl.us/oraweb/owa/www_dbpr2.qry_lic_menu

Auctioneer #22 .... www.state.fl.us/oraweb/owa/www_dbpr2.qry_lic_menu

Bank #05 .... www.dbf.state.fl.us/cf/dogi/Inst_search.cfm

Barber/Barber Assistant/Barber Shop #06 .... www.state.fl.us/oraweb/owa/www_dbpr2.qry_lic_menu

Building Code Administrator #06 .... www.state.fl.us/oraweb/owa/www_dbpr2.qry_lic_menu

Building Contractor #16 .... www.state.fl.us/oraweb/owa/www_dbpr2.qry_lic_menu

Building Inspector #06 .... www.state.fl.us/oraweb/owa/www_dbpr2.qry_lic_menu

Chiropractor #01 .... www.doh.state.fl.us/irm00praes/praslist.asp

Clinical Lab Personnel #01 .... www.doh.state.fl.us/irm00praes/praslist.asp

Collection Agency #05 .... https://ssl.dbf.state.fl.us/cf/lic/pubinqry/pub2/index.cfm

Community Association Manager #06 .... www.state.fl.us/oraweb/owa/www_dbpr2.qry_lic_menu

Construction Businees #16 .... www.state.fl.us/oraweb/owa/www_dbpr2.qry_lic_menu

Contractor, General #16 .... www.state.fl.us/oraweb/owa/www_dbpr2.qry_lic_menu

Cosmetologist, Hair Braider, Nails, Salon #06 ... www.state.fl.us/oraweb/owa/www_dbpr2.qry_lic_menu

Credit Union #05 .... www.dbf.state.fl.us/cf/dogi/Inst_search.cfm

Crematory #06 .... www.state.fl.us/oraweb/owa/www_dbpr2.qry_lic_menu

Dentist/Dental Assistant #01 .... www.doh.state.fl.us/irm00praes/praslist.asp

Dietician/Nutritionist #01 .... www.doh.state.fl.us/irm00praes/praslist.asp

Doctor, Limited License #01 .... www.doh.state.fl.us/irm00praes/praslist.asp

Electrical Contractor #16 .... www.state.fl.us/oraweb/owa/www_dbpr2.qry_lic_menu

Electrologist/Electrologist Facility #01 .... www.doh.state.fl.us/irm00praes/praslist.asp

Embalmer #06 .... www.state.fl.us/oraweb/owa/www_dbpr2.qry_lic_menu

Finance Company, Consumer #05 .... https://ssl.dbf.state.fl.us/cf/lic/pubinqry/pub3/index.cfm

Financial Institution #05 .... www.dbf.state.fl.us/cf/dogi/Inst_search.cfm

Firearms Instructor #18 .... http://licgweb.dos.state.fl.us/access/individual.html

Firearms License, Statewide #18 .... http://licgweb.dos.state.fl.us/access/individual.html

Funeral Director, Funeral Home #06 .... www.state.fl.us/oraweb/owa/www_dbpr2.qry_lic_menu

Geologist/Geology Firm #06 .... www.state.fl.us/oraweb/owa/www_dbpr2.qry_lic_menu

Health Facility #26 .... www.floridahealthstat.com/qs/owa/facilitylocator.facllocator

Hearing Aid Specialist #01 .... www.doh.state.fl.us/irm00praes/praslist.asp

Home Health Care Agency #26 .... www.floridahealthstat.com/qs/owa/facilitylocator.facllocator

Hospitals #26 .... www.floridahealthstat.com/qs/owa/facilitylocator.facllocator

Installment Seller, Retail #05 .... www.dbf.state.fl.us/licensing/

Insurance Adjuster/Agent/Title Agent #14 .... www.doi.state.fl.us/Consumers/Agents_companies/Agents/index.htm

International Bank Office #05 .... www.dbf.state.fl.us/cf/dogi/Inst_search.cfm

Lab Licenses #26 .... www.floridahealthstat.com/qs/owa/facilitylocator.facllocator

Lobbyist/Principal #2 .... www.leg.state.fl.us/Info_Center/index.cfm?Tab=info_center&submenu=1#lobbyist

Lodging Establishment #06 .... www.state.fl.us/oraweb/owa/www_dbpr2.qry_lic_menu

Marriage & Family Therapist #01 .... www.doh.state.fl.us/irm00praes/praslist.asp

Massage Therapist/School/Facility #01 .... www.doh.state.fl.us/irm00praes/praslist.asp

Mechanical Contractor #16 .... www.state.fl.us/oraweb/owa/www_dbpr2.qry_lic_menu

Medical Doctor #01 .... www.doh.state.fl.us/irm00praes/praslist.asp

Medical Faculty Certificate #01 .... www.doh.state.fl.us/irm00praes/praslist.asp

Mental Health Counselor #01 .... www.doh.state.fl.us/irm00praes/praslist.asp

Midwife #01 .... www.doh.state.fl.us/irm00praes/praslist.asp
Mortgage Broker School #05 .... https://ssl.dbf.state.fl.us/cf/lic/mbschools/index.cfm
Mortgage Broker/Firm #05 .... https://ssl.dbf.state.fl.us/cf/lic/pubinqry/pub1/index.cfm
Naturopath #01 .... www.doh.state.fl.us/irm00praes/praslist.asp
Notary Public #19 .... http://notaries.dos.state.fl.us/not001.html
Nuclear Radiology Physicist #01 .... www.doh.state.fl.us/irm00praes/praslist.asp
Nurse #01 .... www.doh.state.fl.us/irm00praes/praslist.asp
Nurse, Practical #01 .... www.doh.state.fl.us/irm00praes/praslist.asp
Nursing Assistant #01 .... www.doh.state.fl.us/irm00praes/praslist.asp
Nursing Home Administrator #01 .... www.doh.state.fl.us/irm00praes/praslist.asp
Nutrition Counselor #01 .... www.doh.state.fl.us/irm00praes/praslist.asp
Occupational Therapist #01 .... www.doh.state.fl.us/irm00praes/praslist.asp
Optician/Optician Apprentice #01 .... www.doh.state.fl.us/irm00praes/praslist.asp
Optometrist #01 .... www.doh.state.fl.us/irm00praes/praslist.asp
Orthotist/Prosthetist #01 .... www.doh.state.fl.us/irm00praes/praslist.asp
Osteopathic Physician/Limited Osteopath #01 .. www.doh.state.fl.us/irm00praes/praslist.asp
Pedorthist #01 .... www.doh.state.fl.us/irm00praes/praslist.asp
Pesticide Applicator (Com., Private, Public) #32 http://doacs.state.fl.us/~aes/pstcert.html
Pesticide Dealer #32 .... http://doacs.state.fl.us/~aes/pstcert.html
Pharmacist, Consulting #01 .... www.doh.state.fl.us/irm00praes/praslist.asp
Pharmacist/Pharmacist Intern #01 .... www.doh.state.fl.us/irm00praes/praslist.asp
Physical Therapist/Assistant #01 .... www.doh.state.fl.us/irm00praes/praslist.asp
Physician Assistant #01 .... www.doh.state.fl.us/irm00praes/praslist.asp
Physicist, Medical #01 .... www.doh.state.fl.us/irm00praes/praslist.asp
Plumbing Contractor #16 .... www.state.fl.us/oraweb/owa/www_dbpr2.qry_lic_menu
Polygraph Examiner #34 .... www.floridapolygraph.org/members.html
Private Investigator/Agency #18 .... http://licgweb.dos.state.fl.us/access/individual.html
Psychologist/Limited License Psychologist #01 . www.doh.state.fl.us/irm00praes/praslist.asp
Public Accountant-CPA #21 .... www.state.fl.us/oraweb/owa/www_dbpr2.qry_lic_menu
Real Estate Appraiser #24 .... www.state.fl.us/oraweb/owa/www_dbpr2.qry_lic_menu
Real Estate Broker/Salesperson #24 .... www.state.fl.us/oraweb/owa/www_dbpr2.qry_lic_menu
Recovery Agent School/Instructor/Manager #18 http://licgweb.dos.state.fl.us/access/agency.html
Recovery Agent/Agency/Intern #18 .... http://licgweb.dos.state.fl.us/access/agency.html
Respiratory Care Therapist/Provider #01 .... www.doh.state.fl.us/irm00praes/praslist.asp
Roofing Contractor #16 .... www.state.fl.us/oraweb/owa/www_dbpr2.qry_lic_menu
Sales Finance Company #05 .... www.dbf.state.fl.us/licensing/
Savings & Loan Association, Charter #05 .... www.dbf.state.fl.us/cf/dogi/Inst_search.cfm
School Psychologist #01 .... www.doh.state.fl.us/irm00praes/praslist.asp
Security Officer School #18 .... http://licgweb.dos.state.fl.us/access/agency.html
Security Officer/Instructor #18 .... http://licgweb.dos.state.fl.us/access/individual.html
Social Worker, Clinical #01 .... www.doh.state.fl.us/irm00praes/praslist.asp
Solar Energy Contractor #16 .... www.state.fl.us/oraweb/owa/www_dbpr2.qry_lic_menu
Speech-Language Pathologist/Audiologist #01 .. www.doh.state.fl.us/irm00praes/praslist.asp
Surveyor, Mapping #06 .... www.state.fl.us/oraweb/owa/www_dbpr2.qry_lic_menu
Swimming Pool/Spa Contractor #16 .... www.state.fl.us/oraweb/owa/www_dbpr2.qry_lic_menu
Talent Agency #06 .... www.state.fl.us/oraweb/owa/www_dbpr2.qry_lic_menu
Therapeutic Radiologic Physician #01 .... www.doh.state.fl.us/irm00praes/praslist.asp
Tobacco Wholesale #06 .... www.state.fl.us/oraweb/owa/www_dbpr2.qry_lic_menu
Trust Company #05 .... www.dbf.state.fl.us/cf/dogi/Inst_search.cfm
Underground Utility Contractor #16 .... www.state.fl.us/oraweb/owa/www_dbpr2.qry_lic_menu
Veterinarian/Veterinary Establishment #06 .... www.state.fl.us/oraweb/owa/www_dbpr2.qry_lic_menu

Licensing Quick Finder

Acupuncturist #01 850-488-0595
Adoption Service #09 850-921-2594
Adult & Foster Care #09 850-921-2594
Air Conditioning Contractor #16 904-727-6530
Alarm System Contractor #06................850-455-6685
Alcoholic Beverage Permit #06 850-487-6793
Ambulance Service #20........................850-487-1911
Animal Registration (Livestock Marks & Brands) #03
....850-922-0187
Architectural Firm #30 850-488-6685
Asbestos Remover/Contractor #16 850-921-6347
Asbestos Surveyor Consultant #16 850-921-6347
Assisted Living Facility #26..................850-487-2515
Athletic Agent #06 850-488-8500
Athletic Trainer #01 850-488-0595
Attorney #23 850-487-1292
Auction Company #22 850-488-5189
Auctioneer #22...................................850-488-5189
Automobile Dealer, New #13 850-488-4958
Automobile Dealer/Sales #13 850-488-4958
Automobile Repossessor #18 850-488-5381
Bail Bondsman #14 850-922-3137
Bank #05 850-410-9805
Barber/Barber Assist./Barber Shop #06 850-488-6888
Boxer #06 850-488-8500
Broker Dealer/Branch Office #05 850-410-9805
Broker/Dealer/Associated Person #05...850-410-9805
Building Code Administrator #06...........850-922-5335
Building Contractor #16 904-727-6530
Building Inspector #06 850-922-5335
Cemetery Lot Salesperson #05..............850-410-9898
Child Care Center #10..........................850-487-3166
Child Care/Child Placing Facility #09 ...850-921-2594
Chiropractor #01 850-488-0595
Clinical Lab Personnel #01 850-488-0595
Clinical Laboratory #26........................850-487-3063
Collection Agency #05..........................850-410-9805
Community Association Mgr. #06...........850-922-5335
Concealed Weapon License #18 850-488-5381
Construction Businees #16...................904-727-6530
Contractor, General #16 904-727-6530
Cosmetologist, Hair Braiders, Nail Specialists, Salons
#06 850-488-5702
Credit Union #05 850-410-9805
Crematory #06 850-488-8690
Day Care Center/Child Care
Center/Nursery School #10 850-487-3166
Dentist/Dental Assistant #01 850-488-0595
Dietician/Nutritionist #01 850-488-0595
Doctor, Limited License #01 850-488-0595
Electrical Contractor #16 850-488-3109
Electrologist/Electrologist Facility #01 ..850-488-0595
Elevator Certificates of Operation #06...904-488-9097
Embalmer #06 850-488-8690
Emergency Medical Technician #20......850-487-1911
Engineer #33 850-521-0500
Engineering Firm #33 850-521-0500
Feed Distributor #32............................850-488-7626
Fertilizer Distributor #32 850-487-2085
Finance Company, Consumer #05.......850-410-9805
Financial Institution #05.......................850-410-9805
Fire Equipment Dealer/Installer #14.....850-922-3172
Firearms Instructor #18 850-488-5381
Firearms License, Statewide #18 850-488-5381

Fishing, Fresh Water, Commercial #25 .904-488-4066
Food Services Establishment #06.........850-922-5335
Foster Family Home #09 850-921-2594
Fumigation Performance Special ID #4 .850-921-4177
Funeral Director, Funeral Home #06 850-488-8690
Geologist/Geology Firm #06 850-488-1105
Guidance Counselor #02 850-488-2317
Health Facility #26...............................850-487-2527
Hearing Aid Specialist #01 850-488-0595
Home Health Care Agency #26 850-414-6010
Hospitals #26......................................850-487-2717
Hotel/Restaurant #06 850-488-7891
In Home Family Day Care Center #10...850-487-3166
Installment Seller, Retail #05 850-410-9805
Insurance Adjuster/Agent/Title Agent #14 ....
....904-922-3137
Interior Design Business/Individual #30.850-488-6685
International Bank Office #05................850-410-9805
Investment Advisor (Credit Union) #05..850-410-9805
Investment-Securities Dealer #05 850-410-9805
Kickboxer #06 850-488-8500
Lab Licenses #26................................850-487-3109
Landscape Architecture, Business & Individual #30
....850-488-6685
Landscape Maint. & Pest Control Mgmt. Company #04
....850-921-4177
Liquor Store #06 850-488-8288
Livestock Hauler #03...........................850-922-0187
Lobbyist/Principal #28 850-922-4990
Lodging Establishment #06 850-922-5335
LPG-Liquefied Petroleum License #32..850-488-3022
Marriage & Family Therapist #01 850-488-0595
Massage Therapist/School/Facility #01.850-488-0595
Mechanical Contractor #16...................904-727-6530
Medical Doctor #01 850-488-0595
Medical Faculty Certificate #01 850-488-0595
Mental Health Counselor #01 850-488-0595
Midwife #01 850-488-0595
Milk Hauler/Tester #31 850-487-1450
Mobile Home Dealer/Broker #13 850-488-4958
Mobile Home Manufacturer #13...........850-488-4958
Money Transmitter #05.........................850-410-9805
Mortgage Broker School #05 850-410-9805
Mortgage Broker/Firm #05...................850-410-9805
Motel/Restaurant #06 904-488-1133
Motel/Restaurant #07 904-488-1133
Nail Specialist #06...............................850-922-5335
Naturopath #01 850-488-0595
Notary Public #19................................850-488-7521
Nuclear Radiology Physicist #01...........850-488-0595
Nurse #01 850-488-0595
Nurse, Practical #01 850-488-0595
Nursing Assistant #01 850-488-0595
Nursing Home Administrator #01 850-488-0595
Nutrition Counselor #01 850-488-0595
Occupational Therapist #01 850-488-0595
Optician/Optician Apprentice #01.........850-488-0595
Optometrist #01 850-488-0595
Organic Certifying Agent #32...............850-488-3863
Orphanage #09 850-921-2594
Orthotist/Prosthetist #01 850-488-0595
Osteopathic Physician/Limited Osteopathic
Physician #01 850-488-0595
Paramedic #20....................................850-487-1911

Pari-Mutuel Wagering #07 850-488-9161
Pari-Mutuel Wagering #06 850-488-9161
Pedorthist #01 850-488-0595
Pest Control Operator #04....................850-921-4177
Pest Control, Structural #04..................850-921-4177
Pesticide Applicator (Commericial, Private, Public) #32
....850-488-6838
Pesticide Dealer #32 850-488-6838
Pet Shop #25 904-488-6253
Pharmacist, Consulting #01 850-488-0595
Pharmacist/Pharmacist Intern #01 850-488-0595
PHPC Public Health Pest Control #04...850-921-4177
Physical Therapist/Assistant #01 850-488-0595
Physician Assistant #01........................850-488-0595
Physicist, Medical #01 850-488-0595
Pilot #06 850-488-0698
Plumbing Contractor #16 904-727-6530
Polygraph Examiner #34 954-321-4264
Private Investigator/Agency #18 850-488-5381
Psychologist/Limited License Psychologist #01 ....
....850-488-0595
Public Accountant-CPA #21.................352-955-2165
Racing, Dog/Horse #06 850-488-9130
Real Estate Appraiser #24 407-245-0800
Real Estate Broker/Salesperson #24 407-245-0800
Recovery Agent School/Instructor/Manager #18..........
....850-488-5381
Recovery Agent/Agency/Intern #18.......850-488-5381
Recreational Vehicle Dealer #13...........850-488-4958
Respiratory Care Therapist/Provider #1 850-488-0595
Roofing Contractor #16 904-727-6530
Sales Finance Company #05...............850-410-9805
Savings & Loan Assoc., Charter #05....850-410-9805
School Administrator/Supervisor #02 850-488-2317
School Educ. Media Specialist #02 850-487-4822
School Principal #02.............................850-488-2317
School Psychologist #01 850-488-0595
Securities Registration #05...................850-410-9805
Security Officer School #18 850-488-5381
Security Officer/Instructor #18 850-488-5381
Seed Dealer #32 850-488-3863
Shorthand Reporter #29 904-488-8628
Social Worker, Clinical #01 850-488-0595
Solar Energy Contractor #16 904-727-6530
Solid Waste Facility Operator #08.........850-922-6104
Speech-Language Pathologist/Audiologist #01...........
....850-488-0595
Surveyor, Mapping #06 850-413-7480
Sweepstakes Operator (Game Promotions) #18............
....850-488-5381
Swimming Pool/Spa Contractor #16......904-727-6530
Talent Agency #06 850-922-5335
Teacher #02...850-487-4822
Therapeutic Radiologic Physician #01...850-488-0595
Timeshare Agent #05 850-410-9805
Tobacco Wholesale #06 850-487-6793
Trust Company #05...............................850-410-9805
Underground Utility Contractor #16 904-727-6530
Veterinarian/Veterinary Establishment #06...............
....850-487-1820
Yacht & Ship Broker/Salesman #06 850-488-1636
Zoo #25 904-488-6253

Licensing Agency Information

#01 Department of Health, 4052 Bald Cypress Way, Tallahassee, FL 32399; 850-488-0595. www.doh.state.flus/mqa
Direct web site URL to search for licensees: www9.myflorida.com/Mqa/PRAES/index.html

#02 Education Center, 325 W Gaines, #701, Tallahassee, FL 32399; 850-201-7400.

#03 Department of Agriculture & Consumer Services, 407 S Calhoun, Mayo Bldg, Rm 332, Tallahassee, FL 32399-0800; 850-922-0187, Fax: 850-487-3641.
http://doacs.state.fl.us/ai/ai.html

#04 Department of Agriculture & Consumer Services, 1203 Government Square Blvd #300, Tallahassee, FL 32301; 850-921-4177, Fax: 850-413-7044.
www.floridatermitehelp.org

#05 Department of Banking & Finance, 101 E Gaines St, Fletcher Bldg #636, Tallahassee, FL 32399-0350; 850-410-9805, Fax: 850-410-9914.
www.dbf.state.fl.us
Direct web site URL to search for licensees: www.dbf.state.fl.us/cf/dogi/Inst_search.cfm

#06 Department of Business & Professional Regulation, 1940 N Monroe St #300, Tallahassee, FL 32399; 850-922-5335, Fax: 850-488-1514.
www.state.fl.us/dbpr

#08 Department of Environmental Regulation, 2600 Blair Stone Rd, Tallahassee, FL 32399-2400; 850-922-6104.
www.dep.state.fl.us

#09 Department of Children & Families, 1317 Winewood Blvd, Bldg 7, #220, Tallahassee, FL 32399-0700; 850-921-2594, Fax: 850-488-0751.
www.state.fl.us/cf_web/
Direct web site URL to search for licensees: www.state.fl.us/cf_web/ This agency provides an informative searchable online list of children available for adoption through them.

#10 Department of Health, 3401 W Tharp, Tallahassee, FL 32303; 850-487-1111, Fax: 850-487-7956.

#13 Department of Highway Safety & Motor Vehicles, 2900 Apalachee Pkwy MS65, Tallahassee, FL 32399-0500; 850-488-4958, Fax: 850-922-9840.
www.hsmv.state.fl.us

#14 Department of Insurance & Treasurer, 200 E Gaines St, Larsen Bldg, Tallahassee, FL 32399; 850-922-3137. www.doi.state.fl.us

#16 Department of Professional Regulation, 7960 Arlington Expwy #300, Jacksonville, FL 32211-7467; 904-727-3689, Fax: 904-727-3677.
www.state.fl.us/dbpr
Direct web site URL to search for licensees: www.state.fl.us/oraweb/owa/www_dbpr2.qry_lic_menu. You can search online using personal name, business name, and license number.

#18 Department of State, 2520 N Monroe St, Tallahassee, FL 32303; 850-488-5381, Fax: 850-487-7950.
http://licgweb.dos.state.fl.us

#19 Department of State, The Capitol Bldg, Rm 1801, Tallahassee, FL 32399-0250; 850-488-7521, Fax: 850-488-1768.
http://notaries.dos.state.fl.us/index.html
Direct web site URL to search for licensees: http://notaries.dos.state.fl.us/not001.html

#20 Emergency Medical Services, 2002D Old St Augustine Rd, Tallahassee, FL 32301-4881; 850-487-1911, Fax: 850-488-2512.
www.doh.state.fl.us/ems
Direct web site URL to search for licensees: www.doh.state.fl.us/ems. You can search online using certification number, name

#21 Department of Business & Professional Regulation, 2610 NW 43rd St, #1A, Gainesville, FL 32606; 352-955-2165, Fax: 352-955-2164.
Direct web site URL to search for licensees: www.state.fl.us/oraweb/owa/www_dbpr2.qry_lic_menu

#22 Department of Business & Professional Regulation, 1940 N Monroe St, Tallahassee, FL 32399; 850-488-5189.
www.state.fl.us/dbpr/prof/auc_index.shtml
Direct web site URL to search for licensees: www.state.fl.us/oraweb/owa/www_dbpr2.qry_lic_menu. You can search online using occupation, then name

#23 Board of Bar Examiners, 1891 Elder Ct, Tallahassee, FL 32399-1750; 850-487-1292.
www.barexam.org/florida
Direct web site URL to search for licensees: www.flabar.org/newflabar/findlawyer.html

#24 Department of Business & Professional Regulation, 400 W Robinson, #N308, Orlando, FL 32801; 407-245-0800.
www.state.fl.us/dbpr

Direct web site URL to search for licensees: www.state.fl.us/oraweb/owa/www_dbpr2.qry_lic_menu. You can search online using personal name, business name, and license number.

#25 Game & Fresh Water Fish Commission, 2590 Executive Center Cir, Tallahassee, FL 32301; 850-488-3641, Fax: 850-414-2628.
www.marinefisheries.org

#26 Facilities Licensing, 2727 Mahan Dr, Tallahassee, FL 32308-5401; 850-487-2528, Fax: 850-410-1512.
www.floridahealthstat.com
Direct web site URL to search for licensees: www.floridahealthstat.com/qs/owa/facilitylocator.f acllocator. You can search online using type and facility name, city, or county

#28 Lobbyist Registration, 111 W Madison St Rm G-68, Tallahassee, FL 32399-1425; 850-922-4990.
Direct web site URL to search for licensees: www.leg.state.fl.us/Info_Center/index.cfm?Tab=in fo_center&submenu=1#lobbyist

#29 , 500 N Duvall, Tallahassee, FL 32399-1900; 850-488-8628.

#30 Department of Professional Regulation, 1940 N Monroe St, Tallahassee, FL 32399-0751; 850-488-6685, Fax: 850-992-2918.
Direct web site URL to search for licensees: www.state.fl.us/dbpr

#31 Department of Agriculture & Consumer Services, 3125 Conner Blvd, Mail Stop C-27, Tallahassee, FL 32399-1650; 850-487-1450, Fax: 850-922-9444.
http://doacs.state.fl.us/~dairy/index.html

#32 Bureau of Compliance Monitoring, 3125 Conner Blvd, Tallahassee, FL 32399-1650; 850-488-3022, Fax: 850-488-8498.
http://doacs.state.fl.us/license.html

#33 Board of Professional Engineers, 1208 Hays Street, Tallahassee, FL 32301; 850-521-0500, Fax: 850-521-0521.
www.fbpe.org
Direct web site URL to search for licensees: www.fbpe.org/pesearch/Pesearch.htm. You can search online using name or PE number.

#34 Florida Polygraph Association, 2601 West Broward Boulevard, Ft. Lauderdale, FL 33311; 954-321-4264, Fax: 954-321-4566.
www.floridapolygraph.org/index.shtml
Direct web site URL to search for licensees: www.floridapolygraph.org/members.html

Florida Federal Courts

The following list indicates the district and division name for each county in the state. If the bankruptcy court location is different from the district court, then the location of the bankruptcy court appears in parentheses.

County/Court Cross Reference

County	District	Division
Alachua	Northern	Gainesville (Tallahassee)
Baker	Middle	Jacksonville
Bay	Northern	Panama City (Tallahassee)
Bradford	Middle	Jacksonville
Brevard	Middle	Orlando
Broward	Southern	Fort Lauderdale (Miami)
Calhoun	Northern	Panama City (Tallahassee)
Charlotte	Middle	Fort Myers (Tampa)
Citrus	Middle	Ocala (Jacksonville)
Clay	Middle	Jacksonville
Columbia	Middle	Jacksonville
Dade	Southern	Miami
De Soto	Middle	Fort Myers (Tampa)
Dixie	Northern	Gainesville (Tallahassee)
Duval	Middle	Jacksonville
Escambia	Northern	Pensacola
Flagler	Middle	Jacksonville
Franklin	Northern	Tallahassee
Gadsden	Northern	Tallahassee
Gilchrist	Northern	Gainesville (Tallahassee)
Glades	Middle	Fort Myers (Tampa)
Gulf	Northern	Panama City (Tallahassee)
Hamilton	Middle	Jacksonville
Hardee	Middle	Tampa
Hendry	Middle	Fort Myers (Tampa)
Hernando	Middle	Tampa
Highlands	Southern	Fort Pierce (Miami)
Hillsborough	Middle	Tampa
Holmes	Northern	Panama City (Tallahassee)
Indian River	Southern	Fort Pierce (Miami)
Jackson	Northern	Panama City (Tallahassee)
Jefferson	Northern	Tallahassee
Lafayette	Northern	Gainesville (Tallahassee)
Lake	Middle	Ocala (Orlando)
Lee	Middle	Fort Myers (Tampa)
Leon	Northern	Tallahassee
Levy	Northern	Gainesville (Tallahassee)
Liberty	Northern	Tallahassee
Madison	Northern	Tallahassee
Manatee	Middle	Tampa
Marion	Middle	Ocala (Jacksonville)
Martin	Southern	Fort Pierce (Miami)
Monroe	Southern	Key West (Miami)
Nassau	Middle	Jacksonville
Okaloosa	Northern	Pensacola
Okeechobee	Southern	Fort Pierce (Miami)
Orange	Middle	Orlando
Osceola	Middle	Orlando
Palm Beach	Southern	W. Palm Beach (Miami)
Pasco	Middle	Tampa
Pinellas	Middle	Tampa
Polk	Middle	Tampa
Putnam	Middle	Jacksonville
Santa Rosa	Northern	Pensacola
Sarasota	Middle	Tampa
Seminole	Middle	Orlando
St. Johns	Middle	Jacksonville
St. Lucie	Southern	Fort Pierce (Miami)
Sumter	Middle	Ocala (Jacksonville)
Suwannee	Middle	Jacksonville
Taylor	Northern	Tallahassee
Union	Middle	Jacksonville
Volusia	Middle	Orlando (Jacksonville)
Wakulla	Northern	Tallahassee
Walton	Northern	Pensacola
Washington	Northern	Panama City (Tallahassee)

US District Court

Middle District of Florida

Fort Myers Division 2110 First St, Room 2-194, Fort Myers, FL 33901 (Courier Address: Use mail address for courier delivery), 941-461-2000.

http://www.flmd.uscourts.gov

Counties: Charlotte, Collier, De Soto, Glades, Hendry, Lee.

Indexing/Storage: Cases are indexed by defendant and plaintiff as well as by case number. New cases are available in the index immediately after filing date. The civil case index is computerized, but the criminal index is not. A card index is maintained. Records are also indexed on microfiche. Open records are located at this court.

Fee & Payment: The fee is $20.00 per item (one party name or case number). Payment may be made by money order, cashier check, personal check. Prepayment is required. Payee: Clerk, US District Court. Certification fee: $7.00 per document. Copy fee: $.50 per page. You are allowed to make your own copies. These copies cost Not Applicable per page.

Phone Search: Docket information is available by phone.

Mail Search: Always enclose a stamped self addressed envelope.

In Person: In person searching is available.

PACER: Sign-up number is 800-676-6856. Access fee is $.60 per minute. Toll-free access: 888-815-8701. Local access: 813-301-5820. Case records are available back to 1989-90. Records are purged three years after case closed. New records are available online after 1 day. PACER is available online at http://pacer.flmd.uscourts.gov.

Jacksonville Division PO Box 53558, Jacksonville, FL 32201 (Courier Address: Suite 110, 311 W Monroe St, Jacksonville, FL 32202), 904-549-1900.

http://www.flmd.uscourts.gov

Counties: Baker, Bradford, Clay, Columbia, Duval, Flagler, Hamilton, Nassau, Putnam, St. Johns, Suwannee, Union.

Indexing/Storage: Cases are indexed by defendant and plaintiff as well as by case number. New cases are available in the index 1 day after filing date. A computer index is maintained. Open records are located at this court.

Fee & Payment: The fee is $20.00 per item (one party name or case number). Payment may be made by money order, cashier check, personal check. Prepayment is required. Payee: Clerk, US District Court. Certification fee: $7.00 per document. Copy fee: $.50 per page. You are allowed to make your own copies. These copies cost $.50 per page.

Phone Search: Searching is not available by phone.

Mail Search: Always enclose a stamped self addressed envelope.

In Person: In person searching is available.

PACER: Sign-up number is 800-676-6856. Access fee is $.60 per minute. Toll-free access: 888-815-8701. Local access: 813-301-5820. Case records are available back to 1989-90. Records are purged three years after case closed. New records are available online after 1 day. PACER is available online at http://pacer.flmd.uscourts.gov.

Ocala Division 207 N W 2nd St, #337, Ocala, FL 34475 (Courier Address: 207 N W 2nd St, #337, Ocala, FL 34475), 352-369-4860.

http://www.flmd.uscourts.gov

Counties: Citrus, Lake, Marion, Sumter.

Indexing/Storage: Cases are indexed by as well as by case number. New cases are available in the index after filing date. Open records are located at the Division.

Fee & Payment: The fee is $20.00 per item (one party name or case number). Payment may be made by money order, cashier check. Business checks are not accepted. Personal checks are not accepted.

Phone Search: Searching is not available by phone.

Mail Search: Always enclose a stamped self addressed envelope.

In Person: In person searching is available.

PACER: Sign-up number is 800-676-6856. Access fee is $.60 per minute. Toll-free access: 888-815-8701. Local access: 813-301-5820. Case records are available back to 1989-90. Records are purged three years after case closed. New records are available online after 1 day. PACER is available online at http://pacer.flmd.uscourts.gov.

Orlando Division Room 218, 80 North Hughey Ave, Orlando, FL 32801 (Courier Address: Use mail address for courier delivery), 407-835-4200.

http://www.flmd.uscourts.gov

Counties: Brevard, Orange, Osceola, Seminole, Volusia.

Indexing/Storage: Cases are indexed by defendant and plaintiff as well as by case number. New cases are available in the index immediately after filing date. A computer index is maintained. Records are stored by case number according to year closed. Open records are located at this court.

Fee & Payment: The fee is $20.00 per item (one party name or case number). Payment may be made by money order, cashier check, personal check. The court will not bill. All checks, except foreign, are accepted. Payee: Clerk, US District Court. Certification fee: $7.00 per document. Copy fee: $.50 per page. You are allowed to make your own copies. These copies cost $.50 per page.

Phone Search: Docket information is available by phone.

Mail Search: Always enclose a stamped self addressed envelope.

In Person: In person searching is available.

PACER: Sign-up number is 800-676-6856. Access fee is $.60 per minute. Toll-free access: 888-815-8701. Local access: 813-301-5820. Case records are available back to 1989-90. Records are purged three years after case closed. New records are available online after 1 day. PACER is available online at http://pacer.flmd.uscourts.gov.

Tampa Division Office of the clerk, 801 N Florida Ave #223, Tampa, FL 33602-4500 (Courier Address: Use mail address for courier delivery), 813-301-5400.

http://www.flmd.uscourts.gov

Counties: Hardee, Hernando, Hillsborough, Manatee, Pasco, Pinellas, Polk, Sarasota.

Indexing/Storage: Cases are indexed by defendant and plaintiff as well as by case number. New cases are available in the index 1 day after filing date. A computer index is maintained. Open records are located at this court.

Fee & Payment: The fee is $20.00 per item (one party name or case number). Payment may be made by money order, cashier check, personal check. Prepayment is required. Payee: Clerk, US District Court. Certification fee: $7.00 per document. Copy fee: $.50 per page. You are allowed to make your own copies. These copies cost $.25 per page.

Phone Search: Only docket information is available by phone.

Mail Search: Always enclose a stamped self addressed envelope.

In Person: In person searching is available.

PACER: Sign-up number is 800-676-6856. Access fee is $.60 per minute. Toll-free access: 888-815-8701. Local access: 813-301-5820. Case records are available back to 1989-90. Records are purged three years after case closed. New records are available online after 1 day. PACER is available online at http://pacer.flmd.uscourts.gov.

US Bankruptcy Court

Middle District of Florida

Jacksonville Division PO Box 559, Jacksonville, FL 32201 (Courier Address: Room 206, 311 W Monroe, Jacksonville, FL 32202), 904-232-2852.

http://www.flmb.uscourts.gov

Counties: Baker, Bradford, Citrus, Clay, Columbia, Duval, Flagler, Hamilton, Marion, Nassau, Putnam, St. Johns, Sumter, Suwannee, Union, Volusia.

Indexing/Storage: Cases are indexed by debtor as well as by case number. New cases are available in the index immediately after filing date. A computer index is maintained. Open records are located at this court. This court has no specific time that they send closed records to the Atlanta Federal Records Center.

Fee & Payment: The fee is $20.00 per item (one party name or case number). Payment may be made by money order, cashier check, business check. Personal checks are not accepted. Prepayment is required. Pacific Photo is the contracted search and copy center for this district. They say it is fine to fax orders to them at 904-355-1062. Payee: Clerk, US Bankruptcy Court. Certification fee: $7.00 per document. Copy fee: $.50 per page.

Phone Search: An automated voice case information service (VCIS) is available.

Mail Search: A stamped self addressed envelope is not required.

In Person: In person searching is available.

PACER: Sign-up number is 800-676-6856. Access fee is $.60 per minute. Local access: 904-232-1311. Case records are available back to 1981.

Records are purged every year. New civil records are available online after 1 week.

Orlando Division Suite 950, 135 W Central Blvd, Orlando, FL 32801 (Courier Address: Use mail address for courier delivery), 407-648-6365.

http://www.flmb.uscourts.gov

Counties: Brevard, Lake, Orange, Osceola, Seminole.

Indexing/Storage: Cases are indexed by debtor and creditors as well as by case number. New cases are available in the index 1-2 days after filing date. A computer index is maintained. Open records are located at this court. This court has no specific time that they send closed records to the Atlanta Federal Records Center.

Fee & Payment: The fee is $20.00 per item (one party name or case number). Payment may be made by money order, cashier check, business check. Personal checks are not accepted. Prepayment is required. Pacific Photo is the contracted search and copy center for this district. Orders may be faxed to them. Payee: Clerk, US Bankruptcy Court. Certification fee: $7.00 per document. Copy fee: $.50 per page.

Phone Search: An automated voice case information service (VCIS) is available.

Mail Search: Always enclose a stamped self addressed envelope.

In Person: In person searching is available.

PACER: Sign-up number is 800-676-6856. Access fee is $.60 per minute. Local access: 407-648-6212. Case records are available back to 1986. Records are never purged. New civil records are available online after 1 day.

Tampa Division 801 N Florida Ave #727, Tampa, FL 33602 (Courier Address: Use mail address for courier delivery), 813-301-5065.

http://www.flmb.uscourts.gov

Counties: Charlotte, Collier, De Soto, Glades, Hardee, Hendry, Hernando, Hillsborough, Lee, Manatee, Pasco, Pinellas, Polk, Sarasota.

Indexing/Storage: Cases are indexed by debtor as well as by case number. New cases are available in the index immediately after filing date. A computer index is maintained. Open records are located at this court. This court has no specific time that they send closed records to the Atlanta Federal Records Center.

Fee & Payment: The fee is $20.00 per item (one party name or case number). Payment may be made by money order, cashier check, business check. Personal checks are not accepted. Prepayment is required. Pacific Photo is the contracted search and copy center for this district. Payee: Clerk, US Bankruptcy Court. Certification fee: $7.00 per document. Copy fee: $.50 per page.

Phone Search: Searching is not available by phone.

Mail Search: Always enclose a stamped self addressed envelope.

In Person: In person searching is available.

PACER: Sign-up number is 800-676-6856. Access fee is $.60 per minute. Local access: 813-301-5206. Case records are available back to 1992. Records are purged every six months. New civil records are available online after 1 day.

US District Court

Northern District of Florida

Gainesville Division 401 SE First Ave, Room 243, Gainesville, FL 32601 (Courier Address: Use mail address for courier delivery), 352-380-2400, Fax: 352-380-2424.

http://www.flnd.uscourts.gov

Counties: Alachua, Dixie, Gilchrist, Lafayette, Levy. Records for cases prior to July 1996 are maintained at the Tallahassee Division.

Indexing/Storage: Cases are indexed by defendant and plaintiff as well as by case number. New cases are available in the index 3 days after filing date. Both computer and card indexes are maintained. Open records are located at this court.

Fee & Payment: The fee is $20.00 per item (one party name or case number). Payment may be made by money order, cashier check, personal check. Prepayment is required. Payee: Clerk, US District Court. Certification fee: $7.00 per document. Copy fee: $.50 per page.

Phone Search: Only 1-3 names may be searched over the phone, and only docket information will be released.

Mail Search: Always enclose a stamped self addressed envelope.

In Person: In person searching is available.

PACER: Sign-up number is 800-676-6856. Access fee is $.60 per minute. Toll-free access: 800-844-0479. Local access: 850-942-8897. Case records are available back to 1992. Records are purged three years after case closed. New records are available online after 2 days. PACER is available online at http://pacer.flnd.uscourts.gov.

Panama City Division 30 W. Government St., Panama City, FL 32401 (Courier Address: Use mail address for courier delivery), 850-769-4556, Fax: 850-769-7528.

http://www.flnd.uscourts.gov

Counties: Bay, Calhoun, Gulf, Holmes, Jackson, Washington.

Indexing/Storage: Cases are indexed by as well as by case number. New cases are available in the index after filing date. Open records are located at the Division.

Fee & Payment: The fee is no charge per item (one party name or case number). Payment may be made by money order, cashier check. Business checks are not accepted. Personal checks are not accepted.

Phone Search: Searching is not available by phone.

Mail Search: Always enclose a stamped self addressed envelope.

In Person: In person searching is available.

PACER: Sign-up number is 800-676-6856. Access fee is $.60 per minute. Toll-free access: 800-844-0479. Local access: 850-942-8897. Case records are available back to 1992. Records are purged three years after case closed. New records are available online after 2 days. PACER is available online at http://pacer.flnd.uscourts.gov.

Pensacola Division US Courthouse, 1 N Palafox St, #226, Pensacola, FL 32501 (Courier Address: Use mail address for courier delivery), 850-435-8440, Fax: 850-433-5972.

http://www.flnd.uscourts.gov

Counties: Escambia, Okaloosa, Santa Rosa, Walton.

Indexing/Storage: Cases are indexed by defendant and plaintiff as well as by case number. New cases are available in the index 2-3 days after filing date. Both computer and card indexes are maintained. Records are indexed on computer as of August 1992. Open records are located at this court. District wide searches are available for information from August 1992 from this division. This division maintains records for the Panama City office.

Fee & Payment: The fee is $20.00 per item (one party name or case number). Payment may be made by money order, cashier check, personal check. Prepayment is required. Payee: Clerk, US District Court. Certification fee: $7.00 per document. Copy fee: $.50 per page.

Phone Search: Only basic information is released over the phone. They will not release all docket information over the phone.

Mail Search: Always enclose a stamped self addressed envelope.

In Person: In person searching is available.

PACER: Sign-up number is 800-676-6856. Access fee is $.60 per minute. Toll-free access: 800-844-0479. Local access: 850-942-8897. Case records are available back to 1992. Records are purged three years after case closed. New records are available online after 2 days. PACER is available online at http://pacer.flnd.uscourts.gov.

Tallahassee Division Suite 122, 110 E Park Ave, Tallahassee, FL 32301 (Courier Address: Use mail address for courier delivery), 850-942-8826, Fax: 850-942-8830.

http://www.flnd.uscourts.gov

Counties: Franklin, Gadsden, Jefferson, Leon, Liberty, Madison, Taylor, Wakulla.

Indexing/Storage: Cases are indexed by defendant and plaintiff as well as by case number. New cases are available in the index immediately after filing date. A computer index is maintained. Records are also indexed by year closed. Open records are located at this court.

Fee & Payment: The fee is $20.00 per item (one party name or case number). Payment may be made by money order, cashier check, personal check. Prepayment required. Payee: Clerk, US District Court. Certification fee: $7.00 per document. Copy fee: $.50 per page.

Phone Search: Basic information about a case requested by name (case number) or by case number (names of parties or their attorneys, date of complaint, or general status) is available by telephone at no charge.

Mail Search: A stamped self addressed envelope is not required.

In Person: In person searching is available.

PACER: Sign-up number is 800-676-6856. Access fee is $.60 per minute. Toll-free access: 800-844-0479. Local access: 850-942-8897. Case records are available back to 1992. Records are purged three years after case closed. New records are available online after 2 days. PACER is available online at http://pacer.flnd.uscourts.gov.

US Bankruptcy Court

Northern District of Florida

Pensacola Division Suite 700, 220 W Garden St, Pensacola, FL 32501 (Courier Address: Use mail address for courier delivery), 850-435-8475.

Counties: Escambia, Okaloosa, Santa Rosa, Walton.

Indexing/Storage: Cases are indexed by debtor as well as by case number. New cases are available in the index 5-7 days after filing date. Both computer and card indexes are maintained. Open records are located at this court.

Fee & Payment: The fee is $20.00 per item (one party name or case number). Payment may be made by money order, cashier check, business check. Personal checks are not accepted. Prepayment is required. Payee: Clerk, US Bankruptcy Court. Certification fee: $7.00 per document. Copy fee: $.50 per page.

Phone Search: Searching is not available by phone.

Mail Search: A stamped self addressed envelope is not required.

In Person: In person searching is available.

PACER: Sign-up number is 904-435-8475. Access fee is $.60 per minute. Toll-free access: 888-765-1751. Local access: 850-942-8897. Use of PC Anywhere V4.0 recommended. Password is bkc. Case records are available back to September 1985. Records are purged when cases are closed. New civil records are available online after 2 days.

Tallahassee Division Room 3120, 227 N Bronough St, Tallahassee, FL 32301-1378 (Courier Address: Use mail address for courier delivery), 850-942-8933.

Counties: Alachua, Bay, Calhoun, Dixie, Franklin, Gadsden, Gilchrist, Gulf, Holmes, Jackson, Jefferson, Lafayette, Leon, Levy, Liberty, Madison, Taylor, Wakulla, Washington.

Indexing/Storage: Cases are indexed by debtor as well as by case number. New cases are available in the index 2-3 days after filing date. A computer index is maintained. Open records are located at this court.

Fee & Payment: The fee is $20.00 per item (one party name or case number). Payment may be made by money order, cashier check, business check. Personal checks are not accepted. Prepayment is required. Payee: Clerk, US Bankruptcy Court. Certification fee: $7.00 per document. Copy fee: $.50 per page.

Phone Search: Searching is not available by phone. Only docket information is available by phone.

Mail Search: Always enclose a stamped self addressed envelope.

In Person: In person searching is available.

PACER: Sign-up number is 800-676-6856. Access fee is $.60 per minute. Toll-free access: 888-765-1752. Local access: 850-942-8815. Use of PC Anywhere V4.0 recommended. Password is bkc. Case records are available back to September 23, 1985. Records are purged every six months. New civil records are available online after 1 day.

US District Court

Southern District of Florida

Fort Lauderdale Division 299 E Broward Blvd, Fort Lauderdale, FL 33301 (Courier Address: Use mail address for courier delivery), 954-769-5400.

http://www.flsd.uscourts.gov

Counties: Broward.

Indexing/Storage: Cases are indexed by defendant and plaintiff as well as by case number. New cases are available in the index immediately after filing date. The full name of any party of the case, case number or case type is required to search for records. Both computer and card indexes are maintained. Civil cases are in the computer from August 1990 to present. Criminal cases are in the computer from January 1992. Cases from 1983 are on microfiche. Cases prior to 1983 are on microfilm. Open records are located at this court. Records that are more than 5 years old are, at the discretion of the clerk, sent to the Atlanta Federal Records Center. Call records department to get location of records.

Fee & Payment: The fee is $20.00 per item (one party name or case number). Payment may be made by money order, cashier check, business check, Visa, Mastercard. Personal checks are not accepted. Prepayment is required. Payee: U.S. Courts. Certification fee: $7.00 per document. Copy fee: $.50 per page. You are allowed to make your own copies. These copies cost $.25 per page. The copy service (954-832-0111) will pull records and make copies for $.25 per copy. Copy machines are also available in the lobby.

Phone Search: Searching is not available by phone. Only docket information is available by phone.

Mail Search: Always enclose a stamped self addressed envelope.

In Person: In person searching is available.

PACER: Sign-up number is 800-676-6856. Access fee is $.60 per minute. Toll-free access: 800-372-8846. Local access: 305-536-7265. Case records are available back to August 1990. Records are purged three years after case closed. New records are available online after 1 day. PACER is available online at http://pacer.flsd.uscourts.gov.

Fort Pierce Division c/o Miami Division, Room 150, 301 N Miami Ave, Miami, FL 33128 (Courier Address: Use mail address for courier delivery), 305-523-5210.

www.flsd.uscourts.gov

Counties: Highlands, Indian River, Martin, Okeechobee, St. Lucie.

Indexing/Storage: Cases are indexed by defendant and plaintiff as well as by case number. New cases are available in the index immediately after filing date. A computer index is maintained. Open records are located at the Division. Records are transferred to the Federal Records Center any time after 5 years at the discretion of the clerk.

Fee & Payment: The fee is $20.00 per item (one party name or case number). Payment may be made by money order, cashier check, personal check. Prepayment is required. Payee: US Court. Certification fee: $7.00 per document. Copy fee: $.50 per page.

Phone Search: Docket information is available by phone.

Mail Search: Always enclose a stamped self addressed envelope.

In Person: In person searching is available.

PACER: Sign-up number is 800-676-6856. Access fee is $.60 per minute. Toll-free access: 800-372-8846. Local access: 305-536-7265. Case records are available back to August 1990. Records are purged three years after case closed. New records are available online after 1 day. PACER is available online at http://pacer.flsd.uscourts.gov.

Key West Division 301 Simonton St., Key West, FL 33040 (Courier Address: Use mail address for courier delivery), 305-295-8100.

www.flsd.uscourts.gov

Counties: Monroe.

Indexing/Storage: Cases are indexed by defendant and plaintiff as well as by case number. New cases are available in the index immediately after filing date. The full name of either party in the case, case number or case type is required to search for records. A computer index is maintained. Open records are located at the Division. Records that are more than 5 years old are, at the discretion of the clerk, are sent to the Atlanta Federal Records Center. Call records department to get location of records.

Fee & Payment: The fee is $20.00 per item (one party name or case number). Payment may be made by money order, cashier check, personal check. Prepayment is required. Payee: U.S. Courts. Certification fee: $7.00 per document. Copy fee: $.50 per page. You are allowed to make your own copies. These copies cost $.50 per page. The copy service will pull records and make copies for $.04 per copy. Copy machines are also available in the lobby.

Phone Search: Searching is not available by phone.

Mail Search: Always enclose a stamped self addressed envelope.

In Person: In person searching is available.

PACER: Sign-up number is 800-676-6856. Access fee is $.60 per minute. Toll-free access: 800-372-8846. Local access: 305-536-7265. Case records are available back to August 1990. Records are purged three years after case closed. New records are available online after 1 day. PACER is available online at http://pacer.flsd.uscourts.gov.

Miami Division Room 150, 301 N Miami Ave, Miami, FL 33128-7788 (Courier Address: Use mail address for courier delivery), 305-523-5700.

http://www.flsd.uscourts.gov

Counties: Dade.

Indexing/Storage: Cases are indexed by defendant and plaintiff as well as by case number. New cases are available in the index 1 day after filing date. The full name of either party in the case, case number or case type is required to search for records. A computer index is maintained. Open records are located at this court. Records that are more than 5 years old are, at the discretion of the clerk, sent to the Atlanta Federal Records Center. Call records department to get location of records.

Fee & Payment: The fee is $20.00 per item (one party name or case number). Payment may be

made by money order, cashier check, personal check, Visa, Mastercard. Prepayment is required. Payee: U.S. Courts. Certification fee: $7.00 per document. Copy fee: $.50 per page. You are allowed to make your own copies. These copies cost $.25 per page. Copy machines are also available in the lobby area of the Records and Docketing Section. There is also an on-site copy service that can pull records and make copies. Call for more information.

Phone Search: Only docket information is available by phone.

Mail Search: Always enclose a stamped self addressed envelope.

In Person: In person searching is available.

PACER: Sign-up number is 800-676-6856. Access fee is $.60 per minute. Toll-free access: 800-372-8846. Local access: 305-536-7265. Case records are available back to August 1990. Records are purged three years after case closed. New records are available online after 1 day. PACER is available online at http://pacer.flsd.uscourts.gov.

West Palm Beach Division Room 402, 701 Clematis St, West Palm Beach, FL 33401 (Courier Address: Use mail address for courier delivery), 561-803-3400.

www.flsd.uscourts.gov

Counties: Palm Beach.

Indexing/Storage: Cases are indexed by defendant and plaintiff as well as by case number. New cases are available in the index immediately after filing date. The full name of either party in the case, case number or case type is required to search for records. A computer index is maintained. Open records are located at this court.

Fee & Payment: The fee is $20.00 per item (one party name or case number). Payment may be made by money order, cashier check, business check, Visa, Mastercard. Personal checks are not accepted. Prepayment is required. Payee: U.S. Courts. Certification fee: $7.00 per document. Copy fee: $.50 per page. You are allowed to make your own copies. These copies cost $.50 per page. A copy service is available to pull records and make copies. Copy machines are also available in the lobby.

Phone Search: Docket information is available by phone.

Mail Search: Always enclose a stamped self addressed envelope.

In Person: In person searching is available.

PACER: Sign-up number is 800-676-6856. Access fee is $.60 per minute. Toll-free access: 800-372-8846. Local access: 305-536-7265. Case records are available back to August 1990. Records are purged three years after case closed. New records are available online after 1 day. PACER is available online at http://pacer.flsd.uscourts.gov.

US Bankruptcy Court

Southern District of Florida

Miami Division Room 1517, 51 SW 1st Ave, Miami, FL 33130 (Courier Address: Use mail address for courier delivery), 305-536-5216.

http://www.flsb.uscourts.gov

Counties: Broward, Dade, Highlands, Indian River, Martin, Monroe, Okeechobee, Palm Beach, St. Lucie. Cases may also be assigned to Fort Lauderdale or to West Palm Beach.

Indexing/Storage: Cases are indexed by debtor and creditors as well as by case number. New cases are available in the index 48 hours after filing date. A computer index is maintained. Open records are located at this court. Open case records may be held in the Fort Lauderdale or West Palm Beach office, depending on the judge assigned.

Fee & Payment: The fee is $20.00 per item (one party name or case number). Payment may be made by money order, cashier check. Business checks are not accepted. Personal checks are not accepted. Prepayment is required. Checks from law firms are accepted. Payee: US Courts. Certification fee: $7.00 per document. Copy fee: $.50 per page.

Phone Search: An automated voice case information service (VCIS) is available. Call VCIS at 800-473-0226 or 305-536-5979.

Mail Search: Always enclose a stamped self addressed envelope.

In Person: In person searching is available.

PACER: Sign-up number is 800-676-6856. Access fee is $.60 per minute. Toll-free access: 888-443-0081. Local access: 305-536-7492. Case records are available back to 1986. Records are purged every six months. New civil records are available online after 1 day. PACER is available online at http://pacer.flsb.uscourts.gov/login.html.

Florida County Courts

Court	Jurisdiction	No. of Courts	How Organized
Circuit Courts*	General	10	20 Circuits
County Courts*	Limited	13	
Combined Courts*		81	

* Profiled in this Sourcebook.

Court	CIVIL								
	Tort	Contract	Real Estate	Min. Claim	Max. Claim	Small Claims	Estate	Eviction	Domestic Relations
Circuit Courts*	X	X	X	$15,000	No Max		X		X
County Courts*	X	X	X	$0	$15,000	$2500		X	

Court	CRIMINAL				
	Felony	Misdemeanor	DWI/DUI	Preliminary Hearing	Juvenile
Circuit Courts*	X				X
County Courts*		X	X	X	

ADMINISTRATION   Office of State Courts Administrator, Supreme Court Bldg, 500 S Duval, Tallahassee, FL, 32399-1900; 850-922-5082, Fax: 850-488-0156. www.flcourts.org/

COURT STRUCTURE   All counties have combined Circuit and County Courts. The Circuit Court is the court of general jurisdiction.

ONLINE ACCESS   There is a statewide, online computer system for internal use only; there is no external access available nor planned currently. However, a number of courts do offer online access to the public.

ADDITIONAL INFORMATION   All courts have one address and switchboard; however, the divisions within the court(s) are completely separate. Requesters should specify which court and which division, e.g., Circuit Civil, County Civil, etc., the request is directed to, even though some counties will automatically check both with one request.

Fees are set by statute and are as follows: Search Fee - $1.00 per name per year; Certification Fee - $1.00 per document plus copy fee; Copy Fee - $1.00 per certified page; $.15 per non-certified page.

Most courts have very lengthy phone recording systems.

Alachua County

Circuit & County Courts PO Box 600, Gainesville, FL 32602; 352-374-3609; Civil phone: 352-338-3207; Criminal phone: 352-491-4400; Fax: 352-338-3201. Hours: 8:30AM-5PM (EST). *Felony, Misdemeanor, Civil, Eviction, Small Claims, Probate.*
http://circuit8.org

Civil Records: Access: Phone, fax, mail, online, in person. Both court and visitors may perform in person searches. Search fee: $1.00 per name per year. Required to search: name, years to search; also helpful: address. Civil cases indexed by defendant, plaintiff. Civil records on computer from 1979, some records on docket books. The Circuit's Civil open cases can be searched free at http://circuit8.org/case/index.html by division; password required Contact court for information. County Clerk online access is available free at www.clerk-alachua-fl.org/clerk/pubrec.html. Records can be searched by name or case number.
Criminal Records: Access: Phone, fax, mail, online, in person. Both court and visitors may perform in person searches. Search fee: $1.00 per name per year. Required to search: name, years to search, DOB; also helpful: address, SSN, race, sex. Criminal records on computer since 1974. The Circuit's criminal open cases can be

searched free on the web at http://circuit8.org/case/index.html by division; password required. Contact court for information.
General Information: Public Access terminal is available. No juvenile, child abuse or sexual battery records released. SASE required. Turnaround time 5 working days. Copy fee: $1.00 per page. Records can be searched by name or case number Certification fee: $1.00. Fee payee: Clerk of Circuit Court. Personal checks accepted. Credit cards accepted: Visa, MasterCard. Visa, MC. Prepayment is required.

Baker County

Circuit & County Courts - Civil 339 E Macclenny Ave, Macclenny, FL 32063; 904-259-0202, 904-259-0209 (Circuit civ); Civil phone: 904-259-0208 (Cty); Probate phone: 904-259-0209; Fax: 904-259-4176. Hours: 8:30AM-5PM (EST). *Civil, Eviction, Small Claims, Probate.*
http://circuit8.org

Civil Records: Access: Mail, in person. Search fee: $1.00 per name per year. Required to search: name, years to search; also helpful: address. Civil cases indexed by defendant, plaintiff. Civil records are computerized since 03/96, prior on index cards and

docket books. **General Information:** Public Access terminal is available. No juvenile, child abuse or sexual battery records released. SASE preferred. Turnaround time 2 days. Copy fee: $1.00 per page. Certification fee: $1.00. Fee payee: Clerk of Circuit Court. Business checks accepted. Prepayment is required.

Circuit & County Courts - Criminal 339 E Macclenny Ave, Macclenny, FL 32063; 904-259-8449; Fax: 904-259-4176. Hours: 8:30AM-5PM (EST). *Felony, Misdemeanor.*
http://circuit8.org

Criminal Records: Access: Mail, in person, online. Only the court performs in person searches; visitors may not. Search fee: $1.00 per name per year. Required to search: name, years to search, DOB. Criminal records on computer since 1989. Some records on docket books. Access to the circuit-wide criminal quick lookup is available at http://circuit8.org/golem/gencrim.html. Account and password is required; restricted usage.
General Information: No juvenile or guardianship records released. SASE required. Turnaround time 1-2 days. Copy fee: $1.00 per page. Certification fee: $1.00. Fee payee: Clerk of Circuit Court. Business checks accepted. Prepayment is required.

Bay County

Circuit Court - Civil PO Box 2269, Panama City, FL 32402; 850-767-5715; Fax: 850-747-5188. Hours: 8AM-5PM (CST). *Civil Actions Over $15,000, Probate.*

www.baycoclerk.com

Civil Records: Access: Phone, fax, mail, in person. Both court and visitors may perform in person searches. Search fee: $1.00 per name per year. Required to search: name, years to search. Civil cases indexed by defendant, plaintiff. Civil records on computer from 1984, on microfiche from 1950 to 1980, archived from 1913 to 1979. Some records on dockets. **General Information:** Public Access terminal is available. No juvenile, adoption, child abuse or sexual battery records released. Turnaround time 2 days. Fax notes: $2.00 per page. Copy fee: $1.00 per page. Certification fee: $1.00. Fee payee: Clerk of Circuit Court. Personal checks accepted. Prepayment is required.

Circuit Court - Criminal PO Box 2269, Panama City, FL 32402; 850-747-5123; Fax: 850-747-5188. Hours: 8AM-4:30PM (CST). *Felony.*

www.baycoclerk.com

Criminal Records: Access: Fax, mail, in person. Both court and visitors may perform in person searches. Search fee: $1.00 per name per year. Required to search: name, years to search, DOB; also helpful: SSN, signed release. Criminal records on computer back to 1986, on microfilm from 1938 to 1982, prior archived. **General Information:** No sealed, juvenile or expunged records released. SASE requested. Turnaround time 3-5 days. Fax notes: $2.00 per document. Copy fee: $1.00 per page. Certification fee: $1.00 per page. Fee payee: Clerk of Circuit Court. Personal checks accepted. Prepayment is required.

County Court - Civil PO Box 2269, Panama City, FL 32402; 850-747-5141; Fax: 850-747-5188. Hours: 8AM-4:30PM (CST). *Civil Actions Under $15,000, Eviction, Small Claims.*

www.baycoclerk.com

Civil Records: Access: Phone, fax, mail, in person. Both court and visitors may perform in person searches. Search fee: $1.00 per name per year. Required to search: name, years to search. Civil cases indexed by defendant, plaintiff. Civil records on computer from 1986, on microfiche from 1950 to 1980, archived from 1913 to 1979. Some records on docket books. **General Information:** Public Access terminal is available. No juvenile, child abuse or sexual battery records released. SASE requested. Turnaround time 2 days. Fax notes: $2.00 per page. Copy fee: $1.00 per page. Certification fee: $1.00. Fee payee: Clerk of Circuit Court. Personal checks accepted. Prepayment is required.

County Court - Misdemeanor PO Box 2269, Panama City, FL 32402; 850-747-5144; Fax: 850-747-5188. Hours: 8AM-4:30PM (CST). *Misdemeanor.*

www.baycoclerk.com

Criminal Records: Access: Phone, fax, mail, in person. Both court and visitors may perform in person searches. Search fee: $1.00 per name per year. Required to search: name, years to search; also helpful: DOB, SSN. Criminal records on computer from 1984, on microfiche from 1938 to 1991, archived from 1938. **General Information:** Public Access terminal is available. No sealed or expunged records released. SASE requested. Turnaround time 7-10 days. Fax notes: $2.00 per document. Copy fee: $1.00 per page. Certification fee: $1.00. Fee payee: Clerk of Circuit Court. Personal checks accepted. Prepayment is required.

Bradford County

Circuit Court PO Drawer B, Starke, FL 32091; 904-964-6280; Fax: 904-964-4454. Hours: 8AM-5PM (EST). *Felony, Civil Actions Over $15,000, Probate.*

http://circuit8.org

Civil Records: Access: Phone, mail, in person. Both court and visitors may perform in person searches. Search fee: $1.00 per name per year. Required to search: name, years to search. Civil cases indexed by defendant, plaintiff. Civil records on computer since late 1987, others on index books.

Criminal Records: Access: Phone, mail, in person, online. Both court and visitors may perform in person searches. Search fee: $1.00 per name per year. Required to search: name, years to search, DOB, SSN. Criminal records on computer since 1989, others on index books. Access to the circuit-wide criminal quick lookup is available at http://circuit8.org/golem/gencrim.html. Account and password is required; restricted usage.

General Information: No juvenile, child abuse or sexual battery records released. SASE required. Turnaround time 1 week. Copy fee: $1.00 per page. Certification fee: $1.00. Fee payee: Clerk at Circuit Court. Business checks accepted. Prepayment is required.

County Court PO Drawer B, Starke, FL 32091; 904-964-6280; Fax: 904-964-4454. Hours: 8AM-5PM (EST). *Misdemeanor, Civil Actions Under $15,000, Eviction, Small Claims.*

www.bradford-co-fla.org

Civil Records: Access: Mail, in person, online. Both court and visitors may perform in person searches. Search fee: $1.00 per name per year. Required to search: name, years to search. Civil cases indexed by defendant, plaintiff. Civil records on computer from 1987. Some records on docket books, some microfilm. Access to court records from the County Clerk should be available some time in 2001 at the web site above.

Criminal Records: Access: Mail, in person, online. Both court and visitors may perform in person searches. Search fee: $1.00 per name per year. Required to search: name, years to search, DOB. Criminal records on computer from 1989. Some records on docket books. Online access to criminal records is the same as civil.

General Information: No juvenile records released. SASE required. Turnaround time 2 days. Copy fee: $1.00 per page. Certification fee: $1.00. Fee payee: Clerk of Court. Business checks accepted. Prepayment is required.

Brevard County

Circuit Court - Civil PO Box 2767, Offical Records Copy Desk, Titusville, FL 32781-2767; 321-264-5245; Fax: 321-264-5246. Hours: 8AM-5PM (EST). *Civil, Eviction, Small Claims, Probate.*

www.clerk.co.brevard.fl.us

Civil Records: Access: Phone, fax, mail, online, in person. Both court and visitors may perform in person searches. Search fee: $1.00 per name per year. Required to search: name, years to search. Civil cases indexed by defendant, plaintiff. Civil records on computer since 1987, on microfiche since early 1900s. Some records on docket books. Access to County Court records are available free from FACTSweb at www.clerk.co.brevard.fl.us/pages/facts1.htm. Online records back to 1988 can be searched by name, case number or citation number. **General Information:** Public Access terminal is available. No juvenile, child abuse or sexual battery victim records released. SASE not required. Turnaround time 1 week. Fax notes: $2.00 for first page, $1.00 each add'l. Fax fee for long distance $3.00 1st page, $1.00 each additional page. Copy fee: $1.00 per page. Certification fee: $1.00. Fee payee:

Circuit Clerk. Personal checks accepted. Check by fax or phone accepted. Credit cards accepted: Visa, MasterCard, Discover. Prepayment is required.

Circuit Court - Felony PO Box 999, 700 S Park Ave, Titusville, FL 32781; 321-264-5350; Fax: 321-264-5395. Hours: 8AM-5PM (EST). *Felony.*

www.clerk.co.brevard.fl.us

Criminal Records: Access: Phone, fax, mail, online, in person. Both court and visitors may perform in person searches. Search fee: $1.00 per name per year. Required to search: name, DOB, SSN. Criminal records on computer since 1988, on microfiche from early 1900s. Some records on docket books. Online access to county criminal court records is available free through FACTSweb at www.clerk.co.brevard.fl.us/pages/facts1.htm. Search by name, case number or citation number.

General Information: Public Access terminal is available. No juvenile, child abuse, sexual battery or adoption records released. SASE not required. Turnaround time 1 week, phone turnaround time same day. Fax notes: $1.00 per page. Fax fee for long distance $2.00. Copy fee: $1.00 per page. Certification fee: $1.00. Fee payee: Circuit Clerk. Personal checks accepted. Credit cards accepted: Visa, MasterCard. Prepayment is required.

County Court - Misdemeanor PO Box 999, 700 S Park Ave, Titusville, FL 32781; 321-264-5350; Fax: 321-264-5395. Hours: 8AM-4:30PM (EST). *Misdemeanor.*

www.clerk.co.brevard.fl.us

Criminal Records: Access: Phone, fax, mail, online, in person. Both court and visitors may perform in person searches. Search fee: $1.00 per name per year. Required to search: name, years to search, DOB; also helpful: SSN, race, sex. Criminal records on computer since 1990, on microfiche from early 1900s. Some records on docket books and index cards. Access to County criminal records are available free from FACTSweb at www.clerk.co.brevard.fl.us/pages/facts1.htm. Online records back to 1988 can be searched by name, case number or citation number.

General Information: Public Access terminal is available. No juvenile, child abuse, sexual battery or adoption records released. SASE not required. Turnaround time 1 week, phone turnaround time 2 days. Fax notes: $1.00 per page. Fax fee for long distance $2.00 for 1st page. Copy fee: $1.00 per page. Certification fee: $1.00. Fee payee: Circuit Clerk. Personal checks accepted. Credit cards accepted: Visa, MasterCard. Prepayment is required.

Broward County

Circuit & County Courts 201 SE 6th St, Ft Lauderdale, FL 33301; 954-765-6565; Probate phone: 954-831-7154; Fax: 954-831-7166. Hours: 9AM-4PM (EST). *Felony, Misdemeanor, Civil, Eviction, Small Claims, Probate.*

www.17th.flcourts.org

Civil Records: Access: Phone, fax, mail, online, in person, email. Both court and visitors may perform in person searches. Search fee: $1.00 per name per year. Add $4.00 for written response (affidavit). Required to search: name, years to search. Civil cases indexed by defendant, plaintiff. Civil records on computer from 1986. Some records on dockets. Will search back 10 years. The county clerk online fee system is being replaced by a web system. The web allows basic information free. More "Detailed information" requires a fee. Search by name or case number or case type. Call 954-831-5654 for info. Also, Limited court records on the County Records Division site are available free at http://205.166.161.20/CRSearch/crSearch.asp. Also, the

Circuit Clerk's recording database is available free at www.clerk-17th-flcourts.org/bccoc/disclaimer.asp.

Criminal Records: Access: Phone, fax, mail, online, in person, email. Both court and visitors may perform in person searches. Search fee: $1.00 per name per year. Add $4.00 for written response (affidavit). Required to search: name, years to search, DOB; also helpful: SSN. Criminal records on computer since 1980. Access to the criminal records on the online pay service or internet is the same as civil.

General Information: Public Access terminal is available. Turnaround time 1-14 days. Copy fee: $1.00 per page. Certification fee: $1.00. Fee payee: Clerk of the Court. Only cashiers checks and money orders accepted.

Calhoun County

Circuit & County Court 425 E Central Ave, Blountstown, FL 32424; 850-674-4545; Fax: 850-674-5553. Hours: 8AM-4PM (CST). *Felony, Misdemeanor, Civil, Eviction, Small Claims, Probate.*

Civil Records: Access: Phone, mail, in person. Both court and visitors may perform in person searches. No search fee. Required to search: name, years to search. Civil cases indexed by defendant, plaintiff. Civil records on computer back to 1986, books from 1970s.

Criminal Records: Access: Phone, mail, in person. Both court and visitors may perform in person searches. No search fee. Required to search: name, years to search. Criminal records on computer back to 1986, on docket books from 1970s.

General Information: No juvenile, child abuse or sexual battery records released. SASE required. Turnaround time 2 days. Fax notes: No fee to fax results. Copy fee: $1.00 per page. Certification fee: $1.00. Fee payee: Clerk of Court. Personal checks accepted. Prepayment is required.

Charlotte County

Circuit & County Courts - Civil Division PO Box 511687, Punta Gorda, FL 33951-1687; 941-637-2279; Fax: 941-637-2116. Hours: 8AM-5PM (EST). *Civil, Eviction, Small Claims, Probate.*

http://co.charlotte.fl.us/clrkinfo/lcerk_default.htm

Civil Records: Access: Mail, in person, online. Both court and visitors may perform in person searches. Search fee: $1.00 per name per year. Required to search: name, years to search. Civil cases indexed by defendant, plaintiff. Civil records on computer back to 1982, on microfiche since 1987. Online access to civil and probate records is available by subscription, see the web site. Original payment is $186.00 ($150 refundable) plus a usage fee based on number of transactions. Allows printing of copies. For more information, call 941-637-2199. **General Information:** Public Access terminal is available. No juvenile, child abuse, sexual battery, adoption records released. SASE requested. Turnaround time 1-2 days. Fax notes: Fee to fax results is $2.00 per page. Copy fee: $1.00 per page. Certification fee: $1.00 per document. Fee payee: Clerk of Circuit Court. Personal checks accepted. Prepayment is required.

Circuit & County Courts - Criminal Division PO Box 511687, Punta Gorda, FL 33951-1687; 941-637-2269; Fax: 941-637-2159. Hours: 8AM-5PM (EST). *Felony, Misdemeanor.*

http://co.charlotte.fl.us/clrkinfo/clerk_default.htm

Criminal Records: Access: Phone, mail, in person, online. Both court and visitors may perform in person searches. Search fee: $1.00 per name per year. Required to search: name, years to search, DOB; also helpful: address, SSN, race, sex. Criminal records on computer since 1985, misdemeanors on index cards, felonies on judgment books, imaging on disc from 1993. Online access to criminal records is available by subscription,

see the web site. Original payment is $186.00 ($150 refundable) plus a usage fee based on number of transactions. Allows printing of copies. For more information, call 941-637-2199.

General Information: Public Access terminal is available. No juvenile, child abuse or sexual battery records released. SASE requested. Turnaround time 1 week. Fax notes: Fee to fax results is $2.00 per page. Copy fee: $1.00 per page. Certification fee: $1.00. Fee payee: Clerk of Circuit Court. Personal checks accepted. Prepayment is required.

Citrus County

Circuit Court 110 N Apopka Rm 101, Inverness, FL 34450; 352-341-6400; Fax: 352-341-6413. Hours: 8AM-5PM (EST). *Felony, Civil Actions Over $15,000, Probate.*

www.clerk.citrus.fl.us

Civil Records: Access: Phone, fax, mail, in person, online. Both court and visitors may perform in person searches. Search fee: $1.00 per name per year. Required to search: name, years to search; also helpful: address. Civil cases indexed by defendant, plaintiff. Civil records on computer from 1989, archived from 1940 to 1991. Some records on docket books. Online access to civil data on the county clerk database is available free at www.clerk.citrus.fl.us/offrsearch.htf. By phone only back to 1989. Indicate on search request the type(s) of cases.

Criminal Records: Access: Phone, fax, mail, in person. Both court and visitors may perform in person searches. Search fee: $1.00 per name per year. Required to search: name, years to search, DOB; also helpful: address, SSN, race, sex. Criminal records on computer from 1989, on microfiche from 1948 to 1987, archived from 1940-1991. By phone only back to 1989.

General Information: Public Access terminal is available. No juvenile, adoption, child abuse or sexual battery records released. SASE required. Turnaround time 1-2 days. Fax notes: $1.00 per page for local; $2.00 per page for long distance. Copy fee: $1.00 per page. Certification fee: $1.00. Fee payee: Clerk of Circuit Court. Personal checks accepted. Prepayment is required.

County Court 110 N Apopka, Rm 101, Inverness, FL 34450; 352-341-6400; Fax: 352-341-6413. Hours: 8AM-5PM (EST). *Misdemeanor, Civil Actions Under $15,000, Eviction, Small Claims.*

www.clerk.citrus.fl.us

Civil Records: Access: Phone, fax, mail, in person. Both court and visitors may perform in person searches. Search fee: $1.00 per name per year. Required to search: name, years to search; also helpful: address. Civil cases indexed by defendant, plaintiff. Civil records on computer from 1990, prior records on docket books. Indicate type of case(s) you are looking for on your search request.

Criminal Records: Access: Mail, in person. Both court and visitors may perform in person searches. Search fee: $1.00 per name per year. Required to search: name, years to search, DOB; also helpful: address, SSN, race, sex. Criminal records on computer from 1990, prior records on docket books.

General Information: Public Access terminal is available. (Criminal only.) No juvenile, child abuse or sexual battery records released. SASE required. Turnaround time 1-3 days. Fax notes: $1.00 per page. Fax fee for long distance $2.00 per page. Copy fee: $1.00 per page. Certification fee: $1.00. Fee payee: Clerk of Circuit Court. Personal checks accepted. Prepayment is required.

Clay County

Circuit Court PO Box 698, Green Cove Springs, FL 32043; 904-284-6302; Fax: 904-284-6390. Hours: 8:30AM-4:30PM (EST). *Felony, Civil Actions Over $15,000, Probate.*

http://clerk.co.clay.fl.us

Civil Records: Access: Mail, online, in person. Both court and visitors may perform in person searches. Search fee: $1.00 per name per year. Required to search: name, years to search; also helpful: address. Civil cases indexed by defendant, plaintiff. Civil records on computer from 1985, prior records on docket books. The clerk of the circuit court provides free access to records from the web site. This has taken the place of the commercial system.

Criminal Records: Access: Mail, in person. Both court and visitors may perform in person searches. Search fee: $1.00 per name per year. Required to search: name, years to search, DOB; also helpful: address, SSN, race, sex. Criminal records (Felony) on computer from 1967, prior records on docket books. The agency hopes to have criminal records online at the web site before the close of 2000. Call 904-284-6371 for details.

General Information: Public Access terminal is available. No juvenile, child abuse or sexual battery records released. Turnaround time 1-3 days. Copy fee: $1.00 per page. Certification fee: $1.00. Fee payee: Clerk of Circuit Court. Only cashiers checks and money orders accepted. Prepayment is required.

County Court PO Box 698, Green Cove Springs, FL 32043; 904-284-6316; Fax: 904-284-6390. Hours: 8:30AM-4:30PM (EST). *Misdemeanor, Civil Actions Under $15,000, Eviction, Small Claims.*

http://clerk.co.clay.fl.us

Civil Records: Access: Mail, online, in person. Both court and visitors may perform in person searches. Search fee: $1.00 per name per year. Required to search: name, years to search; also helpful: address. Civil cases indexed by defendant, plaintiff. Civil records on computer back to 1992, prior records on docket books. Online access is available at no fee from the web site. Click on "Online Information." Online records go back to 1990.

Criminal Records: Access: Mail, in person, online. Both court and visitors may perform in person searches. Search fee: $1.00 per name per year. Required to search: name, years to search, DOB; also helpful: address, SSN, race, sex. Criminal records on computer back to 1992, prior records on docket books. Online access to criminal records is the same as civil.

General Information: Public Access terminal is available. No juvenile, child abuse or sexual battery records released. Turnaround time 1-2 days. Fax notes: Fee to fax results is $2.00 1st page; $1.00 each add'l. Copy fee: $1.00 per page. Certification fee: $1.00. Fee payee: Clerk of Circuit Court. Personal checks accepted. Prepayment is required.

Collier County

Circuit Court PO Box 413044, Naples, FL 34101-3044; 941-732-2646. Hours: 8AM-5PM (EST). *Felony, Civil Actions Over $15,000, Probate.*

www.clerk.collier.fl.us

Civil Records: Access: Mail, online, in person. Both court and visitors may perform in person searches. Search fee: $1.00 per name per year. Required to search: name, years to search. Civil cases indexed by defendant, plaintiff. Civil records on computer from 1990, on microfiche from 1922 to 1994, archived from 1922. The online access system has a $100.00 setup fee, a monthly $10.00 fee and a $.05 per minute access charge. Records include probate, traffic and domestic. For more information, call Judy at 941-774-8339.

Criminal Records: Access: Mail, online, in person. Both court and visitors may perform in person searches. Search fee: $1.00 per name per year. Required to search: name, years to search, DOB; also helpful: SSN. Criminal records on computer from 1990, on microfiche from 1922 to 1994, archived from 1922. Online access to criminal records is the same as civil. Searching is by name for both felony and misdemeanor records. Call 941-774-8339 for more information.

General Information: Public Access terminal is available. No sealed by court or statute records released. Turnaround time within 1 week. Copy fee: $1.00 per page. Certification fee: $1.00. Fee payee: Clerk of Circuit Court. Personal checks accepted. Prepayment is required.

County Court PO Box 413044, Naples, FL 34101-3044; 941-732-2646; Fax: 941-774-8020. Hours: 8AM-5PM (EST). *Misdemeanor, Civil Actions Under $15,000, Eviction, Small Claims.*

www.clerk.collier.fl.us

Civil Records: Access: Mail, online, in person. Both court and visitors may perform in person searches. Search fee: $1.00 per name per year. Required to search: name, years to search; also helpful: address. Civil cases indexed by defendant, plaintiff. Civil records on computer from 1990, on microfiche from 1922 to 1995. The online access system has a $100.00 setup fee, a monthly $10.00 fee and a $.05 per minute access charge. Records include probate, traffic and domestic. For more information, call Judy at 941-774-8339.

Criminal Records: Access: Mail, online, in person. Both court and visitors may perform in person searches. Search fee: $1.00 per name per year. Required to search: name, years to search, DOB; also helpful: address, SSN, race, sex. Criminal records on computer from 1990, on microfiche from 1922 to 1995. Online access to criminal records is the same as civil.

General Information: No juvenile, child abuse or sexual battery records released. SASE required. Turnaround time 1 week. Copy fee: $1.00 per page. Certification fee: $1.00. Fee payee: Clerk of County Court. Personal checks accepted. Prepayment is required.

Columbia County

Circuit & County Courts PO Drawer 2069, Lake City, FL 32056; 386-719-7403. Hours: 8AM-5PM (EST). *Felony, Misdemeanor, Civil, Eviction, Small Claims, Probate.*

Civil Records: Access: Mail, in person, online. Both court and visitors may perform in person searches. Search fee: $1.00 per name per year. Fee is per department. Required to search: name, years to search. Civil cases indexed by defendant, plaintiff. Civil records on computer from 1987, archived from 1800s. DOB and SSN also helpful for searching. Limited online access to the Clerk of Circuit Court's database is available free at www.columbiaclerk.com/Public_R ecords/public_records.html. Search by name, file number or document type.

Criminal Records: Access: In person only. Both court and visitors may perform in person searches. Search fee: $1.00 per name per year. Fee is per department. Required to search: name, years to search, DOB; also helpful: SSN. Criminal records on computer from 1987, archived from 1800s.

General Information: No names of victims of sex related offenses, incompetence or mental health records released. SASE required. Turnaround time 1 day. Fax notes: Fee to fax results is $1.00 per page. Copy fee: $1.00 per page. Certification fee: $1.00. Fee payee: Clerk of Circuit Court. Cashier's check or money orders only. Prepayment is required. Prepayment is required.

Dade County

Circuit & County Courts - Civil 73 W Flagler St, Miami, FL 33130; 305-275-1155; Fax: 305-375-5819. Hours: 9AM-4PM (EST). *Civil, Eviction, Small Claims, Probate.*

http://jud11.flcourts.org

Civil Records: Access: Phone, fax, mail, online, in person. Both court and visitors may perform in person searches. Search fee: $1.00 per name per year. Required to search: name, years to search. Civil cases indexed by defendant, plaintiff. Civil records on computer from 1984, archived from 1836. Microfilm in county recorder's office. Two sources exist. Subscription online access requires a $125.00 setup fee, $52.00 monthly and $.25 per minute after the first 208 minutes each month. Docket information can be searched by case number or name. Call 305-596-8148 for more information. Also, online access to civil court records on the county clerk database are available free at www.metro-dade.com/clerk/Public-Records/disclaimer.asp.

General Information: Public Access terminal is available. No juvenile, child abuse or sexual battery records released. SASE requested. Turnaround time 1 week. Copy fee: $1.00 per page. Certification fee: $1.00. Fee payee: Clerk of Circuit & County Courts. Personal checks accepted. Credit cards accepted: Visa, MasterCard. Visa, MC +$15.00 add'l charge. Prepayment is required.

Circuit & County Courts - Criminal 1351 NW 12th St, Suite 9000, Miami, FL 33125; 305-275-1155; Fax: 305-548-5526. Hours: 9AM-4PM (EST). *Felony, Misdemeanor.*

http://jud11.flcourts.org

Criminal Records: Access: Phone, fax, mail, online, in person. Both court and visitors may perform in person searches. Search fee: $1.00 per year. Required to search: name, years to search, DOB; also helpful: address, SSN, race, sex. Criminal records on computer back to 1971, on microfiche from 1975, archived from 1836. Fees for criminal online access requires a $125.00 setup, $52.00 per month for the first 208 minutes and a $.25 per minute charge thereafter. Searching is by name or case number. Call 305-596-8148 for more information.

General Information: Public Access terminal is available. No juvenile, child abuse or sexual battery records released. SASE required. Turnaround time 10-15 days. Copy fee: $1.00 per page. Certification fee: $1.00. Fee payee: Clerk of Circuit and County Court. Personal checks accepted. Credit cards accepted: Visa, MasterCard. Credit cards accepted in person only. Prepayment is required.

De Soto County

Circuit & County Courts 115 E Oak Street, Arcadia, FL 34266; 863-993-4876; Civil phone: 863-993-4880; Probate phone: 863-993-4880; Fax: 863-993-4669. Hours: 8AM-5PM (EST). *Felony, Misdemeanor, Civil, Eviction, Small Claims, Probate.*

http://12circuit.state.fl.us

Note: County Court & Evictions 863-993-4880.

Civil Records: Access: Phone, fax, mail, in person. Both court and visitors may perform in person searches. Search fee: $1.00 per name per year. Required to search: name, years to search. Civil cases indexed by defendant, plaintiff. Civil records on computer from 1986, on microfiche from 1974, archived from 1887.

Criminal Records: Access: Phone, fax, mail, in person. Both court and visitors may perform in person searches. Search fee: $1.00 per name per year. Required to search: name, years to search, DOB; also helpful: SSN, aliases. Criminal records on computer since 1986, archived since 1887.

General Information: Public Access terminal is available. No juvenile or sex related records released.

SASE requested. Turnaround time 2 days. Fax notes: $1.00 per page. Copy fee: $1.00 per page. Certification fee: $1.00. Fee payee: Clerk of the Court. Personal checks accepted. Prepayment is required.

Dixie County

Circuit & County Courts PO Drawer 1206, Cross City, FL 32628-1206; 352-498-1200; Fax: 352-498-1201. Hours: 9AM-5PM (EST). *Felony, Misdemeanor, Civil, Eviction, Small Claims, Probate.*

Civil Records: Access: Mail, in person. Only the court performs in person searches; visitors may not. Search fee: $1.00 per name per year. Required to search: name, years to search; also helpful: address. Civil cases indexed by defendant, plaintiff. Civil records on computer since 1987.

Criminal Records: Access: Mail, in person. Only the court performs in person searches; visitors may not. Search fee: $1.00 per name per year. Required to search: name, years to search, DOB; also helpful: address, SSN, race, sex. Criminal records on computer since 1989.

General Information: Public Access terminal is available. No juvenile, child abuse or sexual battery records released. SASE required. Turnaround time 1 week. Fax notes: Fee to fax results is $1.00 per page. Copy fee: $1.00 per page. Certification fee: $1.00 per page. Fee payee: Clerk of Circuit Court. Personal checks accepted. Prepayment is required.

Duval County

Circuit & County Courts - Civil Division 330 E Bay St, Jacksonville, FL 32202; 904-630-2039; Fax: 904-630-7506. Hours: 8AM-5PM (EST). *Civil, Eviction, Small Claims, Probate.*

www.coj.net/pub/clerk/default.htm

Civil Records: Access: Fax, mail, online, in person. Both court and visitors may perform in person searches. Search fee: $1.00 per name per year. Required to search: name, years to search; also helpful: address. Civil cases indexed by defendant, plaintiff. Civil records (Circuit) on computer from 1968, county from 1984. County civil on index books from 1975 to 1986, prior on docket books. Circuit civil on index books from 1900s to 1968. Online access requires a $100.00 setup fee, but no access charges. For more information, call Leslie Peterson at 904-630-1212 x5115. Also, court docket sheets are available free at the Clerk of Circuit Court website at www2.coj.net/officialrecords. **General Information:** No juvenile, child abuse or sexual battery records released. Turnaround time for county records 5-7 days, circuit 2-4 days. Fax notes: $1.00 per page. Copy fee: $1.00 per page. Certification fee: $1.00. Fee payee: Clerk of Circuit Court. Business checks accepted. Prepayment is required.

Circuit & County Courts - Criminal Division 330 E Bay St, Rm M106, Jacksonville, FL 32202; 904-630-2070; Fax: 904-630-7505. Hours: 8AM-5PM (EST). *Felony, Misdemeanor.*

www.coj.net/pub/clerk/default.htm

Criminal Records: Access: Mail, online, in person. Visitors must perform in person searches for themselves. No search fee. Required to search: name, years to search, DOB; also helpful: address, SSN, race, sex. Criminal records (Circuit) on computer from 1968, county from 1986. County civil on index books from 1975 to 1986, prior on docket books. Circuit civil on index books from 1900s to 1968. Online access to criminal records requires a $100.00 setup fee, but no access charges. Records go back to 1992. For more information, call Leslie Peterson at 904-630-1212 x5115. Also, court docket sheets are available free at the Clerk of Circuit Court website at www2.coj.net/officialrecords.

General Information: Public Access terminal is available. No juvenile, child abuse or sexual battery records released. SASE helpful. Turnaround time 2-3 days. Copy fee: $1.00 per page. Certification fee: $1.00. Fee payee: Clerk of the Court. Business checks accepted. Prepayment is required.

Escambia County

Circuit & County Courts - Civil Division

190 Governmental Center, Pensacola, FL 32501; 850-595-4170; Civil phone: 850-595-4130 (Circ Ct. Civil); Probate phone: 850-595-4300. Hours: 8AM-5PM (CST). *Civil, Eviction, Small Claims, Probate.*

www.clerk.co.escambia.fl.us

Civil Records: Access: Phone, fax, mail, in person, online. Both court and visitors may perform in person searches. No search fee. Required to search: name, years to search; also helpful: address. Civil cases indexed by defendant, plaintiff. Civil records on computer from mid 1986, prior on index books. Judgments and small claims on microfiche from 1952, evictions from 1973. Online access to county clerk records is available free at www.clerk.co.escambia.fl.us/public_records.html. Search by name, citation, or case number. Small claims, traffic, and marriage data also available. **General Information:** Public Access terminal is available. No juvenile, child abuse, adoption, mental health or sexual battery records released. SASE requested. Turnaround time 1-5 days. Copy fee: $1.00 per page. Certification fee: $1.00. Fee payee: Clerk of Circuit Court. Personal checks accepted. Prepayment is required.

Circuit & County Courts - Criminal Division

190 Governmental Center, Pensacola, FL 32501; 850-595-4150; Fax: 850-595-4198. Hours: 8AM-5PM (CST). *Felony, Misdemeanor.*

www.clerk.co.escambia.fl.us

Note: Misdemeanor records phone is 850-595-4185.

Criminal Records: Access: Fax, mail, in person, online. Only the court performs in person searches; visitors may not. Search fee: $1.00 per name per year. Required to search: name, years to search, DOB; also helpful: address, SSN, race, sex. Criminal records on computer and microfiche from 1973, archived from 1940 to 1972. Online access to county criminal records is available free at www.clerk.co.escambia.fl.us/public_records.html. Search by name, citation, or case number.

General Information: Public Access terminal is available. No juvenile, child abuse, mental health, adoption or sexual battery records released. SASE requested. Turnaround time within 1 week. Fax notes: $1.00 per page. If more than 5 pages $2.00, each additional group of 5 pages charge increases by $1.00, plus phone charge. Copy fee: $1.00 per page. Certification fee: $1.00. Fee payee: Clerk of Circuit Court. Personal checks accepted. Prepayment is required.

Flagler County

Circuit & County Courts

PO Box 787, Bunnell, FL 32110; 386-437-7430; Fax: 386-437-7454. Hours: 8AM-4:30PM (EST). *Felony, Misdemeanor, Civil, Eviction, Small Claims, Probate.*

www.clerk.co.flagler.fl.us

Civil Records: Access: Phone, fax, mail, in person. Both court and visitors may perform in person searches. Search fee: $1.00 per name per year. Required to search: name, years to search; also helpful: address. Civil cases indexed by defendant, plaintiff. Civil records on computer from 1990. All archived from 1917, some on index books.

Criminal Records: Access: Phone, fax, mail, in person. Both court and visitors may perform in person

searches. Search fee: $1.00 per name per year. Required to search: name, years to search, DOB; also helpful: address, SSN, race, sex. Criminal records on computer from 1990. All archived from 1917, some on index books.

General Information: No juvenile, child abuse or sexual battery records released. Turnaround time 3-5 days. Fax notes: $1.00 per page. Copy fee: $1.00 per page. Certification fee: $1.00. Fee payee: Clerk of Circuit Court. Business checks accepted. Prepayment is required.

Franklin County

Circuit & County Courts

33 Market St, Suite 203, Apalachicola, FL 32321; 850-653-8862; Fax: 850-653-2261. Hours: 8:30AM-4:30PM (EST). *Felony, Misdemeanor, Civil, Eviction, Small Claims, Probate.*

www.co.leon.fl.us/court/court.htm

Civil Records: Access: Mail, in person. Both court and visitors may perform in person searches. Search fee: $1.00 per name per year. Required to search: name, years to search; also helpful: address. Civil cases indexed by defendant, plaintiff. Civil records on computer from 3/92.

Criminal Records: Access: Mail, in person. Both court and visitors may perform in person searches. Search fee: $1.00 per name per year. Required to search: name, years to search, DOB; also helpful: address, SSN, race, sex. Criminal records on computer since 1989.

General Information: Public Access terminal is available. No juvenile, child abuse or sexual battery records released. SASE requested. Turnaround time 2-5 days. Copy fee: $1.00 per page. Certification fee: $1.00. Fee payee: Clerk of Circuit Court. In-county personal checks accepted. Prepayment is required.

Gadsden County

Circuit & County Courts - Civil Division

PO Box 1649, Quincy, FL 32353; 850-875-8621; Fax: 850-875-8612. Hours: 8:30AM-5PM (EST). *Civil, Eviction, Small Claims, Probate.*

www.clerk.co.gadsden.fl.us

Civil Records: Access: Phone, fax, mail, online, email, in person. Both court and visitors may perform in person searches. Search fee: $1.00 per name. Required to search: name, years to search. Civil cases indexed by defendant, plaintiff. Civil records on computer since 1984. Online access to civil court records are available free from the County Clerk at www.clerk.co.gadsden.fl.us. **General Information:** Public Access terminal is available. No juvenile, child abuse or sexual battery records released. Turnaround time 1 week. Fax notes: $1.00 per page. Copy fee: $.15 per page. Certification fee: $1.00. Fee payee: Clerk of Circuit Court. Only cashiers checks and money orders accepted. Prepayment is required.

Circuit & County Courts - Criminal Division

112 South Adams St, Quincy, FL 32351; 850-875-8609; Fax: 850-875-7625. Hours: 8:30AM-5PM (EST). *Felony, Misdemeanor.*

www.co.leon.fl.us/court/court.htm

Note: Requests may be sent to PO Box 1649, ZIP is 32353

Criminal Records: Access: Fax, mail, in person. Both court and visitors may perform in person searches. Search fee: $1.00 per name per year. Required to search: name, years to search, DOB; also helpful: SSN. Criminal records on computer from 1984, some on index books and cards.

General Information: Public Access terminal is available. No juvenile or sex offender records released. Turnaround time 3-5 days. Fax notes: $1.00 per page. Copy fee: $.15 per page. Certification fee: $2.00. Fee

payee: Clerk of Circuit Court. Personal checks accepted. Prepayment is required.

Gilchrist County

Circuit & County Courts

Po Box 37, Trenton, FL 32693; 352-463-3170; Fax: 352-463-3166. Hours: 8AM-5PM (EST). *Felony, Misdemeanor, Civil, Eviction, Small Claims, Probate.*

http://circuit8.org

Civil Records: Access: Phone, fax, mail, in person. Both court and visitors may perform in person searches. Search fee: $1.00 per name per year. Add $4.00 for written response (affidavit). Required to search: name, years to search; also helpful: address. Civil cases indexed by defendant, plaintiff. Civil records on computer from 1987, prior on index books.

Criminal Records: Access: Phone, fax, mail, in person, online. Only the court performs in person searches; visitors may not. Search fee: $1.00 per name per year. Add $4.00 for written response (affidavit). Required to search: name, years to search, DOB; also helpful: address, SSN, race, sex. Criminal records on computer since 1989, prior on index books. Access to the circuit-wide criminal quick lookup is available at http://circuit8.org/golem/gencrim.html. Account and password is required; restricted usage.

General Information: No juvenile, child abuse or sexual battery records released. Turnaround time 2-3 days. Fax notes: $1.00 per page. Available for civil only. Copy fee: $1.00 per page. Certification fee: $1.00. Fee payee: Clerk of Circuit Court. Personal checks accepted. Prepayment is required.

Glades County

Circuit & County Courts

PO Box 10, Moore Haven, FL 33471; 863-946-0113; Fax: 863-946-0560. Hours: 8AM-5PM (EST). *Felony, Misdemeanor, Civil, Eviction, Small Claims, Probate.*

Civil Records: Access: Phone, fax, mail, in person. Only the court performs in person searches; visitors may not. Search fee: $1.00 per name per year. Add $4.00 for written response (affidavit). Required to search: name, years to search; also helpful: address. Civil cases indexed by defendant, plaintiff. Civil records on computer from 1991.

Criminal Records: Access: Phone, mail, fax, in person. Only the court performs in person searches; visitors may not. Search fee: $1.00 per name per year. Add $4.00 for written response (affidavit). Required to search: name, years to search, DOB; also helpful: address, SSN, race, sex. Criminal records on computer from 1991.

General Information: No juvenile, child abuse or sexual battery records released. SASE not required. Turnaround time 2-3 days. Copy fee: $1.00 per page. Certification fee: $1.00. Fee payee: Clerk of Circuit Court. Personal checks accepted. Prepayment is required.

Gulf County

Circuit & County Courts

1000 Cecil Costin Blvd, Port St Joe, FL 32456; 850-229-6112; Fax: 850-229-6174. Hours: 9AM-5PM (EST). *Felony, Misdemeanor, Civil, Eviction, Small Claims, Probate.*

Civil Records: Access: Fax, mail, in person. Both court and visitors may perform in person searches. Search fee: $1.00 per name per year. Required to search: name, years to search. Civil cases indexed by defendant, plaintiff. Civil records on computer from 1990.

Criminal Records: Access: Fax, mail, in person. Both court and visitors may perform in person searches. Search fee: $1.00 per name per year. Required to search: name, years to search, DOB; also helpful: SSN. Criminal records on computer from 1990.

General Information: No juvenile, adoption, child abuse or sexual battery records released. SASE required. Turnaround time 1-3 days. Fax notes: $1.50 per page. Copy fee: $.15 per page. Certification fee: $1.00. Fee payee: Clerk of Circuit Court. Personal checks accepted. Prepayment is required.

Hamilton County

Circuit & County Courts 207 NE 1st St #106, Jasper, FL 32052; 904-792-1288; Fax: 904-792-3524. Hours: 8:30AM-4:30PM (EST). *Felony, Misdemeanor, Civil, Eviction, Small Claims, Probate.*

Civil Records: Access: Mail, in person. Both court and visitors may perform in person searches. Search fee: $1.00 per name per year. Required to search: name, years to search; also helpful: address. Civil records on computer from 1/91, county civil from 3/91.

Criminal Records: Access: Mail, in person. Both court and visitors may perform in person searches. Search fee: $1.00 per name per year. Required to search: name, years to search, DOB; also helpful: address, SSN, race, sex. Criminal records on computer-Felony since 3/90, Misdemeanor since 1/89.

General Information: No juvenile, child abuse or sexual battery records released. SASE requested. Turnaround time 2-3 days. Copy fee: $1.00 per page. Certification fee: $1.00. Fee payee: Clerk of Circuit Court. Personal checks accepted. Prepayment is required.

Hardee County

Circuit & County Courts PO Drawer 1749, Wauchula, FL 33873-1749; 863-773-4174; Fax: 863-773-4422. Hours: 8AM-5PM (EST). *Felony, Misdemeanor, Civil, Eviction, Small Claims, Probate.*

http://jud10.flcourts.org

Civil Records: Access: Mail, in person. Both court and visitors may perform in person searches. Search fee: $1.00 per name per year. Required to search: name, years to search; also helpful: address. Civil records on computer from 1984.

Criminal Records: Access: Mail, in person. Both court and visitors may perform in person searches. Search fee: $1.00 per name per year. Required to search: name, years to search, DOB; also helpful: address, SSN, race, sex. Criminal records on computer from 1984.

General Information: Public Access terminal is available. No juvenile, child abuse or sexual battery records released. SASE requested. Turnaround time 3 days. Fax notes: Fee to fax results is $1.00 per page. Copy fee: $1.00 per page. Certification fee: $1.00. Fee payee: Clerk of Circuit Court. Business checks accepted. Prepayment is required.

Hendry County

Circuit & County Courts PO Box 1760, LaBelle, FL 33975-1760; 863-675-5217; Fax: 863-675-5238. Hours: 8:30AM-5PM (EST). *Felony, Misdemeanor, Civil, Eviction, Small Claims, Probate.*

Civil Records: Access: Mail, in person. Both court and visitors may perform in person searches. Search fee: $1.00 per name per year. Required to search: name, years to search; also helpful: address. Civil cases indexed by defendant, plaintiff. Civil records on computer since 5/92, archived from 1923, on microfiche prior to 1989 if filed.

Criminal Records: Access: Mail, in person. Both court and visitors may perform in person searches. Search fee: $1.00 per name per year. Required to search: name, years to search, DOB; also helpful: address, SSN, race, sex. Criminal records on computer since 1989, prior on microfiche, archived since 1923.

General Information: No juvenile, child abuse or sexual battery records released. SASE helpful. Turnaround time varies. Copy fee: $1.00 per page. Certification fee: $1.00. Fee payee: Clerk of Circuit Court. Personal checks accepted. Prepayment is required.

Hernando County

Circuit & County Courts 20 N Main St, Brooksville, FL 34601; 352-754-4201; Fax: 352-754-4247. Hours: 8AM-5PM (EST). *Felony, Misdemeanor, Civil, Eviction, Small Claims, Probate.*

www.co.hernando.fl.us/ccc

Civil Records: Access: Mail, online, in person. Both court and visitors may perform in person searches. Search fee: $1.00 per name per year. Required to search: name, years to search. Civil cases indexed by defendant, plaintiff. Civil records on computer from 1982, archived from late 1800s. Access to the remote online system requires $100 setup, $25 per month and $.10 per minute. A fax back service is available for $1-$1.25 per page. Contact Bob Piercy for more information.

Criminal Records: Access: Mail, online, in person. Both court and visitors may perform in person searches. Search fee: $1.00 per name per year. Required to search: name, years to search, DOB; also helpful: SSN. Criminal records on computer from 1982, archived from late 1800s. Online access to criminal records is the same as civil. Index and docket information is available for felony and misdemeanor records.

General Information: Public Access terminal is available. No juvenile, child abuse or sexual battery records released. Turnaround time approx 5 days. Copy fee: $1.00 per page. Certification fee: $1.00. Fee payee: Clerk of Circuit Court. Personal checks accepted. Prepayment is required.

Highlands County

Circuit & County Courts 590 S Commerce Ave, Sebring, FL 33870-3867; Civil phone: 863-386-6591; Criminal phone: 863-386-6597; Fax: 863-386-6575. Hours: 8AM-4:30PM (EST). *Felony, Misdemeanor, Civil, Eviction, Small Claims, Probate.*

http://jud10.flcourts.org

Civil Records: Access: Mail, in person, online. Both court and visitors may perform in person searches. Search fee: $1.00 per name per year. Required to search: name, years to search. Civil cases indexed by defendant, plaintiff. Civil records on computer since 1992, prior on microfiche and film. Online access to county clerk records is available free at www.clerk.co.highlands.fl.us/index_new.html. Also includes, small claims, probate, and tax deeds.

Criminal Records: Access: Mail, in person. Both court and visitors may perform in person searches. Search fee: $1.00 per name per year. Required to search: name, years to search; also helpful: SSN. Criminal records on computer since 1991, prior on microfiche and film.

General Information: Public Access terminal is available. No juvenile, child abuse or sexual battery records released. Turnaround time 1 week. Copy fee: $1.00 per page. Certification fee: $2.00. Fee payee: Clerk of Courts. Personal checks accepted. Prepayment is required.

Hillsborough

Circuit & County Courts 419 Pierce St, Tampa, FL 33602; 813-276-8100; Fax: 813-272-7707. Hours: 8AM-5PM (EST). *Felony, Misdemeanor, Civil, Eviction, Small Claims, Probate.*

www.hillsclerk.com

Note: Extension for civil is 7252, for criminal is 7802.

Civil Records: Access: Fax, mail, online, in person. Both court and visitors may perform in person searches. Search fee: $1.00 per name per year. Required to search: name, years to search; also helpful: address. Civil cases indexed by defendant, plaintiff. Civil records on computer since 5/85, prior on microfiche since early 1900s. Online access requires a $50.00 set-up/software fee plus initial $50.00 towards access charges of $.25

per minute. Probate, traffic and domestic records are included. Call the help desk at 813-276-8100, Ext. 7000 for more information.

Criminal Records: Access: Fax, mail, online, in person. Both court and visitors may perform in person searches. Search fee: $1.00 per name per year. Required to search: name, years to search, DOB; also helpful: address, SSN, race, sex. Criminal records on computer since 1989, prior on microfiche since 1975, archived from 1953 to 1974. Some felonies on docket books. Online access to criminal records is the same as civil.

General Information: Public Access terminal is available. No juvenile, child abuse or sexual battery records released. Turnaround time 1-2 days. Fax notes: No fee to fax results. Fax account required. Copy fee: $1.00 per page. Certification fee: $1.00. Fee payee: Clerk of Circuit Court. Personal checks accepted. Local personal checks accepted. Prepayment is required.

Holmes County

Circuit & County Courts PO Box 397, Bonifay, FL 32425; 850-547-1100; Fax: 850-547-6630. Hours: 8AM-4PM (CST). *Felony, Misdemeanor, Civil, Eviction, Small Claims, Probate.*

Civil Records: Access: Mail, in person. Both court and visitors may perform in person searches. Search fee: $1.00 per name per year. Required to search: name, years to search; also helpful: address. Civil cases indexed by defendant, plaintiff. Civil records on computer from 10/91, archived from early 1900s.

Criminal Records: Access: Mail, in person. Both court and visitors may perform in person searches. Search fee: $1.00 per name per year. Required to search: name, years to search, DOB; also helpful: address, SSN, race, sex. Criminal records on computer since 1989, prior archived since early 1900s.

General Information: Public Access terminal is available. No juvenile, child abuse or sexual battery records released. SASE required. Turnaround time 1 week. Copy fee: $1.00 per page. Certification fee: $1.00. Fee payee: Holmes County Clerk of Court. Personal checks accepted. Prepayment is required.

Indian River County

Circuit & County Courts PO Box 1028, Vero Beach, FL 32961; 561-770-5185; Fax: 561-770-5008. Hours: 8:30AM-5PM (EST). *Felony, Misdemeanor, Civil, Eviction, Small Claims, Probate.*

Civil Records: Access: Mail, in person, online. Both court and visitors may perform in person searches. Search fee: $1.00 per name per year. Required to search: name, years to search; also helpful: address. Civil cases indexed by defendant, plaintiff. Civil records on computer since 1984, prior on microfiche. Online access to the county recordings index is available free at http://bdc.co.indian-river.fl.us. Records go back to 1983. Full access to court records is available via the clerk's subscription service. Fee is $200.00 per month. For information about free and fee access, call Gary at 561-567-8000 x216.

Criminal Records: Access: Mail, in person, online. Both court and visitors may perform in person searches. Search fee: $1.00 per name per year. Required to search: name, years to search, DOB; also helpful: address, SSN, race, sex. Criminal records on computer (Felony since 1986, Misdemeanor since 1983), both archived since 1925.

General Information: Public Access terminal is available. No juvenile, child abuse or sexual battery records released. SASE helpful. Turnaround time 2 days. Copy fee: $1.00 per page. Certification fee: $1.00. Fee payee: Clerk of Circuit Court. Personal checks accepted. Prepayment is required.

Jackson County

Circuit & County Courts PO Box 510, Marianna, FL 32447; 850-482-9552; Fax: 850-482-7849. Hours: 8AM-4:30PM (CST). *Felony, Misdemeanor, Civil, Eviction, Small Claims, Probate.*

Civil Records: Access: Fax, mail, in person. Both court and visitors may perform in person searches. Search fee: $1.00 per name per year. Required to search: name, years to search; also helpful: address. Civil cases indexed by defendant, plaintiff. Civil records on computer from 1989.

Criminal Records: Access: Fax, mail, in person. Both court and visitors may perform in person searches. Search fee: $1.00 per name per year. Required to search: name, years to search, DOB; also helpful: address, SSN, race, sex. Criminal records on computer since 1989.

General Information: Public Access terminal is available. No juvenile, child abuse or sexual battery records released. SASE helpful. Turnaround time 1-5 days. Fax notes: $3.00 for first page, $1.00 each add'l. Copy fee: $1.00 per page. Certification fee: $1.00. Fee payee: Clerk of Circuit Court. Personal checks accepted. Credit cards accepted: Visa, MasterCard, AmEx. Prepayment is required.

Jefferson County

Circuit & County Courts Jefferson County Courthouse, Rm 10, Monticello, FL 32344; 850-342-0218; Fax: 850-342-0222. Hours: 8AM-5PM (EST). *Felony, Misdemeanor, Civil, Eviction, Small Claims, Probate.*

www.co.leon.fl.us/court/court.htm

Civil Records: Access: Mail, in person. Both court and visitors may perform in person searches. Search fee: $1.00 per name per year. Required to search: name, years to search; also helpful: address. Civil cases indexed by defendant, plaintiff. Civil records on computer since 7/90, prior on dockets.

Criminal Records: Access: Fax, mail, in person. Both court and visitors may perform in person searches. Search fee: $1.00 per name per year. Required to search: name, years to search, DOB; also helpful: address, SSN, race, sex. Criminal records on computer since 1989, prior on microfiche from 1969 to 1980, archived since 1950s, prior to 1950 on dockets.

General Information: Public Access terminal is available. No juvenile, child abuse or sexual battery records released. Turnaround time 1 week. Fax notes: Fee to fax results is $2.00 per page. Copy fee: $1.00 per page. Certification fee: $1.00. Fee payee: Clerk of Circuit Court. Personal checks accepted. Prepayment is required.

Lafayette County

Circuit & County Courts PO Box 88, Mayo, FL 32066; 904-294-1600; Fax: 904-294-4231. Hours: 8AM-5PM (EST). *Felony, Misdemeanor, Civil, Eviction, Small Claims, Probate.*

Civil Records: Access: Phone, mail, in person. Both court and visitors may perform in person searches. No search fee. Required to search: name, years to search; also helpful: address. Civil cases indexed by defendant, plaintiff. Civil records on computer since 1997, on books back to early 1900s.

Criminal Records: Access: Phone, mail, in person. Both court and visitors may perform in person searches. No search fee. Required to search: name, years to search, DOB; also helpful: address, SSN, race, sex. Criminal records computerized since 1989.

General Information: Public Access terminal is available. No juvenile, child abuse or sexual battery records released. SASE required. Turnaround time 5-7 days. Copy fee: $1.00 per page. Certification fee: $1.00.

Fee payee: Clerk of Circuit Court. Personal checks accepted. Prepayment is required.

Lake County

Circuit & County Courts 550 W Main St or PO Box 7800, Tavares, FL 32778; 352-742-4100; Fax: 352-742-4166. Hours: 8:30AM-5PM (EST). *Felony, Misdemeanor, Civil, Eviction, Small Claims, Probate.*

www.lakecountyclerk.org

Civil Records: Access: Fax, mail, in person, online. Both court and visitors may perform in person searches. Search fee: $1.00 per name per year. Required to search: name, years to search; also helpful: address. Civil cases indexed by defendant, plaintiff. Civil records on computer since 1984, county civil on index books since 11/51, circuit civil since 1888. Online access to Clerk of Court Records is available free at www.lakecountyclerk.org/services.asp?subject=Online _Court_Records. County civil records go back to 1985; Circuit records go back to 9/1984. also, marriage licenses back to 2000 are available at the main website. Also, recordings, liens, and judgments on the Circuit Clerk website are available free at www.lakecountyclerk.org/services.asp?subject=Online _Official_Records.

Criminal Records: Access: Fax, mail, in person. Both court and visitors may perform in person searches. Search fee: $1.00 per name per year. Required to search: name, years to search, DOB; also helpful: address, SSN, race, sex. Criminal records on computer since 1983, on microfiche since 1970s, archived since 1920s. Some on index books.

General Information: Public Access terminal is available. No juvenile, child abuse or sexual battery records released. SASE helpful. Turnaround time 7-10 days. Fax notes: $1.00 per page. Copy fee: $1.00 per page. Certification fee: $1.00. Fee payee: Clerk of Circuit Court. Personal checks accepted. Prepayment is required.

Lee County

Circuit & County Courts PO Box 2469, Ft Myers, FL 33902; 941-335-2283. Hours: 7:45AM-5PM (EST). *Felony, Misdemeanor, Civil, Eviction, Small Claims, Probate.*

www.leeclerk.org

Civil Records: Access: Mail, online, in person. Both court and visitors may perform in person searches. Search fee: $1.00 per name per year. Required to search: name, years to search. Civil cases indexed by defendant, plaintiff. Civil records on computer since 1988, prior on microfilm and dockets. The fee system has been replaced by free Internet access at the web site. Registration is required. Online records go back to 1988. Call 941-335-2975 for more information. Includes traffic, felony, misdemeanor, civil, small claims and probate.

Criminal Records: Access: Mail, online, in person. Both court and visitors may perform in person searches. Search fee: $1.00 per name per year. Required to search: name, years to search, DOB; also helpful: address, SSN, race, sex. Criminal records on computer-(Felony since 1978, Misdemeanor since 1986), prior on microfilm. Online access to criminal records is the same as civil.

General Information: Public Access terminal is available. No juvenile, child abuse or sexual offense records released. SASE required. Turnaround time 5 days. Copy fee: $1.00 per page. Certification fee: $1.00. Fee payee: Clerk of Circuit Court. Personal checks accepted. Prepayment is required.

Leon County

Circuit & County Courts PO Box 726, Tallahassee, FL 32302; 850-577-4000; Civil phone: 850-577-4170; Criminal phone: 850-577-4070; Probate phone: 850-577-4180. Hours: 8:30AM-5PM (EST). *Felony, Misdemeanor, Civil, Eviction, Small Claims, Probate.*

www.clerk.leon.fl.us

Civil Records: Access: Mail, online, in person. Both court and visitors may perform in person searches. Search fee: $1.00 per name per year. Required to search: name, years to search; also helpful: address. Civil cases indexed by defendant, plaintiff. Civil records on computer since 8/86, prior on docket books. Also, you may search "High Profile Cases" (re: Election 2000)" at www.clerk.leon.fl.us under "Official Records Search.".

Criminal Records: Access: Mail, online, in person. Both court and visitors may perform in person searches. Search fee: $1.00 per name per year. Required to search: name, years to search, DOB; also helpful: address, SSN, race, sex. Criminal records on computer since 1976, on microfiche since 1937, archived since late 1800s/early 1900s. Online access to criminal records is the same as civil.

General Information: Public Access terminal is available. No juvenile, child abuse or sexual battery records released. SASE helpful. Turnaround time 1-5 days. Copy fee: $1.00 per page. Certification fee: $1.00. Fee payee: Clerk of Circuit Court. Personal checks accepted. Credit cards accepted: Visa, MasterCard. Prepayment is required.

Levy County

Circuit & County Courts PO Box 610, Bronson, FL 32621; 352-486-5100. Hours: 8AM-5PM (EST). *Felony, Misdemeanor, Civil, Eviction, Small Claims, Probate.*

http://circuit8.org

Civil Records: Access: Mail, in person, online. Both court and visitors may perform in person searches. Search fee: $1.00 per name per year. Required to search: name, years to search; also helpful: address. Civil cases indexed by defendant, plaintiff. Civil records on computer from 1986, microfiche to 1981 (in process), prior on docket books. Online access to the Clerk of Circuit Court recording records are available free at www.levyclerk.com/Public_Records/Public_R ecords.html.

Criminal Records: Access: Mail, in person, online. Both court and visitors may perform in person searches. Search fee: $1.00 per name per year. Required to search: name, years to search, DOB, signed release; also helpful: address, SSN, race, sex. Criminal records on computer from 1986 to present, prior on docket books. Access to the circuit-wide criminal quick lookup is available at http://circuit8.org/golem/gencrim.html. Account and password is required; restricted usage.

General Information: Public Access terminal is available. No juvenile, child abuse or sexual battery records released. SASE required. Turnaround time 2-3 days. Copy fee: $1.00 per page. Certification fee: $1.00. Fee payee: Clerk of Circuit Court. Business checks accepted. Prepayment is required.

Liberty County

Circuit & County Courts PO Box 399, Bristol, FL 32321; 850-643-2215; Fax: 850-643-2866. Hours: 8AM-5PM (EST). *Felony, Misdemeanor, Civil, Eviction, Small Claims, Probate.*

www.co.leon.fl.us/court/court.htm

Civil Records: Access: Mail, in person. Both court and visitors may perform in person searches. Search fee: $1.00 per name per year. Required to search: name, years to search; also helpful: address. Civil cases indexed by defendant, plaintiff. Civil records on docket books.

Criminal Records: Access: Mail, in person. Both court and visitors may perform in person searches. Search fee: $1.00 per name per year. Required to search: name, years to search, DOB; also helpful: address, SSN, race, sex. Criminal records on docket books.

General Information: No juvenile, child abuse or sexual battery records released. SASE required. Turnaround time 1 week. Copy fee: $1.00 per page. Certification fee: $1.00. Fee payee: Clerk of Circuit Court. Business checks accepted. Prepayment is required.

Madison County

Circuit & County Courts PO Box 237, Madison, FL 32341; 850-973-1500; Fax: 850-973-2059. Hours: 8AM-5PM (EST). *Felony, Misdemeanor, Civil, Eviction, Small Claims, Probate.*

Civil Records: Access: Phone, mail, in person. Both court and visitors may perform in person searches. Search fee: $1.00 per name per year. Required to search: name, years to search; also helpful: address. Civil cases indexed by defendant, plaintiff. Civil records on computer since 1990, prior on docket books.

Criminal Records: Access: Phone, mail, in person. Both court and visitors may perform in person searches. Search fee: $1.00 per name per year. Required to search: name, years to search, DOB; also helpful: address, SSN, race, sex. Criminal records on computer since 1988, prior on docket books.

General Information: No juvenile, child abuse or sexual battery records released. SASE requested. Turnaround time 1-3 days. Copy fee: $1.00 per page. Certification fee: $1.00. Fee payee: Clerk of Circuit Court. Personal checks accepted. Prepayment is required.

Manatee County

Circuit & County Courts PO Box 25400, Bradenton, FL 34206; 941-749-1800; Fax: 941-741-4082. Hours: 8:30AM-5PM (EST). *Felony, Misdemeanor, Civil, Eviction, Small Claims, Probate.*

www.clerkofcourts.com

Civil Records: Access: Phone, fax, mail, online, in person, email. Both court and visitors may perform in person searches. Search fee: $1.00 per name per year. Required to search: name, years to search; also helpful: address. Civil cases indexed by defendant, plaintiff. Civil records on computer since 9/80, prior on microfilm back to 1972. Court records - dockets and indexes - from the clerk's office are available free at the web site.

Criminal Records: Access: Phone, fax, mail, online, in person, email. Both court and visitors may perform in person searches. Search fee: $1.00 per name per year. Required to search: name, years to search, DOB; also helpful: address, charge, race, sex. Criminal records on computer since 1981, prior on docket books back to 1972. Access to criminal online records is available as of 8/2001; access is the same as civil.

General Information: Public Access terminal is available. No juvenile, adoption, child abuse or sexual battery victim records released. SASE helpful. Turnaround time 2 days. Fax notes: Will not fax results. Copy fee: $1.00 per page. Certification fee: $1.00. Fee payee: Clerk of Circuit Court. Personal checks accepted. Credit cards accepted: Visa, MasterCard. Prepayment is required.

Marion County

Circuit & County Courts PO Box 1030, Ocala, FL 34478; 352-620-3892 (cty civ); Civil phone: 352-620-3891 (Circ); Criminal phone: 352-620-3861; Probate phone: 352-620-3874; Fax: 352-620-3300 (civ); 840-5668 (crim). Hours: 8AM-5PM (EST). *Felony, Misdemeanor, Civil, Eviction, Small Claims, Probate.*

www.marioncountyclerk.org

Civil Records: Access: Fax, mail, in person, online. Both court and visitors may perform in person searches. Search fee: $1.00 per name per year. Required to search: name, years to search; also helpful: address. Civil cases indexed by defendant, plaintiff. Civil records on computer since 1983, on microfiche since 1958. Online access to county clerk civil records is available free online at www.marioncountyclerk.org/Courts/factsweb.htm. Search by name or case number. The site's time default field must be used.

Criminal Records: Access: Fax, mail, in person. Both court and visitors may perform in person searches. Search fee: $1.00 per name per year. Required to search: name, years to search, DOB; also helpful: address, SSN, race, sex. Criminal records on computer. Felonies since 1984, on microfiche from 1950 to 1979, prior on index cards. Misdemeanors since 1983, on microfiche from 1900 to 1982, archived since 1900s, prior on index cards.

General Information: Public Access terminal is available. No juvenile records released. SASE requested. Turnaround time 1-2 weeks. Copy fee: $1.00 per page. Certification fee: $1.00. Fee payee: Clerk of Court. Personal checks accepted. Prepayment is required.

Martin County

Circuit & County Courts PO Box 9016, Stuart, FL 34995; 561-288-5576; Fax: 561-288-5724; 288-5991 (civil). Hours: 8AM-5PM (EST). *Felony, Misdemeanor, Civil, Eviction, Small Claims, Probate.*

www.martin.fl.us/GOVT/co/clerk

Civil Records: Access: Phone, fax, mail, online, in person. Both court and visitors may perform in person searches. Search fee: $1.00 per name per year. Required to search: name, years to search; also helpful: address. Civil cases indexed by defendant, plaintiff. Civil records on computer since 10/86, prior on microfiche and archived. Online access to civil case information on the records division database is available free at http://clerk-web.martin.fl.us/wb_or1. Also includes small claims, recordings, other document types.

Criminal Records: Access: Phone, fax, mail, online, in person. Both court and visitors may perform in person searches. Search fee: $1.00 per name per year. Required to search: name, years to search, DOB; also helpful: address, SSN. Criminal records on computer. Felonies since 1986, on microfiche since 1956, prior on index cards and docket books. Misdemeanors since 1985, on microfiche since 1973, prior on index cards and docket books. Online access to criminal records is the same as civil.

General Information: Public Access terminal is available. No juvenile, child abuse or sexual battery records released. Turnaround time 1 week. Fax notes: $1.25 per page. Copy fee: $1.00 per page. Certification fee: $1.00. Fee payee: Bossier Parish Clerk of Court. Personal checks accepted. Prepayment is required.

Monroe County

Circuit & County Courts 500 Whitehead St, Key West, FL 33040; 305-294-4641; Civil phone: 305-292-3310; Criminal phone: 305-292-3390; Fax: 305-295-3623. Hours: 8:30AM-5PM (EST). *Felony, Misdemeanor, Civil, Eviction, Small Claims, Probate.*

www.co.monroe.fl.us

Civil Records: Access: Mail, fax, in person. Both court and visitors may perform in person searches. Search fee: $1.00 per name per year. Required to search: name, years to search; also helpful: address. Civil cases indexed by defendant, plaintiff. Civil records on computer since 1983, on microfiche since 1972, prior on docket books. Some records purged after 2 years. Probate from 1972.

Criminal Records: Access: Mail, fax, in person. Both court and visitors may perform in person searches. Search fee: $1.00 per name per year. Required to search: name, years to search, DOB; also helpful: address, SSN, race, sex. Criminal records (pending felony and misdemeanors) on computer, others since 1992, non-pending on microfiche since 1945.

General Information: Public Access terminal is available. No juvenile, child abuse or sexual battery records released. SASE helpful. Turnaround time 1-2 weeks. Fax notes: Fee to fax results is $1.00 per page. Copy fee: $1.00 per page. Certification fee: $1.00. Fee payee: Clerk of Circuit Court. Personal checks accepted. Prepayment is required.

Nassau County

Circuit & County Courts PO Box 456, Fernandina Beach, FL 32035; 904-321-5700; Fax: 904-321-5723. Hours: 9AM-5PM (EST). *Felony, Misdemeanor, Civil, Eviction, Small Claims, Probate.*

Civil Records: Access: Phone, fax, mail, in person. Only the court performs in person searches; visitors may not. Search fee: $1.00 per name per year. Required to search: name, years to search; also helpful: address. Civil cases indexed by defendant, plaintiff. Civil records on computer since 1993, on microfiche since 1982, prior on docket books.

Criminal Records: Access: Phone, fax, mail, in person. Only the court performs in person searches; visitors may not. Search fee: $1.00 per name per year. Required to search: name, years to search, DOB; also helpful: address, SSN, race, sex. Criminal records on computer since 1985, on microfiche since 1982, prior on docket books. Past 5 years only can be done on the phone.

General Information: No juvenile, child abuse or sexual battery records released. SASE required. Turnaround time 1 week. Fax notes: $1.00 per page. Copy fee: $1.00 per page. Certification fee: $1.00. Fee payee: Clerk of Circuit Court. Personal checks accepted. Prepayment is required.

Okaloosa County

Circuit & County Courts 1250 Eglin Pkwy, Shalimar, FL 32579; 850-651-7200; Fax: 850-651-7230. Hours: 8AM-5PM (CST). *Felony, Misdemeanor, Civil, Eviction, Small Claims, Probate.*

www.clerkofcourts.cc

Civil Records: Access: Mail, online, in person. Both court and visitors may perform in person searches. Search fee: $6.00 per name. Add $1.00 for each year searched prior to 6/86. Required to search: name, years to search; also helpful: address. Civil cases indexed by defendant, plaintiff. Civil records on computer from 6/86, archived from 1915, prior on index cards. Two options are available. Access to the full online system requires a monthly fee of $100.00. Searching is by name or case number. Records also include probate, traffic and domestic records. For more information, call 850-689-5821. Also, civil records are available free on the internet at www.clerkofcourts.cc/civsearch/civilsearch.asp. Records go back to 1/86. Search civil index by defendant or plaintiff, date, or file type.

Criminal Records: Access: Mail, online, in person. Both court and visitors may perform in person searches. Search fee: $6.00 per name. Add $1.00 for each year searched prior to 6/89. Required to search: name, years to search, DOB; also helpful: address, SSN, race, sex.

...rds on computer from 6/86, archived from ... on index cards. Online access is available ... the fee online system, same as civil. Both ... and misdemeanor indexes can be searched. Also, ... county clerk is planning to place criminal records ... on the Internet at www.clerkofcourts.cc/ orsearch/contract.htm.

General Information: Public Access terminal is available. No juvenile, child abuse or sexual battery records released. SASE required. Turnaround time 1 week. Copy fee: $1.00 per page. Certification fee: $2.00. Fee payee: Clerk of Circuit Court. Personal checks accepted. Prepayment is required.

Okeechobee County

Circuit & County Courts 304 NW 2nd St Rm 101, Okeechobee, FL 34972; 863-763-2131. Hours: 8:30AM-5PM (EST). *Felony, Misdemeanor, Civil, Eviction, Small Claims, Probate.*

Civil Records: Access: Mail, in person. Both court and visitors may perform in person searches. Search fee: $1.00 per name per year. Required to search: name, years to search; also helpful: address. Civil cases indexed by defendant, plaintiff. Civil records on computer since 1990, on index cards from 1983 to 1988.

Criminal Records: Access: Mail, in person. Both court and visitors may perform in person searches. Search fee: $1.00 per name per year. Required to search: name, years to search, DOB; also helpful: address, SSN, race, sex. Criminal records on computer since 1989, on index cards from 1932 to 1988.

General Information: No juvenile, child abuse or sexual battery records released. SASE required. Turnaround time for criminal 2 weeks, civil 1-2 weeks. Copy fee: $1.00 per page. Certification fee: $1.00. Fee payee: Clerk of Circuit Court. Personal checks accepted. Prepayment is required.

Orange County

Circuit & County Courts 425 N Orange Ave, Orlando, FL 32801-1544; 407-836-2060. Hours: 8AM-5PM (EST). *Felony, Misdemeanor, Civil, Eviction, Small Claims, Probate.*

http://orangeclerk.ocfl.net

Note: Mail requests should use room numbers: civil circuit-310; civil county-350; crim circuit-210; crim county-250.

Civil Records: Access: Mail, online, in person. Both court and visitors may perform in person searches. Search fee: $1.00 per name per year. Required to search: name, years to search. Civil cases indexed by defendant, plaintiff. Civil records are on computer as follows: Circuit civil-1992; Domestic civil-1992; probate-1993; traffic-1980. The Teleclerk countywide remote online system requires a $100 one-time fee and $30 per month for unlimited online time. System also includes criminal, probate, traffic and domestic records. For more information, call 407-836-2060.

Criminal Records: Access: Mail, online, in person. Both court and visitors may perform in person searches. Search fee: $1.00 per name per year. Required to search: name, years to search, DOB. Criminal records on computer from 1988. Online access to criminal records is the same as civil.

General Information: Public Access terminal is available. (Available in Records Management Division.) No sex related or adoption records released. SASE helpful. Turnaround time 2 days. Copy fee: $1.00 per page. For more information call 407-836-2064 Certification fee: $1.00. Fee payee: Orange County Clerk of Courts. Personal checks accepted from Orange County only. Prepayment is required.

County Court - Apopka Branch 1111 N Rock Springs Rd, Apopka, FL 32712; 407-654-1030. Hours: 8AM-5PM (EST). *Misdemeanor, Civil Actions Under $15,000, Eviction, Small Claims.*

http://orangeclerk.ocfl.net

Note: Records maintained at Orlando office.

Civil Records: Access: Mail, online, in person. Both court and visitors may perform in person searches. Search fee: $1.00 per name per year. Required to search: name, years to search. Civil cases indexed by defendant, plaintiff. Civil records (Pending) on computer. All dockets on microfilm or microfiche. Some records on index cards. The Teleclerk countywide remote online system requires a $100 one-time fee and $30 per month for unlimited online time. System also includes criminal, probate, traffic and domestic records. For more information, call 407-836-2064.

Criminal Records: Access: Mail, online, in person. Both court and visitors may perform in person searches. Search fee: $5.00 per name. Required to search: name, years to search, DOB; also helpful: SSN. Criminal records (Pending) on computer. All dockets on microfilm or microfiche. Some records on index cards. Online access to criminal records is the same as civil.

General Information: Public Access terminal is available. No sex related or adoption records released. SASE helpful. Turnaround time 2 days. Copy fee: $1.00 per page. Certification fee: $2.00. Fee payee: Clerk of County Court. Personal checks accepted. Prepayment is required.

County Court - NE Orange Division 450 N Lakemont Ave, Winter Park, FL 32792; 407-671-1116. Hours: 8AM-5PM (EST). *Misdemeanor, Civil Actions Under $15,000, Eviction, Small Claims.*

http://orangeclerk.ocfl.net

Civil Records: Access: Phone, mail, online, in person. Only the court performs in person searches; visitors may not. Search fee: $1.00 per name per year. Required to search: name, years to search. Civil cases indexed by defendant, plaintiff. Civil records (Pending) on computer. All dockets on microfilm or microfiche. The Teleclerk countywide remote online system requires a $100 one-time fee and $30 per month for unlimited online time. System also includes criminal, probate, traffic and domestic records. For more information, call 407-836-2060.

Criminal Records: Access: Phone, mail, online, in person. Only the court performs in person searches; visitors may not. Search fee: $1.00 per name per year. Required to search: name, years to search, DOB; also helpful: SSN. Criminal records (Pending) on computer. All dockets on microfilm or microfiche. Online access to criminal records is the same as civil.

General Information: No sex related or adoption records released. SASE helpful. Turnaround time 2 days. Copy fee: $1.00 per page. Certification fee: $1.00. Fee payee: Clerk of County Court. Only cashiers checks and money orders accepted. Prepayment is required.

County Court #3 475 W Story Rd, Ocoee, FL 34761; 407-656-3229. Hours: 8AM-5PM (EST). *Misdemeanor, Civil Actions Under $15,000, Eviction, Small Claims.*

http://orangeclerk.ocfl.net

Civil Records: Access: Mail, online, in person. Both court and visitors may perform in person searches. Search fee: $5.00 per name per year. Required to search: name, years to search. Civil cases indexed by defendant, plaintiff. Civil records (Pending) on computer. All dockets are on microfilm or microfiche. The Teleclerk countywide remote online system requires a $100 one-time fee and $30 per month for unlimited online time. System also includes criminal,

probate, traffic and domestic records. For more information, call 407-836-2060.

Criminal Records: Access: Mail, online, in person. Both court and visitors may perform in person searches. Search fee: $5.00 per name per year. Required to search: name, years to search, DOB; also helpful: SSN. Criminal records (Pending) on computer. All dockets are on microfilm or microfiche. Online access to criminal records is the same as civil.

General Information: No sex related or adoption records released. SASE helpful. Turnaround time 2 days (depending on file). Copy fee: $1.00 per page. Certification fee: $2.00 per page. Fee payee: Clerk of County Court. Personal checks accepted. Credit cards accepted: Visa, MasterCard. Accepted for civil payments only. Prepayment is required.

Osceola County

Circuit Court - Civil 17 S Vernon Ave, Kissimmee, FL 34741; 407-847-1300 #3 X1448. 8:30AM-5PM (EST). *Civil Actions Over $5,000.*

www.ninja9.net

Civil Records: Access: Mail, in person, online. Both court and visitors may perform in person searches. Search fee: $1.00 per name per year. Required to search: name, years to search. Civil cases indexed by defendant, plaintiff. Civil records on computer from 1990, on docket books from 1800s to 1990. Online access to court records on the Clerk of Circuit Court database are available free at www.osceolaclerkcourt.org. **General Information:** No appeal records released. SASE required. Turnaround time 1-2 days. Copy fee: $1.00 per page. Certification fee: $1.00. Fee payee: Clerk of Court. Business checks accepted. Prepayment is required.

Circuit & County Courts - Criminal Division 2 Courthouse Square, Kissimmee, FL 34741; 407-343-3543/3556. Hours: 8:30AM-5PM (EST). *Felony, Misdemeanor.*

www.osceolaclerk.com

Criminal Records: Access: Mail, in person, online. Only the court performs in person searches; visitors may not. Search fee: $1.00 per name per year. Required to search: name, years to search, DOB, SSN. Criminal records on computer back to 1990, on index since 1978, prior on docket books from 1800s to 1978. Online access to criminal records is available free at www.osceolaclerkcourt.org/search.htm. Includes party index and case summary searching.

General Information: Public Access terminal is available. No juvenile or sealed records released. SASE requested. Turnaround time 1 week. Copy fee: $1.00 per page. Certification fee: $1.00. Fee payee: Money orders payable to Clerk of the Court. Business checks accepted. Credit cards accepted, but a surcharge is added. Prepayment is required.

County Court - Civil 17 S Vernon Ave, Kissimmee, FL 34741; 407-847-1300. Hours: 8:30AM-5PM (EST). *Eviction, Small Claims.*

www.osceolaclerk.com

Civil Records: Access: Mail, in person, online. Both court and visitors may perform in person searches. Search fee: $1.00 per name per year. Required to search: name, years to search. Civil cases indexed by defendant, plaintiff. Civil records on computer from 1991, on index cards from 1972 to 1991, on docket books from 1800s to 1972. Online access to court records on the Clerk of Circuit Court database are available free at www.osceolaclerkcourt.org. **General Information:** No juvenile records released. SASE helpful. Turnaround time 1 week. Copy fee: $1.00 per page. Certification fee: $1.00. Fee payee: Clerk of Court. Business checks accepted. Prepayment is required.

Palm Beach County

Circuit Court - Civil Division PO Box 4667, West Palm Beach, FL 33402; 561-355-2986; Fax: 561-355-4643. Hours: 8AM-5PM (EST). *Civil.*

www.pbcountyclerk.com

Civil Records: Access: Phone, mail, online, in person. Both court and visitors may perform in person searches. Search fee: $1.00 per name per year. Required to search: name; years to search; also helpful: address. Civil cases indexed by defendant, plaintiff. Civil records (Circuit) on computer from 1982, prior records on microfiche and dockets. County on computer from 1987, prior on microfilm. Access to the countywide remote online system requires $145 setup and $65 per month fees. Civil index goes back to 1988. Records also include probate, traffic and domestic. Contact Betty Jones at 561-355-6783 for information. Also, online access to the 15th judicial circuit records is available at http://web3172.co.palm-beach.fl.us/aemasp/default.asp. Registration and password is required. **General Information:** Public Access terminal is available. No juvenile, child abuse or sexual battery records released. SASE required. Turnaround time 1 week. Copy fee: $1.00 per page. Certification fee: $1.00. Fee payee: Clerk of Circuit Court. Personal checks accepted. Prepayment is required.

Circuit & County Courts - Criminal Division 205 North Dixie Hwy, West Palm Beach, FL 33401; 561-355-2519; Fax: 561-355-3802. Hours: 8AM-5PM (EST). *Felony, Misdemeanor.*

www.pbcountyclerk.com

Criminal Records: Access: Phone, fax, mail, online, in person. Both court and visitors may perform in person searches. Search fee: $1.00 per name per year. Required to search: name, years to search, DOB, aliases. Criminal records on computer & microfiche (some files) from 1970s, archived from 1920s. Access to the countywide criminal online system requires $145 setup and $65 per month fees. Records also include probate, traffic and domestic. Contact Ms. Kokollari at 561-355-4277 for information. Also, online access to the 15th judicial circuit records is available at http://web3172.co.palm-beach.fl.us/aemasp/default.asp. Registration and password is required. **General Information:** Public Access terminal is available. No juvenile, child abuse or sexual battery records released. SASE not required. Turnaround time 1 day. Copy fee: $1.00 per page. Certification fee: $1.00. Fee payee: Clerk of Circuit Court. Personal checks accepted. Prepayment is required.

County Court - Civil Division PO Box 3406, West Palm Beach, FL 33402; 561-355-2986; Fax: 561-355-4643. Hours: 8AM-5PM (EST). *Eviction, Small Claims.*

www.pbcountyclerk.com

Civil Records: Access: Phone, mail, online, in person. Both court and visitors may perform in person searches. Search fee: $1.00 per name per year. Required to search: name, years to search; also helpful: address. Civil cases indexed by defendant, plaintiff. Civil records (Circuit) on computer from 1982, prior records on microfiche and dockets. County on computer from 1987, prior on microfilm. Access to the countywide remote online system requires $145 setup and $65 per month fees. Civil index goes back to 1988. Records also include probate, traffic and domestic. Contact Betty Jones at 561-355-6783 for information. Also, online access to the 15th judicial circuit records is available at http://web3172.co.palm-beach.fl.us/aemasp/default.asp. Registration and password is required. **General Information:** Public Access terminal is available. No juvenile, child abuse or sexual battery records released. SASE required. Turnaround time 1 week. Copy fee: $1.00 per page. Certification fee: $1.00. Fee payee:

Clerk of Circuit Court. Personal checks accepted. Prepayment is required.

County Court - Probate Division PO Box 4238, West Palm Beach, FL 33402; 561-355-2900. Hours: 8AM-5PM (EST). *Probate.*

Pasco County

Circuit & County Courts - Civil Division 38053 Live Oak Ave, Dade City, FL 33523; 352-521-4482. Hours: 8:30AM-5PM (EST). *Civil, Eviction, Small Claims, Probate.*

www.jud6.org

Civil Records: Access: Mail, online, in person. Both court and visitors may perform in person searches. Search fee: $1.00 per name per year. Required to search: name, years to search. Civil cases indexed by defendant, plaintiff. Civil records on computer from 1985, on docket cards and docket books from 1900s. Online access to Clerk of Circuit Court records via the Internet is to be available in late 2001. Current access to the countywide remote online system requires a $100 deposit, $50 annual fee and $10 monthly minimum. There is a $.10 per screen charge. Probate records also available. Call 352-521-4201 for more information. **General Information:** Public Access terminal is available. No adoption records released. Turnaround time 2-4 days. Copy fee: $1.00 per page. Certification fee: $1.00. Fee payee: Clerk of Court. Personal checks accepted. Prepayment is required.

Circuit & County Courts - Criminal Division 38053 Live Oak Ave, Dade City, FL 33523-3894; 352-521-4491. Hours: 8:30AM-5PM (EST). *Felony, Misdemeanor.*

www.jud6.org

Criminal Records: Access: Mail, online, in person. Both court and visitors may perform in person searches. Search fee: $1.00 per name per year. Required to search: name, years to search, address, DOB; also helpful: SSN. Criminal records on computer since 1978. Access to the countywide criminal online system requires a $100 deposit, $50 annual fee and $10 monthly minimum. There is a $.10 per screen charge. The system is open 24 hours daily. Search by name or case number. Call 352-521-4201 for more information. **General Information:** Public Access terminal is available. No confidential, sealed or juvenile records released. Turnaround time 2-4 days. Copy fee: $1.00 per page. Certification fee: $1.00. Fee payee: Clerk of Courts. Personal checks accepted. Out of state personal checks not accepted. Prepayment is required.

Pinellas County

Circuit & County Courts - Civil Division 315 Court St, Clearwater, FL 33756; 727-464-3267; Fax: 727-464-4070. Hours: 8AM-5PM (EST). *Civil, Eviction, Small Claims, Probate.*

www.jud6.org

Civil Records: Access: Phone, fax, mail, online, in person. Both court and visitors may perform in person searches. Search fee: $1.00 per name per year. Required to search: name, years to search. Civil cases indexed by defendant, plaintiff. Civil records on computer from 1980, on microfiche from 1900s to 1982, older data in warehouse. Access to the countywide remote online system requires a $60 fee plus $.05 per screen. Civil index goes back to 1972. Contact Sue Maskeny at 727-464-3779 for information. Includes probate and traffic records. **General Information:** Public Access terminal is available. No adoption or juvenile records released. SASE helpful. Turnaround time 1 week. Fax notes: $1.00 per page. Copy fee: $1.00 per page. Certification fee: $1.00. Fee payee: Clerk of the Court. Personal checks accepted. Prepayment is required.

Criminal Justice Center Circuit Criminal Court Records, 14250 49th St N, Clearwater, FL 34622; 727-464-6793; Fax: 727-464-6233. Hours: 8AM-5PM (EST). *Felony.*

www.jud6.org

Criminal Records: Access: Phone, fax, mail, online, in person. Both court and visitors may perform in person searches. Search fee: $1.00 per name per year. Required to search: name, years to search, DOB. Criminal records on computer from 1977, on microfilm from 1912 to 1976, on docket books from 1912. Access to the countywide criminal online system requires a $60 fee plus $.05 per screen. Criminal index goes back to 1972. Contact Sue Maskeny at 727-464-3779 for information. **General Information:** Public Access terminal is available. Turnaround time 1 week. Fax notes: $1.00 per page. Copy fee: $1.00 per page. Certification fee: $1.00. Fee payee: Clerk of Circuit Court. Personal checks accepted. Prepayment is required.

County Court - Criminal Division 14250 49th St N, Clearwater, FL 34622-2831; 727-464-7000; Fax: 727-464-7040. Hours: 8AM-5PM (EST). *Misdemeanor.*

www.jud6.org

Criminal Records: Access: Mail, online, in person. Both court and visitors may perform in person searches. Search fee: $1.00 per name per year. Required to search: name, years to search; also helpful: address, DOB, SSN. Criminal records on computer since 10/77, prior on index books. Prior to 1993 on microfilm. Access to the countywide criminal online system requires a $60 fee plus $.05 per screen. Criminal index goes back to 1972. Contact Sue Maskeny at 727-464-3779 for information. **General Information:** Public Access terminal is available. No sealed or non-arrested case records released. Turnaround time 3-5 days. Copy fee: $1.00 per page. Certification fee: $1.00. Fee payee: Clerk of Courts. Personal checks accepted. Prepayment is required.

Polk County

Circuit Court - Civil Division PO Box 9000, Drawer CC2, Bartow, FL 33831-9000; 863-534-4488; Probate phone: 863-534-4478; Fax: 863-534-7707. Hours: 8AM-5PM (EST). *Civil Actions Over $15,000, Probate.*

www.polk-county.net/clerk/clerk.html

Civil Records: Access: Phone, mail, online, in person. Both court and visitors may perform in person searches. Search fee: $1.00 per name per year. Required to search: name. Civil cases indexed by defendant, plaintiff. Civil Records on computer since 1978, on microfiche from 1800s to 1978. Two options are available. Online access to the complete database requires a $150 setup fee and $.15 per minute charge with a $50 minimum per quarter. Call 863-534-7575 for more information. Second, case index information back to 1990 is available free from the County Clerk's web site at www.polk-county.net/clerk/Public_Records/Public_index.html. Includes land and lien searching. **General Information:** No sex related cases, adoption, confidential, victims or child abuse records released. SASE required. Turnaround time 2-3 days. Copy fee: $1.00 per page. Certification fee: $1.00. Fee payee: Clerk of Court. Personal checks accepted. Prepayment is required.

Circuit & County Courts - Felony Division PO Box 9000 Drawer CC9, Bartow, FL 33830; 863-534-4000; Fax: 863-534-4137. Hours: 8AM-5PM (EST). *Felony.*

www.polk-county.net/clerk/clerk.html

Criminal Records: Access: Phone, mail, online, in person. Both court and visitors may perform in person

searches. Search fee: $1.00 per name per year. Required to search: name, years to search, DOB; also helpful: SSN. Criminal records on computer-felonies since 1977, misdemeanors purged periodically. Both on microfiche and archived since 1800s. Two options are available. Online access to the complete database requires a $150 setup fee and $.15 per minute charge with a $50 minimum per quarter. Call 863-534-7575 for more information. Second, case index information back to 1990 is available free from the County Clerk's web site at www.polk-county.net/clerk/Public_Records/Public_index.html.
General Information: Public Access terminal is available. No sex related cases, victims or child abuse released. Turnaround time varies. Indicate on request when record is needed. Copy fee: $1.00 per page. Certification fee: $1.00 per page. Fee payee: Clerk of Circuit Court. Personal checks accepted. Prepayment is required.

Circuit & County Courts - Misdemeanor
Division PO Box 9000 Drawer CC10, Bartow, FL 33831-9000; 863-534-4446; Fax: 863-534-4137. Hours: 8AM-5PM (EST). *Misdemeanor.*

www.polk-county.net/clerk/clerk.html

Criminal Records: Access: Phone, mail, online, in person. Both court and visitors may perform in person searches. Search fee: 3 year search: $4.10; lifetime: $5.10. Required to search: name, years to search, DOB; also helpful: SSN. Criminal records on computer; felonies since 1977, misdemeanors purged periodically. Both on microfiche and archived since 1800s. Two options are available. Online access to the complete database requires a $150 setup fee and $.15 per minute charge with a $50 minimum per quarter. Call 863-534-7575 for more information. Second, case index information back to 1990 is available free from the County Clerk's web site at www.polk-county.net/clerk/Public_Records/Public_index.html.
General Information: Public Access terminal is available. No sex related cases, victims or child abuse released. Turnaround time varies. Indicate on request when record is needed. Copy fee: $1.00 per page. Certification fee: $1.00. Fee payee: Clerk of Circuit Court. Personal checks accepted. Prepayment is required.

County Court - Civil Division PO Box 9000
Drawer CC12, Bartow, FL 33830-9000; 863-534-4556; Fax: 863-534-4089. Hours: 8AM-5PM (EST). *Civil Actions Under $15,000, Eviction, Small Claims.*

www.polk-county.net/clerk/clerk.html

Civil Records: Access: Phone, mail, online, in person. Both court and visitors may perform in person searches. No search fee. Required to search: name, years to search. Civil cases indexed by defendant, plaintiff. Civil records on computer from 1983, on microfiche from 1961 to 1995. Two options are available. Online access to the complete database requires a $150 setup fee and $.15 per minute charge with a $50 minimum per quarter. Call 863-534-7575 for more information. Second, case index information back to 1990 is available free from the County Clerk's web site at www.polk-county.net/clerk/Public_Records/Public_index.html.
Includes land and lien searching. **General Information:** Public Access terminal is available. Turnaround time 1-5 days. Copy fee: $1.00 per page. Certification fee: $1.00. Fee payee: Clerk of Court. Only cashiers checks and money orders accepted. Prepayment is required.

Putnam County
Circuit & County Courts - Civil Division
PO Box 758, Palatka, FL 32178; 386-329-0361; Fax: 386-329-0888. Hours: 8:30AM-5PM (EST). *Civil, Eviction, Small Claims, Probate.*

www.co.putnam.fl.us/clerkofcourt

Civil Records: Both court and visitors may perform in person searches. Search fee: $1.00 per name per year. Required to search: name, years to search. Civil cases indexed by defendant, plaintiff. Civil records on computer from 1984, on microfiche from 1973 to 1984, on index cards and docket books from 1900s to 1973. Access to the countywide remote online system requires a $400 setup fee and $40. monthly charge plus $.05 per minute over 20 hours. Civil records go back to 1984. System includes criminal and real property records. Contact Ryel Christiansen to register. **General Information:** Public Access terminal is available. No juvenile or incompetency records released. SASE requested. Turnaround time 2-3 days. Fax notes: Fee to fax results is $2.25 per page. Copy fee: $1.00 per page. Certification fee: $1.00. Fee payee: Clerk of Court. Personal checks accepted. Prepayment is required.

Circuit & County Courts - Criminal
Division PO Box 758, Palatka, FL 32178; 386-329-0249; Fax: 386-329-0888. Hours: 8:30AM-5PM (EST). *Felony, Misdemeanor.*

www.co.putnam.fl.us/clerkofcourt

Criminal Records: Access: Mail, fax, in person, e-mail. Both court and visitors may perform in person searches. Search fee: $1.00 per name per year. Required to search: name, years to search; also helpful: DOB. Criminal records on computer from 1988, in files from 1930s to 1988. Access to the countywide criminal online system requires a $400 setup fee and $40. monthly charge plus $.05 per minute over 20 hours. Criminal records go back to 1972. System includes civil and real property records. Contact Ryel Christiansen to register.
General Information: Public Access terminal is available. No juvenile records released. Turnaround time 2-3 days. Fax notes: Fee to fax results is $2.25 per page. Copy fee: $1.00 per page. Certification fee: $1.00. Fee payee: Clerk of Circuit Court. Personal checks accepted. Prepayment is required.

Santa Rosa County
Circuit & County Courts - Civil Division
PO Box 472, Milton, FL 32572; 850-623-0135; Fax: 850-626-7248. Hours: 8AM-4:30PM (CST). *Civil, Eviction, Small Claims, Probate.*

http://clerk.co.santa-rosa.fl.us

Civil Records: Access: Fax, mail, in person. Both court and visitors may perform in person searches. Search fee: $1.00 per name per year. Required to search: name, years to search. Civil cases indexed by defendant, plaintiff. Civil records (Circuit) on computer from 1990, archived and on docket books from 1900s. County on computer from 11/92, on microfiche from 1900s, on docket books from early 1900s. **General Information:** Public Access terminal is available. No adoption records released. SASE required. Turnaround time ASAP. Fax notes: $2.00 per page. Copy fee: $1.00 per page. Certification fee: $1.00. Fee payee: Clerk of Courts. Personal checks accepted. Prepayment is required.

Circuit & County Courts - Criminal
Division PO Box 472, Milton, FL 32572; 850-983-1011; Fax: 850-626-5705. Hours: 8AM-4:30PM (CST). *Felony, Misdemeanor.*

http://clerk.co.santa-rosa.fl.us

Criminal Records: Access: Mail, in person. Both court and visitors may perform in person searches. Search

fee: $1.00 per name per year. Required to search: name, years to search, DOB; also helpful: SSN. Criminal records on computer from 1989, felony on index cards from 1925, misdemeanors on docket books from 1900s.
General Information: No records released before sentencing. SASE required. Turnaround time 1-5 days. Fax notes: $2.00 per page. Copy fee: $1.00 per page. Certification fee: $1.00. Fee payee: Clerk's Office. Personal checks accepted. Prepayment is required.

Sarasota County
Circuit & County Courts - Civil Division
PO Box 3079, Sarasota, FL 34230; 941-951-5206. Hours: 8:30AM-5PM (EST). *Civil, Eviction, Small Claims, Probate.*

www.clerk.co.sarasota.fl.us

Civil Records: Access: Mail, online, in person. Both court and visitors may perform in person searches. Search fee: $1.00 per name per year. Required to search: name, years to search. Civil cases indexed by defendant, plaintiff. Civil records on computer from 1983, circuit on docket books from 1900s to 1983, county from 1960s to 1983. Civil case records from the Clerk of the Circuit Court database are available free online at www.clerk.co.sarasota.fl.us/civilapp/civilinq.asp. Criminal, probate and domestic records are also available. Probate court records are available at www.clerk.co.sarasota.fl.us/probapp/probinq.asp.
General Information: Public Access terminal is available. No adoption, mental health, juvenile, or sealed records released. SASE helpful. Turnaround time 1 week. Copy fee: $1.00 per page. Certification fee: $1.00. Fee payee: Clerk of Circuit Court. Personal checks accepted. Credit cards will be accepted as of 07/97. Prepayment is required.

Circuit & County Courts – Criminal
Division PO Box 3079, Sarasota, FL 34230; 941-362-4066. 8:30AM-5PM *Felony, Misdemeanor.*

www.clerk.co.sarasota.fl.us

Criminal Records: Access: Mail, online, in person. Both court and visitors may perform in person searches. Search fee: $1.00 per name per year. Required to search: name, years to search, DOB, SSN. Criminal records on computer since 1983, (circuit) on docket books from 1900s to 1983, (county) on docket books from 1960s to 1983. Criminal case records from the Clerk of the Circuit Court database are available free online at www.clerk.co.sarasota.fl.us/crimdisclaim.htm. Civil, probate and domestic records are also available.
General Information: Public Access terminal is available. No juvenile records released. SASE helpful. Turnaround time 1 week. Copy fee: $1.00 per page. Certification fee: $1.00. Fee payee: Clerk of Circuit Court. Personal checks accepted. Prepayment is required.

Seminole County
Circuit & County Courts - Civil Division
PO Box 8099, Sanford, FL 32772; 407-665-4330; Fax: 407-330-7193. Hours: 8AM-4:30PM (EST). *Civil, Eviction, Small Claims, Probate.*

www.18thcircuit.state.fl.us

Civil Records: Access: Mail, in person, online. Both court and visitors may perform in person searches. Search fee: $1.00 per name per year. Required to search: name, years to search. Civil cases indexed by defendant, plaintiff. Civil records on computer since 1986, on microfiche since 1913. Access to the County Clerk's online records is available free at www.seminoleclerk.org/OfficialRecords. Search by name, case number or document type. **General Information:** Public Access terminal is available. No confidential files pursuant to law or sealed records released. SASE required. Turnaround time 1 week.

Copy fee: $1.00 per page. Certification fee: $1.00. Fee payee: Clerk of the Circuit Court. Personal checks accepted. Prepayment is required.

Circuit & County Courts - Criminal Division
301 N Park Ave, Sanford, FL 32771; 407-665-4356 (Felony) 4377 (Misd). Hours: 8AM-4:30PM (EST). *Felony, Misdemeanor.*

www.seminoleclerk.org

Criminal Records: Access: Mail, in person. Both court and visitors may perform in person searches. Search fee: $1.00 per name per year. Required to search: name, years to search, DOB; also helpful: race, sex. Criminal records on computer from 1986; prior on microfiche.
General Information: Public Access terminal is available. No records of investigations which have not resulted in an arrest released. SASE not required. Turnaround time 2 days for felonies, no set time for misdemeanors. Copy fee: $1.00 per page. Certification fee: $4.00. Fee payee: Clerk of Courts. Business checks accepted. Local personal and company checks allowed. Prepayment is required.

St. Johns County

Circuit & County Courts - Civil Division
PO Drawer 300, St Augustine, FL 32085-0300; 904-823-2333; Fax: 904-823-2294. Hours: 8AM-5PM (EST). *Civil, Eviction, Small Claims, Probate.*

www.co.st-johns.fl.us

Civil Records: Access: Fax, mail, online, in person. Both court and visitors may perform in person searches. Search fee: $1.00 per name per year. Required to search: name, years to search. Civil cases indexed by defendant, plaintiff. Civil records on computer from 1984, on microfiche from 1976 to 1986, on docket books from 1820 to 1983. County on computer from 1991, microfiche from 1983 to 1991, docket books from 1820 to 1983. Access to the countywide remote online system requires a $200 setup fee plus a monthly fee of $50. Searching is by name or case number. Call Mark Dearing at 904-823-2333 x361 for more information. Also, online access to the county Clerk of Circuit Court recording database is available free at www.co.st-johns.fl.us/Const-Officers/Clerk-of-Court/doris/searchdocs.asp. Includes civil and probate records. **General Information:** Public Access terminal is available. No confidential or sealed records released. SASE required. Turnaround time 4-5 days. Fax notes: Long distance: $2.25 for first page, $1.00 each add'l; Local: $1.25 1st page, $1.00 each add'l. Copy fee: $1.00 per page. Certification fee: $1.00. Fee payee: Clerk of Circuit Court. Personal checks accepted. Credit cards accepted: Visa, MasterCard. Prepayment is required.

Circuit & County Courts - Criminal Division
PO Drawer 300, St Augustine, FL 32085-0300; 904-823-2333; Fax: 904-823-2294. Hours: 8AM-5PM (EST). *Felony, Misdemeanor.*

www.co.st-johns.fl.us

Criminal Records: Access: Fax, mail, online, in person. Both court and visitors may perform in person searches. Search fee: $1.00 per name per year. Required to search: name, years to search, DOB; also helpful: address, SSN. Criminal Records on computer. Felony since 1986, Misdemeanor since 1984. Felony on log books from 1950 to 1984. Access to the countywide criminal online system requires a $200 setup fee plus a monthly fee of $50. Searching is by name or case number. Call Mark Dearing at 904-823-2333 x361 for more information.
General Information: Public Access terminal is available. No juvenile or sexual offense records released. SASE required. Turnaround time 4-5 days. Fax notes: Fee to fax results is $1.00 per page. Copy fee: $1.00 per page. Certification fee: $1.00. Fee payee: Clerk of Circuit Court. Personal checks accepted. Credit

cards accepted: Visa, MasterCard. Escrow & billing accounts available to government agencies.

St. Lucie County

Circuit & County Courts - Civil Division
PO Drawer 700, Ft Pierce, FL 34954; 561-462-2758 (Circuit); Civil phone: 561-785-5880 (County; Fax: 561-462-1998 (Circ.) 561-871-5387 (Cty). Hours: 8AM-5PM *Civil, Eviction, Small Claims, Probate.*

www.stlucieco.gov

Civil Records: Access: Mail, in person. Both court and visitors may perform in person searches. Search fee: $1.00 per name per year. Required to search: name, years to search. Civil cases indexed by defendant, plaintiff. Circuit records on computer from 1986, County from 1981. Circuit on microfiche from 1981 to 1986, County from 1981 to 1989. Circuit on docket books from 1900s to 1981, County from 1900s to 1981. Small Claims and County Civil files and microfiche are located at the Courthouse Annex, 250 NW County Club Dr, Pt St. Lucie, FL 34986. **General Information:** Public Access terminal is available. No sealed cases or adoption records released. Turnaround time 1 day. Copy fee: $1.00 per page. Certification fee: $1.00. Fee payee: Clerk of Court. Personal checks accepted. Drivers license & photo ID required. Prepayment is required.

Circuit & County Courts - Criminal Division
PO Drawer 700, Ft Pierce, FL 34954; 561-462-6900; Fax: 561-462-2833. Hours: 8AM-5PM (EST). *Felony, Misdemeanor.*

www.martin.fl.us/GOVT/co/schack

Criminal Records: Access: Fax, mail, in person. Both court and visitors may perform in person searches. Search fee: $1.00 per name per year. Required to search: name, years to search, DOB, signed release; also helpful: address, SSN, race, sex. Criminal records on computer back to 1982, on microfiche to 1960, on books prior to 1900s.
General Information: Public Access terminal is available. No sealed or expunged records released. Turnaround time 1-2 weeks, FAX turnaround time 1-5 days. Fax notes: Fee to fax results is $2.00 per page. Copy fee: $1.00 per page. Certification fee: $2.00. Fee payee: Clerk of Court. Personal checks accepted. Prepayment is required.

Sumter County

Circuit & County Courts - Civil Division
209 N Florida St, Bushnell, FL 33513; 352-793-0215; Fax: 352-568-6608. Hours: 8:30AM-5PM (EST). *Civil, Eviction, Small Claims, Probate.*

Civil Records: Access: Phone, fax, mail, in person. Both court and visitors may perform in person searches. Search fee: $1.00 per name per year. Required to search: name, years to search. Civil cases indexed by defendant, plaintiff. Civil records on computer from 1986 (circuit only), on docket books from 1800s.
General Information: No juvenile or adoption records released. SASE requested. Turnaround time 1 week, phone turnaround 30 min. to 1 hour. Fax notes: $1.00 per page. Copy fee: $1.00 per page. Certification fee: $1.00. Fee payee: Clerk of Circuit Court. Personal checks accepted. Prepayment is required.

Circuit & County Courts - Criminal Division
209 N Florida St, Bushnell, FL 33513; 352-793-0211; Fax: 352-568-6608. Hours: 8:30AM-5PM (EST). *Felony, Misdemeanor.*

Criminal Records: Access: Mail, in person. Only the court performs in person searches; visitors may not. Search fee: $1.00 per name per year. Required to search: name, years to search, DOB. Criminal records (circuit) on computer since 1988, on index books from 1965 to 1988, prior in vaults. County on computer since

1982, on microfiche from 1960 to 1982, on docket books since early 1900s.
General Information: No juvenile records released. SASE requested. Turnaround time 1 week. Fax notes: Fee to fax results is $1.00 per page. Copy fee: $1.00 per page. Certification fee: $1.00. Fee payee: Clerk of Court. Only cashiers checks and money orders accepted. Prepayment is required.

Suwannee County

Circuit & County Courts
200 S Ohio Ave, Live Oak, FL 32060; 904-362-0500; Fax: 904-362-0548. Hours: 8AM-5PM (EST). *Felony, Misdemeanor, Civil, Eviction, Small Claims, Probate.*

www.suwanneeclerkofcourt.com

Civil Records: Access: Mail, in person, online. Both court and visitors may perform in person searches. Search fee: $1.00 per name per year. Fee is per index. Required to search: name, years to search; also helpful: address. Civil cases indexed by defendant, plaintiff. Civil records on computer from 1983, archived from 1859 to 1983. Online access to County Clerk of Circuit Court records is available at the web site. Written requests require prepayment.
Criminal Records: Access: Mail, in person, online. Both court and visitors may perform in person searches. Search fee: $1.00 per name per year. Fee is per index. Required to search: name, years to search, DOB, signed release; also helpful: address, SSN. Criminal records on computer from 1983, archived from 1859 to 1983. Online access to criminal records is the same as civil. Written requests require prepayment.
General Information: Public Access terminal is available. No juvenile or adoption records released. SASE required. Turnaround time 1 week. Copy fee: $1.00 per page. Certification fee: $1.00. Fee payee: Suwannee Court Clerk. Personal checks accepted. Prepayment is required.

Taylor County

Circuit & County Courts
PO Box 620, Perry, FL 32348; 850-838-3506; Fax: 850-838-3549. Hours: 8AM-5PM (EST). *Felony, Misdemeanor, Civil, Eviction, Small Claims, Probate.*

Civil Records: Access: Phone, fax, mail, in person. Only the court performs in person searches; visitors may not. No search fee. Required to search: name, years to search. Civil cases indexed by defendant, plaintiff. Civil records on computer from 1982 to present, on index from 1973 to 1991, prior on index books.
Criminal Records: Access: Phone, fax, mail, in person. Only the court performs in person searches; visitors may not. Search fee: $1.00 per name per year. Required to search: name, years to search, DOB; also helpful: SSN, race, sex. Criminal records on computer from 1982 to present, on index from 1973 to 1991, prior on index books.
General Information: No juvenile records released. SASE helpful. Turnaround time 1 week. Copy fee: $1.00 per page. Certification fee: $1.00. Fee payee: Taylor County Clerk of Court. Business checks accepted. Prepayment is required.

Union County

Circuit & County Courts
Courthouse Rm 103, Lake Butler, FL 32054; 904-496-3711; Fax: 904-496-1718. Hours: 8AM-5PM (EST). *Felony, Misdemeanor, Civil, Eviction, Small Claims, Probate.*

http://circuit8.org

Civil Records: Access: Fax, mail, in person. Both court and visitors may perform in person searches. Search fee: $1.00 per name per year. Required to search: name, years to search. Civil cases indexed by defendant, plaintiff. Civil records on docket books from 1921.

Criminal Records: Access: Fax, mail, in person, online. Both court and visitors may perform in person searches. Search fee: $1.00 per name per year. Required to search: name, years to search, DOB; also helpful: SSN. Criminal records on docket books from 1921. Access to the circuit-wide criminal quick lookup is available at http://circuit8.org/golem/gencrim.html. Account and password is required; restricted usage.

General Information: No juvenile records released. SASE preferred. Turnaround time 2-3 days. Fax notes: $1.00 per page. Copy fee: $1.00 per page. Certification fee: $1.00. Fee payee: Clerk of Court. Personal checks accepted. Prepayment is required.

Volusia County

Circuit & County Courts - Civil Division

PO Box 6043, De Land, FL 32721; 904-736-5915; Fax: 904-822-5711. Hours: 8AM-4:30PM (EST). *Civil, Eviction, Small Claims, Probate.*

http://volusia.org/courts

Civil Records: Access: Fax, mail, online, in person. Both court and visitors may perform in person searches. Search fee: $1.00 per name per year. Required to search: name, years to search. Civil cases indexed by defendant, plaintiff. Civil records on computer from 1986, on docket books from 1863 to 1986. Access to the countywide remote online system requires a $125 setup fee plus a $25 monthly fee. Windows required. Search by name or case number. Call Tom White 904-736-5915 for more information. Criminal, probate and traffic records are also available. **General Information:** Public Access terminal is available. No sealed records released. SASE requested. Turnaround time 1-2 weeks. Fax notes: $1.50 per page. Copy fee: $1.00 per page. Certification fee: $1.00. Fee payee: Clerk of Circuit Court. Personal checks accepted. Prepayment is required.

Circuit & County Courts - Criminal Division

PO Box 6043, De Land, FL 32721-6043; 904-736-5915; Fax: 904-822-5711. Hours: 8AM-4:30PM (EST). *Felony, Misdemeanor.*

http://volusia.org/courts

Criminal Records: Access: Mail, online, in person. Both court and visitors may perform in person searches. Search fee: $1.00 per name per year. Required to search: name, years to search, DOB; also helpful: SSN, race, sex. Criminal records 1982 to present on computer, on microfiche from 1856 to 1988, on docket books prior to 1983. Access to the countywide criminal

online system requires a $125 setup fee plus a $25 monthly. Windows required. Search by name or case number back to 1988. Call 904-822-5710 for more information. Civil, probate and traffic records are also available.

General Information: No confidential, sexual battery and juvenile records released. SASE required. Turnaround time up to 1 week. Fax notes: $1.50 per page. Copy fee: $1.00 per page. Certification fee: $1.00. Fee payee: Clerk of Court. Personal checks accepted. Personal and out of state checks accepted with proper ID. Prepayment is required.

Wakulla County

Circuit & County Courts

3056 Crawfordville Hwy, Crawfordville, FL 32327; 850-926-0905; Fax: 850-926-0938 (Civil); 926-0936 (Crim). Hours: 8AM-5PM (EST). *Felony, Misdemeanor, Civil, Eviction, Small Claims, Probate.*

www.co.leon.fl.us/court/court.htm

Civil Records: Access: Phone, fax, mail, in person. Both court and visitors may perform in person searches. Search fee: $1.00 per name per year. Required to search: name, years to search. Civil cases indexed by defendant, plaintiff. Civil records on computer since 1990, on docket books from 1800s.

Criminal Records: Access: Fax, mail, in person. Both court and visitors may perform in person searches. Search fee: $1.00 per name per year. Required to search: name, years to search, DOB; also helpful: SSN. Criminal records on computer since 1990, on docket books from 1800s. Visitors may review docket books, only court performs name searches.

General Information: No juvenile, adoption records released. SASE helpful. Turnaround time 3-4 days. Fax notes: Fee to fax results is $1.00 per page. Copy fee: $1.00 per page. Certification fee: $1.00. Fee payee: Clerk of Court. Personal checks accepted. Prepayment is required.

Walton County

Circuit & County Courts

PO Box 1260, De Funiak Springs, FL 32435; 850-892-8115; Fax: 850-892-7551. Hours: 8AM-4:30PM (CST). *Felony, Misdemeanor, Civil, Eviction, Small Claims, Probate.*

www.co.walton.fl.us/clerk

Civil Records: Access: Fax, mail, online, in person. Both court and visitors may perform in person searches. Search fee: $1.00 per name per year. Required to

search: name, years to search. Civil cases indexed by defendant, plaintiff. Civil records on computer from 1988, on dockets from 1900s. Access to the county online system requires a setup fee of at least $30 plus $100 monthly. The system includes probate, traffic, domestic and criminal data. Search by name or case number. Call David Langford for more information, 850-892-8115.

Criminal Records: Access: Fax, mail, online, in person. Both court and visitors may perform in person searches. Search fee: $1.00 per name per year. Required to search: name, years to search, DOB. Criminal records on computer from 1988, on dockets from 1900s. Online access to criminal records is the same as civil.

General Information: Public Access terminal is available. No sealed, expunged, or pre-sentence investigation records released. SASE helpful. Turnaround time 24 hours. Fax notes: $1.00 per page. Copy fee: $1.00 per page. Certification fee: $1.00. Fee payee: Clerk of Courts. Personal checks accepted. Prepayment is required.

Washington County

Circuit & County Courts

PO Box 647, Chipley, FL 32428-0647; 850-638-6285; Fax: 850-638-6297. Hours: 8AM-4PM (CST). *Felony, Misdemeanor, Civil, Eviction, Small Claims, Probate.*

Civil Records: Access: Phone, fax, mail, in person. Both court and visitors may perform in person searches. Search fee: $1.00 per name per year. Required to search: name, years to search. Civil cases indexed by defendant, plaintiff. Civil records on computer from 1981, on docket books from 1800s to 1986.

Criminal Records: Access: Phone, fax, mail, in person. Only the court performs in person searches; visitors may not. Search fee: $1.00 per name per year. Required to search: name, years to search. Criminal records on computer from 1981, on docket books from 1800s to 1986.

General Information: Public Access terminal is available. (In the civil department.) No adoption or juvenile records released. SASE requested. Turnaround time 1 day. Copy fee: $1.00 per page. Certification fee: $1.00. Fee payee: Clerk of Court. Business checks accepted. Local personal checks accepted. Prepayment is required.

Florida Recording Offices

ORGANIZATION
67 counties, 67 recording offices. The recording officer is Clerk of the Circuit Court. All transactions are recorded in the "Official Record," a grantor/grantee index. Some counties will search by type of transaction while others will return everything on the index. 57 counties are in the Eastern Time Zone (EST) and 10 are in the Central Time Zone (CST).

REAL ESTATE RECORDS
Any name searched in the "Official Records" will usually include all types of liens and property transfers for that name. Most counties will perform searches. In addition to the usual $1.00 per page copy fee, certification of documents usually cost $1.00 per document. Tax records are located at the Property Appraiser Office.

Note that a number of counties make their real estate records available online.

UCC RECORDS
Financing statements are filed at the state level, and real estate related collateral at the Clerk of the Circuit Court. Until 01/2002, farm related financing was also filed at the clerk's office. All but a few counties will perform UCC searches. Use search request form UCC-11. Search fees are usually $1.00 per debtor name per year searched and include all lien and real estate transactions on record. Copies usually cost $1.00 per page.

TAX LIEN RECORDS
Federal tax liens on personal property of businesses are filed with the Secretary of State. All other federal and state tax liens on personal property are filed with the county Clerk of Circuit Court. Usually tax liens on personal property are filed in the same index with UCC financing statements and real estate transactions. Most counties will perform a tax lien as part of a UCC search. Copies usually cost $1.00 per page.

OTHER LIENS
Judgments, hospital, mechanics, sewer, ambulance.

STATEWIDE ONLINE INFO:
There are numerous county agencies that provide online access to records. Many offer this access free from the web.

Alachua County

County Clerk of the Circuit Court, P.O. Box 600, Gainesville, FL 32602. 352-374-3625; Fax 352-491-4649. http://www.clerk-alachua-fl.org/clerk/pubrec.html Will search UCC records. Tax liens not included in UCC search. RE owner, mortgage, and property transfer searches available. **Online Access:** Property Appraiser, Real Estate, Liens, Vital Records. Online access to the Clerk of Courts recording database are available free at the web site. Records go back to 1/93. Also, search the County Property Search page free online at www.propappr-alachua-fl.org/services/search/search.asp. **Other Phone Numbers:** Treasurer 352-374-3605; Appraiser/Auditor 352-374-5230; Finance Director 352-374-3605.

Baker County

County Clerk of the Circuit Court, 339 East MacClenny Avenue, MacClenny, FL 32063. 904-259-0208; Fax 904-259-4176.
Will search UCC records. Tax liens not included in UCC search. Separate tax lien searches performed at $1.00 per year. RE owner, mortgage, and property transfer searches available. **Other Phone Numbers:** Treasurer 904-259-6880; Appraiser/Auditor 904-259-3191; Elections 904-259-6339.

Bay County

County Clerk of the Circuit Court, P.O. Box 2269, Panama City, FL 32402. 850-747-5104; Fax 850-747-5199. http://bcpa.co.bay.fl.us
Will search UCC records. This agency will not do a tax lien search. Re record owner searches available for 1987 to present. **Online Access:** Property Appraiser. Property information from the County Property Assessor database is available free online at http://bcpa.co.bay.fl.us/database.htm. **Other Phone Numbers:** Appraiser/Auditor 850-784-4095.

Bradford County

County Clerk of the Circuit Court, P.O. Drawer B, Starke, FL 32091. 904-966-6280; Fax 904-964-4454. Will search UCC records. Tax liens not included in UCC search. RE owner, mortgage, and property transfer searches available. **Other Phone Numbers:** Appraiser/Auditor 904-964-6280.

Brevard County

County Clerk of the Circuit Court, P.O. Box 2767, Titusville, FL 32781. 407-264-5244; Fax 407-264-5246. www.clerk.co.brevard.fl.us
Will search UCC records. UCC search includes tax liens if requested. Will search tax records. **Online Access:** Property Appraiser, Real Estate, Liens, Marriage, Recordings. Online access to the Circuit Clerk's tax lien (1981-95), land records (1995 to present) and marriage records is free at www.clerk.co.brevard.fl.us/pages/pubrec9.htm. Also, property records are available free at http://appraiser.co.brevard.fl.us/asp/disclaimer.asp. Search by name or map.

Broward County

County Clerk of the Circuit Court, P.O. Box 14668, Fort Lauderdale, FL 33302. 954-357-7281; Fax 954-357-7267. www.co.broward.fl.us/records1.htm
Will search UCC records. Tax liens not included in UCC search. RE record owner and property searches available. **Online Access:** Property Appraiser, Real Estate, Liens, Recordings. Online access to the county clerk's Public Search database 1978-present is available free at http://205.166.161.20/CRSearch/crSearch.asp. Additionally, professional users may register and receive a password for additional access options. Also, Property Appraiser records are available free online at www.bcpa.net/search.htm. **Other Phone Numbers:** Appraiser/Auditor 954-357-6908.

Calhoun County

County Clerk of the Circuit Court, 425 East Central Avenue, Room 130, Blountstown, FL 32424. 850-674-4545; Fax 850-674-5553.
Will search UCC records. UCC search includes tax liens. RE owner, mortgage, and property transfer searches available. **Other Phone Numbers:** Treasurer 850-674-5636; Appraiser/Auditor 850-647-8242.

Charlotte County

County Clerk of the Circuit Court, P.O. Box 510156, Punta Gorda, FL 33951-0156. 941-637-2245; Fax 941-637-2172. http://www.co.charlotte.fl.us/
Will search UCC records. Tax liens not included in UCC search. RE record owner and mortgage searches available. **Online Access:** Property Appraiser, Real Estate, Liens, Recordings. Property records are available free online at www.ccappraiser.com/record.asp. Sales records are also available here and at the tax collector database, which is free at www.cctaxcol.com/record.asp?. Also, recordings from the county clerk database are available free online at http://208.47.160.70. Search by book/page or grantor/grantee. A subscription service (CASWEB) is also available, which includes images, court records, recordings, etc. Bulk database record purchases, by year, are also available. **Other Phone Numbers:** Appraiser/Auditor 941-743-1488.

Citrus County

County Clerk of the Circuit Court, 110 North Apopka Ave. Room 101, Inverness, FL 34450-4299. 352-341-6468; Fax 352-341-6477. http://www.clerk.citrus.fl.us/
Will search UCC records. UCC search includes tax liens if requested. Will search for any RE records in the official records index. **Online Access:** Property Appraiser, Real Estate, Liens, Recordings, Marriage. Online access to the Clerk of Circuit Court records is available free at www.clerk.citrus.fl.us/offrsearch.htf. Search Marriage License records free online at www.clerk.citrus.fl.us/marrsearch.htf. Search by first and last name. Also, Property records are available free online at www.pa.citrus.fl.us/ccpaask.html. **Other Phone Numbers:** Appraiser/Auditor 352-637-9820.

Clay County

County Clerk of the Circuit Court, P.O. Box 698, Green Cove Springs, FL 32043-0698. 904-284-6300 R/E Recording: 904-284-6362 UCC Recording: 904-284-6362; Fax 904-284-6390. http://clerk.co.clay.fl.us
Will search UCC records. UCC search includes tax liens if requested. Will search for any RE records in official records, except title searches. No search by

phone. **Online Access:** Appraiser, Real Estate, Liens, Recordings. The county clerk of circuit court allows free online access to recording records at http://clerk.co.clay.fl.us/new_search.htm. This replaces the commercial system. Records go back to 1990 Also, the Clay County Property Appraiser's office records are available free at www.ccpao.com/ccpao/ccpao.asp?page=Disclaimer. Search by name, street name and number, or real estate number. Also, search real estate and personal property free on the tax collector database at http://claycountytax.com/Tax_Searchr. **Other Phone Numbers:** Appraiser/Auditor 904-284-6320.

Collier County

County Clerk of the Circuit Court, P.O. Box 413044, Naples, FL 34101-3044. 941-732-2606; Fax 941-774-8003.
Will search UCC records. UCC search includes tax liens if requested. RE owner, mortgage, and property transfer searches available. **Online Access:** Property Appraiser, Real Estate, Liens, Vital Records. Property Appraiser information is free, other data is not. Records on the Property Appraiser database are available free online at www.collierappraiser.com/Disclaimers.asp. Online access to County courts, lien, real estate, and vital records is available by subscription for $100 fee, a $50 deposit, plus $10 monthly plus $.05 per minute. Records include probate, traffic and domestic. Lending agency information is available. For information, contact Judy Stephenson at 941-774-8339. **Other Phone Numbers:** Appraiser/Auditor 941-774-8175.

Columbia County

County Clerk of the Circuit Court, P.O. Box 2069, Lake City, FL 32056-2069. 904-758-1342 R/E Recording: 904-758-1031 UCC Recording: 904-758-1031; Fax 904-758-1337. www.columbiaclerk.com
Will search UCC records. UCC search includes tax liens if requested. RE owner, mortgage, and property transfer searches available. **Online Access:** Real Estate, Liens, Recordings, Probate. Online access to the Clerk of Circuit Courts recording database is available free at www.columbiaclerk.com/Public_Records/public_records.html. Search by name, book/page, file number of document type. **Other Phone Numbers:** Treasurer 904-758-1042; Appraiser/Auditor 904-758-1087; Elections 904-758-1028; Vital Records 904-758-1150.

Dade County

County Clerk of the Circuit Court, P.O. Box 011711, Flagler Station, Miami, FL 33101. 305-275-1155; Fax 305-372-7775. http://www.metro-dade.com/clerk
Will search UCC records. UCC search includes tax liens if requested. RE owner, mortgage, and property transfer searches available. **Online Access:** Property Appraiser, Real Estate, Liens, Recordings, Marriage Records, Tax Records. Three options are available. Record access to 11 databases requires an initial setup fee is $125 and a minimum monthly fee of $52 for 208 minutes of use, $.25 ea. add'l minute. Records date back to 1975. Databases include property appraisal, building permits, tax collection, permit hearings, and others. Contact Jerry Kiernan at 305-596-8148 for information. Second, appraiser records are available free online at www.co.miami-dade.fl.us/pa/record.htm. Search by name, address, folio or map. Third, recorder records are available free online at www.metro-dade.com/clerk/public-records. Search by name, CFN#, plat book, or recording book & page. **Other Phone Numbers:** Appraiser/Auditor 305-375-5447.

De Soto County

County Clerk of the Circuit Court, 115 East Oak St, Arcadia, FL 34266. 863-993-4876; Fax 863-993-4669.
Will search UCC records. UCC search includes tax liens if requested. Will not search real estate records.

Other Phone Numbers: Appraiser/Auditor 863-993-4866.

Dixie County

County Clerk of the Circuit Court, P.O. Box 1206, Cross City, FL 32628. County Clerk of the Circuit Court, R/E and UCC Recording 352-498-1200; Fax 352-498-1201.
Will search UCC records. This agency will not do a tax lien search. Will not search real estate records. **Other Phone Numbers:** Appraiser/Auditor 352-498-1212; Elections 352-498-1216.

Duval County

County Clerk of the Circuit Court, 330 East Bay Street, Courthouse, Jacksonville, FL 32202. 904-630-2043; Fax 904-630-2959. http://www.ci.jax.fl.us
Will search UCC records. RE record owner and mortgage searches available. **Online Access:** Property Appraiser, Real Estate, Liens, Recordings. Online access to the Clerk of Circuit Court and City of Jacksonville Official Records (a grantor/grantee index) is available free at www2.coj.net/officialrecords. Also, the County Property Appraiser offers free access to property records for the County and City of Jacksonville at http://pawww.coj.net/pub/property/lookup.htm. Also, records on County Property (Tax Collector) database are available free online at www2.coj.net/realestate. Also, limited property records on Jacksonville Public Data Depot database are available free online at www.ci.jax.fl.us/pub/depot.htm#prop. **Other Phone Numbers:** Treasurer 904-630-2068; Appraiser/Auditor 904-630-2020.

Escambia County

County Clerk of the Circuit Court, 223 Palafox Place, Old Courthouse, Pensacola, FL 32501. 850-595-3930; Fax 850-595-4827. http://www.clerk.co.escambia.fl.us
Will search UCC records. UCC search includes tax liens if requested. RE owner, mortgage, and property transfer searches available. **Online Access:** Property Appraiser, Real Estate, Liens, Recordings, Marriage Records. Online access to the Clerk of Court Public Records database is available free at http://www.clerk.co.escambia.fl.us/public_records.html. This includes grantor/grantee index and marriage, traffic and court records. Also, online access to the tax collector's Property Tax Inquiry database is available free online at www.co.escambia.fl.us/ectc/taxiq.html. Also, search the property appraiser real estate records at www.escpa.org/searchform.asp. **Other Phone Numbers:** Treasurer 850-436-5200; Appraiser/Auditor 850-436-5260.

Flagler County

County Clerk of the Circuit Court, P.O. Box 787, Bunnell, FL 32010. 904-437-7433; Fax 904-437-7406.
Will search UCC records. Will search for any RE records in general index. **Other Phone Numbers:** Treasurer 904-437-7414; Appraiser/Auditor 904-437-7450.

Franklin County

County Clerk of the Circuit Court, 33 Market Street, Apalachicola, FL 32320. 850-653-8861; Fax 850-653-2261.
Will search UCC records. This agency will not do a tax lien search. Will not search real estate records. **Other Phone Numbers:** Treasurer 850-653-8861; Appraiser/Auditor 850-653-9236.

Gadsden County

County Clerk of the Circuit Court, P.O. Box 1649, Quincy, FL 32353-1649. 850-875-8603; Fax 850-875-8612. http://www.clerk.co.gadsden.fl.us

Will search UCC records. UCC search includes tax liens. Will not search real estate records. **Online Access:** Real Estate, Liens, Recordings, Vital Records. Online access to county clerk records requires a written request sent to the Clerk of the Court. The subscription fee varies, dependent on the level of service. Records date back to 1985. For information, call 850-875-8629. Also, access to the official records index is available free at www.clerk.co.gadsden.fl.us/OfficialRecords/. Index records go back to 1985.

Gilchrist County

County Clerk of the Circuit Court, P.O. Box 37, Trenton, FL 32693. County Clerk of the Circuit Court, R/E and UCC Recording 352-463-3170; Fax 352-463-3166. http://www.co.gilchrist.fl.us/cophone
Will search UCC records. Tax liens not included in UCC search. Will not search real estate records. **Online Access:** Real Estate, Property Appraiser. Online access to the property appraiser database is available free at http://www.ice-systems.net/~gilchrist/PublicPropertySearch.htm. **Other Phone Numbers:** Appraiser/Auditor 352-463-3190; Elections 352-463-3194.

Glades County

County Clerk of the Circuit Court, P.O. Box 10, Moore Haven, FL 33471. County Clerk of the Circuit Court, R/E and UCC Recording 863-946-0113; Fax 863-946-0560.
Will search UCC records. Will search for any RE records on general index. **Other Phone Numbers:** Appraiser/Auditor 863-946-0818.

Gulf County

County Clerk of the Circuit Court, 1000 5th Street, Port St. Joe, FL 32456-1699. 850-229-6113; Fax 850-229-6174.
Will search UCC records. Will search for any RE records in general index for $20.00 per hour plus $1.00 per year **Other Phone Numbers:** Appraiser/Auditor 850-229-6115.

Hamilton County

County Clerk of the Circuit Court, 207 NE 1st Street, Room 106, Jasper, FL 32052. 904-792-1288; Fax 904-792-3524.
Will search UCC records. UCC search includes tax liens if requested. Will search for any RE record in general index. **Other Phone Numbers:** Treasurer 904-792-1288; Appraiser/Auditor 904-792-1284; Elections 904-792-1426; Vital Records 904-792-1288.

Hardee County

County Clerk of the Circuit Court, P.O. Drawer 1749, Wauchula, FL 33873. 863-773-4174; Fax 863-773-4422.
Will search UCC records. This agency will not do a tax lien search. Will not search real estate records. **Other Phone Numbers:** Appraiser/Auditor 863-773-2196.

Hendry County

County Clerk of the Circuit Court, P.O. Box 1760, La Belle, FL 33975-1760. County Clerk of the Circuit Court, R/E and UCC Recording 863-675-5217 UCC Recording: 863-675-5202; Fax 863-675-5238.
Will search UCC records. UCC search includes tax liens. RE owner, mortgage, and property transfer searches available. **Other Phone Numbers:** Treasurer 863-675-5280; Appraiser/Auditor 863-675-5270; Elections 863-675-5231; Vital Records 863-675-5217.

Hernando County

County Clerk of the Circuit Court, 20 North Main, Room 215, Brooksville, FL 34601. 352-754-4201

x214/5 R/E Recording: 352-754-4201 x214 or 215; Fax 352-754-4243. http://www.co.hernando.fl.us
Will search UCC records. Tax liens not included in UCC search. RE record owner and property searches available. **Online Access:** Property Appraiser, Real Estate, Liens, Marriage Records. Remote access cost includes $100 setup, monthly minimum fee and $.10 per minute. A fax back service is available. A deposit is required. For additional information, call 352-754-4201. Lending agency information available. Also, the county now offers 2 levels of the Public Inquiry System Property Appraiser Real Estate database - Easy Search & Real Time Search - free online at www.co.hernando.fl.us/pa/propsearch.htm. Search by owner, address, or parcel key. **Other Phone Numbers:** Treasurer 352-754-4190; Appraiser/Auditor 352-754-4190.

Highlands County

County Clerk of the Circuit Court, 590 South Commerce Avenue, Sebring, FL 33870. County Clerk of the Circuit Court, R/E and UCC Recording 863-402-6590 UCC Recording: 800-822-5436; http://www.clerk.co.highlands.fl.us
Will not search UCC records. This agency will not do a tax lien search. Will not search real estate records. **Online Access:** Property Appraiser, Real Estate, Tax Liens, Recordings. Property Appraiser records are available free online at www.appraiser.co.highlands.fl.us/search.html; Real Estate Property Records and Tangible Personal Property records are available. Online access to deeds, mortgages, judgments from the county recording database are available free at www.clerk.co.highlands.fl.us/owa_highlands/cgi-bin/instrument_search.form.
Records go back to 1983. Also, online access to the county tax collector database is available free at www.collector.co.highlands.fl.us/search/index.html.
Other Phone Numbers: Assessor 863-402-6659; Treasurer 863-402-6685; Appraiser/Auditor 863-402-6661; Elections 863-402-6654; Vital Records 863-402-6040.

Hillsborough County

County Clerk of the Circuit Court, P.O. Box 1110-Recording #313, Tampa, FL 33601-1110. 813-276-8100 x7507; Fax 813-276-2114. http://www.hcpafl.org
Will search UCC records. UCC search includes tax liens. RE owner, mortgage, and property transfer searches available. **Online Access:** Property Appraiser, Real Estate, Liens. Property records are available free online at www.hcpafl.org/disclaimer.html. Select to receive owner information, also legal, sales, value summaries. The County also offers access to county court, real estate, and lien records through a fee online service. Probate, traffic and domestic records included. Access is $.25 per minute or $5.00 per month, whichever is greater, plus a $50.00 one-time set-up fee with software. Contact the help desk at 813-276-8100 X 7000 for more information. **Other Phone Numbers:** Appraiser/Auditor 813-272-6100.

Holmes County

County Clerk of the Circuit Court, P.O. Box 397, Bonifay, FL 32425. 850-547-1102; Fax 850-547-6630.
Will search UCC records. Will not search real estate records. **Other Phone Numbers:** Treasurer 850-547-1115; Appraiser/Auditor 850-547-1113; Elections 850-547-1107.

Indian River County

County Clerk of the Circuit Court, P.O. Box 1028, Vero Beach, FL 32961-1028. 561-770-5185 x184; http://indian-river.fl.us
Will search UCC records. Tax liens not included in UCC search. Will not search real estate records. **Online**

Access: Property Appraiser, Real Estate, Liens, Vital Records. Appraiser information is free, but only some of the recording information is. Appraiser records are available free online at http://indian-river.fl.us/realestate/search.html. Online access to recording indexes on the Clerk of the Circuit Court database are available free at http://bdc.co.indian-river.fl.us. Records go back to 1983. Full real estate, lien and court and vital records are available from the Clerk of the Circuit Court at the fee site, subscription is $200 per month. For information about free and fee access, call Gary at 561-567-8000 x216. **Other Phone Numbers:** Appraiser/Auditor 561-567-8188.

Jackson County

County Clerk of the Circuit Court, P.O. Drawer 510, Marianna, FL 32447. 850-482-9552; Fax 850-482-7849. http://www.jacksoncountyclerk.com
Will not search UCC records. This agency will not do a tax lien search. Will not search real estate records. **Online Access:** Real Estate, Liens, Recording, Marriage, Death, Probate. Online access to the Clerk of Circuit Court Official Records database is available free at www.jacksoncountyclerk.com/records.html. Images will go back to 5/1996. **Other Phone Numbers:** Treasurer 850-482-9653; Appraiser/Auditor 850-482-9646.

Jefferson County

County Clerk of the Circuit Court, Courthouse, Room 10, Monticello, FL 32344. 850-342-0218 x27; Fax 850-342-0222.
Will search UCC records. UCC search includes tax liens if requested. Will not search real estate records. **Other Phone Numbers:** Appraiser/Auditor 850-997-3356.

Lafayette County

County Clerk of the Circuit Court, P.O. Box 88, Mayo, FL 32066. 904-294-1600; Fax 904-294-4231.
Will search UCC records. This agency will not do a tax lien search. Will not search real estate records. **Other Phone Numbers:** Treasurer 904-294-1961; Appraiser/Auditor 904-299-1991.

Lake County

County Clerk of the Circuit Court, P.O. Box 7800, Tavares, FL 32778-7800. 352-742-4114; Fax 352-742-4191. http://www.lakecountyclerk.org
Will search UCC records. UCC search includes tax liens if requested. Will not search real estate records. **Online Access:** Property Appraiser, Real Estate, Liens, Marriage, Recording. The new county clerk official records database is available free online at www.lakecountyclerk.org/services.asp?subject=Online_Official_Records. Records go as far back as 1974. Includes court records. Also, records on the County Property Assessor database are available free online at www.lcpafl.org/agreement.asp. Also, marriage records back to 11/2000 are available at www.lakecountyclerk.org/departments.asp?subject=Marriage_Licenses. **Other Phone Numbers:** Assessor 352-343-9748; Treasurer 352-742-9808; Elections 352-343-9734; Vital Records 352-742-6320; Tax Collector 352-343-9622.

Lee County

County Clerk of the Circuit Court, P.O. Box 2278, Fort Myers, FL 33902-2278. 941-335-2283; http://www.leetc.com/
Will search UCC records. UCC search includes tax liens if requested. RE owner, mortgage, and property transfer searches available. **Online Access:** Property Appraiser, Real Estate, Occupational License. Online access to the appraiser database is available free at www.property-appraiser.lee.fl.us, or the tax roll

database at www.leetc.com/Taxes/default.asp. Also, access to the county "license" database is available at www.leetc.com/OccupationalLicense/default.asp. **Other Phone Numbers:** Appraiser/Auditor 941-335-2283.

Leon County

County Clerk of the Circuit Court, P.O. Box 726, Tallahassee, FL 32302. 850-488-7538; Fax 850-921-1310. http://www.clerk.leon.fl.us
Will search UCC records. Tax liens not included in UCC search. Will search for any Re records in general index. **Online Access:** Property Appraiser, Real Estate, Liens, Marriage Records. Real Estate, lien, and marriage records from the County Clerk are available free online at www.clerk.leon.fl.us. Lending agency information is also available. Property Appraiser database records are available at www.co.leon.fl.us/propappr.prop.htm. **Other Phone Numbers:** Appraiser/Auditor 850-488-6073.

Levy County

County Clerk of the Circuit Court, P.O. Drawer 610, Bronson, FL 32621. 352-486-5229; http://www.levyclerk.com
Will search UCC records. This agency will not do a tax lien search. RE owner, mortgage, and property transfer searches available. **Online Access:** Real Estate, Liens, Recordings. Online access to the Clerk of Circuit Court recording catabase are available free at www.levyclerk.com/Public_Records/Public_Records.html. Search by name, book/page, file number or document type. **Other Phone Numbers:** Appraiser/Auditor 352-486-4311.

Liberty County

County Clerk of the Circuit Court, P.O. Box 399, Bristol, FL 32321. 850-643-2215; Fax 850-643-2866.
Will search UCC records. This agency will not do a tax lien search. Will not search real estate records. **Other Phone Numbers:** Treasurer 850-643-2442; Appraiser/Auditor 850-643-2279.

Madison County

County Clerk of the Circuit Court, P.O. Box 237, Madison, FL 32341-0237. 850-973-1500 R/E Recording: 850-973-1500 x27 UCC Recording: 850-973-1500 x27; Fax 850-973-2059.
Will search UCC records. UCC search includes tax liens if requested. RE owner, mortgage, and property transfer searches available. **Other Phone Numbers:** Appraiser/Auditor 850-973-6133.

Manatee County

County Clerk of the Circuit Court, P.O. Box 25400, Bradenton, FL 34206. 941-741-4041; Fax 941-741-4082. http://www.co.manatee.fl.us
Will search UCC records. UCC search includes tax liens. RE owner, mortgage, and property transfer searches available. **Online Access:** Appraiser, Real Estate, Liens, Vital Records. Several options exist. Real estate and recordings are available free from the Clerk of Circuit Court and Comptroller's database at http://www.clerkofcourts.com/PubRec/RecordedDocs/ormain.htm. Also, Property Appraiser records are available free online at www.manateepao.com. On the third county online system, real estate and vital records are available at no fee to view, but you are limited to 2 hours access. Lending agency information is available. Call Martha Pope at 941-741-4051 for information.

Marion County

County Clerk of the Circuit Court, P.O. Box 1030, Ocala, FL 34478-1030. 352-620-3925; www.marioncountyclerk.org

Will search UCC records. Tax liens not included in UCC search. RE owner, mortgage, and property transfer searches available. **Online Access:** Property Appraiser, Real Estate, Liens, Marriage Records. Records on the County Clerk of Court records database are available free online at www.marion countyclerk.org. Also, records on the Marion County Property Appraiser database are available online free at www.propappr.marion.fl.us. **Other Phone Numbers:** Appraiser/Auditor 352-368-8300.

Martin County

County Clerk of the Circuit Court, P.O. Box 9016, Stuart, FL 34995. County Clerk of the Circuit Court, R/E and UCC Recording 561-288-5554; Fax 561-223-7920. http://www.martin.fl.us/GOVT
Will search UCC records. Tax liens not included in UCC search. RE record owner and mortgage searches available. **Online Access:** Property Appraiser, Real Estate, Liens, Recordings. Online access to the clerk of the circuit court recordings database are available free online at http://clerk-web.martin.fl.us/wb_or1. Also, records on the county property appraiser database are available free online at http://paoweb.martin. fl.us/L1.php3?Page=searches. The county tax collector data files are available free online at www.martin.fl.us/GOVT/co/tax/search. **Other Phone Numbers:** Appraiser/Auditor 561-288-5608; Elections 561-288-5637.

Monroe County

County Clerk of the Circuit Court, P.O. Box 1980, Key West, FL 33041-1980. 305-292-3540; Fax 305-295-3623. http://www.co.monroe.fl.us
Will search UCC records. UCC search includes tax liens. RE owner, mortgage, and property transfer searches available. **Other Phone Numbers:** Treasurer 305-292-3550; Appraiser/Auditor 305-292-3378; Vital Records 305-292-3507.

Nassau County

County Clerk of the Circuit Court, P.O. Box 456, Fernandina, FL 32035. 904-321-5714; Fax 904-321-5723.
Will search UCC records. UCC search includes tax liens if requested. Will not search real estate records. **Other Phone Numbers:** Appraiser/Auditor 904-321-5573.

Official Records Department

County Comptroller, P.O. Box 38, Orlando, FL 32802-0038. County Comptroller, R/E and UCC Recording 407-836-5115; Fax 407-836-5120. http://www.occompt.com
Will search UCC records. UCC search includes tax liens. RE record owner and mortgage searches available. **Online Access:** Property Appraiser, Real Estate, Liens, Marriage Records. Real Estate, Lien, and Marriage records on the county Comptroller database are available free at www.occompt.com/records/or.htm. Lending Agency information is available. Also, property records on the Property Appraiser database are available free at www.ocpafl.org/docs/disclaimer.html. At this main site, click on "Record Searches." Also search Tangible Personal Property records & residential sales. **Other Phone Numbers:** Treasurer 407-836-5715; Appraiser/Auditor 407-836-5000; Elections 407-836-2070; Vital Records 407-623-1182.

Okaloosa County

County Clerk of the Circuit Court, P.O. Drawer 1359, Crestview, FL 32536. 850-689-5847; Fax 850-689-5886. http://www.clerkofcourts.cc/
Will search UCC records. Tax liens not included in UCC search. RE owner, mortgage, and property transfer searches available. **Online Access:** Property

Appraiser, Real Estate, Liens, Recordings, Vital Records. Several databases are available. Access to Okaloosa County online system requires a monthly usage fee of $100. No addresses listed. Lending agency information, traffic and domestic records are. For information, contact Don Howard at 850-689-5821. Online access to land records is available free at http://www.clerkofcourts.cc/orsearch/orframe.asp. Access to marriage records is available free at www.clerkofcourts.cc/marsearch/marriage.asp. Property Appraiser records are available free online at http://propertyappraiser.co.okaloosa.fl.us/property_search.asp. Search by owner name, address, date, district, year built and parcel ID number. **Other Phone Numbers:** Appraiser/Auditor 850-689-5900.

Okeechobee County

County Clerk of the Circuit Court, 304 N.W. 2nd Street, Room 101, Okeechobee, FL 34972. 863-763-2131 R/E Recording: 863-763-0239 UCC Recording: 863-763-0239.
Will search UCC records. This agency will not do a tax lien search. Will search real estate records. Fee is $1.00 per name per year. Will not accept telephone requests. **Other Phone Numbers:** Treasurer 863-763-3421; Appraiser/Auditor 863-763-4422; Elections 863-763-4014; Vital Records 863-462-5819.

Osceola County

County Clerk of the Circuit Court, 2 Courthouse Square, Suite 2000, 17 S. Vernon Ave., Kissimmee, FL 34741-5491. 407-343-3500 x3517 R/E Recording: 407-343-3517 UCC Recording: 407-343-3517; Fax 407-343-3534. http://www.osceolaclerk.com
Will search UCC records. UCC search includes tax liens if requested. RE owner, mortgage, and property transfer searches available. **Online Access:** Real Estate, Property Appraiser. Online access to the county Clerk of Circuit Court database features court records only at this time; see http://www.osceolaclerkcourt.org. Search by party name(s). While property appraiser records are soon to be available free online at www.property-appraiser.com/records.htm, you may currently purchase property data from the county information system database. For information, call 407-343-3700. Data is delivered in either 8mm data cartridges, CD-ROM, or 3.5" diskettes. Fees vary; tax roll data is available for $75.00. Also, land records may be available online at www.osceolaclerkrecording.org. **Other Phone Numbers:** Appraiser/Auditor 407-343-3700; Elections 407-343-3900.

Palm Beach County

County Clerk of the Circuit Court, P.O. Box 4177, West Palm Beach, FL 33402. County Clerk of the Circuit Court, R/E and UCC Recording 561-355-2991; Fax 561-355-2633. http://www.co.palm-beach.fl.us
Will search UCC records. Tax liens not included in UCC search. Search includes all RE records on general index. **Online Access:** Property Appraiser, Real Estate, Liens, Recording, Marriage. Online access to the clerk of cirucit court recording database are available free at www.pbcountyclerk.com/official_records/disclaimer.html. Records go back to 1968; includes marriage records 1979 to present. Name search marriage records online at www.pbcountyclerk.com/servlets/MainServlet?fn=MS. Also, records on the county Property Appraiser database are available free online at www.co.palm-beach.fl.us/papa. **Other Phone Numbers:** Appraiser/Auditor 561-355-2866; Elections 561-355-2650; Vital Records 561-653-2350.

Pasco County

County Clerk of the Circuit Court, 38053 Live Oak Ave., Room 205, Dade City, FL 33523-3894. 352-521-4469; http://pascogov.com

Will search UCC records. RE owner, mortgage, and property transfer searches available. **Online Access:** Property Appraiser, Real Estate, Liens, Marriage Records. Several options are available. Access to real estate, liens, marriage records requires $25 annual fee plus a $50 deposit. Billing rate is $.05 per minute, $.03 evenings. For information, call 352-521-4529. There is a fax back service. Lending agency information is available. Also, property records on the county Property Appraiser database are available free at http://appraiser.pascogov.com. Sales data and maps are also available. And, search tax records free at http://taxcollector.pascogov.com/search/prclsearch.asp. **Other Phone Numbers:** Appraiser/Auditor 352-521-4433.

Pinellas County

County Clerk of the Circuit Court, 315 Court Street, Room 150, Clearwater, FL 33756. 727-464-3204; Fax 727-464-4383. http://clerk.co.pinellas.fl.us/recsonl.htm
Will search UCC records. Tax liens not included in UCC search. RE owner, mortgage, and property transfer searches available. **Online Access:** Property Appraiser, Real estate, Liens, Judgments. Assessor/property records are available free online at www.pao.co.pinellas.fl.us/search2.html. Also, the county clerk of circuit court's recordings are available free online at http://clerk.co.pinellas.fl.us/ori.htm. **Other Phone Numbers:** Appraiser/Auditor 727-464-4814.

Polk County

County Clerk of the Circuit Court, P.O. Box 9000 Drawer CC-8, Bartow, FL 33831-9000. County Clerk of the Circuit Court, R/E and UCC Recording 863-534-4516; Fax 863-534-4008. www.polk-county.net
Will search UCC records. UCC search includes tax liens. Search includes all RE records on general index. **Online Access:** Property Appraiser, Real Estate, Liens, Marriage Records. On the internet, search the county clerk database at www.polk-county.net/clerk/clerk.html for court records, deeds, mortgages, plats, resolutions. For copies of documents, call 863-534-4524. Fee is $1.00 per page. Also, property records from the County Property Appraiser database are available at www.polkpa.org. **Other Phone Numbers:** Appraiser/Auditor 863-534-4700.

Putnam County

County Clerk of the Circuit Court, P.O. Box 758, Palatka, FL 32178-0758. 904-329-0256 R/E Recording: 386-329-0256 UCC Recording: 386-329-0256; Fax 904-329-0889. http://www.co.putnam.fl.us/clerkofcourt
Will search UCC records. RE owner, mortgage, and property transfer searches available. **Online Access:** Real Estate, Liens, Tax Assessor. Access to the county clerk database requires a $400 setup fee and monthly charge of $40 plus $.05 per minute over 20 hours. Includes civil court records and real property records back to 10/1983. For information, call 904-329-0353. **Other Phone Numbers:** Appraiser/Auditor 386-329-0286; Elections 386-329-0455; Vital Records 386-329-0420.

Santa Rosa County

County Clerk of the Circuit Court, P.O. Box 472, Milton, FL 32572. 850-623-0135; Fax 850-626-7248. http://www.srcpa.org
Will search UCC records. UCC search includes tax liens if requested. Will not search real estate records. **Online Access:** Property Appraiser. Property records are available free online. At the main Property Appraiser page, click on "Record Search.". **Other Phone Numbers:** Treasurer 850-623-0135; Appraiser/Auditor 850-623-0135.

Sarasota County

County Clerk of the Circuit Court, P.O. Box 3079, Sarasota, FL 34230. 941-951-5231; www.clerk.co.sarasota.fl.us
Will search UCC records. UCC search includes tax liens if requested. RE record owner and mortgage searches available. **Online Access:** Property Appraiser, Real Estate, Liens, Marriage. Online access to the Clerk of Circuit Court recordings database are available free at www.clerk.co.sarasota.fl.us/online.htm. Includes civil, criminal, and traffic court indexes. Marriage licenses may be searched free by groom/bride name, license number, date of application or ceremony. Probate records are also available. Also, records on the Property Appraiser database are available free online at http://204.193.117.141/scpa_recs.htm. Search by owner, parcel number, address, or instrument type; includes subdivision/condominium sales. **Other Phone Numbers:** Appraiser/Auditor 941-951-5650.

Seminole County

Clerk of the Circuit Court, P.O. Box 8099-Attn Recording Dept, Sanford, FL 32772-8099. 407-65-4336 R/E Recording: 407-665-4409 UCC Recording: 407-65-4409; http://www.seminoleclerk.org
Will search UCC records. This agency will not do a tax lien search. Will not search real estate records. **Online Access:** Property Appraiser, Real Estate, Liens, Recordings. Property appraisal records are available free online at http://ntweb.scpafl.org:8080/owa/owa/seminole_county_selection?. Also, online access to the county clerk of circuit court's recordings database is available free at www.seminoleclerk.org/officialrecords. **Other Phone Numbers:** Appraiser/Auditor 507-665-7502.

St. Johns County

County Clerk of the Circuit Court, P.O. Drawer 300, St. Augustine, FL 32085-0300. County Clerk of the Circuit Court, R/E and UCC Recording 904-823-2333 x330; Fax 904-823-2294. http://www.co.st-johns.fl.us
Will search UCC records. Tax liens included in UCC search if requested. RE record owner and property searches available. **Online Access:** Property Appraiser, Real Estate, Liens, Recordings, Civil. Online access to the county Clerk of Circuit Court recording database is available free at www.co.st-johns.fl.us/Const-Officers/Clerk-of-Court/doris/searchdocs.asp. Search by name, parcel ID, instrument type. Includes civil and probate records, UCCs. **Other Phone Numbers:** Appraiser/Auditor 904-823-2200; Elections 904-823-2238.

St. Lucie County

County Clerk of the Circuit Court, P.O. Box 700, Fort Pierce, FL 34954. 561-462-6928; Fax 561-462-1283. www.stlucieco.gov
Will search UCC records. This agency will not do a tax lien search. Will not search real estate records. **Online Access:** Property Appraiser. Property appriaser records are available free online at www.paslc.org. Click on the "real property database" or "interactive map.". **Other Phone Numbers:** Appraiser/Auditor 561-489-1600.

Sumter County

County Clerk of the Circuit Court, 209 North Florida Street, Room 106, Bushnell, FL 33513. 352-793-0215; Fax 352-793-0218.
Will search UCC records. UCC search includes tax liens if requested. RE record owner and mortgage searches available. **Other Phone Numbers:** Appraiser/Auditor 352-793-0210.

Suwannee County

County Clerk of the Circuit Court, 200 South Ohio Avenue, Live Oak, FL 32060. County Clerk of the Circuit Court, R/E and UCC Recording 386-362-0554; Fax 386-362-0548. http://www.suwanneeclerkofcourt.com
Will search UCC records. Tax liens not included in UCC search. Will not search real estate records. **Online Access:** Real Estate, Liens, Recordings, Property Tax. Online access of the county clerk of circuit database is available free at www.suwanneeclerkofcourt.com/court/kiosk.html. Also, search the tax collector database free at www.suwanneecountytax.com/collectmax/collect30.asp. **Other Phone Numbers:** Treasurer 386-364-3414; Appraiser/Auditor 386-362-1385; Elections 386-362-2616; Vital Records 386-362-0554.

Taylor County

County Clerk of the Circuit Court, P.O. Box 620, Perry, FL 32348. County Clerk of the Circuit Court, R/E and UCC Recording 850-838-3506; Fax 850-838-3549.
Will not search UCC records. This agency will not do a tax lien search. Will not search real estate records. **Other Phone Numbers:** Treasurer 850-838-3517; Appraiser/Auditor 850-838-3511; Elections 850-838-3515; Vital Records 850-838-3506.

Union County

County Clerk of the Circuit Court, State Road 100, Courthouse Room 103, Lake Butler, FL 32054. 386-496-3711; Fax 386-496-1718.

Will search UCC records. UCC search includes tax liens. RE owner, mortgage, and property transfer searches available. **Other Phone Numbers:** Treasurer 386-496-1026; Appraiser/Auditor 386-496-3431; Elections 386-496-2236.

Volusia County

County Clerk of the Circuit Court, P.O. Box 6043, De Land, FL 32721. 904-736-5912; Fax 904-740-5104. http://www.clerk.org
Will search UCC records. Tax liens not included in UCC search. RE record owner searches available. **Online Access:** Property Appraiser, Real Estate, Liens, Vital Records. Property records are available free online at www.clerk.org/publicrecords/or.tshtml. Records go back to 3/1996; will soon have documents back to 1990. Volusia County also offers Real Estate, Lien, and vital records on a commercial Internet site. The initial set up fee is $125, with a flat monthly fee of $25. For information, call 904-822-5710. **Other Phone Numbers:** Appraiser/Auditor 904-736-5902.

Wakulla County

County Clerk of the Circuit Court, Wakulla County Court House, 3056 Crawfordville Hwy, Crawfordville, FL 32327. 850-926-0905 R/E Recording: 850-926-0905 x226 UCC Recording: 850-926-0905 x226; Fax 850-926-0938.
Will search UCC records. Will not search real estate records. **Other Phone Numbers:** Treasurer 850-926-3371; Appraiser/Auditor 850-926-3271.

Walton County

County Clerk of the Circuit Court, P.O.Box 1260, De Funiak Springs, FL 32433. 850-892-8115; Fax 850-892-7551. http://www.co.walton.fl.us/clerk
Will search UCC records. UCC search includes tax liens if requested. RE owner, mortgage, and property transfer searches available. **Online Access:** Real Estate, Liens, Vital Records. Records on the County Clerk database are available free online at www.co.walton.fl.us. This has taken the place of the commercial system. **Other Phone Numbers:** Treasurer 850-892-8121; Appraiser/Auditor 850-892-8123.

Washington County

County Clerk of the Circuit Court, P.O. Box 647, Chipley, FL 32428. 850-638-6285; Fax 850-638-6297.
Will search UCC records. This agency will not do a tax lien search. Will not search real estate records. **Other Phone Numbers:** Treasurer 850-638-6205; Appraiser/Auditor 850-638-6205.

Florida County Locator

You will usually be able to find the city name in the City/County Cross Reference below. In that case, it is a simple matter to determine the county from the cross reference. However, only the official US Postal Service city names are included in this index. There are an additional 40,000 place names that people use in their addresses. Therefore, we have also included a ZIP/City Cross Reference immediately following the City/County Cross Reference.

If you know the ZIP Code but the city name does not appear in the City/County Cross Reference index, look up the ZIP Code in the ZIP/City Cross Reference, find the city name, then look up the city name in the City/County Cross Reference. For example, you want to know the county for an address of Menands, NY 12204. There is no "Menands" in the City/County Cross Reference. The ZIP/City Cross Reference shows that ZIP Codes 12201-12288 are for the city of Albany. Looking back in the City/County Cross Reference, Albany is in Albany County.

City/County Cross Reference

ABMPS Dade
ALACHUA Alachua
ALFORD Jackson
ALTAMONTE SPRINGS Seminole
ALTHA Calhoun
ALTOONA (32702) Lake(84), Marion(16)
ALTURAS Polk
ALVA (33920) Lee(87), Hendry(13)
ANNA MARIA Manatee
ANTHONY Marion
APALACHICOLA Franklin
APO
APOLLO BEACH Hillsborough
APOPKA (32703) Orange(82), Seminole(18)
APOPKA Orange
ARCADIA De Soto
ARCHER (32618) Alachua(74), Levy(26)
ARGYLE Walton
ARIPEKA Pasco
ASTATULA Lake
ASTOR (32102) Lake(85), Volusia(15)
ATLANTIC BEACH Duval
AUBURNDALE Polk
AVON PARK Highlands
BABSON PARK Polk
BAGDAD Santa Rosa
BAKER Okaloosa
BALM Hillsborough
BARBERVILLE Volusia
BARTOW Polk
BASCOM Jackson
BAY PINES Pinellas
BELL Gilchrist
BELLE GLADE Palm Beach
BELLEAIR BEACH Pinellas
BELLEAIR SHORES Pinellas
BELLEVIEW Marion
BEVERLY HILLS Citrus
BIG PINE KEY Monroe
BLOUNTSTOWN Calhoun
BOCA GRANDE Lee
BOCA RATON Palm Beach
BOKEELIA Lee
BONIFAY (32425) Holmes(93), Washington(7)
BONITA SPRINGS (34134) Lee(89), Collier(11)
BONITA SPRINGS Lee
BOSTWICK Putnam
BOWLING GREEN (33834) Hardee(98), Polk(1)
BOYNTON BEACH Palm Beach
BRADENTON Manatee
BRADENTON BEACH Manatee
BRADLEY Polk
BRANDON Hillsborough
BRANFORD (32008) Suwannee(56), Gilchrist(36), Lafayette(7), Dixie(1)
BRISTOL (32321) Liberty(99), Gadsden(1)
BRONSON Levy
BROOKER (32622) Bradford(97), Alachua(3)

BROOKSVILLE Hernando
BROOKSVILLE Pasco
BRYANT Palm Beach
BRYCEVILLE (32009) Nassau(92), Duval(8)
BUNNELL Flagler
BUSHNELL Sumter
CALLAHAN Nassau
CAMPBELLTON Jackson
CANAL POINT (33438) Palm Beach(56), Martin(44)
CANAL POINT Palm Beach
CANDLER Marion
CANTONMENT Escambia
CAPE CANAVERAL Brevard
CAPE CORAL Lee
CAPTIVA Lee
CARRABELLE Franklin
CARYVILLE (32427) Washington(58), Holmes(42)
CASSADAGA (32706) Volusia(90), Osceola(10)
CASSELBERRY Seminole
CEDAR KEY Levy
CENTER HILL Sumter
CENTURY Escambia
CHATTAHOOCHEE Gadsden
CHIEFLAND Levy
CHIPLEY Washington
CHOKOLOSKEE Collier
CHRISTMAS Orange
CITRA Marion
CLARCONA Orange
CLARKSVILLE Calhoun
CLEARWATER Pinellas
CLERMONT Lake
CLEWISTON (33440) Hendry(98), Palm Beach(3)
COCOA Brevard
COCOA BEACH Brevard
COLEMAN Sumter
COPELAND Collier
CORTEZ Manatee
COTTONDALE (32431) Jackson(79), Washington(21)
CRAWFORDVILLE Wakulla
CRESCENT CITY Putnam
CRESTVIEW (32539) Okaloosa(93), Walton(8)
CRESTVIEW Okaloosa
CROSS CITY Dixie
CRYSTAL BEACH Pinellas
CRYSTAL RIVER Citrus
CRYSTAL SPRINGS Pasco
CYPRESS Jackson
DADE CITY (33523) Pasco(83), Hernando(17)
DADE CITY Pasco
DANIA Broward
DAVENPORT (33837) Polk(94), Osceola(6)
DAVENPORT Polk
DAY Lafayette
DAYTONA BEACH Volusia

DE LEON SPRINGS Volusia
DEBARY Volusia
DEERFIELD BEACH Broward
DEFUNIAK SPRINGS Walton
DELAND (32720) Volusia(85), Lake(15)
DELAND Volusia
DELRAY BEACH Palm Beach
DELTONA Volusia
DESTIN (32541) Okaloosa(61), Walton(39)
DESTIN Okaloosa
DOCTORS INLET Clay
DOVER Hillsborough
DUNDEE Polk
DUNEDIN Pinellas
DUNNELLON (34431) Marion(83), Levy(17)
DUNNELLON Citrus
DUNNELLON Marion
DURANT Hillsborough
EAGLE LAKE Polk
EARLETON Alachua
EAST PALATKA Putnam
EASTLAKE WEIR Marion
EASTPOINT Franklin
EATON PARK Polk
EBRO (32437) Washington(83), Bay(17)
EDGEWATER Volusia
EGLIN AFB Okaloosa
ELFERS Pasco
ELKTON St. Johns
ELLENTON Manatee
ENGLEWOOD (34223) Sarasota(73), Charlotte(27)
ENGLEWOOD Charlotte
ENGLEWOOD Sarasota
ESTERO Lee
EUSTIS Lake
EVERGLADES CITY Collier
EVINSTON Alachua
FAIRFIELD Marion
FEDHAVEN Polk
FELDA Hendry
FELLSMERE Indian River
FERNANDINA BEACH Nassau
FERNDALE Lake
FLAGLER BEACH Flagler
FLORAHOME Putnam
FLORAL CITY Citrus
FORT LAUDERDALE Broward
FORT MC COY (32134) Marion(99), Putnam(1)
FORT MEADE Polk
FORT MYERS (33917) Lee(99), Charlotte(1)
FORT MYERS Lee
FORT MYERS BEACH Lee
FORT OGDEN De Soto
FORT PIERCE St. Lucie
FORT WALTON BEACH Okaloosa
FORT WHITE Columbia
FOUNTAIN (32438) Bay(98), Calhoun(1)
FPO
FREEPORT Walton

FROSTPROOF Polk
FRUITLAND PARK Lake
GAINESVILLE Alachua
GENEVA Seminole
GEORGETOWN Putnam
GIBSONTON Hillsborough
GLEN SAINT MARY Baker
GLENWOOD Volusia
GOLDENROD Seminole
GONZALEZ Escambia
GOODLAND Collier
GOTHA Orange
GRACEVILLE (32440) Jackson(89), Holmes(11)
GRAHAM Bradford
GRAND ISLAND Lake
GRAND RIDGE Jackson
GRANDIN Putnam
GRANT Brevard
GREEN COVE SPRINGS (32043) Clay(99), Putnam(1)
GREENSBORO Gadsden
GREENVILLE (32331) Madison(54), Jefferson(37), Taylor(9)
GREENWOOD Jackson
GRETNA Gadsden
GROVELAND Lake
GULF BREEZE (32561) Santa Rosa(83), Escambia(17)
GULF BREEZE Santa Rosa
GULF HAMMOCK Levy
HAINES CITY Polk
HALLANDALE Broward
HAMPTON Bradford
HAROLD Santa Rosa
HASTINGS St. Johns
HAVANA Gadsden
HAWTHORNE (32640) Alachua(68), Putnam(32)
HERNANDO Citrus
HIALEAH Dade
HIGH SPRINGS (32643) Alachua(49), Gilchrist(48), Columbia(3)
HIGH SPRINGS Alachua
HIGHLAND CITY Polk
HILLIARD Nassau
HOBE SOUND Martin
HOLDER Citrus
HOLIDAY Pasco
HOLLISTER Putnam
HOLLYWOOD Broward
HOLMES BEACH Manatee
HOLT (32564) Santa Rosa(90), Okaloosa(10)
HOMELAND Polk
HOMESTEAD Dade
HOMOSASSA Citrus
HOMOSASSA SPRINGS Citrus
HORSESHOE BEACH Dixie
HOSFORD Liberty
HOWEY IN THE HILLS Lake
HUDSON Pasco
HURLBURT FIELD Okaloosa

IMMOKALEE (34142) Collier(99), Hendry(1)
IMMOKALEE Collier
INDIALANTIC Brevard
INDIAN LAKE ESTATES Polk
INDIAN ROCKS BEACH Pinellas
INDIANTOWN Martin
INGLIS (34449) Levy(89), Citrus(11)
INTERCESSION CITY Osceola
INTERLACHEN Putnam
INVERNESS Citrus
ISLAMORADA Monroe
ISLAND GROVE Alachua
ISTACHATTA Hernando
JACKSONVILLE (32234) Duval(77), Clay(22), Nassau(1)
JACKSONVILLE Duval
JACKSONVILLE St. Johns
JACKSONVILLE BEACH Duval
JASPER Hamilton
JAY Santa Rosa
JENNINGS Hamilton
JENSEN BEACH (34957) Martin(82), St. Lucie(18)
JENSEN BEACH Martin
JUPITER (33458) Palm Beach(96), Martin(4)
JUPITER (33469) Palm Beach(65), Martin(35)
JUPITER (33478) Palm Beach(92), Martin(8)
JUPITER Palm Beach
KATHLEEN Polk
KENANSVILLE Osceola
KEY BISCAYNE Dade
KEY COLONY BEACH Monroe
KEY LARGO Monroe
KEY WEST Monroe
KEYSTONE HEIGHTS (32656) Clay(84), Bradford(16)
KILLARNEY Orange
KINARD Calhoun
KISSIMMEE (34747) Osceola(98), Orange(2)
KISSIMMEE (34759) Polk(64), Osceola(36)
KISSIMMEE Osceola
LA CROSSE Alachua
LABELLE (33935) Hendry(98), Glades(2)
LABELLE Hendry
LACOOCHEE Pasco
LADY LAKE (32159) Lake(77), Sumter(23)
LADY LAKE Lake
LAKE ALFRED Polk
LAKE BUTLER (32054) Union(89), Bradford(11)
LAKE CITY (32024) Columbia(76), Suwannee(24)
LAKE CITY Columbia
LAKE COMO Putnam
LAKE GENEVA Clay
LAKE HAMILTON Polk
LAKE HARBOR Palm Beach
LAKE HELEN Volusia
LAKE MARY Seminole
LAKE MONROE Seminole
LAKE PANASOFFKEE Sumter
LAKE PLACID Highlands
LAKE WALES Polk
LAKE WORTH Palm Beach
LAKELAND Polk
LAMONT Jefferson
LANARK VILLAGE Franklin
LAND O LAKES Pasco
LARGO Pinellas
LAUREL Sarasota
LAUREL HILL (32567) Walton(69), Okaloosa(32)
LAWTEY Bradford
LECANTO (34461) Citrus(98), Levy(2)
LECANTO Citrus
LEE Madison
LEESBURG Lake

LEHIGH ACRES Lee
LITHIA (33547) Hillsborough(98), Polk(2)
LIVE OAK Suwannee
LLOYD Jefferson
LOCHLOOSA Alachua
LONG KEY Monroe
LONGBOAT KEY (34228) Sarasota(58), Manatee(42)
LONGWOOD Seminole
LORIDA Highlands
LOUGHMAN Polk
LOWELL Marion
LOXAHATCHEE Palm Beach
LULU Columbia
LUTZ (33549) Hillsborough(73), Pasco(27)
LUTZ Hillsborough
LYNN HAVEN Bay
MACCLENNY Baker
MADISON Madison
MAITLAND (32751) Orange(79), Seminole(21)
MAITLAND Orange
MALABAR Brevard
MALONE Jackson
MANASOTA Manatee
MANGO Hillsborough
MARATHON Monroe
MARATHON SHORES Monroe
MARCO ISLAND Collier
MARIANNA Jackson
MARY ESTHER Okaloosa
MASCOTTE Lake
MAYO Lafayette
MC ALPIN Suwannee
MC DAVID Escambia
MC INTOSH Marion
MELBOURNE Brevard
MELBOURNE BEACH Brevard
MELROSE (32666) Putnam(52), Alachua(20), Bradford(18), Clay(11)
MERRITT ISLAND Brevard
MEXICO BEACH Bay
MIAMI Dade
MICANOPY (32667) Marion(73), Alachua(27)
MICCOSUKEE CPO Leon
MID FLORIDA Seminole
MIDDLEBURG (32068) Clay(88), St. Johns(12)
MIDDLEBURG Clay
MIDWAY Gadsden
MILLIGAN Okaloosa
MILTON Santa Rosa
MIMS (32754) Brevard(92), Volusia(8)
MINNEOLA Lake
MOLINO Escambia
MONTICELLO Jefferson
MONTVERDE Lake
MOORE HAVEN Glades
MORRISTON (32668) Levy(78), Marion(22)
MOSSY HEAD Walton
MOUNT DORA (32757) Lake(94), Orange(6)
MOUNT DORA Lake
MOUNT DORA Orange
MOUNT PLEASANT Gadsden
MULBERRY Polk
MURDOCK Charlotte
MYAKKA CITY Manatee
NALCREST Polk
NAPLES (34119) Collier(98), Lee(2)
NAPLES Collier
NEPTUNE BEACH Duval
NEW PORT RICHEY Pasco
NEW SMYRNA BEACH Volusia
NEWBERRY (32669) Alachua(71), Gilchrist(25), Levy(4)
NICEVILLE (32578) Okaloosa(91), Walton(9)
NICEVILLE Okaloosa
NICHOLS Polk
NOBLETON Hernando

NOCATEE De Soto
NOKOMIS Sarasota
NOMA Holmes
NORTH PALM BEACH Palm Beach
NORTH PORT Sarasota
O BRIEN Suwannee
OAK HILL Volusia
OAKLAND Orange
OCALA Marion
OCHOPEE (33943) Collier(69), Dade(24), Monroe(7)
OCHOPEE (34141) Collier(69), Dade(24), Monroe(7)
OCKLAWAHA Marion
OCOEE Orange
ODESSA (33556) Hillsborough(79), Pasco(21)
OKAHUMPKA Lake
OKEECHOBEE (34972) Okeechobee(98), Osceola(2)
OKEECHOBEE (34974) Okeechobee(90), Glades(4), Martin(3), Highlands(3)
OKEECHOBEE Okeechobee
OLD TOWN (32680) Dixie(85), Gilchrist(15)
OLDSMAR Pinellas
OLUSTEE Baker
ONA Hardee
ONECO Manatee
OPA LOCKA Dade
ORANGE CITY Volusia
ORANGE LAKE Marion
ORANGE PARK (32073) Clay(96), Duval(4)
ORANGE PARK Clay
ORANGE SPRINGS Marion
ORLANDO Brevard
ORLANDO Orange
ORMOND BEACH (32174) Volusia(98), Flagler(2)
ORMOND BEACH Volusia
OSPREY Sarasota
OSTEEN Volusia
OTTER CREEK Levy
OVERSTREET Gulf
OVIEDO Seminole
OXFORD (34484) Sumter(98), Marion(2)
OZONA Pinellas
PAHOKEE Palm Beach
PAISLEY Lake
PALATKA Putnam
PALM BAY Brevard
PALM BEACH Palm Beach
PALM CITY (34990) Martin(95), St. Lucie(5)
PALM CITY Martin
PALM COAST Flagler
PALM HARBOR Pinellas
PALMDALE Glades
PALMETTO Manatee
PANACEA (32346) Wakulla(93), Franklin(7)
PANAMA CITY (32413) Bay(91), Walton(9)
PANAMA CITY Bay
PANAMA CITY BEACH Bay
PARRISH Manatee
PATRICK A F B Brevard
PAXTON Walton
PENNEY FARMS Clay
PENSACOLA Escambia
PERRY Taylor
PIERSON Volusia
PINELAND Lee
PINELLAS PARK Pinellas
PINETTA Madison
PLACIDA Charlotte
PLANT CITY Hillsborough
PLYMOUTH Orange
POINT WASHINGTON Walton
POLK CITY Polk
POMONA PARK Putnam
POMPANO BEACH Broward

PONCE DE LEON (32455) Holmes(87), Walton(13)
PONTE VEDRA BEACH St. Johns
PORT CHARLOTTE Charlotte
PORT ORANGE Volusia
PORT RICHEY Pasco
PORT SAINT JOE Gulf
PORT SAINT LUCIE St. Lucie
PORT SALERNO Martin
PUNTA GORDA Charlotte
PUTNAM HALL Putnam
QUINCY Gadsden
RAIFORD (32083) Union(81), Bradford(19)
REDDICK Marion
RIVER RANCH Polk
RIVERVIEW Hillsborough
ROCKLEDGE Brevard
ROSELAND Indian River
ROTONDA WEST Charlotte
RUSKIN Hillsborough
SAFETY HARBOR Pinellas
SAINT AUGUSTINE St. Johns
SAINT CLOUD Osceola
SAINT JAMES CITY Lee
SAINT LEO Pasco
SAINT MARKS Wakulla
SAINT PETERSBURG Pinellas
SALEM (32356) Taylor(86), Dixie(7), Wakulla(7)
SAN ANTONIO Pasco
SAN MATEO Putnam
SANDERSON Baker
SANFORD Seminole
SANIBEL Lee
SANTA ROSA BEACH Walton
SARASOTA (34243) Manatee(84), Sarasota(16)
SARASOTA Sarasota
SATELLITE BEACH Brevard
SATSUMA Putnam
SCOTTSMOOR Brevard
SEBASTIAN Brevard
SEBASTIAN Indian River
SEBRING Highlands
SEFFNER Hillsborough
SEMINOLE Pinellas
SEVILLE (32190) Volusia(98), Putnam(2)
SHADY GROVE Taylor
SHALIMAR Okaloosa
SHARPES Brevard
SILVER SPRINGS Marion
SNEADS Jackson
SOPCHOPPY Wakulla
SORRENTO Lake
SOUTH BAY Palm Beach
SOUTH FLORIDA Broward
SPARR Marion
SPRING HILL Hernando
STARKE (32091) Bradford(83), Clay(17)
STEINHATCHEE (32359) Taylor(54), Dixie(46)
STUART (34994) Martin(99), St. Lucie(1)
STUART Martin
SUGARLOAF SHORES Monroe
SUMATRA Liberty
SUMMERFIELD Marion
SUMMERLAND KEY Monroe
SUMTERVILLE Sumter
SUN CITY Hillsborough
SUN CITY CENTER Hillsborough
SUNNYSIDE Bay
SUWANNEE Dixie
SYDNEY Hillsborough
TALLAHASSEE Leon
TALLEVAST Manatee
TAMPA Hillsborough
TANGERINE Orange
TARPON SPRINGS Pinellas
TAVARES Lake
TAVERNIER Monroe
TELOGIA (32360) Liberty(80), Citrus(20)
TERRA CEIA Manatee

THONOTOSASSA Hillsborough
TITUSVILLE Brevard
TRENTON (32693) Gilchrist(72), Levy(28)
TRILBY Pasco
UMATILLA (32784) Lake(68), Marion(32)
VALPARAISO Okaloosa
VALRICO Hillsborough
VENICE Sarasota
VENUS (33960) Highlands(88), Glades(12)
VERNON (32462) Washington(69), Walton(19), Bay(12)
VERO BEACH Indian River
WABASSO Indian River
WACISSA Jefferson

WAKULLA SPRINGS Wakulla
WALDO Alachua
WAUCHULA Hardee
WAUSAU Washington
WAVERLY Polk
WEBSTER (33597) Sumter(86), Hernando(13)
WEIRSDALE (32195) Marion(82), Lake(18)
WELAKA Putnam
WELLBORN Suwannee
WEST PALM BEACH Palm Beach
WESTON Broward
WESTVILLE (32464) Holmes(99), Walton(1)

WEWAHITCHKA Gulf
WHITE SPRINGS (32096) Hamilton(83), Suwannee(12), Columbia(5)
WILDWOOD Sumter
WILLISTON (32696) Levy(91), Marion(9)
WIMAUMA Hillsborough
WINDERMERE Orange
WINTER BEACH Indian River
WINTER GARDEN (34787) Orange(97), Lake(3)
WINTER GARDEN Orange
WINTER HAVEN Polk
WINTER PARK (32792) Orange(68), Seminole(32)

WINTER PARK Orange
WINTER SPRINGS Seminole
WOODVILLE Leon
WORTHINGTON SPRINGS Union
YALAHA Lake
YANKEETOWN Levy
YOUNGSTOWN (32466) Bay(97), Washington(3)
YULEE Nassau
ZELLWOOD Orange
ZEPHYRHILLS Pasco
ZOLFO SPRINGS Hardee

ZIP/City Cross Reference

ZIP	City	ZIP	City	ZIP	City	ZIP	City
32004-32004	PONTE VEDRA BEACH	32138-32138	GRANDIN	32350-32350	PINETTA	32539-32539	CRESTVIEW
32007-32007	BOSTWICK	32139-32139	GEORGETOWN	32351-32351	QUINCY	32540-32541	DESTIN
32008-32008	BRANFORD	32140-32140	FLORAHOME	32352-32352	MOUNT PLEASANT	32542-32542	EGLIN AFB
32009-32009	BRYCEVILLE	32141-32141	EDGEWATER	32353-32353	QUINCY	32544-32544	HURLBURT FIELD
32011-32011	CALLAHAN	32142-32142	PALM COAST	32355-32355	SAINT MARKS	32547-32549	FORT WALTON BEACH
32013-32013	DAY	32145-32145	HASTINGS	32356-32356	SALEM	32559-32559	PENSACOLA
32024-32025	LAKE CITY	32147-32147	HOLLISTER	32357-32357	SHADY GROVE	32560-32560	GONZALEZ
32030-32030	DOCTORS INLET	32148-32149	INTERLACHEN	32358-32358	SOPCHOPPY	32561-32562	GULF BREEZE
32033-32033	ELKTON	32151-32151	FLAGLER BEACH	32359-32359	STEINHATCHEE	32563-32563	HAROLD
32034-32035	FERNANDINA BEACH	32157-32157	LAKE COMO	32360-32360	TELOGIA	32564-32564	HOLT
32038-32038	FORT WHITE	32158-32159	LADY LAKE	32361-32361	WACISSA	32565-32565	JAY
32040-32040	GLEN SAINT MARY	32160-32160	LAKE GENEVA	32362-32362	WOODVILLE	32566-32566	GULF BREEZE
32041-32041	YULEE	32164-32164	PALM COAST	32395-32399	TALLAHASSEE	32567-32567	LAUREL HILL
32042-32042	GRAHAM	32168-32170	NEW SMYRNA BEACH	32401-32406	PANAMA CITY	32568-32568	MC DAVID
32043-32043	GREEN COVE SPRINGS	32173-32176	ORMOND BEACH	32407-32407	PANAMA CITY BEACH	32569-32569	MARY ESTHER
32044-32044	HAMPTON	32177-32178	PALATKA	32408-32409	PANAMA CITY	32570-32572	MILTON
32046-32046	HILLIARD	32179-32179	OCKLAWAHA	32410-32410	MEXICO BEACH	32573-32576	PENSACOLA
32050-32050	MIDDLEBURG	32180-32180	PIERSON	32411-32417	PANAMA CITY	32577-32577	MOLINO
32052-32052	JASPER	32181-32181	POMONA PARK	32420-32420	ALFORD	32578-32578	NICEVILLE
32053-32053	JENNINGS	32182-32182	ORANGE SPRINGS	32421-32421	ALTHA	32579-32579	SHALIMAR
32054-32054	LAKE BUTLER	32183-32183	OCKLAWAHA	32422-32422	ARGYLE	32580-32580	VALPARAISO
32055-32056	LAKE CITY	32185-32185	PUTNAM HALL	32423-32423	BASCOM	32581-32582	PENSACOLA
32058-32058	LAWTEY	32187-32187	SAN MATEO	32424-32424	BLOUNTSTOWN	32583-32583	MILTON
32059-32059	LEE	32189-32189	SATSUMA	32425-32425	BONIFAY	32588-32588	NICEVILLE
32060-32060	LIVE OAK	32190-32190	SEVILLE	32426-32426	CAMPBELLTON	32589-32598	PENSACOLA
32061-32061	LULU	32192-32192	SPARR	32427-32427	CARYVILLE	32601-32614	GAINESVILLE
32062-32062	MC ALPIN	32193-32193	WELAKA	32428-32428	CHIPLEY	32615-32616	ALACHUA
32063-32063	MACCLENNY	32195-32195	WEIRSDALE	32430-32430	CLARKSVILLE	32617-32617	ANTHONY
32064-32064	LIVE OAK	32198-32198	DAYTONA BEACH	32431-32431	COTTONDALE	32618-32618	ARCHER
32065-32065	ORANGE PARK	32201-32232	JACKSONVILLE	32432-32432	CYPRESS	32619-32619	BELL
32066-32066	MAYO	32233-32233	ATLANTIC BEACH	32433-32433	DEFUNIAK SPRINGS	32621-32621	BRONSON
32067-32067	ORANGE PARK	32234-32239	JACKSONVILLE	32434-32434	MOSSY HEAD	32622-32622	BROOKER
32068-32068	MIDDLEBURG	32240-32240	JACKSONVILLE BEACH	32435-32435	DEFUNIAK SPRINGS	32625-32625	CEDAR KEY
32071-32071	O BRIEN	32241-32247	JACKSONVILLE	32437-32437	EBRO	32626-32626	CHIEFLAND
32072-32072	OLUSTEE	32250-32250	JACKSONVILLE BEACH	32438-32438	FOUNTAIN	32627-32627	GAINESVILLE
32073-32073	ORANGE PARK	32254-32260	JACKSONVILLE	32439-32439	FREEPORT	32628-32628	CROSS CITY
32079-32079	PENNEY FARMS	32266-32266	NEPTUNE BEACH	32440-32440	GRACEVILLE	32631-32631	EARLETON
32082-32082	PONTE VEDRA BEACH	32267-32297	JACKSONVILLE	32442-32442	GRAND RIDGE	32633-32633	EVINSTON
32083-32083	RAIFORD	32301-32304	TALLAHASSEE	32443-32443	GREENWOOD	32634-32634	FAIRFIELD
32084-32086	SAINT AUGUSTINE	32305-32305	WAKULLA SPRINGS	32444-32444	LYNN HAVEN	32639-32639	GULF HAMMOCK
32087-32087	SANDERSON	32306-32308	TALLAHASSEE	32445-32445	MALONE	32640-32640	HAWTHORNE
32091-32091	STARKE	32309-32309	MICCOSUKEE CPO	32446-32448	MARIANNA	32641-32641	GAINESVILLE
32092-32092	SAINT AUGUSTINE	32310-32317	TALLAHASSEE	32449-32449	KINARD	32643-32643	HIGH SPRINGS
32094-32094	WELLBORN	32320-32320	APALACHICOLA	32452-32452	NOMA	32644-32644	CHIEFLAND
32095-32095	SAINT AUGUSTINE	32321-32321	BRISTOL	32454-32454	POINT WASHINGTON	32648-32648	HORSESHOE BEACH
32096-32096	WHITE SPRINGS	32322-32322	CARRABELLE	32455-32455	PONCE DE LEON	32653-32653	GAINESVILLE
32097-32097	YULEE	32323-32323	LANARK VILLAGE	32456-32457	PORT SAINT JOE	32654-32654	ISLAND GROVE
32099-32099	JACKSONVILLE	32324-32324	CHATTAHOOCHEE	32459-32459	SANTA ROSA BEACH	32655-32655	HIGH SPRINGS
32102-32102	ASTOR	32326-32327	CRAWFORDVILLE	32460-32460	SNEADS	32656-32656	KEYSTONE HEIGHTS
32105-32105	BARBERVILLE	32328-32328	EASTPOINT	32461-32461	SUNNYSIDE	32658-32658	LA CROSSE
32110-32110	BUNNELL	32329-32329	APALACHICOLA	32462-32462	VERNON	32662-32662	LOCHLOOSA
32111-32111	CANDLER	32330-32330	GREENSBORO	32463-32463	WAUSAU	32663-32663	LOWELL
32112-32112	CRESCENT CITY	32331-32331	GREENVILLE	32464-32464	WESTVILLE	32664-32664	MC INTOSH
32113-32113	CITRA	32332-32332	GRETNA	32465-32465	WEWAHITCHKA	32666-32666	MELROSE
32114-32127	DAYTONA BEACH	32333-32333	HAVANA	32466-32466	YOUNGSTOWN	32667-32667	MICANOPY
32129-32129	PORT ORANGE	32334-32334	HOSFORD	32501-32526	PENSACOLA	32668-32668	MORRISTON
32130-32130	DE LEON SPRINGS	32335-32335	SUMATRA	32530-32530	BAGDAD	32669-32669	NEWBERRY
32131-32131	EAST PALATKA	32336-32336	LAMONT	32531-32531	BAKER	32680-32680	OLD TOWN
32132-32132	EDGEWATER	32337-32337	LLOYD	32533-32533	CANTONMENT	32681-32681	ORANGE LAKE
32133-32133	EASTLAKE WEIR	32340-32341	MADISON	32534-32534	PENSACOLA	32683-32683	OTTER CREEK
32134-32134	FORT MC COY	32343-32343	MIDWAY	32535-32535	CENTURY	32686-32686	REDDICK
32135-32135	PALM COAST	32344-32345	MONTICELLO	32536-32536	CRESTVIEW	32692-32692	SUWANNEE
32136-32136	FLAGLER BEACH	32346-32346	PANACEA	32537-32537	MILLIGAN	32693-32693	TRENTON
32137-32137	PALM COAST	32347-32348	PERRY	32538-32538	PAXTON	32694-32694	WALDO

ZIP Range	City	ZIP Range	City	ZIP Range	City	ZIP Range	City
32696-32696	WILLISTON	32959-32959	SHARPES	33539-33544	ZEPHYRHILLS	33916-33919	FORT MYERS
32697-32697	WORTHINGTON	32960-32969	VERO BEACH	33547-33547	LITHIA	33920-33920	ALVA
	SPRINGS	32970-32970	WABASSO	33548-33549	LUTZ	33921-33921	BOCA GRANDE
32701-32701	ALTAMONTE SPRINGS	32971-32971	WINTER BEACH	33550-33550	MANGO	33922-33922	BOKEELIA
32702-32702	ALTOONA	32976-32978	SEBASTIAN	33556-33556	ODESSA	33924-33924	CAPTIVA
32703-32704	APOPKA	33001-33001	LONG KEY	33564-33567	PLANT CITY	33926-33926	COPELAND
32706-32706	CASSADAGA	33002-33002	HIALEAH	33568-33569	RIVERVIEW	33927-33927	PUNTA GORDA
32707-32707	CASSELBERRY	33004-33004	DANIA	33570-33570	RUSKIN	33928-33928	ESTERO
32708-32708	WINTER SPRINGS	33008-33009	HALLANDALE	33571-33571	SUN CITY CENTER	33930-33930	FELDA
32709-32709	CHRISTMAS	33010-33018	HIALEAH	33572-33572	APOLLO BEACH	33931-33932	FORT MYERS BEACH
32710-32710	CLARCONA	33019-33029	HOLLYWOOD	33573-33573	SUN CITY CENTER	33935-33935	LABELLE
32712-32712	APOPKA	33030-33035	HOMESTEAD	33574-33574	SAINT LEO	33936-33936	LEHIGH ACRES
32713-32713	DEBARY	33036-33036	ISLAMORADA	33576-33576	SAN ANTONIO	33938-33938	MURDOCK
32714-32717	ALTAMONTE SPRINGS	33037-33037	KEY LARGO	33583-33584	SEFFNER	33944-33944	PALMDALE
32718-32718	CASSELBERRY	33039-33039	HOMESTEAD	33585-33585	SUMTERVILLE	33945-33945	PINELAND
32719-32719	WINTER SPRINGS	33040-33041	KEY WEST	33586-33586	SUN CITY	33946-33946	PLACIDA
32720-32721	DELAND	33042-33042	SUMMERLAND KEY	33587-33587	SYDNEY	33947-33947	ROTONDA WEST
32722-32722	GLENWOOD	33043-33043	BIG PINE KEY	33592-33592	THONOTOSASSA	33948-33949	PORT CHARLOTTE
32723-32724	DELAND	33044-33044	SUGARLOAF SHORES	33593-33593	TRILBY	33950-33951	PUNTA GORDA
32725-32725	DELTONA	33045-33045	KEY WEST	33594-33595	VALRICO	33952-33954	PORT CHARLOTTE
32726-32727	EUSTIS	33050-33050	MARATHON	33597-33597	WEBSTER	33955-33955	PUNTA GORDA
32728-32728	DELTONA	33051-33051	KEY COLONY BEACH	33598-33598	WIMAUMA	33956-33956	SAINT JAMES CITY
32730-32730	CASSELBERRY	33052-33052	MARATHON SHORES	33601-33697	TAMPA	33957-33957	SANIBEL
32732-32732	GENEVA	33054-33056	OPA LOCKA	33701-33743	SAINT PETERSBURG	33959-33959	BONITA SPRINGS
32733-32733	GOLDENROD	33060-33069	POMPANO BEACH	33744-33744	BAY PINES	33960-33960	VENUS
32735-32735	GRAND ISLAND	33070-33070	TAVERNIER	33747-33747	SAINT PETERSBURG	33965-33965	FORT MYERS
32736-32736	EUSTIS	33071-33077	POMPANO BEACH	33755-33767	CLEARWATER	33970-33972	LEHIGH ACRES
32738-32739	DELTONA	33081-33081	HOLLYWOOD	33770-33771	LARGO	33975-33975	LABELLE
32744-32744	LAKE HELEN	33082-33082	SOUTH FLORIDA	33772-33772	SEMINOLE	33980-33981	PORT CHARLOTTE
32746-32746	LAKE MARY	33083-33084	HOLLYWOOD	33773-33774	LARGO	33982-33983	PUNTA GORDA
32747-32747	LAKE MONROE	33090-33092	HOMESTEAD	33775-33776	SEMINOLE	33990-33993	CAPE CORAL
32750-32750	LONGWOOD	33093-33097	POMPANO BEACH	33777-33779	LARGO	33994-33994	FORT MYERS
32751-32751	MAITLAND	33101-33148	MIAMI	33780-33782	PINELLAS PARK	34101-34120	NAPLES
32752-32752	LONGWOOD	33149-33149	KEY BISCAYNE	33784-33784	SAINT PETERSBURG	34133-34136	BONITA SPRINGS
32754-32754	MIMS	33150-33299	MIAMI	33785-33785	INDIAN ROCKS BEACH	34137-34137	COPELAND
32756-32757	MOUNT DORA	33301-33326	FORT LAUDERDALE	33786-33786	BELLEAIR BEACH	34138-34138	CHOKOLOSKEE
32759-32759	OAK HILL	33327-33327	WESTON	33801-33815	LAKELAND	34139-34139	EVERGLADES CITY
32762-32762	OVIEDO	33328-33394	FORT LAUDERDALE	33820-33820	ALTURAS	34140-34140	GOODLAND
32763-32763	ORANGE CITY	33401-33407	WEST PALM BEACH	33823-33823	AUBURNDALE	34141-34141	OCHOPEE
32764-32764	OSTEEN	33408-33408	NORTH PALM BEACH	33825-33826	AVON PARK	34142-34143	IMMOKALEE
32765-32766	OVIEDO	33409-33422	WEST PALM BEACH	33827-33827	BABSON PARK	34145-34146	MARCO ISLAND
32767-32767	PAISLEY	33424-33426	BOYNTON BEACH	33830-33831	BARTOW	34201-34210	BRADENTON
32768-32768	PLYMOUTH	33427-33429	BOCA RATON	33834-33834	BOWLING GREEN	34215-34215	CORTEZ
32771-32773	SANFORD	33430-33430	BELLE GLADE	33835-33835	BRADLEY	34216-34216	ANNA MARIA
32774-32774	ORANGE CITY	33431-33434	BOCA RATON	33836-33837	DAVENPORT	34217-34217	BRADENTON BEACH
32775-32775	SCOTTSMOOR	33435-33437	BOYNTON BEACH	33838-33838	DUNDEE	34218-34218	HOLMES BEACH
32776-32776	SORRENTO	33438-33438	CANAL POINT	33839-33839	EAGLE LAKE	34219-34219	PARRISH
32777-32777	TANGERINE	33439-33439	BRYANT	33840-33840	EATON PARK	34220-34221	PALMETTO
32778-32778	TAVARES	33440-33440	CLEWISTON	33841-33841	FORT MEADE	34222-34222	ELLENTON
32779-32779	LONGWOOD	33441-33443	DEERFIELD BEACH	33843-33843	FROSTPROOF	34223-34224	ENGLEWOOD
32780-32783	TITUSVILLE	33444-33448	DELRAY BEACH	33844-33845	HAINES CITY	34228-34228	LONGBOAT KEY
32784-32784	UMATILLA	33454-33454	LAKE WORTH	33846-33846	HIGHLAND CITY	34229-34229	OSPREY
32789-32790	WINTER PARK	33455-33455	HOBE SOUND	33847-33847	HOMELAND	34230-34243	SARASOTA
32791-32791	LONGWOOD	33458-33458	JUPITER	33848-33848	INTERCESSION CITY	34250-34250	TERRA CEIA
32792-32793	WINTER PARK	33459-33459	LAKE HARBOR	33849-33849	KATHLEEN	34251-34251	MYAKKA CITY
32794-32794	MAITLAND	33460-33467	LAKE WORTH	33850-33850	LAKE ALFRED	34260-34260	MANASOTA
32795-32795	LAKE MARY	33468-33469	JUPITER	33851-33851	LAKE HAMILTON	34264-34264	ONECO
32796-32796	TITUSVILLE	33470-33470	LOXAHATCHEE	33852-33852	LAKE PLACID	34265-34266	ARCADIA
32798-32798	ZELLWOOD	33471-33471	MOORE HAVEN	33853-33853	LAKE WALES	34267-34267	FORT OGDEN
32799-32799	MID FLORIDA	33474-33474	BOYNTON BEACH	33854-33854	FEDHAVEN	34268-34268	NOCATEE
32801-32899	ORLANDO	33475-33475	HOBE SOUND	33855-33855	INDIAN LAKE ESTATES	34270-34270	TALLEVAST
32901-32902	MELBOURNE	33476-33476	PAHOKEE	33856-33856	NALCREST	34272-34272	LAUREL
32903-32903	INDIALANTIC	33477-33478	JUPITER	33857-33857	LORIDA	34274-34275	NOKOMIS
32904-32904	MELBOURNE	33480-33480	PALM BEACH	33858-33858	LOUGHMAN	34276-34278	SARASOTA
32905-32911	PALM BAY	33481-33481	BOCA RATON	33859-33859	LAKE WALES	34280-34282	BRADENTON
32912-32919	MELBOURNE	33482-33484	DELRAY BEACH	33860-33860	MULBERRY	34284-34285	VENICE
32920-32920	CAPE CANAVERAL	33486-33488	BOCA RATON	33862-33862	LAKE PLACID	34286-34287	NORTH PORT
32922-32924	COCOA	33493-33493	SOUTH BAY	33863-33863	NICHOLS	34292-34293	VENICE
32925-32925	PATRICK A F B	33496-33499	BOCA RATON	33865-33865	ONA	34295-34295	ENGLEWOOD
32926-32927	COCOA	33503-33503	BALM	33867-33867	RIVER RANCH	34420-34421	BELLEVIEW
32931-32932	COCOA BEACH	33509-33511	BRANDON	33868-33868	POLK CITY	34423-34429	CRYSTAL RIVER
32934-32936	MELBOURNE	33513-33513	BUSHNELL	33870-33872	SEBRING	34430-34434	DUNNELLON
32937-32937	SATELLITE BEACH	33514-33514	CENTER HILL	33873-33873	WAUCHULA	34436-34436	FLORAL CITY
32940-32941	MELBOURNE	33521-33521	COLEMAN	33877-33877	WAVERLY	34442-34442	HERNANDO
32948-32948	FELLSMERE	33523-33523	DADE CITY	33880-33888	WINTER HAVEN	34445-34445	HOLDER
32949-32949	GRANT	33524-33524	CRYSTAL SPRINGS	33890-33890	ZOLFO SPRINGS	34446-34446	HOMOSASSA
32950-32950	MALABAR	33525-33526	DADE CITY	33901-33903	FORT MYERS	34447-34447	HOMOSASSA SPRINGS
32951-32951	MELBOURNE BEACH	33527-33527	DOVER	33904-33904	CAPE CORAL	34448-34448	HOMOSASSA
32952-32954	MERRITT ISLAND	33530-33530	DURANT	33905-33908	FORT MYERS	34449-34449	INGLIS
32955-32956	ROCKLEDGE	33534-33534	GIBSONTON	33909-33910	CAPE CORAL	34450-34453	INVERNESS
32957-32957	ROSELAND	33537-33537	LACOOCHEE	33911-33913	FORT MYERS	34460-34461	LECANTO
32958-32958	SEBASTIAN	33538-33538	LAKE PANASOFFKEE	33914-33915	CAPE CORAL	34464-34465	BEVERLY HILLS

34470-34483	OCALA	34667-34667	HUDSON	34731-34731	FRUITLAND PARK	34785-34785	WILDWOOD
34484-34484	OXFORD	34668-34668	PORT RICHEY	34734-34734	GOTHA	34786-34786	WINDERMERE
34487-34487	HOMOSASSA	34669-34669	HUDSON	34736-34736	GROVELAND	34787-34787	WINTER GARDEN
34488-34489	SILVER SPRINGS	34673-34673	PORT RICHEY	34737-34737	HOWEY IN THE HILLS	34788-34789	LEESBURG
34491-34492	SUMMERFIELD	34674-34674	HUDSON	34739-34739	KENANSVILLE	34797-34797	YALAHA
34498-34498	YANKEETOWN	34677-34677	OLDSMAR	34740-34740	KILLARNEY	34945-34951	FORT PIERCE
34601-34605	BROOKSVILLE	34679-34679	ARIPEKA	34741-34747	KISSIMMEE	34952-34953	PORT SAINT LUCIE
34606-34608	SPRING HILL	34680-34680	ELFERS	34748-34749	LEESBURG	34954-34954	FORT PIERCE
34609-34610	BROOKSVILLE	34681-34681	CRYSTAL BEACH	34753-34753	MASCOTTE	34956-34956	INDIANTOWN
34611-34611	SPRING HILL	34682-34685	PALM HARBOR	34755-34755	MINNEOLA	34957-34958	JENSEN BEACH
34613-34614	BROOKSVILLE	34688-34689	TARPON SPRINGS	34756-34756	MONTVERDE	34972-34974	OKEECHOBEE
34615-34630	CLEARWATER	34690-34691	HOLIDAY	34758-34759	KISSIMMEE	34979-34982	FORT PIERCE
34636-34636	ISTACHATTA	34695-34695	SAFETY HARBOR	34760-34760	OAKLAND	34983-34988	PORT SAINT LUCIE
34639-34639	LAND O LAKES	34697-34698	DUNEDIN	34761-34761	OCOEE	34990-34991	PALM CITY
34652-34656	NEW PORT RICHEY	34705-34705	ASTATULA	34762-34762	OKAHUMPKA	34992-34992	PORT SALERNO
34660-34660	OZONA	34711-34712	CLERMONT	34769-34773	SAINT CLOUD	34994-34997	STUART
34661-34661	NOBLETON	34729-34729	FERNDALE	34777-34778	WINTER GARDEN		

Georgia

General Help Numbers:

Governor's Office
203 State Capitol
Atlanta, GA 30334
http://www.ganet.org/governor/
index_flash.html

404-656-1776
Fax 404-657-7332
8AM-4:30PM

Attorney General's Office
40 Capitol Square SW
Atlanta, GA 30334-1300
http://www.ganet.org/ago

404-656-3300
Fax 404-651-9148
8AM-5PM

State Court Administrator
244 Washington St SW, Suite 300
Atlanta, GA 30334
http://www.georgiacourts.org/
aoc/index.html

404-656-5171
Fax 404-651-6449
8:30AM-5PM

State Archives
Archives & History Department
330 Capitol Ave SE
Atlanta, GA 30334
http://www.sos.state.ga.us/archives/default.htm

404-656-2393
Fax 404-657-8427
8 AM - 4:45 PM

State Specifics:

Capital:	Atlanta
	Fulton County
Time Zone:	EST
Number of Counties:	159
Population:	8,186,453
Web Site:	www.state.ga.us

State Agencies

Criminal Records

Georgia Bureau of Investigations, Attn: GCIC, PO Box 370748, Decatur, GA 30037-0748 (Courier: 3121 Panthersville Rd, Decatur, GA 30034); 404-244-2890, 404-244-2878 (Fax), 8AM-4PM.

http://www.ganet.org/gbi

Note: GCIC is the central repository of criminal records for the State. The data includes arrest, disposition, and custodial information for offenses designated as fingerprintable the State AG. Sex offender data is at www.state.ga.us/gbi/disclaim.html.

Indexing & Storage: Records are available from 1972 forward. New records are available for inquiry immediately. Records are indexed on fingerprint cards.

Searching: Records are available to employers, government agencies including licensing agencies, and adoption and foster care providers, otherwise a signed release is required. Include the following in your request-name, set of fingerprints, date of birth, sex, race, Social Security Number. A signed release may be required. The GCIC reports that certain law enforcement agencies, who are online, will access and retrieve records for investigative/background purposes. These agencies have the option of requesting a signed release from subject or including a set of fingerprints. The following data is not released: juvenile records, traffic ticket information or out-of-state or federal charges.

Access by: mail, in person.

Fee & Payment: The fee is $15.00 per name. If the requester wishes to check the FBI file, submit 2 sets of fingerprints and a total search fee of $24.00 per name. Fee payee: Georgia Bureau of Investigations. Prepayment required. Money orders are accepted. No credit cards accepted.

Mail search: Turnaround time: 7 to 10 days. No self addressed stamped envelope is required.

In person search: A $3.00 fee is charged for an "Inspection Challenge" of your own personal record. One should call first at 404-244-2639.

Corporation Records
Limited Partnership Records
Limited Liability Company Records

Secretary of State, Corporation Division, 315 W Tower, #2 ML King Drive, Atlanta, GA 30334-1530; 404-656-2817, 404-651-9059 (Fax), 8AM-5PM.

http://www.sos.state.ga.us/corporations

Note: Trade Names, Fictitious Names, assumed names and DBAs are found at the county level.

Indexing & Storage: Records are available from the 1960s, and earlier if the filer has moved records from the county level to the state level. Indexes are maintained on microfilm and document imaging systems. New records are available for inquiry immediately.

Searching: Date of incorporation, current status and registered name and address available at web site or by phone. Officer names available at web site only. Copies and/or certificates can be ordered by mail or from the web.

Access by: mail, phone, in person, online.

Fee & Payment: There is no fee for a web site search; there is a $10.00 fee for a Certificate of Existence (good standing) or certified copies. Fee payee: Secretary of State. Prepayment required. Web requests must be paid by credit card. Personal checks accepted. Credit cards accepted: MasterCard, Visa, AmEx.

Mail search: Turnaround time: 1 day. No self addressed stamped envelope is required.

Phone search: Same information shown at web site is available over the phone.

In person search: Immediate records only if expedited service fees paid.

Online search: Records are available from the corporation database on the Internet site above or www.ganet.org/services/corp/corpsearch.shtml. The corporate database can be searched by entity name or registered agent for no fee. Online multiple records are available for a fee determined by number of records retrieved. Major credit cards accepted. There's a $10.00 charge for a Certificate of Existence (Good Standing) or certified copy of Corporate Charter. Other services include name reservation, filing procedures, downloading of forms/applications.

Expedited service: Expedited service is available for mail and in person searches. Turnaround time: 24 hours. Add $50.00 per business name.

Trademarks/Servicemarks

Secretary of State, Trademark Division, 2 Martin Luther King, Room 315, W Tower, Atlanta, GA 30334; 404-656-2861, 404-657-6380 (Fax), 8AM-5PM.

http://www.sos.state.ga.us/corporations/trademarks .htm

Note: Applications and filing instructions can be obtained at the web site.

Indexing & Storage: Records are available from the beginning of the Division and are maintained on computer. It takes 2 to 3 days before new records are available for inquiry.

Searching: Search by mark name or description or by owner name or by goods and services.

Access by: mail, phone, in person, online.

Fee & Payment: There is no fee. No credit cards accepted.

Mail search: Turnaround time: 2 to 3 days. No self addressed stamped envelope is required.

Phone search: Records are available by phone.

In person search: They will take your request in person, but they will mail back the records.

Online search: A record database is searchable from the web site.

Uniform Commercial Code

Superior Court Clerks' Cooperative Authority, 1875 Century Blvd, #100, Atlanta, GA 30345; 404-327-9058, 404-327-7877 (Fax), 9AM-5PM.

http://www.gsccca.org

Note: High volume, ongoing requesters can open a "search account" and receive expedited service.

Indexing & Storage: Records are available from 1-1-95, indexed on computer.

Searching: All uniform commercial code filings are filed at the county level. As of January 1, 1995, new UCC filings are indexed statewide (older filings are only available at the county). Submit a UCC-11 to the address above to search new filings. Include the following in your request-debtor name, Social Security or federal employer number. All tax liens are filed at the county level only.

Access by: mail, phone, fax, in person, online.

Fee & Payment: Uncertified copies made by searcher are $.25 each, if copies by this office the fee is $1.00 per page. Certified copies are only available at the county level. A search is $10.00. Fee payee: GSCCCA. Prepayment required. Personal checks accepted. No credit cards accepted.

Mail search: Turnaround time: 1 day. No self addressed stamped envelope is required.

Phone search: This is only for expedited service or for accounts.

Fax search: However, this is only available to established accounts.

Online search: Online access is available for regular, ongoing requesters. There is a monthly charge of $9.95 and a $.25 fee per image. Billing is monthly. The system is open 24 hours daily. The online service also includes real estate indexes and images. Minimum baud rate is 9600; 28.8 is supported. Information from 01/01/95 forward is available. Call 800-304-5175 or 404-327-9058 for a subscription package.

Other access: The entire UCC Central Index System can be purchased on a daily, weekly, biweekly basis. For more information, contact the Director's office.

Federal Tax Liens
State Tax Liens
Records not maintained by a state level agency.

Note: All tax liens are filed at the county level.

Sales Tax Registrations

Sales & Use Tax Division, Taxpayer Services Unit, 270 Washington St SW, Atlanta, GA 30334; 404-651-8651, 404-651-9490 (Fax), 8AM-4:30PM.

http://www2.state.ga.us/departments/dor

Indexing & Storage: Records are available for all active accounts, which are kept on computer. Inactive accounts are on microfilm.

Searching: This agency will only confirm that a business is registered and active, if a tax permit number is provided. A tax number is required to search.

Access by: phone, in person. No searching by mail.

Phone search: No fee for telephone request.

In person search: No fee for request. Generally, the information is returned by mail in two weeks.

Birth Certificates

Department of Human Resources, Vital Records Unit, 2600 Skyland Dr NE, Atlanta, GA 30319; 404-679-4701, 877-572-6343 (Credit Card Line), 404-679-4730 (Fax), 8AM-4PM.

http://health.state.ga.us/programs/vitalrecords

Indexing & Storage: Records are available from 1919 to present. It takes 1 month before new records are available for inquiry. Records are indexed on inhouse computer.

Searching: For investigative purposes or distant relatives, a notarized, signed release form from person of record is required. Include the following in your request-full name, names of parents, mother's maiden name, date of birth, place of birth.

Access by: mail, phone, fax, in person.

Fee & Payment: The fee is $10.00 per record. Add $5.00 per name requested for second copies. Multi year searches are $10.00 per ten years or portions thereof. Fee payee: Georgia Department of Human Resources. Prepayment required. Credit cards accepted: MasterCard, Visa, AmEx, Discover.

Mail search: Turnaround time: 2 to 3 weeks. No self addressed stamped envelope is required.

Phone search: You may make requests using a credit card for an additional $8.95 fee. Turnaround time 2 days.

Fax search: Same criteria as phone searching.

In person search: Turnaround time is usually 30 minutes.

Expedited service: Expedited service is available for mail, phone and fax searches. Turnaround time: overnight delivery. Add $16.00 for overnight service plus use of credit card/fee required.

Death Records

Department of Human Resources, Vital Records Unit, 2600 Skyland Dr NE, Atlanta, GA 30319; 404-679-4701, 877-572-6343 (Credit Card Line), 404-679-4730 (Fax), 8AM-4PM.

http://health.state.ga.us/programs/vitalrecords

Indexing & Storage: Records are available from 1919 to present. It takes 1 month before new records are available for inquiry. Records are indexed on inhouse computer.

Searching: Death certificates are available to the general public. Cause of death is released to next of kin only. Include the following in your request- full name, date of death, place of death. Age at death, sex and race are helpful.

Access by: mail, phone, fax, in person.

Fee & Payment: The fee is $10.00 per name. Add $5.00 per name for second copies. Multi year searches are $10.00 per 10 years or portions thereof. Fee payee: Georgia Department of Human Resources. Prepayment required. Credit cards accepted: MasterCard, Visa, AmEx, Discover.

Mail search: Turnaround time: 2 to 3 weeks. No self addressed stamped envelope is required.

Phone search: You can make requests using a credit card for an additional $8.95 service fee. Turnaround time 2 days.

Fax search: Same criteria as phone searching.

In person search: Turnaround time 30 minutes.

Other access: The death index is available for the years 1919-1998 on microfiche for $50.00.

Expedited service: Expedited service is available for mail, phone and fax searches. Turnaround time: overnight delivery. Add $16.00 for overnight delivery, plus include credit card fee.

Marriage Certificates

Department of Human Resources, Vital Records Unit, 2600 Skyland Dr NE, Atlanta, GA 30319; 404-679-4701, 877-572-6343 (Credit Card Line), 404-679-4730 (Fax), 8AM-4PM.

http://health.state.ga.us/programs/vitalrecords

Indexing & Storage: Records are available from 1952 on. Prior to 1952, records must be obtained from the county probate office. It takes 1 month. before new records are available for inquiry. Records are indexed on inhouse computer.

Searching: Certified copies of marriage licenses are available to the general public; but copies of the marriage application are only issued to bride and groom. Records may not be ordered via e-mail. Include the following in your request-full names of husband and wife, date of marriage, place or county of marriage.

Access by: mail, phone, fax, in person.

Fee & Payment: The search fee is $10.00 per name. Add $5.00 per name requested for second copies. Multi-year search are $10.00 per ten years or portions thereof. Fee payee: Georgia Department of Human Resources. Prepayment required. Credit cards accepted: MasterCard, Visa, AmEx, Discover.

Mail search: Turnaround time: 2 to 3 weeks. No self addressed stamped envelope is required.

Phone search: You can make requests using a credit card for an additional $8.95 fee. Turnaround time 2 days.

Fax search: Same criteria as phone searches.

In person search: Turnaround time 30 minutes.

Other access: The marriage index is available on microfiche for $50.00, the set includes the years 1964-1998.

Expedited service: Expedited service is available for mail, phone and fax searches. Turnaround time: overnight delivery. Add $16.00 for express delivery plus the credit card surcharge.

Divorce Records

Department of Human Resources, Vital Records Unit, 2600 Skyland Dr NE, Atlanta, GA 30319; 404-679-4701, 877-572-6343 (Credit Card Line), 404-679-4730 (Fax), 8AM-4PM.

http://health.state.ga.us/programs/vitalrecords

Note: Divorce records are found at the county of issue. However, this agency will do search to identify the county of record, but cannot issue a record. Certified copies are only available at the county level.

Indexing & Storage: Records are available from the counties.

Access by: mail, phone, fax, in person.

Fee & Payment: The fee is $10.00. Fee payee: GA Department of Human Resources. Personal checks accepted. Credit cards accepted: MasterCard, Visa, AmEx, Discover.

Mail search: Records are available by mail.

Phone search: Requires use of credit card for additional $8.95.

Fax search: Same criteria as phone searches.

Other **access:** Divorce microfiche indexes are available to the public, sold in complete set for the years 1919-1998 for $50.00.

Expedited service: Expedited service is available for fax searches. Add $16.00 for express delivery plus the credit card use fee.

Workers' Compensation Records

State Board of Workers Compensation, 270 Peachtree St, NW, Atlanta, GA 30303-1299; 404-656-3875, 8AM-4:30PM.

http://www.ganet.org/sbwc

Indexing & Storage: Records are available from 1989. Records are maintained for 10 years. Records are indexed on inhouse computer.

Searching: Must have a court order signed by a judge to obtain records from this agency unless you are a party to the case. Include the following in your request-claimant name, Social Security Number.

Access by: mail.

Fee & Payment: The agency will bill for required fees. Fee payee: State Board of Workers Compensation. Personal checks accepted. No credit cards accepted.

Mail search: Turnaround time: 2 to 3 weeks. The fee is $7.00 for the first 10 pages plus $.50 per page for over 10 pages. Certification for a document is $7.00.No self addressed stamped envelope is required. No fee for mail request.

Driver Records

Department of Motor Vehicles, Driver's License Section, MVR Unit, PO Box 1456, Atlanta, GA 30371-2303 (Courier: 959 E Confederate Ave, Atlanta, GA 30316); 404-624-7479, 8AM-3:30PM.

http://www.ganet.org/dps

Note: Copies of tickets are not available from a central depository. It is recommended you go directly to the issuing court.

Indexing & Storage: Records are available for either a 3 year record or a 7 year record. Accident involvement is shown if the driver was cited. The driver's address is part of the record. Surrendered license data is purged after two years if the record is clear. It takes ten days or more before new records are available for inquiry.

Searching: Georgia has strict rules concerning driver record access. If an individual requests a driving record on another, the driver's notarized signature is needed (except for court subpoena). Large requesters must have "bulk-user certificates" on file. The driver's full name and DOB are needed to request a record. The license number is optional.

Access by: mail, in person.

Fee & Payment: $5.00 for a 3 year period; $7.00 for a 7 year period. Fee payee: Department of Public Safety. Prepayment required. No credit cards accepted.

Mail search: Turnaround time: 2 weeks. No self addressed stamped envelope is required.

In person search: Walk-in requesters may receive up to three records while waiting, additional requests are processed overnight. Walk-in requests are also available from the State Patrol Posts.

Other access: Georgia offers magnetic tape processing for high volume users.

Vehicle Ownership
Vehicle Identification

Department of Revenue, Motor Vehicle Division - Research, PO Box 740381, Atlanta, GA 30374-0381; 404-362-6500, 8AM-4:30PM.

http://www2.state.ga.us/Departments/DOR/dmv

Indexing & Storage: Records are available from 1997 forward.

Searching: Records are not open to the general public and are restricted to authorized (notarized) agents or individuals, judgment creditor, tax collector and law enforcement officials, license dealers, etc. Records are only released to casual requesters with notarized consent of the subject

Access by: mail, in person.

Fee & Payment: Fees: $1.00 per record for VIN and title histories; $.50 for a tag search with computer print-out; $1.00 for a tag search with copy of file. Lien information is considered part of the title history. There is a full charge for a "no record found." Fee payee: Department of Revenue. Prepayment required. No credit cards accepted.

Mail search: Turnaround time: 2 weeks. A self addressed stamped envelope is requested.

In person search: Turnaround time is while you wait.

Accident Reports

Department of Public Safety, Accident Reporting Section, PO Box 1456, Atlanta, GA 30371 (Courier: 959 E Confederate Ave, Atlanta, GA 30316); 404-624-7660, 404-624-7835 (Fax), 8AM-4:30PM.

Indexing & Storage: Records are available for 10 years to present. It takes 30 days before new records are available for inquiry.

Searching: Only persons involved in the accident or their legal representative may obtain a copy, unless the subject has given written permission. Include the following in your request-full name, date of accident, location of accident.

Access by: mail, in person.

Fee & Payment: The fee for a report is $5.00. There is no charge for a "no record found." Fee payee: Department of Public Safety. Prepayment required. Cash, money orders, certified checks, and cashier's checks are all accepted. No credit cards accepted.

Mail search: Turnaround time: 1 week to 10 days. No self addressed stamped envelope is required.

In person search: Request must be in writing. Turnaround time is within the hour.

Vessel Ownership
Vessel Registration

Georgia Dept of Natural Resources, 2189 Northlake Parkway Bldg 10 #108, Tucker, GA 30084; 770-414-3338, 770-414-3344 (Fax), 8AM-4:30PM.

http://www.ganet.org.dnr

Note: Liens are at the county level and will not show on records at this location.

Indexing & Storage: Records are available from 1986 to present. Records are indexed on microfiche from 1986 to 1993 and on computer from 1994 to present. All motorized boats must be registered. All sailboats 12 ft or longer must be registered.

Searching: Either the name, registration # or hull # must be submitted.

Access by: mail, phone, fax, in person.

Fee & Payment: There is no search fee.

Mail search: Turnaround time: 1 to 2 weeks. No self addressed stamped envelope is required.

Phone search: Verification only.

Fax search: Same criteria as mail searching.

Legislation Records

General Assembly of Georgia, State Capitol, Atlanta, GA 30334; 404-656-5040 (Senate), 404-656-5015 (House), 404-656-2370 (Archives), 404-656-5043 (Fax), 8:30AM-4:30PM.

http://www.legis.state.ga.us

Indexing & Storage: Records are available from 1967 to present. Records are computerized since 1995, on hard copy 95-2000, and on microfilm 67-94. The older the document, the longer the turnaround time.

Searching: Include the following in your request-bill number, year. Either Senate or House Clerk can look up bills, but to receive copies of documents before 1967, go to respective area. State Archives has copies of all bills and has the same fee arrangement.

Access by: mail, phone, fax, in person, online.

Fee & Payment: The copy fee is $.10 per copy, after the first 100 copies. Fee payee: General Assembly of Georgia. Personal checks accepted. No credit cards accepted.

Mail search: Turnaround time: variable. Address questions to Senate to Room 351, House questions to Room 307.No self addressed stamped envelope is required.

Phone search: You may request bills by phone.

Fax search: Fax searching available.

In person search: You may request bills in person.

Online search: The Internet site listed above has bill information. Also, you can search at http://www.ganet.org/services/leg.

Voter Registration

Secretary of State, Elections Division, 2 Martin Luther King Dr SE, Suite 1104, West Tower, Atlanta, GA 30334; 404-656-2871, 404-651-9531 (Fax), 8AM-5PM.

http://www.sos.state.ga.us/elections

Indexing & Storage: Records are available from 1995, on computer. Data is keyed in by county personnel onto the state computer.

Searching: Records may be ordered in a database format directly from the web site. Include the following in your request-full name, Social Security Number if available, date of birth. All requests must be in writing. Records may be requested at county level, also. The following data is not released: Social Security Numbers or bulk information or lists for commercial purposes.

Access by: mail, fax.

Fee & Payment: There is no fee for individual requests.

Mail search: Turnaround time: 2 to 3 days. No self addressed stamped envelope is required.

Fax search: Fax searching available.

Other access: CDs, Internet files, disks, and paper lists are available for purchase for non-commercial purposes.

GED Certificates

GED Testing Services, 1800 Century Pl #555, Atlanta, GA 30345; 404-679-1644, 8:30AM-4:30PM M-F.

http://www.dtae.org

Searching: To search, all are required: a signed release, name, year of test, date of birth, and Social Security Number.

Access by: mail.

Fee & Payment: The fee for a verification or for a copy of a transcript is $5.00 per record. Fee payee: GED Testing Services. Prepayment required. Money orders are accepted. No credit cards accepted.

Mail search: Turnaround time: 2 weeks. No self · addressed stamped envelope is required.

Hunting License Information
Fishing License Information
Records not maintained by a state level agency.

Note: They do not have a central database. You must contact the vendor where the license was purchased.

Georgia State Licensing Agencies

Licenses Searchable Online

Air Conditioning Contractor #09 .... www.sos.state.ga.us/plb/construct/search.htm
Architect #15 .... www.sos.state.ga.us/plb/architects/search.htm
Athletic Agent #12.. www.sos.state.ga.us/plb/agent/search.htm
Athletic Trainer #16.. www.sos.state.ga.us/plb/trainer/search.htm
Auctioneer #12 .... www.sos.state.ga.us/plb/auctioneer/search.htm
Audiologist #16... www.sos.state.ga.us/plb/speech/search.htm
Bank #17.. www.ganet.org/dbf/other_institutions.html
Barber/Barber Shop #19 .... www.sos.state.ga.us/plb/barber_cosmet/search.htm
Cardiac Technician #41 .... www.medicalboard.state.ga.us/licensure_cert.html
Charity #45... www.sos.state.ga.us/securities/charitysearch.htm
Check Casher/Seller #17 .... www.ganet.org/dbf/other_institutions.html
Chiropractor #18.. www.sos.state.ga.us/plb/chiro/search.htm
Contractor, General #09 .... www.sos.state.ga.us/plb/construct/search.htm
Cosmetologist/Cosmetology Shop #19............................ www.sos.state.ga.us/plb/barber_cosmet/search.htm
Counselor #10 .... www.sos.state.ga.us/plb/counselors/search.htm
Credit Union #17.. www.ganet.org/dbf/other_institutions.html
Dental Hygienist #20.. www.sos.state.ga.us/plb/dentistry/search.htm
Dentist #20 .... www.sos.state.ga.us/plb/dentistry/search.htm
Dietitian #02 .... www.sos.state.ga.us/plb/dietitians/search.htm
EDP - Electronic Data Processors #17 .... www.ganet.org/dbf/other_institutions.html
Electrical Contractor #09..................................... www.sos.state.ga.us/plb/construct/search.htm
Embalmer #12... www.sos.state.ga.us/plb/funeral/search.htm
Engineer #11 .... www.sos.state.ga.us/plb/pels/search.htm
Esthetician #19 .... www.sos.state.ga.us/plb/barber_cosmet/search.htm
Family Therapist #10 .... www.sos.state.ga.us/plb/counselors/search.htm
Forester #36 .... www.sos.state.ga.us/plb/foresters/search.htm
Funeral Director/Apprentice/Establishment #12................. www.sos.state.ga.us/plb/funeral/search.htm
Geologist #44 .... www.sos.state.ga.us/plb/geologists/search.htm
Hearing Aid Dealer/Dispenser #26 .... www.sos.state.ga.us/plb/hearingaid/search.htm
Holding Company/Representative Offices #17.................... www.ganet.org/dbf/other_institutions.html
Hospital Wholesale/Retail Manufacturer #31 .... www.sos.state.ga.us/plb/pharmacy/search.htm
Insurance Agent #08... www.inscomm.state.ga.us/AGENTS/AgentStatus.asp
Interior Designer #15 .... www.sos.state.ga.us/plb/architects/search.htm
Landscape Architect #27....................................... www.sos.state.ga.us/plb/landscape/search.htm
Low Voltage Contractor #09.................................... www.sos.state.ga.us/plb/construct/search.htm
Manicurist #19.. www.sos.state.ga.us/plb/barber_cosmet/search.htm
Marriage Counselor #10.. www.sos.state.ga.us/plb/counselors/search.htm
Medical Doctor #41.. www.medicalboard.state.ga.us/licensure_cert.html
Mortgage Institution #17 .... www.ganet.org/dbf/mortgage.html
Nail Care #19 .... www.sos.state.ga.us/plb/barber_cosmet/search.htm
Nuclear Pharmacist #31.. www.sos.state.ga.us/plb/pharmacy/search.htm
Nurse-LPN #02... www.sos.state.ga.us/plb/lpn/search.htm
Nurse-RN #28.. www.sos.state.ga.us/plb/rn/search.htm
Nursing Home Administrator #16 .... www.sos.state.ga.us/plb/nursinghome/search.htm
Occupational Therapist/Therapist Assistant #02................ www.sos.state.ga.us/plb/ot/search.htm
Optician, Dispensing #21 .... www.sos.state.ga.us/plb/opticians/search.htm
Optometrist #22... www.sos.state.ga.us/plb/optometry/search.htm
Osteopathic Physician #41..................................... www.medicalboard.state.ga.us/licensure_cert.html
Paramedic #41 .... www.medicalboard.state.ga.us/licensure_cert.html
Pesticide Contractor/Applicator/Employee #04 .... www.kellysolutions.com/ga/Applicators/index.htm
Pharmacist #31 .... www.sos.state.ga.us/plb/pharmacy/search.htm
Pharmacy School, Clinic Researcher #31........................ www.sos.state.ga.us/plb/pharmacy/search.htm
Physical Therapist/Therapist Assistant #02 .... www.sos.state.ga.us/plb/pt/search.htm
Physician Assistant #41....................................... www.medicalboard.state.ga.us/licensure_cert.html
Plumber Journeyman/Contractor #09............................. www.sos.state.ga.us/plb/construct/search.htm
Podiatrist #33 .... www.sos.state.ga.us/plb/podiatry/search.htm
Poison Pharmacist #31... www.sos.state.ga.us/plb/pharmacy/search.htm
Private Detective #12... www.sos.state.ga.us/plb/detective/search.htm
Psychologist #16 .... www.sos.state.ga.us/plb/psych/search.htm
Public Accountant-CPA #14..................................... www.sos.state.ga.us/plb/accountancy/search.htm
Respiratory Care Practitioner #41 .... www.medicalboard.state.ga.us/licensure_cert.html
School Librarian #40.. www.sos.state.ga.us/plb/librarians/search.htm
Security Guard #12.. www.sos.state.ga.us/plb/detective/search.htm
Social Worker #10 .... www.sos.state.ga.us/plb/counselors/search.htm

Speech-Language Pathologist #16 .... www.sos.state.ga.us/plb/speech/search.htm
Surveyor #11 .... www.sos.state.ga.us/plb/pels/search.htm
Used Car Dealer #12 .... www.sos.state.ga.us/plb/usedcar/search.htm
Used Car Parts Distributor #12 .... www.sos.state.ga.us/plb/usedcar/search.htm
Utility Contractor #09 .... www.sos.state.ga.us/plb/construct/search.htm
Veterinarian/Veterinary Technician #39 .... www.sos.state.ga.us/plb/veterinary/search.htm
Veterinary Faculty #39 .... www.sos.state.ga.us/plb/veterinary/search.htm
Waste Water System Operator #43 .... www.sos.state.ga.us/plb/water/search.htm
Waste Water Industrial #43 .... www.sos.state.ga.us/plb/water/search.htm
Waste Water Laboratory Analyst #43 .... www.sos.state.ga.us/plb/water/search.htm
Waste Water Treatment/Dist. System Operator #43 .www.sos.state.ga.us/plb/water/search.htm
Water Operator Class 1-3 #43 .... www.sos.state.ga.us/plb/water/search.htm

Licensing Quick Finder

Acupuncturist #41 404-656-3913
Air Conditioning Contractor #09 478-207-1416
Amusement Ride Inspector #48............. 404-656-2966
Animal Technician #39 478-207-1686
Architect #15... 478-207-1400
Athletic Agent #12 478-207-1460
Athletic Trainer #16 478-207-1670
Attorney #47 404-527-8700
Auctioneer #12...................................... 478-207-1460
Audiologist #16 478-207-1670
Bank #17 770-986-1633
Barber/Barber Shop #19....................... 478-207-1430
Boiler Inspector #48 404-656-2966
Cardiac Technician #41 404-656-3923
Cemetery #45 404-656-3920
Charity #45 404-656-3920
Check Casher/Seller #17...................... 770-986-1633
Chiropractor #18 478-207-1686
Contractor, General #09 478-207-1600
Cosmetologist/Cosmetology Shop #19..478-207-1430
Counselor #10 478-207-1670
Court Reporter #01 404-656-6422
Credit Union #17 770-986-1637
Dental Hygienist #20 478-207-1680
Dentist #20 478-207-1680
Dietitian #23.. 404-656-3921
Dietitian #02.. 478-207-1620
EDP - Electronic Data Processors #17..770-986-1633
Electrical Contractor #09 478-207-1416
Elevator Inspector #48.......................... 404-656-2966
Embalmer #12 478-207-1460
Emergency Medical Technician #49...... 404-657-6700
Engineer #11 478-207-1453
Esthetician #19 478-207-1430
Family Therapist #10............................. 478-207-1670
Forester #36 478-207-1400
Funeral Director/Apprentice #12 478-207-1460
Funeral Establishment #12 478-207-1460
Geologist #44.. 478-207-1400
Hearing Aid Dealer/Dispenser #26........ 478-207-1686

Holding Co./Representative Offices #17 770-986-1633
Hospital Wholesale/Retail Mfg. #31....... 478-207-1686
Insurance Adjuster #08......................... 404-656-2101
Insurance Agent #08 404-656-2101
Insurance Counselor #08....................... 404-656-2101
Interior Designer #15............................. 478-207-1400
Investment Advisor (Firm) #45.............. 404-656-3920
Landfill Inspector/Operator #05............. 404-362-2696
Landscape Architect #27 478-207-1400
Liquor Control #06................................. 404-651-9516
Low Voltage Contractor #09 478-207-1416
Manicurist #19 478-207-1430
Marriage Counselor #10........................ 478-207-1670
Medical Doctor #41 404-656-3913
Mortgage Institution #17....................... 770-986-1269
Nail Care #19... 478-207-1430
Notary Public #03.................................. 404-327-6023
Nuclear Pharmacist #31 478-207-1686
Nurse-LPN #02...................................... 478-207-1620
Nurse-RN #28.. 404-657-0775
Nursing Home Administrator #16 478-207-1670
Occupational Therapist/Therapist Assistant #02.........
.... 478-207-1620
Optician, Dispensing #21 478-207-1686
Optometrist #22 478-207-1686
Osteopathic Physician #41 404-656-3913
Paramedic #41....................................... 404-656-3923
Pesticide Applicator #04 404-656-4958
Pesticide Contractor/Employee #04 404-656-4958
Pharmacist #31 478-207-1686
Pharmacy School, Clinic Researcher #31 ....
.... 478-207-1686
Physical Therapist/Therpist Assist. #2.. 478-207-1620
Physician Assistant #41......................... 404-656-3913
Plumber Journeyman/Contractor #09.... 478-207-1416
Podiatrist #33.. 478-207-1686
Poison Pharmacist #31.......................... 478-207-1686
Private Detective #12 478-207-1460
Psychologist #16 478-207-1670
Public Accountant-CPA #14.................. 478-207-1400

Public Adjuster #08 404-656-2101
Real Estate Appraiser #46 404-656-3916
Real Estate Broker #46 404-656-3916
Real Estate Community Assn Mgr #46..404-656-3916
Real Estate Sales Agent #46 404-656-3916
Rebuilder #12 478-207-1460
Respiratory Care Practitioner #41 404-656-3914
Salvage Pool Operator #12 478-207-1460
Salvage Yard Dealer #12....................... 478-207-1460
School Administrator/Supervisor #07 404-657-9000
School Bus Driver #51........................... 404-624-7467
School Counselor #07 404-657-9000
School Librarian #40 478-207-1400
School Media Specialist #07 404-657-9000
School Social Worker #07 404-657-9000
Securities Dealer/Salesperson #45 404-656-3920
Security Agency #12 478-207-1460
Security Guard #12 478-207-1460
Shorthand Court Reporter/Stenomask #01...............
.... 404-656-6422
Social Worker #10................................. 478-207-1670
Speech-Language Pathologist #16 478-207-1670
Surplus Line Broker #08 404-656-2101
Surveyor #11... 478-207-1453
Teacher #07... 404-657-9000
Timber Dealer/Processor #04 404-656-4958
Truck Driver #51.................................... 404-624-7467
Used Car Dealer #12............................. 478-207-1460
Used Car Parts Distributor #12 478-207-1460
Utility Contractor #09............................ 478-207-1416
Veterinarian/Veterinary Technician #39. 478-207-1686
Veterinary Faculty #39........................... 478-207-1686
Waste Water Collection System Operator #43...........
.... 478-207-1670
Waste Water Industrial #43 478-207-1670
Waste Water Laboratory Analyst #43....478-207-1670
Waste Water Treatment/Distribution
System Operator #43 478-207-1670
Water Operator Class 1-3 #43 478-207-1670

Licensing Agency Information

#01 Clerk of the Board, 244 Washington St SW, #550, Atlanta, GA 30334; 404-656-6422, Fax: 404-651-6449.

#02 Examining Boards Division, 237 Coliseum Dr, Macon, GA 31217; 478-207-1620, Fax: 478-207-1633.
www.sos.state.ga.us/plb/lpn
Direct web site URL to search for licensees: www.sos.state.ga.us/plb/lpn/search.htm. You can search online using name and license number.

#03 Clerks Authority, 1875 Century Blvd #100, Atlanta, GA 30345; 404-327-6023, Fax: 404-327-7887.
www2.gsccca.org/Projects/aboutnp.html

#04 Department of Agriculture, Capitol Sq, Rm 550, Atlanta, GA 30334; 404-656-4958, Fax: 404-657-8378.
www.agr.state.ga.us
Direct web site URL to search for licensees: www.kellysolutions.com/ga/Applicators/index.htm

#05 Department of Natural Resources, 4244 International Pky, #104, Atlanta, GA 30354; 404-362-2696, Fax: 404-362-2693.
www.dnr.state.ga.us/EPD

#06 Department of Revenue, 270 Washington Rm 203, Atlanta, GA 30334-0390; 404-651-9516.
www2.state.ga.us/Departments/DOR

#07 Education Department, 1452 Twin Towers East, Atlanta, GA 30334; 404-657-9000.
www.gapsc.com

#08 Licensing Division, 2 Martin Luther King Jr Dr, West Tower, #802, Atlanta, GA 30334; 404-656-2101, Fax: 404-656-0874.

#09 State Construction Industry Licensing Board, 237 Coliseum Dr, Macon, GA 31217; 478-207-1416, Fax: 478-207-1425.
www.sos.state.ga.us/plb/construct
Direct web site URL to search for licensees: www.sos.state.ga.us/plb/construct/search.htm. You can search online using last name or license #

#10 Examining Boards Division, 237 Coliseum Dr, Macon, GA 31217; 478-207-1670, Fax: 478-207-1676.
www.sos.state.ga.us/plb/counselors
Direct web site URL to search for licensees: www.sos.state.ga.us/plb/counselors/search.htm. You can search online using name and license number.

#11 Examining Boards Division, 237 Coliseum Dr, Macon, GA 31217-3858; 478-207-1453, Fax: 478-207-1456.
www.sos.state.ga.us/ebd-pel
Direct web site URL to search for licensees: www.sos.state.ga.us/plb/pels/search.htm. You can search online using name and license number.

#12 Professional Licensing, 237 Coliseum Dr, Macon, GA 31217; 478-207-1460.
www.sos.state.ga.us/plb

#14 Examining Boards Division, 237 Coliseum Dr, Macon, GA 31217; 478-207-1400, Fax: 478-207-1410.
www.sos.state.ga.us
Direct web site URL to search for licensees: www.sos.state.ga.us/plb/accountancy/search.htm

#15 Examining Boards Division, 237 Coliseum Dr, Macon, GA 31217-3858; 478-207-1400, Fax: 478-207-1410.
www.sos.state.ga.us/plb/architects
Direct web site URL to search for licensees: www.sos.state.ga.us/plb/architects/search.htm. Search online using last name and license number.

#16 Examining Boards Division, 237 Coliseum, Macon, GA 31217; 478-207-1670, Fax: 478-207-1676.
www.sos.state.ga.us/pld
Direct web site URL to search for licensees: www.sos.state.ga.us/plb/. You can search online using name and license number.

#17 Department of Banking and Finance, 2990 Brandywine Rd #200, Atlanta, GA 30341; 770-986-1633, Fax: 770-986-1654.
www.ganet.org/dbf/index.html
Direct web site URL to search for licensees: www.ganet.org/dbf/regulated_institutions.html. You can search online using alphabetical lists

#18 Examining Boards Division, 237 Coliseum Dr, Macon, GA 31217; 478-207-1686, Fax: 478-207-1699.
www.sos.state.ga.us/plb/chiro
Direct web site URL to search for licensees: www.sos.state.ga.us/plb/chiro/search.htm. You can search online using name and license number.

#19 Examining Boards Division, 237 Coliseum Drive, Macon, GA 31217; 478-207-1430, Fax: 478-207-1442.
www.sos.state.ga.us/plb/barber_cosmet
Direct web site URL to search for licensees: www.sos.state.ga.us/plb/barber_cosmet/search.htm

#20 Examining Boards Division, 237 Coliseum Drive, Macon, GA 31217-3858; 478-207-1680, Fax: 478-207-1685.

www.sos.state.ga.us/plb/dentistry
Direct web site URL to search for licensees: www.sos.state.ga.us/plb/dentistry/search.htm. You can search online using name and license number.

#21 Examining Boards Division, 237 Coliseum Dr, Macon, GA 31217; 478-207-1686, Fax: 478-207-1699.
www.sos.state.ga.us/plb/opticians
Direct web site URL to search for licensees: www.sos.state.ga.us/plb/opticians/search.htm. You can search online using name and license number.

#22 Examining Boards Division, 237 Coliseum Dr, Macon, GA 31217; 478-207-1686, Fax: 478-207-1699.
www.sos.state.ga.us/plb/optometry
Direct web site URL to search for licensees: www.sos.state.ga.us/plb/optometry/search.htm. Search online using name and license number.

#26 Examining Boards Division, 237 Coliseum Dr, Macon, GA 31217; 478-207-1686, Fax: 478-207-1699.
www.sos.state.ga.us/plb/hearingaid/search.htm
Direct web site URL to search for licensees: www.sos.state.ga.us/plb/hearingaid/search.htm. Search online using name and license number.

#27 Examining Boards Division, 237 Coliseum Dr, Macon, GA 31217-3858; 478-207-1400, Fax: 478-207-1400.
www.sos.state.ga.us/plb/landscape
Direct web site URL to search for licensees: www.sos.state.ga.us/plb/landscape/search.htm. You can search online using name and license number.

#28 Examining Boards Division, 237 Coliseum Dr, Macon, GA 30217-3858; 478-207-1640, Fax: 478-207-1660.
www.sos.state.ga.us/plb/rn
Direct web site URL to search for licensees: www.sos.state.ga.us/plb/rn/search.htm. You can search online using name and license number.

#31 Examining Boards Division, 237 Coliseum Dr, Macon, GA 31217; 478-207-1686, Fax: 478-207-1699.
www.sos.state.ga.us/plb/pharmacy
Direct web site URL to search for licensees: www.sos.state.ga.us/plb/pharmacy/search.htm. You can search online using name and license number.

#33 Examining Boards Division, 237 Coliseum Dr, Macon, GA 31217; 478-207-1686, Fax: 478-207-1699.
www.sos.state.ga.us/plb/podiatry/search.htm
Direct web site URL to search for licensees: www.sos.state.ga.us/plb/podiatry/search.htm. You can search online using name and license number.

#36 Examining Boards Division, 237 Coliseum Dr, Macon, GA 31217-3858; 478-207-1400, Fax: 478-207-1410.
www.sos.state.ga.us/plb/foresters
Direct web site URL to search for licensees: www.sos.state.ga.us/plb/foresters/search.htm. You

can search online using last name and licence number.

#39 Examining Boards Division, 237 Coliseum Dr, Macon, GA 31217; 478-207-1686, Fax: 478-207-1699.
www.sos.state.ga.us/plb/veterinary/search.htm
Direct web site URL to search for licensees: www.sos.state.ga.us/plb/veterinary/search.htm. Search online using name and license number.

#40 Examining Boards Division, 237 Coliseum Dr, Macon, GA 31217; 478-207-1400, Fax: 478-207-1410.
www.sos.state.ga.us/plb/librarians
Direct web site URL to search for licensees: www.sos.state.ga.us/plb/librarians/search.htm

#41 Examining Boards Division, 2 Peachtree St, 10th Fl, Atlanta, GA 30303; 404-656-3913, Fax: 404-656-9723.
www.medicalboard.state.ga.us/

#43 Examining Boards Division, 237 Coliseum Dr, Macon, GA 31217; 478-207-1670, Fax: 478-207-1676.
www.sos.state.ga.us/plb/water
Direct web site URL to search for licensees: www.sos.state.ga.us/plb/water/search.htm. You can search online using name or license number.

#44 Examining Boards Division, 237 Coliseum Dr, Macon, GA 31217; 478-207-1400, Fax: 478-207-1410.
www.sos.state.ga.us/ebd-geologists
Direct web site URL to search for licensees: www.sos.state.ga.us/plb/geologists/search.htm. You can search online using name and license number.

#45 Securities & Business Regulation, 2 Martin Luther King Jr Dr, West Tower, #802, Atlanta, GA 30334-1530; 404-656-3920, Fax: 404-657-8410.
www.sos.state.ga.us/securities

#46 Real Estate Commission/Appraiser Board, 229 Peachtree St NE, International Tower, #100, Atlanta, GA 30303-1605; 404-656-3916, Fax: 404-656-6650.
www.grec.state.ga.us

#47 State Bar of Georgia, 50 Hurt Plaza, 800 The Hurt Bldg, Atlanta, GA 30303; 404-527-8700, Fax: 404-527-8717.
www.gabar.org
Direct web site URL to search for licensees: www.gabar.org/ga_bar/searchpage.html. You can search online using name, city, and state.

#48 Department of Labor, 223 Courtland St NE #301, Atlanta, GA 30303-1751; 404-656-2966.

#49 Emergency Medical Svcs, 47 Trinity Ave SW #104-LOB, Atlanta, GA 30334; 404-657-6700.

#51 Department of Public Safety, PO Box 1456, Atlanta, GA 30371; 404-624-7467, Fax: 404-624-7707.
www.ganet.org/dps

Georgia Federal Courts

The following list indicates the district and division name for each county in the state. If the bankruptcy court location is different from the district court, then the location of the bankruptcy court appears in parentheses.

County/Court Cross Reference

County	District	Division
Appling	Southern	Brunswick (Savannah)
Atkinson	Southern	Waycross (Savannah)
Bacon	Southern	Waycross (Savannah)
Baker	Middle	Albany/Americus (Macon)
Baldwin	Middle	Macon
Banks	Northern	Gainesville
Barrow	Northern	Gainesville
Bartow	Northern	Rome
Ben Hill	Middle	Albany/Americus (Macon)
Berrien	Middle	Valdosta (Columbus)
Bibb	Middle	Macon
Bleckley	Middle	Macon
Brantley	Southern	Waycross (Savannah)
Brooks	Middle	Thomasville (Columbus)
Bryan	Southern	Savannah
Bulloch	Southern	Statesboro (Augusta)
Burke	Southern	Augusta
Butts	Middle	Macon
Calhoun	Middle	Albany/Americus (Macon)
Camden	Southern	Brunswick (Savannah)
Candler	Southern	Statesboro (Augusta)
Carroll	Northern	Newnan
Catoosa	Northern	Rome
Charlton	Southern	Waycross (Savannah)
Chatham	Southern	Savannah
Chattahoochee	Middle	Columbus
Chattooga	Northern	Rome
Cherokee	Northern	Atlanta
Clarke	Middle	Athens (Macon)
Clay	Middle	Columbus
Clayton	Northern	Atlanta
Clinch	Middle	Valdosta (Columbus)
Cobb	Northern	Atlanta
Coffee	Southern	Waycross (Savannah)
Colquitt	Middle	Thomasville (Columbus)
Columbia	Southern	Augusta
Cook	Middle	Valdosta (Columbus)
Coweta	Northern	Newnan
Crawford	Middle	Macon
Crisp	Middle	Albany/Americus (Macon)
Dade	Northern	Rome
Dawson	Northern	Gainesville
De Kalb	Northern	Atlanta
Decatur	Middle	Thomasville (Columbus)
Dodge	Southern	Dublin (Augusta)
Dooly	Middle	Macon
Dougherty	Middle	Albany/Americus (Macon)
Douglas	Northern	Atlanta
Early	Middle	Albany/Americus (Macon)
Echols	Middle	Valdosta (Columbus)
Effingham	Southern	Savannah
Elbert	Middle	Athens (Macon)
Emanuel	Southern	Statesboro (Augusta)
Evans	Southern	Statesboro (Augusta)
Fannin	Northern	Gainesville
Fayette	Northern	Newnan
Floyd	Northern	Rome
Forsyth	Northern	Gainesville
Franklin	Middle	Athens (Macon)
Fulton	Northern	Atlanta
Gilmer	Northern	Gainesville
Glascock	Southern	Augusta
Glynn	Southern	Brunswick (Savannah)
Gordon	Northern	Rome
Grady	Middle	Thomasville (Columbus)
Greene	Middle	Athens (Macon)
Gwinnett	Northern	Atlanta
Habersham	Northern	Gainesville
Hall	Northern	Gainesville
Hancock	Middle	Macon
Haralson	Northern	Newnan
Harris	Middle	Columbus
Hart	Middle	Athens (Macon)
Heard	Northern	Newnan
Henry	Northern	Atlanta
Houston	Middle	Macon
Irwin	Middle	Valdosta (Columbus)
Jackson	Northern	Gainesville
Jasper	Middle	Macon
Jeff Davis	Southern	Brunswick (Savannah)
Jefferson	Southern	Augusta
Jenkins	Southern	Statesboro (Augusta)
Johnson	Southern	Dublin (Augusta)
Jones	Middle	Macon
Lamar	Middle	Macon
Lanier	Middle	Valdosta (Columbus)
Laurens	Southern	Dublin (Augusta)
Lee	Middle	Albany/Americus (Macon)
Liberty	Southern	Savannah
Lincoln	Southern	Augusta
Long	Southern	Brunswick (Savannah)
Lowndes	Middle	Valdosta (Columbus)
Lumpkin	Northern	Gainesville
Macon	Middle	Macon
Madison	Middle	Athens (Macon)
Marion	Middle	Columbus
McDuffie	Southern	Augusta
McIntosh	Southern	Brunswick (Savannah)
Meriwether	Northern	Newnan
Miller	Middle	Albany/Americus (Macon)
Mitchell	Middle	Albany/Americus (Macon)
Monroe	Middle	Macon
Montgomery	Southern	Dublin (Augusta)
Morgan	Middle	Athens (Macon)
Murray	Northern	Rome
Muscogee	Middle	Columbus
Newton	Northern	Atlanta
Oconee	Middle	Athens (Macon)
Oglethorpe	Middle	Athens (Macon)
Paulding	Northern	Rome

Peach	Middle	Macon		Thomas	Middle	Thomasville (Columbus)
Pickens	Northern	Gainesville		Tift	Middle	Valdosta (Columbus)
Pierce	Southern	Waycross (Savannah)		Toombs	Southern	Statesboro (Augusta)
Pike	Northern	Newnan		Towns	Northern	Gainesville
Polk	Northern	Rome		Treutlen	Southern	Dublin (Augusta)
Pulaski	Middle	Macon		Troup	Northern	Newnan
Putnam	Middle	Macon		Turner	Middle	Albany/Americus (Macon)
Quitman	Middle	Columbus		Twiggs	Middle	Macon
Rabun	Northern	Gainesville		Union	Northern	Gainesville
Randolph	Middle	Columbus		Upson	Middle	Macon
Richmond	Southern	Augusta		Walker	Northern	Rome
Rockdale	Northern	Atlanta		Walton	Middle	Athens (Macon)
Schley	Middle	Albany/Americus (Macon)		Ware	Southern	Waycross (Savannah)
Screven	Southern	Statesboro (Augusta)		Warren	Southern	Augusta
Seminole	Middle	Thomasville (Columbus)		Washington	Middle	Macon
Spalding	Northern	Newnan		Wayne	Southern	Brunswick (Savannah)
Stephens	Northern	Gainesville		Webster	Middle	Albany/Americus (Macon)
Stewart	Middle	Columbus		Wheeler	Southern	Dublin (Augusta)
Sumter	Middle	Albany/Americus (Macon)		White	Northern	Gainesville
Talbot	Middle	Columbus		Whitfield	Northern	Rome
Taliaferro	Southern	Augusta		Wilcox	Middle	Macon
Tattnall	Southern	Statesboro (Augusta)		Wilkes	Southern	Augusta
Taylor	Middle	Columbus		Wilkinson	Middle	Macon
Telfair	Southern	Dublin (Augusta)		Worth	Middle	Albany/Americus (Macon)
Terrell	Middle	Albany/Americus (Macon)				

US District Court

Middle District of Georgia

Albany/Americus Division PO Box 1906, Albany, GA 31702 (Courier Address: Room 106, 345 Broad Ave, Albany, GA 31701), 229-430-8432, Fax: 229-430-8538.

http://www.gamd.uscourts.gov

Counties: Baker, Ben Hill, Calhoun, Crisp, Dougherty, Early, Lee, Miller, Mitchell, Schley, Sumter, Terrell, Turner, Webster, Worth. Ben Hill and Crisp were transfered from the Macon Division as of October 1, 1997.

Indexing/Storage: Cases are indexed by defendant and plaintiff as well as by case number. New cases are available in the index immediately after filing date. Both computer and card indexes are maintained. Records are on the computer from 1991. Prior records are indexed on index cards. District wide searches are available from any division in this district for files after 1/91. Open records are located at this court.

Fee & Payment: The fee is $20.00 per item (one party name or case number). Payment may be made by money order, cashier check, in-state business check. Personal checks are not accepted. Prepayment is required. Payee: Clerk, USDC. Certification fee: $7.00 per document. Copy fee: $.50 per page.

Phone Search: Only docket information is available by phone.

Mail Search: Always enclose a stamped self addressed envelope.

In Person: In person searching is available.

PACER: Sign-up number is 800-676-6856. Access fee is $.60 per minute. Toll-free access: 888-234-3839. Local access: 912-752-8170. Case records are available back to January 1991. Records are never purged. New records are available online after 1-2 days. Pacer is available online at http://pacer.gamd.uscourts.gov.

Athens Division PO Box 1106, Athens, GA 30603 (Courier Address: 115 E Hancock Ave, Athens, GA 30601), 706-227-1094, Fax: 706-546-2190.

http://www.gamd.uscourts.gov

Counties: Clarke, Elbert, Franklin, Greene, Hart, Madison, Morgan, Oconee, Oglethorpe, Walton. Closed cases before April 1997 are located in the Macon Division.

Indexing/Storage: Cases are indexed by defendant and plaintiff as well as by case number. New cases are available in the index 2 days after filing date. Both computer and card indexes are maintained. Open records are located at this court.

Fee & Payment: The fee is $20.00 per item (one party name or case number). Payment may be made by money order, cashier check, business check. Personal checks are not accepted. Payee: US District Court. Certification fee: $7.00 per document. Copy fee: $.50 per page.

Phone Search: Searching is not available by phone.

Mail Search: Always enclose a stamped self addressed envelope.

In Person: In person searching is available.

PACER: Sign-up number is 800-676-6856. Access fee is $.60 per minute. Toll-free access: 888-234-3839. Local access: 912-752-8170. Case records are available back to January 1991. Records are never purged. New records are available online after 1-2 days. Pacer is available online at http://pacer.gamd.uscourts.gov.

Columbus Division PO Box 124, Columbus, GA 31902 (Courier Address: Room 216, 120 12th St, Columbus, GA 31901), 706-649-7816.

http://www.gamd.uscourts.gov

Counties: Chattahoochee, Clay, Harris, Marion, Muscogee, Quitman, Randolph, Stewart, Talbot, Taylor.

Indexing/Storage: Cases are indexed by defendant and plaintiff as well as by case number. New cases are available in the index immediately after filing date. Both computer and card indexes are maintained. Open records are located at this court.

Fee & Payment: The fee is $20.00 per item (one party name or case number). Payment may be made by money order, cashier check, business check. Personal checks are not accepted. Prepayment is required. Payee: Clerk, US Courts. Certification fee: $7.00 per document. Copy fee: $.50 per page.

Phone Search: Searching is not available by phone. Only docket information is available by phone.

Mail Search: Always enclose a stamped self addressed envelope.

In Person: In person searching is available.

PACER: Sign-up number is 800-676-6856. Access fee is $.60 per minute. Toll-free access: 888-234-3839. Local access: 912-752-8170. Case records are available back to January 1991. Records are never purged. New records are available online after 1-2 days. Pacer is available online at http://pacer.gamd.uscourts.gov.

Macon Division PO Box 128, Macon, GA 31202-0128 (Courier Address: 475 Mulberry, Suite 216, Macon, GA 31201), 912-752-3497, Fax: 912-752-3496.

http://www.gamd.uscourts.gov

Counties: Baldwin, Ben Hill, Bibb, Bleckley, Butts, Crawford, Crisp, Dooly, Hancock, Houston, Jasper, Jones, Lamar, Macon, Monroe, Peach, Pulaski, Putnam, Twiggs, Upson, Washington, Wilcox, Wilkinson.Athens Division cases closed before April 1997 are also located here.

Indexing/Storage: Cases are indexed by defendant and plaintiff as well as by case number. New cases are available in the index immediately after filing date. Both computer and card indexes are maintained. Records after 1/91 can be searched from any court in this district. Open records are located at this court.

Fee & Payment: The fee is $20.00 per item (one party name or case number). Payment may be made by money order, cashier check, business check. Personal checks are not accepted. Payee: US Courts. Certification fee: $7.00 per document. Copy fee: $.50 per page.

Phone Search: Only docket information is available by phone.

Fax Search: Handled same as mail search. Will fax results at $3.00 per page.

Mail Search: Always enclose a stamped self addressed envelope.

In Person: In person searching is available.

PACER: Sign-up number is 800-676-6856. Access fee is $.60 per minute. Toll-free access: 888-234-3839. Local access: 912-752-8170. Case records are available back to January 1991. Records are never purged. New records are available online after 1-2 days. Pacer is available online at http://pacer.gamd.uscourts.gov.

Thomasville Division c/o Valdosta Division, PO Box 68, Valdosta, GA 31601 (Courier Address: Room 212, 401 N Patterson, Valdosta, GA 31603), 912-226-3651.

http://www.gamd.uscourts.gov

Counties: Brooks, Colquitt, Decatur, Grady, Seminole, Thomas.

Indexing/Storage: Cases are indexed by as well as by case number. New cases are available in the index after filing date. Open records are located at the Division.

Fee & Payment: The fee is $20.00 per item (one party name or case number). Payment may be made by money order, cashier check. Business checks are not accepted. Personal checks are not accepted.

Phone Search: Searching is not available by phone.

Mail Search: Always enclose a stamped self addressed envelope.

In Person: In person searching is available.

PACER: Sign-up number is 800-676-6856. Access fee is $.60 per minute. Toll-free access: 888-234-3839. Local access: 912-752-8170. Case records are available back to January 1991. Records are never purged. New records are available online after 1-2 days. Pacer is available online at http://pacer.gamd.uscourts.gov.

Valdosta Division PO Box 68, Valdosta, GA 31603 (Courier Address: Room 212, 401 N Patterson, Valdosta, GA 31601), 912-242-3616, Fax: 912-244-9547.

http://www.gamd.uscourts.gov

Counties: Berrien, Clinch, Cook, Echols, Irwin, Lanier, Lowndes, Tift.

Indexing/Storage: Cases are indexed by defendant and plaintiff as well as by case number. New cases are available in the index immediately after filing date. A computer index is maintained. Open records are located at this court.

Fee & Payment: The fee is $20.00 per item (one party name or case number). Payment may be

made by money order, cashier check, business check. Personal checks are not accepted. Prepayment is required. Payee: US Courts. Certification fee: $7.00 per document. Copy fee: $.50 per page. You are allowed to make your own copies. These copies cost Not Applicable per page.

Phone Search: Docket information is available by phone.

Mail Search: A stamped self addressed envelope is not required.

In Person: In person searching is available.

PACER: Sign-up number is 800-676-6856. Access fee is $.60 per minute. Toll-free access: 888-234-3839. Local access: 912-752-8170. Case records are available back to January 1991. Records are never purged. New records are available online after 1-2 days. Pacer is available online at http://pacer.gamd.uscourts.gov.

US Bankruptcy Court

Middle District of Georgia

Columbus Division PO Box 2147, Columbus, GA 31902 (Courier Address: 901 Front Ave, 1 Arsenal Pl, Columbus, GA 31902), 706-649-7837.

http://www.gamb.uscourts.gov

Counties: Berrien, Brooks, Chattahoochee, Clay, Clinch, Colquitt, Cook, Decatur, Echols, Grady, Harris, Irwin, Lanier, Lowndes, Marion, Muscogee, Quitman, Randolph, Seminole, Stewart, Talbot, Taylor, Thomas, Tift.

Indexing/Storage: Cases are indexed by debtor as well as by case number. New cases are available in the index immediately after filing date. A computer index is maintained. An alias name of the debtor may be required to search for records. Open records are located at this court.

Fee & Payment: The fee is $20.00 per item (one party name or case number). Payment may be made by money order, cashier check, business check. Personal checks are not accepted. Prepayment is required. Payee: Clerk, US Bankruptcy Court. Certification fee: $7.00 per document. Copy fee: $.50 per page.

Phone Search: Docket information is available by phone. An automated voice case information service (VCIS) is available. Call VCIS at 800-211-3015 or 912-752-8183.

Mail Search: Always enclose a stamped self addressed envelope.

In Person: In person searching is available.

PACER: Sign-up number is 800-676-6856. Access fee is $.60 per minute. Toll-free access: 800-546-7343. Local access: 912-752-3551. Case records are available back to March 1990 (some back to 1985). Records are purged except last 12 months. New civil records are available online after 1 day. PACER is available online at http://pacer.gamb.uscourts.gov.

Macon Division PO Box 1957, Macon, GA 31201 (Courier Address: 433 Cherry St, Macon, GA 31202), 912-752-3506, Fax: 912-752-8157.

http://www.gamb.uscourts.gov

Counties: Baldwin, Baker, Ben Hill, Bibb, Bleckley, Butts, Calhoun, Clarke, Crawford, Crisp, Dooly, Dougherty, Early, Elbert, Franklin, Greene, Hancock, Hart, Houston, Jasper, Jones, Lamar, Lee, Macon, Madison, Miller, Mitchell, Monroe,

Morgan, Oconee, Oglethorpe, Peach, Pulaski, Putnam, Schley, Sumter, Terrell, Turner, Twiggs, Upson, Walton, Washington, Webster, Wilcox, Wilkinson, Worth.

Indexing/Storage: Cases are indexed by debtor and creditors as well as by case number. New cases are available in the index 1-2 days after filing date. Any alias name of the debtor may be required to search for records. A computer index is maintained. Open records are located at this court.

Fee & Payment: The fee is $20.00 per item (one party name or case number). Payment may be made by money order, cashier check, business check. Personal checks are not accepted. Prepayment is required. Payee: Clerk, US Bankruptcy Court. Certification fee: $7.00 per document. Copy fee: $.50 per page.

Phone Search: This court will only search for basic information by phone and limits the number of searches to 3 per phone call. An automated voice case information service (VCIS) is available. Call VCIS at 800-211-3015 or 912-752-8183.

Mail Search: Always enclose a stamped self addressed envelope.

In Person: In person searching is available.

PACER: Sign-up number is 800-676-6856. Access fee is $.60 per minute. Toll-free access: 800-546-7343. Local access: 912-752-3551. Case records are available back to March 1990 (some back to 1985). Records are purged except last 12 months. New civil records are available online after 1 day. PACER is available online at http://pacer.gamb.uscourts.gov.

US District Court

Northern District of Georgia

Atlanta Division 2211 US Courthouse, 75 Spring St SW, Atlanta, GA 30303-3361 (Courier Address: Use mail address for courier delivery), 404-215-1660.

http://www.gand.uscourts.gov

Counties: Cherokee, Clayton, Cobb, De Kalb, Douglas, Fulton, Gwinnett, Henry, Newton, Rockdale.

Indexing/Storage: Cases are indexed by defendant and plaintiff as well as by case number. New cases are available in the index 1 day after filing date. A computer index is maintained. Open records are located at this court.

Fee & Payment: The fee is $20.00 per item (one party name or case number). Payment may be made by money order, cashier check. Business checks are not accepted. Personal checks are not accepted. Prepayment is required. Payee: Clerk, US District Court. Certification fee: $7.00 per document. Copy fee: $.50 per page.

Phone Search: Only docket information is available by phone.

Mail Search: A stamped self addressed envelope is not required.

In Person: In person searching is available.

PACER: Sign-up number is 800-676-6856. Access fee is $.60 per minute. Toll-free access: 800-801-6932. Local access: 404-730-9668. Case records are available back to August 1992. Records are purged on a varied schedule. New records are available online after 1 day. PACER is available online at http://pacer.gand.uscourts.gov.

Gainesville Division Federal Bldg, Room 201, 121 Spring St SE, Gainesville, GA 30501 (Courier Address: Use mail address for courier delivery), 678-450-2760.

http://www.gand.uscourts.gov

Counties: Banks, Barrow, Dawson, Fannin, Forsyth, Gilmer, Habersham, Hall, Jackson, Lumpkin, Pickens, Rabun, Stephens, Towns, Union, White.

Indexing/Storage: Cases are indexed by defendant and plaintiff as well as by case number. New cases are available in the index 24 hours after filing date. A computer index is maintained. Open records are located at this court.

Fee & Payment: The fee is $20.00 per item (one party name or case number). Payment may be made by money order. Business checks are not accepted. Personal checks are not accepted. Prepayment is required. The court will only accept US Postal money orders, law firm checks and cashier's checks. Payee: Clerk, US District Court. Certification fee: $7.00 per document. Copy fee: $.50 per page.

Phone Search: Searching is not available by phone.

Mail Search: Always enclose a stamped self addressed envelope.

In Person: In person searching is available.

PACER: Sign-up number is 800-676-6856. Access fee is $.60 per minute. Toll-free access: 800-801-6932. Local access: 404-730-9668. Case records are available back to August 1992. Records are purged on a varied schedule. New records are available online after 1 day. PACER is available online at http://pacer.gand.uscourts.gov.

Newnan Division PO Box 939, Newnan, GA 30264 (Courier Address: 18 Greenville St, #352, Newnan, GA 30263), 678-423-3060.

http://www.gand.uscourts.gov

Counties: Carroll, Coweta, Fayette, Haralson, Heard, Meriwether, Pike, Spalding, Troup.

Indexing/Storage: Cases are indexed by defendant and plaintiff as well as by case number. New cases are available in the index immediately after filing date. A computer index is maintained. Open records are located at this court.

Fee & Payment: The fee is $20.00 per item (one party name or case number). Payment may be made by money order, cashier check. Business checks are not accepted. Personal checks are not accepted. Prepayment is required. Only attorney firm checks will be accepted. Payee: Clerk, US District Court. Certification fee: $7.00 per document. Copy fee: $.50 per page.

Phone Search: Only docket information is available by phone.

Mail Search: A stamped self addressed envelope is not required.

In Person: In person searching is available.

PACER: Sign-up number is 800-676-6856. Access fee is $.60 per minute. Toll-free access: 800-801-6932. Local access: 404-730-9668. Case records are available back to August 1992. Records are purged on a varied schedule. New records are available online after 1 day. PACER is available online at http://pacer.gand.uscourts.gov.

Rome Division PO Box 1186, Rome, GA 30162-1186 (Courier Address: 600 E 1st St, Room 304, Rome, GA 30161), 706-291-5629.

http://www.gand.uscourts.gov

Counties: Bartow, Catoosa, Chattooga, Dade, Floyd, Gordon, Murray, Paulding, Polk, Walker, Whitfield.

Indexing/Storage: Cases are indexed by defendant and plaintiff as well as by case number. New cases are available in the index immediately after filing date. A computer index is maintained. Records are also indexed on microfiche. Only records prior to 1978 are on index cards. Open records are located at this court.

Fee & Payment: The fee is $20.00 per item (one party name or case number). Payment may be made by money order, cashier check. Business checks are not accepted. Personal checks are not accepted. Prepayment is required. Attorney checks also accepted. Payee: Clerk, US District Court. Certification fee: $7.00 per document. Copy fee: $.50 per page.

Phone Search: Only docket information showing if a suit has been filed, date of filing, and if case is pending or closed will be released over the phone.

Mail Search: Always enclose a stamped self addressed envelope.

In Person: In person searching is available.

PACER: Sign-up number is 800-676-6856. Access fee is $.60 per minute. Toll-free access: 800-801-6932. Local access: 404-730-9668. Case records are available back to August 1992. Records are purged on a varied schedule. New records are available online after 1 day. PACER is available online at http://pacer.gand.uscourts.gov.

US Bankruptcy Court

Northern District of Georgia

Atlanta Division 1340 US Courthouse, 75 Spring St SW, Atlanta, GA 30303-3361 (Courier Address: Use mail address for courier delivery), 404-215-1000.

http://www.ganb.uscourts.gov

Counties: Cherokee, Clayton, Cobb, DeKalb, Douglas, Fulton, Gwinnett, Henry, Newton, Rockdale.

Indexing/Storage: Cases are indexed by debtor as well as by case number. New cases are available in the index 1-2 days after filing date. Both computer and card indexes are maintained. Records are also indexed on microfiche. Open records are located at this court.

Fee & Payment: The fee is $20.00 per item (one party name or case number). Payment may be made by money order, cashier check, business check. Personal checks are not accepted. Prepayment is required. Debtor's checks are not accepted. Payee: Clerk, US Bankruptcy Court. Certification fee: $7.00 per document. Copy fee: $.50 per page.

Phone Search: Docket information is available by phone. An automated voice case information service (VCIS) is available. Call VCIS at 888-510-8284 or 404-730-2866.

Fax Search: Fax requests are handled by a copy service. To set-up a fax request, call the service at 404-681-9125.

Mail Search: Always enclose a stamped self addressed envelope.

In Person: In person searching is available.

PACER: Sign-up number is 800-676-6856. Access fee is $.60 per minute. Toll-free access: 800-436-8395. Local access: 404-730-3264. Case records are available back to August 1986. Records are never purged. New civil records are available online after 2 days.

Electronic Filing: Electronic filing information is available online at http://ecf.ganb.uscourts.gov

Gainesville Division 121 Spring St SE, Room 120, Gainesville, GA 30501 (Courier Address: Use mail address for courier delivery), 678-450-2700.

http://www.ganb.uscourts.gov

Counties: Banks, Barrow, Dawson, Fannin, Forsyth, Gilmer, Habersham, Hall, Jackson, Lumpkin, Pickens, Rabun, Stephens, Towns, Union, White.

Indexing/Storage: Cases are indexed by debtor as well as by case number. New cases are available in the index 1-2 days after filing date. This court maintains index cards on older cases. Both computer and card indexes are maintained. Open records are located at this court.

Fee & Payment: The fee is $20.00 per item (one party name or case number). Payment may be made by money order, cashier check, personal check. Prepayment is required. Debtors checks not accepted. Payee: Clerk, US Bankruptcy Court. Certification fee: $7.00 per document. Copy fee: $.50 per page.

Phone Search: Docket information available by phone. An automated voice case information service (VCIS) is available. Call VCIS at 888-510-8284 or 404-730-2866.

Mail Search: Always enclose a stamped self addressed envelope.

In Person: In person searching is available.

PACER: Sign-up number is 800-676-6856. Access fee is $.60 per minute. Toll-free access: 800-436-8395. Local access: 404-730-3264. Case records are available back to August 1986. Records are never purged. New civil records are available online after 2 days.

Electronic Filing: Electronic filing information is available online at http://ecf.ganb.uscourts.gov

Newnan Division Clerk, PO Box 2328, Newnan, GA 30264 (Courier Address: Room 220, 18 Greenville St, Newnan, GA 30263), 678-423-3000.

http://www.ganb.uscourts.gov

Counties: Carroll, Coweta, Fayette, Haralson, Heard, Meriwether, Pike, Spalding, Troup.

Indexing/Storage: Cases are indexed by debtor as well as by case number. New cases are available in the index 1 day after filing date. A card index is maintained. Records are also indexed on microfiche. Open records are located at this court.

Fee & Payment: The fee is $20.00 per item (one party name or case number). Payment may be made by money order, cashier check, personal check. Prepayment is required. Debtor's checks are not accepted. Payee: Clerk, US Bankruptcy Court. Certification fee: $7.00 per document. Copy fee: $.50 per page.

Phone Search: Only docket information is available by phone. The debtor's address and social security number will not be released. There is no charge if a case number is provided. An automated voice case information service (VCIS) is available. Call VCIS at 888-510-8284 or 404-730-2866.

Mail Search: A stamped self addressed envelope is not required.

In Person: In person searching is available.

PACER: Sign-up number is 800-676-6856. Access fee is $.60 per minute. Toll-free access: 800-436-8395. Local access: 404-730-3264. Case records are available back to August 1986. Records are never purged. New civil records are available online after 2 days.

Electronic Filing: Electronic filing information is available online at http://ecf.ganb.uscourts.gov

Rome Division Clerk, 600 E 1st St, Room 339, Rome, GA 30161-3187 (Courier Address: Use mail address for courier delivery), 706-291-5639.

http://www.ganb.uscourts.gov

Counties: Bartow, Catoosa, Chattooga, Dade, Floyd, Gordon, Murray, Paulding, Polk, Walker, Whitfield.

Indexing/Storage: Cases are indexed by debtor as well as by case number. New cases are available in the index 24 hours after filing date. A card index is maintained. Open records are located at this court.

Fee & Payment: The fee is $20.00 per item (one party name or case number). Payment may be made by money order, cashier check, personal check. Prepayment is required. Payee: Clerk, US Bankruptcy Court. Certification fee: $7.00 per document. Copy fee: $.50 per page.

Phone Search: Docket information is available by phone. An automated voice case information service (VCIS) is available. Call VCIS at 888-510-8284 or 404-730-2866.

Mail Search: Always enclose a stamped self addressed envelope.

In Person: In person searching is available.

PACER: Sign-up number is 800-676-6856. Access fee is $.60 per minute. Toll-free access: 800-436-8395. Local access: 404-730-3264. Case records are available back to August 1986. Records are never purged. New civil records are available online after 2 days.

Electronic Filing: Electronic filing information is available online at http://ecf.ganb.uscourts.gov

US District Court

Southern District of Georgia

Augusta Division PO Box 1130, Augusta, GA 30903 (Courier Address: Use mail address for courier delivery., 500 E Ford St, First Floor,), 706-849-4400.

http://www.gasd.uscourts.gov

Counties: Burke, Columbia, Glascock, Jefferson, Lincoln, McDuffie, Richmond, Taliaferro, Warren, Wilkes.

Indexing/Storage: Cases are indexed by defendant and plaintiff as well as by case number. New cases are available in the index immediately after filing date. Records are alphabetically indexed and stored by chronological case number order. A computer index is maintained. Open records are located at this court.

Fee & Payment: The fee is $20.00 per item (one party name or case number). Payment may be made by money order, cashier check, personal

check. Prepayment is required. Payee: US Courts. Certification fee: $7.00 per document. Copy fee: $.50 per page.

Phone Search: Docket information available by phone.

Mail Search: Always enclose a stamped self addressed envelope.

In Person: In person searching is available.

PACER: Sign-up number is 800-676-6856. Access fee is $.60 per minute. Toll-free access: 800-801-6934. Local access: 912-650-4046. Case records are available back to June 1995. New records are available online after 1 day. PACER is available online at http://pacer.gasd.uscourts.gov.

Brunswick Division PO Box 1636, Brunswick, GA 31521 (Courier Address: Room 222, 801 Glouchester, Brunswick, GA 31520), 912-280-1330.

http://www.gasd.uscourts.gov

Counties: Appling, Camden, Glynn, Jeff Davis, Long, McIntosh, Wayne.

Indexing/Storage: Cases are indexed by defendant and plaintiff as well as by case number. New cases are available in the index immediately after filing date. A computer index is maintained. The records from the last 1 1/2 years are indexed on computer. Prior records are indexed on microfiche. Open records are located at this court.

Fee & Payment: The fee is $20.00 per item (one party name or case number). Payment may be made by money order, cashier check, personal check. Prepayment is required. Payee: Clerk, US District Court. Certification fee: $7.00 per document. Copy fee: $.50 per page.

Phone Search: Only docket information is available by phone.

Mail Search: Always enclose a stamped self addressed envelope.

In Person: In person searching is available.

PACER: Sign-up number is 800-676-6856. Access fee is $.60 per minute. Toll-free access: 800-801-6934. Local access: 912-650-4046. Case records are available back to June 1995. New records are available online after 1 day. PACER is available online at http://pacer.gasd.uscourts.gov.

Dublin Division c/o Augusta Division, PO Box 1130, Augusta, GA 30903 (Courier Address: 500 E Ford St, Augusta, GA 30901), 706-849-4400.

http://www.gasd.uscourts.gov

Counties: Dodge, Johnson, Laurens, Montgomery, Telfair, Treutlen, Wheeler.

Indexing/Storage: Cases are indexed by as well as by case number. New cases are available in the index after filing date. Open records are located at the Division.

Fee & Payment: The fee is no charge per item (one party name or case number). Payment may be made by money order, cashier check. Business checks are not accepted. Personal checks are not accepted.

Phone Search: Searching is not available by phone.

Mail Search: A stamped self addressed envelope is not required.

In Person: In person searching is available.

PACER: Sign-up number is 800-676-6856. Access fee is $.60 per minute. Toll-free access: 800-801-6934. Local access: 912-650-4046. Case

records are available back to June 1995. New records are available online after 1 day. PACER is available online at http://pacer.gasd.uscourts.gov.

Savannah Division PO Box 8286, Savannah, GA 31412 (Courier Address: Room 306, 125 Bull St, Savannah, GA 31401), 912-650-4020, Fax: 912-650-4030.

http://www.gasd.uscourts.gov

Counties: Bryan, Chatham, Effingham, Liberty.

Indexing/Storage: Cases are indexed by defendant and plaintiff as well as by case number. New cases are available in the index immediately after filing date. A computer index is maintained. Records have been indexed on computer from 1992. Prior records are indexed on microfiche. Open records are located at this court.

Fee & Payment: The fee is $20.00 per item (one party name or case number). Payment may be made by money order, cashier check, personal check. Prepayment is required. Payee: Clerk, US District Court. Certification fee: $7.00 per document. Copy fee: $.50 per page.

Phone Search: Searching is not available by phone. Only docket information is available by phone.

Mail Search: A stamped self addressed envelope is not required.

In Person: In person searching is available.

PACER: Sign-up number is 800-676-6856. Access fee is $.60 per minute. Toll-free access: 800-801-6934. Local access: 912-650-4046. Case records are available back to June 1995. New records are available online after 1 day. PACER is available online at http://pacer.gasd.uscourts.gov.

Statesboro Division c/o Savannah Division, PO Box 8286, Savannah, GA 31412 (Courier Address: Use mail address for courier delivery), 912-650-4020.

http://www.gasd.uscourts.gov

Counties: Bulloch, Candler, Emanuel, Evans, Jenkins, Screven, Tattnall, Toombs.

Indexing/Storage: Cases are indexed by as well as by case number. New cases are available in the index after filing date. Open records are located at the Division.

Fee & Payment: The fee is no charge per item (one party name or case number). Payment may be made by money order, cashier check. Business checks are not accepted. Personal checks are not accepted.

Phone Search: Searching is not available by phone.

Mail Search: A stamped self addressed envelope is not required.

In Person: In person searching is available.

PACER: Sign-up number is 800-676-6856. Access fee is $.60 per minute. Toll-free access: 800-801-6934. Local access: 912-650-4046. Case records are available back to June 1995. New records are available online after 1 day. PACER is available online at http://pacer.gasd.uscourts.gov.

Waycross Division c/o Savannah Division, PO Box 8286, Savannah, GA 31412 (Courier Address: Room 306, 125 Bull St, Savannah, GA 31401), 912-650-4020.

http://www.gasd.uscourts.gov

Counties: Atkinson, Bacon, Brantley, Charlton, Coffee, Pierce, Ware.

Indexing/Storage: Cases are indexed by as well as by case number. New cases are available in the index after filing date. Open records are located at the Division.

Fee & Payment: The fee is no charge per item (one party name or case number). Payment may be made by money order, cashier check. Business checks are not accepted. Personal checks are not accepted.

Phone Search: Searching is not available by phone.

Mail Search: A stamped self addressed envelope is not required.

In Person: In person searching is available.

PACER: Sign-up number is 800-676-6856. Access fee is $.60 per minute. Toll-free access: 800-801-6934. Local access: 912-650-4046. Case records are available back to June 1995. New records are available online after 1 day. PACER is available online at http://pacer.gasd.uscourts.gov.

US Bankruptcy Court

Southern District of Georgia

Augusta Division PO Box 1487, Augusta, GA 30903 (Courier Address: 933 Broad St - 3rd Fl, Augusta, GA 30901), 706-724-2421.

http://www.gas.uscourts.gov

Counties: Bulloch, Burke, Candler, Columbia, Dodge, Emanuel, Evans, Glascock, Jefferson, Jenkins, Johnson, Laurens, Lincoln, McDuffie, Montgomery, Richmond, Screven, Taliaferro, Tattnall, Telfair, Toombs, Treutlen, Warren, Wheeler, Wilkes.

Indexing/Storage: Cases are indexed by debtor as well as by case number. New cases are available in the index 24 hours after filing date. A computer index is maintained. Open records are located at this court. District wide searches are available for information from August 1986 from this court. This court handles files for the Statesboro and Dublin divisions as well as the Augusta files.

Fee & Payment: The fee is $20.00 per item (one party name or case number). Payment may be made by money order, cashier check, business check. Personal checks are not accepted. Prepayment is required. Payee: Clerk, US Bankruptcy Court. Certification fee: $7.00 per document. Copy fee: $.50 per page.

Phone Search: If case number is provided over the phone, all docket information will be released.

Mail Search: Always enclose a stamped self addressed envelope.

In Person: In person searching is available.

PACER: Sign-up number is 800-676-6856. Access fee is $.60 per minute. Toll-free access: 800-259-8679. Local access: 912-650-4190. Case records are available back to August 1986. Records are purged annually. New records are available online after. PACER is available online at http://pacer.gasb.uscourts.gov. This appears to be a combination of RACER and PACER; the fee is 7 cents per page.

Savannah Division PO Box 8347, Savannah, GA 31412 (Courier Address: Room 213, 125 Bull St, Savannah, GA 31412), 912-650-4100.

http://www.gas.uscourts.gov

Counties: Appling, Atkinson, Bacon, Brantley, Bryan, Camden, Charlton, Chatham, Coffee, Effingham, Glynn, Jeff Davis, Liberty, Long, McIntosh, Pierce, Ware, Wayne.

Indexing/Storage: Cases are indexed by debtor as well as by case number. New cases are available in the index immediately after filing date. Cases are also indexed by Social Security number. A computer index is maintained. Open records are located at this court. District wide searches are available for information from August 1, 1985 at this court. This court handles files for the Waycross and Brunswick divisions as well as the Savannah files.

Fee & Payment: The fee is $20.00 per item (one party name or case number). Payment may be made by money order, cashier check, business check. Personal checks are not accepted. Prepayment is required. Payee: Clerk, US Bankruptcy Court. Certification fee: $7.00 per document. Copy fee: $.50 per page.

Phone Search: Phone search is limited to information on computer.

Mail Search: A stamped self addressed envelope is not required.

In Person: In person searching is available.

PACER: Sign-up number is 800-676-6856. Access fee is $.60 per minute. Toll-free access: 800-891-9583. Local access: 912-650-4190. Case records are available back to 1988. Records are purged every six months. New civil records are available online after 1 day. PACER is available online at http://pacer.gasb.uscourts.gov. This appears to be a combination of RACER and PACER; the fee is 7 cents per page.

Georgia County Courts

Court	Jurisdiction	No. of Courts	How Organized
Superior Courts*	General	100	48 Circuits
State Courts*	Limited	69	69 Counties
Combined Courts*		43	
Magistrate Courts*	Limited	159	By County
Combined Superior/ Magistrate Court*		17	
Civil Courts*	Limited	2	Bibb, Richmond
County Recorder's Courts	Limited	4	Chatham, DeKalb, Gwinnett, Muscogee
Municipal Court	Municipal	1	Columbus, Moscogee
Municipal Courts	Municipal	474	Includes City Court of Atlanta
Probate Courts*	Probate	159	By County
Juvenile Courts	Special	159	By County

* Profiled in this Sourcebook.

CIVIL									
Court	Tort	Contract	Real Estate	Min. Claim	Max. Claim	Small Claims	Estate	Eviction	Domestic Relations
Superior Courts*	X	X	X	$0	No Max	X		X	X
State Courts*	X	X		$0	No Max	X		X	
Combined Courts*	X	X		$0	No Max	$0		X	
Magistrate Courts*	X	X		$0	$15,000	$15,000		X	
Combined Superior/ Magistrate Court*									
Civil Courts*	X	X		$0	$7500	$7500			
Recorder's Courts									
Municipal Courts									
Probate Courts*							X		
Juvenile Courts									

CRIMINAL					
Court	Felony	Misdemeanor	DWI/DUI	Preliminary Hearing	Juvenile
Superior Courts*	X	X	X	X	
State Courts*		X	X	X	
Combined Courts*				X	
Magistrate Courts*		X		X	
Combined Superior/ Magistrate Court*			X	X	
Civil Courts*				X	
Recorder's Courts		X	X	X	
Municipal Courts		X	X	X	
Probate Courts*		X	X	X	
Juvenile Courts					X

ADMINISTRATION   Court Administrator, 244 Washington St SW, Suite 550, Atlanta, GA, 30334; 404-656-5171, Fax: 404-651-6449. www.georgiacourts.org/aoc/index.html

COURT STRUCTURE   Georgia's Superior Courts are arranged in 48 circuits of general jurisdiction, and these assume the role of a State Court if the county does not have one. The 69 State Courts, like Superior Courts, can conduct jury trials, but are limited jurisidiction. Each county has a Probate, a Juvenile, and a Magistrate Court; the latter has jurisdiction over civil actions under $15,000, also one type of misdemeanor related to passing bad checks. Magistrate Courts also issue arrest warrants and set bond on all felonies. Probate courts can, in certain cases, issue search and arrest warrants, and hear miscellaneous misdemeanors.

ONLINE ACCESS   Cobb County has Internet access to records, but there is no online access available statewide, although one is being planned.

ADDITIONAL INFORMATION   In most Georgia counties, the courts will not perform criminal record searches, and, in many cases, will not do civil record searches. An in-person search or the use of a record retriever is required.

The Georgia Crime Information Center is the felony criminal history state repository.

Appling County

Superior & State Court PO Box 269, Baxley, GA 31513; 912-367-8126. Hours: 8AM-5PM (EST). *Felony, Misdemeanor, Civil.*

Civil Records: Access: In person only. Visitors must perform in person searches for themselves. No search fee. Required to search: name, years to search. Civil cases indexed by defendant, plaintiff. Civil records on docket books back to 1800s.
Criminal Records: Access: In person only. Visitors must perform in person searches for themselves. No search fee. Required to search: name, years to search, DOB; also helpful: SSN, race, sex. Criminal records on docket books back to 1800s.
General Information: No juvenile, adoption, sealed, sexual, mental health or expunged records released. Copy fee: $.25 for first page, $.10 each add'l. Certification fee: $2.50 plus $.50 per page after first. Fee payee: Court Clerk. Personal checks accepted.

Magistrate Court Box 366, Baxley, GA 31515; 912-367-8116; Fax: 912-367-8182. Hours: 8:30AM-5PM (EST). *Civil Actions Under $15,000, Eviction, Small Claims.*

Probate Court 36 S Main St #B, Baxley, GA 31513; 912-367-8114; Fax: 912-367-8166. Hours: 8:30AM-5PM (EST). *Probate.*

Atkinson County

Superior Court PO Box 6, South Main, Courthouse Square, Pearson, GA 31642; 912-422-3343; Fax: 912-422-7025. Hours: 8AM-5PM (EST). *Felony, Misdemeanor, Civil.*

Civil Records: Access: In person only. Visitors must perform in person searches for themselves. No search fee. Required to search: name, years to search. Civil cases indexed by defendant. Civil records in docket books back to 1919.
Criminal Records: Access: In person only. Visitors must perform in person searches for themselves. No search fee. Required to search: name, years to search. Criminal records in docket books back to 1919.
General Information: No juvenile, adoption, sealed, sexual, mental health or expunged records released. Copy fee: $.25 per page. Certification fee: $2.50 plus $.50 per page after first. Fee payee: Clerk of Superior Court. Personal checks accepted. Prepayment is required.

Magistrate Court PO Box 674, Pearson, GA 31642; 912-422-7158; Fax: 912-422-3429. Hours: 9AM-4:30PM (EST). *Civil Actions Under $15,000, Eviction, Small Claims.*

Probate Court PO Box 855, Pearson, GA 31642; 912-422-3552; Fax: 912-422-7842. Hours: 8AM-5PM (EST). *Probate.*

Bacon County

Superior Court PO Box 376, Alma, GA 31510; 912-632-4915. Hours: 9AM-5PM (EST). *Felony, Misdemeanor, Civil.*

Civil Records: Access: Mail, in person. Both court and visitors may perform in person searches. No search fee. Required to search: name, years to search. Civil cases indexed by defendant, plaintiff. Civil records on index from 1918.
Criminal Records: Access: Mail, in person. Both court and visitors may perform in person searches. No search fee. Required to search: name, years to search, DOB; also helpful: SSN, race, sex. Criminal records on index from 1918.
General Information: No juvenile, adoption, sealed, sexual, mental health, expunged or first offender records released. SASE required. Turnaround time 1 week. Copy fee: $.25 per page. Certification fee: $2.50 plus $.50 per page after first. Fee payee: Clerk of Superior Court. Personal checks accepted. Prepayment is required.

Magistrate Court Box 389, Alma, GA 31510; 912-632-5961. Hours: 9AM-5PM (EST). *Civil Actions Under $15,000, Eviction, Small Claims.*

Probate Court PO Box 146, Alma, GA 31510; 912-632-7661; Fax: 912-632-7662. Hours: 9AM-5PM (EST). *Probate.*

Baker County

Superior Court PO Box 10, Governmental Bldg, Newton, GA 31770; 229-734-3004; Fax: 229-734-8822. Hours: 9AM-5PM (EST). *Felony, Misdemeanor, Civil.*

Civil Records: Access: In person only. Visitors must perform in person searches for themselves. No search fee. Required to search: name, years to search. Civil cases indexed by defendant. Civil records on index from 1850.
Criminal Records: Access: In person only. Visitors must perform in person searches for themselves. No search fee. Required to search: name, years to search, DOB; also helpful: SSN, race, sex. Criminal records on index from 1850.
General Information: No juvenile, adoption, sealed, sexual or expunged records released. Copy fee: $.25 per page. Certification fee: $2.50 plus $.50 per page after first. Fee payee: Court Clerk. Personal checks accepted. Prepayment is required.

Magistrate Court Box 535, Newton, GA 31770; 229-734-3009; Fax: 229-734-8822. Hours: 9AM-5PM (EST). *Civil Actions Under $15,000, Eviction, Small Claims.*

Probate Court PO Box 548, Newton, GA 31770; 229-734-3007; Fax: 229-734-8822. Hours: 9AM-5PM M-W & F; 9AM-Noon Th (EST). *Probate.*

Baldwin County

Superior & State Court PO Drawer 987, Milledgeville, GA 31061; 478-445-4007; Fax: 478-445-1404. Hours: 8:30AM-5PM (EST). *Felony, Misdemeanor, Civil.*

Civil Records: Access: In person only. Visitors must perform in person searches for themselves. No search fee. Required to search: name, years to search. Civil cases indexed by defendant, plaintiff. Civil records on docket from 1861; on computer back to 1996.
Criminal Records: Access: In person only. Visitors must perform in person searches for themselves. No search fee. Required to search: name, years to search. Criminal records on docket from 1861; on computer back to 1996.
General Information: Public Access terminal is available. No juvenile, adoption, sealed, sexual, mental health or expunged records released. Copy fee: $.25 per page. Certification fee: $2.50 plus $.50 per page after first. Personal checks accepted. Prepayment is required.

Magistrate Court PO Box 1565, Milledgeville, GA 31061; 478-445-4446; Fax: 478-445-5918. Hours: 8:30AM-5PM (EST). *Civil Actions Under $15,000, Eviction, Small Claims.*

Probate Court PO Box 964, Milledgeville, GA 31061; 478-445-4807; Fax: 478-445-5178. Hours: 8:30AM-5PM (EST). *Probate.*

Banks County

Superior Court PO Box 337, 144 Yorah Homer Road, Homer, GA 30547; 706-677-6240; Fax: 706-677-2337. Hours: 8:30AM-5PM (EST). *Felony, Misdemeanor, Civil.*

Civil Records: Access: In person only. Visitors must perform in person searches for themselves. No search fee. Required to search: name, years to search. Civil cases indexed by defendant, plaintiff. Civil records on docket from 1960.
Criminal Records: Access: In person only. Visitors must perform in person searches for themselves. No search fee. Required to search: name, years to search, DOB, signed release; also helpful: SSN, race, sex. Criminal records on docket from 1960.

General Information: Public Access terminal is available. No juvenile, adoption, sealed, sexual, mental health or expunged records released. Copy fee: $.25 per page. Certification fee: $3.75. Fee payee: Clerk of Superior Court. Personal checks accepted.

Magistrate Court Box 364, Homer, GA 30547; 706-677-6270; Fax: 706-677-6215. Hours: 8:30AM-5PM (EST). *Civil Actions Under $15,000, Eviction, Small Claims.*

Probate Court PO Box 7, Homer, GA 30547; 706-677-6250; Fax: 706-677-2339. Hours: 80AM-5PM (EST). *Probate.*

Barrow County

Superior Court PO Box 1280, Winder, GA 30680; 770-307-3035; Fax: 770-867-4800. Hours: 8AM-5PM (EST). *Felony, Misdemeanor, Civil.*

Civil Records: Access: In person only. Visitors must perform in person searches for themselves. No search fee. Required to search: name, years to search. Civil cases indexed by defendant, plaintiff. Civil records on computer from 1990, docket from 1914.
Criminal Records: Access: In person only. Visitors must perform in person searches for themselves. No search fee. Required to search: name, years to search, DOB; also helpful: SSN, race, sex. Criminal records on computer from 1992, docket from 1914.
General Information: No juvenile, adoption, sealed, sexual, mental health or expunged records released. Copy fee: $.25 per page. Certification fee: $2.50 plus $.50 per page after first. Fee payee: Clerk of Superior Court. Business checks accepted. Prepayment is required.

Magistrate Court 30 N Broad St, Ste 331, Winder, GA 30680; 770-307-3050; Fax: 770-868-1440. Hours: 8AM-5PM (EST). *Civil Actions Under $15,000, Eviction, Small Claims.*

Probate Court Barrow County Courthouse, 30 N Broad St, Winder, GA 30680; 770-867-8981; Fax: 770-867-4800. Hours: 8AM-5PM (EST). *Probate.*

Bartow County

Superior Court 135 W Cherokee #233, Cartersville, GA 30120; 770-387-5025; Fax: 770-387-5611. Hours: 8AM-5PM *Felony, Misdemeanor, Civil.*

Civil Records: Access: In person only. Visitors must perform in person searches for themselves. No search fee. Required to search: name, years to search. Civil cases indexed by defendant, plaintiff. Civil records on computer from 9/92, on books from 1900s.
Criminal Records: Access: In person only. Visitors must perform in person searches for themselves. No search fee. Required to search: name, years to search, address, DOB, SSN, signed release. Criminal records on computer for 10 years, prior on books.
General Information: No juvenile, adoptions or sealed records released. Copy fee: $.25 per page. Certification fee: $2.50 plus $.25 each add'l page. Fee payee: Clerk of Superior Court. Personal checks accepted. Prepayment is required.

Magistrate Court 135 W Cherokee Ave #225, Cartersville, GA 30120; 770-387-5070. Hours: 7AM-5:30PM (EST). *Civil Actions Under $15,000, Eviction, Small Claims.*

Probate Court 135 W Cherokee #243A, Cartersville, GA 30120; 770-387-5075; Fax: 770-387-5074. Hours: 8AM-5PM (EST). *Probate.*

Ben Hill County

Superior Court PO Box 1104, 401 Central, Fitzgerald, GA 31750; 229-426-5135; Fax: 229-426-5487. Hours: 8:30AM-4:30PM (EST). *Felony, Misdemeanor, Civil.*

Civil Records: Access: In person only. Visitors must perform in person searches for themselves. No search fee. Required to search: name, years to search. Civil cases indexed by defendant. Civil records on computer from 1994, archived from 1907, docket 1907.
Criminal Records: Access: In person only. Visitors must perform in person searches for themselves. No search fee. Required to search: name, years to search, signed release; also helpful: DOB, SSN. Criminal records on computer from 1994, archived from 1907, docket 1907.
General Information: No juvenile, adoption, sealed, sexual, mental health or expunged records released. Copy fee: $.25 per page; $1.00 per page if mailed. Certification fee: $2.00 plus $.50 per page. Fee payee: Clerk. Personal checks accepted. Prepayment is required.

Magistrate Court Box 1163, Fitzgerald, GA 31750; 229-426-5140. Hours: 8:30AM-5:30PM (EST). *Civil Actions Under $15,000, Eviction, Small Claims.*

Probate Court 401 E Central Ave, Fitzgerald, GA 31750; 229-426-5137; Fax: 229-426-5486. Hours: 9AM-5PM (EST). *Probate.*

Berrien County

Superior Court 101 E Marion Ave, Ste 3, Nashville, GA 31639; 229-686-5506. Hours: 8AM-5PM (EST). *Felony, Misdemeanor, Civil.*

Civil Records: Access: Mail, in person. Both court and visitors may perform in person searches. No search fee. Required to search: name, years to search. Civil cases indexed by defendant, plaintiff. Civil records on docket back to 1800.
Criminal Records: Access: Mail, in person. Both court and visitors may perform in person searches. No search fee. Required to search: name, years to search, DOB; also helpful: SSN, race, sex. Criminal records on docket back to 1800.
General Information: No juvenile, adoption, sealed, sexual, mental health or expunged records released. Turnaround time same day. Copy fee: $.25 per page. Certification fee: $2.50 plus $.50 per page after first. Fee payee: Court Clerk. Personal checks accepted. Prepayment is required.

Magistrate Court PO Box 103, Nashville, GA 31639; 229-686-7019; Fax: 229-686-6328. Hours: 8:30AM-4:30PM (EST). *Civil Actions Under $15,000, Eviction, Small Claims.*

Probate Court 101 E Marion Ave, Ste 2, Nashville, GA 31639; 229-686-5213; Fax: 229-686-9495. Hours: 7AM-5PM Sun-Sat (EST). *Probate.*

Bibb County

Superior Court PO Box 1015, 601 Mulberry St Rm 216, Macon, GA 31202; 478-749-6527. Hours: 8:30AM-5PM (EST). *Felony, Civil.*

Civil Records: Access: Mail, in person. Both court and visitors may perform in person searches. Search fee: $10.00 per name. Required to search: name, years to search. Civil cases indexed by defendant, plaintiff. Civil records on computer from 1993, on books from 1823.
Criminal Records: Access: Mail, in person. Both court and visitors may perform in person searches. Search fee: $10.00 per name. Required to search: name, years to search, DOB, signed release; also helpful: SSN. Criminal records on computer since 1989.

General Information: No adoption or sealed records released. Turnaround time same day. Copy fee: $.25 per page. Fee is $1.00 if court makes copy. Certification fee: $2.50 plus $.50 per page after first. Fee payee: Superior Court Clerk. Only cashiers checks and money orders accepted. Prepayment is required.

State Court PO Box 5086, Macon, GA 31213-7199; 478-749-6676; Fax: 478-749-6326. Hours: 8AM-5PM (EST). *Misdemeanor, Civil.*

Civil Records: Access: Mail, in person. Both court and visitors may perform in person searches. Search fee: $10.00 per name. Required to search: name, years to search. Civil cases indexed by defendant, plaintiff. Civil records on computer from 1989, docket from 1945.
Criminal Records: Access: Mail, in person. Both court and visitors may perform in person searches. Search fee: $10.00 per name. Required to search: name, years to search, DOB; also helpful: SSN, race, sex. Criminal records on computer from 1989, docket from 1945.
General Information: No juvenile, adoption, sealed, sexual, mental health or expunged records released. SASE required. Turnaround time 1 day. Copy fee: $.30 per page. Certification fee: $2.50 plus $.30 per page. Fee payee: Court Clerk. Business checks accepted. Prepayment is required.

Civil & Magistrate Court PO Box 121, Bibb County Courthouse, Macon, GA 31202-0121; 478-749-6495; Fax: 478-722-5861. Hours: 8AM-5PM (EST). *Civil Actions Under $25,000, Eviction, Small Claims.*

Probate Court 207 Bibb County Courthouse, PO Box 6518, Macon, GA 31208-6518; 478-749-6494; Fax: 478-749-6686. Hours: 8AM-5PM (EST). *Probate.*

Bleckley County

Superior Court 306 SE 2nd St, Cochran, GA 31014; 478-934-3210; Fax: 478-934-3205. Hours: 8:30AM-5PM (EST). *Felony, Misdemeanor, Civil.*

Civil Records: Access: In person only. Visitors must perform in person searches for themselves. No search fee. Required to search: name, years to search. Civil cases indexed by defendant, plaintiff. Civil records archived from 1913, docket from 1913.
Criminal Records: Access: In person only. Visitors must perform in person searches for themselves. No search fee. Required to search: name, years to search, DOB; also helpful: SSN, race, sex. Criminal records archived from 1913, docket from 1913.
General Information: No juvenile, adoption, sealed, sexual, mental health or expunged records released. Copy fee: $.25 per page. Certification fee: $2.50 plus $.50 per page after first. Fee payee: Clerk of the Superior Court. Personal checks not accepted. Prepayment is required.

Magistrate Court 101 Eighth St, Cochran, GA 31014; 478-934-3202; Fax: 478-934-3226. Hours: 8:30AM-5PM (EST). *Civil Actions Under $15,000, Eviction, Small Claims.*

Probate Court 306 SE Second St, Cochran, GA 31014; 478-934-3204; Fax: 478-934-3205. Hours: 8:30AM-5PM (EST). *Probate.*

Brantley County

Superior Court PO Box 1067, 117 Brantley St, Nahunta, GA 31553; 912-462-5635; Fax: 912-462-6247. Hours: 8AM-5PM (EST). *Felony, Misdemeanor, Civil.*

Civil Records: Access: In person only. Visitors must perform in person searches for themselves. No search fee. Required to search: name, years to search. Civil cases indexed by defendant, plaintiff. Civil records on dockets from 1922.

Criminal Records: Access: In person only. Visitors must perform in person searches for themselves. No search fee. Required to search: name, years to search, DOB, SSN, signed release; also helpful: race, sex. Criminal records on dockets from 1922.

General Information: No juvenile, adoption, sealed, 1st offenders, expunged or confidential records released. Copy fee: $.25 per page. Certification fee: $2.50 plus $.50 per page after first. Fee payee: Superior Court Clerk. Personal checks accepted. Prepayment is required.

Magistrate Court PO Box 998, Nahunta, GA 31553; 912-462-6780; Fax: 912-462-5538. Hours: 8AM-4:30PM (EST). *Civil Actions Under $15,000, Eviction, Small Claims.*

Probate Court PO Box 207, Nahunta, GA 31553; 912-462-5192; Fax: 912-462-5538. Hours: 9AM-5PM (EST). *Probate.*

Brooks County

Superior Court PO Box 630, Quitman, GA 31643; 229-263-4747/5150; Fax: 229-263-5050. Hours: 8AM-5PM (EST). *Felony, Misdemeanor, Civil.*

www2.state.ga.us/courts/superior/dca/dca2sohp.htm

Civil Records: Access: In person only. Visitors must perform in person searches for themselves. No search fee. Required to search: name, years to search. Civil cases indexed by defendant, plaintiff. Civil records in books back to 1857.

Criminal Records: Access: In person only. Visitors must perform in person searches for themselves. No search fee. Required to search: name, years to search, DOB; also helpful: SSN, race, sex. Criminal records in books back to 1857.

General Information: No juvenile, adoption, sealed, sexual, mental health or expunged records released. Copy fee: $.25 per page. Certification fee: $2.50 plus $.50 per page after first. Fee payee: Clerk Superior Court. Business checks accepted.

Magistrate Court PO Box 387, Quitman, GA 31643; 229-263-9989; Fax: 229-263-7847. Hours: 8AM-5PM (EST). *Civil Actions Under $15,000, Eviction, Small Claims.*

Probate Court PO Box 665, Quitman, GA 31643; 229-263-5567; Fax: 229-263-7559. Hours: 8:30AM-5PM (EST). *Probate.*

Bryan County

Superior & State Court PO Drawer H, Pembroke, GA 31321; 912-653-3872; Fax: 912-653-3695. Hours: 8AM-5PM (EST). *Felony, Misdemeanor, Civil.*

Civil Records: Access: Mail, in person. Visitors must perform in person searches for themselves. No search fee. Required to search: name, years to search. Civil cases indexed by defendant, plaintiff. Civil records on dockets from 1960, recent records are computerized.

Criminal Records: Access: Mail, in person. Visitors must perform in person searches for themselves. No search fee. Required to search: name, years to search, DOB; also helpful: SSN, race, sex. Criminal records on dockets from 1960, recent records are computerized.

General Information: Public Access terminal is available. No juvenile, adoption, sealed, sexual, mental health or expunged records released. SASE requested. Turnaround time 1-2 days. Copy fee: $.25 per page. Certification fee: $2.50 plus $.25 per page after first. Fee payee: Clerk of Superior & State Court. Personal checks accepted. Prepayment is required.

Magistrate Court Box 927, Pembroke, GA 31321; 912-653-3861; Fax: 912-653-4603. Hours: 8AM-5PM (EST). *Civil Actions Under $15,000, Eviction, Small Claims.*

Probate Court PO Box 418, Pembroke, GA 31321; 912-653-3856; Fax: 912-653-4691. Hours: 8AM-12, 1-5PM (EST). *Probate.*

Bulloch County

Superior & State Court Judicial Annex Bldg, 20 Siebald St, Statesboro, GA 30458; 912-764-9009. Hours: 8:30AM-5PM (EST). *Felony, Misdemeanor, Civil.*

Civil Records: Access: In person only. Visitors must perform in person searches for themselves. No search fee. Required to search: name, years to search. Civil cases indexed by defendant. Civil records on computer from 1991, dockets back to 1796.

Criminal Records: Access: In person only. Visitors must perform in person searches for themselves. No search fee. Required to search: name, years to search. Criminal records on computer from 1991, dockets back to 1796.

General Information: Public Access terminal is available. No juvenile, adoption, sexual, mental health or expunged records released. Copy fee: $.25 per page. Certification fee: $2.50 plus $.50 per page after first. Fee payee: Court Clerk. Personal checks accepted. Prepayment is required.

Magistrate Court Box 1004, Statesboro, GA 30459-1004; 912-764-6458; Fax: 912-489-6731. Hours: 8:30AM-5PM (EST). *Civil Actions Under $15,000, Eviction, Small Claims.*

Probate Court PO Box 1005, Statesboro, GA 30459; 912-489-8749; Fax: 912-764-8740. Hours: 8:30AM-5PM (EST). *Probate.*

Burke County

Superior & State Court PO Box 803, 111 E 6th St, Rm 105, Waynesboro, GA 30830; 706-554-2279; Fax: 706-554-7887. Hours: 9AM-5PM (EST). *Felony, Misdemeanor, Civil.*

Civil Records: Access: In person only. Visitors must perform in person searches for themselves. No search fee. Required to search: name, years to search. Civil cases indexed by defendant. Civil records on minute books back to 1856, indexed on computer since 1996.

Criminal Records: Access: In person only. Visitors must perform in person searches for themselves. No search fee. Required to search: name, years to search, DOB; also helpful: SSN, race, sex. Criminal records on minute books back to 1856, indexed on computer since 1996.

General Information: Public Access terminal is available. No juvenile, adoption, sexual, mental health or expunged records released. Fax notes: Fee to fax results is $1.00 1st page; $.25 each add'l. Copy fee: $.25 per page. Certification fee: $2.50 plus $.50 per page after first. Fee payee: Clerk of Superior Court. Personal checks accepted. Prepayment is required.

Magistrate Court Box 401, Waynesboro, GA 30830; 706-554-4281; Fax: 706-554-0530. Hours: 9AM-5PM (EST). *Civil Actions Under $15,000, Eviction, Small Claims.*

Probate Court PO Box 322, Waynesboro, GA 30830; 706-554-3000; Fax: 706-554-6693. Hours: 9AM-5PM (EST). *Probate.*

Butts County

Superior Court PO Box 320, 26 3rd St, Jackson, GA 30233; 770-775-8215. Hours: 8AM-5PM (EST). *Felony, Misdemeanor, Civil.*

Civil Records: Access: In person only. Visitors must perform in person searches for themselves. No search fee. Required to search: name, years to search. Civil cases indexed by defendant, plaintiff. Civil records on dockets from 1966.

Criminal Records: Access: In person only. Visitors must perform in person searches for themselves. No search fee. Required to search: name, years to search, signed release; also helpful: DOB, SSN, race, sex. Criminal records on dockets from 1966.

General Information: No juvenile, adoption, sexual, mental health or expunged records released. Copy fee: $.25 per page. Certification fee: $2.50 plus $.50 per page. Fee payee: Clerk of Superior Court. Personal checks accepted. Prepayment is required.

Magistrate Court Box 457, Jackson, GA 30233; 770-775-8220; Fax: 770-775-8236. Hours: 8AM-5PM (EST). *Civil Actions Under $15,000, Eviction, Small Claims.*

Probate Court 25 Third Street, #7, Jackson, GA 30233; 770-775-8204; Fax: 770-775-8211. Hours: 8AM-5PM (EST). *Probate.*

Calhoun County

Superior Court PO Box 69, Morgan, GA 31766; 229-849-2715; Fax: 229-849-0072. Hours: 8AM-5PM (EST). *Felony, Misdemeanor, Civil.*

Civil Records: Access: Mail, in person. Both court and visitors may perform in person searches. No search fee. Required to search: name, years to search. Civil cases indexed by defendant, plaintiff. Civil records on dockets back to 1854.

Criminal Records: Access: Mail, in person. Both court and visitors may perform in person searches. No search fee. Required to search: name, years to search, DOB, SSN. Criminal records on dockets back to 1854.

General Information: Public Access terminal is available. No juvenile, adoption, sexual, mental health or expunged records released. SASE required. Turnaround time 1-2 days. Fax notes: $1.50 per fax; no charge to toll-free numbers. Copy fee: $.25 per page. Certification fee: $3.00. Fee payee: Superior Court Clerk. Personal checks accepted. Prepayment is required.

Magistrate & Probate Court PO Box 87, Morgan, GA 31766; 229-849-2115; Fax: 229-849-0072. Hours: 8AM-5PM (EST). *Civil Actions Under $15,000, Eviction, Small Claims, Probate.*

Camden County

Superior Court PO Box 578, 202 E 4th Street, Woodbine, GA 31569; 912-576-5624. Hours: 9AM-5PM (EST). *Felony, Misdemeanor, Civil.*

Civil Records: Access: In person only. Visitors must perform in person searches for themselves. No search fee. Required to search: name, years to search. Civil cases indexed by defendant, plaintiff. Civil records on computer from 1989, on dockets from 1776.

Criminal Records: Access: In person only. Visitors must perform in person searches for themselves. No search fee. Required to search: name, years to search, signed release; also helpful: DOB, SSN. Criminal records on computer from 1989, on dockets from 1776.

General Information: Public Access terminal is available. No juvenile, adoption, sexual or expunged records released. Copy fee: $.25 per page. Certification fee: $2.00 plus $.50 per page after first. Fee payee: Clerk of Superior Court. Personal checks accepted. Prepayment is required.

Magistrate Court Box 386, Woodbine, GA 31569; 912-576-5658. Hours: 9AM-5PM (EST). *Civil Actions Under $15,000, Eviction, Small Claims.*

Probate Court PO Box 818, Woodbine, GA 31569; 912-576-3785; Fax: 912-576-5484. Hours: 9AM-Noon, 1-5PM (EST). *Probate.*

Candler County

Superior & State Court PO Draawer 830, Metter, GA 30439; 912-685-5257; Fax: 912-685-2946. Hours: 8:30AM-5PM (EST). *Felony, Misdemeanor, Civil.*

Civil Records: Access: In person only. Visitors must perform in person searches for themselves. No search fee. Required to search: name, years to search. Civil cases indexed by defendant, plaintiff. Civil records on dockets from 1914.
Criminal Records: Access: In person only. Visitors must perform in person searches for themselves. No search fee. Required to search: name, years to search. Criminal records on dockets from 1914.
General Information: No juvenile, adoption, mental health, expunged or sealed records released. Copy fee: $.25 per page. Certification fee: $2.00 plus $.50 per page. Fee payee: Clerk of Superior & State Court. Personal checks accepted. Prepayment is required.

Magistrate Court Box 682, 349 N Roundtree St, Metter, GA 30439; 912-685-2888; Fax: 912-685-6426. Hours: 9AM-5PM (EST). *Civil Actions Under $15,000, Eviction, Small Claims.*

Probate Court Courthouse Square, Metter, GA 30439; 912-685-2357; Fax: 912-685-5130. Hours: 8AM-5PM (EST). *Probate.*

Carroll County

Superior & State Court PO Box 1620, Carrollton, GA 30117; 770-830-5830; Fax: 770-830-5988. Hours: 8AM-5PM (EST). *Felony, Misdemeanor, Civil.*

Civil Records: Access: Mail, in person. Both court and visitors may perform in person searches. Search fee: $5.00 per name. Required to search: name, years to search. Civil cases indexed by defendant, plaintiff. Civil records on computer from 1986, docket.
Criminal Records: Access: Mail, in person. Both court and visitors may perform in person searches. Search fee: $5.00 per name. Required to search: name, years to search, DOB; also helpful: SSN, race, sex. Criminal records on computer from 1986, docket.
General Information: No juvenile, adoption, sexual, mental health or expunged records released. SASE required. Turnaround time 1 week. Copy fee: $1.00 per page. Certification fee: $2.50 plus $.50 per page after first. Fee payee: Clerk of Superior & State Court. Personal checks accepted. Prepayment is required.

Magistrate Court PO Box 338, Carrollton, GA 30117; 770-830-0116. Hours: 9AM-5PM (EST). *Civil Actions Under $15,000, Eviction, Small Claims.*

Probate Court Carroll County Courthouse, Rm 204, Carrollton, GA 30117; 770-830-5840; Fax: 770-830-5995. Hours: 8AM-5PM (EST). *Probate.*

Catoosa County

Superior & Magistrate Court 875 Lafayette St, Ringgold, GA 30736; 706-935-4231. Hours: 8:30AM-5PM (EST). *Felony, Misdemeanor, Civil, Eviction, Small Claims.*

Civil Records: Access: In person only. Visitors must perform in person searches for themselves. No search fee. Required to search: name, years to search. Civil cases indexed by defendant, plaintiff. Civil records on dockets from 1800.

Criminal Records: Access: In person only. Visitors must perform in person searches for themselves. No search fee. Required to search: name, years to search, DOB; also helpful: SSN, race, sex. Criminal records on dockets from 1800.
General Information: No juvenile, adoption, sexual, mental health or expunged records released. Copy fee: $1.00 per page. Certification fee: $2.50 plus $.50 per page after first. Fee payee: Superior Court - Court Clerk. Personal checks accepted. Prepayment is required.

Probate Court 875 LaFayette St, Justice Bldg, Ringgold, GA 30736; 706-935-3511. Hours: 9AM-5PM (EST). *Probate.*

Charlton County

Superior Court Courthouse, Folkston, GA 31537; 912-496-2354. Hours: 8:30AM-5PM (EST). *Felony, Misdemeanor, Civil.*

Civil Records: Access: Mail, in person. Both court and visitors may perform in person searches. No search fee. Required to search: name, years to search. Civil cases indexed by defendant. Civil records on index from 1954.
Criminal Records: Access: Mail, in person. Both court and visitors may perform in person searches. No search fee. Required to search: name, years to search, DOB, SSN. Criminal records on index from 1954.
General Information: No juvenile, adoption, sexual, mental health or expunged records released. Turnaround time 1 day. Copy fee: $.25 per page. Certification fee: $2.50 plus $.50 per page after first. Fee payee: Court Clerk. Personal checks accepted.

Magistrate Court 608 Pennsylvania Ave, Homeland, GA 31537; 912-496-7332; Fax: 912-496-3747. Hours: 8AM-5PM (EST). *Civil Actions Under $15,000, Eviction, Small Claims.*

Probate Court 100 S 3rd St, Folkston, GA 31537; 912-496-2230; Fax: 912-496-1156. Hours: 8AM-5PM (EST). *Probate.*

Chatham County

Superior Court PO Box 10227, 133 Montgomery St, Savannah, GA 31412; 912-652-7197; Fax: 912-652-7380. Hours: 8AM-5PM (EST). *Felony, Misdemeanor, Civil.*

Civil Records: Access: Mail, in person. Both court and visitors may perform in person searches. No search fee. Required to search: name, years to search. Civil cases indexed by defendant, plaintiff. Civil records on computer from 1984, archived back to 1900, dockets back to 1900s.
Criminal Records: Access: Mail, in person. Both court and visitors may perform in person searches. No search fee. Required to search: name, years to search, signed release; also helpful: DOB, SSN. Criminal records on computer from 1984, archived back to 1900, dockets back to 1900s.
General Information: Public Access terminal is available. No juvenile, adoption or 1st offender records released. SASE requested. Turnaround time 1 week. Copy fee: $.25 per page. Certification fee: $2.00 plus $.50 per page. Fee payee: Court Clerk. Personal checks accepted. Prepayment is required.

State Court County Courthouse 133 Montgomery St, Savannah, GA 31401; 912-652-7224; Fax: 912-652-7229. Hours: 8AM-5PM (EST). *Misdemeanor, Civil.*

www.chathamcourts.org
Civil Records: Access: Mail, fax, in person. Both court and visitors may perform in person searches. No search fee. Required to search: name, years to search, address. Civil cases indexed by defendant, plaintiff. Civil records on computer from 1983, prior on books. Current state court cases only are available free online at

www.chathamcourts.org. Search by name or case number.
Criminal Records: Access: Mail, fax, in person. Both court and visitors may perform in person searches. No search fee. Required to search: name, years to search. Criminal records on computer from 1983, prior on books.
General Information: Public Access terminal is available. No first time criminal offender or sealed civil records released. SASE required. Turnaround time 2 days. Copy fee: $1.00 per page. Certification fee: $2.50 plus $.50 per page. Fee payee: Clerk of State Court. Only cashiers checks and money orders accepted. Prepayment is required.

Magistrate Court 133 Montgomery St Room 303, Savannah, GA 31401; 912-652-7181; Fax: 912-652-7550. Hours: 8AM-5PM (EST). *Civil Actions Under $15,000, Eviction, Small Claims.*

www.chathamcourts.org

Probate Court 133 Montgomery St, Rm 509, PO Box 509, Savannah, GA 31401; 912-652-7264; Fax: 912-652-7262. Hours: 8AM-5PM (EST). *Probate.*

www.chathamcourts.org

Chattahoochee County

Superior & Magistrate Court PO Box 120, Cusseta, GA 31805; 706-989-3424; Fax: 706-989-0396. Hours: 8AM-5PM (EST). *Felony, Misdemeanor, Civil, Eviction, Small Claims.*

Note: Magistrate Court is 706-989-3643.

Civil Records: Access: In person only. Visitors must perform in person searches for themselves. No search fee. Required to search: name, years to search. Civil cases indexed by defendant, plaintiff. Civil records on dockets from 1854.
Criminal Records: Access: In person only. Visitors must perform in person searches for themselves. No search fee. Required to search: name, years to search, DOB; also helpful: SSN, race, sex. Criminal records on dockets from 1854.
General Information: Public Access terminal is available. No juvenile, adoption, sexual, mental health or expunged records released. Copy fee: $.25 per page. Certification fee: $2.50 plus $.50 per page after first. Fee payee: Court Clerk. Business checks accepted. Prepayment is required.

Probate Court PO Box 119, Cusseta, GA 31805; 706-989-3603; Fax: 706-989-2005. Hours: 8AM-Noon, 1-5PM (EST). *Probate.*

Chattooga County

Superior & State Court PO Box 159, Summerville, GA 30747; 706-857-0706. Hours: 8:30AM-5PM (EST). *Felony, Misdemeanor, Civil, Eviction, Small Claims.*

Civil Records: Access: In person only. Visitors must perform in person searches for themselves. No search fee. Required to search: name, years to search. Civil cases indexed by defendant, plaintiff. Civil records on dockets from 1960.
Criminal Records: Access: In person only. Visitors must perform in person searches for themselves. No search fee. Required to search: name, years to search, DOB; also helpful: SSN, race, sex. Criminal records on dockets from 1960.
General Information: No juvenile, adoption, sexual, mental health or expunged records released. Copy fee: $.25 per page. Certification fee: $2.50 plus $.50 per page after first. Fee payee: Clerk of Court. Personal checks accepted. Prepayment is required.

Magistrate Court 10017 Commerce St, Summerville, GA 30747; 706-857-0711; Fax: 706-857-

0675. Hours: 8AM-5PM (EST). *Civil Actions Under $15,000, Eviction, Small Claims.*

Probate Court PO Box 467, Summerville, GA 30747; 706-857-0709; Fax: 706-857-0709. Hours: 8:30AM-Noon, 1-5PM (EST). *Probate.*

Cherokee County

Superior & State Court 990 North St, Ste G170, Canton, GA 30114; 770-479-0538. Hours: 8:30AM-5PM (EST). *Felony, Misdemeanor, Civil.*

http://209.86.240.205/blueridgehp.shtml

Note: This court location also handles juvenile records.

Civil Records: Access: In person only. Visitors must perform in person searches for themselves. No search fee. Required to search: name. Civil cases indexed by defendant, plaintiff. Civil records on computer from 1976, archived 1900-1976, on dockets back to 1900.

Criminal Records: Access: In person only. Both court and visitors may perform in person searches. No search fee. Required to search: name, years to search, DOB; also helpful: SSN, race, sex. Criminal records on computer from 1976, archived 1900-1976, on dockets back to 1900.

General Information: Public Access terminal is available. No juvenile, adoption, sexual, mental health, expunged or confidential records released. Copy fee: $.25 per page. Certification fee: $2.00 plus $.50 per add'l page. Fee payee: Clerk of Court. Only cashiers checks and money orders accepted. Prepayment is required.

Magistrate Court 90 North St #150, Canton, GA 30114; 770-479-8516. Hours: 8:30AM-5PM (EST). *Civil Actions Under $15,000, Eviction, Small Claims.*

Probate Court 90 North St, Rm 340, Canton, GA 30114; 770-479-0541; Fax: 770-479-0567. *Probate.*

Clarke County

Superior & State Court PO Box 1805, Athens, GA 30603; 706-613-3190. Hours: 8AM-5PM (EST). *Felony, Misdemeanor, Civil.*

Civil Records: Access: In person only. Visitors must perform in person searches for themselves. No search fee. Required to search: name, years to search. Civil cases indexed by defendant, plaintiff. Civil records on computer from 1993, docket books from 1801.

Criminal Records: Access: In person only. Visitors must perform in person searches for themselves. No search fee. Required to search: name, years to search, DOB. Criminal records on computer from 1993, docket books from 1801.

General Information: Public Access terminal is available. No juvenile, adoptions, sealed, sexual, mental health or expunged records released. Copy fee: In-house copies are $.25 each; by mail is $1.00 per page. Certification fee: $2.50 plus $.50 per page after first. Fee payee: County Clerk. Personal checks accepted. Prepayment is required.

Magistrate Court PO Box 1868, 325 E Washington St, Athens, GA 30601; 706-613-3310; Fax: 706-613-3314. Hours: 8AM-5PM (EST). *Civil Actions Under $15,000, Eviction, Small Claims.*

Probate Court 325 E Washington St, Rm 215, Athens, GA 30601; 706-613-3320; Fax: 706-613-3323. Hours: 8AM-5PM (EST). *Probate.*

Clay County

Superior Court PO Box 550, Ft Gaines, GA 31751; 229-768-2631; Fax: 229-768-3047. Hours: 8AM-4:30PM *Felony, Misdemeanor, Civil, Eviction.*

Civil Records: Access: In person only. Visitors must perform in person searches for themselves. No search fee. Required to search: name, years to search. Civil cases indexed by defendant, plaintiff. Civil records on computer from 1990, on dockets from 1854.

Criminal Records: Access: In person only. Visitors must perform in person searches for themselves. No search fee. Required to search: name, years to search. Criminal records on computer from 1990, on dockets from 1854.

General Information: Public Access terminal is available. No juvenile, adoption, sexual, mental health or expunged records released. Copy fee: $1.00 per page. Certification fee: $3.00. Fee payee: Superior Court Clerk. Personal checks accepted. Prepayment is required.

Magistrate Court PO Box 73, Ft Gaines, GA 31751; 229-768-2841; Fax: 229-768-3443. Hours: 8AM-4:30PM (EST). *Civil Actions Under $15,000, Eviction, Small Claims.*

Probate Court 210 S Washington, Ft. Gaines, GA 31751; 229-768-2445; Fax: 229-768-2710. Hours: 8AM-4:30PM (EST). *Probate.*

Clayton County

Superior Court 9151 Tara Blvd, Jonesboro, GA 30236-4912; 770-477-3405. Hours: 8AM-5PM (EST). *Felony, Civil.*

www.co.clayton.ga.us/magistrate_superior_court/clerk_of_courts

Civil Records: Access: In person only. Visitors must perform in person searches for themselves. No search fee. Required to search: name, years to search. Civil cases indexed by defendant. Civil records on docket books for all records, on computer from 1992, on microfilm from 1990, archived from 1800-1982, dockets to 1800.

Criminal Records: Access: In person only. Visitors must perform in person searches for themselves. No search fee. Required to search: name, years to search, DOB; also helpful: SSN, race, sex. Criminal record keeping as civil.

General Information: Public Access terminal is available. No adoption, sexual, mental health or expunged records released. Copy fee: $.25 per page. Certification fee: $2.50 plus $.50 per page after first. Fee payee: Clerk of Superior Court. Only cashiers checks and money orders accepted. Attorney checks accepted. Prepayment is required.

State Court 9151 Tara Blvd #1CL181, Jonesboro, GA 30236; 770-477-4522; Criminal phone: 770-477-4522. Hours: 8AM-5PM (EST). *Misdemeanor.*

www.co.clayton.ga.us/state_court/clerk_of_courts

Criminal Records: Access: In person only. Visitors must perform in person searches for themselves. No search fee. Required to search: name, years to search. Criminal records on computer from 1985.

General Information: No juvenile, adoption, sexual, mental health or expunged records released. Copy fee: $.25 per page. Certification fee: $2.50 plus $.50 per page after first. Fee payee: Court Clerk. Business checks accepted.

Magistrate Court 121 S McDonough St, Jonesboro, GA 30236; 770-477-3444; Fax: 770-473-5750. Hours: 8AM-5PM (EST). *Civil Actions Under $15,000, Eviction, Small Claims.*

www.co.clayton.ga.us/magistrate_superior_court/clerk_of_courts

Probate Court 121 S McDonough St, Annex 3, Jonesboro, GA 30236-3694; 770-477-3299; Fax: 770-477-3306. Hours: 8AM-5PM (EST). *Probate.*

www.co.clayton.ga.us/probate_court

Clinch County

Superior & State Court PO Box 433, Homerville, GA 31634; 912-487-5854; Fax: 912-489-3083. Hours: 8AM-5PM *Felony, Misdemeanor, Civil.*

Civil Records: Access: Mail, in person. Both court and visitors may perform in person searches. No search fee. Required to search: name, years to search. Civil cases indexed by defendant, plaintiff. Civil records on dockets from 1900.

Criminal Records: Access: Mail, in person. Both court and visitors may perform in person searches. No search fee. Required to search: name, years to search, DOB; also helpful: SSN, race, sex. Criminal records on dockets from 1900.

General Information: No juvenile, adoption, sexual, mental health or expunged records released. SASE requested. Turnaround time 1-2 days. Copy fee: $.25 per page. Certification fee: $3.00. Fee payee: Court Clerk. Personal checks accepted.

Magistrate Court 100 Court Square, Homerville, GA 31634; 912-487-2514; Fax: 912-487-3658. Hours: 9AM-5PM (EST). *Civil Actions Under $15,000, Eviction, Small Claims.*

Probate Court PO Box 364, Homerville, GA 31634; 912-487-5523; Fax: 912-487-3083. Hours: 9AM-5PM (EST). *Probate.*

Cobb County

Superior Court PO Box 3370, Marietta, GA 30061; 770-528-1300; Fax: 770-528-1382. Hours: 8AM-5PM (EST). *Felony, Misdemeanor, Civil.*

www.cobbgasupctclk.com/index.htm

Civil Records: Access: Online, in person. Visitors must perform in person searches for themselves. No search fee. Required to search: name, years to search. Civil cases indexed by defendant, plaintiff. Civil records on computer from 1982, records on dockets from 1958. Civil or criminal indexes of the Clerk of Superior Court are available free online at the web site. Search by name, type or case number. The data is updated every Friday.

Criminal Records: Access: Mail, online, in person. Visitors must perform in person searches for themselves. No search fee. Required to search: name, years to search, signed release. Criminal records on computer from 1982, Records on dockets from 1958. Online access to criminal records is the same as civil.

General Information: Public Access terminal is available. No juvenile, adoption, sexual, mental health or expunged records released. Fax notes: Will not fax results. Copy fee: $.25 per page. Certification fee: $2.00 plus $.50 per page. Fee payee: Clerk of Superior Court. Personal checks accepted. Prepayment is required.

State Court - Civil & Criminal Divisions 12 East Park Square, Marietta, GA 30090-9630; Civil phone: 770-528-1219; Criminal phone: 770-528-1255. Hours: 8AM-5PM (EST). *Misdemeanor, Civil, Eviction.*

www.cobbstatecourtclerk.com

Civil Records: Access: In person only. Visitors must perform in person searches for themselves. Search fee: No search fee unless offsite (pre-1994), then $7.00. Required to search: name, years to search. Civil cases indexed by defendant, plaintiff. Civil records on computer since 03/10/97, docket books from 1965.

Criminal Records: Access: In person only. Both court and visitors may perform in person searches. Search fee: None unless offsite (pre-1994), then $7.00. Required to search: name, years to search, offense; also helpful: DOB. Criminal records on computer since 05/99, on microfiche 01/81 -04/99.

General Information: Public Access terminal is available. No juvenile, adoption, sexual, mental health, expunged or sealed records released. Copy fee: $.25 per page. Certification fee: $3.00. Fee payee: State Court Clerk. Prepayment is required.

Magistrate Court 32 Waddell St, 3rd Fl, Marietta, GA 30090-9656; 770-528-8931; Fax: 770-528-8947. Hours: 8AM-5PM (EST). *Civil Actions Under $15,000, Small Claims.*

www.cobbmagistratecourt.org

Probate Court 32 Waddell St, Marietta, GA 30060; 770-528-1990; Fax: 770-528-1996. Hours: 8AM-4:30PM (EST). *Probate.*

Coffee County

Superior & State Court 101 S Peterson Ave, Douglas, GA 31533; 912-384-2865. Hours: 8:30AM-5PM (EST). *Felony, Misdemeanor, Civil.*

Civil Records: Access: In person only. Visitors must perform in person searches for themselves. No search fee. Required to search: name. Civil cases indexed by defendant, plaintiff. Civil records on dockets.
Criminal Records: Access: In person only. Visitors must perform in person searches for themselves. No search fee. Required to search: name, years to search. Criminal records on dockets.
General Information: No juvenile, adoption, sexual, mental health or expunged records released. Copy fee: $.25 per page. Certification fee: $3.00. Fee payee: Clerk Superior Court. Business checks accepted.

Magistrate Court 101 S Peterson Ave, Douglas, GA 31533; 912-384-1381; Fax: 912-384-0291. Hours: 8AM-5PM (EST). *Civil Actions Under $15,000, Eviction, Small Claims.*

Probate Court 109 S Peterson Ave, Douglas, GA 31533; 912-384-5213; Fax: 912-384-0291. Hours: 9AM-5PM (EST). *Probate.*

Colquitt County

Superior & State Court PO Box 2827, Moultrie, GA 31776; 229-616-7420. Hours: 8AM-5PM (EST). *Felony, Misdemeanor, Civil.*

www2.state.ga.us/courts/superior/dca/dca2sohp.htm

Civil Records: Access: In person only. Visitors must perform in person searches for themselves. No search fee. Required to search: name, years to search. Civil cases indexed by defendant, plaintiff. Civil records on dockets books.
Criminal Records: Access: In person only. Visitors must perform in person searches for themselves. No search fee. Required to search: name, years to search. Criminal records on dockets books.
General Information: No juvenile, adoption, sexual, mental health or expunged records released. Fax notes: Will not fax results. Copy fee: $.50 per page. Certification fee: $2.00. Fee payee: Court Clerk. Personal checks accepted. Prepayment is required.

Magistrate Court PO Box 70, Moultrie, GA 31776; 229-891-7450; Fax: 229-891-7494. Hours: 8AM-5PM (EST). *Civil Actions Under $15,000, Eviction, Small Claims.*

Probate Court PO Box 264, Moultrie, GA 31776-0264; 229-891-7415; Fax: 229-891-7403. Hours: 8AM-5PM (EST). *Probate.*

Columbia County

Superior Court PO Box 100, Appling, GA 30802; 706-541-1139; Fax: 706-541-4013. Hours: 8AM-5PM (EST). *Felony, Misdemeanor, Civil.*

Civil Records: Access: In person only. Visitors must perform in person searches for themselves. No search fee. Required to search: name, years to search. Civil

cases indexed by plaintiff. Civil records on computer from 1987, prior on docket books.
Criminal Records: Access: In person only. Visitors must perform in person searches for themselves. No search fee. Required to search: name, years to search, DOB; also helpful: SSN, race, sex. Criminal records on computer from 1987, prior on docket books.
General Information: No juvenile, adoption, sexual, mental health or expunged records released. Copy fee: $.25 per page. Certification fee: $2.00. Fee payee: Clerk of Superior Court. Personal checks accepted.

Magistrate Court PO Box 777, Evans, GA 30809; 706-868-3316. Hours: 8AM-5PM (EST). *Civil Actions Under $15,000, Eviction, Small Claims.*

Probate Court PO Box 525, Appling, GA 30802; 706-541-1254; Fax: 706-541-4001. Hours: 8AM-5PM (EST). *Probate.*

Cook County

Superior Court 212 N Hutchinson Ave, Adel, GA 31620; 229-896-7717. Hours: 8:30AM-4:30PM (EST). *Felony, Misdemeanor, Civil.*

Civil Records: Access: Phone, mail, in person. Both court and visitors may perform in person searches. Search fee: $10.00 per name, per five year period. Required to search: name, years to search. Civil cases indexed by defendant. Civil records on dockets books, microfilm.
Criminal Records: Access: Mail, in person. Both court and visitors may perform in person searches. Search fee: $10.00 per name per 5 year period. Required to search: name, years to search, DOB, signed release; also helpful: SSN, race, sex. Criminal records on dockets books, microfilm.
General Information: No juvenile, adoption, sexual, 1st offenders, mental health or expunged records released. SASE not required. Turnaround time same day. Fax notes: Will not fax results. Copy fee: $1.00 per page. Certification fee: $2.50 plus $.50 per page after first. Fee payee: Court Clerk. Business checks accepted. Prepayment is required.

Magistrate Court 212 N Hutchinson Ave, Adel, GA 31620; 229-896-3151; Fax: 229-896-7629. Hours: 8AM-4:30PM (EST). *Civil Actions Under $15,000, Eviction, Small Claims.*

Probate Court 212 N Hutchinson Ave, Adel, GA 31620; 229-896-3941; Fax: 229-896-7629. Hours: 8:30AM-5PM (EST). *Probate.*

Coweta County

Superior Court PO Box 943, 200 Court Square, Newnan, GA 30264; 770-254-2693/2695; Fax: 770-254-3700. Hours: 8AM-5PM (EST). *Felony, Civil.*

Civil Records: Access: Phone, mail, in person. Both court and visitors may perform in person searches. No search fee. Required to search: name, years to search. Civil cases indexed by defendant, plaintiff. Civil records on computer from 1990, dockets books to 1970.
Criminal Records: Access: Phone, mail, in person. Both court and visitors may perform in person searches. No search fee. Required to search: name, years to search, DOB; also helpful: SSN, race, sex. Criminal records on docket books back to 1919. Can only conduct felony searches from 1990 to present.
General Information: Public Access terminal is available. No juvenile, adoption, sexual, mental health or expunged records released. Turnaround time 2 days. Copy fee: $.25 per page. Certification fee: $2.50 plus $.50 per page after first. Fee payee: Clerk of Superior & State Court. Business checks accepted. Prepayment is required.

State Court 9A E Broad St, Newnan, GA 30263; 770-254-2699. Hours: 8AM-5PM (EST). *Misdemeanor, Civil.*

Note: This is a new court in new location as of 5/2001.

Civil Records: Access: Phone, in person. Both court and visitors may perform in person searches. Search fee: None, unless records are off-site (pre-1990), fee is $5.00. Required to search: name, years to search. Civil cases indexed by defendant, plaintiff. Civil records on computer from 1990, dockets books to 1970. No real estate; this court handles family court issues, generally.
Criminal Records: Access: In person only. Both court and visitors may perform in person searches. Search fee: None, but if records are off-site (pre-1990), fee is $5.00. Required to search: name, years to search, DOB. Criminal records on docket books back to 1919; on computer from 1990. Can only conduct felony searches from 1990 to present.
General Information: Public Access terminal is available. No juvenile, adoption, sexual, mental health or expunged records released. Copy fee: $.25 per page. Certification fee: $2.50 plus $.50 per page after first. Fee payee: Clerk of Superior & State Court. Prepayment is required.

Magistrate Court 34 E Broad St, Newnan, GA 30263; 770-254-2610; Fax: 770-254-2606. Hours: 8AM-5PM (EST). *Civil Actions Under $15,000, Eviction, Small Claims.*

Probate Court 22 E Broad St, Newnan, GA 30263; 770-254-2640; Fax: 770-254-2648. Hours: 8AM-5PM (EST). *Probate.*

Crawford County

Superior Court PO Box 1037, Roberta, GA 31058; 478-836-3328. Hours: 9AM-5PM (EST). *Felony, Misdemeanor, Civil.*

Civil Records: Access: In person only. Visitors must perform in person searches for themselves. No search fee. Required to search: name, years to search. Civil cases indexed by defendant, plaintiff. Civil records on dockets books, recent records computerized.
Criminal Records: Access: In person only. Visitors must perform in person searches for themselves. No search fee. Required to search: name, years to search, DOB; also helpful: SSN, race, sex. Criminal records on dockets books, recent records computerized.
General Information: Public Access terminal is available. (Access limited to deeds from 01/99 to present.) No juvenile, adoption, sexual, mental health or expunged records released. Copy fee: $.25 per page. Certification fee: $2.50 plus $.50 per page after first. Fee payee: Clerk of Superior Court. Personal checks accepted. Prepayment is required.

Magistrate Court PO Box 568, Roberta, GA 31078; 478-836-5804; Fax: 478-836-4340. Hours: 8AM-5PM (EST). *Civil Actions Under $15,000, Eviction, Small Claims.*

Probate Court PO Box 1028, Roberta, GA 31078; 478-836-3313. Hours: 8:30AM-4:30PM *Probate.*

Note: The record search fee is $4.00.

Crisp County

Superior & Juvenile Court PO Box 747, Cordele, GA 31010-0747; 229-276-2616. Hours: 8:30AM-5PM (EST). *Felony, Misdemeanor, Civil Actions Over $15,000.*

Civil Records: Access: Mail, in person. Visitors must perform in person searches for themselves. No search fee. Required to search: name, years to search. Civil cases indexed by defendant. Civil records on docket books to 1905.

Criminal Records: Access: Mail, in person. Visitors must perform in person searches for themselves. No search fee. Required to search: name, years to search; also helpful: SSN. Criminal records on docket books to 1905.
General Information: Public Access terminal is available. No juvenile, adoption, sexual, mental health or expunged records released. SASE required. Turnaround time 1-2 days. Fax notes: Fee to fax results is $2.50 first page, $1.00 each add'l. Copy fee: $.25 per page. Certification fee: $2.00 plus $.50 per page. Fee payee: Clerk of Superior Court. Personal checks accepted. Prepayment is required.

Magistrate Court 210 S 7th St Room 102, Cordese, GA 31015; 229-276-2618. Hours: 8:30AM-5PM (EST). *Civil Actions Under $15,000, Eviction, Small Claims.*

Probate Court PO Box 26, Cordele, GA 31010-0026; 229-276-2621; Fax: 229-273-9184. Hours: 9AM-5PM (EST). *Probate.*

Dade County

Superior Court PO Box 417, Trenton, GA 30752; 706-657-4778; Sm Claims 706-657-4113. Hours: 8:30AM-5PM (EST). *Felony, Misdemeanor, Civil, Eviction, Small Claims.*

Civil Records: Access: Phone, fax, mail, in person. Both court and visitors may perform in person searches. No search fee. Required to search: name, years to search. Civil cases indexed by defendant, plaintiff. Civil records on computer back to 1/1999; prior on docket books.
Criminal Records: Access: Mail, fax, in person. Both court and visitors may perform in person searches. Search fee: $5.00 per name. Required to search: name, years to search, DOB; also helpful: SSN, race, sex. Criminal records on computer back to 1/1999; prior on docket books.
General Information: Public Access terminal is available. No juvenile, adoption, sexual, mental health or expunged records released. SASE requested. Turnaround time 1 day. Fax notes: Fee to fax results is $1.00 per page. Copy fee: $1.32 per page. Certification fee: $2.00 plus $.50 per page after first. Fee payee: Superior Court. Personal checks accepted. Prepayment is required.

Magistrate Court PO Box 518, Trenton, GA 31083; 706-657-4113; Fax: 706-657-9618. Hours: 8AM-5PM (EST). *Civil Actions Under $15,000, Eviction, Small Claims.*

Probate Court PO Box 605, Trenton, GA 30752; 706-657-4414; Fax: 706-657-5116. Hours: 8:30AM-5PM (EST). *Probate.*

Dawson County

Superior Court 25 Tucker Ave, #106, Dawsonville, GA 30534; 706-344-3510 X227; Fax: 706-344-3511. Hours: 8AM-5PM (EST). *Felony, Misdemeanor, Civil.*

http://209.86.240.205/dca9nehp.shtml

Civil Records: Access: Phone, mail, fax, in person. Visitors must perform in person searches for themselves. No search fee. Required to search: name, years to search. Civil cases indexed by plaintiff. Civil records on computer back to 1994, prior in dockets books.
Criminal Records: Access: mail, fax, in person. Visitors must perform in person searches for themselves. No search fee. Required to search: name, years to search, DOB; also helpful: SSN, race, sex. Criminal records on computer back to 1994, prior in dockets books.

General Information: Public Access terminal is available. No juvenile, adoption, sexual, mental health or expunged records released. Copy fee: $.25 per page. Certification fee: $2.50. Fee payee: Superior Court. Prepayment is required.

Magistrate Court PO Box 254, Dawsonville, GA 30534; 706-334-3730-8000; Fax: 706-344-3537. Hours: 10AM-8PM M,T; 10AM-2PM W; 8:30AM-5PM F (EST). *Civil Actions Under $15,000, Eviction, Small Claims.*

Probate Court 25 Tucker Ave #211, Dawsonville, GA 30534; 706-344-3580; Fax: 706-265-6155. Hours: 8AM-5PM (EST). *Probate.*

De Kalb County

Superior Court 556 N McDonough St, Decatur, GA 30030; 404-371-2836; Fax: 404-371-2635. Hours: 8:30AM-5PM (EST). *Felony, Misdemeanor, Civil.*

Civil Records: Access: In person only. Visitors must perform in person searches for themselves. No search fee. Required to search: name, years to search. Civil cases indexed by defendant, plaintiff. Civil records on computer from 1988, prior archived.
Criminal Records: Access: In person only. Visitors must perform in person searches for themselves. No search fee. Required to search: name, years to search, DOB; also helpful: SSN, race, sex. Criminal records on computer from 1980, on microfilm from 1947.
General Information: Public Access terminal is available. No juvenile, adoption, sexual, mental health or expunged records released. Copy fee: Copies made by the court are $1.00 per page, do it yourself is $.25 per page. Certification fee: $2.50 plus $.50 per page after first. Fee payee: Clerk of Superior Court. Personal checks accepted. Prepayment is required.

State Court 556 N McDonough St, Decatur, GA 30030; 404-371-2261; Fax: 404-371-3064. Hours: 8:30AM-5PM (EST). *Misdemeanor, Civil.*

www.dekalbstatecourt.net

Civil Records: Access: Mail, in person. Visitors must perform in person searches for themselves. No search fee. Required to search: name, years to search. Civil cases indexed by defendant, plaintiff. Civil records on docket books. The court will perform limited searches.
Criminal Records: Access: In person only. Visitors must perform in person searches for themselves. No search fee. Required to search: name. Criminal records on docket books.
General Information: Public Access terminal is available. Turnaround time 7 days. Copy fee: $.25 per page. Certification fee: $5.00. Fee payee: Court Clerk. Personal checks accepted. Prepayment is required.

Magistrate Court 807 DeKalb County Courthouse, Decatur, GA 30030; 404-371-4766; Fax: 404-371-2986. Hours: 8:30AM-5PM (EST). *Civil Actions Under $15,000, Eviction, Small Claims.*

Probate Court 103 County Courthouse, 556 N McDonough St, Rm 103, Decatur, GA 30030; 404-371-2718; Fax: 404-371-7055. Hours: 8:30AM-4PM (EST). *Probate.*

http://co.dekalb.ga.us/probate

Decatur County

Superior & State Court PO Box 336, Bainbridge, GA 31718; 229-248-3025. Hours: 9AM-5PM (EST). *Felony, Misdemeanor, Civil.*

Civil Records: Access: In person only. Visitors must perform in person searches for themselves. No search fee. Required to search: name, years to search. Civil cases indexed by defendant, plaintiff. Civil records on docket books from 1823; computerized from 1996.

Criminal Records: Access: In person only. Visitors must perform in person searches for themselves. No search fee. Required to search: name, years to search, DOB; also helpful: SSN, race, sex. Criminal records on docket books from 1823; computerized from 1996.
General Information: Public Access terminal is available. No juvenile, adoption, sexual, mental health or expunged records released. Copy fee: $.25 per page. Certification fee: $2.00 plus $.50 per page. Fee payee: Court Clerk. No personal checks accepted.

Magistrate Court 912 Spring Creek Rd Box #3, Bainbridge, GA 31717; 229-248-3014; Fax: 229-248-3862. Hours: 9AM-5PM (EST). *Civil Actions Under $15,000, Eviction, Small Claims.*

Probate Court PO Box 234, Bainbridge, GA 31718; 229-248-3016; Fax: 229-248-3858. Hours: 9AM-5PM (EST). *Probate.*

Dodge County

Superior Court PO Drawer 4276, 5401 Anson Av, Eastman, GA 31023; 478-374-2871. Hours: 9AM-5PM (EST). *Felony, Misdemeanor, Civil.*

Civil Records: Access: In person only. Visitors must perform in person searches for themselves. No search fee. Required to search: name, years to search. Civil cases indexed by defendant. Civil records on docket books.
Criminal Records: Access: In person only. Visitors must perform in person searches for themselves. No search fee. Required to search: name, years to search, DOB, signed release; also helpful: SSN, race, sex. Criminal records on docket books and computer.
General Information: No juvenile, adoption, sexual, mental health or expunged records released. Copy fee: $.25 per page. Certification fee: $2.00 plus $.50 per page after first. Fee payee: Court Clerk. Personal checks accepted. Prepayment is required.

Magistrate Court 5018 Courthouse Circle #202, Eastman, GA 31023; 478-374-5145; Fax: 478-374-5716. Hours: 8:30AM-4:30PM (EST). *Civil Actions Under $15,000, Eviction, Small Claims.*

Probate Court PO Box 514, Eastman, GA 31023; 478-374-3775; Fax: 478-374-9197. Hours: 9AM-Noon, 1-5PM (EST). *Probate.*

Dooly County

Superior Court PO Box 326, Vienna, GA 31092-0326; 229-268-4234; Fax: 229-268-1427. Hours: 8:30AM-5PM (EST). *Felony, Misdemeanor, Civil.*

Civil Records: Access: Fax, mail, in person. Visitors must perform in person searches for themselves. No search fee. Required to search: name, years to search. Civil cases indexed by defendant, plaintiff. Civil records on computer since 1995. Prefer to have public do searches.
Criminal Records: Access: Fax, mail, in person. Visitors must perform in person searches for themselves. No search fee. Required to search: name, years to search, DOB, signed release; also helpful: SSN, race, sex. Criminal records on computer since 1995, docket books prior to 1857. Prefer to have public to perform searches.
General Information: Public Access terminal is available. No juvenile, adoption, sexual, mental health or expunged records released. SASE required. Turnaround time varies. Copy fee: $.25 per page. Certification fee: $2.50. Fee payee: Dooly County Superior Court Clerk. Personal checks accepted. Prepayment is required.

Magistrate Court PO Box 336, Vienna, GA 31092; 229-268-4324. Hours: 8AM-Noon, 1-5PM M,W,F (EST). *Civil Actions Under $15,000, Eviction, Small Claims.*

Probate Court PO Box 304, Vienna, GA 31092; 229-268-4217; Fax: 229-268-6142. Hours: 8AM-5PM M,T,Th,F; 8:30AM-Noon W & Sat or by appointment (EST). *Probate.*

Dougherty County

Superior & State Court PO Box 1827, Albany, GA 31703; 229-431-2198. Hours: 8:30AM-5PM (EST). *Felony, Misdemeanor, Civil.*

www.dougherty.ga.us/dococlk.htm

Civil Records: Access: Online, in person. Visitors must perform in person searches for themselves. No search fee. Required to search: name, years to search. Civil cases indexed by defendant, plaintiff. Civil records on computer from 1992. Access to civil and criminal court docket data is available free at the web site. The same system permits access to probate, UCC, tax, deeds, and death certificate records.

Criminal Records: Access: Online, in person. Visitors must perform in person searches for themselves. No search fee. Required to search: name, years to search; also helpful: SSN. Criminal records on computer from 1992. Online access to criminal records is the same as civil.

General Information: Public Access terminal is available. No juvenile, adoption, sexual, mental health or expunged records released. Copy fee: If court makes copy then $1.00, if yourself then $.25. Certification fee: $3.00 first page then $1.00 each additional. Fee payee: Court Clerk. Personal checks accepted. Prepayment is required.

Magistrate Court PO Box 1827, Albany, GA 31702; 229-431-3216; Fax: 229-434-2692. Hours: 8:30AM-5PM (EST). *Civil Actions Under $15,000, Eviction, Small Claims.*

Probate Court PO Box 1827, Albany, GA 31702; 229-431-2102; Fax: 229-434-2694. Hours: 8:30AM-5PM (EST). *Probate.*

www.dougherty.ga.us/dococlk.htm

Douglas County

Superior Court Douglas County Courthouse, 8700 Hospital Dr, Douglasville, GA 30134; 770-920-7252. Hours: 8AM-5PM (EST). *Felony, Misdemeanor, Civil.*

Civil Records: Access: In person only. Visitors must perform in person searches for themselves. No search fee. Required to search: name, years to search. Civil cases indexed by defendant, plaintiff. Civil records on computer from 1994, prior on docket books.

Criminal Records: Access: In person only. Visitors must perform in person searches for themselves. No search fee. Required to search: name, years to search, DOB, signed release; also helpful: address, SSN. Criminal records on computer from 1994, prior on docket books.

General Information: Public Access terminal is available. No juvenile, adoption, sexual, mental health or expunged records released. Copy fee: $.25 per page. Certification fee: $2.50 plus $.50 per page. Fee payee: Clerk of Superior Court. Personal checks accepted. Prepayment is required.

Magistrate Court PO Box 99, Douglasville, GA 30133; 770-949-1115. Hours: 8AM-5PM (EST). *Civil Actions Under $15,000, Eviction, Small Claims.*

Probate Court 8700 Hospital Dr, Douglasville, GA 30134; 770-920-7249; Fax: 770-920-7381. Hours: 8AM-5PM (EST). *Probate.*

Early County

Superior & State Court PO Box 849, Blakely, GA 31723; 229-723-3033; Fax: 229-723-5246. Hours: 8AM-5PM (EST). *Felony, Misdemeanor, Civil.*

Civil Records: Access: In person only. Visitors must perform in person searches for themselves. No search fee. Required to search: name, years to search. Civil cases indexed by defendant, plaintiff. Civil records on dockets.

Criminal Records: Access: In person only. Visitors must perform in person searches for themselves. No search fee. Required to search: name, years to search, DOB; also helpful: SSN, race, sex. Criminal records on dockets.

General Information: No juvenile, adoption, sexual, mental health or expunged records released. Copy fee: $.50 per page. Certification fee: $2.50 plus $.50 per page after first. Fee payee: Court Clerk. Personal checks accepted. Prepayment is required.

Magistrate Court Early County Courthouse, Rm 8, Blakely, GA 31723; 229-723-3454; Fax: 229-723-5246. Hours: 8AM-5PM (EST). *Civil Actions Under $15,000, Eviction, Small Claims.*

Echols County

Superior Court PO Box 213, Statenville, GA 31648; 229-559-5642; Fax: 229-559-5792. Hours: 8AM-Noon, 1-4:30PM (EST). *Felony, Misdemeanor, Civil.*

www2.state.ga.us/courts/superior/dca/dca2sohp.htm

Civil Records: Access: In person only. Visitors must perform in person searches for themselves. No search fee. Required to search: name, years to search. Civil cases indexed by defendant, plaintiff. Civil records on dockets books.

Criminal Records: Access: In person only. Visitors must perform in person searches for themselves. No search fee. Required to search: name, years to search. Criminal records on dockets books.

General Information: No juvenile, adoption, sexual, mental health or expunged records released. Copy fee: $1.00 per page. Certification fee: Certification $2.00 1st page, $.50 each additional page. Fee payee: Court Clerk. Personal checks accepted. Prepayment is required.

Magistrate & Probate Court PO Box 397, Statenville, GA 31648; 229-559-7526; Fax: 229-559-5792. Hours: 8:30AM-4:30PM (EST). *Civil Actions Under $15,000, Eviction, Small Claims, Probate.*

Effingham County

Superior & State Court PO Box 387, Springfield, GA 31329; 912-754-2118. Hours: 8:30AM-5PM (EST). *Felony, Misdemeanor, Civil.*

Civil Records: Access: Mail, in person. Both court and visitors may perform in person searches. Search fee: $20.00 per name. Required to search: name, years to search. Civil cases indexed by defendant, plaintiff. Civil records on computer from 1991, dockets books.

Criminal Records: Access: Mail, in person. Both court and visitors may perform in person searches. Search fee: $20.00 per name. Required to search: name, years to search, DOB; also helpful: SSN, race, sex. Criminal records on computer from 1991, dockets books.

General Information: No juvenile, adoption, sexual, mental health or expunged records released. SASE required. Turnaround time 3-5 days. Copy fee: $.25 per page. Certification fee: $2.50 plus $.50 per page each add'l. Fee payee: Court Clerk. Business checks accepted. Prepayment is required.

Magistrate Court PO Box 819, Springfield, GA 31329; 912-754-2124; Fax: 912-754-4893. Hours: 8:15AM-4:15PM (EST). *Civil Actions Under $15,000, Eviction, Small Claims.*

Probate Court 901 Pine St, PO Box 387, Springfield, GA 31329; 912-754-2112; Fax: 912-754-3894. Hours: 8:30AM-5PM (EST). *Probate.*

Elbert County

Superior & State Court PO Box 619, Elberton, GA 30635; 706-283-2005; Fax: 706-213-7286. Hours: 8AM-5PM (EST). *Felony, Misdemeanor, Civil.*

Civil Records: Access: In person only. Visitors must perform in person searches for themselves. No search fee. Required to search: name, years to search. Civil cases indexed by defendant, plaintiff. Civil records on computer from 1986 (excluding felonies), dockets books prior.

Criminal Records: Access: In person only. Visitors must perform in person searches for themselves. No search fee. Required to search: name, years to search. Criminal records on computer from 1986 (excluding felonies), dockets books prior.

General Information: Public Access terminal is available. No juvenile, adoption, sexual, mental health or expunged records released. Copy fee: $.25 per page. Certification fee: $2.00 plus $.50 per page. Fee payee: Clerk of Court. Personal checks accepted. Prepayment is required.

Magistrate Court PO Box 763, Elberton, GA 30635; 706-283-2027; Fax: 706-283-2004. Hours: 8AM-5PM (EST). *Civil Actions Under $15,000, Eviction, Small Claims.*

Probate Court Elbert County Courthouse, Elberton, GA 30635; 706-283-2016; Fax: 706-283-8144. Hours: 8AM-5PM (EST). *Probate.*

Emanuel County

Superior & State Court PO Box 627, Swainsboro, GA 30401; 478-237-8911; Fax: 478-237-2173. Hours: 8AM-5PM (EST). *Felony, Misdemeanor, Civil.*

Civil Records: Access: In person only. Visitors must perform in person searches for themselves. No search fee. Required to search: name, years to search. Civil cases indexed by defendant, plaintiff. Civil records computerized since 1999, earlier on dockets books.

Criminal Records: Access: In person only. Visitors must perform in person searches for themselves. No search fee. Required to search: name, years to search, DOB; also helpful: SSN, race, sex. Criminal records computerized since 1999, earlier on dockets books.

General Information: No juvenile, adoption, sexual, mental health or expunged records released. Copy fee: $.25 per page. Certification fee: $2.50 plus $.50 per page. Fee payee: Court Clerk. Personal checks accepted. Prepayment is required.

Magistrate Court 107 N Main St, Swainsboro, GA 30401; 478-237-7278; Fax: 478-237-2593. Hours: 8AM-5PM (EST). *Civil Actions Under $15,000, Eviction, Small Claims.*

Probate Court PO Drawer 70, Swainsboro, GA 30401; 478-237-7091; Fax: 478-237-2633. Hours: 8AM-5PM (EST). *Probate.*

Evans County

Superior & State Court PO Box 845, Claxton, GA 30417; 912-739-3868; Fax: 912-739-2504. Hours: 8AM-5PM (EST). *Felony, Misdemeanor, Civil.*

Civil Records: Access: In person only. Visitors must perform in person searches for themselves. No search fee. Required to search: name, years to search. Civil

cases indexed by defendant, plaintiff. Civil records on computer from 1989, dockets bookstore 1915.

Criminal Records: Access: In person only. Visitors must perform in person searches for themselves. No search fee. Required to search: name, years to search, DOB; also helpful: SSN, race, sex. Criminal records on computer from 1989, dockets books to 1915.

General Information: Public Access terminal is available. No juvenile, adoption, sexual, mental health or expunged records released. Copy fee: $1.00 per page. Certification fee: $2.50 plus $.50 per page after first. Fee payee: Court Clerk. Personal checks accepted. Prepayment is required.

Magistrate Court Courthouse Annex, Rm 7, Freeman St, Claxton, GA 30417; 912-739-3948; Fax: 912-739-8865. Hours: 8AM-5PM (EST). *Civil Actions Under $15,000, Eviction, Small Claims.*

Probate Court 123 W Main St, PO Box 852, Claxton, GA 30417; 912-739-4080; Fax: 912-739-4077. Hours: 8AM-5PM (EST). *Probate.*

Fannin County

Superior Court PO Box 1300, 420 W Main St, Blue Ridge, GA 30513; 706-632-2039. Hours: 9AM-5PM (EST). *Felony, Misdemeanor, Civil.*

http://209.86.240.205/dca9apphp.shtml

Civil Records: Access: In person only. Visitors must perform in person searches for themselves. No search fee. Required to search: name, years to search. Civil cases indexed by defendant, plaintiff. Civil records on docket books.

Criminal Records: Access: In person only. Visitors must perform in person searches for themselves. No search fee. Required to search: name, years to search, DOB, signed release; also helpful: SSN, race, sex. Criminal records on docket books.

General Information: No juvenile, adoption, sexual, mental health or expunged records released. Copy fee: $.25 per page. $1.00 per page if the court make copies. Certification fee: $2.50 plus $.50 per page after first. Fee payee: Court Clerk. Personal checks accepted. Prepayment is required.

Magistrate Court 420 W Main St, #7, Blue Ridge, GA 30513; 706-632-5558; Fax: 706-632-8236. Hours: 9AM-5PM (EST). *Civil Actions Under $15,000, Eviction, Small Claims.*

Probate Court 420 W Main St #2, Blue Ridge, GA 30513; 706-632-3011; Fax: 706-632-7167. Hours: 8AM-5PM (EST). *Probate.*

Fayette County

Superior Court PO Box 130, Fayetteville, GA 30214; 770-461-4703. Hours: 8AM-5PM (EST). *Felony, Misdemeanor, Civil.*

Civil Records: Access: In person only. Visitors must perform in person searches for themselves. No search fee. Required to search: name, years to search. Civil cases indexed by defendant, plaintiff. Civil records on computer since 1989; prior records on dockets books.

Criminal Records: Access: In person only. Visitors must perform in person searches for themselves. No search fee. Required to search: name, years to search, DOB; also helpful: SSN, race, sex. Criminal records on computer since 1989; prior records on dockets books.

General Information: Public Access terminal is available. No juvenile, adoption, sexual, mental health or expunged records released. Copy fee: $.25 per page. Certification fee: $2.00 plus $.50 per page after first. Fee payee: Court Clerk. Only cashiers checks and money orders accepted.

Magistrate Court PO Box 1076, Fayetteville, GA 30214; 770-461-4703. Hours: 8AM-5PM (EST). *Civil Actions Under $15,000, Eviction, Small Claims.*

Probate Court 145 Johnson Ave, Fayetteville, GA 30214; 770-461-9555; Fax: 770-460-8685. Hours: 8AM-5PM (EST). *Probate.*

Floyd County

Superior Court PO Box 1110, #3 Government Plaza #101, Rome, GA 30163; 706-291-5190; Fax: 706-233-0035. Hours: 8AM-5PM (EST). *Felony, Misdemeanor, Civil.*

www.floydsuperiorcourt.org

Civil Records: Access: In person only. Visitors must perform in person searches for themselves. No search fee. Required to search: name, years to search. Civil cases indexed by defendant, plaintiff. Civil records on computer since 11/95; prior on docket books to 1833.

Criminal Records: Access: Fax, mail, in person. Both court and visitors may perform in person searches. No search fee. Required to search: name, years to search, signed release. Criminal records on computer since 02/96; prior on docket books back to 1833. The court will not do name searches.

General Information: Public Access terminal is available. No juvenile, adoption, sexual, mental health or expunged records released. Fax notes: $.50 per page. Copy fee: $.50 per page. Certification fee: $2.00 plus $.50 per page after first. Fee payee: Court Clerk. Personal checks accepted. Prepayment is required.

Magistrate Court 3 Government Plaza, Rm 227, 410 Tribute St, Rm 227, Rome, GA 30161; 706-291-5250; Fax: 706-291-5269. Hours: 9AM-5PM (EST). *Civil Actions Under $15,000, Eviction, Small Claims.*

Probate Court 3 Government Plaza #201, County Administrative Offices, Rome, GA 30162; 706-291-5138; Fax: 706-291-5189. Hours: 8AM-4:30PM (EST). *Probate.*

Forsyth County

Superior & State Court 100 Courthouse Square, Rm 010, Cumming, GA 30040; 770-781-2120. Hours: 8:30AM-5PM (EST). *Felony, Misdemeanor, Civil, Eviction, Small Claims.*

http://209.86.240.205/bellforsythhp.shtml

Civil Records: Access: In person only. Visitors must perform in person searches for themselves. No search fee. Required to search: name, years to search. Civil cases indexed by defendant. Civil records on computer since 03/97; prior records on docket books.

Criminal Records: Access: In person only. Visitors must perform in person searches for themselves. No search fee. Required to search: name, years to search; also helpful: SSN. Criminal records on computer since late 1989.

General Information: No juvenile, adoption, sexual, mental health or expunged records released. Copy fee: $.25 per page. Certification fee: $2.50 plus $.50 per page after first. Fee payee: Court Clerk. Personal checks accepted. Prepayment is required.

Magistrate Court 121 Dahlonega St, Cumming, GA 30040; 770-781-2211; Fax: 770-844-7581. Hours: 8AM-5PM (EST). *Civil Actions Under $15,000, Eviction, Small Claims, Probate.*

Probate Court County Courthouse Annex, Rm 101, 112 W Maple St, Cumming, GA 30130; 770-781-2140; Fax: 770-886-2839. Hours: 8:30AM-5PM (EST). *Probate.*

Franklin County

Superior Court PO Box 70, Carnesville, GA 30521; 706-384-2514. Hours: 8AM-5PM (EST). *Felony, Misdemeanor, Civil.*

Civil Records: Access: In person only. Visitors must perform in person searches for themselves. No search fee. Required to search: name, years to search. Civil cases indexed by defendant, plaintiff. Civil records on computer since 1995; prior records on docket books.

Criminal Records: Access: In person only. Visitors must perform in person searches for themselves. No search fee. Required to search: name, years to search, DOB; also helpful: SSN, race, sex. Criminal records on computer since 1995; prior records on docket books.

General Information: Public Access terminal is available. No juvenile, adoption, sexual, mental health or expunged records released. Copy fee: $.25 per page. Certification fee: $2.50 and $.50 each add'l page. Fee payee: Court Clerk. Personal checks accepted. Prepayment is required.

Magistrate Court PO Box 467, Carnesville, GA 30521; 706-384-7473; Fax: 706-384-4346. Hours: 8AM-5PM (EST). *Civil Actions Under $15,000, Eviction, Small Claims.*

Probate Court PO Box 207, Carnesville, GA 30521; 706-384-2403; Fax: 706-384-4346. Hours: 8AM-4:30PM (EST). *Probate.*

Fulton County

Superior Court 136 Pryor St SW, Rm C-155, Superior Court Clerk, Atlanta, GA 30303; Civil phone: 404-730-5344; Fax: 404-302-3430. Hours: 8:30AM-5PM (EST). *Civil.*

www.fcclk.org

Civil Records: Access: In person only. Both court and visitors may perform in person searches. No search fee. Required to search: name, years to search. Civil cases indexed by defendant, plaintiff. Civil records on computer since 1972. **General Information:** Public Access terminal is available. No juvenile, adoption, sexual, mental health, sealed or expunged records released. Copy fee: $.25 per page. Certification fee: $2.50 for 1st page; $.50 each add'l. Fee payee: Court Clerk. Personal checks accepted. Prepayment is required.

Superior Court 136 Pryor St SW, Rm C-515, Superior Court Clerk, Atlanta, GA 30303; Criminal phone: 404-730-5242; Fax: 404-730-7993. Hours: 8:30AM-5PM (EST). *Felony, Misdemeanor, Eviction.*

www.fcclk.org

Criminal Records: Access: In person only. Visitors must perform in person searches for themselves. No search fee. Required to search: name, years to search, DOB, signed release; also helpful: SSN, race, sex. Criminal records on computer from 1973.

General Information: Public Access terminal is available. No juvenile, adoption, sexual, mental health, sealed or expunged records released. Copy fee: $.25 per page. Certification fee: $2.50 for 1st page; $.50 each add'l. Fee payee: Court Clerk. Personal checks accepted. Prepayment is required.

State Court TG100 Justice Center Tower, 185 Central Ave SW, Atlanta, GA 30303; 404-730-5000; Fax: 404-730-8141 Civil; 335-3521 Criminal. Hours: 8:30AM-5PM (EST). *Misdemeanor, Civil.*

www.fultonstatecourt.com

Civil Records: Access: In person only. Visitors must perform in person searches for themselves. No search fee. Required to search: name, years to search. Civil cases indexed by defendant, plaintiff. Civil records on computer from 1984, dockets books back 20 years.

Criminal Records: Access: In person only. Visitors must perform in person searches for themselves. No search fee. Required to search: name, years to search, DOB; also helpful: SSN, race, aliases, date of offense, sex. Criminal records on computer from 1984, docket books back 30 years. Approximate arrest date helpful.
General Information: Public Access terminal is available. No juvenile, adoption, sexual, mental health or expunged records released. Copy fee: $.25 per page. Certification fee: $2.50 plus $.50 each add'l pg. Fee payee: Court Clerk. Business checks accepted. Prepayment is required.

Magistrate Court 136 Pryor St SW, #C-669, Fulton County Courthouse, Atlanta, GA 30303; 404-730-4552; Civil phone: 404-730-5045; Criminal phone: 404-730-4752; Fax: 404-893-2683. Hours: 8:30AM-5PM (EST). *Civil Actions Under $15,000, Eviction, Small Claims.*

Probate Court 185 Central Ave. SW, T2705 Justice Ctr Tower, Atlanta, GA 30303; 404-730-4690; Fax: 404-730-7998. Hours: 8:30AM-5PM (EST). *Probate.*

Gilmer County

Superior Court #1 Westside Square, Ellijay, GA 30540; 706-635-4462; Fax: 706-635-1462. Hours: 8:30AM-5PM (EST). *Felony, Misdemeanor, Civil.*

http://209.86.240.205/dca9apphp.shtml

Civil Records: Access: In person only. Visitors must perform in person searches for themselves. No search fee. Required to search: name, years to search. Civil cases indexed by defendant, plaintiff. Civil records on docket books and computer.
Criminal Records: Access: In person only. Visitors must perform in person searches for themselves. No search fee. Required to search: name, years to search, signed release; also helpful: DOB, SSN. Criminal records on docket books and computer.
General Information: Public Access terminal is available. No juvenile, adoption, sealed, sexual, mental health, expunged or sealed records released. Copy fee: $.25 per page. Certification fee: $2.50 plus $.50 per page after first. Fee payee: Superior Court Clerk. Personal checks accepted. Prepayment is required.

Magistrate Court #1 Westside Square, Box 5, Ellijay, GA 30540; 706-635-2515; Fax: 706-635-7756. Hours: 8:30AM-5PM (EST). *Civil Actions Under $15,000, Eviction, Small Claims.*

Probate Court One Westside Square, Ellijay, GA 30540; 706-635-4763; Fax: 706-635-1461. Hours: 8:30AM-5PM (EST). *Probate.*

Glascock County

Superior Court PO Box 231, 62 E Main St, Gibson, GA 30810; 706-598-2084; Fax: 706-598-2577. Hours: 8AM-Noon, 1-5PM (EST). *Felony, Misdemeanor, Civil.*

Civil Records: Access: In person only. Visitors must perform in person searches for themselves. No search fee. Required to search: name, years to search. Civil cases indexed by defendant, plaintiff. Civil records on computer from 1990, dockets books.
Criminal Records: Access: In person only. Visitors must perform in person searches for themselves. No search fee. Required to search: name, years to search, DOB; also helpful: SSN, race, sex. Criminal records on computer from 1990, dockets books.
General Information: Public Access terminal is available. No juvenile, adoption, sexual, mental health or expunged records released. Copy fee: $.25 per page. Legal size copies $1.00 per page. Certification fee: $2.00 plus $.50 per page after first. Fee payee: Court

Clerk. Personal checks accepted. Prepayment is required.

Magistrate Court PO Box 201, Gibson, GA 30810; 706-598-2013. Hours: 4-8PM T; 9AM-1PM W & Sat (EST). *Civil Actions Under $15,000, Eviction, Small Claims.*

Probate Court PO Box 64, Gibson, GA 30810; 706-598-3241. Hours: 8AM-Noon, 1-5PM (EST). *Probate.*

Glynn County

Superior Court PO Box 1355, Brunswick, GA 31521; 912-554-7272; Fax: 912-267-5625. Hours: 8:30AM-5PM (EST). *Felony, Civil.*

Civil Records: Access: Phone, fax, mail, in person. Both court and visitors may perform in person searches. No search fee. Required to search: name, years to search. Civil cases indexed by defendant, plaintiff. Civil records on computer back to 1989, archived and in docket books from 1917.
Criminal Records: Access: Phone, fax, mail, in person. Both court and visitors may perform in person searches. No search fee. Required to search: name, years to search, DOB, signed release; also helpful: SSN, race, sex. Criminal records on computer back to 1989.
General Information: No juvenile, adoption, sexual, mental health or expunged records released. SASE requested. Turnaround time 1-3 days. Fax notes: Fee to fax results is $5.00 per document. Copy fee: $.25 per page. If court does copy, fee is $1.00 per page. Certification fee: $2.50 plus $.50 per page after first. Fee payee: Court Clerk. Personal checks accepted. Will bill copy & certification fees.

State Court PO Box 879 (701 H St.), Brunswick, GA 31521; 912-554-7325; Fax: 912-261-3849. Hours: 9AM-5PM (EST). *Misdemeanor, Civil.*

Civil Records: Access: In person only. Visitors must perform in person searches for themselves. No search fee. Required to search: name, years to search. Civil cases indexed by defendant. Civil records on dockets books.
Criminal Records: Access: In person only. Visitors must perform in person searches for themselves. No search fee. Required to search: name, years to search. Criminal records on dockets books.
General Information: Public Access terminal is available. No juvenile, adoption, sexual, mental health or expunged records released. Copy fee: $.25 per page. Certification fee: $2.00 plus $.50 per page. Fee payee: Clerk of State Court. Only cashiers checks and money orders accepted. Prepayment is required.

Magistrate Court PO Box 879, Brunswick, GA 31521; 912-267-5650. Hours: 8:30AM-5PM (EST). *Civil Actions Under $15,000, Eviction, Small Claims.*

Probate Court PO Box 938, Brunswick, GA 31521; 912-554-7231; Fax: 912-466-8001. Hours: 8:30AM-5PM (EST). *Probate.*

Gordon County

Superior Court 100 Wall St #102, Calhoun, GA 30701; 706-629-9533; Fax: 706-629-2139. Hours: 8:30AM-5PM (EST). *Felony, Misdemeanor, Civil.*

Civil Records: Access: Fax, mail, in person. Both court and visitors may perform in person searches. No search fee. Required to search: name, years to search. Civil cases indexed by defendant, plaintiff. Civil records on computer since 03/97; prior records on docket books.
Criminal Records: Access: Fax, mail, in person. Both court and visitors may perform in person searches. No search fee. Required to search: name, years to search. Criminal records on computer since 03/97; prior records on docket books.

General Information: No sealed records released. SASE required. Turnaround time 1-2 days. Copy fee: $1.00 per page. Certification fee: $2.50 plus $.50 per page after first. Fee payee: Superior Court Clerk. Personal checks accepted. Prepayment is required.

Magistrate Court PO Box 1025, 100 Wall St, Calhoun, GA 30703; 706-629-6818 X121/122/143/144. Hours: 8:30AM-5PM (EST). *Civil Actions Under $15,000, Eviction, Small Claims.*

Probate Court PO Box 669, Calhoun, GA 30703; 706-629-7314; Fax: 706-629-4698. Hours: 8:30AM-5PM (EST). *Probate.*

Grady County

Superior Court 250 N Broad St, Box 8, Cairo, GA 31728; 229-377-2912. Hours: 8AM-5PM (EST). *Felony, Misdemeanor, Civil.*

Civil Records: Access: In person only. Court will assist visitors with searches. No search fee. Required to search: name, years to search. Civil cases indexed by defendant, plaintiff. Civil records on computer since 1993; prior records on docket books.
Criminal Records: Access: In person only. Court will assist visitors with searches. No search fee. Required to search: name, years to search. Criminal records on computer since 1993; prior records on docket books.
General Information: Public Access terminal is available. No juvenile or adoption records released. Copy fee: $.25 per page. Certification fee: $2.00 plus $.50 per page. Fee payee: Superior Court Clerk. Personal checks accepted. Prepayment is required.

Magistrate Court 250 N Broad St, Cairo, GA 31728; 229-377-4132; Fax: 229-377-4127. Hours: 8AM-5PM (EST). *Civil Actions Under $15,000, Eviction, Small Claims.*

Probate Court Courthouse, 250 N Broad St, Box 1, Cairo, GA 31728; 229-377-4621; Fax: 229-377-4127. Hours: 8AM-5PM (EST). *Probate.*

Greene County

Superior & Juvenile Court 113 North Main St, #109, Greensboro, GA 30642; 706-453-3340; Fax: 706-453-3341. Hours: 8AM-5PM (EST). *Felony, Misdemeanor, Civil, Eviction, Small Claims.*

Civil Records: Access: In person only. Visitors must perform in person searches for themselves. No search fee. Required to search: name, years to search. Civil cases indexed by defendant, plaintiff. Civil records in books.
Criminal Records: Access: In person only. Visitors must perform in person searches for themselves. No search fee. Required to search: name, years to search; also helpful: SSN. Criminal records in books.
General Information: No juvenile or adoption records released. Copy fee: $.25 per page. Certification fee: Fee is $2.50 plus $.25 per page. Fee payee: Superior Court Clerk. Personal checks accepted. Prepayment is required.

Magistrate & Probate Court 113 N Main St #113, Greensboro, GA 30642; 706-453-3346; Fax: 706-453-7649. Hours: 8AM-5PM (EST). *Civil Actions Under $15,000, Eviction, Small Claims, Probate.*

Gwinnett County

Superior & State Court PO Box 880 (75 Langley Dr.), Lawrenceville, GA 30046; 770-822-8100. Hours: 8AM-5PM (EST). *Felony, Misdemeanor, Civil, Eviction, Small Claims.*

www.gwinnettcourts.com/courts/Supcourt.htm

Civil Records: Access: Online, in person. Visitors must perform in person searches for themselves. No search fee. Required to search: name, years to search. Civil cases indexed by defendant, plaintiff. Civil records on computer from 1990, prior records on card index. Online access to the court case party index is available free online at www.gwinnettcourts.com/misc/casendx.htm. Search by name or case number.

Criminal Records: Access: Online, in person. Visitors must perform in person searches for themselves. No search fee. Required to search: name, years to search. Criminal records on computer from 1990, prior records on card index. Online access to criminal records is the same as civil.

General Information: Public Access terminal is available. No sealed records released. Copy fee: $.25 per page. Certification fee: $2.50 plus $.50 per page. Fee payee: Superior Court Clerk. Personal checks accepted. Prepayment is required.

Magistrate Court 75 Langley Dr, Justice & Admin. Ctr., Lawrenceville, GA 30045-6900; 770-822-8080; Fax: 770-822-8075. Hours: 8AM-5PM (EST). *Civil Actions Under $15,000, Eviction, Small Claims.*

www.gwinnettcourts.com/courts/Magcourt.htm

Probate Court 75 Langley Dr, Justice & Admin. Ctr, Lawrenceville, GA 30045; 770-822-8250; Fax: 770-822-8267. Hours: 8:30AM-4:30PM (EST). *Probate.*

www.gwinnettcourts.com/courts/Procourt.htm

Habersham County

Superior & State Court 555 Monroe St, Unit 35, Clarkesville, GA 30523; 706-754-2923. Hours: 8AM-5PM (EST). *Felony, Misdemeanor, Civil.*

http://209.86.240.205/mountainhp.shtml

Civil Records: Access: In person only. Visitors must perform in person searches for themselves. No search fee. Required to search: name, years to search. Civil cases indexed by defendant, plaintiff. Civil records on index books from 1819.

Criminal Records: Access: In person only. Visitors must perform in person searches for themselves. No search fee. Required to search: name, years to search. Criminal records on index books from 1819.

General Information: Public Access terminal is available. No juvenile, adoption, sexual, mental health or expunged records released. Copy fee: $.25 per page. Certification fee: No cert fee. Fee payee: Court Clerk. Personal checks accepted. Prepayment is required.

Magistrate Court PO Box 738, Cornelia, GA 30531; 706-754-4871. Hours: 8AM-5PM (EST). *Civil Actions Under $15,000, Eviction, Small Claims.*

Probate Court Habersham County Courthouse, PO Box 625, Clarkesville, GA 30523; 706-754-2013; Fax: 706-754-5093. Hours: 8AM-5PM (EST). *Probate.*

Hall County

Superior & State Court PO Box 1336, Gainesville, GA 30503; 770-531-7025; Fax: 770-531-7070; 536-0702 real estate. Hours: 8AM-5PM (EST). *Felony, Misdemeanor, Civil.*

http://209.86.240.205/dca9nehp.shtml

Civil Records: Access: In person only. Visitors must perform in person searches for themselves. No search fee. Required to search: name, years to search. Civil cases indexed by defendant, plaintiff. Civil records on computer from 1989, dockets books from the late 1920s.

Criminal Records: Access: In person only. Visitors must perform in person searches for themselves. No search fee. Required to search: name, years to search. Criminal records on computer from 1989, dockets books from the late 1920s.

General Information: No juvenile, adoption, sexual, mental health or expunged records released. Fax notes: Fee to fax results is $1.00 per page. Copy fee: $1.00 per page. Certification fee: $2.00 plus $.50 per page. Fee payee: Court Clerk. Personal checks accepted. Prepayment is required.

Magistrate Court PO Box 1435, Gainesville, GA 30503; 770-531-6912; Fax: 770-531-6917. Hours: 8AM-5PM (EST). *Civil Actions Under $15,000, Eviction, Small Claims.*

www.hallcounty.org/clerkct.htm

Probate Court Hall County Courthouse, Rm 123, 116 Spring St, Gainesville, GA 30501; 770-531-6923; Fax: 770-531-4946. Hours: 8AM-5PM (EST). *Probate.*

http://hallcountyprobatect.com/clerkct.htm

Note: The search fee is $4.00 per record

Hancock County

Superior Court PO Box 451, Courthouse Square, Sparta, GA 31087; 706-444-6644; Fax: 706-444-6221. Hours: 8AM-5PM, 8AM-Noon Th (EST). *Felony, Misdemeanor, Civil.*

Civil Records: Access: Mail, in person. Both court and visitors may perform in person searches. Search fee: $5.00 per name. Required to search: name, years to search. Civil cases indexed by defendant, plaintiff. Civil records on docket books from 1991.

Criminal Records: Access: Mail, in person. Both court and visitors may perform in person searches. Search fee: $5.00 per name. Required to search: name, years to search, DOB, signed release; also helpful: SSN, race, sex. Criminal records on books since 1991.

General Information: Public Access terminal is available. (Includes deeds, UCCs and notary publics only.) No juvenile, adoptions, sealed, sexual, mental health or expunged records released. SASE required. Turnaround time 1 week. Copy fee: $.25 per page. Certification fee: 2 page doc is $2.50 plus $.25 per page; 3 pages and more are $4.50 plus $.25 per page after 3. Fee payee: Clerk of Superior Court. Personal checks accepted. Prepayment is required.

Magistrate Court 601 Courthouse Square, Sparta, GA 31087; 706-444-6234; Fax: 706-444-6221. Hours: 9AM-5PM (EST). *Civil Actions Under $15,000, Eviction, Small Claims.*

Probate Court 601 Court St, Sparta, GA 31087; 706-444-5343; Fax: 706-444-8024. Hours: 8AM-5PM M-W & F; 8AM-Noon Th (EST). *Probate.*

Haralson County

Superior Court Drawer 849, 4485 Georgia Hwy 120, Buchanan, GA 30113; 770-646-2005; Fax: 770-646-2035. Hours: 8:30AM-5PM (EST). *Felony, Misdemeanor, Civil.*

Civil Records: Access: Mail, in person. Both court and visitors may perform in person searches. No search fee. Required to search: name, years to search. Civil cases indexed by defendant, plaintiff. Civil records on dockets books from the 1800s.

Criminal Records: Access: Mail, in person. Both court and visitors may perform in person searches. No search fee. Required to search: name, years to search, signed release. Criminal records on dockets books from the 1800s.

General Information: No juvenile, adoption, sexual, mental health or expunged records released. SASE required. Turnaround time 1 wk. Copy fee: $.25 per page. Certification fee: $2.50 plus $.50 per page after first. Fee payee: Clerk of Superior Court. Personal checks accepted. Prepayment is required.

Magistrate Court PO Box 1040, Buchanan, GA 30113; 770-646-2025; Fax: 770-646-1508. Hours: 8:30AM-5PM (EST). *Civil Actions Under $15,000, Eviction, Small Claims.*

Probate Court PO Box 620, Buchanan, GA 30113; 770-646-2008; Fax: 770-646-3419. Hours: 8:30AM-5PM (EST). *Probate.*

Harris County

Superior Court PO Box 528, Hamilton, GA 31811; 706-628-4944; Fax: 706-628-7039. Hours: 8AM-5PM (EST). *Felony, Misdemeanor, Civil.*

Civil Records: Access: In person only. Visitors must perform in person searches for themselves. No search fee. Required to search: name, years to search. Civil cases indexed by defendant, plaintiff. Civil records on dockets books from 1827.

Criminal Records: Access: In person only. Visitors must perform in person searches for themselves. No search fee. Required to search: name, years to search, DOB; also helpful: SSN, race, sex. Criminal records on dockets books from 1827.

General Information: Juvenile, adoption, sexual, mental health or expunged records are only released with a signed release. Copy fee: $.25 per page. Certification fee: $2.50 plus $.50 per page after first. Fee payee: Court Clerk. No personal checks accepted. Prepayment is required.

Magistrate Court PO Box 347, Hamilton, GA 31811; 706-628-4977; Fax: 706-628-4221. Hours: 8AM-5PM (EST). *Civil Actions Under $15,000, Eviction, Small Claims.*

Probate Court PO Box 569, Hamilton, GA 31811; 706-628-5038; Fax: 706-628-7322. Hours: 8AM-Noon, 1-5PM (EST). *Probate.*

Hart County

Superior Court PO Box 386, Hartwell, GA 30643; 706-376-7189; Fax: 706-376-1277. Hours: 8:30AM-5PM (EST). *Felony, Misdemeanor, Civil.*

Civil Records: Access: In person only. Visitors must perform in person searches for themselves. No search fee. Required to search: name, years to search. Civil cases indexed by defendant, plaintiff. Civil records on computer back to 1991, dockets books from 1853.

Criminal Records: Access: In person only. Visitors must perform in person searches for themselves. No search fee. Required to search: name, years to search, DOB; also helpful: SSN, race, sex. Criminal records on computer back to 1991, dockets books from 1853.

General Information: Public Access terminal is available. No juvenile, adoption, sexual, mental health or expunged records released. Copy fee: $.25 per page. Certification fee: $2.50 plus $.50 per page after first. Fee payee: Clerk of Court. Personal checks accepted. Prepayment is required.

Magistrate Court PO Box 698, Hartwell, GA 30643; 706-376-6817; Fax: 706-376-6821. Hours: 8:30AM-5PM (EST). *Civil Actions Under $15,000, Eviction, Small Claims.*

Probate Court PO Box 1159, Hartwell, GA 30643; 706-376-2565; Fax: 706-376-9032. Hours: 8:30AM-5PM (EST). *Probate.*

Heard County

Superior Court PO Box 249, Franklin, GA 30217; 706-675-3301. Hours: 8:30AM-5PM (EST). *Felony, Misdemeanor, Civil.*

Civil Records: Access: In person only. Visitors must perform in person searches for themselves. No search fee. Required to search: name, years to search. Civil

cases indexed by defendant, plaintiff. Civil records on docket books from 1800s.

Criminal Records: Access: In person only. Visitors must perform in person searches for themselves. No search fee. Required to search: name, years to search, DOB, signed release; also helpful: SSN, race, sex. Criminal records on docket books from 1800s.

General Information: No juvenile, adoptions, sealed, sexual, mental health or expunged records released. Copy fee: $.25 per page. Certification fee: $2.50 plus $.50 per page after first. Fee payee: Court Clerk. Personal checks accepted. Prepayment is required.

Magistrate Court PO Box 395, Franklin, GA 30217; 706-675-3002; Fax: 706-675-0819. Hours: 8:30AM-5PM (EST). *Civil Actions Under $15,000, Eviction, Small Claims.*

Probate Court PO Box 478, Franklin, GA 30217; 706-675-3353; Fax: 706-675-0819. Hours: 8:30AM-5PM (EST). *Probate.*

Henry County

Superior Court One Courthouse Square, McDonough, GA 30253; 770-954-2121. Hours: 8AM-5PM (EST). *Felony, Misdemeanor, Civil.*

Civil Records: Access: Phone, mail, in person. Visitors must perform in person searches for themselves. No search fee. Required to search: name, years to search. Civil cases indexed by defendant, plaintiff. Civil records on dockets books from 1800s.

Criminal Records: Access: Phone, mail, in person. Visitors must perform in person searches for themselves. No search fee. Required to search: name, years to search, DOB, signed release; also helpful: SSN, race, sex. Criminal records on dockets books from 1800s.

General Information: No juvenile, adoption, sexual, mental health or expunged records released. Fax notes: No fee to fax results. Copy fee: $.25 per page. Certification fee: $2.50 plus $.50 per page thereafter. Fee payee: Clerk of Superior Court. Personal checks accepted. Prepayment is required.

Magistrate Court 30 Atlanta St, McDonough, GA 30253; 770-954-2111; Fax: 770-957-2144. Hours: 8AM-5PM (EST). *Civil Actions Under $15,000, Eviction, Small Claims.*

Probate Court 20 Lawrenceville St, McDonough, GA 30253; 770-954-2303; Fax: 770-954-2308. Hours: 8AM-5PM (EST). *Probate.*

Houston County

Superior Court 800 Carroll St, Perry, GA 31069; 478-987-2170; Fax: 478-987-3252. Hours: 8:30AM-5PM (EST). *Felony, Misdemeanor, Civil.*

Civil Records: Access: Phone, fax, mail, in person. Both court and visitors may perform in person searches. No search fee. Required to search: name, years to search. Civil cases indexed by defendant, plaintiff. Civil records on computer from 1984, dockets books back to 1823.

Criminal Records: Access: Fax, mail, in person. Both court and visitors may perform in person searches. No search fee. Required to search: name, years to search, DOB; also helpful: SSN, race, sex. Criminal records on computer from 1984, dockets books back to 1823.

General Information: Public Access terminal is available. No juvenile, adoption, mental health or expunged records released. Turnaround time 1-2 days. Copy fee: $.25 per page. Certification fee: $2.50 plus $.50 per page after first. Fee payee: Court Clerk. Personal checks accepted. Prepayment is required.

State Court 202 Carl Vinson Pkwy, Warner Robins, GA 31088; 478-542-2105; Fax: 478-542-2077. Hours: 8AM-5PM (EST). *Misdemeanor, Civil.*

Civil Records: Access: Mail, fax, in person. Both court and visitors may perform in person searches. No search fee. Required to search: name, years to search. Civil cases indexed by defendant. Civil records on computer from 1987, dockets books from 1965.

Criminal Records: Access: Mail, fax, in person. Both court and visitors may perform in person searches. No search fee. Required to search: name, years to search, DOB; also helpful: SSN, race, sex. Criminal records on computer from 1987, dockets books from 1965.

General Information: No juvenile, adoption, sexual, mental health or expunged records released. SASE requested. Turnaround time 1 week. Copy fee: $.25 per page. Certification fee: $2.50 plus $.50 per page after first. Fee payee: Court Clerk. Only cashiers checks and money orders accepted. Prepayment is required.

Magistrate Court 1911 Northside Rd, Perry, GA 31069; 478-987-4695; Fax: 478-987-5249. Hours: 8AM-5PM (EST). *Civil Actions Under $15,000, Eviction, Small Claims.*

Probate Court PO Box 1801, Perry, GA 31069; 478-987-2770; Fax: 478-988-4511. Hours: 8AM-4PM (EST). *Probate.*

www.courts.state.wi.us

Irwin County

Superior Court 113 N Irwin Ave, Ocilla, GA 31774; 229-468-5356. Hours: 8AM-5PM (EST). *Felony, Misdemeanor, Civil.*

Civil Records: Access: Phone, mail, in person. Both court and visitors may perform in person searches. No search fee. Required to search: name, years to search. Civil cases indexed by defendant, plaintiff. Civil records on dockets books from 1800s.

Criminal Records: Access: Phone, mail, in person. Both court and visitors may perform in person searches. No search fee. Required to search: name, years to search, DOB, signed release; also helpful: SSN, race, sex. Criminal records on dockets books from 1800s.

General Information: No juvenile, adoption, sexual, mental health or expunged records released. Turnaround time 2 days. Copy fee: $1.00 for first page, $.25 each add'l. Certification fee: $2.50 plus $.50 per page after first. Fee payee: Court Clerk. Personal checks accepted. Prepayment is required.

Magistrate Court 207 S Irwin Ave # 3, Ocilla, GA 31774; 229-468-7671; Fax: 229-468-9672. Hours: 8AM-5PM (EST). *Civil Actions Under $15,000, Eviction, Small Claims.*

Probate Court 310 S Irwin St #101, Ocilla, GA 31774; 229-468-5138; Fax: 229-468-7765. Hours: 8AM-5PM (EST). *Probate.*

Jackson County

Superior & State Court PO Box 7, Jefferson, GA 30549; 706-367-6360; Fax: 706-367-2468. Hours: 8AM-5PM (EST). *Felony, Misdemeanor, Civil.*

Civil Records: Access: In person only. Visitors must perform in person searches for themselves. No search fee. Required to search: name, years to search. Civil cases indexed by defendant, plaintiff. Civil records on computer from 1992, on dockets books from 1800s.

Criminal Records: Access: In person only. Visitors must perform in person searches for themselves. No search fee. Required to search: name, years to search, DOB; also helpful: SSN, race, sex. Criminal records on computer from 1992, on dockets books from 1800s.

General Information: Public Access terminal is available. No juvenile, adoption, sexual, mental health

or expunged records released. Copy fee: $.25 per page. Certification fee: $2.50 plus $.50 per page after first. Fee payee: Court Clerk. Personal checks accepted. Prepayment is required.

Magistrate Court PO Box 751, Commerce, GA 30529; 706-335-6545; Fax: 706-335-5221. Hours: 8AM-5PM (EST). *Civil Actions Under $15,000, Eviction, Small Claims.*

Probate Court 85 Washington St, Jefferson, GA 30549; 706-367-6366; Fax: 706-367-2468. Hours: 8:30AM-5PM (EST). *Probate.*

Jasper County

Superior Court 126 W Green Street, #200, Monticello, GA 31064; 706-468-4901; Fax: 706-468-4946. Hours: 8AM-5PM (EST). *Felony, Misdemeanor, Civil.*

Civil Records: Access: In person only. Visitors must perform in person searches for themselves. No search fee. Required to search: name, years to search. Civil cases indexed by defendant, plaintiff. Civil records on computer from 1990, dockets books from 1807.

Criminal Records: Access: In person only. Visitors must perform in person searches for themselves. No search fee. Required to search: name, years to search, DOB; also helpful: SSN, race, sex. Criminal records on computer from 1990, dockets books from 1807.

General Information: No juvenile, adoption, sexual, mental health or expunged records released. Copy fee: $.25 per page. Certification fee: $2.50 plus $.50 per page after first. Fee payee: Court Clerk. Personal checks accepted.

Magistrate Court 126 W Green St #301, Monticello, GA 31064; 706-468-4909; Fax: 706-468-4928. Hours: 8:30AM-4:30PM (EST). *Civil Actions Under $15,000, Eviction, Small Claims.*

Probate Court Jasper County Courthouse, 126 W Green St #201, Monticello, GA 31064; 706-468-4903; Fax: 706-468-4926. Hours: 8AM-4:30PM (EST). *Probate.*

Jeff Davis County

Superior & State Court PO Box 248, Hazlehurst, GA 31539; 912-375-6615 & 375-0378; Fax: 912-375-6637. Hours: 8AM-5PM (EST). *Felony, Misdemeanor, Civil.*

Civil Records: Access: Fax, mail, in person. Both court and visitors may perform in person searches. No search fee. Required to search: name, years to search. Civil cases indexed by defendant, plaintiff. Civil records on dockets books from 1805, limited records on computer back 3 years.

Criminal Records: Access: Fax, mail, in person. Both court and visitors may perform in person searches. Search fee: $3.00 per name. Required to search: name, years to search. Criminal records on dockets books from 1805, limited records on computer back 3 years.

General Information: No juvenile, confidential, adoption or sealed records released. Turnaround time 1 week, fax immediately. Fax notes: Fee to fax results is $2.00 1st page, $1.00 each add'l. Copy fee: $.25 per page. Certification fee: $2.50 plus $.50 per page after first. Fee payee: Court Clerk. Personal checks accepted.

Magistrate Court PO Box 568, Hazlehurst, GA 31539; 912-375-6630; Fax: 912-375-0378. Hours: 8AM-5PM (EST). *Civil Actions Under $15,000, Eviction, Small Claims.*

Probate Court PO Box 13, Hazlehurst, GA 31539; 912-375-6626. Hours: 9AM-5PM (EST). *Probate.*

Jefferson County

Superior & State Court PO Box 151, Louisville, GA 30434; 478-625-7922; Fax: 478-625-4002. Hours: 9AM-5PM (EST). *Felony, Misdemeanor, Civil.*

Civil Records: Access: Mail, in person. Both court and visitors may perform in person searches. No search fee. Required to search: name, years to search. Civil cases indexed by defendant, plaintiff. Civil records on dockets books from 1865; on computer back to 1995.
Criminal Records: Access: Mail, in person. Both court and visitors may perform in person searches. No search fee. Required to search: name, years to search, DOB or SSN. Criminal records on dockets books from 1865; on computer back to 1995.
General Information: Public Access terminal is available. No juvenile, adoption, sexual, mental health or expunged records released. SASE required. Turnaround time 1 week. Copy fee: $.25 per page. Certification fee: $2.50 plus $1.00 per add'l page. Fee payee: Court Clerk. Personal checks accepted.

Magistrate Court PO Box 749, Louisville, GA 30434; 478-625-8834; Fax: 478-625-9736. Hours: 8AM-5PM (EST). *Civil Actions Under $15,000, Eviction, Small Claims.*

Probate Court PO Box 307, PO Box 307, Louisville, GA 30434; 478-625-3258; Fax: 478-625-9589. Hours: 9AM-4:30PM (EST). *Probate.*

Jenkins County

Superior & State Court PO Box 659, Millen, GA 30442; 478-982-4683; Fax: 478-982-1274. Hours: 8:30AM-5PM (EST). *Felony, Misdemeanor, Civil.*

Civil Records: Access: In person only. Visitors must perform in person searches for themselves. No search fee. Required to search: name, years to search. Civil cases indexed by defendant. Civil records on dockets books.
Criminal Records: Access: In person only. Visitors must perform in person searches for themselves. No search fee. Required to search: name, years to search, DOB; also helpful: SSN, race, sex. Criminal records on dockets books.
General Information: No juvenile, adoption, sexual, mental health or expunged records released. Copy fee: $.25 per page. Certification fee: $2.50 plus $.50 per page after first. Fee payee: Clerk of Court. Prepayment is required.

Magistrate Court PO Box 892, Millen, GA 30442; 478-982-5580; Fax: 478-982-4911. Hours: 8:30AM-5PM (EST). *Civil Actions Under $15,000, Eviction, Small Claims.*

Probate Court PO Box 904, Millen, GA 30442; 478-982-5581; Fax: 478-982-2829. Hours: 8:30AM-5PM (EST). *Probate.*

Johnson County

Superior & Magistrate Court PO Box 321, Wrightsville, GA 31096; 478-864-3484; Fax: 478-864-1343. Hours: 9AM-5PM (EST). *Felony, Misdemeanor, Civil, Eviction, Small Claims.*

Civil Records: Access: In person only. Visitors must perform in person searches for themselves. No search fee. Required to search: name, years to search. Civil cases indexed by defendant, plaintiff. Civil records on computer from 1991, dockets books from 1859.
Criminal Records: Access: In person only. Visitors must perform in person searches for themselves. No search fee. Required to search: name, years to search, DOB; also helpful: SSN, race, sex. Criminal records on computer from 1991, dockets books from 1859.
General Information: No juvenile, adoption, sexual, mental health or expunged records released. Copy fee:

$.25 per page. Certification fee: $3.00. Fee payee: Court Clerk. Personal checks accepted. Prepayment is required.

Probate Court PO Box 321, Wrightsville, GA 31096; 478-864-3484; Fax: 478-864-1343. *Probate.*

Jones County

Superior Court PO Box 39, 110 South Jefferson St, Gray, GA 31032; 478-986-6671/6674. Hours: 8:30AM-4:30PM (EST). *Felony, Misdemeanor, Civil.*

Civil Records: Access: In person only. Visitors must perform in person searches for themselves. No search fee. Required to search: name, years to search. Civil cases indexed by defendant, plaintiff. Civil records on computer since 1989, dockets books from 1800s. The court will fax records not requiring a search, $5.00 minimum.
Criminal Records: Access: In person only. Visitors must perform in person searches for themselves. No search fee. Required to search: name, years to search, signed release. Criminal records on docket books, computerized since 1995.
General Information: No juvenile, adoption, sexual, mental health or expunged records released. Copy fee: $.50 per page. Certification fee: $2.50 plus $.50 per page after first. Fee payee: Superior Court. Personal checks accepted. Prepayment is required.

Magistrate & Probate Court PO Box 1359, Gray, GA 31032; 478-986-6668; Fax: 478-986-1715. Hours: 8:30AM-4:30PM (EST). *Civil Actions Under $15,000, Eviction, Small Claims, Probate.*

Lamar County

Superior Court 326 Thomaston St, Barnesville, GA 30204; 770-358-5145; Fax: 770-358-5149. Hours: 8AM-5PM (EST). *Felony, Misdemeanor, Civil.*

Civil Records: Access: In person only. Only the court performs in person searches; visitors may not. No search fee. Required to search: name, years to search. Civil cases indexed by defendant. Civil records on dockets books from 1921.
Criminal Records: Access: In person only. Only the court performs in person searches; visitors may not. No search fee. Required to search: name, years to search, DOB, offense, date of offense; also helpful: SSN, race, sex. Criminal records on dockets books from 1921.
General Information: No juvenile, adoption, sexual, mental health or expunged records released. Copy fee: $1.00 for first page, $.25 each add'l. Certification fee: $2.50 the first page and $.50 each additional. Fee payee: Court Clerk. Personal checks accepted. Prepayment is required. Will bill copy fees.

Magistrate Court 121 Roberta Dr, Barnesville, GA 30204; 770-358-5154; Fax: 770-358-5214. Hours: 8AM-5PM (EST). *Civil Actions Under $15,000, Eviction, Small Claims.*

Probate Court 326 Thomaston St, Barnesville, GA 30204; 770-358-5155; Fax: 770-358-5348. Hours: 8AM-5PM (EST). *Probate.*

Lanier County

Superior Court County Courthouse, 100 Main St, Lakeland, GA 31635; 229-482-3594; Fax: 229-482-8333. Hours: 8AM-Noon, 1-5PM (EST). *Felony, Misdemeanor, Civil.*

Civil Records: Access: In person only. Visitors must perform in person searches for themselves. No search fee. Required to search: name, years to search. Civil cases indexed by defendant, plaintiff. Civil records on dockets books from 1921; on computer back to 1995.
Criminal Records: Access: In person only. Visitors must perform in person searches for themselves. No search fee. Required to search: name, years to search,

DOB, signed release. Criminal records on dockets books from 1921; on computer back to 1995.
General Information: Public Access terminal is available. No juvenile, adoption, sexual, mental health or expunged records released. Copy fee: $.25 per page. Certification fee: $3.00. Fee payee: Court Clerk. Personal checks accepted. Prepayment is required.

Magistrate Court 100 Main St, County Courthouse, Lakeland, GA 31635; 229-482-2207. Hours: 8AM-5PM (EST). *Civil Actions Under $15,000, Eviction, Small Claims.*

Probate Court County Courthouse, 100 Main St, Lakeland, GA 31635; 229-482-3668; Fax: 229-482-8333. Hours: 8AM-5PM (EST). *Probate.*

Laurens County

Superior & Magistrate Court PO Box 2028, Dublin, GA 31040; 478-272-3210. Hours: 8:30AM-5:30PM (EST). *Felony, Misdemeanor, Civil, Eviction, Small Claims.*

Civil Records: Access: In person only. Visitors must perform in person searches for themselves. No search fee. Required to search: name, years to search. Civil cases indexed by defendant, plaintiff. Civil records on computer from 1992, dockets books from 1800s.
Criminal Records: Access: In person only. Visitors must perform in person searches for themselves. No search fee. Required to search: name, years to search; also helpful: SSN. Criminal records on computer from 1992, dockets books from 1800s.
General Information: No juvenile, adoption, sexual, mental health or expunged records released. Copy fee: $.25 per page. Certification fee: $2.50 plus $.50 per page after first. Fee payee: Court Clerk. Personal checks accepted. Prepayment is required.

Probate Court PO Box 2098, Dublin, GA 31040; 478-272-2566; Fax: 478-277-2932. Hours: 8:30AM-5:30PM (EST). *Probate.*

Lee County

Superior Court PO Box 597, Leesburg, GA 31763; 229-759-6018. Hours: 8AM-5PM (EST). *Felony, Misdemeanor, Civil.*

Civil Records: Access: Mail, in person. Both court and visitors may perform in person searches. No search fee. Required to search: name, years to search. Civil cases indexed by defendant, plaintiff. Civil records on docket books from 1850.
Criminal Records: Access: Mail, in person. Both court and visitors may perform in person searches. Search fee: $5.00. Required to search: name, years to search, DOB; also helpful: SSN, race, sex. Criminal records on docket books from 1850.
General Information: Public Access terminal is available. No juvenile, adoption, sexual, mental health or expunged records released. SASE required. Turnaround time 1 week. Copy fee: $1.00 per page. Certification fee: $2.00 plus $.50 per page after first. Fee payee: Court Clerk. Personal checks accepted. Prepayment is required.

Magistrate Court PO Box 522, Leesburg, GA 31763; 229-759-6016; Fax: 229-759-3303. Hours: 8AM-5PM (EST). *Civil Actions Under $15,000, Eviction, Small Claims.*

Probate Court PO Box 592, Leesburg, GA 31763; 229-759-6005; Fax: 229-759-6032. Hours: 8AM-5PM (EST). *Probate.*

Liberty County

Superior & State Court PO Box 50, Hinesville, GA 31313-0050; 912-876-3625. Hours: 8AM-5PM (EST). *Felony, Misdemeanor, Civil.*

www.libertyco.com

Civil Records: Access: Phone, fax, mail, in person. Both court and visitors may perform in person searches. No search fee. Required to search: name, years to search. Civil cases indexed by defendant, plaintiff. Civil records on computer from 1986, dockets books from 1700s.

Criminal Records: Access: Mail, in person. Both court and visitors may perform in person searches. Search fee: $5.00 per name. Required to search: name, years to search, DOB, signed release; also helpful: SSN, race, sex. Criminal records on computer from 1986, dockets books from 1700s.

General Information: Public Access terminal is available. No juvenile, adoption, sexual, mental health or expunged records released. SASE not required. Turnaround time 1-2 days. Fax notes: Fax fee $5.00 1st 5 pages, $1.00 each additional page. Need prepaid account for fax retrieval. Copy fee: $1.00 per page. Certification fee: $2.50 plus $.50 per page after first. Fee payee: Court Clerk. Business checks accepted. Prepayment is required.

Magistrate Court PO Box 912, Hinesville, GA 31310; 912-368-2063. Hours: 8AM-5PM (EST). *Civil Actions Under $15,000, Eviction, Small Claims.*

www.libertyco.com

Probate Court PO Box 28, Hinesville, GA 31310; 912-876-3635; Fax: 912-876-3589. Hours: 8AM-5PM (EST). *Probate.*

Lincoln County

Superior Court PO Box 340, Lincolnton, GA 30817; 706-359-5505. Hours: 9AM-5PM (EST). *Felony, Misdemeanor, Civil.*

Civil Records: Access: In person only. Visitors must perform in person searches for themselves. No search fee. Required to search: name, years to search. Civil cases indexed by defendant, plaintiff. Civil records on index books from 1800s. There is no public terminal, must search in the books.

Criminal Records: Access: In person only. Visitors must perform in person searches for themselves. No search fee. Required to search: name, years to search. Criminal records on index books from 1800s.

General Information: No adoption or juvenile records released. Copy fee: $.25 per page. Certification fee: $2.50. Fee payee: Superior Court Clerk. Personal checks accepted. Prepayment is required.

Magistrate Court PO Box 205, Lincolnton, GA 30817; 706-359-5519; Fax: 706-359-5027. Hours: 8:30AM-4:30PM (EST). *Civil Actions Under $15,000, Eviction, Small Claims.*

Probate Court PO Box 340, Lincolnton, GA 30817; 706-359-5528; Fax: 706-359-4729. Hours: 9AM-5PM (EST). *Probate.*

Long County

Superior & State Court PO Box 458, Ludowici, GA 31316; 912-545-2123. Hours: 8:30AM-4:30PM (EST). *Felony, Misdemeanor, Civil.*

Civil Records: Access: Mail, in person. Only the court performs in person searches; visitors may not. Search fee: $5.00 per name. Required to search: name, years to search. Civil cases indexed by defendant, plaintiff. Civil records on docket books, archived from 1921.

Criminal Records: Access: Mail, in person. Only the court performs in person searches; visitors may not. Search fee: $5.00 per name. Required to search: name,

years to search, DOB; also helpful: SSN, race, sex. Criminal records on docket books, archived from 1921.

General Information: No juvenile, adoption, sealed, sexual, mental health, expunged or confidential records released. SASE required. Turnaround time 1 week. Copy fee: $.25 per page. Certification fee: $2.50 plus $.50 per page after first. Fee payee: Court Clerk. Business checks accepted. Prepayment is required.

Magistrate & Probate Court PO Box 426, Ludowici, GA 31316; 912-545-2131; Fax: 912-545-2150. Hours: 8:30AM-4:30PM (EST). *Civil Actions Under $15,000, Eviction, Small Claims, Probate.*

Lowndes County

Superior & State Court PO Box 1349, Valdosta, GA 31603; 229-333-5127. Hours: 8AM-5PM (EST). *Felony, Misdemeanor, Civil.*

www2.state.ga.us/courts/superior/dca/dca2sohp.htm

Civil Records: Access: Mail, in person. Both court and visitors may perform in person searches. Search fee: $3.00 per name for mail requests. Required to search: name, years to search. Civil cases indexed by defendant, plaintiff. Civil records on computer from 1990, prior on dockets books.

Criminal Records: Access: In person only. Visitors must perform in person searches for themselves. No search fee. Required to search: name, years to search, DOB; also helpful: SSN, race, sex. Criminal records on computer back to 1984; prior records on docket books.

General Information: Public Access terminal is available. No juvenile, adoption, sexual, mental health or expunged records released. Turnaround time 1 week. Fax notes: Fee to fax results is $.25 per page. Copy fee: $.25 per page. Certification fee: $2.50 plus $.50 per page after first; $5.00 minimum. Fee payee: Court Clerk. Only cashiers checks and money orders accepted. Prepayment is required.

Magistrate Court PO Box 1349, Valdosta, GA 31603; 229-333-5112; Fax: 229-333-7616. Hours: 9AM-5PM (EST). *Civil Actions Under $15,000, Eviction, Small Claims.*

Probate Court PO Box 72, Valdosta, GA 31603; 229-333-5103; Fax: 229-333-7646. Hours: 8AM-5PM (EST). *Probate.*

Lumpkin County

Superior, Juvenile & Magistrate Court 99 Courthouse Hill, Suite D, Dahlonega, GA 30533-0541; 706-864-3736; Fax: 706-864-5298. Hours: 8AM-5PM (EST). *Felony, Misdemeanor, Civil, Eviction, Small Claims.*

http://209.86.240.205/enotahhp.shtml

Note: For Magistrate Court criminal records info, call 706-864-7760.

Civil Records: Access: In person only. Visitors must perform in person searches for themselves. No search fee. Required to search: name, years to search; also helpful: address. Civil cases indexed by defendant, plaintiff. Civil records on computer from 1988, prior on dockets books to 1833.

Criminal Records: Access: In person only. Visitors must perform in person searches for themselves. No search fee. Required to search: name, years to search, DOB; also helpful: address, SSN, race, sex. Criminal records on computer from 1988, prior on dockets books to 1833.

General Information: Public Access terminal is available. No juvenile, adoption, sealed records released. Fax notes: $2.50 for 1st page; $1.00 each add'l. Copy fee: $1.00 per page; $.25 if in person. Certification fee: $2.50 plus $.50 per page after first. Fee payee: Court Clerk. Personal checks accepted. Prepayment is required.

Probate Court 99 Courthouse Hill, Suite C, Dahlonega, GA 30533; 706-864-3847; Fax: 706-864-9271. Hours: 8:30AM-4:30PM (EST). *Probate.*

Macon County

Superior Court PO Box 337, Oglethorpe, GA 31068; 478-472-7661. Hours: 8AM-5PM (EST). *Felony, Misdemeanor, Civil.*

Civil Records: Access: Mail, in person. Both court and visitors may perform in person searches. No search fee. Civil cases indexed by defendant, plaintiff. Civil records on dockets books from 1800s.

Criminal Records: Access: In person only. Both court and visitors may perform in person searches. No search fee. Criminal records on dockets books from 1800s.

General Information: No juvenile, adoption, sexual, mental health or expunged records released. SASE required. Turnaround time 1 week. Fax notes: No fee to fax results. Copy fee: $.25 per page. Certification fee: $2.00. Fee payee: Court Clerk. Business checks accepted. Prepayment is required.

Magistrate Court PO Box 605, Oglethorpe, GA 31068; 478-472-8509; Fax: 478-472-5643. Hours: 8AM-Noon, 1-5PM (EST). *Civil Actions Under $15,000, Eviction, Small Claims.*

Probate Court PO Box 216, Oglethorpe, GA 31068; 478-472-7685. Hours: 8AM-Noon, 1-5PM (EST). *Probate.*

Madison County

Superior Court PO Box 247, Danielsville, GA 30633; 706-795-3352; Fax: 706-795-2209. Hours: 8AM-5PM (EST). *Felony, Misdemeanor, Civil.*

Civil Records: Access: In person only. Visitors must perform in person searches for themselves. No search fee. Required to search: name, years to search. Civil cases indexed by defendant. Civil records on computer since 1976; prior records on dockets books from 1800s.

Criminal Records: Access: In person only. Visitors must perform in person searches for themselves. No search fee. Required to search: name, years to search, DOB; also helpful: SSN, race, sex. Criminal records on computer since 1960.

General Information: Public Access terminal is available. No juvenile, adoption, sexual, mental health or expunged records released. Copy fee: $.25 per page. Certification fee: $2.50 plus $.50 per page after first. Fee payee: Court Clerk. No personal checks accepted. Prepayment is required.

Magistrate Court PO Box 6, Danielsville, GA 30633; 706-795-5679; Fax: 706-795-2222. Hours: 8AM-5PM (EST). *Civil Actions Under $15,000, Eviction, Small Claims.*

Probate Court PO Box 207, Danielsville, GA 30633; 706-795-3354; Fax: 706-795-5933. Hours: 8AM-5PM (EST). *Probate.*

Marion County

Superior Court PO Box 41, Buena Vista, GA 31803; 229-649-7321; Fax: 229-649-7331. Hours: 8:30AM-5PM (EST). *Felony, Misdemeanor, Civil.*

Civil Records: Access: In person only. Visitors must perform in person searches for themselves. No search fee. Required to search: name, years to search. Civil cases indexed by defendant, plaintiff. Civil records on dockets books from 1845.

Criminal Records: Access: In person only. Visitors must perform in person searches for themselves. No search fee. Required to search: name, years to search; also helpful: SSN. Criminal records on dockets books from 1845.

General Information: No juvenile, adoption, sexual, mental health or expunged records released. Copy fee: $.25 per page. Certification fee: $2.50 plus $.50 per page after first. Fee payee: Court Clerk. Personal checks accepted. Prepayment is required.

Magistrate & Probate Court PO Box 207, Buena Vista, GA 31803; 229-649-5542; Fax: 229-649-2059. Hours: 8:30AM-Noon, 1-5PM (EST). *Civil Under $15,000, Eviction, Small Claims, Probate.*

McDuffie County

Superior Court PO Box 158, 337 Main St, Thomson, GA 30824; 706-595-2134. Hours: 8AM-5PM (EST). *Felony, Misdemeanor, Civil.*

Civil Records: Access: In person only. Visitors must perform in person searches for themselves. No search fee. Required to search: name, years to search. Civil cases indexed by defendant, plaintiff. Civil records on computer from 1991, dockets books from 1800s.
Criminal Records: Access: In person only. Visitors must perform in person searches for themselves. No search fee. Required to search: name, years to search, signed release; also helpful: DOB. Civil records on computer from 1991, dockets books from 1800s.
General Information: Public Access terminal is available. No juvenile or adoption records released. Copy fee: $.25 per page self; $1.00 per page assisted. Certification fee: $2.50 plus $.50 per page after first. Fee payee: Clerk Superior Court. Personal checks accepted. Prepayment is required.

Magistrate Court PO Box 252, Thomson, GA 30824; 706-597-2618; Fax: 706-595-2041. Hours: 8AM-5PM (EST). *Civil Actions Under $15,000, Eviction, Small Claims.*

Probate Court PO Box 2028, Thomson, GA 30824; 706-595-2124; Fax: 706-595-4710. Hours: 8AM-5PM (EST). *Probate.*

McIntosh County

Superior & State Court PO Box 1661, Darien, GA 31305; 912-437-6641; Fax: 912-437-6673. Hours: 8AM-4:30PM (EST). *Felony, Misdemeanor, Civil.*

Civil Records: Access: In person only. Visitors must perform in person searches for themselves. No search fee. Required to search: name, years to search. Civil cases indexed by defendant, plaintiff. Civil records on computer from 1991, dockets books from 1800s.
Criminal Records: Access: In person only. Visitors must perform in person searches for themselves. No search fee. Required to search: name, years to search, DOB; also helpful: SSN, race, sex. Criminal records on computer from 1991, dockets books from 1800s.
General Information: Public Access terminal is available. No juvenile, adoption, sexual, mental health or expunged records released. Copy fee: $.25 per page. Certification fee: $2.50 plus $.50 per page after first. Fee payee: Court Clerk. Personal checks accepted. Prepayment is required.

Magistrate Court PO Box 459, Darien, GA 31305; 912-437-4888; Fax: 912-437-2768. Hours: 8AM-4:30PM (EST). *Civil Actions Under $15,000, Eviction, Small Claims.*

Probate Court PO Box 453, Darien, GA 31305; 912-437-6636; Fax: 912-437-6635. Hours: 8AM-5PM (EST). *Probate.*

Meriwether County

Superior Court PO Box 160, Greenville, GA 30222; 706-672-4416; Fax: 706-672-1296. Hours: 9AM-5PM (EST). *Felony, Misdemeanor, Civil.*

Civil Records: Access: In person only. Visitors must perform in person searches for themselves. No search

fee. Required to search: name, years to search. Civil cases indexed by defendant, plaintiff. Civil records on microfilm and computer from 1990, prior on writ and minute books.
Criminal Records: Access: In person only. Visitors must perform in person searches for themselves. No search fee. Required to search: name, years to search, DOB, SSN, signed release. Criminal records computerized since 1991.
General Information: Public Access terminal is available. No juvenile, adoption, sexual, mental health or expunged records released. Fax notes: Fee to fax results is $2.50 first pg; $1.00 each add'l. Copy fee: $.25 per page. Certification fee: $2.50 plus $.50 per page after first. Fee payee: Court Clerk. Business checks accepted.

Magistrate Court PO Box 702, 124 N Court Sq, Greenville, GA 30222; 706-672-1247; Fax: 706-672-1172. Hours: 9AM-4:30PM M,T,TH,F/9AM-11:30PM W (EST). *Civil Actions Under $15,000, Eviction, Small Claims.*

Probate Court PO Box 608, Greenville, GA 30222; 706-672-4952; Fax: 706-672-1886. Hours: 8:30AM-5PM (EST). *Probate.*

Miller County

Superior & State Court PO Box 66, Colquitt, GA 31737; 229-758-4102. Hours: 8AM-5PM (EST). *Felony, Misdemeanor, Civil.*

Civil Records: Access: In person only. Visitors must perform in person searches for themselves. No search fee. Required to search: name, years to search. Civil cases indexed by defendant, plaintiff. Civil records on dockets books from 1800s.
Criminal Records: Access: In person only. Visitors must perform in person searches for themselves. No search fee. Required to search: name, years to search. Criminal records on dockets books from 1800s.
General Information: Public Access terminal is available. No juvenile or adoption records released. Copy fee: $1.00 per page. Certification fee: $2.50 plus $1.00 per page after first. Fee payee: Court Clerk. Business checks accepted. Prepayment is required.

Magistrate & Probate Court 155 S 1st St, Box 110, Box110, Colquitt, GA 31737; 229-758-4110; Fax: 229-758-8133. Hours: 8AM-5PM (EST). *Civil Actions Under $15,000, Small Claims, Probate.*

Mitchell County

Superior & State Court PO Box 427, Camilla, GA 31730; 229-336-2022. Hours: 8:30AM-5PM (EST). *Felony, Misdemeanor, Civil.*

Civil Records: Access: In person only. Visitors must perform in person searches for themselves. No search fee. Required to search: name, years to search. Civil cases indexed by defendant. Civil records on dockets books from 1800s.
Criminal Records: Access: In person only. Visitors must perform in person searches for themselves. No search fee. Required to search: name, years to search, DOB; also helpful: SSN, race, sex. Criminal records on dockets books from 1800s.
General Information: No juvenile, adoption, sexual, mental health or expunged records released. Copy fee: $.25 per page. Certification fee: $2.50 plus $.50 per page after first. Fee payee: Court Clerk. Only cashiers checks and money orders accepted. Prepayment is required.

Magistrate Court PO Box 664, Pelham, GA 31779; 229-294-4460; Fax: 229-294-4951. Hours: 8:30AM-5PM (EST). *Civil Actions Under $15,000, Eviction, Small Claims.*

Probate Court PO Box 229, Camilla, GA 31730; 229-336-2016; Fax: 229-336-2004. Hours: 8:30AM-5PM (EST). *Probate.*

Monroe County

Superior Court PO Box 450, 1 Courthouse Square, Forsyth, GA 31029; 478-994-7022; Fax: 478-994-7053. Hours: 8:30AM-4:30PM (EST). *Felony, Misdemeanor, Civil.*

Civil Records: Access: In person only. Visitors must perform in person searches for themselves. No search fee. Required to search: name, years to search. Civil cases indexed by defendant, plaintiff. Civil records on computer from 1986, dockets books from 1800s.
Criminal Records: Access: Mail, in person. Both court and visitors may perform in person searches. No search fee. Required to search: name, years to search, signed release. Criminal records on computer from 1989.
General Information: Public Access terminal is available. No juvenile, adoption, sexual, mental health or expunged records released. Mail requests not accepted. Turnaround time 1 day. Copy fee: $1.00 per page. Certification fee: $2.50 plus $.50 per page after first. Fee payee: Court Clerk. Personal checks accepted. Prepayment is required.

Magistrate Court PO Box 974, Forsyth, GA 31029; 478-994-7018; Fax: 478-994-7284. Hours: 8:30AM-Noon, 1:30-4:30PM (EST). *Civil Actions Under $15,000, Eviction, Small Claims.*

Probate Court PO Box 187, Forsyth, GA 31029; 478-994-7036; Fax: 478-994-7054. Hours: 8:30AM-4:30PM (EST). *Probate.*

Montgomery County

Superior Court PO Box 311, Mt Vernon, GA 30445; 912-583-4401. Hours: 8AM-5PM (EST). *Felony, Misdemeanor, Civil.*

Civil Records: Access: In person only. Visitors must perform in person searches for themselves. No search fee. Required to search: name, years to search. Civil cases indexed by defendant, plaintiff. Civil records on computer from 1993, on dockets from 1793.
Criminal Records: Access: In person only. Visitors must perform in person searches for themselves. No search fee. Required to search: name, years to search, DOB; also helpful: SSN, race, sex. Criminal records on computer from 1993, on dockets from 1793.
General Information: No juvenile or adoption records released. Fax notes: Fee to fax results is $2.50 per page. Copy fee: $1.00 per page. Certification fee: $2.50 per page. Fee payee: Superior Court Clerk. Personal checks accepted.

Magistrate Court PO Box 174, Mt Vernon, GA 30445; 912-583-2170; Fax: 912-583-4343. Hours: 8AM-5PM (EST). *Civil Actions Under $15,000, Eviction, Small Claims.*

Probate Court PO Box 302, Mt Vernon, GA 30445; 912-583-2681; Fax: 912-583-4343. Hours: 9AM-5PM (EST). *Probate.*

Morgan County

Superior Court PO Box 130, 149 E Jefferson St, Madison, GA 30650; 706-342-3605. Hours: 9AM-5PM (EST). *Felony, Misdemeanor, Civil.*

Civil Records: Access: In person only. Visitors must perform in person searches for themselves. No search fee. Required to search: name, years to search. Civil

cases indexed by defendant, plaintiff. Civil records on computer from 1986, on dockets from 1900s.
Criminal Records: Access: In person only. Visitors must perform in person searches for themselves. No search fee. Required to search: name, years to search, signed release. Criminal records on computer from 1986, on dockets from 1900s.
General Information: Public Access terminal is available. No juvenile, adoption, sexual, mental health or expunged records released. Copy fee: $.25 per page. Certification fee: $2.50 plus $.50 per page after first. Fee payee: Superior Court Clerk. Personal checks accepted. Prepayment is required.

Magistrate Court 149 E Jefferson St, Rm 110, Madison, GA 30650; 706-342-3088; Fax: 706-343-0000. Hours: 8AM-5PM (EST). *Civil Actions Under $15,000, Eviction, Small Claims.*

Probate Court PO Box 857, Madison, GA 30650; 706-342-1373; Fax: 706-342-5085. Hours: 8AM-5PM (EST). *Probate.*

Murray County

Superior Court PO Box 1000, Chatsworth, GA 30705; 706-695-2932. Hours: 8:30AM-5PM (EST). *Felony, Misdemeanor, Civil.*

Civil Records: Access: In person only. Visitors must perform in person searches for themselves. No search fee. Required to search: name, years to search. Civil cases indexed by defendant, plaintiff. Civil records on dockets from 1940, prior to 1940 archived.
Criminal Records: Access: In person only. Visitors must perform in person searches for themselves. No search fee. Required to search: name, years to search, signed release. Criminal records on dockets from 1940, prior to 1940 archived.
General Information: No juvenile, adoption, sexual, mental health or expunged records released. Copy fee: $.25 per page. Certification fee: $2.50 plus $.50 per page after first. Fee payee: Superior Court Clerk. Personal checks accepted. Prepayment is required.

Magistrate Court 121 4th Ave, Chatsworth, GA 30705; 706-695-3021. Hours: 8AM-Noon, 1-5PM (EST). *Civil Actions Under $15,000, Eviction, Small Claims.*

Probate Court 115 Fort St, Chatsworth, GA 30705; 706-695-3812; Fax: 706-517-1340. Hours: 8:30AM-5PM (EST). *Probate.*

Muscogee County

Superior & State Court PO Box 2145, Columbus, GA 31902; 706-653-4351; Fax: 706-653-4359. Hours: 8:30AM-5PM (EST). *Felony, Misdemeanor, Civil.*

Civil Records: Access: Mail, in person. Both court and visitors may perform in person searches. Search fee: $30.00 per name. Required to search: name, years to search. Civil cases indexed by defendant, plaintiff. Civil records on computer from 1989, on dockets from 1919 to 1989.
Criminal Records: Access: Mail, in person. Both court and visitors may perform in person searches. Search fee: $30.00 per name. Required to search: name, years to search, DOB; also helpful: SSN. Criminal records on computer since 1989, on dockets from 1989 to 1957.
General Information: Public Access terminal is available. No adoption, sealed or first offender records released. Turnaround time 1 week. Copy fee: $.25 per page. Certification fee: $2.50 plus $.50 per page after first. Fee payee: Superior Court Clerk. Business checks accepted. Prepayment is required.

Magistrate Court Box 1340, Columbus, GA 31902; 706-571-4870; Fax: 706-571-2010. Hours: 8:30AM-5PM (EST). *Civil Actions Under $15,000, Eviction, Small Claims.*

Probate Court PO Box 1340, Columbus, GA 31902; 706-653-4333. Hours: 8:30AM-4PM (EST). *Probate.*

Newton County

Superior Court 1132 Usher St, Covington, GA 30014; 770-784-2035. Hours: 8AM-5PM (EST). *Felony, Misdemeanor, Civil.*

Civil Records: Access: In person only. Visitors must perform in person searches for themselves. No search fee. Required to search: name, years to search. Civil cases indexed by defendant, plaintiff. Civil records on computer from 1991, on dockets from 1900s.
Criminal Records: Access: In person only. Visitors must perform in person searches for themselves. No search fee. Required to search: name, years to search, signed release. Criminal records on computer from 1991, on dockets from 1900s.
General Information: Public Access terminal is available. No adoption, sexual, mental health or expunged records released. Copy fee: $.25 per page. Certification fee: $2.50 plus $.50 per page after first. Fee payee: Superior Court Clerk. Personal checks accepted. Prepayment is required.

Magistrate & Probate Court 1132 Usher St, Rm 148, Covington, GA 30014; 770-784-2045; Fax: 770-784-2145. Hours: 8AM-5PM (EST). *Civil Actions Under $15,000, Eviction, Small Claims, Probate.*

Oconee County

Superior & Magistrate Courts PO Box 1099, Watkinsville, GA 30677; 706-769-3940; Fax: 706-769-3948. Hours: 8AM-5PM (EST). *Felony, Misdemeanor, Civil, Eviction, Small Claims.*

Civil Records: Access: In person only. Visitors must perform in person searches for themselves. No search fee. Required to search: name, years to search. Civil cases indexed by defendant, plaintiff. Civil records on computer from 1989, on dockets from 1875.
Criminal Records: Access: In person only. Visitors must perform in person searches for themselves. No search fee. Required to search: name, years to search; also helpful: DOB, SSN. Criminal records on computer from 1989, on dockets from 1875.
General Information: No juvenile, adoption, sexual, mental health or expunged records released. Copy fee: $.25 per page. Certification fee: $2.50 plus $.50 per page after first. Fee payee: Superior Court Clerk. Personal checks accepted. Prepayment is required.

Probate Court PO Box 54, Watkinsville, GA 30677; 706-769-3936; Fax: 706-769-3934. Hours: 8AM-5PM (EST). *Probate.*

Oglethorpe County

Superior Court PO Box 68, Lexington, GA 30648; 706-743-5731; Fax: 706-743-5335. Hours: 8AM-5PM (EST). *Felony, Misdemeanor, Civil.*

Civil Records: Access: Mail, in person. Visitors must perform in person searches for themselves. No search fee. Required to search: name, years to search. Civil cases indexed by defendant. Civil records on computer from 1992, on dockets from 1900s.
Criminal Records: Access: In person only. Visitors must perform in person searches for themselves. No search fee. Required to search: name, years to search, DOB; also helpful: SSN, race, sex. Criminal records on computer from 1992, on dockets from 1900s.
General Information: No juvenile or adoption records released. Turnaround time 2-3 days. Copy fee: $.25 per

page. Certification fee: $2.50 plus $.50 per page after first. Fee payee: Superior Court Clerk. Personal checks accepted. Prepayment is required.

Magistrate Court Box 356, Lexington, GA 30648; 706-743-8321; Fax: 706-743-3177. Hours: 8AM-5PM (EST). *Civil Actions Under $15,000, Eviction, Small Claims.*

Probate Court PO Box 7078, Lexington, GA 30648; 706-743-5350; Fax: 706-743-8219. Hours: 8AM-5PM (EST). *Probate.*

Paulding County

Superior Court 11 Courthouse Square, Rm G2, Dallas, GA 30132; 770-443-7529. Hours: 8AM-5PM (EST). *Felony, Misdemeanor, Civil.*

Civil Records: Access: In person only. Visitors must perform in person searches for themselves. No search fee. Required to search: name, years to search. Civil cases indexed by defendant, plaintiff. Civil records on computer from 1990, archived from 1850.
Criminal Records: Access: In person only. Visitors must perform in person searches for themselves. No search fee. Required to search: name, years to search, DOB; also helpful: SSN, race, sex. Criminal records on docket books.
General Information: No juvenile, adoption, sexual, mental health or expunged records released. Copy fee: $.25 per page. Certification fee: $2.50 plus $.50 per page after first. Fee payee: Court Clerk. Personal checks accepted. Prepayment is required.

Magistrate & Probate Court 124 Main St, Dallas, GA 30132; 770-445-2123; Fax: 770-445-1127. Hours: 8AM-5PM (EST). *Civil Actions Under $15,000, Eviction, Small Claims, Probate.*

Probate Court 11 Courthouse Square, Rm 106, Dallas, GA 30132; 770-443-7541; Fax: 770-443-7631. Hours: 8AM-5PM (EST). *Probate.*

Peach County

Superior Court PO Box 389, Ft Valley, GA 31030; 478-825-5331. Hours: 8:30AM-5PM (EST). *Felony, Misdemeanor, Civil.*

Civil Records: Access: Mail, in person. Both court and visitors may perform in person searches. No search fee. Required to search: name, years to search. Civil cases indexed by defendant, plaintiff. Civil records on computer back to 1997; on dockets from 1925.
Criminal Records: Access: Mail, in person. Both court and visitors may perform in person searches. No search fee. Required to search: name, years to search, DOB; also helpful: SSN, race, sex. Criminal records on computer back to 1997; on dockets from 1925.
General Information: No juvenile, adoption, sexual, mental health or expunged records released. SASE required. Turnaround time 1 week. Copy fee: $.25 per page. Certification fee: $3.00. Fee payee: Court Clerk. Personal checks accepted. Prepayment is required.

Magistrate Court 700 Spruce St, Bldg A, Ft Valley, GA 31030; 478-825-2060; Fax: 478-825-1893. Hours: 8AM-5PM (EST). *Civil Actions Under $15,000, Eviction, Small Claims.*

Probate Court PO Box 327, Ft Valley, GA 31030; 478-825-2313; Fax: 478-825-2678. *Probate.*

Pickens County

Superior Court 52 N Main St Ste 102, Jasper, GA 30143; 706-692-2014. Hours: 8AM-5PM (EST). *Felony, Misdemeanor, Civil.*

http://209.86.240.205/dca9apphp.shtml

Civil Records: Access: In person only. Visitors must perform in person searches for themselves. No search fee. Required to search: name, years to search. Civil cases indexed by defendant, plaintiff. Civil records on computer from 1988, dockets from 1854.

Criminal Records: Access: In person only. Visitors must perform in person searches for themselves. No search fee. Required to search: name, years to search, DOB, signed release; also helpful: SSN, race, sex. Criminal records on computer from 1988, dockets from 1854.

General Information: Public Access terminal is available. No juvenile, adoption, sexual, mental health or expunged records released. Copy fee: $.25 per page. $1.00 per page if the court makes the copies. Certification fee: $2.50 plus $.50 per page after first. Fee payee: Court Clerk. Personal checks accepted. Prepayment is required.

Magistrate Court 50 N Main St, Jasper, GA 30143; 706-692-3550; Fax: 706-692-2850. Hours: 8AM-5PM (EST). *Civil Actions Under $15,000, Eviction, Small Claims.*

Probate Court 50 N Main St, Suite C, Jasper, GA 30143; 706-692-2515. Hours: 8AM-Noon, 1-5PM (EST). *Probate.*

Pierce County

Superior Court PO Box 588, Blackshear, GA 31516; 912-449-2020. Hours: 9AM-5PM (EST). *Felony, Misdemeanor, Civil.*

Civil Records: Access: In person only. Visitors must perform in person searches for themselves. No search fee. Required to search: name, years to search. Civil cases indexed by defendant. Civil records on computer from 1991, on index from 1800s.

Criminal Records: Access: In person only. Visitors must perform in person searches for themselves. No search fee. Required to search: name, years to search. Criminal records on computer from 1991, on index from 1800s.

General Information: Copy fee: $.25 per page. Certification fee: $2.50 first page, $.50 each additional. Fee payee: Superior Court Clerk. Personal checks accepted. Prepayment is required.

State Court PO Box 588, Blackshear, GA 31516; 912-449-2020. Hours: 9AM-5PM (EST). *Misdemeanor, Civil.*

Civil Records: Access: In person only. Visitors must perform in person searches for themselves. No search fee. Required to search: name, years to search. Civil cases indexed by defendant, plaintiff. Civil records on computer from 1991, on docket books from 1800s.

Criminal Records: Access: In person only. Visitors must perform in person searches for themselves. No search fee. Required to search: name, years to search, DOB; also helpful: SSN, race, sex. Criminal records on computer from 1991, on docket books from 1800s.

General Information: No juvenile, adoption, sealed, sexual, mental health or expunged records released. Copy fee: If court does copy $.50, if yourself then $.25. Certification fee: $2.50 plus $.50 per page after first. Fee payee: Clerk of Court. Business checks accepted. Prepayment is required.

Magistrate Court 3550 Highway 84 West, Blackshear, GA 31516; 912-449-2027; Fax: 912-449-2103. Hours: 9AM-5PM (EST). *Civil Actions Under $15,000, Eviction, Small Claims.*

Probate Court PO Box 406, Blackshear, GA 31516; 912-449-2029; Fax: 912-449-2024. Hours: 9AM-5PM (EST). *Probate.*

Pike County

Superior Court PO Box 10, Zebulon, GA 30295; 770-567-2000. Hours: 8AM-5PM (EST). *Felony, Misdemeanor, Civil.*

Civil Records: Access: In person only. Visitors must perform in person searches for themselves. No search fee. Required to search: name, years to search. Civil cases indexed by defendant, plaintiff. Civil records on dockets books from 1823.

Criminal Records: Access: In person only. Visitors must perform in person searches for themselves. No search fee. Required to search: name, years to search. Criminal records on dockets books from 1823.

General Information: No juvenile, adoption, sexual, mental health or expunged records released. Copy fee: $.25 per page. Certification fee: $2.50 plus $.50 per page after first. Fee payee: Court Clerk. Personal checks accepted. Prepayment is required.

Magistrate Court PO Box 466, Zebulon, GA 30295; 770-567-2004; Fax: 770-567-2023. Hours: 8AM-5PM (EST). *Civil Actions Under $15,000, Eviction, Small Claims.*

Probate Court PO Box 324, Zebulon, GA 30295; 770-567-8734; Fax: 770-567-2006. Hours: 9AM-5PM (EST). *Probate.*

Polk County

Superior Court PO Box 948, Cedartown, GA 30125; 770-749-2114; Fax: 770-749-2148. Hours: 9AM-5PM (EST). *Felony, Misdemeanor, Civil.*

Civil Records: Access: In person only. Visitors must perform in person searches for themselves. No search fee. Required to search: name, years to search. Civil cases indexed by defendant, plaintiff. Civil records on computer from 1991, alpha indexes from 1930.

Criminal Records: Access: Mail, in person. Visitors must perform in person searches for themselves. No search fee. Required to search: name, years to search, DOB, signed release; also helpful: SSN, race, sex. Criminal records on computer from 1991, alpha indexes from 1930.

General Information: Public Access terminal is available. No juvenile, adoption, sexual, mental health or expunged records released. Fax notes: Fee to fax results is $2.00 per page. Copy fee: $.25 per page. Certification fee: $2.50 plus $.50 per page after first. Fee payee: Court Clerk. Personal checks accepted. Prepayment is required.

Magistrate Court 105 Polk County Courthouse, Cedartown, GA 30125; 770-749-2130; Fax: 770-749-2186. Hours: 9AM-5PM (EST). *Civil Actions Under $15,000, Eviction, Small Claims.*

Probate Court Polk County Courthouse. Rm 102, Cedartown, GA 30125; 770-749-2128; Fax: 770-749-2150. Hours: 9AM-5PM (EST). *Probate.*

Pulaski County

Superior Court PO Box 60, Hawkinsville, GA 31036; 478-783-1911; Fax: 478-892-3308. Hours: 8AM-5PM (EST). *Felony, Misdemeanor, Civil.*

Civil Records: Access: Phone, mail, in person. Both court and visitors may perform in person searches. No search fee. Required to search: name, years to search. Civil cases indexed by defendant, plaintiff. Civil records on computer from 1986, alpha index from early 1800s.

Criminal Records: Access: Mail, in person. Both court and visitors may perform in person searches. No search fee. Required to search: name, years to search, DOB, signed release; also helpful: SSN, race, sex. Criminal records on computer from 1986, alpha index from early 1800s.

General Information: No juvenile, adoption, sexual, mental health or expunged records released. Turnaround time 1 week. Copy fee: $1.00 per page. Certification fee: $.50 per page. Fee payee: Court Clerk. Personal checks accepted. Prepayment is required.

Magistrate Court PO Box 667, Hawkinsville, GA 31036; 478-783-1357; Fax: 478-892-3308. Hours: 8AM-5PM (EST). *Civil Actions Under $15,000, Eviction, Small Claims.*

Probate Court Pulaski County Courthouse, Hawkinsville, GA 31036; 478-783-2061; Fax: 478-783-0696. Hours: 8AM-5PM (EST). *Probate.*

Putnam County

Superior & State Court County Courthouse, Eatonton, GA 31024; 706-485-4501; Fax: 706-485-2515. Hours: 8AM-5PM (EST). *Felony, Misdemeanor, Civil.*

Civil Records: Access: In person only. Visitors must perform in person searches for themselves. No search fee. Required to search: name, years to search. Civil cases indexed by defendant, plaintiff. Civil records on computer since 1997; prior records on dockets to early 1920s.

Criminal Records: Access: In person only. Visitors must perform in person searches for themselves. No search fee. Required to search: name, years to search, DOB; also helpful: SSN, race, sex. Criminal records on computer since 1997; prior records on dockets to early 1920s.

General Information: Public Access terminal is available. No juvenile, adoption, sexual, mental health or expunged records released. Copy fee: $1.00 per page. Certification fee: $3.00. Fee payee: Court Clerk. Personal checks accepted. Prepayment is required.

Magistrate Court 108 S Madison Ave, #101, Eatonton, GA 31024; 706-485-4306; Fax: 706-485-2515. Hours: 8AM-5PM (EST). *Civil Actions Under $15,000, Eviction, Small Claims.*

Probate Court County Courthouse, 100 S Jefferson St, Eatonton, GA 31024; 706-485-5476; Fax: 706-485-2515. Hours: 8AM-5PM (EST). *Probate.*

Quitman County

Superior Court PO Box 307, Georgetown, GA 31754; 229-334-2578. Hours: 8AM-Noon, 1-5PM (EST). *Felony, Misdemeanor, Civil.*

Civil Records: Access: Mail, in person. Both court and visitors may perform in person searches. Search fee: $10.00 per name. Required to search: name, years to search. Civil cases indexed by defendant, plaintiff. Civil records on computer back to 7/1997; indexed on dockets from 1879.

Criminal Records: Access: Mail, in person. Visitors must perform in person searches for themselves. No search fee. Required to search: name, years to search, DOB; also helpful: SSN, race, sex. Criminal records on computer back to 7/1997; indexed on dockets from 1879. The court asks mail requesters to mail the sheriff's office with a $10.00 fee and signed, notarized (subject) request.

General Information: No juvenile, adoption, sexual, mental health or expunged records released. SASE required. Turnaround time 1 day. Fax notes: Fee to fax results is $3.00 1st pg, $1.00 each add'l. Copy fee: $.50 per page. Certification fee: $2.50 1st page and $.50 each additional. Fee payee: Clerk of Superior Court. Personal checks accepted. Prepayment is required.

Magistrate & Probate Court PO Box 297, Georgetown, GA 31754; 229-334-2224; Fax: 229-334-3576. Hours: 8:30AM-5PM (EST). *Civil Actions Under $15,000, Eviction, Small Claims, Probate.*

Rabun County

Superior Court 25 Courthouse Sq #105, Clayton, GA 30525; 706-782-3615; Fax: 706-782-1391. Hours: 8:30AM-5PM (EST). *Felony, Misdemeanor, Civil.*

http://209.86.240.205/mountainhp.shtml

Civil Records: Access: Mail, in person. Visitors must perform in person searches for themselves. No search fee. Required to search: name, years to search. Civil cases indexed by defendant, plaintiff. Civil records on dockets from 1949; on computer since.
Criminal Records: Access: Mail, in person. Visitors must perform in person searches for themselves. No search fee. Required to search: name, years to search, DOB, signed release; also helpful: SSN, race, sex. Criminal records on dockets from 1949; on computer since.
General Information: No juvenile, adoption, sexual, mental health or expunged records released. Fax notes: No fee to fax back results. Copy fee: $.25 per page. Certification fee: $5.00. Fee payee: Court Clerk. Personal checks accepted. Prepayment is required.

Magistrate Court 17 Chechero St, Clayton, GA 30525; 706-782-4285; Fax: 706-782-7317. Hours: 8:30AM-5PM (EST). *Civil Actions Under $15,000, Eviction, Small Claims.*

Probate Court 25 Courthouse Square, Box 15, Clayton, GA 30525; 706-782-3614; Fax: 706-782-9278. Hours: 8:30AM-Noon, 1-5PM (EST). *Probate.*

Randolph County

Superior Court PO Box 98, Cuthbert, GA 31740; 229-732-2216; Fax: 229-732-5881. Hours: 8AM-5PM (EST). *Felony, Misdemeanor, Civil.*

Civil Records: Access: In person only. Visitors must perform in person searches for themselves. No search fee. Required to search: name, years to search. Civil cases indexed by defendant. Civil records on index from 1835.
Criminal Records: Access: In person only. Visitors must perform in person searches for themselves. No search fee. Required to search: name, years to search, DOB; also helpful: SSN, race, sex. Criminal records on index from 1835.
General Information: No juvenile, adoption, sexual, mental health or expunged records released. Copy fee: $.25 per page. Certification fee: $2.00 plus $.50 per page after first. Fee payee: Court Clerk. Personal checks accepted. Prepayment is required.

Magistrate Court PO Box 6, Cuthbert, GA 31740; 229-732-6182; Fax: 229-732-5781. Hours: 9AM-5PM (EST). *Civil Actions Under $15,000, Eviction, Small Claims.*

Probate Court PO Box 424, Cuthbert, GA 31740; 229-732-2671; Fax: 229-732-5781. Hours: 8AM-5PM (EST). *Probate.*

Richmond County

Superior Court 530 Greene St, Augusta, GA 30911; 706-821-2460; Fax: 706-821-2448. Hours: 8:30AM-5PM (EST). *Felony, Misdemeanor, Civil.*

Civil Records: Access: Mail, in person. Visitors must perform in person searches for themselves. No search fee. Required to search: name, years to search. Civil cases indexed by defendant, plaintiff. Civil records on docket books and microfilm from 1940s, real estate from 1986 on computer.

Criminal Records: Access: Mail, in person. Visitors must perform in person searches for themselves. No search fee. Required to search: name, years to search. Criminal records on docket books and microfilm from 1940s, real estate from 1986 on computer.
General Information: No juvenile, adoption, sexual, mental health or expunged records released. SASE requested. Turnaround time 1 week. Copy fee: $.25 per page. Certification fee: $2.50 plus $.50 per page after first. Fee payee: Superior Court Clerk. Business checks accepted. Local checks accepted. Prepayment is required.

State Court 401 Walton Way, #218A, Augusta, GA 30911; 706-821-1233. Hours: 8:30AM-5PM (EST). *Misdemeanor, Civil.*

Civil Records: Access: In person only. Visitors must perform in person searches for themselves. No search fee. Required to search: name, years to search. Civil cases indexed by defendant, plaintiff. Civil records on docket books and microfilm from 1940s, prior archived.
Criminal Records: Access: In person only. Visitors must perform in person searches for themselves. No search fee. Required to search: name, years to search, DOB; also helpful: SSN, race, sex. Criminal records on docket books and microfilm from 1940s, prior archived.
General Information: No juvenile, adoption, sexual, mental health or expunged records released. Copy fee: $.25 per page. Certification fee: $2.50 plus $.50 per page after first. Fee payee: Court Clerk. Only cashiers checks and money orders accepted. Prepayment is required.

Civil & Magistrate Court 530 Greene St, Rm 705, Augusta, GA 30911; 706-821-2370; Fax: 706-821-2381. Hours: 8:30AM-5PM (EST). *Civil Actions Under $45,000, Eviction, Small Claims.*

Civil Records: Access: Phone, mail, in person. Both court and visitors may perform in person searches. No search fee. Required to search: name, years to search. Civil cases indexed by defendant, plaintiff. Civil records on dockets back to 1970s. **General Information:** SASE requested. Turnaround time 1 day. Copy fee: $.25 per page. Certification fee: $5.00. Fee payee: Magistrate Court. Business checks accepted. Prepayment is required.

Probate Court 530 Greene St, Rm 401, Augusta, GA 30911; 706-821-2434; Fax: 706-821-2442. Hours: 8:30AM-5PM (EST). *Probate.*

Rockdale County

Superior Court PO Box 937, 922 Court St, Conyers, GA 30012; 770-929-4021. Hours: 8AM-4:45PM (EST). *Felony, Civil.*

Civil Records: Access: In person only. Visitors must perform in person searches for themselves. No search fee. Required to search: name, years to search. Civil cases indexed by defendant, plaintiff. Civil records on computer back to 1993, in books from 1900.
Criminal Records: Access: In person only. Visitors must perform in person searches for themselves. No search fee. Required to search: name, years to search, signed release. Criminal records on computer back to 1990, in books from 1900.
General Information: Public Access terminal is available. No juvenile, adoption, sexual, mental health or expunged records released. Copy fee: $.25 per page. Certification fee: $2.50 plus $.50 per page after first. Fee payee: Clerk Superior Court. Personal checks accepted. Prepayment is required.

State Court PO Box 938, Conyers, GA 30012; 770-929-4019. Hours: 8AM-4:45PM (EST). *Misdemeanor, Civil.*

Civil Records: Access: In person only. Visitors must perform in person searches for themselves. No search

fee. Required to search: name, years to search. Civil cases indexed by defendant, plaintiff. Civil records on computer from 1994, on dockets to 1994.
Criminal Records: Access: In person only. Visitors must perform in person searches for themselves. No search fee. Required to search: name, years to search. Criminal records on computer from 1990, on dockets from 1987-1990.
General Information: Public Access terminal is available. No juvenile, adoption, sexual, mental health or expunged records released. Copy fee: $.25 per page. Certification fee: $2.50 plus $.50 per page after first. Fee payee: Rockdale State Court. Business checks accepted. Prepayment is required.

Magistrate Court PO Box 289, Conyers, GA 30012; 770-922-5742; Fax: 770-922-4647. Hours: 8:30AM-4:30PM (EST). *Civil Actions Under $15,000, Eviction, Small Claims.*

Note: Court also has jurisdiction for bad checks, arrest warrants, preliminary hearings, and county ordinance violations

Probate Court 922 Court St NE, Rm 107, Conyers, GA 30012; 770-929-4058; Fax: 770-918-6463. Hours: 8:30AM-4:30PM (EST). *Probate.*

Schley County

Superior Court PO Box 7, US Hwy 19-Courthouse Square, Ellaville, GA 31806; 229-937-5581; Fax: 229-937-5047. Hours: 8AM-Noon,1-5PM (EST). *Felony, Misdemeanor, Civil.*

www.gsccca.org

Civil Records: Access: In person only. Visitors must perform in person searches for themselves. No search fee. Required to search: name, years to search. Civil cases indexed by defendant. Civil records in books from 1885.
Criminal Records: Access: In person only. Visitors must perform in person searches for themselves. No search fee. Required to search: name, years to search, DOB, signed release; also helpful: SSN, race, sex. Criminal records in books from 1934.
General Information: No juvenile, adoption, sexual, mental health or expunged records released. Copy fee: $.25 per page. Certification fee: $2.50 plus $.50 per page after first. Fee payee: Clerk Superior Court. Personal checks accepted. Prepayment is required.

Magistrate Court PO Box 43, Ellaville, GA 31806; 229-937-2013; Fax: 229-937-2347. Hours: 8AM-5PM (EST). *Civil Actions Under $15,000, Eviction, Small Claims.*

Probate Court PO Box 385, Ellaville, GA 31806; 229-937-2905; Fax: 229-937-5047. Hours: 8:30AM-Noon, 1-5PM (EST). *Probate.*

Screven County

Superior Court PO Box 156, Sylvania, GA 30467; 912-564-2614; Fax: 912-564-2622. Hours: 8:30AM-5PM (EST). *Felony, Misdemeanor, Civil.*

Civil Records: Access: In person only. Visitors must perform in person searches for themselves. No search fee. Required to search: name, years to search. Civil cases indexed by defendant, plaintiff. Civil records on dockets from 1793.
Criminal Records: Access: In person only. Visitors must perform in person searches for themselves. No search fee. Required to search: name, years to search, DOB; also helpful: SSN, race, sex. Criminal records on dockets from 1793.
General Information: No juvenile or adoption records released. Copy fee: $.25 per page. Certification fee: $3.00. Fee payee: Court Clerk. Personal checks accepted. Prepayment is required.

State Court PO Box 156, Sylvania, GA 30467; 912-564-2614; Fax: 912-564-2622. Hours: 8:30AM-5PM (EST). *Misdemeanor, Civil.*

Civil Records: Access: In person only. Visitors must perform in person searches for themselves. No search fee. Required to search: name, years to search. Civil cases indexed by defendant, plaintiff. Civil records on dockets from 1793.

Criminal Records: Access: In person only. Visitors must perform in person searches for themselves. No search fee. Required to search: name, years to search, DOB; also helpful: SSN, race, sex. Criminal records on dockets from 1793.

General Information: No juvenile, adoption, sexual, mental health or expunged records released. Copy fee: $.25 per page. Certification fee: $3.00. Fee payee: Court Clerk. Personal checks accepted. Prepayment is required.

Magistrate Court 304 Singleton Ave, Sylvania, GA 30467; 912-564-2400. Hours: 8AM-5PM (EST). *Civil Actions Under $15,000, Eviction, Small Claims.*

Probate Court 216 Mims Rd #107, Sylvania, GA 30467; 912-564-2783; Fax: 912-564-9139. Hours: 8:30AM-5PM (EST). *Probate.*

Seminole County

Superior Court PO Box 672, Main St, Donalsonville, GA 31745; 229-524-2525; Fax: 229-524-8883. Hours: 8AM-5PM (EST). *Felony, Misdemeanor, Civil.*

Civil Records: Access: Phone, fax, mail, in person. Both court and visitors may perform in person searches. Search fee: $1.00 per name per year. Required to search: name, years to search. Civil cases indexed by defendant, plaintiff. Civil records on computer from 1994, on dockets from 1921.

Criminal Records: Access: Fax, mail, in person. Both court and visitors may perform in person searches. Search fee: $1.00 per name per year. Required to search: name, years to search, DOB, signed release; also helpful: SSN, race, sex. Criminal records on computer from 1994, on dockets from 1921.

General Information: No juvenile, adoption, sexual, mental health or expunged records released. SASE required. Turnaround time 1 day. Fax notes: $1.00 per page. Copy fee: $1.00 per page. Copy fees are $.25 per page in person. Certification fee: $2.50. Fee payee: Court Clerk. Personal checks accepted. Prepayment is required.

Magistrate & Probate Court Seminole County Courthouse, PO Box 672, Donalsonville, GA 31745; 229-524-5256; Fax: 229-524-8644. Hours: 8AM-5PM (EST). *Civil Actions Under $15,000, Eviction, Small Claims.*

Spalding County

Superior Court PO Box 1046, Griffin, GA 30224; 770-467-4745. Hours: 8AM-5PM (EST). *Felony, Misdemeanor, Civil.*

Civil Records: Access: Mail, in person. Visitors must perform in person searches for themselves. No search fee. Required to search: name, years to search. Civil cases indexed by defendant, plaintiff. Civil records on computer from 1991, on dockets from 1852. Mail for specific case info only, the court will not do name searches.

Criminal Records: Access: Mail, in person. Visitors must perform in person searches for themselves. No search fee. Required to search: name, years to search, DOB; also helpful: SSN, race, sex. Criminal records on computer from 1991, on dockets from 1852. Court will not do name searches, will only do specific case files.

General Information: Public Access terminal is available. No juvenile, adoption, sexual, mental health or expunged records released. SASE required. Turnaround time 2 days. Copy fee: $.25 per page. Certification fee: $2.00, plus $.50 per page. Fee payee: Court Clerk. Personal checks accepted. Prepayment is required.

State Court PO Box 1046, Griffin, GA 30224; 770-467-4745. Hours: 8AM-5PM (EST). *Misdemeanor, Civil.*

Civil Records: Access: In person only. Both court and visitors may perform in person searches. No search fee. Required to search: name, years to search. Civil cases indexed by defendant, plaintiff. Civil records on computer back to 1995; prior records on dockets from 1852. Mail access only for specific case information, no name searching.

Criminal Records: Access: Mail, in person. Both court and visitors may perform in person searches. No search fee. Required to search: name, years to search, DOB; also helpful: SSN, race, sex. Criminal records on computer back to 1995; prior records on dockets from 1852. Mail access for specific case information only, no name searching by the court.

General Information: Public Access terminal is available. No juvenile, adoption, sexual, mental health or expunged records released. SASE required. Turnaround time 2 days. Copy fee: $.25 per page. Certification fee: $2.00. Fee payee: Court Clerk. Business checks accepted. Prepayment is required.

Magistrate Court 132 E Solomon St, Griffin, GA 30223; 770-467-4336; Fax: 770-467-0081. Hours: 8AM-5PM (EST). *Civil Actions Under $15,000, Eviction, Small Claims.*

Probate Court 132 E Solomon St, Griffin, GA 30223; 770-467-4340; Fax: 770-467-4243. Hours: 8AM-5PM (EST). *Probate.*

Stephens County

Superior Court 205 Alexander St N, #202, Toccoa, GA 30577; 706-886-3598; Fax: 706-886-5710. Hours: 8AM-5PM (EST). *Felony, Misdemeanor, Civil.*

Civil Records: Access: Mail, fax, in person. Both court and visitors may perform in person searches. Search fee: $7.50 per name. Required to search: name, years to search. Civil cases indexed by defendant, plaintiff. Civil records on computer back to 1988, on dockets from 1906.

Criminal Records: Access: Mail, fax, in person. Both court and visitors may perform in person searches. Search fee: $7.50 per name. Required to search: name, years to search, DOB, signed release; also helpful: SSN, race, sex. Criminal records on computer back to 1988, on dockets from 1906.

General Information: Public Access terminal is available. No juvenile, adoption, sexual, mental health or expunged records released. Turnaround time 1 day. Fax notes: Fee to fax results pre-paid: $2.00 1st page, $1.00 each add'l. Copy fee: $1.00 per page. Certification fee: $2.50 plus $.50 per page after first. Fee payee: Court Clerk. Personal checks accepted. Prepayment is required.

State Court 205 N Alexander St Rm 202, County Government Building, Toccoa, GA 30577; 706-886-3598/9496. Hours: 8AM-5PM (EST). *Misdemeanor, Civil.*

Civil Records: Access: Mail, in person. Both court and visitors may perform in person searches. Search fee: $7.50 per name. Required to search: name, years to search. Civil cases indexed by defendant, plaintiff. Civil records on computer back to 1988, on dockets from 1906.

Criminal Records: Access: Mail, in person. Both court and visitors may perform in person searches. Search fee: $7.50 per name. Required to search: name, years to search, DOB, signed release; also helpful: SSN, race, sex. Criminal records on computer back to 1988, on dockets from 1906.

General Information: No juvenile, adoption, sexual, mental health or expunged records released. Turnaround time 1 day. Copy fee: $1.00 per page. Certification fee: $2.50 plus $.50 per page after first. Fee payee: Court Clerk. Personal checks accepted. Prepayment is required.

Magistrate Court 204 N Alexander St, Rm 107, Toccoa, GA 30577; 706-886-6205; Fax: 706-886-5569. Hours: 8AM-5PM (EST). *Civil Actions Under $15,000, Eviction, Small Claims.*

http://209.86.240.205/mountainhp.shtml

Probate Court County Courthouse, PO Box 456, Toccoa, GA 30577; 706-886-2828; Fax: 706-886-2631. Hours: 8AM-5PM (EST). *Probate.*

Stewart County

Superior Court PO Box 910, Main St, Lumpkin, GA 31815; 229-838-6220. Hours: 8AM-4:30PM (EST). *Felony, Misdemeanor, Civil.*

Civil Records: Access: In person only. Visitors must perform in person searches for themselves. No search fee. Required to search: name, years to search; also helpful: address. Civil cases indexed by defendant. Civil records in index books.

Criminal Records: Access: In person only. Visitors must perform in person searches for themselves. No search fee. Required to search: name, years to search; also helpful: address, DOB, SSN. Criminal records in index books to 1840s.

General Information: Public Access terminal is available. No juvenile, adoption, sexual, mental health or sealed records are released. Copy fee: $.25 per page. Certification fee: $2.50 plus $.50 per page after first. Fee payee: Clerk of Superior Court. Personal checks accepted.

Magistrate Court PO Box 712, Lumpkin, GA 31815; 229-838-4261; Fax: 229-838-4394. Hours: 8AM-5PM (EST). *Civil Actions Under $15,000, Eviction, Small Claims.*

Probate Court PO Box 876, Lumpkin, GA 31815; 229-838-4394; Fax: 229-838-9084. Hours: 8AM-Noon, 1-5PM (EST). *Probate.*

Sumter County

State Court PO Box 333, Americus, GA 31709; 229-924-5626. Hours: 9AM-5PM (EST). *Misdemeanor, Civil.*

Civil Records: Access: In person only. Visitors must perform in person searches for themselves. No search fee. Required to search: name, years to search. Civil cases indexed by defendant, plaintiff. Civil records on dockets from late 1800s.

Criminal Records: Access: In person only. Visitors must perform in person searches for themselves. No search fee. Required to search: name, years to search, DOB; also helpful: SSN, race, sex. Criminal records on dockets from late 1800s.

General Information: No juvenile, adoption, sealed, sexual, mental health or expunged records released. Copy fee: $.25 per page. Certification fee: $2.50 plus $.50 per page. Fee payee: Court Clerk. Prepayment is required.

Magistrate Court PO Box 563, Americus, GA 31709; 229-924-6699; Fax: 229-931-0407. Hours: 9AM-5PM (EST). *Civil Actions Under $15,000, Eviction, Small Claims.*

Probate Court PO Box 246, Americus, GA 31709; 229-924-7693; Fax: 229-924-2541. Hours: 9AM-5PM (EST). *Probate.*

Talbot County

Superior Court PO Box 325, Talbotton, GA 31827; 706-665-3239; Fax: 706-665-8199. Hours: 9AM-5PM (EST). *Felony, Misdemeanor, Civil.*

Civil Records: Access: In person only. Visitors must perform in person searches for themselves. No search fee. Required to search: name, years to search. Civil cases indexed by defendant, plaintiff. Civil records on dockets from 1827.

Criminal Records: Access: In person only. Visitors must perform in person searches for themselves. No search fee. Required to search: name, years to search. Criminal records on computer since 1991, prior on docket books.

General Information: No juvenile, adoption, sexual, mental health or expunged records released. Copy fee: $.25 per page. Certification fee: $2.00 plus $.50 per page after first. Fee payee: Superior Court. Business checks accepted. Prepayment is required.

Magistrate & Probate Court PO Box 157, Talbotton, GA 31827; 706-665-8866; Fax: 706-665-8199. Hours: 8AM-5PM (EST). *Civil Actions Under $15,000, Eviction, Small Claims, Probate.*

Taliaferro County

Superior Court PO Box 182, Crawfordville, GA 30631; 706-456-2123. Hours: 9AM-5PM (EST). *Felony, Misdemeanor, Civil.*

Civil Records: Access: In person only. Visitors must perform in person searches for themselves. No search fee. Required to search: name, years to search. Civil cases indexed by defendant, plaintiff. Civil records on dockets from 1825.

Criminal Records: Access: In person only. Visitors must perform in person searches for themselves. No search fee. Required to search: name, years to search, DOB; also helpful: SSN, race, sex. Criminal records on dockets from 1825.

General Information: No juvenile, adoption, sexual, mental health or expunged records released. Copy fee: $.25 per page. Certification fee: $2.00. Fee payee: Court Clerk. Personal checks accepted. Prepayment is required.

Magistrate & Probate Court PO Box 264, Crawfordville, GA 30631; 706-456-2253; Fax: 706-456-2904. Hours: 8AM-5PM (EST). *Civil Actions Under $15,000, Eviction, Small Claims, Probate.*

Tattnall County

Superior & State Court PO Box 39, Reidsville, GA 30453; 912-557-6716; Fax: 912-557-4861. Hours: 8AM-5PM (EST). *Felony, Misdemeanor, Civil.*

Civil Records: Access: In person only. Visitors must perform in person searches for themselves. No search fee. Required to search: name, years to search; also helpful: address. Civil cases indexed by defendant, plaintiff. Civil records on computer back to 1990; on dockets from 1800s.

Criminal Records: Access: In person only. Visitors must perform in person searches for themselves. No search fee. Required to search: name, years to search, DOB; also helpful: address, SSN, race, sex. Criminal records on computer back to 1990; on dockets from 1800s.

General Information: Public Access terminal is available. No juvenile, adoption, sexual, mental health or expunged records released. Copy fee: $.25 per page. Certification fee: $3.00 plus $.50 per page after first. Fee payee: Court Clerk. Business checks accepted. Prepayment is required.

Magistrate Court PO Box 513, Reidsville, GA 30453; 912-557-4372; Fax: 912-557-3631. Hours: 8AM-4:30PM (EST). *Civil Actions Under $15,000, Eviction, Small Claims.*

Probate Court PO Box 699, Reidsville, GA 30453; 912-557-6719; Fax: 912-557-3976. Hours: 8:30AM-4:30PM (EST). *Probate.*

Taylor County

Superior Court PO Box 248, Courthouse Square, Butler, GA 31006; 478-862-5594; Fax: 478-862-5334. Hours: 8AM-5PM (EST). *Felony, Misdemeanor, Civil.*

Civil Records: Access: In person only. Both court and visitors may perform in person searches. No search fee. Required to search: name, years to search. Civil cases indexed by defendant, plaintiff. Civil records on computer from 1991, dockets from 1852.

Criminal Records: Access: In person only. Visitors must perform in person searches for themselves. No search fee. Required to search: name, years to search, DOB; also helpful: SSN, race, sex. Criminal records on computer from 1991, dockets from 1852.

General Information: Public Access terminal is available. No juvenile, adoption, sexual, mental health or expunged records released. Copy fee: $.25 per page. $1.00 maximum. Certification fee: $2.00 plus $.50 per page after first. Fee payee: Court Clerk. Personal checks accepted. Prepayment is required.

Magistrate & Probate Court PO Box 536, Butler, GA 31006; 478-862-3357; Fax: 478-862-5334. Hours: 8AM-5PM (EST). *Civil Actions Under $15,000, Eviction, Small Claims, Probate.*

Telfair County

Superior Court Courthouse, 128 Oak St #2, McRae, GA 31055; 229-868-6525; Fax: 229-868-7956. Hours: 8:30AM-4:30PM (EST). *Felony, Misdemeanor, Civil.*

Civil Records: Access: Phone, mail, in person. Visitors must perform in person searches for themselves. No search fee. Required to search: name, years to search. Civil cases indexed by defendant. Civil records on dockets from early 1900s.

Criminal Records: Access: Phone, in person. Visitors must perform in person searches for themselves. No search fee. Required to search: name, years to search, DOB, signed release; also helpful: SSN, race, sex. Criminal records on dockets from early 1900s.

General Information: No juvenile, adoption, sexual, mental health or expunged records released. SASE requested. Turnaround time 1 week. Copy fee: $.25 per page. Certification fee: $3.00. Fee payee: Court Clerk. Personal checks accepted.

Magistrate Court 128 E Oak St #5, McRae, GA 31055; 229-868-6772; Fax: 229-868-7956. Hours: 8:30AM-4:30PM (EST). *Civil Actions Under $15,000, Eviction, Small Claims.*

Probate Court Courthouse Square, Telfair County Courthouse, McRae, GA 31055; 229-868-6038; Fax: 229-868-7956. Hours: 8:30AM-Noon, 1-4:30PM (EST). *Probate.*

Terrell County

Superior Court PO Box 1892, 335 E Lee, Dawson, GA 31742; 229-995-2631. Hours: 8:30AM-5PM (EST). *Felony, Misdemeanor, Civil.*

Civil Records: Access: In person only. Visitors must perform in person searches for themselves. No search fee. Required to search: name, years to search. Civil cases indexed by defendant. Civil records on computer from 1988, dockets books from 1900s.

Criminal Records: Access: In person only. Visitors must perform in person searches for themselves. No search fee. Required to search: name, years to search, DOB, signed release; also helpful: SSN, race, sex. Criminal records on computer from 1988, dockets books from 1900s.

General Information: No juvenile, adoption, sexual, mental health or expunged records released. Copy fee: $.25 per page. Certification fee: $3.00 plus $.50 per page after first. Fee payee: Court Clerk. Business checks accepted. Prepayment is required.

Magistrate Court PO Box 793, Dawson, GA 31742; 229-995-3757; Fax: 229-995-4496. Hours: 8AM-5PM (EST). *Civil Actions Under $15,000, Eviction, Small Claims.*

Probate Court PO Box 67, Dawson, GA 31742; 229-995-5515; Fax: 229-995-4301. *Probate.*

Thomas County

Superior & State Court PO Box 1995, Thomasville, GA 31799; 229-225-4108; Fax: 229-225-4110. Hours: 8AM-5PM (EST). *Felony, Misdemeanor, Civil.*

www.thomascoclerkofcourt.org

Civil Records: Access: In person only. Visitors must perform in person searches for themselves. No search fee. Required to search: name, years to search. Civil cases indexed by defendant, plaintiff. Civil records on computer from 1989, archived from 1826.

Criminal Records: Access: In person only. Visitors must perform in person searches for themselves. No search fee. Required to search: name, years to search, DOB; also helpful: SSN, race, sex.

General Information: Public Access terminal is available. No juvenile, adoption, sexual, mental health or expunged records released. Copy fee: $1.00 per page. Certification fee: $2.00. Fee payee: Court Clerk. Personal checks accepted. Prepayment is required.

Magistrate Court PO Box 879, Thomasville, GA 31799; 229-225-3334; Fax: 229-225-3342. Hours: 8AM-5PM (EST). *Civil Actions Under $15,000, Eviction, Small Claims.*

Probate Court PO Box 1582, Thomasville, GA 31799; 229-225-4116; Fax: 229-227-1698. Hours: 8AM-5PM (EST). *Probate.*

Tift County

Superior & State Court PO Box 354, Tifton, GA 31793; 229-386-7810. Hours: 8AM-5PM (EST). *Felony, Misdemeanor, Civil.*

Civil Records: Access: In person only. Visitors must perform in person searches for themselves. No search fee. Required to search: name, years to search. Civil cases indexed by defendant. Civil records on dockets books from 1905.

Criminal Records: Access: In person only. Visitors must perform in person searches for themselves. No search fee. Required to search: name, years to search, DOB; also helpful: SSN, race, sex. Criminal records on dockets books from 1905.

General Information: No juvenile, adoption, sexual, mental health or expunged records released. Copy fee: $.25 per page. Certification fee: $2.50 plus $.50 per page after first. Fee payee: Court Clerk. Personal checks accepted. Prepayment is required.

Magistrate Court PO Box 214, Tifton, GA 31793; 229-386-7907; Fax: 229-386-7978. Hours: 8AM-5PM (EST). *Civil Actions Under $15,000, Eviction, Small Claims.*

Probate Court PO Box 792, Tifton, GA 31793; 229-386-7936; Fax: 229-386-7913. Hours: 9AM-5PM (EST). *Probate.*

Toombs County

Superior & State Court PO Drawer 530, Lyons, GA 30436; 912-526-3501; Fax: 912-526-1004. Hours: 8:30AM-5PM (EST). *Felony, Misdemeanor, Civil.*

Civil Records: Access: In person only. Visitors must perform in person searches for themselves. No search fee. Required to search: name, years to search. Civil cases indexed by defendant, plaintiff. Civil records on dockets books from 1908, on computer since 1995.
Criminal Records: Access: In person only. Visitors must perform in person searches for themselves. No search fee. Required to search: name, years to search, DOB; also helpful: SSN, race, sex. Criminal records on dockets books from 1908, on computer since 1995.
General Information: No juvenile, adoption, sexual, mental health or expunged records released. Copy fee: $1.00 per page. Certification fee: $2.50 plus $1.00 per page after first. Fee payee: Court Clerk. Personal checks accepted. Prepayment is required.

Magistrate Court PO Box 184, Lyons, GA 30436; 912-526-8984; Fax: 912-526-8985. Hours: 8:30AM-5PM (EST). *Civil Actions Under $15,000, Eviction, Small Claims.*

Probate Court Toombs County Courthouse, Lyons, GA 30436; 912-526-8696; Fax: 912-526-1004. Hours: 8:30AM-5PM (EST). *Probate.*

Towns County

Superior Court 48 River St Suite E, Hiawassee, GA 30546; 706-896-2130. Hours: 8:30AM-4:30PM (EST). *Felony, Misdemeanor, Civil.*

http://209.86.240.205/enotahhp.shtml

Civil Records: Access: Phone, mail, in person. Both court and visitors may perform in person searches. No search fee. Required to search: name, years to search. Civil cases indexed by plaintiff. Civil records on dockets books from 1940.
Criminal Records: Access: Phone, mail, in person. Both court and visitors may perform in person searches. No search fee. Required to search: name, years to search, DOB, signed release; also helpful: SSN, race, sex. Criminal records on docket books, indexed by defendant.
General Information: No juvenile, adoption, sexual, mental health or expunged records released. SASE required. Turnaround time same day. Copy fee: $.25 per page. Certification fee: $2.50 per page. Fee payee: Court Clerk. Personal checks accepted. Prepayment is required.

Magistrate & Probate Court PO Box 549, Hiawassee, GA 30546; 706-896-2203; Fax: 706-896-4491. Hours: 8:30AM-4:30PM (EST). *Civil Actions Under $15,000, Eviction, Small Claims, Probate.*

Treutlen County

Superior & State Court PO Box 356, Soperton, GA 30457; 912-529-4215. Hours: 8AM-5PM (EST). *Felony, Misdemeanor, Civil.*

Civil Records: Access: Mail, in person. Both court and visitors may perform in person searches. No search fee. Required to search: name, years to search. Civil cases indexed by defendant, plaintiff. Civil records on computer from 1991, dockets books from 1919.
Criminal Records: Access: Mail, in person. Both court and visitors may perform in person searches. No search fee. Required to search: name, years to search, DOB; also helpful: SSN, race, sex. Criminal records on computer from 1991, dockets books from 1919.
General Information: Public Access terminal is available. No juvenile, adoption, sexual, mental health or expunged records released. Turnaround time 1-2 days. Copy fee: $.25 per page. Certification fee: $2.50

plus $.50 per page after first. Fee payee: Court Clerk. Personal checks accepted. Prepayment is required.

Magistrate & Probate Court 114 Second St South, Courthhouse Annex, Soperton, GA 30457; 912-529-3342; Fax: 912-529-6838. Hours: 9AM-12; 1-5PM (EST). *Civil Actions Under $15,000, Eviction, Small Claims, Probate.*

Troup County

Superior & State Court 118 Ridley Ave (PO Box 866, 30241), LaGrange, GA 30240; 706-883-1740. Hours: 8AM-5PM (EST). *Felony, Misdemeanor, Civil.*

Civil Records: Access: In person only. Visitors must perform in person searches for themselves. No search fee. Required to search: name, years to search. Civil cases indexed by defendant, plaintiff. Civil records on computer from 1994, on docket books from 1940s.
Criminal Records: Access: In person only. Visitors must perform in person searches for themselves. No search fee. Required to search: name, years to search, DOB; also helpful: SSN, race, sex. Criminal records on computer from 1994, on docket books from 1940s.
General Information: Public Access terminal is available. (UCC & Taxes.) No juvenile, adoption, sexual, mental health or expunged records released. Copy fee: $.25 per page. Certification fee: $2.75 plus $.25 per page. Fee payee: Court Clerk. Personal checks accepted. Prepayment is required.

Magistrate Court 119 Ridley Ave #101, LaGrange, GA 30240; 706-883-1695; Fax: 706-883-1632. Hours: 8AM-5PM (EST). *Civil Actions Under $15,000, Eviction, Small Claims.*

Probate Court 119 Ridley Ave, #201, LaGrange, GA 30240; 706-883-1727; Fax: 706-883-1639. Hours: 8AM-5PM (EST). *Probate.*

Turner County

Superior Court PO Box 106, 219 E College Ave, Ashburn, GA 31714; 229-567-2011; Fax: 229-567-0450. Hours: 8AM-5PM (EST). *Felony, Misdemeanor, Civil.*

Civil Records: Access: In person only. Visitors must perform in person searches for themselves. No search fee. Required to search: name, years to search. Civil cases indexed by defendant, plaintiff. Civil records on docket books, archived from 1905.
Criminal Records: Access: In person only. Visitors must perform in person searches for themselves. No search fee. Required to search: name, years to search, DOB, signed release; also helpful: SSN, race, sex. Criminal records on docket books, archived from 1905.
General Information: No juvenile, adoption, sexual, mental health or expunged records released. Copy fee: $1.00 by court, $.25 if do it yourself. Certification fee: $2.50 plus $1.00 per page after first. Fee payee: Court Clerk. Personal checks accepted. Prepayment is required.

Magistrate Court 219 E College Ave, Rm 2, Ashburn, GA 31714; 229-567-3155. Hours: 9AM-6PM M,T,Th/9AM-4PM F (EST). *Civil Actions Under $15,000, Eviction, Small Claims.*

Probate Court PO Box 2506, Ashburn, GA 31714; 229-567-2151; Fax: 229-567-0358. Hours: 8AM-5PM (EST). *Probate.*

Twiggs County

Superior Court PO Box 228, Jeffersonville, GA 31044; 478-945-3350. Hours: 8AM-5PM (EST). *Felony, Misdemeanor, Civil.*

Civil Records: Access: In person only. Visitors must perform in person searches for themselves. No search fee. Required to search: name, years to search. Civil

cases indexed by defendant, plaintiff. Civil records on computer from 1991, dockets books to 1901.
Criminal Records: Access: In person only. Visitors must perform in person searches for themselves. No search fee. Required to search: name, years to search, DOB, signed release; also helpful: SSN, race, sex. Criminal records on computer from 1991, dockets books to 1901.
General Information: No juvenile, adoption, sexual, mental health or expunged records released. Copy fee: $.25 per page. Certification fee: $2.50 plus $.50 per page after first. Fee payee: Court Clerk. Personal checks accepted. Prepayment is required.

Magistrate Court PO Box 146, Jeffersonville, GA 31044; 478-945-3428; Fax: 478-945-2083. Hours: 9AM-5PM (EST). *Civil Actions Under $15,000, Eviction, Small Claims.*

Probate Court PO Box 307, Jeffersonville, GA 31044; 478-945-3390; Fax: 478-945-6070. Hours: 9AM-5PM (EST). *Probate.*

Union County

Superior Court 114 Courthouse St, Box 5, Blairsville, GA 30512; 706-745-2611; Fax: 706-745-3822. Hours: 8AM-5PM (EST). *Felony, Misdemeanor, Civil.*

http://209.86.240.205/enotahhp.shtml

Civil Records: Access: In person only. Both court and visitors may perform in person searches. No search fee. Required to search: name, years to search. Civil cases indexed by defendant, plaintiff. Civil records on computer from 1988, on dockets from 1936.
Criminal Records: Access: In person only. Both court and visitors may perform in person searches. No search fee. Required to search: name, years to search, DOB, signed release; also helpful: SSN, race, sex. Criminal records on docket books from 1930.
General Information: Public Access terminal is available. No juvenile, adoption, sexual, mental health or expunged records released. Copy fee: $.25 per page. Certification fee: $2.50 plus $.25 per page after first. Fee payee: Court Clerk. Personal checks accepted. Prepayment is required.

Magistrate & Probate Court 114 Courthouse St, # 8, Blairsville, GA 30512; 706-745-2654; Fax: 706-745-9384. Hours: 8AM-4:30PM (EST). *Civil Actions Under $15,000, Eviction, Small Claims, Probate.*

Upson County

Superior Court PO Box 469, Thomaston, GA 30286; 706-647-7835; Fax: 706-647-8999. Hours: 8AM-5PM (EST). *Felony, Misdemeanor, Civil.*

Civil Records: Access: In person only. Visitors must perform in person searches for themselves. No search fee. Required to search: name, years to search. Civil cases indexed by defendant, plaintiff. Civil records on dockets books from 1927; on computer back to 1990.
Criminal Records: Access: In person only. Visitors must perform in person searches for themselves. No search fee. Required to search: name, years to search, DOB; also helpful: SSN, race, sex. Criminal records on docket books from 1937; on computer back to 1990.
General Information: Public Access terminal is available. No juvenile, adoption, sexual, mental health or expunged records released. Copy fee: $.25 per page. Certification fee: $2.50 plus $.50 per page after first. Fee payee: Court Clerk. Personal checks accepted. Prepayment is required.

Magistrate Court PO Box 890, Thomaston, GA 30286; 706-647-6891; Fax: 706-647-1248. Hours: 8AM-5PM (EST). *Civil Actions Under $15,000, Eviction, Small Claims.*

Probate Court PO Box 906, Thomaston, GA 30286; 706-647-7015; Fax: 706-646-7030. Hours: 8AM-5PM (EST). *Probate.*

Walker County

Superior & State Court PO Box 448, LaFayette, GA 30728; 706-638-1772. Hours: 8AM-5PM (EST). *Felony, Misdemeanor, Civil.*

Civil Records: Access: In person only. Visitors must perform in person searches for themselves. No search fee. Required to search: name, years to search. Civil cases indexed by defendant, plaintiff. Civil records on dockets books from 1883.
Criminal Records: Access: In person only. Visitors must perform in person searches for themselves. No search fee. Required to search: name, years to search, DOB; also helpful: SSN, race, sex. Criminal records on dockets books from 1883.
General Information: No juvenile, adoption, sexual, mental health or expunged records released. Copy fee: $.25 per page. Certification fee: $2.00. Fee payee: Court Clerk. Personal checks accepted.

Magistrate Court 102 Napier St, LaFayette, GA 30728; 706-638-1217; Fax: 706-638-1218. Hours: 8AM-5PM (EST). *Civil Actions Under $15,000, Eviction, Small Claims.*

Probate Court PO Box 436, LaFayette, GA 30728; 706-638-2852; Fax: 706-638-2869. Hours: 8AM-5PM (EST). *Probate.*
www.gaprobate.org

Walton County

Superior Court PO Box 745, Monroe, GA 30655; 770-267-1307; Fax: 770-267-1441. Hours: 8:30AM-5PM (EST). *Felony, Misdemeanor, Civil.*

Civil Records: Access: In person only. Visitors must perform in person searches for themselves. No search fee. Required to search: name, years to search. Civil cases indexed by defendant, plaintiff. Civil records on computer from 1986, dockets books from 1900s.
Criminal Records: Access: In person only. Visitors must perform in person searches for themselves. No search fee. Required to search: name, years to search; also helpful: DOB, race, sex. Criminal records on computer from 1986, dockets books from 1900s.
General Information: No juvenile, adoption, sexual, mental health or expunged records released. Copy fee: $.25 per page. Certification fee: $2.50 plus $.50 per page after first. Fee payee: Court Clerk. Personal checks accepted. Prepayment is required.

Magistrate Court PO Box 1188, Monroe, GA 30655; 770-267-1386; Fax: 770-266-1512. Hours: 8:30AM-5PM (EST). *Civil Actions Under $15,000, Eviction, Small Claims.*

Probate Court PO Box 629, Monroe, GA 30655; 770-267-1345; Fax: 770-267-1417. Hours: 8:30AM-5PM (EST). *Probate.*

Note: This location also has traffic and misdemeanor records

Ware County

Superior & State Court PO Box 776, Waycross, GA 31502; 912-287-4340. Hours: 9AM-5PM (EST). *Felony, Misdemeanor, Civil.*

Civil Records: Access: In person only. Visitors must perform in person searches for themselves. No search fee. Required to search: name, years to search. Civil records on computer since 1995; prior records on dockets books from 1874.
Criminal Records: Access: In person only. Visitors must perform in person searches for themselves. No search fee. Required to search: name, years to search, DOB; also helpful: SSN, race, sex. Criminal records on computer since 1995; prior records on dockets books from 1874.
General Information: No juvenile, adoption, sexual, mental health or expunged records released. Copy fee: $.25 per page; $1.00 if court assists. Certification fee: $2.50 plus $.50 per page after first. Fee payee: Court Clerk. Personal checks accepted. Prepayment is required.

Magistrate Court PO Box 17, 201 State St, Rm 102, Waycross, GA 31501; 912-287-4373; Fax: 912-287-4377. Hours: 9AM-5PM (EST). *Civil Actions Under $15,000, Eviction, Small Claims.*

Probate Court Ware County Courthouse, Rm 105, 800 Church St, Waycross, GA 31501; 912-287-4315; Fax: 912-287-4317. Hours: 9AM-5PM (EST). *Probate.*

Warren County

Superior Court PO Box 227, 100 Main St, Warrenton, GA 30828; 706-465-2262; Fax: 706-465-0232. Hours: 8AM-5PM (EST). *Felony, Misdemeanor, Civil.*

Civil Records: Access: In person only. Visitors must perform in person searches for themselves. No search fee. Required to search: name, years to search. Civil cases indexed by defendant, plaintiff. Civil records on dockets books to 1950.
Criminal Records: Access: In person only. Visitors must perform in person searches for themselves. No search fee. Required to search: name, years to search, DOB, signed release; also helpful: SSN, race, sex. Criminal records on dockets books to 1950.
General Information: No juvenile, adoption, sexual, mental health or expunged records released. Copy fee: $.25 per page. Certification fee: $2.50 1st page plus $.50 each add'l page. Fee payee: Court Clerk. Only cashiers checks and money orders accepted. Prepayment is required.

Magistrate Court PO Box 203, Warrenton, GA 30828; 706-465-3123; Fax: 706-465-1300. Hours: 8AM-5PM (EST). *Civil Actions Under $15,000, Eviction, Small Claims.*

Probate Court PO Box 364, Warrenton, GA 30828; 706-465-2227. Hours: 8AM-5PM (EST). *Probate.*

Washington County

Superior & State Court PO Box 231, Sandersville, GA 31082; 478-552-3186. Hours: 9AM-5PM (EST). *Felony, Misdemeanor, Civil.*

Civil Records: Access: Mail, in person. Visitors must perform in person searches for themselves. No search fee. Required to search: name, years to search. Civil cases indexed by defendant, plaintiff. Civil records on dockets books to 1869.
Criminal Records: Access: Mail, in person. Visitors must perform in person searches for themselves. No search fee. Required to search: name, years to search. Criminal records on dockets books to 1869.
General Information: Public Access terminal is available. No juvenile, adoption, sexual, mental health or expunged records released. Copy fee: $.25 per page. Certification fee: $2.00. Fee payee: Court Clerk. Personal checks accepted. Prepayment is required.

Magistrate Court PO Box 1053, Sandersville, GA 31082; 478-552-3591; Fax: 478-552-7424. Hours: 9AM-5PM (EST). *Civil Actions Under $15,000, Eviction, Small Claims.*

Probate Court PO Box 669, Sandersville, GA 31082; 478-552-3304; Fax: 478-552-7424. Hours: 9AM-Noon, 1-5PM (EST). *Probate.*

Wayne County

Superior & State Court PO Box 918, Jesup, GA 31545; 912-427-5930; Fax: 912-427-5939. Hours: 8:30AM-5PM (EST). *Felony, Misdemeanor, Civil.*

Civil Records: Access: In person only. Visitors must perform in person searches for themselves. No search fee. Required to search: name, years to search. Civil cases indexed by defendant, plaintiff. Civil records on computer, on docket books from 1810.
Criminal Records: Access: In person only. Visitors must perform in person searches for themselves. No search fee. Required to search: name, years to search, DOB. Criminal records on computer, on docket books from 1810.
General Information: Public Access terminal is available. No juvenile, adoption, sexual, mental health or expunged records released. Copy fee: $.25 per page. Certification fee: $2.50 plus $.50 per page after first. Fee payee: Superior Court Clerk. Personal checks accepted. Prepayment is required.

Magistrate Court PO Box 27, Jesup, GA 31598; 912-427-5960. Hours: 8:30AM-5PM (EST). *Civil Actions Under $15,000, Eviction, Small Claims.*

Probate Court 174 N Brunswick St, Jesup, GA 31598; 912-427-5940; Fax: 912-427-5944. Hours: 8AM-5PM (EST). *Probate.*

Webster County

Superior Court PO Box 117, Preston, GA 31824; 229-828-3525. Hours: 8AM-4:30PM (EST). *Felony, Misdemeanor, Civil.*

Civil Records: Access: In person only. Visitors must perform in person searches for themselves. No search fee. Required to search: name, years to search. Civil cases indexed by defendant, plaintiff. Civil records on docket books from 1860.
Criminal Records: Access: In person only. Visitors must perform in person searches for themselves. No search fee. Required to search: name, years to search, signed release. Criminal records on docket books from 1860.
General Information: No juvenile, adoption, sexual, mental health or expunged records released. Copy fee: $.25 per page. Certification fee: $2.50 plus $.50 per page after first page. Fee payee: Clerk Superior Court. Personal checks accepted. Prepayment is required.

Magistrate & Probate Court PO Box 135, Preston, GA 31824; 229-828-3615; Fax: 229-828-3616. Hours: 8:30AM-4:30PM (EST). *Civil Actions Under $15,000, Eviction, Small Claims, Probate.*

Note: This court will not give out SSNs

Wheeler County

Superior Court PO Box 38, Alamo, GA 30411; 912-568-7137. Hours: 8AM-4PM (EST). *Felony, Misdemeanor, Civil.*

Civil Records: Access: In person only. Visitors must perform in person searches for themselves. No search fee. Required to search: name, years to search. Civil cases indexed by defendant. Civil records on docket books from 1913.
Criminal Records: Access: In person only. Visitors must perform in person searches for themselves. No search fee. Required to search: name, years to search. Criminal records on docket books from 1913.
General Information: No juvenile or adoption records released. Copy fee: $.25 per page. Certification fee: $2.50 plus $.50 each additional page. Fee payee: Superior Court Clerk. Personal checks accepted. Prepayment is required.

Magistrate & Probate Court PO Box 477, Alamo, GA 30411; 912-568-7133; Fax: 912-568-7131. Hours: 8AM-4PM (EST). *Civil Actions Under $15,000, Eviction, Small Claims, Probate.*

White County

Superior Court 59 S Main St, Ste B, Cleveland, GA 30528; 706-865-2613; Fax: 706-865-7749. Hours: 8:30AM-5PM (EST). *Felony, Misdemeanor, Civil.*

http://209.86.240.205/enotahhp.shtml

Civil Records: Access: In person only. Visitors must perform in person searches for themselves. No search fee. Required to search: name, years to search. Civil cases indexed by defendant, plaintiff. Civil records on computer from 1989, on docket books from 1857.

Criminal Records: Access: In person only. Visitors must perform in person searches for themselves. No search fee. Required to search: name, years to search. Criminal records on computer from 1989, on docket books from 1857. Will accept mail requests only if a case number is provided.

General Information: Public Access terminal is available. No juvenile, adoption, sexual, mental health or expunged records released. Fax notes: Fee to fax results is $1.00 per page. Copy fee: $.25 per page. Certification fee: $2.50 plus $.50 per page after first. Fee payee: Superior Court Clerk. Business checks accepted. Prepayment is required.

Magistrate Court 59 S Main St, Cleveland, GA 30528; 706-865-6636. Hours: 8:30AM-5PM (EST). *Civil Actions Under $15,000, Misdemeanor, Eviction, Small Claims.*

Probate Court 85 S Main St #D, Cleveland, GA 30528; 706-865-4141; Fax: 706-865-1324. Hours: 8:30AM-5PM (EST). *Probate.*

Whitfield County

Superior Court PO Box 868, Dalton, GA 30722; 706-275-7450; Fax: 706-275-7456. Hours: 8AM-5PM (EST). *Felony, Misdemeanor, Civil.*

Civil Records: Access: In person only. Visitors must perform in person searches for themselves. No search fee. Required to search: name, years to search. Civil cases indexed by defendant, plaintiff. Civil records on computer from 1988, on docket books from 1852.

Criminal Records: Access: In person only. Visitors must perform in person searches for themselves. No search fee. Required to search: name, years to search, offense, date of offense. Criminal records on computer from 1988, on docket books from 1852.

General Information: Public Access terminal is available. No juvenile, adoption, sexual, mental health or expunged records released. Copy fee: $.50 per page. Certification fee: $3.00. Fee payee: Superior Court Clerk. Business checks accepted. Prepayment is required.

Magistrate Court PO Box 386, Dalton, GA 30722-0386; 706-278-5052. Hours: 8AM-5PM M-W,

F; 9AM-5PM Th (EST). *Civil Actions Under $15,000, Eviction, Small Claims.*

Probate Court 301 Crawford St, Dalton, GA 30720; 706-275-7400; Fax: 706-275-7486. Hours: 8AM-5PM (EST). *Probate.*

Wilcox County

Superior & Magistrate Courts 103 N Broad St, Abbeville, GA 31001; 229-467-2442; Fax: 229-467-2000. Hours: 9AM-5PM (EST). *Felony, Misdemeanor, Civil, Eviction, Small Claims.*

Civil Records: Access: Mail, in person. Both court and visitors may perform in person searches. No search fee. Required to search: name, years to search. Civil cases indexed by defendant, plaintiff. Civil records on computer since 1995; prior records on docket books from 1950s.

Criminal Records: Access: Mail, in person. Both court and visitors may perform in person searches. No search fee. Required to search: name, years to search, DOB; also helpful: SSN. Criminal records on computer since 1995; prior records on docket books from 1950s.

General Information: No juvenile, adoption, sexual, mental health or expunged records released. Turnaround time 1 week. Copy fee: $.25 per page. Certification fee: $2.50 per page. Fee payee: Superior Court Clerk. Personal checks accepted. Prepayment is required.

Probate Court 103 N Broad St, Abbeville, GA 31001; 229-467-2220; Fax: 229-467-2000. Hours: 9AM-5PM (EST). *Probate.*

Wilkes County

Superior Court 23 E Court St, Rm 205, Washington, GA 30673; 706-678-2423. Hours: 9AM-5PM (EST). *Felony, Misdemeanor, Civil.*

Civil Records: Access: In person only. Visitors must perform in person searches for themselves. No search fee. Required to search: name, years to search. Civil cases indexed by defendant, plaintiff. Civil records on docket books from 1700s.

Criminal Records: Access: In person only. Visitors must perform in person searches for themselves. Search fee: $5.00 per name. Required to search: name, years to search. Criminal records on docket books from 1700s.

General Information: No juvenile or adoption records released. Copy fee: $.25 per page self-serve. Certification fee: $2.50 plus $.50 per page after first. Fee payee: Superior Court Clerk. Personal checks accepted. Prepayment is required.

Magistrate Court 23 E Court St, Rm 427, Washington, GA 30673; 706-678-1881. Hours: 8:30AM-5PM (EST). *Civil Actions Under $15,000, Eviction, Small Claims.*

Probate Court 23 E Court St, Rm 422, Washington, GA 30673; 706-678-2523; Fax: 706-678-4854. Hours: 8:30AM-5PM (EST). *Probate.*

Wilkinson County

Superior Court PO Box 250, Irwinton, GA 31042; 478-946-2221; Fax: 478-946-1497. Hours: 8AM-5PM (EST). *Felony, Misdemeanor, Civil.*

Civil Records: Access: In person only. Visitors must perform in person searches for themselves. No search fee. Required to search: name, years to search. Civil cases indexed by defendant, plaintiff. Civil records on computer from 6/91, on docket books from 1890s.

Criminal Records: Access: In person only. Visitors must perform in person searches for themselves. No search fee. Required to search: name, years to search, DOB. Criminal records on computer from 6/91, on docket books from 1890s. The court will not do searches.

General Information: No juvenile, adoption, sexual, mental health or expunged records released. Copy fee: $.25 per page. Certification fee: $2.50 per page. Fee payee: Superior Court Clerk. Personal checks accepted. Prepayment is required.

Magistrate & Probate Court PO Box 201, Irwinton, GA 31042; 478-946-2222; Fax: 478-946-3767. Hours: 8AM-5PM (EST). *Civil Actions Under $15,000, Eviction, Small Claims, Probate.*

Worth County

Superior & State Court 201 N Main St, Rm 13, Sylvester, GA 31791; 229-776-8205; Fax: 229-776-8205. Hours: 8AM-5PM (EST). *Felony, Misdemeanor, Civil, Eviction, Small Claims.*

Civil Records: Access: In person only. Visitors must perform in person searches for themselves. No search fee. Required to search: name, years to search. Civil cases indexed by defendant, plaintiff. Civil records computerized since 1995, on books since 1880, real estate records from 9/93.

Criminal Records: Access: In person only. Visitors must perform in person searches for themselves. No search fee. Required to search: name, years to search; also helpful: SSN. Criminal records computerized since 1995.

General Information: Public Access terminal is available. No juvenile, adoption, sexual, mental health or expunged records released. Copy fee: $.25 per page. Certification fee: $2.50 plus $.50 per page after first. Fee payee: Superior Court Clerk. Personal checks accepted. Prepayment is required.

Magistrate Court PO Box 64, 201 N Main St, Sylvester, GA 31791; 229-776-8210. Hours: 8:30AM-5PM (EST). *Civil Actions Under $15,000, Eviction, Small Claims.*

Note: All records are maintained at the Superior Court, not here

Probate Court 201 N Main St, Rm 12, Sylvester, GA 31791; 229-776-8207; Fax: 229-776-1540. Hours: 8AM-5PM (EST). *Probate.*

Georgia Recording Offices

ORGANIZATION   159 counties, 159 recording offices. The recording officer is Clerk of Superior Court. All transactions are recorded in a "General Execution Docket." The entire state is in the Eastern Time Zone (EST).

REAL ESTATE RECORDS   Most counties will not perform real estate searches. Copy fees are the same as for UCC. Certification fees are usually $2.00 per document - $1.00 for seal and $1.00 for stamp - plus $.50 per page.

UCC RECORDS   There is no central state agency office for UCC. Financing statements are filed only with the Clerk of Superior Court and one can file in any county. Their system, as of January 1, 1995, merges all new UCC filings into a central statewide database, and allows statewide searching for filings of 01/95 forward from any county office. However, filings prior to that date will remain at the county offices. Only a few counties will perform local UCC searches. Use search request form UCC-11 for local searches. Search fees vary from $2.50 to $25.00 per debtor name. Copies usually cost $.25 per page if you make it and $1.00 per page if the county makes it.

TAX LIEN RECORDS   All tax liens on personal property are filed with the county Clerk of Superior Court in a "General Execution Docket" (grantor/grantee) or "Lien Index." Most counties will not perform tax lien searches. Copy fees are the same as for UCC.

OTHER LIENS   Judgments, hospital, materialman, county tax, lis pendens, child support, labor, mechanics.

STATEWIDE ONLINE INFO: The Georgia Superior Court Clerk's Cooperative Authority (GSCCCA) at http://www2.gsccca.org/search offers access on a subscription basis. The system includes a UCC Index with records back to 1/1995; Real Estate Deed Index back to 1/1999; Notary Public Index and Plat Index. Subscription is $9.95 per month, per user, for unlimited use, and $.25 for each page printed. You may submit UCC Certified Search requests online. The charge for certified searches is $10 per debtor name.

Appling County

County Superior Court Clerk, P.O. Box 269, Baxley, GA 31513. 912-367-8126.
Will search UCC records. This agency will not do a tax lien search. Will not search real estate records. **Other Phone Numbers:** Assessor 912-367-8109; Treasurer 912-367-8100.

Atkinson County

County Superior Court Clerk, P.O. Box 6, Pearson, GA 31642. 912-422-3343; Fax 912-422-3429.
Will search UCC records. This agency will not do a tax lien search. Will not search real estate records. **Other Phone Numbers:** Assessor 912-422-7382.

Bacon County

County Superior Court Clerk, P.O. Box 376, Alma, GA 31510. County Superior Court Clerk, R/E and UCC Recording 912-632-4915; Fax 912-632-6545.
Will not search UCC records. This agency will not do a tax lien search. Will not search real estate records. **Other Phone Numbers:** Assessor 912-632-5215; Treasurer 912-632-5214.

Baker County

County Superior Court Clerk, P.O. Box 10, Newton, GA 31770. 229-734-3004.
Will search UCC records. This agency will not do a tax lien search. Will not search real estate records. **Other Phone Numbers:** Assessor 229-734-3010.

Baldwin County

County Superior Court Clerk, P.O. Drawer 987, Milledgeville, GA 31059. 478-445-6327 R/E Recording: 478-445-4008 UCC Recording: 478-445-4008; Fax 478-445-1404.
Will not search UCC records. This agency will not do a tax lien search. Will not search real estate records. **Other Phone Numbers:** Assessor 478-453-5300; Treasurer 478-434-4791; Appraiser/Auditor 478-445-5300; Elections 478-445-4526; Vital Records 478-445-4807.

Banks County

County Superior Court Clerk, P.O. Box 337, Homer, GA 30547. 706-677-6243 R/E Recording: 706-677-6240 UCC Recording: 706-677-6240; Fax 706-677-2337.
Will search UCC records. This agency will not do a tax lien search. Will do name searches for property and plats only. **Other Phone Numbers:** Assessor 706-677-2320; Treasurer 706-677-6200; Elections 706-677-6250.

Barrow County

County Superior Court Clerk, P.O. Box 1280, Winder, GA 30680. 770-307-3035.
Will not search UCC records. This agency will not do a tax lien search. Will not search real estate records. **Other Phone Numbers:** Assessor 770-307-3108; Treasurer 770-307-3106.

Bartow County

County Superior Court Clerk, 135 W. Cherokee Ave., Suite 233, Cartersville, GA 30120. 770-387-5025; Fax 770-386-0846.
Will search UCC records. This agency will not do a tax lien search. Will not search real estate records. **Other Phone Numbers:** Assessor 770-387-8873.

Ben Hill County

County Superior Court Clerk, P.O. Box 1104, Fitzgerald, GA 31750-1104. 229-426-5135; Fax 229-426-5487.
Will search UCC records. This agency will not do a tax lien search. Will not search real estate records. **Other Phone Numbers:** Assessor 229-4237323.

Berrien County

County Superior Court Clerk, 101 E. Marion Ave. #3, Nashville, GA 31639. 229-686-5506.
Will search UCC records. This agency will not do a tax lien search. Will not search real estate records. **Other Phone Numbers:** Assessor 229-686-2144; Treasurer 229-686-7461.

Bibb County

County Superior Court Clerk, P.O. Box 1015, Macon, GA 31202-1015. 478-749-6527; Fax 478-749-6539.
Will search UCC records. This agency will not do a tax lien search. Will not search real estate records. **Other Phone Numbers:** Assessor 478-742-2254; Treasurer 478-749-6310.

Bleckley County

County Superior Court Clerk, Courthouse, Cochran, GA 31014. 478-934-3210; Fax 478-934-3205.
Will search UCC records. This agency will not do a tax lien search. Will not search real estate records. **Other Phone Numbers:** Assessor 478-934-3209; Treasurer 478-934-3200.

Brantley County

County Superior Court Clerk, P.O. Box 1067, Nahunta, GA 31553. 912-462-5635; Fax 912-462-5538.
Will search UCC records. This agency will not do a tax lien search. Will not search real estate records. **Other Phone Numbers:** Assessor 912-462-5251; Treasurer 912-462-5256.

Brooks County

County Superior Court Clerk, P.O. Box 630, Quitman, GA 31643. County Superior Court Clerk, R/E and UCC Recording 229-263-4747; Fax 229-263-5050.
Will search UCC records. This agency will not do a tax lien search. Will not search real estate records. **Other Phone Numbers:** Assessor 229-263-7920.

Bryan County

County Superior Court Clerk, P.O. Drawer H, Pembroke, GA 31321. 912-653-3872; Fax 912-653-3695.
Will search UCC records. This agency will not do a tax lien search. Will not search real estate records. **Other Phone Numbers:** Assessor 912-653-4681.

Bulloch County

County Superior Court Clerk, Judicial Annex, 20 Siebald St., Statesboro, GA 30458. 912-764-9009.
Will search UCC records. This agency will not do a tax lien search. Will not search real estate records. **Other**

Phone Numbers: Assessor 912-764-2181; Treasurer 912-764-6285.

Burke County

County Superior Court Clerk, P.O. Box 803, Waynesboro, GA 30830-0803. County Superior Court Clerk, R/E and UCC Recording 706-554-2279; Fax 706-554-7887.

Will search UCC records. This agency will not do a tax lien search. Will not search real estate records. **Other Phone Numbers:** Assessor 706-554-2607; Treasurer 706-554-2324; Appraiser/Auditor 706-554-2607; Elections 706-554-7457; Vital Records 706-554-3000.

Butts County

County Superior Court Clerk, P.O. Box 320, Jackson, GA 30233. 770-775-8215; Fax 770-775-8211.

Will search UCC records. This agency will not do a tax lien search. Will not search real estate records. **Other Phone Numbers:** Assessor 770-775-8207; Treasurer 770-775-8200.

Calhoun County

County Superior Court Clerk, P.O. Box 69, Morgan, GA 31766. 229-849-2715; Fax 229-849-0072.

Will search UCC records. This agency will not do a tax lien search. Will not search real estate records. **Other Phone Numbers:** Assessor 229-849-4685; Treasurer 229-849-2970.

Camden County

County Superior Court Clerk, P.O. Box 578, Woodbine, GA 31569-0578. 912-576-5622.

Will search UCC records. This agency will not do a tax lien search. Will not search real estate records. **Other Phone Numbers:** Assessor 912-576-5601; Treasurer 912-576-5601.

Candler County

County Superior Court Clerk, P.O. Drawer 830, Metter, GA 30439. 912-685-5257; Fax 912-685-2160.

Will search UCC records. This agency will not do a tax lien search. Will not search real estate records. **Other Phone Numbers:** Assessor 912-685-6346; Treasurer 912-685-5257.

Carroll County

County Superior Court Clerk, P.O. Box 1620, Carrollton, GA 30117. 770-830-5830; Fax 770-214-3125.

Will search UCC records. This agency will not do a tax lien search. Will not search real estate records. **Other Phone Numbers:** Assessor 770-830-5812; Treasurer 770-830-5801.

Catoosa County

County Superior Court Clerk, 875 Lafayette Street, Courthouse, Ringgold, GA 30736. 706-935-4231.

Will search UCC records. This agency will not do a tax lien search. Will not search real estate records. **Other Phone Numbers:** Assessor 706-965-3772; Treasurer 706-935-2500.

Charlton County

County Superior Court Clerk, Courthouse, 100 S. Third St., Folkston, GA 31537. 912-496-2354; Fax 912-496-3882.

Will search UCC records. This agency will not do a tax lien search. Will not search real estate records. **Other Phone Numbers:** Assessor 912-496-7437.

Chatham County

County Superior Court Clerk, P.O. Box 10227, Savannah, GA 31412. 912-652-7219; Fax 912-652-7380.

Will search UCC records. This agency will not do a tax lien search. Will not search real estate records. **Other Phone Numbers:** Assessor 912-652-7127.

Chattahoochee County

County Superior Court Clerk, P.O. Box 120, Cusseta, GA 31805-0120. 706-989-3424 R/E Recording: 709-989-3424; Fax 706-989-0396.

Will search UCC records. This agency will not do a tax lien search. Will not search real estate records. **Other Phone Numbers:** Assessor 706-989-3249; Elections 706-989-3602; Vital Records 706-989-3603.

Chattooga County

County Superior Court Clerk, P.O. Box 159, Summerville, GA 30747. 706-857-0706.

Will search UCC records. This agency will not do a tax lien search. Will not search real estate records. **Other Phone Numbers:** Assessor 706-857-3819; Treasurer 706-857-0703.

Cherokee County

County Superior Court Clerk, 90 North Street, Suite G-170, Canton, GA 30114. 770-479-0558 UCC Recording: 770-479-6350.

Will search UCC records. This agency will not do a tax lien search. Will not search real estate records. **Other Phone Numbers:** Assessor 770-479-0433; Treasurer 770-479-0425; Elections 770-479-0740; Vital Records 770-479-0541.

Clarke County

County Superior Court Clerk, P.O. Box 1805, Athens, GA 30603. 706-613-3196; Fax 706-613-3189.

Will not search UCC records. This agency will not do a tax lien search. Will not search real estate records. **Other Phone Numbers:** Assessor 706-613-3140; Treasurer 706-613-3040.

Clay County

County Superior Court Clerk, P.O. Box 550, Fort Gaines, GA 31751-0550. 229-768-2631; Fax 229-768-3047.

Will search UCC records. This agency will not do a tax lien search. Will not search real estate records. **Other Phone Numbers:** Assessor 229-768-2000; Treasurer 229-768-2915.

Clayton County

County Superior Court Clerk, 9151 Tara Blvd, Room 202, Jonesboro, GA 30236. 770-477-3395; http://www.co.clayton.ga.us/superior_court/clerk_of_co urts/

Will not search UCC records. This agency will not do a tax lien search. Will not search real estate records. **Online Access:** Real Estate, UCC, Notary. Free online access to Real Estate, UCC, and Notary records available at http://www.co.clayton.ga.us/superior_court/clerk_of_co urts. **Other Phone Numbers:** Assessor 770-447-3285; Tax Commissioner 770-477-3311; Probate Court 770-477-3301;

Clinch County

County Superior Court Clerk, P.O. Box 433, Homerville, GA 31634. 912-487-5854; Fax 912-487-3083.

Will search UCC records. This agency will not do a tax lien search. Will not search real estate records. **Other Phone Numbers:** Assessor 912-487-2561.

Cobb County

County Superior Court Clerk, PO Box 3490, Marietta, GA 30061. 770-528-1363; http://www.cobb gasupctclk.com

Will search UCC records. This agency will not do a tax lien search. Will not search real estate records. **Online Access:** Real Estate, Grantor/Grantee. Property records on the County Superior Court Clerk web site are available free online at www.cobbgasupctclk. com/index.htm. Search by name, address, land description, instrument type, or book & page. You may also search court records. Also, see www2.gsccca.org for online access to Deed and UCC indexes. **Other Phone Numbers:** Assessor 770-528-3100; Treasurer 770-528-8600.

Coffee County

County Superior Court Clerk, Courthouse, 101 S. Peterson Ave., Douglas, GA 31533. 912-384-2865.

Will search UCC records. This agency will not do a tax lien search. Will not search real estate records. **Other Phone Numbers:** Assessor 912-384-2136; Treasurer 912-384-4799.

Colquitt County

County Superior Court Clerk, P.O. Box 2827, Moultrie, GA 31776-2827. 229-891-7420.

Will search UCC records. This agency will not do a tax lien search. Will not search real estate records. **Other Phone Numbers:** Assessor 229-985-9615; Treasurer 229-985-5306.

Columbia County

County Superior Court Clerk, P.O. Box 100, Appling, GA 30802. 706-541-1139; Fax 706-541-4013.

Will not search UCC records. This agency will not do a tax lien search. Will not search real estate records. **Other Phone Numbers:** Assessor 706-541-0920.

Cook County

County Superior Court Clerk, 212 North Hutchinson Avenue, Adel, GA 31620-2497. County Superior Court Clerk, R/E and UCC Recording 229-896-7717.

This agency ony records real estate transactions, not UCC. Will not search real estate records. **Other Phone Numbers:** Assessor 229-896-3665; Elections 229-896-3941.

Coweta County

County Superior Court Clerk, Courthouse, First FLoor, 200 Court Square, Newnan, GA 30263. 770-254-2690; Fax 770-254-3700.

Will search UCC records. This agency will not do a tax lien search. Will not search real estate records. **Other Phone Numbers:** Assessor 770-254-2640.

Crawford County

County Superior Court Clerk, P.O. Box 1037, Roberta, GA 31078-1037. County Superior Court Clerk, R/E and UCC Recording 478-836-3328.

Will not search UCC records. This agency will not do a tax lien search. Will not search real estate records. **Other Phone Numbers:** Assessor 478-836-2800; Treasurer 478-836-3575; Appraiser/Auditor 478-836-2800; Elections 478-836-3575; Vital Records 478-836-3313.

Crisp County

County Superior Court Clerk, P.O. Box 747, Cordele, GA 31010-0747. County Superior Court Clerk, R/E and UCC Recording 229-276-2616; Fax 229-273-5730.

Will not search UCC records. This agency will not do a tax lien search. Will not search real estate records. **Other Phone Numbers:** Assessor 229-276-2635; Treasurer 229-276-2672; Appraiser/Auditor 229-276-2635.

Dade County

County Superior Court Clerk, P.O. Box 417, Trenton, GA 30752. 706-657-4778; Fax 706-657-8284.
Will not search UCC records. This agency will not do a tax lien search. Will not search real estate records. **Other Phone Numbers:** Assessor 706-657-6341; Appraiser/Auditor 706-657-6341; Elections 706-657-4414; Vital Records 706-657-4414.

Dawson County

County Superior Court Clerk, 25 Tucker Ave, #106, Dawsonville, GA 30534-0222. 706-344-3510 R/E Recording: 706-344-3510 x229 UCC Recording: 706-344-3510 x227; Fax 706-344-3511.
Will search UCC records. This agency will not do a tax lien search. Will not search real estate records.

De Kalb County

County Superior Court Clerk, 556 North McDonough Street, Courthouse, Room 208, Decatur, GA 30030. 404-371-2836.
Will search UCC records. This agency will not do a tax lien search. Will not search real estate records. **Other Phone Numbers:** Assessor 404-371-4938.

Decatur County

County Superior Court Clerk, P.O. Box 336, Bainbridge, GA 31718. 229-248-3025; Fax 229-248-3029.
Will search UCC records. This agency will not do a tax lien search. Will not search real estate records. **Other Phone Numbers:** Assessor 229-248-3008; Treasurer 229-248-3030.

Dodge County

County Superior Court Clerk, P.O. Box 4276, Eastman, GA 31023-4276. 478-374-2871.
Will search UCC records. This agency will not do a tax lien search. Will not search real estate records. **Other Phone Numbers:** Assessor 478-374-8122; Treasurer 478-374-3775.

Dooly County

County Superior Court Clerk, P.O. Box 326, Vienna, GA 31092-0326. 229-268-4234; Fax 229-268-6142.
Will search UCC records. This agency will not do a tax lien search. Will not search real estate records. **Other Phone Numbers:** Assessor 229-268-4719; Treasurer 229-268-4228.

Dougherty County

County Superior Court Clerk, P.O. Box 1827, Albany, GA 31701. County Superior Court Clerk, R/E and UCC Recording 229-431-2198; Fax 229-431-2850. http://www.albany.ga.us
Will search UCC records. This agency will not do a tax lien search. Will not search real estate records. **Online Access:** Real Estate, Personal Property, Tax Records. **Other Phone Numbers:** Assessor 229-431-2130; Treasurer 229-431-2130.

Douglas County

County Superior Court Clerk, Douglas County Courthouse, 8700 Hospital Dr., Douglasville, GA 30134. 770-920-7449.
Will search UCC records. This agency will not do a tax lien search. Will not search real estate records. **Other Phone Numbers:** Assessor 770-920-7228.

Early County

County Superior Court Clerk, P.O. Box 849, Blakely, GA 31723. 229-723-3033; Fax 229-723-5246.
Will search UCC records. This agency will not do a tax lien search. Will not search real estate records. **Other

Phone Numbers:** Assessor 229-723-3088; Treasurer 229-723-4024.

Echols County

County Superior Court Clerk, P.O. Box 213, Statenville, GA 31648. 229-559-5642; Fax 229-559-5792.
Will not search UCC records. This agency will not do a tax lien search. Will not search real estate records. **Other Phone Numbers:** Assessor 229-559-7370; Treasurer 229-559-5253; Elections 229-559-7526.

Effingham County

County Superior Court Clerk, P.O. Box 387, Springfield, GA 31329-0387. County Superior Court Clerk, R/E and UCC Recording 912-754-2118.
Will search UCC records. This agency will not do a tax lien search. Will not search real estate records. **Other Phone Numbers:** Assessor 912-754-2125; Elections 912-754-2115; Vital Records 912-754-2112; Tax Commissioner 912-754-2121; Zoning 912-754-2128;

Elbert County

County Superior Court Clerk, P.O. Box 619, Elberton, GA 30635. County Superior Court Clerk, R/E and UCC Recording 706-283-2005; Fax 706-213-7286.
Will not search UCC records. This agency will not do a tax lien search. Will not search real estate records. **Other Phone Numbers:** Assessor 706-283-2008.

Emanuel County

County Superior Court Clerk, P.O. Box 627, Swainsboro, GA 30401. 478-237-8911; Fax 478-237-2173.
Will search UCC records. This agency will not do a tax lien search. Will not search real estate records. **Other Phone Numbers:** Assessor 478-237-3424.

Evans County

County Superior Court Clerk, P.O. Box 845, Claxton, GA 30417. 912-739-3868; Fax 912-739-2504.
Will search UCC records. This agency will not do a tax lien search. Will not search real estate records. **Other Phone Numbers:** Assessor 912-739-3424; Treasurer 912-739-1147; Elections 912-739-0708.

Fannin County

County Superior Court Clerk, P.O. Box 1300, Blue Ridge, GA 30513. 706-632-2039.
Will not search UCC records. This agency will not do a tax lien search. Will not search real estate records. **Other Phone Numbers:** Assessor 706-632-5954; Treasurer 706-632-2645.

Fayette County

County Superior Court Clerk, P.O. Box 130, Fayetteville, GA 30214. County Superior Court Clerk, R/E and UCC Recording 770-461-4703; http://www.admin.co.fayette.ga.us
Will not search UCC records. This agency will not do a tax lien search. Will not search real estate records. **Online Access:** Assessor, Real Estate. Records on the County Assessor database are available free online at www.admin.co.fayette.ga.us/property/propsearch.asp. Also, See www2.gsccca.org for online access to Deed and UCC indexes. **Other Phone Numbers:** Assessor 770-461-6041; Treasurer 770-461-8611.

Floyd County

County Superior Court Clerk, P.O. Box 1110, Rome, GA 30162-1110. 706-291-5190; Fax 706-233-0035.
Will Search UCC records. This agency will not do a tax lien search. Will not search real estate records. **Other Phone Numbers:** Assessor 706-291-5143; Treasurer 706-291-5148.

Forsyth County

County Superior Court Clerk, 100 Courthouse Square, Room 010, Cumming, GA 30040. 770-781-2120; Fax 770-886-2858.
Will search UCC records. This agency will not do a tax lien search. Will not search real estate records. **Other Phone Numbers:** Assessor 770-781-2106.

Franklin County

County Superior Court Clerk, P.O. Box 70, Carnesville, GA 30521. 706-384-2514; Fax 706-384-2185.
Will search UCC records. This agency will not do a tax lien search. Will not search real estate records. **Other Phone Numbers:** Assessor 706-384-3896.

Fulton County

County Superior Court Clerk, 136 Pryor Street, Atlanta, GA 30303. 404-730-5535 R/E Recording: 404-730-5371 UCC Recording: 404-730-5355; Fax 404-730-7993. http://www2.gsccca.org/clerks/displayclerk.asp
Will not search UCC records. This agency will not do a tax lien search. Will not search real estate records. **Other Phone Numbers:** Assessor 404-730-6440; Treasurer 404-730-6100.

Gilmer County

County Superior Court Clerk, 1 West Side Square, Courthouse, Box #30, Ellijay, GA 30540. County Superior Court Clerk, R/E and UCC Recording 706-635-4462; Fax 706-635-1462.
Will not search UCC records. This agency will not do a tax lien search. Will not search real estate records. **Other Phone Numbers:** Assessor 706-635-2703; Treasurer 706-635-4361.

Glascock County

County Superior Court Clerk, P.O. Box 231, Gibson, GA 30810. County Superior Court Clerk, R/E and UCC Recording 706-598-2084; Fax 706-598-2577.
Will search UCC records. This agency will not do a tax lien search. Will not search real estate records. **Other Phone Numbers:** Assessor 706-598-2863; Treasurer 706-598-2671; Elections 706-598-3241.

Glynn County

County Superior Court Clerk, P.O. Box 1355, Brunswick, GA 31521-1355. County Superior Court Clerk, R/E and UCC Recording 912-554-7313; Fax 912-267-5625.
Will not search UCC records. This agency will not do a tax lien search. Will not search real estate records. **Other Phone Numbers:** Assessor 912-267-7093; Treasurer 912-267-5680.

Gordon County

County Superior Court Clerk, Courthouse, Suite 102, 100 Wall St., Calhoun, GA 30701. County Superior Court Clerk, R/E and UCC Recording 706-629-9533; Fax 706-629-2139. www2.gsccca.org
Will search UCC records. This agency will not do a tax lien search. Will not search real estate records. **Other Phone Numbers:** Assessor 706-629-6812; Treasurer 706-629-9242; Elections 706-629-7781; Vital Records 706-629-7314.

Grady County

Superior Court Clerk, 250 North Broad St, Box 8, Box 8, Cairo, GA 31728. Superior Court Clerk, R/E and UCC Recording 229-377-2912.
Will not search UCC records. Public Access terminal is available. Clerk will assist visitors. Will not search real estate records. **Other Phone Numbers:** Assessor 229-377-3325; Registrar 229-377-1897.

Greene County

County Superior Court Clerk, Courthouse, Suite 109, 113 North Main St., Greensboro, GA 30642-1107. 706-453-3340; Fax 706-453-9179.
Will search UCC records. This agency will not do a tax lien search. Will not search real estate records. **Other Phone Numbers:** Assessor 706-453-3355.

Gwinnett County

County Superior Court Clerk, P.O. Box 2050, Lawrenceville, GA 30046. 770-822-8100.
Will search UCC records. This agency will not do a tax lien search. Will not search real estate records. **Online Access:** Property. Records on the County Property database are available free online at www.akanda.com/publicaccess/gwinprof.htm. Also, see www2.gsccca.org for online access to Deed and UCC indexes. **Other Phone Numbers:** Assessor 770-822-7233; Treasurer 770-822-8000.

Habersham County

County Superior Court Clerk, Highway 115, 555 Monroe St., Unit 35, Clarkesville, GA 30523. 706-754-2923; Fax 706-754-8779.
Will search UCC records. This agency will not do a tax lien search. Will not search real estate records. **Other Phone Numbers:** Assessor 706-754-2013.

Hall County

County Superior Court Clerk, P.O. Box 1336, Gainesville, GA 30503-1336. 770-531-7052 R/E Recording: 770-531-7058; Fax 770-536-0702.
Will not search UCC records. This agency will not do a tax lien search. Will not search real estate records. **Other Phone Numbers:** Assessor 770-531-6720; Treasurer 770-531-6950.

Hancock County

County Superior Court Clerk, P.O. Box 451, Sparta, GA 31087. 706-444-6644; Fax 706-444-6221.
Will search UCC records. This agency will not do a tax lien search. Will not search real estate records. **Other Phone Numbers:** Assessor 706-444-5721.

Haralson County

County Superior Court Clerk, P.O. Drawer 849, Buchanan, GA 30113. County Superior Court Clerk, R/E and UCC Recording 770-646-2005; Fax 770-646-2035.
Will search UCC records. This agency will not do a tax lien search. Will not search real estate records. **Other Phone Numbers:** Assessor 770-646-2022; Treasurer 770-646-2022; Appraiser/Auditor 770-646-2022; Vital Records 770-646-2008.

Harris County

County Superior Court Clerk, P.O. Box 528, Hamilton, GA 31811. County Superior Court Clerk, R/E and UCC Recording 706-628-5570; Fax 706-628-7039.
Will search UCC records. This agency will not do a tax lien search. Will not search real estate records. **Other Phone Numbers:** Assessor 706-628-5171; Treasurer 706-628-4958; Elections 706-628-5210; Tax Commissioner 706-628-4843.

Hart County

County Superior Court Clerk, P.O.Box 386, Hartwell, GA 30643. County Superior Court Clerk, R/E and UCC Recording 706-376-7189; Fax 706-376-1277.
Will search UCC records. This agency will not do a tax lien search. Will not search real estate records. **Other Phone Numbers:** Assessor 706-376-3997; Treasurer 706-376-2024; Appraiser/Auditor 706-376-3997; Elections 706-376-2565; Vital Records 706-376-2565.

Heard County

County Superior Court Clerk, P.O. Box 249, Franklin, GA 30217. 706-675-3301; Fax 706-675-0819.
Will search UCC records. This agency will not do a tax lien search. Will not search real estate records. **Other Phone Numbers:** Assessor 706-675-3786.

Henry County

County Superior Court Clerk, Courthouse, #1 Courthouse Square, McDonough, GA 30253. County Superior Court Clerk, R/E and UCC Recording 770-954-2121.
Will not search UCC records. This agency will not do a tax lien search. Will not search real estate records. **Other Phone Numbers:** Assessor 770-954-2420; Treasurer 770-954-2470; Elections 770-954-2069; Vital Records 770-954-2303.

Houston County

County Superior Court Clerk, 800 Carroll Street, Perry, GA 31069. County Superior Court Clerk, R/E and UCC Recording   478-987-2170;   Fax   478-987-3252. http://www.houstoncountyga.com
Will not search UCC records. This agency will not do a tax lien search. Will not search real estate records. **Online Access:** Assessor, Real Estate. Online access to the assessor's Mapguide database is available free at www.assessor.houstoncountyga.org. The Autodesk MapGuide viewer is available to download. Also see www2.gsccca.org for online access to Deed and UCC indexes. **Other Phone Numbers:** Assessor 478-987-3060; Elections 478-987-1973; Marriage/Death/Birth Records 478-987-2770; Divorce Records 478-987-2170;

Irwin County

County Superior Court Clerk, 113 N Irwin Ave, 301 S. Irwin Avenue, Ocilla, GA 31774. 229-468-5356; Fax 229-468-5356.
Will search UCC records. This agency will not do a tax lien search. Will not search real estate records. **Other Phone Numbers:** Assessor 229-468-5514; Treasurer 229-468-5505.

Jackson County

County Superior Court Clerk, P.O. Box 7, Jefferson, GA 30549. 706-367-6360; Fax 706-367-2468.
Will search UCC records. This agency will not do a tax lien search. Will not search real estate records. **Other Phone Numbers:** Assessor 706-367-6330.

Jasper County

County Superior Court Clerk, Courthouse, Monticello, GA 31064. 706-468-4901; Fax 706-468-4946.
Will search UCC records. This agency will not do a tax lien search. Will not search real estate records. **Other Phone Numbers:** Assessor 706-468-4904; Treasurer 706-468-4900.

Jeff Davis County

County Superior Court Clerk, P.O. Box 248, Hazlehurst, GA 31539. 912-375-6615; Fax 912-375-0378.
Will search UCC records. This agency will not do a tax lien search. Will not search real estate records. **Other Phone Numbers:** Assessor 912-375-6624.

Jefferson County

County Superior Court Clerk, P.O. Box 151, Louisville, GA 30434. 478-625-7922; Fax 478-625-9589.
Will search UCC records. This agency will not do a tax lien search. Will not purch real estate records. **Other Phone Numbers:** Assessor 478-625-8209; Treasurer 478-625-7736.

Jenkins County

County Superior Court Clerk, P.O. Box 659, Millen, GA 30442. 478-982-4683; Fax 478-982-1274.
Will search UCC records. This agency will not do a tax lien search. Will not search real estate records. **Other Phone Numbers:** Assessor 478-982-4939; Treasurer 478-982-4925.

Johnson County

County Superior Court Clerk, P.O. Box 321, Wrightsville, GA 31096. 478-864-3484; Fax 478-864-1343.
Will search UCC records. This agency will not do a tax lien search. Will not search real estate records. **Other Phone Numbers:** Assessor 478-864-3325; Treasurer 478-864-2565.

Jones County

County Superior Court Clerk, P.O. Box 39, Gray, GA 31032. 478-986-6671.
Will search UCC records. This agency will not do a tax lien search. Will not search real estate records. **Other Phone Numbers:** Assessor 478-986-6300; Treasurer 478-986-6538.

Lamar County

County Superior Court Clerk, 326 Thomaston Street, Courthouse, Barnesville, GA 30204-1669. 770-358-5145; Fax 770-358-5149.
Will search UCC records. This agency will not do a tax lien search. Will not search real estate records. **Other Phone Numbers:** Assessor 770-358-5161; Treasurer 770-358-5162.

Lanier County

County Superior Court Clerk, County Courthouse, 100 Main Street, Lakeland, GA 31635. 229-482-3594; Fax 229-482-8333.
Will search UCC records. This agency will not do a tax lien search. Will not search real estate records. **Other Phone Numbers:** Assessor 229-482-2090; Treasurer 229-482-3795.

Laurens County

County Superior Court Clerk, P.O. Box 2028, Dublin, GA 31040. 478-272-3210; Fax 478-275-2595.
Will search UCC records. This agency will not do a tax lien search. Will not search real estate records. **Other Phone Numbers:** Assessor 478-272-6443; Treasurer 478-272-6994.

Lee County

County Superior Court Clerk, P.O. Box 597, Leesburg, GA 31763. 229-759-6018.
Will search UCC records. This agency will not do a tax lien search. Will not search real estate records. **Other Phone Numbers:** Assessor 229-759-6010; Treasurer 922912-759-6000.

Liberty County

County Superior Court Clerk, P.O. Box 50, Hinesville, GA 31310. County Superior Court Clerk, R/E and UCC Recording   912-876-3625;   Fax   912-369-5463. http://www.libertyco.com
Will not search UCC records. This agency will not do a tax lien search. Will not search real estate records. **Online Access:** Property, UCCs. See www2.gsccca.org for online access to Deed and UCC indexes. **Other Phone Numbers:** Assessor 912-876-2823; Treasurer 912-876-3389; Vital Records 912-876-3625.

Lincoln County

County Superior Court Clerk, P.O. Box 340, Lincolnton, GA 30817. 706-359-4444.

Will search UCC records. This agency will not do a tax lien search. Will not search real estate records. **Other Phone Numbers:** Assessor 706-359-4444; Treasurer 706-359-4444.

Long County

County Superior Court Clerk, P.O. Box 458, Ludowici, GA 31316. 912-545-2123.
Will search UCC records. UCC search includes tax liens if requested. Will not search real estate records. **Other Phone Numbers:** Assessor 912-545-9111; Treasurer 912-545-2127.

Lowndes County

County Superior Court Clerk, P.O. Box 1349, Valdosta, GA 31601-1349. 229-333-5125; Fax 229-333-7637.
Will search UCC records. This agency will not do a tax lien search. Will not search real estate records. **Other Phone Numbers:** Assessor 229-333-5144; Treasurer 229-333-5106.

Lumpkin County

County Superior Court Clerk, 99 Courthouse Hill, Suite D, Dahlonega, GA 30533-0541. County Superior Court Clerk, R/E and UCC Recording 706-864-3736; Fax 706-864-5298.
Will search UCC records. This agency will not do a tax lien search. Will not search real estate records. **Other Phone Numbers:** Assessor 706-864-2433; Treasurer 706-864-3742; Appraiser/Auditor 706-864-2433; Elections 706-864-6279; Vital Records 706-864-3847.

Macon County

County Superior Court Clerk, P.O. Box 337, Oglethorpe, GA 31068. County Superior Court Clerk, R/E and UCC Recording 478-472-7661; Fax 478-472-4775.
Will search UCC records. This agency will not do a tax lien search. Will not search real estate records. **Other Phone Numbers:** Assessor 478-472-6560; Treasurer 478-472-7031; Appraiser/Auditor 478-472-6560; Elections 478-472-7685; Vital Records 478-472-7685.

Madison County

County Superior Court Clerk, P.O. Box 247, Danielsville, GA 30633. 706-795-3351; Fax 706-795-5668.
Will search UCC records. This agency will not do a tax lien search. Will not search real estate records. **Other Phone Numbers:** Assessor 706-795-3351 x15; Treasurer 706-795-3351 x31.

Marion County

County Superior Court Clerk, P.O. Box 41, Buena Vista, GA 31803. County Superior Court Clerk, R/E and UCC Recording 229-649-7321; Fax 229-649-2059.
Will not search UCC records. This agency will not do a tax lien search. Will not search real estate records. **Other Phone Numbers:** Assessor 229-649-5504; Treasurer 229-649-2603; Appraiser/Auditor 229-649-5504; Elections 229-649-2603; Vital Records 229-649-5542.

McDuffie County

County Superior Court Clerk, P.O. Box 158, Thomson, GA 30824-0150. County Superior Court Clerk, R/E and UCC Recording 706-595-2134; Fax 706-595-9150.
Will not search UCC records. This agency will not do a tax lien search. Will not search real estate records. **Other Phone Numbers:** Assessor 706-595-2128; Treasurer 706-595-2100; Appraiser/Auditor 706-595-2128; Elections 706-595-2105; Vital Records 706-595-2124.

McIntosh County

County Superior Court Clerk, P.O. Box 1661, Darien, GA 31305. 912-437-6641; Fax 912-437-6673.
Will search UCC records. This agency will not do a tax lien search. Will not search real estate records. **Other Phone Numbers:** Assessor 912-437-6663; Treasurer 912-437-6627.

Meriwether County

County Superior Court Clerk, P.O. Box 160, Greenville, GA 30222-0160. 706-672-4416; Fax 706-672-9465.
Will search UCC records. This agency will not do a tax lien search. Will not search real estate records. **Other Phone Numbers:** Assessor 706-672-4222; Treasurer 706-672-4219.

Miller County

County Superior Court Clerk, P.O. Box 66, Colquitt, GA 31737. County Superior Court Clerk, R/E and UCC Recording 229-758-4102; Fax 229-758-6585.
Will not search UCC records. This agency will not do a tax lien search. Will not search real estate records. **Other Phone Numbers:** Assessor 229-758-4100; Treasurer 229-758-4101; Appraiser/Auditor 229-758-4100; Elections 229-758-4118; Vital Records 229-758-4110.

Mitchell County

County Superior Court Clerk, P.O. Box 427, Camilla, GA 31730. 229-336-2022; Fax 229-336-2003.
Will search UCC records. This agency will not do a tax lien search. Will not search real estate records. **Other Phone Numbers:** Assessor 229-336-2005; Treasurer 229-336-2010.

Monroe County

County Superior Court Clerk, P.O. Box 450, Forsyth, GA 31029-0450. 478-994-7022; Fax 478-994-7053.
Will not search UCC records. This agency will not do a tax lien search. Will not search real estate records. **Other Phone Numbers:** Assessor 478-994-7038; Elections 478-994-7036; Vital Records 478-994-7036.

Montgomery County

County Superior Court Clerk, P.O. Box 311, Mount Vernon, GA 30445. 912-583-4401.
Will not search UCC records. This agency will not do a tax lien search. Will not search real estate records. **Other Phone Numbers:** Assessor 912-583-4131; Elections 912-583-2681; Vital Records 912-583-2681.

Morgan County

County Superior Court Clerk, P.O. Box 130, Madison, GA 30650. 706-342-3605.
Will search UCC records. This agency will not do a tax lien search. Will not search real estate records. **Other Phone Numbers:** Assessor 706-342-0551.

Murray County

County Superior Court Clerk, P.O. Box 1000, Chatsworth, GA 30705. 706-695-2932.
Will search UCC records. This agency will not do a tax lien search. Will not search real estate records. **Other Phone Numbers:** Assessor 706-695-2521; Treasurer 706-695-3423.

Muscogee County

County Superior Court Clerk, P.O. Box 2145, Columbus, GA 31902-2145. 706-653-4358 R/E Recording: 706-653-4356 UCC Recording: 706-653-4356; Fax 706-653-4359.
Will search UCC records. This agency will not do a tax lien search. Will not search real estate records. **Other**

Phone Numbers: Assessor 706-653-4398; Treasurer 706-653-4100.

Newton County

County Superior Court Clerk, Newton County Judicial Center, 1132 Usher St., 3rd Floor, Covington, GA 30014. 770-784-2035.
Will search UCC records. This agency will not do a tax lien search. Will not search real estate records. **Other Phone Numbers:** Assessor 770-784-2000.

Oconee County

County Superior Court Clerk, P.O. Box 1099, Watkinsville, GA 30677. 706-769-3940; Fax 706-769-3948.
Will search UCC records. This agency will not do a tax lien search. Will not search real estate records. **Other Phone Numbers:** Assessor 706-769-3921.

Oglethorpe County

County Superior Court Clerk, P.O. Box 68, Lexington, GA 30648-0068. 706-743-5731; Fax 706-743-5335.
http://www.gsccca.org
Will search UCC records. This agency will not do a tax lien search. Will not search real estate records. **Online Access:** UCC, Real Estate. UCC and real estate records are available online from the Oglethorpe County Clerk for a monthly subscription fee of $9.95 plus $.25 per printed page. Guest accounts are available. For information and to open an account, call 404-327-9058. Also, see www2.gsccca.org for online access to Deed and UCC indexes. **Other Phone Numbers:** Assessor 706-743-5166.

Paulding County

County Superior Court Clerk, 11 Courthouse Sq., Room G-2, Dallas, GA 30132. 770-443-7527.
Will search UCC records. This agency will not do a tax lien search. Will not search real estate records. **Other Phone Numbers:** Assessor 770-443-7606.

Peach County

County Superior Court Clerk, P.O. Box 389, Fort Valley, GA 31030. 478-825-5331.
Will not search UCC records. This agency will not do a tax lien search. Will not search real estate records. **Other Phone Numbers:** Assessor 478-825-5924; Treasurer 478-825-2535.

Pickens County

County Superior Court Clerk, P.O. Box 130, Jasper, GA 30143. 706-692-2014.
Will search UCC records. This agency will not do a tax lien search. Will not search real estate records. **Other Phone Numbers:** Assessor 706-692-3556.

Pierce County

County Superior Court Clerk, P.O. Box 588, Blackshear, GA 31516. 912-449-2020.
Will search UCC records. This agency will not do a tax lien search. Will not search real estate records.

Pike County

County Superior Court Clerk, P.O. Box 10, Zebulon, GA 30295. 770-567-2000.
Will search UCC records. This agency will not do a tax lien search. Will not search real estate records.

Polk County

County Superior Court Clerk, P.O. Box 948, Cedartown, GA 30125. 770-749-2114; Fax 770-749-2148.
Will search UCC records. This agency will not do a tax lien search. Will not search real estate records. **Other**

Phone Numbers: Assessor 770-749-2125; Treasurer 770-749-2108.

Pulaski County

Superior Court Clerk, P.O. Box 60, Hawkinsville, GA 31036. Superior Court Clerk, R/E and UCC Recording 478-783-1911; Fax 478-892-3308.
Will not search UCC records. This agency will not do a tax lien search. Will not search real estate records. **Other Phone Numbers:** Assessor 478-783-4154; Treasurer 478-783-2811; Elections 478-783-2061; Vital Records 478-783-2061.

Putnam County

County Superior Court Clerk, Courthouse, 100 S. Jefferson St., Eatonton, GA 31024-1087. 706-485-4501; Fax 706-485-2515.
Will not search UCC records. This agency will not do a tax lien search. Will not search real estate records. **Other Phone Numbers:** Assessor 706-485-6376; Treasurer 706-485-5441.

Quitman County

County Superior Court Clerk, P.O. Box 307, Georgetown, GA 31754. 229-334-2578; Fax 229-334-2151.
Will search UCC records. UCC search includes tax liens if requested. Will not search real estate records.

Rabun County

County Superior Court Clerk, 25 Courthouse Square # 7, Clayton, GA 30525. 706-782-3615; Fax 706-782-7588.
Will search UCC records. Tax liens not included in UCC search. RE owner, mortgage, and property transfer searches available. **Other Phone Numbers:** Assessor 706-782-5068; Treasurer 706-782-3813.

Randolph County

County Superior Court Clerk, P.O. Box 98, Cuthbert, GA 31740. 229-732-2216; Fax 229-732-5881.
Will search UCC records. This agency will not do a tax lien search. Will not search real estate records. **Other Phone Numbers:** Assessor 229-732-2522; Treasurer 229-732-2881.

Richmond County

County Superior Court Clerk, P.O. Box 2046, Augusta, GA 30903. 706-821-2460; Fax 706-821-2448.
Will search UCC records. This agency will not do a tax lien search. Will not search real estate records. **Other Phone Numbers:** Assessor 706-821-2310; Treasurer 706-821-2391.

Rockdale County

County Superior Court Clerk, P.O. Box 937, Conyers, GA 30207. 770-929-4069; Fax 770-860-0381.
Will search UCC records. This agency will not do a tax lien search. Will not search real estate records. **Other Phone Numbers:** Assessor 770-929-4024; Treasurer 770-929-4009.

Schley County

County Superior Court Clerk, P.O. Box 7, Ellaville, GA 31806-0007. County Superior Court Clerk, R/E and UCC Recording 229-937-5581; Fax 229-937-5047.
Will not search UCC records. This agency will not do a tax lien search. Will not search real estate records. **Other Phone Numbers:** Assessor 229-937-2689; Appraiser/Auditor 229-937-2689; Elections 229-937-2905; Vital Records 229-937-2905.

Screven County

County Superior Court Clerk, P.O. Box 156, Sylvania, GA 30467. 912-564-2614; Fax 912-564-2622.

Will search UCC records. This agency will not do a tax lien search. Will not search real estate records.

Seminole County

County Superior Court Clerk, P.O. Box 672, Donalsonville, GA 31745. 229-524-2525; Fax 229-524-8883.
Will not search UCC records. Will not search real estate records. **Other Phone Numbers:** Assessor 229-524-5831.

Spalding County

County Superior Court Clerk, P.O. Box 1046, Griffin, GA 30224. 770-467-4356.
Will search UCC records. This agency will not do a tax lien search. Will not search real estate records. **Other Phone Numbers:** Assessor 770-228-9900 x350.

Stephens County

County Superior Court Clerk, Stephens County Courthouse, 150 West Doyle St., Toccoa, GA 30577-2310. 706-886-9496.
Will search UCC records. This agency will not do a tax lien search. Will not search real estate records. **Other Phone Numbers:** Assessor 706-886-4753.

Stewart County

County Superior Court Clerk, P.O. Box 910, Lumpkin, GA 31815-0910. 229-838-6220.
Will not search UCC records. This agency will not do a tax lien search. Will not search real estate records.

Sumter County

County Superior Court Clerk, P.O. Box 333, Americus, GA 31709. County Superior Court Clerk, R/E and UCC Recording 229-924-5626.
Will not search UCC records. This agency will not do a tax lien search. Will not search real estate records. **Other Phone Numbers:** Assessor 229-924-0313; Treasurer 229-924-3090; Appraiser/Auditor 229-924-0313; Elections 229-924-7693; Vital Records 229-924-3637 (Health Dept).

Talbot County

County Superior Court Clerk, P.O. Box 325, Talbotton, GA 31827-0325. 706-665-3239; Fax 706-665-8637.
Will search UCC records. This agency will not do a tax lien search. Will not search real estate records. **Other Phone Numbers:** Assessor 706-665-3377; Treasurer 706-665-3240.

Taliaferro County

County Superior Court Clerk, P.O. Box 182, Crawfordville, GA 30631. 706-456-2123; Fax 706-456-2749.
Will not search UCC records. This agency will not do a tax lien search. Will not search real estate records. **Other Phone Numbers:** Assessor 706-456-2717; Elections 706-456-2253; Vital Records 706-456-2316.

Tattnall County

County Superior Court Clerk, P.O. Box 39, Reidsville, GA 30453. County Superior Court Clerk, R/E and UCC Recording 912-557-6716; Fax 912-557-4552.
Will search UCC records. This agency will not do a tax lien search. Will not search real estate records. **Other Phone Numbers:** Assessor 912-557-4010; Appraiser/Auditor 912-557-4010; Probate Court 912-557-6917.

Taylor County

County Superior Court Clerk, P.O. Box 248, Butler, GA 31006. 478-862-5594; Fax 478-862-5334.
Will not search UCC records. This agency will not do a tax lien search. Will not search real estate records.

Telfair County

County Superior Court Clerk, 128 E Oak St, Ste. 2, Oak Street, McRae, GA 31055-1604. County Superior Court Clerk, R/E and UCC Recording 229-868-6525; Fax 229-868-7956.
Will not search UCC records. This agency will not do a tax lien search. Will not search real estate records. **Other Phone Numbers:** Assessor 229-868-6772.

Terrell County

County Superior Court Clerk, P.O. Box 189, Dawson, GA 31742. 229-995-2631.
Will not search UCC records. This agency will not do a tax lien search. Will not search real estate records. **Other Phone Numbers:** Assessor 229-995-5210; Treasurer 229-995-5151.

Thomas County

County Superior Court Clerk, P.O. Box 1995, Thomasville, GA 31799. 229-225-4108; Fax 229-225-4110. http://www.thomascoclerkofcourt.org/
Will not search UCC records. This agency will not do a tax lien search. Will not search real estate records. **Other Phone Numbers:** Assessor 229-225-4133; Treasurer 229-225-4133; Appraiser/Auditor 229-225-4133; Elections 229-225-4101; Vital Records 229-226-4241.

Tift County

County Superior Court Clerk, P.O. Box 354, Tifton, GA 31793. 229-386-7810; Fax 229-386-7807.
Will not search UCC records. This agency will not do a tax lien search. Will not search real estate records. **Other Phone Numbers:** Assessor 229-386-7840.

Toombs County

County Superior Court Clerk, P.O. Drawer 530, Lyons, GA 30436. County Superior Court Clerk, R/E and UCC Recording 912-526-3501; Fax 912-526-1015.
Will not search UCC records. This agency will not do a tax lien search. Will not search real estate records. **Other Phone Numbers:** Assessor 912-526-6291; Treasurer 912-526-8575; Appraiser/Auditor 912-526-6291; Elections 912-526-8696.

Towns County

County Superior Court Clerk, 48 River St., Courthouse, Suite E, Hiawassee, GA 30546. County Superior Court Clerk, R/E and UCC Recording 706-896-2130.
Will search UCC records. This agency will not do a tax lien search. Will not search real estate records. **Other Phone Numbers:** Assessor 706-896-3984; Treasurer 706-896-2276; Appraiser/Auditor 706-896-3984; Elections 706-896-4353; Vital Records 706-896-3467.

Treutlen County

County Superior Court Clerk, P.O. Box 356, Soperton, GA 30457. 912-529-4215; Fax 912-529-6364.
Will search UCC records. This agency will not do a tax lien search. Will not search real estate records. **Other Phone Numbers:** Assessor 912-529-4343.

Troup County

County Superior Court Clerk, P.O. Box 866, LaGrange, GA 30241-0866. County Superior Court Clerk, R/E and UCC Recording 706-883-1740.
Will not search UCC records. This agency will not do a tax lien search. Will not search real estate records. **Other Phone Numbers:** Assessor 706-883-1625; Treasurer 706-883-1620.

Turner County

County Superior Court Clerk, P.O. Box 106, Ashburn, GA 31714. 229-567-2011; Fax 229-567-0450.

Will search UCC records. This agency will not do a tax lien search. Will not search real estate records. **Other Phone Numbers:** Assessor 229-567-2334; Treasurer 229-567-3636.

Twiggs County

County Superior Court Clerk, P.O. Box 228, Jeffersonville, GA 31044-0228. 478-945-3350.
Will search UCC records. This agency will not do a tax lien search. Will not search real estate records. **Other Phone Numbers:** Assessor 478-945-3663; Treasurer 478-945-3629.

Union County

County Superior Court Clerk, 114 Courthouse Street, Box 5, Blairsville, GA 30512. 706-745-2611; Fax 706-745-3822.
Will search UCC records. This agency will not do a tax lien search. Will not search real estate records. **Other Phone Numbers:** Assessor 706-745-2280; Treasurer 706-745-2260.

Upson County

County Superior Court Clerk, P.O. Box 469, Thomaston, GA 30286. 706-647-7835; Fax 706-647-8999.
Will search UCC records. This agency will not do a tax lien search. Will not search real estate records. **Other Phone Numbers:** Assessor 706-647-8176; Elections 706-647-7015.

Walker County

County Superior Court Clerk, P.O. Box 448, La Fayette, GA 30728. 706-638-1742.
Will search UCC records. This agency will not do a tax lien search. Will not search real estate records. **Other Phone Numbers:** Assessor 706-638-2929; Treasurer 706-638-2929.

Walton County

County Superior Court Clerk, P.O. Box 745, Monroe, GA 30655. 770-267-1304; Fax 770-267-1441.
Will search UCC records. This agency will not do a tax lien search. Will not search real estate records. **Other Phone Numbers:** Assessor 770-267-1477.

Ware County

County Superior Court Clerk, P.O. Box 776, Waycross, GA 31502-0776. 912-287-4340.
Will search UCC records. This agency will not do a tax lien search. Will not search real estate records. **Other Phone Numbers:** Assessor 912-287-4383; Treasurer 912-287-4305.

Warren County

County Superior Court Clerk, P.O. Box 227, Warrenton, GA 30828. 706-465-2262; Fax 706-465-0232.
Will search UCC records. This agency will not do a tax lien search. Will not search real estate records. **Other Phone Numbers:** Assessor 706-465-3321; Treasurer 706-465-2177.

Washington County

County Superior Court Clerk, P.O. Box 231, Sandersville, GA 31082-0231. County Superior Court Clerk, R/E and UCC Recording 478-552-3186.
Will search UCC records. This agency will not do a tax lien search. Will not search real estate records. **Other Phone Numbers:** Assessor 478-552-2937.

Wayne County

County Superior Court Clerk, P.O. Box 918, Jesup, GA 31598-0918. 912-427-5930; Fax 912-427-5939.
Will search UCC records. This agency will not do a tax lien search. Will not search real estate records. **Other Phone Numbers:** Assessor 912-427-5920; Treasurer 912-427-5900.

Webster County

County Superior Court Clerk, P.O. Box 117, Preston, GA 31824. 229-828-3525.
Will search UCC records. This agency will not do a tax lien search. Will not search real estate records. **Other Phone Numbers:** Assessor 229-828-3690.

Wheeler County

County Superior Court Clerk, P.O. Box 38, Alamo, GA 30411-0038. County Superior Court Clerk, R/E and UCC Recording 912-568-7137; Fax 912-568-7453.
Will search UCC records. This agency will not do a tax lien search. Will not search real estate records. **Other Phone Numbers:** Assessor 912-568-7924; Treasurer 912-568-7131; Elections 912-568-7133; Vital Records 912-568-7161.

White County

County Superior Court Clerk, 59 South Main Street, Courthouse, Suite B, Cleveland, GA 30528. County Superior Court Clerk, R/E and UCC Recording 706-865-2613; Fax 706-865-7749.
This agency will not do a UCC search. Contact GA Superior Court Clerk's Cooperative Authority of search. This agency will not do a tax lien search. Will not search real estate records. **Other Phone Numbers:** Assessor 706-865-5328; Appraiser/Auditor 706-865-5328; Elections 706-865-4141; County Commissioner 706-865-2235.

Whitfield County

County Superior Court Clerk, P.O. Box 868, Dalton, GA 30722. 706-275-7450; Fax 706-275-7456.
Will search UCC records. This agency will not do a tax lien search. Will not search real estate records. **Other Phone Numbers:** Assessor 706-275-7410; Treasurer 706-275-7510.

Wilcox County

County Superior Court Clerk, Courthouse, 103 North Broad St., Abbeville, GA 31001-1000. County Superior Court Clerk, R/E and UCC Recording 229-467-2442; Fax 229-467-2000.
Will not search UCC records. This agency will not do a tax lien search. Will not search real estate records. **Other Phone Numbers:** Assessor 229-467-2428; Appraiser/Auditor 229-467-2028; Elections 229-467-2300; Vital Records 229-467-2220.

Wilkes County

County Superior Court Clerk, 23 East Court Street, Room 205, Washington, GA 30673. County Superior Court Clerk, R/E and UCC Recording 706-678-2423; Fax 706-678-2115.
Will not search UCC records. RE owner, mortgage, and property transfer searches available. **Other Phone Numbers:** Assessor 706-678-7732; Elections 706-678-2523; Vital Records 706-678-2523.

Wilkinson County

County Superior Court Clerk, P.O. Box 250, Irwinton, GA 31042-0250. County Superior Court Clerk, R/E and UCC Recording 478-946-2221; Fax 478-946-1497. www.gsccca.org
Will search UCC records. This agency will not do a tax lien search. Will not search real estate records. **Other Phone Numbers:** Assessor 478-946-2076; Treasurer 478-946-2236 (County Commissioner); Appraiser/Auditor 478-946-2188; Elections 478-946-2222.

Worth County

County Superior Court Clerk, 201 North Main Street, Courthouse, Room 13, Sylvester, GA 31791. 229-776-8205.
Will not search UCC records. This agency will not do a tax lien search. Will not search real estate records. **Other Phone Numbers:** Assessor 229-776-8203; Treasurer 229-776-8204; Elections 229-776-8208; Vital Records 229-776-8207.

Georgia County Locator

You will usually be able to find the city name in the City/County Cross Reference below. In that case, it is a simple matter to determine the county from the cross reference. However, only the official US Postal Service city names are included in this index. There are an additional 40,000 place names that people use in their addresses. Therefore, we have also included a ZIP/City Cross Reference immediately following the City/County Cross Reference.

If you know the ZIP Code but the city name does not appear in the City/County Cross Reference index, look up the ZIP Code in the ZIP/City Cross Reference, find the city name, then look up the city name in the City/County Cross Reference. For example, you want to know the county for an address of Menands, NY 12204. There is no "Menands" in the City/County Cross Reference. The ZIP/City Cross Reference shows that ZIP Codes 12201-12288 are for the city of Albany. Looking back in the City/County Cross Reference, Albany is in Albany County.

City/County Cross Reference

ABBEVILLE Wilcox
ACWORTH (30101) Cobb(84), Bartow(8), Paulding(7)
ACWORTH (30102) Cherokee(52), Bartow(26), Cobb(22)
ADAIRSVILLE (30103) Bartow(61), Gordon(30), Floyd(9)
ADEL Cook
ADRIAN (31002) Emanuel(43), Johnson(31), Laurens(18), Treutlen(9)
AILEY Montgomery
ALAMO (30411) Wheeler(61), Laurens(39)
ALAPAHA Berrien
ALBANY (31701) Dougherty(98), Lee(2)
ALBANY (31705) Dougherty(88), Worth(10), Mitchell(2)
ALBANY (31707) Dougherty(93), Lee(5), Baker(1)
ALBANY Dougherty
ALLENHURST (31301) Liberty(79), Long(21)
ALLENTOWN Wilkinson
ALMA (31510) Bacon(97), Pierce(3)
ALPHARETTA (30004) Fulton(76), Forsyth(17), Cherokee(7)
ALPHARETTA (30005) Fulton(87), Forsyth(13)
ALPHARETTA Fulton
ALSTON Montgomery
ALTO (30510) Habersham(65), Banks(28), Hall(8)
ALTO Habersham
AMBROSE Coffee
AMERICUS Sumter
ANDERSONVILLE (31711) Sumter(84), Macon(15)
APPLING Columbia
ARABI (31712) Crisp(94), Worth(6)
ARAGON (30104) Polk(70), Floyd(26), Bartow(4)
ARGYLE Clinch
ARLINGTON (31713) Calhoun(60), Early(30), Baker(10)
ARMUCHEE (30105) Floyd(94), Chattooga(6)
ARNOLDSVILLE (30619) Oglethorpe(88), Oconee(12)
ASHBURN (31714) Turner(94), Worth(6)
ATHENS (30601) Clarke(98), Jackson(1), Madison(1)
ATHENS (30605) Clarke(99), Oconee(1)
ATHENS (30606) Clarke(92), Oconee(8)
ATHENS (30607) Jackson(64), Clarke(36)
ATHENS Clarke
ATLANTA (30306) Fulton(60), De Kalb(40)
ATLANTA (30307) De Kalb(74), Fulton(27)
ATLANTA (30316) De Kalb(72), Fulton(28)
ATLANTA (30317) De Kalb(99), Fulton(1)
ATLANTA (30319) De Kalb(92), Fulton(8)
ATLANTA (30324) Fulton(82), De Kalb(18)
ATLANTA (30337) Fulton(88), Clayton(13)
ATLANTA (30338) De Kalb(97), Fulton(3)
ATLANTA (30339) Cobb(97), Fulton(3)

ATLANTA (30340) De Kalb(88), Gwinnett(12)
ATLANTA (30349) Fulton(65), Clayton(35)
ATLANTA (30350) Fulton(99), De Kalb(1)
ATLANTA (30354) Fulton(91), Clayton(9)
ATLANTA (30360) De Kalb(79), Gwinnett(21)
ATLANTA De Kalb
ATLANTA Fulton
ATTAPULGUS Decatur
AUBURN (30011) Barrow(81), Gwinnett(19)
AUBURN Barrow
AUGUSTA (30907) Columbia(76), Richmond(24)
AUGUSTA Columbia
AUGUSTA Richmond
AUSTELL (30001) Cobb(93), Douglas(7)
AUSTELL (30106) Cobb(97), Douglas(3)
AUSTELL (30168) Cobb(90), Douglas(10)
AVERA Jefferson
AVONDALE ESTATES De Kalb
AXSON (31624) Atkinson(63), Ware(27), Coffee(11)
BACONTON Mitchell
BAINBRIDGE Decatur
BALDWIN (30511) Banks(97), Habersham(3)
BALL GROUND (30107) Cherokee(86), Pickens(11), Forsyth(3)
BARNESVILLE (30204) Lamar(95), Monroe(3), Upson(2)
BARNEY Brooks
BARTOW (30413) Jefferson(88), Washington(12)
BARWICK Brooks
BAXLEY Appling
BELLVILLE Evans
BERLIN Colquitt
BETHLEHEM (30620) Gwinnett(91), Barrow(8), Walton(2)
BISHOP (30621) Oconee(68), Morgan(32)
BLACKSHEAR Pierce
BLAIRSVILLE Union
BLAKELY (31723) Early(96), Miller(4)
BLOOMINGDALE (31302) Chatham(52), Effingham(48)
BLUE RIDGE Fannin
BLUFFTON (31724) Clay(88), Early(12)
BLYTHE (30805) Burke(54), Richmond(46)
BOGART (30622) Oconee(61), Clarke(30), Jackson(9)
BOLINGBROKE Monroe
BONAIRE Houston
BONEVILLE McDuffie
BOSTON (31626) Thomas(98), Brooks(2)
BOSTWICK Morgan
BOWDON (30108) Carroll(95), Heard(5)
BOWDON JUNCTION Carroll
BOWERSVILLE Hart
BOWMAN (30624) Elbert(79), Hart(13), Madison(9)

BOX SPRINGS (31801) Talbot(57), Muscogee(24), Marion(19)
BRASELTON (30517) Jackson(76), Hall(14), Barrow(5), Gwinnett(5)
BREMEN (30110) Haralson(93), Carroll(7)
BRINSON (31725) Decatur(99), Seminole(1)
BRISTOL (31518) Appling(58), Pierce(38), Wayne(4)
BRONWOOD Terrell
BROOKFIELD Tift
BROOKLET Bulloch
BROOKS (30205) Fayette(52), Spalding(48)
BROXTON (31519) Coffee(99), Jeff Davis(1)
BRUNSWICK Glynn
BUCHANAN (30113) Haralson(88), Polk(12)
BUCKHEAD (30625) Morgan(95), Putnam(5)
BUENA VISTA (31803) Marion(95), Schley(4)
BUFORD (30518) Gwinnett(85), Hall(15)
BUFORD Gwinnett
BUTLER Taylor
BYROMVILLE Dooly
BYRON (31008) Peach(83), Houston(10), Crawford(7)
CADWELL Laurens
CAIRO Grady
CALHOUN (30701) Gordon(99), Floyd(1)
CALHOUN Gordon
CALVARY Grady
CAMAK Warren
CAMILLA Mitchell
CANON (30520) Hart(58), Franklin(43)
CANTON Cherokee
CARLTON (30627) Oglethorpe(86), Madison(14)
CARNESVILLE (30521) Franklin(96), Banks(5)
CARROLLTON Carroll
CARTERSVILLE Bartow
CASSVILLE Bartow
CATAULA Harris
CAVE SPRING (30124) Floyd(95), Polk(5)
CECIL Cook
CEDAR SPRINGS Early
CEDARTOWN (30125) Polk(98), Floyd(2)
CENTERVILLE Houston
CHATSWORTH Murray
CHAUNCEY (31011) Dodge(96), Laurens(4)
CHERRYLOG Gilmer
CHESTER (31012) Dodge(65), Bleckley(32), Laurens(3)
CHESTNUT MOUNTAIN Hall
CHICKAMAUGA (30707) Walker(97), Catoosa(3)
CHULA (31733) Irwin(71), Tift(29)
CISCO Murray
CLARKDALE Cobb

CLARKESVILLE Habersham
CLARKSTON De Kalb
CLAXTON Evans
CLAYTON Rabun
CLERMONT (30527) Hall(94), White(6)
CLEVELAND (30528) White(96), Lumpkin(4)
CLIMAX Decatur
CLINCHFIELD Houston
CLYO Effingham
COBB Sumter
COBBTOWN (30420) Tattnall(50), Candler(48), Evans(2)
COCHRAN (31014) Bleckley(91), Dodge(7), Twiggs(2)
COCHRAN Dodge
COHUTTA (99999) Whitfield(99), Catoosa(1)
COLBERT (30628) Madison(90), Oglethorpe(10)
COLEMAN (31736) Randolph(81), Clay(19)
COLLINS Tattnall
COLQUITT (31737) Miller(95), Decatur(2), Baker(2), Early(1)
COLUMBUS Muscogee
COMER (30629) Madison(90), Oglethorpe(10)
COMMERCE (30529) Jackson(90), Banks(10)
COMMERCE (30530) Jackson(49), Madison(22), Banks(20), Franklin(9)
COMMERCE Jackson
CONCORD Pike
CONLEY (30288) Clayton(50), De Kalb(50)
CONLEY Clayton
CONYERS (30012) Rockdale(97), De Kalb(2)
CONYERS (30013) Rockdale(93), Newton(7)
CONYERS Rockdale
COOLIDGE (31738) Colquitt(69), Thomas(28), Telfair(3)
COOSA Floyd
CORDELE Crisp
CORNELIA Habersham
COTTON Mitchell
COVINGTON (30014) Newton(90), Walton(9), Jasper(1)
COVINGTON Newton
CRANDALL Murray
CRAWFORD Oglethorpe
CRAWFORDVILLE (30631) Taliaferro(91), Wilkes(7), Greene(2)
CRESCENT McIntosh
CULLODEN (31016) Monroe(56), Upson(30), Lamar(11), Crawford(3)
CUMMING (30040) Forsyth(93), Cherokee(7)
CUMMING Forsyth
CUSSETA (31805) Chattahoochee(96), Stewart(4)
CUTHBERT Randolph
DACULA (30019) Gwinnett(97), Walton(2)

DACULA Gwinnett
DAHLONEGA Lumpkin
DAISY Evans
DALLAS (30132) Paulding(98), Cobb(2)
DALTON Whitfield
DAMASCUS (31741) Early(74), Baker(20), Miller(7)
DANIELSVILLE Madison
DANVILLE (31017) Twiggs(76), Wilkinson(17), Bleckley(8)
DARIEN McIntosh
DAVISBORO Washington
DAWSON Terrell
DAWSONVILLE (30534) Dawson(86), Lumpkin(10), Forsyth(3)
DE SOTO (31743) Sumter(88), Lee(12)
DEARING McDuffie
DECATUR De Kalb
DEMOREST Habersham
DENTON Jeff Davis
DEWY ROSE (30634) Elbert(57), Hart(43)
DEXTER Laurens
DILLARD Rabun
DIXIE Brooks
DOERUN (31744) Colquitt(70), Worth(29), Mitchell(1)
DONALSONVILLE (31745) Seminole(96), Miller(3)
DOUGLAS Coffee
DOUGLASVILLE (30134) Douglas(68), Paulding(33)
DOUGLASVILLE Douglas
DOVER Screven
DRY BRANCH (31020) Twiggs(69), Bibb(31)
DU PONT (31630) Clinch(81), Echols(19)
DUBLIN Laurens
DUDLEY (31022) Laurens(96), Bleckley(3)
DULUTH (30097) Fulton(51), Gwinnett(45), Forsyth(4)
DULUTH Gwinnett
EAST ELLIJAY Gilmer
EASTANOLLEE (30538) Stephens(72), Franklin(28)
EASTMAN (31023) Dodge(99), Pulaski(1)
EATONTON Putnam
EDEN Effingham
EDISON (31746) Calhoun(91), Clay(7), Randolph(2)
ELBERTON (30635) Elbert(99), Hart(1)
ELKO Houston
ELLABELL (31308) Bryan(79), Bulloch(21)
ELLAVILLE Schley
ELLENTON Colquitt
ELLENWOOD (30294) De Kalb(39), Clayton(34), Henry(27)
ELLENWOOD Clayton
ELLERSLIE Harris
ELLIJAY Gilmer
EMERSON Bartow
ENIGMA (31749) Berrien(64), Tift(34), Irwin(2)
EPWORTH Fannin
ESOM HILL Polk
ETON Murray
EVANS Columbia
EXPERIMENT Spalding
FAIRBURN (30213) Fulton(87), Fayette(13)
FAIRMOUNT (30139) Gordon(71), Pickens(24), Bartow(5)
FARGO (31631) Clinch(64), Echols(29), Charlton(7)
FARMINGTON Oconee
FAYETTEVILLE (30215) Fayette(93), Clayton(7)
FAYETTEVILLE Fayette
FELTON Haralson
FITZGERALD (31750) Ben Hill(86), Irwin(14)
FLEMING Liberty
FLINTSTONE Walker
FLOVILLA Butts

FLOWERY BRANCH Hall
FOLKSTON (31537) Charlton(94), Camden(6)
FOREST PARK Clayton
FORSYTH Monroe
FORT BENNING Muscogee
FORT GAINES Clay
FORT OGLETHORPE Catoosa
FORT STEWART (31314) Liberty(98), Bryan(2)
FORT STEWART Liberty
FORT VALLEY (31030) Peach(93), Crawford(5), Macon(2)
FORTSON (31808) Harris(67), Muscogee(33)
FOWLSTOWN Decatur
FRANKLIN (30217) Heard(99), Troup(1)
FRANKLIN SPRINGS Franklin
FUNSTON Colquitt
GAINESVILLE (30506) Hall(96), Forsyth(4)
GAINESVILLE Hall
GARFIELD (30425) Emanuel(39), Bulloch(38), Jenkins(23)
GAY Meriwether
GENEVA Talbot
GEORGETOWN (31754) Quitman(90), Clay(10)
GIBSON (30810) Glascock(97), Jefferson(3), Warren(1)
GILLSVILLE (30543) Hall(57), Banks(30), Jackson(13)
GIRARD (30426) Burke(96), Screven(4)
GLENN Heard
GLENNVILLE (30427) Tattnall(95), Long(5)
GLENWOOD (30428) Wheeler(73), Laurens(27)
GOOD HOPE (30641) Walton(82), Morgan(18)
GORDON (31031) Wilkinson(88), Baldwin(10), Twiggs(1), Jones(1)
GOUGH Burke
GRACEWOOD Richmond
GRANTVILLE (30220) Meriwether(75), Coweta(26)
GRAY Jones
GRAYSON Gwinnett
GRAYSVILLE Catoosa
GREENSBORO Greene
GREENVILLE Meriwether
GRIFFIN (30224) Spalding(95), Pike(3), Lamar(2)
GRIFFIN Spalding
GROVETOWN (30813) Columbia(99), Richmond(1)
GUYTON Effingham
HADDOCK (31033) Jones(81), Baldwin(20)
HAGAN Evans
HAHIRA (31632) Lowndes(95), Cook(5)
HAMILTON Harris
HAMPTON (30228) Henry(69), Clayton(25), Spalding(6)
HARALSON Coweta
HARDWICK Baldwin
HARLEM (30814) Columbia(94), McDuffie(6)
HARRISON Washington
HARTSFIELD Colquitt
HARTWELL Hart
HAWKINSVILLE (31036) Pulaski(86), Houston(13)
HAZLEHURST Jeff Davis
HELEN White
HELENA (31037) Telfair(35), Wheeler(35), Dodge(26), Laurens(4)
HEPHZIBAH (30815) Richmond(77), Burke(23)
HIAWASSEE Towns
HIGH SHOALS (30645) Morgan(80), Oconee(20)
HILLSBORO (31038) Jasper(93), Jones(6)
HINESVILLE Liberty
HIRAM (30141) Paulding(88), Cobb(13)

HOBOKEN Brantley
HOGANSVILLE (30230) Troup(76), Heard(12), Meriwether(12)
HOLLY SPRINGS Cherokee
HOMER Banks
HOMERVILLE Clinch
HORTENSE (31543) Wayne(64), Brantley(32), Glynn(4)
HOSCHTON (30548) Jackson(83), Gwinnett(16)
HOWARD Taylor
HULL (30646) Madison(98), Jackson(2)
IDEAL Macon
ILA Madison
INMAN Fayette
IRON CITY (31759) Seminole(96), Miller(3)
IRWINTON (31042) Wilkinson(97), Laurens(3)
IRWINVILLE Irwin
JACKSON (30233) Butts(79), Monroe(15), Henry(3), Lamar(2)
JACKSONVILLE Telfair
JAKIN (31761) Early(97), Seminole(3)
JASPER (30143) Pickens(99), Cherokee(1)
JEFFERSON Jackson
JEFFERSONVILLE (31044) Twiggs(97), Wilkinson(3)
JEKYLL ISLAND Glynn
JENKINSBURG (30234) Butts(81), Henry(19)
JERSEY Walton
JESUP Wayne
JEWELL (31045) Hancock(64), Warren(36)
JONESBORO (30236) Clayton(94), Henry(6)
JONESBORO (30238) Clayton(95), Fayette(5)
JONESBORO Clayton
JULIETTE (31046) Monroe(98), Jones(2)
JUNCTION CITY (31812) Talbot(86), Taylor(14)
KATHLEEN Houston
KENNESAW Cobb
KEYSVILLE (30816) Burke(72), Jefferson(28)
KINGS BAY Camden
KINGSLAND Camden
KINGSTON (30145) Bartow(61), Floyd(39)
KITE (31049) Johnson(54), Emanuel(46)
KNOXVILLE Crawford
LA FAYETTE Walker
LAGRANGE Troup
LAKE PARK (31636) Lowndes(91), Echols(6), Catoosa(3)
LAKELAND (99999) Lanier(98), Clinch(1)
LAKEMONT Rabun
LAVONIA (30553) Franklin(72), Hart(28)
LAWRENCEVILLE Gwinnett
LEARY (31762) Calhoun(51), Baker(49)
LEBANON Cherokee
LEESBURG Lee
LENOX (31637) Cook(53), Berrien(20), Colquitt(18), Tift(9)
LESLIE Sumter
LEXINGTON Oglethorpe
LILBURN Gwinnett
LILLY Dooly
LINCOLNTON (30817) Lincoln(97), McDuffie(2), Wilkes(1)
LINDALE (30147) Floyd(96), Polk(4)
LITHIA SPRINGS Douglas
LITHONIA (30058) De Kalb(67), Gwinnett(30), Rockdale(3)
LITHONIA De Kalb
LIZELLA (31052) Bibb(91), Crawford(10)
LOCUST GROVE (30248) Henry(93), Spalding(5), Butts(2)
LOGANVILLE (30052) Walton(64), Gwinnett(34), Rockdale(1)
LOGANVILLE Gwinnett
LOOKOUT MOUNTAIN (30750) Walker(60), Dade(40)

LOUISVILLE (30434) Jefferson(96), Burke(4)
LOUVALE Stewart
LOVEJOY Clayton
LUDOWICI Long
LULA (30554) Hall(68), Banks(32)
LUMBER CITY (31549) Telfair(75), Wheeler(25)
LUMPKIN Stewart
LUTHERSVILLE Meriwether
LYERLY Chattooga
LYONS (30436) Toombs(94), Emanuel(5)
MABLETON Cobb
MACON (31210) Bibb(89), Monroe(11)
MACON (31211) Bibb(60), Jones(40)
MACON (31217) Bibb(84), Jones(9), Twiggs(8)
MACON (31220) Bibb(76), Monroe(24)
MACON Bibb
MADISON (30650) Morgan(93), Greene(5), Walton(2)
MANASSAS Tattnall
MANCHESTER Meriwether
MANOR Ware
MANSFIELD (30055) Jasper(55), Newton(41), Morgan(4)
MANSFIELD Jasper
MARBLE HILL (30148) Pickens(74), Dawson(26)
MARIETTA Cobb
MARSHALLVILLE Macon
MARTIN (30557) Franklin(70), Stephens(30)
MATTHEWS Jefferson
MAUK (31058) Marion(64), Taylor(36)
MAXEYS Oglethorpe
MAYSVILLE (30558) Jackson(56), Banks(44)
MC CAYSVILLE Fannin
MC INTYRE Wilkinson
MC RAE Telfair
MCDONOUGH (30252) Henry(98), Rockdale(2)
MCDONOUGH Henry
MEANSVILLE (30256) Pike(64), Upson(32), Lamar(4)
MEIGS (31765) Mitchell(48), Thomas(34), Colquitt(18)
MELDRIM Effingham
MENLO (30731) Chattooga(43), Walker(37), Dade(20)
MERIDIAN McIntosh
MERSHON (31551) Pierce(81), Bacon(19)
MESENA Warren
METTER Candler
MIDLAND (31820) Muscogee(88), Harris(12)
MIDVILLE (30441) Emanuel(70), Burke(30)
MIDWAY Liberty
MILAN (31060) Telfair(59), Dodge(42)
MILLEDGEVILLE (31061) Baldwin(94), Putnam(4), Wilkinson(2)
MILLEDGEVILLE Baldwin
MILLEN (30442) Jenkins(94), Burke(4), Screven(2)
MILLWOOD (31552) Ware(91), Coffee(6), Atkinson(3)
MILNER (30257) Lamar(87), Pike(13)
MINERAL BLUFF Fannin
MITCHELL (30820) Glascock(64), Warren(37)
MOLENA (30258) Pike(65), Upson(35)
MONROE Walton
MONTEZUMA (31063) Macon(98), Dooly(2)
MONTICELLO Jasper
MONTROSE (31065) Laurens(90), Bleckley(10)
MORELAND Coweta
MORGAN (31766) Calhoun(94), Randolph(6)

MORGANTON (30560) Fannin(82), Union(18)
MORRIS (31767) Quitman(63), Clay(29), Randolph(5), Stewart(4)
MORROW Clayton
MORVEN Brooks
MOULTRIE Colquitt
MOUNT AIRY Habersham
MOUNT BERRY Floyd
MOUNT VERNON Montgomery
MOUNT ZION Carroll
MOUNTAIN CITY Rabun
MURRAYVILLE (30564) Lumpkin(62), Hall(33), White(6)
MUSELLA (31066) Crawford(57), Bibb(43)
MYSTIC Irwin
NAHUNTA (31553) Brantley(98), Charlton(2)
NASHVILLE Berrien
NAYLOR (31641) Lowndes(85), Lanier(15)
NELSON Cherokee
NEWBORN (30056) Jasper(51), Newton(39), Morgan(10)
NEWBORN Newton
NEWINGTON (30446) Screven(66), Effingham(34)
NEWNAN Coweta
NEWTON Baker
NICHOLLS (31554) Coffee(62), Ware(21), Bacon(17)
NICHOLSON Jackson
NORCROSS (30092) Gwinnett(98), Fulton(2)
NORCROSS Gwinnett
NORMAN PARK (31771) Colquitt(98), Worth(3)
NORRISTOWN Emanuel
NORTH METRO Gwinnett
NORWOOD Warren
NUNEZ Emanuel
OAKFIELD Worth
OAKMAN Gordon
OAKWOOD Hall
OCHLOCKNEE (31773) Thomas(79), Grady(19), Colquitt(2)
OCILLA Irwin
OCONEE (31067) Washington(83), Laurens(17)
ODUM (31555) Wayne(85), Appling(15)
OFFERMAN Pierce
OGLETHORPE Macon
OLIVER Screven
OMAHA Stewart
OMEGA (31775) Colquitt(56), Tift(27), Worth(17)
ORCHARD HILL Spalding
OXFORD (30054) Newton(82), Walton(18)
OXFORD Newton
PALMETTO (30268) Fulton(81), Coweta(19)
PARROTT (31777) Terrell(82), Webster(18)
PATTERSON Pierce
PAVO (31778) Thomas(78), Brooks(18), Colquitt(4)
PEACHTREE CITY Fayette
PEARSON (31642) Atkinson(95), Clinch(3), Coffee(2)
PELHAM Mitchell
PEMBROKE (31321) Bryan(50), Bulloch(50)
PENDERGRASS (30567) Hall(98), Jackson(2)
PERKINS Jenkins
PERRY Houston
PINE LAKE De Kalb
PINE MOUNTAIN (31822) Harris(83), Troup(15), Meriwether(2)
PINE MOUNTAIN VALLEY Harris
PINEHURST Dooly
PINEVIEW (31071) Pulaski(56), Wilcox(43), Dooly(1)

PITTS (31072) Wilcox(87), Crisp(12), Dooly(1)
PLAINFIELD Dodge
PLAINS Sumter
PLAINVILLE (30733) Gordon(92), Floyd(9)
POOLER Chatham
PORTAL Bulloch
PORTERDALE Newton
POULAN Worth
POWDER SPRINGS (30127) Cobb(92), Paulding(8)
POWDER SPRINGS Cobb
PRESTON Webster
PULASKI Candler
PUTNEY Dougherty
QUITMAN Brooks
RABUN GAP Rabun
RANGER (30734) Gordon(73), Pickens(27)
RAY CITY (31645) Lanier(61), Berrien(36), Lowndes(4)
RAYLE (30660) Wilkes(78), Oglethorpe(19), Taliaferro(4)
REBECCA (31783) Turner(50), Irwin(40), Ben Hill(11)
RED OAK Fulton
REDAN De Kalb
REGISTER Bulloch
REIDSVILLE Tattnall
RENTZ Laurens
RESACA (30735) Gordon(71), Murray(21), Whitfield(8)
REX (30273) Clayton(92), Henry(8)
REYNOLDS (31076) Taylor(82), Macon(18)
RHINE (31077) Dodge(52), Telfair(48)
RICEBORO (31323) Liberty(93), Long(7)
RICHLAND (31825) Stewart(88), Webster(12)
RICHMOND HILL Bryan
RINCON Effingham
RINGGOLD (30736) Catoosa(97), Walker(2)
RISING FAWN (30738) Dade(72), Walker(28)
RIVERDALE (30296) Clayton(83), Fulton(10), Fayette(7)
RIVERDALE Clayton
ROBERTA Crawford
ROCHELLE (31079) Wilcox(89), Ben Hill(11)
ROCK SPRING (30739) Walker(88), Catoosa(12)
ROCKLEDGE Laurens
ROCKMART (30153) Polk(86), Paulding(8), Haralson(6)
ROCKY FACE (30740) Whitfield(85), Walker(15)
ROCKY FORD Screven
ROME Floyd
ROOPVILLE (30170) Heard(63), Carroll(38)
ROSSVILLE (30741) Walker(60), Catoosa(40)
ROSWELL (30075) Fulton(81), Cobb(17), Cherokee(1)
ROSWELL Fulton
ROYSTON (30662) Franklin(55), Hart(28), Madison(17), Elbert(1)
RUPERT (31081) Taylor(80), Macon(18), Schley(3)
RUTLEDGE (30663) Morgan(99), Walton(1)
RYDAL (30171) Bartow(77), Gordon(23)
SAINT GEORGE Charlton
SAINT MARYS Camden
SAINT SIMONS ISLAND Glynn
SALE CITY (31784) Mitchell(73), Colquitt(27)
SANDERSVILLE Washington
SAPELO ISLAND McIntosh
SARDIS Burke
SARGENT Coweta
SASSER Terrell

SAUTEE NACOOCHEE (30571) White(97), Habersham(3)
SAVANNAH Chatham
SCOTLAND Telfair
SCOTTDALE De Kalb
SCREVEN Wayne
SEA ISLAND Glynn
SENOIA (30276) Coweta(89), Fayette(6), Meriwether(6)
SEVILLE Wilcox
SHADY DALE Jasper
SHANNON Floyd
SHARON Taliaferro
SHARPSBURG Coweta
SHELLMAN (31786) Randolph(96), Terrell(3), Calhoun(2)
SHILOH (31826) Harris(74), Talbot(26)
SILOAM Greene
SILVER CREEK (30173) Floyd(94), Polk(6)
SMARR Monroe
SMITHVILLE (31787) Lee(90), Sumter(10)
SMYRNA Cobb
SNELLVILLE Gwinnett
SOCIAL CIRCLE (30025) Walton(67), Newton(32), Morgan(2)
SOCIAL CIRCLE Walton
SOPERTON (30457) Treutlen(94), Montgomery(4), Emanuel(2)
SPARKS Cook
SPARTA (31087) Hancock(96), Baldwin(4)
SPRINGFIELD Effingham
STAPLETON (30823) Jefferson(84), Warren(13), Glascock(3), McDuffie(1)
STATENVILLE Echols
STATESBORO Bulloch
STATHAM (30666) Barrow(67), Oconee(25), Jackson(8)
STEPHENS Oglethorpe
STILLMORE Emanuel
STOCKBRIDGE (30281) Henry(90), Rockdale(7), Clayton(3)
STOCKTON (31649) Lanier(95), Echols(5)
STONE MOUNTAIN (30087) De Kalb(56), Gwinnett(44)
STONE MOUNTAIN De Kalb
SUCHES (30572) Union(77), Fannin(22)
SUGAR VALLEY (30746) Gordon(97), Walker(4)
SUMMERTOWN Emanuel
SUMMERVILLE (30747) Chattooga(94), Walker(6)
SUMNER Worth
SUNNY SIDE Spalding
SURRENCY Appling
SUWANEE (30024) Gwinnett(75), Forsyth(24), Fulton(1)
SUWANEE Gwinnett
SWAINSBORO Emanuel
SYCAMORE Turner
SYLVANIA Screven
SYLVESTER (31791) Worth(99), Dougherty(1)
TALBOTTON Talbot
TALKING ROCK (30175) Pickens(58), Gilmer(42)
TALLAPOOSA Haralson
TALLULAH FALLS (30573) Rabun(83), Habersham(17)
TALMO (30575) Jackson(79), Hall(21)
TARRYTOWN (30470) Montgomery(88), Treutlen(12)
TATE Pickens
TAYLORSVILLE (30178) Bartow(82), Polk(18)
TEMPLE (30179) Carroll(45), Haralson(31), Paulding(25)
TENNGA Murray
TENNILLE (31089) Washington(98), Johnson(2)
THE ROCK (30285) Upson(59), Pike(23), Lamar(18)
THOMASTON Upson

THOMASVILLE (31792) Thomas(97), Grady(3)
THOMASVILLE Thomas
THOMSON (30824) McDuffie(98), Columbia(2)
TIFTON Tift
TIGER Rabun
TIGNALL (30668) Wilkes(84), Lincoln(17)
TOCCOA (30577) Stephens(81), Franklin(14), Habersham(5), Banks(1)
TOCCOA Stephens
TOOMSBORO Wilkinson
TOWNSEND McIntosh
TRENTON Dade
TRION (30753) Chattooga(68), Walker(32)
TUCKER (30084) De Kalb(79), Gwinnett(21)
TUCKER De Kalb
TUNNEL HILL (30755) Catoosa(54), Whitfield(46)
TURIN Coweta
TURNERVILLE Habersham
TWIN CITY (30471) Emanuel(80), Bulloch(13), Jenkins(7)
TY TY (31795) Tift(76), Worth(24)
TYBEE ISLAND Chatham
TYRONE Fayette
UNADILLA (31091) Dooly(99), Houston(1)
UNION CITY Fulton
UNION POINT (30669) Greene(79), Oglethorpe(11), Taliaferro(10)
UPATOI (31829) Muscogee(92), Harris(8)
UVALDA (30473) Toombs(62), Montgomery(38)
VALDOSTA (31602) Lowndes(95), Brooks(5)
VALDOSTA (31605) Lowndes(97), Brooks(3)
VALDOSTA Lowndes
VALONA McIntosh
VARNELL Whitfield
VIDALIA (30474) Toombs(88), Montgomery(10), Emanuel(1)
VIDALIA Toombs
VIENNA (31092) Dooly(98), Crisp(2)
VILLA RICA (30180) Carroll(76), Douglas(17), Paulding(7)
WACO (30182) Carroll(66), Haralson(35)
WADLEY Jefferson
WALESKA Cherokee
WALTHOURVILLE Liberty
WARESBORO Ware
WARM SPRINGS Meriwether
WARNER ROBINS Houston
WARRENTON Warren
WARTHEN Washington
WARWICK Worth
WASHINGTON Wilkes
WATKINSVILLE (30677) Oconee(97), Greene(3)
WAVERLY Camden
WAVERLY HALL (31831) Harris(96), Talbot(4)
WAYCROSS (31503) Ware(94), Brantley(5), Pierce(1)
WAYCROSS Ware
WAYNESBORO Burke
WAYNESVILLE (31566) Brantley(52), Camden(48)
WEST GREEN (31567) Jeff Davis(58), Coffee(42)
WEST POINT (31833) Troup(71), Harris(29)
WESTON (31832) Webster(81), Randolph(19)
WHIGHAM Grady
WHITE (30184) Bartow(68), Cherokee(32)
WHITE OAK Camden
WHITE PLAINS (30678) Greene(98), Hancock(2)
WHITESBURG (30185) Carroll(97), Douglas(4)

WILDWOOD Dade
WILEY Rabun
WILLACOOCHEE (31650) Coffee(93), Atkinson(7)
WILLIAMSON (30292) Pike(68), Spalding(32)
WINDER (30680) Barrow(99), Oconee(1)

WINSTON (30187) Douglas(99), Carroll(1)
WINTERVILLE (30683) Clarke(62), Oglethorpe(37), Madison(2)
WOODBINE Camden
WOODBURY Meriwether
WOODLAND Talbot

WOODSTOCK (30188) Cherokee(97), Cobb(3)
WOODSTOCK Cherokee
WRAY (31798) Irwin(87), Ben Hill(7), Coffee(7)
WRENS Jefferson

WRIGHTSVILLE (31096) Johnson(84), Washington(10), Laurens(6)
YATESVILLE (31097) Upson(90), Lamar(7), Monroe(3)
YOUNG HARRIS (30582) Towns(80), Union(20)
ZEBULON Pike

ZIP/City Cross Reference

ZIP	City	ZIP	City	ZIP	City	ZIP	City
30002-30002	AVONDALE ESTATES	30125-30125	CEDARTOWN	30229-30229	HARALSON	30429-30429	HAGAN
30003-30003	NORCROSS	30126-30126	MABLETON	30230-30230	HOGANSVILLE	30434-30434	LOUISVILLE
30004-30005	ALPHARETTA	30127-30127	POWDER SPRINGS	30232-30232	INMAN	30436-30436	LYONS
30006-30008	MARIETTA	30128-30128	CUMMING	30233-30233	JACKSON	30438-30438	MANASSAS
30009-30009	ALPHARETTA	30129-30129	COOSA	30234-30234	JENKINSBURG	30439-30439	METTER
30010-30010	NORCROSS	30130-30131	CUMMING	30235-30235	JERSEY	30441-30441	MIDVILLE
30011-30011	AUBURN	30132-30132	DALLAS	30236-30238	JONESBORO	30442-30442	MILLEN
30012-30013	CONYERS	30133-30135	DOUGLASVILLE	30239-30239	ALPHARETTA	30445-30445	MOUNT VERNON
30014-30016	COVINGTON	30136-30136	DULUTH	30240-30241	LAGRANGE	30446-30446	NEWINGTON
30017-30017	GRAYSON	30137-30137	EMERSON	30243-30246	LAWRENCEVILLE	30447-30447	NORRISTOWN
30018-30018	JERSEY	30138-30138	ESOM HILL	30247-30247	LILBURN	30448-30448	NUNEZ
30019-30019	DACULA	30139-30139	FAIRMOUNT	30248-30248	LOCUST GROVE	30449-30449	OLIVER
30020-30020	CLARKDALE	30140-30140	FELTON	30249-30249	LOGANVILLE	30450-30450	PORTAL
30021-30021	CLARKSTON	30141-30141	HIRAM	30250-30250	LOVEJOY	30451-30451	PULASKI
30022-30023	ALPHARETTA	30142-30142	HOLLY SPRINGS	30251-30251	LUTHERSVILLE	30452-30452	REGISTER
30024-30024	SUWANEE	30143-30143	JASPER	30252-30253	MCDONOUGH	30453-30453	REIDSVILLE
30025-30025	SOCIAL CIRCLE	30144-30144	KENNESAW	30255-30255	MANSFIELD	30454-30454	ROCKLEDGE
30026-30026	DULUTH	30145-30145	KINGSTON	30256-30256	MEANSVILLE	30455-30455	ROCKY FORD
30027-30027	CONLEY	30146-30146	LEBANON	30257-30257	MILNER	30456-30456	SARDIS
30028-30028	CUMMING	30147-30147	LINDALE	30258-30258	MOLENA	30457-30457	SOPERTON
30029-30029	DULUTH	30148-30148	MARBLE HILL	30259-30259	MORELAND	30458-30461	STATESBORO
30030-30037	DECATUR	30149-30149	MOUNT BERRY	30260-30260	MORROW	30464-30464	STILLMORE
30038-30038	LITHONIA	30150-30150	MOUNT ZION	30261-30261	LAGRANGE	30466-30466	SUMMERTOWN
30039-30039	SNELLVILLE	30151-30151	NELSON	30262-30262	NEWBORN	30467-30467	SYLVANIA
30040-30041	CUMMING	30152-30152	KENNESAW	30263-30265	NEWNAN	30470-30470	TARRYTOWN
30042-30046	LAWRENCEVILLE	30153-30153	ROCKMART	30266-30266	ORCHARD HILL	30471-30471	TWIN CITY
30047-30048	LILBURN	30154-30154	DOUGLASVILLE	30267-30267	OXFORD	30473-30473	UVALDA
30049-30049	ELLENWOOD	30155-30155	DULUTH	30268-30268	PALMETTO	30474-30475	VIDALIA
30050-30051	FOREST PARK	30158-30159	NORTH METRO	30269-30269	PEACHTREE CITY	30477-30477	WADLEY
30052-30052	LOGANVILLE	30161-30165	ROME	30270-30270	PORTERDALE	30499-30499	REIDSVILLE
30054-30054	OXFORD	30168-30168	AUSTELL	30271-30271	NEWNAN	30501-30501	GAINESVILLE
30055-30055	MANSFIELD	30170-30170	ROOPVILLE	30272-30272	RED OAK	30502-30502	CHESTNUT MOUNTAIN
30056-30056	NEWBORN	30171-30171	RYDAL	30273-30273	REX	30503-30507	GAINESVILLE
30057-30057	LITHIA SPRINGS	30172-30172	SHANNON	30274-30274	RIVERDALE	30510-30510	ALTO
30058-30058	LITHONIA	30173-30173	SILVER CREEK	30275-30275	SARGENT	30511-30511	BALDWIN
30059-30059	MABLETON	30174-30174	SUWANEE	30276-30276	SENOIA	30512-30512	BLAIRSVILLE
30060-30069	MARIETTA	30175-30175	TALKING ROCK	30277-30277	SHARPSBURG	30513-30513	BLUE RIDGE
30070-30070	PORTERDALE	30176-30176	TALLAPOOSA	30278-30278	SNELLVILLE	30514-30514	BLAIRSVILLE
30071-30071	NORCROSS	30177-30177	TATE	30279-30279	SOCIAL CIRCLE	30515-30515	BUFORD
30072-30072	PINE LAKE	30178-30178	TAYLORSVILLE	30281-30281	STOCKBRIDGE	30516-30516	BOWERSVILLE
30073-30073	POWDER SPRINGS	30179-30179	TEMPLE	30284-30284	SUNNY SIDE	30517-30517	BRASELTON
30074-30074	REDAN	30180-30180	VILLA RICA	30285-30285	THE ROCK	30518-30519	BUFORD
30075-30077	ROSWELL	30182-30182	WACO	30286-30286	THOMASTON	30520-30520	CANON
30078-30078	SNELLVILLE	30183-30183	WALESKA	30287-30287	MORROW	30521-30521	CARNESVILLE
30079-30079	SCOTTDALE	30184-30184	WHITE	30288-30288	CONLEY	30522-30522	CHERRYLOG
30080-30082	SMYRNA	30185-30185	WHITESBURG	30289-30289	TURIN	30523-30523	CLARKESVILLE
30083-30083	STONE MOUNTAIN	30187-30187	WINSTON	30290-30290	TYRONE	30525-30525	CLAYTON
30084-30085	TUCKER	30188-30189	WOODSTOCK	30291-30291	UNION CITY	30527-30527	CLERMONT
30086-30088	STONE MOUNTAIN	30195-30199	DULUTH	30292-30292	WILLIAMSON	30528-30528	CLEVELAND
30089-30089	DECATUR	30201-30202	ALPHARETTA	30293-30293	WOODBURY	30529-30530	COMMERCE
30090-30090	MARIETTA	30203-30203	AUBURN	30294-30294	ELLENWOOD	30531-30531	CORNELIA
30091-30093	NORCROSS	30204-30204	BARNESVILLE	30295-30295	ZEBULON	30533-30533	DAHLONEGA
30094-30094	CONYERS	30205-30205	BROOKS	30296-30296	RIVERDALE	30534-30534	DAWSONVILLE
30095-30099	DULUTH	30206-30206	CONCORD	30297-30298	FOREST PARK	30535-30535	DEMOREST
30101-30102	ACWORTH	30207-30207	CONYERS	30301-30399	ATLANTA	30537-30537	DILLARD
30103-30103	ADAIRSVILLE	30209-30210	COVINGTON	30401-30401	SWAINSBORO	30538-30538	EASTANOLLEE
30104-30104	ARAGON	30211-30211	DACULA	30410-30410	AILEY	30539-30539	EAST ELLIJAY
30105-30105	ARMUCHEE	30212-30212	EXPERIMENT	30411-30411	ALAMO	30540-30540	ELLIJAY
30106-30106	AUSTELL	30213-30213	FAIRBURN	30412-30412	ALSTON	30541-30541	EPWORTH
30107-30107	BALL GROUND	30214-30215	FAYETTEVILLE	30413-30413	BARTOW	30542-30542	FLOWERY BRANCH
30108-30108	BOWDON	30216-30216	FLOVILLA	30414-30414	BELLVILLE	30543-30543	GILLSVILLE
30109-30109	BOWDON JUNCTION	30217-30217	FRANKLIN	30415-30415	BROOKLET	30544-30544	DEMOREST
30110-30110	BREMEN	30218-30218	GAY	30417-30417	CLAXTON	30545-30545	HELEN
30111-30111	CLARKDALE	30219-30219	GLENN	30420-30420	COBBTOWN	30546-30546	HIAWASSEE
30113-30113	BUCHANAN	30220-30220	GRANTVILLE	30421-30421	COLLINS	30547-30547	HOMER
30114-30115	CANTON	30221-30221	GRAYSON	30423-30423	DAISY	30548-30548	HOSCHTON
30116-30119	CARROLLTON	30222-30222	GREENVILLE	30424-30424	DOVER	30549-30549	JEFFERSON
30120-30121	CARTERSVILLE	30223-30224	GRIFFIN	30425-30425	GARFIELD	30552-30552	LAKEMONT
30122-30122	LITHIA SPRINGS	30226-30226	LILBURN	30426-30426	GIRARD	30553-30553	LAVONIA
30123-30123	CASSVILLE	30227-30227	LAWRENCEVILLE	30427-30427	GLENNVILLE	30554-30554	LULA
30124-30124	CAVE SPRING	30228-30228	HAMPTON	30428-30428	GLENWOOD	30555-30555	MC CAYSVILLE

30557-30557	MARTIN	30735-30735	RESACA	31042-31042	IRWINTON	31513-31515	BAXLEY
30558-30558	MAYSVILLE	30736-30736	RINGGOLD	31044-31044	JEFFERSONVILLE	31516-31516	BLACKSHEAR
30559-30559	MINERAL BLUFF	30738-30738	RISING FAWN	31045-31045	JEWELL	31518-31518	BRISTOL
30560-30560	MORGANTON	30739-30739	ROCK SPRING	31046-31046	JULIETTE	31519-31519	BROXTON
30562-30562	MOUNTAIN CITY	30740-30740	ROCKY FACE	31047-31047	KATHLEEN	31520-31521	BRUNSWICK
30563-30563	MOUNT AIRY	30741-30741	ROSSVILLE	31049-31049	KITE	31522-31522	SAINT SIMONS ISLAND
30564-30564	MURRAYVILLE	30742-30742	FORT OGLETHORPE	31050-31050	KNOXVILLE	31523-31525	BRUNSWICK
30565-30565	NICHOLSON	30746-30746	SUGAR VALLEY	31051-31051	LILLY	31527-31527	JEKYLL ISLAND
30566-30566	OAKWOOD	30747-30747	SUMMERVILLE	31052-31052	LIZELLA	31532-31532	DENTON
30567-30567	PENDERGRASS	30750-30750	LOOKOUT MOUNTAIN	31054-31054	MC INTYRE	31533-31535	DOUGLAS
30568-30568	RABUN GAP	30751-30751	TENNGA	31055-31055	MC RAE	31537-31537	FOLKSTON
30571-30571	SAUTEE NACOOCHEE	30752-30752	TRENTON	31057-31057	MARSHALLVILLE	31539-31539	HAZLEHURST
30572-30572	SUCHES	30753-30753	TRION	31058-31058	MAUK	31542-31542	HOBOKEN
30573-30573	TALLULAH FALLS	30755-30755	TUNNEL HILL	31060-31060	MILAN	31543-31543	HORTENSE
30575-30575	TALMO	30756-30756	VARNELL	31061-31062	MILLEDGEVILLE	31544-31544	JACKSONVILLE
30576-30576	TIGER	30757-30757	WILDWOOD	31063-31063	MONTEZUMA	31545-31546	JESUP
30577-30577	TOCCOA	30802-30802	APPLING	31064-31064	MONTICELLO	31547-31547	KINGS BAY
30580-30580	TURNERVILLE	30803-30803	AVERA	31065-31065	MONTROSE	31548-31548	KINGSLAND
30581-30581	WILEY	30805-30805	BLYTHE	31066-31066	MUSELLA	31549-31549	LUMBER CITY
30582-30582	YOUNG HARRIS	30806-30806	BONEVILLE	31067-31067	OCONEE	31550-31550	MANOR
30596-30596	ALTO	30807-30807	CAMAK	31068-31068	OGLETHORPE	31551-31551	MERSHON
30597-30597	DAHLONEGA	30808-30808	DEARING	31069-31069	PERRY	31552-31552	MILLWOOD
30598-30598	TOCCOA	30809-30809	EVANS	31070-31070	PINEHURST	31553-31553	NAHUNTA
30599-30599	COMMERCE	30810-30810	GIBSON	31071-31071	PINEVIEW	31554-31554	NICHOLLS
30601-30613	ATHENS	30811-30811	GOUGH	31072-31072	PITTS	31555-31555	ODUM
30619-30619	ARNOLDSVILLE	30812-30812	GRACEWOOD	31073-31073	PLAINFIELD	31556-31556	OFFERMAN
30620-30620	BETHLEHEM	30813-30813	GROVETOWN	31075-31075	RENTZ	31557-31557	PATTERSON
30621-30621	BISHOP	30814-30814	HARLEM	31076-31076	REYNOLDS	31558-31558	SAINT MARYS
30622-30622	BOGART	30815-30815	HEPHZIBAH	31077-31077	RHINE	31560-31560	SCREVEN
30623-30623	BOSTWICK	30816-30816	KEYSVILLE	31078-31078	ROBERTA	31561-31561	SEA ISLAND
30624-30624	BOWMAN	30817-30817	LINCOLNTON	31079-31079	ROCHELLE	31563-31563	SURRENCY
30625-30625	BUCKHEAD	30818-30818	MATTHEWS	31081-31081	RUPERT	31564-31564	WARESBORO
30627-30627	CARLTON	30819-30819	MESENA	31082-31082	SANDERSVILLE	31565-31565	WAVERLY
30628-30628	COLBERT	30820-30820	MITCHELL	31083-31083	SCOTLAND	31566-31566	WAYNESVILLE
30629-30629	COMER	30821-30821	NORWOOD	31084-31084	SEVILLE	31567-31567	WEST GREEN
30630-30630	CRAWFORD	30822-30822	PERKINS	31085-31085	SHADY DALE	31568-31568	WHITE OAK
30631-30631	CRAWFORDVILLE	30823-30823	STAPLETON	31086-31086	SMARR	31569-31569	WOODBINE
30633-30633	DANIELSVILLE	30824-30824	THOMSON	31087-31087	SPARTA	31598-31599	JESUP
30634-30634	DEWY ROSE	30828-30828	WARRENTON	31088-31088	WARNER ROBINS	31601-31606	VALDOSTA
30635-30635	ELBERTON	30830-30830	WAYNESBORO	31089-31089	TENNILLE	31620-31620	ADEL
30638-30638	FARMINGTON	30833-30833	WRENS	31090-31090	TOOMSBORO	31622-31622	ALAPAHA
30639-30639	FRANKLIN SPRINGS	30901-30999	AUGUSTA	31091-31091	UNADILLA	31623-31623	ARGYLE
30641-30641	GOOD HOPE	31001-31001	ABBEVILLE	31092-31092	VIENNA	31624-31624	AXSON
30642-30642	GREENSBORO	31002-31002	ADRIAN	31093-31093	WARNER ROBINS	31625-31625	BARNEY
30643-30643	HARTWELL	31003-31003	ALLENTOWN	31094-31094	WARTHEN	31626-31626	BOSTON
30645-30645	HIGH SHOALS	31004-31004	BOLINGBROKE	31095-31095	WARNER ROBINS	31627-31627	CECIL
30646-30646	HULL	31005-31005	BONAIRE	31096-31096	WRIGHTSVILLE	31629-31629	DIXIE
30647-30647	ILA	31006-31006	BUTLER	31097-31097	YATESVILLE	31630-31630	DU PONT
30648-30648	LEXINGTON	31007-31007	BYROMVILLE	31098-31099	WARNER ROBINS	31631-31631	FARGO
30650-30650	MADISON	31008-31008	BYRON	31106-31199	ATLANTA	31632-31632	HAHIRA
30655-30656	MONROE	31009-31009	CADWELL	31201-31299	MACON	31634-31634	HOMERVILLE
30660-30660	RAYLE	31010-31010	CORDELE	31301-31301	ALLENHURST	31635-31635	LAKELAND
30662-30662	ROYSTON	31011-31011	CHAUNCEY	31302-31302	BLOOMINGDALE	31636-31636	LAKE PARK
30663-30663	RUTLEDGE	31012-31012	CHESTER	31303-31303	CLYO	31637-31637	LENOX
30664-30664	SHARON	31013-31013	CLINCHFIELD	31304-31304	CRESCENT	31638-31638	MORVEN
30665-30665	SILOAM	31014-31014	COCHRAN	31305-31305	DARIEN	31639-31639	NASHVILLE
30666-30666	STATHAM	31015-31015	CORDELE	31307-31307	EDEN	31641-31641	NAYLOR
30667-30667	STEPHENS	31016-31016	CULLODEN	31308-31308	ELLABELL	31642-31642	PEARSON
30668-30668	TIGNALL	31017-31017	DANVILLE	31309-31309	FLEMING	31643-31643	QUITMAN
30669-30669	UNION POINT	31018-31018	DAVISBORO	31310-31310	HINESVILLE	31645-31645	RAY CITY
30671-30671	MAXEYS	31019-31019	DEXTER	31312-31312	GUYTON	31646-31646	SAINT GEORGE
30673-30673	WASHINGTON	31020-31020	DRY BRANCH	31313-31313	HINESVILLE	31647-31647	SPARKS
30677-30677	WATKINSVILLE	31021-31021	DUBLIN	31314-31315	FORT STEWART	31648-31648	STATENVILLE
30678-30678	WHITE PLAINS	31022-31022	DUDLEY	31316-31316	LUDOWICI	31649-31649	STOCKTON
30680-30680	WINDER	31023-31023	EASTMAN	31318-31318	MELDRIM	31650-31650	WILLACOOCHEE
30683-30683	WINTERVILLE	31024-31024	EATONTON	31319-31319	MERIDIAN	31698-31699	VALDOSTA
30701-30703	CALHOUN	31025-31025	ELKO	31320-31320	MIDWAY	31701-31708	ALBANY
30705-30705	CHATSWORTH	31027-31027	DUBLIN	31321-31321	PEMBROKE	31709-31710	AMERICUS
30707-30707	CHICKAMAUGA	31028-31028	CENTERVILLE	31322-31322	POOLER	31711-31711	ANDERSONVILLE
30708-30708	CISCO	31029-31029	FORSYTH	31323-31323	RICEBORO	31712-31712	ARABI
30710-30710	COHUTTA	31030-31030	FORT VALLEY	31324-31324	RICHMOND HILL	31713-31713	ARLINGTON
30711-30711	CRANDALL	31031-31031	GORDON	31326-31326	RINCON	31714-31714	ASHBURN
30719-30722	DALTON	31032-31032	GRAY	31327-31327	SAPELO ISLAND	31715-31715	ATTAPULGUS
30724-30724	ETON	31033-31033	HADDOCK	31328-31328	TYBEE ISLAND	31716-31716	BACONTON
30725-30725	FLINTSTONE	31034-31034	HARDWICK	31329-31329	SPRINGFIELD	31717-31718	BAINBRIDGE
30726-30726	GRAYSVILLE	31035-31035	HARRISON	31331-31331	TOWNSEND	31720-31720	BARWICK
30728-30728	LA FAYETTE	31036-31036	HAWKINSVILLE	31332-31332	VALONA	31722-31722	BERLIN
30730-30730	LYERLY	31037-31037	HELENA	31333-31333	WALTHOURVILLE	31723-31723	BLAKELY
30731-30731	MENLO	31038-31038	HILLSBORO	31401-31499	SAVANNAH	31724-31724	BLUFFTON
30732-30732	OAKMAN	31039-31039	HOWARD	31501-31503	WAYCROSS	31725-31725	BRINSON
30733-30733	PLAINVILLE	31040-31040	DUBLIN	31510-31510	ALMA	31726-31726	BRONWOOD
30734-30734	RANGER	31041-31041	IDEAL	31512-31512	AMBROSE	31727-31727	BROOKFIELD

31728-31728	CAIRO	31756-31756	HARTSFIELD	31782-31782	PUTNEY	31812-31812	JUNCTION CITY
31729-31729	CALVARY	31757-31758	THOMASVILLE	31783-31783	REBECCA	31814-31814	LOUVALE
31730-31730	CAMILLA	31759-31759	IRON CITY	31784-31784	SALE CITY	31815-31815	LUMPKIN
31732-31732	CEDAR SPRINGS	31760-31760	IRWINVILLE	31785-31785	SASSER	31816-31816	MANCHESTER
31733-31733	CHULA	31761-31761	JAKIN	31786-31786	SHELLMAN	31820-31820	MIDLAND
31734-31734	CLIMAX	31762-31762	LEARY	31787-31787	SMITHVILLE	31821-31821	OMAHA
31735-31735	COBB	31763-31763	LEESBURG	31789-31789	SUMNER	31822-31822	PINE MOUNTAIN
31736-31736	COLEMAN	31764-31764	LESLIE	31790-31790	SYCAMORE	31823-31823	PINE MOUNTAIN VALLEY
31737-31737	COLQUITT	31765-31765	MEIGS	31791-31791	SYLVESTER	31824-31824	PRESTON
31738-31738	COOLIDGE	31766-31766	MORGAN	31792-31792	THOMASVILLE	31825-31825	RICHLAND
31739-31739	COTTON	31767-31767	MORRIS	31793-31794	TIFTON	31826-31826	SHILOH
31740-31740	CUTHBERT	31768-31768	MOULTRIE	31795-31795	TY TY	31827-31827	TALBOTTON
31741-31741	DAMASCUS	31769-31769	MYSTIC	31796-31796	WARWICK	31829-31829	UPATOI
31742-31742	DAWSON	31770-31770	NEWTON	31797-31797	WHIGHAM	31830-31830	WARM SPRINGS
31743-31743	DE SOTO	31771-31771	NORMAN PARK	31798-31798	WRAY	31831-31831	WAVERLY HALL
31744-31744	DOERUN	31772-31772	OAKFIELD	31799-31799	THOMASVILLE	31832-31832	WESTON
31745-31745	DONALSONVILLE	31773-31773	OCHLOCKNEE	31801-31801	BOX SPRINGS	31833-31833	WEST POINT
31746-31746	EDISON	31774-31774	OCILLA	31803-31803	BUENA VISTA	31836-31836	WOODLAND
31747-31747	ELLENTON	31775-31775	OMEGA	31804-31804	CATAULA	31901-31904	COLUMBUS
31749-31749	ENIGMA	31776-31776	MOULTRIE	31805-31805	CUSSETA	31905-31905	FORT BENNING
31750-31750	FITZGERALD	31777-31777	PARROTT	31806-31806	ELLAVILLE	31906-31994	COLUMBUS
31751-31751	FORT GAINES	31778-31778	PAVO	31807-31807	ELLERSLIE	31995-31995	FORT BENNING
31752-31752	FOWLSTOWN	31779-31779	PELHAM	31808-31808	FORTSON	31997-31999	COLUMBUS
31753-31753	FUNSTON	31780-31780	PLAINS	31810-31810	GENEVA	39901-39901	ATLANTA
31754-31754	GEORGETOWN	31781-31781	POULAN	31811-31811	HAMILTON		

Hawaii

General Help Numbers:

Governor's Office
State Capitol
415 S Beretania St
Honolulu, HI 96813
http://gov.state.hi.us

808-586-0034
Fax 808-586-0006
7:45AM-5PM

Attorney General's Office
425 Queen St
Honolulu, HI 96813
http://www.state.hi.us/ag

808-586-1500
Fax 808-586-1239
7:45AM-4:30PM

State Court Administrator
417 S. King St
Honolulu, HI 96813
http://www.state.hi.us/jud

808-539-4900
Fax 808-539-4855
7:45AM-4:30PM

State Archives
Iolani Palace Grounds
Honolulu, HI 96813
http://www.state.hi.us/dags/archives

808-586-0329
Fax 808-586-0330
9AM-4PM

State Specifics:

Capital:

Honolulu
Honolulu County

Time Zone:

HT (Hawaii Standard Time)

Number of Counties:

4

Population:

1,211,537

Web Site:

www.state.hi.us

State Agencies

Criminal Records

Hawaii Criminal Justice Data Center, Liane Moriyama, Administrator, 465 S King St, Room 101, Honolulu, HI 96813; 808-587-3106, 8AM-4PM.

http://www.state.hi.us/hcjdc

Indexing & Storage: Records are available from the 1930's. Records are indexed on inhouse computer.

Searching: They will release only convictions and public sex offender information--arrests without dispositions are not released. Sex offender data is available online at www.ehawaiigov.org/HI_SOR.

Include the following in your request-any aliases, date of birth, Social Security Number.

Access by: mail, in person.

Fee & Payment: The search fee for a name-based criminal record search is $15.00. A fingerprint-based search is $25.00. A public access (convictions only) printout, available only in-person at this office or at main police stations, is $10.00. Fee payee: Hawaii Criminal Justice Data Center. Prepayment required. Money orders and cashiers' checks are the only acceptable methods of payment. No credit cards accepted.

Mail search: Turnaround time: 7 to 10 days. A self addressed stamped envelope is requested.

In person search: The public may access conviction information by computer on-site. Name, SSN, and gender are required. Date of birth is optional. If SSN is unavailable, the staff will do the search.

Corporation Records
Fictitious Name
Limited Partnership Records
Assumed Name
Trademarks/Servicemarks
Limited Liability Company Records
Limited Liability Partnerships

Business Registration Division, PO Box 40, Honolulu, HI 96810 (Courier: 1010 Richard St, 1st Floor, Honolulu, HI 96813); 808-586-2727, 808-586-2733 (Fax), 7:45AM-4:30PM.

http://www.businessregistrations.com

Indexing & Storage: Records are available for active companies only. Inactive companies are archived. New records are available for inquiry immediately. Records are indexed on microfiche, hard copy.

Searching: There are no access restrictions. Records are open to the public. Include the following in your request-full name of business. In addition to the articles of incorporation, corporation records include the following information: Annual Reports, Officers, Directors, DBAs, Prior (merged) names, Inactive and Reserved names.

Access by: mail, phone, fax, in person, online.

Fee & Payment: The copy fee is $.25 per page. There is no search fee. Fee payee: Business Registration Division. Prepayment required. Personal checks accepted. No credit cards accepted.

Mail search: Turnaround time: 2 weeks. A self addressed stamped envelope is requested. No fee for mail request.

Phone search: No fee for telephone request. They will confirm data over the phone or let you know how many copies to prepay.

Fax search: Same criteria as mail searches.

In person search: No fee for request. Turnaround time is while you wait.

Online search: Online access is available through the Internet or via modem dial-up at 808-587-4800. There are no fees, the system is open 24 hours. For assistance during business hours, call 808-586-1919. Also, business names searching is available free online at www.ehawaiigov.com. Tax license searching is available free at www.ehawaiigov.org/serv/taxpayer. Search by name, ID number of DBA name.

Uniform Commercial Code
Federal Tax Liens
State Tax Liens

UCC Division, Bureau of Conveyances, PO Box 2867, Honolulu, HI 96803 (Courier: Dept. of Land & Natural Resources, 1151 Punchbowl St, Honolulu, HI 96813); 808-587-0154, 808-587-0136 (Fax), 7:45AM-4:30PM.

http://www.hawaii.gov/dlnr/bc/bc.html

Indexing & Storage: Records are available from 1845. Records are on microfiche from 1976 to present. It takes 1 day before new records are available for inquiry.

Searching: Use search request form UCC-3. Include the following in your request-debtor name.

A UCC record does not include tax liens; a separate search is required.

Access by: mail, in person.

Fee & Payment: Fees are $25.00 per debtor name plus $5.00 for each financing statement and statement of assignment reported. Copies cost $1.00 per page. Fee payee: Bureau of Conveyances. Prepayment required. An initial fee of $25.00 must be paid in advance, additional fees will be invoiced. Personal checks accepted. No credit cards accepted.

Mail search: Turnaround time: 1 week. A self addressed stamped envelope is requested.

In person search: There is self-service in the public reference room.

Sales Tax Registrations
State does not impose sales tax.

Birth Certificates

State Department of Health, Vital Records Section, PO Box 3378, Honolulu, HI 96801 (Courier: 1250 Punchbowl St, Room 103, Honolulu, HI 96813); 808-586-4533, 808-586-4606 (Fax), 7:45AM-2:30PM.

http://www.hawaii.gov/doh

Indexing & Storage: Records are available from mid 1800's to present. New records are available for inquiry immediately. Records are indexed on microfilm, inhouse computer.

Searching: Must have a signed release form from person of record or immediate family member. Include the following in your request-full name, names of parents, mother's maiden name, date of birth, place of birth, relationship to person of record, reason for information request. Include a daytime phone number in your request. The Vital Records office will call you collect to verify information, if required. If your record is prior to July, 1909, you must know the island of event.

Access by: mail, in person.

Fee & Payment: Fees are $10.00 for first copy and $4.00 for each subsequent copy of same record. Fee payee: State Department of Health. Prepayment required. Money orders, certified checks, and cashier's checks are accepted. No credit cards accepted.

Mail search: Turnaround time: 4 to 6 weeks. No self addressed stamped envelope is required.

In person search: Turnaround time is 10 days or more.

Expedited service: Expedited service is available for mail and phone searches. You must send a pre-paid envelope going to requester.

Death Records

State Department of Health, Vital Records Section, PO Box 3378, Honolulu, HI 96801 (Courier: 1250 Punchbowl St, Room 103, Honolulu, HI 96813); 808-586-4533, 808-586-4606 (Fax), 7:45AM-2:30PM.

http://www.hawaii.gov/doh

Indexing & Storage: Records are available from mid 1800's on, but early records are not complete. New records are available for inquiry immediately. Records are indexed on microfilm, inhouse computer.

Searching: Must have a signed release form from immediate family member. Include the following in your request-full name, date of death, place of death, names of parents, relationship to person of record, reason for information request. Include a daytime phone number in your request. The agency may call you collect to verify information, if required. For records prior to July 1909, you must include the island of the event.

Access by: mail, in person.

Fee & Payment: The fee is $10.00 per record and $4.00 for each subsequent copy of same record. Fee payee: State Department of Health. Prepayment required. Cashier's checks and money orders accepted. No credit cards accepted.

Mail search: Turnaround time: 4 to 6 weeks.

In person search: Turnaround time is 10 days or more.

Marriage Certificates

State Department of Health, Vital Records Section, PO Box 3378, Honolulu, HI 96801 (Courier: 1250 Punchbowl St, Room 103, Honolulu, HI 96813); 808-586-4533, 808-586-4606 (Fax), 7:45AM-2:30PM.

http://www.hawaii.gov/doh

Indexing & Storage: Records are available from mid 1800's to present. New records are available for inquiry immediately. Records are indexed on microfilm, inhouse computer.

Searching: Must have a signed release form from person of record or immediate family member. Include the following in your request-names of husband and wife, wife's maiden name, date of marriage, place or county of marriage, names of parents, relationship to person of record, reason for information request. Include a daytime phone number. The office will call you collect to verify information, if required. For records prior to July 1909, include the island of the event.

Access by: mail, in person.

Fee & Payment: Fee is $10.00 per record and $4.00 for subsequent copy of same record. Fee payee: State Department of Health. Prepayment required. Cashier's check and money orders accepted. No credit cards accepted.

Mail search: Turnaround time: 4 to 6 weeks. No self addressed stamped envelope is required.

In person search: Turnaround time is 10 days or less.

Divorce Records

State Department of Health, Vital Records Section, PO Box 3378, Honolulu, HI 96801 (Courier: 1250 Punchbowl St, Room 103, Honolulu, HI 96813); 808-586-4533, 808-586-4606 (Fax), 7:45AM-2:30PM.

http://www.hawaii.gov/health

Indexing & Storage: Records are available from July 1951 to present. Prior records are held by the clerk of the court granting the decree. New records are available for inquiry immediately. Records are indexed on microfilm, inhouse computer.

Searching: Must have a signed release form from person of record or immediate family member. Include the following in your request-names of husband and wife, date of divorce, place of divorce, relationship to person of record, reason for information request. Include a daytime phone number in your request. This office will call you collect to verify information, if required.

Access by: mail, in person.

Fee & Payment: The fee is $10.00 per record and $4.00 each additional copy of same record. Fee payee: State Department of Health. Prepayment required. Cashier's check and money orders accepted. No credit cards accepted.

Mail search: Turnaround time: 4 to 6 weeks.

In person search: Results are mailed. Turnaround time is same day only if documented emergency.

Workers' Compensation Records

Labor & Industrial Relations, Disability Compensation Division, 830 Punchbowl St, Room 209, Honolulu, HI 96813; 808-586-9174, 808-586-9219 (Fax), 7:45AM-4:30PM.

Indexing & Storage: Records are available for the past 8 years. Prior records are in the State Archives but still must be requested through the Disability Compensation Division. It takes 2 to 4 days from receipt before new records are available for inquiry. Records are indexed on inhouse computer.

Searching: Must have a signed release from injured party or HI circuit court order signed by a judge. Include the following in your request-claimant name, Social Security Number, claim number.

Access by: mail, fax, in person.

Fee & Payment: There is no search fee, copy fee is $.05 per page. Fee payee: Director of Finance. Prepayment required. Personal checks accepted. No credit cards accepted.

Mail search: Turnaround time: 6 to 12 weeks. A self addressed stamped envelope is requested.

Fax search: Same criteria as mail searches.

In person search: In-person requests only saves mail time; results are mailed.

Driver Records

Traffic Violations Bureau, Abstract Section, 1111 Alakea St, Honolulu, HI 96813; 808-538-5560, 7:45AM-9:PM.

http://www.state.hi.us/jud

Note: The Bureau furnishes the record abstracts, but the 4 counties have the responsibility of gathering the records. Copies of tickets are only available from the court where ticket was issued. The fees are $1.00 for first copy, $.50 each additional copy.

Indexing & Storage: Records are available for three years for moving violations, five years for no-faults, and ten years for DUIs. Accidents are only listed if a citation is issued for the accident. The driver's address is screened from the record.

Searching: Casual requesters can obtain records; however, personal information is not released. The driver's full name, DOB and either license number or SSN are needed when ordering.

Access by: mail, in person.

Fee & Payment: The fee is $7.00 per request. There is a full charge even if no record is found. Fee payee: TVB. Prepayment required. The state requires a money order or cashier's check for mail-

in requests; in-person requesters may use cash, credit cards, personal or business checks.

Mail search: Turnaround time: 2 to 3 weeks. A self addressed stamped envelope is requested.

In person search: Walk-in requests can be processed in five to twenty minutes at any District Traffic Court or Traffic Violations Bureau Office.

Other access: Magnetic tape ordering is available in Hawaii for frequent or large orders. The fee is $7.00 per request. Turnaround time is 48 hours.

Accident Reports
Records not maintained by a state level agency.

Note: Accident reports are not available from the state. Records are maintained at the county level at the police departments and only available to those involved.

Vehicle Ownership
Vehicle Identification
Access to Records is Restricted.

Vessel Ownership
Vessel Registration

Land & Natural Resources, Division of Boating & Recreation, 333 Queen St Rm 300, Honolulu, HI 96813; 808-587-1970, 808-587-1977 (Fax), 7:45AM-4:30PM.

http://www.hawaii.gov/dlnr/dbor/dbor.html

Indexing & Storage: Records are available 1950s, computerized since 1994, and on microfiche from 1987 to 1994.

Searching: Requests must be made in writing and must include a statement revealing the purpose for which the information will be used. Name or hull id number or registration number is required for search. The following data is not released: addresses or phone numbers.

Access by: mail, fax, in person.

Fee & Payment: There is no search fee.

Mail search: Turnaround time: 1 to 2 days. No self addressed stamped envelope is required.

Fax search: Same criteria as mail searching.

In person search: Turnaround time is usually the same day.

Legislation Records

Hawaii Legislature, 415 S Beretania St, Honolulu, HI 96813; 808-587-0700 (Bill # and Location), 808-586-6720 (Clerk's Office-Senate), 808-586-6400 (Clerk's Office-House), 808-586-0690 (State Library), 808-587-0720 (Fax), 7AM-6PM.

http://www.capitol.hawaii.gov

Indexing & Storage: Records are available from 1983 to present. Records are indexed on inhouse computer.

Searching: Include the following in your request-bill number, year. Call the first phone number to get bill number and location of bill. Older bills are stored at the State Archives, 808-586-0329. Any

bills that have become Acts can also be found at the library.

Access by: phone, in person, online.

Fee & Payment: There is no search fee nor a copy fee, unless extensive request is made. Records are available by mail.

Phone search: General information is available over the phone, copies can be requested.

Online search: To dial online for current year bill information line, call 808-296-4636. Or, access the information through the Internet site. There is no fee, the system is up 24 hours.

Voter Registration
Records not maintained by a state level agency.

Note: Voter information is maintained by the County Clerks.

GED Certificates

Department of Education, GED Records, 634 Pensacola, #222, Honolulu, HI 96814; 808-594-0170, 808-594-0181 (Fax), 8AM-5PM.

Note: GED certificates are not issued by this agency. Instead, high school diplomas are issued to qualified individuals.

Searching: Include the following in your request-signed release, date of birth, Social Security Number. Knowing the approximate date and location of the test is helpful. The requirements are for both verifications and copies of transcripts.

Access by: mail, fax, in person.

Fee & Payment: Fees are not normally charged unless extensive search time involved. Certain fees will vary, depending on the record location site.

Mail search: Turnaround time: 5 to 10 days. A self addressed stamped envelope is required.

Fax search: Same criteria as mail searching.

In person search: Same criteria as mail searching.

Hunting License Information
Fishing License Information
Access to Records is Restricted

Land & Natural Resources Department, 1151 Punchbowl St, Kalanimokui Bldg, Honolulu, HI 96813; 808-587-0100 (Fishing), 808-587-0166 (Hunting), 808-587-0115 (Fax), 7:45AM-4:30PM.

www.state.hi.us/dlnr

Note: Fishing information is kept by the Aquatic Resources Division; Hunting information by the Division of Forestry & Wildlife. Limited record information is released to the public. Generally, this department's information is only released to law enforcement agencies. There is no "search engine" here.

Hawaii State Licensing Agencies

Licenses Searchable Online

Acupuncturist #04..www.ehawaiigov.org/serv/pvl
Architect #19 ....www.ehawaiigov.org/serv/pvl
Auction #42 ....www.ehawaiigov.org/serv/pvl
Barber Shop #05...www.ehawaiigov.org/serv/pvl
Barber/Barber Apprentice #05 ....www.ehawaiigov.org/serv/pvl
Beauty Operator #05..www.ehawaiigov.org/serv/pvl
Cemetery #42 ....www.ehawaiigov.org/serv/pvl
Chiropractor #06..www.ehawaiigov.org/serv/pvl
Collection Agency #42 ....www.ehawaiigov.org/serv/pvl
Condominium Hotel Operator #34.........................www.ehawaiigov.org/serv/pvl
Condominium Managing Agent #34 ....www.ehawaiigov.org/serv/pvl
Contractor #27...www.ehawaiigov.org/serv/pvl
Contractor, General #33 ....www.ehawaiigov.org/serv/pvl
Dental Hygienist #07..www.ehawaiigov.org/serv/pvl
Dentist #07 ....www.ehawaiigov.org/serv/pvl
Electrician #29...www.ehawaiigov.org/serv/pvl
Electrologist #42..www.ehawaiigov.org/serv/pvl
Elevator Mechanic #29...www.ehawaiigov.org/serv/pvl
Emergency Medical Personnel #13 ....www.ehawaiigov.org/serv/pvl
Employment Agency #42......................................www.ehawaiigov.org/serv/pvl
Engineer #19 ....www.ehawaiigov.org/serv/pvl
Hearing Aid Dealer/Fitter #30..............................www.ehawaiigov.org/serv/pvl
Insurance Adjuster #31..www.ehawaiigov.org/serv/hils
Insurance Agent/Solicitor #31 ....www.ehawaiigov.org/serv/hils
Land Surveyor #42 ....www.ehawaiigov.org/serv/pvl
Landscape Architect #19......................................www.ehawaiigov.org/serv/pvl
Lobbyist #41...www.state.hi.us/ethics/noindex/pubrec.htm
Marriage & Family Therapist #42 ....www.ehawaiigov.org/serv/pvl
Massage Therapist/Establishment #42..................www.ehawaiigov.org/serv/pvl
Mechanic #42 ....www.ehawaiigov.org/serv/pvl
Medical Doctor #13..www.ehawaiigov.org/serv/pvl
Mortgage Broker/Solicitor #42..............................www.ehawaiigov.org/serv/pvl
Motor Vehicle Dealer/Broker/Seller #42................www.ehawaiigov.org/serv/pvl
Motor Vehicle Repair Dealer #42..........................www.ehawaiigov.org/serv/pvl
Naturopathic Physician #10 ....www.ehawaiigov.org/serv/pvl
Nurse #14...www.ehawaiigov.org/serv/pvl
Nursing Home Administrator #12 ....www.ehawaiigov.org/serv/pvl
Occupational Therapist #17 ....www.ehawaiigov.org/serv/pvl
Optician, Dispensing #08.....................................www.ehawaiigov.org/serv/pvl
Optometrist #11...www.odfinder.org/LicSearch.asp
Osteopathic Physician #13...................................www.ehawaiigov.org/serv/pvl
Pest Control Field Rep./Operator #32...................www.ehawaiigov.org/serv/pvl
Pharmacist/Pharmacy #16....................................www.ehawaiigov.org/serv/pvl
Physical Therapist #17...www.ehawaiigov.org/serv/pvl
Physician Assistant #13..www.ehawaiigov.org/serv/pvl
Plumber #29..www.ehawaiigov.org/serv/pvl
Podiatrist #13 ....www.ehawaiigov.org/serv/pvl
Port Pilot #42..www.ehawaiigov.org/serv/pvl
Private Detective/Investigation Agency #18 ....www.ehawaiigov.org/serv/pvl
Psychologist #20 ....www.ehawaiigov.org/serv/pvl
Public Accountant-CPA #21..................................www.ehawaiigov.org/serv/pvl
Real Estate Broker/Salesperson #34 ....www.ehawaiigov.org/serv/pvl
Security Guard/Agency #18 ....www.ehawaiigov.org/serv/pvl
Social Worker #42 ....www.ehawaiigov.org/serv/pvl
Speech Pathologist/Audiologist #22 ....www.ehawaiigov.org/serv/pvl
Timeshare #42..www.ehawaiigov.org/serv/pvl
Travel Agency #42...www.ehawaiigov.org/serv/pvl
Veterinarian #23 ....www.ehawaiigov.org/serv/pvl

Licensing Quick Finder

Acupuncturist #04	808-586-3000
Airport-related Professions #37	808-836-6533
Architect #19	808-587-3222
Attorney #38	808-537-1868
Auction #42	808-586-2699
Bank #28	808-586-2820
Barber Shop #05	808-587-3222
Barber/Barber Apprentice #05	808-587-3222
Beauty Operator #05	808-586-2699
Boxer #24	808-586-2701
Boxing Physician #24	808-586-2701
Boxing Professional #24	808-586-2701
Cable Franchise #26	808-586-2620
Cemetery #42	808-586-2699
Chiropractor #06	808-586-3000
Clinical Lab Director #40	808-453-6653
Clinical Laboratory Cytotechnologist #40	808-453-6653
Clinical Laboratory Technician #40	808-453-6653
Clinical Laboratory Technologist/Specialist #40	808-453-6653
Collection Agency #42	808-586-2699
Condominium Hotel Operator #34	808-587-3222
Condominium Managing Agent #34	808-587-3222
Contractor #27	808-587-3222
Contractor, General #33	808-586-3000
Cosmetologist #05	808-587-3222
Credit Union #28	808-586-2820
Dental Hygienist #07	808-587-3222
Dentist #07	808-587-3222
Drug (Prescription) Dist./ Wholesale #16	808-586-3000
Educational Administrator #35	808-586-3420
Electrician #29	808-587-3295
Electrologist #42	808-586-2699
Elevator Mechanic #29	808-587-3295
Embalmer #43	808-586-8000
Emergency Medical Personnel #13	808-586-3000
Employment Agency #42	808-586-2699
Engineer #19	808-587-3222
Escrow Company #28	808-586-2820
Financial Services Loan Companies (depository & nondepository) #28	808-586-2820
Hearing Aid Dealer/Fitter #30	808-586-3000
Insurance Adjuster #31	808-586-2788
Insurance Agent #31	808-586-2788
Insurance Solicitor #31	808-586-2788
Investment Advisor/Representative #25	808-586-2730
Land Surveyor #42	808-586-2699
Landscape Architect #19	808-587-3222
Lobbyist #41	808-587-0460
Marine License, Commercial #36	808-587-0100
Marriage & Family Therapist #42	808-586-2693
Massage Therapist/Establishment #42	808-586-2699
Mechanic #42	808-586-2701
Medical Doctor #13	808-586-3000
Mortgage Broker/Solicitor #42	808-586-2709
Motor Vehicle Dealer/Broker/Seller #42	808-586-2699
Motor Vehicle Repair Dealer #42	808-586-2699
Naturopathic Physician #10	808-586-3000
Notary Public #03	808-586-1216
Nuclear Medicine Technologist #44	808-586-4700
Nurse #14	808-586-3000
Nurses' Aide #14	808-586-3000
Nursing Home Administrator #12	808-586-3000
Optician, Dispensing #08	808-586-3000
Optometrist #11	808-586-3000
Osteopathic Physician #13	808-586-3000
Pest Control Field Rep./Operator #32	808-587-3295
Pesticide Applicator #02	808-973-9409
Pesticide Applicator, Private #02	808-973-9424
Pesticide Dealer #02	808-973-9424
Pesticide Product #02	808-973-9414
Pharmacy/Pharmacist #16	808-586-3000
Pharmacy, Out-of-State #16	808-586-3000
Physical Therapist #17	808-586-3000
Physician Assistant #13	808-586-3000
Plumber #29	808-587-3295
Podiatrist #13	808-586-2708
Port Pilot #42	808-586-2699
Private Detective #18	808-586-3000
Private Detective/Investigation Agency #18	808-586-3000
Psychologist #20	808-586-3000
Public Accountant-CPA #21	808-586-3222
Radiation Therapist #44	808-586-4700
Radiographer #44	808-586-4700
Real Estate Appraiser #34	808-587-3222
Real Estate Broker/Salesperson #34	808-587-3222
Sanitarian #43	808-586-4576
Savings & Loan Association #28	808-586-2820
Savings Bank #28	808-586-2820
Securities Salesperson #25	808-586-2730
Security Guard/Agency #18	808-586-3000
Shorthand Reporter #01	808-539-4226
Social Worker #42	808-586-2696
Speech Pathologist/Audiologist #22	808-586-3000
Surveyor #19	808-587-3222
Tattoo Artist #43	808-586-8000
Taxi Driver #39	808-733-2540
Teacher #35	808-586-3392
Timeshare #42	808-586-2699
Travel Agency #42	808-586-2699
Trust Company #28	808-586-2820
Veterinarian #23	808-587-3222

Licensing Agency Information

#01 Board of Certified Shorthand Reporters, 777 Punchbowl St, Honolulu, HI 96813; 808-539-4226, Fax: 808-539-4149.

#02 Department of Agriculture, PO Box 22159, Honolulu, HI 96823-2159; 808-973-9401, Fax: 808-973-9410.
www.hawaiiag.org/hdoa

#03 Department of Attorney General, 425 Queen St, Honolulu, HI 96813; 808-586-1500, Fax: 808-586-1205.
www.state.hi.us/ag/notary/content.htm

#04 Department of Commerce & Consumer Affairs, PO Box 3469 (1010 Richards St, 96813), Honolulu, HI 96801; 808-586-2698.
www.state.hi.us/dcca/pvl/areas_acupuncture.html

#05 Department of Commerce & Consumer Affairs, PO Box 3469 (1010 Richards St, 96813), Honolulu, HI 96801; 808-586-3000.

#06 Department of Commerce & Consumer Affairs, PO Box 3469 (1010 Richards St, 96813), Honolulu, HI 96801; 808-586-3000.
www.state.hi.us/dcca/pvl

#07 Department of Commerce & Consumer Affairs, PO Box 3469 (1010 Richards St 96813), Honolulu, HI 96801; 808-586-3000.

#08 Department of Commerce & Consumer Affairs, PO Box 3469 (1010 Richards St, 96813), Honolulu, HI 96801; 808-586-2704, Fax: 808-586-3031.
www.state.hi.us/lrb/gd/gddoc.html

#10 Department of Commerce & Consumer Affairs, PO Box 3469 (1010 Richards St, 96813), Honolulu, HI 96801; 808-586-3000, Fax: 808-586-3031.
www.state.hi.us/dcca/dcca.html

#11 Department of Commerce & Consumer Affairs, PO Box 3469 (1010 Richards St, 96813), Honolulu, HI 96801; 808-586-2694.
Direct web site URL to search for licensees: www.odfinder.org/LicSearch.asp. You can search online using national database by name, city, or state

#12 Department of Commerce & Consumer Affairs, PO Box 3469 (1010 Richards St, 96813), Honolulu, HI 96801; 808-586-2695.
www.state.hi.us/dcca/pvl

#13 Department of Commerce & Consumer Affairs, PO Box 3469 (1010 Richards St, 96813), Honolulu, HI 96801; 808-586-3000.
www.state.hi.us/dcca/pvl

#14 Department of Commerce & Consumer Affairs, PO Box 3469 (1010 Richards St, 96813), Honolulu, HI 96801; 808-586-2695.

#16 Department of Commerce & Consumer Affairs, PO Box 3469 (1010 Richards St, 96813), Honolulu, HI 96801; 808-586-2694.
www.state.hi.us/dcca/dcca.html

#17 Department of Commerce & Consumer Affairs, PO Box 3469 (1010 Richards St, 96813), Honolulu, HI 96801; 808-586-2694.
www.state.hi.us/dcca/dcca.html

#18 Department of Commerce & Consumer Affairs, PO Box 3469 (1010 Richards St, 96813), Honolulu, HI 96801; 808-586-2701, Fax: 808-586-2589.
Direct web site URL to search for licensees: www.ehawaiigov.org/serv/pvl

#19 Department of Commerce & Consumer Affairs, PO Box 3469 (1010 Richards St, 96813), Honolulu, HI 96801; 808-586-3000.

#20 Department of Commerce & Consumer Affairs, PO Box 3469 (1010 Richards St, 96813), Honolulu, HI 96801; 808-586-2693.

#21 Department of Commerce & Consumer Affairs, PO Box 3469 (1010 Richards St, 96813), Honolulu, HI 96801; 808-586-2696, Fax: 808-586-2689.
www.state.hi.us/dcca/divisions.html

#22 Department of Commerce & Consumer Affairs, PO Box 3469 (1010 Richards St, 96813), Honolulu, HI 96801; 808-586-2698.

www.state.hi.us/dcca/pvl

#23 Department of Commerce & Consumer Affairs, PO Box 3469 (1010 Richards St, 96813), Honolulu, HI 96801; 808-586-3000.

#24 Department of Commerce & Consumer Affairs, PO Box 3469 (1010 Richards St, 96813), Honolulu, HI 96801; 808-586-2701, Fax: 808-586-2689.

#25 Department of Commerce & Consumer Affairs, Business Registration Division, PO Box 3469 (1010 Richards St, 96813), Honolulu, HI 96801; 808-586-2820, Fax: 808-586-2733.

#26 Department of Commerce & Consumer Affairs, PO Box 541, Honolulu, HI 96809; 808-586-2620, Fax: 808-586-2625.

#27 Department of Commerce & Consumer Affairs, PO Box 3469 (1010 Richards St, 96813), Honolulu, HI 96801; 808-586-2700, Fax: 808-586-3031.
www.state.hi.us/dcca

#28 Department of Commerce & Consumer Affairs, PO Box 2054, Honolulu, HI 96805; 808-586-2820, Fax: 808-586-2818.
www.state.hi.us/dcca/dfi

#29 Department of Commerce & Consumer Affairs, PO Box 3469 (1010 Richards St, 96813), Honolulu, HI 96801; 808-586-2705.
www.state.hi.us/dcca/ Online searching scheduled for late 2000.

#30 Department of Commerce & Consumer Affairs, PO Box 3469 (1010 Richards St, 96813), Honolulu, HI 96801; 808-586-2698.
www.state.hi.us/dcca/pvl

#31 Department of Commerce & Consumer Affairs, Insurance Division, 250 S King St, 5th Fl, Honolulu, HI 96813; 808-586-2790, Fax: 808-586-2806.
www.ehawaiigov.org
Direct web site URL to search for licensees: www.ehawaiigov.org/serv/hils. You can search online using license number, island, proper name, company name or trade name.

#32 Department of Commerce & Consumer Affairs, PO Box 3469, Honolulu, HI 96801; 808-586-2705.
www.state.hi.us/dcca/

#33 Department of Commerce & Consumer Affairs, PO Box 3469 (1010 Richards St, 96813), Honolulu, HI 96801; 808-586-3000.
www.state.hi.us/dcca/pvl

#34 Department of Commerce & Consumer Affairs, 250 S King St #702, Honolulu, HI 96813; 808-586-2643.
www.state.hi.us/hirec

#35 Department of Education, PO Box 2360, Honolulu, HI 96804; 808-586-3420, Fax: 808-586-3433.

#36 Department of Land & Natural Resources, 1151 Punch Bowl St Rm 330, Honolulu, HI 96813; 808-587-0100, Fax: 808-587-0115.

www.state.hi.us/dlnr/dar

#37 Department of Transportation, Airports Division, Honolulu Intl Airport, Honolulu, HI 96819-1897; 808-836-6533, Fax: 808-836-6682.
www.state.hi.us/dot/airports

#38 Bar Association, 1132 Bishop St #906, Honolulu, HI 96813-2814; 808-586-2660, Fax: 808-521-7936.

#39 Motor Vehicle Licensing Division, 1199 Dillingham St Rm A101, Honolulu, HI 96817; 808-532-7730.

#40 Department of Health, 2725 Waimano Home Rd, Pearl City, HI 96782; 808-453-6653, Fax: 808-453-6662.

#41 Ethics Commission, 1001 Bishop St, Pacific Tower #970, Honolulu, HI 96813; 808-587-0460, Fax: 808-587-0470.
www.state.hi.us/ethics
Direct web site URL to search for licensees: www.state.hi.us/ethics/noindex/pubrec.htm

#42 Department of Commerce & Consumer Affairs, 1010 Richards St, Honolulu, HI 96813; 808-586-2699.

#43 Department of Health, 591 Ala Moana Blvd, Honolulu, HI 96813; 808-586-8000, Fax: 808-586-4729.
www.hawaii.gov/doh

#44 Department of Health, 591 Ala Moana Blvd, Honolulu, HI 96813-4921; 808-586-4700.

Hawaii Federal Courts

The following list indicates the district and division name for each county in the state.

County/Court Cross Reference

Hawaii .... Honolulu
Honolulu .... Honolulu
Kalawao .... Honolulu
Kauai .... Honolulu
Maui .... Honolulu

US District Court

District of Hawaii

Honolulu Division 300 Ala Moana Blvd, Rm C-338, Honolulu, HI 96850 (Courier Address: Use mail address for courier delivery), 808-541-1300, Fax: 808-541-1303.

http://www.hid.uscourts.gov

Counties: All counties.

Indexing/Storage: Cases are indexed by defendant and plaintiff as well as by case number. New cases are available in the index immediately after filing date. Both computer and card indexes are maintained. A microfiche index is also maintained. Open records are located at this court.

Fee & Payment: The fee is $20.00 per item (one party name or case number). Payment may be made by money order, cashier check, personal check. Prepayment is required. Payee: Clerk, US District Court. Certification fee: $7.00 per document. Copy fee: $.50 per page.

Phone Search: Searching is not available by phone.

Mail Search: Always enclose a stamped self addressed envelope.

In Person: In person searching is available.

PACER: Sign-up number is 800-676-6856. Access fee is $.60 per minute. Local access: 808-541-1179. Case records are available back to October 1991. Records are never purged. New civil records are available online after 1 day. New criminal records are available online after 3 days. PACER is available online at http://pacer.hid.uscourts.gov.

US Bankruptcy Court

District of Hawaii

Honolulu Division 1132 Bishop St, Suite 250-L, Honolulu, HI 96813 (Courier Address: Use mail address for courier delivery), 808-522-8100.

http://www.hib.uscourts.gov

Counties: All counties.

Indexing/Storage: Cases are indexed by debtor as well as by case number. New cases are available in the index 24 hours after filing date. Both computer and card indexes are maintained. Open records are located at this court.

Fee & Payment: The fee is $20.00 per item (one party name or case number). Payment may be made by money order, cashier check, personal check. Prepayment is required. Debtor's checks are not accepted. Payee: US Bankruptcy Court. Certification fee: $7.00 per document. Copy fee: $.50 per page. You are allowed to make your own copies. These copies cost $.15 per page.

Phone Search: Only docket information is available by phone.

Mail Search: Always enclose a stamped self addressed envelope.

In Person: In person searching is available.

PACER: Sign-up number is 800-676-6856. Access fee is $.60 per minute. Toll-free access: 888-853-3766. Local access: 808-522-8118. Use of PC Anywhere v4.0 suggested. Case records are available back to 1987. Records are purged varies. New civil records are available online after 1 day.

Hawaii County Courts

Court	Jurisdiction	No. of Courts	How Organized
Circuit Courts*	General	4	4 Circuits
District Courts*	Limited	7	4 Circuits

* Profiled in this Sourcebook.

CIVIL									
Court	Tort	Contract	Real Estate	Min. Claim	Max. Claim	Small Claims	Estate	Eviction	Domestic Relations
Circuit Courts*	X	X	X	$5000/ $10,000	No Max		X		X
District Courts*	X	X	X	$0	$20,000	$2500		X	

CRIMINAL					
Court	Felony	Misdemeanor	DWI/DUI	Preliminary Hearing	Juvenile
Circuit Courts*	X	X	X		X
District Courts*		X	X	X	

ADMINISTRATION   Administrative Director of Courts, Judicial Branch, 417 S King St, Honolulu, HI, 96813; 808-539-4900, Fax: 808-539-4855. www.state.hi.us/jud

COURT STRUCTURE   Hawaii's trial level is comprised of Circuit Courts (with Family Courts) and District Courts. These trial courts function in four judicial circuits: First (Honolulu City/County), Second (Maui/Molokai/Lanai), Third (Hawaii County), and Fifth (Kauai/Niihau.) The Fourth Circuit was merged with the Third in 1943.

Circuit Courts are general jurisdiction and handle all jury trials, felony cases, and civil over $20,000, also probate and guardianship. The exception to to jury trial rule is DUI jury trial cases, which can be conducted in District Court. The District Court handles minor "felonies" (less then 1-yr sentence) and some civil cases up to $20,000, also landlord/tenant and DUI cases.

ONLINE ACCESS   Online access to Circuit Court and family court records first became available free in mid-2000 at http://state.hi.us/jud. Search by name or case number.

ADD'L INFORMATION   Most Hawaii state courts offer a public access terminal to search records at the courthouse.

Hawaii County

3rd Circuit Court Legal Documents Section
PO Box 1007, Hilo, HI 96721-1007; 808-961-7404; Fax: 808-961-7416. Hours: 7:45AM-4:30PM (HT). *Felony, Misdemeanor, Civil Actions Over $5,000, Probate.*

www.state.hi.us/jud/trials1.htm

Civil Records: Access: Mail, in person, online. Both court and visitors may perform in person searches. Search fee: $5.00 per name. Required to search: name, years to search. Civil cases indexed by defendant, plaintiff. Civil records on computer from 1988, index card system prior to 1988. Online access to Circuit Court and family court records is available free at http://166.122.201.51/hod/judstart.htm. Search by name or case number. Records go back to 1984.

Criminal Records: Access: Mail, in person, online. Both court and visitors may perform in person searches. Search fee: $5.00 per name. Required to search: name, years to search. Criminal records on computer from 1988, index card system prior to 1988. Online access to criminal records is the same as civil.

General Information: Public Access terminal is available. No adoption, juvenile, dependencies, confidential records released. SASE required. Turnaround time 2 days depending upon staff coverage. Copy fee: $1.00 for first page, $.50 each add'l. Certification fee: $2.00. Fee payee: Clerk, 3rd Circuit Court. Personal checks accepted. Prepayment is required.

District Court
PO Box 4879, Hilo, HI 96720; 808-961-7470; Fax: 808-961-7447. Hours: 7:45AM-4:30PM (HT). *Misdemeanor, Civil Actions Under $20,000, Eviction, Small Claims.*

www.state.hi.us/jud/trials3.htm

Civil Records: Access: Phone, fax, mail, in person. Only the court performs in person searches; visitors may not. Search fee: $5.00 per name. Required to search: name, years to search, case number; also helpful: address. Civil cases indexed by defendant. Civil records on ledgers from statehood.

Criminal Records: Access: Phone, fax, mail, in person. Only the court performs in person searches; visitors may not. No search fee. Required to search: name, years to search, case number; also helpful: address, DOB, SSN. Criminal records on computer since March 1996. Public access terminal available for criminal abstracts.

General Information: Public Access terminal is available. (Available for criminal abstract record only.) No family court records released. SASE requested. Turnaround time 1 week. Fax notes: $2.00 for first page, $1.00 each add'l. Extra fee for out of state faxing. Call for fee information. Copy fee: $1.00 for first page, $.50 each add'l. Off site storage- usual copy fees plus $5.00. Certification fee: $2.00. Fee payee: Clerk of the District Court. Personal checks accepted. Credit cards accepted: Visa, MasterCard.

Honolulu County

1st Circuit Court
Legal Documents Branch, 777 Punchbowl St, Honolulu, HI 96813; 808-539-4300; Fax: 808-539-4314. Hours: 7:45AM-4:30PM (HT). *Felony, Civil Actions Over $5,000, Probate, Family.*

www.state.hi.us/jud/trials1.htm

Civil Records: Access: Mail, in person, online. Both court and visitors may perform in person searches. Search fee: $5.00 per name. Required to search: name, years to search. Civil cases indexed by defendant, plaintiff. Civil records on computer from 1983, on microfiche and archived from 1900. Online access to Circuit Court & family court records is available free at

http://166.122.201.51/hod/judstart.htm. Search by name or case number. Records go back to 1984.
Criminal Records: Access: Mail, in person, online. Both court and visitors may perform in person searches. Search fee: $5.00 per name. Required to search: name, years to search, DOB; also helpful: SSN. Criminal records on computer from 1983, on microfiche and archived from 1900. Online access to criminal records is the same as civil.
General Information: Public Access terminal is available. No adoptions, paternity or sealed records released. SASE required. Turnaround time same day. Copy fee: $1.00 for first page, $.50 each add'l. Microfilm service fee $5.00; cost of copies $1.00 per page. Certification fee: $2.00. Fee payee: 1st Circuit Court. Business checks accepted. Prepayment is required.

District Court - Civil Division 1111 Alakea St, 3th Floor, Honolulu, HI 96813; 808-538-5151; Fax: 808-538-5444. Hours: 7:45AM-4:30PM (HT). *Civil Actions Under $20,000, Eviction, Small Claims.*

www.state.hi.us/jud/trials3.htm

Civil Records: Access: Phone, mail, in person. Both court and visitors may perform in person searches. Search fee: $5.00 per name. Required to search: name, years to search. Civil cases indexed by defendant. Civil records on computer from 1990; plaintiff index only on computer records. **General Information:** Public Access terminal is available. No sealed records released. SASE required. Turnaround time 1 week. Fax notes: Call for fax fee. Certification fee: No cert fee. Fee payee: District Court of the 1st Circuit. Personal checks accepted. Credit cards accepted: Visa, MasterCard, Discover. Prepayment is required.

District Court - Criminal Division 1111 Alakea St, 9th Floor Records, Honolulu, HI 96813; 808-538-5300 X1686; Fax: 808-538-5309. Hours: 7:45AM-4:30PM (HT). *Misdemeanor.*

www.state.hi.us/jud/trials3.htm

Criminal Records: Access: Fax, mail, in person. Only the court performs in person searches; visitors may not. Search fee: $5.00 per name. Required to search: name, years to search, SSN, signed release, aliases; also helpful: address, DOB.
General Information: No sealed records released. SASE required. Turnaround time 1 week. No copy fee. Certification fee: No cert fee. Fee payee: District Court of the 1st Circuit. Business checks accepted. Prepayment is required.

Kauai County

5th Circuit Court 3059 Umi St Rm #101, Lihue, HI 96766; 808-246-3300; Fax: 808-246-3310. Hours: 7:45AM-4:30PM (HT). *Felony, Misdemeanor, Civil Actions Over $10,000, Probate.*

www.state.hi.us/jud/trials1.htm

Civil Records: Access: Mail, in person, online. Both court and visitors may perform in person searches. Search fee: $5.00 per name. Required to search: name, years to search. Civil cases indexed by defendant. Civil records on computer from 1987, microfiche from 1960. Online access to Circuit Court & family court records is available free at http://166.122.201.51/hod/judstart.htm. Search by name or case number. Records go back to 1984.
Criminal Records: Access: Mail, in person, online. Both court and visitors may perform in person searches. Search fee: $5.00 per name. Required to search: name, years to search, DOB; also helpful: SSN. Criminal

records on computer from 1987, microfiche from 1960. Online access to criminal records is the same as civil.
General Information: Public Access terminal is available. No juvenile, dependencies records released. SASE required. Turnaround time 1 week. Copy fee: $1.00 for first page, $.50 each add'l. Certification fee: $2.00. Fee payee: 5th Circuit Court. Only cashiers checks and money orders accepted. Prepayment is required.

District Court of the 5th Circuit 3059 Umi St, Room 111, Lihue, HI 96766; 808-246-3330; Fax: 808-246-3309. Hours: 7:45AM-4:30PM (HT). *Misdemeanor.*

www.state.hi.us/jud/trials3.htm

Criminal Records: Access: Phone, fax, mail, in person. Only the court performs in person searches; visitors may not. Search fee: $15.00. Required to search: name, years to search, DOB; also helpful: SSN.
General Information: Fax notes: $2.00 for first page, $1.00 each add'l. Copy fee: $1.00 for first page, $.50 each add'l. Certification fee: $2.00.

District Court of the 5th Circuit 4357 Rice St, #101, Lihue, HI 96766; 808-246-3301; Fax: 808-241-7103. Hours: 7:45AM-4:30PM (HT). *Civil Actions Under $20,000, Eviction, Small Claims.*

www.state.hi.us/jud/trials3.htm

Civil Records: Access: Phone, fax, mail, in person. Both court and visitors may perform in person searches. Search fee: $5.00 per case. Required to search: name, years to search. Civil cases indexed by defendant. Civil records on index books. **General Information:** No juvenile records released. SASE requested. Turnaround time 1-7 days. Fax notes: $2.00 for first page, $1.00 each add'l. Copy fee: $1.00 for first page, $.50 each add'l. Certification fee: No cert fee. Fee payee: District Court of the Fifth Circuit. Personal checks accepted. In-state personal check accepted. No third party checks. Credit cards accepted: Visa, MasterCard. Credit cards accepted.

Maui County

2nd Circuit Court 2145 Main St, #106, Wailuku, HI 96793; 808-244-2929; Fax: 808-244-2932. Hours: 7:45AM-4:30PM (HT). *Felony, Misdemeanor, Civil Actions Over $5,000, Probate.*

www.state.hi.us/jud/trials1.htm

Note: This court also covers the counties of Lanai and Molokai.

Civil Records: Access: Mail, in person, online. Both court and visitors may perform in person searches. Search fee: $5.00 per name. Required to search: name, years to search. Civil cases indexed by defendant, plaintiff. Civil records on computer from 10/88, some prior on microfiche. Online access to Circuit Court & family court records is available free at http://166.122.201.51/hod/judstart.htm. Search by name or case number. Records go back to 1984.
Criminal Records: Access: Mail, in person, online. Both court and visitors may perform in person searches. Search fee: $5.00 per name. Required to search: name, years to search; also helpful: DOB, SSN. Criminal records on computer from 10/88, some prior on microfiche. Online access to criminal records is the same as civil.
General Information: Public Access terminal is available. No juvenile or paternity records released. SASE required. Turnaround time 1 week. Fax notes: Fee to fax results is $5.00 1st page, $2.00 each add'l in USA; $2.00 for first and $1.00 each add'l in Hawaii.

Copy fee: File marked pages are $1.00 per page; non-file marked are $.50. Certification fee: $2.00. Fee payee: Clerk, 2nd Circuit Court. Personal checks accepted. Prepayment is required.

Lanai District Court PO Box 631376, Lanai City, HI 96763; 808-565-6447. Hours: 7:45AM-4:30PM (HT). *Misdemeanor, Civil Actions Under $20,000, Eviction, Small Claims.*

www.state.hi.us/jud/trials3.htm

Civil Records: Access: Mail, in person. Only the court performs in person searches; visitors may not. Search fee: $5.00 per search. Required to search: name, years to search. Civil cases indexed by defendant, plaintiff. Civil records on index and docket books back to statehood.
Criminal Records: Access: Mail, in person. Only the court performs in person searches; visitors may not. Search fee: $5.00 per search. Required to search: name, years to search; also helpful: DOB, SSN. Criminal records on computer since 1980.
General Information: Turnaround time 2-3 weeks. Copy fee: $1.00 for first page, $.50 each add'l. Certification fee: $1.00. Fee payee: Lanai District Court. Personal checks accepted. Credit cards accepted: Visa, MasterCard. Prepayment is required.

Molokai District Court PO Box 284, Kaunaka-kai, HI 96748; 808-553-5451; Fax: 808-553-3374. Hours: 7:45AM-4PM (HT). *Misdemeanor, Civil Actions Under $20,000, Eviction, Small Claims.*

www.state.hi.us/jud/trials3.htm

Civil Records: Access: In person only. Only the court performs in person searches; visitors may not. Search fee: $5.00 per name. Required to search: name, years to search. Civil cases indexed by defendant, plaintiff. Civil records on index and docket books back to statehood.
Criminal Records: Access: In person only. Only the court performs in person searches; visitors may not. Search fee: $5.00 per name. Required to search: name, years to search; also helpful: address, DOB, SSN. Criminal records on computer since 1980.
General Information: No juvenile or paternity records released. Copy fee: $1.00 for first page, $.50 each add'l. Certification fee: $5.00. Fee payee: Molokai District Court. Business checks accepted. Prepayment is required.

Wailuku District Court 2145 Main St, Ste 137, Wailuku, HI 96793; 808-244-2800; Fax: 808-244-2849. Hours: 7:45AM-4:30PM (HT). *Misdemeanor, Civil Actions Under $20,000, Eviction, Small Claims.*

www.state.hi.us/jud/trials3.htm

Civil Records: Access: Fax, mail, in person. Only the court performs in person searches; visitors may not. Search fee: $5.00 per name. Required to search: name, years to search; also helpful: address. Civil cases indexed by defendant, plaintiff. Civil records on index and docket books.
Criminal Records: Access: Fax, mail, in person. Only the court performs in person searches; visitors may not. Search fee: $5.00 per name. Required to search: name, years to search, DOB; also helpful: address, SSN. Criminal records on computer since 1980.

General Information: SASE required. Turnaround time 2-3 weeks. Fax notes: $5.00 for first page, $2.00 each add'l. Within HI; $2.00 first page, $1.00 each add'l. Copy fee: $1.00 for first page, $.50 each add'l. Certification fee: No cert fee. Fee payee: District Court 2nd Circuit. Personal checks accepted. Credit cards accepted: Visa, MasterCard. Prepayment is required.

Hawaii Recording Offices

ORGANIZATION

All UCC financing statements, tax liens, and real estate documents are filed centrally with the Bureau of Conveyances located in Honolulu. The entire state is Hawaii Time Zone (HT).

Bureau of Conveyances

Bureau of Conveyances, P.O. Box 2867, Honolulu, HI 96803. 808-587-0154; Fax 808-587-0136.

Will search UCC records. Tax liens not included in UCC search. Will not search real estate records. **Online Access:** Property. Property records on the Honolulu Property Information database are available at http://caro.esri.com/honolulu/prperty.htm.

Hawaii County Locator

You will usually be able to find the city name in the City/County Cross Reference below. In that case, it is a simple matter to determine the county from the cross reference. However, only the official US Postal Service city names are included in this index. There are an additional 40,000 place names that people use in their addresses. Therefore, we have also included a ZIP/City Cross Reference immediately following the City/County Cross Reference.

If you know the ZIP Code but the city name does not appear in the City/County Cross Reference index, look up the ZIP Code in the ZIP/City Cross Reference, find the city name, then look up the city name in the City/County Cross Reference. For example, you want to know the county for an address of Menands, NY 12204. There is no "Menands" in the City/County Cross Reference. The ZIP/City Cross Reference shows that ZIP Codes 12201-12288 are for the city of Albany. Looking back in the City/County Cross Reference, Albany is in Albany County.

City/County Cross Reference

AIEA Honolulu	HONOMU Hawaii	KUALAPUU Maui	PAIA Maui
ANAHOLA Kauai	HOOLEHUA Maui	KULA Maui	PAPAALOA Hawaii
BARBERS POINT N A S Honolulu	KAAAWA Honolulu	KUNIA Honolulu	PAPAIKOU Hawaii
CAMP H M SMITH Honolulu	KAHUKU Honolulu	KURTISTOWN Hawaii	PEARL CITY Honolulu
CAPTAIN COOK Hawaii	KAHULUI Maui	LAHAINA Maui	PEARL HARBOR Honolulu
ELEELE Kauai	KAILUA Honolulu	LAIE Honolulu	PEPEEKEO Hawaii
EWA BEACH Honolulu	KAILUA KONA Hawaii	LANAI CITY Maui	PRINCEVILLE Kauai
FORT SHAFTER Honolulu	KALAHEO Kauai	LAUPAHOEHOE Hawaii	PUKALANI Maui
HAIKU Maui	KALAUPAPA Maui	LAWAI Kauai	PUUNENE Maui
HAKALAU Hawaii	KAMUELA Hawaii	LIHUE Kauai	SCHOFIELD BARRACKS Honolulu
HALEIWA Honolulu	KANEOHE Honolulu	M C B H KANEOHE BAY Honolulu	TRIPLER ARMY MEDICAL CTR Honolulu
HANA Maui	KAPAA Kauai	MAKAWAO Maui	VOLCANO Hawaii
HANALEI Kauai	KAPAAU Hawaii	MAKAWELI Kauai	WAHIAWA Honolulu
HANAMAULU Kauai	KAPOLEI Honolulu	MAUNALOA Maui	WAIALUA Honolulu
HANAPEPE Kauai	KAUMAKANI Kauai	MILILANI Honolulu	WAIANAE Honolulu
HAUULA Honolulu	KAUNAKAKAI Maui	MOUNTAIN VIEW Hawaii	WAIKOLOA Hawaii
HAWAII NATIONAL PARK Hawaii	KEAAU Hawaii	NAALEHU Hawaii	WAILUKU Maui
HAWI Hawaii	KEALAKEKUA Hawaii	NINOLE Hawaii	WAIMANALO Honolulu
HICKAM AFB Honolulu	KEALIA Kauai	OCEAN VIEW Hawaii	WAIMEA Kauai
HILO Hawaii	KEAUHOU Hawaii	OOKALA Hawaii	WAIPAHU Honolulu
HOLUALOA Hawaii	KEKAHA Kauai	PAAUHAU Hawaii	WAKE ISLAND Honolulu
HONAUNAU Hawaii	KIHEI Maui	PAAUILO Hawaii	WHEELER ARMY AIRFIELD Honolulu
HONOKAA Hawaii	KILAUEA Kauai	PAHALA Hawaii	
HONOLULU Honolulu	KOLOA Kauai	PAHOA Hawaii	

ZIP/City Cross Reference

96701-96701	AIEA	96731-96731	KAHUKU	96760-96760	KURTISTOWN	96785-96785	VOLCANO
96703-96703	ANAHOLA	96732-96733	KAHULUI	96761-96761	LAHAINA	96786-96786	WAHIAWA
96704-96704	CAPTAIN COOK	96734-96734	KAILUA	96762-96762	LAIE	96788-96788	PUKALANI
96705-96705	ELEELE	96737-96737	OCEAN VIEW	96763-96763	LANAI CITY	96789-96789	MILILANI
96706-96706	EWA BEACH	96738-96738	WAIKOLOA	96764-96764	LAUPAHOEHOE	96790-96790	KULA
96707-96707	KAPOLEI	96739-96739	KEAUHOU	96765-96765	LAWAI	96791-96791	WAIALUA
96708-96708	HAIKU	96740-96740	KAILUA KONA	96766-96766	LIHUE	96792-96792	WAIANAE
96709-96709	KAPOLEI	96741-96741	KALAHEO	96767-96767	LAHAINA	96793-96793	WAILUKU
96710-96710	HAKALAU	96742-96742	KALAUPAPA	96768-96768	MAKAWAO	96795-96795	WAIMANALO
96712-96712	HALEIWA	96743-96743	KAMUELA	96769-96769	MAKAWELI	96796-96796	WAIMEA
96713-96713	HANA	96744-96744	KANEOHE	96770-96770	MAUNALOA	96797-96797	WAIPAHU
96714-96714	HANALEI	96745-96745	KAILUA KONA	96771-96771	MOUNTAIN VIEW	96801-96850	HONOLULU
96715-96715	HANAMAULU	96746-96746	KAPAA	96772-96772	NAALEHU	96853-96853	HICKAM AFB
96716-96716	HANAPEPE	96747-96747	KAUMAKANI	96773-96773	NINOLE	96854-96854	WHEELER ARMY
96717-96717	HAUULA	96748-96748	KAUNAKAKAI	96774-96774	OOKALA		AIRFIELD
96718-96718	HAWAII NATIONAL PARK	96749-96749	KEAAU	96775-96775	PAAUHAU	96857-96857	SCHOFIELD BARRACKS
96719-96719	HAWI	96750-96750	KEALAKEKUA	96776-96776	PAAUILO	96858-96858	FORT SHAFTER
96720-96721	HILO	96751-96751	KEALIA	96777-96777	PAHALA	96859-96859	TRIPLER ARMY MEDICAL
96722-96722	PRINCEVILLE	96752-96752	KEKAHA	96778-96778	PAHOA		CTR
96725-96725	HOLUALOA	96753-96753	KIHEI	96779-96779	PAIA	96860-96860	PEARL HARBOR
96726-96726	HONAUNAU	96754-96754	KILAUEA	96780-96780	PAPAALOA	96861-96861	CAMP H M SMITH
96727-96727	HONOKAA	96755-96755	KAPAAU	96781-96781	PAPAIKOU	96862-96862	BARBERS POINT N A S
96728-96728	HONOMU	96756-96756	KOLOA	96782-96782	PEARL CITY	96863-96863	M C B H KANEOHE BAY
96729-96729	HOOLEHUA	96757-96757	KUALAPUU	96783-96783	PEPEEKEO	96898-96898	WAKE ISLAND
96730-96730	KAAAWA	96759-96759	KUNIA	96784-96784	PUUNENE		

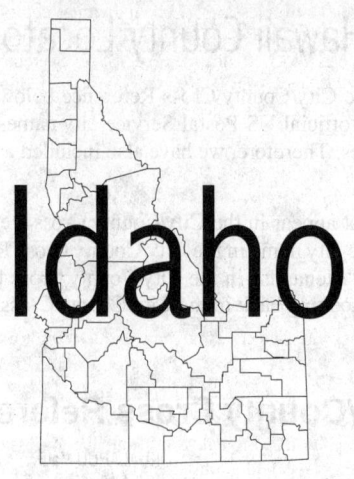

Idaho

General Help Numbers:

Governor's Office
PO Box 83720   208-334-2100
Boise, ID 83720-0034   Fax 208-334-2175
http://www2.state.id.us/gov/govhmpg.htm   8AM-6PM

Attorney General's Office
PO Box 83720   208-334-2400
Boise, ID 83720-0010   Fax 208-334-2530
http://www.state.id.us/ag   8AM-5PM

State Court Administrator
451 W State St, Supreme Court Bldg   208-334-2246
Boise, ID 83720   Fax 208-334-2146
http://www2.state.id.us/judicial   9AM-5PM

State Archives
Historical Library & Archives   208-334-3356
450 N 4th Street   Fax 208-334-3198
Boise, ID 83702-6027   9AM-5PM
http://www2.state.id.us/ishs

State Specifics:

Capital:
Boise
Ada County

Time Zone:
MST*

* Idaho's ten northwestern-most counties are PST:
They are: Benewah, Bonner, Boundary, Clearwater,
Idaho, Kootenai, Latah, Lewis, Nez Perce, Shoshone.

Number of Counties:
44

Population:
1,293,953

Web Site:
www.state.id.us

State Agencies

Criminal Records

State Repository, Bureau of Criminal Identification, PO Box 700, Meridian, ID 83680-0700 (Courier: 700 S Stratford Dr, Meridian, ID 83642); 208-884-7130, 208-884-7193 (Fax), 8AM-5PM.

http://www.isp.state.id.us

Indexing & Storage: Records are available from 1960 on. New records are available for inquiry immediately.

Searching: A signed release is not required; however, a record of an arrest without disposition after 12 months from date of arrest will only be given if signed release presented. Requests without the release will receive all records with

dispositions. Name and DOB are required to search, SSN and alias will aid in identification. Fingerprints may be required to establish positive identification. Fingerprint searches take 5-7 days.

Access by: mail, in person.

Fee & Payment: The $5.00 fee per person for name search only will increase to $10.00 of 07/01/2001. The fee is $10.00 for a fingerprint search. Fee payee: BCI. Prepayment required. Cashier check or money order is preferred form of payment. No credit cards accepted.

Mail search: Turnaround time: 3 to 5 days.

In person search: You may request information in person, but results are still mailed.

Corporation Records
Limited Partnerships
Trademarks/Servicemarks
Limited Liability Company Records
Assumed Name

Secretary of State, Corporation Division, PO Box 83720, Boise, ID 83720-0080 (Courier: 700 W Jefferson, Boise, ID 83720); 208-334-2301, 208-334-2847 (Fax), 8AM-5PM.

http://www.idsos.state.id.us

Note: Effective 1/1/97, fictitious or assumed names are found at this office. (Previously they had recorded at the county level.)

Indexing & Storage: Records are available for all entities. New records are available for inquiry immediately. Records are indexed on inhouse computer.

Searching: Include the following in your request-full name of business, specific records that you need copies of. In addition to the articles of incorporation, corporation records include the following information: Annual Reports, Officers, Directors, Prior names, Inactive and Reserved names, and Filing History. Cross reference of owners/officers is not avail.

Access by: mail, phone, fax, in person, online.

Fee & Payment: There is no search fee. The fee for copies is $.25 per page. Certification is $10.00 as is a Certification of Existence. Fee payee: Secretary of State. Prepayment required. Agency will invoice for payment. Personal checks accepted. No credit cards accepted.

Mail search: Turnaround time: 1 to 2 days. No self addressed stamped envelope is required.

Phone search: There is a limit of 3 entities per call.

Fax search: Copies cost an additional $.50 each if returned by fax.

In person search: Call first to make an appointment so that they can pull file.

Online search: There are 2 systems. To subscribe to PAIS, you must pre-pay. An initial deposit of $25 is requested. There is a monthly subscription of $10.00 and an online usage charge of $.10 per minute. The system is available from 8AM-5PM M-F. This system offers an excellent array of reports and information. Business Entity Searches at www.accessidaho.org/apps/sos/corp/search.html is a free Internet service open 24 hours daily.

Other access: There are a variety of formats and media available for bulk purchase requesters.

Expedited service: Expedited service is available for mail, phone and in person searches. Turnaround time: 1 day. Add $20.00 per document.

Uniform Commercial Code
Federal Tax Liens
State Tax Liens

UCC Division, Secretary of State, PO Box 83720, Boise, ID 83720-0080 (Courier: 700 W Jefferson, Boise, ID 83720); 208-334-3191, 208-334-2847 (Fax), 8AM-5PM.

http://www.idsos.state.id.us

Indexing & Storage: Records are available from 1967. It takes 1 to 2 days before new records are available for inquiry. Records are indexed on inhouse computer.

Searching: Use search request form UCC-4. The search includes federal tax liens, farm filings, and seed and labor filings. There is also an agricultural commodity lien search. Federal tax liens on individuals are filed at the county level. Include the following in your request-debtor name. For state tax liens that closed prior to 01/07/98, one must search at the county. On that date, the state took over the filing and database of state tax liens.

Access by: mail, phone, fax, in person, online.

Fee & Payment: Information request only by type of search is $6.00 per name, two or more file types

is $10.00. Copies are $6.00. Individual copies are available at $1.00 per page. The Commodity lien search is a $5.00 flat fee. Fee payee: Secretary of State. Prepayment is not required, but preferred. Personal checks accepted. No credit cards accepted.

Mail search: Turnaround time: 3 to 5 days. No self addressed stamped envelope is required.

Phone search: They will tell whether a filing exists.

Fax search: Searches can be invoiced. There is an additional fee of $.25 per page.

In person search: You may request information in person.

Online search: AccessIdaho at www.accessidaho.org is the official state site. There is a free limited search, but the professional searchers should subscribe to the commercial service at this site. There is a $75 annual fee and possible transaction fees.

Other access: A summary data file on current filing is available on 4mm data tape.

Expedited service: Expedited service is available for mail and phone searches. The 24 hour service is available for an extra $10.00.

Sales Tax Registrations

Revenue Operations Division, Records Management, PO Box 36, Boise, ID 83722 (Courier: 800 Park, Boise, ID 83722); 208-334-7660, 208-334-7792 (Records Management), 208-334-7650 (Fax), 8AM-5:00PM.

http://www.state.id.us/tax/index.htm

Indexing & Storage: Records are available from 1983. The agency maintains records on computer since 1998 and on microfiche from 1983 to present.

Searching: This agency will only confirm that a business is registered if a tax permit number is provided. They will provide no other information. The only information released is that within public domain. They will also search if provided with a tax permit number, a DBA or an EIN.

Access by: mail, phone, fax, in person, online.

Fee & Payment: There is no search fee, but there is a fee for postage for mail requests or for faxing. Fee payee: ISTC, PO Box 36, Boise, ID 83732. Prepayment required. Personal checks accepted. No credit cards accepted.

Mail search: Turnaround time: 1 to 3 days. The copy fee is $.10 per page, after 20 pages.No self addressed stamped envelope is required.

Phone search: No fee for telephone request. Only general information is released.

Fax search: The fee is $1.00 per page. Turnaround time 24 hours.

In person search: No fee for request.

Online search: E-mail requests are accepted at rmcmichael@tax.state.id.us.

Birth Certificates

Vital Records, PO Box 83720, Boise, ID 83720-0036 (Courier: 450 W State St, 1st Floor, Boise, ID 83702); 208-334-5988, 208-389-9096 (Fax), 8AM-5PM.

http://www2.state.id.us/dhw

Indexing & Storage: Records are available on computer from July 1911 to present.

Searching: Records are confidential for 100 years. Only immediate family or legal representative may receive records as well as those who have a notarized release from persons of record or an immediate family member. Include the following in your request-full name, names of parents, mother's maiden name, date of birth, place of birth, relationship to person of record, reason for information request. Also include a copy of a photo ID and sign the request. The following data is not released: adoption records or sealed records.

Access by: mail, fax, in person.

Fee & Payment: Requesters must include their signature and a copy of a driver's license or photo ID. Fee is $10.00 per name, add $10.00 per name requested for additional copies. Fee payee: Vital Records. Prepayment required. Credit cards accepted for fax requests only. Personal checks accepted. Credit cards accepted: MasterCard, Visa, AmEx, Discover.

Mail search: Turnaround time: 2 to 3 weeks. No self addressed stamped envelope is required.

Fax search: See Expedited Service.

In person search: Monday through Friday, 8:00 a.m. to 5:00 p.m., except holidays.

Expedited service: Expedited service is available for fax searches. The fee is $20.00 plus cost of return Federal Express, if requested. Requests received by noon (MST) will be processed same day or following day if requesting Federal Express delivery; otherwise 1 week turnaround.

Death Records

Vital Records, PO Box 83720, Boise, ID 83720-0036 (Courier: 450 W State St, 1st Floor, Boise, ID 83702); 208-334-5988, 208-389-9096 (Fax), 8AM-5PM.

http://www2.state.id.us/dhw

Indexing & Storage: Records are available from July 1911 to present. Records are indexed on microfilm, inhouse computer.

Searching: Records are confidential for 50 years and are available only to immediate family members or legal representatives or a person who has a notarized release form from persons of record or an immediate family member. Include the following in your request-full name, date of death, place of death, relationship to person of record, reason for information request.

Access by: mail, fax, in person.

Fee & Payment: Include a copy of your driver's license or photo ID and signature with request. The fee is $10.00 per name or additional copy. Fee payee: Vital Records. Prepayment required. Credit cards are accepted with fax requests only. Personal checks accepted. Credit cards accepted: MasterCard, Visa, AmEx, Discover.

Mail search: Turnaround time: 2 to 3 weeks. No self addressed stamped envelope is required.

Fax search: There is an additional $5.00 special handling fee along with a $5.00 Vital Chek fee.

In person search: Monday through Friday, 8 a.m. to 5 p.m., except holidays.

Expedited service: Please add $5.00 for each order requiring priority mailing and/or special handling. This fee is in addition to the cost of FedEx, Postal Express, or Priority Mail.

Marriage Certificates

Vital Records, PO Box 83720, Boise, ID 83720-0036 (Courier: 450 W State St, 1st Floor, Boise, ID 83702); 208-334-5988, 208-389-9096 (Fax).

http://www2.state.id.us/dhw

Indexing & Storage: Records are available from May 1947 to present. Records are indexed on microfilm, inhouse computer.

Searching: Indexes are not available to the public for 50 years. Only immediate family members and legal representatives may obtain recent records, others may obtain records with a notarized release from a family member or person of record. Include the following in your request-names of husband and wife, date of marriage, place or county of marriage.

Access by: mail, fax, in person.

Fee & Payment: Include a copy of a photo ID or driver's license and a signature with request. The fee is $10.00 per name and per each additional copy. Fee payee: Vital Records. Prepayment required. Credit cards accepted with fax requests only. Personal checks accepted. Credit cards accepted: MasterCard, Visa, AmEx, Discover.

Mail search: Turnaround time: 2 to 3 weeks. No self addressed stamped envelope is required.

Fax search: There is an additional $5.00 special handling fee along with a $5.00 VitalChek fee.

In person search: Monday through Friday, 8 a.m. to 5 p.m., except holidays.

Expedited service: Please add $5.00 for each order requiring priority mailing and/or special handling. This fee is in addition to the cost of FedEx, Postal Express, or Priority Mail.

Divorce Records

Vital Records, PO Box 83720, Boise, ID 83720-0036 (Courier: 450 W State St, 1st Floor, Boise, ID 83702); 208-334-5988, 208-389-9096 (Fax), 8AM-5PM.

http://www2.state.id.us/dhw

Note: This agency only maintains certificates of divorce; copies of decrees are available through the court system.

Indexing & Storage: Records are available from May 1947 to present. New records are available for inquiry immediately. Records are indexed on microfilm, inhouse computer.

Searching: Records are not available to the public for 50 years and are available only to immediate family members, legal representatives, and a person with a notarized signed release form from persons of record or immediate family. Include the following in your request-names of husband and wife, date of divorce, place of divorce, relationship.

Access by: mail, fax, in person.

Fee & Payment: Include a copy of a driver's license or photo ID and include a signature with request. The fee is $10.00 per name. Fee payee: Vital Records. Prepayment required. Credit cards are accepted with fax requests only. Personal checks accepted. Credit cards accepted: MasterCard, Visa, AmEx, Discover.

Mail search: Turnaround time: 2 to 3 weeks. No self addressed stamped envelope is required.

Fax search: There is an additional $5.00 special handling fee along with a $5.00 Vital Chek fee.

Expedited service: Please add $5.00 for each order requiring priority mailing and/or special handling. This fee is in addition to the cost of FedEx, Postal Express, or Priority Mail.

Workers' Compensation Records

Industrial Commission of Idaho, Attn: Records Management, PO Box 83720, Boise, ID 83720-0041; 208-334-6000, 208-334-2321 (Fax), 8AM-5PM.

http://www2.state.id.us/iic

Indexing & Storage: Records are available from 1917 on. New records are available for inquiry immediately. Records are indexed on microfilm, index cards, inhouse computer.

Searching: Must have a certified release form if you are not a party to the claim. Pre-employment screening companies must also provide an ADA certification and contingent job offer, and cannot get copies of files, only a work history report. Include the following in your request-claimant name, Social Security Number, date of accident and claim number. It is suggested to use their request form, found on the web site under Benefits Administration`. The following data is not released: psychiatric information.

Access by: mail, fax, in person.

Fee & Payment: Copy costs depend upon file size which are those that exceed 100 copied pages or 50 microfilmed pages. Larger files cost $.05 per page on paper and $.10 per page on microfilm. If file is off site, shipping fees of $2.00 per file apply. Fee payee: Industrial Commission. Charges that total under $5.00 are waived. Personal checks accepted. No credit cards accepted.

Mail search: Turnaround time: 3 days. There is a charge for postage.No self addressed stamped envelope is required.

Fax search: Fax searching available.

In person search: One may request information in person. However, not all files are available the same day because some files are not on site and must be ordered from storage.

Other access: There is no bulk data access as per Idaho law.

Driver Records

Idaho Transportation Department, Driver's Services, PO Box 34, Boise, ID 83731-0034 (Courier: 3311 W State, Boise, ID 83703); 208-334-8736, 208-334-8739 (Fax), 8:30AM-5PM.

http://www2.state.id.us/itd/dmv/ds.htm

Note: Copies of tickets may be available from the address listed above for a $4.00 fee per record.

Indexing & Storage: Records are available for at least 3 years for moving violations, DUIs and suspensions. Accidents are not shown on the record. It takes 1 day from receipt before new records are available for inquiry. Records are normally destroyed after 10 years and archived to tape.

Searching: Personal information is not released to casual requesters unless the requestor claims a valid authorization. The driver's license number and DOB are used for the primary search. If no record is found, a secondary search is performed using the name and DOB, or name and license number. The following data is not released: Social Security Numbers or medical information.

Access by: mail, fax, in person, online.

Fee & Payment: The fee is $4.00 per record. Convenience fees are added for online and batch searches. Fee payee: Idaho Transportation Department. Prepayment required. Ongoing requesters can set up an account. Personal checks accepted. Credit cards accepted: MasterCard, Visa.

Mail search: Turnaround time: 3 to 5 days. Mail-in requesters are asked to use the state form.No self addressed stamped envelope is required.

Fax search: Fax requests for records are accepted, if paid by a credit card or by account. Call 208-334-8761 to set up an account.

In person search: Walk-in requesters may receive up to ten records while they wait, the rest are processed overnight.

Online search: Idaho offers online access (CICS) to the driver license files through its portal provider, Access Idaho. Fee is $5.50 per record. For more information, call 208-332-0102 or visit http://www.accessidaho.org.

Other access: Idaho offers bulk retrieval of basic drivers license information with a signed contract. For information, call 208-334-8601

Vehicle Ownership
Vehicle Identification

Idaho Transportation Department, Vehicle Services, PO Box 34, Boise, ID 83731-0034 (Courier: 3311 W State St, Boise, ID 83707); 208-334-8773, 208-334-8542 (Fax), 8:30AM-5PM.

http://www2.state.id.us/itd/dmv/vs.htm

Indexing & Storage: Records are available from 1981. It takes 1 day before new records are available for inquiry.

Searching: Personal information is not released to casual requesters unless the requestor claims a valid authorization. Submit the name, VIN, license plate number for search, current address is also helpful. The following data is not released: Social Security Numbers or medical records.

Access by: mail, fax, in person, online.

Fee & Payment: The fee is $4.00 for current title with lien information or for a registration search. A complete title history (using the microfilm) is $8.00. Convenience fees are added for online and batch searches. Fee payee: Idaho Transportation Department. Prepayment required. Motor vehicle record accounts may be established by calling 208-334-8761. Personal checks accepted. Credit cards accepted: MasterCard, Visa.

Mail search: Turnaround time: 5 to 10 days. Information request forms are available.No self addressed stamped envelope is required.

Fax search: You may fax a request with a major credit card. Results, except for history records, can returned by fax for no additional fee. Turnaround time is three days.

In person search: You may request information in person here or at any county assessor auto licensing location statewide.

Online search: Idaho offers online and batch access to registration and title files through its portal provider, Access Idaho. Records are $4.00 each plus an additional convenience fee. For more information, call 208-332-0102.

Other access: Idaho offers bulk retrieval of registration, ownership, and vehicle information with a signed contract. For more information, call 208-334-8601.

Accident Reports

Idaho Transportation Department, Office of Highway Safety-Accident Records, PO Box 7129, Boise, ID 83707-1129 (Courier: 3311 W State St, Boise, ID 83707); 208-334-8100, 208-334-4430 (Fax), 8AM-12:00PM; 1PM-5PM.

Indexing & Storage: Records are available from 1970's (on microfilm) to present. Starting in 2000, records are stored on an imaging system. It takes 4 to 5 weeks before new records are available for inquiry.

Searching: Include the following in your request-full name, date of accident, location of accident, driver's license number.

Access by: mail, phone, fax, in person.

Fee & Payment: The fee is $4.00 per report plus handling and tax. Fee payee: Idaho Transportation Department, Financial Control. Do not send a check with a request, you will be billed. Personal checks accepted. No credit cards accepted.

Mail search: Turnaround time: 2 weeks. A self addressed stamped envelope is requested.

Phone search: No fee for telephone request. Fee charged if copies sent. Turnaround time: 2 weeks.

Fax search: Turnaround time 2 weeks.

In person search: It is suggested that walk-in requesters call first before going to department should the state have to locate the records on microfilm.

Other access: Computer files may be purchased with prepaid deposit plus computer charges. However, the file will not contain addresses, citation information, or drivers' license numbers. Annual databases may be purchased.

Vessel Ownership
Vessel Registration

Idaho Parks & Recreation, PO Box 83720, Boise, ID 83720-0065 (Courier: 5657 Warm Springs, Boise, ID 83712); 208-334-4197, 208-334-2639 (Fax), 8AM-5PM.

http://www.idahoparks.org

Note: Liens must be searched at the UCC Division at the Secretary of State office.

Indexing & Storage: Records are available from 1987 to present. Older records are available, but to search them, you must know the registration #. Records are indexed on computer. All boats with motors and/or sails must be registered.

Searching: To search, a signed release is required along with one of the following: owner's name, hull #, or registration #.

Access by: mail, in person.

Fee & Payment: There is no search fee.

Mail search: Turnaround time: 2 to 3 weeks. No self addressed stamped envelope is required.

In person search: This is the preferred method.

Legislation Records

Legislative Services Office, Research and Legislation, PO Box 83720, Boise, ID 83720-0054 (Courier: 700 W Jefferson, Lower Level, East, Boise, ID 83720); 208-334-2475, 208-334-2125 (Fax), 8AM-5PM.

http://www.state.id.us/legislat/legislat.html

Note: Sessions are from January to the end of March.

Indexing & Storage: Records are available from 1971 to present. The current and previous year are available on the Internet.

Searching: Include the following in your request-bill number and year. During session, current bills are in the mailroom on the lower level, State Capitol Bldg.

Access by: mail, phone, fax, in person, online.

Fee & Payment: There is no charge unless the bill is very long. The first 10 pages are free and the fee for pages in excess of 7 is $.20 per page. They will compute the charge. Fee payee: Legislative Services. Will bill for copy charges. Personal checks accepted. No credit cards accepted.

Mail search: Turnaround time: 3 days. Turnaround time may be longer from December through April.No self addressed stamped envelope is required.

Phone search: You may call for information. Information can be returned using your FedEx account number.

Fax search: Same criteria as phone searches. Up to 15 pages can be returned by fax.

In person search: You may request information in person.

Online search: Statutes, bill information, and subject are available from the web site. They also will answer questions via e-mail. (kford@lso.state.id.us)

Voter Registration
Records not maintained by a state level agency.

Note: Records are maintained by the County Clerks. The counties will generally release name address and voting precinct on individual request.

GED Certificates

Department of Education, GED Testing, PO Box 83720, Boise, ID 83720-0027; 208-332-6980, 208-334-4664 (Fax), 8AM-5PM.

http://www.sde.state.id.us

Searching: Include the following in your request-Social Security Number, date of birth. A signed release is necessary for copies of transcripts or for scores.

Access by: mail, phone, fax, in person.

Mail search: Turnaround time: 2 to 3 days. No self addressed stamped envelope is required. No fee for mail request.

Phone search: No fee for telephone request. Verification only over the phone.

Fax search: Turnaround time is 1 day.

In person search: No fee for request. Information is released immediately.

Hunting License Information
Fishing License Information

ID Department of Fish & Game, Licenses Division, PO Box 25, Boise, ID 83707-0025 (Courier: 1075 Park Blvd, Boise, ID 83707); 208-334-3717 (License Department), 208-334-3736 (Enforcement Office), 208-334-2148 (Fax), 8AM-5PM.

http://www.state.id.us/fishgame/fishgame.html

Note: The license division says that if you want an individual name, you must call the Enforcement Office. This office will not release individual records with addresses, they will only confirm is there is a license issued.

Indexing & Storage: Records are available from January 1992 to present.

Searching: Use of their request form is required. Include signature and copy of valid ID.

Access by: mail, phone, in person.

Fee & Payment: There is no fee unless the search is extensive.

Mail search: Turnaround time: variable. No self addressed stamped envelope is required.

Phone search: They will only confirm.

Idaho State Licensing Agencies

Licenses Searchable Online

Attorney #29 .... www2.state.id.us/isb/roster_search.htm

Bank #21 .... http://finance.state.id.us/industry/bank_info.asp

Boiler Inspector #10 .... www.accessidaho.org/public/dbs/safety/search.html

Collection Agency/Collector #21 .... http://finance.state.id.us/industry/statutes_confin.asp?Chapter=CAA

Contractor, Public Works #31 .... www.accessidaho.org/public/dbs/pubworks/search.html

Credit Union #21 .... http://finance.state.id.us/industry/creditunion_section.asp

Dental Hygienist #13 .... www2.state.id.us/isbd/isbdqry.htm

Dentist #13 .... www2.state.id.us/isbd/isbdqry.htm

Electrical Insp./Contr./Appr./Journeyman #10 .... www.accessidaho.org/public/dbs/electrical/search.html

Engineer #17 .... www2.state.id.us/ipels/pelsnumb.htm

Finance Company #21 .... http://finance.state.id.us/consumer/concredit_section.asp

Guide #15 .... www2.state.id.us/oglb/oglbhome.htm

Investment Advisor #21 .... http://finance.state.id.us/industry/securities_resources.asp?resource=IARR

Lobbyist #28 .... www.idsos.state.id.us/elect/lobbyist/lobinfo.htm

Manufactured Commercial Building #10 .... www.accessidaho.org/public/dbs/building/search.html

Manufactured Homes & Housing #10 .... www.accessidaho.org/public/dbs/building/search.html

Manufactured Housing Dealer/Broker/Mfg. #10 .. www.accessidaho.org/public/dbs/building/search.html

Mortgage Broker/Banker #21 .... http://finance.state.id.us/industry/mortgage_section.asp

Mortgage Company #21 .... http://finance.state.id.us/industry/mortgage_section.asp

Optometrist #19 .... www.odfinder.org/LicSearch.asp

Oral Surgeon #13 .... www2.state.id.us/isbd/isbdqry.htm

Orthodontist #13 .... www2.state.id.us/isbd/isbdqry.htm

Outfitter #15 .... www2.state.id.us/oglb/oglbhome.htm

Plumbing Insp./Contr./Appr./Journeyman #10 .... www.accessidaho.org/public/dbs/plumbing/search.html

Public Accountant-CPA #12 .... www2.state.id.us/boa/HTM/license.htm

Public Accountant-LPA #12 .... www2.state.id.us/boa/HTM/license.htm

Savings & Loan Association #21 .... http://finance.state.id.us/industry/bank_section.asp

Securities Broker/Dealer/Seller/Issuer #21 .... http://finance.state.id.us/industry/securities.asp

Surveyor #17 .... www2.state.id.us/ipels/pelsnumb.htm

Trust Company #21 .... http://finance.state.id.us/consumer/bank_info.asp

Licensing Quick Finder

Applicator, Commercial/Private #20 208-332-8500
Aquaculture, Commercial #20 208-332-8500
Architect #19..............................208-334-3233
Artificial Inseminator #20 208-332-8500
Asbestos Worker #10 208-334-2129
Athletic Trainer #30 208-334-2822
Attorney #29 208-344-4500
Bakery #11 208-327-7499
Bank #21 208-332-8005
Barber School Instructor #19 208-334-3233
Barber/Barber Shop/Barber School #19 208-334-3233
Bed & Breakfast #11 208-327-7450
Beekeeper #20.............................208-332-8500
Beer & Wine License, Whlse/Retail #25 208-884-7060
Boiler Inspector #10 208-334-2129
Boiler Safety Code #10....................208-334-2129
Bottling Plant #11 208-327-7450
Boxer #32 208-334-3888
Boxing/Wrestling Event #32 208-334-3888
Boxing/Wrestling Professional #32........208-334-3888
Brewery #25...............................208-334-7060
Brokerage Dealer #12 208-334-2490
Building Inspector #10 208-334-3896
Chemigator #20 208-332-8500
Child Care Institution/Agency #07 208-334-5700
Child Care Licensure #07 208-334-5700
Chiropractor #19 208-334-3233
Clinical Laboratory Registration #02......208-334-2235
Clinical Nurse Specialist #14 ....208-334-3110 X34
Collection Agency/Collector #21 208-332-8002
Commission Merchant #20 208-332-8500
Commodity Dealer #20.....................208-332-8500
Communication Disorders School Specialist #05.......
....208-332-6800
Construction Manager #31 208-334-4057
Consumer Loan Company & Credit Sale #21 ....
....208-332-8002
Contractor, Public Works #31 208-334-4057
Controlled Substance Registrant #16.....208-334-2356
Cosmetologist/Cosmetology Salon#19...208-334-3233
Cosmetology School/Instructor #19...208-334-3233
Counselor #19 208-334-3233
Counselor, Professional #19 208-334-3233
Credit Union #21 208-332-8003
Crematory #03 208-334-3233
Critical Material Handler #11................208-327-7499
Dairy Product Processor, Dairy Farm #20 ....
....208-332-8500
Day Care Center Inspector #11 208-327-7499
Day Care Center/Home #07 208-334-5700
Dental Hygienist #13 208-334-2369
Dentis, Dental Assistant #13.................208-334-2369
Denturist #19 208-334-3233
Dietitian #30...............................208-334-2822
Driller, Rotary #26 208-327-7900
Drug Mfg./Repackager/Whls. #16 208-334-2356
Drug Outlet (i.e. Nursing Home) #16 208-334-2356
Drug Sales, Non-Pharmacy (i.e. Grocery Store) #16
....208-334-2356
Egg Distributor/Grader #20...................208-332-8500
Electrical Inspector/Contractor/Apprentice/Journeyman
#10 208-334-2183
Electrolysis #19..............................208-334-3233
Elevator Installation/Repairmen #10......208-334-2129
Emergency Medical Technician #09......208-334-4000
Engineer #17 208-334-3860

Environmental Health Specialist #19.....208-334-3233
Esthetician #19 208-334-3233
Euthanasia Agency #01....................208-332-8588
Euthanasia Technician #01 208-332-8588
Exceptional Child School Program Advisor #05.........
....208-332-6800
Farm Produce Dealer/Broker #20 208-332-8500
Feed Mfg., Commercial #20................208-332-8500
Fertilizer Mfg., Commercial #20 208-332-8500
Finance Company #21 208-332-8002
Fire Sprinkler System Contractor #23 ..208-334-4370
Fishing, Commercial #22...................208-334-3717
Florist/Nurseryman #20 208-332-8500
Food Processing/Mfg. Plant #11 208-327-7499
Food Warehouse, Cold Storage #11 208-327-7499
Foster Home #07 208-334-5700
Funeral Establishment #03 208-334-3233
Fur Buyer #22 208-334-3717
Game Farm (Commercial Wildlife) #22 .208-334-3717
Geologist #18..............................208-334-2268
Grocery Store #11 208-327-7499
Guide #15 208-327-7380
Hearing Aid Dealer/Fitter #19 208-334-3233
Horse Racing, Evens/Occupation #33...208-884-7080
Hospital #08...............................208-334-5500
Insurance Agent Corporation or Partnership #24 ....
....208-334-4250
Insurance Agent Licensure Examination #24.............
....208-334-4250
Insurance Agent Non-resident #24........208-334-4320
Insurance Broker License #24 208-334-4250
Insurer, Domestic & Mutual #24............208-334-4250
Insurer, Foreign & Alien #24 208-334-4250
Intermediate Care Facility for the Mentally Retarded
#08 208-334-5500
Investment Advisor #21 208-332-8004
Landscape Architect #19 208-334-3233
Liquor License, Retail #25 208-884-7060
Livestock Auction Market #20 208-332-8500
Livestock Brand #25.......................208-884-7070
Loan Agent #12............................208-334-2490
Loan Collection Officer #12 208-334-2490
Lobbyist #28 208-334-2852
Logging #10 208-334-6000
Mammography #02 208-334-2235
Manufactured Commercial Building #10 208-334-3896
Manufactured Homes & Housing #10....208-334-3896
Manufactured Housing Dealer/Broker/Mfg. #10
....208-334-3896
Medical Doctor #30 208-334-2822
Medical Resident #30......................208-334-2822
Midwife Nurse #14 ....208-334-3110 X34
Milk Hauler, Bulk #20 208-332-8500
Milk & Dairy Product Storage/Handling #20..............
....208-332-8500
Mine Safety Training #10...................208-334-2129
Mixer-Loader #20 208-332-8500
Mortgage Broker/Banker #21 208-332-8004
Mortgage Company #21 208-332-8004
Mortician/Mortician Resi. Trainee #03 ...208-334-3233
Notary Public #28..........................208-334-2810
Nurse #14 ....208-334-3110 X34
Nurse Anesthetist #14 ....208-334-3110 X25
Nurse-LPN #14............................208-334-3110
Nursing Assistant #14 208-334-3110
Nursing Care (Skilled) Facility #08........208-334-5500

Nursing Home Administrator #19 208-334-3233
Occupational Therapist/Assistant #30 ...208-334-2822
Optometrist #19 208-334-3233
Oral Surgeon #13..........................208-334-2369
Organic Certification #20 208-332-8500
Orthodontist #13 208-334-2369
Osteopathic Physician #30 208-334-2822
Outfitter #15...............................208-327-7380
Paramedic (EMT) #09......................208-334-4000
Pest Control Consultant #20 208-332-8500
Pesticide Applicator/Operator/Dealer/Mfg. #20 ....
....208-332-8500
Pharmacist,/Intern/Preceptor #16.........208-334-2356
Pharmacy/Drug Store#16 208-334-2356
Pharmacy Mail Service #16 208-334-2356
Physical Therapist/Assistant #30 208-334-2822
Physician Assistant #30....................208-334-2822
Plumbing Inspector/Contractor/Apprentice/Journeyman
#10 208-334-3442
Podiatrist #19 208-334-3233
Police (Peace) Officer #25 208-884-7000
Psychologist #19 208-334-3233
Public Accountant-CPA/LPA #12 ..208-334-2490
Public Commodity Warehouse #20 ...208-332-8500
Radiation Equipment #03 208-334-3945
Real Estate Appraiser #19 208-334-3233
Recreational Vehicle Mfg. #10 208-334-3896
Rehabilitation Facility #08...................208-334-5500
Residential Care Administrator #19........208-334-3233
Residential Care Facility #08 208-334-5500
Residential School #07 208-334-5700
Respiratory Therapist #30 208-334-2822
Restaurant Sanitation Standard #11 208-327-7499
Savings & Loan Association #21 208-332-8005
School Counselor #05 208-332-6800
School Nurse #05..........................208-332-6800
School Principal/Superintendent #05 208-332-6800
Securities Broker/Dealer/Seller/Issuer #21 ....
....208-332-8004
Seed Company #20........................208-332-8500
Septic Tank Pumper #11 208-327-7499
Shooting Preserve #22.....................208-334-3717
Shorthand Reporter #04 208-334-2517
Social Worker #19 208-334-3233
Soil & Plant Amendment Mfg. #20 208-332-8500
Solicitor (Financial) #21.....................208-332-8002
Special Education Director #05.............208-332-6800
Substance Abuse Treatment Ctr. #07 ...208-334-5700
Subsurface Sewage Installer #11.........208-327-7499
Surveyor #17 208-334-3860
Swimming Pool Installer #11................208-327-7499
Taxidermist #22 208-334-3717
Teacher #05...............................208-332-6800
Trapper/Junior Trapper #22 208-334-3736
Trust Company #21 208-332-8005
Utility Regulation #27 208-334-0300
Veterinarian/Veterinary Technician #01.208-332-8588
Veterinary Drug Outlet/Technician #16..208-334-2356
Water Laboratory #02.....................208-334-2235
Water Rights Examiner #26 208-327-7900
Water Well Driller #26 208-327-7900
Weighmaster #20..........................208-332-8500
Winery #25 208-334-7060
Wrestler #32 208-334-3888
X-ray Equipment #02......................208-334-2235

Licensing Agency Information

#01 Board of Veterinary Medicine, PO Box 7249, Boise, ID 83707; 208-332-8588, Fax: 208-334-4062.

#02 Bureau of Laboratories, 2220 Old Penitentiary Rd, Boise, ID 83712; 208-334-2235, Fax: 208-334-2382.

#03 Bureau of Occupational Licenses, 1109 Main St, #220, Boise, ID 83702-5642; 208-334-3233, Fax: 208-334-3945.
www2.state.id.us/ibol The ability to search is planned. Once available, you should be able to access it from the following web address: www2.state.id.us/ibol/mor.htm.

#04 Certified Shorthand Reporters Board, 550 W State St, Boise, ID 83720-0017; 208-334-2517.

#05 Department of Education, PO Box 83720, Boise, ID 83720-0027; 208-332-6800, Fax: 208-334-2094.
www.sde.state.id.us/certification

#07 Department of Health & Welfare, 450 W State St, 5th Fl, Boise, ID 83720; 208-334-5700, Fax: 208-334-6558.
www2.state.id.us/dhw/hwgd_www/contentlist.htm l#Family

#08 Department of Health & Welfare, 1410 N Hilton, Boise, ID 83706-1255; 208-373-0502, Fax: 208-373-0342.
www2.state.id.us/DEQ

#09 Department of Health & Welfare, 590 W Washington, Boise, ID 83702; 208-334-4000, Fax: 208-334-4015.

#10 Division of Building Safety, PO Box 83720, Boise, ID 83720-0048; 208-334-3950, Fax: 208-334-2683.
www2.state.id.us/dbs/dbs_index.html
Direct web site URL to search for licensees: www2.state.id.us/dbs/dbs_index.html

#11 Environmental Health Department, 707 N Armstrong Place, Boise, ID 83704; 208-327-7450, Fax: 208-327-8553.

#12 Board of Accountancy, 1109 Main #470, Boise, ID 83702-0002; 208-334-2490, Fax: 208-334-2615.
www2.state.id.us/boa

#13 Board of Dentistry, PO Box 83720, Boise, ID 83720-0021; 208-334-2369, Fax: 208-334-3247.
www2.state.id.us/isbd
Direct web site URL to search for licensees: www2.state.id.us/isbd/isbdqry.htm. You can search online using status, name, city and license number.

#14 Board of Nursing, 280 N 8th St #210, Boise, ID 83720; 208-334-3110, Fax: 208-334-3262.
www2.state.id.us/ibn/ibnhome.htm

#15 Board of Outfitters & Guides, 1365 N Orchard St, Rm 172, Boise, ID 83706; 208-327-7380, Fax: 208-327-7382.
www2.state.id.us/oglb/oglbhome.htm
Direct web site URL to search for licensees: www2.state.id.us/oglb/oglbhome.htm. You can search online using type and unit. Scroll to the bottom of the page to find the appropriate links for searching.

#16 Board of Pharmacy, 3380 Americana Terr #320, PO Box 83720, Boise, ID 83720-0067; 208-334-2356, Fax: 208-334-3536.
www.state.id.us/bop

#17 Board of Professional Engineers & Surveyors, 600 S Orchard, #A, Boise, ID 83705; 208-334-3860, Fax: 208-334-2008.
www2.state.id.us/ipels/index.htm
Direct web site URL to search for licensees: www2.state.id.us/ipels/pelsnumb.htm. You can search online using name and license number.

#18 Board of Professional Geologists, 550 W State St, Boise, ID 83720-0033; 208-334-2268.

#19 Bureau of Occupational Licenses, 1109 Main St, Owyhee Plaza, #220, Boise, ID 83702; 208-334-3233, Fax: 208-334-3945.
www2.state.id.us/ibol/

#20 Department of Agriculture, 2270 Old Penitentiary Rd, Boise, ID 83712; 208-332-8500.
www.agri.state.id.us/agresource/licensing.htm

#21 Department of Finance, 700 W State St, Boise, ID 83720-0031; 208-332-8000, Fax: 208-332-8098.
http://finance.state.id.us/home.asp

#22 Department of Fish & Game, PO Box 25, Boise, ID 83707; 208-334-3700, Fax: 208-334-2114.

www2.state.id.us/fishgame

#23 Department of Insurance, 700 W State St, 3rd Fl, Boise, ID 83720-0043; 208-334-4370, Fax: 208-334-4375.

#24 ID Department of Insurance, 700 W State St, Boise, ID 83720-0043; 208-334-4250, Fax: 208-334-4398.
www.doi.state.id.us

#25 State Police, PO Box 700, Meridian, ID 83680; 208-884-7000, Fax: 208-884-7098.

#26 Department of Water Resources, 1301 N Orchard St, Boise, ID 83706; 208-327-7900, Fax: 208-327-7866.
www.idwr.state.id.us

#27 Public Utilities Commission, 472 W Washington St, Boise, ID 83702; 208-334-0300, Fax: 208-334-3762.

#28 Secretary of State, Rm 203, Statehouse, PO Box 83720, Boise, ID 83720; 208-334-2300, Fax: 208-334-2282.
www.idsos.state.id.us
Direct web site URL to search for licensees: www.idsos.state.id.us. You can search online using surname, company name

#29 State Bar, PO Box 895, Boise, ID 83701; 208-334-4500, Fax: 208-334-4515.
www2.state.id.us/isb
Direct web site URL to search for licensees: www2.state.id.us/isb/roster_search.htm. You can search online using last name

#30 Board of Medicine, 280 N 8th St #202, Boise, ID 83720-0058; 208-334-2822, Fax: 208-334-2801.

#31 Division of Building Safety, PO Box 83720 (1090 Watertower St, Meridian, ID), Boise, ID 83720-0073; 208-334-4057, Fax: 208-855-9666.
www2.state.id.us/dbs/dbs_index.html

#32 State Athletic Department, 10 S Latah, #208, Boise, ID 83705; 208-334-3888, Fax: 208-345-1145.

#33 Horse Racing Commission, 700 Stratford Dr, Meridian, ID 83642; 208-884-7080, Fax: 208-884-7098.
www2.state.id.us/race

Idaho Federal Courts

The following list indicates the district and division name for each county in the state. If the bankruptcy court location is different from the district court, then the location of the bankruptcy court appears in parentheses.

County/Court Cross Reference

Ada	Boise	Gem	Boise
Adams	Boise	Gooding	Boise
Bannock	Pocatello	Idaho	Pocatello (Moscow)
Bear Lake	Pocatello	Jefferson	Pocatello
Benewah	Coeur d' Alene	Jerome	Boise
Bingham	Pocatello	Kootenai	Coeur d' Alene
Blaine	Boise	Latah	Moscow
Boise	Boise	Lemhi	Pocatello
Bonner	Coeur d' Alene	Lewis	Moscow
Bonneville	Pocatello	Lincoln	Boise
Boundary	Coeur d' Alene	Madison	Pocatello
Butte	Pocatello	Minidoka	Boise
Camas	Boise	Nez Perce	Moscow
Canyon	Boise	Oneida	Pocatello
Caribou	Pocatello	Owyhee	Boise
Cassia	Boise	Payette	Boise
Clark	Pocatello	Power	Pocatello
Clearwater	Moscow	Shoshone	Coeur d' Alene
Custer	Pocatello	Teton	Pocatello
Elmore	Boise	Twin Falls	Boise
Franklin	Pocatello	Valley	Boise
Fremont	Pocatello	Washington	Boise

US District Court

District of Idaho

Boise Division MSC 039, Federal Bldg, 550 W Fort St, Room 400, Boise, ID 83724 (Courier Address: Use mail address for courier delivery), 208-334-1361, Fax: 208-334-9362.

http://www.id.uscourts.gov

Counties: Ada, Adams, Blaine, Boise, Camas, Canyon, Cassia, Elmore, Gem, Gooding, Jerome, Lincoln, Minidoka, Owyhee, Payette, Twin Falls, Valley, Washington.

Indexing/Storage: Cases are indexed by defendant and plaintiff as well as by case number. New cases are available in the index immediately after filing date. Both computer and card indexes are maintained. Open records are located at this court.

Fee & Payment: The fee is $20.00 per item (one party name or case number). Payment may be made by money order, cashier check, personal check. Prepayment is only required for large requests. Payee: US District Court Clerk. Certification fee: $7.00 per document. Copy fee: $.50 per page.

Phone Search: All public information will be released over the phone.

Fax Search: Handled same as mail request. Check with Court Copy Service.

Mail Search: A stamped self addressed envelope is not required.

In Person: In person searching is available.

PACER: Sign-up number is 208-334-9342. Access fee is No charge. Local access: 208-334-9590. Case records are available back to January 1990. Records are purged varies. New civil records are available online after 2 days. New criminal records are available online after 1 day.

Opinions Online: Court opinions are available online at http://www.id.uscourts.gov

Other Online Access: Search records online using RACER. Currently the system is free; visit http://www.id.uscourts.gov/doc.htm.

Coeur d' Alene Division c/o Boise Division, MSD 039, Federal Bldg, 550 W Fort St, Room 400, Boise, ID 83724 (Courier Address: Use mail address for courier delivery), 208-334-1361.

http://www.id.uscourts.gov

Counties: Benewah, Bonner, Boundary, Kootenai, Shoshone.

Indexing/Storage: Cases are indexed by as well as by case number. New cases are available in the index after filing date. Open records are located at the Division.

Fee & Payment: The fee is $20.00 per item (one party name or case number). Payment may be made by money order, cashier check. Business checks are not accepted. Personal checks are not accepted.

Phone Search: Searching is not available by phone.

Mail Search: Always enclose a stamped self addressed envelope.

In Person: In person searching is available.

PACER: Sign-up number is 208-334-9342. Access fee is No charge. Local access: 208-334-9590. Case records are available back to January 1990. Records are purged varies. New civil records are available online after 2 days. New criminal records are available online after 1 day.

Opinions Online: Court opinions are available online at http://www.id.uscourts.gov

Other Online Access: Search records online using RACER. Currently the system is free; visit http://www.id.uscourts.gov/doc.htm.

Moscow Division c/o Boise Division, PO Box 039, Federal Bldg, 550 W Fort St, Boise, ID 83724 (Courier Address: Use mail address for courier delivery), 208-334-1361.

http://www.id.uscourts.gov

Counties: Clearwater, Latah, Lewis, Nez Perce.

Indexing/Storage: Cases are indexed by as well as by case number. New cases are available in the index after filing date. Open records are located at the Division.

Fee & Payment: The fee is $20.00 per item (one party name or case number). Payment may be made by money order, cashier check. Business checks are not accepted. Personal checks are not accepted.

Phone Search: Searching is not available by phone.

Mail Search: Always enclose a stamped self addressed envelope.

In Person: In person searching is available.

PACER: Sign-up number is 208-334-9342. Access fee is No charge. Local access: 208-334-9590. Case records are available back to January 1990. Records are purged varies. New civil records are available online after 2 days. New criminal records are available online after 1 day.

Opinions Online: Court opinions are available online at http://www.id.uscourts.gov

Other Online Access: Search records online using RACER. Currently the system is free; visit http://www.id.uscourts.gov/doc.htm.

Pocatello Division c/o Boise Division, 801 E Sherman, Pocatello, ID 83201 (Courier Address: Use mail address for courier delivery), 208-478-4123.

http://www.id.uscourts.gov

Counties: Bannock, Bear Lake, Bingham, Bonneville, Butte, Caribou, Clark, Custer, Franklin, Fremont, Idaho, Jefferson, Lemhi, Madison, Oneida, Power, Teton.

Indexing/Storage: Cases are indexed by as well as by case number. New cases are available in the index after filing date. Open records are located at the Division.

Fee & Payment: The fee is $20.00 per item (one party name or case number). Payment may be made by money order, cashier check. Business checks are not accepted. Personal checks are not accepted.

Phone Search: Searching is not available by phone.

Mail Search: Always enclose a stamped self addressed envelope.

In Person: In person searching is available.

PACER: Sign-up number is 208-334-9342. Access fee is No charge. Local access: 208-334-9590. Case records are available back to January 1990. Records are purged varies. New civil records are available online after 2 days. New criminal records are available online after 1 day.

Opinions Online: Court opinions are available online at http://www.id.uscourts.gov

Other Online Access: Search records online using RACER. Currently the system is free; visit http://www.id.uscourts.gov/doc.htm.

US Bankruptcy Court

District of Idaho

Boise Division MSC 042, US Courthouse, 550 W Fort St, Room 400, Boise, ID 83724 (Courier Address: Use mail address for courier delivery), 208-334-1074, Fax: 208-334-9362.

http://www.id.uscourts.gov

Counties: Ada, Adams, Blaine, Boise, Camas, Canyon, Cassia, Elmore, Gem, Gooding, Jerome, Lincoln, Minidoka, Owyhee, Payette, Twin Falls, Valley, Washington.

Indexing/Storage: Cases are indexed by debtor as well as by case number. New cases are available in the index immediately after filing date. A computer index is maintained. Open records are located at this court.

Fee & Payment: The fee is $20.00 per item (one party name or case number). Payment may be made by money order, cashier check. Business checks are not accepted. Personal checks are not accepted. Prepayment is required. Make all search and copy arrangements with private vendor Court Copy Services, 208-334-9463. Payee: Coourt Copy Services. Certification fee: $7.00 per document. Copy fee: $.25 per page. The fee for copies made by court personnel is $.50 per page.

Phone Search: Only docket information is available by phone. An automated voice case information service (VCIS) is available.

Fax Search: Fax requests are handled by a copy service. Call 208-334-9463 to arrange a fax request.

Mail Search: A stamped self addressed envelope is not required.

In Person: In person searching is available.

PACER: Sign-up number is 208-334-9342. Access fee is No charge. Local access: 208-334-9895. Case records are available back to September 1990. Records are purged immediately when case closed. New civil records are available online after 1 day.

Opinions Online: Court opinions are available online at http://www.id.uscourts.gov

Other Online Access: Search records online using RACER. Currently the system is free; visit http://www.id.uscourts.gov/doc.htm.

Coeur d' Alene Division 205 N 4th St, 2nd Floor, Coeur d'Alene, ID 83814 (Courier Address: Use mail address for courier delivery), 208-664-4925, Fax: 208-765-0270.

http://www.id.uscourts.gov

Counties: Benewah, Bonner, Boundary, Kootenai, Shoshone.

Indexing/Storage: Cases are indexed by debtor as well as by case number. New cases are available in the index immediately after filing date. A computer index is maintained. Open records are located at this court.

Fee & Payment: The fee is $20.00 per item (one party name or case number). Payment may be made by money order, cashier check, business check. Personal checks are not accepted. Prepayment is required. Payee: US Bankruptcy Court. Certification fee: $7.00 per document. Copy fee: $.50 per page.

Phone Search: Only docket information is available by phone. An automated voice case information service (VCIS) is available.

Fax Search: Fax search handled same as mail.

Mail Search: Always enclose a stamped self addressed envelope.

In Person: In person searching is available.

PACER: Sign-up number is 208-334-9342. Access fee is No charge. Local access: 208-334-9895. Case records are available back to September 1990. Records are purged immediately when case closed. New civil records are available online after 1 day.

Opinions Online: Court opinions are available online at http://www.id.uscourts.gov

Other Online Access: Search records online using RACER. Currently the system is free; visit http://www.id.uscourts.gov/doc.htm.

Moscow Division 220 E 5th St, Moscow, ID 83843 (Courier Address: Use mail address for courier delivery), 208-882-7612, Fax: 208-883-1576.

http://www.id.uscourts.gov

Counties: Clearwater, Idaho, Latah, Lewis, Nez Perce.

Indexing/Storage: Cases are indexed by debtor as well as by case number. New cases are available in the index immediately after filing date. A computer index is maintained. Open records are located at this court.

Fee & Payment: The fee is $20.00 per item (one party name or case number). Payment may be made by money order, cashier check, business check. Personal checks are not accepted. Prepayment is required. Payee: US Bankruptcy Court. Certification fee: $7.00 per document. Copy fee: $.50 per page.

Phone Search: Only docket information is available by phone. An automated voice case information service (VCIS) is available.

Mail Search: Always enclose a stamped self addressed envelope.

In Person: In person searching is available.

PACER: Sign-up number is 208-334-9342. Access fee is No charge. Local access: 208-334-9895. Case records are available back to September 1990. Records are purged immediately when case closed. New civil records are available online after 1 day.

Opinions Online: Court opinions are available online at http://www.id.uscourts.gov

Other Online Access: Search records online using RACER. Currently the system is free; visit http://www.id.uscourts.gov/doc.htm.

Pocatello Division 801 E Sherman, Pocatello, ID 83201 (Courier Address: Use mail address for courier delivery), 208-478-4123, Fax: 208-478-4106.

http://www.id.uscourts.gov

Counties: Bannock, Bear Lake, Bingham, Bonneville, Butte, Caribou, Clark, Custer, Franklin, Fremont, Jefferson, Lemhi, Madison, Oneida, Power, Teton.

Indexing/Storage: Cases are indexed by debtor as well as by case number. New cases are available in the index immediately after filing date. A computer index is maintained. Open records are located at this court. No cases have been sent to the Federal Records Center yet.

Fee & Payment: The fee is $20.00 per item (one party name or case number). Payment may be made by money order, cashier check, business check. Personal checks are not accepted. Copy service will bill after first order. Payee: US Bankruptcy Court. Certification fee: $7.00 per document. Copy fee: $.50 per page.

Phone Search: Only docket information is available by phone. An automated voice case information service (VCIS) is available.

Fax Search: Fax searching available with a deposit account. Call for special procedures. Copy service will fax documents at $.50 per page.

Mail Search: Always enclose a stamped self addressed envelope.

In Person: In person searching is available.

PACER: Sign-up number is 208-334-9342. Access fee is No charge. Local access: 208-334-9895. Case records are available back to September 1990. Records are purged immediately when case closed. New civil records are available online after 1 day.

Opinions Online: Court opinions are available online at http://www.id.uscourts.gov

Other Online Access: Search records online using RACER. Currently the system is free; visit http://www.id.uscourts.gov/doc.htm.

Idaho County Courts

Court	Jurisdiction	No. of Courts	How Organized
District Courts*	General		7 Districts
Magistrates Division*	Limited	3	7 Districts
Combined Courts*		44	

* Profiled in this Sourcebook.

Court	CIVIL								
	Tort	Contract	Real Estate	Min. Claim	Max. Claim	Small Claims	Estate	Eviction	Domestic Relations
District Courts*	X	X	X	$0	No Max				
Magistrates Division*	X	X	X	$0	$10,000	$3000	X	X	X

Court	CRIMINAL				
	Felony	Misdemeanor	DWI/DUI	Preliminary Hearing	Juvenile
District Courts*	X	X	X	X	
Magistrates. Division*			X	X	X

ADMINISTRATION   Administrative Director of Courts, Supreme Court Building, 451 W State St, Boise, ID, 83720; 208-334-2246, Fax: 208-334-2146. www2.state.id.us/judicial/

COURT STRUCTURE   The District Court oversees felony and most civil cases. Small claims are handled by the Magistrate Division of the District Court. Probate is handled by the Magistrate Division of the District Court.

ONLINE ACCESS   There is no statewide computer system offering external access. ISTARS is a statewide intra-court/intra-agency system run and managed by the State Supreme Court. All counties are on ISTARS, and all courts provide public access terminals on-site.

ADDITIONAL INFORMATION   A statewide court administrative rule states that record custodians do not have a duty to "compile or summarize information contained in a record, nor ... to create new records for the requesting party." Under this rule, some courts will not perform searches.

Many courts require a signed release for employment record searches.

The following fees are mandated statewide: Search Fee - none; Certification Fee - $1.00 per document plus copy fee; Copy Fee - $1.00 per page. Not all jurisdictions currently follow these guidelines.

📖 📖 📖 📖 📖 📖 📖

Ada County

District & Magistrate Courts-I 514 W. Jefferson St, Boise, ID 83702-5931; 208-364-2000. Hours: 8:30AM-5PM (MST). *Felony, Civil, Eviction, Small Claims, Probate.*

www2.state.id.us/fourthjudicial

Civil Records: Access: Mail, in person. Both court and visitors may perform in person searches. No search fee. Required to search: name, years to search; also helpful: address. Civil cases indexed by defendant, plaintiff. Civil records on computer since 1985, microfiche and docket books from 1860s.

Criminal Records: Access: Mail, in person. Both court and visitors may perform in person searches. No search fee. Required to search: name, years to search; also helpful: address, DOB, SSN. Criminal records on computer since 1985, microfiche and docket books from 1860s.

General Information: Public Access terminal is available. No juvenile, adoption, child protection

records released. SASE required. Turnaround time 1-7 days. Copy fee: $1.00 per page. Certification fee: $1.00 per page. Fee payee: Ada County. Personal checks accepted.

Ada County Traffic Court 7180 Barrister, Boise, ID 83704; 208-327-5352. Hours: 8AM-5PM (MST). *Misdemeanor.*

www2.state.id.us/fourthjudicial

Criminal Records: Access: Mail, in person. Both court and visitors may perform in person searches. No search fee. Required to search: name, years to search; also helpful: address, DOB, SSN. Criminal records on computer from 1985, microfiche from 1983, docket books back to statehood.

General Information: Public Access terminal is available. No alcohol level or confidential evaluation records released. SASE required. Turnaround time up to 1-2 weeks. Copy fee: $1.00 per page. Certification fee: $1.50. Fee payee: Ada County. Personal checks accepted. Prepayment is required.

Adams County

District & Magistrate Courts PO Box 48, Council, ID 83612; 208-253-4561/4233; Fax: 208-253-4880. Hours: 8AM-5PM (MST). *Felony, Misdemeanor, Civil, Eviction, Small Claims, Probate.*

www.webpak.net/~tca3sec

Civil Records: Access: Fax, mail, in person. Both court and visitors may perform in person searches. No search fee. Required to search: name, years to search. Civil cases indexed by defendant, plaintiff. Civil records on computer back to 1993, microfiche from 1972, docket books from 1911.

Criminal Records: Access: Fax, mail, in person. Both court and visitors may perform in person searches. No search fee. Required to search: name, years to search, signed release, DOB or SSN. Criminal records on computer back to 1993, microfiche from 1972, docket books from 1911. Submit DOB and/or SSN.

General Information: Public Access terminal is available. No juvenile, sealed cases records released.

SASE requested. Turnaround time 2 days. Fax notes: $4.00 per page. Copy fee: $1.00 per page. Certification fee: $1.00. Fee payee: Adams County. Personal checks accepted. Prepayment is required.

Bannock County

District & Magistrate Courts 624 East Center, Pocatello, ID 83205; 208-236-7351, 7352; Civil phone: 208-236-7350; Criminal phone: 208-236-7272; Probate phone: 208-236-7351; Fax: 208-236-7013. Hours: 8AM-5PM (MST). *Felony, Misdemeanor, Civil, Eviction, Small Claims, Probate.*

www.co.bannock.id.us/clkcrt1.htm

Civil Records: Access: Fax, mail, in person. Both court and visitors may perform in person searches. No search fee. Required to search: name, years to search. Civil cases indexed by defendant, plaintiff. Civil records on computer from 1986, on docket books from 1970s.
Criminal Records: Access: Fax, mail, in person. Both court and visitors may perform in person searches. No search fee. Required to search: name, years to search; also helpful: DOB, SSN. Criminal records on computer from 1986, on docket books from 1970s.
General Information: Public Access terminal is available. No adoption, mental, juvenile, termination, domestic violence records released. SASE required. Turnaround time 1 day to 2 weeks. Fax notes: $1.00 per page. Copy fee: $1.00 per page. Certification fee: $.50 per page. Fee payee: Bannock County District Court. Personal checks accepted.

Bear Lake County

District & Magistrate Courts PO Box 190, Paris, ID 83261; 208-945-2208; Fax: 208-945-2780. Hours: 8:30AM-5PM (MST). *Felony, Misdemeanor, Civil, Eviction, Small Claims, Probate.*

Civil Records: Access: Fax, mail, in person. Only the court performs in person searches; visitors may not. No search fee. Required to search: name, years to search. Civil cases indexed by defendant, plaintiff. Civil records on computer from 1991, docket books from early 1900s.
Criminal Records: Access: Fax, mail, in person. Only the court performs in person searches; visitors may not. No search fee. Required to search: name, years to search, DOB, signed release; also helpful: SSN. Criminal records on computer from 1991, docket books from early 1900s.
General Information:. No juvenile, CPA, divorce records released. SASE required. Turnaround time 2-3 days. Fax notes: $1.00 per page. Copy fee: $1.00 per page. Certification fee: $1.50. Fee payee: Clerk of Court. Business checks accepted. Prepayment is required.

Benewah County

District & Magistrate Courts Courthouse, 701 College Ave, St Maries, ID 83861; 208-245-3241; Fax: 208-245-3046. Hours: 9AM-5PM (PST). *Felony, Misdemeanor, Civil, Eviction, Small Claims, Probate.*

Civil Records: Access: Fax, mail, in person. Only the court performs in person searches; visitors may not. No search fee. Required to search: name, years to search. Civil cases indexed by defendant, plaintiff. Civil records on computer from 1991, index cards and docket books from early 1900s.
Criminal Records: Access: Mail, fax, in person. Only the court performs in person searches; visitors may not. Search fee: No search fee. If printout required $.15 per page. Required to search: name, years to search. Criminal records on computer from 1991, index cards and docket books from early 1900s.
General Information:. No juvenile, adoptions, mental commitments or sealed records released. SASE required. Turnaround time 3-5 days. Fax notes: $3.00 for first page, $1.00 each add'l. No fax fee if 800

number provided. Copy fee: $1.00 per page. Certification fee: $1.00. Fee payee: Clerk of Court. Personal checks accepted. Prepayment is required.

Bingham County

District & Magistrate Courts 501 N Maple St, #402, Blackfoot, ID 83221-1700; 208-785-5005 X342(Dist) X267(Magis); Fax: 208-785-8057. Hours: 8AM-Noon, 1-5PM (MST). *Felony, Misdemeanor, Civil, Eviction, Small Claims, Probate.*

Civil Records: Access: Phone, fax, mail, in person. Both court and visitors may perform in person searches. No search fee. Required to search: name, years to search; also helpful: address. Civil cases indexed by defendant, plaintiff. Civil records on computer from 1989, from microfiche from 1865.
Criminal Records: Access: Phone, fax, mail, in person. Both court and visitors may perform in person searches. No search fee. Required to search: name, years to search, signed release; also helpful: address, DOB, SSN. Criminal records on computer from 1989, from microfiche from 1865.
General Information: Public Access terminal is available. No juvenile, adoption, mental records released. SASE required. Turnaround time 1-2 weeks. Fax notes: $1.25 per page. Copy fee: $1.00 per page. Certification fee: $1.00. Fee payee: Clerk of Court. Personal checks accepted. Prepayment is required.

Blaine County

District & Magistrate Courts 201 2nd Ave S #110, Hailey, ID 83333; 208-788-5548; Fax: 208-788-5512. Hours: 9AM-5PM (MST). *Felony, Misdemeanor, Civil, Eviction, Small Claims, Probate.*

Note: The Magistrate Court (Misdemeanor, Small Claims, Eviction, Probate) is in suite #106; Magistrate Court phone is 208-788-5525; fax 208-788-5527.

Civil Records: Access: Phone, fax, mail, in person. Both court and visitors may perform in person searches. No search fee. Required to search: name, years to search. Civil cases indexed by defendant, plaintiff. Civil records on computer from 1992.
Criminal Records: Access: Phone, fax, mail, in person. Both court and visitors may perform in person searches. No search fee. Required to search: name, years to search, DOB, SSN. Criminal records on computer since 1988.
General Information:. No juvenile records released. SASE required. Turnaround time 3-10 days. Fax notes: $1.00 per page. Copy fee: $1.00 per page. Certification fee: $1.00 per document. Fee payee: Clerk of Court. Personal checks accepted. Prepayment is required.

Boise County

District & Magistrate Courts PO Box 126, Idaho City, ID 83631; 208-392-4452; Fax: 208-392-6712. Hours: 8AM-5PM (MST). *Felony, Misdemeanor, Civil, Eviction, Small Claims, Probate.*

Civil Records: Access: In person only. Visitors must perform in person searches for themselves. No search fee. Required to search: name, years to search. Civil cases indexed by defendant, plaintiff. Civil records on computer from 6/90, on docket books from 1863.
Criminal Records: Access: In person only. Visitors must perform in person searches for themselves. No search fee. Required to search: name, years to search, SSN; also helpful: DOB. Criminal records on computer from 6/90, on docket books from 1863.
General Information: Public Access terminal is available. No juvenile, adoption records released. Copy fee: $1.00 per page. Certification fee: $1.50 per page. Fee payee: Boise County. Personal checks accepted. Prepayment is required.

Bonner County

District & Magistrate Courts 215 S. First Ave, Bonner Courthouse, Sandpoint, ID 83864; 208-265-1432; Fax: 208-265-1447. Hours: 9AM-5PM (PST). *Felony, Misdemeanor, Civil, Eviction, Small Claims, Probate.*

Civil Records: Access: Mail, fax, in person. Both court and visitors may perform in person searches. No search fee. Required to search: name, years to search; also helpful: address. Civil cases indexed by defendant, plaintiff. Civil records on computer from 1990, index and docket books from 1907.
Criminal Records: Access: Mail, fax, in person. Both court and visitors may perform in person searches. No search fee. Required to search: name, years to search; also helpful: address, DOB, SSN. Criminal records on computer from 1990, index and docket books from 1907.
General Information: Public Access terminal is available. No juvenile records released. SASE required. Turnaround time 1 week. Fax notes: Fax fee $3.00 per page. Copy fee: $1.00 per page. Certification fee: $1.00. Fee payee: Bonner County Recorder or Clerk. Personal checks accepted. Prepayment is required.

Bonneville County

District & Magistrate Courts 605 N. Capital, Idaho Falls, ID 83402; 208-529-1350; Fax: 208-529-1300. Hours: 8AM-5PM (MST). *Felony, Misdemeanor, Civil, Eviction, Small Claims, Probate.*

www.co.bonneville.id.us

Civil Records: Access: In person only. Visitors must perform in person searches for themselves. No search fee. Required to search: name, years to search. Civil cases indexed by defendant, plaintiff. Civil records on computer from civil from 1991. Docket books by case number ongoing. Actual case records are archived before 10/91.
Criminal Records: Access: In person only. Visitors must perform in person searches for themselves. No search fee. Required to search: name, years to search, DOB, signed release; also helpful: SSN. Criminal misdemeanor records on computer from 1983, felony on computer from 1991, civil from 1991. Criminal on microfiche from 1977, civil from 1923. Docket books by case number ongoing. Actual case records are archived before 10/91.
General Information: Public Access terminal is available. No child protective, protection orders, juvenile, sanity, adoption or termination records released. Copy fee: $1.00 per page. Certification fee: $1.00. Fee payee: Bonneville County. Personal checks accepted. For criminal and traffic records only. Prepayment is required.

Boundary County

District & Magistrate Courts Boundary County Courthouse, PO Box 419, Bonners Ferry, ID 83805; 208-267-5504; Fax: 208-267-7814. Hours: 9AM-5PM (PST). *Felony, Misdemeanor, Civil, Eviction, Small Claims, Probate.*

www.boundary-idaho.com

Civil Records: Access: In person only. Visitors must perform in person searches for themselves. No search fee. Required to search: name, years to search; also helpful: address. Civil cases indexed by defendant, plaintiff. Civil records on computer from 1989; by case number, index books, cards or microfiche by name from early 1900s.
Criminal Records: Access: In person only. Visitors must perform in person searches for themselves. No search fee. Required to search: name, years to search, SSN; also helpful: DOB. Criminal records on computer from 1989; by case number, index books, cards or microfiche by name from early 1900s.

General Information: Public Access terminal is available. No sealed records released. Copy fee: $1.00 per page. Certification fee: $1.00 per page. Fee payee: Clerk of Court. Personal checks accepted. Prepayment is required.

Butte County

District & Magistrate Courts PO Box 737, Arco, ID 83213; 208-527-3021; Fax: 208-527-3448. Hours: 9AM-5PM (MST). *Felony, Misdemeanor, Civil, Eviction, Small Claims, Probate.*

Civil Records: Access: Phone, fax, mail, in person. Both court and visitors may perform in person searches. No search fee. Required to search: name, years to search; also helpful: address. Civil cases indexed by defendant, plaintiff. Civil records on computer from 1989, archives prior. Docket books by case number from early 1910s.
Criminal Records: Access: Phone, fax, mail, in person. Both court and visitors may perform in person searches. No search fee. Required to search: name, years to search; also helpful: address, DOB, SSN. Criminal records on computer from 1989, archives prior. Docket books by case number from early 1910s.
General Information: Public Access terminal is available. No juvenile records released. SASE required. Turnaround time 1 week. Fax notes: Fee to fax results is $1.00 per page. Copy fee: $1.00 per page. Certification fee: $2.50. Fee payee: Butte County Magistrate Court. Personal checks accepted. Prepayment is required.

Camas County

District & Magistrate Courts PO Box 430, Fairfield, ID 83327; 208-764-2238; Fax: 208-764-2349. Hours: 8:30AM-Noon, 1-5PM (MST). *Felony, Misdemeanor, Civil, Eviction, Small Claims, Probate.*

Civil Records: Access: Mail, in person. Both court and visitors may perform in person searches. No search fee. Required to search: name, years to search; also helpful: address. Civil cases indexed by defendant, plaintiff. Civil records from archives from 1917. Register of actions by case number.
Criminal Records: Access: Mail, in person. Both court and visitors may perform in person searches. No search fee. Required to search: name, years to search; also helpful: address, DOB, SSN. Criminal records from archives from 1917. Register of actions by case number.
General Information: Public Access terminal is available. No juvenile or domestic violence records released. SASE required. Turnaround time 1 day. Copy fee: $1.00 per page. Certification fee: $1.00. Fee payee: Camas County Courthouse. Personal checks accepted. Prepayment is required.

Canyon County

District & Magistrate Courts 1115 Albany, Caldwell, ID 83605; Civil phone: 208-454-7570; Criminal phone: 208-454-7571. Hours: 8:30AM-5PM (MST). *Felony, Misdemeanor, Civil, Eviction, Small Claims, Probate.*

www.webpak.net/~tca3sec
Note: A daily court calendar is available at the web site.
Civil Records: Access: In person only. Visitors must perform in person searches for themselves. No search fee. Required to search: name, years to search. Civil cases indexed by defendant, plaintiff. Civil records on computer from 1989, microfiche from 1800s, and docket books.
Criminal Records: Access: In person only. Visitors must perform in person searches for themselves. No search fee. Required to search: name, years to search; also helpful: DOB, SSN. Criminal records on computer from 1989, microfiche from 1800s, and docket books.
General Information: Public Access terminal is available. No adoption, mental, domestic violence

records not released. Copy fee: $1.00 per page. Certification fee: $1.00. Fee payee: Clerk of Court. Only cashiers checks and money orders accepted.

Caribou County

District & Magistrate Courts 159 S. Main, Soda Springs, ID 83276; 208-547-4342; Fax: 208-547-4759. Hours: 9AM-5PM (MST). *Felony, Misdemeanor, Civil, Eviction, Small Claims, Probate.*

Civil Records: Access: Phone, fax, mail, in person. Only the court performs in person searches; visitors may not. No search fee. Required to search: name, years to search. Civil cases indexed by defendant, plaintiff. Civil records on computer from 1989, from archives from 1919 by case number.
Criminal Records: Access: Phone, fax, mail, in person. Only the court performs in person searches; visitors may not. No search fee. Required to search: name, years to search, DOB, SSN; also helpful: address. Criminal records on computer from 1989, from archives from 1919 by case number.
General Information:. No adoption, guardianship records released. SASE required. Turnaround time to 1 week. Fax notes: $2.00 for first page, $1.00 each add'l. Copy fee: $1.00 per page. Certification fee: $1.00. Fee payee: Clerk of Court. Business checks accepted. Out of state checks not accepted. Prepayment is required.

Cassia County

District & Magistrate Courts 1459 Overland, Burley, ID 83318; 208-878-7351 Magistrate; 878-4367 Dist; Fax: 208-878-1003. Hours: 8:30AM-5PM (MST). *Felony, Misdemeanor, Civil, Eviction, Small Claims, Probate.*

www.safelink.net/ccounty/clerkof.htm
Civil Records: Access: Phone, fax, mail, in person. Both court and visitors may perform in person searches. No search fee. Required to search: name, years to search; also helpful: address. Civil cases indexed by defendant, plaintiff. Civil records on computer from 1990, archives from 1900s.
Criminal Records: Access: Fax, mail, in person. Both court and visitors may perform in person searches. No search fee. Required to search: name, years to search; also helpful: address, DOB, SSN. Criminal records on computer from 1990, archives from 1900s.
General Information: Public Access terminal is available. No juvenile, adoption, mental commitment, child protection records released. SASE required. Turnaround time to 1-2 days. Fax notes: $2.50 per page. Copy fee: $1.00 per page. Certification fee: $1.50. Fee payee: Clerk of Court. Personal checks accepted. Prepayment is required.

Clark County

District & Magistrate Courts PO Box 205, DuBois, ID 83423; 208-374-5402; Fax: 208-374-5609. Hours: 9AM-5PM (MST). *Felony, Misdemeanor, Civil, Eviction, Small Claims, Probate.*

Civil Records: Access: Fax, mail, in person. Both court and visitors may perform in person searches. No search fee. Required to search: name, years to search; also helpful: address. Civil cases indexed by defendant, plaintiff. Civil records on computer from 1985, on microfiche for civil judgments and from archives from 1919.
Criminal Records: Access: Fax, mail, in person. Both court and visitors may perform in person searches. No search fee. Required to search: name, years to search; also helpful: address, DOB, SSN. Criminal records on computer from 1985, on microfiche for civil judgments and from archives from 1919.
General Information: Public Access terminal is available. No juvenile, adoption records released. SASE required. Turnaround time 3 days. Fax notes: $.50 per page. Copy fee: $1.00 per page. Certification fee: $2.00.

Fee payee: Clerk of Court. Personal checks accepted. Prepayment is required.

Clearwater County

District & Magistrate Courts PO Box 586, Orofino, ID 83544; 208-476-5596; Fax: 208-476-5159. Hours: 8AM-5PM (PST). *Felony, Misdemeanor, Civil, Eviction, Small Claims, Probate.*

Civil Records: Access: Phone, fax, mail, in person. Only the court performs in person searches; visitors may not. No search fee. Required to search: name, years to search. Civil cases indexed by defendant, plaintiff. Civil records on computer from 8/91, in docket books prior.
Criminal Records: Access: Phone, fax, mail, in person. Only the court performs in person searches; visitors may not. No search fee. Required to search: name, years to search. Criminal records on computer from 8/91, in docket books prior.
General Information:. No juvenile, domestic violence, adoption, social records released. SASE requested. Turnaround time 7 days. Fax notes: $1.00 per page. Copy fee: $1.00 per page. Certification fee: $1.00. Fee payee: Clerk of Court. Business checks accepted. Prepayment is required.

Custer County

District & Magistrate Courts PO Box 385, Challis, ID 83226; 208-879-2359; Fax: 208-879-5246. Hours: 8AM-5PM (MST). *Felony, Misdemeanor, Civil, Eviction, Small Claims, Probate.*

Civil Records: Access: Phone, mail, in person. Only the court performs in person searches; visitors may not. Search fee: $5.00 per name. Required to search: name, years to search. Civil cases indexed by defendant. Civil records on computer from 1989, archived from early 1900s.
Criminal Records: Access: Phone, mail, in person. Only the court performs in person searches; visitors may not. Search fee: $5.00 per name. Required to search: name, years to search, DOB, signed release; also helpful: SSN. Criminal records on computer from 1989, archived from early 1900s.
General Information:. No juvenile, adoption records released. Turnaround time 1 week. Copy fee: $1.00 per page. Certification fee: $1.00 per page. Fee payee: Custer County. Personal checks accepted. Prepayment is required.

Elmore County

District & Magistrate Courts 150 S 4th East, Ste 5, Mountain Home, ID 83647; 208-587-2133 x208; Fax: 208-587-2134. Hours: 9AM-5PM (MST). *Felony, Misdemeanor, Civil, Eviction, Small Claims, Probate.*

Civil Records: Access: In person only. Visitors must perform in person searches for themselves. No search fee. Required to search: name; also helpful: years to search. Civil cases indexed by defendant, plaintiff. Civil records on computer from 1992, on microfiche from 1972, archived from early 1900s.
Criminal Records: Access: In person only. Visitors must perform in person searches for themselves. No search fee. Required to search: name, DOB, signed release; also helpful: years to search, SSN. Criminal records on computer from 1992, on microfiche from 1972, archived from early 1900s.
General Information: Public Access terminal is available. No juvenile, adoption, domestic violence, mental commitment records released. Fax notes: $1.00 per page. Copy fee: $1.00 per page. Certification fee: $1.00 per page. Fee payee: Elmore County. Personal checks accepted. Prepayment is required.

Franklin County

District & Magistrate Courts 39 West Oneida, Preston, ID 83263; 208-852-0877; Fax: 208-852-2926. Hours: 9AM-5PM (MST). *Felony, Misdemeanor, Civil, Eviction, Small Claims, Probate.*

Civil Records: Access: Phone, fax, mail, in person. Both court and visitors may perform in person searches. Search fee: $2.00 per name. Fee is for years prior to 1990. No fee for 1990 to present. Required to search: name, years to search. Civil cases indexed by defendant, plaintiff. Civil records on computer from 1990, on microfiche from 1920, archived from 1920.

Criminal Records: Access: Phone, fax, mail, in person. Both court and visitors may perform in person searches. Search fee: $2.00 per name. Fee is for years prior to 1990. No fee for 1990 to present. Required to search: name, years to search; also helpful: DOB, SSN. Criminal records on computer from 1990, on microfiche from 1920, archived from 1920.

General Information: Public Access terminal is available. No adoption records released. SASE required. Turnaround time 2-3 days. Fax notes: No fee to fax results. Local calls only. Copy fee: $1.00 per page. Certification fee: $1.00. Fee payee: Clerk of Court. Personal checks accepted. Prepayment is required.

Fremont County

District & Magistrate Courts 151 W 1st North, St Anthony, ID 83445; 208-624-7401; Fax: 208-624-4607. Hours: 9AM-5PM (MST). *Felony, Misdemeanor, Civil, Eviction, Small Claims, Probate.*

Civil Records: Access: Phone, fax, mail, in person. Both court and visitors may perform in person searches. No search fee. Required to search: name, years to search; also helpful: address. Civil cases indexed by defendant, plaintiff. Civil records on computer back to 1990, microfiche for last 20 years, prior archives. Thursday is the best day for in person searches.

Criminal Records: Access: Fax, mail, in person. Both court and visitors may perform in person searches. No search fee. Required to search: name, years to search, DOB; also helpful: SSN. Criminal records on computer back to 1990, microfiche for last 20 years, prior archives. Same as civil.

General Information: Public Access terminal is available. No adoption or juvenile records released. SASE required. Turnaround time 1 week. Fax notes: Fee to fax results is $2.00 per page. Copy fee: $1.00 per page. Certification fee: $1.00. Fee payee: Clerk of Court. Personal checks accepted. Prepayment is required.

Gem County

District & Magistrate Courts 415 East Main St, Emmett, ID 83617; 208-365-4561; Fax: 208-365-6172. Hours: 8AM-5PM (MST). *Felony, Misdemeanor, Civil, Eviction, Small Claims, Probate.*

www.webpak.net/~tca3sec

Note: Felony and misdemeanor records in different offices; therefore, a search fee is charged for each.

Civil Records: Access: Mail, in person. Both court and visitors may perform in person searches. Search fee: $5.00 per name. Required to search: name, years to search; also helpful: address. Civil cases indexed by defendant, plaintiff. Civil records on computer from 1990, on microfiche, and archived from 1916.

Criminal Records: Access: Mail, in person. Both court and visitors may perform in person searches. Search fee: $5.00 per name. Required to search: name, years to search; also helpful: address, DOB, SSN. Criminal records on computer from 1990, on microfiche, and archived from 1916.

General Information: Public Access terminal is available. No juvenile, adoption records or domestic

violence released. SASE required. Turnaround time 10 days. Copy fee: $1.00 per page. Certification fee: $1.00 plus $.50 per page. Fee payee: Gem County. Personal checks accepted. Prepayment is required.

Gooding County

District & Magistrate Courts PO Box 477, Gooding, ID 83330; 208-934-4261; Fax: 208-934-4408. Hours: 8AM-5PM (MST). *Felony, Misdemeanor, Civil, Eviction, Small Claims, Probate.*

Civil Records: Access: Phone, fax, mail, in person. Visitors must perform in person searches for themselves. No search fee. Required to search: name, years to search. Civil cases indexed by defendant, plaintiff. Civil records on computer from 1994, on microfiche, docket books from 1860s.

Criminal Records: Access: In person only. Visitors must perform in person searches for themselves. No search fee. Required to search: name, years to search, DOB, SSN. Criminal records on computer from 1994, on microfiche, docket books from 1860s.

General Information: Public Access terminal is available. No juvenile, adoption, domestic violence records released. SASE required. Turnaround time 5-10 days. Fax notes: Fee to fax results is $1.00 per page. Copy fee: $1.00 per page. Certification fee: $1.00. Fee payee: Gooding County Clerk. Personal checks accepted. Prepayment is required.

Idaho County

District & Magistrate Courts 320 West Main, Grangeville, ID 83530; 208-983-2776; Fax: 208-983-2376. Hours: 8:30AM-5PM (PST). *Felony, Misdemeanor, Civil, Eviction, Small Claims, Probate.*

Civil Records: Access: Phone, fax, mail, in person. Only the court performs in person searches; visitors may not. No search fee. Required to search: name, years to search. Civil cases indexed by defendant, plaintiff. Civil records on computer from 1989, on microfiche and archived from late 1800s.

Criminal Records: Access: Phone, fax, mail, in person. Only the court performs in person searches; visitors may not. No search fee. Required to search: name, years to search. Criminal records on computer from 1989, on microfiche and archived from late 1800s.

General Information:. No domestic violence, juvenile, hospitalization, adoption, termination records released. SASE not required. Turnaround time same week. Fax notes: $2.00 per page. Copy fee: $1.00 per page. Certification fee: $1.00. Fee payee: Idaho County. Personal checks accepted. Prepayment is required.

Jefferson County

District & Magistrate Courts PO Box 71, Rigby, ID 83442; 208-745-7736; Fax: 208-745-6636. Hours: 9AM-5PM (MST). *Felony, Misdemeanor, Civil, Eviction, Small Claims, Probate.*

Civil Records: Access: In person only. Both court and visitors may perform in person searches. No search fee. Required to search: name, years to search. Civil cases indexed by defendant, plaintiff. Civil records archived from early 1900s. Type of case also helpful with request.

Criminal Records: Access: In person only. Both court and visitors may perform in person searches. No search fee. Required to search: name, years to search, DOB. Criminal records archived from early 1900s. Type of case also helpful with request.

General Information: Public Access terminal is available. No juvenile, adoption, some domestic records released. Fax notes: $1.00 per page. Copy fee: $1.00 per page. Certification fee: $1.00 per page. Fee payee: Clerk of Court. Personal checks accepted. Prepayment is required.

Jerome County

District & Magistrate Courts 300 N Lincoln St, Jerome, ID 83338; 208-324-8811; Fax: 208-324-2719. Hours: 8:30AM-5PM (MST). *Felony, Misdemeanor, Civil, Eviction, Small Claims, Probate.*

Civil Records: Access: Fax, mail, in person. Both court and visitors may perform in person searches. No search fee. Required to search: name, years to search. Civil cases indexed by defendant, plaintiff. Civil records on computer from 1988, prior on microfiche.

Criminal Records: Access: Fax, mail, in person. Both court and visitors may perform in person searches. No search fee. Required to search: name, years to search, address, DOB, SSN. Criminal records on computer from 1985, civil from 1988, prior on microfiche. Will not do background searches.

General Information:. No juvenile records released. SASE required. Turnaround time 2 days. Fax notes: $3.00 for first page, $2.50 each add'l. Copy fee: $1.00 per page. Certification fee: $1.50 per page. Fee payee: Clerk of Court. Personal checks accepted. Prepayment is required.

Kootenai County

District Court 324 West Garden Ave (PO Box 9000), Coeur d'Alene, ID 83816-9000; Civil phone: 208-769-4430; Criminal phone: 208-769-4440; Fax: 208-664-0639. Hours: 9AM-5PM (PST). *Felony, Misdemeanor, Civil, Eviction, Small Claims, Probate.*

www.co.kootenai.id.us/court

Civil Records: Access: In person, online. Visitors must perform in person searches for themselves. No search fee. Required to search: name, years to search. Civil cases indexed by defendant, plaintiff. Civil records on computer from 1989, on microfiche from 1881, archived from 1819. Online access to court documents is available free at www.co.kootenai.id.us/court/default.asp.

Criminal Records: Access: In person, online. Visitors must perform in person searches for themselves. No search fee. Required to search: name, years to search; also helpful: DOB, SSN. Criminal records on computer from 1989, on microfiche from 1881, archived from 1819. Online access to criminal records same as civil.

General Information: Public Access terminal is available. No sealed, adoption, parental termination, mentally incapacitated records released. Copy fee: $1.00 per page. Certification fee: $1.00. Fee payee: Clerk of Court. Personal checks accepted. Credit cards accepted through official payments 800-530-8189. Prepayment is required.

Latah County

District & Magistrate Courts PO Box 8068, Moscow, ID 83843; 208-883-2255; Fax: 208-883-2259. Hours: 8:30AM-5PM M-W, 8AM-5PM TH,F (PST). *Felony, Misdemeanor, Civil, Eviction, Small Claims, Probate.*

Civil Records: Access: Phone, fax, mail, in person. Only the court performs in person searches; visitors may not. Search fee: $4.00 per name. Required to search: name, years to search; also helpful: address. Civil cases indexed by defendant, plaintiff. Civil records on computer from 1986, archived from May 1888.

Criminal Records: Access: Phone, fax, mail, in person. Only the court performs in person searches; visitors may not. Search fee: $4.00 per name. Required to search: name, years to search; also helpful: address, DOB, SSN. Criminal records on computer from 1986, archived from May 1888.

General Information:. No adoption, juvenile, hospitalization records released. Turnaround time 1-2 days. Copy fee: $1.00 per page. Certification fee: $1.00. Fee payee: Clerk of Court. Personal checks accepted. Prepayment is required.

Lemhi County

District & Magistrate Courts 206 Courthouse Dr, Salmon, ID 83467; 208-756-2815; Fax: 208-756-8424. 8AM-5PM (MST). *Felony, Misdemeanor, Civil, Eviction, Small Claims, Probate.*

Civil Records: Access: Phone, fax, mail, in person. Both court and visitors may perform in person searches. Search fee: $5.00 per name. Required to search: name, years to search; also helpful: address. Civil cases indexed by defendant, plaintiff. Civil records on computer from 1991, on microfiche from 1964, archives from 1869.

Criminal Records: Access: Phone, fax, mail, in person. Both court and visitors may perform in person searches. Search fee: $5.00 per name. Required to search: name, years to search; also helpful: address, DOB, SSN. Criminal records on computer from 1991, on microfiche from 1964, archives from 1869.

General Information: Public Access terminal is available. No PSI, sealed records released. SASE requested. Turnaround time 1 day. Fax notes: Fee to fax results is $1.00 per page. Copy fee: $1.00 per page. Certification fee: $1.00. Fee payee: Lemhi County Clerk. Personal checks accepted. Credit cards accepted: Visa, MasterCard, Discover, AmEx. This is through a service. Prepayment is required.

Lewis County

District & Magistrate Courts 510 Oak St (PO Box 39), Nezperce, ID 83543; 208-937-2251; Fax: 208-937-9223. Hours: 9AM-5PM (PST). *Felony, Misdemeanor, Civil, Eviction, Small Claims, Probate.*

Civil Records: Access: Phone, fax, mail, in person. Both court and visitors may perform in person searches. No search fee. Required to search: name, years to search. Civil cases indexed by defendant, plaintiff. Civil records on computer from 1991, archived from late 1911.

Criminal Records: Access: Phone, fax, mail, in person. Both court and visitors may perform in person searches. No search fee. Required to search: name, years to search; also helpful: DOB, SSN. Criminal records on computer from 1991, archived from late 1911.

General Information:. No juvenile, adoption records released. SASE required. Turnaround time 1 week. Fax notes: $1.00 per page. Copy fee: $1.00 per page. Certification fee: $1.00. Fee payee: Clerk of Court. Only cashiers checks and money orders accepted. Two-party checks not accepted. Prepayment is required.

Lincoln County

District & Magistrate Courts Drawer A, Shoshone, ID 83352; 208-886-2173; Fax: 208-886-2458. Hours: 8:30AM-5PM (MST). *Felony, Misdemeanor, Civil, Eviction, Small Claims, Probate.*

Civil Records: Access: In person only. Visitors must perform in person searches for themselves. No search fee. Required to search: name, years to search. Civil cases indexed by defendant, plaintiff. Civil records on computer from 1991, archives from 1800s.

Criminal Records: Access: In person only. Visitors must perform in person searches for themselves. No search fee. Required to search: name, years to search; also helpful: DOB, SSN. Criminal records on computer from 1991, archives from 1800s.

General Information: Public Access terminal is available. No juvenile, domestic violence, sealed records released. Copy fee: $1.00 per page. Certification fee: $1.00. Fee payee: Lincoln County Courts. Personal checks accepted.

Madison County

District & Magistrate Courts PO Box 389, Rexburg, ID 83440; 208-356-9383; Fax: 208-356-5425. Hours: 9AM-5PM (MST). *Felony, Misdemeanor, Civil, Eviction, Small Claims, Probate.*

Civil Records: Access: In person only. Both court and visitors may perform in person searches. No search fee. Required to search: name, years to search; also helpful: address. Civil cases indexed by defendant, plaintiff. Civil records on computer from 1991, microfiche and archives from early 1900s.

Criminal Records: Access: In person only. Visitors must perform in person searches for themselves. No search fee. Required to search: name, years to search; also helpful: address, DOB, SSN. Criminal records on computer from 1991, microfiche and archives from early 1900s.

General Information: Public Access terminal is available. No juvenile records released. Copy fee: $1.00 per page. Certification fee: $1.00. Fee payee: Clerk of Court. Personal checks accepted. Prepayment required.

Minidoka County

District & Magistrate Courts PO Box 368, Rupert, ID 83350; 208-436-9041 (Dist) 436-7186 (Magis); Fax: 208-436-5857. Hours: 8:30AM-5PM (MST). *Felony, Misdemeanor, Civil, Eviction, Small Claims, Probate.*

Civil Records: Access: Phone, fax, mail, in person. Only the court performs in person searches; visitors may not. No search fee. Required to search: name, years to search. Civil cases indexed by defendant, plaintiff. Civil records on computer from 1989, archives from early 1900s.

Criminal Records: Access: Phone, fax, mail, in person. Only the court performs in person searches; visitors may not. No search fee. Required to search: name, years to search, DOB, SSN, signed release. Criminal records on computer from 1989, archives from early 1900s.

General Information:. No juvenile records released. Turnaround time 1-3 days. Fax notes: $.50 per page. Copy fee: $1.00 per page. Certification fee: $.50 per page. Fee payee: Clerk of Court. Personal checks accepted.

Nez Perce County

District & Magistrate Court PO Box 896 (1230 Main St), Lewiston, ID 83501; 208-799-3040; Fax: 208-799-3058. Hours: 8AM-5PM (PST). *Felony, Misdemeanor, Civil, Eviction, Small Claims, Probate.*

www.co.nezperce.id.us/clerk/clerk.htm

Civil Records: Access: Phone, fax, mail, in person. Both court and visitors may perform in person searches. No search fee. Required to search: name; also helpful: years to search. Civil cases indexed by defendant, plaintiff. Civil records on computer from 1990, microfiche from 1970 and archives from late 1800s.

Criminal Records: Access: Phone, fax, mail, in person. Both court and visitors may perform in person searches. No search fee. Required to search: name, DOB; also helpful: years to search, aliases, SSN. Criminal records on computer from 1990, microfiche from 1970 and archives from late 1800s.

General Information: Public Access terminal is available. SASE not required. Turnaround time 10 day waiting period. Fax notes: $1.00 for first page, plus (if long-distance) $.50 each add'l minute. Copy fee: $1.00 per page. Certification fee: $1.00 per page. Fee payee: Clerk of Court. Personal checks accepted. Prepayment is required.

Oneida County

District & Magistrate Courts 10 Court St, Malad City, ID 83252; 208-766-4285 X111,112,114,105; Fax: 208-766-2990. Hours: 9AM-5PM (MST). *Felony, Misdemeanor, Civil, Eviction, Small Claims, Probate.*

Civil Records: Access: Phone, fax, mail, in person. Both court and visitors may perform in person searches. No search fee. Required to search: name, years to search; also helpful: address. Civil cases indexed by case number, defendant, plaintiff. Civil records on computer from 1990, archives from 1886.

Criminal Records: Access: Phone, fax, mail, in person. Both court and visitors may perform in person searches. No search fee. Required to search: name, years to search; also helpful: address, DOB, SSN. Criminal records on computer from 1990, archives from 1886.

General Information:. No juvenile, adoption records released. SASE requested. Turnaround time 1-2 days. Fax notes: $1.00 per page. Copy fee: $1.00 per page. Certification fee: $1.00. Fee payee: Clerk of Court. Personal checks accepted. Prepayment is required.

Owyhee County

District & Magistrate Courts-I Courthouse, Murphy, ID 83650; 208-495-2806; Fax: 208-495-1226. Hours: 8:30AM-5PM (MST). *Felony, Misdemeanor, Civil, Eviction, Small Claims, Probate.*

www.webpak.net/~tca3sec

Civil Records: Access: Fax, mail, in person. Both court and visitors may perform in person searches. No search fee. Required to search: name, years to search. Civil cases indexed by defendant, plaintiff. Civil records on computer from 1992, archives from 1800s.

Criminal Records: Access: Fax, mail, in person. Both court and visitors may perform in person searches. No search fee. Required to search: name, years to search; also helpful: DOB. Criminal records on computer from 1992, archives from 1800s. Signed release required for search of juvenile records.

General Information:. No adoption, juvenile (except for some that are open), domestic violence records released. Turnaround time 5-7 days. Fax notes: Fee to fax results is $1.00 per page or $5.00 per document. Copy fee: $1.00 per page. Certification fee: $1.00 per page. Fee payee: Owyhee County. Only cashiers checks and money orders accepted. Prepayment is required.

Homedale Magistrate Court 31 W Wyoming, Homedale, ID 83628-3402; 208-337-4540; Fax: 208-337-3035. Hours: 8:30AM-5PM (MST). *Misdemeanor, Civil Actions Under $10,000, Eviction, Small Claims.*

http://owyheecounty.net

Civil Records: Access: In person only. Only the court performs in person searches; visitors may not. No search fee. Required to search: name, years to search; also helpful: address. Civil cases indexed by defendant. Civil records on computer from 1992, archives from 1975.

Criminal Records: Access: In person only. Only the court performs in person searches; visitors may not. No search fee. Required to search: name, years to search; also helpful: address, DOB, SSN. Criminal records on computer from 1992, archives from 1975.

General Information:. No juvenile or mental records released. Fax notes: $5.00 each 1st 2 pages, $2.00 pages 3-10; $.75 each add'l. Copy fee: $1.00 per page. Certification fee: $1.00 per document. Fee payee: Clerk of Court. Prepayment is required.

Payette County

District & Magistrate Courts 1130 3rd Ave N, Payette, ID 83661; 208-642-6000 (Dist) 642-6010(Magis); Fax: 208-642-6011. Hours: 9AM-5PM (MST). *Felony, Misdemeanor, Civil, Eviction, Small Claims, Probate.*

www.webpak.net/~tca3sec

Civil Records: Access: Fax, mail, in person. Both court and visitors may perform in person searches. Search fee: $5.00 per name. Required to search: name, years to search; also helpful: address. Civil cases indexed by defendant, plaintiff. Civil records on computer back to 1992, prior on microfiche or archived from 1917.

Criminal Records: Access: Fax, mail, in person. Both court and visitors may perform in person searches. Search fee: $5.00 per name. Required to search: name, years to search, signed release; also helpful: address, DOB, SSN. Criminal records on computer back to 1992, prior microfiche or archived from 1917.

General Information: Public Access terminal is available. No juvenile, adoption records released. SASE required. Turnaround time 1 day. Fax notes: $3.00 1st page, $.50 each add'l. Copy fee: $1.00 per page. Certification fee: $1.00. Fee payee: Clerk of Court. Personal checks accepted. Prepayment is required.

Power County

District & Magistrate Courts 543 Bannock Ave, American Falls, ID 83211; 208-226-7611 (Dist) 226-7618(Magistrate); Fax: 208-226-7612. Hours: 9AM-5PM (MST). *Felony, Misdemeanor, Civil, Eviction, Small Claims, Probate.*

Civil Records: Access: Phone, fax, mail, in person. Only the court performs in person searches; visitors may not. No search fee. Required to search: name, years to search. Civil cases indexed by defendant. Civil records on computer from 1986, prior archived from early 1900s.

Criminal Records: Access: Phone, fax, mail, in person. Only the court performs in person searches; visitors may not. No search fee. Required to search: name, years to search, DOB, SSN, signed release. Criminal records on computer from 1986, prior archived from early 1900s.

General Information: Public Access terminal is available. No juvenile, mental commitment records released. SASE required. Turnaround time 10 days. Fax notes: $1.00 per page. Copy fee: $1.00 per page. Certification fee: $1.50. Fee payee: Power County Magistrate Court. Personal checks accepted. Prepayment is required.

Shoshone County

District & Magistrate Courts 700 Bank St, Wallace, ID 83873; 208-752-1266; Fax: 208-753-0921. Hours: 9AM-5PM (PST). *Felony, Misdemeanor, Civil, Eviction, Small Claims, Probate.*

Civil Records: Access: Phone, fax, mail, in person. Both court and visitors may perform in person searches. No search fee. Required to search: name, years to search; also helpful: address. Civil cases indexed by defendant, plaintiff. Civil records on computer from 1988, archives from 1971. Juvenile case information not available by fax.

Criminal Records: Access: Phone, mail, in person. Both court and visitors may perform in person searches. No search fee. Required to search: name, years to search; also helpful: address, DOB, SSN. Criminal records on computer from 1988, archives from 1971.

General Information: Public Access terminal is available. (For records since 1995.) No special proceeding, juvenile records released. SASE required.

Turnaround time 1-2 days. Fax notes: $2.00 for first page, $1.00 each add'l. Add $1.00 1st page if long distance. Copy fee: $1.00 per page. Certification fee: $1.00. Fee payee: Clerk of Court. Personal checks accepted. Prepayment is required.

Teton County

District & Magistrate Courts 89 N Main #5, Driggs, ID 83422; 208-354-2239; Fax: 208-354-8496. Hours: 9AM-5PM (MST). *Felony, Misdemeanor, Civil, Eviction, Small Claims, Probate.*

Note: Address and telephone given above are for District Court. If you wish to access only the Magistrate Court and call 208-354-2239.

Civil Records: Access: Phone, fax, mail, in person. Both court and visitors may perform in person searches. Search fee: $5.00 per name. Required to search: name, years to search; also helpful: address. Civil cases indexed by defendant, plaintiff. Civil records on computer from 1992, archives from 1974, I-Star since 1992.

Criminal Records: Access: Phone, fax, mail, in person. Both court and visitors may perform in person searches. Search fee: $5.00 per name. Required to search: name, years to search; also helpful: address, DOB, SSN. Criminal records on computer from 1992, archives from 1974, I-Star since 1993.

General Information: Public Access terminal is available. No juvenile, DV records released. SASE required. Turnaround time 3 days. Fax notes: $2.00 per page. Copy fee: $1.00 per page. Certification fee: $1.00. Fee payee: Clerk of Court. Personal checks accepted. Prepayment is required.

Twin Falls County

District & Magistrate Courts PO Box 126, Twin Falls, ID 83303-0126; 208-736-4013; Fax: 208-736-4155. Hours: 8AM-5PM (MST). *Felony, Misdemeanor, Civil, Eviction, Small Claims, Probate.*

www.co.twin-falls.id.us/5thdistrict

Civil Records: Access: Phone, fax, mail, in person. Both court and visitors may perform in person searches. No search fee. Required to search: name, years to search; also helpful: address. Civil cases indexed by defendant, plaintiff. Civil records on computer from 1989, archives from early 1900s.

Criminal Records: Access: Phone, fax, mail, in person. Both court and visitors may perform in person searches. No search fee. Required to search: name, years to search; also helpful: address, DOB, SSN. Criminal records on computer from 1989, archives from early 1900s.

General Information: Public Access terminal is available. No adoption, termination, juvenile records released. Turnaround time 1-10 days. Fax notes: $2.50 per page. Copy fee: $1.00 per page. Certification fee: $1.00 per page. Fee payee: Court Services. Personal checks accepted. Prepayment is required.

Valley County

District & Magistrate Courts-I PO Box 1350, Cascade, ID 83611; 208-382-7178; Fax: 208-382-7184. Hours: 9AM-5PM (MST). *Felony, Misdemeanor, Civil, Eviction, Small Claims, Probate.*

Civil Records: Access: Phone, fax, mail, in person. Both court and visitors may perform in person searches. Search fee: $5.00. Required to search: name, years to search; also helpful: address. Civil cases indexed by defendant, plaintiff. Civil records on computer from 1990, microfiche and archives from early 1900s.

Criminal Records: Access: Phone, fax, mail, in person. Both court and visitors may perform in person searches. Search fee: $5.00. Required to search: name, years to search; also helpful: address, DOB, SSN. Criminal records on computer from 1990, microfiche and archives from early 1900s.

General Information: Public Access terminal is available. No juvenile records released. SASE required. Turnaround time 1-3 days. Fax notes: No fee to fax results. Copy fee: $1.00 per page. Certification fee: $1.50 per page. Fee payee: Valley County. Personal checks accepted. Two-party or out of country (w/o printed-stamped US Funds) not accepted. Prepayment is required.

Magistrate Court II Valley County Courthouse Annex, 550 Deinhard Lane, McCall, ID 83638; 208-634-8102; Fax: 208-634-4040. Hours: 9AM-5PM (MST). *Misdemeanor, Civil Actions Under $10,000, Eviction, Small Claims.*

Civil Records: Access: Phone, fax, mail, in person. Only the court performs in person searches; visitors may not. No search fee. Required to search: name, years to search; also helpful: address. Civil cases indexed by defendant. Civil records on computer from 1990, archives from 1984.

Criminal Records: Access: Phone, fax, mail, in person. Only the court performs in person searches; visitors may not. No search fee. Required to search: name, years to search; also helpful: address, DOB, SSN. Criminal records on computer from 1990, archives from 1984.

General Information:. No juvenile records released. SASE required. Turnaround time 1-5 days. Fax notes: $5.00 for first page, $2.00 each add'l. Copy fee: $1.00 per page. Certification fee: $1.00 per page. Fee payee: McCall Court. Personal checks accepted.

Washington County

District & Magistrate Courts PO Box 670, Weiser, ID 83672; 208-414-2092; Fax: 208-414-3925. Hours: 8:30AM-5PM (MST). *Felony, Misdemeanor, Civil, Eviction, Small Claims, Probate.*

www.webpak.net/~tca3sec

Civil Records: Access: In person only. Visitors must perform in person searches for themselves. No search fee. Required to search: name. Civil cases indexed by defendant, plaintiff. Civil records on computer from 02/90, archives from late 1800s.

Criminal Records: Access: In person only. Visitors must perform in person searches for themselves. No search fee. Required to search: name, years to search, DOB; also helpful: SSN. Criminal records on computer from 02/90, archives from late 1800s.

General Information: Public Access terminal is available. No juvenile, adoption, hospitalization, child protection-termination of parental rights records released. Copy fee: $1.00 per page. Certification fee: $1.00. Fee payee: Washington County. Local business checks only. Prepayment is required.

Idaho Recording Offices

ORGANIZATION   44 counties, 44 recording offices. The recording officer is County Recorder. Many counties utilize a grantor/grantee index containing all transactions recorded with them. 34 counties are in the Mountain Time Zone (MST), and 10 are in the Pacific Time Zone (PST).

REAL ESTATE RECORDS   Most counties will not perform real estate name searches. Certification of copies usually costs $1.00 per document.

UCC RECORDS   Financing statements are filed at the state level except for real estate related filings. All counties will perform UCC searches. Use search request form UCC-4. Search fees are usually $6.00 per debtor name for a listing of filings and $12.00 per debtor name for a listing plus copies at no additional charge. Separately ordered copies usually cost $1.00 per page.

TAX LIEN RECORDS   Until 07/01/98, state tax liens were filed at the local county recorder. Now they are filed with the Secretary of State who has all active case files. Federal tax liens on personal property of businesses are filed with the Secretary of State. Other federal tax liens are filed with the county recorder. Some counties will perform a combined tax lien search for $5.00 while others will not perform tax lien searches.

OTHER LIENS   Judgments, hospital, labor, mechanics.

Ada County

County Clerk & Recorder, 650 Main Street, Boise, ID 83702-5960. 208-364-2223 R/E Recording: 208-364-2222 UCC Recording: 208-364-2225.
Will search UCC records. UCC search includes tax liens if requested. Will not search real estate records. **Other Phone Numbers:** Assessor 208-364-2400; Treasurer 208-364-2233; Elections 208-364-2323; Vital Records 208-334-5980.

Adams County

County Clerk & Recorder, P.O. Box 48, Council, ID 83612. 208-253-4561; Fax 208-253-4880.
Will search UCC records. This agency will not do a tax lien search. Will not search real estate records. **Other Phone Numbers:** Assessor 208-253-4271; Treasurer 208-253-4263.

Bannock County

County Clerk & Recorder, 624 East Center, Courthouse, Room 211, Pocatello, ID 83201. 208-236-7340; Fax 208-236-7345.
Will search UCC records. UCC search includes tax liens if requested. Will not search real estate records. **Other Phone Numbers:** Assessor 208-236-7260.

Bear Lake County

County Clerk & Recorder, P.O. Box 190, Paris, ID 83261. County Clerk & Recorder, R/E and UCC Recording 208-945-2212; Fax 208-945-2780.
Will search UCC records. Tax liens not included in UCC search. Mortgage searches available. **Other Phone Numbers:** Assessor 208-945-2155; Treasurer 208-945-2130; Elections 208-945-2212; Vital Records 208-945-2212.

Benewah County

County Clerk & Recorder, 701 College, St. Maries, ID 83861. 208-245-3212; Fax 208-245-3046.
Will search UCC records. This agency will not do a tax lien search. Will not search real estate records. **Other Phone Numbers:** Assessor 208-245-2821; Treasurer 208-245-2421.

Bingham County

County Clerk & Recorder, 501 North Maple #205, Blackfoot, ID 83221. 208-785-5005; Fax 208-785-4131.
Will search UCC records. UCC search includes tax liens if requested. Will not search real estate records.

Other Phone Numbers: Assessor 208-785-5005 x216; Treasurer 208-785-5005 x259.

Blaine County

County Clerk & Recorder, Courthouse, Suite 200, 206 1st Ave. South, Hailey, ID 83333. County Clerk & Recorder, R/E and UCC Recording 208-788-5505; Fax 208-788-5501. http://www.co.blaine.id.us
Will search UCC records. UCC search includes tax liens if requested. Mortgage searches available. **Other Phone Numbers:** Assessor 208-788-5535; Treasurer 208-788-5530; Appraiser/Auditor 208-788-5535; Elections 208-788-5510.

Boise County

County Clerk & Recorder, P.O. Box 1300, Idaho City, ID 83631. County Clerk & Recorder, R/E and UCC Recording 208-392-4431; Fax 208-392-4473.
Will search UCC records. This agency will not do a tax lien search. RE owner, mortgage, and property transfer searches available. **Other Phone Numbers:** Assessor 208-392-4415; Treasurer 208-392-4441; Appraiser/Auditor 208-392-4415; Elections 208-392-4431.

Bonner County

County Clerk & Recorder, 215 South First, Sandpoint, ID 83864. 208-265-1432; Fax 208-265-1447.
Will search UCC records. This agency will not do a tax lien search. Will not search real estate records. **Other Phone Numbers:** Assessor 208-265-1440; Treasurer 208-265-1433.

Bonneville County

County Clerk & Recorder, 605 North Capital, Idaho Falls, ID 83402-3582. 208-529-1350 R/E Recording: 208-529-1350 x1350 UCC Recording: 208-529-1350 x1350; Fax 208-529-1353. http://www.co.bonneville.id.us/
Will search UCC records. Tax liens not included in UCC search. Will not search real estate records. **Other Phone Numbers:** Assessor 208-529-1350 x1320; Treasurer 208-529-1350 x1380; Elections 208-529-1350 x1363; Vital Records 208-529-1350 x1350.

Boundary County

County Clerk & Recorder, P.O. Box 419, Bonners Ferry, ID 83805. 208-267-2242; Fax 208-267-7814. http://www.boundary-idaho.com
Will search UCC records. This agency will not do a tax lien search. Will not search real estate records. **Other**

Phone Numbers: Assessor 208-267-3301; Treasurer 208-267-3291.

Butte County

County Clerk & Recorder, P.O. Box 737, Arco, ID 83213. 208-527-3021; Fax 208-527-3295.
Will search UCC records. UCC search includes tax liens. RE owner, mortgage, and property transfer searches available. **Other Phone Numbers:** Assessor 208-527-8288; Treasurer 208-527-3047.

Camas County

County Clerk & Recorder, P.O. Box 430, Fairfield, ID 83327-0430. County Clerk & Recorder, R/E and UCC Recording 208-764-2242; Fax 208-764-2349.
Will search UCC records. This agency will not do a tax lien search. Will not search real estate records. **Other Phone Numbers:** Assessor 208-764-2370; Treasurer 208-764-2126; Appraiser/Auditor 208-764-2370; Elections 208-764-2242; Vital Records 208-764-2242.

Canyon County

County Recorder, 1115 Albany Street, Caldwell, ID 83605. County Recorder, R/E and UCC Recording 208-454-7556.
Will search UCC records. Tax liens not included in UCC search. Will not search real estate records. **Online Access:** Assessor, Property. Online access to the Assessor and Treasurer's databases requires registration and monthly fees. For subscription information, email clane@canyoncounty.org or call 208-454-7401. **Other Phone Numbers:** Assessor 208-454-7431; Treasurer 208-454-7354; Elections 208-454-7562; Vital Records 208-334-5980.

Caribou County

County Clerk & Recorder, P.O. Box 775, Soda Springs, ID 83276-0775. County Clerk & Recorder, R/E and UCC Recording 208-547-4324; Fax 208-547-4759.
Will search UCC records. UCC search includes tax liens if requested. Will not search real estate records. **Other Phone Numbers:** Assessor 208-547-4749; Treasurer 208-547-3726.

Cassia County

County Clerk & Recorder, 1459 Overland Ave., Room 105, Burley, ID 83318. 208-878-5240; Fax 208-878-1003.
Will search UCC records. Tax liens not included in UCC search. Will not search real estate records. **Other Phone Numbers:** Assessor 208-678-3540.

Clark County

County Clerk & Recorder, P.O. Box 205, Dubois, ID 83423. 208-374-5304; Fax 208-374-5609.
Will search UCC records. UCC search includes tax liens if requested. Will not search real estate records. **Other Phone Numbers:** Assessor 208-374-5404.

Clearwater County

County Clerk & Recorder, P.O. Box 586, Orofino, ID 83544-0586. 208-476-5615 R/E Recording: 208-476-5616 UCC Recording: 208-476-5616; Fax 208-476-9315.
Will search UCC records. This agency will not do a tax lien search. Property transfer searches available. **Other Phone Numbers:** Assessor 208-476-4912; Treasurer 208-476-5213; Appraiser/Auditor 208-476-4912; Elections 208-476-5615; Vital Records 208-476-5615.

Custer County

County Clerk & Recorder, P.O. Box 385, Challis, ID 83226. 208-879-2360; Fax 208-879-5246.
Will search UCC records. UCC search includes tax liens if requested. Will not search real estate records. **Other Phone Numbers:** Assessor 208-879-2325; Treasurer 208-879-2330.

Elmore County

County Clerk & Recorder, 150 South 4th East, Suite #3, Mountain Home, ID 83647-3097. County Clerk & Recorder, R/E and UCC Recording 208-587-2130; Fax 208-587-2159.
Will search UCC records. This agency will not do a tax lien search. Will not search real estate records. **Other Phone Numbers:** Assessor 208-587-2126; Treasurer 208-587-2138; Appraiser/Auditor 208-587-2126; Elections 208-587-2130; Vital Records 208-587-2130.

Franklin County

County Clerk & Recorder, 39 West Oneida, Preston, ID 83263. County Clerk & Recorder, R/E and UCC Recording 208-852-1090; Fax 208-852-1094.
Will search UCC records. This agency will not do a tax lien search. Will not search real estate records. **Other Phone Numbers:** Assessor 208-852-1091; Treasurer 208-852-1095; Appraiser/Auditor 208-852-1091; Elections 208-852-1090.

Fremont County

County Clerk & Recorder, 151 West 1st N. Room 12, St. Anthony, ID 83445. County Clerk & Recorder, R/E and UCC Recording 208-624-3148; Fax 208-624-7335.
http://www.co.fremont.id.us/departments/index.htm
Will search UCC records. Tax liens not included in UCC search. Will not search real estate records. **Other Phone Numbers:** Assessor 208-624-7894; Treasurer 208-624-3361; Appraiser/Auditor 208-624-7984; Elections 208-624-7332; Vital Records 208-624-3148; Commissioners 208-624-4271.

Gem County

County Clerk & Recorder, 415 East Main, Emmett, ID 83617. County Clerk & Recorder, R/E and UCC Recording 208-365-4561; Fax 208-365-6172.
Will search UCC records. Tax liens not included in UCC search. Will not search real estate records. **Other Phone Numbers:** Assessor 208-365-2982; Treasurer 208-365-3272; Appraiser/Auditor 208-365-2982 208-365-4561; Elections 208-365-4561; Vital Records 208-334-5980.

Gooding County

County Clerk & Recorder, P.O. Box 417, Gooding, ID 83330. 208-934-4841; Fax 208-934-5085.
Will search UCC records. Tax liens not included in UCC search. Will not search real estate records. **Other**

Phone Numbers: Assessor 208-934-5666; Treasurer 208-935-5673.

Idaho County

County Clerk & Recorder, 320 W. Main, Room 5, Grangeville, ID 83530. 208-983-2751; Fax 208-983-1428.
Will search UCC records. This agency will not do a tax lien search. Will not search real estate records. **Other Phone Numbers:** Assessor 208-983-2742; Treasurer 208-983-2801.

Jefferson County

County Clerk & Recorder, P.O. Box 275, Rigby, ID 83442. 208-745-7756; Fax 208-745-6636.
Will search UCC records. This agency will not do a tax lien search. Will not search real estate records. **Other Phone Numbers:** Assessor 208-745-9215; Treasurer 208-745-9219.

Jerome County

County Clerk & Recorder, 300 North Lincoln, Courthouse, Room 301, Jerome, ID 83338. 208-324-8811 R/E Recording: 208-324-8811 x114 UCC Recording: 208-324-8811 x114; Fax 208-324-2719.
Will search UCC records. State tax liens filed at Secretary of State. Will not search real estate records. **Other Phone Numbers:** Assessor 208-324-8811 x17; Treasurer 208-324-8811 x72.

Kootenai County

County Clerk & Recorder, P.O. Box 9000, Coeur d'Alene, ID 83816-9000. 208-666-8162; http://www.co.kootenai.id.us/default.asp
Will search UCC records. This agency will not do a tax lien search. Will not search real estate records. **Online Access:** Property, Recording, Unclaimed Property. Online access to the county mapping/recording database is available free at http://www.co.kootenai.id.us/publicinfo/default.asp. Click on "Search". **Other Phone Numbers:** Assessor 208-769-4400 x459; Treasurer 208-769-4400 x146.

Latah County

County Clerk & Recorder, P.O. Box 8068, Moscow, ID 83843-0568. 208-882-8580 x379 R/E Recording: 208-882-8580 x3379 UCC Recording: 208-882-8580 x3379; Fax 208-883-7203. http://www.latah.id.us
Will search UCC records. This agency will not do a tax lien search. Will not search real estate records. **Other Phone Numbers:** Assessor 208-882-8580 x3306; Treasurer 208-882-8580 x3343; Appraiser/Auditor 208-882-8580 x3516; Elections 208-883-2278; Vital Records 208-334-5980 (Boise).

Lemhi County

County Clerk & Recorder, 206 Courthouse Drive, Salmon, ID 83467. County Clerk & Recorder, R/E and UCC Recording 208-756-2815; Fax 208-756-8424.
Will search UCC records. UCC search includes tax liens if requested. Will not search real estate records. **Other Phone Numbers:** Assessor 208-756-3116; Treasurer 208-756-2816; Appraiser/Auditor 208-756-3116; Elections 208-756-2815; Vital Records 208-756-2815.

Lewis County

County Clerk & Recorder, P.O. Box 39, Nezperce, ID 83543. 208-937-2661; Fax 208-937-9234.
Will search UCC records. Tax liens not included in UCC search. Will not search real estate records. **Other Phone Numbers:** Assessor 208-937-2261; Treasurer 208-937-2341; Elections 208-937-2661.

Lincoln County

County Clerk & Recorder, P.O. Drawer A, Shoshone, ID 83352-2774. County Clerk & Recorder, R/E and UCC Recording 208-886-7641; Fax 208-886-2707.
Will search UCC records. Tax liens not included in UCC search. Will not search real estate records. **Other Phone Numbers:** Assessor 208-886-2161; Treasurer 208-886-7681; Elections 208-886-7641; Vital Records 208-886-7641.

Madison County

County Clerk & Recorder, P.O. Box 389, Rexburg, ID 83440. County Clerk & Recorder, R/E and UCC Recording 208-356-3662; Fax 208-356-8396.
http://www.co.madison.id.us
Will search UCC records. UCC search includes tax liens. Will not search real estate records. **Other Phone Numbers:** Assessor 208-356-3071; Treasurer 208-356-6871.

Minidoka County

County Clerk & Recorder, P.O. Box 368, Rupert, ID 83350-0474. County Clerk & Recorder, R/E and UCC Recording 208-436-9511; Fax 208-436-0737.
Will search UCC records. This agency will not do a tax lien search. Will not search real estate records. **Other Phone Numbers:** Assessor 208-436-7181; Treasurer 208-436-7188; Appraiser/Auditor 208-436-7181; Elections 208-436-9511.

Nez Perce County

County Clerk & Recorder, P.O. Box 896, Lewiston, ID 83501-0896. 208-799-3020; Fax 208-799-3070.
http://www.co.nezperce.id.us
Will search UCC records. Tax liens not included in UCC search. Will not search real estate records. **Other Phone Numbers:** Assessor 208-799-3010; Treasurer 208-799-3030; Elections 208-799-3020; Vital Records 208-799-3020.

Oneida County

County Clerk & Recorder, 10 Court Street, Malad, ID 83252. 208-766-4116 x100 R/E Recording: 208-76-4116 x100 or 102 UCC Recording: 208-76-4116 x100 or 102; Fax 208-766-2448.
Will search UCC records. This agency will not do a tax lien search. Will not search real estate records. **Other Phone Numbers:** Assessor 208-766-2954; Treasurer 208-766-2962; Appraiser/Auditor 208-766-4116 x109, 106 or 116; Elections 208-76-4116 x100 or 102.

Owyhee County

County Clerk & Recorder, P.O. Box 128, Murphy, ID 83650. County Clerk & Recorder, R/E and UCC Recording 208-495-2421; Fax 208-495-1173.
Will search UCC records. UCC search includes tax liens if requested. Will not search real estate records. **Other Phone Numbers:** Assessor 208-495-2817; Treasurer 208-495-1158; Elections 208-495-2421; Vital Records 208-495-2421.

Payette County

County Clerk & Recorder, P.O. Drawer D, Payette, ID 83661. County Clerk & Recorder, R/E and UCC Recording 208-642-6000; Fax 208-642-6011.
http://www.payettecounty.com
Will search UCC records. This agency will not do a tax lien search. Will not search real estate records. **Other Phone Numbers:** Assessor 208-642-6012; Treasurer 208-642-6005; Appraiser/Auditor 208-642-6012; Elections 208-642-6000.

Power County

County Clerk & Recorder, 543 Bannock, American Falls, ID 83211. County Clerk & Recorder, R/E and

UCC Recording 208-226-7611; Fax 208-226-7612. www.co.power.id.us
Will search UCC records. UCC search includes tax liens if requested. Will not search real estate records. **Other Phone Numbers:** Assessor 208-226-7616; Treasurer 208-226-7614; Elections 208-226-7611; Vital Records 208-226-7611.

Shoshone County

County Clerk & Recorder, Courthouse, Suite 120, 700 Bank St., Wallace, ID 83873-2348. 208-752-1264; Fax 208-753-2711.
Will search UCC records. This agency will not do a tax lien search. RE owner, mortgage, and property transfer searches available. **Other Phone Numbers:** Assessor 208-752-1202.

Teton County

County Clerk & Recorder, 89 North Main #1, Driggs, ID 83422. 208-354-2905; Fax 208-354-8410.
Will search UCC records. UCC search includes tax liens. RE owner, mortgage, and property transfer searches available. **Other Phone Numbers:** Assessor 208-354-2938; Treasurer 208-354-2254.

Twin Falls County

County Clerk & Recorder, P.O. Box 126, Twin Falls, ID 83303-0126. 208-736-4004; Fax 208-736-4182.
Will search UCC records. Tax liens not included in UCC search. Will not search real estate records. **Other Phone Numbers:** Assessor 208-736-4010; Treasurer 208-736-4008.

Valley County

County Clerk & Recorder, P.O. Box 1350, Cascade, ID 83611-1350. 208-382-7100; Fax 208-382-7107.
Will search UCC records. This agency will not do a tax lien search. Will not search real estate records. **Other Phone Numbers:** Assessor 208-382-7126; Treasurer 208-382-7110.

Washington County

County Clerk & Recorder, P.O. Box 670, Weiser, ID 83672-0670. 208-549-2092 R/E Recording: 208-414-2092 UCC Recording: 208-414-2092; Fax 208-549-3925. www.ruralnetwork.net/~wgassr

Will search UCC records. This agency will not do a tax lien search. Will not search real estate records. **Other Phone Numbers:** Assessor 208-549-2000; Treasurer 208-549-0324; Appraiser/Auditor 208-414-2000; Elections 208-414-2092; Vital Records 208-414-2092 (1907-1911 only); Vital Statistics (Boise, ID) 288-334-5988.

Idaho County Locator

You will usually be able to find the city name in the City/County Cross Reference below. In that case, it is a simple matter to determine the county from the cross reference. However, only the official US Postal Service city names are included in this index. There are an additional 40,000 place names that people use in their addresses. Therefore, we have also included a ZIP/City Cross Reference immediately following the City/County Cross Reference.

If you know the ZIP Code but the city name does not appear in the City/County Cross Reference index, look up the ZIP Code in the ZIP/City Cross Reference, find the city name, then look up the city name in the City/County Cross Reference. For example, you want to know the county for an address of Menands, NY 12204. There is no "Menands" in the City/County Cross Reference. The ZIP/City Cross Reference shows that ZIP Codes 12201-12288 are for the city of Albany. Looking back in the City/County Cross Reference, Albany is in Albany County.

City/County Cross Reference

ABERDEEN Bingham
AHSAHKA Clearwater
ALBION Cassia
ALMO Cassia
AMERICAN FALLS Power
ARBON Power
ARCO Butte
ARIMO Bannock
ASHTON Fremont
ATHOL (83801) Kootenai(85), Bonner(15)
ATLANTA Elmore
ATOMIC CITY Bingham
AVERY Shoshone
BANCROFT Caribou
BANKS Boise
BASALT Bingham
BAYVIEW (83803) Kootenai(59), Bonner(41)
BELLEVUE Blaine
BERN Bear Lake
BLACKFOOT Bingham
BLANCHARD Bonner
BLISS Gooding
BLOOMINGTON Bear Lake
BOISE (83706) Ada(98), Boise(2)
BOISE Ada
BONNERS FERRY Boundary
BOVILL Latah
BRUNEAU Owyhee
BUHL Twin Falls
BURLEY Cassia
CALDER Shoshone
CALDWELL (83605) Canyon(98), Payette(2)
CALDWELL Canyon
CAMBRIDGE Washington
CAREY Blaine
CAREYWOOD Bonner
CARMEN Lemhi
CASCADE Valley
CASTLEFORD Twin Falls
CATALDO (83810) Kootenai(98), Shoshone(2)
CHALLIS (83226) Custer(98), Lemhi(2)
CHESTER Fremont
CLARK FORK Bonner
CLARKIA Shoshone
CLAYTON Custer
CLIFTON Franklin
COBALT Lemhi
COCOLALLA Bonner
COEUR D ALENE Kootenai
COLBURN Bonner
CONDA Caribou
COOLIN Bonner
CORRAL Camas
COTTONWOOD Idaho
COUNCIL Adams
CRAIGMONT Lewis
CULDESAC (83524) Nez Perce(86), Lewis(14)
DAYTON Franklin
DEARY Latah
DECLO Cassia
DESMET Benewah
DIETRICH Lincoln
DINGLE Bear Lake
DONNELLY Valley
DOVER Bonner

DOWNEY Bannock
DRIGGS Teton
DUBOIS Clark
EAGLE Ada
EASTPORT Boundary
EDEN Jerome
ELBA Cassia
ELK CITY Idaho
ELK RIVER Clearwater
ELLIS (83235) Custer(73), Lemhi(27)
EMMETT Gem
FAIRFIELD Camas
FELT Teton
FENN Idaho
FERDINAND Idaho
FERNWOOD Benewah
FILER Twin Falls
FIRTH Bingham
FISH HAVEN Bear Lake
FORT HALL Bingham
FRANKLIN Franklin
FRUITLAND Payette
FRUITVALE Adams
GARDEN VALLEY Boise
GENESEE (83832) Latah(85), Nez Perce(15)
GENEVA Bear Lake
GEORGETOWN Bear Lake
GIBBONSVILLE Lemhi
GLENNS FERRY Elmore
GOODING Gooding
GRACE (99999) Caribou(99), Franklin(1)
GRAND VIEW Owyhee
GRANGEVILLE Idaho
GREENCREEK Idaho
GREENLEAF Canyon
HAGERMAN (83332) Gooding(81), Twin Falls(19)
HAILEY Blaine
HAMER Jefferson
HAMMETT Elmore
HANSEN Twin Falls
HARRISON Kootenai
HARVARD Latah
HAYDEN Kootenai
HAZELTON Jerome
HEADQUARTERS Clearwater
HEYBURN (83336) Minidoka(81), Cassia(19)
HILL CITY Camas
HOLBROOK Oneida
HOMEDALE Owyhee
HOPE Bonner
HORSESHOE BEND (83629) Gem(69), Boise(31)
HOWE Butte
HUSTON Canyon
IDAHO CITY Boise
IDAHO FALLS Bonneville
INDIAN VALLEY (83632) Adams(87), Washington(13)
INKOM Bannock
IONA Bonneville
IRWIN Bonneville
ISLAND PARK Fremont
JEROME (83338) Jerome(99), Gooding(1)
JULIAETTA (83535) Latah(65), Nez Perce(35)
KAMIAH (83536) Idaho(73), Lewis(27)

KELLOGG Shoshone
KENDRICK (83537) Latah(52), Nez Perce(36), Clearwater(12)
KETCHUM (83340) Blaine(98), Custer(2)
KIMBERLY Twin Falls
KING HILL Elmore
KINGSTON Shoshone
KOOSKIA Idaho
KOOTENAI Bonner
KUNA (83634) Ada(95), Canyon(5)
LACLEDE Bonner
LAKE FORK Valley
LAPWAI (83540) Nez Perce(99), Benewah(1)
LAVA HOT SPRINGS Bannock
LEADORE (83464) Lemhi(83), Clark(17)
LEMHI Lemhi
LENORE (83541) Nez Perce(51), Clearwater(49)
LETHA Gem
LEWISTON Nez Perce
LEWISVILLE Jefferson
LOWMAN Boise
LUCILE Idaho
MACKAY Custer
MACKS INN Fremont
MALAD CITY Oneida
MALTA Cassia
MARSING Owyhee
MAY (83253) Lemhi(71), Custer(29)
MC CALL Valley
MC CAMMON Bannock
MEDIMONT Kootenai
MELBA (83641) Canyon(70), Owyhee(17), Ada(14)
MENAN (83434) Jefferson(91), Madison(9)
MERIDIAN Ada
MESA Adams
MIDDLETON Canyon
MIDVALE Washington
MINIDOKA Minidoka
MONTEVIEW Jefferson
MONTPELIER Bear Lake
MOORE (83255) Butte(72), Custer(28)
MOORE Butte
MORELAND Bingham
MOSCOW Latah
MOUNTAIN HOME Elmore
MOUNTAIN HOME A F B Elmore
MOYIE SPRINGS Boundary
MULLAN Shoshone
MURPHY Owyhee
MURRAY Shoshone
MURTAUGH (83344) Twin Falls(80), Cassia(21)
NAMPA (83687) Canyon(98), Ada(2)
NAMPA Canyon
NAPLES Boundary
NEW MEADOWS (83654) Adams(98), Idaho(2)
NEW PLYMOUTH Payette
NEWDALE (83436) Madison(56), Teton(28), Fremont(17)
NEZPERCE Lewis
NORDMAN Bonner
NORTH FORK Lemhi
NOTUS Canyon
OAKLEY Cassia
OLA Gem

OLDTOWN Bonner
OROFINO Clearwater
OSBURN Shoshone
OVID Bear Lake
PALISADES Bonneville
PARIS Bear Lake
PARKER Fremont
PARMA (83660) Canyon(90), Payette(10)
PAUL (83347) Lincoln(57), Minidoka(28), Jerome(15)
PAYETTE Payette
PECK Nez Perce
PICABO Blaine
PIERCE Clearwater
PINEHURST Shoshone
PINGREE Bingham
PLACERVILLE Boise
PLUMMER Benewah
POCATELLO (83202) Bannock(96), Bingham(4)
POCATELLO (83204) Bannock(95), Power(5)
POCATELLO Bannock
POLLOCK (83547) Idaho(83), Adams(17)
PONDERAY Bonner
PORTHILL Boundary
POST FALLS Kootenai
POTLATCH Latah
PRESTON Franklin
PRIEST RIVER Bonner
PRINCETON Latah
RATHDRUM Kootenai
REUBENS (83548) Lewis(53), Nez Perce(47)
REXBURG Madison
RICHFIELD Lincoln
RIGBY Jefferson
RIGGINS Idaho
RIRIE (83443) Jefferson(51), Bonneville(49)
ROBERTS Jefferson
ROCKLAND Power
ROGERSON Twin Falls
RUPERT Minidoka
SAGLE Bonner
SAINT ANTHONY Fremont
SAINT CHARLES Bear Lake
SAINT MARIES Benewah
SALMON Lemhi
SAMUELS Bonner
SANDPOINT Bonner
SANTA Benewah
SHELLEY Bingham
SHOSHONE Lincoln
SHOUP Lemhi
SILVERTON Shoshone
SMELTERVILLE Shoshone
SODA SPRINGS (83276) Caribou(91), Bear Lake(9)
SPALDING Nez Perce
SPENCER Clark
SPIRIT LAKE (83869) Kootenai(70), Bonner(30)
SPRINGFIELD Bingham
SQUIRREL Fremont
STANLEY Custer
STAR (83669) Ada(90), Canyon(11)
STITES Idaho
STONE Oneida

SUGAR CITY (83448) Madison(88), Fremont(12)
SUN VALLEY Blaine
SWAN VALLEY Bonneville
SWANLAKE Bannock
SWEET Gem
TENDOY Lemhi
TENSED Benewah

TERRETON Jefferson
TETON (83451) Fremont(64), Madison(36)
TETONIA Teton
THATCHER (83283) Franklin(98), Oneida(2)
TROY Latah
TWIN FALLS Twin Falls
UCON Bonneville

VICTOR Teton
VIOLA Latah
WALLACE Shoshone
WARREN Idaho
WAYAN (83285) Bonneville(52), Caribou(48)
WEIPPE Clearwater
WEISER Washington

WENDELL Gooding
WESTON Franklin
WHITE BIRD Idaho
WILDER Canyon
WINCHESTER Lewis
WORLEY Kootenai
YELLOW PINE Valley

ZIP/City Cross Reference

ZIP	City	ZIP	City	ZIP	City	ZIP	City
83201-83202	POCATELLO	83327-83327	FAIRFIELD	83531-83531	FENN	83672-83672	WEISER
83203-83203	FORT HALL	83328-83328	FILER	83533-83533	GREENCREEK	83676-83676	WILDER
83204-83209	POCATELLO	83330-83330	GOODING	83535-83535	JULIAETTA	83677-83677	YELLOW PINE
83210-83210	ABERDEEN	83332-83332	HAGERMAN	83536-83536	KAMIAH	83680-83680	MERIDIAN
83211-83211	AMERICAN FALLS	83333-83333	HAILEY	83537-83537	KENDRICK	83686-83687	NAMPA
83212-83212	ARBON	83334-83334	HANSEN	83538-83538	COTTONWOOD	83701-83788	BOISE
83213-83213	ARCO	83335-83335	HAZELTON	83539-83539	KOOSKIA	83801-83801	ATHOL
83214-83214	ARIMO	83336-83336	HEYBURN	83540-83540	LAPWAI	83802-83802	AVERY
83215-83215	ATOMIC CITY	83337-83337	HILL CITY	83541-83541	LENORE	83803-83803	BAYVIEW
83217-83217	BANCROFT	83338-83338	JEROME	83542-83542	LUCILE	83804-83804	BLANCHARD
83218-83218	BASALT	83340-83340	KETCHUM	83543-83543	NEZPERCE	83805-83805	BONNERS FERRY
83220-83220	BERN	83341-83341	KIMBERLY	83544-83544	OROFINO	83806-83806	BOVILL
83221-83221	BLACKFOOT	83342-83342	MALTA	83545-83545	PECK	83808-83808	CALDER
83223-83223	BLOOMINGTON	83343-83343	MINIDOKA	83546-83546	PIERCE	83809-83809	CAREYWOOD
83226-83226	CHALLIS	83344-83344	MURTAUGH	83547-83547	POLLOCK	83810-83810	CATALDO
83227-83227	CLAYTON	83346-83346	OAKLEY	83548-83548	REUBENS	83811-83811	CLARK FORK
83228-83228	CLIFTON	83347-83347	PAUL	83549-83549	RIGGINS	83812-83812	CLARKIA
83229-83229	COBALT	83348-83348	PICABO	83551-83551	SPALDING	83813-83813	COCOLALLA
83230-83230	CONDA	83349-83349	RICHFIELD	83552-83552	STITES	83814-83816	COEUR D ALENE
83232-83232	DAYTON	83350-83350	RUPERT	83553-83553	WEIPPE	83821-83821	COOLIN
83233-83233	DINGLE	83352-83352	SHOSHONE	83554-83554	WHITE BIRD	83822-83822	OLDTOWN
83234-83234	DOWNEY	83353-83354	SUN VALLEY	83555-83555	WINCHESTER	83823-83823	DEARY
83235-83235	ELLIS	83355-83355	WENDELL	83601-83601	ATLANTA	83824-83824	DESMET
83236-83236	FIRTH	83401-83415	IDAHO FALLS	83602-83602	BANKS	83825-83825	DOVER
83237-83237	FRANKLIN	83420-83420	ASHTON	83604-83604	BRUNEAU	83826-83826	EASTPORT
83238-83238	GENEVA	83421-83421	CHESTER	83605-83606	CALDWELL	83827-83827	ELK RIVER
83239-83239	GEORGETOWN	83422-83422	DRIGGS	83610-83610	CAMBRIDGE	83830-83830	FERNWOOD
83241-83241	GRACE	83423-83423	DUBOIS	83611-83611	CASCADE	83832-83832	GENESEE
83243-83243	HOLBROOK	83424-83424	FELT	83612-83612	COUNCIL	83833-83833	HARRISON
83244-83244	HOWE	83425-83425	HAMER	83615-83615	DONNELLY	83834-83834	HARVARD
83245-83245	INKOM	83427-83427	IONA	83616-83616	EAGLE	83835-83835	HAYDEN
83246-83246	LAVA HOT SPRINGS	83428-83428	IRWIN	83617-83617	EMMETT	83836-83836	HOPE
83250-83250	MC CAMMON	83429-83429	ISLAND PARK	83619-83619	FRUITLAND	83837-83837	KELLOGG
83251-83251	MACKAY	83431-83431	LEWISVILLE	83620-83620	FRUITVALE	83839-83839	KINGSTON
83252-83252	MALAD CITY	83433-83433	MACKS INN	83622-83622	GARDEN VALLEY	83840-83840	KOOTENAI
83253-83253	MAY	83434-83434	MENAN	83623-83623	GLENNS FERRY	83841-83841	LACLEDE
83254-83254	MONTPELIER	83435-83435	MONTEVIEW	83624-83624	GRAND VIEW	83842-83842	MEDIMONT
83255-83255	MOORE	83436-83436	NEWDALE	83626-83626	GREENLEAF	83843-83844	MOSCOW
83256-83256	MORELAND	83438-83438	PARKER	83627-83627	HAMMETT	83845-83845	MOYIE SPRINGS
83261-83261	PARIS	83440-83441	REXBURG	83628-83628	HOMEDALE	83846-83846	MULLAN
83262-83262	PINGREE	83442-83442	RIGBY	83629-83629	HORSESHOE BEND	83847-83847	NAPLES
83263-83263	PRESTON	83443-83443	RIRIE	83630-83630	HUSTON	83848-83848	NORDMAN
83271-83271	ROCKLAND	83444-83444	ROBERTS	83631-83631	IDAHO CITY	83849-83849	OSBURN
83272-83272	SAINT CHARLES	83445-83445	SAINT ANTHONY	83632-83632	INDIAN VALLEY	83850-83850	PINEHURST
83274-83274	SHELLEY	83446-83446	SPENCER	83633-83633	KING HILL	83851-83851	PLUMMER
83276-83276	SODA SPRINGS	83447-83447	SQUIRREL	83634-83634	KUNA	83852-83852	PONDERAY
83277-83277	SPRINGFIELD	83448-83448	SUGAR CITY	83635-83635	LAKE FORK	83853-83853	PORTHILL
83278-83278	STANLEY	83449-83449	SWAN VALLEY	83636-83636	LETHA	83854-83854	POST FALLS
83280-83280	STONE	83450-83450	TERRETON	83637-83637	LOWMAN	83855-83855	POTLATCH
83281-83281	SWANLAKE	83451-83451	TETON	83638-83638	MC CALL	83856-83856	PRIEST RIVER
83283-83283	THATCHER	83452-83452	TETONIA	83639-83639	MARSING	83857-83857	PRINCETON
83285-83285	WAYAN	83454-83454	UCON	83641-83641	MELBA	83858-83858	RATHDRUM
83286-83286	WESTON	83455-83455	VICTOR	83642-83642	MERIDIAN	83860-83860	SAGLE
83287-83287	FISH HAVEN	83460-83460	REXBURG	83643-83643	MESA	83861-83861	SAINT MARIES
83301-83301	TWIN FALLS	83462-83462	CARMEN	83644-83644	MIDDLETON	83862-83862	SAMUELS
83302-83302	ROGERSON	83463-83463	GIBBONSVILLE	83645-83645	MIDVALE	83864-83864	SANDPOINT
83303-83303	TWIN FALLS	83464-83464	LEADORE	83647-83647	MOUNTAIN HOME	83865-83865	COLBURN
83311-83311	ALBION	83465-83465	LEMHI	83648-83648	MOUNTAIN HOME A F B	83866-83866	SANTA
83312-83312	ALMO	83466-83466	NORTH FORK	83650-83650	MURPHY	83867-83867	SILVERTON
83313-83313	BELLEVUE	83467-83467	SALMON	83651-83653	NAMPA	83868-83868	SMELTERVILLE
83314-83314	BLISS	83468-83468	TENDOY	83654-83654	NEW MEADOWS	83869-83869	SPIRIT LAKE
83316-83316	BUHL	83469-83469	SHOUP	83655-83655	NEW PLYMOUTH	83870-83870	TENSED
83318-83318	BURLEY	83501-83501	LEWISTON	83656-83656	NOTUS	83871-83871	TROY
83320-83320	CAREY	83520-83520	AHSAHKA	83657-83657	OLA	83872-83872	VIOLA
83321-83321	CASTLEFORD	83522-83522	COTTONWOOD	83660-83660	PARMA	83873-83873	WALLACE
83322-83322	CORRAL	83523-83523	CRAIGMONT	83661-83661	PAYETTE	83874-83874	MURRAY
83323-83323	DECLO	83524-83524	CULDESAC	83666-83666	PLACERVILLE	83876-83876	WORLEY
83324-83324	DIETRICH	83525-83525	ELK CITY	83669-83669	STAR	83877-83877	POST FALLS
83325-83325	EDEN	83526-83526	FERDINAND	83670-83670	SWEET		
83326-83326	ELBA	83530-83530	GRANGEVILLE	83671-83671	WARREN		

General Help Numbers:

Governor's Office
207 Statehouse
Springfield, IL 62706
http://www.state.il.us/gov

217-782-0244
Fax 217-524-4049
8:30AM-5PM

Attorney General's Office
500 S 2nd St
Springfield, IL 62706
http://www.ag.state.il.us

217-782-1090
Fax 217-524-4701
8:45AM-4:45PM

State Court Administrator
222 N. Lasalle - 13th Floor
Chicago, IL 60601

312-793-3250
Fax 312-793-1335
8AM-5PM

State Archives
Archives Division
Norton Bldg, Capitol Complex
Springfield, IL 62756
http://www.sos.state.il.us/depts/
archives/arc_home.html

217-782-4682
Fax 217-524-3930
8AM-4:30PM M-F,
8AM-3:30PM SA

State Specifics:

Capital:

Springfield
Sangamon County

Time Zone:

CST

Number of Counties:

102

Population:

12,419,293

Web Site:

www.state.il.us

State Agencies

Criminal Records

Illinois State Police, Bureau of Identification, 260 N Chicago St, Joliet, IL 60432-4075; 815-740-5164, 8AM-4PM M-F.

http://www.state.il.us/isp/isphpage.htm

Note: Sex offender data is available online at http://samnet.isp.state.il.us/ispso2/sex_offenders/frames.htm and may also be available at http://12.17.79.4.

Indexing & Storage: Records are available from 1930's on. New records are available for inquiry immediately. Records are indexed on microfilm, index cards, inhouse computer.

Searching: No records are released without a disposition of conviction. Requester must use the state's Uniform Conviction Information Form signed by person of record. A request for a non-business purpose will be honored. Include the following in your request-name, date of birth, sex, race. Fingerprint cards are an option.

Access by: mail, in person, online.

Fee & Payment: The search fee is $12.00 per form. A fingerprint search is $14.00. Fee payee: Illinois State Police. Prepayment required. Modem users and ongoing UCIA requesters must prepay for records in groups of 35 at a time. Personal checks accepted. No credit cards accepted.

Mail search: Turnaround time: 15 to 20 days. No self addressed stamped envelope is required.

In person search: Going in person saves mailing time only.

Online search: Online access costs $7.00 per name. Upon signing an interagency agreement with ISP and establishing a $200 escrow account, users can submit inquiries over modem. Replies with convictions are returned by mail. Clear records can be returned via e-mail, by request. Modem access is available from 7AM-4PM M-F, excluding holidays. Users must utilize LAPLINK version 6.0 or later. For more information on the Modem Porgram, call 815-740-5164.

Corporation Records
Limited Partnership Records
Trade Names
Assumed Name
Limited Liability Company Records

Department of Business Services, Corporate Department, Howlett Bldg, 3rd Floor, Copy Section, Springfield, IL 62756 (Courier: 501 S 2nd St, Springfield, IL 62756); 217-782-7880, 217-782-4528 (Fax), 8AM-4:30PM.

http://www.sos.state.il.us

Indexing & Storage: Records are available from mid-1800's on. Closed records are stored at the State Archives. Only limited information is available for corporations dissolved before 1986. New records are available for inquiry immediately. Records are indexed on inhouse computer.

Searching: Records are on micro-film from 1984. In-house computer has name of agent, state and date of incorporation, etc. Include the following in your request-full name of business, corporation file number. In addition to the articles of incorporation, corporation records include the following information: Annual Reports, Officers, Directors, Prior (merged) names, Assumed names, and Inactive names.

Access by: mail, phone, in person, online.

Fee & Payment: The search fee is $5.00 per name. Certification is $10.00 which includes search fee. Copies are $.50 per page after the initial $5.00. Fee payee: Secretary of State. Prepayment required. There is an additional $.50 charge to use a credit card. Personal checks accepted. Credit cards accepted: MasterCard, Visa, Discover.

Mail search: Turnaround time: 5 to 7 days. A self addressed stamped envelope is requested.

Phone search: Expedited copy service is available using a credit card.

Online search: The web site gives free access to records, except the web does not offer not-for-profit records. Search Corporate/LLC records at www.cyberdriveillinois.com/departments/business _services/corpstart.html. A commercial access program is also available. Fees vary. Potential users must submit in writing the purpose of the request. Submit to: Sharon Thomas, Dept. of Business Srvs, 330 Howlett Bldg, Springfield, IL 62756. Also, call 217-782-4104 for more information.

Other access: List or bulk file purchases are available. Call 217-782-4101 for more information.

Expedited service: Expedited service is available for mail, phone and fax searches. Turnaround time: 24 hours. Add $25.00 per business name.

Uniform Commercial Code
Federal Tax Liens

Secretary of State, UCC Division, 2nd & Edwards St, Howlett Bldg, Room 030, Springfield, IL 62756; 217-782-7518, 8AM-4:30PM.

http://www.sos.state.il.us

Indexing & Storage: Records are available from 1962. Records are computerized since 1972.

Searching: Use search request form UCC-11. Request searches for federal tax liens on businesses since 1988 separately with a fee of $5.00. Federal tax liens on individuals and all state tax liens are filed at the county level. Include the following in your request-debtor name and address.

Access by: mail, in person.

Fee & Payment: A UCC search is $10.00 per debtor name. A federal tax lien search only is available for $5.00 plus $.50 per page of copies. Copies are $1.00 per page. Fee payee: Secretary of State. Prepayment required. Personal checks accepted. Credit cards accepted: MasterCard, Visa, Discover.

Mail search: Turnaround time: 1 week. A self addressed stamped envelope is requested.

In person search: Documents can be viewed at no charge.

Other access: The entire database can be purchased and the state offers a CD update service for $250 per month.

State Tax Liens
Records not maintained by a state level agency.

Note: All state tax liens are filed at the county.

Sales Tax Registrations

Revenue Department, Taxpayer Services, PO Box 19044, Springfield, IL 62794-9044 (Courier: 101 W Jefferson, Springfield, IL 62702); 800-732-8866, 217-782-3336, 217-782-4217 (Fax), 8AM-5PM.

http://www.revenue.state.il.us

Indexing & Storage: Records are available for all active businesses with the state, records can go back to the 1930s.

Searching: This agency will only confirm that a business is registered if an Illinois business tax number is provided, often, the business name is not enough. They provide no other information. The state tax permit or federal tax ID is also helpful.

Access by: mail, phone, in person.

Fee & Payment: There is no fee. No credit cards accepted.

Mail search: Turnaround time: 7 to 10 days. A self addressed stamped envelope is requested.

Phone search: Will do up to 5 confirmations at a time.

Birth Certificates

IL Department of Public Health, Division of Vital Records, 605 W Jefferson St, Springfield, IL 62702-5097; 217-782-6554, 217-782-6553 (Instructions), 217-523-2648 (Fax), 8AM-5PM, M-F.

http://www.idph.state.il.us/vital/home.htm

Indexing & Storage: Records are available from 1916 to present. It takes up to one month before new records are available for inquiry. Records are indexed on microfiche, inhouse computer.

Searching: Birth records are not considered public records. Copies are available to subject if 18 years old, parents, or legal guardian (with court order). Include the following in your request-full name, date of birth, place of birth, relationship to person of record, names of parents, mother's maiden name. Place of birth can be city or county. Include

name of hospital, if known. The following data is not released: sealed records.

Access by: mail, phone, fax, in person.

Fee & Payment: Fees are $10.00 per name for a computer abstract and $15.00 per name for a certified copy of original. Add $2.00 for each additional copy. Add $6.00 service fee to use a credit card. Fee payee: Illinois Department of Public Health. Prepayment required. Personal checks accepted. Credit cards accepted: MasterCard, Visa, AmEx, Discover.

Mail search: Turnaround time: 15 days. No self addressed stamped envelope is required.

Phone search: Use of credit card is required for extra fee of $6.00. Normal turnaround time is 2 days.

Fax search: Same criteria as phone searching.

In person search: Turnaround time less than 1/2 hour.

Expedited service: Expedited service is available for mail, phone and fax searches. Add $6.00 for using a credit card, $13.00 for express delivery.

Death Records

IL Department of Public Health, Division of Vital Records, 605 W Jefferson St, Springfield, IL 62702-5097; 217-782-6554, 217-782-6553 (Instructions), 217-523-2648 (Fax), 8AM-5PM.

http://www.idph.state.il.us/vital/home.htm

Indexing & Storage: Records are available from 1916 to present. New records are available for inquiry immediately. Records are indexed on microfiche.

Searching: Death records are not considered public documents. Copies are available to person with property rights interest in the record. Once records are 20 years old, they are open for genealogical searches. Include the following in your request-full name, date of death, place of death, relationship to person of record, parents' names, reason for request.

Access by: mail, fax, in person.

Fee & Payment: Fees are $17.00 for a certified Death Certificate. Fee payee: Illinois Department of Public Health. Prepayment required. Personal checks accepted. Credit cards accepted: MasterCard, Visa, AmEx, Discover.

Mail search: Turnaround time: 1 month. No self addressed stamped envelope is required.

Fax search: Same criteria as phone searching.

In person search: There is one day waiting period. If ordered by 2PM, will be available the next day at 10AM.

Expedited service: Expedited service is available for mail, phone and fax searches. The fee is $6.00 for the credit card use and $13.00 for express delivery. If you send your request in by express delivery, they will turnaround in one day.

Marriage Certificates
Divorce Records
Records not maintained by a state level agency.

Note: State will verify marriage or divorce from 1962-present

but will not issue certificate. Verification requests must be in writing and there is a fee of $5.00 per event requested. Records of marriage and divorce are found at the county of issue.

Workers' Compensation Records

Industrial Commission, 100 W Randolph, 8th Floor, Chicago, IL 60601; 312-814-6611, 8:30AM-5PM.

http://www.state.il.us/agency/iic

Note: The web site lists cases that are up for a hearing status.

Indexing & Storage: Records are available on computer from 1982 to present, on microfiche from 1927 to 1981. Settled file copies are kept in Springfield, but must be requested from Chicago. Data is indexed by name and file number. Records are indexed on file folders. Records are normally destroyed after five years.

Searching: Include the following in your request- claimant name, Social Security Number, date of accident. Include case number and company name.

Access by: mail, phone, in person.

Fee & Payment: There is no charge for a small file. For "large files," the office will contact you and suggest you use a record retrieval service. If your request is large enough to warrant the use of a copy service, the service will have its own fees that must be paid by you.

Mail search: Turnaround time: 2 weeks. Send a name as well as any other information you may have, such as company name and date of accident, to determine if any files existA self addressed stamped envelope is requested.

Phone search: Information about a case is accessed by the file number. The staff will do a name search if you have enough information for them to do so.

In person search: There are several public access terminals available in the office.

Driver Records

Abstract Information Unit, Drivers Services Department, 2701 S Dirksen Prky, Springfield, IL 62723; 217-782-2720, 8AM-4:30PM.

http://www.sos.state.il.us

Note: Copies of tickets can be obtained from the county of the incident for $1.00 or copies may be requested at the above address for a fee of $.50 per copy.

Indexing & Storage: Records are available for 4 years for moving violations; 7 years for suspension; lifetime for DWI. Commercial Driver records can go back 10 years for serious violations. It takes 2 weeks before new records are available for inquiry.

Searching: No personal identifiable information is provided on record unless requester is exempt. Exempt requesters include business representatives with a legitimate business need (e.g. insurance, financial institutions, employers, etc.). Include the following in your request-full name, date of birth, sex. There is a 10 day waiting period when requesting an abstract of another individual's driving record unless the requester is "exempt." This is so the person of record can be informed of the name of the requesting individual.

Access by: mail, in person.

Fee & Payment: The fee is $6.00 per record, which includes certification. There is a full charge for a "no record found." Fee payee: Secretary of

State. Prepayment required. Personal checks accepted. No credit cards accepted.

Mail search: Turnaround time: 10 days. No self addressed stamped envelope is required.

In person search: Up to five requests will be processed immediately if requester meets the access requirement (see above). Requests are available from any Driver Services Facility statewide.

Other access: Overnight magnetic tape processing is available to high volume users (there is a 200 request minimum per day). Call (217) 785-2384 for more information.

Vehicle Ownership
Vehicle Identification

Vehicle Services Department, Vehicle Record Inquiry, 501 S 2nd Street #408, Springfield, IL 62756; 217-782-6992, 217-524-0122 (Fax), 8AM-4:30PM.

http://www.sos.state.il.us

Indexing & Storage: Records are available generally for 8 years to present.

Searching: Personal information is not released for non-business purposes. Bulk sales are not permitted for solicitation purposes.

Access by: mail, in person.

Fee & Payment: The fee is $5.00 per record search. Fee payee: Secretary of State. Prepayment required. Personal checks accepted. MasterCard, Visa, Discover accepted.

Mail search: Turnaround time: 4 to 7 days. You may search by mail, but there is a 10 day delay if the requester is not "exempt."A self addressed stamped envelope is requested.

In person search: Walk-in requesters may retrieve data immediately; however, if requester is not exempt there is a 10 day delay.

Other access: The state will sell customized, bulk requests upon approval of purpose and with a signed contract.

Accident Reports (Crash Reports)

Illinois State Police, Patrol Records Unit, 500 Iles Park Place, Ste 200, Springfield, IL 62718; 217-785-0612, 8AM-5PM.

http://www.isp.state.il.us

Note: If crash occurred on IL Tollway System, send check or money order payable to: IL Toll Highway Authority, Attn: State Police District 15, One Authority Drive, Downers Grove, IL 60515.

Indexing & Storage: Records are available from 1976 to present.

Searching: Crash reports are considered public record and are available without restriction. Items needed by the requester include date, names of drivers involved, report number, and an exact location.

Access by: mail, phone, in person.

Fee & Payment: The fee is $5.00 per report or $20.00 for a reconstruction report. Fee payee: Illinois State Police. Prepayment required. Personal checks accepted. No credit cards accepted.

Mail Search: Turnaround time: 7 to 10 days. If requester provides express envelope & label, the request will be returned quicker.A self addressed stamped envelope is requested.

Phone search: You may call to get information, but copies of records are only released with written requests.

In person search: Turnaround time is immediate.

Vessel Ownership
Vessel Registration

Department of Natural Resources, 524 S 2nd St, Springfield, IL 62701; 800-382-1696, 217-782-5016 (Fax), 8AM-5PM.

http://dnr.state.il.us

Note: Lien information will show on the history report.

Indexing & Storage: Records are available from 1982 to the present. Snow mobile records are also available. Records are indexed on computer. All boats must be titled and registered unless if only used on a private lake.

Searching: To search, one of the following is required: name, hull id #, or registration #.

Access by: mail, phone.

Fee & Payment: There is a $5.00 fee for any search, including a title history search. Fee payee: IL Dept of Natural Resources. Prepayment required. Personal checks accepted. No credit cards accepted.

Mail search: Turnaround time: 4 to 6 weeks. No self addressed stamped envelope is required.

Phone search: They will give limited name search and verification information, time permitting.

Legislation Records

Illinois General Assembly, State House, House (or Senate) Bills Division, Springfield, IL 62706; 217-782-3944 (Bill Status Only), 217-782-7017 (Index Div-Older Bills), 217-782-5799 (House Bills), 217-782-9778 (Senate Bills), 217-524-6059 (Fax), 8AM-4:30PM.

http://www.legis.state.il.us

Note: Previous session bills must be obtained from: Senate 217-792-6970; House 217-782-7192. Cost is $.10 per page.

Indexing & Storage: Records are available from 1997 to present on computer. Records are indexed on microfiche.

Searching: Include the following in your request- bill number. For statutes, it is suggested to go to a local law library or visit the Internet site. Complete statutes are not available here.

Access by: mail, phone, in person, online.

Fee & Payment: All copies of documents are considered as certified. There is no search fee, copies are free if from the last two sessions, otherwise $0.10 each. Fee payee: Illinois General Assembly. Personal checks accepted. No credit cards accepted.

Mail search: No self addressed stamped envelope is required.

Phone search: Records are available by phone.

Online search: The Legislative Information System is available for subscription through a standard modem. The sign-up fee is $500.00 which includes 100 free minutes of access. Thereafter, access time is billed at $1.00 per minute. The hours of availability are 8 AM - 10 PM when in session and 8 AM - 5 PM when not in session, M-F. Contact Craig Garret at 217- 782-

4083 to set-up an account. The Internet site offers free access but the state has a disclaimer which says the site should not be relied upon as an official record of action.

Other access: A prepayment of $500.00 is required to obtain a printed copy of all bills.

Voter Registration

Access to Records is Restricted

Board of Elections, 1020 S Spring, Springfield, IL 62704; 217-782-4141, 217-782-5959 (Fax), 8AM-4:30PM.

http://www.elections.state.il.us

Note: The data is not considered public record at the state level and is only available in bulk format to political committees and government agencies. County Clerks control the information at the local level.

GED Certificates

Access to Records is Restricted

State Board of Education, 100 N 1st St, Springfield, IL 62777; 217-782-3370 (Main Number).

Note: All GED information is kept at the county level. You must contact the county where the test was taken. If you need assistance determining which county, contact the State Board of Education at the number listed here.

Hunting License Information
Fishing License Information

Records not maintained by a state level agency.

Note: They do not have a central database. The vendors hold license records.

Illinois State Licensing Agencies

Licenses Searchable Online

Amusement Ride #37 ....www.state.il.us/agency/idol/carn.htm
Architect #11 ....www.dpr.state.il.us/licenselookup/default.asp
Athletic Trainer #11......................................www.dpr.state.il.us/licenselookup/default.asp
Auctioneer #29 ....www.obre.state.il.us/lookup/
Bank #29...www.obre.state.il.us/CBT/REGENTY/BTREG.HTM
Barber #11...www.dpr.state.il.us/licenselookup/default.asp
Check Printer #29 ....www.obre.state.il.us/CBT/REGENTY/BTREG.HTM
Chiropractor #11..www.dpr.state.il.us/licenselookup/default.asp
Collection Agency #11 ....www.dpr.state.il.us/licenselookup/default.asp
Controlled Substance Registrant #11 ....www.dpr.state.il.us/licenselookup/default.asp
Corporate Fiduciary #29 ....www.obre.state.il.us/CBT/REGENTY/BTREG.HTM
Cosmetologist #11...www.dpr.state.il.us/licenselookup/default.asp
Counselor/Clinical Professional Counselor #11 www.dpr.state.il.us/licenselookup/default.asp
Dentist/Dental Hygienist #11 ....www.dpr.state.il.us/licenselookup/default.asp
Dietitian/Nutrition Counselor #11......................www.dpr.state.il.us/licenselookup/default.asp
Drug Distributor, Wholesale #11 ....www.dpr.state.il.us/licenselookup/default.asp
Employee Leasing Company #04....................www.state.il.us/INS/elc.htm
Engineer #11 ....www.dpr.state.il.us/licenselookup/default.asp
Engineer, Structural #11 ....www.dpr.state.il.us/licenselookup/default.asp
Environmental Health Practitioner #11 ....www.dpr.state.il.us/licenselookup/default.asp
Esthetician #11..www.dpr.state.il.us/licenselookup/default.asp
Funeral Director/Embalmer #11 ....www.dpr.state.il.us/licenselookup/default.asp
HMO #04...www.state.il.us/INS/mmcchart.pdf
Interior Designer #11 ....www.dpr.state.il.us/licenselookup/default.asp
Landscape Architect #11...............................www.dpr.state.il.us/licenselookup/default.asp
Lead Contractor #17 ....http://app.idph.state.il.us/Envhealth/Lead/Leadcnt.asp
Lead Risk Assessor/Inspector/Supervisor #17..http://app.idph.state.il.us/Envhealth/lead/Leadinsp.asp
Lead Training Provider #17............................http://app.idph.state.il.us/Envhealth/lead/Leadinsp.asp
Liquor License, Retail/Distributor/Mfg. #25 ....www.state.il.us/distributors/search.htm
Lobbyist #32...www.cyberdriveillinois.com/cgi-bin/index/lobbysrch.s
Long Term Care Insurance Company #04........www.state.il.us/INS/longtermcareframe.htm
Marriage & Family Therapist #11 ....www.dpr.state.il.us/licenselookup/default.asp
Medical Corporation #11................................www.dpr.state.il.us/licenselookup/default.asp
Medical Doctor/Physician Assistant #11 ....www.dpr.state.il.us/licenselookup/default.asp
Mortgage Banker/Broker #29 ....www.obre.state.il.us/RESFIN/liclistc.pdf
Nail Technician #11 ....www.dpr.state.il.us/licenselookup/default.asp
Naprapath #11..www.dpr.state.il.us/licenselookup/default.asp
Nurse #11...www.dpr.state.il.us/licenselookup/default.asp
Nursing Home Administrator #17 ....www.medicare.gov/Nursing/Overview.asp
Occupational Therapist #11 ....www.dpr.state.il.us/licenselookup/default.asp
Optometrist #11...www.dpr.state.il.us/licenselookup/default.asp
Osteopathic Physician #11............................www.dpr.state.il.us/licenselookup/default.asp
Pawnbroker #29...www.obre.state.il.us/CBT/REGENTY/BTREG.HTM
Pharmacist/Pharmacy #11............................www.dpr.state.il.us/licenselookup/default.asp
Physical Therapist #11..................................www.dpr.state.il.us/licenselookup/default.asp
Podiatrist #11 ....www.dpr.state.il.us/licenselookup/default.asp
Polygraph - Deception Detection Examiner #11 www.dpr.state.il.us/licenselookup/default.asp
Private Detective #11 ....www.dpr.state.il.us/licenselookup/default.asp
Private Security Contractor #11 ....www.dpr.state.il.us/licenselookup/default.asp
Psychologist #11 ....www.dpr.state.il.us/licenselookup/default.asp
Public Accountant-CPA #11...........................www.dpr.state.il.us/licenselookup/default.asp
Real Estate Appraiser #29 ....www.obre.state.il.us/lookup/
Real Estate Broker/Salesperson #29 ....www.obre.state.il.us/lookup/
Roofer #11..www.dpr.state.il.us/licenselookup/default.asp
Sawmill #03..www.dnr.state.il.us/conservation/forestry/sawmill.htm
Shorthand Reporter #11.................................www.dpr.state.il.us/licenselookup/default.asp
Social Worker #11 ....www.dpr.state.il.us/licenselookup/default.asp
Speech-Language Pathologist/Audiologist #11.www.dpr.state.il.us/licenselookup/default.asp
Surveyor #11 ....www.dpr.state.il.us/licenselookup/default.asp
Timeshare/Land Sales #29 ....www.obre.state.il.us/lookup/
Trust Company #29 ....www.obre.state.il.us/CBT/REGENTY/BTREG.HTM
Veterinarian #11 ....www.dpr.state.il.us/licenselookup/default.asp

Licensing Quick Finder

Accident Reconstruction Specialist#19..217-782-4540
Alcohol Abuse Counselor #21 217-698-8110
Ambulance Service #13......................217-785-2080
Animal Breeder #06 217-785-3423
Aquaculturist #06 217-785-3423
Architect #11....................................217-785-0800
Asbestos Contractor #17 217-782-3517
Athletic Trainer #11 217-785-0800
Attorney #01....................................217-522-6838
Auctioneer #29.................................312-793-8704
Auctioneer, Vehicle #30.....................217-782-7817
Automotive Parts Recycler #30.............217-782-7817
Bank #29 312-793-3000
Barber #11.......................................217-785-0800
Bilingual Teacher, Transitional #35 217-782-2805
Bingo Operation #18 217-785-5864
Blacksmith #26.................................312-814-2600
Blaster #07 217-782-4970
Boat Operator #05.............................217-782-2138
Boiler Inspector #36 217-782-2696
Boxing/Wrestling Event/Employee #11..217-785-0800
Breath Analyzer Operator #13 217-782-1571
Check Printer #29 312-793-3000
Child Care Facility #02 217-785-2688
Chiropractor #11 217-785-0800
Coal Mine Worker #08........................217-782-6791
Collection Agency #11........................217-785-0800
Controlled Substance Registrant #11....217-785-0800
Coroner (County) #19.........................217-782-4540
Corporate Fiduciary #29 312-793-3000
Correction Officer (County) #19 217-782-4540
Cosmetologist #11 217-785-0800
Counselor/Clinical Prof. Counselor #11.217-785-0800
Criminal Electronic Surveillance Officer #19 ....
....217-782-4540
Cross-Connection Control Device Inspector #24 ....
....217-782-1020
Day Care #02....................................217-785-2688
Dentist/Dental Hygienist #11................217-785-0800
Dietitian/Nutrition Counselor #11..........217-785-0800
Distribution System Operator (Enviromental) #24 ......
....217-782-9720
Driving Instructor #31 847-437-3953
Drug Distributor/Wholesale #11 217-785-0800
Early Childhood Teacher #35 217-782-2805
Emergency Medical Technician #13......217-785-2080
Employee Leasing Company #04 217-782-6366
Employment Agency #23.....................312-793-2810
Engineer #11....................................217-785-0800
Engineer, Structural #11.....................217-785-0800
Environmental Health Practitioner #11 ..217-785-0800
Esthetician #11 217-785-0800
Explosive - General Use #08 217-782-9976
Explosive Magazine Storage #08..........217-782-9976
Firearms Regulation (Firearm Owner's Reg.) #27.......
....217-782-7980
Fish Dealer #06.................................217-785-3423
Fisherman, Commercial #06................217-785-3423
Food Processing Plant/Warehouse#13.217-785-2439
Food Service Sanitation Mgr. #13.........217-785-2439

Funeral Director/Embalmer #11 217-785-0800
Fur Buyer/Tanner/Dyer #05 217-785-3423
Gambling Addiction Counselor #21 217-698-8110
Gambling Employee #20 312-814-4702
Hearing Instrument Dispenser #15........217-782-4733
High School Teacher #35 217-782-2805
HMO #04..217-782-6366
Home Health Aide #13........................217-782-7412
Home Health Care Agency #13 217-782-7412
Horseshoer #26 312-814-2600
Hospital #13......................................217-782-7412
Hunting Area Operator #05..................217-785-3423
Industrial Radiographer #09.................217-785-9913
Insurance Producer #04......................217-782-6366
Interior Designer #11 217-785-0800
Investment Adviser #33 217-785-4929
Laboratory Analysis Technician #13......217-785-8820
Land Sale #11...................................217-785-0800
Landfill Chief Operator #24 217-782-9877
Landscape Architect #11 217-785-0800
Lead Contractor #17...........................217-782-3517
Lead Risk Assessor/Insp./Supvr. #17...217-782-3517
Lead Training Providers #17 217-782-3517
Liquor License, Retail/Dist./Mfg. #25.....312-814-3930
Lobbyist #32.....................................217-782-0705
Long Term Care Insurance Co. #04......217-782-6366
Marriage & Family Therapist #11 217-785-0800
Medical Corporation #11 217-785-0800
Medical Doctor/Physician Assistant#11.217-785-0800
Mental Health Counselor #21 217-698-8110
Mine Engineer/Foreman #08 217-782-6791
Mine Rescue Supervisor/Assistant #08.217-782-6791
Mine Supervisor #08 217-782-6791
Mortgage Banker/Broker #29...............217-793-1409
Motor Vehicle Dealer, New #30 217-782-7817
Nail Technician #11............................217-785-0800
Naprapath #11..................................217-785-0800
Notary Public #32..............................217-782-0641
Nuclear Medicine Technologist #09 217-785-9913
Nurse #11...217-785-0800
Nurses' Aide #13...............................217-785-5133
Nursing Agency #23...........................312-793-1718
Nursing Home #12 217-702-0545
Nursing Home Administrator #17 217-782-0514
Occupational Aide #12 217-782-0545
Occupational Therapist #11 217-785-0800
Optometrist #11 217-785-0800
Osteopathic Physician #11 217-785-0800
Pari-Mutuel Employee #26 312-814-2600
Pawnbroker #29................................312-793-3000
Pest Control Technician/Business/Non-commercial #17
....217-782-4674
Pesticide Applicator #17 217-782-5830
Pharmacist/Pharmacy #11...................217-785-0800
Physical Aide #12..............................217-782-0545
Physical Therapist #11 217-785-0800
Plumber #17 217-524-0791
Plumber Apprentice #13 217-785-1153
Podiatrist #11....................................217-785-0800
Polygraph - Deception Detection Examiner #11 ....

....217-785-0800
Private Detective #11 217-785-0800
Private Security Contractor #11 217-785-0800
Psychologist #11...............................217-785-0800
Public Accountant-CPA #11.................217-785-0800
Racetrack #26...................................312-814-2600
Radiation Therapist #10 217-785-9913
Radiographer #10 217-785-9913
Radon Measurement Specialist #10......217-785-9935
Real Estate Appraiser #29 312-793-8704
Real Estate Broker/Salesperson#29 312-793-8704
Rehabilitation Aide #12.......................217-782-0545
Restaurant & Retail Food Store #17......217-785-2439
Riverboat Employee #20 312-814-4702
Roofer #11..217-785-2439
Salvage Firm #13...............................217-785-2439
Savings & Loan Association #29...........217-782-9043
Savings Bank #29..............................217-782-9043
Sawmill #03 217-782-6431
School Business Official #35 217-782-2805
School Guidance Counselor #35 217-782-2805
School Media Specialist/Librarian #35...217-782-2805
School Nurse #35...............................217-782-2805
School Principal//Superintendent./Administrator #35
....217-782-2805
School Psychologist #35 217-782-2805
Scrap Processor #30 217-782-7817
Securities Dealer/Salesperson #33 217-782-2256
Sewage System Contractor #17 217-782-5830
Sheriff Law Enforcement Officer #19....217-782-4540
Shorthand Reporter #11 217-785-0800
Social Worker #11..............................217-785-0800
Special Teacher #35 217-782-2805
Speech-Language Pathologist/Audiologist #11...........
....217-785-0800
Stock Broker #33 217-782-2256
Substance Abuse Counselor #21..........217-698-8110
Substitute Teacher #35 217-782-2805
Surveyor #11....................................217-785-0800
Tanning Facility #17 217-785-2439
Taxidermist #06 217-785-3423
Teacher #35......................................217-782-2805
Timber Buyer #03..............................217-782-6431
Timeshare #11 217-785-0800
Timeshare/Land Sales #29 312-793-8704
Trust Company #29............................312-793-3000
Underground Shot Firer #08 217-782-6791
Used Vehicle Dealer #30.....................217-782-7817
Vehicle Rebuilder/Repair #30...............217-782-7817
Veterinarian #11................................217-785-0800
Vision & Hearing Screening Technician #15.............
....217-782-4733
Waste Water Treatment Plant Operator #24.............
....217-782-9720
Water Supply Operator #24 217-782-9720
Water Well & Pump Installation Contractor #17.........
....217-782-5830
Water Well Contractor/IDPH #17 217-782-5830
Weighing & Measuring Device Serviceman #22 ....
....217-782-3817

Licensing Agency Information

#01 Attorney Registration & Disciplinary Commission of Supreme Court of IL, 700 E Adams St, Hilton Offices, #201, Springfield, IL 62701; 217-522-6838, Fax: 217-522-2417.

#02 Department of Children & Family Services, 406 E Monroe St, Springfield, IL 62701; 217-785-2509, Fax: 217-785-1052.

#03 Department of Natural Resources, 524 S 2nd St, Springfield, IL 62701-1787; 217-782-6431, Fax: 217-785-8405.
www.dnr.state.il.us

#04 Department of Insurance, 320 W Washington, Springfield, IL 62767-0001; 217-782-4515, Fax: 217-782-5020.
www.state.il.us/INS

#05 Department of Natural Resources, 524 S 2nd St, Springfield, IL 62701; 217-782-2138, Fax: 217-782-5016.
http://dnr.state.il.us

#06 Department of Natural Resources, 524 S 2nd St, Springfield, IL 62701; 217-785-3423, Fax: 217-782-5016.
http://dnr.state.il.us

#08 Department of Natural Resources, 300 W Jefferson St, #300, Springfield, IL 62791; 217-782-9976, Fax: 217-524-4819.
http://dnr.state.il.us/mines/index.html

#09 Department of Nuclear Safety, 1035 Outer Park Dr, Springfield, IL 62704; 217-785-9900, Fax: 217-785-9962.
www.state.il.us/idns/

#11 Department of Professional Regulation, 320 W Washington, 3rd Fl, Springfield, IL 62786; 217-785-0800, Fax: 217-782-7645.
www.dpr.state.il.us
Direct web site URL to search for licensees: www.dpr.state.il.us/licenselookup/default.asp. You can search online using name or license number.

#12 Department of Public Aid, 201 S. Grand Ave, Springfield, IL 62763-0001; 217-782-0545, Fax: 217-524-7114.

#13 Department of Public Health, 525 W Jefferson St 4th Fl, Springfield, IL 62761; 217-782-4977, Fax: 217-782-3987.
www.idph.state.il.us

#15 Department of Public Health, 535 W Jefferson St, Springfield, IL 62761; 217-782-4733, Fax: 217-524-2831.
www.idph.state.il.us

#17 Department of Public Health, 525 W Jefferson St, 3rd Fl, Springfield, IL 62761; 217-782-5830, Fax: 217-785-0253.
www.idph.state.il.us

#18 Department of Revenue, 101 W Jefferson RM3011, Springfield, IL 62794; 217-785-5864.

#19 Law Enforcement & Standards Training Board, 600 S 2nd St, #300, Springfield, IL 62704; 217-782-4540, Fax: 217-524-5350.
www.ptb.state.il.us

#20 Gaming Board, 160 N Lasalle #300, Chicago, IL 60601; 312-814-4700, Fax: 312-814-1581.
www.igb.state.il.us

#21 Counselor Certification Department, 1305 Wabash Ave #L, Springfield, IL 62704-4938; 217-698-8110, Fax: 217-698-8234.
www.iaodapca.org

#22 Department of Agriculture, PO Box 19281, Springfield, IL 62794-9281; 217-782-2172, Fax: 217-524-7801.
www.agr.state.il.us

#23 Department of Labor, 160 N LaSalle, 13th Fl, #C1300, Chicago, IL 60601; 312-793-2800, Fax: 312-793-5257.
www.state.il.us/agency/idol

#24 Environmental Protection Agency, PO Box 19276 (1021 N Grand Ave E), Springfield, IL 62794-9276; 217-782-1020, Fax: 217-782-0075.
www.epa.state.il.us/water/index.html

#25 Freedom of Information Compliance Officer, 100 W Randolph, #5-300, Chicago, IL 60601; 312-814-2206, Fax: 312-814-2241.
www.state.il.us/lcc/default.htm
Direct web site URL to search for licensees: www.state.il.us/distributors/search.htm. You can search online using license year, license class, and license number.

#26 Racing Board, 100 W Randolph, #11-100, Chicago, IL 60601; 312-814-2600, Fax: 312-814-5062.
www.state.il.us/agency/irb

#27 State Police, 100 Iles Park Pl, 103 Armory Bldg, Springfield, IL 62708; 217-782-7980, Fax: 217-785-2821.
www.isp.state.il.us

#29 Office of Banks & Real Estate, 500 E Monroe, Springfield, IL 62701-1509; 217-782-3000, Fax: 217-524-5941.
www.obre.state.il.us
Direct web site URL to search for licensees: www.obre.state.il.us/lookup/. You can search online using name, business name, license #. Lists Real Estate Professions.

#30 Secretary of State, Howlett Bldg, Rm 069, Springfield, IL 62756; 217-782-7817, Fax: 217-524-0120.
www.sos.state.il.us

#31 Secretary of State, 650 Roppolo Dr, Elk Grove, IL 60007; 847-437-3953, Fax: 847-437-3911.

#32 Secretary of State, 111 E Monroe St, Springfield, IL 62756; 217-782-7017, Fax: 217-524-0930.
www.sos.state.il.us

#33 Secretary of State, 520 S 2nd St, Lincoln Tower, #200, Springfield, IL 62701; 217-782-2256, Fax: 217-524-2172.
www.sos.state.il.us
Direct web site URL to search for licensees: www.nasdr.com

#35 Board of Education, 100 N 1st St, Springfield, IL 62777; 217-782-2805, Fax: 217-524-1289.
www.isbe.state.il.us/teachers

#36 State Fire Marshall, 1035 Stevenson Dr, Springfield, IL 62703; 217-785-0969, Fax: 217-782-1062.

#37 Department of Labor, 1 West Old State Capitol Plaza, #300, Springfield, IL 62701; 217-782-9347, Fax: 217-785-8776.
www.state.il.us/agency/idol/carn.htm
Direct web site URL to search for licensees: www.state.il.us/agency/idol/carn.htm

Illinois Federal Courts

The following list indicates the district and division name for each county in the state. If the bankruptcy court location is different from the district court, then the location of the bankruptcy court appears in parentheses.

County/Court Cross Reference

County	District	Division
Adams	Central	Springfield
Alexander	Southern	Benton
Bond	Southern	East St Louis
Boone	Northern	Rockford
Brown	Central	Springfield
Bureau	Central	Peoria
Calhoun	Southern	East St Louis
Carroll	Northern	Rockford
Cass	Central	Springfield
Champaign	Central	Danville/Urbana (Danville)
Christian	Central	Springfield
Clark	Southern	Benton (East St Louis)
Clay	Southern	Benton (East St Louis)
Clinton	Southern	East St Louis
Coles	Central	Danville/Urbana (Danville)
Cook	Northern	Chicago (Eastern)
Crawford	Southern	Benton (East St Louis)
Cumberland	Southern	Benton
De Kalb	Northern	Rockford
De Witt	Central	Springfield
Douglas	Central	Danville/Urbana (Danville)
Du Page	Northern	Chicago (Eastern)
Edgar	Central	Danville/Urbana (Danville)
Edwards	Southern	Benton
Effingham	Southern	Benton (East St Louis)
Fayette	Southern	East St Louis
Ford	Central	Danville/Urbana (Danville)
Franklin	Southern	Benton
Fulton	Central	Peoria
Gallatin	Southern	Benton
Greene	Central	Springfield
Grundy	Northern	Chicago (Eastern)
Hamilton	Southern	Benton
Hancock	Central	Peoria
Hardin	Southern	Benton
Henderson	Central	Rock Island (Peoria)
Henry	Central	Rock Island (Peoria)
Iroquois	Central	Danville/Urbana (Danville)
Jackson	Southern	Benton
Jasper	Southern	Benton (East St Louis)
Jefferson	Southern	Benton
Jersey	Southern	East St Louis
Jo Daviess	Northern	Rockford
Johnson	Southern	Benton
Kane	Northern	Chicago (Eastern)
Kankakee	Central	Danville/Urbana (Danville)
Kendall	Northern	Chicago (Eastern)
Knox	Central	Peoria
La Salle	Northern	Chicago (Eastern)
Lake	Northern	Chicago (Eastern)
Lawrence	Southern	Benton (East St Louis)
Lee	Northern	Rockford
Livingston	Central	Peoria (Danville)
Logan	Central	Springfield
Macon	Central	Danville/Urbana (Spmgfld)
Macoupin	Central	Springfield
Madison	Southern	East St Louis
Marion	Southern	East St Louis
Marshall	Central	Peoria
Mason	Central	Springfield
Massac	Southern	Benton
McDonough	Central	Peoria
McHenry	Northern	Rockford
McLean	Central	Peoria (Springfield)
Menard	Central	Springfield
Mercer	Central	Rock Island (Peoria)
Monroe	Southern	East St Louis
Montgomery	Central	Springfield
Morgan	Central	Springfield
Moultrie	Central	Danville/Urbana (Danville)
Ogle	Northern	Rockford
Peoria	Central	Peoria
Perry	Southern	Benton
Piatt	Central	Danville/Urbana (Danville)
Pike	Central	Springfield
Pope	Southern	Benton
Pulaski	Southern	Benton
Putnam	Central	Peoria
Randolph	Southern	East St Louis
Richland	Southern	Benton (East St Louis)
Rock Island	Central	Rock Island (Peoria)
Saline	Southern	Benton
Sangamon	Central	Springfield
Schuyler	Central	Springfield
Scott	Central	Springfield
Shelby	Central	Springfield
St. Clair	Southern	East St Louis
Stark	Central	Peoria
Stephenson	Northern	Rockford
Tazewell	Central	Peoria
Union	Southern	Benton
Vermilion	Central	Danville/Urbana (Danville)
Wabash	Southern	Benton
Warren	Central	Rock Island (Peoria)
Washington	Southern	East St Louis (Benton)
Wayne	Southern	Benton
White	Southern	Benton
Whiteside	Northern	Rockford
Will	Northern	Chicago (Eastern)
Williamson	Southern	Benton
Winnebago	Northern	Rockford
Woodford	Central	Peoria

US District Court

Central District of Illinois

Danville/Urbana Division 201 S Vine, Room 218, Urbana, IL 61801 (Courier Address: Use mail address for courier delivery), 217-373-5830.

http://www.ilcd.uscourts.gov

Counties: Champaign, Coles, Douglas, Edgar, Ford, Iroquois, Kankakee, Macon, Moultrie, Piatt, Vermilion.

Indexing/Storage: Cases are indexed by defendant and plaintiff as well as by case number. New cases are available in the index immediately after filing date. Both computer and card indexes are maintained. Open records are located at this court. District wide searches are availiable for civil records from October 1989 and criminal records from April 1992 from this court.

Fee & Payment: The fee is $20.00 per item (one party name or case number). Payment may be made by money order, cashier check, business check. Personal checks are not accepted. Prepayment is required. Payee: Clerk, US District Court. Certification fee: $7.00 per document. Copy fee: $.50 per page.

Phone Search: Only docket information is available by phone.

Mail Search: A stamped self addressed envelope is not required.

In Person: In person searching is available.

PACER: Sign-up number is 800-676-6856. Access fee is $.60 per minute. Toll-free access: 800-258-3678. Local access: 217-492-4997. Case records are available back to 1995. Records are purged after 5-7 years. New records are available online after 1 day. PACER is available online at http://pacer.ilcd.uscourts.gov.

Peoria Division US District Clerk's Office, 309 Federal Bldg, 100 NE Monroe St, Peoria, IL 61602 (Courier Address: Use mail address for courier delivery), 309-671-7117.

http://www.ilcd.uscourts.gov

Counties: Bureau, Fulton, Hancock, Knox, Livingston, McDonough, McLean, Marshall, Peoria, Putnam, Stark, Tazewell, Woodford.

Indexing/Storage: Cases are indexed by defendant and plaintiff as well as by case number. New cases are available in the index immediately after filing date. District-wide searches are available for civil cases from November 1989 and for criminal records from April 1992. Both computer and card indexes are maintained. Open records are located at this court.

Fee & Payment: The fee is $20.00 per item (one party name or case number). Payment may be made by money order, cashier check. Business checks are not accepted. Personal checks are not accepted. Prepayment is required. Law firm checks are accepted. Payee: Clerk,US District Court. Certification fee: $7.00 per document. Copy fee: $.50 per page.

Phone Search: Searching not available by phone.

Mail Search: Always enclose a stamped self addressed envelope.

In Person: In person searching is available.

PACER: Sign-up number is 800-676-6856. Access fee is $.60 per minute. Toll-free access: 800-258-3678. Local access: 217-492-4997. Case

records are available back to 1995. Records are purged after 5-7 years. New records are available online after 1 day. PACER is available online at http://pacer.ilcd.uscourts.gov.

Rock Island Division US District Clerk's Office, Room 40, Post Office Bldg, 211 19th St, Rock Island, IL 61201 (Courier Address: Use mail address for courier delivery), 309-793-5778.

http://www.ilcd.uscourts.gov

Counties: Henderson, Henry, Mercer, Rock Island, Warren.

Indexing/Storage: Cases are indexed by defendant and plaintiff as well as by case number. New cases are available in the index immediately after filing date. A computer index is maintained. Open records are located at this court.

Fee & Payment: The fee is $20.00 per item (one party name or case number). Payment may be made by money order, cashier check, business check. Personal checks are not accepted. Prepayment is required. Payee: Clerk of US District Court. Certification fee: $7.00 per document. Copy fee: $.50 per page.

Phone Search: All information that is not sealed is available for release over the phone.

Mail Search: Always enclose a stamped self addressed envelope.

In Person: In person searching is available.

PACER: Sign-up number is 800-676-6856. Access fee is $.60 per minute. Toll-free access: 800-258-3678. Local access: 217-492-4997. Case records are available back to 1995. Records are purged after 5-7 years. New records are available online after 1 day. PACER is available online at http://pacer.ilcd.uscourts.gov.

Springfield Division Clerk, 151 US Courthouse, 600 E Monroe, Springfield, IL 62701 (Courier Address: Use mail address for courier delivery), 217-492-4020.

http://www.ilcd.uscourts.gov

Counties: Adams, Brown, Cass, Christian, De Witt, Greene, Logan, Macoupin, Mason, Menard, Montgomery, Morgan, Pike, Sangamon, Schuyler, Scott, Shelby.

Indexing/Storage: Cases are indexed by defendant and plaintiff as well as by case number. New cases are available in the index immediately after filing date. Both computer and card indexes are maintained. Open records are located at this court. District wide searches are available for civil records from November 1989 and criminal records from 1992 from this court.

Fee & Payment: The fee is $20.00 per item (one party name or case number). Payment may be made by money order, cashier check, business check. Personal checks are not accepted. Prepayment is required. Payee: US District Court Clerk. Certification fee: $7.00 per document. Copy fee: $.50 per page. You are allowed to make your own copies. These copies cost $.50 per page.

Phone Search: Searching not available by phone.

Mail Search: A stamped self addressed envelope is not required.

In Person: In person searching is available.

PACER: Sign-up number is 800-676-6856. Access fee is $.60 per minute. Toll-free access: 800-258-3678. Local access: 217-492-4997. Case records are available back to 1995. Records are purged after 5-7 years. New records are available

online after 1 day. PACER is available online at http://pacer.ilcd.uscourts.gov.

US Bankruptcy Court

Central District of Illinois

Danville Division 201 N Vermilion #130, Danville, IL 61832-4733 (Courier Address: Use mail address for courier delivery), 217-431-4820, Fax: 217-431-2694.

http://www.ilcb.uscourts.gov

Counties: Champaign, Coles, Douglas, Edgar, Ford, Iroquois, Kankakee, Livingston, Moultrie, Piatt, Vermilion.

Indexing/Storage: Cases are indexed by debtor as well as by case number. New cases are available in the index 24 hours after filing date. A computer index is maintained. Open records are located at this court.

Fee & Payment: The fee is $20.00 per item (one party name or case number). Payment may be made by money order, cashier check, business check. Personal checks are not accepted. Prepayment is required. Payee: US Bankruptcy Court. Certification fee: $7.00 per document. Copy fee: $.50 per page.

Phone Search: Docket information available by phone. An automated voice case information service (VCIS) is available. Call VCIS at 800-827-9005 or 217-492-4550.

Fax Search: You may request a fee quotation by fax. Court will add $25.00 if records are in Chicago. Will fax results for $15.00 plus other fees.

Mail Search: Always enclose a stamped self addressed envelope.

In Person: In person searching is available.

PACER: Sign-up number is 800-676-6856. Access fee is $.60 per minute. Toll-free access: 800-454-9893. Local access: 217-492-4260. Case records are available back to 1989-90. Records are purged immediately when case is closed. New civil records are available online after 2 days. PACER is available online at http://pacer.ilcb.uscourts.gov.

Peoria Division 131 Federal Bldg, 100 NE Monroe, Peoria, IL 61602 (Courier Address: Use mail address for courier delivery), 309-671-7035, Fax: 309-671-7076.

http://www.ilcb.uscourts.gov

Counties: Bureau, Fulton, Hancock, Henderson, Henry, Knox, Marshall, McDonough, Mercer, Peoria, Putnam, Rock Island, Stark, Tazewell, Warren, Woodford.

Indexing/Storage: Cases are indexed by debtor as well as by case number. New cases are available in the index 24 hours after filing date. A computer index is maintained. Open records are located at this court.

Fee & Payment: The fee is $20.00 per item (one party name or case number). Payment may be made by money order, cashier check, business check. Personal checks are not accepted. Prepayment is required. A bill can be sent for copies. Payee: US Bankruptcy Court. Certification fee: $7.00 per document. Copy fee: $.50 per page.

Phone Search: An automated voice case information service (VCIS) is available. Call VCIS at 800-827-9005 or 217-492-4550.

Fax Search: You may request a quotation of fees by fax.

Mail Search: Always enclose a stamped self addressed envelope.

In Person: In person searching is available.

PACER: Sign-up number is 800-676-6856. Access fee is $.60 per minute. Toll-free access: 800-454-9893. Local access: 217-492-4260. Case records are available back to 1989-90. Records are purged immediately when case is closed. New civil records are available online after 2 days. PACER is available online at http://pacer.ilcb.uscourts.gov.

Springfield Division 226 US Courthouse, Springfield, IL 62701 (Courier Address: 600 E Monroe St., #226, Springfield, IL 62701), 217-492-4551, Fax: 217-492-4556.

http://www.ilcb.uscourts.gov

Counties: Adams, Brown, Cass, Christian, De Witt, Greene, Logan, Macon, Macoupin, Mason, McLean, Menard, Montgomery, Morgan, Pike, Sangamon, Schuyler, Scott, Shelby.

Indexing/Storage: Cases are indexed by debtor as well as by case number. New cases are available in the index 24 hours after filing date. A computer index is maintained. Open records are located at this court.

Fee & Payment: The fee is $20.00 per item (one party name or case number). Payment may be made by money order, cashier check, business check. Personal checks are not accepted. Prepayment is required. A bill will be sent for copies. Payee: US Bankruptcy Court. Certification fee: $7.00 per document. Copy fee: $.50 per page.

Phone Search: An automated voice case information service (VCIS) is available. Call VCIS at 800-827-9005 or 217-492-4550.

Fax Search: Fax requests are handled the same as mail requests.

Mail Search: Always enclose a stamped self addressed envelope.

In Person: In person searching is available.

PACER: Sign-up number is 800-676-6856. Access fee is $.60 per minute. Toll-free access: 800-454-9893. Local access: 217-492-4260. Case records are available back to 1989-90. Records are purged immediately when case is closed. New civil records are available online after 2 days. PACER is available online at http://pacer.ilcb.uscourts.gov.

US District Court

Northern District of Illinois

Chicago (Eastern) Division 20th Floor, 219 S Dearborn St, Chicago, IL 60604 (Courier Address: Use mail address for courier delivery), 312-435-5698.

http://www.ilnd.uscourts.gov

Counties: Cook, Du Page, Grundy, Kane, Kendall, Lake, La Salle, Will.

Indexing/Storage: Cases are indexed by defendant and plaintiff as well as by case number. New cases are available in the index 2 days after filing date. A computer index is maintained. Records are also indexed on microfiche. Open records are located at this court.

Fee & Payment: The fee is $20.00 per item (one party name or case number). Payment may be

made by money order, cashier check, personal check, Visa, Mastercard. Except for criminal bail bonds, all types of checks or money orders are accepted. Prepayment is required. Credit cards are only accepted in person. Payee: Clerk, US District Court. Certification fee: $7.00 per document. Copy fee: $.50 per page. You are allowed to make your own copies. These copies cost $.25 per page.

Phone Search: Searching is not available by phone. Only docket information is available by phone. Phone inquiries may be made from 8:15AM-5PM.

Mail Search: Always enclose a stamped self addressed envelope.

In Person: In person searching is available.

PACER: Sign-up number is 800-676-6856. Access fee is $.60 per minute. Toll-free access: 800-621-7029. Local access: 312-408-7777. Case records are available back to 1988. Records are purged varies. New records are available online after 1-2 days. If you are a registered PACER subscriber, you can access this court through the Internet at http://pacer.ilnd.uscourts.gov.

Rockford Division Room 211, 211 S Court St, Rockford, IL 61101 (Courier Address: Use mail address for courier delivery), 815-987-4355.

http://www.ilnd.uscourts.gov

Counties: Boone, Carroll, De Kalb, Jo Daviess, Lee, McHenry, Ogle, Stephenson, Whiteside, Winnebago.

Indexing/Storage: Cases are indexed by defendant and plaintiff as well as by case number. New cases are available in the index 1-3 days after filing date. A computer index is maintained. Open records are located at this court.

Fee & Payment: The fee is $20.00 per item (one party name or case number). Payment may be made by money order, cashier check, personal check. Prepayment is required. Payee: Clerk, US District Court. Certification fee: $7.00 per document. Copy fee: $.50 per page.

Phone Search: Searching is not available by phone.

Mail Search: Any indictments, pending information, case numbers and docket sheets (if specifically requested) will be released. A stamped self addressed envelope is not required.

In Person: In person searching is available.

PACER: Sign-up number is 800-676-6856. Access fee is $.60 per minute. Toll-free access: 800-621-7029. Local access: 312-408-7777. Case records are available back to 1988. Records are purged varies. New records are available online after 1-2 days. If you are a registered PACER subscriber, you can access this court through the Internet at http://pacer.ilnd.uscourts.gov.

US Bankruptcy Court

Northern District of Illinois

Chicago (Eastern) Division 219 S Dearborn St, Chicago, IL 60604-1802 (Courier Address: Use mail address for courier delivery), 312-435-5694.

http://www.ilnb.uscourts.gov

Counties: Cook, Du Page, Grundy, Kane, Kendall, La Salle, Lake, Will.

Indexing/Storage: Cases are indexed by debtor as well as by case number. New cases are available in

the index 1 day after filing date. A computer index is maintained. Open records are located at this court.

Fee & Payment: The fee is $20.00 per item (one party name or case number). Payment may be made by money order, cashier check, business check. Personal checks are not accepted. Prepayment is required. Payee: Clerk, US Bankruptcy Court. Certification fee: $7.00 per document. Copy fee: $.50 per page. You are allowed to make your own copies. These copies cost $.28 per page. Copies are available through Ikon Copy Service, 312-913-9508.

Phone Search: If the searcher has a case number, any information contained on the docket will be released. An automated voice case information service (VCIS) is available.

Mail Search: Always enclose a stamped self addressed envelope.

In Person: In person searching is available.

PACER: Sign-up number is 800-676-6856. Access fee is $.60 per minute. Toll-free access: 888-541-1078. Local access: 312-408-5101. Case records are available back to July 1, 1993. Records are never purged. New civil records are available online after 1 day. Online access to PACER/RACER is available at the web site. Access fee is 7 cents per document.

Other Online Access: Free Case Image Viewing is available from 5 a.m. to 11:59 p.m. CST at www.ilnb.uscourts.gov/casenotice.htm. Access fee is 7 cents per page.

Rockford Division Room 110, 211 S Court St, Rockford, IL 61101 (Courier Address: Use mail address for courier delivery), 815-987-4350, Fax: 815-987-4205.

http://www.ilnb.uscourts.gov

Counties: Boone, Carroll, De Kalb, Jo Daviess, Lee, McHenry, Ogle, Stephenson, Whiteside, Winnebago.

Indexing/Storage: Cases are indexed by debtor and creditors as well as by case number. New cases are available in the index immediately after filing date. A computer index is maintained. Open records are located at this court.

Fee & Payment: The fee is $20.00 per item (one party name or case number). Payment may be made by money order, cashier check, personal check. Debtor's checks are not accepted. Payee: Clerk, US Bankruptcy Court. Certification fee: $7.00 per document. Copy fee: $.50 per page.

Phone Search: Only docket information is available by phone. An automated voice case information service (VCIS) is available. Call VCIS at 888-293-3698 or.

Mail Search: Always enclose a stamped self addressed envelope.

In Person: In person searching is available.

PACER: Sign-up number is 800-676-6856. Access fee is $.60 per minute. Local access: 815-987-4489, 815-987-4490. Case records are available back to 1992. New civil records are available online after 1 day. Online access to PACER/RACER is available at the web site. Access fee is 7 cents per document.

Other Online Access: Free Case Image Viewing is available from 5 a.m. to 11:59 p.m. CST at www.ilnb.uscourts.gov/casenotice.htm. Access fee is 7 cents per page.

US District Court

Southern District of Illinois

Benton Division 301 W Main St, Benton, IL 62812 (Courier Address: Use mail address for courier delivery), 618-439-7760.

http://www.ilsd.uscourts.gov

Counties: Alexander, Clark, Clay, Crawford, Cumberland, Edwards, Effingham, Franklin, Gallatin, Hamilton, Hardin, Jackson, Jasper, Jefferson, Johnson, Lawrence, Massac, Perry, Pope, Pulaski, Richland, Saline, Union, Wabash, Wayne, White, Williamson. Cases mayalso be allocated to the Benton Division.

Indexing/Storage: Cases are indexed by defendant and plaintiff as well as by case number. New cases are available in the index immediately after filing date. The name and date are required to search for records. Both computer and card indexes are maintained. Records are also indexed on microfiche. Open records are located at this court.

Fee & Payment: The fee is $20.00 per item (one party name or case number). Payment may be made by money order, cashier check, personal check. Except in an emergency, prepayment is required. Payee: Clerk, US District Court. Certification fee: $7.00 per document. Copy fee: $.50 per page. You are allowed to make your own copies. These copies cost $.50 per page.

Phone Search: Docket information available by phone.

Mail Search: Always enclose a stamped self addressed envelope.

In Person: In person searching is available.

PACER: Sign-up number is 800-676-6856. Access fee is $.60 per minute. Toll-free access: 800-426-7523. Local access: 618-482-9430. Case records are available back to 1985. Records are purged when deemed necessary. New civil records are available online after 1 day. New criminal records are available online after 1-2 days. PACER is available online at http://pacer.ilsd.uscourts.gov.

East St Louis Division PO Box 249, East St Louis, IL 62202 (Courier Address: 750 Missouri Ave, East St Louis, IL 62201), 618-482-9371.

http://www.ilsd.uscourts.gov

Counties: Bond, Calhoun, Clinton, Fayette, Jersey, Madison, Marion, Monroe, Randolph, St. Clair, Washington. Cases for these counties may also be allocated to the Benton Division.

Indexing/Storage: Cases are indexed by defendant and plaintiff as well as by case number. New cases are available in the index immediately after filing date. Name and date are required to search for records. Both computer and card indexes are maintained. Records are also indexed on microfiche. Open records are located at this court.

Fee & Payment: The fee is $20.00 per item (one party name or case number). Payment may be made by money order, cashier check, personal check. Except in an emergency, prepayment is required. Cash is also accepted. Payee: Clerk, US District Court. Certification fee: $7.00 per document. Copy fee: $.50 per page.

Phone Search: Docket information available by phone.

Mail Search: Always enclose a stamped self addressed envelope.

In Person: In person searching is available.

PACER: Sign-up number is 800-676-6856. Access fee is $.60 per minute. Toll-free access: 800-426-7523. Local access: 618-482-9430. Case records are available back to 1985. Records are purged when deemed necessary. New civil records are available online after 1 day. New criminal records are available online after 1-2 days. PACER is available online at http://pacer.ilsd.uscourts.gov.

US Bankruptcy Court

Southern District of Illinois

Benton Division 301 W Main, Benton, IL 62812 (Courier Address: Use mail address for courier delivery), 618-435-2200.

http://www.ilsb.uscourts.gov

Counties: Alexander, Edwards, Franklin, Gallatin, Hamilton, Hardin, Jackson, Jefferson, Johnson, Massac, Perry, Pope, Pulaski, Randolph, Saline, Union, Wabash, Washington, Wayne, White, Williamson.

Indexing/Storage: Cases are indexed by debtor as well as by case number. New cases are available in the index immediately after filing date. Both computer and card indexes are maintained. Open records are located at this court.

Fee & Payment: The fee is $20.00 per item (one party name or case number). Payment may be made by money order, cashier check, business check. Personal checks are not accepted. Prepayment is required. Payee: Clerk, US Bankruptcy Court. Certification fee: $7.00 per document. Copy fee: $.50 per page.

Phone Search: An automated voice case information service (VCIS) is available. Call VCIS at 800-726-5622 or 618-482-9365.

Mail Search: Always enclose a stamped self addressed envelope.

In Person: In person searching is available.

PACER: Sign-up number is 800-676-6856. Access fee is $.60 per minute. Toll-free access: 800-933-9148. Local access: 618-482-9114. Case records are available back to January 1989. Records are purged as deemed necessary. New civil records are available online after 1 day. PACER is available online at http://pacer.ilsb.uscourts.gov.

East St Louis Division PO Box 309, East St Louis, IL 62202-0309 (Courier Address: 750 Missouri Ave, East St Louis, IL 62201), 618-482-9400.

http://www.ilsb.uscourts.gov

Counties: Bond, Calhoun, Clark, Clay, Clinton, Crawford, Cumberland, Effingham, Fayette, Jasper, Jersey, Lawrence, Madison, Marion, Monroe, Richland, St. Clair.

Indexing/Storage: Cases are indexed by debtor as well as by case number. New cases are available in the index 1 working day after filing date. Both computer and card indexes are maintained. Records are also indexed on microfiche. Open records are located at this court. District wide searches are available from this court.

Fee & Payment: The fee is $20.00 per item (one party name or case number). Payment may be made by money order, cashier check, personal check. Prepayment is required. Debtor's checks are not accepted. Payee: Clerk, US Bankruptcy Court. Certification fee: $7.00 per document. Copy fee: $.50 per page.

Phone Search: An automated voice case information service (VCIS) is available. Call VCIS at 800-726-5622 or 618-482-9365.

Mail Search: A stamped self addressed envelope is not required.

In Person: In person searching is available.

PACER: Sign-up number is 800-676-6856. Access fee is $.60 per minute. Toll-free access: 800-933-9148. Local access: 618-482-9114. Case records are available back to January 1989. Records are purged as deemed necessary. New civil records are available online after 1 day. PACER is available online at http://pacer.ilsb.uscourts.gov.

Illinois County Courts

Court	Jurisdiction	No. of Courts	How Organized
Circuit Courts*	General	106	22 Circuits

* Profiled in this Sourcebook.

CIVIL									
Court	Tort	Contract	Real Estate	Min. Claim	Max. Claim	Small Claims	Estate	Eviction	Domestic Relations
Circuit Courts*	X	X	X	$0	No Max	$5000	X	X	X

CRIMINAL					
Court	Felony	Misdemeanor	DWI/DUI	Preliminary Hearing	Juvenile
Circuit Courts*	X	X	X	X	X

ADMINISTRATION Administative Office of Courts, 222 N LaSalle 13th Floor, Chicago, IL, 60601; 312-793-3250, Fax: 312-793-1335.

COURT STRUCTURE Illinois is divided into 22 judicial circuits; 3 are single county: Cook, Du Page (18th Circuit) and Will (12th Circuit). The other 19 circuits consist of 2 or more contiguous counties. The Circuit Court of Cook County is the largest unified court system in the world. Its 2300-person staff handles approximately 2.4 million cases each year. The civil part of the various Circuit Courts in Cook County is divided as follows: under $30,000 are "civil cases" and over $30,000 are "civil law division cases."

Probate is handled by the Circuit Court in all counties.

ONLINE ACCESS While there is no statewide public online system available, a number of Illinois Circuit Courts offer online access.

ADDITIONAL INFORMATION The search fee is set by statute and has three levels based on the county population. The higher the population, the larger the fee. In most courts, both civil and criminal data is on computer from the same starting date. In most Illinois courts the search fee is charged on a per name per year basis.

📖 📖 📖 📖 📖 📖 📖

Adams County

Circuit Court 521 Vermont St, Quincy, IL 62301; 217-277-2100; Fax: 217-277-2116. Hours: 8:30AM-4:30PM (CST). *Felony, Misdemeanor, Civil, Eviction, Small Claims, Probate.*

www.co.adams.il.us

Civil Records: Access: Phone, mail, fax, in person, online, email. Both court and visitors may perform in person searches. Search fee: $2.00 per name. Fee is $4.00 for years prior to 1987. Required to search: name, years to search. Civil cases indexed by defendant, plaintiff. Civil records on computer from 1987, books and index cards from 1920. Online access to 8th Circuit Clerk of Court records is available free at www.circuitclerk.co.adams.il.us/. Search by name, case or docket number.

Criminal Records: Access: Phone, mail, fax, in person, online, email. Both court and visitors may perform in person searches. Search fee: $2.00 per name. Fee is $4.00 for years prior to 1987. Required to search: name, years to search, DOB. Criminal records on computer from 1987, books and index cards from 1920. Online access to criminal records is the same as civil.

General Information: Public Access terminal is available. No juvenile or adoption records released. SASE required. Turnaround time 2-3 days. Copy fee: $1.00 for first page, $.50 each add'l. Certification fee: $2.00. Fee payee: Clerk of Circuit Court. Personal checks accepted. Prepayment is required.

Alexander County

Circuit Court 2000 Washington Ave, Cairo, IL 62914; 618-734-0107; Fax: 618-734-7003. Hours: 8AM-4PM (CST). *Felony, Misdemeanor, Civil, Eviction, Small Claims, Probate.*

Civil Records: Access: Fax, mail, in person. Both court and visitors may perform in person searches. Search fee: $4.00 per name per year. Required to search: name, years to search. Civil cases indexed by defendant, plaintiff. Civil records on computer from 1987, books and index cards from 1800s.

Criminal Records: Access: Fax, mail, in person. Both court and visitors may perform in person searches. Search fee: $4.00 per name per year. Required to search: name. Criminal records on computer from 1987, books and index cards from 1800s.

General Information: Public Access terminal is available. No juvenile or adoption records released. SASE required. Turnaround time 1 day. Copy fee: $1.00 for first page, $.50 each add'l. Certification fee: $2.50. Fee payee: Clerk of Circuit Court. Personal checks accepted. Prepayment is required.

Bond County

Circuit Court 200 W College Ave, Greenville, IL 62246; 618-664-3208; Fax: 618-664-4676. Hours: 8AM-4PM (CST). *Felony, Misdemeanor, Civil, Eviction, Small Claims, Probate.*

www.johnkking.org

Civil Records: Access: Mail, in person. Both court and visitors may perform in person searches. Search fee: $4.00 per name per year. Required to search: name, years to search. Civil cases indexed by defendant, plaintiff. Civil records on computer back to 4/90 and are limited, index books from 1900s.

Criminal Records: Access: Mail, in person. Both court and visitors may perform in person searches. Search fee: $4.00 per name per year. Required to search: name, years to search; also helpful: DOB. Criminal records on computer back to 1987; index books from 1900s.

General Information: Public Access terminal is available. No juvenile or adoption records released. SASE required. Turnaround time 1-2 weeks. Copy fee: $.50 per page. Certification fee: $2.00 plus $.50 per page. Fee payee: Clerk of Circuit Court. Personal checks accepted. Prepayment is required.

Boone County

Circuit Court 601 N Main #303, Belvidere, IL 61008; 815-544-0371. Hours: 8:30AM-5PM (CST). *Felony, Misdemeanor, Civil, Eviction, Small Claims, Probate.*

Civil Records: Access: Mail, in person. Both court and visitors may perform in person searches. Search fee: $4.00 per name per year. Required to search: name, years to search. Civil cases indexed by defendant, plaintiff. Civil records on computer since August, 1993, on index books from 1800s.

Criminal Records: Access: Mail, in person. Both court and visitors may perform in person searches. Search fee: $4.00 per name per year. Required to search: name, years to search, DOB; also helpful: SSN, signed release. Criminal records on computer since August, 1993, on index books from 1800s.

General Information: Public Access terminal is available. No juvenile or adoption records released. SASE required. Turnaround time 1-2 days. Copy fee: $1.00 for first page, $.50 each add'l. Certification fee: $2.00. Fee payee: Clerk of Circuit Court. Only cashiers checks and money orders accepted. Prepayment is required.

Brown County

Circuit Court Brown County Courthouse, 200 Court St, Rm 5, Mt Sterling, IL 62353; 217-773-2713. Hours: 8:30AM-4:30PM (CST). *Felony, Misdemeanor, Civil, Eviction, Small Claims, Probate.*

Civil Records: Access: Phone, fax, mail, in person. Both court and visitors may perform in person searches. Search fee: $4.00 per name per year. Required to search: name, years to search. Civil cases indexed by defendant, plaintiff. Civil records on computer since 1994, on index books from 1830s.

Criminal Records: Access: Phone, fax, mail, in person. Both court and visitors may perform in person searches. Search fee: $4.00 per name per year. Required to search: name, years to search, DOB, signed release. Criminal records on computer since 1994, on index books from 1830s.

General Information: Public Access terminal is available. No juvenile or adoption records released. SASE required. Turnaround time 1 week. Fax notes: $3.00 per page. Copy fee: $.35 per page. Certification fee: $2.00. Fee payee: Clerk of Circuit Court. Only cashiers checks and money orders accepted. Prepayment is required.

Bureau County

Circuit Court 702 S Main, Princeton, IL 61356; 815-872-2001; Fax: 815-872-0027. Hours: 8AM-4PM (CST). *Felony, Misdemeanor, Civil, Eviction, Small Claims, Probate.*

www.bccirclk.gov

Civil Records: Access: Online, in person. Visitors must perform in person searches for themselves. No search fee. Required to search: name, years to search. Civil cases indexed by defendant, plaintiff. Civil records on computer from 8/1988, prior on index books. Online access to judicial circuit records is available to local attorney firms and retrievers. The service is free. Call the Clerk's office for details, 815-872-0027.

Criminal Records: Access: Mail, fax, in person. Both court and visitors may perform in person searches. Search fee: $4.00 per name per year. Required to search: name, years to search, DOB. Criminal records on computer from 8/1988, prior on index books.

General Information: Public Access terminal is available. No juvenile or adoption records released. SASE required. Turnaround time 1 week. Fax notes: Fee to fax results is $2.00 1st pg; $1.00 each add'l. Copy fee: $.25 per page. Certification fee: $2.00. Fee payee: Bureau County Circuit Clerk. Personal checks accepted. Prepayment is required.

Calhoun County

Circuit Court PO Box 486, Hardin, IL 62047; 618-576-2451; Fax: 618-576-9541. Hours: 8:30AM-4:30PM (CST). *Felony, Misdemeanor, Civil, Eviction, Small Claims, Probate.*

Civil Records: Access: Phone, fax, mail, in person. Both court and visitors may perform in person searches. Search fee: $4.00 per name per year. Required to search: name, years to search. Civil cases indexed by

defendant, plaintiff. Civil records on index books from 1800s, computerized since 07/98.

Criminal Records: Access: Phone, fax, mail, in person. Both court and visitors may perform in person searches. Search fee: $4.00 per name per year. Required to search: name, years to search, DOB. Criminal records on index books from 1800s, computerized since 07/98.

General Information: No juvenile or adoption records released. SASE required. Turnaround time 1-2 days. Fax notes: No fee to fax results. Copy fee: $1.00 for first page. $.50 per page, pages 2-19; $.25 each additional page. Certification fee: $2.00. Fee payee: Clerk of Circuit Court. Only cashiers checks and money orders accepted. Prepayment is required.

Carroll County

Circuit Court 301 N Main St, PO Box 32, Mt Carroll, IL 61053; 815-244-0230 X27; Fax: 815-244-3869. Hours: 8:30AM-4:30PM (CST). *Felony, Misdemeanor, Civil, Eviction, Small Claims, Probate.*

Civil Records: Access: Mail, in person. Both court and visitors may perform in person searches. Search fee: $4.00 per name per year. Required to search: name, years to search. Civil cases indexed by defendant. Civil records on computer from 1988, prior on index books. Will respond by fax if possible.

Criminal Records: Access: Mail, in person. Both court and visitors may perform in person searches. Search fee: $4.00 per name per year. Required to search: name, years to search, DOB. Criminal records on computer from 1988, prior on index books. Will respond by fax if possible.

General Information: Public Access terminal is available. No juvenile, mental health or adoption records released. SASE required. Turnaround time 2-3 days. Copy fee: $1.00 for first page, $.50 each add'l. Certification fee: $2.00. Fee payee: Clerk of Circuit Court. Personal checks accepted. Prepayment is required.

Cass County

Circuit Court PO Box 203, Virginia, IL 62691; 217-452-7225. Hours: 8:30AM-4:30PM (CST). *Felony, Misdemeanor, Civil, Eviction, Small Claims, Probate.*

Civil Records: Access: Mail, in person. Both court and visitors may perform in person searches. Search fee: $4.00 per name per year. Required to search: name, years to search. Civil cases indexed by defendant, plaintiff. Civil records on index books from 1800s.

Criminal Records: Access: Mail, in person. Both court and visitors may perform in person searches. Search fee: $4.00 per name per year. Required to search: name, years to search, DOB; also helpful: SSN. Criminal records on index books from 1800s.

General Information: No juvenile or adoption records released. SASE required. Turnaround time 1-2 weeks. Copy fee: $1.00 for first page, $.50 each add'l. Certification fee: $2.00. Fee payee: Cass County Circuit Clerk. Personal checks accepted. Prepayment is required.

Champaign County

Circuit Court 101 E Main, Urbana, IL 61801; Civil phone: 217-384-3725; Criminal phone: 217-384-3727; Fax: 217-384-3879. Hours: 8:30AM-4:30PM *Felony, Misdemeanor, Civil, Eviction, Small Claims, Probate.*

www.cccircuitclerk.com

Civil Records: Access: Mail, online, in person. Both court and visitors may perform in person searches. Search fee: $4.00 per name per year. Required to search: name, years to search. Civil cases indexed by defendant, plaintiff. Civil records on computer from 1986, index books from 1800s. Access to the remote online system called PASS requires a setup fee and annual user fee. Online case records go back to 1992.

Fee is $200 per year plus $25 per user; there are separate reduced fees for law firms and non-profits organizations. Contact Jo Kelly at 217-384-3767 for subscription information.

Criminal Records: Access: Mail, online, in person. Both court and visitors may perform in person searches. Search fee: $4.00 per name per year. Required to search: name, years to search; also helpful: DOB, SSN. Criminal records on computer from 1988, index books from 1800s. Online access to criminal records is the same as civil.

General Information: Public Access terminal is available. No juvenile or adoption records released. SASE required. Turnaround time 1-2 weeks. Copy fee: $.25 per page. Certification fee: $2.00. Fee payee: Clerk of Circuit Court. Personal checks accepted. Prepayment is required.

Christian County

Circuit Court PO Box 617, Taylorville, IL 62568; 217-824-4966; Fax: 217-824-5105. Hours: 8AM-4PM (CST). *Felony, Misdemeanor, Civil, Eviction, Small Claims, Probate.*

Civil Records: Access: Phone, mail, in person. Both court and visitors may perform in person searches. Search fee: $5.00 per name per year. Required to search: name; also helpful: years to search. Civil cases indexed by defendant, plaintiff. Civil records on computer from 1988, index books from 1840.

Criminal Records: Access: Phone, mail, in person. Both court and visitors may perform in person searches. Search fee: $5.00 per name per year. Required to search: name; also helpful: years to search, DOB. Criminal records on computer from 1988, index books from 1840.

General Information: No juvenile or adoption records released. SASE required. Turnaround time 1-2 days. Copy fee: $1.00 for first page, $.50 each add'l. Certification fee: $2.00. Fee payee: Clerk of Circuit Court. Business checks accepted. Prepayment required.

Clark County

Circuit Court PO Box 187, Marshall, IL 62441; 217-826-2811. Hours: 8AM-4PM (CST). *Felony, Misdemeanor, Civil, Eviction, Small Claims, Probate.*

Civil Records: Access: Mail, in person. Both court and visitors may perform in person searches. Search fee: $4.00 per name per year. Required to search: name, years to search; also helpful: address. Civil cases indexed by defendant, plaintiff. Civil records on computer from 1989, index books from 1800s.

Criminal Records: Access: Mail, in person. Both court and visitors may perform in person searches. Search fee: $4.00 per name per year. Required to search: name, years to search, DOB, signed release; also helpful: address, SSN. Criminal records on computer from 1989, index books from 1800s.

General Information: Public Access terminal is available. No juvenile, maternity, or adoption records released. Turnaround time 1 week. Copy fee: $1.00 for first page, $.50 each add'l. After 20 pages, fee is $.25 per page. Certification fee: $2.00. Fee payee: Clerk of Circuit Court. Only cashiers checks and money orders accepted.

Clay County

Circuit Court PO Box 100, Louisville, IL 62858; 618-665-3523; Fax: 618-665-3543. Hours: 8AM-4PM (CST). *Felony, Misdemeanor, Civil, Eviction, Small Claims, Probate.*

Civil Records: Access: Fax, mail, in person. Both court and visitors may perform in person searches. Search fee: $4.00 per name. Fee is $4.00 per year prior to 1988. Required to search: name, years to search. Civil cases indexed by defendant. Civil records on computer from 1988, index books from 1850s.

Criminal Records: Access: Fax, mail, in person. Both court and visitors may perform in person searches. Search fee: $4.00 per name. Fee is $4.00 per year prior to 1988. Required to search: name, years to search; also helpful: DOB. Criminal records on computer from 1988, index books from 1850s.

General Information: Public Access terminal is available. No juvenile or adoption records released. SASE required. Turnaround time 2-3 days. Fax notes: $1.00 for first page, $.50 each add'l 19; $.25 each thereafter. Certification fee: $2.00. Fee payee: Clerk of Circuit Court. Personal checks accepted. Prepayment required.

Clinton County

Circuit Court County Courthouse, PO Box 407, Carlyle, IL 62231; 618-594-2464. Hours: 8AM-4PM (CST). *Felony, Misdemeanor, Civil, Eviction, Small Claims, Probate.*

Civil Records: Access: Mail, in person. Both court and visitors may perform in person searches. Search fee: $10.00 per name. Fee is for 10 year search. Required to search: name, years to search. Civil cases indexed by defendant, plaintiff. Civil records on computer from 1988, index books from 1800s.

Criminal Records: Access: Mail, in person. Both court and visitors may perform in person searches. Search fee: $10.00 per name. Flat fee for 10 year search. Required to search: name, years to search, DOB. Criminal records on computer from 1988, index books from 1800s.

General Information: Public Access terminal is available. No juvenile or adoption records released. SASE required. Turnaround time 2-4 days. Copy fee: $.50 per page. Certification fee: $2.00. Fee payee: Clerk of Circuit Court. Personal checks accepted. Prepayment is required.

Coles County

Circuit Court PO Box 48, Charleston, IL 61920; 217-348-0516. Hours: 8:30AM-4:30PM (CST). *Felony, Misdemeanor, Civil, Eviction, Small Claims, Probate.*

Civil Records: Access: Fax, mail, in person. Both court and visitors may perform in person searches. Search fee: $5.00 per name. Required to search: name, years to search. Civil cases indexed by defendant, plaintiff. Civil records on computer from 1989, index books from 1800s.

Criminal Records: Access: Fax, mail, in person. Both court and visitors may perform in person searches. Search fee: $5.00 per name. Required to search: name, years to search, DOB; also helpful: SSN. Criminal records on computer from 1989, index books from 1800s.

General Information: Public Access terminal is available. No juvenile or adoption records released. SASE required. Turnaround time 1-2 days. Copy fee: $.50 per page. Certification fee: $2.00. Fee payee: Clerk of Circuit Court. Personal checks accepted. Prepayment is required.

Cook County

Circuit Court - Criminal Division 2650 S California Ave, Chicago, IL 60608; Criminal phone: 773-869-3140; Fax: 773-869-4444. Hours: 9AM-5PM (CST). *Felony.*

www.cookcountyclerkofcourt.org

Note: Cases are heard in six district courts within the county and each court has a central index, eventually all criminal case files are maintained here.

Criminal Records: Access: Mail, online, in person. Both court and visitors may perform in person searches. Search fee: $6.00 per name per year. Required to search: name, years to search; also helpful: DOB, SSN.

Criminal records on computer since 1964; prior records on microfiche from 1800s. Online case searching for limited case information, called case snapshots, is available free online at www.cookcounty clerkofcourt.org/Terms/terms.html. Search by name, case number or court date. Information included is parties (up to 3), attorneys, case type, the filing date, the ad damnum (amount of damages sought), division and district, and the most current court date.

General Information: Public Access terminal is available. No juvenile or adoption records released. SASE required. Turnaround time 2 weeks. Copy fee: $2.00 for first page, $.50 each add'l. $.25 per page after 20. Certification fee: $6.00. Fee payee: Clerk of Circuit Court. Personal checks accepted. Personal checks accepted with drivers license# or attorney code. Prepayment is required.

Circuit Court - Civil - Chicago District 1 50 W Washington, Rm 601, Chicago, IL 60602; 312-603-5145; Civil phone: 312-603-5116 (admin); Criminal phone: 312-603-4641; Probate phone: 312-603-6441; Fax: 312-443-4557. Hours: 8:30AM-4:30PM (CST). *Misdemeanor, Civil Action Under $100,000, Eviction, Small Claims, Probate.*

www.cookcountyclerkofcourt.org

Note: Note: Cases are heard in six district courts within the county. Each court has a central index. Eventually all case files are maintained here. Probate is a separate division at the same address.

Civil Records: Access: Phone, mail, online, in person. Both court and visitors may perform in person searches. No search fee. Required to search: name, years to search. Civil cases indexed by defendant, plaintiff. Civil records on computer from 1983, index books from 1800s. Online case searching for limited case information, called case snapshots, is available free online at www.cookcountyclerkofcourt.org/Terms/ terms.html. Search by name, case number or court date. Information included is parties (up to 3), attorneys, case type, the filing date, the ad damnum (amount of damages sought), division and district, and the most current court date. Phone inquiries to court to check status only. Phone record requests can be directed to the Computer Center at 312-603-7586 or 7.

Criminal Records: Access: Phone, mail, online, in person. Visitors must perform in person searches for themselves. No search fee. Required to search: name, years to search, DOB. Misdemeanor records only. Search misdemeanors in person in Room 1006. For online information, see civil. Phone record requests can be directed to the Computer Ctr. at 312-603-7586 or 7.

General Information: Public Access terminal is available. No juvenile or adoption records released. SASE required. Turnaround time 1 week. Copy fee: $2.00 for first page, $.50 each add'l. Certification fee: $6.00. Fee payee: Clerk of Circuit Court. Personal checks accepted. Prepayment is required.

Bridgeview District 5 10220 S 76th Ave Rm 121, Bridgeview Court Bldg, Bridgeview, IL 60453; Civil phone: 708-974-6500; Criminal phone: 708-974-6404. *Felony, Civil Action Under $100,000, Eviction, Small Claims.*

www.cookcountyclerkofcourt.org

Note: Alsip, Bridgeview, Burbank, Countryside, Evergreen Pk, Forest View, Hickory Hills, Hinsdale, Hodgkins, Hometown, Justice, Lagrange, Lemont, Lyons, McCook, Oak Lawn, Orland Hills, Palos Park, Stickney, Summit, West Haven, Willow Springs, Worth.

Civil Records: Access: Online, in person. Visitors must perform in person searches for themselves. No search fee. Required to search: name, years to search. Civil cases indexed by defendant, plaintiff. Civil records computerized since 1985, microfiche to early 1970s.

Limited online case information is available; see Circuit Court - Chicago Division for details.

Criminal Records: Access: Online, in person. Visitors must perform in person searches for themselves. No search fee. Required to search: name.

General Information: Public Access terminal is available. Copy fee: $2.00 for first page, $.50 each add'l. Certification fee: $6.00. Fee payee: Clerk of Circuit Court. Personal checks accepted.

Markham District 6 16501 S Kedzie Pkwy Rm119, Markham, IL 60426-5509; Civil phone: 708-210-4581; Criminal phone: 708-210-4217. *Felony, Civil Action Under $30,000, Eviction, Small Claims.*

www.cookcountyclerkofcourt.org

Blue Is, Burnham, Calumet, Chicago Hgts, Crestwood, Crete, Dixmoor, Dolton, Flossmoor, Glenwood, Harvey, Hazelcrest, Homewood, Lansing, Lynwood, Markham, Matteson, Midlothian, Oak Forest, Posen, Riverdale, Robbins, Sauk Village, Tinley Pk.

Civil Records: Access: Online, in person. Visitors must perform in person searches for themselves. No search fee. Required to search: name. Civil cases indexed by defendant, plaintiff. Civil records computerized since 1989. Limited online case information is available; see Circuit Court - Chicago Division for details.

Criminal Records: Access: Mail, online, in person. Visitors must perform in person searches for themselves. No search fee. Required to search: name, years to search. Online access to criminal records is the same as civil.

General Information: Public Access terminal is available. Turnaround time 2 weeks. Copy fee: $2.00 for first page, $.50 each add'l. Certification fee: $6.00. Fee payee: Clerk of Circuit Court. Personal checks accepted.

Maywood District 4 1500 S Maybrook Dr, Rm 236, Maywood, IL 60153-2410; Civil phone: 708-865-4973; Criminal phone: 708-865-6040. Hours: 9AM-5PM (CST). *Felony, Civil Action Under $100,000, Eviction, Small Claims.*

www.cookcountyclerkofcourt.org

Note: Bellwood, Berkeley, Berwyn, Broadview, Brookfield, Cicero, Elmwood Park, Forest Park, Franklin Park, Hillside, La Grange Park, Maywood, Melrose Park, Northlake, North Riverside, Oak Park, River Forest, River Grove, Riverside, Stone Park, Westchester.

Civil Records: Access: Mail, online, in person. Visitors must perform in person searches for themselves. No search fee. Required to search: name; also helpful: years to search. Civil cases indexed by defendant, plaintiff. Civil records computerized since 1982, docket books to 1970s, prior archived. Limited online case information is available; see Circuit Court - Chicago Div. for details.

Criminal Records: Access: Online, in person. Visitors must perform in person searches for themselves. No search fee. Required to search: name, years to search, DOB. Online access to criminal records same as civil.

General Information: Public Access terminal is available. Turnaround time 1 week. Copy fee: $2.00 for first page, $.50 each add'l. Certification fee: $6.00. Fee payee: Clerk of Circuit Court. Personal checks accepted. Prepayment is required.

Rolling Meadows District 3 2121 Euclid Ave, Rolling Meadows, IL 60008-1566; Civil phone: 847-818-2300; Criminal phone: 847-818-2701. Hours: 8:30AM-4:30PM (CST). *Felony, Civil Action Under $100,000, Eviction, Small Claims.*

www.cookcountyclerkofcourt.org

Note: Arlington Hgts, Barrington, Bartlett, Bensonville, Buffalo Grove, Elgin, Elk Grove Village, Hanover Pk, Harwood Hgts, Inverness, Mt. Prospect, Norridge,

Palatine, Prospect Hgts, Rolling Meadows, Roselle, Rosemont, Schaumburg, Schiller Pk, Wheeling.

Civil Records: Access: Mail, online, in person. Visitors must perform in person searches for themselves. No search fee. Required to search: name; also helpful: years to search. Civil cases indexed by defendant, plaintiff. Civil records are computerized since 1986. Limited online case information is available; see Circuit Court - Chicago Division for details.

Criminal Records: Access: Online, in person. Visitors must perform in person searches for themselves. No search fee. Required to search: name, years to search; also helpful: DOB, SSN. Online access to criminal records is the same as civil.

General Information: Public Access terminal is available. Turnaround time 2 weeks. Copy fee: $2.00 for first page, $.50 each add'l. Certification fee: $6.00. Fee payee: Clerk of Circuit Court. Personal checks accepted.

Skokie District 2 Skokie Court Bldg Rm 136, 5600 Old Orchard Rd, Skokie, IL 60076-1023; 847-470-7250. Hours: 8:30AM-4:30PM (CST). *Misdemeanor, Civil Action Under $100,000, Eviction, Small Claims.*

www.cookcountyclerkofcourt.org

Note: Deerfield, Des Plaines, Evanston, Glencoe, Glenview, Golf, Kenilworth, Lincolnwood, Morton Grove, Niles, Northbrook, Northfield, Park Ridge, Prospect Heights, Skokie, Wilmette, Winnetka.

Civil Records: Access: Phone, mail, online, in person. Visitors must perform in person searches for themselves. Search fee: $6.00 per name per year. Required to search: name, years to search. Civil cases indexed by defendant, plaintiff. Civil records computerized since 1983. Limited online case information is available; see Circuit Court - Chicago Division for details.

Criminal Records: Access: Phone, mail, online, in person. Both court and visitors may perform in person searches. Search fee: $6.00 per name per year. Required to search: name, years to search; also helpful: DOB, SSN. Online access to criminal records same as civil.

General Information: Public Access terminal is available. All records are public. SASE not required. Turnaround time 1 week to 1 month. Copy fee: $2.00 for first page, $.50 each add'l. Certification fee: $6.00. Fee payee: Clerk of Circuit Court. Personal checks accepted. Prepayment is required.

Crawford County

Circuit Court PO Box 655, Robinson, IL 62454-0655; 618-544-3512; Fax: 618-546-5628. Hours: 8AM-4PM (CST). *Felony, Misdemeanor, Civil, Eviction, Small Claims, Probate.*

Civil Records: Access: Fax, mail, in person. Both court and visitors may perform in person searches. Search fee: $4.00 per name per year. Required to search: name, years to search. Civil cases indexed by defendant, plaintiff. Civil records on computer from 1989, index books from 1800s.

Criminal Records: Access: Fax, mail, in person. Both court and visitors may perform in person searches. Search fee: $4.00 per name per year. Required to search: name, years to search, DOB. Criminal records on computer from 1989, index books from 1800s.

General Information: No juvenile or adoption records released. SASE required. Turnaround time up to 1 week. Fax notes: $2.00 per page. Copy fee: $1.00 for first page, $.50 each add'l. Certification fee: $2.00. Fee payee: Circuit Clerk. Personal checks accepted. Prepayment is required.

Cumberland County

Circuit Court PO Box 145, Toledo, IL 62468; 217-849-3601; Fax: 217-849-3183. Hours: 8AM-4PM (CST). *Felony, Misdemeanor, Civil, Eviction, Small Claims, Probate.*

Civil Records: Access: Phone, fax, mail, in person. Both court and visitors may perform in person searches. Search fee: $4.00 per name per year. Required to search: name, years to search. Civil cases indexed by defendant, plaintiff. Civil records on computer from 1990, index books from 1885.

Criminal Records: Access: Phone, fax, mail, in person. Both court and visitors may perform in person searches. Search fee: $4.00 per name per year. Required to search: name, years to search; also helpful: DOB, SSN. Criminal records on computer from 1990, index books from 1885.

General Information: No juvenile or adoption records released. SASE required. Turnaround time up to 1 week. Copy fee: $1.00 for 1st page, $.50 per page next 19, then $.25 per page. Certification fee: $2.00. Fee payee: Clerk of Circuit Court. Only cashiers checks and money orders accepted. Prepayment is required.

De Kalb County

Circuit Court 133 W State St, Sycamore, IL 60178; Civil phone: 815-895-7131; Criminal phone: 815-895-7138; Fax: 815-895-7140. Hours: 8:30AM-4:30PM (CST). *Felony, Misdemeanor, Civil, Eviction, Small Claims, Probate.*

Civil Records: Access: Mail, in person. Both court and visitors may perform in person searches. Search fee: $4.00 per name per year. Required to search: name, years to search; also helpful: address. Civil cases indexed by defendant, plaintiff. Civil records on computer since 9/91, on index books back 60 years. Court planning to offer online access. Call 1-800-307-1100 for more information.

Criminal Records: Access: Mail, in person. Both court and visitors may perform in person searches. Search fee: $4.00 per name per year. Required to search: name, years to search, signed release; also helpful: address, DOB. Criminal records on computer since 9/91, on index books back 60 years. Court planning to offer online access to criminal records. Call 1-800-307-1100 for more information.

General Information: Public Access terminal is available. No juvenile or adoption records released. SASE required. Turnaround time 2 weeks. Copy fee: $1.00 for first page, $.50 each add'l. After 20 pages, copies are $.25 each. Certification fee: $3.50. Fee payee: DeKalb County Circuit Clerk. Personal checks accepted. Credit cards accepted: Visa, MasterCard. Accepted in person only. Prepayment is required.

De Witt County

Circuit Court 201 Washington St, Clinton, IL 61727; 217-935-2195; Fax: 217-935-3310. Hours: 8:30AM-4:30PM (CST). *Felony, Misdemeanor, Civil, Eviction, Small Claims, Probate.*

Civil Records: Access: Mail, fax, in person. Both court and visitors may perform in person searches. Search fee: $4.00 per name per year. Required to search: name, years to search. Civil cases indexed by defendant. Civil records on computer from 1989, index books from 1839.

Criminal Records: Access: Mail, fax, in person. Both court and visitors may perform in person searches. Search fee: $4.00 per name per year. Required to search: name, years to search, DOB. Criminal records on computer from 1989, index books from 1839.

General Information: Public Access terminal is available. No juvenile or adoption records released. SASE required. Turnaround time 1-2 weeks. Copy fee: $.50 for first page, $.25 each add'l. Certification fee:

$2.00. Fee payee: Clerk of Circuit Court. Only cashiers checks and money orders accepted. Prepayment is required.

Douglas County

Circuit Court PO Box 50, Tuscola, IL 61953; 217-253-2352. Hours: 8:30AM-4:30PM (CST). *Felony, Misdemeanor, Civil, Eviction, Small Claims, Probate.*

Civil Records: Access: Mail, in person. Both court and visitors may perform in person searches. Search fee: $4.00 per name per year. Required to search: name, years to search. Civil cases indexed by defendant, plaintiff. Civil records on computer from 1989, index books from 1964.

Criminal Records: Access: Mail, in person. Both court and visitors may perform in person searches. Search fee: $4.00 per name per year. Required to search: name, years to search, DOB; also helpful: SSN. Criminal records on computer from 1989, index books from 1964.

General Information: Public Access terminal is available. No juvenile or adoption records released. SASE required. Turnaround time 1 week. Fax notes: $5.00 for 1st 4 pages; $1.00 each add'l. Copy fee: $1.00 for first page, $.50 each add'l. $.25 per pg after 20 pages. Certification fee: $2.00. Fee payee: Douglas County Circuit Clerk. Personal checks accepted. Prepayment is required.

Du Page County

Circuit Court PO Box 707, Wheaton, IL 60189-0707; Civil phone: 630-682-7100; Criminal phone: 630-682-7080; Fax: 630-682-7082. Hours: 8:30AM-4:30PM (CST). *Felony, Misdemeanor, Civil, Eviction, Small Claims, Probate.*

www.dupageco.org

Civil Records: Access: Phone, mail, in person. Both court and visitors may perform in person searches. Search fee: $4.00 per name per year. Required to search: name, years to search. Civil cases indexed by defendant, plaintiff. Civil records on-line from 1976, microfilm records back to 1939, index records back to 1839. All document files after 01/01/92 are on optical disk.

Criminal Records: Access: Phone, mail, in person. Both court and visitors may perform in person searches. Search fee: $4.00 per name per year. Required to search: name, years to search, DOB. Criminal records on-line from 1976, microfilm records back to 1939, index records back to 1839. All document files after 01/01/92 are on optical disk.

General Information: Public Access terminal is available. No juvenile or adoption records released. SASE required. Turnaround time 1 week. Copy fee: $2.00 for first page, $.50 each add'l. Certification fee: $4.00. Fee payee: Clerk of Circuit Court. Personal checks accepted. Credit cards accepted: Visa, MasterCard. Prepayment is required.

Edgar County

Circuit Court County Courthouse, 115 W Court, Paris, IL 61944; 217-466-7447. Hours: 8AM-4PM (CST). *Felony, Misdemeanor, Civil, Eviction, Small Claims, Probate.*

Civil Records: Access: Mail, in person. Both court and visitors may perform in person searches. Search fee: $4.00 per name per year. Required to search: name, years to search. Civil cases indexed by defendant, plaintiff. Civil records on computer from 1992, index books from 1823.

Criminal Records: Access: In person only. Both court and visitors may perform in person searches. Search fee: $4.00 per name per year. Required to search: Name, years to search, DOB. Criminal records on computer from 1992, index books from 1823.

General Information: No juvenile or adoption records released. SASE required. Turnaround time 1 week. Copy fee: $.50 for first page, $.25 each add'l. Certification fee: $1.00. Fee payee: Janis K Nebergall, Circuit Clerk. Personal checks accepted. Prepayment is required.

Edwards County

Circuit Court County Courthouse, Albion, IL 62806; 618-445-2016; Fax: 618-445-4943. Hours: 8AM-4PM (CST). *Felony, Misdemeanor, Civil, Eviction, Small Claims, Probate.*

Civil Records: Access: Mail, in person. Both court and visitors may perform in person searches. Search fee: $4.00 per name per year. Required to search: name, years to search. Civil cases indexed by defendant. Civil records on computer from 1988, books and index cards from 1815.

Criminal Records: Access: Mail, in person. Both court and visitors may perform in person searches. Search fee: $4.00 per name per year. Required to search: name, years to search, DOB. Criminal records on computer from 1988, index books from 1815.

General Information: Public Access terminal is available. No juvenile or adoption records released. SASE required. Turnaround time 1 week. Copy fee: $.30 per page. Certification fee: $2.00. Fee payee: Clerk of Circuit Court. Only cashiers checks and money orders accepted. Prepayment is required.

Effingham County

Circuit Court 100 E Jefferson, PO Box 586, Effingham, IL 62401; 217-342-4065; Fax: 217-342-6183. Hours: 8AM-4PM (CST). *Felony, Misdemeanor, Civil, Small Claims, Probate.*

Civil Records: Access: Mail, in person. Both court and visitors may perform in person searches. Search fee: $4.00 per name per year. Required to search: name, years to search; also helpful: address. Civil cases indexed by defendant, plaintiff. Civil records on computer from 1988, index books from 1800s.

Criminal Records: Access: Mail, in person. Both court and visitors may perform in person searches. Search fee: $4.00 per name per year. Required to search: name, years to search, DOB; also helpful: address. Criminal records on computer from 1988, index books from 1800s.

General Information: Public Access terminal is available. No juvenile or adoption records released. SASE required. Turnaround time 1 week. Copy fee: $1.00 for first page, $.50 each add'l. $.25 per page after 20. Certification fee: $2.00. Fee payee: Effingham County Circuit Clerk. Business checks accepted. Prepayment is required.

Fayette County

Circuit Court 221 S 7th St, Vandalia, IL 62471; 618-283-5009. Hours: 8AM-4PM (CST). *Felony, Misdemeanor, Civil, Eviction, Small Claims, Probate.*

Civil Records: Access: Phone, mail, fax, in person. Both court and visitors may perform in person searches. Search fee: $4.00 per name per year. Required to search: name, years to search. Civil cases indexed by defendant. Civil records on computer from 1988, index books from 1800s.

Criminal Records: Access: Phone, mail, fax, in person. Both court and visitors may perform in person searches. Search fee: $4.00 per name per year. Required to search: name, years to search, DOB. Criminal records on computer from 1988, index books from 1800s.

General Information: Public Access terminal is available. No juvenile, impounded or adoption records released. SASE required. Turnaround time 1 week. Fax notes: Fee to fax results is $.50 per page. Copy fee: $1.00 for first page, $.50 each add'l. Certification fee:

$1.00. Fee payee: Clerk of Circuit Court. Business checks accepted. Prepayment is required.

Ford County

Circuit Court 200 W State St, Paxton, IL 60957; 217-379-2641; Fax: 217-379-3445. Hours: 8:30AM-4:30PM (CST). *Felony, Misdemeanor, Civil, Eviction, Small Claims, Probate.*

Civil Records: Access: Mail, fax, in person. Both court and visitors may perform in person searches. Search fee: $4.00 per name per year. Required to search: name, years to search. Civil cases indexed by defendant. Civil records on index books from 1800s; recent on computer.

Criminal Records: Access: Mail, fax, in person. Both court and visitors may perform in person searches. Search fee: $4.00 per name per year. Required to search: name, years to search, DOB. Criminal records on index books from 1800s; recent on computer.

General Information: Public Access terminal is available. No juvenile or adoption records released. SASE required. Turnaround time 2 days. Copy fee: $1.00 for first page, $.50 each add'l. after 20 pages then $.25 per page. Certification fee: $2.00. Fee payee: Clerk of Circuit Court. Personal checks accepted. Prepayment is required.

Franklin County

Circuit Court County Courthouse, PO Box 485, Benton, IL 62812; Civil phone: 618-439-2011. Hours: 8AM-4PM (CST). *Felony, Misdemeanor, Civil, Eviction, Small Claims, Probate.*

Civil Records: Access: Mail, in person. Both court and visitors may perform in person searches. Search fee: $4.00 per name per year. Required to search: name, years to search. Civil cases indexed by defendant, plaintiff. Civil records on computer from 1987, index books from 1800s.

Criminal Records: Access: Mail, in person. Both court and visitors may perform in person searches. Search fee: $4.00 per name per year. Required to search: name, years to search, DOB. Criminal records on computer from 1987, index books from 1800s.

General Information: No juvenile or adoption records released. SASE required. Turnaround time 1 week. Copy fee: $1.00 for first page, $.50 each add'l. Certification fee: $2.00. Fee payee: Franklin County Circuit Clerk. Only cashiers checks and money orders accepted. Prepayment is required.

Fulton County

Circuit Court PO Box 152, Lewistown, IL 61542; 309-547-3041; Fax: 309-547-3674. Hours: 8AM-4PM (CST). *Felony, Misdemeanor, Civil, Eviction, Small Claims, Probate.*

Civil Records: Access: Mail, in person. Both court and visitors may perform in person searches. Search fee: $4.00 per name per year. Required to search: name, years to search. Civil cases indexed by defendant, plaintiff. Civil records on computer from 1989, index books from 1800s.

Criminal Records: Access: Mail, in person. Both court and visitors may perform in person searches. Search fee: $4.00 per name per year. Required to search: name, years to search; also helpful: DOB. Criminal records on computer from 1989, index books from 1800s.

General Information: Public Access terminal is available. No juvenile, impounded or adoption records released. SASE required. Turnaround time 1-2 days. Copy fee: $1.00 for first page, $.50 each add'l. Certification fee: $2.00. Fee payee: Fulton County Circuit Clerk. Business checks accepted. Prepayment is required.

Gallatin County

Circuit Court County Courthouse, PO Box 249, Shawneetown, IL 62984; 618-269-3140; Fax: 618-269-4324. Hours: 8AM-4PM (CST). *Felony, Misdemeanor, Civil, Eviction, Small Claims, Probate.*

Civil Records: Access: Fax, mail, in person. Visitors must perform in person searches for themselves. No search fee. Required to search: name, years to search. Civil cases indexed by defendant. Civil records on index books from 1800s.

Criminal Records: Access: Fax, mail, in person. Visitors must perform in person searches for themselves. No search fee. Required to search: name, years to search, DOB, signed release. Criminal records on index books from 1800s.

General Information: No juvenile or adoption records released. SASE required. Turnaround time 1 week. Fax notes: $1.00 per page. Copy fee: $.25 per page. Certification fee: $1.00. Fee payee: Clerk of Circuit Court. Business checks accepted. Prepayment is required.

Greene County

Circuit Court 519 N Main, County Courthouse, Carrollton, IL 62016; 217-942-3421; Fax: 217-942-6211. Hours: 8AM-4PM (CST). *Felony, Misdemeanor, Civil, Eviction, Small Claims, Probate.*

Civil Records: Access: Phone, mail, in person. Both court and visitors may perform in person searches. Search fee: $5.00 per name. Required to search: name, years to search. Civil cases indexed by defendant, plaintiff. Civil records on index books from 1800s.

Criminal Records: Access: Phone, fax, mail, in person. Both court and visitors may perform in person searches. Search fee: $5.00 per name. Required to search: name, years to search, DOB. Criminal records on index books from 1800s. No felonies by phone. Include signed release with felony search requests.

General Information: No juvenile or adoption records released. SASE required. Turnaround time 1-2 days. Fax notes: $.25 per page. Copy fee: $.25 per page. Certification fee: $2.00. Fee payee: Clerk of Circuit Court. Personal checks accepted. Prepayment is required.

Grundy County

Circuit Court PO Box 707, Morris, IL 60450; 815-941-3256; Fax: 815-942-2222. Hours: 8AM-4:30PM (CST). *Felony, Misdemeanor, Civil, Eviction, Small Claims, Probate.*

Civil Records: Access: Mail, online, in person. Both court and visitors may perform in person searches. Search fee: $4.00 per name per year. Required to search: name, years to search. Civil cases indexed by defendant, plaintiff. Civil records on computer back to 1988. Online access to judicial circuit records should be available in 2001 for local attorney firms and retrievers. The service is free. Call the Clerk's office at 815-941-3256 for details.

Criminal Records: Access: Mail, in person. Both court and visitors may perform in person searches. Search fee: $4.00 per name per year. Required to search: name, years to search, DOB, signed release. Criminal records on computer back to 1988.

General Information: Public Access terminal is available. No juvenile or adoption records released. SASE required. Turnaround time 1-2 days. Copy fee: $.50 per page. Certification fee: $2.00. Fee payee: Clerk of Circuit Court. Personal checks accepted. Prepayment is required.

Hamilton County

Circuit Court County Courthouse, McLeansboro, IL 62859; 618-643-3224; Fax: 618-643-3455. Hours: 8AM-4:30PM (CST). *Felony, Misdemeanor, Civil, Eviction, Small Claims, Probate.*

Civil Records: Access: Mail, in person. Both court and visitors may perform in person searches. Search fee: $4.00 per name per year. Required to search: name, years to search. Civil cases indexed by defendant, plaintiff. Civil records on index books from 1800s; computer records go back to 1990.

Criminal Records: Access: Mail, in person. Both court and visitors may perform in person searches. Search fee: $4.00 per name per year. Required to search: name, years to search, DOB. Criminal records on index books from 1800s; computer records go back to 1990.

General Information: No juvenile or adoption records released. SASE required. Turnaround time 1-2 days. Copy fee: $.30 per page. Certification fee: $1.00 per page, $.50 per page for next 19 pages; additional pages $.25. Fee payee: Clerk of Circuit Court. No personal checks accepted. Prepayment is required.

Hancock County

Circuit Court PO Box 189, Carthage, IL 62321; 217-357-2616; Fax: 217-357-2231. Hours: 8AM-4PM (CST). *Felony, Misdemeanor, Civil, Eviction, Small Claims, Probate.*

Civil Records: Access: Mail, in person. Both court and visitors may perform in person searches. Search fee: $15.00 per name per year. Required to search: name, years to search. Civil cases indexed by defendant, plaintiff. Civil records on computer from 1992, index books from 1800s.

Criminal Records: Access: Mail, in person. Both court and visitors may perform in person searches. Search fee: $5.00 per name per year. Required to search: name, years to search, DOB; also helpful: SSN. Criminal records on computer from 1992, index books from 1800s.

General Information: No juvenile or adoption records released. SASE required. Turnaround time 1 week. Copy fee: $.50 per page. Certification fee: $5.00. Fee payee: Clerk of Circuit Court. Personal checks accepted. Prepayment is required.

Hardin County

Circuit Court County Courthouse, Elizabethtown, IL 62931; 618-287-2735; Fax: 618-287-7833. Hours: 8AM-4PM (CST). *Felony, Misdemeanor, Civil, Eviction, Small Claims, Probate.*

Civil Records: Access: Mail, fax, in person. Both court and visitors may perform in person searches. Search fee: $4.00 per name per year. Required to search: name, years to search. Civil cases indexed by defendant, plaintiff. Civil records on computer back to 9/1992; on index books from 1800s.

Criminal Records: Access: Mail, fax, in person. Both court and visitors may perform in person searches. Search fee: $4.00 per name per year. Required to search: name, years to search, DOB. Criminal records on computer back to 9/1992; on index books from 1800s.

General Information: No juvenile or adoption records released. SASE required. Turnaround time 1 week. Fax notes: Fee to fax results is $2.00 for 1st 2 pages; $.50 each add'l page. Copy fee: $.25 per page. Certification fee: $1.00 plus $.50 each add'l page. Fee payee: Circuit Clerk. Only cashiers checks and money orders accepted. Prepayment is required.

Henderson County

Circuit Court County Courthouse, PO Box 546, Oquawka, IL 61469; 309-867-3121; Fax: 309-867-3207. Hours: 8AM-4PM (CST). *Felony, Misdemeanor, Civil, Eviction, Small Claims, Probate.*

Civil Records: Access: Phone, mail, in person. Both court and visitors may perform in person searches. No search fee. Required to search: name, years to search. Civil cases indexed by defendant, plaintiff. Civil records on computer from 1991, index books from 1800s.

Criminal Records: Access: Phone, mail, in person. Both court and visitors may perform in person searches. No search fee. Required to search: name, years to search, DOB; also helpful: SSN. Criminal records on computer from 1991, index books from 1800s.

General Information: Public Access terminal is available. No juvenile or adoption records released. SASE required. Turnaround time 1 day to 1 week. Copy fee: $.25 per page. Certification fee: $1.00 plus $.50 each add'l page. Fee payee: Clerk of Circuit Court. Personal checks accepted. Prepayment is required.

Henry County

Circuit Court Henry County Courthouse, PO Box 9, Cambridge, IL 61238; 309-937-3572. Hours: 8AM-4:30PM (CST). *Felony, Misdemeanor, Civil, Eviction, Small Claims, Probate.*

Civil Records: Access: Mail, in person. Both court and visitors may perform in person searches. Search fee: $4.00 per name per year. Required to search: name, years to search. Civil cases indexed by defendant. Civil records on computer from 1989, index books from 1800s.

Criminal Records: Access: Mail, in person. Both court and visitors may perform in person searches. Search fee: $4.00 per name per year. Required to search: name, middle initial, years to search, DOB; also helpful-last known address. Criminal records on computer from 1989, index books from 1800s.

General Information: Public Access terminal is available. No juvenile or adoption records released. SASE not required. Turnaround time 2 weeks. Copy fee: $.50 per page. Certification fee: $2.00. Fee payee: Clerk of Circuit Court. Only cashiers checks and money orders accepted. Prepayment is required.

Iroquois County

Circuit Court 550 S 10th St, Watseka, IL 60970; 815-432-6950 (6952 Traff) (6991 Ch Supp); Fax: 815-432-6953. Hours: 8:30AM-4:30PM (CST). *Felony, Misdemeanor, Civil, Eviction, Small Claims, Probate.*

Civil Records: Access: Fax, mail, in person. Both court and visitors may perform in person searches. Search fee: $4.00 per name per year. Required to search: name, years to search. Civil cases indexed by defendant. Civil records on index books from 1865.

Criminal Records: Access: Fax, mail, in person. Both court and visitors may perform in person searches. Search fee: $4.00 per name per year. Required to search: name, years to search, DOB. Criminal records on index books from 1865.

General Information: No juvenile or adoption records released. SASE required. Turnaround time 1-2 days. Fax notes: Fee to fax results is $4.00 per document. Copy fee: $.50 per page. Certification fee: $2.00. Fee payee: Clerk of Circuit Court. Personal checks accepted. Prepayment is required.

Jackson County

Circuit Court County Courthouse, 1001 Walnut, PO Box 730, Murphysboro, IL 62966; 618-687-7300. Hours: 8AM-4PM (CST). *Felony, Misdemeanor, Civil, Eviction, Small Claims, Probate.*

www.circuitclerk.co.jackson.il.us

Civil Records: Access: Mail, in person. Both court and visitors may perform in person searches. Search fee: $4.00 per name. Fee is for 1986 to present. $4.00 per year prior to 1986. Required to search: name, years to search. Civil cases indexed by defendant, plaintiff. Civil records on computer from 1986, index books from 1860.

Criminal Records: Access: Mail, in person. Both court and visitors may perform in person searches. Search fee: $4.00 per name. Required to search: name, years to search. Criminal records on computer from 1986, index books from 1860.

General Information: Public Access terminal is available. No juvenile or adoption records released. SASE required. Turnaround time 1-2 weeks. Copy fee: $.50 per page. Certification fee: $2.50. Fee payee: Circuit Clerk. Personal checks accepted. Prepayment is required.

Jasper County

Circuit Court 100 W Jourdan St, Newton, IL 62448; 618-783-2524. Hours: 8AM-4:30PM (CST). *Felony, Misdemeanor, Civil, Eviction, Small Claims, Probate.*

Civil Records: Access: Mail, in person. Both court and visitors may perform in person searches. Search fee: $4.00 per name per year. Required to search: name, years to search; also helpful: address. Civil cases indexed by defendant, plaintiff. Civil records on computer from 1988, index books from 1835.

Criminal Records: Access: Mail, in person. Both court and visitors may perform in person searches. Search fee: $4.00 per name per year. Required to search: name, years to search, DOB, sex, signed release. Criminal records on computer from 1988, index books from 1835.

General Information: No juvenile or adoption records released. SASE required. Turnaround time 1 week. Fax notes: Fee to fax results is $2.00 per document. Copy fee: $.50 per page. Certification fee: $2.00. Fee payee: Clerk of Circuit Court. Personal checks accepted. Prepayment is required.

Jefferson County

Circuit Court PO Box 1266, Mt Vernon, IL 62864; 618-244-8008; Fax: 618-244-8029. Hours: 8AM-5PM (CST). *Felony, Misdemeanor, Civil, Eviction, Small Claims, Probate.*

Civil Records: Access: Phone, fax, mail, in person. Both court and visitors may perform in person searches. No search fee. Required to search: name, years to search. Civil cases indexed by defendant. Civil records on computer from 1988, index books from 1800s. Fax requests must be followed by original, before being processed.

Criminal Records: Access: Phone, fax, mail, in person. Both court and visitors may perform in person searches. Search fee: $8.00. Required to search: name, years to search, DOB. Criminal records on computer from 1988, index books from 1800s.

General Information: No juvenile or adoption records released. SASE required. Turnaround time 1 week. Fax notes: $.25 per page + phone charge. Copy fee: $.25 per page. Certification fee: No certification fee. Fee payee: Clerk of Circuit Court. Only cashiers checks and money orders accepted. Prepayment is required.

Jersey County

Circuit Court 201 W Pearl St, Jerseyville, IL 62052; 618-498-5571; Fax: 618-498-6128. Hours: 8:30AM-4:30PM (CST). *Felony, Misdemeanor, Civil, Eviction, Small Claims, Probate.*

Civil Records: Access: Phone, fax, mail, in person. Both court and visitors may perform in person searches. Search fee: $5.00 per name. Required to search: name, years to search. Civil cases indexed by defendant. Civil records on computer from 1991, index books from 1800s.

Criminal Records: Access: Phone, fax, mail, in person. Both court and visitors may perform in person searches. Search fee: $5.00 per name. Required to search: name, years to search; also helpful: DOB. Criminal records on computer from 1991, index books from 1800s.

General Information: No juvenile or adoption records released. SASE required. Turnaround time 1 week. Copy fee: $.50 per page. Certification fee: $6.00. Fee payee: Clerk of Circuit Court. Personal checks accepted. Prepayment is required.

Jo Daviess County

Circuit Court 330 N Bench St, Galena, IL 61036; 815-777-2295/0037. Hours: 8AM-4PM (CST). *Felony, Misdemeanor, Civil, Eviction, Small Claims, Probate.*

Civil Records: Access: In person only. Visitors must perform in person searches for themselves. No search fee. Required to search: name, years to search. Civil cases indexed by defendant, plaintiff. Civil records on computer since 1992, on index books from 1960; will and probate back to 1850.

Criminal Records: Access: Mail, in person. Both court and visitors may perform in person searches. Search fee: $4.00 per name. Fee is for 1992 to present. Prior to 1992 $4.00 per name per year. Required to search: name, years to search, DOB. Criminal records on computer since 1992, on index books from 1960.

General Information: Public Access terminal is available. No juvenile or adoption records released. SASE required. Turnaround time 1 week. Fax notes: Will not fax results. Copy fee: $.25 per page. Certification fee: $2.00. Fee payee: Circuit Clerk. Business checks accepted. Prepayment is required.

Johnson County

Circuit Court PO Box 517, Vienna, IL 62995; 618-658-4751; Fax: 618-658-2908. Hours: 8AM-4PM (CST). *Felony, Misdemeanor, Civil, Eviction, Small Claims, Probate.*

Civil Records: Access: Mail, in person. Both court and visitors may perform in person searches. Search fee: $4.00 per name per year. Required to search: name, years to search. Civil cases indexed by defendant, plaintiff. Civil records on computer from 1987, index books from 1930s.

Criminal Records: Access: Mail, in person. Both court and visitors may perform in person searches. Search fee: $4.00 per name per year. Required to search: name, years to search, DOB. Criminal records on computer from 1987, index books from 1930s.

General Information: Public Access terminal is available. No juvenile or adoption records released. SASE required. Turnaround time 1 week. Copy fee: $.25. Certification fee: $3.00. Fee payee: Circuit Clerk. Business checks accepted. Prepayment is required.

Kane County

Circuit Court PO Box 112, Geneva, IL 60134; 630-232-3413; Civil phone: 630-208-3323; Criminal phone: 630-208-3319; Fax: 630-208-2172. Hours: 8:30AM-4:30PM (CST). *Felony, Misdemeanor, Civil, Eviction, Small Claims, Probate.*

www.co.kane.il.us/circuitclerk

Civil Records: Access: Phone, fax, mail, in person. Both court and visitors may perform in person searches. Search fee: $4.00 per name per year. Fee is for past 5 years. $8.00 for past 6 years or more. Required to search: name, years to search. Civil cases indexed by defendant, plaintiff. Civil records on computer from 1986, index books from 1800s.

Criminal Records: Access: Phone, fax, mail, in person. Both court and visitors may perform in person searches. Search fee: $4.00 per name per year. Required

to search: name, years to search, DOB. Criminal records on computer past 5-7 years, index books from 1800s. Same as civil.

General Information: Public Access terminal is available. No juvenile, mental health or adoption records released. SASE required. Turnaround time 1 week. Fax notes: $2.00 for first page, $.50 each add'l. Copy fee: $2.00 for first page, $.50 each add'l. Certification fee: $4.00. Judgment orders certification fee $10.00. Fee payee: Clerk of Circuit Court. Personal checks accepted. Credit cards accepted: Visa, MasterCard. Prepayment is required.

Kankakee County

Circuit Court 450 E Court St, County Courthouse, Kankakee, IL 60901; 815-937-2905; Fax: 815-939-8830. Hours: 8:30AM-4:30PM (CST). *Felony, Misdemeanor, Civil, Eviction, Small Claims, Probate.*

Civil Records: Access: Mail, in person. Both court and visitors may perform in person searches. Search fee: $4.00 per name per year. Required to search: name, years to search. Civil cases indexed by defendant, plaintiff. Civil records on computer from 1990, index books from 1800s.

Criminal Records: Access: Mail, in person. Both court and visitors may perform in person searches. Search fee: $4.00 per name per year. Required to search: name, years to search, DOB. Criminal records on computer from 1990, index books from 1800s.

General Information: Public Access terminal is available. No juvenile, impounded, mental health, expunged or adoption records released. SASE required. Turnaround time 1-2 weeks. Copy fee: $1.00 for first page, $.50 each add'l. Certification fee: $2.00. Fee payee: Clerk of Circuit Court. Personal checks accepted. Prepayment is required.

Kendall County

Circuit Court PO Drawer M, 807 W John St, Yorkville, IL 60560; 630-553-4183. Hours: 8AM-4:30PM (CST). *Felony, Misdemeanor, Civil, Eviction, Small Claims, Probate.*

Civil Records: Access: Mail, in person. Both court and visitors may perform in person searches. Search fee: $4.00 per name per year. Required to search: name, years to search. Civil cases indexed by defendant, plaintiff. Civil records on computer since 1992, on index books from 1800s.

Criminal Records: Access: Mail, in person. Both court and visitors may perform in person searches. Search fee: $4.00 per name per year. Required to search: name, years to search, DOB. Criminal records on computer since 1992, on index books from 1800s.

General Information: Public Access terminal is available. No juvenile or adoption records released. SASE required. Turnaround time 2-3 days. Copy fee: $1.00 for first page, $.50 each add'l. $2.00 per page when hard copy printouts when cases are maintained on an automated medium. Certification fee: $2.00. Fee payee: Clerk of Circuit Court. Only cashiers checks and money orders accepted. Prepayment is required.

Knox County

Circuit Court County Courthouse, Galesburg, IL 61401; 309-345-3817; Fax: 309-345-0098. Hours: 8:30AM-4:30PM (CST). *Felony, Misdemeanor, Civil, Eviction, Small Claims, Probate.*

Civil Records: Access: Fax, mail, in person. Both court and visitors may perform in person searches. No search fee. Required to search: name, years to search. Civil cases indexed by defendant, plaintiff. Civil records on index books from 1800s.

Criminal Records: Access: Fax, mail, in person. Both court and visitors may perform in person searches. No search fee. Required to search: name, years to search,

DOB, sex. Criminal records on index books from 1800s.

General Information: No juvenile or adoption records released. SASE not required. Turnaround time 1 week. Copy fee: $1.00 for first page, $.50 each add'l. Certification fee: $2.00. Fee payee: Clerk of Circuit Court. Personal checks accepted. Prepayment is required.

La Salle County

Circuit Court - Civil Division PO Box 617, Ottawa, IL 61350-0617; 815-434-8671; Fax: 815-433-9198. Hours: 8AM-4:30PM (CST). *Civil, Eviction, Small Claims, Probate.*

Civil Records: Access: Mail, online, in person. Both court and visitors may perform in person searches. Search fee: $4.00 per name per year. Required to search: name, years to search. Civil cases indexed by defendant, plaintiff. Some records on computer since late 1980s; prior records on index books from 1800s. Online access to Judicial Circuit records should be available in 2001 for local attorney firms and retrievers. The service is free. Call the Clerk's office at 815-434-8671 for details. **General Information:** Public Access terminal is available. No juvenile or adoption records released. SASE required. Turnaround time 1-2 weeks. Fax notes: No fee to fax results. Copy fee: $1.00 for first page, $.50 each add'l. Certification fee: $2.00. Fee payee: Clerk of Circuit Court. Personal checks accepted. Credit cards accepted: Visa, MasterCard. Prepayment is required.

Circuit Court - Criminal Division 707 Etna Rd, Ottawa, IL 61360; 815-434-8271; Fax: 815-434-8299. Hours: 8AM-4:30PM (CST). *Felony, Misdemeanor.*

www.lasallecounty.com

Criminal Records: Access: Fax, mail, in person. Visitors must perform in person searches for themselves. No search fee. Required to search: name, years to search; also helpful: DOB.

General Information: Public Access terminal is available. No juvenile or adoption records released. SASE required. Turnaround time 1-2 weeks. Fax notes: No fee to fax results. Copy fee: $1.00 for first page, $.50 each add'l. Certification fee: $2.00. Fee payee: Clerk of Circuit Court. Personal checks accepted. Credit cards accepted: Visa, MasterCard. Prepayment is required.

Lake County

Circuit Court 18 N County St, Waukegan, IL 60085; 847-360-6680. Hours: 8:30AM-5PM (CST). *Felony, Misdemeanor, Civil, Eviction, Small Claims, Probate.*

Civil Records: Access: Phone, mail, in person. Both court and visitors may perform in person searches. Search fee: $4.00 per name per year (first year free). Required to search: name, years to search. Civil cases indexed by defendant, plaintiff. Civil records on computer or microfiche from 1968, index books from 1800s.

Criminal Records: Access: Phone, mail, in person. Both court and visitors may perform in person searches. Search fee: $4.00 per name per year (first year free). Required to search: name, years to search, DOB. Criminal records on computer or microfiche from 1968, index books from 1800s.

General Information: Public Access terminal is available. No juvenile or adoption records released. SASE required. Turnaround time 1-2 days. Copy fee: $2.00 for first page, $.50 each add'l. Certification fee: $4.00. Fee payee: Circuit Clerk. No personal checks accepted. Credit cards accepted: Discover. Discover. Prepayment is required.

Lawrence County

Circuit Court County Courthouse, Lawrenceville, IL 62439; 618-943-2815; Fax: 618-943-5205. Hours: 9AM-5PM (CST). *Felony, Misdemeanor, Civil, Eviction, Small Claims, Probate.*

Civil Records: Access: Mail, in person. Both court and visitors may perform in person searches. Search fee: $4.00 per name per year. Required to search: name, years to search, address. Civil cases indexed by defendant, plaintiff. Civil records on computer from 1988, index books from 1800s.

Criminal Records: Access: Mail, in person. Both court and visitors may perform in person searches. Search fee: $4.00 per name per year. Required to search: name, years to search, address, DOB, SSN, signed release. Criminal records on computer from 1988, index books from 1800s.

General Information: No juvenile or adoption records released. SASE required. Turnaround time 2-3 days. Copy fee: $1.00 for first page, $.50 each add'l. Certification fee: $2.00. Fee payee: Clerk of Circuit Court. Only cashiers checks and money orders accepted. Prepayment is required.

Lee County

Circuit Court PO Box 325, Dixon, IL 61021; 815-284-5234. Hours: 8:30AM-4:30PM (CST). *Felony, Misdemeanor, Civil, Eviction, Small Claims, Probate.*

Civil Records: Access: Mail, in person. Both court and visitors may perform in person searches. Search fee: $4.00 per name per year. Required to search: name, years to search. Civil cases indexed by defendant, plaintiff. Civil records on computer from 1989, index books from 1800s.

Criminal Records: Access: Mail, in person. Both court and visitors may perform in person searches. Search fee: $4.00 per name per year. Required to search: name, years to search, DOB; also helpful: SSN. Criminal records on computer from 1989, index books from 1800s.

General Information: Public Access terminal is available. No juvenile, impounded or adoption records released. SASE required. Turnaround time 1 week. Copy fee: $.50 per page. Certification fee: $2.00. Fee payee: Clerk of Circuit Court. Personal checks accepted. Prepayment is required.

Livingston County

Circuit Court 112 W Madison St, Box 320, Pontiac, IL 61764; 815-844-2602. Hours: 8AM-4:30PM (CST). *Felony, Misdemeanor, Civil, Eviction, Small Claims, Probate.*

Civil Records: Access: Mail, in person. Both court and visitors may perform in person searches. Search fee: $4.00 per name per year. Required to search: name, years to search; also helpful: address. Civil cases indexed by defendant, plaintiff. Civil records on computer from 1989 (child support since 1988), index books from 1837.

Criminal Records: Access: Mail, in person. Both court and visitors may perform in person searches. Search fee: $4.00 per name per year. Required to search: name, years to search, DOB, SSN; also helpful: address. Criminal records on computer from 1989 (child support since 1988), index books from 1837. Signed release required for juvenile cases.

General Information: No juvenile, impound or adoption records released. SASE required. Turnaround time 3-5 days. Fax notes: Fee to fax results is $3.00 per fax. Copy fee: $1.00 for 1st pg; $.50 per pg, pages 2-19; $.25 each additional page. Certification fee: $2.00. Fee payee: Livingston County Circuit Clerk. Personal checks accepted. Prepayment is required.

Logan County

Circuit Court County Courthouse, PO Box 158, Lincoln, IL 62656; 217-735-2376; Fax: 217-732-1231. Hours: 8:30AM-4:30PM (CST). *Felony, Misdemeanor, Civil, Eviction, Small Claims, Probate.*

Civil Records: Access: Mail, in person. Both court and visitors may perform in person searches. Search fee: $4.00 per name per year. Required to search: name, years to search. Civil cases indexed by defendant, plaintiff. Civil records on computer from 1990, index books from 1857.

Criminal Records: Access: Mail, in person. Both court and visitors may perform in person searches. Search fee: $4.00 per name per year. Required to search: name, years to search, DOB; also helpful: sex. Criminal records on computer from 1990, index books from 1857.

General Information: Public Access terminal is available. No juvenile or adoption records released. SASE not required. Turnaround time 1 week. Copy fee: $1.00 for first page, $.50 each add'l. After 20 pages, the fee is $.25 per page. Certification fee: $2.00. Fee payee: Carla Bender, Circuit Clerk. Business checks accepted. Prepayment is required.

Macon County

Circuit Court 253 E Wood St, Decatur, IL 62523; 217-424-1454; Fax: 217-424-1350. Hours: 8AM-4:30PM (CST). *Felony, Misdemeanor, Civil, Eviction, Small Claims, Probate.*

www.court.co.macon.il.us

Civil Records: Access: Phone, mail, online, in person. Both court and visitors may perform in person searches. Search fee: $4.00 per name per year. Required to search: name, years to search; also helpful: address. Civil cases indexed by defendant, plaintiff. Civil records on computer from 1989, index books from 1800s. Access to court records is available free online at the web site 24 hours a day. Civil docket information is viewable back to 04/96.

Criminal Records: Access: Phone, mail, online, in person. Both court and visitors may perform in person searches. Search fee: $4.00 per name per year. Required to search: name, years to search; also helpful: address, DOB, SSN. Criminal records on computer from 1989, index books from 1800s. Online access to criminal records is the same as civil; search docket information back to 04/96.

General Information: Public Access terminal is available. No juvenile or adoption records released. SASE required. Turnaround time 1 week. Copy fee: $1.00 for first page, $.50 each add'l. Certification fee: $2.00. Fee payee: Macon County Circuit Clerk. Business checks accepted. Prepayment is required.

Macoupin County

Circuit Court PO Box 197, Carlinville, IL 62626; 217-854-3211; Fax: 217-854-8461. Hours: 8:30AM-4:30PM (CST). *Felony, Misdemeanor, Civil, Eviction, Small Claims, Probate.*

Civil Records: Access: Mail, in person. Both court and visitors may perform in person searches. Search fee: $4.00 per name per year. Required to search: name, years to search. Civil cases indexed by defendant, plaintiff. Civil records on computer from 1994, index books from 1837.

Criminal Records: Access: Mail, in person. Both court and visitors may perform in person searches. Search fee: $4.00 per name per year. Required to search: name, years to search; also helpful: DOB, SSN. Criminal records on computer from 1994, index books from 1837.

General Information: Public Access terminal is available. No juvenile or adoption records released. SASE required. Turnaround time 1 month to 6 weeks.

Copy fee: $1.00 for first page, $.50 each add'l; $.25 for 20+ pages. Certification fee: $2.00. Fee payee: Mike Mathis Circuit Clerk. Personal checks accepted. Prepayment is required.

Madison County

Circuit Court 155 N Main St, Edwardsville, IL 62025; 618-692-6240; Fax: 618-692-0676. Hours: 8AM-5PM (CST). *Felony, Misdemeanor, Civil, Eviction, Small Claims, Probate.*

Civil Records: Access: Mail, in person. Both court and visitors may perform in person searches. Search fee: $4.00 per name per year. Required to search: name, years to search. Civil cases indexed by defendant, plaintiff. Civil records on computer from 1990, index books from 1800s.

Criminal Records: Access: Mail, in person. Both court and visitors may perform in person searches. Search fee: $4.00 per name per year. Required to search: name, years to search, DOB. Criminal records on computer from 1990, index books from 1800s.

General Information: Public Access terminal is available. No juvenile, mental health, adoption records released. SASE required. Turnaround time 2-3 days. Copy fee: $2.00 for 1st pg; $.50 per pg for pgs 2-19; $.25 ea add'l pg. Certification fee: $4.00. Fee payee: Clerk of Circuit Court. Personal checks accepted. Prepayment is required.

Marion County

Circuit Court 100 E Main, PO Box 130, Salem, IL 62881; 618-548-3856; Fax: 618-548-2358. Hours: 8AM-4PM (CST). *Felony, Misdemeanor, Civil, Eviction, Small Claims, Probate.*

Civil Records: Access: In person only. Visitors must perform in person searches for themselves. No search fee. Required to search: name, years to search. Civil cases indexed by defendant, plaintiff. Civil records on computer from 1988, index books from 1800s.

Criminal Records: Access: In person only. Visitors must perform in person searches for themselves. No search fee. Required to search: name, years to search; also helpful: DOB, SSN. Criminal records on computer from 1988, index books from 1800s.

General Information: No juvenile or adoption records released. Copy fee: $1.00 for first page, $.50 each add'l. Certification fee: $2.00. Fee payee: Clerk of Circuit Court. Only cashiers checks and money orders accepted. Will bill to attorneys.

Marshall County

Circuit Court PO Box 328, Lacon, IL 61540-0328; 309-246-6435; Fax: 309-246-2173. Hours: 8:30AM-Noon, 1-4:30PM (CST). *Felony, Misdemeanor, Civil, Eviction, Small Claims, Probate.*

Civil Records: Access: Mail, in person. Both court and visitors may perform in person searches. Search fee: $4.00 per name per year. Required to search: name, years to search. Civil cases indexed by defendant, plaintiff. Civil records on computer from 1988, microfiche since 1964, index books from 1800s.

Criminal Records: Access: Mail, in person. Both court and visitors may perform in person searches. Search fee: $4.00 per name per year. Required to search: name, years to search, DOB. Criminal records on computer from 1988, microfiche since 1964, index books from 1800s.

General Information: Public Access terminal is available. No juvenile or adoption records released. SASE required. Turnaround time 1 week. Copy fee: $.50 per page. Certification fee: $2.00. Fee payee: Clerk of Circuit Court. Personal checks accepted. Prepayment is required.

Mason County

Circuit Court 125 N Plum, Havana, IL 62644; 309-543-6619; Fax: 309-543-4214. Hours: 8AM-4PM (CST). *Felony, Misdemeanor, Civil, Eviction, Small Claims, Probate.*

Civil Records: Access: Mail, in person. Both court and visitors may perform in person searches. Search fee: $4.00 per name per year. Required to search: name, years to search. Civil cases indexed by defendant, plaintiff. Civil records on computer from 1989, index books from 1800s.

Criminal Records: Access: Mail, in person. Both court and visitors may perform in person searches. Search fee: $4.00 per name per year. Required to search: name, years to search, DOB. Criminal records on computer from 1989, index books from 1800s.

General Information: Public Access terminal is available. No juvenile or adoption records released. SASE required. Turnaround time 1 week. Copy fee: $1.00 for first page, $.50 each add'l. Certification fee: $2.00. Fee payee: Clerk of Circuit Court. Only cashiers checks and money orders accepted. Prepayment is required.

Massac County

Circuit Court PO Box 152, Metropolis, IL 62960; 618-524-9359; Fax: 618-524-4850. Hours: 8AM-Noon, 1-4PM (CST). *Felony, Misdemeanor, Civil, Eviction, Small Claims, Probate.*

Civil Records: Access: Phone, mail, in person. Both court and visitors may perform in person searches. Search fee: $4.00 per name per year. Required to search: name, years to search. Civil cases indexed by defendant. Civil records on computer from 1986, index books from 1800s.

Criminal Records: Access: Phone, mail, in person. Both court and visitors may perform in person searches. Search fee: $4.00 per name per year. Required to search: name, years to search, DOB, signed release. Criminal records on computer from 1986, index books from 1800s.

General Information: Public Access terminal is available. No juvenile or adoption records released. SASE required. Turnaround time 5 business days. Copy fee: $.25 per page. Certification fee: $4.00. Fee payee: Clerk of Circuit Court. Only cashiers checks and money orders accepted. Prepayment is required.

McDonough County

Circuit Court County Courthouse, #1 Courthouse Sq, Macomb, IL 61455; 309-837-4889; Fax: 309-833-4493. Hours: 8AM-4PM (CST). *Felony, Misdemeanor, Civil, Eviction, Small Claims, Probate.*

Civil Records: Access: Phone, fax, mail, in person. Both court and visitors may perform in person searches. Search fee: $5.00 per name per year. Required to search: name, years to search. Civil cases indexed by defendant, plaintiff. Civil records on computer from 1991, index books from 1800s.

Criminal Records: Access: Phone, fax, mail, in person. Both court and visitors may perform in person searches. Search fee: $5.00 per name per year. Required to search: name, years to search; also helpful: SSN. Criminal records on computer from 1991, index books from 1800s.

General Information: Public Access terminal is available. No juvenile or adoption records released. SASE required. Turnaround time 1 week. Fax notes: Fee to fax results is $1.50 per page. Copy fee: $.50 per page. Certification fee: $2.00. Fee payee: Clerk of Circuit Court. Personal checks accepted. Prepayment is required.

McHenry County

Circuit Court 2200 N Seminary Ave, Woodstock, IL 60098; 815-334-4307; Fax: 815-338-8583. Hours: 8AM-4:30PM (CST). *Felony, Misdemeanor, Civil, Eviction, Small Claims, Probate.*

www.mchenrycircuitclerk.org

Civil Records: Access: Phone, mail, online, in person. Both court and visitors may perform in person searches. Search fee: $4.00 per name per year. Required to search: name, years to search. Civil cases indexed by defendant, plaintiff. Civil records on computer from 1991, index books from 1800s. Access to records on the remote online system requires a $750 license fee plus $50 per month. Records date back to 1990. Civil, criminal, probate, traffic, and domestic records are available. For more information, call 815-334-4193.

Criminal Records: Access: Phone, mail, online, in person. Both court and visitors may perform in person searches. Search fee: $4.00 per name per year. Required to search: name, years to search, DOB; also helpful: SSN. Criminal records on computer from 1994, index books from 1800s. Online access to criminal records is the same as civil.

General Information: Public Access terminal is available. No juvenile or adoption records released. SASE required. Turnaround time 1 week; criminal same day. Copy fee: $2.00 for first page, $.50 each add'l. Over 20 copies then fee is $.25 per page. Certification fee: $4.00. Fee payee: Clerk of Circuit Court. Personal checks accepted. Credit cards accepted: Visa, MasterCard, Discover. Visa, MC, Discover. Prepayment is required.

McLean County

Circuit Court PO Box 2420, Bloomington, IL 61702-2420; Civil phone: 309-888-5341; Criminal phone: 309-888-5321. Hours: 8:30AM-4:30PM (CST). *Felony, Misdemeanor, Civil, Eviction, Small Claims, Probate.*

www.mclean.gov

Civil Records: Access: Mail, in person. Both court and visitors may perform in person searches. Search fee: $4.00 per name per year. Required to search: name, years to search. Civil cases indexed by defendant, plaintiff. Civil records on computer from 1991, index books from 1800s.

Criminal Records: Access: Mail, in person. Both court and visitors may perform in person searches. Search fee: $4.00 per name per year. Required to search: name, years to search, DOB; also helpful: address, SSN. Criminal records on computer from 1991, index books from 1800s.

General Information: Public Access terminal is available. (Criminal only.) No juvenile or adoption records released. SASE required. Turnaround time 10 days. Copy fee: $1.00 for first page, $.50 each add'l. Certification fee: $2.00. Fee payee: McLean County Circuit Clerk. Personal checks accepted. Prepayment is required.

Menard County

Circuit Court PO Box 466, Petersburg, IL 62675; 217-632-2615. Hours: 8:30AM-4:30PM (CST). *Felony, Misdemeanor, Civil, Eviction, Small Claims, Probate.*

Civil Records: Access: Mail, in person. Both court and visitors may perform in person searches. Search fee: $4.00 per name per year. Required to search: name, years to search. Civil cases indexed by defendant. Civil records on computer from March, 1994, on index books from 1839.

Criminal Records: Access: Mail, in person. Both court and visitors may perform in person searches. Search fee: $4.00 per name per year. Required to search: name,

years to search, DOB. Criminal records on computer from March, 1994, on index books from 1839.

General Information: No juvenile or adoption records released. SASE required. Turnaround time 2 days. Copy fee: $1.00 for first page, $.50 each add'l. Certification fee: $1.00. Fee payee: Clerk of Circuit Court. Only cashiers checks and money orders accepted. Prepayment is required.

Mercer County

Circuit Court PO Box 175, Aledo, IL 61231; 309-582-7122; Fax: 309-582-7121. Hours: 8AM-4PM (CST). *Felony, Misdemeanor, Civil, Eviction, Small Claims, Probate.*

Note: 1988 forward records are available for search on the public access terminal.

Civil Records: Access: Phone, fax, mail, in person. Only the court performs in person searches; visitors may not. Search fee: $5.00 per name per year. Required to search: name, years to search. Civil cases indexed by defendant, plaintiff. Civil records on computer from 1988, index books from 1800s.

Criminal Records: Access: Phone, fax, mail, in person. Only the court performs in person searches; visitors may not. Search fee: $5.00 per name per year. Required to search: name, years to search, DOB. Criminal records on computer from 1988, index books from 1800s.

General Information: Public Access terminal is available. No juvenile or adoption records released. SASE required. Turnaround time 2-3 days. Fax notes: Fee to fax results is $1.00 per page. Copy fee: $.25 per page. Certification fee: $3.00. Fee payee: Clerk of Circuit Court. Business checks accepted. Prepayment is required.

Monroe County

Circuit Court 100 S Main St, Waterloo, IL 62298; 618-939-8681; Fax: 618-939-5132. Hours: 8AM-4:30PM (CST). *Felony, Misdemeanor, Civil, Eviction, Small Claims, Probate.*

http://ns.htc.net/~jacobdj/mcc

Civil Records: Access: Phone, fax, mail, in person. Both court and visitors may perform in person searches. Search fee: $4.00 per name per year. Required to search: name, years to search. Civil cases indexed by defendant, plaintiff. Civil records on computer from 1992, index books from 1818.

Criminal Records: Access: Phone, fax, mail, in person. Both court and visitors may perform in person searches. Search fee: $4.00 per name per year. Required to search: name, years to search, DOB. Criminal records on computer from 1992, index books from 1818.

General Information: Public Access terminal is available. No juvenile or adoption records released. SASE required. Turnaround time 1 week. Fax notes: No fee to fax results. Copy fee: $1.00 for first page, $.50 each add'l. If over 20 pages, fee is $.25 per page (from 20 on). Certification fee: $2.00. Fee payee: Circuit Clerk. Business checks accepted.

Montgomery County

Circuit Court County Courthouse, PO Box C, Hillsboro, IL 62049; 217-532-9546. Hours: 8AM-4PM (CST). *Felony, Misdemeanor, Civil, Eviction, Small Claims, Probate.*

www.courts.montgomery.k12.il.us

Civil Records: Access: Mail, online, in person. Both court and visitors may perform in person searches. Search fee: $4.00 per name per year. Required to search: name, years to search. Civil cases indexed by defendant, plaintiff. Civil records on computer from 1988, index books from 1821, microfiche (probate only) since 1939. Online access to court records is available   at

www.courts.montgomery.k12.il.us/CaseInfo.htm.
Search by name or case number.

Criminal Records: Access: Mail, online, in person. Both court and visitors may perform in person searches. Search fee: $4.00 per name per year. Required to search: name, years to search, DOB. Criminal records on computer from 1988, index books from 1821, microfiche (probate only) since 1939. Online access to criminal records is the same as civil.

General Information: Public Access terminal is available. No juvenile or adoption records released. SASE required. Turnaround time 1 week. Copy fee: $1.00 for first page, $.50 each add'l. Certification fee: $4.00. Fee payee: Clerk of Circuit Court. Only cashiers checks and money orders accepted. Prepayment is required.

Morgan County

Circuit Court 300 W State St, Jacksonville, IL 62650; 217-243-5419; Fax: 217-243-2009. Hours: 8:30AM-4:30PM (CST). *Felony, Misdemeanor, Civil, Eviction, Small Claims, Probate.*

Civil Records: Access: Mail, in person. Both court and visitors may perform in person searches. Search fee: $4.00 per name per year. Required to search: name, years to search. Civil cases indexed by defendant. Civil records on computer from 1990, index books from 1890s.

Criminal Records: Access: Mail, in person. Both court and visitors may perform in person searches. Search fee: $4.00 per name per year. Required to search: name, years to search, DOB. Criminal records on computer from 1990, index books from 1890s.

General Information: Public Access terminal is available. No juvenile or adoption records released. SASE required. Turnaround time 1 week. Fax notes: Fax fee $1.00 first page, $.50 per page thereafter. Copy fee: $1.00 first page, $.50 per page thereafter. Certification fee: $2.00. Fee payee: Clerk of Circuit Court. Only cashiers checks and money orders accepted. Prepayment is required.

Moultrie County

Moultrie County Courthouse 10 S Main, #7, Sullivan, IL 61951; 217-728-4622. Hours: 8:30AM-4:30PM (CST). *Felony, Misdemeanor, Civil, Eviction, Small Claims, Probate.*

www.circuit-clerk.moultrie.il.us

Civil Records: Access: Mail, in person. Both court and visitors may perform in person searches. Search fee: $4.00 per name per year. Required to search: name, years to search. Civil cases indexed by defendant. Civil records on computer from 1990, index books from 1850.

Criminal Records: Access: Mail, in person. Both court and visitors may perform in person searches. Search fee: $4.00 per name per year. Required to search: name, years to search, DOB. Criminal records on computer from 1990, index books from 1850.

General Information: No juvenile or adoption records released. SASE required. Turnaround time 1 week. Copy fee: $.25 per page. Certification fee: $2.00. Fee payee: Clerk of Circuit Court. Business checks accepted. Prepayment is required.

Ogle County

Circuit Court PO Box 337, Oregon, IL 61061; 815-732-1130. Hours: 8:30AM-4:30PM (CST). *Felony, Misdemeanor, Civil, Eviction, Small Claims, Probate.*

www.oglecounty.org

Civil Records: Access: Mail, online, in person. Both court and visitors may perform in person searches. Search fee: $4.00 per name per year. Required to search: name, years to search. Civil cases indexed by defendant, plaintiff. Civil records on computer since

1994; prior records on microfiche last 10 years, index books from 1836. Online access is available through a private company service at www.judici.com. Permission to use the system and sign-up is through the court, or email subscribe@judici.com.

Criminal Records: Access: Mail, online, in person. Both court and visitors may perform in person searches. Search fee: $4.00 per name per year. Required to search: name, years to search, DOB. Criminal records on computer since 1994; prior records on microfiche last 10 years, index books from 1836. Online access to criminal records is the same as civil.

General Information: Public Access terminal is available. No juvenile or adoption records released. SASE required. Turnaround time 2-3 weeks. Copy fee: $1.00 for first page, $.50 each add'l. $.25 per page after 20. Certification fee: $2.00. Fee payee: Clerk of Circuit Court. Only cashiers checks and money orders accepted. Prepayment is required.

Peoria County

Circuit Court 324 Main St, Peoria, IL 61602; 309-672-6953; Fax: 309-677-6228. Hours: 8:30AM-5PM (CST). *Felony, Misdemeanor, Civil, Eviction, Small Claims, Probate.*

Civil Records: Access: Phone, mail, in person. Both court and visitors may perform in person searches. Search fee: $4.00 per name per year. Required to search: name, years to search. Civil cases indexed by defendant, plaintiff. Civil records on computer from 1986 (traffic), from 1987 (civil), archived from 1800s.

Criminal Records: Access: Phone, mail, in person. Both court and visitors may perform in person searches. Search fee: $4.00 per name per year. Required to search: name, years to search, DOB; also helpful: SSN. Criminal records on computer from 1978, archived from 1800s.

General Information: Public Access terminal is available. No juvenile or adoption records released. SASE required. Turnaround time 1 week. Copy fee: $2.00 for first page, $.50 each add'l. Certification fee: $4.00. Fee payee: Clerk of Circuit Court. Personal checks accepted. Credit cards accepted: Visa, MasterCard. Prepayment is required.

Perry County

Circuit Court PO Box 219, Pinckneyville, IL 62274; 618-357-6726. Hours: 8AM-4PM (CST). *Felony, Misdemeanor, Civil, Eviction, Small Claims, Probate.*

Civil Records: Access: Mail, in person. Both court and visitors may perform in person searches. Search fee: $4.00 per name per year. Required to search: name, years to search. Civil cases indexed by defendant, plaintiff. Civil records on computer from 1990, index books from 1800s.

Criminal Records: Access: Mail, in person. Both court and visitors may perform in person searches. Search fee: $4.00 per name per year. Required to search: name, years to search; also helpful: DOB. Criminal records on computer from 1990, index books from 1800s.

General Information: Public Access terminal is available. No juvenile or adoption records released. SASE required. Turnaround time 1 week. Copy fee: $.25 per page. Certification fee: $2.00. Fee payee: Clerk of Circuit Court. Only cashiers checks and money orders accepted. Prepayment is required.

Piatt County

Circuit Court PO Box 288, Monticello, IL 61856; 217-762-4966; Fax: 217-762-8394. Hours: 8:30AM-4:30PM (CST). *Felony, Misdemeanor, Civil, Eviction, Small Claims, Probate.*

www.co.piatt.il.us

Civil Records: Access: Phone, fax, mail, in person. Both court and visitors may perform in person searches.

No search fee. Required to search: name, years to search. Civil cases indexed by defendant, plaintiff. Civil records on computer since 1988, index books from 1800s.

Criminal Records: Access: Phone, fax, mail, in person. Both court and visitors may perform in person searches. No search fee. Required to search: name, years to search, DOB; also helpful: SSN. Criminal records on computer since 1988, index books from 1800s.

General Information: Public Access terminal is available. No juvenile or adoption records released. SASE not required. Turnaround time 2-3 days. Fax notes: $1.00 for first page, $.50 each add'l. Copy fee: $1.00 for first page, $.50 each add'l. Certification fee: $1.00 plus $.50 each add'l page. Fee payee: Clerk of Circuit Court. Business checks accepted. Prepayment is required.

Pike County

Circuit Court Pike County Courthouse, 100 E Washington St, Pittsfield, IL 62363; 217-285-6612; Fax: 217-285-4726. Hours: 8:30AM-4:30PM (CST). *Felony, Misdemeanor, Civil, Eviction, Small Claims, Probate.*

Civil Records: Access: Mail, in person. Both court and visitors may perform in person searches. Search fee: $4.00 per name per year. Required to search: name, years to search. Civil cases indexed by defendant, plaintiff. Civil records on computer since 1992, index books from 1800s.

Criminal Records: Access: Mail, in person. Both court and visitors may perform in person searches. Search fee: $4.00 per name per year. Required to search: name, years to search; also helpful: SSN. Criminal records on computer since 1992, index books from 1800s.

General Information: Public Access terminal is available. No juvenile or adoption records released. SASE required. Turnaround time as soon as possible. Copy fee: $1.00 for first page, $.50 each add'l. $.25 per page after 19 pages. Certification fee: $3.00. Fee payee: Circuit Clerk. Personal checks accepted. Prepayment is required.

Pope County

Circuit Court County Courthouse, Golconda, IL 62938; 618-683-3941; Fax: 618-683-3018. Hours: 8AM-4PM (CST). *Felony, Misdemeanor, Civil, Eviction, Small Claims, Probate.*

Civil Records: Access: Phone, fax, mail, in person. Both court and visitors may perform in person searches. Search fee: $4.00 per name per year. Required to search: name, years to search. Civil cases indexed by defendant. Civil records on computer from 1989, index books from 1800s.

Criminal Records: Access: Phone, fax, mail, in person. Both court and visitors may perform in person searches. Search fee: $4.00 per name per year. Required to search: name, years to search, DOB. Criminal records on computer from 1989, index books from 1800s.

General Information: Public Access terminal is available. No juvenile or adoption records released. SASE required. Turnaround time 2-3 days. Fax notes: $.50 per page. Copy fee: $.25 per page. Certification fee: $2.00. Fee payee: Circuit Clerk. Business checks accepted. Prepayment is required.

Pulaski County

Circuit Court PO Box 88, Mound City, IL 62963; 618-748-9300; Fax: 618-748-9338. Hours: 8AM-4PM (CST). *Felony, Misdemeanor, Civil, Eviction, Small Claims, Probate.*

Civil Records: Access: Mail, in person. Both court and visitors may perform in person searches. Search fee: $4.00 per name. Required to search: name, years to

search. Civil cases indexed by defendant, plaintiff. Civil records on computer since 1987, on books prior.

Criminal Records: Access: Mail, in person. Both court and visitors may perform in person searches. Search fee: $4.00 per name per year. Required to search: name, years to search, signed release; also helpful: DOB, SSN. Criminal records on computer since 1987, on books prior.

General Information: No juvenile, adoption records released. SASE required. Turnaround time 1 week. Copy fee: $1.00 for first page, $.50 each add'l. If over 20 pages, fee becomes $.25 per copy. Certification fee: $2.00. Fee payee: Clerk of Circuit Court. Only cashiers checks and money orders accepted. Prepayment is required.

Putnam County

Circuit Court 120 N 4th St, Hennepin, IL 61327; 815-925-7016; Fax: 815-925-7549. Hours: 9AM-4PM (CST). *Felony, Misdemeanor, Civil, Eviction, Small Claims, Probate.*

Civil Records: Access: Mail, in person. Both court and visitors may perform in person searches. Search fee: $5.00 per name. Fee is per 5 years searched. Required to search: name, years to search. Civil cases indexed by defendant. Civil records on computer from 1991, index books from 1836.

Criminal Records: Access: Mail, in person. Both court and visitors may perform in person searches. Search fee: $5.00 per name. Fee is per 5 years searched. Required to search: name, years to search, DOB. Criminal records on computer from 1991, index books from 1836.

General Information: Public Access terminal is available. No juvenile or adoption records released. SASE required. Turnaround time 3 days. Copy fee: $.50 per page. $.25 per page after 20. Certification fee: $2.00. Fee payee: Clerk of Circuit Court. Only cashiers checks and money orders accepted. Prepayment is required.

Randolph County

Circuit Court County Courthouse, PO Box 329, Chester, IL 62233; 618-826-5000 X150. Hours: 8AM-4PM (CST). *Felony, Misdemeanor, Civil, Eviction, Small Claims, Probate.*

Civil Records: Access: Mail, in person. Both court and visitors may perform in person searches. Search fee: $4.00 per name per year. Required to search: name, years to search. Civil cases indexed by defendant, plaintiff. Civil records on computer from 1992, index books from 1800s. Visitors can search computer index only.

Criminal Records: Access: Mail, in person. Both court and visitors may perform in person searches. Search fee: $4.00 per name per year. Required to search: name, years to search, DOB. Criminal records on computer from 1992, index books from 1800s. Visitors can search computer index only.

General Information: Public Access terminal is available. No juvenile or adoption records released. SASE required. Turnaround time 1-2 days. Copy fee: $.25 per page. Certification fee: $1.00 first page, $.50 each add'l. Fee payee: Clerk of Circuit Court. Business checks accepted. Prepayment is required.

Richland County

Circuit Court 103 W Main #21, Olney, IL 62450; 618-392-2151; Fax: 618-392-5041. Hours: 8AM-4PM (CST). *Felony, Misdemeanor, Civil, Eviction, Small Claims, Probate.*

Civil Records: Access: Mail, in person. Both court and visitors may perform in person searches. Search fee: $4.00 per name per year. Required to search: name, years to search. Civil cases indexed by defendant. Civil records on index books from 1800s.

Criminal Records: Access: Mail, in person. Both court and visitors may perform in person searches. Search fee: $4.00 per name per year. Required to search: name, years to search, DOB. Criminal records on index books from 1800s.

General Information: Public Access terminal is available. No juvenile or adoption records released. SASE required. Turnaround time 1-2 weeks. Copy fee: $1.00 for first page, $.50 each add'l. Certification fee: $.50. Fee payee: Clerk of Circuit Court. Only cashiers checks and money orders accepted. Prepayment is required.

Rock Island County

Circuit Court 210 15th St, PO Box 5230, Rock Island, IL 61204-5230; 309-786-4451; Fax: 309-786-3029. Hours: 8AM-4:30PM (CST). *Felony, Misdemeanor, Civil, Eviction, Small Claims, Probate.* www.co.rock-island.il.us

Civil Records: Access: Mail, online, in person. Both court and visitors may perform in person searches. Search fee: $4.00 per name per year. Required to search: name, years to search. Civil cases indexed by defendant, plaintiff. Civil records on computer from 1989, index books from 1950s. Access to records on the remote online system requires a $200 setup fee plus a $1.00 per minute for access. Civil, criminal, probate, traffic, and domestic records can be accessed by name or case number.

Criminal Records: Access: Fax, mail, online, in person. Both court and visitors may perform in person searches. Search fee: $4.00 per name per year. Required to search: name, years to search, DOB; also helpful: SSN. Criminal records on computer from 1989, index books from 1950s. Online access to criminal records is the same as civil.

General Information: Public Access terminal is available. No juvenile or adoption records released. SASE required. Turnaround time 1 week. Fax notes: $1.00 for first page, $.50 each add'l. Copy fee: $1.00 for first page, $.50 each add'l. Certification fee: $2.00. Fee payee: Circuit Clerks Office. Personal checks accepted. Prepayment is required.

Saline County

Circuit Court County Courthouse, Harrisburg, IL 62946; 618-253-5096 & 253-3904; Fax: 618-252-8438. Hours: 8AM-4PM (CST). *Felony, Misdemeanor, Civil, Eviction, Small Claims, Probate.*

Civil Records: Access: Fax, mail, in person. Both court and visitors may perform in person searches. Search fee: $5.00 per name per year. Required to search: name, years to search. Civil cases indexed by defendant, plaintiff. Civil records on computer back to 1986, index books from 1800s.

Criminal Records: Access: Fax, mail, in person. Both court and visitors may perform in person searches. Search fee: $5.00 per name per year. Required to search: name, years to search, DOB. Criminal records on computer back to 1986, index books from 1800s.

General Information: Public Access terminal is available. No juvenile or adoption records released. SASE required. Turnaround time 1-2 weeks. Fax notes: Fee to fax results is $2.00 1st page, $1.00 each add'l. Copy fee: $1.00 for first page, $.50 each add'l. Certification fee: $2.00. Fee payee: Clerk of Circuit Court. Business checks accepted. Prepayment is required.

Sangamon County

Circuit Court 200 S Ninth St Rm 405, Springfield, IL 62701; 217-753-6674; Fax: 217-753-6665. Hours: 8:30AM-4:30PM (CST). *Felony, Misdemeanor, Civil, Eviction, Small Claims, Probate.*

Civil Records: Access: Fax, mail, in person. Both court and visitors may perform in person searches. Search

fee: $4.00 per name per year. Required to search: name, years to search. Civil cases indexed by defendant, plaintiff. Civil records on computer from 1982, index books from 1800s.

Criminal Records: Access: Fax, mail, in person. Both court and visitors may perform in person searches. Search fee: $4.00 per name per year. Required to search: name, years to search, DOB. Criminal records on computer from 1982, index books from 1800s.

General Information: Public Access terminal is available. No juvenile, mental health, adoption records released. SASE required. Turnaround time 1-2 weeks. Fax notes: No fee to fax results. Copy fee: $1.00 for first page, $.50 each add'l. $.25 per page after 19. Certification fee: $2.00. Fee payee: Circuit Clerk. Personal checks accepted.

Schuyler County

Circuit Court PO Box 80, Rushville, IL 62681; 217-322-4633; Fax: 217-322-6164. Hours: 8AM-4PM (CST). *Felony, Misdemeanor, Civil, Eviction, Small Claims, Probate.*

Civil Records: Access: Mail, in person. Both court and visitors may perform in person searches. Search fee: $4.00 per name per year. Required to search: name, years to search. Civil cases indexed by defendant. Civil records on computer from 1988, index books from 1800s.

Criminal Records: Access: Mail, in person. Both court and visitors may perform in person searches. Search fee: $4.00 per name per year. Required to search: name, years to search, DOB. Criminal records on computer from 1988, index books from 1800s.

General Information: No juvenile or adoption records released. SASE required. Turnaround time 1 week. Fax notes: Fee to fax results is $1.00 per page. Copy fee: $1.00 for first page, $.50 each add'l. $.25 after 20. Certification fee: $2.00. Fee payee: Clerk of Circuit Court. Only cashiers checks and money orders accepted. Prepayment is required.

Scott County

Circuit Court 35 E Market St, Winchester, IL 62694; 217-742-5217; Fax: 217-742-5853. Hours: 8AM-Noon, 1-4PM (CST). *Felony, Misdemeanor, Civil, Eviction, Small Claims, Probate.*

Civil Records: Access: Mail, in person. Both court and visitors may perform in person searches. Search fee: $4.00 per name per year. Required to search: name, years to search. Civil cases indexed by defendant, plaintiff. Civil records on index books from 1800s.

Criminal Records: Access: Mail, in person. Both court and visitors may perform in person searches. Search fee: $4.00 per name per year. Required to search: name, years to search, DOB. Criminal records on index books from 1800s.

General Information: No juvenile or adoption records released. SASE required. Turnaround time 1 week. Copy fee: $1.00 for first page, $.50 each add'l. After 20 pages, copies are $.25 each. Certification fee: $2.00. Fee payee: Clerk of Circuit Court. Only cashiers checks and money orders accepted. Prepayment is required.

Shelby County

Circuit Court County Courthouse, PO Box 469, Shelbyville, IL 62565; 217-774-4212; Fax: 217-774-4109. Hours: 8AM-4PM (CST). *Felony, Misdemeanor, Civil, Eviction, Small Claims, Probate.*

Civil Records: Access: Fax, mail, in person. Search fee: $4.00 per name. Required to search: name, years to search. Civil cases indexed by defendant, plaintiff. Civil records on computer from 1988, index books from 1848.

Criminal Records: Access: Fax, mail, in person. Both court and visitors may perform in person searches. Search fee: $4.00 per name. Required to search: name, years to search, DOB. Criminal records on computer from 1988, index books from 1848.

General Information: Public Access terminal is available. No juvenile or adoption records released. SASE required. Turnaround time 1-2 weeks. Copy fee: $1.00 for first page, $.50 each add'l. Certification fee: $2.00. Fee payee: Circuit Clerk.

St. Clair County

Circuit Court 10 Public Square, Belleville, IL 62220-1623; 618-277-6832; Fax: 618-277-1562. Hours: 9AM-4PM (CST). *Felony, Misdemeanor, Civil, Eviction, Small Claims, Probate.*

Civil Records: Access: Mail, phone, fax, in person. Both court and visitors may perform in person searches. Search fee: $4.00 per name per year. Required to search: name, years to search; also helpful: address. Civil cases indexed by defendant, plaintiff. Civil records on computer from 1990, microfiche from 1800s.

Criminal Records: Access: Mail, phone, fax, in person. Both court and visitors may perform in person searches. Search fee: $4.00 per name per year. Required to search: name, years to search, DOB. Criminal records on computer from 1990, microfiche from 1800s.

General Information: No juvenile or adoption records released. SASE required. Turnaround time 1-2 days. Copy fee: $2.00 for first page, $.50 each add'l. $.25 per pg after 20. Certification fee: $4.00. Fee payee: Clerk of Circuit Court. Only cashiers checks and money orders accepted. Prepayment is required.

Stark County

Circuit Court 130 W Main St, Toulon, IL 61483; 309-286-5941. Hours: 8AM-4:30PM (CST). *Felony, Misdemeanor, Civil, Eviction, Small Claims, Probate.*

Civil Records: Access: Mail, in person. Both court and visitors may perform in person searches. Search fee: $4.00 per name per year. Required to search: name, years to search. Civil cases indexed by defendant. Civil records on index books from 1800s.

Criminal Records: Access: Mail, in person. Both court and visitors may perform in person searches. Search fee: $4.00 per name per year. Required to search: name, years to search, DOB. Criminal records on index books from 1800s.

General Information: No juvenile or adoption records released. SASE required. Turnaround time 2-3 days. Copy fee: $1.00 for first page, $.50 each add'l. Certification fee: $2.00. Fee payee: Clerk of Circuit Court. Personal checks accepted. Prepayment is required.

Stephenson County

Circuit Court 15 N Galena Ave, Freeport, IL 61032; 815-235-8266. Hours: 8:30AM-4:30PM (CST). *Felony, Misdemeanor, Civil, Eviction, Small Claims, Probate.*

Civil Records: Access: Mail, in person. Both court and visitors may perform in person searches. Search fee: $4.00 per name per year. Required to search: name, years to search. Civil cases indexed by defendant, plaintiff. Civil records on computer from 8/1989, index books from 1875.

Criminal Records: Access: Mail, in person. Both court and visitors may perform in person searches. Search fee: $4.00 per name per year. Required to search: name, years to search, DOB. Criminal records on computer from 8/1989, index books from 1875.

General Information: Public Access terminal is available. No juvenile or adoption records released. SASE required. Turnaround time 5-15 days. Copy fee: $1.00 for first page, $.50 each add'l. Certification fee: $2.00. Fee payee: Clerk of Circuit Court. Business checks accepted. Prepayment is required.

Tazewell County

Circuit Court Courthouse, 4th & Court Sts, Pekin, IL 61554; 309-477-2214. Hours: 8:30AM-5PM (CST). *Felony, Misdemeanor, Civil, Small Claims, Probate.*

Civil Records: Access: Mail, in person. Both court and visitors may perform in person searches. Search fee: $4.00 per name per year. Required to search: name, years to search. Civil cases indexed by defendant, plaintiff. Civil records on computer from 02/89 index books from 1800s.

Criminal Records: Access: Mail, in person. Both court and visitors may perform in person searches. Search fee: $4.00 per name per year. Required to search: name, years to search, DOB, signed release. Criminal records on computer from 02/89 index books from 1800s.

General Information: Public Access terminal is available. No juvenile or adoption records released. SASE required. Turnaround time 3-4 days. Copy fee: $1.00 for first page, $.50 each add'l. After 20 pages, $.10 per page. Certification fee: $2.00. Fee payee: Clerk of Circuit Court. Only cashiers checks and money orders accepted. Prepayment is required.

Union County

Circuit Court Union County Courthouse, 309 W Market, Rm 101, Jonesboro, IL 62952; 618-833-5913; Fax: 618-833-5223. Hours: 8AM-Noon,1-4PM (CST). *Felony, Misdemeanor, Civil, Eviction, Small Claims, Probate.*

Civil Records: Access: Fax, mail, in person. Both court and visitors may perform in person searches. Search fee: $4.00 per name per year. Required to search: name, years to search. Civil cases indexed by defendant, plaintiff. Civil records on computer from 1986, index books from 1800s. Public can only search paper records up to 1986. Only court personnel have access to computer records.

Criminal Records: Access: Fax, mail, in person. Both court and visitors may perform in person searches. Search fee: $4.00 per name per year. Required to search: name, years to search; also helpful: DOB. Criminal records on computer from 1986, index books from 1800s. Same search procedures as civil.

General Information: No juvenile or adoption records released. SASE required. Turnaround time 1 week. Fax notes: $5.00 per page. Copy fee: $.25 per page. Certification fee: $1.00. $.50 each page after first. Fee payee: Lorraine Moreland, Circuit Clerk. Business checks accepted. Prepayment is required.

Vermilion County

Circuit Court 7 N Vermilion, Danville, IL 61832; 217-431-2534; Fax: 217-431-2538. Hours: 8:30AM-4:30PM (CST). *Felony, Misdemeanor, Civil, Eviction, Small Claims, Probate.*

Civil Records: Access: Phone, mail, in person. Both court and visitors may perform in person searches. Search fee: $4.00 per name per year. Required to search: name, years to search. Civil cases indexed by defendant, plaintiff. Civil records on computer from 1989; microfilm from March 1949 to May 1989; index books from 1800s.

Criminal Records: Access: Phone, mail, in person. Both court and visitors may perform in person searches. Search fee: $4.00 per name per year. Required to search: name, years to search, DOB; also helpful: SSN. Criminal records on computer from 1989; microfilm from March 1949 to May 1989; index books from 1800s.

General Information: Public Access terminal is available. No juvenile, impounded, mental health or adoption records released. SASE required. Turnaround time 1 week. Copy fee: $1.00 for first page, $.50 each add'l. Certification fee: $4.00. Fee payee: Clerk of Circuit Court. Business checks accepted. Prepayment is required.

Wabash County

Circuit Court PO Box 997, 401 Market St, Mt Carmel, IL 62863; 618-262-5362; Fax: 618-263-4441. Hours: 8AM-5PM (CST). *Felony, Misdemeanor, Civil, Eviction, Small Claims, Probate.*

Civil Records: Access: Mail, in person. Both court and visitors may perform in person searches. Search fee: $4.00 per name per year. Required to search: name, years to search. Civil cases indexed by defendant, plaintiff. Civil records on computer from 1988, index books from 1800s.

Criminal Records: Access: Mail, in person. Both court and visitors may perform in person searches. Search fee: $4.00 per name per year. Required to search: name, years to search, DOB. Criminal records on computer from 1988, index books from 1800s.

General Information: Public Access terminal is available. No juvenile or adoption records released. SASE required. Turnaround time 5 days. Fax notes: Will fax back if all fees prepaid. Copy fee: $.50 for 1st 20 pages; $.25 each add'l. Certification fee: $2.00. Fee payee: Clerk of Circuit Court. Only cashiers checks and money orders accepted. Prepayment is required.

Warren County

Circuit Court 100 W Broadway, Monmouth, IL 61462; 309-734-5179. Hours: 8AM-4:30PM (CST). *Felony, Misdemeanor, Civil, Eviction, Small Claims, Probate.*

Civil Records: Access: Mail, in person. Both court and visitors may perform in person searches. Search fee: $5.00 per name per year. Required to search: name, years to search. Civil cases indexed by defendant. Civil records on computer from 1990, index books from 1800s.

Criminal Records: Access: Mail, in person. Both court and visitors may perform in person searches. Search fee: $5.00 per name per year. Required to search: name, years to search, DOB. Criminal records on computer from 1990, index books from 1800s.

General Information: No juvenile or adoption records released. SASE required. Turnaround time 1-2 weeks. Copy fee: $.50 per page. Certification fee: $2.00. Fee payee: Clerk of Circuit Court. Only cashiers checks and money orders accepted. Prepayment is required.

Washington County

Circuit Court 101 E St Louis St, Nashville, IL 62263; 618-327-4800 X305; Fax: 618-327-3583. Hours: 8AM-4PM (CST). *Felony, Misdemeanor, Civil, Eviction, Small Claims, Probate.*

Civil Records: Access: Mail, in person. Both court and visitors may perform in person searches. Search fee: $5.00 per name per year. Required to search: name, years to search. Civil cases indexed by defendant, plaintiff. Civil records on computer since 1998; 1988 for child support; prior records on index books from 1800s.

Criminal Records: Access: Mail, in person. Both court and visitors may perform in person searches. Search fee: $5.00 per name per year. Required to search: name, years to search; also helpful: DOB. Criminal records on computer since 1998; 1988 for child support; prior records on index books from 1800s.

General Information: No juvenile or adoption records released. SASE required. Turnaround time 3-5 days. Copy fee: $1.00 per page. Certification fee: $2.00. Fee payee: Washington County Circuit Clerk. No personal checks accepted. Will bill to attorneys.

Wayne County

Circuit Court County Courthouse, PO Box 96, Fairfield, IL 62837; 618-842-7684; Fax: 618-842-2556. Hours: 8AM-4:30PM (CST). *Felony, Misdemeanor, Civil, Eviction, Small Claims, Probate.*

Civil Records: Access: Mail, in person. Both court and visitors may perform in person searches. Search fee: $4.00 per name per year. Required to search: name, years to search. Civil cases indexed by defendant, plaintiff. Civil records on computer from 11/88, index books from 1800s.

Criminal Records: Access: Mail, in person. Both court and visitors may perform in person searches. Search fee: $4.00 per name per year. Required to search: name, years to search, DOB. Criminal records computerized since 1990.

General Information: Public Access terminal is available. No juvenile or adoption records released. SASE required. Turnaround time 1 week. Copy fee: $.50 per page. Certification fee: $2.00. Fee payee: Clerk of Circuit Court. Only cashiers checks and money orders accepted. Prepayment is required.

White County

Circuit Court PO Box 310, County Courthouse, Carmi, IL 62821; 618-382-2321; Fax: 618-382-2322. Hours: 8AM-4PM (CST). *Felony, Misdemeanor, Civil, Small Claims, Probate.*

Civil Records: Access: Fax, mail, in person. Both court and visitors may perform in person searches. Search fee: $4.00 per name per year. Required to search: name, years to search. Civil cases indexed by defendant, plaintiff. Civil records on computer from 1991, index books from 1800s.

Criminal Records: Access: Fax, mail, in person. Both court and visitors may perform in person searches. Search fee: $4.00 per name per year. Required to search: name, years to search; also helpful: DOB. Criminal records on computer from 1991, index books from 1800s.

General Information: Public Access terminal is available. No juvenile or adoption records released. SASE required. Turnaround time 1-2 weeks. Fax notes: $2.00 per page. Copy fee: $.25 per page. Certification fee: $1.00 plus $.50 per add'l page. Fee payee: Clerk of Circuit Court. Personal checks accepted. Prepayment is required.

Whiteside County

Circuit Court 200 E Knox St, Morrison, IL 61270-2698; 815-772-5188; Fax: 815-772-5187. Hours: 8:30AM-4:30PM (CST). *Felony, Misdemeanor, Civil, Eviction, Small Claims, Probate.*

Civil Records: Access: Phone, fax, mail, in person. Both court and visitors may perform in person searches. Search fee: $4.00 per name. Required to search: name, years to search. Civil cases indexed by defendant. Civil records on computer from 1989, index books from 1800s.

Criminal Records: Access: Phone, fax, mail, in person. Both court and visitors may perform in person searches. Search fee: $4.00 per name. Required to search: name, years to search, DOB. Criminal records on computer from 1989, index books from 1800s.

General Information: Public Access terminal is available. No juvenile or adoption records released. SASE required. Turnaround time 1 week. Fax notes: No fee to fax results. Local call only. Copy fee: $.25 per page. Certification fee: $2.00. Fee payee: Clerk of Circuit Court. Personal checks accepted. Prepayment is required.

Will County

Circuit Court 14 W Jefferson St, Joliet, IL 60432; 815-727-8592; Fax: 815-727-8896. Hours: 8:30AM-4:30PM (CST). *Felony, Misdemeanor, Civil, Eviction, Small Claims, Probate.*

www.willcountycircuitcourt.com

Civil Records: Access: Fax, mail, in person. Both court and visitors may perform in person searches. Search fee: $4.00 per name per year. Required to search: name, years to search. Civil cases indexed by defendant, plaintiff. Civil records on computer from 1980, index books from 1800s.

Criminal Records: Access: Fax, mail, in person. Both court and visitors may perform in person searches. Search fee: $4.00 per name per year. Required to search: name, years to search, DOB. Criminal records on computer from 1980, index books from 1800s.

General Information: Public Access terminal is available. No juvenile, adoption, mental health records released. SASE required. Turnaround time 2 week. Copy fee: $2.00 for first page, $.50 each add'l. Certification fee: $4.00. Fee payee: Pamela J McGuire, Clerk of Circuit Court. Only cashiers checks and money orders accepted. Prepayment is required.

Williamson County

Circuit Court 200 W Jefferson St, Marion, IL 62959; 618-997-1301 X114. Hours: 8AM-4PM (CST). *Felony, Misdemeanor, Civil, Eviction, Small Claims, Probate.*

Civil Records: Access: Mail, in person. Both court and visitors may perform in person searches. Search fee: $4.00 per name per year. Required to search: name, years to search. Civil cases indexed by defendant, plaintiff. Civil records on computer from 07/86, index books from 1800s.

Criminal Records: Access: Mail, in person. Both court and visitors may perform in person searches. Search fee: $4.00 per name per year. Required to search: name, years to search, DOB. Criminal records on computer from 07/86, index books from 1800s.

General Information: Public Access terminal is available. No juvenile or adoption records released. SASE required. Turnaround time 1 week. Copy fee: $1.00 for first page, $.50 each add'l. Certification fee: $2.00. Fee payee: Clerk of Circuit Court. Business checks accepted. Prepayment is required.

Winnebago County

Circuit Court 400 W State St, Rockford, IL 61101; Civil phone: 815-987-2510; Criminal phone: 815-987-3079/3175; Fax: 815-987-3012. Hours: 8AM-5PM (CST). *Felony, Misdemeanor, Civil, Eviction, Small Claims, Probate.*

Civil Records: Access: Phone, mail, in person. Both court and visitors may perform in person searches. Search fee: $4.00 per name per year. Required to search: name, years to search. Civil cases indexed by defendant, plaintiff. Civil records on computer past 3 years; prior records on index books from 1800s.

Criminal Records: Access: Phone, mail, in person. Both court and visitors may perform in person searches. Search fee: $4.00 per name per year. Required to search: name, years to search, DOB. Criminal records on computer past 3 years; prior records on index books from 1800s.

General Information: Public Access terminal is available. No juvenile, mental or adoption records released. SASE required. Turnaround time 1 week. Copy fee: $2.00 for first page, $.50 each add'l. After 20 pgs, fee is $.25 per pg. Certification fee: $4.00 plus $.50 per add'l page. Fee payee: Clerk of Circuit Court. Only cashiers checks and money orders accepted. Prepayment is required.

Woodford County

Circuit Court County Courthouse, PO Box 284, 115 N Main, Suite 201, Eureka, IL 61530; 309-467-3312. Hours: 8AM-5PM (CST). *Felony, Misdemeanor, Civil, Eviction, Small Claims, Probate.*

Civil Records: Access: Mail, in person. Both court and visitors may perform in person searches. Search fee: $4.00 per name per year. Required to search: name, years to search. Civil cases indexed by defendant, plaintiff. Civil records on computer from 1990, index books from 1800s.

Criminal Records: Access: Mail, in person. Both court and visitors may perform in person searches. Search fee: $4.00 per name per year. Required to search: name, years to search, DOB. Criminal records on computer from 1990, index books from 1800s.

General Information: Public Access terminal is available. No juvenile or adoption records released. SASE required. Turnaround time 2-3 days. Copy fee: $.50 per page. Certification fee: $2.00. Fee payee: Woodford County Circuit Clerk. Personal checks accepted. Prepayment is required.

Illinois Recording Offices

ORGANIZATION   102 counties, 103 recording offices. Cook County hads separate offices for real estate recording and UCC filing until June 30, 2001. As of that date the UCC filing office only searches for, and no longer takes new, UCC filings. The recording officer is Recorder of Deeds. Many counties utilize a grantor/grantee index containing all transactions. The entire state is in the Central Time Zone (CST).

REAL ESTATE RECORDS   Most counties will not perform real estate searches. Cost of certified copies varies widely, but many counties charge the same as the cost of recording the document. Tax records are usually located at the Treasurer's Office.

UCC RECORDS   Financing statements are filed at the state level except for real estate related filings which are filed with the County Recorder. (See above regarding Cook County.) Most counties will perform UCC searches. Use search request form UCC-11. Search fees are usually $10.00 per debtor name/address combination. Copies usually cost $1.00 per page.

TAX LIEN RECORDS   Federal tax liens on personal property of businesses are filed with the Secretary of State. Other federal and all state tax liens on personal property are filed with the County Recorder. Some counties will perform tax lien searches for $5.00-$10.00 per name (state and federal are separate searches in many of these counties) and $1.00 per page of copy.

OTHER LIENS   Judgments, mechanics, contractor, medical, lis pendens, oil & gas, mobile home.

Adams County

County Recorder, P.O. Box 1067, Quincy, IL 62306. County Recorder, R/E and UCC Recording 217-277-2125.
Will search UCC records. This agency will not do a tax lien search. Will not search real estate records. **Other Phone Numbers:** Assessor 217-277-2136; Treasurer 217-277-2248; Elections 217-277-2157; Vital Records 217-277-2158.

Alexander County

County Recorder, 2000 Washington Avenue, Cairo, IL 62914. 618-734-7000; Fax 618-734-7002.
Will search UCC records. Tax liens not included in UCC search. Will not search real estate records. **Other Phone Numbers:** Assessor 618-734-7006; Treasurer 618-734-7009.

Bond County

County Recorder, 203 West College Avenue, Greenville, IL 62246. 618-664-0449; Fax 618-664-9414.
Will search UCC records. UCC search includes tax liens if requested. Will not search real estate records. **Other Phone Numbers:** Assessor 618-664-2848; Treasurer 618-664-0618.

Boone County

County Recorder, 601 North Main Street, Suite 202, Belvidere, IL 61008. 815-544-3103; Fax 815-547-8701.
Will search UCC records. This agency will not do a tax lien search. Will not search real estate records. **Other Phone Numbers:** Assessor 815-544-2958; Treasurer 815-544-2666; Elections 815-544-3103; Vital Records 815-544-3103.

Brown County

County Recorder, Courthouse - Room 4, #1 Court Street, Mount Sterling, IL 62353-1285. County Recorder, R/E and UCC Recording 217-773-3421; Fax 217-773-2233.
Will search UCC records. UCC search includes tax liens if requested. Will not search real estate records. **Other Phone Numbers:** Assessor 217-773-3415; Treasurer 217-773-3133; Elections 217-773-3421; Vital Records 217-773-3421.

Bureau County

County Recorder, 700 South Main St., Courthouse, Princeton, IL 61356. County Recorder, R/E and UCC Recording 815-875-3239; Fax 815-879-4803.
Will search UCC records. This agency will not do a tax lien search. Will not search real estate records. **Other Phone Numbers:** Assessor 815-875-6478; Treasurer 815-875-3241; Elections 815-875-2014; Vital Records 815-875-3239.

Calhoun County

County Clerk & Recorder, P.O. Box 187, Hardin, IL 62047. 618-576-2351; Fax 618-576-2895.
Will search UCC records. UCC search includes tax liens. Mortgage searches available. **Other Phone Numbers:** Assessor 618-576-8041; Treasurer 618-576-2421.

Carroll County

County Recorder, P.O. Box 152, Mount Carroll, IL 61053. 815-244-0223; Fax 815-244-3709.
Will search UCC records. This agency will not do a tax lien search. Will not search real estate records. **Other Phone Numbers:** Assessor 815-244-9171 x257; Treasurer 815-244-9171 x273.

Cass County

County Recorder, 100 E Springfield St, Virginia, IL 62691. 217-452-7217; Fax 217-452-7219.
Will search UCC records. UCC search includes tax liens. Will not search real estate records. **Other Phone Numbers:** Assessor 217-452-7249; Treasurer 217-452-7721.

Champaign County

County Recorder, 1776 E. Washington, Urbana, IL 61802. 217-384-3774; Fax 217-344-1663.
Will search UCC records. UCC search includes only state tax liens if requested Will not search real estate records. **Other Phone Numbers:** Assessor 217-384-3760; Treasurer 217-384-3734.

Christian County

County Recorder, P.O. Box 647, Taylorville, IL 62568. County Recorder, R/E and UCC Recording 217-824-4960; Fax 217-824-5105.

Will search UCC records. This agency will not do a tax lien search. Will not search real estate records. **Other Phone Numbers:** Assessor 217-824-5900; Treasurer 217-824-4889; Elections 217-824-4969; Vital Records 217-824-4969.

Clark County

County Recorder, Courthouse, Marshall, IL 62441. County Recorder, R/E and UCC Recording 217-826-8311.
Will search UCC records. This agency will not do a tax lien search. Will not search real estate records. **Other Phone Numbers:** Assessor 217-826-5815; Treasurer 217-826-5721; Elections 217-826-8311; Vital Records 217-826-8311.

Clay County

County Recorder, P.O. Box 160, Louisville, IL 62858-0160. County Recorder, R/E and UCC Recording 618-665-3626; Fax 618-665-3607.
Will search UCC records. UCC search includes tax liens. RE owner, mortgage, and property transfer searches available. **Other Phone Numbers:** Assessor 618-665-3370; Treasurer 618-665-3727; Elections 618-665-3626; Vital Records 618-665-3626.

Clinton County

County Recorder, P.O. Box 308, Carlyle, IL 62231. County Recorder, R/E and UCC Recording 618-594-2464 UCC Recording: 618-594-0142; Fax 618-594-0195. http://www.clintonco.org/
Will search UCC records. UCC search includes tax liens if requested. Will not search real estate records. **Other Phone Numbers:** Assessor 618-594-3221; Treasurer 618-594-2464; Elections 618-594-2464; Vital Records 618-594-2464.

Coles County

County Recorder, 651 Jackson Ave., Room 122, Charleston, IL 61920. 217-348-7325; Fax 217-348-7337.
Will search UCC records. This agency will not do a tax lien search. Will not search real estate records. **Other Phone Numbers:** Treasurer 217-348-0501.

Cook County

County Clerk, 118 North Clark Street, Room 120, Chicago, IL 60602-1387. 312-603-7524; Fax 312-603-5063. http://www.assessor.co.cook.il.us

Will search UCC records. This agency will not do a tax lien search. See Recorder for real estate records. **Online Access:** Property Tax Records. Records on the County Assessor Residential Assessment Search database are available free online at www.assessor.co.cook.il.us/starsearch.html. Database is offered as a tax assessment comparison service. **Other Phone Numbers:** Assessor 312-443-7550.

Cook County Recorder

County Recorder, 118 North Clark St., Room 230, Chicago, IL 60602. 312-603-5134; Fax 312-603-5063. There are no filings recorded at this office after June 30, 2001. Only records prior to this date can be searched. Will search UCC records, but only real estate related UCC filed here. State tax lien copies-$10.00 uncertified, $20.00 certified. Federal tax lien copies-$2.00 uncertified, $5.00 certified **Other Phone Numbers:** Assessor 312-443-5300; Treasurer 312-443-4436.

Crawford County

County Recorder, P.O. Box 602, Robinson, IL 62454-0602. County Recorder, R/E and UCC Recording 618-546-1212; Fax 618-546-0140. http://www.crawfordcountyclerk.com Will search UCC records. This agency will not do a tax lien search. Will not search real estate records. **Other Phone Numbers:** Assessor 618-546-1212; Treasurer 618-546-1212; Elections 618-546-2590; Vital Records 618-546-1212.

Cumberland County

County Recorder, P.O. Box 146, Toledo, IL 62468. County Recorder, R/E and UCC Recording 217-849-2631; Fax 217-849-2968. Will search UCC records. This agency will not do a tax lien search. Will not search real estate records. **Other Phone Numbers:** Assessor 217-849-3831; Treasurer 217-849-2321; Elections 217-849-2631; Vital Records 217-849-2631.

De Kalb County

County Recorder, 110 East Sycamore Street, Sycamore, IL 60178. 815-895-7156. Will search UCC records. Tax liens not included in UCC search. Will not search real estate records. **Online Access:** Real Estate, Liens. The DeKalb County online system requires a $350 subscription fee, with a per minute charge of $.25, $.50 if printing. Records date back to 1980. Lending agency information is available. For further information, contact Sheila Larson at 815-895-7152. **Other Phone Numbers:** Assessor 815-895-7120; Treasurer 815-895-7112.

De Witt County

County Recorder, P.O. Box 439, Clinton, IL 61727-0439. 217-935-2119; Fax 217-935-4596. Will search UCC records. This agency will not do a tax lien search. Will not search real estate records. **Other Phone Numbers:** Treasurer 217-935-2359.

Douglas County

County Recorder, P.O. Box 467, Tuscola, IL 61953-0467. County Recorder, R/E and UCC Recording 217-253-4410; Fax 217-253-2233. Will search UCC records. This agency will not do a tax lien search. Will not search real estate records. **Other Phone Numbers:** Assessor 217-253-3031; Treasurer 217-253-4011; Elections 217-253-2411; Vital Records 217-253-2411.

Du Page County

County Recorder, P.O. Box 936, Wheaton, IL 60189. 630-682-7200; Fax 630-682-7204. http://www.co.dupage.il.us

Will search UCC records. This agency will not do a tax lien search. Will not search real estate records. **Online Access:** Real Estate, Liens, Tax Assessor Records. For access to the Du Page County database, one must lease a live interface telephone line from a carrier to establish a connection. Additionally, there is a fee of $.05 per transaction. Records date back to 1977. For information, contact Fred Kieltcka at 630-682-7030. **Other Phone Numbers:** Assessor 630-682-7024; Treasurer 630-682-7012; Elections 630-682-7440; Vital Records 630-682-7035.

Edgar County

County Clerk and Recorder, 115 W Court St, Rm J, 115 W. Court St., Paris, IL 61944-1785. County Clerk and Recorder, R/E and UCC Recording 217-466-7433; Fax 217-466-7430. Will search UCC records. UCC search includes tax liens if requested. RE owner, mortgage, and property transfer searches available. **Other Phone Numbers:** Assessor 217-466-5140; Treasurer 217-463-6050; Elections 217-466-7433; Vital Records 217-466-7433.

Edwards County

County Recorder, 50 East Main Street, Courthouse, Albion, IL 62806-1294. 618-445-2115; Fax 618-445-3505. Will search UCC records. UCC search includes tax liens if requested. RE record owner searches available. **Other Phone Numbers:** Assessor 618-445-3591; Treasurer 618-445-3581; Elections 618-445-2115; Vital Records 618-445-2115.

Effingham County

County Clerk & Recorder, P.O. Box 628, Effingham, IL 62401-0628. County Clerk & Recorder, R/E and UCC Recording 217-342-6535; Fax 217-342-3577. http://co.effingham.il.us Will search UCC records. Tax liens not included in UCC search. Will not search real estate records. **Other Phone Numbers:** Assessor 217-324-6711; Treasurer 217-342-6844; Elections 217-342-6535; Vital Records 217-342-6535.

Fayette County

County Recorder, P.O. Box 401, Vandalia, IL 62471-0401. County Recorder, R/E and UCC Recording 618-283-5000; Fax 618-283-5004. Will search UCC records. This agency will not do a tax lien search. Will not search real estate records. **Other Phone Numbers:** Assessor 618-283-5020; Treasurer 618-283-5022; Elections 618-283-5000; Vital Records 618-283-5000.

Ford County

County Recorder, 200 West State Street, Room 101, Paxton, IL 60957. County Recorder, R/E and UCC Recording 217-379-2721; Fax 217-379-3258. www.prairienet.org Will search UCC records. This agency will not do a tax lien search. Will not search real estate records. **Other Phone Numbers:** Assessor 217-379-4132; Treasurer 217-379-2532.

Franklin County

County Clerk & Recorder, P.O. Box 607, Benton, IL 62812. County Clerk & Recorder, R/E and UCC Recording 618-438-3221; Fax 618-439-4119. Will search UCC records. Tax liens not included in UCC search. RE record owner and mortgage searches available. **Other Phone Numbers:** Assessor 618-438-4331; Treasurer 618-438-7311; Elections 618-438-3403; Vital Records 618-438-3221.

Fulton County

County Recorder, P.O. Box 226, Lewistown, IL 61542. 309-547-3041 R/E Recording: 309-547-3041 x43 UCC Recording: 309-547-3041 x43. Will search UCC records. This agency will not do a tax lien search. Will not search real estate records. **Other Phone Numbers:** Assessor 309-547-3041 x58; Treasurer 309-547-3041 x25; Elections 309-547-3041 x704; Vital Records 309-547-3041 x 42.

Gallatin County

County Recorder, P.O. Box 550, Shawneetown, IL 62984. County Recorder, R/E and UCC Recording 618-269-3025; Fax 618-269-3343. Will search UCC records. This agency will not do a tax lien search. Will not search real estate records. **Other Phone Numbers:** Assessor 618-269-3791; Treasurer 618-269-3022; Elections 618-269-3025; Vital Records 618-269-3025.

Greene County

County Recorder, 519 North Main Street, Courthouse, Carrollton, IL 62016-1033. 217-942-5443; Fax 217-942-9323. Will search UCC records. Tax liens not included in UCC search. Will not search real estate records. **Other Phone Numbers:** Assessor 217-942-6412; Treasurer 217-942-5124.

Grundy County

County Recorder, P.O. Box 675, Morris, IL 60450-0675. 815-941-3224; Fax 815-942-2220. Will search UCC records. UCC search includes tax liens if requested. Will not search real estate records. **Other Phone Numbers:** Assessor 815-941-3269; Treasurer 815-941-3215; Elections 815-941-3221; Vital Records 815-941-3222.

Hamilton County

County Recorder, Courthouse, 100 S Jackson St, Room 2, McLeansboro, IL 62859-1489. 618-643-2721. Will search UCC records. UCC search includes tax liens if requested. Will not search real estate records. **Other Phone Numbers:** Treasurer 618-643-3313.

Hancock County

County Recorder, P.O. Box 39, Carthage, IL 62321-0039. County Recorder, R/E and UCC Recording 217-357-3911. Will search UCC records. UCC search includes tax liens if requested. Will not search real estate records. **Other Phone Numbers:** Assessor 217-357-2615; Treasurer 217-357-2624; Elections 217-357-3911; Vital Records 217-357-3911.

Hardin County

County Recorder, P.O. Box 187, Elizabethtown, IL 62931. County Recorder, R/E and UCC Recording 618-287-2251; Fax 618-287-7833. Will search UCC records. UCC search includes tax liens if requested. RE record owner and property searches available. **Other Phone Numbers:** Assessor 618-287-3551; Treasurer 618-287-2053; Elections 618-287-2251; Vital Records 618-287-2251; Other Fax 618-287-2661.

Henderson County

County Recorder, P.O. Box 308, Oquawka, IL 61469-0308. 309-867-2911; Fax 309-867-2033. Will search UCC records. This agency will not do a tax lien search. Will not search real estate records. **Other Phone Numbers:** Assessor 309-867-3291; Treasurer 309-867-3121.

Henry County

County Recorder, 100 South Main, Cambridge, IL 61238. 309-937-3585; Fax 309-937-2796. http://www.henrycty.com/recorder.htm
Will search UCC records. This agency will not do a tax lien search. Will not search real estate records. **Other Phone Numbers:** Assessor 309-937-3570; Treasurer 309-937-3576; Elections 309-937-3492; Vital Records 309-937-3575.

Iroquois County

County Recorder, 1001 East Grant Street, Watseka, IL 60970. 815-432-6962; Fax 815-432-3894.
Will search UCC records. UCC search includes tax liens if requested. Will not search real estate records. **Other Phone Numbers:** Assessor 815-432-6978; Treasurer 815-432-6985.

Jackson County

County Recorder, The Courthouse, 1001 & Walnut, Murphysboro, IL 62966. 618-687-7360.
Will search UCC records. UCC search includes tax liens if requested. Will not search real estate records. **Other Phone Numbers:** Assessor 618-687-7220; Treasurer 618-687-3555.

Jasper County

County Recorder, 100 West Jourdan, Newton, IL 62448. 618-783-3124; Fax 618-783-4137.
Will search UCC records. This agency will not do a tax lien search. Will not search real estate records. **Other Phone Numbers:** Assessor 618-783-8042; Treasurer 618-783-3211.

Jefferson County

County Recorder, Courthouse, 100 S. 10th St., Room 105, Mount Vernon, IL 62864. 618-244-8020.
Will search UCC records. This agency will not do a tax lien search. Will not search real estate records. **Other Phone Numbers:** Assessor 618-244-8016; Treasurer 618-244-8011.

Jersey County

County Recorder, 200 N Lafayette #2, Jerseyville, IL 62052. County Recorder, R/E and UCC Recording 618-498-5571 x117/8; Fax 618-498-6128.
Will search UCC records. Tax liens not included in UCC search. Will not search real estate records. **Other Phone Numbers:** Assessor 618-498-5571 x126; Treasurer 618-498-5571 x110; Elections 618-498-5571 x112; Vital Records 618-498-5571 x113.

Jo Daviess County

County Recorder, 330 North Bench Street, Galena, IL 61036. 815-777-9694; Fax 815-777-3688.
Will search UCC records. This agency will not do a tax lien search. Will do 20-year search regarding to liens for genealogy purposes. **Other Phone Numbers:** Assessor 815-777-1016; Treasurer 815-777-0355.

Johnson County

County Recorder, P.O. Box 96, Vienna, IL 62995. County Recorder, R/E and UCC Recording 618-658-3611; Fax 618-658-2908.
Will search UCC records. UCC search includes tax liens if requested. RE owner, mortgage, and property transfer searches available. **Other Phone Numbers:** Assessor 618-658-8010; Treasurer 618-658-8042; Elections 618-658-3611; Vital Records 618-658-3611.

Kane County

County Recorder, P.O. Box 71, Geneva, IL 60134. 630-232-5935; Fax 630-232-5945.
Will search UCC records. This agency will not do a tax lien search. Will not search real estate records. **Other**

Phone Numbers: Assessor 630-232-3818; Treasurer 630-232-3565.

Kankakee County

County Recorder, 189 East Court Street, Kankakee, IL 60901. County Recorder, R/E and UCC Recording 815-937-2980; Fax 815-937-3657.
Will search UCC records. This agency will not do a tax lien search. Will not search real estate records. **Other Phone Numbers:** Assessor 815-937-2945; Treasurer 815-937-2960; Elections 815-937-2990; Vital Records 815-937-2990.

Kendall County

County Recorder, 111 West Fox Street, Yorkville, IL 60560. 630-553-4112; Fax 630-553-4119.
Will not search UCC records. Will not search tax liens. Will not search real estate records. **Other Phone Numbers:** Assessor 630-553-4146; Treasurer 630-553-4124; Appraiser/Auditor 630-553-4146; Elections 630-553-4105; Vital Records 630-553-4105.

Knox County

County Recorder, County Court House, Galesburg, IL 61401. 309-345-3818; Fax 309-343-7002.
Will search UCC records. This agency will not do a tax lien search. Will not search real estate records. **Other Phone Numbers:** Assessor 309-345-3824; Treasurer 309-345-3863.

La Salle County

County Recorder, P.O. Box 189, Ottawa, IL 61350. 815-434-8226; Fax 815-434-8260. http://www.lasallecounty.org/Final/contents2.htm
Will search UCC records. This agency will not do a tax lien search. Will not search real estate records. **Online Access:** Real Estate, Assessor. Assessor records on the County Assessor database are available free online at www.lasallecounty.org/cidnet/asrpfull.htm. Also, 1999 & 2000 assessment data can be accessed online at www.lasallecounty.org/contents3.htm. **Other Phone Numbers:** Assessor 815-434-8280; Treasurer 815-434-8220; Elections 815-434-8202.

Lake County

County Recorder, 18 North County Street, Courthouse - 2nd Floor, Waukegan, IL 60085-4358. 847-377-2575 R/E Recording: 847-377-2040; Fax 847-625-7200. http://www.co.lake.il.us/recorder
Will search UCC records. This agency will not do a tax lien search. Will not search real estate records. **Other Phone Numbers:** Assessor 847-377-2050; Treasurer 847-377-2323; Elections 847-377-3610; Vital Records 847-377-3610.

Lawrence County

County Recorder, 100 State St, Courthouse, Lawrenceville, IL 62439. County Recorder, R/E and UCC Recording 618-943-5126; Fax 618-943-5205.
Will search UCC records. UCC search includes tax liens if requested. Will not search real estate records. **Other Phone Numbers:** Assessor 618-943-2719; Treasurer 618-943-2016; Elections 618-943-2346; Vital Records 618-943-2346.

Lee County

County Recorder, P.O. Box 329, Dixon, IL 61021-0329. 815-288-3309; Fax 815-288-6492.
Will search UCC records. This agency will not do a tax lien search. Will not search real estate records. **Other Phone Numbers:** Assessor 815-288-4483; Treasurer 815-288-4477.

Livingston County

County Recorder, 112 West Madison, Courthouse, Pontiac, IL 61764-1871. 815-844-2006; Fax 815-842-1844.
Will search UCC records. Tax liens not included in UCC search. Will not search real estate records. **Other Phone Numbers:** Assessor 815-844-5166 x166-7; Treasurer 815-844-5166 x144.

Logan County

County Recorder, P.O. Box 278, Lincoln, IL 62656. 217-732-4148; Fax 217-732-6064.
Will search UCC records. UCC search includes tax liens if requested. Will not search real estate records. **Other Phone Numbers:** Assessor 217-732-9635; Treasurer 217-732-3761.

Macon County

County Recorder, 141 S. Main St., Room 201, Decatur, IL 62523-1293. 217-424-1359; Fax 217-428-2908.
Will search UCC records. UCC search includes tax liens if requested. Will not search real estate records. **Other Phone Numbers:** Assessor 217-424-1364; Treasurer 217-424-1426.

Macoupin County

County Recorder, P.O. Box 107, Carlinville, IL 62626. 217-854-3214; Fax 217-854-8461.
Will search UCC records. UCC search includes tax liens if requested. Will not search real estate records. **Other Phone Numbers:** Assessor 217-854-3214 x205; Treasurer 217-854-3214 x270.

Madison County

County Recorder, P.O. Box 308, Edwardsville, IL 62025-0308. 618-692-7040 x4772; Fax 618-692-9843.
Will search UCC records. UCC search includes tax liens if requested. RE record owner and mortgage searches available. **Other Phone Numbers:** Assessor 618-692-6200 x4569; Treasurer 618-692-6200.

Marion County

County Recorder, P.O. Box 637, Salem, IL 62881. 618-548-3400 R/E Recording: 618-548-3852 UCC Recording: 618-548-3852; Fax 618-548-2226.
Will search UCC records. Will not search real estate records. **Other Phone Numbers:** Assessor 618-548-3853; Treasurer 618-548-3858; Elections 618-548-3400; Vital Records 618-548-3850.

Marshall County

County Recorder, P.O. Box 328, Lacon, IL 61540. County Recorder, R/E and UCC Recording 309-246-6325; Fax 309-246-3667.
Will search UCC records. This agency will not do a tax lien search. Will not search real estate records. **Other Phone Numbers:** Assessor 309-246-2350; Treasurer 309-246-6085; Elections 309-246-6325; Vital Records 309-246-6325.

Mason County

County Recorder, P.O. Box 77, Havana, IL 62644. 309-543-6661; Fax 309-543-2085.
Will search UCC records. This agency will not do a tax lien search. Will not search real estate records. **Other Phone Numbers:** Assessor 309-543-4775; Treasurer 309-543-3359.

Massac County

County Recorder, P.O. Box 429, Metropolis, IL 62960. County Recorder, R/E and UCC Recording 618-524-5213; Fax 618-524-8514.
Will search UCC records. This agency will not do a tax lien search. Will not search real estate records. **Other Phone Numbers:** Assessor 618-524-9632; Treasurer

618-524-5121; Elections 618-524-5213; Vital Records 618-524-5213.

McDonough County

County Recorder, 1 Courthouse Square, Macomb, IL 61455. 309-833-2474; Fax 309-836-3368.
Will search UCC records. This agency will not do a tax lien search. Will not search real estate records. **Other Phone Numbers:** Assessor 309-833-5305; Treasurer 309-833-2032.

McHenry County

County Recorder, 2200 North Seminary Avenue, Room A280, Woodstock, IL 60098. 815-334-4110; Fax 815-338-9612.
Will search UCC records. This agency will not do a tax lien search. Will not search real estate records. **Online Access:** Assessor/Treasurer. Records on the County Treasurer Inquiry site are available free online at http://209.172.155.14/cidnet.publictre1.htm.   **Other Phone Numbers:** Assessor 847-360-6378; Treasurer 815-334-2098.

McLean County

County Recorder, P.O. Box 2400, Bloomington, IL 61702-2400. 309-888-5170; Fax 309-888-5927. http://www.mclean.gov/
Will search UCC records and recorded deeds. This agency will not do a tax lien search. Will not search real estate records. **Online Access:** Assessor/Treasurer. Online access to the county Tax Bill Information Lookup database is available free at www.mclean.gov/TaxLookupMainFirst.asp. No name searching; parcel number or streetname and city required. Also, access to the Township of Normal assessor database is available free at www.normaltownship.org/Assessor/ParcelSearch.php. No name searching; parcel number or address required. **Other Phone Numbers:** Assessor 309-888-5130; Treasurer 309-888-5180; Elections 309-888-5190.

Menard County

County Recorder, P.O. Box 465, Petersburg, IL 62675. 217-632-2415; Fax 217-632-4124.
Will search UCC records. This agency will not do a tax lien search. Will not search real estate records. **Other Phone Numbers:** Assessor 217-632-3201 x25; Treasurer 217-632-2333.

Mercer County

County Recorder, P.O. Box 66, Aledo, IL 61231. 309-582-7021; Fax 309-582-7022.
Will search UCC records. This agency will not do a tax lien search. Will not search real estate records. **Other Phone Numbers:** Assessor 309-582-7814; Treasurer 309-582-2524.

Monroe County

County Recorder, 100 South Main, Courthouse, Waterloo, IL 62298-1399. 618-939-8681; Fax 618-939-8639.
Will search UCC records. This agency will not do a tax lien search. Will not search real estate records. **Other Phone Numbers:** Assessor 618-939-8681 x211; Treasurer 618-939-8681 x213.

Montgomery County

County Recorder, Historic Courthouse, 1 Courthouse Square, Hillsboro, IL 62049-1196. County Recorder, R/E and UCC Recording 217-532-9532; Fax 217-532-9581. www.montgomeryco.com
Will search UCC records. UCC search includes tax liens if requested. RE owner, mortgage, and property transfer searches available. **Other Phone Numbers:**

Assessor 217-532-9595; Treasurer 217-532-9521; Elections 217-532-9530; Vital Records 217-532-9537.

Morgan County

County Recorder, P.O. Box 1387, Jacksonville, IL 62651. 217-243-8581.
Will search UCC records. UCC search includes tax liens if requested. Will not search real estate records. **Other Phone Numbers:** Assessor 217-243-8557; Treasurer 217-243-8581.

Moultrie County

County Recorder, Courthouse, Suite 6, 10 S. Main, Sullivan, IL 61951. County Recorder, R/E and UCC Recording 217-728-4389; Fax 217-728-8178.
Will search UCC records. Tax liens not included in UCC search. Will not search real estate records. **Other Phone Numbers:** Assessor 217-728-4951; Treasurer 217-728-4032; Elections 217-728-4389; Vital Records 217-728-4389.

Ogle County

County Recorder, P.O. Box 357, Oregon, IL 61061. 815-732-1115 x270/1.
Will search UCC records. UCC search includes tax liens if requested. Will not search real estate records. **Other Phone Numbers:** Assessor 815-732-1150 x239, 256, 257, 258 & 305; Treasurer 815-732-1100 x202/201/310 & 286; Elections 815-732-1110 x012/213/281/214 & 215; Vital Records 815-732-1110 x012/213/281/214 & 215.

Peoria County

County Recorder, County Courthouse - Room G04, 324 Main Street, Peoria, IL 61602. 309-672-6090.
Will search UCC records. This agency will not do a tax lien search. Will not search real estate records. **Other Phone Numbers:** Assessor 309-672-6910; Treasurer 309-672-6065.

Perry County

County Recorder, P.O. Box 438, Pinckneyville, IL 62274. 618-357-5116; Fax 618-357-3194.
Will search UCC records. UCC search includes tax liens if requested. Will not search real estate records. **Other Phone Numbers:** Assessor 618-357-2209; Treasurer 618-357-5002.

Piatt County

County Recorder, P.O. Box 558, Monticello, IL 61856-0558. County Recorder, R/E and UCC Recording 217-762-9487; Fax 217-762-7563. www.co.piatt.il.us
Will search UCC records. This agency will not do a tax lien search. Will not search real estate records. **Other Phone Numbers:** Assessor 217-762-4266; Treasurer 217-762-4866; Elections 217-762-9487; Vital Records 217-762-9487.

Pike County

County Recorder, Courthouse, 100 E. Washington St., Pittsfield, IL 62363. County Recorder, R/E and UCC Recording 217-285-6812; Fax 217-285-5820.
Will search UCC records. UCC search includes tax liens if requested. Will not search real estate records. **Other Phone Numbers:** Assessor 217-285-2382; Treasurer 217-285-4218; Elections 217-285-6812; Vital Records 217-285-6812.

Pope County

County Recorder, P.O. Box 216, Golconda, IL 62938. 618-683-4466; Fax 618-683-4466.
Will Search UCC records. UCC search includes tax liens if requested. Will not search real estate records. **Other Phone Numbers:** Assessor 618-683-6231; Treasurer 618-683-5501.

Pulaski County

County Recorder, P.O. Box 109, Mound City, IL 62963. 618-748-9360.
Will search UCC records. This agency will not do a tax lien search. Will not search real estate records. **Other Phone Numbers:** Assessor 618-748-9321; Treasurer 618-748-9322.

Putnam County

County Recorder, P.O. Box 236, Hennepin, IL 61327. 815-925-7129; Fax 815-925-7549.
Will search UCC records. This agency will not do a tax lien search. Will not search real estate records. **Other Phone Numbers:** Treasurer 815-925-7226.

Randolph County

County Recorder, P.O. Box 309, Chester, IL 62233-0309. 618-826-5000 x191; Fax 618-826-3750.
Will search UCC records. Tax liens included with UCC search if requested. Will not search real estate records. **Other Phone Numbers:** Assessor 618-826-5000 x192; Treasurer 618-826-5000 x224.

Richland County

County Recorder, 103 West Main, Courthouse, Olney, IL 62450. 618-392-3111; Fax 618-393-4005.
Will search UCC records. Tax liens not included in UCC search. Will not search real estate records. **Other Phone Numbers:** Assessor 618-395-4387; Treasurer 618-392-8341.

Rock Island County

County Recorder, P.O. Box 3067, Rock Island, IL 61204. 309-786-4451 x357.
Will search UCC records. This agency will not do a tax lien search. Will not search real estate records. **Other Phone Numbers:** Assessor 309-786-4451; Treasurer 309-786-4451.

Saline County

County Recorder, 10 E. Poplar, Harrisburg, IL 62946. 618-253-8197 R/E Recording: 618-253-3073 UCC Recording: 618-253-3073; Fax 618-252-3073.
Will search UCC records. This agency will not do a tax lien search. Will not search real estate records. **Other Phone Numbers:** Assessor 618-252-0691; Treasurer 618-253-6915; Elections 618-253-8197; Vital Records 618-253-8197.

Sangamon County

County Recorder, P.O. Box 669, Springfield, IL 62705-0669. 217-535-3150; Fax 217-535-3159. http://www.co.sangamon.il.us
Will search UCC records. UCC search includes tax liens if requested. Will not search real estate records. **Other Phone Numbers:** Assessor 217-753-6615; Treasurer 217-753-6800.

Schuyler County

County Recorder, P.O. Box 200, Rushville, IL 62681. County Recorder, R/E and UCC Recording 217-322-4734; Fax 217-322-6164.
Will search UCC records. Tax liens not included in UCC search. Will not search real estate records. **Other Phone Numbers:** Assessor 217-322-4432; Treasurer 217-322-3830; Elections 217-322-4734; Vital Records 217-322-4734.

Scott County

County Recorder, Courthouse, Winchester, IL 62694. 217-742-3178; Fax 217-742-5853.
Will search UCC records. UCC search includes tax liens. RE owner, mortgage, and property transfer searches available. **Other Phone Numbers:** Assessor 217-742-5751; Treasurer 217-742-3368.

Shelby County

County Recorder, P.O. Box 230, Shelbyville, IL 62565. 217-774-4421; Fax 217-774-5291.
Will search UCC records. UCC search includes tax liens if requested. RE owner, mortgage, and property transfer searches available. **Other Phone Numbers:** Assessor 217-774-5579; Treasurer 217-774-3841.

St. Clair County

County Recorder, P.O. Box 543, Belleville, IL 62220. 618-277-6600 UCC Recording: 618-277-6600 x2484.
Will search UCC records. Tax liens not included in UCC search. Will not search real estate records. **Other Phone Numbers:** Assessor 618-277-6600 x2509; Treasurer 618-277-6600 x2448; Elections 770-531-6600 x2363.

Stark County

County Recorder, P.O. Box 97, Toulon, IL 61483. County Recorder, R/E and UCC Recording 309-286-5911; Fax 309-286-4039. http://www.starkcourt.org
Will search UCC records. This agency will not do a tax lien search. Will not search real estate records. **Online Access:** Unclaimed Funds. Online access to the county clerk of courts unclaimed funds database are avilable at www.starkcourt.org/cgi-bin/starkcrt/pdfarchive/uf_pdf list.cgi. File is in pdf format. **Other Phone Numbers:** Assessor 309-286-7172; Treasurer 309-286-5901; Elections 309-286-5911; Vital Records 309-286-5911.

Stephenson County

County Recorder, 15 North Galena Ave., Suite 1, Freeport, IL 61032. 815-235-8385.
Will search UCC records. Will not search real estate records. **Other Phone Numbers:** Assessor 815-235-8260; Treasurer 815-235-8264.

Tazewell County

County Recorder, P.O. Box 36, Pekin, IL 61555-0036. 309-477-2210; Fax 309-477-2321.
Will search UCC records. This agency will not do a tax lien search. Will not search real estate records. **Other Phone Numbers:** Assessor 309-477-2275; Treasurer 309-477-2284.

Union County

County Recorder, P.O. Box H, Jonesboro, IL 62952. 618-833-5711; Fax 618-833-8712.
Will search UCC records. This agency will not do a tax lien search. Will not search real estate records. **Other Phone Numbers:** Assessor 618-833-8051; Treasurer 618-833-5621.

Vermilion County

County Recorder, 6 North Vermilion Street, Danville, IL 61832-5877. 217-431-2604; Fax 217-431-7460.
Will search UCC records. This agency will not do a tax lien search. Will not search real estate records. **Other Phone Numbers:** Assessor 217-431-2634; Treasurer 217-431-2631.

Wabash County

County Recorder, P.O. Box 277, Mount Carmel, IL 62863. County Recorder, R/E and UCC Recording 618-262-4561.
Will search UCC records. Tax liens not included in UCC search. RE record owner searches available. **Other Phone Numbers:** Assessor 618-262-4463; Treasurer 618-262-5262.

Warren County

County Recorder, Courthouse, 100 W. Broadway, Monmouth, IL 61462-1797. 309-734-8592; Fax 309-734-7406.
Will search UCC records. UCC search includes tax liens if requested. Will not search real estate records. **Other Phone Numbers:** Assessor 309-734-8561; Treasurer 309-734-8536; Elections 309-734-4612; Vital Records 309-734-8592.

Washington County

County Recorder, County Courthouse, 101 E. St. Louis Street, Nashville, IL 62263-1105. 618-327-4800 x300; Fax 618-327-3582.
Will search UCC records. UCC search includes tax liens if requested. RE owner, mortgage, and property transfer searches available. **Other Phone Numbers:** Assessor 618-327-4800 x325; Treasurer 618-327-4800 x315.

Wayne County

County Recorder, P.O. Box 187, Fairfield, IL 62837. County Recorder, R/E and UCC Recording 618-842-5182; Fax 618-842-6427. http://assessor.wayne.il.us/Index.html
Will search UCC records. UCC search includes tax liens if requested. Will not search real estate records. **Online Access:** Assessor, Property Records. Records on the Wayne Township Assessor Office database are available free online at http://assessor.wayne.il.us/OPID.html. Also, an advanced search feature (fee) is available for subscribers. This includes legal, assessment, sales history, buildings and other information. **Other Phone Numbers:** Assessor 618-842-2582; Treasurer 618-842-5087; Elections 618-842-5182; Vital Records 618-842-5182.

White County

County Recorder, P.O. Box 339, Carmi, IL 62821. 618-382-7211.
Will search UCC records. UCC search includes tax liens if requested. Will not search real estate records. **Other Phone Numbers:** Assessor 618-618-382-721182-2332; Treasurer 618-382-8122; Elections 618-382-7211; Vital Records 618-382-7211.

Whiteside County

County Recorder, 200 East Knox, Morrison, IL 61270. 815-772-5192.
Will search UCC records. This agency will not do a tax lien search. Will not search real estate records. **Other Phone Numbers:** Assessor 815-772-5195; Treasurer 815-772-5196.

Will County

County Recorder, 302 N. Chicago Street, Joliet, IL 60432. 815-740-4637; Fax 815-740-4697.
Will search UCC records. This agency will not do a tax lien search. Will not search real estate records. **Other Phone Numbers:** Assessor 815-740-4648; Treasurer 815-740-4675.

Williamson County

County Recorder, P.O. Box 1108, Marion, IL 62959-1108. 618-997-1301; Fax 618-993-2071.
Will search UCC records. This agency will not do a tax lien search. Will not search real estate records. **Other Phone Numbers:** Assessor 618-997-1301 x164; Treasurer 618-997-1301 x129.

Winnebago County

County Recorder, 404 Elm St., Room 405, Rockford, IL 61101. 815-987-3100; Fax 815-961-3261.
Will search UCC records. UCC search includes tax liens if requested. Will not search real estate records. **Other Phone Numbers:** Assessor 815-987-3025; Treasurer 815-987-3010.

Woodford County

County Recorder, 115 North Main, Courthouse, Room 202, Eureka, IL 61530-1273. County Recorder, R/E and UCC Recording 309-467-2822.
Will search UCC records. This agency will not do a tax lien search. Will not search real estate records. **Other Phone Numbers:** Assessor 309-467-3708; Treasurer 309-467-4621; Elections 309-467-2822; Vital Records 309-467-2822

Illinois County Locator

You will usually be able to find the city name in the City/County Cross Reference below. In that case, it is a simple matter to determine the county from the cross reference. However, only the official US Postal Service city names are included in this index. There are an additional 40,000 place names that people use in their addresses. Therefore, we have also included a ZIP/City Cross Reference immediately following the City/County Cross Reference.

If you know the ZIP Code but the city name does not appear in the City/County Cross Reference index, look up the ZIP Code in the ZIP/City Cross Reference, find the city name, then look up the city name in the City/County Cross Reference. For example, you want to know the county for an address of Menands, NY 12204. There is no "Menands" in the City/County Cross Reference. The ZIP/City Cross Reference shows that ZIP Codes 12201-12288 are for the city of Albany. Looking back in the City/County Cross Reference, Albany is in Albany County.

City/County Cross Reference

ABINGDON (61410) Knox(98), Warren(2)
ADAIR McDonough
ADDIEVILLE Washington
ADDISON Du Page
ADRIAN Hancock
AKIN Franklin
ALBANY Whiteside
ALBERS Clinton
ALBION Edwards
ALDEN McHenry
ALEDO Mercer
ALEXANDER Morgan
ALEXIS (61412) Mercer(80), Warren(20)
ALGONQUIN (60102) McHenry(92), Kane(8)
ALHAMBRA Madison
ALLENDALE (62410) Wabash(98), Lawrence(2)
ALLERTON (61810) Vermilion(68), Douglas(15), Edgar(14), Champaign(3)
ALMA Marion
ALPHA Henry
ALSEY Scott
ALSIP Cook
ALTAMONT (62411) Effingham(98), Fayette(2)
ALTO PASS (62905) Union(78), Jackson(22)
ALTON Madison
ALTONA (61414) Knox(69), Henry(31)
ALVIN Vermilion
AMBOY Lee
AMF OHARE Cook
ANCHOR (61720) McLean(76), Ford(24)
ANCONA Livingston
ANDALUSIA Rock Island
ANDOVER Henry
ANNA Union
ANNAPOLIS (62413) Crawford(94), Clark(6)
ANNAWAN Henry
ANTIOCH Lake
APPLE RIVER Jo Daviess
ARCOLA (61910) Douglas(89), Coles(11)
ARENZVILLE (62611) Cass(79), Morgan(21)
ARGENTA Macon
ARLINGTON Bureau
ARLINGTON HEIGHTS Cook
ARMINGTON (61721) Tazewell(92), Logan(7)
ARMSTRONG Vermilion
AROMA PARK Kankakee
ARROWSMITH McLean
ARTHUR (61911) Douglas(62), Moultrie(34), Coles(3)
ASHKUM Iroquois
ASHLAND (62612) Cass(58), Morgan(41)
ASHLEY (62808) Washington(82), Jefferson(18)
ASHMORE Coles
ASHTON (61006) Lee(69), Ogle(31)

ASSUMPTION (62510) Christian(87), Shelby(13)
ASTORIA Fulton
ATHENS (62613) Menard(93), Logan(5), Sangamon(2)
ATKINSON Henry
ATLANTA (61723) Logan(98), McLean(2)
ATWATER (62511) Macoupin(97), Montgomery(3)
ATWOOD (61913) Douglas(80), Piatt(19)
AUBURN Sangamon
AUGUSTA (62311) Hancock(93), Schuyler(6), Adams(1)
AURORA (60504) Du Page(82), Kane(14), Will(3)
AURORA (60506) Kane(97), Du Page(3)
AURORA Du Page
AURORA Kane
AVA Jackson
AVISTON Clinton
AVON (61415) Fulton(79), Warren(21)
BAILEYVILLE (61007) Ogle(69), Stephenson(31)
BALDWIN Randolph
BARDOLPH McDonough
BARNHILL Wayne
BARRINGTON (60010) Lake(58), Cook(36), McHenry(5)
BARRINGTON Lake
BARRY (62312) Pike(93), Adams(8)
BARSTOW Rock Island
BARTELSO Clinton
BARTLETT (60103) Cook(51), Du Page(49)
BASCO Hancock
BATAVIA Kane
BATCHTOWN Calhoun
BATH Mason
BAYLIS (62314) Pike(90), Adams(9), Brown(2)
BEARDSTOWN Cass
BEASON (62512) Logan(94), De Witt(6)
BEAVERVILLE (60912) Kankakee(53), Iroquois(47)
BECKEMEYER Clinton
BEDFORD PARK Cook
BEECHER (60401) Will(98), Kankakee(2)
BEECHER CITY (62414) Effingham(62), Fayette(28), Shelby(10)
BELKNAP (62908) Massac(55), Johnson(45)
BELLE RIVE (62810) Jefferson(94), Hamilton(4), Wayne(3)
BELLEVILLE St. Clair
BELLFLOWER McLean
BELLMONT Wabash
BELLWOOD Cook
BELVIDERE Boone
BEMENT Piatt
BENLD Macoupin
BENSENVILLE Du Page
BENSON Woodford
BENTON Franklin

BERKELEY Cook
BERWICK Warren
BERWYN Cook
BETHALTO Madison
BETHANY Moultrie
BIG ROCK (60511) Kane(94), De Kalb(5)
BIGGSVILLE Henderson
BINGHAM Fayette
BIRDS Lawrence
BISHOP HILL Henry
BISMARCK Vermilion
BLACKSTONE Livingston
BLANDINSVILLE (61420) McDonough(91), Hancock(9)
BLOOMINGDALE Du Page
BLOOMINGTON McLean
BLUE ISLAND Cook
BLUE MOUND (62513) Macon(76), Christian(24)
BLUFF SPRINGS Cass
BLUFFS (62621) Scott(89), Morgan(11)
BLUFORD (62814) Jefferson(99), Wayne(1)
BOLES Johnson
BOLINGBROOK (60440) Du Page(68), Will(32)
BOLINGBROOK (60490) Du Page(59), Will(41)
BONDVILLE Champaign
BONE GAP Edwards
BONFIELD Kankakee
BONNIE Jefferson
BOODY Macon
BOURBONNAIS Kankakee
BOWEN (62316) Hancock(99), Adams(1)
BRACEVILLE (60407) Will(54), Grundy(45), Kankakee(1)
BRADFORD (61421) Stark(72), Bureau(23), Marshall(5)
BRADLEY Kankakee
BRAIDWOOD Will
BREESE Clinton
BRIDGEPORT Lawrence
BRIDGEVIEW Cook
BRIGHTON (62012) Macoupin(44), Jersey(40), Madison(16)
BRIMFIELD Peoria
BRISTOL Kendall
BROADLANDS (61816) Champaign(97), Douglas(4)
BROCTON (61917) Edgar(97), Douglas(3)
BROOKFIELD Cook
BROOKPORT (62910) Massac(96), Pope(4)
BROUGHTON Hamilton
BROWNING (62624) Schuyler(96), Fulton(5)
BROWNS (62818) Edwards(77), Wabash(23)
BROWNSTOWN Fayette
BRUSSELS Calhoun
BRYANT Fulton

BUCKINGHAM (60917) Kankakee(88), Livingston(12)
BUCKLEY Iroquois
BUCKNER Franklin
BUDA Bureau
BUFFALO Sangamon
BUFFALO GROVE (60089) Lake(50), Cook(50)
BUFFALO PRAIRIE Rock Island
BULPITT Christian
BUNCOMBE (62912) Johnson(55), Union(45)
BUNKER HILL Macoupin
BURBANK Cook
BUREAU Bureau
BURLINGTON Kane
BURNSIDE Hancock
BURNT PRAIRIE (62820) White(83), Wayne(17)
BUSHNELL McDonough
BUTLER Montgomery
BYRON Ogle
CABERY (60919) Ford(43), Livingston(37), Kankakee(21)
CACHE Alexander
CAIRO Alexander
CALEDONIA (61011) Boone(72), Winnebago(29)
CALHOUN Richland
CALUMET CITY Cook
CAMARGO Douglas
CAMBRIA Williamson
CAMBRIDGE Henry
CAMDEN Schuyler
CAMERON Warren
CAMP GROVE Marshall
CAMP POINT Adams
CAMPBELL HILL (62916) Jackson(77), Randolph(14), Perry(9)
CAMPUS Livingston
CANTON Fulton
CANTRALL Sangamon
CAPRON Boone
CARBON CLIFF Rock Island
CARBONDALE (62901) Jackson(89), Williamson(11)
CARBONDALE Jackson
CARLINVILLE Macoupin
CARLOCK (61725) McLean(76), Woodford(24)
CARLYLE Clinton
CARMAN Henderson
CARMI White
CAROL STREAM Du Page
CARPENTERSVILLE Kane
CARRIER MILLS (62917) Saline(89), Williamson(11)
CARROLLTON Greene
CARTERVILLE Williamson
CARTHAGE Hancock
CARY (60013) McHenry(95), Lake(5)
CASEY (62420) Clark(83), Cumberland(15), Coles(1)

CASEYVILLE St. Clair
CASTLETON Stark
CATLIN Vermilion
CAVE IN ROCK Hardin
CEDAR POINT La Salle
CEDARVILLE Stephenson
CENTRALIA (62801) Marion(68),
    Clinton(21), Washington(7), Jefferson(4)
CERRO GORDO Piatt
CHADWICK (61014) Carroll(82),
    Whiteside(18)
CHAMBERSBURG (62323) Pike(92),
    Brown(8)
CHAMPAIGN Champaign
CHANA Ogle
CHANDLERVILLE (62627) Cass(52),
    Mason(48)
CHANNAHON Will
CHAPIN (62628) Morgan(93), Scott(7)
CHARLESTON Coles
CHATHAM Sangamon
CHATSWORTH (60921) Livingston(99),
    Ford(1)
CHEBANSE (60922) Kankakee(64),
    Iroquois(36)
CHENOA (61726) McLean(94),
    Livingston(6)
CHERRY Bureau
CHERRY VALLEY (61016) Winnebago(89),
    Boone(11)
CHESTER Randolph
CHESTERFIELD (62630) Macoupin(96),
    Greene(3), Jersey(1)
CHESTNUT Logan
CHICAGO Cook
CHICAGO HEIGHTS Cook
CHICAGO RIDGE Cook
CHILLICOTHE Peoria
CHRISMAN Edgar
CHRISTOPHER Franklin
CICERO Cook
CISCO (61830) Piatt(87), Macon(13)
CISNE Wayne
CISSNA PARK Iroquois
CLARE De Kalb
CLAREMONT (62421) Richland(95),
    Crawford(4), Lawrence(1)
CLARENDON HILLS Du Page
CLAY (62824) Clay(93), Wayne(7)
CLAYTON (62324) Adams(92), Brown(8)
CLAYTONVILLE Iroquois
CLIFTON Iroquois
CLINTON De Witt
COAL CITY Grundy
COAL VALLEY (61240) Rock Island(78),
    Henry(22)
COATSBURG Adams
COBDEN Union
COELLO Franklin
COFFEEN Montgomery
COLCHESTER (62326) McDonough(98),
    Hancock(2)
COLETA Whiteside
COLFAX McLean
COLLINSVILLE (62234) Madison(91), St.
    Clair(9)
COLLISON Vermilion
COLMAR McDonough
COLONA Henry
COLP Williamson
COLUMBIA (62236) Monroe(94), St.
    Clair(6)
COLUSA Hancock
COMPTON Lee
CONCORD Morgan
CONGERVILLE Woodford
COOKSVILLE McLean
CORDOVA Rock Island
CORNELL Livingston
CORNLAND Logan
CORTLAND De Kalb
COTTAGE HILLS Madison

COULTERVILLE (62237) Randolph(44),
    Washington(30), Perry(26)
COUNTRY CLUB HILLS Cook
COWDEN (62422) Shelby(76), Fayette(23),
    Fulton(1)
CREAL SPRINGS (62922) Williamson(72),
    Johnson(28)
CRESCENT CITY Iroquois
CRESTON Ogle
CRETE Will
CREVE COEUR Tazewell
CROPSEY (61731) McLean(63), Ford(36),
    Livingston(2)
CROSSVILLE White
CRYSTAL LAKE McHenry
CUBA Fulton
CULLOM (60929) Livingston(88), Ford(12)
CUTLER (62238) Perry(97), Randolph(3)
CYPRESS (62923) Johnson(89),
    Pulaski(9), Union(2)
DAHINDA Knox
DAHLGREN (62828) Hamilton(97),
    Wayne(3)
DAKOTA Stephenson
DALE Hamilton
DALLAS CITY (62330) Hancock(92),
    Henderson(8)
DALTON CITY (61925) Moultrie(62),
    Macon(38)
DALZELL Bureau
DANA (61321) La Salle(87), Livingston(6),
    Woodford(5), Marshall(3)
DANFORTH Iroquois
DANVERS (61732) McLean(62),
    Tazewell(38)
DANVILLE Vermilion
DARIEN Du Page
DAVIS (61019) Stephenson(60),
    Winnebago(40)
DAVIS JUNCTION (61020) Ogle(91),
    Winnebago(9)
DAWSON Sangamon
DE KALB De Kalb
DE LAND (61839) Vermilion(54), Piatt(47)
DE SOTO (62924) Jackson(80),
    Williamson(20)
DECATUR Macon
DEER CREEK Tazewell
DEER GROVE Whiteside
DEERE CO GROUP CLAIMS Rock Island
DEERFIELD (60015) Lake(95), Cook(6)
DEERFIELD Cook
DELAVAN Tazewell
DENNISON (62423) Clark(87), Edgar(13)
DEPUE Bureau
DES PLAINES Cook
DEWEY (61840) Champaign(97), Ford(3)
DEWITT De Witt
DIETERICH (62424) Effingham(90),
    Jasper(11)
DIVERNON Sangamon
DIX (62830) Jefferson(94), Marion(6)
DIXON (61021) Lee(90), Ogle(10)
DOLTON Cook
DONGOLA (62926) Union(91), Pulaski(8)
DONNELLSON (62019) Montgomery(75),
    Bond(25)
DONOVAN Iroquois
DORSEY (62021) Madison(99),
    Macoupin(2)
DOVER Bureau
DOW Jersey
DOWELL Jackson
DOWNERS GROVE Du Page
DOWNS McLean
DU BOIS (62831) Washington(91), Perry(8)
DU QUOIN (62832) Perry(97), Jackson(3)
DUNDAS (62425) Richland(87), Jasper(13)
DUNDEE (60118) Kane(98), Cook(2)
DUNFERMLINE Fulton
DUNLAP Peoria
DUPO St. Clair

DURAND Winnebago
DWIGHT (60420) Livingston(93), Grundy(7)
EAGARVILLE Macoupin
EARLVILLE (60518) La Salle(82), De
    Kalb(15), Lee(3)
EAST ALTON Madison
EAST CARONDELET (62240) St. Clair(98),
    Monroe(2)
EAST DUBUQUE Jo Daviess
EAST GALESBURG Knox
EAST LYNN Vermilion
EAST MOLINE Rock Island
EAST PEORIA (61611) Tazewell(87),
    Woodford(14)
EAST SAINT LOUIS St. Clair
EASTON Mason
EDDYVILLE Pope
EDELSTEIN (61526) Peoria(92),
    Marshall(6), Stark(2)
EDGEWOOD (62426) Effingham(68),
    Clay(23), Fayette(10)
EDINBURG Christian
EDWARDS Peoria
EDWARDSVILLE Madison
EFFINGHAM Effingham
EL PASO (61738) Woodford(96),
    McLean(4)
ELBURN Kane
ELCO Alexander
ELDENA Lee
ELDORADO (62930) Saline(98), Gallatin(2)
ELDRED Greene
ELEROY Stephenson
ELGIN (60120) Kane(55), Cook(45)
ELGIN Kane
ELIZABETH (61028) Jo Daviess(98),
    Carroll(2)
ELIZABETHTOWN (62931) Hardin(80),
    Gallatin(20)
ELK GROVE VILLAGE (60007) Cook(96),
    Du Page(4)
ELK GROVE VILLAGE Cook
ELKHART Logan
ELKVILLE Jackson
ELLERY (62833) Edwards(57), Wayne(43)
ELLIOTT Ford
ELLIS GROVE Randolph
ELLISVILLE Fulton
ELLSWORTH McLean
ELMHURST Du Page
ELMWOOD (61529) Peoria(97), Knox(3)
ELMWOOD PARK Cook
ELSAH Jersey
ELVASTON Hancock
ELWIN Macon
ELWOOD Will
EMDEN (62635) Tazewell(58), Logan(42)
EMINGTON Livingston
EMMA White
ENERGY Williamson
ENFIELD (62835) White(94), Hamilton(6)
EOLA Du Page
EQUALITY (62934) Gallatin(69), Saline(31)
ERIE (61250) Whiteside(94), Henry(6)
ESMOND (60129) Ogle(73), De Kalb(27)
ESSEX (60935) Kankakee(98), Will(2)
EUREKA Woodford
EVANSTON Cook
EVANSVILLE Randolph
EVERGREEN PARK Cook
EWING (62836) Franklin(98), Jefferson(2)
FAIRBURY (61739) Livingston(90),
    McLean(10)
FAIRFIELD Wayne
FAIRMOUNT Vermilion
FAIRVIEW Fulton
FAIRVIEW HEIGHTS St. Clair
FARINA (62838) Fayette(53), Clay(24),
    Marion(22), Effingham(1)
FARMER CITY (61842) De Witt(91),
    McLean(9)
FARMERSVILLE Montgomery

FARMINGTON (61531) Fulton(92),
    Peoria(5), Knox(2)
FENTON (61251) Whiteside(99), Rock
    Island(2)
FERRIS Hancock
FIATT Fulton
FIDELITY Jersey
FIELDON (62031) Jersey(94), Greene(6)
FILLMORE Montgomery
FINDLAY Shelby
FISHER (61843) Champaign(93),
    McLean(7)
FITHIAN Vermilion
FLANAGAN Livingston
FLAT ROCK (62427) Crawford(95),
    Lawrence(5)
FLORA Clay
FLOSSMOOR Cook
FOOSLAND (61845) Champaign(77),
    Ford(15), McLean(8)
FOREST CITY Mason
FOREST PARK Cook
FORREST Livingston
FORRESTON Ogle
FORSYTH Macon
FORT SHERIDAN Lake
FOWLER Adams
FOX LAKE Lake
FOX RIVER GROVE McHenry
FOX VALLEY Du Page
FRANKFORT Will
FRANKFORT HEIGHTS Franklin
FRANKLIN (62638) Morgan(99),
    Macoupin(1)
FRANKLIN GROVE (61031) Lee(95),
    Ogle(5)
FRANKLIN PARK Cook
FREDERICK Schuyler
FREEBURG St. Clair
FREEMAN SPUR Williamson
FREEPORT Stephenson
FULTON Whiteside
FULTS Monroe
GALATIA (62935) Saline(98), Hamilton(2)
GALATIA Saline
GALENA Jo Daviess
GALESBURG (61401) Knox(99), Warren(1)
GALESBURG Knox
GALT Whiteside
GALVA (61434) Henry(98), Knox(2)
GARDEN PRAIRIE (61038) Boone(85),
    McHenry(15)
GARDNER Grundy
GAYS (61928) Moultrie(61), Coles(26),
    Shelby(13)
GEFF Wayne
GENESEO Henry
GENEVA Kane
GENOA De Kalb
GEORGETOWN Vermilion
GERLAW Warren
GERMAN VALLEY (61039)
    Stephenson(61), Ogle(39)
GERMANTOWN Clinton
GIBSON CITY (60936) Ford(99),
    Champaign(1)
GIFFORD Champaign
GILBERTS Kane
GILLESPIE Macoupin
GILMAN Iroquois
GILSON Knox
GIRARD (62640) Macoupin(99),
    Montgomery(1)
GLADSTONE Henderson
GLASFORD (61533) Peoria(73), Fulton(27)
GLEN CARBON Madison
GLEN ELLYN Du Page
GLENARM Sangamon
GLENCOE Cook
GLENDALE HEIGHTS Du Page
GLENVIEW Cook
GLENVIEW NAS Cook

GLENWOOD Cook
GODFREY (62035) Madison(95), Jersey(5)
GOLCONDA (62938) Pope(86), Hardin(7), Massac(7)
GOLDEN Adams
GOLDEN EAGLE Calhoun
GOLDEN GATE Wayne
GOLF Cook
GOOD HOPE McDonough
GOODFIELD Woodford
GOODWINE Iroquois
GOREVILLE (62939) Johnson(92), Williamson(5), Union(3)
GORHAM Jackson
GRAFTON Jersey
GRAND CHAIN (62941) Pulaski(56), Massac(44)
GRAND RIDGE La Salle
GRAND TOWER Jackson
GRANITE CITY Madison
GRANT PARK (60940) Kankakee(97), Will(3)
GRANTSBURG (62943) Johnson(78), Massac(18), Pope(4)
GRANVILLE (61326) Putnam(88), La Salle(12)
GRAYMONT Livingston
GRAYSLAKE Lake
GRAYVILLE (62844) White(59), Edwards(41)
GREAT LAKES Lake
GREEN VALLEY (99999) Tazewell(99), Mason(1)
GREENFIELD Greene
GREENUP Cumberland
GREENVIEW Menard
GREENVILLE Bond
GRIDLEY (61744) McLean(90), Livingston(9)
GRIGGSVILLE Pike
GROVELAND Tazewell
GURNEE Lake
HAGARSTOWN Fayette
HAMBURG Calhoun
HAMEL Madison
HAMILTON Hancock
HAMLETSBURG Pope
HAMMOND (61929) Piatt(98), Moultrie(2)
HAMPSHIRE (99999) Kane(99), De Kalb(1)
HAMPTON Rock Island
HANNA CITY Peoria
HANOVER Jo Daviess
HARDIN Calhoun
HARMON (61042) Lee(99), Whiteside(1)
HARRISBURG Saline
HARRISTOWN Macon
HARTFORD Madison
HARTSBURG (62643) Montgomery(62), Logan(38)
HARVARD McHenry
HARVEL (62538) Montgomery(82), Christian(19)
HARVEY Cook
HAVANA (62644) Mason(95), Fulton(5)
HAZEL CREST Cook
HEBRON McHenry
HECKER Monroe
HENDERSON Knox
HENNEPIN Putnam
HENNING Vermilion
HENRY Marshall
HERALD White
HEROD (62947) Saline(44), Hardin(32), Pope(24)
HERRICK (62431) Shelby(69), Fayette(31)
HERRIN Williamson
HERSCHER (60941) Kankakee(96), Iroquois(3), Ford(2)
HETTICK (62649) Macoupin(99), Greene(1)
HEYWORTH (61745) McLean(97), De Witt(3)

HICKORY HILLS Cook
HIDALGO Jasper
HIGHLAND (62249) Madison(95), Clinton(4)
HIGHLAND PARK Lake
HIGHWOOD Lake
HILLSBORO Montgomery
HILLSDALE Rock Island
HILLSIDE Cook
HILLVIEW Greene
HINCKLEY De Kalb
HINDSBORO (61930) Douglas(84), Coles(16)
HINES Cook
HINSDALE (60521) Du Page(89), Cook(11)
HINSDALE (60523) Du Page(98), Cook(2)
HINSDALE Du Page
HOFFMAN Clinton
HOFFMAN ESTATES Cook
HOLCOMB Ogle
HOMER (61849) Champaign(79), Vermilion(21)
HOMETOWN Cook
HOMEWOOD Cook
HOOPESTON (60942) Vermilion(92), Iroquois(9)
HOOPPOLE Henry
HOPEDALE Tazewell
HOPKINS PARK Kankakee
HOYLETON Washington
HUDSON (61748) McLean(98), Woodford(2)
HUEY Clinton
HULL (62343) Pike(94), Adams(6)
HUMBOLDT Coles
HUME Edgar
HUNTLEY (60142) McHenry(80), Kane(20)
HUNTSVILLE Schuyler
HURST Williamson
HUTSONVILLE Crawford
ILLINOIS CITY (61259) Rock Island(98), Mercer(2)
ILLIOPOLIS (62539) Sangamon(93), Macon(6)
INA (62846) Jefferson(96), Franklin(4)
INDIANOLA (61850) Vermilion(98), Edgar(2)
INDUSTRY (61440) McDonough(98), Schuyler(2)
INGLESIDE Lake
INGRAHAM (62434) Jasper(79), Clay(21)
IOLA Clay
IPAVA Fulton
IROQUOIS Iroquois
IRVING Montgomery
IRVINGTON Washington
ISLAND LAKE (60042) Lake(56), McHenry(44)
ITASCA Du Page
IUKA Marion
IVESDALE (61851) Champaign(82), Piatt(14), Douglas(5)
JACKSONVILLE Morgan
JACOB Jackson
JANESVILLE Cumberland
JEFFERSON BANK Peoria
JERSEYVILLE Jersey
JEWETT (62436) Jasper(60), Cumberland(40)
JOHNSONVILLE Wayne
JOHNSTON CITY Williamson
JOLIET Will
JONESBORO Union
JOPPA Massac
JOY (61260) Mercer(93), Rock Island(7)
JUNCTION Gallatin
JUSTICE Cook
KAMPSVILLE (62053) Calhoun(97), Pike(3)
KANE (62054) Greene(86), Jersey(14)
KANEVILLE Kane
KANKAKEE Kankakee

KANSAS (61933) Edgar(84), Clark(13), Coles(2)
KARBERS RIDGE Hardin
KARNAK (62956) Massac(57), Pulaski(43)
KASBEER Bureau
KEENES (62851) Wayne(65), Jefferson(27), Marion(8)
KEENSBURG Wabash
KEITHSBURG (61442) Mercer(94), Henderson(6)
KELL (62853) Marion(98), Jefferson(2)
KEMPTON (60946) Ford(77), Livingston(23)
KENILWORTH Cook
KENNEY (61749) De Witt(79), Logan(22)
KENT (61044) Stephenson(72), Jo Daviess(28)
KEWANEE Henry
KEYESPORT (62253) Bond(54), Clinton(42), Fayette(4)
KILBOURNE Mason
KINCAID Christian
KINDERHOOK Pike
KINGS Ogle
KINGSTON (60145) De Kalb(93), Boone(7)
KINGSTON MINES Peoria
KINMUNDY (62854) Marion(98), Clay(1), Fayette(1)
KINSMAN (60437) Grundy(98), La Salle(3)
KIRKLAND (60146) De Kalb(90), Boone(8), Ogle(1), Winnebago(1)
KIRKWOOD (61447) Warren(91), Henderson(9)
KNOXVILLE Knox
LA FAYETTE (61449) Stark(79), Knox(21)
LA GRANGE Cook
LA GRANGE PARK Cook
LA HARPE (61450) Hancock(61), McDonough(37), Henderson(2)
LA MOILLE (61330) Bureau(70), Lee(30)
LA PLACE Piatt
LA PRAIRIE (62346) Adams(73), Schuyler(24), Hancock(3)
LA ROSE Marshall
LA SALLE La Salle
LACON Marshall
LADD Bureau
LAFOX Kane
LAKE BLUFF Lake
LAKE FOREST Lake
LAKE FORK Logan
LAKE VILLA Lake
LAKE ZURICH Lake
LAKEWOOD Shelby
LANARK Carroll
LANCASTER Wabash
LANE De Witt
LANSING Cook
LATHAM (62543) Logan(72), Macon(28)
LAURA (61451) Peoria(90), Stark(10)
LAWNDALE Logan
LAWRENCEVILLE Lawrence
LE ROY McLean
LEAF RIVER (61047) Ogle(97), Stephenson(2), Winnebago(2)
LEBANON St. Clair
LEE (60530) De Kalb(55), Lee(45)
LEE CENTER Lee
LELAND (60531) La Salle(67), De Kalb(33)
LEMONT (60439) Du Page(73), Cook(24), Will(3)
LENA (61048) Stephenson(97), Jo Daviess(3)
LENZBURG (62255) St. Clair(92), Washington(8)
LEONORE La Salle
LERNA (62440) Coles(71), Cumberland(29)
LEWISTOWN Fulton
LEXINGTON McLean
LIBERTY Adams
LIBERTYVILLE Lake

LIMA Adams
LINCOLN Logan
LINCOLN'S NEW SALEM Menard
LINCOLNSHIRE Lake
LINDENWOOD Ogle
LISLE Du Page
LITCHFIELD (62056) Montgomery(98), Macoupin(2)
LITERBERRY Morgan
LITTLE YORK (61453) Warren(87), Henderson(13)
LITTLETON (61452) Schuyler(83), McDonough(17)
LIVERPOOL Fulton
LIVINGSTON Madison
LOAMI Sangamon
LOCKPORT Will
LODA (60948) Iroquois(89), Ford(11)
LOGAN Franklin
LOMAX Henderson
LOMBARD Du Page
LONDON MILLS Fulton
LONG GROVE Lake
LONG POINT Livingston
LONGVIEW (61852) Champaign(87), Douglas(13)
LOOGOOTEE Fayette
LORAINE (62349) Adams(88), Hancock(12)
LOSTANT (61334) La Salle(96), Putnam(4)
LOUISVILLE (62858) Clay(98), Effingham(2)
LOVEJOY St. Clair
LOVES PARK Winnebago
LOVINGTON (61937) Moultrie(97), Piatt(3)
LOWDER Sangamon
LOWPOINT Woodford
LUDLOW (60949) Champaign(90), Ford(10)
LYNDON Whiteside
LYNN CENTER (61262) Henry(92), Mercer(8)
LYONS Cook
MACEDONIA (62860) Franklin(89), Hamilton(11)
MACHESNEY PARK Winnebago
MACKINAW Tazewell
MACOMB McDonough
MACON Macon
MADISON Madison
MAEYSTOWN Monroe
MAGNOLIA (61336) Putnam(59), Marshall(33), La Salle(9)
MAHOMET (61853) Champaign(98), Piatt(2)
MAKANDA (62958) Jackson(72), Williamson(15), Union(13)
MALDEN Bureau
MALTA De Kalb
MANCHESTER Scott
MANHATTAN Will
MANITO (61546) Mason(90), Tazewell(10)
MANLIUS Bureau
MANSFIELD Piatt
MANTENO (60950) Kankakee(98), Will(2)
MAPLE PARK (60151) Kane(88), De Kalb(12)
MAPLETON Peoria
MAQUON Knox
MARENGO McHenry
MARIETTA (61459) Fulton(60), McDonough(40)
MARINE Madison
MARION Williamson
MARISSA (62257) St. Clair(70), Washington(28), Randolph(2)
MARK Putnam
MAROA Macon
MARSEILLES La Salle
MARSHALL (62441) Clark(98), Edgar(2)
MARTINSVILLE (62442) Clark(99), Crawford(1)

MARTINTON Iroquois
MARYVILLE Madison
MASCOUTAH St. Clair
MASON (62443) Effingham(95), Clay(5)
MASON CITY Mason
MATHERVILLE Mercer
MATTESON Cook
MATTOON Coles
MAUNIE White
MAYWOOD Cook
MAZON Grundy
MC CLURE (62957) Alexander(65), Union(35)
MC CONNELL Stephenson
MC HENRY (60050) McHenry(96), Lake(4)
MC HENRY McHenry
MC LEAN (61754) McLean(95), Logan(5)
MC LEANSBORO Hamilton
MC NABB Putnam
MECHANICSBURG (62545) Sangamon(57), Christian(43)
MEDIA (61460) Henderson(93), Warren(7)
MEDINAH Du Page
MEDORA Jersey
MELROSE PARK Cook
MELVIN (60952) Ford(94), Livingston(6)
MENARD Randolph
MENDON (62351) Adams(77), Hancock(23)
MENDOTA (61342) La Salle(97), Bureau(2), Lee(1)
MEREDOSIA (62665) Morgan(91), Scott(9)
MERNA McLean
METAMORA Woodford
METCALF Edgar
METROPOLIS Massac
MICHAEL Calhoun
MIDDLETOWN (62666) Logan(84), Menard(16)
MIDLOTHIAN Cook
MILAN Rock Island
MILFORD Iroquois
MILL SHOALS White
MILLBROOK Kendall
MILLCREEK Union
MILLEDGEVILLE (61051) Carroll(90), Ogle(8), Whiteside(2)
MILLER CITY Alexander
MILLINGTON Kendall
MILLSTADT St. Clair
MILMINE Piatt
MILTON Pike
MINERAL (61344) Henry(65), Bureau(35)
MINIER Tazewell
MINONK (61760) Woodford(98), Marshall(2)
MINOOKA (60447) Grundy(43), Kendall(36), Will(21)
MOBIL OIL CREDIT CORP Du Page
MODE Shelby
MODESTO (62667) Macoupin(91), Morgan(9)
MODOC Randolph
MOKENA Will
MOLINE Rock Island
MOMENCE Kankakee
MONEE (60449) Will(99), Cook(1)
MONMOUTH Warren
MONROE CENTER (61052) Ogle(92), Winnebago(5), De Kalb(4)
MONTGOMERY (60538) Kane(53), Kendall(47)
MONTGOMERY WARD Du Page
MONTICELLO Piatt
MONTROSE (62445) Jasper(58), Cumberland(37), Effingham(5)
MOOSEHEART Kane
MORO Madison
MORRIS Grundy
MORRISON Whiteside
MORRISONVILLE (62546) Christian(89), Montgomery(11)

MORTON Tazewell
MORTON GROVE Cook
MOSSVILLE Peoria
MOUND CITY Pulaski
MOUNDS Pulaski
MOUNT AUBURN (62547) Christian(98), Macon(2)
MOUNT CARMEL Wabash
MOUNT CARROLL (61053) Carroll(90), Jo Daviess(10)
MOUNT ERIE Wayne
MOUNT MORRIS Ogle
MOUNT OLIVE (62069) Macoupin(97), Montgomery(3)
MOUNT PROSPECT Cook
MOUNT PULASKI Logan
MOUNT STERLING Brown
MOUNT VERNON Jefferson
MOWEAQUA Christian
MOZIER Calhoun
MT ZION Macon
MUDDY Saline
MULBERRY GROVE (62262) Bond(73), Fayette(23), Montgomery(3)
MULKEYTOWN Franklin
MUNCIE Vermilion
MUNDELEIN Lake
MURDOCK Douglas
MURPHYSBORO Jackson
MURRAYVILLE (62668) Morgan(95), Scott(5)
NACHUSA Lee
NAPERVILLE (60564) Will(80), Du Page(21)
NAPERVILLE (60565) Du Page(66), Will(34)
NAPERVILLE Du Page
NASHVILLE Washington
NASON Jefferson
NATIONAL STOCK YARDS St. Clair
NAUVOO Hancock
NEBO (62355) Pike(70), Calhoun(30)
NELSON Lee
NEOGA (62447) Cumberland(88), Shelby(12)
NEPONSET (61345) Bureau(95), Stark(5)
NEW ATHENS (62264) St. Clair(98), Monroe(2)
NEW BADEN (62265) Clinton(92), St. Clair(8)
NEW BEDFORD Bureau
NEW BERLIN Sangamon
NEW BOSTON Mercer
NEW BURNSIDE (62967) Johnson(86), Williamson(14)
NEW CANTON Pike
NEW DOUGLAS (62074) Madison(94), Montgomery(4), Bond(1)
NEW HAVEN (62867) Gallatin(60), White(40)
NEW HOLLAND (62671) Logan(92), Mason(8)
NEW LENOX Will
NEW MEMPHIS Clinton
NEW SALEM Pike
NEW WINDSOR (61465) Mercer(97), Henry(3)
NEWARK (60541) Kendall(90), Grundy(8), La Salle(3)
NEWMAN (61942) Douglas(93), Edgar(7)
NEWTON (62448) Jasper(98), Richland(2)
NIANTIC Macon
NILES Cook
NILWOOD Macoupin
NIOTA Hancock
NOBLE (62868) Richland(98), Wayne(2)
NOKOMIS (62075) Montgomery(96), Christian(4)
NORA Jo Daviess
NORMAL McLean
NORRIS Fulton

NORRIS CITY (62869) White(94), Gallatin(4), Hamilton(2)
NORTH AURORA Kane
NORTH CHICAGO Lake
NORTH HENDERSON (61466) Mercer(97), Warren(3)
NORTHBROOK Cook
O FALLON St. Clair
OAK FOREST Cook
OAK LAWN Cook
OAK PARK Cook
OAKDALE (62268) Washington(95), Perry(5)
OAKFORD (62673) Cass(52), Menard(48)
OAKLAND (61943) Coles(84), Douglas(11), Edgar(5)
OAKLEY Macon
OAKWOOD Vermilion
OBLONG (62449) Crawford(90), Jasper(9)
OCONEE (62553) Shelby(61), Christian(25), Montgomery(14)
ODELL Livingston
ODIN Marion
OGDEN (61859) Champaign(86), Vermilion(14)
OGLESBY La Salle
OHIO (61349) Bureau(38), Cass(31), Lee(31)
OHLMAN Montgomery
OKAWVILLE Washington
OLIVE BRANCH Alexander
OLMSTED Pulaski
OLNEY Richland
OLYMPIA FIELDS Cook
OMAHA Gallatin
ONARGA Iroquois
ONEIDA Knox
OPDYKE Jefferson
OPHEIM Henry
OQUAWKA Henderson
ORANGEVILLE Stephenson
ORAVILLE Jackson
OREANA Macon
OREGON Ogle
ORIENT Franklin
ORION (61273) Henry(64), Rock Island(36)
ORLAND PARK (60467) Cook(91), Will(9)
ORLAND PARK Cook
OSCO Henry
OSWEGO Kendall
OTTAWA La Salle
OWANECO Christian
OZARK (62972) Johnson(96), Williamson(2), Pope(1)
PALATINE (60074) Cook(97), Lake(3)
PALATINE Cook
PALESTINE Crawford
PALMER Christian
PALMYRA Macoupin
PALOMA Adams
PALOS HEIGHTS Cook
PALOS HILLS Cook
PALOS PARK Cook
PANA (62557) Christian(95), Shelby(4), Montgomery(2)
PANAMA Montgomery
PAPINEAU Iroquois
PARIS Edgar
PARK FOREST (60466) Cook(56), Will(45)
PARK RIDGE Cook
PARKERSBURG Richland
PATOKA (62875) Marion(95), Fayette(5)
PATTERSON Greene
PAW PAW Lee
PAWNEE (62558) Sangamon(81), Christian(14), Montgomery(4)
PAXTON (60957) Ford(96), Champaign(3)
PAYSON Adams
PEARL (62361) Pike(98), Calhoun(3)
PEARL CITY (61062) Stephenson(93), Jo Daviess(6)

PECATONICA (61063) Winnebago(90), Stephenson(10)
PEKIN Tazewell
PENFIELD (61862) Champaign(81), Vermilion(19)
PEORIA Peoria
PEOTONE (60468) Will(96), Kankakee(4)
PERCY (62272) Randolph(82), Perry(18)
PERKS Pulaski
PERRY Pike
PERU (61354) La Salle(98), Bureau(2)
PESOTUM (61863) Champaign(95), Douglas(5)
PETERSBURG Menard
PHILO Champaign
PIASA (62079) Macoupin(81), Jersey(19)
PIERRON Bond
PINCKNEYVILLE Perry
PIPER CITY (60959) Ford(93), Livingston(7)
PITTSBURG Williamson
PITTSFIELD Pike
PLAINFIELD Will
PLAINVIEW Macoupin
PLAINVILLE (62365) Adams(98), Pike(2)
PLANO Kendall
PLATO CENTER Kane
PLEASANT HILL (62366) Pike(99), Calhoun(1)
PLEASANT PLAINS Sangamon
PLYMOUTH (62367) Hancock(50), McDonough(43), Schuyler(8)
POCAHONTAS (62275) Madison(44), Bond(39), Clinton(17)
POLO (61064) Ogle(98), Whiteside(1)
POMONA Jackson
PONTIAC Livingston
POPLAR GROVE Boone
PORT BYRON Rock Island
POSEN Cook
POTOMAC Vermilion
PRAIRIE CITY McDonough
PRAIRIE DU ROCHER (62277) Randolph(57), Monroe(43)
PREEMPTION Mercer
PRINCETON Bureau
PRINCEVILLE (61559) Peoria(95), Stark(5)
PROPHETSTOWN (61277) Whiteside(78), Henry(22)
PROSPECT HEIGHTS Cook
PULASKI Pulaski
PUTNAM (61560) Putnam(92), Bureau(6), Marshall(1)
QUINCY Adams
RADOM Washington
RALEIGH Saline
RAMSEY (62080) Fayette(92), Montgomery(7), Shelby(1)
RANKIN (60960) Vermilion(71), Ford(23), Iroquois(3), Champaign(3)
RANSOM (60470) La Salle(88), Grundy(7), Livingston(5)
RANTOUL Champaign
RAPIDS CITY Rock Island
RARITAN Henderson
RAYMOND (62560) Montgomery(97), Macoupin(3)
RED BUD (62278) Randolph(69), Monroe(32)
REDDICK (60961) Kankakee(81), Livingston(15), Grundy(4)
REDMON Edgar
RENAULT Monroe
REYNOLDS (61279) Rock Island(73), Mercer(27)
RICHMOND McHenry
RICHTON PARK Cook
RICHVIEW (62877) Washington(98), Jefferson(3)
RIDGE FARM (61870) Vermilion(92), Edgar(8)
RIDGWAY Gallatin

RIDOTT Stephenson
RINARD Wayne
RINGWOOD McHenry
RIO (61472) Knox(98), Mercer(2)
RIVER FOREST Cook
RIVER GROVE Cook
RIVERDALE Cook
RIVERSIDE Cook
RIVERTON Sangamon
ROANOKE Woodford
ROBBINS Cook
ROBERTS (60962) Ford(95), Livingston(5)
ROBINSON Crawford
ROCHELLE (61068) Ogle(96), Lee(3)
ROCHESTER (62563) Sangamon(81),
   Christian(19)
ROCK CITY Stephenson
ROCK FALLS (61071) Whiteside(99),
   Lee(1)
ROCK ISLAND Rock Island
ROCKBRIDGE Greene
ROCKFORD (61102) Winnebago(98),
   Ogle(2)
ROCKFORD (61107) Winnebago(98),
   Boone(2)
ROCKFORD (61114) Winnebago(95),
   Boone(5)
ROCKFORD Winnebago
ROCKPORT Pike
ROCKTON Winnebago
ROCKWOOD (62280) Jackson(59),
   Randolph(42)
ROLLING MEADOWS Cook
ROME Peoria
ROMEOVILLE Will
ROODHOUSE (62082) Greene(94),
   Scott(5)
ROSAMOND (62083) Christian(58),
   Montgomery(43)
ROSCOE (61073) Winnebago(98),
   Boone(2)
ROSELLE (60172) Du Page(78), Cook(22)
ROSEVILLE (61473) McDonough(66),
   Warren(34)
ROSICLARE Hardin
ROSSVILLE Vermilion
ROUND LAKE Lake
ROXANA Madison
ROYAL Champaign
ROYALTON Franklin
RUSHVILLE Schuyler
RUSSELL Lake
RUTLAND (61358) Marshall(51), La
   Salle(49)
SADORUS (61872) Champaign(91),
   Douglas(10)
SAILOR SPRINGS Clay
SAINT ANNE (60964) Kankakee(94),
   Iroquois(6)
SAINT AUGUSTINE (61474) Knox(93),
   Warren(6), Fulton(1)
SAINT CHARLES Kane
SAINT DAVID Fulton
SAINT ELMO (62458) Fayette(94),
   Effingham(6)
SAINT FRANCISVILLE (62460)
   Lawrence(95), Wabash(5)
SAINT JACOB Madison
SAINT JOSEPH Champaign
SAINT LIBORY St. Clair
SAINT PETER Fayette
SAINTE MARIE Jasper
SALEM Marion
SAN JOSE (62682) Mason(71), Logan(16),
   Tazewell(13)
SANDOVAL (62882) Marion(92), Clinton(8)
SANDWICH (60548) De Kalb(78), La
   Salle(19), Kendall(4)
SAUNEMIN Livingston
SAVANNA (61074) Carroll(98), Jo
   Daviess(2)
SAVOY Champaign

SAWYERVILLE Macoupin
SAYBROOK McLean
SCALES MOUND Jo Daviess
SCHAUMBURG Cook
SCHELLER (62883) Jefferson(62),
   Franklin(31), Perry(7)
SCHILLER PARK Cook
SCIOTA (61475) McDonough(89),
   Warren(11)
SCIOTO MILLS Stephenson
SCOTT AIR FORCE BASE St. Clair
SCOTTVILLE Macoupin
SEATON (61476) Mercer(87),
   Henderson(11), Warren(2)
SEATONVILLE Bureau
SECOR Woodford
SENECA (61360) La Salle(85), Grundy(15)
SERENA La Salle
SESSER Franklin
SEWARD Winnebago
SEYMOUR Champaign
SHABBONA De Kalb
SHANNON (61078) Carroll(79),
   Stephenson(14), Ogle(7)
SHATTUC (62283) Clinton(99), Marion(1)
SHAWNEETOWN Gallatin
SHEFFIELD (61361) Henry(59),
   Bureau(41)
SHELBYVILLE Shelby
SHELDON Iroquois
SHERIDAN La Salle
SHERMAN Sangamon
SHERRARD Mercer
SHIPMAN Macoupin
SHIRLAND Winnebago
SHIRLEY McLean
SHOBONIER (62885) Fayette(95),
   Marion(5)
SHUMWAY (62461) Effingham(93),
   Shelby(7)
SIBLEY Ford
SIDELL (61876) Vermilion(80), Edgar(20)
SIDNEY Champaign
SIGEL (62462) Cumberland(64),
   Shelby(34), Effingham(2)
SILVIS Rock Island
SIMPSON (62985) Johnson(87), Pope(13)
SIMS Wayne
SKOKIE Cook
SMITHBORO Bond
SMITHFIELD Fulton
SMITHSHIRE (61478) Warren(94),
   Henderson(6)
SMITHTON St. Clair
SOLON MILLS McHenry
SOMONAUK (60552) De Kalb(53), La
   Salle(47)
SORENTO (62086) Bond(55),
   Montgomery(42), Madison(4)
SOUTH BELOIT (61080) Winnebago(93),
   Boone(7)
SOUTH ELGIN Kane
SOUTH HOLLAND Cook
SOUTH PEKIN Tazewell
SOUTH ROXANA Madison
SOUTH WILMINGTON Grundy
SPARLAND (61565) Marshall(97),
   Peoria(3)
SPARTA Randolph
SPEER Stark
SPRING GROVE (60081) McHenry(66),
   Lake(34)
SPRING VALLEY Bureau
SPRINGERTON (62887) White(75),
   Hamilton(25)
SPRINGFIELD Sangamon
STANDARD Putnam
STANDARD CITY Macoupin
STANFORD (61774) McLean(99),
   Tazewell(1)
STAUNTON (62088) Macoupin(79),
   Madison(21)

STEELEVILLE Randolph
STEGER Cook
STERLING (61081) Whiteside(98), Lee(2)
STEWARD (99999) Lee(99), De Kalb(1)
STEWARDSON Shelby
STILLMAN VALLEY (61084) Ogle(95),
   Winnebago(5)
STOCKLAND Iroquois
STOCKTON Jo Daviess
STONE PARK Cook
STONEFORT (62987) Saline(61),
   Williamson(33), Pope(7)
STONINGTON Christian
STOY Crawford
STRASBURG Shelby
STRAWN (61775) Livingston(95), Ford(6)
STREAMWOOD Cook
STREATOR (61364) La Salle(90),
   Livingston(10)
STRONGHURST Henderson
SUBLETTE Lee
SUGAR GROVE Kane
SULLIVAN (61951) Moultrie(99), Coles(2)
SUMMER HILL Pike
SUMMERFIELD St. Clair
SUMMIT ARGO Cook
SUMNER (62466) Lawrence(88),
   Crawford(7), Richland(5)
SUTTER (62373) Hancock(97), Adams(3)
SYCAMORE (60178) De Kalb(98), Kane(3)
TABLE GROVE (61482) Knox(42),
   Fulton(30), McDonough(27)
TALLULA Menard
TAMAROA Perry
TAMMS Alexander
TAMPICO (61283) Whiteside(97), Henry(3)
TAYLOR RIDGE Rock Island
TAYLOR SPRINGS Montgomery
TAYLORVILLE Christian
TECHNY Cook
TENNESSEE (62374) McDonough(65),
   Hancock(35)
TEUTOPOLIS (62467) Effingham(85),
   Jasper(9), Cumberland(7)
TEXICO (62889) Jefferson(67), Marion(33)
THAWVILLE (60968) Iroquois(55),
   Ford(44), Livingston(1)
THAYER Sangamon
THEBES Alexander
THOMASBORO Champaign
THOMPSONVILLE (62890) Franklin(67),
   Williamson(24), Saline(7), Hamilton(2)
THOMSON Carroll
THORNTON Cook
TILDEN Randolph
TILTON Vermilion
TIMEWELL (62375) Brown(99), Adams(1)
TINLEY PARK (60477) Cook(98), Will(2)
TISKILWA Bureau
TOLEDO Cumberland
TOLONO Champaign
TOLUCA Marshall
TONICA La Salle
TOPEKA Mason
TOULON (61483) Stark(96), Henry(4)
TOVEY Christian
TOWANDA McLean
TOWER HILL Shelby
TREMONT Tazewell
TRENTON (62293) Clinton(76), St.
   Clair(15), Madison(9)
TRILLA (62469) Cumberland(77),
   Coles(23)
TRIUMPH La Salle
TRIVOLI (61569) Peoria(95), Fulton(5)
TROY (62294) Madison(97), St. Clair(4)
TROY GROVE La Salle
TUNNEL HILL Johnson
TUSCOLA Douglas
ULLIN (62992) Pulaski(98), Alexander(2)
UNION McHenry
UNION HILL Kankakee

UNITY Alexander
URBANA Champaign
URSA Adams
UTICA La Salle
VALIER Franklin
VALMEYER Monroe
VAN ORIN Bureau
VANDALIA Fayette
VARNA Marshall
VENEDY Washington
VENICE (62090) Madison(98), St. Clair(2)
VERGENNES Jackson
VERMILION Edgar
VERMONT (61484) McDonough(78),
   Fulton(20), Schuyler(2)
VERNON (62892) Marion(91), Fayette(9)
VERNON HILLS Lake
VERONA Grundy
VERSAILLES Brown
VICTORIA Knox
VIENNA Johnson
VILLA GROVE (61956) Douglas(99),
   Champaign(1)
VILLA PARK Du Page
VILLA RIDGE Pulaski
VIOLA Mercer
VIRDEN (62690) Macoupin(90),
   Montgomery(6), Sangamon(4)
VIRGIL Kane
VIRGINIA Cass
WADSWORTH Lake
WAGGONER (62572) Montgomery(90),
   Macoupin(10)
WALNUT (61376) Bureau(92), Lee(8)
WALNUT HILL (62893) Marion(59),
   Jefferson(41)
WALSH Randolph
WALSHVILLE Montgomery
WALTONVILLE Jefferson
WAPELLA De Witt
WARREN (61087) Jo Daviess(99),
   Stephenson(1)
WARRENSBURG Macon
WARRENVILLE Du Page
WARSAW (62379) Hancock(99), Adams(1)
WASCO Kane
WASHBURN (61570) Woodford(56),
   Marshall(44)
WASHINGTON Tazewell
WATAGA Knox
WATERLOO (62298) Monroe(92), St.
   Clair(8)
WATERMAN De Kalb
WATSEKA Iroquois
WATSON Effingham
WAUCONDA Lake
WAUKEGAN Lake
WAVERLY (62692) Morgan(77),
   Sangamon(22)
WAYNE Du Page
WAYNE CITY (62895) Wayne(96),
   Hamilton(5)
WAYNESVILLE De Witt
WEDRON La Salle
WELDON (61882) De Witt(99), Piatt(1)
WELLINGTON Iroquois
WENONA (61377) Marshall(82), La
   Salle(18)
WEST BROOKLYN Lee
WEST CHICAGO (60185) Du Page(99),
   Kane(1)
WEST CHICAGO Du Page
WEST FRANKFORT (62896) Franklin(94),
   Williamson(6)
WEST LIBERTY Jasper
WEST POINT Hancock
WEST SALEM (62476) Edwards(91),
   Wabash(6), Lawrence(2), Richland(1)
WEST UNION Clark
WEST YORK (62478) Clark(57),
   Crawford(43)
WESTCHESTER Cook

WESTERN SPRINGS Cook
WESTERVELT Shelby
WESTFIELD (62474) Clark(91), Coles(9)
WESTMONT Du Page
WESTVILLE Vermilion
WHEATON Du Page
WHEELER (62479) Jasper(98),
    Effingham(2)
WHEELING (60090) Cook(99), Lake(1)
WHITE HALL Greene
WHITE HEATH (61884) Piatt(86),
    Champaign(14)
WHITTINGTON Franklin
WILLIAMSFIELD (61489) Knox(89),
    Peoria(10)

WILLIAMSVILLE (62693) Sangamon(83),
    Logan(16)
WILLISVILLE Perry
WILLOW HILL Jasper
WILLOW SPRINGS Cook
WILMETTE Cook
WILMINGTON (60481) Will(98), Grundy(2)
WILSONVILLE Macoupin
WINCHESTER (62694) Scott(79),
    Morgan(21)
WINDSOR Shelby
WINFIELD Du Page
WINNEBAGO Winnebago
WINNETKA Cook
WINSLOW Stephenson

WINTHROP HARBOR Lake
WITT Montgomery
WOLF LAKE Union
WONDER LAKE McHenry
WOOD DALE Du Page
WOOD RIVER Madison
WOODHULL (61490) McDonough(74),
    Henry(24), Knox(2)
WOODLAND Iroquois
WOODLAWN Jefferson
WOODRIDGE Du Page
WOODSON Morgan
WOODSTOCK McHenry
WOOSUNG Ogle
WORDEN Madison

WORTH Cook
WRIGHTS Greene
WYANET Bureau
WYOMING (61491) Stark(95), Marshall(5)
XENIA (62899) Clay(93), Marion(7)
YALE (62481) Jasper(98), Cumberland(2)
YATES CITY Knox
YORKVILLE Kendall
ZEIGLER Franklin
ZION Lake

ZIP/City Cross Reference

60001-60001 ALDEN	60085-60085 WAUKEGAN	60160-60161 MELROSE PARK	60445-60445 MIDLOTHIAN
60002-60002 ANTIOCH	60086-60086 NORTH CHICAGO	60162-60162 HILLSIDE	60446-60446 ROMEOVILLE
60004-60006 ARLINGTON HEIGHTS	60087-60087 WAUKEGAN	60163-60163 BERKELEY	60447-60447 MINOOKA
60007-60007 ELK GROVE VILLAGE	60088-60088 GREAT LAKES	60164-60164 MELROSE PARK	60448-60448 MOKENA
60008-60008 ROLLING MEADOWS	60089-60089 BUFFALO GROVE	60165-60165 STONE PARK	60449-60449 MONEE
60009-60009 ELK GROVE VILLAGE	60090-60090 WHEELING	60168-60168 SCHAUMBURG	60450-60450 MORRIS
60010-60011 BARRINGTON	60091-60091 WILMETTE	60170-60170 PLATO CENTER	60451-60451 NEW LENOX
60012-60012 CRYSTAL LAKE	60092-60092 LIBERTYVILLE	60171-60171 RIVER GROVE	60452-60452 OAK FOREST
60013-60013 CARY	60093-60093 WINNETKA	60172-60172 ROSELLE	60453-60454 OAK LAWN
60014-60014 CRYSTAL LAKE	60094-60095 PALATINE	60173-60173 SCHAUMBURG	60455-60455 BRIDGEVIEW
60015-60015 DEERFIELD	60096-60096 WINTHROP HARBOR	60174-60175 SAINT CHARLES	60456-60456 HOMETOWN
60016-60019 DES PLAINES	60097-60097 WONDER LAKE	60176-60176 SCHILLER PARK	60457-60457 HICKORY HILLS
60020-60020 FOX LAKE	60098-60098 WOODSTOCK	60177-60177 SOUTH ELGIN	60458-60458 JUSTICE
60021-60021 FOX RIVER GROVE	60099-60099 ZION	60178-60178 SYCAMORE	60459-60459 BURBANK
60022-60022 GLENCOE	60101-60101 ADDISON	60179-60179 HOFFMAN ESTATES	60460-60460 ODELL
60025-60025 GLENVIEW	60102-60102 ALGONQUIN	60180-60180 UNION	60461-60461 OLYMPIA FIELDS
60026-60026 GLENVIEW NAS	60103-60103 BARTLETT	60181-60181 VILLA PARK	60462-60462 ORLAND PARK
60029-60029 GOLF	60104-60104 BELLWOOD	60182-60182 VIRGIL	60463-60463 PALOS HEIGHTS
60030-60030 GRAYSLAKE	60105-60106 BENSENVILLE	60183-60183 WASCO	60464-60464 PALOS PARK
60031-60031 GURNEE	60107-60107 STREAMWOOD	60184-60184 WAYNE	60465-60465 PALOS HILLS
60033-60033 HARVARD	60108-60108 BLOOMINGDALE	60185-60186 WEST CHICAGO	60466-60466 PARK FOREST
60034-60034 HEBRON	60109-60109 BURLINGTON	60187-60187 WHEATON	60467-60467 ORLAND PARK
60035-60035 HIGHLAND PARK	60110-60110 CARPENTERSVILLE	60188-60188 CAROL STREAM	60468-60468 PEOTONE
60037-60037 FORT SHERIDAN	60111-60111 CLARE	60189-60189 WHEATON	60469-60469 POSEN
60038-60038 PALATINE	60112-60112 CORTLAND	60190-60190 WINFIELD	60470-60470 RANSOM
60039-60039 CRYSTAL LAKE	60113-60113 CRESTON	60191-60191 WOOD DALE	60471-60471 RICHTON PARK
60040-60040 HIGHWOOD	60114-60114 ADDISON	60192-60196 SCHAUMBURG	60472-60472 ROBBINS
60041-60041 INGLESIDE	60115-60115 DE KALB	60197-60199 CAROL STREAM	60473-60473 SOUTH HOLLAND
60042-60042 ISLAND LAKE	60116-60116 CAROL STREAM	60201-60209 EVANSTON	60474-60474 SOUTH WILMINGTON
60043-60043 KENILWORTH	60117-60117 BLOOMINGDALE	60251-60251 PALATINE	60475-60475 STEGER
60044-60044 LAKE BLUFF	60118-60118 DUNDEE	60301-60304 OAK PARK	60476-60476 THORNTON
60045-60045 LAKE FOREST	60119-60119 ELBURN	60305-60305 RIVER FOREST	60477-60477 TINLEY PARK
60046-60046 LAKE VILLA	60120-60123 ELGIN	60351-60353 CAROL STREAM	60478-60478 COUNTRY CLUB HILLS
60047-60047 LAKE ZURICH	60125-60125 CAROL STREAM	60401-60401 BEECHER	60479-60479 VERONA
60048-60048 LIBERTYVILLE	60126-60126 ELMHURST	60402-60402 BERWYN	60480-60480 WILLOW SPRINGS
60049-60049 LONG GROVE	60128-60128 CAROL STREAM	60406-60406 BLUE ISLAND	60481-60481 WILMINGTON
60050-60051 MC HENRY	60129-60129 ESMOND	60407-60407 BRACEVILLE	60482-60482 WORTH
60053-60053 MORTON GROVE	60130-60130 FOREST PARK	60408-60408 BRAIDWOOD	60490-60490 BOLINGBROOK
60055-60055 PALATINE	60131-60131 FRANKLIN PARK	60409-60409 CALUMET CITY	60499-60499 BEDFORD PARK
60056-60056 MOUNT PROSPECT	60132-60132 CAROL STREAM	60410-60410 CHANNAHON	60501-60501 SUMMIT ARGO
60060-60060 MUNDELEIN	60134-60134 GENEVA	60411-60412 CHICAGO HEIGHTS	60504-60507 AURORA
60061-60061 VERNON HILLS	60135-60135 GENOA	60415-60415 CHICAGO RIDGE	60510-60510 BATAVIA
60062-60062 NORTHBROOK	60136-60136 GILBERTS	60416-60416 COAL CITY	60511-60511 BIG ROCK
60063-60063 DEERFIELD	60137-60138 GLEN ELLYN	60417-60417 CRETE	60512-60512 BRISTOL
60064-60064 NORTH CHICAGO	60139-60139 GLENDALE HEIGHTS	60419-60419 DOLTON	60513-60513 BROOKFIELD
60065-60065 NORTHBROOK	60140-60140 HAMPSHIRE	60420-60420 DWIGHT	60514-60514 CLARENDON HILLS
60067-60067 PALATINE	60141-60141 HINES	60421-60421 ELWOOD	60515-60516 DOWNERS GROVE
60068-60068 PARK RIDGE	60142-60142 HUNTLEY	60422-60422 FLOSSMOOR	60517-60517 WOODRIDGE
60069-60069 LINCOLNSHIRE	60143-60143 ITASCA	60423-60423 FRANKFORT	60518-60518 EARLVILLE
60070-60070 PROSPECT HEIGHTS	60144-60144 KANEVILLE	60424-60424 GARDNER	60519-60519 EOLA
60071-60071 RICHMOND	60145-60145 KINGSTON	60425-60425 GLENWOOD	60520-60520 HINCKLEY
60072-60072 RINGWOOD	60146-60146 KIRKLAND	60426-60426 HARVEY	60521-60523 HINSDALE
60073-60073 ROUND LAKE	60147-60147 LAFOX	60429-60429 HAZEL CREST	60525-60525 LA GRANGE
60074-60074 PALATINE	60148-60148 LOMBARD	60430-60430 HOMEWOOD	60526-60526 LA GRANGE PARK
60075-60075 RUSSELL	60150-60150 MALTA	60431-60436 JOLIET	60527-60527 HINSDALE
60076-60077 SKOKIE	60151-60151 MAPLE PARK	60437-60437 KINSMAN	60530-60530 LEE
60078-60078 PALATINE	60152-60152 MARENGO	60438-60438 LANSING	60531-60531 LELAND
60079-60079 WAUKEGAN	60153-60153 MAYWOOD	60439-60439 LEMONT	60532-60532 LISLE
60080-60080 SOLON MILLS	60154-60154 WESTCHESTER	60440-60440 BOLINGBROOK	60534-60534 LYONS
60081-60081 SPRING GROVE	60155-60155 CAROL STREAM	60441-60441 LOCKPORT	60536-60536 MILLBROOK
60082-60082 TECHNY	60157-60157 MEDINAH	60442-60442 MANHATTAN	60537-60537 MILLINGTON
60083-60083 WADSWORTH	60158-60158 CAROL STREAM	60443-60443 MATTESON	60538-60538 MONTGOMERY
60084-60084 WAUCONDA	60159-60159 SCHAUMBURG	60444-60444 MAZON	60539-60539 MOOSEHEART

ZIP Range	City	ZIP Range	City	ZIP Range	City	ZIP Range	City
60540-60540	NAPERVILLE	60954-60954	MOMENCE	61087-61087	WARREN	61336-61336	MAGNOLIA
60541-60541	NEWARK	60955-60955	ONARGA	61088-61088	WINNEBAGO	61337-61337	MALDEN
60542-60542	NORTH AURORA	60956-60956	PAPINEAU	61089-61089	WINSLOW	61338-61338	MANLIUS
60543-60543	OSWEGO	60957-60957	PAXTON	61091-61091	WOOSUNG	61340-61340	MARK
60544-60544	PLAINFIELD	60959-60959	PIPER CITY	61101-61110	ROCKFORD	61341-61341	MARSEILLES
60545-60545	PLANO	60960-60960	RANKIN	61111-61111	LOVES PARK	61342-61342	MENDOTA
60546-60546	RIVERSIDE	60961-60961	REDDICK	61112-61114	ROCKFORD	61344-61344	MINERAL
60548-60548	SANDWICH	60962-60962	ROBERTS	61115-61115	MACHESNEY PARK	61345-61345	NEPONSET
60549-60549	SERENA	60963-60963	ROSSVILLE	61125-61126	ROCKFORD	61346-61346	NEW BEDFORD
60550-60550	SHABBONA	60964-60964	SAINT ANNE	61130-61132	LOVES PARK	61348-61348	OGLESBY
60551-60551	SHERIDAN	60966-60966	SHELDON	61201-61206	ROCK ISLAND	61349-61349	OHIO
60552-60552	SOMONAUK	60967-60967	STOCKLAND	61230-61230	ALBANY	61350-61350	OTTAWA
60553-60553	STEWARD	60968-60968	THAWVILLE	61231-61231	ALEDO	61353-61353	PAW PAW
60554-60554	SUGAR GROVE	60969-60969	UNION HILL	61232-61232	ANDALUSIA	61354-61354	PERU
60555-60555	WARRENVILLE	60970-60970	WATSEKA	61233-61233	ANDOVER	61356-61356	PRINCETON
60556-60556	WATERMAN	60973-60973	WELLINGTON	61234-61234	ANNAWAN	61358-61358	RUTLAND
60557-60557	WEDRON	60974-60974	WOODLAND	61235-61235	ATKINSON	61359-61359	SEATONVILLE
60558-60558	WESTERN SPRINGS	61001-61001	APPLE RIVER	61236-61236	BARSTOW	61360-61360	SENECA
60559-60559	WESTMONT	61006-61006	ASHTON	61237-61237	BUFFALO PRAIRIE	61361-61361	SHEFFIELD
60560-60560	YORKVILLE	61007-61007	BAILEYVILLE	61238-61238	CAMBRIDGE	61362-61362	SPRING VALLEY
60561-60561	DARIEN	61008-61008	BELVIDERE	61239-61239	CARBON CLIFF	61363-61363	STANDARD
60563-60567	NAPERVILLE	61010-61010	BYRON	61240-61240	COAL VALLEY	61364-61364	STREATOR
60568-60568	AURORA	61011-61011	CALEDONIA	61241-61241	COLONA	61367-61367	SUBLETTE
60570-60570	HINSDALE	61012-61012	CAPRON	61242-61242	CORDOVA	61368-61368	TISKILWA
60572-60572	AURORA	61013-61013	CEDARVILLE	61243-61243	DEER GROVE	61369-61369	TOLUCA
60597-60597	FOX VALLEY	61014-61014	CHADWICK	61244-61244	EAST MOLINE	61370-61370	TONICA
60598-60598	AURORA	61015-61015	CHANA	61250-61250	ERIE	61371-61371	TRIUMPH
60599-60599	FOX VALLEY	61016-61016	CHERRY VALLEY	61251-61251	FENTON	61372-61372	TROY GROVE
60601-60626	CHICAGO	61017-61017	COLETA	61252-61252	FULTON	61373-61373	UTICA
60627-60627	RIVERDALE	61018-61018	DAKOTA	61254-61254	GENESEO	61374-61374	VAN ORIN
60628-60634	CHICAGO	61019-61019	DAVIS	61256-61256	HAMPTON	61375-61375	VARNA
60635-60635	ELMWOOD PARK	61020-61020	DAVIS JUNCTION	61257-61257	HILLSDALE	61376-61376	WALNUT
60636-60649	CHICAGO	61021-61021	DIXON	61258-61258	HOOPPOLE	61377-61377	WENONA
60650-60650	CICERO	61024-61024	DURAND	61259-61259	ILLINOIS CITY	61378-61378	WEST BROOKLYN
60651-60665	CHICAGO	61025-61025	EAST DUBUQUE	61260-61260	JOY	61379-61379	WYANET
60666-60666	AMF OHARE	61027-61027	ELEROY	61261-61261	LYNDON	61401-61402	GALESBURG
60667-60701	CHICAGO	61028-61028	ELIZABETH	61262-61262	LYNN CENTER	61410-61410	ABINGDON
60707-60707	ELMWOOD PARK	61030-61030	FORRESTON	61263-61263	MATHERVILLE	61411-61411	ADAIR
60714-60714	NILES	61031-61031	FRANKLIN GROVE	61264-61264	MILAN	61412-61412	ALEXIS
60803-60803	ALSIP	61032-61032	FREEPORT	61265-61266	MOLINE	61413-61413	ALPHA
60804-60804	CICERO	61036-61036	GALENA	61270-61270	MORRISON	61414-61414	ALTONA
60805-60805	EVERGREEN PARK	61037-61037	GALT	61272-61272	NEW BOSTON	61415-61415	AVON
60827-60827	RIVERDALE	61038-61038	GARDEN PRAIRIE	61273-61273	ORION	61416-61416	BARDOLPH
60901-60902	KANKAKEE	61039-61039	GERMAN VALLEY	61274-61274	OSCO	61417-61417	BERWICK
60910-60910	AROMA PARK	61041-61041	HANOVER	61275-61275	PORT BYRON	61418-61418	BIGGSVILLE
60911-60911	ASHKUM	61042-61042	HARMON	61276-61276	PREEMPTION	61419-61419	BISHOP HILL
60912-60912	BEAVERVILLE	61043-61043	HOLCOMB	61277-61277	PROPHETSTOWN	61420-61420	BLANDINSVILLE
60913-60913	BONFIELD	61044-61044	KENT	61278-61278	RAPIDS CITY	61421-61421	BRADFORD
60914-60914	BOURBONNAIS	61046-61046	LANARK	61279-61279	REYNOLDS	61422-61422	BUSHNELL
60915-60915	BRADLEY	61047-61047	LEAF RIVER	61281-61281	SHERRARD	61423-61423	CAMERON
60917-60917	BUCKINGHAM	61048-61048	LENA	61282-61282	SILVIS	61424-61424	CAMP GROVE
60918-60918	BUCKLEY	61049-61049	LINDENWOOD	61283-61283	TAMPICO	61425-61425	CARMAN
60919-60919	CABERY	61050-61050	MC CONNELL	61284-61284	TAYLOR RIDGE	61426-61426	CASTLETON
60920-60920	CAMPUS	61051-61051	MILLEDGEVILLE	61285-61285	THOMSON	61427-61427	CUBA
60921-60921	CHATSWORTH	61052-61052	MONROE CENTER	61299-61299	ROCK ISLAND	61428-61428	DAHINDA
60922-60922	CHEBANSE	61053-61053	MOUNT CARROLL	61301-61301	LA SALLE	61430-61430	EAST GALESBURG
60924-60924	CISSNA PARK	61054-61054	MOUNT MORRIS	61310-61310	AMBOY	61431-61431	ELLISVILLE
60926-60926	CLAYTONVILLE	61057-61057	NACHUSA	61311-61311	ANCONA	61432-61432	FAIRVIEW
60927-60927	CLIFTON	61058-61058	NELSON	61312-61312	ARLINGTON	61433-61433	FIATT
60928-60928	CRESCENT CITY	61059-61059	NORA	61313-61313	BLACKSTONE	61434-61434	GALVA
60929-60929	CULLOM	61060-61060	ORANGEVILLE	61314-61314	BUDA	61435-61435	GERLAW
60930-60930	DANFORTH	61061-61061	OREGON	61315-61315	BUREAU	61436-61436	GILSON
60931-60931	DONOVAN	61062-61062	PEARL CITY	61316-61316	CEDAR POINT	61437-61437	GLADSTONE
60932-60932	EAST LYNN	61063-61063	PECATONICA	61317-61317	CHERRY	61438-61438	GOOD HOPE
60933-60933	ELLIOTT	61064-61064	POLO	61318-61318	COMPTON	61439-61439	HENDERSON
60934-60934	EMINGTON	61065-61065	POPLAR GROVE	61319-61319	CORNELL	61440-61440	INDUSTRY
60935-60935	ESSEX	61067-61067	RIDOTT	61320-61320	DALZELL	61441-61441	IPAVA
60936-60936	GIBSON CITY	61068-61068	ROCHELLE	61321-61321	DANA	61442-61442	KEITHSBURG
60938-60938	GILMAN	61070-61070	ROCK CITY	61322-61322	DEPUE	61443-61443	KEWANEE
60939-60939	GOODWINE	61071-61071	ROCK FALLS	61323-61323	DOVER	61447-61447	KIRKWOOD
60940-60940	GRANT PARK	61072-61072	ROCKTON	61324-61324	ELDENA	61448-61448	KNOXVILLE
60941-60941	HERSCHER	61073-61073	ROSCOE	61325-61325	GRAND RIDGE	61449-61449	LA FAYETTE
60942-60942	HOOPESTON	61074-61074	SAVANNA	61326-61326	GRANVILLE	61450-61450	LA HARPE
60944-60944	HOPKINS PARK	61075-61075	SCALES MOUND	61327-61327	HENNEPIN	61451-61451	LAURA
60945-60945	IROQUOIS	61076-61076	SCIOTO MILLS	61328-61328	KASBEER	61452-61452	LITTLETON
60946-60946	KEMPTON	61077-61077	SEWARD	61329-61329	LADD	61453-61453	LITTLE YORK
60948-60948	LODA	61078-61078	SHANNON	61330-61330	LA MOILLE	61454-61454	LOMAX
60949-60949	LUDLOW	61079-61079	SHIRLAND	61331-61331	LEE CENTER	61455-61455	MACOMB
60950-60950	MANTENO	61080-61080	SOUTH BELOIT	61332-61332	LEONORE	61458-61458	MAQUON
60951-60951	MARTINTON	61081-61081	STERLING	61333-61333	LONG POINT	61459-61459	MARIETTA
60952-60952	MELVIN	61084-61084	STILLMAN VALLEY	61334-61334	LOSTANT	61460-61460	MEDIA
60953-60953	MILFORD	61085-61085	STOCKTON	61335-61335	MC NABB	61462-61462	MONMOUTH

Zip Range	City	Zip Range	City
61465-61465	NEW WINDSOR	61726-61726	CHENOA
61466-61466	NORTH HENDERSON	61727-61727	CLINTON
61467-61467	ONEIDA	61728-61728	COLFAX
61468-61468	OPHEIM	61729-61729	CONGERVILLE
61469-61469	OQUAWKA	61730-61730	COOKSVILLE
61470-61470	PRAIRIE CITY	61731-61731	CROPSEY
61471-61471	RARITAN	61732-61732	DANVERS
61472-61472	RIO	61733-61733	DEER CREEK
61473-61473	ROSEVILLE	61734-61734	DELAVAN
61474-61474	SAINT AUGUSTINE	61735-61735	DEWITT
61475-61475	SCIOTA	61736-61736	DOWNS
61476-61476	SEATON	61737-61737	ELLSWORTH
61477-61477	SMITHFIELD	61738-61738	EL PASO
61478-61478	SMITHSHIRE	61739-61739	FAIRBURY
61479-61479	SPEER	61740-61740	FLANAGAN
61480-61480	STRONGHURST	61741-61741	FORREST
61482-61482	TABLE GROVE	61742-61742	GOODFIELD
61483-61483	TOULON	61743-61743	GRAYMONT
61484-61484	VERMONT	61744-61744	GRIDLEY
61485-61485	VICTORIA	61745-61745	HEYWORTH
61486-61486	VIOLA	61747-61747	HOPEDALE
61488-61488	WATAGA	61748-61748	HUDSON
61489-61489	WILLIAMSFIELD	61749-61749	KENNEY
61490-61490	WOODHULL	61750-61750	LANE
61491-61491	WYOMING	61751-61751	LAWNDALE
61501-61501	ASTORIA	61752-61752	LE ROY
61516-61516	BENSON	61753-61753	LEXINGTON
61517-61518	BRIMFIELD	61754-61754	MC LEAN
61519-61519	BRYANT	61755-61755	MACKINAW
61520-61520	CANTON	61756-61756	MAROA
61523-61523	CHILLICOTHE	61758-61758	MERNA
61524-61524	DUNFERMLINE	61759-61759	MINIER
61525-61525	DUNLAP	61760-61760	MINONK
61526-61526	EDELSTEIN	61761-61761	NORMAL
61528-61528	EDWARDS	61764-61764	PONTIAC
61529-61529	ELMWOOD	61769-61769	SAUNEMIN
61530-61530	EUREKA	61770-61770	SAYBROOK
61531-61531	FARMINGTON	61771-61771	SECOR
61532-61532	FOREST CITY	61772-61772	SHIRLEY
61533-61533	GLASFORD	61773-61773	SIBLEY
61534-61534	GREEN VALLEY	61774-61774	STANFORD
61535-61535	GROVELAND	61775-61775	STRAWN
61536-61536	HANNA CITY	61776-61776	TOWANDA
61537-61537	HENRY	61777-61777	WAPELLA
61539-61539	KINGSTON MINES	61778-61778	WAYNESVILLE
61540-61540	LACON	61790-61790	NORMAL
61541-61541	LA ROSE	61791-61799	BLOOMINGTON
61542-61542	LEWISTOWN	61801-61803	URBANA
61543-61543	LIVERPOOL	61810-61810	ALLERTON
61544-61544	LONDON MILLS	61811-61811	ALVIN
61545-61545	LOWPOINT	61812-61812	ARMSTRONG
61546-61546	MANITO	61813-61813	BEMENT
61547-61547	MAPLETON	61814-61814	BISMARCK
61548-61548	METAMORA	61815-61815	BONDVILLE
61550-61550	MORTON	61816-61816	BROADLANDS
61552-61552	MOSSVILLE	61817-61817	CATLIN
61553-61553	NORRIS	61818-61818	CERRO GORDO
61554-61558	PEKIN	61820-61826	CHAMPAIGN
61559-61559	PRINCEVILLE	61830-61830	CISCO
61560-61560	PUTNAM	61831-61831	COLLISON
61561-61561	ROANOKE	61832-61832	DANVILLE
61562-61562	ROME	61833-61833	TILTON
61563-61563	SAINT DAVID	61834-61834	DANVILLE
61564-61564	SOUTH PEKIN	61839-61839	DE LAND
61565-61565	SPARLAND	61840-61840	DEWEY
61567-61567	TOPEKA	61841-61841	FAIRMOUNT
61568-61568	TREMONT	61842-61842	FARMER CITY
61569-61569	TRIVOLI	61843-61843	FISHER
61570-61570	WASHBURN	61844-61844	FITHIAN
61571-61571	WASHINGTON	61845-61845	FOOSLAND
61572-61572	YATES CITY	61846-61846	GEORGETOWN
61601-61607	PEORIA	61847-61847	GIFFORD
61610-61610	CREVE COEUR	61848-61848	HENNING
61611-61611	EAST PEORIA	61849-61849	HOMER
61612-61656	PEORIA	61850-61850	INDIANOLA
61701-61710	BLOOMINGTON	61851-61851	IVESDALE
61720-61720	ANCHOR	61852-61852	LONGVIEW
61721-61721	ARMINGTON	61853-61853	MAHOMET
61722-61722	ARROWSMITH	61854-61854	MANSFIELD
61723-61723	ATLANTA	61855-61855	MILMINE
61724-61724	BELLFLOWER	61856-61856	MONTICELLO
61725-61725	CARLOCK	61857-61857	MUNCIE

Zip Range	City	Zip Range	City
61858-61858	OAKWOOD	62046-62046	HAMEL
61859-61859	OGDEN	62047-62047	HARDIN
61862-61862	PENFIELD	62048-62048	HARTFORD
61863-61863	PESOTUM	62049-62049	HILLSBORO
61864-61864	PHILO	62050-62050	HILLVIEW
61865-61865	POTOMAC	62051-62051	IRVING
61866-61866	RANTOUL	62052-62052	JERSEYVILLE
61870-61870	RIDGE FARM	62053-62053	KAMPSVILLE
61871-61871	ROYAL	62054-62054	KANE
61872-61872	SADORUS	62056-62056	LITCHFIELD
61873-61873	SAINT JOSEPH	62058-62058	LIVINGSTON
61874-61874	SAVOY	62059-62059	LOVEJOY
61875-61875	SEYMOUR	62060-62060	MADISON
61876-61876	SIDELL	62061-62061	MARINE
61877-61877	SIDNEY	62062-62062	MARYVILLE
61878-61878	THOMASBORO	62063-62063	MEDORA
61880-61880	TOLONO	62065-62065	MICHAEL
61882-61882	WELDON	62067-62067	MORO
61883-61883	WESTVILLE	62069-62069	MOUNT OLIVE
61884-61884	WHITE HEATH	62070-62070	MOZIER
61910-61910	ARCOLA	62071-62071	NATIONAL STOCK YARDS
61911-61911	ARTHUR	62074-62074	NEW DOUGLAS
61912-61912	ASHMORE	62075-62075	NOKOMIS
61913-61913	ATWOOD	62076-62076	OHLMAN
61914-61914	BETHANY	62077-62077	PANAMA
61917-61917	BROCTON	62078-62078	PATTERSON
61919-61919	CAMARGO	62079-62079	PIASA
61920-61920	CHARLESTON	62080-62080	RAMSEY
61924-61924	CHRISMAN	62081-62081	ROCKBRIDGE
61925-61925	DALTON CITY	62082-62082	ROODHOUSE
61928-61928	GAYS	62083-62083	ROSAMOND
61929-61929	HAMMOND	62084-62084	ROXANA
61930-61930	HINDSBORO	62085-62085	SAWYERVILLE
61931-61931	HUMBOLDT	62086-62086	SORENTO
61932-61932	HUME	62087-62087	SOUTH ROXANA
61933-61933	KANSAS	62088-62088	STAUNTON
61936-61936	LA PLACE	62089-62089	TAYLOR SPRINGS
61937-61937	LOVINGTON	62090-62090	VENICE
61938-61938	MATTOON	62091-62091	WALSHVILLE
61940-61940	METCALF	62092-62092	WHITE HALL
61941-61941	MURDOCK	62093-62093	WILSONVILLE
61942-61942	NEWMAN	62094-62094	WITT
61943-61943	OAKLAND	62095-62095	WOOD RIVER
61944-61944	PARIS	62097-62097	WORDEN
61949-61949	REDMON	62098-62098	WRIGHTS
61951-61951	SULLIVAN	62201-62207	EAST SAINT LOUIS
61953-61953	TUSCOLA	62208-62208	FAIRVIEW HEIGHTS
61955-61955	VERMILION	62214-62214	ADDIEVILLE
61956-61956	VILLA GROVE	62215-62215	ALBERS
61957-61957	WINDSOR	62216-62216	AVISTON
62001-62001	ALHAMBRA	62217-62217	BALDWIN
62002-62002	ALTON	62218-62218	BARTELSO
62006-62006	BATCHTOWN	62219-62219	BECKEMEYER
62009-62009	BENLD	62220-62223	BELLEVILLE
62010-62010	BETHALTO	62224-62224	MASCOUTAH
62011-62011	BINGHAM	62225-62225	SCOTT AIR FORCE BASE
62012-62012	BRIGHTON	62226-62226	BELLEVILLE
62013-62013	BRUSSELS	62230-62230	BREESE
62014-62014	BUNKER HILL	62231-62231	CARLYLE
62015-62015	BUTLER	62232-62232	CASEYVILLE
62016-62016	CARROLLTON	62233-62233	CHESTER
62017-62017	COFFEEN	62234-62234	COLLINSVILLE
62018-62018	COTTAGE HILLS	62236-62236	COLUMBIA
62019-62019	DONNELLSON	62237-62237	COULTERVILLE
62021-62021	DORSEY	62238-62238	CUTLER
62022-62022	DOW	62239-62239	DUPO
62023-62023	EAGARVILLE	62240-62240	EAST CARONDELET
62024-62024	EAST ALTON	62241-62241	ELLIS GROVE
62025-62026	EDWARDSVILLE	62242-62242	EVANSVILLE
62027-62027	ELDRED	62243-62243	FREEBURG
62028-62028	ELSAH	62244-62244	FULTS
62030-62030	FIDELITY	62245-62245	GERMANTOWN
62031-62031	FIELDON	62246-62246	GREENVILLE
62032-62032	FILLMORE	62247-62247	HAGARSTOWN
62033-62033	GILLESPIE	62248-62248	HECKER
62034-62034	GLEN CARBON	62249-62249	HIGHLAND
62035-62035	GODFREY	62250-62250	HOFFMAN
62036-62036	GOLDEN EAGLE	62252-62252	HUEY
62037-62037	GRAFTON	62253-62253	KEYESPORT
62040-62040	GRANITE CITY	62254-62254	LEBANON
62044-62044	GREENFIELD	62255-62255	LENZBURG
62045-62045	HAMBURG		

Zip	Place	Zip	Place	Zip	Place	Zip	Place
62256-62256	MAEYSTOWN	62370-62370	ROCKPORT	62530-62530	DIVERNON	62673-62673	OAKFORD
62257-62257	MARISSA	62373-62373	SUTTER	62531-62531	EDINBURG	62674-62674	PALMYRA
62258-62258	MASCOUTAH	62374-62374	TENNESSEE	62532-62532	ELWIN	62675-62675	PETERSBURG
62259-62259	MENARD	62375-62375	TIMEWELL	62533-62533	FARMERSVILLE	62676-62676	PLAINVIEW
62260-62260	MILLSTADT	62376-62376	URSA	62534-62534	FINDLAY	62677-62677	PLEASANT PLAINS
62261-62261	MODOC	62378-62378	VERSAILLES	62535-62535	FORSYTH	62681-62681	RUSHVILLE
62262-62262	MULBERRY GROVE	62379-62379	WARSAW	62536-62536	GLENARM	62682-62682	SAN JOSE
62263-62263	NASHVILLE	62380-62380	WEST POINT	62537-62537	HARRISTOWN	62683-62683	SCOTTVILLE
62264-62264	NEW ATHENS	62401-62401	EFFINGHAM	62538-62538	HARVEL	62684-62684	SHERMAN
62265-62265	NEW BADEN	62410-62410	ALLENDALE	62539-62539	ILLIOPOLIS	62685-62685	SHIPMAN
62266-62266	NEW MEMPHIS	62411-62411	ALTAMONT	62540-62540	KINCAID	62686-62686	STANDARD CITY
62268-62268	OAKDALE	62413-62413	ANNAPOLIS	62541-62541	LAKE FORK	62688-62688	TALLULA
62269-62269	O FALLON	62414-62414	BEECHER CITY	62543-62543	LATHAM	62689-62689	THAYER
62271-62271	OKAWVILLE	62415-62415	BIRDS	62544-62544	MACON	62690-62690	VIRDEN
62272-62272	PERCY	62417-62417	BRIDGEPORT	62545-62545	MECHANICSBURG	62691-62691	VIRGINIA
62273-62273	PIERRON	62418-62418	BROWNSTOWN	62546-62546	MORRISONVILLE	62692-62692	WAVERLY
62274-62274	PINCKNEYVILLE	62419-62419	CALHOUN	62547-62547	MOUNT AUBURN	62693-62693	WILLIAMSVILLE
62275-62275	POCAHONTAS	62420-62420	CASEY	62548-62548	MOUNT PULASKI	62694-62694	WINCHESTER
62277-62277	PRAIRIE DU ROCHER	62421-62421	CLAREMONT	62549-62549	MT ZION	62695-62695	WOODSON
62278-62278	RED BUD	62422-62422	COWDEN	62550-62550	MOWEAQUA	62701-62796	SPRINGFIELD
62279-62279	RENAULT	62423-62423	DENNISON	62551-62551	NIANTIC	62801-62801	CENTRALIA
62280-62280	ROCKWOOD	62424-62424	DIETERICH	62552-62552	OAKLEY	62803-62803	HOYLETON
62281-62281	SAINT JACOB	62425-62425	DUNDAS	62553-62553	OCONEE	62805-62805	AKIN
62282-62282	SAINT LIBORY	62426-62426	EDGEWOOD	62554-62554	OREANA	62806-62806	ALBION
62283-62283	SHATTUC	62427-62427	FLAT ROCK	62555-62555	OWANECO	62807-62807	ALMA
62284-62284	SMITHBORO	62428-62428	GREENUP	62556-62556	PALMER	62808-62808	ASHLEY
62285-62285	SMITHTON	62431-62431	HERRICK	62557-62557	PANA	62809-62809	BARNHILL
62286-62286	SPARTA	62432-62432	HIDALGO	62558-62558	PAWNEE	62810-62810	BELLE RIVE
62288-62288	STEELEVILLE	62433-62433	HUTSONVILLE	62560-62560	RAYMOND	62811-62811	BELLMONT
62289-62289	SUMMERFIELD	62434-62434	INGRAHAM	62561-62561	RIVERTON	62812-62812	BENTON
62292-62292	TILDEN	62435-62435	JANESVILLE	62563-62563	ROCHESTER	62814-62814	BLUFORD
62293-62293	TRENTON	62436-62436	JEWETT	62565-62565	SHELBYVILLE	62815-62815	BONE GAP
62294-62294	TROY	62438-62438	LAKEWOOD	62567-62567	STONINGTON	62816-62816	BONNIE
62295-62295	VALMEYER	62439-62439	LAWRENCEVILLE	62568-62568	TAYLORVILLE	62817-62817	BROUGHTON
62297-62297	WALSH	62440-62440	LERNA	62570-62570	TOVEY	62818-62818	BROWNS
62298-62298	WATERLOO	62441-62441	MARSHALL	62571-62571	TOWER HILL	62819-62819	BUCKNER
62301-62306	QUINCY	62442-62442	MARTINSVILLE	62572-62572	WAGGONER	62820-62820	BURNT PRAIRIE
62310-62310	ADRIAN	62443-62443	MASON	62573-62573	WARRENSBURG	62821-62821	CARMI
62311-62311	AUGUSTA	62444-62444	MODE	62601-62601	ALEXANDER	62822-62822	CHRISTOPHER
62312-62312	BARRY	62445-62445	MONTROSE	62610-62610	ALSEY	62823-62823	CISNE
62313-62313	BASCO	62446-62446	MOUNT ERIE	62611-62611	ARENZVILLE	62824-62824	CLAY CITY
62314-62314	BAYLIS	62447-62447	NEOGA	62612-62612	ASHLAND	62825-62825	COELLO
62316-62316	BOWEN	62448-62448	NEWTON	62613-62613	ATHENS	62827-62827	CROSSVILLE
62318-62318	BURNSIDE	62449-62449	OBLONG	62615-62615	AUBURN	62828-62828	DAHLGREN
62319-62319	CAMDEN	62450-62450	OLNEY	62617-62617	BATH	62829-62829	DALE
62320-62320	CAMP POINT	62451-62451	PALESTINE	62618-62618	BEARDSTOWN	62830-62830	DIX
62321-62321	CARTHAGE	62452-62452	PARKERSBURG	62621-62621	BLUFFS	62831-62831	DU BOIS
62323-62323	CHAMBERSBURG	62454-62454	ROBINSON	62622-62622	BLUFF SPRINGS	62832-62832	DU QUOIN
62324-62324	CLAYTON	62458-62458	SAINT ELMO	62624-62624	BROWNING	62833-62833	ELLERY
62325-62325	COATSBURG	62459-62459	SAINTE MARIE	62625-62625	CANTRALL	62834-62834	EMMA
62326-62326	COLCHESTER	62460-62460	SAINT FRANCISVILLE	62626-62626	CARLINVILLE	62835-62835	ENFIELD
62329-62329	COLUSA	62461-62461	SHUMWAY	62627-62627	CHANDLERVILLE	62836-62836	EWING
62330-62330	DALLAS CITY	62462-62462	SIGEL	62628-62628	CHAPIN	62837-62837	FAIRFIELD
62334-62334	ELVASTON	62463-62463	STEWARDSON	62629-62629	CHATHAM	62838-62838	FARINA
62336-62336	FERRIS	62464-62464	STOY	62630-62630	CHESTERFIELD	62839-62839	FLORA
62338-62338	FOWLER	62465-62465	STRASBURG	62631-62631	CONCORD	62840-62840	FRANKFORT HEIGHTS
62339-62339	GOLDEN	62466-62466	SUMNER	62633-62633	EASTON	62841-62841	FREEMAN SPUR
62340-62340	GRIGGSVILLE	62467-62467	TEUTOPOLIS	62634-62634	ELKHART	62842-62842	GEFF
62341-62341	HAMILTON	62468-62468	TOLEDO	62635-62635	EMDEN	62843-62843	GOLDEN GATE
62343-62343	HULL	62469-62469	TRILLA	62638-62638	FRANKLIN	62844-62844	GRAYVILLE
62344-62344	HUNTSVILLE	62471-62471	VANDALIA	62639-62639	FREDERICK	62845-62845	HERALD
62345-62345	KINDERHOOK	62473-62473	WATSON	62640-62640	GIRARD	62846-62846	INA
62346-62346	LA PRAIRIE	62474-62474	WESTFIELD	62642-62642	GREENVIEW	62847-62847	IOLA
62347-62347	LIBERTY	62475-62475	WEST LIBERTY	62643-62643	HARTSBURG	62848-62848	IRVINGTON
62348-62348	LIMA	62476-62476	WEST SALEM	62644-62644	HAVANA	62849-62849	IUKA
62349-62349	LORAINE	62477-62477	WEST UNION	62649-62649	HETTICK	62850-62850	JOHNSONVILLE
62351-62351	MENDON	62478-62478	WEST YORK	62650-62651	JACKSONVILLE	62851-62851	KEENES
62352-62352	MILTON	62479-62479	WHEELER	62655-62655	KILBOURNE	62852-62852	KEENSBURG
62353-62353	MOUNT STERLING	62480-62480	WILLOW HILL	62656-62656	LINCOLN	62853-62853	KELL
62354-62354	NAUVOO	62481-62481	YALE	62659-62659	LINCOLN'S NEW SALEM	62854-62854	KINMUNDY
62355-62355	NEBO	62501-62501	ARGENTA	62660-62660	LITERBERRY	62855-62855	LANCASTER
62356-62356	NEW CANTON	62510-62510	ASSUMPTION	62661-62661	LOAMI	62856-62856	LOGAN
62357-62357	NEW SALEM	62511-62511	ATWATER	62662-62662	LOWDER	62857-62857	LOOGOOTEE
62358-62358	NIOTA	62512-62512	BEASON	62663-62663	MANCHESTER	62858-62858	LOUISVILLE
62359-62359	PALOMA	62513-62513	BLUE MOUND	62664-62664	MASON CITY	62859-62859	MC LEANSBORO
62360-62360	PAYSON	62514-62514	BOODY	62665-62665	MEREDOSIA	62860-62860	MACEDONIA
62361-62361	PEARL	62515-62515	BUFFALO	62666-62666	MIDDLETOWN	62861-62861	MAUNIE
62362-62362	PERRY	62517-62517	BULPITT	62667-62667	MODESTO	62862-62862	MILL SHOALS
62363-62363	PITTSFIELD	62518-62518	CHESTNUT	62668-62668	MURRAYVILLE	62863-62863	MOUNT CARMEL
62365-62365	PLAINVILLE	62519-62519	CORNLAND	62670-62670	NEW BERLIN	62864-62864	MOUNT VERNON
62366-62366	PLEASANT HILL	62520-62520	DAWSON	62671-62671	NEW HOLLAND	62865-62865	MULKEYTOWN
62367-62367	PLYMOUTH	62521-62527	DECATUR	62672-62672	NILWOOD	62866-62866	NASON

62867-62867	NEW HAVEN	62898-62898	WOODLAWN	62934-62934	EQUALITY	62967-62967	NEW BURNSIDE
62868-62868	NOBLE	62899-62899	XENIA	62935-62935	GALATIA	62969-62969	OLIVE BRANCH
62869-62869	NORRIS CITY	62901-62903	CARBONDALE	62938-62938	GOLCONDA	62970-62970	OLMSTED
62870-62870	ODIN	62905-62905	ALTO PASS	62939-62939	GOREVILLE	62971-62971	ORAVILLE
62871-62871	OMAHA	62906-62906	ANNA	62940-62940	GORHAM	62972-62972	OZARK
62872-62872	OPDYKE	62907-62907	AVA	62941-62941	GRAND CHAIN	62973-62973	PERKS
62874-62874	ORIENT	62908-62908	BELKNAP	62942-62942	GRAND TOWER	62974-62974	PITTSBURG
62875-62875	PATOKA	62909-62909	BOLES	62943-62943	GRANTSBURG	62975-62975	POMONA
62876-62876	RADOM	62910-62910	BROOKPORT	62944-62944	HAMLETSBURG	62976-62976	PULASKI
62877-62877	RICHVIEW	62912-62912	BUNCOMBE	62946-62946	HARRISBURG	62977-62977	RALEIGH
62878-62878	RINARD	62913-62913	CACHE	62947-62947	HEROD	62979-62979	RIDGWAY
62879-62879	SAILOR SPRINGS	62914-62914	CAIRO	62948-62948	HERRIN	62982-62982	ROSICLARE
62880-62880	SAINT PETER	62915-62915	CAMBRIA	62949-62949	HURST	62983-62983	ROYALTON
62881-62881	SALEM	62916-62916	CAMPBELL HILL	62950-62950	JACOB	62984-62984	SHAWNEETOWN
62882-62882	SANDOVAL	62917-62917	CARRIER MILLS	62951-62951	JOHNSTON CITY	62985-62985	SIMPSON
62883-62883	SCHELLER	62918-62918	CARTERVILLE	62952-62952	JONESBORO	62987-62987	STONEFORT
62884-62884	SESSER	62919-62919	CAVE IN ROCK	62953-62953	JOPPA	62988-62988	TAMMS
62885-62885	SHOBONIER	62920-62920	COBDEN	62954-62954	JUNCTION	62990-62990	THEBES
62886-62886	SIMS	62921-62921	COLP	62955-62955	KARBERS RIDGE	62991-62991	TUNNEL HILL
62887-62887	SPRINGERTON	62922-62922	CREAL SPRINGS	62956-62956	KARNAK	62992-62992	ULLIN
62888-62888	TAMAROA	62923-62923	CYPRESS	62957-62957	MC CLURE	62993-62993	UNITY
62889-62889	TEXICO	62924-62924	DE SOTO	62958-62958	MAKANDA	62994-62994	VERGENNES
62890-62890	THOMPSONVILLE	62926-62926	DONGOLA	62959-62959	MARION	62995-62995	VIENNA
62891-62891	VALIER	62927-62927	DOWELL	62960-62960	METROPOLIS	62996-62996	VILLA RIDGE
62892-62892	VERNON	62928-62928	EDDYVILLE	62961-62961	MILLCREEK	62997-62997	WILLISVILLE
62893-62893	WALNUT HILL	62929-62929	ELCO	62962-62962	MILLER CITY	62998-62998	WOLF LAKE
62894-62894	WALTONVILLE	62930-62930	ELDORADO	62963-62963	MOUND CITY	62999-62999	ZEIGLER
62895-62895	WAYNE CITY	62931-62931	ELIZABETHTOWN	62964-62964	MOUNDS		
62896-62896	WEST FRANKFORT	62932-62932	ELKVILLE	62965-62965	MUDDY		
62897-62897	WHITTINGTON	62933-62933	ENERGY	62966-62966	MURPHYSBORO		

Indiana

General Help Numbers:

Governor's Office
206 State House
Indianapolis, IN 46204
http://www.in.gov/gov

317-232-4567
Fax 317-232-3443
8AM-5PM

Attorney General's Office
402 W Washington, 5th Fl
Indianapolis, IN 46204
http://www.in.gov/attorneygeneral

317-232-6201
Fax 317-232-7979
8:30AM-5PM

State Court Administrator
115 W Washington St, #1080
Indianapolis, IN 46204-3417
http://www.in.gov/judiciary/admin/

317-232-2542
Fax 317-233-6586
8:30AM-4:30PM

State Archives
Commission on Public Records
6400 E 30th St
Indianapolis, IN 46219
http://www.in.gov/icpr

317-591-5222
Fax 317-591-5324
8AM-4:30PM

State Specifics:

Capital:

Indianapolis
Marion County

Time Zone:

EST*
* Indiana's eleven northwestern-most counties are CST:
They are: Gibson, Jasper, Laporte, Lake, Newton, Porter, Posey, Spencer,
Starke, Vanderburgh, Warrick.

Number of Counties:

92

Population:

6,080,485

Web Site:

www.state.in.us

State Agencies

Criminal Records

Indiana State Police, Central Records, IGCN - 100 N Senate Ave Room 302, Indianapolis, IN 46204-2259; 317-232-8266, 8AM-4:30PM.

http://www.state.in.us/isp

Note: Sex offender data is available online at www.state.in.us//cji/html/sexoffender.html.

Indexing & Storage: Records are available from 1935. It takes 10 days before new records are available for inquiry. Records are indexed on inhouse computer.

Searching: Only employers or the subject can request records using State Form 8053. The record

will show all activity, including arrests, dismissals, and convictions. If the charge is over a year old and there is no disposition, the charge will not be released. Include the following in your request-full name, date of birth, sex, race.

Access by: mail, in person.

Fee & Payment: The fee for employers is $7.00 per name. The fee for your own records or for a fingerprint search is $10.00. Fee payee: State of Indiana. Prepayment required. Cash, money orders, and certified checks are accepted. Ongoing requesters may open a monthly billing account. No credit cards accepted.

Mail search: Turnaround time: 5 to 10 working days. Use State Form 8053.

In person search: Search costs $10.00 per individual. Requester must have picture ID, turnaround time is 30 minutes.

Corporation Records
Limited Partnerships
Fictitious Name
Assumed Name
Limited Liability Company Records
Limited Liability Partnerships

Corporation Division, Secretary of State, 302 W Washington St, Room E018, Indianapolis, IN 46204; 317-232-6576, 317-233-3387 (Fax), 8AM-5:30PM M-F.

http://www.state.in.us/sos

Note: This agency also holds Agricultural Cooperative and Business Trust records.

Indexing & Storage: Records are available for all active entities. Corporate reports prior to 1993 may take as long as 6 weeks to retrieve. New records are available for inquiry immediately. Records are indexed on microfilm, inhouse computer, and paper.

Searching: There are no restrictions, all information is public record. Include the following in your request-full name of business, specific records that you need copies of. Other records available include: Annual or Bi-annual Reports, Officers (when applicable), Prior (merged) names, Inactive and Reserved names, Assumed Business names, and Registered Agent and address. Directors information is available, but not by phone.

Access by: mail, phone, in person, online.

Fee & Payment: There is no search fee. Copies cost $1.00 per page plus $15.00 for document certification. Due & Diligent Searches may be ordered for information that cannot be found initially. Fee payee: Secretary of State. Prepayment required. The state will allow pre-paid accounts for filing only. Personal checks accepted. No credit cards accepted.

Mail search: Turnaround time: 4 to 7 days. No pre-payments accepted for mail requests. Due & Diligent searches take 10 business days.No self addressed stamped envelope is required.

Phone search: Limited verification information is available.

In person search: Turnaround time: In by noon, ready by noon the next day. Requests after 12 noon are ready within 2 business days.

Online search: This subscription service is available from the Access Indiana Information Network (AI) gateway on the Internet. There is no fee to view a partial record, but $1.00 to view a screen containing the registered agent and other information. Go to www.ai.org.

Other access: Monthly lists of all new businesses are available online, as are bulk data and specialized searches.

Trademarks/Servicemarks

Secretary of State, Trademark Division, 302 W Washington St, IGC-South, Room E111, Indianapolis, IN 46204; 317-232-6540, 317-233-3675 (Fax), 8:45AM-4:45PM.

http://www.state.in.us/sos

Note: These records are considered public and are available with no restrictions.

Indexing & Storage: Records are available for active trademarks. It takes 2 to 3 days before new records are available for inquiry.

Searching: Search requires trademark/servicemark name or file ID number. It generally takes 2 to 3 days to search for logo/designs, but name searches can be done immediately. If you have the file ID number, it will help.

Access by: mail, phone, fax, in person.

Fee & Payment: Fees: Copies cost $1.00 per page. Fee payee: Secretary of State. Prepayment required. Cash is not accepted. Personal checks accepted. No credit cards accepted.

Mail search: Turnaround time: 2 to 3 days. No self addressed stamped envelope is required.

Phone search: There is a limit to three searches at any one time.

Fax search: There is no fee for fax searches. Turnaround time is 1-3 days.

In person search: You may request information in person.

Other access: The state will release a computer printout of the database. Contact the office for pricing information.

Uniform Commercial Code

UCC Division, Secretary of State, 302 West Washington St, Room E-018, Indianapolis, IN 46204; 317-233-3984, 317-233-3387 (Fax), 8AM-5:30PM.

http://www.in.gov/sos

Indexing & Storage: Records are available 1964, indexed on computer. It takes 3 days before new records are available for inquiry.

Searching: Use the state request form. All tax liens are filed at the county level. Include the following in your request-debtor name. Address is helpful.

Access by: mail, fax, in person, online.

Fee & Payment: The search fee of $5.00 per debtor name. Fee payee: Secretary of State. Personal checks accepted. No credit cards accepted.

Mail search: Turnaround time: 2 days.

Fax search: Results are still mailed in 2 days.

In person search: Turnaround time is 2-5 days.

Online search: Searching is available via the Internet. Plans are underway to offer filing services also.

Federal Tax Liens
State Tax Liens
Records not maintained by a state level agency.

Note: All tax liens are found at the county level.

Sales Tax Registrations

Revenue Department, Taxpayer Services, Government Center N, 100 N Senate Ave, Room N248, Indianapolis, IN 46204; 317-233-4015, 317-232-2103 (Fax), 8:15AM-4:45PM.

http://www.ai.org/dor

Searching: This agency will only confirm whether a company is registered. No other information will

be given about the company. The database is not available for purchase. Include the following in your request-name. They can also search by permit number or federal tax ID.

Access by: mail, phone.

Mail search: Turnaround time: 6 to 12 weeks. No fee for mail request.

Phone search: No fee for telephone request. This is very limited, only one search permitted.

Birth Certificates

State Department of Health, Vital Records Office, PO Box 7125, Indianapolis, IN 46206-7125 (Courier: 2 N. Meridian, Indianapolis, IN 46204), 317-233-2700, 317-233-7210 (Fax), 8:15AM-4:45PM.

Note: The information is also available at each local county health department.

Indexing & Storage: Records are available from October 1907 on and are computerized since 1978. It takes 12 weeks before new records are available for inquiry. Records are indexed on microfilm, index cards, books (volumes).

Searching: Must have a signed release form from person of record or be immediate family member or show direct need. Include the following in your request-full name, names of parents, mother's maiden name, date of birth, place of birth, relationship to person of record, reason for information request.

Access by: mail, phone, fax, in person.

Fee & Payment: If exact date of birth is not known there is an additional fee of $4.00 for each 5 years searched. Add $1.00 per name requested for each additional copy of same record. Fee payee: Indiana State Department of Health. Prepayment required. Personal checks accepted. Credit cards accepted: MasterCard, Visa, AmEx, Discover.

Mail search: Turnaround time: 3 to 4 weeks. Must include a copy of a signature ID with your request.No self addressed stamped envelope is required. Search costs $6.00 for each name in request.

Phone search: Search costs $11.00 for each name in request. Fee includes use of a credit card, which is required.

Fax search: The search costs $6.00 for each name in request, plus an additional $5.00 for the use of a credit card. Turnaround time is 5-10 days.

In person search: Search costs $6.00 for each name in request. It takes about 30 minutes to process the request.

Expedited service: Expedited service is available for mail, phone and fax searches. Turnaround time: 3 to 5 days. The expedited service requires use of a credit card and a $11.85 payment for overnight service.

Death Records

State Department of Health, Vital Records Office, PO Box 7125, Indianapolis, IN 46206-7125 (Courier: 2 N. Meridian, Indianapolis, IN 46204), 317-233-2700, 317-233-7210 (Fax), 8:15AM-4:45PM.

Indexing & Storage: Records are available from 1900 on. Records are indexed on microfilm, index cards, books (volumes).

Searching: This index is not for public review. You must have a signed release from immediate family member. Include a copy of your photo ID with your request. Include the following in your request-full name, date of death, place of death, relationship to person of record, reason for information request.

Access by: mail, phone, fax, in person.

Fee & Payment: If exact date of death is not known, there is a $4.00 fee for each 5 years searched. Add $1.00 per name requested for each additional copy of same record. Fee payee: Indiana State Department of Health. Prepayment required. Personal checks accepted. Credit cards accepted: MasterCard, Visa, AmEx, Discover.

Mail search: Turnaround time: 1 month. No self addressed stamped envelope is required. Search costs $4.00 for each name in request.

Phone search: Search costs $9.00 for each name in request. The fee includes use of a credit card, which is required.

Fax search: Search cost $4.00 for each name in request, plus an additional $5.00 fax fee for the use of a credit card.

In person search: Search costs $4.00 for each name in request.

Expedited service: Expedited service is available for fax searches. Turnaround time: 3 to 5 days. The expedited service requires use of a credit card and $11.85 payment for express delivery.

Marriage Certificates
Divorce Records
Records not maintained by a state level agency.

Note: Marriage and divorce records are found at county of issue. The state tells us that the index can also be found at the Indiana State Library.

Workers' Compensation Records

Workers Compensation Board, 402 W Washington St, Room W196, Indianapolis, IN 46204-2753; 317-232-3808, 8AM-4:30PM.

http://www.state.is.us/wkcomp

Indexing & Storage: Records are available for past 5 years. Records are indexed on inhouse computer.

Searching: Must have a notarized authorization release from claimant or a subpoena to obtain records from this agency. Requests are reviewed by the Executive Secretary who decides whether to release the information. Include the following in your request-claimant name, Social Security Number, date of accident, reason for information request.

Access by: mail.

Fee & Payment: Copies are $.50 per page, there is no search fee. Fee payee: Workers Compensation Board. Personal checks accepted. No credit cards accepted.

Mail search: Turnaround time: variable. No self addressed stamped envelope is required.

Driver Records

BMV-Driving Records, 100 N Senate Ave, Indiana Government Center North, Room N405,

Indianapolis, IN 46204; 317-232-6000 x2, 8:15AM-4:30PM.

http://www.state.in.us/bmv

Note: Copies of tickets are available at the address listed above for a fee of $8.00 per ticket.

Indexing & Storage: Records are available for 7 years (10 years for habitual violators) for moving violations; 10 years for DWIs and suspensions. Accidents reported to the state police appear on the record. It takes 1-3 weeks before new records are available for inquiry.

Searching: Personal information is not disclosed to casual requesters. Further, a driver's Social Security Number, driver's license number or Federal ID number is not disclosed to all non-governmental requesters. The license number or name and DOB are required when ordering a record.

Access by: mail, in person, online.

Fee & Payment: The fee is $4.00 per record, except for online requests. The fee is $8.00 for a certified record. The fee is $12.00 for certified "complete" record and history. Turnaround time is 12 weeks for certified records. Fee payee: Bureau of Motor Vehicles. Prepayment required. Personal checks accepted. No credit cards accepted.

Mail search: Turnaround time: 7 to 10 days. No self addressed stamped envelope is required.

In person search: Up to seven requests are processed at one time for a walk-in requester at the Customer Service Center, 531 Virginia Ave, Indianapolis, IN 46204, Room W160.

Online search: Online access costs $5.00 per record. Access Indiana Information Network (AIIN) is the state owned interactive information and communication system which provides batch and interactive access to driving records. There is an annual $50.00 fee. For more information, call AIIN at 317-233-2010 or go to www.ai.org.

Vehicle Ownership
Vehicle Identification
Vessel Ownership
Vessel Registration

Bureau of Motor Vehicles, Records, 100 N Senate Ave, Room N404, Indianapolis, IN 46204; 317-233-6000, 8:15AM-4:45PM.

http://www.state.in.us/bmv

Indexing & Storage: Records are available for 3 years on computer and up to ten years on microfilm. All motor boats that were valued over $3,000 when new must be titled and registered.

Searching: Casual requesters can obtain records, but no personal information is released on subjects who have opted out. Vehicle owner's SSN, driver's license number, and Federal ID number cannot be disclosed to all non-governmental requesters. There are five types of records available for search; title inquiry, title history, registration inquiry, registration history, and registration copy. The title history will show liens. The title inquiry will show current listed lienholder, also.

Access by: mail, in person, online.

Fee & Payment: For vehicle, the fee is $4.00 per "inquiry" and $8.00 per "history." For watercraft, the fee is $4.00 for all title and registration searches. Fee payee: Bureau of Motor Vehicles. Prepayment required. Personal checks accepted. No credit cards accepted.

Mail search: Turnaround time: within 2 weeks. No self addressed stamped envelope is required.

In person search: Turnaround time depends on availability of personnel. Title histories are not provided on an immediate basis, they must be returned by mail or picked up later.

Online search: The Access Indiana Information network (AIIN) at 317-233-2010 is the state appointed vendor. The fee is $5.00 per record plus an annual fee of $50.00. Visit www.ai.org for more information.

Other access: Bulk record requests are not available from Indiana.

Accident Reports

State Police Department, Vehicle Crash Records Sections, Room N301, Indiana Government Center, Indianapolis, IN 46204; 317-232-8286, 317-232-0652 (Fax), 8AM-4PM.

Note: The only reports released are those of the officers. Indiana operator report forms are not released.

Indexing & Storage: Records are available from 20 years to present. Older records are archived on microfiche. It takes 2 weeks before new records are available for inquiry.

Searching: Include the following in your request-full name, date of accident, location of accident.

Access by: mail, phone, in person.

Fee & Payment: The fee is $3.00 per report. If you are requesting all reports on a per-name basis, there is a $6.81 per hour search fee in addition. Fee payee: Indiana State Police. Prepayment required. Personal checks accepted. No credit cards accepted.

Mail search: Turnaround time: 7 to 10 days. No self addressed stamped envelope is required.

Phone search: You can phone to see if a report is on file before the fee is sent.

In person search: Normal turnaround time is while you wait. If you are requesting all accidents on a "name," this request should be in writing and will take longer.

Other access: For information about bulk file purchasing, contact the Data Section at 317-232-8289.

Legislation Records

Legislative Services Agency, State House, 200 W Washington, Room 301, Indianapolis, IN 46204-2789; 317-232-9856, 8:15AM-4:45PM.

http://www.state.in.us

Note: Sessions start in January. Long sessions (61 days) are in the odd years; short sessions (30 days) are in the even years. Bills prior to 1990 are stored in the State Law Library.

Indexing & Storage: Records are available from 1980 to present.

Searching: Include the following in your request-bill number. Can search on code citation also.

Access by: mail, phone, in person, online.

Fee & Payment: Fees are $.15 per copy plus postage. Fee payee: Legislative Services Agency. Prepayment required. Personal checks accepted. No credit cards accepted.

Mail search: Turnaround time: 1 to 4 days. No self addressed stamped envelope is required.

Phone search: You may request the cost of sending documents, but all requests must be prepaid.

Online search: All legislative information is available over the Internet. The Indiana Code is also available.

Other access: Online access is free.

Voter Registration
Access to Records is Restricted

Elections Commission, 302 Washington, Room E-204, Indianapolis, IN 46204-2767; 317-232-3939, 317-233-6793 (Fax), 8AM-4:30PM.

http://www.state.in.us/sos/elections

Note: This agency will not sell records for commercial or investigative reasons, but will sell data in bulk format for political purposes for $5,000. The SSN is not released. In general, the Circuit Court has records locally. Campaign finance reports are searchable at the web site, which is full of good information about elections in IN.

GED Certificates

Division of Adult Education, GED Testing, State House Rm 229, Indianapolis, IN 46204-2798; 317-232-0522, 317-233-0859 (Fax).

http://ideanet.doe.state.in.us/adulted/adult2.htm

Note: The suggested Release Form is available online at the web site.

Indexing & Storage: It takes two weeks before new records are available for inquiry.

Searching: To search, all of the following are required: a signed release, name, date/year of test, date of birth, Social Security Number, city of test, and a phone number where you can be reached.

Access by: mail, fax.

Fee & Payment: There is no fee. E-mail requests are accepted, but like all requests a signed release is required.

Mail search: Records are available by mail.

Fax search: Records are available by fax.

Hunting License Information
Fishing License Information
Records not maintained by a state level agency.

Note: They do not have a central database. Vendors keep all records.

Indiana State Licensing Agencies

Licenses Searchable Online

Athletic Trainer #09.......................www.state.in.us/hpb/mlvs/index.html
Audiologist #09.............................www.state.in.us/hpb/mlvs/index.html
Child Care Center/Home #10.........www.ai.org/fssa/database/centers.html
Child Care Home #10.....................www.ai.org/fssa/database/homes.html
Chiropractor #09............................www.state.in.us/hpb/mlvs/index.html
Collection Agency #19...................www.state.in.us/serv/sos_securities
Dental Hygienist #09......................www.state.in.us/hpb/mlvs/index.html
Dentist #09...................................www.state.in.us/hpb/mlvs/index.html
Dietitian #09.................................www.state.in.us/hpb/mlvs/index.html
Emergency Medical Technician #09..............www.state.in.us/hpb/mlvs/index.html
Environmental Health #09...............www.state.in.us/hpb/mlvs/index.html
Hazardous Waste Handler/Facility #05..........www.state.in.us/idem/olq/site_information/lists.html
Health Services Administrator #09................www.state.in.us/hpb/mlvs/index.html
Hearing Aid Dealer #09..................www.state.in.us/hpb/mlvs/index.html
Hypnotist #09...............................www.state.in.us/hpb/mlvs/index.html
Insurance Agent/Consultant #07...................www.in.gov/idoi/
Investment Advisor #19..................www.state.in.us/serv/sos_securities
Loan Brokers #19..........................www.state.in.us/serv/sos_securities
Marriage & Family Therapist #09..................www.state.in.us/hpb/mlvs/index.html
Medical Doctor #09........................www.state.in.us/hpb/mlvs/index.html
Mental Health Counselor #09........www.state.in.us/hpb/mlvs/index.html
Midwife Nurse #09.........................www.state.in.us/hpb/mlvs/index.html
Nurse #09.....................................www.state.in.us/hpb/mlvs/index.html
Nurse-LPN/RN #09........................www.state.in.us/hpb/mlvs/index.html
Nursing Home Administrator #09...................www.state.in.us/hpb/mlvs/index.html
Occupational Therapist #09...........www.state.in.us/hpb/mlvs/index.html
Optometrist #09.............................www.state.in.us/hpb/mlvs/index.html
Osteopathic Physician #09.............www.state.in.us/hpb/mlvs/index.html
Pharmacist/Pharmacist Intern #09................www.state.in.us/hpb/mlvs/index.html
Physical Therapist/Therapist Assistant #09....www.state.in.us/hpb/mlvs/index.html
Physician #09................................www.state.in.us/hpb/mlvs/index.html
Physician Assistant #09.................www.state.in.us/hpb/mlvs/index.html
Podiatrist #09...............................www.state.in.us/hpb/mlvs/index.html
Polygraph Examiner #21.................www.indianapolygraphassociation.com
Psychologist #09...........................www.state.in.us/hpb/mlvs/index.html
Respiratory Care Practitioner #09.................www.state.in.us/hpb/mlvs/index.html
Securities Broker/Dealer #19.........www.in.gov/serv/sos_securities
Securities Sales Agent #19............www.in.gov/serv/sos_securities
Social Worker #09..........................www.state.in.us/hpb/mlvs/index.html
Social Worker, Clinical #09.............www.state.in.us/hpb/mlvs/index.html
Solid Waste Facility #05.................www.state.in.us/idem/olq/site_information/lists.html
Speech Pathologist #09.................www.state.in.us/hpb/mlvs/index.html
Teacher #14..................................http://dew4.doe.state.in.us/LIC/license.html
Veterinarian #09............................www.state.in.us/hpb/mlvs/index.html
Waste Tire Processor/Transporter #05...........www.state.in.us/idem/olq/site_information/lists.html
Yard Waste Composting Facility #05..............www.state.in.us/idem/olq/site_information/lists.html

Licensing Quick Finder

Alcoholic Beverage Dist./Retailer/Employee #01 ....
....317-232-2446
Amusement Ride #37 217-782-9347
Architect #18....................................317-232-2980
Asbestos Contractor #04 317-232-8232
Asbestos Disposal Mgr./Worker #04 317-232-8232
Asbestos Inspector/Supervisor/Project Designer #04
....317-232-8232
Asbestos Training Course Provider#04 .317-232-8232
Athletic Trainer #09 317-232-2960
Attorney #15 317-232-1930
Auctioneer #18...................................317-232-2980
Audiologist #09 317-232-2960
Bank & Trust Company #06.................317-232-5846
Barber #18 317-232-2980
Boiler & Pressure Vessel Inspector #8 ..317-232-1921
Boxer #18 317-232-2980
Building & Loan #06 317-232-5851
Check Casher #06 317-232-3955
Child Care Center #10.........................317-232-1144
Child Care Home #10..........................317-232-1144
Chiropractor #09 317-232-2960
Collection Agency #19........................317-232-0093
Consumer Credit Grantor #06..............317-232-5849
Cosmetologist #18 317-232-2980
Credit Union #06 317-232-5851
Dental Hygienist #09 317-232-2960
Dentist #09 317-232-2960
Dietitian #09.....................................317-232-2960
Elevator Safety Contractor #08 317-232-6609
Emergency Medical Technician #09......317-232-2960
Engineer #18 317-232-2980
Environmental Health #09 317-232-2960

Funeral/Cemetery Director #18.............317-232-2980
Grain Bank/Warehouse #12..................317-232-1358
Grain Buyer #12.................................317-232-1360
Hazardous Waste Facility #05 317-232-8603
Hazardous Waste Handler #05 317-232-8603
Health Services Administrator #09 317-232-2960
Hearing Aid Dealer #09 317-232-2960
Horse Racing #13...............................317-233-3119
Hypnotist #09....................................317-232-2960
Insurance Adjuster #07.......................317-232-2414
Insurance Agent/Consultant #07..........317-232-2414
Investment Advisor #19......................317-232-6681
Lender #06 317-232-3955
Livestock Dealer #02..........................317-227-0300
Loan Brokers #19...............................317-232-6681
Lottery Retailer #16............................317-264-4800
Manufactured Home Builder #08...........317-232-1408
Marriage & Family Therapist #09..........317-232-2960
Medical Doctor #09............................317-232-2960
Mental Health Counselor #09 317-232-2960
Midwife Nurse #09.............................317-232-2960
Money Transmitter #06........................317-232-3955
Notary Public #17...............................317-232-6542
Nurse #09..317-232-2960
Nurse-LPN #09 317-232-2960
Nurse-RN #09 317-232-2960
Nursing Home Administrator #09 317-232-2960
Occupational Therapist #09 317-232-2960
Optometrist #09 317-232-2960
Osteopathic Physician #09 317-232-2960
Pawnbroker #06..................................317-232-3955
Pesticide Applicator #03 765-494-1594
Pesticide Technician/Consultant #03 765-494-1594

Pharmacist/Pharmacist Intern #09 317-232-2960
Physical Therapist/Therapist Assistant #09 ....
....317-233-2960
Physician #09 317-232-2960
Physician Assistant #09......................317-232-2960
Plumber #18 317-232-2980
Podiatrist #09 317-232-2960
Polygraph Examiner #21 317-232-8263
Private Detective #18 317-232-2980
Psychologist #09................................317-232-2960
Public Accountant #18........................317-232-2980
Radiologic Technologist #20................317-233-7565
Real Estate Agent #18 317-232-2980
Real Estate Appraiser #18...................317-232-2980
Respiratory Care Practitioner #09 317-232-2960
School Administrator/Principal #14 317-232-9010
School Counselor #14.........................317-232-9010
Securities Broker/Dealer #19 317-232-6690
Securities Sales Agent #19..................317-232-6690
Shorthand Reporter #11 219-756-0702
Social Worker #09..............................317-232-2960
Social Worker, Clinical #09 317-232-2960
Solid Waste Facility #05 317-232-8603
Speech Pathologist #09.......................317-232-2960
Surveyor #18 317-232-2980
Teacher #14.......................................317-232-9010
Underground Storage Tank #08............317-233-3560
Veterinarian #09.................................317-232-2960
Warehouse (Agricultural, etc.) #12........317-232-1358
Waste Tire Processor/Transporter #05..317-232-8603
Waste Water Treatment Plant Operator #05..............
....317-232-8666
Yard Waste Composting Facility #05 317-232-8603

Licensing Agency Information

#01 Alcoholic Beverage Commission, 302 W Washington St, Rm E114, Indianapolis, IN 46204; 317-232-2455, Fax: 317-233-6114.

#02 Licensing/Enforcement Division, 805 Beachway Dr #50, Indianapolis, IN 46224; 317-227-0300, Fax: 317-227-0330.
www.state.in.us/boah/

#03 Department of Biochemistry, Purdue University, West Lafayette, IN 47907; 765-494-1594, Fax: 765-494-4331.
www.isco.purdue.edu

#04 Department of Environmental Management, 100 N. Senate, Indianapolis, IN 46204-6015; 317-232-8603, Fax: 317-232-8406.
www.IN.gov/idem/

#05 Department of Environmental Management, PO Box 6015, Indianapolis, IN 46204-6015; 317-232-8603, Fax: 317-232-8406.
www.state.in.us/idem

#06 Department of Financial Institutions, 402 W Washington St, IGC-S, Rm W066, Indianapolis, IN 46204-2759; 317-232-3955, Fax: 317-232-7655.
www.dfi.state.in.us

#07 Department of Insurance, 311 W Washington St #300, Indianapolis, IN 46204-2787; 317-232-2385, Fax: 317-232-5251.
www.in.gov/idol
Direct web site URL to search for licensees:
www.in.gov/idol/licagent.html

#08 Fire & Building Services, 402 W Washington St, IGS-S, Rm W246, Indianapolis, IN 46204; 317-232-6609, Fax: 317-232-0146.

#09 Health Professions Bureau, 402 W Washington St, #041, Indianapolis, IN 46204-2739; 317-232-2960, Fax: 317-233-4236.
www.ai.org/hpb
Direct web site URL to search for licensees:
www.state.in.us/hpb/mlvs/index.html   To search online, you have to subscribe to AIIN. For more AIIN info, www.state.in.us/premium/about.html

#10 Family and Social Services Administration, 402 W. Washington St., Rm W386, Indianapolis, IN 46201; 317-232-1144.
www.state.in.us/fssa/HTML/CHILD/index.html
Direct web site URL to search for licensees:
www.state.in.us/fssa/index.html. Search online using facility name, city, zip, county, age of child

#11 ISRA President, Karen Price, PO Box 11270, Merrillville, IN 46411; 219-756-0702, Fax: 219-756-1766.

#12 Grain Buyers & Warehouse Licensing Agency, 150 W Market St, Rm 416, Indianapolis, IN 46204-2810; 317-232-1356, Fax: 317-232-1362.
www.IN.gov/igbwla/

#13 Horse Racing Licensing, 150 W Market St, Indianapolis, IN 46204; 317-233-3119, Fax: 317-233-4470. www.IN.gov/ihrc/

#14 Professional Standards Board, 101 W Ohio St, #300, Indianapolis, IN 46204; 317-232-9010, Fax: 317-232-9023. www.state.in.us/psb

#15 Clerk of the Indiana Supreme Court, 217 State House, 20th Fl, Indianapolis, IN 46204; 317-232-1930, Fax: 317-232-8365.
www.IN.gov/judiciary/

#16 Lottery Commission of Indiana, 201 S Capitol Av #1100, Indianapolis, IN 46225; 317-264-4800, Fax: 317-264-4908.
www.hoosierlottery.com/yes.htm

#17 Office of Secretary of State, Statehouse, #201, Indianapolis, IN 46204; 317-232-6542, Fax: 317-233-3283.
www.state.in.us/sos/bus_service/notary/

#18 Professional Licensing Agency, 302 W Washington St, Rm E034, Indianapolis, IN 46204; 317-232-2980, Fax: 31733-5559.
www.IN.gov/pla/

#19 Secretary of State, 302 W Washington RME 111, Indianapolis, IN 46204; 317-232-6681, Fax: 317-233-3675.
www.state.in.us/sos/security/
Direct web site URL to search for licensees:
www.state.in.us/serv/sos_securities. You can search online using name, registration #

#20 Division of End. & Radiologic Health, 2 N Meridian St, 5F, Indianapolis, IN 46204-3003; 317-233-7150.

#21 State Police, 100 N Senate Ave, Government Center N, #302, Indianapolis, IN 46204-2259; 317-232-8263, Fax: 317-232-0652.
www.indianapolygraphassociation.com
Direct web site URL to search for licensees:
www.indianapolygraphassociation.com

Indiana Federal Courts

The following list indicates the district and division name for each county in the state. If the bankruptcy court location is different from the district court, then the location of the bankruptcy court appears in parentheses.

County/Court Cross Reference

County	District	Division
Adams	Northern	Fort Wayne
Allen	Northern	Fort Wayne
Bartholomew	Southern	Indianapolis
Benton	Northern	Lafayette (Hammond at Lafayette)
Blackford	Northern	Fort Wayne
Boone	Southern	Indianapolis
Brown	Southern	Indianapolis
Carroll	Northern	Lafayette (Hammond at Lafayette)
Cass	Northern	South Bend
Clark	Southern	New Albany
Clay	Southern	Terre Haute
Clinton	Southern	Indianapolis
Crawford	Southern	New Albany
Daviess	Southern	Evansville
DeKalb	Northern	Fort Wayne
Dearborn	Southern	New Albany
Decatur	Southern	Indianapolis
Delaware	Southern	Indianapolis
Dubois	Southern	Evansville
Elkhart	Northern	South Bend
Fayette	Southern	Indianapolis
Floyd	Southern	New Albany
Fountain	Southern	Indianapolis
Franklin	Southern	Indianapolis
Fulton	Northern	South Bend
Gibson	Southern	Evansville
Grant	Northern	Fort Wayne
Greene	Southern	Terre Haute
Hamilton	Southern	Indianapolis
Hancock	Southern	Indianapolis
Harrison	Southern	New Albany
Hendricks	Southern	Indianapolis
Henry	Southern	Indianapolis
Howard	Southern	Indianapolis
Huntington	Northern	Fort Wayne
Jackson	Southern	New Albany
Jasper	Northern	Lafayette (Hammond at Lafayette)
Jay	Northern	Fort Wayne
Jefferson	Southern	New Albany
Jennings	Southern	New Albany
Johnson	Southern	Indianapolis
Knox	Southern	Terre Haute
Kosciusko	Northern	South Bend
La Porte	Northern	South Bend
LaGrange	Northern	Fort Wayne
Lake	Northern	Hammond (Hammond. at Gary)
Lawrence	Southern	New Albany
Madison	Southern	Indianapolis
Marion	Southern	Indianapolis
Marshall	Northern	South Bend
Martin	Southern	Evansville
Miami	Northern	South Bend
Monroe	Southern	Indianapolis
Montgomery	Southern	Indianapolis
Morgan	Southern	Indianapolis
Newton	Northern	Lafayette (Hammond at Lafayette)
Noble	Northern	Fort Wayne
Ohio	Southern	New Albany
Orange	Southern	New Albany
Owen	Southern	Terre Haute
Parke	Southern	Terre Haute
Perry	Southern	Evansville
Pike	Southern	Evansville
Porter	Northern	Hammond (Hammond. at Gary)
Posey	Southern	Evansville
Pulaski	Northern	South Bend
Putnam	Southern	Terre Haute
Randolph	Southern	Indianapolis
Ripley	Southern	New Albany
Rush	Southern	Indianapolis
Scott	Southern	New Albany
Shelby	Southern	Indianapolis
Spencer	Southern	Evansville
St. Joseph	Northern	South Bend
Starke	Northern	South Bend
Steuben	Northern	Fort Wayne
Sullivan	Southern	Terre Haute
Switzerland	Southern	New Albany
Tippecanoe	Northern	Lafayette (Hammond at Lafayette)
Tipton	Southern	Indianapolis
Union	Southern	Indianapolis
Vanderburgh	Southern	Evansville
Vermillion	Southern	Terre Haute
Vigo	Southern	Terre Haute
Wabash	Northern	South Bend
Warren	Northern	Lafayette (Hammond at Lafayette)
Warrick	Southern	Evansville
Washington	Southern	New Albany
Wayne	Southern	Indianapolis
Wells	Northern	Fort Wayne
White	Northern	Lafayette (Hammond at Lafayette)
Whitley	Northern	Fort Wayne

US District Court

Northern District of Indiana

Fort Wayne Division Room 1108, Federal Bldg, 1300 S Harrison St, Fort Wayne, IN 46802 (Courier Address: Use mail address for courier delivery), 219-424-7360.

http://www.innd.uscourts.gov

Counties: Adams, Allen, Blackford, DeKalb, Grant, Huntington, Jay, Lagrange, Noble, Steuben, Wells, Whitley.

Indexing/Storage: Cases are indexed by defendant and plaintiff as well as by case number. New cases are available in the index 1-2 days after filing date. Both computer and card indexes are maintained. Open records are located at this court.

Fee & Payment: The fee is $20.00 per item (one party name or case number). Payment may be made by money order, cashier check, personal check. Prepayment is required. Payee: Clerk, US District Court. Certification fee: $7.00 per document. Copy fee: $.50 per page.

Phone Search: Only case names and numbers will be released over the phone.

Mail Search: Always enclose a stamped self addressed envelope.

In Person: In person searching is available.

PACER: Sign-up number is 800-676-6856. Access fee is $.60 per minute. Toll-free access: 800-371-8843. Local access: 219-246-8200. Case records are available back to 1994. Records are purged as deemed necessary. New records are available online after 2 days. PACER is available online at http://pacer.innd.uscourts.gov.

Hammond Division Room 101, 507 State St, Hammond, IN 46320 (Courier Address: Use mail address for courier delivery), 219-937-5235.

http://www.innd.uscourts.gov

Counties: Lake, Porter.

Indexing/Storage: Cases are indexed by defendant and plaintiff as well as by case number. New cases are available in the index 1-3 days after filing date. A computer index is maintained. Open records are located at this court.

Fee & Payment: The fee is $20.00 per item (one party name or case number). Payment may be made by money order, cashier check, personal check. Prepayment is required. Payee: Clerk, US District Court. Certification fee: $7.00 per document. Copy fee: $.50 per page.

Phone Search: Only docket information is available by phone.

Mail Search: Always enclose a stamped self addressed envelope.

In Person: In person searching is available.

PACER: Sign-up number is 800-676-6856. Access fee is $.60 per minute. Toll-free access: 800-371-8843. Local access: 219-246-8200. Case records are available back to 1994. Records are purged as deemed necessary. New records are available online after 2 days. PACER is available online at http://pacer.innd.uscourts.gov.

Lafayette Division PO Box 1498, Lafayette, IN 47902 (Courier Address: 230 N 4th St, Lafayette, IN 47901), 765-420-6250.

http://www.innd.uscourts.gov

Counties: Benton, Carroll, Jasper, Newton, Tippecanoe, Warren, White.

Indexing/Storage: Cases are indexed by defendant and plaintiff as well as by case number. New cases are available in the index 24 hours after filing date. A computer index is maintained. Microfiche is also available. Open records are located at this court.

Fee & Payment: The fee is $20.00 per item (one party name or case number). Payment may be made by money order, cashier check, personal check. Prepayment is required. Payee: Clerk, US District Court. Certification fee: $7.00 per document. Copy fee: $.50 per page.

Phone Search: Only docket information is available by phone.

Fax Search: Will accept fax only to ask if a person is a defendant or plaintiff in any cases.

Mail Search: Always enclose a stamped self addressed envelope.

In Person: In person searching is available.

PACER: Sign-up number is 800-676-6856. Access fee is $.60 per minute. Toll-free access: 800-371-8843. Local access: 219-246-8200. Case records are available back to 1994. Records are purged as deemed necessary. New records are available online after 2 days. PACER is available online at http://pacer.innd.uscourts.gov.

South Bend Division Room 102, 204 S Main, South Bend, IN 46601 (Courier Address: Use mail address for courier delivery), 219-246-8000, Fax: 219-246-8002.

http://www.innd.uscourts.gov

Counties: Cass, Elkhart, Fulton, Kosciusko, La Porte, Marshall, Miami, Pulaski, St. Joseph, Starke, Wabash.

Indexing/Storage: Cases are indexed by defendant and plaintiff as well as by case number. New cases are available in the index 2 days after filing date. A computer index is maintained. Open records are located at this court.

Fee & Payment: The fee is $20.00 per item (one party name or case number). Payment may be made by money order, cashier check, personal check. Prepayment is required. Payee: Clerk, US District Court. Certification fee: $7.00 per document. Copy fee: $.50 per page.

Phone Search: Only docket information is available by phone.

Mail Search: Always enclose a stamped self addressed envelope.

In Person: In person searching is available.

PACER: Sign-up number is 800-676-6856. Access fee is $.60 per minute. Toll-free access: 800-371-8843. Local access: 219-246-8200. Case records are available back to 1994. Records are purged as deemed necessary. New records are available online after 2 days. PACER is available online at http://pacer.innd.uscourts.gov.

US Bankruptcy Court

Northern District of Indiana

Fort Wayne Division PO Box 2547, Fort Wayne, IN 46801-2547 (Courier Address: 1188 Federal Bldg, 1300 S Harrison St, Fort Wayne, IN 46802), 219-420-5100.

http://www.innb.uscourts.gov

Counties: Adams, Allen, Blackford, DeKalb, Grant, Huntington, Jay, Lagrange, Noble, Steuben, Wells, Whitley.

Indexing/Storage: Cases are indexed by debtor and creditors as well as by case number. New cases are available in the index 24 hours after filing date. A computer index is maintained. A card index of debtor names is also maintained. Open records are located at this court. Records in closed cases are only kept locally for a brief period. Records are shipped to the Chicago FRC annually. At the time a case is closed, both the date of filing and the date of closing are factors in determining when the case is shipped.

Fee & Payment: The fee is $20.00 per item (one party name or case number). Payment may be made by money order, cashier check, personal check. Prepayment is required. Debtor's checks are not accepted. Payee: Clerk, US Bankruptcy Court. Certification fee: $7.00 per document. Copy fee: $.50 per page.

Phone Search: Only docket information is available by phone. An automated voice case information service (VCIS) is available. Call VCIS at 800-755-8393 or 219-968-2275.

Mail Search: Always enclose a stamped self addressed envelope.

In Person: In person searching is available.

PACER: Sign-up number is 800-676-6856. Access fee is $.60 per minute. Toll-free access: 888-917-2237. Local access: 219-968-2270. Case records are available back to 1992. Records are purged every 6 months. New civil records are available online after 2 days. PACER is available online at http://pacer.innb.uscourts.gov.

Hammond at Gary Division 221 Federal Bldg, 610 Connecticut St, Gary, IN 46402-2595 (Courier Address: Use mail address for courier delivery), 219-881-3335, Fax: 219-881-3307.

http://www.innb.uscourts.gov

Counties: Lake, Porter.

Indexing/Storage: Cases are indexed by debtor and creditors as well as by case number. New cases are available in the index 24 hours after filing date. A computer index is maintained. Open records are located at this court. Records in closed cases are only kept locally for a brief period. Records are shipped to the FRC twice a year. At the time a case is closed, both the date of filing and the date of closing are factors in determining when the case is shipped.

Fee & Payment: The fee is $20.00 per item (one party name or case number). Payment may be made by money order, cashier check, personal check, Visa or Mastercard. Prepayment is required. Debtor's checks and credit cards are not accepted. Payee: Clerk, US Bankruptcy Court. Certification fee: $7.00 per document. Copy fee: $.50 per page. You are allowed to make your own copies. These copies cost $.15 per page.

Phone Search: Only docket information is available by phone. An automated voice case information service (VCIS) is available. Call VCIS at 800-755-8393 or 219-968-2275.

Mail Search: Always enclose a stamped self addressed envelope.

In Person: In person searching is available.

PACER: Sign-up number is 800-676-6856. Access fee is $.60 per minute. Toll-free access: 888-917-2237. Local access: 219-968-2270. Case records are available back to 1992. Records are purged every 6 months. New civil records are available online after 2 days. PACER is available online at http://pacer.innb.uscourts.gov.

Hammond at Lafayette Division c/o Fort
Wayne Division, PO Box 2547, Fort Wayne, IN 46801-2547 (Courier Address: Use mail address for courier delivery), 219-420-5100.

http://www.innb.uscourts.gov

Counties: Benton, Carroll, Jasper, Newton, Tippecanoe, Warren, White.

Indexing/Storage: Cases are indexed by debtor and collector as well as by case number. New cases are available in the index after filing date. All the files for the Hammond Division at Lafayette are physically kept in the Fort Wayne office. All papers pertaining to Hammond Division at Lafayette cases after the initial filing, including claims, should be sent to the Fort Wayne office. Open records are located at the Division.

Fee & Payment: The fee is $20.00 per item (one party name or case number). Payment may be made by money order, cashier check. Business checks are not accepted. Personal checks are not accepted.

Phone Search: An automated voice case information service (VCIS) is available. Call VCIS at 800-755-8393 or 219-968-2275.

Mail Search: Always enclose a stamped self addressed envelope.

In Person: In person searching is available.

PACER: Sign-up number is 800-676-6856. Access fee is $.60 per minute. Toll-free access: 888-917-2237. Local access: 219-968-2270. Case records are available back to 1992. Records are purged every 6 months. New civil records are available online after 2 days. PACER is available online at http://pacer.innb.uscourts.gov.

South Bend Division PO Box 7003, South
Bend, IN 46634-7003 (Courier Address: 401 S Michigan St, South Bend, IN 46601), 219-968-2100, Fax: 219-968-2205.

http://www.innb.uscourts.gov

Counties: Cass, Elkhart, Fulton, Kosciusko, La Porte, Marshall, Miami, Pulaski, St. Joseph, Starke, Wabash.

Indexing/Storage: Cases are indexed by debtor and creditors as well as by case number. New cases are available in the index 24 hours after filing date. A computer index is maintained. Open records are located at this court. Records in closed cases are only kept locally for a brief period. Records are shipped to the Chicago FRC semi-annually. At the time a case is closed, both the date of filing and the date of closing are factors in determining when the case is shipped.

Fee & Payment: The fee is $20.00 per item (one party name or case number). Payment may be made by money order, cashier check, personal check, Visa or Mastercard. Prepayment is required. Debtor's checks are not accepted. Payee: Clerk, US Bankruptcy Court. Certification fee: $7.00 per document. Copy fee: $.50 per page. You are allowed to make your own copies. These copies cost $.15 per page. A self service copy machine is available.

Phone Search: Only docket information is available by phone. An automated voice case information service (VCIS) is available. Call VCIS at 800-755-8393 or 219-968-2275.

Mail Search: Always enclose a stamped self addressed envelope.

In Person: In person searching is available.

PACER: Sign-up number is 800-676-6856. Access fee is $.60 per minute. Toll-free access: 888-917-2237. Local access: 219-968-2270. Case records are available back to 1992. Records are purged every 6 months. New civil records are available online after 2 days. PACER is available online at http://pacer.innb.uscourts.gov.

US District Court

Southern District of Indiana

Evansville Division 304 Federal Bldg, 101 NW Martin Luther King Blvd, Evansville, IN 47708 (Courier Address: Use mail address for courier delivery), 812-465-6426, Fax: 812-465-6428.

http://www.insd.uscourts.gov

Counties: Daviess, Dubois, Gibson, Martin, Perry, Pike, Posey, Spencer, Vanderburgh, Warrick.

Indexing/Storage: Cases are indexed by defendant and plaintiff as well as by case number. New cases are available in the index immediately after filing date. Cases prior to 1992 are indexed by name only on index cards. Open records are located at this court.

Fee & Payment: The fee is $20.00 per item (one party name or case number). Payment may be made by money order, cashier check, personal check. Prepayment is required. Payee: Clerk, US District Court. Certification fee: $7.00 per document. Copy fee: $.50 per page.

Phone Search: Searching is not available by phone.

Mail Search: A stamped self addressed envelope is not required.

In Person: In person searching is available.

PACER: There is no PACER access to this court.

Other Online Access: Search records using the Internet. Searching is currently free. Visit www.insd.uscourts.gov/casesearch.htm to search.

Indianapolis Division Clerk, Room 105, 46 E Ohio St, Indianapolis, IN 46204 (Courier Address: Use mail address for courier delivery), 317-229-3700, Fax: 317-229-3959.

http://www.insd.uscourts.gov

Counties: Bartholomew, Boone, Brown, Clinton, Decatur, Delaware, Fayette, Fountain, Franklin, Hamilton, Hancock, Hendricks, Henry, Howard, Johnson, Madison, Marion, Monroe, Montgomery, Morgan, Randolph, Rush, Shelby, Tipton, Union, Wayne.

Indexing/Storage: Cases are indexed by defendant and plaintiff as well as by case number. New cases are available in the index 24 hours after filing date. A computer index is maintained. Open records are located at this court. District wide searches are available from this court for cases from 1996 to the present.

Fee & Payment: The fee is $20.00 per item (one party name or case number). Payment may be made by money order. Business checks are not accepted, Visa, Mastercard. Personal checks are not accepted. Prepayment is required. Payee: Clerk, US District Court. Certification fee: $7.00 per document. Copy fee: $.50 per page.

Phone Search: Only information contained on the face of the docket sheet will be released over the phone. Anything from the remaining pages requires that the search fee be paid.

Mail Search: A stamped self addressed envelope is not required.

In Person: In person searching is available.

PACER: There is no PACER access to this court.

Other Online Access: Search records using the Internet. Searching is currently free. Visit www.insd.uscourts.gov/casesearch.htm to search.

New Albany Division Room 210, 121 W Spring St, New Albany, IN 47150 (Courier Address: Use mail address for courier delivery), 812-948-5238, Fax: 812-948-5246.

http://www.insd.uscourts.gov

Counties: Clark, Crawford, Dearborn, Floyd, Harrison, Jackson, Jefferson, Jennings, Lawrence, Ohio, Orange, Ripley, Scott, Switzerland, Washington.

Indexing/Storage: Cases are indexed by defendant and plaintiff as well as by case number. New cases are available in the index immediately after filing date. A card index is maintained. Open records are located at this court. Files may also be in Indianapolis or Evansville.

Fee & Payment: The fee is $20.00 per item (one party name or case number). Payment may be made by money order, cashier check, personal check. Prepayment is required. Payee: Clerk, US District Court. Certification fee: $7.00 per document. Copy fee: $.50 per page.

Phone Search: Searching is not available by phone.

Mail Search: Always enclose a stamped self addressed envelope.

In Person: In person searching is available.

PACER: There is no PACER access to this court.

Other Online Access: Search records using the Internet. Searching is currently free. Visit www.insd.uscourts.gov/casesearch.htm to search.

Terre Haute Division 207 Federal Bldg, 30 N 7th St, Terre Haute, IN 47808 (Courier Address: Use mail address for courier delivery), 812-234-9484.

http://www.insd.uscourts.gov

Counties: Clay, Greene, Knox, Owen, Parke, Putnam, Sullivan, Vermillion, Vigo.

Indexing/Storage: Cases are indexed by defendant and plaintiff as well as by case number. New cases are available in the index immediately after filing date. A computer index is maintained. Open records are located at this court.

Fee & Payment: The fee is $20.00 per item (one party name or case number). Payment may be made by money order, cashier check, personal check. Prepayment is required. Payee: Clerk, US District Court. Certification fee: $7.00 per document. Copy fee: $.50 per page.

Phone Search: All information that is not sealed is available for release over the phone.

Mail Search: Always enclose a stamped self addressed envelope.

In Person: In person searching is available.

PACER: There is no PACER access to court.

Other Online Access: Search records using the Internet. Searching is currently free. Visit www.insd.uscourts.gov/casesearch.htm to search.

US Bankruptcy Court

Southern District of Indiana

Evansville Division 352 Federal Building, 101 NW Martin Luther King Blvd, Evansville, IN 47708 (Courier Address: Use mail address for courier delivery), 812-465-6440, Fax: 812-465-6453.

http://www.insb.uscourts.gov

Counties: Daviess, Dubois, Gibson, Martin, Perry, Pike, Posey, Spencer, Vanderburgh, Warrick.

Indexing/Storage: Cases are indexed by debtor as well as by case number. New cases are available in the index 1-2 days after filing date. Both computer and card indexes are maintained. Open records are located at this court.

Fee & Payment: The fee is $20.00 per item (one party name or case number). Payment may be made by money order, cashier check, personal check. Prepayment is required. Debtor's checks are not accepted. Payee: Clerk, US Bankruptcy Court. Certification fee: $7.00 per document. Copy fee: $.50 per page. You are allowed to make your own copies. These copies cost $.50 per page.

Phone Search: Only docket information is available by phone. An automated voice case information service (VCIS) is available. Call VCIS at 800-335-8003 or.

Mail Search: Always enclose a stamped self addressed envelope.

In Person: In person searching is available.

PACER: Sign-up number is 317-229-3845. Access fee is $.60 per minute. Local access: 317-229-3989, 317-229-3878. NIBS system: First number is for Carbon Copy users and second is for Procomm users. Use of Carbon Copy Plus required. Case records are available back to 1988. Records are purged every 3 months. New civil records are available online after 2-3 days.

Other Online Access: Search records online at http://neworleans.insb.uscourts.gov/public/casesearch.asp. Search using case number, party name, social security number and/or tax ID number. The system is currently free.

Indianapolis Division US Courthouse, Rm 116, 46 E Ohio St, Indianapolis, IN 46204 (Courier Address: Use mail address for courier delivery), 317-229-3800, Fax: 317-229-3801.

http://www.insb.uscourts.gov

Counties: Bartholomew, Boone, Brown, Clinton, Decatur, Delaware, Fayette, Fountain, Franklin, Hamilton, Hancock, Hendricks, Henry, Howard, Johnson, Madison, Marion, Monroe, Montgomery, Morgan, Randolph, Rush, Shelby, Tipton, Union, Wayne.

Indexing/Storage: Cases are indexed by debtor as well as by case number. New cases are available in the index 48 hours after filing date. A computer index is maintained. Records are stored electronically since 1986. Open records are located at this court.

Fee & Payment: The fee is $20.00 per item (one party name or case number). Payment may be made by money order, cashier check, personal check. Checks are accepted from debtors. Payee: Clerk, US Bankruptcy Court (SDIN). Certification fee: $7.00 per document. Copy fee: $.50 per page.

Phone Search: Only docket information is available by phone. An automated voice case information service (VCIS) is available. Call VCIS at 800-335-8003 or.

Mail Search: Always enclose a stamped self addressed envelope.

In Person: In person searching is available.

PACER: Sign-up number is 317-229-3845. Access fee is $.60 per minute. Local access: 317-229-3989, 317-229-3878. NIBS system: First number is for Carbon Copy users and second is for Procomm users. Use of Carbon Copy Plus required. Case records are available back to 1988. Records are purged every 3 months. New civil records are available online after 2-3 days.

Other Online Access: Search records online at http://neworleans.insb.uscourts.gov/public/casesearch.asp. Search using case number, party name, social security number and/or tax ID number. The system is currently free.

New Albany Division US Courthouse, Rm 110, 121 W Spring St, New Albany, IN 47150 (Courier Address: Use mail address for courier delivery), 812-948-5254, Fax: 812-948-5262.

http://www.insb.uscourts.gov

Counties: Clark, Crawford, Dearborn, Floyd, Harrison, Jackson, Jefferson, Jennings, Lawrence, Ohio, Orange, Ripley, Scott, Switzerland, Washington.

Indexing/Storage: Cases are indexed by debtor as well as by case number. New cases are available in the index 48 hours after filing date. A computer index is maintained. Open records are located at this court.

Fee & Payment: The fee is $20.00 per item (one party name or case number). Payment may be made by money order, cashier check, personal check. Checks are not accepted from debtors. Payee: Clerk, US Bankruptcy Court (SDIN). Certification fee: $7.00 per document. Copy fee: $.50 per page.

Phone Search: Only docket information is available by phone. An automated voice case information service (VCIS) is available. Call VCIS at 800-335-8003 or.

Mail Search: Always enclose a stamped self addressed envelope.

In Person: In person searching is available.

PACER: Sign-up number is 317-229-3845. Access fee is $.60 per minute. Local access: 317-229-3989, 317-229-3878. NIBS system: First number is for Carbon Copy users and second is for Procomm users. Use of Carbon Copy Plus required. Case records are available back to 1988. Records are purged every 3 months. New civil records are available online after 2-3 days.

Other Online Access: Search records online at http://neworleans.insb.uscourts.gov/public/casesearch.asp. Search using case number, party name, social security number and/or tax ID number. The system is currently free.

Terre Haute Division Federal Bldg Rm 207, 30 N 7th St, Terre Haute, IN 47808 (Courier Address: Use mail address for courier delivery), 812-238-1550, Fax: 812-238-1831.

http://www.insb.uscourts.gov

Counties: Clay, Greene, Knox, Owen, Parke, Putnam, Sullivan, Vermillion, Vigo.

Indexing/Storage: Cases are indexed by debtor as well as by case number. New cases are available in the index 48 hours after filing date. A computer index is maintained. Records are stored electronically since 1986. Open records are located at this court.

Fee & Payment: The fee is $20.00 per item (one party name or case number). Payment may be made by money order, cashier check, personal check. Prepayment is required. A search fee will only be charged if a detailed search is required. Personal checks are not accepted from debtors. Payee: Clerk, US Bankruptcy Court. Certification fee: $7.00 per document. Copy fee: $.50 per page.

Phone Search: Only docket information is available by phone. An automated voice case information service (VCIS) is available. Call VCIS at 800-335-8003 or.

Mail Search: Always enclose a stamped self addressed envelope.

In Person: In person searching is available.

PACER: Sign-up number is 317-229-3845. Access fee is $.60 per minute. Local access: 317-229-3989, 317-229-3878. NIBS system: First number is for Carbon Copy users and second is for Procomm users. Use of Carbon Copy Plus required. Case records are available back to 1988. Records are purged every 3 months. New civil records are available online after 2-3 days.

Other Online Access: Search records online at http://neworleans.insb.uscourts.gov/public/casesearch.asp. Search using case number, party name, social security number and/or tax ID number. The system is currently free.

Indiana County Courts

Court	Jurisdiction	No. of Courts	How Organized
Circuit Courts*	General	24	
Superior Courts*	General	4	
Combined Courts*		68	
County Courts*	Limited		
Combined Circuit/County*		4	
City Courts	Limited	47	
Small Claims -Marion County	Special	9	
Town Courts	Municipal	25	
Probate Court	Special	1	St. Joseph County

* Profiled in this Sourcebook.

Court	CIVIL								
	Tort	Contract	Real Estate	Min. Claim	Max. Claim	Small Claims	Estate	Eviction	Domestic Relations
Circuit Courts*	X	X	X	$0	No Max	$3000	X		X
Superior Courts*	X	X	X	$0	No Max	$3000	X		X
County Courts*	X	X	X	$0	$10,000	$3000		X	X
City Courts	X	X		$0	$2500			X	X
Small Claims - Marion County						$3000			
Town Courts									X
Probate Court							X		

Court	CRIMINAL				
	Felony	Misdemeanor	DWI/DUI	Preliminary Hearing	Juvenile
Circuit Courts*	X	X	X	X	X
Superior Courts*	X	X	X	X	X
County Courts*	X	X	X	X	
City Courts		X	X	X	
Small Claims - Marion County					
Town Courts		X	X	X	
Probate Court					X

ADMINISTRATION   State Court Administrator, 115 W Washington St Suite 1080, Indianapolis, IN, 46204; 317-232-2542, Fax: 317-233-6586. www.in.gov/judiciary

COURT STRUCTURE   There are 92 judicial circuits with Circuit Courts or Combined Circuit and Superior Courts. In addition, there are 47 City Courts and 25 Town Courts. County courts are gradually being restructured into divisions of the Superior Courts. Note that Small Claims in Marion County are heard at the township and records are maintained at that level. The phone number for the township offices are indicated in Marion County.

ONLINE ACCESS   No online access computer system, internal or external, is available, except for Marion County through CivicNet/Access Indiana Information Network, which is available on the Internet (www.civicnet.net). Account and password are required. No charge for civil court name searches. Fees range from $2.00 to $5.00 for civil case summaries, civil justice name searches, criminal case summaries, and party booking details.

ADDITIONAL INFORMATION

The Circuit Court Clerk/County Clerk in every county is the same individual and is responsible for keeping all county judicial records. However, it is recommended that, when requesting a record, the request indicate which court heard the case (Circuit, Superior, or County).

Many courts are no longer performing searches, especially criminal searches, based on a 7/8/96 statement by the State Board of Accounts.

Certification and copy fees are set by statute as $1.00 per document plus copy fee for certification and $1.00 per page for copies.

📖 📖 📖 📖 📖 📖 📖

Adams County

Circuit & Superior Court 112 S 2nd St, Decatur, IN 46733; 219-724-2600 X206; Fax: 219-724-3848. Hours: 8AM-4:30PM (EST). *Felony, Misdemeanor, Civil, Eviction, Small Claims, Probate.*

Civil Records: Access: In person only. Visitors must perform in person searches for themselves. No search fee. Required to search: name, years to search. Civil cases indexed by defendant, plaintiff. Civil records on computer from 1992, archived from 1876. Some records on index cards.

Criminal Records: Access: In person only. Visitors must perform in person searches for themselves. No search fee. Required to search: name, years to search, DOB; also helpful: SSN. Criminal records on computer from 1992, archived from 1876. Some records on index cards.

General Information: Public Access terminal is available. (Limited information available.) No juvenile, adoption, mental health or sealed records released. Copy fee: $1.00 per page. Certification fee: $2.00 per page. Fee payee: Adams County Clerk. Only cashiers checks and money orders accepted. Prepayment is required.

Allen County

Circuit & Superior Court 715 S. Calhoun St. Rm 200 Courthouse, Ft Wayne, IN 46802; 219-449-7245. Hours: 8AM-4:30PM (EST). *Felony, Misdemeanor, Civil, Eviction, Small Claims, Probate.*
www.co.allen.in.us/clerk/Default.htm

Civil Records: Access: In person only. Visitors must perform in person searches for themselves. No search fee. Required to search: name, years to search. Civil cases indexed by defendant, plaintiff. Recent civil cases on computer; prior records on microfiche, archived and index from 1824.

Criminal Records: Access: In person only. Visitors must perform in person searches for themselves. No search fee. Required to search: name, years to search; also helpful: DOB, SSN. Recent cases on computer; prior records on microfiche, archived and index from 1824.

General Information: Public Access terminal is available. No juvenile, adoption or sealed records released. Copy fee: $1.00 per page. Certification fee: $1.00 per page. Fee payee: Clerk of Allen Circuit Court. Business checks accepted. Prepayment is required.

Bartholomew County

Circuit & Superior Court PO Box 924, Columbus, IN 47202-0924; 812-379-1600; Fax: 812-379-1675. Hours: 8AM-5PM (EST). *Felony, Misdemeanor, Civil, Eviction, Small Claims, Probate.*

Civil Records: Access: In person only. Visitors must perform in person searches for themselves. No search fee. Required to search: name. Civil cases indexed by plaintiff. Civil records on computer from 1985, on microfilm from 1940, on index from 1821.

Criminal Records: Access: Fax, mail, in person. Both court and visitors may perform in person searches. No search fee. Required to search: name, years to search,

DOB; also helpful: SSN, race, sex. Criminal records on computer from 1985, on microfilm from 1940, on index from 1821.

General Information: Public Access terminal is available. No juvenile, mental health, adoption or sealed released. All searches 1985 to present. SASE required. Turnaround time 1 day. Fax notes: $5.00 per page. No fee to fax to 800 number. Copy fee: $1.00 per page. Certification fee: $1.00. Fee payee: Bartholomew County Clerk. Personal checks accepted. Prepayment is required.

Benton County

Circuit Court 706 E 5th St, Suite 37, Fowler, IN 47944-1556; 765-884-0930; Fax: 765-884-0322. Hours: 8:30AM-4PM (EST). *Felony, Misdemeanor, Civil, Eviction, Small Claims, Probate.*
www.bentoncounty.org

Civil Records: Access: In person only. Visitors must perform in person searches for themselves. No search fee. Required to search: name, years to search. Civil cases indexed by defendant, plaintiff. Civil records on computer from 1992, on index books from 1860.

Criminal Records: Access: Mail, in person. Visitors must perform in person searches for themselves. No search fee. Required to search: name, years to search, DOB. Criminal records on computer from 1992, on index books from 1860.

General Information: No juvenile, mental, adoption or sealed released. SASE required. Turnaround time 2-3 days. Copy fee: $1.00 per page. Certification fee: $1.00. Fee payee: Benton County Clerk. Only cashiers checks and money orders accepted. Prepayment is required.

Blackford County

Circuit & County Court 110 W Washington St, Hartford City, IN 47348; 765-348-1130. Hours: 8AM-4PM (EST). *Felony, Misdemeanor, Civil, Eviction, Small Claims, Probate.*

Civil Records: Access: Mail, in person. Both court and visitors may perform in person searches. No search fee. Required to search: name, years to search. Civil cases indexed by defendant, plaintiff. Civil records on computer from 1991, on index from 1800.

Criminal Records: Access: Mail, in person. Both court and visitors may perform in person searches. No search fee. Required to search: name, years to search, DOB; also helpful: SSN. court records on computer from 1991, on index from 1800.

General Information: Public Access terminal is available. No juvenile, mental, adoption or sealed released. Turnaround time 1 week. Copy fee: $1.00 per page. Certification fee: $2.00. Fee payee: Clerk of Blackford County. Business checks accepted. Prepayment is required.

Boone County

Circuit & Superior Court I & II Rm 212, Courthouse Sq, Lebanon, IN 46052; 765-482-3510. Hours: 7AM-4PM (EST). *Felony, Misdemeanor, Civil, Eviction, Small Claims, Probate.*

Civil Records: Access: Mail, in person. Both court and visitors may perform in person searches. No search fee.

Required to search: name, years to search. Civil cases indexed by defendant, plaintiff. Civil records on index from 1900.

Criminal Records: Access: Mail, in person. Both court and visitors may perform in person searches. No search fee. Required to search: name, years to search; also helpful: SSN. Criminal records on index from 1900.

General Information: No juvenile, mental, adoption or sealed released. SASE required. Turnaround time 1 week. Copy fee: $1.00 per page. Certification fee: $1.00. Fee payee: Boone County Clerk. Business checks accepted. Prepayment is required.

Brown County

Circuit Court Box 85, Nashville, IN 47448; 812-988-5510; Fax: 812-988-5515. Hours: 8AM-4PM (EST). *Felony, Misdemeanor, Civil, Eviction, Small Claims, Probate.*

Civil Records: Access: In person only. Visitors must perform in person searches for themselves. No search fee. Required to search: name, years to search. Civil cases indexed by defendant, plaintiff. Civil records on open cases on computer from 1993, in entry books from early 1800s. Records are not indexed by SSN, but SSNs can be viewed.

Criminal Records: Access: In person only. Visitors must perform in person searches for themselves. No search fee. Required to search: name, years to search, DOB; also helpful: SSN. Criminal records on open cases on computer from 1993, in entry books from early 1800s. Records are not indexed by SSN, but SSNs can be viewed.

General Information: Public Access terminal is available. No juvenile, mental, adoption or sealed records released. Copy fee: $1.00 per page. Certification fee: $2.00. Fee payee: County Clerk. Personal checks accepted. Prepayment is required.

Carroll County

Circuit & Superior Court Courthouse, 101 W Main, Delphi, IN 46923; 765-564-4485; Fax: 765-564-6907. Hours: 8AM-5PM M,T,Th,F; 8AM-Noon W (EST). *Felony, Misdemeanor, Civil, Eviction, Small Claims, Probate.*

Civil Records: Access: In person only. Both court and visitors may perform in person searches. No search fee. Required to search: name, years to search. Civil cases indexed by defendant, plaintiff. Civil records archived from 1981, on index from 1828.

Criminal Records: Access: In person only. Visitors must perform in person searches for themselves. No search fee. Required to search: name, years to search. Criminal records archived from 1981, on index from 1828.

General Information: No juvenile, mental, adoption or sealed released. Copy fee: $1.00 per page. Certification fee: $1.00. Fee payee: Carroll County Clerk. Personal checks accepted. Prepayment is required.

Cass County

Circuit & Superior Court 200 Court Park, Logansport, IN 46947; 219-753-7870. Hours: 8AM-4PM (EST). *Felony, Misdemeanor, Civil, Eviction, Small Claims, Probate.*

Civil Records: Access: Mail, in person. Both court and visitors may perform in person searches. No search fee. Required to search: name, years to search. Civil cases indexed by defendant, plaintiff. Civil records on computer from 1989, on index from 1830s.

Criminal Records: Access: Mail, in person. Both court and visitors may perform in person searches. No search fee. Required to search: name, years to search, DOB; also helpful: SSN, signed release. Criminal records on computer from 1989, on index from 1830s.

General Information: Public Access terminal is available. No juvenile, mental, adoption or sealed released. SASE requested. Turnaround time 2 weeks. Fax notes: Fax fee $1.00 per page. Copy fee: $1.00 per page. Fee is for criminal division only. Certification fee: $3.00. Fee payee: Cass County Clerk. Personal checks accepted. Checks accepted up to $10.00 only. Prepayment is required.

Clark County

Circuit, Superior & County Court 501 E Court, Rm 137, Jeffersonville, IN 47130; 812-285-6244. Hours: 8:30AM-4:30PM M-F, 8:30-Noon S (EST). *Felony, Misdemeanor, Civil, Eviction, Small Claims, Probate.*

Civil Records: Access: In person only. Visitors must perform in person searches for themselves. No search fee. Required to search: name, years to search; also helpful: address. Civil cases indexed by defendant, plaintiff. Civil records on computer since 8/92, on index cards from 1900.

Criminal Records: Access: In person only. Visitors must perform in person searches for themselves. No search fee. Required to search: name, years to search; also helpful: DOB, SSN. Criminal records on computer since 8/92, on index cards from 1900.

General Information: Public Access terminal is available. No juvenile, mental, adoption or sealed released. Copy fee: $1.00 per page. Certification fee: $1.00. Fee payee: County Clerk. Business checks accepted. Prepayment is required.

Clay County

Circuit & Superior Court Box 33, Brazil, IN 47834; 812-448-9024. Hours: 8AM-4PM (EST). *Felony, Misdemeanor, Civil, Eviction, Small Claims, Probate.*

Civil Records: Access: Mail, in person. No search fee. Required to search: name, years to search; also helpful: address. Civil cases indexed by defendant, plaintiff. Civil records on index from 1850; on computer to 1995.

Criminal Records: Access: Mail, in person. Visitors must perform in person searches for themselves. No search fee. Required to search: name, years to search, address, DOB; also helpful-SSN, signed release. Criminal records on index from 1850; on computer back to 1995.

General Information: No juvenile, mental, adoption or sealed released. SASE required. Turnaround time 1 week. Copy fee: $1.00 per page. Certification fee: $1.00. Fee payee: County Clerk. Business checks accepted. Prepayment is required.

Clinton County

Circuit & Superior Court 265 Courthouse Square, Frankfort, IN 46041; 765-659-6335. Hours: 8AM-4PM M-TH,8AM-5PM F (EST). *Felony, Misdemeanor, Civil, Eviction, Small Claims, Probate.*

Civil Records: Access: Mail, in person. Both court and visitors may perform in person searches. Search fee: $4.00 per name. Required to search: name, years to search. Civil cases indexed by defendant, plaintiff. Civil records on computer from 1991, on microfiche and index from 1900s.

Criminal Records: Access: Mail, in person. Both court and visitors may perform in person searches. Search fee: $4.00 per name. Required to search: name, years to search, signed release; also helpful: DOB. Criminal records on computer from 1991, on microfiche and index from 1900s.

General Information: Public Access terminal is available. No juvenile, mental, adoption or sealed released. SASE required. Turnaround time 1 week. Copy fee: $1.00 per page. Certification fee: $1.00. Fee payee: County Clerk. Business checks accepted. Prepayment is required.

Crawford County

Circuit Court Box 375, English, IN 47118; 812-338-2565; Fax: 812-338-2507. Hours: 8AM-4PM M,F; 8AM-6PM T-Th (EST). *Felony, Misdemeanor, Civil, Eviction, Small Claims, Probate.*

Civil Records: Access: In person only. Visitors must perform in person searches for themselves. No search fee. Required to search: name, years to search. Civil cases indexed by defendant, plaintiff. Civil records on index from 1900s.

Criminal Records: Access: Fax, mail, in person. Only the court performs in person searches; visitors may not. Search fee: $5.00 per name. Required to search: name, years to search, DOB, SSN, signed release. Criminal records on index from 1900s.

General Information: No juvenile, mental, adoption or sealed released. SASE required. Turnaround time 1 week. Fax notes: No fee to fax results. Copy fee: $1.00 per page. Fee is for criminal division only. Certification fee: $2.00. Fee payee: County Clerk. Business checks accepted. Prepayment is required.

Daviess County

Circuit & Superior Court PO Box 739, Washington, IN 47501; 812-254-8664; Fax: 812-254-8698. Hours: 8AM-4PM (EST). *Felony, Misdemeanor, Civil, Eviction, Small Claims, Probate.*

Civil Records: Access: Mail, in person. Both court and visitors may perform in person searches. No search fee. Required to search: name, years to search. Civil cases indexed by defendant, plaintiff. Civil records on index from 1900s; recent on computer.

Criminal Records: Access: Mail, in person. Both court and visitors may perform in person searches. No search fee. Required to search: name, years to search. Criminal records on index from 1900s; recent on computer.

General Information: Public Access terminal is available. No juvenile, mental, adoption or sealed records released. SASE required. Turnaround time varies. Copy fee: $1.00 per page. Certification fee: $1.00. Fee payee: Daviess County Clerk. Business checks accepted. Prepayment is required.

Dearborn County

Circuit & County Court Courthouse, 215 W High St, Lawrenceburg, IN 47025; 812-537-8867; Fax: 812-537-4295. Hours: 8:30AM-4:30PM (EST). *Felony, Misdemeanor, Civil, Eviction, Small Claims, Probate.*

Civil Records: Access: In person only. Visitors must perform in person searches for themselves. No search fee. Required to search: name, years to search. Civil cases indexed by defendant, plaintiff. Civil records on computer from 1992, on index from 1970s.

Criminal Records: Access: In person only. Visitors must perform in person searches for themselves. No search fee. Required to search: name, years to search, DOB; also helpful: SSN. Criminal records on computer from 1992, on index from 1970s.

General Information: Public Access terminal is available. No juvenile, mental, adoption or sealed records released. Copy fee: $1.00 per page. Fee is for civil division only. Certification fee: $1.00. Fee payee: Circuit Court Clerk. Only cashiers checks and money orders accepted. Prepayment is required.

Decatur County

Circuit & Superior Court 150 Courthouse Square, Suite 244, Greensburg, IN 47240; 812-663-8223/8642; Fax: 812-663-8642. Hours: 8AM-4PM, 8AM-5PM F (EST). *Felony, Misdemeanor, Civil, Eviction, Small Claims, Probate.*

Civil Records: Access: Mail, in person. Visitors must perform in person searches for themselves. No search fee. Required to search: name, years to search. Civil cases indexed by defendant, plaintiff. Civil records on index from 1823.

Criminal Records: Access: Mail, in person. Visitors must perform in person searches for themselves. No search fee. Required to search: name, years to search, DOB; also helpful: SSN. Criminal records on index from 1823.

General Information: No juvenile, mental, adoption or sealed released. Turnaround time 2-7 days. Copy fee: $1.00 per page. Certification fee: $1.00. Fee payee: Decatur County Clerk. Personal checks accepted. Prepayment is required.

DeKalb County

Circuit & Superior Court PO Box 230, Auburn, IN 46706; 219-925-0912; Fax: 219-925-5126. Hours: 8:30AM-4:30PM (EST). *Felony, Misdemeanor, Civil, Eviction, Small Claims, Probate.*

Civil Records: Access: In person only. Visitors must perform in person searches for themselves. No search fee. Required to search: name, years to search. Civil cases indexed by defendant, plaintiff. Civil records on computer from 1987, on index from 1800s.

Criminal Records: Access: In person only. Visitors must perform in person searches for themselves. No search fee. Required to search: name, years to search. Criminal records on computer from 1987, on index from 1800s.

General Information: Public Access terminal is available. No juvenile, mental, adoption or sealed released. Fax notes: Fee to fax results is $1.00 per document plus $1.00 per page. Copy fee: $1.00 per page. Certification fee: $1.00. Fee payee: Court Clerk. Only cashiers checks and money orders accepted. Prepayment is required.

Delaware County

Circuit & Superior Court Box 1089, Muncie, IN 47308; 765-747-7726; Fax: 765-747-7768. Hours: 8:30AM-4:30PM (EST). *Felony, Misdemeanor, Civil, Small Claims, Probate.*

www.dcclerk.org

Civil Records: Access: Phone, fax, mail, in person. Both court and visitors may perform in person searches. No search fee. Required to search: name, years to search. Civil cases indexed by defendant, plaintiff. Civil records on computer from 1989, on microfiche, archived and on index from 1800.

Criminal Records: Access: In person only. Visitors must perform in person searches for themselves. No search fee. Required to search: name, years to search, DOB, SSN. Criminal records on computer from 1989, on microfiche, archived and on index from 1800.

General Information: Public Access terminal is available. No juvenile, mental, adoption or sealed released. Turnaround time 1-2 days. Fax notes: Fee to fax results is $2.00 per page. Copy fee: $.10 per page. Certification fee: $1.00. Fee payee: Court Clerk. Business checks accepted. Prepayment is required.

Dubois County

Circuit & Superior Court 1 Courthouse Square, Jasper, IN 47546; 812-481-7070/7035/7020; Fax: 812-481-7030. Hours: 8AM-4PM (EST). *Felony, Misdemeanor, Civil, Eviction, Small Claims, Probate.*

Civil Records: Access: In person only. Visitors must perform in person searches for themselves. No search fee. Required to search: name; also helpful: years to search. Civil cases indexed by defendant, plaintiff. Civil records on computer to 8\93, on index books to 1930.
Criminal Records: Access: In person only. Visitors must perform in person searches for themselves. No search fee. Required to search: name; also helpful: years to search. Criminal records on computer from 8\93, on index books from 1930.
General Information: Public Access terminal is available. No juvenile, mental, adoption or sealed records released. Copy fee: $.25 per page. Certification fee: $1.00. Fee payee: Court Clerk. Personal checks accepted. Prepayment is required.

Elkhart County

Elkhart Superior Courts 1, 2, 5, 6 315 S Second St, Elkhart, IN 46516; 219-523-2233/2305/2007; Fax: 219-523-2323. Hours: 8AM-4PM M-Th, 8AM-5PM F (EST). *Felony, Misdemeanor, Civil, Eviction, Small Claims, Probate.*

Civil Records: Access: In person only. Visitors must perform in person searches for themselves. No search fee. Required to search: name, years to search. Civil cases indexed by defendant, plaintiff. Civil records archived from 1830; on computer since 1996. Some records on index books.
Criminal Records: Access: In person only. Visitors must perform in person searches for themselves. No search fee. Required to search: name, years to search, DOB; also helpful: SSN. Criminal records archived from 1830; on computer since 1996. Some records on index books.
General Information: Public Access terminal is available. No juvenile, mental, adoption or sealed records released. Certification fee: $1.00. Fee payee: Court Clerk. Personal checks accepted. Prepayment is required.

Goshen Circuit & Superior Courts 3, 4 Courthouse, 101 N. Main St, Goshen, IN 46526; 219-535-6431; Fax: 219-535-6471. Hours: 8AM-4PM M-Th, 8AM-5PM F (EST). *Felony, Misdemeanor, Civil, Eviction, Small Claims, Probate.*

Note: Includes Circuit Court (Rm 204) and Superior Court 3 (Rm 205) and 4 (Rm 105).

Civil Records: Access: In person only. Visitors must perform in person searches for themselves. No search fee. Required to search: name, years to search. Civil cases indexed by defendant, plaintiff. Civil records archived from 1830; on computer since 1996. Some records on index books.
Criminal Records: Access: In person only. Visitors must perform in person searches for themselves. No search fee. Required to search: name, years to search, DOB; also helpful: SSN. Criminal records archived from 1830; on computer since 1996. Some records on index books.
General Information: Public Access terminal is available. No juvenile, mental, adoption or sealed records released. Certification fee: $1.00. Fee payee: Court Clerk. Personal checks accepted. Prepayment is required.

Fayette County

Circuit & Superior Court PO Box 607, Connersville, IN 47331-0607; 765-825-1813. Hours: 8:30AM-4PM (5PM on Wed) (EST). *Felony, Misdemeanor, Civil, Eviction, Small Claims, Probate.*

http://courthouse.co.fayette.in.us

Civil Records: Access: In person only. Visitors must perform in person searches for themselves. No search fee. Required to search: name, years to search. Civil cases indexed by defendant, plaintiff. Civil records on computer from 1988 (Circuit), 1992 (Superior).
Criminal Records: Access: In person only. Visitors must perform in person searches for themselves. No search fee. Required to search: name, years to search. Criminal records on computer from 1988 (Circuit), 1992 (Superior).
General Information: Public Access terminal is available. No juvenile, mental, adoption or sealed released. Copy fee: $1.00 per page. Certification fee: $1.00. Fee payee: Fayette County Clerk. Only cashiers checks and money orders accepted. Prepayment is required.

Floyd County

Circuit, Superior & County Court Box 1056, City County Bldg, New Albany, IN 47150; 812-948-5414; Fax: 812-948-4711. Hours: 8AM-4PM *Felony, Misdemeanor, Civil, Eviction, Small Claims, Probate.*

Civil Records: Access: Mail, in person. No search fee. Required to search: name, years to search. Civil cases indexed by defendant, plaintiff. Civil records on computer from 1988, archived from 1978, on index from 1819.
Criminal Records: Access: Mail, in person. Visitors must perform in person searches for themselves. No search fee. Required to search: name, years to search; also helpful: SSN. Criminal records on computer from 1988, archived from 1978, on index from 1819.
General Information: Public Access terminal is available. No juvenile, mental, adoption or sealed released. SASE required. Turnaround time 1-2 days. Copy fee: $1.00 per page. Certification fee: $1.00. Fee payee: Court Clerk. Personal checks accepted. Prepayment is required.

Fountain County

Circuit Court Box 183, Covington, IN 47932; 765-793-2192; Fax: 765-793-5002. Hours: 8AM-4PM (EST). *Felony, Misdemeanor, Civil, Eviction, Small Claims, Probate.*

Civil Records: Access: Mail, in person. Both court and visitors may perform in person searches. No search fee. Required to search: name, years to search, SSN. Civil cases indexed by defendant, plaintiff. Civil records on computer from 1989.
Criminal Records: Access: Mail, in person. Both court and visitors may perform in person searches. No search fee. Required to search: name, years to search, SSN. Criminal records on computer from 1989.
General Information: Public Access terminal is available. No juvenile, mental, adoption or sealed released. SASE required. Turnaround time 1-2 days if records after 1989, 4-5 days if prior. Copy fee: $1.00 per page. Certification fee: $2.00. Fee payee: Court Clerk. Personal checks accepted. Prepayment is required.

Franklin County

Circuit Court 459 Main, Brookville, IN 47012; 765-647-5111; Fax: 765-647-3224. Hours: 8:30AM-4PM (EST). *Felony, Misdemeanor, Civil, Eviction, Small Claims, Probate.*

Civil Records: Access: In person only. Visitors must perform in person searches for themselves. No search fee. Required to search: name, years to search. Civil

cases indexed by defendant, plaintiff. Civil records on index from 1978.
Criminal Records: Access: In person only. Visitors must perform in person searches for themselves. No search fee. Required to search: name, years to search. Criminal records on index from 1950.
General Information: No juvenile, mental, adoption or sealed released. Copy fee: $.50 per page. Certification fee: $1.00. Fee payee: Court Clerk. Personal checks accepted. Prepayment is required.

Fulton County

Circuit Court 815 Main St, PO Box 524, Rochester, IN 46975; 219-223-2911; Fax: 219-223-8304. Hours: 8AM-4PM M-TH, 8AM-5PM F (EST). *Felony, Misdemeanor, Civil, Eviction, Small Claims, Probate.*

Civil Records: Access: Mail, in person. Both court and visitors may perform in person searches. No search fee. Required to search: name, years to search. Civil cases indexed by defendant, plaintiff. Civil records on computer from 1989, on microfiche, archived and on index from 1845.
Criminal Records: Access: Mail, in person. Both court and visitors may perform in person searches. No search fee. Required to search: name, years to search. Criminal records on computer from 1989, on microfiche, archived and on index from 1845.
General Information: Public Access terminal is available. No juvenile, mental, adoption or sealed released. SASE Required. Turnaround time 3-4 days. Copy fee: $1.00 per page. Certification fee: $1.00. Fee payee: Court Clerk. Business checks accepted. Prepayment is required.

Gibson County

Circuit & Superior Court Courthouse, Princeton, IN 47670; 812-386-6474; Fax: 812-386-5025. Hours: 8AM-4PM (CST). *Felony, Misdemeanor, Civil, Eviction, Small Claims, Probate.*

Civil Records: Access: In person only. Visitors must perform in person searches for themselves. No search fee. Required to search: name, years to search. Civil cases indexed by defendant, plaintiff. Civil records on computer from 1996, on microfiche from 1940, on index from 1813.
Criminal Records: Access: In person only. Visitors must perform in person searches for themselves. No search fee. Required to search: name, years to search. Criminal records on computer from 1996, on microfiche from 1940, on index from 1813.
General Information: Public Access terminal is available. No juvenile, mental, adoption or sealed records released. Fax notes: Fax fee $4.00 per document. Copy fee: $1.00 per page. Certification fee: $1.00. Fee payee: Court Clerk. Prepayment is required.

Grant County

Circuit & Superior Court Courthouse 101 E 4th St, Marion, IN 46952; 765-668-8121; Fax: 765-668-6541. Hours: 8AM-4PM (EST). *Felony, Misdemeanor, Civil, Eviction, Small Claims, Probate.*

Civil Records: Access: In person only. Visitors must perform in person searches for themselves. No search fee. Required to search: name, years to search; also helpful: address. Civil cases indexed by defendant, plaintiff. Civil records on computer from 1989, on index from 1881.
Criminal Records: Access: In person only. Visitors must perform in person searches for themselves. No search fee. Required to search: name, years to search; also helpful: DOB, SSN. Criminal records on computer from 1989, on index from 1881.
General Information: Public Access terminal is available. No juvenile, adoption, mental health or sealed records released. Copy fee: $.10 per page. Certification

fee: $1.00. Fee payee: Court Clerk. Personal checks accepted. Prepayment is required.

Greene County

Circuit & Superior Court PO Box 229, Bloomfield, IN 47424; 812-384-8532; Fax: 812-384-8458. Hours: 8AM-4PM (EST). *Felony, Misdemeanor, Civil, Eviction, Small Claims, Probate.*

Civil Records: Access: In person only. Visitors must perform in person searches for themselves. No search fee. Required to search: name, years to search. Civil cases indexed by defendant, plaintiff. Civil records on computer back to 1989, all other records in books.

Criminal Records: Access: In person only. Visitors must perform in person searches for themselves. No search fee. Required to search: name, years to search. Criminal records on computer back to 1989; prior in books.

General Information: Public Access terminal is available. No juvenile, mental, adoption or sealed released. Copy fee: $1.00 per page. Certification fee: $1.00. Fee payee: Court Clerk. Only cashiers checks and money orders accepted. Prepayment is required.

Hamilton County

Circuit & Superior Court One Hamilton County Square, Suite 106, Noblesville, IN 46060-2233; 317-776-9629; Fax: 317-776-9727. Hours: 8AM-4:30PM (EST). *Felony, Misdemeanor, Civil, Eviction, Small Claims, Probate.*

www.co.hamilton.in.us

Civil Records: Access: In person only. Visitors must perform in person searches for themselves. No search fee. Required to search: name, years to search. Civil cases indexed by defendant, plaintiff. Civil records on computer from 1987, on index from 1840s.

Criminal Records: Access: In person only. Visitors must perform in person searches for themselves. No search fee. Required to search: name, years to search. Criminal records on computer from 1987, on index from 1840s.

General Information: Public Access terminal is available. No juvenile, mental, adoption or sealed released. Copy fee: $.50 per page. Certification fee: $1.00 plus $.50 per page. Fee payee: Court Clerk. Business checks accepted. Prepayment is required.

Hancock County

Circuit & Superior Court 9 E Main St, Rm 201, Greenfield, IN 46140; 317-462-1109; Fax: 317-462-1163. Hours: 8AM-4PM (EST). *Felony, Misdemeanor, Civil, Eviction, Small Claims, Probate.*

Civil Records: Access: Phone, mail, in person. Both court and visitors may perform in person searches. No search fee. Required to search: name, years to search. Civil cases indexed by defendant, plaintiff. Civil records on computer from 07/88, on index and archived from 1883.

Criminal Records: Access: Phone, mail, in person. Both court and visitors may perform in person searches. No search fee. Required to search: name, years to search, DOB; also helpful: SSN. Criminal records on computer from 07/88, on index and archived from 1883.

General Information: Public Access terminal is available. No juvenile, mental, adoption or sealed released. SASE required. Turnaround time 3-7 days, same day or next for phone requests. Copy fee: $1.00 per page for case history, otherwise $.25 per page. Certification fee: $1.00. Fee payee: Court Clerk. Personal checks accepted. Prepayment is required.

Harrison County

Circuit & Superior Court 300 N Capitol, Corydon, IN 47112; 812-738-4289. Hours: 8AM-4PM M,T,Th,F; 8AM-Noon W,S (EST). *Felony, Misdemeanor, Civil, Eviction, Small Claims, Probate.*

Civil Records: Access: Mail, in person. Visitors must perform in person searches for themselves. No search fee. Required to search: name, years to search. Civil cases indexed by defendant, plaintiff. Civil records on index from 1900. Court personnel will only do record searching when they have time, strongly urge using a retriever.

Criminal Records: Access: Mail, in person. Visitors must perform in person searches for themselves. No search fee. Required to search: name, years to search. Criminal records on index from 1900. Court personnel only do record searching when they have time, suggest to use a retriever.

General Information: No juvenile, mental, adoption or sealed released. Turnaround - as time permits. Copy fee: $.50 per page. Certification fee: $2.00. Fee payee: Court Clerk. Only cashiers checks and money orders accepted. Prepayment is required.

Hendricks County

Circuit & Superior Court PO Box 599, Danville, IN 46122; 317-745-9231; Fax: 317-745-9306. Hours: 8AM-4PM (EST). *Felony, Misdemeanor, Civil, Eviction, Small Claims, Probate.*

Civil Records: Access: In person only. Visitors must perform in person searches for themselves. No search fee. Required to search: name, years to search. Civil cases indexed by defendant, plaintiff. Civil records on computer since late 1992, on index from 1800s.

Criminal Records: Access: In person only. Visitors must perform in person searches for themselves. No search fee. Required to search: name, years to search; also helpful: DOB, SSN. Criminal records on computer since late 1992, on index from 1800s.

General Information: No juvenile, mental, adoption or sealed released. Copy fee: $1.00 per page. Certification fee: $1.00. Fee payee: Court Clerk. Business checks accepted. Prepayment is required.

Henry County

Circuit & Superior Court PO Box B, New Castle, IN 47362; 765-529-6401. Hours: 8AM-4PM (EST). *Felony, Misdemeanor, Civil, Eviction, Small Claims, Probate.*

Civil Records: Access: Mail, fax, in person. Both court and visitors may perform in person searches. No search fee. Required to search: name, years to search. Civil cases indexed by plaintiff. Civil records on computer from 1991, archived from 1979, on index from 1976.

Criminal Records: Access: Mail, fax, in person. Both court and visitors may perform in person searches. No search fee. Required to search: name, years to search. Criminal records on computer from 1991, archived from 1979, on index from 1976.

General Information: Public Access terminal is available. No juvenile, mental, adoption or sealed released. SASE Required. Turnaround time 1-2 days. Fax notes: Fax fee $1.00 per document. Copy fee: $1.00 per page. Certification fee: $1.00. Fee payee: County Clerk. Only cashiers checks and money orders accepted. Prepayment is required.

Howard County

Circuit & Superior Court PO Box 9004, Kokomo, IN 46904; 765-456-2204; Fax: 765-456-2267. Hours: 8AM-4PM (EST). *Felony, Misdemeanor, Civil, Eviction, Small Claims, Probate.*

Civil Records: Access: In person only. Visitors must perform in person searches for themselves. No search fee. Required to search: name, years to search. Civil

cases indexed by defendant, plaintiff. Civil records on computer since 1994, on microfiche from early 1800s.

Criminal Records: Access: In person only. Visitors must perform in person searches for themselves. No search fee. Required to search: name, years to search; also helpful: DOB, SSN. Criminal records on computer since 1994, on microfiche from early 1800s.

General Information: Public Access terminal is available. No juvenile, mental, adoption or sealed records released. Copy fee: $.20 per page. Certification fee: $1.00. Fee payee: County Clerk. Only cashiers checks and money orders accepted.

Huntington County

Circuit & Superior Court PO Box 228, Huntington, IN 46750; 219-358-4817. Hours: 8AM-4:30PM (EST). *Felony, Misdemeanor, Civil, Eviction, Small Claims, Probate.*

Civil Records: Access: Phone, mail, in person. Both court and visitors may perform in person searches. No search fee. Required to search: name, years to search. Civil cases indexed by defendant, plaintiff. Civil records on computer from 1990, on microfiche from 1970, on index and archived from 1800s.

Criminal Records: Access: In person only. Visitors must perform in person searches for themselves. No search fee. Required to search: name, years to search. Criminal records on computer from 1990, on microfiche from 1970, on index and archived from 1800s.

General Information: Public Access terminal is available. No juvenile, mental, adoption or sealed released. SASE not required. Turnaround time 1-2 days. Copy fee: $1.00 per page. Certification fee: $1.00. Fee payee: County Clerk. Personal checks not accepted. Prepayment is required.

Jackson County

Circuit Court PO Box 318, Brownstown, IN 47220; 812-358-6117; Fax: 812-358-6197. Hours: 8AM-4:30PM (EST). *Felony, Misdemeanor, Civil, Eviction, Small Claims, Probate.*

Civil Records: Access: Fax, mail, in person. Both court and visitors may perform in person searches. Search fee: $5.00 per name. Required to search: name, years to search. Civil cases indexed by defendant, plaintiff. Civil records on computer from 1989, on index from 1800s.

Criminal Records: Access: Fax, mail, in person. Both court and visitors may perform in person searches. Search fee: $5.00 per name. Required to search: name, years to search; also helpful: DOB, SSN. Criminal records on computer from 1989, on index from 1800s.

General Information: Public Access terminal is available. No juvenile, mental, adoption or sealed released. SASE required. Turnaround time 2-3 days. Fax notes: $5.00 per document; no fee to toll-free number. Copy fee: $1.00 per page. Certification fee: $2.00. Fee payee: Jackson County Clerk. Personal checks accepted.

Superior Court PO Box 788, Seymour, IN 47274; 812-522-9676; Fax: 812-523-6065. Hours: 8AM-4:30PM (EST). *Felony, Misdemeanor, Civil, Eviction, Small Claims.*

Civil Records: Access: Fax, mail, in person. Both court and visitors may perform in person searches. Search fee: $5.00 per name. Required to search: name, years to search. Civil cases indexed by defendant, plaintiff. Civil records on computer from 1989, on index from 1800s.

Criminal Records: Access: Fax, mail, in person. Both court and visitors may perform in person searches. Search fee: $5.00 per name. Required to search: name, years to search; also helpful: DOB, SSN. Criminal records on computer from 1989, on index from 1800s.

General Information: Public Access terminal is available. No juvenile, mental, adoption or sealed released. SASE required. Turnaround time 2-3 days. Fax notes: $5.00 per document; no fee to toll-free number. Copy fee: $1.00 per page. Certification fee: $2.00. Fee payee: Jackson County Clerk. Personal checks accepted.

Jasper County

Circuit Court 115 W Washington, Rensselaer, IN 47978; 219-866-4941. Hours: 8AM-4PM *Felony, Misdemeanor, Civil, Eviction, Small Claims, Probate.*

Note: This court also handles juvenile, paternity and adoption.

Civil Records: Access: Mail, in person. Both court and visitors may perform in person searches. No search fee. Required to search: name, years to search. Civil cases indexed by defendant, plaintiff. County records on computer from 1976, circuit from 1989. Some records on index from 1900s.

Criminal Records: Access: Mail, in person. Both court and visitors may perform in person searches. No search fee. Required to search: name, years to search; also helpful: DOB, SSN. County records on computer from 1976, circuit from 1989. Some records on index from 1900s.

General Information: Public Access terminal is available. No juvenile, mental, adoption or sealed released. SASE required. Turnaround time 1 day. Copy fee: $1.00 per page. Certification fee: $2.00. Fee payee: Jasper County Clerk. Business checks accepted. Prepayment is required.

Superior Court I 115 W Washington St, Rensselaer, IN 47978; 219-866-4922. Hours: 8AM-4PM (CST). *Felony, Misdemeanor, Civil, Probate.*

Civil Records: Access: Mail, in person. Both court and visitors may perform in person searches. No search fee. Required to search: name, years to search. Civil cases indexed by defendant, plaintiff. County records on computer from 1976, circuit from 1989. Some records on index from 1900s.

Criminal Records: Access: Mail, in person. Both court and visitors may perform in person searches. No search fee. Required to search: name, years to search. County records on computer from 1976, circuit from 1989. Some records on index from 1900s.

General Information: Public Access terminal is available. No juvenile, mental, adoption or sealed released. SASE required. Turnaround time 1 day to 1 week. Copy fee: $.50 per page. Non-case related copies are $.10 per page. Certification fee: $1.00. Per page. Fee payee: County Clerk. Only cashiers checks and money orders accepted. Prepayment is required.

Jay County

Circuit & Superior Court Courthouse, Portland, IN 47371; 219-726-4951. Hours: 8:30AM-4:30PM (EST). *Felony, Misdemeanor, Civil, Eviction, Small Claims, Probate.*

Civil Records: Access: Mail, fax, in person. Both court and visitors may perform in person searches. No search fee. Required to search: name, years to search; also helpful: address. Civil cases indexed by defendant, plaintiff. Civil records on computer from 8\94, prior on microfiche from 1979, on index books from 1900.

Criminal Records: Access: Mail, fax, in person. Both court and visitors may perform in person searches. No search fee. Required to search: name, years to search, DOB, SSN; also helpful: address. Criminal records on computer from 8\94, prior on microfiche from 1979, on index books from 1900.

General Information: Public Access terminal is available. No juvenile, mental, adoption or sealed records released. SASE required. Turnaround time 1-2 days. Copy fee: $1.00 per page. Certification fee: $1.00. Fee payee: Court Clerk. Only cashiers checks and money orders accepted. Prepayment is required.

Jefferson County

Circuit & Superior Court Courthouse 300E Main St, Madison, IN 47250; 812-265-8923; Fax: 812-265-8950. Hours: 8AM-4PM (EST). *Felony, Misdemeanor, Civil, Eviction, Small Claims, Probate.*

Civil Records: Access: In person only. Visitors must perform in person searches for themselves. No search fee. Required to search: name, years to search. Civil cases indexed by defendant, plaintiff. Civil records on index from 1975, computerized since 1995.

Criminal Records: Access: In person only. Visitors must perform in person searches for themselves. No search fee. Required to search: Name, years to search, address, DOB, SSN, signed release. Criminal records on index from 1975, computerized since 1995.

General Information: Public Access terminal is available. No juvenile, mental, adoption or sealed released. Fax notes: Fax fee $1.00 per page. Copy fee: $1.00 per page. Certification fee: $1.00. Fee payee: County Clerk. Only cashiers checks and money orders accepted. Prepayment is required.

Jennings County

Circuit Court Courthouse, PO Box 385, Vernon, IN 47282; 812-346-5977. Hours: 8AM-4PM (EST). *Felony, Misdemeanor, Civil, Eviction, Small Claims, Probate.*

Civil Records: Access: Mail, in person. Both court and visitors may perform in person searches. No search fee. Required to search: name, years to search. Civil cases indexed by defendant, plaintiff. Civil records on index from 1930.

Criminal Records: Access: Mail, in person. Both court and visitors may perform in person searches. No search fee. Required to search: name, years to search, DOB; also helpful: SSN. Criminal records on index to 1930.

General Information: No juvenile, mental, adoption or sealed released. SASE required. Turnaround time 2 weeks. Copy fee: $.25 per page. Certification fee: $1.00. Fee payee: County Clerk. Personal checks accepted. Prepayment is required.

Johnson County

Circuit & Superior Court Courthouse, PO Box 368, Franklin, IN 46131; 317-736-3708; Fax: 317-736-3749. Hours: 8AM-4:30PM (EST). *Felony, Misdemeanor, Civil, Eviction, Small Claims, Probate.*

Civil Records: Access: Phone, fax, mail, in person. Both court and visitors may perform in person searches. No search fee. Required to search: name, years to search. Civil cases indexed by defendant, plaintiff. Civil records on computer from 1989, on index from 1968, on microfiche from 1800s.

Criminal Records: Access: Phone, fax, mail, in person. Both court and visitors may perform in person searches. No search fee. Required to search: name, years to search; also helpful: DOB, SSN. Criminal records on computer from 1989, on index from 1968, on microfiche from 1800s.

General Information: Public Access terminal is available. No juvenile, mental, adoption or sealed released. Turnaround time 1-2 days. Fax notes: $1.00 for first page, $.50 each add'l. Copy fee: $1.00 per page. Certification fee: $1.00. Fee payee: County Clerk. Business checks accepted. Prepayment is required.

Knox County

Circuit & Superior Court 101 N 7th St, Vincennes, IN 47591; 812-885-2521. Hours: 8AM-4PM (EST). *Felony, Misdemeanor, Civil, Eviction, Small Claims, Probate.*

Civil Records: Access: Mail, in person. Visitors must perform in person searches for themselves. No search fee. Required to search: name, years to search. Civil

cases indexed by defendant, plaintiff. Civil records on index books from 1800s.

Criminal Records: Access: Mail, in person. Visitors must perform in person searches for themselves. No search fee. Required to search: name, years to search. Criminal records on index books from 1800s.

General Information: No juvenile, mental, adoption or sealed released. Turnaround time 1 week. Copy fee: $1.00 per page. Certification fee: $1.00. Fee payee: Knox County Clerk. Personal checks accepted.

Kosciusko County

Circuit & Superior Court 121 N Lake, Warsaw, IN 46580; 219-372-2331. Hours: 8AM-4PM (EST). *Felony, Misdemeanor, Civil, Eviction, Small Claims, Probate.*

www.indico.net/counties/KOSCIUSKO/GOVERNMENT/clerk.html

Civil Records: Access: Mail, in person. Both court and visitors may perform in person searches. No search fee. Required to search: name, years to search. Civil cases indexed by defendant, plaintiff. Civil records on computer from 10/1/93, general index from 1908.

Criminal Records: Access: Mail, in person. Both court and visitors may perform in person searches. No search fee. Required to search: name, years to search. Criminal records on computer from 10/1/93, general index from 1908.

General Information: Public Access terminal is available. No juvenile, mental, adoption or sealed released. SASE required. Turnaround time 1-3 weeks. Copy fee: $1.00 per page. Certification fee: $1.00. Fee payee: County Clerk. Personal checks accepted. Prepayment is required.

La Porte County

Circuit & Superior Court 813 Lincolnway, La Porte, IN 46350; 219-326-6808. Hours: 8:30AM-5PM (CST). *Felony, Misdemeanor, Civil, Eviction, Probate.*

Civil Records: Access: In person only. Visitors must perform in person searches for themselves. No search fee. Required to search: name, years to search. Civil cases indexed by defendant, plaintiff. Civil records on microfiche and index from 1900.

Criminal Records: Access: In person only. Visitors must perform in person searches for themselves. No search fee. Required to search: name, years to search. Criminal records on microfiche and index from 1900.

General Information: Public Access terminal is available. No juvenile, mental, adoption or sealed released. Copy fee: $1.00 per page. Certification fee: $1.00 per page. Fee payee: Court Clerk. Business checks accepted. Will bill dissolutions.

LaGrange County

Circuit & Superior Court 105 N Detroit St, Courthouse, LaGrange, IN 46761; 219-463-3442. Hours: 8AM-4PM M-TH, 8AM-5PM F (EST). *Felony, Misdemeanor, Civil, Eviction, Small Claims, Probate.*

Civil Records: Access: Phone, mail, in person. Both court and visitors may perform in person searches. No search fee. Required to search: name, years to search. Civil cases indexed by defendant, plaintiff. Civil records on computer from 1990, on books from 1900.

Criminal Records: Access: Phone, mail, in person. Both court and visitors may perform in person searches. No search fee. Required to search: name, years to search; also helpful: DOB, SSN. Criminal records on computer from 1990, on books from 1900.

General Information: No juvenile, mental, adoption or sealed released. SASE requested. Turnaround time 1-2 days from 1/1/90. 30 days if prior to 1/1/90. Copy fee: $1.00 per page. Certification fee: $1.00. Fee payee: LaGrange County Clerk. Personal checks accepted. Prepayment is required.

Lake County

Circuit & Superior Court 2293 N Main St, Courthouse, Crown Point, IN 46307; 219-755-3000. Hours: 8:30AM-4:20PM (CST). *Felony, Misdemeanor, Civil, Eviction, Small Claims, Probate.*

Civil Records: Access: Mail, in person. Both court and visitors may perform in person searches. No search fee. Required to search: name, years to search; also helpful: address. Civil cases indexed by defendant, plaintiff. Civil records on computer and microfiche back to 1983, archived and on index from 1900.

Criminal Records: Access: Mail, in person. Only the court performs in person searches; visitors may not. Search fee: $7.00 per name. Required to search: name, years to search, signed release, DOB, SSN; also helpful: address. Criminal records on computer and microfiche back to 1983. Search requests for background checks are forwarded to the County Bureau of Identification, 775-3316.

General Information: No juvenile, mental, adoption or sealed released. Turnaround time 1 week. Copy fee: $1.00 per page. Certification fee: $2.00. Fee payee: Lake County Clerk. Business checks accepted. Prepayment is required.

Lawrence County

Circuit, Superior & County Court 31 Courthouse, 916 15th St, Bedford, IN 47421; 812-275-7543; Fax: 812-277-2024. Hours: 8:30AM-4:30PM (EST). *Felony, Misdemeanor, Civil, Eviction, Small Claims, Probate.*

Note: Superior Court I is located at 1410 I Street, 812-275-3124. Superior Court II is located at 1420 I Street, 812-275-4161. All small claims are filed in Superior II.

Civil Records: Access: In person only. Visitors must perform in person searches for themselves. No search fee. Required to search: name, years to search. Civil cases indexed by plaintiff. Civil records on computer from 1987, on index from 1817.

Criminal Records: Access: In person only. Visitors must perform in person searches for themselves. No search fee. Required to search: name, years to search, DOB; also helpful: SSN. Criminal records on computer from 1987, on index from 1817.

General Information: No juvenile, mental, adoption or sealed released. Copy fee: $1.00 per page. Certification fee: $1.00. Fee payee: Lawrence County Clerk. Only cashiers checks and money orders accepted. Prepayment is required.

Madison County

Circuit, Superior & County Court PO Box 1277, Anderson, IN 46015-1277; 765-641-9443; Fax: 765-640-4203. Hours: 8AM-4PM (EST). *Felony, Misdemeanor, Civil, Eviction, Small Claims, Probate.*

Civil Records: Access: In person only. Visitors must perform in person searches for themselves. No search fee. Required to search: name, years to search. Civil cases indexed by defendant. Civil records on microfiche and archived from 1950, on index from 1900.

Criminal Records: Access: In person only. Visitors must perform in person searches for themselves. No search fee. Required to search: name, years to search, signed release. Criminal records on microfiche and archived from 1950, on index from 1900.

General Information: Public Access terminal is available. No juvenile, mental, adoption or sealed released. Copy fee: $1.00 per page. Certification fee: $1.00. Fee payee: County Clerk. Business checks accepted. Prepayment is required.

Marion County

Circuit & Superior Court 200 E Washington St, Indianapolis, IN 46204; 317-327-4740; Civil phone: 317-327-4724; Criminal phone: 317-327-4733. Hours: 8AM-4:30PM (EST). *Felony, Misdemeanor, Civil, Probate.*

www.indygov.org/clerk

Note: The Municipal Court of Marion County, once separate, is now part of Superior Court. All records are merged with the Superior Court.

Civil Records: Access: Mail, online, in person. Both court and visitors may perform in person searches. No search fee. Required to search: name, years to search. Civil cases indexed by defendant, plaintiff. Civil records on computer back to 1981, on microfiche, archived and on index from 1912. Small claims records are held by the township in which they were filed; the phone numbers are listed below. Access to the remote online system is available via the internet at www.civicnet.net. The setup fee is $50. Other fees vary by type of record or search.

Criminal Records: Access: Mail, online, in person. Both court and visitors may perform in person searches. Search fee: $7.00 per name. Fee is $3.00 for in person request. Required to search: name, years to search, DOB; also helpful: SSN. Criminal records on computer back to 1981, on microfiche, archived and on index from 1912. Small claims records are held by the township in which they were filed; the phone numbers are listed below. Online access to criminal records is the same as civil. Criminal records go back to 1988.

General Information: Public Access terminal is available. No juvenile, mental, adoption or sealed released. SASE not required. Turnaround time 1-2 days. Fax notes: Will not fax results. Copy fee: $1.00 per page. Certification fee: $1.00. Fee payee: County Clerk. Personal checks accepted.

Marshall County

Circuit & Superior Court 1 & 2 211 W Madison St, Plymouth, IN 46563; 219-936-8922; Fax: 219-936-8893. Hours: 8AM-4PM (EST). *Felony, Misdemeanor, Civil, Eviction, Small Claims, Probate.*

Civil Records: Access: In person only. Visitors must perform in person searches for themselves. No search fee. Required to search: name, years to search; also helpful: address. Civil cases indexed by defendant, plaintiff. Civil records on computer from 1989, on microfiche, archived and on index from 1835.

Criminal Records: Access: Mail, in person. Both court and visitors may perform in person searches. Search fee: $10.00 per name. Required to search: name, years to search, signed release; also helpful: address, DOB, SSN. Criminal records on computer from 1989, on microfiche, archived and on index from 1835.

General Information: Public Access terminal is available. No juvenile, mental, adoption or sealed released. SASE required. Turnaround time within 1 week. Fax notes: Fee to fax results is $1.00 per page; certified 1st page is $2.00. Copy fee: $1.00 per page. Certification fee: $2.00. Fee payee: County Clerk. Business checks accepted. Prepayment is required.

Martin County

Circuit Court PO Box 120 (111 Main St), Shoals, IN 47581; 812-247-3651; Fax: 812-247-2791. Hours: 8AM-4PM (EST). *Felony, Misdemeanor, Civil, Eviction, Small Claims, Probate.*

Civil Records: Access: Phone, mail, fax, in person. Both court and visitors may perform in person searches. No search fee. Required to search: name, years to search. Civil cases indexed by defendant, plaintiff. Civil records on index books.

Criminal Records: Access: Phone, mail, fax, in person. Both court and visitors may perform in person searches. No search fee. Required to search: name, years to search, DOB or SSN. Criminal records on index books.

General Information: No juvenile, mental, adoption, or sealed records released. Turnaround time 4 days. Copy fee: $1.00 per page. Certification fee: $2.00. Fee payee: County Clerk. Business checks accepted. Prepayment is required.

Miami County

Circuit & Superior Court PO Box 184, Peru, IN 46970; 765-472-3901; Fax: 765-472-1778. Hours: 8AM-4PM (EST). *Felony, Misdemeanor, Civil, Eviction, Small Claims, Probate.*

Civil Records: Access: Fax, mail, in person. Both court and visitors may perform in person searches. Search fee: $10.00 per name. Required to search: name, years to search. Civil cases indexed by defendant, plaintiff. Civil records archived from 1900s. Some records on docket books by case number and alpha.

Criminal Records: Access: Fax, mail, in person. Both court and visitors may perform in person searches. Search fee: $10.00 per name. Required to search: name, years to search, DOB, signed release; also helpful: SSN. Criminal records archived from 1900s. Some records on docket books by case number and alpha.

General Information: No juvenile, mental, adoption, or sealed released. Turnaround time 1-2 days. Fax notes: $1.00 per page. No fee for toll free or local calls. Copy fee: $1.00 per page. Certification fee: $1.00. Fee payee: Miami County Clerk. Personal checks accepted. Prepayment is required.

Monroe County

Circuit Court PO Box 547, Bloomington, IN 47402; 812-349-2614; Fax: 812-349-2610. Hours: 8AM-4PM (EST). *Felony, Misdemeanor, Civil, Eviction, Small Claims, Probate.*

Civil Records: Access: Mail, fax, in person. Both court and visitors may perform in person searches. No search fee. Required to search: name, years to search. Civil cases indexed by defendant, plaintiff. Civil records on computer from 1993. Some records on docket books by case number and alpha. In the process of putting records on microfiche.

Criminal Records: Access: Mail, fax, in person. Both court and visitors may perform in person searches. No search fee. Required to search: name, years to search, DOB; also helpful: SSN. Criminal records on computer from 1993. Some records on docket books by case number and alpha. In the process of putting records on microfiche.

General Information: Public Access terminal is available. No juvenile, mental, adoption or sealed released. Turnaround time 48 hours. Fax notes: Fee to fax results is $1.00 per page. Copy fee: $1.00 per page. Certification fee: $1.00. Fee payee: Monroe County Clerk. Personal checks accepted. Prepayment is required.

Montgomery County

Circuit, Superior & County Court PO Box 768, Crawfordsville, IN 47933; 765-364-6430; Fax: 765-364-6355. Hours: 8:30AM-4:30PM (EST). *Felony, Misdemeanor, Civil, Eviction, Small Claims, Probate.*

Civil Records: Access: Phone, fax, mail, in person. Both court and visitors may perform in person searches. No search fee. Required to search: name, years to search. Civil cases indexed by defendant, plaintiff. Civil records on computer from 1990, some on microfiche and docket books, and archived from 1800s. Indicate type(s) of cases sought in search request.

Criminal Records: Access: Mail, fax, in person. Both court and visitors may perform in person searches. No search fee. Required to search: name, years to search, DOB; also helpful: SSN. Criminal records on computer from 1990, some on microfiche and docket books, and archived from 1800s.

General Information: No juvenile, mental, adoption or sealed released. SASE required. Turnaround time 1 week. Fax notes: $1.00 per page. Additional fax fee $3.25. Copy fee: $1.00 per page. Certification fee: $2.00. Fee payee: Montgomery County Clerk. Prepayment is required.

Morgan County

Circuit & Superior Court PO Box 1556, Martinsville, IN 46151; 765-342-1025; Fax: 765-342-1111. Hours: 8AM-4PM (EST). *Felony, Misdemeanor, Civil, Eviction, Small Claims, Probate.*

Civil Records: Access: In person only. Visitors must perform in person searches for themselves. No search fee. Required to search: name, years to search. Civil cases indexed by defendant, plaintiff. Civil records archived from 1970; on computer back to 1993. Some records on index cards.

Criminal Records: Access: In person only. Visitors must perform in person searches for themselves. No search fee. Required to search: name, years to search, DOB; also helpful: SSN, signed release. Criminal records archived from 1970; on microfilm 1992-95, on computer back to 1993.

General Information: Public Access terminal is available. No juvenile, mental, adoption or sealed released. Fax notes: Will not fax results. Certification fee: $1.00 per page. Fee payee: Morgan County Clerk. Personal checks accepted. Prepayment is required.

Newton County

Circuit & Superior Court PO Box 49, Kentland, IN 47951; 219-474-6081. Hours: 8AM-4PM (CST). *Felony, Misdemeanor, Civil, Eviction, Small Claims, Probate.*

Civil Records: Access: Mail, in person. Both court and visitors may perform in person searches. Search fee: $3.00 per name. Required to search: name, years to search. Civil cases indexed by defendant, plaintiff. Civil records on index from 1950, partial on microfiche.

Criminal Records: Access: Mail, in person. Both court and visitors may perform in person searches. Search fee: $3.00 per name. Required to search: name, years to search, DOB; also helpful: SSN. Criminal records on index from 1950, partial on microfiche.

General Information: No juvenile, mental, adoption or sealed records released. SASE required. Turnaround time 1-2 weeks. Copy fee: $1.00 per page. Certification fee: $2.00. Fee payee: Clerk of Newton Circuit Court. Business checks accepted. Prepayment is required.

Noble County

Circuit, Superior & County Court 101 N Orange St, Albion, IN 46701; 219-636-2736; Fax: 219-636-4000. Hours: 8AM-4PM (EST). *Felony, Misdemeanor, Civil, Eviction, Small Claims, Probate.*

Civil Records: Access: Fax, mail, in person. Both court and visitors may perform in person searches. No search fee. Required to search: name, years to search. Civil cases indexed by defendant, plaintiff. Civil records on index cards and docket books to 1859. Preparing computer and microfiche records.

Criminal Records: Access: Fax, mail, in person. Both court and visitors may perform in person searches. No search fee. Required to search: name, years to search; also helpful: DOB, SSN. Criminal records on index cards and docket books to 1859. Preparing computer and microfiche records. Criminal record searches are 10-year only.

General Information: Public Access terminal is available. No juvenile, mental, adoption or sealed released. SASE required. Turnaround time 1 week. Fax notes: Will fax back to toll-free numbers. Copy fee: $1.00 per page. Certification fee: $1.00. Fee payee: Noble County Clerk. No personal checks accepted. Prepayment is required.

Ohio County

Circuit & Superior Court PO Box 185, Rising Sun, IN 47040; 812-438-2610; Fax: 812-438-4590. Hours: 9AM-4PM M,T,Th,F 9AM-Noon S (EST). *Felony, Misdemeanor, Civil, Eviction, Small Claims, Probate.*

Civil Records: Access: Phone, fax, mail, in person. Both court and visitors may perform in person searches. No search fee. Required to search: name, years to search. Civil cases indexed by defendant, plaintiff. Civil records archived from 1844; on computer back to 8/1999.

Criminal Records: Access: In person only. Visitors must perform in person searches for themselves. No search fee. Required to search: name, years to search. Criminal records on computer back to 8/1999.

General Information: Public Access terminal is available. No juvenile, mental, adoption or sealed released. Fax notes: Fee to fax results is $3.00 1st page, $1.00 each add'l. Copy fee: $1.00 per page. Certification fee: $2.00. Fee payee: Ohio County Clerk. Personal checks accepted. Prepayment is required.

Orange County

Circuit & County Court Courthouse, Court St, Paoli, IN 47454; 812-723-2649. Hours: 8AM-4PM (EST). *Felony, Misdemeanor, Civil, Eviction, Small Claims, Probate.*

Note: The physical location of the County Court is 205 E Main Street. The County Court handles misdemeanor, eviction and small claims.

Civil Records: Access: Mail, fax, in person. Both court and visitors may perform in person searches. No search fee. Required to search: name, years to search. Civil cases indexed by defendant, plaintiff. Civil records archived from 1874. Some records on docket books.

Criminal Records: Access: Mail, fax, in person. Both court and visitors may perform in person searches. No search fee. Required to search: name, years to search. Criminal records archived from 1874. Some records on docket books.

General Information: No juvenile, mental, adoption or sealed released. SASE required. Turnaround time 2 weeks. Copy fee: $1.00 per page. Certification fee: $2.00. Fee payee: Orange Circuit Clerk. Only cashiers checks and money orders accepted.

Owen County

Circuit Court PO Box 146, Courthouse, Spencer, IN 47460; 812-829-5015; Fax: 812-829-5028. Hours: 8AM-4PM (EST). *Felony, Misdemeanor, Civil, Eviction, Small Claims, Probate.*

Civil Records: Access: Fax, in person. Visitors must perform in person searches for themselves. No search fee. Required to search: name, years to search. Civil cases indexed by defendant, plaintiff. Civil records archived from 1800s. Some records on docket books.

Criminal Records: Access: Fax, in person. Visitors must perform in person searches for themselves. No search fee. Required to search: name, years to search. Criminal records archived from 1800s. Some records on docket books.

General Information: No juvenile, mental, adoption or sealed records released. Fax notes: No fee to fax results. Copy fee: $1.00 per page. Certification fee: $2.00. Fee payee: Owen County Clerk. Business checks accepted. Prepayment is required.

Parke County

Circuit Court 116 W High St, Rm 204, Rockville, IN 47872; 765-569-5132. Hours: 8AM-4PM (EST). *Felony, Misdemeanor, Civil, Eviction, Small Claims, Probate.*

Civil Records: Access: In person only. Visitors must perform in person searches for themselves. No search fee. Required to search: name, years to search. Civil cases indexed by defendant, plaintiff. Civil records archived from 1880s. Some records on docket books.

Criminal Records: Access: In person only. Visitors must perform in person searches for themselves. No search fee. Required to search: name, years to search. Criminal records archived from 1880s. Some records on docket books.

General Information: No juvenile, mental, adoption or sealed released. Copy fee: $1.00 per page. Certification fee: $2.00. Fee payee: Parke County Clerk. Personal checks not accepted.

Perry County

Circuit Court 2219 Payne St, Courthouse, Tell City, IN 47586; 812-547-3741. Hours: 8AM-4PM (EST). *Felony, Misdemeanor, Civil, Eviction, Small Claims, Probate.*

Civil Records: Access: In person only. Both court and visitors may perform in person searches. No search fee. Required to search: name, years to search. Civil cases indexed by defendant, plaintiff. Civil records archived from 1900s. Some records on dockets.

Criminal Records: Access: In person only. Both court and visitors may perform in person searches. No search fee. Required to search: name, years to search. Criminal records archived from 1900s. Some records on dockets.

General Information: No juvenile, mental, adoption or sealed released. Copy fee: $.50 per page. Certification fee: $1.00. Fee payee: Perry County Clerk. Business checks accepted. Prepayment is required.

Pike County

Circuit Court 801 Main St. Courthouse, Petersburg, IN 47567-1298; 812-354-6025; Fax: 812-354-3552. Hours: 8AM-4PM (EST). *Felony, Misdemeanor, Civil, Eviction, Small Claims, Probate.*

Civil Records: Access: Mail, in person. Both court and visitors may perform in person searches. No search fee. Required to search: name, years to search. Civil cases indexed by defendant, plaintiff. Civil records archived from 1817. Some records on docket books and index file; on computer since.

Criminal Records: Access: Mail, in person. Both court and visitors may perform in person searches. No search fee. Required to search: name, years to search, DOB. Criminal records archived from 1817. Some records on docket books and index file; on computer since.

General Information: No juvenile, mental, adoption or sealed released. SASE required. Turnaround time 1-2 days. Copy fee: $1.00 per page. Certification fee: $2.00. Fee payee: Pike County Clerk. Only cashiers checks and money orders accepted. Prepayment is required.

Porter County

Circuit Court Records Division, Courthouse Suite 217, 16 E Lincolnway, Valparaiso, IN 46383-5659; 219-465-3453; Fax: 219-465-3592. Hours: 8:30AM-4:30PM (CST). *Felony, Misdemeanor, Civil, Eviction, Small Claims, Probate.*

Civil Records: Access: Mail, in person. Both court and visitors may perform in person searches. No search fee. Required to search: name, years to search. Civil cases indexed by defendant, plaintiff. Civil records on computer index from 1990. Circuit Court records kept from 1844, Superior Court records from 1895. Probate records from Circuit Court kept from 1853, Superior Court from 1900.

Criminal Records: Access: Mail, in person. Both court and visitors may perform in person searches. No search fee. Required to search: name, years to search. Criminal records on computer index since 1990. Circuit Court criminal records kept from 1877, Superior Court from 1895.

General Information: Public Access terminal is available. No juvenile, mental, adoption or sealed released. SASE required. Turnaround time 1-2 weeks. Copy fee: $1.00 per page. Certification fee: $1.00. Fee payee: Porter County Clerk. Only cashiers checks and money orders accepted. Prepayment is required.

Superior Court 3560 Willow Creek Dr, Portage, IN 46368; 219-759-2501. Hours: 8:30AM-4:30PM (CST). *Misdemeanor, Civil, Small Claims, Probate.*

Civil Records: Access: Mail, in person. Both court and visitors may perform in person searches. No search fee. Required to search: name, years to search. Civil cases indexed by defendant, plaintiff. Civil records on computer since 1991; prior records on manual index.

Criminal Records: Access: Mail, in person. Both court and visitors may perform in person searches. No search fee. Required to search: name, years to search; also helpful: DOB, SSN. Criminal records on computer since 1991; prior records on manual index.

General Information: Public Access terminal is available. No juvenile, mental, adoption or sealed records released. Fax notes: Fee to fax results is $.79 per page. Copy fee: $2.00 per page. Certification fee: $1.00. Fee payee: Porter County Clerk. Only cashiers checks and money orders accepted. Prepayment is required.

Posey County

Circuit & Superior Court PO Box 606, 300 Main St, Mount Vernon, IN 47620-0606; 812-838-1306; Fax: 812-838-1307. Hours: 8AM-4PM (CST). *Felony, Misdemeanor, Civil, Eviction, Small Claims, Probate.*

Civil Records: Access: In person only. Visitors must perform in person searches for themselves. No search fee. Required to search: name, years to search; also helpful: address. Civil cases indexed by defendant, plaintiff. Civil records on computer since 8/88, prior on docket books.

Criminal Records: Access: In person only. Visitors must perform in person searches for themselves. No search fee. Required to search: name, years to search; also helpful: DOB, SSN. Criminal records on computer since 8/88, prior on docket books.

General Information: Public Access terminal is available. (Available in Superior Court.) No juvenile, mental, adoption or sealed released. Copy fee: $1.00 per page. Certification fee: $1.00. Fee payee: Posey County Clerk. Only cashiers checks and money orders accepted. Prepayment is required.

Pulaski County

Circuit & Superior Court 112 E Main, Room 230, Winamac, IN 46996; 219-946-3313; Fax: 219-946-4953. Hours: 8AM-4PM (EST). *Felony, Misdemeanor, Civil, Eviction, Small Claims, Probate.*

Civil Records: Access: In person only. Visitors must perform in person searches for themselves. No search fee. Required to search: name, years to search. Civil cases indexed by defendant. Civil records archived from 1850s. Some records on docket books. On computer back to 10/2000.

Criminal Records: Access: In person only. Visitors must perform in person searches for themselves. No search fee. Required to search: name, years to search; also helpful: SSN. Criminal records archived from 1850s. Some records on docket books. On computer back to 10/2000.

General Information: Public Access terminal is available. No juvenile, mental, adoption or sealed

records released. Fax notes: Will not fax results. Copy fee: $.50 per page. Certification fee: $2.00. Fee payee: Pulaski County Clerk. Only cashiers checks and money orders accepted. Prepayment is required.

Putnam County

Circuit & Superior Court PO Box 546, Greencastle, IN 46135; 765-653-2648. Hours: 8AM-4PM (EST). *Felony, Misdemeanor, Civil, Eviction, Small Claims, Probate.*

Civil Records: Access: Mail, in person. Both court and visitors may perform in person searches. No search fee. Required to search: name, years to search. Civil cases indexed by defendant, plaintiff. Civil records on index books from 1991, archived from 1800s. Some records on docket books.

Criminal Records: Access: In person only. Visitors must perform in person searches for themselves. No search fee. Required to search: name, years to search; also helpful: DOB, SSN. Criminal records on index books from 1991, archived from 1800s. Some records on docket books.

General Information: No juvenile, mental, adoption or sealed released. Turnaround time 1 week. Copy fee: $1.00 per page. Certification fee: $1.00. Fee payee: Putnam County Clerk. Business checks accepted. Prepayment is required.

Randolph County

Circuit & Superior Court PO Box 230 Courthouse, Winchester, IN 47394-0230; 765-584-7070 X231; Fax: 765-584-2958. Hours: 8AM-4PM (EST). *Felony, Misdemeanor, Civil, Eviction, Small Claims, Probate.*

Civil Records: Access: Fax, mail, in person. Both court and visitors may perform in person searches. No search fee. Required to search: name, years to search. Civil cases indexed by defendant, plaintiff. Civil records archived from early 1800s. Records on docket books and microfiche.

Criminal Records: Access: Fax, mail, in person. Both court and visitors may perform in person searches. No search fee. Required to search: name, years to search. Criminal records archived from early 1800s. Records on docket books and microfiche.

General Information: Public Access terminal is available. No juvenile, mental, adoption or sealed released. SASE required. Turnaround time 3 days. Fax notes: $4.00 for first page, $.75 each add'l. Copy fee: $1.00 per page. Certification fee: $1.00. Fee payee: Randolph County Clerk. Only cashiers checks and money orders accepted. Prepayment is required.

Ripley County

Circuit Court PO BOX 177, Versailles, IN 47042; 812-689-6115. Hours: 8AM-4PM (EST). *Felony, Misdemeanor, Civil, Eviction, Small Claims, Probate.*

Civil Records: Access: Mail, in person. Both court and visitors may perform in person searches. No search fee. Required to search: name, years to search. Civil cases indexed by defendant, plaintiff. Civil records on computer since 1994, archived from 1900s. Some records on docket books.

Criminal Records: Access: Mail, in person. Both court and visitors may perform in person searches. No search fee. Required to search: name, years to search, DOB; also helpful: SSN. Criminal records on computer since 1994, archived from 1900s. Some records on docket books.

General Information: Public Access terminal is available. No juvenile, mental, adoption or sealed records released. Turnaround time 1 week. Copy fee: $1.00 per page. Certification fee: $1.00. Fee payee: Clerk of Ripley Circuit Court. Personal checks accepted. Prepayment is required.

Rush County

Circuit & Superior Court PO Box 429, Rushville, IN 46173; 765-932-2086; Fax: 765-932-2357. Hours: 8AM-4PM (EST). *Felony, Misdemeanor, Civil, Eviction, Small Claims, Probate.*

Civil Records: Access: In person only. Visitors must perform in person searches for themselves. No search fee. Required to search: name, years to search. Civil cases indexed by defendant, plaintiff. Civil records archived from 1822. Some records on docket books.

Criminal Records: Access: In person only. Visitors must perform in person searches for themselves. No search fee. Required to search: name, years to search, DOB; also helpful: SSN, cause number. Criminal records archived from 1822. Some records on docket books.

General Information: No juvenile, mental, adoption or sealed records released. Copy fee: $1.00 per page. Certification fee: $1.00. Fee payee: Rush County Clerk. Business checks accepted. Prepayment is required.

Scott County

Circuit & Superior Court 1 E McClain Ave, #120, Scottsburg, IN 47170; 812-752-8420; Fax: 812-752-5459. Hours: 8:30AM-4:30PM (EST). *Felony, Misdemeanor, Civil, Eviction, Small Claims, Probate.*

Civil Records: Access: In person only. Visitors must perform in person searches for themselves. No search fee. Required to search: name, years to search; also helpful: address. Civil cases indexed by defendant, plaintiff. Civil records on computer from 2/90, on docket books from 1970.

Criminal Records: Access: In person only. Visitors must perform in person searches for themselves. No search fee. Required to search: name, years to search; also helpful: DOB, SSN. Criminal records on computer from 2/90, on docket books from 1970.

General Information: No juvenile, mental, adoption or sealed released. Copy fee: $1.00 per page. Certification fee: $2.00. Fee payee: Scott County Clerk. Business checks accepted. Prepayment is required.

Shelby County

Circuit & Superior Court PO Box 198, Shelbyville, IN 46176; 317-392-6320. Hours: 8AM-4PM (EST). *Felony, Misdemeanor, Civil, Eviction, Small Claims, Probate.*

Civil Records: Access: In person only. Visitors must perform in person searches for themselves. No search fee. Required to search: name, years to search. Civil cases indexed by defendant, plaintiff. Civil records on computer since 07/95.

Criminal Records: Access: In person only. Visitors must perform in person searches for themselves. No search fee. Required to search: name, years to search. Criminal records on computer since 07/95.

General Information: Public Access terminal is available. No juvenile, mental, adoption or sealed released. Copy fee: $1.00 per page. Certification fee: $1.00. Fee payee: Clerk of Court. Personal checks accepted. Prepayment is required.

Spencer County

Circuit Court PO Box 12, Rockport, IN 47635; 812-649-6027; Fax: 812-649-6030. Hours: 8AM-4PM (CST). *Felony, Misdemeanor, Civil, Eviction, Small Claims, Probate.*

Civil Records: Access: In person only. Visitors must perform in person searches for themselves. No search fee. Required to search: name, years to search. Civil cases indexed by defendant, plaintiff. Civil records archived from early 1900s. Some records on docket books. Child support cases on computer.

Criminal Records: Access: In person only. Visitors must perform in person searches for themselves. No

search fee. Required to search: name, years to search. Criminal records archived from early 1900s. Some records on docket books. Child support cases on computer.

General Information: No juvenile, mental, adoption or sealed released. Copy fee: $1.00 per page. Certification fee: $1.00. Fee payee: Spencer Circuit Court. Only cashiers checks and money orders accepted. Prepayment is required.

St. Joseph County

Circuit & Superior Court 101 South Main St, South Bend, IN 46601; 219-235-9635; Fax: 219-235-9838. Hours: 8AM-4:30PM (EST). *Felony, Misdemeanor, Civil, Eviction, Small Claims, Probate.*

Civil Records: Access: Mail, in person. Both court and visitors may perform in person searches. No search fee. Required to search: name, years to search. Civil cases indexed by defendant, plaintiff. Civil records on general index from 1962.

Criminal Records: Access: In person only. Visitors must perform in person searches for themselves. No search fee. Required to search: name, years to search; also helpful: address, DOB, SSN. Criminal records on general index from 1962.

General Information: Public Access terminal is available. No juvenile, mental, adoption or sealed released. SASE required. Turnaround time 1-2 days. Copy fee: $1.00 per page. Certification fee: $1.00. Fee payee: St Joseph County Clerk. Business checks accepted.

Starke County

Circuit Court Courthouse, 53 E Washington St, Knox, IN 46534; 219-772-9128. Hours: 8:30AM-4PM (CST). *Felony, Misdemeanor, Civil, Eviction, Small Claims, Probate.*

Civil Records: Access: In person only. Visitors must perform in person searches for themselves. No search fee. Required to search: name, years to search. Civil cases indexed by defendant, plaintiff. Civil records archived from 1850s. Some records on docket books.

Criminal Records: Access: In person only. Visitors must perform in person searches for themselves. No search fee. Required to search: name, years to search, DOB; also helpful: SSN. Criminal records archived from 1850s. Some records on docket books. Same as civil.

General Information: No juvenile, mental, adoption or sealed released. Copy fee: $1.00 per page. Certification fee: $2.00. Fee payee: Clerk of Stark Circuit Court. Business checks accepted. Prepayment is required.

Steuben County

Circuit & Superior Court Courthouse, 55 S. Public Square, Angola, IN 46703; 219-668-1000 X2240. Hours: 8AM-4:30PM (EST). *Felony, Misdemeanor, Civil, Eviction, Small Claims, Probate.*

Civil Records: Access: In person only. Visitors must perform in person searches for themselves. No search fee. Required to search: name, years to search. Civil cases indexed by defendant, plaintiff. Civil records archived from 1800s. Some records on docket books.

Criminal Records: Access: In person only. Visitors must perform in person searches for themselves. No search fee. Required to search: name, years to search. Criminal records archived from 1800s. Some records on docket books.

General Information: Public Access terminal is available. No juvenile, mental, adoption, some probate, or sealed released. Copy fee: $1.00 per page. Certification fee: $2.00. Fee payee: Steuben County Clerk. Only cashiers checks and money orders accepted. Prepayment is required.

Sullivan County

Circuit & Superior Court Courthouse, 3rd Fl, PO Box 370, Sullivan, IN 47882-0370; 812-268-4657. Hours: 8AM-4PM (EST). *Felony, Misdemeanor, Civil, Eviction, Small Claims, Probate.*

Civil Records: Access: In person only. Both court and visitors may perform in person searches. No search fee. Required to search: name, years to search; also helpful: address. Civil cases indexed by defendant, plaintiff. Civil records on docket books or general index from late 1800's; computerized from 1998.

Criminal Records: Access: In person only. Visitors must perform in person searches for themselves. No search fee. Required to search: name, years to search, DOB, signed release; also helpful: address, SSN. Criminal records on docket books or general index from late 1800's; computerized from 1998.

General Information: Public Access terminal is available. No juvenile, mental, adoption or sealed released. Copy fee: $1.00 per page. Certification fee: $2.00 per page. Fee payee: Sullivan County. Personal checks accepted. Prepayment is required.

Switzerland County

Circuit & Superior Court Courthouse, 212 W Main St, Vevay, IN 47043; 812-427-3175; Fax: 812-427-2017. Hours: 8:30-3:30PM M-W & F *Felony, Misdemeanor, Civil, Eviction, Small Claims, Probate.*

Civil Records: Access: Phone, mail, fax, in person. Both court and visitors may perform in person searches. No search fee. Required to search: name, years to search, DOB. Civil cases indexed by defendant, plaintiff. Civil records archived from 1900s. All records on docket books or general index.

Criminal Records: Access: Phone, mail, fax, in person. Both court and visitors may perform in person searches. No search fee. Required to search: name, years to search, DOB. Criminal records archived from 1900s. All records on docket books or general index.

General Information: No juvenile, mental, adoption or sealed records released. SASE required. Turnaround time varies. Fax fee $2.50 1st page, $.50 per page thereafter. Copy fee: $1.00 per page. Certification fee: $1.00. Fee payee: Switzerland County Clerk. Only cashiers checks and money orders accepted. Prepayment is required.

Tippecanoe County

Circuit, Superior & County Court PO Box 1665, Lafayette, IN 47902; 765-423-9326; Fax: 765-423-9194. Hours: 8AM-4:30PM (EST). *Felony, Misdemeanor, Civil, Eviction, Small Claims, Probate.*

www.county.tippecanoe.in.us

Civil Records: Access: In person, online. Visitors must perform in person searches for themselves. No search fee. Required to search: name, years to search. Civil cases indexed by defendant, plaintiff. Civil records on computer from 1987, on microfiche from 1900. Some records on index and docket books. Online access to court records through CourtView are available free online at http://court.county.tippecanoe.in.us/pa/pa.htm.

Criminal Records: Access: In person, online. Visitors must perform in person searches for themselves. No search fee. Required to search: name, years to search; also helpful: DOB, SSN, sex, signed release. Criminal records on computer from 1987, on microfiche from 1900. Some records on index and docket books. Online access to criminal records is the same as civil.

General Information: Public Access terminal is available. No juvenile, mental, adoption or sealed released. Copy fee: $.50 per page. Certification fee: $1.00. Fee payee: Tippecanoe County Clerk. Business checks accepted. Prepayment is required.

Tipton County

Circuit Court Tipton County Courthouse, Tipton, IN 46072; 765-675-2791; Fax: 765-675-7797. Hours: 8AM-4PM M-Th, 8AM-5PM F (EST). *Felony, Misdemeanor, Civil, Eviction, Small Claims, Probate.*

Civil Records: Access: In person only. Visitors must perform in person searches for themselves. No search fee. Required to search: name, years to search. Civil cases indexed by defendant, plaintiff. Civil records on card file and archived from 1930s.

Criminal Records: Access: In person only. Visitors must perform in person searches for themselves. No search fee. Required to search: name, years to search. Criminal records on card file and archived from 1930s.

General Information: No juvenile, mental, adoption or sealed released. Copy fee: $1.00 per page. Certification fee: $1.00. Fee payee: Tipton County Clerk. Personal checks accepted.

Union County

Circuit Court 26 W Union St, Liberty, IN 47353; 765-458-6121; Fax: 765-458-5263. Hours: 8AM-4PM (EST). *Felony, Misdemeanor, Civil, Eviction, Small Claims, Probate.*

Civil Records: Access: In person only. Both court and visitors may perform in person searches. No search fee. Required to search: name, years to search. Civil cases indexed by defendant, plaintiff. Civil records archived from 1821. Some records on docket or entry books.

Criminal Records: Access: In person only. Both court and visitors may perform in person searches. No search fee. Required to search: name, years to search; also helpful: DOB, SSN. Criminal records archived from 1821. Some records on docket books or entry books.

General Information: No juvenile, mental, adoption or sealed records released. Copy fee: $.25 per page. Certification fee: $1.00. Fee payee: Union County Clerk. Only cashiers checks and money orders accepted. Prepayment is required.

Vanderburgh County

Circuit & Superior Court PO Box 3356, Evansville, IN 47732-3356; 812-435-5160; Fax: 812-435-5849. Hours: 8AM-5PM (CST). *Felony, Misdemeanor, Civil, Eviction, Small Claims, Probate.*

www.countyclerk.evansville.net/newhome

Civil Records: Access: In person only. Visitors must perform in person searches for themselves. No search fee. Required to search: name, years to search. Civil cases indexed by defendant, plaintiff. Civil records on computer back to 1991, archived from 1900s. Some records on index books.

Criminal Records: Access: In person only. Visitors must perform in person searches for themselves. No search fee. Required to search: name, years to search, DOB, SSN. Criminal records on computer back to 1991, archived to 1900s. Some records on index books.

General Information: Public Access terminal is available. No juvenile, mental, adoption or sealed released. Fax notes: Fee to fax results is $2.00 per document plus $1.00 per page. Copy fee: $1.00 per page. Certification fee: $1.00. Fee payee: Vanderburgh County Clerk. Business checks accepted. Prepayment is required.

Vermillion County

Circuit Court PO Box 10, Newport, IN 47966-0010; 765-492-3500. Hours: 8AM-4PM *Felony, Misdemeanor, Civil, Eviction, Small Claims, Probate.*

Civil Records: Access: In person only. Visitors must perform in person searches for themselves. No search fee. Required to search: name. Civil cases indexed by defendant, plaintiff. Pending on computer. Archived from 1800s. Some records on docket books.

Criminal Records: Access: In person only. Visitors must perform in person searches for themselves. No search fee. Required to search: name. Pending on computer. Archived from 1800s. Some records on docket books.

General Information: No juvenile, mental, adoption or sealed released. Copy fee: $1.00 per page. Certification fee: $2.00. Fee payee: Vermillion County Clerk. Business checks accepted. Prepayment required.

Vigo County

Circuit, Superior & County Court 2nd Fl, Courthouse, PO Box 8449, Terre Haute, IN 47807-8449; 812-462-3211. Hours: 8AM-4PM *Felony, Misdemeanor, Civil, Eviction, Small Claims, Probate.*

Civil Records: Access: In person only. Visitors must perform in person searches for themselves. No search fee. Required to search: name, years to search. Civil cases indexed by defendant, plaintiff. Civil records on index books; on computer back to 8/1996.

Criminal Records: Access: In person only. Visitors must perform in person searches for themselves. No search fee. Required to search: name, years to search; also helpful: DOB, SSN. Criminal records on index books; on computer back to 8/1996.

General Information: Public Access terminal is available. No juvenile, mental, adoption or sealed released. Copy fee: $1.00 per page. Certification fee: $1.00. Fee payee: Vigo County Clerk. Only cashiers checks/money orders accepted. Prepayment required.

Wabash County

Circuit & Superior Court One West Hill St, Wabash, IN 46992; 219-563-0661 X30 or X32; Fax: 219-563-3451. Hours: 8AM-4PM (EST). *Felony, Misdemeanor, Civil, Eviction, Small Claims, Probate.*

Civil Records: Access: In person only. Visitors must perform in person searches for themselves. No search fee. Required to search: name, years to search. Civil cases indexed by defendant, plaintiff. Civil records archived from 1800s; on computer since 1989. Some judgments on fee books.

Criminal Records: Access: In person only. Visitors must perform in person searches for themselves. No search fee. Required to search: name, years to search, DOB; also helpful: SSN. Criminal records archived from 1800s; on computer since 1989. Some judgments on fee books.

General Information: Public Access terminal is available. No juvenile, mental, adoption or sealed records released. Fax notes: $3.00 for first page, $2.00 each add'l. Copy fee: $1.00 per page. Certification fee: $1.00. Fee payee: Wabash County Clerk. Business checks accepted.

Warren County

Circuit Court Ste 11, 125 N Monroe, Williamsport, IN 47993; 765-762-3510; Fax: 765-762-7222. Hours: 8AM-4PM (EST). *Felony, Misdemeanor, Civil, Eviction, Small Claims, Probate.*

Civil Records: Access: In person only. Both court and visitors may perform in person searches. No search fee. Required to search: name, years to search. Civil cases indexed by defendant, plaintiff. Civil records archived from 1828. Some records on docket books.

Criminal Records: Access: In person only. Both court and visitors may perform in person searches. No search fee. Required to search: name, years to search, DOB; also helpful: SSN. Criminal records archived from 1828. Some records on docket books.

General Information: No juvenile, mental, adoption or sealed released. Fax notes: Fee to fax results is $1.00 per page. Copy fee: $1.00 per page. Certification fee: $1.00. Fee payee: Warren County Clerk. Personal checks accepted. Prepayment is required.

Warrick County

Circuit & Superior Court One County Square, #200, Boonville, IN 47601; 812-897-6160. Hours: 8AM-4PM (CST). *Felony, Misdemeanor, Civil, Eviction, Small Claims, Probate.*

Civil Records: Access: Phone, mail, in person. Both court and visitors may perform in person searches. No search fee. Required to search: name, years to search. Civil cases indexed by defendant, plaintiff. Civil records on computer from 1987, archived from 1900s. Some records on index books.

Criminal Records: Access: Mail, in person. Both court and visitors may perform in person searches. No search fee. Required to search: name, years to search; also helpful: DOB, SSN. Criminal records on computer from 1987, archived from 1900s. Some on index books.

General Information: No juvenile, mental, adoption or sealed released. SASE required. Turnaround time same day. Copy fee: $1.00 per page. Certification fee: $1.00. Fee payee: Warrick County Clerk. Business checks accepted. Prepayment is required.

Washington County

Circuit & Superior Court Courthouse, 99 Public Sq, Salem, IN 47167; 812-883-1634/5748; Fax: 812-883-1933. 8:30AM-4PM M-Th, 8:30AM-6PM F *Felony, Misdemeanor, Civil, Small Claims, Probate.*

Civil Records: Access: Mail, fax, in person. Both court and visitors may perform in person searches. No search fee. Required to search: name, years to search; also helpful: address. Civil cases indexed by defendant, plaintiff. Civil records on books, archived from 1820. Some records on docket books.

Criminal Records: Access: Mail, fax, in person. Both court and visitors may perform in person searches. No search fee. Required to search: name, years to search; also helpful: address, DOB, SSN. Criminal records on computer from 1980, docket books/archived from 1820.

General Information: No juvenile, mental, adoption or sealed released; no information given out via telephone. SASE required. Turnaround time 1-5 days. Copy fee: $1.00 per page. Certification fee: $1.00. Fee payee: Washington County Clerk. Only cashiers checks and money orders accepted. Prepayment is required.

Wayne County

Circuit & Superior Court Courthouse, 301 E Main Street, Richmond, IN 47374; 765-973-9200; Fax: 765-973-9490. Hours: 8:30AM-5PM M; 8:30AM-4:30PM T-F (EST). *Felony, Misdemeanor, Civil, Eviction, Small Claims, Probate.*

www.co.wayne.in.us/courts

Civil Records: Access: Mail, fax, in person. Both court and visitors may perform in person searches. No search fee. Required to search: name, years to search. Civil cases indexed by defendant, plaintiff. Civil records on computer from 4/90, circuit on microfiche from 1957, superior on microfiche from 1960 to 1971, all archived from 1800s. Some records on dockets. Fax request must be on letterhead.

Criminal Records: Access: Mail, fax, in person. Both court and visitors may perform in person searches. No search fee. Required to search: name, years to search, fax request on letterhead. Criminal records on computer from 4/90, circuit on microfiche from 1957, superior on microfiche from 1960 to 1971, all archived from 1800s. Some records on dockets. Fax must be on letterhead.

General Information: Public Access terminal is available. No juvenile, mental, adoption or sealed released. SASE required. Turnaround time 2-3 days. Fax notes: Will not fax results. Copy fee: $1.00 per page. Certification fee: $1.00. Fee payee: Wayne County Clerk. Personal checks accepted. Prepayment is required.

Wells County

Circuit & Superior Court 102 West Market, Rm 201, Bluffton, IN 46714; 219-824-6479. Hours: 8AM-4:30PM (EST). *Civil, Probate.*

Civil Records: Access: In person only. Visitors must perform in person searches for themselves. No search fee. Required to search: name, years to search. Civil cases indexed by defendant, plaintiff. Civil records archived from 1837. Some records on docket books.

Criminal Records: Access: In person only. Visitors must perform in person searches for themselves. No search fee. Required to search: name, years to search, DOB; also helpful: SSN. Criminal records archived from 1837. Some records on docket books.

General Information: No juvenile, mental, adoption or sealed released. Certification fee: $1.00. Fee payee: Wells County Clerk. Personal checks accepted. Prepayment is required.

White County

Circuit Court PO Box 350, 110 N Main, Monticello, IN 47960; 219-583-7032; Fax: 219-583-1532. Hours: 8AM-4PM (EST). *Civil, Probate.*

Civil Records: Access: In person only. Visitors must perform in person searches for themselves. No search fee. Required to search: name, years to search. Civil cases indexed by defendant, plaintiff. Civil records on indexes and files, some records on docket books.

General Information: No juvenile, mental, adoption or sealed released. Copy fee: $1.00 per page. Certification fee: $1.00. Fee payee: White County Clerk. Personal checks accepted. Prepayment required.

Superior Court PO Box 1005, 110 N Main, Monticello, IN 47960; 219-583-9520; Fax: 219-583-2437. Hours: 8AM-4PM (EST). *Felony, Misdemeanor, Eviction, Small Claims.*

Civil Records: Access: In person only. Both court and visitors may perform in person searches. Court will search only if a date is provided. No search fee. Required to search: name, years to search. Civil cases indexed by defendant, plaintiff. Civil records on indexes and files, some records on docket books.

Criminal Records: Access: In person only. Both court and visitors may perform in person searches. Court will search only if a date is provided. No search fee. Required to search: name, years to search. Criminal records on indexes and files, some on docket books.

General Information: No juvenile, mental, adoption or sealed released. Copy fee: $1.00 per page. Certification fee: $1.00. Fee payee: White County Clerk. Personal checks accepted. Prepayment required.

Whitley County

Circuit & Superior Court 101 W Van Buren, Rm 10, Columbia City, IN 46725; 219-248-3102; Fax: 219-248-3137. Hours: 8AM-4:30PM (EST). *Felony, Misdemeanor, Civil, Eviction, Small Claims, Probate.*

Civil Records: Access: In person only. Visitors must perform in person searches for themselves. No search fee. Required to search: name, years to search. Civil cases indexed by defendant, plaintiff. Civil records on computer from 1999. Some records on docket books.

Criminal Records: Access: In person only. Visitors must perform in person searches for themselves. No search fee. Required to search: name, years to search; also helpful: DOB. Criminal records on computer from 1999. Some records on docket books.

General Information: Public Access terminal is available. No juvenile, mental, adoption or sealed released. Copy fee: $1.00 per page. Certification fee: $1.00. Fee payee: Whitley County Clerk. Only cashiers checks and money orders accepted. Prepayment is required.

Indiana Recording Offices

ORGANIZATION   92 counties, 92 recording offices. The recording officer is County Recorder (Circuit Clerk for state tax liens on personal property). Many counties utilize a "Miscellaneous Index" for tax and other liens. 81 counties are in the Eastern Time Zone (EST), and 11 are in the Central Time Zone (CST).

REAL ESTATE RECORDS   Most counties will not perform real estate name searches. Copies usually cost $1.00 per page, and certification usually costs $5.00 per document.

UCC RECORDS   Financing statements are filed at the state level, except for real estate related collateral, which are filed with the County Recorder. However, prior to 07/2001, consumer goods collateral were also filed at the County Recorder and these older records can be searched there. Starting 07/2002, farm collateral will change form local to state centralized filing. All counties will perform UCC searches. Use search request form UCC-11. Search fees are usually $1.00 per debtor name. Copies usually cost $.50 per page. Most counties also charge $.50 for each financing statement reported on a search.

TAX LIEN RECORDS   All federal tax liens on personal property are filed with the County Recorder. State tax liens on personal property are filed with the Circuit Clerk, who is in a different office from the Recorder. Refer to the County Court section for information about Indiana Circuit Courts. Most counties will not perform tax lien searches.

OTHER LIENS   Judgments, mechanics, hospital, sewer, utility, innkeeper.

STATEWIDE ONLINE INFO: Very few county agencies offer onlice access. The most notable is the subscription service offered by Marion County at www.civicnet.net.

Adams County

County Recorder, Adams County Service Complex, 313 W. Jefferson, Room 240, Decatur, IN 46733. 219-724-2600 R/E Recording: 219-724-2600 x213; Fax 219-724-2815.
Will search UCC records. This agency will not do a federal tax lien search. Will not search real estate records. **Other Phone Numbers:** Assessor 219-724-2600 x225; Treasurer 219-724-2600 x215; Auditor 219-724-2600 x200.

Allen County

County Recorder, 1 East Main Street, City County Building Room 206, Fort Wayne, IN 46802-1890. County Recorder, R/E and UCC Recording 219-449-7165; Fax 219-449-3261.
Will search UCC records. This agency will not do a federal tax lien search. Will not search real estate records. **Other Phone Numbers:** Assessor 219-428-7123; Treasurer 219-428-7693; Elections 219-449-7329; Vital Records 219-449-7147.

Bartholomew County

County Recorder, P.O. Box 1121, Columbus, IN 47202-1121. 812-379-1520.
Will search UCC records. This agency will not do a federal tax lien search. RE record owner searches available.

Benton County

County Recorder, 706 East 5th Street, Suite 24, Fowler, IN 47944-1556. County Recorder, R/E and UCC Recording 765-884-1630; Fax 765-884-2013.
Will search UCC records. Will not search real estate records. **Other Phone Numbers:** Assessor 765-884-1205; Treasurer 765-884-1070; Elections 765-884-0930; Vital Records 765-884-1728.

Blackford County

County Recorder, 110 West Washington Street, Courthouse, Hartford City, IN 47348. County Recorder, R/E and UCC Recording 765-348-2207; Fax 765-348-7222.
Will search UCC records. This agency will not do a federal tax lien search. Will not search real estate

records. **Other Phone Numbers:** Assessor 765-348-1707; Vital Records 765-348-2207.

Boone County

County Recorder, 202 Courthouse Square, Lebanon, IN 46052. 765-482-3070 R/E Recording: 765-482-2940.
Will search UCC records. This agency will not do a federal tax lien search. Will not search real estate records. **Other Phone Numbers:** Assessor 765-482-0140; Treasurer 765-482-2880; Elections 765-482-3510.

Brown County

County Recorder, P.O. Box 86, Nashville, IN 47448. County Recorder, R/E and UCC Recording 812-988-5462; Fax 812-988-5520.
Will search UCC records. This agency will not do a federal tax lien search. Will not search real estate records. **Other Phone Numbers:** Assessor 812-988-5466; Treasurer 812-988-5458.

Carroll County

County Recorder, Court House, 101 West Main St, Delphi, IN 46923-1522. 765-564-2124; Fax 765-564-2576.
Will search UCC records. UCC search includes federal tax liens if requested. Will not search real estate records. **Other Phone Numbers:** Assessor 765-564-3444; Treasurer 765-564-3446.

Cass County

County Recorder, 200 Court Park, Logansport, IN 46947. 219-753-7810.
Will search UCC records. This agency will not do a federal tax lien search. Will not search real estate records. **Other Phone Numbers:** Assessor 219-753-7720; Treasurer 219-753-7720.

Clark County

County Recorder, 501 East Court Avenue, Room 105, Jeffersonville, IN 47130. 812-285-6236.
Will search UCC records. This agency will not do a federal tax lien search. Will not search real estate records. **Other Phone Numbers:** Assessor 812-285-6224; Treasurer 812-285-6205.

Clay County

County Recorder, Courthouse, Room 111, 609 E National Ave., Brazil, IN 47834. County Recorder, R/E and UCC Recording 812-448-9005; Fax 812-446-5095.
Will search UCC records. This agency will not do a federal tax lien search. Will not search real estate records. **Other Phone Numbers:** Assessor 812-448-9013; Treasurer 812-448-9009; Elections 812-448-9023; Vital Records 812-448-9018.

Clinton County

County Recorder, 270 Courthouse Square, Frankfort, IN 46041-1957. 765-659-6320; Fax 765-659-6391.
Will search UCC records. This agency will not do a federal tax lien search. Will not search real estate records. **Other Phone Numbers:** Assessor 765-659-6315; Treasurer 765-659-6325; Elections 765-659-6335.

Crawford County

County Recorder, Courthouse, PO Box 214, English, IN 47118-0214. 812-338-2615; Fax 812-338-2507.
Will search UCC records. This agency will not do a federal tax lien search. Will not search real estate records. **Other Phone Numbers:** Assessor 812-338-2402; Treasurer 812-338-2651.

Daviess County

County Recorder, P.O. Box 793, Washington, IN 47501. 812-254-8675; Fax 812-254-8697.
Will search UCC records. This agency will not do a federal tax lien search. Will not search real estate records. **Other Phone Numbers:** Assessor 812-254-8660; Treasurer 812-254-8677.

Dearborn County

County Recorder, 215 B West High Street, Lawrenceburg, IN 47025. 812-537-1040.
Will search UCC records. This agency will not do a federal tax lien search. Will not search real estate records. **Other Phone Numbers:** Assessor 812-537-8809 x236; Treasurer 812-537-8811.

Decatur County

County Recorder, 150 Courthouse Square, Suite 121, Greensburg, IN 47240. 812-663-4681; Fax 812-663-2407.
Will search UCC records. This agency will not do a federal tax lien search. Will not search real estate records. **Other Phone Numbers:** Assessor 812-663-4860; Treasurer 812-663-4190.

DeKalb County

County Recorder, P.O. Box 810, Auburn, IN 46706. County Recorder, R/E and UCC Recording 219-925-2112; Fax 219-925-5126.
Will search UCC records. This agency will not do a federal tax lien search. Will not search real estate records. **Other Phone Numbers:** Assessor 219-925-1824; Treasurer 219-925-2712; Elections 219-925-0912; Vital Records 219-925-2220.

Delaware County

County Recorder, P.O. Box 1008, Muncie, IN 47308. 765-747-7804.
Will search UCC records. This agency will not do a federal tax lien search. Will not search real estate records. **Other Phone Numbers:** Assessor 765-747-7715.

Dubois County

County Recorder, Room 101, 1 Courthouse Square, Jasper, IN 47546. 812-481-7067; Fax 812-481-7044.
Will search UCC records. This agency will not do a federal tax lien search. Will not search real estate records. **Other Phone Numbers:** Assessor 812-481-7010; Treasurer 812-481-7080.

Elkhart County

County Recorder, P.O. Box 837, Goshen, IN 46527. 219-535-6754 R/E Recording: 219-535-6756; http://www.elkhartcountygov.com/administrative
Will search UCC records. This agency will not do a federal tax lien search. Will not search real estate records. **Online Access:** Real Estate, Liens, Tax Assessor Records. Access to Elkhart County records is available for an annual fee of $50. plus a minimum of $20 per month of use. The minimum fee allows for 2 hours access, and additional use is billed at $10 per hour. Lending agency information is available. For information, contact Nick Cenova at 219-535-6777. **Other Phone Numbers:** Assessor 219-535-6702; Treasurer 219-535-6759; Elections 219-535-6469; Vital Records 219-523-2107; Voter Registration 219-535-6775.

Fayette County

County Recorder, P.O. Box 324, Connersville, IN 47331-0324. 765-825-3051; www/in-map.net/counties/fayette/recorder
Will search UCC records. This agency will not do a federal tax lien search. Will not search real estate records. **Other Phone Numbers:** Assessor 765-825-4931; Treasurer 765-825-1013.

Floyd County

County Recorder, P.O. Box 878, New Albany, IN 47151-0878. 812-948-5430.
Will search UCC records. This agency will not do a federal tax lien search. Will not search real estate records. **Other Phone Numbers:** Assessor 812-948-5420; Treasurer 812-948-5477.

Fountain County

County Recorder, P.O. Box 55, Covington, IN 47932. 765-793-2431; Fax 765-793-5002.
Will search UCC records. This agency will not do a federal tax lien search. Will not search real estate

records. **Other Phone Numbers:** Assessor 765-793-3481; Treasurer 765-793-4821.

Franklin County

County Recorder, 459 Main Street, Brookville, IN 47012-1486. County Recorder, R/E and UCC Recording 765-647-5131.
Will search UCC records. Will not search real estate records. **Other Phone Numbers:** Assessor 765-647-4921; Treasurer 765-647-5121; Elections 765-647-5111; Vital Records 765-647-4322.

Fulton County

County Recorder, 125 E 9th St, Rochester, IN 46975. County Recorder, R/E and UCC Recording 219-223-2914; Fax 219-223-4734.
Will search UCC records. This agency will not do a federal tax lien search. Will not search real estate records. **Other Phone Numbers:** Assessor 219-223-2801; Treasurer 219-223-7705; Vital Records 219-223-2881.

Gibson County

County Recorder, P.O. Box 1078, Princeton, IN 47670. County Recorder, R/E and UCC Recording 812-385-3332; Fax 812-386-9502.
Will search UCC records. This agency will not do a federal tax lien search. Will not search real estate records. **Other Phone Numbers:** Assessor 812-385-5286; Treasurer 812-385-2540; Appraiser/Auditor 812-385-4927; Elections 812-385-8401; Vital Records 812-385-3831.

Grant County

County Recorder, 401 South Adams Street, Marion, IN 46953. 765-668-8871.
Will search UCC records. This agency will not do a federal tax lien search. Will not search real estate records. **Other Phone Numbers:** Assessor 765-668-8871; Treasurer 765-668-8871.

Greene County

County Recorder, P.O. Box 309, Bloomfield, IN 47424. 812-384-2020; Fax 812-384-2044.
Will search UCC records. UCC search includes federal tax liens if requested. RE owner, mortgage, and property transfer searches available. **Other Phone Numbers:** Assessor 812-384-2003.

Hamilton County

County Recorder, Courthouse, 33 N. 9th St, Suite 309, Noblesville, IN 46060. 317-776-9618; Fax 317-776-8200.
Will search UCC records. This agency will not do a federal tax lien search. Will not search real estate records. **Other Phone Numbers:** Assessor 317-776-9614; Treasurer 317-776-9620.

Hancock County

County Recorder, 9 East Main Street, Courthouse, Room 204, Greenfield, IN 46140. 317-462-1142.
Will search UCC records. This agency will not do a federal tax lien search. Will not search real estate records. **Other Phone Numbers:** Assessor 317-462-1102; Treasurer 317-462-1152.

Harrison County

County Recorder, 300 Capitol Avenue, Courthouse, Room 204, Corydon, IN 47112. 812-738-3788; Fax 812-738-1153.
Will search UCC records. This agency will not do a federal tax lien search. Will not search real estate records. **Other Phone Numbers:** Assessor 812-738-4280.

Hendricks County

County Recorder, P.O. Box 86, Danville, IN 46122. 317-745-9224.
Will search UCC records. This agency will not do a federal tax lien search. Will not search real estate records. **Other Phone Numbers:** Assessor 317-745-9207; Treasurer 317-745-9220.

Henry County

County Recorder, 216 S. 12th St., New Castle, IN 47362-4609. 765-529-4304; Fax 765-521-7017.
Will search UCC records. This agency will not do a federal tax lien search. Will not search real estate records. **Other Phone Numbers:** Assessor 765-529-2104.

Howard County

County Recorder, P.O. Box 733, Kokomo, IN 46903-0733. 765-456-2210; Fax 765-456-2259.
Will search UCC records. This agency will not do a federal tax lien search. Will not search real estate records. **Other Phone Numbers:** Assessor 317-456-2211; Treasurer 317-456-2213.

Huntington County

County Recorder, 201 N. Jefferson St., Room 101, Huntington, IN 46750-2841. County Recorder, R/E and UCC Recording 219-358-4848.
Will search UCC records. This agency will not do a federal tax lien search. Will not search real estate records. **Other Phone Numbers:** Assessor 219-358-4802; Treasurer 219-358-4860.

Jackson County

County Recorder, P.O. Box 75, Brownstown, IN 47220. 812-358-6113.
Will search UCC records. Will not search real estate records. **Other Phone Numbers:** Assessor 812-358-6111; Treasurer 812-358-6125.

Jasper County

County Recorder, 115 W. Washington, Courthouse Box 4, Rensselaer, IN 47978-2891. 219-866-4923; Fax 219-866-4940.
Will search UCC records. This agency will not do a federal tax lien search. Will not search real estate records. **Other Phone Numbers:** Assessor 219-866-4194; Treasurer 219-866-4939.

Jay County

County Recorder, 120 West Main Street, Portland, IN 47371. 219-726-4572.
Will search UCC records. This agency will not do a federal tax lien search. Will not search real estate records. **Other Phone Numbers:** Assessor 219-726-4456; Treasurer 219-726-7007.

Jefferson County

County Recorder, Courthouse - Room 104, 300 E. Main St., Madison, IN 47250. 812-265-8903.
Will search UCC records. Will not search real estate records. **Other Phone Numbers:** Assessor 812-265-8905; Treasurer 812-265-8910.

Jennings County

County Recorder, P.O. Box 397, Vernon, IN 47282-0397. 812-346-3152 R/E Recording: 812-346-3053 UCC Recording: 812-346-3053; Fax 812-346-4605.
Will search UCC records. Will not search real estate records. **Other Phone Numbers:** Assessor 812-346-3013; Treasurer 812-346-3060; Appraiser/Auditor 812-346-3021; Elections 812-346-3080; Vital Records 812-346-3024.

Johnson County

County Recorder, P.O. Box 475, Franklin, IN 46131. County Recorder, R/E and UCC Recording 317-736-3718; Fax 317-736-8066.

Will search UCC records. This agency will not do a federal tax lien search. Will not search real estate records. **Other Phone Numbers:** Assessor 317-736-3030; Treasurer 317-736-3711; Elections 317-736-3789; Vital Records 317-736-3775; Assessor County 317-736-3715.

Knox County

County Recorder, Courthouse, 11 N. 7th St., Vincennes, IN 47591. 812-885-2508; Fax 812-886-2414.

Will search UCC records. This agency will not do a federal tax lien search. Will not search real estate records. **Other Phone Numbers:** Assessor 812-885-2513; Treasurer 812-885-2513.

Kosciusko County

County Recorder, 100 West Center Street, Courthouse Room 14, Warsaw, IN 46580. County Recorder, R/E and UCC Recording 219-372-2360; Fax 219-372-2469. Will search UCC records. This agency will not do a federal tax lien search. Will not search real estate records. **Other Phone Numbers:** Assessor 219-372-2310; Treasurer 219-372-2370.

La Porte County

County Recorder, 813 Lincolnway, La Porte, IN 46350-3488. 219-326-6808 R/E Recording: 219-326-6808 x267 UCC Recording: 219-326-6808 x234; Fax 219-326-0828. www.laportecounty.org

Will search UCC records. This agency will not do a federal tax lien search. Will not search real estate records. **Other Phone Numbers:** Assessor 219-326-6808 x233; Treasurer 219-326-6808 x268; Elections 219-326-6808 x465; Vital Records 219-326-6808 x200.

LaGrange County

County Recorder, P.O. Box 214, LaGrange, IN 46761. County Recorder, R/E and UCC Recording 219-499-6320.

Will search UCC records. Will not search real estate records. **Other Phone Numbers:** Assessor 219-499-6319; Treasurer 219-499-6316.

Lake County

County Recorder, 2293 N Main Street, Building A, 2nd Floor, Crown Point, IN 46307. 219-755-3730; Fax 219-755-3257.

Will search UCC records. UCC search includes federal tax liens. RE owner, mortgage, and property transfer searches available. **Other Phone Numbers:** Assessor 219-755-3100; Treasurer 219-755-3760.

Lawrence County

County Recorder, 916 15th St, Rm 21, Room 21, Bedford, IN 47421. 812-275-3245; Fax 812-275-4138. Will search UCC records. This agency will not do a federal tax lien search. Will not search real estate records. **Other Phone Numbers:** Assessor 812-275-4135; Treasurer 812-275-2431.

Madison County

County Recorder, 16 East 9th Street, Anderson, IN 46016. 765-641-9618.

Will search UCC records. This agency will not do a tax lien search. Will not search real estate records. **Other Phone Numbers:** Assessor 765-641-9401; Treasurer 765-641-9645.

Marion County

County Recorder, 200 E. Washington, Suite 721, Indianapolis, IN 46204. 317-327-4020 R/E Recording: 317-327-4018 UCC Recording: 317-327-4015; Fax 317-327-3942.

Will search UCC records. UCC search includes federal tax liens if requested. Property transfer searches available. **Online Access:** Real Estate, Liens. Access to Marion County online records requires a $200 set up fee, plus an escrow balance of at least $100 must be maintained. Additional charges are $.50 per minute, $.25 display charge for first page; $.10 each add'l page. Records date back to 1987; images from 2/24/93. Federal tax liens and UCC information are available. For information, contact Mike Kerner at 317-327-4587. **Other Phone Numbers:** Assessor 317-327-4907; Treasurer 317-327-4040; Auditor 317-327-4646.

Marshall County

County Recorder, 112 West Jefferson Street, Room 201, Plymouth, IN 46563. 219-935-8515.

Will search UCC records. This agency will not do a federal tax lien search. Will not search real estate records. **Other Phone Numbers:** Assessor 219-935-8525.

Martin County

County Recorder, P.O. Box 147, Shoals, IN 47581. 812-247-2420; Fax 812-247-2756.

Will search UCC records. UCC search includes federal tax liens if requested. Will not search real estate records. **Other Phone Numbers:** Assessor 812-247-2070.

Miami County

County Recorder, P.O. Box 597, Peru, IN 46970. 765-472-3901; Fax 765-472-1412.

Will search UCC records. This agency will not do a federal tax lien search. Will not search real estate records.

Monroe County

County Recorder, P.O. Box 1634, Bloomington, IN 47402. 812-349-2520.

Will search UCC records. This agency will not do a federal tax lien search. Will not search real estate records. **Other Phone Numbers:** Assessor 812-333-3502; Treasurer 812-333-3530.

Montgomery County

County Recorder, P.O. Box 865, Crawfordsville, IN 47933. 765-364-6415; Fax 765-364-6404.

Will search UCC records. This agency will not do a federal tax lien search. Will not search real estate records. **Other Phone Numbers:** Assessor 765-364-6420; Treasurer 765-364-6410.

Morgan County

County Recorder, P.O. Box 1653, Martinsville, IN 46151. County Recorder, R/E and UCC Recording 765-342-1077.

Will search UCC records. This agency will not do a federal tax lien search. Will not search real estate records. **Other Phone Numbers:** Assessor 765-342-1065; Treasurer 765-342-1048; Elections 765-342-1029; Vital Records 765-342-6621.

Newton County

County Recorder, 201 N 3rd St, Kentland, IN 47951. 219-474-6081.

Will search UCC records. This agency will not do a federal tax lien search. Mortgage searches available. **Other Phone Numbers:** Assessor 219-474-6081; Treasurer 219-474-6081.

Noble County

County Recorder, 101 North Orange Street, Albion, IN 46701. 219-636-2672; Fax 219-636-3264.

Will search UCC records. Will not search real estate records. **Other Phone Numbers:** Assessor 219-636-2297; Treasurer 219-636-2644.

Ohio County

County Recorder, Courthouse, 413 Main St., Rising Sun, IN 47040. County Recorder, R/E and UCC Recording 812-438-3369; Fax 812-438-4590.

Will search UCC records. This agency will not do a federal tax lien search. Will not search real estate records. **Other Phone Numbers:** Assessor 812-438-3264; Treasurer 812-438-2724; Elections 812-438-2610; Vital Records 812-438-2551.

Orange County

County Recorder, 205 East Main Street, Courthouse, Paoli, IN 47454. 812-723-3600.

Will search UCC records. This agency will not do a federal tax lien search. Will not search real estate records. **Other Phone Numbers:** Assessor 812-723-3600.

Owen County

County Recorder, Courthouse, Spencer, IN 47460. 812-829-5013; Fax 812-829-5014.

Will search UCC records. Will not search real estate records. **Other Phone Numbers:** Assessor 812-829-5018; Treasurer 812-829-5011.

Parke County

County Recorder, 116 W. High St., Room 102, Rockville, IN 47872-1787. County Recorder, R/E and UCC Recording 765-569-3419; Fax 765-569-4037.

Will search UCC records. This agency will not do a federal tax lien search. Will not search real estate records. **Other Phone Numbers:** Assessor 765-569-4036; Treasurer 765-569-3437.

Perry County

County Recorder, 2219 Payne St., Room W2, Tell City, IN 47586-2830. County Recorder, R/E and UCC Recording 812-547-4261; Fax 812-547-6428.

Will search UCC records. Will not search tax liens. Will not search real estate records. **Other Phone Numbers:** Assessor 812-547-5531; Treasurer 812-547-4816; Elections 812-547-3741; Vital Records 812-547-2746.

Pike County

County Recorder, Main Street, Courthouse, Petersburg, IN 47567-1298. 812-354-6747; Fax 812-354-9431.

Will search UCC records. This agency will not do a federal tax lien search. Will not search real estate records. **Other Phone Numbers:** Assessor 812-354-6584; Treasurer 812-354-6363; Elections 812-354-6025; Vital Records 812-354-8797.

Porter County

County Recorder, 155 Indiana Ave, Suite 210, Valparaiso, IN 46383. County Recorder, R/E and UCC Recording 219-465-3465 UCC Recording: 219-465-3374; Fax 219-465-3592.

Will search UCC records. This agency will not do a federal tax lien search. Will not search real estate records. **Other Phone Numbers:** Assessor 219-465-3460; Treasurer 219-465-3470.

Posey County

County Recorder, P.O. Box 9, Mount Vernon, IN 47620. 812-838-1314; Fax 812-838-8563.

Will not search UCC records. This agency will not do a tax lien search. Will not search real estate records. **Other Phone Numbers:** Assessor 812-838-1309; Treasurer 812-838-1316.

Pulaski County

County Recorder, Courthouse - Room 220, 112 E. Main St., Winamac, IN 46996. County Recorder, R/E and UCC Recording 219-946-3844.
Will search UCC records. This agency will not do a state tax lien search. Will not search real estate records. **Other Phone Numbers:** Assessor 219-946-3845; Treasurer 219-946-3632; Elections 219-946-3313; Vital Records 219-946-6080.

Putnam County

County Recorder, Courthouse Square, Room 25, Greencastle, IN 46135. 765-653-5613.
Will search UCC records. Will not search real estate records. **Other Phone Numbers:** Assessor 765-653-4312; Treasurer 765-653-4510.

Randolph County

County Recorder, Courthouse, Room 101, 100 South Main St., Winchester, IN 47394-1899. County Recorder, R/E and UCC Recording 765-584-7300.
Will search UCC records. This agency will not do a federal tax lien search. Will not search real estate records. **Other Phone Numbers:** Assessor 765-584-2427; Treasurer 765-584-0704; Appraiser/Auditor 765-584-7407; Elections 765-584-1155.

Ripley County

County Recorder, P.O. Box 404, Versailles, IN 47042. 812-689-5808.
Will search UCC records. Will not search real estate records. **Other Phone Numbers:** Assessor 812-689-5656; Treasurer 812-689-6352.

Rush County

County Recorder, Courthouse, Room 208, Rushville, IN 46173. 765-932-2388.
Will search UCC records. This agency will not do a federal tax lien search. Will not search real estate records. **Other Phone Numbers:** Assessor 765-932-3242; Treasurer 765-932-2386.

Scott County

County Recorder, 1 E. McClain St., Suite 100, Scottsburg, IN 47170. 812-752-8442; Fax 812-752-7914.
Will search UCC records. This agency will not do a federal tax lien search. Will not search real estate records. **Other Phone Numbers:** Assessor 812-752-8436; Treasurer 812-752-8414.

Shelby County

County Recorder, 407 South Harrison, Courthouse, Shelbyville, IN 46176. 317-392-6370; Fax 317-392-6393.
Will search UCC records. This agency will not do a federal tax lien search. Will not search real estate records. **Other Phone Numbers:** Assessor 317-392-5481; Treasurer 317-392-6375.

Spencer County

County Recorder, Courthouse, 200 Main, Rockport, IN 47635. 812-649-6013; Fax 812-649-6005.
Will search UCC records. This agency will not do a tax lien search. Will not search real estate records. **Other Phone Numbers:** Assessor 812-649-2381; Treasurer 812-649-4556.

St. Joseph County

County Recorder, 227 West Jefferson, Room 321, South Bend, IN 46601. 219-235-9525.
Will search UCC records. This agency will not do a federal tax lien search. Will not search real estate records. **Other Phone Numbers:** Assessor 219-235-9523; Treasurer 219-235-9531.

Starke County

County Recorder, P.O. Box 1, Knox, IN 46534. 219-772-9110 R/E Recording: 219-772-9109 UCC Recording: 219-772-9109; Fax 219-772-9178.
Will search UCC records. This agency will not do a federal tax lien search. Will not search real estate records. **Other Phone Numbers:** Assessor 219-772-9107; Treasurer 219-772-9113.

Steuben County

County Recorder, P.O. Box 397, Angola, IN 46703. 219-668-1000 x1700; Fax 219-665-8483.
Will search UCC records. This agency will not do a federal tax lien search. Will not search real estate records.

Sullivan County

County Recorder, Room 205, 100 Court House Square, Sullivan, IN 47882-1565. 812-268-4844; Fax 812-268-0521.
Will search UCC records. This agency will not do a federal tax lien search. Will not search real estate records. **Other Phone Numbers:** Assessor 812-268-4657.

Switzerland County

County Recorder, Courthouse, 212 West Main, Vevay, IN 47043. 812-427-2544.
Will search UCC records. This agency will not do a federal tax lien search. Will not search real estate records. **Other Phone Numbers:** Assessor 812-427-3379; Treasurer 812-427-3369; Auditor 812-427-3302.

Tippecanoe County

County Recorder, 20 North 3rd Street, Lafayette, IN 47901. 765-423-9353; Fax 765-423-9158. http://county.tippecanoe.in.us/
Will search UCC records. This agency will not do a federal tax lien search. Will not search real estate records. **Online Access:** Property Records. Online access to proeprty information on the county gis-mapping site is available free at http://gis.county.tippecanoe.in.us/gis/app12/index.html. **Other Phone Numbers:** Assessor 765-423-9255.

Tipton County

County Recorder, Courthouse, 101 E. Jefferson St., Tipton, IN 46072. 765-675-4614.
Will search UCC records. This agency will not do a federal tax lien search. Will not search real estate records. **Other Phone Numbers:** Assessor 765-675-6450; Treasurer 765-675-2742.

Union County

County Recorder, 26 West Union Street, Room 106, Liberty, IN 47353. County Recorder, R/E and UCC Recording 765-458-5434; Fax 765-458-5263.
Will search UCC records. This agency will not do a federal tax lien search. Will not search real estate records. **Other Phone Numbers:** Assessor 317-458-5331; Treasurer 317-458-6491.

Vanderburgh County

County Recorder, 231 City-County Admin. Building, 1 NW Martin Luther King, Jr. Blvd., Evansville, IN 47708-1881. County Recorder, R/E and UCC Recording 812-435-5215 UCC Recording: 812-435-5221; Fax 812-435-5580. http://www.assessor.evansville.net
Will search UCC records. This agency will not do a federal tax lien search. Will not search real estate records. **Online Access:** Property Records. Records on the County Assessor Property database are available free online at www.assessor.evansville.net/disclaim.htm. **Other Phone Numbers:** Assessor 812-

435-5273; Treasurer 812-435-5248; Elections 812-435-5160; Vital Records 812-435-5681.

Vermillion County

County Recorder, P.O. Box 145, Newport, IN 47966-0145. 765-492-5003.
Will search UCC records. This agency will not do a federal tax lien search. Will not search real estate records. **Other Phone Numbers:** Assessor 765-492-5004.

Vigo County

County Recorder, 201 Cherry Street, Terre Haute, IN 47807. 812-462-3301; Fax 812-232-2219.
Will search UCC records. This agency will not do a federal tax lien search. Will not search real estate records. **Other Phone Numbers:** Assessor 812-462-3358.

Wabash County

County Recorder, Courthouse, One West Hill St., Wabash, IN 46992. 219-563-0661 x24.
Will search UCC records. This agency will not do a federal tax lien search. Will not search real estate records. **Other Phone Numbers:** Assessor 219-563-0661 x25; Treasurer 219-563-0661.

Warren County

County Recorder, 125 N. Monroe, Courthouse - Suite 10, Williamsport, IN 47993-1162. 765-762-3174; Fax 765-762-7222.
Will search UCC records. UCC search includes federal tax liens if requested. Will not search real estate records. **Other Phone Numbers:** Assessor 765-762-4528; Treasurer 765-762-3562.

Warrick County

County Recorder, P.O. Box 28, Boonville, IN 47601-0028. 812-897-6165; Fax 812-897-6168. http://www.warrickcounty.gov/departments/recorder.htm
Will search UCC records. This agency will not do a federal tax lien search. Will not search real estate records. **Other Phone Numbers:** Assessor 812-897-6125; Treasurer 812-897-6166.

Washington County

County Recorder, Courthouse, Salem, IN 47167. 812-883-4001; Fax 812-883-4020.
Will search UCC records. This agency will not do a federal tax lien search. Will not search real estate records. **Other Phone Numbers:** Assessor 812-883-4000; Treasurer 812-883-3307.

Wayne County

County Recorder, 401 E Main St, County Administration Bldg., 401 E. Main, Richmond, IN 47374. County Recorder, R/E and UCC Recording 765-973-9235; Fax 765-973-9321. http://www.co.wayne.in.us/offices
Will search UCC records. This agency will not do a tax lien search. Will not search real estate records. **Online Access:** Marriage. Marriage records are being added irregularly to the web site at www.co.wayne.in.us/marriage/retrieve.cgi. Records are from 1811 forward, with recent years being added. **Other Phone Numbers:** Assessor 765-973-9228; Treasurer 765-973-9238; Elections 765-973-9226; Vital Records 765-973-9245.

Wells County

County Recorder, Courthouse - Suite 203, 102 W. Market St., Bluffton, IN 46714. 219-824-6507.
Will search UCC records. This agency will not do a federal tax lien search. Will not search real estate

records. **Other Phone Numbers:** Assessor 219-824-6476.

White County

County Recorder, P.O. Box 127, Monticello, IN 47960. 219-583-5912; Fax 219-583-1521.
Will search UCC records. This agency will not do a federal tax lien search. Will not search real estate

records. **Other Phone Numbers:** Assessor 219-583-7755.

Whitley County

County Recorder, Courthouse, 2nd Floor - Room 18, Columbia City, IN 46725. County Recorder, R/E and UCC Recording 219-248-3106; Fax 219-248-3137.

Will search UCC records. This agency will not do a federal tax lien search. Will not search real estate records. **Other Phone Numbers:** Assessor 219-248-3109.

Indiana County Locator

You will usually be able to find the city name in the City/County Cross Reference below. In that case, it is a simple matter to determine the county from the cross reference. However, only the official US Postal Service city names are included in this index. There are an additional 40,000 place names that people use in their addresses. Therefore, we have also included a ZIP/City Cross Reference immediately following the City/County Cross Reference.

If you know the ZIP Code but the city name does not appear in the City/County Cross Reference index, look up the ZIP Code in the ZIP/City Cross Reference, find the city name, then look up the city name in the City/County Cross Reference. For example, you want to know the county for an address of Menands, NY 12204. There is no "Menands" in the City/County Cross Reference. The ZIP/City Cross Reference shows that ZIP Codes 12201-12288 are for the city of Albany. Looking back in the City/County Cross Reference, Albany is in Albany County.

City/County Cross Reference

ADVANCE Boone
AKRON (46910) Fulton(61), Kosciusko(35), Miami(4)
ALAMO Montgomery
ALBANY (47320) Delaware(94), Randolph(5)
ALBION Noble
ALEXANDRIA (46001) Madison(98), Delaware(2)
AMBIA (47917) Warren(59), Benton(41)
AMBOY (46911) Miami(76), Wabash(24)
AMO Hendricks
ANDERSON (46017) Madison(97), Delaware(3)
ANDERSON Madison
ANDREWS (46702) Huntington(92), Wabash(8)
ANGOLA Steuben
ARCADIA Hamilton
ARCOLA Allen
ARGOS (46501) Marshall(97), Fulton(3)
ARLINGTON (46104) Rush(99), Shelby(1)
ASHLEY (46705) DeKalb(72), Steuben(28)
ATHENS Fulton
ATLANTA (46031) Hamilton(53), Tipton(47)
ATTICA (47918) Fountain(74), Warren(25), Tippecanoe(1)
ATWOOD Kosciusko
AUBURN (99999) DeKalb(99), Allen(1)
AURORA Dearborn
AUSTIN (47102) Scott(85), Jackson(15)
AVILLA (46710) Noble(95), DeKalb(5)
AVOCA Lawrence
BAINBRIDGE Putnam
BARGERSVILLE (46106) Johnson(95), Morgan(5)
BATESVILLE Franklin
BATH (47010) Franklin(70), Union(28), Tipton(2)
BATTLE GROUND (47920) Tippecanoe(72), White(17), Carroll(12)
BEDFORD Lawrence
BEECH GROVE Marion
BELLMORE Parke
BENNINGTON Switzerland
BENTONVILLE Fayette
BERNE Adams
BETHLEHEM Clark
BEVERLY SHORES Porter
BICKNELL Knox
BIPPUS Huntington
BIRDSEYE (47513) Dubois(74), Crawford(18), Perry(7), Orange(1)
BLANFORD Vermillion
BLOOMFIELD Greene
BLOOMINGDALE Parke
BLOOMINGTON Monroe
BLUFFTON (46714) Wells(96), Adams(4)
BOGGSTOWN (46110) Shelby(93), Johnson(7)
BOONE GROVE Porter
BOONVILLE (47601) Warrick(98), Spencer(2)

BORDEN (47106) Clark(87), Washington(10), Floyd(3)
BOSTON Wayne
BOSWELL (47921) Benton(78), Warren(22)
BOURBON (46504) Marshall(97), Kosciusko(3)
BOWLING GREEN (47833) Clay(77), Owen(23)
BRADFORD Harrison
BRANCHVILLE Perry
BRAZIL (47834) Clay(93), Vigo(5), Parke(1)
BREMEN (46506) Marshall(88), St. Joseph(12)
BRIDGETON Parke
BRIMFIELD Noble
BRINGHURST Carroll
BRISTOL Elkhart
BRISTOW Perry
BROOK (47922) Newton(94), Jasper(6)
BROOKLYN Morgan
BROOKSTON (47923) White(89), Carroll(11)
BROOKVILLE Franklin
BROWNSBURG Hendricks
BROWNSTOWN Jackson
BROWNSVILLE (47325) Union(79), Fayette(19), Wayne(2)
BRUCEVILLE Knox
BRYANT (47326) Jay(97), Adams(3)
BUCK CREEK Tippecanoe
BUCKSKIN Gibson
BUFFALO White
BUNKER HILL Miami
BURKET Kosciusko
BURLINGTON Carroll
BURNETTSVILLE (47926) White(64), Carroll(34), Cass(2)
BURNEY Decatur
BURROWS Carroll
BUTLER DeKalb
BUTLERVILLE Jennings
CAMBRIDGE CITY (47327) Wayne(95), Henry(4)
CAMBY (46113) Morgan(62), Marion(26), Hendricks(12)
CAMDEN (46917) Carroll(99), Cass(1)
CAMPBELLSBURG (47108) Washington(92), Orange(7)
CANAAN (47224) Jefferson(99), Switzerland(1)
CANNELBURG Daviess
CANNELTON Perry
CARBON (47837) Clay(60), Parke(40)
CARLISLE Sullivan
CARMEL Hamilton
CARTERSBURG Hendricks
CARTHAGE (46115) Rush(95), Hancock(5)
CAYUGA Vermillion
CEDAR GROVE Franklin
CEDAR LAKE Lake
CELESTINE Dubois

CENTERPOINT (47840) Clay(97), Putnam(3)
CENTERVILLE Wayne
CENTRAL Harrison
CHALMERS White
CHANDLER Warrick
CHARLESTOWN Clark
CHARLOTTESVILLE (46117) Hancock(90), Henry(10)
CHESTERTON Porter
CHRISNEY Spencer
CHURUBUSCO (46723) Whitley(64), Allen(24), Noble(13)
CICERO Hamilton
CLARKS HILL (47930) Tippecanoe(70), Montgomery(16), Clinton(14)
CLARKSBURG Decatur
CLARKSVILLE Clark
CLAY CITY (47841) Clay(99), Owen(1)
CLAYPOOL Kosciusko
CLAYTON Hendricks
CLEAR CREEK Monroe
CLIFFORD Bartholomew
CLINTON Vermillion
CLOVERDALE (46120) Putnam(89), Owen(9), Morgan(2)
COAL CITY (47427) Clay(96), Owen(4)
COALMONT Clay
COATESVILLE (46121) Hendricks(61), Putnam(40)
COLBURN Tippecanoe
COLFAX (46035) Clinton(81), Boone(16), Montgomery(3)
COLUMBIA CITY (46725) Whitley(96), Noble(3)
COLUMBUS (47201) Bartholomew(96), Brown(4)
COLUMBUS Bartholomew
COMMISKEY (47227) Jennings(80), Jefferson(20)
CONNERSVILLE Fayette
CONVERSE (46919) Grant(67), Miami(21), Howard(11), Wabash(1)
CORTLAND Jackson
CORUNNA (46730) DeKalb(97), Noble(3)
CORY Clay
CORYDON Harrison
COVINGTON (47932) Fountain(90), Warren(5), Vermillion(5)
CRAIGVILLE (46731) Wells(89), Adams(11)
CRANDALL Harrison
CRANE Martin
CRAWFORDSVILLE Montgomery
CROMWELL (46732) Noble(56), Kosciusko(44)
CROSS PLAINS Ripley
CROTHERSVILLE (47229) Jackson(90), Jennings(10)
CROWN POINT (46307) Lake(99), Porter(2)
CROWN POINT Lake

CULVER (46511) Marshall(80), Starke(11), Fulton(8), Pulaski(2)
CUTLER (46920) Carroll(99), Clinton(1)
CYNTHIANA (47612) Posey(68), Gibson(32)
DALE (47523) Spencer(66), Warrick(30), Dubois(3)
DALEVILLE (47334) Delaware(98), Henry(2)
DANA Vermillion
DANVILLE Hendricks
DARLINGTON Montgomery
DAYTON Tippecanoe
DECATUR Adams
DECKER Knox
DEEDSVILLE Miami
DELONG Fulton
DELPHI Carroll
DEMOTTE (46310) Jasper(76), Newton(24)
DENHAM Pulaski
DENVER (46926) Miami(90), Cass(7), Wabash(3)
DEPAUW Harrison
DEPUTY (47230) Jefferson(92), Jennings(8)
DERBY Perry
DILLSBORO Dearborn
DONALDSON Marshall
DUBLIN Wayne
DUBOIS (47527) Dubois(98), Martin(1)
DUGGER (47848) Sullivan(97), Greene(3)
DUNKIRK (47336) Jay(63), Blackford(20), Delaware(17)
DUNREITH Henry
DUPONT (47231) Jefferson(77), Jennings(23)
DYER Lake
EARL PARK (47942) Benton(96), Newton(4)
EARL PARK Benton
EAST CHICAGO Lake
EAST ENTERPRISE Switzerland
EATON Delaware
ECKERTY Crawford
ECONOMY Wayne
EDINBURGH (46124) Johnson(56), Bartholomew(26), Shelby(18)
EDWARDSPORT (47528) Knox(96), Sullivan(4)
ELBERFELD (47613) Warrick(84), Gibson(15), Vanderburgh(1)
ELIZABETH (47117) Harrison(98), Floyd(2)
ELIZABETHTOWN (47232) Bartholomew(69), Jennings(31)
ELKHART Elkhart
ELLETTSVILLE Monroe
ELNORA (47529) Daviess(96), Greene(4)
ELWOOD (46036) Madison(91), Tipton(9)
EMINENCE Morgan
EMISON Knox
ENGLISH (47118) Crawford(74), Orange(23), Perry(3)

ETNA GREEN (46524) Kosciusko(98), Marshall(2)
EVANSTON Spencer
EVANSVILLE (47712) Vanderburgh(87), Posey(13)
EVANSVILLE Vanderburgh
FAIR OAKS (47943) Jasper(56), Newton(44)
FAIRBANKS Sullivan
FAIRLAND Shelby
FAIRMOUNT (46928) Grant(97), Madison(2)
FALMOUTH (46127) Rush(76), Fayette(24)
FARMERSBURG (47850) Sullivan(83), Vigo(17)
FARMLAND Randolph
FERDINAND (47532) Dubois(86), Spencer(13), Perry(2)
FILLMORE Putnam
FINLY Hancock
FISHERS Hamilton
FLAT ROCK (47234) Shelby(91), Bartholomew(9)
FLORA (46929) Carroll(92), Howard(8)
FLORENCE Switzerland
FLOYDS KNOBS (47119) Floyd(97), Clark(3)
FOLSOMVILLE Warrick
FONTANET Vigo
FOREST Clinton
FORT BRANCH Gibson
FORT RITNER Lawrence
FORT WAYNE (46818) Allen(99), Whitley(1)
FORT WAYNE Allen
FORTVILLE (46040) Hancock(76), Hamilton(17), Madison(7)
FOUNTAIN CITY (47341) Wayne(98), Randolph(2)
FOUNTAINTOWN (46130) Shelby(79), Hancock(21)
FOWLER Benton
FOWLERTON Grant
FRANCESVILLE (47946) Pulaski(84), Jasper(16)
FRANCISCO Gibson
FRANKFORT (46041) Clinton(98), Carroll(2)
FRANKLIN Johnson
FRANKTON Madison
FREDERICKSBURG (47120) Washington(97), Harrison(3)
FREEDOM Owen
FREELANDVILLE Knox
FREETOWN (47235) Jackson(72), Brown(29)
FREMONT Steuben
FRENCH LICK (47432) Orange(88), Dubois(11)
FRIENDSHIP Ripley
FULDA Spencer
FULTON Fulton
GALVESTON (46932) Cass(91), Miami(5), Howard(4)
GARRETT DeKalb
GARY (46403) Lake(98), Porter(2)
GARY Lake
GAS CITY Grant
GASTON (47342) Delaware(97), Grant(2)
GENEVA (46740) Adams(93), Wells(4), Jay(3)
GENTRYVILLE (47537) Spencer(76), Warrick(24)
GEORGETOWN (47122) Floyd(59), Harrison(41)
GLENWOOD (46133) Fayette(57), Rush(43)
GOLDSMITH Tipton
GOODLAND (47948) Newton(68), Jasper(21), Benton(11)
GOSHEN Elkhart

GOSPORT (47433) Owen(37), Monroe(37), Morgan(27)
GRABILL Allen
GRAMMER Bartholomew
GRANDVIEW Spencer
GRANGER (46530) St. Joseph(95), Elkhart(5)
GRANTSBURG Crawford
GRASS CREEK Fulton
GRAYSVILLE Sullivan
GREENCASTLE Putnam
GREENFIELD Hancock
GREENS FORK Wayne
GREENSBORO Henry
GREENSBURG Decatur
GREENTOWN Howard
GREENVILLE (47124) Floyd(67), Harrison(33)
GREENWOOD Johnson
GRIFFIN Posey
GRIFFITH Lake
GRISSOM AFB Miami
GROVERTOWN (46531) Starke(98), Marshall(2)
GUILFORD Dearborn
GWYNNEVILLE Shelby
HAGERSTOWN (47346) Wayne(96), Henry(4)
HAMILTON (46742) Steuben(85), DeKalb(15)
HAMLET (46532) Starke(62), La Porte(38)
HAMMOND Lake
HANNA La Porte
HANOVER Jefferson
HARDINSBURG (47125) Orange(52), Washington(48)
HARLAN (46743) Allen(99), DeKalb(1)
HARMONY Clay
HARRODSBURG Monroe
HARTFORD CITY Blackford
HARTSVILLE (47244) Bartholomew(80), Decatur(20)
HATFIELD Spencer
HAUBSTADT (47639) Gibson(84), Vanderburgh(15), Warrick(2)
HAYDEN Jennings
HAZLETON (47640) Gibson(70), Pike(30)
HEBRON (46341) Porter(78), Lake(19), Jasper(2)
HELMSBURG Brown
HELTONVILLE (47436) Lawrence(87), Monroe(13)
HEMLOCK Howard
HENRYVILLE (47126) Clark(95), Washington(4)
HIGHLAND Lake
HILLISBURG Clinton
HILLSBORO Fountain
HILLSDALE Vermillion
HOAGLAND (46745) Allen(97), Adams(3)
HOBART (46342) Lake(98), Porter(2)
HOBBS Tipton
HOLLAND (47541) Dubois(75), Pike(21), Spencer(3), Warrick(2)
HOLTON (47023) Ripley(55), Franklin(42), Jennings(3)
HOMER Rush
HOPE Bartholomew
HOWE LaGrange
HUDSON (46747) Steuben(78), LaGrange(14), DeKalb(8)
HUNTERTOWN (46748) Allen(95), DeKalb(3), Noble(2)
HUNTINGBURG Dubois
HUNTINGTON Huntington
HURON Lawrence
HYMERA Sullivan
IDAVILLE (47950) White(96), Carroll(4)
INDIANAPOLIS (46229) Marion(94), Hancock(6)
INDIANAPOLIS (46231) Hendricks(63), Marion(37)

INDIANAPOLIS (46234) Marion(59), Hendricks(41)
INDIANAPOLIS (46239) Marion(98), Hancock(2)
INDIANAPOLIS (46256) Marion(95), Hamilton(5)
INDIANAPOLIS (46259) Marion(86), Johnson(7), Shelby(7)
INDIANAPOLIS (46260) Marion(99), Hamilton(1)
INDIANAPOLIS (46278) Marion(94), Hendricks(6)
INDIANAPOLIS Hamilton
INDIANAPOLIS Marion
INGALLS Madison
INGLEFIELD Vanderburgh
IRELAND Dubois
JAMESTOWN (46147) Boone(91), Hendricks(9)
JASONVILLE (47438) Greene(73), Clay(25), Sullivan(2)
JASPER Dubois
JEFFERSONVILLE Clark
JONESBORO Grant
JONESVILLE Bartholomew
JUDSON Parke
KEMPTON (46049) Tipton(92), Clinton(8)
KENDALLVILLE Noble
KENNARD Henry
KENTLAND Newton
KEWANNA (46939) Fulton(88), Pulaski(12)
KEYSTONE Wells
KIMMELL Noble
KINGMAN (47952) Fountain(96), Parke(5)
KINGSBURY La Porte
KINGSFORD HEIGHTS La Porte
KIRKLIN (46050) Clinton(74), Boone(22), Tipton(4)
KNIGHTSTOWN (46148) Henry(84), Rush(16)
KNIGHTSVILLE Clay
KNOX Starke
KOKOMO (46901) Howard(99), Miami(1)
KOKOMO Howard
KOLEEN Greene
KOUTS Porter
KURTZ Jackson
LA CROSSE (46348) La Porte(99), Porter(1)
LA FONTAINE (46940) Wabash(88), Huntington(9), Grant(3)
LA PORTE La Porte
LACONIA Harrison
LADOGA (47954) Montgomery(92), Putnam(7), Hendricks(1)
LAFAYETTE Tippecanoe
LAGRANGE (46761) LaGrange(95), Steuben(5)
LAGRO Wabash
LAKE CICOTT Cass
LAKE STATION Lake
LAKE VILLAGE Newton
LAKETON Wabash
LAKEVILLE (46536) St. Joseph(93), Marshall(8)
LAMAR Spencer
LANDESS Grant
LANESVILLE (47136) Harrison(85), Floyd(16)
LAOTTO (46763) Noble(86), DeKalb(14)
LAPAZ Marshall
LAPEL Madison
LARWILL (46764) Whitley(93), Noble(8)
LAUREL (47024) Franklin(99), Fayette(1)
LAWRENCEBURG Dearborn
LEAVENWORTH (47137) Crawford(98), Perry(1)
LEBANON Boone
LEESBURG Kosciusko
LEITERS FORD Fulton
LEO Allen
LEOPOLD Perry

LEROY Lake
LEWIS (47858) Clay(51), Vigo(32), Sullivan(17)
LEWISVILLE (47352) Rush(52), Henry(47), Fayette(1)
LEXINGTON (47138) Jefferson(53), Scott(45), Clark(1)
LIBERTY (47353) Union(95), Franklin(5)
LIBERTY CENTER (46766) Wells(98), Huntington(2)
LIBERTY MILLS Wabash
LIGONIER (46767) Noble(97), Elkhart(2), LaGrange(2)
LINCOLN CITY Spencer
LINDEN (47955) Montgomery(95), Tippecanoe(5)
LINN GROVE Adams
LINTON Greene
LITTLE YORK Washington
LIZTON Hendricks
LOGANSPORT (46947) Cass(98), Carroll(2)
LOOGOOTEE (47553) Martin(81), Daviess(19)
LOSANTVILLE (47354) Randolph(73), Henry(16), Delaware(6), Wayne(5)
LOWELL Lake
LUCERNE (46950) Cass(96), Fulton(4)
LYNN Randolph
LYNNVILLE (47619) Warrick(92), Gibson(8)
LYONS Greene
MACKEY Gibson
MACY (46951) Miami(52), Fulton(48)
MADISON (47250) Jefferson(97), Ripley(2), Switzerland(1)
MAGNET Perry
MANILLA (46150) Rush(94), Shelby(6)
MARENGO (47140) Orange(54), Crawford(46)
MARIAH HILL Spencer
MARION (46952) Grant(98), Wells(1)
MARION Grant
MARKLE (46770) Wells(82), Huntington(18)
MARKLEVILLE (46056) Madison(77), Hancock(18), Henry(5)
MARSHALL Parke
MARTINSVILLE Morgan
MARYSVILLE Clark
MATTHEWS Grant
MAUCKPORT Harrison
MAXWELL Hancock
MAYS Rush
MC CORDSVILLE (46055) Hancock(79), Hamilton(21)
MECCA Parke
MEDARYVILLE (47957) Pulaski(91), Jasper(9)
MEDORA Jackson
MELLOTT Fountain
MEMPHIS Clark
MENTONE (46539) Kosciusko(91), Fulton(7), Marshall(2)
MEROM Sullivan
MERRILLVILLE Lake
METAMORA Franklin
MEXICO Miami
MIAMI Miami
MICHIGAN CITY (46360) La Porte(94), Porter(6)
MICHIGAN CITY La Porte
MICHIGANTOWN Clinton
MIDDLEBURY (46540) Elkhart(90), LaGrange(10)
MIDDLETOWN (47356) Henry(93), Madison(5), Delaware(2)
MIDLAND Greene
MILAN Ripley
MILFORD (46542) Kosciusko(94), Elkhart(6)
MILL CREEK La Porte

MILLERSBURG (46543) Elkhart(73), LaGrange(26), Noble(2)
MILLHOUSEN Decatur
MILLTOWN (47145) Crawford(94), Washington(5)
MILROY (46156) Rush(95), Decatur(6)
MILTON (47357) Wayne(71), Fayette(24), Madison(6)
MISHAWAKA St. Joseph
MITCHELL (47446) Lawrence(98), Martin(1)
MODOC (47358) Randolph(99), Wayne(1)
MONGO LaGrange
MONON (47959) White(90), Jasper(7), Pulaski(3)
MONROE Adams
MONROE CITY Knox
MONROEVILLE (46773) Allen(90), Adams(10)
MONROVIA Morgan
MONTEREY (46960) Pulaski(67), Starke(26), Fulton(8)
MONTEZUMA Parke
MONTGOMERY Daviess
MONTICELLO (47960) White(90), Carroll(10)
MONTMORENCI Tippecanoe
MONTPELIER (47359) Blackford(88), Wells(12)
MOORELAND (47360) Henry(97), Wayne(3)
MOORES HILL Dearborn
MOORESVILLE (46158) Morgan(88), Hendricks(12)
MORGANTOWN (46160) Brown(53), Morgan(28), Johnson(19)
MOROCCO Newton
MORRIS Ripley
MORRISTOWN (46161) Shelby(79), Hancock(13), Rush(8)
MOUNT AYR Newton
MOUNT PLEASANT Perry
MOUNT SAINT FRANCIS Floyd
MOUNT SUMMIT Henry
MOUNT VERNON Posey
MULBERRY (46058) Clinton(97), Tippecanoe(3)
MUNCIE Delaware
MUNSTER Lake
NABB (47147) Clark(45), Scott(31), Jefferson(25)
NAPOLEON Ripley
NAPPANEE (46550) Elkhart(84), Kosciusko(11), Marshall(4), St. Joseph(1)
NASHVILLE Brown
NEBRASKA Jennings
NEEDHAM (46162) Johnson(59), Shelby(41)
NEW ALBANY Floyd
NEW CARLISLE (46552) La Porte(60), St. Joseph(40)
NEW CASTLE Henry
NEW GOSHEN Vigo
NEW HARMONY Posey
NEW HAVEN Allen
NEW LEBANON Sullivan
NEW LISBON Henry
NEW MARKET Montgomery
NEW MIDDLETOWN Harrison
NEW PALESTINE (46163) Hancock(94), Shelby(6)
NEW PARIS Elkhart
NEW POINT Decatur
NEW RICHMOND (47967) Montgomery(86), Tippecanoe(14)
NEW ROSS (47968) Montgomery(79), Boone(14), Hendricks(7)
NEW SALISBURY Harrison
NEW TRENTON Franklin
NEW WASHINGTON Clark
NEW WAVERLY Cass

NEWBERRY (47449) Greene(93), Daviess(6), Martin(1)
NEWBURGH Warrick
NEWPORT Vermillion
NEWTOWN Fountain
NINEVEH (46164) Brown(70), Johnson(30)
NOBLESVILLE Hamilton
NORMAN (47264) Jackson(87), Lawrence(9), Monroe(4)
NORTH JUDSON (46366) Starke(93), Pulaski(7)
NORTH LIBERTY (46554) St. Joseph(97), La Porte(3)
NORTH MANCHESTER (46962) Wabash(95), Kosciusko(4)
NORTH SALEM (46165) Hendricks(99), Putnam(1)
NORTH VERNON Jennings
NORTH WEBSTER Kosciusko
NOTRE DAME St. Joseph
OAKFORD Howard
OAKLAND CITY (47660) Gibson(87), Pike(13)
OAKTOWN (47561) Knox(79), Sullivan(21)
OAKVILLE Delaware
ODON Daviess
OLDENBURG Franklin
ONWARD Cass
OOLITIC Lawrence
ORA Starke
ORESTES Madison
ORLAND (46776) Steuben(75), LaGrange(25)
ORLEANS (47452) Orange(92), Lawrence(7), Washington(1)
OSCEOLA (46561) St. Joseph(93), Elkhart(7)
OSGOOD Ripley
OSSIAN (46777) Wells(92), Allen(4), Adams(3)
OSSIAN Steuben
OSSIAN Wells
OTISCO Clark
OTTERBEIN (47970) Benton(45), Warren(44), Tippecanoe(12)
OTWELL (47564) Pike(90), Dubois(10)
OWENSBURG Greene
OWENSVILLE Gibson
OXFORD Benton
PALMYRA (47164) Harrison(71), Washington(29)
PAOLI Orange
PARAGON (46166) Morgan(97), Owen(3)
PARIS CROSSING (47270) Jennings(95), Jefferson(5)
PARKER CITY (47368) Randolph(85), Delaware(15)
PATOKA Gibson
PATRICKSBURG Owen
PATRIOT Switzerland
PAXTON Sullivan
PEKIN (47165) Washington(97), Clark(2)
PENCE Warren
PENDLETON (46064) Madison(94), Hancock(5), Hamilton(1)
PENNVILLE (47369) Jay(96), Blackford(4)
PERRYSVILLE Vermillion
PERSHING Wayne
PERU (46970) Miami(93), Cass(6)
PETERSBURG Pike
PETROLEUM Wells
PIERCETON (46562) Kosciusko(84), Noble(9), Whitley(7)
PIERCEVILLE Ripley
PIMENTO (47866) Vigo(93), Sullivan(7)
PINE VILLAGE (47975) Warren(96), Benton(4)
PITTSBORO (46167) Hendricks(98), Boone(2)
PLAINFIELD Hendricks
PLAINVILLE Daviess
PLEASANT LAKE Steuben

PLEASANT MILLS Adams
PLYMOUTH Marshall
POLAND (47868) Owen(66), Clay(29), Putnam(5)
PONETO Wells
PORTAGE Porter
PORTLAND Jay
POSEYVILLE (47633) Posey(96), Vanderburgh(4)
PRAIRIE CREEK Vigo
PRAIRIETON Vigo
PREBLE Adams
PRINCETON Gibson
PUTNAMVILLE Putnam
QUINCY (47456) Owen(49), Morgan(38), Putnam(13)
RAGSDALE Knox
RAMSEY Harrison
REDKEY (47373) Jay(87), Randolph(14)
REELSVILLE (46171) Putnam(98), Clay(2)
REMINGTON (47977) Jasper(78), Benton(21)
RENSSELAER Jasper
REYNOLDS White
RICHLAND Spencer
RICHMOND Wayne
RIDGEVILLE (47380) Randolph(92), Jay(8)
RILEY Vigo
RISING SUN Ohio
ROACHDALE Putnam
ROANN (46974) Wabash(81), Miami(20)
ROANOKE (46783) Huntington(51), Allen(39), Whitley(8), Wells(2)
ROCHESTER Fulton
ROCKFIELD Carroll
ROCKPORT Spencer
ROCKVILLE Parke
ROLLING PRAIRIE La Porte
ROME Perry
ROME CITY Noble
ROMNEY (47981) Tippecanoe(94), Montgomery(6)
ROSEDALE (47874) Vigo(52), Parke(43), Clay(5)
ROSELAWN Newton
ROSSVILLE (46065) Clinton(58), Carroll(42)
ROYAL CENTER (46978) Cass(93), White(3), Pulaski(3)
RUSHVILLE (46173) Rush(98), Franklin(1)
RUSSELLVILLE (46175) Putnam(95), Parke(3), Montgomery(2)
RUSSIAVILLE (46979) Howard(88), Clinton(5), Tipton(4), Carroll(3)
SAINT ANTHONY Dubois
SAINT BERNICE Vermillion
SAINT CROIX (47576) Perry(99), Crawford(2)
SAINT JOE DeKalb
SAINT JOHN Lake
SAINT MARY OF THE WOODS Vigo
SAINT MEINRAD (47577) Spencer(82), Perry(18)
SAINT PAUL (47272) Decatur(72), Shelby(26), Rush(1)
SALAMONIA Jay
SALEM Washington
SAN PIERRE (46374) Starke(87), Pulaski(8), Jasper(5)
SANDBORN (47578) Knox(68), Greene(31), Sullivan(1)
SANDFORD Vigo
SANTA CLAUS Spencer
SARATOGA Randolph
SCHERERVILLE Lake
SCHNEIDER Lake
SCHNELLVILLE Dubois
SCIPIO Jennings
SCOTLAND Greene
SCOTTSBURG (47170) Scott(85), Washington(14)
SEDALIA Clinton

SEELYVILLE Vigo
SELLERSBURG (47172) Clark(87), Floyd(13)
SELMA Delaware
SERVIA Wabash
SEYMOUR (47274) Jackson(94), Bartholomew(3), Jennings(2)
SHARPSVILLE (46068) Tipton(92), Howard(8)
SHELBURN Sullivan
SHELBY Lake
SHELBYVILLE Shelby
SHEPARDSVILLE Vigo
SHERIDAN (46069) Hamilton(63), Boone(32), Clinton(6)
SHIPSHEWANA LaGrange
SHIRLEY (47384) Henry(72), Hancock(28)
SHOALS Martin
SIDNEY Kosciusko
SILVER LAKE (46982) Kosciusko(76), Wabash(20), Fulton(4)
SIMS Grant
SMITHVILLE Monroe
SOLSBERRY (47459) Greene(91), Owen(9)
SOMERSET Wabash
SOMERVILLE Gibson
SOUTH BEND St. Joseph
SOUTH MILFORD LaGrange
SOUTH WHITLEY (46787) Whitley(92), Kosciusko(7)
SPENCER (47460) Owen(98), Monroe(2), Greene(1)
SPENCERVILLE (46788) Allen(62), DeKalb(38)
SPICELAND Henry
SPRINGPORT (47386) Henry(97), Delaware(3)
SPRINGVILLE (47462) Lawrence(63), Monroe(37)
SPURGEON Pike
STANFORD Monroe
STAR CITY (46985) Pulaski(96), White(3)
STATE LINE Warren
STAUNTON Clay
STENDAL Pike
STILESVILLE (46180) Hendricks(64), Morgan(36)
STINESVILLE Monroe
STOCKWELL Tippecanoe
STRAUGHN (47387) Henry(99), Fayette(1)
STROH LaGrange
SULLIVAN Sullivan
SULPHUR (47174) Crawford(96), Perry(4)
SULPHUR SPRINGS Henry
SUMAVA RESORTS Newton
SUMMITVILLE (46070) Madison(95), Delaware(3), Grant(2)
SUNMAN (47041) Ripley(62), Dearborn(39)
SWAYZEE (46986) Grant(98), Howard(2)
SWEETSER Grant
SWITZ CITY Greene
SYRACUSE (46567) Kosciusko(96), Elkhart(4)
TALBOT Benton
TANGIER Parke
TASWELL (47175) Crawford(97), Orange(4)
TAYLORSVILLE Bartholomew
TEFFT Jasper
TELL CITY Perry
TEMPLETON Benton
TENNYSON (47637) Warrick(62), Spencer(38)
TERRE HAUTE Vigo
THAYER Newton
THORNTOWN Boone
TIPPECANOE (46570) Marshall(88), Fulton(12)
TIPTON Tipton
TOBINSPORT Perry
TOPEKA (46571) LaGrange(98), Noble(2)

TRAFALGAR (46181) Johnson(82), Brown(18)
TROY (47588) Spencer(83), Perry(17)
TUNNELTON Lawrence
TWELVE MILE (46988) Cass(98), Fulton(2)
TYNER Marshall
UNDERWOOD (47177) Scott(54), Clark(46)
UNION CITY (47390) Randolph(99), Jay(2)
UNION MILLS (46382) La Porte(99), Lake(1)
UNIONDALE Wells
UNIONVILLE (47468) Brown(57), Monroe(44)
UNIVERSAL Vermillion
UPLAND (46989) Grant(93), Blackford(4), Delaware(3)
URBANA Wabash
VALLONIA (47281) Washington(52), Jackson(48)
VALPARAISO Porter
VAN BUREN (46991) Grant(85), Huntington(13), Wells(3)
VEEDERSBURG Fountain
VELPEN (47590) Pike(92), Dubois(8)
VERNON Jennings
VERSAILLES Ripley

VEVAY Switzerland
VINCENNES Knox
WABASH Wabash
WADESVILLE Posey
WAKARUSA (46573) Elkhart(71), St. Joseph(29)
WALDRON (46182) Shelby(80), Rush(20)
WALKERTON (46574) St. Joseph(39), Marshall(22), Starke(21), La Porte(18)
WALLACE Fountain
WALTON Cass
WANATAH La Porte
WARREN (46792) Huntington(82), Wells(18)
WARSAW Kosciusko
WASHINGTON Daviess
WATERLOO (46793) DeKalb(99), Steuben(1)
WAVELAND (47989) Montgomery(98), Putnam(2)
WAWAKA Noble
WAYNETOWN (47990) Montgomery(90), Fountain(10)
WEBSTER Wayne
WEST BADEN SPRINGS Orange
WEST COLLEGE CORNER Franklin
WEST HARRISON Dearborn

WEST LAFAYETTE Tippecanoe
WEST LEBANON Warren
WEST MIDDLETON Howard
WEST NEWTON Marion
WEST TERRE HAUTE Vigo
WESTFIELD Hamilton
WESTPHALIA Knox
WESTPOINT (47992) Tippecanoe(96), Fountain(4)
WESTPORT (47283) Decatur(93), Bartholomew(4), Jennings(3)
WESTVILLE (46391) La Porte(77), Porter(23)
WHEATFIELD Jasper
WHEATLAND Knox
WHEELER Porter
WHITELAND Johnson
WHITESTOWN Boone
WHITING Lake
WILKINSON (46186) Hancock(96), Henry(4)
WILLIAMS (47470) Lawrence(95), Martin(5)
WILLIAMSBURG (47393) Wayne(72), Randolph(28)
WILLIAMSPORT Warren
WILLOW BRANCH Hancock

WINAMAC Pulaski
WINCHESTER Randolph
WINDFALL (46076) Tipton(95), Howard(5)
WINGATE (47994) Montgomery(67), Fountain(27), Tippecanoe(6)
WINONA LAKE Kosciusko
WINSLOW Pike
WOLCOTT (47995) White(73), Jasper(27)
WOLCOTTVILLE (46795) LaGrange(91), Noble(9)
WOLFLAKE Noble
WOODBURN Allen
WORTHINGTON (47471) Greene(91), Owen(9)
WYATT St. Joseph
YEOMAN Carroll
YODER (46798) Allen(87), Wells(13)
YORKTOWN Delaware
YOUNG AMERICA Cass
ZANESVILLE Allen
ZIONSVILLE (46077) Boone(92), Hamilton(6), Marion(2)

ZIP/City Cross Reference

ZIP	City	ZIP	City	ZIP	City	ZIP	City
46001-46001	ALEXANDRIA	46117-46117	CHARLOTTESVILLE	46301-46301	BEVERLY SHORES	46504-46504	BOURBON
46011-46018	ANDERSON	46118-46118	CLAYTON	46302-46302	BOONE GROVE	46506-46506	BREMEN
46030-46030	ARCADIA	46120-46120	CLOVERDALE	46303-46303	CEDAR LAKE	46507-46507	BRISTOL
46031-46031	ATLANTA	46121-46121	COATESVILLE	46304-46304	CHESTERTON	46508-46508	BURKET
46032-46033	CARMEL	46122-46122	DANVILLE	46307-46308	CROWN POINT	46510-46510	CLAYPOOL
46034-46034	CICERO	46124-46124	EDINBURGH	46310-46310	DEMOTTE	46511-46511	CULVER
46035-46035	COLFAX	46125-46125	EMINENCE	46311-46311	DYER	46513-46513	DONALDSON
46036-46036	ELWOOD	46126-46126	FAIRLAND	46312-46312	EAST CHICAGO	46514-46517	ELKHART
46038-46038	FISHERS	46127-46127	FALMOUTH	46319-46319	GRIFFITH	46524-46524	ETNA GREEN
46039-46039	FOREST	46128-46128	FILLMORE	46320-46320	HAMMOND	46526-46528	GOSHEN
46040-46040	FORTVILLE	46129-46129	FINLY	46321-46321	MUNSTER	46530-46530	GRANGER
46041-46041	FRANKFORT	46130-46130	FOUNTAINTOWN	46322-46322	HIGHLAND	46531-46531	GROVERTOWN
46044-46044	FRANKTON	46131-46131	FRANKLIN	46323-46327	HAMMOND	46532-46532	HAMLET
46045-46045	GOLDSMITH	46133-46133	GLENWOOD	46340-46340	HANNA	46534-46534	KNOX
46046-46046	HILLISBURG	46135-46135	GREENCASTLE	46341-46341	HEBRON	46536-46536	LAKEVILLE
46047-46047	HOBBS	46140-46140	GREENFIELD	46342-46342	HOBART	46537-46537	LAPAZ
46048-46048	INGALLS	46142-46143	GREENWOOD	46345-46345	KINGSBURY	46538-46538	LEESBURG
46049-46049	KEMPTON	46144-46144	GWYNNEVILLE	46346-46346	KINGSFORD HEIGHTS	46539-46539	MENTONE
46050-46050	KIRKLIN	46146-46146	HOMER	46347-46347	KOUTS	46540-46540	MIDDLEBURY
46051-46051	LAPEL	46147-46147	JAMESTOWN	46348-46348	LA CROSSE	46542-46542	MILFORD
46052-46052	LEBANON	46148-46148	KNIGHTSTOWN	46349-46349	LAKE VILLAGE	46543-46543	MILLERSBURG
46055-46055	MC CORDSVILLE	46149-46149	LIZTON	46350-46352	LA PORTE	46544-46546	MISHAWAKA
46056-46056	MARKLEVILLE	46150-46150	MANILLA	46355-46355	LEROY	46550-46550	NAPPANEE
46057-46057	MICHIGANTOWN	46151-46151	MARTINSVILLE	46356-46356	LOWELL	46552-46552	NEW CARLISLE
46058-46058	MULBERRY	46154-46154	MAXWELL	46360-46361	MICHIGAN CITY	46553-46553	NEW PARIS
46060-46061	NOBLESVILLE	46155-46155	MAYS	46365-46365	MILL CREEK	46554-46554	NORTH LIBERTY
46063-46063	ORESTES	46156-46156	MILROY	46366-46366	NORTH JUDSON	46555-46555	NORTH WEBSTER
46064-46064	PENDLETON	46157-46157	MONROVIA	46368-46368	PORTAGE	46556-46556	NOTRE DAME
46065-46065	ROSSVILLE	46158-46158	MOORESVILLE	46371-46371	ROLLING PRAIRIE	46561-46561	OSCEOLA
46067-46067	SEDALIA	46160-46160	MORGANTOWN	46372-46372	ROSELAWN	46562-46562	PIERCETON
46068-46068	SHARPSVILLE	46161-46161	MORRISTOWN	46373-46373	SAINT JOHN	46563-46563	PLYMOUTH
46069-46069	SHERIDAN	46162-46162	NEEDHAM	46374-46374	SAN PIERRE	46565-46565	SHIPSHEWANA
46070-46070	SUMMITVILLE	46163-46163	NEW PALESTINE	46375-46375	SCHERERVILLE	46566-46566	SIDNEY
46071-46071	THORNTOWN	46164-46164	NINEVEH	46376-46376	SCHNEIDER	46567-46567	SYRACUSE
46072-46072	TIPTON	46165-46165	NORTH SALEM	46377-46377	SHELBY	46570-46570	TIPPECANOE
46074-46074	WESTFIELD	46166-46166	PARAGON	46379-46379	SUMAVA RESORTS	46571-46571	TOPEKA
46075-46075	WHITESTOWN	46167-46167	PITTSBORO	46380-46380	TEFFT	46572-46572	TYNER
46076-46076	WINDFALL	46168-46168	PLAINFIELD	46381-46381	THAYER	46573-46573	WAKARUSA
46077-46077	ZIONSVILLE	46170-46170	PUTNAMVILLE	46382-46382	UNION MILLS	46574-46574	WALKERTON
46102-46102	ADVANCE	46171-46171	REELSVILLE	46383-46385	VALPARAISO	46580-46581	WARSAW
46103-46103	AMO	46172-46172	ROACHDALE	46390-46390	WANATAH	46590-46590	WINONA LAKE
46104-46104	ARLINGTON	46173-46173	RUSHVILLE	46391-46391	WESTVILLE	46595-46595	WYATT
46105-46105	BAINBRIDGE	46175-46175	RUSSELLVILLE	46392-46392	WHEATFIELD	46601-46699	SOUTH BEND
46106-46106	BARGERSVILLE	46176-46176	SHELBYVILLE	46393-46393	WHEELER	46701-46701	ALBION
46107-46107	BEECH GROVE	46180-46180	STILESVILLE	46394-46394	WHITING	46702-46702	ANDREWS
46110-46110	BOGGSTOWN	46181-46181	TRAFALGAR	46401-46404	GARY	46703-46703	ANGOLA
46111-46111	BROOKLYN	46182-46182	WALDRON	46405-46405	LAKE STATION	46704-46704	ARCOLA
46112-46112	BROWNSBURG	46183-46183	WEST NEWTON	46406-46409	GARY	46705-46705	ASHLEY
46113-46113	CAMBY	46184-46184	WHITELAND	46410-46411	MERRILLVILLE	46706-46706	AUBURN
46114-46114	CARTERSBURG	46186-46186	WILKINSON	46501-46501	ARGOS	46710-46710	AVILLA
46115-46115	CARTHAGE	46201-46298	INDIANAPOLIS	46502-46502	ATWOOD	46711-46711	BERNE

46713-46713	BIPPUS	46936-46936	GREENTOWN	47110-47110	CENTRAL	47302-47308	MUNCIE
46714-46714	BLUFFTON	46937-46937	HEMLOCK	47111-47111	CHARLESTOWN	47320-47320	ALBANY
46720-46720	BRIMFIELD	46938-46938	JONESBORO	47112-47112	CORYDON	47322-47322	BENTONVILLE
46721-46721	BUTLER	46939-46939	KEWANNA	47114-47114	CRANDALL	47324-47324	BOSTON
46723-46723	CHURUBUSCO	46940-46940	LA FONTAINE	47115-47115	DEPAUW	47325-47325	BROWNSVILLE
46725-46725	COLUMBIA CITY	46941-46941	LAGRO	47116-47116	ECKERTY	47326-47326	BRYANT
46730-46730	CORUNNA	46942-46942	LAKE CICOTT	47117-47117	ELIZABETH	47327-47327	CAMBRIDGE CITY
46731-46731	CRAIGVILLE	46943-46943	LAKETON	47118-47118	ENGLISH	47330-47330	CENTERVILLE
46732-46732	CROMWELL	46945-46945	LEITERS FORD	47119-47119	FLOYDS KNOBS	47331-47331	CONNERSVILLE
46733-46733	DECATUR	46946-46946	LIBERTY MILLS	47120-47120	FREDERICKSBURG	47334-47334	DALEVILLE
46737-46737	FREMONT	46947-46947	LOGANSPORT	47122-47122	GEORGETOWN	47335-47335	DUBLIN
46738-46738	GARRETT	46950-46950	LUCERNE	47123-47123	GRANTSBURG	47336-47336	DUNKIRK
46740-46740	GENEVA	46951-46951	MACY	47124-47124	GREENVILLE	47337-47337	DUNREITH
46741-46741	GRABILL	46952-46953	MARION	47125-47125	HARDINSBURG	47338-47338	EATON
46742-46742	HAMILTON	46957-46957	MATTHEWS	47126-47126	HENRYVILLE	47339-47339	ECONOMY
46743-46743	HARLAN	46958-46958	MEXICO	47129-47129	CLARKSVILLE	47340-47340	FARMLAND
46745-46745	HOAGLAND	46959-46959	MIAMI	47130-47134	JEFFERSONVILLE	47341-47341	FOUNTAIN CITY
46746-46746	HOWE	46960-46960	MONTEREY	47135-47135	LACONIA	47342-47342	GASTON
46747-46747	HUDSON	46961-46961	NEW WAVERLY	47136-47136	LANESVILLE	47344-47344	GREENSBORO
46748-46748	HUNTERTOWN	46962-46962	NORTH MANCHESTER	47137-47137	LEAVENWORTH	47345-47345	GREENS FORK
46750-46750	HUNTINGTON	46965-46965	OAKFORD	47138-47138	LEXINGTON	47346-47346	HAGERSTOWN
46755-46755	KENDALLVILLE	46967-46967	ONWARD	47139-47139	LITTLE YORK	47348-47348	HARTFORD CITY
46759-46759	KEYSTONE	46968-46968	ORA	47140-47140	MARENGO	47351-47351	KENNARD
46760-46760	KIMMELL	46970-46970	PERU	47141-47141	MARYSVILLE	47352-47352	LEWISVILLE
46761-46761	LAGRANGE	46971-46971	GRISSOM AFB	47142-47142	MAUCKPORT	47353-47353	LIBERTY
46763-46763	LAOTTO	46974-46974	ROANN	47143-47143	MEMPHIS	47354-47354	LOSANTVILLE
46764-46764	LARWILL	46975-46975	ROCHESTER	47144-47144	JEFFERSONVILLE	47355-47355	LYNN
46765-46765	LEO	46977-46977	ROCKFIELD	47145-47145	MILLTOWN	47356-47356	MIDDLETOWN
46766-46766	LIBERTY CENTER	46978-46978	ROYAL CENTER	47146-47146	MOUNT SAINT FRANCIS	47357-47357	MILTON
46767-46767	LIGONIER	46979-46979	RUSSIAVILLE	47147-47147	NABB	47358-47358	MODOC
46769-46769	LINN GROVE	46980-46980	SERVIA	47150-47151	NEW ALBANY	47359-47359	MONTPELIER
46770-46770	MARKLE	46982-46982	SILVER LAKE	47160-47160	NEW MIDDLETOWN	47360-47360	MOORELAND
46771-46771	MONGO	46984-46984	SOMERSET	47161-47161	NEW SALISBURY	47361-47361	MOUNT SUMMIT
46772-46772	MONROE	46985-46985	STAR CITY	47162-47162	NEW WASHINGTON	47362-47362	NEW CASTLE
46773-46773	MONROEVILLE	46986-46986	SWAYZEE	47163-47163	OTISCO	47366-47366	NEW LISBON
46774-46774	NEW HAVEN	46987-46987	SWEETSER	47164-47164	PALMYRA	47367-47367	OAKVILLE
46776-46776	ORLAND	46988-46988	TWELVE MILE	47165-47165	PEKIN	47368-47368	PARKER CITY
46777-46777	OSSIAN	46989-46989	UPLAND	47166-47166	RAMSEY	47369-47369	PENNVILLE
46778-46778	PETROLEUM	46990-46990	URBANA	47167-47167	SALEM	47370-47370	PERSHING
46779-46779	PLEASANT LAKE	46991-46991	VAN BUREN	47170-47170	SCOTTSBURG	47371-47371	PORTLAND
46780-46780	PLEASANT MILLS	46992-46992	WABASH	47172-47172	SELLERSBURG	47373-47373	REDKEY
46781-46781	PONETO	46994-46994	WALTON	47174-47174	SULPHUR	47374-47375	RICHMOND
46782-46782	PREBLE	46995-46995	WEST MIDDLETON	47175-47175	TASWELL	47380-47380	RIDGEVILLE
46783-46783	ROANOKE	46996-46996	WINAMAC	47177-47177	UNDERWOOD	47381-47381	SALAMONIA
46784-46784	ROME CITY	46998-46998	YOUNG AMERICA	47199-47199	JEFFERSONVILLE	47382-47382	SARATOGA
46785-46785	SAINT JOE	47001-47001	AURORA	47201-47203	COLUMBUS	47383-47383	SELMA
46786-46786	SOUTH MILFORD	47003-47003	WEST COLLEGE	47220-47220	BROWNSTOWN	47384-47384	SHIRLEY
46787-46787	SOUTH WHITLEY		CORNER	47223-47223	BUTLERVILLE	47385-47385	SPICELAND
46788-46788	SPENCERVILLE	47006-47006	BATESVILLE	47224-47224	CANAAN	47386-47386	SPRINGPORT
46789-46789	STROH	47010-47010	BATH	47225-47225	CLARKSBURG	47387-47387	STRAUGHN
46791-46791	UNIONDALE	47011-47011	BENNINGTON	47226-47226	CLIFFORD	47388-47388	SULPHUR SPRINGS
46792-46792	WARREN	47012-47012	BROOKVILLE	47227-47227	COMMISKEY	47390-47390	UNION CITY
46793-46793	WATERLOO	47016-47016	CEDAR GROVE	47228-47228	CORTLAND	47392-47392	WEBSTER
46794-46794	WAWAKA	47017-47017	CROSS PLAINS	47229-47229	CROTHERSVILLE	47393-47393	WILLIAMSBURG
46795-46795	WOLCOTTVILLE	47018-47018	DILLSBORO	47230-47230	DEPUTY	47394-47394	WINCHESTER
46796-46796	WOLFLAKE	47019-47019	EAST ENTERPRISE	47231-47231	DUPONT	47396-47396	YORKTOWN
46797-46797	WOODBURN	47020-47020	FLORENCE	47232-47232	ELIZABETHTOWN	47401-47408	BLOOMINGTON
46798-46798	YODER	47021-47021	FRIENDSHIP	47234-47234	FLAT ROCK	47420-47420	AVOCA
46799-46799	ZANESVILLE	47022-47022	GUILFORD	47235-47235	FREETOWN	47421-47421	BEDFORD
46801-46899	FORT WAYNE	47023-47023	HOLTON	47236-47236	GRAMMER	47424-47424	BLOOMFIELD
46901-46904	KOKOMO	47024-47024	LAUREL	47240-47240	GREENSBURG	47426-47426	CLEAR CREEK
46910-46910	AKRON	47025-47025	LAWRENCEBURG	47243-47243	HANOVER	47427-47427	COAL CITY
46911-46911	AMBOY	47030-47030	METAMORA	47244-47244	HARTSVILLE	47429-47429	ELLETTSVILLE
46912-46912	ATHENS	47031-47031	MILAN	47245-47245	HAYDEN	47430-47430	FORT RITNER
46913-46913	BRINGHURST	47032-47032	MOORES HILL	47246-47246	HOPE	47431-47431	FREEDOM
46914-46914	BUNKER HILL	47033-47033	MORRIS	47247-47247	JONESVILLE	47432-47432	FRENCH LICK
46915-46915	BURLINGTON	47034-47034	NAPOLEON	47249-47249	KURTZ	47433-47433	GOSPORT
46916-46916	BURROWS	47035-47035	NEW TRENTON	47250-47250	MADISON	47434-47434	HARRODSBURG
46917-46917	CAMDEN	47036-47036	OLDENBURG	47260-47260	MEDORA	47435-47435	HELMSBURG
46919-46919	CONVERSE	47037-47037	OSGOOD	47261-47261	MILLHOUSEN	47436-47436	HELTONVILLE
46920-46920	CUTLER	47038-47038	PATRIOT	47262-47262	NEBRASKA	47437-47437	HURON
46921-46921	DEEDSVILLE	47039-47039	PIERCEVILLE	47263-47263	NEW POINT	47438-47438	JASONVILLE
46922-46922	DELONG	47040-47040	RISING SUN	47264-47264	NORMAN	47439-47439	KOLEEN
46923-46923	DELPHI	47041-47041	SUNMAN	47265-47265	NORTH VERNON	47441-47441	LINTON
46926-46926	DENVER	47042-47042	VERSAILLES	47270-47270	PARIS CROSSING	47443-47443	LYONS
46928-46928	FAIRMOUNT	47043-47043	VEVAY	47272-47272	SAINT PAUL	47445-47445	MIDLAND
46929-46929	FLORA	47060-47060	WEST HARRISON	47273-47273	SCIPIO	47446-47446	MITCHELL
46930-46930	FOWLERTON	47102-47102	AUSTIN	47274-47274	SEYMOUR	47448-47448	NASHVILLE
46931-46931	FULTON	47104-47104	BETHLEHEM	47280-47280	TAYLORSVILLE	47449-47449	NEWBERRY
46932-46932	GALVESTON	47106-47106	BORDEN	47281-47281	VALLONIA	47451-47451	OOLITIC
46933-46933	GAS CITY	47107-47107	BRADFORD	47282-47282	VERNON	47452-47452	ORLEANS
46935-46935	GRASS CREEK	47108-47108	CAMPBELLSBURG	47283-47283	WESTPORT	47453-47453	OWENSBURG

ZIP Range	City	ZIP Range	City	ZIP Range	City	ZIP Range	City
47454-47454	PAOLI	47574-47574	ROME	47837-47837	CARBON	47928-47928	CAYUGA
47455-47455	PATRICKSBURG	47575-47575	SAINT ANTHONY	47838-47838	CARLISLE	47929-47929	CHALMERS
47456-47456	QUINCY	47576-47576	SAINT CROIX	47840-47840	CENTERPOINT	47930-47930	CLARKS HILL
47457-47457	SCOTLAND	47577-47577	SAINT MEINRAD	47841-47841	CLAY CITY	47932-47932	COVINGTON
47458-47458	SMITHVILLE	47578-47578	SANDBORN	47842-47842	CLINTON	47933-47939	CRAWFORDSVILLE
47459-47459	SOLSBERRY	47579-47579	SANTA CLAUS	47845-47845	COALMONT	47940-47940	DARLINGTON
47460-47460	SPENCER	47580-47580	SCHNELLVILLE	47846-47846	CORY	47941-47941	DAYTON
47462-47462	SPRINGVILLE	47581-47581	SHOALS	47847-47847	DANA	47942-47942	EARL PARK
47463-47463	STANFORD	47584-47584	SPURGEON	47848-47848	DUGGER	47943-47943	FAIR OAKS
47464-47464	STINESVILLE	47585-47585	STENDAL	47849-47849	FAIRBANKS	47944-47944	FOWLER
47465-47465	SWITZ CITY	47586-47586	TELL CITY	47850-47850	FARMERSBURG	47946-47946	FRANCESVILLE
47467-47467	TUNNELTON	47588-47588	TROY	47851-47851	FONTANET	47948-47948	GOODLAND
47468-47468	UNIONVILLE	47590-47590	VELPEN	47852-47852	GRAYSVILLE	47949-47949	HILLSBORO
47469-47469	WEST BADEN SPRINGS	47591-47591	VINCENNES	47853-47853	HARMONY	47950-47950	IDAVILLE
47470-47470	WILLIAMS	47596-47596	WESTPHALIA	47854-47854	HILLSDALE	47951-47951	KENTLAND
47471-47471	WORTHINGTON	47597-47597	WHEATLAND	47855-47855	HYMERA	47952-47952	KINGMAN
47490-47490	BLOOMINGTON	47598-47598	WINSLOW	47856-47856	JUDSON	47954-47954	LADOGA
47501-47501	WASHINGTON	47601-47601	BOONVILLE	47857-47857	KNIGHTSVILLE	47955-47955	LINDEN
47512-47512	BICKNELL	47610-47610	CHANDLER	47858-47858	LEWIS	47957-47957	MEDARYVILLE
47513-47513	BIRDSEYE	47611-47611	CHRISNEY	47859-47859	MARSHALL	47958-47958	MELLOTT
47514-47514	BRANCHVILLE	47612-47612	CYNTHIANA	47860-47860	MECCA	47959-47959	MONON
47515-47515	BRISTOW	47613-47613	ELBERFELD	47861-47861	MEROM	47960-47960	MONTICELLO
47516-47516	BRUCEVILLE	47614-47614	FOLSOMVILLE	47862-47862	MONTEZUMA	47962-47962	MONTMORENCI
47519-47519	CANNELBURG	47615-47615	GRANDVIEW	47863-47863	NEW GOSHEN	47963-47963	MOROCCO
47520-47520	CANNELTON	47616-47616	GRIFFIN	47864-47864	NEW LEBANON	47964-47964	MOUNT AYR
47521-47521	CELESTINE	47617-47617	HATFIELD	47865-47865	PAXTON	47965-47965	NEW MARKET
47522-47522	CRANE	47618-47618	INGLEFIELD	47866-47866	PIMENTO	47966-47966	NEWPORT
47523-47523	DALE	47619-47619	LYNNVILLE	47868-47868	POLAND	47967-47967	NEW RICHMOND
47524-47524	DECKER	47620-47620	MOUNT VERNON	47869-47869	PRAIRIE CREEK	47968-47968	NEW ROSS
47525-47525	DERBY	47629-47630	NEWBURGH	47870-47870	PRAIRIETON	47969-47969	NEWTOWN
47527-47527	DUBOIS	47631-47631	NEW HARMONY	47871-47871	RILEY	47970-47970	OTTERBEIN
47528-47528	EDWARDSPORT	47633-47633	POSEYVILLE	47872-47872	ROCKVILLE	47971-47971	OXFORD
47529-47529	ELNORA	47634-47634	RICHLAND	47874-47874	ROSEDALE	47974-47974	PERRYSVILLE
47531-47531	EVANSTON	47635-47635	ROCKPORT	47875-47875	SAINT BERNICE	47975-47975	PINE VILLAGE
47532-47532	FERDINAND	47637-47637	TENNYSON	47876-47876	SAINT MARY OF THE	47976-47976	EARL PARK
47535-47535	FREELANDVILLE	47638-47638	WADESVILLE		WOODS	47977-47977	REMINGTON
47536-47536	FULDA	47639-47639	HAUBSTADT	47878-47878	SEELYVILLE	47978-47978	RENSSELAER
47537-47537	GENTRYVILLE	47640-47640	HAZLETON	47879-47879	SHELBURN	47980-47980	REYNOLDS
47541-47541	HOLLAND	47647-47647	BUCKSKIN	47880-47880	SHEPARDSVILLE	47981-47981	ROMNEY
47542-47542	HUNTINGBURG	47648-47648	FORT BRANCH	47881-47881	STAUNTON	47982-47982	STATE LINE
47545-47545	IRELAND	47649-47649	FRANCISCO	47882-47882	SULLIVAN	47983-47983	STOCKWELL
47546-47546	JASPER	47654-47654	MACKEY	47884-47884	UNIVERSAL	47984-47984	TALBOT
47550-47550	LAMAR	47660-47660	OAKLAND CITY	47885-47885	WEST TERRE HAUTE	47986-47986	TEMPLETON
47551-47551	LEOPOLD	47665-47665	OWENSVILLE	47901-47905	LAFAYETTE	47987-47987	VEEDERSBURG
47552-47552	LINCOLN CITY	47666-47666	PATOKA	47906-47907	WEST LAFAYETTE	47988-47988	WALLACE
47553-47553	LOOGOOTEE	47670-47671	PRINCETON	47916-47916	ALAMO	47989-47989	WAVELAND
47556-47556	MARIAH HILL	47683-47683	SOMERVILLE	47917-47917	AMBIA	47990-47990	WAYNETOWN
47557-47557	MONROE CITY	47701-47750	EVANSVILLE	47918-47918	ATTICA	47991-47991	WEST LEBANON
47558-47558	MONTGOMERY	47801-47814	TERRE HAUTE	47920-47920	BATTLE GROUND	47992-47992	WESTPOINT
47561-47561	OAKTOWN	47830-47830	BELLMORE	47921-47921	BOSWELL	47993-47993	WILLIAMSPORT
47562-47562	ODON	47831-47831	BLANFORD	47922-47922	BROOK	47994-47994	WINGATE
47564-47564	OTWELL	47832-47832	BLOOMINGDALE	47923-47923	BROOKSTON	47995-47995	WOLCOTT
47567-47567	PETERSBURG	47833-47833	BOWLING GREEN	47924-47924	BUCK CREEK	47996-47996	WEST LAFAYETTE
47568-47568	PLAINVILLE	47834-47834	BRAZIL	47925-47925	BUFFALO	47997-47997	YEOMAN
47573-47573	RAGSDALE	47836-47836	BRIDGETON	47926-47926	BURNETTSVILLE		

General Help Numbers:

Governor's Office
State Capitol Bldg   515-281-5211
Des Moines, IA 50319   Fax 515-281-6611
http://www.state.ia.us/governor   8AM-4:30PM

Attorney General's Office
Hoover Bldg   515-281-5164
1305 E Walnut St, 2nd fl   Fax 515-281-4209
Des Moines, IA 50319   8AM-4:30PM
http://www.state.ia.us/government/ag

State Court Administrator
State Capitol   515-281-5241
Des Moines, IA 50319   Fax 515-242-0014
http://www.judicial.state.ia.us/courtadmin 8AM-4:30PM

State Archives
Library/Archives   515-281-5111
600 E. Locust   Fax 515-282-0502
Des Moines, IA 50319-0290   9AM-4:30PM TU-SA
http://www.iowahistory.org   & M (June-Aug)

State Specifics:

Capital:	Des Moines
	Polk County
Time Zone:	CST
Number of Counties:	99
Population:	2,926,324
Web Site:	www.state.ia.us

State Agencies

Criminal Records

Division of Criminal Investigations, Bureau of Identification, Wallace State Office Bldg, Des Moines, IA 50319; 515-281-4776, 515-281-7996, 515-242-6297 (Fax), 8AM-4:30PM.

http://www.state.ia.us/government/dps/dci/crimhist.htm

Note: The Iowa Sex Offender Registry can be searched at http://www.state.ia.us/government/dps/dci/isor.

Indexing & Storage: Records are available until the person is 80 years old or passes away, then records are deleted. There is a computerized index going back to 1935.

Searching: A signed release or waiver is not required, but if not included the reports will not show any arrest over 18 months old without a disposition. If there is no disposition within 4 years of the arrest, the record is expunged. Include the following in your request-date of birth, sex, Social Security Number. Be sure to give the full name. Request Form A is required for each surname. This form can be obtained from the web site, by fax, mail, or in person.

Access by: mail, fax, in person.

Fee & Payment: The fee for a record search is $13.00 per surname checked. If married and maiden names are checked, the fee would be $26.00. Iowa law requires employers to pay the fee for potential employees' record checks. Fee payee: Iowa Division of Criminal Investigation. Payment is required unless pre-arranged billing has been arranged. Ongoing requesters can set up an account with a $500 deposit. Personal checks accepted. Credit cards accepted: MasterCard, Visa.

Mail search: Turnaround time: 1 to 2 days. No self addressed stamped envelope is required.

Fax search: Only those requesters who have opened a pre-paid account may fax.

Expedited service: Expedited service is available for fax searches. Account is required. Turnaround time: same day if possible.

Corporation Records
Limited Liability Company Records
Fictitious Name
Limited Partnership Records
Trademarks/Servicemarks

Secretary of State, Corporation Division, 2nd Floor, Hoover Bldg, Des Moines, IA 50319; 515-281-5204, 515-242-5953 (Fax), 8AM-4:30PM.

http://www.sos.state.ia.us

Indexing & Storage: Records are available from the late 1800s. New records are available for inquiry immediately. Records are indexed on microfilm, inhouse computer, on-line.

Searching: Include the following in your request-full name of business, specific records that you need copies of. In addition to the articles of incorporation, the following information is released: Annual/Biennial Reports, Officers, Directors, DBAs, Prior (merged) names, Inactive and Reserved names.

Access by: mail, phone, fax, in person, online.

Fee & Payment: Copies are $1.00 each. Fee payee: Secretary of State. Prepayment required. A charge account may be established for ongoing requesters. Call 515-281-5204 for more details. Personal checks accepted. Credit cards accepted: MasterCard, Visa.

Mail search: Turnaround time: 2 to 3 days. A self addressed stamped envelope is requested. No fee for mail request.

Phone search: No fee for telephone request. You are restricted to 3 requests per call.

Fax search: Copies cost $1.00 per page, plus $1.00 for each page that is faxed. Turnaround time: 2 days.

In person search: No fee for request.

Online search: The state offers the DataShare On-line System. Fees are $175.00 per year plus $.30 per minute. The system is open 5 AM to 8 PM daily. All records are available, including UCCs. Call 515-281-5204 and ask for Cheryl Allen for more information. Another online option is via the Internet. Access to information is free; however, the data is not as current as the DataShare System.

Other access: The state will sell the records in database format. Call the number listed above and ask for Karen Ubaldo for more information.

Uniform Commercial Code
Federal Tax Liens

UCC Division, Secretary of State, Hoover Bldg, 2nd Floor, Des Moines, IA 50319; 515-281-5204, 515-242-5953 (Other Fax Line), 515-242-6556 (Fax), 8AM-4:30PM.

http://www.sos.state.ia.us/business/services.html

Indexing & Storage: Records are available from 1966 and are computerized. All current records are on optical disk. It takes 1 to 3 days before new records are available for inquiry.

Searching: Use search request form UCC-11. Specify if you also want federal tax liens and include another search fee. Federal tax liens on individuals and all state tax liens are filed at the county level. Include the following in your request-debtor name. Copies of filings may be requested at time of search, but do not ask for copies with your initial request unless you have a charge account.

Access by: mail, phone, fax, in person, online.

Fee & Payment: The fee is $5.00 per debtor name, $6.00 for federal liens. Copies are $1.00 per page. Fee payee: Secretary of State. Prepayment required. Personal checks accepted. Credit cards accepted: MasterCard, Visa.

Mail search: Turnaround time: 1 to 2 days. A self addressed stamped envelope is requested.

Phone search: A telephone search is available with a prepaid or charge account, or with credit card.

Fax search: Turnaround time usually same day, fee is $1.00 per page.

Online search: All information is available online at www.sos.state.ia.us/uccweb. There is no fee.

State Tax Liens
Records not maintained by a state level agency.

Note: Records are found at the county recorder's offices.

Sales Tax Registrations

Department of Revenue, Taxpayer Services Division, Hoover State Office Bldg, Des Moines, IA 50306-0465; 515-281-3114, 515-242-6487 (Fax), 8AM-4PM.

http://www.state.ia.us/tax

Indexing & Storage: Records are available for 5 years. Records are indexed on computer, microfiche.

Searching: This agency will provide any information found on the face of the Tax Permit-business name, business address, and tax permit number. Information not released includes telephone numbers, tax liabilities, taxes collected, officers, federal ID#s, etc. Include the following in your request-business name. They will also search by tax permit number.

Access by: mail, phone, in person.

Fee & Payment: There is no search fee; however, there is a $5.00 copy fee per document. Fee payee: Treasurer State of Iowa. Prepayment required. Personal checks accepted. No credit cards accepted.

Mail search: Turnaround time: 7 to 10 days. No self addressed stamped envelope is required.

Phone search: Limited information is available by phone.

Other access: The agency will provide the database on lists, fees vary from $20 to $45.

Birth Certificates

Iowa Department of Public Health, Bureau of Vital Records, 321 E 12th St, Lucas Bldg, Des Moines,

IA 50319-0075; 515-281-4944, 515-281-5871 (Message Recording), 7AM-4:45PM.

http://www.idph.state.ia.us

Note: All vital records are open for inspection at the county level, usually for a $10.00 fee.

Indexing & Storage: Records are available from 1880 to present. It takes 30 days to 6 weeks before new records are available for inquiry. Records are indexed on microfiche, inhouse computer.

Searching: Adoption records are not released. Include the following in your request-full name, names of parents, mother's maiden name, date of birth, place of birth, relationship to person of record, reason for information request. Must have copy of a photo ID (mail) or a photo ID (in person) to search.

Access by: mail, phone, in person.

Fee & Payment: The search fee is $10.00, There is an additional $5.00 fee to use a credit card. For records 1880 to 1915, a $10.00 per year fee is charged. Fee payee: Iowa Department of Public Health. Prepayment required. Personal checks accepted. Credit cards accepted: MasterCard, Visa, AmEx, Discover.

Mail search: Turnaround time: within 1 month.

Phone search: Records are available by phone.

In person search: Same day service is not available. Turnaround time is 48 hours.

Expedited service: Expedited mail service is available for phone searches. Add $11.00 per package. Must use a credit card which is an extra $5.00. Normal turnaround time is 10-14 days.

Death Records

Iowa Department of Public Health, Vital Records, 321 E 12th St, Lucas Bldg, Des Moines, IA 50319-0075; 515-281-4944, 515-281-5871 (Message Recording), 7AM-4:45PM.

http://www.idph.state.ia.us

Indexing & Storage: Records are available from 1880 to present. From 1880 to 1895 there is no index. It takes up to 60 days before new records are available for inquiry. Records are indexed on microfiche, inhouse computer.

Searching: Include the following in your request-full name, date of death, place of death, relationship to person of record, reason for information request. Must have a copy of a photo ID (mail) or a photo ID (in person) to search.

Access by: mail, phone, in person.

Fee & Payment: The search fee is $10.00 for each index searched. There is an additional $5.00 fee when using a credit card. Fee payee: Iowa Department of Public Health. Prepayment required. Personal checks accepted. Credit cards accepted: MasterCard, Visa, AmEx, Discover.

Mail search: Turnaround time: within 1 month. A self addressed stamped envelope is requested.

Phone search: Records are available by phone.

In person search: Same day service in not available. Turnaround time is 48 hours.

Expedited service: Expedited mail service is available phone searches. Add fee for express delivery. Also, be sure to include the extra credit card fee. Turnaround time is 7-10 days.

Marriage Certificates

Iowa Department of Public Health, Vital Records, 321 E 12th St, Lucas Bldg, Des Moines, IA 50319-0075; 515-281-4944, 515-281-5871 (Message Recording), 7AM-4:45PM.

http://www.idph.state.ia.us

Indexing & Storage: Records are available from 1880. Records from 1880 to 1915 have to be searched by year. 1916 forward are indexed. New records are available for inquiry immediately. Records are indexed on microfiche, inhouse computer.

Searching: Include the following in your request-names of husband and wife, date of marriage, place or county of marriage.

Access by: mail, phone, in person.

Fee & Payment: The search fee is $10.00 per index searched. There is an additional $5.00 fee when using a credit card. Fee payee: Iowa Department of Public Health. Prepayment required. Personal checks accepted. Credit cards accepted: MasterCard, Visa, AmEx, Discover.

Mail search: Turnaround time: within 1 month. A self addressed stamped envelope is requested.

Phone search: Records are available by phone.

In person search: Same day service is not available. Turnaround time is 48 hours.

Expedited service: Expedited mail service is available for phone searches. Add fee for express delivery. Also, there is an additional $5.00 for use of credit card. Turnaround time is 7-10 days.

Divorce Records

Records not maintained by a state level agency.

Note: Divorce records are found at the county court issuing the decree. In general records are available from 1880.

Workers' Compensation Records

Iowa Workforce Development, Division of Workers' Compensation, 1000 E Grand Ave, Des Moines, IA 50319; 515-281-5387, 515-281-6501 (Fax), 8AM-4:30PM.

http://www.state.ia.us/iwd/wc

Note: Regular, ongoing requesters may apply for charge accounts.

Indexing & Storage: Records are available from 1985 to present. It takes 2 weeks before new records are available for inquiry.

Searching: Include the following in your request-claimant name, Social Security Number, place of employment at time of accident. Older records may take as long as 6 weeks to research.

Access by: mail, phone, fax, in person.

Fee & Payment: There is no search fee, copies are $.50 per page. Fee payee: Workers' Compensation. Prepayment required. Personal checks accepted. No credit cards accepted.

Mail search: Turnaround time: 3 to 5 days. A self addressed stamped envelope is requested.

Phone search: No fee for telephone request. They will let you know if a record exists. Limit is 4 requests per day. Callers are required to provide their name, company, and SSN or FEIN

(whichever applicable). These are permanently recorded.

Fax search: Response to fax requests is made by mail.

In person search: Files are available for personal viewing only if requested in advance.

Other access: This agency sells its entire database.

Driver Records

Department of Transportation, Driver Service Records Section, PO Box 9204, Des Moines, IA 50306-9204 (Courier: Park Fair Mall, 100 Euclid, Des Moines, IA 50306); 515-244-9124, 515-237-3152 (Fax), 8AM-4:30PM.

http://www.dot.state.ia.us/mvd/ovs/index.htm

Note: Copies of tickets can be requested from this address for $.50 per copy.

Indexing & Storage: Records are available for 5 to 7 years for moving violations; 12 years for DWIs; 5 to 7 years after closed for suspensions. The driver's address is shown on the record. Accidents are listed, but fault is not shown. It takes 2 to 3 days before new records are available for inquiry.

Searching: Casual requesters may not obtain personal information on the record without consent of the subject. Include the following in your request-full name, driver's license number, date of birth. County sheriffs in Iowa are authorized to furnish copies of driving records, but not all do. There are DOT "Super Stations" in Cedar Rapids, Council Bluff, Davenport, and Sioux City that offer a public access terminal.

Access by: mail, in person.

Fee & Payment: The fee for certified mail-in or walk-in requests and tape-to-tape records is $5.50 per record. There is no charge for a no record found. Fee payee: Treasurer, State of Iowa. Prepayment required. Personal checks accepted. No credit cards accepted.

Mail search: Turnaround time: 4 to 7 days. An account can be established for on-going requesters.No self addressed stamped envelope is required.

In person search: Iowa permits walk-in requesters to view driving records at a terminal. The fee for an on-screen look-up is $1.00 per record for the first 5 records viewed and $2.00 for each additional record viewed. These prints are not considered certified.

Other access: Iowa offers magnetic tape processing for high volume users. Iowa will sell the master data file, without driver history information, as well as a suspension/revocation file. Call Carol Padgett at 515-237-3146 for more information.

Vehicle Ownership
Vehicle Identification

Department of Transportation, Office of Vehicle Services, PO Box 9278, Des Moines, IA 50306-9278 (Courier: Park Fair Mall, 100 Euclid, Des Moines, IA 50306); 515-237-3110, 515-237-3049, 515-237-3181 (Fax), 8AM-4:30PM.

http://www.dot.state.ia.us/mvd/ovs/index.htm

Note: Vehicle lien information is not maintained by this department.

Indexing & Storage: Records are available from 1968-present for registration and title. Title records are indexed on computer from 1986-present.

Searching: Vehicle registration information is released to casual requesters, but personal information not given without consent. The state is in compliance with DPPA. Plate searches will release only the vehicle information.

Access by: mail, phone, fax, in person.

Fee & Payment: Fees: $.50 per certified record; photocopy of record is $.10 per copy; record search-$2.70 per quarter hour or fraction thereof. Fee payee: Iowa Department of Transportation. Prepayment required. Personal checks accepted. No credit cards accepted.

Mail search: Turnaround time: 3 to 5 days. No self addressed stamped envelope is required.

Phone search: Records are available by phone.

Fax search: Fax searching available.

In person search: You may request information in person.

Other access: Iowa makes the entire vehicle file or selected data available for purchase. Weekly updates are also available for those purchasers. For more information, call 515-237-3110.

Accident Reports

Department of Transportation, Office of Driver Services, Park Fair Mall, 100 Euclid, Des Moines, IA 50306; 515-244-9124, 800-532-1121, 515-239-1837 (Fax), 8AM-4:30PM.

http://www.dot.state.ia.us/mvd/ods/index.htm

Indexing & Storage: Records are available for five years.

Searching: Accident reports are available only to the person involved in accident or the person's insurance company or attorney. Include the following in your request-full name, date of accident, location of accident.

Access by: mail, fax, in person.

Fee & Payment: The fee is $4.00 per officer report. Fee payee: Treasurer, State of Iowa. Prepayment required. The state allows regular, ongoing requesters to open a deposit account. Personal checks accepted. No credit cards accepted.

Mail search: Turnaround time: 2 to 3 weeks. No self addressed stamped envelope is required.

Fax search: Same criteria as mail searches.

In person search: Turnaround time for walk-in requesters is generally immediate.

Vessel Ownership
Vessel Registration

Records not maintained by a state level agency.

Note: Vessels are registered at the county level.

Legislation Records

Iowa General Assembly, Legislative Information Office, State Capitol, Des Moines, IA 50319; 515-281-5129, 8AM-4:30PM.

http://www.legis.state.ia.us

Note: For copies of older bills, it is suggested to go to a local law library.

Indexing & Storage: Records are available for the current year. Records are indexed on inhouse computer.

Searching: Include the following in your request-bill number.

Access by: mail, phone, in person, online.

Fee & Payment: There is no fee for copies of current and pending legislation. Fee payee: Treasurer, State of Iowa. Prepayment required. Personal checks accepted. No credit cards accepted.

Mail search: Turnaround time: variable. A maximum of 20 bills will be sent by mail.No self addressed stamped envelope is required.

Phone search: You may request bills by phone or receive status information.

In person search: You may request bills in person.

Online search: Access is available through the Legislative Computer Support Bureau or through their web site.

Other access: The state sells a weekly summary called the Session Brief. The fee is $10.60.

Voter Registration

Secretary of State, Voter Registration Division, Lucas State Office Building, Des Moines, IA 50319; 515-281-5762, 515-242-5953 (Fax), 8AM-4:30PM.

http://www.sos.state.ia.us

Indexing & Storage: Records are available for active records and two elections back for inactive.

Searching: The following data is not released: Social Security Numbers or bulk information or lists for commercial purposes.

Access by: phone, in person.

Fee & Payment: There is no fee for confirmation. No searching by mail.

Phone search: Will only confirm.

In person search: Records may be viewed.

Other access: Information is available, on tape, cartridge, disk or CD for political purposes only. Data can be sorted by any field on the registration file. Fees are determined by cost of production.

GED Certificates

Department of Education, GED Records, Grimes State Office Building, Des Moines, IA 50319-0146; 515-281-7308, 515-281-3636, 515-281-6544 (Fax), 8AM-5PM.

Searching: Include the following in your request-signed release, Social Security Number, date of birth. The year and city of test are also helpful.

Access by: mail, phone, fax, in person.

Fee & Payment: There is a $5.00 fee for a copy (and $3.00 for 2nd copy) of a transcript or a diploma. There is no fee for a verification. Fee payee: IA Department of Education. Prepayment required. Money orders are accepted. No personal checks accepted. No credit cards accepted.

Mail search: Turnaround time: 1 to 3 days. A self addressed stamped envelope is requested.

Phone search: Limited information is available.

Fax search: They will return verification data by fax to local or toll-free numbers.

Hunting License Information
Fishing License Information

Department of Natural Resources, Wallace Building, E 9th & Grand Ave, 4th Floor, Des Moines, IA 50319-0034; 515-281-8688, 515-281-6794 (Fax), 8:15AM-4:15PM.

http://www.state.ia.us

Indexing & Storage: Records are available for current year on computer, past years on microfiche. Records are indexed on inhouse computer.

Searching: Include the following in your request-full name, date of birth, Social Security Number. This agency only maintains records for deer (except bow & free landowners) and turkey.

Access by: mail, phone, in person.

Fee & Payment: There is no charge for a search of one record for personal use. Lists will incur a fee based on length and how search must be done. Fee payee: Iowa Department of Natural Resources. Personal checks accepted. No credit cards accepted.

Mail search: Turnaround time: 1 to 3 days. No self addressed stamped envelope is required.

Phone search: You may call for information.

In person search: You may request information in person.

Iowa State Licensing Agencies

Licenses Searchable Online

Acupuncturist #14 .... www.docboard.org/ia/find_ia.htm
Architect #10 .... www.state.ia.us/government/com/prof/search.htm
Bank #04 .... www.idob.state.ia.us
Credit Union #06 .... www.iacudiv.state.ia.us/Public/fieldofmembership/membersearch.htm
Debt Management Company #04 .... www.idob.state.ia.us/license/lic_default.htm
Delayed Deposit Service Business #04 ..... www.idob.state.ia.us/license/lic_default.htm
Engineer #10 .... www.state.ia.us/government/com/prof/search.htm
Finance Company #04 .... www.idob.state.ia.us/license/lic_default.htm
Landscape Architect #10 .... www.state.ia.us/government/com/prof/lands/lanscros.htm
Medical Doctor #14 .... www.docboard.org/ia/find_ia.htm
Money Transmitter #04 .... www.idob.state.ia.us/license/lic_default.htm
Mortgage Banker/Broker #04 .... www.idob.state.ia.us/license/lic_default.htm
Mortgage Loan Service #04 .... www.idob.state.ia.us/license/lic_default.htm
Notary Public #31 .... www.sos.state.ia.us/NotaryWeb
Optometrist #22 .... www.odfinder.org/LicSearch.asp
Osteopathic Physician #14 .... www.docboard.org/ia/find_ia.htm
Public Accountant-CPA #10 .... www.state.ia.us/government/com/prof/search.htm
Real Estate Appraiser #32 .... www.state.ia.us/government/com/prof/search.htm
Real Estate Broker/Salesperson #10 .... www.state.ia.us/government/com/prof/search.htm
Surveryor #10 .... www.state.ia.us/government/com/prof/search.htm
Trust Company #04 .... www.idob.state.ia.us/license/lic_default.htm

Licensing Quick Finder

Acupuncturist #14 515-281-5171
Adoption Investigator #18 515-281-6220
Alcoholic Beverage Retail/Wholesale/Mfg. #05
.... 515-281-7430
Amusement Ride Inspection #27 515-281-5415
Architect #10 515-281-4126
Asbestos Abatement Contractor/Worker #27 ....
.... 515-281-6175
Asbestos Inspector #27 515-281-6175
Asbestos Project Designer/Mgmt. Planner #27 ....
.... 515-281-6175
Athletic Agent #31 515-281-5204
Athletic Trainer #22 515-281-4401
Attorney #30 515-281-5911
Audiologist #22 515-281-4408
Bank #04 515-281-4014
Barber #22 515-281-4416
Boiler Inspector #27 515-281-6533
Bus Driver #34 515-237-3079
Chiropractor #22 515-281-4287
Contractor #27 515-281-6175
Controlled Substance Registrant #16 515-281-5944
Cosmetologist #22 515-281-4416
Cosmetology Instructor #22 515-281-4416
Credit Union #06 515-281-6514
Day Care #17 515-283-9106
Debt Management Company #04 515-281-4014
Delayed Deposit Service Business #4 ... 515-281-4014
Dental Hygienist #13 515-281-5157
Dentist #13 515-281-5157
Dietitian #22 515-281-6959
Drug Distributor/Wholesaler/Mfg. #16 ... 515-281-5944
Elevator Inspection #27 515-281-5415
Emergency Medical Technician-Paramedic #27 ....
.... 515-281-3239
Engineer #10 515-281-5602
Esthetician #33 515-281-4031
Excursion Boat Gambling #19 515-281-7352
Family Foster Care #17 515-283-9106
Finance Company #04 515-281-4014
First Response Paramedic #27 515-281-4958
Funeral Director #22 515-281-4287
Gambling Excursion #19 515-281-7352

Group Foster Care #17 515-283-9106
Hearing Aid Dealer #22 515-281-6959
Instructional Schools #31 515-281-5204
Instructor-Community College or Voc./Tech. School
#12 800-788-7856
Insurance Agency #07 515-281-7757
Insurance Company #07 515-281-7367
Insurance Producer #07 515-281-7757
Landfill Operator #20 515-281-8688
Landscape Architect #10 515-281-4126
Lottery Retailer #26 515-281-7900
Manicurist #33 515-281-4031
Marriage & Family Therapist #22 515-281-4422
Massage Therapist #22 515-281-6959
Medical Doctor #14 515-281-5171
Mental Health Counselor #22 515-281-4422
Money Transmitter #04 515-281-4014
Mortgage Banker #04 515-281-4014
Mortgage Broker #04 515-281-4014
Mortgage Loan Service #04 515-281-4014
Mortuary Science #22 515-281-4287
Nail Technologist #33 515-281-4031
Notary Public #31 515-281-5204
Nuclear Medicine Technologist #29 515-281-4942
Nurse #15 .... 515-281-3264 or 4826
Nurse, Advance Registered Practice #15 ....
.... 515-281-3264 or 4826
Nurse-LPN #15 .... 515-281-3264 or 4826
Nursing Home Administrator #22 515-281-4401
Occupational Therapist/Assistant #22 ... 515-281-4401
Optometrist #22 515-281-4287
Osteopathic Physician #14 515-281-5171
Pari-Mutuel Wagering Facility #19 515-281-7352
Pesticide Commercial Applicator #03 ... 515-281-5601
Pesticide Dealer/Applicator #03 515-281-5601
Pesticide Private Applicator #03 515-281-4339
Pharmacist/Pharmacist Tech/Intern#16. 515-281-5944
Pharmacy #16 515-281-5944
Physical & Occupational Therapist #22 . 515-281-4401
Physical Therapist/Assistant #22 515-281-4401
Physician Assistant #22 515-242-4408
Podiatrist #22 515-242-4422
Polygraph Examiner #25 515-281-7610

Post-Secondary School #31 515-281-5204
Private Investigator #25 515-281-7610
Private Security Guard #25 515-281-7610
Psychologist #22 515-281-4401
Public Accountant-CPA #10 515-281-4126
Racetrack Worker #19 515-281-7352
Radiation Therapist #29 515-281-4942
Radioactive Material #29 515-281-3478
Radiographer (Medical) #29 515-281-4942
Radon Measurement Specialist #29 515-281-4928
Radon Mitigation Specialist #29 515-281-4928
Real Estate Appraiser #32 515-281-7393
Real Estate Broker/Salesperson #10 ... 515-281-5910
Respiratory Therapist #22 515-281-4408
Riverboat Gambling Worker #19 515-281-7352
School Coach #12 800-788-7856
School Counselor #12 800-788-7856
School Principal/Superintendent #12 800-788-7856
Securities Agent/Broker/Dealer #07 515-281-4441
Sheep Dealer #02 515-281-8601
Shorthand Reporter #30 515-246-8076
Social Worker #22 515-281-4422
Solid Waste Incinerator Operator #20 ... 515-281-8688
Speech Pathologist/Audiologist #22 515-281-4408
Surveryor #10 515-281-5602
Tattoo Artist #22 515-242-5149
Taxi Driver #34 515-237-3079
Teacher #12 800-788-7856
Transient Merchant #31 515-281-5204
Travel Agency #31 515-281-5204
Truck Driver #34 515-237-3079
Trust Company #04 515-281-4014
Veterinarian #02 515-281-5304
Veterinary Technician #02 515-281-5304
Voting Booth #01 515-281-0145
Voting Equipment #01 515-281-0145
Waste Water Lagoon/Treatment Operator #20 ....
.... 515-281-8688
Water Distribution Operator #20 515-281-8688
Water Treatment Operator #20 515-281-8688
Well Driller #20 515-281-8688

Licensing Agency Information

#01 Attn: Sandy Steinbach, Hoover Bldg, 2nd Fl, Des Moines, IA 50319; 515-281-0145, Fax: 515-242-5953.
www.sos.state.ia.us

#02 Department of Agriculture, E 9th & Grand Ave, Wallace Bldg, 2nd Fl, Des Moines, IA 50319; 515-281-7074, Fax: 515-281-3121.

#03 Department of Agriculture, Wallace State Office Bldg, Des Moines, IA 50319; 515-281-5601, Fax: 515-242-6497.
www2.state.ia.us/agriculture/

#04 Department of Commerce, 200 E Grand Ave, Des Moines, IA 50309; 515-281-4014, Fax: 515-281-4862.
www.idob.state.ia.us
Direct web site URL to search for licensees: www.idob.state.ia.us/license/lic_default.htm. You can search online using corporate name, license name, license number or address.

#05 Department of Commerce, 1918 SE Hulsizer Ave, Ankeny, IA 50021; 515-281-7430, Fax: 515-281-7375.
www.iowaabd.com

#06 Department of Commerce, 200 E Grand Ave #370, Des Moines, IA 50309; 515-281-6514, Fax: 515-281-7595.
www.iacudiv.state.ia.us
Direct web site URL to search for licensees: www.iacudiv.state.ia.us/Public/fieldofmembership/membersearch.htm. You can search online using name, credit union #, charter #, city, zip code

#07 IA Insurance Division, 330 Maple St, Des Moines, IA 50319-0065; 515-281-5705, Fax: 515-281-3059.
www.state.ia.us/government/com/ins/agent/agent.htm

#10 Department of Commerce, 1918 SE Hulsizer Ave, Ankeny, IA 50021; 515-281-3183, Fax: 515-281-7411.
www.state.ia.us/proflic
Direct web site URL to search for licensees: www.state.ia.us/government/com/prof/lands/lanscros.htm. You can search online using name.

#12 Department of Education, Grimes State Office Bldg, Des Moines, IA 50319-0147; 515-281-5849, Fax: 515-281-7669.
www.state.ia.us/educate/programs/boee

#13 Board of Dental Examiners, 400 SW 8th St, #D, Des Moines, IA 50309-4687; 515-281-5157, Fax: 515-281-7969.
www.state.ia.us/dentalboard

#14 Department of Health, 400 SW 8th #C, Des Moines, IA 50309-4686; 515-281-5171, Fax: 515-242-5908.
www.docboard.org/ia/ia_home.htm   There   is automated phone system for verification. Call 515-281-5171. There is also direct access to their database   (for   a   fee)   at www.info.state.ia.us/sing/medicalmain.htm.

#15 Department of Health, 1223 E Court Ave, Des Moines, IA 50319; 515-281-3255, Fax: 515-281-4825.
www.state.ia.us/government/nursing/
Direct web site URL to search for licensees: www.state.ia.us/government/nursing/. You can search online using name. IVR telephone verifications available at 515-281-3255

#16 Department of Health, 1209 E Court Ave, Executive Hills West, Des Moines, IA 50319-0187; 515-281-5944, Fax: 515-281-4609.

#17 Department of Human Services, Hoover State Office Bldg, 5th Fl, Des Moines, IA 50319-0114; 515-281-5521, Fax: 515-281-4597.
www.dhs.state.ia.us

#18 Department of Human Services, 1305 E Walnut, Des Moines, IA 50319-0114; 515-281-6220, Fax: 515-281-4597.

#19 Department of Inspections & Appeals, 717 E Court Av #B, Des Moines, IA 50309; 515-281-7352, Fax: 515-242-6560.
www3.state.ia.us/irgc/

#20 Department of Natural Resources, 502 E 9th St, Wallace State Office Bldg, Des Moines, IA 50319-0035; 515-281-8688, Fax: 515-281-6794.
www.state.ia.us/dnr

#22 Department of Public Health, Lucas State Office Bldg, Des Moines, IA 50319; 515-281-7074, Fax: 515-281-3121.

#25 Department of Public Safety, Wallace State Office Bldg, Des Moines, IA 50319; 515-281-7610, Fax: 515-281-8921.

#26 Department of Revenue & Finance, 2015 Grand Av, Des Moines, IA 50312; 515-281-7900, Fax: 515-281-7882.
www.ialottery.com

#27 Division of Labor, 1000 E Grand Ave, Des Moines, IA 50319-0209; 515-281-6175, Fax: 515-281-7995.
www.state.ia.us/iwd/labor/index.html

#29 Department of Public Health, 321 E 12th St, Lucas State Office Bldg, Des Moines, IA 50319-0075; 515-281-3478, Fax: 515-242-6284.

#30 Supreme Court Clerk's Office, Legal Boards, Statehouse, Des Moines, IA 50319; 515-281-5911, Fax: 515-242-6164.
www.judicial.state.ia.us/regs

#31 Office of Secretary of State, Hoover Office Bldg, 2nd Fl, Des Moines, IA 50319; 515-281-5204, Fax: 515-242-5953 or 6556.
www.sos.state.ia.us
Direct web site URL to search for licensees: www.sos.state.ia.us. You can search online using name, business, city, and language.

#32 Real Estate Commission, 1918 SE Hulsizer, Ankeny, IA 50021-3941; 515-281-7393.
www.state.ia.us/government/com/prof/realappr/index.htm
Direct web site URL to search for licensees: www.state.ia.us/government/com/prof/search.htm. You can search online using name and county.

#33 Bureau of Professional Licensure, 321 E 12th St, Lucas State Office Bldg 5th Fl, Des Moines, IA 50319-0075; 515-281-4287.

#34 Department of Transportation, 100 Euclid, Park Fair Mall, Des Moines, IA 50306-9204; 515-237-3079, Fax: 515-237-3152.
www.dot.state.ia.us/mvd/ods/

Iowa Federal Courts

The following list indicates the district and division name for each county in the state. If the bankruptcy court location is different from the district court, then the location of the bankruptcy court appears in parentheses.

County/Court Cross Reference

County	District	Division
Adair	Southern	Council Bluffs (Des Moines)
Adams	Southern	Council Bluffs (Des Moines)
Allamakee	Northern	Dubuque (Cedar Rapids)
Appanoose	Southern	Des Moines (Central)
Audubon	Southern	Council Bluffs (Des Moines)
Benton	Northern	Cedar Rapids
Black Hawk	Northern	Dubuque (Cedar Rapids)
Boone	Southern	Des Moines (Central)
Bremer	Northern	Dubuque (Cedar Rapids)
Buchanan	Northern	Dubuque (Cedar Rapids)
Buena Vista	Northern	Sioux City (Cedar Rapids)
Butler	Northern	Sioux City (Cedar Rapids)
Calhoun	Northern	Sioux City (Cedar Rapids)
Carroll	Northern	Sioux City (Cedar Rapids)
Cass	Southern	Council Bluffs (Des Moines)
Cedar	Northern	Cedar Rapids
Cerro Gordo	Northern	Cedar Rapids
Cherokee	Northern	Sioux City (Cedar Rapids)
Chickasaw	Northern	Dubuque (Cedar Rapids)
Clarke	Southern	Council Bluffs (Des Moines)
Clay	Northern	Sioux City (Cedar Rapids)
Clayton	Northern	Dubuque (Cedar Rapids)
Clinton	Southern	Council Bluffs (Des Moines)
Crawford	Northern	Sioux City (Cedar Rapids)
Dallas	Southern	Des Moines (Central)
Davis	Southern	Des Moines (Central)
Decatur	Southern	Council Bluffs (Des Moines)
Delaware	Northern	Dubuque (Cedar Rapids)
Des Moines	Southern	Des Moines (Central)
Dickinson	Northern	Sioux City (Cedar Rapids)
Dubuque	Northern	Dubuque (Cedar Rapids)
Emmet	Northern	Sioux City (Cedar Rapids)
Fayette	Northern	Dubuque (Cedar Rapids)
Floyd	Northern	Dubuque (Cedar Rapids)
Franklin	Northern	Sioux City (Cedar Rapids)
Fremont	Southern	Council Bluffs (Des Moin
Greene	Southern	Des Moines (Central)
Grundy	Northern	Cedar Rapids
Guthrie	Southern	Des Moines (Central)
Hamilton	Northern	Sioux City (Cedar Rapids)
Hancock	Northern	Sioux City (Cedar Rapids)
Hardin	Northern	Cedar Rapids
Harrison	Southern	Council Bluffs (Des Moines)
Henry	Southern	Davenport (Des Moines)
Howard	Northern	Dubuque (Cedar Rapids)
Humboldt	Northern	Sioux City (Cedar Rapids)
Ida	Northern	Sioux City (Cedar Rapids)
Iowa	Northern	Cedar Rapids
Jackson	Northern	Dubuque (Cedar Rapids)
Jasper	Southern	Des Moines (Central)
Jefferson	Southern	Des Moines (Central)
Johnson	Southern	Davenport (Des Moines)
Jones	Northern	Cedar Rapids
Keokuk	Southern	Des Moines (Central)
Kossuth	Northern	Sioux City (Cedar Rapids)
Lee	Southern	Davenport (Des Moines)
Linn	Northern	Cedar Rapids
Louisa	Southern	Davenport (Des Moines)
Lucas	Southern	Council Bluffs (Des Moines)
Lyon	Northern	Sioux City (Cedar Rapids)
Madison	Southern	Des Moines (Central)
Mahaska	Southern	Des Moines (Central)
Marion	Southern	Des Moines (Central)
Marshall	Southern	Des Moines (Central)
Mills	Southern	Council Bluffs (Des Moines)
Mitchell	Northern	Dubuque (Cedar Rapids)
Monona	Northern	Sioux City (Cedar Rapids)
Monroe	Southern	Des Moines (Central)
Montgomery	Southern	Council Bluffs (Des Moines)
Muscatine	Southern	Davenport (Des Moines)
O'Brien	Northern	Sioux City (Cedar Rapids)
Osceola	Northern	Sioux City (Cedar Rapids)
Page	Southern	Council Bluffs (Des Moines)
Palo Alto	Northern	Sioux City (Cedar Rapids)
Plymouth	Northern	Sioux City (Cedar Rapids)
Pocahontas	Northern	Sioux City (Cedar Rapids)
Polk	Southern	Des Moines (Central)
Pottawattamie	Southern	Council Bluffs (Des Moines)
Poweshiek	Southern	Des Moines (Central)
Ringgold	Southern	Council Bluffs (Des Moines)
Sac	Northern	Sioux City (Cedar Rapids)
Scott	Southern	Davenport (Des Moines)
Shelby	Southern	Council Bluffs (Des Moines)
Sioux	Northern	Sioux City (Cedar Rapids)
Story	Southern	Des Moines (Central)
Tama	Northern	Cedar Rapids
Taylor	Southern	Council Bluffs (Des Moines)
Union	Southern	Council Bluffs (Des Moines)
Van Buren	Southern	Davenport (Des Moines)
Wapello	Southern	Des Moines (Central)
Warren	Southern	Des Moines (Central)
Washington	Southern	Davenport (Des Moines)
Wayne	Southern	Council Bluffs (Des Moines)
Webster	Northern	Sioux City (Cedar Rapids)
Winnebago	Northern	Sioux City (Cedar Rapids)
Winneshiek	Northern	Dubuque (Cedar Rapids)
Woodbury	Northern	Sioux City (Cedar Rapids)
Worth	Northern	Sioux City (Cedar Rapids)
Wright	Northern	Sioux City (Cedar Rapids)

US District Court

Northern District of Iowa

Cedar Rapids Division Court Clerk, PO Box 74710, Cedar Rapids, IA 52407-4710 (Courier Address: Federal Bldg, US Courthouse, 101 1st St SE, Room 313, Cedar Rapids, IA 52401), 319-286-2300.

http://www.iand.uscourts.gov

Counties: Benton, Cedar, Cerro Gordo, Grundy, Hardin, Iowa, Jones, Linn, Tama.

Indexing/Storage: Cases are indexed by defendant and plaintiff as well as by case number. New cases are available in the index immediately after filing date. A computer index is maintained. Open records are located at this court.

Fee & Payment: The fee is $20.00 per item (one party name or case number). Payment may be made by money order, cashier check, personal check. Prepayment is required. Payee: Clerk, US District Court. Certification fee: $7.00 per document. Copy fee: $.50 per page.

Phone Search: Anything that is public record will be released over the phone, but only for one name per call.

Mail Search: A stamped self addressed envelope is not required.

In Person: In person searching is available.

PACER: Sign-up number is 800-676-5856. Access fee is $.60 per minute. Toll-free access: 888-845-4528. Local access: 319-362-3256. Case records are available back to November 1992. New records are available online after 1 day. PACER is available online at http://pacer.iand.uscourts.gov.

Dubuque Division c/o Cedar Rapids Division, PO Box 74710, Cedar Rapids, IA 52407-4710 (Courier Address: Federal Bldg, US Courthouse, 101 1st St SE, Room 313, Cedar Rapids, IA 52401), 319-286-2300.

http://www.iand.uscourts.gov

Counties: Allamakee, Black Hawk, Bremer, Buchanan, Chickasaw, Clayton, Delaware, Dubuque, Fayette, Floyd, Howard, Jackson, Mitchell, Winneshiek.

Indexing/Storage: Cases are indexed by as well as by case number. New cases are available in the index after filing date. Open records are located at the Division.

Fee & Payment: The fee is $20.00 per item (one party name or case number). Payment may be made by money order, cashier check. Business checks are not accepted. Personal checks are not accepted.

Phone Search: Searching is not available by phone.

Mail Search: A stamped self addressed envelope is not required.

In Person: In person searching is available.

PACER: Sign-up number is 800-676-5856. Access fee is $.60 per minute. Toll-free access: 888-845-4528. Local access: 319-362-3256. Case records are available back to November 1992. New records are available online after 1 day. PACER is available online at http://pacer.iand.uscourts.gov.

Sioux City Division Room 301, Federal Bldg, 320 6th St, Sioux City, IA 51101 (Courier Address: Use mail address for courier delivery), 712-233-3900.

http://www.iand.uscourts.gov

Counties: Buena Vista, Cherokee, Clay, Crawford, Dickinson, Ida, Lyon, Monona, O'Brien, Osceola, Plymouth, Sac, Sioux, Woodbury.

Indexing/Storage: Cases are indexed by defendant and plaintiff as well as by case number. New cases are available in the index immediately after filing date. A computer index is maintained. Open records are located at this court.

Fee & Payment: The fee is $20.00 per item (one party name or case number). Payment may be made by money order, cashier check, personal check. Prepayment is required. Payee: Clerk, US District Court. Certification fee: $7.00 per document. Copy fee: $.50 per page.

Phone Search: Only docket information is available by phone.

Mail Search: Always enclose a stamped self addressed envelope.

In Person: In person searching is available.

PACER: Sign-up number is 800-676-5856. Access fee is $.60 per minute. Toll-free access: 888-845-4528. Local access: 319-362-3256. Case records are available back to November 1992. New records are available online after 1 day. PACER is available online at http://pacer.iand.uscourts.gov.

US Bankruptcy Court

Northern District of Iowa

Cedar Rapids Division PO Box 74890, Cedar Rapids, IA 52407-4890 (Courier Address: 8th Floor, 425 2nd St SE, Cedar Rapids, IA 52401), 319-286-2200, Fax: 319-286-2280.

http://www.ianb.uscourts.gov

Counties: Allamakee, Benton, Black Hawk, Bremer, Buchanan, Buena Vista, Butler, Calhoun, Carroll, Cedar, Cerro Gordo, Cherokee, Chickasaw, Clay, Clayton, Crawford, Delaware, Dickinson, Dubuque, Emmet, Fayette, Floyd, Franklin, Grundy, Hamilton, Hancock, Hardin, Howard, Humboldt, Ida, Iowa, Jackson, Jones, Kossuth, Linn, Lyon, Mitchell, Monona, O'Brien, Osceola, Palo Alto, Plymouth, Pocahontas, Sac, Sioux, Tama, Webster, Winnebago, Winneshiek, Woodbury, Worth, Wright.

Indexing/Storage: Cases are indexed by debtor and creditors as well as by case number. New cases are available in the index immediately after filing date. A computer index is maintained. Open records are located at this court. District wide searches are available for information from 1988 to the present from this court. This court handles records for the Sioux City division.

Fee & Payment: The fee is $20.00 per item (one party name or case number). Payment may be made by money order, cashier check, business check, Visa or Mastercard. Personal checks are not accepted. Prepayment is required. Checks are accepted from in-state law firms only. Payee: Clerk, US Bankruptcy Court. Certification fee: $7.00 per document. Copy fee: $.50 per page. You are allowed to make your own copies. These copies cost $.25 per page.

Phone Search: Only minimal information will be released over the phone. Not all docket information will be released. An automated voice case information service (VCIS) is available.

Mail Search: Always enclose a stamped self addressed envelope.

In Person: In person searching is available.

PACER: Sign-up number is. Access fee is. Toll-free access: 800-220-5524. Local access: 319-286-2287. New records are available online after. PACER is available online at http://pacer.ianb.uscourts.gov.

US District Court

Southern District of Iowa

Council Bluffs (Western) Division PO Box 307, Council Bluffs, IA 51502 (Courier Address: Room 313, 8 S 6th St, Council Bluffs, IA 51501), 712-328-0283, Fax: 712-328-1241.

http://www.iasd.uscourts.gov

Counties: Audubon, Cass, Fremont, Harrison, Mills, Montgomery, Page, Pottawattamie, Shelby.

Indexing/Storage: Cases are indexed by defendant and plaintiff as well as by case number. New cases are available in the index immediately after filing date. A computer index is maintained. Open records are located at this court.

Fee & Payment: The fee is $20.00 per item (one party name or case number). Payment may be made by money order, cashier check, personal check. The search fee will be charged only if the clerk's staff is required to spend more than 5 minutes searching. Payee: Clerk, US District Court. Certification fee: $7.00 per document. Copy fee: $.50 per page. You are allowed to make your own copies. These copies cost $.50 per page.

Phone Search: All information available will be released over the phone.

Mail Search: Always enclose a stamped self addressed envelope.

In Person: In person searching is available.

PACER: Sign-up number is 800-676-6856. Access fee is $.60 per minute. Local access: 515-284-6475, 515-284-6478. Case records are available back to mid 1989. Records are purged every six months. New records are available online after 3 days. PACER is available online at http://pacer.iasd.uscourts.gov.

Davenport (Eastern) Division PO Box 256, Davenport, IA 52805 (Courier Address: Room 215, 131 E 4th St, Davenport, IA 52801), 563-322-3223, Fax: 563-322-2962.

http://www.iasd.uscourts.gov

Counties: Henry, Johnson, Lee, Louisa, Muscatine, Scott, Van Buren, Washington.

Indexing/Storage: Cases are indexed by defendant and plaintiff as well as by case number. New cases are available in the index 1 week after filing date. All criminal cases are handled in Des Moines Division. Civil cases are handled here. Both computer and card indexes are maintained. Open records are located at this court.

Fee & Payment: The fee is $20.00 per item (one party name or case number). Payment may be made by money order, cashier check, personal check. Will bill fees. Payee: Clerk, US District Court. Certification fee: $7.00 per document. Copy fee: $.50 per page. You are allowed to make your own copies. These copies cost $.50 per page. You are only allowed to search the index cards.

Phone Search: Docket information available by phone.

Fax Search: Fax requests are processed the same as mail searches. Will fax documents for $3.00 up to 9 pages and $5.00 if more, plus copy fees.

Mail Search: A stamped self addressed envelope is not required.

In Person: In person searching is available.

PACER: Sign-up number is 800-676-6856. Access fee is $.60 per minute. Local access: 515-284-6475, 515-284-6478. Case records are available back to mid 1989. Records are purged every six months. New records are available online after 3 days. PACER is available online at http://pacer.iasd.uscourts.gov.

Des Moines (Central) Division PO Box 9344, Des Moines, IA 50306-9344 (Courier Address: 123 E. Walnut St., Rm. 300, Des Moines, IA 50306-9344), 515-284-6248, Fax: 515-284-6418.

http://www.iasd.uscourts.gov

Counties: Adair, Adams, Appanoose, Boone, Clarke, Clinton, Dallas, Davis, Decatur, Des Moines, Greene, Guthrie, Jasper, Jefferson, Keokuk, Lucas, Madison, Mahaska, Marion, Marshall, Monroe, Polk, Poweshiek, Ringgold, Story, Taylor, Union, Wapello, Warren, Wayne.

Indexing/Storage: Cases are indexed by defendant and plaintiff as well as by case number. New cases are available in the index immediately after filing date. A computer index is maintained. Records are stored by date filed and closed. Open records are located at this court.

Fee & Payment: The fee is $20.00 per item (one party name or case number). Payment may be made by money order, cashier check, personal check. A bill can be sent by mail. Payee: Clerk, US District Court. Certification fee: $7.00 per document. Copy fee: $.50 per page.

Phone Search: Searching is not available by phone. Requests for searches must be in writing.

Fax Search: Fax search handled same as mail. Will fax documents for $3.00 up to 9 pages and $5.00 if more, plus copy fee.

Mail Search: A stamped self addressed envelope is not required.

In Person: In person searching is available.

PACER: Sign-up number is 800-676-6856. Access fee is $.60 per minute. Local access: 515-284-6475, 515-284-6478. Case records are available back to mid 1989. Records are purged every six months. New records are available online after 3 days. PACER is available online at http://pacer.iasd.uscourts.gov.

US Bankruptcy Court
Southern District of Iowa

Des Moines Division PO Box 9264, Des Moines, IA 50306-9264 (Courier Address: 300 US Courthouse Annex, 110 East Court Ave, Des Moines, IA 50309), 515-284-6230, Fax: 515-284-6404.

http://www.iasb.uscourts.gov

Counties: Adair, Adams, Appanoose, Audubon, Boone, Cass, Clarke, Clinton, Dallas, Davis, Decatur, Des Moines, Fremont, Greene, Guthrie, Harrison, Henry, Jasper, Jefferson, Johnson, Keokuk, Lee, Louisa, Lucas, Madison, Mahaska, Marion, Marshall, Mills, Monroe,Montgomery, Muscatine, Page, Polk, Pottawattamie, Poweshiek, Ringgold, Scott, Shelby, Story, Taylor, Union, Van Buren, Wapello, Warren, Washington, Wayne.

Indexing/Storage: Cases are indexed by debtor as well as by case number. New cases are available in the index immediately after filing date. A computer index is maintained. Open records are located at this court.

Fee & Payment: The fee is $20.00 per item (one party name or case number). Payment may be made by money order, cashier check, business check. Personal checks are not accepted. Copy requests must be directed to CopyCat Photocopy Center at 515-288-6843. Payee: CopyCat Photocopy Center. Certification fee: $7.00 per document. Copy fee: $.50 per page.

Phone Search: The information released over the phone is: name, case number, chapter date file, assets, attorney, attorney's telephone number, trustee, judge, status and discharge. Information is available from June 1987. An automated voice case information service (VCIS) is available. Call VCIS at 800-597-5917 or 515-284-6427.

Mail Search: Always enclose a stamped self addressed envelope.

In Person: In person searching is available.

PACER: Sign-up number is 800-676-6856. Access fee is $.60 per minute. Toll-free access: 800-597-5917. Local access: 515-284-6466. Case records are available back to June 1987. Records are purged every six months. New civil records are available online after 1 day.

Other Online Access: Search records on the Internet using RACER at https://racer.iasb.uscourts.gov/perl/bkplog.html. Access fee is 7 cents per page.

Iowa County Courts

Court	Jurisdiction	No. of Courts	How Organized
District Courts*	General	100	8 Districts

* Profiled in this Sourcebook.

Court	CIVIL								
	Tort	Contract	Real Estate	Min. Claim	Max. Claim	Small Claims	Estate	Eviction	Domestic Relations
District Courts*	X	X	X	$0	No Max	$4000	X	X	X

Court	CRIMINAL				
	Felony	Misdemeanor	DWI/DUI	Preliminary Hearing	Juvenile
District Courts*	X	X	X	X	X

ADMINISTRATION
State Court Administrator, State Capitol, Des Moines, IA, 50319; 515-281-5241, Fax: 515-242-0014. www.judicial.state.ia.us

COURT STRUCTURE
The District Court is the court of general jurisdiction. Effective 7/1/95, the Small Claims limit increased to $4000 from $3000.

Vital records were moved from courts to the County Recorder's office in each county.

ONLINE ACCESS
There is a statewide online computer system called the Iowa Court Information System (ICIS), which is for internal use only. There is no public access system.

ADDITIONAL INFORMATION
In most courts, the Certification Fee is $10.00 plus copy fee. Copy Fee is $.50 per page. Most courts do not do searches and recommend either in person searches or use of a record retriever.

Courts that accept written search requests usually require an SASE.

Most courts have a public access terminal for access to that court's records.

Adair County

5th District Court PO Box L, Greenfield, IA 50849; 641-743-2445; Fax: 641-743-2974. Hours: 8AM-4:30PM (CST). *Felony, Misdemeanor, Civil, Eviction, Small Claims, Probate.*

Civil Records: Access: In person only. Visitors must perform in person searches for themselves. No search fee. Required to search: name, years to search. Civil cases indexed by defendant, plaintiff. Civil records on docket books from late 1800s.
Criminal Records: Access: In person only. Visitors must perform in person searches for themselves. No search fee. Required to search: name, years to search, DOB, signed release; also helpful: SSN. Criminal records on docket books from late 1800s.
General Information: Public Access terminal is available. No juvenile, sealed, dissolution of marriage, mental health domestic abuse or deferred records released. Copy fee: $.50 per page. Certification fee: $10.00. Fee payee: Clerk of Court. Personal checks accepted. Prepayment is required.

Adams County

5th District Court Courthouse, PO Box 484, Corning, IA 50841; 641-322-4711; Fax: 641-322-4523. Hours: 8AM-4:30PM (CST). *Felony, Misdemeanor, Civil, Eviction, Small Claims, Probate.*

Civil Records: Access: In person only. Visitors must perform in person searches for themselves. No search fee. Required to search: name, years to search. Civil cases indexed by defendant, plaintiff. Civil records on docket books from late 1800s.

Criminal Records: Access: In person only. Visitors must perform in person searches for themselves. No search fee. Required to search: name, years to search, signed release. Criminal records on docket books from late 1800s.
General Information: Public Access terminal is available. No juvenile, sealed, dissolution of marriage, mental health, domestic abuse or deferred records released. Copy fee: $.50 per page. Certification fee: $10.00. Fee payee: Clerk of Court. Personal checks accepted. Prepayment is required.

Allamakee County

1st District Court PO Box 248, Waukon, IA 52172; 563-568-6351. Hours: 8AM-4:30PM *Felony, Misdemeanor, Civil, Eviction, Small Claims, Probate.*

Civil Records: Access: In person only. Visitors must perform in person searches for themselves. No search fee. Required to search: name, years to search. Civil cases indexed by defendant, plaintiff. All judgments on computer back to 4/1997; on index books back to 1880, probate back to 1852.
Criminal Records: Access: In person only. Visitors must perform in person searches for themselves. No search fee. Required to search: name, years to search, signed release. Criminal records on docket books from 1800s; on computer back to 4/1997.
General Information: Public Access terminal is available. No juvenile, adoption, sealed, dissolution of marriage, mental health, domestic abuse or deferred records released. Copy fee: $.50 per page. Certification fee: $10.00. Fee payee: Clerk of Court. Personal checks accepted. Prepayment is required.

Appanoose County

8th District Court PO Box 400, Centerville, IA 52544; 641-856-6101; Fax: 641-856-2282. Hours: 8AM-4:30PM (CST). *Felony, Misdemeanor, Civil, Eviction, Small Claims, Probate.*

Civil Records: Access: In person only. Visitors must perform in person searches for themselves. No search fee. Required to search: name, years to search. Civil cases indexed by defendant, plaintiff. Civil records on docket books from 1847.
Criminal Records: Access: In person only. Visitors must perform in person searches for themselves. No search fee. Required to search: name, years to search, signed release. Criminal records on docket books from 1847.
General Information: Public Access terminal is available. No juvenile, sealed, dissolution of marriage, mental health, domestic abuse or deferred records released. Copy fee: $.25 per page. Certification fee: $10.00. Fee payee: Clerk of Court. Personal checks accepted. Prepayment is required.

Audubon County

4th District Court 318 Leroy St #6, Audubon, IA 50025; 712-563-4275; Fax: 712-563-4276. Hours: 8AM-4:30PM (CST). *Felony, Misdemeanor, Civil, Eviction, Small Claims, Probate.*

Civil Records: Access: In person only. Visitors must perform in person searches for themselves. No search fee. Required to search: name, years to search; also helpful: address. Civil cases indexed by defendant, plaintiff. Civil records on docket books from 1930s, computerized since 1996.

Criminal Records: Access: In person only. Visitors must perform in person searches for themselves. No search fee. Required to search: name, years to search; also helpful: DOB, SSN, address. Criminal records on docket books from late 1800s.

General Information:. No juvenile, sealed, dissolution of marriage, mental health, domestic abuse or deferred records released. Copy fee: $.50 per page. Certification fee: $10.00. Fee payee: Clerk of Court. Prepayment is required.

Benton County

6th District Court PO Box 719, Vinton, IA 52349; 319-472-2766; Fax: 319-472-2747. Hours: 8AM-4:30PM (CST). *Felony, Misdemeanor, Civil, Eviction, Small Claims, Probate.*

Civil Records: Access: In person only. Visitors must perform in person searches for themselves. No search fee. Required to search: name, years to search. Civil cases indexed by defendant, plaintiff. Civil records on original record books from 1800s, index is on computer since 06/95.

Criminal Records: Access: In person only. Visitors must perform in person searches for themselves. No search fee. Required to search: name, years to search. Criminal records on original record books from 1800s, index is on computer since 06/95.

General Information: Public Access terminal is available. No juvenile, sealed, dissolution of marriage, mental health, domestic abuse or deferred records released. Copy fee: $.25 per page. Certification fee: $10.00. Fee payee: Clerk of Court. Personal checks accepted. Prepayment is required.

Black Hawk County

1st District Court 316 E 5th St, Waterloo, IA 50703; 319-833-3331. Hours: 8AM-4:30PM *Felony, Misdemeanor, Civil, Eviction, Small Claims, Probate.*

Civil Records: Access: In person only. Visitors must perform in person searches for themselves. No search fee. Required to search: name, years to search. Civil cases indexed by defendant, plaintiff. Civil records on computer from 1992, docket books from early 1900s.

Criminal Records: Access: In person only. Visitors must perform in person searches for themselves. No search fee. Required to search: name, years to search; also helpful: DOB, SSN. Criminal records on computer from 1992, docket books from early 1900s.

General Information: Public Access terminal is available. No juvenile, sealed, dissolution of marriage, mental health, domestic abuse or deferred records released. Copy fee: $.50 per page. Certification fee: $10.00. Fee payee: District Court. Personal checks accepted. Prepayment is required.

Boone County

2nd District Court 201 State St, Boone, IA 50036; 515-433-0561; Fax: 515-433-0563. Hours: 8AM-4:30PM (CST). *Felony, Misdemeanor, Civil, Eviction, Small Claims, Probate.*

Civil Records: Access: In person only. Visitors must perform in person searches for themselves. No search fee. Required to search: name, years to search. Civil cases indexed by defendant, plaintiff. Civil records on docket books from 1890s; computerized records go back to 1996.

Criminal Records: Access: In person only. Visitors must perform in person searches for themselves. No search fee. Required to search: name, years to search, offense, date of offense. Criminal records on docket books from 1890s; computerized records back to 1996.

General Information: Public Access terminal is available. No juvenile, sealed, dissolution of marriage, mental health, domestic abuse or deferred

released. Copy fee: $.50 per page. Certification fee: $10.00. Fee payee: Clerk of Court. Personal checks accepted. Prepayment is required.

Bremer County

2nd District Court PO Box 328, Waverly, IA 50677; 319-352-5661; Fax: 319-352-1054. Hours: 8AM-4:30PM (CST). *Felony, Misdemeanor, Civil, Eviction, Small Claims, Probate.*

Note: Public access terminal has records back to 1996 only.

Civil Records: Access: In person only. Visitors must perform in person searches for themselves. No search fee. Required to search: name, years to search. Civil cases indexed by defendant, plaintiff. Civil records on computer since 07/96; prior records on docket books from 1880s.

Criminal Records: Access: In person only. Visitors must perform in person searches for themselves. No search fee. Required to search: name, years to search. Criminal records on computer since 07/96; prior records on docket books from 1800s.

General Information: Public Access terminal is available. No juvenile, sealed, dissolution of marriage, mental health, domestic abuse or deferred records released. Copy fee: $.50 per page. Certification fee: $10.00. Fee payee: Clerk of Court. Personal checks accepted. Credit cards accepted: Visa, MasterCard. Prepayment is required.

Buchanan County

1st District Court PO Box 259, Independence, IA 50644; 319-334-2196; Fax: 319-334-7455. Hours: 8AM-4:30PM (CST). *Felony, Misdemeanor, Civil, Eviction, Small Claims, Probate.*

Civil Records: Access: Mail, in person. Both court and visitors may perform in person searches. No search fee. Required to search: name, years to search. Civil cases indexed by defendant, plaintiff. Civil records on docket books from 1900s.

Criminal Records: Access: Mail, in person. Both court and visitors may perform in person searches. No search fee. Required to search: name, years to search. Criminal records on docket books from 1900s.

General Information:. No juvenile, sealed, dissolution of marriage, mental health, domestic abuse or deferred records released. SASE required. Turnaround time 2 days. Copy fee: $.50 per page. Certification fee: $10.00. Fee payee: Clerk of Court. Personal checks accepted. Credit cards accepted: Visa, MasterCard. Prepayment is required.

Buena Vista County

3rd District Court PO Box 1186, Storm Lake, IA 50588; 712-749-2546; Fax: 712-749-2700. Hours: 8AM-4:30PM (CST). *Felony, Misdemeanor, Civil, Eviction, Small Claims, Probate.*

Civil Records: Access: In person only. Visitors must perform in person searches for themselves. No search fee. Required to search: name, years to search. Civil cases indexed by defendant, plaintiff. Civil records on index cards from early 1900s.

Criminal Records: Access: In person only. Visitors must perform in person searches for themselves. No search fee. Required to search: name, years to search. Criminal records on index cards from early 1900s; computerized records go back to 1994.

General Information: Public Access terminal is available. No juvenile, sealed, dissolution of marriage, mental health, domestic abuse or deferred records released. Copy fee: $.50 per page. Certification fee: $10.00 per document. Fee payee: Clerk of Court. Personal checks accepted. Prepayment is required.

Butler County

2nd District Court PO Box 307, Allison, IA 50602; 319-267-2487; Fax: 319-267-2488. Hours: 8AM-4:30PM (CST). *Felony, Misdemeanor, Civil, Eviction, Small Claims, Probate.*

Civil Records: Access: In person only. Visitors must perform in person searches for themselves. No search fee. Required to search: name, years to search. Civil cases indexed by defendant, plaintiff. Civil records on docket books from 1800s.

Criminal Records: Access: In person only. Visitors must perform in person searches for themselves. No search fee. Required to search: name, years to search. Criminal records on docket books from 1800s.

General Information: Public Access terminal is available. No juvenile, sealed, dissolution of marriage, mental health, domestic abuse or deferred records released. Copy fee: $1.00 for first page, $.50 each add'l. Certification fee: $10.00. Fee payee: Clerk of Court. Personal checks accepted. Prepayment is required.

Calhoun County

2nd District Court Box 273, Rockwell City, IA 50579; 712-297-8122; Fax: 712-297-5082. Hours: 8AM-4:30PM (CST). *Felony, Misdemeanor, Civil, Eviction, Small Claims, Probate.*

Civil Records: Access: In person only. Visitors must perform in person searches for themselves. No search fee. Required to search: name, years to search. Civil cases indexed by defendant, plaintiff. Civil records on docket books from 1880s, computerized since 07/97.

Criminal Records: Access: In person only. Visitors must perform in person searches for themselves. No search fee. Required to search: name, years to search, DOB, signed release; also helpful: SSN. Criminal records on docket books from 1880s, computerized since 07/97.

General Information: Public Access terminal is available. No juvenile, sealed, pending dissolution of marriage, mental health, domestic abuse or deferred records released. Fax notes: No fee to fax results. Copy fee: $.50 per page. Certification fee: $10.00. Fee payee: Clerk of the Court. Personal checks accepted. Visa, MasterCard. Prepayment is required.

Carroll County

2nd District Court PO Box 867, Carroll, IA 51401; 712-792-4327; Fax: 712-792-4328. Hours: 8AM-4:30PM (CST). *Felony, Misdemeanor, Civil, Eviction, Small Claims, Probate.*

Civil Records: Access: In person only. Visitors must perform in person searches for themselves. No search fee. Required to search: name, years to search. Civil cases indexed by defendant, plaintiff. Civil records on index books from 1800s.

Criminal Records: Access: In person only. Visitors must perform in person searches for themselves. No search fee. Required to search: name, years to search. Criminal records on computer from June, 1994, index books from 1800s.

General Information: Public Access terminal is available. No juvenile, sealed, dissolution of marriage, mental health, domestic abuse or deferred records released. Copy fee: $.50 per page. Certification fee: $10.00. Fee payee: Clerk of Court. Personal checks accepted. Credit cards accepted. Prepayment is required.

Cass County

4th District Court 5 W 7th St, Courthouse, Atlantic, IA 50022; 712-243-2105. Hours: 8AM-4:30PM (CST). *Felony, Misdemeanor, Civil, Eviction, Small Claims, Probate.*

Civil Records: Access: In person only. Visitors must perform in person searches for themselves. No search fee. Required to search: name, years to search. Civil cases indexed by defendant, plaintiff. Civil records on docket books from early 1900s; on computer back to 11/1996.

Criminal Records: Access: In person only. Visitors must perform in person searches for themselves. No search fee. Required to search: name, years to search, signed release; also helpful: DOB, SSN. Criminal records on docket books from early 1900s; on computer back to 11/1996.

General Information: Public Access terminal is available. No juvenile, sealed, dissolution of marriage, mental health, domestic abuse or deferred records released. Copy fee: $.50 per page. Certification fee: $10.00. Fee payee: Clerk of Court. Personal checks accepted. Prepayment is required.

Cedar County

7th District Court PO Box 111, Tipton, IA 52772; 563-886-3594. Hours: 8AM-4:30PM (CST). *Felony, Misdemeanor, Civil, Eviction, Small Claims, Probate.*

Civil Records: Access: Mail, in person. Both court and visitors may perform in person searches. Search fee: $10.00 per name. Required to search: name, years to search. Civil cases indexed by defendant, plaintiff. Civil records on computer since 1992; on microfiche and docket books from 1839.

Criminal Records: Access: In person only. Both court and visitors may perform in person searches. Search fee: $10.00 per name. Required to search: name, years to search; also helpful: DOB, SSN, signed release. Criminal records on computer since 1992; on microfiche and docket books from 1839.

General Information: Public Access terminal is available. No juvenile, sealed, dissolution of marriage, mental health, domestic abuse or deferred records released. SASE required. Turnaround time 1 week. Copy fee: $.50 per page. Certification fee: $10.00. Fee payee: Clerk of Court. Only cashiers checks and money orders accepted. Prepayment is required.

Cerro Gordo County

2nd District Court 220 W Washington, Mason City, IA 50401; 641-424-6431. Hours: 8AM-4:30PM (CST). *Felony, Misdemeanor, Civil, Eviction, Small Claims, Probate.*

Civil Records: Access: In person only. Visitors must perform in person searches for themselves. No search fee. Required to search: name, years to search. Civil cases indexed by defendant, plaintiff. Civil records on computer since 1996; prior records on docket books from early 1900s.

Criminal Records: Access: In person only. Visitors must perform in person searches for themselves. No search fee. Required to search: name, years to search; also helpful: DOB, SSN. Criminal records on computer since 4/95; prior records on index cards from 1977.

General Information: Public Access terminal is available. No juvenile, sealed, dissolution of marriage, mental health, domestic abuse or deferred records released. Copy fee: $.50 per page. Certification fee: $10.00. Fee payee: Clerk of Court. Personal checks accepted. Credit cards accepted. Prepayment is required.

Cherokee County

3rd District Court Courthouse Drawer F, Cherokee, IA 51012; 712-225-6744; Fax: 712-225-6749. Hours: 8AM-4:30PM (CST). *Felony, Misdemeanor, Civil, Eviction, Small Claims, Probate.*

Civil Records: Access: In person only. Visitors must perform in person searches for themselves. No search fee. Required to search: name, years to search. Civil cases indexed by defendant, plaintiff. Civil records on docket books from 1800s, indexed on computer since 1997.

Criminal Records: Access: In person only. Visitors must perform in person searches for themselves. No search fee. Required to search: name, years to search. Criminal records index is computerized since 06/90.

General Information: Public Access terminal is available. No juvenile, sealed, dissolution of marriage, mental health, domestic abuse or deferred records released. Copy fee: $.50 per page. Certification fee: $10.00. Fee payee: Clerk of Court. Personal checks accepted. Prepayment is required.

Chickasaw County

1st District Court County Courthouse, 8 E Prospect, New Hampton, IA 50659; 641-394-2106; Fax: 641-394-5106. Hours: 8AM-4:30PM (CST). *Felony, Misdemeanor, Civil, Eviction, Small Claims, Probate.*

Civil Records: Access: In person only. Visitors must perform in person searches for themselves. No search fee. Required to search: name, years to search. Civil cases indexed by defendant, plaintiff. Civil records on docket books from late 1800s; on computer back to 1996.

Criminal Records: Access: In person only. Visitors must perform in person searches for themselves. No search fee. Required to search: name, years to search, signed release. Criminal records on docket books from late 1800s; on computer back to 1996.

General Information: Public Access terminal is available. No juvenile, sealed, dissolution of marriage, adoption, mental health, domestic abuse or deferred records released. Copy fee: $.50. $.25 per page after first 10. Certification fee: $10.00. Fee payee: Clerk of District Court. Personal checks accepted. Prepayment is required.

Clarke County

5th District Court Clarke County Courthouse, Osceola, IA 50213; 641-342-6096; Fax: 641-342-2463. Hours: 8AM-4:30PM (CST). *Felony, Misdemeanor, Civil, Eviction, Small Claims, Probate.*

Civil Records: Access: In person only. Both court and visitors may perform in person searches. No search fee. Required to search: name, years to search. Civil cases indexed by defendant, plaintiff. Civil records on docket books from early 1900s.

Criminal Records: Access: In person only. Both court and visitors may perform in person searches. No search fee. Required to search: name, years to search; also helpful: SSN. Criminal records on docket books from early 1900s.

General Information: Public Access terminal is available. No juvenile, sealed, dissolution of marriage, mental health, domestic abuse or deferred records released. Copy fee: $.25 per page. Certification fee: $10.00. Fee payee: Clerk of Court. Personal checks accepted. Prepayment is required.

Clay County

3rd District Court Courthouse 215 W 4th St, Spencer, IA 51301; 712-262-4335. Hours: 8AM-4:30PM (CST). *Felony, Misdemeanor, Civil, Eviction, Small Claims, Probate.*

Civil Records: Access: In person only. Visitors must perform in person searches for themselves. No search fee. Required to search: name, years to search. Civil cases indexed by defendant, plaintiff. Civil records on microfilm from to 1972 to 1995, docket books from 1800s.

Criminal Records: Access: In person only. Visitors must perform in person searches for themselves. No search fee. Required to search: name, years to search. Criminal records on microfilm from to 1972 to 1995, docket books from 1800s.

General Information: Public Access terminal is available. No juvenile, sealed, pending dissolution of

marriage, mental health, sealed domestic abuse or deferred records released. Copy fee: $.50 per page. Certification fee: $10.00. Fee payee: Clerk of Court. Personal checks accepted. Credit cards accepted: Visa, MasterCard.

Clayton County

1st District Court PO Box 418, Clayton County Courthouse, Elkader, IA 52043; 563-245-2204; Fax: 563-245-2825. Hours: 8AM-4:30PM (CST). *Felony, Misdemeanor, Civil, Eviction, Small Claims, Probate.*

Civil Records: Access: In person only. Visitors must perform in person searches for themselves. No search fee. Required to search: name, years to search. Civil cases indexed by defendant, plaintiff. Civil records on docket books from late 1880s.

Criminal Records: Access: In person only. Visitors must perform in person searches for themselves. No search fee. Required to search: name, years to search. Criminal records on docket books from late 1880s.

General Information: Public Access terminal is available. No juvenile unless child is age 10 or older and offense is considered a public offense, sealed, dissolution of marriage, mental health, domestic abuse or deferred records released. Copy fee: $.50 per page. Certification fee: $10.00. Fee payee: Clerk of Court. Personal checks accepted. Prepayment is required.

Clinton County

7th District Court Courthouse (PO Box 2957), Clinton, IA 52733; 563-243-6210; Fax: 563-243-3655. Hours: 8AM-4:30PM (CST). *Felony, Misdemeanor, Civil, Eviction, Small Claims, Probate.*

Civil Records: Access: In person only. Visitors must perform in person searches for themselves. No search fee. Required to search: name, years to search. Civil cases indexed by defendant. Civil records on computer since 1980, on docket books prior.

Criminal Records: Access: In person only. Visitors must perform in person searches for themselves. No search fee. Required to search: name, years to search, DOB, signed release; also helpful: SSN. Criminal records on computer since 1980, on docket books prior.

General Information: Public Access terminal is available. No juvenile, adoption, sealed, dissolution of marriage before decree, mental health, domestic abuse or deferred records released. Copy fee: $.50 per page. Certification fee: $10.00. Fee payee: Clerk of Court. Personal checks accepted. Credit cards accepted: Visa, MasterCard. Prepayment is required.

Crawford County

3rd District Court 1202 Broadway, Denison, IA 51442; 712-263-2242; Fax: 712-263-5753. Hours: 8AM-4:30PM (CST). *Felony, Misdemeanor, Civil, Eviction, Small Claims, Probate.*

Civil Records: Access: In person only. Visitors must perform in person searches for themselves. No search fee. Required to search: name, years to search. Civil cases indexed by defendant, plaintiff. Civil records available since 1937, on docket books from 1869.

Criminal Records: Access: In person only. Visitors must perform in person searches for themselves. No search fee. Required to search: name, years to search. Criminal records available since 1937, on docket books from 1869.

General Information: Public Access terminal is available. No juvenile, sealed, dissolution of marriage, mental health, domestic abuse or deferred records released. Copy fee: $.50 per page. Certification fee: $10.00. Fee payee: Clerk of Court. Personal checks accepted. Prepayment is required.

Dallas County

5th District Court 801 Court St, Adel, IA 50003; 515-993-5816; Fax: 515-993-4752. Hours: 8AM-4:30PM (CST). *Felony, Misdemeanor, Civil, Eviction, Small Claims, Probate.*

Civil Records: Access: In person only. Visitors must perform in person searches for themselves. No search fee. Required to search: name, years to search. Civil cases indexed by defendant, plaintiff. Civil records on docket books from 1800s.

Criminal Records: Access: In person only. Visitors must perform in person searches for themselves. No search fee. Required to search: name, years to search. Criminal records on docket books from 1800s.

General Information: Public Access terminal is available. No juvenile, sealed, dissolution of marriage, mental health, domestic abuse or deferred records released. Copy fee: $.50 per page. Certification fee: $10.00. Fee payee: Clerk of Court. Personal checks accepted. Prepayment is required.

Davis County

8th District Court Davis County Courthouse, Bloomfield, IA 52537; 641-664-2011; Fax: 641-664-2041. Hours: 8AM-4:30PM (CST). *Felony, Misdemeanor, Civil, Eviction, Small Claims, Probate.*

Civil Records: Access: In person only. Visitors must perform in person searches for themselves. No search fee. Required to search: name, years to search. Civil cases indexed by defendant, plaintiff. Civil records on docket books from late 1800s.

Criminal Records: Access: In person only. Visitors must perform in person searches for themselves. No search fee. Required to search: name, years to search, DOB. Criminal records on docket books from late 1800s.

General Information: Public Access terminal is available. (Records available since 1997.) No juvenile, sealed, dissolution of marriage, mental health, domestic abuse or deferred records released. Copy fee: $.25 per page. Certification fee: $10.00. Fee payee: Clerk of Court. Personal checks accepted. Prepayment is required.

Decatur County

5th District Court 207 N Main St, Leon, IA 50144; 641-446-4331; Fax: 641-446-3759. Hours: 8AM-4:30PM (CST). *Felony, Misdemeanor, Civil, Eviction, Small Claims, Probate.*

Civil Records: Access: Fax, mail, in person. Both court and visitors may perform in person searches. No search fee. Required to search: name, years to search. Civil cases indexed by defendant, plaintiff. Civil records on docket books since 1880; on computer back to 1996.

Criminal Records: Access: Fax, mail, in person. Both court and visitors may perform in person searches. No search fee. Required to search: name, years to search, DOB or SSN. Criminal records on docket books since 1880; on computer back to 1996.

General Information: Public Access terminal is available. No juvenile, sealed, dissolution of marriage, mental health, domestic abuse or deferred records released. SASE required. Turnaround time same day. Fax notes: No fee to fax results. Copy fee: $.25 per page. Certification fee: $10.00. Fee payee: Clerk of Court. Personal checks accepted.

Delaware County

District Court Delaware County Courthouse, PO Box 527, Manchester, IA 52057; 563-927-4942; Fax: 563-927-3074. Hours: 8AM-4:30PM (CST). *Felony, Misdemeanor, Civil, Eviction, Small Claims, Probate.*

Civil Records: Access: In person only. Visitors must perform in person searches for themselves. No search fee. Required to search: name, years to search. Civil

cases indexed by defendant, plaintiff. Civil records on docket books from late 1800s; on computer back to 1996.

Criminal Records: Access: In person only. Visitors must perform in person searches for themselves. No search fee. Required to search: name, years to search. Criminal records on docket books from late 1800s; on computer back to 1996.

General Information: Public Access terminal is available. No juvenile, sealed, dissolution of marriage, mental health, domestic abuse or deferred records released. Copy fee: $.50 per page. Certification fee: $10.00. Fee payee: Clerk of Court. Personal checks accepted. Prepayment is required.

Des Moines County

8th District Court 513 Main St, PO Box 158, Burlington, IA 52601; 319-753-8262/8242; Fax: 319-753-8253. Hours: 8AM-4:30PM (CST). *Felony, Misdemeanor, Civil, Eviction, Small Claims, Probate.*

Civil Records: Access: In person only. Visitors must perform in person searches for themselves. No search fee. Required to search: name, years to search; also helpful: address. Civil cases indexed by defendant, plaintiff. Civil records on computer from July, 1992, docket books prior.

Criminal Records: Access: In person only. Visitors must perform in person searches for themselves. No search fee. Required to search: name, years to search, aliases; also helpful: DOB, SSN. Criminal records on computer from July, 1992, docket books prior.

General Information: Public Access terminal is available. No juvenile, sealed, dissolution of marriage, mental health, domestic abuse or deferred records released. Copy fee: $.25 per page. Certification fee: $10.00. Fee payee: Clerk of Court. Personal checks accepted. Credit cards accepted: Visa, MasterCard.

Dickinson County

3rd District Court PO Drawer O N, Spirit Lake, IA 51360; 712-336-1138; Fax: 712-336-4005. Hours: 8AM-4:30PM (CST). *Felony, Misdemeanor, Civil, Eviction, Small Claims, Probate.*

Civil Records: Access: In person only. Visitors must perform in person searches for themselves. No search fee. Required to search: name, years to search. Civil cases indexed by defendant, plaintiff. Early information on microfiche, docket books from 1800s; computerized back to 1992.

Criminal Records: Access: In person only. Visitors must perform in person searches for themselves. No search fee. Required to search: name, years to search. Criminal records early information on microfiche, docket books from 1800s; computerized back to 1992.

General Information: Public Access terminal is available. No juvenile, sealed, dissolution of marriage, mental health, domestic abuse or deferred records released. Fax notes: No fee to fax results. Copy fee: $.50 per page. Certification fee: $10.00. Fee payee: Clerk of Court. Personal checks accepted.

Dubuque County

1st District Court 720 Central, Dubuque, IA 52001; 563-589-4418. Hours: 8AM-4:30PM (CST). *Felony, Misdemeanor, Civil, Eviction, Small Claims, Probate.*

Civil Records: Access: In person only. Visitors must perform in person searches for themselves. No search fee. Required to search: name, years to search. Civil cases indexed by defendant, plaintiff. Civil records on computer since July, 1994, on docket books from 1900s.

Criminal Records: Access: In person only. Visitors must perform in person searches for themselves. No search fee. Required to search: name, years to search;

also helpful: DOB, SSN. Criminal records on computer since July, 1994, on docket books from 1900s.

General Information: Public Access terminal is available. No juvenile, sealed, dissolution of marriage, mental health, domestic abuse or expunged records released. Copy fee: $.50 per page. Certification fee: $10.00. Fee payee: Clerk of District Court. Local checks accepted. Credit cards accepted: Visa, MasterCard. Prepayment is required.

Emmet County

3rd District Court Emmet County, 609 1st Ave N, Estherville, IA 51334; 712-362-3325. Hours: 8AM-4:30PM (CST). *Felony, Misdemeanor, Civil, Eviction, Small Claims, Probate.*

Civil Records: Access: In person only. Visitors must perform in person searches for themselves. No search fee. Required to search: name, years to search. Civil cases indexed by defendant, plaintiff. Civil records on docket books from 1900s.

Criminal Records: Access: In person only. Visitors must perform in person searches for themselves. No search fee. Required to search: name, years to search. Criminal records on docket books from 1900s.

General Information: Public Access terminal is available. (Records available since 1996.) No juvenile, sealed, dissolution of marriage, mental health, domestic abuse or deferred records released. Copy fee: $.25 per page. Certification fee: $10.00. Fee payee: Clerk of Court. Personal checks accepted.

Fayette County

Fayette County District Court PO Box 458, West Union, IA 52175; 563-422-5694; Fax: 563-422-3137. Hours: 8AM-4:30PM (CST). *Felony, Misdemeanor, Civil, Eviction, Small Claims, Probate, Traffic.*

Civil Records: Access: In person only. Visitors must perform in person searches for themselves. No search fee. Required to search: name, years to search. Civil cases indexed by defendant, plaintiff. Civil records on docket books from 1900s.

Criminal Records: Access: In person only. Visitors must perform in person searches for themselves. No search fee. Required to search: name, years to search. Criminal records on docket books from 1900s; 1940-1960 on CD-ROM. Contact Fayette Co Abstract Co, West Union, IA 52175.

General Information: Public Access terminal is available. No juvenile, sealed, dissolution of marriage, mental health, domestic abuse or deferred records released. Copy fee: $.50 per page. Certification fee: $10.00. Fee payee: Clerk of Court. Personal checks accepted. Prepayment is required.

Floyd County

2nd District Court 101 S Main St, Charles City, IA 50616; 641-228-7777; Fax: 641-228-7772. Hours: 8AM-4:30PM (CST). *Felony, Misdemeanor, Civil, Eviction, Small Claims, Probate.*

Civil Records: Access: In person only. Visitors must perform in person searches for themselves. No search fee. Required to search: name, years to search. Civil cases indexed by defendant, plaintiff. Civil records in docket books, are computerized since 1996.

Criminal Records: Access: In person only. Visitors must perform in person searches for themselves. No search fee. Required to search: name, years to search, DOB, signed release; also helpful: SSN. Criminal records in docket books, are computerized since 1996.

General Information: Public Access terminal is available. No juvenile, sealed, dissolution of marriage, mental health, domestic abuse or deferred records released. Copy fee: $.50 per page. Certification fee: $10.00. Fee payee: Clerk of Court. Personal checks accepted. Credit cards accepted.

Franklin County

2nd Judicial District Court 12 1st Ave NW, PO Box 28, Hampton, IA 50441; 641-456-5626; Fax: 641-456-5628. Hours: 8AM-4:30PM (CST). *Felony, Misdemeanor, Civil, Eviction, Small Claims, Probate.*

Civil Records: Access: In person only. Visitors must perform in person searches for themselves. No search fee. Required to search: name, years to search. Civil cases indexed by defendant, plaintiff. Civil records on microfiche and/or microfilm from 1860 to 1984, on docket books from 1984 to present.

Criminal Records: Access: In person only. Visitors must perform in person searches for themselves. No search fee. Required to search: name, years to search. Criminal records on microfiche and/or microfilm from 1860 to 1984, on docket books from 1984 to present.

General Information: Public Access terminal is available. No juvenile, sealed, dissolution of marriage, mental health, domestic abuse or deferred records released. Copy fee: $.50 per page. Certification fee: $10.00. Fee payee: Clerk of District Court. Personal checks accepted. Credit cards accepted: Visa, MasterCard. Credit cards accepted for traffic fees only. Prepayment is required.

Fremont County

4th District Court PO Box 549, Sidney, IA 51652; 712-374-2232; Fax: 712-374-3330. Hours: 8AM-4:30PM (CST). *Felony, Misdemeanor, Civil, Eviction, Small Claims, Probate.*

Civil Records: Access: In person only. Visitors must perform in person searches for themselves. No search fee. Required to search: name, years to search. Civil cases indexed by defendant, plaintiff. Civil records in docket books and microfiche since 1927.

Criminal Records: Access: In person only. Visitors must perform in person searches for themselves. No search fee. Required to search: name, years to search. Criminal records in docket books and microfiche since 1927.

General Information: Public Access terminal is available. No juvenile, sealed, dissolution of marriage, mental health, domestic abuse or deferred records released. Fax notes: Fee to fax results is $3.00 per document. Copy fee: $.25 per page. Certification fee: $10.00. Fee payee: Clerk of Court. Personal checks accepted. Prepayment is required.

Greene County

2nd District Court Greene County Courthouse, 114 N Chestnut, Jefferson, IA 50129; 515-386-2516. Hours: 8AM-4:30PM (CST). *Felony, Misdemeanor, Civil, Eviction, Small Claims, Probate.*

Civil Records: Access: In person only. Visitors must perform in person searches for themselves. No search fee. Required to search: name, years to search. Civil cases indexed by defendant, plaintiff. Civil records on microfiche from 1981 back to establishment of court, docket books from 1800s.

Criminal Records: Access: In person only. Visitors must perform in person searches for themselves. No search fee. Required to search: name, years to search. Criminal records on microfiche from 1981 back to establishment of court, docket books from 1800s.

General Information: Public Access terminal is available. No juvenile, sealed, dissolution of marriage, mental health, domestic abuse or deferred records released. Copy fee: $.50 per page. Certification fee: $10.00. Fee payee: Clerk of Court. Personal checks accepted. Credit cards accepted: Visa, MasterCard. Credit cards accepted for traffic fees only. Prepayment is required.

Grundy County

1st District Court Grundy County Courthouse, 706 G Ave, Grundy Center, IA 50638; 319-824-5229; Fax: 319-824-3447. Hours: 8AM-4:30PM (CST). *Felony, Misdemeanor, Civil, Eviction, Small Claims, Probate.*

Civil Records: Access: In person only. Visitors must perform in person searches for themselves. No search fee. Required to search: name, years to search. Civil cases indexed by defendant, plaintiff. Civil records on docket books from 1881.

Criminal Records: Access: In person only. Visitors must perform in person searches for themselves. No search fee. Required to search: name, years to search. Criminal records on docket books from 1881.

General Information: Public Access terminal is available. No juvenile, sealed, dissolution of marriage, mental health, domestic abuse or deferred records released. Copy fee: $.50 per page. Certification fee: $10.00. Fee payee: Clerk of Court. Personal checks accepted. Credit cards accepted: Visa, MasterCard. Prepayment is required.

Guthrie County

5th District Court Courthouse, 200 N 5th St, Guthrie Center, IA 50115; 641-747-3415. Hours: 8AM-4:30PM (CST). *Felony, Misdemeanor, Civil, Eviction, Small Claims, Probate.*

Civil Records: Access: In person only. Visitors must perform in person searches for themselves. No search fee. Required to search: name, years to search. Civil cases indexed by defendant, plaintiff. Civil records on computer since 11/96; prior records on docket books from 1880s.

Criminal Records: Access: In person only. Visitors must perform in person searches for themselves. No search fee. Required to search: name, years to search. Criminal records on computer since 11/96; prior records on docket books from 1880s.

General Information: Public Access terminal is available. No juvenile, sealed, dissolution of marriage, mental health, domestic abuse or deferred records released. Copy fee: $.50 per page. Certification fee: $10.00. Fee payee: Clerk of Court. Personal checks accepted. Prepayment is required.

Hamilton County

2nd District Court Courthouse PO Box 845, Webster City, IA 50595; 515-832-9600. Hours: 8AM-4:30PM (CST). *Felony, Misdemeanor, Civil, Eviction, Small Claims, Probate.*

Civil Records: Access: In person only. Visitors must perform in person searches for themselves. No search fee. Required to search: name, years to search. Civil cases indexed by defendant, plaintiff. Civil records on microfiche from 1939, docket books from 1880s.

Criminal Records: Access: In person only. Visitors must perform in person searches for themselves. No search fee. Required to search: name, years to search.

General Information: Public Access terminal is available. No juvenile, sealed, dissolution of marriage, mental health, domestic abuse records released. Copy fee: $.50 per page. Certification fee: $10.00. Fee payee: Clerk of Court. Personal checks accepted. Credit cards accepted. Prepayment is required.

Hancock County

2nd District Court 855 State St, Garner, IA 50438; 641-923-2532; Fax: 641-923-3521. Hours: 8AM-4:30PM (CST). *Felony, Misdemeanor, Civil, Eviction, Small Claims, Probate.*

Civil Records: Access: In person only. Visitors must perform in person searches for themselves. No search fee. Required to search: name, years to search. Civil

cases indexed by defendant, plaintiff. Civil records on docket books from 1880s; on computer since 1997.

Criminal Records: Access: In person only. Visitors must perform in person searches for themselves. No search fee. Required to search: name, years to search. Criminal records on docket books from 1880s; on computer since 1997.

General Information: Public Access terminal is available. No juvenile, sealed, dissolution of marriage, mental health, domestic abuse or deferred records released. Fax notes: Fee to fax results is $1.00 per page. Copy fee: $.50 per page. Certification fee: $10.00. Fee payee: Clerk of Court. Personal checks accepted. Prepayment is required.

Hardin County

2nd District Court Courthouse, PO Box 495, Eldora, IA 50627; 641-858-2328; Fax: 641-858-2320. Hours: 8AM-4:30PM (CST). *Felony, Misdemeanor, Civil, Eviction, Small Claims, Probate.*

Civil Records: Access: In person only. Visitors must perform in person searches for themselves. No search fee. Required to search: name, years to search. Civil cases indexed by defendant, plaintiff. Civil records on docket books from 1880s.

Criminal Records: Access: In person only. Visitors must perform in person searches for themselves. No search fee. Required to search: name, years to search. Criminal records on docket books from 1880s.

General Information: Public Access terminal is available. No juvenile, sealed, dissolution of marriage, mental health, domestic abuse or deferred records released. Copy fee: $.50 per page. Certification fee: $10.00. Fee payee: Clerk of Court. Personal checks accepted. Credit cards accepted: Visa, MasterCard. Prepayment is required.

Harrison County

District Court Court House, Logan, IA 51546; 712-644-2665. Hours: 8AM-4:30PM (CST). *Felony, Misdemeanor, Civil, Eviction, Small Claims, Probate.*

Civil Records: Access: In person only. Visitors must perform in person searches for themselves. No search fee. Required to search: name, years to search. Civil cases indexed by defendant, plaintiff. Civil records on computer; prior on docket books since 1840s in Recorder's office. Recent death and birth certificates on microfiche.

Criminal Records: Access: In person only. Visitors must perform in person searches for themselves. No search fee. Required to search: name, years to search. Criminal records on computer, prior on docket books from 1840s in Recorder's office.

General Information: Public Access terminal is available. No juvenile, sealed, dissolution of marriage, mental health, domestic abuse or deferred records released. Copy fee: $.50 per page. Certification fee: $10.00. Fee payee: Clerk of Court. Personal checks accepted. Prepayment is required.

Henry County

8th District Court PO Box 176, Mount Pleasant, IA 52641; Civil phone: 319-385-2632; Criminal phone: 319-385-3150; Fax: 319-385-4144. Hours: 8AM-4:30PM (CST). *Felony, Misdemeanor, Civil, Eviction, Small Claims, Probate.*

Civil Records: Access: In person only. Visitors must perform in person searches for themselves. No search fee. Required to search: name, years to search. Civil cases indexed by defendant, plaintiff. Civil records on docket books from 1880s.

Criminal Records: Access: In person only. Visitors must perform in person searches for themselves. No search fee. Required to search: name, years to search, DOB; also helpful: address, SSN. Criminal records on docket books from 1880s.

General Information: Public Access terminal is available. No juvenile, sealed, dissolution of marriage, mental health, domestic abuse or deferred records released. Copy fee: $.25 per page. Certification fee: $10.00. Fee payee: Clerk of Court. Personal checks accepted. Prepayment is required.

Howard County

1st District Court Courthouse, 137 N Elm St, Cresco, IA 52136; 563-547-2661. Hours: 8AM-4:30PM (CST). *Felony, Misdemeanor, Civil, Eviction, Small Claims, Probate.*

Civil Records: Access: In person only. Visitors must perform in person searches for themselves. No search fee. Required to search: name, years to search. Civil cases indexed by defendant, plaintiff. Civil records on docket books from 1900s.
Criminal Records: Access: In person only. Visitors must perform in person searches for themselves. No search fee. Required to search: name, years to search, DOB. Criminal records on docket books from 1900s.
General Information:. No juvenile, sealed, dissolution of marriage, mental health, domestic abuse or deferred records released. Copy fee: $.50 per page. Certification fee: $10.00. Fee payee: Clerk of Court. Personal checks accepted. Prepayment is required.

Humboldt County

2nd District Court Courthouse, Dakota City, IA 50529; 515-332-1806; Fax: 515-332-7100. Hours: 8AM-4:30PM (CST). *Felony, Misdemeanor, Civil, Eviction, Small Claims, Probate.*

Civil Records: Access: In person only. Visitors must perform in person searches for themselves. No search fee. Required to search: name, years to search. Civil cases indexed by defendant, plaintiff. Civil records on docket books from early 1900s.
Criminal Records: Access: In person only. Visitors must perform in person searches for themselves. No search fee. Required to search: name, years to search. Criminal records on docket books from early 1900s.
General Information: Public Access terminal is available. No juvenile, sealed, dissolution of marriage, mental health, domestic abuse or deferred records released. Copy fee: $.50 per page. Certification fee: $10.00. Fee payee: Clerk of Court. Personal checks accepted. Prepayment is required.

Ida County

3rd District Court Courthouse, 401 Moorehead St, Ida Grove, IA 51445; 712-364-2628; Fax: 712-364-2699. Hours: 8AM-4:30PM (CST). *Felony, Misdemeanor, Civil, Eviction, Small Claims, Probate.*

Civil Records: Access: In person only. Visitors must perform in person searches for themselves. No search fee. Required to search: name, years to search. Civil cases indexed by defendant, plaintiff. Civil records on docket books from early 1800s.
Criminal Records: Access: In person only. Visitors must perform in person searches for themselves. No search fee. Required to search: name, years to search. Criminal records on docket books from early 1800s.
General Information: Public Access terminal is available. No juvenile, sealed, dissolution of marriage, mental health, domestic abuse or deferred records released. Copy fee: $.50 per page. Certification fee: $10.00. Fee payee: Clerk of Court. Personal checks accepted. Prepayment is required.

Iowa County

6th District Court PO Box 266, Marengo, IA 52301; 319-642-3914. Hours: 8AM-4:30PM (CST). *Felony, Misdemeanor, Civil, Eviction, Small Claims, Probate.*

Civil Records: Access: Mail, in person. Visitors must perform in person searches for themselves. No search fee. Required to search: name, years to search. Civil cases indexed by defendant, plaintiff. Civil records on docket books from early 1800s; on computer back to 2/97.
Criminal Records: Access: Mail, in person. Visitors must perform in person searches for themselves. No search fee. Required to search: name, years to search. Criminal records on docket books from early 1800s; on computer back to 2/1997.
General Information: Public Access terminal is available. No juvenile, sealed, dissolution of marriage, mental health, domestic abuse or deferred records released. Fax notes: Will not fax results. Copy fee: $.50 per page. Certification fee: $10.00. Fee payee: Clerk of Court. Personal checks accepted. Prepayment is required.

Jackson County

7th District Court 201 West Platt, Maquoketa, IA 52060; 563-652-4946; Fax: 563-652-2708. Hours: 8AM-4:30PM (CST). *Felony, Misdemeanor, Civil, Eviction, Small Claims, Probate.*

Civil Records: Access: In person only. Visitors must perform in person searches for themselves. No search fee. Required to search: name, years to search. Civil cases indexed by defendant, plaintiff. Civil records on computer since 1994, on docket books from 1900s.
Criminal Records: Access: In person only. Visitors must perform in person searches for themselves. No search fee. Required to search: name, years to search, DOB; also helpful: SSN. Criminal records on computer since 1994, on docket books from 1900s.
General Information: Public Access terminal is available. No juvenile, sealed, dissolution of marriage, mental health, domestic abuse or deferred records released. Copy fee: $.50 per page. Certification fee: $10.00 per page. Fee payee: Clerk of Court. Personal checks accepted. Prepayment is required.

Jasper County

5th District Court 101 1st Street North, Rm 104, Newton, IA 50208; Civil phone: 641-792-3255; Criminal phone: 641-792-9161; Fax: 641-792-2818. Hours: 8AM-4:30PM (CST). *Felony, Misdemeanor, Civil, Eviction, Small Claims, Probate.*

www.judicial.state.ia.us/decisions/district/d5.asp

Civil Records: Access: In person only. Visitors must perform in person searches for themselves. No search fee. Required to search: name, years to search. Civil cases indexed by defendant, plaintiff. Civil records on computer since 1994, docket books from 1900s.
Criminal Records: Access: In person only. Visitors must perform in person searches for themselves. No search fee. Required to search: name, years to search. Criminal records on computer since 1994, docket books from 1900s.
General Information: Public Access terminal is available. No juvenile, sealed, dissolution of marriage, mental health, or deferred records released. Copy fee: $.50 per page. Certification fee: $10.00. Fee payee: Clerk of Court. Personal checks accepted. Prepayment is required.

Jefferson County

8th District Court PO Box 984, Fairfield, IA 52556; 641-472-3454; Fax: 641-472-9472. Hours: 8AM-4:30PM (CST). *Felony, Misdemeanor, Civil, Eviction, Small Claims, Probate.*

Civil Records: Access: In person only. Visitors must perform in person searches for themselves. No search fee. Required to search: name, years to search. Civil cases indexed by defendant, plaintiff. Civil records on docket books from 1800s.

Criminal Records: Access: In person only. Visitors must perform in person searches for themselves. No search fee. Required to search: name, years to search, DOB. Criminal records on docket books from 1800s.
General Information: Public Access terminal is available. No juvenile, sealed, dissolution of marriage, mental health, domestic abuse or deferred records released. Copy fee: $.25 per page. Certification fee: $10.00. Fee payee: Clerk of Court. Personal checks accepted.

Johnson County

6th District Court PO Box 2510, Iowa City, IA 52244; 319-356-6060. Hours: 8AM-4:30PM (CST). *Felony, Misdemeanor, Civil, Eviction, Small Claims, Probate.*

Civil Records: Access: In person only. Visitors must perform in person searches for themselves. No search fee. Required to search: name, years to search. Civil cases indexed by defendant, plaintiff. Civil records on docket books and microfilm from 1880s.
Criminal Records: Access: In person only. Visitors must perform in person searches for themselves. No search fee. Required to search: name, years to search; also helpful: address, DOB, SSN. Criminal records on docket books and microfilm from 1880s.
General Information: Public Access terminal is available. No juvenile, sealed, dissolution of marriage, mental health, domestic abuse or deferred records released. Copy fee: $.50 per page. Certification fee: $10.00. Fee payee: Clerk of Court. Personal checks accepted.

Jones County

6th District Court PO Box 19, Anamosa, IA 52205; 319-462-4341. Hours: 8AM-4:30PM (CST). *Felony, Misdemeanor, Civil, Eviction, Small Claims, Probate.*

Civil Records: Access: In person only. Visitors must perform in person searches for themselves. No search fee. Required to search: name, years to search. Civil cases indexed by defendant, plaintiff. Civil records on docket books from mid 1800s; dockets on computer back to 6/1997.
Criminal Records: Access: In person only. Visitors must perform in person searches for themselves. No search fee. Required to search: name, years to search. Criminal records on docket books from early 1900s; dockets on computer back to 11/1996.
General Information: Public Access terminal is available. No juvenile, sealed, dissolution of marriage (prior to decree), mental health or deferred records released. Copy fee: $.50 per page. Certification fee: $10.00. Fee payee: Clerk of Court. Personal checks accepted. Prepayment is required.

Keokuk County

8th District Court 101 S. Main, Courthouse, Sigourney, IA 52591; 641-622-2210; Fax: 641-622-2171. Hours: 8AM-4:30PM (CST). *Felony, Misdemeanor, Civil, Eviction, Small Claims, Probate.*

Civil Records: Access: In person only. Visitors must perform in person searches for themselves. No search fee. Required to search: name, years to search. Civil cases indexed by defendant, plaintiff. Civil records on docket books from 1888; on computer back to 2/1997.
Criminal Records: Access: In person only. Visitors must perform in person searches for themselves. No search fee. Required to search: name, years to search. Criminal records on docket books from 1888; on computer back to 2/1997.
General Information: Public Access terminal is available. No juvenile, sealed, dissolution of marriage, mental health, domestic abuse or deferred records released. Copy fee: $.25 per page. Certification fee:

$10.00. Fee payee: Clerk of Court. Personal checks accepted. Prepayment is required.

Kossuth County

3rd District Court Kossuth County Courthouse, 114 W State St, Algona, IA 50511; 515-295-3240. Hours: 8AM-4PM (CST). *Felony, Misdemeanor, Civil, Eviction, Small Claims, Probate.*

Civil Records: Access: In person only. Visitors must perform in person searches for themselves. No search fee. Required to search: name, years to search. Civil cases indexed by defendant, plaintiff. Civil records on computer since 09/97; prior records on dockets.

Criminal Records: Access: In person only. Visitors must perform in person searches for themselves. No search fee. Required to search: name, years to search. Criminal records on computer since 09/97; prior records on dockets.

General Information: Public Access terminal is available. No juvenile, sealed, dissolution of marriage, mental health, domestic abuse or deferred records released. Copy fee: $.50 per page. Certification fee: $10.00. Fee payee: Clerk of Court. Personal checks accepted. Prepayment is required.

Lee County

8th District Court PO Box 1443, Ft Madison, IA 52627; 319-372-3523. Hours: 8AM-4:30PM (CST). *Felony, Misdemeanor, Civil, Eviction, Small Claims, Probate.*

Civil Records: Access: In person only. Visitors must perform in person searches for themselves. No search fee. Required to search: name, years to search. Civil cases indexed by defendant, plaintiff. Civil records on docket books from early 1800s; computerized from 1996.

Criminal Records: Access: In person only. Visitors must perform in person searches for themselves. No search fee. Required to search: name, years to search. Criminal records on docket books from early 1800s; computerized from 1996.

General Information: Public Access terminal is available. No juvenile, sealed, dissolution of marriage, mental health, domestic abuse or deferred records released. Copy fee: $.25 per page. Certification fee: $10.00. Fee payee: Clerk of Court. Personal checks accepted. Prepayment is required.

Linn County

District Court Linn County Courthouse, PO Box 1468, Cedar Rapids, IA 52406-1468; 319-398-3411; Fax: 319-398-3964. Hours: 8AM-4:30PM (CST). *Felony, Misdemeanor, Civil, Eviction, Small Claims, Probate.*

Civil Records: Access: In person only. Visitors must perform in person searches for themselves. No search fee. Required to search: name, years to search. Civil cases indexed by defendant, plaintiff. Civil records on computer from 1995, docket books from early 1900s.

Criminal Records: Access: In person only. Visitors must perform in person searches for themselves. No search fee. Required to search: name, years to search; also helpful: address, DOB. Criminal records on computer since 1993.

General Information: Public Access terminal is available. No juvenile, sealed, pending dissolution of marriage, mental health, domestic abuse or deferred records released. Copy fee: $.50 per page. Certification fee: $10.00. Fee payee: Clerk of Court. Personal checks accepted. Prepayment is required.

Louisa County

8th District Court PO Box 268, Wapello, IA 52653; 319-523-4541; Fax: 319-523-4542. Hours: 8AM-4:30PM (CST). *Felony, Misdemeanor, Civil, Eviction, Small Claims, Probate.*

Civil Records: Access: In person only. Both court and visitors may perform in person searches. No search fee. Required to search: name, years to search. Civil cases indexed by defendant, plaintiff. Civil records on docket books from 1920s, on computer since 02/97.

Criminal Records: Access: In person only. Both court and visitors may perform in person searches. No search fee. Required to search: name, years to search, DOB, signed release; also helpful: SSN. Criminal records on docket books from 1920s, on computer since 02/97.

General Information: Public Access terminal is available. No juvenile, sealed, dissolution of marriage, mental health, domestic abuse or deferred records released. Copy fee: $.25 per page. Certification fee: $10.00. Fee payee: Clerk of Court. Personal checks accepted. Prepayment is required.

Lucas County

5th District Court Courthouse, 916 Braden, Chariton, IA 50049; 641-774-4421; Fax: 641-774-8669. Hours: 8AM-4:30PM (CST). *Felony, Misdemeanor, Civil, Eviction, Small Claims, Probate.*

Civil Records: Access: In person only. Visitors must perform in person searches for themselves. No search fee. Required to search: name, years to search. Civil cases indexed by defendant, plaintiff. Civil records on docket books from 1880s; on computer back to 1997.

Criminal Records: Access: In person only. Visitors must perform in person searches for themselves. No search fee. Required to search: name, years to search; also helpful: SSN. Criminal records on docket books from 1880s; on computer back to 1997.

General Information: Public Access terminal is available. No juvenile, adoption, sealed, dissolution of marriage, mental health, domestic abuse or deferred records released. Fax notes: Fee to fax results is $1.00 per page. Copy fee: $.50 per page. Certification fee: $10.00. Fee payee: Clerk of District Court. Personal checks accepted. Credit cards accepted: Visa, MasterCard. Prepayment is required.

Lyon County

3rd District Court Courthouse, Rock Rapids, IA 51246; 712-472-2623; Fax: 712-472-2422. Hours: 8AM-4:30PM (CST). *Felony, Misdemeanor, Civil, Eviction, Small Claims, Probate.*

Civil Records: Access: In person only. Visitors must perform in person searches for themselves. No search fee. Required to search: name, years to search. Civil cases indexed by defendant, plaintiff. Civil records on docket books from 1880s.

Criminal Records: Access: In person only. Visitors must perform in person searches for themselves. No search fee. Required to search: name, years to search. Criminal records on docket books from 1880s.

General Information: Public Access terminal is available. No juvenile, sealed, dissolution of marriage, mental health, domestic abuse or deferred records released. Copy fee: $.50 per page. Certification fee: $10.00. Fee payee: Clerk of Court. Personal checks accepted.

Madison County

5th District Court PO Box 152, Winterset, IA 50273; 515-462-4451; Fax: 515-462-9825. Hours: 8AM-4:30PM (CST). *Felony, Misdemeanor, Civil, Eviction, Small Claims, Probate.*

Civil Records: Access: In person only. Visitors must perform in person searches for themselves. No search fee. Required to search: name, years to search. Civil cases indexed by plaintiff. Civil records on docket books from 1880s. Misdemeanor records from 1974 to present. Other criminal same record keeping as civil.

Criminal Records: Access: In person only. Visitors must perform in person searches for themselves. No search fee. Required to search: name, years to search;

also helpful: DOB. Criminal records on docket books from 1880s. Misdemeanor records from 1974 to present. Other criminal same record keeping as civil.

General Information: Public Access terminal is available. No juvenile, sealed, dissolution of marriage, mental health, domestic abuse of deferred records released. Copy fee: $.25 per page. Certification fee: $10.00. Fee payee: Clerk of Court. Personal checks accepted. Prepayment is required.

Mahaska County

8th District Court Courthouse, 106 S 1st St, Oskaloosa, IA 52577; 641-673-7786; Fax: 641-672-1256. Hours: 8AM-4:30PM (CST). *Felony, Misdemeanor, Civil, Eviction, Small Claims, Probate.*

Civil Records: Access: In person only. Visitors must perform in person searches for themselves. No search fee. Required to search: name, years to search. Civil cases indexed by defendant, plaintiff. Civil records on docket books from 1880s.

Criminal Records: Access: In person only. Visitors must perform in person searches for themselves. No search fee. Required to search: name, years to search. Criminal records on docket books from 1880s.

General Information: Public Access terminal is available. No juvenile, sealed, dissolution of marriage, mental health, domestic abuse or deferred records released. Copy fee: $.25 per page. Docket Copy Fee: $1.00 per page. Certification fee: $10.00. Fee payee: Clerk of Court. Personal checks accepted. Prepayment is required.

Marion County

5th District Court PO Box 497, Knoxville, IA 50138; 641-828-2207; Fax: 641-828-7580. Hours: 8AM-4:30PM (CST). *Felony, Misdemeanor, Civil, Eviction, Small Claims, Probate.*

Civil Records: Access: In person only. Visitors must perform in person searches for themselves. No search fee. Required to search: name, years to search. Civil cases indexed by defendant, plaintiff. Civil records on computer since 1992, docket books from 1896.

Criminal Records: Access: In person only. Visitors must perform in person searches for themselves. No search fee. Required to search: name, years to search. Criminal records on computer since 1992, docket books from 1896.

General Information:. No juvenile, sealed, dissolution of marriage, mental health, domestic abuse or deferred records released. Copy fee: $.50 per page. Certification fee: $10.00. Fee payee: Clerk of Court. Personal checks accepted. Prepayment is required.

Marshall County

2nd District Court Courthouse, Marshalltown, IA 50158; 641-754-1603; Fax: 641-754-1600. Hours: 8AM-4:30PM (CST). *Felony, Misdemeanor, Civil, Eviction, Small Claims, Probate.*

Civil Records: Access: In person only. Visitors must perform in person searches for themselves. No search fee. Required to search: name, years to search. Civil cases indexed by defendant, plaintiff. Civil records on computer since June, 1994, docket books from late 1800s.

Criminal Records: Access: In person only. Visitors must perform in person searches for themselves. No search fee. Required to search: name, years to search; also helpful: DOB, SSN. Criminal records on computer since August, 1992, docket books from late 1800s.

General Information: Public Access terminal is available. No juvenile, sealed, pending dissolution of marriage, mental health, domestic abuse and deferred records released. Copy fee: $.50 per page. Certification fee: $10.00. Fee payee: Clerk of Court. Personal checks accepted. Credit cards accepted. Prepayment is required.

Mills County

4th District Court 418 Sharp St, Courthouse, Glenwood, IA 51534; 712-527-4880; Fax: 712-527-4936. Hours: 8AM-4:30PM (CST). *Felony, Misdemeanor, Civil, Eviction, Small Claims, Probate.*

Civil Records: Access: In person only. Both court and visitors may perform in person searches. Search fee: $6.00 per name. Required to search: name, years to search. Civil cases indexed by defendant, plaintiff. Civil records on docket books since 1880s.

Criminal Records: Access: In person only. Both court and visitors may perform in person searches. Search fee: $6.00 per name. Required to search: name, years to search, DOB; also helpful: SSN. Criminal records on docket books since 1880s.

General Information: Public Access terminal is available. No juvenile, sealed, dissolution of marriage, mental health, domestic abuse or deferred records released. Copy fee: $.25 per page. Certification fee: $10.00. Fee payee: Clerk of Court. Personal checks accepted. Prepayment is required.

Mitchell County

2nd District Court 508 State St, Osage, IA 50461; 641-732-3726; Fax: 641-732-3728. Hours: 8AM-4:30PM (CST). *Felony, Misdemeanor, Civil, Eviction, Small Claims, Probate.*

Civil Records: Access: In person only. Visitors must perform in person searches for themselves. No search fee. Required to search: name, years to search. Civil cases indexed by defendant, plaintiff. Civil records on docket books from 1880s, computerized since 1997.

Criminal Records: Access: In person only. Visitors must perform in person searches for themselves. No search fee. Required to search: name, years to search, signed release. Criminal records on docket books from 1880s, computerized since 1997.

General Information: Public Access terminal is available. No juvenile, sealed, dissolution of marriage, mental health, domestic abuse or deferred records released. Copy fee: $1.00 per page. Certification fee: $10.00 plus $1.00 per page. Fee payee: Clerk of Court. Personal checks accepted. Prepayment is required.

Monona County

3rd District Court PO Box 14, Onawa, IA 51040; 712-423-2491. Hours: 8AM-4:30PM (CST). *Felony, Misdemeanor, Civil, Eviction, Small Claims, Probate.*

Civil Records: Access: In person only. Visitors must perform in person searches for themselves. No search fee. Required to search: name, years to search. Civil cases indexed by defendant, plaintiff. Civil records on computer since 07/97; prior records on microfiche and docket books from 1880s.

Criminal Records: Access: In person only. Visitors must perform in person searches for themselves. No search fee. Required to search: name, years to search. Criminal records on computer since 07/97; prior records on microfiche and docket books from 1880s.

General Information: Public Access terminal is available. No juvenile, sealed, dissolution of marriage, mental health, domestic abuse or deferred records released. Copy fee: $.50 per page. Certification fee: $10.00. Fee payee: Clerk of Court. Personal checks accepted. Prepayment is required.

Monroe County

8th District Court Courthouse, 10 Benton Ave E, Albia, IA 52531; 641-932-5212; Fax: 641-932-3245. Hours: 8AM-4:30PM (CST). *Felony, Misdemeanor, Civil, Eviction, Small Claims, Probate.*

Civil Records: Access: In person only. Visitors must perform in person searches for themselves. No search fee. Required to search: name, years to search. Civil

cases indexed by defendant, plaintiff. Civil records on docket books from late 1800s.

Criminal Records: Access: In person only. Visitors must perform in person searches for themselves. No search fee. Required to search: name, years to search, DOB, signed release; also helpful: SSN. Criminal records on docket books from late 1800s.

General Information: Public Access terminal is available. No juvenile, sealed, dissolution of marriage, mental health, domestic abuse or deferred records released. Certification fee: $10.00. Fee payee: Clerk of Court. Personal checks accepted. Prepayment is required.

Montgomery County

4th District Court PO Box 469, Red Oak, IA 51566; 712-623-4986. Hours: 8AM-4:30PM (CST). *Felony, Misdemeanor, Civil, Eviction, Small Claims, Probate.*

Civil Records: Access: In person only. Visitors must perform in person searches for themselves. No search fee. Required to search: name, years to search. Civil cases indexed by defendant, plaintiff. Civil records on docket books from 1940, microfiche prior.

Criminal Records: Access: In person only. Visitors must perform in person searches for themselves. No search fee. Required to search: name, years to search, DOB; also helpful: SSN. Criminal records on docket books from 1940, microfiche prior.

General Information: Public Access terminal is available. No juvenile, sealed, dissolution of marriage, mental health or deferred records released. Copy fee: $.50 per page. Certification fee: $10.00. Fee payee: Clerk of Court. Personal checks accepted. Prepayment is required.

Muscatine County

7th District Court PO Box 8010, Courthouse, Muscatine, IA 52761; 563-263-6511; Criminal phone: 563-263-2447; Fax: 563-264-3622. Hours: 8AM-4:30PM (CST). *Felony, Misdemeanor, Civil, Eviction, Small Claims, Probate.*

Civil Records: Access: In person only. Visitors must perform in person searches for themselves. No search fee. Required to search: name, years to search. Civil cases indexed by defendant, plaintiff. Civil records on docket books, on computer since 10/95.

Criminal Records: Access: In person only. Visitors must perform in person searches for themselves. No search fee. Required to search: name, years to search. Criminal Records are computerized since 04/95.

General Information: Public Access terminal is available. No juvenile, sealed, dissolutions of marriage, mental health, domestic abuse or deferred records released. Copy fee: $.50 per page. Certification fee: $10.00. Fee payee: Clerk of Court. Personal checks accepted. Prepayment is required.

O'Brien County

3rd District Court Courthouse Criminal Records, Primghar, IA 51245; 712-757-3255; Fax: 712-757-2965. Hours: 8AM-4:30PM (CST). *Felony, Misdemeanor, Civil, Eviction, Small Claims, Probate.*

www.obriencounty.com

Civil Records: Access: In person only. Visitors must perform in person searches for themselves. No search fee. Required to search: name, years to search. Civil cases indexed by defendant, plaintiff. Civil records on docket books from late 1800s.

Criminal Records: Access: In person only. Visitors must perform in person searches for themselves. No search fee. Required to search: name, years to search; also helpful: DOB, SSN. Criminal records on docket books from late 1800s.

General Information: Public Access terminal is available. No juvenile, sealed, dissolution of marriage,

mental health, domestic abuse or deferred records released. Copy fee: $.50 per page. Certification fee: $10.00. Fee payee: Clerk of Court. Personal checks accepted. Prepayment is required.

Osceola County

3rd District Court Courthouse Criminal Records, Sibley, IA 51249; 712-754-3595; Fax: 712-754-2480. Hours: 8AM-4:30PM (CST). *Felony, Misdemeanor, Civil, Eviction, Small Claims, Probate.*

Civil Records: Access: In person only. Visitors must perform in person searches for themselves. No search fee. Required to search: name, years to search. Civil cases indexed by defendant, plaintiff. Civil records on docket books from 1883; on computer back to 1993.

Criminal Records: Access: In person only. Visitors must perform in person searches for themselves. No search fee. Required to search: name, years to search. Criminal records on docket books from 1883; on computer back to 1993.

General Information: Public Access terminal is available. No juvenile, sealed, dissolution of marriage, mental health, domestic abuse or deferred records released. Copy fee: $.50 per page. Certification fee: $10.00. Fee payee: Clerk of Court. Personal checks accepted.

Page County

4th District Court 112 E Main Box 263, Clarinda, IA 51632; 712-542-3214; Fax: 712-542-5460. Hours: 8AM-4:30PM (CST). *Felony, Misdemeanor, Civil, Eviction, Small Claims, Probate.*

Civil Records: Access: In person only. Visitors must perform in person searches for themselves. No search fee. Required to search: name, years to search. Civil cases indexed by defendant, plaintiff. Civil records on docket books.

Criminal Records: Access: In person only. Visitors must perform in person searches for themselves. No search fee. Required to search: name, years to search. Criminal records on docket books.

General Information: Public Access terminal is available. No juvenile, sealed dissolution of marriage, mental health, domestic abuse or deferred records released. Copy fee: $.50 per page. Certification fee: $10.00. Fee payee: Clerk of District Court. Personal checks accepted. Prepayment is required.

Palo Alto County

3rd District Court PO Box 387, Emmetsburg, IA 50536; 712-852-3603. Hours: 8AM-4:30PM (CST). *Felony, Misdemeanor, Civil, Eviction, Small Claims, Probate.*

Civil Records: Access: In person only. Visitors must perform in person searches for themselves. No search fee. Required to search: name, years to search. Civil cases indexed by defendant, plaintiff. Civil records on docket books from 1800s; computerized from 1997.

Criminal Records: Access: In person only. Visitors must perform in person searches for themselves. No search fee. Required to search: name, years to search, DOB, SSN. Criminal records on docket books from 1800s; computerized from 1997.

General Information: Public Access terminal is available. No juvenile, sealed, dissolution of marriage, mental health, domestic abuse or deferred records released. Copy fee: $.50 per page. Certification fee: $10.00. Fee payee: Clerk of Court. Personal checks accepted. Prepayment is required.

Plymouth County

3rd District Court Courthouse 215-4th Ave SE, Le Mars, IA 51031; 712-546-4215. Hours: 8AM-4:30PM (CST). *Felony, Misdemeanor, Civil, Eviction, Small Claims, Probate.*

Civil Records: Access: In person only. Visitors must perform in person searches for themselves. No search fee. Required to search: name, years to search. Civil cases indexed by defendant, plaintiff. Civil records on docket books from 1895 to 11/92, docket cards from 11/92 to present.

Criminal Records: Access: In person only. Visitors must perform in person searches for themselves. No search fee. Required to search: name, years to search. Criminal records on docket books from 1895 to 11/92, docket cards from 11/92 to present.

General Information: Public Access terminal is available. No juvenile, sealed, dissolution of marriage, mental health, domestic abuse or deferred records released. Copy fee: $.50 per page. Certification fee: $10.00. Fee payee: Clerk of Court. Personal checks accepted. Prepayment is required.

Pocahontas County

2nd District Court Courthouse, 99 Court Square, Pocahontas, IA 50574; 712-335-4208; Fax: 712-335-4608. Hours: 8AM-4:30PM (CST). *Felony, Misdemeanor, Civil, Eviction, Small Claims, Probate.*

Civil Records: Access: In person only. Visitors must perform in person searches for themselves. No search fee. Required to search: name, years to search. Civil cases indexed by defendant, plaintiff. Civil records on docket books from 1880s.

Criminal Records: Access: In person only. Visitors must perform in person searches for themselves. No search fee. Required to search: name, years to search, DOB. Criminal records on docket books from 1880s.

General Information: Public Access terminal is available. No juvenile, sealed, dissolution of marriage, mental health, domestic abuse or deferred records released. Copy fee: $.50 per page. Certification fee: $10.00. Fee payee: Clerk of Court. Personal checks accepted. Prepayment is required.

Polk County

District Court 500 Mulberry St, Rm 201, Des Moines, IA 50309; 515-286-3772; Fax: 515-286-3172 (Civil) 323-5250 (Criminal). Hours: 8AM-4:30PM (CST). *Felony, Misdemeanor, Civil, Eviction, Small Claims, Probate.*

Civil Records: Access: In person only. Visitors must perform in person searches for themselves. No search fee. Required to search: name, years to search; also helpful: address. Civil cases indexed by defendant, plaintiff. Civil records on computer, docket books and index cards from 1880s and microfilm prior to 1970.

Criminal Records: Access: In person only. Visitors must perform in person searches for themselves. No search fee. Required to search: name, years to search, address, DOB; also helpful: SSN. Criminal records on computer, docket books and index cards from 1880s and microfilm prior to 1970.

General Information: Public Access terminal is available. No juvenile, sealed, pending dissolution of marriage, mental health, expunged, domestic abuse or deferred records released. Copy fee: $.25 per page. Microfilm Copy Fee: $4.00 1-8 pages; each add'l pg $.50. Certification fee: $10.00. Fee payee: Clerk of Court. Personal checks accepted. Credit cards accepted: Visa. Prepayment is required.

Pottawattamie County

4th District Court 227 S 6th St, Council Bluffs, IA 51501; 712-328-5604. Hours: 8:30AM-3:30PM (CST). *Felony, Misdemeanor, Civil, Eviction, Small Claims, Probate.*

Civil Records: Access: In person only. Visitors must perform in person searches for themselves. No search fee. Required to search: name, years to search. Civil cases indexed by defendant, plaintiff. Civil records on computer from 1978, index books prior. Records are being microfilmed as load permits.

Criminal Records: Access: In person only. Visitors must perform in person searches for themselves. No search fee. Required to search: name, years to search. Criminal records on computer from 1978, index books prior. Records are being microfilmed as load permits.

General Information:. No juvenile, sealed, pending dissolution of marriage, mental health, domestic abuse or deferred records released. Copy fee: $.25 per page. Certification fee: $10.00. Fee payee: Clerk of Court. Personal checks accepted. Prepayment is required.

Poweshiek County

8th District Court PO Box 218, Montezuma, IA 50171; 641-623-5644; Fax: 641-623-5320. Hours: 8AM-4:30PM (CST). *Felony, Misdemeanor, Civil, Eviction, Small Claims, Probate.*

Civil Records: Access: In person only. Visitors must perform in person searches for themselves. No search fee. Required to search: name, years to search. Civil cases indexed by defendant, plaintiff. Civil records on index cards from 1980, docket books from early 1900s, computer since 7/95.

Criminal Records: Access: In person only. Visitors must perform in person searches for themselves. No search fee. Required to search: name, years to search. Criminal records on computer since 1986, index cards since 1980, docket books from early 1900s.

General Information: Public Access terminal is available. No juvenile, sealed, dissolution of marriage, mental health, domestic abuse or deferred records released. Copy fee: $.25 per page. Certification fee: $10.00. Fee payee: Clerk of Court. Personal checks accepted.

Ringgold County

5th District Court 109 W Madison (PO Box 523), Mount Ayr, IA 50854; 641-464-3234; Fax: 641-464-2478. Hours: 8AM-4:30PM (CST). *Felony, Misdemeanor, Civil, Small Claims, Probate.*

Civil Records: Access: In person only. Visitors must perform in person searches for themselves. No search fee. Required to search: name, years to search. Civil cases indexed by defendant, plaintiff. Civil records on docket books and computer.

Criminal Records: Access: In person only. Visitors must perform in person searches for themselves. No search fee. Required to search: name, years to search. Criminal records on docket books and computer.

General Information: Public Access terminal is available. No juvenile, sealed, pending dissolution of marriage, mental health or deferred records released. Copy fee: $.50 per page. Certification fee: $10.00. Fee payee: Clerk of Court. Personal checks accepted.

Sac County

2nd District Court PO Box 368, Sac City, IA 50583; 712-662-7791. Hours: 8AM-4:30PM (CST). *Felony, Misdemeanor, Civil, Eviction, Small Claims, Probate.*

Civil Records: Access: In person only. Visitors must perform in person searches for themselves. No search fee. Required to search: name. Civil cases indexed by defendant, plaintiff. Civil records on docket books and computer.

Criminal Records: Access: In person only. Visitors must perform in person searches for themselves. No search fee. Required to search: name. Criminal records on docket books and computer.

General Information: Public Access terminal is available. No juvenile, sealed, pending dissolution of marriage, mental health, domestic abuse or deferred records released. Copy fee: $.50 per page. Certification fee: $10.00. Fee payee: Clerk of Court. Personal checks accepted. Prepayment is required.

Scott County

7th District Court 416 W 4th St, Davenport, IA 52801; 563-326-8786. Hours: 8AM-4:30PM (CST). *Felony, Misdemeanor, Civil, Eviction, Small Claims, Probate.*

Civil Records: Access: In person only. Visitors must perform in person searches for themselves. No search fee. Required to search: name, years to search. Civil cases indexed by defendant, plaintiff. Civil records on computer back to 11/1993, docket books prior.

Criminal Records: Access: In person only. Visitors must perform in person searches for themselves. No search fee. Required to search: name, years to search, DOB; also helpful: SSN. Criminal records on computer back to 1992, printouts and docket books prior.

General Information: Public Access terminal is available. No juvenile, sealed, dissolution of marriage, mental health, domestic abuse or deferred records released. Copy fee: $.50 per page. Certification fee: $10.00. Fee payee: Clerk of Court. Personal checks accepted. Prepayment is required.

Shelby County

4th District Court PO Box 431, Harlan, IA 51537; 712-755-5543; Fax: 712-755-2667. Hours: 8AM-4:30PM (CST). *Felony, Misdemeanor, Civil, Eviction, Small Claims, Probate.*

www.shco.org

Civil Records: Access: Mail, in person. Both court and visitors may perform in person searches. Search fee: $5.00 per name. Required to search: name, years to search. Civil cases indexed by defendant, plaintiff. Civil records on original files back to 1969, microfilm prior.

Criminal Records: Access: Mail, in person. Both court and visitors may perform in person searches. Search fee: $5.00 per name. Required to search: name, years to search; also helpful: DOB, SSN. Criminal records on original files back to 1980, microfilm prior.

General Information: Public Access terminal is available. No juvenile, sealed, dissolution of marriage, mental health, domestic abuse or deferred records released. SASE required. Turnaround time same day. Copy fee: $.50 per page. Certification fee: $10.00. Fee payee: Clerk of Court. Personal checks accepted. Prepayment is required.

Sioux County

3rd District Court PO Box 47, Courthouse, Orange City, IA 51041; 712-737-2286; Fax: 712-737-8908. Hours: 8AM-4:30PM (CST). *Felony, Misdemeanor, Civil, Eviction, Small Claims, Probate.*

Civil Records: Access: In person only. Visitors must perform in person searches for themselves. No search fee. Required to search: name, years to search. Civil cases indexed by defendant, plaintiff. Civil records on docket books from 1800s.

Criminal Records: Access: In person only. Visitors must perform in person searches for themselves. No search fee. Required to search: name, years to search, signed release. Criminal records on docket books from 1800s.

General Information: Public Access terminal is available. No juvenile, sealed, dissolution of marriage, mental health, domestic abuse or deferred records released. Copy fee: $.50 per page. Certification fee:

$10.00. Fee payee: Clerk of Court. Personal checks accepted. Prepayment is required.

Story County

2nd District Court PO Box 408, Nevada, IA 50201; 515-382-7410. Hours: 8AM-4:30PM (CST). *Felony, Misdemeanor, Civil, Eviction, Small Claims, Probate.*

Civil Records: Access: In person only. Visitors must perform in person searches for themselves. No search fee. Required to search: name, years to search. Civil cases indexed by defendant, plaintiff. Civil records on docket books from 1900s; on computer back to 1995.
Criminal Records: Access: In person only. Visitors must perform in person searches for themselves. No search fee. Required to search: name, years to search. Criminal records on computer since 1992, prior on docket books.
General Information: Public Access terminal is available. No juvenile, sealed, dissolution of marriage, mental health, domestic abuse or deferred records released. Copy fee: $.50 per page. Certification fee: $10.00. Fee payee: Clerk of Court. Personal checks accepted. Prepayment is required.

Tama County

6th Judicial District Court PO Box 306, Toledo, IA 52342; 641-484-3721; Fax: 641-484-6403. Hours: 8AM-4:30PM (CST). *Felony, Misdemeanor, Civil, Eviction, Small Claims, Probate.*

Civil Records: Access: In person only. Visitors must perform in person searches for themselves. No search fee. Required to search: name, years to search. Civil cases indexed by defendant, plaintiff. Civil records on docket books from 1880s. Magistrate dockets to 1972, prior to 1972, Justice of the Peace.
Criminal Records: Access: In person only. Visitors must perform in person searches for themselves. No search fee. Required to search: name, years to search. Criminal records on docket books from 1880s. Magistrate dockets to 1972, prior to 1972, Justice of the Peace.
General Information: Public Access terminal is available. No juvenile, sealed, dissolution of marriage, mental health, domestic abuse or deferred records released. Copy fee: $.25 per page. Certification fee: $10.00. Fee payee: Clerk of Court. Personal checks accepted. Prepayment is required.

Taylor County

5th District Court Courthouse, Bedford, IA 50833; 712-523-2095; Fax: 712-523-2936. Hours: 8AM-4:30PM (CST). *Felony, Misdemeanor, Civil, Eviction, Small Claims, Probate.*

Civil Records: Access: In person only. Visitors must perform in person searches for themselves. No search fee. Required to search: name, years to search. Civil cases indexed by defendant, plaintiff. Civil records on computer since 11/01/96; prior to 1880s.
Criminal Records: Access: In person only. Visitors must perform in person searches for themselves. No search fee. Required to search: name, years to search. Criminal records on computer since 11/01/96; prior to 1880s.
General Information: Public Access terminal is available. No juvenile, sealed, dissolution of marriage, mental health, domestic abuse or deferred records released. Fax notes: Fee to fax results is $3.00 per document and $.50 per pg. Copy fee: $.50 per page. Certification fee: $10.00. Fee payee: Clerk of Court. Personal checks accepted. Prepayment is required.

Union County

5th District Court Courthouse, Creston, IA 50801; 641-782-7315; Fax: 641-782-8241. Hours: 8AM-4:30PM (CST). *Felony, Misdemeanor, Civil, Eviction, Small Claims, Probate.*

Civil Records: Access: In person only. Visitors must perform in person searches for themselves. No search fee. Required to search: name, years to search. Civil cases indexed by defendant, plaintiff. Civil records on docket books from 1900s; computerized back to 1996.
Criminal Records: Access: In person only. Visitors must perform in person searches for themselves. No search fee. Required to search: name, years to search. Criminal records on docket books from 1900s; computerized back to 1996.
General Information:. No juvenile, sealed, pending dissolution of marriage, mental health, domestic abuse or deferred records released. Fax notes: No fee to fax results. Copy fee: $.50 per page. Certification fee: $10.00. Fee payee: Clerk of Court. Personal checks accepted.

Van Buren County

8th District Court Courthouse Criminal Records, Keosauqua, IA 52565; 319-293-3108; Fax: 319-293-3811. Hours: 8AM-4:30PM (CST). *Felony, Misdemeanor, Civil, Eviction, Small Claims, Probate.*

Note: SSNs currently are shown in the public access terminal, but will be masked by the end of 1999.

Civil Records: Access: In person only. Visitors must perform in person searches for themselves. No search fee. Required to search: name, years to search. Civil cases indexed by defendant, plaintiff. Civil records on docket books from 1837, computerized since 1997.
Criminal Records: Access: In person only. Visitors must perform in person searches for themselves. No search fee. Required to search: name, years to search; also helpful: DOB, SSN. Criminal records on docket books from 1837, computerized since 1997.
General Information: Public Access terminal is available. No sealed, mental health, or sealed records released; will release un-sealed juvenile, marriage dissolution or DA records if after July, 2000. Copy fee: $.25 per page. Certification fee: $10.00. Fee payee: Clerk of Court. Personal checks accepted. Prepayment is required.

Wapello County

8th District Court 101 W 4th, Ottumwa, IA 52501; 641-683-0060. Hours: 8AM-4:30PM (CST). *Felony, Misdemeanor, Civil, Eviction, Small Claims, Probate.*

Note: SSNs are only maintained on a confidential sheet not available to the public.

Civil Records: Access: In person only. Visitors must perform in person searches for themselves. No search fee. Required to search: name, years to search. Civil cases indexed by defendant, plaintiff. Civil records on computer (child support), docket books prior.
Criminal Records: Access: In person only. Visitors must perform in person searches for themselves. No search fee. Required to search: name, years to search, DOB; also helpful: SSN. Criminal records on computer (for 6 months prior), docket books prior.
General Information: Public Access terminal is available. No juvenile, sealed, dissolution of marriage, mental health, domestic abuse or deferred records released. Copy fee: $.25 per page. Certification fee: $10.00. Fee payee: Clerk of Court. Personal checks accepted. Prepayment is required.

Warren County

5th District Court PO Box 379, Indianola, IA 50125; 515-961-1033; Fax: 515-961-1071. Hours: 8AM-4:30PM (CST). *Felony, Misdemeanor, Civil, Eviction, Small Claims, Probate.*

Civil Records: Access: In person only. Both court and visitors may perform in person searches. No search fee. Required to search: name, years to search. Civil cases indexed by defendant, plaintiff. Civil records on computer back to 10/1995; prior on docket books.
Criminal Records: Access: In person only. Both court and visitors may perform in person searches. No search fee. Required to search: name, years to search. Criminal records on computer back to 10/1995; prior on docket books.
General Information: Public Access terminal is available. No juvenile, sealed, dissolution of marriage, mental health, domestic abuse or deferred records released. Copy fee: $.50 per page. Certification fee: $10.00. Fee payee: Clerk of Court. Personal checks accepted. Credit cards accepted.

Washington County

8th District Court PO Box 391, Washington, IA 52353; 319-653-7741; Fax: 319-653-7787. Hours: 8AM-4:30PM (CST). *Felony, Misdemeanor, Civil, Eviction, Small Claims, Probate.*

Civil Records: Access: In person only. Visitors must perform in person searches for themselves. No search fee. Required to search: name, years to search. Civil cases indexed by defendant, plaintiff. Civil records on computer back to 1997, microfilm from 1940, docket books since court inception.
Criminal Records: Access: In person only. Visitors must perform in person searches for themselves. No search fee. Required to search: name, years to search. Criminal records on computer back to 1997, microfilm from 1940, docket books since court inception.
General Information: Public Access terminal is available. No juvenile, sealed, dissolution of marriage, mental health, domestic abuse or deferred records released. Copy fee: $.25 per page. Certification fee: $10.00. Fee payee: Clerk of Court. Personal checks accepted. Prepayment is required.

Wayne County

5th District Court PO Box 424, Corydon, IA 50060; 641-872-2264; Fax: 641-872-2431. Hours: 8AM-4:30PM (CST). *Felony, Misdemeanor, Civil, Eviction, Small Claims, Probate.*

Civil Records: Access: In person only. Visitors must perform in person searches for themselves. No search fee. Required to search: name, years to search. Civil cases indexed by defendant, plaintiff. Civil records on dockets from 1890.
Criminal Records: Access: In person only. Visitors must perform in person searches for themselves. No search fee. Required to search: name, years to search, DOB. Criminal records on dockets from 1890.
General Information: Public Access terminal is available. No juvenile, sealed, dissolution of marriage, mental health, domestic abuse or deferred records released. Copy fee: $.50 per page. Certification fee: $10.00. Fee payee: Clerk of Court. Personal checks accepted. Prepayment is required.

Webster County

2nd District Court 701 Central Ave, Courthouse, Ft Dodge, IA 50501; 515-576-7115. Hours: 8AM-4:30PM (CST). *Felony, Misdemeanor, Civil, Eviction, Small Claims, Probate.*

Civil Records: Access: In person only. Visitors must perform in person searches for themselves. No search fee. Required to search: name, years to search. Civil cases indexed by defendant, plaintiff. Civil records on docket books from 1800s, on computer since 1994.

Criminal Records: Access: In person only. Visitors must perform in person searches for themselves. No search fee. Required to search: name, years to search, signed release. Criminal records on docket books from 1800s, on computer since 1994.

General Information: Public Access terminal is available. No juvenile, sealed, dissolution of marriage, mental health, domestic abuse or deferred records released. Copy fee: $.50 per page. Certification fee: $10.00. Fee payee: Clerk of Court. Personal checks accepted. Prepayment is required.

Winnebago County

2nd District Court 126 W Clark, Box 468, Forest City, IA 50436; 641-585-4520; Fax: 641-585-2615. Hours: 8AM-4:30PM (CST). *Felony, Misdemeanor, Civil, Eviction, Small Claims, Probate.*

Civil Records: Access: In person only. Visitors must perform in person searches for themselves. No search fee. Required to search: name, years to search; also helpful: address. Civil cases indexed by defendant, plaintiff. Civil records on dockets from 1880s; on computer since 9/1997.

Criminal Records: Access: In person only. Visitors must perform in person searches for themselves. No search fee. Required to search: name, years to search, offense, date of offense; also helpful: address, DOB, aliases. Criminal records on dockets from 1940s; on computer since 9/1997.

General Information: Public Access terminal is available. No juvenile, pending or dismissed dissolution of marriage, mental health, domestic abuse, criminal deferred or substance abuse records released. Copy fee: $.50 per page. Certification fee: $10.00. Fee payee: Clerk of Court. Personal checks accepted. Credit cards accepted: Visa, MasterCard. Prepayment is required.

Winneshiek County

1st District Court 201 W Main St, Decorah, IA 52101; 563-382-2469; Fax: 563-382-0603. Hours: 8AM-4:30PM (CST). *Felony, Misdemeanor, Civil, Eviction, Small Claims, Probate.*

Civil Records: Access: In person only. Visitors must perform in person searches for themselves. No search fee. Required to search: name, years to search. Civil cases indexed by defendant, plaintiff. Civil records on computer since 1994, docket books since 1860s.

Criminal Records: Access: In person only. Visitors must perform in person searches for themselves. No search fee. Required to search: name, years to search, signed release. Criminal records on computer since 1992, docket books since 1860s.

General Information: Public Access terminal is available. No juvenile, sealed, dissolution of marriage, mental health, domestic abuse or deferred records released. Copy fee: $.50 per page. Certification fee: $10.00. Fee payee: Clerk of Court. Personal checks accepted.

Woodbury County

3rd District Court Woodbury County Courthouse, 620-Douglas, Rm 101, Sioux City, IA 51101-1248; 712-279-6611; Fax: 712-279-6021. Hours: 8AM-4:30PM (CST). *Felony, Civil, Eviction, Probate.*

Civil Records: Access: In person only. Visitors must perform in person searches for themselves. No search fee. Required to search: name, years to search. Civil cases indexed by defendant, plaintiff. Civil records on index books from early 1900; on computer from 7/95.

Criminal Records: Access: In person only. Visitors must perform in person searches for themselves. No search fee. Required to search: name, years to search. Criminal records on index books from early 1900; on computer from 10/95.

General Information: Public Access terminal is available. No sealed, pending dissolution of marriage, mental health records released. Copy fee: $.50 per page. Certification fee: $10.00. Fee payee: Clerk of Court. Personal checks accepted. Prepayment is required.

3rd District Court 407 7th St, County Clerk at Law Enforcement Ctr, Sioux City, IA 51101; 712-279-6624. Hours: 8AM-4:30PM (CST). *Misdemeanor, Civil, Eviction, Small Claims.*

Civil Records: Access: In person only. Visitors must perform in person searches for themselves. No search fee. Required to search: name, years to search. Civil cases indexed by defendant, plaintiff. Civil records on docket books from early 1900; on computer from 7/95.

Criminal Records: Access: In person only. Visitors must perform in person searches for themselves. No

search fee. Required to search: name, years to search. Criminal Records indexed on computer since 1992; on computer from 7/92.

General Information: Public Access terminal is available. No juvenile records released. Copy fee: $.50 per page. Certification fee: $10.00. Fee payee: Clerk of Court. Personal checks accepted. Prepayment is required.

Worth County

2nd District Court 1000 Central Ave, Northwood, IA 50459; 641-324-2840; Fax: 641-324-2360. Hours: 8AM-4:30PM (CST). *Felony, Misdemeanor, Civil, Eviction, Small Claims, Probate.*

Civil Records: Access: In person only. Visitors must perform in person searches for themselves. No search fee. Required to search: name, years to search. Civil cases indexed by defendant, plaintiff. Civil records on computer and docket books.

Criminal Records: Access: In person only. Visitors must perform in person searches for themselves. No search fee. Required to search: name, years to search. Criminal records on computer and docket books.

General Information: Public Access terminal is available. No juvenile, sealed, dissolution of marriage, mental health, domestic abuse, dismissed, or deferred records released. Copy fee: $.50 per page. Certification fee: $10.00. Fee payee: Clerk of Court. Personal checks accepted. Prepayment is required.

Wright County

2nd District Court PO Box 306, Clarion, IA 50525; 515-532-3113; Fax: 515-532-2343. Hours: 8AM-4:30PM (CST). *Felony, Misdemeanor, Civil, Eviction, Small Claims, Probate.*

Civil Records: Access: In person only. Visitors must perform in person searches for themselves. No search fee. Required to search: name, years to search. Civil cases indexed by defendant, plaintiff. Civil records on docket books from 1880; on computer since 1997.

Criminal Records: Access: In person only. Visitors must perform in person searches for themselves. No search fee. Required to search: name, years to search; also helpful: DOB, SSN. Criminal records on docket books from 1880s; on computer since 1997.

General Information: Public Access terminal is available. No juvenile, sealed, dissolution of marriage, mental health, domestic abuse or deferred records released. Copy fee: $.50 per page. Certification fee: $10.00. Fee payee: Clerk of Court. Personal checks accepted.

Iowa Recording Offices

ORGANIZATION   99 counties, 100 recording offices. Lee County has two recording offices. The recording officer is the County Recorder. Many counties utilize a grantor/grantee index containing all transactions recorded with them. See the notes under the county for how to determine which office is appropriate to search. The entire state is in the Central Time Zone (CST).

REAL ESTATE RECORDS   Most counties are hesitant to perform real estate searches, but some will provide a listing from the grantor/grantee index with the understanding that it is not certified in the sense that a title search is. Certification of copies usually costs $2.00-5.00 per document.

UCC RECORDS   Financing statements are filed at the state level, except for real estate related collateral, which are filed with the County Recorder. However, prior to 07/2001, consumer goods were also filed at the County Recorder and these older records can be searched there. All counties will perform UCC searches. Use search request form UCC-11. Search fees are usually $5.00 per debtor name ($6.00 if the standard UCC-11 form is not used). Copies usually cost $1.00 per page.

TAX LIEN RECORDS   Federal tax liens on personal property of businesses are filed with the Secretary of State. Other federal and all state tax liens on personal property are filed with the County Recorder. County search practices vary widely, but most provide some sort of tax lien search for $6.00 per name.

OTHER LIENS   Home improvement, job service.

Adair County

County Recorder, Courthouse, 400 Public Square, Greenfield, IA 50849. 641-743-2411; Fax 641-743-2565.
Will search UCC records. Tax liens not included in UCC search. RE record owner and mortgage searches available. **Other Phone Numbers:** Assessor 641-745-2531; Treasurer 641-743-2312; Vital Records 641-743-2411.

Adams County

County Recorder, P.O. Box 28, Corning, IA 50841. County Recorder, R/E and UCC Recording 641-322-3744; Fax 641-322-3744.
Will search UCC records. Tax liens not included in UCC search. Will not search real estate records. **Other Phone Numbers:** Assessor 641-322-4312; Treasurer 641-322-3210; Appraiser/Auditor 641-322-3340; Vital Records 641-322-3744.

Allamakee County

County Recorder, 110 Allamakee Street, Courthouse, Waukon, IA 52172-1794. 563-568-2364; Fax 319-568-6419.
Will search UCC records. UCC search includes tax liens. Will not search real estate records. **Other Phone Numbers:** Assessor 563-568-3145; Treasurer 563-568-3793.

Appanoose County

County Recorder, Courthouse, Centerville, IA 52544. 641-856-6103.
Will search UCC records. UCC search includes tax liens if requested. Will not search real estate records. **Other Phone Numbers:** Assessor 641-437-4529; Treasurer 641-856-3097.

Audubon County

County Recorder, 318 Leroy St. #7, Audubon, IA 50025-1255. County Recorder, R/E and UCC Recording 712-563-2119; Fax 712-563-4766.
Will search UCC records. Tax liens not included in UCC search. Will not search real estate records. **Other Phone Numbers:** Assessor 712-563-3418; Treasurer 712-563-2293; Vital Records 712-563-2119.

Benton County

County Recorder, Courthouse, Vinton, IA 52349. 319-472-3309; Fax 319-472-3309.
Will search UCC records. Will not search real estate records. **Other Phone Numbers:** Assessor 319-472-5211; Treasurer 319-472-5211.

Black Hawk County

County Recorder, 316 East 5th Street, Courthouse, Room 208, Waterloo, IA 50703-4774. 319-833-3171 R/E Recording: 319-833-3012 UCC Recording: 319-833-3012; Fax 319-833-3170.
Will search UCC records. Tax liens not included in UCC search. RE owner, mortgage, and property transfer searches available. **Other Phone Numbers:** Assessor 319-833-3006; Treasurer 319-833-3013; Elections 319-833-3123; Vital Records 319-833-3012.

Boone County

County Recorder, 201 State Street, Boone, IA 50036-3987. County Recorder, R/E and UCC Recording 515-433-0514; Fax 515-432-8102.
Will search UCC records. Tax liens not included in UCC search. Mortgage searches available. **Other Phone Numbers:** Assessor 515-433-0508; Elections 515-433-0514; Vital Records 515-433-0514.

Bremer County

County Recorder, 415 E Bremer, 415 E. Bremer Ave., Waverly, IA 50677. 319-352-0401; Fax 319-352-0518.
Will search UCC records. Tax liens not included in UCC search. RE owner, mortgage, and property transfer searches available. Real estate searches by phone, no charge **Other Phone Numbers:** Assessor 319-352-5040; Treasurer 319-352-5040.

Buchanan County

County Recorder, P.O. Box 298, Independence, IA 50644-0298. 319-334-4259 R/E Recording: 319-334-6887 UCC Recording: 319-334-6887; Fax 319-334-7453.
Will search UCC records. UCC search includes tax liens if requested. Will not search real estate records. **Other Phone Numbers:** Assessor 319-334-2706; Treasurer 319-334-4340; Elections 319-334-4109; Vital Records 319-334-6887.

Buena Vista County

County Recorder, P.O. Box 454, Storm Lake, IA 50588. 712-749-2539; Fax 712-749-2539.
Will search UCC records. UCC search includes tax liens. Will not search real estate records. **Other Phone Numbers:** Assessor 712-749-2543; Treasurer 712-749-5533.

Butler County

County Recorder, P.O. Box 346, Allison, IA 50602. 319-267-2735; Fax 319-267-2628.
Will search UCC records. Will not search real estate records. **Other Phone Numbers:** Assessor 319-267-2264.

Calhoun County

County Recorder, Calhoun County Courthouse 416-4th St., Rockwell City, IA 50579. 712-297-8121.
Will search UCC records. Tax liens not included in UCC search. Will not search real estate records.

Carroll County

County Recorder, P.O. Box 782, Carroll, IA 51401-0782. 712-792-3328; Fax 712-792-9493.
Will search UCC records. Tax liens not included in UCC search. Will not search real estate records. **Other Phone Numbers:** Assessor 712-792-9973; Treasurer 712-792-1200.

Cass County

County Recorder, 5 West 7th, Atlantic, IA 50022-1492. 712-243-1692; Fax 712-243-4736.
Will search UCC records. UCC search includes tax liens. Copies are $.50 per page Will not search real estate records. **Other Phone Numbers:** Assessor 712-243-2005; Treasurer 712-243-5503.

Cedar County

County Recorder, 400 Cedar Street, Courthouse, Tipton, IA 52772-1752. County Recorder, R/E and UCC Recording 563-886-2230; Fax 319-886-2095.
Will search UCC records. Will not search real estate records. **Other Phone Numbers:** Assessor 563-886-6413; Treasurer 563-886-2557; Elections 563-886-3168; Vital Records 563-886-2230.

Cerro Gordo County

County Recorder, 220 North Washington, Mason City, IA 50401. County Recorder, R/E and UCC Recording 641-421-3056; Fax 641-421-3154.

Will search UCC records. Tax liens not included in UCC search. RE owner, mortgage, and property transfer searches available. **Other Phone Numbers:** Assessor 641-421-3065; Treasurer 641-421-3037; Elections 641-421-3027; Vital Records 641-421-3056.

Cherokee County

County Recorder, Drawer G, Cherokee, IA 51012. County Recorder, R/E and UCC Recording 712-225-6735; Fax 712-225-6754.

Will search UCC records. UCC search includes tax liens if requested. RE owner, mortgage, and property transfer searches available. **Other Phone Numbers:** Assessor 712-225-6701; Treasurer 712-225-4670; Appraiser/Auditor 712-225-6701; Elections 712-225-6704; Vital Records 712-225-6735.

Chickasaw County

County Recorder, P.O. Box 14, New Hampton, IA 50659. 641-394-2336; Fax 641-394-2816.

Will search UCC records. UCC search includes tax liens if requested. RE owner, mortgage, and property transfer searches available. **Other Phone Numbers:** Assessor 641-394-2813; Treasurer 641-394-2107.

Clarke County

County Recorder, Courthouse, Osceola, IA 50213. 641-342-3313; Fax 641-342-3893.

Will search UCC records. Tax liens not included in UCC search. Separate combined tax lien search-$6.00 first name, $5.00 per additional name. Mortgage searches available. **Other Phone Numbers:** Assessor 641-342-3817; Treasurer 641-342-3311.

Clay County

County Recorder, Administration Building, 300 W. 4th St, #3, Spencer, IA 51301-3806. County Recorder, R/E and UCC Recording 712-262-1081; Fax 712-264-3983.

Will search UCC records. Tax liens not included in UCC search. Will not search real estate records. **Other Phone Numbers:** Assessor 712-262-1986; Treasurer 712-262-2179; Appraiser/Auditor 712-262-1986; Elections 712-262-1569; Vital Records 712-262-1081.

Clayton County

County Recorder, P.O. Box 278, Elkader, IA 52043. County Recorder, R/E and UCC Recording 563-245-2710; Fax 319-245-2353.

Will search UCC records. Tax liens not included in UCC search. RE owner, mortgage, and property transfer searches available. **Other Phone Numbers:** Assessor 563-245-2533; Treasurer 563-245-1807; Elections 563-245-1106; Vital Records 563-245-2710.

Clinton County

County Recorder, P.O. Box 2957, Clinton, IA 52733-2957. 563-244-0565 x0544; Fax 563-242-8412.

Will search UCC records. Will not search real estate records. **Other Phone Numbers:** Assessor 563-242-0569; Treasurer 563-242-0573.

Crawford County

County Recorder, 1202 Broadway, Denison, IA 51442. County Recorder, R/E and UCC Recording 712-263-3643; Fax 712-263-3413.

Will search UCC records. UCC search includes tax liens if requested. Will not search real estate records. **Other Phone Numbers:** Assessor 712-263-3447; Treasurer 712-263-2648; Elections 712-263-3045; Vital Records 712-263-3643.

Dallas County

County Recorder, PO Box 38, Adel, IA 50003-0038. 515-993-5804; Fax 515-933-5790.

Will search UCC records. UCC search includes tax liens if requested. RE owner, mortgage, and property transfer searches available. **Other Phone Numbers:** Assessor 515-993-5802; Treasurer 515-993-5808.

Davis County

County Recorder, Courthouse, Bloomfield, IA 52537. County Recorder, R/E and UCC Recording 641-664-2321; Fax 641-664-3082. davis_co_recorder @hayoo.com

Will search UCC records. UCC search includes tax liens if requested. Will not search real estate records. **Other Phone Numbers:** Assessor 641-664-3101; Treasurer 641-664-2155; Elections 641-664-2101; Vital Records 641-664-2321.

Decatur County

County Recorder, 207 North Main Street, Leon, IA 50144. 641-446-4322; Fax 641-446-7159.

Will search UCC records. RE owner, mortgage, and property transfer searches available. **Other Phone Numbers:** Assessor 641-446-4314.

Delaware County

County Recorder, Courthouse, 301 East Main, Manchester, IA 52057. 563-927-4665; Fax 319-927-6423.

Will search UCC records. Tax liens not included in UCC search. Will not search real estate records. **Other Phone Numbers:** Assessor 563-927-2526; Treasurer 563-927-2845.

Des Moines County

County Recorder, P.O. Box 277, Burlington, IA 52601-0277. County Recorder, R/E and UCC Recording 319-753-8221; Fax 319-753-8721.

Will search UCC records. UCC search includes tax liens if requested. Will not search real estate records. **Other Phone Numbers:** Assessor 319-753-8224; Treasurer 319-753-8252; Appraiser/Auditor 319-753-8255; Elections 319-753-8266; Vital Records 319-753-8221; Motor Vehicle 319-753-8273.

Dickinson County

County Recorder, P.O. Box O.E., Spirit Lake, IA 51360. 712-336-1495; Fax 712-336-2677.

Will search UCC records. Tax liens not included in UCC search. Will not search real estate records. **Other Phone Numbers:** Assessor 712-336-2687; Treasurer 712-336-1205.

Dubuque County

County Recorder, Courthouse, 720 Central #9, Dubuque, IA 52001. County Recorder, R/E and UCC Recording 563-589-4434; Fax 319-589-4484.

Will search UCC records. UCC search includes tax liens if requested. Will not search real estate records. **Other Phone Numbers:** Assessor 563-589-4432; Treasurer 563-589-4436; Elections 563-589-4458; Vital Records 563-589-4434.

Emmet County

County Recorder, 609 1st Avenue North, Estherville, IA 51334. County Recorder, R/E and UCC Recording 712-362-4115; Fax 712-362-7454.

Will search UCC records. Tax liens not included in UCC search. Will not search real estate records. **Online Access:** Real Estate. Online access to real estate records on the county database are available free at http://www.emmet.org/pmc. Also, the GIS mapping database may be searched. Includes parcel report, survey section grid, parcel maps, and more. Search the

"Parcel Data" link by owner name, parcel ID, or address. **Other Phone Numbers:** Assessor 712-362-2609; Treasurer 712-362-3824; Appraiser/Auditor 712-362-2609; Elections 712-362-4261; Vital Records 712-362-4115.

Fayette County

County Recorder, P.O. Box 226, West Union, IA 52175-0226. 563-422-3687; Fax 319-422-9201.

Will search UCC records. Tax liens not included in UCC search. Will not search real estate records. **Other Phone Numbers:** Assessor 563-422-6061 x39; Treasurer 563-422-6061.

Floyd County

County Recorder, Courthouse, 101 S. Main, Charles City, IA 50616. County Recorder, R/E and UCC Recording 641-257-6154; Fax 641-228-6458.

Will search UCC records. UCC search includes tax liens if requested. RE record owner and mortgage searches available. **Other Phone Numbers:** Assessor 641-257-6152; Treasurer 641-257-6118; Elections 641-257-6131; Vital Records 641-257-6154.

Franklin County

County Recorder, P.O. Box 26, Hampton, IA 50441. 641-456-5675; Fax 641-456-1990.

Will search UCC records. UCC search includes tax liens if requested. RE owner, mortgage, and property transfer searches available. **Other Phone Numbers:** Assessor 641-456-5118; Treasurer 641-456-5678.

Fremont County

County Recorder, P.O. Box 295, Sidney, IA 51652. County Recorder, R/E and UCC Recording 712-374-2315; Fax 712-374-2826. http://www.co.fremont.ia.us

Will search UCC records. Tax liens not included in UCC search. Will not search real estate records. **Other Phone Numbers:** Assessor 712-374-2631; Treasurer 712-374-2122; Elections 712-374-2031; Vital Records 712-374-2315.

Greene County

County Recorder, Courthouse, 114 N. Chestnut, Jefferson, IA 50129. 515-386-3716 R/E Recording: 515-386-5670 UCC Recording: 515-386-5670; Fax 515-386-5274.

Will search UCC records. UCC search includes tax liens if requested. Will not search real estate records. **Other Phone Numbers:** Assessor 515-386-5660; Treasurer 515-386-5675; Appraiser/Auditor 515-386-5680.

Grundy County

County Recorder, 706 G Avenue, Grundy Center, IA 50638-1447. County Recorder, R/E and UCC Recording 319-824-3234.

Will search UCC records. Tax liens not included in UCC search. Will not search real estate records. **Other Phone Numbers:** Assessor 319-824-6216; Treasurer 319-824-3412; Elections 319-824-3122; Vital Records 319-824-3234.

Guthrie County

County Recorder, 200 North 5th, Courthouse, Guthrie Center, IA 50115. County Recorder, R/E and UCC Recording 641-747-3412; Fax 641-747-3346.

Will search UCC records. This agency will not do a tax lien search. Will not search real estate records. **Other Phone Numbers:** Assessor 641-747-3319; Treasurer 641-747-3414; Appraiser/Auditor 641-747-3319; Elections 641-747-3619; Vital Records 641-747-3412.

Hamilton County

County Recorder, P.O. Box 126, Webster City, IA 50595-0126. 515-832-9535; Fax 515-833-9525.
Will search UCC records. UCC search includes tax liens if requested. **Other Phone Numbers:** Assessor 515-832-9505; Treasurer 515-832-9542.

Hancock County

County Recorder, 855 State Street, Garner, IA 50438. 641-923-2464; Fax 641-923-3912.
Will search UCC records. UCC search includes tax liens if requested. RE record owner and mortgage searches available. **Other Phone Numbers:** Assessor 641-923-2269; Treasurer 641-923-3122.

Hardin County

County Recorder, P.O. Box 443, Eldora, IA 50627. 641-939-8178; Fax 641-939-8245.
Will search UCC records. Tax liens not included in UCC search. RE owner, mortgage, and property transfer searches available. **Other Phone Numbers:** Assessor 641-939-8100; Treasurer 641-939-8226; Appraiser/Auditor 641-939-8230; Drivers License 641-939-8328.

Harrison County

County Recorder, Courthouse, Logan, IA 51546. 712-644-2545; Fax 712-644-2643.
Will search UCC records. Tax liens not included in UCC search. Will not search real estate records. **Other Phone Numbers:** Assessor 712-644-3101; Treasurer 712-644-2750.

Henry County

County Recorder, P.O. Box 106, Mount Pleasant, IA 52641. 319-385-0765; Fax 319-385-3601.
Will search UCC records. Tax liens not included in UCC search. Will not search real estate records. **Other Phone Numbers:** Assessor 319-385-0750; Treasurer 319-385-0763; Elections 319-385-0756; Vital Records 319-385-0765.

Howard County

County Recorder, Court House, 137 N. Elm, Cresco, IA 52136. 563-547-3621; Fax 319-547-2629.
Will search UCC records. UCC search includes tax liens if requested. RE owner, mortgage, and property transfer searches available. **Other Phone Numbers:** Assessor 563-547-3409; Treasurer 563-547-3860.

Humboldt County

County Recorder, P.O. Box 100, Dakota City, IA 50529-0100. 515-332-3693; Fax 515-332-1738.
Will search UCC records. Tax liens not included in UCC search. RE record owner searches available. **Other Phone Numbers:** Assessor 515-332-1643; Treasurer 515-332-1571.

Ida County

County Recorder, 401 Moorehead, Courthouse, Ida Grove, IA 51445. County Recorder, R/E and UCC Recording 712-364-2220; Fax 712-364-2746.
Will search UCC records. Tax liens not included in UCC search. Will not search real estate records. **Other Phone Numbers:** Assessor 712-364-3622; Treasurer 712-364-2287; Elections 712-364-2620; Vital Records 712-364-2220.

Iowa County

County Recorder, P.O. Box 185, Marengo, IA 52301. County Recorder, R/E and UCC Recording 319-642-3622; Fax 319-642-5562.
Will search UCC records. UCC search includes tax liens if requested. Will not search real estate records. **Other Phone Numbers:** Assessor 319-642-3851; Treasurer 319-642-3672; Elections 319-642-3923; Vital Records 319-642-3622.

Jackson County

County Recorder, 201 West Platt, Maquoketa, IA 52060. County Recorder, R/E and UCC Recording 563-652-2504; Fax 319-652-6460.
Will search UCC records. UCC search includes tax liens if requested. RE owner, mortgage, and property transfer searches available. **Other Phone Numbers:** Assessor 563-652-4935; Treasurer 563-652-5649; Elections 563-652-3144; Vital Records 563-652-2504.

Jasper County

County Recorder, P.O. Box 665, Newton, IA 50208. 641-792-5442; Fax 641-791-3680.
Will search UCC records. Will not search real estate records. **Other Phone Numbers:** Assessor 641-792-6195; Treasurer 641-792-6115.

Jefferson County

County Recorder, 51 West Briggs, Fairfield, IA 52556-2820. 641-472-4331; Fax 641-472-6695.
Will search UCC records. UCC search includes tax liens if requested. State tax lien searches are uncertified and performed at no charge Will not search real estate records. **Other Phone Numbers:** Assessor 641-472-2849; Treasurer 641-472-2349.

Johnson County

County Recorder, 913 S. Dubuque Street, Suite 202, Iowa City, IA 52240-4207. 319-356-6093; Fax 319-339-6181.
Will search UCC records. Will provide list of liens from 11/1/83 on **Other Phone Numbers:** Assessor 319-356-6078; Treasurer 319-356-6087.

Jones County

County Recorder, Courthouse, Room 116, 500 W. Main, Anamosa, IA 52205-1632. County Recorder, R/E and UCC Recording 319-462-2477; Fax 319-462-5802.
Will search UCC records. UCC search includes tax liens if requested. RE owner, mortgage, and property transfer searches available. **Other Phone Numbers:** Assessor 319-462-2671; Treasurer 319-462-3550; Elections 319-462-2282; Vital Records 319-462-2477.

Keokuk County

County Recorder, Courthouse, Sigourney, IA 52591. County Recorder, R/E and UCC Recording 641-622-2540; Fax 641-622-3789.
Will search UCC records. UCC search includes tax liens if requested. Will not search real estate records. **Other Phone Numbers:** Assessor 641-622-2560; Treasurer 641-622-2421; Elections 641-622-2320; Vital Records 641-622-2540.

Kossuth County

County Recorder, 114 West State, Algona, IA 50511. 515-295-5660; Fax 515-295-9304.
Will search UCC records. Tax liens not included in UCC search. Will not search real estate records. **Other Phone Numbers:** Assessor 515-295-3857; Treasurer 515-295-3404.

Lee County (Northern District)

County Recorder, P.O. Box 322, Fort Madison, IA 52627-0322. 319-372-4662; Fax 319-372-7033.
Will search UCC records. Tax liens not included in UCC search. Will not search real estate records. **Other Phone Numbers:** Assessor 319-372-6302; Treasurer 319-372-3405; Elections 319-372-3705; Vital Records 319-372-4662.

Lee County (Southern District)

County Recorder, P.O. Box 160, Keokuk, IA 52632. 319-524-1126; Fax 319-524-1544.
Will search UCC records. Will not search real estate records. **Other Phone Numbers:** Assessor 319-524-1375.

Linn County

County Recorder, P.O. Box 1406, Cedar Rapids, IA 52406-1406. County Recorder, R/E and UCC Recording 319-892-5420; Fax 319-892-5459.
http://www.linncountyrecorder.com
Will search UCC records. Will not search real estate records. **Other Phone Numbers:** Assessor 319-892-5220; Treasurer 319-892-5550; Elections 319-892-5400; Vital Records 319-892-5445.

Louisa County

County Recorder, P.O. Box 264, Wapello, IA 52653-0264. 319-523-5361; Fax 319-523-3713.
Will search UCC records. This agency will not do a tax lien search. Will not search real estate records.

Lucas County

County Recorder, Courthouse, Chariton, IA 50049. 641-774-2413; Fax 641-774-2993.
Will search UCC records. This agency will not do a tax lien search. **Other Phone Numbers:** Assessor 641-774-4411; Treasurer 641-774-5213.

Lyon County

County Recorder, 206 Second Avenue, Courthouse, Rock Rapids, IA 51246. 712-472-2381; Fax 712-472-2381.
Will search UCC records. UCC search includes tax liens if requested. Will not search real estate records. **Other Phone Numbers:** Assessor 712-472-3592; Treasurer 712-472-3703.

Madison County

County Recorder, P.O. Box 152, Winterset, IA 50273-0152. County Recorder, R/E and UCC Recording 515-462-3771; Fax 515-462-5881.
Will search UCC records. Tax liens not included in UCC search. Will not search real estate records. **Other Phone Numbers:** Assessor 515-462-4303; Treasurer 515-462-1542; Elections 515-462-3914; Vital Records 515-462-3771.

Mahaska County

County Recorder, Courthouse, Oskaloosa, IA 52577. County Recorder, R/E and UCC Recording 641-673-8187.
Will search UCC records. UCC search includes tax liens if requested. Will not search real estate records. **Other Phone Numbers:** Assessor 641-673-5805; Treasurer 641-673-5482; Vital Records 641-673-8187.

Marion County

County Recorder, 214 E. Main St., Knoxville, IA 50138. 641-828-2211; Fax 641-842-3593.
Will search UCC records. UCC search includes tax liens if requested. Will not search real estate records. **Other Phone Numbers:** Assessor 641-828-2215; Treasurer 641-828-2211.

Marshall County

County Recorder, Courthouse, 3rd Floor, 1 East Main St., Marshalltown, IA 50158-4915. 6417546-355; Fax 641-754-6321.
Will search UCC records. UCC search includes tax liens if requested. Will not search real estate records. **Other Phone Numbers:** Assessor 641-754-5355; Treasurer 641-754-6366.

Mills County

County Recorder, Courthouse, 418 Sharp St., Glenwood, IA 51534. 712-527-9315.
Will search UCC records. UCC search includes tax liens if requested. **Other Phone Numbers:** Assessor 712-527-4883; Treasurer 712-527-4419.

Mitchell County

County Recorder, 508 State Street, Osage, IA 50461-1250. County Recorder, R/E and UCC Recording 641-732-5861; Fax 641-732-5218.
Will search UCC records. Tax liens not included in UCC search. Will not search real estate records. **Other Phone Numbers:** Assessor 641-732-5861; Treasurer 641-732-5861.

Monona County

County Recorder, P.O. Box 53, Onawa, IA 51040. County Recorder, R/E and UCC Recording 712-423-2575; Fax 712-423-3034.
Will search UCC records. UCC search includes tax liens if requested. RE record owner and mortgage searches available. **Other Phone Numbers:** Assessor 712-423-2271; Treasurer 712-423-2271; Elections 712-423-2191; Vital Records 712-423-2575.

Monroe County

County Recorder, Courthouse, 10 Benton Ave. East, Albia, IA 52531. 641-932-5164; Fax 641932-2863.
Will search UCC records. This agency will not do a tax lien search. RE owner, mortgage, and property transfer searches available. **Other Phone Numbers:** Assessor 641-932-2180; Treasurer 641-932-5011.

Montgomery County

County Recorder, P.O. Box 469, Red Oak, IA 51566. County Recorder, R/E and UCC Recording 712-623-4363; Fax 712-623-8915.
Will search UCC records. Tax liens not included in UCC search. Will not search real estate records. **Other Phone Numbers:** Assessor 712-623-4171; Treasurer 712-623-2392; Appraiser/Auditor 712-623-4171; Elections 712-623-5127; Vital Records 712-623-4363.

Muscatine County

County Recorder, 401 East 3rd Street, Courthouse, Muscatine, IA 52761-4166. County Recorder, R/E and UCC Recording 563-263-7741; Fax 563-263-7248.
Will search UCC records. Tax liens not included in UCC search. Federal tax lien copies are $5.00 per page. RE owner, mortgage, and property transfer searches available. Will FAX copies of legal descriptions **Other Phone Numbers:** Assessor 563-263-7061; Treasurer 563-263-7113; Elections 563-263-5821; Vital Records 563-263-7741.

O'Brien County

County Recorder, P.O. Box 340, Primghar, IA 51245-0340. County Recorder, R/E and UCC Recording 712-757-3045; Fax 712-757-3046. http://www.obrien county.com/government/recorder.htm
Will search UCC records. Tax liens not included in UCC search. Will not search real estate records. **Other Phone Numbers:** Assessor 712-757-3205; Treasurer 712-757-3210 or 4185; Elections 712-757-3225; Vital Records 712-757-3045.

Osceola County

County Recorder, Courthouse, 300 7th Street, Sibley, IA 51249-1695. County Recorder, R/E and UCC Recording 712-754-3345; Fax 712-754-2872. http://www.osceolaclerkcourt.org
Will search UCC records. UCC search includes tax liens if requested. Will not search real estate records. **Other Phone Numbers:** Assessor 712-754-3438;

Treasurer 712-754-3217; Elections 712-754-2241; Vital Records 712-754-3345; Assessor 712-754-3438.

Page County

County Recorder, 112 E. Main St., Courthouse, Clarinda, IA 51632. 712-542-3130; Fax 712-542-5019.
Will search UCC records. UCC search includes tax liens if requested. RE owner, mortgage, and property transfer searches available. **Other Phone Numbers:** Assessor 712-542-5322; Treasurer 712-542-2516.

Palo Alto County

County Recorder, PO Box 248, Emmetsburg, IA 50536. 712-852-3701; Fax 712-852-3704.
Will search UCC records. Tax liens not included in UCC search. Will not search real estate records. **Other Phone Numbers:** Assessor 712-852-3823; Treasurer 712-852-3701.

Plymouth County

County Recorder, Courthouse, 215 4th Ave. SE, Le Mars, IA 51031. 712-546-4020.
Will search UCC records. Tax liens not included in UCC search. Will not search real estate records. **Other Phone Numbers:** Treasurer 712-546-4020.

Pocahontas County

County Recorder, 99 Court Square, Pocahontas, IA 50574-1621. 712-335-4404; Fax 712-335-4502.
Will search UCC records. UCC search includes tax liens. RE owner, mortgage, and property transfer searches available. **Other Phone Numbers:** Assessor 712-335-3142; Treasurer 712-335-4334.

Polk County

County Recorder, 111 Court Avenue, Room 250, County Administration Building, Des Moines, IA 50309. County Recorder, R/E and UCC Recording 515-286-3160; Fax 515-323-5393. http://www.co.polk.ia.us
Will search UCC records. Tax liens not included in UCC search. RE record owner searches available. **Online Access:** Assessor, Property Records. Online access to the Polk County assessor database is available free at www.co.polk.ia.us/departments/assessor/ assessor.htm. Search by property or by sales. **Other Phone Numbers:** Assessor 515-286-3141; Treasurer 515-286-3041; Elections 515-286-3247; Vital Records 515-286-3781.

Pottawattamie County

County Recorder, 227 South Sixth Street, Council Bluffs, IA 51501. 712-328-5612; Fax 712-328-4738. http://www.pottco.org
Will search UCC records. Tax liens not included in UCC search. Will not search real estate records. **Online Access:** Real Estate, Property Records. Records on the Pottawattamie County Courthouse/Council Bluffs property database are available free online. Search by owner name, address, or parcel number. Records of the Pottawattamie County Assessor "Residential Sales" database are available free online at www.pottco.org/htdocs/assessor.html. **Other Phone Numbers:** Assessor 712-328-5617; Treasurer 712-328-5627.

Poweshiek County

County Recorder, P.O. Box 656, Montezuma, IA 50171-0656. County Recorder, R/E and UCC Recording 641-623-5434; Fax 641-623-2928.
Will search UCC records. This agency will not do a tax lien search. Will not search real estate records. **Other Phone Numbers:** Assessor 641-623-5445; Treasurer 641-623-5128; Elections 641-623-5434.

Ringgold County

County Recorder, 109 W Madison #204, Mount Ayr, IA 50854. County Recorder, R/E and UCC Recording 641-464-3231; Fax 641-464-2568.
Will search UCC records. UCC search includes tax liens if requested. Will not search real estate records. **Other Phone Numbers:** Assessor 641-464-3233; Treasurer 641-464-3230; Vital Records 641-464-3231.

Sac County

County Recorder, 100 N. West State St., Sac City, IA 50583. 712-662-7789; Fax 712-662-6298. http://www.saccounty.org/Recorder.html
Will search UCC records. Tax liens not included in UCC search. Will not search real estate records. **Other Phone Numbers:** Assessor 712-662-4492; Treasurer 712-662-7411; Vital Records 712-662-7789.

Scott County

County Recorder, 416 West 4th Street, Davenport, IA 52801-1187. County Recorder, R/E and UCC Recording 563-326-8621; Fax 563-328-3225. http://www.scottcountyiowa.com
Will search UCC records. UCC search includes state tax liens if requested RE record owner and mortgage searches available. Record owner and mortgage search combined as UCC search **Other Phone Numbers:** Assessor 563-326-8635; Treasurer 563-326-8664; Elections 563-326-8631; Vital Records 563-326-8650.

Shelby County

County Recorder, P.O. Box 67, Harlan, IA 51537-0067. County Recorder, R/E and UCC Recording 712-755-5640; Fax 712-755-2519.
Will search UCC records. Tax liens not included in UCC search. Will not search real estate records. **Other Phone Numbers:** Assessor 712-755-5718; Treasurer 712-755-5898; Elections 712-755-3831; Vital Records 712-755-5640.

Sioux County

County Recorder, P.O. Box 48, Orange City, IA 51041. County Recorder, R/E and UCC Recording 712-737-2229; Fax 712-737-2230. http://www.court-house.co.sioux.ia.us
Will search UCC records. UCC search includes tax liens if requested. Will not search real estate records. **Online Access:** Tax Sale. Online access to the Treasurer's delinquent tax list is available free at www.court-house.co.sioux.ia.us/pdf/taxlist.pdf. **Other Phone Numbers:** Assessor 712-737-4274; Treasurer 712-737-3505; Elections 712-737-2216; Vital Records 712-737-2229.

Story County

County Recorder, P.O. Box 55, Nevada, IA 50201-0055. 515-382-7230; Fax 515-382-7326. http://www.storycounty.com/departments.html
Will search UCC records. UCC search includes tax liens if requested. Will not search real estate records. **Online Access:** Assessor. Records on the county assessor database are available free online at www.storyassessor.org/pmc/query.asp. **Other Phone Numbers:** Assessor 515-382-7320; Treasurer 515-382-7330; Appraiser/Auditor 515-382-7322; Elections 515-382-7217; Vital Records 515-382-7237; Deputy Assessor 515-382-7322.

Tama County

County Recorder, P.O. Box 82, Toledo, IA 52342. 641-484-3320.
Will search UCC records. Tax liens not included in UCC search. Will not search real estate records. **Other Phone Numbers:** Assessor 641-484-3545; Treasurer 641-484-3141.

Taylor County

County Recorder, 405 Jefferson St., Courthouse, Bedford, IA 50833. 712-523-2275; Fax 712-523-2274. Will search UCC records. Tax liens not included in UCC search. Will not search real estate records. **Other Phone Numbers:** Assessor 712-523-2444; Treasurer 712-523-2080.

Union County

County Recorder, 301 North Pine Street, Creston, IA 50801. 641-782-7616; Fax 641-782-8404. Will search UCC records. UCC search includes tax liens if requested. RE owner, mortgage, and property transfer searches available. **Other Phone Numbers:** Assessor 641-782-5019; Treasurer 641-782-2319.

Van Buren County

County Recorder, P.O. Box 455, Keosauqua, IA 52565. 319-293-3240; Fax 319-293-3828. Will search UCC records. UCC search includes tax liens. Will not search real estate records. **Other Phone Numbers:** Assessor 319-293-3001; Treasurer 319-293-3110; Vital Records 319-293-3240.

Wapello County

County Recorder, 101 West 4th Street, Ottumwa, IA 52501. 641-683-0045; Fax 641-683-0019. Will search UCC records. UCC search includes tax liens if requested. Will not search real estate records. **Other Phone Numbers:** Assessor 641-683-0083; Treasurer 641-683-0040.

Warren County

County Recorder, 301 N Buxton, #109, Indianola, IA 50125. 515-961-1089. Will search UCC records. Mail requests must include a SASE. Federal tax liens not included in UCC search. Will not search real estate records. **Other Phone Numbers:** Assessor 515-961-1010; Treasurer 515-961-1110.

Washington County

County Recorder, P.O. Box 889, Washington, IA 52353-0889. County Recorder, R/E and UCC Recording 319-653-7727. Will search UCC records. Tax liens not included in UCC search. Mortgage searches available. **Other Phone Numbers:** Assessor 319-653-7709; Treasurer 319-653-7726; Elections 319-653-7777; Vital Records 319-653-7727.

Wayne County

County Recorder, P.O. Box 435, Corydon, IA 50060. County Recorder, R/E and UCC Recording 641-872-1676; Fax 641-872-2843. Will search UCC records. UCC search includes tax liens if requested. RE owner, mortgage, and property transfer searches available. **Other Phone Numbers:** Assessor 641-872-2663; Treasurer 641-872-2515; Vital Records 641-872-1676.

Webster County

County Recorder, P.O. Box 1253, Fort Dodge, IA 50501. 515-576-2401; Fax 515-574-3723. Will search UCC records. UCC search includes tax liens if requested. Will not search real estate records. **Other Phone Numbers:** Assessor 515-573-5871; Treasurer 515-576-2731.

Winnebago County

County Recorder, 126 South Clark Street, Courthouse, Forest City, IA 50436. County Recorder, R/E and UCC Recording 641-585-2094; Fax 641-585-2891. Will search UCC records. Tax liens not included in UCC search. Will not search real estate records. **Other Phone Numbers:** Assessor 641-585-2163; Treasurer 641-585-2322; Appraiser/Auditor 641-585-3412; Vital Records 641-585-2094.

Winneshiek County

County Recorder, 201 West Main Street, Decorah, IA 52101. 563-382-3486; Fax 319-387-4083. Will search UCC records. UCC search includes tax liens if requested. Will not search real estate records. **Other Phone Numbers:** Assessor 563-382-5356; Treasurer 563-382-3753.

Woodbury County

County Recorder, 7th & Douglas Street, Courthouse Room 106, Sioux City, IA 51101. 712-279-6528; Fax 712-252-4921. Will search UCC records. UCC search includes tax liens if requested. Will not search real estate records. **Other Phone Numbers:** Assessor 712-278-6505.

Worth County

County Recorder, 1000 Central Avenue, Northwood, IA 50459. County Recorder, R/E and UCC Recording 641-324-2734; Fax 641-324-2316. Will search UCC records. Tax liens not included in UCC search. Will not search real estate records. **Other Phone Numbers:** Assessor 641-324-1198; Treasurer 641-324-2942; Elections 641-324-2316; Vital Records 641-324-2734.

Wright County

County Recorder, P.O. Box 187, Clarion, IA 50525. County Recorder, R/E and UCC Recording 515-532-3204; http://www.wrightcounty.org/county_offices.htm Will search UCC records. Tax liens not included in UCC search. RE record owner and mortgage searches available. **Other Phone Numbers:** Assessor 515-532-3737; Treasurer 515-532-2691.

Iowa County Locator

You will usually be able to find the city name in the City/County Cross Reference below. In that case, it is a simple matter to determine the county from the cross reference. However, only the official US Postal Service city names are included in this index. There are an additional 40,000 place names that people use in their addresses. Therefore, we have also included a ZIP/City Cross Reference immediately following the City/County Cross Reference.

If you know the ZIP Code but the city name does not appear in the City/County Cross Reference index, look up the ZIP Code in the ZIP/City Cross Reference, find the city name, then look up the city name in the City/County Cross Reference. For example, you want to know the county for an address of Menands, NY 12204. There is no "Menands" in the City/County Cross Reference. The ZIP/City Cross Reference shows that ZIP Codes 12201-12288 are for the city of Albany. Looking back in the City/County Cross Reference, Albany is in Albany County.

City/County Cross Reference

A C NIELSEN CO Clinton
ACKLEY (50601) Hardin(72), Franklin(12), Butler(8), Grundy(8)
ACKWORTH Warren
ADAIR (50002) Adair(77), Guthrie(22)
ADEL Dallas
AFTON Union
AGENCY Wapello
AINSWORTH Washington
AKRON Plymouth
ALBERT CITY (50510) Buena Vista(85), Pocahontas(15)
ALBIA Monroe
ALBION Marshall
ALBURNETT Linn
ALDEN (50006) Hardin(84), Franklin(15)
ALEXANDER (50420) Franklin(85), Wright(10), Story(5)
ALGONA Kossuth
ALLEMAN Polk
ALLENDORF Osceola
ALLERTON Wayne
ALLISON Butler
ALPHA Fayette
ALTA Buena Vista
ALTA VISTA (50603) Chickasaw(87), Howard(13)
ALTON (51003) Sioux(99), Plymouth(1)
ALTOONA Polk
ALVORD Lyon
AMANA (52203) Iowa(85), Johnson(14), Linn(1)
AMANA Iowa
AMES (50014) Story(96), Boone(4)
AMES Story
ANAMOSA Jones
ANDOVER Clinton
ANDREW Jackson
ANITA (50020) Cass(80), Adair(12), Audubon(7), Guthrie(1)
ANKENY Polk
ANTHON Woodbury
APLINGTON (50604) Butler(85), Grundy(16)
ARCADIA Carroll
ARCHER O'Brien
AREDALE (50605) Butler(63), Franklin(38)
ARGYLE Lee
ARION Crawford
ARISPE Union
ARLINGTON (50606) Fayette(94), Clayton(6)
ARMSTRONG (50514) Emmet(76), Kossuth(24)
ARNOLDS PARK Dickinson
ARTHUR (51431) Ida(85), Sac(15)
ASHTON (51232) Osceola(78), Lyon(20), O'Brien(2)
ASPINWALL Crawford
AT AND T Pottawattamie
ATALISSA (52720) Muscatine(77), Cedar(23)
ATKINS Benton

ATLANTIC (50022) Cass(98), Audubon(1)
AUBURN (51433) Sac(62), Calhoun(36), Carroll(2)
AUDUBON Audubon
AURELIA (51005) Cherokee(88), Buena Vista(13)
AURORA (50607) Buchanan(61), Fayette(39)
AUSTINVILLE Butler
AVOCA (51521) Pottawattamie(92), Shelby(8)
AYRSHIRE (50515) Palo Alto(82), Clay(18)
BADGER (50516) Webster(87), Humboldt(13)
BAGLEY (50026) Guthrie(69), Greene(31)
BALDWIN (52207) Jackson(91), Clinton(9)
BANCROFT Kossuth
BARNES CITY (50027) Mahaska(98), Poweshiek(2)
BARNUM Webster
BARTLETT Fremont
BATAVIA (52533) Jefferson(73), Wapello(27)
BATTLE CREEK (51006) Ida(90), Woodbury(10)
BAXTER (99999) Jasper(99), Marshall(1)
BAYARD (50029) Guthrie(97), Greene(3)
BEACON Mahaska
BEACONSFIELD Ringgold
BEAMAN (50609) Grundy(73), Marshall(22), Tama(6)
BEAVER Boone
BEDFORD Taylor
BELLE PLAINE (52208) Benton(94), Iowa(4), Tama(1)
BELLEVUE Jackson
BELMOND Wright
BENNETT Cedar
BENTON Ringgold
BERNARD (52032) Dubuque(79), Jackson(17), Jones(5)
BERWICK Polk
BETTENDORF Scott
BEVINGTON Madison
BIG ROCK Scott
BIRMINGHAM (52535) Van Buren(89), Jefferson(12)
BLAIRSBURG (50034) Hamilton(86), Wright(14)
BLAIRSTOWN (52209) Benton(96), Iowa(4)
BLAKESBURG Wapello
BLANCHARD Page
BLENCOE (51523) Monona(94), Harrison(6)
BLOCKTON Taylor
BLOOMFIELD (52537) Davis(91), Wapello(9)
BLUE GRASS (52726) Scott(92), Muscatine(8)
BODE (50519) Humboldt(65), Kossuth(35)
BONAPARTE Van Buren
BONDURANT Polk

BOONE Boone
BOONEVILLE Dallas
BOUTON (50039) Dallas(97), Boone(3)
BOXHOLM Boone
BOYDEN (51234) Sioux(96), Lyon(4)
BRADDYVILLE Page
BRADFORD Franklin
BRADGATE (50520) Humboldt(95), Pocahontas(5)
BRANDON Buchanan
BRAYTON Audubon
BREDA (51436) Carroll(76), Sac(13), Crawford(11)
BRIDGEWATER (50837) Adair(86), Adams(8), Cass(6)
BRIGHTON (52540) Jefferson(54), Washington(46)
BRISTOW Butler
BRITT Hancock
BRONSON Woodbury
BROOKLYN Poweshiek
BRUNSVILLE Plymouth
BRYANT Clinton
BUCKEYE Hardin
BUCKINGHAM Tama
BUFFALO Scott
BUFFALO CENTER (50424) Winnebago(90), Kossuth(10)
BURLINGTON Des Moines
BURNSIDE Webster
BURR OAK Winneshiek
BURT Kossuth
BUSSEY (50044) Marion(74), Mahaska(21), Monroe(5)
CALAMUS Clinton
CALLENDER Webster
CALMAR (52132) Winneshiek(92), Howard(9)
CALUMET O'Brien
CAMANCHE Clinton
CAMBRIDGE (50046) Story(84), Polk(16)
CANTRIL Van Buren
CARBON Adams
CARLISLE (50047) Warren(82), Polk(18)
CARNARVON Sac
CARPENTER Mitchell
CARROLL Carroll
CARSON Pottawattamie
CARTER LAKE Pottawattamie
CASCADE (52033) Dubuque(59), Jones(42)
CASEY (50048) Guthrie(68), Adair(32)
CASTALIA (52133) Winneshiek(70), Fayette(30)
CASTANA Monona
CEDAR Mahaska
CEDAR FALLS (50613) Black Hawk(98), Grundy(2)
CEDAR FALLS Black Hawk
CEDAR RAPIDS Linn
CENTER JUNCTION Jones
CENTER POINT (52213) Linn(88), Benton(10), Scott(2)

CENTERVILLE Appanoose
CENTRAL CITY Linn
CHAPIN Franklin
CHARITON Lucas
CHARLES CITY Floyd
CHARLOTTE (52731) Clinton(91), Jackson(9)
CHARTER OAK Crawford
CHATSWORTH Sioux
CHELSEA (52215) Tama(82), Poweshiek(18)
CHEROKEE Cherokee
CHESTER Howard
CHILLICOTHE Wapello
CHURDAN (50050) Greene(95), Calhoun(4), Carroll(1)
CHURDAN Greene
CINCINNATI Appanoose
CLARE (50524) Webster(95), Pocahontas(3), Humboldt(2), Wright(1)
CLARENCE (52216) Cedar(89), Jones(11)
CLARINDA Page
CLARION Wright
CLARKSVILLE Butler
CLEAR LAKE Cerro Gordo
CLEARFIELD (50840) Taylor(69), Ringgold(31)
CLEGHORN (51014) Cherokee(99), O'Brien(1)
CLEMONS Marshall
CLERMONT (52135) Fayette(98), Clayton(3)
CLIMBING HILL Woodbury
CLINTON Clinton
CLIO Wayne
CLIVE (50325) Polk(93), Dallas(7)
CLUTIER Tama
COGGON (52218) Linn(86), Delaware(13)
COIN Page
COLESBURG (52035) Clayton(71), Delaware(20), Dubuque(9)
COLFAX Jasper
COLLEGE SPRINGS Page
COLLINS (50055) Story(73), Jasper(25), Marshall(2)
COLO Story
COLUMBIA Marion
COLUMBUS CITY Louisa
COLUMBUS JUNCTION (52738) Louisa(95), Washington(5)
COLWELL Floyd
CONESVILLE (52739) Louisa(70), Muscatine(30)
CONRAD (50621) Grundy(93), Marshall(7)
CONROY Iowa
COON RAPIDS (50058) Carroll(81), Guthrie(11), Audubon(5), Greene(3)
COOPER Greene
CORALVILLE Johnson
CORNING (50841) Adams(94), Taylor(6)
CORRECTIONVILLE (51016) Woodbury(95), Ida(5)

CORWITH (50430) Hancock(65), Kossuth(29), Humboldt(3), Wright(3)
CORYDON Wayne
COULTER Franklin
COUNCIL BLUFFS (51503) Pottawattamie(99), Mills(2)
COUNCIL BLUFFS Pottawattamie
CRAIG Plymouth
CRAWFORDSVILLE (52621) Washington(76), Louisa(22), Henry(2)
CRESCENT Pottawattamie
CRESCO (52136) Howard(93), Winneshiek(7)
CRESTON (50801) Union(95), Adair(3), Adams(3)
CROMWELL Union
CRYSTAL LAKE Hancock
CUMBERLAND (50843) Cass(91), Adams(9)
CUMMING (50061) Warren(43), Madison(30), Polk(16), Dallas(12)
CURLEW Palo Alto
CUSHING (51018) Woodbury(59), Ida(41)
CYLINDER Palo Alto
DAKOTA CITY Humboldt
DALLAS Marion
DALLAS CENTER Dallas
DANA (50064) Greene(86), Boone(14)
DANBURY (51019) Woodbury(82), Ida(9), Crawford(5), Monona(3)
DANVILLE (52623) Des Moines(91), Henry(9)
DAVENPORT Scott
DAVIS CITY Decatur
DAWSON Dallas
DAYTON (50530) Webster(96), Boone(4)
DE SOTO Dallas
DE WITT Clinton
DECATUR Decatur
DECORAH Winneshiek
DEDHAM (51440) Carroll(98), Audubon(3)
DEEP RIVER (52222) Poweshiek(74), Iowa(26)
DEFIANCE (51527) Shelby(85), Crawford(15)
DELAWARE Delaware
DELHI Delaware
DELMAR (52037) Clinton(95), Jackson(6)
DELOIT Crawford
DELPHOS Ringgold
DELTA Keokuk
DENISON Crawford
DENMARK Lee
DENVER Bremer
DERBY (50068) Lucas(85), Wayne(15)
DES MOINES (50311) Polk(99), Wayne(1)
DES MOINES (50312) Polk(99), Wayne(1)
DES MOINES (50314) Polk(99), Wayne(2)
DES MOINES (50320) Polk(89), Warren(11)
DES MOINES Polk
DEWAR Black Hawk
DEXTER (50070) Dallas(36), Guthrie(24), Madison(23), Adair(17)
DIAGONAL (50845) Ringgold(90), Union(10)
DICKENS (51333) Clay(98), Dickinson(2)
DIKE Grundy
DIXON Scott
DOLLIVER Emmet
DONAHUE Scott
DONNELLSON Lee
DOON (51235) Lyon(96), Sioux(4)
DORCHESTER (52140) Allamakee(94), Winneshiek(6)
DOUDS Van Buren
DOUGHERTY (50433) Cerro Gordo(53), Franklin(19), Floyd(18), Butler(9)
DOW CITY Crawford
DOWS (50071) Wright(52), Franklin(48)
DRAKESVILLE (52552) Davis(93), Wapello(8)

DUBUQUE Dubuque
DUMONT (50625) Butler(92), Franklin(8)
DUNCOMBE (50532) Webster(94), Hamilton(5)
DUNDEE Delaware
DUNKERTON Black Hawk
DUNLAP (51529) Harrison(77), Crawford(13), Monona(8), Shelby(2)
DURANGO Dubuque
DURANT (52747) Cedar(80), Scott(20)
DYERSVILLE (52040) Dubuque(88), Delaware(12)
DYSART (52224) Tama(68), Benton(32)
EAGLE GROVE (50533) Wright(97), Humboldt(2), Webster(1)
EARLHAM (50072) Madison(83), Dallas(17)
EARLING Shelby
EARLVILLE Delaware
EARLY Sac
EDDYVILLE (52553) Wapello(53), Mahaska(35), Monroe(12)
EDGEWOOD (52042) Clayton(75), Delaware(25)
ELBERON (52225) Tama(79), Benton(21)
ELDON (52554) Wapello(98), Jefferson(2)
ELDORA (50627) Hardin(95), Grundy(5)
ELDRIDGE Scott
ELGIN (52141) Fayette(71), Clayton(29)
ELK HORN (51531) Shelby(84), Audubon(16)
ELKADER Clayton
ELKHART Polk
ELKPORT Clayton
ELLIOTT (51532) Montgomery(66), Pottawattamie(30), Cass(4)
ELLSTON (50074) Ringgold(93), Union(7)
ELLSWORTH (50075) Hamilton(98), Pocahontas(2)
ELMA (50628) Howard(97), Mitchell(3)
ELWOOD Clinton
ELY (52227) Linn(97), Johnson(3)
EMERSON (51533) Mills(61), Montgomery(40)
EMMETSBURG Palo Alto
EPWORTH Dubuque
ESSEX (51638) Page(97), Montgomery(3)
ESTHERVILLE (51334) Emmet(98), Dickinson(2)
EVANSDALE Black Hawk
EVERLY (51338) Clay(83), Dickinson(17)
EXIRA (50076) Audubon(99), Guthrie(1)
EXLINE Appanoose
FAIRBANK (50629) Buchanan(48), Fayette(22), Black Hawk(17), Bremer(13)
FAIRFAX (52228) Linn(74), Benton(14), Johnson(12)
FAIRFIELD Jefferson
FARLEY Dubuque
FARMERSBURG Clayton
FARMINGTON (52626) Van Buren(70), Lee(30)
FARNHAMVILLE (50538) Calhoun(88), Webster(12)
FARRAGUT Fremont
FAYETTE Fayette
FENTON (50539) Kossuth(79), Palo Alto(21)
FERGUSON Marshall
FERTILE (50434) Cerro Gordo(86), Worth(13)
FESTINA Winneshiek
FLORIS Davis
FLOYD Floyd
FONDA (50540) Pocahontas(82), Calhoun(16), Buena Vista(2), Sac(1)
FONDA Pocahontas
FONTANELLE Adair
FOREST CITY (50436) Winnebago(92), Hancock(8)

FORT ATKINSON (52144) Winneshiek(78), Fayette(13), Chickasaw(9)
FORT DODGE Webster
FORT MADISON Lee
FOSTORIA Clay
FREDERICKSBURG (50630) Chickasaw(93), Bremer(7)
FREDERIKA Bremer
FREMONT (52561) Mahaska(70), Benton(15), Keokuk(14)
FRUITLAND Muscatine
GALT Wright
GALVA (51020) Ida(63), Sac(20), Cherokee(17)
GARBER Clayton
GARDEN CITY Hardin
GARDEN GROVE (50103) Decatur(99), Wayne(1)
GARNAVILLO Clayton
GARNER Hancock
GARRISON Benton
GARWIN (50632) Tama(86), Marshall(14)
GENEVA Franklin
GEORGE Lyon
GIBSON (50104) Keokuk(87), Poweshiek(9), Mahaska(4)
GIFFORD Hardin
GILBERT Story
GILBERTVILLE Black Hawk
GILLETT GROVE Clay
GILMAN (50106) Marshall(71), Jasper(17), Tama(9), Poweshiek(3)
GILMORE CITY (50541) Pocahontas(50), Humboldt(29), Calhoun(21)
GLADBROOK (50635) Tama(96), Marshall(5)
GLENWOOD Mills
GLIDDEN (51443) Carroll(99), Greene(2)
GOLDFIELD (50542) Wright(59), Humboldt(41)
GOODELL Hancock
GOOSE LAKE Clinton
GOWRIE (50543) Webster(97), Greene(3)
GRAETTINGER (51342) Palo Alto(80), Emmet(20)
GRAFTON (50440) Worth(99), Mitchell(2)
GRAND JUNCTION (50107) Greene(95), Boone(4)
GRAND MOUND Clinton
GRAND RIVER (50108) Decatur(84), Clarke(15), Ringgold(1)
GRANDVIEW Louisa
GRANGER (50109) Polk(60), Dallas(40)
GRANT Montgomery
GRANVILLE (51022) Sioux(58), O'Brien(41)
GRAVITY Taylor
GRAY Audubon
GREELEY (52050) Delaware(88), Clayton(12)
GREEN MOUNTAIN Marshall
GREENE (50636) Butler(84), Floyd(16)
GREENFIELD Adair
GREENVILLE Clay
GRIMES (50111) Polk(95), Dallas(5)
GRINNELL (50112) Poweshiek(89), Jasper(12)
GRINNELL Poweshiek
GRISWOLD (51535) Pottawattamie(65), Cass(35)
GRUNDY CENTER Grundy
GRUVER Emmet
GUERNSEY (52221) Poweshiek(86), Iowa(14)
GUTHRIE CENTER Guthrie
GUTTENBERG (52052) Clayton(96), Dubuque(4)
HALBUR Carroll
HALE Jones
HAMBURG Fremont
HAMILTON Marion
HAMLIN (50117) Audubon(98), Guthrie(2)

HAMPTON Franklin
HANCOCK Pottawattamie
HANLONTOWN (50444) Worth(82), Cerro Gordo(17), Winnebago(1)
HANSELL Franklin
HARCOURT Webster
HARDY Humboldt
HARLAN Pottawattamie
HARLAN Shelby
HARPER Keokuk
HARPERS FERRY Allamakee
HARRIS (51345) Osceola(94), Dickinson(6)
HARTFORD Warren
HARTLEY (51346) O'Brien(90), Osceola(7), Clay(4)
HARTWICK (52232) Poweshiek(79), Iowa(21)
HARVEY Marion
HASTINGS Mills
HAVELOCK (50546) Pocahontas(97), Palo Alto(3)
HAVERHILL Marshall
HAWARDEN Sioux
HAWKEYE Fayette
HAYESVILLE Keokuk
HAZLETON Buchanan
HEDRICK (52563) Keokuk(74), Wapello(25), Jefferson(1)
HENDERSON (51541) Mills(69), Pottawattamie(17), Montgomery(14)
HIAWATHA Linn
HIGHLANDVILLE Winneshiek
HILLS Johnson
HILLSBORO (52630) Henry(37), Van Buren(37), Lee(26)
HINTON Plymouth
HOLLAND Grundy
HOLSTEIN (51025) Ida(86), Cherokee(8), Woodbury(5)
HOLY CROSS (52053) Dubuque(80), Clayton(20)
HOMESTEAD (52236) Iowa(98), Johnson(2)
HONEY CREEK Pottawattamie
HOPKINTON (52237) Delaware(98), Dubuque(2)
HORNICK (51026) Woodbury(81), Monona(19)
HOSPERS (51238) Sioux(65), O'Brien(35)
HOUGHTON Lee
HUBBARD (50122) Hardin(99), Story(1)
HUDSON (50643) Black Hawk(93), Grundy(7)
HULL Sioux
HUMBOLDT (50548) Humboldt(98), Webster(2)
HUMESTON (50123) Wayne(83), Lucas(8), Decatur(6), Clarke(4)
HUXLEY (50124) Story(91), Polk(9)
IDA GROVE Ida
IMOGENE (51645) Fremont(53), Mills(34), Page(11), Montgomery(1)
INDEPENDENCE Buchanan
INDIANOLA Warren
INWOOD (51240) Lyon(90), Sioux(10)
IONIA (50645) Chickasaw(97), Floyd(3)
IOWA CITY Johnson
IOWA FALLS (50126) Hardin(97), Franklin(3)
IRA Jasper
IRETON (51027) Sioux(84), Plymouth(16)
IRWIN Shelby
JACKSON JUNCTION Winneshiek
JAMAICA (50128) Guthrie(66), Greene(22), Dallas(13)
JANESVILLE (50647) Black Hawk(94), Bremer(6)
JEFFERSON Greene
JESUP (50648) Buchanan(88), Black Hawk(12)
JEWELL Hamilton
JOHNSTON Polk

JOICE (50446) Worth(74), Winnebago(26)
JOLLEY Calhoun
KALONA Washington
KAMRAR Hamilton
KANAWHA (50447) Hancock(75), Wright(25)
KELLERTON (50133) Ringgold(94), Decatur(6)
KELLEY (50134) Story(82), Boone(18)
KELLOGG Jasper
KENSETT Worth
KENT (50850) Adams(51), Union(49)
KEOKUK Lee
KEOSAUQUA Van Buren
KEOTA (52248) Keokuk(80), Washington(20)
KESLEY Butler
KESWICK (50136) Keokuk(94), Iowa(5), Poweshiek(1)
KEYSTONE Benton
KILLDUFF Jasper
KIMBALLTON (51543) Audubon(82), Shelby(18)
KINGSLEY (51028) Plymouth(82), Woodbury(18)
KINROSS Keokuk
KIRKMAN Shelby
KIRKVILLE Wapello
KIRON (51448) Crawford(65), Sac(19), Ida(16)
KLEMME (50449) Cerro Gordo(66), Hancock(34)
KNIERIM Calhoun
KNOXVILLE Marion
LA MOTTE (52054) Jackson(97), Dubuque(3)
LA PORTE CITY (50651) Black Hawk(94), Benton(6)
LACONA (50139) Warren(65), Marion(20), Lucas(15)
LADORA Iowa
LAKE CITY (51449) Calhoun(97), Carroll(4)
LAKE MILLS (50450) Winnebago(95), Worth(5)
LAKE PARK Dickinson
LAKE VIEW Sac
LAKOTA Kossuth
LAMONI Decatur
LAMONT (50650) Buchanan(70), Fayette(28), Delaware(2)
LANESBORO Carroll
LANGWORTHY Jones
LANSING Allamakee
LARCHWOOD Lyon
LARRABEE (51029) Cherokee(94), O'Brien(6)
LATIMER Franklin
LAUREL (50141) Marshall(53), Jasper(47)
LAURENS (50554) Pocahontas(96), Palo Alto(2)
LAWLER (52154) Chickasaw(95), Howard(5)
LAWTON Woodbury
LE CLAIRE Scott
LE GRAND Marshall
LE MARS Plymouth
LEDYARD Kossuth
LEHIGH Webster
LEIGHTON (50143) Mahaska(98), Marion(2)
LELAND Winnebago
LENOX (50851) Taylor(85), Adams(13)
LEON Decatur
LESTER Lyon
LETTS (52754) Louisa(77), Muscatine(23)
LEWIS (51544) Cass(55), Pottawattamie(45)
LIBERTY CENTER Warren
LIBERTYVILLE Jefferson
LIDDERDALE Carroll
LIME SPRINGS Howard
LINCOLN Tama

LINDEN (50146) Dallas(87), Guthrie(13)
LINEVILLE (50147) Wayne(76), Marion(24)
LINN GROVE (51033) Buena Vista(59), Clay(41)
LISBON (52253) Linn(48), Cedar(26), Jones(17), Johnson(9)
LISCOMB (50148) Marshall(89), Grundy(11)
LITTLE CEDAR Mitchell
LITTLE ROCK (51243) Lyon(91), Osceola(9)
LITTLE SIOUX (51545) Harrison(81), Monona(19)
LITTLEPORT Clayton
LIVERMORE (50558) Humboldt(59), Kossuth(41)
LOCKRIDGE (52635) Jefferson(77), Henry(23)
LOGAN Harrison
LOHRVILLE (51453) Calhoun(91), Carroll(8), Greene(1)
LONE ROCK Kossuth
LONE TREE (52755) Johnson(88), Louisa(11), Muscatine(1)
LONG GROVE (52756) Scott(99), Clinton(1)
LORIMOR (50149) Union(66), Madison(33), Clarke(1)
LOST NATION Clinton
LOVILIA (99999) Monroe(99), Marion(1)
LOW MOOR Clinton
LOWDEN (52255) Cedar(98), Clinton(2)
LU VERNE (50560) Kossuth(81), Humboldt(19)
LUANA (52156) Clayton(83), Allamakee(17)
LUCAS (50151) Warren(70), Lucas(27), Clarke(3)
LUTHER Boone
LUXEMBURG Dubuque
LUZERNE (52257) Benton(99), Iowa(1)
LYNNVILLE (50153) Jasper(91), Mahaska(6), Poweshiek(3)
LYTTON (50561) Calhoun(58), Sac(42)
MACEDONIA Pottawattamie
MACKSBURG (50155) Madison(97), Adair(3)
MADRID (50156) Boone(97), Polk(2), Dallas(1)
MAGNOLIA Harrison
MALCOM Poweshiek
MALLARD (50562) Palo Alto(88), Pocahontas(12)
MALOY Ringgold
MALVERN Mills
MANCHESTER Delaware
MANILLA (51454) Crawford(65), Shelby(35)
MANLY (50456) Worth(96), Cerro Gordo(4)
MANNING (51455) Carroll(85), Crawford(8), Audubon(6), Shelby(1)
MANSON (50563) Calhoun(81), Pocahontas(16), Webster(3)
MAPLETON (51034) Monona(93), Woodbury(6), Crawford(1)
MAQUOKETA (52060) Jackson(98), Clinton(2)
MARATHON Buena Vista
MARBLE ROCK Floyd
MARCUS (51035) Cherokee(96), Plymouth(3), O'Brien(1)
MARENGO (52301) Iowa(98), Benton(2)
MARION Linn
MARNE (51552) Cass(66), Shelby(31), Pottawattamie(3)
MARQUETTE Clayton
MARSHALLTOWN Marshall
MARTELLE (52305) Jones(83), Linn(18)
MARTENSDALE Warren
MARTINSBURG Keokuk
MASON CITY Cerro Gordo

MASONVILLE (50654) Delaware(72), Buchanan(28)
MASSENA (50853) Cass(92), Adams(8)
MATLOCK Sioux
MAURICE Sioux
MAXWELL (50161) Story(61), Polk(38), Jasper(1)
MAY CITY Osceola
MAYNARD Fayette
MC CALLSBURG (50154) Story(91), Hardin(10)
MC CAUSLAND Scott
MC CLELLAND Pottawattamie
MC GREGOR Clayton
MC INTIRE Mitchell
MECHANICSVILLE (52306) Cedar(76), Jones(24)
MEDIAPOLIS Des Moines
MELBOURNE (50162) Marshall(97), Jasper(3)
MELCHER Marion
MELROSE Monroe
MELVIN (51350) Osceola(96), O'Brien(4)
MENLO (50164) Guthrie(64), Adair(36)
MERIDEN Cherokee
MERRILL Plymouth
MESERVEY (50457) Cerro Gordo(49), Hancock(24), Franklin(18), Wright(9)
MIDDLE AMANA Iowa
MIDDLETOWN Des Moines
MILES (52064) Jackson(94), Clinton(7)
MILFORD Dickinson
MILLERSBURG Iowa
MILLERTON Wayne
MILO Warren
MILTON Van Buren
MINBURN Dallas
MINDEN Pottawattamie
MINEOLA Mills
MINGO (50168) Jasper(96), Polk(4)
MISSOURI VALLEY (51555) Harrison(83), Pottawattamie(17)
MITCHELLVILLE (50169) Polk(82), Jasper(18)
MODALE Harrison
MONDAMIN Harrison
MONMOUTH (52309) Jackson(74), Jones(26)
MONONA (52159) Clayton(74), Allamakee(26)
MONROE (50170) Jasper(87), Marion(13)
MONTEZUMA (50171) Poweshiek(98), Mahaska(2)
MONTEZUMA Poweshiek
MONTICELLO Jones
MONTOUR Tama
MONTPELIER Muscatine
MONTROSE Lee
MOORHEAD (51558) Monona(90), Harrison(10)
MOORLAND Webster
MORAVIA Appanoose
MORLEY Jones
MORNING SUN (52640) Louisa(72), Des Moines(28)
MORRISON Grundy
MOSCOW (52760) Muscatine(59), Cedar(41)
MOULTON Appanoose
MOUNT AUBURN Benton
MOUNT AYR Ringgold
MOUNT PLEASANT (52641) Henry(97), Washington(2)
MOUNT STERLING Van Buren
MOUNT UNION (52644) Henry(71), Des Moines(29)
MOUNT VERNON Linn
MOVILLE Woodbury
MURRAY (50174) Clarke(97), Union(3)
MUSCATINE (52761) Muscatine(96), Louisa(4)
MYSTIC Appanoose

NASHUA (50658) Chickasaw(86), Floyd(12), Bremer(2)
NEMAHA Sac
NEOLA (51559) Pottawattamie(94), Harrison(6)
NEVADA Story
NEW ALBIN Allamakee
NEW HAMPTON Chickasaw
NEW HARTFORD (50660) Butler(84), Grundy(15)
NEW LIBERTY (52765) Scott(87), Cedar(14)
NEW LONDON (52645) Henry(87), Des Moines(13)
NEW MARKET (51646) Taylor(99), Page(1)
NEW PROVIDENCE (50206) Hardin(89), Marshall(8), Story(3)
NEW SHARON (50207) Mahaska(98), Poweshiek(2)
NEW VIENNA (52065) Dubuque(83), Delaware(18)
NEW VIRGINIA (50210) Warren(65), Clarke(31), Madison(4)
NEWELL (50568) Buena Vista(91), Sac(8), Pocahontas(1)
NEWHALL Benton
NEWTON Jasper
NICHOLS (52766) Muscatine(93), Johnson(7)
NODAWAY (50857) Adams(73), Taylor(23), Montgomery(4)
NORA SPRINGS (50458) Floyd(62), Cerro Gordo(33), Mitchell(5)
NORTH BUENA VISTA Clayton
NORTH ENGLISH (52316) Iowa(88), Keokuk(12)
NORTH LIBERTY Johnson
NORTH WASHINGTON Chickasaw
NORTHBORO (51647) Page(86), Fremont(14)
NORTHWOOD Worth
NORWALK Warren
NORWAY (52318) Benton(80), Iowa(20)
NUMA Appanoose
OAKDALE Johnson
OAKLAND Pottawattamie
OAKVILLE (52646) Louisa(52), Des Moines(48)
OCHEYEDAN Osceola
ODEBOLT Sac
OELWEIN Fayette
OGDEN Boone
OKOBOJI Dickinson
OLDS Henry
OLIN (52320) Jones(93), Cedar(7)
OLLIE (52576) Keokuk(98), Jefferson(2)
ONAWA Monona
ONSLOW Jones
ORAN Fayette
ORANGE CITY Sioux
ORCHARD (50460) Mitchell(70), Floyd(30)
ORIENT Adair
OSAGE Mitchell
OSCEOLA Clarke
OSKALOOSA Mahaska
OSSIAN (52161) Winneshiek(87), Fayette(13)
OTHO Webster
OTLEY (50214) Marion(98), Jasper(2)
OTO Woodbury
OTTOSEN (52570) Humboldt(67), Kossuth(32), Pocahontas(1)
OTTUMWA Wapello
OXFORD (52322) Johnson(97), Iowa(2)
OXFORD JUNCTION (52323) Jones(84), Clinton(8), Cedar(4), Linn(4)
OYENS Plymouth
PACIFIC JUNCTION (51561) Mills(99), Fremont(1)
PACKWOOD (52580) Jefferson(71), Dubuque(24), Keokuk(5)

PALMER Pocahontas
PALO (52324) Linn(97), Benton(3)
PANAMA (51562) Shelby(97), Harrison(3)
PANORA Guthrie
PARKERSBURG (50665) Butler(77), Grundy(23)
PARNELL (52325) Iowa(83), Johnson(17)
PATON (50217) Greene(82), Boone(13), Webster(6)
PATTERSON Madison
PAULLINA (51046) O'Brien(97), Cherokee(4)
PELLA (50219) Marion(95), Mahaska(6)
PEOSTA Dubuque
PERCIVAL Fremont
PERRY (50220) Dallas(94), Boone(6)
PERSHING Marion
PERSIA (51563) Harrison(98), Shelby(2)
PERU (50222) Madison(98), Clarke(3)
PETERSON (51047) Clay(68), Buena Vista(18), Cherokee(10), O'Brien(5)
PIERSON (51048) Woodbury(72), Cherokee(28)
PILOT GROVE Lee
PILOT MOUND Boone
PISGAH Harrison
PLAINFIELD (50666) Bremer(67), Butler(33)
PLANO Appanoose
PLEASANT VALLEY Scott
PLEASANTVILLE (50225) Marion(84), Warren(16)
PLOVER Pocahontas
PLYMOUTH (50464) Cerro Gordo(77), Worth(20), Mitchell(3)
POCAHONTAS Pocahontas
POLK CITY (50226) Polk(96), Boone(3)
POMEROY (50575) Calhoun(61), Pocahontas(39)
POPEJOY Franklin
PORTSMOUTH (51565) Shelby(77), Harrison(23)
POSTVILLE (52162) Allamakee(52), Clayton(34), Winneshiek(10), Fayette(4)
PRAIRIE CITY (50228) Jasper(96), Polk(2), Marion(2)
PRAIRIEBURG Linn
PRESCOTT (50859) Adams(97), Adair(3)
PRESTON (52069) Jackson(91), Clinton(9)
PRIMGHAR O'Brien
PRINCETON Scott
PROLE (50229) Warren(52), Madison(48)
PROMISE CITY Wayne
PROTIVIN Howard
PULASKI Davis
QUASQUETON Buchanan
QUIMBY Cherokee
RADCLIFFE (50230) Hardin(70), Hamilton(29), Story(2)
RAKE Winnebago
RALSTON Carroll
RANDALIA Fayette
RANDALL Hamilton
RANDOLPH (51649) Fremont(98), Mills(2)
RAYMOND Black Hawk
READLYN Bremer
REASNOR Jasper
RED OAK (51566) Montgomery(98), Page(2)
RED OAK Montgomery
REDDING Ringgold
REDFIELD (50233) Dallas(90), Guthrie(11)
REINBECK (50669) Grundy(90), Tama(10)
REMBRANDT Buena Vista
REMSEN Plymouth
RENWICK (50577) Humboldt(67), Wright(33)
RHODES (50234) Marshall(75), Jasper(25)
RICEVILLE (50466) Howard(53), Mitchell(47)
RICHLAND (52585) Keokuk(72), Washington(21), Jefferson(7)

RICKETTS Crawford
RIDGEWAY Winneshiek
RINARD Calhoun
RINGSTED (50578) Emmet(92), Palo Alto(4), Kossuth(4)
RIPPEY (50235) Greene(92), Boone(5), Dallas(3)
RIVERSIDE (52327) Washington(65), Johnson(33), Louisa(2)
RIVERTON Fremont
ROBINS Linn
ROCK FALLS Cerro Gordo
ROCK RAPIDS Lyon
ROCK VALLEY (51247) Sioux(99), Lyon(1)
ROCKFORD (50468) Floyd(85), Cerro Gordo(15)
ROCKWELL Cerro Gordo
ROCKWELL CITY Calhoun
RODMAN Palo Alto
RODNEY (51051) Monona(93), Woodbury(7)
ROLAND (50236) Story(98), Hamilton(2)
ROLFE (50581) Pocahontas(99), Palo Alto(1)
ROME Henry
ROSE HILL (52586) Mahaska(95), Keokuk(5)
ROWAN (50470) Wright(96), Franklin(4)
ROWLEY Buchanan
ROYAL Clay
RUDD (50471) Floyd(94), Mitchell(6)
RUNNELLS (50237) Polk(87), Jasper(9), Marion(4)
RUSSELL (50238) Lucas(90), Wayne(10)
RUTHVEN (51358) Palo Alto(79), Clay(21)
RUTLAND Humboldt
RYAN Delaware
SABULA (52070) Jackson(89), Clinton(11)
SAC CITY Sac
SAINT ANSGAR (50472) Mitchell(95), Worth(5)
SAINT ANTHONY (50239) Marshall(86), Story(14)
SAINT CHARLES (50240) Madison(76), Warren(24)
SAINT DONATUS Jackson
SAINT LUCAS Fayette
SAINT MARYS Warren
SAINT OLAF Clayton
SAINT PAUL Lee
SALEM (52649) Henry(85), Lee(15)
SALIX Woodbury
SANBORN O'Brien
SCARVILLE Winnebago
SCHALLER (51053) Sac(91), Ida(6), Buena Vista(2)
SCHLESWIG (51461) Crawford(94), Ida(6)
SCOTCH GROVE Jones
SCRANTON (51462) Greene(98), Carroll(3)
SEARSBORO (50242) Poweshiek(94), Jasper(6)
SELMA (52588) Van Buren(97), Jefferson(3)
SERGEANT BLUFF Woodbury
SEYMOUR Wayne
SHAMBAUGH Page
SHANNON CITY (50861) Union(92), Ringgold(8)
SHARPSBURG Taylor
SHEFFIELD (50475) Franklin(76), Cerro Gordo(24)
SHELBY (51570) Pottawattamie(46), Shelby(46), Harrison(9)
SHELDAHL Polk
SHELDON (51201) O'Brien(89), Sioux(10)
SHELL ROCK Butler
SHELLSBURG Benton
SHENANDOAH (51601) Page(86), Fremont(14)
SHENANDOAH Page

SHERRILL (52073) Dubuque(97), Clayton(3)
SIBLEY Osceola
SIDNEY Fremont
SIGOURNEY Keokuk
SILVER CITY (51571) Mills(59), Pottawattamie(41)
SIOUX CENTER Sioux
SIOUX CITY (51108) Woodbury(71), Plymouth(29)
SIOUX CITY (51109) Woodbury(88), Plymouth(12)
SIOUX CITY Woodbury
SIOUX RAPIDS (50585) Buena Vista(66), Clay(34)
SLATER (50244) Story(72), Polk(26), Boone(2)
SLOAN (51055) Woodbury(68), Monona(32)
SMITHLAND (51056) Woodbury(92), Monona(8)
SOLDIER Monona
SOLON Johnson
SOMERS (50586) Calhoun(90), Webster(10)
SOUTH AMANA Iowa
SOUTH ENGLISH Keokuk
SPENCER Clay
SPERRY Des Moines
SPILLVILLE Winneshiek
SPIRIT LAKE Dickinson
SPRAGUEVILLE Jackson
SPRINGBROOK Jackson
SPRINGVILLE Linn
STACYVILLE Mitchell
STANHOPE Hamilton
STANLEY (50671) Fayette(64), Buchanan(36)
STANTON Montgomery
STANWOOD Cedar
STATE CENTER (50247) Marshall(90), Story(10)
STEAMBOAT ROCK (50672) Hardin(91), Grundy(10)
STOCKPORT (52651) Van Buren(78), Jefferson(22)
STOCKTON (52769) Scott(67), Muscatine(32), Henry(2)
STORM LAKE Buena Vista
STORY CITY (50248) Story(89), Hamilton(9), Boone(2)
STOUT Grundy
STRATFORD (50249) Hamilton(77), Webster(15), Boone(8)
STRAWBERRY POINT (52076) Clayton(95), Delaware(3), Fayette(2)
STRUBLE Plymouth
STUART (50250) Guthrie(68), Adair(32)
SULLY Jasper
SUMNER (50674) Bremer(67), Fayette(21), Chickasaw(12)
SUPERIOR Dickinson
SUTHERLAND (51058) O'Brien(96), Clay(3), Cherokee(2)
SWALEDALE Cerro Gordo
SWAN (50252) Warren(60), Marion(40)
SWEA CITY Kossuth
SWEDESBURG Henry
SWISHER (52338) Johnson(94), Linn(7)
TABOR (51653) Fremont(61), Mills(39)
TAINTOR Mahaska
TAMA Tama
TEEDS GROVE Clinton
TEMPLETON (51463) Carroll(98), Audubon(2)
TENNANT Shelby
TERRIL (51364) Dickinson(74), Clay(17), Emmet(10)
THAYER (50254) Union(98), Clarke(2)
THOMPSON Winnebago
THOR (50591) Humboldt(85), Webster(15)
THORNBURG Keokuk

THORNTON (50479) Cerro Gordo(88), Franklin(12)
THURMAN Fremont
TIFFIN Johnson
TINGLEY Ringgold
TIPTON Cedar
TITONKA (50480) Kossuth(95), Hancock(3), Winnebago(2)
TODDVILLE Linn
TOETERVILLE Mitchell
TOLEDO Tama
TORONTO Clinton
TRACY (50256) Marion(80), Mahaska(20)
TRAER Tama
TREYNOR Pottawattamie
TRIPOLI Bremer
TROY MILLS Linn
TRUESDALE Buena Vista
TRURO (50257) Madison(85), Clarke(11), Warren(4)
TURIN Monona
UDELL Appanoose
UNDERWOOD Pottawattamie
UNION (50258) Hardin(77), Marshall(22), Grundy(1)
UNIONVILLE Appanoose
UNIVERSITY PARK Mahaska
URBANA Benton
URBANDALE (50323) Polk(72), Dallas(28)
URBANDALE Polk
UTE (51060) Monona(88), Crawford(12)
VAIL Crawford
VAN HORNE Benton
VAN METER (50261) Dallas(53), Madison(47)
VAN WERT Decatur
VARINA Pocahontas
VENTURA (50482) Cerro Gordo(87), Hancock(13)
VICTOR (52347) Iowa(78), Poweshiek(22)
VILLISCA (50864) Montgomery(82), Page(12), Taylor(4)
VINCENT Webster
VINING Tama
VINTON Benton
VIOLA Linn
VOLGA Clayton
WADENA (52169) Fayette(95), Clayton(5)
WALCOTT (52773) Scott(99), Muscatine(1)
WALFORD Benton
WALKER Linn
WALL LAKE (51466) Sac(93), Carroll(4), Crawford(3)
WALLINGFORD Emmet
WALNUT (51577) Pottawattamie(74), Shelby(25)
WAPELLO Louisa
WASHINGTON Washington
WASHTA (51061) Cherokee(79), Ida(21)
WATERLOO Black Hawk
WATERVILLE Allamakee
WATKINS Benton
WAUCOMA (52171) Fayette(71), Chickasaw(16), Winneshiek(13)
WAUKEE Dallas
WAUKON (52172) Allamakee(99), Winneshiek(1)
WAVERLY Bremer
WAYLAND (52654) Henry(72), Washington(28)
WEBB (51366) Clay(96), Buena Vista(4)
WEBSTER (52355) Keokuk(97), Iowa(4)
WEBSTER CITY Hamilton
WELDON (50264) Clarke(51), Decatur(49)
WELLMAN (52356) Washington(89), Iowa(10), Keokuk(1)
WELLSBURG (50680) Grundy(98), Hardin(2)
WELTON Clinton
WESLEY (50483) Kossuth(79), Hancock(22)
WEST AMANA Iowa

WEST BEND (50597) Kossuth(55), Palo Alto(43), Humboldt(2)
WEST BRANCH (52358) Cedar(82), Johnson(17), Mitchell(1)
WEST BURLINGTON Des Moines
WEST CHESTER Washington
WEST DES MOINES (50266) Polk(89), Dallas(11)
WEST DES MOINES (99999) Polk(99), Dallas(1)
WEST GROVE Davis
WEST LIBERTY Muscatine
WEST POINT (52656) Lee(99), Henry(1)
WEST UNION Fayette

WESTFIELD Plymouth
WESTGATE Fayette
WESTPHALIA Shelby
WESTSIDE (51467) Crawford(73), Carroll(27)
WEVER (52658) Lee(87), Des Moines(13)
WHAT CHEER (50268) Keokuk(95), Mahaska(5)
WHEATLAND (52777) Clinton(93), Cedar(7)
WHITING Monona
WHITTEMORE (50598) Kossuth(77), Palo Alto(23)
WHITTEN Hardin

WILLIAMS (50271) Hamilton(91), Wright(8)
WILLIAMSBURG Iowa
WILLIAMSON Lucas
WILTON (52778) Muscatine(56), Cedar(44)
WINFIELD (52659) Henry(84), Louisa(17)
WINTERSET Madison
WINTHROP Buchanan
WIOTA Cass
WODEN (50484) Hancock(49), Winnebago(48), Kossuth(4)
WOODBINE Harrison
WOODBURN Clarke
WOODWARD (50276) Dallas(73), Boone(27)

WOOLSTOCK (50599) Wright(80), Hamilton(21)
WORTHINGTON (52078) Dubuque(60), Delaware(40)
WYOMING Jones
YALE (50277) Guthrie(81), Dallas(20)
YARMOUTH Des Moines
YORKTOWN Page
ZEARING Story
ZWINGLE (52079) Jackson(64), Dubuque(36)

ZIP/City Cross Reference

50001-50001	ACKWORTH	50103-50103	GARDEN GROVE	50171-50171	MONTEZUMA	50274-50274	WIOTA
50002-50002	ADAIR	50104-50104	GIBSON	50173-50173	MONTOUR	50275-50275	WOODBURN
50003-50003	ADEL	50105-50105	GILBERT	50174-50174	MURRAY	50276-50276	WOODWARD
50005-50005	ALBION	50106-50106	GILMAN	50177-50177	GRINNELL	50277-50277	YALE
50006-50006	ALDEN	50107-50107	GRAND JUNCTION	50197-50198	KNOXVILLE	50278-50278	ZEARING
50007-50007	ALLEMAN	50108-50108	GRAND RIVER	50201-50201	NEVADA	50301-50321	DES MOINES
50008-50008	ALLERTON	50109-50109	GRANGER	50206-50206	NEW PROVIDENCE	50322-50323	URBANDALE
50009-50009	ALTOONA	50110-50110	GRAY	50207-50207	NEW SHARON	50325-50325	CLIVE
50010-50014	AMES	50111-50111	GRIMES	50208-50208	NEWTON	50328-50397	DES MOINES
50015-50015	ANKENY	50112-50112	GRINNELL	50210-50210	NEW VIRGINIA	50398-50398	WEST DES MOINES
50020-50020	ANITA	50115-50115	GUTHRIE CENTER	50211-50211	NORWALK	50401-50402	MASON CITY
50021-50021	ANKENY	50116-50116	HAMILTON	50212-50212	OGDEN	50420-50420	ALEXANDER
50022-50022	ATLANTIC	50117-50117	HAMLIN	50213-50213	OSCEOLA	50421-50421	BELMOND
50025-50025	AUDUBON	50118-50118	HARTFORD	50214-50214	OTLEY	50423-50423	BRITT
50026-50026	BAGLEY	50119-50119	HARVEY	50216-50216	PANORA	50424-50424	BUFFALO CENTER
50027-50027	BARNES CITY	50120-50120	HAVERHILL	50217-50217	PATON	50426-50426	CARPENTER
50028-50028	BAXTER	50122-50122	HUBBARD	50218-50218	PATTERSON	50427-50427	CHAPIN
50029-50029	BAYARD	50123-50123	HUMESTON	50219-50219	PELLA	50428-50428	CLEAR LAKE
50031-50031	BEAVER	50124-50124	HUXLEY	50220-50220	PERRY	50430-50430	CORWITH
50032-50032	BERWICK	50125-50125	INDIANOLA	50222-50222	PERU	50431-50431	COULTER
50033-50033	BEVINGTON	50126-50126	IOWA FALLS	50223-50223	PILOT MOUND	50432-50432	CRYSTAL LAKE
50034-50034	BLAIRSBURG	50127-50127	IRA	50225-50225	PLEASANTVILLE	50433-50433	DOUGHERTY
50035-50035	BONDURANT	50128-50128	JAMAICA	50226-50226	POLK CITY	50434-50434	FERTILE
50036-50037	BOONE	50129-50129	JEFFERSON	50227-50227	POPEJOY	50435-50435	FLOYD
50038-50038	BOONEVILLE	50130-50130	JEWELL	50228-50228	PRAIRIE CITY	50436-50436	FOREST CITY
50039-50039	BOUTON	50131-50131	JOHNSTON	50229-50229	PROLE	50438-50438	GARNER
50040-50040	BOXHOLM	50132-50132	KAMRAR	50230-50230	RADCLIFFE	50439-50439	GOODELL
50041-50041	BRADFORD	50133-50133	KELLERTON	50231-50231	RANDALL	50440-50440	GRAFTON
50042-50042	BRAYTON	50134-50134	KELLEY	50232-50232	REASNOR	50441-50441	HAMPTON
50043-50043	BUCKEYE	50135-50135	KELLOGG	50233-50233	REDFIELD	50444-50444	HANLONTOWN
50044-50044	BUSSEY	50136-50136	KESWICK	50234-50234	RHODES	50446-50446	JOICE
50046-50046	CAMBRIDGE	50137-50137	KILLDUFF	50235-50235	RIPPEY	50447-50447	KANAWHA
50047-50047	CARLISLE	50138-50138	KNOXVILLE	50236-50236	ROLAND	50448-50448	KENSETT
50048-50048	CASEY	50139-50139	LACONA	50237-50237	RUNNELLS	50449-50449	KLEMME
50049-50049	CHARITON	50140-50140	LAMONI	50238-50238	RUSSELL	50450-50450	LAKE MILLS
50050-50050	CHURDAN	50141-50141	LAUREL	50239-50239	SAINT ANTHONY	50451-50451	LAKOTA
50051-50051	CLEMONS	50142-50142	LE GRAND	50240-50240	SAINT CHARLES	50452-50452	LATIMER
50052-50052	CLIO	50143-50143	LEIGHTON	50241-50241	SAINT MARYS	50453-50453	LELAND
50054-50054	COLFAX	50144-50144	LEON	50242-50242	SEARSBORO	50454-50454	LITTLE CEDAR
50055-50055	COLLINS	50145-50145	LIBERTY CENTER	50243-50243	SHELDAHL	50455-50455	MC INTIRE
50056-50056	COLO	50146-50146	LINDEN	50244-50244	SLATER	50456-50456	MANLY
50057-50057	COLUMBIA	50147-50147	LINEVILLE	50246-50246	STANHOPE	50457-50457	MESERVEY
50058-50058	COON RAPIDS	50148-50148	LISCOMB	50247-50247	STATE CENTER	50458-50458	NORA SPRINGS
50059-50059	COOPER	50149-50149	LORIMOR	50248-50248	STORY CITY	50459-50459	NORTHWOOD
50060-50060	CORYDON	50150-50150	LOVILIA	50249-50249	STRATFORD	50460-50460	ORCHARD
50061-50061	CUMMING	50151-50151	LUCAS	50250-50250	STUART	50461-50461	OSAGE
50062-50062	DALLAS	50152-50152	LUTHER	50251-50251	SULLY	50464-50464	PLYMOUTH
50063-50063	DALLAS CENTER	50153-50153	LYNNVILLE	50252-50252	SWAN	50465-50465	RAKE
50064-50064	DANA	50154-50154	MC CALLSBURG	50254-50254	THAYER	50466-50466	RICEVILLE
50065-50065	DAVIS CITY	50155-50155	MACKSBURG	50255-50255	THORNBURG	50467-50467	ROCK FALLS
50066-50066	DAWSON	50156-50156	MADRID	50256-50256	TRACY	50468-50468	ROCKFORD
50067-50067	DECATUR	50157-50157	MALCOM	50257-50257	TRURO	50469-50469	ROCKWELL
50068-50068	DERBY	50158-50158	MARSHALLTOWN	50258-50258	UNION	50470-50470	ROWAN
50069-50069	DE SOTO	50160-50160	MARTENSDALE	50259-50259	GIFFORD	50471-50471	RUDD
50070-50070	DEXTER	50161-50161	MAXWELL	50261-50261	VAN METER	50472-50472	SAINT ANSGAR
50071-50071	DOWS	50162-50162	MELBOURNE	50262-50262	VAN WERT	50473-50473	SCARVILLE
50072-50072	EARLHAM	50163-50163	MELCHER	50263-50263	WAUKEE	50475-50475	SHEFFIELD
50073-50073	ELKHART	50164-50164	MENLO	50264-50264	WELDON	50476-50476	STACYVILLE
50074-50074	ELLSTON	50165-50165	MILLERTON	50265-50266	WEST DES MOINES	50477-50477	SWALEDALE
50075-50075	ELLSWORTH	50166-50166	MILO	50268-50268	WHAT CHEER	50478-50478	THOMPSON
50076-50076	EXIRA	50167-50167	MINBURN	50269-50269	WHITTEN	50479-50479	THORNTON
50078-50078	FERGUSON	50168-50168	MINGO	50271-50271	WILLIAMS	50480-50480	TITONKA
50101-50101	GALT	50169-50169	MITCHELLVILLE	50272-50272	WILLIAMSON	50481-50481	TOETERVILLE
50102-50102	GARDEN CITY	50170-50170	MONROE	50273-50273	WINTERSET	50482-50482	VENTURA

ZIP	Place	ZIP	Place	ZIP	Place	ZIP	Place
50483-50483	WESLEY	50606-50606	ARLINGTON	50848-50848	GRAVITY	51240-51240	INWOOD
50484-50484	WODEN	50607-50607	AURORA	50849-50849	GREENFIELD	51241-51241	LARCHWOOD
50501-50501	FORT DODGE	50608-50608	AUSTINVILLE	50851-50851	LENOX	51242-51242	LESTER
50510-50510	ALBERT CITY	50609-50609	BEAMAN	50853-50853	MASSENA	51243-51243	LITTLE ROCK
50511-50511	ALGONA	50611-50611	BRISTOW	50854-50854	MOUNT AYR	51244-51244	MATLOCK
50514-50514	ARMSTRONG	50612-50612	BUCKINGHAM	50857-50857	NODAWAY	51245-51245	PRIMGHAR
50515-50515	AYRSHIRE	50613-50614	CEDAR FALLS	50858-50858	ORIENT	51246-51246	ROCK RAPIDS
50516-50516	BADGER	50616-50616	CHARLES CITY	50859-50859	PRESCOTT	51247-51247	ROCK VALLEY
50517-50517	BANCROFT	50619-50619	CLARKSVILLE	50860-50860	REDDING	51248-51248	SANBORN
50518-50518	BARNUM	50620-50620	COLWELL	50861-50861	SHANNON CITY	51249-51249	SIBLEY
50519-50519	BODE	50621-50621	CONRAD	50862-50862	SHARPSBURG	51250-51250	SIOUX CENTER
50520-50520	BRADGATE	50622-50622	DENVER	50863-50863	TINGLEY	51301-51301	SPENCER
50521-50521	BURNSIDE	50623-50623	DEWAR	50864-50864	VILLISCA	51330-51330	ALLENDORF
50522-50522	BURT	50624-50624	DIKE	50936-50981	DES MOINES	51331-51331	ARNOLDS PARK
50523-50523	CALLENDER	50625-50625	DUMONT	51001-51001	AKRON	51333-51333	DICKENS
50524-50524	CLARE	50626-50626	DUNKERTON	51002-51002	ALTA	51334-51334	ESTHERVILLE
50525-50525	CLARION	50627-50627	ELDORA	51003-51003	ALTON	51338-51338	EVERLY
50527-50527	CURLEW	50628-50628	ELMA	51004-51004	ANTHON	51340-51340	FOSTORIA
50528-50528	CYLINDER	50629-50629	FAIRBANK	51005-51005	AURELIA	51341-51341	GILLETT GROVE
50529-50529	DAKOTA CITY	50630-50630	FREDERICKSBURG	51006-51006	BATTLE CREEK	51342-51342	GRAETTINGER
50530-50530	DAYTON	50631-50631	FREDERIKA	51007-51007	BRONSON	51343-51343	GREENVILLE
50531-50531	DOLLIVER	50632-50632	GARWIN	51008-51008	BRUNSVILLE	51344-51344	GRUVER
50532-50532	DUNCOMBE	50633-50633	GENEVA	51009-51009	CALUMET	51345-51345	HARRIS
50533-50533	EAGLE GROVE	50634-50634	GILBERTVILLE	51010-51010	CASTANA	51346-51346	HARTLEY
50535-50535	EARLY	50635-50635	GLADBROOK	51011-51011	CHATSWORTH	51347-51347	LAKE PARK
50536-50536	EMMETSBURG	50636-50636	GREENE	51012-51012	CHEROKEE	51349-51349	MAY CITY
50538-50538	FARNHAMVILLE	50638-50638	GRUNDY CENTER	51014-51014	CLEGHORN	51350-51350	MELVIN
50539-50539	FENTON	50641-50641	HAZLETON	51015-51015	CLIMBING HILL	51351-51351	MILFORD
50540-50540	FONDA	50642-50642	HOLLAND	51016-51016	CORRECTIONVILLE	51354-51354	OCHEYEDAN
50541-50541	GILMORE CITY	50643-50643	HUDSON	51017-51017	CRAIG	51355-51355	OKOBOJI
50542-50542	GOLDFIELD	50644-50644	INDEPENDENCE	51018-51018	CUSHING	51357-51357	ROYAL
50543-50543	GOWRIE	50645-50645	IONIA	51019-51019	DANBURY	51358-51358	RUTHVEN
50544-50544	HARCOURT	50647-50647	JANESVILLE	51020-51020	GALVA	51360-51360	SPIRIT LAKE
50545-50545	HARDY	50648-50648	JESUP	51022-51022	GRANVILLE	51363-51363	SUPERIOR
50546-50546	HAVELOCK	50649-50649	KESLEY	51023-51023	HAWARDEN	51364-51364	TERRIL
50548-50548	HUMBOLDT	50650-50650	LAMONT	51024-51024	HINTON	51365-51365	WALLINGFORD
50551-50551	JOLLEY	50651-50651	LA PORTE CITY	51025-51025	HOLSTEIN	51366-51366	WEBB
50552-50552	KNIERIM	50652-50652	LINCOLN	51026-51026	HORNICK	51401-51401	CARROLL
50554-50554	LAURENS	50653-50653	MARBLE ROCK	51027-51027	IRETON	51430-51430	ARCADIA
50556-50556	LEDYARD	50654-50654	MASONVILLE	51028-51028	KINGSLEY	51431-51431	ARTHUR
50557-50557	LEHIGH	50655-50655	MAYNARD	51029-51029	LARRABEE	51432-51432	ASPINWALL
50558-50558	LIVERMORE	50657-50657	MORRISON	51030-51030	LAWTON	51433-51433	AUBURN
50559-50559	LONE ROCK	50658-50658	NASHUA	51031-51031	LE MARS	51436-51436	BREDA
50560-50560	LU VERNE	50659-50659	NEW HAMPTON	51033-51033	LINN GROVE	51439-51439	CHARTER OAK
50561-50561	LYTTON	50660-50660	NEW HARTFORD	51034-51034	MAPLETON	51440-51440	DEDHAM
50562-50562	MALLARD	50661-50661	NORTH WASHINGTON	51035-51035	MARCUS	51441-51441	DELOIT
50563-50563	MANSON	50662-50662	OELWEIN	51036-51036	MAURICE	51442-51442	DENISON
50565-50565	MARATHON	50664-50664	ORAN	51037-51037	MERIDEN	51443-51443	GLIDDEN
50566-50566	MOORLAND	50665-50665	PARKERSBURG	51038-51038	MERRILL	51444-51444	HALBUR
50567-50567	NEMAHA	50666-50666	PLAINFIELD	51039-51039	MOVILLE	51445-51445	IDA GROVE
50568-50568	NEWELL	50667-50667	RAYMOND	51040-51040	ONAWA	51446-51446	IRWIN
50569-50569	OTHO	50668-50668	READLYN	51041-51041	ORANGE CITY	51447-51447	KIRKMAN
50570-50570	OTTOSEN	50669-50669	REINBECK	51044-51044	OTO	51448-51448	KIRON
50571-50571	PALMER	50670-50670	SHELL ROCK	51045-51045	OYENS	51449-51449	LAKE CITY
50573-50573	PLOVER	50671-50671	STANLEY	51046-51046	PAULLINA	51450-51450	LAKE VIEW
50574-50574	POCAHONTAS	50672-50672	STEAMBOAT ROCK	51047-51047	PETERSON	51451-51451	LANESBORO
50575-50575	POMEROY	50673-50673	STOUT	51048-51048	PIERSON	51452-51452	LIDDERDALE
50576-50576	REMBRANDT	50674-50674	SUMNER	51049-51049	QUIMBY	51453-51453	LOHRVILLE
50577-50577	RENWICK	50675-50675	TRAER	51050-51050	REMSEN	51454-51454	MANILLA
50578-50578	RINGSTED	50676-50676	TRIPOLI	51051-51051	RODNEY	51455-51455	MANNING
50579-50579	ROCKWELL CITY	50677-50677	WAVERLY	51052-51052	SALIX	51458-51458	ODEBOLT
50581-50581	ROLFE	50680-50680	WELLSBURG	51053-51053	SCHALLER	51459-51459	RALSTON
50582-50582	RUTLAND	50681-50681	WESTGATE	51054-51054	SERGEANT BLUFF	51460-51460	RICKETTS
50583-50583	SAC CITY	50682-50682	WINTHROP	51055-51055	SLOAN	51461-51461	SCHLESWIG
50585-50585	SIOUX RAPIDS	50701-50706	WATERLOO	51056-51056	SMITHLAND	51462-51462	SCRANTON
50586-50586	SOMERS	50707-50707	EVANSDALE	51057-51057	STRUBLE	51463-51463	TEMPLETON
50587-50587	RINARD	50799-50799	WATERLOO	51058-51058	SUTHERLAND	51465-51465	VAIL
50588-50588	STORM LAKE	50801-50801	CRESTON	51059-51059	TURIN	51466-51466	WALL LAKE
50590-50590	SWEA CITY	50830-50830	AFTON	51060-51060	UTE	51467-51467	WESTSIDE
50591-50591	THOR	50831-50831	ARISPE	51061-51061	WASHTA	51501-51503	COUNCIL BLUFFS
50592-50592	TRUESDALE	50833-50833	BEDFORD	51062-51062	WESTFIELD	51510-51510	CARTER LAKE
50593-50593	VARINA	50835-50835	BENTON	51063-51063	WHITING	51520-51520	ARION
50594-50594	VINCENT	50836-50836	BLOCKTON	51101-51111	SIOUX CITY	51521-51521	AVOCA
50595-50595	WEBSTER CITY	50837-50837	BRIDGEWATER	51201-51201	SHELDON	51523-51523	BLENCOE
50597-50597	WEST BEND	50839-50839	CARBON	51230-51230	ALVORD	51525-51525	CARSON
50598-50598	WHITTEMORE	50840-50840	CLEARFIELD	51231-51231	ARCHER	51526-51526	CRESCENT
50599-50599	WOOLSTOCK	50841-50841	CORNING	51232-51232	ASHTON	51527-51527	DEFIANCE
50601-50601	ACKLEY	50842-50842	CROMWELL	51234-51234	BOYDEN	51528-51528	DOW CITY
50602-50602	ALLISON	50843-50843	CUMBERLAND	51235-51235	DOON	51529-51529	DUNLAP
50603-50603	ALTA VISTA	50845-50845	DIAGONAL	51237-51237	GEORGE	51530-51530	EARLING
50604-50604	APLINGTON	50846-50846	FONTANELLE	51238-51238	HOSPERS	51531-51531	ELK HORN
50605-50605	AREDALE	50847-50847	GRANT	51239-51239	HULL	51532-51532	ELLIOTT

ZIP	City	ZIP	City	ZIP	City	ZIP	City
51533-51533	EMERSON	52049-52049	GARNAVILLO	52225-52225	ELBERON	52501-52501	OTTUMWA
51534-51534	GLENWOOD	52050-52050	GREELEY	52226-52226	ELWOOD	52530-52530	AGENCY
51535-51535	GRISWOLD	52052-52052	GUTTENBERG	52227-52227	ELY	52531-52531	ALBIA
51536-51536	HANCOCK	52053-52053	HOLY CROSS	52228-52228	FAIRFAX	52533-52533	BATAVIA
51537-51537	HARLAN	52054-52054	LA MOTTE	52229-52229	GARRISON	52534-52534	BEACON
51540-51540	HASTINGS	52055-52055	LITTLEPORT	52230-52230	HALE	52535-52535	BIRMINGHAM
51541-51541	HENDERSON	52056-52056	LUXEMBURG	52231-52231	HARPER	52536-52536	BLAKESBURG
51542-51542	HONEY CREEK	52057-52057	MANCHESTER	52232-52232	HARTWICK	52537-52537	BLOOMFIELD
51543-51543	KIMBALLTON	52060-52060	MAQUOKETA	52233-52233	HIAWATHA	52538-52538	WEST GROVE
51544-51544	LEWIS	52064-52064	MILES	52235-52235	HILLS	52540-52540	BRIGHTON
51545-51545	LITTLE SIOUX	52065-52065	NEW VIENNA	52236-52236	HOMESTEAD	52542-52542	CANTRIL
51546-51546	LOGAN	52066-52066	NORTH BUENA VISTA	52237-52237	HOPKINTON	52543-52543	CEDAR
51548-51548	MC CLELLAND	52068-52068	PEOSTA	52240-52240	IOWA CITY	52544-52544	CENTERVILLE
51549-51549	MACEDONIA	52069-52069	PRESTON	52241-52241	CORALVILLE	52548-52548	CHILLICOTHE
51550-51550	MAGNOLIA	52070-52070	SABULA	52242-52246	IOWA CITY	52549-52549	CINCINNATI
51551-51551	MALVERN	52071-52071	SAINT DONATUS	52247-52247	KALONA	52550-52550	DELTA
51552-51552	MARNE	52072-52072	SAINT OLAF	52248-52248	KEOTA	52551-52551	DOUDS
51553-51553	MINDEN	52073-52073	SHERRILL	52249-52249	KEYSTONE	52552-52552	DRAKESVILLE
51554-51554	MINEOLA	52074-52074	SPRAGUEVILLE	52250-52250	KINROSS	52553-52553	EDDYVILLE
51555-51555	MISSOURI VALLEY	52075-52075	SPRINGBROOK	52251-52251	LADORA	52554-52554	ELDON
51556-51556	MODALE	52076-52076	STRAWBERRY POINT	52252-52252	LANGWORTHY	52555-52555	EXLINE
51557-51557	MONDAMIN	52077-52077	VOLGA	52253-52253	LISBON	52556-52557	FAIRFIELD
51558-51558	MOORHEAD	52078-52078	WORTHINGTON	52254-52254	LOST NATION	52560-52560	FLORIS
51559-51559	NEOLA	52079-52079	ZWINGLE	52255-52255	LOWDEN	52561-52561	FREMONT
51560-51560	OAKLAND	52101-52101	DECORAH	52257-52257	LUZERNE	52562-52562	HAYESVILLE
51561-51561	PACIFIC JUNCTION	52130-52130	ALPHA	52301-52301	MARENGO	52563-52563	HEDRICK
51562-51562	PANAMA	52131-52131	BURR OAK	52302-52302	MARION	52565-52565	KEOSAUQUA
51563-51563	PERSIA	52132-52132	CALMAR	52305-52305	MARTELLE	52566-52566	KIRKVILLE
51564-51564	PISGAH	52133-52133	CASTALIA	52306-52306	MECHANICSVILLE	52567-52567	LIBERTYVILLE
51565-51565	PORTSMOUTH	52134-52134	CHESTER	52307-52307	MIDDLE AMANA	52568-52568	MARTINSBURG
51566-51566	RED OAK	52135-52135	CLERMONT	52308-52308	MILLERSBURG	52569-52569	MELROSE
51570-51570	SHELBY	52136-52136	CRESCO	52309-52309	MONMOUTH	52570-52570	MILTON
51571-51571	SILVER CITY	52140-52140	DORCHESTER	52310-52310	MONTICELLO	52571-52571	MORAVIA
51572-51572	SOLDIER	52141-52141	ELGIN	52312-52312	MORLEY	52572-52572	MOULTON
51573-51573	STANTON	52142-52142	FAYETTE	52313-52313	MOUNT AUBURN	52573-52573	MOUNT STERLING
51574-51574	TENNANT	52144-52144	FORT ATKINSON	52314-52314	MOUNT VERNON	52574-52574	MYSTIC
51575-51575	TREYNOR	52146-52146	HARPERS FERRY	52315-52315	NEWHALL	52576-52576	OLLIE
51576-51576	UNDERWOOD	52147-52147	HAWKEYE	52316-52316	NORTH ENGLISH	52577-52577	OSKALOOSA
51577-51577	WALNUT	52149-52149	HIGHLANDVILLE	52317-52317	NORTH LIBERTY	52580-52580	PACKWOOD
51578-51578	WESTPHALIA	52151-52151	LANSING	52318-52318	NORWAY	52581-52581	PLANO
51579-51579	WOODBINE	52154-52154	LAWLER	52319-52319	OAKDALE	52583-52583	PROMISE CITY
51591-51591	RED OAK	52155-52155	LIME SPRINGS	52320-52320	OLIN	52584-52584	PULASKI
51593-51593	HARLAN	52156-52156	LUANA	52321-52321	ONSLOW	52585-52585	RICHLAND
51601-51603	SHENANDOAH	52157-52157	MC GREGOR	52322-52322	OXFORD	52586-52586	ROSE HILL
51630-51630	BLANCHARD	52158-52158	MARQUETTE	52323-52323	OXFORD JUNCTION	52588-52588	SELMA
51631-51631	BRADDYVILLE	52159-52159	MONONA	52324-52324	PALO	52590-52590	SEYMOUR
51632-51632	CLARINDA	52160-52160	NEW ALBIN	52325-52325	PARNELL	52591-52591	SIGOURNEY
51636-51636	COIN	52161-52161	OSSIAN	52326-52326	QUASQUETON	52593-52593	UDELL
51637-51637	COLLEGE SPRINGS	52162-52162	POSTVILLE	52327-52327	RIVERSIDE	52594-52594	UNIONVILLE
51638-51638	ESSEX	52163-52163	PROTIVIN	52328-52328	ROBINS	52595-52595	UNIVERSITY PARK
51639-51639	FARRAGUT	52164-52164	RANDALIA	52329-52329	ROWLEY	52601-52601	BURLINGTON
51640-51640	HAMBURG	52165-52165	RIDGEWAY	52330-52330	RYAN	52619-52619	ARGYLE
51645-51645	IMOGENE	52166-52166	SAINT LUCAS	52331-52331	SCOTCH GROVE	52620-52620	BONAPARTE
51646-51646	NEW MARKET	52168-52168	SPILLVILLE	52332-52332	SHELLSBURG	52621-52621	CRAWFORDSVILLE
51647-51647	NORTHBORO	52169-52169	WADENA	52333-52333	SOLON	52623-52623	DANVILLE
51648-51648	PERCIVAL	52170-52170	WATERVILLE	52334-52334	SOUTH AMANA	52624-52624	DENMARK
51649-51649	RANDOLPH	52171-52171	WAUCOMA	52335-52335	SOUTH ENGLISH	52625-52625	DONNELLSON
51650-51650	RIVERTON	52172-52172	WAUKON	52336-52336	SPRINGVILLE	52626-52626	FARMINGTON
51651-51651	SHAMBAUGH	52175-52175	WEST UNION	52337-52337	STANWOOD	52627-52627	FORT MADISON
51652-51652	SIDNEY	52201-52201	AINSWORTH	52338-52338	SWISHER	52630-52630	HILLSBORO
51653-51653	TABOR	52202-52202	ALBURNETT	52339-52339	TAMA	52631-52631	HOUGHTON
51654-51654	THURMAN	52203-52204	AMANA	52340-52340	TIFFIN	52632-52632	KEOKUK
51656-51656	YORKTOWN	52205-52205	ANAMOSA	52341-52341	TODDVILLE	52635-52635	LOCKRIDGE
52001-52004	DUBUQUE	52206-52206	ATKINS	52342-52342	TOLEDO	52637-52637	MEDIAPOLIS
52030-52030	ANDREW	52207-52207	BALDWIN	52344-52344	TROY MILLS	52638-52638	MIDDLETOWN
52031-52031	BELLEVUE	52208-52208	BELLE PLAINE	52345-52345	URBANA	52639-52639	MONTROSE
52032-52032	BERNARD	52209-52209	BLAIRSTOWN	52346-52346	VAN HORNE	52640-52640	MORNING SUN
52033-52033	CASCADE	52210-52210	BRANDON	52347-52347	VICTOR	52641-52641	MOUNT PLEASANT
52035-52035	COLESBURG	52211-52211	BROOKLYN	52348-52348	VINING	52642-52642	ROME
52036-52036	DELAWARE	52212-52212	CENTER JUNCTION	52349-52349	VINTON	52644-52644	MOUNT UNION
52037-52037	DELMAR	52213-52213	CENTER POINT	52350-52350	VIOLA	52645-52645	NEW LONDON
52038-52038	DUNDEE	52214-52214	CENTRAL CITY	52351-52351	WALFORD	52646-52646	OAKVILLE
52039-52039	DURANGO	52215-52215	CHELSEA	52352-52352	WALKER	52647-52647	OLDS
52040-52040	DYERSVILLE	52216-52216	CLARENCE	52353-52353	WASHINGTON	52648-52648	PILOT GROVE
52041-52041	EARLVILLE	52217-52217	CLUTIER	52354-52354	WATKINS	52649-52649	SALEM
52042-52042	EDGEWOOD	52218-52218	COGGON	52355-52355	WEBSTER	52650-52650	SPERRY
52043-52043	ELKADER	52219-52219	PRAIRIEBURG	52356-52356	WELLMAN	52651-52651	STOCKPORT
52044-52044	ELKPORT	52220-52220	CONROY	52358-52358	WEST BRANCH	52652-52652	SWEDESBURG
52045-52045	EPWORTH	52221-52221	GUERNSEY	52359-52359	WEST CHESTER	52653-52653	WAPELLO
52046-52046	FARLEY	52222-52222	DEEP RIVER	52361-52361	WILLIAMSBURG	52654-52654	WAYLAND
52047-52047	FARMERSBURG	52223-52223	DELHI	52362-52362	WYOMING	52655-52655	WEST BURLINGTON
52048-52048	GARBER	52224-52224	DYSART	52401-52499	CEDAR RAPIDS	52656-52656	WEST POINT

52657-52657	SAINT PAUL	52731-52731	CHARLOTTE	52752-52752	GRANDVIEW	52768-52768	PRINCETON
52658-52658	WEVER	52732-52736	CLINTON	52753-52753	LE CLAIRE	52769-52769	STOCKTON
52659-52659	WINFIELD	52737-52737	COLUMBUS CITY	52754-52754	LETTS	52771-52771	TEEDS GROVE
52660-52660	YARMOUTH	52738-52738	COLUMBUS JUNCTION	52755-52755	LONE TREE	52772-52772	TIPTON
52701-52701	ANDOVER	52739-52739	CONESVILLE	52756-52756	LONG GROVE	52773-52773	WALCOTT
52720-52720	ATALISSA	52742-52742	DE WITT	52757-52757	LOW MOOR	52774-52774	WELTON
52721-52721	BENNETT	52745-52745	DIXON	52758-52758	MC CAUSLAND	52776-52776	WEST LIBERTY
52722-52722	BETTENDORF	52746-52746	DONAHUE	52759-52759	MONTPELIER	52777-52777	WHEATLAND
52726-52726	BLUE GRASS	52747-52747	DURANT	52760-52760	MOSCOW	52778-52778	WILTON
52727-52727	BRYANT	52748-52748	ELDRIDGE	52761-52761	MUSCATINE	52801-52809	DAVENPORT
52728-52728	BUFFALO	52749-52749	FRUITLAND	52765-52765	NEW LIBERTY		
52729-52729	CALAMUS	52750-52750	GOOSE LAKE	52766-52766	NICHOLS		
52730-52730	CAMANCHE	52751-52751	GRAND MOUND	52767-52767	PLEASANT VALLEY		

Kansas

General Help Numbers:

Governor's Office
State Capitol Bldg, Room 212S   785-296-3232
Topeka, KS 66612-1590   Fax 785-296-7973
http://www.ink.org/public/governor   8AM-5PM

Attorney General's Office
Memorial Hall   785-296-2215
120 SW 10th Ave, 2nd Floor   Fax 785-296-6296
Topeka, KS 66612-1597   8AM-5PM
http://www.ink.org/public/ksag

State Court Administrator
Kansas Judicial Center, 301 SW 10th St   785-296-4873
Topeka, KS 66612-1507   Fax 785-296-7076
http://www.kscourts.org   8AM-5PM

State Archives
Library and Archives Division   785-272-8681
6425 SW 6th Ave   Fax 785-272-8682
Topeka, KS 66615-1099   9AM-4:30PM M-SA
http://hs4.kshs.org

State Specifics:

Capital: Topeka
          Shawnee County

Time Zone: CST*
*Kansas' five western-most counties are MST:
They are: Greeley, Hamilton, Kearny, Sherman, Wallace,

Number of Counties: 105

Population: 2,688,418

Web Site: www.accesskansas.org

State Agencies

Criminal Records

Kansas Bureau of Investigation, Criminal Records Division, 1620 SW Tyler, Crim. History Record Sec., Topeka, KS 66612-1837; 785-296-8200, 785-296-6781 (Fax), 8AM-5PM.

http://www.kbi.state.ks.us

Note: Non-criminal justice agencies, organizations, individuals and commercial companies are entitled to receive recorded conviction information. Arrests with no convictions are not shown, unless arrest is less than 12 months old and there is no disposition.

Indexing & Storage: New records are available for inquiry immediately. Records are indexed on Kansas Central Repository database, which is synchronized with the automated fingerprint ID system db.

Searching: Each request must be on a separate "Records Check Request Form." First time requesters must complete a user's agreement. Sex offender data is available online at www.ink.org/cgi-bin/kbi/search.pl. Include the following in your request-full name, sex, race, date of birth, Social Security Number. Turnaround time may be several weeks if the record is not currently automated. The following data is not released:

expunged records, non-conviction information or juvenile records.

Access by: mail, fax.

Fee & Payment: Fees: $10.00 for a name check; $17.00 for fingerprint search. All requests are allowed one additional alias name per person. However, add $5.00 per third and each additional alias name. Fee payee: KBI Records Fees Fund. Prepayment required. Personal checks accepted. No credit cards accepted.

Mail search: Turnaround time: 2 to 4 weeks. A self addressed stamped envelope is requested.

Fax search: Prior arrangement is required, same criteria as mail.

Other access: Currently constructing web site that allows record checks with credit card payment system.

Corporation Records
Limited Partnerships
Limited Liability Company
Records

Secretary of State, Memorial Hall, 120 SW 10th Ave, 1st Floor, Topeka, KS 66612-1594; 785-296-4564, 785-296-4570 (Fax), 8AM-5PM.

http://okwww.kssos.org

Indexing & Storage: Records are available since the applicable laws have been in effect. All Annual Reports before 1995 are at the Historical Society. New records are available for inquiry immediately. Records are indexed on inhouse computer.

Searching: Items not released include confidential annual report balance sheets and copies of extensions. Include the following in your request-full name of business, specific records that you need copies of. In addition to the articles of incorporation, corporation records include the following information: Annual Reports, Officers, Directors and Prior (merged) names. They do not keep Inactive or Reserved names.

Access by: mail, phone, fax, in person, online.

Fee & Payment: Fees: Certificate of good standing - $7.50; letter of status - $5.00; written record search $5.00. Copies are $1.00 per page. Fee payee: Secretary of State. Prepayment required. When requesting by mail, send check for $5.00 or $10.00. They will refund any excess. Prepaid accounts are available. Personal checks accepted. Credit cards accepted: MasterCard, Visa.

Mail search: Turnaround time: 1 to 2 days. No self addressed stamped envelope is required.

Phone search: General information is given without charge.

Fax search: Items can be returned by fax for an additional $2.00 for the first page and $1.00 each additional page.

In person search: No fee for request. Turnaround time 10 minutes.

Online search: Corporate data can be ordered from the Information Network of Kansas (INK), a state sponsored interface at www.ink.org/public/corps. There is no fee to search or view records, but there is a fee to order copies of certificates or good standings. You must also subscribe to INK which entails an annual fee of $60.00 plus an initial subscription fee.

Expedited service: Expedited service is available for fax searches. Turnaround time: same day if possible. Add $20.00 per package.

Trademarks/Servicemarks

Secretary of State, Trademarks/Servicemarks Division, 120 SW 10th Ave, Rm 100, Topeka, KS 66612-1240; 785-296-4564, 785-296-4570 (Fax), 8AM-5PM.

http://www.kssos.org

Indexing & Storage: Records are available from the 1950s, all on computer. It takes 2 to 3 days before new records are available for inquiry.

Searching: All information recorded is available to the public. However, Kansas law prohibits the use of names and/or addresses derived from public record for solicitation purposes. Include the following in your request-trademark/servicemark name, name of owner. The search provides the names and addresses of owners, date of filing, and class code of filing.

Access by: mail, phone, fax, in person.

Fee & Payment: There is no search fee. Copies are $1.00 per page. Certification is $7.50 plus the copy fees. Fee payee: Secretary of State. Prepayment required. The Secretary of State's office offers prepaid accounts for all regular, ongoing requesters. Personal checks accepted. Credit cards accepted: MasterCard, Visa.

Mail search: Turnaround time: 1 to 2 days. A mail request must include the name of trademark/servicemark and/or the owner's name.No self addressed stamped envelope is required. No fee for mail request.

Phone search: No fee for telephone request. They will give you limited information from the computer index.

Fax search: Turnaround time 24 hours.

In person search: No fee for request. If you call ahead of time, they will have information ready when you come in.

Other access: For bulk file purchase, there is a $20-75 program set-up fee, plus $1.00 per page. Files are also available on CD for $40 and $20 program set-up fee.

Expedited service: Expedited service is available for mail, phone and in person searches. Expedited requesters are required to have a pre-paid account, $150 to start.

Uniform Commercial Code
Federal Tax Liens
State Tax Liens

UCC Division, Secretary of State, Memorial Hall, 120 SW 10th Ave, Topeka, KS 66612; 785-296-1849, 785-296-3659 (Fax), 8AM-5PM.

http://www.kssos.org/uccwelc.html

Indexing & Storage: Records are available from 1966 on computer, from 1966 to present on microfiche with exception of electronic filings.

Searching: Use search request form UCC-3. The search includes federal tax liens on businesses. Federal tax liens on individuals can be filed here or at county, all state tax liens are filed at the county level. Include the following in your request-debtor name. You must order copies to receive collateral information. No collateral data is given over the phone.

Access by: mail, phone, fax, in person, online.

Fee & Payment: Copies are $1.00 per page, search varies with type of access. Editor's Note: fees will change in July 2001. Fee payee: Secretary of State. Prepayment required. Personal checks accepted. Credit cards accepted: MasterCard, Visa.

Mail search: Turnaround time: 1 day. A self addressed stamped envelope is requested. Search costs $8.00 per debtor name.

Phone search: Search costs $15.00 per debtor name.

Fax search: Same criteria as mail searching. You can have information returned by fax for an additional $2.00 for the first page and $1.00 each additional page.

In person search: Search costs $8.00 per debtor name. Copies cost $1.00 per page.

Online search: Online service is provided the Information Network of Kansas (INK). The system is open 24 hours daily. There is an annual fee. Network charges are $.10 a minute unless access is through their Internet site at www.ink.org which has no network fee. UCC records are $8.00 per record. This is the same online system used for corporation records. For more information, call INK at 800-4-KANSAS.

Other access: INK also provides records in a bulk or database format.

Sales Tax Registrations
Access to Records is Restricted

Kansas Department of Revenue, Customer Relations, 3rd Floor, Docking State Office Bldg, 915 SW Harrison, Topeka, KS 66612-1588; 785-368-8222, 785-291-3614 (Fax), 7AM-5PM.

http://www.ink.org/public/kdor

Note: Sales tax registration information is considered confidential and not public record.

Birth Certificates

Kansas Department of Health & Environment, Office of Vital Statistics, 900 SW Jackson, #151, Topeka, KS 66612-2221; 785-296-1400, 785-296-3253 (Credit Card Orders), 785-357-4332 (Fax), 8AM-5PM.

http://www.kdhe.state.ks.us/vital

Note: Vital records are not considered public records in Kansas.

Indexing & Storage: Records are available from 1911 to present. Delayed birth registrations from the mid-1800s are available. Records are indexed on microfiche, index cards, inhouse computer.

Searching: Must have a signed release from person of record or have direct interest for personal or property right. Include the following in your request-full name, names of parents, mother's maiden name, date of birth, place of birth, relationship to person of record, reason for information request. Include a daytime phone number.

Access by: mail, phone, fax, in person.

Fee & Payment: The fee is $10.00 for first certified copy; add $5.00 for each additional copy of same record. Fee payee: Vital Statistics. Prepayment required. There is an additional $8.00 VitalChek fee with the use of a credit card. Personal checks accepted. Credit cards accepted: MasterCard, Visa, AmEx, Discover.

Mail search: Turnaround time: 2 to 3 weeks. Include copy of personal ID.A self addressed stamped envelope is requested.

Phone search: You must use a credit card for an additional $8.00 fee. Turnaround time is next business day. Phone service hours are from 8am to 4pm.

Fax search: The fee must include $8.00 for use of a credit card. Turnaround time: 2-3 business days.

In person search: You must complete an application and provide ID. Turnaround time: 20 to 30 minutes.

Expedited service: Expedited service is available for fax searches. Turnaround time: overnight delivery. Overnight mail services for return of documents is available for an additional fee. Requests may require up to 24 business hours to process. Use of credit card required.

Death Records

Kansas State Department of Health & Environment, Office of Vital Statistics, 900 SW Jackson, #151, Topeka, KS 66612-2221; 785-296-1400, 785-296-3253 (Credit Card Orders), 785-357-4332 (Fax), 8AM-5PM.

http://www.kdhe.state.ks.us/vital

Note: Vital records are not considered public records in Kansas.

Indexing & Storage: Records are available from July 1, 1911 to present. New records are available for inquiry immediately. Records are indexed on microfiche, index cards, inhouse computer.

Searching: Must have a signed release from immediate family member or show direct interest for personal or property right. Include the following in your request-full name, date of death, place of death, relationship to person of record, reason for information request. Please include a daytime phone number.

Access by: mail, phone, fax, in person.

Fee & Payment: The search fee is $10.00 for 1 certified copy; add $5.00 per copy requested at the same time. The search fee covers five years, if year not known. Fee payee: Vital Statistics. Prepayment required. Money orders are accepted. There is a $7.00 VitalChek fee for the use of a credit card. Personal checks accepted. Credit cards accepted: MasterCard, Visa, AmEx, Discover.

Mail search: Turnaround time: 3 to 5 days. Must include a personal ID.A self addressed stamped envelope is requested.

Phone search: Use a credit card required for an additional $8.00 fee. Turnaround time is next business day.

Fax search: Same criteria as phone searches.

In person search: Must complete an application and provide personal ID. Turnaround time: 20 to 30 minutes.

Expedited service: Expedited service is available for fax searches. Overnight service is available for an additional fee. Use of credit card required.

Marriage Certificates

Kansas State Department of Health & Environment, Office of Vital Statistics, 900 SW Jackson, #151, Topeka, KS 66612-2221; 785-296-1400, 785-357-4332 (Fax), 8AM-5PM.

http://www.kdhe.state.ks.us/vital

Note: Vital records are not considered public records in Kansas.

Indexing & Storage: Records are available from May 1, 1913 to present. Records prior to 1913 are found at county of issue. Records are computerized from 1993. Records are indexed on microfiche, index cards, inhouse computer.

Searching: Must have a signed release from person of record or have direct interest in personal or property right. Include the following in your request-names of husband and wife, date of marriage, place or county of marriage, relationship to person of record, reason for information request, wife's maiden name. Include a daytime phone number.

Access by: mail, phone, fax, in person.

Fee & Payment: The search fee is $10.00 for 1 certified copy; add $5.00 per name for add'l copy. Fee payee: Vital Statistics. Prepayment required. Money orders are accepted. Personal checks

accepted. Credit cards accepted: MasterCard, Visa, AmEx, Discover.

Mail search: Turnaround time: 3 to 5 days. Must include a personal ID number.A self addressed stamped envelope is requested.

Phone search: You must use a credit card for an additional $8.00 fee. Turnaround time is next business day.

Fax search: Same criteria as phone searches.

In person search: Turnaround time 20 to 30 minutes.

Expedited service: Expedited service is available for fax searches. Overnight mail service is available for an additional fee. Overnight requests may require up to 24 business hours to process. Use of credit card required.

Divorce Records

Kansas State Department of Health & Environment, Office of Vital Statistics, 900 SW Jackson, #151, Topeka, KS 66612-2221; 785-296-1400, 785-296-3253 (Credit Card Orders), 785-357-4332 (Fax), 8AM-5PM.

http://www.kdhe.state.ks.us/vital

Note: The agency will issue a divorce certificate, but a copy of the decree must be ordered from the county of issue.

Indexing & Storage: Records are available from July 1, 1951 to present. Records prior to July 1, 1951 are found at county of issue. New records are available for inquiry immediately. Records are indexed on microfiche, index cards, inhouse computer.

Searching: Must have a signed release from person of record or show direct interest in personal or property right. Include the following in your request-names of husband and wife, date of divorce, relationship to person of record, reason for information request.

Access by: mail, phone, fax, in person.

Fee & Payment: The search fee is $10.00 for 1 certified copy; add $5.00 per additional copy. Fee payee: Vital Statistics. Prepayment required. Money orders are accepted. Personal checks accepted. Credit cards accepted: MasterCard, Visa, AmEx, Discover.

Mail search: Turnaround time: 3 to 5 days. A self addressed stamped envelope is requested.

Phone search: Must use a credit card for an additional $8.00 fee. Turnaround time is next business day.

Fax search: Same criteria as phone searches.

In person search: Turnaround time is 20-30 minutes.

Expedited service: Expedited service is available for fax searches. Overnight mail service is available for an additional fee and may require up to 24 business hours to process. Use of credit card required.

Workers' Compensation Records

Human Resources Department, Workers Compensation Division, 800 SW Jackson, Suite 600, Topeka, KS 66612-1227; 785-296-3441, 800-332-0353 (Claims Advisor), 785-296-0025 (Fax), 8AM-5PM.

http://www.hr.state.ks.us/wc/html/wc.htm

Indexing & Storage: Records are available from the mid-1970's on. New records are available for inquiry immediately. Records are indexed on inhouse computer, file folders.

Searching: Information not released includes financial information submitted by employer, peer review records, records related to safety inspections. Medical records are only released to those authorized by law, and are not open to the general public. Include the following in your request-claimant name, Social Security Number. Employers may receive medical records if a job has been conditionally offered and there is a signed release by the subject.

Access by: mail, phone, fax, in person.

Fee & Payment: There is no search fee.

Mail search: Turnaround time: 1 week to 10 days. No self addressed stamped envelope is required.

Phone search: Records are available by phone.

Fax search: Fax searching available.

In person search: Requests maintained off premises will take 2 days to obtain.

Other access: Release of bulk lists or portions of the database is available per special written request. Call for more information.

Driver Records
Accident Reports

Department of Revenue, Driver Control Bureau, PO Box 12021, Topeka, KS 66612-2021 (Courier: Docking State Office Building, 915 Harrison, 1st Floor, Topeka, KS 66612); 785-296-3671, 785-296-6851 (Fax), 8AM-4:45PM.

http://www.ink.org/public/kdor/dmv/driverinfo.html

Indexing & Storage: Records are available for 3 years for minor violations and 5 years for DWIs. The state does not record speeding violations of 10 mph or less over in a 70 speed zone or 5 mph or less in all other speed zones. It takes 2 to 21 days before new records are available for inquiry.

Searching: Casual requesters cannot obtain records. Statutes prohibit acquiring records for the purpose of obtaining addresses and lists for the sale of property or services. An explanation of intended use may be required. The driver license number and either full name or DOB are required when ordering a driving record. The driver's address will show on the record. For an accident report, include the full name, DOB and/or VIN number, and date of accident. The following data is not released: medical information.

Access by: mail, in person, online.

Fee & Payment: The fee is $5.00 for a walk-in or mail-in request for a driving record. An accident report is available for $3.50 per page. Fee payee: Department of Revenue. Prepayment required. Personal checks accepted. No credit cards accepted.

Mail search: Turnaround time: 2 to 5 days. A self addressed stamped envelope is requested.

In person search: Walk-in requests are usually processed within 30 minutes. Local law enforcement agencies may also honor driving record requests at a higher cost.

Online search: Kansas has contracted with the Information Network of Kansas (INK) (800-452-6727) to service all electronic media requests of driver license histories. INK offers connection through an "800 number" or can be reached via the

Internet at www.ink.org. The fee is $3.50 per record. There is an initial $75 subscription fee and an annual $60 fee to access records from INK. The system is open 24 hours a day, 7 days a week. Batch requests are available at 7:30 am (if ordered by 10 pm the previous day.

Other access: Tape-to-tape request records are available on an overnight basis through INK.

Vehicle Ownership
Vehicle Identification

Division of Vehicles, Title and Registration Bureau, 915 Harrison, Rm 155, Topeka, KS 66612; 785-296-3621, 785-296-3852 (Fax), 7:30AM-4:45PM.

http://www.ink.org/public/kdor/kdorvehicle

Indexing & Storage: Records are available from approximately 1940. Older records are on microfilm, on microfiche from 1970-1987, and computerized since 1988.

Searching: Casual requesters can obtain records, no personal information is released if subject opted out. Records are restricted from purchase for the purpose of obtaining address mail lists for selling property or services. Mail and walk-in search requesters are asked to use Form TR-18.

Access by: mail, in person, online.

Fee & Payment: The fee for a title/registration verification depends on the request mode, noted as below. Fee payee: Kansas Department of Revenue. Prepayment required. Personal checks accepted. No credit cards accepted.

Mail search: Turnaround time: 2 days. The fee for a title or registration verification is $5.00 ($3.50, if your own record). The fee for a title application copy of a vehicle title history is $10.00. A self addressed stamped envelope is requested.

In person search: Inquires are processed while you wait; however, requests must be in writing. Same fees as by mail.

Online search: Online batch inquires are $3.00 per record; online interactive requests are $4.00 per record. See the Driving Records Section for a complete description of the Information Network of Kansas (800-452-6727), the state authorized vendor. There is an initial $75 subscription fee and an annual $60 fee to access records from INK.

Other access: The state has several programs available to sell data in bulk format. Contact Cathy Reardon at the Dept of Revenue's Bureau of Research & Analysis.

Vessel Ownership
Vessel Registration

Kansas Wildlife & Parks Department, Boat Registration, 512 SE 25th Ave, Pratt, KS 67124-8174; 316-672-5911, 316-672-3013 (Fax), 8AM-5PM M-F.

http://www.kdwp.state.ks.us

Note: Liens must be searched at the county level.

Indexing & Storage: Records are available from 1967 to present. Records are indexed on computer. Titles are not required. All motorized or sailboats must be registered.

Searching: All requests must be submitted in writing with specific reason given for the request. No information is released for solicitation purposes. To search, either the hull ID or name is required.

Access by: mail, fax, in person.

Fee & Payment: There is no search fee, unless extensive searching is requested.

Mail search: Turnaround time: 3 weeks. No self addressed stamped envelope is required.

Fax search: Same criteria as mail searching.

Legislation Records

Kansas State Library, Capitol Bldg, 300 SW 10th Ave, Topeka, KS 66612; 785-296-2149, 785-296-6650 (Fax), 8AM-5PM.

http://www.ink.org

Note: A second URL is http://skyways.lib.ks.us/ksl.

Indexing & Storage: Records are available from 1908 to present. Records are on computer since 1991.

Searching: Include either bill number or bill topic.

Access by: mail, phone, fax, in person, online.

Fee & Payment: First 20 pages are free for all searches. Copies are $.10 a page. Fee payee: Kansas State Library. Personal checks accepted. No credit cards accepted.

Mail search: Turnaround time: 1 to 2 days. No self addressed stamped envelope is required. No fee for mail request.

Phone search: No fee for telephone request.

Fax search: Fax searching available.

In person search: No fee for request.

Online search: The web site has bill information for the current session. The site also contains access to the state statutes.

Voter Registration
Access to Records is Restricted

Secretary of State, Department of Elections, 120 SW 10th Street, Topeka, KS 66612; 785-296-4564, 785-291-3051 (Fax), 8AM-5PM.

http://www.kssos.org

Note: Individual records must be searched at the county level. This agency will sell the database on disk, CD or tape format only for political purposes.

GED Certificates

Kansas Board of Regents, GED Records, 700 SW Harrison, Ste 1410, Topeka, KS 66603-3760; 785-296-3191, 785-296-0983 (Fax).

http://www.kansasregents.com

Searching: Include the following in your request- Social Security Number, signed release. Also include the date of the test.

Access by: mail, fax, in person.

Fee & Payment: There is no fee for a verification, the fee for a transcript is $5.00. Fee payee: Kansas Board of Regents. Prepayment required. Cash and money orders are accepted. No credit cards accepted.

Mail search: Turnaround time: 1 week. No self addressed stamped envelope is required.

Fax search: Same criteria as mail searching.

Fishing License Information
Records not maintained by a state level agency.

Hunting License Information

Dept of Wildlife & Parks, Operations Office, Fish & Wildlife, 512 SE 25th Ave, Pratt, KS 67124-8174; 316-672-5911, 316-672-3013 (Fax), 8AM-5PM.

http://www.kdwp.state.ks.us

Indexing & Storage: Records are available for 2 years. Boat statistics are available. Records are indexed on hard copy.

Searching: You can get big game information only. You must submit request in writing indicating what information you require and its intended use. Requests for information to be used for the sale of products or services will not be answered. Include the following in your request- full name, date of birth.

Access by: mail, in person.

Fee & Payment: You must have Department approval. The agency reserves the right to recover costs for voluminous requests.

Mail search: Turnaround time: 1 to 3 days. No self addressed stamped envelope is required.

In person search: You may request information in person.

Kansas State Licensing Agencies

Licenses Searchable Online

Athletic Trainer #10.................................. www.docboard.org/ks/df/kssearch.htm
Chiropractor #10....................................... www.docboard.org/ks/df/kssearch.htm
Insurance Company #22........................... www.ksinsurance.org/company/main.html
Medical Doctor #10.................................. www.docboard.org/ks/df/kssearch.htm
Mortician #11... www.ink.org/public/ksbma/listings.html
Occupational Therapist/Assistant #10 .... www.docboard.org/ks/df/kssearch.htm
Optometrist #26....................................... www.odfinder.org/LicSearch.asp
Osteopathic Physician #10....................... www.docboard.org/ks/df/kssearch.htm
Physical Therapist/Assistant #10 .... www.docboard.org/ks/df/kssearch.htm
Physician Assistant #10........................... www.docboard.org/ks/df/kssearch.htm
Podiatrist #10 .... www.docboard.org/ks/df/kssearch.htm
Public Accountant-CPA #04..................... www.ink.org/public/ksboa
Real Estate Appraiser #28 .... www.ink.org/public/kreab/appraisdir.html
Respiratory Therapist #10........................ www.docboard.org/ks/df/kssearch.htm

Licensing Quick Finder

Abstractor #01 316-544-2311	Funeral Director/Assistant #11 785-296-3980	Physician Assistant #10........................785-296-7413
Adult Care Home Administrator #16......785-296-0061	Funeral Establishment #11 785-296-3980	Podiatrist #10.......................................785-296-7413
Alcohol Vendor License #20 785-296-7015	Geologist #14..785-296-3054	Private Investigator #23........................785-296-4436
Alcohol/Drug Counselor #03................785-296-3240	Hearing Aid Dispenser #09..................620-263-0774	Psychologist #03..................................785-296-3240
Ambulance Attendant #08 785-296-7299	Home Health Aide #16 785-296-1250	Public Accountant-CPA #04..................785-296-2162
Ambulance Service #08........................785-296-7299	Insurance Agent #22.............................785-296-7859	Racing & Wagering Equip./Svcs #25....785-296-5800
Animal Keeper #02...............................785-296-2326	Insurance Company #22 785-296-7859	Racing Concessionaire #25 785-296-5800
Architect #14..785-296-3053	Investment Advisor #29 785-296-3307	Racing Facility Owner/Manager #25 785-296-5800
Athletic Trainer #10 785-296-7413	Landscape Architect #14 785-296-3053	Racing Occupation License #25 785-296-5800
Attorney #18 785-296-8409	Livestock Brand #02..............................785-296-2326	Racing Organization #25.......................785-296-5800
Audiologist #16 785-296-0061	Lobbyist #27 785-296-3488	Real Estate Agent/Salesperson #31......785-296-3411
Barber #05..785-296-2211	Marriage & Family Therapist #03 785-296-3240	Real Estate Appraiser #28 785-271-3373
Body Piercer #06 785-296-3155	Medical Doctor #10................................785-296-7413	Real Estate Broker #31 785-296-3411
Child Care Attendant #30 785-296-1240	Medication Aide #16...............................785-296-1250	Respiratory Therapist #10 785-296-7413
Chiropractor #10 785-296-7413	Mortician #11 785-296-3980	School Administrator #07.......................785-296-2288
Contractor, General #21 785-296-4460	Nail Technician #06................................785-296-3155	School Counselor #07 785-296-2288
Cosmetic Facilities #06.........................785-296-3155	Notary Public #27...................................785-296-2239	School Library Media Specialist #07 785-296-2288
Cosmetologist #06 785-296-3155	Nurse #12..785-296-4929	School Nurse #07..................................785-296-2288
Cosmetology School Instructor #06.......785-296-3155	Nurses' Aide #16....................................785-296-1250	Securities Agent #29 785-296-3307
Counselor, Professional #03.................785-296-3240	Nursing Home Administrator #16............785-296-0061	Securities Broker/Dealer #29 785-296-3307
Dental Hygienist #19 785-273-0780	Occupational Therapist/Assistant #10 ...785-296-7413	Shorthand Reporter #17 785-296-8410
Dentist/Dental Hygienist #19................785-273-0780	Optometrist #26 785-832-9986	Social Worker #03.................................785-296-3240
Dietitian #16...785-296-0061	Osteopathic Physician #10 785-296-7413	Speech/Language Pathologist #16 785-296-0061
Electrologist #06 785-296-3155	Permanent Cosmetic Technician #06....785-296-3155	Surveyor #14 785-296-3053
Embalmer #11 785-296-3980	Pesticide Applicator #24 785-296-2263	Tanning Facility #06 785-296-3155
Emergency Medical Technician #08......785-296-7299	Pesticide Dealer #24 785-296-2263	Tattoo Artist #06....................................785-296-3155
Engineer #14 785-296-3053	Pharmacist #13......................................785-296-8420	Teacher #07...785-296-2288
Esthetics #06 785-296-3155	Physical Therapist/Assistant #10 785-296-7413	Veterinarian #15....................................785-355-8781

Licensing Agency Information

#01 Abstracters Board of Examiners, 525 W Jefferson St, Box 549, 4th Fl, Hugoton, KS 67951-0549; 316-544-2311, Fax: 316-544-8029.

#02 Animal Health Department, 708 S Jackson, Topeka, KS 66603-3714; 785-296-2326, Fax: 785-296-1765.

#03 Behavioral Sciences Regulatory Board, 712 S Kansas, Topeka, KS 66603; 785-296-3240, Fax: 785-296-3112.

#04 Board of Accountancy, 900 SW Jackson, Topeka, KS 66612-1239; 785-296-2162.
www.ink.org/public/ksboa

#05 Board of Barbering, 700 SW Jackson #1002, Topeka, KS 66603; 785-296-2211, Fax: 785-368-7071.

#06 Board of Cosmetology, 714 SW Jackson St #100, Topeka, KS 66603-3722; 785-296-3155, Fax: 785-296-3002.
www.ink.org/public/KBOC

#07 Board of Education, 120 SE 10th Ave, Topeka, KS 66612-1182; 785-296-2288, Fax: 785-296-7933.
www.ksbe.state.ks.us/welcome.html

#08 Board of Emergency Medical Services, 109 SW 6th, Topeka, KS 66603-3826; 785-296-7299, Fax: 785-296-6212.
www.ksbems.org

#09 Board of Examiners for Hearing Aid Dispensers, 600 N St Francis, Wichita, KS 67201-0252; 620-263-0774, Fax: 620-264-2681.

#10 Board of Healing Arts, 235 S Topeka Blvd, Topeka, KS 66603-3059; 785-296-7413, Fax: 785-296-0852.
www.ksbha.org

#11 Board of Mortuary Arts, 700 SW Jackson, #904, Topeka, KS 66603-3733; 785-296-3980, Fax: 785-296-0891.
www.ink.org/public/ksbma
Direct web site URL to search for licensees: www.ink.org/public/ksbma/listings.html

#12 Board of Nursing, 900 SW Jackson, Rm 551 S, Topeka, KS 66612-1230; 785-296-2967, Fax: 785-296-3929.

www.ksbn.org There is a searchable database of licenses available online, but you must be a registered user of INK (Information Network of Kansas).

#13 Board of Pharmacy, 900 Jackson, Landon State Office Bldg, Rm 513, Topeka, KS 66612; 785-296-4056, Fax: 785-296-8420.

#14 Board of Technical Professions, 900 SW Jackson, Rm 507, Topeka, KS 66612-1257; 785-296-3053.
www.state.ks.us/public/ksbtp/roster.html

#15 Board of Veterinary Examiners, PO Box 242 (1003 Lincoln), Wamego, KS 66547-0242; 785-456-8781, Fax: 785-456-8782.
www.ink.org/public/veterinary

#16 Department of Health & Environment, 900 SW Jackson #1051-S, Topeka, KS 66612-1290; 785-296-0056, Fax: 785-296-3075.
www.kdhe.state.ks.us/hoc/index.html

#17 Clerk of Appellate Court, 301 W 10th St, Topeka, KS 66612; 785-296-8410, Fax: 785-296-1028.
www.kscourts.org

#18 Clerk of the Supreme Court, 301 SW 10th Ave, Topeka, KS 66612; 785-296-8409, Fax: 785-296-1028.
www.kscourts.org

#19 Dental Board, 3601 SW 29th St #134, Topeka, KS 66614-2062; 785-273-0780, Fax: 785-273-7545.

#20 Department of Revenue, 200 SE 6th St, 4 Townsite Plaza, #210, Topeka, KS 66603-3512; 785-296-7015, Fax: 785-296-1279.
www.ink.org/public/kdor/abc/

#21 Department of Revenue, 915 SW Harrison St, Topeka, KS 66625-0001; 785-296-3160.
www.ink.org/public/kdor/main.html

#22 Insurance Department, 420 SW 9th, Topeka, KS 66612-1678; 785-296-7859, Fax: 785-368-7019.
www.ksinsurance.org
Direct web site URL to search for licensees: www.ksinsurance.org/company/main.html. You can search online using company name, type,

class, or state Searching is fee but there are fees to download from their database.

#23 Bureau of Investigation, 1620 SW Tyler, Topeka, KS 66612-1837; 785-296-8200, Fax: 785-296-6781.
www.ink.org/public/kbi

#24 Department of Agriculture, 109 SW 9th St, Topeka, KS 66612; 785-296-2263, Fax: 785-296-0673.
www.ink.org/ii/?type=byserv&which=agencies

#25 Racing Commission, 3400 SW Van Buren, Topeka, KS 66611-2228; 785-296-5800, Fax: 785-296-0900.
www.ink.org/public/krc

#26 Board of Examiners in Optometry, 3111 W 6th #A, Lawrence, KS 66049; 785-832-9986, Fax: 785-832-9986.
www.terraworld.net/kssbeo/
Direct web site URL to search for licensees: www.odfinder.org/LicSearch.asp. You can search online using national database by name, city, or state

#27 Office of Secretary of State, 120 SW 10th Ave, Topeka, KS 66612; 785-296-1848, Fax: 785-296-4570.
www.kssos.org

#28 Real Estate Commission, 1100 SW Wanamaker Rd #104, Topeka, KS 66604-3805; 785-271-3373, Fax: 785-271-3370.
www.ink.org/public/kreab/
Direct web site URL to search for licensees: www.ink.org/public/kreab/appraisdir.html. You can search online using name, city, or license number

#29 Securities Commissioner of Kansas, 618 S Kansas 2nd Fl, Topeka, KS 66603-3804; 785-296-3307, Fax: 785-296-6872.
www.ink.org/public/ksecom/

#30 Child Care Licensing & Registration, 900 SW Jackson #260, Topeka, KS 66612; 785-296-1240.

#31 Real Estate Commission, 120 SE 6th, Topeka, KS 66603; 785-296-3411, Fax: 785-296-1771.
www.ink.org/public/krec/

Kansas Federal Courts

The following list indicates the district and division name for each county in the state. If the bankruptcy court location is different from the district court, then the location of the bankruptcy court appears in parentheses.

County/Court Cross Reference

County	Court	County	Court
Allen	Topeka	Linn	Kansas City
Anderson	Topeka	Logan	Wichita
Atchison	Kansas City	Lyon	Topeka
Barber	Wichita	Marion	Topeka
Barton	Wichita	Marshall	Kansas City
Bourbon	Kansas City	McPherson	Wichita
Brown	Kansas City	Meade	Wichita
Butler	Wichita	Miami	Kansas City
Chase	Topeka	Mitchell	Topeka
Chautauqua	Wichita	Montgomery	Wichita
Cherokee	Kansas City	Morris	Topeka
Cheyenne	Wichita	Morton	Wichita
Clark	Wichita	Nemaha	Kansas City
Clay	Topeka	Neosho	Topeka
Cloud	Topeka	Ness	Wichita
Coffey	Topeka	Norton	Wichita
Comanche	Kansas City (Wichita)	Osage	Topeka
Cowley	Wichita	Osborne	Wichita
Crawford	Kansas City	Ottawa	Topeka
Decatur	Wichita	Pawnee	Wichita
Dickinson	Topeka	Phillips	Wichita
Doniphan	Kansas City	Pottawatomie	Topeka
Douglas	Topeka	Pratt	Wichita
Edwards	Wichita	Rawlins	Wichita
Elk	Wichita	Reno	Wichita
Ellis	Wichita	Republic	Topeka
Ellsworth	Wichita	Rice	Wichita
Finney	Wichita	Riley	Topeka
Ford	Wichita	Rooks	Wichita
Franklin	Topeka	Rush	Wichita
Geary	Topeka	Russell	Wichita
Gove	Wichita	Saline	Topeka
Graham	Wichita	Scott	Wichita
Grant	Wichita	Sedgwick	Wichita
Gray	Wichita	Seward	Wichita
Greeley	Wichita	Shawnee	Topeka
Greenwood	Wichita	Sheridan	Wichita
Hamilton	Wichita	Sherman	Wichita
Harper	Wichita	Smith	Wichita
Harvey	Wichita	Stafford	Wichita
Haskell	Wichita	Stanton	Wichita
Hodgeman	Wichita	Stevens	Wichita
Jackson	Topeka	Sumner	Wichita
Jefferson	Wichita	Thomas	Wichita
Jewell	Topeka	Trego	Wichita
Johnson	Kansas City	Wabaunsee	Topeka
Kearny	Wichita	Wallace	Wichita
Kingman	Wichita	Washington	Topeka
Kiowa	Wichita	Wichita	Wichita
Labette	Kansas City	Wilson	Topeka
Lane	Wichita	Woodson	Topeka
Leavenworth	Kansas City	Wyandotte	Kansas City
Lincoln	Topeka		

US District Court

District of Kansas

Kansas City Division Clerk, 500 State Ave, Kansas City, KS 66101 (Courier Address: Use mail address for courier delivery), 913-551-6719.

http://www.ksd.uscourts.gov

Counties: Atchison, Bourbon, Brown, Cherokee, Crawford, Doniphan, Johnson, Labette, Leavenworth, Linn, Marshall, Miami, Nemaha, Wyandotte.

Indexing/Storage: Cases are indexed by defendant and plaintiff as well as by case number. New cases are available in the index immediately after filing date. Both computer and card indexes are maintained. Records are also indexed on microfiche. Open records are located at this court.

Fee & Payment: The fee is no charge per item (one party name or case number). Payment may be made by money order, cashier check, personal check. No search fee is charged unless certification is required. All certification searches are conducted by the Wichita office. Payee: Clerk, US District Court. Certification fee: $7.00 per document. Copy fee: $.50 per page.

Phone Search: Searching is not available by phone. Only docket information will be released over the phone if you have a case number.

Mail Search: A stamped self addressed envelope is not required.

In Person: In person searching is available.

PACER: Sign-up number is 800-676-6856. Access fee is $.60 per minute. Toll-free access: 800-898-3078. Local access: 316-269-6284. Case records are available back to 1991. Records are never purged. New civil records are available online after 2 days. New criminal records are available online after 3 days. PACER is available online at http://pacer.ksd.uscourts.gov.

Topeka Division Clerk, US District Court, Room 490, 444 SE Quincy, Topeka, KS 66683 (Courier Address: Use mail address for courier delivery), 785-295-2610.

http://www.ksd.uscourts.gov

Counties: Allen, Anderson, Chase, Clay, Cloud, Coffey, Dickinson, Douglas, Franklin, Geary, Jackson, Jewell, Lincoln, Lyon, Marion, Mitchell, Morris, Neosho, Osage, Ottawa, Pottawatomie, Republic, Riley, Saline, Shawnee, Wabaunsee, Washington, Wilson, Woodson.

Indexing/Storage: Cases are indexed by defendant and plaintiff as well as by case number. New cases are available in the index 24 hours after filing date. A full name, the case number and a date are very helpful to obtain records. Both computer and card indexes are maintained. Open records are located at this court.

Fee & Payment: The fee is $20.00 per item (one party name or case number). Payment may be made by money order, cashier check, personal check. Prepayment is required. Payee: Clerk of US District Court. Certification fee: $7.00 per document. Copy fee: $.50 per page.

Phone Search: Docket information available by phone.

Mail Search: Always enclose a stamped self addressed envelope.

In Person: In person searching is available.

PACER: Sign-up number is 800-676-6856. Access fee is $.60 per minute. Toll-free access: 800-898-3078. Local access: 316-269-6284. Case records are available back to 1991. Records are never purged. New civil records are available online after 2 days. New criminal records are available online after 3 days. PACER is available online at http://pacer.ksd.uscourts.gov.

Wichita Division 204 US Courthouse, 401 N Market, Wichita, KS 67202-2096 (Courier Address: Use mail address for courier delivery), 316-269-6491.

http://www.ksd.uscourts.gov

Counties: All counties in Kansas. Cases may be heard from counties in the other division.

Indexing/Storage: Cases are indexed by defendant and plaintiff as well as by case number. New cases are available in the index immediately after filing date. Both computer and card indexes are maintained. Records are indexed on the computer since 1990. Prior records are indexed on microfiche or index cards. Open records are located at this court. District wide searches are available from this court.

Fee & Payment: The fee is $20.00 per item (one party name or case number). Payment may be made by money order, cashier check, personal check. Prepayment is required. Payee: Clerk, US District Court. Certification fee: $7.00 per document. Copy fee: $.50 per page.

Phone Search: Will do computer search on one name over the phone.

Mail Search: Always enclose a stamped self addressed envelope.

In Person: In person searching is available.

PACER: Sign-up number is 800-676-6856. Access fee is $.60 per minute. Toll-free access: 800-898-3078. Local access: 316-269-6284. Case records are available back to 1991. Records are never purged. New civil records are available online after 2 days. New criminal records are available online after 3 days. PACER is available online at http://pacer.ksd.uscourts.gov.

US Bankruptcy Court

District of Kansas

Kansas City Division 500 State Ave, Room 161, Kansas City, KS 66101 (Courier Address: Use mail address for courier delivery), 913-551-6732, Fax: 913-551-6715.

http://www.ksb.uscourts.gov

Counties: Atchison, Bourbon, Brown, Cherokee, Comanche, Crawford, Doniphan, Johnson, Labette, Leavenworth, Linn, Marshall, Miami, Nemaha, Wyandotte.

Indexing/Storage: Cases are indexed by debtor as well as by case number. New cases are available in the index 1 day after filing date. Approximate year of filing will also help in the search for files. A computer index is maintained. Bankruptcy searches can be performed from any bankruptcy court in the district for case files from 1989 forward; master listing for pre-1989 cases are available from the Topeka Office. Open records are located at this court.

Fee & Payment: The fee is $20.00 per item (one party name or case number). Payment may be made by money order, cashier check, personal check. Prepayment is required. Debtor's checks are

not accepted. Payee: Clerk of US Bankruptcy Court. Certification fee: $7.00 per document. Copy fee: $.50 per page. You are allowed to make your own copies. These copies cost $.25 per page.

Phone Search: Only docket information is available by phone. An automated voice case information service (VCIS) is available. Call VCIS at 800-827-9028 or 316-269-6668.

Mail Search: Always enclose a stamped self addressed envelope.

In Person: In person searching is available.

PACER: Sign-up number is 800-676-6856. Access fee is $.60 per minute. Toll-free access: 800-613-7052. Local access: 316-269-6258. Case records are available back to 1988. Records are purged every 6 months. New civil records are available online after 1 day. PACER is available online at http://pacer.ksb.uscourts.gov.

Topeka Division 240 US Courthouse, 444 SE Quincy, Topeka, KS 66683 (Courier Address: Use mail address for courier delivery), 785-295-2750, Fax: 785-295-2964.

http://www.ksb.uscourts.gov

Counties: Allen, Anderson, Chase, Clay, Cloud, Coffey, Dickinson, Douglas, Franklin, Geary, Jackson, Jewell, Lincoln, Lyon, Marion, Mitchell, Morris, Neosho, Osage, Ottawa, Pottawatomie, Republic, Riley, Saline, Shawnee, Wabaunsee, Washington, Wilson, Woodson.

Indexing/Storage: Cases are indexed by debtor as well as by case number. New cases are available in the index 1 day after filing date. A computer index is maintained. Approximate year of filing will also help in the search for files. Open records are located at this court.

Fee & Payment: The fee is $20.00 per item (one party name or case number). Payment may be made by money order, cashier check, personal check. Prepayment is required. Debtor's checks are not accepted. Payee: Clerk, US Bankruptcy Court. Certification fee: $7.00 per document. Copy fee: $.50 per page. You are allowed to make your own copies. These copies cost $.25 per page.

Phone Search: Only docket information is available by phone. An automated voice case information service (VCIS) is available. Call VCIS at 800-827-9028 or 316-269-6668.

Mail Search: A stamped self addressed envelope is not required.

In Person: In person searching is available.

PACER: Sign-up number is 800-676-6856. Access fee is $.60 per minute. Toll-free access: 800-613-7052. Local access: 316-269-6258. Case records are available back to 1988. Records are purged every 6 months. New civil records are available online after 1 day. PACER is available online at http://pacer.ksb.uscourts.gov.

Wichita Division 167 US Courthouse, 401 N Market, Wichita, KS 67202 (Courier Address: Use mail address for courier delivery), 316-269-6486, Fax: 316-269-6181.

http://www.ksb.uscourts.gov

Counties: Barber, Barton, Butler, Chautauqua, Cheyenne, Clark, Comanche, Cowley, Decatur, Edwards, Elk, Ellis, Ellsworth, Finney, Ford, Gove, Graham, Grant, Gray, Greeley, Greenwood, Hamilton, Harper, Harvey, Haskell, Hodgeman, Jefferson, Kearny, Kingman, Kiowa,Lane, Logan, Mcpherson, Meade, Montgomery, Morton, Ness, Norton, Osborne, Pawnee, Phillips, Pratt, Rawlins, Reno, Rice, Rooks, Rush, Russell, Scott,

Sedgwick, Seward, Sheridan, Smith, Stafford, Stanton, Stevens, Sumner, Thomas, Trego, Wallace, Wichita.

Indexing/Storage: Cases are indexed by debtor as well as by case number. New cases are available in the index 1 day after filing date. A computer index is maintained. Records are also indexed on microfiche. Open records are located at this court. District wide searches are available from this division.

Fee & Payment: The fee is $20.00 per item (one party name or case number). Payment may be made by money order, cashier check, personal check. Prepayment is required. Payee: Clerk, US Bankruptcy Court. Certification fee: $7.00 per document. Copy fee: $.50 per page. You are allowed to make your own copies. These copies cost $.25 per page.

Phone Search: Only the attorneys, trustees, hearing dates and file dates will be released over the phone. An automated voice case information service (VCIS) is available. Call VCIS at 800-827-9028 or 316-269-6668.

Mail Search: A stamped self addressed envelope is not required.

In Person: In person searching is available.

PACER: Sign-up number is 800-676-6856. Access fee is $.60 per minute. Toll-free access: 800-613-7052. Local access: 620-269-6258. Case records are available back to 1988. Records are purged every 6 months. New civil records are available online after 1 day. PACER is available online at http://pacer.ksb.uscourts.gov.

Kansas County Courts

Court	Jurisdiction	No. of Courts	How Organized
District Courts*	General	109	31 Districts
Municipal Courts	Municipal	350	

* Profiled in this Sourcebook.

	CIVIL								
Court	Tort	Contract	Real Estate	Min. Claim	Max. Claim	Small Claims	Estate	Eviction	Domestic Relations
District Courts*	X	X	X	$0	No Max	$1800	X	X	
Municipal Courts									

	CRIMINAL				
Court	Felony	Misdemeanor	DWI/DUI	Preliminary Hearing	Juvenile
District Courts*	X	X	X	X	X
Municipal Courts			X		

ADMINISTRATION

Judicial Administrator, Kansas Judicial Center, 301 SW 10th St, Topeka, KS, 66612; 785-296-2256, Fax: 785-296-7076. www.kscourts.org

COURT STRUCTURE

The District Court is the court of general jurisdiction. There are 110 courts in 31 districts in 105 counties.

If an individual in Municipal Court wants a jury trial, the request must be filed de novo in a District Court.

ONLINE ACCESS

Commercial online access is available for District Court Records in 4 counties - Johnson, Sedgwick, Shawnee, and Wyandotte - through Access Kansas, part of the Information Network of Kansas (INK) Services. Franklin and Finney counties may be available in early 2002. A user can access INK through their Internet site at www.accesskansas.org or via a dial-up system. The INK subscription fee is $75.00, and the annual renewal fee is $60.00. There is no per minute connect charge, but there is a transaction fee. Other information from INK includes Drivers License, Title, Registration, Lien, and UCC searches. For additional information or a registration packet, call 800-4-KANSAS (800-452-6727).

ADDITIONAL INFORMATION

Five counties - Cowley, Crawford, Labette, Montgomery and Neosho - have two hearing locations, but only one record center, which is the location included in this Sourcebook.

Many Kansas courts do not do criminal record searches and will refer any criminal requests to the Kansas Bureau of Investigation. The Kansas Legislature's Administrative Order 156 (Fall, 2000) allows Courts to charge up to $12.00 per hour for search services, though courts may set their own search fees, if any.

📖 📖 📖 📖 📖 📖

Allen County

District Court PO Box 630, Iola, KS 66749; 620-365-1425; Fax: 620-365-1429. Hours: 8AM-5PM (CST). *Felony, Misdemeanor, Civil, Eviction, Small Claims, Probate.*

Civil Records: Access: Fax, mail, in person, email. Both court and visitors may perform in person searches. Search fee: $12.00 per hour. Required to search: name, years to search. Civil cases indexed by defendant, plaintiff. Civil records on computer from 1993, manual index from 1800s.

Criminal Records: Access: Fax, mail, in person, email. Both court and visitors may perform in person searches. Search fee: $12.00 per hour. Required to search: name, years to search. Criminal records on computer from 1993, manual index from 1800s.

General Information: Public Access terminal is available. No juvenile (under the age of 15), mental health, sealed or expunged records released. Accepts requests via email, but cannot return results by email. SASE required. Turnaround time 1 week. Fax notes:

Fee to fax results is $1.00 per page; $3.00 for 1st page. Copy fee: $.50 per page. Certification fee: $1.00. Fee payee: Clerk of Court. Personal checks accepted. Prepayment is required.

Anderson County

District Court PO Box 305, Garnett, KS 66032; 785-448-6886; Fax: 785-448-3230. Hours: 8AM-5PM (CST). *Felony, Misdemeanor, Civil, Eviction, Small Claims, Probate.*

www.kscourts.org.dstcts/4dstct.htm

Civil Records: Access: Fax, mail, in person, online. Both court and visitors may perform in person searches. No search fee. Required to search: name, years to search. Civil cases indexed by defendant, plaintiff. Civil records on computer from 1977, index books from 1800s. Current court calendars are available free online at www.kscourts.org/dstcts/4andckt.htm.

Criminal Records: Access: In person only. Visitors must perform in person searches for themselves. No search fee. Required to search: name, years to search. Criminal records on computer from 1977, index books

from 1800s. Online access to criminal calendars is the same as civil. For criminal record searches, the court urges requesters to contact the KS Bureau of Investigations.

General Information: Public Access terminal is available. (Not on statewide system.) No juvenile, mental health, sealed or expunged records released. SASE required. Turnaround time same day. Fax notes: $2.00 for first page, $.50 each add'l. Copy fee: $.25 per page. Certification fee: $1.00. Fee payee: District Court. Personal checks accepted.

Atchison County

District Court PO Box 408, Atchison, KS 66002; 913-367-7400; Fax: 913-367-1171. Hours: 8AM-5PM (CST). *Felony, Misdemeanor, Civil, Eviction, Small Claims, Probate.*

Civil Records: Access: Fax, mail, in person. Both court and visitors may perform in person searches. No search fee. Required to search: name, years to search. Civil cases indexed by defendant, plaintiff. Civil records on computer from 1991, microfiche from 1860s, index books from 1900s, archives from 1860s.

Criminal Records: Access: In person only. Visitors must perform in person searches for themselves. No search fee. Required to search: name, years to search; also helpful: SSN. Criminal records on computer from 1991, microfiche from 1860s, index books from 1900s, archives from 1860s.

General Information: Public Access terminal is available. No juvenile, mental health, sealed or expunged records released. SASE required. Turnaround time 1-5 days. Fax notes: $1.25 per page. Copy fee: $.25 per page. Certification fee: $1.00. Fee payee: District Court. Personal checks accepted. Prepayment is required.

Barber County

District Court 118 E Washington, Medicine Lodge, KS 67104; 620-886-5639; Fax: 620-886-5854. Hours: 8AM-Noon,1-5PM (CST). *Felony, Misdemeanor, Civil, Eviction, Small Claims, Probate.*

Civil Records: Access: In person only. Visitors must perform in person searches for themselves. No search fee. Required to search: name, years to search. Civil cases indexed by defendant, plaintiff. Civil records on computer from 1987, microfiche from 1900-1976, index cards from 1800s.

Criminal Records: Access: In person only. Visitors must perform in person searches for themselves. No search fee. Required to search: name, years to search, SSN; also helpful: DOB. Criminal records on computer from 1987, microfiche from 1900-1976, index cards from 1800s.

General Information: Public Access terminal is available. No juvenile, mental health, sealed or expunged records released. Copy fee: $.25 per page. Certification fee: $1.00. Fee payee: District Court. Personal checks accepted.

Barton County

District Court 1400 Main, Rm 306, Great Bend, KS 67530; 620-793-1856; Fax: 620-793-1860. Hours: 8AM-5PM (CST). *Felony, Misdemeanor, Civil, Eviction, Small Claims, Probate.*

Civil Records: Access: Fax, mail, in person. Both court and visitors may perform in person searches. Search fee: $12.00 per hour. Required to search: name, years to search. Civil cases indexed by defendant, plaintiff. Civil records on computer 1990, microfiche and archives from 1800s, index from 1987.

Criminal Records: Access: Fax, mail, in person. Both court and visitors may perform in person searches. Search fee: $12.00 per hour. Required to search: name, years to search. Criminal records on computer 1990, microfiche and archives from 1800s, index from 1987.

General Information: Public Access terminal is available. No juvenile, mental health, sealed or expunged records released. Turnaround time 3 days. Fax notes: No fee to fax results. Copy fee: $.35 per page; $.50 for microfilm copies. Certification fee: No cert fee. Fee payee: Clerk of Court. Personal checks accepted. Prepayment is required.

Bourbon County

District Court PO Box 868, Ft Scott, KS 66701; 620-223-0780; Fax: 620-223-5303. Hours: 8:30AM-4:30PM (CST). *Felony, Misdemeanor, Civil, Eviction, Small Claims, Probate.*

Civil Records: Access: Fax, mail, in person. Both court and visitors may perform in person searches. Search fee: $12.00 per hour. Required to search: name, years to search. Civil cases indexed by defendant, plaintiff. Civil records on computer since 1990, index on computer since 1985.

Criminal Records: Access: Fax, mail, in person. Both court and visitors may perform in person searches.

Search fee: $12.00 per hour. Required to search: name, years to search; also helpful: SSN. Criminal records on computer since 1990, index on computer since 1985.

General Information: Public Access terminal is available. No juvenile, mental health, sealed or expunged records released. SASE required. Turnaround time 3 days. Fax notes: $1.00 per page. Copy fee: $.25 per page. Certification fee: $1.00. Fee payee: Clerk of Court. Personal checks accepted. Prepayment is required.

Brown County

District Court PO Box 417, Hiawatha, KS 66434; 785-742-7481; Fax: 785-742-3506. Hours: 8AM-5PM (CST). *Felony, Misdemeanor, Civil, Eviction, Small Claims, Probate.*

Civil Records: Access: Phone, fax, mail, in person. Both court and visitors may perform in person searches. Search fee: $12.00 per hour. Required to search: name, years to search. Civil cases indexed by defendant, plaintiff. Civil records on computer from 1982, microfiche from 1900s, index books from 1900s.

Criminal Records: Access: Phone, fax, mail, in person. Both court and visitors may perform in person searches. Search fee: $12.00 per hour. Required to search: name, years to search; also helpful: SSN. Criminal records on computer from 1982, microfiche and index books from 1900s.

General Information: Public Access terminal is available. No juvenile, mental health, sealed or expunged records released. SASE required. Turnaround time 1-2 days. Fax notes: Fee to fax results is $1.00 per page. Copy fee: $.50 for first page, $.25 each add'l. Certification fee: $1.00. Fee payee: District Court. Personal checks accepted. Prepayment is required.

Butler County

District Court PO Box 432, El Dorado, KS 67042; 316-322-4370; Fax: 316-321-9486. Hours: 8:30AM-5PM (CST). *Felony, Misdemeanor, Civil, Eviction, Small Claims, Probate.*

Civil Records: Access: In person only. Visitors must perform in person searches for themselves. No search fee. Required to search: name, years to search. Civil cases indexed by defendant, plaintiff. Civil records on computer from 1992, index cards from 1800s.

Criminal Records: Access: In person only. Visitors must perform in person searches for themselves. No search fee. Required to search: name, years to search, SSN. Criminal records on computer from 1992, index cards from 1800s.

General Information: Public Access terminal is available. No juvenile, mental health, sealed or expunged records released. Copy fee: $.25 per page. Certification fee: $1.00. Fee payee: Clerk of District Court. Personal checks accepted. Fax fees billed.

Chase County

District Court PO Box 207, Cottonwood Falls, KS 66845; 620-273-6319; Fax: 620-273-6890. Hours: 8AM-5PM (CST). *Felony, Misdemeanor, Civil, Eviction, Small Claims, Probate.*

Civil Records: Access: In person only. Visitors must perform in person searches for themselves. No search fee. Required to search: name, years to search. Civil cases indexed by defendant, plaintiff. Civil records on computer from late 1990, microfiche from 1860, index books from 1860.

Criminal Records: Access: In person only. Visitors must perform in person searches for themselves. No search fee. Required to search: name, years to search. Criminal records on computer from late 1990, microfiche from 1860, index books from 1860.

General Information: No juvenile, mental health, sealed or expunged records released. Copy fee: $.25 per

---

page. Certification fee: $2.00. Fee payee: District Court. Personal checks accepted. Prepayment is required.

Chautauqua County

District Court 215 N Chautauqua, PO Box 306, Sedan, KS 67361; 620-725-5870; Fax: 620-725-3027. Hours: 8AM-5PM (CST). *Felony, Misdemeanor, Civil, Eviction, Small Claims, Probate.*

Civil Records: Access: Mail, in person. Both court and visitors may perform in person searches. Search fee: $12.00 per hour. Required to search: name, years to search. Civil cases indexed by defendant, plaintiff. Civil records on computer from 1994, archives from 1950, index cards from 1870.

Criminal Records: Access: Mail, in person. Both court and visitors may perform in person searches. Search fee: $12.00 per hour. Required to search: name, years to search; also helpful: DOB. Criminal records on computer from 1994, archives from 1950, index cards from 1870.

General Information: Public Access terminal is available. No juvenile, mental health, sealed or expunged records released. SASE required. Turnaround time 1-2 weeks. Copy fee: $.25 per page. Certification fee: $1.00. Fee payee: District Court. Personal checks accepted.

Cherokee County

District Court PO Box 189, Columbus, KS 66725; 620-429-3880; Fax: 620-429-1130. Hours: 8AM-5PM (CST). *Felony, Misdemeanor, Civil, Eviction, Small Claims, Probate.*

Civil Records: Access: In person only. Visitors must perform in person searches for themselves. No search fee. Required to search: name, years to search. Civil cases indexed by defendant, plaintiff. Civil records on computer from 1990, index books from 1867.

Criminal Records: Access: In person only. Visitors must perform in person searches for themselves. No search fee. Required to search: name, years to search; also helpful: SSN. Criminal records on computer from 1990, index books from 1867.

General Information: Public Access terminal is available. No juvenile, mental health, sealed or expunged records released. Certification fee: $1.00. Fee payee: District Court. Personal checks accepted. Prepayment is required.

Cheyenne County

District Court PO Box 646, St Francis, KS 67756; 785-332-8850; Fax: 785-332-8851. Hours: 8AM-Noon,1-5PM (CST). *Felony, Misdemeanor, Civil, Eviction, Small Claims, Probate.*

Civil Records: Access: Fax, mail, in person. Both court and visitors may perform in person searches. No search fee. Required to search: name, years to search. Civil cases indexed by defendant, plaintiff. Civil records on strip index from 1989, index cards from 1870.

Criminal Records: Access: Fax, mail, in person. Both court and visitors may perform in person searches. No search fee. Required to search: name, years to search. Criminal records on strip index from 1989, index cards from 1870.

General Information: No juvenile, adoptions, mental health, sealed or expunged records released. SASE not required. Turnaround time 2 days. Fax notes: $1.00 per page unless toll free line used. Copy fee: $.25 per page. Certification fee: $1.00. Fee payee: Clerk of Court. Personal checks accepted. Prepayment is required.

Clark County

District Court PO Box 790, Ashland, KS 67831; 620-635-2753; Fax: 620-635-2155. Hours: 8AM-5PM (CST). *Felony, Misdemeanor, Civil, Eviction, Small Claims, Probate.*

www.kscourts.org/dstcts/16dstct.htm

Civil Records: Access: Mail, fax, in person. Both court and visitors may perform in person searches. Search fee: $12.00 per hour. Required to search: name, years to search. Civil cases indexed by defendant, plaintiff. Civil records on computer from 1992 (Child support only), microfiche and archives from 1800s, index cards from 1800s.

Criminal Records: Access: Mail, fax, in person. Both court and visitors may perform in person searches. Search fee: $9.00 per hour (may be no fee if short and a name search). Required to search: name, years to search; also helpful: SSN. Criminal records on index cards.

General Information: No juvenile, mental health, sealed or expunged records released. SASE required. Turnaround time 1 day. Copy fee: $.25 per page. Certification fee: $1.25. Fee payee: District Court. Personal checks accepted. Prepayment is required.

Clay County

District Court PO Box 203, Clay Center, KS 67432; 785-632-3443; Fax: 785-632-2651. Hours: 8AM-5PM (CST). *Felony, Misdemeanor, Civil, Eviction, Small Claims, Probate.*

www.co.riley.ks.us/DistrictCourts/default.htm

Civil Records: Access: Mail, in person. Visitors must perform in person searches for themselves. No search fee. Required to search: name, years to search. Civil cases indexed by defendant, plaintiff. Civil records on computer from July, 1994, index books from late 1800s.

Criminal Records: Access: In person only. Visitors must perform in person searches for themselves. No search fee. Required to search: name. Criminal records on computer from July, 1994, index books from late 1800s.

General Information: Public Access terminal is available. No juvenile, adoption, mental health, sealed or expunged records released. SASE required. Turnaround time 2 days. Copy fee: $.25 per page. Certification fee: $1.00. Fee payee: Clerk of District Court. Personal checks accepted. Prepayment required.

Cloud County

District Court 811 Washington, Concordia, KS 66901; 785-243-8124; Fax: 785-243-8188. Hours: 8:00AM-5PM (CST). *Felony, Misdemeanor, Civil, Eviction, Small Claims, Probate.*

www.kscourts.org/dstcts/12dstct.htm

Civil Records: Access: Phone, fax, mail, in person. Visitors must perform in person searches for themselves. Search fee: $12.00 per hour. Required to search: name, years to search. Civil cases indexed by defendant, plaintiff. Civil records in strip indexes from 1992, index books prior to 1992, index cards to 1800s.

Criminal Records: Access: Fax, mail, in person. Both court and visitors may perform in person searches. Search fee: $12.00 per hour. Required to search: name, years to search; also helpful: SSN. Criminal records in strip indexes from 1992, index books prior to 1992, index cards from 1800s.

General Information: Public Access terminal is available. No juvenile, mental health, sealed or expunged records released. SASE required. Turnaround time 3-4 days. Fax notes: $3.00 per page. Copy fee: $.25 per page. Certification fee: $1.00. Fee payee: Clerk of Court. Personal checks accepted. Prepayment is required.

Coffey County

District Court PO Box 330, Burlington, KS 66839; 620-364-8628; Fax: 620-364-8535. Hours: 8AM-5PM (CST). *Felony, Misdemeanor, Civil, Eviction, Small Claims, Probate.*

www.kscourts.org/dstcts/4dstct.htm

Civil Records: Access: Mail, fax, in person, email, online. Both court and visitors may perform in person searches. Search fee: $12.00 per hour. Required to search: name, years to search. Civil cases indexed by defendant, plaintiff. Civil records on computer back to 1800s, index cards from 1800s. Current court calendars are available free online at www.kscourts.org/dstcts/4codckt.htm. Probate and marriage records are accessible at the web site.

Criminal Records: Access: Mail, fax, in person, email, online. Both court and visitors may perform in person searches. Search fee: $12.00 per hour. Required to search: name, years to search, DOB. Criminal records on computer back to 1800s, index cards from 1800s. Online access to criminal records is the same as civil.

General Information: Public Access terminal is available. No juvenile, mental health, sealed or expunged records released. SASE required. Turnaround time 1 day. Fax notes: Fee to fax results is $2.00 1st page; $.50 each add'l. Copy fee: $.25 per page. Certification fee: $1.00. Fee payee: Clerk of District Court. Personal checks accepted. Prepayment is required.

Comanche County

District Court PO Box 722, Coldwater, KS 67029; 620-582-2182; Fax: 620-582-2603. Hours: 8AM-5PM (CST). *Felony, Misdemeanor, Civil, Eviction, Small Claims, Probate.*

www.kscourts.org/dstcts/16dstct.htm

Civil Records: Access: In person only. Both court and visitors may perform in person searches. No search fee. Required to search: name, years to search. Civil cases indexed by defendant, plaintiff. Civil records on computer since 1992 (child support only), index cards from 1886.

Criminal Records: Access: In person only. Both court and visitors may perform in person searches. No search fee. Required to search: name, years to search; also helpful: SSN. Criminal records on index cards to 1886.

General Information: No juvenile, mental health, sealed or expunged records released. Copy fee: $.25 per page. Certification fee: $1.00. Fee payee: District Court. Personal checks accepted. Prepayment is required.

Cowley County

Arkansas City District Court PO Box 1152, Arkansas City, KS 67005; 620-441-4520; Fax: 620-442-7213. Hours: 8AM-Noon,1-4PM (CST). *Felony, Misdemeanor, Civil, Eviction, Small Claims, Probate.*

Note: This court covers the southern part of the county. All felony records are kept at Winfield.

Civil Records: Access: Mail, in person. Both court and visitors may perform in person searches. Search fee: $12.00 per name. Required to search: name, years to search. Civil cases indexed by defendant, plaintiff. Civil records from 1977. This Court facility has only been in existence since 1977, so no records prior to that date, index cards only. Computer records commencing 1994.

Criminal Records: Access: Mail, in person. Both court and visitors may perform in person searches. Search fee: $12.00 per name. Required to search: name, years to search, SSN. Criminal records from 1977. This Court facility has only been in existence since 1977, so no records prior to that date, index cards only. Computer records commencing 1994.

General Information: Public Access terminal is available. No juvenile, mental health, sealed or

expunged records released. SASE not required. Turnaround time 1 week. Copy fee: $.50 per page. Certification fee: $1.00. Fee payee: Clerk of Court. Personal checks accepted. Prepayment is required.

Winfield District Court PO Box 472, Winfield, KS 67156; 620-221-5470; Fax: 620-221-1097. Hours: 8AM-Noon,1-4PM (CST). *Felony, Misdemeanor, Civil, Eviction, Small Claims, Probate.*

Note: This court covers northern part of county.

Civil Records: Access: Fax, mail, in person. Both court and visitors may perform in person searches. Search fee: $12.00 per hour. Required to search: name, years to search. Civil cases indexed by defendant, plaintiff. Civil records on computer since 1994, index cards from 1874.

Criminal Records: Access: Fax, mail, in person. Both court and visitors may perform in person searches. Search fee: $12.00 per hour. Required to search: name, years to search. Criminal records on computer since 1994, index cards from 1874.

General Information: Public Access terminal is available. No juvenile, mental health, sealed or expunged records released. SASE not required. Turnaround time 1 week. Copy fee: $.50 per page. Certification fee: $1.00. Fee payee: Clerk of Court. Personal checks accepted. Prepayment is required.

Crawford County

Girard District Court PO Box 69, Girard, KS 66743; 620-724-6211; Fax: 620-724-4987. Hours: 8AM-5PM (CST). *Felony, Misdemeanor, Civil, Eviction, Small Claims, Probate.*

Note: Records on computer are maintained here for the Pittsburg District Court as well since 8/92. For prior cases, search both courts separately.

Civil Records: Access: Fax, mail, in person. Both court and visitors may perform in person searches. Search fee: $12.00 per hour. Required to search: name, years to search. Civil cases indexed by defendant, plaintiff. Civil records on computer since August, 1992, microfiche from 1977, index cards from 1977.

Criminal Records: Access: Phone, fax, in person. Both court and visitors may perform in person searches. No search fee. Required to search: name, years to search. Criminal records on computer since August, 1992, microfiche from 1977, index cards from 1977. Employment/work-related mail inquires are referred to the Kansas Bureau of Investigation.

General Information: Public Access terminal is available. No juvenile, mental health, sealed or expunged records released. SASE required. Turnaround time 3 days. Fax notes: $2.50 per page. Copy fee: $.25 per page. Certification fee: $1.00. Fee payee: Clerk of Court. Personal checks accepted. Prepayment is required.

Pittsburg District Court PO Box 1348, Pittsburg, KS 66762; 620-231-0391; Fax: 620-231-0316. Hours: 8AM-5PM (CST). *Felony, Misdemeanor, Civil, Eviction, Small Claims, Probate.*

Note: Records back to 8/92 can be searched at Girard District Court as well; Girard and Pittsburg share a computer system. For cases prior to 8/92, search both courts separately.

Civil Records: Access: Fax, mail, in person. Both court and visitors may perform in person searches. Search fee: $12.00 per hour. Required to search: name, years to search. Civil cases indexed by defendant, plaintiff. Civil records on computer since August, 1992, microfiche from 1977, index cards from 1977.

Criminal Records: Access: Phone, fax, in person. Both court and visitors may perform in person searches. No search fee. Required to search: name, years to search. Criminal records on computer since August, 1992, microfiche from 1977, index cards from 1977.

Employment/work-related mail inquires are referred to the Kansas Bureau of Investigation.

General Information: Public Access terminal is available. No juvenile, mental health, sealed or expunged records released. SASE required. Turnaround time 3 days. Fax notes: $2.50 per page. Copy fee: $.25 per page. Certification fee: $1.00. Fee payee: Clerk of Court. Personal checks accepted. Prepayment is required.

Decatur County

District Court PO Box 89, Oberlin, KS 67749; 785-475-8107; Fax: 785-475-8170. Hours: 8AM-5PM (CST). *Felony, Misdemeanor, Civil, Eviction, Small Claims, Probate.*

Civil Records: Access: In person only. Visitors must perform in person searches for themselves. No search fee. Required to search: name, years to search. Civil cases indexed by defendant, plaintiff. Civil records on index books from 1870.

Criminal Records: Access: In person only. Visitors must perform in person searches for themselves. No search fee. Required to search: name, years to search. Criminal records on index books from 1870.

General Information: No adoption, juvenile, mental health, sealed or expunged records released. Copy fee: $.25 per page. Certification fee: $1.00. Fee payee: Clerk of District Court.

Dickinson County

District Court PO Box 127, Abilene, KS 67410; 785-263-3142; Fax: 785-263-4407. Hours: 8AM-5PM (CST). *Felony, Misdemeanor, Civil, Eviction, Small Claims, Probate.*

Civil Records: Access: Mail, fax, in person, e-mail. Both court and visitors may perform in person searches. Search fee: $12.00 per hour. Required to search: name, years to search. Civil cases indexed by defendant, plaintiff. Civil records on computer since 7/92, on index books prior.

Criminal Records: Access: Mail, fax, in person, e-mail. Both court and visitors may perform in person searches. Search fee: $12.00 per hour. Required to search: name, years to search; also helpful: SSN. Criminal records on computer since 7/92, on index books prior.

General Information: Public Access terminal is available. No juvenile, mental health, sealed or expunged records released. SASE required. Turnaround time 1 week. Fax notes: Fax fee $1.00 per page. Copy fee: $1.00. Fee for first 4 pages. Add $.25 per page thereafter. Certification fee: $1.00. Fee payee: Clerk of District Court. Personal checks accepted. Prepayment is required.

Doniphan County

District Court PO Box 295, Troy, KS 66087; 785-985-3582; Fax: 785-985-2402. Hours: 8AM-5PM (CST). *Felony, Misdemeanor, Civil, Eviction, Small Claims, Probate.*

Civil Records: Access: Phone, fax, mail, in person. Both court and visitors may perform in person searches. Search fee: $12.00 per hour. Required to search: name, years to search. Civil cases indexed by defendant, plaintiff. Civil records on computer since 1992; index cards from 1856.

Criminal Records: Access: Phone, fax, mail, in person. Only the court performs in person searches; visitors may not. Search fee: $12.00 per hour. Required to search: name, years to search; also helpful: address, DOB. Criminal records on computer since 1992; index cards from 1856.

General Information: Public Access terminal is available. No juvenile, mental health, sealed or expunged records released. SASE required. Turnaround time 1-2 days. Fax notes: Fee to fax results is $2.00 per page. Copy fee: $.50 for first page, $.25 each add'l. Certification fee: $1.00. Fee payee: Clerk of Court. Personal checks accepted.

Douglas County

District Court 111 E 11th St, Rm 144, Lawrence, KS 66044-2966; 785-841-7700 X141; Fax: 785-832-5174. Hours: 8:30AM-4PM (CST). *Felony, Misdemeanor, Civil, Eviction, Small Claims, Probate.*

www.douglas-county.com/dcht

Civil Records: Access: Phone, fax, mail, in person, online. Both court and visitors may perform in person searches. Search fee: $12.00 per hour. Required to search: name, years to search. Civil cases indexed by defendant, plaintiff. Civil records on index cards from 1863, archived from 1865 on film, indexed on computer since 1989. Online access via Internet to district court records is available for a $180.00 annual fee and $60.00 set-up fee. For further information and registration, contact Beverly at 785-832-5299. All written requests must include a phone number. In person requests take 48 hours to process, if court does search.

Criminal Records: Access: Phone, fax, mail, in person, online. Both court and visitors may perform in person searches. Search fee: $12.00 per hour. Required to search: name, years to search; also helpful: DOB, SSN. Criminal records on computer from 1989, index cards 1860, archived from 1865. Online access to criminal records is the same as civil. All other background check requests must be in writing.

General Information: Public Access terminal is available. No juvenile, mental health, sealed or expunged records released. SASE not required. Turnaround time 3 days. Fax notes: Fee to fax results is $2.00 per document. Copy fee: $.25 per page. Certification fee: $1.00; Authentications are $2.00 each. Fee payee: Clerk of Court. Personal checks accepted. Prepayment is required.

Edwards County

District Court PO Box 232, Kinsley, KS 67547; 620-659-2442; Fax: 620-659-2998. Hours: 8AM-5PM (CST). *Felony, Misdemeanor, Civil, Eviction, Small Claims, Probate.*

www.kscourts.org/dstcts/24dstct.htm

Civil Records: Access: Mail, in person. Both court and visitors may perform in person searches. No search fee. Required to search: name, years to search. Civil cases indexed by defendant, plaintiff. Civil records on index books from 1800s.

Criminal Records: Access: In person only. Visitors must perform in person searches for themselves. No search fee. Required to search: name, years to search. Criminal records on index books from 1800s.

General Information: No juvenile, adoption, mental health, sealed or expunged records released. SASE required. Turnaround time 1-2 days. Copy fee: $.25 per page. Certification fee: $1.00. Fee payee: Clerk District Court. Personal checks accepted. Prepayment is required.

Elk County

District Court PO Box 306, Howard, KS 67349; 620-374-2370; Fax: 620-374-3531. Hours: 8AM-4:30PM (CST). *Felony, Misdemeanor, Civil, Eviction, Small Claims, Probate.*

Civil Records: Access: In person only. Visitors must perform in person searches for themselves. No search fee. Required to search: name, years to search. Civil cases indexed by defendant, plaintiff. Civil records on index books from 1907.

Criminal Records: Access: In person only. Visitors must perform in person searches for themselves. No search fee. Required to search: name, years to search. Criminal records on index books from 1907.

General Information: No juvenile, mental health, sealed or expunged records released. Copy fee: $.25 per page. Certification fee: $1.00. Fee payee: Clerk of District Court. Personal checks accepted. Prepayment is required.

Ellis County

District Court PO Box 8, Hays, KS 67601; 785-628-9415; Fax: 785-628-8415. Hours: 8AM-5PM (CST). *Felony, Misdemeanor, Civil, Eviction, Small Claims, Probate.*

Civil Records: Access: Mail, in person. Both court and visitors may perform in person searches. No search fee. Required to search: name, years to search. Civil cases indexed by defendant, plaintiff. Civil records on computer from 1991, microfiche from 1900s, index cards from 1800s, archives from 1800s.

Criminal Records: Access: In person only. Visitors must perform in person searches for themselves. No search fee. Required to search: name, years to search. Criminal records on computer from 1991, microfiche from 1900s, index cards from 1800s, archives from 1800s.

General Information: Public Access terminal is available. No juvenile, mental health, sealed or expunged records released. SASE required. Turnaround time 7 days. Copy fee: $.25 per page. Certification fee: $1.00. Fee payee: Clerk of Court. Personal checks accepted. Prepayment is required.

Ellsworth County

District Court 210 N Kansas, Ellsworth, KS 67439-3118; 785-472-3832; Fax: 785-472-5712. Hours: 8AM-5PM (CST). *Felony, Misdemeanor, Civil, Eviction, Small Claims, Probate.*

Civil Records: Access: Phone, fax, mail, in person. Both court and visitors may perform in person searches. No search fee. Required to search: name, years to search. Civil cases indexed by defendant, plaintiff. Civil records on computer from 1994, microfiche from 1900s, books from late 1800s.

Criminal Records: Access: Phone, fax, mail, in person. Both court and visitors may perform in person searches. No search fee. Required to search: name, years to search; also helpful: SSN. Criminal records on computer from 1994, microfiche from 1900s, books from late 1800s.

General Information: No juvenile, mental health, sealed or expunged records released. SASE required. Turnaround time 1-2 days. Fax notes: $.50 per page. Copy fee: $.35 per page. Certification fee: No cert fee. Fee payee: District Court. Personal checks accepted. Prepayment is required.

Finney County

District Court PO Box 798, Garden City, KS 67846; Civil phone: 620-271-6121; Criminal phone: 620-271-6122; Fax: 620-271-6140. Hours: 8AM-4:30PM (CST). *Felony, Misdemeanor, Civil, Eviction, Small Claims, Probate.*

Civil Records: Access: In person only. Visitors must perform in person searches for themselves. No search fee. Required to search: name, years to search. Civil cases indexed by defendant, plaintiff. Civil records on computer from 1991, microfiche from 1900s, index books from 1900s.

Criminal Records: Access: In person only. Visitors must perform in person searches for themselves. No search fee. Required to search: name, years to search. Criminal records on computer from 1991, microfiche from 1900s, index books from 1900s.

General Information: Public Access terminal is available. No juvenile, Mental health, sealed or expunged records released. Copy fee: $.25 per page. Certification fee: $1.00. Fee payee: District Court. Personal checks accepted. Prepayment is required.

Ford County

District Court 101 W Spruce, Dodge City, KS 67801; 620-227-4609; Civil phone: 620-227-4610; Criminal phone: 620-227-4608; Fax: 620-227-6799. Hours: 8AM-5PM (CST). *Felony, Misdemeanor, Civil, Eviction, Small Claims, Probate.*

www.kscourts.org/dstcts/16dstct.htm

Civil Records: Access: Fax, mail, in person. Both court and visitors may perform in person searches. Search fee: $12.00 per hour. Required to search: name, years to search. Civil cases indexed by defendant, plaintiff. Civil records on computer from end of 1991, microfiche from 1900s, index books from 1900s.

Criminal Records: Access: Fax, mail, in person. Both court and visitors may perform in person searches. Search fee: $12 per hour. Required to search: name, years to search, DOB; also helpful: SSN. Criminal records on computer from end of 1991, microfiche from 1900s, index books from 1900s.

General Information: Public Access terminal is available. No juvenile, mental health, sealed or expunged records released. SASE required. Turnaround time 3 days. Fax notes: Fee to fax results is $1.00 per page. Copy fee: $.25 per page. Certification fee: $1.00. Fee payee: Clerk of District Court. Personal checks accepted. Prepayment is required.

Franklin County

District Court PO Box 637, Ottawa, KS 66067; 785-242-6000; Fax: 785-242-5970. Hours: 8AM-12, 1PM-4PM (CST). *Felony, Misdemeanor, Civil, Eviction, Small Claims, Probate.*

www.kscourts.org/dstcts/4dstct.htm

Civil Records: Access: Mail, in person, online. Both court and visitors may perform in person searches. No search fee. Required to search: name, years to search. Civil cases indexed by defendant, plaintiff. Civil records on computer from 1982, index books from 1800s. Current court calendars are available free online at www.kscourts.org/dstcts/4frdckt.htm.

Criminal Records: Access: In person, online. Visitors must perform in person searches for themselves. No search fee. Required to search: name, years to search, SSN. Criminal records on computer from 1982, index books from 1800s. Online access to criminal calendars is the same as civil.

General Information: Public Access terminal is available. No juvenile, mental health, sealed or expunged records released. SASE required. Turnaround time 3-5 days. Copy fee: $.25 per page. Certification fee: $1.00. Fee payee: Clerk of District Court. Personal checks accepted. Prepayment is required.

Geary County

District Court PO Box 1147, Junction City, KS 66441; 785-762-5221; Fax: 785-762-4420. Hours: 8AM-5PM (CST). *Felony, Misdemeanor, Civil, Eviction, Small Claims, Probate.*

Civil Records: Access: Mail, in person, email. Both court and visitors may perform in person searches. Search fee: $12.00 per hour. Required to search: name, years to search. Civil cases indexed by defendant, plaintiff. Civil records on computer from 1992, microfiche, index books and archives from 1894.

Criminal Records: Access: Mail, in person, email. Both court and visitors may perform in person searches. Search fee: $12.00 per hour. Required to search: name, years to search; also helpful: SSN. Criminal records on computer from 1992, microfiche, index books and archives from 1894.

General Information: Public Access terminal is available. No juvenile, adoption, mental health, sealed or expunged records released. SASE not required. Turnaround time 3 days. Fax notes: Fee to fax results is $2.00 per page. Copy fee: $.25 per page. Certification

fee: $1.00. Fee payee: Clerk of Court. Personal checks accepted. Prepayment is required.

Gove County

District Court PO Box 97, Gove, KS 67736; 785-938-2310; Fax: 785-938-2312. Hours: 8AM-Noon, 1-5PM (CST). *Felony, Misdemeanor, Civil, Eviction, Small Claims, Probate.*

Civil Records: Access: Fax, mail, in person. Both court and visitors may perform in person searches. Search fee: $9.00 per hour. Required to search: name, years to search. Civil cases indexed by defendant, plaintiff. Civil records on computer from 1992, index books from 1890 through present.

Criminal Records: Access: Fax, mail, in person. Both court and visitors may perform in person searches. Search fee: $9.00 per hour. Required to search: name, years to search. Criminal records on computer from 1992, index books from 1890 through present.

General Information: No juvenile, mental health, sealed or expunged records released. SASE required. Turnaround time 1-2 days. Fax notes: Fee to fax results is $1.00 per page. Copy fee: $.25 per page. Certification fee: $1.00. Fee payee: Clerk of District Court. Personal checks accepted. Prepayment is required.

Graham County

District Court 410 N Pomeroy, Hill City, KS 67642; 785-421-3458; Fax: 785-421-5463. Hours: 8AM-5PM (CST). *Felony, Misdemeanor, Civil, Eviction, Small Claims, Probate.*

Civil Records: Access: In person, mail. Visitors must perform in person searches for themselves. No search fee. Required to search: name, years to search. Civil cases indexed by defendant, plaintiff. Civil records on index books from 1880s.

Criminal Records: Access: In person, mail. Visitors must perform in person searches for themselves. No search fee. Required to search: name, years to search, DOB; also helpful: SSN. Criminal records on index books from 1880s.

General Information: No juvenile, mental health, sealed or expunged records released. Copy fee: $.25 per page. Certification fee: $1.00. Fee payee: Clerk of District Court. Personal checks accepted. Prepayment is required.

Grant County

District Court 108 S Glenn, Ulysses, KS 67880; 620-356-1526; Fax: 620-353-2131. Hours: 8:30AM-5PM (CST). *Felony, Misdemeanor, Civil, Eviction, Small Claims, Probate.*

Civil Records: Access: In person only. Visitors must perform in person searches for themselves. No search fee. Required to search: name, years to search. Civil cases indexed by defendant, plaintiff. Civil records on computer from 1977, microfiche index from 1880s.

Criminal Records: Access: In person, mail. Visitors must perform in person searches for themselves. No search fee. Required to search: name, years to search. Criminal records on computer from 1977, microfiche index from 1880s. The court refers all searchers to the state Bureau of investigations, including in-person searchers.

General Information: Public Access terminal is available. No juvenile, mental health, sealed or expunged records released. SASE required. Turnaround time same day. Copy fee: $.50 per page. Certification fee: $1.00. Fee payee: District Court. Personal checks accepted. Prepayment is required.

Gray County

District Court PO Box 487, Cimarron, KS 67835; 620-855-3812; Fax: 620-855-7037. Hours: 8AM-5PM (CST). *Felony, Misdemeanor, Civil, Eviction, Small Claims, Probate.*

www.kscourts.org/dstcts/16dstct.htm

Civil Records: Access: Fax, mail, in person. Visitors must perform in person searches for themselves. No search fee. Required to search: name; also helpful: years to search. Civil cases indexed by defendant, plaintiff. Civil records on computer from 1990, index books from 1800s. Fax requests must be pre-paid.

Criminal Records: Access: Fax, mail, in person. Visitors must perform in person searches for themselves. No search fee. Required to search: name, years to search; also helpful: address, DOB. Criminal records on computer from 1990, index books from 1800s. Fax requests must be pre-paid.

General Information: Public Access terminal is available. No juvenile, mental health, sealed or expunged records released. Copy fee: $.50 per page. Certification fee: $1.00. Fee payee: Clerk of District Court. Personal checks accepted.

Greeley County

District Court PO Box 516, Tribune, KS 67879; 620-376-4292. Hours: 8AM-Noon, 1-5PM (MST). *Felony, Misdemeanor, Civil, Eviction, Small Claims, Probate.*

Civil Records: Access: In person only. Visitors must perform in person searches for themselves. No search fee. Required to search: name, years to search. Civil cases indexed by defendant, plaintiff. Civil records on hardcopy index from beginning.

Criminal Records: Access: In person only. Visitors must perform in person searches for themselves. No search fee. Required to search: name, years to search; also helpful: SSN. Criminal records on hardcopy index from beginning.

General Information: Public Access terminal is available. No juvenile, mental health, sealed or expunged records released. Copy fee: $.50 per page. Certification fee: $1.00. Fee payee: Clerk of the District Court. Personal checks accepted. Prepayment is required.

Greenwood County

District Court 311 N Main, Eureka, KS 67045; 620-583-8153; Fax: 620-583-6818. Hours: 8AM-5PM (CST). *Felony, Misdemeanor, Civil, Eviction, Small Claims, Probate.*

Civil Records: Access: Mail, in person. Both court and visitors may perform in person searches. Search fee: $12.00 per hour per hour if search is conducted by court personnel. Required to search: name, years to search. Civil cases indexed by defendant, plaintiff. Civil records on computer from 1983, index cards from 1800s.

Criminal Records: Access: Mail, in person. Both court and visitors may perform in person searches. Search fee: $12.00 per hour if search is performed by court personnel. Required to search: name, years to search. Criminal records on computer from 1993, index cards from 1800s.

General Information: Public Access terminal is available. No juvenile, mental health, sealed or expunged records released. SASE required. Turnaround time 1-2 days. Copy fee: $.25 per page. Certification fee: $1.00. Fee payee: Clerk of Court. Personal checks accepted. Prepayment is required.

Hamilton County

District Court PO Box 745, Syracuse, KS 67878; 620-384-5159; Fax: 620-384-7806. Hours: 8AM-5PM (MST). *Felony, Misdemeanor, Civil, Eviction, Small Claims, Probate.*

Civil Records: Access: In person only. Visitors must perform in person searches for themselves. No search fee. Required to search: name, years to search. Civil cases indexed by defendant, plaintiff. Civil records on computer from 1985, microfiche, archives and index cards from 1880s.
Criminal Records: Access: In person only. Visitors must perform in person searches for themselves. No search fee. Required to search: name, years to search. Criminal records on computer from 1985, microfiche, archives and index cards from 1880s.
General Information: Public Access terminal is available. No juvenile, mental health, sealed or expunged records released. Fax notes: Fee to fax results is $1.00 per page. Copy fee: $.25 per page. Certification fee: $1.00. Fee payee: Clerk of District Court. Personal checks accepted. Prepayment is required.

Harper County

District Court PO Box 467, Anthony, KS 67003; 620-842-3721; Fax: 620-842-5937. Hours: 8AM-Noon, 1-5PM (CST). *Felony, Misdemeanor, Civil, Eviction, Small Claims, Probate.*

Civil Records: Access: Fax, mail, in person. Both court and visitors may perform in person searches. Search fee: $12.00 per hour. Required to search: name, years to search. Civil cases indexed by defendant, plaintiff. Civil records on computer from 1976, microfiche, index books and archives from 1887.
Criminal Records: Access: Fax, mail, in person. Both court and visitors may perform in person searches. Search fee: $12.00 per hour. Required to search: name, years to search, SSN. Criminal records on computer from 1976, microfiche, index books and archives from 1887.
General Information: Public Access terminal is available. No juvenile, mental health, sealed or expunged records released. SASE not required. Turnaround time same day. Fax notes: $1.00 per page. Copy fee: $.25 per page. Certification fee: $1.00. Fee payee: Clerk of District Court. Personal checks accepted.

Harvey County

District Court PO Box 665, Newton, KS 67114-0665; 316-284-6890; Civil phone: 316-284-6894; Criminal phone: 316-284-6896; Fax: 316-283-4601. Hours: 8AM-5PM (CST). *Felony, Misdemeanor, Civil, Eviction, Small Claims, Probate.*

Civil Records: Access: Mail, fax, in person, email. Both court and visitors may perform in person searches. Search fee: $12.00 per hour. Required to search: name, years to search. Civil cases indexed by defendant, plaintiff. Civil records on index books from 1800s; on computer back to 1995.
Criminal Records: Access: Mail, fax, in person, email. Both court and visitors may perform in person searches. Search fee: $12.00 per hour. Required to search: name, years to search, DOB; also helpful-SSN, signed release. Criminal records on index books from 1800s. Call KBI for thorough search.
General Information: Public Access terminal is available. No juvenile, mental health, sealed or expunged records released. SASE not required. Turnaround time 3-5 days. Copy fee: $.50 per page. Certification fee: $1.00. Fee payee: Clerk of District Court. Personal checks accepted.

Haskell County

District Court PO Box 146, Sublette, KS 67877; 620-675-2671; Fax: 620-675-8599. Hours: 8AM-5PM (CST). *Felony, Misdemeanor, Civil, Eviction, Small Claims, Probate.*

Civil Records: Access: Phone, mail, fax, in person. Both court and visitors may perform in person searches. No search fee. Required to search: name, years to search. Civil cases indexed by defendant, plaintiff. Civil records on computer from 1990, index books from 1874.
Criminal Records: Access: Phone, mail, fax, in person. Visitors must perform in person searches for themselves. No search fee. Required to search: name, years to search. Criminal records on computer from 1990, index books from 1874.
General Information: Public Access terminal is available. No juvenile, mental health, sealed or expunged records released. SASE not required. Turnaround time same day. Fax notes: Fax fee is $.25 per page or $3.00 per document. Copy fee: $.25 per page. Certification fee: $1.00. Fee payee: Clerk of District Court. Personal checks accepted. Prepayment is required.

Hodgeman County

District Court PO Box 187, Jetmore, KS 67854; 620-357-6522; Fax: 620-357-6216. Hours: 8:30AM-5PM (CST). *Felony, Misdemeanor, Civil, Eviction, Small Claims, Probate.*

www.kscourts.org/dstcts/24dstct.htm

Civil Records: Access: Phone, fax, mail, in person. Both court and visitors may perform in person searches. No search fee. Required to search: name, years to search. Civil cases indexed by defendant, plaintiff. Civil records on index cards and books from 1800s.
Criminal Records: Access: In person only. Visitors must perform in person searches for themselves. No search fee. Required to search: name, years to search; also helpful: SSN. Criminal records on index cards and books from 1800s.
General Information: No juvenile, mental health, sealed or expunged records released. SASE not required. Turnaround time 1-2 days. Fax notes: $.50 per page. Copy fee: $.25 per page. Certification fee: $1.00. Fee payee: Clerk of Court. Personal checks accepted. Must prepay for mail and fax.

Jackson County

District Court 400 New York Av #311, Holton, KS 66436; 785-364-2191; Fax: 785-364-3804. Hours: 8AM-4:30PM (CST). *Felony, Misdemeanor, Civil, Eviction, Small Claims, Probate.*

Civil Records: Access: In person only. Visitors must perform in person searches for themselves. No search fee. Required to search: name, years to search. Civil cases indexed by defendant, plaintiff. Civil records on index cards from 1800s (working on installation of computer at this time).
Criminal Records: Access: In person only. Visitors must perform in person searches for themselves. No search fee. Required to search: name, years to search. Criminal records on index cards from 1800s (working on installation of computer at this time).
General Information: No juvenile, mental health, sealed or expunged records released. Copy fee: $.25 per page. Certification fee: $1.00. Fee payee: Clerk of District Court. Personal checks accepted.

Jefferson County

District Court PO Box 327, Oskaloosa, KS 66066; 785-863-2461; Fax: 785-863-2369. Hours: 8AM-4:30PM (CST). *Felony, Misdemeanor, Civil, Eviction, Small Claims, Probate.*

Civil Records: Access: In person only. Visitors must perform in person searches for themselves. No search fee. Required to search: name, years to search. Civil cases indexed by defendant, plaintiff. Civil records on computer since 5/94, on index books from 1855.
Criminal Records: Access: In person only. Visitors must perform in person searches for themselves. No search fee. Required to search: name, years to search; also helpful: SSN. Criminal records on index books from 1855.
General Information: Public Access terminal is available. No juvenile, mental health, sealed or expunged records released. Copy fee: $.25 per page. Certification fee: $1.00. Fee payee: District Court. Personal checks accepted. Prepayment is required.

Jewell County

District Court 307 N Commercial, Mankato, KS 66956; 785-378-4030; Fax: 785-378-4035. Hours: 8AM-5PM (CST). *Felony, Misdemeanor, Civil, Eviction, Small Claims, Probate.*

www.kscourts.org/dstcts/12dstct.htm

Civil Records: Access: Phone, fax, mail, in person. Both court and visitors may perform in person searches. Search fee: $12.00 per hour. Required to search: name, years to search. Civil cases indexed by defendant, plaintiff. Civil records on index books from 1871.
Criminal Records: Access: Phone, fax, mail, in person. Both court and visitors may perform in person searches. Search fee: $12.00 per hour. Required to search: name, years to search. Criminal records on index books from 1871.
General Information: No juvenile, mental health, sealed or expunged records released. SASE required. Turnaround time 1-2 days. Fax notes: $3.00 per page. Copy fee: $.25 per page. Certification fee: $1.00. Fee payee: District Court. Personal checks accepted. Prepayment is required.

Johnson County

District Court 100 N Kansas, Olathe, KS 66061; 913-715-3500; Civil phone: 913-715-3400; Criminal phone: 913-715-3460; Fax: 913-715-3481. Hours: 8:30AM-4PM (CST). *Felony, Misdemeanor, Civil, Eviction, Small Claims, Probate.*

www.jocoks.com/jococourts/index.htm
Note: Search requests should be made to the Records Center, phone 913-715-3480.

Civil Records: Access: Fax, mail, online, in person. Both court and visitors may perform in person searches. Search fee: $12.00 per hour. Required to search: name, years to search. Civil cases indexed by defendant, plaintiff. Civil records on computer from 1980, microfiche, archives and index prior. Index online through INK of Kansas. See www.ink.org for subscription information.
Criminal Records: Access: Fax, mail, in person. Both court and visitors may perform in person searches. Search fee: $12.00 per hour. Required to search: name, years to search. Criminal records on computer from 1980, microfiche, archives and index prior. Criminal fax number is 913-715-3481.
General Information: Public Access terminal is available. No juvenile, mental health, sealed or expunged records released. No employment searches. SASE required. Turnaround time 1-2 days if current records, 1-2 weeks for very old document. Fax notes: $2.50 per page. Copy fee: $.50 per page. Copy fee for records prior to 1993 $10.00 flat fee. Certification fee:

$1.00. Fee payee: Clerk of the District Court. Only cashiers checks and money orders accepted. Prepayment is required.

Kearny County

District Court PO Box 64, Lakin, KS 67860; 620-355-6481; Fax: 620-355-7462. Hours: 8AM-Noon,1-5PM (CST). *Felony, Misdemeanor, Civil, Eviction, Small Claims, Probate.*

Civil Records: Access: Mail, in person. Visitors must perform in person searches for themselves. No search fee. Required to search: name, years to search. Civil cases indexed by defendant, plaintiff. Civil records on computer from 1991, index books from 1900s.
Criminal Records: Access: Mail, in person. Visitors must perform in person searches for themselves. No search fee. Required to search: name, years to search, SSN. Criminal records on computer from 1991, index books from 1900s. A case number must be provided with mail search requests.
General Information: Public Access terminal is available. No juvenile, mental health, adoption, sealed or expunged records released. SASE required. Turnaround time 3 days. Copy fee: $.25 per page. Certification fee: $1.00. Fee payee: District Court. Personal checks accepted. Prepayment is required.

Kingman County

District Court PO Box 495 (130 N Spruce St), Kingman, KS 67068; 620-532-5151; Fax: 620-532-2952. Hours: 8AM-Noon, 1-5PM (CST). *Felony, Misdemeanor, Civil, Eviction, Small Claims, Probate.*

Civil Records: Access: Mail, fax, in person. Both court and visitors may perform in person searches. Search fee: $12.00 per hour. Required to search: name, years to search. Civil cases indexed by defendant, plaintiff. Civil records on computer from 1990, microfiche, archives and index cards from 1800s.
Criminal Records: Access: Mail, fax, in person. Both court and visitors may perform in person searches. Search fee: $12.00 per hour. Required to search: name, years to search; also helpful: case type. Criminal records on computer from 1990, microfiche, archives and index cards from 1800s.
General Information: Public Access terminal is available. No juvenile, mental health, sealed or expunged records released. SASE required. Turnaround time 1-2 days. Fax notes: Fee to fax results is $1.00 per page. Copy fee: $.25 per page. Certification fee: $1.00. Fee payee: Clerk of Court. Personal checks accepted. Prepayment is required.

Kiowa County

District Court 211 E Florida, Greensburg, KS 67054; 620-723-3317; Fax: 620-723-2970. Hours: 8AM-5PM (CST). *Felony, Misdemeanor, Civil, Eviction, Small Claims, Probate.*
www.kscourts.org/dstcts/16dstct.htm

Civil Records: Access: Fax, mail, in person. Both court and visitors may perform in person searches. Search fee: $12.00 per hour. Required to search: name, years to search. Civil cases indexed by defendant, plaintiff. Civil records archived and on index books from 1800s; computerized back to 1977.
Criminal Records: Access: Fax, mail, in person. Both court and visitors may perform in person searches. Search fee: $12.00 per hour. Required to search: name, years to search, signed release; also helpful: DOB. Criminal records archived and on index books from 1800s; computerized back to 1977.
General Information: No juvenile, mental health, sealed or expunged records released. SASE required. Turnaround time 7 days. Fax notes: Fee to fax results is $1.00 per page. Copy fee: $.25 per page. Certification fee: $1.00. Fee payee: Clerk of District Court. Personal checks accepted.

Labette County

District Court Courthouse, 517 Merchant, Oswego, KS 67356; 620-795-4533 (620-421-4120 Parsons); Fax: 620-795-3056 (316-421-3633 Parsons). Hours: 8AM-5PM (CST). *Felony, Misdemeanor, Civil, Eviction, Small Claims, Probate.*

Civil Records: Access: Mail, in person. Both court and visitors may perform in person searches. No search fee. Required to search: name, years to search. Civil cases indexed by defendant, plaintiff. Civil records on computer since 1992.
Criminal Records: Access: Mail, in person. Both court and visitors may perform in person searches. No search fee. Required to search: name, years to search; also helpful: DOB, SSN. Criminal records on computer since 1992.
General Information: Public Access terminal is available. no juvenile, adoption, mental health, sealed or expunged records released. Copy fee: $.25 per page. Certification fee: $1.00. Fee payee: Clerk of District Court. Personal checks accepted. Prepayment is required.

District Court 201 South Central, Parsons, KS 67357; 620-421-4120; Fax: 620-421-3633. Hours: 8AM-5PM (CST). *Felony, Misdemeanor, Civil, Eviction, Small Claims, Probate.*

Civil Records: Access: Mail, in person. Both court and visitors may perform in person searches. Search fee: $12.00 per hour. Required to search: name, years to search. Civil cases indexed by defendant, plaintiff. Civil records on computer from 1992, index books from 1874.
Criminal Records: Access: Mail, in person. Both court and visitors may perform in person searches. Search fee: $9.00 per hour. Required to search: name, years to search. Criminal records on computer from 1992, index books from 1874.
General Information: Public Access terminal is available. No juvenile, adoption, mental health, sealed or expunged records released. SASE required. Turnaround time 1-2 days. Copy fee: $.25 per page. Certification fee: $1.00. Fee payee: Clerk of District Court. Personal checks accepted. Prepayment is required.

Lane County

District Court PO Box 188, Dighton, KS 67839; 620-397-2805; Fax: 620-397-5526. Hours: 8AM-5PM (CST). *Felony, Misdemeanor, Civil, Eviction, Small Claims, Probate.*
www.kscourts.org/dstcts/24dstct.htm

Civil Records: Access: Mail, in person. Both court and visitors may perform in person searches. No search fee. Required to search: name, years to search. Civil cases indexed by defendant, plaintiff. Civil records on computer since 1993; prior records from 1800s.
Criminal Records: Access: In person only. Visitors must perform in person searches for themselves. No search fee. Required to search: name, years to search; also helpful: SSN. Criminal records on computer since 1993; prior records from 1800s.
General Information: No juvenile, mental health, sealed or expunged records released. SASE required. Turnaround time 1-2 weeks. Copy fee: $.25 per page. Certification fee: $1.00. Fee payee: Clerk of Court. Personal checks accepted. Prepayment is required.

Leavenworth County

District Court 601 S Third Street, Leavenworth, KS 66048; 913-684-0700; Civil phone: 913-684-0701; Criminal phone: 913-684-0704; Fax: 913-684-0492. Hours: 8AM-5PM (CST). *Felony, Misdemeanor, Civil, Eviction, Small Claims, Probate.*

Civil Records: Access: In person only. Both court and visitors may perform in person searches. No search fee. Required to search: name, years to search. Civil cases indexed by defendant, plaintiff. Civil records on computer from 1990, microfiche and index books from 1960.
Criminal Records: Access: Mail, in person. Both court and visitors may perform in person searches. No search fee. Required to search: name, years to search; also helpful: SSN. Criminal records on computer from 1990, microfiche and index books from 1960.
General Information: Public Access terminal is available. No juvenile, mental health, sealed or expunged records released. SASE required. Turnaround time 1-2 days. Copy fee: $.25 per page. Certification fee: $1.00. Fee payee: Clerk of District Court. Personal checks accepted. Prepayment is required.

Lincoln County

District Court 216 E Lincoln Ave, Lincoln, KS 67455; 785-524-4057; Fax: 785-524-3204. Hours: 8AM-12, 1_5PM (CST). *Felony, Misdemeanor, Civil, Eviction, Small Claims, Probate.*
www.kscourts.org/dstcts/12dstct.htm

Civil Records: Access: Fax, mail, in person. Both court and visitors may perform in person searches. Search fee: $9.00 per hour. Required to search: name; also helpful: years to search. Civil cases indexed by defendant, plaintiff. All records on computer.
Criminal Records: Access: Fax, mail, in person. Both court and visitors may perform in person searches. Search fee: $9.00 per hour. Required to search: name; also helpful: years to search, DOB, SSN. Criminal records on computer since 1980, on index cards from 1880.
General Information: No juvenile, mental health, sealed or expunged records released. SASE required. Turnaround time 3 days. Fax notes: $3.00 per page. Copy fee: $.25 per page. Certification fee: $1.00. Fee payee: Clerk of Court. Personal checks accepted. Prepayment is required.

Linn County

District Court PO Box 350, Mound City, KS 66056-0350; 913-795-2660; Fax: 913-795-2004. Hours: 8AM-5PM (CST). *Felony, Misdemeanor, Civil, Eviction, Small Claims, Probate.*

Civil Records: Access: In person only. Visitors must perform in person searches for themselves. No search fee. Required to search: name, years to search. Civil cases indexed by defendant, plaintiff. Civil records on computer from 1990, archives and index books from 1886.
Criminal Records: Access: In person only. Visitors must perform in person searches for themselves. No search fee. Required to search: name, years to search. Criminal records on computer from 1990, archives and index books from 1886.
General Information: Public Access terminal is available. No juvenile, mental health, sealed or expunged records released. Copy fee: $.25 per page. Certification fee: $1.00. Fee payee: Clerk of District Court. Personal checks accepted. Prepayment is required.

Logan County

District Court 710 W 2nd St, Oakley, KS 67748-1233; 785-672-3654; Fax: 785-672-3517. Hours: 8:30AM-Noon, 1-5PM (CST). *Felony, Misdemeanor, Civil, Eviction, Small Claims, Probate.*

Civil Records: Access: In person only. Visitors must perform in person searches for themselves. No search fee. Required to search: name; also helpful: years to search. Civil cases indexed by defendant, plaintiff. Civil records on computer from 1948, index cards from 1889.
Criminal Records: Access: In person only. Visitors must perform in person searches for themselves. No search fee. Required to search: name; also helpful: SSN, years to search. Criminal records on computer from 1948, index cards from 1889.
General Information: Public Access terminal is available. No juvenile, mental health, sealed or expunged records released. Copy fee: $.25 per page. Certification fee: $1.00. Fee payee: Clerk of District Court. Personal checks accepted. Prepayment is required.

Lyon County

District Court 402 Commercial St, Emporia, KS 66801; 620-342-4950; Fax: 620-342-8005. Hours: 8AM-4PM (CST). *Felony, Misdemeanor, Civil, Eviction, Small Claims, Probate.*

Civil Records: Access: Fax, mail, in person. Both court and visitors may perform in person searches. No search fee. Required to search: name, years to search. Civil cases indexed by defendant, plaintiff.
Criminal Records: Access: In person only. Visitors must perform in person searches for themselves. No search fee. Required to search: name, years to search.
General Information: Public Access terminal is available. No mental health, sealed or expunged records released. Turnaround time 3 days. Fax notes: $1.00 per page. Copy fee: $.50 per page. Certification fee: $2.00. Fee payee: Clerk of District Court. Personal checks accepted. Prepayment is required.

Marion County

District Court PO Box 298, Marion, KS 66861; 620-382-2104; Fax: 620-382-2259. Hours: 8AM-5PM (CST). *Felony, Misdemeanor, Civil, Eviction, Small Claims, Probate.*

Civil Records: Access: In person only. Both court and visitors may perform in person searches. Search fee: $12.00 per hour. Required to search: name, years to search. Civil cases indexed by defendant, plaintiff. Civil records on computer from July, 1992, on index cards from 1800s.
Criminal Records: Access: In person only. Both court and visitors may perform in person searches. Search fee: $12.00 per hour. Required to search: name, years to search. Criminal records on computer from July, 1992, on index cards from 1800s.
General Information: Public Access terminal is available. No juvenile, mental health, sealed or expunged records released. Copy fee: $1.00 per page. Certification fee: $1.00. Fee payee: District Court. Personal checks accepted. Prepayment is required.

Marshall County

District Court PO Box 86, Marysville, KS 66508; 785-562-5301; Fax: 785-562-2458. Hours: 8AM-5PM; Search hours: 8:30AM-4:30PM (CST). *Felony, Misdemeanor, Civil, Eviction, Small Claims, Probate.*

Civil Records: Access: Fax, mail, in person. Both court and visitors may perform in person searches. Search fee: $9.00 per hour. Required to search: name, years to search. Civil cases indexed by defendant, plaintiff. Civil records on computer from 1990, microfiche from 1977 (earlier records on roll-marriage licenses on computer

index 1860s, forward/naturalizations on computer index).
Criminal Records: Access: Fax, mail, in person. Both court and visitors may perform in person searches. Search fee: $9.00 per hour. Required to search: name, years to search. Criminal records on computer from 1988, microfiche from 1977.
General Information: Public Access terminal is available. No juvenile, mental health, sealed or expunged records released. SASE required. Turnaround time 1-2 days. Fax notes: $2.00 for first page, $1.00 each add'l. Prepayment required. Copy fee: $.50 for first page, $.25 each add'l. Certification fee: $1.00. Fee payee: Clerk of Court. Personal checks accepted. Prepayment is required.

McPherson County

District Court PO Box 1106, McPherson, KS 67460; 620-241-3422; Fax: 620-241-1372. Hours: 8AM-5PM (CST). *Felony, Misdemeanor, Civil, Eviction, Small Claims, Probate.*

Civil Records: Access: Mail, in person. Both court and visitors may perform in person searches. Search fee: $12.00 per hour. Required to search: name, years to search. Civil cases indexed by defendant, plaintiff. Civil records on microfilm from 1953, index cards from 1900s.
Criminal Records: Access: Mail, in person. Both court and visitors may perform in person searches. Search fee: $12.00 per hour. Required to search: name, years to search; also helpful: SSN. Criminal records on microfilm from 1953, index cards from 1900s.
General Information: Public Access terminal is available. No juvenile, mental health, sealed or expunged records released. SASE required. Turnaround time 1-3 days. Fax notes: Fax fee $1.00 per page. Copy fee: $.50 per page. Certification fee: $.50 per document. Fee payee: District Court. Personal checks accepted. Prepayment is required.

Meade County

Meade County District Court PO Box 623, Meade, KS 67864; 620-873-8750; Fax: 620-873-8759. Hours: 8AM-5PM (CST). *Felony, Misdemeanor, Civil, Eviction, Small Claims, Probate.*

www.kscourts.org/dstcts/16dstct.htm

Note: All employment background checks requested by mail, phone, or fax are referred to the KBI (state agency for criminal records).

Civil Records: Access: Mail, in person. Both court and visitors may perform in person searches. Search fee: $12.00 per hour. Required to search: name, years to search. Civil cases indexed by defendant, plaintiff. Civil records on computer from 1990, index cards from 1896.
Criminal Records: Access: Mail, in person. Both court and visitors may perform in person searches. Search fee: $12.00 per hour. Required to search: name, years to search. Criminal records on computer from 1990, index cards from 1896.
General Information: Public Access terminal is available. No juvenile, mental health, sealed or expunged records released. SASE required. Turnaround time 1-2 days. Copy fee: $.25 per page. Certification fee: $1.00. Fee payee: Clerk of Court. Only cashiers checks and money orders accepted. Prepayment is required.

Miami County

District Court PO Box 187, Paola, KS 66071; 913-294-3326; Fax: 913-294-2535. Hours: 8AM-4:30PM (CST). *Felony, Misdemeanor, Civil, Eviction, Small Claims, Probate.*

Civil Records: Access: In person only. Both court and visitors may perform in person searches. Search fee: $12.00 per hour. Required to search: name, years to

search. Civil cases indexed by defendant, plaintiff. Civil records on computer from 1984, index cards from 1890s.
Criminal Records: Access: In person only. Both court and visitors may perform in person searches. Search fee: $12.00 per hour. Required to search: name, years to search; also helpful: SSN. Criminal records on computer from 1984, index cards from 1890s.
General Information: Public Access terminal is available. No juvenile, mental health, sealed or expunged records released. Copy fee: $.25 per page. Certification fee: $1.00. Fee payee: District Court. Personal checks accepted. Prepayment is required.

Mitchell County

District Court 115 S Hersey, Beloit, KS 67420; 785-738-3753; Fax: 785-738-4101. Hours: 8AM-5PM (CST). *Felony, Misdemeanor, Civil, Eviction, Small Claims, Probate.*

www.kscourts.org/dstcts/12dstct.htm

Civil Records: Access: Mail, in person. Both court and visitors may perform in person searches. Search fee: $10.00 per hour. Required to search: name, years to search. Civil cases indexed by defendant, plaintiff. Civil records on index cards from 1870.
Criminal Records: Access: Mail, in person. Both court and visitors may perform in person searches. Search fee: $10.00 per hour. Required to search: name, years to search. Criminal records on index cards from 1870.
General Information: No juvenile, mental health, sealed or expunged records released. SASE required. Turnaround time 1-2 days. Copy fee: $.25 per page. Certification fee: $1.00. Fee payee: Clerk of Court. Personal checks accepted. Prepayment is required.

Montgomery County

Independence District Court PO Box 768, Independence, KS 67301; 620-330-1070; Fax: 620-331-6120. Hours: 8AM-5PM (CST). *Felony, Misdemeanor, Civil, Eviction, Small Claims, Probate.*

Note: This court covers civil cases for the northern part of the county. It is suggested to search both courts.

Civil Records: Access: Fax, mail, in person. Both court and visitors may perform in person searches. Search fee: $12.80 per hour. $6.00 minimum. Required to search: name, years to search. Civil cases indexed by defendant, plaintiff. Civil records on computer since 1992, on microfiche from 1870-1930, archives 1930-1992, index cards from 1870.
Criminal Records: Access: Fax, mail, in person. Both court and visitors may perform in person searches. Search fee: $12.80 per hour. $6.00 minimum. Required to search: name, years to search; also helpful: SSN. Criminal records on computer since 1992, on microfiche from 1870-1930, archives 1930-1992, index cards from 1870.
General Information: Public Access terminal is available. No juvenile, adoptions, mental health, sealed or expunged records released. SASE not required. Turnaround time 72 hours. Fax notes: $5.00 for first page, $1.00 each add'l. Copy fee: $.25 per page. Certification fee: $1.00. Fee payee: Clerk of Court. Personal checks accepted. Prepayment is required.

Coffeyville District Court PO Box 409, Coffeyville, KS 67337; 620-251-1060; Fax: 620-251-2734. Hours: 8AM-5PM (CST). *Civil, Eviction, Small Claims, Probate.*

Note: This court covers civil cases for the southern part of the county, although cases can be filed in either court. It is recommended to search both courts

Civil Records: Access: Fax, mail, in person. Both court and visitors may perform in person searches. Search fee: $12.80 per hour; $6.00 minimum. Required to search: name, years to search. Civil cases indexed by defendant, plaintiff. Civil records on computer back to

1992, on paper, fiche, etc. since 1924. **General Information:** Public Access terminal is available. No juvenile, mental health, sealed, adoption, or expunged records released. Turnaround time 72 hours. Fax notes: Fee to fax results is $1.00 per page. Copy fee: $.25 per page. Certification fee: $1.00. Fee payee: Clerk of Court. Personal checks accepted.

Morris County

District Court County Courthouse, Council Grove, KS 66846; 620-767-6838; Fax: 620-767-6488. Hours: 8AM-5PM (CST). *Felony, Misdemeanor, Civil, Eviction, Small Claims, Probate.*

Civil Records: Access: Fax, mail, in person. Both court and visitors may perform in person searches. Search fee: $12.00 per hour. Required to search: name, years to search. Civil cases indexed by defendant, plaintiff. Civil records on computer since 1992, on microfiche, archives and index cards from 1860.
Criminal Records: Access: Fax, mail, in person. Both court and visitors may perform in person searches. Search fee: $12.00 per hour. Required to search: name, years to search. Criminal records on computer since 1992, on microfiche, archives and index cards to 1860.
General Information: Public Access terminal is available. SASE required. Turnaround time 1-2 days. Fax notes: $1.00 per page. Copy fee: $.25 per page. Certification fee: $1.00. Fee payee: Clerk of Court. Personal checks accepted. Prepayment is required.

Morton County

District Court PO Box 825, Elkhart, KS 67950; 620-697-2563; Fax: 620-697-4289. Hours: 8AM-Noon, 1-5PM (CST). *Felony, Misdemeanor, Civil, Eviction, Small Claims, Probate.*

Civil Records: Access: Mail, in person. Both court and visitors may perform in person searches. Search fee: $12.00 per hour. Required to search: name, years to search. Civil cases indexed by defendant, plaintiff. Civil records on computer from 1992, index cards to 1800s.
Criminal Records: Access: Mail, in person. Both court and visitors may perform in person searches. Search fee: $12.00 per hour. Required to search: name, years to search. Criminal records on computer from 1992, index cards from 1800s.
General Information: Public Access terminal is available. No juvenile, mental health, sealed or expunged records released. SASE not required. Turnaround time 1 day. Copy fee: $.25 per page. Certification fee: $1.00. Fee payee: Clerk of Court. Personal checks accepted. Two party checks not accepted. Prepayment is required.

Nemaha County

District Court PO Box 213, Seneca, KS 66538; 785-336-2146; Fax: 785-336-6450. Hours: 8AM-5PM (CST). *Felony, Misdemeanor, Civil, Eviction, Small Claims, Probate.*

Civil Records: Access: Phone, mail, in person. Both court and visitors may perform in person searches. Search fee: $12.00 per hour. Required to search: name, years to search. Civil cases indexed by defendant, plaintiff. Civil records on computer from 1977, index cards from 1870.
Criminal Records: Access: Phone, mail, in person. Both court and visitors may perform in person searches. Search fee: $12.00 per hour. Required to search: name, years to search, SSN. Criminal records on computer from 1977, index cards from 1870.
General Information: No juvenile, mental health, sealed or expunged records released. SASE required. Turnaround time 1-2 days. Fax notes: Fee to fax is $2.00 1st page, $1.00 each add'l. Copy fee: $.25 per page. Certification fee: $1.00. Fee payee: Clerk of District Court. Business checks accepted. Prepayment is required.

Neosho County

Chanute District Court 102 S Lincoln, PO Box 889, Chanute, KS 66720; 620-431-5700; Fax: 620-431-5710. *Felony, Misdemeanor, Civil, Eviction, Small Claims.*

Note: This is a branch court of Erie.

Civil Records: Access: Mail, in person. Both court and visitors may perform in person searches. No search fee. Required to search: name, years to search. Civil cases indexed by defendant, plaintiff. Civil records on computer since 1993; prior back to 1955.
Criminal Records: Access: In person only. Visitors must perform in person searches for themselves. No search fee. Required to search: name, years to search. Criminal records on computer since 1993; prior back to 1955.
General Information: Public Access terminal is available. No juvenile, mental health, sealed or expunged records released. Turnaround time 1-3 days. Fax notes: Fee to fax results is $1.00 per page. Copy fee: $.50 per page. Certification fee: $1.00. Fee payee: Clerk of District Court. Personal checks accepted.

Erie District Court Neosho County Courthouse, PO Box 19, Erie, KS 66733; 620-244-3831; Fax: 620-244-3830. Hours: 8AM-noon, 1-4:30PM (CST). *Felony, Misdemeanor, Civil, Eviction, Small Claims, Probate.*

Note: This is the main court for the county.

Civil Records: Access: Fax, mail, in person. Both court and visitors may perform in person searches. No search fee. Required to search: name, years to search. Civil cases indexed by defendant, plaintiff. Civil records on index cards from 1900s; on computer back to 1993.
Criminal Records: Access: In person only. Visitors must perform in person searches for themselves. No search fee. Required to search: name, years to search, DOB. Criminal records on index cards from 1900s; on computer back to 1993.
General Information: Public Access terminal is available. No juvenile, mental health, sealed or expunged records released. SASE required. Turnaround time 1-2 days. Fax notes: Fee to fax results is $1.00 per page. Copy fee: $.50 per page. Certification fee: $1.00. Fee payee: Clerk of Court. Personal checks accepted. Prepayment is required.

Ness County

District Court PO Box 445, Ness City, KS 67560; 785-798-3693; Fax: 785-798-3348. Hours: 8AM-5PM (CST). *Felony, Misdemeanor, Civil, Eviction, Small Claims, Probate.*

www.kscourts.org/dstcts/24dstct.htm

Civil Records: Access: Fax, mail, in person. Both court and visitors may perform in person searches. No search fee. Required to search: name, years to search. Civil cases indexed by defendant, plaintiff. Civil records on index books from 1885.
Criminal Records: Access: In person only. Visitors must perform in person searches for themselves. No search fee. Required to search: name, years to search. Criminal records on index books from 1885.
General Information: No juvenile, mental health, sealed or expunged records released. SASE not required. Turnaround time 3 days. Fax notes: $1.00 per page. Copy fee: $.25 per page. Certification fee: $1.00. Fee payee: Clerk of Court. Personal checks accepted. Prepayment is required.

Norton County

District Court PO Box 70, Norton, KS 67654; 785-877-5720; Fax: 785-877-5722. Hours: 8AM-5PM (CST). *Felony, Misdemeanor, Civil, Eviction, Small Claims, Probate.*

Civil Records: Access: Mail, in person. Both court and visitors may perform in person searches. Search fee: $12.00. Required to search: name, years to search. Civil cases indexed by defendant, plaintiff. Civil records on index from 1900s.
Criminal Records: Access: Mail, in person. Both court and visitors may perform in person searches. Search fee: $12.00. Required to search: name, years to search. Criminal records on index from 1900s.
General Information: No juvenile, mental health, sealed or expunged records released. SASE required. Turnaround time 1 week. Copy fee: $.25 per page. Certification fee: $1.00. Fee payee: Clerk of District Court. Personal checks accepted. Prepayment is required.

Osage County

District Court PO Box 549, Lyndon, KS 66451; 785-828-4514; Fax: 785-828-4704. Hours: 8AM-Noon,1-4PM (CST). *Felony, Misdemeanor, Civil, Eviction, Small Claims, Probate.*

www.kscourts.org/dstcts/4dstct.htm

Civil Records: Access: Mail, in person, online. Both court and visitors may perform in person searches. Search fee: $12.00 per hour. Required to search: name, years to search. Civil cases indexed by defendant, plaintiff. Civil records on computer from 1980, index cards from 1979. Current court calendars are available free online at www.kscourts.org/dstcts/4osdckt.htm.
Criminal Records: Access: Mail, in person, online. Both court and visitors may perform in person searches. Search fee: $12.00 per hour. Required to search: name, years to search. Criminal records on computer from 1980, index cards from 1979. Online access to criminal records is the same as civil.
General Information: Public Access terminal is available. No juvenile, mental health, sealed or expunged records released. SASE required. Turnaround time 1-2 days. Copy fee: $.25 per page. Certification fee: $1.00. Fee payee: Clerk of Court. Business checks accepted. Prepayment is required.

Osborne County

District Court 423 W Main, PO Box 160, Osborne, KS 67473; 785-346-5911; Fax: 785-246-5992. Hours: 8:30AM-5PM (CST). *Felony, Misdemeanor, Civil, Eviction, Small Claims, Probate.*

Civil Records: Access: In person only. Visitors must perform in person searches for themselves. No search fee. Required to search: name, years to search. Civil cases indexed by defendant, plaintiff. Civil records on microfiche from 1872-1980, index books from 1981, index cards from 1872.
Criminal Records: Access: In person only. Visitors must perform in person searches for themselves. No search fee. Required to search: name, years to search; also helpful: SSN. Criminal records on microfiche from 1872-1980, index books from 1981, index cards from 1872.
General Information: No juvenile, mental health, sealed or expunged records released. Copy fee: $.25 per page. Certification fee: $1.00. Fee payee: Clerk of District Court. Personal checks accepted.

Ottawa County

District Court 307 N Concord, Minneapolis, KS 67467; 785-392-2917. Hours: 8:30AM-5PM (CST). *Felony, Misdemeanor, Civil, Eviction, Small Claims, Probate.*

Civil Records: Access: Mail, in person. Both court and visitors may perform in person searches. Search fee: $12.00 per hour. Required to search: name, years to search. Civil cases indexed by defendant, plaintiff. Civil records on index from 1800s.

Criminal Records: Access: Mail, in person. Both court and visitors may perform in person searches. Search fee: $12.00 per hour. Required to search: name, years to search; also helpful: SSN. Criminal records on index from 1800s.

General Information: No juvenile, mental health, sealed or expunged records released. SASE required. Turnaround time 1 week. Copy fee: $1.00 for first page, $.25 each add'l. Certification fee: $1.00. Fee payee: Clerk of District Court. Personal checks accepted. Prepayment is required.

Pawnee County

District Court PO Box 270, Larned, KS 67550; 620-285-6937; Fax: 620-285-3665. Hours: 8AM-5PM (CST). *Felony, Misdemeanor, Civil, Eviction, Small Claims, Probate.*

www.kscourts.org/dstcts/24dstct.htm

Civil Records: Access: Fax, mail, in person. Both court and visitors may perform in person searches. No search fee. Required to search: name, years to search. Civil cases indexed by defendant, plaintiff. Civil records on computer from 1991, index cards from 1900s.

Criminal Records: Access: In person only. Visitors must perform in person searches for themselves. No search fee. Required to search: name, years to search; also helpful: SSN. Criminal records on computer from 1991, index cards from 1900s.

General Information: No juvenile, mental health, sealed or expunged records released. SASE not required. Turnaround time 1-2 days. Fax notes: $.50 per page. Copy fee: $.25 per page. Certification fee: $1.00. Fee payee: Clerk of District Court. Personal checks accepted. Prepayment is required.

Phillips County

District Court PO Box 564, Phillipsburg, KS 67661; 785-543-6830; Fax: 785-543-6832. Hours: 8AM-5PM (CST). *Felony, Misdemeanor, Civil, Eviction, Small Claims, Probate.*

Civil Records: Access: In person only. Visitors must perform in person searches for themselves. No search fee. Required to search: name, years to search. Civil cases indexed by defendant, plaintiff. Civil records on index from 1900s; on computer back to 1994.

Criminal Records: Access: In person only. Visitors must perform in person searches for themselves. No search fee. Required to search: name, years to search; also helpful: DOB, SSN. Criminal records on index from 1900s; on computer back to 1994.

General Information: No juvenile, mental health, sealed or expunged records released. Fax notes: Fee to fax results is $.50 per page. Copy fee: $.25 per page. Certification fee: $1.00. Fee payee: Clerk of District Court. Personal checks accepted.

Pottawatomie County

District Court PO Box 129, Westmoreland, KS 66549; 785-457-3392; Fax: 785-457-2107. Hours: 8AM-4:30PM (CST). *Felony, Misdemeanor, Civil, Eviction, Small Claims, Probate.*

Civil Records: Access: Fax, mail, in person. Both court and visitors may perform in person searches. No search fee. Required to search: name, years to search. Civil cases indexed by defendant, plaintiff. Civil records

computerized since 1998, on microfiche from 1800s, index from 1800s.

Criminal Records: Access: Fax, mail, in person. Both court and visitors may perform in person searches. No search fee. Required to search: name, years to search; also helpful: SSN. Criminal records computerized since 1998, on microfiche from 1800s, index from 1800s.

General Information: Public Access terminal is available. (Records available since 1995.) No juvenile, mental health, sealed or expunged records released. SASE required. Turnaround time 1-2 days. Fax notes: $2.00 per page. Copy fee: $.25 per page. Certification fee: $2.00. Fee payee: Clerk of District Court. Personal checks accepted.

Pratt County

District Court PO Box 984, Pratt, KS 67124; 620-672-4100; Fax: 620-672-2902. Hours: 8AM-Noon, 1-5PM (CST). *Felony, Misdemeanor, Civil, Eviction, Small Claims, Probate.*

Civil Records: Access: Mail, fax, in person. Both court and visitors may perform in person searches. Search fee: $12.00 per hour. Required to search: name, years to search. Civil cases indexed by defendant, plaintiff. Civil records on computer back to 1988, microfiche, archives, index from 1878.

Criminal Records: Access: Mail, fax, in person. Only the court performs in person searches; visitors may not. Search fee: $12.00 per hour. Required to search: name, years to search, DOB; also helpful: SSN, signed release. Criminal records on computer back to 1988, microfiche, archives, index from 1878.

General Information: Public Access terminal is available. No juvenile, mental health, sealed or expunged records released. SASE required. Turnaround time 1-2 days. Fax notes: Fee to fax results is $.25 per page. Copy fee: $.25 per page. Certification fee: $1.00. Fee payee: Clerk of District Court. Personal checks accepted. Prepayment is required.

Rawlins County

District Court PO Box 257, Atwood, KS 67730; 785-626-3465; Fax: 785-626-3350. Hours: 9AM-5PM (CST). *Felony, Misdemeanor, Civil, Eviction, Small Claims, Probate.*

Civil Records: Access: Fax, mail, in person. Both court and visitors may perform in person searches. No search fee. Required to search: name, years to search. Civil cases indexed by defendant, plaintiff. Civil records on index from 1900s.

Criminal Records: Access: In person only. Visitors must perform in person searches for themselves. No search fee. Required to search: name, years to search; also helpful: SSN. Criminal records on index from 1900s. This agency refers requesters to the Kansas Bureau of Investigations.

General Information: No juvenile, mental health, sealed or expunged records released. SASE required. Turnaround time 3-5 days. Fax notes: $1.00 for first page, $.25 each add'l. Copy fee: $.25 per page. Certification fee: $1.00. Fee payee: Clerk of District Court. Only in state checks accepted. Prepayment is required.

Reno County

District Court 206 W 1st, Hutchinson, KS 67501; 620-694-2956; Fax: 620-694-2958. Hours: 8AM-Noon, 1-5PM (CST). *Felony, Misdemeanor, Civil, Eviction, Small Claims, Probate.*

Civil Records: Access: Mail, in person. Only the court performs in person searches; visitors may not. Search fee: $9.50 per hour. Required to search: name, years to search. Civil cases indexed by defendant, plaintiff. Civil records on computer from 1992, index cards from 1900s.

Criminal Records: Access: Mail, in person. Only the court performs in person searches; visitors may not. Search fee: $9.50 per hour. Required to search: name, years to search, DOB, signed release; also helpful: address, SSN. Criminal records on computer from 1992, index cards from 1900s.

General Information: No mental health, juvenile (some), sealed or expunged records released. SASE required. Turnaround time 3-5 days (in-state); 3-10 days (out-of-state). Fax notes: Will not fax results. Copy fee: $.25 per page. Certification fee: $1.00. Fee payee: Clerk of District Court. Only cashiers checks and money orders accepted. Prepayment is required.

Republic County

District Court PO Box 8, Belleville, KS 66935; 785-527-5691; Fax: 785-527-5029. Hours: 8:30AM-5PM (CST). *Felony, Misdemeanor, Civil, Eviction, Small Claims, Probate.*

www.kscourts.org/dstcts/12dstct.htm

Civil Records: Access: Mail, in person. Both court and visitors may perform in person searches. No search fee. Required to search: name, years to search. Civil cases indexed by defendant, plaintiff. Civil records on computer from 1990, index cards from 1869 for probate.

Criminal Records: Access: In person only. Visitors must perform in person searches for themselves. No search fee. Required to search: name, years to search. Criminal records on computer from 1990, index cards from 1869 for probate.

General Information: No juvenile, mental health, sealed or expunged records released. SASE required. Turnaround time 2-4 weeks. Copy fee: $.25 per page. Certification fee: $1.00. Fee payee: Clerk of Court. Personal checks accepted. Prepayment is required.

Rice County

District Court 101 W Commercial, Lyons, KS 67554; 620-257-2383; Fax: 620-257-3826. Hours: 8:30AM-5PM (CST). *Felony, Misdemeanor, Civil, Eviction, Small Claims, Probate.*

Civil Records: Access: Fax, mail, in person. Only the court performs in person searches; visitors may not. Search fee: $9.00 per hour. Required to search: name, years to search. Civil cases indexed by defendant, plaintiff. Civil records on computer from 1980, index cards from 1880.

Criminal Records: Access: Fax, mail, in person. Only the court performs in person searches; visitors may not. Search fee: $9.00 per hour. Required to search: name, years to search; also helpful: SSN. Criminal records on computer from 1980, index cards from 1880. All criminal searches are referred to the KBI, 1620 SW Tyler, Topeka KS 66601.

General Information: Public Access terminal is available. No juvenile, mental health, sealed or expunged records released. SASE required. Turnaround time 1-3 days. Fax notes: $.50 per page. Copy fee: $1.00 for first page, $.25 each add'l. Certification fee: No cert fee. Fee payee: Clerk of Court. Personal checks accepted. Prepayment is required.

Riley County

District Court PO Box 158, Manhattan, KS 66505-0158; 785-537-6364. Hours: 8:30AM-5PM (CST). *Felony, Misdemeanor, Civil, Eviction, Small Claims, Probate.*

www.co.riley.ks.us/court/default.htm

Civil Records: Access: In person only. Visitors must perform in person searches for themselves. No search fee. Required to search: name, years to search. Civil cases indexed by defendant, plaintiff. Civil records on computer back to 10/93; prior records in index journals.

Criminal Records: Access: In person only. Visitors must perform in person searches for themselves. No search fee. Required to search: name, years to search; also helpful: DOB, SSN. Criminal records on computer back to 1986, microfiche, archives and index cards from 1900s.

General Information: Public Access terminal is available. No juvenile (14 and under), mental health, sealed or expunged records released. Copy fee: $.25 per page. Certification fee: $1.00. Fee payee: Clerk of Court. Personal checks accepted. Prepayment is required.

Rooks County

District Court 115 N Walnut, PO Box 532, Stockton, KS 67669; 785-425-6718; Fax: 785-425-6568. Hours: 8AM-5PM (CST). *Felony, Misdemeanor, Civil, Eviction, Small Claims, Probate.*

Civil Records: Access: Mail, in person. Both court and visitors may perform in person searches. Search fee: $12.00 per hour. Required to search: name, years to search. Civil cases indexed by defendant, plaintiff. Civil records on index cards from 1888; on computer since.

Criminal Records: Access: Mail, in person. Both court and visitors may perform in person searches. Search fee: $12.00 per hour. Required to search: name, years to search; also helpful: DOB, SSN. Criminal records on index cards from 1888; on computer since.

General Information: Public Access terminal is available. No juvenile, adoption, mental health, sealed or expunged records released. SASE required. Turnaround time 1-3 days. Fax notes: Fee to fax results is $1.00 per page. Copy fee: $.25 per page. Certification fee: $2.00. Fee payee: Clerk of Court. Personal checks accepted. Prepayment is required.

Rush County

District Court PO Box 387, La Crosse, KS 67548; 785-222-2718; Fax: 785-222-2748. Hours: 8AM-5PM (CST). *Felony, Misdemeanor, Civil, Eviction, Small Claims, Probate.*

www.kscourts.org/dstcts/24dstct.htm

Civil Records: Access: Phone, fax, mail, in person. Both court and visitors may perform in person searches. No search fee. Required to search: name, years to search. Civil cases indexed by defendant, plaintiff. Civil records on computer from April, 1994, on index from 1800s.

Criminal Records: Access: In person only. Visitors must perform in person searches for themselves. No search fee. Required to search: name, years to search; also helpful: SSN. Criminal records on computer from April, 1994, on index from 1800s.

General Information: No juvenile, mental health, sealed or expunged records released. SASE required. Turnaround time 3 days. Fax notes: Fee to fax results is $.50 per page. Copy fee: $.25 per page. Certification fee: $1.00. Fee payee: Clerk of District Court. Personal checks accepted. Prepayment is required.

Russell County

District Court PO Box 876, Russell, KS 67665; 785-483-5641; Fax: 785-483-2448. Hours: 8AM-5PM (CST). *Felony, Misdemeanor, Civil, Eviction, Small Claims, Probate.*

Civil Records: Access: Fax, mail, in person. Both court and visitors may perform in person searches. Search fee: $12.00 per hour. Required to search: name, years to search. Civil cases indexed by defendant, plaintiff. Civil records on computer from 1990, index cards from 1900s.

Criminal Records: Access: Fax, mail, in person. Both court and visitors may perform in person searches. Search fee: $12.00 per hour. Required to search: name, years to search, DOB. Criminal records on computer from 1990, index cards from 1900s.

General Information: Public Access terminal is available. No juvenile, mental health, sealed or expunged records released. SASE required. Turnaround time 3 days. Fax notes: Fee to fax results is $.50 per page. Copy fee: $.50 per page. Certification fee: No cert fee. Fee payee: Clerk of Court. Personal checks accepted. Prepayment is required.

Saline County

District Court PO Box 1760, Salina, KS 67402-1760; 785-826-6617; Fax: 785-826-7319. Hours: 8:30AM-4PM (CST). *Felony, Misdemeanor, Civil, Eviction, Small Claims, Probate.*

Civil Records: Access: Mail, in person. Both court and visitors may perform in person searches. Search fee: $12.00 per hour. Required to search: name, years to search, address. Civil cases indexed by defendant, plaintiff. Civil records on computer from 1990, index from early 1900s.

Criminal Records: Access: Mail, in person. Both court and visitors may perform in person searches. Search fee: $12.00 per hour. Required to search: name, years to search, address, DOB, SSN, signed release. Criminal records on computer from 1990, index from early 1900s.

General Information: No juvenile, mental health, sealed or expunged records released. SASE not required. Turnaround time 1 week. Copy fee: $.25 per page. Certification fee: $1.00. Fee payee: Clerk of District Court. Personal checks accepted. Prepayment is required.

Scott County

District Court 303 Court, Scott City, KS 67871; 620-872-7208. Hours: 8AM-Noon, 1-5PM (CST). *Felony, Misdemeanor, Civil, Eviction, Small Claims, Probate.*

Civil Records: Access: Mail, in person. No search fee. Required to search: name, years to search. Civil cases indexed by defendant, plaintiff. Civil records on computer back to 1992, index cards from 1980s.

Criminal Records: Access: In person only. Visitors must perform in person searches for themselves. No search fee. Required to search: name, years to search, DOB. Criminal records on computer back to 1992, index cards from 1980s.

General Information: Public Access terminal is available. No juvenile, mental health, sealed or expunged records released. SASE required. Turnaround time 1-2 days. Fax notes: Fee to fax results is $1.00 per page. Copy fee: $.25 per page. Certification fee: $1.00. Fee payee: Clerk of Court. Personal checks accepted. Prepayment is required.

Sedgwick County

District Court 525 N Main, Wichita, KS 67203; 316-383-7302; Civil phone: 316-383-7311; Criminal phone: 316-383-7253; Fax: 316-383-8070 (Civil) 383-8071 (Criminal). Hours: 8AM-5PM (CST). *Felony, Misdemeanor, Civil, Eviction, Small Claims, Probate.*

http://distcrt18.state.ks.us

Civil Records: Access: Fax, mail, online, in person. Both court and visitors may perform in person searches. Search fee: $11.60 per hour. Fee charged if more than 15 minutes. Required to search: name, years to search. Civil cases indexed by defendant, plaintiff. Civil records on computer from 1983, microfiche from 1982, archives from 1977 and index cards from 1900s. Access to the remote online system requires a $225 setup fee, $49 monthly fee and a small transaction fee. The system also includes probate, traffic, domestic, and criminal cases. For more information, call 316-383-7563.

Criminal Records: Access: Fax, mail, online, in person. Both court and visitors may perform in person searches. Search fee: $11.60 per hour. Fee charged if more than 15 minutes. Required to search: name, years

to search. Criminal records on computer from 1983, microfiche from 1982, archives from 1977 and index cards from 1900s. Online access to criminal records is the same as civil.

General Information: Public Access terminal is available. No juvenile, adoption, mental health, sealed or expunged records released. SASE required. Turnaround time 7-10 days. Fax notes: $5.00 for first page, $2.00 each add'l. Copy fee: $.25 per page. Certification fee: $2.00. Fee payee: Clerk of Court. Personal checks accepted. Prepayment is required.

Seward County

District Court 415 N Washington #103, Liberal, KS 67901; 620-626-3265; Fax: 620-626-3302. Hours: 8:30AM-5PM (CST). *Felony, Misdemeanor, Civil, Eviction, Small Claims, Probate.*

Court will do searches on occasion, fee: $12. per hour.

Civil Records: Access: In person only. Visitors must perform in person searches for themselves. No search fee. Required to search: name, years to search. Civil cases indexed by defendant, plaintiff. Civil records on computer back to 1977, index from 1900s.

Criminal Records: Access: In person only. Visitors must perform in person searches for themselves. No search fee. Required to search: name, years to search; also helpful: SSN. Criminal records on computer back to 1977, index from 1900s.

General Information: Public Access terminal is available. No juvenile, mental health, sealed or expunged records released. Fax notes: Fee to fax results is $2.50 1st page, $.50 each add'l. Certification fee: $1.25. Fee payee: Clerk of District Court. Personal checks accepted. Prepayment is required.

Shawnee County

District Court 200 E 7th Rm 209, Topeka, KS 66603; 785-233-8200 X4327; Fax: 785-291-4811. Hours: 8:30AM-5PM (CST). *Felony, Misdemeanor, Civil, Eviction, Small Claims, Probate.*

www.shawneecourt.org

Civil Records: Access: Fax, mail, in person, online. Both court and visitors may perform in person searches. Search fee: $12.00 per hour. Required to search: name, years to search. Civil cases indexed by defendant, plaintiff. Civil records on computer from 1980, microfiche from 1950, archives and index from 1800s. Index online through INK of Kansas. See www.ink.org for subscription information. Also, online access to county court records is available free at www.shawneecourt.org/pa_inst.htm. Also, online access to court record images is available free at www.shawneecourt.org/img_temp.htm.

Criminal Records: Access: Fax, mail, in person, online. Both court and visitors may perform in person searches. Search fee: $12.00 per hour. Required to search: name, years to search, DOB. Criminal records on computer from 1980, microfiche from 1950, archives and index from 1800s. Online access to criminal records is the same as civil.

General Information: Public Access terminal is available. No juvenile, mental health, sealed or expunged records released. SASE not required. Turnaround time 3-4 days. Copy fee: $.50 per page. $1.50 per pg for microfilm copies. Certification fee: $2.50. Fee payee: Clerk of District Court. Personal checks accepted. Prepayment is required.

Sheridan County

District Court PO Box 753, Hoxie, KS 67740; 785-675-3451; Fax: 785-675-2256. Hours: 8:30AM-5PM (CST). *Felony, Misdemeanor, Civil, Eviction, Small Claims, Probate.*

Civil Records: Access: Phone, fax, mail, in person. Both court and visitors may perform in person searches.

Search fee: $12.00 per hour. Required to search: name, years to search. Civil cases indexed by defendant, plaintiff. Civil records on strip index from 1885; on computer since. Mail requests require use of a special form.

Criminal Records: Access: Phone, fax, mail, in person. Both court and visitors may perform in person searches. Search fee: $12.00 per hour. Required to search: name, years to search, signed release. Criminal records on strip index from 1885; on computer since.

General Information: No juvenile, mental health, sealed or expunged records released. SASE required. Turnaround time 1-2 days. Copy fee: $.20 per page. Certification fee: $1.00. Fee payee: Clerk of Court. Personal checks accepted. Prepayment is required.

Sherman County

District Court 813 Broadway Rm 201, Goodland, KS 67735; 785-899-4850; Fax: 785-899-4858. Hours: 8:30AM-5PM (MST). *Felony, Misdemeanor, Civil, Eviction, Small Claims, Probate.*

Civil Records: Access: In person only. Visitors must perform in person searches for themselves. No search fee. Required to search: name, years to search. Civil cases indexed by defendant, plaintiff. Civil records on docket books from 1900s.

Criminal Records: Access: In person only. Visitors must perform in person searches for themselves. No search fee. Required to search: name, years to search; also helpful: SSN. Criminal records on docket books from 1900s.

General Information: No juvenile, mental health, sealed or expunged records released. Copy fee: $.25 per page. Certification fee: $1.00. Fee payee: Clerk of District Court. Personal checks accepted.

Smith County

District Court PO Box 273, Smith Center, KS 66967; 785-282-5140/41; Fax: 785-282-5145. Hours: 8AM-5PM (CST). *Felony, Misdemeanor, Civil, Eviction, Small Claims, Probate.*

Civil Records: Access: In person only. Visitors must perform in person searches for themselves. No search fee. Required to search: name, years to search. Civil cases indexed by defendant, plaintiff. Civil records on index cards from 1873.

Criminal Records: Access: In person only. Visitors must perform in person searches for themselves. No search fee. Required to search: name, years to search; also helpful: SSN. Criminal records on index cards from 1873.

General Information: No juvenile, mental health, sealed or expunged records released. Copy fee: $.25 per page. Certification fee: $1.00. Fee payee: Clerk of Court. Personal checks accepted. Prepayment is required.

Stafford County

District Court PO Box 365, St John, KS 67576; 620-549-3295; Fax: 620-549-3298. Hours: 8AM-5PM (CST). *Felony, Misdemeanor, Civil, Eviction, Small Claims, Probate.*

Civil Records: Access: Phone, mail, fax, in person, email. Both court and visitors may perform in person searches. No search fee. Required to search: name, years to search. Civil cases indexed by defendant, plaintiff. Civil records on computer from 1988, microfiche and index from 1900s.

Criminal Records: Access: In person only. Visitors must perform in person searches for themselves. No search fee. Required to search: name, years to search; also helpful: SSN, signed release. Criminal records on computer from 1988, microfiche and index from 1900s.

General Information: Public Access terminal is available. No juvenile, mental health, sealed or expunged records released. SASE required. Turnaround

time 1-3 days. Copy fee: $.15 per page. Certification fee: No cert fee. Fee payee: Clerk of District Court. Personal checks accepted. Prepayment is required.

Stanton County

District Court PO Box 913, Johnson, KS 67855; 620-492-2180; Fax: 620-492-6410. Hours: 8AM-5PM (CST). *Felony, Misdemeanor, Civil, Eviction, Small Claims, Probate.*

Civil Records: Access: Phone, fax, mail, in person. Both court and visitors may perform in person searches. Search fee: $12.00 per hour. Required to search: name, years to search. Civil cases indexed by defendant, plaintiff. Civil records on computer from 1977, index from 1887.

Criminal Records: Access: Phone, fax, mail, in person. Both court and visitors may perform in person searches. Search fee: $12.00 per hour. Required to search: name, years to search, DOB, SSN. Criminal records on computer from 1977, index from 1887.

General Information: Public Access terminal is available. No juvenile, mental health, sealed or expunged records released. SASE required. Turnaround time 1-3 days. Fax notes: $2.00 for first page, $.50 each add'l. Copy fee: $.25 per page. Certification fee: $1.50. Fee payee: Clerk of District Court. Personal checks accepted. Prepayment is required.

Stevens County

District Court 200 E 6th, Hugoton, KS 67951; 620-544-2484; Fax: 620-544-2528. Hours: 8AM-5PM (CST). *Felony, Misdemeanor, Civil, Eviction, Small Claims, Probate.*

Civil Records: Access: Mail, in person. Both court and visitors may perform in person searches. Search fee: $12.00 per hour. Required to search: name, years to search. Civil cases indexed by defendant, plaintiff. Civil records on computer from 1991, microfiche, archives and index from 1887.

Criminal Records: Access: In person only. Visitors must perform in person searches for themselves. No search fee. Required to search: name, years to search; also helpful: SSN. Criminal records on computer from 1991, microfiche, archives and index from 1887.

General Information: Public Access terminal is available. No juvenile, mental health, sealed or expunged records released. SASE required. Turnaround time 1-3 days. Fax notes: Fee to fax results is $3.00 plus $.25 per page. Copy fee: $.25 per page. Certification fee: $1.25. Fee payee: Clerk of District Court. Personal checks accepted. Must prepay for fax and mail.

Sumner County

District Court PO Box 399, Sumner County Courthouse, Wellington, KS 67152; 620-326-5936; Fax: 620-326-5365. Hours: 8AM-Noon, 1-5PM (CST). *Felony, Misdemeanor, Civil, Eviction, Small Claims, Probate.*

Civil Records: Access: Mail, fax in person. Both court and visitors may perform in person searches. No search fee. Required to search: name, years to search. Civil cases indexed by defendant, plaintiff. Civil records on computer from 1991, index cards from 1800s for probate.

Criminal Records: Access: Mail, fax, in person. Visitors must perform in person searches for themselves. No search fee. Required to search: name, years to search; also helpful: case number. Criminal records on computer from 1991, index cards from 1800s for probate.

General Information: No juvenile, mental health, sealed or expunged records released. SASE not required. Turnaround time 1-3 days. Copy fee: $.25 per page. Certification fee: $2.00. Fee payee: Clerk of Court. Personal checks accepted. Prepayment is preferred.

Thomas County

District Court PO Box 805, Colby, KS 67701; 785-462-4540; Fax: 785-462-2291. Hours: 8:30AM-5PM (CST). *Felony, Misdemeanor, Civil, Eviction, Small Claims, Probate.*

Civil Records: Access: Fax, mail, in person. Both court and visitors may perform in person searches. Search fee: $12.00 per hour. Required to search: name, years to search. Civil cases indexed by defendant, plaintiff. Civil records on index from 1887.

Criminal Records: Access: Fax, mail, in person. Both court and visitors may perform in person searches. Search fee: $12.00 per hour. Required to search: name, years to search, DOB, sex; also helpful: SSN. Criminal records on index from 1887.

General Information: Public Access terminal is available. No juvenile, mental health, sealed or expunged records released. SASE required. Turnaround time varies. Fax notes: $1.00 per page. Copy fee: $.25 per page. Certification fee: $1.00. Fee payee: Clerk. Personal checks accepted. Prepayment is required.

Trego County

District Court 216 N Main, Wakeeney, KS 67672; 785-743-2148; Fax: 785-743-2726. Hours: 8:30AM-5PM (CST). *Felony, Misdemeanor, Civil, Eviction, Small Claims, Probate.*

Civil Records: Access: Mail, in person. Both court and visitors may perform in person searches. Search fee: $12.00 per hour. Required to search: name, years to search. Civil cases indexed by defendant, plaintiff. Civil records on computer since 1996; prior records on card index.

Criminal Records: Access: Mail, in person. Both court and visitors may perform in person searches. Search fee: $12.00 per hour. Required to search: name, years to search; also helpful: DOB, SSN, sex. Criminal records on computer since 1996; prior records on card index.

General Information: No juvenile, mental health, sealed or expunged records released. SASE required. Turnaround time 1-2 weeks. Fax notes: Fee to fax results is $5.00 per document. Copy fee: $.20 per page. Certification fee: $2.00. Fee payee: Clerk of Court. Personal checks accepted. Prepayment is required.

Wabaunsee County

District Court Courthouse, PO Box 278, Alma, KS 66401; 785-765-2406; Fax: 785-765-2487. Hours: 8:30AM-4:30PM (CST). *Felony, Misdemeanor, Civil, Eviction, Small Claims, Probate.*

Civil Records: Access: In person only. Visitors must perform in person searches for themselves. No search fee. Required to search: name, years to search. Civil cases indexed by defendant, plaintiff. Civil records on book index from 1800s; on computer back to 1996.

Criminal Records: Access: In person only. Visitors must perform in person searches for themselves. No search fee. Required to search: name, years to search; also helpful: SSN. Criminal records on book index from 1800s; on computer back to 1996.

General Information: Public Access terminal is available. No juvenile, mental health, sealed or expunged records released. Copy fee: $.25 per page. Certification fee: $1.25. Fee payee: Clerk of District Court. Personal checks accepted.

Wallace County

District Court PO Box 8, Sharon Springs, KS 67758; 785-852-4289; Fax: 785-852-4271. Hours: 8AM-Noon,1-5PM (MST). *Felony, Misdemeanor, Civil, Eviction, Small Claims, Probate.*

Civil Records: Access: Mail, in person. Both court and visitors may perform in person searches. No search fee. Required to search: name; also helpful: years to search. Civil cases indexed by defendant, plaintiff. Civil records on index from 1887. By mail only if requested for a particular case, court will not do name searches.

Criminal Records: Access: In person only. Visitors must perform in person searches for themselves. No search fee. Required to search: name; also helpful: years to search. Criminal records on index from 1887.

General Information: No juvenile offender (under 14 years old), juvenile in need of care, adoption, mental health, sealed or expunged records released. SASE not required. Turnaround time 1-2 days. Copy fee: $.25 per page. Certification fee: $1.00. Fee payee: Clerk of Court. Personal checks accepted. Prepayment is required.

Washington County

District Court Courthouse, 214 C Street, Washington, KS 66968; 785-325-2381; Fax: 785-325-2557. Hours: 8AM-Noon,1-5PM (CST). *Felony, Misdemeanor, Civil, Eviction, Small Claims, Probate.*

www.kscourts.org/dstcts/12dstct.htm

Civil Records: Access: Fax, mail, in person. Both court and visitors may perform in person searches. Search fee: $12.00 per hour. Required to search: name, years to search. Civil cases indexed by defendant, plaintiff. Civil records on card index from 1887; computer to 1995.

Criminal Records: Access: Fax, mail, in person. Both court and visitors may perform in person searches. Search fee: $12.00 per hour. Required to search: name, years to search. Criminal records on card index from 1887; on computer back to 1995.

General Information: No juvenile, mental health, sealed or expunged records released. SASE required. Turnaround time 1-3 weeks. Fax notes: Fee to fax results is $3.00 per page. Copy fee: $.25 per page. Certification fee: $1.00. Fee payee: Clerk of Court. Personal checks accepted. Prepayment is required.

Wichita County

District Court 206 S 4th St, PO Box 968, Leoti, KS 67861; 620-375-4454; Fax: 620-375-2999. Hours: 8AM-5PM (CST). *Felony, Misdemeanor, Civil, Eviction, Small Claims, Probate.*

Note: The District Court for Wichita, KS is in Sedgwick County.

Civil Records: Access: Mail, in person. Both court and visitors may perform in person searches. Search fee: $12.00 per hour. Required to search: name, years to

search. Civil cases indexed by defendant, plaintiff. Civil records on computer from 1993, on index from 1892.

Criminal Records: Access: In person only. Visitors must perform in person searches for themselves. Search fee: $12.00 per hour. Required to search: name, years to search. Criminal records on computer from 1993, on index from 1892. Criminal records are available through the KBI.

General Information: Public Access terminal is available. (Indexed only from 1991.) No juvenile, mental health, sealed or expunged records released. SASE required. Turnaround time 1 week. Copy fee: $.20 per page. Certification fee: $1.00. Fee payee: Clerk of District Court. Personal checks accepted. Prepayment is required.

Wilson County

District Court PO Box 246, Fredonia, KS 66736; 620-378-4533; Fax: 620-378-4531. Hours: 8:30AM-5PM (CST). *Felony, Misdemeanor, Civil, Eviction, Small Claims, Probate.*

Civil Records: Access: Fax, mail, in person. Both court and visitors may perform in person searches. Search fee: $12.00 per hour. Required to search: name, years to search. Civil cases indexed by defendant, plaintiff. Civil records on computer since 1993, index cards from 1864.

Criminal Records: Access: Fax, mail, in person. Both court and visitors may perform in person searches. Search fee: $12.00 per hour. Required to search: name, years to search; also helpful: SSN. Criminal records on computer since 1993, index cards from 1864.

General Information: Public Access terminal is available. No juvenile, mental health, sealed or expunged records released. SASE required. Turnaround time 1-3 weeks. Fax notes: Fee to fax results is $1.00 per page. Copy fee: $.25 per page. Certification fee: $.50. Fee payee: Clerk of Court. Personal checks accepted. Prepayment is required.

Woodson County

District Court PO Box 228, Yates Center, KS 66783; 620-625-8610; Fax: 620-625-8674. Hours: 8AM-Noon,1-5PM (CST). *Felony, Misdemeanor, Civil, Eviction, Small Claims, Probate.*

Civil Records: Access: Fax, mail, in person. Both court and visitors may perform in person searches. No search fee. Required to search: name, years to search. Civil

cases indexed by defendant, plaintiff. Civil records on index from 1880s, on computer since 1993.

Criminal Records: Access: In person only. Visitors must perform in person searches for themselves. No search fee. Required to search: name, years to search. Criminal records on index from 1880s, on computer since 1993. Refer phone inquires to KBI at 785-296-8200.

General Information: Public Access terminal is available. No juvenile (under age 14 years), mental health, sealed or expunged records released. SASE required. Turnaround time 1 day. Fax notes: Fee to fax results is $1.00 per page. Copy fee: $.50 per page. Certification fee: $1.00. Fee payee: District Court. Business checks accepted. Prepayment is required.

Wyandotte County

District Court 710 N 7th St, Kansas City, KS 66101; Civil phone: 913-573-2901; Criminal phone: 913-573-2905; Fax: 913-573-8177. Hours: 8AM-5PM (CST). *Felony, Misdemeanor, Civil, Eviction, Small Claims, Probate.*

Civil Records: Access: Phone, mail, online, in person. Both court and visitors may perform in person searches. No search fee. Required to search: name, years to search. Civil cases indexed by defendant, plaintiff. Civil records on computer from 1975, microfiche, archives and index from 1900s. Access to the remote online system requires specific software and a $20 setup fee. Transactions are $.05 each. For more information call 913-573-2885.

Criminal Records: Access: Online, in person. Visitors must perform in person searches for themselves. No search fee. Required to search: name, years to search, DOB, SSN. Criminal records on computer from 1972, microfiche, archives and index from early 1900s. Online access to criminal records is the same as civil. Refer phone inquires to KBI at 785-296-8200.

General Information: No juvenile, mental health, sealed or expunged records released. SASE required. Turnaround time 1-3 days. Copy fee: $.25 per page. Certification fee: $1.00. Fee payee: Clerk of District Court. Personal checks accepted.

Kansas Recording Offices

ORGANIZATION   105 counties, 105 recording offices. The recording officer is Register of Deeds. Many counties utilize a "Miscellaneous Index" for tax and other liens, separate from real estate records. 100 counties are in the Central Time Zone (CST) and 5 are in the Mountain Time Zone (MST).

REAL ESTATE RECORDS   Most counties will not perform real estate searches, although some will do as an accommodation with the understanding that they are not "certified." Some counties will also do a search based upon legal description to determine owner. Copy fees vary, and certification fees are usually $1.00 per document. Tax records are located at the Appraiser's Office.

UCC RECORDS   Financing statements are filed at the state level, except for real estate related collateral, which are filed with the Register of Deeds. However, prior to 07/2001, consumer goods collateral were also filed at the Register of Deeds and these older records can be searched there. All counties will perform UCC searches. Use search request form UCC-3. Search fees are usually $15.00 per debtor name. Copies usually cost $1.00 per page.

TAX LIEN RECORDS   Federal tax liens on personal property of businesses are filed with the Secretary of State. Other federal tax liens and all state tax liens on personal property are filed with the county Register of Deeds. Most counties automatically include tax liens on personal property with a UCC search. Tax liens on personal property may usually be searched separately for $8.00 per name.

OTHER LIENS   Mechanics, harvesters, lis pendens, threshers.

Allen County
County Register of Deeds, P.O. Box 15, Iola, KS 66749. 620-365-1412; Fax 620-365-1414. www.ksrods.org
Will search UCC records. UCC search includes tax liens. Will not search real estate records. **Other Phone Numbers:** Treasurer 620-365-1409; Appraiser/Auditor 620-365-1415; Elections 620-365-1407; Vital Records 785-296-1400 (Topeka); Clerk of District Court (Marriage, etc.) 620-365-1425; City of Iola Clerk (Birth & Death before 1911) 620-365-4910;

Anderson County
County Register of Deeds, Courthouse, 100 E. 4th Street, Garnett, KS 66032-1503. County Register of Deeds, R/E and UCC Recording 785-448-3715; Fax 785-448-5621.
Will search UCC records. UCC search includes tax liens. Will not search real estate records. **Other Phone Numbers:** Assessor 785-448-6844; Treasurer 785-448-5824; Appraiser/Auditor 785-448-6844; Elections 785-448-6841; Vital Records 785-448-4564.

Atchison County
County Register of Deeds, 423 North 5th St., Courthouse, Atchison, KS 66002-1861. 913-367-2568; Fax 913-367-0227.
Will search UCC records. UCC search includes tax liens if requested. RE owner, mortgage, and property transfer searches available.

Barber County
County Register of Deeds, 120 East Washington Street, Courthouse, Medicine Lodge, KS 67104. 620-886-3981; Fax 620-886-5045.
Will search UCC records. UCC search includes tax liens. Will search real estate records on a limited basis. **Other Phone Numbers:** Assessor 620-886-3723; Treasurer 620-886-3775; Elections 620-886-3961.

Barton County
County Register of Deeds, Courthouse, #205, 1400 Main St., Great Bend, KS 67530-4037. 620-793-1849; Fax 620-793-1990.
Will search UCC records. UCC search includes tax liens. Will not search real estate records. **Other Phone Numbers:** Assessor 620-793-1821; Treasurer 620-793-1827.

Bourbon County
County Register of Deeds, 210 South National, Fort Scott, KS 66701. 620-223-3800 x17; Fax 620-223-5241.
Will search UCC records. UCC search includes tax liens. Will not search real estate records. **Other Phone Numbers:** Assessor 620-223-3800 x16; Treasurer 620-223-3800 x29.

Brown County
County Register of Deeds, Courthouse, 601 Oregon, Hiawatha, KS 66434. County Register of Deeds, R/E and UCC Recording 785-742-3741; Fax 785-742-3255.
Will search UCC records. UCC search includes tax liens. RE record owner and mortgage searches available. **Other Phone Numbers:** Assessor 785-742-7232; Treasurer 785-742-2051; Appraiser/Auditor 785-742-7232; Elections 785-742-2581.

Butler County
County Register of Deeds, 205 West Central, Courthouse, Suite 104, El Dorado, KS 67042. 316-322-4113; Fax 316-321-1011.
Will search UCC records. UCC search includes tax liens if requested. Will not search real estate records. **Other Phone Numbers:** Assessor 316-321-4220; Treasurer 316-322-4210.

Chase County
County Register of Deeds, P.O. Box 59, Cottonwood Falls, KS 66845-0059. County Register of Deeds, R/E and UCC Recording 620-273-6398; Fax 620-273-6617.
Will search UCC records. UCC search includes tax liens if requested. Will not search real estate records. **Other Phone Numbers:** Assessor 620-273-6423; Treasurer 620-273-6493; Appraiser/Auditor 620-273-6306; Elections 620-273-6423; Vital Records 620-273-6398.

Chautauqua County
County Register of Deeds, 215 North Chautauqua, Courthouse, Sedan, KS 67361. 620-725-5830; Fax 620-725-5831.
Will search UCC records. UCC search includes tax liens. Will not search real estate records. **Other Phone Numbers:** Assessor 620-725-3127; Treasurer 620-725-3666.

Cherokee County
County Register of Deeds, P.O. Box 228, Columbus, KS 66725. County Register of Deeds, R/E and UCC Recording 620-429-3777; Fax 620-429-1362.
Will search UCC records. UCC search includes tax liens. Will not search real estate records. **Other Phone Numbers:** Assessor 620-429-3984; Treasurer 620-429-2418; Appraiser/Auditor 620-429-3984; Elections 620-429-8043.

Cheyenne County
County Register of Deeds, P.O. Box 907, St. Francis, KS 67756-0907. 785-332-8820; Fax 785-332-8825.
Will search UCC records. UCC search includes tax liens. Will not search real estate records. **Other Phone Numbers:** Assessor 785-332-8830; Treasurer 785-332-8810; Appraiser/Auditor 785-332-8830; Elections 785-332-8830; Vital Records 785-332-8850.

Clark County
County Register of Deeds, P.O. Box 222, Ashland, KS 67831-0222. County Register of Deeds, R/E and UCC Recording 620-635-2812; Fax 620-635-2393.
Will search UCC records. UCC search includes tax liens. Will not search real estate records. **Other Phone Numbers:** Assessor 620-635-2142; Treasurer 620-635-2745; Appraiser/Auditor 620-635-2142; Elections 620-635-2813.

Clay County
County Register of Deeds, P.O. Box 63, Clay Center, KS 67432. 785-632-3811; Fax 785-632-2651.
Will search UCC records. UCC search includes tax liens. RE owner, mortgage, and property transfer searches available. **Other Phone Numbers:** Assessor 785-632-2800; Treasurer 785-632-3282.

Cloud County
County Register of Deeds, P.O. Box 96, Concordia, KS 66901-0096. 785-243-8121; Fax 785-243-8123.
Will search UCC records. UCC search includes tax liens. Will not search real estate records. **Other Phone Numbers:** Assessor 785-243-8100.

Coffey County

County Register of Deeds, 110 S 6th St, Rm 205 - Courthouse, 110 S. 6th St., Burlington, KS 66839. 620-364-2423.
Will search UCC records. UCC search includes tax liens. Will not search real estate records. **Other Phone Numbers:** Assessor 620-364-8426; Treasurer 620-364-5532.

Comanche County

County Register of Deeds, P.O. Box 576, Coldwater, KS 67029-0576. County Register of Deeds, R/E and UCC Recording 620-582-2152; Fax 620-582-2390.
Will search UCC records. UCC search includes tax liens. Will not search real estate records, but will help walk-ins. **Other Phone Numbers:** Assessor 620-582-2544; Treasurer 620-582-2964; Appraiser/Auditor 620-582-2544; Elections 620-582-2361.

Cowley County

County Register of Deeds, P.O. Box 741, Winfield, KS 67156-0471. 620-221-5461; Fax 620-221-5463.
Will search UCC records. UCC search includes tax liens. Will not search real estate records. **Other Phone Numbers:** Assessor 620-221-5430; Treasurer 620-221-5412.

Crawford County

County Register of Deeds, P.O. Box 44, Girard, KS 66743. 620-724-8218; Fax 620-724-8823.
Will search UCC records. UCC search includes tax liens. RE record owner and mortgage searches available. **Other Phone Numbers:** Assessor 620-724-6431.

Decatur County

County Register of Deeds, P.O. Box 167, Oberlin, KS 67749-0167. County Register of Deeds, R/E and UCC Recording 785-475-8105; Fax 785-475-8150.
Will search UCC records. UCC search includes tax liens. Will not search real estate records. **Other Phone Numbers:** Assessor 785-475-8109; Treasurer 785-475-8103; Appraiser/Auditor 785-475-8109; Elections 785-475-8102; Vital Records 785-475-8105; Clerk of District Court 785-475-8107; Decatur County Clerk 785-475-8102;

Dickinson County

County Register of Deeds, P.O. Box 517, Abilene, KS 67410. 785-263-3073; Fax 785-263-1512.
Will search UCC records. UCC search includes tax liens if requested. RE owner, mortgage, and property transfer searches available. **Other Phone Numbers:** Assessor 785-263-4418; Treasurer 785-263-3231.

Doniphan County

County Register of Deeds, P.O. Box 73, Troy, KS 66087. 785-985-3932; Fax 785-985-3723.
Will search UCC records. UCC search includes tax liens if requested. RE owner, mortgage, and property transfer searches; fee is $6.00 per hour plus $.50 per copy **Other Phone Numbers:** Assessor 785-985-3977; Treasurer 785-985-3831; Elections 785-985-3513.

Douglas County

County Register of Deeds, 1100 Massachusetts, Courthouse, Lawrence, KS 66044-3097. 785-832-5283; Fax 785-841-4036. http://www.douglas-county.com
Will search UCC records. UCC search includes tax liens. Will not search real estate records. **Online Access:** Property Appraiser, Real Estate. Two non-government Internet sites provide free access to records from the Douglas County Assessor. Find County Property Appraiser records at www.douglas-county.com/value. Douglas County property valuations can be found at http://hometown.lawrence.com/valuation/valuation.cgi. **Other Phone Numbers:** Assessor 785-841-7700 x107; Treasurer 785-841-7700.

Edwards County

County Register of Deeds, P.O. Box 264, Kinsley, KS 67547-0364. 620-659-3131; Fax 620-659-2583.
Will search UCC records. UCC search includes tax liens. Will not search real estate records. **Other Phone Numbers:** Assessor 620-659-2406; Treasurer 620-659-3132.

Elk County

County Register of Deeds, P.O. Box 476, Howard, KS 67349-0476. County Register of Deeds, R/E and UCC Recording 620-374-2472; Fax 620-374-2771.
Will search UCC records. UCC search includes tax liens. Will not search real estate records. **Other Phone Numbers:** Assessor 620-374-2832; Treasurer 620-374-2256; Appraiser/Auditor 620-374-2832; Elections 620-374-2490; Vital Records 620-374-2370.

Ellis County

County Register of Deeds, P.O. Box 654, Hays, KS 67601. County Register of Deeds, R/E and UCC Recording 785-628-9450 UCC Recording: 785-628-9451; Fax 785-628-9451. www.ksrods.org
Will search UCC records. UCC search includes tax liens if requested. Will not search real estate records. **Other Phone Numbers:** Assessor 785-628-9400; Treasurer 785-628-9466; Appraiser/Auditor 785-628-9400; Elections 785-628-9410; Vital Records 785-628-9450.

Ellsworth County

County Register of Deeds, 210 N. Kansas, Courthouse, Ellsworth, KS 67439-3118. 785-472-3022; Fax 785-472-4912.
Will search UCC records. UCC search includes tax liens. RE owner, mortgage, and property transfer searches available. **Other Phone Numbers:** Assessor 785-472-3165; Treasurer 785-472-4152.

Finney County

County Register of Deeds, P.O. Box M, Garden City, KS 67846. County Register of Deeds, R/E and UCC Recording 620-272-3520; Fax 620-272-3624. http://www.finneycounty.org/
Will search UCC records. UCC search includes tax liens. Will not search real estate records. **Other Phone Numbers:** Assessor 620-272-3517; Treasurer 620-373-3526; Appraiser/Auditor 620-272-3585; Elections 620-272-3523.

Ford County

County Register of Deeds, P.O. Box 1352, Dodge City, KS 67801-1352. 620-227-4565; Fax 620-227-4699.
Will search UCC records. UCC search includes tax liens. RE owner, mortgage, and property transfer searches available. **Other Phone Numbers:** Assessor 620-227-4516; Treasurer 620-227-4535.

Franklin County

County Register of Deeds, 315 South Main, Courthouse, Room 103, Ottawa, KS 66067-2335. 785-229-3440; Fax 785-229-3419.
Will search UCC records. UCC search includes tax liens. RE record owner searches available. **Other Phone Numbers:** Assessor 785-242-2573; Treasurer 785-242-4201.

Geary County

County Register of Deeds, P.O. Box 927, Junction City, KS 66441-2591. 785-238-5531; Fax 785-238-5419.
Will search UCC records. UCC search includes tax liens. Will not search real estate records. **Other Phone Numbers:** Assessor 785-238-4407; Treasurer 785-238-3912.

Gove County

County Register of Deeds, P.O. Box 116, Gove, KS 67736. County Register of Deeds, R/E and UCC Recording 785-938-4465; Fax 785-938-4486.
Will search UCC records. UCC search includes tax liens if requested. Will search real estate records. **Other Phone Numbers:** Assessor 785-938-2301; Treasurer 785-938-2275; Appraiser/Auditor 785-938-2301; Elections 785-938-2300; Vital Records 785-938-4465.

Graham County

County Register of Deeds, 410 North Pomeroy, Hill City, KS 67642. 785-421-2551; Fax 785-421-5463.
Will search UCC records. UCC search includes tax liens. Will not search real estate records. **Other Phone Numbers:** Assessor 785-674-2196; Treasurer 785-674-2331.

Grant County

County Register of Deeds, 108 S. Glenn, Lower Level, Courthouse, Ulysses, KS 67880. 620-356-1538; Fax 620-356-5379.
Will search UCC records. UCC search includes tax liens. Will not search real estate records. **Other Phone Numbers:** Assessor 620-356-3362; Treasurer 620-356-1551.

Gray County

County Register of Deeds, P.O. Box 487, Cimarron, KS 67835-0487. 620-855-3835; Fax 620-855-3107.
Will search UCC records. UCC search includes tax liens. RE owner, mortgage, and property transfer searches available. **Other Phone Numbers:** Assessor 620-855-3858; Treasurer 620-855-3861; Appraiser/Auditor 620-855-3858; Elections 620-855-3618.

Greeley County

County Register of Deeds, P.O. Box 12, Tribune, KS 67879. 620-376-4275; Fax 620-376-2294.
Will search UCC records. UCC search includes tax liens. Will not search real estate records. **Other Phone Numbers:** Assessor 620-376-4057; Treasurer 620-376-4413.

Greenwood County

County Register of Deeds, Courthouse, 311 N. Main, Eureka, KS 67045-1311. 620-583-8162; Fax 620-583-8124.
Will search UCC records. UCC search includes tax liens. Will search by legal description. **Other Phone Numbers:** Assessor 620-583-7431; Treasurer 620-583-8146.

Hamilton County

County Register of Deeds, P.O. Box 1167, Syracuse, KS 67878. 620-384-6925; Fax 620-384-5853.
Will search UCC records. UCC search includes tax liens. Will not search real estate records. **Other Phone Numbers:** Assessor 620-384-5451; Treasurer 620-384-5522.

Harper County

County Register of Deeds, Courthouse, 201 North Jennings, Anthony, KS 67003. 620-842-5336; Fax 620-842-3455. http://www.harpercounty.org/toc.htm
Will search UCC records. UCC search includes tax liens. Will search by RE record owner as a courtesy. **Other Phone Numbers:** Assessor 620-842-3718; Treasurer 620-842-5191; Elections 620-842-5555.

Harvey County

County Register of Deeds, P.O. Box 687, Newton, KS 67114-0687. County Register of Deeds, R/E & UCC Recording 316-284-6950; Fax 316-284-6951.
Will search UCC records. UCC search includes tax liens if requested. RE owner, mortgage, and property transfer searches available. **Other Phone Numbers:** Assessor 316-284-6815; Treasurer 316-284-6975; Appraiser/Auditor 316-284-6815; Elections 316-284-6842.

Haskell County

County Register of Deeds, P.O. Box 656, Sublette, KS 67877. 620-675-8343.
Will search UCC records. Tax liens included in UCC search and will search separately. Will not search real estate records. **Other Phone Numbers:** Assessor 620-675-8269; Treasurer 620-675-2265.

Hodgeman County

County Register of Deeds, P.O. Box 505, Jetmore, KS 67854-0505. 620-357-8536; Fax 620-357-8300.
Will search UCC records. UCC search includes tax liens. Will not search real estate records. **Other Phone Numbers:** Assessor 620-357-8366; Treasurer 620-357-6236.

Jackson County

County Register of Deeds, Courthouse, Room 203, 415 New York, Holton, KS 66436. 785-364-3591; Fax 785-364-3420.
Will search UCC records. UCC search includes tax liens. Will look up last owner or mortgagor. **Other Phone Numbers:** Assessor 785-364-5256; Treasurer 785-364-3791.

Jefferson County

County Register of Deeds, P.O. Box 352, Oskaloosa, KS 66066-0352. County Register of Deeds, R/E and UCC Recording 785-863-2243; Fax 785-863-2602.
Will search UCC records. UCC search includes tax liens. RE record owner searches, but indexed by location. **Other Phone Numbers:** Assessor 785-863-2080; Treasurer 785-863-2691; Appraiser/Auditor 785-863-2552; Elections 785-863-2272.

Jewell County

County Register of Deeds, 307 North Commercial Street, Courthouse, Mankato, KS 66956-2093. County Register of Deeds, R/E and UCC Recording 785-378-4070; Fax 785-378-4075.
Will search UCC records. This agency will not do a tax lien search. Will not search real estate records. **Other Phone Numbers:** Assessor 785-378-4000; Treasurer 785-378-4090; Appraiser/Auditor 785-378-4000; Elections 785-378-4020.

Johnson County

County Register of Deeds, P.O. Box 700, Olathe, KS 66051. 913-715-2300 x5375; Fax 913-715-2310.
http://www.jocoks.com/appraiser
Will search UCC records. UCC search includes tax liens. Will not search real estate records. **Online Access:** Property Appraiser. Records on the Johnson County Kansas Land Records database are available free online at www.jocoks.com/appraiser/disclaim.html. At the bottom of the Disclaimer page, click on "Yes" under "I understand and accept the above statement.". **Other Phone Numbers:** Assessor 913-764-5335; Treasurer 913-764-8484 x5380.

Kearny County

County Register of Deeds, P.O. Box 42, Lakin, KS 67860. County Register of Deeds, R/E and UCC Recording 620-355-6241; Fax 620-355-7382.

Will search UCC records. UCC search includes Federal tax liens Will not search real estate records. **Other Phone Numbers:** Assessor 620-355-6427; Treasurer 620-355-6372; Appraiser/Auditor 620-355-6427; Elections 620-355-6422.

Kingman County

County Register of Deeds, P.O. Box 461, Kingman, KS 67068. County Register of Deeds, R/E and UCC Recording 620-532-3211; Fax 620-532-2037.
Will search UCC records. Tax liens not included in UCC search. Will not search real estate records. **Other Phone Numbers:** Assessor 620-532-5119; Treasurer 620-532-3461; Appraiser/Auditor 620-532-5119; Elections 620-532-2521.

Kiowa County

County Register of Deeds, 211 East Florida, Greensburg, KS 67054. 620-723-2441; Fax 620-723-1033.
Will search UCC records. UCC search includes tax liens. Will not search real estate records. **Other Phone Numbers:** Assessor 620-723-3366; Treasurer 620-723-2681.

Labette County

County Register of Deeds, Courthouse, 521 Merchant, Oswego, KS 67356. County Register of Deeds, R/E and UCC Recording 620-795-4931; Fax 620-795-2928.
Will search UCC records. UCC search includes tax liens if requested. Will not search real estate records. **Other Phone Numbers:** Assessor 620-795-2548; Treasurer 620-795-2918; Appraiser/Auditor 620-795-2548; Elections 620-795-2138.

Lane County

County Register of Deeds, P.O. Box 805, Dighton, KS 67839-0805. County Register of Deeds, R/E and UCC Recording 620-397-2803; Fax 620-397-5937.
Will search UCC records. UCC search includes tax liens. RE owner, mortgage, and property transfer searches available. **Other Phone Numbers:** Assessor 620-397-2804; Treasurer 620-397-2802; Appraiser/Auditor 620-397-2804; Elections 620-397-5356.

Leavenworth County

County Register of Deeds, 300 Walnut, Room 103, Courthouse, Leavenworth, KS 66048. 913-684-0424; Fax 913-684-0406.
Will search UCC records. UCC search includes tax liens if requested. Will not search real estate records. **Other Phone Numbers:** Assessor 913-684-0440; Treasurer 913-684-0430.

Lincoln County

County Register of Deeds, 216 East Lincoln, Lincoln, KS 67455-2056. 785-524-4657; Fax 785-524-5008.
Will search UCC records. UCC search includes tax liens. Will not search real estate records. **Other Phone Numbers:** Treasurer 785-524-4190; Appraiser/Auditor 785-524-4958; Elections 785-524-4757.

Linn County

County Register of Deeds, P.O. Box 350, Mound City, KS 66056-0350. 913-795-2226; Fax 913-795-2889.
Will search UCC records. UCC search includes tax liens if requested. Will not search real estate records. **Other Phone Numbers:** Assessor 913-795-2536; Treasurer 913-795-2227.

Logan County

County Register of Deeds, 710 West 2nd Street, Courthouse, Oakley, KS 67748. County Register of Deeds, R/E and UCC Recording 785-672-4224; Fax 785-672-3517.

Will search UCC records. Tax liens not included in UCC search. Will not search real estate records. **Other Phone Numbers:** Assessor 785-672-4821; Treasurer 785-672-3216; Appraiser/Auditor 785-672-4821; Elections 785-672-4244; County Clerk 785-672-4244.

Lyon County

County Register of Deeds, 402 Commercial Street, Emporia, KS 66801. County Register of Deeds, R/E and UCC Recording 620-341-3241; Fax 620-342-2652.
Will search UCC records. UCC search includes tax liens. RE record owner and mortgage searches available.

Marion County

County Register of Deeds, P.O. Box 158, Marion, KS 66861-0158. 620-382-2151; Fax 620-382-3420.
Will search UCC records. UCC search includes tax liens if requested. Will not search real estate records. **Other Phone Numbers:** Assessor 620-382-3715.

Marshall County

County Register of Deeds, 1201 Broadway, Courthouse, Marysville, KS 66508. 785-562-3226; Fax 785-562-5685.
Will search UCC records. UCC search includes tax liens. Will not search real estate records. **Other Phone Numbers:** Assessor 785-562-3301; Treasurer 785-562-5363.

McPherson County

County Register of Deeds, P.O. Box 86, McPherson, KS 67460. 620-241-5050; Fax 620-241-1372.
Will search UCC records. UCC search includes tax liens. RE record owner and mortgage searches available. **Other Phone Numbers:** Assessor 620-241-5870; Treasurer 620-241-3664.

Meade County

County Register of Deeds, P.O. Box 399, Meade, KS 67864-0399. 620-873-8705; Fax 620-873-8713.
Will search UCC records. UCC search includes tax liens. Will not search real estate records. **Other Phone Numbers:** Assessor 620-873-8710; Treasurer 620-873-8740; Appraiser/Auditor 620-873-8710; Elections 620-873-8700.

Miami County

County Register of Deeds, 201 S. Pearl St. #101, Paola, KS 66071. 913-294-3716; Fax 913-294-9515.
Will search UCC records. This agency will not do a tax lien search. Will not search real estate records. **Other Phone Numbers:** Assessor 913-294-9311; Treasurer 913-294-2353.

Mitchell County

County Register of Deeds, P.O. Box 6, Beloit, KS 67420. 785-738-3854; Fax 785-738-5844.
Will search UCC records. UCC search includes tax liens if requested. Will search by RE legal description. **Other Phone Numbers:** Assessor 785-738-5061; Treasurer 785-738-3411.

Montgomery County

County Register of Deeds, P.O. Box 647, Independence, KS 67301. 620-331-2180; Fax 620-331-2619.
Will search UCC records. This agency will not do a tax lien search. Will not search real estate records. **Other Phone Numbers:** Assessor 620-331-4510; Treasurer 620-331-3040.

Morris County

County Register of Deeds, Courthouse, Council Grove, KS 66846. 620-767-5614; Fax 620-767-6861.

Will search UCC records. UCC search includes tax liens if requested. Will not search real estate records. **Other Phone Numbers:** Assessor 620-767-5617; Treasurer 620-767-5614.

Morton County

County Register of Deeds, P.O. Box 756, Elkhart, KS 67950-0756. 620-697-2561; Fax 620-697-4386. Will search UCC records. UCC search includes tax liens if requested. Will not search real estate records. **Other Phone Numbers:** Assessor 620-697-2106; Treasurer 620-697-2560.

Nemaha County

County Register of Deeds, P.O. Box 211, Seneca, KS 66538. 785-336-2120; Fax 785-336-3373. Will search UCC records. UCC search includes tax liens if requested. Will not search real estate records. **Other Phone Numbers:** Assessor 785-336-2179; Treasurer 785-336-2106.

Neosho County

County Register of Deeds, P.O. Box 138, Erie, KS 66733-0138. 620-244-3858; Fax 620-244-3860. Will search UCC records. UCC search includes tax liens if requested. Will not search real estate records. **Other Phone Numbers:** Assessor 620-244-3821; Treasurer 620-244-3800.

Ness County

County Register of Deeds, P.O. Box 127, Ness City, KS 67560. 785-798-3127; Fax 785-798-3829. Will search UCC records. UCC search includes tax liens. Will not search real estate records. **Other Phone Numbers:** Assessor 785-798-2777.

Norton County

County Register of Deeds, P.O. Box 70, Norton, KS 67654. County Register of Deeds, R/E and UCC Recording 785-877-5765; Fax 785-877-5703. Will search UCC records. Tax liens not included in UCC search. RE owner, mortgage, and property transfer searches available. **Other Phone Numbers:** Assessor 785-877-5700; Treasurer 785-877-5795.

Osage County

County Register of Deeds, P.O. Box 265, Lyndon, KS 66451-0265. 785-828-4523; Fax 785-828-4749. www.osageco.org Will search UCC records. UCC search includes tax liens if requested. Will not search real estate records. **Other Phone Numbers:** Assessor 913-828-3124; Treasurer 913-828-4923.

Osborne County

County Register of Deeds, P.O. Box 160, Osborne, KS 67473-0160. 785-346-2452; Fax 785-346-5992. Will search UCC records. UCC search includes tax liens. RE owner, mortgage, and property transfer searches available. **Other Phone Numbers:** Assessor 785-346-2310; Treasurer 785-346-2251; Appraiser/Auditor 785-346-2310.

Ottawa County

County Register of Deeds, Courthouse - Suite 220, 307 N. Concord, Minneapolis, KS 67467-2140. 785-392-2078; Fax 785-392-3605. Will search UCC records. Will search by RE name or legal description. **Other Phone Numbers:** Assessor 785-392-3037; Treasurer 785-392-3129.

Pawnee County

County Register of Deeds, Courthouse, 2nd Floor, 715 Broadway St., Larned, KS 67550-3097. County

Register of Deeds, R/E and UCC Recording 620-285-3276; Fax 620-285-3802. Will search UCC records. UCC search includes tax liens. Will look up last deed of record. **Other Phone Numbers:** Assessor 620-285-2915; Treasurer 620-285-3746; Appraiser/Auditor 620-285-2915; Elections 620-285-3721; Vital Records 620-285-6937.

Phillips County

County Register of Deeds, Courthouse, 301 State St., Phillipsburg, KS 67661. 785-543-6875; Fax 785-999-9999. Will search UCC records. UCC search includes tax liens. Will not search real estate records. **Other Phone Numbers:** Assessor 785-543-6810; Treasurer 785-543-6895.

Pottawatomie County

County Register of Deeds, P.O. Box 186, Westmoreland, KS 66549. 785-457-3471; Fax 785-457-3577. Will search UCC records. UCC search includes tax liens. RE record owner and mortgage searches available. **Other Phone Numbers:** Assessor 785-457-3500; Treasurer 785-457-3681.

Pratt County

County Register of Deeds, P.O. Box 873, Pratt, KS 67124. County Register of Deeds, R/E and UCC Recording 620-672-4140; Fax 620-672-9541. www.prattcounty.org Will search UCC records. This agency will not do a tax lien search. Will not search real estate records. **Other Phone Numbers:** Assessor 620-672-4112; Treasurer 620-672-4118; Appraiser/Auditor 620-672-4112; Elections 620-672-4110; District Court (probates & state tax liens) 620-672-4110.

Rawlins County

County Register of Deeds, P.O. Box 201, Atwood, KS 67730. County Register of Deeds, R/E and UCC Recording 785-626-3172; Fax 785-626-9481. Will search UCC records. UCC search includes tax liens. Will not search real estate records. **Other Phone Numbers:** Assessor 785-626-3101; Treasurer 785-626-3331.

Reno County

County Register of Deeds, 206 West First, Hutchinson, KS 67501. 620-694-2942; Fax 620-694-2944. Will search UCC records. UCC search includes tax liens. Will not search real estate records. **Other Phone Numbers:** Assessor 620-694-2915; Treasurer 620-694-2938.

Republic County

County Register of Deeds, P.O. Box 429, Belleville, KS 66935. 785-527-5691 x224; Fax 785-527-2659. Will search UCC records. UCC search includes tax liens. RE record owner and mortgage searches available. **Other Phone Numbers:** Assessor 785-527-5691; Treasurer 785-527-5691.

Rice County

County Register of Deeds, 101 West Commercial, Lyons, KS 67554. 620-257-2931; Fax 620-257-3039. Will search UCC records. UCC search includes tax liens. RE owner, mortgage, and property transfer searches available. **Other Phone Numbers:** Assessor 620-257-3611; Treasurer 620-257-2852.

Riley County

County Register of Deeds, 110 Courthouse Plaza, 5th & Humboldt Sts., Manhattan, KS 66502-6018. County Register of Deeds, R/E and UCC Recording 785-537-

6340; Fax 785-537-6343. http://www.co.riley.ks.us/deeds.html Will search UCC records. This agency will not do a tax lien search. Will not search real estate records. **Other Phone Numbers:** Assessor 785-537-6310; Treasurer 785-537-6320; Appraiser/Auditor 785-537-6310.

Rooks County

County Register of Deeds, 115 North Walnut St., Stockton, KS 67669. 785-425-6291. Will search UCC records. Tax liens not included in UCC search. Will not search real estate records. **Other Phone Numbers:** Assessor 785-425-6262; Treasurer 785-425-6291.

Rush County

County Register of Deeds, P.O. Box 117, La Crosse, KS 67548. 785-222-3312; Fax 785-222-3559. Will search UCC records. UCC search includes tax liens. Will give owner for a property. **Other Phone Numbers:** Assessor 785-222-2659; Treasurer 785-222-3416.

Russell County

County Register of Deeds, PO Box 191, Russell, KS 67665. County Register of Deeds, R/E and UCC Recording 785-483-4612; Fax 785-483-5725. Will search UCC records. UCC search includes tax liens. **Other Phone Numbers:** Assessor 785-483-5551; Treasurer 785-483-2251; Appraiser/Auditor 785-483-5551; Elections 785-483-4641.

Saline County

County Register of Deeds, P.O. Box 5040, Salina, KS 67402-5040. 785-309-5855; Fax 785-309-5856. http://www.co.saline.ks.us Will search UCC records. UCC search includes tax liens. Will not search real estate records. **Other Phone Numbers:** Assessor 785-309-5800; Treasurer 785-309-5860.

Scott County

County Register of Deeds, Courthouse, 303 Court St., Scott City, KS 67871. 620-872-3155; Fax 620-872-7145. Will search UCC records. UCC search includes tax liens. Will do limited real estate record searches. **Other Phone Numbers:** Assessor 620-872-5446; Treasurer 620-872-2640; Appraiser/Auditor 620-872-5446; Elections 620-872-2420.

Sedgwick County

County Register of Deeds, PO Box 3326, Wichita, KS 67201-3326. 316-383-7425; Fax 316-383-8066. http://www.co.sedgwick.ks.us/dept.htm Will search UCC records. UCC search includes tax liens if requested. Will not search real estate records. **Online Access:** Real Estate, Liens, Tax Assessor Records. Records are available two ways. Records on the Sedgwick County online system are available for a set up fee of $225, with a $49 monthly fee, and a per transaction charge of $.03-$.04. Lending agency information is available. For information, call John Zukovich at 316-383-7384. A sex offender registry list is available on the Web at the county departments page. County Treasurer & Appraiser database records are available free online at www.co.sedgwick.ks.us/Appraiser/RealProperty.htm. Search by city, street numbers or street name for property tax/appraisal information. No name searching. **Other Phone Numbers:** Assessor 316-383-7461; Treasurer 316-383-7707.

Seward County

County Register of Deeds, 415 North Washington, Courthouse, Suite 105, Liberal, KS 67901. County Register of Deeds, R/E and UCC Recording 620-626-3220; Fax 620-626-5031.

Will search UCC records. UCC search includes tax liens. Will not search real estate records. **Other Phone Numbers:** Treasurer 620-626-3216; Appraiser/Auditor 620-626-3252; Elections 620-626-3201.

Shawnee County

County Register of Deeds, 200 East 7th Street, Suite 108, Topeka, KS 66603-3932. 785-233-8200 x4021; Fax 785-291-4912.

Will search UCC records. Will not search real estate records. **Other Phone Numbers:** Assessor 785-233-8200 x5151; Treasurer 785-233-8200 x5161.

Sheridan County

County Register of Deeds, P.O. Box 899, Hoxie, KS 67740-0899. 785-675-3741; Fax 785-675-3050.

Will search UCC records. UCC search includes tax liens if requested. RE record owner searches available at no charge. **Other Phone Numbers:** Assessor 785-675-3932; Treasurer 785-675-3622.

Sherman County

County Register of Deeds, 813 Broadway, Room 104, Goodland, KS 67735-3097. 785-899-4845; Fax 785-899-4848.

Will search UCC records. UCC search includes tax liens. Will not search real estate records. **Other Phone Numbers:** Assessor 785-899-4825; Treasurer 785-899-4810; Appraiser/Auditor 785-899-4825; Elections 785-899-4800.

Smith County

County Register of Deeds, 218 South Grant, Smith Center, KS 66967. 785-282-5160; Fax 785-282-6257.

Will search UCC records. Tax liens not included in UCC search. RE owner, mortgage, and property transfer searches available. **Other Phone Numbers:** Assessor 785-282-5100; Treasurer 785-282-5170; Appraiser/Auditor 785-282-5100; Elections 785-282-5110.

Stafford County

County Register of Deeds, 209 North Broadway, Stafford County Courthouse, St. John, KS 67576. 620-549-3505.

Will search UCC records. UCC search includes tax liens. Will not search real estate records. **Other Phone Numbers:** Assessor 620-549-3540; Treasurer 620-549-3508; Appraiser/Auditor 620-549-3540.

Stanton County

County Register of Deeds, P.O. Box 716, Johnson, KS 67855. 620-492-2190; Fax 620-492-2688.

Will search UCC records. UCC search includes tax liens. Will not search real estate records. **Other Phone Numbers:** Assessor 620-492-6896; Treasurer 620-492-2160.

Stevens County

County Register of Deeds, 200 East 6th, Hugoton, KS 67951. County Register of Deeds, R/E and UCC Recording 620-544-2630; Fax 620-544-4081.

Will search UCC records. UCC search includes tax liens if requested. Will search real estate records. **Other Phone Numbers:** Assessor 620-544-2993; Treasurer 620-544-2542; Appraiser/Auditor 620-544-2693; Elections 620-544-2541.

Sumner County

County Register of Deeds, P.O. Box 469, Wellington, KS 67152. County Register of Deeds, R/E and UCC Recording 620-326-2041; Fax 620-326-8172.

Will search UCC records. UCC search includes tax liens if requested. RE owner, mortgage, and property transfer searches available. **Other Phone Numbers:** Assessor 620-326-8986; Treasurer 620-326-3371; Appraiser/Auditor 620-326-8986; Elections 620-326-3395.

Thomas County

County Register of Deeds, 300 North Court, Colby, KS 67701. County Register of Deeds, R/E and UCC Recording 785-462-4535; Fax 785-462-4512.

Will search UCC records. UCC search includes tax liens. Will confirm property owner from legal description **Other Phone Numbers:** Assessor 785-462-4525; Treasurer 785-462-4520; Elections 785-462-4500.

Trego County

County Register of Deeds, 216 Main, WaKeeney, KS 67672-2189. County Register of Deeds, R/E and UCC Recording 785-743-6622; Fax 785-743-2461.

Will search UCC records. UCC search includes tax liens. Will give last owner from legal description. **Other Phone Numbers:** Assessor 785-743-5758; Treasurer 785-743-2001; Appraiser/Auditor 785-743-5758; Elections 785-743-5773.

Wabaunsee County

County Register of Deeds, P.O. Box 278, Alma, KS 66401-0278. County Register of Deeds, R/E and UCC Recording 785-765-3822; Fax 785-765-3992.

Will search UCC records. UCC search includes tax liens. Will not search real estate records. **Other Phone Numbers:** Assessor 785-765-3508; Treasurer 785-765-3812; Elections 785-765-2421; Vital Records 785-765-3822.

Wallace County

County Register of Deeds, P.O. Box 10, Sharon Springs, KS 67758-9998. County Register of Deeds, R/E and UCC Recording 785-852-4283; Fax 785-852-4783.

Will search UCC records. UCC search includes tax liens. Will not search real estate records. **Other Phone Numbers:** Assessor 785-852-4206; Treasurer 785-852-4281; Appraiser/Auditor 785-852-4206; Elections 785-852-4282.

Washington County

County Register of Deeds, 214 C Street, Courthouse, Washington, KS 66968-1928. County Register of Deeds, R/E and UCC Recording 785-325-2286; Fax 785-325-2830.

Will search UCC records. UCC search includes tax liens. Will give RE information at no charge. **Other Phone Numbers:** Assessor 785-325-2236; Treasurer 785-325-2461; Appraiser/Auditor 785-325-2236; Elections 785-325-2974; Vital Records 785-296-1400 (Topeka, KS).

Wichita County

County Register of Deeds, P.O. Box 472, Leoti, KS 67861-0472. County Register of Deeds, R/E and UCC Recording 620-375-2733; Fax 316-375-4350.

Will search UCC records. UCC search includes tax liens. Will not search real estate records. **Other Phone Numbers:** Assessor 620-375-4242; Treasurer 620-375-2715; Appraiser/Auditor 620-375-4242; Elections 620-375-2341.

Wilson County

County Register of Deeds, Courthouse, Room 106, Fredonia, KS 66736-1396. County Register of Deeds, R/E and UCC Recording 620-378-3662; Fax 620-378-4762.

Will search UCC records. UCC search includes tax liens. RE record owner and mortgage searches available at no charge. **Other Phone Numbers:** Assessor 620-378-2187.

Woodson County

County Register of Deeds, 105 W. Rutledge, Room 101, Yates Center, KS 66783-1499. 620-625-8635; Fax 620-625-8670.

Will search UCC records. UCC search includes tax liens. Will not search real estate records. **Other Phone Numbers:** Assessor 620-625-8600; Treasurer 620-625-8650.

Wyandotte County

County Register of Deeds, Courthouse, 710 N. 7th St., Kansas City, KS 66101-3084. 913-573-2841; Fax 913-321-3075.

Will search UCC records. UCC search includes tax liens. Will not search real estate records. **Online Access:** Real Estate, Liens, Property Appraisal Records. County records are available online, and property tax records are available on the Internet. The online services requires a $20 set up fee, with a $5 monthly fee and $.05 each after the first 100 transactions. Lending agency information is available. For information, contact Louise Sachen at 913-573-2885. Records from the County Assessor Tax database are available free on the Internet at www.courthouseusa.com/wyanadd.htm. Search by street number and name, but no name searching. **Other Phone Numbers:** Assessor 913-287-2641.

Kansas County Locator

You will usually be able to find the city name in the City/County Cross Reference below. In that case, it is a simple matter to determine the county from the cross reference. However, only the official US Postal Service city names are included in this index. There are an additional 40,000 place names that people use in their addresses. Therefore, we have also included a ZIP/City Cross Reference immediately following the City/County Cross Reference.

If you know the ZIP Code but the city name does not appear in the City/County Cross Reference index, look up the ZIP Code in the ZIP/City Cross Reference, find the city name, then look up the city name in the City/County Cross Reference. For example, you want to know the county for an address of Menands, NY 12204. There is no "Menands" in the City/County Cross Reference. The ZIP/City Cross Reference shows that ZIP Codes 12201-12288 are for the city of Albany. Looking back in the City/County Cross Reference, Albany is in Albany County.

City/County Cross Reference

ABBYVILLE Reno
ABILENE Dickinson
ADA (67414) Ottawa(95), Lincoln(5)
ADMIRE Lyon
AGENDA Republic
AGRA Phillips
ALBERT (67511) Barton(56), Rush(44)
ALDEN (67512) Rice(94), Reno(6)
ALEXANDER (67513) Rush(95), Pawnee(5)
ALLEN Lyon
ALMA Wabaunsee
ALMENA Norton
ALTA VISTA (66834) Wabaunsee(37), Morris(25), Jackson(22), Geary(15)
ALTAMONT Labette
ALTON (67623) Osborne(99), Smith(1)
ALTOONA Wilson
AMERICUS Lyon
AMES Cloud
ANDALE Sedgwick
ANDOVER Butler
ANTHONY Harper
ARCADIA (66711) Crawford(93), Bourbon(8)
ARGONIA (67004) Sumner(82), Harper(17)
ARKANSAS CITY Cowley
ARLINGTON Reno
ARMA Crawford
ARNOLD (67515) Ness(82), Trego(18)
ASHLAND Clark
ASSARIA (67416) Saline(97), McPherson(4)
ATCHISON (66002) Atchison(92), Leavenworth(6), Doniphan(1), Jefferson(1)
ATHOL Smith
ATLANTA (67008) Cowley(55), Butler(45)
ATTICA (67009) Harper(97), Barber(3)
ATWOOD Rawlins
AUBURN (66402) Shawnee(98), Osage(2)
AUGUSTA Butler
AURORA Cloud
AXTELL (66403) Marshall(93), Nemaha(7)
BAILEYVILLE (66404) Nemaha(95), Marshall(5)
BALDWIN CITY (66006) Douglas(92), Franklin(9)
BARNARD (67418) Lincoln(86), Mitchell(14)
BARNES (66933) Washington(93), Riley(7)
BARTLETT Labette
BASEHOR Leavenworth
BAXTER SPRINGS Cherokee
BAZINE Ness
BEATTIE Marshall
BEAUMONT Butler
BEAVER Barton
BEELER (67518) Ness(73), Lane(27)
BELLE PLAINE Sumner
BELLEVILLE Republic
BELOIT (99999) Mitchell(99), Cloud(1)

BELPRE (67519) Edwards(89), Pawnee(11)
BELVIDERE Kiowa
BELVUE (66407) Wabaunsee(60), Pottawatomie(40)
BENDENA Doniphan
BENEDICT Wilson
BENNINGTON Ottawa
BENTLEY Sedgwick
BENTON (67017) Butler(88), Sedgwick(12)
BERN Nemaha
BERRYTON (66409) Shawnee(83), Douglas(12), Osage(4)
BEVERLY Lincoln
BIRD CITY Cheyenne
BISON Rush
BLUE MOUND (66010) Linn(94), Bourbon(6)
BLUE RAPIDS (66411) Marshall(97), Riley(3)
BLUFF CITY (67018) Harper(91), Sumner(9)
BOGUE Graham
BONNER SPRINGS (66012) Wyandotte(65), Leavenworth(35)
BREMEN (66412) Marshall(94), Washington(6)
BREWSTER (67732) Thomas(67), Sherman(26), Rawlins(6)
BRONSON (66716) Bourbon(92), Allen(8)
BROOKVILLE (67425) Saline(53), Ellsworth(46), Lincoln(1)
BROWNELL (67521) Ness(89), Trego(11)
BUCKLIN (67834) Ford(92), Clark(7)
BUCYRUS (66013) Johnson(54), Miami(46)
BUFFALO (66717) Wilson(96), Woodson(4)
BUHLER (67522) Reno(90), Harvey(10)
BUNKER HILL Russell
BURDEN Cowley
BURDETT (67523) Pawnee(92), Hodgeman(8)
BURDICK (66838) Morris(96), Chase(2), Marion(2)
BURLINGAME (66413) Osage(95), Lyon(4), Wabaunsee(1)
BURLINGTON Coffey
BURNS (66840) Butler(66), Marion(27), Chase(6)
BURR OAK Jewell
BURRTON (67020) Harvey(57), Reno(38), Sedgwick(5)
BUSHTON (67427) Rice(72), Ellsworth(27), Barton(2)
BYERS (67021) Pratt(94), Stafford(6)
CALDWELL Sumner
CAMBRIDGE Cowley
CANEY Montgomery
CANTON (67428) McPherson(98), Marion(2)
CARBONDALE Osage
CARLTON Dickinson
CASSODAY Butler

CATHARINE Ellis
CAWKER CITY (67430) Mitchell(73), Jewell(19), Osborne(5), Smith(3)
CEDAR Smith
CEDAR POINT (66843) Chase(99), Marion(1)
CEDAR VALE (67024) Chautauqua(78), Cowley(22)
CENTERVILLE (66014) Linn(91), Anderson(9)
CENTRALIA Nemaha
CHANUTE (66720) Neosho(96), Wilson(3)
CHAPMAN Dickinson
CHASE Rice
CHAUTAUQUA Chautauqua
CHENEY (67025) Sedgwick(68), Kingman(31)
CHEROKEE Crawford
CHERRYVALE (67335) Montgomery(85), Labette(13), Logan(2)
CHETOPA (67336) Labette(79), Cherokee(21)
CIMARRON Gray
CIRCLEVILLE Jackson
CLAFLIN (67525) Barton(96), Rice(4)
CLAY CENTER (67432) Clay(98), Ottawa(2)
CLAYTON (67629) Norton(81), Decatur(19)
CLEARVIEW CITY Johnson
CLEARWATER (67026) Sedgwick(93), Sumner(8)
CLIFTON (66937) Washington(82), Clay(18)
CLYDE (66938) Cloud(78), Washington(14), Republic(5), Clay(4)
COATS (67028) Pratt(67), Barber(18), Kiowa(15)
CODELL Rooks
COFFEYVILLE (67337) Montgomery(95), Labette(5)
COLBY Thomas
COLDWATER (67029) Comanche(97), Kiowa(3)
COLLYER (67631) Trego(82), Graham(15), Gove(1), Sheridan(1)
COLONY (66015) Anderson(84), Allen(12), Coffey(4)
COLUMBUS Cherokee
COLWICH Sedgwick
CONCORDIA (66901) Cloud(98), Republic(2)
CONWAY SPRINGS (67031) Sumner(96), Sedgwick(4)
COOLIDGE Hamilton
COPELAND (67837) Gray(49), Haskell(42), Meade(9)
CORNING Nemaha
COTTONWOOD FALLS Chase
COUNCIL GROVE (66846) Morris(95), Lyon(5)
COURTLAND (66939) Republic(83), Jewell(17)
COYVILLE Wilson

CRESTLINE Cherokee
CUBA (66940) Republic(99), Washington(1)
CUMMINGS Atchison
CUNNINGHAM (67035) Kingman(74), Pratt(17), Reno(9)
DAMAR (67632) Rooks(89), Graham(11)
DANVILLE Harper
DE SOTO Johnson
DEARING Montgomery
DEERFIELD (67838) Kearny(63), Finney(37)
DELIA Jackson
DELPHOS (67436) Ottawa(89), Cloud(11)
DENISON (66419) Jackson(84), Jefferson(16)
DENNIS Labette
DENNIS THE MENACE Sedgwick
DENTON (66017) Doniphan(98), Brown(2)
DERBY Sedgwick
DEXTER Cowley
DIGHTON (67839) Lane(96), Gove(4)
DODGE CITY Ford
DORRANCE (67634) Russell(97), Barton(3)
DOUGLASS Butler
DOVER Shawnee
DOWNS (67437) Osborne(96), Smith(4)
DRESDEN (67635) Decatur(69), Sheridan(31)
DURHAM Marion
DWIGHT (66849) Morris(62), Jackson(22), Geary(16)
EASTON Leavenworth
EDGERTON (66021) Johnson(73), Miami(25), Douglas(3)
EDMOND (67636) Norton(83), Graham(17)
EDNA Labette
EDSON Sherman
EDWARDSVILLE Wyandotte
EFFINGHAM Atchison
EL DORADO Butler
ELBING Butler
ELK CITY (67344) Montgomery(75), Chautauqua(16), Elk(9)
ELK FALLS Elk
ELKHART Morton
ELLINWOOD (67526) Barton(95), Rice(4)
ELLIS (67637) Ellis(88), Trego(12)
ELLSWORTH Ellsworth
ELMDALE Chase
ELSMORE Allen
ELWOOD Doniphan
EMMETT (66422) Jackson(51), Pottawatomie(50)
EMPORIA Lyon
ENGLEWOOD (67840) Clark(73), Meade(27)
ENSIGN (67841) Gray(74), Ford(26)
ENTERPRISE Dickinson
ERIE Neosho
ESBON Jewell
ESKRIDGE Wabaunsee

EUDORA (66025) Douglas(75), Johnson(25)
EUREKA Greenwood
EVEREST (66424) Brown(83), Atchison(17)
FAIRVIEW Brown
FALL RIVER (67047) Greenwood(62), Elk(21), Wilson(18)
FALUN (67442) Saline(98), McPherson(2)
FARLINGTON Crawford
FLORENCE Marion
FONTANA (66026) Miami(86), Linn(15)
FORD Ford
FORMOSO (66942) Jewell(98), Republic(2)
FORT DODGE Ford
FORT LEAVENWORTH Leavenworth
FORT RILEY Geary
FORT SCOTT Bourbon
FOSTORIA Pottawatomie
FOWLER (67844) Meade(80), Ford(14), Gray(7)
FRANKFORT (66427) Marshall(98), Pottawatomie(2)
FRANKLIN Crawford
FREDONIA Wilson
FREEPORT (67049) Harper(89), Sumner(11)
FRONTENAC Crawford
FULTON (66738) Bourbon(96), Linn(4)
GALENA Cherokee
GALESBURG Neosho
GALVA McPherson
GARDEN CITY Finney
GARDEN PLAIN Sedgwick
GARDNER Johnson
GARFIELD Pawnee
GARLAND Bourbon
GARNETT Anderson
GAS Allen
GAYLORD (67638) Smith(92), Osborne(8)
GEM (67734) Thomas(66), Rawlins(34)
GENESEO (67444) Rice(70), Ellsworth(30)
GEUDA SPRINGS (67051) Sumner(89), Cowley(11)
GIRARD Crawford
GLADE (67639) Phillips(98), Rooks(2)
GLASCO (67445) Cloud(91), Ottawa(9)
GLEN ELDER (67446) Mitchell(91), Jewell(9)
GODDARD Sedgwick
GOESSEL Marion
GOFF Nemaha
GOODLAND Sherman
GORHAM (67640) Russell(72), Ellis(28)
GOVE Gove
GRAINFIELD (67737) Gove(77), Sheridan(23)
GRANTVILLE Jefferson
GREAT BEND Barton
GREELEY (66033) Anderson(69), Franklin(28), Linn(3)
GREEN (67447) Clay(90), Riley(10)
GREENLEAF Washington
GREENSBURG Kiowa
GREENWICH Sedgwick
GRENOLA (67346) Elk(68), Chautauqua(32)
GRIDLEY (66852) Coffey(88), Greenwood(8), Woodson(4)
GRINNELL (67738) Gove(60), Sheridan(40)
GYPSUM (67448) Saline(49), McPherson(27), Dickinson(23)
HADDAM Washington
HALSTEAD Harvey
HAMILTON Greenwood
HANOVER Washington
HANSTON (67849) Hodgeman(98), Ness(2)
HARDTNER Barber
HARLAN Smith
HARPER (67058) Harper(97), Kingman(3)

HARTFORD (66854) Lyon(78), Coffey(21)
HARVEYVILLE (66431) Wabaunsee(88), Shawnee(12)
HAVANA (67347) Montgomery(75), Chautauqua(25)
HAVEN Reno
HAVENSVILLE (66432) Pottawatomie(78), Jackson(20), Nemaha(1)
HAVILAND (67059) Kiowa(68), Edwards(20), Pratt(12)
HAYS Ellis
HAYSVILLE Sedgwick
HAZELTON (67061) Barber(65), Harper(35)
HEALY (67850) Lane(86), Scott(11), Gove(3)
HEPLER (66746) Crawford(84), Bourbon(16)
HERINGTON (67449) Dickinson(82), Morris(18)
HERNDON (67739) Rawlins(88), Decatur(12)
HESSTON Harvey
HIAWATHA Brown
HIGHLAND Doniphan
HILL CITY Graham
HILLSBORO Marion
HILLSDALE Miami
HOISINGTON Barton
HOLCOMB Finney
HOLLENBERG Washington
HOLTON (66436) Jackson(98), Atchison(2)
HOLYROOD (67450) Ellsworth(81), Barton(16), Russell(3)
HOME Marshall
HOPE (67451) Dickinson(99), Marion(1)
HORTON (66439) Brown(83), Jackson(11), Atchison(6)
HOWARD Elk
HOXIE (67740) Sheridan(98), Graham(2)
HOYT (66440) Jackson(97), Shawnee(3)
HUDSON Stafford
HUGOTON Stevens
HUMBOLDT Allen
HUNTER (67452) Mitchell(60), Lincoln(40)
HUTCHINSON Reno
INDEPENDENCE Montgomery
INGALLS (67853) Gray(91), Finney(9)
INMAN (67546) McPherson(87), Rice(8), Reno(5)
IOLA Allen
ISABEL (67065) Barber(53), Pratt(45), Kingman(2)
IUKA Pratt
JAMESTOWN (66948) Cloud(82), Republic(18)
JENNINGS (67643) Decatur(94), Sheridan(6)
JETMORE Hodgeman
JEWELL Jewell
JOHNSON (67855) Stanton(98), Grant(1)
JUNCTION CITY Geary
KALVESTA Finney
KANOPOLIS Ellsworth
KANORADO (66771) Sherman(96), Cheyenne(2), Wallace(2)
KANSAS CITY (66106) Wyandotte(96), Johnson(4)
KANSAS CITY (66109) Wyandotte(98), Leavenworth(2)
KANSAS CITY Wyandotte
KECHI Sedgwick
KENDALL (67857) Hamilton(58), Kearny(42)
KENSINGTON (66951) Smith(87), Phillips(13)
KINCAID (66039) Anderson(92), Allen(4), Linn(3)
KINGMAN (67068) Kingman(99), Reno(2)
KINGSDOWN (67858) Ford(90), Clark(10)
KINSLEY (67547) Edwards(98), Hodgeman(2)

KIOWA Barber
KIRWIN (67644) Phillips(90), Smith(5), Rooks(4), Osborne(1)
KISMET Seward
LA CROSSE Rush
LA CYGNE (66040) Linn(99), Miami(1)
LA HARPE Allen
LAKE CITY Barber
LAKIN Kearny
LAMONT Greenwood
LANCASTER Atchison
LANE Franklin
LANSING Leavenworth
LARNED (67550) Pawnee(98), Stafford(2)
LATHAM (67072) Butler(92), Cowley(7)
LAWRENCE (66044) Douglas(93), Jefferson(4), Leavenworth(3)
LAWRENCE Douglas
LE ROY Coffey
LEAVENWORTH Leavenworth
LEBANON (66952) Smith(96), Jewell(4)
LEBO (66856) Coffey(69), Osage(31)
LECOMPTON (66050) Shawnee(59), Douglas(41)
LEHIGH Marion
LENORA (67645) Norton(74), Graham(26)
LEON Butler
LEONARDVILLE Riley
LEOTI (67861) Wichita(94), Logan(6)
LEVANT (67743) Thomas(97), Rawlins(3)
LEWIS Edwards
LIBERAL Seward
LIBERTY (67351) Montgomery(89), Labette(12)
LIEBENTHAL Rush
LINCOLN Lincoln
LINCOLNVILLE (66858) Marion(95), Chase(5)
LINDSBORG (67456) McPherson(91), Saline(10)
LINN Washington
LINWOOD Leavenworth
LITTLE RIVER Rice
LOGAN (67646) Phillips(76), Rooks(10), Norton(9), Graham(4)
LONG ISLAND (67647) Phillips(99), Norton(1)
LONGFORD (67458) Clay(83), Ottawa(16)
LONGTON (67352) Elk(88), Chautauqua(13)
LORRAINE Ellsworth
LOST SPRINGS (66859) Marion(79), Morris(21)
LOUISBURG Miami
LOUISVILLE Pottawatomie
LUCAS (67648) Russell(72), Osborne(24), Lincoln(3)
LUDELL Rawlins
LURAY (67649) Russell(64), Osborne(36)
LYNDON Osage
LYONS Rice
MACKSVILLE (67557) Stafford(59), Pawnee(18), Pratt(17), Edwards(6)
MADISON (66860) Greenwood(66), Lyon(34)
MAHASKA Washington
MAIZE Sedgwick
MANCHESTER Dickinson
MANHATTAN (66502) Riley(93), Pottawatomie(6)
MANHATTAN (66503) Riley(99), Pottawatomie(1)
MANHATTAN Riley
MANKATO Jewell
MANTER (67862) Stanton(75), Morton(25)
MAPLE CITY Cowley
MAPLE HILL Wabaunsee
MAPLETON (66754) Bourbon(94), Linn(6)
MARIENTHAL Wichita
MARION Marion
MARQUETTE (67464) McPherson(66), Ellsworth(34)

MARYSVILLE Marshall
MATFIELD GREEN Chase
MAYETTA Jackson
MAYFIELD Sumner
MC CONNELL A F B Sedgwick
MC CRACKEN (67556) Rush(67), Ness(17), Ellis(16)
MC CUNE (66753) Crawford(93), Labette(5), Neosho(2)
MC DONALD (67745) Rawlins(76), Cheyenne(24)
MC FARLAND Wabaunsee
MC LOUTH (66054) Jefferson(76), Leavenworth(24)
MCPHERSON McPherson
MEADE Meade
MEDICINE LODGE Barber
MELVERN Osage
MENTOR Saline
MERIDEN (66512) Jefferson(90), Jackson(7), Shawnee(3)
MILAN Sumner
MILFORD Geary
MILTON (67106) Sumner(62), Sedgwick(35), Kingman(3)
MILTONVALE (67466) Cloud(55), Ottawa(24), Clay(21)
MINNEAPOLIS Ottawa
MINNEOLA (67865) Ford(66), Clark(34)
MOLINE (67353) Elk(78), Chautauqua(22)
MONTEZUMA (67867) Gray(95), Meade(5)
MONUMENT (67747) Logan(90), Thomas(10)
MORAN (66755) Allen(97), Bourbon(3)
MORGANVILLE Clay
MORLAND Graham
MORRILL Brown
MORROWVILLE Washington
MOSCOW Stevens
MOUND CITY (66056) Linn(79), Atchison(21)
MOUND VALLEY Labette
MOUNDRIDGE (67107) McPherson(78), Harvey(20), Marshall(2)
MOUNT HOPE (67108) Sedgwick(60), Reno(40)
MULBERRY Crawford
MULLINVILLE Kiowa
MULVANE (67110) Sedgwick(62), Sumner(38)
MUNDEN Republic
MURDOCK Kingman
MUSCOTAH (66058) Jackson(66), Atchison(34)
NARKA (66960) Republic(94), Washington(6)
NASHVILLE (67112) Kingman(88), Barber(13)
NATOMA (67651) Osborne(62), Rooks(31), Ellis(6), Russell(2)
NEAL Greenwood
NEKOMA (67559) Rush(83), Pawnee(17)
NEODESHA (66757) Wilson(95), Montgomery(5)
NEOSHO FALLS (66758) Coffey(76), Woodson(22), Anderson(1), Allen(1)
NEOSHO RAPIDS (66864) Lyon(94), Coffey(6)
NESS CITY Ness
NETAWAKA (66516) Jackson(89), Brown(11)
NEW ALBANY Wilson
NEW ALMELO Norton
NEW CAMBRIA (67470) Saline(89), Ottawa(11)
NEW CENTURY Johnson
NEWTON (67114) Harvey(93), Butler(4), Marion(3)
NICKERSON Reno
NIOTAZE Chautauqua
NORCATUR (67653) Decatur(68), Norton(32)

NORTH NEWTON (67117) McPherson(80), Harvey(20)
NORTON Norton
NORTONVILLE (66060) Atchison(55), Jefferson(46)
NORWAY Republic
NORWICH (67118) Kingman(95), Sedgwick(4)
OAKHILL (67472) Clay(71), Ottawa(29)
OAKLEY (67748) Logan(78), Thomas(16), Gove(6)
OBERLIN (67749) Decatur(99), Rawlins(1)
ODIN Barton
OFFERLE (67563) Edwards(55), Ford(41), Hodgeman(4)
OGALLAH (67656) Trego(93), Graham(7)
OGDEN Riley
OKETO Marshall
OLATHE Johnson
OLMITZ Barton
OLPE Lyon
OLSBURG Pottawatomie
ONAGA (66521) Pottawatomie(93), Nemaha(7)
ONEIDA Nemaha
OPOLIS Crawford
OSAGE CITY (66523) Osage(99), Lyon(1)
OSAWATOMIE (66064) Miami(94), Franklin(6)
OSBORNE Osborne
OSKALOOSA Jefferson
OSWEGO (99999) Labette(99), Cherokee(1)
OTIS (67565) Rush(88), Barton(10), Russell(1)
OTTAWA Franklin
OVERBROOK (66524) Osage(62), Douglas(30), Shawnee(6), Franklin(2)
OXFORD (67119) Sumner(81), Cowley(19)
OZAWKIE Jefferson
PALCO (67657) Rooks(76), Graham(25)
PALMER (66962) Washington(81), Clay(19)
PAOLA Miami
PARADISE (67658) Osborne(60), Russell(40)
PARK (67751) Gove(53), Sheridan(47)
PARKER (66072) Linn(93), Miami(6), Anderson(1)
PARSONS (67357) Labette(92), Neosho(8)
PARTRIDGE Reno
PAWNEE ROCK (67567) Barton(58), Pawnee(26), Stafford(10), Rush(6)
PAXICO Wabaunsee
PEABODY (66866) Marion(93), Harvey(7)
PECK (67120) Sumner(70), Sedgwick(30)
PENOKEE Graham
PERRY Jefferson
PERU Chautauqua
PFEIFER Ellis
PHILLIPSBURG Phillips
PIEDMONT (67122) Greenwood(69), Elk(31)
PIERCEVILLE Finney
PIQUA Woodson
PITTSBURG (66762) Crawford(98), Cherokee(2)
PLAINS Meade
PLAINVILLE (67663) Rooks(98), Ellis(2)
PLEASANTON Linn
PLEVNA Reno
POMONA Franklin
PORTIS (67474) Osborne(84), Smith(17)
POTTER Atchison

POTWIN Butler
POWHATTAN Brown
PRAIRIE VIEW (67664) Phillips(83), Norton(17)
PRATT Pratt
PRESCOTT Linn
PRETTY PRAIRIE (67570) Reno(88), Kingman(12)
PRINCETON Franklin
PROTECTION (67127) Comanche(87), Clark(13)
QUENEMO (66528) Osage(98), Franklin(2)
QUINTER (67752) Gove(93), Sheridan(7)
RAGO Kingman
RAMONA (67475) Marion(61), Dickinson(39)
RANDALL Jewell
RANDOLPH Riley
RANSOM (67572) Ness(84), Trego(16)
RANTOUL (66079) Franklin(94), Miami(6)
RAYMOND (67573) Rice(99), Barton(1)
READING (66868) Lyon(89), Osage(11), Coffey(1)
REDFIELD Bourbon
REPUBLIC Republic
REXFORD (67753) Thomas(62), Sheridan(31), Rawlins(6), Wallace(2)
RICHFIELD Morton
RICHMOND (66080) Franklin(78), Anderson(22)
RILEY Riley
RIVERTON Cherokee
ROBINSON (66532) Brown(76), Doniphan(24)
ROCK (67131) Cowley(97), Butler(3)
ROLLA (67954) Morton(75), Stevens(26)
ROSALIA Butler
ROSE HILL (67133) Butler(99), Sedgwick(1)
ROSSVILLE (66533) Shawnee(96), Jackson(4)
ROXBURY McPherson
ROZEL Pawnee
RUSH CENTER (67575) Rush(97), Pawnee(3)
RUSSELL Russell
RUSSELL SPRINGS Logan
SABETHA (66534) Nemaha(96), Brown(4)
SAINT FRANCIS Cheyenne
SAINT GEORGE Pottawatomie
SAINT JOHN (67576) Stafford(99), Pratt(1)
SAINT MARYS (66536) Pottawatomie(96), Shawnee(2), Wabaunsee(1)
SAINT PAUL Neosho
SALINA Saline
SATANTA (67870) Haskell(76), Grant(19), Seward(4), Sherman(1)
SAVONBURG (66772) Allen(93), Neosho(4), Bourbon(3)
SAWYER (67134) Pratt(89), Barber(11)
SCAMMON Cherokee
SCANDIA Republic
SCHOENCHEN Ellis
SCOTT CITY (67871) Scott(97), Logan(1), Finney(1)
SCRANTON Osage
SEDAN Chautauqua
SEDGWICK (67135) Harvey(61), Sedgwick(39)
SELDEN (67757) Sheridan(58), Decatur(38), Thomas(4)
SENECA Nemaha
SEVERY (67137) Greenwood(87), Elk(13)
SEWARD Stafford

SHARON (67138) Barber(98), Harper(2)
SHARON SPRINGS Wallace
SHAWNEE MISSION Johnson
SHIELDS (67874) Lane(87), Gove(13)
SILVER LAKE (66539) Shawnee(98), Jackson(2)
SIMPSON Mitchell
SMITH CENTER Smith
SMOLAN Saline
SOLDIER (66540) Jackson(96), Nemaha(4)
SOLOMON (67480) Dickinson(56), Ottawa(31), Saline(13)
SOUTH HAVEN Sumner
SOUTH HUTCHINSON Reno
SPEARVILLE (67876) Ford(92), Hodgeman(8)
SPIVEY Kingman
SPRING HILL (66083) Johnson(60), Miami(40)
STAFFORD Stafford
STARK (66775) Neosho(98), Bourbon(2)
STERLING (67579) Rice(82), Reno(18)
STILWELL Johnson
STOCKTON Rooks
STRONG CITY Chase
STUDLEY (67759) Sheridan(89), Graham(11)
STUTTGART Phillips
SUBLETTE Haskell
SUMMERFIELD Marshall
SUN CITY Barber
SYCAMORE Montgomery
SYLVAN GROVE (67481) Lincoln(98), Russell(3)
SYLVIA Reno
SYRACUSE (67878) Hamilton(86), Stanton(14)
TALMAGE Dickinson
TAMPA Marion
TECUMSEH Shawnee
TESCOTT (67484) Ottawa(83), Saline(15), Lincoln(2)
THAYER (66776) Neosho(87), Wilson(11), Labette(1)
TIMKEN (67582) Rush(99), Pawnee(1)
TIPTON (67485) Osborne(54), Mitchell(47)
TONGANOXIE Leavenworth
TOPEKA (66610) Shawnee(99), Wabaunsee(1)
TOPEKA (66615) Shawnee(94), Wabaunsee(6)
TOPEKA (66617) Shawnee(91), Jefferson(9)
TOPEKA Shawnee
TORONTO (66777) Woodson(94), Greenwood(5), Wilson(1)
TOWANDA Butler
TREECE Cherokee
TRIBUNE Greeley
TROY Doniphan
TURON (67583) Reno(51), Pratt(43), Stafford(7)
TURON Pratt
TYRO Montgomery
UDALL (67146) Cowley(89), Sumner(11)
ULYSSES (67880) Grant(99), Kearny(1)
UNIONTOWN Bourbon
UTICA (67584) Ness(65), Lane(13), Trego(12), Gove(10)
VALLEY CENTER (67147) Sedgwick(99), Harvey(2)
VALLEY FALLS (66088) Jefferson(98), Atchison(2)
VASSAR Osage

VERMILLION (66544) Marshall(95), Nemaha(5)
VICTORIA Ellis
VIOLA Sedgwick
VIRGIL (66870) Greenwood(96), Woodson(4)
VLIETS Marshall
WA KEENEY (67672) Trego(98), Graham(2)
WAKARUSA (66546) Shawnee(86), Osage(14)
WAKEFIELD (67487) Clay(90), Dickinson(7), Geary(3)
WALDO (67673) Russell(83), Osborne(17)
WALDRON Harper
WALKER Ellis
WALLACE (67761) Wallace(58), Logan(42)
WALNUT (66780) Bourbon(66), Neosho(18), Crawford(16)
WALTON (67151) Harvey(86), Marion(14)
WAMEGO (66547) Pottawatomie(95), Wabaunsee(5)
WASHINGTON Washington
WATERVILLE (66548) Marshall(98), Washington(1)
WATHENA Doniphan
WAVERLY (66871) Coffey(97), Osage(4)
WEBBER Jewell
WEIR (66781) Cherokee(98), Crawford(2)
WELDA (66091) Anderson(98), Franklin(2)
WELLINGTON Sumner
WELLS Ottawa
WELLSVILLE (66092) Franklin(65), Miami(26), Douglas(9)
WESKAN Wallace
WEST MINERAL Cherokee
WESTMORELAND Pottawatomie
WESTPHALIA (66093) Anderson(66), Coffey(34)
WETMORE (66550) Nemaha(83), Jackson(12), Brown(5)
WHEATON (66551) Pottawatomie(99), Marshall(1)
WHITE CITY (66872) Morris(96), Geary(4)
WHITE CLOUD (66094) Doniphan(61), Brown(39)
WHITEWATER (67154) Butler(89), Harvey(11)
WHITING Jackson
WICHITA (67228) Sedgwick(98), Butler(3)
WICHITA (67230) Sedgwick(97), Butler(3)
WICHITA Sedgwick
WILLIAMSBURG (66095) Franklin(90), Anderson(10)
WILMORE (67155) Comanche(85), Kiowa(15)
WILSEY Morris
WILSON (67490) Ellsworth(83), Russell(13), Lincoln(4)
WINCHESTER Jefferson
WINDOM (67491) McPherson(78), Rice(22)
WINFIELD Cowley
WINONA (67764) Logan(83), Thomas(17)
WOODBINE Dickinson
WOODSTON (67675) Rooks(99), Osborne(2)
WRIGHT Ford
YATES CENTER Woodson
YODER Reno
ZENDA (67159) Kingman(83), Harper(17)
ZURICH (67676) Rooks(90), Ellis(10)

ZIP/City Cross Reference

66002-66002	ATCHISON	66409-66409	BERRYTON	66713-66713	BAXTER SPRINGS
66006-66006	BALDWIN CITY	66411-66411	BLUE RAPIDS	66714-66714	BENEDICT
66007-66007	BASEHOR	66412-66412	BREMEN	66716-66716	BRONSON
66008-66008	BENDENA	66413-66413	BURLINGAME	66717-66717	BUFFALO
66010-66010	BLUE MOUND	66414-66414	CARBONDALE	66720-66720	CHANUTE
66012-66012	BONNER SPRINGS	66415-66415	CENTRALIA	66724-66724	CHEROKEE
66013-66013	BUCYRUS	66416-66416	CIRCLEVILLE	66725-66725	COLUMBUS
66014-66014	CENTERVILLE	66417-66417	CORNING	66727-66727	COYVILLE
66015-66015	COLONY	66418-66418	DELIA	66728-66728	CRESTLINE
66016-66016	CUMMINGS	66419-66419	DENISON	66732-66732	ELSMORE
66017-66017	DENTON	66420-66420	DOVER	66733-66733	ERIE
66018-66018	DE SOTO	66422-66422	EMMETT	66734-66734	FARLINGTON
66019-66019	CLEARVIEW CITY	66423-66423	ESKRIDGE	66735-66735	FRANKLIN
66020-66020	EASTON	66424-66424	EVEREST	66736-66736	FREDONIA
66021-66021	EDGERTON	66425-66425	FAIRVIEW	66738-66738	FULTON
66023-66023	EFFINGHAM	66426-66426	FOSTORIA	66739-66739	GALENA
66024-66024	ELWOOD	66427-66427	FRANKFORT	66740-66740	GALESBURG
66025-66025	EUDORA	66428-66428	GOFF	66741-66741	GARLAND
66026-66026	FONTANA	66429-66429	GRANTVILLE	66742-66742	GAS
66027-66027	FORT LEAVENWORTH	66431-66431	HARVEYVILLE	66743-66743	GIRARD
66030-66030	GARDNER	66432-66432	HAVENSVILLE	66746-66746	HEPLER
66031-66031	NEW CENTURY	66434-66434	HIAWATHA	66748-66748	HUMBOLDT
66032-66032	GARNETT	66436-66436	HOLTON	66749-66749	IOLA
66033-66033	GREELEY	66438-66438	HOME	66751-66751	LA HARPE
66035-66035	HIGHLAND	66439-66439	HORTON	66753-66753	MC CUNE
66036-66036	HILLSDALE	66440-66440	HOYT	66754-66754	MAPLETON
66039-66039	KINCAID	66441-66441	JUNCTION CITY	66755-66755	MORAN
66040-66040	LA CYGNE	66442-66442	FORT RILEY	66756-66756	MULBERRY
66041-66041	LANCASTER	66449-66449	LEONARDVILLE	66757-66757	NEODESHA
66042-66042	LANE	66450-66450	LOUISVILLE	66758-66758	NEOSHO FALLS
66043-66043	LANSING	66451-66451	LYNDON	66759-66759	NEW ALBANY
66044-66047	LAWRENCE	66501-66501	MC FARLAND	66760-66760	OPOLIS
66048-66048	LEAVENWORTH	66502-66506	MANHATTAN	66761-66761	PIQUA
66049-66049	LAWRENCE	66507-66507	MAPLE HILL	66762-66762	PITTSBURG
66050-66050	LECOMPTON	66508-66508	MARYSVILLE	66763-66763	FRONTENAC
66051-66051	OLATHE	66509-66509	MAYETTA	66767-66767	PRESCOTT
66052-66052	LINWOOD	66510-66510	MELVERN	66769-66769	REDFIELD
66053-66053	LOUISBURG	66512-66512	MERIDEN	66770-66770	RIVERTON
66054-66054	MC LOUTH	66514-66514	MILFORD	66771-66771	SAINT PAUL
66056-66056	MOUND CITY	66515-66515	MORRILL	66772-66772	SAVONBURG
66058-66058	MUSCOTAH	66516-66516	NETAWAKA	66773-66773	SCAMMON
66060-66060	NORTONVILLE	66517-66517	OGDEN	66775-66775	STARK
66061-66063	OLATHE	66518-66518	OKETO	66776-66776	THAYER
66064-66064	OSAWATOMIE	66520-66520	OLSBURG	66777-66777	TORONTO
66066-66066	OSKALOOSA	66521-66521	ONAGA	66778-66778	TREECE
66067-66067	OTTAWA	66522-66522	ONEIDA	66779-66779	UNIONTOWN
66070-66070	OZAWKIE	66523-66523	OSAGE CITY	66780-66780	WALNUT
66071-66071	PAOLA	66524-66524	OVERBROOK	66781-66781	WEIR
66072-66072	PARKER	66526-66526	PAXICO	66782-66782	WEST MINERAL
66073-66073	PERRY	66527-66527	POWHATTAN	66783-66783	YATES CENTER
66075-66075	PLEASANTON	66528-66528	QUENEMO	66801-66801	EMPORIA
66076-66076	POMONA	66531-66531	RILEY	66830-66830	ADMIRE
66077-66077	POTTER	66532-66532	ROBINSON	66833-66833	ALLEN
66078-66078	PRINCETON	66533-66533	ROSSVILLE	66834-66834	ALTA VISTA
66079-66079	RANTOUL	66534-66534	SABETHA	66835-66835	AMERICUS
66080-66080	RICHMOND	66535-66535	SAINT GEORGE	66838-66838	BURDICK
66083-66083	SPRING HILL	66536-66536	SAINT MARYS	66839-66839	BURLINGTON
66085-66085	STILWELL	66537-66537	SCRANTON	66840-66840	BURNS
66086-66086	TONGANOXIE	66538-66538	SENECA	66842-66842	CASSODAY
66087-66087	TROY	66539-66539	SILVER LAKE	66843-66843	CEDAR POINT
66088-66088	VALLEY FALLS	66540-66540	SOLDIER	66845-66845	COTTONWOOD FALLS
66090-66090	WATHENA	66541-66541	SUMMERFIELD	66846-66846	COUNCIL GROVE
66091-66091	WELDA	66542-66542	TECUMSEH	66849-66849	DWIGHT
66092-66092	WELLSVILLE	66543-66543	VASSAR	66850-66850	ELMDALE
66093-66093	WESTPHALIA	66544-66544	VERMILLION	66851-66851	FLORENCE
66094-66094	WHITE CLOUD	66546-66546	WAKARUSA	66852-66852	GRIDLEY
66095-66095	WILLIAMSBURG	66547-66547	WAMEGO	66853-66853	HAMILTON
66097-66097	WINCHESTER	66548-66548	WATERVILLE	66854-66854	HARTFORD
66101-66112	KANSAS CITY	66549-66549	WESTMORELAND	66855-66855	LAMONT
66113-66113	EDWARDSVILLE	66550-66550	WETMORE	66856-66856	LEBO
66115-66160	KANSAS CITY	66551-66551	WHEATON	66857-66857	LE ROY
66201-66286	SHAWNEE MISSION	66552-66552	WHITING	66858-66858	LINCOLNVILLE
66401-66401	ALMA	66554-66554	RANDOLPH	66859-66859	LOST SPRINGS
66402-66402	AUBURN	66555-66555	MARYSVILLE	66860-66860	MADISON
66403-66403	AXTELL	66601-66699	TOPEKA	66861-66861	MARION
66404-66404	BAILEYVILLE	66701-66701	FORT SCOTT	66862-66862	MATFIELD GREEN
66406-66406	BEATTIE	66710-66710	ALTOONA	66863-66863	NEAL
66407-66407	BELVUE	66711-66711	ARCADIA	66864-66864	NEOSHO RAPIDS
66408-66408	BERN	66712-66712	ARMA	66865-66865	OLPE

66866-66866	PEABODY
66868-66868	READING
66869-66869	STRONG CITY
66870-66870	VIRGIL
66871-66871	WAVERLY
66872-66872	WHITE CITY
66873-66873	WILSEY
66901-66901	CONCORDIA
66930-66930	AGENDA
66932-66932	ATHOL
66933-66933	BARNES
66935-66935	BELLEVILLE
66936-66936	BURR OAK
66937-66937	CLIFTON
66938-66938	CLYDE
66939-66939	COURTLAND
66940-66940	CUBA
66941-66941	ESBON
66942-66942	FORMOSO
66943-66943	GREENLEAF
66944-66944	HADDAM
66945-66945	HANOVER
66946-66946	HOLLENBERG
66948-66948	JAMESTOWN
66949-66949	JEWELL
66951-66951	KENSINGTON
66952-66952	LEBANON
66953-66953	LINN
66955-66955	MAHASKA
66956-66956	MANKATO
66958-66958	MORROWVILLE
66959-66959	MUNDEN
66960-66960	NARKA
66961-66961	NORWAY
66962-66962	PALMER
66963-66963	RANDALL
66964-66964	REPUBLIC
66966-66966	SCANDIA
66967-66967	SMITH CENTER
66968-66968	WASHINGTON
66970-66970	WEBBER
67001-67001	ANDALE
67002-67002	ANDOVER
67003-67003	ANTHONY
67004-67004	ARGONIA
67005-67005	ARKANSAS CITY
67008-67008	ATLANTA
67009-67009	ATTICA
67010-67010	AUGUSTA
67012-67012	BEAUMONT
67013-67013	BELLE PLAINE
67016-67016	BENTLEY
67017-67017	BENTON
67018-67018	BLUFF CITY
67019-67019	BURDEN
67020-67020	BURRTON
67021-67021	BYERS
67022-67022	CALDWELL
67023-67023	CAMBRIDGE
67024-67024	CEDAR VALE
67025-67025	CHENEY
67026-67026	CLEARWATER
67028-67028	COATS
67029-67029	COLDWATER
67030-67030	COLWICH
67031-67031	CONWAY SPRINGS
67035-67035	CUNNINGHAM
67036-67036	DANVILLE
67037-67037	DERBY
67038-67038	DEXTER
67039-67039	DOUGLASS
67041-67041	ELBING
67042-67042	EL DORADO
67045-67045	EUREKA
67047-67047	FALL RIVER
67049-67049	FREEPORT
67050-67050	GARDEN PLAIN
67051-67051	GEUDA SPRINGS
67052-67052	GODDARD

ZIP	City	ZIP	City	ZIP	City	ZIP	City
67053-67053	GOESSEL	67351-67351	LIBERTY	67522-67522	BUHLER	67672-67672	WA KEENEY
67054-67054	GREENSBURG	67352-67352	LONGTON	67523-67523	BURDETT	67673-67673	WALDO
67055-67055	GREENWICH	67353-67353	MOLINE	67524-67524	CHASE	67674-67674	WALKER
67056-67056	HALSTEAD	67354-67354	MOUND VALLEY	67525-67525	CLAFLIN	67675-67675	WOODSTON
67057-67057	HARDTNER	67355-67355	NIOTAZE	67526-67526	ELLINWOOD	67701-67701	COLBY
67058-67058	HARPER	67356-67356	OSWEGO	67529-67529	GARFIELD	67730-67730	ATWOOD
67059-67059	HAVILAND	67357-67357	PARSONS	67530-67530	GREAT BEND	67731-67731	BIRD CITY
67060-67060	HAYSVILLE	67360-67360	PERU	67543-67543	HAVEN	67732-67732	BREWSTER
67061-67061	HAZELTON	67361-67361	SEDAN	67544-67544	HOISINGTON	67733-67733	EDSON
67062-67062	HESSTON	67363-67363	SYCAMORE	67545-67545	HUDSON	67734-67734	GEM
67063-67063	HILLSBORO	67364-67364	TYRO	67546-67546	INMAN	67735-67735	GOODLAND
67065-67065	ISABEL	67401-67402	SALINA	67547-67547	KINSLEY	67736-67736	GOVE
67066-67066	IUKA	67410-67410	ABILENE	67548-67548	LA CROSSE	67737-67737	GRAINFIELD
67067-67067	KECHI	67414-67414	ADA	67550-67550	LARNED	67738-67738	GRINNELL
67068-67068	KINGMAN	67416-67416	ASSARIA	67552-67552	LEWIS	67739-67739	HERNDON
67070-67070	KIOWA	67417-67417	AURORA	67553-67553	LIEBENTHAL	67740-67740	HOXIE
67071-67071	LAKE CITY	67418-67418	BARNARD	67554-67554	LYONS	67741-67741	KANORADO
67072-67072	LATHAM	67420-67420	BELOIT	67556-67556	MC CRACKEN	67743-67743	LEVANT
67073-67073	LEHIGH	67422-67422	BENNINGTON	67557-67557	MACKSVILLE	67744-67744	LUDELL
67074-67074	LEON	67423-67423	BEVERLY	67559-67559	NEKOMA	67745-67745	MC DONALD
67101-67101	MAIZE	67425-67425	BROOKVILLE	67560-67560	NESS CITY	67747-67747	MONUMENT
67102-67102	MAPLE CITY	67427-67427	BUSHTON	67561-67561	NICKERSON	67748-67748	OAKLEY
67103-67103	MAYFIELD	67428-67428	CANTON	67563-67563	OFFERLE	67749-67749	OBERLIN
67104-67104	MEDICINE LODGE	67430-67430	CAWKER CITY	67564-67564	OLMITZ	67751-67751	PARK
67105-67105	MILAN	67431-67431	CHAPMAN	67565-67565	OTIS	67752-67752	QUINTER
67106-67106	MILTON	67432-67432	CLAY CENTER	67566-67566	PARTRIDGE	67753-67753	REXFORD
67107-67107	MOUNDRIDGE	67436-67436	DELPHOS	67567-67567	PAWNEE ROCK	67755-67755	RUSSELL SPRINGS
67108-67108	MOUNT HOPE	67437-67437	DOWNS	67568-67568	PLEVNA	67756-67756	SAINT FRANCIS
67109-67109	MULLINVILLE	67438-67438	DURHAM	67570-67570	PRETTY PRAIRIE	67757-67757	SELDEN
67110-67110	MULVANE	67439-67439	ELLSWORTH	67572-67572	RANSOM	67758-67758	SHARON SPRINGS
67111-67111	MURDOCK	67441-67441	ENTERPRISE	67573-67573	RAYMOND	67761-67761	WALLACE
67112-67112	NASHVILLE	67442-67442	FALUN	67574-67574	ROZEL	67762-67762	WESKAN
67114-67114	NEWTON	67443-67443	GALVA	67575-67575	RUSH CENTER	67764-67764	WINONA
67117-67117	NORTH NEWTON	67444-67444	GENESEO	67576-67576	SAINT JOHN	67801-67801	DODGE CITY
67118-67118	NORWICH	67445-67445	GLASCO	67578-67578	STAFFORD	67831-67831	ASHLAND
67119-67119	OXFORD	67446-67446	GLEN ELDER	67579-67579	STERLING	67834-67834	BUCKLIN
67120-67120	PECK	67447-67447	GREEN	67581-67581	SYLVIA	67835-67835	CIMARRON
67122-67122	PIEDMONT	67448-67448	GYPSUM	67583-67583	TURON	67836-67836	COOLIDGE
67123-67123	POTWIN	67449-67449	HERINGTON	67584-67584	UTICA	67837-67837	COPELAND
67124-67124	PRATT	67450-67450	HOLYROOD	67585-67585	YODER	67838-67838	DEERFIELD
67127-67127	PROTECTION	67451-67451	HOPE	67601-67601	HAYS	67839-67839	DIGHTON
67128-67128	RAGO	67452-67452	HUNTER	67621-67621	AGRA	67840-67840	ENGLEWOOD
67131-67131	ROCK	67454-67454	KANOPOLIS	67622-67622	ALMENA	67841-67841	ENSIGN
67132-67132	ROSALIA	67455-67455	LINCOLN	67623-67623	ALTON	67842-67842	FORD
67133-67133	ROSE HILL	67456-67456	LINDSBORG	67625-67625	BOGUE	67844-67844	FOWLER
67134-67134	SAWYER	67457-67457	LITTLE RIVER	67626-67626	BUNKER HILL	67846-67846	GARDEN CITY
67135-67135	SEDGWICK	67458-67458	LONGFORD	67627-67627	CATHARINE	67849-67849	HANSTON
67137-67137	SEVERY	67459-67459	LORRAINE	67628-67628	CEDAR	67850-67850	HEALY
67138-67138	SHARON	67460-67460	MCPHERSON	67629-67629	CLAYTON	67851-67851	HOLCOMB
67140-67140	SOUTH HAVEN	67464-67464	MARQUETTE	67631-67631	COLLYER	67853-67853	INGALLS
67142-67142	SPIVEY	67466-67466	MILTONVALE	67632-67632	DAMAR	67854-67854	JETMORE
67143-67143	SUN CITY	67467-67467	MINNEAPOLIS	67634-67634	DORRANCE	67855-67855	JOHNSON
67144-67144	TOWANDA	67468-67468	MORGANVILLE	67635-67635	DRESDEN	67856-67856	KALVESTA
67146-67146	UDALL	67470-67470	NEW CAMBRIA	67637-67637	ELLIS	67857-67857	KENDALL
67147-67147	VALLEY CENTER	67473-67473	OSBORNE	67638-67638	GAYLORD	67858-67858	KINGSDOWN
67149-67149	VIOLA	67474-67474	PORTIS	67639-67639	GLADE	67859-67859	KISMET
67150-67150	WALDRON	67475-67475	RAMONA	67640-67640	GORHAM	67860-67860	LAKIN
67151-67151	WALTON	67476-67476	ROXBURY	67642-67642	HILL CITY	67861-67861	LEOTI
67152-67152	WELLINGTON	67478-67478	SIMPSON	67643-67643	JENNINGS	67862-67862	MANTER
67154-67154	WHITEWATER	67480-67480	SOLOMON	67644-67644	KIRWIN	67863-67863	MARIENTHAL
67155-67155	WILMORE	67481-67481	SYLVAN GROVE	67645-67645	LENORA	67864-67864	MEADE
67156-67156	WINFIELD	67482-67482	TALMAGE	67646-67646	LOGAN	67865-67865	MINNEOLA
67159-67159	ZENDA	67483-67483	TAMPA	67647-67647	LONG ISLAND	67867-67867	MONTEZUMA
67201-67220	WICHITA	67484-67484	TESCOTT	67648-67648	LUCAS	67868-67868	PIERCEVILLE
67221-67221	MC CONNELL A F B	67485-67485	TIPTON	67649-67649	LURAY	67869-67869	PLAINS
67223-67278	WICHITA	67487-67487	WAKEFIELD	67650-67650	MORLAND	67870-67870	SATANTA
67301-67301	INDEPENDENCE	67490-67490	WILSON	67651-67651	NATOMA	67871-67871	SCOTT CITY
67330-67330	ALTAMONT	67491-67491	WINDOM	67653-67653	NORCATUR	67876-67876	SPEARVILLE
67332-67332	BARTLETT	67492-67492	WOODBINE	67654-67654	NORTON	67877-67877	SUBLETTE
67333-67333	CANEY	67501-67504	HUTCHINSON	67656-67656	OGALLAH	67878-67878	SYRACUSE
67334-67334	CHAUTAUQUA	67505-67505	SOUTH HUTCHINSON	67657-67657	PALCO	67879-67879	TRIBUNE
67335-67335	CHERRYVALE	67510-67510	ABBYVILLE	67658-67658	PARADISE	67880-67880	ULYSSES
67336-67336	CHETOPA	67511-67511	ALBERT	67659-67659	PENOKEE	67882-67882	WRIGHT
67337-67337	COFFEYVILLE	67512-67512	ALDEN	67660-67660	PFEIFER	67901-67905	LIBERAL
67340-67340	DEARING	67513-67513	ALEXANDER	67661-67661	PHILLIPSBURG	67950-67950	ELKHART
67341-67341	DENNIS	67514-67514	ARLINGTON	67663-67663	PLAINVILLE	67951-67951	HUGOTON
67342-67342	EDNA	67515-67515	ARNOLD	67664-67664	PRAIRIE VIEW	67952-67952	MOSCOW
67344-67344	ELK CITY	67516-67516	BAZINE	67665-67665	RUSSELL	67953-67953	RICHFIELD
67345-67345	ELK FALLS	67518-67518	BEELER	67667-67667	SCHOENCHEN	67954-67954	ROLLA
67346-67346	GRENOLA	67519-67519	BELPRE	67669-67669	STOCKTON		
67347-67347	HAVANA	67520-67520	BISON	67670-67670	STUTTGART		
67349-67349	HOWARD	67521-67521	BROWNELL	67671-67671	VICTORIA		

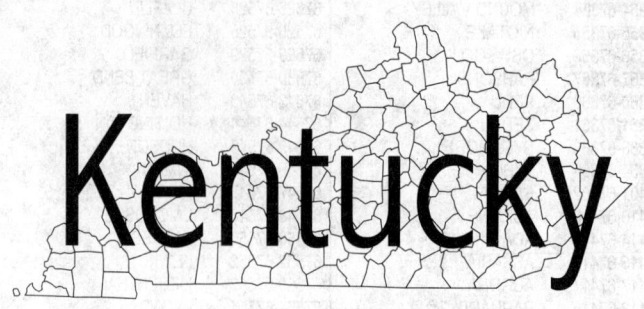

Kentucky

General Help Numbers:

Governor's Office

700 Capitol Ave, Room 100   502-564-2611
Frankfort, KY 40601   Fax 502-564-2517
http://gov.state.ky.us   7:30AM-5PM

Attorney General's Office

700 Capitol Ave, Ste. 118   502-696-5300
Frankfort, KY 40601   Fax 502-573-8317
http://www.law.state.ky.us   8AM-5PM

State Court Administrator

100 Mill Creek Park   502-573-2350
Frankfort, KY 40601   Fax 502-695-1759
http://www.kycourts.net   8AM-4:30PM

State Archives

300 Coffee Tree Rd   502-564-8300
Frankfort, KY 40601   Fax 502-564-5773
http://www.kdla.state.ky.us 8AM-4PM T-SA

State Specifics:

Capital: Frankfort
                                            Franklin County

Time Zone: EST*
  * Kentucky's forty western-most counties are CST: They are:
  Adair, Allen, Ballard, Barren, Breckinridge, Butler, Caldwell,
  Calloway, Carlisle, Christian, Clinton, Crittenden, Cumberland,
  Daviess, Edmonson, Fulton, Graves, Grayson, Hancock, Hart,
  Henderson, Hickman, Hopkins, Livingstone, Logan, Marshall,
  McCracken, McLean, Metcalfe, Monroe, Muhlenberg, Ohio, Russell,
  Simpson, Todd, Trigg, Union, Warren, Wayne, Webster.

Number of Counties: 120

Population: 4,041,769

Web Site: www.kydirect.net

State Agencies

Criminal Records

Kentucky State Police, Records Branch, 1250 Louisville Rd, Frankfort, KY 40601; 502-227-8713, 502-227-8734 (Fax), 8AM-4PM.

http://www.state.ky.us/agencies/ksp/ksphome.htm

Note: Kentucky courts at the local level will not do criminal searches and refer all requesters to the Administrative Office of Courts in Frankfort, then to KY State Police who will do record checks for $10.00 per name.

Indexing & Storage: Records are available from 1952 on for criminal records. It takes a minimum of 30 days before new records are available for inquiry. Records are indexed on inhouse computer, fingerprint cards.

Searching: Access only as mandated by Kentucky Revised Statutes. Requests accepted for employment purposes, nursing homes and adoptive/foster parent background searches. Include the following in your request-full name, date of birth, Social Security Number, reason for information request. A signed release is also required. Statistical information about criminal offenses and accidents is available from 1971 on. The following data is not released: juvenile records, dismissals or pending cases.

Access by: mail, in person.

Fee & Payment: The fee is $10.00 per name. Fee payee: Kentucky State Treasurer. Prepayment required. Personal checks accepted. No credit cards accepted.

Mail search: Turnaround time: 2 to 3 weeks. A self addressed stamped envelope is requested.

In person search: Turnaround time is while you wait. There is a limit of 5 searches.

Corporation Records
Limited Partnerships
Assumed Name
Limited Liability Company Records

Secretary of State, Corporate Records, PO Box 718, Frankfort, KY 40602-0718 (Courier: 700

Capitol Ave, Room 156, Frankfort, KY 40601); 502-564-7330, 502-564-4075 (Fax), 8AM-4PM.

http://www.sos.state.ky.us

Indexing & Storage: Records are available from the 1977 forward on computer index. Hard copies are on microfilm. Records inactive by 1976 are archived and it takes 2 weeks to research. New records are available for inquiry immediately.

Searching: Computer records are limited, they contain name, dates, current registered agent and initial incorporators and initial directors. They do contain current lists of officers and directors when available. Include the following in your request-full name of business.

Access by: mail, phone, in person, online.

Fee & Payment: There is no search fee, but there is a $5.00 certification fee. Copies are $1.00 (minimum) for up to first to 10 pages, and $.10 per each additional page. Pages can be certified for $.50 each. A Certificate of Good Standing is $10.00. Fee payee: Secretary of State. Prepayment required. Send at least $1.00 in the mail for copies. If certified copies are needed, call first. Personal checks accepted. No credit cards accepted.

Mail search: Turnaround time: 2 to 3 days. No self addressed stamped envelope is required.

Phone search: Only information on the computer system is released over the phone.

In person search: Turnaround time while you wait. If you order 5 or more, they will mail the records to you.

Online search: The Internet site, open 24 hours, has a searchable database with over 340,000 KY businesses. The site also offers downloading of filing forms.

Other access: Monthly lists of new corporations are available for $10.00 per month.

Trademarks/Servicemarks

Secretary of State, Legal Department, 700 Capitol Ave, Room 86, Frankfort, KY 40601; 502-564-2848 x442, 502-564-1484 (Fax), 8AM-4:30PM.

http://www.sos.state.ky.us

Searching: Include the trademark/servicemark name or applicant name or certification number.

Access by: mail, in person.

Fee & Payment: There is no fee, unless extensive searching is required. Fee payee: KY State Treasurer. Prepayment required. Personal checks accepted. No credit cards accepted.

Mail search: Turnaround time: 1 week. A self addressed stamped envelope is requested.

Uniform Commercial Code

UCC Division, Secretary of State, PO Box 1470, Frankfort, KY 40602-0718 (Courier: State Capitol Bldg, Rm 79, Frankfort, KY 40601); 502-564-2848, 502-564-5687 (Fax), 8AM-4:30PM.

http://www.sos.state.ky.us

Note: Important--UCC statements filed at the county clerks office on or before 01/04/99 plus all out-of-state debtor filings are available from this agency. All tax liens are filed at the county level.

Searching: Records are open; however, this agency does not conduct searches itself. You must contact a search company or do in-person. Mail requests are referred to the county level. Include the following in your request-debtor name.

Access by: in person, online.

Fee & Payment: There is no search fee. The copy fee is a minimum of $1.00 which includes the first 10 pages, then $.10 per page thereafter. Fee payee: KY State Treasurer. Personal checks accepted. No credit cards accepted. No searching by mail.

Online search: The Kentucky Lien Information Search System is offered free of charge at the web site. Search by debtor name, secured party name, location or date of filing, or county identification number.

Federal Tax Liens
State Tax Liens
Records not maintained by a state level agency.
Note: All tax liens are at the county level.

Sales Tax Registrations

Revenue Cabinet, Tax Compliance Department, Sales Tax Section, Station 53, PO Box 181, Frankfort, KY 40602-0181 (Courier: 200 Fair Oaks, Bldg 2, Frankfort, KY 40602); 502-564-5170, 502-564-2041 (Fax), 8AM-4:30PM.

http://www.state.ky.us/agencies/revenue/revhome.htm

Indexing & Storage: Records are available from the 1970's. Records are indexed on computer from 1996 to present; on microfilm from 1985 to 1995.

Searching: This agency will only confirm if a business is registered, and they will confirm if a tax permit exists. They will provide no other information. Include the following in your request-business name, owner name and address, federal employer identification number. They will also search by tax permit number.

Access by: mail, phone, in person.

Mail search: Turnaround time: 2 to 3 months. A self addressed stamped envelope is requested. No fee for mail request.

Phone search: No fee for telephone request.

In person search: No fee for request.

Birth Certificates

Department for Public Health, Vital Statistics, 275 E Main St - IE-A, Frankfort, KY 40621-0001; 502-564-4212, 502-227-0032 (Fax), 8AM-4PM.

http://publichealth.state.ky.us/vital.htm

Indexing & Storage: Records are available from 1911 to present. It takes 1 month before new records are available for inquiry. Records are indexed on microfiche, inhouse computer, books (volumes).

Searching: Include the following in your request-full name, names of parents, mother's maiden name, date of birth, place of birth. Provide a daytime phone number.

Access by: mail, phone, fax, in person.

Fee & Payment: Searches are $9.00 per name. Add $5.00 if using a credit card. Fee payee: Kentucky State Treasurer. Prepayment required. Personal checks accepted. Credit cards accepted: MasterCard, Visa, AmEx, Discover.

Mail search: Turnaround time: 3 to 4 weeks. No self addressed stamped envelope is required.

Phone search: Must use a credit card (add $5.00 fee) for a phone request. Turnaround time is 3 to 5 days.

Fax search: Same fees as telephone search.

In person search: Turnaround time 1 1/2 hour.

Expedited service: Expedited service is available for mail, phone and fax searches. Turnaround time: overnight delivery. Add $11.75 per package. Also, be sure to include extra credit card use fee.

Death Records

Department for Public Health, Vital Statistics, 275 E Main St - IE-A, Frankfort, KY 40621-0001; 502-564-4212, 502-227-0032 (Fax), 8AM-3PM.

http://publichealth.state.ky.us/vital.htm

Indexing & Storage: Records are available from 1911 on. It takes 1 month before new records are available for inquiry. Records are indexed on microfiche, inhouse computer, books (volumes).

Searching: Include the following in your request-full name, date of death, place of death. Provide a daytime phone number.

Access by: mail, phone, fax, in person, online.

Fee & Payment: The fee is $6.00 per name. Fee payee: Kentucky State Treasurer. Prepayment required. Personal checks accepted. Credit cards accepted: MasterCard, Visa, AmEx, Discover.

Mail search: Turnaround time: 3 to 4 weeks. No self addressed stamped envelope is required.

Phone search: Must use a credit card (add $5.00 fee) to make phone request. Turnaround time is 2-3 days.

Fax search: Same fees and turnaround time as telephone requests.

In person search: Turnaround time 1 1/2 hour.

Online search: In cooperation with the University of Kentucky, there is a searchable death index at http://ukcc.uky.edu:80/~vitalrec. This is for non-commercial use only. Records are from 1911 through 1992.

Expedited service: Expedited service is available for mail, phone and fax searches. Turnaround time: overnight delivery. Add $11.75 per package. Also, be sure to include extra credit card use fee.

Marriage Certificates

Department for Public Health, Vital Statistics, 275 E Main St - IE-A, Frankfort, KY 40621-0001; 502-564-4212, 502-227-0032 (Fax), 8AM-3PM.

http://publichealth.state.ky.us/vital.htm

Indexing & Storage: Records are available from June 1958 to present. It takes 1 to 2 months before new records are available for inquiry. Records are indexed on microfiche, inhouse computer, books (volumes).

Searching: Include the following in your request-names of husband and wife, date of marriage, place or county of marriage. Must also include where marriage license was obtained and a daytime phone number.

Access by: mail, phone, fax, in person, online.

Fee & Payment: The fee is $6.00 per name. Fee payee: Kentucky State Treasurer. Prepayment required. Personal checks accepted. Credit cards accepted: MasterCard, Visa, AmEx, Discover.

Mail search: Turnaround time: 3 to 4 weeks. No self addressed stamped envelope is required.

Phone search: Must use a credit card (add $5.00 fee) for a phone request. Turnaround time is 3 to 5 days.

Fax search: Same criteria as phone orders.

In person search: Turnaround time 1 1/2 hour.

Online search: In cooperation with the University of Kentucky, a searchable index is available on the Internet at http://ukcc.uky.edu:80/~vitalrec. The index runs from 1973 through 1993. This is for non-commercial use only.

Other access: Contact Libraries and Archives.

Expedited service: Expedited service is available for mail, phone and fax searches. Turnaround time: overnight delivery. Add $11.75 per package. Also, be sure to include extra credit card use fee.

Divorce Records

Department for Public Health, Vital Statistics, 275 E Main St - IE-A, Frankfort, KY 40621-0001; 502-564-4212, 502-227-0032 (Fax), 8AM-3PM.

http://publichealth.state.ky.us/vital.htm

Indexing & Storage: Records are available from June, 1958 to present. It takes 1 to 2 months before new records are available for inquiry. Records are indexed on microfiche, inhouse computer, books (volumes).

Searching: Include the following in your request-names of husband and wife, date of divorce, place of divorce. Provide a daytime phone number.

Access by: mail, phone, fax, in person, online.

Fee & Payment: The fee is $6.00 per name. Fee payee: Kentucky State Treasurer. Prepayment required. Personal checks accepted. Credit cards accepted: MasterCard, Visa, AmEx, Discover.

Mail search: Turnaround time: 3 to 4 weeks. No self addressed stamped envelope is required.

Phone search: Must use a credit card (add $5.00 fee) for a phone request. Turnaround time 3-5 days.

Fax search: Same criteria as phone requests.

In person search: Turnaround time 1 1/2 hour.

Online search: In cooperation with the University of Kentucky, there is a searchable index on the Internet at http://ukcc.uky.edu:80/~vitalrec. This is for non-commercial use only. The index is for 1973-1993.

Other access: Contact Libraries and Archives.

Expedited service: Expedited service is available for mail, phone and fax searches. Turnaround time: overnight delivery. Add $11.75 per package.

Workers' Compensation Records

Kentucky Department of Workers' Claims, Perimeter Park West, 1270 Louisville Rd, Bldg C, Frankfort, KY 40601; 502-564-5550, 502-564-5732 (Fax), 8AM-4:30PM.

http://www.state.ky/us/agencies/labor/wkrclaims.htm

Indexing & Storage: Records are available from 1982 to present on computer. New records are available for inquiry immediately.

Searching: Must have a signed release from claimant only for copies of first report. Otherwise, information is open to the public per KRS 61.870 through 61.884. Include the following in your request-claimant name, Social Security Number, date of accident, place of employment at time of accident. The following data is not released: Social Security Numbers, addresses or personal information (height, weight, sex, eye color, etc.).

Access by: mail, fax, in person.

Fee & Payment: Fees are $.50 per page from microfilm and photocopies are $.10 per page. Fee payee: Kentucky State Treasurer. Payment may be submitted at the time records are picked up. Otherwise, an invoice will be mailed at the end of the month. Personal checks accepted. No credit cards accepted.

Mail search: Turnaround time: 2 to 4 weeks. Requests are processed in order by the date received.A self addressed stamped envelope is requested.

Fax search: Fax requests are processed by date of receipt same as requests that are mailed.

In person search: The office will have the records ready for you if you call ahead first and make an appointment.

Other access: A listing of file contents may be requested. Call for details.

Driver Records

Division of Driver Licensing, State Office Bldg, MVRS, 501 High Street, 2nd Floor, Frankfort, KY 40622; 502-564-6800 x2250, 502-564-5787 (Fax), 8AM-4:30PM.

http://www.kytc.state.ky.us

Note: Requests for copies of tickets must be submitted in writing to; Cabinets Record Custodian, Department of Administrative Services, State Office Building, Frankfort 40622. There is a $.10 fee per document.

Indexing & Storage: Records are available for 3 years for moving violations, DWIs and suspensions. Accidents are not reported. Any entry over 3 years old is "masked for insurance and employers." Records of surrendered licenses are available for 3 years. Records computer indexed for past 5 years.

Searching: There is no opt out. Casual requesters can obtain record information, but no personal information is provided. The SSN can be used as the DL#. That number, the full name and DOB are needed when ordering. The driver's address is not included as part of the search report without a release from the driver.

Access by: mail, in person, online.

Fee & Payment: The fee is $3.00 per record. Fee payee: Kentucky State Treasurer. Prepayment required. Personal checks accepted. No credit cards accepted.

Mail search: Turnaround time: 3 days.

In person search: Walk-in requesters may receive up to 5 records immediately at the address listed above or at any one of 11 field offices in the state.

Online search: This is a batch method for higher volume users. There is a minimum order of 150 requests per batch. Input received by 3 PM will be available the next morning. Either the DL# or SSN is needed for ordering. The state will bill monthly. Fee is $3.00 per record.

Other access: The state will sell its entire database of driver license names and addresses to certain vendors. Records are not available for commercial purposes.

Vehicle Ownership
Vehicle Identification

Department of Motor Vehicles, Division of Motor Vehicle Licensing, State Office Bldg, 3rd Floor, Frankfort, KY 40622; 502-564-4076 (Title History), 502-564-3298 (Other Requests), 502-564-1686 (Fax), 8AM-4:30PM.

http://www.kytc.state.ky.us

Indexing & Storage: Records are available from 1978 years to present, but generally only last 10 years released. Records are indexed on computer from 1983 to present, and on microfiche from 1978 to 1982. It takes 1-4 weeks before new records are available for inquiry.

Searching: Vehicle and ownership records are made available to the public; however, personal information is not released to the general public or for marketing purposes without consent. This agency will not do a search by SSN.

Access by: mail, in person, online.

Fee & Payment: The fee is $2.00 per record request. The state reports current lien information. There is a full charge for a "no record found." Fee payee: Division of Motor Vehicles. Prepayment required. Cash and money orders are accepted. Personal checks accepted. No credit cards accepted.

Mail search: Turnaround time: 5 to 10 days. A self addressed stamped envelope is requested.

In person search: Turnaround time is while you wait (typically, 15 minutes to 1 hour).

Online search: Online access costs $2.00 per record. The online mode is interactive. Title, lien and registration searches are available. Records include those for mobile homes. For more information, contact Gale Warfield at 502-564-4076.

Other access: Kentucky has the ability to supply customized bulk delivery of vehicle registration information. The request must be in writing with the intended use outlined. For more information, call 502- 564-3298.

Accident Reports

Department of State Police, Records Section, 1250 Louisville Rd, Frankfort, KY 40601; 502-227-8700, 502-227-8734 (Fax), 8AM-4:30PM.

http://www.state.ky.us/agencies/ksp/ksphome.htm

Indexing & Storage: Records are available from 4 years back at this location. However, there is limited access to accident reports less than 2 years old. It is suggested to go to the agency that filed the report for the record.

Searching: Some requests must be made through "open records." Detailed listing of accidents at specific location without personal identifying information is available for a fee with a written request. For more information phone 502-226-2169 for details. Search requirements include the exact date, county, roadway and mile post, and the driver's name and DOB. All requests must be in writing.

Access by: mail.

Fee & Payment: The charge is $.10 per page with a $.20 minimum. Fee payee: KY State Treasurer. Prepayment required. Personal checks accepted. No credit cards accepted.

Mail search: Turnaround time: 2 to 3 weeks. A self addressed stamped envelope is requested.

Other access: Specific accident statistics may be obtained by phoning the statistics coordinator.

Vessel Ownership
Vessel Registration

Division of Motor Vehicle Licensing, Vessel Titles and Registration, State Office Building, 3rd Floor, Frankfort, KY 40622; 502-564-5301, 8AM-5PM.

http://www.kytc.state.ky.us

Indexing & Storage: Records are available for titles from 1990, for registration from 1985. Prior records are kept by Circuit Clerks. Only motorized vessels must be titled and registered.

Searching: Personal information is not released to casual requesters. The hull number, title number or KY number must be submitted.

Access by: mail, in person.

Fee & Payment: The fee is $2.00 per record. Fee payee: Kentucky State Treasurer. Prepayment required. No credit cards accepted.

Mail search: Turnaround time: 1 week.

In person search: Most of the time results will be mailed.

Legislation Records

Kentucky General Assembly, Legislative Research Commission, 700 Capitol Ave, Room 300, Frankfort, KY 40601; 502-372-7181 (Bill Status Only), 502-564-8100 x323 (Bill Room), 502-564-8100 x340 (LRC Library), 502-223-5094 (Fax), 8AM-4:30PM.

http://www.lrc.state.ky.us

Indexing & Storage: Records are available from 1986 on computer, and from 1950 in hard copy. Kentucky Acts from 1820 to present are available in hard copy. Records are indexed on inhouse computer.

Searching: Include the following in your request-bill number.

Access by: mail, phone, fax, in person, online.

Fee & Payment: Minimum fee $1.00. Fees over $1.00 are invoiced. You pay postage/UPS charges over 8 ounces. Copies are $.15 each. Fee payee: LRC. Personal checks accepted. No credit cards accepted.

Mail search: Turnaround time: variable.

Phone search: Records are available by phone.

Fax search: The fee is $.65 per page.

Online search: The web site has an extensive searching mechanism for bills, actions, summaries, and statutes.

Voter Registration

State Board of Elections, 140 Walnut, Frankfort, KY 40601; 502-573-7100, 502-573-4369 (Fax), 8AM-4:30PM.

http://www.sos.state.ky.us/elecdiv.htm

Note: Written requests are always required; agency is required to respond within 3 days. Bulk data is available for political purposes only. For individual searches, it is best to go to the county level.

Searching: The state will provide verification of records and voting histories upon receipt of a written request. The SSN or DOB is required when doing a verification. The following data is not released: Social Security Numbers, bulk information or information to ineligible persons, pursuant to state statutes.

Access by: mail, fax, in person.

Fee & Payment: There is no search fee. There is a $.10 per page copy fee.

Mail search: Turnaround time: 3 business days. Turnaround time is longer for information exempted by statute.

Fax search: Records are available by fax.

In person search: Records may be ordered (with written request) and picked up in person. Law allows for 3 business day turnaround. In person searching is not allowed.

Other access: Data is available on CD-rom, labels or lists for eligible persons, pursuant to state statutes

GED Certificates

Dept for Adult Education and Literacy, GED Program, Capitol Plaza Tower, 500 Mero St, 3rd Fl, Frankfort, KY 40601; 502-564-5117, 502-564-5436 (Fax).

http://adulted.state.ky.us

Searching: To verify or to get copy of transcript or diploma, all of the following is required: a signed release, name, date/year of test, date of birth, Social Security Number, and city of test.

Access by: mail, fax, in person.

Fee & Payment: There is no fee for verification. Copies of transcript or duplicate diplomas are $5.00 each. Fee payee: KY State Treasurer. Prepayment required. Money orders are accepted, personal checks are not. No credit cards accepted.

Mail search: Turnaround time is 1 week. No self addressed stamped envelope is required.

Fax search: Same criteria as mail searching.

In person search: In person searchers must bring a photo id. Turnaround time: Same day.

Hunting License Information
Fishing License Information

Fish & Wildlife Resources Department, Division of Administrative Services, 1 Game Farm Rd, Arnold Mitchell Bldg, Frankfort, KY 40601; 502-564-4224, 502-564-6508 (Fax), 8AM-4:30PM.

http://kdfwr.state.ky.us

Note: A database has been created, starting in 1996. Records are not released without written request and for good reason. Records are not available for commercial mail lists. Older records are archived in boxes. Record retrieval extremely difficult.

Indexing & Storage: Records are available for the past two years (actual copies). Prior records are archived and not readily available. It takes 16 days before new records are available for inquiry. Records are indexed on hard copy.

Searching: Requests must be in writing and addressed to the Commissioner's Office. The general public cannot receive records, beyond the type of license issued. Include the following in your request-full name, Social Security Number.

Access by: mail, in person.

Fee & Payment: Fees will vary by type of request.

Mail search: Records are available by mail.

Kentucky State Licensing Agencies

Licenses Searchable Online

Architect #07	http://kybera.com/roster.shtml
Engineer #39	http://kyboels.state.ky.us/roster.htm
Engineer/Land Surveyor Firm #39	http://kyboels.state.ky.us/roster.htm
Geologist #15	www.state.ky.us/agencies/finance/boards/geology/pages/geol.html
Mortgage Broker #18	www.dfi.state.ky.us/aspscripts/mort_brokers.asp
Mortgage Loan Company #18	www.dfi.state.ky.us/aspscripts/mort_company.asp
Optometrist #11	http://web.state.ky.us/GBC/LicenseSearch.asp?AGY=8
Physical Therapist #38	http://web.state.ky.us/gbc/LicenseSearch.asp?AGY=4
Physical Therapist Assistant #38	http://web.state.ky.us/gbc/LicenseSearch.asp?AGY=4
Public Accountant-CPA #03	http://cpa.state.ky.us/Locate.html
Real Estate Broker #33	http://web.state.ky.us/krecweb/LicenseeLookUp.asp
Real Estate Brokerage/Firm #33	http://web.state.ky.us/krecweb/FirmLookUp.asp
Real Estate Sales Associate #33	http://web.state.ky.us/krecweb/LicenseeLookUp.asp
Surveyor #39	http://kyboels.state.ky.us/roster.htm

Licensing Quick Finder

Animal Technician #15	502-564-3296
Architect #07	859-246-2069
Art Therapist #15	502-564-3296
Athletic Manager #15	502-564-3296
Athletic Trainer #15	502-564-3296
Attorney #02	502-564-3795
Auction House Operator #04	502-339-9453
Auctioneer/Auctioneer Apprentice #04	502-339-9453
Bank #18	502-573-3390
Barber #05	502-429-8841
Blacksmith #31	859-246-2040
Boiler Contractor #26	502-564-3626
Boiler Inspector/Installer #26	502-564-3626
Boxer #15	502-564-3296
Broker/Dealer Agent #18	502-573-3390
Building Inspector #26	502-564-8090
Check Seller/Casher #18	502-573-3390
Child Care Facility #13	502-564-2800
Chiropractor #35	888-605-1368
Compost Operator #24	502-565-6716
Coroner #17	859-622-6165
Cosmetologist #37	502-564-4262
Counselor, Professional #15	502-564-3296
Dental Hygienist #06	502-423-0573
Dental Laboratory #06	502-423-0573
Dental Laboratory Technician #06	502-423-0573
Dentist #06	502-423-0573
Dietitian/Nutritionist #15	502-564-3296
Drinking Water Treatment/Distribution System Operator #29	502-564-3410
Driver Training Instructor #42	502-226-7404
Drug Mfg./Wholesaler #12	502-573-1580
Electrical Contractor #26	502-564-3626
Electrical Inspector #26	502-564-3626
Elevator Inspector #26	502-564-3626
Embalmer #36	502-241-3918
Emergency Medical Technician-Basic #14	502-564-8950
Emergency Medical Technician-First Response #14	502-564-8950
Engineer #39	502-573-2680
Engineer/Land Surveyor Firm #39	502-573-2680
Fire Alarm System Inspector #26	502-564-3626
Fire Protection Sprinkler Installer #26	502-564-3626
Fire Suppression System Inspt. #26	502-564-8090
Fishing, Commercial #20	800-858-1549
Funeral Director #36	502-241-3918
Fur Buyer #20	800-858-1549
Fur Processor #20	800-858-1549
Geologist #15	502-564-3296 x227
Guide, Hunting & Fishing #20	800-858-1549
Health Care Facility #13	502-564-2800
Hearing Instrument Specialist #15	502-564-3296
Horse Claiming License #31	859-246-2040
Horse Farm Manager/Agent #31	859-246-2040
Horse Owner/Trainer/Asst. Trainer #31	829-246-2040
Horse Racing Occupation License #31	859-246-2040
Horse Racing Official/Autho. Agent #31	859-246-2040
Horse Veterinarian/Veterinary Asst. #31	859-246-2040
Horse Veterinary Dental Technician #31	859-246-2040
Insurance Adjuster #21	502-564-3630
Insurance Agent #21	502-564-3630
Insurance Consultant #21	502-564-3630
Insurance Solicitor #21	502-564-3630
Investment Advisor/Representative #18	502-573-3390
Jockey Agent #31	859-246-2040
Jockey/Jockey Apprentice #31	859-246-2040
Lake Operator #20	800-858-1549
Landfarm Operator #24	502-564-6716
Landfill Operator/Manager #24	502-564-6716
Law Enforcement Training Instrct. #17	859-622-6165
Liquor License #01	502-573-4850
Livestock Auctioneer, Limited #04	502-339-9453
Loan Company #18	502-573-3390
Malt Beverage Distributor #01	502-573-4850
Marriage & Family Therapist #15	502-564-3296
Medical Doctor/Surgeon #41	502-429-8046
Midwife Nurse #09	502-329-7000
Milk Sampler/Weigher/Tester#43	859-257-2785
Mine Safety Instructor #22	859-246-2026
Miner #22	859-246-2026
Mining Blaster #22	859-246-2026
Mining Fire Boss #22	859-246-2026
Mining Foreman/Inspector #22	859-246-2026
Mortgage Broker #18	502-573-3390
Mortgage Loan Company #18	502-573-3390
Nail Technician #37	502-564-4262
Notary Public #30	502-564-3490
Nurse #09	502-329-7000
Nurse Anesthetist #09	502-329-7000
Nurse Clinical Specialist #09	502-329-7000
Nurse-RN/LPN #09	502-329-7000
Nurses' Aide Instructor #09	502-329-7048
Nursing Home Administrator #15	502-564-3296
Occupational Therapist/Assistant #15	502-564-3296
Ophthalmic Dispenser/Optician/Apprentice #10	502-564-3296
Optometrist #11	859-246-2744
Osteopathic Physician #41	502-429-8046
Paramedic #14	502-564-8950
Pari-Mutuel Employee #31	859-246-2040
Pesticide Applicator #16	502-564-7274
Pesticide Dealer #16	502-564-7274
Pesticide Exterminator #16	502-564-7274
Pharmacy/Pharmacist #12	502-573-1580
Physical Therapist #38	502-327-8497
Physical Therapist Assistant #38	502-327-8497
Physician Assistant #41	502-429-8046
Plans & Specifications Inspector #26	502-564-8090
Plumber #26	502-564-3580
Podiatrist #27	207-759-0007
Police Officer #17	859-622-6165
Polygraph Examiner/Examiner Trainee #28	502-564-4756
Property Valuation Administrator #34	502-564-8338
Proprietary Education School #15	502-564-3296
Psychologist #15	502-564-3296
Public Accountant-CPA #03	502-595-3037
Racetrack Occupation (vendors, etc.) #31	859-246-2040
Racing Association Employee #31	859-246-2040
Radiation Operator #44	502-564-3700
Real Estate Appraiser #32	502-573-0091
Real Estate Broker #33	502-425-4273
Real Estate Brokerage/Firm #33	502-425-4273
Real Estate Sales Associate #33	502-425-4273
Rehabilitation Counselor #23	502-564-6745
Respiratory Care Practitioner #15	502-564-3296
Respiratory Therapist #15	502-564-3296
Sanitarian #45	502-564-7398
Savings & Loan #18	502-573-3390
School Administrator #25	502-573-4606
School Bus Driver #46	502-564-4718
School Guidance Counselor #25	502-573-4606
School Media Librarian #25	502-573-4606
School Nurse #25	502-573-4606
School Social Worker/Psychologist 25	502-573-4606
Securities Agent #18	502-573-3370
Securities Broker/Dealer #18	502-573-3370
Septic System Installer, Onsite #45	502-564-4856
Sexual Assault Nurse Examiner #09	502-329-7000
Social Worker #15	502-564-3296
Speech-Language Pathologist/Audiologist #15	502-564-3296 x227
Stable Employee #31	859-246-2040
Surveyor #39	502-573-2680
Taxidermist #20	800-858-1549
Teacher #25	502-573-4606
Tobacco Auctioneer, Limited #04	502-339-9453
Vendor/Vendor Employee #31	859-246-2040
Veterinarian #15	502-564-3296
Waste Water System Operator #29	502-564-3410
Water Well Driller #29	502-564-3410
Wrestler #15	502-564-3296

Licensing Agency Information

#01 Alcoholic Beverage Control Department, 1003 Twilight Trail, #A2, Frankfort, KY 40601; 502-564-4850, Fax: 502-564-1442.

#02 Bar Association, 514 W Main St, Frankfort, KY 40601-1883; 502-564-3795, Fax: 502-564-3225.
www.kybar.org

#03 Board of Accountancy, 332 W Broadway, #310, Louisville, KY 40202; 502-595-3037, Fax: 502-595-4281.
http://cpa.state.ky.us
Direct web site URL to search for licensees: www.state.ky.us/agencies/boa/Locate.html. You can search online using name and address. The online search is actually e-mail based, meaning that you visit the URL listed, enter the search criteria, and an e-mail is sent to the board. The results of your inquiry are e-mailed to you.

#04 Board of Auctioneers, 9112 Leesgate Rd, Louisville, KY 40222-5089; 502-339-9453, Fax: 502-423-1854.

#05 Board of Barbering, 9114 Leesgate Rd, #6, Louisville, KY 40222-5055; 502-429-8841, Fax: 502-429-5223.

#06 Board of Dentistry, 10101 Linn Station Rd, #540, Louisville, KY 40223; 502-423-0573, Fax: 502-423-1239.

#07 Board of Examiners & Registration of Architects, 841 Corporate Dr, #200B, Lexington, KY 40503; 859-246-2069, Fax: 859-246-2431.
http://kybera.com/
Direct web site URL to search for licensees: http://kybera.com/roster.shtml. You can search online using name, city, other

#09 Board of Nursing, 312 Whittington Pky, #300, Louisville, KY 40222-5172; 502-329-7000, Fax: 502-329-7011.
www.kbn.state.ky.us/index.htm

#10 Division of Occupations and Professions, PO Box 456, Frankfort, KY 40602; 502-564-3296 x227, Fax: 502-564-4818.

#11 Board of Optometric Examiners, 301 E Main St #850, Lexington, KY 40507-1578; 859-246-2744, Fax: 859-246-2746.
http://optometry.state.ky.us
Direct web site URL to search for licensees: http://web.state.ky.us/GBC/LicenseSearch.asp?AGY=8. You can search online using name and license number.

#12 Board of Pharmacy, 1024 Capital Center Dr, #210, Frankfort, KY 40601-8204; 502-573-1580, Fax: 502-573-1582.

#13 Division of Licensing & Regulations, CHR Bldg, 4th Fl East, Frankfort, KY 40621-0001; 502-564-2800, Fax: 502-564-6546.
www.cfc-chs.chr.state.ky.us

#14 Cabinet for Health Services, 275 Main St, Frankfort, KY 40621; 502-564-8950, Fax: 502-564-6533.
http://publichealth.state.ky.us/ems.htm

#15 Department of Administration, PO Box 1360, Frankfort, KY 40602; 502-564-3296, Fax: 502-564-4818.
www.state.ky.us/agencies/finance/occupations

#16 Department of Agriculture, 100 Fair Oak Ln, 5th Fl, Frankfort, KY 40601; 502-564-7274, Fax: 502-564-3773.
www.kyagr.com

#17 Department of Criminal Justice Training, 3137 Kit Carson Dr, Richmond, KY 40475-3137; 859-622-6165, Fax: 859-622-2740.
www.jus.state.ky.us

#18 Department of Financial Institutions, 1025 Capitol Center Dr #200, Frankfort, KY 40601; 800-223-3390, Fax: 502-573-8787.
www.dfi.state.ky.us

#20 Department of Fish & Wildlife, 1 Game Farm Rd, Frankfort, KY 40601; 800-858-1549, Fax: 502-564-9136.
www.kdfwr.state.ky.us

#21 Department of Insurance, PO Box 517, 215 W Main St, Frankfort, KY 40602-0517; 502-564-3630.
www.doi.state.ky.us/kentucky/

#22 Department of Mines & Minerals, PO Box 2244, Frankfort, KY 40602-2244; 502-573-0140, Fax: 502-573-0152.
www.caer.uky.edu/kdmm/homepage.htm

#23 Department of Vocational Rehabilitation, 209 St Clair St, Frankfort, KY 40601; 502-564-4440, Fax: 502-564-6745.
http://kydvr.state.ky.us

#24 Division of Waste Management, 14 Reilly Rd, Frankfort, KY 40601; 502-564-6716, Fax: 502-564-4049.
www.nr.state.ky.us/nrepc/dep/waste/dwmhome.htm

#25 Education Department, 1025 Capitol Center Dr, Frankfort, KY 40601; 502-573-4606, Fax: 502-573-4606.
www.kde.state.ky.us

#26 Buildings & Construction Department, 1047 US 127 S, #1, Frankfort, KY 40601; 502-564-8044.
www.state.ky.us/agencies/cppr/housing/hbchome.htm

#27 Board of Podiatry, 906B South 12th St, Murray, KY 42071-2949; 270-759-0007, Fax: 270-753-0684.

#28 State Police, 1250 Louisville Rd, Frankfort, KY 40601; 502-564-4756, Fax: 502-564-5956.
www.state.ky.us/agencies/ksp/ksphome.htm

#29 Division of Water, 14 Reilly Rd, Frankfort Office Park, Frankfort, KY 40601; 502-564-3410, Fax: 502-564-9720.
http://water.nr.state.ky.us/dow/dwhome.htm

#30 Office of Secretary of State, Capitol Bldg, Frankfort, KY 40602-0821; 502-564-3490 x413, Fax: 502-564-4075.
www.kysos.com

#31 National Horse Center - Bldg B, 4063 Iron Works Pike, Lexington, KY 40511; 859-246-2040, Fax: 859-246-2039.

#32 Real Estate Appraisers Board, 1025 Capitol Center Dr #100, Frankfort, KY 40601-8205; 502-573-0091, Fax: 502-573-0093.

#33 Real Estate Commission, 10200 Linn Station Rd, #201, Louisville, KY 40223; 502-425-4273, Fax: 502-426-2717.
www.krec.net
Direct web site URL to search for licensees: http://web.state.ky.us/krecweb. You can search online using name.

#34 Department of Property Taxation, 200 Fair Oaks, Frankfort, KY 40620; 502-564-8338, Fax: 502-564-8368.
www.revenue.state.ky.ys/contact.htm

#35 Board of Chiropractic Examiners, 209 S Green St (PO Box 183), Glasgow, KY 42142-0183; 270-651-2522, Fax: 270-651-8784.

#36 Board of Embalmers & Funeral Directors, PO Box 324, Crestwood, KY 40014; 502-241-3918, Fax: 502-241-4297.

#37 Board of Hairdressers & Cosmetologists, 111 St James Court #A, Frankfort, KY 40601; 502-564-4262, Fax: 502-564-0481.

#38 Board of Physical Therapy, 9110 Leesgate Rd, #6, Louisville, KY 40222-5159; 502-327-8497, Fax: 502-423-0934.
http://kbpt.state.ky.us
Direct web site URL to search for licensees: http://web.state.ky.us/gbc/LicenseSearch.asp?AGY=4. You can search online using last name or license number

#39 Professional Engineers & Land Surveyors, Board of Licensure, 160 Democrat Dr, Frankfort, KY 40601; 502-573-2680, Fax: 502-573-6687.
http://kyboels.state.ky.us/
Direct web site URL to search for licensees: http://kyboels.state.ky.us/roster.htm. You can search online using name.

#41 Board of Medical Licensure, 310 Whittington Pky, #1B, Louisville, KY 40222; 502-429-8046, Fax: 502-429-9923.

#42 State Police Driver Testing Section, 919 Versailles Rd, Frankfort, KY 40601; 502-226-7404, Fax: 502-226-7412.

#43 Division of Regulatory Services, 103 Regulatory Service Bldg, Lexington, KY 40546-0275; 859-257-2785, Fax: 859-323-9931.
www.rs.uky.edu

#44 Radiation Health & Toxic Agents, 275 E Main St, Frankfort, KY 40621; 502-564-3700, Fax: 502-564-6533.

#45 Department for Public Health, 275 E Main, 2nd Fl E, HS 2EA, Frankfort, KY 40621; 502-564-7398, Fax: 502-564-6533.

#46 Department of Education, 500 Mero St 15th Fl, Frankfort, KY 40601; 502-564-4718, Fax: 502-564-9574.
www.kde.state.ky.us

Kentucky Federal Courts

The following list indicates the district and division name for each county in the state. If the bankruptcy court location is different from the district court, then the location of the bankruptcy court appears in parentheses.

County/Court Cross Reference

County	District	Division
Adair	Western	Bowling Green (Louisville)
Allen	Western	Bowling Green (Louisville)
Anderson	Eastern	Frankfort (Lexington)
Ballard	Western	Paducah (Louisville)
Barren	Western	Bowling Green (Louisville)
Bath	Eastern	Lexington
Bell	Eastern	London (Lexington)
Boone	Eastern	Covington (Lexington)
Bourbon	Eastern	Lexington
Boyd	Eastern	Ashland (Lexington)
Boyle	Eastern	Lexington
Bracken	Eastern	Covington (Lexington)
Breathitt	Eastern	Pikeville (Lexington)
Breckinridge	Western	Louisville
Bullitt	Western	Louisville
Butler	Western	Bowling Green (Louisville)
Caldwell	Western	Paducah (Louisville)
Calloway	Western	Paducah (Louisville)
Campbell	Eastern	Covington (Lexington)
Carlisle	Western	Paducah (Louisville)
Carroll	Eastern	Frankfort (Lexington)
Carter	Eastern	Ashland (Lexington)
Casey	Western	Bowling Green (Louisville)
Christian	Western	Paducah (Louisville)
Clark	Eastern	Lexington
Clay	Eastern	London (Lexington)
Clinton	Western	Bowling Green (Louisville)
Crittenden	Western	Paducah (Louisville)
Cumberland	Western	Bowling Green (Louisville)
Daviess	Western	Owensboro (Louisville)
Edmonson	Western	Bowling Green (Louisville)
Elliott	Eastern	Ashland (Lexington)
Estill	Eastern	Lexington
Fayette	Eastern	Lexington
Fleming	Eastern	Lexington
Floyd	Eastern	Pikeville (Lexington)
Franklin	Eastern	Frankfort (Lexington)
Fulton	Western	Paducah (Louisville)
Gallatin	Eastern	Covington (Lexington)
Garrard	Eastern	Lexington
Grant	Eastern	Covington (Lexington)
Graves	Western	Paducah (Louisville)
Grayson	Western	Owensboro (Louisville)
Green	Western	Bowling Green (Louisville)
Greenup	Eastern	Ashland (Lexington)
Hancock	Western	Owensboro (Louisville)
Hardin	Western	Louisville
Harlan	Eastern	London (Lexington)
Harrison	Eastern	Lexington
Hart	Western	Bowling Green (Louisville)
Henderson	Western	Owensboro (Louisville)
Henry	Eastern	Frankfort (Lexington)
Hickman	Western	Paducah (Louisville)
Hopkins	Western	Owensboro (Louisville)
Jackson	Eastern	London (Lexington)
Jefferson	Western	Louisville
Jessamine	Eastern	Lexington
Johnson	Eastern	Pikeville (Lexington)
Kenton	Eastern	Covington (Lexington)
Knott	Eastern	Pikeville (Lexington)
Knox	Eastern	London (Lexington)
Larue	Western	Louisville
Laurel	Eastern	London (Lexington)
Lawrence	Eastern	Ashland (Lexington)
Lee	Eastern	Lexington
Leslie	Eastern	London (Lexington)
Letcher	Eastern	Pikeville (Lexington)
Lewis	Eastern	Ashland (Lexington)
Lincoln	Eastern	Lexington
Livingston	Western	Paducah (Louisville)
Logan	Western	Bowling Green (Louisville)
Lyon	Western	Paducah (Louisville)
Madison	Eastern	Lexington
Magoffin	Eastern	Pikeville (Lexington)
Marion	Western	Louisville
Marshall	Western	Paducah (Louisville)
Martin	Eastern	Pikeville (Lexington)
Mason	Eastern	Covington (Lexington)
McCracken	Western	Paducah (Louisville)
McCreary	Eastern	London (Lexington)
McLean	Western	Owensboro (Louisville)
Meade	Western	Louisville
Menifee	Eastern	Lexington
Mercer	Eastern	Lexington
Metcalfe	Western	Bowling Green (Louisville)
Monroe	Western	Bowling Green (Louisville)
Montgomery	Eastern	Lexington
Morgan	Eastern	Ashland (Lexington)
Muhlenberg	Western	Owensboro (Louisville)
Nelson	Western	Louisville
Nicholas	Eastern	Lexington
Ohio	Western	Owensboro (Louisville)
Oldham	Western	Louisville
Owen	Eastern	Frankfort (Lexington)
Owsley	Eastern	London (Lexington)
Pendleton	Eastern	Covington (Lexington)
Perry	Eastern	Pikeville (Lexington)
Pike	Eastern	Pikeville (Lexington)
Powell	Eastern	Lexington
Pulaski	Eastern	London (Lexington)
Robertson	Eastern	Covington (Lexington)
Rockcastle	Eastern	London (Lexington)
Rowan	Eastern	Ashland (Lexington)
Russell	Western	Bowling Green (Louisville)

Scott	Eastern	Lexington	
Shelby	Eastern	Frankfort (Lexington)	
Simpson	Western	Bowling Green (Louisville)	
Spencer	Western	Louisville	
Taylor	Western	Bowling Green (Louisville)	
Todd	Western	Bowling Green (Louisville)	
Trigg	Western	Paducah (Louisville)	
Trimble	Eastern	Frankfort (Lexington)	

Union	Western	Owensboro (Louisville)
Warren	Western	Bowling Green (Louisville)
Washington	Western	Louisville
Wayne	Eastern	London (Lexington)
Webster	Western	Owensboro (Louisville)
Whitley	Eastern	London (Lexington)
Wolfe	Eastern	Lexington
Woodford	Eastern	Lexington

US District Court

Eastern District of Kentucky

Ashland Division Suite 336, 1405 Greenup Ave, Ashland, KY 41101 (Courier Address: Use mail address for courier delivery), 606-329-8652.

http://www.kyed.uscourts.gov

Counties: Boyd, Carter, Elliott, Greenup, Lawrence, Lewis, Morgan, Rowan.

Indexing/Storage: Cases are indexed by defendant and plaintiff as well as by case number. New cases are available in the index 1-2 days after filing date. Lexington Division has a master index for the district. Both computer and card indexes are maintained. The index is computerized from 1992. Open records are located at this court.

Fee & Payment: The fee is $20.00 per item (one party name or case number). Payment may be made by money order, cashier check, personal check. Prepayment is required. Payee: Clerk, USDC. Certification fee: $7.00 per document. Copy fee: $.50 per page.

Phone Search: Only docket information from active cases will be released over the phone.

Mail Search: A stamped self addressed envelope is not required.

In Person: In person searching is available.

PACER: Sign-up number is 800-676-6856. Access fee is $.60 per minute. Toll-free access: 800-361-0442. Local access: 859-233-2787. Case records are available back to September 1991. Records are never purged. New records are available online after 1 day. PACER is available online at http://pacer.kyed.uscourts.gov.

Covington Division Clerk, PO Box 1073, Covington, KY 41012 (Courier Address: US Courthouse, Room 201, 35 W 5th St, Covington, KY 41011), 859-392-7925.

http://www.kyed.uscourts.gov

Counties: Boone, Bracken, Campbell, Gallatin, Grant, Kenton, Mason, Pendleton, Robertson.

Indexing/Storage: Cases are indexed by defendant and plaintiff as well as by case number. New cases are available in the index immediately after filing date. Both computer and card indexes are maintained. Open records are located at this court.

Fee & Payment: The fee is $20.00 per item (one party name or case number). Payment may be made by money order, cashier check, personal check. Prepayment is required. The turnaround time for written requests varies. Payee: Clerk, US District Court. Certification fee: $7.00 per document. Copy fee: $.50 per page.

Phone Search: Searching is not available by phone.

Mail Search: Always enclose a stamped self addressed envelope.

In Person: In person searching is available.

PACER: Sign-up number is 800-676-6856. Access fee is $.60 per minute. Toll-free access: 800-361-0442. Local access: 859-233-2787. Case records are available back to September 1991. Records are never purged. New records are available online after 1 day. PACER is available online at http://pacer.kyed.uscourts.gov.

Frankfort Division Room 313, 330 W Broadway, Frankfort, KY 40601 (Courier Address: Use mail address for courier delivery), 502-223-5225.

http://www.kyed.uscourts.gov

Counties: Anderson, Carroll, Franklin, Henry, Owen, Shelby, Trimble.

Indexing/Storage: Cases are indexed by defendant and plaintiff as well as by case number. New cases are available in the index immediately after filing date. Both computer and card indexes are maintained. Records have been indexed on computer since January, 1993. Open records are located at this court.

Fee & Payment: The fee is $20.00 per item (one party name or case number). Payment may be made by money order, cashier check, personal check. Prepayment is required. Payee: Clerk, US District Court. Certification fee: $7.00 per document. Copy fee: $.50 per page.

Phone Search: Only docket information is available by phone.

Mail Search: A stamped self addressed envelope is not required.

In Person: In person searching is available.

PACER: Sign-up number is 800-676-6856. Access fee is $.60 per minute. Toll-free access: 800-361-0442. Local access: 606-233-2787. Case records are available back to September 1991. Records are never purged. New records are available online after 1 day. PACER is available online at http://pacer.kyed.uscourts.gov.

Lexington Division PO Box 3074, Lexington, KY 40588 (Courier Address: Room 206, 101 Barr St, Lexington, KY 40507), 859-233-2503.

http://www.kyed.uscourts.gov

Counties: Bath, Bourbon, Boyle, Clark, Estill, Fayette, Fleming, Garrard, Harrison, Jessamine, Lee, Lincoln, Madison, Menifee, Mercer, Montgomery, Nicholas, Powell, Scott, Wolfe, Woodford. Lee and Wolfe counties were part of the Pikeville Divisionbefore 10/31/92. Perry became part of Pikeville after 1992.

Indexing/Storage: Cases are indexed by defendant and plaintiff as well as by case number. New cases are available in the index 24 hours after filing date. Both computer and card indexes are maintained. Civil cases filed after October 1, 1992 are on the computer. Cases prior to October 1992 are on index cards. Open records are located at this court.

Fee & Payment: The fee is $20.00 per item (one party name or case number). Payment may be made by money order, cashier check, personal check. Prepayment is required. Payee: Clerk, USDC. Certification fee: $7.00 per document. Copy fee: $.50 per page.

Phone Search: Only docket information from active cases will be released over the phone.

Mail Search: A stamped self addressed envelope is not required.

In Person: In person searching is available.

PACER: Sign-up number is 800-676-6856. Access fee is $.60 per minute. Toll-free access: 800-361-0442. Local access: 859-233-2787. Case records are available back to September 1991. Records are never purged. New records are available online after 1 day. PACER is available online at http://pacer.kyed.uscourts.gov.

London Division PO Box 5121, London, KY 40745-5121 (Courier Address: 124 US Courthouse, 300 S Main, London, KY 40741), 606-864-5137.

http://www.kyed.uscourts.gov

Counties: Bell, Clay, Harlan, Jackson, Knox, Laurel, Leslie, McCreary, Owsley, Pulaski, Rockcastle, Wayne, Whitley.

Indexing/Storage: Cases are indexed by defendant and plaintiff as well as by case number. New cases are available in the index 1 day after filing date. A computer index is maintained. Open records are located at this court.

Fee & Payment: The fee is $20.00 per item (one party name or case number). Payment may be made by money order, cashier check, personal check. Prepayment is required. Payee: Clerk, USDC. Certification fee: $7.00 per document. Copy fee: $.50 per page.

Phone Search: Only docket information is available by phone.

Mail Search: Always enclose a stamped self addressed envelope.

In Person: In person searching is available.

PACER: Sign-up number is 800-676-6856. Access fee is $.60 per minute. Toll-free access: 800-361-0442. Local access: 859-233-2787. Case records are available back to September 1991. Records are never purged. New records are available online after 1 day. PACER is available online at http://pacer.kyed.uscourts.gov.

Pikeville Division Office of the clerk, 203 Federal Bldg, 110 Main St, Pikeville, KY 41501 (Courier Address: Use mail address for courier delivery), 606-437-6160.

http://www.kyed.uscourts.gov

Counties: Breathitt, Floyd, Johnson, Knott, Letcher, Magoffin, Martin, Perry, Pike. Lee and Wolfe Counties were part of this division until 10/31/92, when they were moved to the Lexington Division.

Indexing/Storage: Cases are indexed by defendant and plaintiff as well as by case number. New cases are available in the index immediately after filing date. A computer index is maintained. Open records are located at this court.

Fee & Payment: The fee is $20.00 per item (one party name or case number). Payment may be made by money order, cashier check, personal check. Prepayment required except for Kentucky attorneys. Payee: Clerk, US District Court. Certification fee: $7.00 per document. Copy fee: $.50 per page. You are allowed to make your own copies. These copies cost $.50 per page.

Phone Search: Only the date the case was filed and the status of the case will be released over the phone.

Mail Search: A stamped self addressed envelope is not required.

In Person: In person searching is available.

PACER: Sign-up number is 800-676-6856. Access fee is $.60 per minute. Toll-free access: 800-361-0442. Local access: 859-233-2787. Case records are available back to September 1991. Records are never purged. New records are available online after 1 day. PACER is available online at http://pacer.kyed.uscourts.gov.

US Bankruptcy Court

Eastern District of Kentucky

Lexington Division PO Box 1111, Lexington, KY 40589-1111 (Courier Address: Community Trust Bldg, Suite 202, 100 E Vine St, Lexington, KY 40507), 859-233-2608.

http://www.kyeb.uscourts.gov

Counties: Anderson, Bath, Bell, Boone, Bourbon, Boyd, Boyle, Bracken, Breathitt, Campbell, Carroll, Carter, Clark, Clay, Elliott, Estill, Fayette, Fleming, Floyd, Franklin, Gallatin, Garrard, Grant, Greenup, Harlan, Harrison, Henry, Jackson, Jessamine, Johnson,Kenton, Knott, Knox, Laurel, Lawrence, Lee, Leslie, Letcher, Lewis, Lincoln, Madison, Magoffin, Martin, Mason, McCreary, Menifee, Mercer, Montgomery, Morgan, Nicholas, Owen, Owsley, Pendleton, Perry, Pike, Powell, Pulaski, Robertson, Rockcastle, Rowan,Scott, Shelby, Trimble, Wayne, Whitley, Wolfe, Woodford.

Indexing/Storage: Cases are indexed by debtor as well as by case number. New cases are available in the index 3 days after filing date. Both computer and card indexes are maintained. Open records are located at this court.

Fee & Payment: The fee is $20.00 per item (one party name or case number). Payment may be made by money order, cashier check, business check. Personal checks are not accepted. Prepayment is required (excluding pauper filings). Payee: Clerk, US Bankruptcy Court. Certification fee: $7.00 per document. Copy fee: $.50 per page.

You are allowed to make your own copies. These copies cost $.15 per page.

Phone Search: Only docket information is available by phone. An automated voice case information service (VCIS) is available. Call VCIS at 800-998-2650 or 606-233-2650.

Mail Search: Always enclose a stamped self addressed envelope.

In Person: In person searching is available.

PACER: Sign-up number is 800-676-6856. Access fee is $.60 per minute. Toll-free access: 800-497-2777. Local access: 859-233-2777. Case records are available back to July 1992. Records are purged every six months. New civil records are available online after 1 day. PACER is available online at http://pacer.kyeb.uscourts.gov.

US District Court

Western District of Kentucky

Bowling Green Division US District Court, 241 E Main St, Room 120, Bowling Green, KY 42101-2175 (Courier Address: Use mail address for courier delivery), 270-781-1110, Fax: 270-842-2836.

http://www.kywd.uscourts.gov

Counties: Adair, Allen, Barren, Butler, Casey, Clinton, Cumberland, Edmonson, Green, Hart, Logan, Metcalfe, Monroe, Russell, Simpson, Taylor, Todd, Warren.

Indexing/Storage: Cases are indexed by defendant and plaintiff as well as by case number. New cases are available in the index 1-2 days after filing date. Both computer and card indexes are maintained. Open records are located at this court.

Fee & Payment: The fee is $20.00 per item (one party name or case number). Payment may be made by money order, cashier check, personal check. Prepayment is required. Payee: Clerk, US District Court. Certification fee: $7.00 per document. Copy fee: $.50 per page. You are allowed to make your own copies. These copies cost $.50 per page.

Phone Search: Only docket information is available by phone.

Mail Search: Always enclose a stamped self addressed envelope.

In Person: In person searching is available.

PACER: Sign-up number is 800-676-6856. Access fee is $.60 per minute. Local access: 502-588-3260, 502-588-3261. Case records are available back to 1992. New records are available online after 1 day. PACER is available online at http://207.41.14.16/ndefault.html.

Electronic Filing: Electronic filing information is available online at www.kywd.uscourts.gov/scripts/usdckyw/ecf/ecf2.pl

Opinions Online: Court opinions are available online at http://www.kywd.uscourts.gov

Louisville Division Clerk, US District Court, 450 US Courthouse, 601 W Broadway, Louisville, KY 40202 (Courier Address: Use mail address for courier delivery), 502-625-3500, Fax: 502-625-3880.

http://www.kywd.uscourts.gov

Counties: Breckinridge, Bullitt, Hardin, Jefferson, Larue, Marion, Meade, Nelson, Oldham, Spencer, Washington.

Indexing/Storage: Cases are indexed by defendant and plaintiff as well as by case number. New cases are available in the index immediately after filing date. Both computer and card indexes are maintained. Records are indexed on index cards from 1938 to 1979. Records are indexed on microfiche from 1979 to 4/92. Records after 4/92 are on the automated system. Open records are located at this court. District wide searches are available from this court for information from 1938.

Fee & Payment: The fee is $20.00 per item (one party name or case number). Payment may be made by money order, cashier check, personal check. Prepayment is required. Payee: Clerk, US District Court. Certification fee: $7.00 per document. Copy fee: $.50 per page.

Phone Search: Searching is not available by phone. Only docket information is available by phone.

Mail Search: Always enclose a stamped self addressed envelope.

In Person: In person searching is available.

PACER: Sign-up number is 800-676-6856. Access fee is $.60 per minute. Local access: 502-588-3260, 502-588-3261. Case records are available back to 1992. New records are available online after 1 day. PACER is available online at http://38.244.24.105/webpacer.html.

Electronic Filing: Electronic filing information is available online at www.kywd.uscourts.gov/scripts/usdckyw/ecf/ecf2.pl

Opinions Online: Court opinions are available online at http://www.kywd.uscourts.gov

Owensboro Division Federal Bldg, Room 126, 423 Frederica St, Owensboro, KY 42301 (Courier Address: Use mail address for courier delivery), 270-683-0221, Fax: 502-685-4601.

http://www.kywd.uscourts.gov

Counties: Daviess, Grayson, Hancock, Henderson, Hopkins, McLean, Muhlenberg, Ohio, Union, Webster.

Indexing/Storage: Cases are indexed by defendant and plaintiff as well as by case number. New cases are available in the index 1-2 days after filing date. The court needs the correct name, date and/or criminal or civil case number to search for a record. A computer index is maintained. Open records are located at this court.

Fee & Payment: The fee is $20.00 per item (one party name or case number). Payment may be made by money order, cashier check, personal check. The court will only bill to in state searchers. Payee: Clerk, US District Court. Certification fee: $7.00 per document. Copy fee: $.50 per page. You are allowed to make your own copies. These copies cost $.50 per page.

Phone Search: Only docket information is available by phone.

Mail Search: A stamped self addressed envelope is not required.

In Person: In person searching is available.

PACER: Sign-up number is 800-676-6856. Access fee is $.60 per minute. Local access: 502-588-3260, 502-588-3261. Case records are available back to 1992. New records are available online after 1 day. PACER is available online at http://38.244.24.105/webpacer.html.

Electronic Filing: Electronic filing information is available online at www.kywd.uscourts.gov/scripts/usdckyw/ecf/ecf2.pl

Opinions Online: Court opinions are available online at http://www.kywd.uscourts.gov

Paducah Division 127 Federal Building, 501 Broadway, Paducah, KY 42001 (Courier Address: Use mail address for courier delivery), 270-443-1337, Fax: 270-442-1919.

http://www.kywd.uscourts.gov

Counties: Ballard, Caldwell, Calloway, Carlisle, Christian, Crittenden, Fulton, Graves, Hickman, Livingston, Lyon, McCracken, Marshall, Trigg.

Indexing/Storage: Cases are indexed by defendant and plaintiff as well as by case number. New cases are available in the index 1-2 days after filing date. Both computer and card indexes are maintained. Open records are located at this court.

Fee & Payment: The fee is $20.00 per item (one party name or case number). Payment may be made by money order, cashier check, personal check. Prepayment is required. Payee: Clerk, US District Court. Certification fee: $7.00 per document. Copy fee: $.50 per page. You are allowed to make your own copies. These copies cost $.50 per page.

Phone Search: Only docket information is available by phone.

Fax Search: You may fax for a fee quote.

Mail Search: Always enclose a stamped self addressed envelope.

In Person: In person searching is available.

PACER: Sign-up number is 800-676-6856. Access fee is $.60 per minute. Local access: 502-588-3260, 502-588-3261. Case records are available back to 1992. New records are available online after 1 day. PACER is available online at http://38.244.24.105/webpacer.html.

Electronic Filing: Electronic filing information is available online at www.kywd.uscourts.gov/scripts/usdckyw/ecf/ecf2.pl

Opinions Online: Court opinions are available online at http://www.kywd.uscourts.gov

US Bankruptcy Court
Western District of Kentucky

Louisville Division 546 US Courthouse, 601 W Broadway, Louisville, KY 40202 (Courier Address: Use mail address for courier delivery), 502-627-5800.

http://www.kywb.uscourts.gov

Counties: Adair, Allen, Ballard, Barren, Breckinridge, Bullitt, Butler, Caldwell, Calloway, Carlisle, Casey, Christian, Clinton, Crittenden, Cumberland, Daviess, Edmonson, Fulton, Graves, Grayson, Green, Hancock, Hardin, Hart, Henderson, Hickman, Hopkins,Jefferson, Larue, Livingston, Logan, Lyon, Marion, Marshall, McCracken, McLean, Meade, Metcalfe, Monroe, Muhlenberg, Nelson, Ohio, Oldham, Russell,

Simpson, Spencer, Taylor, Todd, Trigg, Union, Warren, Washington, Webster.

Indexing/Storage: Cases are indexed by debtor as well as by case number. New cases are available in the index 1-2 days after filing date. A card index is maintained. Open records are located at this court. District wide searches are available from this division. This division maintains records for all of the divisions in this district.

Fee & Payment: The fee is $20.00 per item (one party name or case number). Payment may be made by money order, cashier check. Business checks are not accepted. Personal checks are not accepted. Prepayment is required. Payee: Clerk, US Bankruptcy Court. Certification fee: $7.00 per document. Copy fee: $.50 per page.

Phone Search: Only docket information is available by phone. An automated voice case information service (VCIS) is available. Call VCIS at 800-263-9385 or 502-625-7391.

Mail Search: Always enclose a stamped self addressed envelope.

In Person: In person searching is available.

PACER: Sign-up number is 800-676-6856. Access fee is $.60 per minute. Toll-free access: 800-263-9389. Local access: 502-627-5664. Case records are available back to July 1992. Records are purged every six months. New civil records are available online after 1-2 days. PACER is available online at http://pacer.kywb.uscourts.gov.

Kentucky County Courts

Court	Jurisdiction	No. of Courts	How Organized
Circuit Courts*	General	19	56 Judicial Circuits
District Courts*	Limited	19	59 Judicial Districts
Combined*		102	

* Profiled in this Sourcebook.

				CIVIL					
Court	Tort	Contract	Real Estate	Min. Claim	Max. Claim	Small Claims	Estate	Eviction	Domestic Relations
Circuit Courts*	X	X	X	$4000	No Max				X
District Courts*	X	X	X	$0	$4000	$1500	X	X	X

			CRIMINAL		
Court	Felony	Misdemeanor	DWI/DUI	Preliminary Hearing	Juvenile
Circuit Courts*	X				
District Courts*		X	X	X	X

ADMINISTRATION
Administrative Office of Courts, 100 Mill Creek Park, Frankfort, KY, 40601; 502-573-2350, Fax: 502-573-1448. http://www.kycourts.net/aoc/default.htm

COURT STRUCTURE
The Circuit Court is the court of general jurisdiction and the District Court is the limited jurisdiction court. Most of Kentucky's counties combined the courts into one location and records are co-mingled.

ONLINE ACCESS
There are statewide, online computer systems called SUSTAIN and KyCourts available for internal judicial/state agency use only. No courts offer online access.

ADDITIONAL INFORMATION
Until 1978, county judges handled all cases; therefore, in many cases, District and Circuit Court records go back only to 1978. Records prior to that time are archived.

Many courts refer requests for criminal searches to the Administrative Office of Courts (AOC - 502-573-2350 or 800-928-6381) due to lack of personnel for searching at the court level. AOC maintains records on an internal system called COURTNET, which contains information on opening, closing, proceedings, disposition, and parties to including individual defendants. Felony convictions are accessible back to 1978, and Misdemeanors back five years. The required Release Form is available from the AOC at the numbers above. A check or money order for the Search Fee of $10.00 per requested individual ($5.00 fee if non-profit or if you are the individual) is payable to the State Treasurer of Kentucky. A SASE and a second postage-attached envelope must accompany the request.

Adair County

Circuit & District Court 500 Public Square, Suite 6, Columbia, KY 42728; 270-384-2626; Fax: 270-384-4299. Hours: 8AM-4PM (CST). *Felony, Misdemeanor, Civil, Eviction, Small Claims, Probate.*
Civil Records: Access: Mail, in person. Both court and visitors may perform in person searches. No search fee. Required to search: name, years to search. Civil records on computer since June 1993, prior records on docket books since 1978.
Criminal Records: Access: Mail, in person. Both court and visitors may perform in person searches. No search fee. Required to search: name, years to search, SSN. Criminal records on computer since June 1993, prior records on docket books since 1978.
General Information: Public Access terminal is available. No adoption, mental, juvenile, or sealed records released. SASE required. Turnaround time same day. Copy fee: $.15 per page. Certification fee: No cert fee. Fee payee: Circuit Clerk. Personal checks accepted.

Allen County

Circuit & District Court Box 477, Scottsville, KY 42164; 270-237-3561. Hours: 8AM-4:30PM (CST). *Felony, Misdemeanor, Civil, Eviction, Small Claims, Probate.*
Civil Records: Access: In person only. Visitors must perform in person searches for themselves. No search fee. Required to search: name, years to search. Civil cases indexed by defendant, plaintiff. Civil records on computer since 1992, records on index cards from 1978 to 1992, prior records on books.
Criminal Records: Access: In person only. Visitors must perform in person searches for themselves. No search fee. Required to search: name, years to search; also helpful: SSN. Criminal records on computer since 1992, records on index cards from 1978 to 1992, prior records on books. Court recommends that criminal search requests be directed to the State of Kentucky AOC, 502-573-2350.
General Information: Public Access terminal is available. No adoption, mental, juvenile, or sealed records released. Fax notes: Fee to fax results is $1.00 per page, first page; $2.00 each add'l. Copy fee: $.15 per page. Certification fee: $1.00. Fee payee: Circuit Clerk. Personal checks accepted. Prepayment is required.

Anderson County

Circuit Court Courthouse 151 S Main St, Lawrenceburg, KY 40342; 502-839-3508. Hours: 8:30AM-5PM *Felony, Civil Actions Over $4,000.*
Civil Records: Access: In person only. Only the court performs in person searches; visitors may not. No search fee. Required to search: name, years to search. Civil cases indexed by defendant, plaintiff. Civil records

on computer since August 1994, prior records on docket books since 1978.

Criminal Records: Access: In person only. Visitors must perform in person searches for themselves. No search fee. Required to search: name, years to search; also helpful: DOB, SSN. All record requests are referred to the state agency at 502-573-2350.

General Information:. No adoption, mental, juvenile, or sealed records released. Certification fee: $1.00. Fee payee: Clerk of Circuit Clerk. Personal checks accepted. Prepayment is required.

District Court 151 S Main, Lawrenceburg, KY 40342; 502-839-5445. Hours: 8:30AM-5PM M-TH, 8:30AM-6PM F (EST). *Misdemeanor, Civil Actions Under $4,000, Eviction, Small Claims, Probate.*

Civil Records: Access: In person only. Only the court performs in person searches; visitors may not. No search fee. Required to search: name, years to search. Civil cases indexed by defendant, plaintiff. Civil records on computer since August 1994, prior records on index cards.

Criminal Records: Access: In person only. Visitors must perform in person searches for themselves. No search fee. Required to search: name, years to search; also helpful: DOB, SSN. All requests are referred to Pre-trial Services at 800-928-6381. You may call them to perform the search for you.

General Information:. No adoption, mental, juvenile, or sealed records released. Copy fee: $.15 per page. Certification fee: $1.00. Fee payee: Anderson County District Court. Business checks accepted. Prepayment is required.

Ballard County

Circuit & District Court Box 265, Wickliffe, KY 42087; 270-335-5123; Fax: 270-335-3849. Hours: 8AM-4PM (CST). *Felony, Misdemeanor, Civil, Eviction, Small Claims, Probate.*

Civil Records: Access: Mail, fax, in person. Both court and visitors may perform in person searches. No search fee. Required to search: name, years to search. Civil cases indexed by defendant, plaintiff. Civil records on computer since 1992, prior records on books to 1978.

Criminal Records: Access: In person only. Visitors must perform in person searches for themselves. No search fee. Required to search: name, years to search, DOB. Criminal records on computer since 1992, prior records on books to 1978.

General Information: Public Access terminal is available. No adoption, mental, juvenile, or sealed records released. SASE required. Turnaround time 2 days. Fax notes: Fee to fax results is $2.00 per page. Copy fee: $.15 per page. Certification fee: $1.50. Fee payee: Circuit Clerk. Only cashiers checks and money orders accepted. Prepayment is required.

Barren County

Circuit & District Court PO Box 1359, Glasgow, KY 42142-1359; 270-651-3763; Fax: 270-651-6203. Hours: 8AM-4:30PM (CST). *Felony, Misdemeanor, Civil, Eviction, Small Claims, Probate.*

Civil Records: Access: In person only. Visitors must perform in person searches for themselves. No search fee. Required to search: name, years to search. Civil cases indexed by defendant, plaintiff. Civil records on computer back to 10/1991, prior records on index books since 1800s.

Criminal Records: Access: In person only. Visitors must perform in person searches for themselves. No search fee. Required to search: name, years to search, DOB; also helpful: SSN. Criminal records on computer back to 10/1991, prior on index books since 1800s.

General Information: Public Access terminal is available. No adoption, mental, juvenile, or sealed records released. Copy fee: $.15 per page. Certification

fee: $1.00. Fee payee: Circuit Clerk. Personal checks accepted. Prepayment is required.

Bath County

Circuit & District Court Box 558, Owingsville, KY 40360; 606-674-2186 X6821; Fax: 606-674-3996. Hours: 8AM-4PM (EST). *Felony, Misdemeanor, Civil, Eviction, Small Claims, Probate.*

Civil Records: Access: In person only. Visitors must perform in person searches for themselves. No search fee. Required to search: name, years to search. Civil cases indexed by defendant, plaintiff. Civil records computerized since 1994, on docket books since 1978, prior records archived.

Criminal Records: Access: In person only. Visitors must perform in person searches for themselves. No search fee. Required to search: name, years to search, DOB, SSN. Criminal records computerized since 1994, on docket books since 1978, prior records archived.

General Information: Public Access terminal is available. No adoption, mental, juvenile, or sealed records released. Copy fee: $.15 per page. Certification fee: $1.00. Fee payee: Circuit Clerk. Personal checks accepted. Prepayment is required.

Bell County

Circuit & District Court Box 307, Pineville, KY 40977; 606-337-2942/9900; Fax: 606-337-8850. Hours: 8:30AM-4PM (EST). *Felony, Misdemeanor, Civil, Eviction, Small Claims, Probate.*

Civil Records: Access: Phone, mail, in person. Both court and visitors may perform in person searches. No search fee. Required to search: name, years to search. Civil cases indexed by defendant, plaintiff. Civil records on computer since 1991, prior on docket books to 1978.

Criminal Records: Access: Phone, mail, in person. Both court and visitors may perform in person searches. No search fee. Required to search: name, years to search. Criminal records on computer since 1991, prior records on docket books since 1978.

General Information: Public Access terminal is available. No adoption, mental, juvenile, or sealed records released. SASE required. Copy fee: $.15 per page. Certification fee: $3.00. Fee payee: Circuit Clerk. Personal checks accepted. Prepayment is required.

Boone County

Circuit & District Court Box 480, Burlington, KY 41005; 859-334-2237; Fax: 859-586-9413. Hours: 8:30AM-5:30PM (EST). *Felony, Misdemeanor, Civil, Eviction, Small Claims, Probate.*

Civil Records: Access: Mail, in person. Both court and visitors may perform in person searches. No search fee. Required to search: name, years to search. Civil cases indexed by defendant, plaintiff. Civil records on computer since July 1990, on index card file since 1978, prior records on books.

Criminal Records: Access: In person only. Visitors must perform in person searches for themselves. No search fee. Required to search: name, years to search; also helpful: SSN. Criminal records on computer since July 1990, on index card file since 1978, prior on books.

General Information:. No adoption, mental, juvenile, or sealed records released. SASE required. Copy fee: $.15 per page. Certification fee: $1.00. Fee payee: Circuit Clerk. Only cashiers checks and money orders accepted.

Bourbon County

Circuit & District Court Box 740, Paris, KY 40361; 859-987-2624. Hours: 8:30AM-4:30PM M-TH, 8:30AM-6PM F (EST). *Felony, Misdemeanor, Civil, Eviction, Small Claims, Probate.*

Civil Records: Access: In person only. Visitors must perform in person searches for themselves. No search

fee. Required to search: name, years to search. Civil cases indexed by defendant, plaintiff. Civil records on computer since November 1991, prior records on books.

Criminal Records: Access: In person only. Visitors must perform in person searches for themselves. No search fee. Required to search: name, years to search; also helpful: SSN. Criminal records on computer since November 1991, prior records on books.

General Information: Public Access terminal is available. No adoption, mental, juvenile, or sealed records released. Copy fee: District Ct documents are $.15 per page, Circuit Ct $.25 per page. Certification fee: $1.00. Fee payee: Circuit Clerk. Personal checks accepted. Prepayment is required.

Boyd County

Circuit & District Court Box 694, Catlettsburg, KY 41129-0694; 606-739-4131; Fax: 606-739-5793. Hours: 8:30AM-4PM (EST). *Felony, Misdemeanor, Civil, Eviction, Small Claims, Probate.*

Civil Records: Access: In person only. Visitors must perform in person searches for themselves. No search fee. Required to search: name, years to search. Civil cases indexed by defendant, plaintiff. Civil records on computer since 1991, prior records on index cards since 1975.

Criminal Records: Access: In person only. Visitors must perform in person searches for themselves. No search fee. Required to search: name, years to search, signed release; also helpful: DOB, SSN. Criminal records on computer since 1991, on index cards since 1978; misdemeanor & traffic from 1987.

General Information: Public Access terminal is available. No adoption, mental, juvenile, or sealed records released. Copy fee: $.15 per page. Certification fee: $1.00. Fee payee: Circuit Clerk. Personal checks accepted. Prepayment is required.

Boyle County

Circuit Court Courthouse, Main St, Danville, KY 40422; 859-239-7442; Fax: 859-239-7807. Hours: 8AM-5PM (EST). *Felony, Civil Actions Over $4,000.*

Civil Records: Access: Phone, mail, in person. Both court and visitors may perform in person searches. No search fee. Required to search: name, years to search. Civil cases indexed by defendant, plaintiff. Civil records on computer since 08/91, prior records on index cards.

Criminal Records: Access: Fax, mail, in person. Both court and visitors may perform in person searches. No search fee. Required to search: name, years to search, DOB, SSN. Criminal records on computer since 08/91, prior records on index cards.

General Information: Public Access terminal is available. No adoption, mental, juvenile, or sealed records released. SASE required. Turnaround time 2-4 days. Copy fee: $.15 per page. Certification fee: $1.00. Fee payee: Circuit Clerk. Personal checks accepted. Prepayment is required.

District Court Courthouse, 3rd Floor, Danville, KY 40422; 859-239-7362; Fax: 859-236-9807. Hours: 8AM-4:30PM (EST). *Misdemeanor, Civil Actions Under $4,000, Eviction, Small Claims, Probate.*

Civil Records: Access: Mail, fax, in person. Both court and visitors may perform in person searches. No search fee. Required to search: name, years to search. Civil cases indexed by defendant, plaintiff. Civil records on computer since August 1991, prior records on index cards since 1978.

Criminal Records: Access: Mail, fax, in person. Both court and visitors may perform in person searches. No search fee. Required to search: name, DOB, SSN. Criminal records on computer since 08/91; prior records on card index.

General Information: Public Access terminal is available. No adoption, mental, juvenile, or sealed records released. SASE required. Turnaround time 3-4 days. Fax notes: Fee to fax results is $2.00 per page. Copy fee: $.15 per page. Certification fee: $1.00. Fee payee: District Clerk. Personal checks accepted. Prepayment is required.

Bracken County

Circuit & District Court PO Box 205, Brooksville, KY 41004-0205; 606-735-3328; Fax: 606-735-3900. Hours: 9AM-4PM M,T,TH,F, 9AM-Noon W & Sat (EST). *Felony, Misdemeanor, Civil, Eviction, Small Claims, Probate.*

Civil Records: Access: Mail, in person. Both court and visitors may perform in person searches. No search fee. Required to search: name, years to search. Civil cases indexed by defendant, plaintiff. Civil records on computer since 1993, prior records on docket books since the 1800s.

Criminal Records: Access: In person only. Visitors must perform in person searches for themselves. No search fee. Required to search: name, years to search; also helpful: SSN. Criminal records on computer since 1993, prior records on docket books since the 1800s.

General Information: Public Access terminal is available. No adoption, mental, juvenile, or sealed records released. SASE required. Copy fee: $.15 per page. Certification fee: $1.00. Fee payee: Circuit Clerk. Prepayment is required.

Breathitt County

Circuit & District Court 1137 Main St, Jackson, KY 41339; 606-666-5768; Fax: 606-666-4893. Hours: 8AM-4PM M,T,TH,F; 8AM-Noon W; 9AM-Noon Sat (EST). *Felony, Misdemeanor, Civil, Eviction, Small Claims, Probate.*

Civil Records: Access: Phone, mail, in person. Both court and visitors may perform in person searches. No search fee. Required to search: name, years to search. Civil cases indexed by defendant, plaintiff. Civil records in files since 1987.

Criminal Records: Access: Phone, mail, in person. Both court and visitors may perform in person searches. No search fee. Required to search: name, years to search, DOB, SSN, signed release. Criminal records in files since 1987.

General Information: Public Access terminal is available. No adoption, mental, juvenile, or sealed records released. SASE required. Turnaround time 2-3 days. Copy fee: $.25 per page. Certification fee: $1.00. Fee payee: Circuit Clerk. Personal checks accepted. Prepayment is required.

Breckinridge County

Circuit & District Court Box 111, Hardinsburg, KY 40143; 270-756-2239; Fax: 270-756-1129. Hours: 8AM-4PM (CST). *Felony, Misdemeanor, Civil, Eviction, Small Claims, Probate.*

Civil Records: Access: In person only. Visitors must perform in person searches for themselves. No search fee. Required to search: name, years to search. Civil cases indexed by defendant, plaintiff. Civil records on computer back to 8/1994, on index cards since 1978, prior records on docket books since the 1800s.

Criminal Records: Access: In person only. Visitors must perform in person searches for themselves. No search fee. Required to search: name, years to search, DOB, SSN. Criminal records on computer back to 8/1994, on index cards since 1978, prior records on docket books since the 1800s.

General Information: Public Access terminal is available. No adoption, mental, juvenile, or sealed records released. Fax notes: Fee to fax results is $2.00 per page. Copy fee: $.15 per page. Certification fee:

$1.00. Fee payee: Circuit Clerk. Personal checks accepted. Prepayment is required.

Bullitt County

Circuit & District Court Box 746, Shephardsville, KY 40165; 502-543-7104; Fax: 502-543-7158. Hours: 8AM-4PM (EST). *Felony, Misdemeanor, Civil, Eviction, Small Claims, Probate.*

Civil Records: Access: Fax, mail, in person. Both court and visitors may perform in person searches. Search fee: $1.00 per name. Required to search: name. Civil cases indexed by defendant, plaintiff. Civil records on computer since 11/91, prior records on index cards since the 1800s.

Criminal Records: Access: Fax, mail, in person. Both court and visitors may perform in person searches. Search fee: $1.00 per name. Required to search: name, years to search, DOB, SSN. Criminal records on computer since 11/91, prior records on index cards since the 1800s. Access by mail with authorization.

General Information: Public Access terminal is available. No adoption, mental, juvenile, or sealed records released. SASE required. Turnaround time 1-2 days. Fax notes: $1.00 per page. Send copy of check with fax. Copy fee: $.15 per page. Certification fee: $1.00. Fee payee: Circuit Clerk. Personal checks accepted. Prepayment is required.

Butler County

Circuit & District Court Box 625, Morgantown, KY 42261; 270-526-5631. Hours: 8AM-4:30PM M-F; 9AM-Noon Sat (CST). *Felony, Misdemeanor, Civil, Eviction, Small Claims, Probate.*

Civil Records: Access: Mail, in person. No search fee. Required to search: name, years to search. Civil cases indexed by defendant, plaintiff. Civil records on computer since 1993, prior records on index cards since the 1800s.

Criminal Records: Access: Mail, in person. Both court and visitors may perform in person searches. No search fee. Required to search: name, years to search, DOB; also helpful: SSN. Criminal records on computer since 1993, prior records on index cards since the 1800s.

General Information: Public Access terminal is available. No adoption, mental, juvenile, or sealed records released. SASE required. Turnaround time 1 week. Copy fee: $.25 per page. Certification fee: No cert fee. Fee payee: Circuit Clerk. Personal checks accepted. Prepayment is required.

Caldwell County

Circuit & District Court 105 West Court Sq, Princeton, KY 42445; 270-365-6884; Fax: 270-365-9171. Hours: 8AM-4PM (CST). *Felony, Misdemeanor, Civil, Eviction, Small Claims, Probate.*

Civil Records: Access: Mail, fax, in person. Visitors must perform in person searches for themselves. No search fee. Required to search: name, years to search. Civil cases indexed by defendant, plaintiff. Civil records on index cards; on computer since 09/94.

Criminal Records: Access: Fax, in person. Visitors must perform in person searches for themselves. No search fee. Required to search: name, years to search; also helpful: DOB, SSN. Criminal records on index cards; on computer since 09/94.

General Information: Public Access terminal is available. No adoption, mental, juvenile, or sealed records released. SASE required. Turnaround time 2 days. Fax notes: $2.00 for first page, $1.00 each add'l. Copy fee: $.15 per page. Copy request must include postage. Certification fee: $1.00. Fee payee: Circuit Clerk. Personal checks accepted. Prepayment is required.

Calloway County

Circuit & District Court 312 N 4th St, Murray, KY 42071; 270-753-2714; Fax: 270-759-9822. Hours: 8AM-4:30PM (CST). *Felony, Misdemeanor, Civil, Eviction, Small Claims, Probate.*

Civil Records: Access: Mail, in person. Both court and visitors may perform in person searches. No search fee. Required to search: name, years to search. Civil cases indexed by defendant, plaintiff. Civil records on computer since 06/92, on index cards since 1978. Prior to 1978 records are archived in Frankfort.

Criminal Records: Access: In person only. Visitors must perform in person searches for themselves. No search fee. Required to search: name, years to search, DOB; also helpful: SSN. Criminal records on computer since 06/92, on index cards since 1978. Prior to 1978 records are archived in Frankfort.

General Information: Public Access terminal is available. No adoption, mental, juvenile, or sealed records released. SASE required. Turnaround time 2-4 days. Copy fee: $.20 per page. Certification fee: $1.50. Fee payee: Circuit Clerk. Personal checks accepted. Prepayment is required.

Campbell County

Circuit Court 330 York St Rm 8, Newport, KY 41071; 859-292-6314; Fax: 859-431-0816. Hours: 8:30AM-4PM *Felony, Civil Actions Over $4,000.*

Civil Records: Access: In person only. Visitors must perform in person searches for themselves. No search fee. Required to search: name, years to search. Civil cases indexed by defendant, plaintiff. Civil records on computer since 1992, prior on index cards since 1978.

Criminal Records: Access: In person only. Visitors must perform in person searches for themselves. No search fee. Required to search: name, years to search; also helpful: SSN. Criminal records on computer since 1992, prior records on index cards since 1978.

General Information: Public Access terminal is available. No adoption, mental, juvenile, or sealed records released. Copy fee: $.15 per page. Certification fee: $1.50. Fee payee: Campbell Circuit Court. Personal checks accepted. Prepayment is required.

District Court 600 Columbia St, Newport, KY 41071-1816; 859-292-6305; Fax: 859-292-6593. Hours: 8:30AM-4PM (EST). *Misdemeanor, Civil Actions Under $4,000, Eviction, Small Claims, Probate.*

Civil Records: Access: Mail, in person. Both court and visitors may perform in person searches. No search fee. Required to search: name, years to search. Civil cases indexed by defendant, plaintiff. Civil records on computer since 1992, prior records on index cards.

Criminal Records: Access: In person only. Visitors must perform in person searches for themselves. No search fee. Required to search: name, years to search, SSN. Criminal records on computer since 1992, prior records on index cards.

General Information: Public Access terminal is available. No adoption, mental, juvenile, or sealed records released. SASE required. Turnaround time 7 days. Copy fee: $.15 per page. Certification fee: $1.00. Fee payee: District Clerk. Business checks accepted. Prepayment is required.

Carlisle County

Circuit & District Court Box 337, Bardwell, KY 42023; 270-628-5425; Fax: 270-628-5456. Hours: 8AM-4PM (CST). *Felony, Misdemeanor, Civil, Eviction, Small Claims, Probate.*

Civil Records: Access: Phone, fax, mail, in person. Both court and visitors may perform in person searches. No search fee. Required to search: name, years to search. Civil cases indexed by defendant, plaintiff. Civil records on computer since May 1993, records on docket books since 1978, prior records archived.

Criminal Records: Access: Phone, fax, mail, in person. Both court and visitors may perform in person searches. No search fee. Required to search: name, years to search. Criminal records on computer since May 1993, records on docket books since 1978, prior records archived.

General Information:. No adoption, mental, juvenile, or sealed records released. SASE required. Turnaround time 1-5 days. Copy fee: $.15 per page. Certification fee: $1.15. Fee payee: Circuit Clerk. Personal checks accepted. Prepayment is required.

Carroll County

Circuit & District Court 802 Clay St, Carrollton, KY 41008; 502-732-4305. Hours: 8AM-4:30PM (EST). *Felony, Misdemeanor, Civil, Eviction, Small Claims, Probate.*

Civil Records: Access: Phone, mail, in person. Both court and visitors may perform in person searches. No search fee. Required to search: name, years to search. Civil cases indexed by defendant, plaintiff. Civil records on computer since 1994, on docket books since 1980. Records before 1980 are archived in Frankfurt.

Criminal Records: Access: Phone, mail, in person. Both court and visitors may perform in person searches. No search fee. Required to search: name, years to search, DOB; also helpful: SSN. Criminal records on computer since 1994, on docket books since 1980. Records before 1980 are archived in Frankfurt.

General Information: Public Access terminal is available. No adoption, mental, juvenile, or sealed records released. SASE required. Turnaround time 2-4 days. Copy fee: $.15 per page. Certification fee: $1.00. Fee payee: Circuit Clerk. Personal checks accepted. Prepayment is required.

Carter County

Circuit Court 300 W Main St, Rm 308, Grayson, KY 41143; 606-474-5191; Fax: 606-474-8826. Hours: 8:30AM-4PM M-F; 9AM-Noon Sat (EST). *Felony, Civil Actions Over $4,000.*

Civil Records: Access: Mail, in person. Both court and visitors may perform in person searches. No search fee. Required to search: name, years to search. Civil cases indexed by defendant, plaintiff. Civil records on computer since 1994, records archived since 1978, prior records are archived.

Criminal Records: Access: In person only. Both court and visitors may perform in person searches. No search fee. Required to search: name, years to search, DOB, SSN. Criminal records on computer since 1994, records archived since 1978, prior records are archived.

General Information: Public Access terminal is available. No adoption, mental, juvenile, or sealed records released. SASE required. Turnaround time 1-2 days. Copy fee: $.15 per page. Certification fee: $2.00. Fee payee: Carter County Circuit Clerk. Prepayment is required.

District Court Courthouse, Rm 203, 300 West Main, Grayson, KY 41143; 606-474-6572; Fax: 606-474-8584. Hours: 8AM-4PM (EST). *Misdemeanor, Civil Actions Under $4,000, Eviction, Small Claims, Probate.*

Civil Records: Access: Mail, in person. Both court and visitors may perform in person searches. No search fee. Required to search: name, years to search. Civil cases indexed by defendant, plaintiff. Civil records on computer since 1994, prior records on index cards.

Criminal Records: Access: In person only. Visitors must perform in person searches for themselves. No search fee. Required to search: name, years to search, DOB; also helpful: SSN. Criminal records on computer since 1994, prior records on index cards.

General Information: Public Access terminal is available. No adoption, mental, juvenile, or sealed records released. SASE required. Turnaround time 2-4 days. Copy fee: $.15 per page. Certification fee: $1.00. Fee payee: District Clerk. Personal checks accepted. Prepayment is required.

Casey County

Circuit & District Court PO Box 147, Liberty, KY 42539; 606-787-6510. Hours: 8AM-4:30PM M & F, 8AM-4PM Tu-W-Th, 8AM-Noon Sat (EST). *Felony, Misdemeanor, Civil, Eviction, Small Claims, Probate.*

Note: This court asks all pre-trial record requests go to the Administrative office of the Courts in Frankfort.

Civil Records: Access: Mail, in person. Both court and visitors may perform in person searches. No search fee. Required to search: name, years to search. Civil cases indexed by defendant, plaintiff. Civil records on index cards since 1978, prior records archived.

Criminal Records: Access: In person only. Visitors must perform in person searches for themselves. No search fee. Required to search: name, years to search; also helpful: SSN. Criminal records on index cards since 1978, prior records archived.

General Information: Public Access terminal is available. No adoption, mental, juvenile, or sealed records released. SASE required. Turnaround time 1-2 days. Copy fee: $.15 per page. Certification fee: $1.50. Fee payee: Circuit Clerk. Personal checks accepted. Prepayment is required.

Christian County

Circuit & District Court 511 S Main St Rm 301, Hopkinsville, KY 42240-2368; 270-889-6539; Fax: 270-889-6564. Hours: 8AM-4:30PM (CST). *Felony, Misdemeanor, Civil, Eviction, Small Claims, Probate.*

Civil Records: Access: Mail, in person. Both court and visitors may perform in person searches. No search fee. Required to search: name, years to search. Civil cases indexed by defendant, plaintiff. Civil records on computer since 1991, prior records on index cards since 1978.

Criminal Records: Access: In person only. Visitors must perform in person searches for themselves. No search fee. Required to search: name, years to search; also helpful: DOB, SSN. Criminal records on computer since 1991, prior records on index cards since 1978.

General Information: Public Access terminal is available. No adoption, mental, juvenile, or sealed records released. SASE required. Turnaround time 2-4 days. Copy fee: $.15 per page. Certification fee: $1.00. Fee payee: Circuit Clerk. Personal checks accepted. Prepayment is required.

Clark County

Circuit Court Box 687, Winchester, KY 40392; 859-737-7264. Hours: 8AM-4PM (EST). *Felony, Civil Actions Over $4,000.*

Civil Records: Access: Mail, in person. Both court and visitors may perform in person searches. No search fee. Required to search: name, years to search; also helpful: address. Civil cases indexed by defendant, plaintiff. Civil records on computer since 1989, on index cards since 1950, prior records archived since the 1700s.

Criminal Records: Access: In person only. Visitors must perform in person searches for themselves. No search fee. Required to search: name, years to search; also helpful: address, DOB, SSN. Criminal records on computer since 1989, on index cards since 1950, prior records archived since the 1700s.

General Information: Public Access terminal is available. No adoption, mental, juvenile, or sealed records released. SASE required. Turnaround time 2-4 days. Copy fee: $.25 per page. Certification fee: $1.00.

Fee payee: Circuit Clerk. Personal checks accepted. Prepayment is required.

District Court PO Box 687, Winchester, KY 40392-0687; 859-737-7141; Fax: 859-737-7005. Hours: 8AM-4PM (EST). *Misdemeanor, Civil Actions Under $4,000, Eviction, Small Claims, Probate.*

Civil Records: Access: Mail, fax, in person. Both court and visitors may perform in person searches. No search fee. Required to search: name, years to search. Civil cases indexed by defendant, plaintiff. Civil records on computer since 1989, on docket books since 1978, prior records on archived.

Criminal Records: Access: Mail, fax, in person. Both court and visitors may perform in person searches. No search fee. Required to search: name, years to search; also helpful: DOB, SSN. Criminal records on computer since 1989, on docket books since 1978, prior records on archived.

General Information: Public Access terminal is available. No adoption, mental, juvenile, or sealed records released. SASE required. Turnaround time 1-3 days. Copy fee: $.25 per page. Certification fee: $1.00. Fee payee: District Clerk. Personal checks accepted. Prepayment is required.

Clay County

Circuit & District Court 316 Main Street, #108, Manchester, KY 40962; 606-598-3663; Fax: 606-598-4047. Hours: 8AM-4PM (EST). *Felony, Misdemeanor, Civil, Eviction, Small Claims, Probate.*

Civil Records: Access: In person only. Visitors must perform in person searches for themselves. No search fee. Required to search: name, years to search. Civil cases indexed by defendant, plaintiff. Civil records on computer back to 1992, on index cards since 1978, prior records archived.

Criminal Records: Access: In person only. Visitors must perform in person searches for themselves. No search fee. Required to search: name, years to search, DOB; also helpful: SSN. Criminal records on computer back to 1992, on index cards since 1978, prior records archived.

General Information: Public Access terminal is available. No adoption, mental, juvenile, or sealed records released. Copy fee: $.15 per page. Certification fee: $1.00 per page. Fee payee: Circuit Clerk. Personal checks accepted. Prepayment is required.

Clinton County

Circuit & District Court Courthouse 2nd Fl, Albany, KY 42602; 606-387-6424; Fax: 606-387-8154. Hours: 8AM-4PM M-F; 8AM-Noon Sat (CST). *Felony, Misdemeanor, Civil, Eviction, Small Claims, Probate.*

Civil Records: Access: Phone, mail, in person. Both court and visitors may perform in person searches. No search fee. Required to search: name, years to search. Civil cases indexed by defendant, plaintiff. Civil records on computer since 08/92, on docket books since 1978, prior records archived.

Criminal Records: Access: Phone, mail, in person. Both court and visitors may perform in person searches. No search fee. Required to search: name, years to search, SSN; also helpful: DOB. Criminal records on computer since 08/92, on docket books since 1978, prior records archived.

General Information: Public Access terminal is available. No adoption, mental, juvenile, or sealed records released. SASE required. Turnaround time 5 days. Copy fee: $.15 per page. Certification fee: $1.00. Fee payee: Circuit Clerk. Personal checks accepted. Prepayment is required.

Crittenden County

Circuit & District Court 107 S Main, Marion, KY 42064; 270-965-4200. Hours: 8AM-4:30PM (CST). *Felony, Misdemeanor, Civil, Eviction, Small Claims, Probate.*

Civil Records: Access: Mail, in person. Both court and visitors may perform in person searches. No search fee. Required to search: name, years to search. Civil cases indexed by defendant, plaintiff. Civil records on index cards since 1977; on computer back to 9/94.

Criminal Records: Access: In person only. Visitors must perform in person searches for themselves. No search fee. Required to search: name, years to search. Criminal records on index cards since 1977; on computer back to 9/94.

General Information: Public Access terminal is available. No adoption, mental, juvenile, or sealed records released. SASE required. Turnaround time 10 days. Fax notes: Fee to fax results is $2.00 1st page; $1.00 each add'l. Copy fee: $.15 per page. Certification fee: $1.00. Fee payee: Circuit Clerk. Checks not accepted. Prepayment is required.

Cumberland County

Circuit & District Court Box 395, Burkesville, KY 42717; 270-864-2611. Hours: 8AM-4PM (CST). *Felony, Misdemeanor, Civil, Eviction, Small Claims, Probate.*

Civil Records: Access: Mail, fax, in person. Both court and visitors may perform in person searches. No search fee. Required to search: name, years to search. Civil cases indexed by defendant, plaintiff. Civil records on computer back to 06/93, on docket cards from 1978, prior records archived.

Criminal Records: Access: Mail, fax, in person. Both court and visitors may perform in person searches. No search fee. Required to search: name, years to search, DOB; also helpful: SSN. Criminal records on computer back to 06/93, on docket cards from 1978, prior records archived.

General Information: Public Access terminal is available. No adoption, mental, juvenile, or sealed records released. SASE required. Turnaround time 3-5 days. Fax notes: Fee to fax results is $2.00 and $1.00 per page. Copy fee: $.15 per page. Certification fee: $1.00. Fee payee: Circuit Clerk. Personal checks accepted. Prepayment is required.

Daviess County

Circuit & District Court Box 277, Owensboro, KY 42302; 270-687-7333. Hours: 8AM-4PM (CST). *Felony, Misdemeanor, Civil, Eviction, Small Claims, Probate.*

Civil Records: Access: In person only. Visitors must perform in person searches for themselves. No search fee. Required to search: name, years to search. Civil cases indexed by defendant, plaintiff. Civil records on computer since 04/91, on index cards since 1978, prior records on docket books since 1809. Search in person only on Tuesday or Thursday.

Criminal Records: Access: In person only. Visitors must perform in person searches for themselves. No search fee. Required to search: name, years to search, DOB, SSN. Criminal records on computer since 04/91, on index cards since 1978, prior records on docket books since 1809. Search in person only on Tuesday or Thursday.

General Information: Public Access terminal is available. No adoption, mental, juvenile, or sealed records released. Copy fee: $.15 per page. Certification fee: $1.00. Fee payee: Circuit Clerk. Business checks accepted. Prepayment is required.

Edmonson County

Circuit & District Court Box 739, Brownsville, KY 42210; 270-597-2584; Fax: 270-597-2884. Hours: 8AM-4:30PM M-W,F; 8AM-Noon Th,S (CST). *Felony, Misdemeanor, Civil, Eviction, Small Claims, Probate.*

Civil Records: Access: In person only. Visitors must perform in person searches for themselves. No search fee. Required to search: name, years to search, address. Civil cases indexed by defendant, plaintiff. Civil records computerized since 1995, on index cards and docket books from 1800s.

Criminal Records: Access: In person only. Visitors must perform in person searches for themselves. No search fee. Required to search: name, years to search, DOB, SSN. Criminal records computerized since 1995, on index cards and docket books from 1800s.

General Information:. No adoption, mental, juvenile, or sealed records released. Copy fee: $.15 per page. Certification fee: $1.00. Fee payee: Circuit Clerk. Personal checks accepted. Prepayment is required.

Elliott County

Circuit & District Court Box 788, Sandy Hook, KY 41171; 606-738-5238; Fax: 606-738-6962. Hours: 8AM-4PM M-F; 9AM-Noon Sat (EST). *Felony, Misdemeanor, Civil, Eviction, Small Claims, Probate.*

Civil Records: Access: Phone, mail, in person. Both court and visitors may perform in person searches. No search fee. Required to search: name, years to search. Civil cases indexed by defendant, plaintiff. Civil records on computer since October 1992, prior records on index cards since 1978.

Criminal Records: Access: Phone, mail, in person. Both court and visitors may perform in person searches. No search fee. Required to search: name, years to search; also helpful: SSN. Criminal records on computer since October 1992, prior records on index cards since 1978.

General Information: Public Access terminal is available. No adoption, mental, juvenile, or sealed records released. SASE required. Turnaround time 1-2 days. Copy fee: $.15 per page. Certification fee: $1.00. Fee payee: Circuit Clerk. Personal checks accepted. Prepayment is required.

Estill County

Circuit & District Court 130 Main St, Rm 207, Irvine, KY 40336; 606-723-3970; Fax: 606-723-1158. Hours: 8AM-4PM (EST). *Felony, Misdemeanor, Civil, Eviction, Small Claims, Probate.*

Civil Records: Access: Phone, fax, mail, in person. Both court and visitors may perform in person searches. No search fee. Required to search: name, years to search. Civil cases indexed by defendant, plaintiff. Civil records on index cards.

Criminal Records: Access: Phone, fax, mail, in person. Both court and visitors may perform in person searches. No search fee. Required to search: name, years to search, DOB; also helpful: SSN. Criminal records on index cards.

General Information: Public Access terminal is available. No adoption, mental, juvenile, or sealed records released. SASE required. Turnaround time 2-4 days. Fax notes: $1.00 per page. Copy fee: $.15 per page. Certification fee: $1.00. Fee payee: Circuit Clerk. Personal checks accepted. Prepayment is required.

Fayette County

Circuit Court - Criminal & Civil Divisions 215 W Main (Civil-Rm 200), Lexington, KY 40507; Civil phone: 859-246-2141; Criminal phone: 859-246-2224. Hours: 8:30AM-4:30PM (EST). *Felony, Civil Actions Over $4,000.*

Civil Records: Access: Mail, in person. Both court and visitors may perform in person searches. Search fee: $5.00 per name. Required to search: name, years to search. Civil cases indexed by defendant, plaintiff. Civil records on computer since April 1993, on index cards since 1978, prior records on books and archived.

Criminal Records: Access: Mail, in person. Both court and visitors may perform in person searches. Search fee: $5.00 per name. Required to search: name, years to search; also helpful: DOB, SSN. Criminal records on computer since April 1993, on index cards since 1978, prior records on books and archived.

General Information: Public Access terminal is available. No adoption, juvenile, mental, or sealed records released. SASE required. Turnaround time 1-2 days. Copy fee: $.50 per page. Certification fee: $1.50. Fee payee: Fayette County Circuit Clerk. No personal checks accepted. Prepayment is required.

District Court - Criminal & Civil 140 N ML King Blvd (Criminal), 136 N ML King Blvd (Civil), Lexington, KY 40507; Civil phone: 859-246-2240; Criminal phone: 859-246-2228. Hours: 8AM-4PM (EST). *Misdemeanor, Civil Actions Under $4,000, Eviction, Small Claims, Probate.*

Civil Records: Access: Mail, in person. Both court and visitors may perform in person searches. No search fee. Required to search: name, years to search. Civil cases indexed by defendant, plaintiff. Civil records on computer since 1992, prior on index cards since 1977.

Criminal Records: Access: Mail, in person. Both court and visitors may perform in person searches. No search fee. Required to search: name, years to search, DOB; also helpful: SSN. Criminal records on computer since 1977.

General Information: Public Access terminal is available. No adoption, mental, juvenile, or sealed records released. SASE required. Turnaround time 3 days. Copy fee: $.25 per page. Certification fee: $1.00. Fee payee: District Clerk. Personal checks accepted. Prepayment is required.

Fleming County

Circuit & District Court Courthouse 100 Court Square, Flemingsburg, KY 41041; 606-845-7011; Fax: 606-849-2400. Hours: 8AM-4:30PM (EST). *Felony, Misdemeanor, Civil, Eviction, Small Claims, Probate.*

Civil Records: Access: Phone, fax, mail, in person. Both court and visitors may perform in person searches. No search fee. Required to search: name, years to search. Civil cases indexed by defendant, plaintiff. Civil records on computer since May 1994, prior records on index cards since 1978.

Criminal Records: Access: In person only. Both court and visitors may perform in person searches. No search fee. Required to search: name, years to search, DOB; also helpful: SSN. Criminal records on computer since May 1994, prior records on index cards since 1978.

General Information: Public Access terminal is available. No adoption, mental, juvenile, or sealed records released. SASE required. Turnaround time 1-2 days. Fax notes: $1.00 per page. Copy fee: $.15 per page. Certification fee: $1.00. Fee payee: Circuit Clerk. Personal checks accepted. Prepayment is required.

Floyd County

Circuit Court PO Bix 3368, (127 S Lake Dr), Prestonsburg, KY 41653-3368; 606-886-3090; Fax: 606-886-9075. Hours: 8AM-4PM (EST). *Felony, Civil Actions Over $4,000.*

Civil Records: Access: Mail, in person. Both court and visitors may perform in person searches. No search fee. Required to search: name, years to search. Civil cases indexed by defendant, plaintiff. Civil records on computer since September 1991, prior records on index cards since 1978.

Criminal Records: Access: Mail, in person. Both court and visitors may perform in person searches. No search fee. Required to search: name, years to search, DOB, SSN. Criminal records on computer since September 1991, prior records on index cards since 1978.

General Information:. No adoption, mental, juvenile, or sealed records released. SASE required. Turnaround time 2-4 days. Copy fee: $.25 per page. Certification fee: $1.00. Fee payee: Clerk of Circuit Court. Personal checks accepted. Prepayment is required.

District Court PO Box 3368, (127 S Lake Dr), Prestonsburg, KY 41653-3368; 606-886-9114. Hours: 8AM-4PM (EST). *Misdemeanor, Small Claims.*

Note: Small claims can be reached at 606-886-2124

Criminal Records: Access: Phone, mail, in person. Only the court performs in person searches; visitors may not. No search fee. Required to search: name, years to search; also helpful: SSN. Criminal records on computer since 1991, prior records in index cards since 1989. Records are only kept for five years in this office.

General Information:. No adoption, mental, juvenile, or sealed records released. SASE required. Turnaround time 2-4 days. Copy fee: $.15 per page. Certification fee: $1.75. Fee payee: Floyd District Court. Personal checks accepted. Prepayment is required.

Franklin County

Circuit Court Box 678, Frankfort, KY 40602; 502-564-8380; Fax: 502-564-8188. Hours: 8AM-4:30PM (EST). *Felony, Civil Actions Over $4,000.*

Civil Records: Access: Fax, mail, in person. Both court and visitors may perform in person searches. No search fee. Required to search: name, years to search. Civil cases indexed by defendant, plaintiff. Civil records on computer since 1990, prior on index cards since 1978.

Criminal Records: Access: Fax, in person. Visitors must perform in person searches for themselves. No search fee. Required to search: name, years to search, DOB, SSN. Criminal records on computer since 1990, prior records on index cards since 1978. All requests are referred to the state Administrator's Office of Courts.

General Information: Public Access terminal is available. No adoption, mental, juvenile, or sealed records released. SASE required. Turnaround time 2 days. Fax notes: $2.00 for first page, $1.00 each add'l. Copy fee: $.15 per page. Certification fee: $1.00. Fee payee: Circuit Clerk. Personal checks accepted. Prepayment is required.

District Court Box 678, Frankfort, KY 40601; 502-564-7013; Fax: 502-564-8188. Hours: 8AM-4:30PM (EST). *Misdemeanor, Civil Actions Under $4,000, Eviction, Small Claims, Probate.*

Civil Records: Access: In person only. Visitors must perform in person searches for themselves. No search fee. Required to search: name, years to search. Civil cases indexed by defendant, plaintiff. Civil records on computer since 1990, records on index cards since 1978, prior archived.

Criminal Records: Access: In person only. Visitors must perform in person searches for themselves. No search fee. Required to search: name, years to search, DOB. Criminal records on computer since 1990, records on index cards since 1978, prior archived.

General Information: Public Access terminal is available. No adoption, mental, juvenile, or sealed records released. Copy fee: $.15 per page. Certification fee: $1.00. Fee payee: Franklin Circuit Clerk. Personal checks accepted. Prepayment is required.

Fulton County

Circuit & District Court Box 198, Hickman, KY 42050; 270-236-3944; Fax: 270-236-3729. Hours: 8:30AM-4PM (CST). *Felony, Misdemeanor, Civil, Eviction, Small Claims, Probate.*

Civil Records: Access: Mail, in person. Both court and visitors may perform in person searches. No search fee. Required to search: name, years to search. Civil cases indexed by defendant, plaintiff. Civil records on index and archived since 1843.

Criminal Records: Access: In person only. Visitors must perform in person searches for themselves. No search fee. Required to search: name, years to search. Criminal records on index and archived since 1843.

General Information: Public Access terminal is available. No adoption, mental, juvenile, or sealed records released. SASE required. Copy fee: $.15 per page. Certification fee: $1.00. Fee payee: Circuit Clerk. Personal checks accepted. Prepayment is required.

Gallatin County

Circuit Court Box 256, Warsaw, KY 41095; 859-567-5241. Hours: 8AM-5PM M,T,Th,F; Closed W (EST). *Felony, Civil Actions Over $4,000.*

Civil Records: Access: Mail, in person. Both court and visitors may perform in person searches. No search fee. Required to search: name, years to search. Civil cases indexed by defendant, plaintiff. Civil records on index cards since 1978.

Criminal Records: Access: Mail, in person. Both court and visitors may perform in person searches. No search fee. Required to search: name, years to search; also helpful: SSN. Criminal records on index cards to 1978.

General Information: Public Access terminal is available. No adoption, mental, juvenile, or sealed records released. SASE required. Turnaround time 4 days. Copy fee: $.15 per page. Certification fee: $1.00. Fee payee: Circuit Clerk. Personal checks accepted. Prepayment is required.

District Court Box 256, Warsaw, KY 41095; 859-567-2388. Hours: 8AM-5PM T,Th,F; 8AM-6PM M; 8AM-Noon Sat (EST). *Misdemeanor, Civil Actions Under $4,000, Eviction, Small Claims, Probate.*

Civil Records: Access: Mail, in person. Both court and visitors may perform in person searches. No search fee. Required to search: name, years to search. Civil cases indexed by defendant, plaintiff. Civil records on computer since November 1994, prior records on index cards since 1978.

Criminal Records: Access: Mail, in person. Both court and visitors may perform in person searches. No search fee. Required to search: name, years to search, DOB; also helpful: SSN. Criminal records on computer since November 1994, prior records on index cards to 1978.

General Information: Public Access terminal is available. No adoption, mental, juvenile, or sealed records released. Turnaround time 1-2 days. Copy fee: $.15 per page. Certification fee: $1.00. Fee payee: District Clerk. Personal checks accepted. Prepayment is required.

Garrard County

Circuit & District Court 7 Public Square, Courthouse Annex, Lancaster, KY 40444; 859-792-6032; Fax: 859-792-6414. Hours: 8AM-4PM M,T,TH,F, 8AM-Noon Wed & Sat (EST). *Felony, Misdemeanor, Civil, Eviction, Small Claims, Probate.*

Civil Records: Access: In person only. Visitors must perform in person searches for themselves. No search fee. Required to search: name, years to search. Civil cases indexed by defendant, plaintiff. Civil records in index since 1978.

Criminal Records: Access: In person only. Visitors must perform in person searches for themselves. No search fee. Required to search: name, years to search; also helpful: address, DOB, SSN. Criminal records in index since 1978.

General Information: Public Access terminal is available. No adoption, mental, juvenile, or sealed records released. Copy fee: $.15 per page. Certification fee: $1.00. Fee payee: Circuit Clerk. Personal checks accepted. Prepayment is required.

Grant County

Circuit & District Court Courthouse 101 N Main, Williamstown, KY 41097; 859-824-4467. Hours: 8AM-4PM (EST). *Felony, Misdemeanor, Civil, Eviction, Small Claims, Probate.*

Civil Records: Access: In person only. Visitors must perform in person searches for themselves. No search fee. Required to search: name, years to search. Civil cases indexed by defendant, plaintiff. Civil records on computer since 1992, prior records on index cards since 1978.

Criminal Records: Access: In person only. Visitors must perform in person searches for themselves. No search fee. Required to search: name, years to search, DOB; also helpful: SSN. Criminal records on computer since 1992, prior records on index cards since 1978.

General Information: Public Access terminal is available. No adoption, mental, juvenile, or sealed records released. Copy fee: $.15 per page. Certification fee: $1.00. Fee payee: Circuit Clerk. Personal checks accepted. Prepayment is required.

Graves County

Circuit & District Court Courthouse 100 E Broadway, Mayfield, KY 42066; 270-247-1733; Fax: 270-247-7358. Hours: 8AM-4:30PM (CST). *Felony, Misdemeanor, Civil, Eviction, Small Claims, Probate.*

Civil Records: Access: In person only. Visitors must perform in person searches for themselves. No search fee. Required to search: name, years to search. Civil cases indexed by defendant, plaintiff. Civil records on computer since June, 1994, prior records on index cards since 1978.

Criminal Records: Access: In person only. Visitors must perform in person searches for themselves. No search fee. Required to search: name, years to search, DOB; also helpful: SSN. Criminal records on computer since June, 1994, prior records on index cards since 1978.

General Information:. No adoption, mental, juvenile, or sealed records released. Copy fee: $.25 per page. Certification fee: $1.00. Fee payee: Circuit Clerk. Personal checks accepted. Prepayment is required.

Grayson County

Circuit & District Court 125 E White Oak, Leitchfield, KY 42754; 270-259-3040; Fax: 270-259-9866. Hours: 8AM-4PM M-F; 8AM-Noon Sat (CST). *Felony, Misdemeanor, Civil, Eviction, Small Claims, Probate.*

Civil Records: Access: Mail, in person. Both court and visitors may perform in person searches. Search fee: $10.00 per name. Required to search: name, years to search. Civil cases indexed by defendant, plaintiff. Civil records on computer since 05/94, prior records on index cards since 1978.

Criminal Records: Access: Mail, in person. Both court and visitors may perform in person searches. Search fee: $10.00. Required to search: name, years to search; also helpful: DOB, SSN. Criminal records on computer since 05/94, prior records on index cards since 1978.

General Information: Public Access terminal is available. No adoption, mental, juvenile, or sealed records released. SASE required. Turnaround time 2 days. Copy fee: $.15 per page. Certification fee: $1.50. Fee payee: Circuit Clerk. Personal checks accepted. Prepayment is required.

Green County

Circuit & District Court 203 W Court St, Greensburg, KY 42743; 270-932-5631; Fax: 270-932-6468. Hours: 8AM-4PM M-W, F; 8AM-12:30PM Sat (EST). *Felony, Misdemeanor, Civil, Eviction, Small Claims, Probate.*

Civil Records: Access: Fax, mail, in person. Both court and visitors may perform in person searches. No search fee. Required to search: name, years to search; also helpful: address. Civil cases indexed by defendant, plaintiff. Civil records on index cards since 1978.

Criminal Records: Access: Fax, mail, in person. Both court and visitors may perform in person searches. No search fee. Required to search: name, years to search; also helpful: address, DOB, SSN. Criminal records on index cards since 1978.

General Information: Public Access terminal is available. No adoption, mental, juvenile, or sealed records released. SASE required. Turnaround time 1-2 days. Fax notes: No fee to fax results. Will only fax to 800 numbers. Copy fee: $.15 per page. Certification fee: $1.00. Fee payee: Circuit Clerk. Personal checks accepted. Prepayment is required.

Greenup County

Circuit & District Court Courthouse Annex, Greenup, KY 41144; 606-473-9869; Fax: 606-473-7388. Hours: 9AM-4:30PM M-F (EST). *Felony, Misdemeanor, Civil, Eviction, Small Claims, Probate.*

Civil Records: Access: In person only. Both court and visitors may perform in person searches. No search fee. Required to search: name, years to search. Civil cases indexed by defendant, plaintiff. Civil records on computer since 1990, prior records on index cards since 1978.

Criminal Records: Access: In person only. Visitors must perform in person searches for themselves. No search fee. Required to search: name, years to search, DOB; also helpful: SSN. Criminal records on computer since 1990, prior records on index cards since 1978.

General Information: Public Access terminal is available. No adoption, mental, juvenile, or sealed records released. Fax notes: Fee to fax results is $2.00 1st page, $1.00 each add'l. Copy fee: $.15 per page. Certification fee: $1.00. Fee payee: Circuit Clerk. Personal checks accepted. Prepayment is required.

Hancock County

Circuit & District Court Courthouse, PO Box 250, Hawesville, KY 42348; 270-927-8144; Fax: 270-927-8629. Hours: 8AM-4PM M,T,W,F; 8AM-5:30PM Th (CST). *Felony, Misdemeanor, Civil, Eviction, Small Claims, Probate.*

Civil Records: Access: Mail, fax, in person. Both court and visitors may perform in person searches. No search fee. Required to search: name, years to search. Civil cases indexed by defendant, plaintiff. Civil records on computer since August, 1994, prior records on index cards.

Criminal Records: Access: Mail, fax, in person. Both court and visitors may perform in person searches. No search fee. Required to search: name, years to search, DOB; also helpful: SSN. Criminal records on computer since August, 1994, prior records on index cards.

General Information: Public Access terminal is available. No adoption, mental, juvenile, or sealed records released. SASE required. Turnaround time 1-2 days. Fax notes: Fee to fax results is $2.00 first page; $1.00 each add'l. Copy fee: $.15 per page. Certification

fee: $1.00. Fee payee: Circuit Clerk. Personal checks accepted. Prepayment is required.

Hardin County

Circuit & District Court Hardin County Justice Center, 120 E Dixie Ave, Elizabethtown, KY 42701; 270-766-5000; Fax: 270-766-5243. Hours: 8AM-4:30PM; (EST). *Felony, Misdemeanor, Civil, Eviction, Small Claims, Probate.*

Civil Records: Access: In person only. Visitors must perform in person searches for themselves. No search fee. Required to search: name, years to search. Civil cases indexed by defendant, plaintiff. Civil records on computer since 03/28/94, prior records on index cards since 1978.

Criminal Records: Access: In person only. Visitors must perform in person searches for themselves. No search fee. Required to search: name, years to search, DOB. Criminal records on computer since 03/28/94, prior records on index cards since 1978.

General Information: Public Access terminal is available. No adoption, mental, juvenile, or sealed records released. Fax notes: Fee to fax results is $2.00 1st page; $1.00 each add'l. Copy fee: $.15 per page. Certification fee: $1.00. Fee payee: Circuit Clerk. Personal checks accepted. Prepayment is required.

Radcliff District Court 220 Freedom Way, Radcliff, KY 40160; 270-351-1299; Fax: 270-351-1301. Hours: 8:30AM-12, 12:20-4PM (EST). *Probate, Eviction.*

Harlan County

Circuit & District Court Box 190, Harlan, KY 40831; 606-573-2680. Hours: 8AM-4:30PM (EST). *Felony, Misdemeanor, Civil, Eviction, Small Claims, Probate.*

Civil Records: Access: In person only. Visitors must perform in person searches for themselves. No search fee. Required to search: name, years to search. Civil cases indexed by defendant, plaintiff. Civil records on computer since August, 1991, on index cards since 1978, records prior to 1983 are archived in Frankfort.

Criminal Records: Access: In person only. Visitors must perform in person searches for themselves. No search fee. Required to search: name, years to search, DOB; also helpful: SSN. Criminal records on computer since August, 1991, on index cards since 1978, records prior to 1983 are archived in Frankfort.

General Information: Public Access terminal is available. No adoption, mental, juvenile, sealed or domestic violence records released. Fax notes: $2.00 fee to fax 1st page; $1.00 each add'l. Copy fee: $.25 per page. Certification fee: $3.50. Fee payee: Circuit Clerk. Personal checks accepted. Prepayment is required.

Harrison County

Circuit & District Court Courthouse Box 10, Cynthiana, KY 41031; 859-234-1914. Hours: 8:30AM-4:30PM M-F, 9AM-12PM Sat (EST). *Felony, Misdemeanor, Civil, Eviction, Small Claims, Probate.*

Civil Records: Access: Mail, in person. Both court and visitors may perform in person searches. No search fee. Required to search: name, years to search. Civil cases indexed by defendant, plaintiff. Civil records on index cards since 1978 (circuit only); on computer back to 1995; others back to 1953.

Criminal Records: Access: In person only. Visitors must perform in person searches for themselves. No search fee. Required to search: name, years to search, DOB; also helpful: SSN. Criminal records on index cards since 1978 (circuit only); on computer back to 1995; others back to 1953.

General Information: Public Access terminal is available. No adoption, mental, juvenile, or sealed records released. SASE required. Turnaround time 2-4

days. Copy fee: $.15 per page. Certification fee: $1.00. Fee payee: Circuit Clerk. Personal checks accepted. Prepayment is required.

Hart County

Circuit & District Court Box 248, Munfordville, KY 42765; 270-524-5181. Hours: 8AM-4PM M-F; 9AM-Noon Sat (CST). *Felony, Misdemeanor, Civil, Eviction, Small Claims, Probate.*

Civil Records: Access: In person only. Visitors must perform in person searches for themselves. No search fee. Required to search: name, years to search; also helpful: address. Civil cases indexed by defendant, plaintiff. Civil records on index cards since 1978, computerized since 03/95.

Criminal Records: Access: In person only. Visitors must perform in person searches for themselves. No search fee. Required to search: name, years to search, DOB, SSN; also helpful: address. Criminal records on index cards since 1978, computerized since 03/95.

General Information: Public Access terminal is available. No adoption, mental, juvenile, or sealed records released. Copy fee: $.15 per page. Certification fee: $1.00. Fee payee: Circuit Clerk. Business checks accepted. Prepayment is required.

Henderson County

Circuit & District Court PO Box 675, Henderson, KY 42420; 270-826-2405/1566; Fax: 270-827-5932; 831-2710 (District). Hours: 8AM-6PM M; 8AM-4:30PM T-F *Felony, Civil Actions Over $4,000.*

Civil Records: Access: In person only. Visitors must perform in person searches for themselves. No search fee. Required to search: name, years to search. Civil cases indexed by defendant, plaintiff. Civil records on computer from March, 1991, records on index cards from 1978 to March, 1991.

Criminal Records: Access: In person only. Visitors must perform in person searches for themselves. No search fee. Required to search: name, years to search, DOB; also helpful: SSN. Criminal records on computer from March, 1991, records on index cards from 1978 to March, 1991.

General Information:. No adoption, mental, juvenile, or sealed records released. Copy fee: $.15 per page. Certification fee: $1.00. Fee payee: Circuit Clerk. Personal checks accepted. Prepayment is required.

Henry County

Circuit & District Court PO Box 359, New Castle, KY 40050; 502-845-7551; Fax: 502-845-6738. Hours: 8AM-4:30PM M-F (EST). *Felony, Misdemeanor, Civil, Eviction, Small Claims, Probate.*

Civil Records: Access: In person only. Visitors must perform in person searches for themselves. No search fee. Required to search: name, years to search. Civil cases indexed by defendant, plaintiff. Civil records on computer since May, 1994, records on docket books since 1800s.

Criminal Records: Access: In person only. Visitors must perform in person searches for themselves. No search fee. Required to search: name, years to search; also helpful: SSN. Criminal records on computer since May, 1994, records on docket books since 1800s.

General Information: Public Access terminal is available. No adoption, mental, juvenile, or sealed records released. Copy fee: $.15 per page. Certification fee: $1.00. Fee payee: Circuit Clerk. Personal checks accepted. Prepayment is required.

Hickman County

Circuit & District Court 109 S Washington St, Clinton, KY 42031; 270-653-3901; Fax: 270-653-3989. Hours: 8AM-4PM (CST). *Felony, Misdemeanor, Civil, Eviction, Small Claims, Probate.*

Civil Records: Access: Mail, in person. Both court and visitors may perform in person searches. No search fee. Required to search: name, years to search. Civil cases indexed by defendant, plaintiff. Civil records on computer from June, 1994 to present, on index from 1978 to June, 1994. If court does search, request must be in writing.

Criminal Records: Access: Mail, in person. Both court and visitors may perform in person searches. No search fee. Required to search: name, years to search, DOB; also helpful: SSN. Criminal records on computer from June, 1994 to present, on index from 1978 to June, 1994. Requests must be in writing.

General Information: Public Access terminal is available. No adoption, mental, juvenile, or sealed records released. SASE required. Turnaround time same day. Fax notes: Fee to fax results is $2.00 1st pg; $1.00 each add'l. Copy fee: $.15 per page. Certification fee: $1.00. Fee payee: Circuit Clerk. Personal checks accepted. Prepayment is required.

Hopkins County

Circuit & District Court Courthouse 30 S Main St, Madisonville, KY 42431; 270-824-7502; Fax: 270-824-7032. Hours: 8AM-4PM (CST). *Felony, Misdemeanor, Civil, Eviction, Small Claims, Probate.*

Civil Records: Access: In person only. Visitors must perform in person searches for themselves. No search fee. Required to search: name, years to search. Civil cases indexed by defendant, plaintiff. Civil records on computer back to 6/1991; on index cards from 1978 to 1991.

Criminal Records: Access: In person only. Visitors must perform in person searches for themselves. No search fee. Required to search: name, years to search, signed release; also helpful: DOB, SSN. Criminal records on computer back to 6/1991, on index cards from 1978 to 1991.

General Information: Public Access terminal is available. No adoption, mental, juvenile, or sealed records released. Fax notes: Fee to fax results is $2.00 1st page; $1.00 each add'l. Copy fee: $.15 per page. Certification fee: $1.00. Fee payee: Circuit Clerk. Personal checks accepted. Prepayment is required.

Jackson County

Circuit Court PO Box 84, McKee, KY 40447; 606-287-7783; Fax: 606-287-3277. Hours: 8AM-4PM M-F 8AM-Noon Sat (EST). *Felony, Civil Actions Over $4,000.*

Civil Records: Access: Fax, mail, in person. Both court and visitors may perform in person searches. No search fee. Required to search: name, years to search; also helpful: address. Civil cases indexed by defendant, plaintiff. Civil records on computer from May, 1993 to present, on index cards from 1978 to 1993.

Criminal Records: Access: Fax, mail, in person. Both court and visitors may perform in person searches. No search fee. Required to search: name, years to search, DOB; also helpful: SSN. Criminal records on computer from May, 1993 to present, on index cards from 1978 to 1993.

General Information: Public Access terminal is available. No adoption, mental, juvenile, or sealed records released. SASE required. Turnaround time 2 days. Fax notes: $1.00 per page. Copy fee: $.15 per page. Certification fee: $1.00. Fee payee: Jackson County Circuit Clerk. Personal checks accepted.

District Court PO Box 84, McKee, KY 40447; 606-287-8651; Fax: 606-287-3277. Hours: 8AM-4PM M-F; 8AM-Noon Sat (EST). *Misdemeanor, Civil Actions Under $4,000, Eviction, Small Claims, Probate.*

Civil Records: Access: Fax, mail, in person. Both court and visitors may perform in person searches. No search fee. Required to search: name, years to search. Civil cases indexed by defendant, plaintiff. Civil records on computer from May, 1993 to present, on index cards from 1978.

Criminal Records: Access: Fax, mail, in person. Both court and visitors may perform in person searches. No search fee. Required to search: name, years to search, DOB; also helpful: SSN. Criminal records on computer from May, 1993 to present, on index cards from 1990.

General Information: Public Access terminal is available. No adoption, mental, juvenile, or sealed records released. SASE required. Turnaround time 1 week. Copy fee: $.15 per page. Certification fee: $1.00. Fee payee: Jackson County District Clerk. Personal checks accepted. Prepayment is required.

Jefferson County

Circuit & District Court Hall of Justice 600 W Jefferson St, Louisville, KY 40202; 502-595-3064; Fax: 502-595-4629. *Felony, Misdemeanor, Civil, Eviction, Small Claims, Probate.*

Civil Records: Access: Phone, mail, in person. Both court and visitors may perform in person searches. No search fee. Required to search: name, years to search. Civil cases indexed by defendant, plaintiff. Civil records on computer from 1988 to present, on index cards from 1978 to 1988.

Criminal Records: Access: Mail, in person. Both court and visitors may perform in person searches. No search fee. Required to search: name, years to search; also helpful: DOB, SSN. Criminal records on computer from 1988 to present, on index cards from 1978 to 1988.

General Information: Public Access terminal is available. No adoption, mental, juvenile, or sealed records released. SASE not required. Turnaround time 3 days. Copy fee: $.15 per page. Certification fee: $1.00. Fee payee: Circuit Clerk. Personal checks accepted. Credit cards accepted. Accepted for District Criminal Traffic. Prepayment is required.

Jessamine County

Circuit Court 107 N Main St, Nicholasville, KY 40356; 859-885-4531. Hours: 8AM-4:30PM M-W, F; 8AM-12PM TH (EST). *Felony, Civil Actions Over $4,000.*

Civil Records: Access: Mail, in person. Both court and visitors may perform in person searches. No search fee. Required to search: name, years to search. Civil cases indexed by defendant, plaintiff. Civil records on computer from June, 1992 to present, on index cards from 1978 to 1992.

Criminal Records: Access: Mail, in person. Both court and visitors may perform in person searches. No search fee. Required to search: name, years to search, DOB; also helpful: SSN. Criminal records on computer from June, 1992 to present, on index cards from 1978 to 1992.

General Information:. No adoption, mental, juvenile, or sealed records released. SASE required. Turnaround time 1-2 days or refer to A.O.C. in Frankfort. Copy fee: $.15 per page. Certification fee: $1.00. Fee payee: Jessamine Circuit Clerk. Personal checks accepted. Prepayment is required.

District Court 107 N Main St, Nicholasville, KY 40356; 859-887-1005; Fax: 859-887-0425. Hours: 8AM-4:30PM M-W; 8AM-Noon TH; 8AM-4PM F (EST). *Misdemeanor, Civil Actions Under $4,000, Eviction, Small Claims, Probate.*

Civil Records: Access: Mail, in person. Both court and visitors may perform in person searches. No search fee. Required to search: name, years to search. Civil cases indexed by defendant, plaintiff. Civil records on computer since 1992, on file cards prior.

Criminal Records: Access: Mail, in person. Both court and visitors may perform in person searches. No search fee. Required to search: name, years to search; also helpful: DOB, SSN. Criminal records on computer since 1992, on file cards prior.

General Information: Public Access terminal is available. No adoption, mental, juvenile, or sealed records released. SASE required. Turnaround time 2-4 days. Copy fee: $.15 per page. Certification fee: $1.00. Fee payee: Circuit Clerk. Personal checks accepted. Prepayment is required.

Johnson County

Circuit & District Court Box 1405, Paintsville, KY 41240; 606-789-5181; Fax: 606-789-5611. Hours: 8AM-4:30PM; 8:30AM-Noon Sat Driver's license only (EST). *Felony, Misdemeanor, Civil, Eviction, Small Claims, Probate.*

Civil Records: Access: Phone, mail, in person. Both court and visitors may perform in person searches. No search fee. Required to search: name, years to search. Civil cases indexed by defendant, plaintiff. Civil records on computer since 09/88, on index cards from 1978 to 1988, books from 1843 to 1978. From 1988 and prior files are at the archives in Frankfort.

Criminal Records: Access: In person only. Visitors must perform in person searches for themselves. No search fee. Required to search: name, years to search, DOB, SSN. Criminal records on computer since 09/88, on index cards from 1978 to 1988, books from 1843 to 1978. From 1988 and prior files are at the archives in Frankfort. Court will not conduct searches. Contact AOC for statewide search by mail.

General Information: Public Access terminal is available. No adoption, mental, juvenile, or sealed records released. SASE required. Turnaround time at least 3 days. Copy fee: $.15 per page. Certification fee: $2.50. Fee payee: Circuit Clerk. Personal checks accepted. Prepayment is required.

Kenton County

Circuit Court 230 Madison Ave (PO Box 669), Covington, KY 41011; 859-292-6521; Fax: 859-292-6611. Hours: 8AM-5PM (EST). *Felony, Civil Actions Over $4,000.*

http://www.aoc.state.ky.us/kenton

Civil Records: Access: Mail, in person. Both court and visitors may perform in person searches. No search fee. Required to search: name, years to search. Civil cases indexed by defendant, plaintiff. Civil records on computer from 06/89 to present, on index cards from 1800s.

Criminal Records: Access: In person only. Visitors must perform in person searches for themselves. No search fee. Required to search: name, years to search, DOB; also helpful: SSN. Criminal records on computer from 4/90 to present, on index cards from 1800s.

General Information: Public Access terminal is available. No adoption, mental, juvenile, or sealed records released. SASE required. Turnaround time 1-2 days. Copy fee: $.15 per page. Certification fee: $1.00. Fee payee: Kenton Circuit Clerk. Prepayment is required.

District Court 230 Madison Ave, 3rd Fl, Covington, KY 41011; 859-292-6523; Fax: 859-292-6611. Hours: 7AM-5PM *Misdemeanor, Civil Actions Under $4,000, Eviction, Small Claims, Probate.*

http://www.aoc.state.ky.us/kenton

Civil Records: Access: Mail, in person. Only the court performs in person searches; visitors may not. No search fee. Required to search: name, years to search. Civil cases indexed by defendant, plaintiff. Civil records on computer back to 1989, on index cards from 1983.

Criminal Records: Access: In person only. Visitors must perform in person searches for themselves. No search fee. Required to search: name, years to search DOB; also helpful: SSN. Criminal records on computer from 05/91 to present, index cards for the last 5 years.

General Information: Public Access terminal is available. No adoption, mental, juvenile, or sealed records released. SASE required. Turnaround time 1 week. Fax notes: Fee to fax results is $3.00 per document. Copy fee: $.15 per page. Certification fee: $1.00. Fee payee: Circuit Clerk. Business checks accepted. Prepayment is required.

Knott County

Circuit & District Court PO Box 1317, Hindman, KY 41822; 606-785-5021. Hours: 8AM-4PM (EST). *Felony, Misdemeanor, Civil, Eviction, Small Claims, Probate.*

Civil Records: Access: Fax, mail, in person. Both court and visitors may perform in person searches. No search fee. Required to search: name, years to search. Civil cases indexed by defendant, plaintiff. Civil records in index files.

Criminal Records: Access: Fax, mail, in person. Both court and visitors may perform in person searches. No search fee. Required to search: name, years to search; also helpful: DOB, SSN. Criminal records in index files.

General Information: Public Access terminal is available. No adoption, mental, juvenile, or sealed records released. SASE required. Turnaround time 2-4 days. Copy fee: $.15 per page. Certification fee: $2.50. Fee payee: Circuit Clerk. Personal checks accepted. Prepayment is required.

Knox County

Circuit & District Court PO Box 760, Barbourville, KY 40906; 606-546-3075 (Circuit) 546-3232 (Dist); Fax: 606-546-7949. Hours: 8AM-4:30PM M-F; 8AM-noon Sat (EST). *Felony, Misdemeanor, Civil, Eviction, Small Claims, Probate.*

Civil Records: Access: In person only. Visitors must perform in person searches for themselves. No search fee. Required to search: name, years to search. Civil cases indexed by defendant, plaintiff. Civil records go back to 1975; on computer back to 07/92.

Criminal Records: Access: In person only. Visitors must perform in person searches for themselves. No search fee. Required to search: name, years to search, DOB; also helpful: SSN. Criminal records go back to 1975; on computer back to 07/92.

General Information: Public Access terminal is available. No adoption, mental, juvenile, or sealed records released. Fax notes: Fee to fax results is $.15 per page. Copy fee: $.15 per page. Certification fee: $1.00 per page. Fee payee: Circuit Clerk. Personal checks accepted. Prepayment is required.

Larue County

Circuit & District Court Courthouse Annex, PO Box 191, Hodgenville, KY 42748; 270-358-3421; Fax: 270-358-3731. Hours: 8AM-4PM (EST). *Felony, Misdemeanor, Civil, Eviction, Small Claims, Probate.*

Civil Records: Access: Fax, mail, in person. Both court and visitors may perform in person searches. No search

fee. Required to search: name, years to search. Civil cases indexed by defendant, plaintiff. Civil records on computer since 1995.

Criminal Records: Access: Fax, mail, in person. Both court and visitors may perform in person searches. No search fee. Required to search: name, years to search, DOB; also helpful: SSN. Criminal records on computer since 1995.

General Information: Public Access terminal is available. No adoption, mental, juvenile, or sealed records released. SASE required. Turnaround time 2 days. Fax notes: No fee to fax results. Copy fee: $.15 per page. Certification fee: No cert fee. Fee payee: Circuit Clerk. Personal checks accepted. Prepayment is required.

Laurel County

Circuit & District Court Box 1798, London, KY 40743-1798; 606-864-2863; Fax: 606-864-8264. Hours: 8AM-4PM (EST). *Felony, Misdemeanor, Civil, Eviction, Small Claims, Probate.*

Civil Records: Access: In person only. Visitors must perform in person searches for themselves. No search fee. Required to search: name, years to search. Civil cases indexed by defendant, plaintiff. Civil records on computer and index books.

Criminal Records: Access: In person only. Visitors must perform in person searches for themselves. No search fee. Required to search: name, years to search, DOB, SSN. Criminal records on computer and index books.

General Information: Public Access terminal is available. No adoption, mental, juvenile, or sealed records released. Copy fee: $.15 per page. Certification fee: $1.00. Fee payee: Circuit Clerk. Personal checks accepted. Prepayment is required.

Lawrence County

Circuit & District Court Courthouse, PO Box 212, Louisa, KY 41230; 606-638-4215; Fax: 606-638-0264. Hours: 8:30AM-4:30PM M-F 8:30AM-Noon Sat (EST). *Felony, Misdemeanor, Civil, Eviction, Small Claims, Probate.*

Civil Records: Access: Mail, in person. Both court and visitors may perform in person searches. No search fee. Required to search: name, years to search. Civil cases indexed by defendant, plaintiff. Civil records on computer from 11/94, index cards from 1978.

Criminal Records: Access: Mail, in person. Both court and visitors may perform in person searches. No search fee. Required to search: name, years to search; also helpful: DOB, SSN. Criminal records on computer from 11/94, index cards from 1978.

General Information: Public Access terminal is available. No adoption, mental, juvenile, or sealed records released. SASE required. Turnaround time within 1 week. Copy fee: $.15 per page. Certification fee: $1.00. Fee payee: Circuit Clerk. Personal checks accepted.

Lee County

Circuit & District Court Box E, Beattyville, KY 41311; 606-464-8400; Fax: 606-464-0144. Hours: 8AM-4PM M-F; 8:30AM-11:30AM Sat (EST). *Felony, Misdemeanor, Civil, Eviction, Small Claims, Probate.*

Civil Records: Access: In person only. Visitors must perform in person searches for themselves. No search fee. Required to search: name, years to search. Civil cases indexed by defendant, plaintiff. Civil records on computer from 09/94 to present, on index cards from 1978.

Criminal Records: Access: In person only. Visitors must perform in person searches for themselves. No search fee. Required to search: name, years to search,

DOB; also helpful: SSN. Criminal records on computer from 09/94 to present, on index cards from 1978.

General Information: Public Access terminal is available. No adoption, mental, juvenile, or sealed records released. Copy fee: $.15 per page. Certification fee: $5.00. Fee payee: Circuit Clerk. Only cashiers checks and money orders accepted. Attorney checks accepted. Prepayment is required.

Leslie County

Circuit & District Court Box 1750, Hyden, KY 41749; 606-672-2505; Fax: 606-672-5128. Hours: 8AM-5PM M; 8AM-4PM T-F; 8AM-Noon Sat (EST). *Felony, Misdemeanor, Civil, Eviction, Small Claims, Probate.*

Civil Records: Access: Phone, fax, mail, in person. Both court and visitors may perform in person searches. No search fee. Required to search: name, years to search. Civil cases indexed by plaintiff. Civil records on computer and index books.

Criminal Records: Access: In person only. Visitors must perform in person searches for themselves. No search fee. Required to search: name, years to search; also helpful: address, DOB, SSN. Criminal records on computer and index books.

General Information: Public Access terminal is available. No adoption, mental, juvenile, or sealed records released. SASE required. Turnaround time 2-4 days. Fax notes: $2.00 for first page, $1.00 each add'l. Copy fee: $.15 per page. Certification fee: $1.00. Fee payee: Circuit Clerk. Personal checks accepted. Prepayment is required.

Letcher County

Circuit & District Court 156 W Main St, #201, Whitesburg, KY 41858; 606-633-7559/8810; Fax: 606-633-5864. Hours: 8:30AM-4PM M-F 8:30AM-12PM first Sat of month (EST). *Felony, Misdemeanor, Civil, Eviction, Small Claims, Probate.*

Civil Records: Access: Fax, mail, in person. Both court and visitors may perform in person searches. No search fee. Required to search: name, years to search; also helpful: address. Civil cases indexed by defendant, plaintiff. Civil records on computer from 11/1991 to present, on index books from 1986 to 1991. Files maintained in office. Records from 1985 to 1800s in archives in Frankfort.

Criminal Records: Access: In person only. Visitors must perform in person searches for themselves. No search fee. Required to search: name, years to search, DOB, SSN; also helpful: address. Criminal records on computer from 11/1991 to present, on index books from 1986 to 1991. Files maintained in office. Records from 1985 to 1800s in archives in Frankfort. Contact AOC for statewide search by mail.

General Information: Public Access terminal is available. No adoption, mental, juvenile, or sealed records released. SASE required. Turnaround time 2-4 days. Fax notes: $2.00 for first page, $1.00 each add'l. Copy fee: $.15 per page. Certification fee: $1.00. Fee payee: Circuit Clerk. Personal checks accepted. Prepayment is required.

Lewis County

Circuit & District Court PO Box 70, Vanceburg, KY 41179; 606-796-3053; Fax: 606-796-3030. Hours: 8AM-4:30PM M,T,Th,F 8:30-Noon W,Sat (EST). *Felony, Misdemeanor, Civil, Eviction, Small Claims, Probate.*

Civil Records: Access: Mail, in person. Both court and visitors may perform in person searches. No search fee. Required to search: name, years to search. Civil cases indexed by defendant, plaintiff. Civil records on index cards from 1978 to present. Plans to go onto computer in 1995.

Criminal Records: Access: Mail, in person. Both court and visitors may perform in person searches. No search fee. Required to search: name, years to search, DOB; also helpful: SSN. Criminal records on index cards from 1978 to present. Plans to go onto computer in 1995.

General Information: Public Access terminal is available. No adoption, mental, juvenile, or sealed records released. SASE required. Turnaround time within 1 week. Copy fee: $.15 per page. Certification fee: $1.00. Fee payee: Circuit Clerk. Personal checks accepted. Prepayment is required.

Lincoln County

Circuit & District Court 101 E Main, Stanford, KY 40484; 606-365-2535; Fax: 606-365-3389. Hours: 8AM-4PM; 9AM-12PM Sat. (EST). *Felony, Misdemeanor, Civil, Eviction, Small Claims, Probate.*

Civil Records: Access: In person only. Visitors must perform in person searches for themselves. No search fee. Required to search: name, years to search. Civil cases indexed by defendant, plaintiff. Civil records on computer from 05/94, index cards prior, archived from 978 to 1900.

Criminal Records: Access: In person only. Visitors must perform in person searches for themselves. No search fee. Required to search: name, years to search; also helpful: SSN. Criminal records on computer from 05/94, index cards prior, archived from 978 to 1900.

General Information: Public Access terminal is available. No adoption, mental, juvenile, or sealed records released. Copy fee: $.25 per page. Certification fee: No cert fee. Fee payee: Circuit Clerk. Personal checks accepted.

Livingston County

Circuit & District Court PO Box 160, Smithland, KY 42081; 270-928-2172. Hours: 8AM-6PM M 8AM-4PM T-F (CST). *Felony, Misdemeanor, Civil, Eviction, Small Claims, Probate.*

Civil Records: Access: In person only. Visitors must perform in person searches for themselves. No search fee. Required to search: name, years to search. Civil cases indexed by defendant, plaintiff. Civil records on computer from 1993 to present, index cards prior, archived from 1799 to 1851.

Criminal Records: Access: In person only. Visitors must perform in person searches for themselves. No search fee. Required to search: name, years to search, DOB; also helpful: SSN. Criminal records on computer from 1993 to present, index cards prior, archived from 1799 to 1851.

General Information: Public Access terminal is available. No adoption, mental, juvenile, or sealed records released. Copy fee: $.15 per page. Certification fee: $1.00. Fee payee: Circuit Clerk. Personal checks accepted. Prepayment is required.

Logan County

Circuit Court Box 420, Russellville, KY 42276-0420; 270-726-2424; Fax: 270-726-7893. Hours: 8AM-4:30PM M-Th; 8AM-5PM F (CST). *Felony, Civil Actions Over $4,000.*

Civil Records: Access: In person only. Visitors must perform in person searches for themselves. No search fee. Required to search: name, years to search. Civil cases indexed by defendant, plaintiff. Civil records on computer from April, 1992 to present, on index card from 1978 to 1992.

Criminal Records: Access: In person only. Visitors must perform in person searches for themselves. No search fee. Required to search: name, years to search, DOB, SSN. Criminal records on computer from April, 1992 to present, on index card from 1978 to 1992.

General Information: Public Access terminal is available. No adoptions, mental, juvenile or sealed records released. Copy fee: $.15 per page. Certification

fee: $3.00. Fee payee: Circuit Clerk. Only cashiers checks and money orders accepted. Prepayment is required.

District Court Box 420, Russellville, KY 42276; 270-726-3107; Fax: 270-726-7893. Hours: 8AM-4:30PM (CST). *Misdemeanor, Civil Actions Under $4,000, Eviction, Small Claims, Probate.*

Civil Records: Access: In person only. Visitors must perform in person searches for themselves. No search fee. Required to search: name, years to search. Civil cases indexed by defendant, plaintiff. Civil records on computer since 1992, index cards from 1978 to 1992.

Criminal Records: Access: In person only. Visitors must perform in person searches for themselves. No search fee. Required to search: name, years to search, DOB; also helpful: SSN. Criminal records on computer since 1992, index cards from 1978 to 1992.

General Information: Public Access terminal is available. No adoption, mental, juvenile, or sealed records released. Copy fee: $.15 per page. Certification fee: $1.00. Fee payee: Logan Circuit Clerk. Personal checks accepted. Prepayment is required.

Lyon County

Circuit & District Court Box 565, Eddyville, KY 42038; 270-388-7231. Hours: 8AM-4PM (CST). *Felony, Misdemeanor, Civil, Eviction, Small Claims, Probate.*

Civil Records: Access: In person only. Visitors must perform in person searches for themselves. No search fee. Required to search: name, years to search. Civil cases indexed by defendant, plaintiff. Civil records on computer from 11/94 to present, on index cards from 1978 to 1994.

Criminal Records: Access: In person only. Visitors must perform in person searches for themselves. No search fee. Required to search: name, years to search, DOB; also helpful: SSN. Criminal records on computer from 11/94 to present, on index cards from 1978 to 1994.

General Information: Public Access terminal is available. No adoption, mental, juvenile, or sealed records released. Copy fee: $.15 per page. Certification fee: No cert fee. Fee payee: Circuit Clerk. Personal checks accepted. Prepayment is required.

Madison County

Circuit Court PO Box 813, Richmond, KY 40476-0813; 859-624-4793. Hours: 8AM-4PM (EST). *Felony, Civil Actions Over $4,000.*

Civil Records: Access: In person only. Visitors must perform in person searches for themselves. No search fee. Required to search: name, years to search. Civil cases indexed by defendant, plaintiff. Civil records on computer from December, 1990 to present, on index cards from 1978 to 1990, on ledger books 1965 to 1978.

Criminal Records: Access: In person only. Visitors must perform in person searches for themselves. No search fee. Required to search: name, years to search; also helpful: DOB, SSN. Criminal records on computer from December, 1990 to present, on index cards from 1978 to 1990, on ledger books from 1965 to 1978. Contact AOC for statewide searches by mail.

General Information: Public Access terminal is available. No adoption, mental, juvenile, or sealed records released. Copy fee: $.15 per page. Certification fee: $2.00. Fee payee: Madison Circuit Clerk. Personal checks accepted. Prepayment is required.

District Court Madison Hall of Justice, 351 West Main St, Richmond, KY 40475; 859-624-4722; Fax: 859-624-4746. Hours: 8AM-4PM (EST). *Misdemeanor, Civil Actions Under $4,000, Eviction, Small Claims, Probate.*

Civil Records: Access: Fax, mail, in person. Both court and visitors may perform in person searches. No search

fee. Required to search: name, years to search. Civil cases indexed by defendant. Civil records on computer since 11/1990; prior on index cards.

Criminal Records: Access: In person only. Both court and visitors may perform in person searches. No search fee. Required to search: name, years to search, DOB; also helpful: SSN. Criminal records on computer since 11/1990.

General Information: Public Access terminal is available. No adoption, mental, juvenile, or sealed records released. SASE required. Turnaround time 1 week. Fax notes: Fee to fax results for $2.00 per page. Copy fee: $.15 per page. Certification fee: $1.00. Fee payee: Circuit Clerk. Personal checks accepted. Prepayment is required.

Magoffin County

Circuit & District Court Box 147, Salyersville, KY 41465; 606-349-2215; Fax: 606-349-2209. Hours: 8AM-4PM (EST). *Felony, Misdemeanor, Civil, Eviction, Small Claims, Probate.*

Civil Records: Access: Fax, mail, in person. Both court and visitors may perform in person searches. No search fee. Required to search: name, years to search. Civil cases indexed by defendant, plaintiff. Civil records on computer from March, 1993 to present, on index cards from 1978 to 1993.

Criminal Records: Access: Fax, mail, in person. Both court and visitors may perform in person searches. No search fee. Required to search: name, years to search, DOB; also helpful: SSN. Criminal records on computer from March, 1993 to present, on index cards from 1978 to 1993.

General Information: Public Access terminal is available. No adoption, mental, juvenile, or sealed records released. SASE required. Turnaround time 3 days. Fax notes: $2.00 for first page, $1.00 each add'l. Copy fee: $.15 per page. Certification fee: $1.50. Fee payee: Circuit Clerk. Personal checks accepted. Prepayment is required.

Marion County

Circuit & District Court 120 W Main St, Suite B, Lebanon, KY 40033; 270-692-2681. Hours: 8:30AM-4:30PM M-F; 8:30AM-Noon Sat (EST). *Felony, Misdemeanor, Civil, Eviction, Small Claims, Probate.*

Civil Records: Access: In person only. Visitors must perform in person searches for themselves. No search fee. Required to search: name, years to search. Civil cases indexed by defendant, plaintiff. Civil records on computer from May, 1993 to present, on index cards from 1978 to 1993.

Criminal Records: Access: In person only. Visitors must perform in person searches for themselves. No search fee. Required to search: name, years to search; also helpful: SSN. Criminal records on computer from May, 1993 to present, on index cards from 1978 to 1993.

General Information: Public Access terminal is available. No adoption, mental, juvenile, or sealed records released. Copy fee: $.15 per page. Certification fee: $1.00. Fee payee: Circuit Clerk. Personal checks accepted. Prepayment is required.

Marshall County

Circuit & District Court 1101 Main St, Benton, KY 42025; 270-527-3883/1721; Fax: 270-527-5865. Hours: 8AM-4:30PM (CST). *Felony, Misdemeanor, Civil, Eviction, Small Claims, Probate.*

Civil Records: Access: Phone, fax, mail, in person. Both court and visitors may perform in person searches. No search fee. Required to search: name, years to search. Civil cases indexed by defendant, plaintiff. Civil records on computer since August, 1992 to present, on index books from 1978 to 1992.

Criminal Records: Access: Phone, fax, mail, in person. Both court and visitors may perform in person searches. No search fee. Required to search: name, years to search, DOB; also helpful: SSN. Criminal records on computer since August, 1992 to present, on index books from 1978 to 1992.

General Information: Public Access terminal is available. No adoption, mental, juvenile, or sealed records released. SASE required. Turnaround time 3 days. Fax notes: $2.00 for first page, $1.00 each add'l. Copy fee: $.15 per page. Certification fee: $1.00. Fee payee: Circuit Clerk. Personal checks accepted. Prepayment is required.

Martin County

Circuit & District Court Box 430, Inez, KY 41224; 606-298-3508; Fax: 606-298-4202. Hours: 8AM-4:30PM M-TH, 8AM-5:30PM F, 9AM-Noon Sat (EST). *Felony, Misdemeanor, Civil, Eviction, Small Claims, Probate.*

Civil Records: Access: Mail, in person. Both court and visitors may perform in person searches. No search fee. Required to search: name, years to search. Civil cases indexed by defendant, plaintiff. Civil records on computer since April, 1994, District on index books since 1987, Circuit on index books since 1978, prior records on docket books.

Criminal Records: Access: In person only. Visitors must perform in person searches for themselves. No search fee. Required to search: name, years to search; also helpful: DOB, SSN. Criminal records on computer since April, 1994, District on index books since 1987, Circuit on index books since 1978, prior records on docket books.

General Information: Public Access terminal is available. No adoption, mental, juvenile, or sealed records released. SASE not required. Turnaround time 4 days. Copy fee: $.15 per page. Return postage required. Certification fee: $1.00. Fee payee: Circuit Clerk. Personal checks accepted. Prepayment is required.

Mason County

Circuit Court 100 W 3rd St, Maysville, KY 41056; 606-564-4340; Fax: 606-564-0932. Hours: 8:30AM-4:30PM (EST). *Felony, Civil Actions Over $4,000.*

Civil Records: Access: In person only. Visitors must perform in person searches for themselves. No search fee. Required to search: name, years to search. Civil cases indexed by defendant, plaintiff. Civil records on computer back to 4/1994, records on index books since 1929, prior records archived from 1798.

Criminal Records: Access: In person only. Visitors must perform in person searches for themselves. No search fee. Required to search: name, years to search. Criminal records on computer back to 4/1994, records on index books since 1929, prior archived from 1798.

General Information: Public Access terminal is available. No adoption, mental, juvenile, or sealed records released. Fax notes: Fee to fax results is $1.00 per page. Copy fee: $.15 per page. Certification fee: $1.00 per page. Fee payee: Kentucky State Treasurer. Personal checks accepted. Prepayment is required.

District Court 100 W 3rd St, Maysville, KY 41056; 606-564-4011; Fax: 606-564-0932. Hours: 8:30AM-4:30PM (EST). *Misdemeanor, Civil Actions Under $4000, Eviction, Small Claims, Probate.*

Civil Records: Access: In person only. Visitors must perform in person searches for themselves. No search fee. Required to search: name, years to search. Civil cases indexed by defendant, plaintiff. Civil records on computer since April, 1994, prior records on index books from 1978.

Criminal Records: Access: In person only. Visitors must perform in person searches for themselves. No search fee. Required to search: name, years to search.

Criminal records on computer since April, 1994, prior records on index books from 1983.

General Information: Public Access terminal is available. No adoption, mental, juvenile, or sealed records released. Copy fee: $.15 per page. Certification fee: $1.00. Fee payee: Kentucky State Treasurer. Personal checks accepted. Prepayment is required.

McCracken County

Circuit Court Box 1455, Paducah, KY 42002-1455; 270-575-7280. Hours: 8:30AM-5:30PM M, 8:30AM-4:30PM T-F (CST). *Felony, Civil Actions Over $4,000.*

Note: Visitors may only search from 2PM-4PM on Thursday.

Civil Records: Access: Mail, in person. Both court and visitors may perform in person searches. No search fee. Required to search: name, years to search. Civil cases indexed by defendant, plaintiff. Civil records on computer since September 1991, prior records on index cards since 1978.

Criminal Records: Access: Mail, in person. Both court and visitors may perform in person searches. No search fee. Required to search: name, years to search; also helpful: DOB, SSN. Criminal records on computer since September 1991, prior records on index cards since 1978.

General Information: Public Access terminal is available. No adoption, mental, juvenile, or sealed records released. SASE required. Turnaround time 1-2 days. Copy fee: $.15 per page. Certification fee: $1.00. Fee payee: Circuit Clerk. Personal checks accepted. Prepayment is required.

District Court Box 1436, Paducah, KY 42001; 270-575-7270. Hours: 8:30AM-4:30PM (CST). *Misdemeanor, Civil Actions Under $4,000, Eviction, Small Claims, Probate.*

Civil Records: Access: In person only. No search fee. Required to search: name, years to search. Civil cases indexed by defendant, plaintiff. Civil records on computer since 1991, on index books since 1982, prior records archived from the 1900s. Visitors may search only from 2PM to 4PM on Thursday.

Criminal Records: Access: In person only. Both court and visitors may perform in person searches. No search fee. Required to search: name, years to search; also helpful: SSN. Criminal records on computer since 1991, on index books since 1982, prior records archived from the 1900s.

General Information: Public Access terminal is available. No adoption, mental, juvenile, or sealed records released. Copy fee: $.15 per page. Certification fee: $1.00. Fee payee: District Clerk. Personal checks accepted. Prepayment is required.

McCreary County

Circuit & District Court Box 40, Whitley City, KY 42653; 606-376-5041; Fax: 606-376-8844. Hours: 8AM-4:30PM (EST). *Felony, Misdemeanor, Civil, Eviction, Small Claims, Probate.*

Civil Records: Access: Mail, in person. Both court and visitors may perform in person searches. No search fee. Required to search: name, years to search; also helpful: address. Civil cases indexed by defendant, plaintiff. Civil records go back to 1992; on computer back to 1995.

Criminal Records: Access: Mail, in person. Both court and visitors may perform in person searches. No search fee. Required to search: name, years to search, DOB, SSN; also helpful: address. Criminal records go back to 1992; on computer back to 1995.

General Information: Public Access terminal is available. No adoption, mental, juvenile, or sealed records released. SASE required. Copy fee: $.15 per page. Certification fee: $1.00. Fee payee: Circuit Clerk. Personal checks accepted. Prepayment is required.

McLean County

Circuit & District Court Box 145, Calhoun, KY 42327; 270-273-3966; Fax: 270-273-3791. Hours: 8AM-4:30PM M-F; 9AM-Noon Sat (CST). *Felony, Misdemeanor, Civil, Eviction, Small Claims, Probate.*

Civil Records: Access: Mail, in person. Only the court performs in person searches; visitors may not. No search fee. Required to search: name, years to search. Civil cases indexed by defendant, plaintiff. Civil records on computer since 1991, prior records on index cards since 1978.

Criminal Records: Access: In person only. Visitors must perform in person searches for themselves. No search fee. Required to search: name, years to search, DOB; also helpful: SSN. Criminal records on computer since 1991, prior records on index cards since 1978. The court refers all written requests to the Administrative Office of Courts in Frankfort.

General Information:. No adoption, mental, juvenile, or sealed records released. SASE required. Turnaround time 7 days. Copy fee: $.15 per page. Certification fee: $1.00. Fee payee: Circuit Clerk. Personal checks accepted. Prepayment is required.

Meade County

Circuit & District Court Courthouse, Brandenburg, KY 40108; 270-422-4961; Fax: 270-422-2147. Hours: 8AM-4:30AM (EST). *Felony, Misdemeanor, Civil, Eviction, Small Claims, Probate.*

Note: This court asks all record requests go to the Administrative office of the Courts in Frankfort.

Civil Records: Access: In person only. Visitors must perform in person searches for themselves. No search fee. Required to search: name, years to search. Civil cases indexed by defendant, plaintiff. Civil records on computer since 2/95, prior on index cards.

Criminal Records: Access: In person only. Visitors must perform in person searches for themselves. No search fee. Required to search: name, years to search. Criminal records on computer to 2/95, prior on cards.

General Information: Public Access terminal is available. No adoption, mental, juvenile, or sealed records released. Copy fee: $.15 per page. Certification fee: No cert fee. Fee payee: Circuit Clerk. Personal checks accepted.

Menifee County

Circuit & District Court Box 172, Frenchburg, KY 40322; 606-768-2461; Fax: 606-768-2462. Hours: 8:30AM-4PM (EST). *Felony, Misdemeanor, Civil, Eviction, Small Claims, Probate.*

Civil Records: Access: Fax, mail, in person. Both court and visitors may perform in person searches. No search fee. Required to search: name, years to search. Civil cases indexed by defendant, plaintiff. Civil records on index cards from 1978 to present.

Criminal Records: Access: Fax, mail, in person. Both court and visitors may perform in person searches. No search fee. Required to search: name, years to search. Criminal records on index cards from 1978 to present.

General Information: Public Access terminal is available. No adoption, mental, juvenile, or sealed records released. SASE required. Turnaround time 1-3 days. Fax notes: $2.00 for first page, $1.00 each add'l. Copy fee: $.25 per page. Certification fee: $1.00. Fee payee: Circuit Clerk. Prepayment is required.

Mercer County

Circuit & District Court Courthouse, 224 Main St S, Harrodsburg, KY 40330-1696; 859-734-6306; Fax: 859-734-9159. 8AM-4:30PM (EST). *Felony, Misdemeanor, Civil, Eviction, Small Claims, Probate.*

Civil Records: Access: In person only. Visitors must perform in person searches for themselves. No search fee. Required to search: name, years to search. Civil

cases indexed by defendant, plaintiff. Civil records on computer back to 1993; prior in index books.

Criminal Records: Access: In person only. Visitors must perform in person searches for themselves. No search fee. Required to search: name, years to search; also helpful: DOB, SSN. Criminal records on computer back to 1993; prior in index books.

General Information: Public Access terminal is available. No adoption, mental, juvenile, or sealed records released. Certification fee: $1.00. Payee: Circuit Clerk. Personal checks accepted. Prepayment required.

Metcalfe County

Circuit & District Court Box 485, Edmonton, KY 42129; 270-432-3663; Fax: 270-432-4437. Hours: 8AM-4PM (CST). *Felony, Misdemeanor, Civil, Eviction, Small Claims, Probate.*

Civil Records: Access: Phone, fax, mail, in person. Both court and visitors may perform in person searches. No search fee. Required to search: name, years to search. Civil cases indexed by defendant, plaintiff. Civil records on computer since 1992, prior records on index cards since 1978.

Criminal Records: Access: Phone, fax, mail, in person. Both court and visitors may perform in person searches. No search fee. Required to search: name, years to search; also helpful: DOB, SSN, sex. Criminal records on computer since 1992, prior records on index cards since 1978.

General Information: Public Access terminal is available. No adoption, mental, juvenile, or sealed records released. SASE required. Turnaround time 1-2 days. Fax notes: Fee to fax results is $2.00 1st page; $1.00 each add'l. Copy fee: $.15 per page. Certification fee: $1.00. Fee payee: Circuit Clerk. Personal checks accepted. Prepayment is required.

Monroe County

Circuit & District Court Box 245, Tompkinsville, KY 42167; 270-487-5480; Fax: 270-487-0068. Hours: 8AM-4PM (CST). *Felony, Misdemeanor, Civil, Eviction, Small Claims, Probate.*

Civil Records: Access: Phone, mail, in person. Both court and visitors may perform in person searches. No search fee. Required to search: name, years to search. Civil cases indexed by defendant, plaintiff. Civil records kept in files.

Criminal Records: Access: Phone, mail, in person. Both court and visitors may perform in person searches. No search fee. Required to search: name, years to search. Criminal records kept in files.

General Information: Public Access terminal is available. No adoption, mental, juvenile, or sealed records released. SASE required. Turnaround time 1 week. Copy fee: $.15 per page. Certification fee: $1.00. Fee payee: Circuit Clerk. Personal checks accepted. Prepayment is required.

Montgomery County

Circuit & District Court Courthouse, One Court St (PO Box 327), Mt Sterling, KY 40353; 859-498-5966; Fax: 859-498-9341. 8:30AM-4PM *Felony, Misdemeanor, Civil, Eviction, Small Claims, Probate.*

Civil Records: Access: Mail, in person. Both court and visitors may perform in person searches. No search fee. Required to search: name, years to search. Civil cases indexed by defendant, plaintiff. Civil records on computer since August, 1991, on index cards from 1978-1991, prior records on docket books.

Criminal Records: Access: Mail, in person. Both court and visitors may perform in person searches. No search fee. Required to search: name, years to search. Criminal records on computer since August, 1991, on index cards from 1978-1991, prior records on docket books.

General Information: Public Access terminal is available. No adoption, mental, juvenile, or sealed

records released. SASE required. Turnaround time 1-2 days. Copy fee: $.15 per page. Certification fee: $1.00. Fee payee: Circuit Clerk. Personal checks accepted. Prepayment is required.

Morgan County

Circuit & District Court Box 85, West Liberty, KY 41472; 606-743-3763; Fax: 606-743-2633. Hours: 8AM-4PM (EST). *Felony, Misdemeanor, Civil, Eviction, Small Claims, Probate.*

Civil Records: Access: Mail, in person. Both court and visitors may perform in person searches. No search fee. Required to search: name, years to search. Civil cases indexed by defendant, plaintiff. Civil records on computer back to 9/1993; index books back to 1921.

Criminal Records: Access: Mail, in person. Both court and visitors may perform in person searches. No search fee. Required to search: name, years to search. Criminal records on computer to 9/1993; index books to 1921.

General Information: Public Access terminal is available. No adoption, mental, juvenile, or sealed records released. Turnaround time 1 day. Fax notes: Will not fax results. Copy fee: $.15 per page. Certification fee: Certification $2.00 1st page, $1.00 each additional page. Fee payee: Circuit Clerk. Personal checks accepted. Prepayment is required.

Muhlenberg County

Circuit Court Box 776, Greenville, KY 42345; 270-338-4850 (Felony); Fax: 270-338-7482. Hours: 8AM-4PM (CST). *Felony, Civil Actions Over $4,000.*

Civil Records: Access: In person only. Visitors must perform in person searches for themselves. No search fee. Required to search: name, years to search. Civil cases indexed by defendant, plaintiff. Civil records on computer since May, 1992, records on index since 1932, prior records archived since 1940.

Criminal Records: Access: In person only. Visitors must perform in person searches for themselves. No search fee. Required to search: name, years to search, SSN; also helpful: DOB. Criminal records on computer since May, 1992, records on index since 1932, prior records archived since 1940.

General Information: Public Access terminal is available. No adoption, mental, juvenile, or sealed records released. Copy fee: $.15 per page. Certification fee: $1.00. Fee payee: Circuit Clerk. Personal checks accepted. Prepayment is required.

District Court Box 274, Greenville, KY 42345; 270-338-0995; Fax: 270-338-7482. Hours: 8AM-4PM (CST). *Misdemeanor, Civil Actions Under $4,000, Eviction, Small Claims, Probate.*

Civil Records: Access: In person only. Both court and visitors may perform in person searches. No search fee. Required to search: name, years to search. Civil cases indexed by defendant, plaintiff. Civil records on computer since 1992, prior records on index books.

Criminal Records: Access: In person only. Visitors must perform in person searches for themselves. No search fee. Required to search: name, years to search. Criminal records on computer since 1992, prior records on index books.

General Information: Public Access terminal is available. No adoption, mental, juvenile, or sealed records released. Copy fee: $.15 per page. Certification fee: $1.00. Fee payee: District Clerk. Personal checks accepted. Prepayment is required.

Nelson County

Circuit & District Court Box 845, Bardstown, KY 40004; 502-348-3648. Hours: 8:30AM-4:30PM (EST). *Felony, Misdemeanor, Civil, Eviction, Small Claims, Probate.*

Civil Records: Access: Mail, in person. Both court and visitors may perform in person searches. No search fee.

Required to search: name, years to search. Civil cases indexed by defendant, plaintiff. Civil records on computer since 1990, on index since 1978, prior records archived from 1940.

Criminal Records: Access: Mail, in person. Both court and visitors may perform in person searches. No search fee. Required to search: name, years to search, DOB; also helpful: SSN. Criminal records on computer since 1990, on index since 1978, prior archived from 1940.

General Information: Public Access terminal is available. No adoption, mental, juvenile, domestic violence or sealed records released. Turnaround time 2 weeks. Copy fee: $.15 per page. Certification fee: $1.00. Fee payee: Circuit Clerk. Personal checks accepted. Prepayment is required.

Nicholas County

Circuit & District Court PO Box 109, Carlisle, KY 40311; 859-289-2336; Fax: 859-289-6141. Hours: 8:30AM-4:30PM M-F (EST). *Felony, Misdemeanor, Civil, Eviction, Small Claims, Probate.*

Civil Records: Access: Fax, mail, in person. Both court and visitors may perform in person searches. No search fee. Required to search: name, years to search. Civil cases indexed by defendant, plaintiff. Civil records on computer since March, 1993, prior records on index cards. Request must be in writing.

Criminal Records: Access: Fax, mail, in person. Both court and visitors may perform in person searches. No search fee. Required to search: name, years to search. Criminal records on computer since March, 1993, prior records on index cards. Request must be in writing.

General Information: Public Access terminal is available. No adoption, mental, juvenile, or sealed records released. SASE required. Turnaround time 1-2 days. Fax notes: No fee to fax results. Copy fee: $.15 per page. Certification fee: $1.00. Fee payee: Circuit Clerk. Personal checks accepted. Prepayment required.

Ohio County

Circuit & District Court 130 E Washington, Ste 300, Hartford, KY 42347; 270-298-3671; Fax: 270-298-9565. Hours: 8:30AM-4:30PM (CST). *Felony, Misdemeanor, Civil, Eviction, Small Claims, Probate.*

Civil Records: Access: In person only. Visitors must perform in person searches for themselves. No search fee. Required to search: name, years to search. Civil cases indexed by defendant, plaintiff. Civil records on computer since 10/91, Circuit court on index books since the 1800s, District court on index books since 1987 and prior records are archived.

Criminal Records: Access: In person only. Visitors must perform in person searches for themselves. No search fee. Required to search: name, years to search. Criminal records on computer since 10/91, Circuit court on index books since the 1800s, District court on index books since 1987 and prior records are archived.

General Information: Public Access terminal is available. No adoption, mental, juvenile, or sealed records released. Copy fee: $.15 per page. Will not mail. Certification fee: $1.00. Fee payee: Circuit Clerk. No personal checks accepted. Prepayment is required.

Oldham County

Circuit & District Court 100 W Main St, La Grange, KY 40031; 502-222-9837; Fax: 502-222-3047. Hours: 8AM-4PM (EST). *Felony, Misdemeanor, Civil, Eviction, Small Claims, Probate.*

Note: Criminal record requests are referred to the Administrative office of the Courts in Frankfort.

Civil Records: Access: In person only. Visitors must perform in person searches for themselves. No search fee. Required to search: name, years to search. Civil cases indexed by defendant, plaintiff. Civil records on computer since 1991, on index books since 1978, prior records archived since 1800s.

Criminal Records: Access: In person only. Visitors must perform in person searches for themselves. No search fee. Required to search: name, years to search; also helpful: SSN. Criminal records on computer since 1991, index books to 1978, prior archived since 1800s.

General Information: Public Access terminal is available. No adoption, mental, juvenile, or sealed records released. Fax notes: Fee to fax results is $2.00 per page. Copy fee: $.15 per page. Certification fee: $1.00. Fee payee: Circuit Clerk. Personal checks accepted. Prepayment is required. Fee to fax results if $1.00 per document plus $.20 per page.

Owen County

Circuit & District Court Box 473, Owenton, KY 40359; 502-484-2232; Fax: 502-484-0625. Hours: 8AM-4PM (EST). *Felony, Misdemeanor, Civil, Eviction, Small Claims, Probate.*

Civil Records: Access: Fax, mail, in person. Both court and visitors may perform in person searches. No search fee. Required to search: name, years to search. Civil cases indexed by defendant, plaintiff. Civil records on computer since 1992, prior records on index books since 1946. Cases before 1978 at state archives.

Criminal Records: Access: Fax, mail, in person. Both court and visitors may perform in person searches. No search fee. Required to search: name, years to search, DOB, SSN. Criminal records on computer since 1992, prior records on index books since 1946. Cases before 1978 transferred to state archives. Court suggests statewide search through A.O.C. at 502-573-2350.

General Information:. No adoption, mental, juvenile, or sealed records released. Turnaround time 1 week. Copy fee: $.15 per page. Certification fee: $1.00. Fee payee: Circuit Clerk. Personal checks accepted. Prepayment is required.

Owsley County

Circuit & District Court Box 130, Booneville, KY 41314; 606-593-6226; Fax: 606-593-6343. Hours: 8AM-4PM M-F, 8AM-Noon Sat (EST). *Felony, Misdemeanor, Civil, Eviction, Small Claims, Probate.*

Civil Records: Access: In person only. Visitors must perform in person searches for themselves. No search fee. Required to search: name, years to search. Civil cases indexed by defendant, plaintiff. Civil records on computer since 10/1994, prior records on index cards since 1978.

Criminal Records: Access: In person only. Visitors must perform in person searches for themselves. No search fee. Required to search: name, years to search, DOB or SSN. Criminal records on computer since 10/1994, prior records on index cards since 1978.

General Information: Public Access terminal is available. No adoption, mental, juvenile, or sealed records released. Fax notes: Fee to fax results is $2.00 1st page, $1.00 each add'l. Copy fee: $.15 per page. Certification fee: $1.00. Fee payee: Circuit Clerk. Personal checks accepted. Prepayment is required.

Pendleton County

Circuit & District Court PO Box 69, Falmouth, KY 41040; 859-654-3347. Hours: 8AM-4PM *Felony, Misdemeanor, Civil, Eviction, Small Claims, Probate.*

Civil Records: Access: Mail, in person. Both court and visitors may perform in person searches. No search fee. Required to search: name, years to search. Civil cases indexed by defendant, plaintiff. Civil records on computer since July, 1994, prior records on index books since 1978.

Criminal Records: Access: In person only. Both court and visitors may perform in person searches. No search fee. Required to search: name, years to search. Criminal records on computer since July, 1994, prior records on index books since 1978.

General Information:. No adoption, mental, juvenile, or sealed records released. SASE not required. Copy fee: $.15 per page. Certification fee: $1.00. Fee payee: Circuit Clerk. Personal checks accepted. Prepayment is required.

Perry County

Circuit Court Box 7433, Hazard, KY 41701; 606-435-6000. Hours: 8AM-4PM (EST). *Felony, Civil Actions Over $4,000.*

Civil Records: Access: Phone, mail, in person. Both court and visitors may perform in person searches. No search fee. Required to search: name, years to search. Civil cases indexed by defendant, plaintiff. Civil records on computer since October, 1991, prior records on index cards since 1978.

Criminal Records: Access: Phone, mail, in person. Both court and visitors may perform in person searches. No search fee. Required to search: name, years to search. Criminal records on computer since October, 1991, prior records on index cards since 1978.

General Information: Public Access terminal is available. No adoption, mental, juvenile, or sealed records released. SASE required. Turnaround time approximately 1 week. Copy fee: $.15 per page. Certification fee: $1.00. Fee payee: Circuit Clerk. Personal checks accepted. Prepayment is required.

District Court Box 7433, Hazard, KY 41702; 606-435-6002. 8AM-4PM *Misdemeanor, Civil Actions Under $4,000, Eviction, Small Claims, Probate.*

Civil Records: Access: Mail, in person. No search fee. Required to search: name, years to search. Civil cases indexed by defendant, plaintiff. Civil records on computer since 1991, records on index books since 1978, prior records archived since 1900s.

Criminal Records: Access: Mail, in person. Both court and visitors may perform in person searches. No search fee. Required to search: name, years to search. Criminal records on computer since 1991, records on index books since 1978, prior records archived since 1900s.

General Information: Public Access terminal is available. No adoption, mental, juvenile, or sealed records released. SASE required. Turnaround time minimum 2 days. Copy fee: $.15 per page. Certification fee: $1.00. Fee payee: District Clerk. Personal checks accepted. Prepayment is required.

Pike County

Circuit & District Court PO Box 1002, Pikeville, KY 41502; 606-433-7557; Fax: 606-433-7044. Hours: 8AM-4:30PM (EST). *Felony, Misdemeanor, Civil, Eviction, Small Claims, Probate.*

Civil Records: Access: Mail, in person. Both court and visitors may perform in person searches. No search fee. Required to search: name, years to search. Civil cases indexed by defendant, plaintiff. Civil records on computer since March, 1994, prior records on index cards from 1978.

Criminal Records: Access: In person only. Visitors must perform in person searches for themselves. No search fee. Required to search: name, years to search. Criminal records on computer since March, 1994, prior records on index cards from 1978.

General Information: Public Access terminal is available. No adoption, mental, juvenile, or sealed records released. SASE required. Turnaround time 3 days. Copy fee: $.15 per page. Certification fee: $1.00. Fee payee: Circuit Clerk. Personal checks accepted. Prepayment is required.

Powell County

Circuit & District Court Box 578, Stanton, KY 40380; 606-663-4141; Fax: 606-663-2710. Hours: 8AM-4PM M,T,W,F, 8AM-Noon Th & Sat *Felony, Misdemeanor, Civil, Eviction, Small Claims, Probate.*

Civil Records: Access: Mail, in person. Both court and visitors may perform in person searches. No search fee. Required to search: name, years to search. Civil cases indexed by defendant, plaintiff. Civil records on computer since 1993, prior on index cards since 1978.

Criminal Records: Access: Mail, in person. Both court and visitors may perform in person searches. No search fee. Required to search: name, years to search, DOB; also helpful: SSN. Criminal records on computer since 1993, prior records on index cards since 1978.

General Information: Public Access terminal is available. No adoption, mental, juvenile, or sealed records released. SASE required. Turnaround time varies. Copy fee: $.15 per page. Certification fee: $1.00. Fee payee: Circuit Clerk. Personal checks accepted. Prepayment is required.

Pulaski County

Circuit & District Court Box 664, Somerset, KY 42502; 606-677-4029; Fax: 606-677-4002. Hours: 8AM-4:30PM M-F, 8AM-Noon Sat (EST). *Felony, Misdemeanor, Civil, Eviction, Small Claims, Probate.*

Civil Records: Access: In person only. Visitors must perform in person searches for themselves. No search fee. Required to search: name, years to search. Civil cases indexed by defendant, plaintiff. Civil records on computer since 1991, prior on index books from 1978.

Criminal Records: Access: In person only. Visitors must perform in person searches for themselves. No search fee. Required to search: name, years to search. Criminal records on computer since 1991, prior records on index books from 1978.

General Information: Public Access terminal is available. No adoption, mental, juvenile, or sealed records released. Copy fee: $.15 per page. Certification fee: $1.00. Fee payee: Circuit Clerk. Personal checks accepted. Prepayment is required.

Robertson County

Circuit & District Court PO Box 63 (211 Court St), Mt Olivet, KY 41064; 606-724-5993; Fax: 606-724-5721. Hours: 8:30AM-4:30PM (EST). *Felony, Misdemeanor, Civil, Eviction, Small Claims, Probate.*

Note: The physical location is 211 Court Street.

Civil Records: Access: In person only. Visitors must perform in person searches for themselves. No search fee. Required to search: name, years to search. Civil cases indexed by defendant, plaintiff. Civil records on computer, index cards, older records at Frankfort.

Criminal Records: Access: In person only. Visitors must perform in person searches for themselves. No search fee. Required to search: name, years to search; also helpful: DOB, SSN. Criminal records on computer, index cards, older records archived at Frankfort.

General Information: Public Access terminal is available. No adoption, mental, juvenile, or sealed records released. Copy fee: $.15 per page. Certification fee: $1.00. Fee payee: Circuit Clerk. Personal checks accepted. Prepayment is required.

Rockcastle County

Circuit & District Court Courthouse Annex, 1st Fl, 205 E Main St., Mt Vernon, KY 40456; 606-256-2581. Hours: 8AM-4PM M-W & F; 8AM-6PM Th; 8:30AM-Noon Sat (EST). *Felony, Misdemeanor, Civil, Eviction, Small Claims, Probate.*

Civil Records: Access: Mail, in person. Both court and visitors may perform in person searches. No search fee. Required to search: name, years to search. Civil cases indexed by defendant, plaintiff. Civil records on computer since 1991, index cards from 1978 to 1990, prior are archived at Frankfort.

Criminal Records: Access: In person only. Visitors must perform in person searches for themselves. No search fee. Required to search: name, years to search, DOB; also helpful: SSN. Criminal Records from 1991 to present are available. A form is available to request a criminal history through AOC, Retrieval Services. This court will provide a form via mail if provided a SASE. **General Information:** Public Access terminal is available. No adoption, mental, juvenile, or sealed records released. SASE requires. Turnaround time 3 days. Copy fee: $.15 per page. Certification fee: $1.00 plus copy fee per page. Fee payee: Circuit Clerk. Personal checks accepted. Prepayment is required.

Rowan County

Circuit & District Court 627 E Main, Morehead, KY 40351-1398; 606-784-4574; Fax: 606-784-1899. Hours: 8:30AM-4:30PM M-F 8:30AM-12PM SAT (EST). *Felony, Misdemeanor, Civil, Eviction, Small Claims, Probate.*

Civil Records: Access: In person only. Visitors must perform in person searches for themselves. No search fee. Required to search: name, years to search. Civil cases indexed by defendant, plaintiff. Civil records on computer to 1991, cards to 1989, archived from 1900.
Criminal Records: Access: In person only. Visitors must perform in person searches for themselves. No search fee. Required to search: name, years to search. Criminal records on computer from 1991, index cards from 1989, archived from 1900.
General Information: Public Access terminal is available. No adoption, mental, juvenile, or sealed records released. Copy fee: $.15 per page. Certification fee: No cert fee. Fee payee: Circuit Clerk. Only cashiers checks and money orders accepted. Prepayment is required.

Russell County

Circuit & District Court 410 Monument Square, Suite 203, Jamestown, KY 42629; 270-343-2185; Fax: 270-343-5808. Hours: 8AM-4:30PM M-F 8AM-Noon Sat (CST). *Felony, Misdemeanor, Civil, Eviction, Small Claims, Probate.*

Civil Records: Access: In person only. Visitors must perform in person searches for themselves. No search fee. Required to search: name, years to search. Civil cases indexed by defendant, plaintiff. Civil records on computer from August, 1994, index cards from 1978-1994, prior archived at Frankfort.
Criminal Records: Access: In person only. Visitors must perform in person searches for themselves. No search fee. Required to search: name, years to search. Criminal records on computer from August, 1994, index cards from 1978-1994, prior at Frankfort.
General Information: Public Access terminal is available. No adoption, mental, juvenile, or sealed records released. Copy fee: $.15 per page. Certification fee: $1.00. Fee payee: Circuit Clerk. Personal checks accepted. Prepayment is required.

Scott County

Circuit & District Court 119 N Hamilton, Georgetown, KY 40324; 502-863-0474. Hours: 8AM-4:30PM (EST). *Felony, Misdemeanor, Civil, Eviction, Small Claims, Probate.*

Civil Records: Access: Mail, in person. Both court and visitors may perform in person searches. No search fee. Required to search: name, years to search. Civil cases indexed by defendant, plaintiff. Civil records on computer since 1992, index cards from 1978 to 1992, in books prior.
Criminal Records: Access: Mail, in person. Both court and visitors may perform in person searches. No search fee. Required to search: name, years to search; also helpful: SSN. Criminal records on computer since 1992, index cards from 1978 to 1992, in books prior.
General Information: Public Access terminal is available. No adoption, mental, juvenile, paternity and domestic violence records released. SASE required. Turnaround time varies. Copy fee: $.15 per page.

Certification fee: $1.00. Fee payee: Circuit Clerk. Personal checks accepted. Prepayment is required.

Shelby County

Circuit & District Court 501 Main St, Shelbyville, KY 40065; 502-633-1289; Civil phone: 502-633-4736 (Dist Ct); Fax: 502-633-0146 (633-6421 Dist Ct fax). Hours: 8:30AM-4:30PM (EST). *Felony, Misdemeanor, Civil, Eviction, Small Claims, Probate.*

Civil Records: Access: Fax, mail, in person. Both court and visitors may perform in person searches. No search fee. Required to search: name, years to search. Civil cases indexed by defendant, plaintiff. Civil records on computer back to 1991; index cards from 1978 to 1991.
Criminal Records: Access: In person only. Visitors must perform in person searches for themselves. No search fee. Required to search: name, years to search, DOB. Criminal records on computer back to 1991; index cards from 1978 to 1991.
General Information: Public Access terminal is available. No adoption, mental, juvenile, or sealed records released. SASE required. Turnaround time 3-5 days. Copy fee: $.15 per page. Certification fee: $1.00. Fee payee: Circuit Clerk. Personal checks accepted. Prepayment is required.

Simpson County

Circuit & District Court Box 261, Franklin, KY 42135-0261; 270-586-8910/4241; Fax: 270-586-0265. Hours: 8AM-4PM (CST). *Felony, Misdemeanor, Civil, Eviction, Small Claims, Probate.*

Civil Records: Access: Mail, in person. Both court and visitors may perform in person searches. No search fee. Required to search: name, years to search. Civil cases indexed by defendant, plaintiff. Civil records on computer since 1993, manual prior to 1993.
Criminal Records: Access: Mail, in person. Both court and visitors may perform in person searches. No search fee. Required to search: name, years to search, DOB, SSN. Criminal records on computer since 1993, card index 1978-1992.
General Information: Public Access terminal is available. No adoption, mental, juvenile, or sealed records released. SASE required. Turnaround time 1 week. Copy fee: $.25 per page. Certification fee: $1.25. Fee payee: Circuit Clerk. Only cashiers checks and money orders accepted. Prepayment is required.

Spencer County

Circuit & District Court Box 282, Taylorsville, KY 40071; 502-477-3220; Fax: 502-477-9368. Hours: 7:45AM-4PM (EST). *Felony, Misdemeanor, Civil, Eviction, Small Claims, Probate.*

Civil Records: Access: Mail, in person. Visitors must perform in person searches for themselves. No search fee. Required to search: name, years to search. Civil cases indexed by defendant, plaintiff. Civil records on computer from 08/94 to present, index cards from 1978 to 1994.
Criminal Records: Access: Mail, in person. Visitors must perform in person searches for themselves. No search fee. Required to search: name, years to search, DOB; also helpful: SSN. Criminal records on computer from 08/94 to present, index cards from 1978 to 1994.
General Information: Public Access terminal is available. No adoption, mental, juvenile, or sealed records released. SASE required. Turnaround time 1-4 days. Copy fee: $.15 per page. Certification fee: $1.00. Fee payee: Circuit Clerk. Personal checks accepted. Prepayment is required.

Taylor County

Circuit & District Court 203 N Court Courthouse, Campbellsville, KY 42718; 270-465-6686; Fax: 270-789-4356. Hours: 8AM-4:30PM *Felony, Misdemeanor, Civil, Eviction, Small Claims, Probate.*

Civil Records: Access: In person only. Both court and visitors may perform in person searches. No search fee. Required to search: name, years to search. Civil cases indexed by defendant, plaintiff. Civil records on computer from 1993, index cards from 1978 to 1993.
Criminal Records: Access: In person only. Visitors must perform in person searches for themselves. No search fee. Required to search: name, years to search, DOB, SSN. Criminal records on computer from 1993 to present, index cards from 1978 to 1993.
General Information: Public Access terminal is available. No adoption, mental, juvenile, or sealed records released. Copy fee: $.15 per page. Certification fee: $1.00. Fee payee: Circuit Clerk. Personal checks accepted. Prepayment is required.

Todd County

Circuit & District Court Box 337, Elkton, KY 42220; 270-265-5631; Fax: 270-265-2122. Hours: 8AM-4:30PM (CST). *Felony, Misdemeanor, Civil, Eviction, Small Claims, Probate.*

Civil Records: Access: In person only. Visitors must perform in person searches for themselves. No search fee. Required to search: name, years to search. Civil cases indexed by defendant, plaintiff. Civil records on computer since January, 1993, index cards from 1978-1993, index books prior to 1978.
Criminal Records: Access: In person only. Visitors must perform in person searches for themselves. No search fee. Required to search: name, years to search. Criminal records on computer since January, 1993, index cards from 1978-1993, index books prior to 1978.
General Information: Public Access terminal is available. No adoption, mental, juvenile, or sealed records released. Copy fee: $.15 per page. Certification fee: $1.50. Fee payee: Circuit Clerk. Personal checks accepted. Prepayment is required.

Trigg County

Circuit & District Court Box 673, Cadiz, KY 42211; 270-522-6270. Hours: 8AM-4PM M-F 9AM-11:30AM 1st SAT of each month (CST). *Felony, Misdemeanor, Civil, Eviction, Small Claims, Probate.*

Civil Records: Access: In person only. Visitors must perform in person searches for themselves. No search fee. Required to search: name, years to search. Civil cases indexed by defendant, plaintiff. Civil records on computer from April, 1993 to present, index cards from 1978 to 1993.
Criminal Records: Access: In person only. Visitors must perform in person searches for themselves. No search fee. Required to search: name, years to search, DOB; also helpful: SSN. Criminal records on computer from April, 1993 to present, index cards 1978 to 1993.
General Information: Public Access terminal is available. No adoption, mental, juvenile, or sealed records released. Copy fee: $.15 per page. Certification fee: $1.00. Fee payee: Circuit Clerk. Only cashiers checks and money orders accepted.

Trimble County

Circuit & District Court Box 248, Bedford, KY 40006; 502-255-3213, 502-255-3525 (District); Fax: 502-255-4953. Hours: 8AM-4:30PM M,T,Th,F 8AM-Noon Sat (EST). *Felony, Misdemeanor, Civil, Eviction, Small Claims, Probate.*

Civil Records: Access: Mail, in person. Both court and visitors may perform in person searches. No search fee. Required to search: name, years to search. Civil cases indexed by defendant, plaintiff. Civil records on computer and in folders from 1993 to present, folders 1978 to 1992, archives prior to 1978.
Criminal Records: Access: In person only. Visitors must perform in person searches for themselves. No search fee. Required to search: name, years to search, DOB; also helpful: SSN. Criminal records on computer

and in folders from 1993 to present, folders 1978 to 1992, archives prior to 1978.

General Information: Public Access terminal is available. No adoption, mental, juvenile, or sealed records released. SASE required. Turnaround time 2-4 days. Copy fee: $.15 per page. Certification fee: $1.00. Fee payee: Circuit Clerk. Only cashiers checks and money orders accepted. Prepayment is required.

Union County

Circuit & District Court Box 59, Morganfield, KY 42437; 270-389-0800/0804; Fax: 270-389-9887. Hours: 8AM-4PM (No searches performed on Thursday) (CST). *Felony, Misdemeanor, Civil, Eviction, Small Claims, Probate.*

Civil Records: Access: Mail, in person. Both court and visitors may perform in person searches. No search fee. Required to search: name, years to search. Civil cases indexed by defendant, plaintiff. Civil records on computer since June, 1994 (new records only); prior on index cards and archived.

Criminal Records: Access: In person only. Visitors must perform in person searches for themselves. No search fee. Required to search: name, years to search, DOB, SSN. Criminal records on computer since June, 1994 (new records only); prior on index cards and archived. Contact AOC for statewide search by mail (criminal requests to be acquired through Pre-Trial Svcs, Frankfort).

General Information: Public Access terminal is available. No adoption, mental, juvenile, or sealed records released. SASE required. Turnaround time 2-4 days. Copy fee: $.15 per page. Certification fee: $1.00. Fee payee: Circuit Clerk. Business checks accepted. Prepayment is required.

Warren County

Circuit & District Court 1001 Center St #102, Bowling Green, KY 42101-2184; 270-746-7400; Fax: 270-746-7501. Hours: 8:AM-4:30PM (CST). *Felony, Misdemeanor, Civil, Eviction, Small Claims, Probate.*

Civil Records: Access: In person only. Visitors must perform in person searches for themselves. No search fee. Required to search: name, years to search. Civil cases indexed by defendant, plaintiff. Civil records on computer since 1989.

Criminal Records: Access: In person only. Visitors must perform in person searches for themselves. No search fee. Required to search: name, years to search; also helpful: DOB, SSN. Criminal records on computer since 1990.

General Information: Public Access terminal is available. No adoption, mental, juvenile, or sealed records released. Fax notes: Fee to fax results is $1.00 per page, $2.00 for 1st page. Copy fee: $.15 per page. Certification fee: $1.00. Fee payee: Circuit Clerk. Personal checks accepted. Prepayment is required.

Washington County

Circuit & District Court PO Box 346, Springfield, KY 40069; 859-336-3761; Fax: 859-336-9824. Hours: 8AM-4:30PM; 8:30-12 on Sat (EST). *Felony, Misdemeanor, Civil, Eviction, Small Claims, Probate.*

Civil Records: Access: Mail, in person. Both court and visitors may perform in person searches. No search fee. Required to search: name, years to search. Civil cases indexed by defendant, plaintiff. Civil records on computer, index cards and archived.

Criminal Records: Access: Mail, in person. Both court and visitors may perform in person searches. No search

fee. Required to search: name, years to search, DOB. Criminal records on computer, index cards, archived.

General Information: Public Access terminal is available. No adoption, mental, juvenile, or sealed records released. SASE not required. Turnaround time 2-4 days. Copy fee: $.15 per page. Add postage. Certification fee: $1.00. Fee payee: Circuit Clerk. Personal checks accepted. Prepayment is required.

Wayne County

Circuit & District Court 109 N Main St, #2, Monticello, KY 42633-1458; 606-348-5841; Fax: 606-348-4225. Hours: 8AM-4:15PM M-F; 8:30AM-Noon Sat (CST). *Felony, Misdemeanor, Civil, Eviction, Small Claims, Probate.*

Civil Records: Access: Mail, in person. Both court and visitors may perform in person searches. No search fee. Required to search: name, years to search. Civil cases indexed by defendant, plaintiff. Civil records on computer from 10/92 to present, index cards from 1978 to 1992.

Criminal Records: Access: Mail, in person. Both court and visitors may perform in person searches. No search fee. Required to search: name, years to search; also helpful: DOB, SSN. Criminal records on computer from 10/92 to present, index cards from 1978 to 1992.

General Information: Public Access terminal is available. No adoption, mental, juvenile, or sealed records released. SASE required. Turnaround time 5 days. Copy fee: $.15 per page. Certification fee: $1.00. Fee payee: Circuit Clerk. Personal checks accepted. Prepayment is required.

Webster County

Circuit & District Court Box 290 (25 US Hiway 41A South), Dixon, KY 42409; 270-639-9160; Fax: 270-639-6757. Hours: 8AM-4PM (CST). *Felony, Misdemeanor, Civil, Eviction, Small Claims, Probate.*

Civil Records: Access: Fax, mail, in person. Both court and visitors may perform in person searches. No search fee. Required to search: name, years to search. Civil cases indexed by defendant, plaintiff. Civil records in office from 1978 to present, prior records are at Frankfort archives.

Criminal Records: Access: Fax, mail, in person. Both court and visitors may perform in person searches. No search fee. Required to search: name, years to search. Criminal records in office from 1978 to present, prior records are at Frankfort archives.

General Information: Public Access terminal is available. No adoption, mental, juvenile, or sealed records released. SASE required. Turnaround time 1 day. Fax notes: $2.00 for first page, $1.00 each add'l. Copy fee: $.15 per page. Certification fee: $1.00. Fee payee: Circuit Clerk. Personal checks accepted. Prepayment is required.

Whitley County

Corbin Circuit & District Court 805 S Main St, Corbin, KY 40701; 606-523-1085; Fax: 606-523-2049. Hours: 8AM-4PM (EST). *Felony, Misdemeanor, Civil, Eviction, Small Claims, Probate.*

Civil Records: Access: Mail, in person. Both court and visitors may perform in person searches. No search fee. Required to search: name, years to search. Civil cases indexed by defendant, plaintiff. Civil records on computer from 1993 to present, index books prior.

Criminal Records: Access: In person only. Visitors must perform in person searches for themselves. No search fee. Required to search: name, years to search. Criminal records on computer from 1993 to present, index books prior.

General Information: Public Access terminal is available. No adoption, mental, juvenile or sealed records released. SASE requested. Turnaround time 1-2 days. Copy fee: $.15 per page. Certification fee: $1.50. Fee payee: Whitley District Court. Personal checks accepted.

Williamsburg Circuit & District Court Box 329, Williamsburg, KY 40769; 606-549-5162/2973. Hours: 8AM-4PM (EST). *Felony, Misdemeanor, Civil, Eviction, Small Claims, Probate.*

Civil Records: Access: In person only. Visitors must perform in person searches for themselves. No search fee. Required to search: name, years to search. Civil cases indexed by defendant, plaintiff. Civil records on computer from 1993 to present, index cards from 1978 to 1993.

Criminal Records: Access: In person only. Visitors must perform in person searches for themselves. No search fee. Required to search: name, years to search; also helpful: DOB, SSN. Criminal records on computer from 1993 to present, index cards from 1978 to 1993.

General Information: Public Access terminal is available. No adoption, mental, juvenile, or sealed records released. Copy fee: $.15 per page. Certification fee: $1.00. Fee payee: Whitley Circuit Clerk. Personal checks accepted. Prepayment is required.

Wolfe County

Circuit & District Court Box 296, Campton, KY 41301; 606-668-3736; Fax: 606-668-3198. Hours: 8:30AM-4:30PM (EST). *Felony, Misdemeanor, Civil, Eviction, Small Claims, Probate.*

Civil Records: Access: Mail, in person. Both court and visitors may perform in person searches. No search fee. Required to search: name, years to search. Civil cases indexed by defendant, plaintiff. Civil records on computer from 1992 to present, index books prior.

Criminal Records: Access: Mail, in person. Both court and visitors may perform in person searches. No search fee. Required to search: name, years to search; also helpful: DOB, SSN. Criminal records on computer from 1992 to present, index books prior.

General Information: Public Access terminal is available. No adoption, mental, juvenile, or sealed records released. SASE required. Turnaround time same day. Copy fee: $.15 per page. Certification fee: $1.00. Fee payee: Circuit Clerk. Personal checks accepted. Prepayment is required.

Woodford County

Circuit & District Court 130 Court St, Versailles, KY 40383; 859-873-3711. Hours: 8AM-4PM M-Th; 8AM-6PM F (EST). *Felony, Misdemeanor, Civil, Eviction, Small Claims, Probate.*

Civil Records: Access: In person only. Visitors must perform in person searches for themselves. No search fee. Required to search: name, years to search. Civil cases indexed by defendant, plaintiff. Civil records on computer from 02/91 to present, index cards from 1978 to 1991.

Criminal Records: Access: In person only. Visitors must perform in person searches for themselves. No search fee. Required to search: name, years to search; also helpful: SSN. Criminal records on computer from 02/91 to present, index cards from 1978 to 1991.

General Information:. No adoption, mental, juvenile, or sealed records released. Copy fee: $.15 per page. Certification fee: $1.00. Fee payee: Circuit Clerk. Personal checks accepted. Prepayment is required.

Kentucky Recording Offices

ORGANIZATION   120 counties, 122 recording offices. The recording officer is County Clerk. Kenton County has two recording offices. Jefferson County hads a separate office for UCC filing until June 30, 2001; that office now only searches for filings up to that date. 80 counties are in the Eastern Time Zone (EST) and 40 are in the Central Time Zone (CST)

REAL ESTATE RECORDS   Most counties will not perform real estate searches. Copy fees vary. Certification fee is usually $5 per document. Tax records are maintained by the Property Valuation Administrator, designated "Assessor" in this section.

UCC RECORDS   Under revised Article 9, Kentucky changes from a "local filing state" to a "central filing state" with the Sec. Of State's office. Collateral on non-resident debtors were always filed at the state level. Rela estate related UCC is still found at the County Clerk's offcie. Many counties will not perform UCC searches. Use search request form UCC-11. Search fees are usually $5.00 per debtor name, and copy fees vary widely.

TAX LIEN RECORDS   All federal and state tax liens on personal property are filed with the County Clerk, often in an "Encumbrance Book." Most counties will not perform tax lien searches.

OTHER LIENS   Judgments, motor vehicle, mechanics, lis pendens, bail bond

Adair County

County Clerk, 424 Public Square, Columbia, KY 42728. 270-384-2801; Fax 270-384-4805. Will search UCC records. This agency will not do a tax lien search. Will not search real estate records. **Other Phone Numbers:** Assessor 270-384-3673.

Allen County

County Clerk, 201 West Main Street, Room 6, Scottsville, KY 42164. 270-237-3706; Fax 270-237-9206. Will search UCC records. This agency will not do a tax lien search. Will not search real estate records. **Other Phone Numbers:** Assessor 270-237-3711.

Anderson County

County Clerk, 151 South Main, Lawrenceburg, KY 40342. 502-839-3041; Fax 502-839-3043. Will search UCC records. This agency will not do a tax lien search. Will not search real estate records. **Other Phone Numbers:** Assessor 502-839-4061.

Ballard County

County Clerk, P.O. Box 145, Wickliffe, KY 42087. 270-335-5168; Fax 270-335-3081. Will search UCC records. UCC search includes tax liens if requested. Mortgage searches available. **Other Phone Numbers:** Assessor 270-335-3400; Treasurer 270-335-5776.

Barren County

County Clerk, 924 Happy Valley Rd., Suite A, Glasgow, KY 42141-2812. 270-651-5200; Fax 270-651-1083. Will search UCC records. This agency will not do a tax lien search. Will not search real estate records. **Other Phone Numbers:** Assessor 270-651-2026.

Bath County

County Clerk, P.O. Box 609, Owingsville, KY 40360. 606-674-2613; Fax 606-674-2613. Will search UCC records. UCC search includes tax liens if requested. RE record owner and mortgage searches available.

Bell County

County Clerk, P.O. Box 156, Pineville, KY 40977. 606-337-6143; Fax 606-337-5415. Will search UCC records. This agency will not do a tax lien search. Will not search real estate records. **Other Phone Numbers:** Assessor 606-337-2720; Treasurer 606-337-2497.

Boone County

County Clerk, P.O. Box 874, Burlington, KY 41005. 859-334-2137; Fax 859-334-2193. http://www.boonecountyclerk.com Will search UCC records. This agency will not do a tax lien search. Will not search real estate records. **Online Access:** Real Estate, Lines, UCCs, Assessor, Marriage. Online access to the county clerk database is available through eCCLIX, a fee-based service; $200.00 sign-up and $65.00 monthly. Records go back to 1989; images to 1998. For information, see the web site or call 502-266-9445. **Other Phone Numbers:** Assessor 859-334-2236; Treasurer 859-334-2150.

Bourbon County

County Clerk, P.O. Box 312, Paris, KY 40362-0312. 859-987-2142; Fax 859-987-5660. Will search UCC records. This agency will not do a tax lien search. Will not search real estate records. **Other Phone Numbers:** Assessor 859-987-2152.

Boyd County

County Clerk, P.O. Box 523, Catlettsburg, KY 41129. 606-739-5116; Fax 606-739-6357. Will search UCC records. This agency will not do a tax lien search. Will not search real estate records. **Online Access:** Real Estate, Liens. Access to the County Clerk online records requires a $10 monthly usage fee. The system operates 24 hours daily; records date back to 1/1979. Lending agency information is available. For information, contact Maxine Selbee or Kathy Fisher at 606-739-5166. **Other Phone Numbers:** Assessor 606-739-5173; Treasurer 606-739-4242.

Boyle County

County Clerk, 321 W. Main St., Room 123, Danville, KY 40422-1837. County Clerk, R/E and UCC Recording 859-238-1112; Fax 859-238-1114. Will search UCC records. UCC search includes tax liens if requested. Will not search real estate records. **Other Phone Numbers:** Assessor 859-238-1104; Treasurer 859-238-1118; Vital Records 502-564-4212 (Frankfort, KY).

Bracken County

County Clerk, P.O. Box 147, Brooksville, KY 41004-0147. County Clerk, R/E and UCC Recording 606-735-2952; Fax 606-735-2925. Will search UCC records. This agency will not do a tax lien search. Will not search real estate records. **Other Phone Numbers:** Assessor 606-735-2228; Treasurer 606-735-2125; Appraiser/Auditor 606-735-2228; Elections 606-735-2952606-735-2952.

Breathitt County

County Clerk, 1137 Main Street, Jackson, KY 41339. County Clerk, R/E and UCC Recording 606-666-3810; Fax 606-666-3807. Will search UCC records. This agency will not do a tax lien search. Will not search real estate records. **Other Phone Numbers:** Treasurer 606-666-4268; Elections 606-666-3810.

Breckinridge County

County Clerk, P.O. Box 538, Hardinsburg, KY 40143. County Clerk, R/E and UCC Recording 270-756-6166 UCC Recording: 270-756-2246; Fax 270-756-1569. Will not search UCC records. This agency will not do a tax lien search. Will not search real estate records. **Other Phone Numbers:** Assessor 270-756-5154; Treasurer 270-756-2269; Elections 270-756-2246.

Bullitt County

County Clerk, P.O. Box 6, Shepherdsville, KY 40165-0006. 502-543-2513; Fax 502-543-9121. Will search UCC records. This agency will not do a tax lien search. Will not search real estate records.

Butler County

County Clerk, P.O. Box 449, Morgantown, KY 42261. 270-526-5676; Fax 270-526-2658. Will not search UCC records. This agency will not do a tax lien search. Will not search real estate records.

Caldwell County

County Clerk, 100 E Market Street, Rm 3, Courthouse - Room 3, Princeton, KY 42445. 270-365-6754; Fax 270-365-7447. Will search UCC records. This agency will not do a tax lien search. Will not search real estate records. **Other Phone Numbers:** Assessor 270-365-7227; Treasurer 270-365-9776; Elections 270-365-6754.

Calloway County

County Clerk, 101 South 5th Street, Murray, KY 42071-2569. 270-753-3923; Fax 270-759-9611.
Will search UCC records. This agency will not do a tax lien search. Will not search real estate records. **Other Phone Numbers:** Assessor 270-753-3482.

Campbell County

County Clerk, 4th and York Streets, Courthouse, Newport, KY 41071. 859-292-3850 R/E Recording: 859-292-3845; Fax 859-292-3887.
Will search UCC records. This agency will not do a tax lien search. Will not search real estate records. **Other Phone Numbers:** Assessor 859-292-3871; Treasurer 859-292-3838; Appraiser/Auditor 859-292-3871; Elections 859-292-3885.

Carlisle County

County Clerk, P.O. Box 176, Bardwell, KY 42023. 270-628-3233; Fax 270-628-0191.
Will search UCC records. Will not search real estate records. **Other Phone Numbers:** Assessor 270-628-5498; Treasurer 270-628-3922.

Carroll County

County Clerk, 440 Main Street, Court House, Carrollton, KY 41008. County Clerk, R/E and UCC Recording 502-732-7005; Fax 502-732-7007.
Will search UCC records. Tax liens not included in UCC search. Will not search real estate records. **Other Phone Numbers:** Assessor 502-732-5448; Treasurer 502-732-7000; Elections 502-732-7005.

Carter County

County Clerk, 300 W. Main St., Room 232, Grayson, KY 41143. County Clerk, R/E and UCC Recording 606-474-5188; Fax 606-474-6883.
Will search UCC records. This agency will not do a tax lien search. Will not search real estate records. **Other Phone Numbers:** Assessor 606-474-5663; Treasurer 606-474-9551; Elections 606-474-5188; Vital Records 606-474-5188.

Casey County

County Clerk, Box 310, Liberty, KY 42539. 606-787-6471; Fax 606-787-9155.
Will search UCC records. This agency will not do a tax lien search. Will not search real estate records. **Other Phone Numbers:** Assessor 606-787-7621.

Christian County

County Clerk, 511 South Main, Hopkinsville, KY 42240. 270-887-4105 R/E Recording: 270-887-4109; Fax 270-887-4186.
Will search UCC records. This agency will not do a tax lien search. Will not search real estate records. **Other Phone Numbers:** Assessor 270-887-4115; Treasurer 270-887-4103; Appraiser/Auditor 270-887-4115; Elections 270-887-4105.

Clark County

County Clerk, P.O. Box 4060, Winchester, KY 40392. 859-745-0280 R/E Recording: 859-745-0282; Fax 859-745-4251.
Will search UCC records. This agency will not do a tax lien search. Will not search real estate records. **Other Phone Numbers:** Assessor 859-745-0270; Treasurer 859-745-0200; Elections 859-745-0280; Vital Records 859-745-0282.

Clay County

County Clerk, 316 Main Street, Suite 143, Manchester, KY 40962. 606-598-2544; Fax 606-598-7199.

Will search UCC records. Will not search real estate records. **Other Phone Numbers:** Assessor 606-598-3832; Treasurer 606-598-2071.

Clinton County

County Clerk, 212 Washington Street, Courthouse, Albany, KY 42602. County Clerk, R/E and UCC Recording 606-387-5943; Fax 606-387-5258.
Will search UCC records. This agency will not do a tax lien search. Will not search real estate records. **Other Phone Numbers:** Treasurer 606-387-5234; Elections 606-387-5943; Vital Records 606-387-5943.

Crittenden County

County Clerk, 107 South Main, Courthouse, Suite 203, Marion, KY 42064. 270-965-3403; Fax 270-965-3447.
Will search UCC records. This agency will not do a tax lien search. Will not search real estate records. **Other Phone Numbers:** Assessor 270-965-4598.

Cumberland County

County Clerk, P.O. Box 275, Burkesville, KY 42717. County Clerk, R/E and UCC Recording 270-864-3726; Fax 270-864-5884.
Will search UCC records. This agency will not do a tax lien search. Will not search real estate records. **Other Phone Numbers:** Assessor 270-864-5161; Treasurer 270-864-3444; Elections 270-864-3726.

Daviess County

County Clerk, P.O. Box 609, Owensboro, KY 42302. 270-685-8420; Fax 270-685-2431.
Will search UCC records. This agency will not do a tax lien search. Will not search real estate records. **Other Phone Numbers:** Assessor 270-685-8474; Treasurer 270-685-8424.

Edmonson County

County Clerk, P.O. Box 830, Brownsville, KY 42210-0830. County Clerk, R/E and UCC Recording 270-597-2624; Fax 270-597-9714.
Will search UCC records. This agency will not do a tax lien search. Will not search real estate records. **Other Phone Numbers:** Assessor 270-597-2381; Treasurer 270-597-2819; Elections 270-597-2624; Vital Records 270-597-2624.

Elliott County

County Clerk, P.O. Box 225, Sandy Hook, KY 41171-0225. 606-738-5421; Fax 606-738-4462.
Will search UCC records. Tax liens not included in UCC search. Will not search real estate records. **Other Phone Numbers:** Assessor 606-738-5090; Treasurer 606-738-5821.

Estill County

County Clerk, P.O. BOX 59, Irvine, KY 40336. 606-723-5156; Fax 606-723-5108.
Will search UCC records. UCC search includes tax liens if requested. RE owner, mortgage, and property transfer searches available. **Other Phone Numbers:** Assessor 606-723-4569.

Fayette County

County Clerk, 162 East Main Street, Lexington, KY 40507-1334. 859-253-3344.
Will search UCC records. This agency will not do a tax lien search. Will not search real estate records. **Other Phone Numbers:** Assessor 859-254-2722; Treasurer 859-258-3300.

Fleming County

County Clerk, Court Square, Flemingsburg, KY 41041. 606-845-8461; Fax 606-845-0212.

Will search UCC records. This agency will not do a tax lien search. Will not search real estate records. **Other Phone Numbers:** Assessor 606-845-8801; Treasurer 606-845-8801.

Floyd County

County Clerk, P.O. Box 1089, Prestonsburg, KY 41653-5089. 606-886-3816; Fax 606-886-8089.
Will search UCC records. This agency will not do a tax lien search. Will not search real estate records. **Other Phone Numbers:** Assessor 606-886-9622.

Franklin County

County Clerk, P.O. Box 338, Frankfort, KY 40602. 502-875-8703 R/E Recording: 502-875-8710; Fax 502-875-8718. http://www.franklincountyclerk.org
Will search UCC records. This agency will not do a tax lien search. Will not search real estate records. **Other Phone Numbers:** Treasurer 502-875-8747; Elections 502-875-8704; Vital Records 502-875-8702.

Fulton County

County Clerk, P.O. Box 126, Hickman, KY 42050. 270-236-2061; Fax 270-236-2522.
Will search UCC records. RE owner, mortgage, and property transfer searches available. **Other Phone Numbers:** Assessor 270-236-2548; Treasurer 270-236-2594.

Gallatin County

County Clerk, P.O. Box 1309, Warsaw, KY 41095. 859-567-5411; Fax 859-567-5444.
Will search UCC records. This agency will not do a tax lien search. Will not search real estate records. **Other Phone Numbers:** Assessor 859-567-5621; Treasurer 859-567-5691; Elections 859-567-5411.

Garrard County

County Clerk, Courthouse Building, Lancaster, KY 40444. 859-792-3071; Fax 859-792-2010.
Berea, KY addresses may be in Madison County, and parts of Crab Orchard are in Lincoln County. Will search UCC records. UCC search includes tax liens if requested. RE owner, mortgage, and property transfer searches available. **Other Phone Numbers:** Assessor 859-792-3291.

Grant County

County Clerk, Courthouse Basement, Room 15, 101 N. Main St., Williamstown, KY 41097. 859-824-3321; Fax 859-824-3367.
Will search UCC records. This agency will not do a tax lien search. Will not search real estate records. **Other Phone Numbers:** Assessor 859-824-6511; Treasurer 859-824-7561.

Graves County

County Clerk, Courthouse, Mayfield, KY 42066. 270-247-1676 R/E Recording: 270-247-1697; Fax 270-247-1274.
Will search UCC records. Tax liens not included in UCC search. Will not search real estate records. **Other Phone Numbers:** Assessor 270-247-3301; Treasurer 270-247-3626; Elections 270-247-1676.

Grayson County

County Clerk, 10 Public Square, Leitchfield, KY 42754. County Clerk, R/E and UCC Recording 270-259-5295 UCC Recording: 270-259-3201; Fax 270-259-9264.
Will search UCC records. Will not search real estate records. **Other Phone Numbers:** Assessor 270-259-4838; Treasurer 270-259-5000; Elections 270-259-3201; Vital Records 270-259-5295.

Green County

County Clerk, 203 West Court Street, Greensburg, KY 42743. 270-932-5386; Fax 270-932-6241.
Will search UCC records. UCC search includes tax liens if requested. Will not search real estate records. **Other Phone Numbers:** Assessor 270-932-7518; Treasurer 270-932-4024.

Greenup County

County Clerk, P.O. Box 686, Greenup, KY 41144-0686. County Clerk, R/E & UCC Recording 606-473-7396; Fax 606-473-5354.
Will search UCC records. This agency will not do a tax lien search. Will not search real estate records. **Other Phone Numbers:** Assessor 606-473-9984; Treasurer 606-473-5350; Elections 606-473-7396; Vital Records 606-473-7396.

Hancock County

County Clerk, P.O. Box 146, Hawesville, KY 42348. 270-927-6117; Fax 270-927-8639.
Will search UCC records. This agency will not do a tax lien search. Will not search real estate records. **Other Phone Numbers:** Assessor 270-927-6846; Treasurer 270-927-8101.

Hardin County

County Clerk, P.O. Box 1030, Elizabethtown, KY 42702. 270-765-4116 R/E Recording: 270-765-2171; Fax 270-769-2682.
Will search UCC records. This agency will not do a tax lien search. Will not search real estate records. **Other Phone Numbers:** Assessor 270-765-2129; Treasurer 270-765-2350; Elections 270-765-6762; Vital Records 270-765-2171.

Harlan County

County Clerk, P.O. Box 670, Harlan, KY 40831-0670. County Clerk, R/E and UCC Recording 606-573-3636; Fax 606-573-0064.
Will search UCC records. This agency will not do a tax lien search. Will not search real estate records. **Other Phone Numbers:** Assessor 606-573-1990; Treasurer 606-573-4771.

Harrison County

County Clerk, 190 West Pike Street, Cynthiana, KY 41031-1397. 859-234-7130; Fax 859-234-8049.
Will search UCC records. This agency will not do a tax lien search. Will not search real estate records. **Other Phone Numbers:** Assessor 859-234-7113; Treasurer 859-234-7136.

Hart County

County Clerk, P.O. Box 277, Munfordville, KY 42765. County Clerk, R/E and UCC Recording 270-524-2751; Fax 270-524-0458.
Will search UCC records. This agency will not do a tax lien search. Will not search real estate records. **Other Phone Numbers:** Assessor 270-524-2321; Treasurer 270-524-9474.

Henderson County

County Clerk, P.O. Box 374, Henderson, KY 42419-0374. County Clerk, R/E and UCC Recording 270-826-3906; Fax 270-826-9677.
Will search UCC records. This agency will not do a tax lien search. Will not search real estate records. **Other Phone Numbers:** Assessor 270-827-6024; Treasurer 270-826-3233; Appraiser/Auditor 270-826-6024; Elections 270-826-3906.

Henry County

County Clerk, P.O. Box 615, New Castle, KY 40050-0615. 502-845-5705; Fax 502-845-5708.

Will search UCC records. This agency will not do a tax lien search. Will not search real estate records.

Hickman County

County Clerk, Courthouse, 110 E. Clay, Clinton, KY 42031-1296. 270-653-2131; Fax 270-653-4248.
Will search UCC records. This agency will not do a tax lien search. Will not search real estate records. **Other Phone Numbers:** Assessor 270-653-5521; Treasurer 270-653-6195; Elections 270-653-2131; Vital Records 270-653-6110.

Hopkins County

County Clerk, 10 S Main St, Madisonville, KY 42431. County Clerk, R/E and UCC Recording 270-821-7361 UCC Recording: 270-825-5001; Fax 270-825-7000.
Will search UCC records. This agency will not do a tax lien search. Will not search real estate records. **Other Phone Numbers:** Assessor 270-825-3092; Treasurer 270-825-2666.

Jackson County

County Clerk, P.O. Box 700, McKee, KY 40447-0700. 606-287-7800; Fax 606-287-4505.
Will search UCC records. This agency will not do a tax lien search. Will not search real estate records. **Other Phone Numbers:** Assessor 606-287-7634; Treasurer 606-287-8562.

Jefferson County Clerk

County Clerk, P.O. Box 35339, Louisville, KY 40232-5339. 502-574-6427; Fax 502-574-6041.
Will search UCC records. This agency will not do a tax lien search. See Recorder for real estate records. **Other Phone Numbers:** Assessor 502-574-6380.

Jefferson County Recorder

County Clerk, 527 W Jefferson St, Rm 204, Louisville, KY 40202. County Clerk, R/E and UCC Recording 502-574-5785 UCC Recording: 502-574-6130; Fax 502-574-8130.
Will search UCC records, but only real estate related UCC filed here. This agency will not do a tax lien search. Will not search real estate records.

Jessamine County

County Clerk, 101 North Main Street, Nicholasville, KY 40356-1270. County Clerk, R/E and UCC Recording 859-885-4161; Fax 859-885-5837.
Will search UCC records. This agency will not do a tax lien search. Will not search real estate records. **Other Phone Numbers:** Assessor 859-885-4931; Treasurer 859-885-4500; Elections 859-885-4161.

Johnson County

County Clerk, Courthouse, Court St., Paintsville, KY 41240. 606-789-2557; Fax 606-789-2559.
Will search UCC records. UCC search includes tax liens. RE owner, mortgage, and property transfer searches available. **Other Phone Numbers:** Assessor 606-789-2564.

Kenton County (1st District)

County Clerk, P.O. Box 1109, Covington, KY 41012. 859-491-0702; Fax 859-491-4515. http://www.kentonpva.com/
Will search UCC records. This agency will not do a tax lien search. Will not search real estate records. **Online Access:** Property Appraiser. Online access to the county Property Valuation database is available free at www.kentonpva.com/pvacat/catsearch.htm. **Other Phone Numbers:** Assessor 859-491-2728; Treasurer 859-491-2800.

Kenton County (2nd District)

County Clerk, P.O. Box 38, Independence, KY 41051. 859-356-9272; Fax 859-356-9278. http://www.kentonpva.com/
2nd District includes property south of Banklick Creek. 1st District includes property north of Banklick Creek. Will search UCC records. This agency will not do a tax lien search. Will search real estate records. **Online Access:** Property Appraiser. Online access to the county Property Valuation database is available free at www.kentonpva.com/pvacat/catsearch.htm. **Other Phone Numbers:** Assessor 859-491-2728; Treasurer 859-356-4942.

Knott County

County Clerk, P.O. Box 446, Hindman, KY 41822. 606-785-5651; Fax 606-785-0996.
Will search UCC records. UCC search includes tax liens if requested with extra fee RE owner, mortgage, and property transfer searches available. **Other Phone Numbers:** Assessor 606-785-5569; Treasurer 606-785-5592.

Knox County

County Clerk, 401 Court Square, Suite 102, Barbourville, KY 40906. 606-546-3568; Fax 606-546-3589.
Will search UCC records. This agency will not do a tax lien search. Will not search real estate records. **Other Phone Numbers:** Assessor 606-546-4113.

Larue County

County Clerk, 209 W. High St., Hodgenville, KY 42748. 270-358-3544; Fax 270-358-4528.
Will search UCC records. Tax liens not included in UCC search. RE owner, mortgage, and property transfer searches available. **Other Phone Numbers:** Assessor 270-358-4202; Treasurer 270-358-4400.

Laurel County

County Clerk, 101 South Main, Courthouse, London, KY 40741. 606-864-5158; Fax 606-864-7369.
Will search UCC records. This agency will not do a tax lien search. Will not search real estate records. **Other Phone Numbers:** Assessor 606-864-2889.

Lawrence County

County Clerk, 122 South Main Cross Street, Louisa, KY 41230. County Clerk, R/E and UCC Recording 606-638-4108 UCC Recording: 606-638-0504; Fax 606-638-0638.
Will search UCC records. This agency will not do a tax lien search. Will not search real estate records. **Other Phone Numbers:** Assessor 606-638-4743; Treasurer 606-638-4102.

Lee County

County Clerk, P.O. Box 551, Beattyville, KY 41311. 606-464-4115; Fax 606-464-4102.
Will search UCC records. This agency will not do a tax lien search. Will not search real estate records. **Other Phone Numbers:** Assessor 606-464-4105; Treasurer 606-464-4100.

Leslie County

County Clerk, P.O. Box 916, Hyden, KY 41749-0916. 606-672-2193; Fax 606-672-4264.
Will search UCC records. This agency will not do a tax lien search. Will not search real estate records. **Other Phone Numbers:** Assessor 606-672-2456.

Letcher County

County Clerk, P.O. Box 28, Whitesburg, KY 41858. 606-633-2432; Fax 606-632-9282.

Will search UCC records. This agency will not do a tax lien search. Will not search real estate records. **Other Phone Numbers:** Assessor 606-633-2182.

Lewis County

County Clerk, P.O. Box 129, Vanceburg, KY 41179-0129. County Clerk, R/E and UCC Recording 606-796-3062; Fax 606-796-6511.
Will search UCC records. UCC search includes tax liens if requested. RE record owner and mortgage searches available. **Other Phone Numbers:** Assessor 606-796-2622; Treasurer 606-796-2722; Elections 606-796-2311; Vital Records 606-796-3062.

Lincoln County

County Clerk, 102 East Main, Courthouse, Stanford, KY 40484. 606-365-4570 R/E Recording: 606-365-4520; Fax 606-365-4572.
Will search UCC records. This agency will not do a tax lien search. Will not search real estate records. **Other Phone Numbers:** Assessor 606-365-4550; Treasurer 606-365-4590; Elections 606-365-4570.

Livingston County

County Clerk, P.O. Box 400, Smithland, KY 42081-0400. 270-928-2162; Fax 270-928-2162.
Will search UCC records. This agency will not do a tax lien search. Will not search real estate records. **Other Phone Numbers:** Assessor 270-928-2524.

Logan County

County Clerk, P.O. Box 358, Russellville, KY 42276-0358. 270-726-6061; Fax 270-726-4355.
Will search UCC records. UCC search includes tax liens if requested. Will not search real estate records. **Other Phone Numbers:** Assessor 270-726-8334; Treasurer 270-726-2167.

Lyon County

County Clerk, P.O. Box 310, Eddyville, KY 42038. County Clerk, R/E and UCC Recording 270-388-2331; Fax 270-388-0634.
Will search UCC records. This agency will not do a tax lien search. Will not search real estate records. **Other Phone Numbers:** Assessor 270-388-7271; Treasurer 270-388-7193; Elections 270-388-2331.

Madison County

County Clerk, 101 W. Main Street, County Court House, Richmond, KY 40475-1415. 859-624-4704; Fax 859-624-8474.
Will search UCC records. This agency will not do a tax lien search. Will not search real estate records.

Magoffin County

County Clerk, P.O. Box 530, Salyersville, KY 41465. County Clerk, R/E and UCC Recording 606-349-2216; Fax 606-349-2328.
Will search UCC records. This agency will not do a tax lien search. Will not search real estate records. **Other Phone Numbers:** Assessor 606-349-6198; Treasurer 606-349-2313; Elections 606-349-6194; Vital Records 606-349-2216.

Marion County

County Clerk, Courthouse, Suite 3, 120 W. Main St., Lebanon, KY 40033. 270-692-2651; Fax 270-692-9811.
Will search UCC records. This agency will not do a tax lien search. Will not search real estate records. **Other Phone Numbers:** Assessor 270-692-3401; Treasurer 270-692-3451.

Marshall County

County Clerk, Courthouse, 1101 Main St., Benton, KY 42025. 270-527-4740; Fax 270-527-4738.
Will not search UCC records. Will not search real estate records. **Other Phone Numbers:** Assessor 270-527-4728.

Martin County

County Clerk, P.O. Box 460, Inez, KY 41224-0485. 606-298-2810; Fax 606-298-0143.
Will search UCC records. This agency will not do a tax lien search. Will not search real estate records. **Other Phone Numbers:** Assessor 606-298-2808.

Mason County

County Clerk, P.O. Box 234, Maysville, KY 41056. 606-564-3341; Fax 606-564-8979.
Will search UCC records. This agency will not do a tax lien search. Will not search real estate records. **Other Phone Numbers:** Assessor 606-564-3700; Treasurer 606-564-6381.

McCracken County

County Clerk, P.O. Box 609, Paducah, KY 42002-0609. 270-444-4700; Fax 270-444-4704.
Will search UCC records. This agency will not do a tax lien search. Will not search real estate records. **Other Phone Numbers:** Assessor 270-444-4712; Treasurer 270-444-4725.

McCreary County

County Clerk, P.O. Box 699, Whitley City, KY 42653. 606-376-2411; Fax 606-376-3898.
Will search UCC records. UCC search includes tax liens if requested. Will not search real estate records. **Other Phone Numbers:** Assessor 606-376-2514.

McLean County

County Clerk, P.O. Box 57, Calhoun, KY 42327-0057. County Clerk, R/E and UCC Recording 270-273-3082; Fax 270-273-5084.
Will search UCC records. This agency will not do a tax lien search. Will not search real estate records. **Other Phone Numbers:** Assessor 270-273-3291; Treasurer 270-273-9964; Elections 270-273-3082.

Meade County

County Clerk, P.O. Box 614, Brandenburg, KY 40108. 270-422-2152; Fax 270-422-2158.
Will search UCC records. This agency will not do a tax lien search. Will not search real estate records. **Other Phone Numbers:** Assessor 270-422-2178.

Menifee County

County Clerk, P.O. Box 123, Frenchburg, KY 40322-0123. County Clerk, R/E and UCC Recording 606-768-3512; Fax 606-768-2144.
Will search UCC records. This agency will not do a tax lien search. Will not search real estate records. **Other Phone Numbers:** Assessor 606-768-3514; Treasurer 606-768-3514; Elections 606-768-3512; Vital Records 606-768-3512.

Mercer County

County Clerk, P.O. Box 426, Harrodsburg, KY 40330. 859-734-6313; Fax 859-734-6309.
Will search UCC records. UCC search includes tax liens if requested. Will not search real estate records. **Other Phone Numbers:** Assessor 859-734-6330.

Metcalfe County

County Clerk, P.O. Box 25, Edmonton, KY 42129. 270-432-4821; Fax 270-432-5176.

Will search UCC records. This agency will not do a tax lien search. Will not search real estate records. **Other Phone Numbers:** Assessor 270-432-3162; Treasurer 270-432-3181.

Monroe County

County Clerk, P.O. Box 188, Tompkinsville, KY 42167. County Clerk, R/E and UCC Recording 270-487-5471; Fax 270-487-5976.
Will search UCC records. UCC search includes tax liens. Will not search real estate records. **Other Phone Numbers:** Assessor 270-487-6401; Treasurer 270-487-5505; Elections 270-487-5471.

Montgomery County

County Clerk, P.O. Box 414, Mount Sterling, KY 40353. County Clerk, R/E and UCC Recording 859-498-8700; Fax 859-498-8729.
Will search UCC records. This agency will not do a tax lien search. Will not search real estate records. **Other Phone Numbers:** Assessor 859-498-8710; Treasurer 859-498-8703.

Morgan County

County Clerk, P.O. Box 26, West Liberty, KY 41472. County Clerk, R/E and UCC Recording 606-743-3949; Fax 606-743-2111.
Will search UCC records. This agency will not do a tax lien search. Will not search real estate records. **Other Phone Numbers:** Assessor 606-743-3349; Treasurer 606-743-3195; Appraiser/Auditor 606-743-3349; Elections 606-743-3949; Vital Records 606-743-3949.

Muhlenberg County

County Clerk, P.O. Box 525, Greenville, KY 42345. 270-338-1441; Fax 270-338-1774.
Will search UCC records. UCC search includes tax liens if requested. Will not search real estate records. **Other Phone Numbers:** Assessor 270-338-4664.

Nelson County

County Clerk, P.O. Box 312, Bardstown, KY 40004. County Clerk, R/E and UCC Recording 502-348-1830 UCC Recording: 502-348-1828; Fax 502-348-1822.
Will search UCC records. Will not search real estate records. **Other Phone Numbers:** Assessor 502-348-1810; Treasurer 502-348-1800; Appraiser/Auditor 502-348-1810; Elections 502-348-1829; Vital Records 502-564-4212.

Nicholas County

County Clerk, P.O. Box 227, Carlisle, KY 40311. 859-289-3730; Fax 859-289-3709.
Will search UCC records. UCC search includes tax liens if requested. Will not search real estate records. **Other Phone Numbers:** Assessor 859-289-3735; Treasurer 859-289-3725; Elections 859-289-3730.

Ohio County

County Clerk, P.O. Box 85, Hartford, KY 42347. 270-298-4422; Fax 270-298-4425.
Will search UCC records. This agency will not do a tax lien search. Will not search real estate records. **Other Phone Numbers:** Assessor 270-298-3692.

Oldham County

County Clerk, 100 West Jefferson Street, LaGrange, KY 40031. 502-222-9311; Fax 502-222-3208. http://oldhamcounty.state.ky.us
Will search UCC records. This agency will not do a tax lien search. Will not search real estate records. **Online Access:** Real Estate, Liens, UCC, Assessor, Marriage. Online access to the county clerk database is available through eCCLIX, a fee-based service; $200.00 sign-up and $65.00 monthly. Records go back, generally, to

1980. UCC images to 2/97. Real estate instruments back to 1/95. Marriages back to 1977. For information, call 502-222-9311. For information, see the web site or call 502-266-9445. **Other Phone Numbers:** Assessor 502-222-9320.

Owen County

County Clerk, P.O. Box 338, Owenton, KY 40359-0338. County Clerk, R/E and UCC Recording 502-484-2213; Fax 502-484-1002.
Will search UCC records. This agency will not do a tax lien search. Will not search real estate records. **Other Phone Numbers:** Assessor 502-484-5172; Treasurer 502-484-3557; Elections 502-484-2213; Vital Records 502-484-2213.

Owsley County

County Clerk, P.O. Box 500, Booneville, KY 41314. 606-593-5735; Fax 606-593-5737.
Will search UCC records. UCC search includes tax liens if requested. Will not search real estate records. **Other Phone Numbers:** Assessor 606-593-6265; Treasurer 606-593-6202.

Pendleton County

County Clerk, P.O. Box 112, Falmouth, KY 41040. County Clerk, R/E and UCC Recording 859-654-3380; Fax 859-654-5600.
Will search UCC records. UCC search includes tax liens if requested. Will not search real estate records. **Other Phone Numbers:** Assessor 859-654-6055; Treasurer 859-654-4321; Appraiser/Auditor 859-654-3380; Elections 859-654-3380.

Perry County

County Clerk, P.O. Box 150, Hazard, KY 41702. 606-436-4614; Fax 606-439-0557.
Will search UCC records. Tax liens not included in UCC search. Will not search real estate records. **Other Phone Numbers:** Assessor 606-436-4914; Treasurer 606-436-1816.

Pike County

County Clerk, P.O. Box 631, Pikeville, KY 41502-0631. 606-432-6240; Fax 606-432-6222.
Will search UCC records. This agency will not do a tax lien search. Will not search real estate records. **Other Phone Numbers:** Assessor 606-432-6201.

Powell County

County Clerk, P.O. Box 548, Stanton, KY 40380. County Clerk, R/E and UCC Recording 606-663-6444; Fax 606-663-6406.
Will search UCC records. This agency will not do a tax lien search. Will not search real estate records. **Other Phone Numbers:** Assessor 606-663-4184; Treasurer 606-663-2834; Appraiser/Auditor 606-663-4184; Vital Records 502-564-4212.

Pulaski County

County Clerk, P.O. Box 724, Somerset, KY 42502. 606-679-3652 R/E Recording: 606-679-2042 UCC Recording: 606-679-2042; Fax 606-678-0073.
Will search UCC records. This agency will not do a tax lien search. Will not search real estate records. **Other Phone Numbers:** Assessor 606-679-1812; Treasurer 606-679-1311; Elections 606-679-3652; Vital Records 606-679-3652.

Robertson County

County Clerk, P.O. Box 75, Mount Olivet, KY 41064. 606-724-5212; Fax 606-724-5022.
Will search UCC records. UCC search includes tax liens if requested. Will not search real estate records.

Other Phone Numbers: Assessor 606-724-5213; Treasurer 606-724-5403.

Rockcastle County

County Clerk, P.O. Box 365, Mount Vernon, KY 40456. 606-256-2831; Fax 606-256-4302.
Will search UCC records. This agency will not do a tax lien search. Will not search real estate records. **Other Phone Numbers:** Assessor 606-256-4194; Treasurer 606-256-3623.

Rowan County

County Clerk, Courthouse - 2nd Floor, 627 E. Main Street, Morehead, KY 40351. 606-784-5212; Fax 606-784-2923.
Will search UCC records. This agency will not do a tax lien search. Will not search real estate records. **Other Phone Numbers:** Assessor 606-784-5517; Treasurer 606-784-4211.

Russell County

County Clerk, P.O. Box 579, Jamestown, KY 42629-0579. 270-343-2125; Fax 270-343-4700.
Will search UCC records. This agency will not do a tax lien search. Will not search real estate records. **Other Phone Numbers:** Assessor 270-343-4395; Treasurer 270-343-2112.

Scott County

County Clerk, Courthouse, 101 E. Main St., Georgetown, KY 40324-1794. 502-863-7875; Fax 502-863-7898.
Will search UCC records. This agency will not do a tax lien search. Will not search real estate records. **Other Phone Numbers:** Assessor 502-863-7885; Treasurer 502-863-7850.

Shelby County

County Clerk, P.O. Box 819, Shelbyville, KY 40066-0819. 502-633-4410; Fax 502-633-7887.
Will search UCC records. This agency will not do a tax lien search. Will not search real estate records. **Other Phone Numbers:** Assessor 502-633-4403; Treasurer 502-633-1220.

Simpson County

County Clerk, P.O. Box 268, Franklin, KY 42135-0268. 270-586-8161; Fax 270-586-6464.
Will search UCC records. This agency will not do a tax lien search. Will not search real estate records. **Other Phone Numbers:** Assessor 502-586-4261; Treasurer 502-586-7184.

Spencer County

County Clerk, P.O. Box 544, Taylorsville, KY 40071. 502-477-3215; Fax 502-477-3216.
Will search UCC records. This agency will not do a tax lien search. Will not search real estate records. **Other Phone Numbers:** Assessor 502-477-3207; Treasurer 502-477-3211.

Taylor County

County Clerk, 203 North Court Street, Suite # 5, Campbellsville, KY 42718-2298. 270-465-6677; Fax 270-789-1144.
Will search UCC records. This agency will not do a tax lien search. Will not search real estate records. **Other Phone Numbers:** Assessor 270-465-5811; Treasurer 270-789-1008.

Todd County

County Clerk, P.O. Box 307, Elkton, KY 42220. 270-265-2363; Fax 270-265-2588.
Will search UCC records. This agency will not do a tax lien search. Will not search real estate records. **Other**

Phone Numbers: Assessor 270-265-5614; Treasurer 270-265-2451.

Trigg County

County Clerk, P.O. Box 1310, Cadiz, KY 42211. 270-522-6661; Fax 270-522-6662.
Will search UCC records. This agency will not do a tax lien search. Will not search real estate records. **Other Phone Numbers:** Assessor 270-522-6661; Treasurer 270-522-8459.

Trimble County

County Clerk, P.O. Box 262, Bedford, KY 40006-0262. County Clerk, R/E and UCC Recording 502-255-7174; Fax 502-255-7045.
Will search UCC records. This agency will not do a tax lien search. Will not search real estate records. **Other Phone Numbers:** Assessor 502-255-3592; Elections 502-255-7174; Vital Records 502-255-7174.

Union County

County Clerk, P.O. Box 119, Morganfield, KY 42437-0119. 270-389-1334; Fax 270-389-9135.
Will search UCC records. This agency will not do a tax lien search. Will not search real estate records. **Other Phone Numbers:** Assessor 270-389-1933.

Warren County

County Clerk, P.O. Box 478, Bowling Green, KY 42102-0478. County Clerk, R/E and UCC Recording 270-842-9416; Fax 270-843-5319. http://warren county.state.ky.us
Will search UCC records. This agency will not do a tax lien search. Will not search real estate records. **Online Access:** Real Estate, Liens, UCCs, Assessor, Marriage. Online access to the county clerk database is available through eCCLIX, a fee-based service; $200.00 sign-up and $65.00 monthly. Records go back to 1989; images to 1998. For information, see the web site or call 502-266-9445. **Other Phone Numbers:** Assessor 270-842-3268; Treasurer 270-842-5805; Elections 270-842-5306; Vital Records 270-842-9416.

Washington County

County Clerk, P.O. Box 446, Springfield, KY 40069. 859-336-5425; Fax 859-336-5408.
Will search UCC records. Tax liens not included in UCC search. RE record owner and mortgage searches available. **Other Phone Numbers:** Assessor 859-336-5420.

Wayne County

County Clerk, P.O. Box 565, Monticello, KY 42633. County Clerk, R/E and UCC Recording 606-348-6661; Fax 606-348-8303.
Will search UCC records. This agency will not do a tax lien search. Will not search real estate records. **Other Phone Numbers:** Assessor 606-348-6621; Treasurer 606-348-8411.

Webster County

County Clerk, P.O. Box 19, Dixon, KY 42409-0019. 270-639-7006; Fax 270-639-7029.
Will search UCC records. This agency will not do a tax lien search. Will not search real estate records. **Other Phone Numbers:** Assessor 270-639-7016; Treasurer 270-639-5042.

Whitley County

County Clerk, P.O. Box 8, Williamsburg, KY 40769. 606-549-6002; Fax 606-549-2790.
Will search UCC records. This agency will not do a tax lien search. Will not search real estate records.

Wolfe County

County Clerk, P.O. Box 400, Campton, KY 41301. County Clerk, R/E and UCC Recording 606-668-3515; Fax 606-668-3492.

Will search UCC records. This agency will not do a tax lien search. Will not search real estate records. **Other Phone Numbers:** Assessor 606-668-6923; Treasurer 606-668-4060; Appraiser/Auditor 606-668-6925; Elections 606-668-3515; Vital Records 606-668-4212.

Woodford County

County Clerk, Courthouse - Room 120, 103 S. Main St., Versailles, KY 40383. 859-873-3421; Fax 859-873-6985.

Will search UCC records. This agency will not do a tax lien search. Will not search real estate records. **Other Phone Numbers:** Assessor 859-873-4101; Treasurer 859-873-6122; Elections 859-873-3421.

Kentucky County Locator

You will usually be able to find the city name in the City/County Cross Reference below. In that case, it is a simple matter to determine the county from the cross reference. However, only the official US Postal Service city names are included in this index. There are an additional 40,000 place names that people use in their addresses. Therefore, we have also included a ZIP/City Cross Reference immediately following the City/County Cross Reference.

If you know the ZIP Code but the city name does not appear in the City/County Cross Reference index, look up the ZIP Code in the ZIP/City Cross Reference, find the city name, then look up the city name in the City/County Cross Reference. For example, you want to know the county for an address of Menands, NY 12204. There is no "Menands" in the City/County Cross Reference. The ZIP/City Cross Reference shows that ZIP Codes 12201-12288 are for the city of Albany. Looking back in the City/County Cross Reference, Albany is in Albany County.

City/County Cross Reference

AARON (42601) Clinton(97), Russell(3)
ABERDEEN Butler
ACORN Pulaski
ADAIRVILLE (42202) Logan(94),
   Simpson(6)
ADAMS Lawrence
ADOLPHUS Allen
AGES BROOKSIDE Harlan
ALBANY Clinton
ALEXANDRIA Campbell
ALLEGRE Todd
ALLEN Floyd
ALLENSVILLE (42204) Todd(70),
   Logan(30)
ALLOCK Perry
ALMO Calloway
ALPHA (42603) Clinton(67), Wayne(33)
ALTRO Breathitt
ALVATON (42122) Warren(95), Allen(6)
AMBURGEY Knott
ANNVILLE (40402) Jackson(99), Clay(1)
ARGILLITE Greenup
ARJAY Bell
ARLINGTON (42021) Carlisle(73),
   Hickman(27)
ARTEMUS Knox
ARY Perry
ASHCAMP Pike
ASHER Leslie
ASHLAND (41101) Boyd(94), Greenup(6)
ASHLAND Boyd
ATHOL Breathitt
AUBURN (42206) Logan(90), Simpson(7),
   Warren(3)
AUGUSTA Bracken
AUSTIN Barren
AUXIER Floyd
AVAWAM Perry
AXTEL Breckinridge
BAGDAD (40003) Shelby(87), Franklin(13)
BAKERTON (42711) Cumberland(92),
   Adair(8)
BANDANA Ballard
BANNER Floyd
BARBOURVILLE Knox
BARDSTOWN Nelson
BARDWELL Carlisle
BARLOW Ballard
BASKETT Henderson
BATTLETOWN Meade
BAXTER Harlan
BAYS Breathitt
BEAR BRANCH Leslie
BEATTYVILLE Lee
BEAUMONT Metcalfe
BEAUTY Martin
BEAVER Floyd
BEAVER DAM (42320) Ohio(98), Butler(2)
BEDFORD (40006) Trimble(98), Carroll(2)
BEE SPRING Edmonson
BEECH CREEK Muhlenberg
BEECH GROVE McLean
BEECHMONT Muhlenberg

BELCHER Pike
BELFRY Pike
BELLEVUE Campbell
BELTON Muhlenberg
BENHAM Harlan
BENTON (42025) Marshall(97),
   Calloway(2), Graves(1)
BEREA (40403) Madison(94),
   Rockcastle(3), Garrard(2)
BEREA Madison
BERRY (41003) Grant(47), Harrison(45),
   Pendleton(8)
BETHANY Wolfe
BETHEL Bath
BETHELRIDGE Casey
BETHLEHEM Henry
BETSY LAYNE (41605) Floyd(97), Pike(3)
BEULAH HEIGHTS McCreary
BEVERLY (40913) Bell(94), Clay(6)
BEVINSVILLE Floyd
BIG CLIFTY (42712) Grayson(59),
   Hardin(41)
BIG CREEK Clay
BIG LAUREL (40808) Leslie(57),
   Harlan(43)
BIG SPRING (40106) Breckinridge(91),
   Hardin(10)
BIGHILL Madison
BIMBLE Knox
BLACKEY Letcher
BLACKFORD Webster
BLAINE Lawrence
BLANDVILLE Ballard
BLEDSOE (40810) Harlan(94), Leslie(6)
BLOOMFIELD (40008) Nelson(83),
   Spencer(16)
BLUE RIVER Floyd
BLUEHOLE Clay
BOAZ (42027) Graves(93), McCracken(7)
BOND Jackson
BONNIEVILLE Hart
BONNYMAN Perry
BOONEVILLE (41314) Owsley(72),
   Breathitt(28)
BOONS CAMP Johnson
BOSTON Nelson
BOW (42714) Cumberland(93), Clinton(7)
BOWEN Powell
BOWLING GREEN (42101) Warren(98),
   Edmonson(2)
BOWLING GREEN Warren
BRADFORDSVILLE (40009) Marion(75),
   Casey(17), Taylor(8)
BRANDENBURG Meade
BREEDING (42715) Adair(89), Metcalfe(7),
   Cumberland(4)
BREMEN Muhlenberg
BRINKLEY Knott
BRODHEAD (40409) Rockcastle(94),
   Lincoln(5), Pulaski(1)
BRONSTON (42518) Pulaski(97),
   Wayne(3)
BROOKLYN Butler

BROOKS (40109) Bullitt(98), Jefferson(2)
BROOKSVILLE Bracken
BROWDER Muhlenberg
BROWNS FORK Perry
BROWNSVILLE Edmonson
BRUIN Elliott
BRYANTS STORE Knox
BRYANTSVILLE Garrard
BUCKHORN Perry
BUCKNER Oldham
BUFFALO (42716) Larue(75), Green(20),
   Taylor(5)
BULAN (41722) Perry(64), Knott(36)
BURDINE Letcher
BURGIN Mercer
BURKESVILLE Cumberland
BURKHART Wolfe
BURLINGTON Boone
BURNA Livingston
BURNSIDE Pulaski
BURNWELL Pike
BUSH Laurel
BUSKIRK Morgan
BUSY (41723) Perry(75), Leslie(25)
BUTLER Pendleton
BYPRO Floyd
CADIZ Trigg
CALHOUN (42327) McLean(98),
   Daviess(2)
CALIFORNIA Campbell
CALVERT CITY Marshall
CALVIN Bell
CAMP DIX Lewis
CAMPBELLSBURG (40011) Henry(79),
   Trimble(17), Carroll(4)
CAMPBELLSVILLE (42718) Taylor(96),
   Marion(2), Green(2)
CAMPBELLSVILLE Taylor
CAMPTON (41301) Wolfe(89), Breathitt(6),
   Lee(4), Powell(1)
CANADA Pike
CANE VALLEY Adair
CANEY Morgan
CANEYVILLE (42721) Grayson(91),
   Butler(5), Edmonson(4)
CANMER Hart
CANNEL CITY Morgan
CANNON Knox
CANOE Breathitt
CANTON Trigg
CARLISLE (40311) Nicholas(91),
   Bourbon(8), Bath(1)
CARRIE Knott
CARROLLTON Carroll
CARTER Carter
CARVER Magoffin
CASEY CREEKG (42723) Adair(62),
   Taylor(32), Casey(6)
CATLETTSBURG (41129) Boyd(98),
   Lawrence(2)
CAVE CITY (42127) Barren(93), Hart(7)
CAWOOD Harlan
CECILIA Hardin

CENTER (42214) Metcalfe(79), Green(21)
CENTERTOWN Ohio
CENTRAL CITY Muhlenberg
CERULEAN (42215) Trigg(61),
   Christian(38)
CHAPLIN Nelson
CHAPPELL Leslie
CHAVIES Perry
CINDA Leslie
CISCO Magoffin
CLARKSON Grayson
CLAY (42404) Webster(91), Union(10)
CLAY CITY Powell
CLAYHOLE Breathitt
CLEARFIELD Rowan
CLEATON Muhlenberg
CLERMONT Bullitt
CLIFTY Todd
CLINTON Hickman
CLOSPLINT Harlan
CLOVERPORT Breckinridge
COALGOOD Harlan
COBHILL Estill
COLDIRON Harlan
COLUMBIA Adair
COLUMBUS Hickman
COMBS Perry
CONCORD Lewis
CONFLUENCE Leslie
CONLEY Magoffin
CONSTANCE Boone
CONSTANTINE Breckinridge
CONWAY Rockcastle
COOPERSVILLE Wayne
CORBIN (40701) Whitley(58), Laurel(29),
   Knox(13)
CORBIN Whitley
CORINTH (41010) Grant(70), Owen(27),
   Harrison(3)
CORNETTSVILLE (41731) Perry(85),
   Letcher(15)
CORYDON (99999) Henderson(99),
   Webster(1)
COTTLE Morgan
COVINGTON Kenton
COXS CREEK (40013) Nelson(75),
   Bullitt(15), Spencer(9)
CRAB ORCHARD (40419) Lincoln(68),
   Garrard(16), Rockcastle(9), Pulaski(7)
CRANKS Harlan
CRAYNE Crittenden
CRAYNOR Floyd
CRESTWOOD Oldham
CRITTENDEN (41030) Grant(67),
   Boone(33)
CROCKETT Morgan
CROFTON Christian
CROMONA Letcher
CROMWELL (42333) Ohio(86), Butler(14)
CROWN Letcher
CRYSTAL (40420) Lee(83), Estill(17)
CUB RUN (42729) Hart(75), Edmonson(25)
CULVER Elliott

CUMBERLAND (40823) Harlan(99), Letcher(1)
CUNDIFF Adair
CUNNINGHAM (42035) Carlisle(58), Graves(42)
CURDSVILLE Daviess
CUSTER Breckinridge
CUTSHIN Leslie
CYNTHIANA Harrison
DABOLT Jackson
DAISY Perry
DANA Floyd
DANVILLE Boyle
DAVID Floyd
DAWSON SPRINGS (42408) Hopkins(88), Caldwell(9), Christian(3)
DAYHOIT Harlan
DAYTON Campbell
DE MOSSVILLE Pendleton
DEANE (41812) Knott(77), Letcher(23)
DEBORD Martin
DECOY (41321) Knott(80), Breathitt(20)
DEFOE Henry
DELPHIA Perry
DELTA Wayne
DEMA Knott
DENNISTON Menifee
DENTON (41132) Carter(96), Lawrence(3), Boyd(1)
DENVER Johnson
DEWITT Knox
DEXTER (42036) Calloway(99), Marshall(1)
DICE Perry
DINGUS Morgan
DIXON Webster
DIZNEY Harlan
DORTON Pike
DOVER (41034) Mason(97), Bracken(3)
DRAFFIN Pike
DRAKE Warren
DRAKESBORO Muhlenberg
DREYFUS Madison
DRIFT Floyd
DRY RIDGE Grant
DUBRE (42731) Cumberland(84), Metcalfe(16)
DUNBAR Butler
DUNDEE Ohio
DUNMOR (42339) Muhlenberg(93), Butler(7)
DUNNVILLE (42528) Casey(97), Russell(3)
DWALE Floyd
DWARF Perry
DYCUSBURG Crittenden
EARLINGTON Hopkins
EAST BERNSTADT Laurel
EAST POINT (41216) Floyd(66), Johnson(34)
EASTERN Floyd
EASTVIEW Hardin
EASTWOOD Jefferson
EDDYVILLE Lyon
EDMONTON (42129) Metcalfe(94), Adair(6)
EDNA Magoffin
EGYPT Jackson
EIGHTY EIGHT Barren
EKRON Meade
ELIZABETHTOWN Hardin
ELIZAVILLE Fleming
ELK HORN (42733) Taylor(76), Casey(23), Adair(1)
ELKFORK Morgan
ELKHORN CITY Pike
ELKTON (42220) Todd(98), Muhlenberg(2)
ELLIOTTVILLE Rowan
ELSIE Magoffin
EMERSON Lewis
EMINENCE (40019) Henry(98), Shelby(2)
EMLYN Whitley
EMMA Floyd

EMMALENA Knott
ENDICOTT Floyd
EOLIA Letcher
ERILINE Clay
ERLANGER Kenton
ERMINE Letcher
ESSIE (40827) Leslie(96), Adair(4)
ESTILL Floyd
ETOILE Barren
EUBANK (42567) Pulaski(86), Lincoln(14)
EVARTS Harlan
EWING Fleming
EZEL Morgan
FAIRDALE Jefferson
FAIRFIELD Nelson
FAIRPLAY Adair
FAIRVIEW Christian
FALCON Magoffin
FALL ROCK Clay
FALLS OF ROUGH (40119) Grayson(59), Breckinridge(39), Ohio(2)
FALMOUTH Pendleton
FANCY FARM (42039) Graves(54), Hickman(28), Carlisle(18)
FARMERS Rowan
FARMINGTON (42040) Graves(78), Calloway(22)
FAUBUSH (42532) Pulaski(59), Russell(35), Wayne(6)
FEDSCREEK Pike
FERGUSON Pulaski
FILLMORE Lee
FINCHVILLE Shelby
FINLEY (42736) Taylor(57), Marion(43)
FIREBRICK Lewis
FISHERVILLE (40023) Jefferson(59), Spencer(38), Shelby(3)
FISTY Knott
FLAT FORK Magoffin
FLAT LICK Knox
FLATGAP Johnson
FLATWOODS Greenup
FLEMINGSBURG Fleming
FLORENCE Boone
FOGERTOWN Clay
FORD Clark
FORDS BRANCH Pike
FORDSVILLE (42343) Ohio(68), Hancock(31)
FOREST HILLS Pike
FORT CAMPBELL Christian
FORT KNOX Hardin
FORT THOMAS Campbell
FOSTER Bracken
FOUNTAIN RUN (42133) Monroe(49), Barren(32), Allen(19)
FOURMILE Knox
FRAKES (40940) Bell(64), Whitley(36)
FRANKFORT (40601) Franklin(97), Woodford(2), Shelby(1)
FRANKFORT Franklin
FRANKLIN (42134) Simpson(94), Allen(5)
FRANKLIN Simpson
FRAZER Wayne
FREDONIA (42411) Caldwell(57), Crittenden(38), Lyon(5)
FREDVILLE Magoffin
FREEBURN Pike
FRENCHBURG Menifee
FRITZ Magoffin
FT MITCHELL Kenton
FUGET Johnson
FULTON (42041) Fulton(72), Graves(17), Hickman(11)
GALVESTON Floyd
GAMALIEL Monroe
GAPVILLE Magoffin
GARFIELD (40140) Breckinridge(85), Hardin(15)
GARNER Knott
GARRARD Clay
GARRETT (41630) Knott(55), Floyd(45)

GARRISON (41141) Lewis(61), Greenup(25), Carter(14)
GAYS CREEK Perry
GEORGETOWN Scott
GERMANTOWN (41044) Bracken(51), Mason(50)
GHENT Carroll
GILBERTSVILLE Marshall
GILLMORE Wolfe
GIRDLER Knox
GLASGOW Barren
GLENCOE (41046) Grant(74), Gallatin(26)
GLENDALE Hardin
GLENS FORK (42741) Adair(93), Russell(8)
GLENVIEW Jefferson
GOODY Pike
GOOSE ROCK Clay
GORDON Letcher
GOSHEN Oldham
GRACEY (42232) Christian(77), Trigg(23)
GRADYVILLE Adair
GRAHAM Muhlenberg
GRAHN Carter
GRAND RIVERS Livingston
GRATZ Owen
GRAVEL SWITCH (40328) Marion(46), Boyle(32), Casey(20), Washington(2)
GRAY (40734) Knox(87), Laurel(13)
GRAY HAWK Jackson
GRAYS KNOB Harlan
GRAYSON (41143) Carter(99), Greenup(1)
GREEN HALL Owsley
GREEN ROAD Knox
GREENSBURG (42743) Green(97), Adair(2), Taylor(2)
GREENUP Greenup
GREENVILLE Muhlenberg
GRETHEL Floyd
GULSTON Harlan
GUNLOCK Magoffin
GUSTON (40142) Meade(96), Breckinridge(4)
GUTHRIE Todd
GYPSY Magoffin
HADDIX Breathitt
HADLEY Warren
HAGERHILL Johnson
HALDEMAN Rowan
HALFWAY Allen
HALLIE Letcher
HALO Floyd
HAMLIN Calloway
HAMPTON Livingston
HANSON Hopkins
HAPPY Perry
HARDBURLY Perry
HARDIN (42048) Marshall(95), Calloway(5)
HARDINSBURG Breckinridge
HARDY Pike
HARDYVILLE (42746) Hart(80), Green(12), Metcalfe(8)
HARLAN Harlan
HARNED Breckinridge
HAROLD Floyd
HARRODS CREEK Jefferson
HARRODSBURG (40330) Mercer(96), Washington(4)
HARTFORD Ohio
HAWESVILLE (42348) Hancock(98), Daviess(2)
HAZARD (41701) Perry(91), Knott(9)
HAZARD Perry
HAZEL Calloway
HAZEL GREEN (41332) Wolfe(82), Morgan(18)
HEBRON Boone
HEIDELBERG Lee
HEIDRICK Knox
HELLIER Pike
HELTON (40840) Leslie(77), Harlan(23)
HENDERSON Henderson

HENDRICKS Magoffin
HERD Jackson
HERNDON (42236) Christian(86), Trigg(15)
HESTAND (42151) Monroe(97), Metcalfe(3)
HI HAT Floyd
HICKMAN Fulton
HICKORY Graves
HILLSBORO Fleming
HIMA Clay
HINDMAN Knott
HINKLE Knox
HIPPO Floyd
HISEVILLE Barren
HITCHINS Carter
HODGENVILLE Larue
HOLLAND Allen
HOLLYBUSH Knott
HOLMES MILL Harlan
HONAKER Floyd
HOPE (40334) Bath(87), Montgomery(13)
HOPKINSVILLE Christian
HORSE BRANCH (42349) Ohio(82), Grayson(18)
HORSE CAVE (42749) Hart(94), Metcalfe(4), Barren(2)
HOSKINSTON Leslie
HOWARDSTOWN (40028) Nelson(84), Larue(16)
HUDDY Pike
HUDSON Breckinridge
HUEYSVILLE (41640) Knott(80), Floyd(20)
HUFF Edmonson
HULEN Bell
HUNTER Floyd
HUNTSVILLE Butler
HUSTONVILLE (40437) Lincoln(69), Casey(31)
HYDEN Leslie
INDEPENDENCE Kenton
INEZ Martin
INGLE Pulaski
INGRAM Bell
INSKO Morgan
IRVINE (40336) Estill(98), Lee(1)
IRVINGTON (40146) Breckinridge(98), Meade(2)
ISLAND McLean
ISLAND CITY Owsley
ISOM Letcher
ISONVILLE Elliott
IVEL Floyd
IVYTON Magoffin
JACKHORN Letcher
JACKSON (41339) Breathitt(94), Knott(6)
JACOBS Carter
JAMBOREE Pike
JAMESTOWN Russell
JEFF Perry
JEFFERSONVILLE Montgomery
JENKINS (41537) Letcher(97), Pike(3)
JEREMIAH Letcher
JETSON Butler
JOB Martin
JOHNS RUN Carter
JONANCY Pike
JONESVILLE Grant
JUNCTION CITY Boyle
KEATON Johnson
KEAVY Laurel
KEENE Jessamine
KEITH Harlan
KENTON Kenton
KENVIR Harlan
KERBY KNOB Jackson
KETTLE Cumberland
KETTLE ISLAND Bell
KEVIL (42053) McCracken(53), Ballard(47)
KIMPER Pike
KINGS MOUNTAIN (40442) Lincoln(64), Casey(36)

KIRKSEY (42054) Calloway(80), Marshall(14), Graves(6)
KITE Knott
KNIFLEY Adair
KNOB LICK (42154) Metcalfe(86), Barren(14)
KONA Letcher
KRYPTON (41754) Perry(97), Leslie(3)
KUTTAWA Lyon
LA CENTER Ballard
LA FAYETTE Christian
LA GRANGE (40031) Oldham(95), Henry(5)
LA GRANGE Oldham
LACKEY (41643) Knott(84), Floyd(16)
LAMB (42155) Barren(61), Monroe(39)
LAMBRIC Breathitt
LAMERO Rockcastle
LANCASTER (40444) Garrard(97), Lincoln(3)
LANCASTER Garrard
LANGLEY Floyd
LATONIA Kenton
LAWRENCEBURG Anderson
LEANDER Johnson
LEATHERWOOD Perry
LEBANON Marion
LEBANON JUNCTION (40150) Bullitt(78), Hardin(22)
LEBURN Knott
LEDBETTER Livingston
LEE CITY Wolfe
LEECO Lee
LEITCHFIELD (42754) Grayson(94), Breckinridge(6)
LEITCHFIELD Grayson
LEJUNIOR Harlan
LENOX Morgan
LEROSE Owsley
LETCHER Letcher
LEWISBURG (42256) Logan(86), Todd(10), Butler(3), Muhlenberg(1)
LEWISPORT (42351) Hancock(92), Daviess(8)
LEXINGTON (40509) Fayette(98), Clark(2)
LEXINGTON (40511) Fayette(98), Scott(1)
LEXINGTON (40514) Fayette(94), Jessamine(7)
LEXINGTON (40516) Fayette(85), Bourbon(15)
LEXINGTON Fayette
LIBERTY Casey
LICK CREEK Pike
LILY Laurel
LINDSEYVILLE Edmonson
LINEFORK Letcher
LITTCARR Knott
LITTLE Breathitt
LIVERMORE (42352) McLean(95), Ohio(5)
LIVINGSTON (40445) Rockcastle(98), Laurel(2)
LLOYD Greenup
LOCKPORT Henry
LOLA Livingston
LONDON Laurel
LONE Lee
LOOKOUT Pike
LORETTO (40037) Marion(75), Washington(17), Nelson(8)
LOST CREEK (41348) Breathitt(77), Perry(23)
LOUISA (41230) Lawrence(98), Martin(2)
LOUISVILLE (40229) Jefferson(62), Bullitt(38)
LOUISVILLE (40241) Jefferson(98), Oldham(2)
LOUISVILLE (40245) Jefferson(88), Shelby(11), Oldham(1)
LOUISVILLE (40272) Jefferson(99), Bullitt(2)
LOUISVILLE (40299) Jefferson(98), Bullitt(2)

LOUISVILLE Jefferson
LOVELACEVILLE Ballard
LOVELY Martin
LOWES Graves
LOWMANSVILLE (41232) Lawrence(68), Johnson(32)
LOYALL Harlan
LUCAS Barren
LYNCH Harlan
LYNNVILLE Graves
MACEDONIA Breathitt
MACEO Daviess
MACKVILLE Washington
MADISONVILLE Hopkins
MAGNOLIA (42757) Hart(53), Larue(39), Green(8)
MAJESTIC Pike
MALLIE Knott
MALONE Morgan
MAMMOTH CAVE Edmonson
MANCHESTER Clay
MANITOU Hopkins
MANNSVILLE Taylor
MAPLE MOUNT Daviess
MARIBA Menifee
MARION Crittenden
MARROWBONE Cumberland
MARSHALLVILLE Magoffin
MARSHES SIDING McCreary
MARTHA (41159) Lawrence(93), Johnson(8)
MARTIN Floyd
MARY ALICE (40964) Harlan(93), Adair(7)
MARYDELL Laurel
MASON Grant
MASONIC HOME Jefferson
MAYFIELD Graves
MAYKING Letcher
MAYSLICK Mason
MAYSVILLE Mason
MAZIE Lawrence
MC ANDREWS Pike
MC CARR Pike
MC COMBS (41545) Pike(90), Floyd(10)
MC DANIELS Breckinridge
MC DOWELL Floyd
MC HENRY Ohio
MC KEE (40447) Jackson(97), Rockcastle(2), Estill(1)
MC KINNEY Lincoln
MC QUADY Breckinridge
MC ROBERTS Letcher
MC VEIGH Pike
MEALLY Johnson
MEANS (40346) Menifee(81), Bath(11), Montgomery(9)
MELBER (42069) Graves(90), McCracken(9), Carlisle(1)
MELBOURNE Campbell
MELVIN Floyd
MIDDLEBURG Casey
MIDDLESBORO Bell
MIDWAY (40347) Woodford(92), Franklin(4), Scott(3)
MILBURN Carlisle
MILFORD Bracken
MILL SPRINGS Wayne
MILLERSBURG Bourbon
MILLS Knox
MILLSTONE Letcher
MILLTOWN Adair
MILLWOOD Grayson
MILTON (40045) Trimble(86), Carroll(14)
MIMA Morgan
MINERVA Mason
MINNIE Floyd
MIRACLE Bell
MISTLETOE Owsley
MITCHELLSBURG Boyle
MIZE Morgan
MONTICELLO Wayne
MONTPELIER Adair

MOON Morgan
MOOREFIELD Nicholas
MOORMAN Muhlenberg
MOREHEAD Rowan
MORGANFIELD (42437) Union(98), Webster(2)
MORGANTOWN Butler
MORNING VIEW Kenton
MORRILL Jackson
MORTONS GAP Hopkins
MOUNT EDEN (40046) Spencer(59), Anderson(37), Shelby(4)
MOUNT HERMON Monroe
MOUNT OLIVET Robertson
MOUNT SHERMAN (42764) Green(52), Larue(48)
MOUNT STERLING (40353) Montgomery(98), Clark(1)
MOUNT VERNON Rockcastle
MOUNT WASHINGTON Bullitt
MOUSIE Knott
MOUTHCARD Pike
MOZELLE Leslie
MULDRAUGH Meade
MUNFORDVILLE Hart
MURRAY Calloway
MUSES MILLS Fleming
MYRA Pike
NANCY (42544) Pulaski(72), Wayne(18), Russell(9)
NARROWS Ohio
NAZARETH Nelson
NEAFUS Grayson
NEBO (42441) Hopkins(95), Webster(5)
NELSE Pike
NEON (41840) Letcher(98), Knott(2)
NERINX Marion
NEVISDALE Whitley
NEW CASTLE Henry
NEW CONCORD Calloway
NEW HAVEN (40051) Nelson(84), Larue(16)
NEW HOPE (40052) Nelson(86), Larue(12), Marion(2)
NEW LIBERTY Owen
NEWPORT Campbell
NICHOLASVILLE Jessamine
NOCTOR Breathitt
NORTH MIDDLETOWN Bourbon
NORTONVILLE (42442) Hopkins(95), Christian(5)
OAK GROVE Christian
OAKLAND Warren
OAKVILLE Logan
OFFUTT Johnson
OIL SPRINGS Johnson
OLATON (42361) Ohio(88), Grayson(12)
OLD LANDING Lee
OLDTOWN Greenup
OLIVE HILL (41164) Carter(97), Elliott(3)
OLLIE Edmonson
OLMSTEAD (42265) Logan(90), Todd(10)
OLYMPIA Bath
ONEIDA Clay
OPHIR Morgan
ORLANDO Rockcastle
OVEN FORK Letcher
OWENSBORO Daviess
OWENTON Owen
OWINGSVILLE (40360) Bath(94), Montgomery(6)
PADUCAH McCracken
PAINT LICK (40461) Garrard(61), Madison(39)
PAINTSVILLE Johnson
PARIS Bourbon
PARK CITY (42160) Barren(80), Edmonson(20)
PARKERS LAKE McCreary
PARKSVILLE (40464) Boyle(92), Casey(8)
PARROT Jackson
PARTRIDGE Letcher

PATHFORK Harlan
PAW PAW Pike
PAYNEVILLE (40157) Meade(99), Breckinridge(1)
PELLVILLE Hancock
PEMBROKE (42266) Christian(93), Todd(7)
PENDLETON (40055) Trimble(45), Henry(40), Oldham(16)
PENROD Muhlenberg
PEOPLES Jackson
PERRY PARK Owen
PERRYVILLE (40468) Boyle(93), Washington(4), Mercer(2)
PETERSBURG Boone
PEWEE VALLEY Oldham
PEYTONSBURG Cumberland
PHELPS Pike
PHILPOT (42366) Daviess(94), Hancock(4), Ohio(3)
PHYLLIS Pike
PIKEVILLE Pike
PILGRIM Martin
PINE KNOT McCreary
PINE RIDGE (41360) Wolfe(85), Powell(15)
PINE TOP Knott
PINEVILLE Bell
PINSONFORK Pike
PIPPA PASSES Knott
PITTSBURG Laurel
PLANK Clay
PLEASUREVILLE (40057) Henry(89), Shelby(11)
PLUMMERS LANDING Fleming
POMEROYTON Menifee
POOLE Webster
PORT ROYAL Henry
POWDERLY Muhlenberg
PREMIUM Letcher
PRESTON Bath
PRESTONSBURG Floyd
PRIMROSE Lee
PRINCETON (42445) Caldwell(93), Lyon(3), Hopkins(2), Trigg(2)
PRINTER Floyd
PROSPECT (40059) Jefferson(67), Oldham(33)
PROVIDENCE (42450) Webster(91), Hopkins(5), Crittenden(5)
PROVO Butler
PRYSE Estill
PUTNEY Harlan
QUALITY (42268) Butler(73), Logan(27)
QUICKSAND Breathitt
QUINCY Lewis
RACCOON Pike
RADCLIFF Hardin
RANSOM Pike
RAVEN Knott
RAVENNA Estill
RAYWICK Marion
REDFOX Knott
REED Henderson
REGINA Pike
RENFRO VALLEY Rockcastle
REVELO McCreary
REYNOLDS STATION (42368) Hancock(78), Ohio(22)
RHODELIA (40161) Meade(90), Breckinridge(11)
RICETOWN Owsley
RICHARDSON Lawrence
RICHARDSVILLE Warren
RICHMOND Madison
RINEYVILLE Hardin
RIVER (41254) Johnson(95), Lawrence(5)
ROARK Leslie
ROBARDS (42452) Henderson(85), Webster(16)
ROBINSON CREEK Pike
ROCHESTER Butler
ROCKFIELD (42274) Warren(92), Logan(8)

ROCKHOLDS (40759) Whitley(91), Knox(9)
ROCKHOUSE Pike
ROCKPORT Ohio
ROCKY HILL Edmonson
ROCKYBRANCH Wayne
ROGERS Wolfe
ROSINE Ohio
ROUNDHILL (42275) Butler(71), Edmonson(30)
ROUSSEAU Breathitt
ROWDY Perry
ROWLETTS Hart
ROXANA Letcher
ROYALTON Magoffin
RUMSEY McLean
RUSH (41168) Carter(72), Boyd(27)
RUSSELL Greenup
RUSSELL SPRINGS (42642) Russell(91), Adair(6), Casey(2)
RUSSELLVILLE Logan
SACRAMENTO (42372) Muhlenberg(51), McLean(50)
SADIEVILLE (40370) Scott(75), Harrison(26)
SAINT CATHARINE Washington
SAINT CHARLES Hopkins
SAINT FRANCIS Marion
SAINT HELENS Lee
SAINT JOSEPH Daviess
SAINT MARY Marion
SAINT PAUL Lewis
SALDEE Breathitt
SALEM (42078) Livingston(62), Crittenden(38)
SALT LICK (40371) Bath(92), Menifee(8)
SALVISA (40372) Mercer(94), Anderson(6)
SALYERSVILLE (41465) Magoffin(98), Floyd(2)
SANDERS Carroll
SANDGAP Jackson
SANDY HOOK Elliott
SASSAFRAS Knott
SAUL Perry
SAWYER McCreary
SCALF Knox
SCIENCE HILL Pulaski
SCOTTSVILLE Allen
SCUDDY Perry
SE REE Breckinridge
SEBREE Webster
SECO Letcher
SEDALIA Graves
SEITZ Magoffin
SEXTONS CREEK (40983) Clay(67), Owsley(33)
SHARON GROVE Todd
SHARPSBURG (40374) Bath(91), Bourbon(5), Nicholas(4)
SHELBIANA Pike
SHELBY GAP Pike
SHELBYVILLE Shelby
SHEPHERDSVILLE Bullitt
SHOPVILLE Pulaski
SIDNEY Pike
SILER (40763) Whitley(80), Bell(20)
SILVER GROVE Campbell
SILVERHILL Morgan
SIMPSONVILLE Shelby

SITKA Johnson
SIZEROCK Leslie
SLADE Powell
SLAUGHTERS (42456) Webster(72), Hopkins(28)
SLEMP Perry
SLOANS VALLEY Pulaski
SMILAX Leslie
SMITH Harlan
SMITH MILLS Henderson
SMITHFIELD (40068) Henry(87), Shelby(8), Oldham(5)
SMITHLAND Livingston
SMITHS GROVE (42171) Warren(49), Edmonson(29), Barren(23)
SOLDIER Carter
SOMERSET Pulaski
SONORA (42776) Hardin(67), Larue(34)
SOUTH CARROLLTON Muhlenberg
SOUTH PORTSMOUTH Greenup
SOUTH SHORE Greenup
SOUTH UNION Logan
SOUTH WILLIAMSON Pike
SPARTA (41086) Owen(52), Gallatin(48)
SPEIGHT Pike
SPOTTSVILLE Henderson
SPRING LICK Grayson
SPRINGFIELD Washington
STAB Pulaski
STAFFORDSVILLE Johnson
STAMBAUGH Johnson
STAMPING GROUND (40379) Scott(82), Owen(14), Franklin(5)
STANFORD Lincoln
STANLEY Daviess
STANTON (40380) Powell(97), Estill(3)
STANVILLE (41659) Floyd(97), Pike(3)
STEARNS McCreary
STEELE Pike
STEFF Grayson
STEPHENS Elliott
STEPHENSBURG Hardin
STEPHENSPORT Breckinridge
STEUBENVILLE Wayne
STINNETT Leslie
STONE Pike
STONEY FORK (40988) Bell(54), Harlan(46)
STOPOVER Pike
STRUNK McCreary
STURGIS (42459) Union(94), Crittenden(6)
SULLIVAN Union
SULPHUR Henry
SUMMER SHADE (42166) Metcalfe(72), Barren(16), Monroe(13)
SUMMERSVILLE (42782) Green(95), Hart(5)
SUMMIT Hardin
SUNFISH Edmonson
SWAMP BRANCH Johnson
SWEEDEN Edmonson
SYMSONIA (42082) Graves(74), Marshall(23), McCracken(3)
TALBERT Breathitt
TALCUM (41765) Knott(86), Perry(14)
TALLEGA Lee
TATEVILLE Pulaski
TAYLORSVILLE (40071) Spencer(80), Bullitt(18), Shelby(2)

TEABERRY Floyd
THELMA Johnson
THORNTON Letcher
THOUSANDSTICKS Leslie
THREEFORKS Martin
TILINE Livingston
TOLER Pike
TOLLESBORO Lewis
TOLU Crittenden
TOMAHAWK Martin
TOMPKINSVILLE Monroe
TOPMOST Knott
TOTZ Harlan
TRAM Floyd
TRENTON (42286) Todd(96), Christian(4)
TROSPER Knox
TURKEY CREEK (41570) Pike(96), Martin(4)
TURNERS STATION (40075) Henry(72), Carroll(28)
TUTOR KEY Johnson
TYNER (40486) Jackson(97), Clay(3)
TYPO Perry
ULYSSES Lawrence
UNION Boone
UNION STAR Breckinridge
UNIONTOWN (42461) Union(97), Henderson(3)
UPTON (42784) Hardin(53), Larue(28), Hart(19)
UTICA (42376) Daviess(74), Ohio(20), McLean(6)
VAN LEAR Johnson
VANCEBURG (41179) Lewis(94), Carter(6)
VANCLEVE Breathitt
VARNEY Pike
VENTRESS Hardin
VERONA Boone
VERSAILLES (40383) Woodford(99), Jessamine(2)
VERSAILLES Woodford
VEST Knott
VICCO (41773) Perry(63), Knott(37)
VINCENT Owsley
VINE GROVE (40175) Hardin(65), Meade(35)
VIPER Perry
VIRGIE Pike
VOLGA Johnson
WACO (40385) Madison(98), Estill(3)
WADDY (40076) Shelby(72), Franklin(16), Anderson(10), Spencer(2)
WALKER Knox
WALLINGFORD Fleming
WALLINS CREEK Harlan
WALNUT GROVE Pulaski
WALTON (41094) Boone(99), Kenton(1)
WANETA Jackson
WARBRANCH Leslie
WARFIELD Martin
WARSAW (41095) Gallatin(96), Boone(4)
WASHINGTON Mason
WATER VALLEY (42085) Graves(69), Hickman(31)
WATERVIEW Cumberland
WAVERLY (42462) Union(91), Henderson(10)
WAX Grayson
WAYLAND Floyd

WAYNESBURG (40489) Lincoln(80), Pulaski(12), Casey(8)
WEBBVILLE (41180) Lawrence(54), Carter(45), Elliott(1)
WEBSTER (40176) Breckinridge(66), Meade(34)
WEEKSBURY Floyd
WELCHS CREEK Butler
WELLINGTON Menifee
WENDOVER Leslie
WEST LIBERTY (41472) Morgan(98), Elliott(2)
WEST LOUISVILLE Daviess
WEST PADUCAH McCracken
WEST POINT (40177) Hardin(91), Bullitt(7), Jefferson(2)
WEST PRESTONSBURG Floyd
WEST SOMERSET Pulaski
WEST VAN LEAR Johnson
WESTPORT Oldham
WESTVIEW Breckinridge
WHEATCROFT Webster
WHEATLEY Owen
WHEELWRIGHT Floyd
WHICK Breathitt
WHITE MILLS Hardin
WHITE OAK Morgan
WHITE PLAINS (42464) Hopkins(74), Muhlenberg(17), Christian(10)
WHITEHOUSE Johnson
WHITESBURG Letcher
WHITESVILLE (42378) Daviess(53), Ohio(47)
WHITLEY CITY McCreary
WICKLIFFE Ballard
WIDECREEK Breathitt
WILDIE Rockcastle
WILLARD Carter
WILLIAMSBURG Whitley
WILLIAMSPORT Johnson
WILLIAMSTOWN Grant
WILLISBURG (40078) Washington(96), Mercer(2), Anderson(2)
WILLOW SHADE Metcalfe
WILMORE (40390) Jessamine(98), Woodford(2)
WINCHESTER Clark
WIND CAVE Jackson
WINDSOR (42565) Casey(99), Russell(1)
WINDY Wayne
WINGO (42088) Graves(85), Hickman(15)
WINSTON Estill
WITTENSVILLE Johnson
WOODBINE (40771) Knox(84), Whitley(16)
WOODBURN (42170) Warren(64), Simpson(36)
WOODBURY Butler
WOODMAN Pike
WOOLLUM Knox
WOOTON Leslie
WORTHINGTON Greenup
WORTHVILLE (41098) Owen(96), Carroll(4)
WRIGLEY Morgan
YEADDISS Leslie
YERKES Perry
YOSEMITE Casey
ZACHARIAH Lee
ZOE Lee

ZIP/City Cross Reference

40003-40003	BAGDAD	40013-40013	COXS CREEK	40027-40027	HARRODS CREEK	40047-40047	MOUNT WASHINGTON
40004-40004	BARDSTOWN	40014-40014	CRESTWOOD	40031-40032	LA GRANGE	40048-40048	NAZARETH
40006-40006	BEDFORD	40018-40018	EASTWOOD	40033-40033	LEBANON	40049-40049	NERINX
40007-40007	BETHLEHEM	40019-40019	EMINENCE	40036-40036	LOCKPORT	40050-40050	NEW CASTLE
40008-40008	BLOOMFIELD	40020-40020	FAIRFIELD	40037-40037	LORETTO	40051-40051	NEW HAVEN
40009-40009	BRADFORDSVILLE	40022-40022	FINCHVILLE	40040-40040	MACKVILLE	40052-40052	NEW HOPE
40010-40010	BUCKNER	40023-40023	FISHERVILLE	40041-40041	MASONIC HOME	40055-40055	PENDLETON
40011-40011	CAMPBELLSBURG	40025-40025	GLENVIEW	40045-40045	MILTON	40056-40056	PEWEE VALLEY
40012-40012	CHAPLIN	40026-40026	GOSHEN	40046-40046	MOUNT EDEN	40057-40057	PLEASUREVILLE

40058-40058	PORT ROYAL	40360-40360	OWINGSVILLE	40825-40825	DIZNEY	41034-41034	DOVER
40059-40059	PROSPECT	40361-40362	PARIS	40826-40826	EOLIA	41035-41035	DRY RIDGE
40060-40060	RAYWICK	40363-40363	PERRY PARK	40827-40827	ESSIE	41037-41037	ELIZAVILLE
40061-40061	SAINT CATHARINE	40366-40366	PRESTON	40828-40828	EVARTS	41039-41039	EWING
40062-40062	SAINT FRANCIS	40370-40370	SADIEVILLE	40829-40829	GRAYS KNOB	41040-41040	FALMOUTH
40063-40063	SAINT MARY	40371-40371	SALT LICK	40830-40830	GULSTON	41041-41041	FLEMINGSBURG
40065-40066	SHELBYVILLE	40372-40372	SALVISA	40831-40831	HARLAN	41042-41042	FLORENCE
40067-40067	SIMPSONVILLE	40374-40374	SHARPSBURG	40840-40840	HELTON	41043-41043	FOSTER
40068-40068	SMITHFIELD	40376-40376	SLADE	40843-40843	HOLMES MILL	41044-41044	GERMANTOWN
40069-40069	SPRINGFIELD	40379-40379	STAMPING GROUND	40844-40844	HOSKINSTON	41045-41045	GHENT
40070-40070	SULPHUR	40380-40380	STANTON	40845-40845	HULEN	41046-41046	GLENCOE
40071-40071	TAYLORSVILLE	40383-40384	VERSAILLES	40847-40847	KENVIR	41048-41048	HEBRON
40075-40075	TURNERS STATION	40385-40385	WACO	40849-40849	LEJUNIOR	41049-41049	HILLSBORO
40076-40076	WADDY	40386-40386	VERSAILLES	40854-40854	LOYALL	41051-41051	INDEPENDENCE
40077-40077	WESTPORT	40387-40387	WELLINGTON	40855-40855	LYNCH	41052-41052	JONESVILLE
40078-40078	WILLISBURG	40390-40390	WILMORE	40856-40856	MIRACLE	41053-41053	KENTON
40104-40104	BATTLETOWN	40391-40392	WINCHESTER	40858-40858	MOZELLE	41054-41054	MASON
40106-40106	BIG SPRING	40402-40402	ANNVILLE	40862-40862	PARTRIDGE	41055-41055	MAYSLICK
40107-40107	BOSTON	40403-40404	BEREA	40863-40863	PATHFORK	41056-41056	MAYSVILLE
40108-40108	BRANDENBURG	40405-40405	BIGHILL	40865-40865	PUTNEY	41059-41059	MELBOURNE
40109-40109	BROOKS	40409-40409	BRODHEAD	40867-40867	SMITH	41061-41061	MILFORD
40110-40110	CLERMONT	40410-40410	BRYANTSVILLE	40868-40868	STINNETT	41062-41062	MINERVA
40111-40111	CLOVERPORT	40419-40419	CRAB ORCHARD	40870-40870	TOTZ	41063-41063	MORNING VIEW
40115-40115	CUSTER	40421-40421	DABOI T	40873 40873	WALLINS CREEK	41064-41064	MOUNT OLIVET
40117-40117	EKRON	40422-40423	DANVILLE	40874-40874	WARBRANCH	41065-41065	MUSES MILLS
40118-40118	FAIRDALE	40434-40434	GRAY HAWK	40902-40902	ARJAY	41071-41072	NEWPORT
40119-40119	FALLS OF ROUGH	40437-40437	HUSTONVILLE	40903-40903	ARTEMUS	41073-41073	BELLEVUE
40121-40121	FORT KNOX	40440-40440	JUNCTION CITY	40906-40906	BARBOURVILLE	41074-41074	DAYTON
40140-40140	GARFIELD	40442-40442	KINGS MOUNTAIN	40913-40913	BEVERLY	41075-41075	FORT THOMAS
40142-40142	GUSTON	40444-40444	LANCASTER	40914-40914	BIG CREEK	41076-41076	NEWPORT
40143-40143	HARDINSBURG	40445-40445	LIVINGSTON	40915-40915	BIMBLE	41080-41080	PETERSBURG
40144-40144	HARNED	40446-40446	LANCASTER	40921-40921	BRYANTS STORE	41081-41081	PLUMMERS LANDING
40145-40145	HUDSON	40447-40447	MC KEE	40923-40923	CANNON	41083-41083	SANDERS
40146-40146	IRVINGTON	40448-40448	MC KINNEY	40927-40927	CLOSPLINT	41085-41085	SILVER GROVE
40150-40150	LEBANON JUNCTION	40452-40452	MITCHELLSBURG	40930-40930	DEWITT	41086-41086	SPARTA
40152-40152	MC DANIELS	40456-40456	MOUNT VERNON	40931-40931	ERILINE	41091-41091	UNION
40153-40153	MC QUADY	40460-40460	ORLANDO	40932-40932	FALL ROCK	41092-41092	VERONA
40155-40155	MULDRAUGH	40461-40461	PAINT LICK	40935-40935	FLAT LICK	41093-41093	WALLINGFORD
40157-40157	PAYNEVILLE	40464-40464	PARKSVILLE	40939-40939	FOURMILE	41094-41094	WALTON
40159-40160	RADCLIFF	40467-40467	PEOPLES	40940-40940	FRAKES	41095-41095	WARSAW
40161-40161	RHODELIA	40468-40468	PERRYVILLE	40941-40941	GARRARD	41096-41096	WASHINGTON
40162-40162	RINEYVILLE	40472-40472	RAVENNA	40943-40943	GIRDLER	41097-41097	WILLIAMSTOWN
40164-40164	SE REE	40473-40473	RENFRO VALLEY	40944-40944	GOOSE ROCK	41098-41098	WORTHVILLE
40165-40165	SHEPHERDSVILLE	40475-40476	RICHMOND	40946-40946	GREEN ROAD	41099-41099	NEWPORT
40170-40170	STEPHENSPORT	40481-40481	SANDGAP	40949-40949	HEIDRICK	41101-41114	ASHLAND
40171-40171	UNION STAR	40484-40484	STANFORD	40951-40951	HIMA	41121-41121	ARGILLITE
40175-40175	VINE GROVE	40486-40486	TYNER	40953-40953	HINKLE	41124-41124	BLAINE
40176-40176	WEBSTER	40488-40488	WANETA	40955-40955	INGRAM	41125-41125	BRUIN
40177-40177	WEST POINT	40489-40489	WAYNESBURG	40958-40958	KETTLE ISLAND	41127-41127	CAMP DIX
40178-40178	WESTVIEW	40492-40492	WILDIE	40962-40962	MANCHESTER	41128-41128	CARTER
40201-40299	LOUISVILLE	40495-40495	WINSTON	40964-40964	MARY ALICE	41129-41129	CATLETTSBURG
40309-40309	BOWEN	40501-40596	LEXINGTON	40965-40965	MIDDLESBORO	41131-41131	CONCORD
40310-40310	BURGIN	40601-40622	FRANKFORT	40972-40972	ONEIDA	41132-41132	DENTON
40311-40311	CARLISLE	40701-40702	CORBIN	40977-40977	PINEVILLE	41135-41135	EMERSON
40312-40312	CLAY CITY	40724-40724	BUSH	40979-40979	ROARK	41137-41137	FIREBRICK
40313-40313	CLEARFIELD	40729-40729	EAST BERNSTADT	40981-40981	SAUL	41139-41139	FLATWOODS
40316-40316	DENNISTON	40730-40730	EMLYN	40982-40982	SCALF	41141-41141	GARRISON
40317-40317	ELLIOTTVILLE	40734-40734	GRAY	40983-40983	SEXTONS CREEK	41142-41142	GRAHN
40319-40319	FARMERS	40737-40737	KEAVY	40988-40988	STONEY FORK	41143-41143	GRAYSON
40320-40320	FORD	40740-40740	LILY	40995-40995	TROSPER	41144-41144	GREENUP
40322-40322	FRENCHBURG	40741-40745	LONDON	40997-40997	WALKER	41146-41146	HITCHINS
40324-40324	GEORGETOWN	40751-40751	MARYDELL	40999-40999	WOOLLUM	41149-41149	ISONVILLE
40328-40328	GRAVEL SWITCH	40754-40754	NEVISDALE	41001-41001	ALEXANDRIA	41150-41150	JACOBS
40329-40329	HALDEMAN	40755-40755	PITTSBURG	41002-41002	AUGUSTA	41156-41156	LLOYD
40330-40330	HARRODSBURG	40759-40759	ROCKHOLDS	41003-41003	BERRY	41159-41159	MARTHA
40334-40334	HOPE	40763-40763	SILER	41004-41004	BROOKSVILLE	41160-41160	MAZIE
40336-40336	IRVINE	40769-40769	WILLIAMSBURG	41005-41005	BURLINGTON	41164-41164	OLIVE HILL
40337-40337	JEFFERSONVILLE	40771-40771	WOODBINE	41006-41006	BUTLER	41166-41166	QUINCY
40339-40339	KEENE	40801-40801	AGES BROOKSIDE	41007-41007	CALIFORNIA	41168-41168	RUSH
40340-40340	NICHOLASVILLE	40803-40803	ASHER	41008-41008	CARROLLTON	41169-41169	RUSSELL
40342-40342	LAWRENCEBURG	40806-40806	BAXTER	41009-41009	CONSTANCE	41170-41170	SAINT PAUL
40346-40346	MEANS	40807-40807	BENHAM	41010-41010	CORINTH	41171-41171	SANDY HOOK
40347-40347	MIDWAY	40808-40808	BIG LAUREL	41011-41014	COVINGTON	41173-41173	SOLDIER
40348-40348	MILLERSBURG	40810-40810	BLEDSOE	41015-41015	LATONIA	41174-41174	SOUTH PORTSMOUTH
40350-40350	MOOREFIELD	40813-40813	CALVIN	41016-41016	COVINGTON	41175-41175	SOUTH SHORE
40351-40351	MOREHEAD	40815-40815	CAWOOD	41017-41017	FT MITCHELL	41179-41179	VANCEBURG
40353-40353	MOUNT STERLING	40816-40816	CHAPPELL	41018-41018	ERLANGER	41180-41180	WEBBVILLE
40355-40355	NEW LIBERTY	40818-40818	COALGOOD	41019-41019	COVINGTON	41181-41181	WILLARD
40356-40356	NICHOLASVILLE	40819-40819	COLDIRON	41022-41022	FLORENCE	41183-41183	WORTHINGTON
40357-40357	NORTH MIDDLETOWN	40820-40820	CRANKS	41030-41030	CRITTENDEN	41189-41189	TOLLESBORO
40358-40358	OLYMPIA	40823-40823	CUMBERLAND	41031-41031	CYNTHIANA	41201-41201	ADAMS
40359-40359	OWENTON	40824-40824	DAYHOIT	41033-41033	DE MOSSVILLE	41203-41203	BEAUTY

Code	City	Code	City	Code	City	Code	City
41204-41204	BOONS CAMP	41517-41517	BURDINE	41721-41721	BUCKHORN	42039-42039	FANCY FARM
41214-41214	DEBORD	41519-41519	CANADA	41722-41722	BULAN	42040-42040	FARMINGTON
41215-41215	DENVER	41520-41520	DORTON	41723-41723	BUSY	42041-42041	FULTON
41216-41216	EAST POINT	41522-41522	ELKHORN CITY	41725-41725	CARRIE	42044-42044	GILBERTSVILLE
41219-41219	FLATGAP	41524-41524	FEDSCREEK	41727-41727	CHAVIES	42045-42045	GRAND RIVERS
41222-41222	HAGERHILL	41526-41526	FORDS BRANCH	41729-41729	COMBS	42046-42046	HAMLIN
41224-41224	INEZ	41527-41527	FOREST HILLS	41730-41730	CONFLUENCE	42047-42047	HAMPTON
41226-41226	KEATON	41528-41528	FREEBURN	41731-41731	CORNETTSVILLE	42048-42048	HARDIN
41228-41228	LEANDER	41531-41531	HARDY	41735-41735	DELPHIA	42049-42049	HAZEL
41230-41230	LOUISA	41534-41534	HELLIER	41736-41736	DICE	42050-42050	HICKMAN
41231-41231	LOVELY	41535-41535	HUDDY	41739-41739	DWARF	42051-42051	HICKORY
41232-41232	LOWMANSVILLE	41536-41536	JAMBOREE	41740-41740	EMMALENA	42053-42053	KEVIL
41234-41234	MEALLY	41537-41537	JENKINS	41743-41743	FISTY	42054-42054	KIRKSEY
41238-41238	OIL SPRINGS	41538-41538	JONANCY	41745-41745	GAYS CREEK	42055-42055	KUTTAWA
41240-41240	PAINTSVILLE	41539-41539	KIMPER	41746-41746	HAPPY	42056-42056	LA CENTER
41250-41250	PILGRIM	41540-41540	LICK CREEK	41747-41747	HARDBURLY	42058-42058	LEDBETTER
41254-41254	RIVER	41542-41542	LOOKOUT	41749-41749	HYDEN	42060-42060	LOVELACEVILLE
41255-41255	SITKA	41543-41543	MC ANDREWS	41751-41751	JEFF	42061-42061	LOWES
41256-41256	STAFFORDSVILLE	41544-41544	MC CARR	41754-41754	KRYPTON	42063-42063	LYNNVILLE
41257-41257	STAMBAUGH	41546-41546	MC VEIGH	41759-41759	SASSAFRAS	42064-42064	MARION
41260-41260	THELMA	41547-41547	MAJESTIC	41760-41760	SCUDDY	42066-42066	MAYFIELD
41262-41262	TOMAHAWK	41548-41548	MOUTHCARD	41762-41762	SIZEROCK	42069-42069	MELBER
41263-41263	TUTOR KEY	41549-41549	MYRA	41763-41763	SLEMP	42070-42070	MILBURN
41264-41264	ULYSSES	41553-41553	PHELPS	41764-41764	SMILAX	42071-42071	MURRAY
41265-41265	VAN LEAR	41554-41554	PHYLLIS	41766-41766	THOUSANDSTICKS	42076-42076	NEW CONCORD
41267-41267	WARFIELD	41555-41555	PINSONFORK	41772-41772	VEST	42078-42078	SALEM
41268-41268	WEST VAN LEAR	41557-41557	RACCOON	41773-41773	VICCO	42079-42079	SEDALIA
41269-41269	WHITEHOUSE	41558-41558	RANSOM	41774-41774	VIPER	42081-42081	SMITHLAND
41271-41271	WILLIAMSPORT	41559-41559	REGINA	41775-41775	WENDOVER	42082-42082	SYMSONIA
41274-41274	WITTENSVILLE	41560-41560	ROBINSON CREEK	41776-41776	WOOTON	42083-42083	TILINE
41301-41301	CAMPTON	41561-41561	ROCKHOUSE	41777-41777	YEADDISS	42084-42084	TOLU
41307-41307	ATHOL	41562-41562	SHELBIANA	41778-41778	YERKES	42085-42085	WATER VALLEY
41310-41310	BAYS	41563-41563	SHELBY GAP	41804-41804	BLACKEY	42086-42086	WEST PADUCAH
41311-41311	BEATTYVILLE	41564-41564	SIDNEY	41810-41810	CROMONA	42087-42087	WICKLIFFE
41313-41313	BETHANY	41566-41566	STEELE	41812-41812	DEANE	42088-42088	WINGO
41314-41314	BOONEVILLE	41567-41567	STONE	41815-41815	ERMINE	42101-42104	BOWLING GREEN
41317-41317	CLAYHOLE	41568-41568	STOPOVER	41817-41817	GARNER	42120-42120	ADOLPHUS
41332-41332	HAZEL GREEN	41569-41569	TOLER	41819-41819	GORDON	42122-42122	ALVATON
41333-41333	HEIDELBERG	41571-41571	VARNEY	41821-41821	HALLIE	42123-42123	AUSTIN
41338-41338	ISLAND CITY	41572-41572	VIRGIE	41822-41822	HINDMAN	42124-42124	BEAUMONT
41339-41339	JACKSON	41601-41601	ALLEN	41824-41824	ISOM	42127-42127	CAVE CITY
41342-41342	LEE CITY	41602-41602	AUXIER	41825-41825	JACKHORN	42128-42128	DRAKE
41344-41344	LEROSE	41603-41603	BANNER	41826-41826	JEREMIAH	42129-42129	EDMONTON
41347-41347	LONE	41604-41604	BEAVER	41828-41828	KITE	42130-42130	EIGHTY EIGHT
41348-41348	LOST CREEK	41605-41605	BETSY LAYNE	41831-41831	LEBURN	42131-42131	ETOILE
41351-41351	MISTLETOE	41606-41606	BEVINSVILLE	41832-41832	LETCHER	42133-42133	FOUNTAIN RUN
41352-41352	MIZE	41607-41607	BLUE RIVER	41833-41833	LINEFORK	42134-42135	FRANKLIN
41360-41360	PINE RIDGE	41612-41612	BYPRO	41834-41834	LITTCARR	42140-42140	GAMALIEL
41362-41362	PRIMROSE	41615-41615	DANA	41835-41835	MC ROBERTS	42141-42142	GLASGOW
41364-41364	RICETOWN	41616-41616	DAVID	41836-41836	MALLIE	42150-42150	HALFWAY
41365-41365	ROGERS	41619-41619	DRIFT	41837-41837	MAYKING	42151-42151	HESTAND
41366-41366	ROUSSEAU	41621-41621	DWALE	41838-41838	MILLSTONE	42152-42152	HISEVILLE
41367-41367	ROWDY	41622-41622	EASTERN	41839-41839	MOUSIE	42153-42153	HOLLAND
41368-41368	SAINT HELENS	41626-41626	ENDICOTT	41840-41840	NEON	42154-42154	KNOB LICK
41377-41377	TALBERT	41630-41630	GARRETT	41843-41843	PINE TOP	42156-42156	LUCAS
41385-41385	VANCLEVE	41631-41631	GRETHEL	41844-41844	PIPPA PASSES	42157-42157	MOUNT HERMON
41386-41386	VINCENT	41632-41632	GUNLOCK	41845-41845	PREMIUM	42159-42159	OAKLAND
41390-41390	WHICK	41635-41635	HAROLD	41847-41847	REDFOX	42160-42160	PARK CITY
41397-41397	ZOE	41636-41636	HI HAT	41848-41848	ROXANA	42163-42163	ROCKY HILL
41408-41408	CANNEL CITY	41639-41639	HONAKER	41849-41849	SECO	42164-42164	SCOTTSVILLE
41410-41410	CISCO	41640-41640	HUEYSVILLE	41855-41855	THORNTON	42166-42166	SUMMER SHADE
41413-41413	CROCKETT	41642-41642	IVEL	41858-41858	WHITESBURG	42167-42167	TOMPKINSVILLE
41419-41419	EDNA	41643-41643	LACKEY	41859-41859	DEMA	42170-42170	WOODBURN
41421-41421	ELKFORK	41645-41645	LANGLEY	41861-41861	RAVEN	42171-42171	SMITHS GROVE
41422-41422	ELSIE	41647-41647	MC DOWELL	41862-41862	TOPMOST	42201-42201	ABERDEEN
41425-41425	EZEL	41649-41649	MARTIN	42001-42001	PADUCAH	42202-42202	ADAIRVILLE
41426-41426	FALCON	41650-41650	MELVIN	42020-42020	ALMO	42203-42203	ALLEGRE
41427-41427	FLAT FORK	41651-41651	MINNIE	42021-42021	ARLINGTON	42204-42204	ALLENSVILLE
41433-41433	GAPVILLE	41653-41653	PRESTONSBURG	42022-42022	BANDANA	42206-42206	AUBURN
41444-41444	IVYTON	41655-41655	PRINTER	42023-42023	BARDWELL	42207-42207	BEE SPRING
41451-41451	MALONE	41659-41659	STANVILLE	42024-42024	BARLOW	42209-42209	BROOKLYN
41452-41452	MARSHALLVILLE	41660-41660	TEABERRY	42025-42025	BENTON	42210-42210	BROWNSVILLE
41459-41459	OPHIR	41663-41663	TRAM	42027-42027	BOAZ	42211-42211	CADIZ
41464-41464	ROYALTON	41666-41666	WAYLAND	42028-42028	BURNA	42214-42214	CENTER
41465-41465	SALYERSVILLE	41667-41667	WEEKSBURY	42029-42029	CALVERT CITY	42215-42215	CERULEAN
41472-41472	WEST LIBERTY	41668-41668	WEST PRESTONSBURG	42031-42031	CLINTON	42216-42216	CLIFTY
41477-41477	WRIGLEY	41669-41669	WHEELWRIGHT	42032-42032	COLUMBUS	42217-42217	CROFTON
41501-41502	PIKEVILLE	41701-41702	HAZARD	42033-42033	CRAYNE	42219-42219	DUNBAR
41503-41503	SOUTH WILLIAMSON	41712-41712	ARY	42035-42035	CUNNINGHAM	42220-42220	ELKTON
41512-41512	ASHCAMP	41713-41713	AVAWAM	42036-42036	DEXTER	42221-42221	FAIRVIEW
41513-41513	BELCHER	41714-41714	BEAR BRANCH	42037-42037	DYCUSBURG	42223-42223	FORT CAMPBELL
41514-41514	BELFRY	41719-41719	BONNYMAN	42038-42038	EDDYVILLE	42232-42232	GRACEY

42234-42234 GUTHRIE	42344-42344 GRAHAM	42450-42450 PROVIDENCE	42711-42711 BAKERTON
42235-42235 HADLEY	42345-42345 GREENVILLE	42451-42451 REED	42712-42712 BIG CLIFTY
42236-42236 HERNDON	42347-42347 HARTFORD	42452-42452 ROBARDS	42713-42713 BONNIEVILLE
42240-42241 HOPKINSVILLE	42348-42348 HAWESVILLE	42453-42453 SAINT CHARLES	42715-42715 BREEDING
42251-42251 HUNTSVILLE	42349-42349 HORSE BRANCH	42455-42455 SEBREE	42716-42716 BUFFALO
42252-42252 JETSON	42350-42350 ISLAND	42456-42456 SLAUGHTERS	42717-42717 BURKESVILLE
42254-42254 LA FAYETTE	42351-42351 LEWISPORT	42457-42457 SMITH MILLS	42718-42719 CAMPBELLSVILLE
42256-42256 LEWISBURG	42352-42352 LIVERMORE	42458-42458 SPOTTSVILLE	42720-42720 CANE VALLEY
42257-42257 LINDSEYVILLE	42354-42354 MC HENRY	42459-42459 STURGIS	42721-42721 CANEYVILLE
42259-42259 MAMMOTH CAVE	42355-42355 MACEO	42460-42460 SULLIVAN	42722-42722 CANMER
42261-42261 MORGANTOWN	42356-42356 MAPLE MOUNT	42461-42461 UNIONTOWN	42724-42724 CECILIA
42262-42262 OAK GROVE	42361-42361 OLATON	42462-42462 WAVERLY	42726-42726 CLARKSON
42265-42265 OLMSTEAD	42364-42364 PELLVILLE	42463-42463 WHEATCROFT	42728-42728 COLUMBIA
42266-42266 PEMBROKE	42365-42365 PENROD	42464-42464 WHITE PLAINS	42729-42729 CUB RUN
42267-42267 PROVO	42366-42366 PHILPOT	42501-42503 SOMERSET	42731-42731 DUBRE
42270-42270 RICHARDSVILLE	42367-42367 POWDERLY	42516-42516 BETHELRIDGE	42732-42732 EASTVIEW
42273-42273 ROCHESTER	42368-42368 REYNOLDS STATION	42518-42518 BRONSTON	42733-42733 ELK HORN
42274-42274 ROCKFIELD	42369-42369 ROCKPORT	42519-42519 BURNSIDE	42735-42735 FAIRPLAY
42275-42275 ROUNDHILL	42370-42370 ROSINE	42528-42528 DUNNVILLE	42740-42740 GLENDALE
42276-42276 RUSSELLVILLE	42371-42371 RUMSEY	42533-42533 FERGUSON	42741-42741 GLENS FORK
42280-42280 SHARON GROVE	42372-42372 SACRAMENTO	42539-42539 LIBERTY	42742-42742 GRADYVILLE
42283-42283 SOUTH UNION	42374-42374 SOUTH CARROLLTON	42541-42541 MIDDLEBURG	42743-42743 GREENSBURG
42285-42285 SWEEDEN	42375-42375 STANLEY	42544-42544 NANCY	42746-42746 HARDYVILLE
42286-42286 TRENTON	42376-42376 UTICA	42553-42553 SCIENCE HILL	42748-42748 HODGENVILLE
42287-42287 WELCHS CREEK	42377-42377 WEST LOUISVILLE	42555-42555 SLOANS VALLEY	42749-42749 HORSE CAVE
42288-42288 WOODBURY	42378-42378 WHITESVILLE	42558-42558 TATEVILLE	42753-42753 KNIFLEY
42301-42304 OWENSBORO	42402-42402 BASKETT	42564-42564 WEST SOMERSET	42754-42755 LEITCHFIELD
42320-42320 BEAVER DAM	42403-42403 BLACKFORD	42565-42565 WINDSOR	42757-42757 MAGNOLIA
42321-42321 BEECH CREEK	42404-42404 CLAY	42566-42566 YOSEMITE	42758-42758 MANNSVILLE
42322-42322 BEECH GROVE	42406-42406 CORYDON	42567-42567 EUBANK	42759-42759 MARROWBONE
42323-42323 BEECHMONT	42408-42408 DAWSON SPRINGS	42602-42602 ALBANY	42761-42761 MILLTOWN
42324-42324 BELTON	42409-42409 DIXON	42603-42603 ALPHA	42762-42762 MILLWOOD
42325-42325 BREMEN	42410-42410 EARLINGTON	42629-42629 JAMESTOWN	42764-42764 MOUNT SHERMAN
42326-42326 BROWDER	42411-42411 FREDONIA	42631-42631 MARSHES SIDING	42765-42765 MUNFORDVILLE
42327-42327 CALHOUN	42413-42413 HANSON	42632-42632 MILL SPRINGS	42776-42776 SONORA
42328-42328 CENTERTOWN	42419-42420 HENDERSON	42633-42633 MONTICELLO	42780-42780 STEFF
42330-42330 CENTRAL CITY	42431-42431 MADISONVILLE	42634-42634 PARKERS LAKE	42782-42782 SUMMERSVILLE
42332-42332 CLEATON	42436-42436 MANITOU	42635-42635 PINE KNOT	42783-42783 SUMMIT
42333-42333 CROMWELL	42437-42437 MORGANFIELD	42638-42638 REVELO	42784-42784 UPTON
42334-42334 CURDSVILLE	42440-42440 MORTONS GAP	42642-42642 RUSSELL SPRINGS	42786-42786 WATERVIEW
42337-42337 DRAKESBORO	42441-42441 NEBO	42647-42647 STEARNS	42788-42788 WHITE MILLS
42338-42338 DUNDEE	42442-42442 NORTONVILLE	42649-42649 STRUNK	
42339-42339 DUNMOR	42444-42444 POOLE	42653-42653 WHITLEY CITY	
42343-42343 FORDSVILLE	42445-42445 PRINCETON	42701-42702 ELIZABETHTOWN	

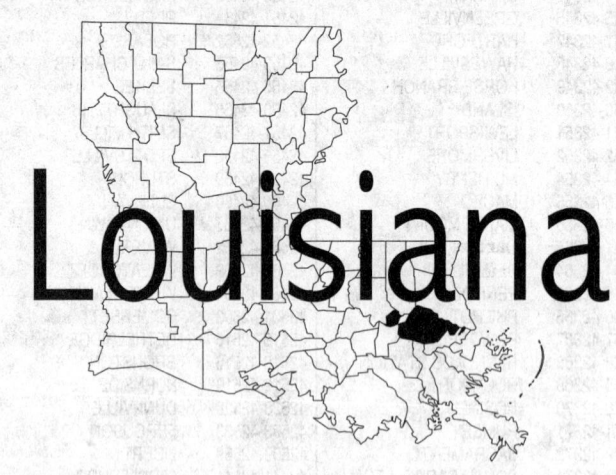

Louisiana

General Help Numbers:

Governor's Office
PO Box 94004
Baton Rouge, LA 70804-9004
http://www.gov.state.la.us

225-342-0991
Fax 225-342-7099
8AM-5PM

Attorney General's Office
LA Department of Justice
PO Box 94005
Baton Rouge, LA 70804-9005
http://www.ag.state.la.us

225-342-7013
Fax 225-342-7335
8:30AM-5PM

State Court Administrator
Judicial Council of the Supreme Court
1555 Poydras Street, Suite 1540
New Orleans, LA 70112-1814
http://www.lajao.org

504-568-5747

9AM-5PM

State Archives
Division of Archives, Records Mgt, & History   225-922-1000
3851 Essen Lane
Baton Rouge, LA 70809-2137
http://www.sec.state.la.us/archives/archives/archives-index.htm

Fax 225-922-0433
8AM-4:30PM,
9-5 SA 1-5 SU

State Specifics:

Capital:	Baton Rouge, East Baton Rouge Parish
Time Zone:	CST
Number of Parishes:	64
Population:	4,468,976
Web Site:	www.state.la.us

State Agencies

Criminal Records

State Police, Bureau of Criminal Identification, 265 S Foster, Baton Rouge, LA 70806; 225-925-6095, 225-925-7005 (Fax), 8AM-4:30PM.

http://www.lsp.org

Note: Records are available for employment screening purposes only if the employment falls under a state statute requiring a criminal record check. Sex offender and child predator data is

available online at www.lasocpr.lsp.org/Static/Search.htm.

Indexing & Storage: Records are available from the early 1900's. Records are indexed by name on computer from 1974 to present.

Searching: Records are not available to the public in general or to employers who do not qualify under a specific legislative act (such as childcare or schools). Include the following in your request-set of fingerprints, signed release. The following

data is not released: pending records or juvenile records.

Access by: mail, in person.

Fee & Payment: Fees vary by type of requester. Dealing with children or health care is $10; dealing with state licensing boards is $10 to no charge. We recommend calling first. Fee payee: State Police. Prepayment required. Business checks, cashiers' checks, and money orders are accepted. No credit cards accepted.

Mail search: Turnaround time: 30 days. No self addressed stamped envelope is required.

Corporation Records
Limited Partnership Records
Limited Liability Company Records
Trademarks/Servicemarks

Commercial Division, Corporation Department, PO Box 94125, Baton Rouge, LA 70804-9125 (Courier: 3851 Essen Lane, Baton Rouge, LA 70809); 225-925-4704, 225-925-4726 (Fax), 8AM-4:30PM.

http://www.sec.state.la.us

Note: Fictitious Names and Assumed Names are found at the parish level.

Indexing & Storage: Records are available from mid-1800s. New records are available for inquiry immediately. Records are indexed on microfilm, inhouse computer, index cards, on-line.

Searching: Include the following in your request-full name of business. In addition to the articles of incorporation, corporation records include the following information: Annual Reports, Officers, Directors, Prior (merged) names, Inactive names, Reserved names and (possibly) US Tax ID number.

Access by: mail, phone, fax, in person, online.

Fee & Payment: The search fee is $10.00. Copies cost $10.00 without amendments and $20.00 with amendments and a fee of $.25 per page after 40 pages for specific query searches on computer. Fee payee: Secretary of State. Prepayment required. Personal checks accepted. Credit cards accepted: MasterCard, Visa, AmEx.

Mail search: Turnaround time: 5 to 10 working days. No self addressed stamped envelope is required.

Phone search: You may call for information; however, only limited information is available.

Fax search: There is an additional $1.00 per page fee if returned by fax. Turnaround time is 5 to 10 working days.

In person search: There is a free public access terminal.

Online search: There are 2 ways to go: free on the Internet or pay. Free but limited information is available on the web site; go to "Commercial Division, Corporations Section," then "Search Corporations Database." The pay system is $360 per year for unlimited access. Almost any communications software will work with up to a 14,400 baud rate. The system is open from 6:30 am to 11pm. For more information, call Brenda Wright at (225) 922-1475.

Other access: The state offers corporation, LLC, partnership, and trademark information on tape cartridges. For more info, call 225-925-4792.

Expedited service: Expedited service is available for mail and phone searches. Turnaround time: 1 day. Add $20.00 per business name.

Uniform Commercial Code

Secretary of State, UCC Records, PO Box 94125, Baton Rouge, LA 70804-9125; 800-256-3758, 225-342-9011 (Fax), 8AM-4:30PM.

http://www.sec.state.la.us/comm/ucc-index.htm

Note: The statewide index of UCC filings is available in each parish office. All tax liens and financial statements are filed at the parish level. IRS liens show up on UCC records. Records CANNOT be obtained from this office, except via the online system.

Indexing & Storage: Records are available for all active listings. Records are indexed on computer since 1990. It takes 2 days before new records are available for inquiry.

Searching: All filing information including debtor names, property descriptions, and subsequent filings and amendments are available. Mail-in requests are sent to the parish involved.

Access by: online.

Fee & Payment: Fees are only for the online service. Fee payee: Secretary of State. Prepayment required. The payment information outlined here applies only to online access. Personal checks accepted. Credit cards accepted: MasterCard, Visa. Records are available by mail.

Online search: An annual $400 fee gives unlimited access to UCC filing information. The dial-up service is open from 6:30 AM to 11 PM daily. Minimum baud rate is 9600. Most any software communications program can be configured to work. For further information, call Brenda Wright at 225-922-1475, or visit the web site.

Federal Tax Liens
State Tax Liens
Records not maintained by a state level agency.

Note: Records are filed with the Clerk of Court at the parish level.

Sales Tax Registrations
Access to Records is Restricted

Revenue and Tax Department, Sales Tax Division, PO Box 201, Baton Rouge, LA 70821-0201 (Courier: 330 N Ardenwwod Blvd, Baton Rouge, LA 70806); 225-925-7356, 225-925-3860 (Fax), 8AM-4:30PM.

http://www.rev.state.la.us

Note: This agency will only provide registration information to the registrant itself.

Birth Certificates

Vital Records Registry, Office of Public Health, PO Box 60630, New Orleans, LA 70160 (Courier: 325 Loyola Ave Room 102, New Orleans, LA 70112); 504-568-5152, 504-568-5167 (For adoptions), 504-568-5391 (Fax), 8AM-4PM.

http://www.dhh.state.la.us/OPH/VITAL/index.htm

Note: Some certificates (all types of vital records) contain information at the bottom of the document that is confidential and not released to anyone. This information is used for statistical purposes and varies depending on legislative action.

Indexing & Storage: Records are available from 1914 on. Birth records for only the City of New Orleans are available from 1900 on. Records older than 100 years should be ordered from the State Archives. New records are available for inquiry immediately. Records are indexed on microfiche, index cards, inhouse computer.

Searching: Birth certificates are considered confidential for 100 years. Requesters must be related to the person of record or have a signed release. Include the following in your request-full name, names of parents, mother's maiden name, date of birth, place of birth, relationship to person of record, reason for information request. Older records must be searched at the State Archives 225-922-1184.

Access by: mail, fax, in person.

Fee & Payment: A "long form" birth certificate is $15.00, while a "birth card" is $9.00. Fee payee: Vital Records Registry. Prepayment required. Credit cards are not accepted for mail requests. Personal checks accepted. Credit cards accepted: MasterCard, Visa.

Mail search: Turnaround time: 3 weeks. No self addressed stamped envelope is required.

Fax search: Fax requests are with a credit card number only. See expedited service.

In person search: Photo ID required, turnaround time immediate.

Expedited service: Expedited service is available for mail, fax, and phone searches. Turnaround time: 24 to 48 hours. Add $15.50 per packageplus additional 2.5% for use of credit card. You must include written authorization to charge document fee and shipment fee to your credit card. The extra fee is over overnight delivery.

Death Records

Vital Records Registry, Office of Public Health, PO Box 60630, New Orleans, LA 70160 (Courier: 325 Loyola Ave Room 102, New Orleans, LA 70112); 504-568-5152, 504-568-5273 (Corrections), 504-568-5391 (Fax), 8AM-4PM.

http://www.dhh.state.la.us/OPH/vrinfo.htm

Indexing & Storage: Records are available from 1950 on. Older records must be obtained from the State Archives. New records are available for inquiry immediately. Records are indexed on microfiche, index cards, inhouse computer.

Searching: Death records are considered confidential for 50 years. Must show how related or have a signed release from immediate family member if for investigative purposes. Include the following in your request-full name, date of death, place of death, relationship to person of record, reason for information request. Records older than 50 years must be searched at the State Archives 225-922-1184.

Access by: mail, fax, in person.

Fee & Payment: The search fee is $5.00. Fee payee: Department of Vital Records. Prepayment required. Credit cards accepted for fax and in person requests only. Personal checks accepted. Credit cards accepted: MasterCard, Visa.

Mail search: Turnaround time: 3 weeks. No self addressed stamped envelope is required.

Fax search: Fax requests require use of credit card and are charged expedited fees.

In person search: In person search requires a photo ID. Turnaround time usually 45 minutes.

Expedited service: Expedited service is available for mail and phone searches. Turnaround time: 24 to 48 hours. Add $15.50 per package, add 2.5% for use of credit card. You must include written authorization to charge document fee and shipping fee to credit card.

Marriage Certificates
Divorce Records
Records not maintained by a state level agency.

Note: Only Orleans Parish marriage records are available from 1948 on at the VR Registry for a fee of $5.00 same search criteria as others. Include name of bride (maiden)

groom and date of marriage. Other marriage records and all divorce records are only found at parish of issue. Marriage Records older than 50 years are open to the public.

Workers' Compensation Records

Department of Labor, Office of Workers' Compensation, PO Box 94040, Baton Rouge, LA 70804-9040 (Courier: LA Department of Labor, Office of Workers' Compensation, Baton Rouge, LA 70802); 225-342-2056, 225-342-7582 (Fax), 8AM-5PM.

http://www.laworks.net

Note: For partial information, and to determine if a record exists, and if you have the name and SSN, see the Other Access section below.

Indexing & Storage: Records are available from 1983 to present on microfilm. Only cases on file are those where the employee lost 7 days or more of work and/or had disputed issues resolved or settlements approved. New records are available for inquiry immediately. Records are indexed on microfilm.

Searching: Most records are considered confidential. Public records include decisions, awards, or orders in disputed cases. No records are released until "copy" charges are paid. Include the following in your request-claimant name, Social Security Number, date of accident, reason for information request, specific records that you need copies of. All record requests must be in writing. The following data is not released: pending records.

Access by: mail, phone, fax, in person.

Fee & Payment: Copies are $.25 per page, $1.00 to certify, there is no fee to search. Fee payee: Workers' Compensation Administrative Fund. Prepayment required. Cash is not accepted. Personal checks accepted. No credit cards accepted.

Mail search: Turnaround time: 7 to 10 days.

Phone search: With a name and SSN (required), you may use the "Easy Call" Interactive Voice Response System at 225-342-8731 for partial public information, especially to determine if a record exists.

Fax search: Records can be requested by fax at no extra fee.

In person search: If you request in person, the turnaround time is shortened only by the mail time.

Other access: With a name and SSN (required), you may use the "Easy Call" Interactive Voice Response System at 225-342-8731 for partial public information, especially to determine if a record exists. Enter 1-4-1-2-2 after the phone answers.

Driver Records

Dept of Public Safety and Corrections, Office of Motor Vehicles, PO Box 64886, Baton Rouge, LA

70896 (Courier: 109 S Foster Dr, Baton Rouge, LA 70806); 877-368-5463, 225-925-6388, 225-925-6915 (Fax), 8AM-4:30PM.

http://www.dps.state.la.us/omv/home.html

Note: Copies of tickets may be obtained from the address listed above. The fee is $5.00 per page.

Indexing & Storage: Records are available for 3 years for moving violations, 10 years from date of conviction for DWIs and 5 or 10 years for suspensions. Accidents are reported, but fault is not shown. It takes 2 to 3 weeks before new records are available for inquiry.

Searching: Casual requesters can obtain driving records with proper release form signed by subject. Include the following in your request-driver's license number, full name, date of birth. It is sometimes helpful to include the race or sex when requesting a record.

Access by: mail, in person, online.

Fee & Payment: The fee for mail-in or walk-in requests is $15.00 per name. The fee for online or tape requests is $6.00. Fee payee: Office of Motor Vehicles. Prepayment required. No credit cards accepted.

Mail search: Turnaround time: 10 working days. No self addressed stamped envelope is required.

In person search: Walk-in requesters may "view" a record for no charge. Casual requesters must present signed form. The fee is for the hard copy. Records can be requested from the Motor Vehicle Offices in New Orleans, Lake Charles, Monroe, Baton Rouge, Shreveport, and Alexandria.

Online search: Online, interactive mode is available from 7 AM to 9:30 PM daily. There is a minimum order requirement of 2,000 requests per month. A bond or large deposit is required. Fee is $6.00 per record. For more information, call 225-925-6032. There are plans to convert to an Internet based system later in 2001.

Other access: Tape ordering is available for batch delivery. Bulk database sales are available to permissible users.

Vehicle Ownership
Vehicle Identification

Department of Public Safety & Corrections, Office of Motor Vehicles, PO Box 64886, Baton Rouge, LA 70896 (Courier: 109 S Foster Dr, Baton Rouge, LA 70806); 225-922-6146, 877-368-5463, 225-925-3979 (Fax), 8AM-4PM.

http://www.dps.state.la.us/dmv/home.html

Indexing & Storage: Records are available from the 1950's (only if plate or title is known). Records indexed on computer from 1970 to present and 1970 to 1998 on microfiche, if active.

Searching: Casual requesters can obtain records, but personal information is not released without consent of subject. The state requires a written request stating the nature of the inquiry. The following data is not released: Social Security Numbers.

Access by: mail, fax, in person, online.

Fee & Payment: The current fee for VIN, registration, and plate checks is $10.00 per record. Fee payee: Office of Motor Vehicles. Prepayment required. Personal checks accepted. No credit cards accepted.

Mail search: Turnaround time: within 2 weeks. Mail searches require license plate number or

vehicle identification number (VIN).A self addressed stamped envelope is requested.

Fax search: Requesters must be pre-approved. The fee is $10.00 per record. Turnaround time: 5-10 working days.

In person search: You may request information in person.

Online search: Online access costs $6.00 per record. Minimum usage is 2,000 requests per month. The online system operates similar to the system for driving records. For more information: Dept. of Public Safety and Corrections, PO Box 66614, Baton Rouge, LA 70896; 225-925-6032.

Other access: Louisiana offers bulk retrieval of vehicle and license data. A letter of agreement must be signed and the purpose of the request expressed. Further resale of the data is prohibited.

Accident Reports

Louisiana State Police, Accident Records, PO Box 66614, Baton Rouge, LA 70896 (Courier: 265 S Foster Blvd, Baton Rouge, LA 70806); 225-925-6157, 225-925-4922 (Fax), 8AM-4:30PM.

Indexing & Storage: Records are available from 1980's to present. It takes 2 to 3 weeks before new records are available for inquiry.

Searching: The driver name(s), date of accident and parish are needed when ordering.

Access by: mail, in person.

Fee & Payment: The fee is $7.50 per record. Fee payee: Louisiana State Police. Prepayment required. Personal checks are not accepted. No credit cards accepted.

Mail search: Turnaround time: 10 working days. A self addressed stamped envelope is requested.

In person search: Turnaround time is while you wait, if personnel not busy.

Vessel Ownership
Vessel Registration

Department of Wildlife & Fisheries, PO Box 14796, Baton Rouge, LA 70898 (Courier: 2000 Quail Road, Baton Rouge, LA 70898); 225-765-2898, 225-763-5421 (Fax), 8:15AM-4:15PM.

http://www.wlf.state.la.us

Note: Lien information is found at the parish level.

Indexing & Storage: Records are available from 1960 to present. Record are indexed on computer from the 1970s to present. All motorized boats and sailboats over 12 ft must be registered.

Searching: The hull ID # is not released. To search, one of the following is required: Louisiana #, name, or hull ID #, and from whom boat was acquired. Records are subject to DPPA and 14 permissible uses. Records are not released to the general public unless subject has given permission.

Access by: mail.

Fee & Payment: There is no fee. Fee payee: Department of Wildlife and Fisheries. Prepayment required. Payments are only required for list purchases. Personal checks accepted. No credit cards accepted.

Mail search: Turnaround time: 7 to 10 days. No self addressed stamped envelope is required.

Other access: Records can be purchased in bulk in a variety of media formats. There is a $100.00 minimum deposit, the fee is $.05 per record.

Legislation Records

Louisiana House (Senate) Representative, State Capitol, 2nd Floor, PO Box 44486, Baton Rouge, LA 70804; 225-342-2456 (Information Help Desk), 225-342-2365 (Senate Documents (Room 205)), 225-342-6458 (House Documents (Room 207)), 800-256-3793 (General Information, In-state), 8AM-5PM.

http://www.legis.state.la.us

Note: Sessions are from the last Monday in April for 60 days in even numbered years, In March for 85 days in odd numbered years. The PO Box above is for the House; the PO Box for Senate bills is 94183.

Indexing & Storage: Records are available from 1952 to present, 1997 forward is on Internet. Records are indexed on microfiche.

Searching: Include the following in your request-bill number, year. Call first on the passed bills for location on microfiche. Pending bills are available in hard copy.

Access by: mail, phone, fax, in person, online.

Fee & Payment: Copies are $.25 per page. Fee payee: LA Legislative Document Services. Will send invoices. Personal checks accepted. No credit cards accepted.

Mail search: Turnaround time: same day if possible. A minimum of $1.50 postage applies.No self addressed stamped envelope is required.

Phone search: A minimum of $1.50 for postage applies.

Fax search: The fee is $1.00 per page for items returned by fax.

In person search: No fee for request.

Online search: The Internet site has a wealth of information about sessions and bills from 1997 forward.

Voter Registration

Department of Elections & Registration, PO Box 14179, Baton Rouge, LA 70898-4179; 225-925-7885, 225-925-1841 (Fax), 8AM-5PM.

http://www.laelections.org

Note: Although the information is public record, individual searching must be done at the parish level through the Parish Registrar of Voters.

Indexing & Storage: Records are available for all currently registered voters.

Searching: The following data is not released: Social Security Numbers or phone numbers.

Access by:. No searching by mail.

Other access: The state will sell the database statewide or by parish. Media formats include disk, tape, labels, CD, and lists. There are no restrictions regarding purchasing for marketing purposes. Call 225-925-7873 for more information.

GED Certificates

Division of Audit Education & Training, PO Box 94064, Baton Rouge, LA 70804-9064; 225-342-0444 (Main Number), 225-219-4439 (Fax).

Searching: To search, you must use their form, which may be requested via phone, fax, or mail.

Access by: mail, fax, in person.

Fee & Payment: There is no fee.

Mail search: Turnaround time 2 weeks.No self addressed stamped envelope is required.

Fax search: Results of a fax search will be mailed, same criteria as mail searches.

In person search: In person searchers must have a photo ID. Turnaround time: Immediate.

Hunting License Information
Fishing License Information

Wildlife & Fisheries Department, License Division, PO Box 98000, Baton Rouge, LA 70898-9000 (Courier: 2000 Quail Dr, Baton Rouge, LA 70808); 225-765-2881, 225-765-3150 (Fax), 8:15AM-4:15PM.

http://www.wlf.state.la.us

Note: Their central database has been modified an is now supplied by the DMV. All license information is subject to the DPPA under US Code 18. At present, not all 14 permissible uses are readily available and use of a subpoena is suggested.

Indexing & Storage: Records are available from 1987 and are on computer.

Searching: The following data is not released: Social Security Numbers.

Access by: Records are available by mail.

Louisiana State Licensing Agencies

Licenses Searchable Online

Acupuncturist #20...www.lsbme.org/bmeSearch/licenseesearch.asp
Athletic Trainer #20...www.lsbme.org/bmeSearch/licenseesearch.asp
Bank #32..www.ofi.state.la.us/newbanks.htm
Bond For Deed Agency #32..............................www.ofi.state.la.us/newbfd.htm
Check Casher #32..www.ofi.state.la.us/newcheckcash.htm
Clinical Lab Personnel #20................................www.lsbme.org/bmeSearch/licenseesearch.asp
Collection Agency #32.......................................www.ofi.state.la.us/newcolagn.htm
Consumer Credit Grantor #32...........................www.ofi.state.la.us/newliclen.htm
Counselor, Professional (LPC) #46..................www.lpcboard.org/lpc_alpha_list.htm
Credit Repair Agency #32..................................www.ofi.state.la.us/newcredrep.htm
Credit Union #32...www.ofi.state.la.us/newcus.htm
Dental Hygienist #09..www.lsbd.org/fpDentistSearch.asp
Dentist #09...www.lsbd.org/dentistsearch.asp
Drug Distributor, Wholesale #64.......................http://host.ntg.com/ldwdd/search.asp
Engineer #40..www.lapels.com/indv_reg.html
Exercise Physiologist, Clinical #20...................www.lsbme.org/bmeSearch/licenseesearch.asp
Insurance Agent/Broker #33..............................www.ldi.state.la.us/searchforms/searchform.asp
Insurance Agent-LHA/PC #33...........................www.ldi.state.la.us/searchforms/searchform.asp
Land Surveyor #40...www.lapels.com/indv_reg.html
Lender #32..www.ofi.state.la.us/newliclen.htm
Lobbyist #66...www.ethics.state.la.us/lobs.htm
Medical Doctor #20..www.lsbme.org/bmeSearch/licenseesearch.asp
Midwife #20..www.lsbme.org/bmeSearch/licenseesearch.asp
Mortgage Lender/Broker, Residential #32.........www.ofi.state.la.us/newrml.htm
Notary Public #54...www.sec.state.la.us/notary-pub/NTRINQ.htm
Notification Filer #32..www.ofi.state.la.us/newnotif.htm
Occupational Therapist/Technologist #20..........www.lsbme.org/bmeSearch/licenseesearch.asp
Optometrist #22..www.odfinder.org/LicSearch.asp
Osteopathic Physician #20................................www.lsbme.org/bmeSearch/licenseesearch.asp
Pawnbroker #32..www.ofi.state.la.us/newpawn.htm
Physician Assistant #20.....................................www.lsbme.org/bmeSearch/licenseesearch.asp
Podiatrist #20..www.lsbme.org/bmeSearch/licenseesearch.asp
Radiologic Technologist, Private #20.................www.lsbme.org/bmeSearch/licenseesearch.asp
Respiratory Therapist/Therapy Technician #20..www.lsbme.org/bmeSearch/licenseesearch.asp
Savings & Loan #32..www.ofi.state.la.us/newcus.htm
Solicitor #33...www.ldi.state.la.us/searchforms/searchform.asp
Thrift & Loan Company #32................................www.ofi.state.la.us/newthrift.htm
Vocational Rehabilitative Counselor #63...........www.lrcboard.org/licensee_database.asp

Licensing Quick Finder

Acupuncturist #20 504-524-6820	Blood Alcohol Analyst #01 225-925-6216	225-756-3404
Adult Day Care #35 225-022-0015	Boiler Inspector/Installer #55 225-925-4344	Counselor, Professional (LPC) #46 225-765-2515
Adult Education Instructor #42 225-342-3490	Bond For Deed Agency #32 225-925-4660	Credit Repair Agency #32 225-925-4660
Adult Residential Care #35 225-022-0015	Boxing/Wrestling Personnel #27 337-828-7154	Credit Union #32 225-925-4660
Agricultural Consultant #56 225-925-3787	Burglar Alarm Contractor #55 225-925-6766	Day Care Facilities #35 225-922-0015
Alcoholic Beverage Vendor #03 225-925-4041	Cemetery #02 504-838-5267	Dental Hygienist #09 504-568-8574
Amusement Ride/Attraction Inspector #55	Check Casher #32 225-925-4660	Dentist #09 504-568-8574
....225-925-7045	Check Seller #32 225-925-4660	Dietitian #13 225-763-5490
Amusement Ride/Attraction Owner/Operator #55	Chemical Engineer #40 225-925-6291	Drug Distributor, Wholesale #64 225-295-8567
....225-925-7045	Child Nutrition Program Supervisor #42 225-342-3490	Electrical Engineer #40 225-925-6291
Appraiser #29 225-925-4771	Child Residential Care #35 225-022-0015	Electrologist #10 318-463-6180
Arborist/Utility Arborist #39 225-925-7772	Chiropractor #07 225-765-2322	Electronics Repairman; Radio/TV/Recording Device
Architect/Architectural Firm #50 225-925-4802	Clinical Lab Personnel #20 504-524-6820	#34 225-231-4710
Art Therapist #42 225-342-3490	Collection Agency #32 225-925-4660	Embalmer #12 504-838-5109
Athletic Trainer #20 504-524-6820	Compulsive Gambler Counselor #28 225-927-7600	Emergency Medical Technician #20 504-524-6820
Attorney #49 504-566-1600	Consumer Credit Grantor #32 225-925-4667	Emergency Shelter #35 225-922-0015
Auctioneer/Auction Company #44 225-922-2329	Contractor (Residential/Commercial) #41	Engineer/ Engineer Intern #40 225-925-6291
Bank #32 225-925-4660	225-765-2301	Environmental Engineer #40 225-925-6291
Barber/Barber Shop/Instructor/School #04	Contractor, General #30 504-736-7125	Equine Dentist #45 225-342-2176
....225-925-1701	Cosmetologist/Cosmetology Instructor #08	Esthetician #08 225-756-3404

Euthanasia Technician #45 225-342-2176
Exercise Physiologist, Clinical #20 504-524-6820
Explosives Dealer/Handler #38 225-925-6178
Family Support #35 225-022-0015
Fire Alarm Contractor #55 225-925-6766
Fire Extinguisher Contractor #55.........225-925-6766
Fire Protection Sprinkler Contractor #55225-925-6766
Fire Suppression Contractor #55 225-925-6766
Florist, Retail/Wholesale #39 225-925-7772
Foster Care/Adoption Care #35 225-922-0015
Funeral Director/Establishment #12 504-838-5109
Funeral Home Internship/Work Permit #12................
....504-838-5109
Guidance Counselor #42 225-342-3490
Hearing Aid Dealer #19 318-362-3014
Horse Owner/Trainer #52 504-483-4000
Horse Racing #52 504-483-4000
Horse Racing-related Profession (Groom, Plater, etc.)
#52 504-483-4000
Horticulturist #39 225-925-7772
Infant Intervention Services #35............225-022-0015
Insurance Agent/Broker #33 225-342-0860
Insurance Agent-LHA/PC #33..............225-342-0860
Interior Designer #14...........................225-298-1283
Investment Advisor #53........................225-925-4660
Jockey/Apprentice/Jockey Agent #52....504-483-4000
Juvenile Detention #35.........................225-022-0015
Land Surveying Intern #40....................225-925-6291
Land Surveyor #40...............................225-925-6291
Landscape Architect #39 225-925-7772
Landscape Contractor #39 225-925-7772
Lender #32 225-925-4660
Livestock Branding #43 225-925-3962
Loan Broker #32 225-925-4660
Lobbyist #66 225-992-1400
Lottery #47...225-297-2000
Lottery Claims Center #48 504-889-0031
Manicurist #08 225-756-3404
Manufactured Home Installer/Developer #55............
....225-925-4911
Manufactured Home Mfg. #55 225-925-4911
Manufactured Housing Dealer/Salesman #55
....225-925-4911

Massage Therapist #62 225-658-8941
Maternity Home #35 225-922-0015
Medical Doctor #20 504-524-6820
Medical Gas Piping Installer #51.........504-826-2382
Midwife #20 504-524-6820
Montessori Teacher #42 225-342-3490
Mortgage Lender/Broker, Residential #32 ....
....225-925-4662
Motor Vehicle Agent/Salesman # 59 504-838-5207
Motor Vehicle Dealer; New/Used #59 504-838-5207
Motor Vehicle Inspector #01 225-925-6984
Motor Vehicle Leasing/Rental Company # 59............
....504-838-5207
Motor Vehicle Sales Finance Company #59 ....
....504-838-5207
Music Therapist #42 225-342-3490
Notary Public #54.................................225-342-4981
Notification Filer #32............................225-992-0634
Nuclear Engineer #40...........................225-925-6291
Nuclear Medicine Technologist #16 504-838-5231
Nurse #21...504-838-5332
Nurse (Practical) School #25 504-568-6480
Nurse, Student #21 504-838-5332
Nurse-LPN #25 504-568-6480
Nurses' Aide #36 225-925-4132
Nursing Home Administrator #36 225-925-4132
Nursing School #21..............................504-838-5332
Nutritionist #13 225-763-5490
Occupational Therapist/Technologist #20................
....504-524-6820
Optometrist #22 318-335-2989
Osteopathic Physician #20 504-524-6820
Pari-Mutuel Employee #52 504-483-4000
Pawnbroker #32 225-925-4660
Payday Lender #32 225-925-4660
Personal Care Attendant #35................225-922-0015
Pesticide Applicator/Operator#31..........225-925-3787
Pesticide Dealer #56 225-925-3796
Pharmacist/Pharmacy #23....................225-925-6496
Physical Therapist/Therapist Asst #24 ..337-262-1043
Physician Assistant #20.......................504-524-6820
Plumber Journeyman/Master #51 504-826-2382
Podiatrist #20.......................................504-524-6820

Polygraph Examiner #57 504-389-3836
Prevention Specialist (Social Work)#28.225-927-7600
Private Investigator/PI Company #58 225-763-3556
Private Security #26 225-295-8486
Psychologist #15 225-763-3935
Public Accountant-CPA #05..................504-566-1244
Radiation Therapy Technologist #16 504-838-5231
Radio & TV Technician #40 225-925-6291
Radiographer #16 504-838-5231
Radiologic Technologist #16.................504-838-5231
Radiologic Technologist, Private #20 504-524-6820
Reading Specialist #42.........................225-342-3490
Real Estate Broker/Salesperson #60 225-925-4771
Respiratory Therapist/Therapy Technician #20 ....
....504-524-6820
Respite Care #35 225-022-0015
Sanitarian #17......................................318-676-7489
Savings & Loan #32 225-925-4660
School Counselor/Librarian/Nurse/Principal #42.........
....225-342-3490
School Psychologist #42 225-342-3490
School Superintendent, Parish or City #42 ....
....225-342-3490
School Therapist #42 225-342-3490
Securities Dealer/Salesperson #53 225-925-4660
Security Guard #26 225-295-8486
Shorthand Reporter #37 225-925-7671
Social Worker #06 225-763-5470
Solicitor #33 225-342-0860
Speech Pathologist/Audiologist #18 225-763-5480
Speech/Language/Hearing Teacher #42 ....
....225-342-3490
Substance Abuse Counselor #28..........225-927-7600
Supervised Independent Living #35 225-022-0015
Surveyor #40 225-925-6291
Teacher, Temporary #42 225-342-3490
Teacher/Teacher's Aide #11 225-342-3490
Thrift & Loan Company #32..................225-925-4660
Timeshare Interest Salesperson #60......225-925-4771
Used Vehicle Salesperson #61 225-925-3870
Veterinarian/Veterinary Technician#45..225-342-2176
Vocational Rehabilitative Counselor#63 225-922-1435
Water Supply Piping #51 504-826-2382

Licensing Agency Information

#01 State Police Safety & Enforcement, PO Box 66614, Baton Rouge, LA 70896; 225-925-6984, Fax: 225-925-3966.

#02 Cemetery Board, 2901 Ridgelake Dr, #101, Metairie, LA 70002-4946; 504-838-5267, Fax: 504-838-5289.

#03 Board of Alcohol & Tobacco, PO Box 66404, Baton Rouge, LA 70896-6404; 225-925-4041, Fax: 225-925-3975.
www.atcla.com/home.cfm

#04 Board of Barber Examiners, PO Box 14029, Baton Rouge, LA 70898-4029; 225-925-1701, Fax: 225-925-1703.
www.barber-cosmos.com

#05 Board of Certified Public Accountants, 601 Poydras St, #1770, New Orleans, LA 70130; 504-566-1244, Fax: 504-566-1252.

#06 Board of Certified Social Work Examiners, 11930 Perkins Rd, #B, Baton Rouge, LA 70810; 225-763-5470, Fax: 225-763-5400.
www.labswe.org

#07 Board of Chiropractic Examiners, 8621 Summa Ave, Baton Rouge, LA 70809; 225-765-2322, Fax: 225-765-2640.
www.dhh.state.la.us/boards.htm

#08 Board of Cosmetology, 11622 Sunbelt Court, Baton Rouge, LA 70809; 225-756-3404, Fax: 225-756-3410/3109.

#09 Board of Dentistry, 365 Canal Street, Suite 2680, New Orleans, LA 70112; 504-568-8574, Fax: 504-568-8598.
www.lsbd.org
Direct web site URL to search for licensees: www.lsbd.org/DentistSearch.asp. You can search online using name or license #

#10 Board of Electrolysis Examiners, PO Box 67, DeRidder, LA 70634-0067; 318-463-6180, Fax: 318-463-3991.

#11 Board of Elementary & Secondary Education, 626 N 4th St, Baton Rouge, LA 70804-9064; 225-342-3490, Fax: 225-342-3499.
www.doe.state.la.us

#12 Board of Embalmers & Funeral Directors, 3500 N Causeway Blvd, #1232, New Orleans, LA 70002; 504-838-5109, Fax: 504-838-5112.
www.lsbefd.state.la.us

#13 Board of Examiners of Dietitics & Nutrition, 11930 Perkins Rd, #B, Baton Rouge, LA 70810; 225-763-5490, Fax: 225-763-5400.

#14 Board of Examiners of Interior Designers, 2900 Westfork Dr #200, Baton Rouge, LA 70827-0004; 225-298-1283, Fax: 225-925-1892.

#15 Board of Examiners of Psychologists, 8280 YMCA Plaza Dr, Bldg 8B, Baton Rouge, LA 70810; 225-763-3935, Fax: 225-763-3968.
www.lsbep.org
Direct web site URL to search for licensees: www.lsbep.org. You can search online using A list of current members is available on the web site, updated infrequently.

#16 Board of Examiners of Radiologic Technologists, 3108 Cleary Ave, #207, Metairie, LA 70002; 504-838-5231, Fax: 504-780-1740.

#17 Board of Examiners of Sanitarians, 1525 Fairfield Ave, Rm 569, Shreveport, LA 71101-4388; 318-676-7489, Fax: 318-676-7560.

#18 Board of Examiners of Speech/Language Pathology & Audiology, 11930 Perkins Rd, #B, Baton Rouge, LA 70810; 225-763-5480, Fax: 225-763-5400.
www.lbespa.org/

#19 Board of Hearing Aid Dealers, 2205 Liberty St, Monroe, LA 71211-6016; 318-362-3014, Fax: 318-362-3019.

#20 Executive Director, 630 Camp St, New Orleans, LA 70130; 504-524-6820, auto response: dial 1, Fax: 504-568-8893.
www.lsbme.org

Direct web site URL to search for licensees: www.lsbme.org/bmeSearch/licenseesearch.asp

#21 Board of Nursing, 3510 N Causeway Blvd, #501, Metairie, LA 70002; 504-838-5332, Fax: 504-838-5349.
www.lsbn.state.la.us

#22 Board of Optometry Examiners, 115 B N 13th St, Oakdale, LA 71463; 318-335-2989, Fax: 318-335-2989.
Direct web site URL to search for licensees: www.odfinder.org/LicSearch.asp. You can search online using national database by name, city or state.

#23 Board of Pharmacy, 5615 Corporate Blvd, #8E, Baton Rouge, LA 70808; 225-925-6496, Fax: 225-925-6499.
www.labp.com

#24 Board of Physical Therapy Examiners, 714 E Kaliste Saloom Rd #D2, Lafayette, LA 70508; 337-262-1043, Fax: 337-262-1054.
www.laptboard.org

#25 Board of Practical Nurse Examiners, 3421 N Causeway Blvd #203, Metairie, LA 70002-3711; 504-838-5791, Fax: 504-838-5279.
www.lsbpne.com

#26 Board of Private Security Examiners, PO Box 86510, Baton Rouge, LA 70879-6510; 225-295-8486, Fax: 225-295-8498.

#27 Boxing & Wrestling Commission, PO Box 251, Franklin, LA 70538; 337-828-7154.

#28 Board of Certification for Substance Abuse Counselors, 4637 Jamestown #2A, Baton Rouge, LA 70808; 225-927-7600, Fax: 225-927-8150.
www.lsbcsac.org

#29 Real Estate Appraisers State Board of Certification, PO Box 14785, Baton Rouge, LA 70898; 225-925-4771, Fax: 225-925-4431.
www.lreasbc.state.la.us

#30 Contractors Licensing Board, 1221 Elmwood Pk Blvd, New Orleans, LA 70141; 504-736-7125, Fax: 504-736-7125 *Key.

#32 Department of Economic Development, 8660 United Plaza Blvd, 2nd Floor, Baton Rouge, LA 70809; 225-925-4660, Fax: 225-925-4548.
www.ofi.state.la.us

#33 Department of Insurance, 950 N 5th, Baton Rouge, LA 70802; 225-342-0860, Fax: 225-342-3078.
www.ldi.state.la.us

#34 Radio And Television Technicians Board, 6554 Florida Boulevard #109, Baton Rouge, LA 70806; 225-231-4710.

#35 Department of Social Services, PO Box 3078, Baton Rouge, LA 70821; 225-922-0015, Fax: 225-922-0014.
www.dss.state.la.us/offos/html/licensing.html

#36 Examiners of Nursing Facility Administrators, 5615 Corporate Blvd, #8D, Baton Rouge, LA 70808; 225-922-0009, Fax: 225-922-0006.

#37 Examiners of Certified Shorthand Reporters, PO Box 3257, Baton Rouge, LA 70821-3257; 225-925-7671, Fax: 225-925-7672.

www.lacourtreporterboard.com

#38 Explosives Control Unit, PO Box 66614, Mail Stop 21, Baton Rouge, LA 70896; 225-925-6178 x208, Fax: 225-925-4048.
www.dps.state.la.us/lsp

#39 Department of Agriculture, PO Box 3596, Baton Rouge, LA 70821-3596; 225-925-7772, Fax: 225-925-3760.

#40 Professional Engineers & Land Surveying Board, 9643 Brookline Ave #121, Baton Rouge, LA 70809-1433; 225-925-6291, Fax: 225-925-6292.
www.lapels.com
Direct web site URL to search for licensees: www.lapels.com/indv_reg.html. You can search online using alphabetical lists

#41 Licensing Board for Contractors, PO Box 14419, Baton Rouge, LA 70898-4419; 225-765-2301, Fax: 225-765-2431.

#42 Department of Education, 626 N 4th St, Baton Rouge, LA 70804-9064; 225-342-3490, Fax: 225-342-3499.
www.doe.state.la.us

#43 LA Dept of Agriculture & Forestry, PO Box 1951 (5825 Florida Blvd, 70806), Baton Rouge, LA 70821; 225-925-3962, Fax: 225-925-4103.
www.ldaf.state.la.us

#44 Auctioneers Licensing Board, 8017 Jefferson Hwy, #A-2, Baton Rouge, LA 70809; 225-922-2329, Fax: 225-925-1892.

#45 Board of Veterinary Medicine, 263 3rd St, #104, Baton Rouge, LA 70801; 225-342-2176, Fax: 225-342-2142.

#46 Licensed Professional Counselors, 8631 Summa Ave, #A, Baton Rouge, LA 70809; 225-765-2515, Fax: 225-765-2514.
www.lpcboard.org
Direct web site URL to search for licensees: www.lpcboard.org/lpc_alpha_list.htm

#47 Lottery Corporation, 11200 Industriplex, #190, Baton Rouge, LA 70809; 225-297-2000, Fax: 225-297-2005.
www.lalottery.com

#48 Lottery Corporation, 2222 Clearview Parkway, Metairie, LA 70001; 504-889-0031, Fax: 504-889-0490.
www.louisianalottery.com

#49 State Bar Association, 601 St Charles Av, New Orleans, LA 70130; 504-566-1600, Fax: 504-566-0930.
www.lsba.org

#50 Board of Architectural Examiners, 8017 Jefferson Hwy B-2, Baton Rouge, LA 70809; 225-925-4802, Fax: 225-925-4804.
www.lastbdarchs.com
Direct web site URL to search for licensees: www.lastbdarchs.com/roster.htm. You can search online using name.

#51 Plumbing Board, 2714 Canal St, #512, New Orleans, LA 70119; 504-826-2382, Fax: 504-826-2175.

#52 Racing Commission, 320 N Carrollton Ave, #2B, New Orleans, LA 70119-5100; 504-483-4000, Fax: 504-483-4898.
www.lded.state.la.us/new/lrc/lrcmain.htm

#53 Securities, PO Box 94095 (8660 United Plaza Blvd, 2nd Fl), Baton Rouge, LA 70804; 225-925-4660, Fax: 225-925-4548.
www.ofi.state.la.us

#54 Office of Secretary of State, PO Box 94125, Baton Rouge, LA 70804-9125; 225-342-4981, Fax: 225-342-2066.
www.sec.state.la.us/notary-pub/notary.htm
Direct web site URL to search for licensees: www.sec.state.la.us/notary-pub/NTRINQ.htm. You can search online using alpha or zip code

#55 Office of the State Fire Marshall, 5150 Florida Blvd, Baton Rouge, LA 70806; 225-925-4911; 800-256-5452, Fax: 225-925-4241.
www.dps.state.la.us/sfm/

#56 Agricultural & Environmental Sciences, 5825 Florida Blvd, Baton Rouge, LA 70806; 225-925-3796, Fax: 225-925-3760.
www.ldaf.state.la.us

#57 Polygraph Board, 9746 W Wheaton Circle, New Orleans, LA 70127-2236; 504-389-3836.

#58 Board of Private Investigators Examiners, 2051 Silverside Dr. #109, Baton Rouge, LA 70808; 225-763-3556, Fax: 225-763-3536.
www.lsbpie.com/

#59 Motor Vehicle Commission, 3519 12th Street, Metairie, LA 70002-3427; 504-838-5207.

#60 Real Estate Commission, 9071 Interline Ave, Baton Rouge, LA 70809; 225-925-4771, Fax: 225-925-4431.
www.lrec.state.la.us

#61 Used Motor Vehicle & Parts Commission, 3132 Valley Creek Drive, Baton Rouge, LA 70808; 225-925-3870, Fax: 225-925-3869.

#62 Professional Licensing Boards, 4707 Main St, Zachary, LA 70791; 225-658-8941, Fax: 225-658-8946.
www.lsbmt.org

#63 Board of Examiners, PO Box 41594, Baton Rouge, LA 70801; 225-922-1435, Fax: 225-922-1352. www.lrcboard.org

#64 Board of Wholesale Drug Distributors, 12046 Justice Ave, #C, Baton Rouge, LA 70816; 225-295-8567, Fax: 225-295-8568.
www.lsbwdd.org
Direct web site URL to search for licensees: http://host.ntg.com/ldwdd/search.asp. You can search online using name of licensee, dba, or license number.

#66 Ethics Board, 8401 United Plaza Blvd #200, Baton Rouge, LA 70809; 225-992-1400 1-800-842-6630, Fax: 225-922-1414.
www.ethics.state.la.us
Direct web site URL to search for licensees: www.ethics.state.la.us/lobs.htm. You can search online using Lobbyist and company list; lists are updated irregularly.

Louisiana Federal Courts

The following list indicates the district and division name for each Parish in the state. If the bankruptcy court location is different from the district court, then the location of the bankruptcy court appears in parentheses.

Parish/Court Cross Reference

Acadia Parish	Western	Lafayette (Lafayette-Opelousas)	Madison Parish	Western	Monroe
Allen Parish	Western	Lake Charles	Morehouse Parish	Western	Monroe
Ascension Parish	Middle	Baton Rouge	Natchitoches Parish	Western	Alexandria
Assumption Parish	Eastern	New Orleans	Orleans Parish	Eastern	New Orleans
Avoyelles Parish	Western	Alexandria	Ouachita Parish	Western	Monroe
Beauregard Parish	Western	Lake Charles	Plaquemines Parish	Eastern	New Orleans
Bienville Parish	Western	Shreveport	Pointe Coupee Parish	Middle	Baton Rouge
Bossier Parish	Western	Shreveport	Rapides Parish	Western	Alexandria
Caddo Parish	Western	Shreveport	Red River Parish	Western	Shreveport
Calcasieu Parish	Western	Lake Charles	Richland Parish	Western	Monroe
Caldwell Parish	Western	Monroe	Sabine Parish	Western	Shreveport
Cameron Parish	Western	Lake Charles	St. Bernard Parish	Eastern	New Orleans
Catahoula Parish	Western	Alexandria	St. Charles Parish	Eastern	New Orleans
Claiborne Parish	Western	Shreveport	St. Helena Parish	Middle	Baton Rouge
Concordia Parish	Western	Alexandria	St. James Parish	Eastern	New Orleans
De Soto Parish	Western	Shreveport	St. John the Baptist Parish	Parish	EasternNew Orleans
East Baton Rouge Parish	Parish	Middle Baton Rouge	St. Landry Parish	Western	Lafayette (Lafayette-Opelousas)
East Carroll Parish	Western	Monroe	St. Martin Parish	Western	Lafayette (Lafayette-Opelousas)
East Feliciana Parish	Middle	Baton Rouge	St. Mary Parish	Western	Lafayette (Lafayette-Opelousas)
Evangeline Parish	Western	Lafayette (Lafayette-Opelousas)	St. Tammany Parish	Eastern	New Orleans
Franklin Parish	Western	Monroe	Tangipahoa Parish	Eastern	New Orleans
Grant Parish	Western	Alexandria	Tensas Parish	Western	Monroe
Iberia Parish	Western	Lafayette (Lafayette-Opelousas)	Terrebonne Parish	Eastern	New Orleans
Iberville Parish	Middle	Baton Rouge	Union Parish	Western	Monroe
Jackson Parish	Western	Monroe	Vermilion Parish	Western	Lafayette (Lafayette-Opelousas)
Jefferson Davis Parish	Western	Lake Charles	Vernon Parish	Western	Alexandria
Jefferson Parish	Eastern	New Orleans	Washington Parish	Eastern	New Orleans
La Salle Parish	Western	Alexandria	Webster Parish	Western	Shreveport
Lafayette Parish	Western	Lafayette (Lafayette-Opelousas)	West Baton Rouge Parish	Parish	Middle Baton Rouge
Lafourche Parish	Eastern	New Orleans	West Carroll Parish	Western	Monroe
Lincoln Parish	Western	Monroe	West Feliciana Parish	Middle	Baton Rouge
Livingston Parish	Middle	Baton Rouge	Winn Parish	Western	Alexandria

US District Court

Eastern District of Louisiana

New Orleans Division Clerk, Room 151, 500 Camp St, New Orleans, LA 70130 (Courier Address: Use mail address for courier delivery), 504-589-7650, Fax: 504-589-7189.

http://www.laed.uscourts.gov

Counties: Assumption Parish, Jefferson Parish, Lafourche Parish, Orleans Parish, Plaquemines Parish, St. Bernard Parish, St. Charles Parish, St. James Parish, St. John the Baptist Parish, St. Tammany Parish, Tangipahoa Parish, Terrebonne Parish, Washington Parish.

Indexing/Storage: Cases are indexed by defendant and plaintiff as well as by case number. New cases are available in the index 1-2 days after filing date. Both computer and card indexes are maintained. Open records are located at this court.

Fee & Payment: The fee is $20.00 per item (one party name or case number). Payment may be made by money order, cashier check, personal check. Prepayment is required. Payee: Clerk, US District Court. Certification fee: $7.00 per document. Copy fee: $.50 per page.

Phone Search: Searching is not available by phone. Only docket information is available by phone.

Mail Search: Always enclose a stamped self addressed envelope.

In Person: In person searching is available.

PACER: Sign-up number is 800-676-6856. Access fee is $.60 per minute. Toll-free access: 888-257-1175. Local access: 504-589-6714. Case records are available back to 1989. Records are purged every six months. New records are available online after 1-2 days. PACER is available online at http://pacer.laed.uscourts.gov.

US Bankruptcy Court

Eastern District of Louisiana

New Orleans Division Hale Boggs Federal Bldg, 501 Magazine St, #601, New Orleans, LA 70130 (Courier Address: Use mail address for courier delivery), 504-589-7878.

http://www.laeb.uscourts.gov

Counties: Assumption Parish, Jefferson Parish, Lafourche Parish, Orleans Parish, Plaquemines Parish, St. Bernard Parish, St. Charles Parish, St. James Parish, St. John the Baptist Parish, St. Tammany Parish, Tangipahoa Parish, Terrebonne Parish, Washington Parish.

Indexing/Storage: Cases are indexed by debtor as well as by case number. New cases are available in the index 2 days after filing date. Both computer and card indexes are maintained. Records are also indexed on microfiche. Open records are located at this court. District wide searches are available from this court from November 1985 for information in the computer and from 1979 to 1985 on card index.

Fee & Payment: The fee is $20.00 per item (one party name or case number). Payment may be made by money order, cashier check, business check. Personal checks are not accepted. Prepayment is required. Payee: Clerk, US Bankruptcy Court. Certification fee: $7.00 per document. Copy fee: $.50 per page.

Phone Search: Information is available from 9:00 to 10:30 a.m. and 1:00 to 2:30 p.m. over the phone. There is no fee for case status information. Only docket information will be released. An automated voice case information service (VCIS) is available.

Mail Search: Always enclose a stamped self addressed envelope.

In Person: In person searching is available.

PACER: Sign-up number is 800-676-6856. Access fee is $.60 per minute. Toll-free access: 800-743-2464. Local access: 504-589-6761. Case records are available back to 1985. Records are purged every six months. New civil records are available online after 2 days. PACER is available online at http://pacer.laeb.uscourts.gov.

US District Court
Middle District of Louisiana

Baton Rouge Division PO Box 2630, Baton Rouge, LA 70821-2630 (Courier Address: 777 Florida St., #139, Baton Rouge, LA 70801), 225-389-3500, Fax: 225-389-3501.

http://www.lamd.uscourts.gov

Counties: Ascension Parish, East Baton Rouge Parish, East Feliciana Parish, Iberville Parish, Livingston Parish, Pointe Coupee Parish, St. Helena Parish, West Baton Rouge Parish, West Feliciana Parish.

Indexing/Storage: Cases are indexed by defendant and plaintiff as well as by case number. New cases are available in the index immediately after filing date. A computer index is maintained. Index prior to 1992 is on microfiche and computer. Open records are located at this court.

Fee & Payment: The fee is $20.00 per item (one party name or case number). Payment may be made by money order, cashier check, business check, Visa, Mastercard. Personal checks are not accepted. Prepayment is required. The court has no billing procedures. Payee: Clerk, US District Court. Certification fee: $7.00 per document. Copy fee: $.50 per page. You are allowed to make your own copies. These copies cost $.25 per page. A coin operated copier is installed for the public.

Phone Search: Only docket information is available by phone. If the information is at the Federal Records Center, the court will provide the information needed to review a record.

Mail Search: A stamped self addressed envelope is not required.

In Person: In person searching is available.

PACER: Sign-up number is 800-676-6856. Access fee is $.60 per minute. Toll-free access: 800-616-8757. Local access: 225-389-3547. Case records are available back to October 1993. New records are available online after 1 day. PACER is available online at http://pacer.lamd.uscourts.gov.

US Bankruptcy Court
Middle District of Louisiana

Baton Rouge Division Room 119, 707 Florida St, Baton Rouge, LA 70801 (Courier Address: Use mail address for courier delivery), 225-389-0211.

http://www.lamb.uscourts.gov

Counties: Ascension Parish, East Baton Rouge Parish, East Feliciana Parish, Iberville Parish, Livingston Parish, Pointe Coupee Parish, St. Helena Parish, West Baton Rouge Parish, West Feliciana Parish.

Indexing/Storage: Cases are indexed by debtor and creditors as well as by case number. New cases are available in the index immediately after filing date. A computer index is maintained. Open records are located at this court.

Fee & Payment: The fee is $20.00 per item (one party name or case number). Payment may be made by money order, cashier check, business check. Personal checks are not accepted. Prepayment is required. Payee: Clerk, US Bankruptcy Court. Certification fee: $7.00 per document. Copy fee: $.50 per page. You are allowed to make your own copies. These copies cost $.25 per page.

Phone Search: Only docket information is available by phone. An automated voice case information service (VCIS) is available.

Mail Search: Always enclose a stamped self addressed envelope.

In Person: In person searching is available.

PACER: Sign-up number is 800-676-6856. Access fee is. Case records are available back to May 15, 1992. New civil records are available online after 1 day. PACER is available online at http://pacer.lamb.uscourts.gov.

Electronic Filing: Electronic filing information is available online at https://ecf.lamb.uscourts.gov

US District Court
Western District of Louisiana

Alexandria Division PO Box 1269, Alexandria, LA 71309 (Courier Address: 515 Murray, Alexandria, LA 71301), 318-473-7415, Fax: 318-473-7345.

http://www.lawd.uscourts.gov

Counties: Avoyelles Parish, Catahoula Parish, Concordia Parish, Grant Parish, La Salle Parish, Natchitoches Parish, Rapides Parish, Winn Parish.

Indexing/Storage: Cases are indexed by defendant and plaintiff as well as by case number. New cases are available in the index 3 days after filing date. A computer index is maintained. Open records are located at this court.

Fee & Payment: The fee is $20.00 per item (one party name or case number). Payment may be made by money order, cashier check, personal check. Prepayment is required. Payee: Clerk, US District Court. Certification fee: $7.00 per document. Copy fee: $.50 per page.

Phone Search: Only docket information is available by phone.

Mail Search: Always enclose a stamped self addressed envelope.

In Person: In person searching is available.

PACER: Sign-up number is 800-676-6856. Access fee is $.60 per minute. Toll-free access: 888-263-2679. Local access: 318-676-3958. Case records are available back to October 1993. Records are purged as deemed necessary. New records are available online after 1 day. PACER is available online at https://pacer.lawd.uscourts.gov.

Lafayette Division Room 113, Federal Bldg, 705 Jefferson St, Lafayette, LA 70501 (Courier Address: Use mail address for courier delivery), 337-593-5000.

http://www.lawd.uscourts.gov

Counties: Acadia Parish, Evangeline Parish, Iberia Parish, Lafayette Parish, St. Landry Parish, St. Martin Parish, St. Mary Parish, Vermilion Parish.

Indexing/Storage: Cases are indexed by defendant and plaintiff as well as by case number. New cases are available in the index 1 day after filing date. A computer index is maintained. Open records are located at this court.

Fee & Payment: The fee is no charge per item (one party name or case number). Payment may be made by money order, cashier check, business check. Personal checks are not accepted. Prepayment is required. Payee: Clerk, US District Court. Certification fee: $7.00 per document. Copy fee: $.50 per page.

Phone Search: Only docket information is available by phone.

Mail Search: Certified name searches can only be performed from the Shreveport office. A stamped self addressed envelope is not required.

In Person: In person searching is available.

PACER: Sign-up number is 800-676-6856. Access fee is $.60 per minute. Toll-free access: 888-263-2679. Local access: 318-676-3958. Case records are available back to October 1993. Records are purged as deemed necessary. New records are available online after 1 day. PACER is available online at https://pacer.lawd.uscourts.gov.

Lake Charles Division 611 Broad St, Suite 188, Lake Charles, LA 70601 (Courier Address: Use mail address for courier delivery), 337-437-3870.

http://www.lawd.uscourts.gov

Counties: Allen Parish, Beauregard Parish, Calcasieu Parish, Cameron Parish, Jefferson Davis Parish, Vernon Parish.

Indexing/Storage: Cases are indexed by defendant and plaintiff as well as by case number. New cases are available in the index 3 days after filing date. A computer index is maintained. Open records are located at this court.

Fee & Payment: The fee is $20.00 per item (one party name or case number). Payment may be made by money order, cashier check, business check. Personal checks are not accepted. Prepayment is required. Payee: Clerk, US District Court. Certification fee: $7.00 per document. Copy fee: $.50 per page.

Phone Search: Only docket information is available by phone.

Mail Search: Always enclose a stamped self addressed envelope.

In Person: In person searching is available.

PACER: Sign-up number is 800-676-6856. Access fee is $.60 per minute. Toll-free access: 888-263-2679. Local access: 318-676-3958. Case records are available back to October 1993.

Records are purged as deemed necessary. New records are available online after 1 day. PACER is available online at https://pacer.lawd.uscourts.gov.

Monroe Division
PO Drawer 3087, Monroe, LA 71210 (Courier Address: Room 215, 201 Jackson St, Monroe, LA 71201), 318-322-6740.

http://www.lawd.uscourts.gov

Counties: Caldwell Parish, East Carroll Parish, Franklin Parish, Jackson Parish, Lincoln Parish, Madison Parish, Morehouse Parish, Ouachita Parish, Richland Parish, Tensas Parish, Union Parish, West Carroll Parish.

Indexing/Storage: Cases are indexed by defendant and plaintiff as well as by case number. New cases are available in the index 3 days after filing date. The Shreveport computerized index is used for searching. A computer index is maintained. Open records are located at this court. This division has been without a judge since 1996, and may not be getting one. Therefore, there are very few case records held here any longer. It is recommended to search at the Shreveport division.

Fee & Payment: The fee is $20.00 per item (one party name or case number). Payment may be made by money order, cashier check, business check. Personal checks are not accepted. Prepayment is required. Payee: Clerk, US District Court. Certification fee: $7.00 per document. Copy fee: $.50 per page.

Phone Search: Only docket information is available by phone.

Mail Search: Always enclose a stamped self addressed envelope.

In Person: In person searching is available.

PACER: Sign-up number is 800-676-6856. Access fee is $.60 per minute. Toll-free access: 888-263-2679. Local access: 318-676-3958. Case records are available back to October 1993. Records are purged as deemed necessary. New records are available online after 1 day. PACER is available online at https://pacer.lawd.uscourts.gov.

Shreveport Division
US Courthouse, Suite 1167, 300 Fannin St, Shreveport, LA 71101-3083 (Courier Address: Use mail address for courier delivery), 318-676-4273.

http://www.lawd.uscourts.gov

Counties: Bienville Parish, Bossier Parish, Caddo Parish, Claiborne Parish, De Soto Parish, Red River Parish, Sabine Parish, Webster Parish.

Indexing/Storage: Cases are indexed by defendant and plaintiff as well as by case number. New cases are available in the index immediately after filing date. A computer index is maintained. On computer are cases that were filed in 1977 or later. Copies from closed records in cases filed in 1977 or later are available from microfiche located at this court. Open records are located at this court.

Fee & Payment: The fee is $20.00 per item (one party name or case number). Payment may be made by money order, cashier check, business check. Personal checks are not accepted. Prepayment is required. Payee: Clerk, US District Court. Certification fee: $7.00 per document. Copy fee: $.50 per page.

Phone Search: Only docket information is available by phone. If the information is at the Federal Records Center, the court will provide the information needed to review a record.

Mail Search: A stamped self addressed envelope is not required.

In Person: In person searching is available.

PACER: Sign-up number is 800-676-6856. Access fee is $.60 per minute. Toll-free access: 888-263-2679. Local access: 318-676-3958. Case records are available back to October 1993. Records are purged as deemed necessary. New records are available online after 1 day. PACER is available online at https://pacer.lawd.uscourts.gov.

US Bankruptcy Court
Western District of Louisiana

Alexandria Division
300 Jackson St, Suite 116, Alexandria, LA 71301-8357 (Courier Address: Hemenway Bldg, 300 Jackson St, Alexandria, LA 71301), 318-445-1890.

http://www.lawb.uscourts.gov

Counties: Avoyelles Parish, Catahoula Parish, Concordia Parish, Grant Parish, La Salle Parish, Natchitoches Parish, Rapides Parish, Vernon Parish, Winn Parish.

Indexing/Storage: Cases are indexed by debtor as well as by case number. New cases are available in the index 1 day after filing date. Chapter 7 and 11 cases from the Monroe Division are now at this court. Chapter 12 and Chapter 13 continue to be handled by Shreveport. A computer index is maintained. Open records are located at this court.

Fee & Payment: The fee is $20.00 per item (one party name or case number). Payment may be made by money order, cashier check, personal check. A copy service will also do the search and copies at $5.00 for the search fee and $.25 per page plus cost of postage. The copy service will bill law firms. Payee: Clerk, US Bankruptcy Court or copy service. Certification fee: $7.00 per document. The fee for copies made by court personnel is $.50 per page.

Phone Search: Only docket information is available by phone. An automated voice case information service (VCIS) is available. Call VCIS at 800-326-4026 or 318-676-4234.

Mail Search: A stamped self addressed envelope is not required.

In Person: In person searching is available.

PACER: Sign-up number is 800-676-6856. Access fee is $.60 per minute. Toll-free access: 888-523-1976. Local access: 318-676-4235. Case records are available back to 1992. New civil records are available online after 1 day. PACER is available online at http://pacer.lawb.uscourts.gov.

Lafayette-Opelousas Division
PO Box J, Opelousas, LA 70571-1909 (Courier Address: Room 205, 231 S Union, Opelousas, LA 70570), 318-948-3451, Fax: 318-948-4426.

http://www.lawb.uscourts.gov

Counties: Acadia Parish, Evangeline Parish, Iberia Parish, Lafayette Parish, St. Landry Parish, St. Martin Parish, St. Mary Parish, Vermilion Parish.

Indexing/Storage: Cases are indexed by debtor as well as by case number. New cases are available in the index 1 day after filing date. Both computer and card indexes are maintained. Records are indexed on index cards for pre-1987 files only. Records are also indexed on microfiche. Open records are located at this court. District wide searches are available for information from January 1, 1986 from this division. This office

handles case records for the Lake Charles Division also.

Fee & Payment: The fee is $20.00 per item (one party name or case number). Payment may be made by money order, cashier check, business check. Personal checks are not accepted. Prepayment is required. Payee: Clerk, US Bankruptcy Court. Certification fee: $7.00 per document. Copy fee: $.50 per page.

Phone Search: Only docket information is available by phone. An automated voice case information service (VCIS) is available. Call VCIS at 800-326-4026 or 318-676-4234.

Mail Search: A stamped self addressed envelope is not required.

In Person: In person searching is available.

PACER: Sign-up number is 800-676-6856. Access fee is $.60 per minute. Toll-free access: 888-523-1976. Local access: 318-676-4235. Case records are available back to 1992. New civil records are available online after 1 day. PACER is available online at http://pacer.lawb.uscourts.gov.

Lake Charles Division
c/o Lafayette-Opelousas Division, PO Box J, Opelousas, LA 70571-1909 (Courier Address: Room 205, 250 S Union, Opelousas, LA 70570), 318-948-3451.

http://www.lawb.uscourts.gov

Counties: Allen Parish, Beauregard Parish, Calcasieu Parish, Cameron Parish, Jefferson Davis Parish.

Indexing/Storage: Cases are indexed by as well as by case number. New cases are available in the index after filing date. Open records are located at the Division.

Fee & Payment: The fee is no charge per item (one party name or case number). Payment may be made by money order, cashier check. Business checks are not accepted. Personal checks are not accepted.

Phone Search: An automated voice case information service (VCIS) is available. Call VCIS at 800-326-4026 or 318-676-4234.

Mail Search: A stamped self addressed envelope is not required.

In Person: In person searching is available.

PACER: Sign-up number is 800-676-6856. Access fee is $.60 per minute. Toll-free access: 888-523-1976. Local access: 318-676-4235. Case records are available back to 1992. New civil records are available online after 1 day. PACER is available online at http://pacer.lawb.uscourts.gov.

Monroe Division
c/o Shreveport Division, Suite 2201, 300 Fannin St, Shreveport, LA 71101 (Courier Address: Use mail address for courier delivery), 318-676-4267.

http://www.lawb.uscourts.gov

Counties: Caldwell Parish, East Carroll Parish, Franklin Parish, Jackson Parish, Lincoln Parish, Madison Parish, Morehouse Parish, Ouachita Parish, Richland Parish, Tensas Parish, Union Parish, West Carroll Parish.

Indexing/Storage: Cases are indexed by as well as by case number. New cases are available in the index after filing date. This court is an unmanned office. Cases are housed as follows: Chapter 7 and Chapter 11 cases to Alexandria; Chapter 12 and Chapter 13 cases to Shreveport. Open records are located at the Division.

Fee & Payment: The fee is no charge per item (one party name or case number). Payment may be made by money order. Business checks are not accepted. Personal checks are not accepted.

Mail Search: Always enclose a stamped self addressed envelope.

Phone Search: An automated voice case information service (VCIS) is available. Call VCIS at 800-326-4026 or 318-676-4234.

In Person: In person searching is available.

PACER: Sign-up number is 800-676-6856. Access fee is $.60 per minute. Toll-free access: 888-523-1976. Local access: 318-676-4235. Case records are available back to 1992. New civil records are available online after 1 day. PACER is available online at http://pacer.lawb.uscourts.gov.

Shreveport Division Suite 2201, 300 Fannin St, Shreveport, LA 71101-3089 (Courier Address: Use mail address for courier delivery), 318-676-4267.

http://www.lawb.uscourts.gov

Counties: Bienville Parish, Bossier Parish, Caddo Parish, Claiborne Parish, De Soto Parish, Red River Parish, Sabine Parish, Webster Parish.

Indexing/Storage: Cases are indexed by as well as by case number. New cases are available in the index immediately after filing date. A computer index is maintained. Open records are located at this court.

Fee & Payment: The fee is $20.00 per item (one party name or case number). Payment may be made by money order, business check. Personal

checks are not accepted. Prepayment is required. Debtor's checks are not accepted. Payee: Clerk, US Bankruptcy Court. Certification fee: $7.00 per document. Copy fee: $.50 per page.

Phone Search: An automated voice case information service (VCIS) is available. Call VCIS at 800-326-4026 or 318-676-4234.

Mail Search: Always enclose a stamped self addressed envelope.

In Person: In person searching is available.

PACER: Sign-up number is 800-676-6856. Access fee is $.60 per minute. Toll-free access: 888-523-1976. Local access: 318-676-4235. Case records are available back to 1992. New civil records are available online after 1 day. PACER is available online at http://pacer.lawb.uscourts.gov.

Louisiana Parish Courts

Court	Jurisdiction	No. of Courts	How Organized
District Courts*	General	65	42 Districts
New Orleans City Court*	Limited	1	City of New Orleans
City and Parish Courts	Limited	52	
Justice of the Peace Courts	Municipal	390	
Mayor's Courts	Municipal	250	
Family Court	Special	1	Baton Rouge
Juvenile Courts	Special	4	

* Profiled in this Sourcebook.

CIVIL									
Court	Tort	Contract	Real Estate	Min. Claim	Max. Claim	Small Claims	Estate	Eviction	Domestic Relations
District Courts*	X	X	X	$0	No Max		X		X
New Orleans City Court*	X	X	X	$0	$20,000	$2000			X
City and Parish Courts	X	X	X	$0	$15,000	$2000		X	X
Justice of the Peace Courts	X	X	X	$0	$2000	$2000		X	
Mayor's Courts									
Family Court									X
Juvenile Courts									X

CRIMINAL					
Court	Felony	Misdemeanor	DWI/DUI	Preliminary Hearing	Juvenile
District Courts*	X	X	X		X
New Orleans City Court*		X	X	X	X
City and Parish Courts		X	X	X	X
Justice of the Peace Courts					
Mayor's Courts					
Family Court					X
Juvenile Courts					X

ADMINISTRATION   Judicial Administrator, Judicial Council of the Supreme Court, 1555 Poydras St #1540, New Orleans, LA, 70112; 504-568-5747, Fax: 504-568-5687. www.lasc.org

COURT STRUCTURE   A District Court Clerk in each Parish holds all the records for that Parish. Each Parish has its own clerk and courthouse. A municipality may have a Mayor's Court; the mayor may hold trials, but nothing over $30.00, and there are no records.

ONLINE ACCESS   The online computer system, Case Management Information System (CMIS), is operating and development is continuing. It is for internal use only; there is no plan to permit online access to the public. However, Supreme Court opinions are currently available.

There are a number of Parishes that do offer a means of remote online access to the public.

Acadia Parish

15th District Court PO Box 922, Crowley, LA 70527; 337-788-8881; Fax: 337-788-1048. Hours: 8:30AM-4:30PM (CST). *Felony, Misdemeanor, Civil, Probate.*

www.acadiaparishclerk.com

Civil Records: Access: Phone, fax, mail, in person. Both court and visitors may perform in person searches. Search fee: $11.00 per name per year. Required to search: name, years to search. Civil cases indexed by defendant, plaintiff. Civil records on computer from 1979, archived from 1800s. Copy of check must be faxed with request.
Criminal Records: Access: Phone, fax, mail, in person. Both court and visitors may perform in person searches. Search fee: $11.00 per name per year. Required to search: name, years to search, DOB; also helpful: SSN. Criminal records on computer from 1979, archived from 1800s. Copy of check must be included in the fax request.
General Information: No adoption or juvenile records released. SASE required. Turnaround time 1-2 days. Fax notes: Fee to fax results is $6.00 1st page, $2.00 for any add'l pages. Copy fee: $2.00 per page. Certification fee: $6.00. Fee payee: Acadia Parish Clerk of Court. Personal checks accepted. Prepayment is required.

Allen Parish

33rd District Court PO Box 248, Oberlin, LA 70655; 337-639-4351; Fax: 337-639-2030. Hours: 8AM-4:30PM *Felony, Misdemeanor, Civil, Probate.*

Civil Records: Access: Fax, mail, in person. Both court and visitors may perform in person searches. Search fee: $10.00 per name. Fee is for a 10 year search. Required to search: name, years to search. Civil cases indexed by defendant, plaintiff. Civil records archived back to 1913; on computer back to.
Criminal Records: Access: Mail, in person. Both court and visitors may perform in person searches. Search fee: $10.00 per name. Fee is for a 10 year search. Required to search: name, years to search, DOB, SSN. Criminal records archived back to 1913; on computer also.
General Information: Public Access terminal is available. No adoption or juvenile records released. SASE requested. Turnaround time 2 days. Fax notes: Fee to fax results is $2.00 per page. Copy fee: $1.00 per page. Certification fee: $2.00. Fee payee: Allen Parish Clerk of Court. Personal checks accepted. Prepayment is required.

Ascension Parish

23rd District Court PO Box 192, Donaldsonville, LA 70346; 225-473-9866; Fax: 225-473-8641. Hours: 8:30AM-4:30PM (CST). *Felony, Misdemeanor, Civil, Probate.*

Civil Records: Access: Fax, mail, in person. Both court and visitors may perform in person searches. Search fee: $10.00 per name. Required to search: name, years to search. Civil cases indexed by defendant, plaintiff. Civil records on computer from 1987, index books back to 1800s, property tax to 1994, mortgage since 11/77.
Criminal Records: Access: Fax, mail, in person. Both court and visitors may perform in person searches. Search fee: $10.00 per name. Required to search: name, years to search, DOB; also helpful: SSN. Criminal Records computerized since 11/86.
General Information: Public Access terminal is available. No adoption or juvenile records released. SASE requested. Turnaround time 2 days. Fax notes: $5.00 for first page, $1.00 each add'l. Add $5.00 on search fee if request by fax. Copy fee: $1.00 per page. Certification fee: $3.00. Fee payee: Ascension Parish Clerk of Court. Personal checks accepted. Prepayment is required.

Assumption Parish

23rd District Court PO Box 249, Napoleonville, LA 70390; 985-369-6653; Fax: 985-369-2032. Hours: 8:30AM-4:30PM (CST). *Felony, Misdemeanor, Civil, Probate.*

Civil Records: Access: Fax, mail, in person. Both court and visitors may perform in person searches. Search fee: $10.00 per name. Required to search: name, years to search. Civil cases indexed by defendant, plaintiff. Civil records archived back to 1800s; on computer back to 1994.
Criminal Records: Access: Fax, mail, in person. Both court and visitors may perform in person searches. Search fee: $10.00 per name. Required to search: name, years to search, DOB. Criminal records archived back to 1800s; on computer back to 1994.
General Information: Public Access terminal is available. No adoption or juvenile records released. SASE requested. Turnaround time 1 day. Fax notes: $2.00 for first page, $1.00 each add'l. Copy fee: $1.00 per page. Certification fee: $4.00. Fee payee: Assumption Parish Clerk of Court. Personal checks accepted. Prepayment is required.

Avoyelles Parish

12th District Court PO Box 219, Marksville, LA 71351; 318-253-7523. Hours: 8:30AM-4:30PM (CST). *Felony, Misdemeanor, Civil, Probate.*

Civil Records: Access: Mail, in person. Both court and visitors may perform in person searches. Search fee: $10.00 per name. Required to search: name, years to search. Civil cases indexed by defendant, plaintiff. Civil records on computer from 1985, microfiche back to 1800s.
Criminal Records: Access: Mail, in person. Both court and visitors may perform in person searches. Search fee: $10.00 per name. Required to search: name, years to search, DOB; also helpful: SSN. Criminal records on computer from 1985, microfiche back to 1800s.
General Information: No adoption or juvenile records released. SASE not required. Turnaround time 1 day. Copy fee: $1.00 per page. Certification fee: $3.00 per page. Fee payee: Clerk of Court. Personal checks accepted. Prepayment is required.

Beauregard Parish

36th District Court PO Box 1148, DeRidder, LA 70634; 337-463-8595; Fax: 337-462-3916. Hours: 8AM-4:30PM (CST). *Felony, Misdemeanor, Civil, Probate.*

Civil Records: Access: Mail, in person. Both court and visitors may perform in person searches. Search fee: $15.00 per name. Fee is per 10 years searched. Required to search: name, years to search. Civil cases indexed by defendant, plaintiff. Civil records on computer since 1985, archived from 1913.
Criminal Records: Access: Mail, in person. Both court and visitors may perform in person searches. Search fee: $15.00 per name. Fee is per 10 years searched. Required to search: name, years to search, DOB; also helpful: SSN. Criminal records on computer since 1985, archived from 1913.
General Information: No adoption or juvenile records released. SASE required. Turnaround time 1 wk. Copy fee: $.50 per page. Certification fee: $2.25. Fee payee: Clerk of Court. Personal checks accepted. Prepayment is required.

Bienville Parish

2nd District Court 100 Courthouse Dr, Rm 100, Arcadia, LA 71001; 318-263-2123; Fax: 318-263-7426. Hours: 8:30AM-4:30PM (CST). *Felony, Misdemeanor, Civil, Probate.*

www.bienvilleparish.org/clerk

Civil Records: Access: Fax, mail, in person. Both court and visitors may perform in person searches. Search fee: $10.00 per name. Required to search: name, years to search. Civil cases indexed by defendant, plaintiff. Civil records on computer from 1991, index books prior.
Criminal Records: Access: Fax, mail, in person. Both court and visitors may perform in person searches. Search fee: $10.00 per name. Required to search: name, years to search, DOB; also helpful: SSN. Criminal records on computer from 1991, index books prior.
General Information: No adoption or juvenile records released. SASE not required. Turnaround time 2-3 days. Fax notes: $3.00 fee plus $.50 per page. Copy fee: $.50 per page. Certification fee: $2.50. Fee payee: Clerk of Court. Personal checks accepted. Prepayment is required.

Bossier Parish

26th District Court PO Box 430, Benton, LA 71006; 318-965-2336; Fax: 318-965-2713. Hours: 8:30AM-4:30PM (CST). *Felony, Misdemeanor, Civil, Probate.*

www.ebrclerkofcourt.org

Civil Records: Access: Mail, online, in person. Both court and visitors may perform in person searches. Search fee: $15.00 per name. Required to search: name, years to search. Civil cases indexed by defendant, plaintiff. Civil records on computer from 1987, index books back to 1843. Access to the Parish Clerk of Court online records requires a $100 setup fee and a $15 monthly minimum plus $.33 per minute if you view, $.50 if you print. Civil, criminal, probate (1988 forward), traffic and domestic index information is available by name or case number. Call 225-389-5295 for more information.
Criminal Records: Access: Mail, online, in person. Both court and visitors may perform in person searches. Search fee: $15.00 per name. Required to search: name, years to search. Criminal records on computer since 1982. Online access to criminal records same as civil.
General Information: Public Access terminal is available. No adoption or juvenile records released. SASE requested. Turnaround time 4-5 days. Copy fee: $.50 per page. Certification fee: $2.00. Fee payee: Clerk of Court. Business checks accepted. Prepayment is required.

Caddo Parish

1st District Court 501 Texas St, Rm 103, Shreveport, LA 71101-5408; 318-226-6780; Fax: 318-227-9080. Hours: 8:30AM-5PM (CST). *Felony, Misdemeanor, Civil, Probate.*

www.caddoclerk.com

Civil Records: Access: Mail, in person, online. Both court and visitors may perform in person searches. Search fee: $10.00 per name. Fee is $5.00 for second name on same search request. Required to search: name, years to search. Civil cases indexed by defendant, plaintiff. Civil records on computer from 1984. Online access to civil records back to 1994 and name index back to 1984 are available through the county dial-up service. Registration and $50 set-up fee and $30 monthly usage fee is required. Marriage and recording information is also available. For information and sign-up, call 318-226-6918.
Criminal Records: Access: Mail, in person, online. Both court and visitors may perform in person searches. Search fee: $10.00 per name. Fee is $5.00 for second name on same search request. Required to search: name, years to search, DOB; also helpful: SSN. Criminal records on computer from 1984. Online access to criminal records is the same as civil. Online criminal name index goes back to 1980; minutes to 1984. Current calendar is also available.

General Information: Public Access terminal is available. No adoption or juvenile records released. SASE required. Turnaround time 1-2 days. Copy fee: $.50 per page. Certification fee: $2.00. Fee payee: Clerk of Court. Personal checks accepted. Prepayment is required.

Calcasieu Parish

14th District Court PO Box 1030, Lake Charles, LA 70602; 337-437-3550; Fax: 337-437-3350/3833. Hours: 8:30AM-4:30PM (CST). *Felony, Misdemeanor, Civil, Probate.*

Civil Records: Access: Fax, mail, in person. Both court and visitors may perform in person searches. Search fee: $10.00 per name. Additional fee of $2.00 per year after 1st 10 years. Required to search: name, years to search. Civil cases indexed by defendant, plaintiff. Civil records on computer since 1987.

Criminal Records: Access: Mail, in person. Both court and visitors may perform in person searches. Search fee: $10.00 per name. Additional fee of $2.00 per year after 1st 10 years. Required to search: name, years to search, DOB; also helpful: SSN. Criminal records on computer since 1987.

General Information: Public Access terminal is available. No adoption or juvenile records released. SASE required. Turnaround time 1 wk. Fax notes: $7.00 for first page, $2.00 each add'l. Fax available for civil division only. Copy fee: $1.00 per page. Certification fee: $5.00. Fee payee: Clerk of Court. Personal checks accepted. Prepayment is required.

Caldwell Parish

37th District Court PO Box 1327, Columbia, LA 71418; 318-649-2272; Fax: 318-649-2037. Hours: 8AM-4:30PM *Felony, Misdemeanor, Civil, Probate.*

Note: All record requests must be in writing.

Civil Records: Access: Fax, mail, in person. Both court and visitors may perform in person searches. Search fee: $10.00 per name. Required to search: name, years to search. Civil cases indexed by defendant, plaintiff. Civil records on books from 1970, computerized 11/84.

Criminal Records: Access: Mail, in person. Only the court performs in person searches; visitors may not. Search fee: $10.00 per name. Required to search: name, years to search, DOB; also helpful: SSN. Criminal Records kept on books since 1970.

General Information: No adoption or juvenile records released. SASE not required. Turnaround time 1 week. Fax notes: $3.00 for first page, $1.00 each add'l. Copy fee: $1.00 per page. Certification fee: $2.00 plus $1.00 per page. Fee payee: Clerk of Court. Personal checks accepted. Prepayment is required.

Cameron Parish

38th District Court PO Box 549, Cameron, LA 70631; 337-775-5316; Fax: 337-775-7172. Hours: 8:30AM-4:30PM (CST). *Felony, Misdemeanor, Civil, Probate.*

Civil Records: Access: Phone, mail, fax, in person. Both court and visitors may perform in person searches. Search fee: $10.00. Required to search: name, years to search. Civil cases indexed by defendant, plaintiff. Civil records from 1874; on computer back to 1968.

Criminal Records: Access: Fax, mail, in person. Only the court performs in person searches; visitors may not. Search fee: $10.00 per name. Required to search: name, years to search, DOB. Criminal records from 1874; on computer back to 1968.

General Information: No adoption, interdiction or juvenile records released. SASE required. Turnaround time 2 days. Fax notes: Fee to fax results $1.00 per page plus cert fee. Copy fee: $1.00 per page. Certification fee: $5.00. Fee payee: Cameron Parish Clerk of Court. Personal checks accepted.

Catahoula Parish

7th District Court PO Box 198, Harrisonburg, LA 71340; 318-744-5222; Fax: 318-744-5488. Hours: 8AM-4:30PM (CST). *Felony, Misdemeanor, Civil, Probate.*

Civil Records: Access: Mail, in person. Both court and visitors may perform in person searches. Search fee: $25.00 per name. Fee is for 10 year search. Required to search: name, years to search. Civil cases indexed by defendant, plaintiff. Civil records minute entries back to 1800s.

Criminal Records: Access: Mail, in person. Both court and visitors may perform in person searches. Search fee: $25.00 per name. Fee is for 10 year search. Required to search: name, years to search, DOB. Criminal records minute entries back to 1800s.

General Information: No adoption or juvenile records released. SASE required. Turnaround time 1-2 weeks. Copy fee: $1.00 per page. Certification fee: $5.00. Fee payee: Clerk of Court. Personal checks accepted. Prepayment is required.

Claiborne Parish

2nd District Court PO Box 330, Homer, LA 71040; 318-927-9601; Fax: 318-927-2345. Hours: 8:30AM-4:30PM (CST). *Felony, Misdemeanor, Civil, Probate.*

Civil Records: Access: Mail, in person. Both court and visitors may perform in person searches. Search fee: $10.00 per name. Required to search: name, years to search. Civil cases indexed by defendant, plaintiff. Civil records on index books back to early 1900s.

Criminal Records: Access: Mail, in person. Both court and visitors may perform in person searches. Search fee: $10.00 per name. Required to search: name, years to search, DOB; also helpful: SSN. Criminal records on computer 1993 forward.

General Information: No adoption or juvenile records released. SASE required. Turnaround time 1-2 days. Fax notes: Fee to fax results is $10.00 per document. Copy fee: $1.00 per page. Certification fee: $2.50. Fee payee: Clerk of Court. Personal checks accepted. Prepayment is required.

Concordia Parish

7th District Court PO Box 790, Vidalia, LA 71373; 318-336-4204; Fax: 318-336-8217. Hours: 8:30AM-4:30PM (CST). *Felony, Misdemeanor, Civil, Probate.*

Civil Records: Access: Fax, mail, in person. Both court and visitors may perform in person searches. Search fee: $25.00 per name. Required to search: name, years to search. Civil cases indexed by defendant, plaintiff. Civil records on computer from 1983, index books back to 1800s.

Criminal Records: Access: Mail, in person. Both court and visitors may perform in person searches. Search fee: $25.00 per name. Required to search: name, years to search, DOB; also helpful: SSN. Criminal records on computer from 1983, index books back to 1800s.

General Information: Public Access terminal is available. No adoption or juvenile records released. SASE not required. Turnaround time 3-4 days. Fax notes: $5.00 per document. Fax available for civil division only. Copy fee: $1.00 per page. Certification fee: $6.50. Fee payee: Clerk of Court. Personal checks accepted. Prepayment is required.

De Soto Parish

11th District Court PO Box 1206, Mansfield, LA 71052; 318-872-3110; Fax: 318-872-4202. Hours: 8AM-4:30PM (CST). *Felony, Misdemeanor, Civil, Probate.*

Civil Records: Access: Mail, in person. Both court and visitors may perform in person searches. Search fee:

$10.00 per name. Required to search: name, years to search. Civil cases indexed by defendant, plaintiff. Civil records on computer from 1991, index books back to 1843.

Criminal Records: Access: Mail, in person. Both court and visitors may perform in person searches. Search fee: $10.00 per name. Required to search: name, years to search, DOB. Criminal records on computer since 1991, archived or in books prior.

General Information: Public Access terminal is available. No adoption or juvenile records released. SASE Required. Turnaround time 1-2 days. Fax notes: Fee to fax results is $1.00 per page. Copy fee: $1.00 per page. Certification fee: $3.50. Fee payee: Clerk of Court. Prepayment is required.

East Baton Rouge Parish

19th District Court PO Box 1991, Baton Rouge, LA 70821; 225-389-3950; Fax: 225-389-3392. Hours: 7:30AM-5:30PM (CST). *Felony, Misdemeanor, Civil, Probate.*

www.ebrclerkofcourt.org

Civil Records: Access: Fax, mail, online, in person. Both court and visitors may perform in person searches. Search fee: Search fee is determined by the years searched. Required to search: name, years to search. Civil cases indexed by defendant, plaintiff. Civil records in index books from 1942. Online access to the clerk's database is available by subscription. Civil record indexes go back to 1988; case tracking of civil and probate back to 1991. Setup fee is $100.00 plus $15.00 per month plus per-minute usage charges. VS Com software required. Call the MIS Dept at 225-389-5295 for information or visit the web site.

Criminal Records: Access: Mail, online, in person. Both court and visitors may perform in person searches. Search fee: $20.00 per name. Required to search: name, years to search, DOB; also helpful: SSN. Criminal records in index books from 1942; on computer back to 1990. Online access to criminal records is the same as civil. Criminal case tracking goes back to 8/1990.

General Information: Public Access terminal is available. No adoption or juvenile records released. Fax notes: Fee to fax results is $5.00 per document and $.50 per page. Copy fee: $.50 per page. Criminal record copy fee is $1.00 per page. Certification fee: $2.20.

East Carroll Parish

6th District Court 400 1st St, Lake Providence, LA 71254; 318-559-2388. Hours: 8:30AM-4:30PM (CST). *Felony, Misdemeanor, Civil, Probate.*

Civil Records: Access: Mail, in person. Both court and visitors may perform in person searches. Search fee: $10.00 per name. Required to search: name, years to search. Civil cases indexed by defendant, plaintiff. Civil records on index books back to 1832.

Criminal Records: Access: Mail, in person. Both court and visitors may perform in person searches. Search fee: $10.00 per name. Required to search: name, years to search, DOB; also helpful: SSN. Criminal records on index books back to 1832.

General Information: No adoption or juvenile records released. SASE required. Turnaround time same day. Copy fee: $1.00 per page. Certification fee: $2.00. Fee payee: Clerk of Court. Personal checks accepted. Prepayment is required.

East Feliciana Parish

20th District Court PO Box 599, Clinton, LA 70722; 225-683-5145; Fax: 225-683-3556. Hours: 8AM-4:30PM (CST). *Felony, Misdemeanor, Civil, Probate.*

Civil Records: Access: Fax, mail, in person. Both court and visitors may perform in person searches. Search fee: $10.00 per name per ten years. Required to search: name, years to search; also helpful: address. Civil cases indexed by defendant, plaintiff. Civil records on computer from 1988, index books back to 1800s. State which years to search.

Criminal Records: Access: Fax, mail, in person. Both court and visitors may perform in person searches. Search fee: $10.00 per name. Required to search: name, years to search; also helpful: address, DOB. Criminal records on computer from 1988, index books back to 1800s. State which years to search.

General Information: Public Access terminal is available. No adoption or juvenile records released. SASE required. Turnaround time 1-2 days. Fax notes: $5.00 for first page, $1.00 each add'l. Copy fee: $1.00 per page. Certification fee: $5.00. Fee payee: Clerk of Court. Personal checks accepted. Prepayment is required.

Evangeline Parish

13th District Court PO Drawer 347, Ville Platte, LA 70586; 337-363-5671; Fax: 337-363-5780. Hours: 8AM-4:30PM (CST). *Felony, Misdemeanor, Civil, Probate.*

Civil Records: Access: Fax, mail, in person. Both court and visitors may perform in person searches. Search fee: $10.00 per name. Fee is for first 7 years searched. Add $2.00 per additional year. Required to search: name, years to search. Civil cases indexed by defendant, plaintiff. Civil records on computer back to 1/1/89; prior records archived from 1911.

Criminal Records: Access: Fax, mail, in person. Both court and visitors may perform in person searches. Search fee: $10.00 per name. Fee is for first 7 years searched. Add $2.00 per additional year. Required to search: name, years to search; also helpful: DOB, SSN. Criminal records on computer back to 11/1/97, prior records archived from 1911.

General Information: Public Access terminal is available. No adoption or juvenile records released. Turnaround time 1-2 days. Fax notes: $5.00 for first page, $2.00 each add'l. Copy fee: $.75 per page. Certification fee: $2.00 per page. Fee payee: Clerk of Court. Personal checks accepted. Prepayment is required.

Franklin Parish

5th District Court PO Box 431, Winnsboro, LA 71295; 318-435-5133; Fax: 318-435-5134. Hours: 8:30AM-4:30PM (CST). *Felony, Misdemeanor, Civil, Probate.*

Civil Records: Access: Mail, in person. Both court and visitors may perform in person searches. Search fee: $10.00 per name. Required to search: name, years to search. Civil cases indexed by defendant, plaintiff. Civil records on computer from 1988, index books back to 1843.

Criminal Records: Access: Mail, in person. Both court and visitors may perform in person searches. Search fee: $10.00 per name. Fee includes 10 year search. Required to search: name, years to search, DOB; also helpful: SSN. Criminal records on computer since 1995.

General Information: No adoption or juvenile records released. SASE required. Turnaround time 1-2 days. Fax notes: $5.00 for first page, $1.00 each add'l. Copy fee: $1.00 per page. Certification fee: $2.00. Fee payee: Clerk of Court. Business checks accepted. Prepayment is required.

Grant Parish

35th District Court PO Box 263, Colfax, LA 71417; 318-627-3246. Hours: 8:30AM-4:30PM (CST). *Felony, Misdemeanor, Civil, Probate.*

Civil Records: Access: Phone, mail, in person. Only the court performs in person searches; visitors may not. Search fee: $5.00 per name. Required to search: name, years to search. Civil cases indexed by defendant,

plaintiff. Civil records on computer from 1990, index books back to 1878.

Criminal Records: Access: Phone, mail, in person. Only the court performs in person searches; visitors may not. Search fee: $5.00 per name. Required to search: name, years to search, DOB; also helpful: SSN. Criminal records on computer since 1996.

General Information: No adoption or juvenile records released without approval of a judge. SASE required. Turnaround time 1-2 days. Copy fee: $.75 per page. Certification fee: $5.00. Fee payee: Grant Parish Clerk of Court. Personal checks accepted.

Iberia Parish

16th District Court PO Drawer 12010, New Iberia, LA 70562-2010; 337-365-7282; Fax: 337-365-0737. Hours: 8:30AM-4:30PM (CST). *Felony, Misdemeanor, Civil, Probate.*

Civil Records: Access: Phone, fax, mail, online, in person. Both court and visitors may perform in person searches. Search fee: $10.00 per name. Required to search: name, years to search; also helpful: address. Civil cases indexed by defendant, plaintiff. Civil records on computer from 1974, index books back to 1800s. Access to the remote online system requires a $50 monthly fee. Search civil or probate records by name or case number. Call Mike Thibodeaux at 337-365-7282 for more information.

Criminal Records: Access: Mail, in person. Both court and visitors may perform in person searches. Search fee: $10.00 per name. Required to search: name, years to search, DOB; also helpful: address, SSN. Criminal records on computer from 1974, index books back to 1800s.

General Information: Public Access terminal is available. No adoption or juvenile records released. SASE required. Turnaround time 1-2 days. Fax notes: Fee to fax results is $1.50 per page. Copy fee: $.50 per page. Certification fee: $5.50. Fee payee: Clerk of Court. Personal checks accepted. Prepayment required.

Iberville Parish

18th District Court PO Box 423, Plaquemine, LA 70764; 225-687-5160; Fax: 225-687-5260. Hours: 8:30AM-4:30PM (CST). *Felony, Misdemeanor, Civil, Probate.*

Civil Records: Access: Fax, mail, in person. Both court and visitors may perform in person searches. Search fee: $10.00 per name. Required to search: name, years to search. Civil cases indexed by defendant, plaintiff. Civil records on books back to 1800s.

Criminal Records: Access: Fax, mail, in person. Both court and visitors may perform in person searches. Search fee: $10.00 per name. Required to search: name, years to search, DOB; also helpful: SSN. Criminal records on books back to 1800s.

General Information: No adoption or juvenile records released. SASE required. Turnaround time 1-2 days. Fax notes: Fee to fax results is $5.00 1st page, $2.00 each add'l. Copy fee: $.75 per page. Certification fee: $4.00. Fee payee: Clerk of Court. Personal checks accepted. Prepayment is required.

Jackson Parish

2nd District Court PO Drawer 730, Jonesboro, LA 71251; 318-259-2424; Fax: 318-395-0386. Hours: 8:30AM-4:30PM (CST). *Felony, Misdemeanor, Civil, Probate.*

Civil Records: Access: Phone, mail, in person. Both court and visitors may perform in person searches. Search fee: $10.00 per name. Fee is per 10 years searched. Required to search: name, years to search. Civil cases indexed by defendant, plaintiff. Civil records on index books from 1880 and on computer since 1988.

Criminal Records: Access: Phone, mail, in person. Both court and visitors may perform in person searches.

Search fee: $10.00 per name. Fee is per 10 years searched. Required to search: name, years to search, DOB; also helpful: SSN. Criminal records on computer since 1988.

General Information: Public Access terminal is available. No adoption or juvenile records released. SASE required. Turnaround time 1-2 days. Copy fee: $1.00 per page. Certification fee: $2.50. Fee payee: Clerk of Court. Personal checks accepted. Prepayment is required.

Jefferson Davis Parish

31st District Court PO Box 799, Jennings, LA 70546; 337-824-1160; Fax: 337-824-1354. Hours: 8:30AM-4:30PM (CST). *Felony, Misdemeanor, Civil, Probate.*

Civil Records: Access: Mail, in person. Both court and visitors may perform in person searches. Search fee: $10.00 per name. Required to search: name, years to search; also helpful: address. Civil cases indexed by defendant, plaintiff. Civil records archived from 1913, on computer back to 1991.

Criminal Records: Access: Mail, in person. Both court and visitors may perform in person searches. Search fee: $10.00 per name. Required to search: name, years to search; also helpful: DOB, SSN. Criminal records archived from 1913, on computer back to 1991. Include city of residence of subject in your search request.

General Information: No adoption or juvenile records released. SASE not required. Turnaround time 2 days. Fax notes: Fee to fax results is $1.00 per page. Copy fee: $1.00 per page. Certification fee: $4.00. Fee payee: Clerk of Court. Personal checks accepted. Prepayment is required.

Jefferson Parish

24th District Court PO Box 10, Gretna, LA 70053; 504-364-2992; Fax: 504-364-3797. Hours: 8:30AM-4:30PM (CST). *Felony, Misdemeanor, Civil, Probate.*

www.clerkofcourt.co.jefferson.la.us

Civil Records: Access: Fax, mail, online, in person. Both court and visitors may perform in person searches. Search fee: $20.00 per name per year. Required to search: name, years to search. Civil cases indexed by defendant, plaintiff. Civil records on computer from 1986, in index books back to 1972, prior records archived. Online access is available through a dial-up service. Initiation fee is $200, plus $85.00 monthly and $.25 per minute usage fee. Includes recordings, marriage index, and assessor rolls. For further information and sign-up, call 504-364-2908 or visit the web site and click on "Jeffnet.".

Criminal Records: Access: Fax, mail, online, in person. Both court and visitors may perform in person searches. Search fee: $10.00 per name. Required to search: name, years to search, DOB; also helpful: SSN. Criminal records on computer from 1994 to present, active cases are in books from 1972. Online access is via a dial-up service, see civil.

General Information: Public Access terminal is available. No adoption, juvenile or grand jury records released. Turnaround time 1-2 days. Fax notes: $5.00 for first page, $1.00 each add'l. Copy fee: $.75 per page. Add postage. Certification fee: $1.25 per page. Fee payee: Clerk of Court. Personal checks accepted. Out of state personal checks not accepted. Prepayment is required.

La Salle Parish

28th District Court PO Box 1316, Jena, LA 71342; 318-992-2158; Fax: 318-992-2157. Hours: 8:30AM-4:30PM (CST). *Felony, Misdemeanor, Civil, Probate.*

Civil Records: Access: Phone, fax, mail, in person. Both court and visitors may perform in person searches.

Search fee: $17.00 per name. Fee is for 10 year search per name with certificate. Required to search: name, years to search. Civil cases indexed by defendant, plaintiff. Civil records archived from 1916; on computer since 1993.
Criminal Records: Access: Phone, fax, mail, in person. Both court and visitors may perform in person searches. Search fee: $17.00 per name per year. Fee is for 10 year search per name with certificate. Required to search: name, years to search, DOB; also helpful: SSN. Criminal records archived from 1916; on computer since 1993.
General Information: Public Access terminal is available. No adoption or juvenile records released. SASE not required. Turnaround time 1-2 wks, will release info sooner by phone. Fax notes: Fee to fax results is $10.00 per document. Copy fee: $1.00 per page. Certification fee: $3.30 plus $1.10 per add'l page. Fee payee: Clerk of Court. Personal checks accepted. Prepayment is required.

Lafayette Parish

15th District Court PO Box 2009, Lafayette, LA 70502; 337-233-0150; Fax: 337-269-6392. Hours: 8:30AM-4:30PM (CST). *Felony, Misdemeanor, Civil, Probate.*
www.lafayetteparishclerk.com
Civil Records: Access: Phone, fax, mail, online, in person. Both court and visitors may perform in person searches. Search fee: $11.00 per name. Required to search: name, years to search. Civil cases indexed by defendant, plaintiff. Civil records archived from 1923; on computer back to 1986. Access to the remote online system requires a $100 setup fee plus $15 per month and $.50 per minute. Civil index goes back to 1986. For more information, call Derek Comeaux at 337-291-6433.
Criminal Records: Access: Phone, fax, mail, online, in person. Both court and visitors may perform in person searches. Search fee: $11.00 per name. Required to search: name, years to search, DOB. Criminal records archived from 1966; on computer back to 1986. Online access to criminal records is the same as civil.
General Information: Public Access terminal is available. No adoption or juvenile records released. SASE not required. Turnaround time 1-2 days. Copy fee: $.50 per page. Certification fee: The fee is $1.00 for criminal records and $5.00 for civil. Fee payee: Clerk of Court. Personal checks accepted. Prepayment is required.

Lafourche Parish

17th District Court PO Box 818, Thibodaux, LA 70302; 985-447-4841; Fax: 985-447-5800. Hours: 8:30AM-4:30PM (CST). *Felony, Misdemeanor, Civil, Probate.*
Civil Records: Access: Fax, mail, in person. Both court and visitors may perform in person searches. Search fee: $15.00 per name. Fee is for 10 year search. Required to search: name, years to search. Civil cases indexed by defendant, plaintiff. Civil records on computer from 1982, microfiche from 1968, index books back to 1800s.
Criminal Records: Access: Fax, mail, in person. Both court and visitors may perform in person searches. Search fee: $15.00 per name. Fee is for 10 year search. Required to search: name, years to search, DOB; also helpful: SSN, race, sex. Criminal records on computer from 1982, microfiche to 1968, index books to 1800s.
General Information: Public Access terminal is available. No adoption or juvenile records released. SASE requested. Turnaround time 1-2 days. Fax notes: $5.00 for first page, $1.00 each add'l. Copy fee: $.55 per page. Certification fee: Minimum certification fee with copies is $3.30. Fee payee: Lafourche Parish Clerk of

Court. Personal checks accepted. Prepayment is required.

Lincoln Parish

3rd District Court PO Box 924, Ruston, LA 71273-0924; 318-251-5130; Fax: 318-255-6004. Hours: 8:30AM-4:30PM (CST). *Felony, Misdemeanor, Civil, Probate.*
Civil Records: Access: Mail, in person. Both court and visitors may perform in person searches. Search fee: $10.00 per name. Fee is per 10 years searched. Required to search: name, years to search. Civil cases indexed by defendant, plaintiff. Civil records on computer since 1985, index books back to 1800s.
Criminal Records: Access: Mail, in person. Both court and visitors may perform in person searches. Search fee: $10.00 per name. Fee is per 10 years searched. Required to search: name, years to search, DOB; also helpful: SSN. Criminal records on computer since 1992.
General Information: Public Access terminal is available. No adoption or juvenile records released. SASE not required. Turnaround time 1-2 days. Fax notes: Fee to fax results is $5.00 for 1st page, $1.00 each add'l. Copy fee: $1.00 per page. Certification fee: $2.00. Fee payee: Clerk of Court. Personal checks accepted. Prepayment is required.

Livingston Parish

21st District Court PO Box 1150, Livingston, LA 70754; 225-686-2216. Hours: 8AM-4:30PM (CST). *Felony, Misdemeanor, Civil, Probate.*
Civil Records: Access: In person only. Visitors must perform in person searches for themselves. No search fee. Required to search: name, years to search. Civil cases indexed by defendant, plaintiff. Civil records on index books since 1800s.
Criminal Records: Access: In person only. Visitors must perform in person searches for themselves. No search fee. Required to search: name, years to search, DOB; also helpful: SSN, race, sex. Criminal records on index books since 1800s.
General Information: Public Access terminal is available. No adoption or juvenile records released. Copy fee: $1.00 per page. Certification fee: $5.00. Fee payee: 21st District Court. Personal checks accepted. Prepayment is required.

Madison Parish

6th District Court PO Box 1710, Tallulah, LA 71282; 318-574-0655; Fax: 318-574-0656. Hours: 8:30AM-4:30PM (CST). *Felony, Misdemeanor, Civil, Probate.*
Civil Records: Access: Phone, mail, in person. Both court and visitors may perform in person searches. Search fee: $10.00 per name. Required to search: name, years to search. Civil cases indexed by defendant, plaintiff. Civil records kept on computer since 7/93.
Criminal Records: Access: Phone, mail, in person. Both court and visitors may perform in person searches. Search fee: $10.00 per name. Required to search: name, years to search, DOB; also helpful: SSN. Criminal records on index.
General Information: No adoption or juvenile records released. SASE required. Turnaround time 1-2 days. No copy fee. Certification fee: $5.50. Fee does not include any copy fees. Fee payee: Clerk of Court. Personal checks accepted. Prepayment is required.

Morehouse Parish

4th District Court PO Box 1543, Bastrop, LA 71221; 318-281-3343/3346/3349; Fax: 318-281-3775. Hours: 8:30AM-4:30PM (CST). *Felony, Misdemeanor, Civil, Probate.*
Civil Records: Access: Phone, fax, mail, in person. Both court and visitors may perform in person searches.

Search fee: $15.00 per name. Fee is per 10 years searched. Required to search: name, years to search; also helpful: address. Civil cases indexed by defendant, plaintiff. Civil records on computer since 1987, in books since 1898, some on microfilm.
Criminal Records: Access: Phone, fax, mail, in person. Both court and visitors may perform in person searches. Search fee: $15.00 per name. Fee is per 10 years searched. Required to search: name, years to search, DOB; also helpful: address, SSN. Criminal records in books since 1926 and on microfilm since 1974.
General Information: Public Access terminal is available. No adoption, juvenile or judicial commitment records released. SASE required. Turnaround time 2-3 days. Fax notes: $5.00 for first page, $1.00 each add'l. Copy fee: $1.00 per page. Certification fee: $2.50. Fee payee: Clerk of Court. Personal checks accepted. Prepayment is required.

Natchitoches Parish

10th District Court PO Box 476, Natchitoches, LA 71458; 318-352-8152; Fax: 318-352-9321. Hours: 8:15AM-4:30PM (CST). *Felony, Misdemeanor, Civil, Probate.*
Civil Records: Access: Phone, fax, mail, in person. Both court and visitors may perform in person searches. Search fee: $10.00 per name. Required to search: name, years to search. Civil cases indexed by defendant, plaintiff. Civil records on computer back to 6/1991, archived from 1950, index books back to 1800s.
Criminal Records: Access: Phone, fax, mail, in person. Both court and visitors may perform in person searches. Search fee: $10.00 per name. Required to search: name, years to search, DOB; also helpful: SSN. Criminal records on computer back to 6/1991, archived from 1950, index books back to 1800s.
General Information: Public Access terminal is available. No adoption or juvenile records released. SASE required. Turnaround time 1 week. Fax notes: $5.00 1st page, $2.00 each add'l. Fax available for civil division only. Copy fee: $1.00 per page. Certification fee: $5.00. Fee payee: Clerk of Court. Personal checks accepted. Prepayment is required.

Orleans Parish

Civil District Court 421 Loyola Ave, Rm 402, New Orleans, LA 70112; 504-592-9100 X122; Fax: 504-592-9128. Hours: 8AM-5PM *Civil, Probate.*
www.orleanscdc.gov
Civil Records: Access: Phone, mail, online, in person. Both court and visitors may perform in person searches. No search fee. Required to search: name, years to search. Civil cases indexed by defendant, plaintiff. Civil records on computer since 1985, in books back to early 1800s. CDC Remote provides access to civil cases from 1985 and First City Court cases as well as parish mortgage and conveyance indexes. The fee is $250 per year. Call 504-592-9264 for more information. **General Information:** Public Access terminal is available. No adoptions or juvenile released. SASE required. Turnaround time 1-2 days. Copy fee: $.75 per page. Certification fee: $2.00 per document. Fee payee: Clerk of Court. Only cashiers checks and money orders accepted. Prepayment is required.

New Orleans City Court 421 Loyola Ave, Rm 201, New Orleans, LA 70112; 504-592-9155; Fax: 504-592-9281. Hours: 8:30AM-4PM (CST). *Civil Actions Under $20,000, Small Claims.*
www.orleanscdc.gov/fcc.htm
Civil Records: Access: Mail, online, in person. Both court and visitors may perform in person searches. No search fee. Required to search: name, years to search. Civil cases indexed by defendant, plaintiff. Civil records on computer back to 1988. CDC Remote provides

access to First City Court cases from 1988 as well as civil cases, parish mortgage and conveyance indexes. The fee is $250 per year. Call 504-592-9264 for more information. **General Information:** Public Access terminal is available. No sealed records released. SASE requested. Turnaround time 5-10 days. Copy fee: $1.00 per page. Certification fee: $3.00. Fee payee: New Orleans First City Court. Personal checks accepted. Credit cards accepted: Visa, MasterCard. Prepayment is required.

4th District Court - Criminal Division
2700 Tulane Ave, Rm 115, New Orleans, LA 70119; 504-827-3520; Fax: 504-827-3385. Hours: 8:15AM-3:30PM (CST). *Felony, Misdemeanor.*

Criminal Records: Access: Mail, in person. Both court and visitors may perform in person searches. Search fee: $10.00 per name. Expedited search available for $20.00 per name. Required to search: name, years to search, DOB; also helpful: SSN. Criminal records on computer past 8 years, books and files go back to early 1900s.
General Information: Public Access terminal is available. No adoption or juvenile records released. SASE required. Turnaround time 2 days. No copy fee. Certification fee: $1.50 per page. Fee payee: Clerk of Court. Business checks accepted. Prepayment is required.

Ouachita Parish

4th District Court
PO Box 1862, Monroe, LA 71210-1862; 318-327-1444; Fax: 318-327-1462. Hours: 8:30AM-5PM (CST). *Felony, Misdemeanor, Civil, Probate.*

Civil Records: Access: Fax, mail, in person. Both court and visitors may perform in person searches. Search fee: $10.00 per name. Required to search: name, years to search. Civil cases indexed by defendant, plaintiff. Civil records on computer from 1991, index books back to 1800s.
Criminal Records: Access: Fax, mail, in person. Both court and visitors may perform in person searches. Search fee: $10.00 per name. Required to search: name, years to search, DOB; also helpful: SSN. Criminal records on computer from 1991, index books back to 1800s.
General Information: No adoption or juvenile records released. SASE required. Turnaround time 1-2 days. Fax notes: $2.00 for first page, $1.00 each add'l. Copy fee: $.50 per page. Certification fee: $2.00. Fee payee: Clerk of Court. Business checks accepted. Checks accepted up to $50.00. Prepayment is required.

Plaquemines Parish

25th District Court
PO Box 129, Pointe A La Hache, LA 70082; 985-333-4377; Fax: 985-333-9202. Hours: 8:30AM-4:30PM (CST). *Felony, Misdemeanor, Civil, Probate.*

Civil Records: Access: In person only. Visitors must perform in person searches for themselves. No search fee. Required to search: name, years to search. Civil cases indexed by defendant, plaintiff. Civil records on index books back to 1800s.
Criminal Records: Access: In person only. Visitors must perform in person searches for themselves. No search fee. Required to search: name, years to search, DOB. Criminal records on index books back to 1966.
General Information: No adoption or juvenile records released. Copy fee: $.50 per page. Certification fee: $3.00. Fee payee: Clerk of Court. Personal checks accepted. Prepayment is required.

Pointe Coupee Parish

18th District Court
PO Box 86, New Roads, LA 70760; 225-638-9596. Hours: 8:30AM-4:30PM (CST). *Felony, Misdemeanor, Civil, Probate.*

Civil Records: Access: Mail, in person. Both court and visitors may perform in person searches. No search fee. Required to search: name, years to search. Civil cases indexed by defendant, plaintiff. Civil records on index books back to 1800s.
Criminal Records: Access: In person only. Visitors must perform in person searches for themselves. No search fee. Required to search: name, years to search, DOB; also helpful: SSN. Criminal records on index books back to 1800s.
General Information: No adoption or juvenile records released. SASE not required. Turnaround time 2 weeks. Copy fee: $1.25 per page. Certification fee: $5.00. Fee payee: Clerk of Court. Personal checks accepted. Prepayment is required.

Rapides Parish

9th District Court
PO Box 952, Alexandria, LA 71309; 318-473-8153; Fax: 318-473-4667. Hours: 8:30AM-4:30PM (CST). *Felony, Misdemeanor, Civil, Probate.*

Civil Records: Access: Mail, in person. Both court and visitors may perform in person searches. Search fee: $11.00 per name. Fee is per separate index. Required to search: name, years to search. Civil cases indexed by defendant, plaintiff. Civil records on index books since 1864, civil in computer since 1985.
Criminal Records: Access: Mail, in person. Both court and visitors may perform in person searches. Search fee: $11.00 per name. Fee is per separate index. Required to search: name, years to search, DOB; also helpful: SSN. Criminal records on computer since 1984; prior records in index books back to 1864.
General Information: Public Access terminal is available. No adoption, juvenile, or judicial commitment records released. SASE not required. Turnaround time 2-4 days. Copy fee: $.50 per page. Certification fee: $2.00. Fee payee: Rapides Parish Clerk of Court. Personal checks accepted. Prepayment is required.

Red River Parish

39th District Court
PO Box 485, Coushatta, LA 71019; 318-932-6741. Hours: 8:30AM-4:30PM (CST). *Felony, Misdemeanor, Civil, Probate.*

Civil Records: Access: Mail, in person. Both court and visitors may perform in person searches. Search fee: $10.00 per name. Required to search: name, years to search. Civil cases indexed by defendant, plaintiff. Civil records on index books.
Criminal Records: Access: Mail, in person. Only the court performs in person searches; visitors may not. Search fee: $10.00 per name. Required to search: name, years to search, DOB; also helpful: SSN. The index is kept in the DA's office.
General Information: No adoption or juvenile records released. SASE required. Turnaround time 1-2 days. Copy fee: $1.00 per page. Certification fee: $5.00. Fee payee: Clerk of Court. Personal checks accepted. Prepayment is required.

Richland Parish

5th District Court
PO Box 119, Rayville, LA 71269; 318-728-4171. Hours: 8:30AM-4:30PM (CST). *Felony, Misdemeanor, Civil, Probate.*

Civil Records: Access: Mail, in person. Both court and visitors may perform in person searches. Search fee: $10.00 per name. Required to search: name, years to search. Civil cases indexed by defendant, plaintiff. Civil records on since 1/94, prior on books to 1800s.

Criminal Records: Access: Mail, in person. Both court and visitors may perform in person searches. Search fee: $10.00 per name. Required to search: name, years to search, DOB, SSN. Criminal records on since 1/94, prior on books to 1800s.
General Information: No adoption or juvenile records released. SASE required. Turnaround time 1-2 days. Copy fee: $1.00 per page. Certification fee: $3.00. Fee payee: Clerk of Court. Personal checks accepted. Prepayment is required.

Sabine Parish

11th District Court
PO Box 419, Many, LA 71449; 318-256-6223; Fax: 318-256-9037. Hours: 8AM-4:30PM (CST). *Felony, Misdemeanor, Civil, Probate.*

Civil Records: Access: Fax, mail, in person. Both court and visitors may perform in person searches. Search fee: $10.00 per name. Required to search: name, years to search. Civil cases indexed by defendant, plaintiff. Civil records on index books back to 1843's.
Criminal Records: Access: Fax, mail, in person. Both court and visitors may perform in person searches. Search fee: $10.00 per name. Required to search: name, years to search. Criminal Records available for 10 years.´
General Information: Public Access terminal is available. No adoption or juvenile records released. SASE required. Turnaround time 5-10 days. Fax notes: $5.00 for first page, $2.00 each add'l. Copy fee: $1.25 per page. Certification fee: $4.00. Fee payee: Sabine Parish Clerk. Personal checks accepted. Prepayment is required.

St. Bernard Parish

34th District Court
PO Box 1746, Chalmette, LA 70044; 504-271-3434. Hours: 8:30AM-4:30PM (CST). *Felony, Misdemeanor, Civil, Probate.*

Civil Records: Access: Mail, in person. Both court and visitors may perform in person searches. Search fee: $5.00 per name. Fee is per 10 years searched. Required to search: name, years to search. Civil cases indexed by defendant, plaintiff. Civil records on index books back to 1800s, on computer since 1989.
Criminal Records: Access: Mail, in person. Both court and visitors may perform in person searches. Search fee: $5.00 per name. Fee is per 10 years searched. Required to search: name, years to search, DOB; also helpful: SSN. Criminal records on index books back to 1800s, on computer since 1989.
General Information: Public Access terminal is available. No adoption or juvenile. SASE required. Turnaround time 2-3 days. Copy fee: $1.00 per page. Certification fee: $5.00. Fee payee: Clerk of Court. Personal checks accepted. Prepayment is required.

St. Charles Parish

29th District Court
PO Box 424, Hahnville, LA 70057; 985-783-6632; Fax: 985-783-2005. Hours: 8:30AM-4:30PM (CST). *Felony, Misdemeanor, Civil, Probate.*

Civil Records: Access: Mail, in person. Both court and visitors may perform in person searches. Search fee: $5.00 per name. Required to search: name, years to search. Civil cases indexed by defendant, plaintiff. Civil records on computer back to 1981, on index books back to 1800s.
Criminal Records: Access: Mail, in person. Both court and visitors may perform in person searches. Search fee: $5.00 per name. Required to search: name, years to search, DOB; also helpful: SSN, race, sex. Criminal records on computer back to 1981, on index books back to 1800s.
General Information: Public Access terminal is available. No adoption or juvenile records released. Turnaround time 1 day. Fax notes: Fee to fax results is

$4.00 per document. Copy fee: $.50 per page. Certification fee: $2.00 per page. Fee payee: Clerk of Court. Personal checks accepted. Prepayment is required.

St. Helena Parish

21st District Court PO Box 308, Greensburg, LA 70441; 225-222-4514. Hours: 8:30AM-4:30PM (CST). *Felony, Misdemeanor, Civil, Probate.*

Civil Records: Access: Phone, mail, fax, in person. Both court and visitors may perform in person searches. Search fee: $10.00 per name. Required to search: name, years to search. Civil cases indexed by defendant, plaintiff. Civil records on index books back to 1800s.
Criminal Records: Access: Mail, in person. Both court and visitors may perform in person searches. Search fee: $10.00 per name. Required to search: name, years to search, DOB; also helpful: SSN. Criminal records on index books back to 1800s.
General Information: No adoption or juvenile records released. SASE required. Turnaround time 1-2 days. Fax notes: Fee to fax results is $2.00 per page. No copy fee. Certification fee: $5.00. Fee payee: Clerk of Court. Personal checks accepted.

St. James Parish

23rd District Court PO Box 63, Convent, LA 70723; 225-562-7496; Fax: 504-562-2383. Hours: 8AM-4:30PM (CST). *Felony, Misdemeanor, Civil, Probate.*

Civil Records: Access: Mail, in person. Both court and visitors may perform in person searches. Search fee: $15.00 per name. Required to search: name, years to search. Civil cases indexed by defendant, plaintiff. Civil records on index books back to early 1900s; on computer back to 1988.
Criminal Records: Access: Mail, in person. Both court and visitors may perform in person searches. Search fee: $15.00 per name. Required to search: name, years to search, DOB. Criminal records on index books back to early 1900s; on computer back to 1990.
General Information: Public Access terminal is available. No adoption or juvenile records released. SASE required. Turnaround time 1-2 days. Copy fee: $.75 per page. Certification fee: $5.00. Fee payee: Clerk of Court. Only cashiers checks and money orders accepted. Prepayment is required.

St. John the Baptist Parish

40th District Court PO Box 280, Edgard, LA 70049; 985-497-3331; Fax: 985-497-3972. Hours: 8:30AM-4:30PM (CST). *Felony, Misdemeanor, Civil, Probate.*

Civil Records: Access: Mail, fax, in person. Both court and visitors may perform in person searches. Search fee: $5.00 per name. Fee is for first 5 years. Add $1.00 per additional year. Required to search: name, years to search. Civil cases indexed by defendant, plaintiff. Civil records on computer since 1983.
Criminal Records: Access: Mail, fax, in person. Both court and visitors may perform in person searches. Search fee: $5.00 per name. Fee is for first 5 years. Add $1.00 per additional year. Required to search: name, years to search, DOB; also helpful: SSN. Felony records on computer since 1983, misdemeanors since 3/91.
General Information: Public Access terminal is available. No adoption or juvenile records released. SASE required. Turnaround time 3-4 days. Fax notes: Fee to fax results is $5.00 per page. Copy fee: $1.00 per page. Certification fee: $5.50. Fee payee: Clerk of Court. Personal checks accepted. Prepayment is required.

St. Landry Parish

27th District Court PO Box 750, Courthouse, Opelousas, LA 70570; 337-942-5606; Fax: 337-948-1653. Hours: 8AM-4:30PM (CST). *Felony, Misdemeanor, Civil, Probate.*
www.stlandry.org/CourtsDivision.html
Civil Records: Access: Mail, fax, in person. Both court and visitors may perform in person searches. Search fee: $15.00 per name. Additional $1.00 fee per year after 1st 10 years. Required to search: name, years to search. Civil cases indexed by defendant, plaintiff. Civil records on index books back to 1800s, on computer back to 1992.
Criminal Records: Access: Mail, fax, in person. Both court and visitors may perform in person searches. Search fee: $15.00 per name. Additional $1.00 fee per year after 1st 10 years. Required to search: name, years to search, DOB; also helpful: SSN. Criminal records on index books back to 1800s, on computer back to 1992.
General Information: Public Access terminal is available. (Public terminal only allows access to civil records.) No adoption or juvenile records released. SASE required. Turnaround time 1-2 days. Fax notes: Fee to fax results is $5.00 1st page, $1.00 each add'l. Copy fee: $.75 per page. Certification fee: $5.50. Fee payee: Clerk of Court. Personal checks accepted. Prepayment is required.

St. Martin Parish

16th District Court PO Box 308, St. Martinville, LA 70582; 337-394-2210; Fax: 337-394-7772. Hours: 8:30AM-4:30PM (CST). *Felony, Misdemeanor, Civil, Probate.*

Civil Records: Access: Fax, mail, in person. Both court and visitors may perform in person searches. Search fee: $10.00 per name. Required to search: name, years to search; also helpful: address. Civil cases indexed by defendant, plaintiff. Civil records archived from 1760, on computer since 1990.
Criminal Records: Access: Fax, mail, in person. Both court and visitors may perform in person searches. Search fee: $10.00 per name. Required to search: name, years to search, DOB; also helpful: address, SSN. Criminal records archived from 1760, on computer since 1990.
General Information: Public Access terminal is available. No adoption, sealed records, expunged or juvenile records released. SASE required. Turnaround time 1-2 days. Fax notes: $.75 per page. Copy fee: $.50 per page. Certification fee: $6.00. Fee payee: Clerk of Court. Personal checks accepted. Prepayment is required.

St. Mary Parish

16th District Court PO Box 1231, Franklin, LA 70538; 337-828-4100 X200; Fax: 337-828-2509. Hours: 8:30AM-4:30PM (CST). *Felony, Misdemeanor, Civil, Probate.*

Civil Records: Access: In person only. Visitors must perform in person searches for themselves. No search fee. Required to search: name, years to search. Civil cases indexed by defendant, plaintiff. Civil records on index books back to 1800s.
Criminal Records: Access: In person only. Visitors must perform in person searches for themselves. No search fee. Required to search: name, years to search, DOB; also helpful: SSN. Criminal records on index books back to 1800s.
General Information: No adoption or juvenile records released. Copy fee: $1.00 per page. Certification fee: $5.00. Fee payee: St. Mary Parish Clerk of Court. Personal checks accepted. Prepayment is required.

St. Tammany Parish

22nd District Court PO Box 1090, Covington, LA 70434; 985-898-2430. Hours: 8:30AM-4:30PM (CST). *Felony, Misdemeanor, Civil, Probate.*
http://stp.pa.st-tammany.la.us/othergov/clerk
Civil Records: Access: Mail, in person, online. Both court and visitors may perform in person searches. Search fee: $10.00 per name. Required to search: name, years to search. Civil cases indexed by defendant, plaintiff. Civil records on index books back to 1800s, on computer since 1967. Remote online access to civil records is available from the Clerk of Court; fee is $.20 per minute with a $100 initial setup fee. Modem and PC Anywhere is required. For information, call Khristy Howell at 985-898-2491.
Criminal Records: Access: Mail, in person, online. Both court and visitors may perform in person searches. Search fee: $10.00 per name. Required to search: name, years to search, DOB; also helpful: SSN. Criminal records on computer since 10/87. Remote online access to criminal records is the same as civil.
General Information: Public Access terminal is available. No adoption or juvenile records released. SASE required. Turnaround time 2-3 days. Copy fee: $1.00 per page. Certification fee: $2.00 per document. Fee payee: Clerk of Court. Personal checks accepted. Prepayment is required.

Tangipahoa Parish

21st District Court PO Box 667, Amite, LA 70422; 985-748-4146; Fax: 985-748-6503. 8:30AM-4:30PM (CST). *Felony, Misdemeanor, Civil, Probate.*
www.tangiclerk.org
Civil Records: Access: Phone, fax, mail, in person, online, email. Both court and visitors may perform in person searches. Search fee: $10.00 per name. Required to search: name, years to search. Civil cases indexed by defendant, plaintiff. Civil records archived back to early 1900s; on computer back to 1980. Online access to Parish notarial records is available by subscription; visit the web site for or call Alison Theard at 985-549-1611.
Criminal Records: Access: Phone, fax, mail, in person, email. Both court and visitors may perform in person searches. Search fee: $10.00 per name. Required to search: name, years to search, DOB; also helpful: SSN. Criminal records archived back to early 1900s; on computer back to 1980.
General Information: Public Access terminal is available. No adoption or juvenile records released. SASE required. Turnaround time 3-4 days. Fax notes: Fee to fax results is $5.00 1st page, $1.00 each add'l. Copy fee: $1.00 per page. Certification fee: $5.50. Fee payee: Clerk of Court. Personal checks accepted. Prepayment is required.

Tensas Parish

6th District Court PO Box 78, St. Joseph, LA 71366; 318-766-3921. Hours: 8:30AM-4:30PM (CST). *Felony, Misdemeanor, Civil, Probate.*

Civil Records: Access: In person only. Visitors must perform in person searches for themselves. No search fee. Required to search: name, years to search. Civil cases indexed by defendant, plaintiff. Civil records archived back to 1800s, on computer since mid-1998.
Criminal Records: Access: In person only. Visitors must perform in person searches for themselves. No search fee. Required to search: name, years to search; also helpful: DOB, SSN. Criminal records on computer since 1998; archived back to 1800s.
General Information: No adoption or juvenile records released. Fax notes: Fee to fax results is $5.00 per document. Certification fee: $5.50. Fee payee: Clerk of Court. Personal checks accepted. Prepayment is required.

Terrebonne Parish

32nd District Court PO Box 1569, Houma, LA 70361; 985-868-5660. Hours: 8:30AM-4:30PM (CST). *Felony, Misdemeanor, Civil, Probate.*

Civil Records: Access: Mail, in person. Both court and visitors may perform in person searches. Search fee: $15.00 per name. Required to search: name, years to search. Civil cases indexed by defendant, plaintiff. Civil records on computer since 1986, in books to 1823.

Criminal Records: Access: Mail, in person. Both court and visitors may perform in person searches. Search fee: $15.00 per name. Required to search: name, years to search, DOB; also helpful: SSN, race, sex. Criminal records archived to 1800s.

General Information: No adoption or juvenile records released. SASE required. Turnaround time 2-3 days. Fax notes: Fee to fax results is $2.00 per page. Copy fee: $.75 per page. Certification fee: $6.00. Fee payee: Terrebonne Parish Clerk of Court. Personal checks accepted. Prepayment is required.

Union Parish

3rd District Court Courthouse Bldg, 100 E Bayou #105, Farmerville, LA 71241; 318-368-3055; Fax: 318-368-2487. Hours: 8:30AM-4:30PM (CST). *Felony, Misdemeanor, Civil, Probate.*

Civil Records: Access: Mail, in person. Search fee: $5.00 per name. Required to search: name, years to search. Civil cases indexed by defendant, plaintiff. Civil records on index books back to 1839.

Criminal Records: Access: Mail, fax, in person. Both court and visitors may perform in person searches. Search fee: $10.00 per name. Required to search: name, years to search, SSN. Criminal records on index books back to 1839; computerized records go back to 1982.

General Information: No adoption or juvenile records released. SASE required. Turnaround time 2-3 days. Fax notes: $3.00 fee per document. Copy fee: $.75 per page. Certification fee: $2.00. Fee payee: Clerk of Court. Personal checks accepted. Prepayment required.

Vermilion Parish

15th District Court 100 N. State St, #101, Abbeville, LA 70511-0790; 337-898-1992; Fax: 337-898-0404. Hours: 8:30AM-4:30PM (CST). *Felony, Misdemeanor, Civil, Probate.*

Civil Records: Access: Phone, fax, mail, in person. Both court and visitors may perform in person searches. Search fee: $12.00 per name. Fee for second name on same search request is $6.50. Required to search: name, years to search. Civil cases indexed by defendant, plaintiff. Civil records on computer since 1982, in books since 1885, on microfilm since 1885.

Criminal Records: Access: Phone, fax, mail, in person. Both court and visitors may perform in person searches. Search fee: $12.00 per name. Fee for second name on same search request is $6.50. Required to search: name, years to search, DOB; also helpful: SSN, race, sex. Criminal records on computer since 1982, in books since 1885, on microfilm since 1885.

General Information: Public Access terminal is available. No adoption or juvenile records released. SASE required. Turnaround time 1-2 days after payment. Fax notes: $2.00 for first page, $1.00 each add'l. Copy fee: $1.00 per page. Certification fee: $5.00. Fee payee: Vermilion Parish Clerk of Court. Personal checks accepted. Prepayment is required.

Vernon Parish

30th District Court PO Box 40, Leesville, LA 71496; 337-238-1384; Fax: 337-238-9902. Hours: 8AM-4:30PM *Felony, Misdemeanor, Civil, Probate.*

Civil Records: Access: Mail, in person. Both court and visitors may perform in person searches. Search fee: $10.00 per name. Required to search: name, years to

search. Civil cases indexed by defendant, plaintiff. Civil records on computer from November 1985, archived back to 1900.

Criminal Records: Access: Mail, in person. Both court and visitors may perform in person searches. Search fee: $10.00 per name. Required to search: name, years to search, DOB. Criminal records on computer from November 1985, archived back to 1900.

General Information: Public Access terminal is available. No adoption or juvenile records released. SASE required. Turnaround time same day. Copy fee: $1.25 per page. Certification fee: $3.00. Fee payee: Clerk of Court. Personal checks accepted. Prepayment is required.

Washington Parish

22nd District Court PO Box 607, Franklinton, LA 70438; 985-839-4663/7821. Hours: 8AM-4:30PM (CST). *Felony, Misdemeanor, Civil, Probate.*

Civil Records: Access: Mail, in person. Both court and visitors may perform in person searches. Search fee: $10.00 per name. Required to search: name, years to search. Civil cases indexed by defendant, plaintiff. Civil records on computer from August 1989, archived April 1967, index books back to 1800s.

Criminal Records: Access: Mail, in person. Both court and visitors may perform in person searches. Search fee: $10.00 per name. Required to search: name, years to search, DOB, SSN. Criminal records on computer from August 1989, archived April 1967, index books back to 1800s.

General Information: No adoption or juvenile records released. SASE requested. Turnaround time 1-2 days. Copy fee: $1.00 per page. Certification fee: $5.00. Fee payee: Washington Parish Clerk of Court. Personal checks accepted. Prepayment is required.

Webster Parish

26th District Court PO Box 370, Minden, LA 71058-0370; 318-371-0366; Fax: 318-371-0226. 8:30AM-4:30PM *Felony, Misdemeanor, Civil, Probate.*

Civil Records: Access: Fax, mail, in person. Both court and visitors may perform in person searches. Search fee: $10.00 per name. Required to search: name, years to search. Civil cases indexed by defendant, plaintiff. Civil records archived to 1800s, on computer to 1986.

Criminal Records: Access: Fax, mail, in person. Both court and visitors may perform in person searches. Search fee: $10.00 per name. Required to search: name; also helpful: years to search. Criminal records not on computer, in books to 1800s.

General Information: No adoption or juvenile records released. SASE not required. Turnaround time 2-3 days. Fax notes: $5.00 per page. Copy fee: $1.00 per page. Certification fee: $5.00. Fee payee: Clerk of Court. Personal checks accepted. Prepayment is required.

West Baton Rouge Parish

18th District Court PO Box 107, Port Allen, LA 70767; 225-383-0378. Hours: 8:30AM-4:30PM (CST). *Felony, Misdemeanor, Civil, Probate.*

Civil Records: Access: Phone, mail, in person. Both court and visitors may perform in person searches. Search fee: $10.00 per name. Required to search: name, years to search. Civil cases indexed by defendant, plaintiff. Civil records on computer from 1983.

Criminal Records: Access: Phone, mail, in person. Both court and visitors may perform in person searches. Search fee: $10.00 per name. Required to search: name, years to search, DOB; also helpful: SSN. Criminal records on computer from 1983.

General Information: No adoption or juvenile records released. SASE required. Turnaround time 1-2 days. Copy fee: $.50 per page. Certification fee: $2.00. Fee

payee: Clerk of Court. Personal checks accepted. Prepayment is required.

West Carroll Parish

5th District Court PO Box 1078, Oak Grove, LA 71263; 318-428-3281. Hours: 8:30AM-4:30PM (CST). *Felony, Misdemeanor, Civil, Probate.*

Civil Records: Access: Mail, in person. Both court and visitors may perform in person searches. Search fee: $1.00 per name per year. Required to search: name, years to search. Civil cases indexed by defendant, plaintiff. Civil records on index books back to 1800s.

Criminal Records: Access: Mail, in person. Both court and visitors may perform in person searches. Search fee: $1.00 per name per year. Required to search: name, years to search, DOB. Criminal records on index books back to 1800s.

General Information: No adoption or juvenile records released. SASE required. Turnaround time 1-2 days. Copy fee: $1.00 per page. Certification fee: $3.00. Fee payee: Clerk of Court. Only cashiers checks and money orders accepted. Prepayment is required.

West Feliciana Parish

20th District Court PO Box 1843, St Francisville, LA 70775; 225-635-3794; Fax: 225-635-3770. Hours: 8:30AM-4:30PM (CST). *Felony, Misdemeanor, Civil, Probate.*

Civil Records: Access: Mail, in person. Both court and visitors may perform in person searches. Search fee: $10.00 per name. Fee is per 5 years searched. Required to search: name, years to search; also helpful: address. Civil cases indexed by defendant, plaintiff. Civil records on computer from 1984, index books back to 1800s.

Criminal Records: Access: Mail, in person. Both court and visitors may perform in person searches. Search fee: $10.00 per name. Fee is per 5 years searched. Required to search: name, years to search, DOB; also helpful: address. Criminal records on computer since 1992; prior on cards and dockets back to 1800s.

General Information: No adoption, juvenile or juvenile records released. SASE required. Turnaround time 3-5 days. Copy fee: $1.00 per page. Certification fee: $5.00. Fee payee: Clerk of Court. Business checks accepted. Prepayment is required.

Winn Parish

8th District Court 100 Main St, #103, Winnfield, LA 71483; 318-628-3515. Hours: 8AM-4:30PM (CST). *Felony, Misdemeanor, Civil, Probate.*

Civil Records: Access: Mail, in person. Both court and visitors may perform in person searches. Search fee: $15.00 per name. Fee is for 10 year search. Required to search: name, years to search, address. Civil cases indexed by defendant, plaintiff. Civil records on books from 1886 to present, on computer from 1988, mortgages since 1981, conveyances since 1993.

Criminal Records: Access: Mail, in person. Both court and visitors may perform in person searches. Search fee: $15.00 per name. Fee is for 10 year search. Required to search: name, years to search, address, DOB; also helpful: SSN. Criminal records in books since 1886, computerized since 1997.

General Information: No adoption or juvenile records released. SASE required. Turnaround time 2-3 days. Fax notes: Fee to fax results is $5.00 per document and $1.00 per page. Copy fee: $1.00 per page. Certification fee: $5.00. Fee payee: Winn Parish Clerk of Court. Personal checks accepted. Prepayment is required.

Louisiana Recording Offices

ORGANIZATION   64 parishes (not counties), 64 recording offices. One parish, St. Martin, has two non-contiguous segments. The recording officer is the Clerk of Court. Many parishes include tax and other non-UCC liens in their mortgage records. The entire state is in the Central Time Zone (CST).

REAL ESTATE RECORDS   Most parishes will perform a mortgage search. Some will provide a record owner search. Copy and certification fees vary widely.

UCC RECORDS   Financing statements are filed with the Clerk of Court in any parish in the state and are entered onto a statewide computerized database of UCC financing statements available for searching at any parish office. All parishes perform UCC searches for $15.00 per debtor name. Use search request form UCC-11. Copy fees are $.50-1.00 per page.

TAX LIEN RECORDS   All federal and state tax liens are filed with the Clerk of Court. Parishes usually file tax liens on personal property in their UCC or mortgage records, and most will perform tax lien searches for varying fees. Some parishes will automatically include tax liens on personal property in a mortgage certificate search.

OTHER LIENS   Judgments, labor, material, hospital.

Acadia Parish

Clerk of Court, P.O. Box 922, Crowley, LA 70526. 337-788-8881; Fax 337-788-1048. http://www.acadiaparishclerk.com
Will search UCC records. This agency will not do a tax lien search. Will provide mortgage certificates **Other Phone Numbers:** Assessor 337-788-8871; Treasurer 337-788-8800.

Allen Parish

Clerk of Court, P.O. Box 248, Oberlin, LA 70655. 337-639-4351; Fax 337-639-2030.
Will search UCC records. Tax liens not included in UCC search. RE owner, mortgage, and property transfer searches available. **Other Phone Numbers:** Assessor 337-639-4391.

Ascension Parish

Clerk of Court, P.O. Box 192, Donaldsonville, LA 70346. 225-473-9866; Fax 225-473-8641.
Will search UCC records. UCC search includes tax liens if requested. RE record owner and mortgage searches available. **Other Phone Numbers:** Assessor 225-473-9239.

Assumption Parish

Clerk of Court, P.O. Drawer 249, Napoleonville, LA 70390. 985-369-6653; Fax 985-369-2032.
Will search UCC records. UCC search includes tax liens if requested. RE record owner and mortgage searches available. **Other Phone Numbers:** Assessor 985-369-6385; Register of Voters 985-369-7347.

Avoyelles Parish

Clerk of Court, P.O. Box 196, Marksville, LA 71351. 318-253-7523; Fax 318-253-4614.
Will search UCC records. UCC search includes tax liens if requested. Will not search real estate records. **Other Phone Numbers:** Assessor 318-253-4507; Treasurer 318-253-9208.

Beauregard Parish

Clerk of Court, P.O. Box 100, De Ridder, LA 70634. 337-463-8595; Fax 337-462-3916.
Will search UCC records. Tax liens not included in UCC search. RE owner, mortgage, and property transfer searches available. **Other Phone Numbers:** Assessor 337-463-8945.

Bienville Parish

Clerk of Court, 100 Courthouse Dr, Rm 100, Room 100, Arcadia, LA 71001-3600. 318-263-2123; Fax 318-263-7426.
Will search UCC records. Tax liens not included in UCC search. RE owner, mortgage, and property transfer searches available. **Other Phone Numbers:** Assessor 318-263-2214; Treasurer 318-263-2019.

Bossier Parish

Clerk of Court, P.O. Box 430, Benton, LA 71006. 318-965-2336; http://www.ebrclerkofcourt.org
Will search UCC records. UCC search includes tax liens. Mortgage searches available. **Online Access:** Mortgage, Marriage Records. Records on the Parish Clerk of Courts database are available online for a $15 monthly fee and $.33 per minute, $.50 if you retrieve or print. Includes conveyance and mortgage record indexes from the previous 2 years to present. Also, marriage and court records from 1988 to present. Contact the MIS department at 225-389-5295. **Other Phone Numbers:** Assessor 318-965-2213.

Caddo Parish

Clerk of Court, 501 Texas Street, Room 103, Shreveport, LA 71101-5408. 318-226-6783 R/E Recording: 318-226-6790; Fax 318-227-9080. http://www.caddoclerk.com
Will search UCC records. Tax liens not included in UCC search. Will not search real estate records. **Online Access:** Real Estate, Liens, Marriage. Access to the Parish online records requires a $50 set up fee plus a $30 monthly fee. Mortgages and indirect conveyances date back to 1981; direct conveyances date back to 1914. Lending agency information available. UCCs are at Sec. of State. Marriage licenses go back to 1937. For system information, contact Susan Twohig at 318-226-6523. **Other Phone Numbers:** Assessor 318-226-6702; Treasurer 318-226-6900; Elections 318-226-6788.

Calcasieu Parish

Clerk of Court, P.O. Box 1030, Lake Charles, LA 70601-1030. 337-437-3550; Fax 337-437-3350.
Will search UCC records. UCC search includes tax liens. RE record owner and mortgage searches available. **Other Phone Numbers:** Assessor 337-437-3461; Treasurer 337-437-3680.

Caldwell Parish

Clerk of Court, P.O. Box 1327, Columbia, LA 71418. 318-649-2272; Fax 318-649-2037.
Will search UCC records. Tax liens not included in UCC search. Mortgage searches available. **Other Phone Numbers:** Assessor 318-649-2636; Treasurer 318-649-2681.

Cameron Parish

Clerk of Court, P.O. Box 549, Cameron, LA 70631. Clerk of Court, R/E and UCC Recording 337-775-5316; Fax 337-775-7172.
Will search UCC records. UCC search includes tax liens if requested. RE owner, mortgage, and property transfer searches available. **Other Phone Numbers:** Assessor 337-775-5416; Treasurer 337-775-5718; Elections 337-775-5316; Vital Records 337-775-5316.

Catahoula Parish

Clerk of Court, P.O. Box 198, Harrisonburg, LA 71340. 318-744-5497; Fax 318-744-5488.
Will search UCC records. Tax liens not included in UCC search. Mortgage searches available. **Other Phone Numbers:** Assessor 318-744-5291.

Claiborne Parish

Clerk of Court, P.O. Box 330, Homer, LA 71040. 318-927-9601; Fax 318-927-2345.
Will search UCC records. Tax liens not included in UCC search. Mortgage certificate searches (includes tax liens) are $16.50 for first name, $5.50 each add'l. **Other Phone Numbers:** Assessor 318-927-3022; Treasurer 318-927-2222.

Concordia Parish

Clerk of Court, Courthouse, P.O. Box 790, Vidalia, LA 71373. 318-336-4204.
Will search UCC records. UCC search includes tax liens. Mortgage searches available. **Other Phone Numbers:** Assessor 318-336-5122.

De Soto Parish

Clerk of Court, P.O. Box 1206, Mansfield, LA 71052. 318-872-3110; Fax 318-872-4202.
Will search UCC records. UCC search includes tax liens if requested. RE owner, mortgage, and property transfer searches available. **Other Phone Numbers:** Assessor 318-872-3610.

East Baton Rouge Parish

Clerk of Court, P.O. Box 1991, Baton Rouge, LA 70821-1991. 225-389-3985; Fax 225-389-3392. http://www.ebrclerkofcourt.org
Will search UCC records. UCC search includes tax liens if requested. RE owner, mortgage, and property transfer searches available. **Online Access:** Real Estate, Liens. Access to online records requires a $100 set up fee with a $5 monthly fee and $.33 per minute of use. Four years worth of data is kept active on the system. Lending agency information is available. For information, contact Wendy Gibbs at 225-398-5295. UCC information is located at the Secretary of State. **Other Phone Numbers:** Assessor 225-389-3920; Treasurer 225-389-3276.

East Carroll Parish

Clerk of Court, 400 First Street, Lake Providence, LA 71254. 318-559-2399.
Will search UCC records. Tax liens not included in UCC search. RE owner, mortgage, and property transfer searches available. **Other Phone Numbers:** Assessor 318-559-2850; Treasurer 318-559-2000.

East Feliciana Parish

Clerk of Court, P.O. Drawer 599, Clinton, LA 70722. 225-683-5145; Fax 225-683-3556.
Will search UCC records. Tax liens not included in UCC search. Mortgage searches available. Property description required **Other Phone Numbers:** Assessor 225-683-8945.

Evangeline Parish

Clerk of Court, P.O. Drawer 347, Ville Platte, LA 70586. Clerk of Court, R/E and UCC Recording 337-363-5671; Fax 337-363-5780.
Will search UCC records. Tax liens not included in UCC search. Mortgage searches available. **Other Phone Numbers:** Assessor 337-363-4310; Treasurer 337-363-5651.

Franklin Parish

Clerk of Court, P.O. Box 1564, Winnsboro, LA 71295. Clerk of Court, R/E and UCC Recording 318-435-5133; Fax 318-435-5134.
Will search UCC records. Tax liens not included in UCC search. Mortgage searches available. Property description required **Other Phone Numbers:** Assessor 318-435-5390.

Grant Parish

Clerk of Court, P.O. Box 263, Colfax, LA 71417. 318-627-3246; Fax 318-627-3201.
Will search UCC records. Tax liens not included in UCC search. Mortgage searches available. **Other Phone Numbers:** Assessor 318-627-5471.

Iberia Parish

Clerk of Court, P.O. Drawer 12010, New Iberia, LA 70562-2010. 337-365-7282; Fax 337-365-0737.
Will search UCC records. Tax liens not included in UCC search. RE owner, mortgage, and property transfer searches available. **Online Access:** Real Estate, Liens, Marriage Records, Divorce Records. Access to the Parish online records requires a $50 monthly usage fee. Records date back to 1959. Lending agency information is available. System includes court records. For information, contact Mike Thibodeaux at 337-365-7282. **Other Phone Numbers:** Assessor 337-369-4415; Treasurer 337-685-4720.

Iberville Parish

Clerk of Court, P.O. Box 423, Plaquemine, LA 70765-0423. 225-687-5160; Fax 225-687-5260.
Will search UCC records. Tax liens not included in UCC search. Mortgage searches available. **Other Phone Numbers:** Assessor 225-687-3568.

Jackson Parish

Clerk of Court, P.O. Drawer 730, Jonesboro, LA 71251. Clerk of Court, R/E and UCC Recording 318-259-2424; Fax 318-395-0386.
Will search UCC records. Tax liens not included in UCC search. Tax liens will automatically show on a mortgage certificate. RE record owner and mortgage searches available. **Other Phone Numbers:** Assessor 318-259-2151; Elections 318-259-2424; Police Jury 318-259-2361.

Jefferson Davis Parish

Clerk of Court, P.O. Box 799, Jennings, LA 70546-0799. 337-824-1160/1161.
Will search UCC records. UCC search includes tax liens if requested. RE record owner and mortgage searches available. **Other Phone Numbers:** Assessor 337-824-3451.

Jefferson Parish

Clerk of Court, P.O. Box 10, Gretna, LA 70054-0010. 504-364-2907; Fax 504-364-3836. http://www.clerkofcourt.co.jefferson.la.us
Will search UCC records. Tax liens not included in UCC search, but tax liens are included with other lien searches. Mortgage and property transfer searches available. **Online Access:** Real Estate, Assessor, Marriage, Civil. Online access to the clerk's JeffNet database is available by subscription; set-up fee is $200.00 plus $8.50 monthly and $.25 per minute. Mortgage and convenyance images go back to 1990; index to 1967. Marriage and assessor records go back to 1992. For information, visit www.clerkofcourt.co.jefferson.la.us/jeffnet.htm or call the Court Information Systems at 504-364-2908.

La Salle Parish

Clerk of Court, P.O. Box 1316, Jena, LA 71342. Clerk of Court, R/E and UCC Recording 318-992-2158; Fax 318-992-2157.
Will search UCC records. UCC search includes tax liens if requested. Separate combined tax lien search-$12.00 first name, $5.50 per additional name RE record owner and mortgage searches available. **Other Phone Numbers:** Assessor 318-992-8256; Appraiser/Auditor 318-992-2211; Elections 318-992-2158; Vital Records 318-992-2158.

Lafayette Parish

Clerk of Court, P.O. Box 2009, Lafayette, LA 70502. 337-233-0150; Fax 337-269-6392. http://www.lafayettecourthouse.com
Will search UCC records. UCC search includes tax liens if requested. Mortgage searches available. **Online Access:** Real Estate, Liens. Access to Parish online records requires a $100 set up fee plus $15 per month and $.50 per minute. Conveyances date back to 1936; mortgages to 1948; other records to 1986. Lending agency information is available. For information, contact Derek Comeaux at 337-291-6433. Tax and UCC lien information is for this parish only. **Other Phone Numbers:** Assessor 337-267-7080.

Lafourche Parish

Clerk of Court, P.O. Box 818, Thibodaux, LA 70302. Clerk of Court, R/E and UCC Recording 985-447-4841; Fax 985-447-5800.
Will search UCC records. Tax liens not included in UCC search. Will not search real estate records. **Other Phone Numbers:** Assessor 985-447-7242; Treasurer 985-447-4841; Elections 985-447-4841.

Lincoln Parish

Clerk of Court, P.O. Box 924, Ruston, LA 71273-0924. Clerk of Court, R/E and UCC Recording 318-251-5130; Fax 318-255-6004.
Will search UCC records. Tax liens not included in UCC search. Separate combined tax lien search-$11.00 first name, $5.50 per additional name Mortgage searches available. **Other Phone Numbers:** Assessor 318-251-5140.

Livingston Parish

Clerk of Court, P.O. Box 1150, Livingston, LA 70754. 225-686-2216; Fax 225-686-1867.
Will search UCC records. UCC search includes tax liens if requested. Will not search real estate records. **Other Phone Numbers:** Assessor 225-686-7278.

Madison Parish

Clerk of Court, P.O. Box 1710, Tallulah, LA 71282. 318-574-0655; Fax 318-574-3961.
Will search UCC records. This agency will not do a tax lien search. Mortgage searches available. **Other Phone Numbers:** Assessor 318-574-0117.

Morehouse Parish

Clerk of Court, P.O. Box 1543, Bastrop, LA 71221-1543. Clerk of Court, R/E and UCC Recording 318-281-3343; Fax 318-281-3775.
Will search UCC records. Tax liens not included in UCC search. RE record owner and mortgage searches available. **Online Access:** Real Estate, Liens. Remote online access will be available in 2001. The service and fees will be similar to the Lafayette Parish. **Other Phone Numbers:** Assessor 318-281-1802; Vital Records 318-568-5050.

Natchitoches Parish

Clerk of Court, P.O. Box 476, Natchitoches, LA 71458-0476. 318-352-8152; Fax 318-352-9321.
Will search UCC records. Tax liens not included in UCC search. RE owner, mortgage, and property transfer searches available. **Other Phone Numbers:** Assessor 318-352-2377.

Orleans Parish

Clerk of Court, 421 Loyola Avenue, B-1, Civil Court Building, New Orleans, LA 70112. 504-592-9189; Fax 504-592-9192.
Will search UCC records. UCC search includes tax liens. Additional $5.00 fee for general combined and state tax lien searches Re record owner and property transfer searches available. **Online Access:** Real Estate, Liens. Access to the Parish online records requires a set up fee and $300 deposit for 1,200 minutes of usage, plus $.25 per minute. Records date back to 9/1987. No lending agency information is available. For information, contact John Rabb at 504-592-9264. **Other Phone Numbers:** Assessor 504-592-7050.

Ouachita Parish

Clerk of Court, P.O. Box 1862, Monroe, LA 71210-1862. 318-327-1444; Fax 318-327-1462.
Will search UCC records. UCC search includes tax liens. Mortgage searches available. **Other Phone Numbers:** Assessor 318-327-1300.

Plaquemines Parish

Clerk of Court, P.O. Box 129, Pointe a la Hache, LA 70082. Clerk of Court, R/E and UCC Recording 985-333-4377; Fax 985-333-9202.
Will search UCC records. UCC search includes tax liens. RE record owner and property searches available. **Other Phone Numbers:** Assessor 985-333-4331; Elections 985-333-4377.

Pointe Coupee Parish

Clerk of Court, P.O. Box 86, New Roads, LA 70760. 225-638-9596; Fax 225-638-9590.
Will search UCC records. Tax liens not included in UCC search. RE owner, mortgage, and property transfer searches available. **Other Phone Numbers:** Assessor 225-638-7077; Treasurer 504-638-9556.

Rapides Parish

Clerk of Court, P.O. Box 952, Alexandria, LA 71309. Clerk of Court, R/E and UCC Recording 318-473-8153; Fax 318-473-4667.
Will search UCC records. UCC search includes tax liens if requested. RE record owner and mortgage searches available. **Other Phone Numbers:** Assessor 318-448-8511; Elections 318-473-6770.

Red River Parish

Clerk of Court, P.O. Box 485, Coushatta, LA 71019-0485. 318-932-6741.
Will search UCC records. UCC search includes tax liens if requested. Mortgage searches available.

Richland Parish

Clerk of Court, P.O. Box 119, Rayville, LA 71269. 318-728-4171; Fax 318-728-7020.
Will search UCC records. UCC search includes tax liens if requested. Mortgage searches available. **Other Phone Numbers:** Assessor 318-728-4491.

Sabine Parish

Clerk of Court, P.O. Box 419, Many, LA 71449. Clerk of Court, R/E and UCC Recording 318-256-6223; Fax 318-256-9037.
Will search UCC records. Tax liens not included in UCC search. RE owner, mortgage, and property transfer searches available. **Other Phone Numbers:** Assessor 318-256-3482; Treasurer 318-256-5637; Sheriff 318-256-9241.

St. Bernard Parish

Clerk of Court, P.O. Box 1746, Chalmette, LA 70044. Clerk of Court, R/E and UCC Recording 504-271-3434.
Will search UCC records. UCC search includes tax liens if requested. Mortgage and property transfer searches available. **Other Phone Numbers:** Assessor 504-279-6379; Elections 504-271-3434.

St. Charles Parish

Clerk of Court, P.O. Box 424, Hahnville, LA 70057. 985-783-6632.
Will search UCC records. UCC search includes tax liens if requested. Separate combined tax lien search-$12.00 first name, $5.00 each additional name Mortgage searches available. **Other Phone Numbers:** Assessor 985-783-6281.

St. Helena Parish

Clerk of Court, P.O. Box 308, Greensburg, LA 70441-0308. 225-222-4514; Fax 225-222-3443.
Will search UCC records. UCC search includes tax liens if requested. Re record owner search costs $12.00 per name. Mortgage searches performed at $26.50 per name. **Other Phone Numbers:** Assessor 225-222-4540.

St. James Parish

Clerk of Court, P.O. Box 63, Convent, LA 70723. 225-562-2270; Fax 225-562-2383.
Will search UCC records. Tax liens not included in UCC search. RE owner, mortgage, and property transfer searches available. **Other Phone Numbers:** Assessor 225-562-2250; Treasurer 504-562-2300.

St. John the Baptist Parish

Clerk of Court, P.O. Box 280, Edgard, LA 70049-0280. 985-497-3331 R/E Recording: 985-497-8836 x246 UCC Recording: 985-497-8836 x249; Fax 985-497-3972.
Will search UCC records. Tax liens not included in UCC search. Separate combined tax lien search-$12.00 first name, $6.00 each additional name. RE owner, mortgage, and property transfer searches available. **Other Phone Numbers:** Assessor 985-497-8788.

St. Landry Parish

Clerk of Court, P.O. Box 750, Opelousas, LA 70571-0750. 337-942-5606; Fax 337-948-7265.
Will search UCC records. Tax liens not included in UCC search. Separate combined tax lien search-$11.00 first name, $5.00 each additional name. RE owner, mortgage, and property transfer searches available. **Other Phone Numbers:** Assessor 337-942-2316; Treasurer 337-948-6516.

St. Martin Parish

Clerk of Court, P.O. Box 308, St. Martinville, LA 70582. 337-394-2210; Fax 337-394-7772.
Will search UCC records. Tax liens not included in UCC search. RE owner, mortgage, and property transfer searches available. **Other Phone Numbers:** Assessor 337-394-2208; Treasurer 337-394-2200; Elections 337-394-2210; Vital Records 337-394-2210.

St. Mary Parish

Clerk of Court, P.O. Box 1231, Franklin, LA 70538. 318-828-4100 x200; Fax 318-828-2509.
Will search UCC records. UCC search includes tax liens. RE owner, mortgage, and property transfer searches available. **Other Phone Numbers:** Assessor 318-828-4100 x250.

St. Tammany Parish

Clerk of Court, P.O. Box 1090, Covington, LA 70434. 985-898-2430; http://stp.pa.st-tammany.la.us
Will search UCC records. Tax liens not included in UCC search. Separate combined tax lien search-$12.00 first name, $6.50 each additional name. RE owner, mortgage, and property transfer searches available. **Online Access:** Real Estate, Liens. Access to online records requires a $100 set up fee, plus $.30 per minute of use. Records date back to 1961; viewable images on conveyances back to 1985; mortgages to 8/93. For information, contact Mark Cohn at 504-898-2890 or Christy Howell at 504-898-2491. UCC lien information is with the Secretary of State. **Other Phone Numbers:** Assessor 985-892-6150.

Tangipahoa Parish

Clerk of Court, P.O. Box 667, Amite, LA 70422. 985-549-1611 R/E Recording: 985-549-1612; Fax 985-748-6503. http://www.tangiclerk.org
Will search UCC records. Tax liens not included in UCC search. Separate combined tax lien search-$12.50 first name, $6.50 each additional name. Mortgage searches available. **Online Access:** Real Estate, Liens, Recording, Civil. Access to Parish online records requires registration and a $55 monthly fee. Record dates vary though most indexes go back to 1990. Lending agency information is available. For information, contact Alison Carona at 504-549-1611. Also, a mapping feature is being developed that includes assessor basic information; access will be free.

Tensas Parish

Clerk of Court, P.O. Box 78, St. Joseph, LA 71366. 225-766-3921; Fax 225-222-3443.
Will search UCC records. Tax liens not included in UCC search. RE owner, mortgage, and property transfer searches available. **Other Phone Numbers:** Assessor 225-766-3501.

Terrebonne Parish

Clerk of Court, P.O. Box 1569, Houma, LA 70361. 985-868-5660.
Will search UCC records. Tax liens not included in UCC search. RE owner, mortgage, and property transfer searches available.

Union Parish

Clerk of Court, Courthouse, 100 E. Bayou, Suite 105, Farmerville, LA 71241. 318-368-3055; Fax 318-368-3861.
Will search UCC records. Tax liens not included in UCC search. RE record owner and mortgage searches available. **Other Phone Numbers:** Assessor 318-368-3232.

Vermilion Parish

Clerk of Court, 100 N State St #101, Abbeville, LA 70510. Clerk of Court, R/E and UCC Recording 337-898-1992; Fax 337-898-0404.
Will search UCC records. Tax liens not included in UCC search. RE owner, mortgage, and property transfer searches available. **Other Phone Numbers:** Assessor 337-893-2837; Treasurer 337-898-4300; Appraiser/Auditor 337-898-2837; Elections 337-898-1992; Vital Records 337-898-1992.

Vernon Parish

Clerk of Court, P.O. Box 40, Leesville, LA 71496-0040. 337-238-1384 R/E Recording: 337-238-4824; Fax 337-238-9902.
Will search UCC records. UCC search includes tax liens if requested. Mortgage searches available. **Other Phone Numbers:** Assessor 337-293-2167; Elections 337-238-1384.

Washington Parish

Clerk of Court, P.O. Box 607, Franklinton, LA 70438. 985-839-4663.
Will search UCC records. Tax liens not included in UCC search. RE owner, mortgage, and property transfer searches available. **Other Phone Numbers:** Assessor 985-839-2280.

Webster Parish

Clerk of Court, P.O. Box 370, Minden, LA 71058-0370. Clerk of Court, R/E and UCC Recording 318-371-0366; Fax 318-371-0226.
Will search UCC records. UCC search includes tax liens if requested. Separate combined tax lien search-$25.00 first name, $5.00 each additional name RE record owner searches available. **Other Phone Numbers:** Assessor 318-377-9311; Elections 318-371-0366.

West Baton Rouge Parish

Clerk of Court, P.O. Box 107, Port Allen, LA 70767. Clerk of Court, R/E and UCC Recording 225-383-0378; Fax 225-383-3694.
Will search UCC records. Tax liens not included in UCC search. RE owner, mortgage, and property transfer searches available. **Other Phone Numbers:** Assessor 225-344-6777.

West Carroll Parish

Clerk of Court, P.O. Box 1078, Oak Grove, LA 71263. Clerk of Court, R/E and UCC Recording 318-428-3281; Fax 318-428-9896.
Will search UCC records. UCC search includes tax liens. Mortgage searches available. **Other Phone Numbers:** Assessor 318-428-2371.

West Feliciana Parish

Clerk of Court, P.O. Box 1843, St. Francisville, LA 70775. 225-635-3794; Fax 225-635-3770.
Will search UCC records. Tax liens not included in UCC search. RE owner, mortgage, and property transfer searches available. **Other Phone Numbers:** Assessor 225-635-3350.

Winn Parish

Clerk of Court, Courthouse, Room 103, 100 Main St., Winnfield, LA 71483. 318-628-3515; Fax 318-628-2753.
Will search UCC records. Tax liens not included in UCC search. RE owner, mortgage, and property transfer searches available. **Other Phone Numbers:** Assessor 318-628-3267; Treasurer 318-628-5824.

Louisiana County Locator

You will usually be able to find the city name in the City/Parish Cross Reference below. In that case, it is a simple matter to determine the county from the cross reference. However, only the official US Postal Service city names are included in this index. There are an additional 40,000 place names that people use in their addresses. Therefore, we have also included a ZIP/City Cross Reference immediately following the City/Parish Cross Reference.

If you know the ZIP Code but the city name does not appear in the City/Parish Cross Reference index, look up the ZIP Code in the ZIP/City Cross Reference, find the city name, then look up the city name in the City/Parish Cross Reference. For example, you want to know the county for an address of Menands, NY 12204. There is no "Menands" in the City/Parish Cross Reference. The ZIP/City Cross Reference shows that ZIP Codes 12201-12288 are for the city of Albany. Looking back in the City/Parish Cross Reference, Albany is in Albany Parish.

City/Parish Cross Reference

ABBEVILLE Vermilion Parish
ABITA SPRINGS St. Tammany Parish
ACME Concordia Parish
ADDIS West Baton Rouge Parish
AIMWELL Catahoula Parish
AKERS Tangipahoa Parish
ALBANY Livingston Parish
ALEXANDRIA Rapides Parish
AMA St. Charles Parish
AMELIA St. Mary Parish
AMITE (70422) Tangipahoa Parish(80), St. Helena Parish(20)
ANACOCO Vernon Parish
ANGIE Washington Parish
ANGOLA West Feliciana Parish
ARABI St. Bernard Parish
ARCADIA (71001) Bienville Parish(68), Claiborne Parish(16), Lincoln Parish(16)
ARCHIBALD Richland Parish
ARNAUDVILLE (70512) St. Landry Parish(59), St. Martin Parish(41)
ASHLAND Natchitoches Parish
ATHENS Claiborne Parish
ATLANTA (71404) Grant Parish(51), Winn Parish(49)
AVERY ISLAND Iberia Parish
BAKER East Baton Rouge Parish
BALDWIN St. Mary Parish
BALL Rapides Parish
BARATARIA Jefferson Parish
BARKSDALE AFB Bossier Parish
BASILE (70515) Acadia Parish(73), Evangeline Parish(28)
BASKIN Franklin Parish
BASTROP Morehouse Parish
BATCHELOR Pointe Coupee Parish
BATON ROUGE East Baton Rouge Parish
BATON ROUGE East Baton Rouge Parish Parish
BAYOU GOULA Iberville Parish
BELCHER Caddo Parish
BELL CITY (70630) Calcasieu Parish(68), Cameron Parish(32)
BELLE CHASSE Plaquemines Parish
BELLE ROSE Assumption Parish
BELMONT Sabine Parish
BENTLEY Grant Parish
BENTON Bossier Parish
BERNICE (71222) Union Parish(85), Claiborne Parish(15)
BERWICK St. Mary Parish
BETHANY Caddo Parish
BIENVILLE Bienville Parish
BIG BEND Avoyelles Parish
BLANCHARD Caddo Parish
BLANKS Pointe Coupee Parish
BOGALUSA (70427) Washington Parish(97), St. Tammany Parish(3)
BOGALUSA Washington Parish
BONITA Morehouse Parish
BOOTHVILLE Plaquemines Parish
BORDELONVILLE Avoyelles Parish
BOSSIER CITY Bossier Parish

BOURG (70343) Terrebonne Parish(82), Lafourche Parish(18)
BOUTTE St. Charles Parish
BOYCE Rapides Parish
BRAITHWAITE Plaquemines Parish
BRANCH Acadia Parish
BREAUX BRIDGE St. Martin Parish
BRITTANY Ascension Parish
BROUSSARD (70518) Lafayette Parish(99), St. Martin Parish(1)
BRUSLY West Baton Rouge Parish
BRYCELAND Bienville Parish
BUCKEYE Rapides Parish
BUECHE West Baton Rouge Parish
BUNKIE (71322) Avoyelles Parish(87), St. Landry Parish(12), Rapides Parish(2)
BURAS Plaquemines Parish
BURNSIDE Ascension Parish
BUSH St. Tammany Parish
CADE St. Martin Parish
CALHOUN Ouachita Parish
CALVIN Winn Parish
CAMERON Cameron Parish
CAMPTI Natchitoches Parish
CARENCRO Lafayette Parish
CARLISLE Plaquemines Parish
CARVILLE Iberville Parish
CASTOR Bienville Parish
CECILIA St. Martin Parish
CENTER POINT (71323) Avoyelles Parish(98), Rapides Parish(2)
CENTERVILLE St. Mary Parish
CHALMETTE St. Bernard Parish
CHARENTON St. Mary Parish
CHASE Franklin Parish
CHATAIGNIER Evangeline Parish
CHATHAM Jackson Parish
CHAUVIN Terrebonne Parish
CHENEYVILLE Rapides Parish
CHOPIN Natchitoches Parish
CHOUDRANT (71227) Lincoln Parish(58), Jackson Parish(33), Ouachita Parish(9)
CHURCH POINT (70525) Acadia Parish(83), St. Landry Parish(17)
CLARENCE Natchitoches Parish
CLARKS Caldwell Parish
CLAYTON (71326) Catahoula Parish(51), Concordia Parish(47), Tensas Parish(1)
CLINTON (70722) East Feliciana Parish(97), East Baton Rouge Parish(3)
CLOUTIERVILLE Natchitoches Parish
COLFAX Grant Parish
COLLINSTON (71229) Morehouse Parish(81), Ouachita Parish(19)
COLUMBIA (71418) Caldwell Parish(88), Richland Parish(8), Ouachita Parish(4)
CONVENT St. James Parish
CONVERSE Sabine Parish
COTTON VALLEY Webster Parish
COTTONPORT Avoyelles Parish
COUSHATTA (71019) Red River Parish(97), Natchitoches Parish(3)
COVINGTON St. Tammany Parish

CREOLE Cameron Parish
CRESTON Natchitoches Parish
CROWLEY Acadia Parish
CROWVILLE Franklin Parish
CULLEN Webster Parish
CUT OFF Lafourche Parish
CYPRESS Natchitoches Parish
DARROW Ascension Parish
DAVANT Plaquemines Parish
DELCAMBRE (70528) Vermilion Parish(70), Iberia Parish(31)
DELHI (71232) Richland Parish(67), Franklin Parish(25), Madison Parish(8)
DELTA Madison Parish
DENHAM SPRINGS (70706) Livingston Parish(94), St. Helena Parish(6)
DENHAM SPRINGS Livingston Parish
DEQUINCY Calcasieu Parish
DERIDDER (70634) Beauregard Parish(92), Vernon Parish(8)
DERRY Natchitoches Parish
DES ALLEMANDS (70030) St. Charles Parish(89), Lafourche Parish(11)
DESTREHAN St. Charles Parish
DEVILLE (71328) Rapides Parish(87), Avoyelles Parish(13)
DODSON (71422) Winn Parish(99), Jackson Parish(1)
DONALDSONVILLE Ascension Parish
DONNER Terrebonne Parish
DOWNSVILLE (71234) Union Parish(80), Ouachita Parish(13), Lincoln Parish(7)
DOYLINE Webster Parish
DRY CREEK (70637) Beauregard Parish(77), Allen Parish(23)
DRY PRONG Grant Parish
DUBACH (71235) Lincoln Parish(98), Claiborne Parish(2)
DUBBERLY Webster Parish
DULAC Terrebonne Parish
DUPLESSIS Ascension Parish
DUPONT Avoyelles Parish
DUSON Lafayette Parish
EAST POINT Red River Parish
ECHO Rapides Parish
EDGARD St. John the Baptist Parish
EFFIE Avoyelles Parish
EGAN Acadia Parish
ELIZABETH Allen Parish
ELM GROVE Bossier Parish
ELMER Rapides Parish
ELTON (70532) Jefferson Davis Parish(82), Allen Parish(18)
EMPIRE Plaquemines Parish
ENTERPRISE (71425) Catahoula Parish(91), Rapides Parish(9)
EPPS (71237) West Carroll Parish(88), East Carroll Parish(9), Madison Parish(3)
ERATH Vermilion Parish
EROS (71238) Jackson Parish(52), Ouachita Parish(48)
ERWINVILLE (70729) West Baton Rouge Parish(89), Pointe Coupee Parish(11)

ESTHERWOOD Acadia Parish
ETHEL East Feliciana Parish
EUNICE (70535) St. Landry Parish(95), Acadia Parish(4)
EVANGELINE Acadia Parish
EVANS Vernon Parish
EVERGREEN Avoyelles Parish
EXTENSION Franklin Parish
FAIRBANKS Ouachita Parish
FARMERVILLE Union Parish
FENTON Jefferson Davis Parish
FERRIDAY Concordia Parish
FISHER Sabine Parish
FLATWOODS (71427) Rapides Parish(76), Natchitoches Parish(24)
FLORA Natchitoches Parish
FLORIEN Sabine Parish
FLUKER (70436) Tangipahoa Parish(87), St. Helena Parish(13)
FOLSOM St. Tammany Parish
FORDOCHE Pointe Coupee Parish
FOREST West Carroll Parish
FOREST HILL Rapides Parish
FORT NECESSITY Franklin Parish
FRANKLIN St. Mary Parish
FRANKLINTON Washington Parish
FRENCH SETTLEMENT Livingston Parish
FRIERSON De Soto Parish
FROGMORE Concordia Parish
FULLERTON Vernon Parish Parish
GALLIANO Lafourche Parish
GARDEN CITY St. Mary Parish
GARDNER Rapides Parish
GARYVILLE St. John the Baptist Parish
GEISMAR Ascension Parish
GEORGETOWN Grant Parish
GHEENS Lafourche Parish
GIBSLAND Bienville Parish
GIBSON Terrebonne Parish
GILBERT Franklin Parish
GILLIAM Caddo Parish
GLENMORA Rapides Parish
GLOSTER De Soto Parish
GLYNN (70736) Pointe Coupee Parish(98), West Baton Rouge Parish(2)
GOLDEN MEADOW Lafourche Parish
GOLDONNA (71031) Natchitoches Parish(52), Winn Parish(49)
GONZALES Ascension Parish
GORUM Natchitoches Parish
GOUDEAU Avoyelles Parish
GRAMBLING Lincoln Parish
GRAMERCY St. James Parish
GRAND CANE De Soto Parish
GRAND CHENIER Cameron Parish
GRAND COTEAU St. Landry Parish
GRAND ISLE Jefferson Parish
GRANT Allen Parish
GRAY Terrebonne Parish
GRAYSON (71435) Caldwell Parish(96), Catahoula Parish(2), La Salle Parish(2)
GREENSBURG St. Helena Parish

GREENWELL SPRINGS East Baton Rouge Parish
GREENWOOD Caddo Parish
GRETNA Jefferson Parish
GROSSE TETE Iberville Parish
GUEYDAN (70542) Vermilion Parish(96), Cameron Parish(4)
HACKBERRY Cameron Parish
HAHNVILLE St. Charles Parish
HALL SUMMIT Red River Parish
HAMBURG Avoyelles Parish
HAMMOND (70403) Tangipahoa Parish(96), Livingston Parish(4)
HAMMOND Tangipahoa Parish
HARMON Red River Parish
HARRISONBURG Catahoula Parish
HARVEY Jefferson Parish
HAUGHTON Bossier Parish
HAYES Calcasieu Parish
HAYNESVILLE Claiborne Parish
HEBERT Caldwell Parish
HEFLIN (71039) Webster Parish(84), Bienville Parish(16)
HESSMER Avoyelles Parish
HESTER St. James Parish
HICKS Vernon Parish
HINESTON (71438) Rapides Parish(81), Vernon Parish(19)
HODGE Jackson Parish
HOLDEN (70744) Livingston Parish(99), St. Helena Parish(1)
HOMER Claiborne Parish
HORNBECK (71439) Vernon Parish(76), Sabine Parish(24)
HOSSTON Caddo Parish
HOUMA (70364) Terrebonne Parish(86), Lafourche Parish(14)
HOUMA Terrebonne Parish
HUSSER Tangipahoa Parish
IDA Caddo Parish
INDEPENDENCE (70443) Tangipahoa Parish(50), Livingston Parish(41), St. Helena Parish(9)
INNIS Pointe Coupee Parish
IOTA Acadia Parish
IOWA Calcasieu Parish
JACKSON (70748) East Feliciana Parish(76), West Feliciana Parish(22), East Baton Rouge Parish(3)
JAMESTOWN Bienville Parish
JARREAU Pointe Coupee Parish
JEANERETTE (70544) Iberia Parish(82), St. Mary Parish(18)
JENA La Salle Parish
JENNINGS (70546) Jefferson Davis Parish(97), Acadia Parish(3)
JIGGER Franklin Parish
JONES Morehouse Parish
JONESBORO (71251) Jackson Parish(98), Bienville Parish(2)
JONESVILLE (71343) Catahoula Parish(80), Concordia Parish(20)
JOYCE Winn Parish
KAPLAN Vermilion Parish
KEATCHIE De Soto Parish
KEITHVILLE Caddo Parish
KELLY (71441) Caldwell Parish(73), La Salle Parish(27)
KENNER Jefferson Parish
KENTWOOD (70444) Tangipahoa Parish(84), St. Helena Parish(16)
KILBOURNE West Carroll Parish
KILLONA St. Charles Parish
KINDER (70648) Allen Parish(99), Jefferson Davis Parish(1)
KRAEMER Lafourche Parish
KROTZ SPRINGS St. Landry Parish
KURTHWOOD Vernon Parish
LA PLACE (70068) St. John the Baptist Parish(94), St. Charles Parish(6)
LA PLACE St. John the Baptist Parish
LABADIEVILLE Assumption Parish

LABARRE Pointe Coupee Parish
LACAMP Vernon Parish
LACASSINE Jefferson Davis Parish
LACOMBE St. Tammany Parish
LAFAYETTE Lafayette Parish
LAFITTE Jefferson Parish
LAKE ARTHUR (70549) Jefferson Davis Parish(98), Cameron Parish(3)
LAKE CHARLES (70607) Calcasieu Parish(92), Cameron Parish(8)
LAKE CHARLES Calcasieu Parish
LAKE PROVIDENCE East Carroll Parish
LAKELAND Pointe Coupee Parish
LAROSE Lafourche Parish
LARTO Catahoula Parish
LAWTELL St. Landry Parish
LE MOYEN St. Landry Parish
LEANDER Vernon Parish
LEBEAU St. Landry Parish
LEBLANC Allen Parish
LECOMPTE Rapides Parish
LEESVILLE Vernon Parish
LENA (71447) Natchitoches Parish(53), Rapides Parish(47)
LEONVILLE St. Landry Parish
LETTSWORTH Pointe Coupee Parish
LIBUSE Rapides Parish
LILLIE Union Parish
LISBON Claiborne Parish
LIVINGSTON Livingston Parish
LIVONIA Pointe Coupee Parish
LOCKPORT Lafourche Parish
LOGANSPORT De Soto Parish
LONGLEAF Rapides Parish
LONGSTREET De Soto Parish
LONGVILLE Beauregard Parish
LORANGER Tangipahoa Parish
LOREAUVILLE Iberia Parish
LOTTIE Pointe Coupee Parish
LULING St. Charles Parish
LUTCHER St. James Parish
LYDIA Iberia Parish
MADISONVILLE St. Tammany Parish
MAMOU Evangeline Parish
MANDEVILLE St. Tammany Parish
MANGHAM Richland Parish
MANSFIELD De Soto Parish
MANSURA Avoyelles Parish
MANY Sabine Parish
MARINGOUIN Iberville Parish
MARION Union Parish
MARKSVILLE Avoyelles Parish
MARRERO Jefferson Parish
MARTHAVILLE (71450) Natchitoches Parish(67), Sabine Parish(33)
MATHEWS Lafourche Parish
MAUREPAS (70449) Livingston Parish(98), Ascension Parish(2)
MAURICE (70555) Vermilion Parish(88), Lafayette Parish(12)
MELDER Rapides Parish
MELROSE Natchitoches Parish
MELVILLE St. Landry Parish
MER ROUGE Morehouse Parish
MERAUX St. Bernard Parish
MERMENTAU Acadia Parish
MERRYVILLE Beauregard Parish
METAIRIE Jefferson Parish
MILTON Lafayette Parish
MINDEN Webster Parish
MIRA Caddo Parish
MITTIE Allen Parish
MODESTE Ascension Parish Parish
MONROE (71202) Ouachita Parish(99), Caldwell Parish(1)
MONROE Ouachita Parish
MONTEGUT (70377) Terrebonne Parish(87), Lafourche Parish(13)
MONTEREY Concordia Parish
MONTGOMERY (71454) Grant Parish(80), Winn Parish(20)
MOORINGSPORT Caddo Parish

MORA (71455) Rapides Parish(99), Natchitoches Parish(1)
MOREAUVILLE Avoyelles Parish
MORGAN CITY (70380) St. Mary Parish(91), Assumption Parish(9)
MORGAN CITY St. Mary Parish
MORGANZA Pointe Coupee Parish
MORROW (71356) St. Landry Parish(55), Avoyelles Parish(45)
MORSE Acadia Parish
MOUNT AIRY (70076) St. Charles Parish(95), St. John the Baptist Parish(5)
MOUNT HERMON Washington Parish
NAPOLEONVILLE Assumption Parish
NATALBANY Tangipahoa Parish
NATCHEZ Natchitoches Parish
NATCHITOCHES (71457) Natchitoches Parish(97), Winn Parish(3)
NATCHITOCHES Natchitoches Parish
NEGREET Sabine Parish
NEW IBERIA Iberia Parish
NEW ORLEANS Jefferson Parish
NEW ORLEANS Orleans Parish
NEW ROADS Pointe Coupee Parish
NEW SARPY St. Charles Parish
NEWELLTON Tensas Parish
NEWLLANO Vernon Parish
NOBLE Sabine Parish
NORCO St. Charles Parish
NORWOOD East Feliciana Parish
OAK GROVE West Carroll Parish
OAK RIDGE (71264) Morehouse Parish(77), Richland Parish(23)
OAKDALE (71463) Allen Parish(94), Rapides Parish(5), Evangeline Parish(1)
OBERLIN Allen Parish
OIL CITY Caddo Parish
OLLA (71465) La Salle Parish(82), Winn Parish(10), Caldwell Parish(7), Catahoula Parish(1)
OPELOUSAS St. Landry Parish
OSCAR Pointe Coupee Parish
OTIS Rapides Parish
PAINCOURTVILLE Assumption Parish
PALMETTO St. Landry Parish
PARADIS St. Charles Parish
PATTERSON St. Mary Parish
PAULINA St. James Parish
PEARL RIVER St. Tammany Parish
PELICAN De Soto Parish
PERRY Vermilion Parish
PIERRE PART (70339) Assumption Parish(92), St. Martin Parish(8)
PILOTTOWN Plaquemines Parish
PINE GROVE St. Helena Parish
PINE PRAIRIE Evangeline Parish
PINEVILLE (71360) Rapides Parish(98), Avoyelles Parish(2)
PINEVILLE Rapides Parish
PINEVILLE Rapides Parish Parish
PIONEER West Carroll Parish
PITKIN (70656) Vernon Parish(64), Rapides Parish(21), Allen Parish(15)
PLAIN DEALING Bossier Parish
PLAQUEMINE Iberville Parish
PLATTENVILLE Assumption Parish
PLAUCHEVILLE Avoyelles Parish
PLEASANT HILL Sabine Parish
POINTE A LA HACHE Plaquemines Parish
POLLOCK Grant Parish
PONCHATOULA Tangipahoa Parish
PORT ALLEN West Baton Rouge Parish
PORT BARRE St. Landry Parish
PORT SULPHUR Plaquemines Parish
POWHATAN Natchitoches Parish
PRAIRIEVILLE Ascension Parish
PRIDE East Baton Rouge Parish
PRINCETON Bossier Parish
PROVENCAL Natchitoches Parish
QUITMAN (71268) Jackson Parish(71), Bienville Parish(30)
RACELAND Lafourche Parish

RAGLEY (70657) Beauregard Parish(86), Allen Parish(14)
RAYNE (70578) Acadia Parish(91), Vermilion Parish(5), Lafayette Parish(4)
RAYVILLE Richland Parish
REDDELL Evangeline Parish
REEVES Allen Parish
RESERVE St. John the Baptist Parish
RHINEHART Catahoula Parish
RINGGOLD (71068) Bienville Parish(94), Red River Parish(6)
ROANOKE Jefferson Davis Parish
ROBELINE (71469) Natchitoches Parish(76), Sabine Parish(24)
ROBERT Tangipahoa Parish
RODESSA Caddo Parish
ROSA St. Landry Parish
ROSEDALE Iberville Parish
ROSELAND Tangipahoa Parish
ROSEPINE Vernon Parish
ROUGON Pointe Coupee Parish
RUBY Rapides Parish
RUSTON (71270) Lincoln Parish(93), Jackson Parish(7)
RUSTON Lincoln Parish
SAINT AMANT Ascension Parish
SAINT BENEDICT St. Tammany Parish
SAINT BERNARD St. Bernard Parish
SAINT FRANCISVILLE West Feliciana Parish
SAINT GABRIEL Iberville Parish
SAINT JAMES St. James Parish
SAINT JOSEPH Tensas Parish
SAINT LANDRY Evangeline Parish
SAINT MARTINVILLE St. Martin Parish
SAINT MAURICE Winn Parish
SAINT ROSE St. Charles Parish
SALINE (71070) Natchitoches Parish(55), Bienville Parish(46)
SAREPTA (71071) Webster Parish(95), Bossier Parish(5)
SCHRIEVER Terrebonne Parish
SCOTT (70583) Lafayette Parish(94), Acadia Parish(7)
SHONGALOO Webster Parish
SHREVEPORT (71104) Caddo Parish(99), Bossier Parish(1)
SHREVEPORT (71115) Caddo Parish(96), Red River Parish(4)
SHREVEPORT Caddo Parish
SIBLEY Webster Parish
SICILY ISLAND Catahoula Parish
SIEPER Rapides Parish
SIKES Winn Parish
SIMMESPORT Avoyelles Parish
SIMPSON Vernon Parish
SIMSBORO Lincoln Parish
SINGER Beauregard Parish
SLAGLE Vernon Parish
SLAUGHTER East Feliciana Parish
SLIDELL St. Tammany Parish
SONDHEIMER (71276) Madison Parish(56), East Carroll Parish(44)
SORRENTO Ascension Parish
SPEARSVILLE Union Parish
SPRINGFIELD (70462) Livingston Parish(88), Tangipahoa Parish(12)
SPRINGHILL (71075) Webster Parish(99), Bossier Parish(1)
STARKS Calcasieu Parish
START Richland Parish
STERLINGTON (71280) Ouachita Parish(56), Union Parish(44)
STONEWALL De Soto Parish
SUGARTOWN Beauregard Parish
SULPHUR Calcasieu Parish
SUMMERFIELD Claiborne Parish
SUN St. Tammany Parish
SUNSET St. Landry Parish
SUNSHINE Iberville Parish
SWARTZ Ouachita Parish
TALISHEEK St. Tammany Parish

TALLULAH Madison Parish
TANGIPAHOA Tangipahoa Parish
TAYLOR Bienville Parish
THERIOT Terrebonne Parish
THIBODAUX (70301) Lafourche Parish(96), Terrebonne Parish(4)
THIBODAUX Lafourche Parish
TICKFAW Tangipahoa Parish
TIOGA Rapides Parish
TORBERT Pointe Coupee Parish
TRANSYLVANIA East Carroll Parish
TROUT La Salle Parish

TULLOS (71479) Winn Parish(75), La Salle Parish(25)
TUNICA West Feliciana Parish
TURKEY CREEK Evangeline Parish
UNCLE SAM St. James Parish
URANIA La Salle Parish
VACHERIE (70090) St. James Parish(77), St. John the Baptist Parish(23)
VENICE Plaquemines Parish
VENTRESS Pointe Coupee Parish
VERDA Grant Parish
VICK Avoyelles Parish
VIDALIA Concordia Parish

VILLE PLATTE Evangeline Parish
VINTON Calcasieu Parish
VIOLET St. Bernard Parish
VIVIAN Caddo Parish
WAKEFIELD West Feliciana Parish
WALKER Livingston Parish
WASHINGTON St. Landry Parish
WATERPROOF Tensas Parish
WATSON Livingston Parish
WELSH Jefferson Davis Parish
WEST MONROE Ouachita Parish
WESTLAKE Calcasieu Parish
WESTWEGO Jefferson Parish

WEYANOKE West Feliciana Parish
WHITE CASTLE Iberville Parish
WILDSVILLE Concordia Parish
WILSON East Feliciana Parish
WINNFIELD Winn Parish
WINNSBORO Franklin Parish
WISNER Franklin Parish
WOODWORTH Rapides Parish
YOUNGSVILLE Lafayette Parish
ZACHARY East Baton Rouge Parish
ZWOLLE Sabine Parish

ZIP/City Cross Reference

70001-70011	METAIRIE	70359-70359	GRAY	70521-70521	CECILIA	70648-70648	KINDER
70030-70030	DES ALLEMANDS	70360-70364	HOUMA	70522-70522	CENTERVILLE	70650-70650	LACASSINE
70031-70031	AMA	70371-70371	KRAEMER	70523-70523	CHARENTON	70651-70651	LEBLANC
70032-70032	ARABI	70372-70372	LABADIEVILLE	70524-70524	CHATAIGNIER	70652-70652	LONGVILLE
70033-70033	METAIRIE	70373-70373	LAROSE	70525-70525	CHURCH POINT	70653-70653	MERRYVILLE
70036-70036	BARATARIA	70374-70374	LOCKPORT	70526-70527	CROWLEY	70654-70654	MITTIE
70037-70037	BELLE CHASSE	70375-70375	MATHEWS	70528-70528	DELCAMBRE	70655-70655	OBERLIN
70038-70038	BOOTHVILLE	70376-70376	MODESTE	70529-70529	DUSON	70656-70656	PITKIN
70039-70039	BOUTTE	70377-70377	MONTEGUT	70531-70531	EGAN	70657-70657	RAGLEY
70040-70040	BRAITHWAITE	70380-70381	MORGAN CITY	70532-70532	ELTON	70658-70658	REEVES
70041-70041	BURAS	70390-70390	NAPOLEONVILLE	70533-70533	ERATH	70659-70659	ROSEPINE
70042-70042	CARLISLE	70391-70391	PAINCOURTVILLE	70534-70534	ESTHERWOOD	70660-70660	SINGER
70043-70044	CHALMETTE	70392-70392	PATTERSON	70535-70535	EUNICE	70661-70661	STARKS
70046-70046	DAVANT	70393-70393	PLATTENVILLE	70537-70537	EVANGELINE	70662-70662	SUGARTOWN
70047-70047	DESTREHAN	70394-70394	RACELAND	70538-70538	FRANKLIN	70663-70665	SULPHUR
70049-70049	EDGARD	70395-70395	SCHRIEVER	70540-70540	GARDEN CITY	70668-70668	VINTON
70050-70050	EMPIRE	70397-70397	THERIOT	70541-70541	GRAND COTEAU	70669-70669	WESTLAKE
70051-70051	GARYVILLE	70401-70404	HAMMOND	70542-70542	GUEYDAN	70704-70704	BAKER
70052-70052	GRAMERCY	70420-70420	ABITA SPRINGS	70543-70543	IOTA	70706-70706	DENHAM SPRINGS
70053-70054	GRETNA	70421-70421	AKERS	70544-70544	JEANERETTE	70707-70707	GONZALES
70055-70055	METAIRIE	70422-70422	AMITE	70546-70546	JENNINGS	70710-70710	ADDIS
70056-70056	GRETNA	70426-70426	ANGIE	70548-70548	KAPLAN	70711-70711	ALBANY
70057-70057	HAHNVILLE	70427-70429	BOGALUSA	70549-70549	LAKE ARTHUR	70712-70712	ANGOLA
70058-70059	HARVEY	70431-70431	BUSH	70550-70550	LAWTELL	70714-70714	BAKER
70060-70060	METAIRIE	70433-70435	COVINGTON	70551-70551	LEONVILLE	70715-70715	BATCHELOR
70062-70065	KENNER	70436-70436	FLUKER	70552-70552	LOREAUVILLE	70716-70716	BAYOU GOULA
70066-70066	KILLONA	70437-70437	FOLSOM	70554-70554	MAMOU	70717-70717	BLANKS
70067-70067	LAFITTE	70438-70438	FRANKLINTON	70555-70555	MAURICE	70718-70718	BRITTANY
70068-70069	LA PLACE	70441-70441	GREENSBURG	70556-70556	MERMENTAU	70719-70719	BRUSLY
70070-70070	LULING	70442-70442	HUSSER	70558-70558	MILTON	70720-70720	BUECHE
70071-70071	LUTCHER	70443-70443	INDEPENDENCE	70559-70559	MORSE	70721-70721	CARVILLE
70072-70073	MARRERO	70444-70444	KENTWOOD	70560-70563	NEW IBERIA	70722-70722	CLINTON
70075-70075	MERAUX	70445-70445	LACOMBE	70569-70569	LYDIA	70723-70723	CONVENT
70076-70076	MOUNT AIRY	70446-70446	LORANGER	70570-70571	OPELOUSAS	70725-70725	DARROW
70078-70078	NEW SARPY	70447-70447	MADISONVILLE	70575-70575	PERRY	70726-70727	DENHAM SPRINGS
70079-70079	NORCO	70448-70448	MANDEVILLE	70576-70576	PINE PRAIRIE	70728-70728	DUPLESSIS
70080-70080	PARADIS	70449-70449	MAUREPAS	70577-70577	PORT BARRE	70729-70729	ERWINVILLE
70081-70081	PILOTTOWN	70450-70450	MOUNT HERMON	70578-70578	RAYNE	70730-70730	ETHEL
70082-70082	POINTE A LA HACHE	70451-70451	NATALBANY	70580-70580	REDDELL	70732-70732	FORDOCHE
70083-70083	PORT SULPHUR	70452-70452	PEARL RIVER	70581-70581	ROANOKE	70733-70733	FRENCH SETTLEMENT
70084-70084	RESERVE	70453-70453	PINE GROVE	70582-70582	SAINT MARTINVILLE	70734-70734	GEISMAR
70085-70085	SAINT BERNARD	70454-70454	PONCHATOULA	70583-70583	SCOTT	70736-70736	GLYNN
70086-70086	SAINT JAMES	70455-70455	ROBERT	70584-70584	SUNSET	70737-70737	GONZALES
70087-70087	SAINT ROSE	70456-70456	ROSELAND	70585-70585	TURKEY CREEK	70738-70738	BURNSIDE
70090-70090	VACHERIE	70457-70457	SAINT BENEDICT	70586-70586	VILLE PLATTE	70739-70739	GREENWELL SPRINGS
70091-70091	VENICE	70458-70461	SLIDELL	70589-70589	WASHINGTON	70740-70740	GROSSE TETE
70092-70092	VIOLET	70462-70462	SPRINGFIELD	70591-70591	WELSH	70743-70743	HESTER
70094-70096	WESTWEGO	70463-70463	SUN	70592-70592	YOUNGSVILLE	70744-70744	HOLDEN
70112-70195	NEW ORLEANS	70464-70464	TALISHEEK	70593-70593	LAFAYETTE	70747-70747	INNIS
70301-70310	THIBODAUX	70465-70465	TANGIPAHOA	70601-70629	LAKE CHARLES	70748-70748	JACKSON
70339-70339	PIERRE PART	70466-70466	TICKFAW	70630-70630	BELL CITY	70749-70749	JARREAU
70340-70340	AMELIA	70467-70467	ANGIE	70631-70631	CAMERON	70750-70750	KROTZ SPRINGS
70341-70341	BELLE ROSE	70469-70469	SLIDELL	70632-70632	CREOLE	70751-70751	LABARRE
70342-70342	BERWICK	70470-70471	MANDEVILLE	70633-70633	DEQUINCY	70752-70752	LAKELAND
70343-70343	BOURG	70501-70509	LAFAYETTE	70634-70634	DERIDDER	70753-70753	LETTSWORTH
70344-70344	CHAUVIN	70510-70511	ABBEVILLE	70637-70637	DRY CREEK	70754-70754	LIVINGSTON
70345-70345	CUT OFF	70512-70512	ARNAUDVILLE	70638-70638	ELIZABETH	70755-70755	LIVONIA
70346-70346	DONALDSONVILLE	70513-70513	AVERY ISLAND	70639-70639	EVANS	70756-70756	LOTTIE
70352-70352	DONNER	70514-70514	BALDWIN	70640-70640	FENTON	70757-70757	MARINGOUIN
70353-70353	DULAC	70515-70515	BASILE	70642-70642	FULLERTON	70759-70759	MORGANZA
70354-70354	GALLIANO	70516-70516	BRANCH	70643-70643	GRAND CHENIER	70760-70760	NEW ROADS
70355-70355	GHEENS	70517-70517	BREAUX BRIDGE	70644-70644	GRANT	70761-70761	NORWOOD
70356-70356	GIBSON	70518-70518	BROUSSARD	70645-70645	HACKBERRY	70762-70762	OSCAR
70357-70357	GOLDEN MEADOW	70519-70519	CADE	70646-70646	HAYES	70763-70763	PAULINA
70358-70358	GRAND ISLE	70520-70520	CARENCRO	70647-70647	IOWA	70764-70765	PLAQUEMINE

70767-70767	PORT ALLEN	71060-71060	MOORINGSPORT	71276-71276	SONDHEIMER	71411-71411	CAMPTI
70769-70769	PRAIRIEVILLE	71061-71061	OIL CITY	71277-71277	SPEARSVILLE	71414-71414	CLARENCE
70770-70770	PRIDE	71063-71063	PELICAN	71279-71279	START	71415-71415	CLARKS
70772-70772	ROSEDALE	71064-71064	PLAIN DEALING	71280-71280	STERLINGTON	71416-71416	CLOUTIERVILLE
70773-70773	ROUGON	71065-71065	PLEASANT HILL	71281-71281	SWARTZ	71417-71417	COLFAX
70774-70774	SAINT AMANT	71066-71066	POWHATAN	71282-71284	TALLULAH	71418-71418	COLUMBIA
70775-70775	SAINT FRANCISVILLE	71067-71067	PRINCETON	71286-71286	TRANSYLVANIA	71419-71419	CONVERSE
70776-70776	SAINT GABRIEL	71068-71068	RINGGOLD	71291-71294	WEST MONROE	71422-71422	DODSON
70777-70777	SLAUGHTER	71069-71069	RODESSA	71295-71295	WINNSBORO	71423-71423	DRY PRONG
70778-70778	SORRENTO	71070-71070	SALINE	71301-71315	ALEXANDRIA	71424-71424	ELMER
70780-70780	SUNSHINE	71071-71071	SAREPTA	71316-71316	ACME	71425-71425	ENTERPRISE
70781-70781	TORBERT	71072-71072	SHONGALOO	71320-71320	BORDELONVILLE	71426-71426	FISHER
70782-70782	TUNICA	71073-71073	SIBLEY	71322-71322	BUNKIE	71427-71427	FLATWOODS
70783-70783	VENTRESS	71075-71075	SPRINGHILL	71323-71323	CENTER POINT	71428-71428	FLORA
70784-70784	WAKEFIELD	71078-71078	STONEWALL	71324-71324	CHASE	71429-71429	FLORIEN
70785-70785	WALKER	71079-71079	SUMMERFIELD	71325-71325	CHENEYVILLE	71430-71430	FOREST HILL
70786-70786	WATSON	71080-71080	TAYLOR	71326-71326	CLAYTON	71431-71431	GARDNER
70787-70787	WEYANOKE	71082-71082	VIVIAN	71327-71327	COTTONPORT	71432-71432	GEORGETOWN
70788-70788	WHITE CASTLE	71101-71109	SHREVEPORT	71328-71328	DEVILLE	71433-71433	GLENMORA
70789-70789	WILSON	71110-71110	BARKSDALE AFB	71329-71329	DUPONT	71434-71434	GORUM
70791-70791	ZACHARY	71111-71113	BOSSIER CITY	71330-71330	ECHO	71435-71435	GRAYSON
70792-70792	UNCLE SAM	71115-71166	SHREVEPORT	71331-71331	EFFIE	71438-71438	HINESTON
70801-70898	BATON ROUGE	71171-71172	BOSSIER CITY	71333-71333	EVERGREEN	71439-71439	HORNBECK
71001-71001	ARCADIA	71201-71213	MONROE	71334-71334	FERRIDAY	71440-71440	JOYCE
71002-71002	ASHLAND	71218-71218	ARCHIBALD	71336-71336	GILBERT	71441-71441	KELLY
71003-71003	ATHENS	71219-71219	BASKIN	71339-71339	HAMBURG	71443-71443	KURTHWOOD
71004-71004	BELCHER	71220-71221	BASTROP	71340-71340	HARRISONBURG	71444-71444	LACAMP
71006-71006	BENTON	71222-71222	BERNICE	71341-71341	HESSMER	71446-71446	LEESVILLE
71007-71007	BETHANY	71223-71223	BONITA	71342-71342	JENA	71447-71447	LENA
71008-71008	BIENVILLE	71225-71225	CALHOUN	71343-71343	JONESVILLE	71448-71448	LONGLEAF
71009-71009	BLANCHARD	71226-71226	CHATHAM	71345-71345	LEBEAU	71449-71449	MANY
71016-71016	CASTOR	71227-71227	CHOUDRANT	71346-71346	LECOMPTE	71450-71450	MARTHAVILLE
71018-71018	COTTON VALLEY	71229-71229	COLLINSTON	71348-71348	LIBUSE	71452-71452	MELROSE
71019-71019	COUSHATTA	71230-71230	CROWVILLE	71350-71350	MANSURA	71454-71454	MONTGOMERY
71021-71021	CULLEN	71232-71232	DELHI	71351-71351	MARKSVILLE	71455-71455	MORA
71023-71023	DOYLINE	71233-71233	DELTA	71353-71353	MELVILLE	71456-71456	NATCHEZ
71024-71024	DUBBERLY	71234-71234	DOWNSVILLE	71354-71354	MONTEREY	71457-71458	NATCHITOCHES
71025-71025	EAST POINT	71235-71235	DUBACH	71355-71355	MOREAUVILLE	71459-71459	LEESVILLE
71027-71027	FRIERSON	71237-71237	EPPS	71356-71356	MORROW	71460-71460	NEGREET
71028-71028	GIBSLAND	71238-71238	EROS	71357-71357	NEWELLTON	71461-71461	NEWLLANO
71029-71029	GILLIAM	71240-71240	FAIRBANKS	71358-71358	PALMETTO	71462-71462	NOBLE
71030-71030	GLOSTER	71241-71241	FARMERVILLE	71359-71361	PINEVILLE	71463-71463	OAKDALE
71031-71031	GOLDONNA	71242-71242	FOREST	71362-71362	PLAUCHEVILLE	71465-71465	OLLA
71032-71032	GRAND CANE	71243-71243	FORT NECESSITY	71363-71363	RHINEHART	71466-71466	OTIS
71033-71033	GREENWOOD	71245-71245	GRAMBLING	71365-71365	RUBY	71467-71467	POLLOCK
71034-71034	HALL SUMMIT	71247-71247	HODGE	71366-71366	SAINT JOSEPH	71468-71468	PROVENCAL
71036-71036	HARMON	71249-71249	JIGGER	71367-71367	SAINT LANDRY	71469-71469	ROBELINE
71037-71037	HAUGHTON	71250-71250	JONES	71368-71368	SICILY ISLAND	71471-71471	SAINT MAURICE
71038-71038	HAYNESVILLE	71251-71251	JONESBORO	71369-71369	SIMMESPORT	71472-71472	SIEPER
71039-71039	HEFLIN	71253-71253	KILBOURNE	71371-71371	TROUT	71473-71473	SIKES
71040-71040	HOMER	71254-71254	LAKE PROVIDENCE	71373-71373	VIDALIA	71474-71474	SIMPSON
71043-71043	HOSSTON	71256-71256	LILLIE	71375-71375	WATERPROOF	71475-71475	SLAGLE
71044-71044	IDA	71259-71259	MANGHAM	71377-71377	WILDSVILLE	71477-71477	TIOGA
71045-71045	JAMESTOWN	71260-71260	MARION	71378-71378	WISNER	71479-71479	TULLOS
71046-71046	KEATCHIE	71261-71261	MER ROUGE	71401-71401	AIMWELL	71480-71480	URANIA
71047-71047	KEITHVILLE	71263-71263	OAK GROVE	71403-71403	ANACOCO	71481-71481	VERDA
71048-71048	LISBON	71264-71264	OAK RIDGE	71404-71404	ATLANTA	71483-71483	WINNFIELD
71049-71049	LOGANSPORT	71266-71266	PIONEER	71405-71405	BALL	71485-71485	WOODWORTH
71050-71050	LONGSTREET	71268-71268	QUITMAN	71406-71406	BELMONT	71486-71486	ZWOLLE
71051-71051	ELM GROVE	71269-71269	RAYVILLE	71407-71407	BENTLEY	71496-71496	LEESVILLE
71052-71052	MANSFIELD	71270-71273	RUSTON	71409-71409	BOYCE	71497-71497	NATCHITOCHES
71055-71058	MINDEN	71275-71275	SIMSBORO	71410-71410	CALVIN		

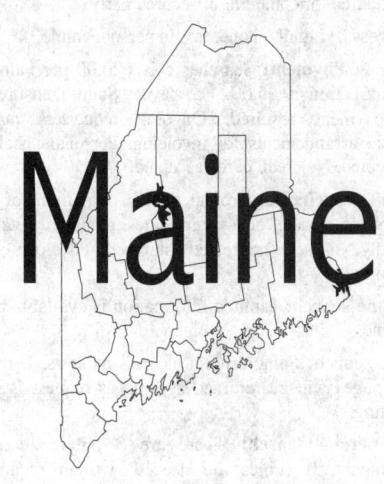

Maine

General Help Numbers:

Governor's Office

1 State House Station, Room 236
Augusta, ME 04333-0001
http://www.state.me.us/governor

207-287-3531
Fax 207-287-1034
7:30AM-5:30PM

Attorney General's Office

6 State House Station
Augusta, ME 04333
http://www.state.me.us/ag

207-626-8800
Fax 207-626-8828
8AM-5PM

State Court Administrator

PO Box 4820
Portland, ME 04112
http://www.courts.state.me.us

207-822-0792
Fax 207-822-0781
8AM-4PM

State Archives

84 State House Station
Augusta, ME 04333-0084
http://www.state.me.us/sos/arc

207-287-5795
Fax 207-287-5739
8:30AM-4PM

State Specifics:

Capital:	Augusta
	Kennebec County
Time Zone:	EST
Number of Counties:	16
Population:	1,274,923
Web Site:	www.state.me.us

State Agencies

Criminal Records

Maine State Police, State Bureau of Identification, 42 State House Station, Augusta, ME 04333; 207-624-7009, 207-624-7088 (Fax), 8AM-5PM.

http://www.state.me.us/dps

Indexing & Storage: Records are available from 1937 on. It takes 1 to 2 days before new records are available for inquiry.

Searching: All convictions and all pending cases less than 1 year old are reported. Requests must be in writing. Submit one name per page (otherwise list could be held or sent back). Include the following in your request-name, date of birth, any aliases. Include maiden name for females. Also include purpose of the inquiry and name and address of requester. The following data is not released: juvenile records.

Access by: mail, in person.

Fee & Payment: Prepayment required. Fee payee: Treasurer, State of Maine. Personal checks accepted. No credit cards accepted.

Mail search: Normal turnaround time is less than one week, those records with "hits" may take slightly longer to process. A self addressed stamped envelope is requested. Search costs $8.00 per individual.

In person search: Search costs $8.00 per individual. This only saves mail-in time; records are returned by mail.

Corporation Records
Limited Partnerships
Trademarks/Servicemarks
Assumed Name
Limited Liability Company Records
Limited Liability Partnerships

Secretary of State, Reports & Information Division, 101 State House Station, Augusta, ME 04333-0101; 207-624-7752, 207-624-7736 (Main Number), 207-287-5874 (Fax), 8AM-5PM.

http://www.state.me.us/sos/cec/corp

Indexing & Storage: Records are available from 1700's on. The older records are in law books. Records on the in-house computer are for all active and some inactive corporations. New records are available for inquiry immediately. Records are indexed on index cards, inhouse computer.

Searching: Include the following in your request-full name of business, specific records that you need copies of. In addition to the articles of incorporation, corporation records include the following information: Annual Reports (back to 1972), Officers, Directors, Prior (merged) names, Inactive and Reserved names.

Access by: mail, phone, in person, online.

Fee & Payment: Copies are $2.00 per page if plain and $5.00 if certified. A Good Standing is $25.00 short form, $35.00 long form and $10.00 if not for profit. Fee payee: Secretary of State. They will invoice for copies. Personal checks accepted. No credit cards accepted.

Mail search: Turnaround time: 1 week. There is a fee of $5.00 per name for information without copies.No self addressed stamped envelope is required.

Phone search: They will provide names and addresses of officers and directors over the phone.

Online search: The Internet site gives basic information about the entity including address, corp ID, agent, and status.

Other access: Lists of new entities filed with this office are available monthly.

Expedited service: Expedited service is available for mail and phone searches. Turnaround time: 24 hours. Add $50.00 per business name. For immediate service, the fee is $100.

Uniform Commercial Code
Federal Tax Liens
State Tax Liens

UCC Filing Section, Secretary of State, 101 State House Station, Augusta, ME 04333-0101 (Courier: Burton McCross State Office Bldg, 109 Sewell St, 4th Fl, Augusta, ME 04333); 207-624-7760, 207-287-5874 (Fax), 8AM-5PM.

http://www.state.me.us/sos/cec/corp/ucc.htm#fi111

Indexing & Storage: Records are available from 1964. Records are computerized since 1993. Records are indexed on inhouse computer.

Searching: Use search request form UCC-11 when needed for certification or a form fabricated by this office. The search includes both federal and state tax liens. Include the following in your request-debtor name. Try to include a middle initial in your request. Searching is done by index

number or debtor name only. They will not search by address or collateral or secured party.

Access by: mail, phone, fax, in person, online.

Fee & Payment: Searches cost $20.00 per name. Certification is $5.00. Fee payee: State Treasurer. Prepayment required. Ongoing requesters may make arrangements for invoicing. Personal checks accepted. No credit cards accepted.

Mail search: Turnaround time: a maximum of 5 days. If update or certain dates requested, state boldly.No self addressed stamped envelope is required.

Phone search: Limited information is available by phone.

Fax search: Same criteria as mail requests. Up to 15 pages will be returned as long as request is in writing.

In person search: There are 3 public access terminals. If copies are needed, written request required and fees apply.

Online search: Online access is available at https://www.informe.org/ucc/search/begin.shtml. There is a free name search, and reports may be ordered online, also.

Other access: Farm products - buyers reports, secured party available in bulk.

Expedited service: Expedited service is available for mail and phone searches. Turnaround time: 1 day. Add $10.00 per name. Write and highlight the word "Expedite" on the search request. For immediate turnaround, the fee is $25.00.

Sales Tax Registrations

Maine Revenue Services, Sales, Fuel & Special Tax Division, 24 State House Station, Augusta, ME 04333; 207-287-2336, 207-287-6628 (Fax), 8AM-4PM.

http://janus.state.me.us/revenue

Indexing & Storage: Records are available from 1993, on computer. It takes up to 2 months before new records are available for inquiry.

Searching: This agency will only confirm that a business is registered. They will provide no other information. Include the following in your request-business name. They will also search by tax permit number or federal ID.

Access by: mail, phone, fax, in person.

Mail search: Turnaround time: 7 to 10 days. A self addressed stamped envelope is requested. No fee for mail request.

Phone search: No fee for telephone request.

Fax search: Same criteria as mail searching.

In person search: No fee for request.

Birth Certificates

Maine Department of Human Services, Vital Records, 221 State St, Station 11, Augusta, ME 04333-0011; 207-287-3181, 877-523-2659, 207-287-1093 (Fax), 8AM-5PM.

http://www.state.me.us/dhs/welcome.htm

Note: The web site has a link to VitalChek for online ordering.

Indexing & Storage: Records are available from 1923 to present. Maine State Archives has records prior to 1923 (call 207-287-5795). Records are indexed on computer from 1975 to present, and on microfiche from 1892 to present. Records are indexed on books (volumes).

Searching: Must give relationship to person of record and reason for request. Confidential information will not be released except to the person listed on the birth certificate. Include the following in your request-full name, names of parents, mother's maiden name, date of birth, place of birth. Also include your daytime phone number with the request. The following data is not released: illegitimate births or adoption records.

Access by: mail, phone, in person, online.

Fee & Payment: $10.00 fee for certified copy or $6.00 for an uncertified copy. Add $4.00 per name for additional copy of same record. A five year search will be conducted. Fee payee: Treasurer, State of Maine. Prepayment required. Personal checks accepted. Credit cards accepted: MasterCard, Visa, AmEx, Discover.

Mail search: Turnaround time: 1 to 2 weeks. Specific dates are needed to search as well as names (if available).

Phone search: See expedited service.

In person search: Turnaround time is while you wait.

Online search: Pre-1892 records are available at the Internet at www.state.me.us/sos/geneology/homepage.html.

Other access: Birth lists are available, excluding restricted information.

Expedited service: Expedited service is available for mail, phone and fax searches. Turnaround time: overnight delivery. Add $9.95 plus $15.50 courier fee. Use of credit card is required.

Death Records

Maine Department of Human Services, Vital Records, 221 State St, Station 11, Augusta, ME 04333-0011; 207-287-3181, 877-523-2659, 207-287-1093 (Fax), 8AM-5PM.

http://www.state.me.us/dhs/welcome.htm

Note: The web site has a link to VitalChek for online ordering.

Indexing & Storage: Records are available from 1923 to present. Maine State Archives has records prior to 1923 (call 207-287-5795). Records are indexed on computer from 1975 to present, and on microfiche from 1892 to present. Records are indexed on books (volumes).

Searching: Access to cause of death is restricted to those with a legitimate interest in the information. All information on certificate of death is confidential, except name, age, date of death, as well as city/town where death occurred. Include the following in your request-full name, date of death, place of death, relationship to person of record.

Access by: mail, in person, online.

Fee & Payment: Certified copies are $10.00 per copy and uncertified records are $6.00 each. Add $4.00 per name for each additional copy. A five year search will be conducted. Fee payee: Treasurer, State of Maine. Prepayment required. Personal checks accepted. Credit cards accepted: MasterCard, Visa, AmEx, Discover.

Mail search: Turnaround time: 1 to 2 weeks. When requesting a search, keep in mind that records are filed by the date of the death, and then by name.

In person search: Turnaround time is while you wait.

Online search: Both old and newer records are available at www.state.me.us/sos/arc/geneology/omepage.html. Death History records from the Maine State Archives are also available at http://thor.ddp.state.me.us/archives.plsql/archdev.death_archinve.search_form.

Other access: Bulk file purchases are available, with the exclusion of restricted data.

Expedited service: Expedited service is available for mail, phone and fax searches. Turnaround time: overnight delivery. Add $9.95 plus $15.50 for delivery. Use of creidt card required.

Marriage Certificates

Maine Department of Human Services, Vital Records, 221 State St, Station 11, Augusta, ME 04333-0011; 207-287-3181, 877-523-2659 (Expedited Srv), 207-287-1093 (Fax), 8AM-5PM.

http://www.state.me.us/dhs/welcome.htm

Note: The web site has a link to VitalChek for online ordering.

Indexing & Storage: Records are available from 1923 to present. Maine State Archives has records prior to 1923 (call 207-287-5795). Records are indexed on microfiche from 1892 to present. Records are indexed on books (volumes).

Searching: Must give relationship to persons of record and reason for request. Data recorded in the section of the certificate specified as confidential is not released (i.e. race, education, etc.). Include the following in your request-names of husband and wife, date of marriage, place or county of marriage.

Access by: mail, phone, in person, online.

Fee & Payment: Certified copies cost $10.00 per copy and non-certified copies are $6.00 each. Add $4.00 per name per extra copy. A five year search will be conducted. Fee payee: Treasurer, State of Maine. Prepayment required. Personal checks accepted. Credit cards accepted: MasterCard, Visa, AmEx, Discover.

Mail search: Turnaround time: 1 to 2 weeks.

Phone search: See expedited service.

In person search: Turnaround time is while you wait.

Online search: Records are available at www.state.me.us/sos/arc/geneology/homepage.html from 1892-1966 and 1976-1996. Marriage History records from the Maine State Archives are available at http://thor/ddp/state.me.us.

Other access: Bulk file purchasing is available, with restricted data excluded.

Expedited service: Expedited service is available for mail, phone and fax searches. Turnaround time: overnight delivery. Add $9.95 plus $15.50 for courier per package. Use of credit card is required. Make this check out to Federal Express.

Divorce Records

Maine Department of Human Services, Office of Vital Records, 221 State St, Station 11, Augusta, ME 04333-0011; 207-287-3181, 877-523-2659 (Expedited Srv), 207-287-1093 (Fax), 8AM-5PM.

http://www.state.me.us/dhs/welcome.htm

Note: The web site has a link to VitalChek for online ordering.

Indexing & Storage: Records are available from 1923 to present. Maine State Archives has records prior to 1923, call 207-287-5795. It takes 1 month before new records are available for inquiry. Records are indexed on books (volumes).

Searching: Must give relationship to persons of record and reason for request. Include the following in your request-names of husband and wife, date of divorce, place of divorce.

Access by: mail, phone, in person.

Fee & Payment: Certified copies cost $10.00 per copy. Non-certified copies are $6.00 each. Add $4.00 per name for each additional copy. Fee payee: Treasurer, State of Maine. Prepayment required. Personal checks accepted. Credit cards accepted: MasterCard, Visa, AmEx, Discover.

Mail search: Turnaround time: 1 to 2 weeks.

Phone search: See expedited service.

In person search: Turnaround time is while you wait.

Other access: Index information is available for bulk purchase.

Expedited service: Expedited service is available for phone requests. Turnaround time: overnight delivery. Add $9.95 plus courier charge of $15.50 per package. Use of credit card required.

Workers' Compensation Records

Workers Compensation Board, 27 State House Station, Augusta, ME 04333-0027; 207-287-7071, 207-287-5895 (Fax), 7:30AM-5PM.

http://janus.state.me.us/wcb

Indexing & Storage: Records are available from 1984, indexed on computer.

Searching: Records are considered confidential and are released "on a need-to-know basis." Include purpose of your request. Include the following in your request-claimant name, Social Security Number, reason for information request. The following data is not released: personal information (height, weight, sex, eye color, etc.) or Social Security Numbers.

Access by: mail, in person.

Fee & Payment: The research fee is $5.00. Copies are $.50 per page. Fee payee: State of Maine, Workers' Compensation Board. When remitting payment, please include invoice number on your check. Personal checks accepted. No credit cards accepted.

Mail search: Turnaround time: 3 to 4 weeks. Requests should be addressed to: Linda Larrabee, Workers' Compensation Board, 27 State House Station, Augusta, ME 04333-0027.A self addressed stamped envelope is requested.

In person search: Requests must still be in writing and prior approval is suggested.

Other access: Computer data is available, but requests are screened for purpose.

Driver Records

Bureau of Motor Vehicles, Driver License Services, 29 State House Station, Augusta, ME 04333-0029; 207-624-9000, 8AM-5PM.

http://www.state.me.us/sos/bmv

Indexing & Storage: Records are available for 3 years for moving violations, DWIs and 3 years after the reinstatement of suspensions. Accidents are indicated on the record. It takes up to 30 days before new records are available for inquiry.

Searching: Driving records and ticket information is released per DPPA guidelines. Personal information is not available to the general public unless the subject opts in, or a signed release is presented. The full name and DOB are required for a search. The driver's license number is optional. The following data is not released: medical information.

Access by: mail, fax, in person, online.

Fee & Payment: The fee is $5.00 for a non-certified record and $6.00 for a certified record. A "no record found" incurs a full charge, except for walk-in requesters. Fee payee: Secretary of State. Prepayment required. Personal checks accepted. No credit cards accepted.

Mail search: Turnaround time: 3 days. No self addressed stamped envelope is required.

Fax search: The cost is $7.00 and results are returned by mail.

In person search: Up to 5 requests can be obtained in-person immediately; additional requests are available the next day.

Online search: Access is through InforME via the Internet. There is a $50.00 annual fee and records are $5.00 per request. Visit the web site for details and sign-up or call 207-621-2600. The state offers "Driver Cross Check" - a program of notification when activity occurs on a specific record.

Other access: Maine will sell statewide or customized lists of license drivers via magnetic tape and other media for high volume users. Call 207-621-2600 for details.

Vehicle Ownership
Vehicle Identification

Department of Motor Vehicles, Registration Section, 29 State House Station, Augusta, ME 04333-0029; 207-624-9000 x52149, 207-624-9204 (Fax), 8AM-5PM M-F.

http://www.state.me.us/sos/bmv/bmv.htm

Indexing & Storage: Records are available from 1977. It takes up to 30 days before new records are available for inquiry.

Searching: Casual requesters can obtain records, but personal information is not included unless the subject given authorization. Opt-in is available. Include the following in your request-full name, VIN, license plate number. The vehicle owner's DOB is helpful when requesting ownership information.

Access by: mail, phone, fax, in person, online.

Fee & Payment: Fees: $6.00 for certified record; $5.00 for uncertified record. Will also fax record back for an additional $2.00. Fee payee: Secretary of State. Prepayment required. Personal checks accepted. No credit cards accepted.

Mail search: Turnaround time: 5 days. No self addressed stamped envelope is required.

Phone search: Telephone searching is available for parties who establish an account. They are billed monthly.

Fax search: Established accounts may order by fax, and then have data returned by fax for an additional $2.00.

Online search: Maine offers online access to title and registration records via PC and modem. The system is open 24 hours daily. To set up an account, call 207-624-9264. Fee is $5.00 per record, annual registration is $50.00.

Accident Reports

Maine State Police, Traffic Division, Station 20, Augusta, ME 04333-0020 (Courier: 397 Water St, Gardiner, ME 04345); 207-624-8944, 207-624-8945 (Fax), 7:30AM-4PM.

http://www.state.me.us/dps/msp

Indexing & Storage: Records are available from 1975. Most records are on microfilm. It takes up to 30 days before new records are available for inquiry.

Searching: Most accident records are public information. All requests must be in writing. Include the following in your request-full name, date of birth, date of accident, location of accident. Be sure to order by the operator's name, not by vehicle owner name.

Access by: mail, in person.

Fee & Payment: The fee is $5.00 per copy for Police Traffic report, $10.00 for an Officers Investigative Report (fatality involved), $10.00 for an Accident Reconstruction Report, and $10.00 for a Vehicle Autopsy Report. Fee payee: Maine State Police. Prepayment required. Personal checks accepted. No credit cards accepted.

Mail search: Turnaround time: 7 days. No self addressed stamped envelope is required.

In person search: Turnaround time is usually immediate for walk-in requesters.

Vessel Ownership
Vessel Registration

Dept of Inland Fisheries & Wildlife, 41 State House Station, Augusta, ME 04333-0041; 207-287-5231, 207-287-8094 (Fax), 8AM-5PM.

http://www.state.me.us/ifw

Note: Liens are not recorded here and must be searched with UCCs.

Indexing & Storage: Records are available from 1993 to present for registrations that have been continuously renewed. Older records on microfiche are archived, and require payment of a $25.00 search fee. There are no titles, all motorized boats must be registered. Records are indexed on computer. Older records on microfiche and archived.

Searching: Submit the name, registration number and serial number.

Access by: mail, phone, fax, in person.

Fee & Payment: The search fee is $5.00 per record. A boat history fee is $25.00. Fee payee:

Treasurer, State of Maine. Prepayment required. Credit cards accepted: MasterCard, Visa.

Mail search: Turnaround time: 2-3 weeks. No self addressed stamped envelope is required.

Phone search: Results will only be given verbally, unless payment is arranged using a credit card.

Fax search: Turnaround time is within 72 hours. A credit card must be used for all fax searches.

In person search: There is no search fee, but copies are $2.00 each.

Other access: The agency offers record access via tape, labels or printed lists.

Legislation Records

Maine Legislature, 2 State House Station, Legislative Document Room, Augusta, ME 04333-0002; 207-287-1692 (Bill Status or LD #), 207-287-1408 (Document Room), 207-287-1456 (Fax), 8AM-5PM.

http://janus.state.me.us/legis

Note: Older passed bills are found at the State Law Library, 207-287-1600.

Indexing & Storage: Records are available for the current session only.

Searching: Include the following in your request-bill number. A paid document service is available. Will express any results at searcher's expense.

Access by: mail, phone, in person, online.

Fee & Payment: There is no search fee or copy fee.

Mail search: Turnaround time: variable. No self addressed stamped envelope is required.

Phone search: There is a limit of 15 bills per phone call.

Online search: The web site offers bills, status, and access to text of state laws.

Other access: A weekly list of LDs (legislative documents) is available.

Voter Registration
Records not maintained by a state level agency.

Note: The data is considered public record in Maine but can only be accessed at the municipality level.

GED Certificates

Dept of Education, Attn: GED, 23 State House Station, Augusta, ME 04333; 207-624-6752, 207-624-6731 (Fax).

http://janus.state.me.us/education

Searching: Requests for transcripts must be in writing. To verify, all of the following is required: name, date of birth, and Social Security Number. For transcripts, a signed release is required.

Access by: mail, phone, fax, in person, online.

Fee & Payment: There are no fees.

Mail search: Turnaround time 1-2 days. No self addressed stamped envelope is required.

Phone search: You can do a verification over the phone.

Fax search: Turnaround time 1-2 days.

In person search: Turnaround time: Immediate.

Online search: E-mail requests can be made by sending e-mail to: lisataylor@state&me.us

Hunting License Information
Fishing License Information

Inland Fisheries & Wildlife Department, Licensing Division, 284 State St, Augusta, ME 04333; 207-287-5209, 207-287-8094 (Fax), 8AM-5PM.

http://www.state.me.us/ifw

Note: The state is in the process of computerizing license data. Licenses are issued by Town Clerks and approved businesses and forwarded monthly to this department.

Indexing & Storage: Records are available from 1996 to present. It takes at least 3 months before new records are available for inquiry. Records are indexed on inhouse computer.

Searching: All information is considered open to the public. Include the following in your request-full name, date of birth, address.

Access by: mail, phone, in person.

Fee & Payment: Individual searches are completed for $5.00 each. Fee payee: Treasurer, State of Maine. Prepayment required. Credit cards accepted: MasterCard, Visa.

Mail search: Turnaround time: 7 business days. No self addressed stamped envelope is required.

Phone search: Credit card required.

Other access: Bulk data purchases are available at a cost of $.05 per name. Call InfoME at 207-621-2600.

Maine State Licensing Agencies

Licenses Searchable Online

ATV-All-Terrain Vehicle #11 .... www.state.me.us/ifw/index.html
Bank #14 .... www.state.me.us/pfr/bkg/mebanks.htm
Credit Union #14 .... www.state.me.us/pfr/bkg/mebanks.htm
Employee Leasing Company #15 .... www.state.me.us/pfr/ins/emplease.htm
Health Maintenance Organization #15 .... www.state.me.us/pfr/ins/inshmo.htm
Lobbyist #01 .... www.lobbyist.net/Maine/MAILOB.htm
Medical Doctor #23 .... www.docboard.org/me/df/mesearch.htm
Notary Public #24 .... www.state.me.us/sos/cec/rcn/notary/notlist.htm
Optometrist #18 .... www.odfinder.org/LicSearch.asp
Osteopathic Physician/Physician Assistant #26. www.docboard.org/me-osteo
Osteopathic Resident/Intern #26 .... www.docboard.org/me-osteo
Preferred Provider Organization #15 .... www.state.me.us/pfr/ins/insppo.htm
Savings & Loan #14 .... www.state.me.us/pfr/bkg/mebanks.htm
Snowmobile #11 .... www.state.me.us/ifw/index.html
Trust Company #14 .... www.state.me.us/pfr/bkg/mebanks.htm
Utilization Review Entity #15 .... www.state.me.us/pfr/ins/insmedur.htm
Watercraft #11 .... www.state.me.us/ifw/index.html

Licensing Quick Finder

Acupuncturist #13 207-624-8632	First Responder #10 207-287-3953	Pesticide Applicator #03 207-287-2731
Adult Care Home #09 207-624-5250	Forester #13 207-624-8628	Pesticide Dealer #03 207-287-2731
Adult Day Services #09 207-624-5250	Funeral Home #13 207-624-8603	Pharmacist #13 207-624-8616
Aesthetician #13 207-624-8603	Funeral Service #13 207-624-8611	Physical Therapist #13 207-624-8628
Air Quality Control (Business) #05 207-287-2437	Geologist & Soil Scientist #13 207-624-8616	Physician Assistant #23 207-287-3601
Alcohol & Drug Abuse Counselor #13 ...207-624-8603	Hazardous Material/Solid Waste Operator #06	Pilot #13 207-624-8620
Alcoholic Beverage Distributor #21 207-624-8745	207-287-7865	Plumber #13 207-624-8628
Ambulance Attendant #20 207-287-3953	Health Maintenance Organization #15 ...207-624-8475	Podiatrist #13 207-624-8626
Ambulatory Surgical Center #09 207-624-5443	Hearing Aid Dealer/Fitter #13 207-624-8628	Polygraph Examiner #20 207-624-7074
Animal Medical Technician #13 207-624-8603	Home Health Agencies #09 207-624-5443	Preferred Provider Organization #15 207-624-8475
Appraiser, Residential Real Estate #13 .207-624-8616	Home Health Care Service Agency#9 ...207-624-5443	Private Investigator #25 207-624-8775
Architect #13 207-624-8522	Hospice #09 207-624-5443	Psychologist #13 207-624-8628
Assisted Living Facility #09 207-624-5250	Hospital #09 207-624-5443	Public Accountant-CPA #13 207-582-8627
Athletic Trainer #13 207-624-8624	Insurance Advisor #13 207-624-8603	Radiologic Technician #13 207-624-8628
Attorney #22 207-623-1121	Insurance Agent #13 207-624-8603	Real Estate Appraiser, General #13 207-624-8616
ATV-All-Terrain Vehicle #11 207-287-2043	Intermediate Care Facility for the Mentally Retarded	Real Estate Appraiser/Trainee #13 207-624-8616
Auctioneer #13 207-624-8521	#09 207-624-5443	Real Estate Broker #13 207-624-8603
Bank #14 207-624-8648	Investment Advisor #13 207-624-8603	Renal Disease (End Stage) Facility #9 .207-624-5443
Barber #13 207-624-8620	Itinerant Vendor #13 207-624-8624	Residential Child Care Provider #07 207-287-5060
Bedding/Upholstering/Furniture/Stuffed Toy Mfg. #12	Kickboxer #13 207-624-8603	Respiratory Care Therapist #13 207-624-8616
....207-624-6411	Landscape Architect #13 207-624-8616	Savings & Loan #14 207-624-8648
Beekeeper #03 207-287-3117	Library Media Specialist #04 207-287-5944	School Guidance Counselor #04 207-287-5944
Boiler Contractor #13 207-624-8615	Loan Broker #13 207-624-8603	School Library Media Specialist #04 207-287-5944
Boxer #13 207-624-8521	Lobbyist #01 207-287-6221	School Principal #04 207-287-5944
Charitable Solicitation #13 207-624-8624	Lottery Combined Vendor #21 207-287-6824	School Superintendent #04 207-287-5944
Chiropractor #13 207-624-8634	Lottery Retailer #02 207-287-6824	Sea Urchin Harvester #27 207-624-6550
Cosmetologist #13 207-624-8620	Lottery Vending #21 207-287-6824	Seaweed Harvester #27 207-624-6550
Counselor #13 207-624-8626	Manicurist #13 207-624-8603	Security Company (Guard/Alarm) #25 ...207-624-8775
Credit Union #14 207-624-8648	Manufactured Housing #13 207-582-8612	Self Insurance Company #15 207-624-8475
Dental Hygienist #16 207-287-3333	Marriage & Family Therapist #13 207-624-8634	Snowmobile #11 207-287-2043
Dental Radiographer #16 207-287-3333	Massage Therapist #13 207-624-8603	Social Worker #13 207-624-8631
Dentist #16 207-287-3333	Medical Doctor #23 207-287-3601	Soil Scientist #13 207-624-8603
Denturist #16 207-287-3333	Notary Public #24 207-624-7650	Speech Pathologist/Audiologist #13 207-624-8634
Dietitian #13 207-624-8611	Nurse #08 207-287-1133	Sprinkler Inspector #20 207-287-3473
Drug Analyzer #07 207-287-3201	Nursing Home #09 207-624-5443	Substance Abuse Counselor #13 207-624-8634
Electrician #13 207-624-8611	Nursing Home Administrator #13 207-624-8611	Surveyor #13 207-624-8611
Electrologist #07 207-287-5338	Occupational Therapist #13 207-624-8616	Tattoo Artist #07 207-287-3201
Elevator/Tramway Contractor #13 207-624-8615	Oil & Solid Fuel #13 207-624-8631	Taxidermist #11 207-287-2751
Emergency Medical Technician #10 207-287-3953	Optometrist #18 207-624-8691	Teacher #04 207-287-5944
Employee Leasing Company #15 207-624-8475	Osteopathic Physician Extender #26 207-287-2480	Trust Company #14 207-624-8648
Engineer #17 207-287-3236	Osteopathic Physician/Physician Assistant #26	Utilitization Review Entitity #15 207-624-8475
Firearm Permit (Non-resident, Concealed) #25	207-287-2480	Veterinarian #13 207-624-8628
....207-624-8775	Osteopathic Resident/Intern #26 207-287-2480	Veterinary Technician #13 207-624-8603
Firearm Permit (Resident, Concealed) #25	Paramedic #10 207-287-3953	Watercraft #11 207-287-2043
....207-624-8775	Pastoral Counselor #13 207-624-8634	

Licensing Agency Information

#01 Registrar, State House Station 135, Augusta, ME 04333; 207-287-6221, Fax: 207-287-6775. www.state.me.us/ethics

#02 Department of Administrative & Financial Services, 8 State House Station, Augusta, ME 04333-0008; 207-287-6824, Fax: 207-287-6769. www.mainelottery.com

#03 Department of Agriculture, Food & Rural Resources, 280 State House Station, Augusta, ME 04332-0028; 207-287-2731, Fax: 207-287-7548. www.state.me.us/agriculture/pesticides/

#04 Department of Education, 23 State House Station, Augusta Complex, Augusta, ME 04333-0023; 207-287-5944, Fax: 207-287-3910. www.state.me.us/agencies.htm

#05 Department of Environmental Protection, 17 State House Station, Augusta, ME 04333-0017; 207-287-2437, Fax: 207-287-7641. www.state.me.us/dep/home.htm

#06 Department of Environmental Protection, State House Station 17, Augusta, ME 04333; 207-287-7865, Fax: 207-287-7826. www.state.me.us/agencies.htm

#07 Department of Human Services, 221 State St, 11 State House Station, Augusta, ME 04333-0011; 207-287-5060, Fax: 207-287-5282. www.state.me.us/dhs/

#08 Department of Professional & Financial Regulation, 24 Stone Street, # 158 State House Station, Augusta, ME 04333-0158; 207-287-1133, Fax: 207-287-1149. www.state.me.us/nursingbd

#09 Department of Human Services, 35 SHS, Augusta, ME 04333; 207-624-5443, Fax: 207-624-5378. www.state.me.us/pfr/olr/

#10 Department of Public Safety, 16 Edison Dr, Augusta, ME 04333; 207-287-3953, Fax: 207-289-6251.

www.state.me.us/dps/ems

#11 Department of Inland Fisheries & Wildlife, 284 State St, 41 Statehouse Station, Augusta, ME 04333-0041; 207-287-8000, Fax: 207-287-8094. www.state.me.us/ifw/index.html Direct web site URL to search for licensees: www.state.me.us/ifw/index.html. You can search online using name.

#12 Department of Labor, 45 State House Station, Augusta, ME 04333-0045; 207-624-6411, Fax: 207-624-6449. http://janus.state.me.us/labor

#13 Department of Professional & Financial Regulation, 35 State House Station, Augusta, ME 04333-0035; 207-624-8500, Fax: 207-624-8637. www.state.me.us/pfr/olr

#14 Department of Professional & Financial Regulation, 36 State House Station, Augusta, ME 04333-0036; 207-624-8570, Fax: 207-624-8590. www.mainebankingreg.org

#15 Department of Professional & Financial Regulation, State House Station 34, Augusta, ME 04333-0034; 207-624-8475, Fax: 207-624-8599. www.state.me.us/pfr/ins/inshome2.htm

#16 Board of Dental Examiners, 143 Statehouse Station, 2 Bangor St, Augusta, ME 04333-0143; 207-287-3333, Fax: 207-287-8140.

#17 Department of Professional & Financial Regulation, 92 State House Station, Augusta, ME 04333; 207-287-3236, Fax: 207-626-2309. www.state.me.us/pfr/auxboards/enghome.htm

#18 Department of Professional & Financial Regulation, 113 State House Station, Augusta, ME 04333; 207-624-8691, Fax: 207-624-8691. Direct web site URL to search for licensees: www.odfinder.org/LicSearch.asp. You can search online using national database by name, city, or state.

#20 Department of Public Safety, 18 Meadow Rd, 104 State House Station, Augusta, ME 04333-0042; 207-624-7094, Fax: 207-624-7088. www.state.me.us/dps

#21 Department of Public Safety, 164 State House Station, Augusta, ME 04333; 207-624-8745, Fax: 207-624-8767.

#22 Board of Bar Examiners, PO Box 30, Augusta, ME 04332-0030; 207-623-2464, Fax: 207-623-4175.

#23 Medical Doctor & Physician Assistant Licensing & Investigation, 137 State House Station, Augusta, ME 04333; 207-287-3601, Fax: 207-287-6590. www.docboard.org/me/df/find_me.htm

#24 Secretary of State, Div of Elections & Commissions, 101 State House Station, Augusta, ME 04333-0101; 207-624-7650, Fax: 207-287-6545. www.state.me.us/sos/cec/rcn/notary/not.htm Direct web site URL to search for licensees: www.state.me.us/sos/cec/rcn/notary/not.htm. You can search online using town, name, and county.

#25 State Police Licensing Division, 164 State House Station, Augusta, ME 04333; 207-624-8775, Fax: 207-624-8767.

#26 State of Maine, 142 State House Station, Augusta, ME 04333-0142; 207-287-2480, Fax: 207-287-2480. Direct web site URL to search for licensees: www.docboard.org/me-osteo/. You can search online using name or license number.

#27 Department of Marine Resources, 21 State House Station, Hallowell Annex-Baker Bldg, Augusta, ME 04333-0021; 207-624-6550.

Maine Federal Courts

The following list indicates the district and division name for each county in the state. If the bankruptcy court location is different from the district court, then the location of the bankruptcy court appears in parentheses.

County/Court Cross Reference

Androscoggin	Portland	Oxford	Portland
Aroostook	Bangor	Penobscot	Bangor
Cumberland	Portland	Piscataquis	Bangor
Franklin	Bangor	Sagadahoc	Portland
Hancock	Bangor	Somerset	Bangor
Kennebec	Bangor	Waldo	Bangor
Knox	Portland (Bangor)	Washington	Bangor
Lincoln	Portland (Bangor)	York	Portland

US District Court

Bangor Division Court Clerk, PO Box 1007, Bangor, ME 04402-1007 (Courier Address: Room 357, 202 Harlow St, Bangor, ME 04401), 207-945-0575, Fax: 207-945-0362.

http://www.med.uscourts.gov

Counties: Aroostook, Franklin, Hancock, Kennebec, Penobscot, Piscataquis, Somerset, Waldo, Washington.

Indexing/Storage: Cases are indexed by defendant and plaintiff as well as by case number. New cases are available in the index immediately after filing date. A computer index is maintained. Records are indexed and stored by year, then docket number for case files and by name for electronic index system. Open records are located at this court.

Fee & Payment: The fee is $20.00 per item (one party name or case number). Payment may be made by money order, cashier check, personal check. Prepayment is required. Payee: Clerk, US District Court. Certification fee: $7.00 per document. Copy fee: $.50 per page.

Phone Search: Any public record information will be released over the phone including the accession number.

Mail Search: A stamped self addressed envelope is not required.

In Person: In person searching is available.

PACER: Sign-up number is 800-676-6856. Access fee is $.60 per minute. Toll-free access: 800-260-9774. Local access: 207-780-3392. Case records are available back to August 1991. Records are purged every 6 months. New records are available online after 1 day. PACER is available online at https://pacer.med.uscourts.gov.

Portland Division Court Clerk, 156 Federal St, Portland, ME 04101 (Courier Address: Use mail address for courier delivery), 207-780-3356, Fax: 207-780-3772.

http://www.med.uscourts.gov

Counties: Androscoggin, Cumberland, Knox, Lincoln, Oxford, Sagadahoc, York.

Indexing/Storage: Cases are indexed by defendant and plaintiff as well as by case number. New cases are available in the index immediately after filing date. A computer index is maintained. Records are indexed and stored by year, then docket number for case files and by name for electronic index system. Open records are located at this court.

Fee & Payment: The fee is $20.00 per item (one party name or case number). Payment may be made by money order, cashier check, personal check. Prepayment is required. Payee: Clerk, US District Court. Certification fee: $7.00 per document. Copy fee: $.50 per page.

Phone Search: Public record information will be released over phone including accession numbers.

Mail Search: A stamped self addressed envelope is not required.

In Person: In person searching is available.

PACER: Sign-up number is 800-676-6856. Access fee is $.60 per minute. Toll-free access: 800-260-9774. Local access: 207-780-3392. Case records are available back to August 1991. Records are purged every 6 months. New records are available online after 1 day. PACER is available online at https://pacer.med.uscourts.gov.

US Bankruptcy Court

Bangor Division PO Box 1109, Bangor, ME 04402-1109 (Courier Address: 202 Harlow St, Bangor, ME 04401), 207-945-0348, Fax: 207-945-0304.

http://www.meb.uscourts.gov

Counties: Aroostook, Franklin, Hancock, Kennebec, Knox, Lincoln, Penobscot, Piscataquis, Somerset, Waldo, Washington.

Indexing/Storage: Cases are indexed by debtor as well as by case number. New cases are available in the index immediately after filing date. A computer index is maintained. Archived records are available within 2 weeks of shipment to the archives. Open records are located at this court. The length of time records are retained depends on space; files are usually retained 3 years before being sent to the Boston Federal Records Center.

Fee & Payment: The fee is $20.00 per item (one party name or case number). Payment may be made by money order, cashier check, business check. Personal checks are not accepted. Prepayment is required. Payee: United States Courts. Certification fee: $7.00 per document. Copy fee: $.50 per page.

Phone Search: An automated voice case information service (VCIS) is available. Call VCIS at 800-650-7253 or 207-780-3755.

Mail Search: A stamped self addressed envelope is not required.

In Person: In person searching is available.

PACER: Sign-up number is 800-676-6856. Access fee is $.60 per minute. Toll-free access: 800-733-8797. Local access: 207-780-3268. Case records are available back to December 1988. Records are purged every two years. New civil records are available online after 1 day. PACER is available online at http://pacer.meb.uscourts.gov.

Portland Division 537 Congress St, Portland, ME 04101 (Courier Address: P.O. Box 17575, Portland, ME 04112-8575), 207-780-3482, Fax: 207-780-3679.

http://www.meb.uscourts.gov

Counties: Androscoggin, Cumberland, Oxford, Sagadahoc, York.

Indexing/Storage: Cases are indexed by debtor as well as by case number. New cases are available in the index immediately after filing date. Searches for cases filed prior to 1988 require the debtor's name. Automated searches require either the case number or debtor's name. A computer index is maintained. Records from the court are available from the court immediately after docketing. Information through VCIS and Pacer is available 24 hours after docketing. Open records are located at this court.

Fee & Payment: The fee is $20.00 per item (one party name or case number). Payment may be made by money order, cashier check, business check. Personal checks are not accepted. Prepayment is required for individual requesters. Payee: US Bankruptcy Court. Certification fee: $7.00 per document. Copy fee: $.50 per page.

Phone Search: Only docket information is available by phone. An automated voice case information service (VCIS) is available. Call VCIS at 800-650-7253 or 207-780-3755.

Mail Search: Always enclose a stamped self addressed envelope.

In Person: In person searching is available.

PACER: Sign-up number is 800-676-6856. Access fee is $.60 per minute. Toll-free access: 800-733-8797. Local access: 207-780-3268. Case records are available back to December 1988. Records are purged every two years. New civil records are available online after 1 day. PACER is available online at http://pacer.meb.uscourts.gov.

Maine County Courts

Court	Jurisdiction	No. of Courts	How Organized
Superior Courts*	General	17	16 Counties
District Courts*	Limited	31	13 Districts
Probate Courts*	Special	16	

* Profiled in this Sourcebook.

	CIVIL								
Court	Tort	Contract	Real Estate	Min. Claim	Max. Claim	Small Claims	Estate	Eviction	Domestic Relations
Superior Courts*	X	X	X	No Min	No Max				X
District Courts*	X	X	X	No Min	No Max	$4500		X	X
Probate Courts*							X		X

	CRIMINAL				
Court	Felony	Misdemeanor	DWI/DUI	Preliminary Hearing	Juvenile
Superior Courts*	X	X	X	X	
District Courts*	X	X	X	X	X
Probate Courts*					

ADMINISTRATION
State Court Administrator, PO Box 4820, Portland, ME, 04112; 207-822-0792, Fax: 207-822-0781. www.state.me.us/courts

COURT STRUCTURE
The Superior Court is the court of general jurisdiction. Prior to year 2001, District Courts accepted civil cases involving claims less than $30,000. Now, District Courts have jurisdiction concurrent with that of the Superior Court for all civil actions except those cases vested in the Superior Court by statute.

Both Superior and District Courts handle "misdemeanor" and "felony" cases, with jury trials being held in Superior Court only. Superior Court has exclusive jurisdiction over pleas or trials for murder cases.

The small claims limit was raised from $3000 to $4500 as of 7/1/1997.

ONLINE ACCESS
Development of a judicial computer system is in use statewide for all criminal and certain civil case types. The remainder of civil case types will be available statewide in the near future. The system is initially for judicial and law enforcement agencies and will not include public access in the near term.

Some counties are online through a private vendor.

ADDITIONAL INFORMATION
Mail requests for full criminal history record information are returned to the sender, referring them to the State Bureau of Investigation or the Bureau of Motor Vehicles, in most courts. Mail requests that make a specific inquiry related to an identified case are responded to in writing, with appropriate copy and attestation fees.

Telephone requests for information will only be provided to parties to the case and criminal justice agencies.

PROBATE COURTS
Probate Courts are part of the county court system, not the state system. Even though the Probate Court may be housed with other state courts, it is on a different phone system and calls may not be transferred.

Androscoggin County

Androscoggin Superior Court PO Box 3660, Auburn, ME 04212-3660; 207-783-5450. Hours: 8AM-4:30PM (EST). *Felony, Misdemeanor, Civil Actions.*

Civil Records: Access: Phone, mail, in person. Only the court performs in person searches; visitors may not. No search fee. Required to search: name, years to search; also helpful: address. Civil cases indexed by defendant, plaintiff. Civil records on index cards since 1977, docket books from 1961-1977.

Criminal Records: Access: In person only. Visitors must perform in person searches for themselves. No search fee. Required to search: name, years to search; also helpful: DOB. Criminal records go back to 1920s; on computer back to 1997.

General Information: No adoption, juvenile, impounded by judge, certain domestic matters. SASE required. Turnaround time 1 week. Copy fee: $1.00 per page. Certification fee: $1.00. Fee payee: Androscoggin Superior Court. Personal checks accepted. Prepayment is required.

Lewiston District Court - South 8 PO Box 1345, 85 Park St, Lewiston, ME 04243; 207-783-5401. Hours: 8AM-4PM (EST). *Misdemeanor, Civil Actions, Eviction, Small Claims.*

Civil Records: Access: Mail, in person. Both court and visitors may perform in person searches. No search fee. Required to search: name, years to search; also helpful: address. Civil cases indexed by defendant. Civil records on docket books from 1956-1987; on computer back to 1987.

Criminal Records: Access: Mail, in person. Both court and visitors may perform in person searches. No search fee. Required to search: name, years to search, DOB; also helpful: address, SSN. Criminal records on computer back to 1987, docket books from 1956-1987.

General Information: Public Access terminal is available. No juvenile, protective custody records released. SASE required. Turnaround time 1-2 days. Fax notes: Fee to fax results is $1.00 per page. Copy fee: $1.00 per page. Certification fee: $1.00. Fee payee: Maine District Court. Personal checks accepted. Prepayment is required.

North Androscoggin District Court 11 2 Main St, Livermore Falls, ME 04254; 207-897-3800. Hours: 8AM-4PM T-Th (EST). *Misdemeanor, Civil Actions, Eviction, Small Claims.*

Civil Records: Access: Mail, in person. Both court and visitors may perform in person searches. No search fee. Required to search: name, years to search, DOB. Civil cases indexed by defendant. Civil records on docket books.

Criminal Records: Access: Mail, in person. Only the court performs in person searches; visitors may not. No search fee. Required to search: name, years to search; also helpful: DOB. Criminal records on computer since 1988, prior on docket books.

General Information: No juvenile, protective custody records released. SASE requested. Turnaround time up to 1 week. Copy fee: $1.00 per page. Certification fee: $1.00. Fee payee: Maine District Court. Personal checks accepted. Prepayment is required.

Probate Court 2 Turner St, Auburn, ME 04210; 207-782-0281; Fax: 207-782-1135. Hours: 8:30AM-5PM (EST). *Probate.*

Aroostook County

Caribou Superior Court 144 Sweden St, Suite 101, Caribou, ME 04736; 207-498-8125. Hours: 8AM-4PM (EST). *Felony, Misdemeanor, Civil Actions.*

Civil Records: Access: Mail, in person. Only the court performs in person searches; visitors may not. No search fee. Required to search: name, years to search. Civil cases indexed by defendant, plaintiff. Civil records on docket books since 1951. All cases 1990 forward stored in Caribou Court.

Criminal Records: Access: Mail, in person. Only the court performs in person searches; visitors may not. No search fee. Required to search: name, years to search; also helpful: DOB. Criminal records on docket books since 1951. All cases 1990 forward stored in Caribou Court.

General Information: No juvenile, protective custody records released. SASE required. Turnaround time 1 week. Copy fee: $1.00 per page. Certification fee: $2.00. Fee payee: Treasurer, State of Maine or Superior Court. Personal checks accepted. Prepayment required.

Houlton Superior Court PO Box 457, Houlton, ME 04730; 207-532-6563. Hours: 8AM-4PM (EST). *Felony, Misdemeanor, Civil Actions.*

Civil Records: Access: Mail, in person. Both court and visitors may perform in person searches. No search fee. Required to search: name, years to search. Civil cases indexed by defendant, plaintiff. Civil records on docket books 1960-89. Non-pending closed case records are stored at the Houlton Court 1960-89.

Criminal Records: Access: Mail, in person. Both court and visitors may perform in person searches. No search fee. Required to search: name, years to search, DOB. Criminal records on docket books 1960-89. Non-pending closed case records are stored at the Houlton Court 1960-89.

General Information: No juvenile or protective custody records released. SASE required. Turnaround time 2-3 days. Copy fee: $2.00 for first page, $.50 each add'l. Certification fee: $2.00. Fee payee: Maine Superior Court. No personal checks accepted. Prepayment is required.

Caribou District Court - East 1 144 Sweden St, Caribou, ME 04736; 207-493-3144. Hours: 8AM-4PM (EST). *Misdemeanor, Civil Actions, Eviction, Small Claims.*

Civil Records: Access: Mail, in person. Only the court performs in person searches; visitors may not. No search fee. Required to search: name, years to search. Civil cases indexed by defendant. Civil records on docket books since 1963.

Criminal Records: Access: In person only. Visitors must perform in person searches for themselves. No search fee. Required to search: name, years to search; also helpful: DOB. Criminal records on computer since 1987 (includes traffic), docket books since 1963.

General Information: Public Access terminal is available. No juvenile or child protective records released. SASE required. Turnaround time 1 week. Copy fee: $1.00 per page. Certification fee: $2.00 plus $1.00 each additional page. Fee payee: Maine District Court. Personal checks accepted. Prepayment is required.

District Court 2 PO Box 794 (27 Riverside Dr), Presque Isle, ME 04769; 207-764-2055. Hours: 8AM-4PM (EST). *Misdemeanor, Civil Actions, Eviction, Small Claims.*

Civil Records: Access: Mail, in person. Both court and visitors may perform in person searches. No search fee. Required to search: name, years to search. Civil cases indexed by defendant. Civil records on computer since 1987, docket books since 1962.

Criminal Records: Access: In person only. Visitors must perform in person searches for themselves. No search fee. Required to search: name, years to search; also helpful: DOB. Criminal records on computer since 1987, docket books since 1962.

General Information: Public Access terminal is available. No juvenile or child protective records released. SASE required. Turnaround time 1 week. Copy fee: $1.00 per page. Include $1.00 for postage or SASE. Certification fee: $1.00. Fee payee: Maine District Court. Personal checks accepted. Prepayment is required.

Fort Kent District Court - District 1 Division of Western Aroostook, PO Box 473, Fort Kent, ME 04743; 207-834-5003. Hours: 8AM-4PM (EST). *Misdemeanor, Civil Actions, Eviction, Small Claims.*

Civil Records: Access: Phone, mail, in person. Both court and visitors may perform in person searches. No search fee. Required to search: name, years to search. Civil cases indexed by defendant, plaintiff. Few civil records are computerized.

Criminal Records: Access: Phone, mail, in person. Both court and visitors may perform in person searches. No search fee. Required to search: name, years to search. Criminal records on computer from 1988, on docket books from 1960-1988.

General Information: No juvenile, protective custody, impounded, mental health records released. SASE required. Turnaround time 2-3 days. Copy fee: $1.00 per page. Certification fee: $1.00. Fee payee: Maine District Court. Personal checks accepted. Prepayment is required.

Houlton District Court - South 2 PO Box 457, Houlton, ME 04730; 207-532-2147. Hours: 8AM-4PM (EST). *Misdemeanor, Civil Actions, Eviction, Small Claims.*

Civil Records: Access: Mail, in person. Only the court performs in person searches; visitors may not. No search fee. Required to search: name, years to search; also helpful: address. Civil cases indexed by defendant, plaintiff. Civil records on docket books since 1960.

Criminal Records: Access: Mail, in person. Only the court performs in person searches; visitors may not. No search fee. Required to search: name, years to search; also helpful: address, DOB. Criminal records on computer since June 1987, docket books since 1960.

General Information: Public Access terminal is available. (Records available since June 1987.) No Juvenile or protective custody records released. SASE required. Turnaround time 2-3 days. Copy fee: $1.00 per page. Certification fee: $1.00. Fee payee: Maine District Court. Personal checks accepted. Prepayment is required.

Madawaska District Court - West PO Box 127, 645 E Main St, Madawaska, ME 04756; 207-728-4700. Hours: 8AM-4PM M,T,F (EST). *Misdemeanor, Civil Actions, Eviction, Small Claims.*

Civil Records: Access: Phone, mail, in person. Only the court performs in person searches; visitors may not. No search fee. Required to search: name, years to search. Civil cases indexed by defendant, plaintiff. Civil records on docket books from 1966-67.

Criminal Records: Access: Phone, mail, in person. Only the court performs in person searches; visitors may not. No search fee. Required to search: name, years to search; also helpful: DOB or SSN. Criminal records on computer since 1988, docket books from 1966-67.

General Information: No juvenile, protected custody, impounded or mental health records released. SASE required. Turnaround time 2-3 days. Copy fee: $1.00 per page. Additional fee $1.00 if no SASE. Certification fee: $1.00. Fee payee: Maine District Court. Personal checks accepted. Prepayment is required.

Probate Court 26 Court St #103, Houlton, ME 04730; 207-532-1502. Hours: 8AM-4:30PM *Probate.*

Cumberland County

Superior Court - Civil PO Box 287-DTS, Portland, ME 04112; 207-822-4105. Hours: 8AM-4:30PM (EST). *Civil Actions.*

Civil Records: Access: Phone, mail, in person. Both court and visitors may perform in person searches. No search fee. Required to search: name, years to search. Civil cases indexed by defendant, plaintiff. Civil records on index cards since 1900s.
General Information: No juvenile, medical malpractice, impounded records released. SASE required. Turnaround time 1 day to 1 week. Copy fee: $1.00 per page. Include $1.00 for postage unless pre-paid envelope already enclosed. Certification fee: $1.00. Fee payee: Superior Court. Personal checks accepted. Prepayment is required.

Superior Court - Criminal PO Box 287, Portland, ME 04112; 207-822-4113. Hours: 8AM-4:30PM (EST). *Felony, Misdemeanor.*

Criminal Records: Access: In person only. Both court and visitors may perform in person searches. No search fee. Required to search: name, years to search, DOB. Criminal records on index cards since 1900s, some records form 08/98 to present are computerized.
General Information: No juvenile records released. SASE required. Turnaround time 2-3 days. Fax notes: Fee to fax results is $1.00 per page. Copy fee: $1.00 per page. Certification fee: $1.00. Fee payee: Clerk of Courts. Personal checks accepted. Prepayment required.

Portland District Court - South 9 Civil PO Box 412, 205 Newbury St, Portland, ME 04112; 207-822-4200. Hours: 8AM-4:30PM (EST). *Civil Actions, Eviction, Small Claims.*

Note: Also see Sagadahoc District Court, which handles cases from eastern Cumberland County. Also see Brighton District Court which handles cases from western Cumberland County.

Civil Records: Access: In person. Both court and visitors may perform in person searches. No search fee. Required to search: name, years to search. Civil cases indexed by defendant. Civil records go back ten years, small claims and eviction five years.
General Information: No child custody records released. SASE required. Turnaround time 1 week. Copy fee: $1.00 per page. Certification fee: $1.00. Fee payee: Maine District Court. Personal checks accepted. Prepayment is required.

Portland District Court - South 9 Criminal PO Box 412, Portland, ME 04112; 207-822-4204. Hours: 8AM-4:30PM (EST). *Misdemeanor.*

Criminal Records: Access: In person only. Visitors may perform in person searches for themselves. Search fee: No search fee. Required to search: name, years to search, DOB, offense, date of offense. Criminal records on computer back to 09/86, prior records archived.
General Information: No impounded records released. SASE required. Turnaround time 3-4 days. Fax notes: Will not fax results. Copy fee: $1.00 per page. Certification fee: $1.00. Fee payee: Maine District Court. Personal checks accepted. Prepayment is required.

Bath District Court - East 6, Cumberland County, ME. *Misdemeanor, Civil Actions, Eviction, Small Claims.*

Note: Combined with West Bath District Court 6 in Sagadahoc County.

Bridgton District Court - North 9 2 Chase Common, Bridgton, ME 04009; 207-647-3535. Hours: 8AM-4PM (EST). *Misdemeanor, Civil Actions, Eviction, Small Claims.*

Civil Records: Access: Phone, mail, in person. Visitors must perform in person searches for themselves. Search fee: $1.00 per page (copy fee). Required to search: name, years to search. Civil cases indexed by defendant. Civil records on docket books since 1960; on computer back to 1986.
Criminal Records: Access: Phone, mail, in person. Visitors must perform in person searches for themselves. Search fee: $1.00 per page (copy fee). Required to search: name, years to search; also helpful: DOB. Criminal records on computer back to 1986, docket books since 1960.
General Information: Public Access terminal is available. (Criminal only.) No juvenile, protective custody, financial affidavits, impounded or domestic records released. Copy fee: $1.00 per page. Certification fee: $1.00. Fee payee: Maine District Court. Personal checks accepted. Prepayment is required.

Probate Court 142 Federal St, Portland, ME 04101-4196; 207-871-8382. Hours: 8:30AM-4:30PM (EST). *Probate.*

Franklin County

Superior Court 38 Main St, Farmington, ME 04938; 207-778-3346; Fax: 207-778-8261. Hours: 8AM-4PM *Felony, Misdemeanor, Civil Actions.*

Civil Records: Access: Mail, phone, in person. Both court and visitors may perform in person searches. No search fee. Required to search: name, years to search. Civil cases indexed by defendant, plaintiff. Civil records on docket books and index cards since 1900s.
Criminal Records: Access: In person only. Visitors must perform in person searches for themselves. No search fee. Required to search: name, years to search; also helpful: DOB, SSN. Criminal records on docket books and index cards since 1900s.
General Information: No juvenile, impounded or medical malpractice records released. Copy fee: $1.00 per page. Certification fee: $1.00. Fee payee: Superior Court. Personal checks accepted. Prepayment required.

Franklin District Court 12 129 Main St, Farmington, ME 04938; 207-778-8200. Hours: 8AM-4PM (EST). *Misdemeanor, Civil Actions, Eviction, Small Claims.*

Civil Records: Access: In person only. Visitors must perform in person searches for themselves. No search fee. Required to search: name, years to search. Civil cases indexed by defendant. Civil records on docket books since 1965 (index cards in front).
Criminal Records: Access: Mail, in person. Visitors must perform in person searches for themselves. Search fee: $1.00 per name. Required to search: name, years to search, DOB. Criminal records on computer since 1987, on docket books since 1965 (index cards in front).
General Information: No impounded records released. Copy fee: $1.00 per page. Certification fee: $1.00. Fee payee: Maine District Court. Personal checks accepted. Prepayment is required.

Probate Court County Courthouse, 140 Main St, Farmington, ME 04938; 207-778-5888; Fax: 207-778-5899. Hours: 8:30AM-4PM (EST). *Probate.*

Hancock County

Superior Court 50 State St, Ellsworth, ME 04605-1926; 207-667-7176. Hours: 8AM-4PM (EST). *Felony, Misdemeanor, Civil Actions.*

Civil Records: Access: In person. Only the court performs in person searches; visitors may not. No search fee. Required to search: name, years to search.

Civil cases indexed by defendant, plaintiff. Civil records on card files since 1960.
Criminal Records: Access: In person. Only the court performs in person searches; visitors may not. No search fee. Required to search: name, years to search, DOB. Criminal records on card files since 1960.
General Information: No protective custody records released. Mail requests not accepted. Copy fee: $1.00 per page. Certification fee: $1.00. Fee payee: State of Maine. Personal checks accepted. Prepayment is required.

Bar Harbor District Court - South 5 93 Cottage St, Bar Harbor, ME 04609; 207-288-3082. Hours: 8AM-4PM (EST). *Misdemeanor, Civil Actions, Eviction, Small Claims.*

Civil Records: Access: Mail, in person. Both court and visitors may perform in person searches. Search fee: $1.00 per name. Required to search: name, years to search. Civil cases indexed by defendant, plaintiff. Civil records on docket books since 1970.
Criminal Records: Access: Mail, in person. Both court and visitors may perform in person searches. Search fee: $1.00 per name. Required to search: name, years to search, DOB. Criminal records on computer since 1987, on docket books since 1970.
General Information: Public Access terminal is available. No juvenile or impounded records released. SASE required. Turnaround time 2-3 days. Copy fee: $1.00 per page. Certification fee: $1.00. Fee payee: Maine District Court. Personal checks accepted. Prepayment is required.

Ellsworth District Court - Central 5 50 State St #2, Ellsworth, ME 04605; 207-667-7141. Hours: 8AM-4PM (EST). *Misdemeanor, Civil Actions, Eviction, Small Claims.*

Civil Records: Access: Mail, in person. Both court and visitors may perform in person searches. No search fee. Required to search: name, years to search. Civil cases indexed by defendant, plaintiff. Need to know names of both parties to search. Civil records on docket books since 1965; on computer back to 5/1987.
Criminal Records: Access: Mail, in person. Both court and visitors may perform in person searches. No search fee. Required to search: name, years to search, DOB. Criminal records on computer back to 1987, docket books since 1965. The court will allow no access to criminal records.
General Information: No juvenile, child protection, adoption or mental health records released. SASE required. Turnaround time 1 week. Fax notes: Will not fax results. Copy fee: $1.00 per page. Certification fee: $2.00. Fee payee: Maine District Court. Personal checks accepted. Prepayment is required.

Probate Court 50 State St, Ellsworth, ME 04605; 207-667-8434. Hours: 8:30AM-4PM (EST). *Probate.*

Kennebec County

Superior Court 95 State St, Clerk of Court, Augusta, ME 04330; 207-622-9357. Hours: 8AM-4PM (EST). *Felony, Misdemeanor, Civil Actions.*

Civil Records: Access: Mail, in person. Only the court performs in person searches; visitors may not. No search fee. Required to search: name, years to search. Civil cases indexed by defendant, plaintiff. Civil records on index cards since 1977, docket books since 1950, on computer 2 years.
Criminal Records: Access: In person only. Visitors must perform in person searches for themselves. No search fee. Required to search: name, years to search; also helpful: DOB, docket number. Criminal records on index cards since 1977, docket books since 1950, on computer 2 years.
General Information: No protective custody records released. SASE not required. Turnaround time 1 week.

Copy fee: $1.00 per page. Certification fee: $1.00. Fee payee: Treasurer State of Maine. Personal checks accepted. Prepayment is required.

Maine District Court 7 Division of Southern Kennebec, 145 State St, Augusta, ME 04330-7495; 207-287-8075. Hours: 8AM-4PM (EST). *Misdemeanor, Civil Actions, Eviction, Small Claims.*

Civil Records: Access: Mail, in person. Both court and visitors may perform in person searches. No search fee. Required to search: name, years to search. Civil cases indexed by defendant. Civil records on docket books since 1963.

Criminal Records: Access: Mail, in person. Both court and visitors may perform in person searches. No search fee. Required to search: name, years to search, DOB; also helpful: SSN. Criminal records on computer since 1987, docket books since 1963.

General Information: No juvenile, mental health, protective custody and closed proceeding case records released. Turnaround time 1 week. Copy fee: $1.00 per page. Certification fee: $1.00. Fee payee: Maine District Court. Personal checks accepted. Prepayment required.

Waterville District Court - District 7 18 Colby St, PO Box 397, Waterville, ME 04903; 207-873-2103. Hours: 8AM-4PM (EST). *Misdemeanor, Civil Actions, Eviction, Small Claims.*

Civil Records: Access: Mail, in person. Both court and visitors may perform in person searches. No search fee. Required to search: name, years to search; also helpful: address. Civil cases indexed by defendant. Civil records on docket books from 1956-1998; computer since 1998.

Criminal Records: Access: Mail, in person. Both court and visitors may perform in person searches. No search fee. Required to search: name, years to search, DOB; also helpful: address, SSN. Criminal records on computer since 1987, docket books from 1979-1987.

General Information: No juvenile, protective custody records released. Court reserves the right to restrict the number of record requests. SASE required. Turnaround time 1 week. Copy fee: $1.00 per page. Certification fee: $1.00. Fee payee: Maine. Personal checks accepted. Prepayment is required.

Probate Court 95 State St, Augusta, ME 04330; 207-622-7558; Fax: 207-621-1639. Hours: 8AM-4PM (EST). *Probate.*

www.datamaine.com/probate

Knox County

Superior Court 62 Union St, Rockland, ME 04841-2836; 207-594-2576. Hours: 8AM-4PM (EST). *Felony, Misdemeanor, Civil Actions.*

Civil Records: Access: Phone, mail, in person. Both court and visitors may perform in person searches. No search fee. Required to search: name, years to search. Civil cases indexed by defendant, plaintiff. Civil records on docket books since 1930s, index cards (in office) since mid-1970s; on computer back to 1999.

Criminal Records: Access: In person only. Visitors must perform in person searches for themselves. No search fee. Required to search: name, years to search; also helpful: DOB. Criminal records on docket books since 1930s, index cards (in office) since mid-1970s; on computer back to 1999.

General Information: No Impounded or pre-sentence records released. SASE not required. Turnaround time 1 week. Fax notes: Will not fax results. Copy fee: $1.00 per page. Certification fee: $1.00 per document. Fee payee: State Treasurer. Personal checks accepted. Prepayment is required.

District Court 6 62 Union St, Rockland, ME 04841; 207-596-2240. Hours: 8AM-4PM (EST). *Misdemeanor, Civil Actions, Eviction, Small Claims.*

Civil Records: Access: Phone, mail, in person. Both court and visitors may perform in person searches. No search fee. Required to search: name, years to search. Civil cases indexed by defendant, plaintiff. Civil records on docket books.

Criminal Records: Access: Phone, mail, in person. Both court and visitors may perform in person searches. No search fee. Required to search: name, years to search, DOB. Criminal records on docket books.

General Information: Public Access terminal is available. No impounded records released. SASE required. Turnaround time 1 week. Copy fee: $1.00 per page. Certification fee: $1.00. Fee payee: Maine District Court. Personal checks accepted. Prepayment required.

Probate Court 62 Union St, Rockland, ME 04841; 207-594-0427; Fax: 207-594-0443. Hours: 8AM-4PM (EST). *Probate.*

http://knoxcounty.midcoast.com

Lincoln County

Lincoln County Superior Court High St, PO Box 249, Wiscasset, ME 04578; 207-882-7517; Fax: 207-882-7741. Hours: 8AM-4PM (EST). *Felony, Misdemeanor, Civil Actions.*

www.co.lincoln.me.us

Civil Records: Access: Mail, in person. Only the court performs in person searches; visitors may not. No search fee. Required to search: name, years to search. Civil cases indexed by defendant, plaintiff. Civil records on docket books and index cards since 1960s.

Criminal Records: Access: Mail, in person. Only the court performs in person searches; visitors may not. No search fee. Required to search: name, years to search, DOB. Criminal records on docket books and index cards since 1960s.

General Information: No protective custody records released. SASE not required. Copy fee: $1.00 per page. Certification fee: $2.00. Personal checks accepted. Prepayment is required.

District Court 6 32 High St, PO Box 249, Wiscasset, ME 04578; 207-882-6363; Fax: 207-882-5980. Hours: 8AM-4PM (EST). *Misdemeanor, Civil Actions, Eviction, Small Claims.*

www.co.lincoln.me.us

Civil Records: Access: Phone, mail, in person. Both court and visitors may perform in person searches. No search fee. Required to search: name, years to search. Civil cases indexed by defendant, plaintiff. Civil records on docket books since 1965; on computer back to 1987.

Criminal Records: Access: Mail, in person. Only the court performs in person searches; visitors may not. No search fee. Required to search: name, years to search, DOB or SSN. Criminal records on computer back to 1987, docket books since 1960.

General Information: No juvenile, child protective or impounded records released. SASE required. Turnaround time 1 week. Copy fee: $1.00 per page. Certification fee: $5.00. Fee payee: Maine District Court. Personal checks accepted. Prepayment required.

Probate Court High St, PO Box 249, Wiscasset, ME 04578; 207-882-7392; Fax: 207-882-4324. Hours: 8AM-4PM (EST). *Probate.*

www.co.lincoln.me.us/dep.html

Oxford County

Superior Court Courthouse, 26 Western Ave, PO Box 179, South Paris, ME 04281-0179; 207-743-8936; Fax: 207-743-0544. Hours: 8AM-4PM (EST). *Felony, Misdemeanor, Civil Actions.*

Civil Records: Access: Mail, in person. Both court and visitors may perform in person searches. No search fee. Required to search: name, years to search. Civil cases indexed by defendant, plaintiff. Civil records on docket books since 1951.

Criminal Records: Access: In person only. Both court and visitors may perform in person searches. No search fee. Required to search: name, years to search; also helpful: DOB. Criminal records on docket books since 1951.

General Information: No protective custody or protection from abuse records released. SASE required. Turnaround time 3-4 days. Copy fee: $1.00 per page. Certification fee: $1.00. Fee payee: Clerk of Superior Court. Personal checks accepted.

Rumford District Court - North 11 Municipal Bldg, 145 Congress St, Rumford, ME 04276; 207-364-7171. Hours: 8AM-4PM (EST). *Misdemeanor, Civil Actions, Eviction, Small Claims.*

Civil Records: Access: Mail, in person. Both court and visitors may perform in person searches. No search fee. Required to search: name, years to search. Civil cases indexed by defendant, plaintiff. Civil records on docket books since 1966.

Criminal Records: Access: Mail, in person. Both court and visitors may perform in person searches. No search fee. Required to search: name, years to search, DOB. Criminal records on computer since March 1988, docket books since 1966.

General Information: No impounded records released. SASE required. Turnaround time 1 week. Copy fee: $1.00 per page. Certification fee: $2.00. Fee payee: Maine District Court. Personal checks accepted.

South Paris District Court - South 11 26 Western Ave, South Paris, ME 04281; 207-743-8942. Hours: 8AM-4PM (EST). *Misdemeanor, Civil Actions, Eviction, Small Claims.*

Civil Records: Access: Mail, in person. Only the court performs in person searches; visitors may not. No search fee. Required to search: name, years to search. Civil cases indexed by defendant. Civil records on docket books back 5 years.

Criminal Records: Access: Mail, in person. Both court and visitors may perform in person searches. No search fee. Required to search: name, years to search; also helpful: DOB. Criminal records on computer 1988-4/1999, docket books back 5 years. Records after 4/99 cannot be accessed on the public access computer; request a search in writing.

General Information: Public Access terminal is available. (Criminal only.) No juvenile or child protective records released. SASE required. Turnaround time 1-2 days. Copy fee: $1.00 per page. Certification fee: $1.00. Fee payee: Maine District Court. Personal checks accepted. Prepayment is required.

Probate Court 26 Western Ave, PO Box 179, South Paris, ME 04281; 207-743-6671; Fax: 207-743-2656. Hours: 8AM-4PM (EST). *Probate.*

Penobscot County

Superior Court 97 Hammond St, Bangor, ME 04401; 207-947-0751. Hours: 8AM-4:30PM (EST). *Felony, Misdemeanor, Civil Actions.*

Civil Records: Access: Mail, in person. Only the court performs in person searches; visitors may not. No search fee. Required to search: name, years to search. Civil cases indexed by defendant, plaintiff. Civil records on docket books since 1975; on computer back to 1998; archived back to 1927.

Criminal Records: Access: In person only. Only the court performs in person searches; visitors may not. No search fee. Required to search: name, years to search, DOB. Criminal records on docket books since 1975; on computer back to 1998; archived back to 1927.

General Information: No impounded records released. SASE required. Copy fee: $1.00 per page. Certification fee: $1.00. Fee payee: Treasurer, State of Maine. Personal checks accepted. Prepayment required.

Bangor District Court 73 Hammond St, Bangor, ME 04401; 207-941-3040. Hours: 8AM-4PM (EST). *Misdemeanor, Civil Actions, Eviction, Small Claims.*

Civil Records: Access: Mail, in person. Both court and visitors may perform in person searches. No search fee. Required to search: name, years to search. Civil cases indexed by defendant. Civil records on docket books since 1962. Court suggests using central state repository.

Criminal Records: Access: Mail, in person. Both court and visitors may perform in person searches. No search fee. Required to search: name, years to search; also helpful: DOB. Criminal records on computer since late 1986, docket books since 1962.

General Information: Public Access terminal is available. (Criminal only.) No protective custody records released. SASE required. Turnaround time 1 week. Copy fee: $1.00 per page. Certification fee: $1.00. Fee payee: Maine District Court. Personal checks accepted. Prepayment is required.

Central District Court - Central 13 66 Maine St, Lincoln, ME 04457; 207-794-8512. Hours: 8AM-4PM (EST). *Misdemeanor, Civil Actions, Eviction, Small Claims.*

Civil Records: Access: In person only. Only the court performs in person searches; visitors may not. No search fee. Required to search: name, years to search. Civil cases indexed by defendant. Civil records on docket books since 1964.

Criminal Records: Access: In person only. Only the court performs in person searches; visitors may not. No search fee. Required to search: name, years to search, DOB. Criminal records on computer since 1987, docket books since 1964.

General Information: Public Access terminal is available. No juvenile or protective custody records released. Copy fee: $1.00 per page. Certification fee: $1.00. Fee payee: Maine District Court. Personal checks accepted. Prepayment is required.

Millinocket District Court - North 13 207 Penobscot Ave, Millinocket, ME 04462; 207-723-4786. Hours: 8AM-4PM (EST). *Misdemeanor, Civil Actions, Eviction, Small Claims.*

Civil Records: Access: Mail, in person. Visitors must perform in person searches for themselves. No search fee. Required to search: name, years to search. Civil cases indexed by defendant, plaintiff. Civil records on docket books since 1964.

Criminal Records: Access: Mail, in person. Both court and visitors may perform in person searches. No search fee. Required to search: name, years to search, DOB. Criminal records on computer since 1987, docket books since 1964.

General Information: No juvenile or protective custody records released. SASE required. Turnaround time 1 week. Copy fee: $1.00 per page. Certification fee: $1.00. Fee payee: Maine District Court. Personal checks accepted. Prepayment is required.

Newport District Court - West 3 12 Water St, Newport, ME 04953; 207-368-5778. Hours: 8AM-4PM (EST). *Misdemeanor, Civil Actions, Eviction, Small Claims.*

Civil Records: Access: Mail, in person. Both court and visitors may perform in person searches. No search fee. Required to search: name, years to search. Civil cases indexed by defendant, plaintiff. Civil records on docket books back to 1965.

Criminal Records: Access: Mail, in person. Both court and visitors may perform in person searches. No search fee. Required to search: name, years to search, DOB. Criminal records on computer back to 1987, docket books since 1965.

General Information: Public Access terminal is available. No impounded records released. SASE required. Turnaround time 1 week. Copy fee: $1.00 per page. Certification fee: $1.00. Fee payee: Maine District Court. Personal checks accepted. Prepayment required.

Probate Court 97 Hammond St, Bangor, ME 04401-4996; 207-942-8769; Fax: 207-941-8499. Hours: 8AM-4:30PM (EST). *Probate.*

Piscataquis County

Superior Court 51 E Main St, Dover-Foxcroft, ME 04426; 207-564-8419; Fax: 207-564-3363. Hours: 8AM-4PM *Felony, Misdemeanor, Civil Actions.*

Civil Records: Access: Mail, in person. Only the court performs in person searches; visitors may not. No search fee. Required to search: name, years to search. Civil cases indexed by defendant, plaintiff. Civil records on docket books since 1960.

Criminal Records: Access: Mail, in person. Only the court performs in person searches; visitors may not. No search fee. Required to search: name, years to search; also helpful: DOB. Criminal records on docket books since 1960.

General Information: No pre-sentence report records released. SASE required. Turnaround time 1 week. Copy fee: $1.00 per page. Certification fee: $1.00. Fee payee: State of Maine Superior Court. Personal checks accepted. Prepayment is required.

District Court 13 59 E Main St, Dover-Foxcroft, ME 04426; 207-564-2240. Hours: 8AM-4PM (EST). *Misdemeanor, Civil Actions, Eviction, Small Claims.*

Civil Records: Access: Mail, in person. Both court and visitors may perform in person searches. No search fee. Required to search: name, years to search. Civil cases indexed by defendant, plaintiff. Civil records on docket books since 1963.

Criminal Records: Access: Mail, in person. Both court and visitors may perform in person searches. No search fee. Required to search: name, years to search; also helpful: DOB. Criminal records on computer since 1987, docket books since 1963.

General Information: No protective custody or juvenile records released. SASE required. Turnaround time 1 week. Copy fee: $1.00 per page. Certification fee: $1.00. Fee payee: Maine District Court. Personal checks accepted. Prepayment is required.

Probate Court 51 E Main St, Dover-Foxcroft, ME 04426; 207-564-2431; Fax: 207-564-3022. Hours: 8:30AM-4PM (EST). *Probate.*

Sagadahoc County

Superior Court 752 High St, PO Box 246, Bath, ME 04530; 207-443-9733. Hours: 8AM-4:30PM (EST). *Felony, Misdemeanor, Civil Actions.*

Civil Records: Access: In person only. Visitors must perform in person searches for themselves. No search fee. Required to search: name, years to search. Civil cases indexed by defendant, plaintiff. Civil records on docket books since 1900s.

Criminal Records: Access: In person only. Visitors must perform in person searches for themselves. No search fee. Required to search: name, years to search. Criminal records on docket books since 1900s.

General Information: No impounded records released. Copy fee: $1.00 per page. Certification fee: $1.00. Fee payee: Clerk of Superior Court. Only cashiers checks and money orders accepted. Prepayment is required.

West Bath District Court 6 RR 1, Box 310, New Meadows Rd, Bath, ME 04530; 207-442-0200. Hours: 8AM-4PM (EST). *Misdemeanor, Civil Actions, Eviction, Small Claims.*

Note: This court handles the eastern part of Cumberland County & all of Sagadahoc County.

Civil Records: Access: In person only. Both court and visitors may perform in person searches. No search fee. Required to search: name, years to search. Civil cases indexed by defendant, plaintiff. Civil records on docket books since 1980's; prior archived.

Criminal Records: Access: In person only. Both court and visitors may perform in person searches. No search fee. Required to search: name, years to search; also helpful: DOB. Criminal records on computer since 1987, docket books back to 1975; prior archived. Search requests are referred to central state repository.

General Information: No protective custody or juvenile records released. Copy fee: $1.00 per page. Certification fee: $1.00. Fee payee: Maine District Court. Personal checks accepted. Prepayment required.

Probate Court 752 High St, PO Box 246, Bath, ME 04530; 207-443-8218; Fax: 207-443-8217. Hours: 8:30AM-4:30PM (EST). *Probate.*

Somerset County

Superior Court PO Box 725, Skowhegan, ME 04976; 207-474-5161. Hours: 8AM-4PM (EST). *Felony, Misdemeanor, Civil Actions.*

Civil Records: Access: In person only. Visitors must perform in person searches for themselves. No search fee. Required to search: name, years to search. Civil cases indexed by defendant, plaintiff. Civil records archived in Augusta back to 1800s, docket books and index cards back to 1900s.

Criminal Records: Access: In person only. Visitors must perform in person searches for themselves. No search fee. Required to search: name, years to search; also helpful: DOB. Criminal records archived in Augusta back to 1800s, docket books and index cards back to 1900s; on computer back to 1998.

General Information: No impounded, present investigations, psychological evaluations or child support records released. Copy fee: $1.00 per page. Certification fee: $1.00. Fee payee: Clerk of Superior Court. Personal checks accepted. Prepayment is required.

District Court 12 PO Box 525, 47 Court St, Skowhegan, ME 04976; 207-474-9518. Hours: 8AM-4PM (EST). *Misdemeanor, Civil Actions, Eviction, Small Claims.*

Civil Records: Access: Mail, in person. Both court and visitors may perform in person searches. No search fee. Required to search: name, years to search. Civil cases

indexed by defendant. Civil records on docket books since 1960s, divorces since 1970s.

Criminal Records: Access: Mail, in person. Both court and visitors may perform in person searches. No search fee. Required to search: name, years to search; also helpful: DOB. Criminal records on computer since 1987, docket books since 1960s.

General Information: Public Access terminal is available. (Criminal only.) No juvenile records released. SASE required. Turnaround time 2-4 weeks. Copy fee: $1.00 per page. Certification fee: $1.00. Fee payee: Maine District Court. Personal checks accepted. Prepayment is required.

Probate Court Court St, Skowhegan, ME 04976; 207-474-3322. 8:30AM-4:30PM (EST). *Probate.*

Waldo County

Superior Court 137 Church St, PO Box 188, Belfast, ME 04915; 207-338-1940; Fax: 207-338-1086. 8AM-4PM *Felony, Misdemeanor, Civil Actions.*

Civil Records: Access: Mail, fax, in person. Only the court performs in person searches; visitors may not. No search fee. Required to search: name, years to search. Civil cases indexed by defendant, plaintiff. Civil records archived back to 1980 (not in office), on docket books since 1980; on computer back to 1998.

Criminal Records: Access: Mail, fax, in person. Only the court performs in person searches; visitors may not. No search fee. Required to search: name, years to search, DOB. Criminal records archived back to 1975 (not in office), on docket books since 1975; on computer back to 1998.

General Information: No protective custody records released. SASE required. Turnaround time 1 week. Fax notes: Will fax results to toll free numbers only. Copy fee: $1.00 per page. Certification fee: $1.00 per document. Fee payee: State Treasurer. Personal checks accepted. Prepayment is required.

District Court 5 PO Box 382, 103 Church St, Belfast, ME 04915; 207-338-3107. Hours: 8AM-4PM (EST). *Misdemeanor, Civil Actions, Eviction, Small Claims.*

Civil Records: Access: Mail, in person. Both court and visitors may perform in person searches. No search fee. Required to search: name, years to search. Civil cases indexed by defendant, plaintiff. Civil records on docket books since 1966.

Criminal Records: Access: Mail, in person. Both court and visitors may perform in person searches. No search fee. Required to search: name, years to search, DOB. Criminal records on computer since 1987, docket books since 1966.

General Information: No juvenile or impounded records released. SASE required. Turnaround time 1 week. Copy fee: $1.00 per page. Certification fee: $1.00. Fee payee: Maine District Court. Personal checks accepted.

Probate Court 172 High St, PO Box 323, Belfast, ME 04915-0323; 207-338-2780; Fax: 207-338-6360. Hours: 8AM-4PM (EST). *Probate.*

Washington County

Superior Court Clerk of Court, PO Box 526, Machias, ME 04654; 207-255-3326. Hours: 8AM-4PM (EST). *Felony, Misdemeanor, Civil.*

Civil Records: Access: Mail, in person. Both court and visitors may perform in person searches. No search fee. Required to search: name, years to search. Civil cases

indexed by defendant, plaintiff. Civil records on docket books and index cards since 1930s.

Criminal Records: Access: Mail, in person. Both court and visitors may perform in person searches. No search fee. Required to search: name, years to search, DOB. Criminal records on docket books/index cards to 1930s.

General Information: No impounded records released. SASE required. Turnaround time 1 week. Copy fee: $1.00 per page. Certification fee: $1.00. Fee payee: Treasurer, State of Maine. Personal checks accepted. Prepayment is required.

Calais District Court - North 4 PO Box 929, Calais, ME 04619; 207-454-2055; TTY# 207-454-0085. Hours: 8AM-4PM (EST). *Misdemeanor, Civil Actions, Eviction, Small Claims.*

Civil Records: Access: In person only. Visitors must perform in person searches for themselves. No search fee. Required to search: name, years to search. Civil cases indexed by defendant, plaintiff. Civil records on docket books since 1964.

Criminal Records: Access: In person only. Visitors must perform in person searches for themselves. No search fee. Required to search: name, years to search, DOB. Criminal records on computer since 1987, docket books since 1964.

General Information: Public Access terminal is available. No juvenile or protective custody records released. Copy fee: $1.00 per page. Certification fee: $1.00. Fee payee: Maine District Court. Personal checks accepted. Prepayment is required.

Maine District Court 4 47 Court St, PO Box 297, Machias, ME 04654; 207-255-3044. Hours: 8AM-4PM *Misdemeanor, Civil Actions, Eviction, Small Claims.*

Civil Records: Access: Mail, in person. Both court and visitors may perform in person searches. No search fee. Required to search: name, years to search. Civil cases indexed by defendant, plaintiff. Civil records on docket books since 1964; on computer 1987-1999.

Criminal Records: Access: Mail, in person. Both court and visitors may perform in person searches. No search fee. Required to search: name, years to search, DOB. Criminal records on computer 1987-1999, docket books since 1964.

General Information: Public Access terminal is available. No protective custody or juvenile records released. SASE required. Turnaround time 4 days. Copy fee: $1.00 per page. Add $1.00 processing fee. Certification fee: $1.00. Fee payee: Maine District Court. Personal checks accepted. Prepayment required.

Probate Court PO Box 297, Machias, ME 04654; 207-255-6591. Hours: 8AM-4PM (EST). *Probate.*

York County

Superior Court Clerk of Court, PO Box 160, Alfred, ME 04002; 207-324-5122. Hours: 8AM-4:30PM (EST). *Felony, Misdemeanor, Civil Actions.*

Civil Records: Access: In person only. Visitors must perform in person searches for themselves. No search fee. Required to search: name, years to search. Civil cases indexed by defendant, plaintiff. Civil records on docket books since 1930.

Criminal Records: Access: In person only. Visitors must perform in person searches for themselves. No search fee. Required to search: name, years to search, DOB. Criminal records on docket books since 1930.

General Information: No juvenile, or protective custody records released. Copy fee: $1.00 per page.

Add $1.00 handling fee. Certification fee: $1.00. Fee payee: Clerk of Courts. Only cashiers checks and money orders accepted. Prepayment is required.

Biddeford District Court - East 10 25 Adams St, Biddeford, ME 04005; 207-283-1147. Hours: 8AM-4PM (EST). *Misdemeanor, Civil Actions, Eviction, Small Claims.*

Civil Records: Access: In person only. Visitors must perform in person searches for themselves. No search fee. Required to search: name, years to search. Civil cases indexed by defendant. Civil records on docket books since 1989. Court will do up to 3 searches.

Criminal Records: Access: In person only. Visitors must perform in person searches for themselves. No search fee. Required to search: name, years to search; also helpful: DOB. Criminal records on computer since 1986. Court will do up to 3 searches.

General Information: No child protection or juvenile records released. Copy fee: $1.00 per page. Certification fee: $1.00. Fee payee: Maine District Court. Personal checks accepted. Prepayment is required.

Springvale District Court - West 10 PO Box 95, Butler St, Springvale, ME 04083; 207-324-6737. Hours: 8AM-4PM (EST). *Misdemeanor, Civil Actions, Eviction, Small Claims.*

Civil Records: Access: In person only. Visitors must perform in person searches for themselves. No search fee. Required to search: name, years to search. Civil cases indexed by defendant. Civil records on docket books since 1965.

Criminal Records: Access: Mail, in person. Only the court performs in person searches; visitors may not. No search fee. Required to search: name, years to search, DOB. Criminal records on computer since 1987, dockets books since 1965.

General Information: No impounded, juvenile, mental health or protective custody records released. SASE required. Turnaround time 3-4 days. Copy fee: $1.00 per page. Certification fee: $1.00. Fee payee: Maine District Court. Personal checks accepted. Prepayment is required.

York District Court - South 10 PO Box 770, Chase's Pond Rd, York, ME 03909-0770; 207-363-1230. Hours: 8AM-4PM (EST). *Misdemeanor, Civil Actions, Eviction, Small Claims.*

Civil Records: Access: Mail, in person. Visitors must perform in person searches for themselves. Search fee: Court will perform search if name, year and book are provided, $1.00 per page (copy fee). Required to search: name, years to search. Civil cases indexed by defendant, plaintiff. Civil records on docket books since 1975; on computer back to 1985.

Criminal Records: Access: In person only. Visitors must perform in person searches for themselves. Search fee: Court will perform search if name, year and book are provided, $1.00 per page (copy fee). Required to search: name, years to search, DOB. Criminal records on computer back to 1985, docket books since 1975.

General Information: No impounded, juvenile and protective custody records released. Copy fee: $1.00 per page. Certification fee: $2.00. Fee payee: Maine District Court. Personal checks accepted. Prepayment is required.

Probate Court PO Box 399, 45 Kennebunk Rd, Alfred, ME 04002; 207-324-1577; Fax: 207-324-0163. Hours: 8:30AM-4:30PM (EST). *Probate.*

Maine Recording Offices

ORGANIZATION   16 counties, 17 recording offices. The recording officer is County Register of Deeds. Counties maintain a general index of all transactions recorded. Aroostock and Oxford Counties each have two recording offices. There are no county assessors; each town has its own. The entire state is in the Eastern Time Zone (EST).

REAL ESTATE RECORDS   Counties do not usually perform real estate name searches, but some will look up a name informally. Copy and certification fees vary widely. Assessor and tax records are located at the town/city level.

UCC RECORDS   Financing statements are filed at the state level, except for real estate related filings, which are filed only with the Register of Deeds. Counties do not perform UCC searches. Copy fees are usually $1.00 per page.

TAX LIEN RECORDS   All tax liens on personal property are filed with the Secretary of State. All tax liens on real property are filed with the Register of Deeds.

OTHER LIENS   Municipal, bail bond, mechanics.

Androscoggin County

County Register of Deeds, 2 Turner Street, Courthouse, Auburn, ME 04210-5978. County Register of Deeds, R/E and UCC Recording 207-782-0191; Fax 207-784-3163.
Will not search UCC records. This agency will not do a tax lien search. Will not search real estate records. **Online Access:** Real Estate, Tax Liens. Online access to the Registry index is available for a $50.00 annual fee and $.25 per minute. Indexes go back to 1976. For information and sign-up, contact Jeanine at 207-782-0191. **Other Phone Numbers:** Treasurer 207-784-7491.

Aroostook County (North Dist.)

County Register of Deeds, P.O. Box 47, Fort Kent, ME 04743. County Register of Deeds, R/E and UCC Recording 207-834-3925; Fax 207-834-3138.
http://www.aroostook.me.us/indexhome.html
Will not search UCC records. This agency will not do a tax lien search. Will not search real estate records. **Other Phone Numbers:** Assessor 207-834-3090; Treasurer 207-834-3318; Vital Records 207-834-3090.

Aroostook County (South Dist.)

County Register of Deeds, 26 Court St., Suite 102, Houlton, ME 04730. 207-532-1500 R/E Recording: 207-834-3925; Fax 207-532-1506. http://www.aroostook.me.us/indexhome.html
All locations from New Sweden south file in this office. Will not search UCC records. This agency will not do a tax lien search. Will not search real estate records.

Cumberland County

County Register of Deeds, P.O. Box 7230, Portland, ME 04112. 207-871-8389; Fax 207-772-4162.
Will search UCC records. This agency will not do a tax lien search. Will not search real estate records. **Online Access:** Assessor. Records on the Cape Elizabeth Town Assessor database are available free online at www.capeelizabeth.com/taxdata.html. Search by owner name, road and house number for Cape Elizabeth Town. Records on the Freeport Town Assessor property database are available free online at www.freeportmaine.com/assessordb/db.cgi.   **Other Phone Numbers:** Assessor 207-874-8486.

Franklin County

County Register of Deeds, 140 Main Street, Courthouse, Farmington, ME 04938-1818. 207-778-5889; Fax 207-778-5899.
Will not search UCC records. This agency will not do a tax lien search. Will not search real estate records.

Hancock County

County Register of Deeds, P.O. Box 784, Ellsworth, ME 04605. County Register of Deeds, R/E and UCC Recording 207-667-8353; Fax 207-667-1410.
http://www.co.hancock.me.us/deeds2.html
Will search UCC records. This agency will not do a tax lien search. Will not search real estate records. **Online Access:** Real Estate, Lines, UCC, Recording. Online access to the county registry of deeds database at www.registryofdeeds.com requires registration. Viewing of records back to 1790 is free, but $1.25 per page to print. Register online. For information, visit www.registryofdeeds.com or call 888-833-3979.

Kennebec County

County Register of Deeds, P.O. Box 1053, Augusta, ME 04332-1053. 207-622-0431; Fax 207-622-1598.
Will search UCC records. This agency will not do a tax lien search. Will not search real estate records. **Online Access:** Assessor. Records on the Winslow Town Property Records database are available free online at www.winslowmaine.org. Records on the Town of Waterville Assessor's Database are available free online at http://140.239.211.227/watervilleme/. User ID is required; registration is free.

Knox County

County Register of Deeds, 62 Union Street, Rockland, ME 04841. 207-594-0422; Fax 207-594-0446.
Will not search UCC records. This agency will not do a tax lien search. Will not search real estate records. **Other Phone Numbers:** Assessor 207-594-0420.

Lincoln County

County Register of Deeds, P.O. Box 249, 32 High St., Wiscasset, ME 04578-0249. 207-882-7515; Fax 207-882-4061. Will search UCC records. This agency will not do a tax lien search, nor search real estate records.

Oxford County

County Register of Deeds, P.O. Box 179, South Paris, ME 04281-0179. 207-743-6211; Fax 207-743-2656.
File in this office for all towns EXCEPT the following: Brownfield, Denmark, Fryeburg, Hiram, Lovell, Porter, Stoneham, Stow, and Sweden. Will search UCC records. This agency will not do a tax lien search. Will not search real estate records. **Other Phone Numbers:** Assessor 207-539-4431.

Penobscot County

County Register of Deeds, P.O. Box 2070, Bangor, ME 04402-2070. 207-942-8797; Fax 207-945-4920.
Will not search UCC records. This agency will not do a tax lien search. Will not search real estate records.

Piscataquis County

County Register of Deeds, 51 East Main Street, Dover-Foxcroft, ME 04426. 207-564-2411; Fax 207-564-7708.
Will not search UCC records. This agency will not do a tax lien search. Will not search real estate records. **Other Phone Numbers:** Assessor 207-564-3318.

Sagadahoc County

County Register of Deeds, P.O. Box 246, Bath, ME 04530. 207-443-8214; Fax 207-443-8216. http://www.cityofbath.com
Will not search UCC records. Will check a name for recent recording. This agency will not do a tax lien search. Will not search real estate records. **Online Access:** Assessor. Records on the City of Bath Assessor database are available free online at www.cityofbath.com/assessing/INDEX.HTM.

Somerset County

County Register of Deeds, P.O. Box 248, Skowhegan, ME 04976-0248. 207-474-3421; Fax 207-474-2793.
Will not search UCC records. This agency will not do a tax lien search. Will not search real estate records.

Waldo County

County Register of Deeds, P.O. Box D, Belfast, ME 04915. 207-338-1710; Fax 207-338-6360.
Will not search UCC records. This agency will not do a tax lien search. Will not search real estate records.

Washington County

County Register of Deeds, P.O. Box 297, Machias, ME 04654-0297. 207-255-6512; Fax 207-255-3838.
Will search UCC records. This agency will not do a tax lien search. Will not search real estate records. **Other Phone Numbers:** Assessor 207-255-6621.

York County

County Register of Deeds, P.O. Box 339, Alfred, ME 04002-0339. 207-324-1576; Fax 207-324-2886.
http://www.raynorshyn.com/yorknet
Will search UCC records. This agency will not do a tax lien search. Will not search real estate records. **Online Access:** Assessor. Records on the Town of York Assessor Database Lookup are available free online at www.raynorshyn.com/yorknet/accsel.cfm Records on the Town of Eliot Assessor database are available free online at http://140.239.211.227/edliotme/. Search by street name & number, map/block/lot/unit, or account number. Records on Kennebunk Town Property Records db are available free online at www.kennebunk.maine.org/assessing/database/database.html.

Maine County Locator

You will usually be able to find the city name in the City/County Cross. Reference below. In that case, it is a simple matter to determine the county from the cross reference. However, only the official US Postal Service city names are included in this index. There are an additional 40,000 place names that people use in their addresses. Therefore, we have also included a ZIP/City Cross. Reference immediately following the City/County Cross. Reference.

If you know the ZIP Code but the city name does not appear in the City/County Cross. Reference index, look up the ZIP Code in the ZIP/City Cross. Reference, find the city name, then look up the city name in the City/County Cross. Reference. For example, you want to know the county for an address of Menands, NY 12204. There is no "Menands" in the City/County Cross. Reference. The ZIP/City Cross. Reference shows that ZIP Codes 12201-12288 are for the city of Albany. Looking back in the City/County Cross. Reference, Albany is in Albany County.

City/County Cross Reference

ABBOT VILLAGE Piscataquis
ACTON York
ADDISON Washington
ALBION Kennebec
ALFRED York
ALNA Lincoln
ANDOVER Oxford
ANSON Somerset
ASHLAND Aroostook
ATHENS Somerset
ATLANTIC Hancock
AUBURN Androscoggin
AUGUSTA Kennebec
AURORA Hancock
BAILEY ISLAND Cumberland
BANGOR Penobscot
BAR HARBOR Hancock
BAR MILLS York
BASS HARBOR Hancock
BATH Sagadahoc
BAYVILLE Lincoln
BEALS Washington
BELFAST Waldo
BELGRADE Kennebec
BELGRADE LAKES Kennebec
BENEDICTA Aroostook
BERNARD Hancock
BERWICK York
BETHEL Oxford
BIDDEFORD York
BIDDEFORD POOL York
BINGHAM Somerset
BIRCH HARBOR Hancock
BLAINE Aroostook
BLUE HILL Hancock
BLUE HILL FALLS Hancock
BOOTHBAY Lincoln
BOOTHBAY HARBOR Lincoln
BOWDOINHAM Sagadahoc
BRADFORD (04410) Penobscot(97),
   Piscataquis(3)
BRADLEY Penobscot
BREMEN Lincoln
BREWER Penobscot
BRIDGEWATER Aroostook
BRIDGTON Cumberland
BRISTOL Lincoln
BROOKLIN Hancock
BROOKS Waldo
BROOKSVILLE Hancock
BROOKTON Washington
BROWNFIELD Oxford
BROWNVILLE Piscataquis
BROWNVILLE JUNCTION Piscataquis
BRUNSWICK Cumberland
BRYANT POND Oxford
BUCKFIELD Oxford
BUCKS HARBOR Washington
BUCKSPORT (04416) Hancock(89),
   Waldo(11)
BURLINGTON Penobscot
BURNHAM Waldo
BUSTINS ISLAND Cumberland

CALAIS Washington
CAMBRIDGE (04923) Somerset(97),
   Piscataquis(3)
CAMDEN Knox
CANAAN Somerset
CANTON Oxford
CAPE ELIZABETH Cumberland
CAPE NEDDICK York
CAPE PORPOISE York
CARATUNK Somerset
CARDVILLE Penobscot
CARIBOU Aroostook
CARMEL Penobscot
CASCO Cumberland
CASTINE Hancock
CENTER LOVELL Oxford
CHAMBERLAIN Lincoln
CHARLESTON Penobscot
CHEBEAGUE ISLAND Cumberland
CHERRYFIELD (04622) Washington(98),
   Hancock(2)
CHINA Kennebec
CLAYTON LAKE Aroostook
CLIFF ISLAND Cumberland
CLINTON Kennebec
COLUMBIA FALLS Washington
COOPERS MILLS Lincoln
COREA Hancock
CORINNA Penobscot
CORNISH York
COSTIGAN Penobscot
CRANBERRY ISLES Hancock
CROUSEVILLE Aroostook
CUMBERLAND CENTER Cumberland
CUMBERLAND FORESIDE Cumberland
CUSHING Knox
CUTLER Washington
DAMARISCOTTA Lincoln
DANFORTH Washington
DANVILLE Androscoggin
DEER ISLE Hancock
DENMARK Oxford
DENNYSVILLE Washington
DETROIT Somerset
DEXTER (04930) Penobscot(96),
   Somerset(4)
DIXFIELD Oxford
DIXMONT Penobscot
DOVER FOXCROFT Piscataquis
DRESDEN Lincoln
DRYDEN Franklin
DURHAM Androscoggin
EAGLE LAKE Aroostook
EAST ANDOVER Oxford
EAST BALDWIN Cumberland
EAST BLUE HILL Hancock
EAST BOOTHBAY Lincoln
EAST CORINTH Penobscot
EAST DIXFIELD Franklin
EAST LIVERMORE Androscoggin
EAST MACHIAS Washington
EAST MILLINOCKET Penobscot
EAST NEWPORT Penobscot

EAST ORLAND Hancock
EAST PARSONFIELD York
EAST POLAND Androscoggin
EAST STONEHAM Oxford
EAST VASSALBORO Kennebec
EAST WATERBORO York
EAST WATERFORD Oxford
EAST WILTON Franklin
EAST WINTHROP Kennebec
EASTON Aroostook
EASTPORT Washington
EDDINGTON Penobscot
EDGECOMB Lincoln
ELIOT York
ELLSWORTH Hancock
ENFIELD Penobscot
ESTCOURT STATION Aroostook
ETNA Penobscot
EUSTIS Franklin
EXETER Penobscot
FAIRFIELD (04937) Kennebec(99),
   Somerset(1)
FALMOUTH Cumberland
FARMINGDALE Kennebec
FARMINGTON Franklin
FARMINGTON FALLS Franklin
FORT FAIRFIELD Aroostook
FORT KENT Aroostook
FORT KENT MILLS Aroostook
FRANKFORT Waldo
FRANKLIN Hancock
FREEDOM Waldo
FREEPORT Cumberland
FRENCHBORO Hancock
FRENCHVILLE Aroostook
FRIENDSHIP Knox
FRYE Oxford
FRYEBURG Oxford
GARDINER Kennebec
GARLAND Penobscot
GEORGETOWN Sagadahoc
GLEN COVE Knox
GORHAM Cumberland
GOULDSBORO Hancock
GRAND ISLE Aroostook
GRAND LAKE STREAM Washington
GRAY Cumberland
GREENE Androscoggin
GREENVILLE Piscataquis
GREENVILLE JUNCTION (04442)
   Piscataquis(86), Somerset(14)
GROVE Washington
GUILFORD Piscataquis
HALLOWELL Kennebec
HAMPDEN Penobscot
HANCOCK Hancock
HANOVER Oxford
HARBORSIDE Hancock
HARMONY Somerset
HARPSWELL Cumberland
HARRINGTON Washington
HARRISON Cumberland
HARTLAND Somerset

HAYNESVILLE Aroostook
HEBRON Oxford
HINCKLEY Somerset
HIRAM Oxford
HOLDEN (04429) Penobscot(98),
   Hancock(2)
HOLLIS CENTER York
HOPE Knox
HOULTON Aroostook
HOWLAND Penobscot
HUDSON Penobscot
HULLS COVE Hancock
ISLAND FALLS Aroostook
ISLE AU HAUT Knox
ISLE OF SPRINGS Lincoln
ISLESBORO Waldo
ISLESFORD Hancock
JACKMAN Somerset
JAY Franklin
JEFFERSON Lincoln
JONESBORO Washington
JONESPORT Washington
KENDUSKEAG Penobscot
KENNEBUNK York
KENNEBUNKPORT York
KENTS HILL Kennebec
KINGFIELD Franklin
KINGMAN Penobscot
KITTERY York
KITTERY POINT York
LAGRANGE (04453) Penobscot(90),
   Piscataquis(10)
LAMBERT LAKE Washington
LEBANON York
LEE Penobscot
LEEDS Androscoggin
LEVANT Penobscot
LEWISTON Androscoggin
LIBERTY (04949) Waldo(80), Knox(20)
LILLE Aroostook
LIMERICK York
LIMESTONE Aroostook
LIMINGTON York
LINCOLN Penobscot
LINCOLN CENTER Penobscot
LINCOLNVILLE Waldo
LINCOLNVILLE CENTER Waldo
LISBON Androscoggin
LISBON CENTER Androscoggin
LISBON FALLS Androscoggin
LITCHFIELD Kennebec
LITTLE DEER ISLE Hancock
LIVERMORE Androscoggin
LIVERMORE FALLS Androscoggin
LOCKE MILLS Oxford
LONG ISLAND Cumberland
LOVELL Oxford
LUBEC Washington
MACHIAS Washington
MACHIASPORT Washington
MADAWASKA Aroostook
MADISON Somerset
MANCHESTER Kennebec

MANSET Hancock
MAPLETON Aroostook
MARS HILL Aroostook
MASARDIS Aroostook
MATINICUS Knox
MATTAWAMKEAG Penobscot
MECHANIC FALLS Androscoggin
MEDDYBEMPS Washington
MEDWAY Penobscot
MEREPOINT Cumberland
MEXICO Oxford
MILBRIDGE Washington
MILFORD Penobscot
MILLINOCKET Penobscot
MILO (04463) Piscataquis(98),
    Penobscot(2)
MINOT Androscoggin
MINTURN Hancock
MONHEGAN Lincoln
MONMOUTH Kennebec
MONROE Waldo
MONSON Piscataquis
MONTICELLO Aroostook
MOODY York
MORRILL Waldo
MOUNT DESERT Hancock
MOUNT VERNON Kennebec
NAPLES Cumberland
NEW GLOUCESTER Cumberland
NEW HARBOR Lincoln
NEW LIMERICK Aroostook
NEW PORTLAND Somerset
NEW SHARON (04955) Franklin(96),
    Kennebec(3), Somerset(1)
NEW SWEDEN Aroostook
NEW VINEYARD Franklin
NEWAGEN Lincoln
NEWCASTLE Lincoln
NEWFIELD York
NEWPORT (04953) Penobscot(99),
    Somerset(1)
NEWRY Oxford
NOBLEBORO Lincoln
NORRIDGEWOCK Somerset
NORTH AMITY Aroostook
NORTH ANSON Somerset
NORTH BERWICK York
NORTH BRIDGTON Cumberland
NORTH BROOKLIN Hancock
NORTH FRYEBURG Oxford
NORTH HAVEN Knox
NORTH JAY Franklin
NORTH MONMOUTH Kennebec
NORTH NEW PORTLAND Somerset
NORTH SHAPLEIGH York
NORTH TURNER Androscoggin
NORTH VASSALBORO Kennebec
NORTH WATERBORO York
NORTH WATERFORD Oxford
NORTH YARMOUTH Cumberland
NORTHEAST HARBOR Hancock
NORWAY Oxford
OAKFIELD Aroostook
OAKLAND Kennebec
OCEAN PARK York
OGUNQUIT York
OLAMON Penobscot

OLD ORCHARD BEACH York
OLD TOWN Penobscot
OQUOSSOC (04964) Franklin(94),
    Oxford(6)
ORIENT Aroostook
ORLAND Hancock
ORONO Penobscot
ORRINGTON Penobscot
ORRS ISLAND Cumberland
OTTER CREEK Hancock
OWLS HEAD Knox
OXBOW Aroostook
OXFORD Oxford
PALERMO Waldo
PALMYRA Somerset
PARIS Oxford
PARSONSFIELD York
PASSADUMKEAG Penobscot
PATTEN (04765) Penobscot(97),
    Aroostook(3)
PEAKS ISLAND Cumberland
PEJEPSCOT Sagadahoc
PEMAQUID Lincoln
PEMBROKE Washington
PENOBSCOT Hancock
PERHAM Aroostook
PERRY Washington
PERU Oxford
PHILLIPS Franklin
PHIPPSBURG Sagadahoc
PITTSFIELD Somerset
PLAISTED Aroostook
PLYMOUTH Penobscot
POLAND Androscoggin
PORT CLYDE Knox
PORTAGE Aroostook
PORTER Oxford
PORTLAND Cumberland
POWNAL Cumberland
PRESQUE ISLE Aroostook
PRINCETON Washington
PROSPECT HARBOR Hancock
QUIMBY Aroostook
RANDOLPH Kennebec
RANGELEY Franklin
RAYMOND Cumberland
READFIELD Kennebec
RICHMOND Sagadahoc
ROBBINSTON Washington
ROCKLAND Knox
ROCKPORT Knox
ROCKWOOD (04478) Somerset(86),
    Piscataquis(14)
ROUND POND Lincoln
ROXBURY Oxford
RUMFORD Oxford
RUMFORD CENTER Oxford
RUMFORD POINT Oxford
SABATTUS Androscoggin
SACO York
SAINT AGATHA Aroostook
SAINT ALBANS Somerset
SAINT DAVID Aroostook
SAINT FRANCIS Aroostook
SAINT GEORGE Knox
SALSBURY COVE Hancock
SANDY POINT Waldo

SANFORD York
SANGERVILLE Piscataquis
SARGENTVILLE Hancock
SCARBOROUGH Cumberland
SEAL COVE Hancock
SEAL HARBOR Hancock
SEARSMONT Waldo
SEARSPORT Waldo
SEBAGO Cumberland
SEBAGO LAKE Cumberland
SEBASCO ESTATES Sagadahoc
SEBEC Piscataquis
SEDGWICK Hancock
SHAPLEIGH York
SHAWMUT Somerset
SHERIDAN Aroostook
SHERMAN MILLS Aroostook
SHERMAN STATION (04777)
    Penobscot(73), Aroostook(27)
SHIRLEY MILLS Piscataquis
SINCLAIR Aroostook
SKOWHEGAN Somerset
SMALL POINT Sagadahoc
SMITHFIELD Somerset
SMYRNA MILLS Aroostook
SOLDIER POND Aroostook
SOLON Somerset
SORRENTO Hancock
SOUTH BERWICK York
SOUTH BRISTOL Lincoln
SOUTH CASCO Cumberland
SOUTH CHINA Kennebec
SOUTH FREEPORT Cumberland
SOUTH GARDINER Kennebec
SOUTH GOULDSBORO Hancock
SOUTH HIRAM Oxford
SOUTH PARIS Oxford
SOUTH PORTLAND Cumberland
SOUTH THOMASTON Knox
SOUTH WATERFORD Oxford
SOUTH WINDHAM Cumberland
SOUTHWEST HARBOR Hancock
SPRINGFIELD Penobscot
SPRINGVALE York
SPRUCE HEAD Knox
SQUIRREL ISLAND Lincoln
STACYVILLE Penobscot
STANDISH Cumberland
STEEP FALLS Cumberland
STETSON Penobscot
STEUBEN Washington
STILLWATER Penobscot
STOCKHOLM Aroostook
STOCKTON SPRINGS Waldo
STONINGTON Hancock
STRATTON Franklin
STRONG Franklin
SULLIVAN Hancock
SUMNER Oxford
SUNSET Hancock
SURRY Hancock
SWANS ISLAND Hancock
TEMPLE Franklin
TENANTS HARBOR Knox
THOMASTON Knox
THORNDIKE Waldo
TOPSFIELD Washington

TOPSHAM Sagadahoc
TREVETT Lincoln
TROY Waldo
TURNER Androscoggin
TURNER CENTER Androscoggin
UNION Knox
UNITY Waldo
UPPER FRENCHVILLE Aroostook
VAN BUREN Aroostook
VANCEBORO Washington
VASSALBORO Kennebec
VIENNA Kennebec
VINALHAVEN Knox
WAITE Washington
WALDOBORO Lincoln
WALPOLE Lincoln
WARREN Knox
WASHBURN Aroostook
WASHINGTON Knox
WATERBORO York
WATERFORD Oxford
WATERVILLE Kennebec
WAYNE Kennebec
WEEKS MILLS Kennebec
WELD Franklin
WELLS York
WESLEY Washington
WEST BALDWIN Cumberland
WEST BETHEL Oxford
WEST BOOTHBAY HARBOR Lincoln
WEST BOWDOIN Sagadahoc
WEST BUXTON York
WEST ENFIELD Penobscot
WEST FARMINGTON Franklin
WEST FORKS Somerset
WEST KENNEBUNK York
WEST MINOT Androscoggin
WEST NEWFIELD York
WEST PARIS Oxford
WEST POLAND Androscoggin
WEST ROCKPORT Knox
WEST SOUTHPORT Lincoln
WEST TREMONT Hancock
WESTBROOK Cumberland
WESTFIELD Aroostook
WHITEFIELD Lincoln
WHITING Washington
WHITNEYVILLE Washington
WILTON Franklin
WINDHAM Cumberland
WINDSOR Kennebec
WINN Penobscot
WINTER HARBOR Hancock
WINTERPORT Waldo
WINTERVILLE Aroostook
WINTHROP Kennebec
WISCASSET Lincoln
WOODLAND Washington
WOOLWICH Sagadahoc
WYTOPITLOCK Aroostook
YARMOUTH Cumberland
YORK York
YORK BEACH York
YORK HARBOR York

ZIP/City Cross Reference

03901-03901 BERWICK	04001-04001 ACTON	04013-04013 BUSTINS ISLAND	04028-04028 EAST PARSONFIELD
03902-03902 CAPE NEDDICK	04002-04002 ALFRED	04014-04014 CAPE PORPOISE	04029-04029 SEBAGO
03903-03903 ELIOT	04003-04003 BAILEY ISLAND	04015-04015 CASCO	04030-04030 EAST WATERBORO
03904-03904 KITTERY	04004-04004 BAR MILLS	04016-04016 CENTER LOVELL	04032-04034 FREEPORT
03905-03905 KITTERY POINT	04005-04005 BIDDEFORD	04017-04017 CHEBEAGUE ISLAND	04037-04037 FRYEBURG
03906-03906 NORTH BERWICK	04006-04006 BIDDEFORD POOL	04019-04019 CLIFF ISLAND	04038-04038 GORHAM
03907-03907 OGUNQUIT	04007-04007 BIDDEFORD	04020-04020 CORNISH	04039-04039 GRAY
03908-03908 SOUTH BERWICK	04008-04008 BOWDOINHAM	04021-04021 CUMBERLAND CENTER	04040-04040 HARRISON
03909-03909 YORK	04009-04009 BRIDGTON	04022-04022 DENMARK	04041-04041 HIRAM
03910-03910 YORK BEACH	04010-04010 BROWNFIELD	04024-04024 EAST BALDWIN	04042-04042 HOLLIS CENTER
03911-03911 YORK HARBOR	04011-04011 BRUNSWICK	04027-04027 LEBANON	04043-04043 KENNEBUNK

ZIP	Town
04046-04046	KENNEBUNKPORT
04047-04047	PARSONSFIELD
04048-04048	LIMERICK
04049-04049	LIMINGTON
04050-04050	LONG ISLAND
04051-04051	LOVELL
04053-04053	MEREPOINT
04054-04054	MOODY
04055-04055	NAPLES
04056-04056	NEWFIELD
04057-04057	NORTH BRIDGTON
04061-04061	NORTH WATERBORO
04062-04062	WINDHAM
04063-04063	OCEAN PARK
04064-04064	OLD ORCHARD BEACH
04066-04066	ORRS ISLAND
04068-04068	PORTER
04069-04069	POWNAL
04070-04070	SCARBOROUGH
04071-04071	RAYMOND
04072-04072	SACO
04073-04073	SANFORD
04074-04074	SCARBOROUGH
04075-04075	SEBAGO LAKE
04076-04076	SHAPLEIGH
04077-04077	SOUTH CASCO
04078-04078	SOUTH FREEPORT
04079-04079	HARPSWELL
04081-04081	SOUTH WATERFORD
04082-04082	SOUTH WINDHAM
04083-04083	SPRINGVALE
04084-04084	STANDISH
04085-04085	STEEP FALLS
04086-04086	TOPSHAM
04087-04087	WATERBORO
04088-04088	WATERFORD
04090-04090	WELLS
04091-04091	WEST BALDWIN
04092-04092	WESTBROOK
04093-04093	WEST BUXTON
04094-04094	WEST KENNEBUNK
04095-04095	WEST NEWFIELD
04096-04096	YARMOUTH
04097-04097	NORTH YARMOUTH
04098-04098	WESTBROOK
04101-04104	PORTLAND
04105-04105	FALMOUTH
04106-04106	SOUTH PORTLAND
04107-04107	CAPE ELIZABETH
04108-04108	PEAKS ISLAND
04109-04109	PORTLAND
04110-04110	CUMBERLAND FORESIDE
04112-04112	PORTLAND
04116-04116	SOUTH PORTLAND
04122-04124	PORTLAND
04210-04212	AUBURN
04216-04216	ANDOVER
04217-04217	BETHEL
04219-04219	BRYANT POND
04220-04220	BUCKFIELD
04221-04221	CANTON
04222-04222	DURHAM
04223-04223	DANVILLE
04224-04224	DIXFIELD
04225-04225	DRYDEN
04226-04226	EAST ANDOVER
04227-04227	EAST DIXFIELD
04228-04228	EAST LIVERMORE
04230-04230	EAST POLAND
04231-04231	EAST STONEHAM
04234-04234	EAST WILTON
04236-04236	GREENE
04237-04237	HANOVER
04238-04238	HEBRON
04239-04239	JAY
04240-04243	LEWISTON
04250-04250	LISBON
04252-04252	LISBON FALLS
04253-04253	LIVERMORE
04254-04254	LIVERMORE FALLS
04255-04255	LOCKE MILLS
04256-04256	MECHANIC FALLS
04257-04257	MEXICO
04258-04258	MINOT
04259-04259	MONMOUTH
04260-04260	NEW GLOUCESTER
04261-04261	NEWRY
04262-04262	NORTH JAY
04263-04263	LEEDS
04265-04265	NORTH MONMOUTH
04266-04266	NORTH TURNER
04267-04267	NORTH WATERFORD
04268-04268	NORWAY
04270-04270	OXFORD
04271-04271	PARIS
04274-04274	POLAND
04275-04275	ROXBURY
04276-04276	RUMFORD
04278-04278	RUMFORD CENTER
04279-04279	RUMFORD POINT
04280-04280	SABATTUS
04281-04281	SOUTH PARIS
04282-04282	TURNER
04283-04283	TURNER CENTER
04284-04284	WAYNE
04285-04285	WELD
04286-04286	WEST BETHEL
04287-04287	WEST BOWDOIN
04288-04288	WEST MINOT
04289-04289	WEST PARIS
04290-04290	PERU
04291-04291	WEST POLAND
04292-04292	SUMNER
04294-04294	WILTON
04330-04338	AUGUSTA
04341-04341	COOPERS MILLS
04342-04342	DRESDEN
04343-04343	EAST WINTHROP
04344-04344	FARMINGDALE
04345-04345	GARDINER
04346-04346	RANDOLPH
04347-04347	HALLOWELL
04348-04348	JEFFERSON
04349-04349	KENTS HILL
04350-04350	LITCHFIELD
04351-04351	MANCHESTER
04352-04352	MOUNT VERNON
04353-04353	WHITEFIELD
04354-04354	PALERMO
04355-04355	READFIELD
04357-04357	RICHMOND
04358-04358	SOUTH CHINA
04359-04359	SOUTH GARDINER
04360-04360	VIENNA
04361-04361	WEEKS MILLS
04363-04363	WINDSOR
04364-04364	WINTHROP
04401-04402	BANGOR
04406-04406	ABBOT VILLAGE
04408-04408	AURORA
04410-04410	BRADFORD
04411-04411	BRADLEY
04412-04412	BREWER
04413-04413	BROOKTON
04414-04414	BROWNVILLE
04415-04415	BROWNVILLE JUNCTION
04416-04416	BUCKSPORT
04417-04417	BURLINGTON
04418-04418	CARDVILLE
04419-04419	CARMEL
04420-04421	CASTINE
04422-04422	CHARLESTON
04423-04423	COSTIGAN
04424-04424	DANFORTH
04426-04426	DOVER FOXCROFT
04427-04427	EAST CORINTH
04428-04428	EDDINGTON
04429-04429	HOLDEN
04430-04430	EAST MILLINOCKET
04431-04431	EAST ORLAND
04434-04434	ETNA
04435-04435	EXETER
04438-04438	FRANKFORT
04441-04441	GREENVILLE
04442-04442	GREENVILLE JUNCTION
04443-04443	GUILFORD
04444-04444	HAMPDEN
04448-04448	HOWLAND
04449-04449	HUDSON
04450-04450	KENDUSKEAG
04451-04451	KINGMAN
04453-04453	LAGRANGE
04454-04454	LAMBERT LAKE
04455-04455	LEE
04456-04456	LEVANT
04457-04457	LINCOLN
04459-04459	MATTAWAMKEAG
04460-04460	MEDWAY
04461-04461	MILFORD
04462-04462	MILLINOCKET
04463-04463	MILO
04464-04464	MONSON
04467-04467	OLAMON
04468-04468	OLD TOWN
04469-04469	ORONO
04471-04471	ORIENT
04472-04472	ORLAND
04473-04473	ORONO
04474-04474	ORRINGTON
04475-04475	PASSADUMKEAG
04476-04476	PENOBSCOT
04478-04478	ROCKWOOD
04479-04479	SANGERVILLE
04481-04481	SEBEC
04485-04485	SHIRLEY MILLS
04487-04487	SPRINGFIELD
04488-04488	STETSON
04489-04489	STILLWATER
04490-04490	TOPSFIELD
04491-04491	VANCEBORO
04492-04492	WAITE
04493-04493	WEST ENFIELD
04495-04495	WINN
04496-04496	WINTERPORT
04497-04497	WYTOPITLOCK
04530-04530	BATH
04535-04535	ALNA
04536-04536	BAYVILLE
04537-04537	BOOTHBAY
04538-04538	BOOTHBAY HARBOR
04539-04539	BRISTOL
04541-04541	CHAMBERLAIN
04543-04543	DAMARISCOTTA
04544-04544	EAST BOOTHBAY
04547-04547	FRIENDSHIP
04548-04548	GEORGETOWN
04549-04549	ISLE OF SPRINGS
04551-04551	BREMEN
04552-04552	NEWAGEN
04553-04553	NEWCASTLE
04554-04554	NEW HARBOR
04555-04555	NOBLEBORO
04556-04556	EDGECOMB
04558-04558	PEMAQUID
04562-04562	PHIPPSBURG
04563-04563	CUSHING
04564-04564	ROUND POND
04565-04565	SEBASCO ESTATES
04567-04567	SMALL POINT
04568-04568	SOUTH BRISTOL
04570-04570	SQUIRREL ISLAND
04571-04571	TREVETT
04572-04572	WALDOBORO
04573-04573	WALPOLE
04574-04574	WASHINGTON
04575-04575	WEST BOOTHBAY HARBOR
04576-04576	WEST SOUTHPORT
04578-04578	WISCASSET
04579-04579	WOOLWICH
04605-04605	ELLSWORTH
04606-04606	ADDISON
04607-04607	GOULDSBORO
04609-04609	BAR HARBOR
04611-04611	BEALS
04612-04612	BERNARD
04613-04613	BIRCH HARBOR
04614-04614	BLUE HILL
04615-04615	BLUE HILL FALLS
04616-04616	BROOKLIN
04617-04617	BROOKSVILLE
04619-04619	CALAIS
04622-04622	CHERRYFIELD
04623-04623	COLUMBIA FALLS
04624-04624	COREA
04625-04625	CRANBERRY ISLES
04626-04626	CUTLER
04627-04627	DEER ISLE
04628-04628	DENNYSVILLE
04629-04629	EAST BLUE HILL
04630-04630	EAST MACHIAS
04631-04631	EASTPORT
04634-04634	FRANKLIN
04635-04635	FRENCHBORO
04637-04637	GRAND LAKE STREAM
04640-04640	HANCOCK
04642-04642	HARBORSIDE
04643-04643	HARRINGTON
04644-04644	HULLS COVE
04645-04645	ISLE AU HAUT
04646-04646	ISLESFORD
04648-04648	JONESBORO
04649-04649	JONESPORT
04650-04650	LITTLE DEER ISLE
04652-04652	LUBEC
04653-04653	BASS HARBOR
04654-04654	MACHIAS
04655-04655	MACHIASPORT
04656-04656	MANSET
04657-04657	MEDDYBEMPS
04658-04658	MILBRIDGE
04659-04659	MINTURN
04660-04660	MOUNT DESERT
04662-04662	NORTHEAST HARBOR
04664-04664	SULLIVAN
04665-04665	OTTER CREEK
04666-04666	PEMBROKE
04667-04667	PERRY
04668-04668	PRINCETON
04669-04669	PROSPECT HARBOR
04671-04671	ROBBINSTON
04672-04672	SALSBURY COVE
04673-04673	SARGENTVILLE
04674-04674	SEAL COVE
04675-04675	SEAL HARBOR
04676-04676	SEDGWICK
04677-04677	SORRENTO
04679-04679	SOUTHWEST HARBOR
04680-04680	STEUBEN
04681-04681	STONINGTON
04683-04683	SUNSET
04684-04684	SURRY
04685-04685	SWANS ISLAND
04686-04686	WESLEY
04690-04690	WEST TREMONT
04691-04691	WHITING
04693-04693	WINTER HARBOR
04694-04694	WOODLAND
04730-04730	HOULTON
04732-04732	ASHLAND
04733-04733	BENEDICTA
04734-04734	BLAINE
04735-04735	BRIDGEWATER
04736-04736	CARIBOU
04737-04737	CLAYTON LAKE
04738-04738	CROUSEVILLE
04739-04739	EAGLE LAKE
04740-04740	EASTON
04741-04741	ESTCOURT STATION
04742-04742	FORT FAIRFIELD
04743-04743	FORT KENT
04744-04744	FORT KENT MILLS
04745-04745	FRENCHVILLE
04746-04746	GRAND ISLE
04747-04747	ISLAND FALLS
04750-04751	LIMESTONE
04756-04756	MADAWASKA

04757-04757	MAPLETON	04846-04846	GLEN COVE	04923-04923	CAMBRIDGE	04957-04957	NORRIDGEWOCK
04758-04758	MARS HILL	04847-04847	HOPE	04924-04924	CANAAN	04958-04958	NORTH ANSON
04759-04759	MASARDIS	04848-04848	ISLESBORO	04925-04925	CARATUNK	04961-04961	NORTH NEW PORTLAND
04760-04760	MONTICELLO	04849-04849	LINCOLNVILLE	04926-04926	CHINA	04962-04962	NORTH VASSALBORO
04761-04761	NEW LIMERICK	04850-04850	LINCOLNVILLE CENTER	04927-04927	CLINTON	04963-04963	OAKLAND
04762-04762	NEW SWEDEN	04851-04851	MATINICUS	04928-04928	CORINNA	04964-04964	OQUOSSOC
04763-04763	OAKFIELD	04852-04852	MONHEGAN	04929-04929	DETROIT	04965-04965	PALMYRA
04764-04764	OXBOW	04853-04853	NORTH HAVEN	04930-04930	DEXTER	04966-04966	PHILLIPS
04765-04765	PATTEN	04854-04854	OWLS HEAD	04932-04932	DIXMONT	04967-04967	PITTSFIELD
04766-04766	PERHAM	04855-04855	PORT CLYDE	04933-04933	EAST NEWPORT	04969-04969	PLYMOUTH
04768-04768	PORTAGE	04856-04856	ROCKPORT	04935-04935	EAST VASSALBORO	04970-04970	RANGELEY
04769-04769	PRESQUE ISLE	04857-04857	SAINT GEORGE	04936-04936	EUSTIS	04971-04971	SAINT ALBANS
04770-04770	QUIMBY	04858-04858	SOUTH THOMASTON	04937-04937	FAIRFIELD	04972-04972	SANDY POINT
04772-04772	SAINT AGATHA	04859-04859	SPRUCE HEAD	04938-04938	FARMINGTON	04973-04973	SEARSMONT
04773-04773	SAINT DAVID	04860-04860	TENANTS HARBOR	04939-04939	GARLAND	04974-04974	SEARSPORT
04774-04774	SAINT FRANCIS	04861-04861	THOMASTON	04940-04940	FARMINGTON FALLS	04975-04975	SHAWMUT
04775-04775	SHERIDAN	04862-04862	UNION	04941-04941	FREEDOM	04976-04976	SKOWHEGAN
04776-04776	SHERMAN MILLS	04863-04863	VINALHAVEN	04942-04942	HARMONY	04978-04978	SMITHFIELD
04777-04777	SHERMAN STATION	04864-04864	WARREN	04943-04943	HARTLAND	04979-04979	SOLON
04779-04779	SINCLAIR	04865-04865	WEST ROCKPORT	04944-04944	HINCKLEY	04981-04981	STOCKTON SPRINGS
04780-04780	SMYRNA MILLS	04901-04903	WATERVILLE	04945-04945	JACKMAN	04982-04982	STRATTON
04781-04781	SOLDIER POND	04910-04910	ALBION	04947-04947	KINGFIELD	04983-04983	STRONG
04782-04782	STACYVILLE	04911-04911	ANSON	04949-04949	LIBERTY	04984-04984	TEMPLE
04783-04783	STOCKHOLM	04912-04912	ATHENS	04950-04950	MADISON	04985-04985	WEST FORKS
04785-04785	VAN BUREN	04915-04915	BELFAST	04951-04951	MONROE	04986-04986	THORNDIKE
04786-04786	WASHBURN	04917-04917	BELGRADE	04952-04952	MORRILL	04987-04987	TROY
04787-04787	WESTFIELD	04918-04918	BELGRADE LAKES	04953-04953	NEWPORT	04988-04988	UNITY
04788-04788	WINTERVILLE	04920-04920	BINGHAM	04954-04954	NEW PORTLAND	04989-04989	VASSALBORO
04841-04841	ROCKLAND	04921-04921	BROOKS	04955-04955	NEW SHARON	04992-04992	WEST FARMINGTON
04843-04843	CAMDEN	04922-04922	BURNHAM	04956-04956	NEW VINEYARD		

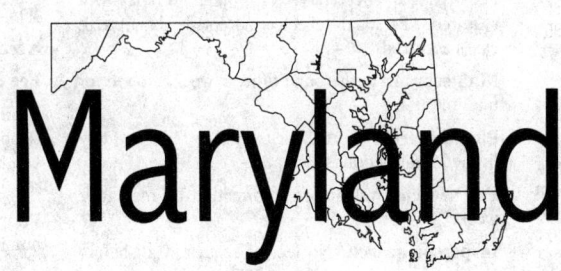

Maryland

General Help Numbers:

Governor's Office

State House
Annapolis, MD 21401
http://www.gov.state.md.us

410-974-3901
Fax 410-974-3275
9AM-5PM

Attorney General's Office

200 St Paul Place, 16th Floor
Baltimore, MD 21202
http://www.oag.state.md.us

410-576-6300
Fax 410-576-6404
8AM-5PM

State Court Administrator

580 Taylor Ave
Annapolis, MD 21401
http://www.courts.state.md.us

410-260-1400
Fax 410-974-2066
8AM-5PM

State Archives

Hall of Records
350 Rowe Blvd
Annapolis, MD 21401
http://www.mdarchives.state.md.us

410-260-6400
Fax 410-974-3895
8AM-4:30PM TU-FR;
8:30-4:30 SA

State Specifics:

Capital:

Annapolis
Anne Arundel County

Time Zone:

EST

Number of Counties:

23

Population:

5,296,486

Web Site:

www.mec.state.md.us

State Agencies

Criminal Records

Criminal Justice Information System, Public Safety & Correctional Records, PO Box 5743, Pikeville, MD 21282-5743 (Courier: 6776 Reisterstown Rd, Rm 200, Pikeville, MD 21208); 410-764-4501, 888-795-0011, 410-974-2169 (Fax), 8AM-3:30PM.

Note: All private parties must first write to this office and receive a "petition package" and then apply for a petition number. Employers and investigative firms are eligible to apply for this petition number.

Indexing & Storage: Records are available from 1978.

Searching: All arrests are released, even those without dispositions. Include the following in your request-signed release, set of fingerprints. Requesters must also submit a copy of their photo ID.

Access by: mail, online.

Fee & Payment: The fee is $18.00 per request. Fee payee: CJIS. Prepayment required. Money orders and cashier's checks are preferred. Personal checks accepted. No credit cards accepted.

Mail search: Turnaround time: 2 to 4 weeks.

Online search: The State Court Administrator's office has online access to criminal records from all state district courts, 3 circuit courts, and 1 city court. The system is available 24 hours daily. There is a one-time $50 fee to register and a $5.00 per hour fee. Land records may also be accessed from this system. Call 410-260-1031 for a sign-up package.

Corporation Records
Limited Partnerships
Trade Names
Limited Liability Company Records
Fictitious Name
Limited Liability Partnerships

Department of Assessments and Taxation, Corporations Division, 301 W Preston St, Room 801, Baltimore, MD 21201; 410-767-1340, 410-767-1330 (Charter Information), 410-333-7097 (Fax), 8AM-4:30PM.

http://www.dat.state.md.us/bsfd

Indexing & Storage: Records are available from 1908 on. New records are available for inquiry immediately. Records are indexed on inhouse computer.

Searching: Officers and directors info is not immediately available. Include the following in your request-full name of business, corporation file number. The following is available; the Articles of Incorporation, Annual Reports, Officers, Directors, DBA's, Prior (merged) names, Inactive and Reserved names.

Access by: mail, phone, fax, in person, online.

Fee & Payment: An abstract of corporate records is $6.00, A Good Standing is $6.00 or $12.00 if long form is needed. Copies are $1.00 per page plus $6.00 to certify. Fee payee: SDAT. Prepayment required. Personal checks accepted. Credit cards accepted: MasterCard, Visa.

Mail search: Turnaround time: 7 days. Officer and director information takes 2 weeks. Expedited service will improve turnaround time for mail or fax requests.No self addressed stamped envelope is required.

Phone search: Charter information includes date of incorporation, agent, and status. They will let you know how many pages if you wish to order copies.

Fax search: This is considered expedited service, see below.

In person search: The office closes at 5 PM for searchers. Public access terminals are available.

Online search: The web site offers free searching for corporate name and trade name records. The site also includes real estate (cannot search by name) and UCC records.

Other access: The state will release information in a bulk output format. Contact Dave Brown at (410) 561-9600 for details.

Expedited service: Expedited service is available for mail, phone and fax searches. Turnaround time: 2 days. There is an additional $20.00 fee to expedite a copy or $9.00 to expedite a certificate. A credit card must be used if requesting by fax.

Trademarks/Servicemarks

Secretary of State, Trademarks Division, State House, Annapolis, MD 21401; 410-974-5531 x2, 410-974-5527 (Fax), 9AM-5PM.

http://www.sos.state.md.us

Indexing & Storage: Records are available for the past 10 years. New records are available for inquiry immediately. Records are indexed on inhouse computer.

Searching: Include the following in your request-trademark/servicemark name.

Access by: mail, phone, fax, in person, online.

Fee & Payment: There is no search fee. Certification is $5.00, copies are $.25 per page. Fee payee: Secretary of State. Prepayment required. Personal checks accepted. No credit cards accepted.

Mail search: Turnaround time: 1 week. No fee for mail request.

Phone search: No fee for telephone request. Only limited information is available.

Fax search: Will return information by mail in 1 week.

In person search: No fee for request. Call before visiting.

Online search: Online searching is available at the Internet site. Search can be by keyword in the description field, the service or product, the owner, the classification, or the mark name or keyword in the mark name. The site offers application forms to register, renew, or assign trade and service marks, and general information about registration. Click on "Trade & Service Marks."

Other access: A computer printout of all marks registered, renewed or assigned within a 3 month period is available for $.05 per trademark.

Uniform Commercial Code
Federal Tax Liens
State Tax Liens

UCC Division, Department of Assessments & Taxation, 301 West Preston St, Baltimore, MD 21201; 410-767-1340, 410-333-7097 (Fax), 8AM-4:30PM.

http://www.dat.state.md.us/bsfd

Note: This agency will not do a search, you must come in person, hire a retriever, or buy the database.

Indexing & Storage: Records are available for all active files.

Searching: All tax liens (filed at the county level) prior to 1995 will not show on the UCC records. From 1995 forward, all are filed with the state and will show.

Access by: in person, online.

Fee & Payment: There is no search fee, copy fee is $1.00 per page. Fee payee: SDAT. Prepayment required. Personal checks accepted. No credit cards accepted. No searching by mail.

In person search: Records can be viewed at no charge on public access terminals.

Online search: The Internet site offers free access to UCC index information. There is also a related site offering access to real property data for the whole state at www.dat.state.md.us/realprop.

Other access: The agency has available for sale copies of public release master data files including corporation, real estate, and UCC. In addition, they can produce customized files on paper or disk. Visit the web site for more information.

Sales Tax Registrations

Taxpayer Services, Revenue Administration Division, 301 W Preston St #206, Baltimore, MD 21201; 410-767-1313, 410-767-1571 (Fax), 8AM-5PM.

http://www.comp.state.md.us

Indexing & Storage: Records are available on a computer index for the past 4 years of applicants.

Searching: This agency will only confirm that a business's number is valid and confirm the name and address of the business. They will provide no other information. The business name and federal ID# or SSN of owner is required to search.

Access by: mail, phone.

Fee & Payment: There are no fees.

Mail search: Turnaround time: 7 working days. Records are not returned by mail, they will call you.No self addressed stamped envelope is required.

Phone search: Call only if you have the permit number.

Birth Certificates

Department of Health, Division of Vital Records, PO Box 68760, Baltimore, MD 21215-0020 (Courier: 6550 Reisterstown Plaza, Baltimore, MD 21205); 410-764-3038, 410-764-3170 (Order), 410-318-6119 (Recording), 410-358-7381 (Fax), 8AM-4PM M-F; 3rd Saturday of each month.

http://www.dhmh.state.md.us

Indexing & Storage: Records are available from 1898 to present for all counties and 1878 to present for City of Baltimore. For prior records, contact the city/county associated with the record in question. It takes 6-8 weeks before new records are available for inquiry. Records are indexed on index cards.

Searching: Must have a notarized signed release form from person of record or mother or father. Include the following in your request-full name, names of parents, mother's maiden name, date of birth, place of birth, relationship to person of record.

Access by: mail, phone, fax, in person.

Fee & Payment: The search fee is $6.00. Only fax, phone and expedited requesters may use a credit card and there is an additional $7.00 fee. Fee payee: Division of Vital Records. Prepayment required. Cash is accepted for walk in requesters only. Personal checks accepted. Credit cards accepted: MasterCard, Visa, AmEx, Discover.

Mail search: Turnaround time: 2 to 4 weeks. A self addressed stamped envelope is requested.

Phone search: Credit card prepayment required. Turnaround time is 2-3 days.

Fax search: Same criteria as phone searches.

In person search: Turnaround time is same day (typically, 45 minutes to 1 hour). Walk in requesters may pay with cash. Presentation of photo ID is required for walk in requesters.

Expedited service: Expedited service is available for mail, phone and fax searches. Turnaround time: 2 days. Add $12.00 per package. Credit card prepayment and fee required.

Death Records

Department of Health, Division of Vital Records, PO Box 68760, Baltimore, MD 21215-0020 (Courier: 6550 Reisterstown Plaza, Baltimore, MD 21215); 410-764-3038, 410-764-3170 (Order), 410-318-6119 (Recording), 410-358-7381 (Fax), 8AM-4PM M-F; 3rd Saturday of each month.

http://www.dhmh.state.md.us

Indexing & Storage: Records are available from 1969 to present. For records prior to 1969 contact Maryland State Archives, 410-260-6429. New records are available for inquiry immediately. Records are indexed on index cards.

Searching: Must have a signed release form from immediate family member. A signature is required from the requester. Include the following in your request-full name, date of death, place of death, relationship to person of record, reason for information request. Include copy of photo ID with request.

Access by: mail, phone, fax, in person.

Fee & Payment: The search fee is $6.00. Only phone, fax and expedited requesters may use a credit card for an extra $7.00 fee. Fee payee: Division of Vital Records. Prepayment required. Personal checks, M.O.s accepted. Credit cards accepted: MasterCard, Visa, AmEx, Discover.

Mail search: Turnaround time: 2 to 4 weeks. A self addressed stamped envelope is requested.

Phone search: Credit card pre-payment required. Turnaround time is 2-3 days.

Fax search: Same criteria as phone searches.

In person search: Turnaround time is same day.

Expedited service: Expedited service is available for mail, phone and fax searches. Turnaround time: 2 days. Add $12.00 per package for express delivery. Use of credit card and fee is required, also.

Marriage Certificates

Department of Health, Division of Vital Records, PO Box 68760, Baltimore, MD 21215-0020 (Courier: 6550 Reisterstown Plaza, Baltimore, MD 21215); 410-764-3038, 410-764-3170 (Order), 410-318-6119 (Recording), 410-358-7381 (Fax), 8AM-4PM M-F; 3rd Saturday of each month.

http://www.dhmh.state.md.us

Indexing & Storage: Records are available from June 1951 to present. It takes 6 months before new records are available for inquiry. Records are indexed on computer.

Searching: Must have a notarized signed release form from persons of record or authorized representative. Include the following in your request-names of husband and wife, date of marriage, place or county of marriage. Include copy of photo ID with request.

Access by: mail, phone, fax, in person.

Fee & Payment: The search fee is $6.00. Only phone, fax and expedited requesters may use a credit card for an additional fee of $7.00. Fee payee: Division of Vital Records. Prepayment required. Personal checks & M.O.s accepted. Credit cards accepted: MasterCard, Visa, AmEx, Discover.

Mail search: Turnaround time: 2 to 3 weeks. A self addressed stamped envelope is requested.

Phone search: Credit Card prepayment required. Turnaround time is 2-3 days.

Fax search: Same search criteria as phone searches.

In person search: Turnaround time same day.

Expedited service: Expedited service is available for mail, phone and fax searches. Turnaround time: 2 days. Add $12.00 per package for express delivery. Use of credit card and fee is required, also.

Divorce Records

Department of Health, Division of Vital Records, PO Box 68760, Baltimore, MD 21215-0020 (Courier: 6550 Reisterstown Plaza, Baltimore, MD 21215); 410-764-3038, 410-318-6119

(Recording), 800-832-3277, 410-358-7381 (Fax), 8AM-4PM M-F; 3rd Saturday of each month.

http://www.dhmh.state.md.us

Indexing & Storage: Records are available from July 1961 to present. New records are available for inquiry immediately. Records are indexed on index cards. 1983-84 indexes are not available for searching.

Searching: Must have a notarized release form from persons of record or authorized agent. Include the following in your request-names of husband and wife, date of divorce, year divorce case began.

Access by: mail, fax, in person.

Fee & Payment: There is no fee to receive a Verification of Report of Divorce and Absolute Annulment. The clerk of the court issuing the decree holds the actual hard copy record.

Mail search: Turnaround time: 2 to 3 weeks.

Fax search: No searching by fax.

In person search: Turnaround time same day.

Workers' Compensation Records

Workers Compensation Commission, 10 E Baltimore St, Baltimore, MD 21202; 410-864-5100, 410-864-5101 (Fax), 8AM-4:30PM.

http://www.charm.net/~wcc

Indexing & Storage: Records are available for past 10 years are on computer. New records are available for inquiry immediately. Records are indexed on microfilm, inhouse computer.

Searching: Include the following in your request-claimant name, Social Security Number, date of accident, place of employment at time of accident. The claim number helps. The following data is not released: medical records.

Access by: mail, phone, in person, online.

Fee & Payment: Fee for copies is $.50 per page. There is no search fee. Fee payee: Workers Compensation Commission. Prepayment required. Personal checks accepted. No credit cards accepted.

Mail search: Turnaround time: 1 week. For copies of documents, the claimant's authorization is needed. A self addressed stamped envelope is requested.

Phone search: Limited verification information is available by phone for three names only per call.

In person search: Turnaround time while you wait.

Online search: Request for online hook-up must be in writing on letterhead. There is no search fee, but there is a $7.00 set-up fee, $5.00 monthly fee and a $.01-03 per minute connect fee assessed by Verizon or other provider. The system is open 24 hours a day to only in-state accounts. Write to the Commission at address above, care of Information Technology Division, or call Lili Joseph at 410-864-5119.

Other access: This agency will sell its entire database depending on the use of the purchaser. Contact the commission for further information.

Driver Records

MVA, Driver Records Unit, 6601 Ritchie Hwy, NE, Glen Burnie, MD 21062; 410-787-7758, 8:15AM-4:30PM.

http://www.mva.state.md.us

Note: Copies of tickets can be obtained from the MD District Court/MATS, 1750 Forest Dr, Annapolis, 21401. There is no charge for ticket copies, but a self addressed stamped envelope is advised.

Indexing & Storage: Records are available for 3 years for moving violations, 10 years for DWIs, and 5 years for suspensions. Law requires a request from the driver to have violations purged from the driving record. Accidents are indicated. It takes 5 to 10 days before new records are available for inquiry.

Searching: Casual requesters may obtain records with personal information only with consent of subject. Records may not be resold or used for direct mail advertising or selling. The driver's license number or the name and DOB are needed for a search.

Access by: mail, in person, online.

Fee & Payment: The fee for a driving record is $5.00. There is an additional $5.00 if you wish to have the record certified. Fee payee: MVA. Prepayment required. Credit cards are not accepted for mail requests. Personal checks accepted. Credit cards accepted: MasterCard, Visa.

Mail search: Turnaround time: 2 to 3 days. MVA offices statewide will also accept mail-in requests for records. A self addressed stamped envelope is requested.

In person search: Up to 20 requests will be processed in-person, additional requests are available the next day. In-person inquires may be processed at over 25 Motor Vehicle offices throughout the state.

Online search: The network is available 6 days a week, twenty-four hours a day to qualified and bonded individuals and businesses. Access is through PC and modem at up to 9600 baud. The communication network is the Public Data Network (Bell Atlantic). Fee is $5.00 per record.

Vehicle Ownership
Vehicle Identification

Department of Motor Vehicles, Vehicle Registration Division, Room 204, 6601 Ritchie Hwy, NE, Glen Burnie, MD 21062; 410-768-7520, 410-768-7653 (Fax), 8:15AM-4:30PM.

http://www.mva.state.md.us

Indexing & Storage: Records are available from 1920. It takes 5 to 10 days before new records are available for inquiry.

Searching: All vehicle/ownership records are open to the public; however, personal information is not released to casual requesters without consent of subject. The following data is not released: medical information.

Access by: mail, in person, online.

Fee & Payment: Fees are $7.00 for non-certified records and $10.00 for certified records. Fee payee: MVA. Prepayment required. Credit cards are only accepted for walk-in requesters. Personal checks accepted. Credit cards accepted: MasterCard, Visa.

Mail search: Turnaround time: 3 to 5 days. Requester can provide prepaid express mail package for faster service.No self addressed stamped envelope is required.

In person search: Turnaround time is generally in a few minutes.

Online search: The state offers vehicle and ownership data over the same online network utilized for driving record searches. Fee is $7.00 per record and line charges will be incurred. For more information, call 410-768-7234.

Accident Reports

Maryland State Police, Central Records Division, 1711 Belmont Ave, Baltimore, MD 21244; 410-298-3390, 410-298-3198 (Fax), 8AM-5PM.

Note: This agency does not have reports for the City of Baltimore. Call 410-396-2359 for those reports.

Indexing & Storage: Records are available for 5 years. Records are computer indexed from 1995 to present.

Searching: If a fatality was involved, please so state in the request. Copies of accident reports investigated by the state police and other police agencies may be requested by giving the date of incident and driver name(s).

Access by: mail, in person.

Fee & Payment: The search fee is $4.00 which includes all copies and is non-refundable. Fee payee: Maryland State Police. Prepayment required. Personal checks accepted. No credit cards accepted.

Mail search: Turnaround time: 3 to 5 weeks. A self addressed stamped envelope is requested.

Vessel Ownership
Vessel Registration

Dept of Natural Resources, Licensing & Registration Service, 580 Taylor Ave, Annapolis, MD 21401; 410-260-8200, 8:30AM-4:30PM.

http://www.dnr.state.md.us

Indexing & Storage: Records are available from the 1960s to the present. This is a title state: all motorized boats must be titled and registered. Records are on indexed on microfiche from the 1960s to the present, and on computer for the last 4 years.

Searching: Lien records are not searchable. However, the Department will indicate with a "yes" or "no" when asked if a lien exists. To search, one of the following is required: Maryland boat #, tidal fish license #, or name and address of boat owner/license holder. There are five additional Regional Service Centers in the state that will process record requests.

Access by: mail, in person.

Fee & Payment: Certified true copies are $10.00 each. Microfiche history files are $5.00 each.

Current computer file copies are $5.00 each. Fee payee: DNR. Prepayment required. Personal checks accepted. No credit cards accepted.

Mail search: Turnaround time: 7 to 10 days. No self addressed stamped envelope is required.

In person search: Turnaround time is immediate, unless historical records needed.

Other access: Bulk lists are available through Marine Trades Association of Maryland at (410) 269-0741.

Legislation Records

Maryland General Assembly, Dept of Legislative Services, 90 State Circle, Annapolis, MD 21401-1991; 410-946-5400 (Bill Status Only), 410-946-5010, 800-492-7122 (In-state), 410-946-5405 (Fax), 8AM-5PM.

http://mlis.state.md.us

Indexing & Storage: Records are available from 1991 to present on computer and to 1990 on hard copy only. Records are indexed on inhouse computer, hard copy.

Searching: Include the following in your request- bill number.

Access by: mail, phone, in person, online.

Fee & Payment: The copy fee is $.15 per page. Fee payee: Maryland General Assembly. Prepayment required. Personal checks accepted. No credit cards accepted.

Mail search: Turnaround time: variable. The first 10 pages are free. No fee for mail request.

Phone search: No fee for telephone request.

In person search: No fee for request.

Online search: The Internet site has complete information regarding bills and status.

Voter Registration
Access to Records is Restricted

State Board of Elections, PO Box 6486, Annapolis, MD 21401-0486 (Courier: 151 West Street, #200, Annapolis, MD 21401); 410-269-2840, 800-222-8683, 410-974-2019 (Fax), 8AM-5PM.

http://www.elections.state.md.us

Note: This agency is authorized to sell voter registration lists in bulk media format for 5 of its 24 local jurisdictions. Purchaser must be a MD registered voter. Lists cannot be used for commercial solicitation. The web site offers a

wealth of information, including access to the campaign finance database.

GED Certificates

State Department of Education, GED Office, 200 W Baltimore St, Baltimore, MD 21201; 410-767-0538, 410-333-8435 (Fax), 8:30AM-5PM.

http://www.umbc.edu/alrc

Indexing & Storage: It takes 30 days before new records are available for inquiry.

Searching: Include the following in your request- date of birth, Social Security Number, signed release.

Access by: mail, fax, in person.

Fee & Payment: The fee is $5.00 for a copy of a transcript. Fee payee: GED Office. Prepayment required. Personal checks accepted. No credit cards accepted.

Mail search: Turnaround time: 3 to 5 days. No self addressed stamped envelope is required.

Fax search: Results are returned by mail.

In person search: Results can be picked up at office (around the corner) at 4 N Liberty, between the hours of 10AM and 1PM.

Hunting License Information
Fishing License Information

Department of Natural Resources, Licensing & Registration Service, 580 Taylor Ave, Annapolis, MD 21401; 410-260-8200, 410-260-8217 (Fax), 8AM-4:30PM.

http://www.dnr.state.md.us

Note: They have a central paper database. Records are organized by the 400+ vendors where the license was purchased making it difficult to search. However, the agency is in the process of automating the license data and a database may be available soon.

Searching: Name searches are not permitted at this time.

Access by: in person. No searching by mail.

In person search: No fee for request. The state will help, if someone wants to look through paper records.

Other access: The agency will sell an annual tape of commercial fishing licenses, including names and addresses. The fee is $175.00. Licensees have the option of opting out. Call Mrs. Johnston at 410-260-8237 for details.

Maryland State Licensing Agencies

Licenses Searchable Online

Architectural Partnership/Corporation #12 .... www.dllr.state.md.us/query/arch.html
Barber #08 .... www.dllr.state.md.us/query/barber.html
Charity #28 .... www.sos.state.md.us/sos/charity/html/search.html
Contractor #10 .... www.dllr.state.md.us/query/home_imprv.html
Cosmetologist/Nail Technician/Esthetician/Makeup Artist #08 www.dllr.state.md.us/query/cosmet.html
Electrician, Master #12 .... www.dllr.state.md.us/query/master_elec.html
Engineer, Examining #12 .... www.dllr.state.md.us/query/stat_eng.html
Engineer, Professional #12 .... www.dllr.state.md.us/query/prof_eng.html
Forester #12 .... www.dllr.state.md.us/query/forester.html
Fund Raisering Counsel #28 .... www.sos.state.md.us/sos/charity/html/psfrclist.html
Home Improvement #12 .... www.dllr.state.md.us/query/home_imprv.html
Home Improvement Salesperson #10 .... www.dllr.state.md.us/query/home_imprv.html
HVACR Contractor #12 .... www.dllr.state.md.us/query/hvacr.html
Interior Designer #12 .... www.dllr.state.md.us/query/cert_int_des.html
Land Surveyor #12 .... www.dllr.state.md.us/query/land_surv.html
Landscape Architect #12 .... www.dllr.state.md.us/query/land_arch.html
Medical Doctor #22 .... www.docboard.org/md/df/mdsearch.htm
Optometrist #22 .... www.odfinder.org/LicSearch.asp
Plumber #12 .... www.dllr.state.md.us/query/plumb.html
Polygraph Examiner #32 .... http://polygraph.org/states/mpa/Members.htm
Precious Metals & Gem Dealer/Secondhand #12 .... www.dllr.state.md.us/query/sec_hand_deal.html
Public Accountant-CPA #12 .... www.dllr.state.md.us/query/cpa.html
Real Estate Agent #15 .... www.dllr.state.md.us/query/Maryland.html
Real Estate Appraiser #11 .... www.dllr.state.md.us/query/real_est_app.html
Solicitor, Professional #28 .... www.sos.state.md.us/sos/charity/html/psfrclist.html
Subcontractor #10 .... www.dllr.state.md.us/query/home_imprv.html

Licensing Quick Finder

Acupuncturist #22 410-764-4766	Handgun Permittee #27 410-799-0191	Polygraph Examiner #32 410-987-6665
Airport #19 410-859-7064	Harness Racing #09 410-230-6330	Precious Metals & Gem Dealer #12 410-333-4640
Airport License #19 410-859-7064	Hazardous Waste #06 410-631-3344	Private Investigator #27 410-799-0191
Alarm Technician #27 410-799-0190	Hearing Aid Dispenser #22 410-764-4792	Psychologist #22 410-764-4787
Architect #30 410-333-6322	Home Improvement #12 410-333-6200	Psychometrist (Education) #05 410-767-0412
Architectural Partnership/Corp. #12 410-333-6322	Home Improvement Salesperson #10 ... 410-230-6231	Public Accountant-CPA #12 410-333-6325
Asbestos Abatement Company #06 410-631-3200	Horse Racing #09 410-230-6330	Pump Installer #06 410-631-3167
Atheltic Agent #16 410-333-6315	HVACR Contractor #12 410-333-6200	Pupil Personnel Worker #05 410-767-0412
Attorney #03 410-260-1950	Insurance Agent #21 410-468-2383	Radiation Therapy Technician #22 410-764-4775
Audiologist #22 410-764-4725	Insurance Broker/Advisor #21 410-468-2383	Reading Specialist #05 410-767-0412
Bail Bondsman #21 410-468-2383	Interior Designer #12 410-333-6322	Reading Teacher #05 410-767-0412
Barber #08 410-230-6320	Investment Adviser/Representative #29 410-576-7784	Real Estate Agent #15 410-333-6230
Boxer/Boxing Professional #17 410-333-6315	Land Surveyor #12 410-333-6322	Real Estate Appraiser #11 410-230-6231
Bus Driver #18 410-768-7232	Landscape Architect #12 410-333-6322	Referee #14 410-333-6315
Charity #28 410-974-5521	Lead Inspectors/Contractors #06 410-631-3167	Respiratory Care Practitioner #22 410-764-4775
Chiropractor/Chiropractic Assistant #22 410-764-2965	Limosine Driver #18 410-768-7232	Sanitarian #06 410-631-3167
Collection Agency #14 410-333-6820	Massage Therapist #22 410-764-2431	School Admin./Superintendent #05 410-767-0412
Contractor #10 410-230-6231	Medical Doctor #22 410-764-4761	School Library Media Generalist/Specialist #05 ....
Cosmetologist/Nail Technician #08 410-230-6320	Mining Foreman/Fire Boss #06 410-631-3609	 410-767-0412
Counselor #22 410-764-4732	Mortgage Broker #13 410-333-6830	School Psychologist #05 410-767-0412
Day Care Provider #02 410-321-2216	Mortician #22 410-764-4792	Securities Broker/Dealer/Agent #29 410-576-6494
Dental Assistant #22 410-764-4730	Notary Public #28 410-974-5520	Security Guard #27 410-799-0191
Dental Hygienist #22 410-764-4730	Nurse-RN-LPN #24 410-585-1979	Sewage Treatment #06 410-631-3609
Dentist #22 410-764-4730	Nursing Assistant #24 410-585-1990	Social Worker #22 410-764-4788
Dietitian/Nutritionist #22 410-764-4733	Nursing Home Administrator #22 410-764-4750	Solicitor, Professional #28 410-974-5534
Electrician, Master #12 410-230-6231	Occupational Therapist/Assistant #22 ... 410-764-2964	Speech Pathologist #22 410-764-4725
Electrologist #07 410-764-4702	Optometrist #22 410-764-4725	Subcontractor #10 410-230-6231
Embalmer #22 410-764-4792	Pesticide Applicator/Operator #04 410-841-5710	Taxi Driver #18 410-768-7232
Engineer, Examining/Professional #12 .. 410-230-6231	Pesticide Business/Dealer #04 410-841-5710	Taxicab #31 410-767-8000
Esthetician/Makeup Artist #08 410-230-6320	Pesticide Consultant #04 410-841-5710	Teacher #05 410-767-0412
Forester #12 410-230-6231	Pharmacist #22 410-764-4755	Truck Driver #18 410-768-7232
Foster Care Provider #26 410-767-7903	Physical Therapist #22 410-764-4752	Veterinarian #01 410-841-5862
Franchises, Bus. Opportunities,	Physical Therapist Assistant #22 410-764-4752	Veterinary Hospital #01 410-841-5862
Multi-level Mktng Programs #29 410-576-7785	Pilot #12 410-333-6329	Waste Water Treatment Plant Superintendent #06 .....
Fund Raisering Counsel #28 410-974-5534	Plant Broker/Dealer #04 410-841-5710	 410-631-3609
Funeral Director/Establishment #22 410-764-4792	Plumber #12 410-230-6231	Water Conditioner Installer #06 410-631-3167
Grain Dealer #04 410-841-5710	Podiatrist #22 410-764-4785	Well Driller #06 410-631-3167
Guidance Counselor #05 410-767-0412	Police Officer, Special #27 410-799-0191	

Licensing Agency Information

#01 Board of Veterinary Medical Examiners, 50 Harry S Truman Pky, Annapolis, MD 21401; 410-841-5862, Fax: 410-841-5999.
www.mda.state.md.us/vet/begin.htm

#02 Child Care Administration, Region 3, 409 Washignton Ave LL8, Towson, MD 21204; 410-321-2216, Fax: 410-321-2240.
www.dhr.state.md.us/cca-home.htm

#03 Client Security Trust Fund, 251 Rowe Blvd 3rd Fl, Annapolis, MD 21401; 410-260-1950, Fax: 410-260-1954.
www.cstf.org

#04 Department of Agriculture, 50 Harry S Truman Pky, Annapolis, MD 21401; 410-841-5710, Fax: 410-841-2765.
www.mda.state.md.us/geninfo/genera10.htm

#05 Department of Education, 200 W Baltimore St, Baltimore, MD 21201-2595; 410-767-0412, Fax: 410-333-8963.
www.msde.state.md.us/certification/certification.html
Direct web site URL to search for licensees:
www.msde.state.md.us/certification/certification.html

#06 Department of Environment, 2500 Broenig Hwy, Baltimore, MD 21224; 410-631-3000, Fax: 410-633-0456.
www.mde.state.md.us

#07 Department of Health & Mental Hygiene, 4201 Patterson Av Room 316, Baltimore, MD 21215; 410-764-4702, Fax: 410-358-0836.

#08 Department of Labor, Licensing & Regulation, 500 N Calvert St, 3rd Fl, Baltimore, MD 21202; 410-230-6220, Fax: 410-230-6314.
www.dllr.state.md.us/occprof/barber.html
Direct web site URL to search for licensees: www.dllr.state.md.us/query/barber.html (or) cosmet.html. You can search online using name, home address, shop name, and shop location.

#09 Department of Labor, Licensing & Regulation, 500 N Calvert St, Baltimore, MD 21202; 410-333-6200, Fax: 410-333-8308.
www.dllr.state.md.us

#10 Department of Licensing & Regulation, 500 N Calvert St, #306, Baltimore, MD 21202-3651; 410-333-6200.

www.dllr.state.md.us/occprof/homeim.html
Direct web site URL to search for licensees: www.dllr.state.md.us/query/home_imprv.html. You can search online using personal name, trade name, trade location, and disciplinary action.

#11 Department of Labor, Licensing & Regulation, 500 N Calvert St, Baltimore, MD 21202; 410-333-6200, Fax: 410-333-1229.
www.dllr.state.md.us/occprof/reappr.html
Direct web site URL to search for licensees: www.dllr.state.md.us/query/real_est_app.html. You can search online using name, location, and disciplinary action.

#12 Department of Licensing & Regulation, 500 N Calvert St, Baltimore, MD 21202; 410-333-6200, Fax: 410-333-1229.

#13 Department of Licensing & Regulation, 500 N Calvert St, #402, Baltimore, MD 21202; 410-333-6200, Fax: 410-333-1229.
www.dllr.state.md.us/license/fin_reg/mortlend/mdfinreg.html

#14 Department of Licensing & Regulation, 500 N Calvert St, 4th Fl, Baltimore, MD 21202; 410-333-6200, Fax: 410-333-1229.
www.dllr.state.md.us/

#15 Department of Licensing & Regulation, 500 N Calvert St, 3rd Fl, Baltimore, MD 21202-3551; 410-333-6230, Fax: 410-333-0851.
www.dllr.state.md.us/occprof/recomm.html
Direct web site URL to search for licensees: www.dllr.state.md.us/query/Maryland.htm. You can search online using name, location, and disciplinary action.

#16 Department of Licensing & Regulation, 500 N Calvert St, Rm 304, Baltimore, MD 21202; 410-230-6271, Fax: 410-333-1229.
www.dllr.state.md.us/license/occprof/sportag.html

#17 Department of Licensing & Regulation, 500 N Calvert St, 2nd Fl, Baltimore, MD 21202; 410-333-6200, Fax: 410-333-6314.
www.dllr.state.md.us/license/occprof/athlet.html

#18 Department of Transportation, 6601 Ritchie Hwy NE, Glen Burnie, MD 21062; 410-768-7232, Fax: 410-333-6088.

#19 Department of Transportation, PO Box 8766, BWI Airport, Baltimore, MD 21240; 410-859-7064, Fax: 410-859-7287.

#21 Licensing & Regulation, 525 St Paul Pl, Baltimore, MD 21202; 410-468-2383, Fax: 410-468-2399.
www.mdinsurance.state.md.us

#22 Licensing Boards, 4201 Patterson Ave, Baltimore, MD 21215-2299; 410-764-2431, Fax: 410-358-6571.
Direct web site URL to search for licensees: www.docboard.org/md/df/mdsearch.htm. You can search online using last name, license #, or town

#24 Board of Nursing, 4140 Patterson Ave, Baltimore, MD 21215; 410-585-1900, Fax: 410-358-3530.
www.dhmh.state.md.us/mbn Alternate web site is www.mdon.org. There is a telephone voice response system called IVR at 410-585-1978. Online search available late in 2000.

#26 Commission on Human Relations, Foster Care Review Board, 311 W Saratoga, Baltimore, MD 21201; 410-767-7903, Fax: 410-333-6693.

#27 State Police, 7751 Washington Blvd, Jessup, MD 20794; 410-799-0191, Fax: 410-799-5934.
www.inform.umd.edu:8080/UMS+State/MD_Resources/MDSP/index.html

#28 Office of Secretary of State, Statehouse, Annapolis, MD 21401; 410-974-5521, Fax: 410-974-5190.
www.sos.state.md.us

#29 Securities Division, 200 St. Paul Place, 25th Fl, Baltimore, MD 21202; 410-576-6360, Fax: 410-576-6532.
www.oag.state.md.us/Securities/index.htm

#30 Board of Architects, 500 N Calvert St 3rd Fl, Baltimore, MD 21202-2272; 410-333-6322.

#31 Public Service Commission, 6 St Paul St, Baltimore, MD 21202; 410-767-8000.

#32 Polygraph Association, PO Box 882, Millersville, MD 21108; 410-987-6665.
http://polygraph.org/states/mpa/
Direct web site URL to search for licensees: http://polygraph.org/states/mpa/Members.htm

Maryland Federal Courts

The following list indicates the district and division name for each county in the state. If the bankruptcy court location is different from the district court, then the location of the bankruptcy court appears in parentheses.

County/Court Cross Reference

Allegany	Baltimore	Harford	Baltimore
Anne Arundel	Baltimore	Howard	Baltimore
Baltimore	Baltimore	Kent	Baltimore
Baltimore City City	Baltimore	Montgomery	Greenbelt
Calvert	Greenbelt	Prince George's	Greenbelt
Caroline	Baltimore	Queen Anne's	Baltimore
Carroll	Baltimore	Somerset	Baltimore
Cecil	Baltimore	St. Mary's	Greenbelt
Charles	Greenbelt	Talbot	Baltimore
Dorchester	Baltimore	Washington	Baltimore
Frederick	Baltimore	Wicomico	Baltimore
Garrett	Baltimore	Worcester	Baltimore

US District Court

Northern District of Maryland

Baltimore Division Clerk, 4th Floor, Room 4415, 101 W Lombard St, Baltimore, MD 21201 (Courier Address: Use mail address for courier delivery), 410-962-2600.

http://www.mdd.uscourts.gov

Counties: Allegany, Anne Arundel, Baltimore, City of Baltimore, Caroline, Carroll, Cecil, Dorchester, Frederick, Garrett, Harford, Howard, Kent, Queen Anne's, Somerset, Talbot, Washington, Wicomico, Worcester.

Indexing/Storage: Cases are indexed by defendant and plaintiff as well as by case number. New cases are available in the index 1-2 days after filing date. Both computer and card indexes are maintained. Open records are located at this court.

Fee & Payment: The fee is $20.00 per item (one party name or case number). Payment may be made by money order, cashier check, personal check. Prepayment is required. Payee: Clerk, USDC. Certification fee: $7.00 per document. Copy fee: $.50 per page.

Phone Search: The court will verify questions over the phone, but will not read long dockets.

Mail Search: Always enclose a stamped self addressed envelope.

In Person: In person searching is available.

PACER: Sign-up number is 800-676-6856. Access fee is $.60 per minute. Toll-free access: 800-241-2259. Local access: 410-962-1812. Case records are available back to October 1990. Records are purged every six months. New records are available online after 1 day. PACER is available online at http://pacer.mdd.uscourts.gov.

Opinions Online: Court opinions are available online at http://www.mdd.uscourts.gov

US Bankruptcy Court

Northern District of Maryland

Baltimore Division 8308 US Courthouse, 101 W Lombard St, Baltimore, MD 21201 (Courier Address: Use mail address for courier delivery), 410-962-2688.

http://www.mdb.uscourts.gov

Counties: Anne Arundel, Baltimore, City of Baltimore, Caroline, Carroll, Cecil, Dorchester, Harford, Howard, Kent, Queen Anne's, Somerset, Talbot, Wicomico, Worcester.

Indexing/Storage: Cases are indexed by debtor as well as by case number. New cases are available in the index 2 days after filing date. The name and/or case number of the debtor(s) as well as specific identification of the pleading involved are required to search for a record. A computer index is maintained. Open records are located at this court. Closed files are retained for the existing year as well as the previous calendar year.

Fee & Payment: The fee is $20.00 per item (one party name or case number). Payment may be made by money order, cashier check. Business checks are not accepted. Personal checks are not accepted. Non-certified copy work is available from an on-site vendor, Document Technology, which charges $.30 per page for copies. Call 410-837-0409 for information. Payee: Clerk, US Bankruptcy Court. Certification fee: $7.00 per document. Copy fee: $.50 per page.

Phone Search: Only docket information is available by phone. An automated voice case information service (VCIS) is available. Call VCIS at 800-829-0145 or 410-962-0733.

Mail Search: A stamped self addressed envelope is not required.

In Person: In person searching is available.

PACER: Sign-up number is 800-676-6856. Access fee is $.60 per minute. Toll-free access: 800-927-0474. Local access: 410-962-0776. Case records are available back to mid 1991. Records are purged every six months. New civil records are available online after 2 days. PACER is available online at http://pacer.mdb.uscourts.gov.

US District Court

Southern District of Maryland

Greenbelt Division Clerk, Room 240, 6500 Cherrywood Lane, Greenbelt, MD 20770 (Courier Address: Use mail address for courier delivery), 301-344-0660.

http://www.mdd.uscourts.gov

Counties: Calvert, Charles, Montgomery, Prince George's, St. Mary's.

Indexing/Storage: Cases are indexed by defendant and plaintiff as well as by case number. New cases are available in the index 3 days after filing date. Both computer and card indexes are maintained. Case records indexed on computer since 1990. Open records are located at this court.

Fee & Payment: The fee is $20.00 per item (one party name or case number). Payment may be made by money order, cashier check, personal check. Prepayment is required. Payee: Clerk, USDC. Certification fee: $7.00 per document. Copy fee: $.50 per page.

Phone Search: The court will verify information over the phone, but will not read long dockets.

Fax Search: To arrange a fax request, contact the court's copy service, Office Solutions, at 301-982-4682.

Mail Search: An outside copy service, Office Solutions, 301-982-4682, is contracted to do all searching and copies. Always enclose a stamped self addressed envelope.

In Person: In person searching is available.

PACER: Sign-up number is 800-676-6856. Access fee is $.60 per minute. Toll-free access: 800-241-2259. Local access: 410-962-1812. Case records are available back to October 1990. Records are purged every six months. New records are available online after 1 day. PACER is available online at http://pacer.mdd.uscourts.gov.

Opinions Online: Court opinions are available online at http://www.mdd.uscourts.gov

US Bankruptcy Court

Southern District of Maryland

Greenbelt Division 6500 Cherrywood Ln, #300, Greenbelt, MD 20770 (Courier Address: Use mail address for courier delivery), 301-344-8018.

http://www.mdb.uscourts.gov

Counties: Allegany, Calvert, Charles, Frederick, Garrett, Montgomery, Prince George's, St. Mary's, Washington.

Indexing/Storage: Cases are indexed by debtor as well as by case number. New cases are available in the index 2-3 days after filing date. A computer index is maintained. The name and/or case number of the debtor(s) as well as specific identification of the pleading involved are required to search for a record. Open records are located at this court.

Fee & Payment: The fee is $20.00 per item (one party name or case number). Payment may be made by money order, cashier check, personal check. The copy fee for in house copy work (4 pages or less and copies that need to be certified) is $.50 per page and is done on an "as time permits" basis. Copy work of 5 pages or more is done off premises at a cost of $.35 per page. Payee: Clerk, US Bankruptcy Court. Certification fee: $7.00 per document.

Phone Search: Only docket information is available by phone. An automated voice case information service (VCIS) is available. Call VCIS at 800-829-0145 or 410-962-0733.

Mail Search: Open cases are searched by IKON Office Solutions, 301-982-4682. A stamped self addressed envelope is not required.

In Person: In person searching is available.

PACER: Sign-up number is 800-676-6856. Access fee is $.60 per minute. Toll-free access: 800-927-0474. Local access: 410-962-0776. Case records are available back to mid 1991. Records are purged every six months. New civil records are available online after 2 days. PACER is available online at http://pacer.mdb.uscourts.gov.

Maryland County Courts

Court	Jurisdiction	No. of Courts	How Organized
Circuit Courts*	General	25	8 Circuits
District Courts*	Limited	26	12 Districts
Orphan's Courts*	Probate	24	Register of Wills

* Profiled in this Sourcebook.

Court	CIVIL								
	Tort	Contract	Real Estate	Min. Claim	Max. Claim	Small Claims	Estate	Eviction	Domestic Relations
Circuit Courts*	X	X	X	$25000	No Max				X
District Courts*	X	X	X	$2500	$25000	$2500		X	X
Orphan's Courts*							X		

Court	CRIMINAL				
	Felony	Misdemeanor	DWI/DUI	Preliminary Hearing	Juvenile
Circuit Courts*	X	X			X
District Courts*		X	X	X	X
Orphan's Courts*					

ADMINISTRATION

Court Administrator, Administrative Office of the Courts, 361 Rowe Blvd, Courts of Appeal Building, Annapolis, MD, 21401; 410-260-1400, Fax: 410-974-2169.

www.courts.state.md.us

COURT STRUCTURE

The Ciruit court is the highest court of record. Effective 10/1/98, the civil judgment limit increased from $20,000 to $25,000 at the District Court level.

Certain categories of minor felonies are handled by the District Courts. However, all misdemeanors and felonies that require a jury trial are handled by Circuit Courts.

ONLINE ACCESS

An online computer system called the Judicial Information System (JIS) or (SJIS) provides access to civil and criminal case information from the following:

    All District Courts - All civil and all misdemeanors

    Circuit Courts Civil - All Circuit Courts are online through JIS except Montgomery and Prince George who have their own systems.

    Circuit Courts Criminal - Three courts are on JIS - Anne Arundel, Carroll county, and Baltimore City Court

Inquiries may be made to: the District Court traffic system for case information data, calendar information data, court schedule data, or officer schedule data; the District Court criminal system for case information data or calendar caseload data; the District Court civil system for case information data, attorney name and address data; the land records system for land and plat records. The one-time fee for JIS access is $50.00, which must be included with the application, and there is a charge of $5.00 per hour for access time, with a $10.00 minimum per month. For additional information or to receive a registration packet, write or call Judicial Information Systems, Security Administrator, 2661 Riva Rd., Suite 900, Annapolis, MD 21401, 410-260-1031.

PROBATE COURTS

The Circuit Court handles Probate in Montgomery and Harford counties. In other counties, probate is handled by the Register of Wills and is a county, not a court, function.

Allegany County

4th Judicial Circuit Court 30 Washington St, PO Box 359, Cumberland, MD 21502; 301-777-5922; Fax: 301-777-2100. Hours: 8AM-4:30PM (EST). *Felony, Misdemeanor, Civil Actions Over $25,000.*

Civil Records: Access: Phone, fax, mail, online, in person. Visitors must perform in person searches for themselves. No search fee. Required to search: name, years to search. Civil cases indexed by defendant, plaintiff. Civil records on computer since 11/92, archived and indexed from 1790. Online access available through SJIS. See state introduction or visit www.courts.state.md.us.
Criminal Records: Access: In person only. Visitors must perform in person searches for themselves. No search fee. Required to search: name, years to search; also helpful: DOB. Criminal records on computer since 9/99, archived and indexed from 1790.
General Information: Public Access terminal is available. No adoptions, juvenile, sealed, expunged or mental records released. SASE required. Copy fee: $.50 per page. Certification fee: $5.00 per instrument. Fee payee: Circuit Court. Personal checks accepted. Prepayment is required.

District Court 3 Pershing St, 2nd Floor, Cumberland, MD 21502; 301-777-2105. Hours: 8:30AM-4:30PM (EST). *Misdemeanor, Civil Actions Under $25,000, Eviction, Small Claims.*

Civil Records: Access: Mail, online, in person. Both court and visitors may perform in person searches. No search fee. Required to search: name, years to search. Civil cases indexed by defendant. Civil records on computer from 1990, on index books from 1970. Online access available through SJIS. See state introduction or visit www.courts.state.md.us. Court will only conduct a search if requester provides case number.
Criminal Records: Access: Mail, online, in person. Both court and visitors may perform in person searches. No search fee. Required to search: name, years to search, signed release; also helpful: SSN. Criminal records on computer from 1980, index books. Online access to criminal records is the same as civil. Court requires a case number for a search.
General Information: No adoptions, juvenile, sealed, expunged or mental records released. SASE required. Turnaround time 7 days. Copy fee: $.25 per page. Certification fee: $5.00 per page. Fee payee: District Court of MD. Personal checks accepted. Prepayment is required.

Register of Wills Courthouse, 30 Washington St, Rm 2, Cumberland, MD 21502; 301-724-3760, 888-724-0148 in MD; Fax: 301-724-1249. Hours: 8AM-4:30PM (EST). *Probate.*

www.registers.state.md.us/county/al/html/allegany.html

Anne Arundel County

5th Judicial Circuit Court Box 71, Annapolis, MD 21404; 410-222-1397. Hours: 8:30AM-4:30PM (EST). *Felony, Misdemeanor, Civil Actions Over $25,000.*

Civil Records: Access: Phone, mail, online, in person. Both court and visitors may perform in person searches. No search fee. Required to search: name, years to search. Civil cases indexed by defendant, plaintiff. Civil records on computer from 1991, on index from 1900. Online access available through SJIS. See state introduction or visit www.courts.state.md.us.
Criminal Records: Access: Phone, mail, online, in person. Both court and visitors may perform in person searches. No search fee. Required to search: name, years to search; also helpful: SSN. Criminal records on computer from 1988, indexed from 1960, archived from

1900. Online access to criminal records is the same as civil.
General Information: Public Access terminal is available. No adoptions, juvenile, sealed, expunged or mental records released. SASE required. Turnaround time 1 week. Copy fee: $.50 per page. Certification fee: $5.00. Fee payee: Clerk of Circuit Court. Personal checks accepted. Prepayment is required.

District Court 251 Rowe Blvd, #141, Annapolis, MD 21401; 410-260-1370. Hours: 8:30AM-4:30PM (EST). *Misdemeanor, Civil Actions Under $25,000, Eviction, Small Claims.*

Civil Records: Access: Mail, online, in person. Both court and visitors may perform in person searches. No search fee. Required to search: name, years to search. Civil cases indexed by defendant. Civil records on computer from 1982, archived and indexed from 1900s. Online access available through SJIS. See state introduction or visit www.courts.state.md.us.
Criminal Records: Access: Mail, online, in person. Both court and visitors may perform in person searches. No search fee. Required to search: name, years to search; also helpful: SSN. Criminal records on computer from 1982, archived and indexed from 1900s. Online access to criminal records is the same as civil.
General Information: Public Access terminal is available. SASE required. Turnaround time 1 day. Copy fee: $.25 per page. Certification fee: $5.00. Fee payee: District Court. Personal checks accepted. Prepayment is required.

Register of Wills PO Box 2368 (44 Calvert St), Annapolis, MD 21404-2368; 410-222-1430, 800-679-6665 in MD; Fax: 410-222-1467. Hours: 8:30AM-4PM (EST). *Probate.*

www.registers.state.md.us/county/aa/html/annearundel.html

Note: Wills only, no genealogy searches

Baltimore County

3rd Judicial Circuit Court 401 Bosley Ave, 2nd Floor, Towson, MD 21204; 410-887-2601. Hours: 8:30AM-4:30PM (EST). *Felony, Misdemeanor, Civil Actions Over $25,000.*

Civil Records: Access: Online, in person. Visitors must perform in person searches for themselves. No search fee. Required to search: name, years to search; also helpful: address. Civil cases indexed by defendant, plaintiff. Civil records in books, file jackets. Online access available through SJIS. See state introduction or visit www.courts.state.md.us.
Criminal Records: Access: In person only. Visitors must perform in person searches for themselves. No search fee. Required to search: name, years to search; also helpful: address, DOB, SSN. Criminal records on computer from 1984, prior on books.
General Information: Public Access terminal is available. (Civil only.) No adoptions, juvenile, sealed, expunged or mental records released. Copy fee: $.50 per page. Certification fee: $5.00 per page. Fee payee: Suzanne Mensh, Clerk. Personal checks accepted. Out of state checks not accepted. Prepayment is required.

District Court 120 E Chesapeake Ave, Towson, MD 21286-5307; 410-512-2000; Criminal phone: 410-512-2101. Hours: 8:30AM-4:30PM (EST). *Misdemeanor, Civil Actions Under $25,000, Eviction, Small Claims.*

Civil Records: Access: Online, in person. Visitors must perform in person searches for themselves. No search fee. Required to search: name, years to search; also helpful: address. Civil cases indexed by defendant, plaintiff. Civil records on computer from 1985, on microfiche from 1971, archived from 1970, on card

index from 1971. Online access available through SJIS. See state introduction or visit www.courts.state.md.us.
Criminal Records: Access: Online, in person. Visitors must perform in person searches for themselves. No search fee. Required to search: name, years to search. Criminal records on computer since 1981. Online access to criminal records is the same as civil.
General Information: Public Access terminal is available. No adoptions, juvenile, sealed, expunged or mental records released. Copy fee: $.25 per page. Certification fee: $5.00. Fee payee: District Court of MD. Personal checks accepted. Prepayment is required.

Register of Wills 401 Bosley Ave, Mail Stop 3507, Towson, MD 21204-4403; 410-887-6685, 888-642-5387 in MD; Fax: 410-583-2517. Hours: 8AM-4:30PM (EST). *Probate.*

www.registers.state.md.us/county/ba/html/baltimore.html

Baltimore City

8th Judicial Circuit Court - Civil Division 111 N Calvert, Rm 409, Baltimore, MD 21202; 410-333-3716. Hours: 8:30AM-4:30PM (EST). *Civil Actions Over $25,000.*

Civil Records: Access: Phone, mail, online, in person. Both court and visitors may perform in person searches. No search fee. Required to search: name, years to search; also helpful: address. Civil cases indexed by defendant. Civil records on computer from 1983. Online access available through SJIS. See state introduction or visit www.courts.state.md.us. Court conducts searches on a limited basis.
General Information: Public Access terminal is available. No adoptions, juvenile, sealed, expunged or mental records released. SASE not required. Turnaround time 5 days. Copy fee: $.50 per page. Certification fee: $5.00. Fee payee: Clerk of the Circuit Court. Business checks accepted. Prepayment is required.

8th Judicial Circuit Court - Criminal Division 110 N Calvert Rm 200, Baltimore, MD 21202; 410-333-3750. Hours: 8:30AM-4:30PM (EST). *Felony, Misdemeanor.*

Criminal Records: Access: Online, in person. Visitors must perform in person searches for themselves. No search fee. Required to search: name, years to search; also helpful: address, DOB. Criminal records on computer from 1994, on microfilm from 1973. Online access available through SJIS. See state introduction or visit www.courts.state.md.us.
General Information: Public Access terminal is available. No adoptions, juvenile, sealed, expunged or mental records released. Copy fee: $.50 per page. Certification fee: $5.00. Fee payee: Clerk of Circuit Court. Business checks accepted.

District Court - Civil Division 501 E Fayette St, Baltimore, MD 21202; 410-878-8900. Hours: 8:30AM-4:30PM (EST). *Civil Actions Under $25,000, Eviction, Small Claims.*

Civil Records: Access: Mail, online, in person. No search fee. Required to search: name, years to search. Civil cases indexed by defendant. Civil records on computer from 1986, on card index from 1971. Online access available through SJIS. See state introduction or visit www.courts.state.md.us.
General Information: Public Access terminal is available. No medical or sealed records released. SASE required. Turnaround time 1-2 days. Copy fee: $.25 per page. Certification fee: $5.00. Fee payee: District Court of MD. Personal checks accepted. Prepayment is required.

District Court - Criminal Division 1400 E North Ave, Baltimore, MD 21213; 410-554-4227. Hours: 8AM-4:30PM (EST). *Misdemeanor.*

Criminal Records: Access: Mail, online, in person. Both court and visitors may perform in person searches. No search fee. Required to search: name, years to search; also helpful: SSN. Criminal records on computer from 1983, prior on index cards from 1970. Online access to criminal records is the same as civil.

General Information: Public Access terminal is available. No adoptions, juvenile, sealed, expunged, medical or mental records released. SASE required. Turnaround time 1 week. Copy fee: $.25 per page. Certification fee: $5.00. Fee payee: District Court. Personal checks accepted. Prepayment is required.

Register of Wills Courthouse East, 111 N Calvert St, Rm 352, Baltimore, MD 21202; 410-752-5131, 888-876-0035 in MD; Fax: 410-752-3494. Hours: 8AM-4:30PM (EST). *Probate.*

www.registers.state.md.us/city/bc/html/baltimorecity.html

Calvert County

7th Judicial Circuit Court 175 Main St Courthouse, Prince Frederick, MD 20678; 410-535-1660. Hours: 8:30AM-4:30PM (EST). *Felony, Misdemeanor, Civil Actions Over $25,000.*

www.courts.state.md.us/clerks/calvert

Civil Records: Access: Online, in person. Visitors must perform in person searches for themselves. No search fee. Required to search: name, years to search. Civil cases indexed by defendant, plaintiff. Civil records on computer back to 10/1997, prior on index books. Online access available through SJIS. See state introduction or visit www.courts.state.md.us.

Criminal Records: Access: In person only. Visitors must perform in person searches for themselves. No search fee. Required to search: name, years to search; also helpful: SSN. Criminal records on computer from 4/2000; prior in books.

General Information: Public Access terminal is available. No adoptions, juvenile, sealed, expunged or mental records released. Copy fee: $.50 per page. Certification fee: $5.00. Fee payee: Clerk of Circuit Court. Personal checks accepted. Prepayment is required.

District Court 200 Duke St Rm 2200, Prince Frederick, MD 20678; 410-535-8800. Hours: 8:30AM-4:30PM (EST). *Misdemeanor, Civil Actions Under $25,000, Eviction, Small Claims.*

Civil Records: Access: Mail, in person. Both court and visitors may perform in person searches. No search fee. Required to search: name; also helpful: address. Civil cases indexed by defendant. Civil records on computer from mid-80s, archived from 1971 to 1981, prior on Cott index. Online access available through SJIS. See state introduction or visit www.courts.state.md.us.

Criminal Records: Access: In person only. Both court and visitors may perform in person searches. No search fee. Required to search: name; also helpful: address, DOB. Criminal records on computer from 1981, archived from 1971-1981, prior on cott index. Online access to criminal records is the same as civil.

General Information: Public Access terminal is available. (Criminal & Traffic.) No adoptions, juvenile, sealed, expunged or mental records released. SASE required. Turnaround time 1-3o days. Copy fee: $.25 per page. Certification fee: $5.00. Fee payee: District Court of Maryland. Personal checks accepted. Prepayment is required.

Register of Wills Courthouse, 175 Main St, Prince Frederick, MD 20678; 410-535-0121, 888-374-0015 in MD; Fax: 410-414-3952. Hours: 8:30AM-4:30PM (EST). *Probate.*

www.registers.state.md.us/county/cv/html/calvert.html

Caroline County

2nd Judicial Circuit Court Box 458, Denton, MD 21629; 410-479-1811; Fax: 410-479-1142. Hours: 8:30AM-4:30PM (EST). *Felony, Misdemeanor, Civil Actions Over $25,000.*

Note: Misdemeanor case records held at District Court until appealed, then stored at Circuit Court.

Civil Records: Access: Online, in person. Visitors must perform in person searches for themselves. No search fee. Required to search: name, years to search; also helpful: address. Civil cases indexed by defendant, plaintiff. Civil records on computer from 4/93, card index from 1774. Online access available through SJIS. See state introduction or visit www.courts.state.md.us.

Criminal Records: Access: In person only. Visitors must perform in person searches for themselves. No search fee. Required to search: name, years to search; also helpful: address, DOB, SSN. Criminal records on computer from 4/93, card index from 1774.

General Information: Public Access terminal is available. No adoptions, juvenile, sealed, expunged or mental records released. Copy fee: $.50 per page. Certification fee: $5.00. Fee payee: F Dale Minner, Clerk. Personal checks accepted. Prepayment is required.

District Court 207 S 3rd St, Denton, MD 21629; 410-479-5800; Fax: 410-479-5808. Hours: 8AM-4:30PM (EST). *Misdemeanor, Civil Actions Under $25,000, Eviction, Small Claims.*

Civil Records: Access: Online, in person. Visitors must perform in person searches for themselves. No search fee. Required to search: name, years to search; also helpful: address. Civil cases indexed by defendant. Civil records on cards from 1971, archived. Online access available through SJIS. See state introduction or visit www.courts.state.md.us.

Criminal Records: Access: Online, in person. Visitors must perform in person searches for themselves. No search fee. Required to search: name, years to search; also helpful: address, DOB, SSN. Criminal records on cards from 1971, archived. Online access to criminal records is the same as civil.

General Information: No adoptions, juvenile, sealed, expunged or mental records released. Certification fee: $5.00. Fee payee: District Court. Personal checks accepted. Prepayment is required.

Register of Wills County Courthouse, 109 Market St, Rm 108, PO Box 416, Denton, MD 21629; 410-479-0717, 888-786-0019 in MD; Fax: 410-479-4983. Hours: 8AM-4:30PM (EST). *Probate.*

www.registers.state.md.us/county/ca/html/caroline.html

Carroll County

5th Judicial Circuit Court 55 N Court Street, Westminster, MD 21157; 410-386-2642; Fax: 410-876-0822. Hours: 8:30AM-4:30PM (EST). *Felony, Misdemeanor, Civil Actions Over $25,000.*

Civil Records: Access: Online, in person. Visitors must perform in person searches for themselves. No search fee. Required to search: name; also helpful: years to search. Civil cases indexed by defendant, plaintiff. Civil records on computer from 1990, on card books from 1837 to 1990. Online access available through SJIS. See state introduction or visit www.courts.state.md.us.

Criminal Records: Access: Online, in person. Visitors must perform in person searches for themselves. No search fee. Required to search: name; also helpful: years to search. Criminal records on computer from 1990, on

card books from 1837 to 1990. Online access to criminal records is the same as civil.

General Information: Public Access terminal is available. No adoptions, juvenile, sealed, expunged or mental records released. Copy fee: $.50 per page. Certification fee: $5.00 per document. Fee payee: Clerk of Court. Personal checks accepted. Credit cards accepted: Visa, MasterCard.

District Court 55 N Court St, Westminster, MD 21157; 410-386-2365. Hours: 8:30AM-4:30PM (EST). *Misdemeanor, Civil Actions Under $25,000, Eviction, Small Claims.*

Civil Records: Access: Online, in person. Visitors must perform in person searches for themselves. No search fee. Required to search: name, years to search. Civil cases indexed by defendant, plaintiff. Civil records on computer back to 1984; on card index from 1971. Online access available through SJIS. See state introduction or visit www.courts.state.md.us.

Criminal Records: Access: Online, in person. Visitors must perform in person searches for themselves. No search fee. Required to search: name, years to search; also helpful: DOB, SSN. Criminal records on computer back to 1984; on card index from 1971. Online access to criminal records is the same as civil.

General Information: Public Access terminal is available. No adoptions, juvenile, sealed, expunged or mental records released. Copy fee: $.25 per page. Certification fee: $5.00 per document. Fee payee: District Court. Personal checks accepted. Prepayment is required.

Register of Wills 55 N Court St, Rm 104, Westminster, MD 21157; 410-848-2586, 888-876-0034 in MD; Fax: 410-876-0657. Hours: 8:30AM-4:30PM (EST). *Probate.*

www.registers.state.md.us/county/cr/html/carroll.html

Cecil County

2nd Judicial Circuit Court 129 E Main St, Rm 108, Elkton, MD 21921; 410-996-5373; Fax: 410-392-6032. Hours: 8:30AM-4:30PM (EST). *Felony, Misdemeanor, Civil Actions Over $25,000.*

Civil Records: Access: Online, in person. Visitors must perform in person searches for themselves. No search fee. Required to search: name, years to search. Civil cases indexed by defendant. Civil records on card index from 1948. Online access available through SJIS. See state introduction or visit www.courts.state.md.us.

Criminal Records: Access: Online, in person. Visitors must perform in person searches for themselves. No search fee. Required to search: name, years to search; also helpful: DOB, SSN. Criminal records on card index from 1948. Online access to criminal records is the same as civil.

General Information: No adoptions, juvenile, sealed, expunged or mental records released. Certification fee: $5.00 per page. Fee payee: Clerk of Court. Personal checks accepted. Prepayment is required.

District Court 170 E Main St, Elkton, MD 21921; 410-996-0700. Hours: 8:30AM-4:30PM (EST). *Misdemeanor, Civil Actions Under $25,000, Eviction, Small Claims.*

Civil Records: Access: Online, in person. Visitors must perform in person searches for themselves. No search fee. Required to search: name, years to search. Civil cases indexed by defendant. Civil records on computer from 1983, on card index from 1973. Online access available through SJIS. See state introduction or visit www.courts.state.md.us.

Criminal Records: Access: Online, in person. Visitors must perform in person searches for themselves. No search fee. Required to search: name, years to search. Criminal records on computer from 1983, on card index from 1973. Online access to criminal records is the same as civil.

General Information: Public Access terminal is available. No adoptions, juvenile, sealed, expunged or mental records released. Copy fee: $.25 per page. Certification fee: $5.00. Fee payee: District Court. Personal checks accepted. Prepayment is required.

Register of Wills County Courthouse, Suite 101, PO Box 468, Elkton, MD 21922; 410-398-2737, 888-398-0301 in MD; Fax: 410-620-3849. Hours: 8:30AM-4:30PM (EST). *Probate.*

www.registers.state.md.us/county/ce/html/cecil.html

Charles County

Circuit Court for Charles County PO Box 970, La Plata, MD 20646; 301-932-3201. Hours: 8:30AM-4:30PM (EST). *Felony, Misdemeanor, Civil Actions Over $25,000.*

Civil Records: Access: Online, in person. Visitors must perform in person searches for themselves. No search fee. Required to search: name, years to search. Civil cases indexed by defendant, plaintiff. Civil records on index books from 1950, on computer back to 1996. Online access available through SJIS. See state introduction or visit www.courts.state.md.us.

Criminal Records: Access: In person only. Visitors must perform in person searches for themselves. No search fee. Required to search: name, years to search. Criminal records on index books from 1950, on computer back to 1996.

General Information: Public Access terminal is available. No adoptions, juvenile, sealed, expunged or medical records released. Copy fee: $.50 per page. Certification fee: $5.00. Fee payee: Clerk of the Circuit Court. Personal checks accepted. Prepayment is required.

District Court PO Box 3070, La Plata, MD 20646; 301-932-3300; Civil phone: 301-932-3290; Criminal phone: 301-932-3295. Hours: 8:30AM-4:30PM (EST). *Misdemeanor, Civil Actions Under $25,000, Eviction, Small Claims.*

Civil Records: Access: Online, in person. Visitors must perform in person searches for themselves. No search fee. Required to search: name, years to search. Civil cases indexed by defendant, plaintiff. Civil records on computer from 1987, on card index from 1980. Online access available through SJIS. See state introduction or visit www.courts.state.md.us.

Criminal Records: Access: Online, in person. Visitors must perform in person searches for themselves. No search fee. Required to search: name, years to search. Criminal records on computer from 1984, on card index from 1980, from 09/98 on public access terminal. Online access to criminal records is the same as civil.

General Information: Public Access terminal is available. (For civil inquiry.) No confidential info, unserved warrants, medical records released. Copy fee: $.25 per page. Certification fee: $5.00. Fee payee: District Court. Personal checks accepted. Prepayment is required.

Register of Wills Box 3080 (Courthouse, 200 E Charles St), La Plata, MD 20646; 301-932-3345, 888-256-0054 in MD; Fax: 301-932-3349. Hours: 8:30AM-4:30PM (EST). *Probate.*

www.registers.state.md.us/county/ch/html/charles.html

Dorchester County

1st Judicial Circuit Court Box 150, Cambridge, MD 21613; 410-228-0481. Hours: 8:30AM-4:30PM (EST). *Felony, Misdemeanor, Civil Actions Over $25,000.*

Civil Records: Access: Online, in person. Visitors must perform in person searches for themselves. No search

fee. Required to search: name, years to search. Civil cases indexed by defendant, plaintiff. Civil records on computer from 1984. Online access available through SJIS. See state introduction or visit www.courts.state.md.us.

Criminal Records: Access: In person only. Visitors must perform in person searches for themselves. No search fee. Required to search: name, years to search. Criminal records on computer from 1984.

General Information: Public Access terminal is available. No adoptions, juvenile, sealed, expunged or mental records released. Copy fee: $.25 per page. Certification fee: $5.00. Fee payee: Clerk of Circuit Court.

District Court Box 547, Cambridge, MD 21613; 410-221-2580. Hours: 8:30AM-4:30PM (EST). *Misdemeanor, Civil Actions Under $25,000, Eviction, Small Claims.*

Civil Records: Access: Online, in person. Visitors must perform in person searches for themselves. No search fee. Required to search: name, years to search; also helpful: address. Civil cases indexed by defendant. Civil records archived and indexed from 1971. Online access available through SJIS. See state introduction or visit www.courts.state.md.us.

Criminal Records: Access: Online, in person. Visitors must perform in person searches for themselves. No search fee. Required to search: name, years to search; also helpful: address, DOB, SSN. Criminal records on card index from 1971. Online access to criminal records is the same as civil.

General Information: Public Access terminal is available. No adoptions, sealed, juvenile, expunged or mental records released. Certification fee: $5.00 per page. Fee payee: District Court. Personal checks accepted. Prepayment is required.

Register of Wills 206 High St, Cambridge, MD 21613; 410-228-4181, 888-242-6257 in MD; Fax: 410-228-4988. Hours: 8AM-4:30PM; Public hours 8:30AM-4:30PM (EST). *Probate.*

www.registers.state.md.us/county/do/html/dorchester.html

Frederick County

6th Judicial Circuit Court 100 W Patrick St, Frederick, MD 21701; 301-694-1972. Hours: 8AM-4:30PM (EST). *Felony, Misdemeanor, Civil Actions Over $25,000.*

Civil Records: Access: Online, in person. Visitors must perform in person searches for themselves. No search fee. Required to search: name, years to search. Civil cases indexed by defendant, plaintiff. Civil records on computer from 08/94, prior on card books. Online access available through SJIS. See state introduction or visit www.courts.state.md.us.

Criminal Records: Access: In person only. Visitors must perform in person searches for themselves. No search fee. Required to search: name, years to search. Criminal records on computer from 12/81, prior on index books.

General Information: Public Access terminal is available. No adoptions, juvenile, sealed, expunged or mental records released. Copy fee: $.50 per page. Certification fee: $5.00. Fee payee: Clerk of Circuit Court. Personal checks accepted. Prepayment is required.

District Court 100 W Patrick St, Frederick, MD 21701; 301-694-2000. Hours: 8:30AM-4:30PM (EST). *Misdemeanor, Civil Actions Under $25,000, Eviction, Small Claims.*

Civil Records: Access: Phone, mail, online, in person. Both court and visitors may perform in person searches. No search fee. Required to search: name; also helpful: years to search. Civil cases indexed by defendant,

plaintiff. Civil records on computer and microfiche from 1982, archived and on card index from 1971. Online access available through SJIS. See state introduction or visit www.courts.state.md.us.

Criminal Records: Access: Phone, mail, online, in person. Both court and visitors may perform in person searches. No search fee. Required to search: name, DOB; also helpful: years to search. Criminal records on computer and microfiche from 1982, archived and on card index from 1971. Online access to criminal records is the same as civil.

General Information: Public Access terminal is available. No adoptions, juvenile, sealed, expunged or mental records released. SASE not required. Turnaround time 30 days. Copy fee: $1.00 per page. Certification fee: $5.00. Fee payee: District Court. Personal checks accepted. Credit cards accepted: Visa, MasterCard, AmEx. Prepayment is required.

Register of Wills 100 W Patrick St, Frederick, MD 21701; 301-663-3722, 888-258-0526; Fax: 301-846-0744. Hours: 8AM-4:30PM (EST). *Probate.*

www.registers.state.md.us/county/fr/html/frederick.html

Garrett County

4th Judicial Circuit Court PO Box 447, Oakland, MD 21550; 301-334-1937; Fax: 301-334-5017. Hours: 8:30AM-4:30PM (EST). *Felony, Misdemeanor, Civil Actions Over $25,000.*

Civil Records: Access: Mail, online, in person. No search fee. Required to search: name, years to search. Civil cases indexed by defendant, plaintiff. Civil records on computer since 11/97. Online access available through SJIS. See state introduction or visit www.courts.state.md.us.

Criminal Records: Access: Mail, in person. Both court and visitors may perform in person searches. No search fee. Required to search: name, years to search, DOB. Criminal records on computer since 11/97.

General Information: Public Access terminal is available. No adoptions, juvenile, sealed, expunged or mental records released. SASE not required. Turnaround time 1 day. Copy fee: $.50 per page. Certification fee: $5.00 per page. Fee payee: David K Martin, Clerk. Personal checks accepted. Prepayment is required.

District Court 205 S 3rd St, Oakland, MD 21550; 301-334-8164. Hours: 8:30AM-4:30PM (EST). *Misdemeanor, Civil Actions Under $25,000, Eviction, Small Claims.*

www.courts.state.md.us/district/dcgarrett.html

Civil Records: Access: Mail, online, in person. Both court and visitors may perform in person searches. No search fee. Required to search: name, years to search. Civil cases indexed by defendant. Civil records on computer from 1990, on index books from 1971. Online access available through SJIS. See state introduction or visit www.courts.state.md.us.

Criminal Records: Access: Online, in person. Visitors must perform in person searches for themselves. No search fee. Required to search: name, years to search, DOB. Criminal records on computer from 1981. Online access to criminal records is the same as civil.

General Information: No adoptions, juvenile, sealed, expunged or mental records released. SASE required. Turnaround time 1 week. Copy fee: $.25 per page. Certification fee: $5.00 per page. Fee payee: District Court. Personal checks accepted. Prepayment is required.

Register of Wills Courthouse, 313 E Alder St, Room 103, Oakland, MD 21550; 301-334-1999, 888-334-2203 in MD; Fax: 301-334-1984. Hours: 8AM-4:30PM (EST). *Probate.*

www.registers.state.md.us/county/ga/html/garrett.html

Harford County

3rd Judicial Circuit 20 W Courtland St, Bel Air, MD 21014; 410-638-3426. Hours: 8:30AM-4:30PM (EST). *Felony, Misdemeanor, Civil Actions Over $25,000.*

www.courts.state.md.us

Civil Records: Access: Online, in person. Visitors must perform in person searches for themselves. No search fee. Required to search: name, years to search; also helpful: address. Civil cases indexed by defendant, plaintiff. Civil records on computer since 08/92 and on books prior. Online access available through SJIS. See state introduction or visit www.courts.state.md.us.
Criminal Records: Access: In person only. Visitors must perform in person searches for themselves. No search fee. Required to search: name, years to search; also helpful: DOB. Criminal records on computer since 08/92 and on books prior.
General Information: Public Access terminal is available. No adoptions, presentence investigations, juvenile, sealed, expunged or mental records released. Copy fee: $.50 per page. Certification fee: $5.00. Fee payee: Clerk of the Circuit Court. Only cashiers checks and money orders accepted. Prepayment is required.

District Court 2 S Bond St, Bel Air, MD 21014; 410-838-2300. Hours: 8:30AM-4:30PM (EST). *Misdemeanor, Civil Actions Under $25,000, Eviction, Small Claims.*

Civil Records: Access: Mail, online, in person. Both court and visitors may perform in person searches. No search fee. Required to search: name, years to search. Civil cases indexed by defendant. Civil records on computer from 1981, on microfiche from 1972, archived from 1900. Online access available through SJIS. See state introduction or visit www.courts.state.md.us.
Criminal Records: Access: Mail, online, in person. Both court and visitors may perform in person searches. No search fee. Required to search: name, years to search; also helpful: address, DOB. Criminal records on computer from 1981, on microfiche from 1972, archived from 1900. Online access to criminal records is the same as civil.
General Information: Public Access terminal is available. No adoptions, motor vehicle, juvenile, sealed, expunged or mental records released. SASE required. Turnaround time 3-4 days. Copy fee: $.25 per page. Certification fee: $5.00. Fee payee: District Court of MD. Personal checks accepted. Credit cards accepted: Visa. Prepayment is required.

Register of Wills 20 W Courtland St, Room 304, Bel Air, MD 21014; 410-638-3275, 888-258-0525 in MD; Fax: 410-893-3177. Hours: 8:30AM-4:30PM (EST). *Probate.*

www.registers.state.md.us/county/ha/html/harford.html

Howard County

5th Judicial Circuit Court 8360 Court Ave, Ellicott City, MD 21043; 410-313-2111. Hours: 8:30AM-4:30PM (EST). *Felony, Misdemeanor, Civil Actions Over $25,000.*
Civil Records: Access: Online, in person. Visitors must perform in person searches for themselves. No search fee. Required to search: name, years to search; also helpful: address. Civil cases indexed by defendant, plaintiff. Civil records on computer from 1984, archived from 1900, on card index from 1900. Online access available through SJIS. See state introduction or visit www.courts.state.md.us.
Criminal Records: Access: In person only. Visitors must perform in person searches for themselves. No search fee. Required to search: name, years to search; also helpful: address, DOB, SSN. Criminal records on card index.

General Information: Public Access terminal is available. No adoptions, juvenile, sealed, expunged or mental records released. Certification fee: $5.00 per page. Payee: Office of Clerk. Personal checks accepted.

District Court 3451 Courthouse Dr, Ellicott City, MD 21043; 410-461-0200. Hours: 8:30AM-4:30PM (EST). *Misdemeanor, Civil Actions Under $25,000, Eviction, Small Claims.*

Civil Records: Access: Mail, online, in person. Both court and visitors may perform in person searches. No search fee. Required to search: name, years to search. Civil cases indexed by defendant. Civil records on computer from 1989, on card index prior. Online access available through SJIS. See state introduction or visit www.courts.state.md.us.
Criminal Records: Access: Mail, online, in person. Both court and visitors may perform in person searches. No search fee. Required to search: name, years to search. Criminal records on computer from 1989, on card index prior. Online access to criminal records is the same as civil.
General Information: Public Access terminal is available. No adoptions, juvenile, sealed, expunged or mental records released. SASE required if return receipt requested. Turnaround time before 1989 4-6 weeks, 1989-present 7 days. Copy fee: $.25 per page. Certification: $5.00. Fee payee: District Court of MD. Personal checks accepted. Credit cards accepted: Visa.

Register of Wills 8360 Court Ave, Ellicott City, MD 21043; 410-313-2133, 888-848-0136 in MD; Fax: 410-313-3409. Hours: 8:30AM-4:30PM *Probate.*

www.registers.state.md.us/county/ho/html/howard.html

Kent County

2nd Judicial Circuit Court 103 N Cross St Courthouse, Chestertown, MD 21620; 410-778-7460; Fax: 410-778-7412. Hours: 8:30AM-4:30PM (EST). *Felony, Misdemeanor, Civil Actions Over $25,000.*

www.courts.state.md.us/clerks/kent/records.html

Civil Records: Access: Online, in person. Visitors must perform in person searches for themselves. No search fee. Required to search: name, years to search. Civil cases indexed by defendant, plaintiff. Civil records on computer from 1991, on card index from 1656. Online access available through SJIS. See state introduction or visit www.courts.state.md.us.
Criminal Records: Access: Online, in person. Visitors must perform in person searches for themselves. No search fee. Required to search: name, years to search; also helpful: DOB, SSN. Criminal records on computer from 1991, on card index from 1656. Online access to criminal records is the same as civil.
General Information: Public Access terminal is available. No adoptions, juvenile, sealed, expunged or mental records released. Copy fee: $.50 per page. Certification fee: $5.00. Fee payee: Mark L Mumford, Clerk. Personal checks accepted. Prepayment required.

District Court 103 N Cross St, Chestertown, MD 21620; 410-810-3362; Fax: 410-810-3361. Hours: 8:30AM-4:30PM (EST). *Misdemeanor, Civil Actions Under $25,000, Eviction, Small Claims.*

Civil Records: Access: Online, in person. Visitors must perform in person searches for themselves. No search fee. Required to search: name, years to search. Civil cases indexed by defendant. Civil records on computer from 1989; on card index from 1971. Online access available through SJIS. See state introduction or visit www.courts.state.md.us.
Criminal Records: Access: Online, in person. Visitors must perform in person searches for themselves. No search fee. Required to search: name, years to search, DOB. Criminal records on computer from 1988, on card index from 1971. Online access to criminal records is the same as civil.

General Information: No sealed, expunged, mental records or judge's notes released. Copy fee: $.25 per page. Certification fee: $5.00 per page. Fee payee: District Court of MD. Personal checks accepted. Credit cards accepted: Visa, Discover.

Register of Wills 103 N Cross St, Chestertown, MD 21620; 410-778-7466, 888-778-0179 in MD; Fax: 410-778-2466. Hours: 8AM-4:30PM (EST). *Probate.*

www.registers.state.md.us/county/ke/html/kent.html

Montgomery County

6th Judicial Circuit Court 50 Maryland Ave, Rockville, MD 20850; 240-777-9466. Hours: 8:30AM-4:30PM (EST). *Felony, Misdemeanor, Civil Actions Over $25,000.*

www.co.mo.md.us/judicial

Civil Records: Access: In person only. Visitors must perform in person searches for themselves. No search fee. Required to search: name, years to search; also helpful: case number. Civil cases indexed by defendant, plaintiff. Civil records on computer from 1977, archived from 1900, on card index from 1977.
Criminal Records: Access: In person only. Visitors must perform in person searches for themselves. No search fee. Required to search: name, years to search; also helpful: case number. Criminal records on computer from 1977, archived from 1900, on card index from 1977.
General Information: Public Access terminal is available. No adoptions, juvenile, sealed, expunged or mental records released. Copy fee: $.50. Certification fee: $5.00. Plus $.50 per page. Fee payee: Clerk of Circuit Court. Personal checks accepted. Prepayment is required.

District Court 8665 Georgia Ave, Silver Spring, MD 20910; 301-608-0660. Hours: 8:30AM-4:30PM (EST). *Misdemeanor, Civil Actions Under $25,000, Eviction, Small Claims.*

Civil Records: Access: Mail, online, in person. Both court and visitors may perform in person searches. No search fee. Required to search: name, years to search. Civil cases indexed by defendant, plaintiff. Civil records on computer from 1986, on card index and case folder. Online access available through SJIS. See state introduction or visit www.courts.state.md.us.
Criminal Records: Access: Mail, online, in person. Both court and visitors may perform in person searches. No search fee. Required to search: name, years to search. Criminal records on computer, index book and case folder. Online access to criminal records is the same as civil.
General Information: Public Access terminal is available. No juvenile, sealed, expunged or mental records or judge's notes released. SASE required. Turnaround time 2-4 weeks. Copy fee: $.25 per page. Certification fee: $5.00. Fee payee: District Court. Personal checks accepted. Prepayment is required.

Rockville District Court 27 Courthouse Square, Rockville, MD 20850; Civil phone: 301-279-1500; Criminal phone: 301-279-1565. Hours: 8:30AM-4:30PM (EST). *Misdemeanor, Civil Actions Under $25,000, Eviction, Small Claims.*

Civil Records: Access: Mail, online, in person. Both court and visitors may perform in person searches. No search fee. Required to search: name, years to search. Civil cases indexed by defendant. Civil records on computer from 1986, prior in case folder. Online access available through SJIS. See state introduction or visit www.courts.state.md.us.
Criminal Records: Access: Mail, online, in person. Both court and visitors may perform in person searches. No search fee. Required to search: name, years to search; also helpful: DOB, SSN. Criminal records on

computer, case folder, index book. Online access to criminal records is the same as civil.

General Information: Public Access terminal is available. No juvenile, sealed, expunged, mental records or judge's notes released. SASE required. Turnaround time 2-4 weeks. Copy fee: $.25 per page. Certification fee: $5.00 per page. Fee payee: District Court. Personal checks accepted. Prepayment is required.

Register of Wills Judicial Center, 50 Maryland Ave, #322, Rockville, MD 20850; 240-777-9680, 888-892-2180 in MD. Hours: 8:30AM-4:30PM *Probate.*

www.registers.state.md.us/county/mo/html/montgomery.html

Prince George's County

7th Judicial Circuit Court 14735 Main St, Upper Marlboro, MD 20772; Civil phone: 301-952-3240; Criminal phone: 301-952-3344. Hours: 8:30AM-4:30PM (EST). *Felony, Misdemeanor, Civil Actions Over $25,000.*

Civil Records: Access: Mail, in person. Visitors must perform in person searches for themselves. No search fee. Required to search: name, years to search. Civil cases indexed by defendant, plaintiff. Civil records on computer from 1981, on microfiche from 1979, on card index prior.

Criminal Records: Access: Mail, in person. Visitors must perform in person searches for themselves. No search fee. Required to search: name, years to search, DOB; also helpful: SSN. Criminal records on computer from 1981, on microfiche to 1979, on card index prior.

General Information: No adoptions, juvenile, sealed, expunged or mental records released. SASE not required. Copy fee: $.50 per page. Certification fee: $5.00 per page. Fee payee: Clerk of Circuit Court. Personal checks accepted. Prepayment is required.

District Court 14735 Main St, Rm 173B, Upper Marlboro, MD 20772; 301-952-4080. Hours: 8:30AM-4:30PM (EST). *Misdemeanor, Civil Actions Under $25,000, Eviction, Small Claims.*

Civil Records: Access: Mail, online, in person. No search fee. Required to search: name, years to search. Civil cases indexed by defendant. Civil records on computer from 1988, on card index from 1970. Online access available through SJIS. See state introduction or visit www.courts.state.md.us.

Criminal Records: Access: Mail, online, in person. Visitors must perform in person searches for themselves. No search fee. Required to search: name, years to search. Criminal records on computer from 1984, on cards from 1970. Online access to criminal records is the same as civil.

General Information: Public Access terminal is available. No adoptions, juvenile, sealed, expunged or mental records released. SASE required. Turnaround time 1-2 weeks. Copy fee: $.25 per page. Certification fee: $5.00 per page. Fee payee: District Court of Maryland. Personal checks accepted. Prepayment is required.

Register of Wills 14735 Main St., Room 306, Upper Marlboro, MD 20772; 301-952-3250, 888-464-4219 in MD; Fax: 301-952-4489. Hours: 8:30AM-4:30PM (EST). *Probate.*

www.registers.state.md.us/county/pg/html/princegeorges.html

Queen Anne's County

2nd Judicial Circuit Court Courthouse, 100 Courthouse Sq, Centreville, MD 21617; 410-758-1773. Hours: 8:30AM-4:30PM (EST). *Felony, Misdemeanor, Civil Actions Over $25,000.*

Note: Misdemeanor case files at District Court until appealed by jury trial.

Civil Records: Access: Online, in person. Visitors must perform in person searches for themselves. No search fee. Required to search: name, years to search. Civil cases indexed by defendant, plaintiff. Civil records on computer from 11/92; on index books from 1978. Online access available through SJIS. See state introduction or visit www.courts.state.md.us.

Criminal Records: Access: Online, in person. Visitors must perform in person searches for themselves. No search fee. Required to search: name, years to search, SSN. Criminal records on computer from 11/92; on index books from 1978. Online access to criminal records is the same as civil.

General Information: Public Access terminal is available. No adoptions, juvenile, sealed, expunged or mental records released. Certification fee: $5.00. Fee payee: Clerk of Circuit Court. Personal checks accepted. Prepayment is required.

District Court 120 Broadway, Centreville, MD 21617; 410-758-5200. Hours: 8:30AM-4:30PM (EST). *Misdemeanor, Civil Actions Under $25,000, Eviction, Small Claims.*

Civil Records: Access: Online, in person. Visitors must perform in person searches for themselves. No search fee. Required to search: name, years to search; also helpful: address. Civil cases indexed by defendant. Civil records on computer from 1988, archived from 1974, prior on index books. Online access available through SJIS. See state intro. or visit www.courts.state.md.us.

Criminal Records: Access: Online, in person. Visitors must perform in person searches for themselves. No search fee. Required to search: name, years to search; also helpful: address, DOB, SSN. Criminal records on computer from 1981, prior on index books. Online access to criminal records is the same as civil.

General Information: Public Access terminal is available. No adoptions, juvenile, sealed, expunged or mental records released. Certification fee: $5.00. Fee payee: District Court of Maryland. Personal checks accepted. Credit cards accepted: Visa, Discover.

Register of Wills Liberty Bldg, 107 N Liberty St #220, PO Box 59, Centreville, MD 21617; 410-758-0585, 888-758-0010 in MD; Fax: 410-758-4408. Hours: 8AM-4:30PM (EST). *Probate.*

www.registers.state.md.us/county/qa/html/queenannes.html

Somerset County

1st Judicial Circuit Court PO Box 99, Princess Anne, MD 21853; 410-651-1555; Fax: 410-651-1048. Hours: 8:30AM-4:30PM (EST). *Felony, Misdemeanor, Civil Actions Over $25,000.*

Civil Records: Access: Online, in person. Visitors must perform in person searches for themselves. No search fee. Required to search: name, years to search; also helpful: address. Civil cases indexed by defendant, plaintiff. Civil records on computer from 9/93; prior archived and on index books. Online access available through SJIS. See state introduction or visit www.courts.state.md.us.

Criminal Records: Access: In person only. Visitors must perform in person searches for themselves. No search fee. Required to search: name, years to search; also helpful: address, DOB, SSN. Criminal records on computer from 9/93; prior archived and on index books.

General Information: Public Access terminal is available. No adoptions, juvenile, sealed, expunged or mental records released. Copy fee: $.50 per page. Certification fee: $5.00. Fee payee: Clerk of Circuit Court. Personal checks accepted. Prepayment required.

District Court 11559 Somerset Ave, Princess Anne, MD 21853; 410-651-2713. Hours: 8:30AM-4:30PM (EST). *Misdemeanor, Civil Actions Under $25,000, Eviction, Small Claims.*

Note: Misdemeanor cases go to Circuit Court if preliminary hearing waived. Records held at court where trial heard.

Civil Records: Access: Online, in person. Visitors must perform in person searches for themselves. No search fee. Required to search: name, years to search. Civil cases indexed by defendant, plaintiff. Civil records on computer from 1987, archived and on index books from 1971. Online access available through SJIS. See state introduction or visit www.courts.state.md.us.

Criminal Records: Access: Online, in person. Visitors must perform in person searches for themselves. No search fee. Required to search: name, years to search; also helpful: SSN. Criminal records on computer from 1987, archived and on index books from 1971. Online access to criminal records is the same as civil.

General Information: Public Access terminal is available. No adoptions, juvenile, sealed, expunged or mental records released. Copy fee: $.50 per page. Certification fee: $5.00. Fee payee: District Court. Personal checks accepted. Prepayment is required.

Register of Wills 30512 Prince William St, Princess Anne, MD 21853; 410-651-1696, 888-758-0039 in MD; Fax: 410-651-3873. Hours: 8:30AM-4:30PM (EST). *Probate.*

www.registers.state.md.us/county/so/html/somerset.html

St. Mary's County

7th Judicial Circuit Court PO Box 676, Leonardtown, MD 20650; 301-475-5621. Hours: 8:30AM-4:30PM (EST). *Felony, Misdemeanor, Civil Actions Over $25,000.*

Civil Records: Access: Online, in person. Visitors must perform in person searches for themselves. No search fee. Required to search: name, years to search. Civil cases indexed by defendant, plaintiff. Civil records on computer from 1987, on card index from 1970. Online access available through SJIS. See state introduction or visit www.courts.state.md.us.

Criminal Records: Access: In person only. Visitors must perform in person searches for themselves. No search fee. Required to search: name, years to search; also helpful: SSN. Criminal records on computer from 1987, on card index from 1970.

General Information: Public Access terminal is available. No adoptions, juvenile, sealed, expunged or mental records released. Copy fee: $.50 per page. Certification fee: $5.00. Fee payee: Clerk of the Circuit Court. Personal checks accepted. Prepayment required.

District Court Carter State Office Bldg, 23110 Leonard Hall Dr, PO Box 653, Leonardtown, MD 20650; 301-475-4530; Fax: 301-475-4535. Hours: 8:30AM-4:30PM (EST). *Misdemeanor, Civil Actions Under $25,000, Eviction, Small Claims.*

Civil Records: Access: Online, in person. Visitors must perform in person searches for themselves. No search fee. Required to search: name, years to search. Civil cases indexed by defendant. Civil records on computer from 1985, archived from 1979. Online access available through SJIS. See state introduction or visit www.courts.state.md.us.

Criminal Records: Access: Online, in person. Visitors must perform in person searches for themselves. No search fee. Required to search: name, years to search; also helpful: DOB. Criminal records on computer from 1985, archived from 1979. Online access to criminal records is the same as civil.

General Information: Public Access terminal is available. No adoptions, juvenile, sealed, expunged or mental records released. Copy fee: $.25 per page. Certification fee: $10.00. Fee payee: District Court of Maryland. Personal checks accepted.

Register of Wills 41605 Court House Drive, Leonardtown, MD 20650; 301-475-5566, 888-475-4821 in MD; Fax: 301-475-4968. Hours: 8:30AM-4:30PM (EST). *Probate.*

www.registers.state.md.us/county/sm/html/stmarys.html

Talbot County

Circuit Court PO Box 723, Easton, MD 21601; 410-822-2611; Fax: 410-820-8168. Hours: 8:30AM-4:30PM (EST). *Felony, Misdemeanor, Civil Actions Over $25,000.*

Civil Records: Access: Online, in person. Visitors must perform in person searches for themselves. No search fee. Required to search: name, years to search; also helpful: address. Civil cases indexed by defendant, plaintiff. Civil records on card index from 1993. Online access available through SJIS. See state introduction or visit www.courts.state.md.us.
Criminal Records: Access: In person only. Visitors must perform in person searches for themselves. No search fee. Required to search: name, years to search; also helpful: address, DOB, SSN. Criminal records on card index from 1993.
General Information: Public Access terminal is available. No adoptions, juvenile, sealed, expunged or mental records released. Copy fee: $.50 per page. Certification fee: $5.00. Fee payee: Maryann Shorall, Clerk of Court. Personal checks accepted. Prepayment is required.

District Court 108 W Dover St, Easton, MD 21601; 410-822-2750; Fax: 410-822-1607. Hours: 8:30AM-4:30PM (EST). *Misdemeanor, Civil Actions Under $25,000, Eviction, Small Claims.*

Civil Records: Access: Online, in person. Visitors must perform in person searches for themselves. No search fee. Required to search: name, years to search. Civil cases indexed by defendant. Civil records on computer from 1988, archived and on card index from 1971. Online access available through SJIS. See state introduction or visit www.courts.state.md.us.
Criminal Records: Access: Online, in person. Visitors must perform in person searches for themselves. No search fee. Required to search: name, years to search. Criminal records on computer from 1984. Online access to criminal records is the same as civil.
General Information: No adoptions, juvenile, sealed, expunged or mental records released. Copy fee: $.25 per page. Certification fee: $5.00. Fee payee: District Court of MD. Personal checks accepted.

Register of Wills Courthouse, 11 N Washington St, Easton, MD 21601; 410-770-6700, 888-822-0039 in MD; Fax: 410-822-5452. Hours: 8AM-4:30PM (EST). *Probate.*

www.registers.state.md.us/county/ta/html/talbot.html

Washington County

Washington County Circuit Court Box 229, Hagerstown, MD 21741; 301-733-8660; Fax: 301-791-1151. Hours: 8:30AM-4:30PM (EST). *Felony, Misdemeanor, Civil Actions Over $25,000.*

Civil Records: Access: Online, in person. Visitors must perform in person searches for themselves. No search fee. Required to search: name, years to search. Civil cases indexed by defendant. Civil records on case files, docket books. Online access available through SJIS. See state introduction or visit www.courts.state.md.us.
Criminal Records: Access: In person only. Visitors must perform in person searches for themselves. No search fee. Required to search: name, years to search; also helpful: DOB. Criminal records on case files, docket books.
General Information: Public Access terminal is available. No adoptions, juvenile, sealed, expunged or

mental records released. Copy fee: $.50 per page. Certification fee: $5.00. Fee payee: Clerk of Circuit Court. Personal checks accepted. Prepayment required.

District Court 36 W Antietam St, Hagerstown, MD 21740; 240-420-4600. Hours: 8:30AM-4:30PM (EST). *Misdemeanor, Civil Actions Under $25,000, Eviction, Small Claims.*

Civil Records: Access: Phone, mail, online, in person. Both court and visitors may perform in person searches. No search fee. Required to search: name, years to search; also helpful: address. Civil cases indexed by defendant. Civil records on computer from 1986, archived and on index books from 1971. Online access available through SJIS. See state introduction or visit www.courts.state.md.us.
Criminal Records: Access: Online, in person. Visitors must perform in person searches for themselves. No search fee. Required to search: name, years to search; also helpful: address, DOB, SSN, case number. Criminal records on computer from 1982, on index books from 1971. Online access to criminal records is the same as civil.
General Information: Public Access terminal is available. No adoptions, juvenile, sealed, expunged or mental records released. SASE required. Turnaround time less than 30 days. Copy fee: $.25 per page. Certification fee: $5.00. Fee payee: District Court. Personal checks accepted. Credit cards accepted: Visa, Discover. Prepayment is required.

Register of Wills 95 W Washington, Hagerstown, MD 21740; 301-739-3612, 888-739-0013 in MD; Fax: 301-733-8636. Hours: 8:30AM-4:30PM (EST). *Probate.*

www.registers.state.md.us/county/wa/html/washington.html

Wicomico County

1st Judicial Circuit Court PO Box 198, Salisbury, MD 21803-0198; 410-543-6551; Fax: 410-548-5150. Hours: 8:30AM-4:30PM (EST). *Felony, Misdemeanor, Civil Actions Over $25,000.*

Civil Records: Access: Phone, mail, online, in person. Both court and visitors may perform in person searches. No search fee. Required to search: name, years to search. Civil cases indexed by defendant, plaintiff. Civil records on books since 1867, cases filed after 05/93 on computer. Online access available through SJIS. See state introduction or visit www.courts.state.md.us. All phone requests must include case number.
Criminal Records: Access: Phone, mail, in person. Both court and visitors may perform in person searches. No search fee. Required to search: name, years to search; also helpful: DOB, SSN. Criminal records on books since 1867, cases filed after 05/93 on computer. Phone requests must include case number.
General Information: Public Access terminal is available. No adoptions, juvenile, sealed, expunged or mental records released. SASE not required. Turnaround time 1-2 days. Copy fee: $.50 per page. Certification fee: $5.00. Fee payee: Clerk of Circuit Court. Personal checks accepted. Out of state checks not accepted. Prepayment is required.

District Court 201 Baptist St, Salisbury, MD 21801; 410-543-6600. Hours: 8:30AM-4:30PM (EST). *Misdemeanor, Civil Actions Under $25,000, Eviction, Small Claims.*

Civil Records: Access: Online, in person. Visitors must perform in person searches for themselves. No search fee. Required to search: name, years to search; also helpful: address. Civil cases indexed by defendant, plaintiff. Civil records on computer go back to 1985, archived from 1984, on card index from 1976. Online

access available through SJIS. See state introduction or visit www.courts.state.md.us.
Criminal Records: Access: Online, in person. Visitors must perform in person searches for themselves. No search fee. Required to search: name, years to search; also helpful: address, DOB. Criminal records go back to 1971; on computer back 1983. Online access to criminal records is the same as civil.
General Information: Public Access terminal is available. No adoptions, juvenile, sealed, expunged or mental records released. Copy fee: $.50. Certification fee: $5.00. Fee payee: District Court. Personal checks accepted. Prepayment is required.

Register of Wills 101 N Division St, Room 102, Salisbury, MD 21803; 410-543-6635, 888-786-0018 in MD; Fax: 410-334-3440. Hours: 8:30AM-4:30PM (EST). *Probate.*

www.registers.state.md.us/county/wi/html/wicomico.html

Worcester County

1st Judicial Circuit Court Box 40, Snow Hill, MD 21863; Civil phone: 410-632-1222; Criminal phone: 410-632-1235. Hours: 8:30AM-4:30PM (EST). *Felony, Misdemeanor, Civil Actions Over $25,000.*

Civil Records: Access: Online, in person. Visitors must perform in person searches for themselves. No search fee. Required to search: name, years to search. Civil cases indexed by defendant. Civil records on computer since 7/93, on docket books prior. Online access available through SJIS. See state introduction or visit www.courts.state.md.us.
Criminal Records: Access: In person only. Visitors must perform in person searches for themselves. No search fee. Required to search: name, years to search. Criminal records on computer since 7/93, on docket books prior.
General Information: Public Access terminal is available. No adoptions, juvenile, sealed or expunged records released. Copy fee: $.50 per page. Certification fee: $5.00. Fee payee: Clerk of Circuit Court. Personal checks accepted. Will bill copy fees to Maryland attorneys.

District Court 301 Commerce St, Snow Hill, MD 21863-1007; 410-632-2525; Fax: 410-632-2718. Hours: 8:30AM-4:30PM (EST). *Misdemeanor, Civil Actions Under $25,000, Eviction, Small Claims.*

Civil Records: Access: Online, in person. Visitors must perform in person searches for themselves. No search fee. Required to search: name, years to search; also helpful: address. Civil cases indexed by defendant. Civil records on computer since 1988. Online access available through SJIS. See state introduction or visit www.courts.state.md.us.
Criminal Records: Access: Online, in person. Visitors must perform in person searches for themselves. No search fee. Required to search: name, years to search; also helpful: address, DOB, SSN. Criminal records on computer since 1982. Online access to criminal records is the same as civil.
General Information: Public Access terminal is available. No sealed or juvenile records released. Copy fee: $.50 per page. Certification fee: $5.00 per page. Fee payee: District Court. Personal checks accepted. Prepayment is required.

Register of Wills Courthouse, 1 W Market St, Room 102, Snow Hill, MD 21863-1074; 410-632-1529, 888-256-0047 in MD; Fax: 410-632-5600. Hours: 8AM-4:30PM (EST). *Probate.*

www.registers.state.md.us/county/wo/html/worcester.html

Maryland Recording Offices

ORGANIZATION
23 counties and one independent city, 24 recording offices. The recording officer is Clerk of the Circuit Court. Baltimore City has a recording office separate from the county of Baltimore. See the City/County Locator section at the end of this chapter for ZIP Codes that include both the city and the county. The entire state is in the Eastern Time Zone (EST).

REAL ESTATE RECORDS
Counties will not perform real estate searches. Copies usually cost $.50 per page, and certification fees $5.00 per document.

UCC RECORDS
This was a dual filing state until July 1995. As of July 1995, all new UCC filings except for consumer goods, farm related and real estate related filings were submitted only to the central filing office. Starting July 2001, only real estate related filing are submitted to the Clerk of Circuit Court.

TAX LIEN RECORDS
All tax liens are filed with the county Clerk of Circuit Court. Counties will not perform name searches.

OTHER LIENS
Judgment, mechanics, county, hospital, condominium.

Allegany County

County Clerk of the Circuit Court, P.O. Box 359, Cumberland, MD 21502. 301-777-5922; Fax 301-777-2100.
Will search UCC records. This agency will not do a tax lien search. Will not search real estate records. **Other Phone Numbers:** Assessor 301-777-2108; Treasurer 301-777-5965.

Anne Arundel County

County Clerk of the Circuit Court, P.O. Box 71, Annapolis, MD 21404. 410-222-1425; Fax 410-222-1087.
Will search UCC records. This agency will not do a tax lien search. Will not search real estate records. **Other Phone Numbers:** Assessor 410-974-5727.

Baltimore City

City Clerk, 100 North Calvert Street, Room 610, Baltimore, MD 21202. 410-333-3760.
Will search UCC records. This agency will not do a tax lien search. Will not search real estate records. **Other Phone Numbers:** Assessor 401-512-4900.

Baltimore County

County Clerk of the Circuit Court, P.O. Box 6754, Baltimore, MD 21285. 410-887-2652; Fax 410-887-3062.
Will search UCC records. This agency will not do a tax lien search. Will not search real estate records. **Other Phone Numbers:** Assessor 410-321-2294.

Calvert County

County Clerk of the Circuit Court, 175 Main Street, Courthouse, Prince Frederick, MD 20678. 410-535-1660 R/E Recording: 410-535-1600 x269 UCC Recording: 410-535-1600 x269.
Will search UCC records. This agency will not do a tax lien search. Will not search real estate records. **Other Phone Numbers:** Assessor 410-535-8850; Treasurer 410-535-1600 x272.

Caroline County

County Clerk of the Circuit Court, P.O. Box 458, Denton, MD 21629. 410-479-1811; Fax 410-479-1142.
Will search UCC records. This agency will not do a tax lien search. Will not search real estate records. **Other Phone Numbers:** Assessor 410-479-5950; Treasurer 410-479-0410.

Carroll County

County Clerk of the Circuit Court, 55 North Court Street, Room G8, Westminster, MD 21157. 410-386-2022; Fax 410-876-0822.
Will search UCC records. This agency will not do a tax lien search. Will not search real estate records. **Other Phone Numbers:** Assessor 410-857-0600; Treasurer 410-386-2971; Appraiser/Auditor 410-857-0600.

Cecil County

County Clerk of the Circuit Court, 129 East Main St., Room 108, Elkton, MD 21921-5971. 410-996-5375.
Will search UCC records. This agency will not do a tax lien search. Will not search real estate records. **Other Phone Numbers:** Assessor 410-996-0525; Treasurer 410-996-5394.

Charles County

County Clerk of the Circuit Court, P.O. Box 970, La Plata, MD 20646. 301-932-3255.
Will not search UCC records. This agency will not do a tax lien search. Will not search real estate records. **Other Phone Numbers:** Assessor 301-932-2440; Treasurer 301-645-0685; Elections 301-934-8962.

Dorchester County

County Clerk of the Circuit Court, P.O. Box 150, Cambridge, MD 21613. 410-228-0481.
Will search UCC records. This agency will not do a tax lien search. Will not search real estate records. **Other Phone Numbers:** Assessor 410-228-3380.

Frederick County

County Clerk of the Circuit Court, 100 West Patrick Street, Frederick, MD 21701. 301-694-1964; Fax 301-846-2245.
Will search UCC records. This agency will not do a tax lien search. Will not search real estate records. **Other Phone Numbers:** Assessor 301-694-2040; Treasurer 301-694-1111.

Garrett County

County Clerk of the Circuit Court, P.O. Box 447, Oakland, MD 21550-0447. 301-334-1937; Fax 301-334-5017.
Will search UCC records. This agency will not do a tax lien search. Will not search real estate records. **Other Phone Numbers:** Assessor 301-334-1950; Treasurer 301-334-1965.

Harford County

County Clerk of the Circuit Court, 20 West Courtland Street, Bel Air, MD 21014. 410-638-3244.
Will not search UCC records. This agency will not do a tax lien search. Will not search real estate records. **Other Phone Numbers:** Assessor 410-838-4800; Treasurer 410-638-3269.

Howard County

County Clerk of the Circuit Court, 8360 Court Avenue, Ellicott City, MD 21043. 410-313-2111.
Will search UCC records. This agency will not do a tax lien search. Will not search real estate records. **Other Phone Numbers:** Assessor 410-461-0135.

Kent County

County Clerk of the Circuit Court, Courthouse, 103 N. Cross St., Chestertown, MD 21620. 410-778-7431.
Will search UCC records. This agency will not do a tax lien search. Will not search real estate records. **Other Phone Numbers:** Assessor 401-778-7447.

Montgomery County

County Clerk of the Circuit Court, 50 Maryland Ave., County Courthouse, Rockville, MD 20850. 301-217-7116; Fax 301-217-1635.
Will search UCC records. This agency will not do a tax lien search. Will not search real estate records. **Other Phone Numbers:** Assessor 301-279-1701; Treasurer 301-217-1070.

Prince George's County

County Clerk of the Circuit Court, 14735 Main Street, Upper Marlboro, MD 20772. 301-952-3352.
Will search UCC records. This agency will not do a tax lien search. Will not search real estate records. **Other Phone Numbers:** Assessor 301-952-2500; Treasurer 301-952-3946.

Queen Anne's County

County Clerk of the Circuit Court, 100 Court House Square, Centreville, MD 21617. 410-758-1773.
Will search UCC records. This agency will not do a tax lien search. Will not search real estate records. **Other Phone Numbers:** Assessor 410-758-5030; Treasurer 410-758-0414.

Somerset County

County Clerk of the Circuit Court, P.O. Box 99, Princess Anne, MD 21853. 410-651-1555; Fax 410-651-1048.

Will search UCC records. This agency will not do a tax lien search. Will not search real estate records. **Other Phone Numbers:** Assessor 410-651-0868; Treasurer 410-651-0440; Vital Records 410-651-1555.

St. Mary's County

County Clerk of the Circuit Court, P.O. Box 676, Leonardtown, MD 20650. 301-475-4567 R/E Recording: 301-475-4554.

Will search UCC records. This agency will not do a tax lien search. Will not search real estate records. **Other Phone Numbers:** Assessor 301-475-4610; Treasurer 301-475-4473.

Talbot County

County Clerk of the Circuit Court, P.O. Box 723, Easton, MD 21601. 410-822-2611; Fax 410-820-8168.

Will search UCC records. This agency will not do a tax lien search. Will not search real estate records. **Other Phone Numbers:** Assessor 401-819-5920.

Washington County

County Clerk of the Circuit Court, P.O. Box 229, Hagerstown, MD 21741-0229. 301-733-8660; Fax 301-791-1151.

Will search UCC records. This agency will not do a tax lien search. Will not search real estate records. **Other Phone Numbers:** Assessor 301-791-3050; Treasurer 301-733-3170.

Wicomico County

County Clerk of the Circuit Court, P.O. Box 198, Salisbury, MD 21803-0198. 410-543-6551.

Will search UCC records. This agency will not do a tax lien search. Will not search real estate records. **Other Phone Numbers:** Assessor 410-543-6623.

Worcester County

County Clerk of the Circuit Court, P.O. Box 40, Snow Hill, MD 21863-0040. 410-632-1221.

Will not search UCC records. This agency will not do a tax lien search. Will not search real estate records. **Other Phone Numbers:** Assessor 410-632-1194.

Maryland County Locator

You will usually be able to find the city name in the City/County Cross Reference below. In that case, it is a simple matter to determine the county from the cross reference. However, only the official US Postal Service city names are included in this index. There are an additional 40,000 place names that people use in their addresses. Therefore, we have also included a ZIP/City Cross Reference immediately following the City/County Cross Reference.

If you know the ZIP Code but the city name does not appear in the City/County Cross Reference index, look up the ZIP Code in the ZIP/City Cross Reference, find the city name, then look up the city name in the City/County Cross. Reference. For example, you want to know the county for an address of Menands, NY 12204. There is no "Menands" in the City/County Cross Reference. The ZIP/City Cross Reference shows that ZIP Codes 12201-12288 are for the city of Albany. Looking back in the City/County Cross Reference, Albany is in Albany County.

City/County Cross Reference

ABELL St. Mary's
ABERDEEN Harford
ABERDEEN PROVING GROUND Harford
ABINGDON Harford
ACCIDENT Garrett
ACCOKEEK (20607) Prince George's(99), Charles(1)
ADAMSTOWN Frederick
ALESIA (21107) Carroll(59), Baltimore(41)
ALLEN Wicomico
ANDREWS AIR FORCE BASE Prince George's
ANNAPOLIS Anne Arundel
ANNAPOLIS JUNCTION (20701) Howard(85), Anne Arundel(15)
AQUASCO Prince George's
ARNOLD Anne Arundel
ASHTON Montgomery
AVENUE St. Mary's
BALDWIN (21013) Baltimore(68), Harford(32)
BALTIMORE (21206) Baltimore City(83), Baltimore(17)
BALTIMORE (21209) Baltimore(52), Baltimore City(49)
BALTIMORE (21210) Baltimore City(93), Baltimore(7)
BALTIMORE (21212) Baltimore City(63), Baltimore(37)
BALTIMORE (21215) Baltimore City(91), Baltimore(10)
BALTIMORE (21224) Baltimore City(85), Baltimore(15)
BALTIMORE (21229) Baltimore City(83), Baltimore(17)
BALTIMORE (21239) Baltimore City(80), Baltimore(20)
BALTIMORE Anne Arundel
BALTIMORE Baltimore
BALTIMORE Baltimore City
BARCLAY Queen Anne's
BARNESVILLE Montgomery
BARSTOW Calvert
BARTON (21521) Allegany(72), Garrett(28)
BEALLSVILLE Montgomery
BEL AIR Harford
BEL ALTON Charles
BELCAMP Harford
BELTSVILLE Prince George's
BENEDICT Charles
BENSON Harford
BERLIN Worcester
BETHESDA Montgomery
BETHLEHEM Caroline
BETTERTON Kent
BIG POOL Washington
BISHOPVILLE Worcester
BITTINGER Garrett
BIVALVE Wicomico
BLADENSBURG Prince George's
BLOOMINGTON Garrett
BOONSBORO Washington
BORING Baltimore

BOWIE Prince George's
BOYDS Montgomery
BOZMAN Talbot
BRADDOCK HEIGHTS Frederick
BRADSHAW Baltimore
BRANDYWINE (20613) Prince George's(92), Charles(8)
BRENTWOOD Prince George's
BRINKLOW Montgomery
BROOKEVILLE (20833) Montgomery(97), Howard(3)
BROOKLANDVILLE Baltimore
BROOKLYN (21225) Baltimore City(54), Anne Arundel(46)
BROOMES ISLAND Calvert
BROWNSVILLE Washington
BRUNSWICK Frederick
BRYANS ROAD Charles
BRYANTOWN Charles
BUCKEYSTOWN Frederick
BURKITTSVILLE Frederick
BURTONSVILLE Montgomery
BUSHWOOD St. Mary's
BUTLER Baltimore
CABIN JOHN Montgomery
CALIFORNIA St. Mary's
CALLAWAY St. Mary's
CAMBRIDGE Dorchester
CAPITOL HEIGHTS Montgomery
CAPITOL HEIGHTS Prince George's
CARDIFF Harford
CASCADE (21719) Washington(99), Frederick(1)
CATONSVILLE Baltimore
CAVETOWN Washington
CECILTON Cecil
CENTREVILLE Queen Anne's
CHANCE Somerset
CHAPTICO St. Mary's
CHARLESTOWN Cecil
CHARLOTTE HALL (20622) Charles(67), St. Mary's(33)
CHASE Baltimore
CHELTENHAM Prince George's
CHESAPEAKE BEACH Calvert
CHESAPEAKE CITY Cecil
CHESTER Queen Anne's
CHESTERTOWN Kent
CHESTERTOWN Queen Anne's
CHEVY CHASE Montgomery
CHEWSVILLE Washington
CHILDS Cecil
CHURCH CREEK Dorchester
CHURCH HILL Queen Anne's
CHURCHTON Anne Arundel
CHURCHVILLE Harford
CLAIBORNE Talbot
CLARKSBURG (20871) Montgomery(90), Frederick(10)
CLARKSVILLE Howard
CLEAR SPRING Washington
CLEMENTS St. Mary's
CLINTON Prince George's

COBB ISLAND Charles
COCKEYSVILLE Baltimore
COLLEGE PARK Prince George's
COLORA Cecil
COLTONS POINT St. Mary's
COLUMBIA Howard
COMPTON St. Mary's
CONOWINGO Cecil
COOKSVILLE Howard
CORDOVA Talbot
CORRIGANVILLE Allegany
CRAPO Dorchester
CRISFIELD Somerset
CROCHERON Dorchester
CROFTON Anne Arundel
CROWNSVILLE Anne Arundel
CRUMPTON Queen Anne's
CUMBERLAND Allegany
CURTIS BAY (21226) Baltimore City(59), Anne Arundel(41)
DAMASCUS Montgomery
DAMERON St. Mary's
DAMES QUARTER Somerset
DARLINGTON Harford
DAVIDSONVILLE Anne Arundel
DAYTON Howard
DEAL ISLAND Somerset
DEALE Anne Arundel
DELMAR Wicomico
DENTON Caroline
DERWOOD Montgomery
DETOUR Carroll
DICKERSON (20842) Montgomery(86), Frederick(14)
DISTRICT HEIGHTS Prince George's
DOWELL Calvert
DRAYDEN St. Mary's
DUNDALK (21222) Baltimore(97), Baltimore City(3)
DUNKIRK (20754) Calvert(85), Anne Arundel(15)
EARLEVILLE Cecil
EAST NEW MARKET Dorchester
EASTON Talbot
ECKHART MINES Allegany
EDEN (21822) Worcester(94), Somerset(6)
EDGEWATER Anne Arundel
EDGEWOOD Harford
ELK MILLS Cecil
ELKRIDGE (99999) Howard(99), Carroll(1)
ELKTON Cecil
ELLERSLIE Allegany
ELLICOTT CITY (21043) Howard(98), Baltimore(2)
ELLICOTT CITY Howard
EMMITSBURG Frederick
ESSEX Baltimore
EWELL Somerset
FAIRPLAY Washington
FALLSTON Harford
FAULKNER Charles
FEDERALSBURG Caroline
FINKSBURG Carroll

FISHING CREEK Dorchester
FLINTSTONE Allegany
FOREST HILL Harford
FORK Baltimore
FORT GEORGE G MEADE Anne Arundel
FORT HOWARD Baltimore
FORT WASHINGTON Prince George's
FREDERICK Frederick
FREELAND Baltimore
FRIENDSHIP Anne Arundel
FRIENDSVILLE Garrett
FROSTBURG (21532) Allegany(84), Garrett(16)
FRUITLAND Wicomico
FULTON Howard
FUNKSTOWN Washington
GAITHER Carroll
GAITHERSBURG Montgomery
GALENA Kent
GALESVILLE Anne Arundel
GAMBRILLS Anne Arundel
GAPLAND Washington
GARRETT PARK Montgomery
GARRISON Baltimore
GEORGETOWN Cecil
GERMANTOWN Montgomery
GIBSON ISLAND Anne Arundel
GIRDLETREE Worcester
GLEN ARM Baltimore
GLEN BURNIE Anne Arundel
GLEN ECHO Montgomery
GLENELG Howard
GLENN DALE Prince George's
GLENWOOD Howard
GLYNDON Baltimore
GOLDSBORO Caroline
GRANTSVILLE Garrett
GRASONVILLE Queen Anne's
GREAT MILLS St. Mary's
GREENBELT Prince George's
GREENSBORO Caroline
GUNPOWDER Harford
GWYNN OAK (21207) Baltimore(66), Baltimore City(34)
GWYNN OAK Baltimore
HAGERSTOWN Washington
HALETHORPE (21227) Baltimore(95), Baltimore City(5)
HAMPSTEAD Carroll
HANCOCK Washington
HANOVER (21076) Anne Arundel(91), Howard(9)
HANOVER Anne Arundel
HARMANS Anne Arundel
HARWOOD Anne Arundel
HAVRE DE GRACE Harford
HEBRON Wicomico
HELEN St. Mary's
HENDERSON Caroline
HENRYTON Carroll
HIGHLAND (20777) Howard(95), Montgomery(5)
HILLSBORO Caroline

HOLLYWOOD St. Mary's
HUGHESVILLE Charles
HUNT VALLEY Baltimore
HUNTINGTOWN Calvert
HURLOCK Dorchester
HYATTSVILLE (20783) Prince
   George's(98), Montgomery(2)
HYATTSVILLE Prince George's
HYDES (21082) Baltimore(96), Harford(4)
IJAMSVILLE Frederick
INDIAN HEAD Charles
INGLESIDE Queen Anne's
IRONSIDES Charles
ISSUE Charles
JARRETTSVILLE Harford
JEFFERSON Frederick
JESSUP (20794) Howard(84), Anne
   Arundel(16)
JOPPA Harford
KEEDYSVILLE Washington
KENNEDYVILLE Kent
KENSINGTON Montgomery
KEYMAR (21757) Frederick(51),
   Carroll(49)
KINGSVILLE (21087) Baltimore(86),
   Harford(14)
KITZMILLER Garrett
KNOXVILLE (21758) Frederick(56),
   Washington(45)
LA PLATA Charles
LADIESBURG Frederick
LANHAM Prince George's
LAUREL Anne Arundel
LAUREL Howard
LAUREL Prince George's
LEONARDTOWN St. Mary's
LEXINGTON PARK St. Mary's
LIBERTYTOWN Frederick
LINEBORO Carroll
LINKWOOD Dorchester
LINTHICUM HEIGHTS Anne Arundel
LINWOOD Carroll
LISBON Howard
LITTLE ORLEANS Allegany
LONACONING (21539) Allegany(69),
   Garrett(31)
LONG GREEN Baltimore
LOTHIAN Anne Arundel
LOVEVILLE St. Mary's
LUKE Allegany
LUSBY Calvert
LUTHERVILLE TIMONIUM Baltimore
LYNCH Kent
MADISON Dorchester
MAGNOLIA Harford
MANCHESTER (21102) Carroll(98),
   Baltimore(2)
MANOKIN Somerset
MARBURY Charles
MARDELA SPRINGS Wicomico
MARION STATION Somerset
MARRIOTTSVILLE (21104) Howard(48),
   Carroll(43), Baltimore(9)
MARYDEL Caroline
MARYLAND LINE Baltimore
MASSEY Kent
MAUGANSVILLE Washington
MAYO Anne Arundel
MC HENRY Garrett

MCDANIEL Talbot
MECHANICSVILLE (20659) St. Mary's(98),
   Charles(2)
MIDDLE RIVER Baltimore
MIDDLEBURG Carroll
MIDDLETOWN Frederick
MIDLAND Allegany
MIDLOTHIAN Allegany
MILLERSVILLE Anne Arundel
MILLINGTON Kent
MONKTON (21111) Baltimore(87),
   Harford(13)
MONROVIA Frederick
MONTGOMERY VILLAGE Montgomery
MORGANZA St. Mary's
MOUNT AIRY (21771) Frederick(46),
   Carroll(36), Howard(15), Montgomery(2)
MOUNT RAINIER Prince George's
MOUNT SAVAGE Allegany
MOUNT VICTORIA Charles
MYERSVILLE Frederick
NANJEMOY Charles
NANTICOKE Wicomico
NEAVITT Talbot
NEW MARKET Frederick
NEW MIDWAY Frederick
NEW WINDSOR (21776) Carroll(83),
   Frederick(17)
NEWARK Worcester
NEWBURG Charles
NEWCOMB Talbot
NIKEP Allegany
NORTH BEACH (20714) Calvert(89), Anne
   Arundel(11)
NORTH EAST Cecil
NOTTINGHAM Baltimore
OAKLAND Garrett
OCEAN CITY Worcester
ODENTON Anne Arundel
OLDTOWN Allegany
OLNEY Montgomery
OWINGS Calvert
OWINGS MILLS Baltimore
OXFORD Talbot
OXON HILL Prince George's
PARK HALL St. Mary's
PARKTON Baltimore
PARKVILLE (21234) Baltimore(89),
   Baltimore City(11)
PARSONSBURG Wicomico
PASADENA Anne Arundel
PATUXENT RIVER St. Mary's
PERRY HALL Baltimore
PERRY POINT Cecil
PERRYMAN Harford
PERRYVILLE Cecil
PHOENIX Baltimore
PIKESVILLE (21208) Baltimore(93),
   Baltimore City(7)
PINEY POINT St. Mary's
PINTO Allegany
PITTSVILLE Wicomico
POCOMOKE CITY (21851) Worcester(88),
   Somerset(12)
POINT OF ROCKS Frederick
POMFRET Charles
POOLESVILLE Montgomery
PORT DEPOSIT Cecil
PORT REPUBLIC Calvert

PORT TOBACCO Charles
POTOMAC Montgomery
POWELLVILLE Wicomico
PRESTON Caroline
PRINCE FREDERICK Calvert
PRINCESS ANNE Somerset
PYLESVILLE Harford
QUANTICO Wicomico
QUEEN ANNE Queen Anne's
QUEENSTOWN Queen Anne's
RANDALLSTOWN Baltimore
RAWLINGS Allegany
REHOBETH Somerset
REISTERSTOWN (21136) Baltimore(97),
   Carroll(3)
RHODES POINT Somerset
RHODESDALE Dorchester
RIDERWOOD Baltimore
RIDGE St. Mary's
RIDGELY Caroline
RISING SUN Cecil
RIVA Anne Arundel
RIVERDALE Prince George's
ROCK HALL Kent
ROCK POINT Charles
ROCKVILLE Montgomery
ROCKY RIDGE Frederick
ROHRERSVILLE Washington
ROSEDALE (21237) Baltimore(96),
   Baltimore City(4)
ROYAL OAK Talbot
SABILLASVILLE (21780) Frederick(94),
   Washington(6)
SAINT INIGOES St. Mary's
SAINT JAMES (21781) Frederick(50),
   Washington(50)
SAINT LEONARD Calvert
SAINT MARYS CITY St. Mary's
SAINT MICHAELS Talbot
SALISBURY Wicomico
SANDY SPRING Montgomery
SAVAGE Howard
SCOTLAND St. Mary's
SECRETARY Dorchester
SEVERN Anne Arundel
SEVERNA PARK Anne Arundel
SHADY SIDE Anne Arundel
SHARPSBURG Washington
SHARPTOWN Wicomico
SHERWOOD Talbot
SHOWELL Worcester
SILVER SPRING (20903) Montgomery(85),
   Prince George's(15)
SILVER SPRING Montgomery
SIMPSONVILLE Howard
SMITHSBURG (21783) Washington(76),
   Frederick(24)
SNOW HILL Worcester
SOLOMONS Calvert
SOUTHERN MD FACILITY Prince
   George's
SPARKS GLENCOE Baltimore
SPARROWS POINT Baltimore
SPENCERVILLE Montgomery
SPRING GAP Allegany
STEVENSON Baltimore
STEVENSVILLE Queen Anne's
STILL POND Kent
STOCKTON Worcester

STREET Harford
SUBURB MARYLAND FAC Montgomery
SUDLERSVILLE Queen Anne's
SUITLAND Prince George's
SUNDERLAND Calvert
SWANTON Garrett
SYKESVILLE (21784) Carroll(94),
   Howard(6)
TAKOMA PARK (20912) Montgomery(92),
   Prince George's(8)
TAKOMA PARK Prince George's
TALL TIMBERS St. Mary's
TANEYTOWN (21787) Carroll(90),
   Frederick(10)
TAYLORS ISLAND Dorchester
TEMPLE HILLS Prince George's
TEMPLEVILLE Caroline
THURMONT Frederick
TILGHMAN Talbot
TODDVILLE Dorchester
TOWSON Baltimore
TRACYS LANDING Anne Arundel
TRAPPE Talbot
TUSCARORA Frederick
TYASKIN Wicomico
TYLERTON Somerset
UNION BRIDGE (21791) Frederick(52),
   Carroll(48)
UNIONVILLE Frederick
UPPER FAIRMOUNT Somerset
UPPER FALLS Baltimore
UPPER HILL Somerset
UPPER MARLBORO Prince George's
UPPERCO (21155) Baltimore(92),
   Carroll(8)
VALLEY LEE St. Mary's
VIENNA Dorchester
WALDORF (20601) Charles(95), Prince
   George's(5)
WALDORF Charles
WALKERSVILLE Frederick
WARWICK Cecil
WASHINGTON Prince George's
WASHINGTON GROVE Montgomery
WELCOME Charles
WENONA Somerset
WEST FRIENDSHIP Howard
WEST RIVER Anne Arundel
WESTERNPORT Allegany
WESTMINSTER Carroll
WESTOVER Somerset
WHALEYVILLE Worcester
WHITE HALL (21161) Baltimore(60),
   Harford(40)
WHITE MARSH Baltimore
WHITE PLAINS Charles
WHITEFORD Harford
WILLARDS Wicomico
WILLIAMSPORT Washington
WINGATE Dorchester
WITTMAN Talbot
WOODBINE (21797) Howard(62),
   Carroll(38)
WOODSBORO Frederick
WOODSTOCK (21163) Baltimore(71),
   Howard(29)
WOOLFORD Dorchester
WORTON Kent
WYE MILLS Talbot

ZIP/City Cross Reference

ZIP Range	City	ZIP Range	City	ZIP Range	City	ZIP Range	City
20601-20604	WALDORF	20615-20615	BROOMES ISLAND	20624-20624	CLEMENTS	20635-20635	HELEN
20606-20606	ABELL	20616-20616	BRYANS ROAD	20625-20625	COBB ISLAND	20636-20636	HOLLYWOOD
20607-20607	ACCOKEEK	20617-20617	BRYANTOWN	20626-20626	COLTONS POINT	20637-20637	HUGHESVILLE
20608-20608	AQUASCO	20618-20618	BUSHWOOD	20627-20627	COMPTON	20639-20639	HUNTINGTOWN
20609-20609	AVENUE	20619-20619	CALIFORNIA	20628-20628	DAMERON	20640-20640	INDIAN HEAD
20610-20610	BARSTOW	20620-20620	CALLAWAY	20629-20629	DOWELL	20643-20643	IRONSIDES
20611-20611	BEL ALTON	20621-20621	CHAPTICO	20630-20630	DRAYDEN	20645-20645	ISSUE
20612-20612	BENEDICT	20622-20622	CHARLOTTE HALL	20632-20632	FAULKNER	20646-20646	LA PLATA
20613-20613	BRANDYWINE	20623-20623	CHELTENHAM	20634-20634	GREAT MILLS	20650-20650	LEONARDTOWN

ZIP Range	City
20653-20653	LEXINGTON PARK
20656-20656	LOVEVILLE
20657-20657	LUSBY
20658-20658	MARBURY
20659-20659	MECHANICSVILLE
20660-20660	MORGANZA
20661-20661	MOUNT VICTORIA
20662-20662	NANJEMOY
20664-20664	NEWBURG
20667-20667	PARK HALL
20670-20670	PATUXENT RIVER
20674-20674	PINEY POINT
20675-20675	POMFRET
20676-20676	PORT REPUBLIC
20677-20677	PORT TOBACCO
20678-20678	PRINCE FREDERICK
20680-20680	RIDGE
20682-20682	ROCK POINT
20684-20684	SAINT INIGOES
20685-20685	SAINT LEONARD
20686-20686	SAINT MARYS CITY
20687-20687	SCOTLAND
20688-20688	SOLOMONS
20689-20689	SUNDERLAND
20690-20690	TALL TIMBERS
20692-20692	VALLEY LEE
20693-20693	WELCOME
20695-20695	WHITE PLAINS
20697-20697	SOUTHERN MD FACILITY
20701-20701	ANNAPOLIS JUNCTION
20703-20703	LANHAM
20704-20705	BELTSVILLE
20706-20706	LANHAM
20707-20709	LAUREL
20710-20710	BLADENSBURG
20711-20711	LOTHIAN
20712-20712	MOUNT RAINIER
20714-20714	NORTH BEACH
20715-20721	BOWIE
20722-20722	BRENTWOOD
20723-20726	LAUREL
20731-20731	CAPITOL HEIGHTS
20732-20732	CHESAPEAKE BEACH
20733-20733	CHURCHTON
20735-20735	CLINTON
20736-20736	OWINGS
20737-20738	RIVERDALE
20740-20742	COLLEGE PARK
20743-20743	CAPITOL HEIGHTS
20744-20744	FORT WASHINGTON
20745-20745	OXON HILL
20746-20746	SUITLAND
20747-20747	DISTRICT HEIGHTS
20748-20748	TEMPLE HILLS
20749-20749	FORT WASHINGTON
20750-20750	OXON HILL
20751-20751	DEALE
20752-20752	SUITLAND
20753-20753	DISTRICT HEIGHTS
20754-20754	DUNKIRK
20755-20755	FORT GEORGE G MEADE
20757-20757	TEMPLE HILLS
20758-20758	FRIENDSHIP
20759-20759	FULTON
20762-20762	ANDREWS AIR FORCE BASE
20763-20763	SAVAGE
20764-20764	SHADY SIDE
20765-20765	GALESVILLE
20768-20768	GREENBELT
20769-20769	GLENN DALE
20770-20771	GREENBELT
20772-20775	UPPER MARLBORO
20776-20776	HARWOOD
20777-20777	HIGHLAND
20778-20778	WEST RIVER
20779-20779	TRACYS LANDING
20781-20788	HYATTSVILLE
20790-20791	CAPITOL HEIGHTS
20794-20794	JESSUP
20797-20797	SOUTHERN MD FACILITY
20799-20799	CAPITOL HEIGHTS
20800-20800	SUBURB MARYLAND FAC
20812-20812	GLEN ECHO
20813-20814	BETHESDA
20815-20815	CHEVY CHASE
20816-20817	BETHESDA
20818-20818	CABIN JOHN
20824-20824	BETHESDA
20825-20825	CHEVY CHASE
20827-20827	BETHESDA
20830-20832	OLNEY
20833-20833	BROOKEVILLE
20837-20837	POOLESVILLE
20838-20838	BARNESVILLE
20839-20839	BEALLSVILLE
20841-20841	BOYDS
20842-20842	DICKERSON
20847-20853	ROCKVILLE
20854-20854	POTOMAC
20855-20855	DERWOOD
20857-20857	ROCKVILLE
20859-20859	POTOMAC
20860-20860	SANDY SPRING
20861-20861	ASHTON
20862-20862	BRINKLOW
20866-20866	BURTONSVILLE
20868-20868	SPENCERVILLE
20871-20871	CLARKSBURG
20872-20872	DAMASCUS
20874-20876	GERMANTOWN
20877-20879	GAITHERSBURG
20880-20880	WASHINGTON GROVE
20882-20885	GAITHERSBURG
20886-20886	MONTGOMERY VILLAGE
20889-20889	BETHESDA
20890-20890	SUBURB MARYLAND FAC
20891-20891	KENSINGTON
20892-20894	BETHESDA
20895-20895	KENSINGTON
20896-20896	GARRETT PARK
20897-20897	SUBURB MARYLAND FAC
20898-20899	GAITHERSBURG
20901-20911	SILVER SPRING
20912-20913	TAKOMA PARK
20914-20997	SILVER SPRING
21001-21001	ABERDEEN
21005-21005	ABERDEEN PROVING GROUND
21009-21009	ABINGDON
21010-21010	GUNPOWDER
21012-21012	ARNOLD
21013-21013	BALDWIN
21014-21015	BEL AIR
21017-21017	BELCAMP
21018-21018	BENSON
21020-21020	BORING
21021-21021	BRADSHAW
21022-21022	BROOKLANDVILLE
21023-21023	BUTLER
21024-21024	CARDIFF
21027-21027	CHASE
21028-21028	CHURCHVILLE
21029-21029	CLARKSVILLE
21030-21030	COCKEYSVILLE
21031-21031	HUNT VALLEY
21032-21032	CROWNSVILLE
21034-21034	DARLINGTON
21035-21035	DAVIDSONVILLE
21036-21036	DAYTON
21037-21037	EDGEWATER
21040-21040	EDGEWOOD
21041-21043	ELLICOTT CITY
21044-21046	COLUMBIA
21047-21047	FALLSTON
21048-21048	FINKSBURG
21050-21050	FOREST HILL
21051-21051	FORK
21052-21052	FORT HOWARD
21053-21053	FREELAND
21054-21054	GAMBRILLS
21055-21055	GARRISON
21056-21056	GIBSON ISLAND
21057-21057	GLEN ARM
21060-21062	GLEN BURNIE
21071-21071	GLYNDON
21074-21074	HAMPSTEAD
21075-21075	ELKRIDGE
21076-21076	HANOVER
21077-21077	HARMANS
21078-21078	HAVRE DE GRACE
21080-21080	HENRYTON
21082-21082	HYDES
21084-21084	JARRETTSVILLE
21085-21085	JOPPA
21087-21087	KINGSVILLE
21088-21088	LINEBORO
21090-21090	LINTHICUM HEIGHTS
21092-21092	LONG GREEN
21093-21094	LUTHERVILLE TIMONIUM
21098-21098	HANOVER
21101-21101	MAGNOLIA
21102-21102	MANCHESTER
21104-21104	MARRIOTTSVILLE
21105-21105	MARYLAND LINE
21106-21106	MAYO
21108-21108	MILLERSVILLE
21111-21111	MONKTON
21113-21113	ODENTON
21114-21114	CROFTON
21117-21117	OWINGS MILLS
21120-21120	PARKTON
21122-21123	PASADENA
21128-21128	PERRY HALL
21130-21130	PERRYMAN
21131-21131	PHOENIX
21132-21132	PYLESVILLE
21133-21133	RANDALLSTOWN
21136-21136	REISTERSTOWN
21139-21139	RIDERWOOD
21140-21140	RIVA
21144-21144	SEVERN
21146-21146	SEVERNA PARK
21150-21150	SIMPSONVILLE
21152-21152	SPARKS GLENCOE
21153-21153	STEVENSON
21154-21154	STREET
21155-21155	UPPERCO
21156-21156	UPPER FALLS
21157-21158	WESTMINSTER
21160-21160	WHITEFORD
21161-21161	WHITE HALL
21162-21162	WHITE MARSH
21163-21163	WOODSTOCK
21201-21203	BALTIMORE
21204-21204	TOWSON
21205-21206	BALTIMORE
21207-21207	GWYNN OAK
21208-21208	PIKESVILLE
21209-21218	BALTIMORE
21219-21219	SPARROWS POINT
21220-21220	MIDDLE RIVER
21221-21221	ESSEX
21222-21222	DUNDALK
21223-21224	BALTIMORE
21225-21225	BROOKLYN
21226-21226	CURTIS BAY
21227-21227	HALETHORPE
21228-21228	CATONSVILLE
21229-21233	BALTIMORE
21234-21234	PARKVILLE
21235-21235	BALTIMORE
21236-21236	NOTTINGHAM
21237-21237	ROSEDALE
21239-21241	BALTIMORE
21244-21244	GWYNN OAK
21250-21285	BALTIMORE
21286-21286	TOWSON
21287-21298	BALTIMORE
21401-21412	ANNAPOLIS
21501-21505	CUMBERLAND
21520-21520	ACCIDENT
21521-21521	BARTON
21522-21522	BITTINGER
21523-21523	BLOOMINGTON
21524-21524	CORRIGANVILLE
21528-21528	ECKHART MINES
21529-21529	ELLERSLIE
21530-21530	FLINTSTONE
21531-21531	FRIENDSVILLE
21532-21532	FROSTBURG
21536-21536	GRANTSVILLE
21538-21538	KITZMILLER
21539-21539	LONACONING
21540-21540	LUKE
21541-21541	MC HENRY
21542-21542	MIDLAND
21543-21543	MIDLOTHIAN
21545-21545	MOUNT SAVAGE
21550-21550	OAKLAND
21555-21555	OLDTOWN
21556-21556	PINTO
21557-21557	RAWLINGS
21560-21560	SPRING GAP
21561-21561	SWANTON
21562-21562	WESTERNPORT
21601-21606	EASTON
21607-21607	BARCLAY
21609-21609	BETHLEHEM
21610-21610	BETTERTON
21612-21612	BOZMAN
21613-21613	CAMBRIDGE
21617-21617	CENTREVILLE
21619-21619	CHESTER
21620-21620	CHESTERTOWN
21622-21622	CHURCH CREEK
21623-21623	CHURCH HILL
21624-21624	CLAIBORNE
21625-21625	CORDOVA
21626-21626	CRAPO
21627-21627	CROCHERON
21628-21628	CRUMPTON
21629-21629	DENTON
21631-21631	EAST NEW MARKET
21632-21632	FEDERALSBURG
21634-21634	FISHING CREEK
21635-21635	GALENA
21636-21636	GOLDSBORO
21638-21638	GRASONVILLE
21639-21639	GREENSBORO
21640-21640	HENDERSON
21641-21641	HILLSBORO
21643-21643	HURLOCK
21644-21644	INGLESIDE
21645-21645	KENNEDYVILLE
21647-21647	MCDANIEL
21648-21648	MADISON
21649-21649	MARYDEL
21650-21650	MASSEY
21651-21651	MILLINGTON
21652-21652	NEAVITT
21653-21653	NEWCOMB
21654-21654	OXFORD
21655-21655	PRESTON
21656-21656	CHURCH HILL
21657-21657	QUEEN ANNE
21658-21658	QUEENSTOWN
21659-21659	RHODESDALE
21660-21660	RIDGELY
21661-21661	ROCK HALL
21662-21662	ROYAL OAK
21663-21663	SAINT MICHAELS
21664-21664	SECRETARY
21665-21665	SHERWOOD
21666-21666	STEVENSVILLE
21667-21667	STILL POND
21668-21668	SUDLERSVILLE
21669-21669	TAYLORS ISLAND
21670-21670	TEMPLEVILLE
21671-21671	TILGHMAN
21672-21672	TODDVILLE
21673-21673	TRAPPE
21675-21675	WINGATE
21676-21676	WITTMAN

21677-21677	WOOLFORD	21758-21758	KNOXVILLE	21798-21798	WOODSBORO	21863-21863	SNOW HILL
21678-21678	WORTON	21759-21759	LADIESBURG	21801-21804	SALISBURY	21864-21864	STOCKTON
21679-21679	WYE MILLS	21762-21762	LIBERTYTOWN	21810-21810	ALLEN	21865-21865	TYASKIN
21681-21688	RIDGELY	21764-21764	LINWOOD	21811-21811	BERLIN	21866-21866	TYLERTON
21690-21690	CHESTERTOWN	21765-21765	LISBON	21813-21813	BISHOPVILLE	21867-21867	UPPER FAIRMOUNT
21701-21709	FREDERICK	21766-21766	LITTLE ORLEANS	21814-21814	BIVALVE	21869-21869	VIENNA
21710-21710	ADAMSTOWN	21767-21767	MAUGANSVILLE	21816-21816	CHANCE	21870-21870	WENONA
21711-21711	BIG POOL	21769-21769	MIDDLETOWN	21817-21817	CRISFIELD	21871-21871	WESTOVER
21713-21713	BOONSBORO	21770-21770	MONROVIA	21820-21820	DAMES QUARTER	21872-21872	WHALEYVILLE
21714-21714	BRADDOCK HEIGHTS	21771-21771	MOUNT AIRY	21821-21821	DEAL ISLAND	21874-21874	WILLARDS
21715-21715	BROWNSVILLE	21773-21773	MYERSVILLE	21822-21822	EDEN	21875-21875	DELMAR
21716-21716	BRUNSWICK	21774-21774	NEW MARKET	21824-21824	EWELL	21890-21890	WESTOVER
21717-21717	BUCKEYSTOWN	21775-21775	NEW MIDWAY	21826-21826	FRUITLAND	21901-21901	NORTH EAST
21718-21718	BURKITTSVILLE	21776-21776	NEW WINDSOR	21829-21829	GIRDLETREE	21902-21902	PERRY POINT
21719-21719	CASCADE	21777-21777	POINT OF ROCKS	21830-21830	HEBRON	21903-21903	PERRYVILLE
21720-21720	CAVETOWN	21778-21778	ROCKY RIDGE	21835-21835	LINKWOOD	21904-21904	PORT DEPOSIT
21721-21721	CHEWSVILLE	21779-21779	ROHRERSVILLE	21836-21836	MANOKIN	21911-21911	RISING SUN
21722-21722	CLEAR SPRING	21780-21780	SABILLASVILLE	21837-21837	MARDELA SPRINGS	21912-21912	WARWICK
21723-21723	COOKSVILLE	21781-21781	SAINT JAMES	21838-21838	MARION STATION	21913-21913	CECILTON
21727-21727	EMMITSBURG	21782-21782	SHARPSBURG	21840-21840	NANTICOKE	21914-21914	CHARLESTOWN
21733-21733	FAIRPLAY	21783-21783	SMITHSBURG	21841-21841	NEWARK	21915-21915	CHESAPEAKE CITY
21734-21734	FUNKSTOWN	21784-21784	SYKESVILLE	21842-21843	OCEAN CITY	21916-21916	CHILDS
21736-21736	GAPLAND	21787-21787	TANEYTOWN	21849-21849	PARSONSBURG	21917-21917	COLORA
21737-21737	GLENELG	21788-21788	THURMONT	21850-21850	PITTSVILLE	21918-21918	CONOWINGO
21738-21738	GLENWOOD	21790-21790	TUSCARORA	21851-21851	POCOMOKE CITY	21919-21919	EARLEVILLE
21740-21749	HAGERSTOWN	21791-21791	UNION BRIDGE	21852-21852	POWELLVILLE	21920-21920	ELK MILLS
21750-21750	HANCOCK	21792-21792	UNIONVILLE	21853-21853	PRINCESS ANNE	21921-21922	ELKTON
21754-21754	IJAMSVILLE	21793-21793	WALKERSVILLE	21856-21856	QUANTICO	21930-21930	GEORGETOWN
21755-21755	JEFFERSON	21794-21794	WEST FRIENDSHIP	21857-21857	REHOBETH		
21756-21756	KEEDYSVILLE	21795-21795	WILLIAMSPORT	21861-21861	SHARPTOWN		
21757-21757	KEYMAR	21797-21797	WOODBINE	21862-21862	SHOWELL		

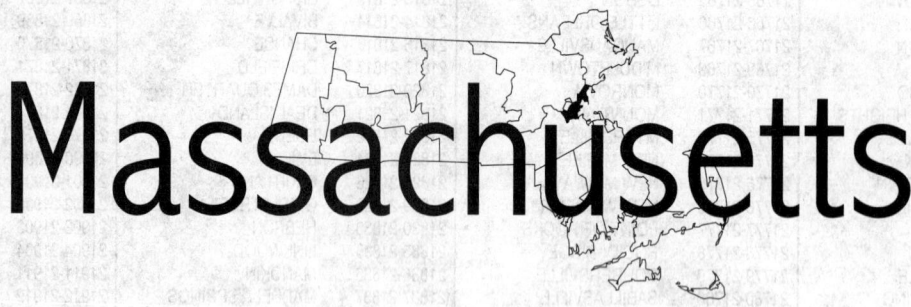

Massachusetts

General Help Numbers:

Governor's Office

State House, Room 360   617-727-6250
Boston, MA 02133   Fax 617-727-9725
http://www.state.ma.us/gov   8AM-6PM

Attorney General's Office

One Ashburton Place, Room 2010   617-727-2200
Boston, MA 02108-1698   Fax 617-727-5768
http://www.ago.state.ma.us   9AM-5PM

State Court Administrator

2 Center Plaza, Room 540   617-742-8575
Boston, MA 02108   Fax 617-742-0968
www.state.ma.us/courts/admin/index.html   8:30AM-5PM

State Archives

Archives Division   617-727-2816
220 Morrissey Blvd   Fax 617-288-8429
Boston, MA 02125   9AM-5PM M-F; 9-3 SA
http://www.state.ma.us/sec/arc

State Specifics:

Capital:	Boston
	Suffolk County
Time Zone:	EST
Number of Counties:	14
Population:	6,349,097
Web Site:	www.state.ma.us

State Agencies

Criminal Records

Criminal History Systems Board, 200 Arlington Street, #2200, Chelsea, MA 02150; 617-660-4600, 617-660-4613 (Fax), 9AM-5PM.

http://www.state.ma.us/chsb/pubs.htm

Note: There are 3 searches offered: Personal; Certified Agency; and Publicly Accessible (PUBAC). Certified Agency requests are pre-approved via statute or by the Board. PUBAC is open to the public.

Indexing & Storage: Records are available for at least 50 years. New records are available for

inquiry immediately. Records are indexed on inhouse computer, file folders.

Searching: PUBAC requesters are limited to adult records. The crime must include a sentence of 5 years or more OR sentenced and convicted for any term if, at the time of request, the subject is on probation or has been released within 2 years of felony conviction Include the following in your request-name, date of birth. The Certified Agency record includes all conviction and all open or pending actions. The Personal request (on one's self) requires a notarized signature.

Access by: mail.

Fee & Payment: The Personal request is free. The Certified Agency request is $10.00. The PUBAC request is $25.00. No fingerprints are used, thus no fingerprint fees. Fee payee: The Commonwealth of Massachusetts. Prepayment required. Personal checks accepted. No credit cards accepted.

Mail search: Turnaround time: 2 weeks. A self addressed stamped envelope is requested.

Corporation Records
Trademarks/Servicemarks
Limited Liability Partnerships
Limited Partnership Records

Secretary of the Commonwealth, Corporation Division, One Ashburton Pl, 17th Floor, Boston, MA 02108; 617-727-9640 (Corporations), 617-727-2850 (Records), 617-727-8329 (Trademarks), 617-727-9440 (Forms request line), 617-742-4538 (Fax), 8:45AM-5PM.

http://www.state.ma.us/sec/cor/coridx.htm

Indexing & Storage: Records are available for corporations and business entities organized since 1978 on computer. Corporations and business entities organized prior to 1978 may or may not be available. Annual reports are maintained for 10 years. New records are available for inquiry immediately. Records are indexed on microfilm, inhouse computer.

Searching: Include the following in your request-full name of business. In addition to the articles of incorporation, corporation records include the following information: Annual Reports, Officers and Directors names and addresses, Prior (merged) names, Inactive and Reserved names and US Tax ID numbers.

Access by: mail, phone, in person, online.

Fee & Payment: Uncertified copies cost $.20 per page. Certified copies cost $7.00 for the first page and $2.00 for each additional page. Certified copies of articles of incorporation are $12.00 per organization. Fee payee: Commonwealth of Massachusetts. Prepayment required. Personal checks accepted. No credit cards accepted.

Mail search: Turnaround time: 3 to 5 days. A self addressed stamped envelope is requested.

Phone search: No fee for telephone request. Telephone room hours are 8:45AM-5PM.

In person search: Turnaround time: while you wait.

Online search: The agency offers "Direct Access." The annual subscription fee is $149.00 and there is a $.40 a minute access fee. System is available from 8 AM to 10 PM. This system also provides UCC record data. Call 617-727-7655 for a sign-up packet.

Uniform Commercial Code
State Tax Liens

UCC Division, Secretary of the Commonwealth, One Ashburton Pl, Room 1711, Boston, MA 02108; 617-727-2860, 900-555-4500 (Computer Prints), 900-555-4600 (Copies), 8:45AM-5PM.

http://www.state.ma.us/sec

Indexing & Storage: Records are available from 09/01/81 on computer and 01/01/84 on microfiche. Records are indexed on inhouse computer.

Searching: Use search request form UCC-11. Federal tax liens are filed at the US District Courts, PO & Courthouse Bldg, Boston, MA 02109 (617-233-9152). A list of state tax liens is available here, but must be searched in person separately from UCC filings. Include the following in your request-debtor name. Only active filings are available.

Access by: mail, phone, fax, in person, online.

Fee & Payment: Information listing only is $5.00. Search with copies is $15.00 for first 15 pages, $1.00 per page of copies after 15. State tax liens

cost $0.20 per copy made. The state does not certify any state tax lien. Fee payee: Commonwealth of Massachusetts. Prepayment required. Personal checks accepted. No credit cards accepted.

Mail search: Turnaround time: 2 days. Information requests are available.

Phone search: See expedited service.

Fax search: Results can be returned by fax, if arrangements are made, only by 900 calls. Call number above for more information. Essentially the fee is $20.00 per search.

In person search: You may request information in person, but turnaround time for certified documents is 24 hours. You may search on an in-house public terminal.

Online search: "Direct Access" is available for $149 per year plus a $.40 per minute network fee. The system is open from 8 AM to 9:50 PM. Call 617-727-7655 to obtain information packet.

Other access: Microfiche may be purchased.

Expedited service: Expedited service is available for fax searches. Turnaround time: 24 hours. A 24 hours express search of financial statements (900-555-4600) is $50.00. An express search of computer printouts is $25.00 per debtor name (900-555-4500), from 10AM-4PM.

Sales Tax Registrations

Revenue Department, Taxpayer Assistance Office, PO Box 7010, Boston, MA 02204 (Courier: 200 Arlington Street, 4th Floor, Chelsea, MA 02150); 617-887-6100, 8AM-5PM.

http://www.state.ma.us/dor

Note: There are actually 6 offices in the state that will allow walk-in researchers. The office in Chelsea will not let you in the building.

Searching: This agency will only confirm that a business is registered. They will provide no other information. Include the following in your request-business name. They will also search by tax permit number.

Access by: mail, phone, fax, in person.

Mail search: Turnaround time: 5 to 10 days. A self addressed stamped envelope is requested. No fee for mail request.

Phone search: No fee for telephone request.

Fax search: They ask that you call first to get the number, they do not wish to publish their fax number.

In person search: No fee for request.

Birth Certificates

Registry of Vital Records and Statistics, 150 Mt. Vernon St, 1st FL, Dorchester, MA 02125; 617-740-2600, 617-740-2606, 8:45AM-4:45PM.

http://www.state.ma.us/dph/vitrecs.htm

Indexing & Storage: Records are available from 1906 to present. Records from 1841 to 1905 are located at the Massachusetts Archives, 220 Morrissey Blvd., Boston, MA 02125. Records prior to 1841 are located at the town/city level. It takes 6 months before new records are available for inquiry.

Searching: Access to out-of-wedlock birth records and health information is strictly limited. A court order is required for adopted children's records. Otherwise, records are open. Include the following in your request-full name, names of parents,

mother's maiden name, date of birth, place of birth. Must present a photo ID or provide a copy of a photo ID to search. Phone and fax searchers must give exact place and date of event.

Access by: mail, phone, fax, in person.

Fee & Payment: Prepayment required. Fee payee: Commonwealth of Massachusetts. Personal checks accepted. Credit cards accepted: MasterCard, Visa, AmEx, Discover.

Mail search: Turnaround time: 3 to 4 weeks. A self addressed stamped envelope is requested. Search costs $11.00 for each 10 years searched.

Phone search: Search costs $19.00 for each 10 years searched. Must use a credit card.

Fax search: Search costs $19.00 for each 10 years searched. Must use a credit card.

In person search: Search costs $6.00 for each 10 years searched. Turnaround time is immediate. You can also do your own searching of records. First 20 minutes is free, then there is a $3.00 fee. The research center is open 9AM-12PM and 2PM-4:30PM, M-F.

Expedited service: Expedited service is available for mail, phone and fax searches. Turnaround time: 2 days. Use of credit card required, add $16.00 for express delivery.

Death Records

Registry of Vital Records and Statistics, 150 Mt Vernon St, 1st FL, Dorchester, MA 02125; 617-740-2600, 617-740-2606, 8:45AM-4:45PM.

http://www.state.ma.us/dph/vitrecs.htm

Indexing & Storage: Records are available from 1906 to present. Prior records at State Archives to 1841. It takes 4 months before new records are available for inquiry.

Searching: Fetal death records are not available. A court order is required to access the originals of amended records. Include the following in your request-full name, date of death, place of death. Name of spouse and age at time of death will help facilitate the search. Phone and fax requesters must supply exact place and date of event.

Access by: mail, phone, fax, in person.

Fee & Payment: Prepayment required. Fee payee: Commonwealth of Massachusetts. Personal checks accepted. Credit cards accepted: MasterCard, Visa, AmEx, Discover.

Mail search: Turnaround time: 3 to 4 weeks. A self addressed stamped envelope is requested. Search costs $11.00 for each 10 years searched.

Phone search: Search costs $19.00 per record. You must use a credit card.

Fax search: Same criteria as phone searches.

In person search: Search costs $6.00 for each 10 years searched. There is a research center open 9AM-12PM and 2PM-4:30PM M-F. Searching is free the first 20 minutes, then it is $3.00 per hour.

Expedited service: Expedited service is available for mail, phone and fax searches. Turnaround time: 2 days. Add $16.00 for express delivery. Use of credit card required.

Marriage Certificates

Registry of Vital Records and Statistics, 150 Mt Vernon St, 1st FL, Dorchester, MA 02125; 617-740-2600, 617-740-2606, 8:45AM-4:45PM.

http://www.state.ma.us/dph/vitrecs.htm

Indexing & Storage: Records are available from 1906 to present. Prior records to 1841 are at State Archives. It takes 5 months before new records are available for inquiry.

Searching: A court order is required for originals of amended records. Include the following in your request-names of husband and wife, date of marriage, place or county of marriage. Phone or fax searchers must submit exact place and date of event. Also helpful is parents' names.

Access by: mail, phone, fax, in person.

Fee & Payment: Prepayment required. Fee payee: Commonwealth of Massachusetts. Personal checks accepted. Credit cards accepted: MasterCard, Visa, AmEx, Discover.

Mail search: Turnaround time: 3 to 4 weeks. A self addressed stamped envelope is requested. Search costs $11.00 for each 10 years searched.

Phone search: Search costs $19.00 per record. You must use a credit card.

Fax search: Same search criteria as phone searching.

In person search: Search costs $6.00 for each 10 years searched. There is a research center open from 9AM-12PM and 2PM-4:30PM, M-F. The first 20 minutes are free, then a $3.00 per hour fee is charged.

Expedited service: Expedited service is available for mail, phone and fax searches. Turnaround time: 2 days. Add $16.00 for express delivery. Use of credit card required.

Divorce Records

Registry of Vital Records and Statistics, 150 Mt. Vernon St, 1st FL, Dorchester, MA 02125; 617-740-2600, 617-740-2606.

http://www.state.ma.us/dph/vitrecs.htm

Note: Divorce records are found at county of issue. However, this agency maintains an index from 1952 to present. The state will do a search for free by mail only to determine the county.

Access by:. Records are available by mail.

Workers' Compensation Records

Keeper of Records, Department of Industrial Accidents, 600 Washington St, 7th Floor, Boston, MA 02111; 617-727-4900 x301, 617-727-1161 (Fax), 8AM-4PM.

http://www.state.ma.us/dia

Indexing & Storage: Records are available from 1994 on, and prior records located at State Archives. The index is computerized since 1981. Earlier records may be researched via microfiche for an index number. Records are indexed on inhouse computer.

Searching: You need a signed release from claimant to receive data regarding medical records, DOB, and SSN. Include the following in your request-claimant name, Social Security Number, date of injury, employer, insurance carrier, and other pertinent information. E-mail address is infodesk@dia.state.ma.us. The following data is not released: medical records, date of birth or Social Security Numbers.

Access by: mail, in person.

Fee & Payment: There is a standard fee of $3.00 prior to release of record(s). Add $.20 per page and $.50 per page if computer generate. Fee payee: Commonwealth of Massachusetts. Prepayment

required. Personal checks accepted. No credit cards accepted.

Mail search: Turnaround time: 2 weeks. No self addressed stamped envelope is required.

In person search: All requests must be in writing.

Driver Records-Registry

Registry of Motor Vehicles, Driver Control Unit, Box 199150, Roxbury, MA 02119-9100; 617-351-9213 (Registry), 617-351-9219 (Fax), 8AM-4:30PM M-T-W-F; 8AM-7PM TH.

http://www.state.ma.us/rmv

Note: The driving records provided by the Registry are for employment or general business use. Both the Registry and the Merit Rating Board use the same database of driving record histories.

Indexing & Storage: Records are available for 6 years plus current year for moving violations. It takes 1 week before new records are available for inquiry.

Searching: Casual requesters can only obtain records without personal information. Include the following in your request-full name, driver's license number, date of birth. The address of the requester should also be included. The following data is not released: bulk information or lists for commercial purposes.

Access by: mail, phone, in person.

Fee & Payment: The fee is $10.00 per record. Fee payee: Registry of Motor Vehicles. Prepayment required. Personal checks accepted. No credit cards accepted.

Mail search: Turnaround time: 10 working days. No self addressed stamped envelope is required.

Phone search: The Registry offers a phone-in request line at 617-351-4500. Orders can be paid with a credit card, results are mailed.

In person search: Up to 10 requests will be processed immediately; the rest are available the next day. You may request a record from any field office.

Driver Records-Insurance

Merit Rating Board, Attn: Driving Records, PO Box 199100, Boston, MA 02119-9100; 617-351-4400, 617-351-9660 (Fax), 8:45AM-5:00PM.

http://www.state.ma.us/rmv

Note: The Merit Rating Board processes driving records for the insurance industry in accordance with state statutes.

Indexing & Storage: Records are available for 6 years for moving violations and at fault accidents (process date). The license number and name are validated against the Registry license file.

Searching: These records do not show revocation or suspension action. Include the following in your request-driver's license number, full name, date of birth. All requests must be on the agency form.

Access by: mail, in person.

Fee & Payment: The fee is $10.00 per record. Fee payee: Commonwealth of Massachusetts. Prepayment required. Personal checks accepted. No credit cards accepted.

Mail search: Turnaround time: 2 days. No self addressed stamped envelope is required.

In person search: Turnaround time while you wait.

Other access: The Merit Rating Board provides both on-line and tape inquiry to the insurance industry for rating and issuance of new and renewal automobile insurance policies. Per statute, this method of retrieval is not open to the public.

Vehicle Ownership
Vehicle Identification

Registry of Motor Vehicles, Customer Assistance-Mail List Dept., PO Box 199100, Boston, MA 02119-9100; 617-351-9384, 617-351-9524 (Fax), 8AM-4:30PM.

http://www.state.ma.us/rmv

Indexing & Storage: Records are available from the 1940's for licenses, from 1963 for registrations and names. Records are computerized from 1986.

Searching: In general, license, ownership, and registration information is available to the public. Personal information is not available to casual requesters without consent. The state does not do VIN look-ups. Lien information is provided as part of the record.

Access by: mail, fax, in person, online.

Fee & Payment: The current fee is $5.00 for per record request if on computer, $10.00 if on microfiche. Fee payee: Commonwealth of Massachusetts. Prepayment required. Personal checks accepted. No credit cards accepted.

Mail search: Turnaround time: 7 to 10 days. A self addressed stamped envelope is requested.

Fax search: Records are available by fax.

In person search: In person requesters may get computer records immediately, microfiche records take 3 days.

Online search: Searching is limited to Massachusetts based insurance companies and agents for the purpose of issuing or renewing insurance. This system is not open to the public. There is no fee, but line charges will be incurred.

Other access: The state offers an extensive array of customized bulk record requests. For further information, contact the Production Control Office.

Accident Reports

Accident Records Section, Registry of Motor Vehicles, PO Box 199100, Roxbury, MA 02119-9100; 617-351-9434, 617-351-9401 (Fax), 8:45AM-5PM.

http://www.state.ma.us/rmv

Note: Accident reports may also be obtained from the local police department in the investigating jurisdiction. Normal fee is $1.00 per page.

Indexing & Storage: Records are available for 2 years to present. Records are indexed on computer.

Searching: Criminal Offender Record Information (CORI) will not be released. Items required for search include; full name, date of accident, location of accident, and license or registration number.

Access by: mail, in person.

Fee & Payment: The charge is $10.00 per report. Fee payee: Registry of Motor Vehicles. Prepayment required. Personal checks accepted. No credit cards accepted.

Mail search: Turnaround time: 7 to 10 days.

In person search: Walk-in location is Copley Place, Tower One, 5th Floor, Boston, MA 02116. Turnaround time is immediate if on system.

Vessel Ownership
Vessel Registration

Massachusetts Environmental Police, 251 Causeway Street, #101, Boston, MA 02114; 617-626-1610, 617-626-1630 (Fax), 8:45AM-5PM.

Indexing & Storage: Records are available from 1988 to present. All motor powered boats and jet skis must be registered with this agency. All boats over 14ft must be titled. Records are indexed on computer.

Searching: To search, you need name and registration or hull number. The following data is not released: Social Security Numbers or phone numbers.

Access by: mail, fax.

Fee & Payment: There is no search fee.

Mail search: Turnaround time: 1 week. No self addressed stamped envelope is required.

Fax search: Turnaround time is usually 5 minutes.

Other access: To obtain printed lists or tapes, contact Andy Petrie.

Legislation Records

Massachusetts General Court, State House, Beacon St, Room 428 (Document Room), Boston, MA 02133; 617-722-2860 (Document Room), 9AM-5PM.

http://www.state.ma.us/legis.legis.htm

Indexing & Storage: Records are available for usually two years on computer. Older years are available from the State House Library at 617-727-2590. Records are computer indexed from 1995 to present.

Searching: The document room only has information on current bills. Include the following in your request-bill number, date of debate.

Access by: mail, phone, in person, online.

Fee & Payment: There is no fee.

Mail search: Turnaround time: same day if possible. A self addressed stamped envelope is requested.

Phone search: Records are available by phone.

In person search: Turnaround time same day.

Online search: The web site has bill information for the current session and the previous session.

Other access: The state does make available a listing of all bills filed and several bulletins; call 617-722-2340 for more information.

Voter Registration
Records not maintained by a state level agency.

Note: Records are maintained at the local city and town level. In general

they are open to the public.

GED Certificates

Massachusetts Dept of Education, GED Processing, 350 Main St, Malden, MA 02148; 781-338-6636, 781-338-3391, 781-338-3391 (Fax).

http://www.doe.mass.edu/ged

Searching: They will not release copies of transcripts (you must go to the educational institution). This agency will verify or confirm receipt of GED diploma information. All of the following are required: a signed release, date of birth, and Social Security Number. The year and the name of institution are also helpful.

Access by: mail, fax, in person.

Fee & Payment: The fee is $5.00 per verification or letter of certification. Fee payee: Commonwealth of Massachusetts. Prepayment required. Only money orders or business checks are accepted. No credit cards accepted.

Mail search: Turnaround time 2-5 days.No self addressed stamped envelope is required.

Fax search: Fax is only available to companies and educational institutions.

In person search: Turnaround time can be immediate, depending on workload.

Hunting License Information
Fishing License Information

Division of Fisheries & Wildlife, 251 Causeway St #S400, Boston, MA 02114-2104; 617-626-1590, 617-626-1517 (Fax), 8:45AM-5PM.

http://www.state.ma.us/dfwele

Indexing & Storage: Records are available for 1 year back only. Older records are maintained at one of several locations off premises and take longer to research.

Searching: All requests must be in writing and on their form. You may call to request the form. Need to know the store where license was purchased and month it was purchased. They are filed by license number only.

Access by: mail, in person.

Fee & Payment: There is no search fee.

Mail search: Turnaround time: same day if possible. No self addressed stamped envelope is required.

In person search: You must complete their form.

Massachusetts State Licensing Agencies

Licenses Searchable Online

Alarm (Burglar & Fire) Installer #07 .... http://license.reg.state.ma.us/pubLic/licque.asp?color=red&Board=EL

Allied Health Professions #07 .... http://license.reg.state.ma.us/pubLic/licque.asp?color=red&Board=AH

Allied Mental Health & Human Svcs Prof. #7 http://license.reg.state.ma.us/pubLic/licque.asp?query=personal&color=red&board=MH

Amusement Device Inspector #27 .... www.state.ma.us/dps/Lic_srch.htm

Architect #42 .... http://license.reg.state.ma.us/pubLic/licque.asp?color=red&Board=AR

Athletic Trainer #07 .... http://license.reg.state.ma.us/pubLic/licque.asp?color=red&Board=AH

Attorney #02 .... www.state.ma.us/obcbbo/bboreg/

Auctioneer School #43 .... www.state.ma.us/standards/auc-sch.htm

Audiologist #07 .... http://license.reg.state.ma.us/pubLic/licque.asp?color=red&Board=SP

Barber #07 .... http://license.reg.state.ma.us/pubLic/licque.asp?color=red&Board=BR

Barber Shop #07 .... http://license.reg.state.ma.us/pubLic/licque.asp?color=red&Board=BR

Boxer #50 .... www.state.ma.us/mbc/ranking.htm

Building Inspector/Local Inspector #03 ...... www.state.ma.us/bbrs/bocert.PDF

Building Producer #03 .... www.state.ma.us/bbrs/mfg98.pdf

Chiropractor #07 .... http://license.reg.state.ma.us/pubLic/licque.asp?color=red&Board=CH

Concrete Technician #03 .... www.state.ma.us/bbrs/programs.htm

Concrete Testing Laboratory #03 .... www.state.ma.us/bbrs/programs.htm

Construction Supervisor #18 .... www.state.ma.us/bbrs/cslsearch.htm

Cosmetologist (Hairdresser, Manicurist, Aesthetician) #07
.... http://license.reg.state.ma.us/pubLic/licque.asp?color=red&Board=HD

Day Care Center #52 .... www.qualitychildcare.org/

Dental Hygienist #07 .... http://license.reg.state.ma.us/pubLic/licque.asp?color=red&Board=DN

Dentist #07 .... http://license.reg.state.ma.us/pubLic/licque.asp?color=red&Board=DN

Water Supply (Drinking) Facility Operator #7 http://license.reg.state.ma.us/pubLic/licque.asp?color=red&Board=DW

Educational Psychologist #07 .... http://license.reg.state.ma.us/pubLic/licque.asp?query=personal&color=red&board=MH

Electrician #07 .... http://license.reg.state.ma.us/pubLic/licque.asp?color=red&Board=EL

Electrologist #07 .... http://license.reg.state.ma.us/pubLic/licque.asp?color=red&Board=ET

Embalmer #40 .... http://license.reg.state.ma.us/pubLic/licque.asp?color=red&Board=EM

Engineer #07 .... http://license.reg.state.ma.us/pubLic/licque.asp?color=red&Board=EN

Family Child Care Provider #52 .... www.qualitychildcare.org/

Fire Protection System Contractor/Fitter #27 www.state.ma.us/dps/Lic_srch.htm

Firemen / Engineer #27 .... www.state.ma.us/dps/Lic_srch.htm

Funeral Director #40 .... http://license.reg.state.ma.us/pubLic/licque.asp?color=red&Board=EM

Gas Fitter #07 .... http://license.reg.state.ma.us/pubLic/licque.asp?color=red&Board=PL

Health Officer (Certified) #12 .... http://license.reg.state.ma.us/pubLic/licque.asp?color=red&Board=HO

HMO #38 .... www.state.ma.us/doi/Consumer/css_health_HMO.html

Hoisting Machinery (Forklift, etc.) Oper. #27 .. www.state.ma.us/dps/Lic_srch.htm

Home Improvement Contractor #18 .... www.state.ma.us/bbrs/Hicsearch.htm

Inspector of Boilers/Pressure Vessels #27. www.state.ma.us/dps/Lic_srch.htm

Insurance, Domestic/Foreign Company #38 www.state.ma.us/doi/companies/companies_home.html

Land Surveyor #07 .... http://license.reg.state.ma.us/pubLic/licque.asp?color=red&Board=EN

Landscape Architect #42 .... http://license.reg.state.ma.us/pubLic/licque.asp?color=red&Board=LA

Lobbyist #21 .... www.state.ma.us/scripts/sec/pre/search.asp

Lumber Producer, Native #03 .... www.state.ma.us/bbrs/lumber99.PDF

Marriage & Family Therapist #07 .... http://license.reg.state.ma.us/pubLic/licque.asp?query=personal&color=red&board=MH

Medical Doctor #53 .... www.docboard.org/ma/df/masearch.htm

Mental Health Counselor #07 .... http://license.reg.state.ma.us/pubLic/licque.asp?query=personal&color=red&board=MH

Nuclear Power Plant Engineer/Operator #27 www.state.ma.us/dps/Lic_srch.htm

Nurse (LPN, RN, Midwife) #07 .... http://license.reg.state.ma.us/pubLic/licque.asp?color=red&Board=RN

Nursing Home Administrator #12 .... http://license.reg.state.ma.us/pubLic/licque.asp?color=red&Board=NH
Nursing Home/Rest Home #45.................. www.medicare.gov/nhcompare/home.asp
Occupational Therapist/Assistant #07 .... http://license.reg.state.ma.us/pubLic/licque.asp?color=red&Board=AH
Oil Burner Technician/Contractor #27 .... www.state.ma.us/dps/Lic_srch.htm
Optician, Dispensing #07 .... http://license.reg.state.ma.us/pubLic/licque.asp?color=red&Board=DO
Optometrist #07.. http://license.reg.state.ma.us/pubLic/licque.asp?color=red&Board=OP
Pharmacist #07 .... http://license.reg.state.ma.us/pubLic/licque.asp?color=red&Board=PH
Physical Therapist/Assistant #07 .... http://license.reg.state.ma.us/pubLic/licque.asp?color=red&Board=AH
Physician Assistant #13 .... http://license.reg.state.ma.us/pubLic/licque.asp?color=red&Board=AP
Pipefitter #27 .... www.state.ma.us/dps/Lic_srch.htm
Plumber #07 .... http://license.reg.state.ma.us/pubLic/licque.asp?color=red&Board=PL
Podiatrist #07 .... http://license.reg.state.ma.us/pubLic/licque.asp?color=red&Board=PD
Psychologist/Provider #13......................... http://license.reg.state.ma.us/pubLic/licque.asp?color=red&Board=PY
Public Accountant-CPA #07 .... http://license.reg.state.ma.us/pubLic/licque.asp?color=red&Board=PA
Radio & TV Repair Technician #07 .... http://license.reg.state.ma.us/pubLic/licque.asp?color=red&Board=TV
Real Estate Appraiser #07 .... http://license.reg.state.ma.us/pubLic/licque.asp?color=red&Board=RA
Real Estate Broker/Salesperson #07 .... http://license.reg.state.ma.us/pubLic/licque.asp?color=red&Board=RE
Refrigeration Technician/Contractor #27 ... www.state.ma.us/dps/Lic_srch.htm
Rehabilitation Therapist #07 .... http://license.reg.state.ma.us/pubLic/licque.asp?query=personal&color=red&board=MH
Respiratory Care Therapist #07 .... http://license.reg.state.ma.us/pubLic/licque.asp?color=red&Board=RC
Sanitarian #42 .... http://license.reg.state.ma.us/pubLic/licque.asp?color=red&Board=SA
Social Worker #07 .... http://license.reg.state.ma.us/pubLic/licque.asp?color=red&Board=SW
Speech-Language Pathologist #07............ http://license.reg.state.ma.us/pubLic/licque.asp?color=red&Board=SP
Veterinarian #07 .... http://license.reg.state.ma.us/pubLic/licque.asp?color=red&Board=VT

Licensing Quick Finder

Acupuncturist #05 617-727-3086
Aerial Passenger Cable Car #27.. 617-727-3200 x662
Aesthetician #07 617-727-9940
Agent, Entertainment #27 617-727-3296
Aircraft #46 617-973-8883
Airline Transportation/Warehouse #01 ..617-727-3040
Airport Manager #46..............................617-973-8883
Alarm (Burglar & Fire) Installer #07 617-727-9931
Alcoholic Beverage Mfg./Whlse #15......617-727-3040
Alcoholic Beverage Solicitor #15...........617-727-3040
Allied Health Profession #07 617-727-3071
Allied Mental Health & Human Svcs Professional #07
....617-727-3071
Ambulance Service #14.........................617-284-8300
Ambulatory Surgical Center #45 617-753-8000
Amusement Device Insp. #27 ...... 617-727-3200 x607
Appraiser (MVD) #47..............................617-521-7453
Architect #42 617-727-3072
Asbestos & Lead Abatement #24..........617-727-7047
Athletic Trainer #07 617-727-3071
Attorney #02 617-728-8800
Auctioneer #43.......................................617-727-3480
Auctioneer School #43 617-727-3480
Audiologist #07 617-727-1747
Automobile Dealer #48 .... 617-956-1500 X501
Automobile Sales Financer #48 ...617-956-1500 X501
Bank & Savings Institution #35 617-956-1500
Bank, Cooperative #35...........................617-956-1500
Bank #35...617-956-1500
Barber #07..617-727-7367
Barber Shop #07....................................617-727-7367
Birthing Center #45 617-753-8000
Blood Bank #45......................................617-753-8000
Boiler Engineer #27 617-727-3200
Boxer #50 .... 617-727-3200 x657
Boxing Physician #50 .... 617-727-3200 x657
Boxing Professional #50.............. 617-727-3200 x657
Brokerage Firm #49 617-727-3548
Building Inspector/Local Inspector #03..617-727-7532

Building Producer #03 617-727-7532
Bus Driver-Motor Coach #31 617-305-3559
Cattle Dealer/Transporter #19 ..... 617-727-3018 x158
Chair Lift #27 .... 617-727-3200 x662
Chiropractor #07 617-727-3093
Cigarette Seller #32 617-887-5090
Clinic #45 617-753-8000
Collection Agency #35...........................617-956-1500
Concrete Technician #03........................617-727-7532
Concrete Testing Laboratory #03..........617-727-7532
Construction Supervisor #18.....617-727-7532 x25205
Consumer Credit Grantor #35...............617-956-1500
Cosmetologist (Hairdresser, Manicurist, Aesthetician)
#07 617-727-9940
Credit Union #35 617-956-1500
Day Care Center #52 617-626-2010
Day Care Center Teacher/Director #52 .617-626-2010
Dental Examiner #41 617-727-9928
Dental Hygienist #07 617-727-9928
Dentist #07 617-727-9928
Drug/Alcoholism Facility/Program #01 ...617-727-3040
Educational Psychologist #07 617-727-3071
Electrician #07 617-727-9931
Electrologist #07 617-727-9957
Elevator Construction/Maintenance #27 ....
....617-727-3200 x25238
Elevator Operator #27 ....617-727-3200 x25238
Embalmer #40 617-727-1718
Emergency Medical Technician #14......617-284-8300
Employment Agency, Placement/Temporary #22 ....
....617-727-3696
Engineer #07 617-727-9957
Exterminator #19........................ 617-727-3020 x104
Family Child Care Assistant #52 617-626-2010
Family Child Care Provider #52 617-626-2010
Finfishing, Commercial #34 617-626-1520
Fire Protection Sprinkler System Contractor/Fitter #27
.... 617-727-3200 x607

Firemen / Engineer #27 .... 617-727-3200 x607
Funeral Director #40..............................617-727-1718
Fur Buyer #34 617-626-1590
Gas Fitter #07 617-727-9952
Gas Station Owner #43 617-727-3480
Guard Dog/Hearing Dog Business #19 ....
.... 617-727-3018 x157
Hairdresser #07 617-727-9940
Health Officer (Certified) #12 617-727-9925
HMO #38..617-521-7794
Hoisting Machinery (Forklift, Hydraulic, Crane)
Operator #27............................. 617-727-3200 x607
Home Improvement Contractor #18 617-727-7532
x25207
Horse (Equine) Dealer #19 .... 617-727-3018 x168
Horse/Greyhound #16 617-568-3336
Hospice #45...617-753-8000
Hospital #45...617-753-8000
Boiler/Pressure Vessel Insp #27 .. 617-727-3200 x607
Insurance Advisor/Adjuster #38 617-727-7189
Insurance Agent/Broker #38 617-727-7189
Insurance, Domestic/Foreign Company #38..............
....617-321-7391
Jockey #16 617-568-3336
Justice of the Peace #44 ....617-727-2795 X3
Laboratory (Medical-related) #45 617-753-8000
Land Surveyor #07.................................617-727-9957
Landscape Architect #42 617-727-3072
Lead Inspector #24 617-727-7047
Library Media Specialist #17 ....781-338-3000 x6600
Loan Company, Small #48 ....617-956-1500 X501
Lobbyist #21 617-878-3434
Lobstering #34 617-626-1520
Lumber Producer, Native #03 617-727-3636
Mammography Radiologic Technologist #26 ....
....617-727-6214
Manicurist #07 617-727-9940
Marriage & Family Therapist #07 617-727-3071

Medical Doctor #53 617-727-3086
Mental Health Counselor #07 617-727-3071
Milk Plant #19 ....617-727-3018 x174
Modeling Industry/Agency #22..............617-727-3696
Mortgage Broker/Lender #48 ....617-956-1500 X501
Motion Picture Operator #27.....617-727-3200 x25223
Motor Vehicle Repair Shop (Auto Body/Glass/etc.) #43
....617-727-3480
Nanny Agency #22 617-727-3696
Notary Public #44.........................617-727-2795 X1
Nuclear Medicine Technologist (Radiologic
  Technologist-Nuclear Medicine) #26..617-727-6214
Nuclear Power Plant Engineer/Operator #27 ....
....617-727-3200 x607
Nurse (LPN, RN, Midwife) #07..............617-727-9961
Nursery #19 617-626-1801
Nursery Agent #19 617-626-1801
Nurses' Aide in Long-term Care Facility #45..............
....617-753-8143
Nursing Home Administrator #12 617-727-9925
Nursing Home/Rest Home #45 617-753-8000
Occupational Therapist/Assistant #07 617-727-3071
Oil Burner Tech./Contractor #27 .. 617-727-3200 x607
Optician, Dispensing #07 617-727-3093
Optometrist #07 617-727-3093
Out-Patient Rehabilitation Facility #45...617-753-8000
Owner/Trainer (Horse/Greyhound) #16.617-568-3336
Pasteurization Plant #19.............. 617-727-3018 x174
Peddler/Hawker #43............................617-727-3480
Personal Agent #27....................617-727-3200 x637
Pesticide Applicator/Dealer #19 617-626-1777

Pet Shop #19.......................... 617-727-3018 x158
Pharmacist #07 617-727-9953
Physical Therapist/Assistant #07 617-727-3071
Physician Assistant #13......................617-727-3069
Pipefitter #27............................ 617-727-3200 x607
Plumber #07 617-727-9952
Podiatrist #07 617-727-1747
Private Detective #33 978-538-6128
Private Investigator #33........................978-538-6128
Psychologist/Provider #13....................617-727-9925
Public Accountant-CPA #07..................617-727-1806
Racetrack (Horse/Greyhound) #16 617-727-2581
Radiation Therapy-Radiologic Technologist #26........
....617-727-6214
Radio & TV Repair Technician #07 617-727-3074
Radiographer #26 617-727-6214
Radiologic Technologist #26.................617-727-6214
Radon Specialist #26 617-727-6214
Railroad Transportation/Warehouse #1.617-727-3040
Real Estate Appraiser #07 617-727-3055
Real Estate Broker/Salesperson #07 617-727-2373
Refrigeration Tech./Contr. #27..... 617-727-3200 x607
Rehabilitation Therapist #07 617-727-3071
Renal Dialysis (End Stage) #45 617-753-8000
Respiratory Care Therapist #07.............617-727-1747
Riding Instructor #19 .... 617-727-3018 x161
Riding School #19 .... 617-727-3018 x161
Sales Finance Company #48........617-956-1500 X501
Sanitarian #42....................................617-727-3072
School Administrator #17............781-338-3000 x6600
School Bus #31...................................617-305-3559

School Guidance Counselor #17 781-338-3000 x6600
Seafood Dealer #34 617-626-1520
Securities Agent #49 617-727-3548
Securities Broker/Dealer #49 617-727-3548
Security Guard Agency #33 978-538-6128
Shellfishing, Commercial #34 617-626-1520
Simulcast & Inter-Track Wagering #16..617-727-2581
Ski Tow #27 .... 617-727-3200 x662
Skimobile #27 .... 617-727-3200 x662
Social Worker #07 617-727-3073
Speech-Language Pathologist #07 617-727-1747
Stable (Horse & Buggy Operator) #19.....................
....617-727-3018 x161
Steamship Transportation/Warehouse #01 ....
....617-727-3040
Stock Broker #49................................617-727-3548
Swine Dealer #19...................... 617-727-3018 x158
Taxidermist #34 617-626-1590
Teacher #17...............................781-338-3000 x6600
Theatrical Booking Agent #27...... 617-727-3200 x637
Ticket Broker #27................................617-727-3296
Ticket Reseller #27 .... 617-727-3200 x637
Tramway Inspector #27............... 617-727-3200 x662
Trapping #34 617-626-1590
Trust Company #35.............................617-956-1500
Vending Machine #25..........................617-522-6712
Vendor, Transient #43 617-727-3480
Veterinarian #07 617-727-3080
Water Supply (Drinking) Facilities Operator #07 ....
....617-727-3074
Weights & Measures #43.....................617-727-3480

Licensing Agency Information

01 Division of Substance Abuse Services, 239 Causeway St #200, Boston, MA 02114-2130; 617-727-3040, Fax: 617-727-1258.

02 Board of Overseers Registry Dept, 75 Federal St, 5th Fl, Boston, MA 02110; 617-728-8800, Fax: 617-357-1872.
www.state.ma.us/obcbbo/bboreg/
Direct web site URL to search for licensees: www.state.ma.us/obcbbo/bboreg/. You can search online using name. Registry gives attorney name, office and residence address

03 Board of Building Regulations & Standards, 1 Ashburton Place, Rm 2133, Boston, MA 02108; 617-727-7532, Fax: 617-727-1754.
www.state.ma.us/eops/index.htm
Direct web site URL to search for licensees: www.state.ma.us/bbrs/programs.htm. You can search online using aslphabetical list

05 Committee on Acupuncture, 10 West St, 3rd Fl, Boston, MA 02111; 617-727-3086, Fax: 617-357-8453.
www.massmedboard.org/acupuncture.htm
Direct web site URL to search for licensees: www.docboard.org/ma/df/masearch.htm. You can search online using name and town name.

07 Division of Registration, 239 Causeway St #400, Boston, MA 02114-2130; 617-727-3074, Fax: 617-727-2197.
www.state.ma.us/reg/home.htm
Direct web site URL to search for licensees: http://license.reg.state.ma.us/pubLic/licque.asp. You can search online using license number, name, city, state and ZIP Code.

12 Division of Registration, 239 Causeway St #400, Boston, MA 02114-2130; 617-727-9925, Fax: 617-727-2366.
www.state.ma.us/reg/home.htm

Direct web site URL to search for licensees: http://license.reg.state.ma.us/pubLic/licque.asp. You can search online using license number, name, city, state and ZIP Code.

13 Division of Registration, 100 Cambridge St, 15th Fl, Boston, MA 02202; 617-727-3074, Fax: 617-727-2197.
www.state.ma.us/reg/boards.htm#P
Direct web site URL to search for licensees: http://license.reg.state.ma.us/pubLic/licque.asp. You can search online using name, city, ZIP Code, and license number.

14 Office of Emergency Medical Services, 56 Roland St, Boston, MA 02129; 617-284-8300, Fax: 617-284-8350.
www.state.ma.us/dph/oems

15 Consumer Department, 236 Causeway St #239, Boston, MA 02114-2130; 617-727-3040, Fax: 617-727-1258.

16 Consumer Department, 1 Ashburton Place, 13th Fl, Rm 1313, Boston, MA 02108; 617-727-2581, Fax: 617-227-6062.
www.state.ma.us/src

17 Division of Educational Personnel, 350 Main St, Malven, MA 02148; 781-338-3000 x6600, Fax: 781-338-3391.
www.doe.mass.edu/cert

18 Home Improvement Contractor/Construction Supervisor Licensing, 1 Ashburton Pl, Rm 1301, Boston, MA 02108; 617-727-7532.
www.state.ma.us/bbrs/programs.htm
Direct web site URL to search for licensees: www.state.ma.us/bbrs/programs.htm. You can search online using name, city/town, license #

19 Department of Food & Agriculture, 251 Causeway St, 5th Fl, Boston, MA 02114-2151; 617-626-1700, Fax: 617-626-1850.

www.massdfa.org/pesticide.htm

21 Secretary of the Commonwealth, One Ashburton Place, Room 1719, Boston, MA 02108; 617-878-3434, Fax: 617-727-5914.
www.state.ma.us/sec/pre/prelob/lobidx.htm
Direct web site URL to search for licensees: www.state.ma.us/scripts/sec/pre/search.asp. Search online using agent last name, employer, and year.

22 Licensing Division, 100 Cambridge St, 11th Fl, Boston, MA 02202; 617-727-3696, Fax: 617-727-7568.

24 Department of Occupational Safety, Licensing Division, 399 Washington St, 5th Fl, Boston, MA 02100-5212; 617-727-7047, Fax: 617-727-7568.
www.state.ma.us/dos

25 Department of Public Health, 305 S St, Jamaica Plain, MA 02130; 617-522-3700, Fax: 617-753-8436.
www.state.ma.us/dph

26 Radiation Control Program, 305 South St, Jamaica Plain, MA 02130; 617-522-3700, Fax: 617-727-2098.
www.state.ma.us/dph

27 Department of Public Safety, 1 Ashburton Pl, 13th Fl, Rm 1301, Boston, MA 02108; 617-727-3200 x623, Fax: 617-248-0813.
www.state.ma.us/dps

31 Department of Telecommunications and Energy, 1 South Sta #2, Boston, MA 02110-2208; 617-305-3559, Fax: 617-478-2598.

32 Department of Revenue, PO Box 7012, Boston, MA 02204; 617-887-5090, Fax: 617-887-5039.
www.dor.state.ma.us

33 Department of State Police, 485 Maple St, Danvers, MA 01923; 978-538-6128, Fax: 978-538-6021.
www.state.ma.us/msp/

34 Department of Fisheries, Wildlife & Environmental Enforcement, 251 Causeway St #S-400, Boston, MA 02114-2104; 617-626-1500, Fax: 617-626-1505.
www.state.ma.us/dfwele/dpt_toc.htm

35 Division of Banks & Loan Agencies, 1 South Station, 3rd FL, Boston, MA 02110; 617-956-1500, Fax: 617-956-1597.
www.state.ma.us/dob

38 Division of Insurance, 470 Atlantic Ave, Boston, MA 02110-2223; 617-521-7794, Fax: 617-521-7772.
www.state.ma.us/doi
Direct web site URL to search for licensees: www.state.ma.us/doi/doi_site_alt.html.   Search online using site map to locate directory lists

40 Division of Registration, 239 Causeway St #400, Boston, MA 02114-2130; 617-727-3074, Fax: 617-727-2197.
www.state.ma.us/reg/boards/em/default.htm
Direct web site URL to search for licensees: http://license.reg.state.ma.us/pubLic/licque.asp?color=red&Board=EM. You can search online using name, city, ZIP Code, and license number.

42 Division of Regulation of Architecture, 239 Causeway St #500, Boston, MA 02114; 617-727-3072, Fax: 617-727-2197.
www.state.ma.us/reg/boards/ar/default.htm
Direct web site URL to search for licensees: http://license.reg.state.ma.us/pubLic/licque.asp?color=red&Board=AR. You can search online using name, state, ZIP Code, and license number.

43 Executive Office of Public Safety, 1 Ashburton Pl, Boston, MA 02108; 617-727-3480, Fax: 617-727-5705.
www.state.ma.us/standards
Direct web site URL to search for licensees: www.state.ma.us/standards/license.htm.   You can search online using alphabetical lists

44 Governor's Council, State House, Rm 184, Boston, MA 02133; 617-727-2795.
www.state.ma.us/gov/govco.htm

45 Department of Public Health, 10 West St, 5th Fl, Boston, MA 02111; 617-753-8000, Fax: 617-753-8095.
www.state.ma.us/dph/hcqskel.htm

46 Massachusetts Aeronautics Commission, 10 Park Plaza, Rm 6620, Boston, MA 02116-3966; 617-973-8881, Fax: 617-973-8889.

47 Division of Insurance, 1 South Station, 5th Fl, Boston, MA 02110; 617-521-7446, Fax: 617-521-7772.

www.state.ma.us/doi

48 Division of Banks, 1 South Station, 3rd Fl, Boston, MA 02110; 617-956-1500 x501, Fax: 617-956-1599.
www.state.ma.us/dob

49 Securities Division, McCormack Bldg, 17th Fl, Boston, MA 02108; 617-727-3548, Fax: 617-248-0177.
www.state.ma.us/sec/sct/sctidx.htm

50 Boxing Commission, 1 Ashburton Pl Rm 1301, Boston, MA 02108; 617-727-3200 x657, Fax: 617-727-5732.
www.state.ma.us/dps/Boxing.htm
Direct web site URL to search for licensees: www.state.ma.us/mbc/ranking.htm.   You can search online using boxer ranking lists

52 Executive Office of Human Svcs, 1 Ashburton Pl Rm 1105, Boston, MA 02108-1518; 617-626-2010.
www.qualitychildcare.org
Direct web site URL to search for licensees: www.qualitychildcare.org/provider_search.htm

53 Board of Registration in Medicine, 10 West St, Boston, MA 02111; 617-727-3086.
www.massmedboard.org.

Massachusetts Federal Courts

The following list indicates the district and division name for each county in the state. If the bankruptcy court location is different from the district court, then the location of the bankruptcy court appears in parentheses.

County/Court Cross Reference

Barnstable .... Boston

Berkshire .... Springfield (Worcester)

Bristol .... Boston

Dukes .... Boston

Essex .... Boston

Franklin .... Springfield (Worcester)

Hampden .... Springfield (Worcester)

Hampshire .... Springfield (Worcester)

Middlesex .... Boston

Nantucket .... Boston

Norfolk .... Boston

Plymouth .... Boston

Suffolk .... Boston

Worcester .... Worcester

US District Court

District of Massachusetts

Boston Division US Courthouse, 1 Courthouse Way, Boston, MA 02210 (Courier Address: Use mail address for courier delivery), 617-748-9152, Fax: 617-748-9096.

http://www.mad.uscourts.gov

Counties: Barnstable, Bristol, Dukes, Essex, Middlesex, Nantucket, Norfolk, Plymouth, Suffolk.

Indexing/Storage: Cases are indexed by defendant and plaintiff as well as by case number. New cases are available in the index 1 day to 1 week after filing date. A computer index is maintained. The civil and criminal database dates from the early 1900's until the present. Records are available when they are not in the possession of the judge or his/her clerks. Open records are located at this court.

Fee & Payment: The fee is $20.00 per item (one party name or case number). Payment may be made by money order, cashier check, personal check. Prepayment is required. Payee: Clerk, US District Court. Certification fee: $7.00 per document. Copy fee: $.50 per page. You are allowed to make your own copies. These copies cost $.25 per page.

Phone Search: Searching is not available by phone.

Mail Search: A stamped self addressed envelope is not required.

In Person: In person searching is available.

PACER: Sign-up number is 800-676-6856. Access fee is $.60 per minute. Toll-free access: 888-399-4639. Local access: 617-748-4294. Case records are available back to January 1990. Records are purged every 12 months. New records are available online after 1 day. PACER is available online at http://pacer.mad.uscourts.gov.

Springfield Division 1550 Main St, Springfield, MA 01103 (Courier Address: Use mail address for courier delivery), 413-785-0214, Fax: 413-785-0204.

http://www.mad.uscourts.gov

Counties: Berkshire, Franklin, Hampden, Hampshire.

Indexing/Storage: Cases are indexed by defendant and plaintiff as well as by case number. New cases are available in the index immediately after filing date. There is a microfiche index for pre-1989 cases. A computer index is maintained. The civil and criminal database dates from July 1979. Open records are located at this court. Records are not available when they are in the possession of a judge or a judge's clerk.

Fee & Payment: The fee is $20.00 per item (one party name or case number). Payment may be made by money order, cashier check, personal check. Will bill if total fee is less than $25.00. Payee: Clerk, US District Court. Certification fee: $7.00 per document. Copy fee: $.50 per page.

Phone Search: Docket information available over the phone if Clerk has time.

Fax Search: Will charge for fax search request only if copies and certification requested. Will fax results at $.50 per page.

Mail Search: A stamped self addressed envelope is not required.

In Person: In person searching is available.

PACER: Sign-up number is 800-676-6856. Access fee is $.60 per minute. Toll-free access: 888-399-4639. Local access: 617-748-4294. Case records are available back to January 1990. Records are purged every 12 months. New records are available online after 1 day. PACER is available online at http://pacer.mad.uscourts.gov.

Worcester Division 595 Main St., Room 502, Worcester, MA 01608 (Courier Address: Use mail address for courier delivery), 508-793-0552.

http://www.mad.uscourts.gov

Counties: Worcester.

Indexing/Storage: Cases are indexed by defendant and plaintiff as well as by case number. New cases are available in the index immediately after filing date. Indexes are on computer from 1988 and on microfiche from 1981. Earlier indexes are in storage from the early 1900's. Open records are located at this court. Records are not available when in the possession of a judge or the judge's clerks.

Fee & Payment: The fee is $20.00 per item (one party name or case number). Payment may be made by money order, cashier check, personal check. Payee: Clerk, US District Court. Certification fee: $7.00 per document. Copy fee: $.50 per page.

Phone Search: Only docket information available by telephone.

Fax Search: Invoice will be sent with copies of records for a fax request.

Mail Search: Always enclose a stamped self addressed envelope.

In Person: In person searching is available.

PACER: Sign-up number is 800-676-6856. Access fee is $.60 per minute. Toll-free access: 888-399-4639. Local access: 617-748-4294. Case records are available back to January 1990. Records are purged every 12 months. New records are available online after 1 day. PACER is available online at http://pacer.mad.uscourts.gov.

US Bankruptcy Court

District of Massachusetts

Boston Division Room 1101, 10 Causeway, Boston, MA 02222-1074 (Courier Address: Use mail address for courier delivery), 617-565-6051, Fax: 617-565-6087.

http://www.mab.uscourts.gov

Counties: Barnstable, Bristol, Dukes, Essex (except towns assigned to Worcester Division), Nantucket, Norfolk (except towns assigned to Worcester Division), Plymouth, Suffolk, and the following towns in Middlesex: Arlington, Belmont, Burlington, Everett,Lexington, Malden, Medford, Melrose, Newton, North Reading, Reading, Stoneham, Wakefield, Waltham, Watertown, Wilmington, Winchester and Woburn.

Indexing/Storage: Cases are indexed by debtor as well as by case number. New cases are available in the index immediately after filing date. A computer index is maintained. Open records are located at this court.

Fee & Payment: The fee is $20.00 per item (one party name or case number). Payment may be made by money order, cashier check, personal check. Copy fees will be billed after the search is completed. Checks are not accepted from debtors. Payee: US Bankruptcy Court. Certification fee: $7.00 per document. Copy fee: $.50 per page. You are allowed to make your own copies. These copies cost $.50 per page.

Phone Search: Only general information will be released over the phone. An automated voice case information service (VCIS) is available. Call VCIS at 888-201-3572 or 617-565-6025.

Fax Search: Fax requests are processed the same as mail requests.

Mail Search: Always enclose a stamped self addressed envelope.

In Person: In person searching is available.

PACER: Sign-up number is 800-676-6856. Access fee is $.60 per minute. Toll-free access: 888-201-3571. Local access: 617-565-6021. Case records are available back to April 1, 1987. Records are purged every 12 months. New civil records are available online after 1 day. PACER is available online at http://pacer.mab.uscourts.gov.

Worcester Division 595 Main St, Room 211, Worcester, MA 01608 (Courier Address: Use mail address for courier delivery), 508-770-8900, Fax: 508-793-0541.

http://www.mab.uscourts.gov

Counties: Berkshire, Franklin, Hampden, Hampshire, Middlesex (except the towns assigned to the Boston Division), Worcester and the following towns: in Essex-Andover, Haverhill, Lawrence, Methuen and North Andover; in Norfolk-Bellingham, Franklin, Medway, Millis and Norfolk.

Indexing/Storage: Cases are indexed by debtor as well as by case number. New cases are available in the index immediately after filing date. A computer index is maintained. Open records are located at this court.

Fee & Payment: The fee is $20.00 per item (one party name or case number). Payment may be made by money order, cashier check, personal check. Prepayment is required. Checks are not accepted from debtors. Payee: US Bankruptcy Court. Certification fee: $7.00 per document. Copy fee: $.50 per page. You are allowed to make your own copies. These copies cost $.25 per page.

Phone Search: Only docket information is available by phone. An automated voice case information service (VCIS) is available. Call VCIS at 888-201-3572 or 617-565-6025.

Mail Search: A stamped self addressed envelope is not required.

In Person: In person searching is available.

PACER: Sign-up number is 800-676-6856. Access fee is $.60 per minute. Toll-free access: 888-201-3571. Local access: 617-565-6021. Case records are available back to April 1, 1987. Records are purged every 12 months. New civil records are available online after 1 day. PACER is available online at http://pacer.mab.uscourts.gov.

Massachusetts County Courts

Court	Jurisdiction	No. of Courts	How Organized
Superior Courts*	General	19	14 Counties
District Courts*	General	68	68 Geographic Divisions
Boston Municipal Court*	General	1	
Housing Courts	General	7	
Probate and Family Courts*	Probate	15	14 Counties
Juvenile Courts	Special	7	
Land Court	Special	1	

* Profiled in this Sourcebook.

Court	CIVIL								
	Tort	Contract	Real Estate	Min. Claim	Max. Claim	Small Claims	Estate	Eviction	Domestic Relations
Superior Courts*	X	X	X	$25,000	No Max				
District Courts*	X	X	X	$0	No Max	$2000	X	X	X
Boston Municipal Court*	X	X	X	$0	No Max	$2000			X
Housing Courts			X	$0	No Max	$2000			
Probate and Family Courts*							X		X
Juvenile Courts									
Land Court			X						

Court	CRIMINAL				
	Felony	Misdemeanor	DWI/DUI	Preliminary Hearing	Juvenile
Superior Courts*	X				
District Courts*	X	X	X	X	X
Boston Municipal Court*		X	X		
Housing Courts		X		X	
Probate and Family Courts*					
Juvenile Courts					X
Land Court					

ADMINISTRATION   Chief Justice for Administration and Management, 2 Center Plaza, Room 540, Boston, MA, 02108; 617-742-8575, Fax: 617-742-0968. www.state.ma.us/courts/admin/index.html

COURT STRUCTURE   The various court sections are called "Departments." While Superior and District Courts have concurrent jurisdiction in civil cases, the practice is to assign cases less than $25,000 to the District Court and those over $25,000 to Superior Court. In addition to misdemeanors, District Courts and Boston Municipal Courts have jurisdiction over certain minor felonies.

ONLINE ACCESS   Online access to records on the statewide Trial Courts Information Center web site is available to attorneys and law firms at www.ma-trialcourts.org. Contact Peter Nylin by email at nylin_p@jud.state.ma.us. Site is updated daily.

PROBATE COURTS   There are more than 20 Probate and Family Court locations in MA - one per county plus two each in Bristol, plus a Middlesex satellite in Cambridge and Lawrence.

Barnstable County

Superior Court 3195 Main St, PO Box 425, Barnstable, MA 02630; 508-375-6684. Hours: 8:30AM-4:30PM (EST). *Felony, Civil Actions Over $25,000.*

Note: Their public access terminal is connected to the statewide Superior Court system.

Civil Records: Access: Mail, in person. Both court and visitors may perform in person searches. No search fee. Required to search: name, years to search; also helpful: address. Civil cases indexed by defendant, plaintiff. Civil records on computer back to 1/2001; on index cards from 1985 and books from 1830s.

Criminal Records: Access: Mail, in person, online. Both court and visitors may perform in person searches. No search fee. Required to search: name, years to search, DOB; also helpful: address, SSN. Criminal records on computer back to 1/2001; on index cards from 1985 and books from 1830s. Online access is records on the Trial Courts Information Center web site is available to attorneys and law firms at www.ma-trialcourts.org. See state introduction for more information.

General Information: Public Access terminal is available. No victims names released. SASE not required. Copy fee: $.50 per page. Certification fee: $1.50. Fee payee: Barnstable Superior Court. Business checks accepted. Prepayment is required.

Barnstable District Court Route 6A, PO Box 427, Barnstable, MA 02630; 508-362-2511. Hours: 8:30AM-4:30PM (EST). *Felony, Misdemeanor, Civil, Eviction, Small Claims.*

Civil Records: Access: Phone, mail, in person. Only the court performs in person searches; visitors may not. No search fee. Required to search: name, years to search. Civil cases indexed by defendant, plaintiff. Civil records on index cards and docket books.

Criminal Records: Access: Phone, mail, in person. Only the court performs in person searches; visitors may not. No search fee. Required to search: name, years to search; also helpful: DOB. Criminal records on computer since 1996; prior records on index cards and docket books.

General Information: No impounded records released. Turnaround time 1-2 weeks. Copy fee: $.50 per page. Certification fee: $1.50. Fee payee: District Court. Only cashiers checks and money orders accepted. Prepayment is required.

Orleans District Court 237 Rock Harbor Rd, Orleans, MA 02653; 508-255-4700. Hours: 8:30AM-4:30PM (EST). *Felony, Misdemeanor, Civil, Eviction, Small Claims.*

Note: Includes Brewster, Chatham, Dennis, Eastham, Orleans, Truro, Wellfleet, Harwich, and Provincetown.

Civil Records: Access: In person only. Visitors must perform in person searches for themselves. No search fee. Required to search: name, years to search. Civil cases indexed by defendant, plaintiff. Civil records kept in storage from 1978. Some prior records destroyed.

Criminal Records: Access: In person only. Visitors must perform in person searches for themselves. No search fee. Required to search: name, years to search. Criminal records kept in storage from 1978. Some prior records destroyed.

General Information: No impounded records released. Copy fee: $.50 per page. Certification fee: $1.50. Fee payee: Orleans District Court. Personal checks accepted. Prepayment is required.

Probate & Family Court PO Box 346, Barnstable, MA 02630; 508-375-6600; Fax: 508-362-3662. Hours: 8:30AM-4:30PM (EST). *Probate.*

Berkshire County

Superior Court 76 East St, Pittsfield, MA 01201; 413-499-7487; Fax: 413-442-9190. Hours: 8:30AM-4:30PM (EST). *Felony, Civil Actions Over $25,000.*

Civil Records: Access: Mail, in person. Both court and visitors may perform in person searches. No search fee. Required to search: name, years to search. Civil cases indexed by defendant, plaintiff. Civil records on index cards from 1980s and books from 1700s.

Criminal Records: Access: Mail, in person. Both court and visitors may perform in person searches. No search fee. Required to search: name, years to search, DOB, SSN. Criminal records on index cards from 1980s and books from 1700s.

General Information: No impounded records released. Turnaround time 1 week. Copy fee: $.50 per page. Certification fee: $1.50. Fee payee: Clerk of Superior Court. Personal checks accepted. Prepayment is required.

North Berkshire District Court #28 City Hall - 10 Main St, North Adams, MA 01247; 413-663-5339; Fax: 413-664-7209. Hours: 8AM-4:30PM (EST). *Felony, Misdemeanor, Civil, Eviction, Small Claims.*

Note: Handles cases for Clarksburg, Florida, Hancock, New Ashford, North Adams, and Williamstown.

Civil Records: Access: Phone, fax, mail, in person. Only the court performs in person searches; visitors may not. No search fee. Required to search: name, years to search. Civil cases indexed by defendant, plaintiff. Civil records on index cards from 1983, docket books to 1900.

Criminal Records: Access: Phone, fax, mail, in person. Only the court performs in person searches; visitors may not. No search fee. Required to search: name, years to search; also helpful: DOB. Criminal records on index cards from 1983, docket books to 1900.

General Information: No impounded records released. Turnaround time 1-2 weeks. Copy fee: $.50 per page. Certification fee: $1.50. Fee payee: District Court. Business checks accepted. Prepayment is required.

North Berkshire District Court #30 65 Park St, Adams, MA 01220; 413-743-0021; Fax: 413-743-4848. Hours: 8AM-4:30PM (EST). *Felony, Misdemeanor, Civil, Eviction, Small Claims.*

Note: Handles cases for Adams, Cheshire, Savoy, and Windsor.

Civil Records: Access: Mail, fax, in person. Only the court performs in person searches; visitors may not. No search fee. Required to search: name, years to search; also helpful: address. Civil cases indexed by defendant, plaintiff. Civil records on index cards from 1990, small claims from 1988. Prior stored.

Criminal Records: Access: Mail, fax, in person. Only the court performs in person searches; visitors may not. No search fee. Required to search: name, years to search; also helpful: DOB, SSN. Criminal records on computer since 1976/77, lists on docket books until 1985.

General Information: No juvenile, mental health, impounded case records released. SASE required. Turnaround time 7 days. Copy fee: $.50 per page. Certification fee: $1.50. Fee payee: District Court. No personal checks accepted. Prepayment is required.

Pittsfield District Court #27 24 Wendell Ave, Pittsfield, MA 01201; 413-442-5468; Fax: 413-499-7327. Hours: 8:30AM-4:30PM (EST). *Felony, Misdemeanor, Civil, Eviction, Small Claims.*

Civil Records: Access: Phone, mail, in person. Only the court performs in person searches; visitors may not. No search fee. Required to search: name, years to

search. Civil cases indexed by defendant, plaintiff. Civil records on docket books.

Criminal Records: Access: Phone, mail, in person. Only the court performs in person searches; visitors may not. No search fee. Required to search: name, years to search; also helpful: DOB. Criminal records on docket books.

General Information: No juvenile or sealed records released. SASE required. Turnaround time 1-2 weeks. Copy fee: $.50 per page. Certification fee: $1.50. Fee payee: Pittsfield District Court. Personal checks accepted. Prepayment is required.

South Berkshire District Court 9 Gilmore Ave, Great Barrington, MA 01230; 413-528-3520; Fax: 413-528-0757. Hours: 8AM-4PM (EST). *Felony, Misdemeanor, Civil, Eviction, Small Claims.*

Civil Records: Access: Fax, mail, in person. Both court and visitors may perform in person searches. No search fee. Required to search: name, years to search. Civil cases indexed by defendant, plaintiff. Civil records on index cards from 1984, docket books to 1900. Court will only perform search if given the docket number.

Criminal Records: Access: Fax, mail, in person. Only the court performs in person searches; visitors may not. No search fee. Required to search: name, years to search. Criminal records on index cards from 1984, docket books to 1900. Court will only do search if given docket number.

General Information: No juvenile, impounded records released. SASE required. Turnaround time 1-2 weeks. Copy fee: $.50 per page. Certification fee: $1.50. Fee payee: District Court. Personal checks accepted. Prepayment is required.

Probate & Family Court 44 Bank Row, Pittsfield, MA 01201; 413-442-6941; Fax: 413-443-3430. Hours: 8:30AM-4PM (EST). *Probate.*

Bristol County

Superior Court - Taunton 9 Court St, Taunton, MA 02780; 508-823-6588 X1. Hours: 8AM-4:30PM (EST). *Felony, Civil Actions Over $25,000.*

Civil Records: Access: Mail, in person. Both court and visitors may perform in person searches. No search fee. Required to search: name, years to search. Civil cases indexed by defendant, plaintiff. Civil records on computer link to Boston from 1985, index books from 1935.

Criminal Records: Access: Mail, in person. Both court and visitors may perform in person searches. No search fee. Required to search: name, years to search; also helpful: DOB. Criminal records on computer link to Boston from 1985, index books from 1935.

General Information: Public Access terminal is available. No impounded records released. Turnaround time 2 weeks. Copy fee: $.50 per page. Certification fee: $1.50. Fee payee: Clerk of Superior Court of Bristol County. Personal checks accepted. Prepayment is required.

Attleboro District Court 34 Courthouse, 88 N Main St, Attleboro, MA 02703; 508-222-5900; Fax: 508-223-3916. Hours: 8AM-4:30PM (EST). *Felony, Misdemeanor, Civil, Eviction, Small Claims.*

Civil Records: Access: Phone, mail, in person. Only the court performs in person searches; visitors may not. No search fee. Required to search: name, years to search. Civil cases indexed by defendant, plaintiff. Civil records on computer since 1995; prior records on index cards from 1983, docket books from 1900.

Criminal Records: Access: Phone, mail, in person. Only the court performs in person searches; visitors may not. No search fee. Required to search: name, years to search, DOB, SSN. Criminal records on computer since 1995; prior records on index cards from 1983, docket books from 1900.

General Information: No impounded records released. Turnaround time 1-2 weeks. Copy fee: $.50 per page. Certification fee: $1.50. Fee payee: District Court, Attleboro District Court. Business checks accepted. Prepayment is required.

Fall River District Court 45 Rock St, Fall River, MA 02720; 508-679-8161; Fax: 508-675-5477. Hours: 8AM-4:30PM (EST). *Felony, Misdemeanor, Civil, Eviction, Small Claims.*

Civil Records: Access: In person only. Visitors must perform in person searches for themselves. No search fee. Required to search: name, years to search. Civil cases indexed by defendant, plaintiff. Civil records on index on computer from 1989, on docket books in vault from 1985.

Criminal Records: Access: Mail, in person. Only the court performs in person searches; visitors may not. No search fee. Required to search: name, years to search, DOB or SSN. Criminal records on index on computer from 1989, on docket books in vault from 1985.

General Information: No sealed, minor, confidential address records released. SASE requested. Turnaround time 1-2 weeks. Fax notes: Fee to fax results is $.50 per page. Copy fee: $.50 per page. Certification fee: $1.00 per page. Fee payee: District Court. Only cashiers checks and money orders accepted. Prepayment is required.

New Bedford District Court 33 75 N 6th St, New Bedford, MA 02740; 508-999-9700. Hours: 8:30AM-4PM (EST). *Felony, Misdemeanor, Civil, Eviction, Small Claims.*

Civil Records: Access: Mail, in person. Only the court performs in person searches; visitors may not. No search fee. Required to search: name, years to search. Civil cases indexed by defendant, plaintiff. Civil records filed from 1989, prior on docket books; on computer back to 1995.

Criminal Records: Access: Mail, in person. Only the court performs in person searches; visitors may not. No search fee. Required to search: name, years to search, DOB; also helpful: SSN. Criminal records filed from 1989, prior on docket books; on computer back to 1995. Searches are limited to pending charges, this agency recommends searching elsewhere for closed case files.

General Information: No impounded records released. Turnaround time 1-2 weeks. Copy fee: $.50 per page. Certification fee: $1.50. Fee payee: District Court. Business checks accepted. Prepayment is required.

Taunton District Court 15 Court St, Taunton, MA 02780; 508-824-4032; Fax: 508-824-2282. Hours: 8AM-4:30PM (EST). *Felony, Misdemeanor, Civil, Eviction, Small Claims.*

Civil Records: Access: Phone, mail, in person. Only the court performs in person searches; visitors may not. No search fee. Required to search: name, years to search. Civil cases indexed by defendant, plaintiff. Civil records on index cards for 6 years.

Criminal Records: Access: Phone, mail, in person. Only the court performs in person searches; visitors may not. No search fee. Required to search: name, years to search, DOB. Criminal records on index cards for 6 years.

General Information: Turnaround time 1-2 days. Copy fee: $.50 per page. Certification fee: $1.50. Fee payee: District Court. Personal checks accepted. Prepayment is required.

New Bedford Probate & Family Court 505 Pleasant St, New Bedford, MA 02740; 508-999-5249; Fax: 508-991-7421. Hours: 8AM-4:30PM (EST). *Probate.*

Taunton Probate & Family Court 11 Court St, PO Box 567, Taunton, MA 02780; 508-824-4004. Hours: 8AM-4:30PM (EST). *Probate.*

Dukes County

Superior Court PO Box 1267, Edgartown, MA 02539; 508-627-4668; Fax: 508-627-7571. Hours: 8AM-4PM (EST). *Felony, Civil Actions Over $25,000.*

Civil Records: Access: Mail, in person. Both court and visitors may perform in person searches. No search fee. Required to search: name, years to search. Civil cases indexed by defendant, plaintiff. Civil records on index cards from 1976 and books from 1695.

Criminal Records: Access: Mail, in person. Both court and visitors may perform in person searches. No search fee. Required to search: name, years to search. Criminal records on index cards from 1976 and books from 1695.

General Information: No sealed records released. SASE required. Turnaround time 1-2 days. Copy fee: $.50 per page. Certification fee: $1.50. Fee payee: Clerk of Superior Court. Personal checks accepted. Prepayment is required.

Edgartown District Court PO Box 1284, Courthouse, 81 Main St, Edgartown, MA 02539-1284; 508-627-3751/4622. Hours: 8:30AM-4:30PM (EST). *Felony, Misdemeanor, Civil, Eviction, Small Claims.*

Civil Records: Access: In person only. Only the court performs in person searches; visitors may not. No search fee. Required to search: name, years to search. Civil cases indexed by defendant, plaintiff. Civil records on index cards from 1983, docket books to 1900.

Criminal Records: Access: In person only. Only the court performs in person searches; visitors may not. No search fee. Required to search: name, years to search, DOB; also helpful: SSN. Criminal records on index cards from 1983, docket books to 1900.

General Information: No sealed records released. Copy fee: $.50 per page. Certification fee: $1.50. Fee payee: District Court. Personal checks accepted. Prepayment is required.

Probate & Family Court PO Box 237, Rm 104, 1st Fl, Edgartown, MA 02539; 508-627-4703; Fax: 508-627-7664. Hours: 8:30AM-4:30PM (EST). *Probate.*

Essex County

Superior Court - Lawrence 43 Appleton Way, Lawrence, MA 01840; 978-687-7463. Hours: 8AM-4:30PM (EST). *Civil Actions Over $25,000.*

Note: Index cards are found in the Salem office (records prior to 1985)

Civil Records: Access: Mail, in person. Both court and visitors may perform in person searches. No search fee. Required to search: name, years to search. Civil cases indexed by defendant, plaintiff. Civil records on computer since 1985; prior records on index cards in Salem office. **General Information:** Public Access terminal is available. No impounded records released. Turnaround time 1-2 days. Copy fee: $.50 per page. Certification fee: $1.50. Fee payee: Clerk of Superior Court. Personal checks accepted. Prepayment is required.

Superior Court - Newburyport 145 High St, Newburyport, MA 01950; 978-462-4474. Hours: 8AM-4:30PM (EST). *Felony, Civil Actions Over $25,000.*

Note: All finished criminal record files are in Salem and civil case records Session A in Salem, Session B in Newburyport and Session C & D in Lawrence.

Civil Records: Access: Mail, in person. Both court and visitors may perform in person searches. No search fee. Required to search: name, years to search. Civil cases indexed by defendant, plaintiff. Civil records on computer back to 1988.

Criminal Records: Access: Mail, in person. Both court and visitors may perform in person searches. No search fee. Required to search: name, years to search.

General Information: No impounded records released. Turnaround time 1-2 days. Copy fee: $.50 per page. Certification fee: $1.50. Fee payee: Clerk of Superior Court. Personal checks accepted. Prepayment is required.

Superior Court - Salem 34 Federal St, Salem, MA 01970; 978-744-5500; Civil phone: X223; Criminal phone: X343; Fax: 978-741-0691 (civ); 978-825-9989 (crim). Hours: 8:00AM-4:30PM (EST). *Felony, Civil Actions Over $25,000.*

Civil Records: Access: Mail, in person. Visitors must perform in person searches for themselves. No search fee. Required to search: name, years to search. Civil cases indexed by defendant, plaintiff. Civil records are entered on computer for civil actions from all three Superior courts in this county. Computer records go back to 1985.

Criminal Records: Access: In person only. Visitors must perform in person searches for themselves. No search fee. Required to search: name, years to search. Criminal records are entered on computer for civil actions from all three Superior courts in this county. Computer records go back to 1985.

General Information: Public Access terminal is available. Impounded cases are not released. Turnaround time 1-2 days. Fax notes: Fee to fax results is $1.50 per page. Copy fee: $.50 per page. Certification fee: $1.50. Fee payee: Clerk of Superior Court. Personal checks accepted. Prepayment is required.

Haverhill District Court PO Box 1389, Haverhill, MA 01831; 978-373-4151; Fax: 978-521-6886. Hours: 8:30AM-4:30PM (EST). *Felony, Misdemeanor, Civil, Eviction, Small Claims.*

Civil Records: Access: Phone, fax, mail, in person. Both court and visitors may perform in person searches. No search fee. Required to search: name, years to search. Civil cases indexed by defendant, plaintiff. Civil records on index cards from 1983. Non-active in storage.

Criminal Records: Access: Phone, fax, mail, in person. Both court and visitors may perform in person searches. No search fee. Required to search: name, years to search; also helpful: DOB. Criminal records on index cards from 1983. Non-active in storage.

General Information: No juvenile, sealed cases, confidential records released. SASE required. Turnaround time 1-2 weeks. Copy fee: $.50 per page. Certification fee: $1.50. Fee payee: District Court. Personal checks accepted. Prepayment is required.

Ipswich District Court 30 South Main St, PO Box 246, Ipswich, MA 01938; 978-356-2681; Fax: 978-356-4396. Hours: 8:30AM-4:30PM (EST). *Felony, Misdemeanor, Civil, Eviction, Small Claims.*

Civil Records: Access: In person only. Visitors must perform in person searches for themselves. No search fee. Required to search: name, years to search. Civil cases indexed by defendant, plaintiff. Civil records on index cards, small claims from 1984, civil from 1964. Civil on docket books from 1970.

Criminal Records: Access: In person only. Visitors must perform in person searches for themselves. No search fee. Required to search: name, years to search; also helpful: DOB. Criminal records on index cards from 1979.

General Information: No juvenile records released. Copy fee: $.50 per page. Certification fee: Certification fee is $1.50 per page. Fee payee: District Court. Personal checks accepted. Prepayment is required.

Lawrence District Court 381 Common St, Lawrence, MA 01840; 978-687-7184; Civil phone: 978-689-2810. Hours: 8AM-4:30PM (EST). *Felony, Misdemeanor, Civil, Eviction, Small Claims.*

Civil Records: Access: Mail, in person. Both court and visitors may perform in person searches. No search fee. Required to search: name, years to search. Civil cases indexed by defendant, plaintiff. Civil records on index cards from 1983, docket books from 1900, on computer since 1990.

Criminal Records: Access: Mail, in person. Only the court performs in person searches; visitors may not. No search fee. Required to search: name, years to search, DOB; also helpful: address, SSN. Criminal records on index cards from 1983, docket books from 1900, on computer since 1990.

General Information: No medical, police reports, impounded, juvenile records released. SASE requested. Turnaround time 1-2 weeks. Copy fee: $.50 per page. Certification fee: $1.50. Fee payee: District Court. Personal checks accepted. Prepayment is required.

Lynn District Court 580 Essex St, Lynn, MA 01901; 781-598-5200. Hours: 8AM-4:30PM (EST). *Felony, Misdemeanor, Civil, Eviction, Small Claims.*

Civil Records: Access: Mail, in person. Both court and visitors may perform in person searches. No search fee. Required to search: name, years to search. Civil cases indexed by defendant, plaintiff. Civil records on index cards from 1983, docket books from approx 1900. Records older than 15 years are difficult to find and may take longer.

Criminal Records: Access: Mail, in person. Only the court performs in person searches; visitors may not. No search fee. Required to search: name, years to search; also helpful: DOB, SSN. Criminal records on index cards from 1983, docket books from approx 1900. Records older than 15 years are difficult to find and may take longer.

General Information: No juvenile, impounded or sealed records released. Copy fee: $.50 per page. Certification fee: $1.50. Fee payee: District Court. Personal checks accepted. Prepayment is required.

Newburyport District Court 22 188 State St, Newburyport, MA 01950; 978-462-2652. Hours: 8:30AM-4:30PM (EST). *Felony, Misdemeanor, Civil, Eviction, Small Claims.*

Civil Records: Access: Phone, mail, in person. Both court and visitors may perform in person searches. No search fee. Required to search: name, years to search. Civil cases indexed by defendant, plaintiff. Civil records on index cards from 1983, prior archived in Worcester.

Criminal Records: Access: Phone, mail, in person. Only the court performs in person searches; visitors may not. No search fee. Required to search: name, years to search, DOB. Criminal records on index cards from 1983, prior archived in Worcester.

General Information: No juvenile or impounded records released. Turnaround time 1-2 weeks. Copy fee: $.50 per page. Certification fee: $1.50. Fee payee: District Court. Personal checks accepted. Prepayment is required.

Peabody District Court 86 PO Box 666, Peabody, MA 01960; 978-532-3100. Hours: 8:30AM-4:30PM (EST). *Felony, Misdemeanor, Civil, Eviction, Small Claims.*

Civil Records: Access: Phone, mail, in person. Only the court performs in person searches; visitors may not. No search fee. Required to search: name, years to search. Civil cases indexed by defendant, plaintiff. Civil records stored in office for 10 years, prior stored in basement and are difficult to find.

Criminal Records: Access: Phone, mail, in person. Only the court performs in person searches; visitors may not. No search fee. Required to search: name, years

to search, DOB. Criminal records stored in office for 10 years, prior stored in basement and are difficult to find.

General Information: No juvenile or impounded records released. Turnaround time 1-2 weeks. Copy fee: $.50 per page. Certification fee: $1.50. Fee payee: District Court. Personal checks accepted. Prepayment is required.

Salem District Court 36 65 Washington St, Salem, MA 01970; 978-744-1167. Hours: 8:30AM-4:30PM (EST). *Felony, Misdemeanor, Civil, Eviction, Small Claims.*

Civil Records: Access: Mail, in person. Only the court performs in person searches; visitors may not. No search fee. Required to search: name, years to search. Civil cases indexed by defendant, plaintiff. Civil records on index cards and docket books.

Criminal Records: Access: Mail, in person. Only the court performs in person searches; visitors may not. No search fee. Required to search: name, years to search, DOB, SSN. Criminal records on index cards and docket books.

General Information: No juvenile or impounded records released. Turnaround time 1-2 weeks. Copy fee: $.50 per page. Certification fee: $1.50. Fee payee: District Court. Personal checks accepted. Prepayment is required.

Probate & Family Court 36 Federal St, Salem, MA 01970; 978-744-1020; Fax: 978-741-2957. Hours: 8:00AM-4:30PM (EST). *Probate.*

Franklin County

Superior Court PO Box 1573, Greenfield, MA 01302; 413-774-5535; Fax: 413-774-4770. Hours: 8:30AM-4:30PM (EST). *Felony, Civil Actions Over $25,000.*

Civil Records: Access: Fax, in person. Both court and visitors may perform in person searches. No search fee. Required to search: name, years to search. Civil cases indexed by defendant, plaintiff. Civil records in files; on computer back 2 years.

Criminal Records: Access: Fax, in person. Only the court performs in person searches; visitors may not. No search fee. Required to search: name, years to search, DOB. Criminal records in files; on computer back 2 years.

General Information: Public Access terminal is available. No impounded or juvenile records released. Fax notes: Fee to fax results is $1.50 per page. Copy fee: $.50 per page. Certification fee: $1.50 per page. Fee payee: Franklin County Superior Court. Personal checks accepted. Prepayment is required.

Greenfield District Court 425 Main St, Greenfield, MA 01301; 413-774-5533; Fax: 413-774-5328. Hours: 8:30AM-4:30PM (EST). *Felony, Misdemeanor, Civil, Eviction, Small Claims.*

Civil Records: Access: In person only. Both court and visitors may perform in person searches. No search fee. Required to search: name, years to search. Civil cases indexed by defendant, plaintiff. Civil records on docket books or index cards; on computer back to 1998.

Criminal Records: Access: In person only. Both court and visitors may perform in person searches. No search fee. Required to search: name, years to search, DOB. Criminal records on docket books or index cards; on computer back to 1998.

General Information: No juvenile records released. Copy fee: $.50 per page. Certification fee: $1.50. Fee payee: Greenfield District Court. Personal checks accepted. Prepayment is required.

Orange District Court #42 One Court Square, Orange, MA 01364; 978-544-8277; Fax: 978-544-5204. Hours: 8:30AM-4:30PM (EST). *Felony, Misdemeanor, Civil, Eviction, Small Claims.*

Civil Records: Access: Phone, mail, in person. Both court and visitors may perform in person searches. No search fee. Required to search: name, years to search. Civil cases indexed by defendant, plaintiff. Civil records on docket books from 1975.

Criminal Records: Access: Phone, mail, in person. Only the court performs in person searches; visitors may not. No search fee. Required to search: name, years to search. Criminal records on docket books from 1975.

General Information: No juvenile records released. Turnaround time 1-2 weeks. Copy fee: $.50 per page. Certification fee: $1.50 per page. Fee payee: District Court. Personal checks accepted. Prepayment is required.

Probate & Family Court PO Box 590, Greenfield, MA 01302; 413-774-7011; Fax: 413-774-3829. Hours: 8AM-4:30PM (EST). *Probate.*

http://aotweb.jud.state.ma.us

Hampden County

Superior Court 50 State St, PO Box 559, Springfield, MA 01102-0559; 413-735-6016; Fax: 413-737-1611. Hours: 8:30AM-4:30PM (EST). *Felony, Civil Actions Over $25,000.*

Civil Records: Access: Phone, mail, in person. Both court and visitors may perform in person searches. No search fee. Required to search: name, years to search. Civil cases indexed by defendant, plaintiff. Civil records on computer from 1989 to present; prior on index cards from 1930s, books from 1812.

Criminal Records: Access: In person only. Both court and visitors may perform in person searches. No search fee. Required to search: name, years to search. Criminal records on computer from 1989 to present; prior on index cards from 1930s, books from 1812.

General Information: Public Access terminal is available. No impounded case records released. SASE requested. Turnaround time 1 week. Copy fee: $.50 per page. Certification fee: $1.50. Fee payee: Clerk of Superior Court. Personal checks accepted. Prepayment is required.

Chicopee District Court #20 30 Church St, Chicopee, MA 01020; 413-598-0099; Fax: 413-598-8176. Hours: 8AM-4PM (EST). *Felony, Misdemeanor, Civil, Eviction, Small Claims.*

Civil Records: Access: Phone, fax, mail, in person. Both court and visitors may perform in person searches. No search fee. Required to search: name, years to search. Civil cases indexed by defendant, plaintiff. Civil records on index cards from 1983, docket books to 1900.

Criminal Records: Access: Phone, mail, in person. Both court and visitors may perform in person searches. No search fee. Required to search: name, years to search, DOB. Criminal records on index cards from 1983, docket books to 1900.

General Information: No juvenile records released. Turnaround time 1-2 weeks. Fax notes: Fee to fax results is $.50 per page. Copy fee: $.50 per page. Certification fee: $1.50. Fee payee: District Court. Personal checks accepted. Prepayment is required.

Holyoke District Court 20 Court Sq, Holyoke, MA 01041-5075; 413-538-9710; Fax: 413-533-7165. Hours: 8:30AM-4:30PM (EST). *Felony, Misdemeanor, Civil, Eviction, Small Claims.*

Civil Records: Access: Phone, mail, fax, in person. Both court and visitors may perform in person searches. No search fee. Required to search: name, years to search. Civil cases indexed by defendant, plaintiff. Civil records on index cards and docket books since 1976; on computer back to 1989.

Criminal Records: Access: Fax, mail, in person. Both court and visitors may perform in person searches. No search fee. Required to search: name, years to search, DOB or SSN, signed release. Criminal records on index cards and docket books since 1976; on computer back to1 1989.

General Information: No juvenile, sealed records released. SASE requested. Turnaround time 1-2 weeks. Copy fee: $.50 per page. Certification fee: $1.50. Fee payee: District Court. Only cashiers checks and money orders accepted. Prepayment is required.

Palmer District Court 235 Sykes St, Palmer, MA 01069; 413-283-8916; Fax: 413-283-6775. Hours: 8:30AM-4:30PM (EST). *Felony, Misdemeanor, Civil, Eviction, Small Claims.*

Civil Records: Access: In person only. Both court and visitors may perform in person searches. No search fee. Required to search: name, years to search. Civil cases indexed by defendant, plaintiff. Civil records on index cards for 10 years.

Criminal Records: Access: In person only. Both court and visitors may perform in person searches. No search fee. Required to search: name, years to search. Criminal records on index cards for 10 years.

General Information: No sealed or juvenile records released. Copy fee: $.50 per page. Certification fee: $1.50. Fee payee: District Court. Personal checks accepted. Prepayment is required.

Springfield District Court 50 State St, Springfield, MA 01103; 413-748-7613; Civil phone: 413-748-8659; Criminal phone: 413-748-7982; Fax: 413-747-4841. Hours: 8:00AM-4:30PM (EST). *Felony, Misdemeanor, Civil, Eviction, Small Claims.*

Civil Records: Access: Phone, mail, in person. Both court and visitors may perform in person searches. No search fee. Required to search: name, years to search. Civil cases indexed by defendant, plaintiff. Civil records on index cards.

Criminal Records: Access: Phone, mail, in person. Both court and visitors may perform in person searches. No search fee. Required to search: name, years to search. Criminal records on index cards.

General Information: No sealed, expunged, or adoption records released. Turnaround time 1-2 weeks. Copy fee: $.50 per page. Certification fee: $1.50. Fee payee: District Court. Business checks accepted. Prepayment is required.

Westfield District Court 27 Washington St, Westfield, MA 01085; 413-568-8946; Fax: 413-568-4863. Hours: 8AM-4PM (EST). *Felony, Misdemeanor, Civil, Eviction, Small Claims.*

Civil Records: Access: Mail, in person. Both court and visitors may perform in person searches. No search fee. Required to search: name, years to search. Civil cases indexed by defendant, plaintiff. Civil records on index cards and in files.

Criminal Records: Access: Mail, in person. Both court and visitors may perform in person searches. No search fee. Required to search: name, years to search. Criminal records on index cards and in files.

General Information: No sealed or juvenile records released. Turnaround time 1-2 weeks. Copy fee: $.50 per page. Certification fee: $1.50. Fee payee: District Court. Personal checks accepted. Prepayment is required.

Probate & Family Court 50 State St, Springfield, MA 01103-0559; 413-748-7759; Fax: 413-781-5605. Hours: 8AM-4:25PM (EST). *Probate.*

Hampshire County

Superior Court PO Box 1119, Northampton, MA 01061; 413-584-5810 x331; Fax: 413-586-8217. Hours: 9AM-4PM (EST). *Felony, Civil Actions Over $25,000.*

Civil Records: Access: Mail, fax, in person. Both court and visitors may perform in person searches. No search fee. Required to search: name, years to search. Civil cases indexed by defendant, plaintiff. Civil records in files, index cards from 1800s; on computer back to 1983.

Criminal Records: Access: Mail, fax, in person. Both court and visitors may perform in person searches. No search fee. Required to search: name, years to search. Criminal records in files, index cards from 1800s; on computer back to 1983.

General Information: Public Access terminal is available. (Civil only.) No impounded case records released. Turnaround time 1 week. Copy fee: $.50 per page. Certification fee: $10.00. Fee payee: Clerk of Superior Court. Personal checks accepted. Prepayment is required.

Northampton District Court Courthouse, 15 Gothic St, Northampton, MA 01060; 413-584-7400/7405 413-584-7776; Criminal phone: 413-584-7400; Fax: 413-586-1980. Hours: 8:30AM-4PM (EST). *Felony, Misdemeanor, Civil, Eviction, Small Claims.*

Civil Records: Access: Phone, fax, mail, in person. Only the court performs in person searches; visitors may not. No search fee. Required to search: name, years to search, address. Civil cases indexed by defendant, plaintiff. Civil records on index cards and docket books.

Criminal Records: Access: Fax, mail, in person. Only the court performs in person searches; visitors may not. No search fee. Required to search: name, years to search, DOB, signed release; also helpful-SSN. Criminal records on index cards and docket books.

General Information: No CHINS-care & protection, show cause-mental health records released. SASE requested. Turnaround time 1-2 weeks. Fax notes: No fee to fax results. Copy fee: $.50 per page. Certification fee: $1.50 per page. Fee payee: District Court. Personal checks accepted. Prepayment is required.

Ware District Court PO Box 300, Ware, MA 01082; 413-967-3301; Fax: 413-967-7986. Hours: 8AM-4:30PM (EST). *Felony, Misdemeanor, Civil, Eviction, Small Claims.*

Civil Records: Access: Phone, fax, mail, in person. Only the court performs in person searches; visitors may not. No search fee. Required to search: name, years to search. Civil cases indexed by defendant, plaintiff. Civil records on index cards or docket books. Some records sent to archives in Worcester.

Criminal Records: Access: Phone, fax, mail, in person. Only the court performs in person searches; visitors may not. No search fee. Required to search: name, years to search; also helpful: DOB, SSN. Criminal records on index cards or docket books. Some records sent to archives in Worcester.

General Information: No sealed, impounded, confidential or juvenile records released. Turnaround time 1-2 weeks. Copy fee: $.50 per page. Certification fee: $1.50. Fee payee: Ware District Court. Personal checks accepted. Prepayment is required.

Probate & Family Court 33 King St #3, Northampton, MA 01060; 413-586-8500; Fax: 413-584-1132. Hours: 8:45AM-4:30PM (EST). *Probate.*

Middlesex County

Superior Court - East Cambridge 40 Thorndike St, East Cambridge, MA 02141; 617-494-4010. Hours: 8:30AM-4:30PM (EST). *Felony, Civil Actions Over $25,000.*

Note: The court is planning to have Internet access.

Civil Records: Access: Mail, in person. Both court and visitors may perform in person searches. No search fee. Required to search: name, years to search; also helpful: address. Civil cases indexed by defendant, plaintiff. Civil records on computer from 1986, rest on card indexes to 1986.

Criminal Records: Access: Mail, in person. Both court and visitors may perform in person searches. No search fee. Required to search: name, years to search; also helpful: address. Criminal records on computer back to 1991, rest on card indexes to 1986.

General Information: Public Access terminal is available. No impounded or those restricted by statute records released. Turnaround time 3-5 days for criminal records. Copy fee: $.50 per page. Certification fee: $1.50. Fee payee: Clerk of Superior Court. Personal checks accepted. Prepayment is required.

Superior Court - Lowell 360 Gorham St, Lowell, MA 01852; 978-453-0201. Hours: 8:30AM-4:30PM (EST). *Felony, Civil Actions Over $25,000.*

Civil Records: Access: Mail, in person. Both court and visitors may perform in person searches. No search fee. Required to search: name, years to search. Civil cases indexed by defendant, plaintiff. Civil records on computer since 1990; prior records kept at East Cambridge Middlesex Superior Court, 40 Thorndike, Cambridge, MA 02141.

Criminal Records: Access: Mail, in person. Both court and visitors may perform in person searches. No search fee. Required to search: name, years to search. Criminal records on computer since 1990; prior records kept at East Cambridge Middlesex Superior Court, 40 Thorndike, Cambridge, MA 02141.

General Information: Turnaround time 1-2 days. Copy fee: $.50 per page. Certification fee: $1.50. Fee payee: Clerk of Superior Court. Personal checks accepted. Prepayment is required.

Ayer District Court 25 E Main St, Ayer, MA 01432; 978-772-2100; Fax: 978-772-5345. Hours: 8:30AM-4:30PM (EST). *Felony, Misdemeanor, Civil, Eviction, Small Claims.*

Civil Records: Access: Mail, in person. No search fee. Required to search: name, years to search. Civil cases indexed by defendant, plaintiff. Civil records on index cards from 1977 to present; only required to keep records 20 years. DOB required on subject.

Criminal Records: Access: Phone, mail, in person. Both court and visitors may perform in person searches. No search fee. Required to search: name, years to search, DOB. Criminal records on index cards from 1977 to 1995, computerized 1996 forward; Only required to keep records 10 years. Access by phone may be limited.

General Information: Juvenile records not released. Turnaround time 1-2 weeks. Copy fee: $.50 per page. Certification fee: $1.50. Fee payee: Ayer District Court. Personal checks accepted. Prepayment is required.

Cambridge District Court 52 PO Box 338, East Cambridge, MA 02141; 617-494-4310; Probate phone: 617-494-5233. Hours: 8:30AM-4:30PM (EST). *Felony, Misdemeanor, Civil, Eviction, Small Claims, Probate.*

Civil Records: Access: Mail, in person. Both court and visitors may perform in person searches. No search fee. Required to search: name, years to search. Civil cases indexed by defendant, plaintiff. Civil records on index cards or docket books. State law requires records be retained for 10 years.

Criminal Records: Access: In person only. Visitors must perform in person searches for themselves. No search fee. Required to search: name, years to search, DOB. Criminal records on index cards or docket books. State law requires records be retained for 10 years.

General Information: No sealed or juvenile records released. Turnaround time 1-2 weeks. Copy fee: $.50 per page. Certification fee: $1.50. Fee payee: District Court. Personal checks accepted. Prepayment is required.

Concord District Court 47 305 Walden St, Concord, MA 01742; 978-369-0500. Hours: 8:30AM-4:30PM (EST). *Felony, Misdemeanor, Civil, Eviction, Small Claims.*

Civil Records: Access: Mail, in person. Both court and visitors may perform in person searches. No search fee. Required to search: name, years to search; also helpful: address. Civil cases indexed by defendant, plaintiff. Civil records on computer from 1991, index cards and books from 1950, archived from 1643. In person searches performed from 1-2PM only.

Criminal Records: Access: Mail, in person. Both court and visitors may perform in person searches. No search fee. Required to search: name, years to search; also helpful: address, DOB, SSN. Criminal records on computer from 1991, index cards and books from 1950, archived from 1643. In person searches performed from 1-2PM only.

General Information: No impounded files released. SASE requested. Turnaround time 1 week. Copy fee: $.50 per page. Certification fee: $1.50. Fee payee: Commonwealth of Massachusetts. Personal checks accepted. Prepayment is required.

Framingham District Court 600 Concord St (PO Box 1669), Framingham, MA 01701; 508-875-7461. Hours: 8:30AM-4:30PM (EST). *Felony, Misdemeanor, Civil, Eviction, Small Claims.*

Civil Records: Access: Mail, in person. Both court and visitors may perform in person searches. No search fee. Required to search: name, years to search. Civil cases indexed by defendant, plaintiff. Civil records on index cards or docket books back to 1900; on computer back to 1986. Special form required for mail request.

Criminal Records: Access: Mail, in person. Both court and visitors may perform in person searches. No search fee. Required to search: name, years to search. Criminal records on index cards or docket books back to 1900; on computer back to 1986. Special form required for mail request.

General Information: No sealed, expunged or juvenile records released. Copy fee: $1.50 per page. Certification fee: $1.50 per page. Fee payee: District Court. Only cashiers checks and money orders accepted. Prepayment is required.

Lowell District Court 41 Hurd St, Lowell, MA 01852; 978-459-4101; Civil phone: x235; Criminal phone: x204. Hours: 8:30AM-4:30PM (EST). *Felony, Misdemeanor, Civil, Eviction, Small Claims.*

Civil Records: Access: In person only. Visitors must perform in person searches for themselves. No search fee. Required to search: name, years to search. Civil cases indexed by defendant, plaintiff. Civil records on index cards or docket books. Records retained for 10 years.

Criminal Records: Access: Mail, in person. Visitors must perform in person searches for themselves. No search fee. Required to search: name, years to search, DOB. Criminal records on index cards or docket books. Records retained for 10 years.

General Information: No impounded records released. Copy fee: $.50 per page. Certification fee:

$1.50. Fee payee: District Court, Lowell Division. Business checks accepted. Prepayment is required.

Malden District Court 89 Summer St., Malden, MA 02148; 781-322-7500. Hours: 8:30AM-4:30PM (EST). *Felony, Misdemeanor, Civil, Eviction, Small Claims.*

Civil Records: Access: Phone, mail, in person. Only the court performs in person searches; visitors may not. No search fee. Required to search: name, years to search. Civil cases indexed by defendant, plaintiff. Civil records on index cards or docket books back to 1970; on computer back to 1992.

Criminal Records: Access: Phone, mail, in person. Both court and visitors may perform in person searches. No search fee. Required to search: name, years to search, DOB. Criminal records on index cards or docket books back to 1970; on computer back to 1992.

General Information: No juvenile records released. Turnaround time 1-2 weeks. Copy fee: $.50 per page. Certification fee: $10.00. Fee payee: District Court. Personal checks accepted. Prepayment is required.

Marlborough District Court 21 45 Williams St, Marlborough, MA 01752; 508-485-3700. Hours: 8AM-4:30PM (EST). *Felony, Misdemeanor, Civil, Eviction, Small Claims.*

Civil Records: Access: Phone, mail, in person. Both court and visitors may perform in person searches. No search fee. Required to search: name, years to search. Civil cases indexed by defendant, plaintiff. Civil records on index cards or docket books. State law requires records be retained for 10 years.

Criminal Records: Access: Phone, mail, in person. Both court and visitors may perform in person searches. No search fee. Required to search: name, years to search, DOB. Criminal records on index cards or docket books. State law requires records be retained for 10 years.

General Information: No juvenile records released. Turnaround time 1-2 weeks. Copy fee: $.50 per page. Certification fee: $1.50. Fee payee: District Court. Personal checks accepted. Prepayment is required.

Natick District Court 117 E Central, Natick, MA 01760; 508-653-4332. Hours: 8:30AM-4:30PM (EST). *Felony, Misdemeanor, Civil, Eviction, Small Claims.*

Civil Records: Access: Phone, mail, in person. Only the court performs in person searches; visitors may not. No search fee. Required to search: name, years to search. Civil cases indexed by defendant, plaintiff. Civil records on index cards and docket books, back for 10 years.

Criminal Records: Access: Phone, mail, in person. Only the court performs in person searches; visitors may not. No search fee. Required to search: name, years to search, DOB. Criminal records on index cards and docket books, back for 10 years.

General Information: No juvenile records released. Turnaround time 1-2 weeks. Copy fee: $.50 per page. Certification fee: $1.50. Fee payee: District Court. Personal checks accepted. Prepayment is required.

Newton District Court 121 Third St, East Cambridge, MA 02141; 617-494-0102. Hours: 8:30AM-4:30PM (EST). *Felony, Misdemeanor, Civil, Eviction, Small Claims.*

www.state.ma.us/courts/courtsandjudges/courts/newton districtmain.html

Note: After renovations, the court is expected to return to 1309 Washington, West Newton 02141 on or near June 4, 2003.

Civil Records: Access: Phone, mail, in person. Both court and visitors may perform in person searches. No search fee. Required to search: name, years to search. Civil cases indexed by defendant, plaintiff. Civil records on index cards back to 1930.

Criminal Records: Access: Phone, mail, in person. Both court and visitors may perform in person searches. No search fee. Required to search: name, years to search. Criminal records on index books back to 1930.

General Information: No juvenile, (some) 209-A cases or mental health records released. Turnaround time 1 week. Copy fee: $.50 per page. Certification fee: $1.50. Fee payee: District Court of Newton. Personal checks accepted.

Somerville District Court 175 Fellsway, Somerville, MA 02145; 617-666-8000. Hours: 8:30AM-4:30PM (EST). *Felony, Misdemeanor, Civil, Eviction, Small Claims.*

Civil Records: Access: Phone, mail, in person. Only the court performs in person searches; visitors may not. No search fee. Required to search: name, years to search. Civil cases indexed by defendant, plaintiff. Civil records on index cards or docket books. State law requires records be retained for 10 years.

Criminal Records: Access: Phone, mail, in person. Only the court performs in person searches; visitors may not. No search fee. Required to search: name, years to search, DOB. Criminal records on computer since 1997; prior records on index cards or docket books. State law requires records be retained for 10 years.

General Information: No juvenile or impounded records released. Turnaround time 1-2 weeks. Copy fee: $.50 per page. Certification fee: $1.50. Fee payee: District Court. Personal checks accepted. Prepayment is required.

Waltham District Court 51 38 Linden St, Waltham, MA 02154; 781-894-4500. Hours: 8:30AM-4:30PM (EST). *Felony, Misdemeanor, Civil, Eviction, Small Claims.*

Civil Records: Access: Mail, in person. Both court and visitors may perform in person searches. No search fee. Required to search: name, years to search. Civil cases indexed by defendant, plaintiff. Civil records on index cards and docket books, back for 10 years.

Criminal Records: Access: Mail, in person. Both court and visitors may perform in person searches. No search fee. Required to search: name, years to search; also helpful: DOB. Criminal records on index cards and docket books, back for 10 years.

General Information: Public Access terminal is available. No juvenile records released. Turnaround time 1 week. Copy fee: $.50 per page. Certification fee: $1.50. Fee payee: District Court. No personal checks. Prepayment is required.

Woburn District Court 53 30 Pleasant St, Woburn, MA 01801; 781-935-4000. Hours: 8:30AM-4:30PM (EST). *Felony, Misdemeanor, Civil, Eviction, Small Claims.*

Civil Records: Access: Mail, in person. Both court and visitors may perform in person searches. No search fee. Required to search: name, years to search. Civil cases indexed by defendant, plaintiff. Civil records on index cards, computer listing or docket books back 30 years.

Criminal Records: Access: Mail, in person. Only the court performs in person searches; visitors may not. No search fee. Required to search: name, years to search; also helpful: DOB. Criminal records on index cards, computer listing or docket books back 30 years.

General Information: Public Access terminal is available. (For records since 1996.) No statutorily non-public records released. SASE requested. Turnaround time 1-2 weeks. Copy fee: $.50 per page. Certification fee: $1.50. Fee payee: District Court. Personal checks accepted. Prepayment is required.

Probate & Family Court 208 Cambridge St, PO Box 410480, East Cambridge, MA 02141-0005; 617-768-5800; Fax: 617-225-0781. Hours: 8AM-4PM (EST). *Probate.*

Nantucket County

Superior Court PO Box 967, Nantucket, MA 02554; 508-228-2559; Fax: 508-228-3725. Hours: 8:30AM-4PM (EST). *Felony, Civil Actions Over $25,000.*

Civil Records: Access: Phone, fax, mail, in person. Both court and visitors may perform in person searches. No search fee. Required to search: name, years to search. Civil cases indexed by defendant, plaintiff. Civil records on index books from 1762.

Criminal Records: Access: Phone, fax, mail, in person. Both court and visitors may perform in person searches. No search fee. Required to search: name, years to search. Criminal records on index books from 1762.

General Information: No impounded records released. SASE required. Turnaround time 1 week. Fax notes: No fee to fax results. In-state faxing only. Copy fee: $.50 per page. Certification fee: $1.50. Fee payee: Nantucket Superior Court. Personal checks accepted. Prepayment is required.

Nantucket District Court 16 Broad Street, PO Box 1800, Nantucket, MA 02554; 508-228-0460. Hours: 8AM-4PM (EST). *Felony, Misdemeanor, Civil, Eviction, Small Claims.*

Civil Records: Access: In person only. Visitors must perform in person searches for themselves. No search fee. Required to search: name, years to search. Civil cases indexed by defendant, plaintiff. Civil records on index cards or docket books. State law requires records be retained for 10 years.

Criminal Records: Access: In person only. Visitors must perform in person searches for themselves. No search fee. Required to search: name, years to search. Criminal records on index cards or docket books. State law requires records be retained for 10 years.

General Information: Copy fee: $.50 per page. Certification fee: $1.50. Fee payee: Nantucket District Court. Prepayment is required.

Probate & Family Court PO Box 1116, Nantucket, MA 02554; 508-228-2669; Fax: 508-228-3662. Hours: 8:30AM-4PM (EST). *Probate.*

Norfolk County

Superior Court 650 High St, Dedham, MA 02026; 781-326-1600; Civil phone: X1; Criminal phone: X2; Fax: 781-326-3871(Civ); 781-320-9726(Crim). Hours: 8:30AM-4:30PM (EST). *Felony, Civil Actions Over $25,000.*

Civil Records: Access: Phone, mail, in person. Both court and visitors may perform in person searches. No search fee. Required to search: name, years to search. Civil cases indexed by defendant, plaintiff. Civil records on index books from 1900, on computer back to 9/2000.

Criminal Records: Access: Mail, in person. Visitors must perform in person searches for themselves. No search fee. Required to search: name, years to search; also helpful: address, DOB, SSN. Criminal records on index books from 1900; on computer back to 9/2000.

General Information: No impounded records released. No one may view a file of a sex-related crime without authorization from a judge. SASE not required. Turnaround time 1 week, 1-2 days for criminal phone in requests. Copy fee: $.50 per page. Certification fee: $1.50. Fee payee: Clerk of Superior Court. Personal checks accepted for copies only. Prepayment is required.

Brookline District Court 360 Washington St, Brookline, MA 02146; 617-232-4660; Fax: 617-739-0734. Hours: 8:30AM-4:30PM (EST). *Felony, Misdemeanor, Civil, Eviction, Small Claims.*

Civil Records: Access: Mail, in person. Both court and visitors may perform in person searches. No search fee. Required to search: name, years to search. Civil cases indexed by defendant, plaintiff. Civil records on index cards and docket books back for 10 years.

Criminal Records: Access: Mail, in person. Only the court performs in person searches; visitors may not. No search fee. Required to search: name, years to search; also helpful: DOB. Criminal records on index cards and docket books back for 10 years.

General Information: No sealed case records released. Turnaround time 1-2 weeks. Copy fee: $.50 per page. Certification fee: $1.50. Fee payee: Brookline District Court. Personal checks accepted. Prepayment is required.

Dedham District Court 631 High St, Dedham, MA 02026; 781-329-4777. Hours: 8:15AM-4:30PM *Felony, Misdemeanor, Civil, Eviction, Small Claims.*

Civil Records: Access: In person only. Visitors must perform in person searches for themselves. No search fee. Required to search: name, years to search. Civil cases indexed by defendant, plaintiff. Civil records on computer since 1997, and on index cards or docket books prior to that. State law requires records be retained for 10 years.

Criminal Records: Access: In person only. Visitors must perform in person searches for themselves. No search fee. Required to search: name, years to search. Criminal records on computer since 1997, and on index cards or docket books prior to that. State law requires records be retained for 10 years. Access is available after 10AM.

General Information: No juvenile records released. Copy fee: $.50 per page. Certification fee: $1.50. Fee payee: District Court. Personal checks accepted. Prepayment is required.

Quincy District Court One Dennis Ryan Parkway, Quincy, MA 02169; 617-471-1650. Hours: 8:30AM-4:30PM (EST). *Felony, Misdemeanor, Civil, Eviction, Small Claims.*

Civil Records: Access: In person only. Visitors must perform in person searches for themselves. No search fee. Required to search: name, years to search. Civil cases indexed by defendant, plaintiff. Civil records on index cards or docket books. State law requires records be retained for 10 years.

Criminal Records: Access: In person only. Visitors must perform in person searches for themselves. No search fee. Required to search: name, years to search; also helpful: DOB. Criminal records on computer since 1996; prior records on index cards or docket books. State law requires records be retained for 10 years.

General Information: No juvenile records released. Copy fee: $.50 per page. Certification fee: $1.50. Fee payee: District Court. Only cashiers checks and money orders accepted. Prepayment is required.

Stoughton District Court 1288 Central St, Stoughton, MA 02072; 781-344-2131. Hours: 8:30AM-4:30PM (EST). *Felony, Misdemeanor, Civil, Eviction, Small Claims.*

Civil Records: Access: Mail, in person. Both court and visitors may perform in person searches. No search fee. Required to search: name, years to search. Civil cases indexed by defendant, plaintiff. Civil records on index cards or docket books for 10 years or more.

Criminal Records: Access: Mail, in person. Only the court performs in person searches; visitors may not. No search fee. Required to search: name, years to search; also helpful: DOB. Criminal records on computer since 1996; prior records on index cards or docket books for 10 years or more.

General Information: No juvenile records released. Turnaround time 1 week. Copy fee: $.50 per page. Certification fee: $1.50. Fee payee: District Court. Personal checks accepted. Prepayment is required.

Wrentham District Court 60 East Street, Wrentham, MA 02093; 508-384-3106; Fax: 508-384-5052. Hours: 8:30AM-4:30PM (EST). *Felony, Misdemeanor, Civil, Eviction, Small Claims.*

Civil Records: Access: In person. Both court and visitors may perform in person searches. No search fee. Required to search: name, years to search. Civil cases indexed by defendant, plaintiff. Civil records on computer since 1995; prior on index cards or docket books. Records retained for 10 years.

Criminal Records: Access: In person. Both court and visitors may perform in person searches. No search fee. Required to search: name, years to search; also helpful: DOB. Criminal records on computer since 1995; prior on index cards or docket books. Records retained for 10 years.

General Information: No show cause hearing or juvenile records released. Mail requests not accepted. Copy fee: $.50 per page. Certification fee: $1.50 per page. Fee payee: District Court. Personal checks accepted. Prepayment is required.

Probate & Family Court 649 High St, PO Box 269, Dedham, MA 02027; 781-326-7200; Fax: 781-326-5575. Hours: 8AM-4:30PM (EST). *Probate.*

Plymouth County

Superior Court - Brockton 72 Belmont St, Brockton, MA 02401; 508-583-8250. Hours: 8:30AM-4:30PM (EST). *Felony, Civil Actions Over $25,000.*

Civil Records: Access: Mail, in person. Both court and visitors may perform in person searches. No search fee. Required to search: name, years to search. Civil cases indexed by defendant, plaintiff. Civil records for current civil cases are here, closed case are in Plymouth, some pending.

Criminal Records: Access: Mail, in person. Both court and visitors may perform in person searches. No search fee. Required to search: name, years to search. Criminal records for current civil cases are here, closed case are in Plymouth, some pending.

General Information: No impounded records released. Turnaround time 1-2 days. Copy fee: $.50 per page. Certification fee: $1.50. Fee payee: Clerk of Superior Court. Personal checks accepted. Prepayment is required.

Superior Court - Plymouth Court St, Plymouth, MA 02360; 508-747-6911. Hours: 8:30AM-4:30PM (EST). *Felony, Civil Actions Over $25,000.*

Civil Records: Access: Mail, in person. Only the court performs in person searches; visitors may not. No search fee. Required to search: name, years to search. Civil cases indexed by defendant, plaintiff. Civil records for all closed cases are kept here.

Criminal Records: Access: Mail, in person. Only the court performs in person searches; visitors may not. No search fee. Required to search: name, years to search. Criminal records 10 years or older are here, for recent cases go to the Superior Court in Brockton.

General Information: No impounded records released. Turnaround time 1 week, immediate four phone requests. Copy fee: $.50 per page. Certification fee: $1.50. Fee payee: Clerk of Superior Court. Personal checks accepted. Prepayment is required.

Brockton District Court PO Box 7610 (215 Main St.), Brockton, MA 02303-7610; 508-587-8000. 8:30AM-4:30PM (EST). *Felony, Misdemeanor, Civil, Eviction, Small Claims.*

Civil Records: Access: Mail, in person. Both court and visitors may perform in person searches. No search fee. Required to search: name, years to search. Civil cases indexed by defendant, plaintiff. Civil records on index cards or docket books, retained for 10 years.

Criminal Records: Access: Mail, in person. Both court and visitors may perform in person searches. No search fee. Required to search: name, years to search; also helpful: DOB. Criminal records on index cards or docket books, retained for 10 years.

General Information: No juvenile or impounded records released. Turnaround time 1-2 weeks. Copy fee: $.50 per page. Certification fee: $1.50. Fee payee: District Court. Personal checks accepted. Prepayment is required.

Hingham District Court 28 George Washington Blvd, Hingham, MA 02043; 781-749-7000; Fax: 781-740-8390. Hours: 8:30AM-4:30PM (EST). *Felony, Misdemeanor, Civil, Eviction, Small Claims.*

Civil Records: Access: Mail, in person. Only the court performs in person searches; visitors may not. No search fee. Required to search: name, years to search. Civil cases indexed by defendant, plaintiff. Civil records on index cards or docket books, retained for 10 years or more.

Criminal Records: Access: Mail, in person. Only the court performs in person searches; visitors may not. No search fee. Required to search: name, years to search; also helpful: DOB. Criminal records on index cards or docket books, retained for 10 years or more.

General Information: No juvenile records released. Turnaround time 1-2 weeks. Copy fee: $.50 per page. Certification fee: $1.50. Fee payee: District Court. Personal checks accepted. Prepayment is required.

Plymouth 3rd District Court Courthouse, South Russell St, Plymouth, MA 02360; 508-747-0500. Hours: 8:30AM-4:30PM *Felony, Misdemeanor, Civil, Eviction, Small Claims.*

Civil Records: Access: Mail, in person. Both court and visitors may perform in person searches. No search fee. Required to search: name, years to search. Civil cases indexed by defendant, plaintiff. Civil records on index cards or docket books. State law requires records be retained for 10 years. Visitors can only access the index cards.

Criminal Records: Access: Mail, in person. Both court and visitors may perform in person searches. No search fee. Required to search: name, years to search; also helpful: DOB. Criminal records on index cards or docket books. State law requires records be retained for 10 years. Visitors can only access the index cards.

General Information: No juvenile or impounded records released. Turnaround time 3-4 days. Copy fee: $.50 per page. Certification fee: $1.50. Fee payee: Plymouth District Court. Personal checks accepted. Prepayment is required.

Wareham District Court 2200 Cranberry Hwy, Junction Routes 28 & 58, West Wareham, MA 02576; 508-295-8300; Fax: 508-291-6376. Hours: 8:30AM-4:30PM (EST). *Felony, Misdemeanor, Civil, Eviction, Small Claims.*

Civil Records: Access: Phone, mail, in person. Both court and visitors may perform in person searches. No search fee. Required to search: name, years to search. Civil cases indexed by defendant, plaintiff. Civil records on index cards or docket books. State law requires records be retained for 10 years.

Criminal Records: Access: Phone, mail, in person. Only the court performs in person searches; visitors may not. No search fee. Required to search: name, years

to search; also helpful: DOB. Criminal records on index cards or docket books. State law requires records be retained for 10 years.

General Information: No juvenile records released. SASE requested. Turnaround time 1-2 weeks. Copy fee: $.50 per page. Certification fee: $1.50. Fee payee: District Court. Personal checks accepted. Prepayment is required.

Probate & Family Court 11 Russell, PO Box 3640, Plymouth, MA 02361; 508-747-6204; Fax: 508-746-6846. Hours: 8:30AM-4PM (EST). *Probate.*

Suffolk County

Superior Court - Civil 90 Devonshire St, Rm 810, Boston, MA 02109; 617-788-7677. Hours: 8:30AM-5PM (EST). *Civil.*

Civil Records: Access: Mail, in person. Both court and visitors may perform in person searches. No search fee. Required to search: name, years to search. Civil cases indexed by defendant, plaintiff. Civil records on computer from 1991, index cards and books from 1860.

General Information: Public Access terminal is available. No impounded records released. Turnaround time 1 week. Copy fee: $.50 per page. Certification fee: $1.50. Fee payee: Clerk of Superior Court. Business checks accepted. Prepayment is required.

Superior Court - Criminal 90 Devonshire St #607, USPO & Courthouse, Boston, MA 02109; 617-788-8160; Fax: 617-788-7798. Hours: 9AM-5PM (EST). *Felony.*

Criminal Records: Access: Mail, fax, in person. Both court and visitors may perform in person searches. No search fee. Required to search: name, years to search. Criminal records on computer back to 1991, index cards and books from 1950, archived from 1864.

General Information: Public Access terminal is available. Turnaround time 1-2 weeks. Copy fee: $.50 per page. Certification fee: $1.50. Fee payee: Superior Court. Personal checks accepted. Prepayment is required.

Brighton District Court 52 Academy Hill Rd, Brighton, MA 02135; 617-782-6521; Fax: 617-254-2127. Hours: 8:30AM-4:30PM (EST). *Felony, Misdemeanor, Civil, Eviction, Small Claims.*

Civil Records: Access: Phone, mail, in person. Both court and visitors may perform in person searches. No search fee. Required to search: name, years to search. Civil cases indexed by defendant, plaintiff. Civil records on index cards or docket books. State law requires records be retained for 10 years.

Criminal Records: Access: Phone, mail, in person. Both court and visitors may perform in person searches. No search fee. Required to search: name, years to search. Criminal records on index cards or docket books. State law requires records be retained for 10 years.

General Information: No sealed or impounded records released. Turnaround time 1-2 weeks. Copy fee: $.50 per page. Certification fee: $1.50 per page. Fee payee: District Court. Personal checks accepted. Prepayment is required.

Charlestown District Court 3 City Square, Charlestown, MA 02129; 617-242-5400; Fax: 617-242-1677. Hours: 8:30AM-4:30PM (EST). *Felony, Misdemeanor, Civil, Eviction, Small Claims.*

Civil Records: Access: Fax, mail, in person. Only the court performs in person searches; visitors may not. No search fee. Required to search: name, years to search. Civil cases indexed by defendant, plaintiff. Civil records on index cards or docket books. State law requires records be retained for 10 years.

Criminal Records: Access: Fax, mail, in person. Only the court performs in person searches; visitors may not.

No search fee. Required to search: name, years to search; also helpful: DOB. Criminal records on index cards or docket books. State law requires records be retained for 10 years.

General Information: No juvenile records released. Turnaround time 1-2 weeks. Copy fee: $.50 per page. Certification fee: $1.50. Fee payee: District Court. Personal checks accepted. Prepayment is required.

Chelsea District Court 120 Broadway, Chelsea, MA 02150-2606; 617-660-9400; Fax: 617-621-9215. Hours: 8:30AM-4:30PM (EST). *Felony, Misdemeanor, Civil, Eviction, Small Claims.*

Civil Records: Access: Phone, mail, in person. Both court and visitors may perform in person searches. No search fee. Required to search: name, years to search. Civil cases indexed by defendant, plaintiff. Civil records on index cards or docket books back to 1900; on computer back to 1990.

Criminal Records: Access: Phone, mail, in person. Both court and visitors may perform in person searches. No search fee. Required to search: name, years to search; also helpful: address, DOB. Criminal records on index cards or docket books back to 1900; on computer back to 1990.

General Information: No closed cases, impounded, sealed, mental health commitment, alcoholic or victim of sexual offense records released. SASE required. Turnaround time 1-2 weeks. Copy fee: $.50 per page. Certification fee: $1.50. Fee payee: District Court. Personal checks accepted. Prepayment is required.

Dorchester District Court 510 Washington St, Dorchester, MA 02124; 617-288-9500. Hours: 8:30AM-4:30PM (EST). *Felony, Misdemeanor, Civil, Eviction, Small Claims.*

Civil Records: Access: Mail, in person. Both court and visitors may perform in person searches. No search fee. Required to search: name, years to search. Civil cases indexed by defendant, plaintiff. Civil records on index cards or docket books. State law requires records be retained for 20 years.

Criminal Records: Access: Mail, in person. Only the court performs in person searches; visitors may not. No search fee. Required to search: name, years to search, DOB. Criminal records on index cards or docket books; later on computer. State law requires records be retained for 20 years.

General Information: No juvenile records released. Turnaround time 1-2 weeks. Copy fee: $.50 per page. Certification fee: $1.50. Fee payee: District Court. Personal checks accepted. Prepayment is required.

East Boston District Court 37 Meridian St, East Boston, MA 02128; 617-569-7550; Fax: 617-561-4988. Hours: 8:30AM-4:30PM (EST). *Misdemeanor, Civil Actions Under $25,000, Eviction, Small Claims.*

Civil Records: Access: Mail, in person. Both court and visitors may perform in person searches. No search fee. Required to search: name, years to search. Civil cases indexed by defendant, plaintiff. Civil records on index cards or docket books. State law requires records be retained for 10 years.

Criminal Records: Access: Mail, in person. Both court and visitors may perform in person searches. No search fee. Required to search: name, years to search. Criminal records on index cards or docket books. State law requires records be retained for 10 years.

General Information: No juvenile records released. Turnaround time 1-2 weeks. Copy fee: $.50 per page. Certification fee: $1.50. Fee payee: District Court. Personal checks accepted. Prepayment is required.

Roxbury District Court 85 Warren St, Roxbury, MA 02119; 617-427-7000; Fax: 617-442-0615. Hours: 8:30AM-4:30PM (EST). *Felony, Misdemeanor, Civil, Eviction, Small Claims.*

Civil Records: Access: Phone, fax, mail, in person. Both court and visitors may perform in person searches. No search fee. Required to search: name, years to search. Civil cases indexed by defendant, plaintiff. Civil records on index cards or docket books since 1981; on computer back to 1999. State law requires records be retained for 10 years.

Criminal Records: Access: Phone, fax, mail, in person. Both court and visitors may perform in person searches. No search fee. Required to search: name, years to search, DOB; also helpful: address. Criminal records on index cards or docket books since 1981; on computer back to 1999. State law requires records be retained for 10 years.

General Information: Public Access terminal is available. No juvenile records released. Turnaround time 1-2 weeks. Fax notes: Fee to fax results is $1.00 per page. Copy fee: $1.00 per page. Certification fee: $1.50. Fee payee: District Court. Prepayment required.

South Boston District Court 535 East Broadway, South Boston, MA 02127; 617-268-9292/9293; Fax: 617-268-7321. Hours: 8:30AM-4:30PM (EST). *Felony, Misdemeanor, Civil, Eviction, Small Claims.*

Civil Records: Access: In person only. Visitors must perform in person searches for themselves. No search fee. Required to search: name, years to search, address. Civil cases indexed by defendant, plaintiff. Civil records on index cards or docket books. Records go back 20 years; two on computer.

Criminal Records: Access: In person only. Visitors must perform in person searches for themselves. No search fee. Required to search: name, years to search, address, DOB. Criminal records on index cards or docket books. Records go back 20 years; two on computer.

General Information: No juvenile or medical records released. Copy fee: $.50 per page. Certification fee: $1.50. Fee payee: District Court. Personal checks accepted. Prepayment is required.

Suffolk County Courthouse Boston Municipal Court 55 Pemberpon Square, Boston, MA 02108; 617-725-8000; Civil phone: 617-725-8404; Criminal phone: 617-725-8460. Hours: 8:30AM-4:30PM (EST). *Misdemeanor, Civil, Small Claims.*

Civil Records: Access: Mail, in person. Both court and visitors may perform in person searches. No search fee. Required to search: name, years to search. Civil cases indexed by defendant, plaintiff. Civil records on computer from 1995 to present, and only court searches those records. Public can search prior records on index cards and look-up. State law requires records be retained for 10 years.

Criminal Records: Access: Mail, in person. Both court and visitors may perform in person searches. No search fee. Required to search: name, years to search; also helpful: DOB. Criminal records on computer from 1995 to present, and only court searches those records. Public can search prior records on index cards and look-up. State law requires records be retained for 10 years.

General Information: No impounded records released. Turnaround time 1-2 weeks. Copy fee: $.50 per page. Certification fee: $1.50. Fee payee: District Court. Personal checks accepted. Prepayment required.

West Roxbury District Court Courthouse, 445 Arborway, Jamaica Plain, MA 02130; 617-971-1200. Hours: 8:30AM-4:30PM (EST). *Felony, Misdemeanor, Civil, Eviction, Small Claims.*

Civil Records: Access: Mail, in person. Only the court performs in person searches; visitors may not. No search fee. Required to search: name, years to search; also helpful: address. Civil cases indexed by defendant, plaintiff. Civil records on index cards or docket books.

State law requires records be retained for 10 years. Include type of civil action to be searched.

Criminal Records: Access: Mail, in person. Only the court performs in person searches; visitors may not. No search fee. Required to search: name, years to search; also helpful: DOB. Criminal records on index cards or docket books. State law requires records be retained for 10 years.

General Information: No juvenile records released. Turnaround time 1-2 weeks. Copy fee: $.50 per page. Certification fee: $1.50. Fee payee: District Court. Personal checks accepted. Prepayment is required.

Probate & Family Court 24 New Chardon St, Boston, MA 02114-4703; 617-788-8300; Fax: 617-788-8926. Hours: 8:30AM-4:30PM (EST). *Probate.*

Worcester County

Superior Court 2 Main St Rm 21, Worcester, MA 01608; 508-770-1899. Hours: 8AM-4:30PM (EST). *Felony, Civil Actions Over $25,000.*

Civil Records: Access: Mail, in person. Both court and visitors may perform in person searches. No search fee. Required to search: name, years to search. Civil cases indexed by defendant, plaintiff. Civil records on computer from 1990, index books from 1900.

Criminal Records: Access: Mail, in person. Both court and visitors may perform in person searches. No search fee. Required to search: name, years to search. Criminal records on computer from 1990, index books from 1900.

General Information: Public Access terminal is available. No impounded or juvenile records released. Turnaround time 1 week. Copy fee: $.50 per page. Certification fee: $1.50. Fee payee: Clerk of Superior Court. Personal checks accepted. Prepayment is required.

Clinton District Court 300 Boylston St, Clinton, MA 01510; 978-368-7811; Fax: 978-368-7827. Hours: 8:30AM-4:30PM (EST). *Felony, Misdemeanor, Civil, Eviction, Small Claims.*

Civil Records: Access: Mail, in person. Only the court performs in person searches; visitors may not. No search fee. Required to search: name, years to search; also helpful: DOB, SSN. Civil cases indexed by defendant, plaintiff. Civil records on index cards or docket books back to 1968. State law requires records be retained for 20 years.

Criminal Records: Access: Mail, in person. Only the court performs in person searches; visitors may not. No search fee. Required to search: name, years to search, address, DOB, SSN, signed release. Criminal records on index cards or docket books back to 1978. State law requires records be retained for 20 years.

General Information: No juvenile records released. SASE required. Turnaround time 1-2 weeks. Copy fee: $1.00 per page. Certification fee: $1.50 per page. Fee payee: District Court Clerk Magistrate. Prepayment is required.

Dudley District Court 64 PO Box 100, Dudley, MA 01571; 508-943-7123; Fax: 508-949-0015. Hours: 8AM-4:30PM (EST). *Felony, Misdemeanor, Civil, Eviction, Small Claims.*

Civil Records: Access: Phone, mail, in person. Both court and visitors may perform in person searches. No search fee. Required to search: name, years to search. Civil cases indexed by defendant, plaintiff. Civil records on index cards or docket books. State law requires records be retained for 10 years.

Criminal Records: Access: Phone, mail, in person. Both court and visitors may perform in person searches. No search fee. Required to search: name, years to search, DOB. Criminal records on computer since 06/96; prior records on index cards or docket books. State law requires records be retained for 10 years.

General Information: No juvenile records released. SASE not required. Turnaround time 1-2 weeks. Copy fee: $.50 per page. Certification fee: $1.50. Fee payee: District Court. Business checks accepted. Prepayment is required.

Fitchburg District Court 16 100 Elm St, Fitchburg, MA 01420; 978-345-2111; Fax: 978-342-2461. Hours: 8:30AM-4:30PM (EST). *Felony, Misdemeanor, Civil, Eviction, Small Claims.*

Civil Records: Access: In person only. Visitors must perform in person searches for themselves. No search fee. Required to search: name, years to search. Civil cases indexed by defendant, plaintiff. Civil records on index cards or docket books back 10 years.

Criminal Records: Access: In person only. Visitors must perform in person searches for themselves. No search fee. Required to search: name, years to search. Criminal records on index cards or docket books back 10 years; on computer back to 1994.

General Information: No juvenile or mental health records released. Copy fee: $.50 per page. Certification fee: $1.50. Fee payee: District Court. Personal checks accepted. Prepayment is required.

Gardner District Court 108 Matthews St, PO Box 40, Gardner, MA 01440-0040; 978-632-2373; Fax: 978-630-3902. Hours: 8:30AM-4:30PM (EST). *Felony, Misdemeanor, Civil, Small Claims.*

Civil Records: Access: Phone, fax, mail, in person. Both court and visitors may perform in person searches. No search fee. Required to search: name, years to search, address. Civil cases indexed by defendant, plaintiff. Civil records on index cards or docket books. State law requires records be retained for 10 years.

Criminal Records: Access: Phone, fax, mail, in person. Both court and visitors may perform in person searches. No search fee. Required to search: name, years to search, DOB. Criminal records on index cards or docket books. State law requires records be retained for 10 years.

General Information: No juvenile records released. Turnaround time 1-2 weeks, quicker for phone and FAX verifications. Fax notes: No fee to fax results. Copy fee: $.50 per page. Certification fee: $1.50. Fee payee: District Court. Personal checks accepted. Prepayment is required.

Leominster District Court 25 School St, Leominster, MA 01453; 978-537-3722; Fax: 978-537-3970. Hours: 8:30AM-4:30PM (EST). *Felony, Misdemeanor, Civil, Eviction, Small Claims.*

Civil Records: Access: Phone, mail, in person. Both court and visitors may perform in person searches. No search fee. Required to search: name, years to search. Civil cases indexed by defendant, plaintiff. Civil records on index cards or docket books. State law requires records be retained for 10 years.

Criminal Records: Access: Phone, mail, in person. Both court and visitors may perform in person searches. No search fee. Required to search: name, years to search; also helpful: DOB. Criminal records on computer since 1987; Prior records on index cards or docket books. State law requires records be retained for 10 years.

General Information: No juvenile or impounded records released. Turnaround time 1-2 weeks. Copy fee: $.50 per page. Certification fee: $1.50. Fee payee: District Court. Personal checks accepted. Prepayment is required.

Milford District Court PO Box 370, Milford, MA 01757; 508-473-1260. Hours: 8:30AM-4:30PM (EST). *Felony, Misdemeanor, Civil, Eviction, Small Claims.*

Civil Records: Access: In person only. Both court and visitors may perform in person searches. No search fee. Required to search: name, years to search. Civil cases indexed by defendant, plaintiff. Civil records on index cards or docket books. State law requires records be retained for 10 years. Some indexes can only be searches by court.

Criminal Records: Access: In person only. Both court and visitors may perform in person searches. No search fee. Required to search: name, years to search, DOB; also helpful: SSN, aliases. Criminal records on computer since 1995; prior records on index cards & docket books; some indexes only searchable by court.

General Information: No mental health, impounded, alcohol, commitment, sexual abuse victim, waivers of fees or costs for indigents, delinquency, C & P, CHINS, 209A minor or 209A address records released. Copy fee: $.50 per page. Certification fee: $1.50. Fee payee: District Court. Business checks accepted. Prepayment is required.

Spencer District Court 544 E Main St, East Brookfield, MA 01515-1701; 508-885-6305/6306; Fax: 508-885-7623. Hours: 8:30AM-4:30PM (EST). *Felony, Misdemeanor, Civil, Eviction, Small Claims.*

Civil Records: Access: Mail, in person. Both court and visitors may perform in person searches. No search fee. Required to search: name, years to search. Civil cases indexed by defendant, plaintiff. Civil records on index cards or docket books. State law requires records be retained for 10 years.

Criminal Records: Access: Mail, in person. Both court and visitors may perform in person searches. No search fee. Required to search: name, years to search; also helpful: DOB. Criminal records on index cards or docket books. State law requires records be retained for 10 years.

General Information: No juvenile, mental health records released. SASE requested. Turnaround time 1-2 weeks, strongly suggest to use a retriever when possible. Copy fee: $.50 per page. Certification fee: $1.50. Fee payee: District Court. Personal checks accepted. Prepayment is required.

Uxbridge District Court PO Box 580, Uxbridge, MA 01569; 508-278-2454; Fax: 508-278-2929. Hours: 8:30AM-4:30PM (EST). *Felony, Misdemeanor, Civil, Eviction, Small Claims.*

Civil Records: Access: Mail, in person. Only the court performs in person searches; visitors may not. No search fee. Required to search: name, years to search.

Civil cases indexed by defendant, plaintiff. Civil records on index cards or docket books. State law requires records be retained for 10 years.

Criminal Records: Access: Mail, in person. Only the court performs in person searches; visitors may not. No search fee. Required to search: name, years to search; also helpful: DOB. Criminal records on index cards or docket books. State law requires records be retained for 10 years.

General Information: Turnaround time 1-2 weeks. Copy fee: $.50 per page. Certification fee: $1.50. Fee payee: District Court. Personal checks accepted. Prepayment is required.

Westborough District Court 175 Milk St, Westborough, MA 01581; 508-366-8266; Fax: 508-366-8268. Hours: 8AM-4:30PM (EST). *Felony, Misdemeanor, Civil, Eviction, Small Claims.*

Civil Records: Access: Mail, in person. Both court and visitors may perform in person searches. No search fee. Required to search: name, years to search. Civil cases indexed by defendant, plaintiff. Civil records go back to 1986, on books and cards.

Criminal Records: Access: Mail, in person. Both court and visitors may perform in person searches. No search fee. Required to search: name, years to search; also helpful: DOB. Criminal records go back to 1986, on books and cards.

General Information: No impounded, juvenile records released. SASE required. Turnaround time 5 days. Copy fee: $.50 per page. Certification fee: $1.50. Fee payee: District Court Westborough Division. Personal checks accepted. Prepayment is required.

Winchendon District Court 80 Central St, Winchendon, MA 01475; 978-297-0156; Fax: 978-297-0161. Hours: 8:30AM-4:30PM (EST). *Felony, Misdemeanor, Civil, Eviction, Small Claims.*

Civil Records: Access: Phone, mail, in person. Both court and visitors may perform in person searches. No search fee. Required to search: name, years to search. Civil cases indexed by defendant, plaintiff. Civil records on index cards or docket books. State law requires records be retained for 10 years.

Criminal Records: Access: Phone, mail, in person. Both court and visitors may perform in person searches. No search fee. Required to search: name, years to

search; also helpful: DOB. Criminal records on index cards or docket books. State law requires records be retained for 10 years.

General Information: Turnaround time 1-2 weeks. Copy fee: $.50 per page. Certification fee: $10.00. Fee payee: District Court. Personal checks accepted. Prepayment is required.

Worcester District Court 50 Harvard St, Worcester, MA 01608; 508-757-8350; Fax: 508-797-0716. Hours: 8AM-4:30PM (EST). *Felony, Misdemeanor, Civil, Eviction, Small Claims.*

Civil Records: Access: Mail, in person. Only the court performs in person searches; visitors may not. No search fee. Required to search: name, years to search. Civil cases indexed by defendant, plaintiff. Civil records on index cards or docket books. State law requires records be retained for 10 years.

Criminal Records: Access: Mail, in person. Only the court performs in person searches; visitors may not. No search fee. Required to search: name, years to search. Criminal records on computer since 1996; prior records on docket books. State law requires records be retained for 10 years.

General Information: No sealed, expunged, adoption or sex offense records released. Turnaround time 1-2 weeks. Copy fee: $.50 per page. Certification fee: $1.50. Fee payee: District Court. Personal checks accepted. Prepayment is required.

Probate & Family Court 2 Main St, Worcester, MA 01608; 508-770-0825 x217; Fax: 508-752-6138. Hours: 8AM-4:30PM (EST). *Probate.*

Massachusetts Recording Offices

ORGANIZATION

14 counties, 312 towns, and 39 cities; 21 recording offices and 365 UCC filing offices. Each town/city profile indicates the county in which the town/city is located. Filing locations vary depending upon the type of document, as noted below. Berkshire and Bristol counties each has three recording offices. Essex, Middlesex and Worcester counties each has two recording offices. Cities/towns bearing the same name as a county are Barnstable, Essex, Franklin, Hampden, Nantucket, Norfolk, Plymouth, and Worcester. Some UCC financing statements on personal property collateral are were submitted to cities/towns until June 30, 2001, while real estate recording is handled by the counties. Recording officers are Town/City Clerk (UCC), County Register of Deeds (real estate), and Clerk of US District Court (federal tax liens). The entire state is in the Eastern Time Zone (EST).

REAL ESTATE RECORDS

Real estate records are located at the county level. Each town/city profile indicates the county in which the town/city is located. Counties will not perform searches. Copy fee with certification is usually $.75 per page. Each town also has Assessor/Tax Collector/Treasurer offices from which real estate ownership and tax information is available.

UCC RECORDS

This was a dual filing state. Until July 1, 2001, financing statements were usually filed both with the Town/City clerk and at the state level, except for real estate related collateral, which is recorded at the county Register of Deeds. Now, all filing are at the state except for the real estate related collateral. Most all recording offices perform searches. Use search request form UCC-11. Search fees are usually $10.00 per debtor name. Copy fees vary widely.

TAX LIEN RECORDS

Federal tax liens on personal property were filed with the Town/City Clerks prior to 1970. Since that time, federal tax liens on personal property are filed with the US District Court in Boston as well as with the towns/cities. Following is how to search the central index for federal tax liens - Address:

US District Court (617-748-9152)

1 Courthouse Way.

Boston, MA 02110

The federal tax liens are indexed here on a computer system. Searches are available by mail or in person. Do not use the telephone. The court suggests including the Social Security number and/or address of individual names in your search request in order to narrow the results. A mail search costs $15.00 and will take about two weeks. Copies are included. Make your check payable to Clerk, US District Court. You can do the search yourself at no charge on their public computer terminal.

State tax liens on personal property are filed with the Town/City Clerk or Tax Collector. All tax liens against real estate are filed with the county Register of Deeds. Some towns file state tax liens on personal property with the UCC index and include tax liens on personal property automatically with a UCC search. Others will perform a separate state tax lien search, usually for a fee of $10.00 plus $1.00 per page of copies.

OTHER LIENS

Medical, town/city tax, child support.

STATEWIDE ONLINE INFO:

A number of towns offer online access via the Internet to the Assessor records for no charge.

Abington Town

Town Clerk, 500 Gliniewicz Way, Abington, MA 02351. 781-982-2112 R/E Recording: 781-982-2107; Fax 781-982-2138.
Will search UCC records. This agency will not do a tax lien search. Real estate records located in Plymouth County. **Other Phone Numbers:** Assessor 781-982-2107; Treasurer 781-982-2131; Appraiser/Auditor 781-982-2107; Elections 781-982-2112; Vital Records 781-982-2112.

Acton Town

Town Clerk, 472 Main Street, Town Hall, Acton, MA 01720. 978-264-9615 R/E Recording: 978-264-9618; Fax 978-264-9630. http://www.town.acton.ma.us
Will search UCC records. UCC search includes tax liens. Real estate records located in Middlesex County. **Other Phone Numbers:** Assessor 978-264-9622; Treasurer 978-264-9612; Vital Records 978-264-9615.

Acushnet Town

Town Clerk, 122 Main Street, Town Hall, Acushnet, MA 02743. 508-998-0215; Fax 508-998-0203.

Will search UCC records. Tax liens not included in UCC search. Real estate records located in Bristol County. **Other Phone Numbers:** Assessor 508-998-0205; Treasurer 508-998-0212; Vital Records 508-998-0215.

Adams Town

Town Clerk, 8 Park Street, Adams, MA 01220. 413-743-8320; Fax 413-743-8316.
Will search UCC records. Tax liens not included in UCC search. Real estate records located in Berkshire County. **Other Phone Numbers:** Assessor 413-743-8350.

Agawam Town

Town Clerk, 36 Main St., Agawam, MA 01001-1837. 413-786-0400 x215; Fax 413-786-9927. www.agawam.ma.us
Will search UCC records. This agency will not do a tax lien search. Real estate records located in Hampden County. **Online Access:** Property Assessment Data. Online access to Property Assessment Data is available free at http://www.patriotproperties.com/agawam/Default.asp?br=exp&vr=5. **Other Phone Numbers:**

Assessor 413-786-0400 x205; Treasurer 413-786-0400 x221; Elections 413-786-0400 x215; Vital Records 413-786-0400 x216.

Alford Town

Town Clerk, Town Hall, 5 Alford Center Road, Alford, MA 01230-8914. 413-528-4536; Fax 413-528-4581.
Will search UCC records. This agency will not do a tax lien search. Real estate records located in Berkshire County.

Amesbury Town

Town Clerk, 62 Friend Street, Town Hall, Amesbury, MA 01913. 978-388-8100; Fax 978-388-8150.
Will search UCC records prior to 7/1/01 only. This agency will not do a tax lien search. RE owner, mortgage, and property transfer searches available. Real estate records located in Essex County. **Other Phone Numbers:** Assessor 978-388-8102; Treasurer 978-388-8105; Elections 978-388-8100; Vital Records 978-388-8100.

Amherst Town

Town Clerk, Town Hall, 4 Boltwood Ave., Amherst, MA 01002. 413-256-4035; Fax 413-256-2504. Will search UCC records. This agency will not do a tax lien search. Real estate records located in Hampshire County. **Other Phone Numbers:** Assessor 413-256-4024.

Andover Town

Town Clerk, 36 Bartlet Street, Andover, MA 01810-3882. 978-623-8256; Fax 978-623-8221. Will search UCC records. This agency will not do a tax lien search. Real estate records located in Essex County. **Online Access:** Assessor. Property tax records on the Assessor's database are available free online at www.town.andover.ma.us/assess/values.htm.

Arlington Town

Town Clerk, 730 Mass Ave, Town Hall, Arlington, MA 02476-9109. 781-316-3073 R/E Recording: 781-316-3051 UCC Recording: 781-316-3051; Fax 781-316-3079. http://www.town.arlington.ma.us/arthalli.htm Will search UCC records. Tax liens included in UCC search. Real estate records located in Middlesex County. **Online Access:** Assessor. Online access to the town assessor database is available free at http://arlserver.town.arlington.ma.us/property.html. **Other Phone Numbers:** Assessor 781-316-3051; Treasurer 781-316-3031; Appraiser/Auditor 781-316-3051; Elections 781-316-3070; Vital Records 781-316-3070.

Ashburnham Town

Town Clerk, 54 Willard Rd., Ashburnham, MA 01430. 978-827-4102; Fax 978-827-4105. Will search UCC records. UCC search includes tax liens if requested. Real estate records located in Worcester County. **Other Phone Numbers:** Assessor 978-827-4100; Treasurer 978-827-4102; Appraiser/Auditor 978-827-4101; Elections 978-827-4102; Vital Records 978-827-4102.

Ashby Town

Town Clerk, 895 Main St., Ashby, MA 01431. 978-386-2424; Fax 978-386-2490. Will search UCC records. This agency will not do a tax lien search. Real estate records located in Middlesex County. **Other Phone Numbers:** Assessor 978-386-2427; Treasurer 978-386-2424.

Ashfield Town

Town Clerk, P.O. Box 595, Ashfield, MA 01330-0595. 413-628-4441; Fax 413-628-4588. Will search UCC records. UCC search includes tax liens if requested. Real estate records located in Franklin County. **Other Phone Numbers:** Assessor 413-628-4439; Treasurer 413-628-4441; Elections 413-628-4441; Vital Records 413-628-4441.

Ashland Town

Town Clerk, 101 Main Street, Town Hall, Ashland, MA 01721. 508-881-0101; Fax 508-881-0102. http://www.ashlandmass.com/ Will search UCC records. UCC search includes tax liens. Real estate records located in Middlesex County. **Other Phone Numbers:** Assessor 508-881-0104; Treasurer 508-881-0107; Elections 508-881-0101; Vital Records 508-881-0101.

Athol Town

Town Clerk, 584 Main Street, Athol, MA 01331. 978-249-4551; Fax 978-249-2491. Will search UCC records. UCC search includes tax liens. Real estate records located in Worcester County. **Other Phone Numbers:** Assessor 978-249-3880;

Treasurer 978-249-3374; Elections 978-249-4551; Vital Records 978-249-4551.

Attleboro City

City Clerk, 77 Park Street, City Hall, Attleboro, MA 02703. 508-223-2222; Fax 508-222-3046. Will search UCC records. UCC search includes tax liens if requested. Real estate records located in Bristol County. **Other Phone Numbers:** Assessor 508-223-2222 x3135; Treasurer 508-223-2222 x3214; Elections 508-223-2222 x3271; Vital Records 508-223-2222 x3111.

Auburn Town

Town Clerk, 104 Central Street, Auburn, MA 01501. 508-832-7701; Fax 508-832-6145. Will search UCC records. UCC search includes tax liens. Real estate records located in Worcester County. **Other Phone Numbers:** Assessor 508-832-7708; Treasurer 508-832-7700.

Avon Town

Town Clerk, Buckley Center, Avon, MA 02322. 508-588-0414; Fax 508-559-0209. Will search UCC records. UCC search includes tax liens. Real estate records located in Norfolk County. **Other Phone Numbers:** Assessor 508-588-0414; Treasurer 508-588-0414.

Ayer Town

Town Clerk, P.O. Box 308, Ayer, MA 01432. 978-772-8215; Fax 978-772-8222. Will search UCC records. Tax liens included in UCC search if requested. Real estate records located in Middlesex County. **Other Phone Numbers:** Assessor 978-772-8211; Treasurer 978-772-8216.

Barnstable County

County Register of Deeds, P.O. Box 368, Barnstable, MA 02630. 508-362-7733; Fax 508-362-5065. http://www.bcrd.co.barnstable.ma.us Will search UCC records, but only real estate related UCC filed here. Tax liens included in UCC search if requested. Will not search real estate records. **Online Access:** Real Estate, Liens. Access to County records requires a $50 annual fee, plus $.50 per minute of use. Records date back to 1976. Lending agency information is available. For information, contact Janet Hoben at 508-362-7733.

Barnstable Town

Town Clerk, 367 Main St., Hyannis, MA 02601. 508-862-4044 R/E Recording: 508-362-7733 UCC Recording: 508-862-4094; Fax 508-790-6326. http://www.town.barnstable.ma.us Hyannis, ZIP Code 02601, is located here, as well as the villages of Barnstable, West Barnstable, Centerville, Cotuit, Osterville and Marstons Mills. Will search UCC records. Tax liens included in UCC search if requested. Real estate records located in Barnstable County. **Online Access:** Assessor. Town of Barnstable Assessor records are available free online at http://town.barnstable.ma.us/Information_01/Assessment/asse_online_db.htm. Email questions or comments to webadm@town.barnstable.ma.us or call the Assessing Dept. at 508-862-4022. **Other Phone Numbers:** Assessor 508-862-4022; Treasurer 508-862-4653; Elections 508-862-4044; Vital Records 508-862-4095.

Barre Town

Town Clerk, P.O. Box 418, Barre, MA 01005. 978-355-5003; Fax 978-355-5032. Will search UCC records. UCC search includes tax liens if requested. Real estate records located in Worcester County. **Other Phone Numbers:** Assessor

978-355-5010; Treasurer 978-355-5000; Elections 978-355-5003; Vital Records 978-355-5003.

Becket Town

Town Clerk, Virginia Andrews, 557 Main St., Becket, MA 01223. 413-623-8934; Fax 413-623-6036. Will search UCC records. UCC search includes tax liens if requested. Real estate records located in Berkshire County. **Other Phone Numbers:** Assessor 413-623-8934; Treasurer 413-623-8934; Appraiser/Auditor 413-623-8934; Elections 413-623-8934; Vital Records 413-623-8934.

Bedford Town

Town Clerk, 10 Mudge Way, Town Hall, Bedford, MA 01730-0083. 781-275-0083; Fax 781-687-6157. Will search UCC records. UCC search includes tax liens if requested. Real estate records located in Middlesex County. **Other Phone Numbers:** Assessor 781-275-0046; Treasurer 781-275-8996.

Belchertown Town

Town Clerk, P.O. Box 607, Belchertown, MA 01007-0607. 413-323-0400; Fax 413-323-0411. Will search UCC records. UCC search includes tax liens if requested. Real estate records located in Hampshire County. **Other Phone Numbers:** Assessor 413-323-0413.

Bellingham Town

Town Clerk, P.O. Box 367, Bellingham, MA 02019-0367. 508-966-5827; Fax 508-966-5804. Will search UCC records. This agency will not do a tax lien search. Real estate records located in Norfolk County. **Other Phone Numbers:** Assessor 508-966-5825; Treasurer 508-966-5828; Elections 508-966-5827; Vital Records 508-966-5827.

Belmont Town

Town Clerk, 455 Concord Avenue, Town Hall, Belmont, MA 02178-2514. 617-489-8201 UCC Recording: 617-489-8200; Fax 617-489-2185. http://www.belmont.ma.us Will search UCC records. This agency will not do a tax lien search. Real estate records located in Middlesex County. **Other Phone Numbers:** Assessor 617-489-8231; Treasurer 617-489-8234; Elections 617-489-8201; Vital Records 617-489-8200.

Berkley Town

Town Clerk, 1 N. Main Street, Berkley, MA 02779. 508-822-3348; Fax 508-822-3511. Will search UCC records. UCC search includes tax liens if requested. Real estate records located in Bristol County. **Other Phone Numbers:** Assessor 508-822-7955.

Berkshire County (Middle District)

County Register of Deeds, 44 Bank Row, Pittsfield, MA 01201. 413-443-7438; Fax 413-448-6025. Will search UCC records, but only real estate related UCC filed here. This agency will not do a tax lien search. Will not search real estate records. **Online Access:** Real Estate, Liens. For online access information, see Berkshire County Southern District.

Berkshire County (Northern District)

County Register of Deeds, 65 Park Street, Suite 1, Adams, MA 01220. 413-743-0035; Fax 413-743-1003. www.ben.net/~nbrd Will not search UCC records, but only real estate related UCC filed here. This agency will not do a tax lien search. Will not search real estate records. **Online Access:** Real Estate, Liens. For online access information, see Berkshire County Middle District. **Other Phone Numbers:** Assessor 413-743-8350 (Town of Adams); Treasurer 413-743-8390 (Town of Adams); Vital Records 413-743-8320 (Town of Adams).

Berkshire County (Southern District)

County Register of Deeds, 334 Main Street, Great Barrington, MA 01230. 413-528-0146; Fax 413-528-6878.
Will search UCC records, but only real estate related UCC filed here. This agency will not do a tax lien search. Will not search real estate records. **Online Access:** Real Estate, Liens. Access to the County records requires a on-time $100 signup and $.50 per minute of use. System provides access to all three District Recorder's records; records date back to 1985. Searchable indexes: recorded land, plans, registered land. Lending agency information available. For information, contact Sharon Henault at 413-443-7438. **Other Phone Numbers:** Assessor 413-637-5502.

Berlin Town

Town Clerk, 23 Linden St, Box 8, Berlin, MA 01503. 978-838-2931; Fax 978-838-0014.
Will search UCC records. UCC search includes tax liens if requested. Real estate records located in Worcester County. **Other Phone Numbers:** Assessor 978-838-2256; Treasurer 978-838-0344; Tax Collector 978-838-2765.

Bernardston Town

Town Clerk, PO Box 504, Bernardston, MA 01337-0435. 413-648-5400 R/E Recording: 413-648-5407; Fax 413-648-5408.
Will search UCC records. UCC search includes tax liens if requested. Real estate records located in Franklin County. **Other Phone Numbers:** Assessor 413-648-5407; Treasurer 413-648-5400; Elections 413-648-5400; Vital Records 413-648-5400; Tax Collector 413-648-5401.

Beverly City

City Clerk, 191 Cabot Street, Beverly, MA 01915-1031. 978-921-6000 x164; Fax 978-921-8511.
Will search UCC records. This agency will not do a tax lien search. Real estate records located in Essex County. **Other Phone Numbers:** Assessor 978-921-6003; Treasurer 978-921-6135.

Billerica Town

Town Clerk, 365 Boston Road, Town Hall, Billerica, MA 01821-1885. 978-671-0924; Fax 978-663-6510.
Will search UCC records. This agency will not do a tax lien search. Real estate records located in Middlesex County.

Blackstone Town

Town Clerk, Municipal Center, 15 St. Paul Street, Blackstone, MA 01504-2295. 508-883-1500 x146; Fax 508-883-7043.
Will search UCC records. Tax liens not included in UCC search. Real estate records located in Worcester County.

Blandford Town

Town Clerk, P.O. Box 101, Blandford, MA 01008. 413-848-2747; Fax 413-848-0908.
Will search UCC records. UCC search includes tax liens if requested. Real estate records located in Hampden County. **Other Phone Numbers:** Assessor 413-848-2782.

Bolton Town

Town Clerk, P.O. Box 278, Bolton, MA 01740. 978-779-2771; Fax 978-779-5461. www.bolton.ma.us
Will search UCC records. Tax liens not included in UCC search. Real estate records located in Worcester County. **Other Phone Numbers:** Assessor 978-779-5556.

Boston City

City Clerk, City Hall, Room 601, 1 City Hall Plaza, Boston, MA 02201. 617-635-4600; Fax 617-635-4658. http://www.ci.boston.ma.us/assessing
Will search UCC records. UCC search includes tax liens if requested. Real estate records located in Suffolk County. **Online Access:** Assessor. Records on the City of Boston Assessor database are available free online at www.ci.boston.ma.us/assessing/search.asp. **Other Phone Numbers:** Assessor 617-635-4287.

Bourne Town

Town Clerk, 24 Perry Avenue, Town Hall, Buzzards Bay, MA 02532. 508-759-0613 UCC Recording: 508-759-0600; Fax 508-759-8026.
Will search UCC records. UCC search includes tax liens if requested. Real estate records located in Barnstable County. **Other Phone Numbers:** Assessor 508-759-0600; Treasurer 508-759-0600; Appraiser/Auditor 508-759-0600; Elections 508-759-0600; Vital Records 508-759-0600.

Boxborough Town

Town Clerk, 29 Middle Road, Boxborough, MA 01719-1499. Town Clerk, R/E and UCC Recording 978-263-1116; Fax 978-264-3127.
Will search UCC records. UCC search includes tax liens. Real estate records located in Middlesex County. **Other Phone Numbers:** Assessor 978-263-1116; Treasurer 978-263-1116; Appraiser/Auditor 978-263-1116; Elections 978-263-1116; Vital Records 978-263-1116.

Boxford Town

Town Clerk, 28 Middleton Road, Boxford, MA 01921. 978-887-0806; Fax 978-887-3546.
Will search UCC records. UCC search includes tax liens if requested. Real estate records located in Essex County. **Other Phone Numbers:** Assessor 978-887-3674; Treasurer 978-887-0806.

Boylston Town

Town Clerk, 45 Main Street, Boylston, MA 01505. 508-869-2234; Fax 508-869-6210.
Will search UCC records. Tax liens included in UCC search if requested. Real estate records located in Worcester County. **Other Phone Numbers:** Assessor 508-869-6543; Treasurer 508-869-2972; Elections 508-869-2234.

Braintree Town

Town Clerk, 1 JFK Memorial Drive, Braintree, MA 02184-6498. 781-794-8000 x8241; Fax 781-794-8259.
Will search UCC records. UCC search includes tax liens if requested. Real estate records located in Norfolk County.

Brewster Town

Town Clerk, 2198 Main Street, Brewster, MA 02631. 508-896-4506; Fax 508-896-8089.
Will search UCC records. UCC search includes tax liens if requested. Real estate records located in Barnstable County. **Other Phone Numbers:** Assessor 508-896-3701 x22.

Bridgewater Town

Town Clerk, Town Hall, 64 Central Square, Bridgewater, MA 02324. Town Clerk, R/E and UCC Recording 508-697-0921; Fax 508-697-0941.
Will search UCC records. UCC search includes tax liens. Real estate records located in Plymouth County. **Other Phone Numbers:** Assessor 508-697-0928; Treasurer 508-697-0923; Elections 508-697-0922; Vital Records 508-697-0921.

Brimfield Town

Town Clerk, P.O. Box 508, Brimfield, MA 01010. 413-245-4101; Fax 413-245-4107.
Will search UCC records. UCC search includes tax liens if requested. Real estate records located in Hampden County. **Other Phone Numbers:** Assessor 413-245-4100.

Bristol County (Fall River District)

County Register of Deeds, 441 North Main Street, Fall River, MA 02720. 508-673-1651; Fax 508-673-7633.
Will search UCC records, but only real estate related UCC filed here. This agency will not do a tax lien search. Will not search real estate records. **Online Access:** Real Estate, Liens. For online access information, see Bristol County Southern District.

Bristol County (Northern District)

County Register of Deeds, 11 Court Street, Taunton, MA 02780-0248. 508-822-0502; Fax 508-880-4975.
Will search UCC records, but only real estate related UCC filed here. This agency will not do a tax lien search. Will not search real estate records. **Online Access:** Real Estate, Liens. For online access information, see Bristol County Southern District. **Other Phone Numbers:** Treasurer 508-824-4028.

Bristol County (Southern District)

County Register of Deeds, 25 North 6th Street, New Bedford, MA 02740. 508-993-2605; Fax 508-997-4250.
Will search UCC records, but only real estate related UCC filed here. This agency will not do a tax lien search. Will not search real estate records. **Online Access:** Real Estate, Liens. Access to County records requires a $100 set up fee and $.50 per minute of use. All three districts are on this system; the record dates vary by district. Lending agency information is available. For information, contact Rosemary at 508-993-2605. **Other Phone Numbers:** Assessor 508-979-1440; Treasurer 508-979-1430.

Brockton City

City Clerk, 45 School Street, Brockton, MA 02401. 508-580-7114; Fax 508-580-7104.
Will search UCC records. This agency will not do a tax lien search. Real estate records located in Plymouth County.

Brookfield Town

Town Clerk, 6 Central St., Brookfield, MA 01506. 508-867-8004 R/E Recording: 508-867-3171; Fax 508-867-5091.
Will search UCC records. Tax liens included in UCC search if requested. Real estate records located in Worcester County. **Other Phone Numbers:** Assessor 508-867-3171; Treasurer 508-867-8004; Elections 508-867-8004; Vital Records 508-867-8004.

Brookline Town

Town Clerk, 333 Washington Street, Town Hall, Brookline, MA 02445. 617-730-2010 R/E Recording: 617-730-2020; Fax 617-730-2043. http://www.town.brookline.ma.us/Assessors

Will search UCC records. Tax liens included in UCC search if requested. Real estate records located in Norfolk County. **Online Access:** Assessor. Records on the Town of Brookline Assessors database are available free online at www.town.brookline.ma.us/Assessors/property.asp. **Other Phone Numbers:** Assessor 617-730-2060; Treasurer 617-730-2020; Elections 617-730-2010; Vital Records 617-730-2010.

Buckland Town

Town Clerk, P.O. Box 159, Buckland, MA 01338. 413-625-8572; Fax 413-625-8570.
Postal designation "Shelburne Falls" is not a town. It refers either to Shelburne or Buckland. Will search UCC records. This agency will not do a tax lien search. Real estate records located in Franklin County. **Other Phone Numbers:** Assessor 413-625-2335; Treasurer 413-625-9474; Elections 413-625-8572; Vital Records 413-625-8572.

Burlington Town

Town Clerk, 29 Center Street, Town Hall, Burlington, MA 01803. 781-270-1660; Fax 781-270-1608.
Will search UCC records. UCC search includes tax liens if requested. Real estate records located in Middlesex County. **Other Phone Numbers:** Assessor 781-270-1650.

Cambridge City

City Clerk, 795 Massachusetts Ave., City Hall, Room 103, Cambridge, MA 02139. 617-349-4260; Fax 617-349-4269. http://www2.ci.cambridge.ma.us/assessor
Will search UCC records. This agency will not do a tax lien search. Real estate records located in Middlesex County. **Online Access:** Assessor. Records on the City of Cambridge Assessor database are available free online at www2.ci.cambridge.ma.us/assessor/index.html.

Canton Town

Town Clerk, 801 Washington Street, Memorial Hall, Canton, MA 02021. 781-821-5013; Fax 781-821-5016.
Will search UCC records. Tax liens included in UCC search if requested. Real estate records located in Norfolk County. **Other Phone Numbers:** Assessor 781-821-5008; Treasurer 781-821-5006; Elections 781-821-5013; Vital Records 781-821-5013.

Carlisle Town

Town Clerk, P.O. Box 827, Carlisle, MA 01741. 978-369-6155; Fax 978-371-0594.
Will search UCC records. This agency will not do a tax lien search. Real estate records located in Middlesex County. **Other Phone Numbers:** Assessor 978-369-0392; Treasurer 978-369-5557; Appraiser/Auditor 978-369-0392; Elections 978-369-6155; Vital Records 978-369-6155.

Carver Town

Town Clerk, P.O. Box 67, Carver, MA 02330. 508-866-3403; Fax 508-866-3408.
Will search UCC records. This agency will not do a tax lien search, records kept in Treasurer's Office Real estate records located in Plymouth County. **Other Phone Numbers:** Treasurer 508-866-3435.

Charlemont Town

Town Clerk, P.O. Box 605, Charlemont, MA 01339-0605. 413-625-6157; Fax 413-339-0329.
Will search UCC records. This agency will not do a tax lien search. Real estate records located in Franklin County. **Other Phone Numbers:** Assessor 413-339-8586; Treasurer 413-625-1097; Elections 413-625-

6157; Vital Records 413-625-6157; Tax Lien/Tax Collector 413-339-5707.

Charlton Town

Town Clerk, 37 Main Street, Charlton, MA 01507. 508-248-2249; Fax 508-248-2073.
Will search UCC records. UCC search includes tax liens if requested. Real estate records located in Worcester County.

Chatham Town

Town Clerk, 549 Main Street, Chatham, MA 02633. 508-945-5101; Fax 508-945-3550.
Will search UCC records. Telephone requests for UCC searches cannot be honored - written requests please. Tax liens included in UCC search if requested. Real estate records located in Barnstable County. **Other Phone Numbers:** Assessor 508-945-5103; Treasurer 508-945-5108; Vital Records 508-945-5101.

Chelmsford Town

Town Clerk, 50 Billerica Road, Chelmsford, MA 01824. 978-250-5205; Fax 978-840-5208. http://www.townhall.chelmsford.ma.us
Will search UCC records. Tax liens not included in UCC search. Real estate records located in Middlesex County. **Other Phone Numbers:** Assessor 978-250-5220; Treasurer 978-250-5210; Elections 978-250-5205; Vital Records 978-250-5205.

Chelsea City

City Clerk, 500 Broadway, City Hall Room 209, Chelsea, MA 02150. 617-889-8226 R/E Recording: 617-889-8213; Fax 617-889-8367.
Will search UCC records. Tax liens included in UCC search if requested. Real estate records located in Suffolk County. **Other Phone Numbers:** Assessor 617-889-8213; Treasurer 617-889-8210 617-889-8226; Appraiser/Auditor 617-889-8213; Elections 617-889-8226; Vital Records 617-889-8226.

Cheshire Town

Town Clerk, 80 Church Street, P.O. Box S, Cheshire, MA 01225. 413-743-1690; Fax 413-743-0389.
Will search UCC records. This agency will not do a tax lien search. Real estate records located in Berkshire County. **Other Phone Numbers:** Assessor 413-743-1690.

Chester Town

Town Clerk, Town Hall, Chester, MA 01011. 413-354-6603; Fax 413-354-2268.
Will search UCC records. This agency will not do a tax lien search. Real estate records located in Hampden County. **Other Phone Numbers:** Assessor 413-354-6357; Treasurer 413-354-7761.

Chesterfield Town

Town Clerk, Davenport Bldg., 422 Main Rd., Chesterfield, MA 01012-0033. 413-296-4741; Fax 413-296-4394.
Will search UCC records. UCC search includes tax liens. Real estate records located in Hampshire County. **Other Phone Numbers:** Assessor 413-296-4010; Treasurer 413-296-4771; Elections 413-296-4741; Vital Records 413-296-4741.

Chicopee City

City Clerk, Market Square, City Hall, Chicopee, MA 01013. 413-594-4711; Fax 413-594-2057.
Will search UCC records. UCC search includes tax liens. Real estate records located in Hampden County.

Chilmark Town

Town Clerk, P.O. Box 119, Chilmark, MA 02535-0119. 508-645-2107; Fax 508-645-2110. http://www.ci.chilmark.ma.us
Will search UCC records. This agency will not do a tax lien search. Real estate records located in Dukes County. **Other Phone Numbers:** Assessor 508-645-2102.

Clarksburg Town

Town Clerk, 111 River Road, Town Hall, Clarksburg, MA 01247. 413-663-8247; Fax 413-664-6575.
Will search UCC records. UCC search includes tax liens. Real estate records located in Berkshire County. **Other Phone Numbers:** Assessor 413-663-8255; Treasurer 413-663-7940; Elections 413-663-7940; Vital Records 413-663-8247.

Clinton Town

Town Clerk, 242 Church Street, Clinton, MA 01510. 978-365-4119; Fax 978-895-4130.
Will search UCC records. Tax liens included in UCC search if requested. Real estate records located in Worcester County. **Other Phone Numbers:** Assessor 978-365-4117; Treasurer 978-365-4129; Elections 978-365-4119; Vital Records 978-365-4119.

Cohasset Town

Town Clerk, 41 Highland Avenue, Cohasset, MA 02025-1814. 781-383-4100; Fax 781-383-1561.
Will search UCC records. This agency will not do a tax lien search. Real estate records located in Norfolk County. **Other Phone Numbers:** Assessor 781-383-4114; Treasurer 781-383-4102; Elections 781-383-4100; Vital Records 781-383-4100.

Colrain Town

Town Clerk, P.O. Box 31, Colrain, MA 01340-0031. 413-624-3454; Fax 413-624-8852.
Will search UCC records. Tax liens included in UCC search. Real estate records located in Franklin County. **Other Phone Numbers:** Assessor 413-624-3356; Treasurer 413-624-3454.

Concord Town

Town Clerk, P.O. Box 535, Concord, MA 01742. 978-318-3080; Fax 978-318-3093. http://www.concordnet.org
Will search UCC records. UCC search includes tax liens. Real estate records located in Middlesex County. **Other Phone Numbers:** Assessor 978-318-3070; Treasurer 978-318-3050; Appraiser/Auditor 978-318-3070; Elections 978-318-3080; Vital Records 978-318-3080.

Conway Town

Town Clerk, P.O. Box 240, Conway, MA 01341. 413-369-4235; Fax 413-369-4237.
Will search UCC records. This agency will not do a tax lien search. Real estate records located in Franklin County. **Other Phone Numbers:** Assessor 413-369-4773; Treasurer 413-369-4235.

Cummington Town

Town Clerk, 585 Berkshire Trail, Cummington, MA 01026. 413-634-5458; Fax 413-634-5568.
Will search UCC records. Tax liens not included in UCC search. Real estate records located in Hampshire County. **Other Phone Numbers:** Assessor 413-634-5354.

Dalton Town

Town Clerk, 462 Main Street, Town Hall, Dalton, MA 01226. 413-684-6103 x14; Fax 413-684-6107.

Will search UCC records. UCC search includes tax liens. Real estate records located in Berkshire County. **Other Phone Numbers:** Assessor 413-684-6105; Treasurer 413-684-6111 x18; Elections 413-684-6103 x15; Vital Records 413-684-6103 x15.

Danvers Town

Town Clerk, 1 Sylvan Street, Town Hall, Danvers, MA 01923. 978-777-0001; Fax 978-777-1025.
Will search UCC records. This agency will not do a tax lien search. Real estate records located in Essex County.

Dartmouth Town

Town Clerk, P.O. Box 79399, Dartmouth, MA 02747. Town Clerk, R/E and UCC Recording 508-910-1809 UCC Recording: 508-910-1800; Fax 508-910-1894. http://www.town.dartmouth.ma.us/town_hall.htm
Will search UCC records. Tax liens not included in UCC search. Real estate records located in Bristol County. **Other Phone Numbers:** Assessor 508-910-1809; Treasurer 508-910-1802; Elections 508-910-1800; Vital Records 508-910-1800.

Dedham Town

Town Clerk, P.O. Box 306, Dedham, MA 02027. 781-326-1638 UCC Recording: 781-326-8247; Fax 781-461-5992.
Will search UCC records. This agency will not do a tax lien search. Real estate records located in Norfolk County. **Online Access:** Assessor. Property records on the Assessor's database are available free online at http://data.visionappraisal.com/dedhamma/.
Registration is required for full access; registration is free. **Other Phone Numbers:** Assessor 781-326-8247.

Deerfield Town

Town Clerk, 8 Conway St., South Deerfield, MA 01373. 413-665-2130; Fax 413-665-7275.
Will search UCC records. Tax liens included in UCC search if requested. Real estate records located in Franklin County. **Other Phone Numbers:** Assessor 413-665-7184; Treasurer 413-665-2130.

Dennis Town

Town Clerk, P.O. Box 1419, South Dennis, MA 02660-1419. 508-760-6115 R/E Recording: 508-362-2511 UCC Recording: 508-760-6112; Fax 508-394-8309.
Will search UCC records. Tax liens not included in UCC search. Real estate records located in Barnstable County. **Other Phone Numbers:** Assessor 508-760-6142; Treasurer 508-760-6117; Appraiser/Auditor 508-760-6141; Elections 508-760-6112; Vital Records 508-760-6112.

Dighton Town

Town Clerk, 979 Somerset Avenue, Dighton, MA 02715-0465. Town Clerk, R/E and UCC Recording 508-669-5411; Fax 508-669-5667.
Will search UCC records. This agency will not do a tax lien search. Real estate records located in Bristol County. **Other Phone Numbers:** Assessor 508-669-5043; Treasurer 508-669-5411; Elections 508-669-5411; Vital Records 508-669-5411.

Douglas Town

Town Clerk, 29 Depot St., Municipal Center, Douglas, MA 01516. 508-476-4000 x355 R/E Recording: 508-476-4000 x353; Fax 508-476-4012.
Will search UCC records. Tax liens not included in UCC search. Real estate records located in Worcester County. **Other Phone Numbers:** Assessor 508-476-4000 x353; Treasurer 508-476-4000 x356; Elections 508-476-4000 x355; Vital Records 508-476-4000 x355.

Dover Town

Town Clerk, P.O. Box 250, Dover, MA 02030-0250. 508-785-1719 R/E Recording: 508-785-0726; Fax 508-785-2341. http://www.doverma.org/townclerk.htm
Will search UCC records. Tax liens not included in UCC search. Real estate records located in Norfolk County. **Other Phone Numbers:** Assessor 508-785-0726; Treasurer 508-785-0057; Elections 508-785-1719; Vital Records 508-785-1719.

Dracut Town

Town Clerk, 62 Arlington Street, Room 4, Dracut, MA 01826. 978-453-0951; Fax 978-452-7924.
Will search UCC records. Tax liens not included in UCC search. Real estate records located in Middlesex County.

Dudley Town

Town Clerk, 40 Schofield Ave, Town Hall, 40 Schofield Ave., Dudley, MA 01571. 508-949-8004; Fax 508-949-7115.
Will search UCC records. UCC search includes tax liens. Real estate records located in Worcester County. **Other Phone Numbers:** Assessor 508-949-8006; Treasurer 508-949-8002; Appraiser/Auditor 508-949-8001; Elections 508-949-8004; Vital Records 508-949-8004.

Dukes County

County Register of Deeds, P.O. Box 5231, Edgartown, MA 02539. County Register of Deeds, R/E and UCC Recording 508-627-4025; Fax 508-627-7821.
This county is comprised of 6 towns-there is no County Assessor, Appraiser, Elections, etc. Will not search UCC records. This agency will not do a tax lien search. Will not search real estate records.

Dunstable Town

Town Clerk, 511 Main St., Dunstable, MA 01827. 978-649-4514; Fax 978-649-2205.
Will search UCC records. This agency will not do a tax lien search. Real estate records located in Middlesex County. **Other Phone Numbers:** Assessor 978-649-3257; Treasurer 978-649-3257; Elections 978-649-4514; Vital Records 978-649-4514.

Duxbury Town

Town Clerk, 878 Tremont Street, Duxbury, MA 02332-4499. 781-934-1100 x150; Fax 781-934-9278.
Will search UCC records. UCC search includes tax liens if requested. Include $5.00 search fee Real estate records located in Plymouth County. **Other Phone Numbers:** Assessor 781-934-1109; Treasurer 781-934-1102.

East Bridgewater Town

Town Clerk, P.O. Box 387, East Bridgewater, MA 02333. 508-378-1606; Fax 508-378-1638.
Will search UCC records. UCC search includes tax liens. Real estate records located in Plymouth County.

East Brookfield Town

Town Clerk, Town Hall, East Brookfield, MA 01515. Town Clerk, R/E and UCC Recording 508-867-6769; Fax 508-867-4190.
Will search UCC records. This agency will not do a tax lien search. Real estate records located in Worcester County. **Other Phone Numbers:** Assessor 508-867-6769; Treasurer 508-867-6769; Elections 508-867-6769; Vital Records 508-867-6769.

East Longmeadow Town

Town Clerk, 60 Center Square, East Longmeadow, MA 01028-2446. 413-525-5400; Fax 413-525-1025.

Will search UCC records. Tax liens not included in UCC search. Real estate records located in Hampden County. **Other Phone Numbers:** Assessor 413-525-5425; Treasurer 413-525-5400.

Eastham Town

Town Clerk, 2500 State Highway, Eastham, MA 02642. 508-240-5900 x223.
Will search UCC records. UCC search includes tax liens if requested. Real estate records located in Barnstable County. **Other Phone Numbers:** Assessor 508-255-0333.

Easthampton City

City Clerk, 43 Main Street, Town Hall, Room 1, Easthampton, MA 01027. 413-529-1460 R/E Recording: 413-529-1401; Fax 413-529-1488.
Will search UCC records. UCC search includes tax liens if requested. Real estate records located in Hampshire County. **Other Phone Numbers:** Assessor 413-529-1401; Treasurer 413-529-1416; Elections 413-529-1460; Vital Records 413-529-1460.

Easton Town

Town Clerk, 136 Elm Street, North Easton, MA 02356-0129. 508-230-3335 R/E Recording: 508-230-3416; Fax 508-230-3438. http://www.easton.ma.us
Will search UCC records. Tax liens included in UCC search if requested. Real estate records located in Bristol County. **Other Phone Numbers:** Assessor 508-230-3416; Treasurer 508-230-3358; Elections 508-230-3335; Vital Records 508-230-3335.

Edgartown Town

Town Clerk, P.O.Box 35, Edgartown, MA 02539-0035. 508-627-6110 R/E Recording: 508-627-4025; Fax 508-627-6123.
Will search UCC records. UCC search includes tax liens if requested. Real estate records located in Dukes County. **Other Phone Numbers:** Assessor 508-627-6140; Treasurer 508-627-6130; Elections 508-627-6110; Vital Records 508-627-6110.

Egremont Town

Town Clerk, P.O. Box 56, North Egremont/ So. Egremont, MA 01258-0056. 413-528-0182; Fax 413-528-5465.
Will search UCC records. UCC search includes tax liens if requested. Real estate records located in Berkshire County. **Other Phone Numbers:** Assessor 413-528-0182.

Erving Town

Town Clerk, Town Hall, 12 E. Main St., Erving, MA 01344. 978-544-3636 X102; Fax 978-544-5436.
Will search UCC records. UCC search includes tax liens if requested. Real estate records located in Franklin County. **Other Phone Numbers:** Assessor 978-544-3636 X107; Treasurer 978-544-3636 X104.

Essex County (Northern District)

County Register of Deeds, 381 Common Street, Lawrence, MA 01840. 978-683-2745; Fax 978-688-4679. http://www.lawrencedeeds.com
Will search UCC records, but only real estate related UCC filed here. Tax liens included in UCC search if requested. Will not search real estate records. **Online Access:** Real Estate, Liens. For online access information, see Andover Town and Essex County Southern District. **Other Phone Numbers:** Assessor 978-683-2745; Treasurer 978-683-2745.

Essex County (Southern District)

County Register of Deeds, 36 Federal Street, Salem, MA 01970. 978-741-0201; Fax 978-744-5865.

Will search UCC records, but only real estate related UCC filed here. This agency will not do a tax lien search. Will not search real estate records. **Online Access:** Real Estate, Liens. Access to the Essex County online records requires a $25 deposit, with a $.25 per minute charge for use. Records date back to 1981. Lending agency information is available. For information, contact David Burke at 978-683-2745. Records on the Essex County South Registry of Deeds database are available free on the Internet at http://207.244.88.10/deedsonline.asp. Images start 1/1992; records back to 1/1984. Search by grantee/grantor, town & date, street, or book & page. **Other Phone Numbers:** Assessor 978-741-0200.

Essex Town

Town Clerk, Town Hall, Martin St., Essex, MA 01929. 978-768-7111.
Do not confuse Essex Town with Essex County. UCC records are filed with the Town/City Clerk, real estate records are at the county level with the Register of Deeds. Will search UCC records. This agency will not do a tax lien search. Real estate records located in Essex County.

Everett City

City Clerk, City Hall, Room 10, Everett, MA 02149. 617-394-2228; Fax 617-387-5770.
Will search UCC records. Tax liens not included in UCC search. Real estate records located in Middlesex County. **Other Phone Numbers:** Assessor 617-394-2205; Treasurer 617-394-2315; Elections 617-394-2229; Vital Records 617-394-2225; Registrar of Voters 617-394-2295.

Fairhaven Town

Town Clerk, 40 Center Street, Fairhaven, MA 02719-2999. 508-979-4025; Fax 508-979-4079.
Will search UCC records. UCC search includes tax liens. Real estate records located in Bristol County. **Other Phone Numbers:** Assessor 508-979-4018; Treasurer 508-979-4026; Elections 508-979-4025; Vital Records 508-979-4025.

Fall River City

City Clerk, One Government Center, Fall River, MA 02722. 508-324-2220; Fax 508-324-2211.
Will search UCC records. Tax liens not included in UCC search. Real estate records located in Bristol County. **Other Phone Numbers:** Assessor 508-324-2300; Treasurer 508-324-2260; Elections 508-324-2630; Vital Records 508-324-2220.

Falmouth Town

Town Clerk, P.O. Box 904, Falmouth, MA 02541. 508-548-7611 R/E Recording: 508-495-7675 UCC Recording: 508-495-7357; Fax 508-457-2511. http://www.town.falmouth.ma.us
Will search UCC records. This agency will not do a tax lien search. Real estate records located in Barnstable County. **Online Access:** Assessor. Records on the Town of Falmouth Assessor database are available free by experiment on the Internet at www.town.falmouth.ma.us/propinq.html. Provides owner, address, and valuation only. **Other Phone Numbers:** Assessor 508-495-7377; Treasurer 508-495-7362; Elections 508-495-7358; Vital Records 508-495-7357; Switchboard 508-548-7611.

Fitchburg City

City Clerk, 718 Main Street, Fitchburg, MA 01420-3198. 978-345-9592; Fax 978-345-9595.
Will search UCC records. This agency will not do a tax lien search. Real estate records located in Worcester County. **Other Phone Numbers:** Assessor 978-345-9562.

Florida Town

Town Clerk, Town Hall, 20 South St, Drury, MA 01343. 413-664-6685; Fax 413-664-8640.
Will search UCC records. UCC search includes tax liens if requested. Real estate records located in Berkshire County. **Other Phone Numbers:** Assessor 413-662-2448; Treasurer 413-663-9851.

Foxborough Town

Town Clerk, 40 South Street, Foxborough, MA 02035-2397. 508-543-1208 R/E Recording: 508-543-1215; Fax 508-543-6278.
Will search UCC records. UCC search includes tax liens. Real estate records located in Norfolk County. **Other Phone Numbers:** Assessor 508-543-1215; Treasurer 508-543-1216; Elections 508-543-1208; Vital Records 508-543-1208; Main Number 508-543-1200.

Framingham Town

Town Clerk, Memorial Building - Room 105, 150 Concord St., Framingham, MA 01702-8374. 508-620-4863; Fax 508-620-5910.
Will search UCC records. UCC search includes tax liens if requested. Real estate records located in Middlesex County. **Other Phone Numbers:** Assessor 508-620-4858; Treasurer 508-620-4866.

Franklin County

County Register of Deeds, P.O. Box 1495, Greenfield, MA 01302-1495. 413-772-0239; Fax 413-774-7150.
Will not search UCC records. This agency will not do a tax lien search. Will not search real estate records. **Other Phone Numbers:** Treasurer 413-774-4804.

Franklin Town

Town Clerk, Municipal Building, 150 Emmons Street, Franklin, MA 02038. 508-520-4900; Fax 508-520-4903.
Will search UCC records. Tax liens included in UCC search. Real estate records located in Franklin County. **Other Phone Numbers:** Assessor 508-520-4920; Treasurer 508-520-4950.

Freetown Town

Town Clerk, P.O. Box 438, Assonet, MA 02702. 508-644-2203 R/E Recording: 508-644-2205; Fax 508-644-9826. http://town.freetown.ma.us/tg/
Will search UCC records. Real estate records located in Bristol County. **Other Phone Numbers:** Assessor 508-644-2205; Treasurer 508-644-2204; Appraiser/Auditor 508-644-2205; Elections 508-644-2203; Vital Records 508-644-2203.

Gardner City

City Clerk, 95 Pleasant Street, City Hall Room 118, Gardner, MA 01440. 978-630-4008; Fax 978-630-2520.
Will search UCC records. Tax liens included in UCC search if requested. Real estate records located in Worcester County. **Other Phone Numbers:** Assessor 978-630-4004; Treasurer 978-630-4016.

Gay Head Town

Town Clerk, 65 State Rd, Aquinnah, MA 02535. 508-645-2306; Fax 508-645-2310.
The Town of Aquinnah was formerly known as Gay Head. Will search UCC records. This agency will not do a tax lien search. Real estate records located in Dukes County.

Georgetown Town

Town Clerk, 1 Library Street, Georgetown, MA 01833. 978-352-5711 R/E Recording: 978-352-5708; Fax 978-352-5725.

Will search UCC records. This agency will not do a tax lien search. Real estate records located in Essex County. **Other Phone Numbers:** Appraiser/Auditor 978-352-5708; Elections 978-352-5711; Vital Records 978-352-5711.

Gill Town

Town Clerk, Town Clerk's Office, 325 Main Road, Gill, MA 01376. 413-863-8103; Fax 413-863-9347.
Will search UCC records. This agency will not do a tax lien search. Real estate records located in Franklin County. **Other Phone Numbers:** Assessor 413-863-8103.

Gloucester City

City Clerk, 9 Dale Avenue, Gloucester, MA 01930-5998. 978-281-9720; Fax 978-281-8472. http://www.ci.gloucester.ma.us
Will search UCC records. UCC search includes tax liens if requested. Real estate records located in Essex County. **Other Phone Numbers:** Assessor 978-281-9715; Treasurer 978-281-9707; Elections 978-281-9720; Vital Records 978-281-9720.

Goshen Town

Town Clerk, P.O. Box 124, Goshen, MA 01032-0124. 413-268-8236; Fax 413-268-8237.
Will search UCC records. This agency will not do a tax lien search. Real estate records located in Hampshire County. **Other Phone Numbers:** Assessor 413-268-7856; Treasurer 413-268-7760; Elections 413-268-8236; Vital Records 413-268-8236.

Gosnold Town

Town Clerk, Town Hall, Gosnold, MA 02713. 508-990-7408; Fax 508-990-7408.
Will search UCC records. This agency will not do a tax lien search. Real estate records located in Dukes County. **Other Phone Numbers:** Assessor 508-990-7101; Treasurer 508-990-7101.

Grafton Town

Town Clerk, Municipal Center, 30 Providence Road, Grafton, MA 01519-1186. 508-839-4722 UCC Recording: 508-839-5335 x195; Fax 508-839-4602.
Will search UCC records. UCC search includes tax liens. Real estate records located in Worcester County. **Other Phone Numbers:** Assessor 508-839-5335 x165; Treasurer 508-839-5335 x170
508-839-5335 x170; Elections 508-839-5335 x195; Vital Records 508-839-5335 x195.

Granby Town

Town Clerk, 250 State St., Kellogg Hall, Granby, MA 01033. 413-467-7178 R/E Recording: 413-584-3637; Fax 413-467-2080.
Will search UCC records. This agency will not do a tax lien search. Real estate records located in Hampshire County. **Other Phone Numbers:** Assessor 413-467-7196; Treasurer 413-467-7176; Elections 413-467-7178; Vital Records 413-467-7178.

Granville Town

Town Clerk, P.O. Box 247, Granville, MA 01034-0247. Town Clerk, R/E and UCC Recording 413-357-8585; Fax 413-357-6002.
Will search UCC records. UCC search includes tax liens. Real estate records located in Hampden County. **Other Phone Numbers:** Assessor 413-357-8585; Treasurer 413-357-8585; Elections 413-357-8585; Vital Records 413-357-8585.

Great Barrington Town

Town Clerk, 334 Main Street, Great Barrington, MA 01230-1802. 413-528-3140 R/E Recording: 413-528-0146; Fax 413-528-2290.
Will search UCC records. This agency will not do a tax lien search. Real estate records located in Berkshire County. **Other Phone Numbers:** Assessor 413-528-2220; Treasurer 413-528-1025; Elections 413-528-3140; Vital Records 413-528-3140; Selectman 413-528-1619.

Greenfield Town

Town Clerk, 14 Court Square, Town Hall, Greenfield, MA 01301. 413-772-1555; Fax 413-772-1542.
Will search UCC records. UCC search includes tax liens if requested. Real estate records located in Franklin County. **Other Phone Numbers:** Assessor 413-772-1506.

Groton Town

Town Clerk, Town Hall, 173 Main St., Groton, MA 01450. 978-448-1100; Fax 978-448-2030. http://www.groton.ma.us/
Will search UCC records. This agency will not do a tax lien search. Real estate records located in Middlesex County. **Other Phone Numbers:** Assessor 978-448-1127; Treasurer 978-448-1103; Elections 978-448-1100; Vital Records 978-448-1100.

Groveland Town

Town Clerk, Town Hall, Groveland, MA 01830. Town Clerk, R/E and UCC Recording 978-372-6861 UCC Recording: 978-372-5005; Fax 978-469-5006.
Will search UCC records. This agency will not do a tax lien search. Real estate records located in Essex County. **Other Phone Numbers:** Assessor 978-372-8528; Treasurer 978-372-6861; Elections 978-372-5005; Vital Records 978-372-5005.

Hadley Town

Town Clerk, 100 Middle Street, Hadley, MA 01035-9517. 413-584-1590; Fax 413-586-5661. http://www.hadleyma.org
Will search UCC records. UCC search includes tax liens if requested. Real estate records located in Hampshire County. **Other Phone Numbers:** Assessor 413-586-6320; Treasurer 413-586-3354.

Halifax Town

Town Clerk, 499 Plymouth Street, Halifax, MA 02338-1395. 781-293-7970; Fax 781-294-7684.
Will search UCC records. Tax liens not included in UCC search. Real estate records located in Plymouth County. **Other Phone Numbers:** Assessor 781-293-5960; Treasurer 781-293-8348; Appraiser/Auditor 781-293-5960; Elections 781-293-7970; Vital Records 781-293-7970.

Hamilton Town

Town Clerk, P.O. Box 429, Hamilton, MA 01936. 978-468-5570; Fax 978-468-2682. http://www.town.hamilton.ma.us/
Will search UCC records. UCC search includes tax liens if requested. Real estate records located in Essex County. **Other Phone Numbers:** Assessor 508-468-5574; Treasurer 508-468-5575; Appraiser/Auditor 508-468-5574; Elections 508-468-5570; Vital Records 508-468-5570; Selectmen 508-468-5572.

Hampden County

County Register of Deeds, 50 State Street, Hall of Justice, Springfield, MA 01103. 413-748-8622; Fax 413-731-8190.
Will search UCC records, but only real estate related UCC filed here. This agency will not do a tax lien search. Will not search real estate records. **Online Access:** Real Estate, Liens. Access to County online records requires a $50 annual fee and $.50 per minute of use. Records date back to 1965. Lending agency information is available. Searchable indexes are bankruptcy (from PACER), unregistered land site and registered land site. For information, contact Donna Brown at 413-748-7945.

Hampden Town

Town Clerk, P.O. Box 351, Hampden, MA 01036. 413-566-3214; Fax 413-566-2010.
Will search UCC records. Tax liens included in UCC search if requested. Real estate records located in Hampden County. **Other Phone Numbers:** Assessor 413-566-3223; Treasurer 413-566-2401.

Hampshire County

County Register of Deeds, 33 King Street, Hall of Records, Northampton, MA 01060. 413-584-3637; Fax 413-584-4136.
Will not search UCC records. Only real estate related UCC filed here. This agency will not do a tax lien search. Will not search real estate records. **Online Access:** Real Estate, Liens. Access to County Register of Deeds online records requires a $100 annual fee and $.50 per minute of use, $.60 for out-of-state. Records date back to 9/2/1986. Lending agency information is available. For information, contact MaryAnn Foster at 413-584-3637.

Hancock Town

Town Clerk, 3650 Hancock Rd., Hancock, MA 01237-1097. Town Clerk, R/E and UCC Recording 413-738-5225; Fax 413-738-5310.
Will search UCC records. Tax liens included in UCC search if requested. Real estate records located in Berkshire County. **Other Phone Numbers:** Assessor 413-738-5225; Treasurer 413-738-5225; Elections 413-738-5225; Vital Records 413-738-5225.

Hanover Town

Town Clerk, 550 Hanover Street, Hanover, MA 02339-2217. 781-826-2691; Fax 781-826-5950.
Will search UCC records. This agency will not do a tax lien search. Real estate records located in Plymouth County. **Other Phone Numbers:** Assessor 781-826-6401; Treasurer 781-826-3571; Vital Records 781-826-2691.

Hanson Town

Town Clerk, Town Hall, 542 Liberty St., Hanson, MA 02341. 781-293-2772; Fax 781-294-0884.
Will search UCC records. Tax liens not included in UCC search. Real estate records located in Plymouth County. **Other Phone Numbers:** Assessor 781-293-5259; Treasurer 781-293-2422; Appraiser/Auditor 781-293-5259; Elections 781-293-2772; Vital Records 781-293-2772.

Hardwick Town

Town Clerk, P.O. Box 575, Gilbertville, MA 01031-0575. 413-477-6197; Fax 413-477-6703.
Will search UCC records. UCC search includes tax liens if requested. Real estate records located in Worcester County.

Harvard Town

Town Clerk, Town Hall, 13 Ayer Rd., Harvard, MA 01451-1458. 978-456-4100 UCC Recording: 978-456-4100 x16; Fax 978-456-4113. http://www.harvard.ma.us/townclerk.htm
The Village of Still River is in the Town of Harvard. UCC records are filed with the Town/City Clerk, real estate records are at the county level with the Register of Deeds. Will search UCC records. UCC search includes tax liens. Real estate records located in Worcester County. **Other Phone Numbers:** Assessor 978-456-4100; Treasurer 978-456-4100; Elections 978-456-4100 x16; Vital Records 978-456-4100 x16.

Harwich Town

Town Clerk, 732 Main Street, Harwich, MA 02645-2717. Town Clerk, R/E and UCC Recording 508-430-7516; Fax 508-432-5039.
Will search UCC records. This agency will not do a tax lien search. Real estate records located in Barnstable County. **Other Phone Numbers:** Assessor 508-430-7503; Treasurer 508-430-7501; Appraiser/Auditor 508-430-7503; Elections 508-430-7516; Vital Records 508-430-7516; Board of Selectmen 508-430-7513.

Hatfield Town

Town Clerk, 59 Main Street, Hatfield, MA 01038-9702. 413-247-0492; Fax 413-347-5029.
Will search UCC records. UCC search includes tax liens. Real estate records located in Hampshire County. **Other Phone Numbers:** Assessor 413-247-0322.

Haverhill City

City Clerk, 4 Summer Street, City Hall, Room 118, Haverhill, MA 01830-5880. 978-374-2312; Fax 978-373-8490.
Will search UCC records. UCC search includes tax liens if requested. Real estate records located in Essex County. **Other Phone Numbers:** Assessor 978-347-2316; Treasurer 978-374-2320; Elections 978-374-2312; Vital Records 978-374-2312.

Hawley Town

Town Clerk, Town Hall, Hawley, MA 01339. 413-339-5518; Fax 413-339-4959.
Will search UCC records. This agency will not do a tax lien search. Real estate records located in Franklin County. **Other Phone Numbers:** Assessor 413-339-5518; Treasurer 413-339-4231; Elections 413-339-5531; Vital Records 413-339-5531.

Heath Town

Town Clerk, Town Hall, 1 E. Main St., Heath, MA 01346. 413-337-4934; Fax 413-337-8542.
Will search UCC records. Tax liens included in UCC search if requested. Real estate records located in Franklin County. **Other Phone Numbers:** Assessor 413-337-4934; Treasurer 413-337-4934.

Hingham Town

Town Clerk, 210 Central St, Hingham, MA 02043. 781-741-1410; Fax 781-740-0239.
Will search UCC records. This agency will not do a tax lien search. Real estate records located in Plymouth County. **Other Phone Numbers:** Assessor 781-741-1455; Treasurer 781-741-1408; Appraiser/Auditor 781-741-1455; Elections 781-741-1410; Vital Records 781-741-1410.

Hinsdale Town

Town Clerk, Town Hall, P.O. Box 803, Hinsdale, MA 01235. 413-655-2301 R/E Recording: 413-443-7438; Fax 413-655-8807.
Will search UCC records. Tax liens included in UCC search if requested. Real estate records located in Berkshire County. **Other Phone Numbers:** Assessor 413-655-2300; Treasurer 413-655-2306; Appraiser/Auditor 413-655-2300; Elections 413-655-2301; Vital Records 413-655-2301.

Holbrook Town

Town Clerk, Town Hall, Holbrook, MA 02343-1502. 781-767-4314; Fax 781-767-0705.

Will search UCC records. This agency will not do a tax lien search. Real estate records located in Norfolk County. **Other Phone Numbers:** Assessor 781-767-4315; Treasurer 781-767-4316; Elections 781-767-4314; Vital Records 781-767-4314.

Holden Town

Town Clerk, 1196 Main Street, Town Hall, Holden, MA 01520-1092. 508-829-0265; Fax 508-829-0252. http://140.239.211.227/HOLDENMA
Will search UCC records. Tax liens included in UCC search if requested. Real estate records located in Worcester County. **Online Access:** Real Estate, Property Tax. Online Access to the Town assessor's database is available free at http://140.239.211.227/HOLDENMA. Registration is required; sign-up is free. **Other Phone Numbers:** Assessor 508-829-0223; Treasurer 508-829-0235.

Holland Town

Town Clerk, 27 Sturbridge Rd, Holland, MA 01521-9712. 413-245-7108; Fax 413-245-7037.
Will search UCC records. This agency will not do a tax lien search. Real estate records located in Hampden County.

Holliston Town

Town Clerk, 703 Washington Street, Holliston, MA 01746. 508-429-0601; Fax 508-429-0684. www.holliston.ma.us
Will search UCC records. UCC search includes tax liens. Real estate records located in Middlesex County. **Other Phone Numbers:** Assessor 508-429-0604; Treasurer 508-429-0602; Vital Records 508-429-0601.

Holyoke City

City Clerk, City Hall, Holyoke, MA 01040. 413-534-2166; Fax 413-534-2322. http://www.ci.holyoke.ma.us/
Will search UCC records. UCC search includes tax liens if requested. Real estate records located in Hampden County. **Online Access:** Tax Assessor. Online access to property valuations on the tax accessor database are available free at www.ci.holyoke.ma.us/Assesment.asp. No name searching. **Other Phone Numbers:** Assessor 413-534-2180; Treasurer 413-534-2153; Appraiser/Auditor 413-534-2166; Elections 413-534-2166.

Hopedale Town

Town Clerk, P.O. Box 7, Hopedale, MA 01747. 508-634-2211; Fax 508-634-2200.
Will search UCC records. UCC search includes tax liens if requested. Real estate records located in Worcester County. **Other Phone Numbers:** Assessor 508-634-2201; Treasurer 508-634-2203; Elections 508-634-2211.

Hopkinton Town

Town Clerk, 18 Main Street, Hopkinton, MA 01748-1260. 508-497-9710; Fax 508-497-9702.
Will search UCC records. Tax liens not included in UCC search. Real estate records located in Middlesex County. **Other Phone Numbers:** Assessor 508-497-9720.

Hubbardston Town

Town Clerk, P.O. Box H, Hubbardston, MA 01452. 978-928-5244; Fax 978-928-1402.
Will search UCC records. Tax liens not included in UCC search. Real estate records located in Worcester County. **Other Phone Numbers:** Assessor 978-928-1400; Treasurer 978-928-1401; Elections 978-928-5244; Vital Records 978-928-5244.

Hudson Town

Town Clerk, 78 Main Street, Town Hall, Hudson, MA 01749. 978-568-9615.
Will search UCC records. UCC search includes tax liens. Real estate records located in Middlesex County. **Other Phone Numbers:** Assessor 978-568-9620; Treasurer 978-568-9605; Elections 978-568-9615; Vital Records 978-568-9615.

Hull Town

Town Clerk, Town Hall, Hull, MA 02045. 781-925-2262; Fax 781-925-0224.
Will search UCC records. Tax liens not included in UCC search. Real estate records located in Plymouth County. **Other Phone Numbers:** Assessor 781-925-2205.

Huntington Town

Town Clerk, Office of Town Clerk, 50 Searle Rd., Huntington, MA 01050. 413-667-3260; Fax 413-667-8859.
Will search UCC records. UCC search includes tax liens if requested. Real estate records located in Hampshire County. **Other Phone Numbers:** Assessor 413-667-3501; Treasurer 413-667-3500.

Ipswich Town

Town Clerk, 25 Green St, 30 South Main St., Ipswich, MA 01938-2357. 978-356-6600; Fax 978-356-6616.
Will search UCC records. Tax liens not included in UCC search. Real estate records located in Essex County. **Other Phone Numbers:** Assessor 978-356-6603; Treasurer 978-356-6601; Elections 978-356-6600.

Kingston Town

Town Clerk, P.O. Drawer E, Kingston, MA 02364. 781-585-0502; Fax 781-585-0542.
Will search UCC records. Real estate records located in Plymouth County. **Other Phone Numbers:** Assessor 781-585-0509; Treasurer 781-585-0508; Elections 781-585-0502; Vital Records 781-585-0502.

Lakeville Town

Town Clerk, 346 Bedford Street, Lakeville, MA 02347. 508-946-8814; Fax 508-946-0112.
Will search UCC records. UCC search includes tax liens if requested. Real estate records located in Plymouth County. **Other Phone Numbers:** Assessor 508-947-4428; Treasurer 508-946-8801; Appraiser/Auditor 508-947-4428.

Lancaster Town

Town Clerk, Town Hall, Box 97, 695 Main St., Lancaster, MA 01523-0097. 978-365-2542 R/E Recording: 978-365-9562; Fax 978-368-4005.
Will search UCC records. This agency will not do a tax lien search. Real estate records located in Worcester County. **Other Phone Numbers:** Assessor 978-365-9562; Treasurer 978-365-6115; Appraiser/Auditor 978-365-9562; Elections 978-365-2542; Vital Records 978-365-2542.

Lanesborough Town

Town Clerk, P.O. Box 1492, Lanesborough, MA 01237. 413-442-1351; Fax 413-443-5811.
Will search UCC records. UCC search includes tax liens if requested. Real estate records located in Berkshire County. **Other Phone Numbers:** Assessor 413-442-8622; Treasurer 413-442-1167; Elections 413-442-1351; Vital Records 413-442-1351.

Lawrence City

City Clerk, 200 Common Street, Lawrence, MA 01840. 978-794-5803 R/E Recording: 978-683-2745; Fax 978-

557-0285. http://www.cityoflawrence.com/Departments.asp
Will search UCC records. This agency will not do a tax lien search. Real estate records located in Essex County Registry of Deeds, 381 Common St, Lawrence MA 01840. **Other Phone Numbers:** Assessor 978-794-5790; Treasurer 978-794-5843; Elections 978-794-5807; Vital Records 978-794-5803.

Lee Town

Town Clerk, Town Hall, 32 Main St., Lee, MA 01238. 413-243-5505; Fax 413-243-5507.
Will search UCC records. UCC search includes tax liens. Real estate records located in Berkshire County. **Other Phone Numbers:** Assessor 413-243-5512; Treasurer 413-243-5506; Elections 413-243-5505; Vital Records 413-243-5505.

Leicester Town

Town Clerk, 3 Washburn Square, Leicester, MA 01524. 508-892-7011; Fax 508-892-7070.
Will search UCC records. Tax liens included in UCC search if requested. Real estate records located in Worcester County. **Other Phone Numbers:** Assessor 508-365-2542; Treasurer 508-365-2542.

Lenox Town

Town Clerk, 6 Walker Street, Town Hall, Lenox, MA 01240-2718. 413-637-5506; Fax 413-637-5518.
Will search UCC records. This agency will not do a tax lien search. Real estate records located in Berkshire County.

Leominster City

City Clerk, 25 West Street, Leominster, MA 01453. 978-534-7536; Fax 978-534-7546.
Will search UCC records. UCC search includes tax liens if requested. Real estate records located in Worcester County. **Online Access:** Assessor. Property tax records on the Assessor's database are available free online at http://140.239.211.227/leominsterma. User ID is required; registration is free. **Other Phone Numbers:** Assessor 978-534-7531.

Leverett Town

Town Clerk, P.O. Box 178, Leverett, MA 01054. 413-548-9150; Fax 413-548-9150.
Will search UCC records. This agency will not do a tax lien search. Real estate records located in Franklin County.

Lexington Town

Town Clerk, 1625 Massachusetts Avenue, Town Office Building, Lexington, MA 02420. 781-862-0500 x270; Fax 781-861-2754.
Will search UCC records. Tax liens not included in UCC search. Real estate records located in Middlesex County. **Other Phone Numbers:** Assessor 617-861-2703.

Leyden Town

Town Clerk, Town Hall, Leyden, MA 01337. 413-774-7769; Fax 413-772-0146.
Will search UCC records. UCC search includes tax liens if requested. Real estate records located in Franklin County. **Other Phone Numbers:** Assessor 413-774-4111; Treasurer 413-774-4111; Elections 413-774-7769; Vital Records 413-774-7769.

Lincoln Town

Town Clerk, P.O. Box 6353, Lincoln Center, MA 01773-6353. 781-259-2607; Fax 781-259-1677. http://www.ifor.com/lincoln
Will search UCC records. This agency will not do a tax lien search. Real estate records located in Middlesex

County. **Other Phone Numbers:** Assessor 781-259-2611; Treasurer 781-259-2606; Elections 781-259-2607; Vital Records 781-259-2607.

Littleton Town

Town Clerk, P.O. Box 1305, Littleton, MA 01460. 978-952-2314;   Fax   978-952-2321. http://www.littletonma.org
Will search UCC records. UCC search includes tax liens if requested. Real estate records located in Middlesex County. **Other Phone Numbers:** Assessor 978-952-2309; Treasurer 978-952-2306; Elections 978-952-2314; Vital Records 978-952-2314.

Longmeadow Town

Town Clerk, Town Hall, 20 Williams Street, Longmeadow, MA 01106. 413-567-1066; Fax 413-565-4112.
Will search UCC records. UCC search includes tax liens. Real estate records located in Hampden County. **Other Phone Numbers:** Assessor 413-567-1251; Treasurer 413-567-1066.

Lowell City

City Clerk, City Hall, 375 Merrimack Street, Lowell, MA 01852. 978-970-4161; Fax 978-970-4162.
Will search UCC records. UCC search includes tax liens if requested. Real estate records located in Middlesex County. **Online Access:** Assessor. Property tax records on the Assessor's database are available free online at http://140.239.211.227/LowellMA. **Other Phone Numbers:** Assessor 978-970-4200; Treasurer 978-970-4224.

Ludlow Town

Town Clerk, 488 Chapin Street, Ludlow, MA 01056. 413-583-5610 R/E Recording: 413-583-5608; Fax 413-583-5603.
Will search UCC records. Tax liens included in UCC search if requested. Real estate records located in Hampden County. **Other Phone Numbers:** Assessor 413-583-5608; Treasurer 413-583-5616; Elections 413-583-5610; Vital Records 413-583-5610.

Lunenburg Town

Town Clerk, P.O. Box 135, Lunenburg, MA 01462. 978-582-4131; Fax 978-582-4148.
Will search UCC records. Tax liens not included in UCC search. Real estate records located in Worcester County. **Other Phone Numbers:** Assessor 978-582-4145; Treasurer 978-582-4130; Elections 978-582-4132; Vital Records 978-582-4131.

Lynn City

City Clerk, 3 City Hall Square, Lynn, MA 01901. 781-598-4000; Fax 781-477-7032.
Will search UCC records. Tax liens at Tax Collector's Office. Real estate records located in Essex County.

Lynnfield Town

Town Clerk, 55 Summer Street, Lynnfield, MA 01940-1823. 781-334-3128; Fax 781-334-0014.
Will search UCC records. Tax liens included in UCC search if requested. Real estate records located in Essex County. **Other Phone Numbers:** Assessor 781-334-2231; Treasurer 781-334-7663; Elections 781-334-3128; Vital Records 781-334-3128.

Malden City

City Clerk, 200 Pleasant Street, City Hall, Malden, MA 02148. 781-397-7116; Fax 781-388-0610.
Will search UCC records. Tax liens not included in UCC search. Real estate records located in Middlesex County. **Other Phone Numbers:** Assessor 781-397-7100.

Manchester-by-the-Sea Town

Town Clerk, Town Hall, Manchester-by-the Sea, MA 01944-1399. 978-526-2040; Fax 978-526-2001. http://www.manchester.ma.us/town.html
Will search UCC records. This agency will not do a tax lien search. Real estate records located in Essex County. **Other Phone Numbers:** Assessor 978-526-2010; Treasurer 978-526-2030; Elections 978-526-2040; Vital Records 978-526-2040.

Mansfield Town

Town Clerk, Town Hall, 6 Park Row, Mansfield, MA 02048-2433. 508-261-7345; Fax 508-261-1083.
Will search UCC records. UCC search includes tax liens. Real estate records located in Bristol County. **Other Phone Numbers:** Assessor 508-261-7350; Treasurer 508-261-7340; Appraiser/Auditor 508-261-7350; Elections 508-261-7345; Vital Records 508-261-7345.

Marblehead Town

Town Clerk, Abbot Hall, Marblehead, MA 01945. 781-631-0528; Fax 781-631-8571.
Will search UCC records. This agency will not do a tax lien search. Real estate records located in Essex County. **Other Phone Numbers:** Assessor 781-631-0236; Treasurer 781-631-1033.

Marion Town

Town Clerk, 2 Spring Street, Marion, MA 02738. 508-748-3502;   Fax   508-748-2845.   http://www.townofmarion.org
Will search UCC records. Tax liens included in UCC search if requested. Real estate records located in Plymouth County. **Other Phone Numbers:** Assessor 508-748-3510; Treasurer 508-748-3505.

Marlborough City

City Clerk, 140 Main Street, Marlborough, MA 01752-3812. 508-460-3775; Fax 508-624-6504.
Will search UCC records. This agency will not do a tax lien search. Real estate records located in Middlesex County. **Other Phone Numbers:** Assessor 508-460-3779; Treasurer 508-460-3730; Appraiser/Auditor 508-460-3779; Elections 508-460-3775; Vital Records 508-460-3775.

Marshfield Town

Town Clerk, Town Hall, Marshfield, MA 02050. 781-834-5540; Fax 781-837-7163.
Will search UCC records. UCC search includes tax liens. Real estate records located in Plymouth County. **Other Phone Numbers:** Assessor 781-834-5585; Treasurer 781-834-5545; Elections 781-834-5540; Vital Records 781-834-5540.

Mashpee Town

Town Clerk, Town Hall, 16 Great Neck Rd. N., Mashpee, MA 02649. 508-539-1400 x561 R/E Recording: 508-539-1400 x537; Fax 508-539-1403. http://www.capecod.net/mashpee
Will search UCC records. UCC search includes tax liens if requested. Real estate records located in Barnstable County. **Online Access:** Assessor. Records on the Town of Mashpee Assessor database are available free online at www.capecode.net/mashpee/assess. **Other Phone Numbers:** Assessor 508-539-1400 x529; Treasurer 508-539-1400 x537; Appraiser/Auditor 508-539-1400 x529; Elections 508-539-1400 x561; Vital Records 508-539-1400 x561.

Mattapoisett Town

Town Clerk, P.O. Box 89, Mattapoisett, MA 02739-0089. 508-758-4103; Fax 508-758-3030.

Will search UCC records. Tax liens included in UCC search if requested. Real estate records located in Plymouth County. **Other Phone Numbers:** Assessor 508-758-4106; Treasurer 508-758-4108.

Maynard Town

Town Clerk, 195 Main Street, Town Hall, Maynard, MA 01754-2575. 978-897-1000 R/E Recording: 978-897-1005; Fax 978-897-8457.
Will search UCC records. Tax liens not included in UCC search. Real estate records located in Middlesex County. **Other Phone Numbers:** Assessor 978-897-1004; Treasurer 978-897-1005; Appraiser/Auditor 978-897-1007; Elections 978-897-1000; Vital Records 978-897-1000.

Medfield Town

Town Clerk, Town Hall, 459 Main St., Medfield, MA 02052. 508-359-8505 R/E Recording: 508-359-8505 x630; Fax 508-359-6182. http://www.town.medfield.net
Will search UCC records. UCC search includes tax liens if requested. Real estate records located in Norfolk County. **Other Phone Numbers:** Treasurer 508-359-8505 X625.

Medford City

City Clerk, 85 George P. Hassett Drive, City Clerk, Medford, MA 02155. 781-393-2425; Fax 781-391-1895. http://www.medford.org
Will search UCC records. This agency will not do a tax lien search. Real estate records located in Middlesex County. **Online Access:** Assessor. **Other Phone Numbers:** Assessor 781-393-2435; Treasurer 781-393-2550; Elections 781-393-2491; Vital Records 781-393-2425.

Medway Town

Town Clerk, 155 Village St., Medway, MA 02053. 508-533-3204; Fax 508-533-3287.
Will search UCC records. UCC search includes tax liens if requested. Real estate records located in Norfolk County. **Other Phone Numbers:** Assessor 508-533-3203; Treasurer 508-533-3205.

Melrose City

City Clerk, P.O. Box C, Melrose, MA 02176. 781-665-2225.
Will search UCC records. This agency will not do a tax lien search. Real estate records located in Middlesex County.

Mendon Town

Town Clerk, P.O. Box 54, Mendon, MA 01756-0054. 508-473-1085;   Fax   508-478-8241. http://www.mendonma.net
Will search UCC records. UCC search includes tax liens if requested. Real estate records located in Worcester County. **Other Phone Numbers:** Assessor 508-473-2738; Treasurer 508-473-6410; Elections 508-473-1085; Vital Records 508-473-1085.

Merrimac Town

Town Clerk, 2 School Street, Merrimac, MA 01860. 978-346-8013; Fax 978-346-0522.
Will search UCC records. UCC search includes tax liens if requested. Real estate records located in Essex County. **Other Phone Numbers:** Assessor 978-346-9022.

Methuen City

City Clerk, 41 Pleasant St., Room 112, Methuen, MA 01844. 978-794-3213 R/E Recording: 978-794-3219; Fax 978-794-7509. http://www.ci.methuen.ma.us/

Will search UCC records. UCC search includes tax liens if requested. Real estate records located in Essex County at Northern Essex Register of Deeds, Lawrence, MA. **Other Phone Numbers:** Assessor 978-794-3219; Treasurer 978-794-3205; Appraiser/Auditor 978-794-3220; Elections 978-794-3213; Vital Records 978-794-3213.

Middleborough Town

Town Clerk, 20 Centre St., 1st Floor, Middleborough, MA 02346. 508-946-2415 R/E Recording: 508-946-2410; Fax 508-946-2308.
Will search UCC records. This agency will not do a tax lien search. Real estate records located in Plymouth County. **Other Phone Numbers:** Assessor 508-946-2410; Treasurer 508-946-2411; Appraiser/Auditor 508-946-2410; Elections 508-946-2415; Vital Records 508-946-2415.

Middlefield Town

Town Clerk, P.O. Box 265, Middlefield, MA 01243. Town Clerk, R/E and UCC Recording 413-623-8966; Fax 413-623-6108.
Will search UCC records. This agency will not do a tax lien search. Real estate records located in Hampshire County. **Other Phone Numbers:** Assessor 413-623-8966; Treasurer 413-623-8966; Appraiser/Auditor 413-623-8966; Elections 413-623-8966.

Middlesex County (Northern District)

County Register of Deeds, 360 Gorham Street, Lowell, MA 01852. 978-322-9000; Fax 978-322-9001. http://www.tiac.net/users/nmrd
Will search UCC records, but only real estate related UCC filed here. This agency will not do a tax lien search. Will not search real estate records. **Online Access:** Real Estate, Liens. Access to the Telesearch online system with North District records requires a $100 set up fee, plus $50 deposit, and $.20 per minute of use. Wang software is $95. Records date back to 1976. A fax back service is available. For information, contact customer service at 978-458-8474.

Middlesex County (Southern District)

County Register of Deeds, 208 Cambridge Street, East Cambridge, MA 02141. 617-494-4500.
Will search UCC records, but only real estate related UCC filed here. This agency will not do a tax lien search. Will not search real estate records. **Online Access:** Real Estate, Liens. Access to the LandTrack online system with Southern District records requires a $100 annual fee, plus $.50 per minute of use. Lending agency information is available as is a fax back service for documents. For information, contact Grace Abruzzio at 617-494-4510.

Middleton Town

Town Clerk, Memorial Hall, Middleton, MA 01949. 978-774-6927.
Will search UCC records. This agency will not do a tax lien search. Real estate records located in Essex County. **Other Phone Numbers:** Assessor 978-774-2099; Treasurer 978-774-8327; Elections 978-774-6927; Vital Records 978-774-6927.

Milford Town

Town Clerk, 52 Main Street, Milford, MA 01757. 508-634-2307; Fax 508-634-2324.
Will search UCC records. UCC search includes tax liens if requested. Real estate records located in Worcester County. **Other Phone Numbers:** Assessor 508-634-2306.

Millbury Town

Town Clerk, 127 Elm Street, Municipal Office Building, Millbury, MA 01527. 508-865-9110 R/E Recording: 508-865-9121.
Will search UCC records. UCC search includes tax liens. Real estate records located in Worcester County. **Other Phone Numbers:** Assessor 508-865-4732; Treasurer 508-865-8040; Elections 508-865-9110; Vital Records 508-865-9110.

Millis Town

Town Clerk, P.O. Box 181, Millis, MA 02054. 508-376-8011; Fax 508-376-2941.
Will search UCC records. This agency will not do a tax lien search. Real estate records located in Norfolk County.

Millville Town

Town Clerk, P.O. Box 703, Millville, MA 01529-0703. 508-883-5849; Fax 508-883-2994.
Will search UCC records. UCC search includes tax liens if requested. Real estate records located in Worcester County. **Other Phone Numbers:** Assessor 508-883-5031; Treasurer 508-883-7449; Elections 508-883-5849; Vital Records 508-883-5849.

Milton Town

Town Clerk, 525 Canton Avenue, Town Hall, Milton, MA 02186. 617-696-5414.
Will search UCC records. Tax liens included in UCC search if requested. Real estate records located in Norfolk County. **Other Phone Numbers:** Assessor 617-696-5400; Treasurer 617-696-5319.

Monroe Town

Town Clerk, P.O. Box 6, Monroe, MA 01350. Town Clerk, R/E and UCC Recording 413-424-5272; Fax 413-424-5272.
Will search UCC records. Tax liens included in UCC search if requested. Real estate records located in Franklin County. **Other Phone Numbers:** Assessor 413-424-5272; Treasurer 413-424-5272.

Monson Town

Town Clerk, 110 Main St. #4, Monson, MA 01057-1332. 413-267-4115; Fax 413-267-3726.
Will search UCC records. UCC search includes tax liens if requested. Real estate records located in Hampden County. **Other Phone Numbers:** Assessor 413-267-4120; Treasurer 413-267-4125; Appraiser/Auditor 413-267-4120; Elections 413-267-4115; Vital Records 413-267-4115.

Montague Town

Town Clerk, 1 Avenue A, Turners Falls, MA 01376-1128. 413-863-3211; Fax 413-863-3224.
Will search UCC records. Tax liens included in UCC search if requested. Real estate records located in Franklin County. **Other Phone Numbers:** Assessor 413-863-4654; Treasurer 413-863-3207; Elections 413-863-3211; Vital Records 413-863-3211.

Monterey Town

Town Clerk, Town Hall, Monterey, MA 01245. 413-528-5175; Fax 413-528-9452.
Will search UCC records. Tax liens included in UCC search if requested. Real estate records located in Berkshire County. **Other Phone Numbers:** Assessor 413-528-6481; Treasurer 413-528-1443; Elections 413-528-5175; Vital Records 413-528-5175.

Montgomery Town

Town Clerk, Town Hall, Montgomery, MA 01085. 413-862-4478; Fax 413-862-3204.

Will search UCC records. This agency will not do a tax lien search. Real estate records located in Hampden County. **Other Phone Numbers:** Assessor 413-862-3101; Treasurer 413-862-3911.

Mt. Washington Town

Town Clerk, 118 East St., Mt. Washington, MA 01258. 413-528-2839; Fax 413-528-2839.
Will search UCC records. This agency will not do a tax lien search. Real estate records located in Berkshire County. **Other Phone Numbers:** Assessor 413-528-2839; Treasurer 413-528-2839; Elections 413-528-2839; Vital Records 413-528-2839.

Nahant Town

Town Clerk, Town Hall, Nahant, MA 01908-0075. 781-581-0018; Fax 781-593-0340.
Will search UCC records. UCC search includes tax liens. Real estate records located in Essex County. **Other Phone Numbers:** Assessor 781-581-0212; Treasurer 781-581-0018; Appraiser/Auditor 781-581-0212; Elections 781-581-0018; Town Accountant 781-581-0099.

Nantucket County

County Register of Deeds, 16 Broad Street, Nantucket, MA 02554. 508-228-7250; Fax 508-325-5331. http://www.nantucketdeeds.com
Will not search UCC records, but only real estate related UCC filed here. This agency will not do a tax lien search. Will not search real estate records. **Other Phone Numbers:** Assessor 508-228-7211; Treasurer 508-228-7265; Elections 508-228-7217; Vital Records 508-228-7217.

Nantucket Town

Town Clerk, Town & County Building, 16 Broad Street, Nantucket, MA 02554. 508-228-7217 R/E Recording: 508-228-7250; Fax 508-325-5313. www.town.nantucket.ma.us
Will search UCC records. UCC search includes tax liens if requested. Real estate records located in Nantucket County. **Other Phone Numbers:** Assessor 508-228-7211; Treasurer 508-325-5314; Elections 508-228-7217; Vital Records 508-228-7255; 508-228-7255.

Natick Town

Town Clerk, 13 East Central Street, Natick, MA 01760. 508-647-6400 UCC Recording: 508-647-6430.
Will search UCC records. UCC search includes tax liens. Real estate records located in Middlesex County. **Online Access:** Property. **Other Phone Numbers:** Assessor 508-647-6420; Treasurer 508-647-6425; Appraiser/Auditor 508-647-6420; Elections 508-647-6430; Vital Records 508-647-6430.

Needham Town

Town Clerk, P.O. Box 663, Needham, MA 02192. 781-455-7510; Fax 781-449-4569. http://www.town.needham.ma.us
Will search UCC records. This agency will not do a tax lien search. Real estate records located in Norfolk County. **Other Phone Numbers:** Assessor 781-455-7507; Treasurer 781-455-7504; Appraiser/Auditor 781-455-7507; Elections 781-455-7501; Vital Records 781-455-7501.

New Ashford Town

Town Clerk, 142 Beach Hill Road, New Ashford, MA 01237. 413-458-5461; Fax 413-458-5461.
Will search UCC records. UCC search includes tax liens if requested. Real estate records located in Berkshire County. **Other Phone Numbers:** Assessor 413-743-9154.

New Bedford City

City Clerk, 133 William Street, New Bedford, MA 02740. 508-979-1450; Fax 508-991-6225. http://www.ci.new-bedford.ma.us/Nav3.htm
Will search UCC records. Tax liens not included in UCC search. Real estate records located in Bristol County. **Online Access:** Property, Assessor. Online access to the assessor's proeprty database is available free at www.ci.new-bedford.ma.us/Assessors/Real PropertyLookup.htm. **Other Phone Numbers:** Assessor 508-979-1440; Treasurer 508-979-1430.

New Braintree Town

Town Clerk, 1750 Hardwick Rd., New Braintree, MA 01531. 413-477-8772; Fax 508-867-6316.
Will search UCC records. UCC search includes tax liens if requested. Real estate records located in Worcester County. **Other Phone Numbers:** Assessor 413-867-2071; Treasurer 413-867-2434.

New Marlborough Town

Town Clerk, P.O. Box 99, Mill River, MA 01244. 413-229-8116; Fax 413-229-6674.
Will search UCC records. This agency will not do a tax lien search. Real estate records located in Berkshire County. **Other Phone Numbers:** Assessor 413-229-8926; Treasurer 413-229-8963; Vital Records 413-229-8116.

New Salem Town

Town Clerk, Town Hall, 15 S. Main St., New Salem, MA 01355. 978-544-2731; Fax 978-544-5775.
Will search UCC records. Tax liens included in UCC search if requested. Real estate records located in Franklin County.

Newbury Town

Town Clerk, 25 High Road, Newbury, MA 01951-4799. 978-462-2332; Fax 978-465-3064.
Will search UCC records. UCC search includes tax liens if requested. Real estate records located in Essex County. **Other Phone Numbers:** Assessor 978-465-0211; Treasurer 978-465-0862.

Newburyport City

City Clerk, 60 Pleasant Street, Newburyport, MA 01950. 978-465-4407; Fax 978-465-4452.
Will search UCC records. Real estate records located in Essex County. **Other Phone Numbers:** Assessor 978-465-4403; Treasurer 978-465-4415; Elections 978-465-4407; Vital Records 978-465-4407.

Newton City

City Clerk, 1000 Commonwealth Avenue, Newton Center, MA 02159. 617-552-7030; Fax 617-964-2333. http://www.ci.newton.ma.us
Will search UCC records. Tax liens included in UCC search if requested. Real estate records located in Middlesex County. **Online Access:** Assessor. Records on the City of Newton Fiscal 1998 Assessment database are available free at www.ci.newton.ma.us/ GIS/Assessors/Default.asp. Data represents market value as of 1/1/1997. **Other Phone Numbers:** Assessor 617-552-7065; Treasurer 617-552-7080.

Norfolk County

County Register of Deeds, P.O. Box 69, Dedham, MA 02027-0069. County Register of Deeds, R/E and UCC Recording 781-461-6122; Fax 781-326-4742. www.norfolkdeeds.org
Will not search UCC records, but only real estate related UCC filed here. This agency will not do a tax lien search. Will not search real estate records. **Online Access:** Real Estate, Liens. Access to county online records requires a $25 set up fee, plus $1 fee for the first

minute and $.50 per minute thereafter per session. The system is only accessible in Massachusetts. Lending agency information is available. For information, contact Pam at 781-461-6116.

Norfolk Town

Town Clerk, P.O. Box 216, Norfolk, MA 02056. 508-528-1400; Fax 508-520-3250.
Will search UCC records. Tax liens included in UCC search. Real estate records located in Norfolk County. **Other Phone Numbers:** Assessor 508-528-1120; Treasurer 508-528-2478.

North Adams City

City Clerk, 10 Main Street, North Adams, MA 01247. 413-662-3015 R/E Recording: 413-743-0035 North; 443-7438 Cent.; 528-0146 South.
Will search UCC records. UCC Form 11 must accompany a search request. Real estate records located in Berkshire County. **Other Phone Numbers:** Assessor 413-662-3012; Treasurer 413-662-3044; Elections 413-662-3015; Vital Records 413-662-3015.

North Andover Town

Town Clerk, 120 Main Street, North Andover, MA 01845. 978-688-9501; Fax 978-688-9556.
Will search UCC records. UCC search includes tax liens if requested. Real estate records located in Essex County. **Other Phone Numbers:** Assessor 978-682-6483; Treasurer 978-682-6483.

North Attleborough Town

Town Clerk, P.O. Box 871, North Attleborough, MA 02761-0871. 508-699-0108 R/E Recording: 508-822-3081; Fax 508-699-2354.
Will search UCC records. UCC search includes tax liens if requested. Real estate records located in Bristol County. **Other Phone Numbers:** Assessor 508-699-0117; Treasurer 508-699-0114; Elections 508-699-0106; Vital Records 508-699-0108.

North Brookfield Town

Town Clerk, 185 No. Main St., North Brookfield, MA 01535. 508-867-0203; Fax 508-867-0249.
Will search UCC records. UCC search includes tax liens if requested. Real estate records located in Worcester County. **Other Phone Numbers:** Assessor 508-867-0209; Treasurer 508-867-0204; Elections 508-867-0203; Vital Records 508-867-0203.

North Reading Town

Town Clerk, 235 North Street, North Reading, MA 01864-1294. 978-664-6030 R/E Recording: 978-664-6021; Fax 978-664-6048.
Will search UCC records. This agency will not do a tax lien search. Real estate records located in Middlesex County. **Other Phone Numbers:** Assessor 978-664-6021; Treasurer 978-664-6019; Appraiser/Auditor 978-664-6021; Elections 978-664-6030; Vital Records 978-664-6030.

Northampton City

City Clerk, 210 Main Street, Northampton, MA 01060. 413-587-1224; Fax 413-587-1264.
Will search UCC records. UCC search includes tax liens if requested. Real estate records located in Hampshire County. **Other Phone Numbers:** Assessor 413-586-6950 x200.

Northborough Town

Town Clerk, 63 Main Street, Northborough, MA 01532-1994. 508-393-5001; Fax 508-393-6996.
Will search UCC records. UCC search includes tax liens if requested. Real estate records located in

Worcester County. **Other Phone Numbers:** Assessor 508-393-5005; Treasurer 508-393-5045.

Northbridge Town

Town Clerk, Town Hall, 7 Main St., Whitinsville, MA 01588. 508-234-2001; Fax 508-234-7640.
Will search UCC records. UCC search includes tax liens if requested. Real estate records located in Worcester County. **Other Phone Numbers:** Assessor 508-234-2740; Treasurer 508-234-5432.

Northfield Town

Town Clerk, Town Hall, Northfield, MA 01360. 413-498-2901; Fax 413-498-5103.
Will search UCC records. Tax liens included in UCC search. Real estate records located in Franklin County. **Other Phone Numbers:** Assessor 413-498-2901; Treasurer 413-498-2901.

Norton Town

Town Clerk, 70 East Main Street, Town Hall, Norton, MA 02766. 508-285-0231; Fax 508-285-0297.
Will search UCC records. Tax liens included in UCC search if requested. Real estate records located in Bristol County. **Other Phone Numbers:** Assessor 508-285-0270; Treasurer 508-285-0223; Vital Records 508-285-0230.

Norwell Town

Town Clerk, P.O. Box 295, Norwell, MA 02061-0295. 781-659-8072 R/E Recording: 781-659-8014; Fax 781-659-7795.
Will search UCC records. Tax liens included in UCC search if requested. Real estate records located in Plymouth County. **Other Phone Numbers:** Assessor 781-659-8014; Treasurer 781-659-8070; Elections 781-659-8072; Vital Records 781-659-8072.

Norwood Town

Town Clerk, P.O. Box 40, Norwood, MA 02062. 781-762-1240 x193 UCC Recording: 781-762-1240; Fax 781-762-0954.
Will search UCC records. Tax liens included in UCC search if requested. Real estate records located in Norfolk County. **Other Phone Numbers:** Assessor 781-762-1240; Treasurer 781-762-1240; Elections 781-762-1240; Vital Records 781-762-1240.

Oak Bluffs Town

Town Clerk, P.O. Box 2490, Oak Bluffs, MA 02557-2490. 508-693-5515; Fax 508-696-7736.
Will search UCC records. Tax liens not included in UCC search. Real estate records located in Dukes County. **Other Phone Numbers:** Assessor 508-693-5519; Treasurer 508-693-5514; Elections 508-693-5515; Vital Records 508-693-5515.

Oakham Town

Town Clerk, P.O. Box 222, Oakham, MA 01068-0222. 508-882-5549; Fax 508-882-3060.
Will search UCC records. This agency will not do a tax lien search. Real estate records located in Worcester County. **Other Phone Numbers:** Assessor 508-882-5549; Treasurer 508-882-5549.

Orange Town

Town Clerk, 6 Prospect Street, Orange, MA 01364. 978-544-2254; Fax 978-544-1120.
Will search UCC records. This agency will not do a tax lien search. Real estate records located in Franklin County. **Other Phone Numbers:** Assessor 978-544-1108; Treasurer 978-544-1103; Elections 978-544-2254; Vital Records 978-544-2254.

Orleans Town

Town Clerk, 19 School Road, Orleans, MA 02653-3699. 508-240-3700 UCC Recording: 508-240-3700 x304; Fax 508-240-3388.
Will search UCC records. UCC search includes tax liens if requested. Real estate records located in Barnstable County. **Other Phone Numbers:** Assessor 508-240-3700 x331; Treasurer 508-240-3700 x323.

Otis Town

Town Clerk, P.O. Box 237, Otis, MA 01253. 413-269-0101; Fax 413-269-0111.
Will search UCC records. This agency will not do a tax lien search. Real estate records located in Berkshire County. **Other Phone Numbers:** Assessor 413-269-0102; Treasurer 413-269-0108; Elections 413-269-0101; Vital Records 413-269-0101.

Oxford Town

Town Clerk, 325 Main Street, Oxford, MA 01540. 508-987-6032; Fax 508-987-6048. http://www.town.oxford.ma.us
Will search UCC records. Tax liens included in UCC search if requested. Real estate records located in Worcester County. **Other Phone Numbers:** Assessor 508-987-6036; Treasurer 508-987-6038; Elections 508-987-6032; Vital Records 508-987-6032.

Palmer Town

Town Clerk, Palmer Town Building, Palmer, MA 01069-1198. 413-283-2608; Fax 413-283-2637.
Will search UCC records. Real estate records located in Hampden County. **Other Phone Numbers:** Assessor 413-283-2607; Treasurer 413-283-2600.

Paxton Town

Town Clerk, 697 Pleasant Street, Paxton, MA 01612. 508-799-7347 x13; Fax 508-797-0966.
Will search UCC records. UCC search includes tax liens if requested. Real estate records located in Worcester County. **Other Phone Numbers:** Assessor 508-799-7231 x16.

Peabody City

City Clerk, 24 Lowell Street, City Hall, Peabody, MA 01960. 978-532-3000; Fax 978-531-0098.
Will search UCC records. This agency will not do a tax lien search. Real estate records located in Essex County.

Pelham Town

Town Clerk, Rhodes Building, 351 Amherst Rd., Pelham, MA 01002-9753. 413-253-7129; Fax 413-256-1061.
Will search UCC records. UCC search includes tax liens if requested. Real estate records located in Hampshire County. **Other Phone Numbers:** Assessor 413-253-7129; Treasurer 413-253-2267; Elections 413-253-7129; Vital Records 413-253-7129.

Pembroke Town

Town Clerk, 100 Center Street, Pembroke, MA 02359. 781-293-7211.
Will search UCC records. This agency will not do a tax lien search. Real estate records located in Plymouth County. **Other Phone Numbers:** Assessor 781-293-2393; Treasurer 781-293-3893; Appraiser/Auditor 781-293-2393; Elections 781-293-7211; Vital Records 781-293-7211; Town Administrator 781-293-3844.

Pepperell Town

Town Clerk, 1 Main Street, Town Hall, Pepperell, MA 01463-1644. 978-433-0339; Fax 978-433-0338. www.town.pepperell.ma.us
Will search UCC records. UCC search includes tax liens if requested. Real estate records located in Middlesex County. **Other Phone Numbers:** Assessor 978-433-0322; Treasurer 978-433-0337; Elections 978-433-0339; Vital Records 978-433-0339.

Peru Town

Town Clerk, 4 North Rd, Peru, MA 01235-9803. 413-655-8326 UCC Recording: 413-655-8312; Fax 413-655-8312.
Will search UCC records. Tax liens not included in UCC search. Real estate records located in Berkshire County. **Other Phone Numbers:** Assessor 413-655-8312; Treasurer 413-655-8312; Elections 413-655-8326; Vital Records 413-655-8326.

Petersham Town

Town Clerk, P.O. Box 486, Petersham, MA 01366. 978-724-6649; Fax 978-724-3501.
Will search UCC records. This agency will not do a tax lien search. Real estate records located in Worcester County. **Other Phone Numbers:** Assessor 978-724-6658; Treasurer 978-724-8813; Elections 978-724-6649; Vital Records 978-724-6649.

Phillipston Town

Town Clerk, 50 The Common, Phillipston, MA 01331. 978-249-1733 R/E Recording: 978-249-1732; Fax 978-249-3356.
Will search UCC records. This agency will not do a tax lien search. Real estate records located in Worcester County. **Other Phone Numbers:** Assessor 978-249-1732; Treasurer 978-249-3415; Appraiser/Auditor 978-249-1732; Elections 978-249-1733; Vital Records 978-249-1733; General Town Hall 978-249-6828.

Pittsfield City

City Clerk, 70 Allen Street, City Hall, Pittsfield, MA 01201. 413-499-9361; Fax 413-499-9363. http://www.pittsfield-ma.org
Will search UCC records. UCC search includes tax liens if requested. Real estate records located in Berkshire County Register of Deeds 413-443-7438 **Other Phone Numbers:** Assessor 413-499-9445; Treasurer 413-499-9466; Elections 413-499-9460; Vital Records 413-499-9361.

Plainfield Town

Town Clerk, 344 Main Street, Plainfield, MA 01070. 413-634-5417; Fax 413-634-5683.
Will search UCC records. This agency will not do a tax lien search. Real estate records located in Hampshire County. **Other Phone Numbers:** Assessor 413-634-5420; Treasurer 413-634-5420; Elections 413-634-5417; Vital Records 413-634-5417.

Plainville Town

Town Clerk, P.O. Box 1717, Plainville, MA 02762. 508-695-3142 x20 R/E Recording: 508-695-3142 x14 UCC Recording: 508-695-3142 x19; Fax 508-695-1857.
Will search UCC records. Tax liens included in UCC search if requested. Real estate records located in Norfolk County. **Other Phone Numbers:** Assessor 508-695-3142 x14; Treasurer 508-695-3142 x17,18; Elections 508-695-3142 x19; Vital Records 508-695-3142 x19.

Plymouth County

County Register of Deeds, P.O. Box 3535, Plymouth, MA 02361. 508-830-9200; Fax 508-830-9280.
Will search UCC records, but only real estate related UCC filed here. This agency will not do a tax lien search. Will not search real estate records. **Online Access:** Real Estate, Liens. Access to Online Titleview for Plymouth County records requires a usage charge of $.60 per minute of use. Records date back to 1971.

Lending agency information is available. A fax back service is $3 plus $1 per page in county, $4. plus $1 per page, outside. For information, call 508-830-9287.

Plymouth Town

Town Clerk, 11 Lincoln Street, Plymouth, MA 02360-3386. 508-830-4050; Fax 508-830-4062.
Will search UCC records. UCC search includes tax liens if requested. Real estate records located in Plymouth County. **Other Phone Numbers:** Assessor 508-830-4020; Treasurer 508-830-4051; Elections 508-830-4050; Vital Records 508-830-4052.

Plympton Town

Town Clerk, P.O. Box 153, Plympton, MA 02367-0153. 781-585-3220; Fax 781-582-1505.
Will search UCC records. This agency will not do a tax lien search. Real estate records located in Plymouth County. **Other Phone Numbers:** Assessor 781-585-3227; Treasurer 781-585-0409.

Princeton Town

Town Clerk, 6 Town Hall Drive, Princeton, MA 01541-1137. 978-464-2103; Fax 978-464-2106. http://town.princeton.ma.us
Will search UCC records. Tax liens included in UCC search if requested. Real estate records located in Worcester County. **Other Phone Numbers:** Assessor 978-464-2104; Treasurer 978-464-2105; Elections 978-464-2103; Vital Records 978-464-2103; Switchboard 978-464-2100.

Provincetown Town

Town Clerk, 260 Commercial Street, Provincetown, MA 02657. 508-487-7013; Fax 508-487-9560. http://www.provincetowngov.org
Will search UCC records. UCC search includes tax liens if requested. Real estate records located in Barnstable County. **Online Access:** Assessor. Records on the Provincetown Assessor database are available free online at www.provincetowngov.org/assessor.html. **Other Phone Numbers:** Assessor 508-487-7017; Treasurer 508-487-7015; Elections 508-487-7013; Vital Records 508-487-7013.

Quincy City

City Clerk, 1305 Hancock Street, City Hall, Quincy, MA 02169. 617-376-1136; Fax 617-376-1139.
Will search UCC records. UCC search includes tax liens. Real estate records located in Norfolk County. **Other Phone Numbers:** Assessor 617-376-1178.

Randolph Town

Town Clerk, 41 S. Main St., Randolph, MA 02368. 781-961-0900; Fax 781-961-0919.
Will search UCC records. This agency will not do a tax lien search. Real estate records located in Norfolk County. **Other Phone Numbers:** Assessor 781-961-0906; Treasurer 781-961-0934.

Raynham Town

Town Clerk, 53 Orchard Street, Raynham, MA 02767-1320. 508-824-2700; Fax 508-823-1812.
Will search UCC records. This agency will not do a tax lien search. Real estate records located in Bristol County. **Other Phone Numbers:** Assessor 508-824-2704; Treasurer 508-824-2702; Vital Records 508-824-2701.

Reading Town

Town Clerk, 16 Lowell Street, Reading, MA 01867. 781-942-9050 UCC Recording: 781-942-9049; Fax 781-942-9070. http://www.ci.reading.ma.us/depts.htm
Will search UCC records. Real estate records located in Middlesex County. **Online Access:** Assessor. Records

on the Town of Reading Assessor database are available free online at www.ziplink.net/~reading1/assessor.htm. **Other Phone Numbers:** Assessor 781-942-9027; Treasurer 781-942-9032; Elections 781-942-9050; Vital Records 781-942-9048.

Rehoboth Town

Town Clerk, 148 Peck Street, Rehoboth, MA 02769-3099. 508-252-6502; Fax 508-252-5342.
Will search UCC records. UCC search includes tax liens if requested. Real estate records located in Bristol County. **Other Phone Numbers:** Assessor 508-252-3352.

Revere City

City Clerk, 281 Broadway, City Hall, Revere, MA 02151-5087. 781-286-8160; Fax 781-286-8135.
Will search UCC records. Tax liens included in UCC search if requested. Real estate records located in Suffolk County. **Other Phone Numbers:** Assessor 781-286-8169; Treasurer 781-286-8136.

Richmond Town

Town Clerk, P.O. Box 81, Richmond, MA 01254. 413-698-3315; Fax 413-698-3272.
Will search UCC records. Real estate records located in Berkshire County. **Other Phone Numbers:** Treasurer 413-698-3355.

Rochester Town

Town Clerk, Town Hall, 1 Constitution Way, Rochester, MA 02770. 508-763-3871; Fax 508-763-4892.
Will search UCC records. Tax liens not included in UCC search. Real estate records located in Plymouth County.

Rockland Town

Town Clerk, 242 Union Street, Rockland, MA 02370. 781-871-1892 R/E Recording: 781-871-0137.
Will search UCC records. This agency will not do a tax lien search. Real estate records located in Plymouth County. **Other Phone Numbers:** Assessor 781-871-0137; Treasurer 781-871-1895; Appraiser/Auditor 781-871-0137; Elections 781-871-1892; Vital Records 781-871-1892.

Rockport Town

Town Clerk, P.O. Box 429, Rockport, MA 01966. 978-546-6894; Fax 978-546-3562.
Will search UCC records. This agency will not do a tax lien search. Real estate records located in Essex County. **Other Phone Numbers:** Assessor 978-546-2011; Treasurer 978-546-6648.

Rowe Town

Town Clerk, Town Hall, Rowe, MA 01367. 413-339-5520; Fax 413-339-5316.
Will search UCC records. UCC search includes tax liens if requested. Real estate records located in Berkshire County. **Other Phone Numbers:** Assessor 413-339-5520; Treasurer 413-339-5520; Vital Records 413-339-4446.

Rowley Town

Town Clerk, P.O. Box 351, Rowley, MA 01969-0351. 978-948-2081; Fax 978-948-2162.
Will search UCC records. This agency will not do a tax lien search. Real estate records located in Essex County.

Royalston Town

Town Clerk, P.O. Box 118, Royalston, MA 01368-0118. 978-249-0493; Fax 978-575-0493.

Will search UCC records. This agency will not do a tax lien search. Real estate records located in Worcester County.

Russell Town

Town Clerk, Town Hall, Russell, MA 01071. 413-862-3265; Fax 413-862-3103.
Will search UCC records. This agency will not do a tax lien search. Real estate records located in Hampden County.

Rutland Town

Town Clerk, 250 Main Street, Rutland, MA 01543. 508-886-4104; Fax 508-886-2929.
Will search UCC records. This agency will not do a tax lien search. Real estate records located in Worcester County. **Other Phone Numbers:** Assessor 508-886-4101; Treasurer 508-886-4103.

Salem City

City Clerk, City Hall, 93 Washington, Salem, MA 01970-3593. 978-745-9595; Fax 978-740-9209.
Will search UCC records. This agency will not do a tax lien search. Real estate records located in Essex County. **Other Phone Numbers:** Assessor 978-745-9595 x261.

Salisbury Town

Town Clerk, 5 Beach Rd, Salisbury, MA 01952. 978-462-7591; Fax 978-462-4176.
Will search UCC records. This agency will not do a tax lien search. Real estate records located in Essex County. **Other Phone Numbers:** Assessor 978-462-7591; Treasurer 978-465-0331; Vital Records 978-462-7591.

Sandisfield Town

Town Clerk, P.O. Box 163, Sandisfield, MA 01255. 413-258-4711 R/E Recording: 413-258-4701 UCC Recording: 413-258-4075; Fax 413-258-4225.
Will search UCC records. Tax liens not included in UCC search. Real estate records located in Berkshire County. **Other Phone Numbers:** Assessor 413-258-4701; Treasurer 413-258-8102; Appraiser/Auditor 413-258-4701; Elections 413-258-4075; Vital Records 413-258-4075; Selectmen 413-258-4711.

Sandwich Town

Town Clerk, 145 Main Street, Sandwich, MA 02563. 508-888-0340; Fax 508-888-2497.
Will search UCC records. UCC search includes tax liens if requested. Real estate records located in Barnstable County. **Other Phone Numbers:** Assessor 508-888-0157; Treasurer 508-888-6508; Elections 508-888-0340; Vital Records 508-888-0340.

Saugus Town

Town Clerk, 298 Central Street, Town Hall, Saugus, MA 01906. 781-231-4101; Fax 781-231-4109. www.saugus.net
Will search UCC records. This agency will not do a tax lien search. Real estate records located in Essex County. **Other Phone Numbers:** Assessor 781-231-4130; Treasurer 781-231-4135.

Savoy Town

Town Clerk, 720 Main Rd., Savoy, MA 01256. 413-743-3759; Fax 413-743-4292.
Will search UCC records. This agency will not do a tax lien search. Real estate records located in Berkshire County. **Other Phone Numbers:** Assessor 413-743-4290; Treasurer 413-743-4290; Elections 413-743-3759; Vital Records 413-743-3759.

Scituate Town

Town Clerk, Town Hall, 600 C. J. Cushing Way, Scituate, MA 02066. 781-545-8744; Fax 781-545-8704.
Will search UCC records. Real estate records located in Plymouth County. **Other Phone Numbers:** Assessor 781-545-8713.

Seekonk Town

Town Clerk, 100 Peck Street, Seekonk, MA 02771. 508-336-2920; Fax 508-336-0764.
Will search UCC records. Tax liens included in UCC search. Real estate records located in Bristol County.

Sharon Town

Town Clerk, 90 South Main Street, Town Hall, Sharon, MA 02067. 781-784-1505; Fax 781-784-1503.
Will search UCC records. UCC search includes tax liens. Real estate records located in Norfolk County. **Other Phone Numbers:** Assessor 781-784-1507; Treasurer 781-784-1500; Elections 781-784-1505; Vital Records 781-784-1505.

Sheffield Town

Town Clerk, P.O. Box 175, Sheffield, MA 01257. 413-229-8752; Fax 413-229-7010.
Will search UCC records. This agency will not do a tax lien search. Real estate records located in Berkshire County. **Other Phone Numbers:** Assessor 413-229-7001; Treasurer 413-229-7007; Elections 413-229-8752; Vital Records 413-229-8752.

Shelburne Town

Town Clerk, Town Hall, 51 Bridge St., Shelburne, MA 01370. 413-625-0301; Fax 413-625-0303.
Will search UCC records. Tax liens included in UCC search if requested. Real estate records located in Franklin County. **Other Phone Numbers:** Assessor 413-625-0301; Treasurer 413-625-0301.

Sherborn Town

Town Clerk, P.O. Box 186, Sherborn, MA 01770-0186. 508-651-7853; Fax 508-651-7854. http://members.aol.com/sherbornma
Will search UCC records. UCC search includes tax liens if requested. Real estate records located in Middlesex County. **Other Phone Numbers:** Assessor 508-651-7857; Treasurer 508-651-7859; Appraiser/Auditor 508-651-7857; Elections 508-651-7853; Vital Records 508-651-7853.

Shirley Town

Town Clerk, P.O. Box 782, Shirley, MA 01464. 978-425-2610; Fax 978-425-2602.
Will search UCC records. Tax liens included in UCC search if requested. Real estate records located in Middlesex County. **Other Phone Numbers:** Assessor 978-425-2613; Treasurer 978-425-2604; Vital Records 978-425-2610.

Shrewsbury Town

Town Clerk, 100 Maple Ave, Town Hall, Shrewsbury, MA 01545. 508-841-8507; Fax 508-842-0587.
Will search UCC records. UCC search includes tax liens. Real estate records located in Worcester County. **Other Phone Numbers:** Assessor 508-841-8501; Treasurer 508-841-8509; Elections 508-841-8507; Vital Records 508-841-8507.

Shutesbury Town

Town Clerk, P.O. Box 326, Shutesbury, MA 01072-0326. 413-259-1204 R/E Recording: 413-259-3790; Fax 413-259-1107. www.shutesbury.org
Will search UCC records. This agency will not do a tax lien search. Real estate records located in Franklin

County. **Other Phone Numbers:** Assessor 413-259-3790; Treasurer 413-259-1801; Elections 413-259-1204; Vital Records 413-259-1204.

Somerset Town

Town Clerk, 140 Wood Street, Somerset, MA 02726. 508-646-2818; Fax 508-646-2802.
Will search UCC records. This agency will not do a tax lien search. Real estate records located in Bristol County. **Other Phone Numbers:** Assessor 508-646-2824; Treasurer 508-646-2822; Vital Records 508-646-2818.

Somerville City

City Clerk, 93 Highland Avenue, Somerville, MA 02143. 617-625-6600 x4100; Fax 617-625-4239.
Will search UCC records. This agency will not do a tax lien search. Real estate records located in Middlesex County. **Other Phone Numbers:** Assessor 617-625-6600 x3100; Vital Records 617-625-6600 x4100.

South Hadley Town

Town Clerk, 116 Main Street, South Hadley, MA 01075-2833. 413-538-5023; Fax 413-538-7565.
Will search UCC records. Real estate records located in Hampshire County. **Other Phone Numbers:** Assessor 413-538-5027.

Southampton Town

Town Clerk, P.O. Box 276, Southampton, MA 01073. 413-527-8392; Fax 413-529-1006.
Will search UCC records. Tax liens not included in UCC search. Real estate records located in Hampshire County. **Other Phone Numbers:** Assessor 413-527-4741; Treasurer 413-527-4920; Elections 413-527-8392; Selectman's 413-529-0106.

Southborough Town

Town Clerk, 17 Common St, Town Hall, Southborough, MA 01772-9109. 508-485-0710; Fax 508-480-0161.
Will search UCC records. UCC search includes tax liens if requested. Real estate records located in Worcester County. **Other Phone Numbers:** Assessor 508-485-0710; Treasurer 508-485-0710; Elections 508-485-0710; Vital Records 508-485-0710.

Southbridge Town

Town Clerk, 41 Elm Street, Southbridge, MA 01550. 508-764-5408; Fax 508-764-5425.
Will search UCC records. This agency will not do a tax lien search. Real estate records located in Worcester County. **Other Phone Numbers:** Assessor 508-764-5404; Treasurer 508-764-5401; Elections 508-764-5408; Vital Records 508-764-5408.

Southwick Town

Town Clerk, Town Hall, 11 Depot St., Southwick, MA 01077. 413-569-5504; Fax 413-569-5001.
Will search UCC records. UCC search includes tax liens if requested. Real estate records located in Hampden County.

Spencer Town

Town Clerk, 157 Main Street, Town Hall, Spencer, MA 01562-2197. 508-885-7500; Fax 508-885-7528.
Will search UCC records. Tax liens included in UCC search. Real estate records located in Worcester County. **Other Phone Numbers:** Assessor 508-885-7520; Treasurer 508-885-7510; Elections 508-885-7500; Vital Records 508-885-7500.

Springfield City

City Clerk, 36 Court Street, Springfield, MA 01103. 413-787-6094.

Will search UCC records. Real estate records located in Hampden County. **Other Phone Numbers:** Assessor 413-787-6160; Treasurer 413-787-6130.

Sterling Town

Town Clerk, Mary Ellen Butterick Municipal Bldg, 1 Park St., Sterling, MA 01564. 978-422-8111; Fax 978-422-0289.
Will search UCC records. UCC search includes tax liens if requested. Real estate records located in Worcester County. **Other Phone Numbers:** Assessor 978-422-8113; Treasurer 978-422-3028; Elections 978-422-8111; Vital Records 978-422-8111.

Stockbridge Town

Town Clerk, P.O. Box 417, Stockbridge, MA 01262-0417. 413-298-4568; Fax 413-298-4485.
Will search UCC records. UCC search includes tax liens if requested. Real estate records located in Berkshire County. **Other Phone Numbers:** Assessor 413-298-3509; Treasurer 413-298-4534; Elections 413-298-4568; Vital Records 413-298-4568.

Stoneham Town

Town Clerk, 35 Central Street, Stoneham, MA 02180. 781-279-2650; Fax 781-279-2653.
Will search UCC records. Real estate records located in Middlesex County.

Stoughton Town

Town Clerk, 10 Pearl Street, Town Hall, Stoughton, MA 02072. 781-341-1300; Fax 781-344-5048.
Will search UCC records. Tax liens included in UCC search if requested. Real estate records located in Norfolk County. **Other Phone Numbers:** Treasurer 781-341-1300.

Stow Town

Town Clerk, Town Building, 380 Great Road, Stow, MA 01775. 978-897-4514; Fax 978-897-4534.
Will search UCC records. UCC search includes tax liens if requested. Real estate records located in Middlesex County. **Other Phone Numbers:** Assessor 978-897-4597; Treasurer 978-897-2834.

Sturbridge Town

Town Clerk, 308 Main, Sturbridge, MA 01566. 508-347-2510 R/E Recording: 508-347-2503; Fax 508-347-5886.
Will search UCC records. UCC search includes tax liens if requested. Real estate records located in Worcester County. **Other Phone Numbers:** Assessor 508-347-2503; Treasurer 508-347-2509; Elections 508-347-2510; Vital Records 508-347-2510.

Sudbury Town

Town Clerk, 322 Concord Road, Sudbury, MA 01776-1800. 978-443-8891 x351; Fax 978-443-0264.
http://www.town.sudbury.ma.us/services
Will search UCC records. This agency will not do a tax lien search. Real estate records located in Middlesex County. **Other Phone Numbers:** Assessor 978-443-8891 x393.

Suffolk County

County Register of Deeds, P. O. Box 9660, Boston, MA 02114-9660. 617-788-8575; Fax 617-720-4163.
Will search UCC records, but only real estate related UCC filed here. This agency will not do a tax lien search. Will not search real estate records. **Online Access:** Real Estate, Liens, Deeds. Searchs on the Registry of Deeds site are free; real estate/liens on the county online system is not. Access to the County online system requires a written request submitted to Paul R Tierney, Register of Deeds, POB 9660, Boston

MA 02114. Online charges are $.50 per minute of use. A fax back service is available. Records on the County Registry of Deeds database are available free on the Internet at www.suffolkdeeds.com/search/default.asp. Search by name, corporation, and grantor/grantee. Recorded land records begin 1979; Registered land, 1983.

Sunderland Town

Town Clerk, 12 School St., Sunderland, MA 01375-9503. 413-665-1442 R/E Recording: 413-665-1445; Fax 413-665-1446.
Will search UCC records. UCC search includes tax liens if requested. Real estate records located in Franklin County. **Other Phone Numbers:** Assessor 413-665-1445; Treasurer 413-665-1444; Elections 413-665-1442; Vital Records 413-665-1442.

Sutton Town

Town Clerk, Town Hall, 4 Uxbridge Rd., Sutton, MA 01590. 508-865-8725; Fax 508-865-8721.
Will search UCC records. This agency will not do a tax lien search. Real estate records located in Worcester County.

Swampscott Town

Town Clerk, Town Hall, 22 Monument Ave., Swampscott, MA 01907. 781-596-8856; Fax 781-596-8870. http://www.swampscott.org/government.htm
Will search UCC records. Tax liens not included in UCC search. Real estate records located in Essex County. **Online Access:** Assessor, Real Estate. Online access to the Assessor's Property Valuation List fy-2000 if available free at www.swampscott.org/assessor%20file.xls. This is a lenghty MS-Excel file. Search the name column: Contol+F then enter name information, then "Find Next.". **Other Phone Numbers:** Assessor 781-596-8858; Elections 781-596-8855; Vital Records 781-596-8856.

Swansea Town

Town Clerk, 81 Main Street, Town Hall, Swansea, MA 02777. 508-678-9389.
Will search UCC records. UCC search includes tax liens if requested. Real estate records located in Bristol County. **Other Phone Numbers:** Assessor 508-678-6702; Treasurer 508-678-6489; Elections 508-678-9389; Vital Records 508-678-9389.

Taunton City

City Clerk, 15 Summer Street, City Hall, Taunton, MA 02780. 508-821-1024 R/E Recording: 508-822-0502; Fax 508-821-1098.
Will search UCC records. UCC search includes tax liens if requested. Real estate records located in Bristol County. **Other Phone Numbers:** Assessor 508-821-1011; Treasurer 508-821-1057; Elections 508-821-1044; Vital Records 508-821-1024.

Templeton Town

Town Clerk, Town Office Building, 9 Main St., Otter River, MA 01436. 978-939-8466; Fax 978-939-2125.
Will search UCC records. UCC search includes tax liens if requested. Real estate records located in Worcester County.

Tewksbury Town

Town Clerk, 1009 Main Street, Town Hall, Tewksbury, MA 01876-2796. 978-640-4355; Fax 978-640-4302.
Will search UCC records. UCC search includes tax liens. Real estate records located in Middlesex County. **Other Phone Numbers:** Assessor 978-640-4330; Treasurer 978-640-4340; Elections 978-640-4355; Vital Records 978-640-4355.

Tisbury Town

Town Clerk, P.O. Box 606, Tisbury, MA 02568-0606. 508-696-4215; Fax 508-693-5876. http://www.ci.tisbury.ma.us
Will search UCC records. This agency will not do a tax lien search. Real estate records located in Dukes County. **Other Phone Numbers:** Assessor 508-696-4206; Treasurer 508-696-4250; Elections 508-696-4215; Vital Records 508-696-4215.

Tolland Town

Town Clerk, 241 W. Granville Rd, Tolland, MA 01034. 413-259-4794; Fax 413-258-4048.
Will search UCC records. This agency will not do a tax lien search. Real estate records located in Hampden County. **Other Phone Numbers:** Assessor 413-259-4794; Treasurer 413-259-4794; Elections 413-259-4794; Vital Records 413-259-4794.

Topsfield Town

Town Clerk, 8 West Common Street, Town Hall, Topsfield, MA 01983. 978-887-1505; Fax 978-887-1502.
Will search UCC records. Tax liens not included in UCC search. Real estate records located in Essex County. **Other Phone Numbers:** Assessor 978-887-1514.

Townsend Town

Town Clerk, Memorial Hall, 272 Main Street, Townsend, MA 01469. 978-597-1704; Fax 978-597-8135.
Will search UCC records. UCC search includes tax liens if requested. Real estate records located in Middlesex County. **Other Phone Numbers:** Assessor 978-597-6612; Treasurer 978-597-1708; Elections 978-597-1704; Vital Records 978-597-1704.

Truro Town

Town Clerk, P.O. Box 2012, Truro, MA 02666-2012. 508-349-3860; Fax 508-349-7720.
Will search UCC records. Real estate records located in Barnstable County. **Other Phone Numbers:** Assessor 508-349-9248; Treasurer 508-349-3860.

Tyngsborough Town

Town Clerk, 25 Bryants Lane, Tyngsborough, MA 01879. 978-649-2300 x129; Fax 978-649-2301.
Will search UCC records. This agency will not do a tax lien search. Real estate records located in Middlesex County. **Other Phone Numbers:** Assessor 978-649-2300 x121; Treasurer 978-649-2300 x125; Elections 978-649-2300 x129.

Tyringham Town

Town Clerk, Main Road, Tyringham, MA 01264. 413-243-1749; Fax 413-243-4942.
Will search UCC records. This agency will not do a tax lien search. Real estate records located in Berkshire County.

Upton Town

Town Clerk, Box 969, Upton, MA 01568. 508-529-3565 R/E Recording: Worcester Cty Registry of Deeds; Fax 508-529-1010. www.upton.ma.us
Will search UCC records. This agency will not do a tax lien search. Real estate records located in Worcester County. **Other Phone Numbers:** Assessor 508-529-1002; Treasurer 508-529-3737; Elections 508-529-3565; Vital Records 508-529-3565.

Uxbridge Town

Town Clerk, 21 South Main Street, Uxbridge, MA 01569. 508-278-8608; Fax 508-278-8605.
Will search UCC records. UCC search includes tax liens if requested. Real estate records located in Worcester County.

Wakefield Town

Town Clerk, 1 Lafayette Street, Town Hall, Wakefield, MA 01880-2383. 781-246-6383 R/E Recording: 781-246-6380; Fax 781-246-4155.
Will search UCC records. Tax liens not included in UCC search. Real estate records located in Middlesex County. **Other Phone Numbers:** Assessor 781-246-5159; Treasurer 781-246-6340; Elections 781-246-6384; Vital Records 781-246-6383; Town Adm./Selectmen 781-246-6390.

Wales Town

Town Clerk, P.O. Box 834, Wales, MA 01081-0834. 413-245-7571; Fax 413-245-3261.
Will search UCC records. UCC search includes tax liens if requested. Real estate records located in Hampden County. **Other Phone Numbers:** Assessor 413-245-3260; Treasurer 413-245-3260; Vital Records 413-245-7571.

Walpole Town

Town Clerk, 135 School Street, Town Hall, Walpole, MA 02081-2898. 508-660-7297 UCC Recording: 508-660-7296; Fax 508-660-7303. http://www.walpole.ma.us
Will search UCC records. UCC search includes tax liens. Real estate records located in Norfolk County. **Other Phone Numbers:** Assessor 508-660-7314; Treasurer 508-660-7311; Elections 508-660-7296; Vital Records 508-660-7296.

Waltham City

City Clerk, 610 Main Street, Waltham, MA 02452. 781-314-3120; Fax 781-314-3130. http://www.city.waltham.ma.us
Will search UCC records. UCC search includes tax liens. Real estate records located in Middlesex County. **Online Access:** Assessor. Records on the City of Waltham Assessor database are available free online at www.city.waltham.ma.us/assessors/caveat.htm. **Other Phone Numbers:** Assessor 781-314-3200; Treasurer 781-314-3250; Elections 781-314-3120; Vital Records 781-314-3120.

Ware Town

Town Clerk, 126 Main Street, Ware, MA 01082. 413-967-4471 UCC Recording: 413-967-4471 x104; Fax 413-967-9600.
Will search UCC records. This agency will not do a tax lien search. Real estate records located in Hampshire County. **Other Phone Numbers:** Assessor 413-967-9610; Treasurer 413-967-4471; Vital Records 413-967-4471 x104.

Wareham Town

Town Clerk, 54 Marion Road, Wareham, MA 02571. 508-291-3140 R/E Recording: 508-830-9200; Fax 508-291-3116.
Will search UCC records. Tax liens included in UCC search if requested. Real estate records located in Plymouth County. **Other Phone Numbers:** Assessor 508-291-3160; Treasurer 508-291-3100 x3146; Elections 508-291-3140; Vital Records 508-291-3140.

Warren Town

Town Clerk, P.O. Box 603, Warren, MA 01083-0603. 413-436-5702; Fax 413-436-9754.
Will Search UCC records. Tax liens included in UCC search. Real estate records located in Middlesex County. **Other Phone Numbers:** Assessor 413-436-5703; Treasurer 413-436-5700.

Warwick Town

Town Clerk, Town Hall, 12 Athol Rd., Warwick, MA 01378. 978-544-8304; Fax 978-544-6499.
Will search UCC records. This agency will not do a tax lien search. Real estate records located in Franklin County. **Other Phone Numbers:** Assessor 978-544-8304; Treasurer 978-544-3845; Vital Records 978-544-8304.

Washington Town

Town Clerk, Town Hall Route 8, GA094, Washington, MA 01223. 413-623-8878; Fax 413-623-2116.
Will search UCC records. UCC search includes tax liens if requested. Real estate records located in Berkshire County. **Other Phone Numbers:** Assessor 413-623-6446.

Watertown Town

Town Clerk, 149 Main Street, Administration Building, Watertown, MA 02472. 617-972-6486; Fax 617-972-6595.
Will search UCC records. This agency will not do a tax lien search. Real estate records located in Middlesex County. **Online Access:** Assessor. Records on the Watertown Town Online Assessed Values site are available free online at www.townonline.com/watertown/realestate/assessments/index.html. **Other Phone Numbers:** Assessor 617-972-6410; Treasurer 617-972-6450; Elections 617-972-6488; Vital Records 617-972-6486.

Wayland Town

Town Clerk, 41 Cochituate Road, Wayland, MA 01778-2697. 508-358-3630; Fax 508-358-3627. http://www.wayland.ma.us/townadministration.html
Will search UCC records. This agency will not do a tax lien search. Real estate records located in Middlesex County. **Online Access:** Assessor. Property tax records on the Assessor's database are available free online at www.wayland.ma.us/assess-reval99.htm. Also, the read only tax assessor information is available through a private company's site at www.myproperty records.com/univers. **Other Phone Numbers:** Assessor 508-358-3658; Treasurer 508-358-3635; Appraiser/Auditor 508-358-3658; Elections 508-358-3631; Vital Records 508-358-3630.

Webster Town

Town Clerk, P.O. Box 193, Webster, MA 01570. 508-949-3850 R/E Recording: 508-949-3810; Fax 508-949-3888.
Will search UCC records. UCC search includes tax liens if requested. Real estate records located in Worcester County. **Other Phone Numbers:** Assessor 508-949-3810; Treasurer 508-949-3820; Elections 508-949-3850; Vital Records 508-949-3850.

Wellesley Town

Town Clerk, P.O.Box 812850, Wellesley, MA 02181-0026. 781-431-1019 x250; Fax 781-239-1043. http://www.ci.wellesley.ma.us/town/index.html
Will search UCC records. Real estate records located in Norfolk County. **Online Access:** Assessor. Property tax records on the Assessor's database are available free online at www.ci.wellesley.ma.us/asr/index.html. **Other Phone Numbers:** Assessor 781-431-1019.

Wellfleet Town

Town Clerk, 300 Main Street, Wellfleet, MA 02667. 508-349-0301; Fax 508-349-0317.
Will search UCC records. UCC search includes tax liens if requested. Real estate records located in Barnstable County. **Other Phone Numbers:** Assessor 508-349-0304.

Wendell Town

Town Clerk, 270 Wendell Depot Rd., Wendell Depot, MA 01380. 978-544-6682.
Will search UCC records. This agency will not do a tax lien search. Real estate records located in Franklin County.

Wenham Town

Town Clerk, Town Hall, 138 Main St., Wenham, MA 01984. 978-468-5520; Fax 978-468-6164.
Will search UCC records. Tax liens included with UCC search if requested. Real estate records located in Essex County. **Other Phone Numbers:** Assessor 978-468-5524; Treasurer 978-468-5525; Elections 978-468-5520; Vital Records 978-468-5520.

West Boylston Town

Town Clerk, 120 Prescott Street, West Boylston, MA 01583. Town Clerk, R/E and UCC Recording 508-835-6240; Fax 508-835-4102. http://www.west boylston.com
Will search UCC records. This agency will not do a tax lien search. Real estate records located in Worcester County. **Online Access:** Assessor. Online access to the town assessor Valuations Listings is available free at www.westboylston.com/ASSESS/Assessors1.htm. Files are searchable by street and include owner names. **Other Phone Numbers:** Assessor 508-835-6093; Treasurer 508-835-6092; Elections 508-835-6240; Vital Records 508-835-6240.

West Bridgewater Town

Town Clerk, 65 North Main Street, Town Hall, West Bridgewater, MA 02379-1734. 508-894-1200; Fax 508-894-1210.
Bridgewater, East Bridgewater and West Bridgewater are separate towns. UCC records are filed with the Town/City Clerk, real estate records are at the county level with the Register of Deeds. Will search UCC records. This agency will not do a tax lien search. Real estate records located in Plymouth County.

West Brookfield Town

Town Clerk, P.O. Box 372, West Brookfield, MA 01585. 508-867-1415; Fax 508-867-1401.
Will search UCC records. UCC search includes tax liens if requested. Real estate records located in Worcester County. **Other Phone Numbers:** Assessor 508-867-1402.

West Newbury Town

Town Clerk, Town Office Bldg., 381 Main St., West Newbury, MA 01985-1499. 978-363-1100 x15 UCC Recording: 978-363-1100 x10; Fax 978-363-1117. http://www.westnewbury.com
Will search UCC records. UCC search includes tax liens if requested. Real estate records located in Essex County. **Other Phone Numbers:** Assessor 978-363-1100 x17; Treasurer 978-363-1100 x13; Elections 978-363-1100 x15; Vital Records 978-363-1100 x10.

West Springfield Town

Town Clerk, 26 Central Street, Town Hall, West Springfield, MA 01089-2779. 413-263-3012 R/E Recording: 413-263-3055.
Will search UCC records. This agency will not do a tax lien search. Real estate records located in Hampden County. **Other Phone Numbers:** Assessor 413-263-3055; Treasurer 413-263-3004; Elections 413-263-3012; Vital Records 413-263-3012.

West Stockbridge Town

Town Clerk, P.O. Box 163, West Stockbridge, MA 01266. 413-232-0300; Fax 413-232-0318.

Will search UCC records. UCC search includes tax liens if requested. Real estate records located in Berkshire County. **Other Phone Numbers:** Assessor 413-232-0303; Treasurer 413-232-0316; Elections 413-232-0300; Vital Records 413-232-0300.

West Tisbury Town

Town Clerk, Box 278, West Tisbury, MA 02575-0278. 508-696-0148; Fax 508-696-0103.
Will search UCC records. UCC search includes tax liens. Real estate records located in Dukes County. **Other Phone Numbers:** Assessor 508-693-9733; Treasurer 508-696-0108; Elections 508-696-0148; Vital Records 508-696-0148.

Westborough Town

Town Clerk, 34 West Main Street, Town Hall, Westborough, MA 01581-1998. 508-366-3020; Fax 508-366-3099.
Will search UCC records. UCC search includes tax liens if requested. Real estate records located in Worcester County. **Other Phone Numbers:** Assessor 508-366-3010; Treasurer 508-366-3025; Elections 508-366-3020; Vital Records 508-366-3020.

Westfield City

City Clerk, 59 Court Street, Westfield, MA 01085-3574. 413-572-6235; Fax 413-564-3114. www.ci.westfield.ma.us
Will search UCC records. This agency will not do a tax lien search. Real estate records located in Hampden County. **Online Access:** Assessor. Property tax records on the Assessor's database are available free online at www.ci.westfield.ma.us/realest/rea00.htm. **Other Phone Numbers:** Assessor 413-572-6222; Treasurer 413-572-6230; Appraiser/Auditor 413-572-6222; Elections 413-572-6266; Vital Records 413-572-6236.

Westford Town

Town Clerk, 55 Main Street, Town Hall, Westford, MA 01886. 978-692-5515; Fax 978-692-9607.
Will search UCC records. UCC search includes tax liens if requested. Real estate records located in Middlesex County. **Other Phone Numbers:** Assessor 978-692-5504; Treasurer 978-692-5506; Elections 978-692-5515; Vital Records 978-652-5515.

Westhampton Town

Town Clerk, Town Hall, Westhampton, MA 01027. 413-527-0463; Fax 413-527-8655.
Will search UCC records. This agency will not do a tax lien search. Real estate records located in Hampshire County.

Westminster Town

Town Clerk, P.O. Box 456, Westminster, MA 01473. 978-874-7406; Fax 978-874-7411. www.westminster-ma.org
Will search UCC records. Tax liens included in UCC search. Real estate records located in Worcester County. **Other Phone Numbers:** Assessor 978-874-7401; Treasurer 978-874-7403; Elections 978-874-7406; Vital Records 978-874-7406.

Weston Town

Town Clerk, PO Box 378, Weston, MA 02493. 781-893-7320; Fax 781-891-3697. http://www.weston.org
Will search UCC records. This agency will not do a tax lien search. Real estate records located in Registry of Deeds, Southern Middlesex District located at 208 Cambridge St, Cambridge, MA 02141-0001. **Other Phone Numbers:** Assessor 781-893-7320 x313; Treasurer 781-893-7320 x316; Elections 781-893-7320 x303; Vital Records 781-893-7320 x303.

Westport Town

Town Clerk, Town Hall, 816 Main Rd., Westport, MA 02790. 508-636-1000 R/E Recording: 508-993-2605 (Registry of Deeds in New Bedford); Fax 508-636-1147.
Will search UCC records. Tax liens not included in UCC search. Real estate records located in Bristol County. **Other Phone Numbers:** Assessor 508-636-1012; Treasurer 508-636-1007; Elections 508-636-1001; Vital Records 508-636-1000; Selectmen 508-636-1003.

Westwood Town

Town Clerk, 580 High Street, Westwood, MA 02090. 781-326-3964; Fax 781-329-8030.
Will search UCC records. Tax liens not included in UCC search. Real estate records located in Norfolk County. **Other Phone Numbers:** Assessor 781-326-6450.

Weymouth Town

Town Clerk, 75 Middle Street, Town Hall, East Weymouth, MA 02189. 781-335-2000; Fax 781-335-3283.
Will search UCC records. Real estate records located in Norfolk County. **Other Phone Numbers:** Assessor 781-335-2000; Treasurer 781-335-2000.

Whately Town

Town Clerk, 218 Chestnut Plain Rd., Whately, MA 01093-0002. 413-665-0054; Fax 413-665-9560.
Will search UCC records. UCC search includes tax liens if requested. Real estate records located in Franklin County. **Other Phone Numbers:** Assessor 413-665-3470; Treasurer 413-665-2595; Elections 413-665-0054; Vital Records 413-665-0054.

Whitman Town

Town Clerk, P.O. Box 426, Whitman, MA 02382. 781-447-7607; Fax 781-447-7318.
Will search UCC records. UCC search includes tax liens if requested. Real estate records located in Plymouth County. **Other Phone Numbers:** Assessor 781-447-7617; Treasurer 781-447-7609.

Wilbraham Town

Town Clerk, 240 Springfield Street, Wilbraham, MA 01095. 413-596-2809; Fax 413-596-2830.
Will search UCC records. UCC search includes tax liens if requested. Real estate records located in Hampden County. **Other Phone Numbers:** Assessor 413-596-2818.

Williamsburg Town

Town Clerk, P.O. Box 447, Haydenville, MA 01039-0447. 413-268-8402; Fax 413-268-8409.
Will search UCC records. Real estate records located in Hampshire County. **Other Phone Numbers:** Assessor 413-268-8403; Treasurer 413-268-8419.

Williamstown Town

Town Clerk, 31 North Street, Williamstown, MA 01267. 413-458-9341 R/E Recording: 413-743-0035; Fax 413-458-4839. http://www.williamstown.net
Will search UCC records. UCC search includes tax liens. Real estate records located in Berkshire County. **Other Phone Numbers:** Assessor 413-458-9342; Treasurer 413-458-9342; Elections 413-458-9341; Vital Records 413-458-9341.

Wilmington Town

Town Clerk, 121 Glen Road, Town Hall, Wilmington, MA 01887. 978-658-2030 R/E Recording: 978-658-3531; Fax 978-658-3334. http://www.town.wilmington.ma.us

Will search UCC records. Tax liens included in UCC search if requested. Real estate records located in Middlesex County. **Other Phone Numbers:** Assessor 978-658-3675; Treasurer 978-658-3531; Appraiser/Auditor 978-658-3675; Elections 978-658-2030.

Winchendon Town

Town Clerk, 109 Front Street, Winchendon, MA 01475. 978-297-2766; Fax 978-297-1616.
Will search UCC records. Tax liens not included in UCC search. Real estate records located in Worcester County. **Other Phone Numbers:** Assessor 978-297-0155; Treasurer 978-297-0152.

Winchester Town

Town Clerk, 71 Mount Vernon Street, Town Hall, Winchester, MA 01890. 781-721-7130; Fax 781-721-1153.
Will search UCC records. Real estate records located in Middlesex County. **Other Phone Numbers:** Assessor 781-721-7111; Treasurer 781-721-7123.

Windsor Town

Town Clerk, 3 Hinsdale Rd., Windsor, MA 01270. 413-684-3977; Fax 413-684-1585.
Will search UCC records. This agency will not do a tax lien search. Real estate records located in Berkshire County. **Other Phone Numbers:** Assessor 413-684-3811; Treasurer 413-684-3811; Appraiser/Auditor 413-684-3811; Elections 413-684-3977; Vital Records 413-684-3977.

Winthrop Town

Town Clerk, Town Hall, Winthrop, MA 02152-3156. 617-846-1742; Fax 617-846-5458.
Will search UCC records. Tax liens included in UCC search if requested. Real estate records located in Suffolk County. **Other Phone Numbers:** Assessor 617-846-2716; Treasurer 617-846-3226.

Woburn City

City Clerk, 10 Common Street, Woburn, MA 01801-4197. 781-932-4453; Fax 781-932-4455.

Will search UCC records. UCC search includes tax liens. Real estate records located in Middlesex County.

Worcester City

City Clerk, 455 Main Street, City Hall - Room 206, Worcester, MA 01608. 508-799-1121; Fax 508-799-1194.
Will search UCC records. Real estate records located in Worcester County. **Online Access:** Real Estate, Liens. Access to the "Landtrack System" for Worcester District records requires a $50 annual fee plus $.25 per minute of use. Index records date back to 1966. Images are viewable from 1974 onward. Lending agency info is available. Fax back service is available for $.50 per page. For information, contact Joe Ursoleo at 508-798-7713 X233. **Other Phone Numbers:** Assessor 508-799-1112; Treasurer 508-799-1077.

Worcester County (Northern District)

County Register of Deeds, P.O. Box 983, Fitchburg, MA 01420. 978-342-2637; Fax 978-345-2865. http://www.state.ma.us/nwrod
Will not search UCC records. This agency will not do a tax lien search. Will not search real estate records. **Online Access:** Real Estate, Liens. Access to the "Northfield" online service requires $50 annually, plus $.25 per minute of use. Records date back to 1983. Viewable images are available back to 1995. Lending agency information is available. A fax back service is available. For information, contact Ruth Piermarini at 978-342-2637. **Other Phone Numbers:** Assessor 508-799-1098.

Worcester County (Worcester District)

County Register of Deeds, 2 Main Street, Courthouse, Worcester, MA 01608. 508-798-7717; Fax 508-753-1338.
Will search UCC records, but only real estate related UCC filed here. This agency will not do a tax lien search. Will not search real estate records. **Online Access:** Real Estate, Property Tax. Records on the Town of Holden assessor's database are available free

online at http://140.239.211.227/HOLDENMA. Registration is required; sign-up is free. **Other Phone Numbers:** Assessor 508-799-1000; Treasurer 508-798-2441.

Worthington Town

Town Clerk, Town Hall, Worthington, MA 01098-0247. 413-238-5578; Fax 413-238-5579.
Will search UCC records. This agency will not do a tax lien search. Real estate records located in Hampshire County. **Other Phone Numbers:** Assessor 413-238-5578; Treasurer 413-238-5577.

Wrentham Town

Town Clerk, 79 South Street, Wrentham, MA 02093. 508-384-5415; Fax 508-384-5434.
Will search UCC records. This agency will not do a tax lien search. Real estate records located in Norfolk County. **Other Phone Numbers:** Assessor 508-384-5408; Treasurer 508-384-5413; Elections 508-384-5415; Vital Records 508-384-5415.

Yarmouth Town

Town Clerk, 1146 Route 28, Town Hall, South Yarmouth, MA 02664. 508-398-2231 R/E Recording: 508-362-7733 x106 UCC Recording: 508-398-2231 x216; Fax 508-398-2365. http://www.Yarmouthcapecod.org
Will search UCC records. Tax liens included in UCC search if requested. Real estate records located in Barnstable County. **Online Access:** Assessor. Records on the Assessor's database are available free online at http://140.239.211.227/yarmouthma. User ID number is required is required to access the full database; registration is free. Non-registered users can access a limited set of data. **Other Phone Numbers:** Assessor 508-398-2231 x221; Treasurer 508-398-2231 x219; Elections 508-398-2231 x216; Vital Records 508-398-2231 x216.

Massachusetts County Locator

You will usually be able to find the city name in the City/County Cross Reference below. In that case, it is a simple matter to determine the county from the cross reference. However, only the official US Postal Service city names are included in this index. There are an additional 40,000 place names that people use in their addresses. Therefore, we have also included a ZIP/City Cross Reference immediately following the City/County Cross Reference.

If you know the ZIP Code but the city name does not appear in the City/County Cross Reference index, look up the ZIP Code in the ZIP/City Cross Reference, find the city name, then look up the city name in the City/County Cross Reference. For example, you want to know the county for an address of Menands, NY 12204. There is no "Menands" in the City/County Cross Reference. The ZIP/City Cross Reference shows that ZIP Codes 12201-12288 are for the city of Albany. Looking back in the City/County Cross Reference, Albany is in Albany County.

City/County Cross Reference

ABINGTON Plymouth
ACCORD Plymouth
ACTON Middlesex
ACUSHNET Bristol
ADAMS Berkshire
AGAWAM Hampden
ALLSTON Suffolk
AMESBURY Essex
AMHERST Hampshire
ANDOVER Essex
ARLINGTON Middlesex
ARLINGTON HEIGHTS Middlesex
ASHBURNHAM Worcester
ASHBY Middlesex
ASHFIELD Franklin
ASHLAND Middlesex
ASHLEY FALLS Berkshire
ASSONET Bristol
ATHOL Worcester
ATTLEBORO Bristol
ATTLEBORO FALLS Bristol
AUBURN Worcester
AUBURNDALE Middlesex
AVON Norfolk
AYER (01432) Middlesex(73),
    Worcester(27)
BABSON PARK Norfolk
BALDWINVILLE Worcester
BAR CODE MCCORMACK Suffolk
BARNSTABLE Barnstable
BARRE Worcester
BECKET Berkshire
BEDFORD Middlesex
BELCHERTOWN Hampshire
BELLINGHAM Norfolk
BELMONT Middlesex
BERKLEY Bristol
BERKSHIRE Berkshire
BERLIN Worcester
BERNARDSTON Franklin
BEVERLY Essex
BILLERICA Middlesex
BLACKSTONE Worcester
BLANDFORD Hampden
BOLTON Worcester
BONDSVILLE Hampden
BOSTON Middlesex
BOSTON Suffolk
BOXBOROUGH Middlesex
BOXFORD Essex
BOYLSTON Worcester
BRAINTREE Norfolk
BRAINTREE Suffolk
BRANT ROCK Plymouth
BREWSTER Barnstable
BRIDGEWATER Plymouth
BRIGHTON Suffolk
BRIMFIELD Hampden
BROCKTON Plymouth
BROOKFIELD Worcester
BROOKLINE Norfolk
BROOKLINE VILLAGE Norfolk
BRYANTVILLE Plymouth

BUCKLAND Franklin
BURLINGTON Middlesex
BUZZARDS BAY (02532) Barnstable(75),
    Plymouth(25)
BUZZARDS BAY Barnstable
BYFIELD Essex
CAMBRIDGE Middlesex
CANTON Norfolk
CARLISLE Middlesex
CARVER Plymouth
CATAUMET (02534) Barnstable(92),
    Dukes(8)
CENTERVILLE Barnstable
CHARLEMONT Franklin
CHARLESTOWN Suffolk
CHARLTON Worcester
CHARLTON CITY Worcester
CHARLTON DEPOT Worcester
CHARTLEY Bristol
CHATHAM Barnstable
CHELMSFORD Middlesex
CHELSEA Suffolk
CHERRY VALLEY Worcester
CHESHIRE Berkshire
CHESTER (01011) Berkshire(70),
    Hampden(30)
CHESTERFIELD Hampshire
CHESTNUT HILL Middlesex
CHICOPEE Hampden
CHILMARK Dukes
CLINTON Worcester
COHASSET Norfolk
COLRAIN Franklin
CONCORD Middlesex
CONWAY Franklin
COTUIT Barnstable
CUMMAQUID Barnstable
CUMMINGTON Hampshire
CUTTYHUNK Dukes
DALTON Berkshire
DANVERS Essex
DARTMOUTH Bristol
DEDHAM Norfolk
DEERFIELD Franklin
DENNIS Barnstable
DENNIS PORT Barnstable
DIGHTON Bristol
DOUGLAS Worcester
DOVER Norfolk
DRACUT Middlesex
DRURY (01343) Berkshire(96), Franklin(4)
DUDLEY Worcester
DUNSTABLE Middlesex
DUXBURY Plymouth
EAST BRIDGEWATER Plymouth
EAST BROOKFIELD Worcester
EAST DENNIS Barnstable
EAST FALMOUTH Barnstable
EAST FREETOWN Bristol
EAST LONGMEADOW Hampden
EAST MANSFIELD Bristol
EAST ORLEANS Barnstable
EAST OTIS Berkshire

EAST PRINCETON Worcester
EAST SANDWICH Barnstable
EAST TAUNTON Bristol
EAST TEMPLETON Worcester
EAST WALPOLE Norfolk
EAST WAREHAM Plymouth
EASTHAM Barnstable
EASTHAMPTON Hampshire
EASTON Bristol
EDGARTOWN Dukes
ELMWOOD Plymouth
ERVING Franklin
ESSEX Essex
EVERETT Middlesex
FAIRHAVEN Bristol
FALL RIVER Bristol
FALMOUTH Barnstable
FAYVILLE Worcester
FEEDING HILLS Hampden
FISKDALE Worcester
FITCHBURG Worcester
FLORENCE Hampshire
FORESTDALE Barnstable
FORT DEVENS (01433) Worcester(53),
    Middlesex(47)
FOXBORO Norfolk
FRAMINGHAM Middlesex
FRANKLIN Norfolk
GARDNER Worcester
GEORGETOWN Essex
GILBERTVILLE Worcester
GLENDALE Berkshire
GLOUCESTER Essex
GOSHEN Hampshire
GRAFTON Worcester
GRANBY Hampshire
GRANVILLE Hampden
GREAT BARRINGTON Berkshire
GREEN HARBOR Plymouth
GREENBUSH Plymouth
GREENFIELD Franklin
GROTON Middlesex
GROVELAND Essex
HADLEY Hampshire
HALIFAX Plymouth
HAMILTON Essex
HAMPDEN Hampden
HANOVER (02339) Plymouth(99),
    Norfolk(1)
HANSCOM AFB Middlesex
HANSON Plymouth
HARDWICK Worcester
HARVARD Worcester
HARWICH Barnstable
HARWICH PORT Barnstable
HATFIELD Hampshire
HATHORNE Essex
HAVERHILL Essex
HAYDENVILLE Hampshire
HEATH Franklin
HINGHAM Plymouth
HINSDALE Berkshire
HOLBROOK Norfolk

HOLDEN Worcester
HOLLAND Hampden
HOLLISTON Middlesex
HOLYOKE Hampden
HOPEDALE Worcester
HOPKINTON Middlesex
HOUSATONIC Berkshire
HUBBARDSTON Worcester
HUDSON Middlesex
HULL Plymouth
HUMAROCK Plymouth
HUNTINGTON (01050) Hampshire(99),
    Hampden(1)
HYANNIS Barnstable
HYANNIS PORT Barnstable
HYDE PARK Suffolk
INDIAN ORCHARD Hampden
IPSWICH Essex
JAMAICA PLAIN Suffolk
JEFFERSON Worcester
KINGSTON Plymouth
LAKE PLEASANT Franklin
LAKEVILLE Plymouth
LANCASTER Worcester
LANESBORO Berkshire
LAWRENCE Essex
LEE Berkshire
LEEDS Hampshire
LEICESTER Worcester
LENOX Berkshire
LENOX DALE Berkshire
LEOMINSTER Worcester
LEVERETT Franklin
LEXINGTON Middlesex
LINCOLN Middlesex
LINWOOD Worcester
LITTLETON Middlesex
LONGMEADOW Hampden
LOWELL Middlesex
LUDLOW Hampden
LUNENBURG Worcester
LYNN Essex
LYNNFIELD Essex
MALDEN Middlesex
MANCHAUG Worcester
MANCHESTER Essex
MANOMET Plymouth
MANSFIELD Bristol
MARBLEHEAD Essex
MARION Plymouth
MARLBOROUGH Middlesex
MARSHFIELD Plymouth
MARSHFIELD HILLS Plymouth
MARSTONS MILLS Barnstable
MASHPEE Barnstable
MATTAPAN Suffolk
MATTAPOISETT Plymouth
MAYNARD Middlesex
MEDFIELD Norfolk
MEDFORD Middlesex
MEDWAY Norfolk
MELROSE Middlesex
MENDON Worcester

MENEMSHA Dukes
MERRIMAC Essex
METHUEN Essex
MIDDLEBORO Plymouth
MIDDLEFIELD Hampshire
MIDDLETON Essex
MILFORD Worcester
MILL RIVER Berkshire
MILLBURY Worcester
MILLIS Norfolk
MILLVILLE Worcester
MILTON Norfolk
MILTON VILLAGE Norfolk
MINOT Plymouth
MONPONSETT Plymouth
MONROE BRIDGE Franklin
MONSON Hampden
MONTAGUE Franklin
MONTEREY Berkshire
MONUMENT BEACH (02553) Barnstable(92), Dukes(8)
NAHANT Essex
NANTUCKET Nantucket
NATICK Middlesex
NEEDHAM Norfolk
NEW BEDFORD Bristol
NEW BRAINTREE Worcester
NEW SALEM Franklin
NEWBURY Essex
NEWBURYPORT Essex
NEWTON Middlesex
NORFOLK Norfolk
NORTH ADAMS Berkshire
NORTH AMHERST Hampshire
NORTH ANDOVER Essex
NORTH ATTLEBORO Bristol
NORTH BILLERICA Middlesex
NORTH BROOKFIELD Worcester
NORTH CARVER Plymouth
NORTH CHATHAM Barnstable
NORTH CHELMSFORD Middlesex
NORTH DARTMOUTH Bristol
NORTH DIGHTON Bristol
NORTH EASTHAM Barnstable
NORTH EASTON Bristol
NORTH EGREMONT Berkshire
NORTH FALMOUTH Barnstable
NORTH GRAFTON Worcester
NORTH HATFIELD Hampshire
NORTH MARSHFIELD Plymouth
NORTH OXFORD Worcester
NORTH PEMBROKE Plymouth
NORTH READING Middlesex
NORTH SCITUATE Plymouth
NORTH TRURO Barnstable
NORTH UXBRIDGE Worcester
NORTHAMPTON Hampshire
NORTHBOROUGH Worcester
NORTHBRIDGE Worcester
NORTHFIELD Franklin
NORTON Bristol
NORWELL Plymouth
NORWOOD Norfolk
NUTTING LAKE Middlesex
OAK BLUFFS Dukes
OAKDALE Worcester

OAKHAM Worcester
OCEAN BLUFF Plymouth
ONSET Plymouth
ORANGE Franklin
ORLEANS Barnstable
OSTERVILLE Barnstable
OTIS Berkshire
OXFORD Worcester
PALMER Hampden
PAXTON Worcester
PEABODY Essex
PEMBROKE Plymouth
PEPPERELL Middlesex
PETERSHAM (01366) Franklin(50), Worcester(50)
PINEHURST Middlesex
PITTSFIELD Berkshire
PLAINFIELD Hampshire
PLAINVILLE (02762) Norfolk(99), Bristol(1)
PLYMOUTH Plymouth
PLYMPTON Plymouth
POCASSET Barnstable
PRIDES CROSSING Essex
PRINCETON Worcester
PROVINCETOWN Barnstable
QUINCY Norfolk
RANDOLPH Norfolk
RAYNHAM Bristol
RAYNHAM CENTER Bristol
READING Middlesex
READVILLE Suffolk
REHOBOTH Bristol
REVERE Suffolk
RICHMOND Berkshire
ROCHDALE Worcester
ROCHESTER (02770) Plymouth(98), Bristol(2)
ROCKLAND Plymouth
ROCKPORT Essex
ROSLINDALE Suffolk
ROWE Franklin
ROWLEY Essex
ROYALSTON (01368) Worcester(99), Franklin(1)
RUSSELL Hampden
RUTLAND Worcester
SAGAMORE Barnstable
SAGAMORE BEACH Barnstable
SALEM Essex
SALISBURY Essex
SANDISFIELD Berkshire
SANDWICH Barnstable
SAUGUS Essex
SAVOY Berkshire
SCITUATE Plymouth
SEARS ROEBUCK Suffolk
SEEKONK Bristol
SHARON Norfolk
SHATTUCKVILLE Franklin
SHEFFIELD Berkshire
SHELBURNE FALLS Franklin
SHELDONVILLE Norfolk
SHERBORN Middlesex
SHIRLEY Middlesex
SHREWSBURY Worcester
SHUTESBURY Franklin

SIASCONSET Nantucket
SILVER BEACH Barnstable
SOMERSET Bristol
SOMERVILLE Middlesex
SOUTH BARRE Worcester
SOUTH CARVER Plymouth
SOUTH CHATHAM Barnstable
SOUTH DARTMOUTH Bristol
SOUTH DEERFIELD Franklin
SOUTH DENNIS Barnstable
SOUTH EASTON Bristol
SOUTH EGREMONT Berkshire
SOUTH GRAFTON Worcester
SOUTH HADLEY Hampshire
SOUTH HAMILTON Essex
SOUTH HARWICH Barnstable
SOUTH LANCASTER Worcester
SOUTH LEE Berkshire
SOUTH ORLEANS Barnstable
SOUTH WALPOLE Norfolk
SOUTH WELLFLEET Barnstable
SOUTH YARMOUTH Barnstable
SOUTHAMPTON Hampshire
SOUTHBOROUGH Worcester
SOUTHBRIDGE Worcester
SOUTHFIELD Berkshire
SOUTHWICK Hampden
SPENCER Worcester
SPRINGFIELD Hampden
STERLING Worcester
STILL RIVER Worcester
STOCKBRIDGE Berkshire
STONEHAM Middlesex
STOUGHTON Norfolk
STOW Middlesex
STURBRIDGE Worcester
SUDBURY Middlesex
SUNDERLAND Franklin
SUTTON Worcester
SWAMPSCOTT Essex
SWANSEA Bristol
TAUNTON Bristol
TEMPLETON Worcester
TEWKSBURY Middlesex
THORNDIKE Hampden
THREE RIVERS Hampden
TOPSFIELD Essex
TOWNSEND Middlesex
TRURO Barnstable
TURNERS FALLS Franklin
TYNGSBORO Middlesex
TYRINGHAM Berkshire
UPTON Worcester
UXBRIDGE Worcester
VILLAGE OF NAGOG WOODS Middlesex
VINEYARD HAVEN Dukes
WABAN Middlesex
WAKEFIELD Middlesex
WALES Hampden
WALPOLE Norfolk
WALTHAM Middlesex
WARE Hampshire
WAREHAM Plymouth
WARREN (01083) Worcester(96), Middlesex(4)
WARWICK Franklin

WATERTOWN Middlesex
WAVERLEY Middlesex
WAYLAND Middlesex
WEBSTER Worcester
WELLESLEY Norfolk
WELLFLEET Barnstable
WENDELL Franklin
WENDELL DEPOT Franklin
WENHAM Essex
WEST BARNSTABLE Barnstable
WEST BOXFORD Essex
WEST BOYLSTON Worcester
WEST BRIDGEWATER Plymouth
WEST BROOKFIELD Worcester
WEST CHATHAM Barnstable
WEST CHESTERFIELD Hampshire
WEST DENNIS Barnstable
WEST FALMOUTH Barnstable
WEST GROTON Middlesex
WEST HARWICH Barnstable
WEST HATFIELD (01088) Worcester(98), Hampshire(2)
WEST HYANNISPORT Barnstable
WEST MEDFORD Middlesex
WEST MILLBURY Worcester
WEST NEWBURY Essex
WEST ROXBURY Suffolk
WEST SPRINGFIELD Hampden
WEST STOCKBRIDGE Berkshire
WEST TISBURY Dukes
WEST TOWNSEND Middlesex
WEST WAREHAM Plymouth
WEST WARREN Worcester
WEST YARMOUTH Barnstable
WESTBOROUGH Worcester
WESTFIELD Hampden
WESTFORD Middlesex
WESTMINSTER Worcester
WESTON Middlesex
WESTPORT Bristol
WESTPORT POINT Bristol
WESTWOOD Norfolk
WEYMOUTH Norfolk
WHATELY Franklin
WHEELWRIGHT Worcester
WHITE HORSE BEACH Plymouth
WHITINSVILLE Worcester
WHITMAN Plymouth
WILBRAHAM Hampden
WILLIAMSBURG Hampshire
WILLIAMSTOWN Berkshire
WILMINGTON Middlesex
WINCHENDON Worcester
WINCHENDON SPRINGS Worcester
WINCHESTER Middlesex
WINDSOR (01270) Franklin(82), Berkshire(18)
WINTHROP Suffolk
WOBURN Middlesex
WOODS HOLE Barnstable
WOODVILLE Middlesex
WORCESTER Worcester
WORONOCO Hampden
WORTHINGTON Hampshire
WRENTHAM Norfolk
YARMOUTH PORT Barnstable

ZIP/City Cross Reference

ZIP Range	City	ZIP Range	City	ZIP Range	City	ZIP Range	City
01001-01001	AGAWAM	01028-01028	EAST LONGMEADOW	01040-01041	HOLYOKE	01069-01069	PALMER
01002-01004	AMHERST	01029-01029	EAST OTIS	01050-01050	HUNTINGTON	01070-01070	PLAINFIELD
01005-01005	BARRE	01030-01030	FEEDING HILLS	01053-01053	LEEDS	01071-01071	RUSSELL
01007-01007	BELCHERTOWN	01031-01031	GILBERTVILLE	01054-01054	LEVERETT	01072-01072	SHUTESBURY
01008-01008	BLANDFORD	01032-01032	GOSHEN	01056-01056	LUDLOW	01073-01073	SOUTHAMPTON
01009-01009	BONDSVILLE	01033-01033	GRANBY	01057-01057	MONSON	01074-01074	SOUTH BARRE
01010-01010	BRIMFIELD	01034-01034	GRANVILLE	01059-01059	NORTH AMHERST	01075-01075	SOUTH HADLEY
01011-01011	CHESTER	01035-01035	HADLEY	01060-01061	NORTHAMPTON	01077-01077	SOUTHWICK
01012-01012	CHESTERFIELD	01036-01036	HAMPDEN	01062-01062	FLORENCE	01079-01079	THORNDIKE
01013-01022	CHICOPEE	01037-01037	HARDWICK	01063-01063	NORTHAMPTON	01080-01080	THREE RIVERS
01026-01026	CUMMINGTON	01038-01038	HATFIELD	01066-01066	NORTH HATFIELD	01081-01081	WALES
01027-01027	EASTHAMPTON	01039-01039	HAYDENVILLE	01068-01068	OAKHAM	01082-01082	WARE

Zip	Town	Zip	Town	Zip	Town	Zip	Town
01083-01083	WARREN	01380-01380	WENDELL DEPOT	01718-01718	VILLAGE OF NAGOG WOODS	01951-01951	NEWBURY
01084-01084	WEST CHESTERFIELD	01420-01420	FITCHBURG			01952-01952	SALISBURY
01085-01086	WESTFIELD	01430-01430	ASHBURNHAM	01719-01719	BOXBOROUGH	01960-01961	PEABODY
01088-01088	WEST HATFIELD	01431-01431	ASHBY	01720-01720	ACTON	01965-01965	PRIDES CROSSING
01089-01090	WEST SPRINGFIELD	01432-01432	AYER	01721-01721	ASHLAND	01966-01966	ROCKPORT
01092-01092	WEST WARREN	01436-01436	BALDWINVILLE	01730-01730	BEDFORD	01969-01969	ROWLEY
01093-01093	WHATELY	01438-01438	EAST TEMPLETON	01731-01731	HANSCOM AFB	01970-01971	SALEM
01094-01094	WHEELWRIGHT	01440-01441	GARDNER	01740-01740	BOLTON	01982-01982	SOUTH HAMILTON
01095-01095	WILBRAHAM	01450-01450	GROTON	01741-01741	CARLISLE	01983-01983	TOPSFIELD
01096-01096	WILLIAMSBURG	01451-01451	HARVARD	01742-01742	CONCORD	01984-01984	WENHAM
01097-01097	WORONOCO	01452-01452	HUBBARDSTON	01745-01745	FAYVILLE	01985-01985	WEST NEWBURY
01098-01098	WORTHINGTON	01453-01453	LEOMINSTER	01746-01746	HOLLISTON	02018-02018	ACCORD
01101-01105	SPRINGFIELD	01460-01460	LITTLETON	01747-01747	HOPEDALE	02019-02019	BELLINGHAM
01106-01106	LONGMEADOW	01462-01462	LUNENBURG	01748-01748	HOPKINTON	02020-02020	BRANT ROCK
01107-01115	SPRINGFIELD	01463-01463	PEPPERELL	01749-01749	HUDSON	02021-02021	CANTON
01116-01116	LONGMEADOW	01464-01464	SHIRLEY	01752-01752	MARLBOROUGH	02025-02025	COHASSET
01118-01144	SPRINGFIELD	01467-01467	STILL RIVER	01754-01754	MAYNARD	02026-02027	DEDHAM
01151-01151	INDIAN ORCHARD	01468-01468	TEMPLETON	01756-01756	MENDON	02030-02030	DOVER
01152-01199	SPRINGFIELD	01469-01469	TOWNSEND	01757-01757	MILFORD	02031-02031	EAST MANSFIELD
01201-01203	PITTSFIELD	01470-01471	GROTON	01760-01760	NATICK	02032-02032	EAST WALPOLE
01220-01220	ADAMS	01472-01472	WEST GROTON	01770-01770	SHERBORN	02035-02035	FOXBORO
01222-01222	ASHLEY FALLS	01473-01473	WESTMINSTER	01772-01772	SOUTHBOROUGH	02038-02038	FRANKLIN
01223-01223	BECKET	01474-01474	WEST TOWNSEND	01773-01773	LINCOLN	02040-02040	GREENBUSH
01224-01224	BERKSHIRE	01475-01475	WINCHENDON	01775-01775	STOW	02041-02041	GREEN HARBOR
01225-01225	CHESHIRE	01477-01477	WINCHENDON SPRINGS	01776-01776	SUDBURY	02043-02044	HINGHAM
01226-01227	DALTON	01501-01501	AUBURN	01778-01778	WAYLAND	02045-02045	HULL
01229-01229	GLENDALE	01503-01503	BERLIN	01784-01784	WOODVILLE	02047-02047	HUMAROCK
01230-01230	GREAT BARRINGTON	01504-01504	BLACKSTONE	01801-01801	WOBURN	02048-02048	MANSFIELD
01235-01235	HINSDALE	01505-01505	BOYLSTON	01803-01805	BURLINGTON	02050-02050	MARSHFIELD
01236-01236	HOUSATONIC	01506-01506	BROOKFIELD	01806-01808	WOBURN	02051-02051	MARSHFIELD HILLS
01237-01237	LANESBORO	01507-01507	CHARLTON	01810-01812	ANDOVER	02052-02052	MEDFIELD
01238-01238	LEE	01508-01508	CHARLTON CITY	01813-01815	WOBURN	02053-02053	MEDWAY
01240-01240	LENOX	01509-01509	CHARLTON DEPOT	01821-01822	BILLERICA	02054-02054	MILLIS
01242-01242	LENOX DALE	01510-01510	CLINTON	01824-01824	CHELMSFORD	02055-02055	MINOT
01243-01243	MIDDLEFIELD	01515-01515	EAST BROOKFIELD	01826-01826	DRACUT	02056-02056	NORFOLK
01244-01244	MILL RIVER	01516-01516	DOUGLAS	01827-01827	DUNSTABLE	02059-02059	NORTH MARSHFIELD
01245-01245	MONTEREY	01517-01517	EAST PRINCETON	01830-01832	HAVERHILL	02060-02060	NORTH SCITUATE
01247-01247	NORTH ADAMS	01518-01518	FISKDALE	01833-01833	GEORGETOWN	02061-02061	NORWELL
01252-01252	NORTH EGREMONT	01519-01519	GRAFTON	01834-01834	GROVELAND	02062-02062	NORWOOD
01253-01253	OTIS	01520-01520	HOLDEN	01835-01835	HAVERHILL	02065-02065	OCEAN BLUFF
01254-01254	RICHMOND	01521-01521	HOLLAND	01840-01843	LAWRENCE	02066-02066	SCITUATE
01255-01255	SANDISFIELD	01522-01522	JEFFERSON	01844-01844	METHUEN	02067-02067	SHARON
01256-01256	SAVOY	01523-01523	LANCASTER	01845-01845	NORTH ANDOVER	02070-02070	SHELDONVILLE
01257-01257	SHEFFIELD	01524-01524	LEICESTER	01850-01854	LOWELL	02071-02071	SOUTH WALPOLE
01258-01258	SOUTH EGREMONT	01525-01525	LINWOOD	01860-01860	MERRIMAC	02072-02072	STOUGHTON
01259-01259	SOUTHFIELD	01526-01526	MANCHAUG	01862-01862	NORTH BILLERICA	02081-02081	WALPOLE
01260-01260	SOUTH LEE	01527-01527	MILLBURY	01863-01863	NORTH CHELMSFORD	02090-02090	WESTWOOD
01262-01263	STOCKBRIDGE	01529-01529	MILLVILLE	01864-01864	NORTH READING	02093-02093	WRENTHAM
01264-01264	TYRINGHAM	01531-01531	NEW BRAINTREE	01865-01865	NUTTING LAKE	02101-02125	BOSTON
01266-01266	WEST STOCKBRIDGE	01532-01532	NORTHBOROUGH	01866-01866	PINEHURST	02126-02126	MATTAPAN
01267-01267	WILLIAMSTOWN	01534-01534	NORTHBRIDGE	01867-01867	READING	02127-02128	BOSTON
01270-01270	WINDSOR	01535-01535	NORTH BROOKFIELD	01876-01876	TEWKSBURY	02129-02129	CHARLESTOWN
01301-01302	GREENFIELD	01536-01536	NORTH GRAFTON	01879-01879	TYNGSBORO	02130-02130	JAMAICA PLAIN
01330-01330	ASHFIELD	01537-01537	NORTH OXFORD	01880-01880	WAKEFIELD	02131-02131	ROSLINDALE
01331-01331	ATHOL	01538-01538	NORTH UXBRIDGE	01885-01885	WEST BOXFORD	02132-02132	WEST ROXBURY
01337-01337	BERNARDSTON	01539-01539	OAKDALE	01886-01886	WESTFORD	02133-02133	BOSTON
01338-01338	BUCKLAND	01540-01540	OXFORD	01887-01887	WILMINGTON	02134-02134	ALLSTON
01339-01339	CHARLEMONT	01541-01541	PRINCETON	01888-01888	WOBURN	02135-02135	BRIGHTON
01340-01340	COLRAIN	01542-01542	ROCHDALE	01889-01889	NORTH READING	02136-02136	HYDE PARK
01341-01341	CONWAY	01543-01543	RUTLAND	01890-01890	WINCHESTER	02137-02137	READVILLE
01342-01342	DEERFIELD	01545-01546	SHREWSBURY	01899-01899	ANDOVER	02138-02142	CAMBRIDGE
01343-01343	DRURY	01550-01550	SOUTHBRIDGE	01901-01905	LYNN	02143-02145	SOMERVILLE
01344-01344	ERVING	01560-01560	SOUTH GRAFTON	01906-01906	SAUGUS	02146-02146	BROOKLINE
01346-01346	HEATH	01561-01561	SOUTH LANCASTER	01907-01907	SWAMPSCOTT	02147-02147	BROOKLINE VILLAGE
01347-01347	LAKE PLEASANT	01562-01562	SPENCER	01908-01908	NAHANT	02148-02148	MALDEN
01349-01349	TURNERS FALLS	01564-01564	STERLING	01910-01910	LYNN	02149-02149	EVERETT
01350-01350	MONROE BRIDGE	01566-01566	STURBRIDGE	01913-01913	AMESBURY	02150-02150	CHELSEA
01351-01351	MONTAGUE	01568-01568	UPTON	01915-01915	BEVERLY	02151-02151	REVERE
01354-01354	NORTHFIELD	01569-01569	UXBRIDGE	01921-01921	BOXFORD	02152-02152	WINTHROP
01355-01355	NEW SALEM	01570-01570	WEBSTER	01922-01922	BYFIELD	02153-02153	MEDFORD
01360-01360	NORTHFIELD	01571-01571	DUDLEY	01923-01923	DANVERS	02154-02154	WALTHAM
01364-01364	ORANGE	01580-01582	WESTBOROUGH	01929-01929	ESSEX	02155-02155	MEDFORD
01366-01366	PETERSHAM	01583-01583	WEST BOYLSTON	01930-01931	GLOUCESTER	02156-02156	WEST MEDFORD
01367-01367	ROWE	01585-01585	WEST BROOKFIELD	01936-01936	HAMILTON	02157-02157	BABSON PARK
01368-01368	ROYALSTON	01586-01586	WEST MILLBURY	01937-01937	HATHORNE	02158-02162	NEWTON
01369-01369	SHATTUCKVILLE	01588-01588	WHITINSVILLE	01938-01938	IPSWICH	02163-02163	BOSTON
01370-01370	SHELBURNE FALLS	01590-01590	SUTTON	01940-01940	LYNNFIELD	02164-02165	NEWTON
01373-01373	SOUTH DEERFIELD	01601-01610	WORCESTER	01944-01944	MANCHESTER	02166-02166	AUBURNDALE
01375-01375	SUNDERLAND	01611-01611	CHERRY VALLEY	01945-01945	MARBLEHEAD	02167-02167	CHESTNUT HILL
01376-01376	TURNERS FALLS	01612-01612	PAXTON	01947-01947	SALEM	02168-02168	WABAN
01378-01378	WARWICK	01613-01655	WORCESTER	01949-01949	MIDDLETON	02169-02171	QUINCY
01379-01379	WENDELL	01701-01705	FRAMINGHAM	01950-01950	NEWBURYPORT	02172-02172	WATERTOWN

02173-02173	LEXINGTON	02348-02349	MIDDLEBORO	02571-02571	WAREHAM	02669-02669	WEST CHATHAM
02174-02174	ARLINGTON	02350-02350	MONPONSETT	02573-02573	VINEYARD HAVEN	02670-02670	WEST DENNIS
02175-02175	ARLINGTON HEIGHTS	02351-02351	ABINGTON	02574-02574	WEST FALMOUTH	02671-02671	WEST HARWICH
02176-02177	MELROSE	02355-02355	NORTH CARVER	02575-02575	WEST TISBURY	02672-02672	WEST HYANNISPORT
02178-02178	BELMONT	02356-02357	NORTH EASTON	02576-02576	WEST WAREHAM	02673-02673	WEST YARMOUTH
02179-02179	WAVERLEY	02358-02358	NORTH PEMBROKE	02584-02584	NANTUCKET	02675-02675	YARMOUTH PORT
02180-02180	STONEHAM	02359-02359	PEMBROKE	02601-02601	HYANNIS	02702-02702	ASSONET
02181-02181	WELLESLEY	02360-02363	PLYMOUTH	02630-02630	BARNSTABLE	02703-02703	ATTLEBORO
02184-02185	BRAINTREE	02364-02364	KINGSTON	02631-02631	BREWSTER	02712-02712	CHARTLEY
02186-02186	MILTON	02366-02366	SOUTH CARVER	02632-02632	CENTERVILLE	02713-02713	CUTTYHUNK
02187-02187	MILTON VILLAGE	02367-02367	PLYMPTON	02633-02633	CHATHAM	02714-02714	DARTMOUTH
02188-02191	WEYMOUTH	02368-02368	RANDOLPH	02634-02634	CENTERVILLE	02715-02715	DIGHTON
02192-02192	NEEDHAM	02370-02370	ROCKLAND	02635-02635	COTUIT	02717-02717	EAST FREETOWN
02193-02193	WESTON	02375-02375	SOUTH EASTON	02636-02636	CENTERVILLE	02718-02718	EAST TAUNTON
02194-02194	NEEDHAM	02379-02379	WEST BRIDGEWATER	02637-02637	CUMMAQUID	02719-02719	FAIRHAVEN
02195-02195	NEWTON	02381-02381	WHITE HORSE BEACH	02638-02638	DENNIS	02720-02724	FALL RIVER
02196-02222	BOSTON	02382-02382	WHITMAN	02639-02639	DENNIS PORT	02725-02726	SOMERSET
02238-02239	CAMBRIDGE	02401-02499	BROCKTON	02641-02641	EAST DENNIS	02738-02738	MARION
02241-02241	BOSTON	02532-02532	BUZZARDS BAY	02642-02642	EASTHAM	02739-02739	MATTAPOISETT
02254-02254	WALTHAM	02534-02534	CATAUMET	02643-02643	EAST ORLEANS	02740-02742	NEW BEDFORD
02258-02258	NEWTON	02535-02535	CHILMARK	02644-02644	FORESTDALE	02743-02743	ACUSHNET
02266-02266	BOSTON	02536-02536	EAST FALMOUTH	02645-02645	HARWICH	02744-02746	NEW BEDFORD
02269-02269	QUINCY	02537-02537	EAST SANDWICH	02646-02646	HARWICH PORT	02747-02747	NORTH DARTMOUTH
02272-02277	WATERTOWN	02538-02538	EAST WAREHAM	02647-02647	HYANNIS PORT	02748-02748	SOUTH DARTMOUTH
02293-02297	BOSTON	02539-02539	EDGARTOWN	02648-02648	MARSTONS MILLS	02754-02754	NORTH DIGHTON
02322-02322	AVON	02540-02541	FALMOUTH	02649-02649	MASHPEE	02760-02761	NORTH ATTLEBORO
02324-02325	BRIDGEWATER	02542-02542	BUZZARDS BAY	02650-02650	NORTH CHATHAM	02762-02762	PLAINVILLE
02327-02327	BRYANTVILLE	02543-02543	WOODS HOLE	02651-02651	NORTH EASTHAM	02763-02763	ATTLEBORO FALLS
02330-02330	CARVER	02552-02552	MENEMSHA	02652-02652	NORTH TRURO	02764-02764	NORTH DIGHTON
02331-02332	DUXBURY	02553-02553	MONUMENT BEACH	02653-02653	ORLEANS	02766-02766	NORTON
02333-02333	EAST BRIDGEWATER	02554-02554	NANTUCKET	02655-02655	OSTERVILLE	02767-02767	RAYNHAM
02334-02334	EASTON	02556-02556	NORTH FALMOUTH	02657-02657	PROVINCETOWN	02768-02768	RAYNHAM CENTER
02337-02337	ELMWOOD	02557-02557	OAK BLUFFS	02659-02659	SOUTH CHATHAM	02769-02769	REHOBOTH
02338-02338	HALIFAX	02558-02558	ONSET	02660-02660	SOUTH DENNIS	02770-02770	ROCHESTER
02339-02339	HANOVER	02559-02559	POCASSET	02661-02661	SOUTH HARWICH	02771-02771	SEEKONK
02341-02341	HANSON	02561-02561	SAGAMORE	02662-02662	SOUTH ORLEANS	02777-02777	SWANSEA
02343-02343	HOLBROOK	02562-02562	SAGAMORE BEACH	02663-02663	SOUTH WELLFLEET	02779-02779	BERKLEY
02344-02344	MIDDLEBORO	02563-02563	SANDWICH	02664-02664	SOUTH YARMOUTH	02780-02780	TAUNTON
02345-02345	MANOMET	02564-02564	SIASCONSET	02666-02666	TRURO	02790-02790	WESTPORT
02346-02346	MIDDLEBORO	02565-02565	SILVER BEACH	02667-02667	WELLFLEET	02791-02791	WESTPORT POINT
02347-02347	LAKEVILLE	02568-02568	VINEYARD HAVEN	02668-02668	WEST BARNSTABLE	05501-05544	ANDOVER

Michigan

General Help Numbers:

Governor's Office

PO Box 30013   517-373-7858
Lansing, MI 48909   Fax 517-335-6863
www.michigan.gov/gov   8AM-5PM

Attorney General's Office

PO Box 30212   517-373-1110
Lansing, MI 48909   Fax 517-373-3042
www.ag.state.mi.us   8AM-5PM

State Court Administrator

309 N Washington Sq   517-373-2222
Lansing, MI 48909   Fax 517-373-2112
www.supremecourt.state.mi.us   8:30AM-5PM

State Archives

Michigan Historical Center   517-373-1408
Michigan Library & Historical Ctr   Fax 517-241-1658
717 W Allegan   10AM-4PM
Lansing, MI 48918-1837
www.sos.state.mi.us/history/archive

State Specifics:

Capital: Lansing
     Ingham County

Time Zone: EST*

* Four north-western Michigan counties are CST:
They are: Dickinson, Gogebic, Iron, Menominee.

Number of Counties: 83

Population: 9,938,444

Web Site: www.state.mi.us

State Agencies

Criminal Records

Michigan State Police, Ident. Section, Criminal Justice Information Center, 7150 Harris Dr, Lansing, MI 48913; 517-322-5531, 517-322-0635 (Fax), 8AM-5PM.

www.msp.state.mi.us

Note: Non-profit organizations may submit a copy of Federal Form 501C3 in lieu of payment for a name search. Sex offender data is available online at www.mipsor.state.mi.us.

Indexing & Storage: Records are available until the subject's DOB indicates 99 years or a death is reported. It takes 6 to 8 weeks before new records are available for inquiry. Records are indexed on inhouse computer.

Searching: Include the following in your request-full name, sex, race, date of birth. A SSN or maiden-previous name is very helpful. Records can be searched with or without a fingerprint card. The following data is not released: non-conviction information.

Access by: mail, fax, online.

Fee & Payment: The search fee is $5.00 per name without a fingerprint card, $15.00 with a fingerprint card, and $39.00 with state and FBI fingerprint cards. Fee payee: State of Michigan.

Prepayment required. Payment required in advance unless a prepaid account has been arranged with Division cashier. Personal checks accepted. Credit cards will be accepted for online access.

Mail search: Turnaround time: 2 to 4 weeks.

Fax search: The state will permit ongoing requesters to set up a pre-paid account and submit requests by fax, but this may be discontinued later in 2001.

Online search: Online access is limited to businesses that are ongoing requesters. Access is via the Internet, credit cards are required. To set up an account, call 517-322-5546

Corporation Records
Limited Liability Company Records
Limited Partnership Records
Assumed Name

Department of Consumer & Industry Svcs, Corporation & Land ve. Bureau, PO Box 30054, Lansing, MI 48909-7554 (Courier: 6546 Mercantile Way, Lansing, MI 48910); 517-241-6470, 517-334-8329 (Fax), 8AM-noon, 1-5PM.

www.cis.state.mi.us/bcs/corp

Note: Forms, policies, and procedures may be viewed at their web site. The fax listed above is for record requests. The fax for copies or certificates is 517-334-7145.

Indexing & Storage: Records are available from the first corporation in Michigan. Older records were indexed on cards. The index to records for active entities are maintained on computer. It takes 24 hours or less before new records are available for inquiry.

Searching: Include the following in your request-full name of business, corporation file number. The directors are only listed on the annual report.

Access by: mail, phone, fax, in person, online.

Fee & Payment: There is no search fee. The minimum charge for copies is $6.00 per record and $1.00 per page if over 6 pages. The minimum charge for a certificate is $10.00. Fee payee: State of Michigan. Credit cards are accepted for in person requests only. Personal checks accepted. Credit cards accepted: MasterCard, Visa.

Mail search: Turnaround time: 5 to 7 days. There is no fee unless copies or certificates are needed, then there is a minimum $6.00 fee.No self addressed stamped envelope is required. Copies cost $1.00 per page.

Phone search: You can order copies or certificates.

Fax search: Only current database records are available by fax.

In person search: The agency has a public access terminal for viewing records.

Online search: Search by compnay name or file number for records of domestic corporations, limited liability companies, and limited partnerships and of foreign corporations, and limited partnerships qualified to transact business in the state. On the web at www.cis.state.mi.us/bcs_corp/sr_corp.asp.

Other access: The database is for sale on tape or microfiche.

Trademarks/Servicemarks

Department of Consumer & Industry Srvs, Securities Examination Division, PO Box 30054, Lansing, MI 48909-7554 (Courier: 6546 Mercantile Way, Lansing, MI 48910); 517-241-6000, 8AM-5PM.

www.cis.state.mi.us/corp

Note: This agency will not do record checks (unless you are applying for a mark). They suggest several outside firms to come in person.

Indexing & Storage: Records are available for current records. The index is available since 1990.

Access by: phone, in person. No mail searching.

Phone search: No fee for telephone request. Limited - words only, no designs.

In person search: No fee for request. There is a public access terminal. They strongly urge to call in first and schedule usage time.

Uniform Commercial Code
Federal Tax Liens
State Tax Liens

UCC Section, Department of State, PO Box 30197, Lansing, MI 48909-7697 (Courier: 7064 Crowner Dr, Dimondale, MI 48821); 517-322-1144, 517-322-5434 (Fax), 8AM-5PM.

www.sos.state.mi.us

Indexing & Storage: Records are available from 1964. Records are computerized since 1990. It takes 7 to 10 days before new records are available for inquiry.

Searching: Use search request form UCC-11. The search includes federal and state tax liens on businesses. Federal and state tax liens on individuals are filed at the county level. Include the following in your request-debtor name.

Access by: mail, phone, fax, in person.

Fee & Payment: The search fee is $6.00. The copy fee is $2.00. Certification (official seal) is an additional $6.00. Fee payee: State of Michigan. Prepayment required. Personal checks accepted. No credit cards accepted.

Mail search: Turnaround time: 1 week. A self addressed stamped envelope is requested.

Phone search: Phone searching is available on a prepaid account basis, results are returned by mail.

Fax search: See expedited services.

In person search: Must be scheduled in advance and subject to availability of equipment.

Expedited service: Expedited service is available for an additional $25.00 fee. Expedited searches are provided on a prepaid account basis at $25.00 + $6.00 per debtor name. If request is received by 11 AM, search is mailed that same day.

Sales Tax Registrations
Records not maintained by a state level agency.

Note: The agency has recently determined it will not release information to the public nor verify or confirm data.

Birth Certificates

Department of Community Health, Vital Records Requests, PO Box 30721, Lansing, MI 48909 (Courier: 3423 Martin Luther King, Jr Blvd, Lansing, MI 48909); 517-335-8656 (Instructions), 517-335-8666 (Request Unit), 517-321-5884 (Fax), 8AM-5PM.

www.mdch.state.mi.us/Pha/Osr/vitframe.htm

Note: Note: Any Michigan vital record can be "verified" for a fee of $4.00. Verification is only for names, date and place of filing.

Indexing & Storage: Records are available from 1867 on. It takes 90 to 120 days after birth before new records are available for inquiry. Records are indexed on microfiche, inhouse computer.

Searching: Certified copies of birth records are only issued to the individual to whom the record pertains, the parent(s) named on the record, an heir, legal guardian or legal rep. of an eligible person, or through court order Records over 110 yrs old are open Include the following in your request-full name, names of parents, mother's maiden name, date of birth, place of birth, relationship to person of record. The signature and relationship to the subject are required items on the request form. The following data is not released: sealed records.

Access by: mail, phone, in person, online.

Fee & Payment: The fee is $13.00 per name for every 3 years searched. The fee is $4.00 for each additional year. Additional copies of the same record are $4.00 each. Use of a credit card is additional $5.00. An "Authenticated Copy" is available for $16.00. Fee payee: State of Michigan. Prepayment required. Personal checks accepted. Credit cards accepted: MasterCard, Visa, AmEx, Discover.

Mail search: Turnaround time: 2 to 3 weeks. No self addressed stamped envelope is required.

Phone search: You can use a credit card when ordering by phone.

In person search: Turnaround time up to 3 hours. Counter closes at 3:30 PM.

Online search: Records may be ordered from the web site. Step-by-step instructions given, use of credit card required.

Expedited service: Expedited service is available for mail, phone, and online searches. The total fee is $32.50 (includes express delivery) and payment must be on credit card. Turnaround is next day if ordered by noon.

Death Records

Department of Health, Vital Records Requests, PO Box 30721, Lansing, MI 48909 (Courier: 3423 Martin Luther King, Jr Blvd, Lansing, MI 48909); 517-335-8656 (Instructions), 517-335-8666 (Request Unit), 517-321-5884 (Fax), 8AM-5PM.

www.mdch.state.mi.us/Pha/Osr/vitframe.htm

Indexing & Storage: Records are available from 1867 to present. New records are available for inquiry immediately. Records are indexed on microfiche, inhouse computer.

Searching: Records are open to the public. Include the following in your request-full name, date of death, place of death, relationship to person of record. The following data is not released: sealed records.

Access by: mail, phone, in person, online.

Fee & Payment: The fee for a certified copy is $13.00 for a 3 year search, add $4.00 for each additional year searched. Add $4.00 per name per copy for additional copies. Use of credit card is additional $5.00 fee. Fee payee: State of Michigan. Prepayment required. Personal checks, money orders accepted. Credit cards accepted: MasterCard, Visa, AmEx, Discover.

Mail search: Turnaround time: 2 to 3 weeks. No self addressed stamped envelope is required.

Phone search: Credit cards are accepted over the phone for an additional fee.

In person search: Turnaround time 2-3 hours. Counter closes at 3:30 PM.

Online search: Records may be ordered from the web. Use of a credit card is required. Records are returned by mail or express delivery. If problems, call 800-255-2414.

Expedited service: Expedited service is available for mail, phone and online searches. The total fee is $32.50 (includes express delivery) and a credit card is required. Turnaround time is 24 hours if order in by noon.

Marriage Certificates

Department of Health, Vital Records Requests, PO Box 30721, Lansing, MI 48909 (Courier: 3423 Martin Luther King, Jr Blvd, Lansing, MI 48909); 517-335-8656 (Instructions), 517-335-8666 (Requests Unit), 517-321-5884 (Fax), 8AM-5PM.

www.mdch.state.mi.us/pha/osr/vitframe.htm

Indexing & Storage: Records are available from 1867 to present. New records are available for inquiry immediately. Records are indexed on microfiche, inhouse computer.

Searching: Records are open to the public. There is no bride index for the years 1950 thru 1975. Include the following in your request-names of husband and wife, date of marriage, place or county of marriage, relationship to person of record. The following data is not released: sealed records.

Access by: mail, phone, in person, online.

Fee & Payment: The fee for a certified copy is $13.00 which includes 3 years searched. Each additional year searched is another $4.00. Additional copies of the same record are $4.00 each. use of credit card is an additional $5.00 fee. Fee payee: State of Michigan. Prepayment required. Personal checks accepted. Credit cards accepted: MasterCard, Visa, AmEx, Discover.

Mail search: Turnaround time: 2 to 3 weeks. No self addressed stamped envelope is required.

Phone search: You can order by credit card over the phone.

In person search: Turnaround time up to 3 hours minutes. Counter closes at 3:30 PM.

Online search: Records can be ordered from the web site, credit card is required.

Expedited service: Expedited service is available for mail and phone searches. The total fee is $32.50 (includes express delivery) and use of a credit card is required. Turnaround time is 24 hours if ordered by noon.

Divorce Records

Department of Health, Vital Records Requests, PO Box 30721, Lansing, MI 48909 (Courier: 3423 Martin Luther King, Jr Blvd, Lansing, MI 48909); 517-335-8656 (Instructions), 517-335-8666 (Requests Unit), 517-321-5884 (Fax), 8AM-5PM.

www.mdch.state.mi.us/pha/osr/vitframe.htm

Indexing & Storage: Records are available from 1897 to present. New records are available for inquiry immediately. Records are indexed on microfiche, inhouse computer.

Searching: Records are open to the public. There are no divorce records for Detroit for 1973 and 1974. There is no "wife index" available prior to 1978. Include the following in your request-names of husband and wife, date of divorce, year divorce case began, case number (if known), relationship to person of record.

Access by: mail, phone, in person.

Fee & Payment: The fee for a certified copy is $13.00, which includes 3 years searched. Each additional year is another $4.00. Extra copies of the same record are $4.00 each. Use of a credit card is an additional $5.00. Fee payee: State of Michigan. Prepayment required. Personal checks accepted. Credit cards accepted: MasterCard, Visa, AmEx, Discover.

Mail search: Turnaround time: 2 to 3 weeks. No self addressed stamped envelope is required.

Phone search: You can order over the phone by credit card.

In person search: Turnaround time 45 minutes. Counter closes at 3:30 PM.

Expedited service: Expedited service is available for mail, phone and fax searches. The total fee is $32.50 (includes express delivery), use of credit card is required. Turnaround time is overnight if ordered by noon.

Workers' Compensation Records

Department of Consumer & Industry Services, Bureau of Workers Disability Compensation, 7150 Harris Dr, Lansing, MI 48909; 517-322-1884, 888-396-5041, 517-322-1808 (Fax), 8AM-5PM.

www.cis.state.mi.us/wkrcomp/bwdc

Note: In person requests are discouraged due to confidentiality of records and records may not be on site. Injured employee may review their own records, but should call first and make arrangements.

Indexing & Storage: Records are available from 1981 on computer and from 1976 to 1981 records on microfilm. You can request by fax, but results are mailed.

Searching: Request must be in writing and cannot be for pre-employment screening. Only litigated cases are released. Include the following in your request-claimant name, Social Security Number.

Access by: mail.

Fee & Payment: Fee is $.25 per page plus postage and research labor cost if over 30 pages. Fee payee: Consumer & Industry Services, Bureau of Workers Dist. Comp. Personal checks accepted. No credit cards accepted.

Mail search: Turnaround time: 1 to 2 weeks. Turnaround time may be longer if records must be searched at archives.No self addressed stamped envelope is required.

Driver Records

Department of State Police, Record Look-up Unit, 7064 Crowner Dr, Lansing, MI 48918; 517-322-1624, 517-322-1181 (Fax), 8AM-4:45PM.

www.sos.state.mi.us/dv

Note: Copies of court abstracts of convictions may be purchased at the same address for a fee of $6.55 per copy. Copies of tickets must be obtained from the courts involved.

Indexing & Storage: Records are available for 7 years from conviction date; unless there is an alcohol or controlled substance conviction which will remain on record for 10 years. Accidents are reported on the record only if the driver is cited. It takes 14 days before new records are available for inquiry.

Searching: Casual requesters can only obtain records without personal information.

Access by: mail, phone, fax, in person, online.

Fee & Payment: The fee for obtaining a record is $6.55 per search. If certification is needed, there is an additional $1.00 fee. Fee payee: State of Michigan. The fee may accompany the request for mail-in, or a bill can be sent with the records. There is a full charge for a "no record found." Credit cards are accepted for fax and phone requests only. Personal checks accepted. Credit cards accepted: MasterCard, Visa.

Mail search: Turnaround time: 10 working days. No self addressed stamped envelope is required.

Phone search: Phone requesting is available for pre-approved accounts and government agencies or with a credit card.

Fax search: Established accounts can order by fax, results are returned by mail.

In person search: Search costs $6.55 per record. Turnaround time is up to 14 days (they mail the record back) unless you are the actual driver, then the record is immediately available.

Online search: Online ordering is available on an interactive basis. The system is open 7 days a week. Ordering is by DL or name and DOB. An account must be established and billing is monthly. Access is also available from the Internet. Fee is $6.55 per record. For more information, call Carol Lycos at 517-322-1591.

Other access: Magnetic tape inquiry is available. Also, the state offers the license file for bulk purchase. Customized runs are $64 per thousand records; the complete database can be purchased for $16 per thousand. A $10,000 surety bond is required.

Vehicle Ownership
Vehicle Identification
Vessel Ownership
Vessel Registration

Department of State Police, Record Look-up Unit, 7064 Crowner Dr, Lansing, MI 48918; 517-322-1624, 517-322-1181 (Fax), 8AM-4:45PM.

www.sos.state.mi.us/dv

Indexing & Storage: Records are available for 10 years to present for vehicle information and 3 years to present for registration information. Vessel titles are on computer since 1974. All motorized boats must be registered, if 20 ft or over they must also be titled. It takes 14 days before new records are available for inquiry.

Searching: Requests for vehicle and ownership records must be submitted in writing with a statement of intended use. Large volume users or fax requesters must be pre-approved. There is no opt out provision.

Access by: mail, phone, fax, in person, online.

Fee & Payment: The fee is $6.55 per transaction. Normal searching requires the plate or VIN number. Records to be accessed include mobile homes and boats. Copy fee is $1.00 per record. Fee payee: State of Michigan. The fee may accompany the request for mail-in, or a bill can be sent with the records. Requests made by fax will be sent a bill with the records. There is a full charge for a "no record found." Personal checks accepted. Credit cards accepted: MasterCard, Visa.

Mail search: Turnaround time: 10 days. A self addressed stamped envelope is requested.

Phone search: Call-in requests are for established, approved accounts only. Records may be mailed or faxed back. They will usually also accept a credit card.

Fax search: Established accounts may order by fax and receive results by fax.

In person search: You can make your request in person, but they will mail back the records in 4 or 5 days. Requests must be in writing.

Online search: Online searching is single inquiry and requires a VIN or plate number. A $25,000 surety bond is required. Fee is $6.55 per record. Direct dialup or Internet access is offered. For more information, call Carol Lycos at 517-322-1591.

Other access: Michigan offers bulk retrieval from the VIN and plate database. A written request letter, stating purpose, must be approved. A surety bond is required upon approval. Please call 517-241-2781.

Accident Reports

Department of State Police, Criminal Justice Information Center, 7150 Harris Dr, Lansing, MI 48913; 517-322-5509, 517-323-5350 (Fax), 8AM-5PM.

www.msp.state.mi.us

Indexing & Storage: Records are available from 1983 to present for state police records. UD10's for all law enforcement agencies in Michigan are available for the current year plus 2 years back, first page only. It takes 3 to 4 weeks before new records are available for inquiry.

Searching: Include the following in your request-full name, date of accident, location of accident.

Access by: mail, in person.

Fee & Payment: Fee is $5.00 per report. Fee payee: State of Michigan. Prepayment required. Personal checks accepted. No credit cards accepted.

Mail search: Turnaround time: 10 days. A self addressed stamped envelope is requested.

In person search: You may request information in person, but it is discouraged.

Legislation Records

Michigan Legislature Document Room, State Capitol, PO Box 30036, Lansing, MI 48909 (Courier: North Capitol Annex, Lansing, MI 48909); 517-373-0169, 8:30AM-5PM.

www.michiganlegislature.org

Note: Older passed bills found at the State Law Library, 517-373-0630.

Indexing & Storage: Records are available from 1997 on computer.

Searching: Search by bill number, sponsor or subject.

Access by: mail, phone, in person, online.

Fee & Payment: There are no fees involved. No credit cards accepted.

Mail search: Turnaround time: 1 day. No self addressed stamped envelope is required.

Phone search: Only current and past session information is available.

Online search: Access is available from their Internet site. Adobe Acrobat Reader is required. Information available includes status of bills, bill text, joint resolution text, journals, calendars, session and committee schedules, and MI complied laws.

Voter Registration
Records not maintained by a state level agency.

Note: The city or township keeps all records. In general
the records are open to the public.

GED Certificates

MI Department of Career Development, Adult Education - GED Testing, PO Box 30714, Lansing, MI 48909 (Courier: 201 N Washington Square, 5th Fl, Lansing, MI 48933-8214); 517-373-1692, 517-335-3461 (Fax), 8AM-5PM.

www.mdcd.org/Core/AdultED1.html

Indexing & Storage: Records are available 3/1969 to present.

Searching: To search, include the SSN, DOB and date and location of test. For a copy of a transcript, also include a signed release.

Access by: mail, phone, fax, in person.

Fee & Payment: There are no fees.

Mail search: Turnaround time: 1 week. No self addressed stamped envelope is required.

Phone search: You request a verification by leaving a message and the agency will call back with the information.

Fax search: Same criteria as mail searching.

In person search: The building is also known as the Victor Building

Hunting License Information
Fishing License Information
Access to Records is Restricted

Dept of Natural Resources, E-Commerce, PO Box 30181, Lansing, MI 48909 (Courier: 530 W Allegan St, Lansing, MI 48933); 517-373-1204, 517-373-0784 (Fax), 8AM-5PM.

Note: Hunting and fishing license information is no longer released. All FOIA requests are now being denied because it is personal information.

Michigan State Licensing Agencies

Licenses Searchable Online

Ambulance Attendant #10 .... www.cis.state.mi.us/verify.htm
Amusement Ride #08 .... www.cis.state.mi.us/verify.htm
Architect #08 .... www.cis.state.mi.us/verify.htm
Assessor #25 .... www.treas.state.mi.us/localgov/Assessor/certlevellist.html
Athletic Control #08 .... www.cis.state.mi.us/verify.htm
Attorney (State Bar) #27 .... www.michbar.org/framemaker.cfm?content_dir=member&content=content.html
Aviation Medical Examiner #24 .... www.mdot.state.mi.us/aero/resources/ame.htm
Barber #08 .... www.cis.state.mi.us/verify.htm
Carnival #08 .... www.cis.state.mi.us/verify.htm
Cemetery #08 .... www.cis.state.mi.us/verify.htm
Child Caring Institution #26 .... www.cis.state.mi.us/brs/cwl/cwllist.htm
Child Welfare Agency (Child Placing) #26 .... www.cis.state.mi.us/brs/cwl/cwllist.htm
Chiropractor #15 .... www.cis.state.mi.us/free/
Collection Manager #08 .... www.cis.state.mi.us/verify.htm
Community Planner #08 .... www.cis.state.mi.us/verify.htm
Cosmetologist #08 .... www.cis.state.mi.us/verify.htm
Counselor #15 .... www.cis.state.mi.us/free/
Dentist/Dental Assistant #15 .... www.cis.state.mi.us/free/
Emergency Medical Personnel #15 .... www.cis.state.mi.us/free/
EMT-Advanced/Specialist/Instructor #10 .... www.cis.state.mi.us/verify.htm
Employment Agency #08 .... www.cis.state.mi.us/verify.htm
Engineer #09 .... www.cis.state.mi.us/verify.htm
Foster Care Facility/Adult Camp #13 .... www.michigan.gov/emi/1,1303,7-102-117_401_459---CI,00.html
Foster Care Program #21 .... www.cis.state.mi.us/verify.htm
Foster Family Home #21 .... www.cis.state.mi.us/verify.htm
Funeral Salesperson (Prepaid Funeral) #09 ...... www.cis.state.mi.us/verify.htm
Hearing Aid Dealer #08 .... www.cis.state.mi.us/verify.htm
Hygenist, Dental #15 .... www.cis.state.mi.us/free/
Mammography Facility #15 .... www.cis.state.mi.us/bhs_car/sr_mam.asp
Marriage & Family Therapist #15 .... www.cis.state.mi.us/free/
Medical Doctor #15 .... www.cis.state.mi.us/free/
Medical First Responder #10 .... www.cis.state.mi.us/free/
Mortuary Science #08 .... www.cis.state.mi.us/verify.htm
Notary Public #22 .... www.sos.state.mi.us/greatse/notaries/notaries.html
Nurse #15 .... www.cis.state.mi.us/free/
Nurses' Aide #15 .... www.cis.state.mi.us/free/
Nursing Home #08 .... www.cis.state.mi.us/bhs_car/sr_car.asp
Nursing Home Administrator #08 .... www.cis.state.mi.us/verify.htm
Occularist #08 .... www.cis.state.mi.us/verify.htm
Optometrist #15 .... www.cis.state.mi.us/free/
Osteopathic Physician #15 .... www.cis.state.mi.us/free/
Paramedic #10 .... www.cis.state.mi.us/verify.htm
Pharmacist #15 .... www.cis.state.mi.us/free/
Physical Therapist #15 .... www.cis.state.mi.us/free/
Physician Assistant #15 .... www.cis.state.mi.us/free/
Pilot Examiner #24 .... www.mdot.state.mi.us/aero/resources/dpe.htm
Podiatrist #15 .... www.cis.state.mi.us/free/
Polygraph Examiner #08 .... www.cis.state.mi.us/verify.htm
Psychologist #15 .... www.cis.state.mi.us/free/
Public Accountant-CPA #08 .... www.cis.state.mi.us/verify.htm
Real Estate Broker/Salesperson #09 .... www.cis.state.mi.us/verify.htm
Sanitarian #15 .... www.cis.state.mi.us/free/
Social Worker #15 .... www.cis.state.mi.us/free/
Social Worker #08 .... www.cis.state.mi.us/verify.htm
Surveyor, Professional #09 .... www.cis.state.mi.us/verify.htm
Veterinarian/Veterinary Technician #15 .... www.cis.state.mi.us/free/

Licensing Quick Finder

Adoption Service #13	517-373-4021
Aeronautics #24	517-335-9719
Alarm System Service #23	517-336-3440
Ambulance Attendant #10	517-241-3018
Amusement Ride #08	517-241-9265
Architect #08	517-241-9253
Asbestos Accreditation, Individual #11	517-322-1320
Asbestos Licensing #11	517-322-1320
Assessor #25	517-373-8320
Athletic Control #08	517-241-9246
Attorney (State Bar) #27	517-372-9030
Automobile Dealer/Mechanic/Repair Facility #28	517-373-9082
Aviation Medical Examiner #24	517-335-9943
Bank & Trust Company #14	517-373-6950
Barber #08	517-241-9261
Bingo Operation, Special or Weekly #1	517-335-5781
Boiler Repairer #07	517-241-9334
Boilermaker (Installer) #07	517-241-9334
Camp, Children's #13	517-373-8300
Carnival #08	517-241-9265
Cemetery #08	517-241-9244
Charitable Gaming (Supplier) #01	517-335-5781
Child Caring Institution #26	517-373-8383
Child Day Care #13	517-373-8300
Child Welfare Agency (Child Placing Agency) #26	517-373-8383
Children's Camp/Adult Camp #26	517-373-0697
Chiropractor #15	900-555-8374
Collection Manager #08	517-241-9258
Community Planner #08	517-241-9253
Corrections Officer #18	517-335-1426
Cosmetologist #08	517-373-9234
Counselor #15	900-555-8374
Credit Union #14	517-373-6930
Dentist/Dental Assistant #15	900-555-8374
Electrician (various types) #07	517-241-9320
Elevator Service #07	517-241-9337
Emergency Medical Personnel #15	900-555-8374
Emergency Medical Technician/Advanced/ Specialist/Instructor #10	517-241-3018
Employment Agency #08	517-241-9246
Engineer #09	517-241-9253
Family/Group Day Care #13	517-373-8300
Food Licensing #02	517-373-1060
Foster Care Facility/Adult Camp #13	517-373-8300
Foster Care Program #21	517-335-6108
Foster Care, Child #13	517-373-8300
Foster Family Home #21	517-335-6108
Funeral Salesperson (Prepaid Funeral Contract Reg.) #09	517-241-9252
Guidance Counselor #19	517-373-6505
Health Facilities/Laboratory #15	517-241-2648
Hearing Aid Dealer #08	517-241-9234
Hygenist, Dental #15	900-555-8374
Insurance Adjuster #05	517-373-0234
Insurance Agent/Counselor/Solicitor/Administrator #05	517-373-0234
Investment Adviser #12	517-334-6215
Liquor Dist./Wholesale/Mfg. #06	517-322-1420
Liquor Licensing Director #06	517-322-1408
Lottery Retailer #01	517-335-5619
Mammography Facility #15	517-241-1989
Manufactured Home Community #16	517-241-6300
Manufactured Home Installer/Services/Retailer #16	517-241-6300
Marriage & Family Therapist #15	900-555-8374
Mechanical Construction #07	517-241-9325
Medical Doctor #15	900-555-8374
Medical First Responder #10	517-241-3018
Millionaire Party-Vegas Night (Gaming) #01	517-335-5781
Mortuary Science #08	517-241-9252
Notary Public #22	517-373-2531
Nurse #15	900-555-8374
Nurses' Aide #15	900-555-8374
Nursing Home #08	517-335-4403
Nursing Home Administrator #08	517-335-4403
Occularist #08	517-241-9234
Optometrist #15	900-555-8374
Osteopathic Physician #15	900-555-8374
Paramedic #10	517-241-3018
Pesticide Licensing #02	517-373-1087
Pharmacist #15	900-555-8374
Physical Therapist #15	900-555-8374
Physician Assistant #15	900-555-8374
Pilot Examiner #24	517-335-9943
Plumber #07	517-241-9304
Podiatrist #15	900-555-8374
Polygraph Examiner #08	517-241-9234
Private Detective #23	517-336-3440
Private Security/Security Arrest Authority #23	517-336-3440
Psychologist #15	900-555-8374
Public Accountant-CPA #08	517-373-0682
Pump Installer #20	517-335-8299
Racing #04	734-462-2400
Raffle #01	517-335-5781
Railroad Commission #23	517-336-3440
Real Estate Broker/Salesperson #09	517-241-9288
Sanitarian #15	900-555-8374
School Librarian #19	517-373-6505
Securities Agent #17	517-334-6211
Securities Agent #12	517-334-6215
Securities Broker/Dealer #12	517-334-6215
Social Worker #08	517-241-9245
Social Worker #15	900-555-8374
Surveyor, Professional #09	517-241-9253
Teacher #19	517-373-6505
Veterinarian/Veterinary Technician #15	900-555-8374
Well Contractor #20	517-335-8299

Licensing Agency Information

#01 Bureau of State Lottery, PO Box 3023 (101 E Hillsdale), Lansing, MI 48909; 517-335-5781, Fax: 517-373-6863.
www.state.mi.us/milottery

#02 Department of Agriculture, Ottawa Bldg, 4th Fl, Lansing, MI 48909; 517-373-1060, Fax: 517-373-3333.
www.state.mi.us

#04 Department of Agriculture, 37650 Professional Center Dr, Livonia, MI 48154-1100; 734-462-2400, Fax: 734-462-2429.
www.state.mi.us

#05 Department of Commerce, PO Box 23127, Lansing, MI 48909-3127; 517-373-0234, Fax: 517-335-4978.
www.cis.state.mi.us/ofis/ofis.htm

#06 Department of Consumer & Industry Services, PO Box 30005, 7150 Harris Dr, Lansing, MI 48909-7505; 517-322-1345, Fax: 517-322-6137.
www.cis.state.mi.us/lcc

#07 Department of Consumer & Industry Services, 2501 Woodlake Cir, Okemos, MI 48864; 517-241-9302, Fax: 517-241-9308.
www.cis.state.mi.us/bcc

#08 Department of Consumer & Industry Services, PO Box 30018, Lansing, MI 48909; 517-241-9288, Fax: 517-241-9280.
www.cis.state.mi.us
Direct web site URL to search for licensees:
www.cis.state.mi.us/verify.htm

#09 Department of Consumer & Industry Services, 2501 Woodlake Cir, Okemos, MI 48864; 517-373-0580, Fax: 517-373-2795.
www.cis.state.mi.us
Direct web site URL to search for licensees:
www.cis.state.mi.us/verify.htm

#10 Department of Consumer & Industry Services, 525 W Ottawa, Lansing, MI 48909; 517-241-3018, Fax: 517-241-2895.
Direct web site URL to search for licensees:
www.cis.state.mi.us/verify.htm

#11 Department of Consumer & Industry Services, PO Box 30671, Lansing, MI 48909-8171; 517-322-1320, Fax: 517-322-1713.
www.cis.state.mi.us/bsr/divisions/occ/asbestos.htm

#12 Department of Consumer & Industry Services, PO Box 30222, Lansing, MI 48909; 517-334-6200, Fax: 517-334-7813.
www.cis.state.mi.us/tmp/corps.htm

#13 Department of Consumer & Industry Services, 525 W Ottawa, Lansing, MI 48909; 517-373-1820, Fax: 517-333-6121.
www.state.mi.us

#14 Department of Consumer & Industry Services, PO Box 30224, Lansing, MI 48909; 517-373-3460, Fax: 517-335-0908.
www.commerce.state.mi.us/ofis/home.htm

#15 Department of Consumer & Industry Services, 611 W Ottawa, 1st Fl, Lansing, MI 48909-8170; 517-335-0918, Fax: 517-373-2179.
www.cis.state.mi.us./bhser
Direct web site URL to search for licensees: www.cis.state.mi.us/free. You can search online using name or license number.

#16 Department of Consumer & Industry Services, PO Box 30703, Lansing, MI 48909; 517-241-6300, Fax: 517-241-6301.
www.cis.state.mi.us/tmp/corps.htm

#18 Department of Corrections, 206 E Michigan Ave, Lansing, MI 48933; 517-335-1426.

#19 Department of Education, Hannah Bldg, 3rd Fl, Lansing, MI 48909; 517-373-3310, Fax: 517-373-0542.
www.state.mi.us/mde/off/ppc/

#20 Department of Environmental Quality, 3423 N Martin Luther King Jr Blvd, Lansing, MI 48909-8130; 517-335-8299, Fax: 517-335-9434.

#21 Department of Consumer & Industry Services, 7109 W Saginaw, 2nd Floor, Lansing, MI 48909-8150; 517-335-6108.
www.cis.state.mi.us/brs

Direct web site URL to search for licensees:
www.cis.state.mi.us/verify.htm

#22 Department of State, 717 W Allegan St, Lansing, MI 48918; 517-373-2531, Fax: 517-373-3706.
www.sos.state.mi.us/greatse/index.html
Direct web site URL to search for licensees:
www.sos.state.mi.us/greatse/notaries/notaries.html
. You can search online using only lists counrty clerks

#23 Department of State Police, 4000 Collins Rd, Lansing, MI 48909; 517-336-3440, Fax: 517-336-3441.
www.state.mi.us

#24 Department of Transportation, 2700 E Airport Service Dr, Lansing, MI 48906; 517-335-9943, Fax: 517-321-6522.
www.mdot.state.mi.us/aero

#25 Department of Treasury, Treasury Bldg, Lansing, MI 48922; 517-373-3200, Fax: 517-373-3553.
www.treas.state.mi.us/localgov/Assessor/assessorind.htm
Direct web site URL to search for licensees:
www.treas.state.mi.us/localgov/Assessor/certlevellist.html

#26 Michigan Department of Consumer & Industry Services, 7109 W Saginaw, 2nd Fl, Lansing, MI 48909-8150; 517-373-8383, Fax: 517-335-6121.
www.cis.state.mi.us/brs
Direct web site URL to search for licensees:
www.cis.state.mi.us/brs/cwl/cwllist.htm. You can search online using name of facility

#27 State Bar, 306 Townsend, Lansing, MI 48933; 517-372-9030, Fax: 517-482-6248.
www.michbar.org
Direct web site URL to search for licensees:
www.michbar.org/framemaker.cfm?content_dir=member&content=content.html

#28 Business Licensing Section, 208 N Capitol Ave, Lansing, MI 48918; 517-373-9082, Fax: 517-373-0964.
www.sos.state.mi.us/bar

Michigan Federal Courts

The following list indicates the district and division name for each county in the state. If the bankruptcy court location is different from the district court, then the location of the bankruptcy court appears in parentheses.

County/Court Cross Reference

County	District	Division
Alcona	Eastern	Bay City
Alger	Western	Marquette-Northern (Marquette)
Allegan	Western	Kalamazoo (Grand Rapids)
Alpena	Eastern	Bay City
Antrim	Western	Grand Rapids
Arenac	Eastern	Bay City
Baraga	Western	Marquette-Northern (Marquette)
Barry	Western	Grand Rapids
Bay	Eastern	Bay City
Benzie	Western	Grand Rapids
Berrien	Western	Kalamazoo (Grand Rapids)
Branch	Western	Lansing (Grand Rapids)
Calhoun	Western	Kalamazoo (Grand Rapids)
Cass	Western	Kalamazoo (Grand Rapids)
Charlevoix	Western	Grand Rapids
Cheboygan	Eastern	Bay City
Chippewa	Western	Marquette-Northern (Marquette)
Clare	Eastern	Bay City
Clinton	Western	Lansing (Grand Rapids)
Crawford	Eastern	Bay City
Delta	Western	Marquette-Northern (Marquette)
Dickinson	Western	Marquette-Northern (Marquette)
Eaton	Western	Lansing (Grand Rapids)
Emmet	Western	Grand Rapids
Genesee	Eastern	Flint
Gladwin	Eastern	Bay City
Gogebic	Western	Marquette-Northern (Marquette)
Grand Traverse	Western	Grand Rapids
Gratiot	Eastern	Bay City
Hillsdale	Western	Lansing (Grand Rapids)
Houghton	Western	Marquette-Northern (Marquette)
Huron	Eastern	Bay City
Ingham	Western	Lansing (Grand Rapids)
Ionia	Western	Grand Rapids
Iosco	Eastern	Bay City
Iron	Western	Marquette-Northern (Marquette)
Isabella	Eastern	Bay City
Jackson	Eastern	Ann Arbor (Detroit)
Kalamazoo	Western	Kalamazoo (Grand Rapids)
Kalkaska	Western	Grand Rapids
Kent	Western	Grand Rapids
Keweenaw	Western	Marquette-Northern (Marquette)
Lake	Western	Grand Rapids
Lapeer	Eastern	Flint
Leelanau	Western	Grand Rapids
Lenawee	Eastern	Ann Arbor (Detroit)
Livingston	Eastern	Flint
Luce	Western	Marquette-Northern (Marquette)
Mackinac	Western	Marquette-Northern (Marquette)
Macomb	Eastern	Detroit
Manistee	Western	Grand Rapids
Marquette	Western	Marquette-Northern (Marquette)
Mason	Western	Grand Rapids
Mecosta	Western	Grand Rapids
Menominee	Western	Marquette-Northern (Marquette)
Midland	Eastern	Bay City
Missaukee	Western	Grand Rapids
Monroe	Eastern	Ann Arbor (Detroit)
Montcalm	Western	Grand Rapids
Montmorency	Eastern	Bay City
Muskegon	Western	Grand Rapids
Newaygo	Western	Grand Rapids
Oakland	Eastern	Ann Arbor (Detroit)
Oceana	Western	Grand Rapids
Ogemaw	Eastern	Bay City
Ontonagon	Western	Marquette-Northern (Marquette)
Osceola	Western	Grand Rapids
Oscoda	Eastern	Bay City
Otsego	Eastern	Bay City
Ottawa	Western	Grand Rapids
Presque Isle	Eastern	Bay City
Roscommon	Eastern	Bay City
Saginaw	Eastern	Bay City
Sanilac	Eastern	Detroit
Schoolcraft	Western	Marquette-Northern (Marquette)
Shiawassee	Eastern	Flint
St. Clair	Eastern	Detroit
St. Joseph	Western	Kalamazoo (Grand Rapids)
Tuscola	Eastern	Bay City
Van Buren	Western	Kalamazoo (Grand Rapids)
Washtenaw	Eastern	Ann Arbor (Detroit)
Wayne	Eastern	Detroit
Wexford	Western	Grand Rapids

US District Court

Eastern District of Michigan

Ann Arbor Division PO Box 8199, Ann Arbor, MI 48107 (Courier Address: 200 E Liberty, Room 120, Ann Arbor, MI 48104), 734-741-2380, Fax: 734-741-2065.

http://www.mied.uscourts.gov

Counties: Jackson, Lenawee, Monroe, Oakland, Washtenaw, Wayne. Civil cases in these counties are assigned randomly to the Detroit, Flint or Port Huron Divisions. Case files are maintained where the case is assigned.

Indexing/Storage: Cases are indexed by defendant and plaintiff as well as by case number. New cases are available in the index immediately after filing date. A computer index is maintained. Open records are located at this court.

Fee & Payment: The fee is $20.00 per item (one party name or case number). Payment may be made by money order, cashier check, personal check. Prepayment is required. Payee: Clerk, US District Court. Certification fee: $7.00 per document. Copy fee: $.50 per page.

Phone Search: Only docket information is available by phone.

Mail Search: Always enclose a stamped self addressed envelope.

In Person: In person searching is available.

PACER: Sign-up number is 800-676-6856. Access fee is $.60 per minute. Toll-free access: 800-229-8015. Local access: 313-234-5376. Case records are available back to 1988. New records are available online after 2 days. PACER is available online at http://pacer.mied.uscourts.gov.

Bay City Division 1000 Washington Ave Rm 304, PO Box 913, Bay City, MI 48707 (Courier Address: Use mail address for courier delivery), 989-894-8800, Fax: 989-894-8804.

http://www.mied.uscourts.gov

Counties: Alcona, Alpena, Arenac, Bay, Cheboygan, Clare, Crawford, Gladwin, Gratiot, Huron, Iosco, Isabella, Midland, Montmorency, Ogemaw, Oscoda, Otsego, Presque Isle, Roscommon, Saginaw, Tuscola.

Indexing/Storage: Cases are indexed by defendant and plaintiff as well as by case number. New cases are available in the index 24 hours after filing date. Both computer and card indexes are maintained. Records are also indexed on microfiche. Open records are located at this court. District wide searches are available for information from 1985 from this division.

Fee & Payment: The fee is $20.00 per item (one party name or case number). Payment may be made by money order, cashier check, personal check. Prepayment is required. Payee: Clerk, US District Court. Certification fee: $7.00 per document. Copy fee: $.50 per page.

Phone Search: Only docket information is available by phone.

Mail Search: Always enclose a stamped self addressed envelope.

In Person: In person searching is available.

PACER: Sign-up number is 800-676-6856. Access fee is $.60 per minute. Toll-free access: 800-229-8015. Local access: 313-234-5376. Case records are available back to 1988. New records

are available online after 2 days. PACER is available online at http://pacer.mied.uscourts.gov.

Detroit Division 231 W Lafayette Blvd, Detroit, MI 48226 (Courier Address: Use mail address for courier delivery), 313-234-5050, Fax: 313-234-5393.

http://www.mied.uscourts.gov

Counties: Macomb, St. Clair, Sanilac. Civil cases for these counties are assigned randomly among the Flint, Ann Arbor and Detroit divisions. Port Huron cases may also be assigned here. Case files are kept where the case is assigned.

Indexing/Storage: Cases are indexed by defendant and plaintiff as well as by case number. New cases are available in the index 2 days after filing date. Both computer and card indexes are maintained. A card index is maintained for older cases. Open records are located at this court. Court is in process of adding older records to the PACER system.

Fee & Payment: The fee is $20.00 per item (one party name or case number). Payment may be made by money order, cashier check, personal check. Prepayment is required for all copying. All checks should be made out for the exact amount. Payee: Clerk, US District Court. Certification fee: $7.00 per document. Copy fee: $.50 per page.

Phone Search: Only docket information on active cases will be released over the phone.

Fax Search: Court will call with costs.

Mail Search: A stamped self addressed envelope is not required.

In Person: In person searching is available.

PACER: Sign-up number is 800-676-6856. Access fee is $.60 per minute. Toll-free access: 800-229-8015. Local access: 313-234-5376. Case records are available back to 1988. New records are available online after 2 days. PACER is available online at http://pacer.mied.uscourts.gov.

Flint Division Clerk, Federal Bldg, Room 140, 600 Church St, Flint, MI 48502 (Courier Address: Use mail address for courier delivery), 810-341-7840.

Counties: Genesee, Lapeer, Livingston, Shiawassee. This office handles all criminal cases for these counties. Civil cases are assigned randomly among the Detroit, Ann Arbor and Flint divisions.

Indexing/Storage: Cases are indexed by defendant and plaintiff as well as by case number. New cases are available in the index 2-5 days after filing date. As of July 3, 1995, cases from these counties may also be assigned to Detroit, Ann Arbor or Port Huron. Case files are maintained where the case is handled. Both computer and card indexes are maintained. Records are also indexed on microfiche. The only records indexed on index cards are old Flint cases. Open records are located at this court. District wide searches are available from this division. The date the information is available varies.

Fee & Payment: The fee is $20.00 per item (one party name or case number). Payment may be made by money order, cashier check, personal check. Prepayment is required. Payee: Clerk, US District Court. Certification fee: $7.00 per document. Copy fee: $.50 per page.

Phone Search: Only general information and a reasonable number of requests will be released over the phone. All docket information will not be released.

Mail Search: A stamped self addressed envelope is not required.

In Person: In person searching is available.

PACER: Sign-up number is 800-676-6856. Access fee is $.60 per minute. Toll-free access: 800-229-8015. Local access: 313-234-5376. Case records are available back to 1988. New records are available online after 2 days. PACER is available online at http://pacer.mied.uscourts.gov.

US Bankruptcy Court

Eastern District of Michigan

Bay City Division PO Box 911, Bay City, MI 48707 (Courier Address: 111 1st St, Bay City, MI 48708), 989-894-8840.

http://www.mieb.uscourts.gov

Counties: Alcona, Alpena, Arenac, Bay, Cheboygan, Clare, Crawford, Gladwin, Gratiot, Huron, Iosco, Isabella, Midland, Montmorency, Ogemaw, Oscoda, Otsego, Presque Isle, Roscommon, Saginaw, Tuscola.

Indexing/Storage: Cases are indexed by debtor as well as by case number. New cases are available in the index immediately after filing date. Both computer and card indexes are maintained. Open records are located at this court. District wide searches are available from this division for records filed on or after 10/1/92.

Fee & Payment: The fee is $20.00 per item (one party name or case number). Payment may be made by money order, cashier check, personal check. Prepayment is required. Payee: US Bankruptcy Court. Certification fee: $7.00 per document. Copy fee: $.50 per page.

Phone Search: Use VCIS to obtain docket information. An automated voice case information service (VCIS) is available. Call VCIS at 877-422-3066 or 313-961-4940.

Mail Search: Always enclose a stamped self addressed envelope.

In Person: In person searching is available.

PACER: Sign-up number is 800-676-6856. Access fee is $.60 per minute. Toll-free access: 800-498-5061. Local access: 313-961-4934. Case records are available back to October 1, 1992. New civil records are available online after 1-2 days. PACER is available online at http://pacer.mieb.uscourts.gov.

Detroit Division Clerk, 21st Floor, 211 W Fort St, Detroit, MI 48226 (Courier Address: Use mail address for courier delivery), 313-234-0065.

http://www.mieb.uscourts.gov

Counties: Jackson, Lenawee, Macomb, Monroe, Oakland, Sanilac, St. Clair, Washtenaw, Wayne.

Indexing/Storage: Cases are indexed by debtor as well as by case number. New cases are available in the index immediately after filing date. A computer index is maintained. Open records are located at this court. District wide searches are available from this division for records filed on or after 10/1/92.

Fee & Payment: The fee is $20.00 per item (one party name or case number). Payment may be made by money order, cashier check, business check. Personal checks are not accepted. Prepayment is required. Payee: US Bankruptcy Court. Certification fee: $7.00 per document. Copy fee: $.50 per page.

Phone Search: Only the case number, case name, filing date, chapter, 341 date, attorney and trustee names will be released. An automated voice case information service (VCIS) is available. Call VCIS at 877-422-3066 or 313-961-4940.

Mail Search: Always enclose a stamped self addressed envelope.

In Person: In person searching is available.

PACER: Sign-up number is 800-676-6856. Access fee is $.60 per minute. Toll-free access: 800-498-5061. Local access: 313-961-4934. Case records are available back to October 1, 1992. New civil records are available online after 1-2 days. PACER is available online at http://pacer.mieb.uscourts.gov.

Flint Division
226 W 2nd St, Flint, MI 48502 (Courier Address: Use mail address for courier delivery), 810-235-4126.

http://www.mieb.uscourts.gov

Counties: Genesee, Lapeer, Livingston, Shiawassee.

Indexing/Storage: Cases are indexed by debtor as well as by case number. New cases are available in the index immediately after filing date. Both computer and card indexes are maintained. Open records are located at this court. District wide searches are available from this division for records filed on or after 10/1/92.

Fee & Payment: The fee is $20.00 per item (one party name or case number). Payment may be made by money order, cashier check, business check. Personal checks are not accepted. Prepayment is required. Payee: Clerk, US Bankruptcy Court. Certification fee: $7.00 per document. Copy fee: $.50 per page.

Phone Search: Only the case number, case name, filing date, chapter, 341 date, attorney and trustee names will be released. An automated voice case information service (VCIS) is available. Call VCIS at 877-422-3066 or 313-961-4940.

Mail Search: Always enclose a stamped self addressed envelope.

In Person: In person searching is available.

PACER: Sign-up number is 800-676-6856. Access fee is $.60 per minute. Toll-free access: 800-498-5061. Local access: 313-961-4934. Case records are available back to October 1, 1992. New civil records are available online after 1-2 days. PACER is available online at http://pacer.mieb.uscourts.gov.

US District Court
Western District of Michigan

Grand Rapids Division
PO Box 3310, Grand Rapids, MI 49501 (Courier Address: Gerald Ford Federal Building, 110 Michigan St NW, Rm 299, Grand Rapids, MI 49503), 616-456-2693.

http://www.miwd.uscourts.gov

Counties: Antrim, Barry, Benzie, Charlevoix, Emmet, Grand Traverse, Ionia, Kalkaska, Kent, Lake, Leelanau, Manistee, Mason, Mecosta, Missaukee, Montcalm, Muskegon, Newaygo, Oceana, Osceola, Ottawa, Wexford. The Lansing and Kalamazoo Divisions also handle casesfrom these counties.

Indexing/Storage: Cases are indexed by defendant and plaintiff as well as by case number. New cases are available in the index 24-48 hours

after filing date. Both computer and card indexes are maintained. Open records are located at this court. Cases in these counties may also be tried in the Kalamazoo or Lansing courts.

Fee & Payment: The fee is $20.00 per item (one party name or case number). Payment may be made by money order, cashier check, personal check. Will bill businesses and law firms for search and copy fees only; otherwise, prepayment is required. Payee: Clerk, US District Court. Certification fee: $7.00 per document. Copy fee: $.50 per page.

Phone Search: Only docket information is available by phone.

Mail Search: Always enclose a stamped self addressed envelope.

In Person: In person searching is available.

PACER: Sign-up number is 800-676-6856. Access fee is $.60 per minute. Toll-free access: 800-547-6398. Local access: 616-732-2765. Case records are available back to September 1989. Records are never purged. New records are available online after 1-2 days. PACER is available online at http://pacer.miwd.uscourts.gov.

Electronic Filing: Electronic filing information is available online at https://ecf.miwd.uscourts.gov

Kalamazoo Division
410 W Michigan, Rm B-35, Kalamazoo, MI 49007 (Courier Address: Use mail address for courier delivery), 616-349-2922.

http://www.miwd.uscourts.gov

Counties: Allegan, Berrien, Calhoun, Cass, Kalamazoo, St. Joseph, Van Buren. Also handle cases from the counties in the Grand Rapids Division.

Indexing/Storage: Cases are indexed by defendant and plaintiff as well as by case number. New cases are available in the index 24-48 hours after filing date. Both computer and card indexes are maintained. Open records are located at this court.

Fee & Payment: The fee is $20.00 per item (one party name or case number). Payment may be made by money order, cashier check, personal check, Visa, Mastercard. Prepayment is required, except for law firms. Payee: Clerk, US District Court. Certification fee: $7.00 per document. Copy fee: $.50 per page.

Phone Search: Only docket information is available by phone.

Mail Search: Always enclose a stamped self addressed envelope.

In Person: In person searching is available.

PACER: Sign-up number is 800-676-6856. Access fee is $.60 per minute. Toll-free access: 800-547-6398. Local access: 616-732-2765. Case records are available back to September 1989. Records are never purged. New records are available online after 1-2 days. PACER is available online at http://pacer.miwd.uscourts.gov.

Electronic Filing: Electronic filing information is available online at https://ecf.miwd.uscourts.gov

Lansing Division
113 Federal Building, 315 W Allegan, Rm 101, Lansing, MI 48933 (Courier Address: Use mail address for courier delivery), 517-377-1559.

http://www.miwd.uscourts.gov

Counties: Branch, Clinton, Eaton, Hillsdale, Ingham. Also handle cases from the counties in the Grand Rapids Division.

Indexing/Storage: Cases are indexed by defendant and plaintiff as well as by case number. New cases are available in the index 24-48 hours after filing date. Both computer and card indexes are maintained. Open records are located at this court.

Fee & Payment: The fee is $20.00 per item (one party name or case number). Payment may be made by money order, cashier check, personal check, Visa, Mastercard. Prepayment is required except from businesses and law firms. Payee: Clerk, US District Court. Certification fee: $7.00 per document. Copy fee: $.50 per page.

Phone Search: Only docket information is available by phone.

Mail Search: Always enclose a stamped self addressed envelope.

In Person: In person searching is available.

PACER: Sign-up number is 800-676-6856. Access fee is $.60 per minute. Toll-free access: 800-547-6398. Local access: 616-732-2765. Case records are available back to September 1989. Records are never purged. New records are available online after 1-2 days. PACER is available online at http://pacer.miwd.uscourts.gov.

Electronic Filing: Electronic filing information is available online at https://ecf.miwd.uscourts.gov

Marquette-Northern Division
PO Box 909, Marquette, MI 49855 (Courier Address: 202 W Washington, Room 229, Marquette, MI 49855), 906-226-2117, Fax: 906-226-6735.

http://www.miwd.uscourts.gov

Counties: Alger, Baraga, Chippewa, Delta, Dickinson, Gogebic, Houghton, Iron, Keweenaw, Luce, Mackinac, Marquette, Menominee, Ontonagon, Schoolcraft.

Indexing/Storage: Cases are indexed by defendant and plaintiff as well as by case number. New cases are available in the index 24-48 hours after filing date. Both computer and card indexes are maintained. Open records are located at this court.

Fee & Payment: The fee is $20.00 per item (one party name or case number). Payment may be made by money order, cashier check, personal check, Visa, Mastercard. Prepayment is required, except from businesses and law firms. Payee: Clerk, US District Court. Certification fee: $7.00 per document. Copy fee: $.50 per page.

Phone Search: Use a credit card for telephone searching. Copies will be mailed.

Mail Search: A stamped self addressed envelope is not required.

In Person: In person searching is available.

PACER: Sign-up number is 800-676-6856. Access fee is $.60 per minute. Toll-free access: 800-547-6398. Local access: 616-732-2765. Case records are available back to September 1989. Records are never purged. New records are available online after 1-2 days. PACER is available online at http://pacer.miwd.uscourts.gov.

Electronic Filing: Electronic filing information is available online at https://ecf.miwd.uscourts.gov

US Bankruptcy Court

Western District of Michigan

Grand Rapids Division PO Box 3310, Grand Rapids, MI 49501 (Courier Address: 110 Michigan NW, Grand Rapids, MI 49503), 616-456-2693, Fax: 616-456-2919.

http://www.miwb.uscourts.gov

Counties: Allegan, Antrim, Barry, Benzie, Berrien, Branch, Calhoun, Cass, Charlevoix, Clinton, Eaton, Emmet, Grand Traverse, Hillsdale, Ingham, Ionia, Kalamazoo, Kalkaska, Kent, Lake, Leelanau, Manistee, Mason, Mecosta, Missaukee, Montcalm, Muskegon, Newaygo,Oceana, Osceola, Ottawa, St. Joseph, Van Buren, Wexford.

Indexing/Storage: Cases are indexed by debtor and creditors as well as by case number. New cases are available in the index immediately after filing date. A computer index is maintained. Records are on the computer from 1990. Open records are located at this court.

Fee & Payment: The fee is $20.00 per item (one party name or case number). Payment may be made by money order, cashier check, personal check, Visa or Mastercard. Will bill for charges less than $10.00. Checks will not be accepted from debtors. Payee: US Bankruptcy Court. Certification fee: $7.00 per document. Copy fee: $.50 per page.

Phone Search: The court will only verify by phone whether a case was filed. An automated voice case information service (VCIS) is available.

Fax Search: Will accept fax requests for $15.00 in advance. Will fax back results of a search.

Mail Search: Always enclose a stamped self addressed envelope.

In Person: In person searching is available.

PACER: Sign-up number is 800-676-6856. Access fee is $.60 per minute. Toll-free access: 800-526-0342. Local access: 616-456-2415. Case records are available back to September 1989. Records are purged six months after case closed. New civil records are available online after 1 day. PACER is available online at http://pacer.miwb.uscourts.gov.

Marquette Division PO Box 909, Marquette, MI 49855 (Courier Address: 202 W Washington, Room 314, Marquette, MI 49855), 906-226-2117, Fax: 906-226-7388.

http://www.miwb.uscourts.gov

Counties: Alger, Baraga, Chippewa, Delta, Dickinson, Gogebic, Houghton, Iron, Keweenaw, Luce, Mackinac, Marquette, Menominee, Ontonagon, Schoolcraft.

Indexing/Storage: Cases are indexed by debtor as well as by case number. New cases are available in the index immediately after filing date. A computer index is maintained. Records are on

computer from 1990. Open records are located at this court.

Fee & Payment: The fee is $20.00 per item (one party name or case number). Payment may be made by money order, cashier check, personal check, Visa or Mastercard. Court will bill for charges totaling less than $10.00. Checks from a debtor are not accepted. Payee: US Bankruptcy Court. Certification fee: $7.00 per document. Copy fee: $.50 per page.

Phone Search: The court will only verify by phone if a case is filed. An automated voice case information service (VCIS) is available.

Fax Search: Will accept searches by fax with a credit card. Will fax copies at $.50 per page plus search fee.

Mail Search: For the fee, the following items will be sent: Case number, list of creditors, and when the first meeting of creditors is scheduled. A stamped self addressed envelope is not required.

In Person: In person searching is available.

PACER: Sign-up number is 800-676-6856. Access fee is $.60 per minute. Toll-free access: 800-526-0342. Local access: 616-456-2415. Case records are available back to September 1989. Records are purged six months after case closed. New civil records are available online after 1 day. PACER records are available online at http://pacer.miwb.uscourts.gov.

Michigan County Courts

Court	Jurisdiction	No. of Courts	How Organized
Circuit Courts*	General	83	57 Circuits
District Courts*	Limited	150	101 Districts
Municipal Courts	Municipal	5	
Probate Courts*	Probate	82	

* Profiled in this Sourcebook.

Court	CIVIL								
	Tort	Contract	Real Estate	Min. Claim	Max. Claim	Small Claims	Estate	Eviction	Domestic Relations
Circuit Courts*	X	X	X	$25,000	No Max				X
District Courts*	X	X	X	$0	$25,000	$1750		X	
Municipal Courts	X	X	X	$0	$1500	$1750			
Probate Courts*							X		

Court	CRIMINAL				
	Felony	Misdemeanor	DWI/DUI	Preliminary Hearing	Juvenile
Circuit Courts*	X				X
District Courts*		X	X	X	
Municipal Courts		X	X	X	
Probate Courts*					

ADMINISTRATION State Court Administrator, 309 N. Washington Sq, PO Box 30048, Lansing, MI, 48909; 517-373-2222, Fax: 517-373-2112. www.supremecourt.state.mi.us

COURT STRUCTURE The Circuit Court is the court of general jurisdiction. District Courts and Municipal Courts have jurisdiction over certain minor felonies and handle all preliminary hearings.

There is a Court of Claims in Lansing that is a function of the 30th Circuit Court with jurisdiction over claims against the state of Michigan.

A Recorder's Court in Detroit was abolished as of October 1, 1997.

As of January 1, 1998, the Family Division of the Circuit Court was created. Domestic relations actions and juvenile cases, including criminal and abuse/neglect, formerly adjudicated in the Probate Court, were transferred to the Family Division of the Circuit Court. Mental health and estate cases continue to be handled by the Probate Courts.

As of January 1, 1998, the limit for civil actions brought in District Court was raised from $10,000 to $25,000. The minimum for civil actions brought in Circuit Court was also raised to $25,000 at that time.

ONLINE ACCESS There is a wide range of online computerization of the judicial system from "none" to "fairly complete," but there is no statewide court records network. Some Michigan courts provide public access terminals in clerk's offices, and some courts are developing off-site electronic filing and searching capability. A few offer remote online to the public. The Criminal Justice Information Center (CJIC), the repository for MI criminal record info, offers online access, but the requester must be a business. Results are available in seconds; fee is $5.00 per name. For more information, call 517-322-5546.

ADDITIONAL INFORMATION Court records are considered public except for specific categories: controlled substances, spousal abuse, Holmes youthful trainee, parental kidnapping, set aside convictions and probation, and sealed records. Courts will, however, affirm that cases exist and provide case numbers.

Some courts will not perform criminal searches. Rather, they refer requests to the State Police.

Note that costs, search requirements, and procedures vary widely because each jurisdiction may create its own administrative orders.

Alcona County

26th Circuit Court PO Box 308, Harrisville, MI 48740; 989-724-6807; Fax: 989-724-5838. Hours: 8:30AM-Noon, 1-4:30PM (EST). *Felony, Civil Actions Over $25,000.*

Civil Records: Access: Phone, mail, in person. Only the court performs in person searches; visitors may not. No search fee. Required to search: name, years to search. Civil cases indexed by defendant, plaintiff. Civil records on computer since 1990, pleading headings in books since 1869.

Criminal Records: Access: Phone, mail, in person. Only the court performs in person searches; visitors may not. No search fee. Required to search: name, years to search, DOB. Criminal records on computer since 1990, pleading headings in books since 1869.

General Information: No suppressed, juvenile, sex offenders, mental health, or adoption records released. SASE required. Turnaround time 1-2 days. Copy fee: $1.00 per page. Certification fee: $10.00 plus $1.00 per page after first. Fee payee: Alcona County Clerk. Personal checks accepted. Prepayment is required.

82nd District Court PO Box 385, Harrisville, MI 48740; 989-724-5313; Fax: 989-724-5397. Hours: 8:30AM-4:30PM (EST). *Misdemeanor, Civil Actions Under $25,000, Eviction, Small Claims.*

Civil Records: Access: Phone, fax, mail, in person. Both court and visitors may perform in person searches. Search fee: $2.00. Required to search: name, years to search. Civil cases indexed by defendant, plaintiff. Civil records on books since 1980; on computer to 1997.

Criminal Records: Access: Fax, mail, in person. Both court and visitors may perform in person searches. Search fee: $2.00. Required to search: name, years to search, DOB; also helpful: SSN. Criminal records on books since 1980; on computer back to 1997.

General Information: No suppressed, juvenile, sex offenders, mental health, or adoption records released. SASE required. Turnaround time 1 week. Fax notes: Fee to fax results is $10.00 1st page, $1.00 each add'l. Copy fee: $1.00 per page. Certification fee: $15.00. Fee payee: 82nd District Court. Personal checks accepted. Prepayment is required.

Probate Court PO Box 328, Harrisville, MI 48740; 989-724-6880; Fax: 989-724-6397. Hours: 8:30AM-4:30PM (EST). *Probate.*

Alger County

11th Circuit Court 101 Court St, PO Box 538, Munising, MI 49862; 906-387-2076; Fax: 906-387-2156. Hours: 8AM-4PM (EST). *Felony, Civil Actions Over $25,000.*

www.courts.net/mi/alger.htm

Civil Records: Access: Phone, mail, in person. Only the court performs in person searches; visitors may not. No search fee. Required to search: name, years to search. Civil cases indexed by defendant, plaintiff. Civil records on index books.

Criminal Records: Access: Phone, mail, in person. Only the court performs in person searches; visitors may not. No search fee. Required to search: name, years to search. Criminal records on index books.

General Information: No juvenile, sex offenders, mental health, or adoption records released. Turnaround time 1 week. Copy fee: $1.00 per page. Certification fee: $10.00 plus $1.00 per page after first. Fee payee: Alger County Clerk. Personal checks accepted.

93rd District Court PO Box 186, Munising, MI 49862; 906-387-3879; Fax: 906-387-2688. Hours: 8AM-4PM (EST). *Misdemeanor, Civil Actions Under $25,000, Eviction, Small Claims.*

Civil Records: Access: Fax, mail, in person. Only the court performs in person searches; visitors may not. No search fee. Required to search: name, years to search. Civil cases indexed by defendant, plaintiff. Civil records on index books from 1984.

Criminal Records: Access: Fax, mail, in person. Only the court performs in person searches; visitors may not. No search fee. Required to search: name, years to search, DOB. Criminal records on index books from 1984.

General Information: No suppressed records released. SASE required. Turnaround time 5-7 days. Copy fee: $.25 per page. Certification fee: $15.00. Fee payee: District Court. Business checks accepted.

Probate Court 101 Court St, Munising, MI 49862; 906-387-2080; Fax: 906-387-2200. Hours: 8AM-Noon, 1-4PM (EST). *Probate.*

Allegan County

48th Circuit Court 113 Chestnut St, Allegan, MI 49010; 616-673-0300; Fax: 616-673-0298. Hours: 8AM-5PM (EST). *Felony, Civil Actions Over $25,000.*

Civil Records: Access: Mail, in person. Only the court performs in person searches; visitors may not. No search fee. Required to search: name, years to search. Civil cases indexed by defendant, plaintiff. Civil records on computer since 1985.

Criminal Records: Access: Mail, in person. Only the court performs in person searches; visitors may not. No search fee. Required to search: name, years to search, DOB; also helpful: SSN. Criminal records on computer since 1985.

General Information: No suppressed, juvenile, sex offenders, mental health, or adoption records released. SASE required. Turnaround time 1-7 days. Copy fee: $1.00 per page. Certification fee: $10.00. Fee payee: Allegan County Clerk. Personal checks accepted. Visa, MasterCard accepted for fax filings only. Prepayment is required.

57th District Court 113 Chestnut St, Allegan, MI 49010; 616-673-0400. Hours: 8AM-5PM (EST). *Misdemeanor, Civil Actions Under $25,000, Eviction, Small Claims.*

Civil Records: Access: In person only. Both court and visitors may perform in person searches. No search fee. Required to search: name, years to search. Civil cases indexed by defendant, plaintiff. Civil records on index books.

Criminal Records: Access: In person only. Both court and visitors may perform in person searches. No search fee. Required to search: name, years to search, DOB. Criminal records on index books.

General Information: Public Access terminal is available. No suppressed or sex offenders records released. Copy fee: $1.00 per page.

Probate Court 2243 33rd St, Allegan, MI 49010; 616-673-0250; Fax: 616-673-2200. Hours: 8AM-5PM (EST). *Probate.*

Alpena County

26th Circuit Court 720 West Chisholm, Alpena, MI 49707; 989-356-0115; Fax: 989-356-6559. Hours: 8:30AM-4:30PM (EST). *Felony, Civil Actions Over $25,000.*

Civil Records: Access: Fax, mail, in person. Only the court performs in person searches; visitors may not. Search fee: $5.00 per name. Required to search: name, years to search. Civil cases indexed by defendant, plaintiff. Civil records on computer since 1988, prior on docket books.

Criminal Records: Access: Fax, mail, in person. Only the court performs in person searches; visitors may not. Search fee: $5.00 per name. Required to search: name, years to search. Criminal records on computer since 1988; prior on docket books.

General Information: No suppressed, juvenile, sex offenders, mental health, or adoption records released. SASE required. Turnaround time 3-4 days. Fax notes: Fax fee $5.00 per document plus $1.00 per page. Copy fee: $1.00 per page. Certification fee: $10.00 plus $1.00 per page after first. Fee payee: County Clerk. Personal checks accepted. Prepayment is required.

88th District Court 719 West Chisholm #3, Alpena, MI 49707; 989-354-3330; Fax: 989-358-9127. Hours: 8:30AM-4:30PM (EST). *Misdemeanor, Civil Actions Under $25,000, Eviction, Small Claims.*

Civil Records: Access: Fax, mail, in person. Only the court performs in person searches; visitors may not. No search fee. Required to search: name, years to search. Civil cases indexed by defendant, plaintiff. Civil records on computer back to 1989, prior on cards back to 1970s.

Criminal Records: Access: Fax, mail, in person. Only the court performs in person searches; visitors may not. No search fee. Required to search: name, years to search, DOB; also helpful: SSN. Criminal records on computer back to 1989, prior on cards back to 1970s.

General Information: No suppressed, juvenile, sex offenders, mental health, or adoption records released. SASE required. Turnaround time 1-2 days. Copy fee: $1.00 per page. Certification fee: No cert fee. Fee payee: 88th District Court. Only cashiers checks and money orders accepted. Prepayment is required.

Probate Court 719 West Chisholm St, Alpena, MI 49707; 989-354-8785; Fax: 989-356-3665. Hours: 8:30AM-4:30PM (EST). *Probate.*

Antrim County

13th Circuit Court PO Box 520, Bellaire, MI 49615; 231-533-6353; Fax: 231-533-6935. Hours: 8:30AM-5PM *Felony, Civil Actions Over $25,000.*

Civil Records: Access: Fax, mail, in person. Both court and visitors may perform in person searches. Search fee: $5.00 per name. Required to search: name, years to search. Civil cases indexed by defendant, plaintiff. Civil records on computer since 1977, prior on books. Only court can search on computer, in person searchers may look at old records on docket books.

Criminal Records: Access: Fax, mail, in person. Both court and visitors may perform in person searches. Search fee: $5.00 per name. Required to search: name, years to search; also helpful: SSN, DOB. Criminal records on books from 1800s, on computer since 1997. Only court can search on computer, in person searchers may review old docket books.

General Information: No suppressed, juvenile, sex offenders, mental health, or adoption records released. SASE required. Turnaround time 1 week. Fax notes: $5.00 per document. Copy fee: $1.00 per page. Certification fee: $10.00 plus $1.00 per page. Fee payee: Antrim County Clerk. Prepayment is required.

86th District Court PO Box 597, Bellaire, MI 49615; 231-533-6441; Fax: 231-533-6322. Hours: 8AM-4:30PM (EST). *Misdemeanor, Civil Actions Under $25,000, Eviction, Small Claims.*

Civil Records: Access: Fax, mail, in person. Only the court performs in person searches; visitors may not. No search fee. Required to search: name, years to search. Civil cases indexed by defendant, plaintiff. Civil records on computer since 1985, prior on cards.

Criminal Records: Access: Fax, mail, in person. Only the court performs in person searches; visitors may not. No search fee. Required to search: name, years to search, DOB; also helpful: SSN. Criminal records on computer since 1985, prior on cards.

General Information: No suppressed, sex offenders records released. SASE not required. Turnaround time same day. Copy fee: $.30 per page. Certification fee: $10.00. Fee payee: District Court. Business checks accepted. Prepayment is required.

Probate Court 205 Cayuga St, PO Box 130, Bellaire, MI 49615; 231-533-6681; Fax: 231-533-6600. Hours: 8:30AM-4:30PM (EST). *Probate.*

Arenac County

34th Circuit Court 120 N Grove St, PO Box 747, Standish, MI 48658; 989-846-9186; Fax: 989-846-6757. Hours: 8:30AM-5PM (EST). *Felony, Civil Actions Over $25,000.*

Civil Records: Access: Mail, in person. Only the court performs in person searches; visitors may not. Search fee: $5.00 per name. Required to search: name, years to search. Civil cases indexed by defendant, plaintiff. Civil records on computer back to 1990, prior on index books.

Criminal Records: Access: Mail, in person. Only the court performs in person searches; visitors may not. Search fee: $5.00 per name. Required to search: name, years to search, DOB; also helpful: SSN. Criminal records on computer back to 1990, prior on index books.

General Information: No suppressed, juvenile, mental health, or adoption records released. SASE required. Turnaround time 1-5 days. Fax notes: Will not fax results. Copy fee: $1.00 per page. Certification fee: $10.00 plus $1.00 per page after first. Fee payee: Arenac County Clerk. Personal checks accepted. Prepayment is required.

81st District Court PO Box 129, Standish, MI 48658; 989-846-9538; Fax: 989-846-2008. Hours: 8:30AM-5PM (EST). *Misdemeanor, Civil Actions Under $25,000, Eviction, Small Claims.*

Civil Records: Access: Phone, fax, mail, in person. Only the court performs in person searches; visitors may not. No search fee. Required to search: name, years to search. Civil cases indexed by defendant, plaintiff. Civil records on computer since 1990, prior on docket books.

Criminal Records: Access: Phone, fax, mail, in person. Only the court performs in person searches; visitors may not. No search fee. Required to search: name, years to search, DOB; also helpful: SSN. Criminal records on computer since 1990, prior on cards by name.

General Information: No suppressed, juvenile, sex offenders, mental health, or adoption records released. SASE required. Turnaround time 5 days. Fax notes: $2.00 for first page, $.50 each add'l. No charge for fax cover sheet. Copy fee: $.25 per page. Certification fee: No cert fee. Fee payee: 81st District Court. Personal checks accepted. Prepayment is required.

Probate Court 120 N Grove, PO Box 666, Standish, MI 48658; 989-846-6941; Fax: 989-846-6757. Hours: 9AM-5PM (EST). *Probate.*

Baraga County

12th Circuit Court 16 North 3rd St, L'Anse, MI 49946; 906-524-6183; Fax: 906-524-6186. Hours: 8:30AM-4:30PM (EST). *Felony, Civil Actions Over $25,000.*

Civil Records: Access: Phone, mail, in person. Both court and visitors may perform in person searches. No search fee. Required to search: name, years to search.

Civil cases indexed by defendant, plaintiff. Civil records on docket books and are not computerized.

Criminal Records: Access: Phone, mail, in person. Both court and visitors may perform in person searches. No search fee. Required to search: name, years to search, DOB; also helpful: SSN. Criminal records on docket books and are not computerized.

General Information: No suppressed records released. SASE required. Turnaround time same day. Copy fee: $2.00 per page. Certification fee: $10.00 plus $2.00 per page after first. Fee payee: County Clerk. Personal checks accepted. Prepayment is required.

97th District Court 16 North 3rd St, L'Anse, MI 49946; 906-524-6109; Fax: 906-524-6186. Hours: 8:30AM-Noon,1-4:30PM (EST). *Misdemeanor, Civil Actions Under $25,000, Eviction, Small Claims.*

Civil Records: Access: Mail, in person. Only the court performs in person searches; visitors may not. Search fee: $5.00 per name. Required to search: name, years to search. Civil cases indexed by defendant, plaintiff. Civil records listed on docket books since 1968.

Criminal Records: Access: Mail, in person. Only the court performs in person searches; visitors may not. Search fee: $5.00 per name. Required to search: name, years to search, DOB; also helpful: SSN. Criminal records listed on docket books since 1968.

General Information: No suppressed, sex offenders records released. SASE requested. Turnaround time 2-3 days. Copy fee: $5.00 per page. Certification fee: $10.00 plus $1.00 per page after first. Fee payee: 97th District Court. Personal checks accepted. Prepayment is required.

Probate Court County Courthouse, 16 N 3rd St, L'Anse, MI 49946; 906-524-6390; Fax: 906-524-6186. Hours: 8:30AM-Noon, 1-4:30PM (EST). *Probate.*

Barry County

5th Circuit Court 220 West State St, Hastings, MI 49058; 616-948-4810; Fax: 616-945-0209. Hours: 8AM-5PM (EST). *Felony, Civil Actions Over $25,000.*

Civil Records: Access: Fax, mail, in person. Only the court performs in person searches; visitors may not. Search fee: $5.00 per name. Required to search: name, years to search. Civil cases indexed by defendant, plaintiff. Civil records on computer since 1992, card index back to 1977, prior on books.

Criminal Records: Access: Fax, mail, in person. Only the court performs in person searches; visitors may not. Search fee: $5.00 per name. Required to search: name, years to search, DOB; also helpful: SSN. Criminal records on computer since 1992, card index back to 1977, prior on books.

General Information: No suppressed, juvenile, sex offenders, mental health, or adoption records released. SASE required. Turnaround time 2 days. Fax notes: $1.00 per page. Copy fee: $1.00 per page. Certification fee: $10.00. Fee payee: County Clerk. Personal checks accepted. Prepayment is required.

56B District Court 220 West Court St, Suite 202, Hastings, MI 49058; 616-945-1404; Fax: 616-948-3314. Hours: 8AM-5PM (EST). *Misdemeanor, Civil Actions Under $25,000, Eviction, Small Claims.*

Civil Records: Access: Phone, fax, mail, in person. Only the court performs in person searches; visitors may not. Search fee: $5.00 per name. Required to search: name, years to search. Civil cases indexed by defendant, plaintiff. Civil records on computer since 1990, prior on index books.

Criminal Records: Access: Phone, fax, mail, in person. Only the court performs in person searches; visitors may not. Search fee: $5.00 per name. Required to search: name, years to search, DOB; also helpful: SSN. Criminal records on computer since 1990, prior on index books.

General Information: No suppressed, sex offenders, or mental health records released. SASE required. Turnaround time 2 days. Fax notes: $1.00 per page. Copy fee: $.25 per page. Certification fee: $10.00 plus $1.00 per page after first. Fee payee: 56B District Court. Personal checks accepted. Prepayment is required.

Probate Court 220 West Court St, Suite 302, Hastings, MI 49058; 616-948-4842; Fax: 616-948-3322. Hours: 8AM-5PM (EST). *Probate.*

Bay County

18th Circuit Court 1230 Washington Ave, Bay City, MI 48708; 989-895-2066; Fax: 989-895-4099. Hours: 8AM-5PM (EST). *Felony, Civil Actions Over $25,000.*

Civil Records: Access: Phone, fax, mail, in person. Only the court performs in person searches; visitors may not. No search fee. Required to search: name, years to search. Civil cases indexed by defendant, plaintiff. Civil records on computer for the last since 1986.

Criminal Records: Access: Phone, fax, mail, in person. Only the court performs in person searches; visitors may not. No search fee. Required to search: name, years to search, DOB. Criminal records on computer for the last since 1986.

General Information: No suppressed records released. SASE requested. Turnaround time same day. Copy fee: $.25 per page. Certification fee: $10.00. Fee payee: County Clerk. Personal checks accepted. Prepayment is required.

74th District Court 1230 Washington Ave, Bay City, MI 48708; 989-895-4232; Fax: 989-895-4233. Hours: 8AM-5PM (EST). *Misdemeanor, Civil Actions Under $25,000, Eviction, Small Claims.*

Civil Records: Access: In person only. Visitors must perform in person searches for themselves. No search fee. Required to search: name, years to search. Civil cases indexed by defendant, plaintiff. Civil records on computer since 1992, listed on index cards prior.

Criminal Records: Access: In person only. Visitors must perform in person searches for themselves. No search fee. Required to search: name, years to search, DOB; also helpful: SSN. Criminal records on computer since 1992, listed on index cards prior.

General Information: No suppressed, juvenile, sex offenders, mental health, or adoption records released. Copy fee: $1.00 per page. Certification fee: $10.00. Fee payee: 74th District Court. Personal checks accepted. Prepayment is required.

Probate Court 1230 Washington, Ste 715, Bay City, MI 48708; 989-895-4205; Fax: 989-895-4194. Hours: 8AM-5PM; Summer hours 7:30AM-4PM (EST). *Probate.*

Benzie County

19th Circuit Court PO Box 377, Beulah, MI 49617; 231-882-9671 & 800-315-3593; Fax: 231-882-5941. Hours: 8AM-5PM (EST). *Felony, Civil Actions Over $25,000.*

Civil Records: Access: Phone, fax, mail, in person. Both court and visitors may perform in person searches. No search fee. Required to search: name, years to search. Civil cases indexed by defendant, plaintiff. Civil records on computer since 1980, prior on docket books.

Criminal Records: Access: Phone, fax, mail, in person. Both court and visitors may perform in person searches. No search fee. Required to search: name, years to search. Criminal records on computer since 1980, prior listed in docket books.

General Information: Public Access terminal is available. No suppressed or home-youthful training case records released. SASE not available. Turnaround time 1-2 days. Fax notes: $3.00 for first page, $1.00 each add'l. Copy fee: $.50 per page. Certification fee: $10.00

plus $1.00 per page after first. Fee payee: Benzie County Clerk. Personal checks accepted. Prepayment is required.

85th District Court
PO Box 377, Beulah, MI 49617; 800-759-5175 231-882-0019; Fax: 231-882-0022. Hours: 9AM-5PM (EST). *Misdemeanor, Civil Actions Under $25,000, Eviction, Small Claims.*

Civil Records: Access: Fax, mail, in person. Only the court performs in person searches; visitors may not. Search fee: $3.00 per name. Required to search: name, years to search. Civil cases indexed by defendant, plaintiff. Civil records on computer back to 1990, prior on cards to 1965.

Criminal Records: Access: Fax, mail, in person. Only the court performs in person searches; visitors may not. Search fee: $3.00 per name. Required to search: name, years to search, DOB; also helpful: SSN. Criminal records on computer back to 1990, prior on cards to 1965.

General Information: Public Access terminal is available. No suppressed, juvenile, sex offenders, mental health, or adoption records released. SASE required. Turnaround time 1 week. Fax notes: $3.00 for first page, $1.00 each add'l. Copy fee: $1.00 per page. Certification fee: $10.00. Fee payee: 85th District Court. Personal checks accepted. Out of state checks not accepted. Prepayment is required.

Probate Court
448 Court Place, County Gov't Ctr., PO Box 377, Beulah, MI 49617; 231-882-9675; Fax: 231-882-5987. Hours: 8:30AM-Noon, 1-5PM (EST). *Probate.*

Berrien County

2nd Circuit Court
811 Port St, St Joseph, MI 49085; 616-983-7111 X8574; Fax: 616-982-8647. Hours: 8:30AM-4PM (EST). *Felony, Civil Actions Over $25,000.*

Civil Records: Access: Mail, in person. Only the court performs in person searches; visitors may not. Search fee: $5.00 per name. Required to search: name, years to search. Civil cases indexed by defendant, plaintiff. Civil records on computer since 1981, prior on books (domestic) back to 1835, (civil & criminal) back to 1837.

Criminal Records: Access: Mail, in person. Only the court performs in person searches; visitors may not. Search fee: $5.00 per name. Required to search: name, years to search, DOB; also helpful: SSN. Criminal records on computer since 1981, prior on books (domestic) back to 1835, (civil & criminal) back to 1837.

General Information: No suppressed, juvenile, sex offenders, mental health, or adoption records released. SASE required. Turnaround time 2-3 days. Copy fee: $1.00 per page. Certification fee: $10.00 plus $1.00 per page after first. Fee payee: Berrien County Clerk. Personal checks accepted. Prepayment is required.

5th District Court - Trial Court Criminal Division
Attn: Records, 811 Port St, St Joseph, MI 49085; 616-983-7111; Fax: 616-982-8643. Hours: 8:30AM-4PM (EST). *Misdemeanor, Civil Actions Under $25,000, Eviction, Small Claims.*

www.berriencounty.org

Civil Records: Access: Mail, in person. Only the court performs in person searches; visitors may not. Search fee: $5.00 per name. Required to search: name, years to search; also helpful: address. Civil cases indexed by defendant, plaintiff. Civil records on computer since 1988, on logs from 1976-87, on index cards from 1969-75. Will do civil record check searches for only seven years.

Criminal Records: Access: Mail, in person. Only the court performs in person searches; visitors may not. Search fee: $5.00 per name. Required to search: name,

years to search, DOB; also helpful: address, SSN. Criminal records on computer back ten years, on microfiche back to 1970.

General Information: No suppressed or mental health records released. SASE not required. Turnaround time 5 days. Copy fee: $1.00 per page. Certification fee: $10.00 plus $1.00 per page after first. Fee payee: 5th District Court. Personal checks accepted. Prepayment is required.

Probate Court
811 Port St., St Joseph, MI 49085; 616-983-7111 X8365; Fax: 616-982-8644. Hours: 8:30AM-5PM (EST). *Probate.*

Branch County

15th Circuit Court
31 Division St, Coldwater, MI 49036; 517-279-4306; Fax: 517-278-5627. Hours: 9AM-5PM (EST). *Felony, Civil Actions Over $25,000.*

www.co.branch.mi.us

Civil Records: Access: Mail, in person. Both court and visitors may perform in person searches. Search fee: $1.00 per name per year. Required to search: name, years to search. Civil cases indexed by defendant, plaintiff. Civil records on computer since 1988, prior in books back to 1830s.

Criminal Records: Access: Mail, in person. Both court and visitors may perform in person searches. Search fee: $1.00 per name per year. Required to search: name, years to search, DOB. Criminal records on computer since 1988, prior in books back to 1830s.

General Information: No suppressed records released. SASE not required. Turnaround time 1-5 days. Copy fee: $1.00 per page. Certification fee: $10.00 plus $1.00 per page. Fee payee: Branch County Clerk. Business checks accepted. Prepayment is required.

3A District Court
31 Division St., Coldwater, MI 49036; 517-279-4308; Fax: 517-279-4333. Hours: 8AM-5PM (EST). *Misdemeanor, Civil Actions Under $25,000, Eviction, Small Claims.*

www.branchcountycourts.com

Civil Records: Access: Phone, mail, in person. Only the court performs in person searches; visitors may not. Search fee: $10.00 per name. Required to search: name, years to search. Civil cases indexed by defendant, plaintiff. Civil records on computer since June 1991, prior on index books.

Criminal Records: Access: Phone, mail, in person. Only the court performs in person searches; visitors may not. Search fee: $10.00 per name. Required to search: name, years to search, DOB; also helpful: SSN. Criminal records on computer since Oct. 1988.

General Information: No suppressed, juvenile, sex offenders, mental health, or adoption records released. SASE requested. Turnaround time immediate if possible, otherwise 2-3 days. Copy fee: $1.00 per page. Certification fee: $10.00. Fee payee: 3A District Court. Personal checks accepted. Credit cards accepted. Prepayment is required.

Probate Court
31 Division St., Coldwater, MI 49036; 517-279-4318; Fax: 517-278-4130. Hours: 9AM-Noon, 1-5PM (EST). *Probate.*

Calhoun County

37th Circuit Court
161 East Michigan, Battle Creek, MI 49014-4066; 616-969-6518. Hours: 8AM-5PM (EST). *Felony, Civil Actions Over $25,000.*

http://courts.co.calhoun.mi.us

Civil Records: Access: Mail, in person. Both court and visitors may perform in person searches. Search fee: $5.00 per name. Required to search: name, years to search. Civil cases indexed by defendant, plaintiff. Civil records on computer since 1984, prior on microfilm. The court will provide case number, filed date, case

title, case status, and date of final judgment for the search fee.

Criminal Records: Access: In person only. Both court and visitors may perform in person searches. Search fee: $5.00 per name. Required to search: name, years to search, DOB; also helpful: SSN. Criminal records on computer since 1984, prior on microfilm. The court refers requests to the State Police (517-322-5531). Searcher may view public court file if case number known.

General Information: No suppressed, juvenile, sex offenders, mental health, or adoption records released. SASE required. Turnaround time 1 week. Copy fee: $1.00 per page. Certification fee: $10.00 plus $1.00 per page after first. Fee payee: 37th Circuit Court Clerk. Personal checks accepted. Prepayment is required.

10th District Court
161 E Michigan Ave, Battle Creek, MI 49014; 616-969-6666; Fax: 616-969-6663. Hours: 8:00AM-4PM (EST). *Misdemeanor, Civil Actions Under $25,000, Eviction, Small Claims.*

Civil Records: Access: in person only. Visitors must perform in person searches for themselves. No search fee. Required to search: name, years to search. Civil cases indexed by defendant, plaintiff. Civil records on computer since 1986, prior on docket books. Public access terminal searches back to 10/1997. Fax requests must be signed.

Criminal Records: Access: In person only. Visitors must perform in person searches for themselves. No search fee. Required to search: name, years to search, DOB. Criminal records on computer since 1986, prior on docket books. Public access terminal searches back to 10/1997. Fax requests must be signed.

General Information: Public Access terminal is available. No suppressed, juvenile, sex offenders, mental health, or adoption records released. Copy fee: $.25 per page. Certification fee: $10.00 plus $1.00 per page after first. Fee payee: 10th District Court. Personal checks accepted. Credit cards accepted: Visa, MasterCard. Prepayment is required.

10th District Court - Marshall Branch
161 E Michigan, Battle Creek, MI 49014; 616-969-6666; Fax: 616-969-6663. Hours: 8AM-4PM (EST). *Misdemeanor, Civil Actions Under $25,000, Eviction, Small Claims.*

Note: Marshall branch records and administration are now located in Battle Creek.

Civil Records: Access: In person only. Visitors must perform in person searches for themselves. No search fee. Required to search: name, years to search. Civil cases indexed by defendant, plaintiff. Civil records on computer since 1997, prior on books.

Criminal Records: Access: In person only. Visitors must perform in person searches for themselves. No search fee. Required to search: name, years to search, DOB; also helpful: SSN. Criminal records on computer since 1997, prior on books.

General Information: Public Access terminal is available. No suppressed, sex offenders, mental health, or adoption records released. Copy fee: $.25 per page. Certification fee: $10.00 plus $1.00 per page after first. Prepayment is required.

Probate Court
Justice Center, 161 E Michigan Ave, Battle Creek, MI 49014; 616-969-6794; Fax: 616-969-6797. Hours: 8AM-5PM (EST). *Probate.*

Cass County

43rd Circuit Court
120 North Broadway, File Room, Cassopolis, MI 49031; 616-445-4416 X3201; Fax: 616-445-4406. Hours: 8AM-5PM (EST). *Felony, Civil Actions Over $25,000.*

Civil Records: Access: Fax, mail, in person. Both court and visitors may perform in person searches. No search fee. Required to search: name, years to search. Civil cases indexed by defendant, plaintiff. Civil records on computer since 1989, in books since 1963.

Criminal Records: Access: Fax, mail, in person. Both court and visitors may perform in person searches. No search fee. Required to search: name, years to search, DOB; also helpful: SSN. Criminal records on computer since 1989, in books since 1963.

General Information: No suppressed, juvenile, sex offenders, mental health, or adoption records released. SASE helpful. Turnaround time 2 weeks. Fax notes: No fee to fax back to an 800 number. Copy fee: $1.00 per page. Certification fee: $10.00. Fee payee: Cass County Clerk. Business checks accepted. Prepayment is required.

4th District Court 110 North Broadway, Cassopolis, MI 49031; 616-445-4424; Fax: 616-445-4486. Hours: 8AM-5PM (EST). *Misdemeanor, Civil Actions Under $25,000, Eviction, Small Claims.*

Civil Records: Access: Phone, mail, in person. Both court and visitors may perform in person searches. No search fee. Required to search: name, years to search; also helpful: address. Civil cases indexed by defendant, plaintiff. Civil records on computer since 1988, indexed on cards prior. You can fax requests, but results will not be returned by fax.

Criminal Records: Access: Phone, mail, in person. Both court and visitors may perform in person searches. No search fee. Required to search: name, years to search, DOB; also helpful: address. Criminal records on computer since 1988, indexed on cards prior. You can fax requests, but results will not be returned by fax.

General Information: No suppressed, juvenile, sex offenders, mental health, or adoption records released. SASE not required. Turnaround time 2 weeks. Copy fee: $1.00 for first page, $.10 each add'l. Certification fee: $10.00 plus $1.00 per page after first. Fee payee: 4th District Court. Personal checks accepted. Prepayment is required.

Probate Court 110 North Broadway, Rm 202, Cassopolis, MI 49031; 616-445-4454; Fax: 616-445-4453. Hours: 8AM-Noon, 1-5PM (EST). *Probate.*

Charlevoix County

33rd Circuit Court 203 Antrim St, Charlevoix, MI 49720; 231-547-7200; Fax: 231-547-7217. Hours: 9AM-5PM (EST). *Felony, Civil Actions Over $25,000.*

Civil Records: Access: Mail, in person. Only the court performs in person searches; visitors may not. No search fee. Required to search: name, years to search. Civil cases indexed by defendant, plaintiff. Civil records on computer from 1991, microfiche and archives from 1868.

Criminal Records: Access: Mail, in person. Only the court performs in person searches; visitors may not. No search fee. Required to search: name, years to search, DOB; also helpful: SSN. Criminal records on computer from 1991, microfiche and archives from 1868.

General Information: No suppressed, juvenile, adoption records released. SASE requested. Turnaround time 1 week. Copy fee: $1.00 per page. Certification fee: $10.00. Fee payee: Charlevoix County Clerk. Personal checks accepted. Prepayment is required.

90th District Court 301 State St, Court Bldg, Charlevoix, MI 49720; 231-547-7227; Fax: 231-547-7253. Hours: 9AM-5PM (EST). *Misdemeanor, Civil Actions Under $25,000, Eviction, Small Claims.*

Civil Records: Access: Phone, mail, fax, in person. Both court and visitors may perform in person searches. No search fee. Required to search: name, years to search. Civil cases indexed by defendant, plaintiff. Civil records on computer back to 1987, listed on index cards to 1963.

Criminal Records: Access: Mail, fax, in person. Both court and visitors may perform in person searches. No

search fee. Required to search: name, years to search, DOB. Criminal records on computer back to 1987, listed on index cards to 1963.

General Information: Public Access terminal is available. No suppressed records released. SASE helpful. Turnaround time 1-2 days. Copy fee: $1.00 per page. Fee payee: 90th District Court. Personal checks accepted. Prepayment is required.

Probate Court 301 State St, County Bldg, Charlevoix, MI 49720; 231-547-7214; Fax: 231-547-7256. Hours: 9AM-5PM (EST). *Probate.*

Note: Shares the same judge with Emmet County Probate Court.

Cheboygan County

53rd Circuit Court PO Box 70, Cheboygan, MI 49721; 231-627-8808. Hours: 8:30AM-5PM (EST). *Felony, Civil Actions Over $25,000.*

Civil Records: Access: Phone, mail, in person. Only the court performs in person searches; visitors may not. No search fee. Required to search: name, years to search. Civil cases indexed by defendant, plaintiff. Civil records on computer from 1985, index cards from 1886.

Criminal Records: Access: Phone, mail, in person. Only the court performs in person searches; visitors may not. No search fee. Required to search: name, years to search, DOB. Criminal records on computer from 1985, index cards from 1886.

General Information: No suppressed records released. SASE requested. Turnaround time 3-4 days. Copy fee: $1.00 for first page, $.20 each add'l. Certification fee: $10.00 plus $1.00 each additional page. Fee payee: County Clerk. Personal checks accepted. Prepayment is required.

89th District Court PO Box 70, Cheboygan, MI 49721; 231-627-8809; Fax: 231-627-8444. Hours: 8:30AM-4PM (EST). *Misdemeanor, Civil Actions Under $25,000, Eviction, Small Claims.*

Civil Records: Access: Phone, fax, mail, in person. Only the court performs in person searches; visitors may not. No search fee. Required to search: name, years to search. Civil cases indexed by defendant, plaintiff. Civil records on computer since 1988, microfilmed prior.

Criminal Records: Access: Phone, fax, mail, in person. Only the court performs in person searches; visitors may not. No search fee. Required to search: name, years to search, DOB, SSN. Criminal records on computer since 1986.

General Information: No suppressed, juvenile, sex offenders, mental health, or adoption records released. SASE required. Turnaround time 3-4 days. Fax notes: No fee to fax results. Copy fee: $1.00 per page. Certification fee: $10.00 plus $1.00 per page after first. Fee payee: 89th District Court. Personal checks accepted. Prepayment is required.

Probate Court 870 S Main St, PO Box 70, Cheboygan, MI 49721; 231-627-8823; Fax: 231-627-8868. Hours: 9AM-5PM (EST). *Probate.*

Chippewa County

50th Circuit Court 319 Court St, Sault Ste Marie, MI 49783; 906-635-6300; Fax: 906-635-6851. Hours: 8AM-5PM (EST). *Felony, Civil Actions Over $25,000.*

Civil Records: Access: Mail, in person. Only the court performs in person searches; visitors may not. Search fee: $5.00 per name. Fee is for 10 year search. Required to search: name, years to search. Civil cases indexed by defendant, plaintiff. Civil records on computer since 1990, prior on index books.

Criminal Records: Access: Mail, in person. Only the court performs in person searches; visitors may not. Search fee: $5.00 per name. Fee is for 10 year search. Required to search: name, years to search, DOB; also

helpful: SSN. Criminal records on computer since 1990, prior on index books.

General Information: No suppressed, juvenile, sex offenders, mental health, or adoption records released. SASA not required. Turnaround time 1-2 days. Copy fee: $1.00 per page. Certification fee: $10.00 plus $1.00 per page after first. Fee payee: County Clerk. Personal checks accepted. Prepayment is required.

91st District Court 325 Court St, Sault Ste Marie, MI 49783; 906-635-6320; Fax: 906-635-7605. Hours: 9AM-4:30PM (EST). *Misdemeanor, Civil Actions Under $25,000, Eviction, Small Claims.*

Note: Call before faxing for instructions.

Civil Records: Access: Mail, fax, in person. Both court and visitors may perform in person searches. Search fee: $5.00 per name. Required to search: name, years to search. Civil cases indexed by defendant, plaintiff. Civil records on computer since 1989, prior on index books to 1968.

Criminal Records: Access: Mail, fax, in person. Both court and visitors may perform in person searches. Search fee: $5.00 per name. Required to search: name, years to search, DOB; also helpful: SSN. Criminal records on computer since 1989, prior on index books to 1968.

General Information: Public Access terminal is available. No suppressed, juvenile, sex offenders, mental health, or adoption records released. SASE required. Turnaround time 10 days. Copy fee: $1.00 per page. Certification fee: $10.00. Only cashiers checks and money orders accepted. Prepayment is required.

Probate Court 319 Court St., Sault Ste Marie, MI 49783; 906-635-6314; Fax: 906-635-6852. Hours: 9AM-5PM (EST). *Probate.*

Clare County

55th Circuit Court 225 West Main St, PO Box 438, Harrison, MI 48625; 989-539-7131; Fax: 989-539-6616. Hours: 8AM-4:30PM (EST). *Felony, Civil Actions Over $25,000.*

Civil Records: Access: Mail, in person. Only the court performs in person searches; visitors may not. Search fee: $5.00 per name. Add $1.00 per year if more than five. Required to search: name, years to search. Civil cases indexed by defendant, plaintiff. Civil records on computer since 1992, on books from 1925.

Criminal Records: Access: Mail, in person. Only the court performs in person searches; visitors may not. Search fee: $5.00 per name. Add $1.00 per year if more than five. Required to search: name, years to search, DOB; also helpful: SSN. Criminal records on computer since 1992, on books from 1925.

General Information: No suppressed, juvenile, sex offenders, mental health, or adoption records released. SASE required. Turnaround time 1-5 days. Copy fee: $1.00 per page. Certification fee: $10.00 per document plus $1.00 per page. Fee payee: Clare County Clerk. Personal checks accepted. Prepayment is required.

80th District Court 225 W. Main St, Harrison, MI 48625; 989-539-7173; Fax: 989-539-4036. Hours: 8AM-4:30PM (EST). *Misdemeanor, Civil Actions Under $25,000, Eviction, Small Claims.*

Civil Records: Access: Mail, in person. Both court and visitors may perform in person searches. No search fee. Required to search: name, years to search. Civil cases indexed by defendant, plaintiff. Civil records on computer since 1988.

Criminal Records: Access: Mail, in person. Only the court performs in person searches; visitors may not. No search fee. Required to search: name, years to search, DOB. Criminal records on computer since 1988.

General Information: No suppressed, juvenile, sex offenders, mental health, or adoption records released. SASE required. Turnaround time 1-2 days. Copy fee:

$1.00 per page. Certification fee: No cert fee. Fee payee: 80th District Court. Personal checks accepted. Prepayment is required.

Probate Court 225 W. Main St., PO Box 96, Harrison, MI 48625; 989-539-7109. Hours: 8AM-4:30PM (EST). *Probate.*

Note: This is combined with Gladwin County Probate Court.

Clinton County

29th Circuit Court PO Box 69, St Johns, MI 48879-0069; 989-224-5140; Fax: 989-224-5254. Hours: 8AM-5PM (EST). *Felony, Civil Actions Over $25,000.*

www.clinton-county.org

Civil Records: Access: Mail, in person. Both court and visitors may perform in person searches. Search fee: $10.00 per name. Fee is for 10 year search. Required to search: name, years to search. Civil cases indexed by defendant, plaintiff. Civil records in calendar books since 1800s, some on microfiche; on computer since.

Criminal Records: Access: Mail, in person. Both court and visitors may perform in person searches. Search fee: $10.00 per name. Fee is for 10 year search. Required to search: name, years to search; also helpful: DOB. Criminal records in calendar books since 1800s, some on microfiche; on computer since.

General Information: No suppressed or non public records released. SASE required. Turnaround time 24 hrs. Copy fee: $1.00 per page. Certification fee: $10.00 plus $1.00 per page. Fee payee: Clinton County Clerk. Personal checks accepted. Prepayment is required.

65th District Court 100 E State St, St Johns, MI 48879-1571; 989-224-5150; Fax: 989-224-5154. Hours: 8AM-5PM (EST). *Misdemeanor, Civil Actions Under $25,000, Eviction, Small Claims.*

Civil Records: Access: Mail, in person. Both court and visitors may perform in person searches. No search fee. Required to search: name, years to search. Civil cases indexed by defendant, plaintiff. Civil records on computer since 1989-90.

Criminal Records: Access: Mail, in person. Both court and visitors may perform in person searches. No search fee. Required to search: name, years to search, DOB, SSN. Criminal records on computer since 1986.

General Information: No suppressed, juvenile, sex offenders, mental health, or adoption records released. SASE required. Turnaround time 1 week. Copy fee: $.25 per page. Certification fee: No cert fee. Fee payee: 65th District Court. Personal checks accepted. Prepayment is required.

Probate Court 101 E State St, St Johns, MI 48879; 989-224-5190; Fax: 989-224-5254. Hours: 8AM Noon, 1-5PM (EST). *Probate.*

www.clinton-county.org

Crawford County

46th Circuit Court 200 West Michigan Ave, Grayling, MI 49738; 989-348-2841; Fax: 989-344-3223. Hours: 8AM-4:30PM (EST). *Felony, Civil Actions Over $25,000.*

www.Circuit46.org

Civil Records: Access: Mail, in person, online. No search fee. Required to search: name, years to search. Civil cases indexed by defendant, plaintiff. Civil records on computer since 1990, prior on books. Online access to court case records (open or closed cases for 90 days only) is available free at www.circuit46.org/Cases/cases.html. Search by name.

Criminal Records: Access: Mail, in person, online. Both court and visitors may perform in person searches. No search fee. Required to search: name, years to search, DOB. Criminal records on computer since 1990,

prior on books. Online access to criminal records is the same as civil.

General Information: No suppressed records released. SASE required. Turnaround time 2-3 days. Copy fee: $1.00 per page. Certification fee: $10.00 plus $1.00 per page after first. Fee payee: Crawford County. Personal checks accepted. Prepayment is required.

83rd District Court 200 West Michigan Ave., Grayling, MI 49738; 989-348-2841 X242; Fax: 989-344-3290. Hours: 8AM-4:30PM (EST). *Misdemeanor, Civil Actions Under $25,000, Eviction, Small Claims.*

www.Circuit46.org

Civil Records: Access: Phone, mail, fax, in person, online. Only the court performs in person searches; visitors may not. No search fee. Required to search: name, years to search. Civil cases indexed by defendant, plaintiff. Civil records on computer since 1990, books from 1969. Online access to court case records (open or closed cases for 90 days only) is available free at www.circuit46.org/Cases/cases.html. Search by name.

Criminal Records: Access: Phone, mail, fax, in person, online. Only the court performs in person searches; visitors may not. No search fee. Required to search: name, years to search, DOB. Criminal records on computer since 1989. Online access to criminal records is the same as civil.

General Information: No suppressed, juvenile, sex offenders, mental health, or adoption records released. SASE not required. Turnaround time 1-4 days. Copy fee: $.25 per page. Certification fee: $10.00 plus $1.00 each additional page. Fee payee: Crawford County 83rd District Court. Personal checks accepted. Credit cards accepted: Visa, MasterCard. Prepayment is required.

Probate Court 200 N Michigan Ave., Grayling, MI 49738; 989-348-2841 X237; Fax: 989-348-7582. Hours: 8:30AM-4:30PM (EST). *Probate.*

www.Circuit46.org

Delta County

47th Circuit Court 310 Ludington St, Escanaba, MI 49829; 906-789-5105; Fax: 906-789-5196. Hours: 8AM-4PM (EST). *Felony, Civil Actions Over $25,000.*

Civil Records: Access: Mail, in person. Both court and visitors may perform in person searches. Search fee: $5.00 per name. Required to search: name; also helpful: years to search, address. Civil cases indexed by defendant, plaintiff. Civil records on computer from 1989, archived into 1800s.

Criminal Records: Access: Mail, in person. Both court and visitors may perform in person searches. Search fee: $5.00 per name. Required to search: name; also helpful: years to search, DOB, SSN. Criminal records on computer from 1989, archived into 1800s.

General Information: No suppressed, juvenile, sex offenders, mental health, or adoption records released. SASE required. Turnaround time same day. Copy fee: $.25 per page. Certification fee: $10.00 plus $1.00 per page after first. Fee payee: Delta County. Personal checks accepted. Prepayment is required.

94th District Court 310 Ludington St., Escanaba, MI 49829; 906-789-5106; Fax: 906-789-5198. Hours: 8AM-4PM (EST). *Misdemeanor, Civil Actions Under $25,000, Eviction, Small Claims.*

Civil Records: Access: Mail, in person. Only the court performs in person searches; visitors may not. No search fee. Required to search: name, years to search; also helpful: address. Civil cases indexed by defendant, plaintiff. Civil records on computer back to 1988, prior on books to 1968.

Criminal Records: Access: Mail, in person. Only the court performs in person searches; visitors may not. Search fee: $5.00 per name. Required to search: name, years to search, DOB; also helpful: address, SSN.

Criminal records on computer back to 1988, prior on books to 1968.

General Information: No suppressed, juvenile, sex offenders, mental health, or adoption records released. SASE required. Turnaround time 3 days. Copy fee: $.25 per page. Certification fee: $10.00. Fee payee: 94th District Court. Personal checks accepted. Prepayment is required.

Probate Court 310 Ludington St., Escanaba, MI 49829; 906-789-5112; Fax: 906-789-5140. Hours: 8AM-Noon, 1-4PM (EST). *Probate.*

Dickinson County

41st Circuit Court PO Box 609, Iron Mountain, MI 49801; 906-774-0988; Fax: 906-774-4660. Hours: 8AM-4:30PM (CST). *Felony, Civil Actions Over $25,000.*

Civil Records: Access: Mail, in person. Both court and visitors may perform in person searches. Search fee: $15.00 per name. Fee is for 10 year search. Required to search: name, years to search. Civil cases indexed by defendant, plaintiff. Civil records on docket books since 1891; on computer since.

Criminal Records: Access: Mail, in person. Both court and visitors may perform in person searches. Search fee: $5.00 per name. Fee is for 10 year search. Required to search: name, years to search, DOB; also helpful: SSN. Criminal records on docket books since 1891; on computer since.

General Information: No suppressed, juvenile, sex offenders, mental health, or adoption records released. SASE required. Turnaround time 1-2 days. Fax notes: Fee to fax results is $1.50 per page. Copy fee: $.15 per page. Certification fee: $10.00 plus $1.00 per page. Fee payee: County Clerk. Business checks accepted. Prepayment is required.

95 B District Court County Courthouse, PO Box 609, Iron Mountain, MI 49801; 906-774-0506; Fax: 906-774-3686. Hours: 8AM-4:30PM (CST). *Misdemeanor, Civil Actions Under $25,000, Eviction, Small Claims.*

Note: May require a signed release for certain records.

Civil Records: Access: Mail, fax, in person. Both court and visitors may perform in person searches. Search fee: $5.00 per name if pre-2/1995. Required to search: name, years to search; also helpful: address. Civil cases indexed by defendant, plaintiff. Civil records on index cards from 1981; on computer back to 2/1995.

Criminal Records: Access: Mail, fax, in person. Both court and visitors may perform in person searches. Search fee: $5.00 per name if pre-2/1995. Required to search: name, years to search, DOB; also helpful: address, SSN. Criminal records on index cards from 1981; on computer back to 2/1995.

General Information: No suppressed, juvenile, sex offenders, mental health, or adoption records released. Turnaround time 1 week. Copy fee: $1.00 per page. Certification fee: $10.00. Fee payee: 95-B District Court. Only cashiers checks and money orders accepted. Prepayment is required.

Probate Court PO Box 609, Iron Mountain, MI 49801; 906-774-1555; Fax: 906-774-1561. Hours: 8AM-4:30PM (CST). *Probate.*

Eaton County

56th Circuit Court 1045 Independence Blvd, Charlotte, MI 48813; 517-543-7500 X396; Fax: 517-543-4475. Hours: 8AM-5PM (EST). *Felony, Civil Actions Over $25,000.*

www.co.eaton.mi.us/COURTS/COURTS.HTM

Civil Records: Access: Phone, fax, mail, in person. Both court and visitors may perform in person searches. Search fee: $5.00 per name. Required to search: name, years to search. Civil cases indexed by defendant, plaintiff. Civil records on computer back to 1988, microfilm since 1930s, books from 1848.

Criminal Records: Access: Fax, mail, in person. Both court and visitors may perform in person searches. Search fee: $5.00 per name. Required to search: name, years to search, DOB; also helpful: SSN. Criminal records on computer back to 1985, microfilm since 1930s, books from 1860s.

General Information: No suppressed, juvenile, sex offenders, mental health, or adoption records released. SASE required. Turnaround time 1-3 days. Copy fee: $1.00 for first page, $.50 each add'l. Certification fee: $10.00. Fee payee: Eaton County Circuit Court Clerk. Personal checks accepted. Prepayment is required.

56th District Court 1045 Independence Blvd, Charlotte, MI 48813; 517-543-7500; Civil phone: X294; Criminal phone: X282; Fax: 517-543-7377. Hours: 8AM-5PM (EST). *Misdemeanor, Civil Actions Under $25,000, Eviction, Small Claims.*

www.co.eaton.mi.us/COURTS/COURTS.HTM

Note: A more complete criminal record check may be requested in writing through Mich. State Police Central Records Bureau, call 517-322-5531 for further information.

Civil Records: Access: Mail, fax, in person. Both court and visitors may perform in person searches. No search fee. Required to search: name, years to search. Civil records on computer back to 1990; prior in books.

Criminal Records: Access: In person only. Visitors must perform in person searches for themselves. No search fee. Required to search: name, years to search, DOB; also helpful: SSN. Criminal records on computer since 1990, prior on books.

General Information: Public Access terminal is available. No suppressed, juvenile, sex offenders, mental health, or adoption records released. SASE required. Turnaround time 2-3 days. Copy fee: $.25 per page. Certification fee: $10.00. Fee payee: 56th District Court. Personal checks accepted. Prepayment is required.

Emmet County

57th Circuit Court 200 Division St, Petoskey, MI 49770; 231-348-1744; Fax: 231-348-0633. Hours: 8AM-5PM (EST). *Felony, Civil Actions Over $25,000.*

www.co.emmet.mi.us

Civil Records: Access: Mail, in person. Only the court performs in person searches; visitors may not. Search fee: $5.00 per name. Required to search: name, years to search. Civil cases indexed by defendant, plaintiff. Civil records on computer from 1867 to present.

Criminal Records: Access: Mail, in person. Only the court performs in person searches; visitors may not. Search fee: $5.00 per name. Required to search: name, years to search, DOB. Criminal records on computer from 1867 to present.

General Information: No suppressed records released. SASE required. Turnaround time 5 days. Copy fee: $1.00 per page. Certification fee: $10.00. Fee payee: Emmet County Clerk. Personal checks accepted. Credit cards accepted: Visa, MasterCard. Prepayment is required.

90th District Court 200 Division St., Petoskey, MI 49770; 231-348-1750; Fax: 231-348-0616. Hours: 8AM-5PM (EST). *Misdemeanor, Civil Actions Under $25,000, Eviction, Small Claims.*

Civil Records: Access: Fax, mail, in person. Only the court performs in person searches; visitors may not. No search fee. Required to search: name, years to search. Civil cases indexed by defendant, plaintiff. Civil records on computer since 1981, prior listed in books.

Criminal Records: Access: Fax, mail, in person. Only the court performs in person searches; visitors may not.

No search fee. Required to search: name, years to search, DOB; also helpful: SSN. Criminal records on computer since 1981, prior listed in books.

General Information: No suppressed, juvenile, sex offenders, mental health, or adoption records released. Turnaround time 2-3 days. Fax notes: $6.00 for first page, $1.00 each add'l. Copy fee: $2.00 per page. Fee is for non-parties. Certification fee: $10.00. Fee payee: 90th District Court. Business checks accepted. Prepayment is required.

Probate Court 200 Division St., Petoskey, MI 49770; 231-348-1707; Fax: 231-348-0672. Hours: 8AM-5PM (EST). *Probate.*

Note: Shares the same judge with Charlevoix County Probate Court.

Genesee County

7th Circuit Court 900 South Saginaw, Flint, MI 48502; 810-257-3220. Hours: 8AM-5PM (EST). *Felony, Civil Actions Over $25,000.*

Civil Records: Access: Mail, in person. Both court and visitors may perform in person searches. Search fee: $5.00 per name. Required to search: name, years to search. Civil cases indexed by defendant, plaintiff. Civil records on computer since 1978, prior on index cards.

Criminal Records: Access: Mail, in person. Both court and visitors may perform in person searches. Search fee: $5.00 per name. Required to search: name, years to search, DOB; also helpful: SSN, sex. Criminal records on computer since 1978, prior on index cards.

General Information: Public Access terminal is available. No suppressed, juvenile, adoption, or mental health records released. SASE required. Turnaround time 1-2 weeks. Copy fee: $1.00 per page. Certification fee: $10.00. Fee payee: Genesee County Clerk. Prepayment is required.

67th District Court 630 South Saginaw, Flint, MI 48502; 810-257-3170. Hours: 8AM-4PM (EST). *Misdemeanor, Civil Actions Under $25,000, Eviction, Small Claims.*

Civil Records: Access: Mail, in person. Only the court performs in person searches; visitors may not. No search fee. Required to search: name, years to search; also helpful: address. Civil cases indexed by defendant, plaintiff. Civil records on computer since 1983, on microfilm since 1969, prior archived.

Criminal Records: Access: Mail, in person. Only the court performs in person searches; visitors may not. No search fee. Required to search: name, years to search, DOB, offense; also helpful: address, SSN. Criminal records on computer since 1983, on microfilm since 1969, prior archived.

General Information: No drug related case records released. SASE helpful. Turnaround time 1 week. Copy fee: $1.00 per page. Certification fee: $10.00. Fee payee: 67th District Court. Only cashiers checks and money orders accepted. Prepayment is required.

Probate Court 919 Beach St, Flint, MI 48502; 810-257-3528; Fax: 810-257-3299. Hours: 8AM-4PM (EST). *Probate.*

Gladwin County

55th Circuit Court 401 West Cedar, Gladwin, MI 48624; 989-426-7351; Fax: 989-426-6917. Hours: 8:30AM-4:30PM (EST). *Felony, Civil Actions Over $25,000.*

Civil Records: Access: Fax, mail, in person. Both court and visitors may perform in person searches. No search fee. Required to search: name, years to search. Civil cases indexed by defendant, plaintiff. Civil records on computer since 1994, prior on books.

Criminal Records: Access: Fax, mail, in person. Both court and visitors may perform in person searches. No search fee. Required to search: name, years to search,

DOB; also helpful: SSN. Criminal records on computer since 1994, prior on books.

General Information: No suppressed, juvenile, sex offenders, mental health, or adoption records released. SASE required. Turnaround time 2-3 days. Copy fee: $1.00 per page. Certification fee: $10.00 plus $1.00 per page after first. Fee payee: Gladwin County Clerk. Personal checks accepted. Prepayment is required.

80th District Court 401 West Cedar, Gladwin, MI 48624; 989-426-9207; Fax: 989-246-0894. Hours: 8:30AM-4:30PM (EST). *Misdemeanor, Civil Actions Under $25,000, Eviction, Small Claims.*

Civil Records: Access: Mail, fax, in person. Only the court performs in person searches; visitors may not. No search fee. Required to search: name, years to search. Civil cases indexed by defendant, plaintiff. Civil records on computer since 1988, prior on index cards and docket books, archived to late 1968.

Criminal Records: Access: Mail, fax, in person. Only the court performs in person searches; visitors may not. No search fee. Required to search: name, years to search, DOB; also helpful: SSN. Criminal records on computer since 1988, prior on index cards and docket books, archived to late 1968.

General Information: No suppressed, juvenile, sex offenders, mental health, or adoption records released. SASE required. Turnaround time same day when possible. Copy fee: $2.00 per page. Certification fee: $10.00 plus $1.00 per page after first. Fee payee: 80th District Court. Personal checks accepted. Prepayment is required.

Probate Court 401 West Cedar, Gladwin, MI 48624; 989-426-7451; Fax: 989-426-5478. Hours: 8:30AM-4:30PM (EST). *Probate.*

Note: This is combined with Clare County Probate Court.

Gogebic County

32nd Circuit Court 200 North Moore St, Bessemer, MI 49911; 906-663-4518; Fax: 906-663-4660. Hours: 8:30AM-4:30PM (CST). *Felony, Civil Actions Over $25,000.*

Civil Records: Access: Mail, in person. Both court and visitors may perform in person searches. Search fee: $5.00 per name. Required to search: name, years to search. Civil cases indexed by defendant, plaintiff. Civil records in books since 1887.

Criminal Records: Access: Mail, in person. Both court and visitors may perform in person searches. Search fee: $5.00 per name. Required to search: name, years to search, DOB; also helpful: SSN. Criminal records in books since 1887.

General Information: No suppressed, juvenile, sex offenders, mental health, or adoption records released. SASE requested. Turnaround time 1-2 days. Copy fee: $1.00 per page. Certification fee: $10.00. Fee payee: Gogebic County Clerk's Office. Personal checks accepted. Prepayment is required.

98th District Court 200 North Moore St, Bessemer, MI 49911; 906-663-4611; Fax: 906-663-4660. Hours: 8:30AM-4PM (CST). *Misdemeanor, Civil Actions Under $25,000, Eviction, Small Claims.*

Civil Records: Access: Mail, in person. Only the court performs in person searches; visitors may not. Search fee: $5.00 per name. Required to search: name, years to search. Civil cases indexed by defendant, plaintiff. Civil records on computer since 6/88.

Criminal Records: Access: Mail, in person. Only the court performs in person searches; visitors may not. Search fee: $5.00 per name. Required to search: name, years to search, DOB, SSN. Criminal records on computer since 6/88.

General Information: No suppressed, juvenile, sex offenders, mental health, or adoption records released.

SASE not required. Turnaround time 10 days. Copy fee: $1.00 per page. Certification fee: $10.00 plus $1.00 per page after first. Fee payee: District Court. Business checks accepted. Prepayment is required.

Probate Court 200 North Moore St., Bessemer, MI 49911; 906-667-0421; Fax: 906-663-4660. Hours: 8:30AM-Noon, 1-4:30PM (CST). *Probate.*

Grand Traverse County

13th Circuit Court 328 Washington St, Traverse City, MI 49684; 231-922-4710. Hours: 8AM-5PM (EST). *Felony, Civil Actions Over $25,000.*

Civil Records: Access: Phone, mail, in person. Both court and visitors may perform in person searches. No search fee. Required to search: name, years to search. Civil cases indexed by defendant, plaintiff. Civil records on computer since 1971, prior on books since 1859.

Criminal Records: Access: Phone, mail, in person. Both court and visitors may perform in person searches. No search fee. Required to search: name, years to search; also helpful: DOB, SSN. Criminal records on computer since 1981.

General Information: No suppressed records released. SASE required. Turnaround time 1 week. Copy fee: $1.00 for first page, $.25 each add'l. Certification fee: $10.00 plus $1.00 per page after first. Fee payee: 13th Circuit Court. Personal checks accepted. Prepayment is required.

86th District Court 328 Washington St., Traverse City, MI 49684; 231-922-4580; Fax: 231-922-4454. Hours: 8AM-5PM (EST). *Misdemeanor, Civil Actions Under $25,000, Eviction, Small Claims.*

Civil Records: Access: Phone, mail, in person. Only the court performs in person searches; visitors may not. No search fee. Required to search: name, years to search. Civil cases indexed by defendant, plaintiff. Civil records on computer since 1988, prior on books.

Criminal Records: Access: Phone, mail, in person. Only the court performs in person searches; visitors may not. No search fee. Required to search: name, years to search, DOB; also helpful: SSN. Most criminal records on computer.

General Information: No suppressed, juvenile, sex offenders, mental health, or adoption records released. SASE required. Turnaround time 2-3 days. Copy fee: $.25 per page. Certification fee: $10.00. Fee payee: 86th District Court. Business checks accepted. Prepayment is required.

Probate Court 400 Boardman St, Traverse City, MI 49684; 231-922-4640; Fax: 231-922-6893. Hours: 8AM-5PM (EST). *Probate.*

Gratiot County

29th Circuit Court 214 East Center St, Ithaca, MI 48847; 989-875-5215. Hours: 8:30AM-5PM (EST). *Felony, Civil Actions Over $25,000.*

Civil Records: Access: Mail, in person. Only the court performs in person searches; visitors may not. Search fee: $10.00 per name. Fee is for 5 years, $1.00 each additional year. Required to search: name, years to search. Civil cases indexed by defendant, plaintiff.

Criminal Records: Access: Mail, in person. Only the court performs in person searches; visitors may not. Search fee: $10.00 per name. Fee is for 5 years, $1.00 each additional year. Required to search: name, years to search.

General Information: No suppressed, juvenile, sex offenders, mental health, or adoption records released. SASE required. Turnaround time 1-3 days. Copy fee: $1.00 per page. Certification fee: $10.00. Fee payee: Gratiot County Clerk. Personal checks accepted. Prepayment is required.

65-B District Court 245 East Newark St, Ithaca, MI 48847; 989-875-5240; Fax: 989-875-5290. Hours: 8AM-4:30PM (EST). *Misdemeanor, Civil Actions Under $25,000, Eviction, Small Claims.*

Civil Records: Access: In person only. Visitors must perform in person searches for themselves. No search fee. Required to search: name, years to search. Civil cases indexed by defendant, plaintiff. Civil records on index books from 1969 to present.

Criminal Records: Access: In person only. Visitors must perform in person searches for themselves. No search fee. Required to search: name, years to search, DOB; also helpful: SSN. Criminal records on computer since 02/20/96.

General Information: No non-public records released. Copy fee: $1.00 per page. Certification fee: $10.00 plus $1.00 per page after first. Fee payee: 65B District Court. Personal checks accepted. Prepayment is required.

Probate Court 214 E Center St, PO Box 217, Ithaca, MI 48847; 989-875-5231; Fax: 989-875-5331. Hours: 8:30AM-5PM (EST). *Probate.*

Hillsdale County

1st Circuit Court 29 North Howell, Hillsdale, MI 49242; 517-437-3391; Fax: 517-437-3392. Hours: 8:30AM-5PM *Felony, Civil Actions Over $25,000.*

Civil Records: Access: Mail, in person. Only the court performs in person searches; visitors may not. Search fee: $1.00 per name per year. Required to search: name, years to search. Civil cases indexed by defendant, plaintiff. Civil records on computer back to 1985, prior on docket books, archived to 1844.

Criminal Records: Access: Mail, in person. Only the court performs in person searches; visitors may not. Search fee: $1.00 per name per year. Required to search: name, years to search, DOB; also helpful: SSN. Criminal records on computer back to 1985, prior on docket books, archived to 1844.

General Information: No suppressed, juvenile, sex offenders, mental health, or adoption records released. SASE required. Turnaround time 2-3 days. Copy fee: $1.00 per page. Certification fee: $10.00. Fee payee: Hillsdale County Clerk. Personal checks accepted. Out-of-state personal checks not accepted. Prepayment is required.

2nd District Court 49 North Howell, Hillsdale, MI 49242; 517-437-7329; Fax: 517-437-2908. Hours: 8AM-4:30PM; 8AM-5PM Traffic (EST). *Misdemeanor, Civil Actions Under $25,000, Eviction, Small Claims.*

Civil Records: Access: Phone, mail, in person. Both court and visitors may perform in person searches. Search fee: $10.00. Required to search: name, years to search. Civil cases indexed by defendant, plaintiff. Civil records kept in docket books back to 1969; on computer since. A request in writing may be required.

Criminal Records: Access: Phone, mail, in person. Only the court performs in person searches; visitors may not. Search fee: $10.00. Required to search: name, years to search, DOB; also helpful: SSN. Criminal records kept in docket books back to 1969; on computer since.

General Information: No suppressed records released. Turnaround time 1 week. Copy fee: $.15 per page. Certification fee: $10.00 plus $1.00 each add'l page. Fee payee: Hillsdale District Court. Personal checks accepted. Prepayment is required.

Probate Court 29 North Howell, Hillsdale, MI 49242; 517-437-4643. Hours: 8:30AM-Noon, 1-5PM (EST). *Probate.*

Houghton County

12th Circuit Court 401 East Houghton Ave, Houghton, MI 49931; 906-482-5420. Hours: 8AM-4:30PM (EST). *Felony, Civil Actions Over $25,000.*

Civil Records: Access: Mail, in person. Only the court performs in person searches; visitors may not. No search fee. Required to search: name, years to search. Civil cases indexed by defendant, plaintiff. Civil records kept on docket books, cards; computerized as of 1997.

Criminal Records: Access: Mail, in person. Only the court performs in person searches; visitors may not. No search fee. Required to search: name, years to search, DOB; also helpful: SSN. Criminal records kept on docket books, cards; are computerized as of 1997.

General Information: No suppressed, juvenile, sex offenders, mental health, or adoption records released. SASE required. Turnaround time 1-2 days. Copy fee: $1.00 per page. Certification fee: $10.00 plus $1.00 per page after first. Fee payee: Clerk of Circuit Court. Personal checks accepted. Prepayment is required.

97th District Court 401 East Houghton Ave., Houghton, MI 49931; 906-482-4980; Fax: 906-482-5270. Hours: 8AM-4:30PM (EST). *Misdemeanor, Civil Actions Under $25,000, Eviction, Small Claims.*

Civil Records: Access: Mail, fax, in person. Both court and visitors may perform in person searches. Search fee: $5.00 per name. Required to search: name, years to search; also helpful: address. Civil cases indexed by defendant, plaintiff. Civil records listed in "Registers of Actions." Records on computer back to 1998; others back to 1969.

Criminal Records: Access: Mail, fax, in person. Both court and visitors may perform in person searches. Search fee: $5.00 per name. Required to search: name, years to search, DOB; also helpful: address, SSN. Criminal records listed in "Registers of Actions." Records on computer back to 1998; others back to 1969.

General Information: No conviction records released. SASE required. Turnaround time 1 week. Copy fee: $1.00 for first page, $.25 each add'l. Certification fee: $10.00 plus $1.00 per page after first. Fee payee: 97th District Court. Business checks accepted. Prepayment is required.

Probate Court 401 E. Houghton Ave., Houghton, MI 49931; 906-482-3120; Fax: 906-487-5964. Hours: 8AM-4:30PM (EST). *Probate.*

Huron County

52nd Circuit Court 250 East Huron Ave, Bad Axe, MI 48413; 989-269-9942; Fax: 989-269-6160. Hours: 8:30AM-5PM (EST). *Felony, Civil Actions Over $25,000.*

Civil Records: Access: Phone, mail, in person. Both court and visitors may perform in person searches. Search fee: $5.00 per name. Required to search: name, years to search. Civil cases indexed by defendant, plaintiff. Civil records on computer since 1992, prior on books to 1867.

Criminal Records: Access: Phone, mail, in person. Both court and visitors may perform in person searches. Search fee: $5.00 per name. Required to search: name, years to search, DOB; also helpful: SSN. Criminal records on computer since 1992, prior on books to 1867.

General Information: No suppressed, juvenile, sex offenders, mental health, or adoption records released. SASE required. Turnaround time 2-3 days. Copy fee: $1.00 per page. Certification fee: $10.00 plus $1.00 per page after first. Fee payee: Huron County Clerk. No personal checks accepted. Prepayment is required.

73B District Court 250 East Huron Ave., Bad Axe, MI 48413; 989-269-9987; Fax: 989-269-6167. Hours: 8:30AM-5PM (EST). *Misdemeanor, Civil Actions Under $25,000, Eviction, Small Claims.*

Civil Records: Access: Phone, fax, mail, in person. Only the court performs in person searches; visitors may not. Search fee: $5.00 per name. Required to search: name, years to search. Civil cases indexed by defendant, plaintiff. Civil records on computer since June 1992, prior on books since 1969.

Criminal Records: Access: Phone, fax, mail, in person. Only the court performs in person searches; visitors may not. Search fee: $5.00 per name. Required to search: name, years to search, DOB; also helpful: SSN. Criminal records on computer since June 1992, prior on books since 1969.

General Information: No suppressed, juvenile, sex offenders, mental health, or adoption records released. SASE required. Turnaround time 1-5 days. Fax notes: No fee to fax results. Copy fee: $1.00 per page. Certification fee: No cert fee. Fee payee: 73B District Court. Business checks accepted. Prepayment is required.

Probate Court 250 E. Huron Ave., Bad Axe, MI 48413; 989-269-9944; Fax: 989-269-0004. Hours: 8:30AM-Noon, 1-5PM (EST). *Probate.*

Ingham County

30th Circuit Court 313 W. Kalamazoo (PO Box 40771), Lansing, MI 48933; 517-483-6500; Fax: 517-483-6501. Hours: 9AM-Noon, 1-5PM M,T,Th,F; 8AM-Noon, 1-5PM W (EST). *Felony, Civil Actions Over $25,000.*

Civil Records: Access: Phone, mail, in person. Both court and visitors may perform in person searches. No search fee. Required to search: name, years to search. Civil cases indexed by defendant, plaintiff. Civil records on computer since 1986.

Criminal Records: Access: Phone, mail, in person. Both court and visitors may perform in person searches. No search fee. Required to search: name, years to search; also helpful: DOB. Criminal records on computer since 1986.

General Information: All circuit Court files are public record unless specifically suppressed by Judge. SASE not required. Turnaround time 1-2 days, unless file is in storage then 1 week. Copy fee: $.50 per page 1st 10 pages, each additional page $.20 per page. Certification fee: $10.00 plus $1.00 per page after first. Fee payee: Ingham County Circuit Court. Personal checks accepted. Prepayment is required.

54 A District Court 124 West Michigan Ave, Lansing, MI 48933; 517-483-4433; Civil phone: 517-483-4426; Criminal phone: 517-483-4445; Fax: 517-483-4108. Hours: 8AM-4:35PM (EST). *Misdemeanor, Civil Actions Under $25,000, Eviction, Small Claims.*

Note: This court covers the city of Lansing.

Civil Records: Access: In person only. Visitors must perform in person searches for themselves. No search fee. Required to search: name, years to search. Civil cases indexed by defendant, plaintiff. Civil records on computer since 1990, microfiche from 1985, prior archived.

Criminal Records: Access: In person only. Visitors must perform in person searches for themselves. No search fee. Required to search: name, years to search, DOB, offense, date of offense; also helpful: SSN. Criminal records on computer since 1990, microfiche from 1985, prior archived.

General Information: Public Access terminal is available. No suppressed, juvenile, sex offenders, mental health, or adoption, non-public records released. Copy fee: $.50 per page. Certification fee: $10.00 plus $1.00 per page after first. Fee payee: 54A District Court.

No personal checks accepted. Credit cards accepted: Visa, MasterCard. Prepayment is required.

54 B District Court 101 Linden, East Lansing, MI 48823; 517-351-7000; Civil phone: 517-351-1730; Criminal phone: 517-336-8630; Fax: 517-351-3371. Hours: 8AM-4:30PM (EST). *Misdemeanor, Civil Actions Under $25,000, Eviction, Small Claims.*

Note: This court covers the city of East Lansing.

Civil Records: Access: Mail, in person. Both court and visitors may perform in person searches. No search fee. Required to search: name, years to search. Civil cases indexed by defendant, plaintiff. Civil records on computer since 1991, ROA's are kept indefinitely.

Criminal Records: Access: Mail, in person. Both court and visitors may perform in person searches. No search fee. Required to search: name, years to search, DOB; also helpful: case number. Criminal records on computer since 1989, files stored prior.

General Information: Public Access terminal is available. No suppressed, juvenile, sex offenders, mental health, or adoption records released. Turnaround time up 1 hour to 1 week, depends on availability. Copy fee: $.25 per page. Certification fee: $10.00 plus $1.00 per page after first. Fee payee: 54-B District Court. Personal checks accepted. Two party or payroll checks not allowed. Credit cards accepted: Visa, MC, Discover. Debit card. Prepayment is required.

55th District Court 700 Buhl, Mason, MI 48854; 517-676-8400. Hours: 8:30AM-4:30PM (EST). *Misdemeanor, Civil Actions Under $25,000, Eviction, Small Claims.*

Note: This court covers all of Ingham County except for Lansing and East Lansing.

Civil Records: Access: Mail, in person. Both court and visitors may perform in person searches. No search fee. Required to search: name, years to search. Civil records on computer since 11/91, prior listed in index books.

Criminal Records: Access: Mail, in person. Both court and visitors may perform in person searches. No search fee. Required to search: name, years to search, DOB; also helpful: SSN. Criminal records on computer since 1994, prior on books.

General Information: No suppressed, juvenile, sex offenders, mental health, or adoption records released. SASE required. Turnaround time 5 days. Copy fee: $1.00 per page. Certification fee: $10.00 plus $1.00 each additional page. Fee payee: 55th District court. Personal checks accepted. Prepayment is required.

Ingham County Probate Court PO Box 176, Mason, MI 48854; 517-676-7276; Fax: 517-676-7344. Hours: 8AM-Noon, 1-5PM (EST). *Probate.*

Lansing Probate Court 303 West Kalamazoo, Lansing, MI 48933; 517-483-6300; Fax: 517-483-6150. Hours: 8AM-Noon, 1-5PM (EST). *Probate.*

Ionia County

8th Circuit Court 100 Main, Ionia, MI 48846; 616-527-5322; Fax: 616-527-5323. Hours: 8:30AM-5PM (EST). *Felony, Civil Actions Over $25,000.*

www.ioniacounty.org

Civil Records: Access: Phone, fax, mail, in person. Only the court performs in person searches; visitors may not. No search fee. Required to search: name, years to search. Civil cases indexed by defendant, plaintiff. Civil records on computer since 7/91; prior records kept in books and files, archived to 1800s.

Criminal Records: Access: Phone, fax, mail, in person. Only the court performs in person searches; visitors may not. No search fee. Required to search: name, years to search; also helpful: DOB, SSN. Criminal records on computer since 6/84; in books and files prior.

General Information: No suppressed records released. SASE not required. Turnaround time 1 week. Fax notes: $1.00 per page. Copy fee: $1.00 per page. Certification fee: $10.00 plus $1.00 per page after first. Fee payee: Ionia County Clerk. Personal checks accepted. Prepayment is required.

64 A District Court 101 West Main, Ionia, MI 48846; 616-527-5346; Fax: 616-527-5343. Hours: 7:45AM-5:30PM (EST). *Misdemeanor, Civil Actions Under $25,000, Eviction, Small Claims.*

Civil Records: Access: Fax, mail, in person. Only the court performs in person searches; visitors may not. Search fee: $3.00 per name. Required to search: name, years to search. Civil cases indexed by defendant, plaintiff. Civil records in files and books available since 1969. Fax request must be followed up by originals.

Criminal Records: Access: Fax, mail, in person. Only the court performs in person searches; visitors may not. Search fee: $3.00 per name. Required to search: name, years to search, DOB; also helpful: address. Criminal records in files and books available since 1969. Fax must be followed up by originals.

General Information: No suppressed, juvenile, sex offenders, mental health, or adoption records released. SASE requested. Turnaround time 10 days. Copy fee: $.50 per page. Certification fee: $10.00 plus $1.00 per page after first. Fee payee: 64-A District Court. Personal checks accepted. Prepayment is required.

Probate Court 100 Main, Ionia, MI 48846; 616-527-5326; Fax: 616-527-5321. Hours: 8:30AM-5PM (EST). *Probate.*

Iosco County

23rd Circuit Court PO Box 838, Tawas City, MI 48764; 989-362-3497; Fax: 989-362-1444. Hours: 9AM-5PM (EST). *Felony, Civil Actions Over $25,000.*

Civil Records: Access: Phone, mail, in person. Both court and visitors may perform in person searches. No search fee. Required to search: name, years to search. Civil records on computer since 1987, prior on books.

Criminal Records: Access: Phone, mail, in person. Both court and visitors may perform in person searches. No search fee. Required to search: name, years to search, DOB; also helpful: SSN. Criminal records on computer since 1983.

General Information: No suppressed, parental waivers, mental health, or adoption records released. SASE not required. Turnaround time 1 week. Copy fee: $.25 per page. Certification fee: $10.00 plus $1.00 per page after first. Fee payee: Iosco County Clerk. Only cashiers checks and money orders accepted. Prepayment is required.

81st District Court PO Box 388, Tawas City, MI 48764; 989-362-4441; Fax: 989-362-3494. Hours: 8AM-5PM (EST). *Misdemeanor, Civil Actions Under $25,000, Eviction, Small Claims.*

Civil Records: Access: Mail, in person. Only the court performs in person searches; visitors may not. No search fee. Required to search: name, years to search. Civil cases indexed by defendant, plaintiff. Civil records on computer since 1987, prior on books.

Criminal Records: Access: Mail, in person. Only the court performs in person searches; visitors may not. No search fee. Required to search: name, years to search, DOB; also helpful: SSN. Criminal records on computer since 1987, prior on books.

General Information: No suppressed, juvenile, sex offenders, mental health, or adoption records released. SASE required. Turnaround time 2-3 days. Copy fee: $2.00 for first page, $.50 each add'l. Certification fee: $10.00 plus $1.00 per page after first. Fee payee: 81st District Court. Personal checks accepted. Prepayment is required.

Probate Court PO Box 421, Tawas City, MI 48764; 989-362-3991; Fax: 989-362-1459. Hours: 8AM-5PM (EST). *Probate.*

Iron County

41st Circuit Court 2 South 6th St, Crystal Falls, MI 49920; 906-875-3221; Fax: 906-875-6675. Hours: 8AM-4PM (CST). *Felony, Civil Actions Over $25,000.*

Civil Records: Access: Fax, mail, in person. Only the court performs in person searches; visitors may not. Search fee: $5.00 per name. Required to search: name, years to search. Civil cases indexed by defendant, plaintiff. Most records on books,; microfiche 1958-67.

Criminal Records: Access: Fax, mail, in person. Only the court performs in person searches; visitors may not. Search fee: $5.00 per name. Required to search: name, years to search, DOB; also helpful: SSN. Most records on books, on microfiche 1958-67.

General Information: No suppressed, juvenile, sex offenders, mental health, or adoption records released. SASE required. Turnaround time 2-3 days. Fax notes: $1.50 per page. Copy fee: $.25 per page. Certification fee: $10.00 plus $1.00 per page after first. Fee payee: Iron County Clerk. Personal checks accepted. Prepayment is required.

95 B District Court 2 South 6th St., Crystal Falls, MI 49920; 906-875-0619; Fax: 906-875-6775. Hours: 8AM-4PM (CST). *Misdemeanor, Civil Actions Under $25,000, Eviction, Small Claims.*

Civil Records: Access: Mail, in person. Only the court performs in person searches; visitors may not. Search fee: $5.00. Required to search: name, years to search. Civil cases indexed by defendant, plaintiff. Civil records computerized since 1999, earlier records index kept on cards, accessible from 1982.

Criminal Records: Access: Mail, in person. Only the court performs in person searches; visitors may not. Search fee: $5.00. Required to search: name, years to search, DOB; also helpful: SSN. Criminal records computerized since 1999, earlier records index kept on cards, accessible from 1982.

General Information: No suppressed, juvenile, sex offenders, mental health, or adoption records released. SASE required. Turnaround time 1 week. Copy fee: $.25 per page. Certification fee: $10.00 plus $1.00 per page after first. Fee payee: 95-B District Court. Personal checks accepted. Prepayment is required.

Probate Court 2 South 6th St, Suite 10, Crystal Falls, MI 49920; 906-875-3121; Fax: 906-875-6775. Hours: 8AM-Noon, 12:30-4PM (CST). *Probate.*

Isabella County

21st Circuit Court 200 North Main St, Mount Pleasant, MI 48858; 989-772-0911 X259. Hours: 8AM-4:30PM (EST). *Felony, Civil Actions Over $25,000.*

Civil Records: Access: Mail, in person. Both court and visitors may perform in person searches. Search fee: $5.00 from 1980 to present. Prior years $1.00 per year. Required to search: name, years to search. Civil cases indexed by defendant, plaintiff. Civil records on computer since 1980, archived from 1900.

Criminal Records: Access: Mail, in person. Both court and visitors may perform in person searches. Search fee: $5.00 from 1980 to present. Prior years $1.00 per year. Required to search: name, years to search, DOB; also helpful: SSN. Criminal records on computer since 1980, archived from 1900.

General Information: No suppressed, juvenile, sex offenders, mental health, or adoption records released. Turnaround time 1-2 weeks. Copy fee: $10.00 for first page, $1.00 each add'l. Certification fee: $10.00 plus $1.00 per page after first. Fee payee: County Clerk. Personal checks accepted. Prepayment is required.

76th District Court 200 North Main St., Mount Pleasant, MI 48858; 989-772-0911 X320; Fax: 989-773-2419. Hours: 8AM-4:30PM (EST). *Misdemeanor, Civil Actions Under $25,000, Eviction, Small Claims.*

Civil Records: Access: Mail, in person. Both court and visitors may perform in person searches. Search fee: $5.00 per name. Required to search: name, years to search. Civil cases indexed by defendant, plaintiff. Civil records on computer since 1988, on books since 1960s.

Criminal Records: Access: Mail, in person. Both court and visitors may perform in person searches. Search fee: $5.00 per name. Required to search: name, years to search, DOB; also helpful: SSN. Criminal records on computer since 1988, on books since 1960s.

General Information: No suppressed, juvenile, sex offenders, mental health, or adoption records released. SASE required. Turnaround time 5-7 days. Copy fee: $1.00 per page. Certification fee: $10.00 plus $1.00 per page after first. Fee payee: 76th District Court. Business checks accepted. Prepayment is required.

Probate Court 200 N Main St, Mount Pleasant, MI 48858; 989-772-0911 X310; Fax: 989-773-2419. Hours: 8AM-4:30PM (EST). *Probate.*

Jackson County

4th Circuit Court 312 South Jackson St, Jackson, MI 49201; 517-788-4268. Hours: 8AM-5PM (EST). *Felony, Civil Actions Over $25,000.*

www.co.jackson.mi.us

Civil Records: Access: Phone, mail, in person. Only the court performs in person searches; visitors may not. Search fee: $10.50 per hour. Required to search: name, years to search. Civil cases indexed by defendant, plaintiff. Civil records on computer since 1982, prior on index cards and docket books since 1800s.

Criminal Records: Access: Phone, mail, in person. Only the court performs in person searches; visitors may not. Search fee: $10.50 per hour. Required to search: name, years to search; also helpful: DOB, SSN. Criminal records on computer since 1982, prior on index cards and docket books since 1800s.

General Information: No adoption or juvenile records released. Turnaround time 1 week. Copy fee: $.25 per page. Certification fee: $10.00 plus $1.00 per page after first. Fee payee: Jackson County Clerk. Only cashiers checks and money orders accepted. Credit cards accepted: Visa, MasterCard. Prepayment of fax and mail service required. Fees billed to Attorney's.

12th District Court 312 South Jackson St., Jackson, MI 49201; 517-788-4260; Fax: 517-788-4262. Hours: 7AM-6PM (EST). *Misdemeanor, Civil Actions Under $25,000, Eviction, Small Claims.*

www.d12.com

Civil Records: Access: Fax, mail, in person. Only the court performs in person searches; visitors may not. No search fee. Required to search: name, years to search. Civil cases indexed by defendant, plaintiff. Civil records on computer since 1986; microfilm to 1969.

Criminal Records: Access: Fax, mail, in person. Only the court performs in person searches; visitors may not. No search fee. Required to search: name, years to search, DOB; also helpful: SSN. Criminal records on computer since 1986; microfilm from 1969.

General Information: No suppressed, juvenile, sex offenders, mental health, or probation records released. Turnaround time 5 days. Fax notes: $5.00 for first page, $1.00 each add'l. Copy fee: $.25 per page. Certification fee: $10.00 plus $1.00 per page after first. Fee payee: 12th District Court. Personal checks accepted. Third party checks not allowed. Prepayment is required.

Probate Court 312 S Jackson St, 1st Fl, Jackson, MI 49201; 517-788-4290. Hours: 8AM-5PM (EST). *Probate.*

Kalamazoo County

9th Circuit Court 227 West Michigan Ave, Kalamazoo, MI 49007; 616-383-8837. Hours: 9AM-4PM (EST). *Felony, Civil Actions Over $25,000.*

Civil Records: Access: Mail, in person. Visitors must perform in person searches for themselves. No search fee. Required to search: name, years to search. Civil cases indexed by defendant, plaintiff. Civil records stored as hard copies, some records kept off-site.

Criminal Records: Access: Mail, in person. Visitors must perform in person searches for themselves. No search fee. Required to search: name, years to search, DOB. Criminal records stored as hard copies, some records kept off-site.

General Information: No suppressed or non-public records released. Turnaround time 2 days. Copy fee: $1.00 per page. Certification fee: $13.00. Fee payee: Circuit Court Clerk. Personal checks accepted. Prepayment is required.

8th District Court 227 West Michigan St., Kalamazoo, MI 49007; 616-384-8171; Fax: 616-384-8047. Hours: 8:30AM-4PM (EST). *Misdemeanor, Civil Actions Under $25,000, Eviction, Small Claims.*

Note: This court covers the areas in Kalamazoo County not handled by the 9th Circuit Courts.

Civil Records: Access: Fax, mail, in person. Both court and visitors may perform in person searches. No search fee. Required to search: name, years to search, address. Civil cases indexed by defendant, plaintiff. Civil records on computer since 1991, prior on books.

Criminal Records: Access: Fax, mail, in person. Both court and visitors may perform in person searches. No search fee. Required to search: name, years to search, DOB; also helpful: SSN. Criminal records on computer since 1991, prior on books.

General Information: Public Access terminal is available. No suppressed or non-public records released. SASE requested. Turnaround time 2 days. Fax notes: No fee to fax results. Copy fee: $.50 per page. Certification fee: $10.00. Fee payee: 8th District Court. Personal checks accepted. Credit cards accepted: Visa, MasterCard. Prepayment is required.

8th District Court Division 1 416 S. Rose, Kalamazoo, MI 49007; 616-384-8020; Fax: 616-383-8899. Hours: 8AM-4:15PM (EST). *Misdemeanor, Civil Actions Under $25,000, Eviction, Small Claims.*

Note: This court covers city of Kalamazoo.

Civil Records: Access: Fax, mail, in person. Both court and visitors may perform in person searches. No search fee. Required to search: name, years to search. Civil cases indexed by defendant, plaintiff. Civil records on computer since 1988, prior on index books.

Criminal Records: Access: Fax, mail, in person. Both court and visitors may perform in person searches. No search fee. Required to search: name, years to search, DOB; also helpful: SSN. Criminal records on computer since 1988, prior on index books.

General Information: No suppressed records released. SASE not required. Turnaround time 1-3 days. Copy fee: $.50 per page. Certification fee: $10.00. Fee payee: 8th District Court. Personal checks accepted. Credit cards accepted: Visa, MasterCard.

8th District Court Division 2 - South 7810 Shaver Rd., Portage, MI 49002; 616-383-6460; Fax: 616-321-3645. Hours: 8AM-4:30PM (EST). *Misdemeanor, Civil Actions Under $25,000, Eviction, Small Claims.*

Note: This court covers Kalamazoo County South of N Avenue (Kilgore Rd).

Civil Records: Access: Mail, in person. Only the court performs in person searches; visitors may not. Search fee: $20.00 per name if prior to 1992. Required to search: name, years to search. Civil cases indexed by defendant, plaintiff. Civil records on computer since 1992, prior on index books.

Criminal Records: Access: Mail, in person. Only the court performs in person searches; visitors may not. Search fee: $20.00 per name if prior to 1992. Required to search: name, years to search, DOB; also helpful: SSN. Criminal records on computer since 1992, prior on index books.

General Information: Public Access terminal is available. No suppressed, juvenile, sex offenders, mental health, or adoption records released. SASE required. Turnaround time 5 days. Fax notes: Fee to fax results is $1.00 per page. Copy fee: $.50 per page. Certification fee: $10.00 plus $1.00 per page after first. Fee payee: 8th District Court. Personal checks accepted. Prepayment is required.

Probate Court 227 West Michigan Ave., Kalamazoo, MI 49007; 616-383-8666/8933; Fax: 616-383-8685. Hours: 9AM-Noon, 1-5PM M; 8AM-Noon, 1-5PM T-F (EST). *Probate.*

Kalkaska County

46th Circuit Court PO Box 10, Kalkaska, MI 49646; 231-258-3300. Hours: 9AM-5PM (EST). *Felony, Civil Actions Over $25,000.*

www.Circuit46.org

Civil Records: Access: Mail, in person, online. Only the court performs in person searches; visitors may not. Search fee: $5.00 per name. Required to search: name, years to search. Civil cases indexed by defendant, plaintiff. Civil records on computer since 1989, prior on books, indexed to 1800s. Online access to court case records (open or closed cases for 90 days only) is available free at www.circuit46.org/Cases/cases.html.

Criminal Records: Access: Mail, in person, online. Only the court performs in person searches; visitors may not. Search fee: $5.00 per name. Required to search: name, years to search, DOB; also helpful: SSN. Criminal records on computer since 1989, prior on books, indexed to 1800s. Online access to criminal records is the same as civil.

General Information: No suppressed records released. SASE required. Turnaround time 2-3 days. Copy fee: $.30 per page. Certification fee: $10.00 plus $1.00 per page. Fee payee: County Clerk. Personal checks accepted. Prepayment is required.

46th Circuit Trial Court - District Court PO Box 780, Kalkaska, MI 49646; 231-258-9031; Fax: 231-258-2424. Hours: 8AM-4:30PM (EST). *Misdemeanor, Civil Actions Under $25,000, Eviction, Small Claims.*

www.Circuit46.org

Civil Records: Access: Phone, mail, in person, online. Only the court performs in person searches; visitors may not. No search fee. Required to search: name, years to search. Civil cases indexed by defendant, plaintiff. Civil records on computer since 1989, prior on books. Online access to court case records (open or closed cases for 90 days only) is available free at www.circuit46.org/Cases/cases.html. Search by name.

Criminal Records: Access: Phone, mail, in person, online. Only the court performs in person searches; visitors may not. No search fee. Required to search: name, years to search, DOB. Criminal records on computer since 1989, prior on books. Online access to criminal records is the same as civil.

General Information: Public Access terminal is available. No suppressed records released. SASE required. Turnaround time 4 days. Copy fee: $1.00 per page. Certification fee: $10.00 plus $1.00 per page after first. Fee payee: 46th Circuit Trial Court. Personal checks accepted. Prepayment is required.

Circuit Trial Court - Probate Division 605 North Birch, PO Box 780, Kalkaska, MI 49646; 231-258-3330; Fax: 231-258-3329. Hours: 9AM-Noon, 1-5PM (EST). *Probate.*

www.Circuit46.org

Kent County

17th Circuit Court 333 Monroe Ave NW, Grand Rapids, MI 49503; 616-336-3679; Fax: 616-336-3349. Hours: 8AM-5PM (EST). *Felony, Civil Actions Over $25,000.*

www.co.kent.mi.us/courts.htm

Civil Records: Access: Mail, in person. Only the court performs in person searches; visitors may not. Search fee: $5.00 per name. Required to search: name, years to search. Civil cases indexed by defendant, plaintiff. Civil records on computer since 1986, prior on books.

Criminal Records: Access: Mail, in person. Only the court performs in person searches; visitors may not. Search fee: $5.00 per name. Required to search: name, years to search, DOB. Criminal records on computer since 1986, prior on books.

General Information: No suppressed records released. SASE not required. Turnaround time 2-3 days. Copy fee: $1.00 per page. Certification fee: $10.00 plus $1.00 per page after first. Fee payee: Kent County Clerk. Personal checks accepted. Prepayment required.

59th District Court - Grandville & Walker 3181 Wilson Ave SW, Grandville, MI 49418; 616-538-9660; Fax: 616-538-5144. Hours: 8:30AM-Noon, 1-5PM (EST). *Misdemeanor, Civil Actions Under $25,000, Eviction, Small Claims.*

Civil Records: Access: Mail, in person. Only the court performs in person searches; visitors may not. Search fee: $1.00 per name. Add $.50 per year requested. Required to search: name, years to search; also helpful: address. Civil cases indexed by defendant, plaintiff. Civil records on computer from 1986, docket books and cards prior.

Criminal Records: Access: Mail, in person. Only the court performs in person searches; visitors may not. Search fee: $1.00 per name. Add $.50 per year requested. Required to search: name, years to search, DOB; also helpful: address, SSN. Criminal records on computer from 1986, docket books and cards prior.

General Information: No suppressed, juvenile, sex offenders, mental health, or adoption records released. SASE required. Turnaround time varies. Copy fee: $1.00 per page. Certification fee: $10.00 plus $1.00 per page after first. Fee payee: 59th District Court. Personal checks accepted. Prepayment is required.

61st District Court - Grand Rapids 333 Monroe Ave NW, Grand Rapids, MI 49503; 616-456-3370; Fax: 616-456-3311. Hours: 7:45AM-4:45PM (EST). *Misdemeanor, Civil Actions Under $25,000, Eviction, Small Claims.*

Civil Records: Access: Mail, in person. Only the court performs in person searches; visitors may not. No search fee. Required to search: name, years to search. Civil cases indexed by defendant, plaintiff. Civil records kept in files and books.

Criminal Records: Access: Mail, in person. Only the court performs in person searches; visitors may not. Search fee: $1.00 per name per year. Required to search: name, years to search, DOB; also helpful: SSN. Criminal records are automated from 1985, microfiche from 1980.

General Information: No suppressed, juvenile, sex offenders, mental health, or adoption records released. SASE not required. Turnaround time 7-10 days. Copy fee: $1.00 for first page, $.50 each add'l. Certification fee: $10.00 plus $1.00 per page after first. Fee payee: 61st District Court. Personal checks accepted. Prepayment of mail service required.

62 A District Court - Wyoming 2650 De Hoop Ave SW, Wyoming, MI 49509; 616-530-7385; Fax: 616-249-3419. Hours: 8AM-5PM (EST). *Misdemeanor, Civil Actions Under $25,000, Eviction, Small Claims.*

www.ci.wyoming.mi.us/court/index.htm

Civil Records: Access: Mail, fax, in person. Both court and visitors may perform in person searches. Search fee: $1.00 per name & $.50 per year. Required to search: name, years to search. Civil cases indexed by defendant, plaintiff. Civil records kept on docket books since 1980; on computer back to 1997. The judge must approve all requests from collection agencies.

Criminal Records: Access: Mail, fax, in person. Both court and visitors may perform in person searches. Search fee: $1.00 per name & $.50 per year. Required to search: name, years to search, DOB; also helpful: SSN. Criminal records kept on docket books since 1980; on computer back to 1997. The court suggests mail requests be sent to the state police.

General Information: Public Access terminal is available. No suppressed, juvenile, sex offenders, mental health, or adoption records released. SASE required. Turnaround time 2-3 days. Fax notes: Will not fax results. Copy fee: $1.00 per page. Certification fee: $10.00 plus $1.00 per page after first. Fee payee: 62 A District Court. Personal checks accepted. Credit cards accepted: Visa. Accepted in person only. Prepayment is required.

62 B District Court - Kentwood PO Box 8848, Kentwood, MI 49518; 616-698-9310; Fax: 616-698-8199. Hours: 8AM-5PM (EST). *Misdemeanor, Civil Actions Under $25,000, Eviction, Small Claims.*

Civil Records: Access: Mail, in person. Only the court performs in person searches; visitors may not. Search fee: $5.00 per name. Required to search: name, years to search. Civil cases indexed by defendant, plaintiff. Civil records on computer since 11/88, prior on books.

Criminal Records: Access: Fax, mail, in person. Only the court performs in person searches; visitors may not. Search fee: $5.00 per name. Required to search: name, years to search, DOB. Criminal records on computer since 11/88, prior on books.

General Information: No suppressed, juvenile, sex offenders, mental health, or adoption records released. SASE required. Turnaround time 1-2 days. Copy fee: $2.00 for first page, $.25 each add'l. Certification fee: $15.00. Fee payee: 62 B District Court. Personal checks accepted. Prepayment is required.

63rd District Court - 1st Division 105 Maple St, Rockford, MI 49341; 616-866-1576; Fax: 616-866-3080. Hours: 8AM-5PM (EST). *Misdemeanor, Civil Actions Under $25,000, Eviction, Small Claims.*

Civil Records: Access: Mail, in person. Both court and visitors may perform in person searches. No search fee. Required to search: name, years to search. Civil cases indexed by defendant, plaintiff. Civil records on computer since 8/94, prior on books.

Criminal Records: Access: Mail, in person. Both court and visitors may perform in person searches. No search fee. Required to search: name, years to search, DOB; also helpful: SSN. Criminal records on computer since 8/94, prior on books.

General Information: Public Access terminal is available. No suppressed, juvenile, sex offenders, mental health, or adoption records released. SASE required. Turnaround time 1 week. Copy fee: $1.00 per page. Certification fee: $10.00. Fee payee: 63rd District Court. Personal checks accepted. Prepayment is required.

Probate Court 320 Ottawa Ave. NW, Grand Rapids, MI 49503; 616-336-3630; Fax: 616-336-3574. Hours: 8:30AM-5PM (EST). *Probate.*

Keweenaw County

12th Circuit Court HCl Box 607, Eagle River, MI 49950-9744; 906-337-2229; Fax: 906-337-2795. Hours: 9AM-4PM (EST). *Felony, Civil Actions Over $25,000.*

Civil Records: Access: Mail, in person. Only the court performs in person searches; visitors may not. No search fee. Required to search: name, years to search. Civil cases indexed by defendant, plaintiff. Civil records kept on index books.
Criminal Records: Access: Mail, in person. Only the court performs in person searches; visitors may not. No search fee. Required to search: name, years to search, DOB. Criminal records kept on index books.
General Information: No suppressed, juvenile, sex offenders, mental health, or adoption records released. SASE required. Turnaround time 1-2 days. Copy fee: $.50 per page. Certification fee: $10.00. Fee payee: Keweenaw County. Personal checks accepted. Prepayment is required.

97th District Court HCl Box 607, Eagle River, MI 49950; 906-337-2229; Fax: 906-337-2795. Hours: 9AM-4PM (EST). *Misdemeanor, Civil Actions Under $25,000, Eviction, Small Claims.*

Civil Records: Access: Fax, mail, in person. Only the court performs in person searches; visitors may not. No search fee. Required to search: name, years to search. Civil cases indexed by defendant, plaintiff. Civil records kept on books to 1975. Results cannot be faxed.
Criminal Records: Access: Fax, mail, in person. Only the court performs in person searches; visitors may not. No search fee. Required to search: name, years to search, DOB; also helpful: SSN. Criminal records kept on books to 1975. Results cannot be faxed.
General Information: No suppressed, juvenile, sex offenders, mental health, or adoption records released. SASE required. Turnaround time 1-2 days. Copy fee: $.50 per page. Certification fee: $10.00. Fee payee: Keweenaw County. Personal checks accepted. Prepayment is required.

Probate Court HC1 Box 607, Courthouse, Eagle River, MI 49924; 906-337-1927; Fax: 906-337-2795. Hours: 9AM-4PM (EST). *Probate.*

Lake County

Lake County Trial Court PO Box 1330, Baldwin, MI 49304; 231-745-4614. Hours: 8AM-Noon, 1-5PM (EST). *Felony, Misdemeanor, Civil Actions, Eviction, Small Claims.*

Civil Records: Access: Mail, in person. Only the court performs in person searches; visitors may not. Search fee: $5.00 per name per year. Required to search: name, years to search. Civil cases indexed by defendant, plaintiff. Civil records on computer since 7/89, prior on books.
Criminal Records: Access: Mail, in person. Only the court performs in person searches; visitors may not. Search fee: $5.00 per name per year. Required to search: name, years to search, DOB; also helpful: SSN. Criminal records on computer to 7/89, prior on books.
General Information: No suppressed, juvenile, sex offenders, mental health, or adoption records released. SASE not required. Turnaround time 1-2 days. Copy fee: $1.00 per page. Certification fee: $10.00. Fee payee: Lake County Trial Court. Personal checks accepted. Prepayment is required.

Lake County Trial Court PO Box 1330, Baldwin, MI 49304; 231-745-4614; Fax: 231-745-2241. Hours: 8:30AM-5PM (EST). *Probate.*

Lapeer County

40th Circuit Court 255 Clay St, Lapeer, MI 48446; 810-667-0358. Hours: 8AM-5PM (EST). *Felony, Civil Actions Over $25,000.*

Civil Records: Access: Mail, in person. Visitors must perform in person searches for themselves. Search fee: $5.00 search fee covers 10 year span. Required to search: name, years to search. Civil cases indexed by defendant, plaintiff. Civil records on computer since 1994, prior on index cards.
Criminal Records: Access: Mail, in person. Visitors must perform in person searches for themselves. Search fee: $5.00 search fee covers 10 year span. Required to search: name, years to search, DOB, sex. Criminal records on computer since 1996, prior on index cards.
General Information: Public Access terminal is available. No suppressed records released. SASE required. Turnaround time 1-3 days. Copy fee: $1.00 per page. Certification fee: $10.00 plus $1.00 per page after first. Fee payee: 40th Circuit Court. Personal checks accepted. Prepayment is required.

71 A District Court 255 Clay St., Lapeer, MI 48446; 810-667-0300. Hours: 8AM-5PM (EST). *Misdemeanor, Civil Actions Under $25,000, Eviction, Small Claims.*

Civil Records: Access: Mail, in person. Only the court performs in person searches; visitors may not. Search fee: $5.00 per name. Required to search: name, years to search. Civil cases indexed by defendant, plaintiff. Civil records on computer since 1992, cards and dockets from 1969.
Criminal Records: Access: Mail, in person. Only the court performs in person searches; visitors may not. Search fee: $5.00 per name. Required to search: name, years to search, DOB; also helpful: SSN. Criminal records on computer since 1992, cards and dockets from 1969.
General Information: No suppressed, juvenile, sex offenders, mental health, or adoption records released. SASE requires. Turnaround time 10 days. Copy fee: $1.00 per page. Certification fee: $10.00 plus $1.00 per page after first. Fee payee: 71 A District Court. Personal checks accepted. Third party checks not accepted. Prepayment is required.

Probate Court 255 Clay St., Lapeer, MI 48446; 810-667-0261; Fax: 810-667-0390. Hours: 8AM-5PM (EST). *Probate.*

Leelanau County

13th Circuit Court PO Box 467, Leland, MI 49654; 231-256-9824; Fax: 231-256-8295. Hours: 9AM-5PM (EST). *Felony, Civil Actions Over $25,000.*

Civil Records: Access: Mail, fax, in person. Both court and visitors may perform in person searches. Search fee: $3.00 per name. Required to search: name, years to search. Civil cases indexed by defendant, plaintiff. Civil records on computer since 1/93, prior on docket books.
Criminal Records: Access: Mail, fax, in person. Both court and visitors may perform in person searches. Search fee: $3.00 per name. Required to search: name, years to search. Criminal records on computer since 1/97; prior records on books.
General Information: No suppressed, juvenile, sex offenders, mental health, or adoption records released. SASE required. Turnaround time 2-3 days. Copy fee: $.50 per page. Certification fee: $10.00 plus $1.00 per page after first. Fee payee: County Clerk. Personal checks accepted. Prepayment is required.

86th District Court
86th District Court PO Box 486, Leland, MI 49654; 231-256-8250; Fax: 231-256-8275. Hours: 8AM-4PM (EST). *Misdemeanor, Civil Actions Under $25,000, Eviction, Small Claims.*

Civil Records: Access: Fax, mail, in person. Only the court performs in person searches; visitors may not. No search fee. Required to search: name, years to search. Civil cases indexed by defendant, plaintiff. Civil records on computer since 1991, prior on books to 1969.
Criminal Records: Access: Phone, fax, mail, in person. Only the court performs in person searches; visitors may not. No search fee. Required to search: name, years to search, DOB; also helpful: SSN. Criminal records on computer since 1991, prior on books to 1969.
General Information: No suppressed, sex offenders records released. SASE requested. Turnaround time 3 days. Fax notes: $.25 per page. Copy fee: $.25 per page. Certification fee: $10.00. Fee payee: 86th District Court. Business checks accepted. Prepayment is required.

Probate Court/Juvenile Division PO Box 595, Leland, MI 49654; 231-256-9803; Fax: 231-256-9845. Hours: 9AM-5PM (EST). *Probate.*

Lenawee County

39th Circuit Court 425 North Main St, Adrian, MI 49221; 517-264-4597. Hours: 8AM-4:30PM (EST). *Felony, Civil Actions Over $25,000.*

Civil Records: Access: Mail, in person. Only the court performs in person searches; visitors may not. Search fee: $10.00 per name. Fee is for ten years. Required to search: name, years to search. Civil records on computer back to 1/89, prior on books.
Criminal Records: Access: Mail, in person. Only the court performs in person searches; visitors may not. Search fee: $10.00 per name. Fee is for 10 years. Required to search: name, years to search. Criminal records on computer back to 1/89, prior on books.
General Information: No suppressed, juvenile, sex offenders, mental health, or adoption records released. SASE helpful. Turnaround time 1-2 days. Copy fee: $.50 per page. Certification fee: $10.00. Fee payee: Lenawee County Clerk or 39th Circuit Court. Personal checks accepted. Prepayment is required.

2A District Court 425 North Main St., Adrian, MI 49221; 517-264-4673 & 264-4668; Fax: 517-264-4665 Probation; 264-4681. Hours: 8AM-4:30PM (EST). *Misdemeanor, Civil Actions Under $25,000, Eviction, Small Claims.*

Civil Records: Access: Fax, mail, in person. Both court and visitors may perform in person searches. Search fee: $10.00 per name. Required to search: name, years to search. Civil cases indexed by defendant, plaintiff. Civil records on computer since 1988, prior on index books, cards and microfilm back to 1969.
Criminal Records: Access: In person only. Both court and visitors may perform in person searches. Search fee: $10.00 per name. Required to search: name, years to search, DOB. Criminal records on computer since 1988, prior on index books, cards/microfilm to 1969.
General Information: No suppressed, juvenile, sex offenders, mental health, or adoption records released. SASE required. Turnaround time 1 week. Copy fee: $.25 per page. Certification fee: $10.00. Fee payee: 2A District Court. Personal checks accepted. Prepayment is required.

Probate Court 425 North Main St., Adrian, MI 49221; 517-264-4614; Fax: 517-264-4616. Hours: 8AM-4:30PM (EST). *Probate.*

Livingston County

44th Circuit Court 204 South Highlander Way #5, Howell, MI 48843; 517-546-9816. Hours: 8AM-5PM (EST). *Felony, Civil Actions Over $25,000.*

Note: Juvenile Unit records are at 517-546-1500.

Civil Records: Access: Mail, in person. Both court and visitors may perform in person searches. No search fee. Required to search: name, years to search. Civil cases indexed by defendant, plaintiff. Civil records computerized from 1987, on microfiche and archived from 1900s.

Criminal Records: Access: Mail, in person. Both court and visitors may perform in person searches. No search fee. Required to search: name, years to search. Criminal records computerized from 1987, microfiche and archived from 1900s.

General Information: Public Access terminal is available. All records released, none are restricted. SASE required. Turnaround time 5 days. Copy fee: $1.00 per page. Certification fee: $10.00 plus $1.00 ea add'l pg. Fee payee: Livingston County Clerk. Personal checks accepted. Out of state checks not accepted. Prepayment is required.

53 A District Court 204 South Highlander Way #1, Howell, MI 48843; 517-548-1000; Fax: 517-548-9445. Hours: 8AM-5PM (EST). *Misdemeanor, Civil Actions Under $25,000, Eviction, Small Claims.*

http://co.livingston.mi.us/DistrictCourt

Civil Records: Access: Mail, in person. Only the court performs in person searches; visitors may not. No search fee. Required to search: name, years to search; also helpful: address. Civil cases indexed by defendant, plaintiff. Civil records on computer since 1982.

Criminal Records: Access: Mail, in person. Only the court performs in person searches; visitors may not. No search fee. Required to search: name, years to search, DOB; also helpful: address, SSN. Criminal records on computer since 1982.

General Information: Public Access terminal is available. No suppressed, juvenile, sex offenders, mental health, or adoption records released. SASE preferred. Turnaround time 1 week. Copy fee: $1.00 for first page, $.50 each add'l. Certification fee: $10.00. Fee payee: 53 District Court. Personal checks accepted. Prepayment is required.

53 B District Court 224 N First, Brighton, MI 48116; 810-229-6615; Fax: 810-229-1770. Hours: 8AM-4:45PM (EST). *Misdemeanor, Civil Actions Under $25,000, Eviction, Small Claims.*

http://co.livingston.mi.us/DistrictCourt53Brighton

Civil Records: Access: Mail, in person. Only the court performs in person searches; visitors may not. No search fee. Required to search: name, years to search. Civil cases indexed by defendant, plaintiff. Civil records on computer since 1985, prior on index books.

Criminal Records: Access: Mail, in person. Only the court performs in person searches; visitors may not. No search fee. Required to search: name, years to search, DOB; also helpful: SSN. Criminal records on computer since 1985, prior on index books.

General Information: No suppressed, juvenile, sex offenders, mental health, or adoption records released. SASE required. Turnaround time 1 week. Copy fee: $1.00 for first page, $.50 each add'l. Certification fee: $10.00. Fee payee: 53rd District Court. Personal checks accepted.

Probate Court 200 E. Grand River, Howell, MI 48843; 517-546-3750; Fax: 517-546-3731. Hours: 8AM-5PM (EST). *Probate.*

Luce County

11th Circuit Court 407 W Harrie, Newberry, MI 49868; 906-293-5521; Fax: 906-293-0050. Hours: 8AM-4PM (EST). *Felony, Civil Actions Over $25,000.*

Civil Records: Access: Mail, in person. Only the court performs in person searches; visitors may not. No search fee. Required to search: name, years to search. Civil cases indexed by defendant, plaintiff. Civil records listed on cards since 1876.

Criminal Records: Access: Mail, in person. Only the court performs in person searches; visitors may not. No search fee. Required to search: name, years to search, DOB. Criminal records listed on cards since 1876.

General Information: No suppressed, juvenile, sex offenders, mental health, or adoption records released. SASE required. Turnaround time 4-5 days. Copy fee: $1.00 per page. Certification fee: $10.00. Fee payee: 11th Circuit Court. Personal checks accepted. Prepayment is required.

92nd District Court 407 W Harrie, Newberry, MI 49868; 906-293-5531; Fax: 906-293-3581. Hours: 8AM-4PM (EST). *Misdemeanor, Civil Actions Under $25,000, Eviction, Small Claims.*

Civil Records: Access: Phone, fax, mail, in person. Only the court performs in person searches; visitors may not. No search fee. Required to search: name, years to search. Civil cases indexed by defendant, plaintiff. Civil records to 1969, some on computer.

Criminal Records: Access: Phone, fax, mail, in person. Only the court performs in person searches; visitors may not. No search fee. Required to search: name, years to search, DOB; also helpful: SSN. Criminal records to 1969, some on computer.

General Information: SASE preferred. Turnaround time 1 week. Fax notes: $1.00 per page. Copy fee: $1.00 per page. Certification fee: No cert fee. Fee payee: 92nd District Court. In-state personal checks accepted. Prepayment is required.

Probate Court 407 W. Harrie, Newberry, MI 49868; 906-293-5601; Fax: 906-293-3581. Hours: 8AM-Noon, 1-4PM (EST). *Probate.*

Note: This is a combined court with Mackinac County Probate Court.

Mackinac County

50th Circuit Court 100 S Marley St, Rm 10, St Ignace, MI 49781; 906-643-7300; Fax: 906-643-7302. Hours: 8:30AM-4:30PM (EST). *Felony, Civil Actions Over $25,000.*

Civil Records: Access: Mail, in person. Both court and visitors may perform in person searches. No search fee. Required to search: name, years to search. Civil cases indexed by defendant, plaintiff. Civil records on docket book; on computer back to 1998.

Criminal Records: Access: In person only. Visitors must perform in person searches for themselves. Search fee: Record checks are referred to the state police. Required to search: name, years to search, DOB. Criminal records on docket book; on computer back to 1998.

General Information: No suppressed, juvenile, sex offenders, mental health, or adoption records released. SASE required. Turnaround time 10 days. Copy fee: $1.00 per page. Certification fee: $10.00 plus $1.00 per page after first. Fee payee: County Clerk. Personal checks accepted. Prepayment is required.

92nd District Court 100 South Marley, Room 55, St Ignace, MI 49781; 906-643-7321; Fax: 906-643-7302. Hours: 8:30AM-4:30PM (EST). *Misdemeanor, Civil Actions Under $25,000, Eviction, Small Claims.*

Civil Records: Access: Mail, in person. No search fee. Required to search: name, years to search. Civil cases

indexed by defendant. Civil records on computer since 11/92, prior in files.

Criminal Records: Access: Mail, in person. Both court and visitors may perform in person searches. No search fee. Required to search: name, years to search, DOB. Criminal records on computer since 11/92, prior in files.

General Information: No suppressed, juvenile, sex offenders, mental health, or adoption records released. SASE required. Turnaround time 1 week. No copy fee. Certification fee: No cert fee. Personal checks accepted.

Probate Court 100 Marley St, St Ignace, MI 49781; 906-643-7303; Fax: 906-643-7302. Hours: 8:30AM-Noon, 1-4:30PM (EST). *Probate.*

Note: This is a combined court with Luce County Probate Court.

Macomb County

16th Circuit Court 40 N Main St, Mount Clemens, MI 48043; 810-469-5208. Hours: 8AM-4:30PM (EST). *Felony, Civil Actions Over $25,000.*

www.macomb.lib.mi.us/sabaugh

Civil Records: Access: Mail, in person. Both court and visitors may perform in person searches. Search fee: $1.00 per name per year. Required to search: name, years to search. Civil cases indexed by defendant, plaintiff. Civil records on computer since 1977, on microfiche to 1969, prior to 1800s archived.

Criminal Records: Access: Mail, in person. Both court and visitors may perform in person searches. Search fee: $1.00 per name per year. Required to search: name, years to search; also helpful: DOB. Criminal records on computer since 1977, on microfiche to 1969, prior to 1800s archived.

General Information: Public Access terminal is available. No suppressed, juvenile, sex offenders, mental health, or adoption records released. Turnaround time 1 week. Copy fee: $.40 per page. Certification fee: $10.00 plus $1.00 per page after first. Fee payee: Macomb County Clerk. Personal checks accepted. Credit cards accepted: Visa, MasterCard. Prepayment is required.

37th District Court - Warren & Center Line 8300 Common Rd., Warren, MI 48093; 810-574-4928; Fax: 810-547-4932. Hours: 8:30AM-4:30PM (EST). *Misdemeanor, Civil Actions Under $25,000, Eviction, Small Claims.*

Civil Records: Access: Mail, in person. Only the court performs in person searches; visitors may not. No search fee. Required to search: name, years to search. Civil cases indexed by defendant, plaintiff. Civil records on computer since 1992, prior on index cards.

Criminal Records: Access: Mail, in person. Only the court performs in person searches; visitors may not. No search fee. Required to search: name, years to search, DOB; also helpful: SSN. Criminal records on computer since 1992, prior on index cards.

General Information: No suppressed, juvenile, sex offenders, mental health, or adoption records released. SASE not required. Turnaround time 2 weeks. Copy fee: $.25 per page. Certification fee: $10.00. Fee payee: 37th District Court. Personal checks accepted. Prepayment is required.

39th District Court - Roseville & Frasier 29733 Gratiot Ave, Roseville, MI 48066; 810-773-2010; Fax: 810-774-3310. Hours: 8AM-4:30PM (EST). *Misdemeanor, Civil Actions Under $25,000, Eviction, Small Claims.*

Civil Records: Access: Mail, in person. Only the court performs in person searches; visitors may not. No search fee. Required to search: name, years to search. Civil cases indexed by defendant, plaintiff. Civil records on computer since 1985, prior on microfilm.

Criminal Records: Access: Mail, in person. Only the court performs in person searches; visitors may not. No search fee. Required to search: name, years to search, DOB; also helpful: SSN. Criminal records on computer since 1985, prior on microfilm.

General Information: No suppressed, juvenile, sex offenders, mental health, or adoption records released. SASE not required. Turnaround time 1-2 days. Copy fee: $1.00 per page. Certification fee: $6.00. Fee payee: 39th District Court. Personal checks accepted.

40th District Court - St. Clair Shores 27701

Jefferson, St. Clair Shores, MI 48081; 810-445-5281; Civil phone: 810-445-5282; Criminal phone: 810-445-5288; Fax: 810-445-4003. Hours: 8:30AM-5PM (EST). *Misdemeanor, Civil Actions Under $25,000, Eviction, Small Claims.*

Civil Records: Access: Mail, in person. Both court and visitors may perform in person searches. No search fee. Required to search: name, years to search. Civil cases indexed by defendant, plaintiff. Civil records on computer since 1991; prior records on index books.

Criminal Records: Access: Mail, in person. Both court and visitors may perform in person searches. No search fee. Required to search: name, years to search, DOB; also helpful: SSN. Criminal records on computer since 1991; prior records on index books. Mail requests must have case number.

General Information: Public Access terminal is available. No suppressed, juvenile, sex offenders, mental health, or adoption records released. Turnaround time 2 weeks. Copy fee: $1.00 for first page, $.30 each add'l. Certification fee: No cert fee. Fee payee: 40th District Court. Personal checks accepted. Prepayment of mail search required.

41 A District Court - Shelby 51660 Van Dyke,

Shelby Township, MI 48316; 810-739-7325; Fax: 810-726-4555; 997-6172 (Civil). Hours: 8AM-4:30PM (EST). *Misdemeanor, Civil Actions Under $25,000, Eviction, Small Claims.*

Civil Records: Access: Mail, in person. Both court and visitors may perform in person searches. No search fee. Required to search: name, years to search. Civil cases indexed by defendant, plaintiff. Civil records on computer since 1992, prior on index cards.

Criminal Records: Access: Mail, in person. Both court and visitors may perform in person searches. No search fee. Required to search: name, years to search, DOB. Criminal records on computer since 1992, prior on index cards.

General Information: Public Access terminal is available. (Available Friday afternoons by appointment only.) No suppressed, sex offenders, mental health records released. SASE required. Turnaround time 10 days. Copy fee: $.50 per page. Certification fee: $10.00. Fee payee: 41A District Court. Personal checks accepted. Credit cards accepted. Prepayment is required.

41 A District Court - Sterling Heights

40111 Dodge Park, Sterling Heights, MI 48313; 810-446-2500. Hours: 8:30AM-4:30PM (EST). *Misdemeanor, Civil Actions Under $25,000, Eviction, Small Claims.*

Civil Records: Access: Mail, in person. Only the court performs in person searches; visitors may not. No search fee. Required to search: name, years to search. Civil cases indexed by defendant, plaintiff. Civil records on computer since 1986; prior records on books.

Criminal Records: Access: Mail, in person. Only the court performs in person searches; visitors may not. No search fee. Required to search: name, years to search, DOB; also helpful: SSN. Criminal records on computer since 1986; prior records on books.

General Information: No suppressed, juvenile, sex offenders, mental health, or adoption records released. SASE required. Turnaround time 1 week. Copy fee: $.50 per page. Certification fee: $10.00. Fee payee:

Clerk of Court. Personal checks accepted. Prepayment is required.

41 B District Court - Clinton TWP 40700

Romeo Plank Rd, Clinton Township, MI 48038-2951; 810-286-8010; Fax: 810-228-2555. Hours: 8:30AM-4:30PM (EST). *Misdemeanor, Civil Actions Under $25,000, Eviction, Small Claims.*

Civil Records: Access: Mail, in person. Only the court performs in person searches; visitors may not. No search fee. Required to search: name, years to search. Civil cases indexed by defendant, plaintiff. Civil records on computer back to 1988, prior on microfilm to 1970s.

Criminal Records: Access: Mail, in person. Only the court performs in person searches; visitors may not. No search fee. Required to search: name, years to search, DOB; also helpful: SSN. Criminal records on computer back to 1988, prior on microfilm to 1970s.

General Information: No suppressed, juvenile, sex offenders, mental health, or adoption records released. SASE required. Copy fee: $.50 per page. Certification fee: $10.00. Fee payee: 41 B District Court. Only cashiers checks and money orders accepted. Credit cards accepted: Visa, MasterCard. Prepayment is required.

42nd District Court Division 1 14713 Thirty-

three Mile Rd., PO Box 6, Romeo, MI 48065; 810-752-9679; Fax: 810-469-5515. Hours: 8:30AM-5PM (EST). *Misdemeanor, Civil Actions Under $25,000, Eviction, Small Claims.*

Civil Records: Access: Mail, in person. Only the court performs in person searches; visitors may not. Search fee: $10.00 per name. Required to search: name, years to search. Civil cases indexed by defendant, plaintiff. Civil records on computer since 1990, prior on index books.

Criminal Records: Access: Mail, in person. Only the court performs in person searches; visitors may not. Search fee: $10.00 per name. Required to search: name, years to search, DOB; also helpful: SSN, sex, signed release. Criminal records on computer since 1990, prior on index books.

General Information: SASE requested. Turnaround time 2-3 days. Copy fee: $.35 per page. Certification fee: $10.00. Fee payee: 42-1 District Court. Personal checks accepted. Prepayment is required.

42nd District Court Division 2 (Lenox, Chesterfield) 36540 Green St, New Baltimore, MI

48047; Civil phone: 810-725-9266; Criminal phone: 810-725-9520; Fax: 810-469-5516. Hours: 8:30AM-5PM (EST). *Misdemeanor, Civil Actions Under $25,000, Eviction, Small Claims.*

Civil Records: Access: Mail, in person. Only the court performs in person searches; visitors may not. No search fee. Required to search: name, years to search. Civil cases indexed by defendant, plaintiff. Civil records on computer since 1990, prior on index cards.

Criminal Records: Access: Mail, in person. Only the court performs in person searches; visitors may not. No search fee. Required to search: name, years to search, DOB; also helpful: SSN. Criminal records on computer since 1990, prior on index cards.

General Information: No suppressed, juvenile, sex offenders, mental health, or adoption records released. SASE required. Turnaround time 1 week. Copy fee: $.50 per page. Certification fee: $1.00 per page. Fee payee: 42nd District Court. Personal checks accepted. Prepayment of mail search required.

41 B District Court - Mt Clemens 1 Crocker

Blvd, Mount Clemens, MI 48043; 810-469-6870; Fax: 810-469-5037. Hours: 8AM-4:30PM (EST). *Civil Actions Under $25,000, Eviction, Small Claims.*

Civil Records: Access: Mail, fax, in person. Only the court performs in person searches; visitors may not. No search fee. Required to search: name, years to search;

also helpful-DOB, case number. Civil cases indexed by defendant, plaintiff. Civil records on computer back to 1996; prior on books back to 1940.

General Information: No suppressed, juvenile, sex offenders, mental health, or adoption records released. SASE required. Turnaround time 3 days. Copy fee: $.25 per page. Certification fee: No cert fee. Fee payee: 41 B District Court. Business checks accepted. Credit cards accepted. Prepayment is required.

Probate Court 21850 Dumham, Mount Clemens, MI 48043-1075; 810-469-5290. Hours: 8:30AM-5PM (EST). *Probate.*

Manistee County

19th Circuit Court 415 3rd St, Manistee, MI

49660; 231-723-3331; Fax: 231-723-1492. Hours: 8:30AM-Noon, 1-5PM (EST). *Felony, Civil Actions Over $25,000.*

Civil Records: Access: Mail, in person. Only the court performs in person searches; visitors may not. Search fee: $5.00 per name. Required to search: name, years to search. Civil cases indexed by defendant, plaintiff. Civil records on computer since 7/90, index books from 1867.

Criminal Records: Access: Mail, in person. Only the court performs in person searches; visitors may not. Search fee: $5.00 per name. Required to search: name, years to search, DOB. Criminal records on computer since 7/90, index books from 1867.

General Information: No suppressed, juvenile, sex offenders, mental health, or adoption records released. SASE required. Turnaround time 2-3 days. Fax notes: Fee to fax results is $1.00 per page. Copy fee: $.25 per page. Certification fee: $10.00 plus $1.00 each add'l page. Fee payee: Manistee County Clerk. Personal checks accepted. Prepayment is required.

85th District Court 415 3rd St, Manistee, MI

49660; 231-723-5010; Fax: 231-723-1491. Hours: 8:30AM-5PM (EST). *Misdemeanor, Civil Actions Under $25,000, Eviction, Small Claims.*

Civil Records: Access: Fax, mail, in person. Both court and visitors may perform in person searches. Search fee: $1.00 per name. Required to search: name, years to search. Civil cases indexed by defendant, plaintiff. Civil records on computer since 4/89, prior on index books.

Criminal Records: Access: Fax, mail, in person. Both court and visitors may perform in person searches. Search fee: $1.00 per name. Required to search: name, years to search, DOB. Criminal records on computer since 4/89, prior on index books.

General Information: No suppressed, juvenile, sex offenders, mental health, or adoption records released. SASE required. Turnaround time 5-7 days. Copy fee: $1.00 per page. Certification fee: $10.00. Fee payee: 85th District Court. Personal checks accepted. Prepayment is required.

Probate Court 415 3rd St, Manistee, MI 49660; 231-723-3261; Fax: 231-723-1492. Hours: 8:30AM-Noon, 1-5PM (EST). *Probate.*

Marquette County

25th Circuit Court 234 W Baraga, Marquette, MI

49855; 906-225-8330; Fax: 906-228-1572. Hours: 8AM-5PM (EST). *Felony, Civil Actions Over $25,000.*

Civil Records: Access: Mail, in person. Only the court performs in person searches; visitors may not. Search fee: $5.00 per name. Required to search: name, years to search. Civil cases indexed by defendant, plaintiff. Civil records on books since 1852, on computer from 04/95.

Criminal Records: Access: Mail, in person. Only the court performs in person searches; visitors may not. Search fee: $5.00 per name. Required to search: name, years to search, DOB. Criminal records on books since 1852, on computer from 04/95.

General Information: Public Access terminal is available. No suppressed, juvenile, sex offenders, mental health, or adoption records released. Turnaround time 2-3 business days. Copy fee: $1.00 per page. Certification fee: $10.00 plus $1.00 per page after first. Fee payee: County Clerk. Personal checks accepted. Prepayment is required.

96th District Court County Courthouse, Marquette, MI 49855; 906-225-8235; Fax: 906-225-8255. Hours: 8:30AM-5PM (EST). *Misdemeanor, Civil Actions Under $25,000, Eviction, Small Claims.*

Civil Records: Access: Fax, mail, in person. Both court and visitors may perform in person searches. Search fee: $5.00 per name. Required to search: name, years to search; also helpful: address. Civil cases indexed by defendant, plaintiff. Civil records on computer since 1987, prior on docket books.

Criminal Records: Access: Fax, mail, in person. Both court and visitors may perform in person searches. Search fee: $5.00 per name. Required to search: name, years to search, DOB; also helpful: SSN, offense. Criminal records on computer since 1987, prior on docket books.

General Information: Public Access terminal is available. No suppressed records released. SASE required. Turnaround time 1-2 weeks. Fax notes: No fee to fax results. Copy fee: $1.00 per page. Certification fee: $10.00 plus $1.00 per page after first. Fee payee: 96th District Court. Business checks accepted. Prepayment is required.

Probate Court 234 W Baraga, Marquette, MI 49855; 906-225-8300; Fax: 906-225-8293. Hours: 8AM-5PM (EST). *Probate.*

Mason County

51st Circuit Court 304 E Ludington Ave, Ludington, MI 49431; 231-845-1445; Fax: 231-843-1972. Hours: 9AM-5PM (EST). *Felony, Civil Actions Over $25,000.*

Civil Records: Access: Phone, mail, in person. Only the court performs in person searches; visitors may not. No search fee. Required to search: name, years to search. Civil cases indexed by defendant, plaintiff. Civil records on file since 1867.

Criminal Records: Access: Phone, mail, in person. Only the court performs in person searches; visitors may not. No search fee. Required to search: name, years to search, DOB; also helpful: SSN. Criminal records on file since 1867.

General Information: No suppressed, juvenile, sex offenders, mental health, or adoption records released. SASE required. Turnaround time 1 week. Copy fee: $1.00 per page. Certification fee: $10.00. Fee payee: Mason County Clerk. Personal checks accepted. Prepayment of mail service required.

79th District Court County Court, Ludington, MI 49431; 231-843-4130; Fax: 231-845-7779. Hours: 8AM-5PM (EST). *Misdemeanor, Civil Actions Under $25,000, Eviction, Small Claims.*

Civil Records: Access: Fax, mail, in person. Only the court performs in person searches; visitors may not. Search fee: $5.00 per name. Required to search: name, years to search. Civil cases indexed by defendant, plaintiff. Civil records on Register of Action Docket Cards, computerized since 10/96.

Criminal Records: Access: Fax, mail, in person. Only the court performs in person searches; visitors may not. Search fee: $5.00 per name. Required to search: name, years to search, DOB. Criminal records on Register of Action Docket Cards, computerized since 10/96.

General Information: No suppressed, juvenile, sex offenders, mental health, or adoption records released. SASE required. Turnaround time 2 days. Fax notes: No fee to fax results. Local calls only. Copy fee: $1.00 per

page. Certification fee: $10.00 plus $1.00 per page after first. Fee payee: 79th District Court. Only cashiers checks and money orders accepted.

Probate Court PO Box 186, Ludington, MI 49431; 231-843-8666; Fax: 231-843-1972. Hours: 9AM-Noon, 1-5PM (EST). *Probate.*

Mecosta County

49th Circuit Court 400 Elm, Big Rapids, MI 49307; 231-592-0783; Fax: 231-592-0193. Hours: 8:30AM-5PM (EST). *Felony, Civil Actions Over $25,000.*

Civil Records: Access: Phone, fax, mail, in person. Only the court performs in person searches; visitors may not. No search fee. Required to search: name, years to search. Civil cases indexed by defendant, plaintiff. Civil records on computer since 10/70, archived and microfiche since 1900s. Brief information only by phone.

Criminal Records: Access: Phone, fax, mail, in person. Only the court performs in person searches; visitors may not. No search fee. Required to search: name, years to search. Criminal records on computer since 10/70, archived and microfiche since 1900s. Brief info only by phone.

General Information: No suppressed, juvenile, mental health, or adoption records released. SASE requested. Turnaround time 1 week. Copy fee: $1.00 per page. Certification fee: $10.00. Fee payee: Mecosta County Clerk. Personal checks accepted. Prepayment is required.

77th District Court 400 Elm, Big Rapids, MI 49307; 231-592-0799; Fax: 231-796-2180. Hours: 8:30AM-4:30PM (EST). *Misdemeanor, Civil Actions Under $25,000, Eviction, Small Claims.*

Civil Records: Access: Mail, in person. Only the court performs in person searches; visitors may not. Search fee: $10.00 per name. Required to search: name, years to search. Civil cases indexed by defendant, plaintiff. Civil records on computer for 10 years, archived and microfiche prior.

Criminal Records: Access: Mail, in person. Only the court performs in person searches; visitors may not. Search fee: $10.00 per name. Required to search: name, years to search, DOB. Criminal records on computer for 10 years, archived and microfiche prior. Signed release required for employment screening.

General Information: No suppressed, juvenile, sex offenders, mental health, or adoption records released. SASE not required. Turnaround time 7 days. Copy fee: $1.00 per page. Certification fee: $10.00. Fee payee: 77th District Court. Business checks accepted. Prepayment is required.

Probate Court 400 Elm St, PO Box 820, Big Rapids, MI 49307; 231-592-0135; Fax: 231-592-0191. Hours: 8:30AM-5PM (EST). *Probate.*

Note: Shares the same judge with Osceola County Probate Court.

Menominee County

41st Circuit Court 839 10th Ave, Menominee, MI 49858; 906-863-9968; Fax: 906-863-8839. Hours: 8AM-4:30PM (CST). *Felony, Civil Actions Over $25,000.*

Civil Records: Access: Mail, in person. Only the court performs in person searches; visitors may not. Search fee: $1.00 per name per year. Required to search: name, years to search. Civil cases indexed by defendant, plaintiff. Civil records kept by docket entry in file folders; also on computer back to 1998.

Criminal Records: Access: Mail, in person. Only the court performs in person searches; visitors may not. Search fee: $5.00 per name for first 7 years, then $1.00 each additional year. Required to search: name, years to

search, DOB; also helpful: SSN. Criminal records kept by docket entry in file folders; also on computer back to 1998.

General Information: No suppressed, juvenile, sex offenders, mental health, or adoption records released. Turnaround time 2-3 days. Fax notes: Fee to fax results is $3.00 1st page, $1.00 each add'l. Copy fee: $1.00 per page. Certification fee: $10.00 plus $1.00 per page after first. Fee payee: 41st Circuit Court. Personal checks accepted. Prepayment is required.

95 A District Court 839 10th Ave, Menominee, MI 49858; 906-863-8532; Fax: 906-863-2023. Hours: 8AM-4:30PM (CST). *Misdemeanor, Civil Actions Under $25,000, Eviction, Small Claims.*

Civil Records: Access: Fax, mail, in person. Both court and visitors may perform in person searches. Search fee: $5.00 per name. Required to search: name, years to search. Civil cases indexed by defendant, plaintiff. Civil records on index books since 1969.

Criminal Records: Access: Fax, mail, in person. Only the court performs in person searches; visitors may not. Search fee: $5.00 per name. Required to search: name, years to search, DOB. Criminal records on index books since 1969.

General Information: No suppressed, juvenile, sex offenders, mental health, or adoption records released. SASE required. Turnaround time 1 week. Fax notes: $.20 per page. Copy fee: $.20 per page. Certification fee: $10.00. Fee payee: District Court 95A. Personal checks accepted. Prepayment is required.

Probate Court 839 10th Ave., Menominee, MI 49858; 906-863-2634; Fax: 906-863-8839. Hours: 8AM-4:30PM (CST). *Probate.*

Midland County

42nd Circuit Court Courthouse, 301 W Main St, Midland, MI 48640; 989-832-6735; Fax: 989-832-6610. Hours: 8AM-5PM (EST). *Felony, Civil Actions Over $25,000.*

Civil Records: Access: Phone, mail, in person. Only the court performs in person searches; visitors may not. No search fee. Required to search: name, years to search. Civil cases indexed by defendant, plaintiff. Civil records on computer from 1986, prior on books since 1800s.

Criminal Records: Access: Phone, mail, in person. Only the court performs in person searches; visitors may not. No search fee. Required to search: name, years to search, DOB. Criminal records on computer from 1986, prior on books since 1800s.

General Information: No suppressed records released. SASE required. Turnaround time same day. Copy fee: $1.00 per page. Certification fee: $10.00 plus $1.00 per page after first. Fee payee: Clerk of Circuit Court. Personal checks accepted. Prepayment is required.

75th District Court - Civil Division 301 W Main St, Midland, MI 48640; 989-832-6701. Hours: 8:30AM-4:30PM (EST). *Civil Actions Under $25,000, Eviction, Small Claims.*

Note: Small Claims can be reached at 517-832-6717

Civil Records: Access: Mail, in person. Only the court performs in person searches; visitors may not. Search fee: $1.00 per name per year. Required to search: name, years to search; also helpful: address. Civil cases indexed by defendant, plaintiff. Civil records on computer since 06/89; on index books until 06/89.

General Information: No suppressed, juvenile, sex offenders, mental health, or adoption records released. SASE not required. Turnaround time 5-7 days. Copy fee: $.25 per page. Certification fee: Certification $10.00 for the first page, additional pages $1.00 each. Fee payee: 75th District Court. Personal checks accepted. Prepayment is required.

75th District Court - Criminal Division 301 W Main St, Midland, MI 48640-5183; 989-832-6702 (6714-traffic). Hours: 8:30AM-4:30PM (EST). *Misdemeanor.*

Criminal Records: Access: Mail, in person. Only the court performs in person searches; visitors may not. Search fee: $1.00 per name per year. $5.00 minimum. Required to search: name, years to search, DOB. Criminal records on computer since 1991, prior on docket books and paper index.

General Information: No suppressed, sex offenders or mental health records released. SASE not required. Turnaround time 2 weeks. Copy fee: $1.00 per page. Certification fee: $10.00. Fee payee: 75th District Court. Personal checks accepted.

Probate Court 301 W Main St, Midland, MI 48640; 989-832-6880; Fax: 989-832-6607. Hours: 8AM-5PM (EST). *Probate.*

Missaukee County

28th Circuit Court PO Box 800, Lake City, MI 49651; 231-839-4967; Fax: 231-839-3684. Hours: 9AM-5PM (EST). *Felony, Civil Actions Over $25,000.*

Civil Records: Access: Phone, fax, mail, in person. Both court and visitors may perform in person searches. Search fee: $5.00 per name. Required to search: name, years to search. Civil cases indexed by defendant, plaintiff. Civil records on computer to 1990, prior on books.

Criminal Records: Access: Phone, fax, mail, in person. Both court and visitors may perform in person searches. Search fee: $5.00 per name. Required to search: name, years to search; also helpful: DOB, SSN. Criminal records on computer to 1990, prior on books.

General Information: Public Access terminal is available. No suppressed, juvenile, sex offenders, mental health, or adoption records released. SASE not required. Turnaround time 2 days. Fax notes: $5.00 for first page, $1.00 each add'l. Copy fee: $1.00 per page. Certification fee: $10.00. Fee payee: Missaukee County Clerk. Personal checks accepted. Prepayment is required.

84th District Court PO Box 800, Lake City, MI 49651; 231-839-4590. Hours: 9AM-5PM (EST). *Misdemeanor, Civil Actions Under $25,000, Eviction, Small Claims.*

Civil Records: Access: Mail, in person. Both court and visitors may perform in person searches. Search fee: $5.00 per name. Required to search: name, years to search. Civil cases indexed by defendant, plaintiff. Civil records on computer since 1989.

Criminal Records: Access: Mail, in person. Both court and visitors may perform in person searches. Search fee: $5.00 per name. Required to search: name, years to search, DOB, SSN. Criminal records on computer to 1988.

General Information: No suppressed, juvenile, sex offenders, mental health, or adoption records released. SASE required. Turnaround time 1 week. Copy fee: $1.00 per page. Certification fee: $10.00 plus $1.00 per page after first. Fee payee: District Court. Personal checks accepted. Prepayment is required.

Probate Court PO Box 800, Lake City, MI 49651; 231-839-2266; Fax: 231-839-5856. Hours: 9AM-Noon, 1-5PM (EST). *Probate.*

Monroe County

38th Circuit Court 106 E 1st St, Monroe, MI 48161; 734-240-7020; Fax: 734-240-7266. Hours: 8:30AM-5PM (EST). *Felony, Civil Actions Over $25,000.*

www.co.monroe.mi.us/Courts/index.html

Civil Records: Access: Mail, fax, in person. Both court and visitors may perform in person searches. Search fee: $8.00 per name. Fee is per name per 5 years. Required to search: name, years to search. Civil cases indexed by defendant, plaintiff. Civil records on computer back to 1990; prior on docket books.

Criminal Records: Access: Mail, fax, in person. Both court and visitors may perform in person searches. Search fee: $8.00 per name. Fee is per name per 5 years. Required to search: name, years to search, DOB. Criminal records on computer back to 1990; prior on docket books.

General Information: Public Access terminal is available. No suppressed records released. SASE required. Turnaround time same day. Copy fee: $1.00 per page. Certification fee: $10.00. Fee payee: 38th Circuit Court. Personal checks accepted. Prepayment is required.

1st District Court 106 E 1st St, Monroe, MI 48161; 734-240-7075; Fax: 734-240-7098. Hours: 8AM-5PM (EST). *Misdemeanor, Civil Actions Under $25,000, Eviction, Small Claims.*

www.co.monroe.mi.us/DistrictCourt/index.htm

Civil Records: Access: Mail, in person. Only the court performs in person searches; visitors may not. No search fee. Required to search: name, years to search, address. Civil cases indexed by defendant, plaintiff. Civil records on computer since 1990; prior records on microfiche.

Criminal Records: Access: Mail, in person. Only the court performs in person searches; visitors may not. No search fee. Required to search: name, years to search, DOB; also helpful: address, SSN. Criminal records on computer since 1990; prior records on microfiche.

General Information: No suppressed, juvenile, sex offenders, mental health, or adoption records released. Turnaround time 1 week. Copy fee: $1.00 per page. Certification fee: $10.00 per page. Fee payee: 1st District Court. Business checks accepted. Prepayment is required.

Probate Court 106 E 1st St, Monroe, MI 48161; 734-243-7018. Hours: 8AM-Noon, 1-5PM *Probate.*

www.co.monroe.mi.us/Courts/index.html

Montcalm County

8th Circuit Court PO Box 368, Stanton, MI 48888; 989-831-7339; Fax: 989-831-7474. Hours: 8AM-5PM (EST). *Felony, Civil Actions Over $25,000.*

Note: The office closes for lunch for one hour.

Civil Records: Access: Mail, in person. Only the court performs in person searches; visitors may not. Search fee: $5.00 for 5 years then $1.00 for each additional year searched. Required to search: name, years to search. Civil cases indexed by defendant, plaintiff. Civil records on docket books.

Criminal Records: Access: Mail, in person. Only the court performs in person searches; visitors may not. Search fee: Same fees as civil. Required to search: name, years to search, DOB. Criminal records on docket books.

General Information: No suppressed, juvenile, sex offenders, mental health, adoption, birth or DD214 records released. Turnaround time 1-3 days. Copy fee: $1.00 per page. Certification fee: $10.00 plus $1.00 per page after first. Fee payee: Montcalm County Clerk. Personal checks accepted. Prepayment is required.

64 B District Court 617 N State Rd #D, Stanton, MI 48888; 989-831-7450; Fax: 989-831-4747. Hours: 8AM-5PM (EST). *Misdemeanor, Civil Actions Under $25,000, Eviction, Small Claims.*

Civil Records: Access: Mail, in person. Only the court performs in person searches; visitors may not. No search fee. Required to search: name, years to search.

Civil cases indexed by defendant, plaintiff. Civil records on computer since 1989, prior on books and microfiche.

Criminal Records: Access: Mail, in person. Only the court performs in person searches; visitors may not. No search fee. Required to search: name, years to search, DOB; also helpful: SSN. Criminal records on computer since 1989, prior on books and microfiche.

General Information: No suppressed records released. SASE required. Turnaround time 14 days. Copy fee: $.50 per page. Certification fee: $10.00 plus $1.00 each add'l pg. Fee payee: 64 B District Court. Personal checks accepted. Prepayment is required.

Probate Court 211 W Main St, PO Box 309, Stanton, MI 48888; 989-831-7316; Fax: 989-831-7314. Hours: 8AM-5PM (EST). *Probate.*

Montmorency County

26th Circuit Court PO Box 789, Atlanta, MI 49709; 989-785-4794; Fax: 989-785-2662. Hours: 8:30AM-Noon, 1-4:30PM (EST). *Felony, Civil Actions Over $25,000.*

Note: A Board ruling regarding search fee changes is pending.

Civil Records: Access: Phone, fax, mail, in person. Both court and visitors may perform in person searches. No search fee. Required to search: name, years to search. Civil cases indexed by defendant, plaintiff. Civil records on computer since 1990, prior on books since 1940s, microfiche to 1970.

Criminal Records: Access: Phone, fax, mail, in person. Both court and visitors may perform in person searches. No search fee. Required to search: name, years to search; also helpful: DOB. Criminal records on computer since 1990, prior on books since 1940s.

General Information: No suppressed, mental health, birth certificate (except to heir or parent) adoption records released. Turnaround time 3-4 days. Fax notes: $1.00 per page. Copy fee: $1.00 per page. Certification fee: $10.00 plus $1.00 each additional page. Fee payee: County Clerk. Personal checks accepted. Prepayment is required.

88th District Court County Courthouse, PO Box 789, Atlanta, MI 49709; 989-785-3122; Fax: 989-785-2376. Hours: 8:30AM-Noon, 1-4:30PM (EST). *Misdemeanor, Civil Actions Under $25,000, Eviction, Small Claims.*

Civil Records: Access: Mail, fax, in person. Only the court performs in person searches; visitors may not. Search fee: $5.00 per name. Required to search: name, years to search; also helpful: address. Civil cases indexed by defendant, plaintiff. Civil records on computer back to 1990, prior on books and card file since 1969.

Criminal Records: Access: Mail, fax, in person. Only the court performs in person searches; visitors may not. Search fee: $5.00 per name. Required to search: name, years to search, DOB; also helpful: address, SSN, signed release. Criminal records on computer back to 1990, prior on books and card file since 1969.

General Information: No suppressed, juvenile, sex offenders, mental health, or adoption records released. SASE required. Turnaround time 1-3 days. Fax notes: Fee to fax results is $1.00 per document plus $1.00 per page. Copy fee: $1.00 per page. Certification fee: $10.00. Fee payee: 88th District Court-Montmorency County. Personal checks accepted. Prepayment is required.

Probate Court PO Box 789, Atlanta, MI 49709-0789; 989-785-4403; Fax: 989-785-2605. *Probate.*

Muskegon County

14th Circuit Court County Bldg, 6th Floor, 990 Terrace St, Muskegon, MI 49442; 231-724-6251; Fax: 231-724-6695. Hours: 8AM-5PM (EST). *Felony, Civil Actions Over $25,000.*

Civil Records: Access: Phone, mail, fax, in person. Both court and visitors may perform in person searches. No search fee. Required to search: name, years to search. Civil cases indexed by defendant, plaintiff. Civil records on computer back to 1984, prior on books since 1853.

Criminal Records: Access: Phone, mail, fax, in person. Both court and visitors may perform in person searches. No search fee. Required to search: name, years to search, DOB; also helpful: SSN. Criminal records on computer to 1984, prior on books to 1853.

General Information: Public Access terminal is available. No suppressed, juvenile, sex offenders, mental health, or adoption records released. SASE requires. Turnaround time 2-3 days. Fax notes: Fee to fax results is $1.00 per page. Copy fee: $1.00 per page. Certification fee: $10.00 plus $1.00 per page after first. Fee payee: Circuit Court Records. Personal checks accepted. Prepayment is required.

60th District Court 990 Terrace, 1st Floor, Muskegon, MI 49442; 231-724-6250; Fax: 231-724-3489. Hours: 8:30AM-4:45PM (EST). *Misdemeanor, Civil Actions Under $25,000, Eviction, Small Claims.*

Civil Records: Access: Mail, in person. Both court and visitors may perform in person searches. No search fee. Required to search: name, years to search. Civil cases indexed by defendant, plaintiff. Civil records on computer since 5/93, prior on hard copy.

Criminal Records: Access: Mail, in person. Only the court performs in person searches; visitors may not. No search fee. Required to search: name, years to search, DOB. Criminal records on computer since 5/93, prior on hard copy.

General Information: Public Access terminal is available. No suppressed, juvenile, sex offenders, mental health, or adoption records released. SASE required. Turnaround time 3 days. Copy fee: $1.00 per page. Certification fee: $10.00. Fee payee: 60th District Court. Personal checks accepted. Prepayment required.

Probate Court 990 Terrace St, 5th Floor, Muskegon, MI 49442; 231-724-6241; Fax: 231-724-6232. Hours: 8AM-5PM (EST). *Probate.*

Newaygo County

27th Circuit Court PO Box 885, White Cloud, MI 49349-0885; 231-689-7269; Fax: 231-689-7007. Hours: 8AM-noon; 1-5PM (EST). *Felony, Civil Actions Over $25,000.*

Civil Records: Access: Mail, fax, in person. Only the court performs in person searches; visitors may not. No search fee. Required to search: name, years to search. Civil cases indexed by defendant, plaintiff. Civil records archived since 1880s; on computer since 7/1994.

Criminal Records: Access: Mail, fax, in person. Only the court performs in person searches; visitors may not. No search fee. Required to search: name, years to search; also helpful: DOB. Criminal records archived since 1880s; on computer since 7/1994.

General Information: No suppressed records released. SASE requested. Turnaround time 2-5 days. Fax notes: Will fax results to toll-free numbers only. Copy fee: $1.00 per page. Certification fee: $10.00 plus $1.00 per page after first. Fee payee: Newaygo County Circuit Court. Personal checks accepted. Prepayment is required.

78th District Court 1092 Newell St, White Cloud, MI 49349; 231-689-7257; Fax: 231-689-7258. Hours: 8AM-noon, 1-5PM (EST). *Misdemeanor, Civil Actions Under $25,000, Eviction, Small Claims.*

Civil Records: Access: Fax, mail, in person. Both court and visitors may perform in person searches. No search fee. Required to search: name, years to search; also helpful: address. Civil cases indexed by defendant, plaintiff. Civil records on computer since 7/27/89, prior in folders.

Criminal Records: Access: Fax, mail, in person. Both court and visitors may perform in person searches. No search fee. Required to search: name, years to search, DOB; also helpful: address, SSN. Criminal records on computer since 7/27/89, prior in folders.

General Information: Public Access terminal is available. No suppressed records released. SASE required. Turnaround time 7-10 days. Fax notes: No fee to fax results. Copy fee: $1.00 per page. Certification fee: $10.00 plus $1.00 per page after first. Fee payee: 78th District Court. Personal checks accepted. Prepayment is required.

Probate Court PO Box 885 (1092 Newell St.), White Cloud, MI 49349; 231-689-7270; Fax: 231-689-7276. Hours: 8AM-Noon, 1-5PM (EST). *Probate.*

Oakland County

6th Circuit Court 1200 N Telegraph Rd, Pontiac, MI 48341; 248-858-0581. Hours: 8:30AM-4:30PM (EST). *Felony, Civil Actions Over $25,000.*

www.co.oakland.mi.us/c_serv/oakcourts

Civil Records: Access: Mail, in person. Both court and visitors may perform in person searches. Search fee: $1.00 per name. Required to search: name, years to search. Civil cases indexed by defendant, plaintiff. Civil records on computer since 1963, prior on microfilm & books.

Criminal Records: Access: Mail, in person. Both court and visitors may perform in person searches. Search fee: $1.00 per name. Required to search: name; also helpful: years to search, DOB, SSN. Criminal records on computer since 1963, prior on microfilm & books.

General Information: Public Access terminal is available. No suppressed, non-public, sex offenders or mental health records released. SASE required. Turnaround time 7 days. Copy fee: $.25 per page. Certification fee: $10.00 plus $1.00 per page after first. Fee payee: Circuit Court. Personal checks accepted. Credit cards accepted: Visa, MasterCard for mail orders.

43rd District Court 43 E Nine Mile Rd, Hazel Park, MI 48030; 248-547-3034; Fax: 248-546-4088. Hours: 8:30AM-5PM (EST). *Misdemeanor, Civil Actions Under $25,000, Eviction, Small Claims.*

Civil Records: Access: Mail, in person. Both court and visitors may perform in person searches. No search fee. Required to search: name, years to search. Civil cases indexed by defendant, plaintiff. Civil records on computer since 1989, prior on books since 1970.

Criminal Records: Access: Mail, in person. Both court and visitors may perform in person searches. No search fee. Required to search: name, years to search, DOB; also helpful: SSN. Criminal records on computer since 1989, prior on books since 1970.

General Information: No suppressed, juvenile, sex offenders, mental health, or adoption records released. SASE not required. Turnaround time 3 days. Copy fee: $.25 per page. Certification fee: $10.00. Fee payee: 43rd District Court. Only cashiers checks and money orders accepted. Prepayment is required.

44th District Court - Royal Oak 400 E Eleven Mile Rd, Box 20, Royal Oak, MI 48068; 248-246-3600; Fax: 248-246-3601. Hours: 8AM-4:30PM (EST). *Misdemeanor, Civil Actions Under $25,000, Eviction, Small Claims.*

Civil Records: Access: Mail, in person. Both court and visitors may perform in person searches. Search fee: $10.00 per name. Required to search: name, years to search. Civil cases indexed by defendant, plaintiff. Civil records on computer since 1980s, prior on docket books and index cards.

Criminal Records: Access: Mail, in person. Both court and visitors may perform in person searches. Search fee: $10.00 per name. Required to search: name, years to search, DOB, signed release, offense; also helpful: address. Criminal records on computer since 1980s, prior on docket books and index cards.

General Information: No suppressed, juvenile, sex offenders, mental health, or adoption records released. SASE required. Turnaround time 5 days. Copy fee: $1.00 per page. Certification fee: $10.00 plus $1.00 per page after first. Fee payee: 44th District Court. Personal checks accepted. Prepayment is required.

45 A District Court - Berkley 3338 Coolidge, Berkley, MI 48072; 248-544-3300; Fax: 248-546-2416. Hours: 8:30AM-4:30PM (EST). *Misdemeanor, Civil Actions Under $25,000, Eviction, Small Claims.*

Civil Records: Access: Mail, in person. Only the court performs in person searches; visitors may not. No search fee. Required to search: name, years to search. Civil cases indexed by defendant, plaintiff. Civil records on computer since 1986, prior on books.

Criminal Records: Access: Mail, in person. Only the court performs in person searches; visitors may not. No search fee. Required to search: name, years to search, DOB; also helpful: SSN. Criminal records on computer since 1986, prior on books.

General Information: No suppressed records released. SASE required. Turnaround time 1 week. Copy fee: $1.00 per page. Certification fee: $10.00 plus $1.00 per page after first. Fee payee: 45 A District Court. Personal checks accepted. Prepayment is required.

45 B District Court 13600 Oak Park Blvd, Oak Park, MI 48237; 248-691-7440; Fax: 248-691-7158. Hours: 9AM-5PM (EST). *Misdemeanor, Civil Actions Under $25,000, Eviction, Small Claims.*

Note: Court covers Huntington Woods, Oak Park, Pleasant Ridge, and Royal Oak Township.

Civil Records: Access: Mail, in person. Only the court performs in person searches; visitors may not. No search fee. Required to search: name, years to search. Civil cases indexed by defendant, plaintiff. Civil records on computer back to 1986, prior on docket books and index cards.

Criminal Records: Access: Mail, in person. Only the court performs in person searches; visitors may not. No search fee. Required to search: name, years to search, DOB; also helpful: SSN. Criminal records on computer back to 1986, prior on docket books and index cards.

General Information: Public Access terminal is available. No suppressed records released. Turnaround time varies. Copy fee: $1.00 per page. Certification fee: $10.00. Fee payee: 45 B District Court. Business checks accepted.

46th District Court 26000 Evergreen Rd, Southfield, MI 48076; 248-354-9506; Civil phone: 248-354-9370; Criminal phone: 248-354-9368; Fax: 248-354-5315. Hours: 8AM-4:45PM (counter) (EST). *Misdemeanor, Civil Actions Under $25,000, Eviction, Small Claims.*

www.46districtcourt.com

Civil Records: Access: Mail, in person. Both court and visitors may perform in person searches. No search fee. Required to search: name, years to search. Civil cases

indexed by defendant, plaintiff. Civil records prior to 1990 are on microfilm; most recent records are computerized.

Criminal Records: Access: Mail, in person. Both court and visitors may perform in person searches. Court will search only 1990 to present with case # provided. No search fee. Required to search: name, years to search, DOB. Criminal records on computer since 1991, prior on microfiche.

General Information: No suppressed, juvenile, sex offenders, mental health, or adoption records released. SASE requested. Turnaround time varies. Copy fee: $.25 per page. Certification fee: $10.00 plus $1.00 per page after first. Fee payee: 46th District Court. Personal checks accepted. Credit cards accepted: Discover. Prepayment is required.

47th District Court - Farmington, Farmington Hills
32795 W Ten Mile Rd, Farmington, MI 48336; 248-477-5630; Fax: 248-477-2441. Hours: 8:30AM-4:30PM; 'til 6:30PM 3rd Tues each month (EST). *Misdemeanor, Civil Actions Under $25,000, Eviction, Small Claims.*

Civil Records: Access: Mail, fax, in person. No search fee. Required to search: name, years to search. Civil cases indexed by defendant, plaintiff. Civil records on computer since 7/19/93; prior on microfiche since 1975.
Criminal Records: Access: Mail, fax, in person. Visitors must perform in person searches for themselves. No search fee. Required to search: name, years to search, DOB; also helpful: SSN, offense. Criminal records on computer since 7/19/93; prior on microfiche since 1975.
General Information: Public Access terminal is available. No suppressed, sex offenders or mental health records released. SASE required. Turnaround time varies. Copy fee: $1.00 per page. Certification fee: $10.00 plus $1.00 per page after first. Fee payee: 47th District Court. Personal checks accepted. Credit cards accepted: Visa, MasterCard.

48th District Court
4280 Telegraph Rd, Bloomfield Hills, MI 48302; 248-647-1141; Fax: 248-647-8955. Hours: 8:30AM-4:30PM (EST). *Misdemeanor, Civil Actions Under $25,000, Eviction, Small Claims.*

Civil Records: Access: Phone, mail, in person. Both court and visitors may perform in person searches. No search fee. Required to search: name, years to search, address. Civil cases indexed by defendant, plaintiff. Civil records on computer to 1980, prior on index cards.
Criminal Records: Access: Phone, mail, in person. Both court and visitors may perform in person searches. No search fee. Required to search: name, years to search, address, DOB; also helpful: SSN. Criminal records on computer since 1980, prior on index cards.
General Information: Public Access terminal is available. No suppressed, juvenile, sex offenders, mental health, victim or adoption records released. Turnaround time varies. Copy fee: $.50 per page. Certification fee: $10.00 plus $1.00 per page after first. Fee payee: 48th District Court. Personal checks accepted. Credit cards accepted: Visa, MasterCard. Debit Card accepted. Prepayment is required.

51st District Court - Waterford
5100 Civic Center Dr, Waterford, MI 48329; 248-674-4655. Hours: 8:30AM-4:45PM (EST). *Misdemeanor, Civil Actions Under $25,000, Eviction, Small Claims.*

Civil Records: Access: Mail, in person. Only the court performs in person searches; visitors may not. Search fee: $2.00 per name. Required to search: name, years to search. Civil cases indexed by defendant, plaintiff. Civil records on computer since 1980s, prior on docket books and index cards.
Criminal Records: Access: Mail, in person. Only the court performs in person searches; visitors may not. No

search fee. Required to search: name, years to search, DOB; also helpful: SSN. Criminal records on computer since 1980s, prior on docket books and index cards.
General Information: No suppressed, juvenile, sex offenders, mental health, or adoption records released. Turnaround time 10 days. Copy fee: $.25 per page. Certification fee: $10.00. Fee payee: 51st District Court. Personal checks accepted. Credit cards accepted: Visa, MasterCard. Prepayment is required.

52nd District Court - Division 1
48150 Grand River, Novi, MI 48374; Civil phone: 248-305-6080; Criminal phone: 248-305-6460. Hours: 8:30AM-4:30PM (EST). *Misdemeanor, Civil Actions Under $25,000, Eviction, Small Claims.*

www.52-1districtcourt.com

Civil Records: Access: Mail, in person. Only the court performs in person searches; visitors may not. No search fee. Required to search: name, years to search. Civil cases indexed by defendant, plaintiff. Civil records on computer since 1984, prior on books.
Criminal Records: Access: Mail, in person. Only the court performs in person searches; visitors may not. No search fee. Required to search: name, years to search; also helpful: DOB. Criminal records on computer since 1984, prior on books.
General Information: Public Access terminal is available. No suppressed, juvenile, sex offenders or mental health records released. SASE required. Turnaround time 1 month. Copy fee: $1.00 per page. Certification fee: $10.00. Fee payee: 52-1 District Court. Personal checks accepted. Credit cards accepted: Visa, MasterCard. In state only. Prepayment is required.

52nd District Court - Division 2
5850 Lorac, Clarkston, MI 48346; Civil phone: 248-625-4994; Criminal phone: 248-625-4888; Fax: 248-625-5602. Hours: 8:30AM-4:30PM (EST). *Misdemeanor, Civil Actions Under $25,000, Eviction, Small Claims.*

Note: Court covers Springfield, Holly, Groveland, Brandon, Independence, Clarkston & Ortonville.

Civil Records: Access: Phone, fax, mail, in person. Only the court performs in person searches; visitors may not. No search fee. Required to search: name, years to search. Civil cases indexed by defendant, plaintiff. Civil records on computer since 1982, prior on microfiche since 1976.
Criminal Records: Access: Phone, fax, mail, in person. Only the court performs in person searches; visitors may not. No search fee. Required to search: name, years to search, DOB; also helpful: SSN. Criminal records on computer since 1982, prior on microfiche since 1976.
General Information: No suppressed, juvenile or sex offender records released. Turnaround time 3-5 days. Copy fee: $1.00 per page. Certification fee: $10.00 plus $1.00 per page after first. Fee payee: 52-2 District Court. Personal checks accepted. Credit cards accepted: Visa, MasterCard. Prepayment is required.

52nd District Court - Division 3
135 Barclay Circle, Rochester Hills, MI 48307; 248-853-5553; Fax: 248-853-3277. Hours: 8:30AM-4:30PM (EST). *Misdemeanor, Civil Actions Under $25,000, Eviction, Small Claims.*

Civil Records: Access: Phone, mail, in person. Visitors must perform in person searches for themselves. No search fee. Required to search: name; also helpful: years to search. Civil cases indexed by defendant, plaintiff. Civil records on computer for 10 years, prior on docket books and index cards.
Criminal Records: Access: Phone, mail, in person. Visitors must perform in person searches for themselves. No search fee. Required to search: name; also helpful: years to search, DOB. Criminal records on computer for 10 years, prior on docket books and index cards.

General Information: No suppressed records released. Turnaround time varies. Copy fee: $1.00 per page. Certification fee: $10.00. Fee payee: 52-3 District Court. Personal checks accepted. Credit cards accepted: Visa, MasterCard. In person only. Prepayment is required.

52nd District Court - Division 4 (Troy, Clawson)
520 W Big Beaver Rd, Troy, MI 48084; 248-528-0400; Fax: 248-528-3588. Hours: 8:15AM-4:15PM (EST). *Misdemeanor, Civil Actions Under $25,000, Eviction, Small Claims.*

Civil Records: Access: Mail, in person. Both court and visitors may perform in person searches. No search fee. Required to search: name, years to search. Civil cases indexed by defendant, plaintiff.
Criminal Records: Access: Phone, fax, mail, in person. Only the court performs in person searches; visitors may not. No search fee. Required to search: name; also helpful: years to search, DOB, SSN. Criminal records.
General Information: No suppressed, juvenile, sex offenders, mental health, or adoption records released. SASE required. Turnaround time 1 week. Fax notes: No fee to fax results. Fax for criminal records and local calls only. Copy fee: $1.00 per page. Certification fee: $10.00. Fee payee: 52-4 District Court. Personal checks accepted. Credit cards accepted: Visa, MasterCard. Prepayment is required.

50th District Court - Pontiac Civil Division
70 N Saganaw, Pontiac, MI 48342; 248-857-8090; Fax: 248-857-6028. Hours: 8:30AM-5PM *Civil Actions Under $25,000, Eviction, Small Claims.*

Civil Records: Access: Mail, in person. Both court and visitors may perform in person searches. No search fee. Required to search: name, years to search. Civil cases indexed by defendant, plaintiff. Civil records on computer since 1985.
General Information: Public Access terminal is available. No suppressed, juvenile, sex offenders, mental health, or adoption records released. Turnaround time 3-4 days. Copy fee: $1.00 per page. Certification fee: $10.00. Fee payee: 50th District Court. Personal checks accepted. Prepayment is required.

50th District Court - Pontiac Criminal Division
70 N Saganaw, Pontiac, MI 48342; 248-857-8027; Fax: 248-857-6028. Hours: 8:30AM-5PM (EST). *Misdemeanor.*

Criminal Records: Access: Mail, in person. Both court and visitors may perform in person searches. No search fee. Required to search: name, years to search, DOB; also helpful: SSN. Criminal records on computer since 1984, prior on index cards since 1975.
General Information: Public Access terminal is available. No suppressed, juvenile, sex offenders, mental health, or adoption records released. Turnaround time 2-3 days. Copy fee: $1.00 per page. Certification fee: $10.00. Fee payee: 50th District Court. Business checks accepted. Prepayment is required.

Probate Court
1200 N Telegraph Rd, 1st Fl, Oakland County Complex, East Wing, Pontiac, MI 48341; 248-858-0260; Fax: 248-452-2016. Hours: 8:30AM-5PM (EST). *Probate.*

Oceana County

27th Circuit Court
100 State Street, #M-34, Hart, MI 49420; 231-873-3977. Hours: 9AM-Noon,1-5PM (EST). *Felony, Civil Actions Over $25,000.*

Civil Records: Access: Mail, in person. Only the court performs in person searches; visitors may not. Search fee: $5.00 per name. Required to search: name, years to search. Civil cases indexed by defendant, plaintiff. Civil records on computer since 1994.

Criminal Records: Access: Mail, in person. Only the court performs in person searches; visitors may not. Search fee: $5.00 per name. Required to search: name, years to search; also helpful: DOB. Criminal records on computer since 1994.

General Information: No suppressed, juvenile, sex offenders, mental health, or adoption records released. SASE requested. Turnaround time same day. Copy fee: $10.00 for first page, $1.00 each add'l. Certification fee: $10.00 plus $1.00 per page after first. Fee payee: Oceana County Circuit Court. Personal checks accepted. Prepayment is required.

79th District Court PO Box 471, Hart, MI 49420; 231-873-4530; Fax: 231-873-1861. Hours: 8AM-5PM (EST). *Misdemeanor, Civil Actions Under $25,000, Eviction, Small Claims.*

Civil Records: Access: Mail, in person. Only the court performs in person searches; visitors may not. Search fee: $5.00 per name. Required to search: name, years to search. Civil cases indexed by plaintiff. Civil records on file cards and in file folders since 1967; on computer back to 1999.

Criminal Records: Access: Mail, in person. Only the court performs in person searches; visitors may not. Search fee: $5.00 per name. Required to search: name, years to search, DOB. Criminal records on file cards and in file folders since 1967; on computer to 1999.

General Information: No suppressed records released. SASE not required. Turnaround time same day. Copy fee: $1.00 per page. Certification fee: $10.00 plus $1.00 per page after first. Fee payee: 79th District Court. No personal checks accepted. Prepayment is required.

Probate Court County Bldg, 100 S State St, Suite M-34, Hart, MI 49420; 231-873-3666; Fax: 231-873-4177. Hours: 9AM-Noon, 1-5PM (EST). *Probate.*

Ogemaw County

34th Circuit Court 806 W Houghton, West Branch, MI 48661; 989-345-0215; Fax: 989-345-7223. Hours: 8:30AM-4:30PM (EST). *Felony, Civil Actions Over $25,000.*

Civil Records: Access: Phone, fax, mail, in person. Only the court performs in person searches; visitors may not. Search fee: $10.00 per name. Fee is for search prior to 1993. Required to search: name, years to search. Civil cases indexed by defendant, plaintiff. Civil records on index cards since 1970, library books in vault since 1960; on computer back to 1993.

Criminal Records: Access: Phone, fax, mail, in person. Only the court performs in person searches; visitors may not. Search fee: $10.00 per name. Fee is for search prior to 1993. Required to search: name, years to search, DOB; also helpful: SSN. Criminal records on index cards since 1970, library books in vault since 1960; on computer back to 1993.

General Information: No suppressed, juvenile, sex offenders, mental health, or adoption records released. SASE required. Turnaround time 1-3 weeks. Fax notes: $2.00 for first page, $1.00 each add'l. Copy fee: $.50 per page. Certification fee: $10.00 plus $1.00 per page. Fee payee: 34th Circuit Court. Personal checks accepted. Prepayment is required.

82nd District Court PO Box 365, West Branch, MI 48661; 989-345-5040; Fax: 989-345-5910. Hours: 8:30AM-4:30PM (EST). *Misdemeanor, Civil Actions Under $25,000, Eviction, Small Claims.*

Civil Records: Access: Fax, mail, in person. Only the court performs in person searches; visitors may not. Search fee: $2.00 per name. Required to search: name, years to search. Civil cases indexed by defendant, plaintiff. Civil records on computer since 1990, prior on books since 1969.

Criminal Records: Access: Fax, mail, in person. Only the court performs in person searches; visitors may not.

Search fee: $2.00 per name. Required to search: name, years to search, DOB. Criminal records on computer since 1990, prior on books since 1969.

General Information: No suppressed records released. SASE requested. Turnaround time 2-3 days. Fax notes: No fee to fax results. Copy fee: $.50 per page. Certification fee: $10.00. Fee payee: 82nd District Court. Personal checks accepted. Prepayment of mail search required.

Probate Court County Courthouse, Rm 203, 806 W Houghton Ave, West Branch, MI 48661; 989-345-0145; Fax: 989-345-5901. Hours: 8:30AM-Noon, 1-4:30PM (EST). *Probate.*

Ontonagon County

32nd Circuit Court 725 Greenland Rd, Ontonagon, MI 49953; 906-884-4255; Fax: 906-884-2916. Hours: 8:30AM-4:30PM (EST). *Felony, Civil Actions Over $25,000.*

Civil Records: Access: Mail, fax, in person. Both court and visitors may perform in person searches. No search fee. Required to search: name, years to search. Civil cases indexed by defendant, plaintiff. Civil records on index cards and in folders.

Criminal Records: Access: Mail, fax, in person. Both court and visitors may perform in person searches. No search fee. Required to search: name, years to search. Criminal records on index cards and in folders.

General Information: No suppressed records released. SASE not required. Turnaround time 2-3 days. Copy fee: $1.00 per page. Certification fee: $10.00. Fee payee: County Clerk. Personal checks accepted. Prepayment is required.

98th District Court 725 Greenland Rd, Ontonagon, MI 49953; 906-884-2865; Fax: 906-884-2916. Hours: 8:30AM-4:30PM (EST). *Misdemeanor, Civil Actions Under $25,000, Eviction, Small Claims.*

Civil Records: Access: Mail, in person. Only the court performs in person searches; visitors may not. No search fee. Required to search: name, years to search. Civil cases indexed by defendant, plaintiff. Civil records kept for 10 years the destroyed.

Criminal Records: Access: Mail, in person. Only the court performs in person searches; visitors may not. No search fee. Required to search: name, years to search, DOB; also helpful: SSN. Criminal records kept for 10 years the destroyed.

General Information: No suppressed records released. SASE required. Turnaround time 1 week. Fax notes: Fee to fax results is $5.00 per document. Copy fee: $1.00 per page. Certification fee: $10.00 plus $1.00 per page. Fee payee: 98th District Court. Business checks accepted.

Probate Court 725 Greenland Rd, Ontonagon, MI 49953; 906-884-4117; Fax: 906-884-2916. Hours: 8:30AM-4:30PM (EST). *Probate.*

Osceola County

49th Circuit Court 310 W Upton, Reed City, MI 49677; 231-832-6103; Fax: 231-832-6149. Hours: 9AM-5PM (EST). *Felony, Civil Actions Over $25,000.*

Civil Records: Access: Phone, fax, mail, in person. Both court and visitors may perform in person searches. No search fee. Required to search: name, years to search. Civil cases indexed by defendant, plaintiff. Civil records on computer since 1992, prior on docket books.

Criminal Records: Access: Phone, fax, mail, in person. Both court and visitors may perform in person searches. No search fee. Required to search: name, years to search, DOB. Criminal records on computer since 1992, prior on docket books.

General Information: No suppressed or adoption records released. SASE required. Turnaround time 1-2 days. Fax notes: Fax fee $1.00 1st 5 pages, each

additional page $.50. Copy fee: $1.00 per page. Certification fee: $10.00 plus $1.00 per page after first. Fee payee: 49th Circuit Court. Personal checks accepted. Prepayment is required.

77th District Court 410 W Upton, Reed City, MI 49677; 231-832-6155; Fax: 231-832-9190. Hours: 8:30AM-4:30PM (EST). *Misdemeanor, Civil Actions Under $25,000, Eviction, Small Claims.*

Civil Records: Access: Mail, in person. Only the court performs in person searches; visitors may not. No search fee. Required to search: name, years to search. Civil cases indexed by defendant, plaintiff. Civil records on computer since 6/91, prior on index cards.

Criminal Records: Access: Mail, in person. Only the court performs in person searches; visitors may not. No search fee. Required to search: name, years to search, DOB. Criminal records on computer since 6/91, prior on index cards.

General Information: No suppressed records released. SASE required. Turnaround time 2 days. Copy fee: $1.00 per page. Certification fee: $10.00 plus $1.00 per page after first. Fee payee: 77th District Court. Only cashiers checks and money orders accepted. Prepayment is required.

Probate Court 410 W Upton, Reed City, MI 49677; 231-832-6124; Fax: 231-832-9190. Hours: 8:30AM-Noon, 1-4:30PM (EST). *Probate.*

Note: Shares the same judge with Mecosta County Probate Court.

Oscoda County

23rd Circuit Court PO Box 399, 311 Morenci Ave, Mio, MI 48647; 989-826-1110; Fax: 989-826-1136. Hours: 8:30AM-4:30PM (EST). *Felony, Civil Actions Over $25,000.*

Civil Records: Access: Mail, in person. Only the court performs in person searches; visitors may not. Search fee: $15.00 per name per year. Required to search: name, years to search. Civil cases indexed by defendant, plaintiff. Civil records on computer since 1989, prior on docket books.

Criminal Records: Access: Mail, in person. Only the court performs in person searches; visitors may not. Search fee: $15.00 per name per year. Required to search: name, years to search, DOB. Criminal records on computer since 1989, prior on docket books.

General Information: No suppressed records released. SASE required. Turnaround time 2-3 weeks. Copy fee: $.25 per page. Certification fee: $10.00 plus $1.00 per page after first. Fee payee: Oscoda County Clerk. Personal checks accepted. Prepayment is required.

82nd District Court PO Box 399, Mio, MI 48647; 989-826-1106. Hours: 8:30AM-4:30PM (EST). *Misdemeanor, Civil Actions Under $25,000, Eviction, Small Claims.*

Civil Records: Access: Mail, in person. Only the court performs in person searches; visitors may not. Search fee: $2.00 per name. Required to search: name, years to search. Civil cases indexed by defendant, plaintiff. Civil records on computer back to 1990, prior on index cards.

Criminal Records: Access: Mail, in person. Only the court performs in person searches; visitors may not. Search fee: $2.00 per name. Required to search: name, years to search, DOB; also helpful: SSN. Criminal records on computer back to 1990, prior on index cards.

General Information: No suppressed records released. SASE required. Turnaround time 1-2 days. Copy fee: $.50 per page. Certification fee: $10.00 plus $1.00 per page after first. Fee payee: 82nd District Court. Personal checks accepted.

Probate Court PO Box 399, Mio, MI 48647; 989-826-1107; Fax: 989-826-1126 or 826-3518. Hours: 8:30AM-Noon, 1-4:30PM (EST). *Probate.*

Otsego County

46th Circuit Court 225 Main St, Gaylord, MI 49735; 989-732-6484; Fax: 989-732-1562. Hours: 8AM-4:30PM (EST). *Felony, Civil Actions Over $25,000.*

www.Circuit46.org

Civil Records: Access: Phone, mail, in person, online. Both court and visitors may perform in person searches. No search fee. Required to search: name, years to search. Civil records on computer since 1988, prior on indexes since 1800s. Online access to court case records (closed cases for 90 days only) is available free at www.circuit46.org/Cases/cases.html. Search by name.
Criminal Records: Access: Phone, mail, in person, online. Both court and visitors may perform in person searches. No search fee. Required to search: name, years to search, DOB. Criminal records on computer since 1988, prior on indexes since 1800s. Online access to criminal records is the same as civil.
General Information: Public Access terminal is available. No suppressed, juvenile, mental health, or adoption records released. SASE required. Turnaround time varies. Copy fee: $1.00 per page. Certification fee: $10.00. Fee payee: Otsego County Clerk. Personal checks accepted. Prepayment is required.

46th Circuit Trial Court - District Court 800 Livingston Blvd, #1C, Gaylord, MI 49735; 989-732-6486; Fax: 989-732-5130. Hours: 8AM-4:30PM (EST). *Misdemeanor, Civil Actions Under $25,000, Eviction, Small Claims.*

www.circuit46.org

Civil Records: Access: Mail, in person, online. Both court and visitors may perform in person searches. No search fee. Required to search: name, years to search. Civil cases indexed by defendant, plaintiff. Civil records on computer since 1985, prior index cards. Online access to court case records (closed cases for 90 days only) is available free at www.circuit46.org/Cases/cases.html. Search by name.
Criminal Records: Access: Mail, in person, online. Both court and visitors may perform in person searches. No search fee. Required to search: name, years to search, DOB. Criminal records on computer since 1985, prior index cards. Online access to criminal records is the same as civil.
General Information: Public Access terminal is available. No suppressed records released. SASE required. Turnaround time 4 days. Copy fee: $1.00 per page. Certification fee: $10.00 plus $1.00 per page after first. Fee payee: 87th District Court. Personal checks accepted. Prepayment is required.

Probate Court 225 W Main St, Gaylord, MI 49735; 989-732-6484 X339; Fax: 989-732-1562. Hours: 8AM-4:30PM (EST). *Probate.*

www.Circuit46.org

Note: Free record searching online at web site

Ottawa County

20th Circuit Court 414 Washington Ave, Grand Haven, MI 49417; 616-846-8310; Fax: 616-846-8138. Hours: 8AM-5PM (EST). *Felony, Civil Actions Over $25,000.*

Civil Records: Access: Mail, in person. Both court and visitors may perform in person searches. No search fee. Required to search: name, years to search. Civil cases indexed by defendant, plaintiff. Civil records on computer since June, 1984.
Criminal Records: Access: Mail, in person. Both court and visitors may perform in person searches. No search

fee. Required to search: name, years to search, DOB; also helpful: SSN. Criminal records on computer since 1990.
General Information: Public Access terminal is available. No suppressed, juvenile, sex offenders, mental health, or adoption records released. SASE requested. Turnaround time 2-3 days, phone search turnaround time 24 hours. Copy fee: $.50 per page. Certification fee: $10.00 plus $1.00 per page. Fee payee: Ottawa County Clerk. Personal checks accepted. Prepayment is required.

58th District Court - Grand Haven 414 Washington Ave, Grand Haven, MI 49417; 616-846-8280; Fax: 616-846-8291. Hours: 8AM-5PM (EST). *Misdemeanor, Civil Actions Under $25,000, Eviction, Small Claims.*

Civil Records: Access: Mail, in person. Only the court performs in person searches; visitors may not. No search fee. Required to search: name, years to search. Civil cases indexed by defendant, plaintiff. Civil records on computer back to 1993, prior on index cards since 1969.
Criminal Records: Access: Mail, in person. Only the court performs in person searches; visitors may not. No search fee. Required to search: name, years to search, DOB. Criminal records on computer back to 1990, prior on index cards since 1969.
General Information: Public Access terminal is available. No suppressed records released. SASE required. Turnaround time 4 days. Fax notes: Fee to fax results is $.25 per page. Copy fee: $.25 per page. Certification fee: $10.00 plus $1.00 per page after first. Fee payee: 58th District Court. Personal checks accepted. Out of state checks not accepted. Prepayment is required.

58th District Court - Holland 57 W 8th St, Holland, MI 49423; 616-392-6991; Fax: 616-392-5013. Hours: 8AM-5PM (EST). *Misdemeanor, Civil Actions Under $25,000, Eviction, Small Claims.*

Civil Records: Access: Mail, in person. Only the court performs in person searches; visitors may not. No search fee. Required to search: name, years to search. Civil cases indexed by defendant, plaintiff. Civil records on computer since 1988, prior on books since 1969.
Criminal Records: Access: Mail, in person. Only the court performs in person searches; visitors may not. No search fee. Required to search: name, years to search, DOB; also helpful: SSN. Criminal records on computer since 1988, prior on books since 1969.
General Information: No suppressed records released. SASE required. Turnaround time varies. Copy fee: $.25 per page. Certification fee: $10.00 plus $1.00 per page after first. Fee payee: 58th District Court. Personal checks accepted. Out of state checks not accepted. Prepayment is required.

58th District Court - Hudsonville 3100 Port Sheldon, Hudsonville, MI 49426; 616-662-3100; Fax: 616-669-2950. Hours: 8AM-noon; 1-5PM (EST). *Misdemeanor, Civil Actions Under $25,000, Eviction, Small Claims.*

Civil Records: Access: Mail, in person. Only the court performs in person searches; visitors may not. No search fee. Required to search: name, years to search; also helpful: address. Civil cases indexed by defendant, plaintiff. Civil records on computer since July, 1993, prior on index file.
Criminal Records: Access: Mail, in person. Only the court performs in person searches; visitors may not. No search fee. Required to search: name, years to search, DOB; also helpful: address. Criminal records on computer since 1990.
General Information: No suppressed records released. SASE not required. Turnaround time 2 days. Copy fee: $.25 per page. Certification fee: $10.00. Fee payee: 58th District Court. Personal checks accepted.

Probate Court 12120 Fillmore St, West Olive, MI 49460; 616-786-4110; Fax: 616-786-4154. Hours: 8AM-5PM (EST). *Probate.*

Presque Isle County

26th Circuit Court PO Box 110, Rogers City, MI 49779; 989-734-3288; Fax: 989-734-7635. Hours: 9AM-5PM (EST). *Felony, Civil Actions Over $25,000.*

Civil Records: Access: Phone, fax, mail, in person. Only the court performs in person searches; visitors may not. No search fee. Required to search: name, years to search. Civil cases indexed by defendant, plaintiff. Civil records on docket books since 1800s.
Criminal Records: Access: Phone, fax, mail, in person. Only the court performs in person searches; visitors may not. No search fee. Required to search: name, years to search, DOB. Criminal records on docket books since 1800s.
General Information: No suppressed, juvenile, sex offenders, mental health, or adoption records released. SASE required. Turnaround time 1 week. Copy fee: $1.00 per page. Certification fee: $10.00 plus $1.00 per page after first. Fee payee: Presque Isle County Clerk. Personal checks accepted. Prepayment is required.

89th District Court PO Box 110, Rogers City, MI 49779; 989-734-2411; Fax: 989-734-3400. Hours: 8:30AM-4:30PM (EST). *Misdemeanor, Civil Actions Under $25,000, Eviction, Small Claims.*

Civil Records: Access: Mail, in person. Only the court performs in person searches; visitors may not. No search fee. Required to search: name, years to search. Civil cases indexed by defendant, plaintiff. Civil records on computer since 6/94, prior on index books.
Criminal Records: Access: Mail, in person. Only the court performs in person searches; visitors may not. No search fee. Required to search: name, years to search, DOB. Criminal records on computer since 6/94, prior on index books.
General Information: No suppressed records released. SASE required. Turnaround time 2 weeks. Copy fee: $1.00 for first page, $.25 each add'l. Certification fee: $10.00 plus $1.00 per page after first. Fee payee: 89th District Court. Personal checks accepted.

Probate Court 151 Huron Ave, PO Box 110, Rogers City, MI 49779; 989-734-3268; Fax: 989-734-4420. Hours: 8:30AM-4:30PM (EST). *Probate.*

Roscommon County

34th Circuit Court PO Box 98, Roscommon, MI 48653; 989-275-1902; Fax: 989-275-0602. Hours: 8:30AM-4:30PM (EST). *Felony, Civil Actions Over $25,000.*

Civil Records: Access: Fax, mail, in person. Only the court performs in person searches; visitors may not. Search fee: $5.00 per name. Required to search: name, years to search. Civil records on computer since 3/94, prior on docket books and cards.
Criminal Records: Access: Fax, mail, in person. Only the court performs in person searches; visitors may not. Search fee: $5.00 per name. Required to search: name, years to search, DOB. Criminal records on computer since 3/94, prior on docket books and cards.
General Information: No suppressed, sex offenders or mental health records released. SASE required. Turnaround time 24 hours. Fax notes: Fee to fax results is $3.00 1st page, $1.00 each add'l. Copy fee: $.50 per page. Certification fee: $10.00 plus $1.00 per page after first. Fee payee: 34th Circuit Court. Personal checks accepted. Prepayment is required.

83rd District Court PO Box 189, Roscommon, MI 48653; 989-275-5312; Fax: 989-275-6033. Hours: 8:30AM-4:30PM (EST). *Misdemeanor, Civil Actions Under $25,000, Eviction, Small Claims.*

Civil Records: Access: Phone, fax, mail, in person. Only the court performs in person searches; visitors may not. No search fee. Required to search: name, years to search. Civil cases indexed by defendant, plaintiff. Civil records on computer since 1988, prior on index cards since 1969.

Criminal Records: Access: Phone, fax, mail, in person. Only the court performs in person searches; visitors may not. No search fee. Required to search: name, years to search, DOB; also helpful: SSN. Criminal records on computer since 1988, prior on index cards since 1969.

General Information: No suppressed, juvenile, sex offenders, mental health, or adoption records released. Turnaround time same day. Fax notes: No fee to fax results. Copy fee: $.50 per page. Certification fee: No cert fee. Fee payee: 83rd District Court. Personal checks accepted. Prepayment is required.

Probate Court PO Box 607, Roscommon, MI 48653; 989-275-5221; Fax: 989-275-8537. Hours: 8:30AM-4:30PM (EST). *Probate.*

Saginaw County

10th Circuit Court 111 S Michigan Ave, Saginaw, MI 48602; 989-790-5544; Fax: 989-790-8254. Hours: 8AM-5:00PM (EST). *Felony, Civil Actions Over $25,000.*

Civil Records: Access: Mail, in person. Both court and visitors may perform in person searches. No search fee. Required to search: name, years to search; also helpful: address. Civil cases indexed by defendant, plaintiff. Civil records on computer since 1985, prior on index books.

Criminal Records: Access: Mail, in person. Both court and visitors may perform in person searches. No search fee. Required to search: name, years to search, DOB; also helpful: address, SSN. Criminal records on computer since 1985, prior on index books.

General Information: Public Access terminal is available. No suppressed, sex offenders or mental health records released. SASE required. Turnaround time 2 days. Copy fee: $1.00 per page. Certification fee: $10.00 plus $1.00 per page after first. Fee payee: Saginaw County Clerk. Personal checks accepted.

70th District Court - Civil Division 111 S Michigan Ave, Saginaw, MI 48602; 989-790-5380; Fax: 989-790-5589. Hours: 8AM-4:45PM (EST). *Civil Actions Under $25,000, Eviction, Small Claims.*

Civil Records: Access: Mail, in person. Only the court performs in person searches; visitors may not. Search fee: $5.00 per name. Required to search: name, years to search. Civil cases indexed by defendant, plaintiff. Civil records on computer since 1982, prior on docket books.

General Information: No suppressed records released. SASE required. Turnaround time 1 week. Copy fee: $1.00 per page. Certification fee: $10.00. Fee payee: 70th District court. Personal checks accepted. Prepayment is required.

70th District Court - Criminal Division 111 S Michigan Ave, Saginaw, MI 48602; 989-790-5385; Fax: 989-790-5589. Hours: 8AM-4:45PM (EST). *Misdemeanor.*

Criminal Records: Access: Fax, mail, in person. Only the court performs in person searches; visitors may not. Search fee: $5.00 per name. Required to search: name, years to search, DOB, signed release; also helpful: address. Criminal records on computer back to 1987, prior on microfiche since 1976.

General Information: No suppressed, juvenile, sex offenders, mental health, or adoption records released. Turnaround time 1 week. Copy fee: $1.00 per page. Certification fee: $10.00. Fee payee: 70th District Court. Business checks accepted. Credit cards accepted: Visa, MasterCard. Prepayment is required.

Probate Court 111 S Michigan St, Saginaw, MI 48602; 989-790-5320; Fax: 989-790-5328. Hours: 8AM-5PM (EST). *Probate.*

Sanilac County

24th Circuit Court 60 W Sanilac, Rm 203, Sandusky, MI 48471; 810-648-3212; Fax: 810-648-5466. Hours: 8AM-4:30PM (EST). *Felony, Civil Actions Over $25,000.*

Civil Records: Access: Mail, in person. Both court and visitors may perform in person searches. Search fee: $5.00 per name. Required to search: name, years to search. Civil cases indexed by defendant, plaintiff. Civil records on computer since 1993.

Criminal Records: Access: Mail, in person. Both court and visitors may perform in person searches. Search fee: $5.00 per name. Required to search: name, years to search. Criminal records on computer since 1993.

General Information: Public Access terminal is available. No suppressed, juvenile, sex offenders, mental health, or adoption records released. SASE required. Turnaround time 2-3 days. Copy fee: $1.00 per page. Certification fee: $10.00. Fee payee: Sanilac County Clerk. Personal checks accepted. Prepayment is required.

73rd District Court 60 W Sanilac, Sandusky, MI 48471; 810-648-3250. Hours: 8AM-4:30PM (EST). *Misdemeanor, Civil Actions Under $25,000, Eviction, Small Claims.*

Civil Records: Access: Mail, in person. Only the court performs in person searches; visitors may not. Search fee: $1.00 per name per year. Required to search: name, years to search; also helpful: address. Civil cases indexed by defendant, plaintiff. Civil records on computer back to 1989, prior on docket books to 1969.

Criminal Records: Access: Mail, in person. Only the court performs in person searches; visitors may not. Search fee: $1.00 per name per year. Required to search: name, years to search, DOB; also helpful: address. Criminal records on computer back to 1989, prior on docket books to 1969.

General Information: No suppressed records released. SASE required. Turnaround time 1 week. Copy fee: $1.00 per page. Certification fee: $10.00 plus $1.00 per page after first. Fee payee: 73rd District Court. Personal checks accepted. Prepayment required.

Probate Court 60 W Sanilac Ave., Po Box 128, Sandusky, MI 48471; 810-648-3221; Fax: 810-648-2900. Hours: 8AM-Noon, 1-4:30PM (EST). *Probate.*

Schoolcraft County

11th Circuit Court 300 Walnut St, Rm 164, Manistique, MI 49854; 906-341-3618. Hours: 8AM-4PM (EST). *Felony, Civil Actions Over $25,000.*

Civil Records: Access: Phone, fax, mail, in person. Both court and visitors may perform in person searches. No search fee. Required to search: name, years to search. Civil cases indexed by defendant, plaintiff. Civil records on docket books and index since 1881.

Criminal Records: Access: Phone, fax, mail, in person. Both court and visitors may perform in person searches. No search fee. Required to search: name, years to search. Criminal records on docket books and index since 1881.

General Information: No suppressed, juvenile, sex offenders, mental health, or adoption records released. SASE requested. Turnaround time 2-3 days. Copy fee: $1.00 per page. Certification fee: $10.00. Fee payee: Schoolcraft County Clerk. Personal checks accepted. Prepayment is required.

93rd District Court 300 Walnut St, Rm 135, Manistique, MI 49854; 906-341-3630; Fax: 906-341-8006. Hours: 8AM-4PM (EST). *Misdemeanor, Civil Actions Under $25,000, Eviction, Small Claims.*

Civil Records: Access: Mail, in person. Both court and visitors may perform in person searches. Search fee: $10.00. Required to search: name, years to search. Civil cases indexed by defendant, plaintiff. Civil records kept on index cards.

Criminal Records: Access: Mail, in person. Only the court performs in person searches; visitors may not. Search fee: $10.00. Required to search: name, years to search, DOB; also helpful: SSN. Criminal records kept on index cards.

General Information: No suppressed, sex offenders or mental health records released. SASE required. Turnaround time 2-3 days. Copy fee: $.25 per page. Certification fee: $10.00 plus $1.00 per page after first. Fee payee: 93rd District Court. Business checks accepted. Prepayment is required.

Probate Court 300 Walnut St, Manistique, MI 49854; 906-341-3641; Fax: 906-341-3627. Hours: 8AM-Noon, 1-4PM (EST). *Probate.*

Shiawassee County

35th Circuit Court 208 N Shiawassee St, Corunna, MI 48817; 989-743-2262; Fax: 989-743-2241. Hours: 8AM-5PM (EST). *Felony, Civil Actions Over $25,000.*

Civil Records: Access: Phone, fax, mail, in person. Both court and visitors may perform in person searches. Search fee: $1.00 per name per year. Required to search: name, years to search. Civil cases indexed by defendant, plaintiff. Civil records on computer since 09/87, prior on docket books and cards.

Criminal Records: Access: Phone, fax, mail, in person. Both court and visitors may perform in person searches. Search fee: $1.00 per name per year. Required to search: name, years to search, DOB. Criminal records on computer since 10/93.

General Information: No suppressed records released. SASE required. Turnaround time 1 week. Copy fee: $1.00 per page. Certification fee: $10.00. Fee payee: 35th Circuit Court. Personal checks accepted. Prepayment is required.

66th District Court 110 E Mack St, Corunna, MI 48817; 989-743-2395. Hours: 8AM-5PM (EST). *Misdemeanor, Civil Actions Under $25,000, Eviction, Small Claims.*

Civil Records: Access: Phone, mail, in person. Only the court performs in person searches; visitors may not. Search fee: $10.00 per hour. Required to search: name, years to search. Civil cases indexed by defendant, plaintiff. Civil records on computer since 1995, prior on microfiche.

Criminal Records: Access: Phone, mail, in person. Only the court performs in person searches; visitors may not. Search fee: $10.00 per hour. Required to search: name, years to search, DOB. Case number required for pre-1995 research. Criminal records on computer since 1995, prior on microfiche.

General Information: No suppressed records released. SASE required. Turnaround time 1 week. Copy fee: $1.00 per page. Certification fee: $10.00. Fee payee: 66th District Court. Personal checks accepted.

Probate Court 110 E Mack St, Corunna, MI 48817; 989-743-2211; Fax: 989-743-2349. Hours: 8AM-5PM (EST). *Probate.*

St. Clair County

31st Circuit Court 201 McMorran Blvd, Port Huron, MI 48060; 810-985-2200; Fax: 810-985-4796. Hours: 8AM-4:30PM (EST). *Felony, Civil Actions Over $25,000.*

Civil Records: Access: Mail, fax, in person. Both court and visitors may perform in person searches. No search fee. Required to search: name, years to search; also helpful: address. Civil cases indexed by defendant, plaintiff. Civil records on computer back to 1987.

Criminal Records: Access: Mail, fax, in person. Both court and visitors may perform in person searches. No search fee. Required to search: name, years to search, DOB; also helpful: address. Criminal records on computer back to 1987.

General Information: Public Access terminal is available. No suppressed, juvenile, mental health, or adoption records released. SASE required. Turnaround time 24 hours. Copy fee: $1.00 per page. Certification fee: $10.00. Fee payee: St. Clair Clerk of Court. Only cashiers checks and money orders accepted. In state checks allowed. Prepayment is required.

72nd District Court 201 McMorran Rd, Port Huron, MI 48060; Civil phone: 810-985-2077; Criminal phone: 810-985-2072. Hours: 8AM-4:30PM (EST). *Misdemeanor, Civil Actions Under $25,000, Eviction, Small Claims.*

Civil Records: Access: In person only. Visitors must perform in person searches for themselves. No search fee. Required to search: name, years to search. Civil cases indexed by defendant, plaintiff. Civil records on computer since 1987, prior on docket books.

Criminal Records: Access: in person only. Visitors must perform in person searches for themselves. No search fee. Required to search: name, years to search, DOB; also helpful: SSN. Criminal records on computer since 1987, prior on docket books.

General Information: No suppressed records released. Copy fee: $1.00 per page. Certification fee: $10.00. Fee payee: 72nd District Court. Personal checks accepted. Prepayment is required.

Probate Court 201 McMorran Blvd Rm 216, Port Huron, MI 48060; 810-985-2066; Fax: 810-985-2179. Hours: 8AM-4:30PM (EST). *Probate.*

St. Joseph County

45th Circuit Court PO Box 189, Centreville, MI 49032; 616-467-5531; Fax: 616-467-5628. Hours: 9AM-5PM (EST). *Felony, Civil Actions Over $25,000.*

Civil Records: Access: Mail, in person. Only the court performs in person searches; visitors may not. Search fee: $1.00 per name per year. For records prior to 1988, fee is $1.00 per year searched. Required to search: name, years to search. Civil cases indexed by defendant, plaintiff. Civil records on computer since 1988, prior on books from 1900, earlier in archives.

Criminal Records: Access: Mail, in person. Only the court performs in person searches; visitors may not. Search fee: $1.00 per name per year. For records prior to 1988, fee is $10.00 per year searched. Required to search: name, years to search. Criminal records on computer since 1988, prior on books from 1900, earlier in archives.

General Information: No suppressed records released. SASE not required. Turnaround time same day. Copy fee: $1.00 per page. Certification fee: $10.00. Fee payee: St. Joseph County Clerk. Business checks accepted. Prepayment is required.

3-B District Court PO Box 67, Centreville, MI 49032; 616-467-5627. Hours: 8AM-5PM (EST). *Misdemeanor, Civil Actions Under $25,000, Eviction, Small Claims.*

Civil Records: Access: Phone, mail, in person. Both court and visitors may perform in person searches. No search fee. Required to search: name, years to search; also helpful: address. Civil cases indexed by defendant, plaintiff. Civil records on computer since 1987, prior in archives. Phone search access limited.

Criminal Records: Access: Fax, mail, in person. Both court and visitors may perform in person searches. No search fee. Required to search: name, years to search, DOB, date of offense. Criminal records on computer

since 1987, prior in archives. Signed release required for some searches.

General Information: Public Access terminal is available. No suppressed records released. Turnaround time 2 weeks. Copy fee: $.15 per page. Certification fee: $10.00 plus $1.00 each additional page. Fee payee: 3-B District Court. Business checks accepted.

Probate Court PO Box 190, Centreville, MI 49032; 616-467-5538; Fax: 616-467-5560. Hours: 8AM-5PM (EST). *Probate.*

Tuscola County

54th Circuit Court 440 N State St, Caro, MI 48723; 989-672-3780; Fax: 989-672-4266. Hours: 8AM-Noon, 1-3:30PM (EST). *Felony, Civil Actions Over $25,000.*

Civil Records: Access: Mail, in person. Only the court performs in person searches; visitors may not. Search fee: $5.00 per name. Fee is $1.00 for each year prior to 1989. Required to search: name, years to search. Civil cases indexed by defendant, plaintiff. Civil records on computer since 1989, prior on books since beginning.

Criminal Records: Access: Mail, in person. Only the court performs in person searches; visitors may not. Search fee: $5.00 per name. Fee is $1.00 for each year prior to 1989. Required to search: name, years to search, DOB; also helpful: SSN. Criminal records on computer since 1989, prior on books since beginning.

General Information: No suppressed, juvenile, sex offenders, mental health, or adoption records released. SASE required. Turnaround time 3-4 days. Copy fee: $1.00 per page. Certification fee: $10.00 plus $1.00 per page after first. Fee payee: County Clerk. Personal checks not accepted. Prepayment is required.

71 B District Court 440 N State St., Caro, MI 48723; 989-672-3800; Fax: 989-673-0451. Hours: 8AM-4:30PM (EST). *Misdemeanor, Civil Actions Under $25,000, Eviction, Small Claims.*

Civil Records: Access: Phone, mail, in person. Both court and visitors may perform in person searches. No search fee. Required to search: name, years to search. Civil cases indexed by defendant, plaintiff. Civil records on computer since 1991, prior on cards.

Criminal Records: Access: Phone, mail, in person. Both court and visitors may perform in person searches. No search fee. Required to search: name, years to search, DOB; also helpful: SSN. Criminal records on computer since 1991; others back to 1969.

General Information: No suppressed records released. SASE not required. Copy fee: $.50 per page. Certification fee: $10.00 plus $1.00 per page after first. Fee payee: 71bDistrict Court. Personal checks accepted.

Probate Court 440 N State St, Caro, MI 48723; 989-672-3850; Fax: 989-672-4266. Hours: 8AM-Noon, 1-4:30PM (EST). *Probate.*

Van Buren County

36th Circuit Court 212 Paw Paw St, Paw Paw, MI 49079; 616-657-8218. Hours: 8:30AM-5PM (EST). *Felony, Civil Actions Over $25,000.*

Civil Records: Access: Mail, in person. Only the court performs in person searches; visitors may not. Search fee: $1.00 per name per year. Fee includes combined civil and criminal search. Required to search: name, years to search. Civil cases indexed by defendant, plaintiff. Civil records on computer back to 1990, prior on docket books since 1800s.

Criminal Records: Access: Mail, in person. Only the court performs in person searches; visitors may not. Search fee: $1.00 per name per year. Required to search: name, years to search, DOB, signed release. Criminal records on computer back to 1990, prior on docket books since 1800s.

General Information: No suppressed, sex offender records released. SASE required. Turnaround time 1 day. Fax notes: Will phone with results if a toll-free number is provided. Copy fee: $1.00 per page. Certification fee: $10.00 plus $1.00 per page after first. Fee payee: Van Buren County Clerk. Personal checks accepted. Prepayment is required.

7th District Court 212 Paw Paw St, Paw Paw, MI 49079; 616-657-8222; Fax: 616-657-7573. Hours: 9AM-4:30PM (EST). *Misdemeanor, Civil Actions Under $25,000, Eviction, Small Claims.*

Civil Records: Access: Mail, in person. Both court and visitors may perform in person searches. Search fee: $5.00 per name. Required to search: name, years to search. Civil cases indexed by defendant, plaintiff. Civil records kept in file folder.

Criminal Records: Access: Mail, in person. Both court and visitors may perform in person searches. Search fee: $5.00 per name. Required to search: name, years to search, DOB, SSN. Criminal records kept in file folder.

General Information: No suppressed records released. SASE required. Turnaround time 1-2 days. Copy fee: $.25 per page. Certification fee: $10.00. Fee payee: 7th District Court. No personal checks accepted. Prepayment is required.

7th District Court - West Division 1007 E Wells, PO Box 311, South Haven, MI 49090; 616-637-5258; Fax: 616-637-9169. Hours: 8:30AM-4:30PM (EST). *Misdemeanor, Civil Actions Under $25,000, Eviction, Small Claims.*

Civil Records: Access: Mail, in person. Only the court performs in person searches; visitors may not. Search fee: $1.00 per name. Required to search: name, years to search. Civil cases indexed by defendant, plaintiff. Civil records on computer since 1991, prior on index cards since 1982.

Criminal Records: Access: Mail, in person. Only the court performs in person searches; visitors may not. Search fee: $1.00 per name. Required to search: name, years to search, DOB; also helpful: SSN. Criminal records on computer since 1991, prior on index cards since 1982.

General Information: No suppressed, juvenile, sex offenders, mental health, or adoption records released. Turnaround time 3 days. Copy fee: $.25 per page. Certification fee: $10.00 plus $1.00 per page after first. Fee payee: 7th District Court. Personal checks accepted. Prepayment is required.

Probate Court 212 Paw Paw St, Paw Paw, MI 49079; 616-657-8225; Fax: 616-657-7573. Hours: 8:30AM-5PM (EST). *Probate.*

Washtenaw County

22nd Circuit Court PO Box 8645, Ann Arbor, MI 48107-8645; 734-994-2507. Hours: 8:30AM-4:30PM (EST). *Felony, Civil Actions Over $25,000.*

www.co.washtenaw.mi.us/depts/courts/index.htm

Civil Records: Access: Mail, in person. Both court and visitors may perform in person searches. Search fee: $5.00 per name from 1979 to present; $1.00 per name per year prior to 1979. Required to search: name, years to search. Civil cases indexed by defendant, plaintiff. Civil records kept as originals in file folders.

Criminal Records: Access: Mail, in person. Both court and visitors may perform in person searches. Search fee: Same fees as civil. Required to search: name, years to search, DOB. Criminal records kept as originals in file folders.

General Information: Public Access terminal is available. No suppressed records released. SASE required. Turnaround time 2 or 3 days. Copy fee: $.25 per page. Certification fee: $10.00 plus $1.00 per page. Fee payee: Circuit Court Clerk. Personal checks accepted. Prepayment is required.

14A-1 District Court 4133 Washtenaw, Ann Arbor, MI 48107-8645; 734-971-6050; Fax: 734-971-5018. Hours: 8AM-4:30PM (EST). *Misdemeanor, Civil Actions Under $25,000, Eviction, Small Claims.*

Civil Records: Access: Mail, in person. Both court and visitors may perform in person searches. No search fee. Required to search: name, years to search. Civil cases indexed by defendant, plaintiff. Civil records on computer since 1985, prior on index cards.

Criminal Records: Access: Mail, in person. Both court and visitors may perform in person searches. No search fee. Required to search: name, years to search, DOB, SSN. Criminal records on computer since 1985, prior on index cards.

General Information: Public Access terminal is available. No suppressed records released. SASE required. Turnaround time 1-2 weeks. Copy fee: $.25 per page. Certification fee: $10.00 plus $1.00 per page. Fee payee: 14 A-1 District Court. Personal checks accepted. Prepayment is required.

14th District Court A-2 415 W Michigan Ave, Ypsilanti, MI 48197; 734-484-6690; Fax: 734-484-6697. Hours: 8AM-4:30PM (EST). *Misdemeanor, Civil Actions Under $25,000, Eviction, Small Claims.*

Civil Records: Access: Mail, in person. Only the court performs in person searches; visitors may not. No search fee. Required to search: name, years to search. Civil cases indexed by defendant, plaintiff. Civil records on computer since 1985, prior on file cards since 1969. Specific docket information must be given, the court will not do name searches.

Criminal Records: Access: Mail, in person. Only the court performs in person searches; visitors may not. No search fee. Required to search: name, years to search, DOB; also helpful: SSN. Criminal records on computer since 1985, prior on file cards since 1969. The court will not do name searches.

General Information: No suppressed, juvenile, sex offenders, mental health, or adoption records released. SASE requested. Turnaround time 1 week, phone turnaround time immediate to 2 days. Copy fee: $.25 per page. Certification fee: $10.00 plus $1.00 per page. Fee payee: 14 A-2 District Court. Personal checks accepted. Prepayment is required.

14th District Court A-3 122 S Main St, Chelsea, MI 48118; 734-475-8606; Fax: 734-475-0460. Hours: 8AM-4:30PM (EST). *Misdemeanor, Civil Actions Under $25,000, Eviction, Small Claims.*

Civil Records: Access: Mail, fax, in person. Only the court performs in person searches; visitors may not. No search fee. Required to search: name, years to search. Civil cases indexed by defendant, plaintiff. Civil records on computer since 1986; prior on index cards.

Criminal Records: Access: Mail, fax, in person. Only the court performs in person searches; visitors may not. No search fee. Required to search: name, years to search, DOB; also helpful: SSN. Criminal records on computer since 1986; prior on index cards.

General Information: Public Access terminal is available. No suppressed records released. SASE required. Copy fee: $.25 per page. Certification fee: $10.00. Fee payee: 14th District Court. Personal checks accepted. Prepayment is required.

14th District Court A-4 122 S Main, Chelsea, MI 48118; 734-475-8606; Fax: 734-475-0460. Hours: 8AM-4:30PM M-F (Office), 8AM-3:30PM M-F (Phone) (EST). *Misdemeanor, Civil Actions Under $25,000, Eviction, Small Claims.*

Civil Records: Access: Mail, fax, in person. Only the court performs in person searches; visitors may not. No search fee. Required to search: name, years to search. Civil cases indexed by defendant, plaintiff. Civil records on computer since 1986, prior on index cards.

Criminal Records: Access: Mail, fax, in person. Only the court performs in person searches; visitors may not. No search fee. Required to search: name, years to search, DOB; also helpful: SSN. Criminal records on computer since 1986, prior on index cards.

General Information: No suppressed records released. SASE required. Turnaround time 1 week. Copy fee: $.25 per page. Certification fee: $11.00. Fee payee: 14 A-4 District Court. Personal checks accepted. Credit cards accepted. Prepayment is required.

14th District Court B - Civil Division 7200 S Huron River Dr, Ypsilanti, MI 48197; 734-483-5300; Fax: 734-483-3630. Hours: 8AM-5PM (EST). *Civil Actions Under $25,000, Eviction, Small Claims.*

Civil Records: Access: Mail, in person. Only the court performs in person searches; visitors may not. No search fee. Required to search: name, years to search. Civil cases indexed by defendant, plaintiff. Civil records on computer since 1990, prior on card files from 1985-1989.

General Information: No suppressed, juvenile, sex offenders, probation, mental health, or adoption records released. SASE not required. Turnaround time 1 week, phone turnaround time 1 day. Copy fee: $.50 per page. Certification fee: $10.00. Fee payee: 14-B District Court. Business checks accepted. Credit cards accepted. Prepayment is required.

14th District Court B - Criminal Division 7200 S Huron River Dr, Ypsilanti, MI 48197; 734-483-1333; Fax: 734-483-3630. Hours: 8AM-5PM (EST). *Misdemeanor.*

Criminal Records: Access: Mail, in person. Only the court performs in person searches; visitors may not. No search fee. Required to search: name, years to search, DOB; also helpful: SSN. Criminal records on computer since 1990, prior records kept by name.

General Information: No suppressed, probation, juvenile, sex offenders, probation, mental health, or adoption records released. SASE not required. Turnaround time 1 week, phone turnaround time 1 day. Copy fee: $.50 per page. Certification fee: $10.00. Fee payee: 14-B District Court. Personal checks accepted. Credit cards accepted.

15th District Court - Civil Division 101 E Huron, Box 8650, Ann Arbor, MI 48107; 734-994-2749; Fax: 734-994-2617. Hours: 8:30AM-4:30PM *Civil Actions Under $25,000, Eviction, Small Claims.*

www.co.washtenaw.mi.us/depts/courts/index.htm

Civil Records: Access: Phone, fax, mail, in person. Both court and visitors may perform in person searches. No search fee. Required to search: name, years to search. Civil cases indexed by defendant, plaintiff. Civil records on computer since 1990, prior on docket books.

General Information: No suppressed records released. SASE required. Turnaround time 2-3 days. Copy fee: $.25 per page. Certification fee: $10.00. Fee payee: 15th District Court. Personal checks accepted. Credit cards accepted: Visa, MasterCard, Discover. Prepayment is required.

15th District Court - Criminal Division 101 E Huron, Box 8650, Ann Arbor, MI 48107-8650; 734-994-2745; Criminal phone: 734-994-2746; Fax: 734-994-2617. Hours: 8AM-4:30PM (EST). *Misdemeanor, Traffic.*

www.co.washtenaw.mi.us/depts/courts/index.htm

Criminal Records: Access: Mail, fax, in person. Both court and visitors may perform in person searches. No search fee. Required to search: name, years to search, DOB; also helpful: SSN, offense. Criminal records on computer since 1996; prior on docket cards since 1965. The court will not do a name search. Either a case number or charge and incident date is required.

General Information: Public Access terminal is available. (Limited information available.) No suppressed, juvenile, sex offenders, mental health, or adoption records released. SASE required. Turnaround time 2-3 days. Copy fee: $.25 per page. Certification fee: $10.00. Fee payee: 15th District Court. Only cashiers checks and money orders accepted. Credit cards accepted: Visa, MasterCard, Discover. Prepayment is required.

Probate Court PO Box 8645, Ann Arbor, MI 48107; 734-994-2474; Fax: 734-996-3033. Hours: 8:30AM-4:30PM (EST). *Probate.*

www.co.washtenaw.mi.us/depts/courts/index.htm

Wayne County

3rd Circuit Court 201 County Building, 2 Woodward, Detroit, MI 48226; 313-224-5509. Hours: 8AM-4:30PM (EST). *Civil Actions Over $25,000.*

Civil Records: Access: Phone, mail, in person. Both court and visitors may perform in person searches. No search fee. Required to search: name, years to search. Civil cases indexed by defendant, plaintiff. Civil records on computer since 1984, prior on index cards.

General Information: Public Access terminal is available. No suppressed records released. SASE required. Turnaround time 1 week. Copy fee: $.25 per page. Certification fee: $10.00 plus $1.00 per page. Fee payee: 3rd Circuit Court. Business checks accepted. Prepayment is required.

Frank Murphy Hall of Justice 1441 St Antoine, Detroit, MI 48226; 313-224-2500; Fax: 313-224-2786. Hours: 8AM-4:30PM (EST). *Felony.*

Criminal Records: Access: Mail, in person. Both court and visitors may perform in person searches. Search fee: $2.25 per name. Required to search: name, years to search, DOB; also helpful: SSN, city where crime occurred, aliases. Criminal records on computer since mid 1974, prior on microfiche through 1976, archives off-site 1800s to 1995.

General Information: Public Access terminal is available. No suppressed, juvenile, sex offenders, mental health, or adoption records released. SASE required. Turnaround time 3-4 days. Fax notes: Fee to fax results is $2.00 per page. Copy fee: $1.00 per page. Certification fee: $10.00 plus $1.00 per page after 1st. Fee payee: Wayne County Clerk. Prepayment is required.

36th District Court - Civil (Detroit) 421 Madison Ave, Detroit, MI 48226; 313-965-5794; Civil phone: 313-965-5794; Fax: 313-965-4059. Hours: 8AM-4:30PM (EST). *Civil Actions Under $25,000, Eviction, Small Claims.*

Civil Records: Access: In person only. Visitors must perform in person searches for themselves. No search fee. Required to search: name, years to search, address. Civil cases indexed by defendant, plaintiff. Civil records on computer since 1985, prior kept in file folders.

General Information: Public Access terminal is available. No suppressed records released. Copy fee: $1.00 per page. Certification fee: $10.00 plus $1.00 per page after first. Fee payee: 36th District Court. Personal checks accepted. Credit cards accepted: Visa, MasterCard.

16th District Court 15140 Farmington Rd, Livonia, MI 48154-5498; 734-466-2500; 466-2550 Probation; Civil phone: X3541; Criminal phone: X3452. Hours: 8:30AM-4:30PM (EST). *Misdemeanor, Civil Actions Under $25,000, Eviction, Small Claims.*

Civil Records: Access: Mail, in person. Both court and visitors may perform in person searches. No search fee. Required to search: name, years to search. Civil cases

indexed by defendant, plaintiff. Civil records on computer since 1990, prior on microfiche.

Criminal Records: Access: In person only. Visitors must perform in person searches for themselves. No search fee. Required to search: name, years to search, DOB; also helpful: offense, date of offense, case number. Criminal records on computer since 1991, prior on microfiche. General searches not performed.

General Information: Public Access terminal is available. (Civil only.) No suppressed records released. SASE required. Turnaround time 1 week. Copy fee: $1.00 per page. Certification fee: $10.00. Fee payee: 16th District Court. Personal checks accepted. Prepayment is required.

17th District Court 15111 Beech-Daly Rd, Redford, MI 48239; 313-538-8244; Fax: 313-538-3468. Hours: 8:30AM-4:15PM (EST). *Misdemeanor, Civil Actions Under $25,000, Eviction, Small Claims.*

Civil Records: Access: Mail, in person. Only the court performs in person searches; visitors may not. No search fee. Required to search: name, years to search. Civil cases indexed by defendant, plaintiff. Civil records on computer since 1990, prior on index cards.

Criminal Records: Access: Mail, in person. Only the court performs in person searches; visitors may not. No search fee. Required to search: name, years to search, DOB, SSN. Criminal records on computer since 1990, prior on index cards.

General Information: No suppressed, child and spousal abuse records released. SASE required. Turnaround time 2 days. Copy fee: $1.00 per page. Certification fee: $10.00. Fee payee: 17th District Court. Personal checks accepted. Credit cards accepted: Visa, MasterCard. ATM cards accepted. Prepayment is required.

18th District Court 36675 Ford Rd, Westland, MI 48185; 734-595-8720; Fax: 734-595-0160. Hours: 8:30AM-4PM M,F; 8:30AM-5:30PM T,W; 8:30AM-6PM Th (EST). *Misdemeanor, Civil Actions Under $25,000, Eviction, Small Claims.*

www.18thdistrictcourt.com

Civil Records: Access: Mail, in person. Only the court performs in person searches; visitors may not. Search fee: $10.00 per name. Required to search: name, years to search; also helpful: case number or title. Civil cases indexed by defendant, plaintiff. Civil records on computer since 1987, prior on microfilm.

Criminal Records: Access: Mail, in person. Only the court performs in person searches; visitors may not. Search fee: $10.00 per name. Required to search: name, years to search, DOB; also helpful: case number. Criminal records on computer since 1987, prior on microfilm.

General Information: No suppressed records released. SASE required. Turnaround time 1-2 weeks. Copy fee: $1.00 per page. Certification fee: $10.00. Fee payee: 18th District Court. Personal checks accepted. Prepayment is required.

19th District Court 16077 Michigan Ave, Dearborn, MI 48126; 313-943-2056; Fax: 313-943-3071. Hours: 8AM-4:30PM (EST). *Misdemeanor, Civil Actions Under $25,000, Eviction, Small Claims.*

www.cityofdearborn.org

Civil Records: Access: Fax, mail, in person. Only the court performs in person searches; visitors may not. No search fee. Required to search: name, years to search. Civil cases indexed by defendant, plaintiff. Civil records on computer since 1986.

Criminal Records: Access: Fax, mail, in person. Only the court performs in person searches; visitors may not. No search fee. Required to search: name, years to search, DOB, offense, date of offense. Criminal records on computer since 1987, prior on docket books.

General Information: No suppressed records released. SASE helpful. Copy fee: $1.00 per page. Certification fee: $10.00. Fee payee: 19th District Court. Only cashiers checks and money orders accepted. Credit cards accepted: Visa, MasterCard. Prepayment is required.

20th District Court 6045 Fenton, Dearborn Heights, MI 48127; 313-277-7480; Fax: 313-277-7141. Hours: 9AM-5PM (EST). *Misdemeanor, Civil Actions Under $25,000, Eviction, Small Claims.*

Civil Records: Access: Mail, in person. Only the court performs in person searches; visitors may not. No search fee. Required to search: name, years to search; also helpful: address. Civil cases indexed by defendant, plaintiff. Civil records on computer since April 1991, prior records on microfiche or books.

Criminal Records: Access: Mail, in person. Only the court performs in person searches; visitors may not. No search fee. Required to search: name, years to search, DOB; also helpful: SSN. Criminal records on computer since April 1991, prior records on microfiche or books.

General Information: No suppressed, juvenile, sex offenders, mental health, or adoption records released. SASE required. Turnaround time 1 week-10 days. Copy fee: $1.00 per page. Certification fee: $10.00. Fee payee: 20th District Court. Business checks accepted. Credit cards accepted: Visa, MasterCard. Prepayment is required.

21st District Court 6000 Middlebelt Rd, Garden City, MI 48135; 734-525-8805; Fax: 734-421-4797. Hours: 8:30AM-4:30PM (EST). *Misdemeanor, Civil Actions Under $25,000, Eviction, Small Claims.*

Civil Records: Access: Mail, in person. Only the court performs in person searches; visitors may not. No search fee. Required to search: name, years to search. Civil cases indexed by defendant, plaintiff. Civil records on computer back to 1989, prior on books, microfilm, and cards. In person searchers must fill out a "File/copy Request Form.".

Criminal Records: Access: Mail, in person. Only the court performs in person searches; visitors may not. No search fee. Required to search: name, years to search, DOB; also helpful: SSN. Criminal records on computer back to 1989, prior on books, microfilm, and cards. In person searchers must fill out a "File/copy Request Form.".

General Information: No suppressed records released. SASE required. Turnaround time 1-2 days. Copy fee: $1.00 per page. Certification fee: No cert fee. Fee payee: 21st District Court. Personal checks accepted. Prepayment is required.

22nd District Court 27331 S River Park Dr, Inkster, MI 48141; 313-277-8200; Fax: 313-277-8221. Hours: 8:30AM-4:30PM (EST). *Misdemeanor, Civil Actions Under $25,000, Eviction, Small Claims.*

Civil Records: Access: Mail, in person. Only the court performs in person searches; visitors may not. No search fee. Required to search: name, years to search. Civil cases indexed by defendant, plaintiff. Civil records on computer since 1985, prior on docket books.

Criminal Records: Access: Mail, in person. Only the court performs in person searches; visitors may not. No search fee. Required to search: name, years to search, DOB; also helpful: SSN. Criminal records on computer since 1985, prior on books.

General Information: No suppressed records released. SASE required. Turnaround time 2 weeks. Copy fee: $.25 per page. Certification fee: $10.00. Fee payee: 22nd District Court. Personal checks accepted. Prepayment is required.

23rd District Court 23511 Goddard Rd, Taylor, MI 48180; 734-374-1334; Fax: 734-374-1303. Hours: 8:15AM-4:30PM (EST). *Misdemeanor, Civil Actions Under $25,000, Eviction, Small Claims.*

Civil Records: Access: Mail, in person. Only the court performs in person searches; visitors may not. No search fee. Required to search: name, years to search. Civil cases indexed by defendant, plaintiff. Civil records on computer since 1993, prior on books.

Criminal Records: Access: Mail, in person. Only the court performs in person searches; visitors may not. No search fee. Required to search: name, years to search, DOB; also helpful: SSN. Criminal records on computer since 1993, prior on index cards.

General Information: No suppressed, sexual abuse or drug abuse records released. SASE not required. Turnaround time 1-2 days. Copy fee: $1.00 per page. Certification fee: $10.00. Fee payee: 23rd District Court. Personal checks accepted. Prepayment required.

24th District Court - Allen Park & Melvindale 6515 Roosevelt, Allen Park, MI 48101-2524; 313-928-0535; Fax: 313-928-1860. Hours: 8:30AM-4:30PM (EST). *Misdemeanor, Civil Actions Under $25,000, Eviction, Small Claims.*

www.24thdiscourt.org

Civil Records: Access: Fax, mail, in person. Only the court performs in person searches; visitors may not. No search fee. Required to search: name, years to search. Civil cases indexed by defendant, plaintiff. Civil records on computer since 1990, prior stored as hard-copies.

Criminal Records: Access: Fax, mail, in person. Only the court performs in person searches; visitors may not. No search fee. Required to search: name, years to search, DOB; also helpful: SSN. Criminal records on computer since 1990, prior stored as hard-copies.

General Information: No non-public records, including driving and probation records, released. SASE required if return mail requested. Turnaround time 1 week. Copy fee: $.50 per page. Certification fee: $10.00. Fee payee: 24th District Court. Personal checks accepted. Prepayment is required.

25th District Court 1475 Cleophus, Lincoln Park, MI 48146; 313-382-8603; Civil phone: 313-382-9317; Criminal phone: 313-382-8600; Fax: 313-382-9361. Hours: 9AM-4:30PM (EST). *Misdemeanor, Civil Actions Under $25,000, Eviction, Small Claims.*

Civil Records: Access: Mail, in person. Only the court performs in person searches; visitors may not. No search fee. Required to search: name, years to search. Civil cases indexed by defendant, plaintiff. Civil records on computer since 1988, prior stored as hard-copies.

Criminal Records: Access: Mail, in person. Only the court performs in person searches; visitors may not. No search fee. Required to search: name, years to search, DOB. Criminal records on computer since 1987, prior on docket books and cards.

General Information: No suppressed or expunged records released. SASE required. Turnaround time 1 week. Copy fee: $1.00 per page. Certification fee: $11.00. Fee payee: 25th District Court. Personal checks accepted. Credit cards accepted: Visa, MasterCard. Prepayment is required.

26-1 District Court 10600 W Jefferson, River Rouge, MI 48218; 313-842-7819; Fax: 313-842-5923. Hours: 8:30AM-4:30PM (EST). *Misdemeanor, Civil Actions Under $25,000, Eviction, Small Claims.*

Civil Records: Access: Mail, in person. Only the court performs in person searches; visitors may not. No search fee. Required to search: name, years to search. Civil cases indexed by defendant, plaintiff. Civil records on computer since 11/93; prior records on cards.

Criminal Records: Access: Mail, in person. Only the court performs in person searches; visitors may not. No search fee. Required to search: name, years to search,

DOB. Criminal records on computer since 1993, prior on index cards.

General Information: Public Access terminal is available. No suppressed records released. SASE required. Turnaround time 1 week. Copy fee: $1.00 per page. Certification fee: No cert fee. Fee payee: 26-1 District Court. No personal checks accepted. Prepayment is required.

26-2 District Court 3869 W Jefferson, Ecorse, MI 48229; 313-386-7900; Fax: 313-386-4316. Hours: 9AM-4PM (EST). *Misdemeanor, Civil Actions Under $25,000, Eviction, Small Claims.*

Civil Records: Access: Mail, in person. Only the court performs in person searches; visitors may not. No search fee. Required to search: name, years to search. Civil cases indexed by defendant, plaintiff. Civil records on computer since 1992, prior on index cards.

Criminal Records: Access: Mail, in person. Only the court performs in person searches; visitors may not. No search fee. Required to search: name, years to search, DOB; also helpful: SSN. Criminal records on computer since 1992, prior on index cards.

General Information: No suppressed records released. SASE not required. Turnaround time 1 week. Copy fee: $.50 per page. Certification fee: $10.00. Fee payee: 26-2 District Court. Business checks accepted.

27-1 District Court 2015 Biddle Ave, Wyandotte, MI 48192; 734-324-4475; Fax: 734-324-4472. Hours: 8:30AM-4:30PM (EST). *Misdemeanor, Civil Actions Under $25,000, Eviction, Small Claims.*

Civil Records: Access: Mail, in person. Only the court performs in person searches; visitors may not. No search fee. Required to search: name, years to search. Civil cases indexed by defendant, plaintiff. Civil records on computer since 1988, prior on index cards.

Criminal Records: Access: Mail, in person. Only the court performs in person searches; visitors may not. No search fee. Required to search: name, years to search, DOB. Criminal records on computer since 1988, prior on index cards.

General Information: No suppressed records released. SASE required. Turnaround time 1 week. Copy fee: $1.00 per page. Certification fee: $10.00 plus $1.00 per page after first. Fee payee: 27-1 District Court. Personal checks accepted. Prepayment required.

27-2 District Court 14100 Civic Park Dr, Riverview, MI 48192; 734-281-4204. Hours: 8:30AM-4:30PM (EST). *Misdemeanor, Civil Actions Under $25,000, Eviction, Small Claims.*

Civil Records: Access: Mail, in person. Both court and visitors may perform in person searches. No search fee. Required to search: name, years to search. Civil cases indexed by defendant, plaintiff. Civil records on computer since 1993.

Criminal Records: Access: Mail, in person. Both court and visitors may perform in person searches. No search fee. Required to search: name, years to search, DOB. Criminal records on computer since 1993.

General Information: No suppressed records released. Turnaround time 1 week. Copy fee: $1.00 per page. Certification fee: $10.00 plus $1.00 per page after first. Fee payee: 27-2 District Court. Personal checks accepted. Prepayment is required.

28th District Court 14720 Reaume Parkway, Southgate, MI 48195; Civil phone: 734-246-1366; Criminal phone: 734-246-1360; Fax: 734-246-1405. Hours: 8:30AM-4:30PM (EST). *Misdemeanor, Civil Actions Under $25,000, Eviction, Small Claims.*

Civil Records: Access: In person only. Both court and visitors may perform in person searches. No search fee. Required to search: name, years to search; also helpful: address. Civil cases indexed by defendant, plaintiff. Civil records on computer since 1987, prior on card files by party.

Criminal Records: Access: In person only. Only the court performs in person searches; visitors may not. No search fee. Required to search: name, years to search, DOB; also helpful: address, SSN.

General Information: No suppressed, probation, juvenile, sex offenders, mental health, or adoption records released. Copy fee: $1.00 per page. Certification fee: $10.00. Fee payee: 28th District Court. Only cashiers checks and money orders accepted. Credit cards accepted: Visa, MasterCard. In person only. Prepayment is required.

29th District Court 34808 Sims Ave, Wayne, MI 48184; 734-722-5220; Fax: 734-722-7003. Hours: 8AM-4:30PM (EST). *Misdemeanor, Civil Actions Under $25,000, Eviction, Small Claims.*

Civil Records: Access: Mail, in person. Only the court performs in person searches; visitors may not. No search fee. Required to search: name, years to search. Civil cases indexed by defendant, plaintiff. Civil records on computer since 1990.

Criminal Records: Access: Mail, in person. Only the court performs in person searches; visitors may not. No search fee. Required to search: name, years to search, DOB; also helpful: address, SSN. Criminal records on computer since 1990.

General Information: No suppressed, juvenile, sex offenders, mental health, or adoption records released. SASE required. Turnaround time 1 week, phone turnaround time 1 day. Copy fee: $.50 per page. Certification fee: $25.00. Fee payee: 29th District Court. Personal checks accepted. Credit cards accepted: Visa, MasterCard. Prepayment is required.

30th District Court 28 Gerard Ave, Highland Park, MI 48203; 313-252-0300; Fax: 313-865-1115. Hours: 8AM-4:30PM (EST). *Misdemeanor, Civil Actions Under $25,000, Eviction, Small Claims.*

Civil Records: Access: Mail, in person. Both court and visitors may perform in person searches. Search fee: $5.00 per name. Required to search: name, years to search. Civil cases indexed by defendant, plaintiff. Civil records on computer since 1989, prior on index cards or docket books.

Criminal Records: Access: Mail, in person. Both court and visitors may perform in person searches. Search fee: $5.00 per name. Required to search: name, years to search, DOB. Criminal records on computer since 1989, prior on index cards or docket books.

General Information: No suppressed records released. SASE required. Turnaround time 1 week. Copy fee: $1.00 per page. Certification fee: $5.00. Fee payee: 30th District Court. Prepayment is required.

31st District Court 3401 Evaline Ave, Hamtramck, MI 48212; 313-876-7710; Fax: 313-876-7724. Hours: 8AM-4PM (EST). *Misdemeanor, Civil Actions Under $25,000, Eviction, Small Claims.*

Civil Records: Access: Mail, in person. Only the court performs in person searches; visitors may not. No search fee. Required to search: name, years to search. Civil cases indexed by defendant, plaintiff. Civil records on computer since 1989, prior on index cards.

Criminal Records: Access: Mail, in person. Only the court performs in person searches; visitors may not. No search fee. Required to search: name, years to search, DOB. Criminal records on computer since 1989, prior on index cards.

General Information: No suppressed records released. SASE required. Turnaround time 1-2 days. Copy fee: $1.00 per page. Certification fee: $10.00 plus $1.00 per page after first. Fee payee: 31st District Court. Personal checks accepted. Prepayment is required.

32 A District Court 19617 Harper Ave, Harper Woods, MI 48225; 313-343-2590; Fax: 313-343-2594. Hours: 8:30AM-4:30PM (EST). *Misdemeanor, Civil Actions Under $25,000, Small Claims.*

Civil Records: Access: Phone, fax, mail, in person. Only the court performs in person searches; visitors may not. No search fee. Required to search: name, years to search. Civil cases indexed by defendant, plaintiff. Civil records indexed by name and case number on computer, microfiche, and paper.

Criminal Records: Access: Phone, fax, mail, in person. Only the court performs in person searches; visitors may not. No search fee. Required to search: name, years to search. Criminal records indexed by name and case number on computer, microfiche, and paper.

General Information: No suppressed records released. SASE requested. Turnaround time same day. Fax notes: No fee to fax results. Copy fee: $.50 per page. Certification fee: No cert fee. Fee payee: 32A District Court. Personal checks accepted. Credit cards accepted: Visa, MasterCard. Prepayment is required.

33rd District Court 19000 Van Horn Rd, Woodhaven, MI 48183; Civil phone: 734-671-0225; Criminal phone: 734-671-0201; Fax: 734-671-0307. Hours: 8:30AM-4:30PM (EST). *Misdemeanor, Civil Actions Under $25,000, Eviction, Small Claims.*

Civil Records: Access: Mail, in person. Only the court performs in person searches; visitors may not. No search fee. Required to search: name, years to search; also helpful: address. Civil cases indexed by defendant, plaintiff. Civil records on computer since 1995, prior on microfilm and microfiche.

Criminal Records: Access: Mail, in person. Only the court performs in person searches; visitors may not. No search fee. Required to search: name, years to search, DOB; also helpful: address. Criminal records on computer since 1995, prior on microfilm and microfiche.

General Information: No suppressed records released. SASE required. Turnaround time 1-5 days. Copy fee: $.25 per page. Certification fee: $10.00 plus $1.00 per page after first. Fee payee: 33rd District Court. Business checks accepted. Credit cards accepted: Visa, MasterCard. Prepayment is required.

34th District Court 11131 S Wayne Rd, Romulus, MI 48174; 734-941-4462; Fax: 734-941-7530. Hours: 8:30AM-4PM (EST). *Misdemeanor, Civil Actions Under $25,000, Eviction, Small Claims.*

Civil Records: Access: Mail, in person. Only the court performs in person searches; visitors may not. No search fee. Required to search: name, years to search. Civil cases indexed by defendant, plaintiff. Civil records on computer since 1984, prior on index cards and docket books.

Criminal Records: Access: Mail, in person. Only the court performs in person searches; visitors may not. No search fee. Required to search: name, years to search, DOB; also helpful: SSN. Criminal records on computer since 1984, prior on index cards and docket books.

General Information: No suppressed records released. SASE required. Turnaround time 1 week. Copy fee: $1.00 per page. Certification fee: $10.00 per page. Fee payee: 34th District Court. Personal checks accepted. Prepayment is required.

35th District Court 660 Plymouth Rd, Plymouth, MI 48170; 734-459-4740; Fax: 734-454-9303. Hours: 8:30AM-4:25PM (EST). *Misdemeanor, Civil Actions Under $25,000, Eviction, Small Claims.*

www.35thdistrictcourt.org

Civil Records: Access: Mail, in person. Both court and visitors may perform in person searches. No search fee. Required to search: name, years to search. Civil cases

indexed by defendant, plaintiff. Civil records on computer since 1990; prior records archived.

Criminal Records: Access: Mail, in person. Both court and visitors may perform in person searches. No search fee. Required to search: name, years to search, DOB; also helpful: SSN, sex, signed release. Criminal records on computer since 1990; prior records archived.

General Information: Public Access terminal is available. No suppressed, juvenile, sex offenders, mental health, or adoption records released. Turnaround time 1 week. Fax notes: Fee to fax results is $1.00 per document. Copy fee: $1.00 per page. Certification fee: $10.00. Fee payee: 35th District Court. Personal checks accepted. Third party checks not allowed. Debit cards accepted. Prepayment is required.

Wexford County

28th Circuit Court PO Box 490, Cadillac, MI 49601; 231-779-9450. Hours: 8:30AM-5PM (EST). *Felony, Civil Actions Over $25,000.*

Civil Records: Access: Mail, in person. Only the court performs in person searches; visitors may not. Search fee: $1.00 per name. Required to search: name, years to search. Civil cases indexed by defendant, plaintiff. Civil records on computer since 1977.

Criminal Records: Access: Mail, in person. Only the court performs in person searches; visitors may not. Search fee: $1.00 per name. Required to search: name, years to search. Criminal records on computer since 1977.

General Information: No suppressed, YTA files, juvenile, sex offenders, mental health, or adoption records released. SASE required. Turnaround time same day. Copy fee: $1.00 per page. Certification fee: $10.00. Fee payee: Wexford County Clerk. Only cashiers checks and money orders accepted. Prepayment is required.

84th District Court 501 S Garfield, Cadillac, MI 49601; 231-779-9515; Fax: 231-779-9485. Hours: 8:30AM-5PM (EST). *Misdemeanor, Civil Actions Under $25,000, Eviction, Small Claims.*

Civil Records: Access: Phone, fax, mail, in person. Both court and visitors may perform in person searches. Search fee: $1.00 per name. Required to search: name, years to search. Civil cases indexed by defendant, plaintiff. Civil records on computer since 1984; on index from 1969 to 1984.

Criminal Records: Access: Mail, fax, in person. Both court and visitors may perform in person searches. Search fee: $1.00 per name. Required to search: name, years to search, DOB; also helpful: SSN. Criminal records on computer since 1984; prior records on blue cards.

General Information: No suppressed, juvenile, sex offenders, mental health, or adoption records released. SASE required. Turnaround time 1 week. Copy fee: $1.00 per page. Certification fee: $10.00. Fee payee: 84th District Court. Personal checks accepted. Prepayment is required.

Probate Court 503 S Garfield, Cadillac, MI 49601; 231-779-9510; Fax: 231-779-9485. Hours: 8:30AM-5PM (EST). *Probate.*

Michigan Recording Offices

ORGANIZATION	83 counties, 83 recording offices. The recording officer is County Register of Deeds. 79 counties are in the Eastern Time Zone (EST) and 4 are in the Central Time Zone (CST).
REAL ESTATE RECORDS	Some counties will perform real estate searches. Copies usually cost $1.00 per page. and certification fees vary. Ownership records are located at the Equalization Office, designated "Assessor" in this section. Tax records are located at the Treasurer's Office.
UCC RECORDS	Financing statements are filed at the state level, except for real estate related collateral, which are filed with the County Register. However, prior to 07/2001, consumer goods and farm collateral were also filed at the County Register and these older records can be searched there. All counties will perform UCC searches. Use search request form UCC-11. Search fees are usually $3.00 per debtor name if federal tax identification number or Social Security Number are given, or $6.00 without the number. Copies usually cost $1.00 per page.
TAX LIEN RECORDS	Federal and state tax liens on personal property of businesses are filed with the Secretary of State. Other federal and state tax liens are filed with the Register of Deeds. Most counties search each tax lien index separately. Some charge one fee to search both, while others charge a separate fee for each one. When combining a UCC and tax lien search, total fee is usually $9.00 for all three searches. Some counties require tax identification number as well as name to do a search. Copy fees are usually $1.00 per page.
OTHER LIENS	Construction, lis pendens.

Alcona County

County Register of Deeds, P.O. Box 269, Harrisville, MI 48740-0269. County Register of Deeds, R/E and UCC Recording 989-724-6802; Fax 989-724-5684.
Will search UCC records prior to 7/2001. Search UCC records filed after 7/2001 at the Sec. of State's office only. UCC search includes tax liens if requested. Will not search real estate records. **Other Phone Numbers:** Assessor 989-724-6223; Treasurer 989-724-5140; Elections 989-724-6807; Vital Records 989-724-6807.

Alger County

County Register of Deeds, P.O. Box 538, Munising, MI 49862. 906-387-2076; Fax 906-387-2156.
Will search UCC records prior to 7/2001 and current fixture (land) files. UCC search includes tax liens if requested. Will not search real estate records. **Other Phone Numbers:** Assessor 906-387-2567; Treasurer 906-387-4535.

Allegan County

County Register of Deeds, 113 Chestnut Street, County Court House, Allegan, MI 49010-1360. County Register of Deeds, R/E and UCC Recording 616-673-0390 UCC Recording: 616-673-0390 x3280; Fax 616-673-0289.
Will search UCC records. UCC search includes tax liens if requested. Will not search real estate records. **Other Phone Numbers:** Assessor 616-673-0230.

Alpena County

County Register of Deeds, 720 West Chisholm Street, Courthouse, Alpena, MI 49707-2487. 989-356-3887; Fax 989-356-6559.
Will search UCC records prior to 7/2001 and current fixture (land) files. UCC search includes tax liens if requested. Will not search real estate records. **Other Phone Numbers:** Assessor 989-356-2015; Treasurer 989-356-1751.

Antrim County

County Register of Deeds, P.O. Box 376, Bellaire, MI 49615. County Register of Deeds, R/E and UCC Recording 231-533-6683; Fax 231-533-8317.
Will search UCC records prior to 7/2001 and current fixture (land) files. UCC search includes tax liens if requested. Will not search real estate records. **Other**

Phone Numbers: Assessor 231-533-6320; Treasurer 231-533-6720.

Arenac County

County Register of Deeds, P.O. Box 296, Standish, MI 48658. 989-846-9201 R/E Recording: 517-846-9201.
Will search UCC records prior to 7/2001 and current fixture (land) files. This agency will not do a tax lien search. Will not search real estate records. **Other Phone Numbers:** Assessor 517-846-6246.

Baraga County

County Register of Deeds, Courthouse, 16 N. 3rd St., L'Anse, MI 49946-1085. 906-524-6183; Fax 906-524-6186.
Will search UCC records prior to 7/2001 and current fixture (land) files. UCC search includes tax liens if requested. Will not search real estate records. **Other Phone Numbers:** Assessor 906-524-7331; Treasurer 906-524-7773; Elections 906-524-6183; Vital Records 906-524-6183.

Barry County

County Register of Deeds, P.O. Box 7, Hastings, MI 49058-0007. County Register of Deeds, R/E and UCC Recording 616-948-4824; Fax 616-948-4820.
www.barrycounty.org
Will search UCC records prior to 7/2001 and current fixture (land) files. After 7/2001 all new recordings (UCCs) will need to be searched through the Michigan Secretary of State. UCC search includes tax liens. Will not search real estate records. **Other Phone Numbers:** Assessor 616-948-4821; Treasurer 616-948-4818; Elections 616-948-4810; Vital Records 616-948-4810.

Bay County

County Register of Deeds, 515 Center Avenue, Bay City, MI 48708-5994. County Register of Deeds, R/E and UCC Recording 989-895-4228; Fax 989-895-4296.
Will search UCC records. UCC search includes tax liens. Will not search real estate records. **Other Phone Numbers:** Assessor 989-895-4075; Treasurer 989-895-4285; Vital Records 989-895-4280.

Benzie County

County Register of Deeds, P.O. Box 398, Beulah, MI 49617. 231-882-0016; Fax 231-882-0167.
Will search UCC records prior to 7/2001 and current fixture (land) files. Tax liens not included in UCC

search. Will not search real estate records unless specific document specified, $1.00 minimum. **Other Phone Numbers:** Assessor 231-882-0015; Treasurer 231-882-0011.

Berrien County

County Register of Deeds, Berrien County Administration Center, 701 Main St., St. Joseph, MI 49085. 616-983-7111 x8562 R/E Recording: 616-983-7111; Fax 616-982-8659.
Will search UCC records prior to 7/2001 and current fixture (land) files. UCC search includes tax liens if requested. **Other Phone Numbers:** Assessor 616-983-7111 x8215; Treasurer 616-983-7111 x8208.

Branch County

County Register of Deeds, 570 Marshall Rd, Ste. C, Coldwater, MI 49036. County Register of Deeds, R/E and UCC Recording 517-279-4320.
Will search UCC records prior to 7/2001 and current fixture (land) files. UCC search includes tax liens. Will not search real estate records. **Other Phone Numbers:** Assessor 517-279-4312; Treasurer 517-279-8411.

Calhoun County

County Register of Deeds, 315 West Green Street, Marshall, MI 49068. 616-781-0718; Fax 616-781-0721.
http://co.calhoun.mi.us
Will search UCC records prior to 7/2001 and current fixture (land) files. UCC search includes tax liens if requested. Will not search real estate records. **Other Phone Numbers:** Assessor 616-781-0745; Treasurer 616-969-6910/616-781-0807; Elections 616-781-0988; Vital Records 616-781-0718.

Cass County

County Register of Deeds, P.O. Box 355, Cassopolis, MI 49031-0355. County Register of Deeds, R/E and UCC Recording 616-445-4464; Fax 616-445-4406.
http://www.casscountymi.org
Will search UCC records prior to 7/2001 and current fixture (land) files. UCC search includes tax liens if requested with extra fee Will not search real estate records. **Other Phone Numbers:** Assessor 616-445-4432; Treasurer 616-445-4468; Elections 616-445-4464; Vital Records 616-445-4464.

Charlevoix County

County Register of Deeds, 301 State Street, County Building, Charlevoix, MI 49720. 231-547-7204; Fax 231-547-7246.
Will search UCC records prior to 7/2001 and current fixture (land) files. UCC search includes tax liens if requested. Will not search real estate records. **Other Phone Numbers:** Assessor 231-547-7230; Treasurer 231-547-7202.

Cheboygan County

County Register of Deeds, P.O. Box 70, Cheboygan, MI 49721. 231-627-8866; Fax 231-627-8453.
Will search UCC records prior to 7/2001 and current fixture (land) files. Will not search real estate records. **Other Phone Numbers:** Assessor 231-627-8845; Treasurer 231-627-8821; Elections 231-627-8808; Vital Records 231-627-8808.

Chippewa County

County Register of Deeds, Courthouse, 319 Court St., Sault Ste. Marie, MI 49783. County Register of Deeds, R/E and UCC Recording 906-635-6312; Fax 906-635-6855.
Will search UCC records prior to 7/2001 and current fixture (land) files. UCC search includes tax liens if requested with $6.00 extra per type of tax lien Will not search real estate records. **Other Phone Numbers:** Assessor 906-635-6304; Treasurer 906-635-6308; Elections 906-635-6300; Vital Records 906-635-6300.

Clare County

County Register of Deeds, P.O. Box 438, Harrison, MI 48625. County Register of Deeds, R/E and UCC Recording 989-539-7131; Fax 989-539-6616.
Will search UCC records. UCC search includes tax liens if requested. Mortgage searches available. **Other Phone Numbers:** Assessor 989-539-7894; Treasurer 989-539-7801; Elections 989-539-7131; Vital Records 989-539-7131.

Clinton County

County Register of Deeds, P.O. Box 435, St. Johns, MI 48879-0435. County Register of Deeds, R/E and UCC Recording 989-224-5270; Fax 989-224-5102.
Will search UCC records prior to 7/2001 and current fixture (land) files. UCC search includes tax liens if requested, with extra fees Will not search real estate records. **Other Phone Numbers:** Assessor 989-224-5170; Treasurer 989-224-5280.

Crawford County

County Register of Deeds, 200 West Michigan, Grayling, MI 49738. 989-348-2841 R/E Recording: 989-344-3203 UCC Recording: 989-344-3203; Fax 989-344-3223.
Will search UCC records prior to 7/2001 and current fixture (land) files. UCC search includes tax liens if requested. Will not search real estate records. **Other Phone Numbers:** Assessor 989-344-3235; Treasurer 989-344-3229; Appraiser/Auditor 989-344-3234; Elections 989-344-3200; Vital Records 989-344-3207.

Delta County

County Register of Deeds, 310 Ludington Street, Suite 104, Escanaba, MI 49829-4039. County Register of Deeds, R/E and UCC Recording 906-789-5116; Fax 906-789-5196.
Will search UCC records. Tax liens not included in UCC search. RE owner, mortgage, and property transfer searches available. **Other Phone Numbers:** Assessor 906-789-5109; Treasurer 906-789-5117; Appraiser/Auditor 906-789-5109; Elections 906-789-5105; Vital Records 906-789-5105; Clerk/Registrar FAX 906-789-5196.

Dickinson County

County Register of Deeds, P.O. Box 609, Iron Mountain, MI 49801. 906-774-0955; Fax 906-774-4660.
Will search UCC records prior to 7/2001 and current fixture (land) files. UCC search includes tax liens if requested. Will not search real estate records. **Other Phone Numbers:** Assessor 906-774-2515; Treasurer 906-774-8130.

Eaton County

County Register of Deeds, 1045 Independence Blvd., Room 104, Charlotte, MI 48813-1095. 517-543-7500 x232 R/E Recording: 517-543-7500; Fax 517-543-7377. http://www.co.eaton.mi.us/cntsrv/online.htm
Will search UCC records prior to 7/2001 and current fixture (land) files. UCC search includes tax liens. Will not search real estate records. **Online Access:** Assessor, Tax Records. Two levels of service are available on the County Online Data Service site. For free information, click on the Free Limited Public Information on the main page; then, on the Access System Page, at "User" enter PUBLIC. For "password," enter PUBLIC. The more sophisticated, restricted "Enhanced Records Access" requires registration, a password, and an associated fee. Access fees are billable monthly and can be prepaid to cover usage for any length of time. **Other Phone Numbers:** Assessor 517-543-7500 x236; Treasurer 517-543-7500 x210.

Emmet County

County Register of Deeds, 200 Division, Petoskey, MI 49770. 231-348-1761; Fax 231-348-0633.
Will search UCC records prior to 7/2001 and current fixture (land) files. UCC search includes tax liens if requested. Will not search real estate records. **Other Phone Numbers:** Assessor 231-348-1708; Treasurer 231-348-1715.

Genesee County

County Register of Deeds, 1101 Beach Street, Administration Building, Flint, MI 48502. 810-257-3060; Fax 810-768-7965.
Will search UCC records prior to 7/2001 and current fixture (land) files. UCC search includes tax liens if requested. Will not search real estate records. **Other Phone Numbers:** Assessor 810-257-3017; Treasurer 810-257-3059.

Gladwin County

County Register of Deeds, 401 West Cedar Ave., Ste 7, Gladwin, MI 48624-2093. 989-426-7551.
Will search UCC records prior to 7/2001 and current fixture (land) files. UCC search includes tax liens if requested. Will not search real estate records. **Other Phone Numbers:** Assessor 989-426-9327; Treasurer 989-426-7351.

Gogebic County

County Register of Deeds, Courthouse, 200 N. Moore St., Bessemer, MI 49911. County Register of Deeds, R/E and UCC Recording 906-667-0381; Fax 906-663-4660.
Will search UCC records prior to 7/2001 and current fixture (land) files. UCC search includes tax liens if requested. RE owner, mortgage, and property transfer searches available. **Other Phone Numbers:** Assessor 906-663-4414; Treasurer 906-667-4517; Elections 906-667-4518; Vital Records 906-667-4518.

Grand Traverse County

County Register of Deeds, 400 Boardman Avenue, Traverse City, MI 49684-2577. 231-922-4750; Fax 231-922-4658.

Gratiot County

County Register of Deeds, P.O. Box 5, Ithaca, MI 48847. 989-875-5217.
Will search UCC records. RE record owner searches available. **Other Phone Numbers:** Assessor 989-875-5203; Treasurer 989-875-5220.

Hillsdale County

County Register of Deeds, Courthouse, 29 N Howell, Rm 3, 29 N. Howell, Room 3, Hillsdale, MI 49242. 517-437-2231; Fax 517-437-3139. http://www.co.hillsdale.mi.us/
Will search UCC records prior to 7/2001 and current fixture (land) files. UCC search includes tax liens if requested. Will not search real estate records. **Other Phone Numbers:** Assessor 517-439-9166; Treasurer 517-437-4700; Elections 517-437-3391; Vital Records 517-437-3391.

Houghton County

County Register of Deeds, 401 East Houghton Avenue, Houghton, MI 49931. 906-482-1311; Fax 906-483-0364.
Will search UCC records prior to 7/2001 and current fixture (land) files. UCC search includes tax liens if requested. Will search for last owner by property location. **Other Phone Numbers:** Assessor 906-482-0250; Treasurer 906-482-0560.

Huron County

County Register of Deeds, P.O. Box 126, Bad Axe, MI 48413. 989-269-9941.
Will search UCC records prior to 7/2001 and current fixture (land) files. UCC search includes tax liens if requested. Will not search real estate records. **Other Phone Numbers:** Assessor 989-269-6497; Treasurer 989-269-9238.

Ingham County

County Register of Deeds, P.O. Box 195, Mason, MI 48854-0195. County Register of Deeds, R/E and UCC Recording 517-676-7216 UCC Recording: 517-676-7224; Fax 517-676-7287. http://www.ingham.org/rd/rodindex.htm
Will search UCC records prior to 7/2001 and current fixture (land) files. This agency will not do a tax lien search. Will not search real estate records. **Online Access:** Assumed Business Names. County DBA and co-partnership listings are available free online at www.ingham.org/CL/dbalists.htm. **Other Phone Numbers:** Assessor 517-676-7212; Treasurer 517-676-7220; Elections 517-676-7205; Vital Records 517-676-7201.

Ionia County

County Register of Deeds, P.O. Box 35, Ionia, MI 48846. 616-527-5320; Fax 616-527-5380. http://www.ioniacounty.org
Will search UCC records prior to 7/2001 and current fixture (land) files. UCC search includes tax liens if requested. Will not search real estate records. **Other Phone Numbers:** Assessor 616-527-5376; Treasurer 616-527-5329.

Iosco County

County Register of Deeds, P.O. Box 367, Tawas City, MI 48764. County Register of Deeds, R/E and UCC Recording 989-362-2021; Fax 989-984-1101.

Will search UCC records prior to 7/2001 and current fixture (land) files. Tax liens not included in UCC search. Will search grantor/grantee or mortgagor/mortgagee. **Other Phone Numbers:** Assessor 231-922-4772; Treasurer 231-922-4735.

Will search UCC records prior to 7/2001 and current fixture (land) files. UCC search includes tax liens if requested. RE owner, mortgage, and property transfer searches available only over phone or in person **Other Phone Numbers:** Assessor 989-362-5801; Treasurer 989-362-4409; Elections 989-362-3497; Vital Records 989-362-3497.

Iron County

County Register of Deeds, 2 S. Sixth Street, Ste. 11, Courthouse Annex, Suite 11, Crystal Falls, MI 49920-1413. 906-875-3321; Fax 906-875-0658.
Will search UCC records prior to 7/2001 and current fixture (land) files. UCC search includes tax liens if requested. Will not search real estate records. **Other Phone Numbers:** Assessor 906-875-6502; Treasurer 906-875-3362.

Isabella County

County Register of Deeds, 200 North Main Street, Mt. Pleasant, MI 48858. County Register of Deeds, R/E and UCC Recording 989-772-0911 x253; Fax 989-773-7431.
Will search UCC records prior to 7/2001 and current fixture (land) files. UCC search includes tax liens if requested. Will not search real estate records. **Other Phone Numbers:** Assessor 989-772-0911 x242; Treasurer 989-772-0911 x254; Elections 989-772-0911 x259; Vital Records 989-772-0911 x259.

Jackson County

County Register of Deeds, 120 West Michigan Avenue, 11th Floor, Jackson, MI 49201. 517-788-4350; Fax 517-788-4686.
Will search UCC records prior to 7/2001 and current fixture (land) files. UCC search includes tax liens if requested. Will not search real estate records. **Online Access:** Real Estate, Liens. Access to county online records requires pre-payment and $1 per minute of use (this may be revised). Records date back to 1985. Indexes include grantor/grantee, deeds, mortgage information. Lending agency information is available. Vital records will be added to the system when it is upgraded. For information, contact Mindy at 517-768-6682. **Other Phone Numbers:** Assessor 517-788-4378; Treasurer 517-788-4418.

Kalamazoo County

County Register of Deeds, 201 West Kalamazoo Avenue, Kalamazoo, MI 49007. 616-383-8970.
Will search UCC records prior to 7/2001 and current fixture (land) files. This agency will not do a tax lien search. Will not search real estate records. **Other Phone Numbers:** Assessor 616-383-8960; Treasurer 616-383-8124.

Kalkaska County

County Register of Deeds, P.O. Box 780, Kalkaska, MI 49646. 231-258-3315; Fax 231-258-3318.
Will search UCC records prior to 7/2001 and current fixture (land) files. UCC search includes tax liens. Mortgage searches available. **Other Phone Numbers:** Assessor 231-258-3340; Treasurer 231-258-3310.

Kent County

County Register of Deeds, 300 Monroe Avenue NW, Grand Rapids, MI 49503-2286. 616-336-3558;
http://www.co.kent.mi.us/dept.htm
Will search UCC records prior to 7/2001 and current fixture (land) files. UCC search includes tax liens. Will not search real estate records. **Online Access:** Assessor. Records on the Walker City Assessing Dept. database are available free online at www.ci.walker. mi.us/Services/Assessor/AssessingData/DataIntro.html. In most cases, sales and permit histories go back to 1993. Database contains residential assessment and

structural information. Also, records on the Alpine Charter Township Assessment database are available free online at http://alpine.data-web.net. Search by parcel number or street name. **Other Phone Numbers:** Assessor 616-336-3527; Treasurer 616-336-0762.

Keweenaw County

County Register of Deeds, HC 1 Box 607, Eagle River, MI 49924-9700. County Register of Deeds, R/E and UCC Recording 906-337-2229; Fax 906-337-2795.
Will search UCC records. UCC search includes tax liens if requested. Will not search real estate records. **Other Phone Numbers:** Assessor 906-337-3471; Treasurer 906-337-1625.

Lake County

County Register of Deeds, Drawer B, Baldwin, MI 49304. County Register of Deeds, R/E and UCC Recording 231-745-4641; Fax 231-745-2241. www.michigan.gov
Will search UCC records prior to 7/2001 and current fixture (land) files. UCC search includes tax liens if requested. Will not search real estate records. **Other Phone Numbers:** Assessor 231-745-2723; Treasurer 231-745-4622; Appraiser/Auditor 231-745-4641; Elections 231-745-4641; Vital Records 231-745-2725.

Lapeer County

County Register of Deeds, 279 North Court Street, Lapeer, MI 48446. 810-667-0211; Fax 810-667-0293.
Will search UCC records prior to 7/2001 and current fixture (land) files. UCC search includes tax liens if requested. Will not search real estate records. **Other Phone Numbers:** Assessor 810-667-0228; Treasurer 810-667-0239.

Leelanau County

County Register of Deeds, P.O. Box 595, Leland, MI 49654. 231-256-9682; Fax 231-256-8149.
Will search UCC records prior to 7/2001 and current fixture (land) files. UCC search includes tax liens if requested. Will not search real estate records. **Other Phone Numbers:** Assessor 231-256-9823; Treasurer 231-256-9838.

Lenawee County

County Register of Deeds, 301 N. Main St., Adrian, MI 49221. County Register of Deeds, R/E and UCC Recording 517-264-4538 UCC Recording: 517-264-4540; Fax 517-264-4543.
Will search UCC records. UCC search includes tax liens if requested. Will not search real estate records. **Other Phone Numbers:** Assessor 517-264-4522; Treasurer 517-264-4554.

Livingston County

County Register of Deeds, P.O. Box 197, Howell, MI 48844. 517-546-0270; Fax 517-546-5966.
Will search UCC records prior to 7/2001 and current fixture (land) files. UCC search includes tax liens. Will not search real estate records. **Online Access:** Real Estate, Liens, Tas Assessor Records. Access to County online records is available for occasional users, and a dedicated line is available for $1200 for professional users. Annual fee for occasional use is $400, plus $.000043 per second. Records date back to 1984. Lending agency information is available. For information, contact Judy Epley at 517-546-2530. **Other Phone Numbers:** Assessor 517-546-4182; Treasurer 517-546-7010.

Luce County

County Register of Deeds, County Government Building, Newberry, MI 49868. County Register of

Deeds, R/E and UCC Recording 906-293-5521; Fax 906-293-0050.
Will search UCC records. RE record owner and mortgage searches available. **Other Phone Numbers:** Assessor 906-293-5611; Treasurer 906-293-8171; Elections 906-293-5521; Vital Records 906-293-5521.

Mackinac County

County Register of Deeds, 100 Marley Street, Saint Ignace, MI 49781. 906-643-7306; Fax 906-643-7302.
Will search UCC records prior to 7/2001 and current fixture (land) files. UCC search includes tax liens if requested. Will not search real estate records. **Other Phone Numbers:** Assessor 906-643-7310; Treasurer 906-643-7317.

Macomb County

County Register of Deeds, 10 North Main, Mt. Clemens, MI 48043. County Register of Deeds, R/E and UCC Recording 810-469-5342; Fax 810-469-5130. http://www.co.macomb.mi.us
Will search UCC records prior to 7/2001 and current fixture (land) files. UCC search includes tax liens. RE record owner and mortgage searching available. **Online Access:** Business Registration, Death Records. Business registration information - owner name, address, type and filing date - is available free online at http://macomb.mcntv.com/businessnames. Search by full or partial company name. County death records are available free online at http://macomb.mcntv.com/deathrecords. Search by name or apx. date. Also, County Recorder records are available from a private online source at www.landaccess.com; Fees and registration required. Also, Clinton Township Assessor records are available free online at www.clintontownship.com/assprd.htm. Enter user name: "clintwp" and password "assessor". **Other Phone Numbers:** Assessor 810-469-5190; Treasurer 810-469-5190; Elections 810-469-5209; Vital Records 810-469-5120.

Manistee County

County Register of Deeds, 415 Third Street, Courthouse, Manistee, MI 49660-1606. 231-723-2146; Fax 231-723-9069.
Will search UCC records prior to 7/2001 and current fixture (land) files. Tax liens not included in UCC search. Will not search real estate records. **Other Phone Numbers:** Assessor 231-723-5957.

Marquette County

County Register of Deeds, 234 West Baraga Avenue, C-105, Marquette, MI 49855. 906-225-8415; Fax 906-225-8203.
Will search UCC records prior to 7/2001 and current fixture (land) files. UCC search includes tax liens if requested. Will not search real estate records. **Other Phone Numbers:** Assessor 906-225-8405; Treasurer 906-228-1565.

Mason County

County Register of Deeds, P.O. Box 57, Ludington, MI 49431-0057. 231-843-4466; Fax 231-843-1972.
Will search UCC records prior to 7/2001 and current fixture (land) files. Will not search real estate records. **Other Phone Numbers:** Assessor 231-845-6288; Treasurer 231-845-8411.

Mecosta County

County Register of Deeds, P.O. Box 718, Big Rapids, MI 49307. 231-592-0148.
Will search UCC records prior to 7/2001 and current fixture (land) files. UCC search includes tax liens if requested. Will not search real estate records. **Other Phone Numbers:** Assessor 231-592-0108; Treasurer 231-592-0169.

Menominee County

Register of Deeds, 839 10th Ave, 839 10th Ave., Menominee, MI 49858. 906-863-2822; Fax 906-863-8839.
Will search UCC records prior to 7/2001 and current fixture (land) files. Tax liens not included in UCC search. Property transfer searches available. Real estate search fee is $16.00 per hour, minimum of $4.00. **Other Phone Numbers:** Assessor 906-863-2685; Treasurer 906-863-5548; Elections 906-863-9968; Vital Records 906-863-9968.

Midland County

County Register of Deeds, 220 West Ellsworth Street, County Services Building, Midland, MI 48640-5194. 989-832-6820 R/E Recording: 517-832-6820; Fax 989-832-6608.
Will search UCC records prior to 7/2001 and current fixture (land) files. This agency will not do a tax lien search. Will not search real estate records. **Other Phone Numbers:** Assessor 517-837-3334; Treasurer 989-832-6850.

Missaukee County

County Register of Deeds, P.O. Box 800, Lake City, MI 49651. 231-839-4967; Fax 231-839-3684.
Will search UCC records prior to 7/2001 and current fixture (land) files. UCC search includes tax liens if requested. Will search RE records 1990 forward on computer. **Other Phone Numbers:** Assessor 231-839-2702; Treasurer 231-839-2169.

Monroe County

County Register of Deeds, 51 S Macomb St, Monroe, MI 48161. 734-240-7390.
Will search UCC records prior to 7/2001 and current fixture (land) files. UCC search includes tax liens if requested. Will not search real estate records. **Other Phone Numbers:** Assessor 734-240-7235; Treasurer 734-240-7365.

Montcalm County

County Register of Deeds, P.O. Box 368, Stanton, MI 48888. 989-831-7337 R/E Recording: 517-831-7337; Fax 989-831-7320.
Will search UCC records prior to 7/2001 and current fixture (land) files. UCC search includes tax liens if requested. Searches available for records after 1/88 for last owner from property location. **Online Access:** Real Estate, Liens. Two online options are available. To view the index, the monthly fee is $250. To view both the index and document image, the monthly fee is $650. Records date back to 1/1/1988. Lending agency information is available. For information, contact Laurie Wilson at 517-831-7321. **Other Phone Numbers:** Assessor 989-831-5226 x203; Treasurer 989-831-5226 x234.

Montmorency County

County Register of Deeds, P.O. Box 789, Atlanta, MI 49709. County Register of Deeds, R/E and UCC Recording 989-785-3374; Fax 989-785-2825.
Will search UCC records prior to 7/2001 and current fixture (land) files. UCC search includes tax liens if requested. Will not search real estate records. **Other Phone Numbers:** Assessor 989-785-3411; Treasurer 989-785-4769; Elections 989-785-3374; Vital Records 989-785-3374.

Muskegon County

County Register of Deeds, 990 Terrace St., Muskegon, MI 49442. 231-724-6271; Fax 231-724-6842.
Will search UCC records prior to 7/2001 and current fixture (land) files. UCC search includes tax liens if requested. RE record owner and mortgage searches available. **Other Phone Numbers:** Assessor 231-724-6386; Treasurer 231-724-6261.

Newaygo County

County Register of Deeds, P.O. Box 885, White Cloud, MI 49349. County Register of Deeds, R/E and UCC Recording 231-689-7246; Fax 231-689-7205.
Will search UCC records prior to 7/2001 and current fixture (land) files. UCC search includes tax liens if requested. Will not search real estate records. **Other Phone Numbers:** Assessor 231-689-7240; Treasurer 231-689-7230; Elections 231-689-7235; Vital Records 231-689-7235.

Oakland County

County Register of Deeds, 1200 North Telegraph Road, Dept 480, Pontiac, MI 48341-0480. 248-858-0599 R/E Recording: 248-858-0581; http://www.co.oakland.mi.us
Will search UCC records prior to 7/2001 and current fixture (land) files. UCC search includes tax liens if requested. Will not search real estate records. **Online Access:** Real Estate, Property Tax, Tax Liens. Online access to Access Oakland property information is available by subscription. Available monthly or per use. For information or sign-up, visit www.co.oakland.mi.us (click on "@cess Oakland") or call Information Services at 248-858-0861. Also, County Recorder records are accessible through a private online service at www.landaccess.com; Fees and registration are required. **Other Phone Numbers:** Assessor 248-858-0740; Treasurer 248-858-0599.

Oceana County

County Register of Deeds, P.O. Box 111, Hart, MI 49420. 231-873-4158 R/E Recording: 231-87304158.
Will search UCC records prior to 7/2001 and current fixture (land) files. UCC search includes tax liens if requested. Will not search real estate records. **Other Phone Numbers:** Assessor 231-873-4609; Treasurer 231-873-3980.

Ogemaw County

County Register of Deeds, 806 West Houghton Ave, Room 104, West Branch, MI 48661. County Register of Deeds, R/E and UCC Recording 989-345-0728; Fax 989-345-6221.
Will search UCC records prior to 7/2001 and current fixture (land) files. UCC search includes tax liens if requested. Will not search real estate records. **Other Phone Numbers:** Assessor 989-345-0328; Treasurer 989-345-0084; Elections 989-345-0215; Vital Records 989-345-0215.

Ontonagon County

County Register of Deeds, 725 Greenland Road, Ontonagon, MI 49953-1492. County Register of Deeds, R/E and UCC Recording 906-884-4255; Fax 906-884-2916.
Will search UCC records prior to 7/2001 and current fixture (land) files. UCC search includes tax liens. Will search RE name index. **Other Phone Numbers:** Assessor 906-884-2765; Treasurer 906-884-4665; Appraiser/Auditor 906-884-2765; Elections 906-884-4255; Vital Records 906-884-2806.

Osceola County

County Register of Deeds, 301 W Upton Ave., Reed City, MI 49677-0208. 231-832-6113.
Will search UCC records prior to 7/2001 and current fixture (land) files. UCC search includes tax liens. Will not search real estate records. **Other Phone Numbers:** Assessor 231-832-6119; Treasurer 231-832-6110.

Oscoda County

County Register of Deeds, P.O. Box 399, Mio, MI 48647. 989-826-1116; Fax 989-826-3657.
Will search UCC records prior to 7/2001 and current fixture (land) files. Tax liens not included in UCC search. Will not search real estate records. **Other Phone Numbers:** Assessor 989-826-1113; Treasurer 989-826-3241 x112.

Otsego County

County Register of Deeds, 225 West Main St, Rm 110, Room 108, Gaylord, MI 49735. 989-732-6484 x301/2 R/E Recording: 989-732-6484 x301; Fax 989-732-1562.
Will search UCC records prior to 7/2001 and current fixture (land) files. Tax liens included in UCC search with extra fees. Will not search real estate records. **Other Phone Numbers:** Assessor 989-732-6484 x315; Treasurer 989-732-6484 x311; Elections 989-732-6484 x392; Vital Records 989-732-6484 x303.

Ottawa County

County Register of Deeds, P.O. Box 265, Grand Haven, MI 49417-0265. 616-846-8240 R/E Recording: 616-846-8310;   Fax   616-846-8131. http://www.co.ottawa.mi.us/rod.html
Will search UCC records prior to 7/2001 and current fixture (land) files. UCC search includes tax liens if requested. Will not search real estate records. **Other Phone Numbers:** Assessor 616-738-4826; Treasurer 616-846-8230; Elections 616-846-8231; Vital Records 616-846-8231.

Presque Isle County

County Register of Deeds, P.O. Box 110, Rogers City, MI 49779-0110. 989-734-2676 R/E Recording: 517-734-2676; Fax 989-734-0506.
Will search UCC records prior to 7/2001 and current fixture (land) files. UCC search includes tax liens if requested. Will not search real estate records. **Other Phone Numbers:** Assessor 989-734-3810; Treasurer 989-734-4075.

Roscommon County

County Register of Deeds, P.O. Box 98, Roscommon, MI 48653. 989-275-5931 R/E Recording: 517-275-5931; Fax 989-275-8640.
Will search UCC records prior to 7/2001 and current fixture (land) files. UCC search includes tax liens if requested. Will not search real estate records. **Other Phone Numbers:** Assessor 989-275-8121 x5754; Treasurer 989-275-5823; Elections 989-275-5923; Vital Records 989-275-5923.

Saginaw County

County Register of Deeds, 111 South Michigan Avenue, Saginaw, MI 48602. 989-790-5270; Fax 989-790-5278.
Will search UCC records prior to 7/2001 and current fixture (land) files. UCC search includes tax liens if requested. RE record owner searches available. **Online Access:** Assessor. Records on the Saginaw Charter Township Assessor's Property Data Page are available free online at www.sagtwp.org/pt_scripts/search.cfm. Search by address, tax roll number, or owner name. **Other Phone Numbers:** Assessor 989-790-5260; Treasurer 989-790-5225.

Sanilac County

County Register of Deeds, Box 168, Sandusky, MI 48471-0168. 810-648-2313 R/E Recording: 810-6482313 UCC Recording: 810-648-1213; Fax 810-648-5461.
Will search UCC records prior to 7/2001 and current fixture (land) files. UCC search includes tax liens if

requested. RE record owner and property searches available. **Other Phone Numbers:** Assessor 810-648-2955; Treasurer 810-648-2127; Elections 810-648-3212; Vital Records 810-648-3212.

Schoolcraft County

County Register of Deeds, 300 Walnut Street, Room 164, Manistique, MI 49854. 906-341-3618; Fax 906-341-5680.

Will search UCC records prior to 7/2001 and current fixture (land) files. This agency will not do a tax lien search. Will not search real estate records. **Other Phone Numbers:** Assessor 906-341-3677; Treasurer 906-341-3622.

Shiawassee County

County Register of Deeds, P.O. Box 103, Corunna, MI 48817. 989-743-2216 R/E Recording: 517-743-2216; Fax 989-743-2459.

Will search UCC records prior to 7/2001 and current fixture (land) files. UCC search includes tax liens if requested. Will not search real estate records. **Other Phone Numbers:** Assessor 989-743-2263; Treasurer 989-743-2224.

St. Clair County

County Register of Deeds, 201 McMorran Blvd., Room 116, Port Huron, MI 48060. 810-985-2275; Fax 810-985-4297.

Will search UCC records prior to 7/2001 and current fixture (land) files. UCC search includes tax liens if requested. Will not search real estate records. **Other Phone Numbers:** Assessor 810-985-6925; Treasurer 810-985-2295.

St. Joseph County

County Register of Deeds, P.O. Box 388, Centreville, MI 49032-0388. 616-467-5553 x553 R/E Recording: 616-467-5553; Fax 616-467-5628.

Will search UCC records prior to 7/2001 and current fixture (land) files. UCC search includes tax liens if requested. Tax number required Will not search real estate records. **Other Phone Numbers:** Assessor 616-467-5576; Treasurer 616-467-5581.

Tuscola County

County Register of Deeds, 440 North State Street, Caro, MI 48723. 989-672-3840; Fax 989-672-4266.

Will search UCC records prior to 7/2001 and current fixture (land) files. UCC search includes tax liens if requested. Will not search real estate records. **Other Phone Numbers:** Assessor 989-673-5999 x251; Treasurer 989-673-5999 x300.

Van Buren County

County Register of Deeds, 219 Paw Paw Street, #102, Paw Paw, MI 49079. County Register of Deeds, R/E and UCC Recording 616-657-8242; Fax 616-657-7573.

Will search UCC records prior to 7/2001 and current fixture (land) files. UCC search includes tax liens if requested. Will not search real estate records. **Other Phone Numbers:** Assessor 616-657-8234; Treasurer 616-657-8228; Elections 616-657-8218; Vital Records 616-657-8218.

Washtenaw County

County Register of Deeds, P.O. Box 8645, Ann Arbor, MI 48107. 734-222-6700 R/E Recording: 734-222-6710 UCC Recording: 734-222-6710; Fax 734-222-6528. http://www.co.washtenaw.mi.us/DEPTS/CLERK.HTM

Will search UCC records prior to 7/2001 and current fixture (land) files. UCC search includes tax liens if requested. Will not search real estate records. **Other Phone Numbers:** Assessor 734-994-2511; Treasurer 734-994-2520; Elections 734-222-6730; Vital Records 734-222-6700.

Wayne County

County Register of Deeds, 400 Monroe, Room 620, Detroit, MI 48226. 313-224-5860 R/E Recording: 313-224-5854; Fax 313-224-5884.

Will search UCC records prior to 7/2001 and current fixture (land) files. UCC search includes tax liens if requested. RE owner, mortgage, and property transfer searches available. $15.00 for last owner search by property location **Online Access:** Assessor. Records on the City of Dearborn Residential Property Assessment Database are available free online at http://dev.todaylink.net/asp/cityofdearborn/dbnCitySearch.asp. Search by street name and number. **Other Phone Numbers:** Assessor 313-224-2326; Treasurer 313-224-5990.

Wexford County

County Register of Deeds, 437 East Division Street, Cadillac, MI 49601. 231-779-9455; Fax 231-779-0292. Will search UCC records prior to 7/2001 and current fixture (land) files. UCC search includes tax liens if requested. Will not search real estate records. **Other Phone Numbers:** Assessor 231-779-9531; Treasurer 231-779-9475.

Michigan County Locator

You will usually be able to find the city name in the City/County Cross Reference below. In that case, it is a simple matter to determine the county from the cross reference. However, only the official US Postal Service city names are included in this index. There are an additional 40,000 place names that people use in their addresses. Therefore, we have also included a ZIP/City Cross Reference immediately following the City/County Cross Reference.

If you know the ZIP Code but the city name does not appear in the City/County Cross Reference index, look up the ZIP Code in the ZIP/City Cross Reference, find the city name, then look up the city name in the City/County Cross Reference. For example, you want to know the county for an address of Menands, NY 12204. There is no "Menands" in the City/County Cross Reference. The ZIP/City Cross Reference shows that ZIP Codes 12201-12288 are for the city of Albany. Looking back in the City/County Cross Reference, Albany is in Albany County.

City/County Cross Reference

ACME Grand Traverse
ADA Kent
ADDISON Lenawee
ADRIAN Lenawee
AFTON Cheboygan
AHMEEK Keweenaw
AKRON Tuscola
ALANSON (49706) Emmet(82),
   Cheboygan(18)
ALBA Antrim
ALBION Calhoun
ALDEN (49612) Antrim(73), Kalkaska(27)
ALGER (48610) Ogemaw(36), Arenac(33),
   Gladwin(32)
ALGONAC St. Clair
ALLEGAN Allegan
ALLEN Hillsdale
ALLEN PARK Wayne
ALLENDALE Ottawa
ALLENTON St. Clair
ALLOUEZ Keweenaw
ALMA Gratiot
ALMONT Lapeer
ALPENA (49707) Alpena(98), Presque
   Isle(3)
ALPHA Iron
ALTO Kent
AMASA Iron
ANCHORVILLE St. Clair
ANN ARBOR Washtenaw
APPLEGATE Sanilac
ARCADIA (49613) Manistee(76),
   Benzie(24)
ARGYLE Sanilac
ARMADA (48005) Macomb(96), St. Clair(4)
ARNOLD Marquette
ASHLEY Gratiot
ATHENS (49011) Calhoun(96), Branch(2),
   St. Joseph(2)
ATLANTA Montmorency
ATLANTIC MINE Houghton
ATLAS Genesee
ATTICA Lapeer
AU GRES Arenac
AU TRAIN Alger
AUBURN Bay
AUBURN HILLS Oakland
AUGUSTA Kalamazoo
AVOCA St. Clair
AZALIA Monroe
BAD AXE Huron
BAILEY (49303) Muskegon(89),
   Newaygo(10), Kent(1)
BALDWIN Lake
BANCROFT Shiawassee
BANGOR Van Buren
BANNISTER (48807) Gratiot(76),
   Saginaw(24)
BARAGA Baraga
BARBEAU Chippewa
BARK RIVER (49807) Delta(45),
   Dickinson(35), Menominee(20)
BARODA Berrien

BARRYTON (49305) Mecosta(92),
   Isabella(8)
BARTON CITY Alcona
BATH Clinton
BATTLE CREEK (49016) Calhoun(98),
   Kalamazoo(2)
BATTLE CREEK (49017) Calhoun(95),
   Barry(5)
BATTLE CREEK Calhoun
BAY CITY Bay
BAY PORT Huron
BAY SHORE Charlevoix
BEAR LAKE Manistee
BEAVER ISLAND Charlevoix
BEAVERTON (48612) Gladwin(96),
   Clare(2), Midland(2)
BEDFORD Calhoun
BELDING Ionia
BELLAIRE Antrim
BELLEVILLE Wayne
BELLEVUE (49021) Eaton(69), Barry(24),
   Calhoun(7)
BELMONT Kent
BENTLEY (48613) Bay(87), Gladwin(11),
   Arenac(2)
BENTON HARBOR (49022) Berrien(99),
   Van Buren(1)
BENTON HARBOR Berrien
BENZONIA (49616) Benzie(98),
   Manistee(2)
BERGLAND Ontonagon
BERKLEY Oakland
BERRIEN CENTER (49102) Berrien(96),
   Cass(5)
BERRIEN SPRINGS Berrien
BESSEMER Gogebic
BEULAH Benzie
BIG BAY Marquette
BIG RAPIDS (49307) Mecosta(97),
   Newaygo(3)
BIRCH RUN (48415) Saginaw(96),
   Tuscola(2), Genesee(1)
BIRMINGHAM Oakland
BITELY (49309) Newaygo(94), Lake(6)
BLACK RIVER Alcona
BLANCHARD (49310) Isabella(58),
   Mecosta(39), Montcalm(3)
BLISSFIELD Lenawee
BLOOMFIELD HILLS Oakland
BLOOMINGDALE (49026) Van Buren(88),
   Allegan(12)
BOON Wexford
BOYNE CITY (49712) Charlevoix(98),
   Antrim(2)
BOYNE FALLS (49713) Charlevoix(91),
   Emmet(9)
BRADLEY Allegan
BRANCH (49402) Lake(47), Mason(45),
   Oceana(8)
BRANT Saginaw
BRECKENRIDGE (48615) Gratiot(72),
   Midland(28)
BREEDSVILLE Van Buren

BRETHREN Manistee
BRIDGEPORT Saginaw
BRIDGEWATER Washtenaw
BRIDGMAN Berrien
BRIGHTON Livingston
BRIMLEY Chippewa
BRITTON (49229) Lenawee(89),
   Monroe(9), Washtenaw(3)
BROHMAN Newaygo
BRONSON Branch
BROOKLYN Jackson
BROWN CITY (48416) Sanilac(61),
   Lapeer(36), St. Clair(3)
BRUCE CROSSING Ontonagon
BRUNSWICK (49313) Muskegon(78),
   Newaygo(22)
BRUTUS (49716) Emmet(64),
   Cheboygan(36)
BUCHANAN Berrien
BUCKLEY (49620) Wexford(60), Grand
   Traverse(40)
BURLINGTON Calhoun
BURNIPS Allegan
BURR OAK (49030) St. Joseph(92),
   Branch(8)
BURT Saginaw
BURT LAKE Cheboygan
BURTON Genesee
BYRON (48418) Shiawassee(60),
   Genesee(30), Livingston(10)
BYRON CENTER (49315) Kent(93),
   Ottawa(4), Allegan(3)
CADILLAC Wexford
CADMUS Lenawee
CALEDONIA (49316) Kent(88), Allegan(9),
   Barry(3)
CALUMET Houghton
CAMDEN Hillsdale
CANNONSBURG Kent
CANTON Wayne
CAPAC (48014) St. Clair(98), Lapeer(2)
CARLETON Monroe
CARNEY Menominee
CARO Tuscola
CARP LAKE (49718) Emmet(67),
   Cheboygan(33)
CARROLLTON Saginaw
CARSON CITY (48811) Montcalm(68),
   Gratiot(32)
CARSONVILLE Sanilac
CASCO St. Clair
CASEVILLE Huron
CASNOVIA (49318) Muskegon(70),
   Newaygo(18), Kent(12)
CASPIAN Iron
CASS CITY (48726) Tuscola(85),
   Sanilac(12), Huron(3)
CASSOPOLIS Cass
CEDAR Leelanau
CEDAR LAKE Montcalm
CEDAR RIVER Menominee
CEDAR SPRINGS Kent
CEDARVILLE Mackinac

CEMENT CITY (49233) Lenawee(77),
   Jackson(23)
CENTER LINE Macomb
CENTRAL LAKE Antrim
CENTREVILLE St. Joseph
CERESCO Calhoun
CHAMPION Marquette
CHANNING Dickinson
CHARLEVOIX (49720) Charlevoix(98),
   Antrim(2)
CHARLOTTE Eaton
CHASE Lake
CHASSELL Houghton
CHATHAM Alger
CHEBOYGAN Cheboygan
CHELSEA Washtenaw
CHESANING (48616) Saginaw(99),
   Shiawassee(1)
CHIPPEWA LAKE Mecosta
CLARE (48617) Clare(79), Isabella(21)
CLARKLAKE Jackson
CLARKSTON Oakland
CLARKSVILLE (48815) Ionia(96), Kent(4)
CLAWSON Oakland
CLAYTON Lenawee
CLIFFORD (48727) Lapeer(60),
   Tuscola(40)
CLIMAX Kalamazoo
CLINTON (49236) Lenawee(83),
   Washtenaw(18)
CLINTON TOWNSHIP Macomb
CLIO (48420) Genesee(98), Tuscola(2)
CLOVERDALE Barry
COHOCTAH Livingston
COLDWATER Branch
COLEMAN (48618) Midland(84),
   Isabella(13), Gladwin(3)
COLOMA (49038) Berrien(93), Van
   Buren(7)
COLON (49040) St. Joseph(99), Branch(1)
COLUMBIAVILLE (48421) Lapeer(96),
   Genesee(4)
COLUMBUS St. Clair
COMINS (48619) Oscoda(77),
   Montmorency(23)
COMMERCE TOWNSHIP Oakland
COMSTOCK Kalamazoo
COMSTOCK PARK Kent
CONCORD Jackson
CONKLIN (49403) Ottawa(90),
   Muskegon(5), Kent(5)
CONSTANTINE St. Joseph
CONWAY Emmet
COOKS (49817) Schoolcraft(83), Delta(17)
COOPERSVILLE (49404) Ottawa(97),
   Muskegon(3)
COPEMISH (49625) Manistee(93),
   Wexford(7)
COPPER CITY Houghton
COPPER HARBOR Keweenaw
CORAL Montcalm
CORNELL (49818) Delta(93), Marquette(8)
CORUNNA Shiawassee

COVERT Van Buren
COVINGTON Baraga
CROSS VILLAGE Emmet
CROSWELL Sanilac
CRYSTAL (48818) Montcalm(99), Gratiot(1)
CRYSTAL FALLS Iron
CURRAN (48728) Alcona(86), Oscoda(14)
CURTIS Mackinac
CUSTER Mason
DAFTER Chippewa
DAGGETT Menominee
DANSVILLE Ingham
DAVISBURG Oakland
DAVISON (99999) Genesee(99), Lapeer(1)
DE TOUR VILLAGE Chippewa
DEARBORN Wayne
DEARBORN HEIGHTS Wayne
DECATUR (49045) Van Buren(92), Cass(8)
DECKER (48426) Sanilac(94), Tuscola(6)
DECKERVILLE Sanilac
DEERFIELD Lenawee
DEERTON (49822) Alger(98), Marquette(2)
DEFORD (48729) Tuscola(99), Sanilac(1)
DELTON Barry
DETROIT Wayne
DEWITT Clinton
DEXTER Washtenaw
DIMONDALE (48821) Eaton(95), Ingham(5)
DODGEVILLE Houghton
DOLLAR BAY Houghton
DORR (49323) Allegan(97), Kent(3)
DOUGLAS Allegan
DOWAGIAC (49047) Cass(94), Van Buren(6)
DOWLING Barry
DRAYTON PLAINS Oakland
DRUMMOND ISLAND Chippewa
DRYDEN Lapeer
DUNDEE Monroe
DURAND (48429) Shiawassee(99), Genesee(1)
EAGLE Clinton
EAGLE RIVER Keweenaw
EAST CHINA St. Clair
EAST JORDAN (49727) Charlevoix(70), Antrim(30)
EAST LANSING (48823) Ingham(98), Clinton(2)
EAST LANSING Ingham
EAST LEROY Calhoun
EAST TAWAS Iosco
EASTLAKE Manistee
EASTPOINTE Macomb
EASTPORT Antrim
EATON RAPIDS (48827) Eaton(94), Ingham(6)
EAU CLAIRE (49111) Berrien(85), Cass(15)
EBEN JUNCTION Alger
ECKERMAN Chippewa
ECORSE Wayne
EDENVILLE Midland
EDMORE (48829) Montcalm(99), Isabella(1)
EDWARDSBURG Cass
ELBERTA Benzie
ELK RAPIDS Antrim
ELKTON Huron
ELLSWORTH (49729) Antrim(86), Charlevoix(14)
ELM HALL Gratiot
ELMIRA (49730) Antrim(73), Otsego(21), Charlevoix(6)
ELSIE (48831) Clinton(52), Shiawassee(25), Saginaw(19), Gratiot(4)
ELWELL Gratiot
EMMETT St. Clair
EMPIRE (49630) Leelanau(98), Benzie(3)
ENGADINE Mackinac
ERIE Monroe

ESCANABA Delta
ESSEXVILLE Bay
EUREKA Clinton
EVART (49631) Osceola(92), Mecosta(8)
EWEN Ontonagon
FAIR HAVEN St. Clair
FAIRGROVE Tuscola
FAIRVIEW Oscoda
FALMOUTH Missaukee
FARMINGTON Oakland
FARWELL (48622) Clare(81), Isabella(19)
FELCH Dickinson
FENNVILLE Allegan
FENTON (48430) Genesee(78), Livingston(17), Oakland(5)
FENWICK (48834) Montcalm(60), Ionia(40)
FERNDALE Oakland
FERRYSBURG Ottawa
FIFE LAKE (49633) Kalkaska(60), Grand Traverse(32), Wexford(6), Missaukee(3)
FILER CITY Manistee
FILION Huron
FLAT ROCK Wayne
FLINT Genesee
FLUSHING Genesee
FORESTVILLE Sanilac
FORT GRATIOT St. Clair
FOSTER CITY Dickinson
FOSTORIA (48435) Tuscola(55), Lapeer(45)
FOUNTAIN Mason
FOWLER (48835) Clinton(99), Gratiot(1)
FOWLERVILLE Livingston
FRANKENMUTH (48734) Saginaw(98), Tuscola(2)
FRANKENMUTH Saginaw
FRANKFORT Benzie
FRANKLIN Oakland
FRASER Macomb
FREDERIC (49733) Crawford(74), Otsego(26)
FREE SOIL (49411) Mason(98), Manistee(2)
FREELAND (48623) Saginaw(79), Midland(11), Bay(10)
FREEPORT (49325) Barry(75), Ionia(14), Kent(10)
FREMONT (49412) Newaygo(98), Oceana(2)
FREMONT Newaygo
FRONTIER Hillsdale
FRUITPORT (49415) Muskegon(89), Ottawa(11)
FULTON (49052) Kalamazoo(79), Calhoun(17), St. Joseph(5)
GAASTRA Iron
GAGETOWN (48735) Tuscola(64), Huron(36)
GAINES (48436) Genesee(96), Shiawassee(4)
GALESBURG Kalamazoo
GALIEN Berrien
GARDEN (99999) Delta(99), Schoolcraft(1)
GARDEN CITY Wayne
GAYLORD Otsego
GENESEE Genesee
GERMFASK (49836) Schoolcraft(52), Mackinac(48)
GILFORD Tuscola
GLADSTONE Delta
GLADWIN (48624) Gladwin(92), Clare(6), Roscommon(2)
GLEN ARBOR Leelanau
GLENN Allegan
GLENNIE (48737) Alcona(91), Iosco(9)
GOBLES (49055) Van Buren(93), Allegan(7)
GOETZVILLE Chippewa
GOOD HART Emmet
GOODELLS St. Clair
GOODRICH (48438) Genesee(86), Lapeer(14)

GOULD CITY Mackinac
GOWEN (49326) Kent(74), Montcalm(26)
GRAND BLANC Genesee
GRAND HAVEN Ottawa
GRAND JUNCTION (49056) Van Buren(73), Allegan(27)
GRAND LEDGE (48837) Eaton(90), Clinton(9)
GRAND MARAIS Alger
GRAND RAPIDS (49544) Kent(79), Ottawa(21)
GRAND RAPIDS Kent
GRANDVILLE (49418) Kent(84), Ottawa(16)
GRANDVILLE Kent
GRANT Newaygo
GRASS LAKE (49240) Jackson(92), Washtenaw(8)
GRAWN Grand Traverse
GRAYLING (49738) Crawford(96), Kalkaska(4)
GRAYLING Crawford
GREENBUSH (48738) Alcona(89), Iosco(11)
GREENLAND Ontonagon
GREENVILLE (48838) Montcalm(91), Kent(9)
GREGORY (48137) Livingston(99), Washtenaw(1)
GROSSE ILE Wayne
GROSSE POINTE Wayne
GULLIVER Schoolcraft
GWINN Marquette
HADLEY Lapeer
HAGAR SHORES Berrien
HALE (48739) Iosco(76), Ogemaw(25)
HAMBURG Livingston
HAMILTON Allegan
HAMTRAMCK Wayne
HANCOCK Houghton
HANOVER Jackson
HARBERT Berrien
HARBOR BEACH Huron
HARBOR SPRINGS Emmet
HARPER WOODS Wayne
HARRIETTA (49638) Wexford(90), Manistee(10)
HARRIS Menominee
HARRISON Clare
HARRISON TOWNSHIP Macomb
HARRISVILLE Alcona
HARSENS ISLAND St. Clair
HART Oceana
HARTFORD Van Buren
HARTLAND Livingston
HASLETT (48840) Ingham(96), Clinton(4)
HASTINGS Barry
HAWKS Presque Isle
HAZEL PARK Oakland
HEMLOCK (48626) Saginaw(94), Midland(6)
HENDERSON (48841) Shiawassee(78), Saginaw(22)
HERMANSVILLE Menominee
HERRON Alpena
HERSEY (49639) Osceola(87), Mecosta(13)
HESPERIA (49421) Oceana(72), Newaygo(28)
HESSEL Mackinac
HICKORY CORNERS (49060) Barry(95), Kalamazoo(5)
HIGGINS LAKE Roscommon
HIGHLAND Oakland
HIGHLAND PARK Wayne
HILLMAN (49746) Montmorency(91), Alpena(9)
HILLSDALE Hillsdale
HOLLAND (49423) Ottawa(71), Allegan(29)
HOLLAND Ottawa
HOLLY (48442) Oakland(98), Genesee(2)
HOLT Ingham

HOLTON (49425) Muskegon(81), Oceana(13), Newaygo(7)
HOMER Calhoun
HONOR Benzie
HOPE (48628) Midland(81), Gladwin(19)
HOPKINS Allegan
HORTON (49246) Jackson(98), Hillsdale(2)
HOUGHTON Houghton
HOUGHTON LAKE Roscommon
HOUGHTON LAKE HEIGHTS Roscommon
HOWARD CITY (49329) Montcalm(87), Newaygo(13)
HOWELL Livingston
HUBBARD LAKE (49747) Alpena(56), Alcona(44)
HUBBARDSTON (48845) Ionia(53), Clinton(23), Montcalm(16), Gratiot(8)
HUBBELL Houghton
HUDSON (49247) Lenawee(72), Hillsdale(29)
HUDSONVILLE Ottawa
HULBERT Chippewa
HUNTINGTON WOODS Oakland
IDA Monroe
IDLEWILD Lake
IMLAY CITY (48444) Lapeer(99), St. Clair(1)
INDIAN RIVER Cheboygan
INGALLS Menominee
INKSTER Wayne
INTERLOCHEN (49643) Grand Traverse(75), Benzie(25)
IONIA Ionia
IRON MOUNTAIN Dickinson
IRON RIVER Iron
IRONS (49644) Lake(92), Manistee(7)
IRONWOOD Gogebic
ISHPEMING Marquette
ITHACA Gratiot
JACKSON Jackson
JAMESTOWN Ottawa
JASPER Lenawee
JEDDO (48032) St. Clair(81), Sanilac(19)
JENISON Ottawa
JEROME (49249) Hillsdale(93), Jackson(7)
JOHANNESBURG (49751) Otsego(86), Montmorency(14)
JONES Cass
JONESVILLE Hillsdale
KALAMAZOO Kalamazoo
KALEVA Manistee
KALKASKA Kalkaska
KARLIN Grand Traverse
KAWKAWLIN Bay
KEARSARGE Houghton
KEEGO HARBOR Oakland
KENDALL Van Buren
KENT CITY (49330) Kent(92), Newaygo(5), Muskegon(2), Ottawa(2)
KENTON Houghton
KEWADIN Antrim
KINCHELOE Chippewa
KINDE Huron
KINGSFORD Dickinson
KINGSLEY (49649) Grand Traverse(96), Wexford(4)
KINGSTON (48741) Tuscola(93), Sanilac(7)
KINROSS Chippewa
LA SALLE Monroe
LACHINE Alpena
LACOTA Van Buren
LAINGSBURG (48848) Shiawassee(69), Clinton(31)
LAKE (48632) Clare(74), Isabella(24), Osceola(2)
LAKE ANN Benzie
LAKE CITY Missaukee
LAKE GEORGE Clare
LAKE LEELANAU Leelanau
LAKE LINDEN (49945) Houghton(97), Keweenaw(3)

LAKE ODESSA (48849) Ionia(82), Barry(15), Eaton(3)
LAKE ORION Oakland
LAKELAND Livingston
LAKESIDE Berrien
LAKEVIEW (48850) Montcalm(81), Mecosta(19)
LAKEVILLE Oakland
LAMBERTVILLE Monroe
LAMONT Ottawa
LANSE Baraga
LANSING (48906) Ingham(63), Clinton(35), Eaton(2)
LANSING (48911) Ingham(86), Eaton(14)
LANSING (48917) Eaton(80), Ingham(21)
LANSING Eaton
LANSING Ingham
LAPEER Lapeer
LAWRENCE Van Buren
LAWTON Van Buren
LELAND Leelanau
LENNON (48449) Shiawassee(56), Genesee(44)
LEONARD Oakland
LEONIDAS St. Joseph
LEROY (49655) Osceola(98), Lake(2)
LESLIE Ingham
LEVERING (49755) Emmet(66), Cheboygan(34)
LEWISTON (49756) Montmorency(73), Oscoda(27)
LEXINGTON Sanilac
LINCOLN Alcona
LINCOLN PARK Wayne
LINDEN (48451) Genesee(92), Livingston(8)
LINWOOD Bay
LITCHFIELD Hillsdale
LITTLE LAKE Marquette
LIVONIA Wayne
LONG LAKE (48743) Iosco(93), Ogemaw(7)
LORETTO Dickinson
LOWELL (49331) Kent(92), Ionia(8)
LUDINGTON Mason
LUNA PIER Monroe
LUPTON Ogemaw
LUTHER Lake
LUZERNE Oscoda
LYONS Ionia
MACATAWA Ottawa
MACKINAC ISLAND Mackinac
MACKINAW CITY Cheboygan
MACOMB Macomb
MADISON HEIGHTS Oakland
MANCELONA (49659) Antrim(81), Kalkaska(19)
MANCHESTER Washtenaw
MANISTEE (49660) Manistee(97), Mason(3)
MANISTIQUE (49854) Schoolcraft(99), Delta(1)
MANITOU BEACH Lenawee
MANTON (49663) Wexford(79), Missaukee(21)
MAPLE CITY Leelanau
MAPLE RAPIDS Clinton
MARCELLUS (49067) Cass(66), St. Joseph(24), Van Buren(10)
MARENISCO (49947) Gogebic(85), Ontonagon(15)
MARINE CITY St. Clair
MARION (49665) Osceola(86), Clare(10), Missaukee(4)
MARLETTE (48453) Sanilac(98), Tuscola(2)
MARNE (49435) Ottawa(96), Kent(4)
MARQUETTE Marquette
MARSHALL Calhoun
MARTIN Allegan
MARYSVILLE St. Clair
MASON Ingham

MASS CITY Ontonagon
MATTAWAN (49071) Van Buren(81), Kalamazoo(19)
MAYBEE Monroe
MAYFIELD Grand Traverse
MAYVILLE (48744) Tuscola(88), Lapeer(12)
MC BAIN Missaukee
MC MILLAN (49853) Luce(96), Mackinac(4)
MCBRIDES Montcalm
MEARS Oceana
MECOSTA Mecosta
MELVIN (99999) Sanilac(99), Tuscola(1)
MELVINDALE Wayne
MEMPHIS (48041) St. Clair(79), Macomb(21)
MENDON St. Joseph
MENOMINEE Menominee
MERRILL (48637) Saginaw(70), Midland(15), Gratiot(15)
MERRITT Missaukee
MESICK (49668) Wexford(98), Manistee(2)
METAMORA Lapeer
MICHIGAMME (49861) Baraga(70), Marquette(30)
MICHIGAN CENTER Jackson
MIDDLETON Gratiot
MIDDLEVILLE (49333) Barry(96), Kent(3)
MIDLAND (48642) Midland(97), Bay(3)
MIDLAND Midland
MIKADO (48745) Alcona(93), Iosco(7)
MILAN (48160) Monroe(97), Washtenaw(3)
MILFORD (48380) Oakland(73), Livingston(27)
MILFORD Oakland
MILLBROOK Mecosta
MILLERSBURG Presque Isle
MILLINGTON (48746) Tuscola(93), Genesee(7)
MINDEN CITY (48456) Sanilac(79), Huron(21)
MIO Oscoda
MOHAWK Keweenaw
MOLINE Allegan
MONROE Monroe
MONTAGUE (49437) Muskegon(81), Oceana(19)
MONTGOMERY (49255) Branch(96), Hillsdale(4)
MONTROSE (48457) Genesee(74), Saginaw(26)
MORAN Mackinac
MORENCI Lenawee
MORLEY (49336) Mecosta(92), Montcalm(9)
MORRICE Shiawassee
MOSCOW Hillsdale
MOSHERVILLE Hillsdale
MOUNT CLEMENS Macomb
MOUNT MORRIS Genesee
MOUNT PLEASANT Isabella
MUIR Ionia
MULLETT LAKE Cheboygan
MULLIKEN (48861) Eaton(88), Ionia(12)
MUNGER (48747) Bay(94), Saginaw(6)
MUNISING Alger
MUNITH Jackson
MUSKEGON Muskegon
NADEAU Menominee
NAHMA Delta
NAPOLEON Jackson
NASHVILLE (49073) Barry(90), Eaton(10)
NATIONAL CITY Iosco
NATIONAL MINE Marquette
NAUBINWAY Mackinac
NAZARETH Kalamazoo
NEGAUNEE Marquette
NEW BALTIMORE Macomb
NEW BOSTON Wayne
NEW BUFFALO Berrien
NEW ERA Oceana
NEW HAVEN Macomb

NEW HUDSON Oakland
NEW LOTHROP (48460) Shiawassee(62), Saginaw(36), Genesee(2)
NEW RICHMOND Allegan
NEW TROY Berrien
NEWAYGO (49337) Newaygo(97), Mecosta(2), Montcalm(2)
NEWBERRY Luce
NEWPORT Monroe
NILES (49120) Berrien(84), Cass(16)
NILES Berrien
NISULA Houghton
NORTH ADAMS Hillsdale
NORTH BRANCH Lapeer
NORTH STAR Gratiot
NORTH STREET St. Clair
NORTHLAND Marquette
NORTHPORT Leelanau
NORTHVILLE (48167) Wayne(64), Oakland(31), Washtenaw(5)
NORVELL Jackson
NORWAY Dickinson
NOTTAWA St. Joseph
NOVI Oakland
NUNICA (49448) Ottawa(83), Muskegon(17)
OAK GROVE Livingston
OAK PARK Oakland
OAKLAND Oakland
OAKLEY (48649) Saginaw(94), Shiawassee(6)
ODEN Emmet
OKEMOS Ingham
OLD MISSION Grand Traverse
OLIVET (49076) Eaton(69), Calhoun(31)
OMENA Leelanau
OMER Arenac
ONAWAY (49765) Presque Isle(68), Cheboygan(32)
ONEKAMA Manistee
ONONDAGA (49264) Ingham(71), Jackson(22), Eaton(7)
ONSTED Lenawee
ONTONAGON Ontonagon
ORLEANS Ionia
ORTONVILLE (48462) Oakland(95), Lapeer(3), Genesee(1)
OSCODA Iosco
OSHTEMO Kalamazoo
OSSEO Hillsdale
OSSINEKE Alpena
OTISVILLE (99999) Genesee(99), Lapeer(1)
OTSEGO (49078) Allegan(97), Van Buren(2), Kalamazoo(2)
OTTAWA LAKE (49267) Monroe(87), Lenawee(13)
OTTER LAKE (48464) Lapeer(80), Tuscola(15), Genesee(5)
OVID (48866) Clinton(62), Shiawassee(38)
OWENDALE Huron
OWOSSO Shiawassee
OXFORD (48371) Oakland(94), Lapeer(6)
OXFORD Oakland
PAINESDALE Houghton
PALMER Marquette
PALMS Sanilac
PALMYRA Lenawee
PALO Ionia
PARADISE Chippewa
PARIS (49338) Mecosta(56), Newaygo(37), Osceola(7)
PARMA Jackson
PAW PAW Van Buren
PECK Sanilac
PELKIE (49958) Houghton(65), Baraga(35)
PELLSTON (49769) Emmet(82), Cheboygan(18)
PENTWATER (49449) Oceana(78), Mason(22)
PERKINS Delta
PERRINTON Gratiot

PERRONVILLE (49873) Menominee(86), Dickinson(14)
PERRY (48872) Shiawassee(91), Ingham(8), Livingston(1)
PETERSBURG Monroe
PETOSKEY Emmet
PEWAMO (48873) Ionia(62), Clinton(38)
PICKFORD (49774) Chippewa(88), Mackinac(12)
PIERSON Montcalm
PIGEON Huron
PINCKNEY Livingston
PINCONNING (48650) Bay(95), Arenac(5)
PITTSFORD Hillsdale
PLAINWELL (49080) Allegan(70), Barry(19), Kalamazoo(11)
PLEASANT LAKE Jackson
PLEASANT RIDGE Oakland
PLYMOUTH (48170) Wayne(96), Washtenaw(4)
POINTE AUX PINS Mackinac
POMPEII Gratiot
PONTIAC Oakland
PORT AUSTIN Huron
PORT HOPE Huron
PORT HURON St. Clair
PORT SANILAC Sanilac
PORTAGE Kalamazoo
PORTLAND (48875) Ionia(93), Clinton(7)
POSEN (49776) Presque Isle(75), Alpena(25)
POTTERVILLE Eaton
POWERS Menominee
PRATTVILLE Hillsdale
PRESCOTT Ogemaw
PRESQUE ISLE Presque Isle
PRUDENVILLE Roscommon
PULLMAN Allegan
QUINCY (49082) Branch(94), Hillsdale(6)
QUINNESEC Dickinson
RALPH Dickinson
RAMSAY Gogebic
RAPID CITY (49676) Kalkaska(59), Antrim(41)
RAPID RIVER (49878) Delta(96), Alger(4)
RAVENNA (49451) Muskegon(96), Ottawa(4)
RAY Macomb
READING Hillsdale
REDFORD Wayne
REED CITY (49677) Osceola(83), Lake(14), Newaygo(3)
REESE (48757) Tuscola(67), Saginaw(30), Bay(4)
REMUS (49340) Mecosta(69), Isabella(31)
REPUBLIC (49879) Marquette(99), Iron(1)
RHODES (48652) Gladwin(61), Bay(22), Midland(17)
RICHLAND Kalamazoo
RICHMOND Macomb
RICHVILLE Tuscola
RIDGEWAY Lenawee
RIGA (49276) Lenawee(71), Monroe(29)
RIVER ROUGE Wayne
RIVERDALE (48877) Gratiot(58), Montcalm(32), Isabella(10)
RIVERSIDE Berrien
RIVES JUNCTION Jackson
ROCHESTER (48306) Oakland(98), Macomb(2)
ROCHESTER Oakland
ROCK (49880) Delta(67), Marquette(33)
ROCKFORD Kent
ROCKLAND Ontonagon
ROCKWOOD Wayne
RODNEY Mecosta
ROGERS CITY Presque Isle
ROLLIN Lenawee
ROMEO Macomb
ROMULUS Wayne
ROSCOMMON (48653) Roscommon(80), Crawford(20)

ROSE CITY (48654) Ogemaw(77), Oscoda(23)
ROSEBUSH Isabella
ROSEVILLE Macomb
ROTHBURY Oceana
ROYAL OAK Oakland
RUDYARD (49780) Chippewa(94), Mackinac(6)
RUMELY Alger
RUTH (48470) Huron(99), Sanilac(1)
SAGINAW Saginaw
SAGOLA Dickinson
SAINT CHARLES Saginaw
SAINT CLAIR St. Clair
SAINT CLAIR SHORES Macomb
SAINT HELEN Roscommon
SAINT IGNACE Mackinac
SAINT JOHNS Clinton
SAINT JOSEPH Berrien
SAINT LOUIS (48880) Gratiot(93), Midland(7)
SALEM Washtenaw
SALINE Washtenaw
SAMARIA Monroe
SAND CREEK Lenawee
SAND LAKE (49343) Kent(58), Newaygo(26), Montcalm(16)
SANDUSKY Sanilac
SANFORD Midland
SARANAC Ionia
SAUGATUCK Allegan
SAULT SAINTE MARIE Chippewa
SAWYER Berrien
SCHOOLCRAFT (49087) Kalamazoo(95), Van Buren(4)
SCOTTS Kalamazoo
SCOTTVILLE Mason
SEARS Osceola
SEBEWAING (48759) Huron(99), Tuscola(1)
SENECA Lenawee
SENEY (49883) Schoolcraft(75), Alger(25)
SHAFTSBURG Shiawassee
SHELBY Oceana
SHELBYVILLE (49344) Allegan(57), Barry(43)
SHEPHERD (48883) Isabella(76), Midland(22), Gratiot(2)
SHERIDAN Montcalm
SHERWOOD Branch
SHINGLETON Alger
SIDNAW Houghton
SIDNEY Montcalm
SILVERWOOD (48760) Tuscola(62), Lapeer(38)

SIX LAKES (48886) Montcalm(97), Mecosta(3)
SKANDIA (49885) Marquette(80), Alger(20)
SKANEE Baraga
SMITHS CREEK St. Clair
SMYRNA Ionia
SNOVER Sanilac
SODUS Berrien
SOMERSET Hillsdale
SOMERSET CENTER Hillsdale
SOUTH BOARDMAN Kalkaska
SOUTH BRANCH (48761) Iosco(38), Ogemaw(30), Alcona(28), Oscoda(4)
SOUTH HAVEN (49090) Van Buren(96), Allegan(5)
SOUTH LYON (48178) Oakland(68), Livingston(21), Washtenaw(11)
SOUTH RANGE Houghton
SOUTH ROCKWOOD Monroe
SOUTHFIELD Oakland
SOUTHGATE Wayne
SPALDING Menominee
SPARTA Kent
SPRING ARBOR Jackson
SPRING LAKE (49456) Ottawa(96), Muskegon(4)
SPRINGPORT (49284) Jackson(57), Calhoun(32), Eaton(11)
SPRUCE (48762) Alcona(89), Alpena(11)
STALWART Chippewa
STAMBAUGH Iron
STANDISH (48658) Arenac(95), Bay(5)
STANTON Montcalm
STANWOOD Mecosta
STEPHENSON Menominee
STERLING (48659) Arenac(96), Bay(4)
STERLING HEIGHTS Macomb
STEVENSVILLE Berrien
STOCKBRIDGE (49285) Ingham(84), Jackson(7), Livingston(5), Washtenaw(4)
STRONGS Chippewa
STURGIS St. Joseph
SUMNER (48889) Gratiot(98), Montcalm(2)
SUNFIELD (48890) Eaton(57), Ionia(43)
SUTTONS BAY Leelanau
SWARTZ CREEK Genesee
TAWAS CITY (48763) Iosco(97), Arenac(3)
TAWAS CITY Iosco
TAYLOR Wayne
TECUMSEH Lenawee
TEKONSHA (49092) Calhoun(82), Branch(18)
TEMPERANCE Monroe
THOMPSONVILLE (49683) Benzie(62), Manistee(32), Grand Traverse(6)

THREE OAKS Berrien
THREE RIVERS St. Joseph
TIPTON Lenawee
TOIVOLA (49965) Houghton(87), Ontonagon(13)
TOPINABEE Cheboygan
TOWER Cheboygan
TRAUNIK Alger
TRAVERSE CITY (49684) Grand Traverse(77), Leelanau(23)
TRAVERSE CITY Grand Traverse
TRENARY Alger
TRENTON Wayne
TROUT CREEK (49967) Ontonagon(87), Houghton(13)
TROUT LAKE Chippewa
TROY Oakland
TRUFANT (49347) Montcalm(94), Kent(7)
TURNER (48765) Arenac(69), Iosco(31)
TUSCOLA Tuscola
TUSTIN (49688) Osceola(93), Lake(5), Wexford(3)
TWIN LAKE Muskegon
TWINING (48766) Arenac(97), Iosco(3)
UBLY (48475) Huron(58), Sanilac(42)
UNION Cass
UNION CITY (49094) Branch(99), Calhoun(1)
UNION LAKE Oakland
UNION PIER Berrien
UNIONVILLE (48767) Tuscola(97), Huron(3)
UNIVERSITY CENTER Bay
UTICA Macomb
VANDALIA Cass
VANDERBILT (49795) Otsego(81), Cheboygan(17), Charlevoix(2)
VASSAR Tuscola
VERMONTVILLE Eaton
VERNON Shiawassee
VESTABURG (48891) Montcalm(99), Isabella(1)
VICKSBURG (49097) Kalamazoo(99), St. Joseph(2)
VULCAN (49892) Dickinson(76), Menominee(24)
WABANINGO Muskegon
WAKEFIELD Gogebic
WALDRON Hillsdale
WALHALLA Mason
WALKERVILLE (49459) Oceana(92), Newaygo(9)
WALLACE Menominee
WALLED LAKE Oakland
WALLOON LAKE Charlevoix

WARREN Macomb
WASHINGTON Macomb
WATERFORD Oakland
WATERS Otsego
WATERSMEET Gogebic
WATERVLIET (49098) Berrien(89), Van Buren(11)
WATTON Baraga
WAYLAND (49348) Allegan(83), Barry(17)
WAYNE Wayne
WEBBERVILLE (48892) Ingham(77), Livingston(23)
WEIDMAN Isabella
WELLS Delta
WELLSTON (49689) Manistee(85), Wexford(15)
WEST BLOOMFIELD Oakland
WEST BRANCH Ogemaw
WEST OLIVE Ottawa
WESTLAND Wayne
WESTON Lenawee
WESTPHALIA Clinton
WETMORE (49895) Alger(70), Delta(24), Schoolcraft(7)
WHEELER (48662) Gratiot(85), Midland(15)
WHITE CLOUD Newaygo
WHITE LAKE Oakland
WHITE PIGEON (49099) St. Joseph(89), Cass(11)
WHITE PINE Ontonagon
WHITEHALL Muskegon
WHITMORE LAKE (48189) Washtenaw(57), Livingston(43)
WHITTAKER Washtenaw
WHITTEMORE (48770) Iosco(95), Arenac(3), Ogemaw(2)
WILLIAMSBURG (49690) Grand Traverse(88), Antrim(7), Kalkaska(6)
WILLIAMSTON Ingham
WILLIS Washtenaw
WILSON Menominee
WINN Isabella
WIXOM Oakland
WOLVERINE Cheboygan
WOODLAND Barry
WYANDOTTE Wayne
YALE (48097) St. Clair(83), Sanilac(17)
YPSILANTI Washtenaw
ZEELAND Ottawa

ZIP/City Cross Reference

48001-48001	ALGONAC	48038-48038	CLINTON TOWNSHIP	48069-48069	PLEASANT RIDGE	48116-48116	BRIGHTON
48002-48002	ALLENTON	48039-48039	MARINE CITY	48070-48070	HUNTINGTON WOODS	48117-48117	CARLETON
48003-48003	ALMONT	48040-48040	MARYSVILLE	48071-48071	MADISON HEIGHTS	48118-48118	CHELSEA
48004-48004	ANCHORVILLE	48041-48041	MEMPHIS	48072-48072	BERKLEY	48120-48121	DEARBORN
48005-48005	ARMADA	48042-48042	MACOMB	48073-48073	ROYAL OAK	48122-48122	MELVINDALE
48006-48006	AVOCA	48043-48043	MOUNT CLEMENS	48074-48074	SMITHS CREEK	48123-48124	DEARBORN
48007-48007	TROY	48044-48044	MACOMB	48075-48076	SOUTHFIELD	48125-48125	DEARBORN HEIGHTS
48009-48012	BIRMINGHAM	48045-48045	HARRISON TOWNSHIP	48079-48079	SAINT CLAIR	48126-48126	DEARBORN
48014-48014	CAPAC	48046-48046	MOUNT CLEMENS	48080-48082	SAINT CLAIR SHORES	48127-48127	DEARBORN HEIGHTS
48015-48015	CENTER LINE	48047-48047	NEW BALTIMORE	48083-48084	TROY	48128-48128	DEARBORN
48017-48017	CLAWSON	48048-48048	NEW HAVEN	48086-48086	SOUTHFIELD	48130-48130	DEXTER
48021-48021	EASTPOINTE	48049-48049	NORTH STREET	48089-48093	WARREN	48131-48131	DUNDEE
48022-48022	EMMETT	48050-48050	NEW HAVEN	48094-48095	WASHINGTON	48133-48133	ERIE
48023-48023	FAIR HAVEN	48051-48051	NEW BALTIMORE	48096-48096	RAY	48134-48134	FLAT ROCK
48025-48025	FRANKLIN	48054-48054	EAST CHINA	48097-48097	YALE	48135-48136	GARDEN CITY
48026-48026	FRASER	48059-48059	FORT GRATIOT	48098-48099	TROY	48137-48137	GREGORY
48027-48027	GOODELLS	48060-48061	PORT HURON	48101-48101	ALLEN PARK	48138-48138	GROSSE ILE
48028-48028	HARSENS ISLAND	48062-48062	RICHMOND	48103-48109	ANN ARBOR	48139-48139	HAMBURG
48030-48030	HAZEL PARK	48063-48063	COLUMBUS	48110-48110	AZALIA	48140-48140	IDA
48032-48032	JEDDO	48064-48064	CASCO	48111-48112	BELLEVILLE	48141-48141	INKSTER
48034-48034	SOUTHFIELD	48065-48065	ROMEO	48113-48113	ANN ARBOR	48143-48143	LAKELAND
48035-48036	CLINTON TOWNSHIP	48066-48066	ROSEVILLE	48114-48114	BRIGHTON	48144-48144	LAMBERTVILLE
48037-48037	SOUTHFIELD	48067-48068	ROYAL OAK	48115-48115	BRIDGEWATER	48145-48145	LA SALLE

Range	City	Range	City	Range	City	Range	City
48146-48146	LINCOLN PARK	48410-48410	ARGYLE	48630-48630	HOUGHTON LAKE HEIGHTS	48806-48806	ASHLEY
48150-48154	LIVONIA	48411-48411	ATLAS			48807-48807	BANNISTER
48157-48157	LUNA PIER	48412-48412	ATTICA	48631-48631	KAWKAWLIN	48808-48808	BATH
48158-48158	MANCHESTER	48413-48413	BAD AXE	48632-48632	LAKE	48809-48809	BELDING
48159-48159	MAYBEE	48414-48414	BANCROFT	48633-48633	LAKE GEORGE	48811-48811	CARSON CITY
48160-48160	MILAN	48415-48415	BIRCH RUN	48634-48634	LINWOOD	48812-48812	CEDAR LAKE
48161-48162	MONROE	48416-48416	BROWN CITY	48635-48635	LUPTON	48813-48813	CHARLOTTE
48164-48164	NEW BOSTON	48417-48417	BURT	48636-48636	LUZERNE	48815-48815	CLARKSVILLE
48165-48165	NEW HUDSON	48418-48418	BYRON	48637-48637	MERRILL	48816-48816	COHOCTAH
48166-48166	NEWPORT	48419-48419	CARSONVILLE	48640-48642	MIDLAND	48817-48817	CORUNNA
48167-48167	NORTHVILLE	48420-48420	CLIO	48647-48647	MIO	48818-48818	CRYSTAL
48169-48169	PINCKNEY	48421-48421	COLUMBIAVILLE	48649-48649	OAKLEY	48819-48819	DANSVILLE
48170-48170	PLYMOUTH	48422-48422	CROSWELL	48650-48650	PINCONNING	48820-48820	DEWITT
48173-48173	ROCKWOOD	48423-48423	DAVISON	48651-48651	PRUDENVILLE	48821-48821	DIMONDALE
48174-48174	ROMULUS	48426-48426	DECKER	48652-48652	RHODES	48822-48822	EAGLE
48175-48175	SALEM	48427-48427	DECKERVILLE	48653-48653	ROSCOMMON	48823-48826	EAST LANSING
48176-48176	SALINE	48428-48428	DRYDEN	48654-48654	ROSE CITY	48827-48827	EATON RAPIDS
48177-48177	SAMARIA	48429-48429	DURAND	48655-48655	SAINT CHARLES	48829-48829	EDMORE
48178-48178	SOUTH LYON	48430-48430	FENTON	48656-48656	SAINT HELEN	48830-48830	ELM HALL
48179-48179	SOUTH ROCKWOOD	48432-48432	FILION	48657-48657	SANFORD	48831-48831	ELSIE
48180-48180	TAYLOR	48433-48433	FLUSHING	48658-48658	STANDISH	48832-48832	ELWELL
48182-48182	TEMPERANCE	48434-48434	FORESTVILLE	48659-48659	STERLING	48833-48833	EUREKA
48183-48183	TRENTON	48435-48435	FOSTORIA	48661-48661	WEST BRANCH	48834-48834	FENWICK
48184-48184	WAYNE	48436-48436	GAINES	48662-48662	WHEELER	48835-48835	FOWLER
48185-48186	WESTLAND	48437-48437	GENESEE	48663-48663	SAGINAW	48836-48836	FOWLERVILLE
48187-48188	CANTON	48438-48438	GOODRICH	48667-48686	MIDLAND	48837-48837	GRAND LEDGE
48189-48189	WHITMORE LAKE	48439-48439	GRAND BLANC	48701-48701	AKRON	48838-48838	GREENVILLE
48190-48190	WHITTAKER	48440-48440	HADLEY	48703-48703	AU GRES	48840-48840	HASLETT
48191-48191	WILLIS	48441-48441	HARBOR BEACH	48705-48705	BARTON CITY	48841-48841	HENDERSON
48192-48192	WYANDOTTE	48442-48442	HOLLY	48706-48708	BAY CITY	48842-48842	HOLT
48195-48195	SOUTHGATE	48444-48444	IMLAY CITY	48710-48710	UNIVERSITY CENTER	48843-48844	HOWELL
48197-48198	YPSILANTI	48445-48445	KINDE	48720-48720	BAY PORT	48845-48845	HUBBARDSTON
48201-48202	DETROIT	48446-48446	LAPEER	48721-48721	BLACK RIVER	48846-48846	IONIA
48203-48203	HIGHLAND PARK	48449-48449	LENNON	48722-48722	BRIDGEPORT	48847-48847	ITHACA
48204-48211	DETROIT	48450-48450	LEXINGTON	48723-48723	CARO	48848-48848	LAINGSBURG
48212-48212	HAMTRAMCK	48451-48451	LINDEN	48724-48724	CARROLLTON	48849-48849	LAKE ODESSA
48213-48217	DETROIT	48453-48453	MARLETTE	48725-48725	CASEVILLE	48850-48850	LAKEVIEW
48218-48218	RIVER ROUGE	48454-48454	MELVIN	48726-48726	CASS CITY	48851-48851	LYONS
48219-48219	DETROIT	48455-48455	METAMORA	48727-48727	CLIFFORD	48852-48852	MCBRIDES
48220-48220	FERNDALE	48456-48456	MINDEN CITY	48728-48728	CURRAN	48853-48853	MAPLE RAPIDS
48221-48224	DETROIT	48457-48457	MONTROSE	48729-48729	DEFORD	48854-48854	MASON
48225-48225	HARPER WOODS	48458-48458	MOUNT MORRIS	48730-48730	EAST TAWAS	48856-48856	MIDDLETON
48226-48228	DETROIT	48460-48460	NEW LOTHROP	48731-48731	ELKTON	48857-48857	MORRICE
48229-48229	ECORSE	48461-48461	NORTH BRANCH	48732-48732	ESSEXVILLE	48858-48859	MOUNT PLEASANT
48230-48230	GROSSE POINTE	48462-48462	ORTONVILLE	48733-48733	FAIRGROVE	48860-48860	MUIR
48231-48235	DETROIT	48463-48463	OTISVILLE	48734-48734	FRANKENMUTH	48861-48861	MULLIKEN
48236-48236	GROSSE POINTE	48464-48464	OTTER LAKE	48735-48735	GAGETOWN	48862-48862	NORTH STAR
48237-48237	OAK PARK	48465-48465	PALMS	48736-48736	GILFORD	48863-48863	OAK GROVE
48238-48238	DETROIT	48466-48466	PECK	48737-48737	GLENNIE	48864-48864	OKEMOS
48239-48240	REDFORD	48467-48467	PORT AUSTIN	48738-48738	GREENBUSH	48865-48865	ORLEANS
48242-48299	DETROIT	48468-48468	PORT HOPE	48739-48739	HALE	48866-48866	OVID
48301-48304	BLOOMFIELD HILLS	48469-48469	PORT SANILAC	48740-48740	HARRISVILLE	48867-48867	OWOSSO
48306-48309	ROCHESTER	48470-48470	RUTH	48741-48741	KINGSTON	48870-48870	PALO
48310-48314	STERLING HEIGHTS	48471-48471	SANDUSKY	48742-48742	LINCOLN	48871-48871	PERRINTON
48315-48318	UTICA	48472-48472	SNOVER	48743-48743	LONG LAKE	48872-48872	PERRY
48320-48320	KEEGO HARBOR	48473-48473	SWARTZ CREEK	48744-48744	MAYVILLE	48873-48873	PEWAMO
48321-48321	AUBURN HILLS	48475-48475	UBLY	48745-48745	MIKADO	48874-48874	POMPEII
48322-48325	WEST BLOOMFIELD	48476-48476	VERNON	48746-48746	MILLINGTON	48875-48875	PORTLAND
48326-48326	AUBURN HILLS	48501-48507	FLINT	48747-48747	MUNGER	48876-48876	POTTERVILLE
48327-48329	WATERFORD	48509-48529	BURTON	48748-48748	NATIONAL CITY	48877-48877	RIVERDALE
48330-48330	DRAYTON PLAINS	48531-48559	FLINT	48749-48749	OMER	48878-48878	ROSEBUSH
48331-48336	FARMINGTON	48601-48609	SAGINAW	48750-48753	OSCODA	48879-48879	SAINT JOHNS
48340-48343	PONTIAC	48610-48610	ALGER	48754-48754	OWENDALE	48880-48880	SAINT LOUIS
48346-48348	CLARKSTON	48611-48611	AUBURN	48755-48755	PIGEON	48881-48881	SARANAC
48350-48350	DAVISBURG	48612-48612	BEAVERTON	48756-48756	PRESCOTT	48882-48882	SHAFTSBURG
48353-48353	HARTLAND	48613-48613	BENTLEY	48757-48757	REESE	48883-48883	SHEPHERD
48356-48357	HIGHLAND	48614-48614	BRANT	48758-48758	RICHVILLE	48884-48884	SHERIDAN
48359-48362	LAKE ORION	48615-48615	BRECKENRIDGE	48759-48759	SEBEWAING	48885-48885	SIDNEY
48363-48363	OAKLAND	48616-48616	CHESANING	48760-48760	SILVERWOOD	48886-48886	SIX LAKES
48366-48366	LAKEVILLE	48617-48617	CLARE	48761-48761	SOUTH BRANCH	48887-48887	SMYRNA
48367-48367	LEONARD	48618-48618	COLEMAN	48762-48762	SPRUCE	48888-48888	STANTON
48370-48371	OXFORD	48619-48619	COMINS	48763-48764	TAWAS CITY	48889-48889	SUMNER
48374-48377	NOVI	48620-48620	EDENVILLE	48765-48765	TURNER	48890-48890	SUNFIELD
48380-48381	MILFORD	48621-48621	FAIRVIEW	48766-48766	TWINING	48891-48891	VESTABURG
48382-48382	COMMERCE TOWNSHIP	48622-48622	FARWELL	48767-48767	UNIONVILLE	48892-48892	WEBBERVILLE
48383-48386	WHITE LAKE	48623-48623	FREELAND	48768-48768	VASSAR	48893-48893	WEIDMAN
48387-48387	UNION LAKE	48624-48624	GLADWIN	48769-48769	TUSCOLA	48894-48894	WESTPHALIA
48390-48391	WALLED LAKE	48625-48625	HARRISON	48770-48770	WHITTEMORE	48895-48895	WILLIAMSTON
48393-48393	WIXOM	48626-48626	HEMLOCK	48787-48787	FRANKENMUTH	48896-48896	WINN
48397-48397	WARREN	48627-48627	HIGGINS LAKE	48801-48802	ALMA	48897-48897	WOODLAND
48398-48398	CLAWSON	48628-48628	HOPE	48804-48804	MOUNT PLEASANT	48901-48980	LANSING
48401-48401	APPLEGATE	48629-48629	HOUGHTON LAKE	48805-48805	OKEMOS	49001-49001	KALAMAZOO

ZIP	City	ZIP	City	ZIP	City	ZIP	City
49002-49002	PORTAGE	49107-49107	BUCHANAN	49306-49306	BELMONT	49457-49457	TWIN LAKE
49003-49009	KALAMAZOO	49111-49111	EAU CLAIRE	49307-49307	BIG RAPIDS	49458-49458	WALHALLA
49010-49010	ALLEGAN	49112-49112	EDWARDSBURG	49309-49309	BITELY	49459-49459	WALKERVILLE
49011-49011	ATHENS	49113-49113	GALIEN	49310-49310	BLANCHARD	49460-49460	WEST OLIVE
49012-49012	AUGUSTA	49115-49115	HARBERT	49311-49311	BRADLEY	49461-49461	WHITEHALL
49013-49013	BANGOR	49116-49116	LAKESIDE	49312-49312	BROHMAN	49463-49463	WABANINGO
49014-49018	BATTLE CREEK	49117-49117	NEW BUFFALO	49314-49314	BURNIPS	49464-49464	ZEELAND
49019-49019	KALAMAZOO	49119-49119	NEW TROY	49315-49315	BYRON CENTER	49468-49468	GRANDVILLE
49020-49020	BEDFORD	49120-49121	NILES	49316-49316	CALEDONIA	49501-49599	GRAND RAPIDS
49021-49021	BELLEVUE	49125-49125	SAWYER	49317-49317	CANNONSBURG	49601-49601	CADILLAC
49022-49023	BENTON HARBOR	49126-49126	SODUS	49318-49318	CASNOVIA	49610-49610	ACME
49024-49024	PORTAGE	49127-49127	STEVENSVILLE	49319-49319	CEDAR SPRINGS	49611-49611	ALBA
49026-49026	BLOOMINGDALE	49128-49128	THREE OAKS	49320-49320	CHIPPEWA LAKE	49612-49612	ALDEN
49027-49027	BREEDSVILLE	49129-49129	UNION PIER	49321-49321	COMSTOCK PARK	49613-49613	ARCADIA
49028-49028	BRONSON	49130-49130	UNION	49322-49322	CORAL	49614-49614	BEAR LAKE
49029-49029	BURLINGTON	49201-49204	JACKSON	49323-49323	DORR	49615-49615	BELLAIRE
49030-49030	BURR OAK	49220-49220	ADDISON	49325-49325	FREEPORT	49616-49616	BENZONIA
49031-49031	CASSOPOLIS	49221-49221	ADRIAN	49326-49326	GOWEN	49617-49617	BEULAH
49032-49032	CENTREVILLE	49224-49224	ALBION	49327-49327	GRANT	49618-49618	BOON
49033-49033	CERESCO	49227-49227	ALLEN	49328-49328	HOPKINS	49619-49619	BRETHREN
49034-49034	CLIMAX	49228-49228	BLISSFIELD	49329-49329	HOWARD CITY	49620-49620	BUCKLEY
49035-49035	CLOVERDALE	49229-49229	BRITTON	49330-49330	KENT CITY	49621-49621	CEDAR
49036-49036	COLDWATER	49230-49230	BROOKLYN	49331-49331	LOWELL	49622-49622	CENTRAL LAKE
49038-49038	COLOMA	49232-49232	CAMDEN	49332-49332	MECOSTA	49623-49623	CHASE
49039-49039	HAGAR SHORES	49233-49233	CEMENT CITY	49333-49333	MIDDLEVILLE	49625-49625	COPEMISH
49040-49040	COLON	49234-49234	CLARKLAKE	49335-49335	MOLINE	49626-49626	EASTLAKE
49041-49041	COMSTOCK	49235-49235	CLAYTON	49336-49336	MORLEY	49627-49627	EASTPORT
49042-49042	CONSTANTINE	49236-49236	CLINTON	49337-49337	NEWAYGO	49628-49628	ELBERTA
49043-49043	COVERT	49237-49237	CONCORD	49338-49338	PARIS	49629-49629	ELK RAPIDS
49045-49045	DECATUR	49238-49238	DEERFIELD	49339-49339	PIERSON	49630-49630	EMPIRE
49046-49046	DELTON	49239-49239	FRONTIER	49340-49340	REMUS	49631-49631	EVART
49047-49047	DOWAGIAC	49240-49240	GRASS LAKE	49341-49341	ROCKFORD	49632-49632	FALMOUTH
49050-49050	DOWLING	49241-49241	HANOVER	49342-49342	RODNEY	49633-49633	FIFE LAKE
49051-49051	EAST LEROY	49242-49242	HILLSDALE	49343-49343	SAND LAKE	49634-49634	FILER CITY
49052-49052	FULTON	49245-49245	HOMER	49344-49344	SHELBYVILLE	49635-49635	FRANKFORT
49053-49053	GALESBURG	49246-49246	HORTON	49345-49345	SPARTA	49636-49636	GLEN ARBOR
49055-49055	GOBLES	49247-49247	HUDSON	49346-49346	STANWOOD	49637-49637	GRAWN
49056-49056	GRAND JUNCTION	49248-49248	JASPER	49347-49347	TRUFANT	49638-49638	HARRIETTA
49057-49057	HARTFORD	49249-49249	JEROME	49348-49348	WAYLAND	49639-49639	HERSEY
49058-49058	HASTINGS	49250-49250	JONESVILLE	49349-49349	WHITE CLOUD	49640-49640	HONOR
49060-49060	HICKORY CORNERS	49251-49251	LESLIE	49351-49351	ROCKFORD	49642-49642	IDLEWILD
49061-49061	JONES	49252-49252	LITCHFIELD	49355-49357	ADA	49643-49643	INTERLOCHEN
49062-49062	KENDALL	49253-49253	MANITOU BEACH	49401-49401	ALLENDALE	49644-49644	IRONS
49063-49063	LACOTA	49254-49254	MICHIGAN CENTER	49402-49402	BRANCH	49645-49645	KALEVA
49064-49064	LAWRENCE	49255-49255	MONTGOMERY	49403-49403	CONKLIN	49646-49646	KALKASKA
49065-49065	LAWTON	49256-49256	MORENCI	49404-49404	COOPERSVILLE	49648-49648	KEWADIN
49066-49066	LEONIDAS	49257-49257	MOSCOW	49405-49405	CUSTER	49649-49649	KINGSLEY
49067-49067	MARCELLUS	49258-49258	MOSHERVILLE	49406-49406	DOUGLAS	49650-49650	LAKE ANN
49068-49069	MARSHALL	49259-49259	MUNITH	49408-49408	FENNVILLE	49651-49651	LAKE CITY
49070-49070	MARTIN	49261-49261	NAPOLEON	49409-49409	FERRYSBURG	49653-49653	LAKE LEELANAU
49071-49071	MATTAWAN	49262-49262	NORTH ADAMS	49410-49410	FOUNTAIN	49654-49654	LELAND
49072-49072	MENDON	49263-49263	NORVELL	49411-49411	FREE SOIL	49655-49655	LEROY
49073-49073	NASHVILLE	49264-49264	ONONDAGA	49412-49413	FREMONT	49656-49656	LUTHER
49074-49074	NAZARETH	49265-49265	ONSTED	49415-49415	FRUITPORT	49657-49657	MC BAIN
49075-49075	NOTTAWA	49266-49266	OSSEO	49416-49416	GLENN	49659-49659	MANCELONA
49076-49076	OLIVET	49267-49267	OTTAWA LAKE	49417-49417	GRAND HAVEN	49660-49660	MANISTEE
49077-49077	OSHTEMO	49268-49268	PALMYRA	49418-49418	GRANDVILLE	49663-49663	MANTON
49078-49078	OTSEGO	49269-49269	PARMA	49419-49419	HAMILTON	49664-49664	MAPLE CITY
49079-49079	PAW PAW	49270-49270	PETERSBURG	49420-49420	HART	49665-49665	MARION
49080-49080	PLAINWELL	49271-49271	PITTSFORD	49421-49421	HESPERIA	49666-49666	MAYFIELD
49081-49081	PORTAGE	49272-49272	PLEASANT LAKE	49422-49424	HOLLAND	49667-49667	MERRITT
49082-49082	QUINCY	49274-49274	READING	49425-49425	HOLTON	49668-49668	MESICK
49083-49083	RICHLAND	49275-49275	RIDGEWAY	49426-49426	HUDSONVILLE	49670-49670	NORTHPORT
49084-49084	RIVERSIDE	49276-49276	RIGA	49427-49427	JAMESTOWN	49673-49673	OLD MISSION
49085-49085	SAINT JOSEPH	49277-49277	RIVES JUNCTION	49428-49429	JENISON	49674-49674	OMENA
49087-49087	SCHOOLCRAFT	49278-49278	ROLLIN	49430-49430	LAMONT	49675-49675	ONEKAMA
49088-49088	SCOTTS	49279-49279	SAND CREEK	49431-49431	LUDINGTON	49676-49676	RAPID CITY
49089-49089	SHERWOOD	49280-49280	SENECA	49434-49434	MACATAWA	49677-49677	REED CITY
49090-49090	SOUTH HAVEN	49281-49281	SOMERSET	49435-49435	MARNE	49679-49679	SEARS
49091-49091	STURGIS	49282-49282	SOMERSET CENTER	49436-49436	MEARS	49680-49680	SOUTH BOARDMAN
49092-49092	TEKONSHA	49283-49283	SPRING ARBOR	49437-49437	MONTAGUE	49682-49682	SUTTONS BAY
49093-49093	THREE RIVERS	49284-49284	SPRINGPORT	49440-49445	MUSKEGON	49683-49683	THOMPSONVILLE
49094-49094	UNION CITY	49285-49285	STOCKBRIDGE	49446-49446	NEW ERA	49684-49686	TRAVERSE CITY
49095-49095	VANDALIA	49286-49286	TECUMSEH	49448-49448	NUNICA	49688-49688	TUSTIN
49096-49096	VERMONTVILLE	49287-49287	TIPTON	49449-49449	PENTWATER	49689-49689	WELLSTON
49097-49097	VICKSBURG	49288-49288	WALDRON	49450-49450	PULLMAN	49690-49690	WILLIAMSBURG
49098-49098	WATERVLIET	49289-49289	WESTON	49451-49451	RAVENNA	49696-49696	TRAVERSE CITY
49099-49099	WHITE PIGEON	49301-49301	ADA	49452-49452	ROTHBURY	49701-49701	MACKINAW CITY
49101-49101	BARODA	49302-49302	ALTO	49453-49453	SAUGATUCK	49705-49705	AFTON
49102-49102	BERRIEN CENTER	49303-49303	BAILEY	49454-49454	SCOTTVILLE	49706-49706	ALANSON
49103-49104	BERRIEN SPRINGS	49304-49304	BALDWIN	49455-49455	SHELBY	49707-49707	ALPENA
49106-49106	BRIDGMAN	49305-49305	BARRYTON	49456-49456	SPRING LAKE	49709-49709	ATLANTA

49710-49710	BARBEAU	49769-49769	PELLSTON	49837-49837	GLADSTONE	49905-49905	ATLANTIC MINE
49711-49711	BAY SHORE	49770-49770	PETOSKEY	49838-49838	GOULD CITY	49908-49908	BARAGA
49712-49712	BOYNE CITY	49774-49774	PICKFORD	49839-49839	GRAND MARAIS	49910-49910	BERGLAND
49713-49713	BOYNE FALLS	49775-49775	POINTE AUX PINS	49840-49840	GULLIVER	49911-49911	BESSEMER
49715-49715	BRIMLEY	49776-49776	POSEN	49841-49841	GWINN	49912-49912	BRUCE CROSSING
49716-49716	BRUTUS	49777-49777	PRESQUE ISLE	49845-49845	HARRIS	49913-49913	CALUMET
49717-49717	BURT LAKE	49778-49778	BRIMLEY	49847-49847	HERMANSVILLE	49915-49915	CASPIAN
49718-49718	CARP LAKE	49779-49779	ROGERS CITY	49848-49848	INGALLS	49916-49916	CHASSELL
49719-49719	CEDARVILLE	49780-49780	RUDYARD	49849-49849	ISHPEMING	49917-49917	COPPER CITY
49720-49720	CHARLEVOIX	49781-49781	SAINT IGNACE	49852-49852	LORETTO	49918-49918	COPPER HARBOR
49721-49721	CHEBOYGAN	49782-49782	BEAVER ISLAND	49853-49853	MC MILLAN	49919-49919	COVINGTON
49722-49722	CONWAY	49783-49783	SAULT SAINTE MARIE	49854-49854	MANISTIQUE	49920-49920	CRYSTAL FALLS
49723-49723	CROSS VILLAGE	49784-49788	KINCHELOE	49855-49855	MARQUETTE	49921-49921	DODGEVILLE
49724-49724	DAFTER	49790-49790	STRONGS	49858-49858	MENOMINEE	49922-49922	DOLLAR BAY
49725-49725	DE TOUR VILLAGE	49791-49791	TOPINABEE	49861-49861	MICHIGAMME	49924-49924	EAGLE RIVER
49726-49726	DRUMMOND ISLAND	49792-49792	TOWER	49862-49862	MUNISING	49925-49925	EWEN
49727-49727	EAST JORDAN	49793-49793	TROUT LAKE	49863-49863	NADEAU	49927-49927	GAASTRA
49728-49728	ECKERMAN	49795-49795	VANDERBILT	49864-49864	NAHMA	49929-49929	GREENLAND
49729-49729	ELLSWORTH	49796-49796	WALLOON LAKE	49865-49865	NATIONAL MINE	49930-49930	HANCOCK
49730-49730	ELMIRA	49797-49797	WATERS	49866-49866	NEGAUNEE	49931-49931	HOUGHTON
49733-49733	FREDERIC	49799-49799	WOLVERINE	49868-49868	NEWBERRY	49934-49934	HUBBELL
49734-49734	GAYLORD	49801-49801	IRON MOUNTAIN	49869-49869	NORTHLAND	49935-49935	IRON RIVER
49736-49736	GOETZVILLE	49802-49802	KINGSFORD	49870-49870	NORWAY	49938-49938	IRONWOOD
49737-49737	GOOD HART	49805-49805	ALLOUEZ	49871-49871	PALMER	49942-49942	KEARSARGE
49738-49738	GRAYLING	49806-49806	AU TRAIN	49872-49872	PERKINS	49943-49943	KENTON
49740-49740	HARBOR SPRINGS	49807-49807	BARK RIVER	49873-49873	PERRONVILLE	49945-49945	LAKE LINDEN
49743-49743	HAWKS	49808-49808	BIG BAY	49874-49874	POWERS	49946-49946	LANSE
49744-49744	HERRON	49812-49812	CARNEY	49876-49876	QUINNESEC	49947-49947	MARENISCO
49745-49745	HESSEL	49813-49813	CEDAR RIVER	49877-49877	RALPH	49948-49948	MASS CITY
49746-49746	HILLMAN	49814-49814	CHAMPION	49878-49878	RAPID RIVER	49950-49950	MOHAWK
49747-49747	HUBBARD LAKE	49815-49815	CHANNING	49879-49879	REPUBLIC	49952-49952	NISULA
49748-49748	HULBERT	49816-49816	CHATHAM	49880-49880	ROCK	49953-49953	ONTONAGON
49749-49749	INDIAN RIVER	49817-49817	COOKS	49881-49881	SAGOLA	49955-49955	PAINESDALE
49751-49751	JOHANNESBURG	49818-49818	CORNELL	49883-49883	SENEY	49958-49958	PELKIE
49752-49752	KINROSS	49819-49819	ARNOLD	49884-49884	SHINGLETON	49959-49959	RAMSAY
49753-49753	LACHINE	49820-49820	CURTIS	49885-49885	SKANDIA	49960-49960	ROCKLAND
49755-49755	LEVERING	49821-49821	DAGGETT	49886-49886	SPALDING	49961-49961	SIDNAW
49756-49756	LEWISTON	49822-49822	DEERTON	49887-49887	STEPHENSON	49962-49962	SKANEE
49757-49757	MACKINAC ISLAND	49825-49825	EBEN JUNCTION	49891-49891	TRENARY	49963-49963	SOUTH RANGE
49759-49759	MILLERSBURG	49826-49826	RUMELY	49892-49892	VULCAN	49964-49964	STAMBAUGH
49760-49760	MORAN	49827-49827	ENGADINE	49893-49893	WALLACE	49965-49965	TOIVOLA
49761-49761	MULLETT LAKE	49829-49829	ESCANABA	49894-49894	WELLS	49967-49967	TROUT CREEK
49762-49762	NAUBINWAY	49831-49831	FELCH	49895-49895	WETMORE	49968-49968	WAKEFIELD
49764-49764	ODEN	49833-49833	LITTLE LAKE	49896-49896	WILSON	49969-49969	WATERSMEET
49765-49765	ONAWAY	49834-49834	FOSTER CITY	49901-49901	AHMEEK	49970-49970	WATTON
49766-49766	OSSINEKE	49835-49835	GARDEN	49902-49902	ALPHA	49971-49971	WHITE PINE
49768-49768	PARADISE	49836-49836	GERMFASK	49903-49903	AMASA		

Minnesota

General Help Numbers:

Governor's Office
130 State Capitol Bldg, 75 Constitution Ave 651-296-3391
St Paul, MN 55155   Fax 651-296-2089
http://www.mainserver.state.mn.us/governor 7:30AM-5PM

Attorney General's Office
1400 NCL Tower   651-296-3353
445 Minnesota St   Fax 651-297-4193
St Paul, MN 55101   8AM-5PM
http://www.ag.state.mn.us/

State Court Administrator
135 Minnesota Judicial Center, 25 Constitution Ave   651-296-2474
St Paul, MN 55155   Fax 651-297-5636
http://www.courts.state.mn.us   8AM-4:30PM

State Archives
Division of Library & Archives   651-296-6126
345 Kellogg Blvd West   Fax 651-297-7436
St Paul, MN 55102-1906   9AM-5PM M-SA;
http://www.mnhs.org   till 9PM TU

State Specifics:

Capital: St. Paul
                                          Ramsey County

Time Zone: CST

Number of Counties: 87

Population: 4,919,479

Web Site: www.state.mn.us

State Agencies

Criminal Records

Bureau of Criminal Apprehension, Criminal Justice Information Systems, 1246 University Ave, St Paul, MN 55104; 651-642-0670, 8:15AM-4PM.

http://www.dps.state.mn.us/bca

Indexing & Storage: Records are available from 1924. New records are available for inquiry immediately. Records are indexed on microfilm, inhouse computer.

Searching: For most requesters, to obtain the entire adult history, including all arrests, you must have a notarized release form signed by person of record. To get a 15 year record of convictions only, a consent form is not required. Include the following in your request-name, date of birth, and sex. The following data is not released: juvenile records.

Access by: mail, in person.

Fee & Payment: The fee for the full adult history is $15.00, for non-profits the fee is $8.00. The fee for the 15 year record is $4.00. Non-profits have a reduced fee, call first. Fee payee: BCA. Prepayment required. Business checks, personal checks, money orders and certified funds are accepted. No credit cards accepted.

Mail search: Turnaround time: 1 to 2 weeks. A self addressed stamped envelope is requested.

In person search: Turnaround time is 2 days, unless you are the person of record, then it is immediate. Public access (15 year search) is also immediate.

Other access: A public database is available on CD-ROM. Monthly updates can be purchased. Data is in ASCII format and is raw data. Fee is $250.00.

Corporation Records
Limited Liability Company Records
Assumed Name
Trademarks/Servicemarks
Limited Partnerships

Business Records Services, Secretary of State, 180 State Office Bldg, 100 Constitution Ave, St Paul, MN 55155-1299; 651-296-2803 (Information), 651-297-7067 (Fax), 8AM-4:30PM.

http://www.sos.state.mn.us

Indexing & Storage: Records are available from 1850's on. All records are indexed together. It takes one day before new records are available for inquiry.

Searching: Part II of foreign corporation annual reports are not released. Include the following in your request-full name of business, corporation file number. In addition to articles of incorporation, corporation records include the following information: Annual Reports, Prior (merged) names, Inactive and Reserved names.

Access by: mail, phone, in person, online.

Fee & Payment: There is no search fee. Certification is $5.00 per copy. Copies are $1.00 per page. Fee payee: Secretary of State. Prepayment required. Personal checks accepted. No credit cards accepted.

Mail search: Turnaround time: 1 to 2 days. No self addressed stamped envelope is required.

Phone search: Limited verification information, only on corporation data, is given over the phone.

In person search: You may make copies at $6.00 per business name. There is no fee to view the database or microfilm. However, if you walk-in and wish copies immediately, there is an additional $20.00 fee.

Online search: The Internet site permits free look-ups of "business" names. The program is called Direct Access and is available 24 hours. There is an annual subscription fee of $50.00. Records are $1-4, depending on item needed. Please call 651-297-9096 for more information.

Other access: Information can be purchased in bulk format. Call 651-297-9100 for more information.

Uniform Commercial Code
Federal Tax Liens
State Tax Liens

UCC Division, Secretary of State, 180 State Office Bldg, St Paul, MN 55155-1299; 651-296-2803, 651-297-5844 (Fax), 8AM-4:30PM.

http://www.sos.state.mn.us

Indexing & Storage: Records are available from 1987 on computer. Records on microfiche from 1966 to present. Records are indexed on inhouse computer.

Searching: Use search request form UCC-11 for UCC filings. Use a separate UCC-12 request form to obtain federal and state tax liens on businesses. All tax liens on individuals are filed at the county level. Include the following in your request-debtor name.

Access by: mail, in person, online.

Fee & Payment: Search using approved form is $15.00; other forms $20.00. The search fee includes all copies. Fee payee: Secretary of State. Prepayment required. Personal checks accepted. Credit cards accepted.

Mail search: Turnaround time: 2 to 3 days. A self addressed stamped envelope is requested.

In person search: A free public access terminal is available.

Online search: There is a free look-up available from the web site. A comprehensive commercial program called Direct Access is available 24 hours. There is a subscription fee is $50.00 per year, plus $3.00 per UCC search or $4.00 per business search. Call 651-297-9097 for more information.

Other access: The state will provide information in bulk form on paper, CD or disk. Call 651-296-2803 for more information.

Sales Tax Registrations

Minnesota Department of Revenue, Sales & Use Tax Division, 600 N Robert Street MS:6330, St Paul, MN 55146-6330; 651-296-6181, 651-282-5225 (To Register), 651-296-1938 (Fax), 7:30AM-4:30PM.

http://www.taxes.state.mn.us

Indexing & Storage: Records are available for current registration records only. Records have been computerized since 1992.

Searching: This agency will only confirm that a business is registered, business name and location, and date permit was issued. They will provide no other information. Include the following in your request-business name. They also require the MN business identification number.

Access by: mail, phone, fax, in person.

Fee & Payment: There is no fee. No credit cards accepted.

Mail search: Turnaround time: 7 days. No self addressed stamped envelope is required.

Phone search: Turnaround time for a written reply is approximately 7 days from the request date.

Fax search: Fax searching available.

Birth Certificates

Minnesota Department of Health, Vital Records, PO Box 9441, Minneapolis, MN 55440-9441 (Courier: 717 Delaware St SE, Minneapolis, MN 55414); 612-676-5120, 612-331-5776 (Fax), 8AM-4:30PM.

http://www.health.state.mn.us

Note: For information pertaining to adoption records, call 612-676-5129.

Indexing & Storage: Records are available from 1900 on. Prior records must be obtained from the county level. It takes 3 months before new records are available for inquiry. Records are indexed on microfiche, inhouse computer, depending on years.

Searching: As of 08/01/2000, only those with a "tangible interest" may request a certified record, anyone may order a non-certified record. Out of wedlock birth certificates require a notarized release from parent or child if 18 years or older. Include the following in your request-full name, date of birth, place of birth, names of parents, mother's maiden name. Also, requester's signature must be notarized.

Access by: mail, fax, in person.

Fee & Payment: Fees are: $11.00 for a non-certified copy, $14.00 for a certified copy and $8.00 for an additional certified copy of the same name. Fee payee: Minnesota Department of Health. Prepayment required. Credit cards may be used for fax requesters. Personal checks accepted. Credit cards accepted: MasterCard, Visa, AmEx, Discover.

Mail search: Turnaround time: 6 to 8 weeks. No self addressed stamped envelope is required.

Fax search: See expedited services.

In person search: Turnaround time is 10 to 20 minutes.

Expedited service: Expedited service is available for fax searches. Turnaround time: 4 weeks. Use of credit card required. Add $5.00 for use of credit card and $14.00 for overnight delivery.

Death Records

Minnesota Department of Health, Section of Vital Records, PO Box 9441, Minneapolis, MN 55440-9441 (Courier: 717 Delaware St SE, Minneapolis, MN 55414); 612-676-5120, 612-331-5776 (Fax), 8AM-4:30PM.

http://www.health.state.mn.us

Indexing & Storage: Records are available from 1908 on. Prior records must be obtained at the county level. It takes 3 months before new records are available for inquiry.

Searching: As of 08/01/2000, only those with a "tangible interest" may request a certified record. Those without such interest made receive non-certified. Include the following in your request-full name, date of death, place of death. Also, requester's signature must be notarized. If date or place not known, include last year known to be alive.

Access by: mail, fax, in person.

Fee & Payment: The search fees are $11.00 for a certified record on non-certified, and $5.00 for certified identical copy of same name. Fee payee: Minnesota Department of Health. Prepayment required. Credit cards may be used for ordering by fax only. Personal checks accepted. Credit cards accepted: MasterCard, Visa, AmEx, Discover.

Mail search: Turnaround time: 6 to 8 weeks. No self addressed stamped envelope is required.

Fax search: See expedited services.

In person search: Turnaround time is 10 to 20 minutes.

Expedited service: Expedited service is available for fax searches. Turnaround time: 4 weeks. Use of credit card is required. Add $5.00 for credit card and $14.00 for overnight express.

Marriage Certificates
Divorce Records
Records not maintained by a state level agency.

Note: Marriage and divorce records are found at the county level. The Section of Vital Records has an index and they will direct you to the proper county (Marriage since 1958.

Divorce since 1970). Call the Section of Vital Records at 651-676-5120.

Workers' Compensation Records

Labor & Industry Department, Workers Compensation Division - Records Section, 443 Lafayette Rd, St Paul, MN 55155; 651-296-6845, 651-215-0170 (Fax), 8AM-4:30PM.

http://www.doli.state.mn.us/workcomp.html

Indexing & Storage: Records are available on microfilm or image for 50 years after file closure. Paper records are available for 50 years. New records are available for inquiry immediately. Records are indexed on microfilm, microfiche, inhouse computer. Records are normally destroyed after 19 years old or more.

Searching: Must have a signed release from claimant to obtain all files. Include the following in your request-claimant name, Social Security Number, date of injury, employer. Include any and all dates of injury in your request.

Access by: mail, phone, in person.

Fee & Payment: There is no search fee. Copies are $.65 each. Add 6.5% tax and postage. There is a $6.00 fee for records retrieved from archives. Fee payee: Department of Labor & Industry. Prepayment required. Personal checks accepted. No credit cards accepted.

Mail search: Turnaround time: 2 to 4 weeks. No self addressed stamped envelope is required.

Phone search: Phone searching is limited to employees involved within a case.

In person search: If you request in person, they will mail requested copies.

Driver Records

Driver & Vehicle Services, Records Section, 445 Minnesota St, #180, St Paul, MN 55101; 651-296-6911, 8AM-4:30PM.

http://www.dps.state.mn.us/dvs/index.html

Note: Copies of tickets can be requested from the same address. The fee is $4.00 per record, $5.00 if certified.

Indexing & Storage: Records are available for 5 years minimum for moving violations and suspensions; 10 years for open revocation; retained indefinitely for DWIs for 2 or more convictions. Accidents and up to 10 mph over in a 55 zone on interstate roads are not shown. It takes no more than 15 days before new records are available for inquiry.

Searching: A casual requester can only receive the driver's address with consent of driver. The driver's license number or full name and DOB is required for a search. Surrendered licenses will be purged after one year if clear; after five years if the record has convictions. The following data is not released: medical information.

Access by: Mail, in person, online.

Fee & Payment: Fees: $5.50 per certified record; $4.50 per non-certified record. Fee payee:

Department of Public Safety. Prepayment required. Personal checks accepted. No credit cards accepted.

Mail search: Turnaround time: 1 week. No self addressed stamped envelope is required.

In person search: Up to 3 requests will be processed for walk-in requesters, the rest are available the next day.

Online search: Online access costs $2.50 per record. Online inquiries can be processed either as interactive or as batch files (overnight) 24 hours a day, 7 days a week. Requesters operate from a "bank." Records are accessed by either DL number or full name and DOB. Call 651-297-1714 for more information.

Other access: Minnesota will sell its entire database of driving record information with monthly updates. Customized request sorts are available. Fees vary by type with programming and computer time and are quite reasonable.

Vehicle Ownership
Vehicle Identification

Driver & Vehicle Services, Records Section, 445 Minnesota St, St Paul, MN 55101; 651-296-6911 (General Information), 8AM-4:30PM.

http://www.dps.state.mn.us/dvs/index.html

Indexing & Storage: Records are available for past 7 years. It takes 5 days before new records are available for inquiry.

Searching: The state places no restrictions on obtaining vehicle or ownership information; however, the licensee has the option to restrict access to his/her record from sale to mail list vendors or to individual requesters not on DPPA approval list.

Access by: mail, in person, online.

Fee & Payment: The fee is $4.50 per record for current information and $5.50 per certified copy for mail or walk-in requesters. Fee payee: Department of Public Safety. Prepayment required. Personal checks accepted. No credit cards accepted.

Mail search: Turnaround time: 1 week. A self addressed stamped envelope is requested.

In person search: Turnaround time is immediate for walk-in requesters.

Online search: Online access costs $2.50 per record. There is an additional monthly charge for dial-in access. The system is the same as described for driving record requests. It is open 24 hours a day, 7 days a week. Lien information is included. Call 651-297-1714 for more information.

Accident Reports

Driver & Vehicle Services, Accident Records, 445 Minnesota St, Suite 181, St Paul, MN 55101-5181; 651-296-2060, 651-282-2360 (Fax), 8AM-4:30PM.

Indexing & Storage: Records are available from 1992 to 2002 on microfilm, and from 1992 to present can be located by computer. It takes 3 weeks from date of accident before new records are available for inquiry.

Searching: Police reports may be obtained with the written and signed authorization from the person involved in the accident. Include the following in your request-date of accident, full name, date of birth, driver's license number. Records are indexed by driver names.

Access by: mail, fax, in person.

Fee & Payment: The fee is $4 per police report. Fee payee: DVS. Prepayment required. Personal checks accepted. No credit cards accepted.

Mail search: Turnaround time: 1 week. A self addressed stamped envelope is requested.

Fax search: Fax requests require an account with the agency. Turnaround time 3 days if the request is received after the file has become available.

In person search: Walk-in requesters may obtain copies of accident reports with the authorization of the individual(s) involved in the accident. Turnaround time: while you wait (typically, 5 to 10 minutes).

Vessel Ownership
Vessel Registration

Department of Natural Resources, Information, Education & Licensing Bureau, 500 Lafayette Rd, St Paul, MN 55155-4026; 651-296-2316, 800-285-2000, 651-297-8851 (Fax), 8AM-4:30PM.

http://www.dnr.state.mn.us

Note: Lien information shows on title records obtained at this agency.

Indexing & Storage: Records are available for the last 15 years. Records are maintained for watercraft, snow mobiles, and off-highway vehicles (all terrain) and off-highway motorcycles. A watercraft must be titled if over 16 ft and 1980 model or newer, registered if over 9 ft.

Searching: The name and hull number or registration number is required to complete a search.

Access by: mail, phone, fax, in person.

Fee & Payment: There is no search fee.

Mail search: Turnaround time: 2 weeks.

Phone search: Up to 2 names may be searched over the phone.

Fax search: Same criteria as mail searching.

In person search: Turnaround time is usually immediate.

Other access: Bulk requests are offered in several media types. Call 651-297-4928 for more information.

Legislation Records

Minnesota Legislature, State Capitol, House-Room 211, Senate-Room 231, St Paul, MN 55155; 651-296-2887 (Senate Bills), 651-296-6646 (House Bill Status), 651-296-2314 (House Bill Copies), 651-296-2146 (House Information), 651-296-1563 (Fax), 8AM-5PM.

http://www.leg.state.mn.us

Note: When sessions, the hours are extended to 5:30 PM. Sessions start in January in odd numbered years and in February in even numbered years.

Indexing & Storage: Records are available for current session only. For Senate bill status & general legis. questions, call 651-296-0504; Senate bill copies, 651-296-2343. For historical records, call the legislative reference library at 612-296-3398, and there will be a fee involved. Records are indexed on inhouse computer, hard copy.

Searching: Include the following in your request-bill number.

Access by: mail, phone, in person, online.

Fee & Payment: There is no search fee. There is no expedited service; however, they will help requesters who have their own Federal Express account.

Mail search: Turnaround time: variable. No self addressed stamped envelope is required.

Phone search: No fee for telephone request.

In person search: No fee for request.

Online search: Information available through the Internet site includes full text of bills, status, previous 4 years of bills, and bill tracking.

Voter Registration
Access to Records is Restricted

Secretary of State, Elections Division, 180 State Office Bldg, 100 Constitution Ave, St Paul, MN 55155; 651-215-1440, 651-296-9073 (Fax), 8AM-4:30PM.

http://www.sos.state.mn.us

Note: Records are sold by the state only for political, election, or government purposes and only to MN registered voters. Some counties will honor record requests.

GED Certificates

Department of Children, Families & Learning, GED Testing, 1500 Highway 36 West, Roseville, MN 55113; 651-582-8445, 651-582-8496 (Fax), 7AM-3:30PM.

http://cfl.state.mn.us

Searching: The SSN and year of the test are needed to search. A signed release is needed for a copy of a transcript, scores or graduation verification.

Access by: mail, phone, fax.

Mail search: Turnaround time: 1 to 2 days. No self addressed stamped envelope is required. No fee for mail request.

Phone search: No fee for telephone request. For verification only.

Fax search: Same criteria as mail searching.

Hunting License Information
Fishing License Information

Fish & Wildlife Division, DNR Information Center, 500 Lafayette Rd, St Paul, MN 55155-4040; 651-296-6157, 651-297-3618 (Fax), 8AM-4:30PM.

http://www.dnr.state.mn.us

Indexing & Storage: Records are available on computer from 1979 for doe, turkey - Spring permits; 1985 for moose, 1982 for bear and 1990 for turkey-Fall permits.

Searching: Records are open to public; all information is released. Include the following in your request-full name, date of birth. The driver's license is also helpful.

Access by: mail, phone, fax, in person.

Fee & Payment: There is no search fee. Fee payee: DNR. Prepayment required. Personal checks accepted. No credit cards accepted.

Mail search: Turnaround time: 1 to 3 days. No self addressed stamped envelope is required.

Phone search: They will confirm information over the phone.

Fax search: They will confirm information, turnaround time is 1 week.

Other access: They have mailing lists available for purchase. Call 651-297-8023 for details.

Minnesota State Licensing Agencies

Licenses Searchable Online

Acupuncturist #09 .... www.docboard.org/mn/df/mndf.htm

Alarm & Com. System Contractor/Installer #06 .... www.electricity.state.mn.us/Elec_lic/index.html

Architect #37 .... www.aelslagid.state.mn.us/roster.html

Athletic Trainer #09 .... www.docboard.org/mn/df/mndf.htm

Auditor #39 .... www.boa.state.mn.us/

Bingo Operation #35 .... www.gcb.state.mn.us/

Building Contractors, Residential #23 .... www.commerce.state.mn.us/pages/Contractors/BuilderList.htm

Chiropractor #04 .... www.mn-chiroboard.state.mn.us/main-licensing.htm

Crematory #27 .... www.health.state.mn.us/divs/hpsc/mortsci/finda.htm

Electrician #06 .... www.electricity.state.mn.us/Elec_lic/index.html

Engineer #37 .... www.aelslagid.state.mn.us/roster.html

Funeral Establishment #27 .... www.health.state.mn.us/divs/hpsc/mortsci/finda.htm

Gambling Equipment Dist./Mfg. #35 .... www.gcb.state.mn.us/

Gambling, Lawful Organization #35 .... www.gcb.state.mn.us/

Geologist #37 .... www.aelslagid.state.mn.us/roster.html

Grain Licensing #21 .... www2.mda.state.mn.us/webapp/lis/default.jsp

Insurance Agent/Salesman #23 .... licensing.commerce@state.mn.us

Interior Designer #37 .... www.aelslagid.state.mn.us/roster.html

Landscape Architect #37 .... www.aelslagid.state.mn.us/roster.html

Liquor On-sale Retail #34 .... www.dps.state.mn.us/alcgamb/alcenf/liquorlic/liquorlic.html

Liquor Store, On-sale Retail Municipal #34 .... www.dps.state.mn.us/alcgamb/alcenf/liquorlic/liquorlic.html

Livestock Dealer/Market #21 .... www2.mda.state.mn.us/webapp/lis/default.jsp

Livestock Weighing #21 .... www2.mda.state.mn.us/webapp/lis/default.jsp

Lobbyist #19 .... www.cfboard.state.mn.us/lobby/index.html

Lottery Retailer #42 .... www.lottery.state.mn.us/retailer/lookup.html

LPA #39 .... www.boa.state.mn.us/

Medical Doctor #09 .... www.docboard.org/mn/df/mndf.htm

Midwife #09 .... www.docboard.org/mn/df/mndf.htm

Notary Public #23 .... licensing.commerce@state.mn.us

Optometrist #11 .... www.odfinder.org/LicSearch.asp

Pesticide Applicator Company #22 .... www2.mda.state.mn.us/webapp/lis/pestappdefault.jsp

Pesticide Applicator, Private #22 .... www.mda.state.mn.us/privapp/default.asp

Physical Therapist #09 .... www.docboard.org/mn/df/mndf.htm

Physician Assistant #09 .... www.docboard.org/mn/df/mndf.htm

Political Candidate #19 .... www.cfboard.state.mn.us/legcand.html

Public Accountant-CPA #39 .... www.boa.state.mn.us/

Real Estate Broker/Dealer #23 .... license.commerce@state.mn.us

Respiratory Care Practitioner #09 .... www.docboard.org/mn/df/mndf.htm

Securities/Investment Advisor #23 .... securities.commerce@state.mn.us

Soil Scientist #37 .... www.aelslagid.state.mn.us/roster.html

Surgeon #09 .... www.docboard.org/mn/df/mndf.htm

Surveyor #37 .... www.aelslagid.state.mn.us/roster.html

Teacher #17 .... http://cfl.state.mn.us/licen/licinfo.html

Underground Storage Tank Contractor/Spvr. #43 .. www.pca.state.mn.us/cleanup/ust.html#certification

Weather Modifier #21 .... www2.mda.state.mn.us/webapp/lis/default.jsp

Licensing Quick Finder

Abstractor/Abstractor Company #25 800-657-3978
Acupuncturist #09 612-617-2130
Adoption/Guardianship Agency #31 651-296-0584
Alarm & Com. System Contractor/Installer #06...........
....651-642-0800
Alcohol/Drug Counselor #29 651-282-5619
All-Terrain Vehicle Registration #32 651-296-2316
Amateur Boxing Coach/Referee/Show #03 ....
....651-296-2501
Ambulance Service/Personnel #28 612-627-6000
Applicant Background Study & Investigation #30.......
....651-296-3971
Architect #37 651-297-2208
Asbestos Abatement Contractor/Worker #26...........
....651-215-0900
Assessor, Senior Accredited #01 651-296-0209
Assessor, State Accredited #01 651-296-0209
Assessor/Assessor Specialist #01 651-296-0209
Athletic Trainer #09 612-617-2130
Attorney #40 651-296-2254
Audiologist #29 651-282-5629
Auditor #39 651-296-7937
Bank #24 651-297-3779
Barber #02 651-642-0489
Bingo Operation #35 651-639-4000
Boat & Canoe Registration #32............651-296-2316
Boat Title #32 651-297-2316
Boats for Hire #36 651-289-5080
Boiler Inspector #36 651-296-4531
Bondsman (Insurance) #23 651-296-6319
Boxer #03 651-296-2501
Boxing Cornermen #03.......................651-296-2501
Building Contractors, Residential #23 ...651-296-6319
Chemical Dependency Prof. #30...........651-582-1832
Child Care Facility #31 651-296-3971
Children's Service #30.........................651-297-3840
Chiropractor #04 612-617-2223
Consumer Credit/Credit Union/Savings Assoc. #24 ....
....651-296-2297
Cosmetologist #23 651-296-6319
Cosmetology School/Shop #23.............651-296-6319
County Fair #41 952-496-7950
Credit Union #24 651-296-2297
Crematory #27 651-282-3829
Dental Assistant #05 612-617-2250
Dental Hygienist #05 612-617-2250
Dentist #05 612-617-2250
Developmental Disabilities License #30 651-582-1998
Dietitian #46......................................612-617-2175
Electrician #06 651-642-0800

Elevator Inspector #36.........................651-297-1644
Emergency Medical Technician #28......612-627-6000
Employment Agency Counselor #36 651-296-2282
Employment Agency Manager #36 651-296-2282
Engineer #37 651-296-2388
Esthetician #23 651-296-6319
Food Manager #26..............................651-215-0870
Foster Care Program #31 651-296-3971
Funeral Director #27............................651-282-3829
Funeral Establishment #27 651-282-3829
Gambling Equipment Dist./Mfg. #35......651-639-4000
Gambling, Lawful Organization #35 651-639-4000
Geologist #37 651-296-2388
Grain Licensing #21 651-296-2980
Hearing Aid Dispenser #29 651-282-5620
High Pressure Inspector #36 651-296-4531
Insurance Agent/Salesman #23 651-296-6319
Interior Designer #37 651-296-2388
Kick Karate Professional #03 651-296-2501
Landscape Architect #37 651-296-2388
Liquor and Wine Offsale Retail #34.......651-296-9519
Liquor Consumption & Display Information #34 ....
....651-296-6439
Liquor On-sale Retail #34 651-296-6939
Liquor Store, On-sale Retail Municipal #34..............
....651-215-6209
Liquor Wholesaler/Mfg./Labeler/Importer #34 ....
....651-296-6939
Livestock Dealer/Market #21 651-297-5509
Livestock Weighing #21.......................651-296-2980
Lobbyist #19 651-296-5148
Lottery Retailer #42 651-635-8119
LPA #39...651-296-7937
Manicurist #23 800-657-3978
Manufactured Home Installer #38 651-296-8458
Manufactured Home Mfg./Dealer #38 ...651-296-4628
Manufactured Structures Section #38 ...651-296-4628
Marriage & Family Therapist #08 612-617-2220
Medical Doctor #09 612-617-2130
Mental Health Practitioneers, Unlicensed #29 ....
....651-282-5621
Mental Health, Chemical Depend. #30 ..651-582-1990
Midwife #09 612-617-2130
Mortgage Originators/Servicers, Residential #24 ....
....651-282-9855
Mortician #27 651-282-3829
Notary Public #23...............................651-296-6319
Nurse-LPN/RN #10.............................612-617-2270
Nursing Home Administrator #07 612-617-2117
Nutritionist #46...................................612-617-2175

Occupational Therapist/Assistant #29 ...651-282-5624
Off-Highway Motorcycle #32.................651-296-2316
Off-Road Vehicle #32 651-296-2316
Optometrist #11 612-617-2173
Pesticide Applicator Company #22 651-296-6121
Pesticide Applicator, Private #22...........651-296-6121
Pharmacist #13..................................612-617-2201
Physical Therapist #09 612-617-2130
Physician Assistant #09 612-617-2130
Plumber #26 651-215-0836
Podiatrist #14 612-617-2200
Police (Peace) Officer, Full/Part Time #12...............
....651-643-3060
Political Candidate #19........................651-296-5148
Private Detective #44 651-215-1753
Private Investigator #44.......................651-215-1753
Psychological Practitioner #15 651-617-2230
Psychologist #15................................651-617-2230
Public Accountant-CPA #39.................651-296-7937
Racetrack/Card Club Operator #41 952-496-7950
Racing (Racing Class "A"- Owners of Track) #41 ....
....952-496-7950
Racing/Card Club Occupational #41 952-496-7950
Real Estate Broker/Dealer #23 651-296-6319
Referee (Fight Event) #03 651-296-2501
Residential Remodeler/Contractor #23..651-296-6319
Respiratory Care Practitioner #09 612-617-2130
Sanitarian #26....................................651-215-0870
Securities/Investment Advisor #23 651-296-2083
Security Agent/Protective Agent #44.....651-215-1753
Snowmobile Registration #32 651-296-2316
Social Worker #16 612-617-2100
Soil Scientist #37 651-296-2388
Speech-Language Pathologist #29 651-282-5629
Surgeon #09 612-617-2130
Surveyor #37 651-296-2388
Teacher #17.......................................651-582-8691
Underground Storage Tank Contractor/Supervisor #43 ...
....651-297-8616
Veterinarian #18.................................612-617-2170
Waste Disposal Facility Inspector #43...651-296-7162
Waste Water Disposal Facility Operator #43 ....
....651-296-7162
Water Conditioning Installer/Contractor #26 ....
....651-215-0836
Water Supply Operator #26 651-215-0770
Water Well Contractor #26 651-215-0811
Watercraft #32....................................651-296-2316
Weather Modifier #21 651-296-0591
X-ray Operator #20 651-215-0941

Licensing Agency Information

#01 Board of Assessors, Mail Station 3340, St Paul, MN 55146-3340; 651-296-0209, Fax: 651-297-2166.

#02 Board of Barber Examiners, 1885 University Ave W, #335, St Paul, MN 55104-3403; 651-642-0489, Fax: 651-649-5997.

#03 Board of Boxing, 133 E 7th St, St Paul, MN 55101; 651-296-2501, Fax: 651-297-5310.

#04 Board of Chiropractic Examiners, 2829 University Ave SE, Minneapolis, MN 55414-3220; 612-617-2222, Fax: 612-617-2224.
www.mn-chiroboard.state.mn.us
Direct web site URL to search for licensees: www.mn-chiroboard.state.mn.us/main-licensing.htm. You can search online using alphabetical lists

#05 Board of Dentistry, 2829 University Ave SE, #450, Minneapolis, MN 55414; 612-617-2250, Fax: 612-617-2260.
www.dentalboard.state.mn.us/

#06 Board of Electricity, 1821 University - RM S-128, St Paul, MN 55104; 651-642-0800, Fax: 651-642-0441.
www.electricity.state.mn.us
Direct web site URL to search for licensees: www.electricity.state.mn.us/Elec_lic/index.html

#07 Board of Examiners for Nursing Home Administrators, 2829 University Ave SE #440, Minneapolis, MN 55414; 612-617-2117, Fax: 612-617-2119.
www.benha.state.mn.us

#08 Board of Marriage & Family Therapy, 2829 University Ave SE #330, Minneapolis, MN 55414-3222; 612-617-2220, Fax: 612-617-2221.
www.bmft.state.mn.us

#09 Board of Medical Practice, 2829 University Ave SE, #400, Minneapolis, MN 55414-3246; 612-617-2130, Fax: 612-617-2166.
www.bmp.state.mn.us
Direct web site URL to search for licensees: www.docboard.org/mn/df/mndf.htm. You can search online using name, town name, and license number.

#10 Board of Nursing, 2829 University Ave SE, #500, Minneapolis, MN 55414-3253; 612-617-2181, Fax: 612-617-2190.
www.nursingboard.state.mn.us

#11 Board of Optometry, 2829 University Av SE #550, Minneapolis, MN 55414; 612-617-2173, Fax: 612-617-2174.
Direct web site URL to search for licensees: www.odfinder.org/LicSearch.asp. You can search online using national database by name, city or state.

#12 Board of Peace Officers Standards & Training, 1600 University Av #200, St Paul, MN 55104-3825; 651-643-3060, Fax: 651-643-3072.
www.dps.state.mn.us/post/

#13 Board of Pharmacy, 2829 University Ave SE, #530, Minneapolis, MN 55414-3251; 612-617-2201, Fax: 651-617-2212.
www.phcybrd.state.mn.us

#14 Board of Podiatric Medicine, 2829 University Av SE #430, Minneapolis, MN 55414; 612-617-2200, Fax: 612-617-2698.

#15 Board of Psychology, 2829 University Ave. SE, #320, Minneapolis, MN 55414-3237; 612-612-2230, Fax: 612-617-2240.

#16 Board of Social Work, 2829 University Ave SE, #340, Minneapolis, MN 55414-3239; 612-617-2100, Fax: 612-617-2103.
www.socialwork.state.mn.us

#17 Licensing Unit, 1500 Highway 36 W, Roseville, MN 55113; 651-582-8691, Fax: 651-582-8809.
http://cfl.state.mn.us/teachbrd
Direct web site URL to search for licensees: http://cfl.state.mn.us/licen/licinfo.html. You can search online using file folder number or first & last name

#18 Board of Veterinary Medicine, 2829 University Ave SE, Minneapolis, MN 55414; 612-617-2170, Fax: 612-617-2172.

#19 Division of Plant Health, 638 Cedar St, Centennial Bld, 1st Fl, St Paul, MN 55155; 651-296-5148, Fax: 651-296-1722.
www.cfboard.state.mn.us
Direct web site URL to search for licensees: www.cfboard.state.mn.us/

#20 Department of Health, 121 E 7th Pl #220, St Paul, MN 55101; 651-215-0930, Fax: 651-215-0976.

#21 Department of Agriculture, 90 W Plato Blvd, St Paul, MN 55107; 651-297-2980, Fax: 651-297-2504.
www.mda.state.mn.us
Direct web site URL to search for licensees: www2.mda.state.mn.us/webapp/lis/default.jsp

#22 Department of Agriculture, 90 W Plato Blvd, St Paul, MN 55107; 651-296-6121, Fax: 651-297-2271.
www.mda.state.mn.us
Direct web site URL to search for licensees: www.mda.state.mn.us/lis/default.htm

#23 Department of Commerce, 85 7th Pl E #500, St Paul, MN 55101-2198; 800-657-3978, Fax: 651-296-8591.
www.commerce.state.mn.us

#24 Department of Commerce, 133 E 7th St, St Paul, MN 55101; 651-296-2135, Fax: 651-296-8591.
www.commerce.state.mn.us

#25 Department of Commerce, 85 7th Pl E #600, St Paul, MN 55101-2198; 800-657-3978.
www.commerce.state.mn.us/pages/RealEstateMain.htm

#26 Department of Health, 121 E 7th Pl #230, St Paul, MN 55164-0975; 651-215-0900, Fax: 651-215-0975.
www.health.state.mn.us/divs/eh/eh.html

#27 Department of Health, PO Box 64975, St Paul, MN 55164-0975; 651-282-3829, Fax: 651-282-3839.
www.health.state.mn.us/divs/hpsc/mortsci/mortsci.htm
Direct web site URL to search for licensees: www.health.state.mn.us/divs/hpsc/mortsci/finda.htm Online searching is under construction

#28 Emergency Medical Services, 2829 University Av SE #310, Minneapolis, MN 55414-3222; 612-627-6000, Fax: 612-627-5442.
www.emsrb@state.mn.us

#29 Health Occupation Programs, 121 E 7th Pl #450, Metro Square Bldg, St Paul, MN 55164-0975; 651-282-6366, Fax: 651-282-5628.
www.health.state.mn.us/divs/hpsc/hop/home/homepg.html
Direct web site URL to search for licensees: www.health.state.mn.us/divs/hpsc/hop/home/homepg.html Online searching is under construction at the web site.

#30 Department of Human Services, 444 Lafayette Rd, St Paul, MN 55155; 651-296-6117, Fax: 651-297-1490.
www.dhs.state.mn.us

#31 Department of Human Services, 444 Lafayette Rd, St Paul, MN 55155; 651-296-6117, Fax: 651-297-1490.
www.dhs.state.mn.us

#32 Department of Natural Resources, 500 Lafayette Rd, St Paul, MN 55155; 651-296-2316, Fax: 651-297-8851.
www.dnr.state.mn.us/license_bureau/licenses.html

#33 Department of Public Safety, 444 Cedar St, #133, St Paul, MN 55101-5133; 651-296-6159, Fax: 651-297-5259.
www.dps.state.mn.us/alcgamb/alcgamb.html

#34 Department of Public Safety, 444 Cedar St #133, St Paul, MN 55101-5133; 651-296-6159, Fax: 651-297-5259.
www.dps.state.mn.us/alcgamb/alcenf/alcenf.html

Direct web site URL to search for licensees: www.dps.state.mn.us/alcgamb/alcenf/liquorlic/liquorlic.html. You can search online using licensee, business name, city - for liquor licenses Also, search the liquor license database at www.dps.state.mn.us/alcgamb/New_Folder/search1.asp.

#35 Gambling Control Board, 1711 W County B, #300 South, Roseville, MN 55113; 651-639-4000.
www.gcb.state.mn.us
Direct web site URL to search for licensees: www.gcb.state.mn.us. You can search online using alphabetical lists

#36 Labor & Industry, 443 Lafayette Rd, St Paul, MN 55155-4304; 651-296-4531, Fax: 651-296-1140.
www.doli.state.mn.us/

#37 Board of AELSLAGID, 85 E 7th Pl #160, St Paul, MN 55101; 651-296-2388, Fax: 651-297-5310.
www.aelslagid.state.mn.us
Direct web site URL to search for licensees: www.aelslagid.state.mn.us/lic.html. You can search online using extractable lists, searchable by various criteria

#38 Building Codes & Standards Division, 408 Metro Square Bldg, St Paul, MN 55101-2181; 800-657-3944, Fax: 651-297-1973.
www.admin.state.mn.us/buildingcodes

#39 Board of Accountancy, 8 SE 7th Pl #125, St Paul, MN 55101; 651-296-7937, Fax: 651-282-2644.
www.boa.state.mn.us/

#40 Judicial Center, 25 Constitution Ave #110, St Paul, MN 55155; 651-297-1800, Fax: 651-297-4149.
www.ble.state.mn.us

#41 Racing Commission, PO Box 630, Shakopee, MN 55379; 952-496-7950, Fax: 952-496-7954.
www.mnrace.commission.state.mn.us/

#42 State Lottery, 2645 Long Lake Rd, Roseville, MN 55113; 651-635-8100, Fax: 651-297-7498.
www.lottery.state.mn.us
Direct web site URL to search for licensees: www.lottery.state.mn.us/retailer/lookup.html. You can search online using city or zip code

#43 Pollution Control Agency, 520 Lafayette Rd N, St Paul, MN 55155-4194; 651-297-8367, Fax: 651-282-6247.
www.pca.state.mn.us/netscape4.html

#44 Private Detective & Protective Agent Services Board, 445 Minnesota St, St Paul, MN 55101-5530; 651-215-1753, Fax: 651-296-7096.
www.dps.state.mn.us/pdb/

#46 Board of Dietetics & Nutrition Practice, 2829 University Ave SE #555, Minneapolis, MN 55414-3250; 612-617-2175.

Minnesota Federal Courts

The following list indicates the district and division name for each county in the state. If the bankruptcy court location is different from the district court, then the location of the bankruptcy court appears in parentheses.

County/Court Cross Reference

County	Court		County	Court
Aitkin	Duluth		Martin	Minneapolis (St Paul)
Anoka	Minneapolis		McLeod	Minneapolis
Becker	Minneapolis (Fergus Falls)		Meeker	Minneapolis
Beltrami	Minneapolis (Fergus Falls)		Mille Lacs	Duluth
Benton	Duluth		Morrison	Duluth
Big Stone	Minneapolis (Fergus Falls)		Mower	Minneapolis (St Paul)
Blue Earth	Minneapolis (St Paul)		Murray	Minneapolis (St Paul)
Brown	Minneapolis (St Paul)		Nicollet	Minneapolis (St Paul)
Carlton	Duluth		Nobles	Minneapolis (St Paul)
Carver	Minneapolis		Norman	Minneapolis (Fergus Falls)
Cass	Duluth		Olmsted	Minneapolis (St Paul)
Chippewa	Minneapolis		Otter Tail	Minneapolis (Fergus Falls)
Chisago	Minneapolis (St Paul)		Pennington	Minneapolis (Fergus Falls)
Clay	Minneapolis (Fergus Falls)		Pine	Duluth
Clearwater	Minneapolis (Fergus Falls)		Pipestone	Minneapolis (St Paul)
Cook	Duluth		Polk	Minneapolis (Fergus Falls)
Cottonwood	Minneapolis (St Paul)		Pope	Minneapolis (Fergus Falls)
Crow Wing	Duluth		Ramsey	St Paul
Dakota	Minneapolis (St Paul)		Red Lake	Minneapolis (Fergus Falls)
Dodge	Minneapolis (St Paul)		Redwood	Minneapolis (St Paul)
Douglas	Minneapolis (Fergus Falls)		Renville	Minneapolis
Faribault	Minneapolis (St Paul)		Rice	Minneapolis (St Paul)
Fillmore	Minneapolis (St Paul)		Rock	Minneapolis (St Paul)
Freeborn	Minneapolis (St Paul)		Roseau	Minneapolis (Fergus Falls)
Goodhue	Minneapolis (St Paul)		Scott	Minneapolis (St Paul)
Grant	Minneapolis (Fergus Falls)		Sherburne	Minneapolis
Hennepin	Minneapolis		Sibley	Minneapolis (St Paul)
Houston	Minneapolis (St Paul)		St. Louis	Duluth
Hubbard	Minneapolis (Fergus Falls)		Stearns	Minneapolis (Fergus Falls)
Isanti	Minneapolis		Steele	Minneapolis (St Paul)
Itasca	Duluth		Stevens	Minneapolis (Fergus Falls)
Jackson	Minneapolis (St Paul)		Swift	Minneapolis
Kanabec	Duluth		Todd	Minneapolis (Fergus Falls)
Kandiyohi	Minneapolis		Traverse	Minneapolis (Fergus Falls)
Kittson	Minneapolis (Fergus Falls)		Wabasha	Minneapolis (St Paul)
Koochiching	Duluth		Wadena	Minneapolis (Fergus Falls)
Lac qui Parle	Minneapolis (St Paul)		Waseca	Minneapolis (St Paul)
Lake	Duluth		Washington	Minneapolis (St Paul)
Lake of the Woods	Minneapolis (Fergus Falls)		Watonwan	Minneapolis (St Paul)
Le Sueur	Minneapolis (St Paul)		Wilkin	Minneapolis (Fergus Falls)
Lincoln	Minneapolis (St Paul)		Winona	Minneapolis (St Paul)
Lyon	Minneapolis (St Paul)		Wright	Minneapolis
Mahnomen	Minneapolis (Fergus Falls)		Yellow Medicine	Minneapolis (St Paul)
Marshall	Minneapolis (Fergus Falls)			

US District Court

District of Minnesota

Duluth Division Clerk's Office, 417 Federal Bldg, Duluth, MN 55802 (Courier Address: Use mail address for courier delivery), 218-529-3500, Fax: 218-529-3505.

http://www.mnd.uscourts.gov

Counties: Aitkin, Becker*, Beltrami*, Benton, Big Stone*, Carlton, Cass, Clay*, Clearwater*, Cook, Crow Wing, Douglas*, Grant*, Hubbard*, Itasca, Kanabec, Kittson*, Koochiching, Lake, Lake of the Woods*, Mahnomen*, Marshall*, Mille Lacs, Morrison, Norman*, Otter*,Tail, Pennington*, Pine, Polk*, Pope*, Red Lake*, Roseau*, Stearns*, Stevens*, St. Louis, Todd*, Traverse*, Wadena*, Wilkin*. From March 1, 1995, to 1998, cases from the counties marked with an asterisk (*) were heard here.Before and after that period, cases were and are allocated between St. Paul and Minneapolis.

Indexing/Storage: Cases are indexed by defendant and plaintiff as well as by case number. New cases are available in the index immediately after filing date. A computer index is maintained. Open records are located at this court.

Fee & Payment: The fee is $20.00 per item (one party name or case number). Payment may be made by money order, cashier check, personal check. Prepayment is required. Payee: Clerk, US District Court. Certification fee: $7.00 per document. Copy fee: $.50 per page.

Phone Search: Only docket information is available by phone.

Mail Search: A stamped self addressed envelope is not required.

In Person: In person searching is available.

PACER: Sign-up number is 800-676-6856. Access fee is. Case records are available back to February 1990. New records are available online after 1 day. PACER is available online at http://pacer.mnd.uscourts.gov.

Minneapolis Division Court Clerk, Room 202, 300 S 4th St, Minneapolis, MN 55415 (Courier Address: Use mail address for courier delivery), 612-664-5000, Fax: 612-664-5033.

http://www.mnd.uscourts.gov

Counties: All counties not covered by the Duluth Division. Cases are allocated between Minneapolis and St Paul.

Indexing/Storage: Cases are indexed by defendant and plaintiff as well as by case number. New cases are available in the index immediately after filing date. Both computer and card indexes are maintained. Records are also indexed on microfiche. Open records are located at this court.

Fee & Payment: The fee is $20.00 per item (one party name or case number). Payment may be made by money order, cashier check, personal check. Prepayment is required. Payee: Clerk, US District Court. Certification fee: $7.00 per document. Copy fee: $.50 per page.

Phone Search: The case number and parties involved will be released over the phone.

Mail Search: A stamped self addressed envelope is not required.

In Person: In person searching is available.

PACER: Sign-up number is 800-676-6856. Access fee is. Case records are available back to February 1990. New records are available online after 1 day. PACER is available online at http://pacer.mnd.uscourts.gov.

St Paul Division 700 Federal Bldg, 316 N Robert, St Paul, MN 55101 (Courier Address: Use mail address for courier delivery), 651-848-1100, Fax: 651-848-1109.

http://www.mnd.uscourts.gov

Counties: All counties not covered by the Duluth Division. Cases are allocated between Minneapolis and St Paul.

Indexing/Storage: Cases are indexed by defendant and plaintiff as well as by case number. New cases are available in the index immediately after filing date. Both computer and card indexes are maintained. Records are also indexed on microfiche. Open records are located at this court.

Fee & Payment: The fee is $20.00 per item (one party name or case number). Payment may be made by money order, cashier check, personal check. Prepayment is required. Payee: Clerk, US District Court. Certification fee: $7.00 per document. Copy fee: $.50 per page.

Phone Search: Only the case number and parties involved will be released over the phone.

Fax Search: Fax requests will be accepted, but results that involve copies will not be faxed or mailed back until after payment has been received.

Mail Search: A stamped self addressed envelope is not required.

In Person: In person searching is available.

PACER: Sign-up number is 800-676-6856. Access fee is. Case records are available back to February 1990. New records are available online after 1 day. PACER is available online at http://pacer.mnd.uscourts.gov.

US Bankruptcy Court

District of Minnesota

Duluth Division 416 US Courthouse, 515 W 1st St, Duluth, MN 55802 (Courier Address: Use mail address for courier delivery), 218-529-3600.

http://www.mnb.uscourts.gov

Counties: Aitkin, Benton, Carlton, Cass, Cook, Crow Wing, Itasca, Kanabec, Koochiching, Lake, Mille Lacs, Morrison, Pine, St. Louis. A petition commencing Chapter 11 or 12 proceedings may initially be filed in any of the four divisons, but may be assigned toanother division.

Indexing/Storage: Cases are indexed by debtor as well as by case number. New cases are available in the index 1-2 days after filing date. Chapter 7 and 13 cases in Benton, Kanabec, Mille Lacs, Morrison and Pine may also be filed in St. Paul. A computer index is maintained. Open records are located at this court.

Fee & Payment: The fee is $20.00 per item (one party name or case number). Payment may be made by money order, personal check. Prepayment is required. Payee: Clerk, US Bankruptcy Court. Certification fee: $7.00 per document. Copy fee: $.50 per page. You are allowed to make your own copies. These copies cost $.15 per page.

Phone Search: Only basic information is released over the phone. An automated voice case information service (VCIS) is available. Call VCIS at 800-959-9002 or 612-664-5302.

Mail Search: A stamped self addressed envelope is not required.

In Person: In person searching is available.

PACER: Sign-up number is 800-676-6856. Access fee is $.60 per minute. Local access: 651-848-1096. Case records are available back to January 1993. Records are purged up to April 1996. New civil records are available online after 1 day.

Other Online Access: Search records using the Internet. Searching is currently free.

Fergus Falls Division 204 US Courthouse, 118 S Mill St, Fergus Falls, MN 56537 (Courier Address: Use mail address for courier delivery), 218-739-4671.

http://www.mnb.uscourts.gov

Counties: Becker, Beltrami, Big Stone, Clay, Clearwater, Douglas, Grant, Hubbard, Kittson, Lake of the Woods, Mahnomen, Marshall, Norman, Otter Tail, Pennington, Polk, Pope, Red Lake, Roseau, Stearns, Stevens, Todd, Traverse, Wadena, Wilkin. A petition commencingChapter 11 or 12 proceedings may be filed initially in any of the four divisions, but may then be assigned to another division.

Indexing/Storage: Cases are indexed by debtor as well as by case number. New cases are available in the index immediately after filing date. A computer index is maintained. Open records are located at this court.

Fee & Payment: The fee is $20.00 per item (one party name or case number). Payment may be made by money order, cashier check, personal check. Prepayment is required. Payee: US Bankruptcy Court. Certification fee: $7.00 per document. Copy fee: $.50 per page.

Phone Search: Only docket information is available by phone. An automated voice case information service (VCIS) is available. Call VCIS at 800-959-9002 or 612-664-5302.

Mail Search: A stamped self addressed envelope is not required.

In Person: In person searching is available.

PACER: Sign-up number is 800-676-6856. Access fee is $.60 per minute. Local access: 651-848-1096. Case records are available back to January 1993. Records are purged up to April 1996. New civil records are available online after 1 day.

Other Online Access: Search records using the Internet. Searching is currently free.

Minneapolis Division 301 US Courthouse, 300 S 4th St, Minneapolis, MN 55415 (Courier Address: Use mail address for courier delivery), 612-664-5200.

http://www.mnb.uscourts.gov

Counties: Anoka, Carver, Chippewa, Hennepin, Isanti, Kandiyohi, McLeod, Meeker, Renville, Sherburne, Swift, Wright. Initial petitions for Chapter 11 or 12 may be filed initially at any of the four divisions, but may then be assigned to a judge in another division.

Indexing/Storage: Cases are indexed by as well as by case number. New cases are available in the index immediately after filing date. A computer index is maintained. Records are also indexed on microfiche. Open records are located at this court. District wide searches are available for information from January 2, 1992 from this court. This division holds closed cases from St. Paul for 4 years (no indexing available at this office).

Fee & Payment: The fee is $20.00 per item (one party name or case number). Payment may be made by money order, cashier check, personal check. Prepayment is required. Payee: Clerk, US Bankruptcy Court. Certification fee: $7.00 per document. Copy fee: $.50 per page. You are allowed to make your own copies. These copies cost $.15 per page.

Phone Search: Only basic information is released over the phone. An automated voice case information service (VCIS) is available. Call VCIS at 800-959-9002 or 612-664-5302.

Mail Search: A stamped self addressed envelope is not required.

In Person: In person searching is available.

PACER: Sign-up number is 800-676-6856. Access fee is $.60 per minute. Local access: 651-848-1096. Case records are available back to January 1993. Records are purged up to April 1996. New civil records are available online after 1 day.

Other Online Access: Search records using the Internet. Searching is currently free.

St Paul Division 200 US Courthouse, 316 N Robert St, St Paul, MN 55101 (Courier Address: Use mail address for courier delivery), 651-848-1000.

http://www.mnb.uscourts.gov

Counties: Blue Earth, Brown, Chisago, Cottonwood, Dakota, Dodge, Faribault, Fillmore, Freeborn, Goodhue, Houston, Jackson, Lac qui Parle, Le Sueur, Lincoln, Lyon, Martin, Mower, Murray, Nicollet, Nobles, Olmsted, Pipestone, Ramsey, Redwood, Rice, Rock, Scott,Sibley, Steele, Wabasha, Waseca, Washington, Watonwan, Winona, Yellow Medicine. Cases from Benton, Kanabec, Mille Lacs, Morrison and Pine may also be heard here. A petition commencing Chapter 11 or 12 proceedings may be filed initially with any of thefour divisions, but may then be assigned to another division.

Indexing/Storage: Cases are indexed by debtor as well as by case number. New cases are available in the index 1 day after filing date. A computer index is maintained. Open records are located at this court.

Fee & Payment: The fee is $20.00 per item (one party name or case number). Payment may be made by money order, cashier check, personal check. Payee: Clerk, US Bankruptcy Court. Certification fee: $7.00 per document. Copy fee: $.50 per page. You are allowed to make your own copies. These copies cost $.15 per page.

Phone Search: Only docket information is available by phone. An automated voice case information service (VCIS) is available. Call VCIS at 800-959-9002 or 612-664-5302.

Mail Search: A stamped self addressed envelope is not required.

In Person: In person searching is available.

PACER: Sign-up number is 800-676-6856. Access fee is $.60 per minute. Local access: 651-848-1096. Case records are available back to January 1993. Records are purged up to April 1996. New civil records are available online after 1 day.

Other Online Access: Search records using the Internet. Searching is currently free.

Minnesota County Courts

Court	Jurisdiction	No. of Courts	How Organized
District Courts*	General	97	10 Districts

* Profiled in this Sourcebook.

CIVIL									
Court	Tort	Contract	Real Estate	Min. Claim	Max. Claim	Small Claims	Estate	Eviction	Domestic Relations
Circuit Courts*	X	X	X	$0	No Max	$7500	X	X	X

CRIMINAL					
Court	Felony	Misdemeanor	DWI/DUI	Preliminary Hearing	Juvenile
Circuit Courts*	X	X	X		X

ADMINISTRATION   State Court Adminstrator, 135 Minn. Judicial Center, 25 Constitution Ave, St Paul, MN, 55155; 651-296-2474, Fax: 651-297-5636. www.courts.state.mn.us

COURT STRUCTURE   There are 97 District Courts comprising 10 judicial districts. Effective July 1, 1996, the limit for small claims was raised from $5000 to $7500.

ONLINE ACCESS   There is an online system in place that allows internal and external access. Some criminal information is available online from St Paul through the Bureau of Criminal Apprehension (BCA), 1246 University Ave, St. Paul, MN 55104. Additional information is available from BCA by calling 651-642-0670.

ADDITIONAL INFORMATION   Statewide certification and copy fees are as follows: Certification Fee: $10.00 per document, Copy Fee: $5.00 per document (not per page).

An exact name is required to search, e.g., a request for "Robert Smith" will not result in finding "Bob Smith." The requester must request both names and pay two search and copy fees.

When a search is permitted by "plaintiff or defendant," most jurisdictions stated that a case is indexed by only the 1st plaintiff or defendant, and a 2nd or 3rd party would not be sufficient to search.

The 3rd, 5th, 8th and 10th Judicial Districts no longer will perform criminal record searches for the public.

Most courts take personal checks. Exceptions are noted.

Aitkin County

9th Judicial District Court 209 Second St NW, Aitkin, MN 56431; 218-927-7350; Fax: 218-927-4535. Hours: 8AM-4:30PM (CST). *Felony, Misdemeanor, Civil, Eviction, Small Claims, Probate.*

Civil Records: Access: Mail, in person. Both court and visitors may perform in person searches. Search fee: $5.00 per name. Required to search: name, years to search. Civil cases indexed by defendant, plaintiff. Civil records on computer from 2/90, cards to 1982, index books prior.

Criminal Records: Access: Mail, in person. Both court and visitors may perform in person searches. Search fee: $5.00 per name. Required to search: name, years to search, DOB. Criminal records on computer from 2/90, cards to 1982, index books prior.

General Information: Public Access terminal is available. No adoption, juvenile, sex offender or sealed records released. SASE required. Turnaround time 1 week. Copy fee: $5.00 per document. Certification fee: $10.00. Fee payee: Aitkin District Court. Personal checks accepted. Prepayment is required.

Anoka County

10th Judicial District Court 325 E Main St, Anoka, MN 55303; 763-422-7350; Criminal phone: 763-422-7385; Fax: 763-422-6919. Hours: 8AM-4:30PM (CST). *Felony, Misdemeanor, Civil, Eviction, Small Claims, Probate.*

Civil Records: Access: In person only. Visitors must perform in person searches for themselves. No search fee. Required to search: name, years to search. Civil cases indexed by defendant, plaintiff. Civil records on computer from 1985, prior on microfiche.

Criminal Records: Access: In person only. Visitors must perform in person searches for themselves. No search fee. Required to search: name, years to search, DOB; also helpful: SSN. Criminal records on computer from 1985, prior on microfiche.

General Information: Public Access terminal is available. No adoption, juvenile, sex offender or sealed records released. Copy fee: $5.00 per document. Certification fee: $10.00. Fee payee: Court Administrator. Personal checks accepted. Credit cards accepted: Visa, MasterCard. Prepayment is required.

Becker County

7th Judicial District Court PO Box 787, Detroit Lakes, MN 56502; 218-846-7305; Fax: 218-847-7620. Hours: 8AM-4:30PM (CST). *Felony, Misdemeanor, Civil, Eviction, Small Claims, Probate.*

Civil Records: Access: Phone, fax, mail, in person. Both court and visitors may perform in person searches. No search fee. Required to search: name; also helpful: years to search. Civil cases indexed by defendant, plaintiff. Civil records on computer from 8/86, prior on books from 1891.

Criminal Records: Access: In person only. Visitors must perform in person searches for themselves. No search fee. Required to search: name, years to search. Criminal records on computer from 8/86, prior on books from 1891.

General Information: Public Access terminal is available. No adoption, juvenile, sex offender or sealed records released. SASE required. Turnaround time same day. Fax notes: $5.00 per document. Copy fee: $5.00 per document. Certification fee: $10.00. Fee payee: Becker County. Personal checks accepted. Prepayment is required.

Beltrami County

District Court 619 Beltrami Ave NW, Suite 10, Bemidji, MN 56601; 218-759-4531; Fax: 218-759-4209. Hours: 8AM-4:30PM (CST). *Felony, Misdemeanor, Civil, Eviction, Small Claims, Probate.*

Civil Records: Access: Mail, in person. Both court and visitors may perform in person searches. Search fee: $5.00 per name. Required to search: name, years to search. Civil cases indexed by defendant, plaintiff. Civil records on computer back to 1983.

Criminal Records: Access: Mail, in person. Both court and visitors may perform in person searches. Search fee: $5.00 per name. Required to search: name, DOB. Criminal records on computer back to 1983.

General Information: Public Access terminal is available. No adoption, juvenile, sex offender or sealed records released. SASE not required. Turnaround time 1-2 days. Copy fee: $5.00 per document. Certification fee: $10.00. Fee payee: Court Administrator. Personal checks accepted. Prepayment is required.

Benton County

7th Judicial District Court 615 Highway 23, PO Box 189, Foley, MN 563290189; 320-968-5205; Fax: 320-968-5353. Hours: 8AM-4:30PM (CST). *Felony, Misdemeanor, Civil, Eviction, Small Claims, Probate.*

Civil Records: Access: In person only. Visitors must perform in person searches for themselves. No search fee. Required to search: name, years to search. Civil cases indexed by defendant, plaintiff. Civil records on computer from 1986.

Criminal Records: Access: In person only. Visitors must perform in person searches for themselves. No search fee. Required to search: name, years to search, DOB. Criminal records on computer from 1986.

General Information: Public Access terminal is available. No adoption, juvenile records released. Copy fee: $5.00 per document. Certification fee: $10.00. Fee payee: Court Administrator. Personal checks accepted. Prepayment is required.

Big Stone County

8th Judicial District Court 20 SE 2nd St, Ortonville, MN 56278; 320-839-2536; Fax: 320-839-2537. Hours: 8AM-4:30PM (CST). *Felony, Misdemeanor, Civil, Eviction, Small Claims, Probate.*

http://courtnet.courts.state.mn.us/dist08

Civil Records: Access: Mail, in person. Both court and visitors may perform in person searches. No search fee. Required to search: name, years to search. Civil cases indexed by defendant, plaintiff. Civil records on computer from 1989, prior on cards and in books.

Criminal Records: Access: In person only. Visitors must perform in person searches for themselves. No search fee. Required to search: name, years to search, DOB; also helpful: SSN. Criminal records on computer from 1989, prior on cards and in books.

General Information: Public Access terminal is available. No adoption, juvenile, sex offender or sealed records released. SASE required. Turnaround time 3 days. Copy fee: $5.00 per document. Certification fee: $10.00. Fee payee: Court Administrator. Personal checks accepted. Prepayment is required.

Blue Earth County

5th Judicial District Court 204 S 5th St (PO Box 0347), Mankato, MN 56002-0347; 507-389-8310; Fax: 507-389-8437. Hours: 8AM-5PM (CST). *Felony, Misdemeanor, Civil, Eviction, Small Claims, Probate.*

Civil Records: Access: Mail, in person. Both court and visitors may perform in person searches. No search fee. Required to search: name, years to search. Civil cases

indexed by defendant, plaintiff. Civil records on computer from 8/85, prior in books and cards.

Criminal Records: Access: In person only. Visitors must perform in person searches for themselves. No search fee. Required to search: name, years to search; also helpful: DOB. Criminal records on computer from 8/85, prior in books and cards. The county forwards mail requests to tate Bureau of Criminal Apprehension.

General Information: Public Access terminal is available. No juvenile, adoption, sealed records released. SASE not required. Turnaround time is same day. Copy fee: $5.00 per document. Certification fee: $10.00. Fee payee: Court Administrator. Personal checks accepted. Prepayment is required.

Brown County

5th Judicial District Court PO Box 248, New Ulm, MN 56073-0248; 507-233-6670; Fax: 507-359-9562. Hours: 8AM-5PM (CST). *Felony, Misdemeanor, Civil, Eviction, Small Claims, Probate.*

Civil Records: Access: Mail, in person. Both court and visitors may perform in person searches. No search fee. Required to search: name, years to search. Civil cases indexed by defendant, plaintiff. Civil records on computer from 1988, microfiche 1981-1988, prior on books.

Criminal Records: Access: In person only. Visitors must perform in person searches for themselves. No search fee. Required to search: name, years to search. Criminal records on computer from 1988, microfiche 1981-1988, prior on books. Requests must be made to the state Bureau of Criminal Apprehension.

General Information: Public Access terminal is available. No adoption, juvenile, sex offender or sealed records released. SASE required. Turnaround time 3 days. Fax notes: Fee to fax results is $5.00. Copy fee: $5.00 per document. Certification fee: $10.00. Fee payee: Court Administrator. Personal checks accepted. Credit cards accepted: Visa, MasterCard. Prepayment is required.

Carlton County

6th Judicial District Court PO Box 190, Carlton, MN 55718; 218-384-4281; Fax: 218-384-9182. Hours: 8AM-4PM (CST). *Felony, Misdemeanor, Civil, Eviction, Small Claims, Probate.*

www.6courts.com

Civil Records: Access: Mail, in person. Both court and visitors may perform in person searches. No search fee. Required to search: name, years to search; also helpful: address. Civil cases indexed by defendant, plaintiff. Civil records on computer from 1985, in books from 1900.

Criminal Records: Access: In person only. Visitors must perform in person searches for themselves. No search fee. Required to search: name, years to search; also helpful: address, DOB. Criminal records on computer from 1985, in books from 1900.

General Information: Public Access terminal is available. No adoption, juvenile, sex offender or sealed records released. SASE required. Turnaround time 1 day. Copy fee: $5.00 per document. Certification fee: $10.00. Fee payee: Court Administrator. Personal checks accepted. Prepayment is required.

Carver County

1st Judicial District Court 600 E 4th St, Box 4, Chaska, MN 55318-2183; 952-361-1420; Fax: 952-361-1491. Hours: 8AM-4:30PM (CST). *Felony, Misdemeanor, Civil, Eviction, Small Claims, Probate.*

Civil Records: Access: Mail, in person. Both court and visitors may perform in person searches. Search fee: $5.00 per name. Required to search: name, years to search. Civil cases indexed by defendant, plaintiff. Civil records on computer from 2/92, prior on books.

Criminal Records: Access: Mail, in person. Both court and visitors may perform in person searches. Search fee: $5.00 per name. Required to search: name, years to search, DOB. Criminal records on computer from 2/92, prior on books.

General Information: Public Access terminal is available. No adoption, juvenile, sex offender or sealed records released. SASE not required. Turnaround time 3-4 days. Copy fee: $5.00 per document. Certification fee: $10.00. Fee payee: Court Administrator. Personal checks accepted. Prepayment is required.

Cass County

9th Judicial District Court 300 Minnesota Ave, PO Box 3000, Walker, MN 56484; 218-547-7200; Fax: 218-547-1904. Hours: 8AM-4:30PM (CST). *Felony, Misdemeanor, Civil, Eviction, Small Claims, Probate.*

Civil Records: Access: Mail, in person. Both court and visitors may perform in person searches. Search fee: $5.00 per name. Required to search: name, years to search; also helpful: address. Civil cases indexed by defendant, plaintiff. Civil records on computer from mid-1990, on index cards from 1983-1990, on books to 1983, cards to 1900.

Criminal Records: Access: Mail, in person. Both court and visitors may perform in person searches. Search fee: $5.00 per name. Required to search: name, years to search, DOB; also helpful: address. Criminal records on computer from mid-1990, on index cards from 1983-1990, on books to 1983; cards to 1900.

General Information: Public Access terminal is available. No adoption, juvenile or sealed records released. SASE required. Turnaround time up to 2 weeks. Fax notes: Fee to fax results is $5.00 per document. Copy fee: $5.00 per document. Certification fee: $10.00. Fee payee: District Court. Personal checks accepted. Prepayment is required.

Chippewa County

8th Judicial District Court PO Box 697, Montevideo, MN 56265; 320-269-7774; Fax: 320-269-7733. Hours: 8AM-4:30PM (CST). *Felony, Misdemeanor, Civil, Eviction, Small Claims, Probate.*

http://courtnet.courts.state.mn.us/dist08

Civil Records: Access: Mail, in person. Only the court performs in person searches; visitors may not. No search fee. Required to search: name, years to search. Civil cases indexed by defendant, plaintiff. Civil records on computer from 1988, in books from 1870.

Criminal Records: Access: In person only. Visitors must perform in person searches for themselves. No search fee. Required to search: name, years to search, DOB. Criminal records on computer from 1988, in books from 1870.

General Information:. No adoption, juvenile, sex offender or sealed records released. SASE required. Turnaround time same day. Copy fee: $5.00 per page. Certification fee: $10.00. Fee payee: Court Administrator. Personal checks accepted. Prepayment is required.

Chisago County

10th Judicial District Court 313 N Main St, Rm 358, Center City, MN 55012; 651-257-1300; Fax: 651-257-0359. Hours: 8AM-4:30PM (CST). *Felony, Misdemeanor, Civil, Eviction, Small Claims, Probate.*

Civil Records: Access: Mail, in person. Both court and visitors may perform in person searches. No search fee. Required to search: name, years to search. Civil cases indexed by defendant, plaintiff. Civil records on computer from 1984, prior on index cards.

Criminal Records: Access: In person only. Visitors must perform in person searches for themselves. No search fee. Required to search: name, years to search; also helpful: DOB. Criminal records on computer from 1984, prior on index cards.

General Information: Public Access terminal is available. No adoption, juvenile, sex offender or sealed records released. SASE required. Turnaround time 1-2 days. Copy fee: $5.00 per document. Certification fee: $10.00. Fee payee: Court Administrator. Personal checks accepted. Prepayment is required.

Clay County

7th Judicial District Court PO Box 280, Moorhead, MN 56561; 218-299-5065; Fax: 218-299-7307. Hours: 8AM-4:30PM (CST). *Felony, Misdemeanor, Civil, Eviction, Small Claims, Probate.*

Civil Records: Access: Mail, in person. Both court and visitors may perform in person searches. No search fee. Required to search: name; also helpful: years to search. Civil cases indexed by defendant, plaintiff. Civil records on computer from 1982; prior on microfiche and microfilm.

Criminal Records: Access: In person only. Visitors must perform in person searches for themselves. No search fee. Required to search: name, DOB; also helpful: years to search, SSN. Criminal records on computer from 1982; prior on microfiche and microfilm. Court no longer performs searches as of July 1, 1997.

General Information: Public Access terminal is available. No adoption, juvenile, sex offender or sealed records released. SASE required. Turnaround time 3 days. Copy fee: $5.00 per document. Certification fee: $10.00. Fee payee: Court Administrator. Personal checks accepted. Prepayment is required.

Clearwater County

9th Judicial District Court 213 Main Ave North, Bagley, MN 56621; 218-694-6177; Fax: 218-694-6213. Hours: 8AM-4:30PM (CST). *Felony, Misdemeanor, Civil, Eviction, Small Claims, Probate.*

Civil Records: Access: Phone, mail, fax, in person. Both court and visitors may perform in person searches. Search fee: $5.00 per name, by court. Required to search: name, years to search. Civil cases indexed by defendant, plaintiff. Civil records on computer from 1990, on cards and books prior back to 1903.

Criminal Records: Access: Phone, mail, fax, in person. Both court and visitors may perform in person searches. Search fee: $5.00 per name, by court. Required to search: name, years to search; also helpful: DOB. Criminal records on computer from 1990, on cards and books prior back to 1903.

General Information: Public Access terminal is available. No adoption, juvenile or sealed records released. SASE not required. Turnaround time 3-5 days. Copy fee: $5.00 per document. Certification fee: $10.00. Fee payee: Court Administrator. Personal checks accepted. Prepayment is required.

Cook County

6th Judicial District Court Po Box 1150, Grand Marais, MN 55604-1150; 218-387-3000; Fax: 218-387-3007. Hours: 8AM-4PM (CST). *Felony, Misdemeanor, Civil, Eviction, Small Claims, Probate.*

www.6courts.com

Civil Records: Access: In person only. Both court and visitors may perform in person searches. No search fee. Required to search: name, years to search. Civil cases indexed by defendant, plaintiff. Civil records on computer back to 2/91, prior on card files.

Criminal Records: Access: In person only. Visitors must perform in person searches for themselves. No search fee. Required to search: name, years to search, DOB. Criminal records on computer back to 2/91, prior on card files.

General Information: Public Access terminal is available. No adoption, juvenile, sex offender or sealed records released. Fax notes: Fee to fax results is $5.00 per document. Copy fee: $5.00 per document.

Certification fee: $10.00. Fee payee: Court Administrator. Business checks accepted. Prepayment is required.

Cottonwood County

5th Judicial District Court PO Box 97, Windom, MN 56101; 507-831-4551; Fax: 507-831-1425. Hours: 8AM-4:30PM (CST). *Felony, Misdemeanor, Civil, Eviction, Small Claims, Probate.*

Civil Records: Access: Mail, fax, in person. Only the court performs in person searches; visitors may not. No search fee. Required to search: name; also helpful: years to search. Civil cases indexed by defendant, plaintiff. Civil records on computer back to 1989, judgments on card file, probate on microfilm.

Criminal Records: Access: Mail, fax, in person. Both court and visitors may perform in person searches. No search fee. Required to search: name, years to search, DOB, signed release; also helpful: SSN. Criminal records on computer back to 1989; prior records on card file. Court will only do searches if caseload permits.

General Information: Public Access terminal is available. No adoption, juvenile, sex offender or sealed records released. SASE required. Turnaround time 2-3 days. Copy fee: $5.00 per document. Certification fee: $10.00. Fee payee: Court Administrator. Personal checks accepted. Prepayment is required.

Crow Wing County

District Court 326 Laurel St, Brainerd, MN 56401; 218-824-1310; Fax: 218-824-1311. Hours: 8AM-5PM (CST). *Felony, Misdemeanor, Civil, Eviction, Small Claims, Probate.*

Civil Records: Access: Mail, in person. Both court and visitors may perform in person searches. Search fee: $5.00 per name. Required to search: name, years to search. Civil cases indexed by defendant, plaintiff. Civil records on computer to 1989, prior in books from 1873.

Criminal Records: Access: Mail, in person. Both court and visitors may perform in person searches. Search fee: $5.00 per name. Required to search: name, years to search; also helpful: DOB. Criminal records on computer from 1989, prior in books from 1873.

General Information: Public Access terminal is available. No adoption, juvenile, sex offender or sealed records released. SASE required. Turnaround time 7-14 days. Copy fee: $5.00 per document. Certification fee: $10.00. Fee payee: Court Administrator. Personal checks accepted. Prepayment is required.

Dakota County

1st Judicial District Court - Apple Valley 14955 Galaxie Ave, Apple Valley, MN 55124; 952-891-7256; Fax: 952-891-7285. Hours: 8AM-4:30PM (CST). *Felony, Misdemeanor, Civil, Eviction, Small Claims.*

www.co.dakota.mn.us/courts/index.htm

Civil Records: Access: In person only. Visitors must perform in person searches for themselves. No search fee. Required to search: name, years to search. Civil cases indexed by defendant, plaintiff. Civil records on computer back to 1988, prior in files to 1986.

Criminal Records: Access: In person only. Visitors must perform in person searches for themselves. No search fee. Required to search: name, years to search, DOB; also helpful: SSN. Criminal records on computer back to 1988, prior in files to 1986.

General Information: Public Access terminal is available. No adoption, juvenile, sex offender or sealed records released. Fax notes: Will not fax results. Copy fee: $5.00 per document. Certification fee: $10.00 per document. Fee payee: District Court. Personal checks accepted. Prepayment is required.

1st Judicial District Court - South St Paul

125 3rd Ave North, South St Paul, MN 55075; 651-554-3270; Fax: 651-554-3271. Hours: 8AM-4:30PM (CST). *Felony, Misdemeanor, Civil, Eviction, Small Claims, Probate.*

www.co.dakota.mn.us/courts/index.htm

Civil Records: Access: In person only. Visitors must perform in person searches for themselves. No search fee. Required to search: name, years to search. Civil records on computer from 12/87, prior on ledgers.

Criminal Records: Access: In person only. Visitors must perform in person searches for themselves. No search fee. Required to search: name, years to search. Criminal records on computer from 12/87, prior on ledgers.

General Information:. No adoption, juvenile, sex offender or sealed records released. Copy fee: $5.00 per document. Certification fee: $10.00. Fee payee: Court Administrator. Personal checks accepted. Prepayment is required.

District Court Judicial Center, 1560 Hwy 55, Hastings, MN 55033; 651-438-8100; Fax: 651-438-8162. Hours: 8AM-4:30PM (CST). *Felony, Misdemeanor, Civil, Eviction, Small Claims, Probate.*

www.co.dakota.mn.us/courts

Civil Records: Access: In person only. Visitors must perform in person searches for themselves. No search fee. Required to search: name, years to search. Civil cases indexed by defendant, plaintiff. Civil records on computer from 1/88, on ledgers prior.

Criminal Records: Access: In person only. Visitors must perform in person searches for themselves. No search fee. Required to search: name, years to search. Criminal records on computer to 1/88, on ledgers prior.

General Information: Public Access terminal is available. No adoption, juvenile, sealed records released. Copy fee: $5.00 per document. Certification fee: $10.00. Fee payee: District Court. Personal checks accepted. Prepayment is required.

Dodge County

3rd Judicial District Court PO Box 96, Mantorville, MN 55955; 507-635-6260; Fax: 507-635-6271. Hours: 8AM-4:30PM (CST). *Felony, Misdemeanor, Civil, Eviction, Small Claims, Probate.*

Civil Records: Access: Fax, mail, in person. Both court and visitors may perform in person searches. No search fee. Required to search: name, years to search. Civil cases indexed by defendant, plaintiff. Civil records on computer back to 1984, on cards from 1984, on books from 1972.

Criminal Records: Access: In person only. Visitors must perform in person searches for themselves. No search fee. Required to search: name, years to search, DOB. Criminal records on computer back to 1984, on cards from 1984, on books from 1972.

General Information: Public Access terminal is available. No adoption, juvenile, sex offender or sealed records released. SASE required. Turnaround time 1-2 days. Fax notes: Fee to fax results is $5.00 per document. Copy fee: $5.00 per document. Certification fee: $10.00. Fee payee: Court Administrator. Personal checks accepted. Prepayment is required.

Douglas County

7th Judicial District Court 305 8th Ave West, Alexandria, MN 56308; 320-762-3882; Fax: 320-762-8863. Hours: 8AM-4:30PM (CST). *Felony, Misdemeanor, Civil, Eviction, Small Claims, Probate.*

Civil Records: Access: Mail, in person. Both court and visitors may perform in person searches. Search fee: $5.00 per name. Required to search: name, years to search. Civil cases indexed by defendant, plaintiff. Civil records on computer from 1987, on microfiche from

1951, books prior. The books are grouped by letter, but not alphabetized.

Criminal Records: Access: In person only. Both court and visitors may perform in person searches. Search fee: $5.00 per name. Required to search: name. Criminal records on computer from 1987, on microfiche from 1951, books prior. The books are grouped by letter, but not alphabetized.

General Information: Public Access terminal is available. No adoption, juvenile or sealed records released. SASE required. Turnaround time 1-7 days. Copy fee: $5.00 per document. Certification fee: $10.00. Fee payee: Court Administrator. Personal checks accepted. Prepayment is required.

Faribault County

5th Judicial District Court PO Box 130, Blue Earth, MN 56013; 507-526-6273; Fax: 507-526-3054. Hours: 8AM-4:30PM (CST). *Felony, Misdemeanor, Civil, Eviction, Small Claims, Probate.*

Civil Records: Access: Mail, in person. Only the court performs in person searches; visitors may not. No search fee. Required to search: name, years to search. Civil cases indexed by defendant, plaintiff. Civil records on computer from 1989, in books from 1870.

Criminal Records: Access: In person only. Visitors must perform in person searches for themselves. No search fee. Required to search: name, years to search; also helpful: DOB. Criminal records on computer from 1989, in books from 1870. The county suggests sending requests to the state Bureau of Criminal Apprehension.

General Information: Public Access terminal is available. No adoption, juvenile, sex offender or sealed records released. SASE required. Turnaround time 7 days or less. Copy fee: $5.00 per document. Certification fee: $10.00. Fee payee: Court Administrator. Personal checks accepted. Prepayment is required.

Fillmore County

3rd Judicial District Court 101 Fillmore St, PO Box 436, Preston, MN 55965; 507-765-4483; Fax: 507-765-4571. Hours: 8AM-4:30PM (CST). *Felony, Misdemeanor, Civil, Eviction, Small Claims, Probate.*

www.courts.state.mn.us/districts/third/fillmore/index.html

Civil Records: Access: Mail, in person. Both court and visitors may perform in person searches. No search fee. Required to search: name, years to search. Civil cases indexed by defendant, plaintiff. Civil records on computer from 1990, books from 1860s.

Criminal Records: Access: In person only. Visitors must perform in person searches for themselves. No search fee. Required to search: name, years to search, DOB. Criminal records on computer from 1990, books from 1860s.

General Information: Public Access terminal is available. No adoption, juvenile or sealed records released. SASE not required. Turnaround time 1-2 days. Copy fee: $5.00 per document. Certification fee: $10.00. Fee payee: Court Administrator. Personal checks accepted. Prepayment is required.

Freeborn County

3rd Judicial District Court 411 S Broadway, Albert Lea, MN 56007; 507-377-5153; Fax: 507-377-5260. Hours: 8AM-5PM (CST). *Felony, Misdemeanor, Civil, Eviction, Small Claims, Probate.*

Civil Records: Access: Mail, in person. Both court and visitors may perform in person searches. No search fee. Required to search: name, years to search. Civil cases indexed by defendant, plaintiff. Civil records on computer from 11/89.

Criminal Records: Access: In person only. Visitors must perform in person searches for themselves. No

search fee. Required to search: name, years to search, DOB. Criminal records on computer from 11/89.

General Information: Public Access terminal is available. No adoption, juvenile, sex offender or sealed records released. SASE required. Turnaround time 3-5 days. Copy fee: $5.00 per document. Certification fee: $10.00. Fee payee: Court Administrator. Personal checks accepted. Prepayment is required.

Goodhue County

1st Judicial District Court PO Box 408 (454 W 6th St), Red Wing, MN 55066; 651-267-4800; Fax: 651-267-4989. Hours: 8AM-4:30PM (CST). *Felony, Misdemeanor, Civil, Eviction, Small Claims, Probate.*

Civil Records: Access: Mail, in person. Both court and visitors may perform in person searches. No search fee. Required to search: name, years to search. Civil cases indexed by defendant, plaintiff. Civil records on computer from 3/92, prior records on docket books.

Criminal Records: Access: In person only. Visitors must perform in person searches for themselves. No search fee. Required to search: name. Criminal records on computer from 3/92, prior records on docket books.

General Information: Public Access terminal is available. No adoption, juvenile, sex offender or sealed records released. SASE required. Turnaround time same day. Copy fee: $5.00 per document. Certification fee: $10.00. Fee payee: Court Administrator. Personal checks accepted. Prepayment is required.

Grant County

8th Judicial District Court PO Box 1007 (10 2nd St NE), Elbow Lake, MN 56531; 218-685-4825. Hours: 8AM-4PM (CST). *Felony, Misdemeanor, Civil, Eviction, Small Claims, Probate.*

http://courtnet.courts.state.mn.us/dist08

Civil Records: Access: Mail, in person. Visitors must perform in person searches for themselves. No search fee. Required to search: name, years to search. Civil cases indexed by defendant, plaintiff. Civil records on computer from 6/89, on cards from 1930, prior at Historical Society.

Criminal Records: Access: In person only. Visitors must perform in person searches for themselves. No search fee. Required to search: name, years to search; also helpful: DOB. Criminal records on computer from 6/89, on cards from 1930, prior at Historical Society.

General Information: Public Access terminal is available. No adoption, juvenile, sex offender or sealed records released. SASE required. Turnaround time 1-2 days. Fax notes: Fee to fax results is $5.00 per document. Copy fee: $5.00 per document. Certification fee: $10.00. Fee payee: Court Administrator. Personal checks accepted. Prepayment is required.

Hennepin County

4th Judicial District Court - Division 1

Civil 1251 C Government Center, 300 S 6th St, Minneapolis, MN 55487; 612-348-3164; Fax: 612-348-2131. Hours: 8AM-4:30PM (CST). *Civil.*

www.co.hennepin.mn.us/courts/court.htm

Civil Records: Access: Fax, mail, in person. Both court and visitors may perform in person searches. No search fee. Required to search: name, years to search. Civil cases indexed by defendant, plaintiff. Civil records on computer from 1978, prior on microfilm.

General Information: Public Access terminal is available. No sex offender or sealed records released, domestic abuse and paternity cases are limited. SASE required. Turnaround time 7-10 days. Copy fee: $.50 per document. Certification fee: $10.00. Fee payee: Court Administrator. Personal checks accepted. Prepayment is required.

4th Judicial District Court - Division 1

Criminal 300 S 6th St, Minneapolis, MN 55487; 612-348-2612; Fax: 612-317-6134. Hours: 8AM-4:30PM (CST). *Felony, Misdemeanor.*

www.co.hennepin.mn.us/courts/court.htm

Criminal Records: Access: Fax, mail, in person. Both court and visitors may perform in person searches. Search fee: $5.00 per name if no record found; otherwise $10.00 per name. Required to search: name, years to search, DOB. Same record keeping as civil.

General Information: Public Access terminal is available. No adoption, juvenile, sex offender or sealed records released. SASE required. Turnaround time 7-10 days. Copy fee: $5.00 per document. Certification fee: $10.00. Fee payee: Court Administrator. Personal checks accepted. Prepayment is required.

4th Judicial District Court - Division 2

Brookdale 6125 Shingle Creek Pkwy, Brooklyn Center, MN 55430; 763-569-2799; Fax: 763-569-3697. Hours: 7:45AM-4:30PM (CST). *Misdemeanor, Eviction, Small Claims.*

www.co.hennepin.mn.us/courts/court.htm

Civil Records: Access: Mail, fax, in person. Search fee: $5.00 per name. Required to search: name, years to search. Civil cases indexed by defendant.

Criminal Records: Access: Mail, fax, in person. Both court and visitors may perform in person searches. Search fee: $5.00 per name. Required to search: name, years to search, DOB. Criminal records on computer since 1987.

General Information: Public Access terminal is available. No juvenile court, unlawful detainers or sealed records released. SASE required. Turnaround time 1-7 days. Copy fee: $5.00 per document. Certification fee: $10.00. Fee payee: Hennepin County District Court. Personal checks accepted. Prepayment is required.

4th Judicial District Court - Division 3

Ridgedale 12601 Ridgedale Dr, Minnetonka, MN 55305; 952-541-7000; Fax: 952-541-6297. Hours: 8AM-4:30PM *Misdemeanor, Eviction, Small Claims.*

www.co.hennepin.mn.us/courts/court.htm

Civil Records: Access: Mail, in person. Both court and visitors may perform in person searches. Search fee: $5.00 per name. Required to search: name, years to search. Civil cases indexed by defendant. Civil records on computer.

Criminal Records: Access: Mail, in person. Both court and visitors may perform in person searches. Search fee: $5.00 per name. Required to search: name, years to search; also helpful: DOB. Criminal records on computer since 1989; prior records on microfiche.

General Information: Public Access terminal is available. (Limited information available.) No police reports, juvenile or sealed records released. SASE required. Turnaround time 3-4 weeks. Copy fee: $5.00 per document. Certification fee: $10.00. Fee payee: Hennepin County District Court. Personal checks accepted. Prepayment is required.

4th Judicial District Court - Division 4

Southdale 7009 York Ave South, Edina, MN 55435; 952-830-4877, 830-4905; Fax: 952-830-4993. Hours: 8AM-4:30PM (CST). *Misdemeanor.*

www.co.hennepin.mn.us/courts/court.htm

Criminal Records: Access: In person only. Visitors must perform in person searches for themselves. No search fee. Required to search: name, years to search, DOB; also helpful: offense, date of offense. Criminal records on computer since late 1970s, felonies on computer earlier. In person search with court assistance $10.00.

General Information: Public Access terminal is available. (Criminal & Traffic.) No juvenile or sealed records released. Copy fee: $5.00 per document. Certification fee: $10.00. Fee payee: Hennepin County District Court. Personal checks accepted. Prepayment is required.

4th Judicial District Court - Division 1
C400 Government Center, 300 S 6th St, Minneapolis, MN 55487; 612-348-3244; Fax: 612-348-5799. Hours: 7AM-5PM (CST). *Probate.*

www.co.hennepin.mn.us/courts/court.htm

Houston County

3rd Judicial District Court 304 S Marshall, Rm 204, Caledonia, MN 55921; 507-725-5806; Fax: 507-725-5550. Hours: 8AM-4:30PM (CST). *Felony, Misdemeanor, Civil, Eviction, Small Claims, Probate.*

www.courts.state.mn.us/districts/third/newpage4.htm

Civil Records: Access: Fax, mail, in person. Visitors must perform in person searches for themselves. No search fee. Required to search: name, years to search, DOB. Civil cases indexed by defendant, plaintiff. Civil records on computer from 8/89, prior on cards and books. Probate on microfilm to 1982.

Criminal Records: Access: In person only. Visitors must perform in person searches for themselves. No search fee. Required to search: name, years to search; also helpful: DOB. Criminal records on computer from 8/89, prior on cards and books. Probate on microfilm to 1982.

General Information: Public Access terminal is available. No adoption, juvenile, sex offender or sealed records released. SASE required. Turnaround time 2 days. Fax notes: $5.00 per document. Copy fee: $5.00 per document. Certification fee: $10.00. Fee payee: Court Administrator. Personal checks accepted. Prepayment is required.

Hubbard County

9th Judicial District Court 301 Court St, Park Rapids, MN 56470; 218-732-3573; Fax: 218-732-0137. Hours: 8AM-4:30PM (CST). *Felony, Misdemeanor, Civil, Eviction, Small Claims, Probate.*

Civil Records: Access: Mail, in person. Both court and visitors may perform in person searches. Search fee: $5.00 per name. Required to search: name, years to search. Civil cases indexed by defendant, plaintiff. Civil records on computer since 1990, prior on index cards.

Criminal Records: Access: Mail, in person. Both court and visitors may perform in person searches. Search fee: $5.00 per name. Required to search: name, DOB. Criminal records on computer since 1990, prior on index cards.

General Information: Public Access terminal is available. No adoption, juvenile, sex offender or sealed records released. SASE required. Turnaround time 1 week. Copy fee: $5.00 per document. Certification fee: $10.00. Fee payee: Court Administrator. Personal checks accepted. Prepayment is required.

Isanti County

10th Judicial District Court 555 18th Ave SW, Cambridge, MN 55008-9386; 763-689-2292; Fax: 763-689-8340. Hours: 8AM-4:30PM (CST). *Felony, Misdemeanor, Civil, Eviction, Small Claims, Probate.*

Civil Records: Access: Mail, in person. Both court and visitors may perform in person searches. No search fee. Required to search: name, years to search. Civil cases indexed by defendant, plaintiff. Civil records on computer from 12/84, prior on microfiche.

Criminal Records: Access: In person only. Visitors must perform in person searches for themselves. No search fee. Required to search: name, years to search. Criminal records on computer from 12/84, prior on microfiche.

General Information: Public Access terminal is available. No adoption, juvenile, sex offender or sealed

records released. SASE required. Turnaround time 2 days. Fax notes: Will fax free to local or toll-free numbers. Copy fee: $5.00 per document. Certification fee: $10.00. Fee payee: Court Administrator. Personal checks accepted. Prepayment is required.

Itasca County

9th Judicial District Court 123 4th St NE, Grand Rapids, MN 55744-2600; 218-327-2870; Fax: 218-327-2897. Hours: 8AM-4PM (CST). *Felony, Misdemeanor, Civil, Eviction, Small Claims, Probate.*

Civil Records: Access: Mail, in person. Only the court performs in person searches; visitors may not. Search fee: $5.00 per name. Required to search: name, years to search, DOB. Civil cases indexed by defendant, plaintiff. Civil records on computer from 4-87, on microfiche to 1982, on books prior.

Criminal Records: Access: Mail, in person. Only the court performs in person searches; visitors may not. Search fee: $5.00 per name. Required to search: name, years to search, DOB. Criminal records on computer from 4-87, on microfiche to 1982, on books prior.

General Information: Public Access terminal is available. No adoption, juvenile, sex offender or sealed records released. SASE required. Turnaround time 7-14 days, 24 hours required to pull from off-site storage. Fax notes: Fee to fax results is $5.00 per document. Copy fee: $5.00 per document. Certification fee: $10.00. Fee payee: Court Administrator. Personal checks accepted. Prepayment is required.

Jackson County

5th Judicial District Court PO Box 177, Jackson, MN 56143; 507-847-4400; Fax: 507-847-5433. Hours: 8:30AM-4:30PM (CST). *Felony, Misdemeanor, Civil, Eviction, Small Claims, Probate.*

Civil Records: Access: Fax, mail, in person. Both court and visitors may perform in person searches. No search fee. Required to search: name, years to search, address. Civil cases indexed by defendant, plaintiff. Civil records on computer to 5/89. Probate on microfiche from 1870.

Criminal Records: Access: Fax, mail, in person. Visitors must perform in person searches for themselves. No search fee. Required to search: name, years to search, DOB. Criminal records on computer from 5/89. Probate on microfiche from 1870.

General Information: Public Access terminal is available. No adoption, juvenile, sex offender or sealed records released. SASE required. Turnaround time 2-3 days. Fax notes: Fax fee 1-5 pages $5.00, each additional page $1.00. Copy fee: $5.00 per document. Certification fee: $10.00. Fee payee: Court Administrator. Personal checks accepted. Prepayment is required.

Kanabec County

10th Judicial District Court 18 North Vine, Mora, MN 55051; 320-679-6400; Fax: 320-679-6411. Hours: 8AM-4PM (CST). *Felony, Misdemeanor, Civil, Eviction, Small Claims, Probate.*

Civil Records: Access: In person only. Visitors must perform in person searches for themselves. No search fee. Required to search: name, years to search. Civil cases indexed by defendant, plaintiff. Civil records on computer from 1986, prior on books and microfiche.

Criminal Records: Access: In person only. Visitors must perform in person searches for themselves. No search fee. Required to search: name, years to search; also helpful: DOB. Criminal records on computer from 1986, prior on books and microfiche.

General Information: Public Access terminal is available. No adoption, juvenile or sealed records released. Copy fee: $5.00 per document. Certification fee: $10.00. Fee payee: Court Administrator. Personal checks accepted. Prepayment is required.

Kandiyohi County

8th Judicial District Court 505 Becker Ave SW, Willmar, MN 56201; 320-231-6206; Fax: 320-231-6276. Hours: 8AM-4:30PM (CST). *Felony, Misdemeanor, Civil, Eviction, Small Claims, Probate.*

http://courtnet.courts.state.mn.us/dist08

Civil Records: Access: In person only. Both court and visitors may perform in person searches. No search fee. Required to search: name, years to search. Civil cases indexed by defendant, plaintiff. Civil records on computer from 1986, prior on microfilm.

Criminal Records: Access: In person only. Visitors must perform in person searches for themselves. No search fee. Required to search: name, years to search, DOB; also helpful: SSN. Criminal records on computer from 1986, prior on microfilm.

General Information: Public Access terminal is available. No adoption, juvenile, sex offender or sealed records released. Copy fee: $5.00 per document. Certification fee: $10.00. Fee payee: Court Administrator. Personal checks accepted. Prepayment is required.

Kittson County

9th Judicial District Court PO Box 39, Hallock, MN 56728; 218-843-3632; Fax: 218-843-3634. Hours: 8:30AM-4:30PM (CST). *Felony, Misdemeanor, Civil, Eviction, Small Claims, Probate.*

Civil Records: Access: Fax, mail, in person. Both court and visitors may perform in person searches. Search fee: $5.00 per name. Will charge $20.00 per hour for extensive searches. Required to search: name, years to search. Civil cases indexed by defendant, plaintiff. Civil records on computer from 9/90, prior on books and index cards. Visitors may look at judgment docket.

Criminal Records: Access: Fax, mail, in person. Only the court performs in person searches; visitors may not. Search fee: $5.00 per name. Will charge $20.00 per hour for extensive searches. Required to search: name, years to search, DOB, offense. Criminal records on computer from 9/90, prior on books and index cards.

General Information:. No adoption, juvenile, sex offender or sealed records released. SASE required. Turnaround time 1-2 days. Fax notes: No fee to fax results. Copy fee: $5.00 per document. Certification fee: $10.00. Fee payee: Court Administrator. Personal checks accepted. Prepayment is required.

Koochiching County

9th Judicial District Court Court House, 715 4th St, International Falls, MN 56649; 218-283-1160; Fax: 218-283-1162. Hours: 8AM-4PM (CST). *Felony, Misdemeanor, Civil, Eviction, Small Claims, Probate.*

Civil Records: Access: Mail, in person. Both court and visitors may perform in person searches. Search fee: $5.00 per name. Required to search: name, years to search. Civil cases indexed by defendant, plaintiff. Civil records on computer from 9/90, on TCIS cards from 1984, on books from 1906.

Criminal Records: Access: Mail, in person. Both court and visitors may perform in person searches. Search fee: $5.00 per name. Required to search: name, years to search, DOB. Criminal records on computer from 9/90, on TCIS cards from 1984, on books from 1906.

General Information: Public Access terminal is available. No adoption, juvenile, sex offender or sealed records released. SASE required. Turnaround time 1 week. Fax notes: Fee to fax results is $5.00 per document. Copy fee: $5.00 per document. Certification fee: $10.00. Fee payee: Court Administrator. Personal checks accepted. Prepayment is required.

Lac qui Parle County

8th Judicial District Court PO Box 36, Madison, MN 56256; 320-598-3536; Fax: 320-598-3915. Hours: 8:30AM-4:30PM (CST). *Felony, Misdemeanor, Civil, Eviction, Small Claims, Probate.*

http://courtnet.courts.state.mn.us/dist08

Civil Records: Access: Fax, mail, in person. Only the court performs in person searches; visitors may not. Search fee: $5.00 per name. Required to search: name, years to search. Civil cases indexed by defendant, plaintiff. Civil records on computer from 1988, prior on index cards.

Criminal Records: Access: Fax, mail, in person. Only the court performs in person searches; visitors may not. Search fee: $5.00 per name. Required to search: name, years to search, DOB; also helpful: SSN. Criminal records on computer from 1988, prior on index cards.

General Information:. No adoption, juvenile, sex offender or sealed records released. SASE required. Turnaround time 1-3 days. Fax notes: $5.00 per document. Copy fee: $5.00 per document. Certification fee: $10.00. Fee payee: Court Administrator. Personal checks accepted. Prepayment is required.

Lake County

6th Judicial District Court 601 3rd Ave, Two Harbors, MN 55616; 218-834-8330; Fax: 218-834-8397. Hours: 8AM-4:30PM (CST). *Felony, Misdemeanor, Civil, Eviction, Small Claims, Probate.*

www.6courts.com

Civil Records: Access: Fax, mail, in person. Both court and visitors may perform in person searches. No search fee. Required to search: name, years to search. Civil cases indexed by defendant, plaintiff. Civil records on computer back to 1991, prior on index cards.

Criminal Records: Access: In person only. Visitors must perform in person searches for themselves. No search fee. Required to search: name, years to search, DOB. Criminal records on computer back to 1991, prior on index cards.

General Information: Public Access terminal is available. No adoption, juvenile, sex offender or sealed records released. SASE required. Turnaround time 1 day. Fax notes: Fee to fax results is $5.00 per document. Copy fee: $5.00 per document. Certification fee: $10.00. Fee payee: Court Administrator. Personal checks accepted. Credit cards accepted: Visa, MasterCard. Prepayment is required.

Lake of the Woods County

9th Judicial District Court PO Box 808, Baudette, MN 56623; 218-634-1451; Fax: 218-634-9444. Hours: 7:30AM-4PM (CST). *Felony, Misdemeanor, Civil, Eviction, Small Claims, Probate.*

Civil Records: Access: Fax, mail, in person. Both court and visitors may perform in person searches. Search fee: $10.00 per name. Required to search: name, years to search. Civil records on computer back to 1990; on microfilm to 1923.

Criminal Records: Access: Fax, mail, in person. Only the court performs in person searches; visitors may not. Search fee: $10.00 per name. Required to search: name, years to search, DOB. Criminal records on computer back to 1990; on microfilm back to 1923.

General Information:. No adoption, juvenile, sex offender or sealed records released. SASE not required. Turnaround time 2 days, no phone searches. Fax notes: No fee to fax results. Copy fee: $5.00 per document. Certification fee: $10.00. Fee payee: Court Administrator. Personal checks accepted. Prepayment is required.

Le Sueur County

1st Judicial District Court 88 S Park Ave, Le Center, MN 56057; 507-357-2251; Fax: 507-357-6375. Hours: 8AM-4:30PM (CST). *Felony, Misdemeanor, Civil, Eviction, Small Claims, Probate.*

Civil Records: Access: In person only. Visitors must perform in person searches for themselves. No search fee. Required to search: name, years to search. Civil cases indexed by defendant, plaintiff. Civil records on computer from 1992, prior on books.

Criminal Records: Access: In person only. Visitors must perform in person searches for themselves. No search fee. Required to search: name, years to search, DOB, signed release. Criminal records on computer from 1992, prior on books.

General Information: Public Access terminal is available. No adoption, juvenile, sex offender or sealed records released. Fax notes: No fee to fax results. Copy fee: $5.00 per document. Certification fee: $10.00. Fee payee: Court Administrator. Personal checks accepted. Prepayment is required.

Lincoln County

5th Judicial District Court PO Box 15, Ivanhoe, MN 56142-0015; 507-694-1355; Fax: 507-694-1717. Hours: 8:30AM-Noon,1-4:30PM (CST). *Felony, Misdemeanor, Civil, Eviction, Small Claims, Probate.*

Civil Records: Access: Mail, in person. Only the court performs in person searches; visitors may not. No search fee. Required to search: name, years to search. Civil cases indexed by defendant, plaintiff. Civil records on computer from 1989, on TCIS from 12/82, on books from late 1800.

Criminal Records: Access: In person only. Visitors must perform in person searches for themselves. No search fee. Required to search: name, years to search, DOB. Criminal records on computer from 1989, on TCIS from 12/82, on books from late 1800. All written requests for criminal record information is referred to the Bureau of Criminal Apprehension (state agency). Call first for form, 650-642-0670.

General Information: Public Access terminal is available. No adoption, juvenile, sex offender or sealed records released. SASE required. Turnaround time 1 week. Fax notes: Fee to fax results is $5.00 per document. Copy fee: $5.00 per document. Certification fee: $10.00. Fee payee: Court Administrator. Personal checks accepted. Prepayment is required.

Lyon County

5th Judicial District Court 607 W Main, Marshall, MN 56258; 507-537-6734; Fax: 507-537-6150. Hours: 8:30AM-4:30PM (CST). *Felony, Misdemeanor, Civil, Eviction, Small Claims, Probate.*

Civil Records: Access: Mail, in person. Both court and visitors may perform in person searches. No search fee. Required to search: name, years to search. Civil cases indexed by defendant, plaintiff. Civil records on computer from 1987, prior on index cards.

Criminal Records: Access: In person only. Visitors must perform in person searches for themselves. No search fee. The court requires sending requests to the state Bureau of Criminal Apprehension.

General Information: Public Access terminal is available. No adoption, juvenile, sex offender or sealed records released. SASE required. Copy fee: $5.00 per document. Certification fee: $10.00. Fee payee: Court Administrator. Personal checks accepted. Credit cards accepted: Visa, MasterCard. Prepayment is required.

Mahnomen County

9th Judicial District Court PO Box 459, Mahnomen, MN 56557; 218-935-2251; Fax: 218-935-2851. Hours: 8AM-4:30PM (CST). *Felony, Misdemeanor, Civil, Eviction, Small Claims, Probate.*

Civil Records: Access: Mail, in person. Only the court performs in person searches; visitors may not. Search fee: $5.00 per name. Required to search: name, years to search. Civil cases indexed by defendant, plaintiff. Civil records on computer from 8/90, prior on books from 1907.

Criminal Records: Access: Mail, in person. Only the court performs in person searches; visitors may not. Search fee: $5.00 per name. Required to search: name, years to search. Criminal records on computer from 8/90, prior on books from 1907.

General Information:. No adoption, juvenile, sex offender or sealed records released. SASE required. Turnaround time 1-5 days. Copy fee: $5.00 per document. Certification fee: $10.00. Fee payee: Court Administrator. Personal checks accepted. Prepayment is required.

Marshall County

9th Judicial District Court 208 E Colvin, Warren, MN 56762; 218-745-4921; Fax: 218-745-4343. Hours: 8AM-4:30PM (CST). *Felony, Misdemeanor, Civil, Eviction, Small Claims, Probate.*

Civil Records: Access: Mail, in person. Only the court performs in person searches; visitors may not. Search fee: $5.00 per name. Required to search: name, years to search; also helpful: address. Civil cases indexed by defendant, plaintiff. Civil records on computer from 5/90, on cards from 1982, on books from 1885.

Criminal Records: Access: Mail, in person. Only the court performs in person searches; visitors may not. Search fee: $5.00 per name. Required to search: name, years to search; also helpful: address, DOB. Criminal records on computer from 5/90, on cards from 1982, on books from 1885.

General Information: Public Access terminal is available. No adoption, juvenile, sex offender or sealed records released. SASE required. Turnaround time same day. Copy fee: $5.00 per document. Certification fee: $10.00. Fee payee: Court Administrator. Personal checks accepted. Prepayment is required.

Martin County

5th Judicial District Court 201 Lake Ave, Rm 304, Fairmont, MN 56031; 507-238-3205; Fax: 507-238-1913. Hours: 8AM-5PM (CST). *Felony, Misdemeanor, Civil, Eviction, Small Claims, Probate.*

Civil Records: Access: Mail, in person. Both court and visitors may perform in person searches. No search fee. Required to search: name, years to search; also helpful: address. Civil cases indexed by defendant, plaintiff. Civil records on computer from 7/89, on cards from 1986, on books from 1800s.

Criminal Records: Access: In person only. Visitors must perform in person searches for themselves. No search fee. Required to search: name, years to search, DOB; also helpful: address, SSN. Criminal records on computer from 7/89, on cards from 1986, on books from 1800s. The court suggests sending requests to the state Bureau of Criminal Apprehension.

General Information: Public Access terminal is available. No adoption, juvenile, sex offender or sealed records released. SASE required. Turnaround time 1-2 weeks. Copy fee: $5.00 per document. Certification fee: $10.00. Fee payee: Court Administrator. Personal checks accepted. Credit cards accepted: Visa, MasterCard. Prepayment is required.

McLeod County

1st Judicial District Court 830 E 11th, Glencoe, MN 55336; 320-864-5551. Hours: 8AM-4:30PM (CST). *Felony, Misdemeanor, Civil, Eviction, Small Claims, Probate.*

Civil Records: Access: Mail, in person. No search fee. Required to search: name, years to search. Civil records on computer from 4/92, prior on books.

Criminal Records: Access: In person only. Visitors must perform in person searches for themselves. No search fee. Required to search: name, years to search. Criminal records on computer from 4/92, prior on books.

General Information: Public Access terminal is available. No adoption, juvenile, sex offender or sealed records released. SASE required. Copy fee: $5.00 per document. Certification fee: $10.00. Fee payee: Court Administrator. Personal checks accepted. Prepayment is required.

Meeker County

8th Judicial District Court 325 N Sibley, Litchfield, MN 55355; 320-693-5230; Fax: 320-693-5254. Hours: 8AM-4:30PM (CST). *Felony, Misdemeanor, Civil, Eviction, Small Claims, Probate.*

http://courtnet.courts.state.mn.us/dist08

Civil Records: Access: Fax, mail, in person. Both court and visitors may perform in person searches. No search fee. Required to search: name; also helpful: years to search, address. Civil cases indexed by defendant, plaintiff. Civil records on computer from 11/88, prior on index cards.

Criminal Records: Access: In person only. Visitors must perform in person searches for themselves. No search fee. Required to search: name; also helpful: years to search, DOB. Criminal records on computer from 11/88, prior on index cards.

General Information: Public Access terminal is available. No adoption, juvenile, sex offender or sealed records released. SASE required. Turnaround time 3 days. Fax notes: $5.00 per document. Copy fee: $5.00 per document. Certification fee: $10.00. Fee payee: Court Administrator. Personal checks accepted. Prepayment is required.

Mille Lacs County

7th Judicial District Court Courthouse, Milaca, MN 56353; 320-983-8313; Fax: 320-983-8384. Hours: 8AM-4:30PM (CST). *Felony, Misdemeanor, Civil, Eviction, Small Claims, Probate.*

Civil Records: Access: Fax, mail, in person. Both court and visitors may perform in person searches. No search fee. Required to search: name, years to search. Civil records on computer from 4/86, cards from 1981, books prior.

Criminal Records: Access: Fax, in person. Visitors must perform in person searches for themselves. No search fee. Required to search: name, years to search. Criminal records on computer from 4/86, cards from 1981, books prior.

General Information: Public Access terminal is available. No adoption, juvenile, sex offender or sealed records released. SASE required. Turnaround time 1 week. Fax notes: $5.00 per document. Copy fee: $5.00 per document. Certification fee: $10.00. Fee payee: District Court. Personal checks accepted. Prepayment is required.

Morrison County

7th Judicial District Court 213 SE 1st Ave, Little Falls, MN 56345; 320-632-0325; Fax: 320-632-0340. Hours: 8AM-4:30PM (CST). *Felony, Misdemeanor, Civil, Eviction, Small Claims, Probate.*

Civil Records: Access: Fax, mail, in person. Both court and visitors may perform in person searches. No search

fee. Required to search: name, years to search. Civil cases indexed by defendant, plaintiff. Civil records on computer from 5/86, prior on cards and books.

Criminal Records: Access: In person only. Visitors must perform in person searches for themselves. No search fee. Required to search: name, years to search, DOB. Criminal records on computer from 5/86, prior on cards and books.

General Information: Public Access terminal is available. No adoption, juvenile, sex offender or sealed records released. SASE required. Turnaround time 2-3 days. Fax notes: $5.00 per document. Copy fee: $5.00 per document. Certification fee: $10.00. Fee payee: Court Administrator. Personal checks accepted. Prepayment is required.

Mower County

Mower County District Court 201 1st St NE, Austin, MN 55912; 507-437-9465; Fax: 507-437-9471. Hours: 8AM-5PM (CST). *Felony, Misdemeanor, Civil, Eviction, Small Claims, Probate.*

Civil Records: Access: Mail, in person. Both court and visitors may perform in person searches. No search fee. Required to search: name, years to search. Civil cases indexed by defendant, plaintiff. Civil records on computer from 1989.

Criminal Records: Access: In person only. Visitors must perform in person searches for themselves. No search fee. Required to search: name, years to search, DOB. Criminal records on computer from 1989. Effective July 1, 1997, this court will no longer conduct criminal record searches.

General Information:. No adoption, juvenile, paternity or sealed records released. SASE required. Turnaround time 2-3 weeks for civil, 3-4 days for criminal. Copy fee: $5.00 per document. Certification fee: $10.00. Fee payee: Court Administrator. Personal checks accepted. Prepayment is required.

Murray County

5th Judicial District Court PO Box 57, Slayton, MN 56172-0057; 507-836-6163; Fax: 507-836-6019. Hours: 8AM-5PM (CST). *Felony, Misdemeanor, Civil, Eviction, Small Claims, Probate.*

Civil Records: Access: Fax, mail, in person. Both court and visitors may perform in person searches. No search fee. Required to search: name, years to search. Civil cases indexed by defendant, plaintiff. Civil records on computer from 7/88.

Criminal Records: Access: In person only. Visitors must perform in person searches for themselves. No search fee. Required to search: name, years to search; also helpful: SSN. Criminal records on computer from 7/88. The court suggests sending requests to the state Bureau of Criminal Apprehension.

General Information:. No adoption, juvenile, or sealed records released. SASE required. Turnaround time 5 days. Fax notes: $5.00 per document. Copy fee: $5.00 per document. Certification fee: $10.00. Fee payee: Court Administrator. Personal checks accepted. Prepayment is required.

Nicollet County

5th Judicial District Court PO Box 496, St Peter, MN 56082; 507-931-6800; Fax: 507-931-4278. Hours: 8AM-5PM (CST). *Felony, Misdemeanor, Civil, Eviction, Small Claims, Probate.*

Note: Records for this county can also be found at the District Court Branch in North Mankato.

Civil Records: Access: Mail, in person. Both court and visitors may perform in person searches. No search fee. Required to search: name, years to search. Civil cases indexed by defendant, plaintiff. Civil records on computer from 9/25/88, on books from 1890. The civil records prior to 9/25/88 for the entire county are located here.

Criminal Records: Access: In person only. Both court and visitors may perform in person searches. No search fee. Required to search: name, years to search, DOB. Criminal records on computer since 9/25/88. Prior records for this court only are located here on books and cards.

General Information: Public Access terminal is available. No adoption, juvenile, sex offender or sealed records released. SASE required. Turnaround time 2 days. Copy fee: $5.00 per document. Certification fee: $10.00. Fee payee: Court Administrator. Personal checks accepted. Prepayment is required.

District Court - Branch PO Box 2055, North Mankato, MN 56002-2055; 507-625-3149; Fax: 507-345-1273. Hours: 8AM-5PM (CST). *Felony, Misdemeanor, Civil, Eviction, Small Claims, Probate.*

Note: Phone number for traffic is 507-625-7795.

Civil Records: Access: Mail, in person. Both court and visitors may perform in person searches. No search fee. Required to search: name, years to search. Civil cases indexed by defendant, plaintiff. Civil records on computer from 10/2/1988, prior in St Peters office.

Criminal Records: Access: In person only. Visitors must perform in person searches for themselves. No search fee. Required to search: name, years to search, DOB; also helpful: SSN. Criminal records for both courts are on computer since 9/25/88. Prior records are here for only this branch.

General Information: Public Access terminal is available. No adoption, juvenile, sex offender or sealed records released. SASE required. Turnaround time 2 days. Copy fee: $5.00 per document. Certification fee: $10.00. Fee payee: District Court. Personal checks accepted. Prepayment is required.

Nobles County

5th Judicial District Court PO Box 547, Worthington, MN 56187; 507-372-8263; Fax: 507-372-4994. Hours: 8AM-4:30PM (CST). *Felony, Misdemeanor, Civil, Eviction, Small Claims, Probate.*

Civil Records: Access: Mail, in person. Both court and visitors may perform in person searches. No search fee. Required to search: name, years to search. Civil cases indexed by defendant, plaintiff. Civil records on computer from 7/88, on books and index cards prior.

Criminal Records: Access: In person only. Visitors must perform in person searches for themselves. No search fee. Required to search: name, years to search; also helpful: SSN. Criminal records on computer from 7/88, on books and index cards prior. The court suggests sending requests to the state Bureau of Criminal Apprehension.

General Information: Public Access terminal is available. No adoption, juvenile, sex offender or sealed records released. SASE required. Turnaround time 1 week. Copy fee: $5.00 per document. Certification fee: $10.00. Fee payee: Court Administrator. Personal checks accepted. Credit cards accepted: Visa, MasterCard. In person only. Prepayment is required.

Norman County

9th Judicial District Court 16 3rd Ave E, Ada, MN 56510-0146; 218-784-7131; Fax: 218-784-3110. Hours: 8:30AM-4:30PM (CST). *Felony, Misdemeanor, Civil, Eviction, Small Claims, Probate.*

Civil Records: Access: Mail, in person. Both court and visitors may perform in person searches. Search fee: $5.00 per name. Required to search: name, years to search. Civil records on computer since 5/90, prior on index cards.

Criminal Records: Access: Mail, in person. Both court and visitors may perform in person searches. Search fee: $5.00 per name. Required to search: name, years to search, DOB. Criminal records on computer since 5/90, prior on index cards.

General Information:. No adoption, juvenile, sex offender or sealed records released. SASE required. Turnaround time 1-5 days. Copy fee: $5.00 per document. Certification fee: $10.00. Fee payee: Court Administrator. Business checks accepted. Prepayment is required.

Olmsted County

Olmsted County District Court 151 4th St SE, Rochester, MN 55904; 507-285-8210; Fax: 507-285-8996. Hours: 8AM-5PM (CST). *Felony, Misdemeanor, Civil, Eviction, Small Claims, Probate, Juvenile.*

www.courts.state.mn.us/districts/third/newpage6.htm

Civil Records: Access: Mail, in person. Both court and visitors may perform in person searches. No search fee. Required to search: name, years to search. Civil cases indexed by defendant, plaintiff. Civil records on computer from mid-1989, prior on index cards.
Criminal Records: Access: In person only. Visitors must perform in person searches for themselves. No search fee. Required to search: name, DOB. Criminal records on computer to mid-1989, prior on index cards.
General Information: Public Access terminal is available. No adoption, juvenile, sex offender or sealed records released. SASE required. Turnaround time 2-7 days. Copy fee: $5.00 per document. Certification fee: $10.00. Fee payee: Court Administrator. Personal checks accepted. Credit cards accepted: Visa, MasterCard, Discover. Prepayment is required.

Otter Tail County

Otter Tail County District Court PO Box 417, Fergus Falls, MN 56538-0417; 218-739-2271; Fax: 218-739-4983. Hours: 8AM-5PM (CST). *Felony, Misdemeanor, Civil, Eviction, Small Claims, Probate.*

Civil Records: Access: Mail, in person. Both court and visitors may perform in person searches. No search fee. Required to search: name; also helpful: years to search. Civil cases indexed by defendant, plaintiff. Civil records on computer from 1987, prior on index books.
Criminal Records: Access: In person only. Visitors must perform in person searches for themselves. No search fee. Required to search: name, years to search, DOB; also helpful: address. Criminal records on computer from 1987, prior on index books.
General Information: Public Access terminal is available. No adoption, juvenile, sex offender or sealed records released. SASE required. Turnaround time 2-3 days. Copy fee: $5.00 per document. Certification fee: $10.00. Fee payee: Court Administrator. Personal checks accepted. Prepayment is required.

Pennington County

9th Judicial District Court PO Box 619, Thief River Falls, MN 56701; 218-681-7023; Fax: 218-681-0907. Hours: 8AM-4:30PM (CST). *Felony, Misdemeanor, Civil, Eviction, Small Claims, Probate.*

Civil Records: Access: Mail, in person. Both court and visitors may perform in person searches. Search fee: $5.00 per name. Required to search: name, years to search. Civil cases indexed by defendant, plaintiff. Civil records on computer back to 1990, prior on TCIS cards and books to 1911.
Criminal Records: Access: Mail, in person. Both court and visitors may perform in person searches. Search fee: $5.00 per name. Required to search: name, years to search, DOB. Criminal records on computer back to 1990, prior on TCIS cards and books to 1911.
General Information: Public Access terminal is available. No adoption, juvenile, sex offender or sealed records released. SASE required. Turnaround time 1 day. Copy fee: $5.00 per document. Certification fee: $10.00. Fee payee: Court Administrator. Personal checks accepted. Prepayment is required.

Pine County

10th Judicial District Court 315 Main St S., Pine City, MN 55063; 320-629-5634. Hours: 8AM-4:30PM (CST). *Felony, Misdemeanor, Civil, Eviction, Small Claims, Probate.*

Civil Records: Access: Mail, in person. Visitors must perform in person searches for themselves. No search fee. Required to search: name, years to search. Civil records on computer from 2/85.
Criminal Records: Access: In person only. Visitors must perform in person searches for themselves. No search fee. Required to search: name, years to search. Criminal records on computer from 2/85.
General Information: Public Access terminal is available. No adoption, juvenile, sex offender or sealed records released. SASE required. Turnaround time 7-9 days. Copy fee: $5.00 per document. Certification fee: $10.00. Fee payee: Court Administrator. Personal checks accepted. Prepayment is required.

Pipestone County

5th Judicial District Court 416 S Hiawatha Ave (PO Box 337), Pipestone, MN 56164; 507-825-6730; Fax: 507-825-6733. Hours: 8:30AM-4:30PM (CST). *Felony, Misdemeanor, Civil, Eviction, Small Claims, Probate.*

Civil Records: Access: Mail, in person. Both court and visitors may perform in person searches. No search fee. Required to search: name, years to search. Civil cases indexed by defendant, plaintiff. Civil records on computer from 1989, prior on books.
Criminal Records: Access: In person only. Visitors must perform in person searches for themselves. No search fee. Required to search: name, years to search. Criminal records on computer from 1989, prior on books. The court suggests sending requests to the state Bureau of Criminal Apprehension.
General Information: Public Access terminal is available. No adoption, juvenile, sex offender victims or sealed records released. SASE required. Turnaround time 1 week. Copy fee: $5.00 per document. Certification fee: $10.00. Fee payee: Court Administrator. Personal checks accepted. Prepayment is required.

Polk County

9th Judicial District Court Court Administrator, 612 N Broadway #301, Crookston, MN 56716; 218-281-2332; Fax: 218-281-2204. Hours: 8AM-4:30PM (CST). *Felony, Misdemeanor, Civil, Eviction, Small Claims, Probate.*

Civil Records: Access: Mail, in person. Both court and visitors may perform in person searches. Search fee: $5.00 per name. Required to search: name, years to search. Civil cases indexed by defendant, plaintiff. Civil records on computer from 1990, prior on index cards or books.
Criminal Records: Access: Mail, in person. Both court and visitors may perform in person searches. Search fee: $5.00 per name. Required to search: name, years to search, DOB. Criminal records on computer from 1990, prior on index cards or books.
General Information: Public Access terminal is available. No adoption, non-felony under age 16 juvenile or sealed records released. SASE required. Turnaround time 3-5 days. Copy fee: $5.00 per document. Certification fee: $10.00. Fee payee: Court Administrator. Personal checks accepted. Credit cards accepted. Prepayment is required.

Pope County

8th Judicial District Court 130 E Minnesota Ave, Glenwood, MN 56334; 320-634-5222. Hours: 8AM-4:30PM (CST). *Felony, Misdemeanor, Civil, Eviction, Small Claims, Probate.*

http://courtnet.courts.state.mn.us/dist08

Civil Records: Access: Mail, in person. No search fee. Required to search: name, years to search. Civil cases indexed by defendant, plaintiff. Civil records on computer from 2/89, prior on TCIS cards ad books.
Criminal Records: Access: In person only. Visitors must perform in person searches for themselves. No search fee. Required to search: name, years to search. Criminal records on computer from 2/89, prior on TCIS cards ad books.
General Information: Public Access terminal is available. No adoption, juvenile, sex offender or sealed records released. SASE required. Turnaround time 1-2 days. Copy fee: $5.00 per document. Certification fee: $10.00. Fee payee: Court Administrator. Personal checks accepted. Prepayment is required.

Ramsey County

2nd Judicial District Court 15 W Kellogg, Rm 1700, St Paul, MN 55102; Civil phone: 651-266-8253; Criminal phone: 651-266-8180; Fax: 651-266-8278 civ.; 266-8172 crim. Hours: 8AM-4:30PM (CST). *Felony, Misdemeanor, Civil, Probate.*

www.co.ramsey.mn.us/courts/index.htm

Civil Records: Access: Mail, in person. Both court and visitors may perform in person searches. No search fee. Required to search: name, years to search. Civil cases indexed by defendant. Civil records on computer from 5/88, prior on books.
Criminal Records: Access: In person only. Visitors must perform in person searches for themselves. No search fee. Required to search: name, years to search; also helpful: DOB. Criminal records on computer from 5/88, prior on books.
General Information: Public Access terminal is available. No adoption, juvenile, sex offender or sealed records released. SASE required. Turnaround time 3-5 days. Copy fee: $5.00 per document. Certification fee: $10.00. Fee payee: Court Administrator. Personal checks accepted. Prepayment is required.

2nd Judicial District Court - Maplewood Area 2785 White Bear Ave, Maplewood, MN 55109; 651-777-9111; Fax: 651-777-3970. Hours: 8AM-4:30PM (CST). *Misdemeanor.*

www.co.ramsey.mn.us/courts/index.htm

Criminal Records: Access: In person only. Visitors must perform in person searches for themselves. No search fee. Required to search: name; also helpful: address, DOB, offense, date of offense. Criminal records on computer from 11/90, prior on books or index cards.
General Information: Public Access terminal is available. No adoption, juvenile, sex offender victim, sealed or medical records released. Copy fee: $5.00 per document. Certification fee: $10.00. Fee payee: Ramsey County District Court. Personal checks accepted. Credit cards accepted: Visa, MasterCard, Discover. Not accepted over the phone. Prepayment is required.

2nd Judicial District Court - New Brighton Area 803 Old Hiway 8 NW, New Brighton, MN 55112; 651-636-7101; Fax: 651-635-0722. Hours: 8AM-4:30PM (CST). *Misdemeanor.*

www.co.ramsey.mn.us/courts/index.htm

Criminal Records: Access: In person only. Visitors must perform in person searches for themselves. No search fee. Required to search: name, years to search, DOB; also helpful-address, offense. Criminal records on computer from 11/90. Gross misdemeanor files microfilmed, index cards.

General Information: Public Access terminal is available. No adoption, juvenile, sex offender victim, sealed or medical records released. SASE required. Fax notes: $5.00 per document. Copy fee: $5.00 per document. Certification fee: $10.00. Fee payee: District Court. Personal checks accepted. Credit cards accepted: Visa, MasterCard, Discover.

Red Lake County

9th Judicial District Court PO Box 339, Red Lake Falls, MN 56750; 218-253-4281; Fax: 218-253-4287. Hours: 9AM-5PM (CST). *Felony, Misdemeanor, Civil, Eviction, Small Claims, Probate.*

Civil Records: Access: Mail, in person. Both court and visitors may perform in person searches. Search fee: $5.00 per name. Required to search: name, years to search. Civil cases indexed by defendant, plaintiff. Civil records on computer and microfiche from 1990, on books from 1897.

Criminal Records: Access: Mail, in person. Only the court performs in person searches; visitors may not. Search fee: $5.00 per name. Required to search: name, years to search, DOB. Criminal records on computer and microfiche from 1990, on books from 1897.

General Information:. No adoption, juvenile, sex offender or sealed records released. SASE required. Turnaround time 1 week. Copy fee: $5.00 per document. Certification fee: $10.00. Fee payee: Court Administrator. Personal checks accepted. Prepayment is required.

Redwood County

5th Judicial District Court PO Box 130, Redwood Falls, MN 56283; 507-637-4020; Fax: 507-637-4021. Hours: 8AM-4:30PM (CST). *Felony, Misdemeanor, Civil, Eviction, Small Claims, Probate.*

Civil Records: Access: Mail, in person. Both court and visitors may perform in person searches. No search fee. Required to search: name, years to search. Civil cases indexed by defendant, plaintiff. Civil records on computer from 11/88, prior on card and books.

Criminal Records: Access: In person only. Visitors must perform in person searches for themselves. No search fee. Required to search: name, years to search. Criminal records on computer from 11/88, prior on card and books. No felony or gross misdemeanor searches will be performed.

General Information: Public Access terminal is available. No adoption, juvenile, sex offender or sealed records released. SASE required. Turnaround time 2-3 days. Copy fee: $5.00 per document. Certification fee: $10.00. Fee payee: Court Administrator. Personal checks accepted. Prepayment is required.

Renville County

8th Judicial District Court 500 E DePue Ave, 3rd level, Olivia, MN 56277; 320-523-3680; Fax: 320-523-3689. Hours: 8AM-4:30PM (CST). *Felony, Misdemeanor, Civil, Eviction, Small Claims, Probate.*
http://courtnet.courts.state.mn.us/dist08

Civil Records: Access: Mail, in person. Visitors must perform in person searches for themselves. No search fee. Required to search: name, years to search. Civil cases indexed by defendant, plaintiff. Civil records on computer from 1988, prior on index cards.

Criminal Records: Access: In person only. Visitors must perform in person searches for themselves. No search fee. Required to search: name. Criminal records on computer from 1988, prior on index cards.

General Information: Public Access terminal is available. No adoption, juvenile, sex offender, criminal or sealed records released. SASE required. Turnaround time 1-5 days. Copy fee: $5.00 per document. Certification fee: $10.00. Fee payee: Court

Administrator. Personal checks accepted. Prepayment is required.

Rice County

3rd Judicial District Court 218 NW 3rd St, Suite 300, Faribault, MN 55021; 507-332-6107; Fax: 507-332-6199. Hours: 8AM-4:30PM (CST). *Felony, Misdemeanor, Civil, Eviction, Small Claims, Probate.*

Civil Records: Access: Mail, in person. Both court and visitors may perform in person searches. No search fee. Required to search: name, years to search. Civil cases indexed by defendant, plaintiff. Civil records on computer from 1990, prior on index cards.

Criminal Records: Access: In person only. Visitors must perform in person searches for themselves. No search fee. Required to search: name, years to search; also helpful: SSN. Criminal records on computer from 1990, prior on index cards.

General Information: Public Access terminal is available. No adoption, juvenile, sex offender or sealed records released. SASE required. Turnaround time 1-2 days. Copy fee: $5.00 per document. Certification fee: $10.00. Fee payee: Court Administrator. Personal checks accepted. Prepayment is required.

Rock County

5th Judicial District Court PO Box 745, Luverne, MN 56156; 507-283-5020; Fax: 507-283-5017. Hours: 8AM-5PM (CST). *Felony, Misdemeanor, Civil, Eviction, Small Claims, Probate.*

Civil Records: Access: Mail, in person. Only the court performs in person searches on computer; visitors may not. Visitors may search in books for records prior to 1985. Search fee: $10.00 per name. Required to search: name, years to search. Civil cases indexed by defendant, plaintiff. Civil records on computer from 1989, prior on books.

Criminal Records: Access: Mail, in person. Only the court performs in person searches on computer; visitors may not. Visitors may search in books for records prior to 1985. Search fee: $10.00. Required to search: name, years to search; also helpful: SSN. Criminal records on computer from 1989, prior on books. The court will provide address for the state Bureau of Criminal Apprehension for complete record searches.

General Information:. No adoption, juvenile, sex offender or sealed records released. SASE required. Turnaround time same day if possible. Copy fee: $5.00 per document. Certification fee: $10.00. Fee payee: Court Administrator. Personal checks accepted. Prepayment is required.

Roseau County

9th Judicial District Court 606 5th Ave SW Rm 20, Roseau, MN 56751; 218-463-2541; Fax: 218-463-1889. Hours: 8AM-4:30PM (CST). *Felony, Misdemeanor, Civil, Eviction, Small Claims, Probate.*

Civil Records: Access: Mail, in person. Both court and visitors may perform in person searches. Search fee: $5.00 per name. Required to search: name, years to search. Civil cases indexed by defendant, plaintiff. Civil records on computer back to 1990, prior on index cards.

Criminal Records: Access: Mail, in person. Both court and visitors may perform in person searches. Search fee: $5.00 per name. Required to search: name, years to search; also helpful: DOB. Criminal records on computer back to 1990, prior on index cards.

General Information: Public Access terminal is available. No adoption, juvenile, paternity or sealed records released. SASE required. Turnaround time same day if possible. Copy fee: $5.00 per document. Certification fee: $10.00. Fee payee: Court Administrator. Personal checks accepted. Prepayment is required.

Scott County

1st Judicial District Court Scott County Justice Center, 200 Fourth Ave W, Shakopee, MN 55379; 952-496-8200; Fax: 952-496-8211. Hours: 8AM-4:30PM (CST). *Felony, Misdemeanor, Civil, Eviction, Small Claims, Probate.*

Civil Records: Access: Mail, in person. Both court and visitors may perform in person searches. No search fee. Required to search: name, years to search. Civil cases indexed by defendant, plaintiff. Civil records on computer from 1981, prior on books.

Criminal Records: Access: In person only. Visitors must perform in person searches for themselves. No search fee. Required to search: name, years to search, DOB. Criminal records on computer from 1981, prior on books.

General Information: Public Access terminal is available. No adoption, juvenile or sealed records released. SASE required. Turnaround time 1-2 days. Copy fee: $5.00 per document. Certification fee: $10.00. Fee payee: Scott County. Personal checks accepted. Prepayment is required.

Sherburne County

10th Judicial District Court Sherburne County Government Center, 13880 Hwy #10, Elk River, MN 55330-4608; 763-241-2800; Fax: 763-241-2816. Hours: 8AM-5PM (CST). *Felony, Misdemeanor, Civil, Eviction, Small Claims, Probate.*

Civil Records: Access: Mail, in person. Both court and visitors may perform in person searches. No search fee. Required to search: name, years to search. Civil cases indexed by defendant, plaintiff. Civil records on computer from 02/85, prior on books.

Criminal Records: Access: In person only. Visitors must perform in person searches for themselves. No search fee. Required to search: name, years to search, DOB. Criminal records on computer from 02/85, prior on books.

General Information: Public Access terminal is available. No adoption, juvenile, confidential or sealed records released. SASE required. Turnaround time 5 days. Copy fee: $5.00 per document. Certification fee: $10.00. Fee payee: Court Administrator. Personal checks accepted. Prepayment is required.

Sibley County

1st Judicial District Court PO Box 867, Gaylord, MN 55334; 507-237-4051; Fax: 507-237-4062. Hours: 8AM-5PM (CST). *Felony, Misdemeanor, Civil, Eviction, Small Claims, Probate.*

Civil Records: Access: Mail, in person. Both court and visitors may perform in person searches. Search fee: $5.00 per name. Required to search: name, years to search. Civil cases indexed by defendant, plaintiff. Civil records on computer from 5/92, prior on books.

Criminal Records: Access: Mail, in person. Both court and visitors may perform in person searches. Search fee: $5.00 per name. Required to search: name, years to search, DOB. Criminal records on computer from 5/92, prior on books.

General Information: Public Access terminal is available. No adoption, juvenile or sealed records released. SASE required. Turnaround time 1-2 week. Fax notes: Fee to fax results is $5.00 per document. Copy fee: $5.00 per document. Certification fee: $10.00 per document. Fee payee: Court Administrator. Personal checks accepted. Prepayment is required.

St. Louis County

6th Judicial District Court 100 N 5th Ave W, Rm 320, Duluth, MN 55802-1294; Civil phone: 218-726-2431; Criminal phone: 218-726-2500; Probate phone: 218-726-2500; Fax: 218-726-2473. Hours: 8AM-4:30PM (CST). *Felony, Misdemeanor, Civil, Eviction, Small Claims, Probate.*

www.6courts.com

Note: All three St Louis County courts can access computer records for the county and direct you to the appropriate court to get the physical file.

Civil Records: Access: Mail, in person. No search fee. Required to search: name, years to search. Civil records on computer from 1976.

Criminal Records: Access: In person only. Visitors must perform in person searches for themselves. No search fee. Required to search: name. Criminal records on computer from 1976.

General Information: Public Access terminal is available. No adoption, juvenile, juvenile victim of sex offense, sealed records released. SASE not required. Turnaround time 5 days. Copy fee: $5.00 per document. Certification fee: $10.00. Fee payee: Court Administrator. Personal checks accepted. Prepayment is required.

6th Judicial District Court - Hibbing Branch 1810 12th Ave East, Hibbing, MN 55746; 218-262-0100; Fax: 218-262-0219. Hours: 8AM-4:30PM (CST). *Felony, Misdemeanor, Civil, Eviction, Small Claims, Probate.*

www.courts.state.mn.us/districts/sixth/index.html

Note: All three St Louis County courts can access county computer records and direct you to the appropriate court for the physical file.

Civil Records: Access: Mail, in person. Both court and visitors may perform in person searches. No search fee. Required to search: name, years to search. Civil cases indexed by defendant, plaintiff. Civil records on computer from 1985, prior on card or books.

Criminal Records: Access: Mail, in person. Visitors must perform in person searches for themselves. No search fee. Required to search: name, years to search. Criminal records on computer from 1985, prior on card or books.

General Information: Public Access terminal is available. No adoption, juvenile, sex offender or sealed records released. SASE required. Turnaround time 2 days. Copy fee: $5.00 per document. Certification fee: $10.00. Fee payee: Court Administrator. Personal checks accepted. Prepayment is required.

6th Judicial District Court - Virginia Branch 300 S 5th Ave, Virginia, MN 55792; 218-749-7106; Fax: 218-749-7109. Hours: 8AM-4:30PM (CST). *Felony, Misdemeanor, Civil, Eviction, Small Claims, Probate.*

www.6courts.com

Note: All three St Louis County courts can access computer records for the county and direct you to the appropriate court for the physical files.

Civil Records: Access: Mail, in person. Both court and visitors may perform in person searches. No search fee. Required to search: name, years to search. Civil cases indexed by defendant, plaintiff. Civil records on computer back to 1991, prior on books.

Criminal Records: Access: In person only. Visitors must perform in person searches for themselves. No search fee. Required to search: name, years to search, DOB. Criminal records on computer back to 1991, prior on books.

General Information: Public Access terminal is available. No adoption, juvenile, sex offender or sealed records released. SASE required. Turnaround time 2-3

days. Copy fee: $5.00 per document. Certification fee: $10.00. Fee payee: Court Administrator. Personal checks accepted. Prepayment is required.

Stearns County

Stearns County District Court 725 Courthouse Square, St Cloud, MN 56303; 320-656-3620; Fax: 320-656-3626. Hours: 8AM-4:30PM (CST). *Felony, Misdemeanor, Civil, Small Claims, Eviction, Probate.*

www.co.stearns.mn.us/departments/other/court/index.htm

Civil Records: Access: Mail, in person. Both court and visitors may perform in person searches. No search fee. Required to search: name, years to search. Civil cases indexed by defendant, plaintiff. Civil records on computer from 1984, on books from the 1920s.

Criminal Records: Access: In person only. Visitors must perform in person searches for themselves. No search fee. Required to search: name, years to search, DOB. Criminal records on computer from 1984, on books from the 1920s.

General Information: Public Access terminal is available. No adoption, juvenile, sex offender or sealed records released. SASE not required. Turnaround time 1-2 days. Copy fee: $5.00 per document. Certification fee: $10.00. Fee payee: District Court. Personal checks accepted. Credit cards accepted: Visa, MasterCard, Discover. Prepayment is required.

Steele County

3rd Judicial District Court PO Box 487, Owatonna, MN 55060; 507-444-7700; Fax: 507-444-7491. Hours: 8AM-5PM (CST). *Felony, Misdemeanor, Civil, Eviction, Small Claims, Probate.*

Civil Records: Access: Mail, in person. Both court and visitors may perform in person searches. No search fee. Required to search: name, years to search. Civil cases indexed by defendant, plaintiff. Civil records on computer from 1990, on books from 1870.

Criminal Records: Access: In person only. Visitors must perform in person searches for themselves. No search fee. Required to search: name, years to search; also helpful: SSN. Criminal records on computer from 1990, on books from 1870.

General Information: Public Access terminal is available. No adoption, juvenile, sex offender or sealed records released. SASE required. Turnaround time 1-3 days. Copy fee: $5.00 per document. Certification fee: $10.00. Fee payee: Court Administrator. Personal checks accepted. Prepayment is required.

Stevens County

8th Judicial District Court PO Box 530, Morris, MN 56267; 320-589-7287; Fax: 320-589-7288. Hours: 8AM-4:30PM (8AM-4PM Summer hours) (CST). *Felony, Misdemeanor, Civil, Eviction, Small Claims, Probate.*

http://courtnet.courts.state.mn.us/dist08

Civil Records: Access: Mail, in person. Only the court performs in person searches; visitors may not. Search fee: $5.00 per name. Required to search: name, years to search. Civil cases indexed by defendant, plaintiff. Civil records on computer from 2/89, on cards from 5/86, on books from 1900.

Criminal Records: Access: In person only. Only the court performs in person searches; visitors may not. No search fee. Required to search: name, years to search. Criminal records on computer from 2/89, on cards from 5/86, on books from 1900. For access to criminal history information, the court recommends the BCA at 651-642-0610.

General Information:. No adoption, juvenile, sex offender or sealed records released. SASE required. Turnaround time 1-2 days. Copy fee: $5.00 per

document. Certification fee: $10.00. Fee payee: Court Administrator. Personal checks accepted. Prepayment is required.

Swift County

8th Judicial District Court PO Box 110, Benson, MN 56215; 320-843-2744; Fax: 320-843-4124. Hours: 8AM-4:30PM (CST). *Felony, Misdemeanor, Civil, Eviction, Small Claims, Probate.*

http://courtnet.courts.state.mn.us/dist08

Civil Records: Access: Phone, mail, in person. Both court and visitors may perform in person searches. No search fee. Required to search: name, years to search. Civil cases indexed by defendant, plaintiff. Civil records on computer from 8-88, prior in files and books from 1800s.

Criminal Records: Access: In person only. Visitors must perform in person searches for themselves. No search fee. Required to search: name, years to search; also helpful: DOB. Criminal records on computer from 8-88, prior in files and books from 1800s.

General Information:. No adoption, juvenile, minor victim of sex offense, sealed records released. SASE required. Turnaround time 1 week. Copy fee: $5.00 per document. Certification fee: $10.00. Fee payee: Court Administrator. Personal checks accepted. Prepayment is required.

Todd County

7th Judicial District Court 221 1st Ave South, Long Prairie, MN 56347; 320-732-7800; Fax: 320-732-2506. Hours: 8AM-4:30PM (CST). *Felony, Misdemeanor, Civil, Eviction, Small Claims, Probate.*

Civil Records: Access: Mail, in person. Both court and visitors may perform in person searches. No search fee. Required to search: name, years to search, address. Civil cases indexed by defendant, plaintiff. Civil records on computer 7/86, prior on index cards and books.

Criminal Records: Access: In person only. Visitors must perform in person searches for themselves. No search fee. Required to search: name, years to search, address, DOB; also helpful: SSN. Criminal records on computer 7/86, prior on index cards and books.

General Information: Public Access terminal is available. No adoption, juvenile or sealed records released. SASE required. Turnaround time 3-4 days. Fax notes: Fee to fax results is $5.00 per document. Copy fee: $5.00 per document. Certification fee: $10.00. Fee payee: Court Administrator. Personal checks accepted. Prepayment is required.

Traverse County

8th Judicial District Court PO Box 867, 702 2nd Ave N, Wheaton, MN 56296; 320-563-4343; Fax: 320-563-4311. Hours: 8AM-Noon, 12:30-4:30PM (CST). *Felony, Misdemeanor, Civil, Eviction, Small Claims, Probate.*

http://courtnet.courts.state.mn.us/dist08

Civil Records: Access: Mail, in person. Both court and visitors may perform in person searches. No search fee. Required to search: name, years to search. Civil cases indexed by defendant, plaintiff. Civil records on computer from 6/89, prior on index cards and books. Only judgment searches accepted by mail.

Criminal Records: Access: In person only. Visitors must perform in person searches for themselves. No search fee. Required to search: name, years to search. Criminal records on computer from 6/89, prior on index cards and books.

General Information:. No adoption, juvenile, sex offender or sealed records released. SASE required. Turnaround time 1 day. Copy fee: $5.00 per document. Certification fee: $10.00. Fee payee: Court Administrator. Personal checks accepted. Prepayment is required.

Wabasha County

3rd Judicial District Court 625 Jefferson Ave, Wabasha, MN 55981; 651-565-3579; Fax: 651-565-3160. Hours: 8AM-4PM (CST). *Felony, Misdemeanor, Civil, Eviction, Small Claims, Probate.*

www.co.wabasha.mn.us

Civil Records: Access: Phone, mail, in person. Both court and visitors may perform in person searches. No search fee. Required to search: name, years to search. Civil cases indexed by defendant, plaintiff. Civil records on computer from 6/89, prior on index cards and books.

Criminal Records: Access: In person only. Visitors must perform in person searches for themselves. No search fee. Required to search: name, years to search; also helpful: DOB. Criminal records on computer from 6/89, prior on index cards and books.

General Information: Public Access terminal is available. No adoption, juvenile, sex offender or sealed records released. SASE required. Turnaround time same day usually. Fax notes: Fee to fax results is $5.00 first page; $1.00 each add'l. Copy fee: $5.00 per document. Certification fee: $10.00. Fee payee: Wabasha District Court. Personal checks accepted. Prepayment is required.

Wadena County

7th Judicial District Court County Courthouse, 415 South Jefferson St, Wadena, MN 56482; 218-631-7634; Fax: 218-631-7635. Hours: 8AM-4:30PM (CST). *Felony, Misdemeanor, Civil, Eviction, Small Claims, Probate.*

Civil Records: Access: In person only. Both court and visitors may perform in person searches. No search fee. Required to search: name, years to search. Civil cases indexed by defendant, plaintiff. Civil records on computer from 7/86; prior on books, cards and microfiche.

Criminal Records: Access: In person only. Visitors must perform in person searches for themselves. No search fee. Required to search: name, years to search, DOB; also helpful: address. Criminal records on computer from 7/86; prior on books, cards and microfiche.

General Information: Public Access terminal is available. No adoption, juvenile, or sealed records released. Copy fee: $5.00 per document. Certification fee: $10.00. Fee payee: Court Administrator. Personal checks accepted. Prepayment is required.

Waseca County

3rd Judicial District Court 307 N State St, Waseca, MN 56093; 507-835-0540; Fax: 507-835-0633. Hours: 8AM-4:30PM (CST). *Felony, Misdemeanor, Civil, Eviction, Small Claims, Probate.*

Civil Records: Access: Mail, in person. Both court and visitors may perform in person searches. No search fee. Required to search: name, years to search. Civil cases indexed by defendant, plaintiff. Civil records on computer from 1990, prior on TCIS cards and books.

Criminal Records: Access: In person only. Visitors must perform in person searches for themselves. No search fee. Required to search: name, years to search, DOB. Criminal records on computer from 1990, prior on TCIS cards and books.

General Information: Public Access terminal is available. No adoption, juvenile, sex offender victim or sealed records released. SASE required. Turnaround time 2 days. Copy fee: $5.00 per document. Certification fee: $10.00. Fee payee: Court Administrator. Personal checks accepted. Prepayment is required.

Washington County

10th Judicial District Court 14949 62nd St North, PO Box 3802, Stillwater, MN 55082-3802; 651-430-6263; Fax: 651-430-6300. Hours: 7:30AM-5PM (CST). *Felony, Misdemeanor, Civil, Eviction, Small Claims, Probate.*

www.co.washington.mn.us/crtadmn.htm

Civil Records: Access: Mail, in person. Both court and visitors may perform in person searches. No search fee. Required to search: name, years to search. Civil cases indexed by defendant, plaintiff. Civil records on computer back to 12/83, prior on books.

Criminal Records: Access: In person only. Visitors must perform in person searches for themselves. No search fee. Required to search: name, years to search, DOB. Criminal records on computer back to 12/83, prior on books. Fax & mail access limited to statute requirements.

General Information: Public Access terminal is available. No adoption, juvenile, sex offender or sealed records released. SASE required. Turnaround time 1 week. Copy fee: $5.00 per document. Certification fee: $10.00. Fee payee: Court Administrator. Personal checks accepted. Credit cards accepted: Visa, MasterCard. Prepayment is required.

Watonwan County

5th Judicial District Court PO Box 518, St James, MN 56081; 507-375-1236; Fax: 507-375-5010. Hours: 8AM-5PM (CST). *Felony, Misdemeanor, Civil, Eviction, Small Claims, Probate.*

Civil Records: Access: Mail, in person. Both court and visitors may perform in person searches. No search fee. Required to search: name, years to search. Civil cases indexed by defendant, plaintiff. Civil records on computer from 5/89, prior on index cards.

Criminal Records: Access: In person only. Visitors must perform in person searches for themselves. No search fee. Required to search: name, years to search; also helpful: DOB. Criminal records on computer from 5/89, prior on index cards. A signed release is necessary if court does search.

General Information: Public Access terminal is available. No adoption, juvenile, sex offender or sealed records released. SASE required. Fax notes: Fee to fax is $5.00 per page. Copy fee: $5.00 per document. Certification fee: $10.00. Fee payee: Court Administrator. Personal checks accepted. Prepayment is required.

Wilkin County

8th Judicial District Court PO Box 219, Breckenridge, MN 56520; 218-643-7172; Fax: 218-643-7167. Hours: 8AM-4:30PM (CST). *Felony, Misdemeanor, Civil, Eviction, Small Claims, Probate.*

http://courtnet.courts.state.mn.us/dist08

Civil Records: Access: Mail, in person. Both court and visitors may perform in person searches. No search fee. Required to search: name; also helpful: years to search. Civil cases indexed by defendant, plaintiff. Civil records on computer from 1989, prior on books.

Criminal Records: Access: In person only. Visitors must perform in person searches for themselves. No search fee. Required to search: name; also helpful: years to search. Criminal records on computer from 1989, prior on books.

General Information: Public Access terminal is available. (Not in complete use at this time.) No adoption, juvenile, sex offender or sealed records released. SASE required. Turnaround time 3-5 days. Copy fee: $5.00 per document. Certification fee:

$10.00. Fee payee: Court Administrator. Personal checks accepted. Prepayment is required.

Winona County

3rd Judicial District Court 171 West 3rd St, Winona, MN 55987; 507-457-6385; Fax: 507-457-6392. Hours: 8AM-4:30PM (CST). *Felony, Misdemeanor, Civil, Eviction, Small Claims, Probate.*

www.courts.state.mn.us/districts/third/winona.htm

Civil Records: Access: Mail, in person. Both court and visitors may perform in person searches. No search fee. Required to search: name, years to search. Civil cases indexed by defendant, plaintiff. Civil records on computer from 1986, on books from 1888.

Criminal Records: Access: In person only. Visitors must perform in person searches for themselves. No search fee. Required to search: name, years to search, DOB. Criminal records on computer from 1986, on books from 1888.

General Information: Public Access terminal is available. No adoption, juvenile, sex offender or sealed records released. SASE not required. Turnaround time 5-10 working days. Copy fee: $5.00 per document. Certification fee: $10.00. Fee payee: Court Administrator. Personal checks accepted. Prepayment required.

Wright County

10th Judicial District Court 10 NW 2nd St, Room 201, Buffalo, MN 55313-1192; 763-682-7549; Fax: 763-682-7300. Hours: 8AM-4:30PM (CST). *Felony, Misdemeanor, Civil, Eviction, Small Claims, Probate.*

Civil Records: Access: In person only. Both court and visitors may perform in person searches. No search fee. Required to search: name, years to search. Civil cases indexed by defendant, plaintiff. Civil records on computer from 8/84, prior on books, cards & microfiche.

Criminal Records: Access: In person only. Visitors must perform in person searches for themselves. No search fee. Required to search: name, years to search; also helpful: DOB. Criminal records on computer from 8/84, prior on books, cards & microfiche.

General Information: Public Access terminal is available. No adoption, juvenile, confidential or sealed records released. Copy fee: $5.00 per document. Certification fee: $10.00. Fee payee: Court Administrator. Personal checks accepted. Prepayment is required.

Yellow Medicine County

8th Judicial District Court 415 9th Ave, Granite Falls, MN 56241; 320-564-3325; Fax: 320-564-4435. Hours: 8AM-4PM (CST). *Felony, Misdemeanor, Civil, Eviction, Small Claims, Probate.*

http://courtnet.courts.state.mn.us/dist08

Civil Records: Access: Mail, in person. Both court and visitors may perform in person searches. No search fee. Required to search: name, years to search; also helpful: address. Civil cases indexed by defendant, plaintiff. Civil records on computer from 1988.

Criminal Records: Access: In person only. Visitors must perform in person searches for themselves. No search fee. Required to search: name, years to search. Criminal records on computer from 1988.

General Information: Public Access terminal is available. No adoption, juvenile or sealed records released. SASE required. Turnaround time 2-3 days. Copy fee: $5.00 per document. Certification fee: $10.00. Fee payee: Court Administrator. Personal checks accepted. Prepayment is required.

Minnesota Recording Offices

ORGANIZATION	87 counties, 87 recording offices. The recording officer is County Recorder. The entire state is in the Central Time Zone (CST).
REAL ESTATE RECORDS	Many Minnesota counties will perform real estate searches, especially short questions over the telephone. Copy fees vary, but do not apply to certified copies. Certification fees are usually $1.00 per page with a minimum of $5.00.
UCC RECORDS	Until July 2001, Minnesota maintained a centralized database of financing statements filed at the state level and all counties entered all non-real estate filings into the central statewide database which was accessible from any county office. Now, the only filings recorded by the County Recorder are real estate related collateral. All counties will perform UCC searches. Use search request form UCC-11. Search fees are usually $15.00 per debtor name if the standard UCC-12 request form is used, or $20.00 if a nonstandard form is used. A UCC search can include tax liens. The search fee usually includes 10 listings or copies. Additional copies usually cost $1.00 per page.
TAX LIEN RECORDS	Federal and state tax liens on personal property of businesses are filed with the Secretary of State. Other federal and state tax liens are filed with the County Recorder. A special search form UCC-12 is used for separate tax lien searches. Some counties search each tax lien index separately. Some charge one $15.00 fee to search both indexes, but others charge a separate fee for each index searched. Search and copy fees vary widely.
OTHER LIENS	Mechanics, hospital, judgment, attorneys.

Aitkin County

County Recorder, 209 Second Street NW, Aitkin, MN 56431. County Recorder, R/E and UCC Recording 218-927-7336; Fax 218-927-7324.
Will search UCC records. Tax liens not included in UCC search. RE owner, mortgage, and property transfer searches available. **Other Phone Numbers:** Assessor 218-927-7327; Treasurer 218-927-7325; Elections 218-927-7354; Vital Records 218-927-7336; Marriage Records 218-927-7325.

Anoka County

County Recorder, 2100 3rd Ave., Anoka, MN 55303-2265. 763-323-5416 R/E Recording: 763-323-5413; Fax 763-323-5421. http://www2.co.hennepin.mn.us
Will search UCC records. UCC search includes tax liens if requested. Will not search real estate records. **Online Access:** Real Estate, Tax Assessor Records. Access to the County online records requires an annual fee of $35 and a $25 monthly fee and $.25 per transaction. Records date back to 1995. Lending agency information is available. For information, contact Pam LeBlanc at 763-323-5424. **Other Phone Numbers:** Assessor 763-323-5400; Treasurer 763-323-5400.

Becker County

County Recorder, P.O. Box 595, Detroit Lakes, MN 56502-0595. County Recorder, R/E and UCC Recording 218-846-7304; Fax 218-846-7323. www.beckercounty.com
Will search UCC records. Standard form is UCC-11. UCC search includes tax liens if requested. RE owner, mortgage, and property searches by phone, (very restricted) but are uncertified. **Other Phone Numbers:** Assessor 218-846-7300; Treasurer 218-846-7311; Elections 218-846-7301; Vital Records 218-846-7304.

Beltrami County

County Recorder, 619 Beltrami Ave. NW, Courthouse, Bemidji, MN 56601. 218-759-4170; Fax 218-759-4527.
Will search UCC records. UCC search includes tax liens if requested. Will not search real estate records. **Other Phone Numbers:** Assessor 218-759-4114; Treasurer 218-759-4175.

Benton County

County Recorder, P.O. Box 129, Foley, MN 56329. 320-968-5037 R/E Recording: 320-968-6254; Fax 320-968-5329.
Will search UCC records. UCC search includes tax liens if requested. Will not search real estate records. **Other Phone Numbers:** Assessor 320-968-5019; Treasurer 320-968-5006; Vital Records 320-968-5037.

Big Stone County

County Recorder, P.O. Box 218, Ortonville, MN 56278. 320-839-2308; Fax 320-839-2308.
Will search UCC records. UCC tax liens will be done on UCC 12 form. Will not search real estate records. **Other Phone Numbers:** Assessor 320-839-3272; Treasurer 320-839-3445.

Blue Earth County

County Recorder, P.O. Box 3567, Mankato, MN 56002-3567. 507-389-8251 R/E Recording: 507-389-8222; Fax 507-389-8808.
Will search UCC records. Tax liens not included in UCC search. RE owner, mortgage, and property transfer searches available. Legal description required **Other Phone Numbers:** Assessor 507-389-8257; Treasurer 507-389-8237.

Brown County

County Recorder, P.O. Box 248, New Ulm, MN 56073-0248. County Recorder, R/E and UCC Recording 507-233-6653 UCC Recording: 507-233-6657; Fax 507-359-1430. http://www.co.brown.mn.us
Will search UCC records. Tax liens not included in UCC search. RE owner, mortgage, and property transfer searches available. **Other Phone Numbers:** Assessor 507-233-6609; Treasurer 507-233-6617; Appraiser/Auditor 507-233-6609; Elections 507-233-6617; Vital Records 507-233-6657.

Carlton County

County Recorder, Box 70, Carlton, MN 55718. 218-384-9122 R/E Recording: 218-384-9126 UCC Recording: 218-384-9156; Fax 218-384-9157.
Will search UCC records. Tax liens not included in UCC search. RE owner, mortgage, and property transfer searches available. $20.00 for two hour search, and $10.00 per additional hour up to four. Legal description required **Other Phone Numbers:** Assessor 218-384-4281; Treasurer 218-384-4281; Vital Records 218-384-9156.

Carver County

County Recorder, Carver County Govt Center, Admin Bldg, 600 East Fourth St, Chaska, MN 55318-2158. 952-361-1930 R/E Recording: 952-361-1935; Fax 952-361-1931. http://www.co.carver.mn.us
Will search UCC records. Tax liens not included in UCC search. Will not search real estate records. **Online Access:** Property Tax Records. Records on the County Property Tax Information database are available free online at www.co.carvr.mn.us/Prop_Tax/default.asp. Information is updated bi-monthly. **Other Phone Numbers:** Assessor 952-361-1960; Treasurer 952-361-1980.

Cass County

County Recorder, P.O. Box 3000, Walker, MN 56484. 218-547-7381 R/E Recording: 218-547-3300; Fax 218-547-2440.
Will search UCC records. Tax liens not included in UCC search. Will not search real estate records. **Other Phone Numbers:** Assessor 218-547-3300; Treasurer 218-547-3300.

Chippewa County

County Recorder, 629 No. 11th St., Montevideo, MN 56265. 320-269-9431 R/E Recording: 320-269-7447; Fax 320-269-7168.
Will search UCC records. Tax liens not included in UCC search. RE owner, mortgage, and property transfer searches available. **Other Phone Numbers:** Assessor 320-269-7696; Treasurer 320-269-7347; Vital Records 320-269-9431.

Chisago County

County Recorder, Government Center, Room/Box 277, 313 N. Main St., Center City, MN 55012-9663. 651-213-0438 R/E Recording: 651-257-1300; Fax 651-213-0454.

Will search UCC records. Tax liens not included in UCC search. Will not search real estate records. **Other Phone Numbers:** Assessor 651-213-0401.

Clay County

County Recorder, P.O. Box 280, Moorhead, MN 56561-0280. County Recorder, R/E and UCC Recording 218-299-5031; Fax 218-299-7500. http://www.co.clay.mn.us
Will search UCC records. Requests must be on nationally approved forms. Tax liens not included in UCC search. Will not search real estate records. **Online Access:** Real Estate. The county online GIS mapping service provides property record searching, but by parcel number only. County Recorder records may be available at the web site in the near future. **Other Phone Numbers:** Assessor 218-299-5017; Treasurer 218-299-5011; Elections 218-299-5006; Vital Records 218-299-5031.

Clearwater County

County Recorder, 213 Main Avenue North, Dept. 207, Bagley, MN 56621. 218-694-6129; Fax 218-694-6244. Will search UCC records. UCC search includes tax liens if requested. RE record owner searches available. Charges only required if forms are filled out and signed. **Other Phone Numbers:** Assessor 218-694-6260; Treasurer 218-694-6130.

Cook County

County Recorder, P.O. Box 1150, Grand Marais, MN 55604-1150. 218-387-3000 R/E Recording: 218-387-2282 UCC Recording: 218-387-3000 x160/161; Fax 218-387-2610.
Will search UCC records. RE owner, mortgage, and property transfer searches available. **Other Phone Numbers:** Assessor 218-387-3000 x150-153; Treasurer 218-387-3000; Vital Records 218-387-3000 x160/161.

Cottonwood County

County Recorder, P.O. Box 326, Windom, MN 56101. 507-831-1458 R/E Recording: 507-831-1905; Fax 507-831-3675.
Will search UCC records. Tax liens not included in UCC search. RE owner, mortgage, and property transfer searches available. Possible charge for lengthy searches **Other Phone Numbers:** Assessor 507-831-2458; Treasurer 507-831-1342; Elections 507-831-1905; Vital Records 507-831-1458.

Crow Wing County

County Recorder, P.O. Box 383, Brainerd, MN 56401. 218-828-3965; Fax 218-825-1808.
Will search UCC records. Tax liens not included in UCC search. RE owner, mortgage, and property transfer searches available. Possible charge for lengthy searches **Other Phone Numbers:** Assessor 218-828-3954; Treasurer 218-828-3953.

Dakota County

County Recorder, 1590 Highway 55, Hastings, MN 55033. 651-438-4355; Fax 651-438-8176. http://www.co.dakota.mn.us
Will search UCC records. Tax liens not included in UCC search. No charge for verbal search. Will not search real estate records. **Online Access:** Real Estate, Assessor. Records on the County Real Estate Inquiry database are available free online at www.co.dakota.mn.us/assessor/real_estate_inquiry.htm. Information includes items such as address, estimated value, taxes, last sale price, building details. **Other Phone Numbers:** Assessor 651-438-4200; Treasurer 651-438-4360.

Dodge County

County Recorder, P.O. Box 128, Mantorville, MN 55955-0128. County Recorder, R/E and UCC Recording 507-635-6250; Fax 507-635-6265. http://www.co.dodge.mn.us
Will search UCC records. UCC search includes tax liens if requested. RE record owner and mortgage searches available. Phone searches are uncertified. **Other Phone Numbers:** Assessor 507-635-6245; Treasurer 507-635-6240; Vital Records 507-635-6250.

Douglas County

County Recorder, 305 8th Avenue West, Courthouse, Alexandria, MN 56308. 320-762-3877 R/E Recording: 320-762-2381; Fax 320-762-2389.
Will search UCC records. Tax liens not included in UCC search. Property transfer searches available. Legal description required. **Other Phone Numbers:** Assessor 320-762-3854; Treasurer 320-762-3077; Vital Records 320-762-3877.

Faribault County

County Recorder, P.O. Box 130, Blue Earth, MN 56013. 507-526-6252 R/E Recording: 507-526-5147; Fax 507-526-6227.
Will search UCC records. UCC search includes tax liens if requested. Will give last document of record. **Other Phone Numbers:** Assessor 507-526-6201; Treasurer 507-526-6260; Appraiser/Auditor 507-526-6201; Elections 507-526-6212; Vital Records 507-526-6252.

Fillmore County

County Recorder, Box 465, Preston, MN 55965-0465. 507-765-3852 R/E Recording: 507-765-4701; Fax 507-765-4571.
Will search UCC records. This agency will do a tax lien search, fee is $5.00 per name. RE owner, mortgage, and property transfer searches available. **Other Phone Numbers:** Assessor 507-765-3868; Treasurer 507-765-3811; Elections 507-765-4701; Vital Records 507-765-5339.

Freeborn County

County Recorder, 411 South Broadway, Court House, Albert Lea, MN 56007-4506. 507-377-5130 R/E Recording: 507-377-5116; Fax 507-377-5260.
Will search UCC records. Tax liens not included in UCC search. Will not search real estate records. **Other Phone Numbers:** Assessor 507-377-5176; Treasurer 507-377-5117.

Goodhue County

County Recorder, Box 408, Red Wing, MN 55066. 651-385-3149 R/E Recording: 651-385-8261; Fax 651-385-3039.
Will search UCC records. Tax liens not included in UCC search. Will not search real estate records. **Other Phone Numbers:** Assessor 651-385-3006; Treasurer 651-385-3032.

Grant County

County Recorder, 10th Second Street NE, Courthouse, Elbow Lake, MN 56531-4300. 218-685-4133; Fax 218-685-4521.
Will search UCC records. Tax liens not included in UCC search. RE owner, mortgage, and property transfer searches available. Legal description required

Hennepin County

County Recorder, 300 South 6th Street, 8-A Government Center, Minneapolis, MN 55487. 612-348-3049 R/E Recording: 612-348-3050; http://www2.co.hennepin.mn.us

Will search UCC records. UCC search includes tax liens if requested. Will not search real estate records. **Online Access:** Real Estate, Liens. Three options are available. Access to Hennepin County online records requires a $35 annual fee with a charge of $5 per hour from 7AM-7PM, or $4.15 per hour at other times. Records date back to 1988. Only UCC & lending agency information is available. Property tax info is at the Treasurer office. For information, contact Jerry Erickson at 612-348-3856. Records on the County Property Information Search database are available free on the Internet at www2.co.hennepin.mn.us/pins/main.htm. Search by Property ID #, address, or addition name. An Automated phone system is also available; 612-348-3011. **Other Phone Numbers:** Assessor 612-348-3046.

Houston County

County Recorder, P.O. Box 29, Caledonia, MN 55921-0029. County Recorder, R/E and UCC Recording 507-725-5813; Fax 507-725-2647.
Will search UCC records. UCC search includes tax liens if requested. RE owner, mortgage, and property transfer searches available. **Other Phone Numbers:** Assessor 507-725-5801; Treasurer 507-725-5815; Elections 507-725-5803; Vital Records 507-725-5813.

Hubbard County

County Recorder, Courthouse, Park Rapids, MN 56470. 218-732-3552 R/E Recording: 218-732-3196. Will search UCC records. RE owner, mortgage, and property transfer searches available. Legal description required **Other Phone Numbers:** Assessor 218-732-3452; Treasurer 218-732-4348.

Isanti County

County Recorder, Courthouse, Cambridge, MN 55008. 763-689-1191 R/E Recording: 612-689-1191.
Will search UCC records. Tax liens not included in UCC search. Property transfer searches available. Legal description required.

Itasca County

County Recorder, 123 NE 4th Street, Grand Rapids, MN 55744-2600. County Recorder, R/E and UCC Recording 218-327-2856; Fax 218-327-0689.
Will search UCC records. Tax liens not included in UCC search. RE record owner and mortgage searches available. $12.00 per hour labor charge on all searches **Other Phone Numbers:** Assessor 218-327-2861; Appraiser/Auditor 218-327-2860; Vital Records 218-327-2856.

Jackson County

County Recorder, Jackson County Recorder P.O. Box 209, Jackson, MN 56143. County Recorder, R/E and UCC Recording 507-847-2580; Fax 507-847-4718.
Will search UCC records. UCC search includes tax liens if requested. RE owner, mortgage, and property transfer searches available. Legal description required **Other Phone Numbers:** Assessor 507-847-4033; Treasurer 507-847-2763; Elections 507-847-2763; Vital Records 507-847-2580.

Kanabec County

County Recorder, 18 North Vine Street, Mora, MN 55051. 320-679-6466 R/E Recording: 320-679-1441; Fax 320-679-6431.
Will search UCC records. Tax liens not included in UCC search. RE owner, mortgage, and property transfer searches available. Legal description required **Other Phone Numbers:** Assessor 320-679-3381; Treasurer 320-679-1951.

Kandiyohi County

County Recorder, P.O. Box 736, Willmar, MN 56201-0736. County Recorder, R/E and UCC Recording 320-231-6223 UCC Recording: 320-231-6224; Fax 320-231-6284.

Will search UCC records. This agency will not do a tax lien search. Will search real estate records. **Other Phone Numbers:** Assessor 320-231-6200; Treasurer 320-231-6202; Appraiser/Auditor 320-231-6202; Vital Records 320-231-6532.

Kittson County

County Recorder, P.O. Box 639, Hallock, MN 56728. 218-843-2842; Fax 218-843-2020.

Will search UCC records. Tax liens not included in UCC search. RE owner, mortgage, and property transfer searches available. Legal description required **Other Phone Numbers:** Assessor 218-843-3615; Treasurer 218-843-3432.

Koochiching County

County Recorder, Courthouse, 715 4th St., International Falls, MN 56649. 218-283-1190 R/E Recording: 218-283-6290 UCC Recording: 218-283-1193; Fax 218-283-1194.

Will search UCC records. Tax liens not included in UCC search. Will not search real estate records. **Other Phone Numbers:** Assessor 218-283-1120; Treasurer 218-283-1112; Elections 218-283-1101; Vital Records 218-283-1190.

Lac qui Parle County

County Recorder, P.O. Box 132, Madison, MN 56256-0132. 320-598-3724.

Will search UCC records. Tax liens not included in UCC search. RE owner, mortgage, and property transfer searches available. **Other Phone Numbers:** Assessor 320-598-3187; Treasurer 320-598-3648.

Lake County

County Recorder, 601 Third Avenue, Two Harbors, MN 55616. County Recorder, R/E and UCC Recording 218-834-8347; Fax 218-834-8365.

Will search UCC records. UCC search includes tax liens if requested. Will not search real estate records. **Other Phone Numbers:** Assessor 218-834-8313; Treasurer 218-834-8344; Elections 218-834-8318; Vital Records 218-834-8301.

Lake of the Woods County

County Recorder, P.O. Box 808, Baudette, MN 56623. 218-634-1902; Fax 218-634-2509.

Will search UCC records. Tax liens not included in UCC search. Will not search real estate records. **Other Phone Numbers:** Assessor 218-634-2536; Treasurer 218-634-2361.

Le Sueur County

County Recorder, 88 South Park Avenue, Courthouse, Le Center, MN 56057-1620. 507-357-2251; Fax 507-357-6375.

Will search UCC records. Tax liens not included in UCC search. RE record owner and mortgage searches available. **Other Phone Numbers:** Assessor 507-357-2257.

Lincoln County

County Recorder, P.O. Box 119, Ivanhoe, MN 56142. 507-694-1360; Fax 507-694-1198.

Will search UCC records. UCC search includes tax liens if requested. RE owner, mortgage, and property transfer searches available. **Other Phone Numbers:** Treasurer 507-694-1550.

Lyon County

County Recorder, 607 West Main Street, Marshall, MN 56258. 507-537-6722; Fax 507-537-6091.

Will search UCC records. UCC search includes tax liens if requested. Only telephone searches performed for RE. For certified copies by mail, include $2.50 postage

Mahnomen County

County Recorder, P.O. Box 380, Mahnomen, MN 56557. 218-935-5528; Fax 218-935-5946.

Will search UCC records. Tax liens not included in UCC search. RE owner, mortgage, and property transfer searches available.

Marshall County

County Recorder, 208 East Colvin, Warren, MN 56762. 218-745-4801 R/E Recording: 218-745-4851; Fax 218-745-4343.

Will search UCC records. Tax liens not included in UCC search. $10.00 per hour minimum RE research fee. **Other Phone Numbers:** Assessor 218-745-5331; Treasurer 218-745-4831.

Martin County

County Recorder, P.O. Box 785, Fairmont, MN 56031-0785. 507-238-3213; Fax 507-238-3259.

Will search UCC records. Tax liens not included in UCC search. RE owner, mortgage, and property transfer searches available. Legal description required **Other Phone Numbers:** Assessor 507-238-3210; Treasurer 507-238-3211.

McLeod County

County Recorder, P.O. Box 127, Glencoe, MN 55336. 320-864-5551; Fax 320-864-1295.

Will search UCC records. Tax liens not included in UCC search. RE owner, mortgage, and property transfer searches available. **Other Phone Numbers:** Assessor 320-864-1254; Treasurer 320-864-1203; Vital Records 320-864-1234.

Meeker County

County Recorder, 325 North Sibley Avenue, Courthouse, Litchfield, MN 55355. 320-693-5440 R/E Recording: 320-693-6112; Fax 320-693-5444.

Will search UCC records. Tax liens not included in UCC search. RE owner, mortgage, and property transfer searches available. **Other Phone Numbers:** Assessor 320-693-5205; Treasurer 320-693-5345; Elections 320-693-5212; Vital Records 320-693-5345.

Mille Lacs County

County Recorder, 635 2nd Street S.E., Milaca, MN 56353. 320-983-8309 R/E Recording: 320-983-3146 UCC Recording: 320-983-8326; Fax 320-983-8388.

Will search UCC records with written UCCII request. Tax liens not included in UCC search. Will not search real estate records. **Other Phone Numbers:** Assessor 320-983-8311; Treasurer 320-983-8310; Appraiser/Auditor 320-983-8281; Elections 320-983-8301; Vital Records 320-983-8236.

Morrison County

County Recorder, Administration Building, 213 SE 1st Ave., Little Falls, MN 56345. 320-632-0145 R/E Recording: 320-632-2941 UCC Recording: 320-632-0142; Fax 320-632-0141. http://www.co.morrison.mn.us/wsite/index.htm

Will search UCC records. Tax liens not included in UCC search. RE owner, mortgage, and property transfer searches available. Charge only for lengthy searches **Other Phone Numbers:** Assessor 320-632-0100; Treasurer 320-632-0151; Appraiser/Auditor 320-632-0101; Elections 320-632-0132; Vital Records 320-632-0146.

Mower County

County Recorder, 201 First Street NE, Austin, MN 55912-3475. 507-437-9446 R/E Recording: 507-437-9535; Fax 507-437-9471.

Payments must be paid in advance or an account set up with a security deposit for copies mailed or faxed. Will search UCC records. This agency will do a tax lien search, fee is $15.00 per name. Will not search real estate records. **Other Phone Numbers:** Assessor 507-437-9440; Treasurer 507-437-9456; Appraiser/Auditor 507-437-9440; Elections 507-437-9536; Vital Records 507-437-9456; Information 507-437-9493.

Murray County

County Recorder, P.O. Box 57, Slayton, MN 56172-0057. 507-836-6148 x144 R/E Recording: 507-836-6163; Fax 507-836-8904.

Will search UCC records. Tax liens not included in UCC search. RE owner, mortgage, and property transfer searches available. **Other Phone Numbers:** Assessor 507-836-6148 x151; Treasurer 507-836-6148 x149.

Nicollet County

County Recorder, P.O. Box 493, St. Peter, MN 56082-0493. County Recorder, R/E and UCC Recording 507-931-6800; Fax 507-931-9220.

Will search UCC records. Tax liens not included in UCC search. Will search real estate records, but only tract information for one year. **Other Phone Numbers:** Assessor 507-931-6800; Treasurer 507-931-6800; Elections 507-931-6800.

Nobles County

County Recorder, P.O. Box 757, Worthington, MN 56187. 507-372-8236; Fax 507-372-8223.

Will search UCC records. Tax liens not included in UCC search. Will not search real estate records. **Other Phone Numbers:** Assessor 507-372-8234; Treasurer 507-372-8231.

Norman County

County Recorder, P.O. Box 146, Ada, MN 56510. 218-784-5481 R/E Recording: 218-784-4422; Fax 218-784-2399.

Will search UCC records. UCC search includes tax liens if requested. RE owner, mortgage, and property transfer searches available. **Other Phone Numbers:** Assessor 218-784-5487; Treasurer 218-784-5473; Elections 218-784-5471; Vital Records 218-784-5481.

Olmsted County

Property Records & Licensing, 151 4th St. SE, Rochester, MN 55904. 507-285-8194 R/E Recording: 507-285-8195 UCC Recording: 507-285-8204; Fax 507-287-7186. www.olmstedcounty.com

Will search UCC records. RE owner, mortgage, and property transfer searches available. **Other Phone Numbers:** Assessor 507-285-8124; Treasurer 507-285-8197; Elections 507-287-2118; Vital Records 507-287-1444.

Otter Tail County

County Recorder, P.O. Box 867, Fergus Falls, MN 56538. 218-739-2271.

Will search UCC records. Tax liens not included in UCC search. RE owner, mortgage, and property transfer searches available.

Pennington County

County Recorder, P.O. Box 616, Thief River Falls, MN 56701. 218-683-7027 R/E Recording: 218-681-2522; Fax 218-683-7026.

Will search UCC records. Tax liens not included in UCC search. Will give recent RE documents related to a property location. **Other Phone Numbers:** Assessor 218-681-3843; Treasurer 218-681-4044.

Pine County

County Recorder, Courthouse, 315 Sixth St., Suite 3, Pine City, MN 55063. 320-629-5665 R/E Recording: 320-629-6781; Fax 320-629-7319.

Will search UCC records. Tax liens not included in UCC search. Will not search real estate records. **Other Phone Numbers:** Assessor 320-629-6781 x150; Treasurer 320-629-6781 x138.

Pipestone County

County Recorder, 416 S. Hiawatha Ave., Pipestone, MN 56164. 507-825-6755 R/E Recording: 507-825-4494; Fax 507-825-6741.

Will search UCC records. Tax liens not included in UCC search. Will not search real estate records. **Other Phone Numbers:** Assessor 507-823-3446; Treasurer 507-825-4588.

Polk County

County Recorder, P.O. Box 397, Crookston, MN 56716. 218-281-3464; Fax 218-281-2204.

Will search UCC records. Tax liens not included in UCC search. Will not search real estate records. **Other Phone Numbers:** Assessor 218-281-4186.

Pope County

County Recorder, 130 East Minnesota, Glenwood, MN 56334. 320-634-5723; Fax 320-634-3087.

Will search UCC records. Tax liens not included in UCC search. RE owner, mortgage, and property transfer searches available. **Other Phone Numbers:** Assessor 320-634-5728.

Ramsey County

County Recorder, 50 West Kellogg Blvd., Suite 812 RCGC-W, St. Paul, MN 55102-1693. 651-266-2060 R/E Recording: 612-266-2060.

Will search UCC records. Tax liens not included in UCC search. Will give owner for a property location. **Other Phone Numbers:** Assessor 612-266-2000.

Red Lake County

County Recorder, Box 3, Red Lake Falls, MN 56750-0003. County Recorder, R/E and UCC Recording 218-253-2997; Fax 218-253-4894.

Will search UCC records. Tax liens not included in UCC search. RE owner, mortgage, and property transfer searches available. **Other Phone Numbers:** Assessor 218-253-2596; Treasurer 218-253-2797; Vital Records 218-253-2997.

Redwood County

County Recorder, P.O. Box 130, Redwood Falls, MN 56283. 507-637-4032 R/E Recording: 507-637-8325; Fax 507-637-4064.

Will search UCC records. UCC search includes tax liens if requested. Will not search real estate records. **Other Phone Numbers:** Assessor 507-637-5345.

Renville County

County Recorder, Olivia, MN 56277-1396. County Recorder, R/E and UCC Recording 320-523-3669; Fax 320-523-3679.

http://www.co.renville.mn.us/html/offices.html

Will search UCC records. Tax liens not included in UCC search. Will not search real estate records. **Other**

Phone Numbers: Assessor 320-523-3645; Treasurer 320-523-3676; Appraiser/Auditor 320-523-3645; Elections 320-523-2071; Vital Records 320-523-3669.

Rice County

County Recorder, 320 NW 3rd St., Suite 10, Faribault, MN 55021-6146. 507-332-6114 R/E Recording: 507-332-6100; Fax 507-332-5999.

Will search UCC records. UCC search includes tax liens if requested. RE owner, mortgage, and property transfer searches available. **Other Phone Numbers:** Assessor 507-332-6102; Treasurer 507-332-6104; Appraiser/Auditor 507-332-6102; Elections 507-332-6104; Vital Records 507-332-6114.

Rock County

County Recorder, P.O. Box 509, Luverne, MN 56156. 507-283-5014 R/E Recording: 507-283-9177; Fax 507-283-1343.

Will search UCC records. UCC search includes tax liens if requested. RE record owner and mortgage searches available. **Other Phone Numbers:** Assessor 507-283-5022; Treasurer 507-283-5055; Elections 507-283-5060; Vital Records 507-283-5060.

Roseau County

County Recorder, 606 5th Ave. SW, Room 170, Roseau, MN 56751-1477. County Recorder, R/E and UCC Recording 218-463-2061.

Will search UCC records. Tax liens not included in UCC search. Will not search real estate records. **Other Phone Numbers:** Assessor 218-463-1861; Treasurer 218-463-1215; Elections 218-463-1282; Vital Records 218-463-1215.

Scott County

County Recorder, 200 Fourth Avenue W., Shakopee, MN 55379. County Recorder, R/E and UCC Recording 952-496-8150; Fax 952-496-8138. http://www.co.scott.mn.us/

Will search UCC records. Tax liens not included in UCC search. Will not search real estate records. **Other Phone Numbers:** Assessor 952-496-8150; Treasurer 952-496-8150; Appraiser/Auditor 952-496-8150; Elections 952-496-8161; Vital Records 952-496-8150.

Sherburne County

County Recorder, 13880 Highway 10, Elk River, MN 55330. 763-241-2915 R/E Recording: 800-719-2826 UCC Recording: 800-719-2826; Fax 763-241-2995. www.co.sherburne.mn.us

Will search UCC records. UCC search includes tax liens if requested. RE owner, mortgage, and property transfer searches available. **Online Access:** Real Estate, Tax Assessor Records. Records from the county tax assessor database are available free online at www.hometimes.com/Communities/Taxes/TaxSearch/Shurburne/index.html. **Other Phone Numbers:** Assessor 800-438-0577; Treasurer 800-438-0575; Vital Records 800-719-2826.

Sibley County

County Recorder, P.O. Box 44, Gaylord, MN 55334-0044. 507-237-4080 R/E Recording: 507-237-2369; Fax 507-237-4062. http://co.sibley.mn.us

Will search UCC records. UCC search includes tax liens if requested. RE record owner searches available. **Other Phone Numbers:** Assessor 507-237-5541; Treasurer 507-237-2820; Elections 507-237-4070; Vital Records 507-237-4080.

St. Louis County

County Recorder, P.O. Box 157, Duluth, MN 55801-0157. County Recorder, R/E and UCC Recording 218-726-2677; Fax 218-725-5052.

Will search UCC records. Tax liens not included in UCC search. Will not search real estate records. **Online Access:** Real Estate, Property Tax. Online access to the Auditor and Recorder's tax records for tax professionals database is available by subscription. Fee is $100 quarterly; password provided. For information or sign-up, contact Pam Palen at 218-726-2380 or email to palenp@co.st-louis.mn.us or visit www.co.st-louis.mn.us/auditorsoffice/subscription.pdf. **Other Phone Numbers:** Assessor 218-726-2304; Treasurer 218-726-2380; Appraiser/Auditor 218-726-2304; Elections 218-726-2304; Vital Records 218-726-2559; Torrens Division 218-726-2680.

Stearns County

County Recorder, 705 Courthouse Square, Administration Center, Room 131, St. Cloud, MN 56303. 320-656-3855 R/E Recording: 320-259-3855; Fax 320-656-3916.

Will search UCC records. Tax liens not included in UCC search. Will not search real estate records. **Online Access:** Real Estate, Tax Assessor Records. Records from the county tax assessor database are available free online at www.hometimes.com/Communities/Taxes/TaxSearch/index.html. **Other Phone Numbers:** Assessor 320-656-3680; Treasurer 320-656-3870.

Steele County

County Recorder, P.O. Box 890, Owatonna, MN 55060. County Recorder, R/E and UCC Recording 507-444-7450; Fax 507-444-7470.

Will search UCC records. Tax liens not included in UCC search. Will not search real estate records. **Other Phone Numbers:** Assessor 507-444-7435; Treasurer 507-444-7420; Elections 507-444-7410; Vital Records 507-444-7490.

Stevens County

County Recorder, P.O. Box 530, Morris, MN 56267. 320-589-7414; Fax 320-589-2036.

Will search UCC records. Tax liens not included in UCC search. RE owner, mortgage, and property transfer searches available. **Other Phone Numbers:** Assessor 320-589-7407; Treasurer 320-589-7418.

Swift County

County Recorder, P.O. Box 246, Benson, MN 56215. 320-843-3377 R/E Recording: 612-843-3377; Fax 320-843-2275.

Will search UCC records. Tax liens not included in UCC search. Will not search real estate records. **Other Phone Numbers:** Assessor 320-842-5891.

Todd County

County Recorder, 221 First Avenue South, Suite 300, Long Prairie, MN 56347-1391. County Recorder, R/E and UCC Recording 320-732-4428; Fax 320-732-4001. http://www.co.todd.mn.us/contacts.htm

Will search UCC records. Tax liens not included in UCC search. Will not search real estate records. **Other Phone Numbers:** Assessor 320-732-4430; Treasurer 320-732-4471; Vital Records 320-732-4428.

Traverse County

County Recorder, P.O. Box 487, Wheaton, MN 56296-0487. 320-563-4622 R/E Recording: 320-563-4242; Fax 320-563-4424.

Will search UCC records. Tax liens not included in UCC search. RE owner, mortgage, and property transfer searches available. Searcher performed by phone are free, but are uncertified **Other Phone Numbers:** Assessor 320-563-4113; Treasurer 320-563-4616.

Wabasha County

County Recorder, 625 Jefferson Avenue, Wabasha, MN 55981. 651-565-3623 R/E Recording: 612-565-3623; Fax 651-565-2774.

Will search UCC records. UCC search includes tax liens if requested. RE record owner and mortgage searches available. **Other Phone Numbers:** Assessor 651-565-3669; Treasurer 651-565-3669.

Wadena County

County Recorder, P.O. Box 415, Wadena, MN 56482. 218-631-7622 R/E Recording: 218-631-2425; Fax 218-631-5709. http://www.co.wadena.mn.us/record.htm

Will search UCC records. Tax liens not included in UCC search. Will not search real estate records. **Other Phone Numbers:** Assessor 218-631-7628; Treasurer 218-631-7621; Appraiser/Auditor 218-631-7628; Elections 218-631-7650; Vital Records 218-631-7788; Auditor 218-631-7785.

Waseca County

County Recorder, 307 North State Street, Waseca, MN 56093. 507-835-0670 R/E Recording: 5-7-835-0670; Fax 507-835-0633.

Will search UCC records. Tax liens not included in UCC search. Will not search real estate records. **Other Phone Numbers:** Assessor 507-835-0640.

Washington County

County Recorder, 14900 North 61st Street, P.O. Box 6, Stillwater, MN 55082. 651-430-6755; Fax 651-430-6753. http://www.co.washington.mn.us

Will search UCC records. Tax liens not included in UCC search. RE owner, mortgage, and property transfer searches available. **Online Access:** Real Estate, Liens, Tax Assessor. Access to county online records requires a $250 set up fee; no fees apply to Recorder office information. Records date back 3 years. Lending agency information is available, but UCC information is on a separate system. For information, contact Larry Haseman at 651-430-6423. Also, online access to property tax records is available free at https://washington.mn.ezgov.com/ezproperty/review_search.jsp; no name searching - property ID or address required. **Other Phone Numbers:** Assessor 651-430-6090; Treasurer 651-430-6175.

Watonwan County

County Recorder, P.O. Box 518, St. James, MN 56081. 507-375-1216 R/E Recording: 507-375-3341.

Will search UCC records. Tax liens not included in UCC search. RE owner, mortgage, and property transfer searches available. **Other Phone Numbers:** Assessor 507-375-1205; Treasurer 507-375-1213.

Wilkin County

County Recorder, P.O. Box 29, Breckenridge, MN 56520. 218-643-7164 R/E Recording: 218-643-4012; Fax 218-643-7170. http://www.co.wilkin.mn.us/recorder.asp

Will search UCC records. Tax liens not included in UCC search. RE owner, mortgage, and property transfer searches available. **Other Phone Numbers:** Assessor 218-643-7162; Treasurer 218-643-7112; Vital Records 218-643-7164.

Winona County

County Recorder, 171 West 3rd Street, Winona, MN 55987-3102. 507-457-6340; Fax 507-457-6469.

Will search UCC records. Tax liens not included in UCC search. RE owner, mortgage, and property transfer searches available. **Other Phone Numbers:** Assessor 507-457-6300; Treasurer 507-457-6450.

Wright County

County Recorder, 10 2nd Street NW, Room 210, Buffalo, MN 55313-1196. 763-682-7357 R/E Recording: 763-682-3900 UCC Recording: 763-682-7360; Fax 763-684-4558. www.co.wright.mn.us

Will search UCC records. Tax liens not included in UCC search. RE owner, mortgage, and property transfer searches available. **Other Phone Numbers:** Assessor 763-682-7368; Treasurer 763-682-7573.

Yellow Medicine County

County Recorder, 415 9th Avenue, Courthouse, Granite Falls, MN 56241. 320-564-2529 R/E Recording: 320-564-3132; Fax 320-564-3670.

Will search UCC records. Tax liens not included in UCC search. Will not search real estate records. **Other Phone Numbers:** Assessor 320-564-3678; Treasurer 320-564-3231.

Minnesota County Locator

You will usually be able to find the city name in the City/County Cross Reference below. In that case, it is a simple matter to determine the county from the cross reference. However, only the official US Postal Service city names are included in this index. There are an additional 40,000 place names that people use in their addresses. Therefore, we have also included a ZIP/City Cross Reference immediately following the City/County Cross Reference.

If you know the ZIP Code but the city name does not appear in the City/County Cross Reference index, look up the ZIP Code in the ZIP/City Cross Reference, find the city name, then look up the city name in the City/County Cross Reference. For example, you want to know the county for an address of Menands, NY 12204. There is no "Menands" in the City/County Cross Reference. The ZIP/City Cross Reference shows that ZIP Codes 12201-12288 are for the city of Albany. Looking back in the City/County Cross Reference, Albany is in Albany County.

City/County Cross Reference

ADA Norman
ADAMS Mower
ADOLPH St. Louis
ADRIAN Nobles
AFTON Washington
AH GWAH CHING Cass
AITKIN (56431) Aitkin(96), Crow Wing(4)
AKELEY (56433) Hubbard(51), Cass(49)
ALBANY (56307) Stearns(99), Morrison(2)
ALBERT LEA Freeborn
ALBERTA (56207) Stevens(96), Swift(4)
ALBERTVILLE Wright
ALBORN St. Louis
ALDEN (56009) Freeborn(98), Faribault(2)
ALDRICH Wadena
ALEXANDRIA Douglas
ALMELUND Chisago
ALPHA Jackson
ALTURA (55910) Winona(82), Wabasha(18)
ALVARADO (56710) Marshall(86), Polk(14)
AMBOY (56010) Blue Earth(96), Faribault(3), Martin(1)
AMIRET Lyon
ANGLE INLET Lake of the Woods
ANGORA St. Louis
ANGUS Polk
ANNANDALE Wright
ANOKA Anoka
APPLETON (56208) Swift(95), Lac qui Parle(3), Big Stone(1)
ARCO Lincoln
ARGYLE Marshall
ARLINGTON Sibley
ASHBY (56309) Grant(61), Otter Tail(30), Douglas(9)
ASKOV Pine
ATWATER (56209) Kandiyohi(83), Meeker(17)
AUDUBON Becker
AURORA St. Louis
AUSTIN (55912) Mower(98), Freeborn(2)
AVOCA Murray
AVON Stearns
BABBITT St. Louis
BACKUS (56435) Cass(97), Crow Wing(2)
BADGER Roseau
BAGLEY (56621) Clearwater(98), Polk(2)
BAKER Clay
BALATON (56115) Murray(53), Lyon(47)
BANGOR Pope
BARNESVILLE (56514) Clay(89), Wilkin(10)
BARNUM Carlton
BARRETT Grant
BARRY Big Stone
BATTLE LAKE Otter Tail
BAUDETTE (56623) Lake of the Woods(61), Koochiching(39)
BAXTER Crow Wing
BAYPORT Washington
BEARDSLEY (56211) Big Stone(66), Traverse(35)

BEAVER BAY Lake
BEAVER CREEK Rock
BECIDA Hubbard
BECKER Sherburne
BEJOU (56516) Mahnomen(74), Norman(26)
BELGRADE (56312) Stearns(67), Kandiyohi(33)
BELLE PLAINE (56011) Scott(89), Sibley(5), Carver(3), Le Sueur(3)
BELLINGHAM Lac qui Parle
BELTRAMI (56517) Polk(97), Norman(3)
BELVIEW (56214) Redwood(93), Yellow Medicine(7)
BEMIDJI (56601) Beltrami(98), Hubbard(2)
BEMIDJI Beltrami
BENA Cass
BENEDICT Hubbard
BENSON (56215) Swift(97), Pope(3)
BEROUN Pine
BERTHA (56437) Todd(90), Otter Tail(10)
BETHEL (55005) Anoka(96), Isanti(4)
BIG FALLS Koochiching
BIG LAKE Sherburne
BIGELOW (56117) Nobles(55), Sibley(45)
BIGFORK Itasca
BINGHAM LAKE (56118) Cottonwood(93), Jackson(8)
BIRCHDALE Koochiching
BIRD ISLAND Renville
BIWABIK St. Louis
BLACKDUCK (56630) Beltrami(84), Itasca(16)
BLOMKEST Kandiyohi
BLOOMING PRAIRIE (55917) Steele(83), Dodge(12), Mower(4)
BLUE EARTH (56013) Faribault(99), Martin(1)
BLUFFTON Otter Tail
BOCK Mille Lacs
BORUP (56519) Norman(63), Clay(38)
BOVEY Itasca
BOWLUS (56314) Morrison(97), Stearns(4)
BOWSTRING Itasca
BOY RIVER Cass
BOYD (56218) Lac qui Parle(59), Yellow Medicine(41)
BRAHAM (55006) Isanti(43), Kanabec(39), Pine(13), Chisago(6)
BRAINERD (56401) Crow Wing(96), Cass(4)
BRANDON (56315) Douglas(92), Otter Tail(8)
BRECKENRIDGE Wilkin
BREWSTER (56119) Nobles(67), Jackson(33)
BRICELYN Faribault
BRIMSON (55602) St. Louis(88), Lake(12)
BRITT St. Louis
BROOK PARK (55007) Pine(69), Kanabec(31)
BROOKS (56715) Red Lake(96), Polk(4)
BROOKSTON St. Louis

BROOTEN (56316) Pope(48), Stearns(39), Kandiyohi(12)
BROWERVILLE Todd
BROWNS VALLEY (56219) Traverse(62), Olmsted(37), Big Stone(1)
BROWNSDALE Mower
BROWNSVILLE Houston
BROWNTON McLeod
BRUNO Pine
BUCKMAN Morrison
BUFFALO Wright
BUFFALO LAKE (55314) Renville(85), Sibley(15)
BUHL St. Louis
BURNSVILLE Dakota
BURTRUM (56318) Todd(51), Morrison(49)
BUTTERFIELD Watonwan
BYRON Olmsted
CALEDONIA Houston
CALLAWAY Becker
CALUMET Itasca
CAMBRIDGE Isanti
CAMPBELL (56522) Wilkin(85), Otter Tail(12), Grant(3)
CANBY (56220) Yellow Medicine(85), Lac qui Parle(9), Lincoln(6)
CANNON FALLS (55009) Goodhue(92), Dakota(8)
CANTON Fillmore
CANYON St. Louis
CARLOS (56319) Douglas(87), Todd(13)
CARLTON Carlton
CARVER Carver
CASS LAKE (56633) Cass(72), Hubbard(14), Beltrami(14)
CASTLE ROCK Dakota
CEDAR Anoka
CENTER CITY Chisago
CEYLON Martin
CHAMPLIN Hennepin
CHANDLER (56122) Murray(97), Nobles(3)
CHANHASSEN Carver
CHASKA Carver
CHATFIELD (55923) Fillmore(52), Olmsted(48)
CHISAGO CITY Chisago
CHISHOLM St. Louis
CHOKIO (56221) Stevens(90), Big Stone(8), Traverse(2)
CIRCLE PINES Anoka
CLARA CITY Chippewa
CLAREMONT (55924) Dodge(57), Steele(43)
CLARISSA Todd
CLARKFIELD Yellow Medicine
CLARKS GROVE Freeborn
CLEAR LAKE Sherburne
CLEARBROOK (56634) Clearwater(55), Polk(45)
CLEARWATER (55320) Wright(83), Stearns(17)
CLEMENTS Redwood
CLEVELAND Le Sueur

CLIMAX Polk
CLINTON Big Stone
CLITHERALL Otter Tail
CLONTARF (56226) Swift(65), Pope(36)
CLOQUET (55720) Carlton(92), St. Louis(8)
COHASSET Itasca
COKATO Wright
COLD SPRING Stearns
COLERAINE Itasca
COLLEGEVILLE Stearns
COLOGNE Carver
COMFREY (56019) Brown(73), Cottonwood(25), Watonwan(3)
COMSTOCK Clay
CONGER Freeborn
COOK (55723) St. Louis(95), Itasca(5)
COOK (55788) Itasca(78), St. Louis(22)
CORRELL Big Stone
COSMOS (56228) Meeker(98), Renville(3)
COTTAGE GROVE Washington
COTTON St. Louis
COTTONWOOD (56229) Lyon(87), Yellow Medicine(14)
COURTLAND Nicollet
CRANE LAKE St. Louis
CROMWELL Carlton
CROOKSTON Polk
CROSBY Crow Wing
CROSSLAKE Crow Wing
CRYSTAL BAY Hennepin
CULVER St. Louis
CURRIE Murray
CUSHING (56443) Morrison(93), Todd(7)
CYRUS (56323) Pope(91), Stevens(9)
DAKOTA Winona
DALBO Isanti
DALTON (56324) Otter Tail(97), Grant(3)
DANUBE Renville
DANVERS Swift
DARFUR Watonwan
DARWIN Meeker
DASSEL (55325) Meeker(96), Wright(4)
DAWSON Lac qui Parle
DAYTON Hennepin
DE GRAFF (56233) Swift(82), Chippewa(18)
DEBS Beltrami
DEER CREEK Otter Tail
DEER RIVER (56636) Itasca(94), Cass(6)
DEERWOOD Crow Wing
DELANO (55328) Wright(89), Hennepin(6), Carver(5)
DELAVAN Faribault
DELFT Cottonwood
DENHAM Pine
DENHAM St. Louis
DENNISON (55018) Goodhue(87), Rice(12), Dakota(1)
DENT Otter Tail
DETROIT LAKES (56501) Becker(97), Otter Tail(3)
DETROIT LAKES Becker

DEXTER Mower
DILWORTH Clay
DODGE CENTER Dodge
DONALDSON Kittson
DONNELLY Stevens
DOVER Olmsted
DOVRAY Murray
DULUTH (55810) St. Louis(98), Carlton(2)
DULUTH St. Louis
DUMONT (56236) Traverse(54), Big Stone(46)
DUNDAS Rice
DUNDEE (56126) Nobles(65), Cottonwood(19), Murray(12), Jackson(4)
DUNNELL (56127) Martin(83), Jackson(17)
DUQUETTE Pine
EAGLE BEND (56446) Todd(86), Douglas(8), Otter Tail(6)
EAGLE LAKE Blue Earth
EAST GRAND FORKS Polk
EASTON Faribault
ECHO Yellow Medicine
EDEN PRAIRIE Hennepin
EDEN VALLEY (55329) Stearns(64), Meeker(36)
EDGERTON (56128) Pipestone(78), Rock(9), Nobles(7), Murray(6)
EFFIE (56639) Itasca(83), Koochiching(17)
EITZEN Houston
ELBOW LAKE Grant
ELGIN (55932) Olmsted(50), Wabasha(50)
ELIZABETH Otter Tail
ELK RIVER (55330) Sherburne(75), Wright(19), Anoka(6)
ELKO (55020) Scott(99), Rice(1)
ELKTON Mower
ELLENDALE (56026) Steele(69), Freeborn(18), Olmsted(12), Waseca(1)
ELLSWORTH (56129) Nobles(75), Rock(14), Lyon(11)
ELMORE (56027) Faribault(67), Olmsted(31), Martin(2)
ELROSA Stearns
ELY (55731) St. Louis(95), Lake(5)
ELYSIAN (56028) Le Sueur(84), Waseca(16)
EMBARRASS St. Louis
EMILY Crow Wing
EMMONS Freeborn
ERHARD Otter Tail
ERSKINE (56535) Polk(96), Red Lake(4)
ESKO (55733) Carlton(97), St. Louis(3)
ESSIG Brown
EUCLID Polk
EVAN (56238) Redwood(75), Brown(25)
EVANSVILLE (56326) Douglas(90), Otter Tail(8), Grant(2)
EVELETH St. Louis
EXCELSIOR (55331) Hennepin(77), Carver(23)
EYOTA Olmsted
FAIRFAX (55332) Renville(87), Nicollet(13)
FAIRMONT Martin
FARIBAULT Rice
FARMINGTON Dakota
FARWELL (56327) Douglas(58), Pope(42)
FEDERAL DAM Cass
FELTON Clay
FERGUS FALLS Otter Tail
FERTILE (56540) Polk(91), Norman(9)
FIFTY LAKES Crow Wing
FINLAND Lake
FINLAYSON (55735) Pine(79), Aitkin(21)
FISHER Polk
FLENSBURG Morrison
FLOM Norman
FLOODWOOD St. Louis
FOLEY (56329) Benton(89), Morrison(11)
FORBES St. Louis
FOREST LAKE (55025) Washington(81), Anoka(13), Chisago(6)

FORESTON (56330) Mille Lacs(85), Benton(15)
FORT RIPLEY (56449) Crow Wing(82), Morrison(18)
FOSSTON (56542) Polk(94), Mahnomen(6)
FOUNTAIN Fillmore
FOXHOME Wilkin
FRANKLIN (55333) Renville(92), Redwood(7), Brown(1)
FRAZEE (56544) Becker(85), Otter Tail(15)
FREEBORN Freeborn
FREEPORT (56331) Stearns(95), Morrison(4), Todd(1)
FRONTENAC Goodhue
FROST Faribault
FULDA (56131) Murray(96), Nobles(4)
GARDEN CITY Blue Earth
GARFIELD Douglas
GARRISON (56450) Mille Lacs(67), Crow Wing(34)
GARVIN (56132) Lyon(73), Murray(27)
GARY Norman
GATZKE Marshall
GAYLORD (55334) Sibley(94), Nicollet(6)
GENEVA Freeborn
GEORGETOWN Clay
GHENT Lyon
GIBBON (55335) Sibley(85), Nicollet(15)
GILBERT St. Louis
GILMAN Benton
GLENCOE (55336) McLeod(96), Sibley(4)
GLENVILLE Freeborn
GLENWOOD (56334) Pope(98), Douglas(2)
GLYNDON Clay
GONVICK (56644) Clearwater(96), Polk(4)
GOOD THUNDER Blue Earth
GOODHUE (55027) Goodhue(98), Wabasha(2)
GOODLAND Itasca
GOODRIDGE (56725) Pennington(74), Marshall(26)
GRACEVILLE (56240) Big Stone(80), Traverse(20)
GRANADA (56039) Martin(95), Faribault(5)
GRAND MARAIS Cook
GRAND MEADOW Mower
GRAND PORTAGE (55605) Cook(71), Lyon(29)
GRAND RAPIDS Itasca
GRANDY Isanti
GRANGER Fillmore
GRANITE FALLS (56241) Yellow Medicine(80), Chippewa(17), Renville(3)
GRASSTON (55030) Pine(89), Kanabec(11)
GREEN ISLE (55338) Sibley(86), Carver(14)
GREENBUSH Roseau
GREENWALD Stearns
GREY EAGLE (56336) Todd(96), Stearns(3), Morrison(2)
GROVE CITY Meeker
GRYGLA (56727) Beltrami(58), Marshall(42)
GULLY (56646) Polk(89), Clearwater(11)
HACKENSACK Cass
HADLEY Murray
HALLOCK Kittson
HALMA Kittson
HALSTAD Norman
HAMBURG (55339) Carver(79), Sibley(21)
HAMEL Hennepin
HAMMOND Wabasha
HAMPTON Dakota
HANCOCK (56244) Stevens(67), Pope(28), Swift(5)
HANLEY FALLS Yellow Medicine
HANOVER (55341) Wright(98), Hennepin(2)
HANSKA (56041) Brown(94), Watonwan(3), Blue Earth(3)

HARDWICK Rock
HARMONY Fillmore
HARRIS (55032) Chisago(99), Isanti(1)
HARTLAND (56042) Freeborn(85), Waseca(12), Steele(3)
HASTINGS (55033) Dakota(93), Washington(7)
HAWICK Kandiyohi
HAWLEY Clay
HAYFIELD (55940) Dodge(80), Olmsted(18), Mower(1)
HAYWARD Freeborn
HAZEL RUN Yellow Medicine
HECTOR (55342) Renville(92), Sibley(5), Kandiyohi(2), Meeker(1)
HENDERSON (56044) Sibley(94), Scott(7)
HENDRICKS (56136) Lincoln(70), Dodge(30)
HENDRUM Norman
HENNING Otter Tail
HENRIETTE Pine
HERMAN (56248) Grant(81), Stevens(11), Traverse(7)
HERON LAKE (56137) Jackson(46), Nobles(33), Cottonwood(21)
HEWITT (56453) Todd(71), Otter Tail(29)
HIBBING (55746) St. Louis(96), Itasca(4)
HIBBING St. Louis
HILL CITY (55748) Aitkin(86), Itasca(14)
HILLMAN (56338) Morrison(95), Crow Wing(5)
HILLS (56138) Rock(95), Lyon(4), Mower(1)
HINCKLEY (55037) Pine(95), Kanabec(5)
HINES Beltrami
HITTERDAL (56552) Clay(81), Becker(19)
HOFFMAN (56339) Grant(80), Douglas(20)
HOKAH Houston
HOLDINGFORD (56340) Stearns(82), Morrison(18)
HOLLAND Pipestone
HOLLANDALE Freeborn
HOLLOWAY Swift
HOLMES CITY Douglas
HOLYOKE (55749) Carlton(98), Pine(2)
HOMER (55942) Winona(86), Olmsted(14)
HOPE Steele
HOPKINS Hennepin
HOUSTON (55943) Houston(84), Winona(15)
HOVLAND Cook
HOWARD LAKE Hennepin
HOWARD LAKE Wright
HOYT LAKES St. Louis
HUGO (55038) Washington(64), Anoka(36)
HUMBOLDT Kittson
HUNTLEY Faribault
HUTCHINSON (55350) McLeod(96), Meeker(4)
IHLEN Pipestone
INTERNATIONAL FALLS Koochiching
INVER GROVE HEIGHTS Dakota
IONA Murray
IRON St. Louis
IRONTON Crow Wing
ISABELLA Lake
ISANTI Isanti
ISLE (56342) Mille Lacs(59), Aitkin(21), Kanabec(20)
IVANHOE Lincoln
JACKSON Jackson
JACOBSON (55752) Aitkin(90), Itasca(10)
JANESVILLE Waseca
JASPER (56144) Rock(48), Pipestone(40), Murray(10), Mower(2)
JEFFERS Cottonwood
JENKINS Crow Wing
JOHNSON (56250) Big Stone(71), Traverse(29)
JORDAN Scott
KANARANZI (56146) Nobles(95), Rock(5)
KANDIYOHI Kandiyohi

KARLSTAD (56732) Kittson(91), Marshall(6), Roseau(3)
KASOTA Le Sueur
KASSON (55944) Dodge(96), Olmsted(4)
KEEWATIN Itasca
KELLIHER Beltrami
KELLOGG Wabasha
KELSEY St. Louis
KENNEDY Kittson
KENNETH (56147) Rock(93), Nobles(7)
KENSINGTON (56343) Douglas(80), Pope(16), Stevens(4)
KENT Wilkin
KENYON (55946) Goodhue(84), Rice(13), Steele(2), Dodge(1)
KERKHOVEN (56252) Kandiyohi(56), Swift(33), Chippewa(11)
KERRICK (55756) Pine(96), Carlton(4)
KETTLE RIVER Carlton
KIESTER (56051) Faribault(99), Freeborn(2)
KILKENNY (56052) Le Sueur(60), Rice(40)
KIMBALL (55353) Stearns(77), Meeker(23)
KINNEY St. Louis
KLOSSNER Nicollet
KNIFE RIVER Lake
LA CRESCENT (55947) Houston(90), Winona(10)
LA SALLE Watonwan
LAFAYETTE (56054) Nicollet(86), Sibley(14)
LAKE BENTON (56149) Lincoln(95), Pipestone(5)
LAKE BRONSON Kittson
LAKE CITY (55041) Wabasha(80), Goodhue(20)
LAKE CRYSTAL Blue Earth
LAKE ELMO Washington
LAKE GEORGE Hubbard
LAKE HUBERT Crow Wing
LAKE ITASCA Clearwater
LAKE LILLIAN Kandiyohi
LAKE PARK (56554) Becker(94), Clay(6)
LAKE WILSON Murray
LAKEFIELD Jackson
LAKELAND Washington
LAKEVILLE (55044) Dakota(86), Scott(14)
LAMBERTON (56152) Redwood(88), Cottonwood(12)
LANCASTER (56735) Kittson(98), Roseau(3)
LANESBORO Fillmore
LANSING Mower
LAPORTE Hubbard
LASTRUP Morrison
LE CENTER Le Sueur
LE ROY (55951) Mower(64), Marshall(15), (12), Fillmore(9)
LE SUEUR (56058) Le Sueur(91), Sibley(7), Nicollet(2)
LENGBY (56651) Mahnomen(60), Polk(40)
LEONARD (56652) Clearwater(97), Beltrami(3)
LEOTA Nobles
LESTER PRAIRIE McLeod
LEWISTON Winona
LEWISVILLE (56060) Watonwan(93), Blue Earth(8)
LINDSTROM Chisago
LISMORE Nobles
LITCHFIELD Meeker
LITTLE FALLS Morrison
LITTLEFORK Koochiching
LOMAN Koochiching
LONDON Freeborn
LONG LAKE Hennepin
LONG PRAIRIE (56347) Todd(98), Morrison(2)
LONG PRAIRIE Todd
LONGVILLE Cass
LONSDALE Rice
LORETTO Hennepin

LOUISBURG Lac qui Parle
LOWRY (56349) Pope(77), Douglas(23)
LUCAN Redwood
LUTSEN Cook
LUVERNE Rock
LYLE (55953) Mower(64), Rice(32), Freeborn(4)
LYND Lyon
MABEL (55954) Fillmore(96), Houston(4)
MADELIA (56062) Watonwan(91), Blue Earth(8), Brown(2)
MADISON Lac qui Parle
MADISON LAKE (56063) Blue Earth(57), Le Sueur(29), Waseca(14)
MAGNOLIA (56158) Rock(94), Nobles(6)
MAHNOMEN (56557) Mahnomen(96), Norman(3), Clearwater(2)
MAHTOWA Carlton
MAKINEN St. Louis
MANCHESTER Freeborn
MANHATTAN BEACH Crow Wing
MANKATO Blue Earth
MANKATO Nicollet
MANTORVILLE Dodge
MAPLE LAKE Wright
MAPLE PLAIN Hennepin
MAPLE PLAIN Wright
MAPLETON (56065) Blue Earth(93), Faribault(4), Waseca(3)
MARBLE Itasca
MARCELL Itasca
MARGIE Koochiching
MARIETTA (56257) Lac qui Parle(87), Dodge(10), Grant(3)
MARINE ON SAINT CROIX Washington
MARSHALL (56258) Lyon(99), Redwood(1)
MAX Itasca
MAYER Carver
MAYNARD (56260) Chippewa(90), Renville(10)
MAZEPPA (55956) Wabasha(73), Goodhue(25), Olmsted(1)
MC GRATH Aitkin
MC KINLEY St. Louis
MCGREGOR Aitkin
MCINTOSH Polk
MEADOWLANDS St. Louis
MEDFORD (55049) Steele(92), Rice(8)
MELROSE Stearns
MELRUDE St. Louis
MENAHGA (56464) Wadena(55), Becker(28), Hubbard(15), Otter Tail(3)
MENDOTA Dakota
MENTOR (56736) Polk(87), Red Lake(13)
MERIDEN (56067) Waseca(69), Steele(31)
MERRIFIELD Crow Wing
MIDDLE RIVER Marshall
MILACA (56353) Mille Lacs(97), Isanti(3)
MILAN (56262) Chippewa(90), Swift(10)
MILLVILLE Wabasha
MILROY (56263) Redwood(89), Lyon(11)
MILTONA (56354) Douglas(99), Todd(1)
MINNEAPOLIS (55421) Anoka(87), Ramsey(11), Hennepin(1)
MINNEAPOLIS (55449) Anoka(93), Ramsey(4), Hennepin(3)
MINNEAPOLIS Anoka
MINNEAPOLIS Carver
MINNEAPOLIS Hennepin
MINNEOTA (56264) Lyon(99), Yellow Medicine(1)
MINNESOTA CITY Winona
MINNESOTA LAKE (56068) Faribault(44), Waseca(41), Blue Earth(15)
MINNETONKA Hennepin
MINNETONKA BEACH Hennepin
MIZPAH Koochiching
MONTEVIDEO (56265) Chippewa(93), Lac qui Parle(5), Yellow Medicine(2)
MONTGOMERY (56069) Le Sueur(69), Rice(31)
MONTICELLO Carver

MONTICELLO Wright
MONTROSE (55363) Wright(97), Carver(3)
MOORHEAD Clay
MOOSE LAKE (55767) Carlton(94), Pine(6)
MORA Kanabec
MORGAN (56266) Redwood(88), Brown(12)
MORRIS Stevens
MORRISTOWN (55052) Rice(91), Waseca(8), Steele(2)
MORTON (56270) Renville(61), Redwood(39)
MOTLEY (56466) Morrison(76), Cass(19), Todd(5)
MOUND Hennepin
MOUNTAIN IRON St. Louis
MOUNTAIN LAKE (56159) Cottonwood(96), Jackson(3)
MURDOCK (56271) Swift(83), Chippewa(17)
MYRTLE Freeborn
NASHUA (56565) Wilkin(82), Grant(19)
NASHWAUK Itasca
NASSAU Lac qui Parle
NAVARRE Hennepin
NAYTAHWAUSH Mahnomen
NELSON Douglas
NERSTRAND (55053) Rice(80), Goodhue(20)
NETT LAKE St. Louis
NEVIS Hubbard
NEW AUBURN Sibley
NEW GERMANY (55367) Carver(98), McLeod(2)
NEW LONDON Kandiyohi
NEW MARKET Scott
NEW MUNICH Stearns
NEW PRAGUE (56071) Scott(59), Le Sueur(38), Rice(4)
NEW RICHLAND (56072) Waseca(94), Steele(4), Freeborn(2)
NEW ULM (56073) Brown(94), Nicollet(5), Blue Earth(1)
NEW YORK MILLS Otter Tail
NEWFOLDEN Marshall
NEWPORT Washington
NICOLLET Nicollet
NIELSVILLE (56568) Polk(85), Norman(15)
NIMROD Wadena
NISSWA (56468) Crow Wing(73), Cass(27)
NORCROSS (56274) Grant(69), Traverse(32)
NORTH BRANCH (55056) Chisago(74), Isanti(26)
NORTHFIELD (55057) Rice(83), Dakota(17)
NORTHOME (56661) Koochiching(72), Itasca(22), Beltrami(6)
NORTHROP Martin
NORWOOD (55368) Carver(96), McLeod(2), Hennepin(2)
NORWOOD Carver
NOYES Kittson
OAK ISLAND Lake of the Woods
OAK PARK (56357) Benton(88), Mille Lacs(12)
OAKLAND Freeborn
ODESSA (56276) Big Stone(64), Lac qui Parle(36)
ODIN (56160) Watonwan(43), Martin(37), Jackson(20)
OGEMA Becker
OGILVIE (56358) Kanabec(81), Mille Lacs(19), Isanti(1)
OKABENA Jackson
OKLEE (56742) Red Lake(65), Pennington(33), Polk(2)
OLIVIA Renville
ONAMIA Mille Lacs
ORMSBY (56162) Martin(65), Watonwan(36)
ORONOCO Olmsted

ORR (55771) St. Louis(91), Koochiching(9)
ORTONVILLE Big Stone
OSAGE Becker
OSAKIS (56360) Douglas(54), Todd(46)
OSLO (56744) Marshall(84), Polk(16)
OSSEO Hennepin
OSTRANDER (55961) Mower(60), Fillmore(40)
OTISCO Waseca
OTTERTAIL Otter Tail
OUTING Cass
OWATONNA Steele
PALISADE Aitkin
PARK RAPIDS (56470) Hubbard(95), Becker(5)
PARKERS PRAIRIE (56361) Otter Tail(77), Douglas(23)
PARKVILLE St. Louis
PAYNESVILLE (56362) Stearns(88), Meeker(9), Kandiyohi(3)
PEASE Mille Lacs
PELICAN RAPIDS (56572) Otter Tail(97), Becker(2)
PEMBERTON (56078) Waseca(68), Blue Earth(33)
PENGILLY Itasca
PENNINGTON Beltrami
PENNOCK Kandiyohi
PEQUOT LAKES (56472) Crow Wing(85), Cass(15)
PERHAM Otter Tail
PERLEY (56574) Norman(98), Clay(2)
PETERSON (55962) Fillmore(95), Winona(6)
PIERZ (56364) Morrison(97), Crow Wing(3)
PILLAGER Cass
PINE CITY Pine
PINE ISLAND (55963) Goodhue(55), Olmsted(37), Dodge(9)
PINE RIVER (56474) Cass(81), Crow Wing(19)
PIPESTONE (56164) Pipestone(94), Murray(6)
PITT Lake of the Woods
PLAINVIEW (55964) Wabasha(96), Olmsted(2), Winona(2)
PLATO McLeod
PLUMMER (56748) Red Lake(83), Pennington(17)
PONEMAH Beltrami
PONSFORD Becker
PORTER (56280) Yellow Medicine(67), Lincoln(33)
PRESTON Fillmore
PRINCETON (55371) Mille Lacs(66), Sherburne(16), Isanti(13), Benton(5)
PRINSBURG Kandiyohi
PRIOR LAKE Scott
PUPOSKY Beltrami
RACINE (55967) Mower(98), Fillmore(2)
RANDALL Morrison
RANDOLPH (55065) Dakota(96), Goodhue(4)
RANIER Koochiching
RAY (56669) Koochiching(66), St. Louis(34)
RAYMOND (56282) Kandiyohi(80), Chippewa(20)
READING Nobles
READS LANDING Wabasha
RED LAKE FALLS (56750) Red Lake(93), Polk(4), Pennington(3)
RED WING Goodhue
REDBY Beltrami
REDLAKE Beltrami
REDWOOD FALLS (56283) Redwood(97), Renville(3)
REMER Cass
RENVILLE (56284) Renville(72), Kandiyohi(22), Redwood(6)
REVERE (56166) Redwood(74), Cottonwood(26)

RICE (56367) Benton(81), Stearns(19)
RICHMOND Stearns
RICHVILLE Otter Tail
RICHWOOD Becker
ROCHERT Becker
ROCHESTER Olmsted
ROCK CREEK Pine
ROCKFORD (55373) Wright(63), Hennepin(37)
ROCKVILLE Stearns
ROGERS (55374) Hennepin(70), Wright(30)
ROLLINGSTONE Winona
ROOSEVELT (56673) Lake of the Woods(60), Roseau(40)
ROSCOE Stearns
ROSE CREEK Mower
ROSEAU Roseau
ROSEMOUNT Dakota
ROTHSAY (56579) Wilkin(78), Otter Tail(22)
ROUND LAKE (56167) Nobles(63), Jackson(36), Sibley(1)
ROYALTON (56373) Morrison(91), Benton(10)
RUSH CITY (55069) Chisago(94), Pine(6)
RUSHFORD (55971) Fillmore(81), Winona(12), Houston(7)
RUSHMORE Nobles
RUSSELL (56169) Lyon(99), Wright(1)
RUTHTON (56170) Pipestone(65), Murray(28), Lyon(6), Lincoln(2)
RUTLEDGE Pine
SABIN Clay
SACRED HEART (56285) Renville(98), Chippewa(2)
SAGINAW St. Louis
SAINT BONIFACIUS Hennepin
SAINT CHARLES (55972) Winona(86), Olmsted(15)
SAINT CLAIR Blue Earth
SAINT CLOUD (56304) Sherburne(51), Benton(49)
SAINT CLOUD Stearns
SAINT FRANCIS (55070) Anoka(88), Isanti(12)
SAINT HILAIRE (56754) Pennington(92), Red Lake(8)
SAINT JAMES (99999) Watonwan(99), Brown(1)
SAINT JOSEPH Stearns
SAINT LEO Yellow Medicine
SAINT MARTIN Stearns
SAINT MICHAEL Wright
SAINT PAUL (55110) Ramsey(84), Washington(15), Anoka(1)
SAINT PAUL (55118) Dakota(99), Ramsey(1)
SAINT PAUL (55125) Washington(98), Dakota(2)
SAINT PAUL (55126) Ramsey(99), Anoka(1)
SAINT PAUL Dakota
SAINT PAUL Hennepin
SAINT PAUL Ramsey
SAINT PAUL Washington
SAINT PAUL PARK Washington
SAINT PETER (56082) Nicollet(96), Le Sueur(4)
SAINT STEPHEN Stearns
SAINT VINCENT Kittson
SALOL Roseau
SANBORN (56083) Redwood(78), Cottonwood(15), Brown(8)
SANDSTONE (55072) Pine(87), Kanabec(12), Aitkin(1)
SANTIAGO Sherburne
SARGEANT (55973) Mower(94), Dodge(6)
SARTELL (56377) Stearns(68), Benton(32)
SAUK CENTRE (56378) Stearns(86), Todd(14)

SAUK RAPIDS (56379) Benton(98), Stearns(2)
SAUM Beltrami
SAVAGE Scott
SAWYER Carlton
SCANDIA (55073) Washington(67), Chisago(33)
SCHROEDER Cook
SEAFORTH Redwood
SEARLES Brown
SEBEKA (56477) Wadena(73), Otter Tail(23), Cass(4)
SHAFER Chisago
SHAKOPEE Scott
SHELLY Norman
SHERBURN Martin
SHEVLIN (56676) Clearwater(52), Beltrami(48)
SIDE LAKE St. Louis
SILVER BAY Lake
SILVER CREEK Wright
SILVER LAKE (55381) McLeod(98), Martin(1)
SLAYTON Murray
SLEEPY EYE (56085) Brown(96), Redwood(4)
SOLWAY (56678) Beltrami(97), Clearwater(3)
SOUDAN St. Louis
SOUTH HAVEN (55382) Wright(53), Stearns(37), Meeker(9)
SOUTH INTERNATIONAL FALLS Koochiching
SOUTH SAINT PAUL Dakota
SPICER Kandiyohi
SPRING GROVE (55974) Houston(95), Fillmore(3), Becker(2)
SPRING LAKE Itasca
SPRING PARK Hennepin
SPRING VALLEY (55975) Fillmore(95), Mower(5)
SPRINGFIELD (56087) Brown(87), Redwood(13)
SQUAW LAKE Itasca
STACY (55079) Chisago(46), Anoka(32), Isanti(22)
STACY Washington
STANCHFIELD (55080) Isanti(64), Chisago(36)
STAPLES (56479) Todd(71), Wadena(23), Cass(6)
STARBUCK Pope
STEEN (56173) Rock(77), Lyon(23)
STEPHEN (56757) Marshall(98), Kittson(2)

STEWART (55385) McLeod(75), Renville(19), Sibley(6)
STEWARTVILLE (55976) Olmsted(98), Fillmore(1)
STILLWATER Washington
STOCKTON (55988) Winona(91), Olmsted(9)
STORDEN Cottonwood
STRANDQUIST Marshall
STRATHCONA (56759) Roseau(72), Marshall(28)
STURGEON LAKE (55783) Pine(90), Carlton(8), Aitkin(2)
SUNBURG (56289) Kandiyohi(74), Swift(24), Pope(2)
SWAN RIVER Itasca
SWANVILLE (56382) Morrison(82), Todd(18)
SWATARA Aitkin
SWIFT Roseau
TACONITE Itasca
TALMOON Itasca
TAMARACK (55787) Aitkin(53), Carlton(47)
TAOPI Mower
TAUNTON (56291) Lyon(62), Yellow Medicine(26), Lincoln(12)
TAYLORS FALLS Chisago
TENSTRIKE Beltrami
THEILMAN Wabasha
THIEF RIVER FALLS (56701) Pennington(96), Marshall(4)
TINTAH (56583) Traverse(72), Wilkin(28)
TOFTE Cook
TOWER St. Louis
TRACY (56175) Lyon(80), Redwood(12), Murray(8)
TRAIL (56684) Polk(48), Pennington(41), Red Lake(11)
TRIMONT Martin
TROSKY Pipestone
TRUMAN (56088) Martin(73), Watonwan(20), Blue Earth(8)
TWIG St. Louis
TWIN LAKES Freeborn
TWIN VALLEY (56584) Norman(99), Clay(1)
TWO HARBORS (55616) Lake(99), St. Louis(1)
TYLER (56178) Lincoln(91), Lyon(9)
ULEN (56585) Clay(75), Becker(23), Norman(2)
UNDERWOOD Otter Tail
UPSALA Morrison
UTICA (55979) Winona(96), Fillmore(4)

VERDI (56179) Lincoln(92), Pipestone(8)
VERGAS Otter Tail
VERMILLION Dakota
VERNDALE (56481) Wadena(79), Todd(18), Cass(3)
VERNON CENTER Blue Earth
VESTA (56292) Redwood(97), Yellow Medicine(3)
VICTORIA Carver
VIKING (56760) Marshall(98), Pennington(3)
VILLARD (56385) Pope(85), Stearns(8), Douglas(8)
VINING Otter Tail
VIRGINIA St. Louis
WABASHA Wabasha
WABASSO Redwood
WACONIA (55387) Carver(98), Hennepin(2)
WADENA (56482) Wadena(88), Otter Tail(12)
WAHKON Mille Lacs
WAITE PARK Stearns
WALDORF Waseca
WALKER (56484) Cass(97), Hubbard(3)
WALNUT GROVE (56180) Redwood(78), Murray(15), Cottonwood(7)
WALTERS (56092) Faribault(93), Freeborn(7)
WALTHAM (55982) Mower(98), Dodge(2)
WANAMINGO Goodhue
WANDA Redwood
WANNASKA Roseau
WARBA Itasca
WARREN (56762) Marshall(91), Polk(9)
WARROAD Roseau
WARSAW Rice
WASECA (56093) Waseca(94), Steele(5)
WASKISH Beltrami
WATERTOWN (55388) Carver(74), Wright(24), Hennepin(2)
WATERVILLE (56096) Le Sueur(88), Waseca(7), Rice(6)
WATKINS (55389) Meeker(78), Stearns(22)
WATSON Chippewa
WAUBUN (56589) Mahnomen(74), Becker(26)
WAVERLY Wright
WAWINA Itasca
WAYZATA Hennepin
WEBSTER (55088) Rice(67), Scott(32), Dakota(1)
WELCH (55089) Goodhue(92), Dakota(8)

WELCOME Martin
WELLS (56097) Faribault(94), Waseca(3), Freeborn(3)
WENDELL (56590) Grant(99), Otter Tail(2)
WEST CONCORD (55985) Dodge(88), Goodhue(8), Steele(4)
WEST UNION Todd
WESTBROOK (56183) Cottonwood(90), Murray(10)
WHALAN Fillmore
WHEATON Traverse
WHIPHOLT Cass
WHITE EARTH Becker
WILLERNIE Washington
WILLIAMS Lake of the Woods
WILLMAR Kandiyohi
WILLOW RIVER Pine
WILMONT Nobles
WILTON Beltrami
WINDOM (56101) Cottonwood(91), Jackson(9)
WINGER (56592) Polk(94), Mahnomen(6)
WINNEBAGO (56098) Faribault(94), Martin(6)
WINONA Winona
WINSTED (55395) McLeod(91), Carver(7), Wright(2)
WINTHROP (55396) Sibley(98), McLeod(1)
WINTON St. Louis
WIRT Itasca
WOLF LAKE Becker
WOLVERTON Wilkin
WOOD LAKE (56297) Yellow Medicine(92), Redwood(6), Lyon(2)
WOODSTOCK (56186) Murray(54), Pipestone(46)
WORTHINGTON (56187) Nobles(99), Jackson(1)
WRENSHALL (55797) Carlton(93), Pine(7)
WRIGHT Carlton
WYKOFF Fillmore
WYOMING (55092) Chisago(54), Anoka(46)
YOUNG AMERICA Carver
YOUNG AMERICA Hennepin
ZIM St. Louis
ZIMMERMAN (55398) Sherburne(90), Isanti(10)
ZUMBRO FALLS (55991) Wabasha(90), Olmsted(10)
ZUMBROTA Goodhue

ZIP/City Cross Reference

ZIP	City	ZIP	City	ZIP	City	ZIP	City
55001-55001	AFTON	55030-55030	GRASSTON	55060-55060	OWATONNA	55101-55146	SAINT PAUL
55002-55002	ALMELUND	55031-55031	HAMPTON	55063-55063	PINE CITY	55150-55150	MENDOTA
55003-55003	BAYPORT	55032-55032	HARRIS	55065-55065	RANDOLPH	55155-55191	SAINT PAUL
55005-55005	BETHEL	55033-55033	HASTINGS	55066-55066	RED WING	55301-55301	ALBERTVILLE
55006-55006	BRAHAM	55036-55036	HENRIETTE	55067-55067	ROCK CREEK	55302-55302	ANNANDALE
55007-55007	BROOK PARK	55037-55037	HINCKLEY	55068-55068	ROSEMOUNT	55303-55304	ANOKA
55008-55008	CAMBRIDGE	55038-55038	HUGO	55069-55069	RUSH CITY	55305-55305	HOPKINS
55009-55009	CANNON FALLS	55040-55040	ISANTI	55070-55070	SAINT FRANCIS	55306-55306	BURNSVILLE
55010-55010	CASTLE ROCK	55041-55041	LAKE CITY	55071-55071	SAINT PAUL PARK	55307-55307	ARLINGTON
55011-55011	CEDAR	55042-55042	LAKE ELMO	55072-55072	SANDSTONE	55308-55308	BECKER
55012-55012	CENTER CITY	55043-55043	LAKELAND	55073-55073	SCANDIA	55309-55309	BIG LAKE
55013-55013	CHISAGO CITY	55044-55044	LAKEVILLE	55074-55074	SHAFER	55310-55310	BIRD ISLAND
55014-55014	CIRCLE PINES	55045-55045	LINDSTROM	55075-55075	SOUTH SAINT PAUL	55311-55311	OSSEO
55016-55016	COTTAGE GROVE	55046-55046	LONSDALE	55076-55077	INVER GROVE HEIGHTS	55312-55312	BROWNTON
55017-55017	DALBO	55047-55047	MARINE ON SAINT	55078-55079	STACY	55313-55313	BUFFALO
55018-55018	DENNISON		CROIX	55080-55080	STANCHFIELD	55314-55314	BUFFALO LAKE
55019-55019	DUNDAS	55049-55049	MEDFORD	55082-55083	STILLWATER	55315-55315	CARVER
55020-55020	ELKO	55051-55051	MORA	55084-55084	TAYLORS FALLS	55316-55316	CHAMPLIN
55021-55021	FARIBAULT	55052-55052	MORRISTOWN	55085-55085	VERMILLION	55317-55317	CHANHASSEN
55024-55024	FARMINGTON	55053-55053	NERSTRAND	55087-55087	WARSAW	55318-55318	CHASKA
55025-55025	FOREST LAKE	55054-55054	NEW MARKET	55088-55088	WEBSTER	55319-55319	CLEAR LAKE
55026-55026	FRONTENAC	55055-55055	NEWPORT	55089-55089	WELCH	55320-55320	CLEARWATER
55027-55027	GOODHUE	55056-55056	NORTH BRANCH	55090-55090	WILLERNIE	55321-55321	COKATO
55029-55029	GRANDY	55057-55057	NORTHFIELD	55092-55092	WYOMING	55322-55322	COLOGNE

ZIP Range	City	ZIP Range	City	ZIP Range	City	ZIP Range	City
55323-55323	CRYSTAL BAY	55569-55569	OSSEO	55777-55777	VIRGINIA	55987-55987	WINONA
55324-55324	DARWIN	55570-55572	MAPLE PLAIN	55779-55779	SAGINAW	55988-55988	STOCKTON
55325-55325	DASSEL	55573-55573	YOUNG AMERICA	55780-55780	SAWYER	55990-55990	WYKOFF
55327-55327	DAYTON	55574-55574	MAPLE PLAIN	55781-55781	SIDE LAKE	55991-55991	ZUMBRO FALLS
55328-55328	DELANO	55575-55575	HOWARD LAKE	55782-55782	SOUDAN	55992-55992	ZUMBROTA
55329-55329	EDEN VALLEY	55576-55579	MAPLE PLAIN	55783-55783	STURGEON LAKE	56001-56006	MANKATO
55330-55330	ELK RIVER	55580-55582	MONTICELLO	55784-55784	SWAN RIVER	56007-56007	ALBERT LEA
55331-55331	EXCELSIOR	55583-55583	NORWOOD	55785-55785	SWATARA	56009-56009	ALDEN
55332-55332	FAIRFAX	55584-55591	MONTICELLO	55786-55786	TACONITE	56010-56010	AMBOY
55333-55333	FRANKLIN	55592-55593	MAPLE PLAIN	55787-55787	TAMARACK	56011-56011	BELLE PLAINE
55334-55334	GAYLORD	55594-55594	YOUNG AMERICA	55790-55790	TOWER	56013-56013	BLUE EARTH
55335-55335	GIBBON	55595-55599	LORETTO	55791-55791	TWIG	56014-56014	BRICELYN
55336-55336	GLENCOE	55601-55601	BEAVER BAY	55792-55792	VIRGINIA	56016-56016	CLARKS GROVE
55337-55337	BURNSVILLE	55602-55602	BRIMSON	55793-55793	WARBA	56017-56017	CLEVELAND
55338-55338	GREEN ISLE	55603-55603	FINLAND	55795-55795	WILLOW RIVER	56019-56019	COMFREY
55339-55339	HAMBURG	55604-55604	GRAND MARAIS	55796-55796	WINTON	56020-56020	CONGER
55340-55340	HAMEL	55605-55605	GRAND PORTAGE	55797-55797	WRENSHALL	56021-56021	COURTLAND
55341-55341	HANOVER	55606-55606	HOVLAND	55798-55798	WRIGHT	56022-56022	DARFUR
55342-55342	HECTOR	55607-55607	ISABELLA	55801-55816	DULUTH	56023-56023	DELAVAN
55343-55343	HOPKINS	55609-55609	KNIFE RIVER	55901-55906	ROCHESTER	56024-56024	EAGLE LAKE
55344-55344	EDEN PRAIRIE	55612-55612	LUTSEN	55909-55909	ADAMS	56025-56025	EASTON
55345-55345	MINNETONKA	55613-55613	SCHROEDER	55910-55910	ALTURA	56026-56026	ELLENDALE
55346-55347	EDEN PRAIRIE	55614-55614	SILVER BAY	55912-55912	AUSTIN	56027-56027	ELMORE
55348-55348	MAPLE PLAIN	55615-55615	TOFTE	55917-55917	BLOOMING PRAIRIE	56028-56028	ELYSIAN
55349-55349	HOWARD LAKE	55616-55616	TWO HARBORS	55918-55918	BROWNSDALE	56029-56029	EMMONS
55350-55350	HUTCHINSON	55701-55701	ADOLPH	55919-55919	BROWNSVILLE	56030-56030	ESSIG
55352-55352	JORDAN	55702-55702	ALBORN	55920-55920	BYRON	56031-56031	FAIRMONT
55353-55353	KIMBALL	55703-55703	ANGORA	55921-55921	CALEDONIA	56032-56032	FREEBORN
55354-55354	LESTER PRAIRIE	55704-55704	ASKOV	55922-55922	CANTON	56033-56033	FROST
55355-55355	LITCHFIELD	55705-55705	AURORA	55923-55923	CHATFIELD	56034-56034	GARDEN CITY
55356-55356	LONG LAKE	55706-55706	BABBITT	55924-55924	CLAREMONT	56035-56035	GENEVA
55357-55357	LORETTO	55707-55707	BARNUM	55925-55925	DAKOTA	56036-56036	GLENVILLE
55358-55358	MAPLE LAKE	55708-55708	BIWABIK	55926-55926	DEXTER	56037-56037	GOOD THUNDER
55359-55359	MAPLE PLAIN	55709-55709	BOVEY	55927-55927	DODGE CENTER	56039-56039	GRANADA
55360-55360	MAYER	55710-55710	BRITT	55929-55929	DOVER	56041-56041	HANSKA
55361-55361	MINNETONKA BEACH	55711-55711	BROOKSTON	55931-55931	EITZEN	56042-56042	HARTLAND
55362-55362	MONTICELLO	55712-55712	BRUNO	55932-55932	ELGIN	56043-56043	HAYWARD
55363-55363	MONTROSE	55713-55713	BUHL	55933-55933	ELKTON	56044-56044	HENDERSON
55364-55364	MOUND	55716-55716	CALUMET	55934-55934	EYOTA	56045-56045	HOLLANDALE
55365-55365	MONTICELLO	55717-55717	CANYON	55935-55935	FOUNTAIN	56046-56046	HOPE
55366-55366	NEW AUBURN	55718-55718	CARLTON	55936-55936	GRAND MEADOW	56047-56047	HUNTLEY
55367-55367	NEW GERMANY	55719-55719	CHISHOLM	55939-55939	HARMONY	56048-56048	JANESVILLE
55368-55368	NORWOOD	55720-55720	CLOQUET	55940-55940	HAYFIELD	56050-56050	KASOTA
55369-55369	OSSEO	55721-55721	COHASSET	55941-55941	HOKAH	56051-56051	KIESTER
55370-55370	PLATO	55722-55722	COLERAINE	55942-55942	HOMER	56052-56052	KILKENNY
55371-55371	PRINCETON	55723-55723	COOK	55943-55943	HOUSTON	56054-56054	LAFAYETTE
55372-55372	PRIOR LAKE	55724-55724	COTTON	55944-55944	KASSON	56055-56055	LAKE CRYSTAL
55373-55373	ROCKFORD	55725-55725	CRANE LAKE	55945-55945	KELLOGG	56056-56056	LA SALLE
55374-55374	ROGERS	55726-55726	CROMWELL	55946-55946	KENYON	56057-56057	LE CENTER
55375-55375	SAINT BONIFACIUS	55729-55729	DUQUETTE	55947-55947	LA CRESCENT	56058-56058	LE SUEUR
55376-55376	SAINT MICHAEL	55730-55730	GRAND RAPIDS	55949-55949	LANESBORO	56060-56060	LEWISVILLE
55377-55377	SANTIAGO	55731-55731	ELY	55950-55950	LANSING	56062-56062	MADELIA
55378-55378	SAVAGE	55732-55732	EMBARRASS	55951-55951	LE ROY	56063-56063	MADISON LAKE
55379-55379	SHAKOPEE	55733-55733	ESKO	55952-55952	LEWISTON	56064-56064	MANCHESTER
55380-55380	SILVER CREEK	55734-55734	EVELETH	55953-55953	LYLE	56065-56065	MAPLETON
55381-55381	SILVER LAKE	55735-55735	FINLAYSON	55954-55954	MABEL	56068-56068	MINNESOTA LAKE
55382-55382	SOUTH HAVEN	55736-55736	FLOODWOOD	55955-55955	MANTORVILLE	56069-56069	MONTGOMERY
55383-55383	NORWOOD	55738-55738	FORBES	55956-55956	MAZEPPA	56071-56071	NEW PRAGUE
55384-55384	SPRING PARK	55741-55741	GILBERT	55957-55957	MILLVILLE	56072-56072	NEW RICHLAND
55385-55385	STEWART	55742-55742	GOODLAND	55959-55959	MINNESOTA CITY	56073-56073	NEW ULM
55386-55386	VICTORIA	55744-55745	GRAND RAPIDS	55960-55960	ORONOCO	56074-56074	NICOLLET
55387-55387	WACONIA	55746-55747	HIBBING	55961-55961	OSTRANDER	56075-56075	NORTHROP
55388-55388	WATERTOWN	55748-55748	HILL CITY	55962-55962	PETERSON	56076-56076	OAKLAND
55389-55389	WATKINS	55749-55749	HOLYOKE	55963-55963	PINE ISLAND	56078-56078	PEMBERTON
55390-55390	WAVERLY	55750-55750	HOYT LAKES	55964-55964	PLAINVIEW	56080-56080	SAINT CLAIR
55391-55391	WAYZATA	55751-55751	IRON	55965-55965	PRESTON	56081-56081	SAINT JAMES
55392-55392	NAVARRE	55752-55752	JACOBSON	55967-55967	RACINE	56082-56082	SAINT PETER
55393-55393	MAPLE PLAIN	55753-55753	KEEWATIN	55968-55968	READS LANDING	56083-56083	SANBORN
55394-55394	YOUNG AMERICA	55756-55756	KERRICK	55969-55969	ROLLINGSTONE	56084-56084	SEARLES
55395-55395	WINSTED	55757-55757	KETTLE RIVER	55970-55970	ROSE CREEK	56085-56085	SLEEPY EYE
55396-55396	WINTHROP	55758-55758	KINNEY	55971-55971	RUSHFORD	56087-56087	SPRINGFIELD
55397-55397	YOUNG AMERICA	55760-55760	MCGREGOR	55972-55972	SAINT CHARLES	56088-56088	TRUMAN
55398-55398	ZIMMERMAN	55763-55763	MAKINEN	55973-55973	SARGEANT	56089-56089	TWIN LAKES
55399-55399	YOUNG AMERICA	55764-55764	MARBLE	55974-55974	SPRING GROVE	56090-56090	VERNON CENTER
55401-55488	MINNEAPOLIS	55765-55765	MEADOWLANDS	55975-55975	SPRING VALLEY	56091-56091	WALDORF
55550-55560	YOUNG AMERICA	55766-55766	MELRUDE	55976-55976	STEWARTVILLE	56093-56093	WASECA
55561-55561	MONTICELLO	55767-55767	MOOSE LAKE	55977-55977	TAOPI	56096-56096	WATERVILLE
55562-55562	YOUNG AMERICA	55768-55768	MOUNTAIN IRON	55979-55979	UTICA	56097-56097	WELLS
55563-55563	MONTICELLO	55769-55769	NASHWAUK	55981-55981	WABASHA	56098-56098	WINNEBAGO
55564-55564	YOUNG AMERICA	55771-55771	ORR	55982-55982	WALTHAM	56101-56101	WINDOM
55565-55565	MONTICELLO	55772-55772	NETT LAKE	55983-55983	WANAMINGO	56110-56110	ADRIAN
55566-55568	YOUNG AMERICA	55775-55775	PENGILLY	55985-55985	WEST CONCORD	56111-56111	ALPHA

ZIP Range	Place	ZIP Range	Place	ZIP Range	Place	ZIP Range	Place
56113-56113	ARCO	56225-56225	CLINTON	56330-56330	FORESTON	56467-56467	NEVIS
56114-56114	AVOCA	56226-56226	CLONTARF	56331-56331	FREEPORT	56468-56468	NISSWA
56115-56115	BALATON	56227-56227	CORRELL	56332-56332	GARFIELD	56469-56469	PALISADE
56116-56116	BEAVER CREEK	56228-56228	COSMOS	56333-56333	GILMAN	56470-56470	PARK RAPIDS
56117-56117	BIGELOW	56229-56229	COTTONWOOD	56334-56334	GLENWOOD	56472-56472	PEQUOT LAKES
56118-56118	BINGHAM LAKE	56230-56230	DANUBE	56335-56335	GREENWALD	56473-56473	PILLAGER
56119-56119	BREWSTER	56231-56231	DANVERS	56336-56336	GREY EAGLE	56474-56474	PINE RIVER
56120-56120	BUTTERFIELD	56232-56232	DAWSON	56338-56338	HILLMAN	56475-56475	RANDALL
56121-56121	CEYLON	56235-56235	DONNELLY	56339-56339	HOFFMAN	56477-56477	SEBEKA
56122-56122	CHANDLER	56236-56236	DUMONT	56340-56340	HOLDINGFORD	56478-56478	NIMROD
56123-56123	CURRIE	56237-56237	ECHO	56341-56341	HOLMES CITY	56479-56479	STAPLES
56125-56125	DOVRAY	56239-56239	GHENT	56342-56342	ISLE	56481-56481	VERNDALE
56127-56127	DUNNELL	56240-56240	GRACEVILLE	56343-56343	KENSINGTON	56482-56482	WADENA
56128-56128	EDGERTON	56241-56241	GRANITE FALLS	56344-56344	LASTRUP	56484-56484	WALKER
56129-56129	ELLSWORTH	56243-56243	GROVE CITY	56345-56345	LITTLE FALLS	56501-56502	DETROIT LAKES
56131-56131	FULDA	56244-56244	HANCOCK	56347-56347	LONG PRAIRIE	56510-56510	ADA
56132-56132	GARVIN	56245-56245	HANLEY FALLS	56349-56349	LOWRY	56511-56511	AUDUBON
56134-56134	HARDWICK	56246-56246	HAWICK	56350-56350	MC GRATH	56513-56513	BAKER
56136-56136	HENDRICKS	56248-56248	HERMAN	56352-56352	MELROSE	56514-56514	BARNESVILLE
56137-56137	HERON LAKE	56249-56249	HOLLOWAY	56353-56353	MILACA	56515-56515	BATTLE LAKE
56138-56138	HILLS	56251-56251	KANDIYOHI	56354-56354	MILTONA	56516-56516	BEJOU
56139-56139	HOLLAND	56252-56252	KERKHOVEN	56355-56355	NELSON	56517-56517	BELTRAMI
56140-56140	IHLEN	56253-56253	LAKE LILLIAN	56356-56356	NEW MUNICH	56518-56518	BLUFFTON
56141-56141	IONA	56255-56255	LUCAN	56357-56357	OAK PARK	56519-56519	BORUP
56142-56142	IVANHOE	56256-56256	MADISON	56358-56358	OGILVIE	56520-56520	BRECKENRIDGE
56143-56143	JACKSON	56257-56257	MARIETTA	56359-56359	ONAMIA	56521-56521	CALLAWAY
56144-56144	JASPER	56258-56258	MARSHALL	56360-56360	OSAKIS	56522-56522	CAMPBELL
56145-56145	JEFFERS	56260-56260	MAYNARD	56361-56361	PARKERS PRAIRIE	56523-56523	CLIMAX
56146-56146	KANARANZI	56262-56262	MILAN	56362-56362	PAYNESVILLE	56524-56524	CLITHERALL
56147-56147	KENNETH	56263-56263	MILROY	56363-56363	PEASE	56525-56525	COMSTOCK
56149-56149	LAKE BENTON	56264-56264	MINNEOTA	56364-56364	PIERZ	56527-56527	DEER CREEK
56150-56150	LAKEFIELD	56265-56265	MONTEVIDEO	56367-56367	RICE	56528-56528	DENT
56151-56151	LAKE WILSON	56266-56266	MORGAN	56368-56368	RICHMOND	56529-56529	DILWORTH
56152-56152	LAMBERTON	56267-56267	MORRIS	56369-56369	ROCKVILLE	56531-56531	ELBOW LAKE
56153-56153	LEOTA	56270-56270	MORTON	56371-56371	ROSCOE	56533-56533	ELIZABETH
56155-56155	LISMORE	56271-56271	MURDOCK	56372-56372	SAINT CLOUD	56534-56534	ERHARD
56156-56156	LUVERNE	56272-56272	NASSAU	56373-56373	ROYALTON	56535-56535	ERSKINE
56157-56157	LYND	56273-56273	NEW LONDON	56374-56374	SAINT JOSEPH	56536-56536	FELTON
56158-56158	MAGNOLIA	56274-56274	NORCROSS	56375-56375	SAINT STEPHEN	56537-56538	FERGUS FALLS
56159-56159	MOUNTAIN LAKE	56276-56276	ODESSA	56376-56376	SAINT MARTIN	56540-56540	FERTILE
56160-56160	ODIN	56277-56277	OLIVIA	56377-56377	SARTELL	56541-56541	FLOM
56161-56161	OKABENA	56278-56278	ORTONVILLE	56378-56378	SAUK CENTRE	56542-56542	FOSSTON
56162-56162	ORMSBY	56279-56279	PENNOCK	56379-56379	SAUK RAPIDS	56543-56543	FOXHOME
56164-56164	PIPESTONE	56280-56280	PORTER	56381-56381	STARBUCK	56544-56544	FRAZEE
56165-56165	READING	56281-56281	PRINSBURG	56382-56382	SWANVILLE	56545-56545	GARY
56166-56166	REVERE	56282-56282	RAYMOND	56384-56384	UPSALA	56546-56546	GEORGETOWN
56167-56167	ROUND LAKE	56283-56283	REDWOOD FALLS	56385-56385	VILLARD	56547-56547	GLYNDON
56168-56168	RUSHMORE	56284-56284	RENVILLE	56386-56386	WAHKON	56548-56548	HALSTAD
56169-56169	RUSSELL	56285-56285	SACRED HEART	56387-56387	WAITE PARK	56549-56549	HAWLEY
56170-56170	RUTHTON	56287-56287	SEAFORTH	56389-56389	WEST UNION	56550-56550	HENDRUM
56171-56171	SHERBURN	56288-56288	SPICER	56393-56398	SAINT CLOUD	56551-56551	HENNING
56172-56172	SLAYTON	56289-56289	SUNBURG	56401-56401	BRAINERD	56552-56552	HITTERDAL
56173-56173	STEEN	56291-56291	TAUNTON	56425-56425	BAXTER	56553-56553	KENT
56174-56174	STORDEN	56292-56292	VESTA	56430-56430	AH GWAH CHING	56554-56554	LAKE PARK
56175-56175	TRACY	56293-56293	WABASSO	56431-56431	AITKIN	56556-56556	MCINTOSH
56176-56176	TRIMONT	56294-56294	WANDA	56433-56433	AKELEY	56557-56557	MAHNOMEN
56177-56177	TROSKY	56295-56295	WATSON	56434-56434	ALDRICH	56560-56563	MOORHEAD
56178-56178	TYLER	56296-56296	WHEATON	56435-56435	BACKUS	56565-56565	NASHUA
56179-56179	VERDI	56297-56297	WOOD LAKE	56436-56436	BENEDICT	56566-56566	NAYTAHWAUSH
56180-56180	WALNUT GROVE	56301-56304	SAINT CLOUD	56437-56437	BERTHA	56567-56567	NEW YORK MILLS
56181-56181	WELCOME	56307-56307	ALBANY	56438-56438	BROWERVILLE	56568-56568	NIELSVILLE
56183-56183	WESTBROOK	56308-56308	ALEXANDRIA	56440-56440	CLARISSA	56569-56569	OGEMA
56185-56185	WILMONT	56309-56309	ASHBY	56441-56441	CROSBY	56570-56570	OSAGE
56186-56186	WOODSTOCK	56310-56310	AVON	56442-56442	CROSSLAKE	56571-56571	OTTERTAIL
56187-56187	WORTHINGTON	56311-56311	BARRETT	56443-56443	CUSHING	56572-56572	PELICAN RAPIDS
56201-56201	WILLMAR	56312-56312	BELGRADE	56444-56444	DEERWOOD	56573-56573	PERHAM
56207-56207	ALBERTA	56313-56313	BOCK	56446-56446	EAGLE BEND	56574-56574	PERLEY
56208-56208	APPLETON	56314-56314	BOWLUS	56447-56447	EMILY	56575-56575	PONSFORD
56209-56209	ATWATER	56315-56315	BRANDON	56448-56448	FIFTY LAKES	56576-56576	RICHVILLE
56210-56210	BARRY	56316-56316	BROOTEN	56449-56449	FORT RIPLEY	56577-56577	RICHWOOD
56211-56211	BEARDSLEY	56317-56317	BUCKMAN	56450-56450	GARRISON	56578-56578	ROCHERT
56212-56212	BELLINGHAM	56318-56318	BURTRUM	56452-56452	HACKENSACK	56579-56579	ROTHSAY
56214-56214	BELVIEW	56319-56319	CARLOS	56453-56453	HEWITT	56580-56580	SABIN
56215-56215	BENSON	56320-56320	COLD SPRING	56455-56455	IRONTON	56581-56581	SHELLY
56216-56216	BLOMKEST	56321-56321	COLLEGEVILLE	56456-56456	JENKINS	56583-56583	TINTAH
56218-56218	BOYD	56323-56323	CYRUS	56458-56458	LAKE GEORGE	56584-56584	TWIN VALLEY
56219-56219	BROWNS VALLEY	56324-56324	DALTON	56459-56459	LAKE HUBERT	56585-56585	ULEN
56220-56220	CANBY	56325-56325	ELROSA	56460-56460	LAKE ITASCA	56586-56586	UNDERWOOD
56221-56221	CHOKIO	56326-56326	EVANSVILLE	56461-56461	LAPORTE	56587-56587	VERGAS
56222-56222	CLARA CITY	56327-56327	FARWELL	56464-56464	MENAHGA	56588-56588	VINING
56223-56223	CLARKFIELD	56328-56328	FLENSBURG	56465-56465	MERRIFIELD	56589-56589	WAUBUN
56224-56224	CLEMENTS	56329-56329	FOLEY	56466-56466	MOTLEY	56590-56590	WENDELL

56591-56591	WHITE EARTH	56652-56652	LEONARD	56682-56682	SWIFT	56731-56731	HUMBOLDT
56592-56592	WINGER	56653-56653	LITTLEFORK	56683-56683	TENSTRIKE	56732-56732	KARLSTAD
56593-56593	WOLF LAKE	56654-56654	LOMAN	56684-56684	TRAIL	56733-56733	KENNEDY
56594-56594	WOLVERTON	56655-56655	LONGVILLE	56685-56685	WASKISH	56734-56734	LAKE BRONSON
56601-56619	BEMIDJI	56657-56657	MARCELL	56686-56686	WILLIAMS	56735-56735	LANCASTER
56621-56621	BAGLEY	56658-56658	MARGIE	56687-56687	WILTON	56736-56736	MENTOR
56623-56623	BAUDETTE	56659-56659	MAX	56688-56688	WIRT	56737-56737	MIDDLE RIVER
56626-56626	BENA	56660-56660	MIZPAH	56701-56701	THIEF RIVER FALLS	56738-56738	NEWFOLDEN
56627-56627	BIG FALLS	56661-56661	NORTHOME	56710-56710	ALVARADO	56740-56740	NOYES
56628-56628	BIGFORK	56662-56662	OUTING	56711-56711	ANGLE INLET	56741-56741	OAK ISLAND
56629-56629	BIRCHDALE	56663-56663	PENNINGTON	56712-56712	ANGUS	56742-56742	OKLEE
56630-56630	BLACKDUCK	56666-56666	PONEMAH	56713-56713	ARGYLE	56744-56744	OSLO
56631-56631	BOWSTRING	56667-56667	PUPOSKY	56714-56714	BADGER	56748-56748	PLUMMER
56633-56633	CASS LAKE	56668-56668	RANIER	56715-56715	BROOKS	56750-56750	RED LAKE FALLS
56634-56634	CLEARBROOK	56669-56669	RAY	56716-56716	CROOKSTON	56751-56751	ROSEAU
56636-56636	DEER RIVER	56670-56670	REDBY	56720-56720	DONALDSON	56754-56754	SAINT HILAIRE
56637-56637	TALMOON	56671-56671	REDLAKE	56721-56721	EAST GRAND FORKS	56755-56755	SAINT VINCENT
56639-56639	EFFIE	56672-56672	REMER	56722-56722	EUCLID	56756-56756	SALOL
56641-56641	FEDERAL DAM	56673-56673	ROOSEVELT	56723-56723	FISHER	56757-56757	STEPHEN
56644-56644	GONVICK	56676-56676	SHEVLIN	56724-56724	GATZKE	56758-56758	STRANDQUIST
56646-56646	GULLY	56678-56678	SOLWAY	56725-56725	GOODRIDGE	56759-56759	STRATHCONA
56647-56647	HINES	56679-56679	SOUTH INTERNATIONAL	56726-56726	GREENBUSH	56760-56760	VIKING
56649-56649	INTERNATIONAL FALLS		FALLS	56727-56727	GRYGLA	56761-56761	WANNASKA
56650-56650	KELLIHER	56680-56680	SPRING LAKE	56728-56728	HALLOCK	56762-56762	WARREN
56651-56651	LENGBY	56681-56681	SQUAW LAKE	56729-56729	HALMA	56763-56763	WARROAD

Mississippi

General Help Numbers:

Governor's Office

PO Box 139
Jackson, MS 39205-0139
http://www.governor.state.ms.us

601-359-3150
Fax 601-359-3741
8AM-5PM

Attorney General's Office

PO Box 220
Jackson, MS 39201-0220
http://www.ago.state.ms.us

601-359-3680
Fax 601-359-3796
8AM-5PM

State Court Administrator

Supreme Court, Box 117
Jackson, MS 39205
http://www.mssc.state.ms.us

601-354-7406
Fax 601-354-7459
8AM-5PM

State Archives

Archives & Library Division
PO Box 571
Jackson, MS 39205-0571
http://www.mdah.state.ms.us

601-359-6850
Fax 601-359-6975

8AM-5PM TU-F;
8AM-1PM SA

State Specifics:

Capital:

Jackson
Hinds County

Time Zone:

CST

Number of Counties:

82

Population:

2,844,658

Web Site:

www.state.ms.us/its/msportal.nsf/
WebForm/Government?OpenDocument

State Agencies

Criminal Records

Access to Records is Restricted

Criminal Information Center, Dept. of Public Safety, PO Box 958, Jackson, MS 39205; 601-933-2600.

Note: Mississippi does permit the public to access their central state repository of criminal records. They suggest that you obtain information at the county level.

Corporation Records
Limited Partnership Records
Limited Liability Company Records
Trademarks/Servicemarks

Corporation Commission, Secretary of State, PO Box 136, Jackson, MS 39205-0136 (Courier: 202 N Congress, Suite 601, Jackson, MS 39201); 601-

359-1633, 800-256-3494, 601-359-1607 (Fax), 8AM-5PM.

http://www.sos.state.ms.us

Indexing & Storage: Records are available from the 1800's, computerized since 1995. New records are available for inquiry immediately. Records are indexed on microfilm, inhouse computer.

Searching: Include the following in your request-full name of business. In addition to the articles of incorporation, corporation records include the following information: Annual Reports, Officers, Directors, Prior (merged) names, Inactive and Reserved names. The following data is not released: federal id numbers or phone numbers.

Access by: mail, phone, fax, in person, online.

Fee & Payment: There is no search fee. The certification fee is $10.00 per package. Copies are $1.00 per page. Fee payee: Secretary of State. Prepayment required. You must prepay if the invoice amount is over $50.00. If under $50.00 they will invoice. Personal checks accepted. Credit cards accepted: MasterCard, Visa.

Mail search: Turnaround time: 1 to 2 days.

Phone search: Will only verify if record exists.

Fax search: Requests only are accepted, will return to toll-free fax numbers.

In person search: Computer screen prints are free.

Online search: The system is called "CorpSnap" and is available from the Internet. There is no fee to view records, including officers and registered agents.

Other access: The Data Division offers bulk release of information on paper or disk.

Uniform Commercial Code
Federal Tax Liens

Business Services Division, Secretary of State, PO Box 136, Jackson, MS 39205-0136 (Courier: 202 N Congress St, Suite 601, Union Planters Bank Bldg, Jackson, MS 39201); 601-359-1633, 800-256-3494, 601-359-1607 (Fax), 8AM-5PM.

http://www.sos.state.ms.us

Indexing & Storage: Records are available from 1968. Records are computerized since 1987. Records are indexed on inhouse computer.

Searching: Use search request form UCC-11. The search includes federal tax liens on businesses. Federal tax liens on individuals and all state tax liens are filed at the county level. Include the following in your request-debtor name.

Access by: mail, phone, fax, in person, online.

Fee & Payment: The search fee is $5.00, copies are $2.00 each, financing statements are $2.00 each. Fee payee: Secretary of State. Prepayment required. The state offers ACH accounts for regular requesters. Personal checks accepted. Credit cards accepted: MasterCard, Visa.

Mail search: Turnaround time: 1 day. No self addressed stamped envelope is required.

Phone search: Limited information is released over the phone.

Fax search: Requester must first set-up a prepaid account.

Online search: The PC system is called "Success" and is open 24 hours daily. There is a $250 set-up fee and usage fee of $.10 per screen. Users can access via the Internet to avoid any toll charges. Customers are billed quarterly. For more information, call Burrell Brown at 601-359-1633.

Other access: A monthly list of farm liens is available for purchase.

State Tax Liens
Records not maintained by a state level agency.

Note: All state tax liens are filed at the county level.

Sales Tax Registrations

Revenue Bureau, Sales Tax Division, PO Box 22828, Jackson, MS 39225-2828 (Courier: 1577 Springridge Rd, Raymond, MS 39154); 601-923-7000, 601-923-7300 (Fax), 8AM-5PM.

http://www.mstc.state.ms.us

Indexing & Storage: Records are available for the most current 3 years and are computerized.

Searching: The agency will only verify if a business is registered and will not release ownership data. Include the following in your request-business name. They will also search by tax permit number.

Access by: mail, phone, fax, in person.

Fee & Payment: Prepayment required. Fee payee: Revenue Bureau. Personal checks accepted. No credit cards accepted.

Mail search: Turnaround time: 5 to 10 working days. No self addressed stamped envelope is required. No fee for mail request. Copies cost $2.00 per page.

Phone search: No fee for telephone request.

Fax search: Same criteria as phone or mail searches.

In person search: No fee for request. Copies cost $2.00 per page.

Birth Certificates

State Department of Health, Vital Statistics & Records, PO Box 1700, Jackson, MS 39215-1700 (Courier: 571 Stadium Dr, Jackson, MS 39216); 601-576-7960, 601-576-7988, 601-576-7505 (Fax), 7:30AM-5PM.

http://www.msdh.state.ms.us/phs/index.htm

Indexing & Storage: Records are available from November 1, 1912 to present. New records are available for inquiry immediately. Records are indexed on microfiche, inhouse computer.

Searching: Employers need written release form from person of record. Records are not public access documents, they are only available to persons with legitimate and tangible interest. Include the following in your request-full name, names of parents, mother's maiden name, date of birth, place of birth, relationship to person of record, reason for information request. The following data is not released: original records of adoption.

Access by: mail, phone, fax, in person.

Fee & Payment: The $7.00 fee is for the short form. The fee for the long form certified is $12.00, plus is a $3.00 per for each additional copy. There is a $7.00 charge for no record found. Fee payee: Mississippi State Department of Health. Prepayment required. Use credit card for phone and/or expedited service only. Personal checks accepted only if in-state. Credit cards accepted: MasterCard, Visa, AmEx, Discover.

Mail search: Turnaround time: 7 to 10 days. No self addressed stamped envelope is required.

Phone search: Must use a credit card for an additional $5.00 fee. Turnaround time is same or next day.

Fax search: Same criteria as phone searches.

In person search: Turnaround time for Short Form-while you wait, Long Form-next day mail.

Expedited service: Expedited service is available for mail, phone and fax searches. Turnaround time: overnight delivery. Add a $5.00 credit card fee and $12.75 for overnight shipping.

Death Records

State Department of Health, Vital Statistics & Records, PO Box 1700, Jackson, MS 39215-1700 (Courier: 571 Stadium Dr, Jackson, MS 39216); 601-576-7960, 601-576-7988, 601-576-7505 (Fax), 7:30AM-5PM.

http://www.msdh.state.ms.us/phs/index.htm

Indexing & Storage: Records are available from November 1, 1912 to present. New records are available for inquiry immediately. Records are indexed on microfiche, inhouse computer.

Searching: Employers need written release form from immediate family member. Records are not considered public access documents. They are only available to persons with legitimate and tangible interest. Include the following in your request-full name, date of death, place of death, Social Security Number, relationship to person of record, reason for information request.

Access by: mail, phone, fax, in person.

Fee & Payment: Fee is $10.00 if you want a certified copy, and an additional $2.00 for each additional copy ordered at same time. If no record is found, the fee is $6.00. Fee payee: Mississippi State Department of Health. Prepayment required. Use credit cards for phone, fax and/or expedited service only. Credit cards accepted: MasterCard, Visa, AmEx, Discover.

Mail search: Turnaround time: 7 to 10 days. No self addressed stamped envelope is required.

Phone search: Turnaround time 2-3 days. Must use a credit card for an additional fee of $5.00.

Fax search: Same criteria as phone searching.

In person search: Turnaround time next day mail.

Expedited service: Expedited service is available for mail, phone and fax searches. Turnaround time: 1 day. Add $5.00 for use of credit card and $12.75 for overnight shipping.

Marriage Certificates

State Department of Health, Vital Statistics & Records, PO Box 1700, Jackson, MS 39215-1700 (Courier: 571 Stadium Dr, Jackson, MS 39216); 601-576-7960, 601-576-7988, 601-576-7505 (Fax), 7:30AM-5PM.

http://www.msdh.state.ms.us/phs/index.htm

Note: Records are also available at the county level, including those records from 1938 to 1942.

Indexing & Storage: Records are available from January 1926 to June 1938 and January 1942 to present. New records are available for inquiry immediately. Records are indexed on microfiche, inhouse computer.

Searching: Employers need written release from persons of record. Records are not considered public access documents. They are only available to persons with legitimate and tangible interest. Include the following in your request-names of husband and wife, date of marriage, place or county of marriage, relationship to person of record, reason for information request, wife's maiden name.

Access by: mail, phone, fax, in person.

Fee & Payment: The fee is $10.00 and $2.00 for each additional copy ordered at same time. If record not found fee is $6.00. Fee payee: Mississippi State Department of Health. Prepayment required. Use credit cards for phone, fax and/or expedited service only. Personal checks accepted only if in-state. Credit cards accepted: MasterCard, Visa, AmEx, Discover.

Mail search: Turnaround time: 4 to 7 days. No self addressed stamped envelope is required.

Phone search: Turnaround time 2-3 days. Must use a credit card for an additional $5.00 fee.

Fax search: Same criteria as phone searching.

In person search: Search costs $10.00 per request. Turnaround time next day mail.

Expedited service: Expedited service is available for mail, phone and fax searches. Turnaround time: 1 day. Add $5.00 for use of credit card and $12.75 for overnight delivery.

Divorce Records

State Department of Health, Vital Statistics, PO Box 1700, Jackson, MS 39215-1700 (Courier: 571 Stadium Dr, Jackson, MS 39216); 601-576-7960, 601-576-7988, 601-576-7505 (Fax), 7:30AM-5PM.

http://www.msdh.state.ms.us/phs/index.htm

Note: The state maintains a state-wide index and can refer to book and page number in county records. Requests for copies must be made to the county of record.

Indexing & Storage: Records are available from 1930 to present in county of record. This office will only confirm that a record exists and where. New records are available for inquiry immediately. Records are indexed on microfiche, inhouse computer.

Searching: Employers need written release form from person of record. Records are not public access documents and are available only to persons with legitimate and tangible interest. Include the following in your request-names of husband and wife, date of divorce, year divorce case began, case number (if known), relationship to person of record, reason for information request.

Access by: mail, phone, fax, in person.

Fee & Payment: The fee to do an index search is $6.00. Copies are not released from this agency. Fee payee: Mississippi State Department of Health. Prepayment required. Personal checks accepted if in-state. Credit cards accepted: MasterCard, Visa, AmEx, Discover.

Mail search: Turnaround time: 1 to 3 days. No self addressed stamped envelope is required.

Phone search: Use of credit card, for an additional $5.00 fee, required.

Fax search: Same criteria as phone searching.

In person search: Turnaround time next day mail.

Expedited service: Expedited service is available for mail, phone and fax searches. Turnaround time: 1 day. Add $5.00 for use of credit card and $12.75 for overnight delivery.

Workers' Compensation Records

Workers Compensation Commission, PO Box 5300, Jackson, MS 39296-5300 (Courier: 1428 Lakeland Dr, Jackson, MS 39216); 601-987-4200, 8AM-5PM.

http://www.mwcc.state.ms.us

Indexing & Storage: Records are available for 10 years back to present. New records are available for inquiry immediately. Records are indexed on inhouse computer.

Searching: All requests must be in writing. Claimant's attorney must have contract or medical authorization. Employer/carrier must be party to action to obtain records. They do not conduct searches for pre-employment screening. Include the following in your request-claimant name, Social Security Number, docket number, place of employment at time of accident.

Access by: mail, in person, online.

Fee & Payment: Copy fee is $.50 with a $5.00 minimum, there is no search fee. Fee payee: Mississippi Workers' Compensation Commission. They will invoice. Personal checks accepted. No credit cards accepted.

Mail search: Turnaround time: 3 to 4 working days. No self addressed stamped envelope is required.

In person search: Anyone can come in to view. Medical information is not made available and copies cannot be made unless there is written authorization by party of record.

Online search: The First Report of Injury is available via the web. There is no fee, but users must register.

Other access: A first report of injury database is available on CD-ROM for $500.00.

Accident Reports

Safety Responsibility, Accident Records, PO Box 958, Jackson, MS 39205 (Courier: 1900 E Woodrow Wilson, Jackson, MS 39216); 601-987-1278, 601-987-1261 (Fax), 8AM-5PM.

Note: The above address is for Highway Patrol accident investigations only. Reports require authorization from person involved. You must go to the agency that did the investigation for reports not found with the Highway Patrol.

Indexing & Storage: Records are available for 3 years to present on computer. Records are on microfiche from 1990 to present.

Searching: Must have authorization from individuals involved in the accident. Accident reports are only available to persons involved, their legal counsel and their insurance representative. Include the following in your request-date of accident, location of accident, full name. Requests must be in writing.

Access by: mail.

Fee & Payment: The fee is $10.00 per record. Fee payee: Department of Public Safety. Prepayment required. Personal checks accepted. No credit cards accepted.

Mail search: Turnaround time: 5 days. A self addressed stamped envelope is requested.

Driver Records

Department of Public Safety, Driver Records, PO Box 958, Jackson, MS 39205 (Courier: 1900 E Woodrow Wilson, Jackson, MS 39216); 601-987-1274, 8AM-5PM.

http://www.dps.state.ms.us

Note: Copies of tickets may be obtained from the same address for a fee of $5.00 per record. A pre-addressed, stamped envelope is advised.

Indexing & Storage: Records are available for 3 years for moving violations, DUIs and suspensions. Accidents appear on driving records. The driver's address is provided on the record. It takes 45 days or more before new records are available for inquiry.

Searching: Casual requesters can obtain personal information only with consent of subject. The driver's full name, license number, and/or DOB are needed when ordering. The magnetic tape system requires only the driver's last name and number (first name and DOB are optional). Surrendered license records can only be obtained by a manual search.

Access by: mail, in person, online.

Fee & Payment: The fee is $7.00 per request. Fee payee: Department of Public Safety. Prepayment required. Personal checks accepted. No credit cards accepted.

Mail search: Turnaround time: 2 days. A self addressed stamped envelope is requested.

In person search: Walk-in requesters may submit up to 10 requests for immediate delivery; the rest are available the next day.

Online search: Both interactive and batch delivery is offer for high volume users only. Billing is monthly. Hook-up is through the Advantis System, fees apply. Lookup is by name only-not by driver license number. Fee is $7.00 per record. For more information, call 601-987-1337.

Other access: Overnight batch delivery by tape is available. The state will sell the driver record file (without histories) to private or commercial parties.

Vehicle Ownership
Vehicle Identification

Mississippi State Tax Commission, Registration Department, PO Box 1140, Jackson, MS 39215 (Courier: 1577 Springridge Rd, Raymond, MS 39154); 601-923-7143, 601-923-7134 (Fax), 8AM-5PM.

http://www.mstc.state.ms.us/mvl/main.htm

Note: Please note that title information (liens, histories) requests are processed by a different section than registration information. For mail requests, use PO Box 1033 for the Title Department.

Indexing & Storage: Records are available from July 1, 1969 to present. Records are computer indexed from July 1, 1969 to present, and on microfiche from July 1, 1969 to present.

Searching: Personal information is not released to casual requesters without consent from the subject. The turnaround time will be one week longer if the request requires a search farther back than 5 years.

Access by: mail, in person.

Fee & Payment: Fees are $4.50 per search for title, $1.00 per search for VIN or registration, and $2.00 for lien history. Fee payee: Mississippi State Tax Commission. Prepayment required. No cash will be accepted for mail requests. Personal checks accepted. No credit cards accepted.

Mail search: Turnaround time: 2 days. A self addressed stamped envelope is requested.

In person search: Turnaround time is immediate.

Other access: Mississippi offers some standardized files as well as some customization for bulk requesters of VIN and registration information. For more information, contact MLVB at the address listed above.

Vessel Ownership
Vessel Registration

Dept of Wildlife, Fisheries, & Parks, PO Box 451, Jackson, MS 39205; 601-432-2070, 601-364-2048 (Fax), 8AM-5PM.

http://www.mdwfp.com

Note: Liens are recorded if the vessel has been titled. Starting July 1998, boats are titled at the option of the owner/lender.

Indexing & Storage: Records are available from 1981 to present. Records are indexed on computer from 1985 to present. All motorized boats and all sailboats must be registered. It takes 2 weeks or so before new records are available for inquiry.

Searching: The name or DL number or MS number or hull number is required to search.

Access by: mail, phone, fax, in person.

Fee & Payment: There is no search fee.

Mail search: Turnaround time is the same day, except during the summer, which can take 3-4 weeks.A self addressed stamped envelope is requested.

Phone search: Records are available by phone.

Fax search: Results will be mailed back usually the same day.

In person search: Turnaround time is usually immediate.

Other access: The state makes records available on printed lists and magnetic tapes. Fees vary.

Legislation Records

Mississippi Legislature, PO Box 1018, Jackson, MS 39215 (Courier: New Capitol, 3rd Floor, Jackson, MS 39215-1018), 601-359-3229 (Senate), 601-359-3358 (House), 8:30AM-5PM.

http://www.ls.state.ms.us

Note: The room number for Senate documents is 308, the room number for House documents is 305. The session begins the 1st Tuesday after the 1st Monday in January and usually lasts 3 months.

Indexing & Storage: Records are available from the beginning of the Legislature. Bills from 1991 to present are on computer, prior bills are in file books. New records are available for inquiry immediately. Records are indexed on inhouse computer, books (volumes).

Searching: Include the following in your request-bill number.

Access by: mail, phone, fax, in person, online.

Fee & Payment: No charges for copies or searches.

Mail search: Turnaround time: same day. No self addressed stamped envelope is required.

Phone search: Records are available by phone.

Fax search: Same day service is available.

Online search: The Internet site has an excellent bill status and measure information program. Data includes current and the previous year.

Voter Registration
Access to Records is Restricted

Secretary of State, Elections Division, PO Box 136, Jackson, MS 39205; 800-829-6786, 601-359-1350, 601-359-5019 (Fax), 8AM-5PM.

http://www.sos.state.ms.us/elections/elections.html

Note: Records are open to the public, but must be obtained at the county level.

GED Certificates

State Board for Community & Jr Colleges, GED Office, 3825 Ridgewood Rd, Jackson, MS 39211; 601-432-6338, 601-432-6363 (Fax), 8AM-5PM.

http://www.sbcjc.cc.ms.us

Searching: Transcripts are only available by written request. To search, all of the following is required: a signed release, name, date of birth, and Social Security Number. If known, the diploma number is helpful.

Access by: mail, fax, in person.

Fee & Payment: There is no fee for either a verification or a transcript.

Mail search: Turnaround time is 3 days.No self addressed stamped envelope is required.

Fax search: Same criteria as mail searching.

In person search: In person searchers must have a picture ID. Turnaround time: 2-3 minutes for a verification.

Hunting License Information
Fishing License Information

Department of Wildlife, Fisheries & Parks, PO Box 451, Jackson, MS 39205; 601-432-2055 (License Division), 601-432-2041 (Data Processing Div), 601-432-2071 (Fax), 8AM-5PM.

http://www.mdwfp.com

Indexing & Storage: Records are available for present data only.

Searching: Records are open to the public. They hold records on "sportsman" license holders which is a combination of hunting and fishing. Temporary license information is not maintained. You can search using the name or driver's license number.

Access by: mail, phone, fax, in person.

Fee & Payment: There is no search fee.

Mail search: Turnaround time: 10 days. No self addressed stamped envelope is required.

Phone search: Records are available by phone.

Fax search: Same criteria as mail searches.

In person search: You can make the request in person but they will mail back your response.

Other access: They have available mailing lists. For a print-out the cost is $550.00 for all the names and addresses; for magnetic tape the cost is $300.00 plus $20.00 for the tape. You can provide your own tape; call first to find out type and how many tapes needed.

Mississippi State Licensing Agencies

Licenses Searchable Online

Appraiser #30 .... www.mrec.state.ms.us/asp/findappraiser.asp
Architect #03 .... www.archbd.state.ms.us/aroster.htm
Attorney #27 .... www.mslawyer.com/index.html
Attorney Firm #27 .... www.mslawyer.com/LawFirms/
Child Care Facility #40 .... www.msdh.state.ms.us/childcare/childfind.htm
Contractor, General #06 .... www.msboc.state.ms.us/Search.cfm
Dental Hygienist #08 .... www.msbde.state.ms.us
Dental Radiologist #08 .... www.msbde.state.ms.us
Dentist #08 .... www.msbde.state.ms.us
Engineer #09 .... http://dsitspe01.its.state.ms.us/pepls/EngSurveyors.nsf
HMO #25 .... www.doi.state.ms.us/hmolist.pdf
Insurance Company #25 .... www.doi.state.ms.us/compdir.html
Landscape Architect #03 .... www.archbd.state.ms.us/lroster.htm
Lobbyist #31 .... www.sos.state.ms.us/elections/Lobbyists/Lobbyist_Dir.html
Long Term Care Insurance Company #25 ...... www.doi.state.ms.us/ltclist.html
Notary Public #31 .... www.sos.state.ms.us/busserv/notaries/NotarySearch.html
Optometrist #15 .... www.odfinder.org/LicSearch.asp
Real Estate Appraiser #30 .... www.mrec.state.ms.us/asp/findappraiser.asp
Real Estate Broker #34 .... www.mrec.state.ms.us/asp/findrealtor.asp
Real Estate Salesperson #34 .... www.mrec.state.ms.us/asp/findrealtor.asp
Surveyor #09 .... http://dsitspe01.its.state.ms.us/pepls/EngSurveyors.nsf

Licensing Quick Finder

Air Monitor #22 601-961-5100
Alcohol Beverage Employee #26 601-856-1330
Alcoholic Beverage Retailer #02 601-856-1330
Animal/Veterinary Technician #29 662-324-9380
Appraiser #30 601-932-6770
Architect #03 601-359-6020
Asbestos Contractor/Inspector #22 601-961-5100
Asbestos Project Designer/Mgmt. Planner #22
.... 601-961-5100
Asbestos Supervisor #22 601-961-5100
Asbestos Worker #22 601-961-5100
Athletic Trainer #37 601-576-7260
Attorney #27 601-948-4471
Attorney Firm #27 601-948-4471
Bank #04 601-359-1031
Barber Instructor/School #05 601-359-1015
Barber/Barber Shop #05 601-359-1015
Beauty Shop/Salon #07 601-987-6837
Boiler & Pressure Vessel Inspector #37 601-576-7917
Camp, Youth #40 601-576-7613
Child Care Facility #40 601-576-7613
Chiropractor #35 662-773-4478
Contractor, General #06 601-354-6161
Cosmetologist #07 601-987-6837
Cosmetology Instructor #07 601-987-6837
Counselor, Licensed Professional #10 .. 601-359-6630
CPA-Certified Public Accountant #19 601-354-7320
Dental Hygienist #08 601-944-9622
Dental Radiologist #08 601-944-9622
Dentist #08 601-944-9622
Dietitian #37 601-576-7260

Emergency Medical Technician #37 601-576-7681
Engineer #09 601-359-6160
Esthetician #07 601-987-6837
Eye Enucleator #37 601-576-7260
Finance Company #04 601-359-1031
Fishing, Commercial #24 601-432-2400
Funeral Director #11 601-354-6903
Funeral Service Practitioner #11 601-354-6903
Gaming #26 601-351-2800
Health Facility #41 601-576-7300
Hearing Aid Dealer (Specialist) #37 601-576-7260
HMO #25 601-359-3582
Insurance Company #25 601-359-3582
Insurance Sales Agent #25 601-359-3582
Insurance Solicitor/Advisor #25 601-359-3582
Landscape Architect #03 601-359-6020
Liquor Control #02 601-856-1310
Lobbyist #31 601-359-6353
Long Term Care Insurance Company #25 ...
.... 601-359-3582
Manicurist #07 601-987-6837
Marriage & Family Therapist #28 601-987-6806
Medical Doctor #12 601-987-3079
Mortgage Lender/Company #04 601-359-1031
Notary Public #31 601-359-1615
Nurse #13 601-987-6858
Nurse-LPN #13 601-987-6858
Nursing Home Administrator #14 601-364-2310
Occupational Therapist/Assistant #33 .. 601-576-7260
Optometrist #15 601-853-4338
Osteopathic Physician #12 601-987-3079

Pawn Shop #04 601-359-1031
Pharmacist #16 601-345-6750
Pharmacy #16 601-345-6750
Pharmacy Intern #16 601-345-6750
Pharmacy Technician #16 601-345-6750
Physical Therapist/Assistant #33 601-576-7260
Podiatrist #12 601-987-3079
Polygraph Examiner #17 601-987-1596
Psychologist #18 601-321-4621
Radiation Technician #37 601-576-7260
Real Estate Appraiser #30 601-932-6770
Real Estate Broker #34 601-932-9191
Real Estate Salesperson #34 601-932-9191
Savings Institution #04 601-359-1031
School Administrator #36 601-359-3483
Securities Agent #32 601-359-6363
Securities Broker/Dealer #32 601-359-6363
Septic Tank Installer #37 601-576-7260
Shorthand Reporter #20 601-354-6580
Social Worker #28 601-987-6806
Speech Pathologist/Audiologist #39 ... 601-987-4153
Speech-Language Pathologist/Audiologist #21 ..
.... 601-576-7260
Surveyor #09 601-359-6160
Tattoo Artist #37 601-576-7260
Teacher #36 601-359-3483
Title & Loan Company #04 601-359-1031
Veterinarian #29 662-324-9380
Veterinary Facility #29 662-324-9380

Licensing Agency Information

#02 Office of Alcoholic Beverage Control, PO Box 540, Madison, MS 39110-0540; 601-856-1330, Fax: 601-856-1390.
www.mstc.state.ms.us

#03 Board of Architecture, 239 N Lamarr St, Rm 502, Jackson, MS 39201-1311; 601-359-6020, Fax: 601-359-6011.
www.archbd.state.ms.us
Direct web site URL to search for licensees: www.archbd.state.ms.us/aroster.htm

#04 Department of Banking & Consumer Finance, 501 NW St, 901 Woolfolk Bldg, Ste. A, Jackson, MS 39202; 601-359-1031, Fax: 601-359-3557.
www.dbcf.state.ms.us/review.htm

#05 Board of Barber Examiners, 510 George St, Rm 240, Jackson, MS 39205; 601-359-1015, Fax: 601-359-1050.

#06 Board of Contractors, 2001 Airport Rd. #101, Jackson, MS 39208; 601-354-6161, Fax: 601-354-6715.
www.state.nu.us/vetbo
Direct web site URL to search for licensees: www.msboc.state.ms.us/Search.cfm. You can search online using company name, type, dba, class code, county, or license number

#07 Board of Cosmetology, PO Box 55689, Jackson, MS 39296-5689; 601-987-6837, Fax: 601-987-6840.

#08 Board of Dental Examiners, 600 E Amitest #100, Jackson, MS 39060; 601-944-9622, Fax: 601-924-9623 or 9624.
www.msbde.state.ms.us
Direct web site URL to search for licensees: www.msbde.state.ms.us

#09 Board of Engineers & Land Surveyors, 239 N Lamar St, 501 Robert E Lee Bldg, Jackson, MS 39201; 601-359-6160, Fax: 601-359-6159.
www.pepls.state.ms.us
Direct web site URL to search for licensees: http://dsitspe01.its.state.ms.us/pepls/EngSurveyors.nsf. You can search online using last name or city

#10 Board of Examiners for Licensed Professional Counselors, 1101 Robert E Lee Bldg, 239 N Lamar St, Jackson, MS 39201; 601-359-6630, Fax: 601-359-6295.

#11 Board of Funeral Service, 1307 E Fortification St, Jackson, MS 39202; 601-354-6903, Fax: 601-354-6934.
www.msfuneralboard.com The web site will soon list funeral homes.

#12 Board of Medical Licensure, 2600 Insurance Center Dr #2008, Jackson, MS 39216; 601-987-3079, Fax: 601-987-4159.
www.msbml.state.ms.us

#13 Board of Nursing, 1935 Lakeland Dr #B, Jackson, MS 39216; 601-987-4188, Fax: 601-364-2352.

#14 Board of Nursing Home Administrators, 1400 Lakeover Rd #120, Jackson, MS 39213; 601-364-2310, Fax: 601-364-2306.

#15 Board of Optometry, PO Box 12370, Jackson, MS 39236; 601-853-4338, Fax: 601-853-0336.
www.msoptometry.org
Direct web site URL to search for licensees: www.odfinder.org/LicSearch.asp. You can search online using national database by name, city or state.

#16 Board of Pharmacy, 625 N State St, #202, Jackson, MS 39225-4507; 601-354-6750, Fax: 601-354-6071.
www.mbp.state.ms.us

#17 Board of Polygraph Examiners, PO Box 958, Jackson, MS 39205; 601-987-1596.

#18 Board of Psychology, 4273 I-55 N. #104, Jackson, MS 39206-6157; 601-321-4621, Fax: 601-321-4628.

#19 Board of Public Accountancy, 653 N State St, Jackson, MS 39202; 601-354-7320, Fax: 601-354-7290.
www.msbpa.state.ms.us

#20 Board of Certified Court Reporters, PO Box 369 (656 N State St, Jackson, MS 39205; 601-354-6580, Fax: 601-354-6058.
www.mssc.state.ms.us

#21 Department of Health, PO Box 1700 (570 Woodrow Wilson, 39216), Jackson, MS 39215-1700; 601-576-7260, Fax: 601-576-7267.
www.msdh.state.ms.us

#22 Department of Environmental Quality, PO Box 10385, Jackson, MS 39289-0385; 601-961-5171, Fax: 601-354-6612.
www.deq.state.ms.us/domino/pcweb.nsf

#24 Department of Wildlife, Fisheries & Parks, 1505 Eastover Dr, Jackson, MS 39211-6322; 601-432-2400, Fax: 601-432-2024.
www.mdwfp.com

#25 Insurance Department, 1804 Sillers Bldg, 550 High St, Jackson, MS 39205; 601-359-3569, Fax: 601-359-2474.
www.doi.state.ms.us/agents.html

#26 Gaming Commission, 200 E Pearl St, Jackson, MS 39205; 601-351-2800, Fax: 601-351-2817.
www.msgaming.com

#27 Board of Bar Admissions, PO Box 2168, Jackson, MS 39225; 601-948-4471, Fax: 601-355-8635.
www.msbar.org/index.htm
Direct web site URL to search for licensees: www.mslawyer.com/index.html. You can search online using name, city, address, phone, fax, practice area, or e-mail address.

#28 Marriage & Family Therapists, PO Box 4508, Jackson, MS 39296-4508; 601-987-6806, Fax: 601-987-6808.

#29 Board of Veterinary Medicine, 209 S Lafayette, Starkville, MS 39759; 662-324-9380, Fax: 662-324-9380.

#30 Real Estate Appraiser, 5176 Keele St, Jackson, MS 39236-2685; 601-932-6770, Fax: 601-932-2990.
www.mrec.state.ms.us/default.asp
Direct web site URL to search for licensees: www.mrec.state.ms.us/asp/findappraiser.asp

#31 Office of Secretary of State, PO Box 136, Jackson, MS 39205-0136; 601-359-1350, Fax: 601-359-1499.
www.sos.state.ms.us
Direct web site URL to search for licensees: www.sos.state.ms.us/. You can search online using name, employer

#32 Office of Secretary of State, PO Box 136 (202 N Congress), Jackson, MS 39205-0136; 601-359-6363, Fax: 601-359-2663.

#33 Professional Licensure Division, PO Box 1700, Jackson, MS 39215-1700; 601-576-7260, Fax: 601-576-7267.

#34 Real Estate Commission, PO Box 12685 (2506 Lakeland Dr, #300), Jackson, MS 39236; 601-932-9191, Fax: 601-932-2990.
www.mrec.state.ms.us/default.asp
Direct web site URL to search for licensees: www.mrec.state.ms.us/asp/findrealtor.asp

#35 Board of Chiropractic Examiners, PO Box 775, Louisville, MS 39339; 662-773-4478, Fax: 662-773-4433.

#36 Department of Education, 359 N West Street, Jackson, MS 39201; 601-359-3483, Fax: 601-359-2778.
http://mde.k12.ms.us

#37 Department of Health, 570 E Woodrow Wilson, Jackson, MS 39215; 601-576-7917, Fax: 601-576-7923.
www.msdh.state.ms.us

#40 Department of Health, 570 E Woodrow Wilson, Jackson, MS 39215; 601-576-7613.
www.msdh.state.ms.us
Direct web site URL to search for licensees: www.msdh.state.ms.us/childcare/youthfind.htm

#41 Department of Health, Health Facilities Licensure & Certification, (PO Box 1700), Jackson, MS 39215-1700; 601-576-7300, Fax: 601-576-7350.
www.msdh.state.ms.us

Mississippi Federal Courts

The following list indicates the district and division name for each county in the state. If the bankruptcy court location is different from the district court, then the location of the bankruptcy court appears in parentheses.

County/Court Cross Reference

County	District	Division
Adams	Southern	Vicksburg (Jackson)
Alcorn	Northern	Aberdeen-Eastern (Aberdeen)
Amite	Southern	Jackson
Attala	Northern	Aberdeen-Eastern (Aberdeen)
Benton	Northern	Oxford-Northern (Aberdeen)
Bolivar	Northern	Clarksdale/Delta (Aberdeen)
Calhoun	Northern	Oxford-Northern (Aberdeen)
Carroll	Northern	Greenville (Aberdeen)
Chickasaw	Northern	Aberdeen-Eastern (Aberdeen)
Choctaw	Northern	Aberdeen-Eastern (Aberdeen)
Claiborne	Southern	Vicksburg (Jackson)
Clarke	Southern	Meridian (Biloxi)
Clay	Northern	Aberdeen-Eastern (Aberdeen)
Coahoma	Northern	Clarksdale/Delta (Aberdeen)
Copiah	Southern	Jackson
Covington	Southern	Hattiesburg (Biloxi)
De Soto	Northern	Clarksdale/Delta (Aberdeen)
Forrest	Southern	Hattiesburg (Biloxi)
Franklin	Southern	Jackson
George	Southern	Biloxi-Southern (Biloxi)
Greene	Southern	Hattiesburg (Biloxi)
Grenada	Northern	Oxford-Northern (Aberdeen)
Hancock	Southern	Biloxi-Southern (Biloxi)
Harrison	Southern	Biloxi-Southern (Biloxi)
Hinds	Southern	Jackson
Holmes	Southern	Jackson
Humphreys	Northern	Greenville (Aberdeen)
Issaquena	Southern	Vicksburg (Jackson)
Itawamba	Northern	Aberdeen-Eastern (Aberdeen)
Jackson	Southern	Biloxi-Southern (Biloxi)
Jasper	Southern	Meridian (Biloxi)
Jefferson	Southern	Vicksburg (Jackson)
Jefferson Davis	Southern	Hattiesburg (Biloxi)
Jones	Southern	Hattiesburg (Biloxi)
Kemper	Southern	Meridian (Biloxi)
Lafayette	Northern	Oxford-Northern (Aberdeen)
Lamar	Southern	Hattiesburg (Biloxi)
Lauderdale	Southern	Meridian (Biloxi)
Lawrence	Southern	Hattiesburg (Biloxi)
Leake	Southern	Jackson
Lee	Northern	Aberdeen-Eastern (Aberdeen)
Leflore	Northern	Greenville (Aberdeen)
Lincoln	Southern	Jackson
Lowndes	Northern	Aberdeen-Eastern (Aberdeen)
Madison	Southern	Jackson
Marion	Southern	Hattiesburg (Jackson)
Marshall	Northern	Oxford-Northern (Aberdeen)
Monroe	Northern	Aberdeen-Eastern (Aberdeen)
Montgomery	Northern	Oxford-Northern (Aberdeen)
Neshoba	Southern	Meridian (Biloxi)
Newton	Southern	Meridian (Biloxi)
Noxubee	Southern	Meridian (Biloxi)
Oktibbeha	Northern	Aberdeen-Eastern (Aberdeen)
Panola	Northern	Clarksdale/Delta (Aberdeen)
Pearl River	Southern	Biloxi-Southern (Biloxi)
Perry	Southern	Hattiesburg (Biloxi)
Pike	Southern	Jackson
Pontotoc	Northern	Oxford-Northern (Aberdeen)
Prentiss	Northern	Aberdeen-Eastern (Aberdeen)
Quitman	Northern	Clarksdale/Delta (Aberdeen)
Rankin	Southern	Jackson
Scott	Southern	Jackson
Sharkey	Southern	Vicksburg (Jackson)
Simpson	Southern	Jackson
Smith	Southern	Jackson
Stone	Southern	Biloxi-Southern (Biloxi)
Sunflower	Northern	Greenville (Aberdeen)
Tallahatchie	Northern	Clarksdale/Delta (Aberdeen)
Tate	Northern	Clarksdale/Delta (Aberdeen)
Tippah	Northern	Oxford-Northern (Aberdeen)
Tishomingo	Northern	Aberdeen-Eastern (Aberdeen)
Tunica	Northern	Clarksdale/Delta (Aberdeen)
Union	Northern	Oxford-Northern (Aberdeen)
Walthall	Southern	Hattiesburg (Biloxi)
Warren	Southern	Vicksburg (Jackson)
Washington	Northern	Greenville (Aberdeen)
Wayne	Southern	Meridian (Biloxi)
Webster	Northern	Oxford-Northern (Aberdeen)
Wilkinson	Southern	Vicksburg (Jackson)
Winston	Northern	Aberdeen-Eastern (Aberdeen)
Yalobusha	Northern	Oxford-Northern (Aberdeen)
Yazoo	Southern	Vicksburg (Jackson)

US District Court

Northern District of Mississippi

Aberdeen-Eastern Division PO Box 704, Aberdeen, MS 39730 (Courier Address: 301 W Commerce, Room 310, Aberdeen, MS 39730), 662-369-4952.

http://www.msnd.uscourts.gov

Counties: Alcorn, Attala, Chickasaw, Choctaw, Clay, Itawamba, Lee, Lowndes, Monroe, Oktibbeha, Prentiss, Tishomingo, Winston.

Indexing/Storage: Cases are indexed by defendant and plaintiff as well as by case number. New cases are available in the index 48 hours after filing date. Both computer and card indexes are maintained. Open records are located at this court.

Fee & Payment: The fee is $20.00 per item (one party name or case number). Payment may be made by money order, cashier check, personal check. Prepayment is required. Payee: Clerk, US District Court. Certification fee: $7.00 per document. Copy fee: $.50 per page. You are allowed to make your own copies. These copies cost $.25 per page.

Phone Search: Searching is not available by phone. If a case number is provided over the phone, the court will verify that the case number is correct.

Mail Search: Always enclose a stamped self addressed envelope.

In Person: In person searching is available.

PACER: Sign-up number is 800-676-6856. Access fee is $.60 per minute. Toll-free access: 888-227-0558. Local access: 662-236-4706. Case records are available back to 1990. Records are purged every six months. New records are available online after 1 day. PACER is available online at http://pacer.msnd.uscourts.gov.

Opinions Online: Court opinions are available online at http://sunset.backbone.olemiss.edu/~llibcoll/ndms

Clarksdale/Delta Division c/o Oxford-Northern Division, PO Box 727, Oxford, MS 38655 (Courier Address: Suite 369, 911 Jackson Ave, Oxford, MS 38655), 662-234-1971.

http://www.msnd.uscourts.gov

Counties: Bolivar, Coahoma, De Soto, Panola, Quitman, Tallahatchie, Tate, Tunica.

Indexing/Storage: Cases are indexed by as well as by case number. New cases are available in the index after filing date. Open records are located at the Division.

Fee & Payment: The fee is no charge per item (one party name or case number). Payment may be made by money order, cashier check. Business checks are not accepted. Personal checks are not accepted.

Phone Search: Searching not available by phone.

Mail Search: A stamped self addressed envelope is not required.

In Person: In person searching is available.

PACER: Sign-up number is 800-676-6856. Access fee is $.60 per minute. Toll-free access: 888-227-0558. Local access: 662-236-4706. Case records are available back to 1990. Records are purged every six months. New records are available online after 1 day. PACER is available online at http://pacer.msnd.uscourts.gov.

Opinions Online: Court opinions are available online at http://sunset.backbone.olemiss.edu/~lilibcoll/ndms

Greenville Division PO Box 190, Greenville, MS 38702-0190 (Courier Address: US Post Office & Federal Bldg, 305 Main, Greenville, MS 38701), 662-335-1651, Fax: 662-332-4292.

http://www.msnd.uscourts.gov

Counties: Carroll, Humphreys, Leflore, Sunflower, Washington.

Indexing/Storage: Cases are indexed by defendant and plaintiff as well as by case number. New cases are available in the index immediately after filing date. A computer index is maintained. Open records are located at this court.

Fee & Payment: The fee is $20.00 per item (one party name or case number). Payment may be made by money order, cashier check, personal check. Prepayment is required. Payee: Clerk, US District Court. Certification fee: $7.00 per document. Copy fee: $.50 per page. You are allowed to make your own copies. These copies cost $.25 per page.

Phone Search: Only docket information based on case number is available by phone.

Mail Search: Always enclose a stamped self addressed envelope.

In Person: In person searching is available.

PACER: Sign-up number is 800-676-6856. Access fee is $.60 per minute. Toll-free access: 888-227-0558. Local access: 662-236-4706. Case records are available back to 1990. Records are

purged every six months. New records are available online after 1 day. PACER is available online at http://pacer.msnd.uscourts.gov.

Opinions Online: Court opinions are available online at http://sunset.backbone.olemiss.edu/~lilibcoll/ndms

Oxford-Northern Division PO Box 727, Oxford, MS 38655 (Courier Address: Suite 369, 911 Jackson Ave, Oxford, MS 38655), 662-234-1971.

http://www.msnd.uscourts.gov

Counties: Benton, Calhoun, Grenada, Lafayette, Marshall, Montgomery, Pontotoc, Tippah, Union, Webster, Yalobusha.

Indexing/Storage: Cases are indexed by defendant and plaintiff as well as by case number. New cases are available in the index 48 hours after filing date. Both computer and card indexes are maintained. Records are also indexed on microfiche. Open records are located at this court. Civil records are sent to the Atlanta Federal Records Center 5 years after closing. Criminal records are sent to the Atlanta Federal Records Ce10 years after closing. All criminal records for the Delta Division (Clarksdale) are maintained in this office.

Fee & Payment: The fee is $20.00 per item (one party name or case number). Payment may be made by money order, cashier check, personal check. Prepayment is required. Payee: Clerk, US District Court. Certification fee: $7.00 per document. Copy fee: $.50 per page. You are allowed to make your own copies. These copies cost $.25 per page.

Phone Search: Searching is not available by phone. If a case number is provided over the phone, the court will verify that the case number is correct.

Mail Search: Always enclose a stamped self addressed envelope.

In Person: In person searching is available.

PACER: Sign-up number is 800-676-6856. Access fee is $.60 per minute. Toll-free access: 888-227-0558. Local access: 662-236-4706. Case records are available back to 1990. Records are purged every six months. New records are available online after 1 day. PACER is available online at http://pacer.msnd.uscourts.gov.

Opinions Online: Court opinions are available online at http://sunset.backbone.olemiss.edu/~lilibcoll/ndms

US Bankruptcy Court

Northern District of Mississippi

Aberdeen Division PO Drawer 867, Aberdeen, MS 39730-0867 (Courier Address: 205 Federal Bldg, 301 W. Commerce St, Aberdeen, MS 39730), 662-369-2596.

http://www.msnb.uscourts.gov

Counties: Alcorn, Attala, Benton, Bolivar, Calhoun, Carroll, Chickasaw, Choctaw, Clay, Coahoma, De Soto, Grenada, Humphreys, Itawamba, Lafayette, Lee, Leflore, Lowndes, Marshall, Monroe, Montgomery, Oktibbeha, Panola, Pontotoc, Prentiss, Quitman, Sunflower, Tallahatchie, Tate, Tippah, Tishomingo, Tunica, Union, Washington, Webster, Winston, Yalobusha.

Indexing/Storage: Cases are indexed by debtor as well as by case number. New cases are available in the index 1-2 days after filing date. A computer index is maintained. Open records are located at this court.

Fee & Payment: The fee is $20.00 per item (one party name or case number). Payment may be made by money order, cashier check, personal check. Prepayment is required. Payee: Clerk, US Bankruptcy Court, Northern District. Certification fee: $7.00 per document. Copy fee: $.50 per page. You are allowed to make your own copies. These copies cost $.50 per page. The $15.00 charge is per name or item. You may not take case files from the court for copies.

Phone Search: Only docket information is available by phone. An automated voice case information service (VCIS) is available. Call VCIS at 800-392-8653 or.

Mail Search: Always enclose a stamped self addressed envelope.

In Person: In person searching is available.

PACER: Sign-up number is 800-676-6856. Access fee is $.60 per minute. Toll-free access: 888-372-5709. Local access: 662-369-9805. Case records are available back to April 1, 1987. Records are purged every 6 months. New civil records are available online after 2 days. PACER is available online at http://pacer.msnb.uscourts.gov.

US District Court

Southern District of Mississippi

Biloxi-Southern Division Room 243, 725 Dr. Martin Luther King Jr. Blvd, Biloxi, MS 39530 (Courier Address: Use mail address for courier delivery), 228-432-8623, Fax: 601-436-9632.

http://www.mssd.uscourts.gov

Counties: George, Hancock, Harrison, Jackson, Pearl River, Stone.

Indexing/Storage: Cases are indexed by defendant and plaintiff as well as by case number. New cases are available in the index 48 hours after filing date. Both computer and card indexes are maintained. Open records are located at this court.

Fee & Payment: The fee is $20.00 per item (one party name or case number). Payment may be made by money order, cashier check, personal check. Prepayment is required. Payee: Clerk, US District Court. Certification fee: $7.00 per document. Copy fee: $.50 per page. You are allowed to make your own copies. These copies cost $.25 per page.

Phone Search: Searching is not available by phone. Only docket information is available by phone.

Mail Search: Always enclose a stamped self addressed envelope.

In Person: In person searching is available.

PACER: Sign-up number is 800-676-6856. Access fee is. Toll-free access: 800-839-6425. Local access: 601-965-5141. Case records are available back to 1992. New records are available online after 2 days. PACER is available online at http://pacer.mssd.uscourts.gov.

Hattiesburg Division Suite 200, 701 Main St, Hattiesburg, MS 39401 (Courier Address: Use mail address for courier delivery), 601-583-2433.

http://www.mssd.uscourts.gov

Counties: Covington, Forrest, Greene, Jefferson Davis, Jones, Lamar, Lawrence, Marion, Perry, Walthall.

Indexing/Storage: Cases are indexed by defendant and plaintiff as well as by case number. New cases are available in the index 48 hours after filing date. Both computer and card indexes are maintained. Open records are located at this court.

Fee & Payment: The fee is $20.00 per item (one party name or case number). Payment may be made by money order, cashier check, personal check. Prepayment is required. Payee: Clerk, US District Court. Certification fee: $7.00 per document. Copy fee: $.50 per page. You are allowed to make your own copies. These copies cost $.25 per page.

Phone Search: Only docket information is available by case number over the phone.

Mail Search: Always enclose a stamped self addressed envelope.

In Person: In person searching is available.

PACER: Sign-up number is 800-676-6856. Access fee is. Toll-free access: 800-839-6425. Local access: 601-965-5141. Case records are available back to 1992. New records are available online after 2 days. PACER is available online at http://pacer.mssd.uscourts.gov.

Jackson Division Suite 316, 245 E Capitol St, Jackson, MS 39201 (Courier Address: Use mail address for courier delivery), 601-965-4439.

http://www.mssd.uscourts.gov

Counties: Amite, Copiah, Franklin, Hinds, Holmes, Leake, Lincoln, Madison, Pike, Rankin, Scott, Simpson, Smith.

Indexing/Storage: Cases are indexed by defendant and plaintiff as well as by case number. New cases are available in the index 48 hours after filing date. Both computer and card indexes are maintained. Microfiche index also maintained. Open records are located at this court.

Fee & Payment: The fee is $20.00 per item (one party name or case number). Payment may be made by money order, cashier check, personal check. Prepayment is required. Payee: Clerk, US District Court. Certification fee: $7.00 per document. Copy fee: $.50 per page. You are allowed to make your own copies. These copies cost $.25 per page.

Phone Search: Searching is not available by phone.

Mail Search: Always enclose a stamped self addressed envelope.

In Person: In person searching is available.

PACER: Sign-up number is 800-676-6856. Access fee is. Toll-free access: 800-839-6425. Local access: 601-965-5141. Case records are available back to 1992. New records are available online after 2 days. PACER is available online at http://pacer.mssd.uscourts.gov.

Meridian Division c/o Jackson Division, Suite 316, 245 E Capitol St, Jackson, MS 39201 (Courier Address: Use mail address for courier delivery), 601-965-4439.

http://www.mssd.uscourts.gov

Counties: Clarke, Jasper, Kemper, Lauderdale, Neshoba, Newton, Noxubee, Wayne.

Indexing/Storage: Cases are indexed by defendant and plaintiff as well as by case number. New cases are available in the index after filing date. Open records are located at the Division.

Fee & Payment: The fee is $20.00 per item (one party name or case number). Payment may be made by money order, cashier check. Business checks are not accepted. Personal checks are not accepted. Certification fee: $7.00 per document. Copy fee: $.50 per page.

Phone Search: Searching is not available by phone.

Mail Search: Always enclose a stamped self addressed envelope.

In Person: In person searching is available.

PACER: Sign-up number is 800-676-6856. Access fee is. Toll-free access: 800-839-6425. Local access: 601-965-5141. Case records are available back to 1992. New records are available online after 2 days. PACER is available online at http://pacer.mssd.uscourts.gov.

Vicksburg Division c/o Jackson Division, Suite 316, 245 E Capitol St, Jackson, MS 39201 (Courier Address: Use mail address for courier delivery), 601-965-4439.

http://www.mssd.uscourts.gov

Counties: Adams, Claiborne, Issaquena, Jefferson, Sharkey, Warren, Wilkinson, Yazoo.

Indexing/Storage: Cases are indexed by as well as by case number. New cases are available in the index after filing date. Open records are located at the Division.

Fee & Payment: The fee is $20.00 per item (one party name or case number). Payment may be made by money order, cashier check. Business checks are not accepted. Personal checks are not accepted. Certification fee: $7.00 per document. Copy fee: $.50 per page.

Mail Search: Always enclose a stamped self addressed envelope.

hone Search:

In Person: In person searching is available.

PACER: Sign-up number is 800-676-6856. Access fee is. Toll-free access: 800-839-6425. Local access: 601-965-5141. Case records are available back to 1992. New records are available online after 2 days. PACER is available online at http://pacer.mssd.uscourts.gov.

US Bankruptcy Court

Southern District of Mississippi

Biloxi Division Room 117, 725 Dr. Martin Luther King Jr. Blvd, Biloxi, MS 39530 (Courier Address: Use mail address for courier delivery), 228-432-5542.

http://www.mssb.uscourts.gov

Counties: Clarke, Covington, Forrest, George, Greene, Hancock, Harrison, Jackson, Jasper, Jefferson Davis, Jones, Kemper, Lamar, Lauderdale, Lawrence, Marion, Neshoba, Newton, Noxubee, Pearl River, Perry, Stone, Walthall, Wayne.

Indexing/Storage: Cases are indexed by debtor as well as by case number. New cases are available in the index a few hours after filing date. Both computer and card indexes are maintained. Open records are located at this court.

Fee & Payment: The fee is $20.00 per item (one party name or case number). Payment may be made by money order, cashier check, personal check. Prepayment is required. Payee: Clerk, US Bankruptcy Court. Certification fee: $7.00 per document. Copy fee: $.50 per page.

Phone Search: An automated voice case information service (VCIS) is available. Call VCIS at 800-293-2723 or 601-435-2905.

Mail Search: Always enclose a stamped self addressed envelope.

In Person: In person searching is available.

PACER: Sign-up number is 800-676-6856. Access fee is $.60 per minute. Toll-free access: 800-223-1078. Local access: 601-965-6103. Use of PC Anywhere V4.0 recommended. Case records are available back to 1986. New civil records are available online after 1 day.

Jackson Division PO Box 2448, Jackson, MS 39225-2448 (Courier Address: 100 E Capitol St, Jackson, MS 39201), 601-965-5301.

http://www.mssb.uscourts.gov

Counties: Adams, Amite, Claiborne, Copiah, Franklin, Hinds, Holmes, Issaquena, Jefferson, Leake, Lincoln, Madison, Pike, Rankin, Scott, Sharkey, Simpson, Smith, Warren, Wilkinson, Yazoo.

Indexing/Storage: Cases are indexed by debtor as well as by case number. New cases are available in the index a few hours after filing date. Both computer and card indexes are maintained. Open records are located at this court.

Fee & Payment: The fee is $20.00 per item (one party name or case number). Payment may be made by money order, cashier check, personal check. Prepayment is required. Payee: Clerk, US Bankruptcy Court. Certification fee: $7.00 per document. Copy fee: $.50 per page.

Phone Search: An automated voice case information service (VCIS) is available. Call VCIS at 800-601-8859 or 601-965-6106.

Mail Search: Always enclose a stamped self addressed envelope.

In Person: In person searching is available.

PACER: Sign-up number is 800-676-6856. Access fee is $.60 per minute. Toll-free access: 800-223-1078. Local access: 601-965-6103. Use of PC Anywhere V4.0 recommended. New records are available online after.

Mississippi County Courts

Court	Jurisdiction	No. of Courts	How Organized
Circuit Courts*	General	70	22 Districts
County Courts*	Limited	3	19 Counties
Combined Courts*		20	
Chancery Courts*	General	91	20 Districts
Justice Courts	Limited	88	
Municipal Courts	Municipal	154	
Family Court	Special	1	

* Profiled in this Sourcebook.

Court	CIVIL								
	Tort	Contract	Real Estate	Min. Claim	Max. Claim	Small Claims	Estate	Eviction	Domestic Relations
Circuit Courts*	X	X	X	$2500	No Max			X	X
County Courts*	X	X	X	$0	$75,000			X	X
Combined Courts*									
Chancery Court*	X	X	X	$0	No Max		X		X
Justice Courts*	X	X	X	$0	$2500	$2500		X	
Municipal Courts								X	
Family Court									X

Court	CRIMINAL				
	Felony	Misdemeanor	DWI/DUI	Preliminary Hearing	Juvenile
Circuit Courts*	X				
County Courts*		X	X	X	X
Combined Courts*					
Chancery Court*					X
Justice Courts*		X	X	X	
Municipal Courts		X	X	X	
Family Court					X

ADMINISTRATION
Court Administrator, Supreme Court, Box 117, Jackson, MS, 39205; 601-359-3697, Fax: 601-359-2443. www.mssc.state.ms.us

COURT STRUCTURE
The court of general jurisdiction is the Circuit Court with 70 courts in 22 districts. Justice Courts were first created in 1984, replacing the Justice of the Peace. Prior to 1984, records were kept separately by each Justice of the Peace, so the location of such records today is often unknown. Probate is handled by the Chancery Courts, as are property matters.

ONLINE ACCESS
A statewide online computer system is in use internally for court personnel. There are plans underway to make this system available to the public. For further details, call Susan Anthony at 601-354-7449. The web site allows the public to search the Mississippi Supreme Court and Court of Appeals Decisions

ADDITIONAL INFORMATION
A number of Mississippi counties have two Circuit Court Districts. A search of either court in such a county will include the index from the other court.

Full Name is a search requirement for all courts. DOB and SSN are very helpful for differentiating between like-named individuals.

Adams County

Circuit & County Court PO Box 1224, Natchez, MS 39121; 601-446-6326; Fax: 601-445-7955. Hours: 8AM-5PM (CST). *Felony, Misdemeanor, Civil Actions Over $2,500.*

Civil Records: Access: Phone, fax, mail, in person. Both court and visitors may perform in person searches. Search fee: $10.00 per name. Required to search: name, years to search. Civil cases indexed by defendant, plaintiff. Civil records on computer; docket books to 1950s; records stored in basement to 1799.

Criminal Records: Access: Mail, in person. Both court and visitors may perform in person searches. Search fee: $10.00 per name. Required to search: name, years to search; also helpful: SSN. Criminal records on computer; docket books to 1950s; records stored in basement to 1799.

General Information: No sealed, adoptions, mental health, juvenile, sex, or expunged records released. Turnaround time 1-2 days if on computer. Copy fee: $1.00 per page. Certification fee: No cert fee. Fee payee: Circuit Clerk. Personal checks accepted. Prepayment is required.

Justice Court 115 S Wall, Natchez, MS 39120; 601-446-6326; Fax: 601-445-7955. Hours: 8AM-5PM (CST). *Misdemeanor, Civil Actions Under $2,500, Eviction, Small Claims.*

Chancery Court PO Box 1006, Natchez, MS 39121; 601-446-6684; Fax: 601-445-7913. Hours: 8AM-5PM (CST). *Probate.*

Alcorn County

Circuit Court PO Box 430 Attn: Circuit Clerk, Corinth, MS 38835; 662-286-7740; Fax: 662-286-7767. Hours: 8AM-5PM (CST). *Felony, Civil Actions Over $2,500.*

Civil Records: Access: Mail, fax, in person. Both court and visitors may perform in person searches. Search fee: $10.00 per name. Required to search: name, years to search. Civil cases indexed by defendant, plaintiff. Civil records on docket books from the 1930s.

Criminal Records: Access: Mail, fax, in person. Both court and visitors may perform in person searches. Search fee: $10.00 per name. Required to search: name, years to search, DOB; also helpful: SSN, sex. Criminal records on docket books from the 1930s.

General Information: No sealed, adoptions, mental health, juvenile, sex, or expunged records released. SASE required. Turnaround time varies. Fax notes: Fee to fax results is $10.00 per document. Copy fee: $.50 per page. Certification fee: No cert fee. Fee payee: Circuit Clerk. Personal checks accepted. Prepayment is required.

Justice Court PO Box 226, Corinth, MS 38834; 662-286-7776; Fax: 662-286-2157. Hours: 8AM-5PM (CST). *Misdemeanor, Civil Actions Under $2,500, Eviction, Small Claims.*

Chancery Court PO Box 69, Corinth, MS 38835-0069; 662-286-7702; Fax: 662-286-7706. *Probate.*

Amite County

Circuit Court PO Box 312, Liberty, MS 39645; 601-657-8932; Fax: 601-657-1082. Hours: 8AM-5PM (CST). *Felony, Civil Actions Over $2,500.*

Civil Records: Access: Phone, fax, mail, in person. Both court and visitors may perform in person searches. Search fee: $10.00 per name. Required to search: name, years to search. Civil cases indexed by defendant, plaintiff. Civil records on docket books since 1976; on computer back to 1990.

Criminal Records: Access: Fax, mail, in person. Both court and visitors may perform in person searches.

Search fee: $10.00 per name. Required to search: name, years to search, DOB; also helpful: SSN. Criminal records on docket books since 1976; on computer back to 1990.

General Information: No sealed, adoptions, mental health, juvenile, sex, or expunged records released. SASE required. Turnaround time same day. Fax notes: $3.00. Copy fee: $1.00 per page. Certification fee: $10.00. Fee payee: Circuit Clerk. Personal checks accepted.

Justice Court PO Box 362, Liberty, MS 39645; 601-657-4527; Fax: 601-657-4527. Hours: 8AM-5PM (CST). *Misdemeanor, Civil Actions Under $2,500, Eviction, Small Claims.*

Chancery Court PO Box 680, Liberty, MS 39645; 601-657-8022; Fax: 601-657-8288. Hours: 8AM-5PM (CST). *Probate.*

Attala County

Circuit Court Courthouse, Kosciusko, MS 39090; 662-289-1471; Fax: 662-289-7666. Hours: 8AM-5PM (CST). *Felony, Civil Actions Over $2,500.*

Civil Records: Access: Fax, mail, in person. Both court and visitors may perform in person searches. Search fee: $10.00 per name. Required to search: name, years to search. Civil cases indexed by defendant, plaintiff. Civil records kept on docket books since 1915.

Criminal Records: Access: Fax, mail, in person. Both court and visitors may perform in person searches. Search fee: $10.00 per name. Required to search: name, years to search, DOB; also helpful: SSN. Criminal records kept on docket books since 1915.

General Information: No sealed, adoptions, mental health, juvenile, sex, or expunged records released. SASE required. Turnaround time same day. Fax notes: $.50 per page. Copy fee: $.50 per page. Certification fee: $1.00. Fee payee: Circuit Clerk. Business checks accepted. Prepayment is required.

Justice Court 100 Courthouse, #4, Kosciusko, MS 39090; 662-289-7272; Fax: 662-289-0105. Hours: 8AM-5PM (CST). *Misdemeanor, Civil Actions Under $2,500, Eviction, Small Claims.*

Chancery Court 230 W. Washington, Kosciusko, MS 39090; 662-289-2921; Fax: 662-289-7662. Hours: 8AM-5PM (CST). *Probate.*

Benton County

Circuit Court PO Box 262, Ashland, MS 38603; 662-224-6310; Fax: 662-224-6312. Hours: 8AM-5PM (CST). *Felony, Civil Actions Over $2,500.*

Civil Records: Access: Mail, in person. Both court and visitors may perform in person searches. Search fee: $10.00 per name. Required to search: name, years to search, address. Civil cases indexed by defendant, plaintiff. Civil records kept on index books since 1871.

Criminal Records: Access: Mail, in person. Both court and visitors may perform in person searches. Search fee: $10.00 per name. Required to search: name, years to search, DOB; also helpful: SSN. Criminal records kept on index books since 1871.

General Information: No sealed, adoptions, mental health, juvenile, sex, or expunged records released. Turnaround time same day. Copy fee: $.50 per page. Certification fee: $1.00. Fee payee: Circuit Court. Only cashiers checks and money orders accepted. Prepayment is required.

Justice Court PO Box 152, Ashland, MS 38603; 662-224-6320; Fax: 662-224-6313. Hours: 8AM-5PM (CST). *Misdemeanor, Civil Actions Under $2,500, Eviction, Small Claims.*

Chancery Court PO Box 218, Ashland, MS 38603; 662-224-6300; Fax: 662-224-6303. Hours: 8AM-5PM (CST). *Probate.*

Bolivar County

Circuit & County Court - 1st District PO Box 205, Rosedale, MS 38769; 662-759-6521. Hours: 8AM-5PM (CST). *Felony, Misdemeanor, Civil.*

Civil Records: Access: In person only. Visitors must perform in person searches for themselves. No search fee. Required to search: name, years to search. Civil cases indexed by defendant, plaintiff. Civil records on docket books since 1900s.

Criminal Records: Access: Mail, in person. Both court and visitors may perform in person searches. Search fee: $10.00 per name. Fee is for 7 year search. Required to search: name, years to search. Criminal records on docket books since 1900s.

General Information: No sealed, juvenile, sex, or expunged records released. Turnaround time 2-3 days. Copy fee: $.50 per page. Certification fee: $1.50. Fee payee: Circuit Clerk. Personal checks accepted. Prepayment is required.

Circuit & County Court - 2nd District PO Box 670, Cleveland, MS 38732; 662-843-2061; Fax: 662-846-2943. Hours: 8AM-5PM (CST). *Felony, Misdemeanor, Civil.*

Civil Records: Access: In person only. Visitors must perform in person searches for themselves. No search fee. Required to search: name, years to search. Civil cases indexed by defendant, plaintiff. Civil records on docket books since 1940.

Criminal Records: Access: Mail, in person. Both court and visitors may perform in person searches. Search fee: $10.00 per name. Fee is for 7 year search. Required to search: name, years to search. Criminal records on docket books since 1940.

General Information: No sealed, juvenile or expunged records released. Turnaround time 2-3 days. Copy fee: $.50 per page. Certification fee: $1.50. Fee payee: Circuit Clerk. Personal checks accepted. Prepayment is required.

Justice Court PO Box 1507, Cleveland, MS 38732; 662-843-4008; Fax: 662-846-6783. Hours: 8:00AM-5:00PM (CST). *Misdemeanor, Civil Actions Under $2,500, Eviction, Small Claims.*

Cleveland Chancery Court PO Box 789, Cleveland, MS 38732; 662-843-2071; Fax: 662-846-5880. Hours: 8AM-5PM (CST). *Probate.*

Rosedale Chancery Court PO Box 238, Rosedale, MS 38769; 662-759-3762; Fax: 662-759-3467. Hours: 8AM-Noon, 1-5PM (CST). *Probate.*

Calhoun County

Circuit Court PO Box 25, Pittsboro, MS 38951; 662-412-3101; Fax: 662-412-3103. Hours: 8AM-5PM (CST). *Felony, Civil Actions Over $2,500.*

Civil Records: Access: Mail, in person. Both court and visitors may perform in person searches. Search fee: $10.00 per name. Required to search: name, years to search. Civil cases indexed by defendant, plaintiff. Civil records on docket books since 1923.

Criminal Records: Access: Mail, in person. Both court and visitors may perform in person searches. Search fee: $10.00 per name. Required to search: name, years to search, DOB; also helpful: SSN. Criminal records on docket books since 1923.

General Information: No sealed, adoptions, mental health, juvenile, sex, or expunged records released. SASE not required. Turnaround time same day, phone search info released when payment is received. Fax notes: Fee to fax results is $2.00 per page. Copy fee: $1.00 per page. Certification fee: $1.50. Fee payee:

Circuit Clerk. Personal checks accepted. Prepayment is required.

Justice Court PO Box 7, Pittsboro, MS 38951; 662-412-3134; Fax: 662-412-3136. Hours: 8AM-5PM (CST). *Misdemeanor, Civil Actions Under $2,500, Eviction, Small Claims.*

Chancery Court PO Box 8, Pittsboro, MS 38951; 662-412-3117; Fax: 662-412-3128. Hours: 8AM-5PM (CST). *Probate.*

Carroll County

Circuit Court PO Box 6, Vaiden, MS 39176; 662-464-5476; Fax: 662-464-7745. Hours: 8AM-5PM (CST). *Felony, Civil Actions Over $2,500.*

Civil Records: Access: Mail, in person. Both court and visitors may perform in person searches. Search fee: $10.00 per name. Required to search: name, years to search. Civil cases indexed by defendant, plaintiff. Civil records on books since 1900s.
Criminal Records: Access: Mail, in person. Both court and visitors may perform in person searches. Search fee: $10.00 per name. Required to search: name, years to search; also helpful: SSN. Criminal records on books since 1900s.
General Information: No adoptions, mental health or juvenile records released. Turnaround time 2 days. Copy fee: $.50 per page. Certification fee: $2.00. Fee payee: Circuit Court. Personal checks accepted. Prepayment is required.

Justice Court PO Box 10, Carrollton, MS 38917; 662-237-9285; Fax: 662-237-9286. Hours: 8AM-4PM (CST). *Misdemeanor, Civil Actions Under $2,500, Eviction, Small Claims.*

Chancery Court PO Box 60, Carrollton, MS 38917; 662-237-9274; Fax: 662-237-9642. Hours: 8AM-12; 1-5PM (CST). *Probate.*

Chickasaw County

Circuit Court - 1st District 1 Pinson Sq, Rm 2, Houston, MS 38851; 662-456-2331; Fax: 662-456-5295. Hours: 8AM-5PM (CST). *Felony, Civil Actions Over $2,500.*

Civil Records: Access: Fax, mail, in person. Both court and visitors may perform in person searches. Search fee: $10.00 per name. There is no fee if the visitor performs the search. Required to search: name, years to search; also helpful: address. Civil cases indexed by defendant, plaintiff. Civil records on docket books since mid-1800s.
Criminal Records: Access: Fax, mail, in person. Both court and visitors may perform in person searches. Search fee: $10.00 per name. Required to search: name, years to search, DOB; also helpful: address, SSN. Criminal records on docket books since mid-1800s.
General Information: Public Access terminal is available. No sealed, adoptions, mental health, juvenile, sex, or expunged records released. SASE required. Turnaround time 2-3 days. Fax notes: $1.00 per page. Copy fee: $.25 if visitor does; $1.00 if court does. Certification fee: $1.00 plus $.50 per page after first. Fee payee: Circuit Clerk. Business checks accepted. Prepayment is required.

Circuit Court - 2nd District Courthouse, Okolona, MS 38860; 662-447-2838; Fax: 662-447-5024. Hours: 8AM-5PM (CST). *Felony, Civil Actions Over $2,500.*

Civil Records: Access: Fax, mail, in person. Both court and visitors may perform in person searches. Search fee: $10.00 per name. Required to search: name, years to search; also helpful: address. Civil cases indexed by defendant, plaintiff. Civil records on docket books.

Criminal Records: Access: Fax, mail, in person. Both court and visitors may perform in person searches. Search fee: $10.00 per name. Required to search: name, years to search, DOB; also helpful: SSN. Criminal records on books.
General Information: No sealed, adoptions, mental health, juvenile, sex, or expunged records released. SASE required. Turnaround time 2-3 days. Copy fee: $.50 per page. Certification fee: $1.00 plus $.50 per page after first. Fee payee: Circuit Clerk. Business checks accepted. Prepayment is required.

Justice Court Courthouse, Houston, MS 38851; 662-456-3941; Fax: 662-456-5295. Hours: 8AM-5PM (CST). *Misdemeanor, Civil Actions Under $2,500, Eviction, Small Claims.*

Justice Court District 2 234 W Main, Rm 207, Okolona, MS 38860; 662-447-3402. *Misdemeanor, Civil Actions Under $2,500, Eviction, Small Claims.*

Chancery Court Courthouse Bldg, 1 Pinson Square, Houston, MS 38851; 662-456-2513; Fax: 662-456-5295. *Probate.*

Chancery Court 234 W Main, Rm 201, Okolona, MS 38860-1438; 662-447-2092; Fax: 662-447-5024. *Probate.*

Choctaw County

Circuit Court PO Box 34, Ackerman, MS 39735; 662-285-6245; Fax: 662-285-2196. Hours: 8AM-5PM (CST). *Felony, Civil Actions Over $2,500.*

Civil Records: Access: Mail, in person. Both court and visitors may perform in person searches. Search fee: $10.00 per name. Required to search: name, years to search. Civil cases indexed by defendant, plaintiff. Civil records in books back to 1926.
Criminal Records: Access: Mail, in person. Both court and visitors may perform in person searches. Search fee: $10.00 per name. Same fee for in person search. Required to search: name, years to search; also helpful: DOB, SSN. Criminal records in books back to 1926.
General Information: No sealed, adoptions, mental health, juvenile, sex, or expunged records released. SASE required. Turnaround time 14 days legal maximum. Copy fee: $1.00 per page. Certification fee: $1.00. Fee payee: Choctaw County Circuit Clerk. Personal checks accepted. Prepayment is required.

Justice Court PO Box 357, Ackerman, MS 39735; 662-285-3599; Fax: 662-285-3444. Hours: 8AM-5PM (CST). *Misdemeanor, Civil Actions Under $2,500, Eviction, Small Claims.*

Chancery Court PO Box 250, Ackerman, MS 39735; 662-285-6329; Fax: 662-285-3444. Hours: 8AM-5PM (CST). *Probate.*

Claiborne County

Circuit Court PO Box 549, Port Gibson, MS 39150; 601-437-5841. Hours: 8AM-5PM (CST). *Felony, Civil Actions Over $2,500.*

Civil Records: Access: Mail, in person. Both court and visitors may perform in person searches. Search fee: $10.00 per name. Required to search: name, years to search, address. Civil cases indexed by defendant, plaintiff. Civil records on docket books since 1820.
Criminal Records: Access: Mail, in person. Both court and visitors may perform in person searches. Search fee: $10.00 per name. Required to search: name, years to search, address, DOB, signed release. Criminal records on docket books since 1820.
General Information: No sealed, adoptions, mental health, juvenile, sex, or expunged records released. Turnaround time varies. Copy fee: $1.00 per page. Certification fee: $1.50. Fee payee: Sammie L Good,

Circuit Clerk. Personal checks accepted. Prepayment is required.

Justice Court PO Box 497, Port Gibson, MS 39150; 601-437-4478. Hours: 8AM-5PM (CST). *Misdemeanor, Civil Actions Under $2,500, Eviction, Small Claims.*

Chancery Court PO Box 449, Port Gibson, MS 39150; 601-437-4992; Fax: 601-437-3137. Hours: 8AM-5PM (CST). *Probate.*

Clarke County

Circuit Court PO Box 216, Quitman, MS 39355; 601-776-3111; Fax: 601-776-1001. Hours: 8AM-5PM (CST). *Felony, Civil Actions Over $2,500.*

Civil Records: Access: Fax, mail, in person. Both court and visitors may perform in person searches. Search fee: $10.00 per name. Required to search: name, years to search; also helpful: address. Civil cases indexed by defendant, plaintiff. Civil records kept on docket books since 1950s.
Criminal Records: Access: Fax, mail, in person. Both court and visitors may perform in person searches. Search fee: $10.00 per name. Required to search: name, years to search; also helpful: address, DOB, SSN, sex. Criminal records kept on docket books since 1950s.
General Information: No sealed, adoptions, mental health, juvenile, sex, or expunged records released. Turnaround time 1 day. Fax notes: No fee to fax results. No copy fee. Certification fee: $1.50. Fee payee: Circuit Clerk. Personal checks accepted. Prepayment is required.

Justice Court PO Box 4, Quitman, MS 39355; 601-776-5371. Hours: 8AM-5PM (CST). *Misdemeanor, Civil Actions Under $2,500, Eviction, Small Claims.*

Chancery Court PO Box 689, Quitman, MS 39355; 601-776-2126. Hours: 8AM-5PM *Probate.*

Clay County

Circuit Court PO Box 364, West Point, MS 39773; 662-494-3384; Fax: 662-495-2057. Hours: 8AM-5PM (CST). *Felony, Civil Actions Over $2,500.*

Civil Records: Access: Phone, mail, in person, online. Both court and visitors may perform in person searches. Search fee: $10.00 per name. Required to search: name, years to search. Civil cases indexed by defendant, plaintiff. Civil records on docket books back to 1962; archived since mid-1800s. Online access to circuit court dockets is available by subscription at www.recordsusa.com/Mississippi/ClayCnMS.htm. Credit card, username and password is required; choose either monthly or per-use plan. Visit the web site or call Lisa at 601-264-7701 for information.
Criminal Records: Access: Mail, in person, online. Both court and visitors may perform in person searches. Search fee: $10.00 per name. Required to search: name, years to search, address, DOB; also helpful: SSN. Criminal records on docket books back to 1962; archived since mid-1800s. Online access to criminal dockets is the same as civil.
General Information: No sealed, adoptions, mental health, juvenile, sex, or expunged records released. SASE required. Turnaround time same day. Copy fee: $.50 per page. Certification fee: $10.00. Fee payee: Clay County Circuit Clerk. Personal checks accepted. Prepayment is required.

Justice Court PO Box 674, West Point, MS 39773; 662-494-6141; Fax: 662-494-4034. Hours: 8AM-5PM (CST). *Misdemeanor, Civil Actions Under $2,500, Eviction, Small Claims.*

Chancery Court PO Box 815, West Point, MS 39773; 662-494-3124. Hours: 8AM-5PM (CST). *Probate.*

Coahoma County

Circuit & County Court PO Box 849, Clarksdale, MS 38614-0849; 662-624-3014; Fax: 662-624-3075. Hours: 8AM-5PM (CST). *Felony, Civil.*

Civil Records: Access: Fax, mail, in person. Both court and visitors may perform in person searches. Search fee: $10.00 per name. Required to search: name, years to search, address. Civil cases indexed by defendant, plaintiff. Civil records on docket since 1836.

Criminal Records: Access: Fax, mail, in person. Both court and visitors may perform in person searches. Search fee: $10.00 per name. Required to search: name, years to search, DOB, signed release; also helpful: address, SSN. Criminal records on docket since 1836.

General Information: No sealed, adoptions, mental health, juvenile, sex, or expunged records released. SASE not required. Turnaround time 2 days. Fax notes: No fee to fax results. Copy fee: $.50 per page. Certification fee: $1.00. Fee payee: Circuit Clerk. Personal checks accepted. Prepayment is required.

Justice Court 144 Ritch, Clarksdale, MS 38614; 662-624-3060. Hours: 8AM-5PM (CST). *Misdemeanor, Civil Actions Under $2,500, Eviction, Small Claims.*

Chancery Court PO Box 98, Clarksdale, MS 38614; 662-624-3000; Fax: 662-624-3029. Hours: 8AM-5PM (CST). *Probate.*

Copiah County

Circuit Court PO Box 467, Hazlehurst, MS 39083; 601-894-1241; Fax: 601-894-3026. Hours: 8AM-5PM (CST). *Felony, Civil Actions Over $2,500.*

Civil Records: Access: Fax, mail, in person. Both court and visitors may perform in person searches. Search fee: $6.00 per name. Required to search: name, years to search. Civil cases indexed by defendant. Civil records on docket books since late 1800s.

Criminal Records: Access: Fax, mail, in person. Both court and visitors may perform in person searches. Search fee: $6.00 per name. Required to search: name, years to search; also helpful: DOB, SSN. Criminal records on docket books since late 1800s.

General Information: No sealed, adoptions, mental health, juvenile, sex, or expunged records released. Turnaround time 1-2 days. Fax notes: No fee to fax results. Copy fee: $.50 per page. Certification fee: $1.50. Fee payee: Circuit Clerk. Business checks accepted. Prepayment is required.

Justice Court PO Box 798, Hazlehurst, MS 39083; 601-894-3218; Fax: 601-894-6038. Hours: 8:00AM-5:00PM (CST). *Misdemeanor, Civil Actions Under $2,500, Eviction, Small Claims.*

Chancery Court 121 S Lowe St, Hazlehurst, MS 39083; 601-894-3021; Fax: 601-894-4081. Hours: 8AM-5PM (CST). *Probate.*

Covington County

Circuit Court PO Box 667, Collins, MS 39428; 601-765-6506; Fax: 601-765-5012. Hours: 8AM-5PM (CST). *Felony, Civil Actions Over $2,500.*

Civil Records: Access: Fax, mail, in person. Both court and visitors may perform in person searches. Search fee: $10.00 per name. Required to search: name, years to search. Civil cases indexed by defendant, plaintiff. Civil records on docket books since 1915.

Criminal Records: Access: Fax, mail, in person. Both court and visitors may perform in person searches. Search fee: $10.00 per name. Required to search: name,

years to search, DOB; also helpful: SSN. Criminal records on docket books since 1915.

General Information: No sealed, adoptions, mental health, juvenile, sex, or expunged records released. Turnaround time 2-3 days. Fax notes: No fee to fax results. Copy fee: $.50 for first page, $.25 each add'l. Certification fee: $3.00. Fee payee: Circuit Clerk. Personal checks accepted. Prepayment is required.

Justice Court PO Box 665, Collins, MS 39428; 601-765-6581. Hours: 8AM-5PM (CST). *Misdemeanor, Civil Actions Under $2,500, Eviction, Small Claims.*

Chancery Court PO Box 1679, Collins, MS 39428; 601-765-4242; Fax: 601-765-1052. Hours: 8AM-5PM (CST). *Probate.*

De Soto County

Circuit & County Court 2535 Hwy 51 South, Hernando, MS 38632; 662-429-1325. Hours: 8AM-5PM (CST). *Felony, Misdemeanor, Civil.*

Civil Records: Access: Fax, mail, in person. Both court and visitors may perform in person searches. Search fee: $10.00 per name. Required to search: name, years to search; also helpful: address. Civil cases indexed by defendant, plaintiff. Civil records on docket books since 1972.

Criminal Records: Access: Fax, mail, in person. Both court and visitors may perform in person searches. Search fee: $10.00 per name. Required to search: name, years to search, DOB; also helpful: SSN. Criminal records on docket books since 1972.

General Information: No sealed, adoptions, mental health, juvenile, sex, or expunged records released. Turnaround time 1-2 days. Copy fee: $.50 per page. Certification fee: $2.50. Fee payee: Circuit Clerk. Personal checks accepted. Prepayment is required.

Justice Court 8525 Highway 51 North, Southaven, MS 38671; 662-393-5810; Fax: 662-393-5859. Hours: 8AM-5PM (CST). *Misdemeanor, Civil Actions Under $2,500, Eviction, Small Claims.*

Chancery Court 2535 Hwy 51 South, (PO Box 949), Hernando, MS 38632; 662-429-1320; Fax: 662-429-1311. Hours: 8AM-5PM (CST). *Probate.*

Forrest County

Circuit & County Court PO Box 992, Hattiesburg, MS 39403; 601-582-3213; Fax: 601-545-6065. Hours: 8AM-5PM (CST). *Felony, Misdemeanor, Civil.*

Civil Records: Access: Phone, mail, in person. Both court and visitors may perform in person searches. Search fee: $10.00 per name. Required to search: name, years to search; also helpful: address. Civil cases indexed by defendant, plaintiff. Civil records on docket books since 1900s. Limited phone access.

Criminal Records: Access: Mail, in person. Both court and visitors may perform in person searches. Search fee: $10.00 per name. Required to search: name, years to search, DOB, SSN; also helpful: address. Criminal records on docket books since 1900s; on computer since 1995.

General Information: No juvenile or expunged records released. Turnaround time 10 days. Copy fee: $.50 per page. Certification fee: $1.50. Fee payee: Circuit Clerk. Business checks accepted. Attorney's checks accepted. Prior approval required.

Justice Court 316 Forrest St, Hattiesburg, MS 39401; 601-544-3136; Fax: 601-545-6114. Hours: 8AM-5PM (CST). *Misdemeanor, Civil Actions Under $2,500, Eviction, Small Claims.*

Chancery Court PO Box 951, Hattiesburg, MS 39403; 601-545-6040. Hours: 8AM-5PM (CST). *Probate.*

Franklin County

Circuit Court PO Box 267, Meadville, MS 39653; 601-384-2320; Fax: 601-384-8244. Hours: 8AM-5PM (CST). *Felony, Civil Actions Over $2,500.*

Civil Records: Access: Phone, fax, mail, in person. Both court and visitors may perform in person searches. Search fee: $10.00 per name. Required to search: name, years to search. Civil cases indexed by defendant, plaintiff. Civil records on books since 1944.

Criminal Records: Access: Fax, mail, in person. Both court and visitors may perform in person searches. Search fee: $10.00 per name. Required to search: name, years to search, DOB or SSN; also helpful: address. Criminal records on books since 1944.

General Information: No sealed, adoptions, mental health, juvenile, sex, or expunged records released. Turnaround time 2-3 days. Copy fee: $1.00 per page. Certification fee: $.50. Fee payee: Circuit Clerk. Personal checks accepted. Prepayment is required.

Justice Court PO Box 365, Meadville, MS 39653; 601-384-2002. Hours: 8AM-5PM (CST). *Misdemeanor, Civil Actions Under $2,500, Eviction, Small Claims.*

Chancery Court PO Box 297, Meadville, MS 39653; 601-384-2330; Fax: 601-384-5864. Hours: 8AM-5PM (CST). *Probate.*

George County

Circuit Court 355 Cox St, Suite C, Lucedale, MS 39452; 601-947-4881; Fax: 601-947-8804. Hours: 8AM-5PM M-F, 9AM-12PM Sat (CST). *Felony, Civil Actions Over $2,500.*

Civil Records: Access: Fax, mail, in person. Both court and visitors may perform in person searches. Search fee: $10.00 per name. Required to search: name, years to search. Civil cases indexed by defendant, plaintiff. Civil records on docket books since 1910.

Criminal Records: Access: Fax, mail, in person. Both court and visitors may perform in person searches. Search fee: $10.00 per name. Required to search: name, years to search; also helpful: SSN. Criminal records on docket books since 1910.

General Information: No sealed, adoptions, mental health, juvenile, sex, or expunged records released. SASE requested. Turnaround time 1-2 days. Fax notes: No fee to fax results. Copy fee: $.50 per page. Certification fee: $2.00 plus $1.00 each additional page. Fee payee: Circuit Clerk. Personal checks accepted.

Justice Court 356 A Cox St, Lucedale, MS 39452; 601-947-4834. Hours: 8AM-5PM (CST). *Misdemeanor, Civil Actions Under $2,500, Eviction, Small Claims.*

Chancery Court 355 Cox St, Suite A, Lucedale, MS 39452; 601-947-4801; Fax: 601-947-1300. Hours: 8AM-5PM (CST). *Probate.*

Greene County

Circuit Court PO Box 310, Leakesville, MS 39451; 601-394-2379; Fax: 601-394-2334. Hours: 8AM-5PM M-F (CST). *Felony, Civil Actions Over $2,500.*

Civil Records: Access: Phone, fax, mail, in person. Both court and visitors may perform in person searches. Search fee: $10.00 per name. Required to search: name, years to search; also helpful: address. Civil cases indexed by defendant, plaintiff. Civil records on docket books since early 1900s.

Criminal Records: Access: Phone, fax, mail, in person. Both court and visitors may perform in person searches. Search fee: $10.00 per name. Required to search: name, years to search; also helpful: SSN. Criminal records on docket books since early 1900s. Misdemeanor records are kept in Greene County Justice Court, 601-394-2347.

General Information: No sealed, adoptions, mental health, juvenile, sex, or expunged records released. SASE requested. Turnaround time 1-2 days. Fax notes: No fee to fax results. Copy fee: $.50 per page. Certification fee: $1.00. Fee payee: Circuit Clerk. Personal checks accepted. Prepayment is required.

Justice Court PO Box 547, Leakesville, MS 39451; 601-394-2347; Fax: 601-394-5939. Hours: 8AM-5PM (CST). *Misdemeanor, Civil Actions Under $2,500, Eviction, Small Claims.*

Chancery Court PO Box 610, Leakesville, MS 39451; 601-394-2377. Hours: 8AM-5PM (CST). *Probate.*

Grenada County

Circuit Court PO Box 1517, Grenada, MS 38902-1517; 662-226-1941; Fax: 662-227-2865. Hours: 8AM-5PM (CST). *Felony, Civil Actions Over $2,500.*

Civil Records: Access: In person only. Visitors must perform in person searches for themselves. No search fee. Required to search: name, years to search. Civil cases indexed by defendant, plaintiff. Civil records on docket books since mid-1970s.

Criminal Records: Access: In person only. Visitors must perform in person searches for themselves. No search fee. Required to search: name, years to search. Criminal records on docket books since mid-1970s.

General Information: Public Access terminal is available. (Judgment roll on terminal from 1996.) No sealed, juvenile, or expunged records released. Copy fee: $.50 per page. Certification fee: $1.50. Fee payee: Circuit Clerk. No personal checks accepted. Prepayment is required.

Justice Court 16 First St, Grenada, MS 38901; 662-226-3331. Hours: 8AM-5PM (CST). *Misdemeanor, Civil Actions Under $2,500, Eviction, Small Claims.*

Chancery Court PO Box 1208, Grenada, MS 38902; 662-226-1821; Fax: 662-226-0427. Hours: 8AM-5PM (CST). *Probate.*

Hancock County

Circuit Court PO Box 249, 152 Main Street, Bay St. Louis, MS 39520; 228-467-5265; Fax: 228-467-2779. Hours: 8AM-5PM (CST). *Felony, Civil Actions Over $2,500.*

Civil Records: Access: Mail, in person. Both court and visitors may perform in person searches. Search fee: $10.00 per name. Required to search: name, years to search. Civil cases indexed by defendant, plaintiff. Civil records on docket books since 1975.

Criminal Records: Access: Mail, in person. Both court and visitors may perform in person searches. Search fee: $10.00 per name. Required to search: name, years to search, DOB; also helpful: SSN. Criminal records on docket books since 1918.

General Information: No sealed, adoptions, mental health, juvenile, sex, or expunged records released. Turnaround time 1 week. Copy fee: $.50 per page. Certification fee: $1.50 per page. Fee payee: Circuit Clerk. Personal checks accepted. Prepayment is required.

Justice Court 306 Hwy 90, Bay St. Louis, MS 39520; 228-467-5573. Hours: 8AM-5PM (CST). *Misdemeanor, Civil Actions Under $2,500, Eviction, Small Claims.*

Chancery Court PO Box 429 Bay St., Bay St. Louis, MS 39520; 228-467-5404; Fax: 228-467-3159. Hours: 8AM-5PM (CST). *Probate.*

Harrison County

Circuit Court - 1st District PO Box 998, Gulfport, MS 39502; 228-865-4147; Fax: 228-865-4009. Hours: 8AM-5PM (CST). *Felony, Civil Actions Over $75,000.*

Civil Records: Access: Mail, in person. Both court and visitors may perform in person searches. Search fee: $10.00 per name. Required to search: name, years to search. Civil cases indexed by defendant, plaintiff. Civil records on computer back to 7/1991, prior on docket books, older records are archived.

Criminal Records: Access: Mail, in person. Both court and visitors may perform in person searches. Search fee: $10.00 per name. Required to search: name, years to search, DOB; also helpful: SSN. Criminal records on computer back to 7/1991, prior on docket books, older records are archived.

General Information: Public Access terminal is available. No sealed, adoptions, mental health, juvenile, sex, or expunged records released. SASE requested. Turnaround time 1-2 days. Copy fee: $.50 per page. Certification fee: $1.00. Fee payee: Circuit Clerk. Business checks accepted. Prepayment is required.

Circuit Court - 2nd District PO Box 235, Biloxi, MS 39533; 228-435-8258; Fax: 228-435-8277. Hours: 8AM-5PM (CST). *Felony, Civil Actions Over $75,000.*

Civil Records: Access: Fax, mail, in person. Both court and visitors may perform in person searches. Search fee: $10.00 per name. Required to search: name, years to search. Civil cases indexed by defendant, plaintiff. Civil records on computer since July 1991.

Criminal Records: Access: Fax, mail, in person. Both court and visitors may perform in person searches. Search fee: $10.00 per name. Required to search: name, years to search, DOB; also helpful: SSN. Criminal records on computer since July 1991.

General Information: Public Access terminal is available. No sealed or expunged records released. SASE required. Turnaround time 3 days. Fax notes: $.50 per page. Copy fee: $.50 per page. Certification fee: $1.00. Fee payee: Circuit Clerk. Business checks accepted. Attorney's checks accepted. Prepayment is required.

County Court - 1st District PO Box 998, Gulfport, MS 39502; 228-865-4097; Fax: 228-865-4099. Hours: 8AM-5PM (CST). *Misdemeanor, Civil Actions Under $75,000.*

Civil Records: Access: Mail, in person. Both court and visitors may perform in person searches. Search fee: $10.00 per name. Required to search: name, years to search. Civil cases indexed by defendant, plaintiff. Civil records on computer since 1991, prior on docket books since early 1900s.

Criminal Records: Access: Mail, in person. Both court and visitors may perform in person searches. Search fee: $10.00 per name. Required to search: name, years to search; also helpful: DOB. Criminal records on computer since 1991, prior on docket books since early 1900s.

General Information: Public Access terminal is available. No sealed, adoptions, mental health, juvenile, sex, or expunged records released. Turnaround time 1-2 days. Copy fee: $.50 per page. Certification fee: $1.00. Fee payee: County Clerk. Business checks accepted. Prepayment is required.

County Court - 2nd District PO Box 235, Biloxi, MS 39533; 228-435-8294/8232; Fax: 228-435-8277. Hours: 8AM-5PM (CST). *Misdemeanor, Civil Actions Under $75,000.*

Civil Records: Access: Fax, mail, in person. Both court and visitors may perform in person searches. Search fee: $10.00 per name. Required to search: name, years to search. Civil cases indexed by defendant, plaintiff. Civil records on computer since July 1991, prior on books.

Criminal Records: Access: Fax, mail, in person. Both court and visitors may perform in person searches. Search fee: $10.00 per name. Required to search: name, years to search, DOB; also helpful: SSN, aliases. Criminal records on computer since July 1991, prior on books.

General Information: Public Access terminal is available. No sealed or expunged records released. SASE required. Turnaround time 3 days. Fax notes: No fee to fax results. Copy fee: $.50 per page. Certification fee: $1.00. Fee payee: Circuit Clerk. Business checks accepted. Attorney's checks accepted. Prepayment is required.

Justice Court PO Box 1754, Gulfport, MS 39502; Civil phone: 228-865-4193; Criminal phone: 228-865-4214; Fax: 228-865-4216. Hours: 8AM-5PM (CST). *Misdemeanor, Civil Actions Under $2,500, Eviction, Small Claims.*

Biloxi Chancery Court PO Box 544, Biloxi, MS 39533; 228-435-8220; Fax: 228-435-8251. Hours: 8AM-Noon, 1-5PM (CST). *Probate.*

Gulfport Chancery Court PO Drawer CC, Gulfport, MS 39502; 228-865-4092; Fax: 228-865-1646. Hours: 8AM-Noon, 1-5PM (CST). *Probate.*

Hinds County

Circuit & County Court - 1st District PO Box 327, Jackson, MS 39205; 601-968-6628. Hours: 8AM-5PM (CST). *Felony, Misdemeanor, Civil.*

Civil Records: Access: Mail, in person. Both court and visitors may perform in person searches. Search fee: $9.00 per name. Required to search: name, years to search. Civil cases indexed by defendant, plaintiff. Civil records on docket books back to 1900s.

Criminal Records: Access: Mail, in person. Both court and visitors may perform in person searches. Search fee: $9.00 per name. Required to search: name, years to search, DOB; also helpful: SSN. Criminal records on docket books back to 1900s.

General Information: Public Access terminal is available. No sealed, adoptions, mental health, juvenile, sex, or expunged records released. Turnaround time 14 days. Copy fee: $.50 per page. Certification fee: No cert fee. Fee payee: Circuit Clerk. Personal checks accepted. Prepayment is required.

Circuit & County Court - 2nd District PO Box 999, Raymond, MS 39154; 601-968-6653. Hours: 8AM-Noon, 1-5PM (CST). *Felony, Misdemeanor, Civil.*

Civil Records: Access: Mail, in person. Both court and visitors may perform in person searches. Search fee: $9.00 per name. Required to search: name, years to search. Civil cases indexed by defendant, plaintiff. Civil records on computer since 1994, prior on docket books since late 1800s.

Criminal Records: Access: Mail, in person. Both court and visitors may perform in person searches. Search fee: $9.00 per name. Required to search: name, years to search; also helpful: DOB, SSN. Criminal records on computer to 1994, prior on docket books to late 1800s.

General Information: No sealed, adoptions, mental health, juvenile, sex, expunged or some preliminary criminal records released. SASE not required.

Turnaround time 1 week. Copy fee: $.50 per page. Certification fee: $1.50. Fee payee: Circuit Clerk. Personal checks accepted. Prepayment is required.

Justice Court 407 E Pascagoula, 3rd floor, PO Box 3490, Jackson, MS 39207; 601-968-6781; Fax: 601-973-5532. Hours: 8AM-Noon, 1-5PM *Misdemeanor, Civil Actions Under $2,500, Eviction, Small Claims.*

Jackson Chancery Court PO Box 686, Jackson, MS 39205; 601-968-6540; Fax: 601-973-5554. Hours: 8AM-5PM (CST). *Probate.*

Raymond Chancery Court PO Box 88, Raymond, MS 39154; 601-857-8055; Fax: 601-857-4953. Hours: 8AM-5PM (CST). *Probate.*

Holmes County

Circuit Court PO Box 718, Lexington, MS 39095; 662-834-2476; Fax: 662-834-3870. Hours: 8AM-5PM (CST). *Felony, Civil Actions Over $2,500.*

Civil Records: Access: Fax, mail, in person. Both court and visitors may perform in person searches. Search fee: $10.00 per name. Required to search: name, years to search. Civil cases indexed by defendant, plaintiff. Civil records on docket books since 1940s.

Criminal Records: Access: Fax, mail, in person. Both court and visitors may perform in person searches. Search fee: $10.00 per name. Required to search: name, years to search; also helpful: DOB, SSN. Criminal records on docket books since 1940s.

General Information: Public Access terminal is available. No sealed or expunged records released. Turnaround time 1-2 days. Fax notes: $.25 per page. Copy fee: $1.00 per page. Certification fee: $1.50. Fee payee: Holmes County Circuit Clerk. Business checks accepted. Prepayment is required.

Justice Court PO Box 99, Lexington, MS 39095; 662-834-4565. Hours: 8AM-Noon, 1-5PM (CST). *Misdemeanor, Civil Actions Under $2,500, Eviction, Small Claims.*

Chancery Court PO Box 239, Lexington, MS 39095; 662-834-2508; Fax: 662-834-3020. Hours: 8AM-5PM (CST). *Probate.*

Humphreys County

Circuit Court PO Box 696, Belzoni, MS 39038; 662-247-3065; Fax: 662-247-3906. Hours: 8AM-5PM (CST). *Felony, Civil Actions Over $2,500.*

Civil Records: Access: Fax, mail, in person. Both court and visitors may perform in person searches. Search fee: $10.00 per name. Required to search: name, years to search. Civil cases indexed by defendant, plaintiff. Civil records on books since 1918.

Criminal Records: Access: Fax, mail, in person. Both court and visitors may perform in person searches. Search fee: $10.00 per name. Required to search: name, years to search; also helpful: DOB, SSN. Criminal records on books since 1918.

General Information: No sealed, adoptions, mental health, juvenile, sex, or expunged records released. SASE not required. Turnaround time 1 day, phone turnaround 30 minutes. Fax notes: $.50 per page. Copy fee: $1.00 per page. Certification fee: Certification is included in search fee, unless you do search yourself then $1.00. Fee payee: Circuit Clerk. Personal checks accepted. Prepayment is required.

Justice Court 102 Castleman St, Belzoni, MS 39038; 662-247-4337; Fax: 662-247-1095. Hours: 8AM-Noon, 1-5PM (CST). *Misdemeanor, Civil Actions Under $2,500, Eviction, Small Claims.*

Chancery Court PO Box 547, Belzoni, MS 39038; 662-247-1740; Fax: 662-247-1010. Hours: 8AM-Noon, 1-5PM (CST). *Probate.*

Issaquena County

Circuit Court PO Box 27, Mayersville, MS 39113; 662-873-2761. Hours: 8AM-5PM (CST). *Felony, Civil Actions Over $2,500.*

Civil Records: Access: Mail, in person. Both court and visitors may perform in person searches. Search fee: $20.00 per name. Required to search: name, years to search. Civil cases indexed by defendant, plaintiff. Civil records on docket books since 1846.

Criminal Records: Access: Mail, in person. Both court and visitors may perform in person searches. Search fee: $20.00 per name. Required to search: name, years to search; also helpful: DOB, SSN. Criminal records on docket books since 1846.

General Information: No sealed, adoptions, mental health, juvenile, sex, or expunged records released. Turnaround time 1 week. Copy fee: $.50 per page. Certification fee: $1.00. Fee payee: Circuit Clerk. Personal checks accepted. Prepayment is required.

Justice Court PO Box 58, Mayersville, MS 39113; 662-873-6287. Hours: 8AM-Noon, 1-5PM (CST). *Misdemeanor, Civil Actions Under $2,500, Eviction, Small Claims.*

Chancery Court PO Box 27, Mayersville, MS 39113; 662-873-2761; Fax: 662-873-2061. Hours: 8AM-5PM (CST). *Probate.*

Itawamba County

Circuit Court 201 W Main, Fulton, MS 38843; 662-862-3511; Fax: 662-862-4006. Hours: 8AM-5PM (CST). *Felony, Civil Actions Over $2,500.*

Civil Records: Access: Phone, fax, mail, in person. Both court and visitors may perform in person searches. No search fee. Required to search: name, years to search. Civil cases indexed by defendant, plaintiff. Civil records on books since 1940s.

Criminal Records: Access: Phone, fax, mail, in person. Both court and visitors may perform in person searches. No search fee. Required to search: name, years to search, DOB; also helpful: SSN. Criminal records on books since 1940s.

General Information: Public Access terminal is available. sex or expunged records released. SASE required. Turnaround time 1 day. Fax notes: No fee to fax results. No copy fee. Certification fee: No cert fee. Business checks accepted.

Justice Court 201 W Main, Fulton, MS 38843; 662-862-4315; Fax: 662-862-5805. Hours: 8AM-Noon, 1-5PM (CST). *Misdemeanor, Civil Actions Under $2,500, Eviction, Small Claims.*

Chancery Court 201 W Main, Fulton, MS 38843; 662-862-3421; Fax: 662-862-3421. Hours: 8AM-5PM M-F; 8AM-Noon Sat (CST). *Probate.*

Jackson County

Circuit Court PO Box 998, Pascagoula, MS 39568-0998; 228-769-3025; Fax: 228-769-3180. Hours: 8AM-5PM (CST). *Felony, Civil.*

Civil Records: Access: Mail, in person. Both court and visitors may perform in person searches. Search fee: $10.00 per name per 10 years searched. Required to search: name, years to search. Civil cases indexed by defendant, plaintiff. Civil records on computer back to 1993, prior on docket books since 1920s.

Criminal Records: Access: Mail, in person. Both court and visitors may perform in person searches. Search fee: $10.00 per name, per 10 years searched. Required to search: name, years to search, DOB; also helpful: SSN. Criminal records on computer back to 1992, prior on docket books since 1920s.

General Information: Public Access terminal is available. No sealed or expunged records released.

SASE required. Turnaround time varies. Fax notes: $2.00 per page. Copy fee: $1.0 per page. Certification fee: $2.50. Fee payee: Circuit Clerk. Business checks accepted. Prepayment is required.

County Court PO Box 998, Pascagoula, MS 39568; 228-769-3181. Hours: 8AM-5PM (CST). *Misdemeanor, Civil Actions Under $75,000.*

Civil Records: Access: Phone, mail, in person. Both court and visitors may perform in person searches. Search fee: $10.00 per name. Required to search: name, years to search. Civil cases indexed by defendant, plaintiff. Civil records on docket books since 1940s; on computer back to 1992.

Criminal Records: Access: Mail, in person. Both court and visitors may perform in person searches. Search fee: $10.00 per name. Required to search: name, years to search, DOB. Criminal records on docket books since 1940s; on computer back to 1992.

General Information: Public Access terminal is available. No sealed, adoptions, mental health, juvenile, sex, or expunged records released. Turnaround time 1 week. Copy fee: $1.00 per page. Certification fee: $2.50. Fee payee: Clerk of County Court. Only cashiers checks and money orders accepted. Prepayment is required.

Justice Court 5343 Jefferson St, Moss Point, MS 39563; 228-769-3080; Civil phone: 228-769-3085; Fax: 228-769-3364. Hours: 8AM-5PM (CST). *Misdemeanor, Civil Actions Under $2,500, Eviction, Small Claims.*

www.co.jackson.ms.us

Chancery Court PO Box 998, Pascagoula, MS 39568; 228-769-3124; Fax: 228-769-3397. Hours: 8AM-5PM (CST). *Probate.*

Jasper County

Circuit Court - 1st District PO Box 58, Paulding, MS 39348; 601-727-4941; Fax: 601-727-4475. Hours: 8AM-5PM (CST). *Felony, Civil Actions Over $2,500.*

Civil Records: Access: Fax, mail, in person. Both court and visitors may perform in person searches. Search fee: $10.00 per name. Fee includes a search of both districts in the county. Required to search: name, years to search. Civil cases indexed by defendant, plaintiff. Civil records on docket books since 1932.

Criminal Records: Access: Fax, mail, in person. Both court and visitors may perform in person searches. Search fee: $10.00 per name. Fee includes a search of both districts in the county. Required to search: name, years to search; also helpful: DOB, SSN. Criminal records on docket books since 1932.

General Information: No sealed or expunged records released. Turnaround time 1 week. Fax notes: $5.00 per document. Copy fee: $.50 per page. Certification fee: $1.50. Fee payee: Circuit Clerk. Personal checks accepted. Prepayment is required.

Circuit Court - 2nd District PO Box 447, Bay Springs, MS 39422; 601-764-2245; Fax: 601-764-3078. Hours: 8AM-5PM (CST). *Felony, Civil Actions Over $2,500.*

Civil Records: Access: Mail, in person. Both court and visitors may perform in person searches. Search fee: $10.00 per name. Fee includes a search of both districts in the county. Required to search: name, years to search. Civil cases indexed by defendant, plaintiff. Civil records on docket books since 1932.

Criminal Records: Access: Mail, in person. Both court and visitors may perform in person searches. Search fee: $10.00 per name. Fee includes a search of both districts in the county. Required to search: name, years to search; also helpful: SSN. Criminal records on docket books since 1932.

General Information: No sealed, adoptions, mental health, juvenile, sex, or expunged records released. SASE requested. Turnaround time 1 day. Copy fee: $.50 per page. Certification fee: $1.50. Fee payee: Circuit Clerk. Personal checks accepted.

Justice Court PO Box 1054, Bay Springs, MS 39422; 601-764-2065; Fax: 601-764-3402. Hours: 8AM-Noon, 1-5PM (CST). *Misdemeanor, Civil Actions Under $2,500, Eviction, Small Claims.*

Note: This Justice Court houses all the Justices for Jasper County.

Bay Springs Chancery Court PO Box 1047, Bay Springs, MS 39422; 601-764-3368; Fax: 601-764-3026. Hours: 8AM-5PM (CST). *Probate.*

Paulding Chancery Court PO Box 38, Paulding, MS 39348; 601-727-4941; Fax: 601-727-4475. Hours: 8AM-5PM (CST). *Probate.*

Jefferson County

Circuit Court PO Box 305, Fayette, MS 39069; 601-786-3422; Fax: 601-786-9676. Hours: 8AM-5PM (CST). *Felony, Civil Actions Over $2,500.*

Civil Records: Access: Phone, mail, in person. Both court and visitors may perform in person searches. Search fee: $10.00 per name. Required to search: name, years to search, DOB; also helpful: SSN, sex, signed release. Civil cases indexed by defendant, plaintiff. Civil records on docket books since 1966, prior archived.
Criminal Records: Access: Phone, mail, in person. Both court and visitors may perform in person searches. Search fee: $10.00 per name. Required to search: name, years to search, DOB; also helpful: SSN. Criminal records on docket books since 1971, prior archived.
General Information: No sealed, adoptions, mental health, juvenile, sex, or expunged records released. SASE required. Turnaround time same day. Copy fee: $.50 per page. Certification fee: $1.50. Fee payee: Jefferson County Circuit Court. Business checks accepted. Prepayment is required.

Justice Court PO Box 1047, Fayette, MS 39069; 601-786-8594; Fax: 601-786-6017. Hours: 8AM-5PM (CST). *Misdemeanor, Civil Actions Under $2,500, Eviction, Small Claims.*

Chancery Court PO Box 145, Fayette, MS 39069; 601-786-3021; Fax: 601-786-6009. Hours: 8AM-5PM (CST). *Probate.*

Jefferson Davis County

Circuit Court PO Box 1082, Prentiss, MS 39474; 601-792-4231; Fax: 601-792-4957. Hours: 8AM-5PM (CST). *Felony, Civil Actions Over $2,500.*

Civil Records: Access: Phone, fax, mail, in person. Both court and visitors may perform in person searches. Search fee: $10.00 per name. Required to search: name, years to search. Civil cases indexed by defendant, plaintiff. Civil records on docket books since 1907.
Criminal Records: Access: Phone, fax, mail, in person. Both court and visitors may perform in person searches. Search fee: $10.00 per name. Required to search: name, years to search; also helpful: SSN. Criminal records on docket books since 1907.
General Information: No sealed, adoptions, mental health, juvenile, sex, or expunged records released. Turnaround time 1-2 days. Fax notes: Fee to fax results is $1.00 per page. Copy fee: $1.00 per page. Certification fee: $2.00. Fee payee: Circuit Clerk. Personal checks accepted. Prepayment is required.

Justice Court PO Box 1407, Prentiss, MS 39474; 601-792-5129. Hours: 8AM-Noon, 1-5PM (CST). *Misdemeanor, Civil Actions Under $2,500, Eviction, Small Claims.*

Chancery Court PO Box 1137, Prentiss, MS 39474; 601-792-4204; Fax: 601-792-2894. Hours: 8AM-5PM (CST). *Probate.*

Jones County

Circuit & County Court - 1st District 101 N. Court St., Suite B, Ellisville, MS 39437; 601-477-8538. Hours: 8AM-5PM (CST). *Felony, Misdemeanor, Civil.*

Civil Records: Access: In person only. Visitors must perform in person searches for themselves. No search fee. Required to search: name, years to search. Civil cases indexed by defendant, plaintiff. Civil records on docket books since 1960s.
Criminal Records: Access: Mail, fax, in person. Both court and visitors may perform in person searches. Search fee: $10.00 per name. Required to search: name, years to search. Criminal records on docket books since 1960s.
General Information: No sealed, adoptions, mental health, juvenile, sex, or expunged records released. Turnaround time 1-2 days. Copy fee: $.50 per page. Certification fee: $1.00. Fee payee: Circuit Clerk. Personal checks accepted. Prepayment is required.

Circuit & County Court - 2nd District PO Box 1336, Laurel, MS 39441; 601-425-2556. Hours: 8AM-5PM (CST). *Felony, Misdemeanor, Civil.*

Civil Records: Access: In person only. Visitors must perform in person searches for themselves. No search fee. Required to search: name, years to search. Civil cases indexed by defendant, plaintiff. Civil records on docket books since 1960s.
Criminal Records: Access: Mail, in person. Both court and visitors may perform in person searches. Search fee: $10.00 per name. Fee is per district. Required to search: name, years to search; also helpful: SSN. Criminal records on docket books since 1960s.
General Information: No sealed or Juvenile Youth Court records released. Turnaround time 2 days. Copy fee: $.50 per page. Certification fee: $1.00. Fee payee: Jones County Circuit Clerk. Personal checks accepted. Prepayment is required.

Justice Court PO Box 1997, Laurel, MS 39441; 601-428-3137; Fax: 601-428-0526. Hours: 8AM-Noon, 1-5PM (CST). *Misdemeanor, Civil Actions Under $2,500, Eviction, Small Claims.*

Note: This Justice Court houses all the Justices for Jones County.

Ellisville Chancery Court 101-D Court St., Ellisville, MS 39437; 601-477-3307. Hours: 8AM-Noon, 1-5PM (CST). *Probate.*

Laurel Chancery Court PO Box 1468, Laurel, MS 39441; 601-428-0527; Fax: 601-428-3610. Hours: 8AM-5PM (CST). *Probate.*

www.chancery19thms.com

Kemper County

Circuit Court PO Box 130, De Kalb, MS 39328; 601-743-2224; Fax: 601-743-4173. Hours: 8AM-5PM (CST). *Felony, Civil Actions Over $2,500.*

Civil Records: Access: Phone, fax, mail, in person. Both court and visitors may perform in person searches. Search fee: $10.00 per name. Required to search: name, years to search, address. Civil cases indexed by defendant, plaintiff. Civil records on docket books since 1960s.
Criminal Records: Access: Phone, fax, mail, in person. Both court and visitors may perform in person searches. Search fee: $10.00 per name. Required to search: name, years to search, address, DOB; also helpful: SSN. Criminal records on docket books since 1960s.

General Information: No sealed, adoptions, mental health, juvenile, sex, or expunged records released. Turnaround time 1 week. Fax notes: $.25 per page. Copy fee: $.25 per page. Certification fee: No cert fee. Fee payee: Circuit Clerk. Business checks accepted. Prepayment is required.

Justice Court PO Box 661, De Kalb, MS 39328; 601-743-2793; Fax: 601-743-4893. Hours: 8AM-5PM (CST). *Misdemeanor, Civil Actions Under $2,500, Eviction, Small Claims.*

Chancery Court PO Box 188, De Kalb, MS 39328; 601-743-2460; Fax: 601-743-2789. Hours: 8AM-5PM (CST). *Probate.*

Lafayette County

Circuit Court LaFayette County Courthouse, One Couerthouse Sq, Suite 201, Oxford, MS 38655; 662-234-4951; Fax: 662-236-0238. Hours: 8AM-5PM (CST). *Felony, Civil Actions Over $2,500.*

Civil Records: Access: Mail, in person. Both court and visitors may perform in person searches. Search fee: $10.00 per name. Fee is per 10 years searched. Required to search: name, years to search; also helpful: address. Civil cases indexed by defendant, plaintiff. Civil records on docket books from 1900; on computer back to 1995.
Criminal Records: Access: Mail, in person. Both court and visitors may perform in person searches. Search fee: $10.00 per name. Fee is per 10 years searched. Required to search: name, years to search, DOB; also helpful: address, SSN. Criminal records on docket books from 1900, on computer back to 1995.
General Information: Public Access terminal is available. No sealed, adoptions, mental health, juvenile, sex, or expunged records released. Turnaround time 1-2 days. Copy fee: $1.00 per page. Certification fee: $1.50. Fee payee: Circuit Clerk. Business checks accepted. Prepayment is required.

Justice Court 1219 Monroe, Oxford, MS 38655; 662-234-1545; Fax: 662-238-7990. Hours: 8AM-5PM (CST). *Misdemeanor, Civil Actions Under $2,500, Eviction, Small Claims.*

Chancery Court PO Box 1240, Oxford, MS 38655; 662-234-2131; Fax: 662-234-5402. Hours: 8AM-5PM (CST). *Probate.*

Lamar County

Circuit Court PO Box 369, Purvis, MS 39475; 601-794-8504; Fax: 601-794-3905. Hours: 8AM-5PM (CST). *Felony, Civil Actions Over $2,500.*

Civil Records: Access: Mail, in person. Both court and visitors may perform in person searches. Search fee: $10.00 per name. Required to search: name, years to search. Civil cases indexed by defendant, plaintiff. Civil records on docket books since 1904.
Criminal Records: Access: Mail, in person. Both court and visitors may perform in person searches. Search fee: $10.00 per name. Required to search: name, years to search; also helpful: SSN. Criminal records on docket books since 1904.
General Information: No sealed, adoptions, mental health, juvenile, sex, or expunged records released. SASE requested. Turnaround time 1-2 days. Copy fee: $1.00 per page. Certification fee: No cert fee. Fee payee: Circuit Clerk. Business checks accepted. Prepayment is required.

Justice Court PO Box 1010, Purvis, MS 39475; 601-794-2950; Fax: 601-794-1076. Hours: 8AM-5PM (CST). *Misdemeanor, Civil Actions Under $2,500, Eviction, Small Claims.*

Chancery Court PO Box 247, Purvis, MS 39475; 601-794-8504; Fax: 601-794-3903. Hours: 8AM-5PM (CST). *Probate.*

Lauderdale County

Circuit & County Court PO Box 1005, Meridian, MS 39302-1005; 601-482-9738; Fax: 601-484-3970. Hours: 8AM-5PM (CST). *Felony, Civil Actions Over $2,500.*

Note: County Court can be reached at 601-482-9715.

Civil Records: Access: Phone, mail, fax, in person. Both court and visitors may perform in person searches. Search fee: $10.00 per name. Required to search: name, years to search, SSN. Civil cases indexed by defendant, plaintiff. Civil records on docket books back to 1950s, on computer back to 1992. Court will only search computer records.
Criminal Records: Access: Mail, fax, in person. Both court and visitors may perform in person searches. Search fee: $10.00 per name. Required to search: name, years to search, DOB; also helpful: SSN. Criminal records on computer (Felony) back to 1965.
General Information: Public Access terminal is available. No sealed, adoptions, mental health, juvenile, sex, or expunged records released. SASE not required. Turnaround time 1 week, phone turnaround time 1 week. Fax notes: Will not fax results. Copy fee: $.50 per page. Certification fee: No cert fee. Fee payee: Circuit Clerk. Business checks accepted. Will bill complete files to attorneys.

Justice Court PO Box 5126, Meridian, MS 39302; 601-482-9879; Fax: 601-482-9813. Hours: 8AM-5PM (CST). *Misdemeanor, Civil Actions Under $2,500, Eviction, Small Claims.*

Chancery Court PO Box 1587, Meridian, MS 39302; 601-482-9701; Fax: 601-486-4920. Hours: 8AM-Noon, 1-5PM (CST). *Probate.*

Lawrence County

Circuit Court PO Box 1249, Monticello, MS 39654; 601-587-4791; Fax: 601-587-0750. Hours: 8AM-5PM (CST). *Felony, Civil Actions Over $2,500.*

Civil Records: Access: Phone, fax, mail, in person. Both court and visitors may perform in person searches. Search fee: $10.00 per name. Required to search: name, years to search; also helpful: address. Civil cases indexed by defendant, plaintiff. Civil records on docket books since 1977. For fax request send copy of check for fee.
Criminal Records: Access: Phone, fax, mail, in person. Both court and visitors may perform in person searches. Search fee: $10.00 per name. Required to search: name, years to search, DOB; also helpful: address, SSN. Criminal records on docket books since 1977. For fax request send copy of check for fee.
General Information: No sealed, adoptions, mental health, juvenile, sex, or expunged records released. SASE requested. Turnaround time 1 week, phone turnaround time 1-2 days. Fax notes: $10.00 per document. No copy fee. Certification fee: $1.50. Fee payee: Circuit Clerk. Personal checks accepted. Prepayment is required.

Justice Court PO Box 903, Monticello, MS 39654; 601-587-7183; Fax: 601-587-0755. Hours: 8AM-5PM (CST). *Misdemeanor, Civil Actions Under $2,500, Eviction, Small Claims.*

Chancery Court 517 Broad St, Courthouse Sq, PO Box 821, Monticello, MS 39654; 601-587-7162; Fax: 601-587-0767. Hours: 8AM-5PM (CST). *Probate.*

Leake County

Circuit Court PO Box 67, Carthage, MS 39051; 601-267-8357; Fax: 601-267-8889. Hours: 8AM-5PM (CST). *Felony, Civil Actions Over $2,500.*

Civil Records: Access: In person only. Visitors must perform in person searches for themselves. No search fee. Required to search: name, years to search. Civil cases indexed by defendant, plaintiff. Civil records on docket books since 1970s.
Criminal Records: Access: Mail, in person. Both court and visitors may perform in person searches. Search fee: $10.00 per name. Required to search: name, years to search, DOB; also helpful: SSN. Criminal records on docket books since 1970s.
General Information: Public Access terminal is available. (Voting & Judgments only.) No sealed, adoptions, mental health, juvenile, sex, or expunged records released. SASE required. Turnaround time 1-2 days. Copy fee: $.50 per page. Certification fee: $1.50. Fee payee: Circuit Clerk. Prepayment is required.

Justice Court PO Box 69, Carthage, MS 39051; 601-267-5677; Fax: 601-267-6134. Hours: 8:00AM-5:00PM (CST). *Misdemeanor, Civil Actions Under $2,500, Eviction, Small Claims.*

Chancery Court PO Box 72, Carthage, MS 39051; 601-267-7371; Fax: 601-267-6137. Hours: 8AM-5PM (CST). *Probate.*

Lee County

Circuit & County Court Circuit Court-PO Box 762, County Court - PO Box 736, Tupelo, MS 38802; 662-841-9022/9023(Circuit) 9730 (County); Fax: 662-680-6079. Hours: 8AM-5PM (CST). *Felony, Civil Actions Over $2,500.*

Civil Records: Access: Mail, in person. Both court and visitors may perform in person searches. Search fee: $10.00 per name. Required to search: name, years to search. Civil cases indexed by defendant, plaintiff. Circuit records on computer since 1990, others on docket books since 1987. County records not on computer.
Criminal Records: Access: Mail, in person. Both court and visitors may perform in person searches. Search fee: $10.00 per name. Required to search: name, years to search; also helpful: DOB, SSN. Circuit records on computer since 1990, others on docket books since 1987. County records not on computer.
General Information: No sealed or expunged records released. SASE required. Turnaround time 1-2 days. Copy fee: $.25 per page. Certification fee: $1.50. Fee payee: Lee County & Circuit Court. Business checks accepted. Prepayment is required.

Justice Court PO Box 108, Tupelo, MS 38802; 662-841-9014; Fax: 662-680-6021. Hours: 8AM-5PM (CST). *Misdemeanor, Civil Actions Under $2,500, Eviction, Small Claims.*

Chancery Court PO Box 7127, Tupelo, MS 38802; 662-841-9100; Fax: 662-680-6091. Hours: 8AM-5PM (CST). *Probate.*

Leflore County

Circuit & County Court PO Box 1953, Greenwood, MS 38935-1953; 662-453-1041; Fax: 662-455-1278. Hours: 8AM-5PM (CST). *Felony, Civil Actions Over $2,500.*

Civil Records: Access: Fax, mail, in person. Both court and visitors may perform in person searches. Search fee: $10.00 per name. Required to search: name, years to search. Civil cases indexed by defendant, plaintiff. Civil records on computer since 1994; prior records on docket books since mid-1800s.
Criminal Records: Access: Fax, mail, in person. Both court and visitors may perform in person searches. Search fee: $10.00 per name. Required to search: name, years to search; also helpful: DOB, SSN. Criminal records on computer since 1994; prior records on docket books since mid-1800s.
General Information: Public Access terminal is available. No sealed or expunged records released. Turnaround time 1-2 days. Fax notes: Call for fax fee. Copy fee: $.50 per page. Certification fee: $1.50. Fee payee: Circuit Clerk. Personal checks accepted. Prepayment is required.

Justice Court PO Box 8056, Greenwood, MS 38935; 662-453-1605. Hours: 8AM-5PM (CST). *Misdemeanor, Civil Actions Under $2,500, Eviction, Small Claims.*

Chancery Court PO Box 250, Greenwood, MS 38935-0250; 662-453-1041; 453-1432 (court admin); Fax: 662-455-7959. Hours: 8AM-5PM (CST). *Probate.*

Lincoln County

Circuit Court PO Box 357, Brookhaven, MS 39602; 601-835-3435; Fax: 601-835-3482. Hours: 8AM-5PM (CST). *Felony, Civil Actions Over $2,500.*

Civil Records: Access: Fax, mail, in person. Both court and visitors may perform in person searches. Search fee: $10.00 per name. Required to search: name, years to search. Civil cases indexed by defendant, plaintiff. Civil records on computer since 1986, prior on docket books.
Criminal Records: Access: Fax, mail, in person. Both court and visitors may perform in person searches. Search fee: $10.00 per name. Required to search: name, years to search; also helpful: DOB, SSN. Criminal records on computer since 1986, prior on docket books.
General Information: Public Access terminal is available. No sealed or expunged records released. Turnaround time 1-2 days. Fax notes: $10.00 per document. Copy fee: $.50 per page. Certification fee: $1.00. Fee payee: Circuit Clerk. Personal checks accepted. Out of state checks not accepted. Prepayment is required.

Justice Court PO Box 767, Brookhaven, MS 39602; 601-835-3474. Hours: 8:00AM-5:00PM (CST). *Misdemeanor, Civil Actions Under $2,500, Eviction, Small Claims.*

Chancery Court PO Box 555, Brookhaven, MS 39602; 601-835-3412; Fax: 601-835-3423. Hours: 8AM-5PM (CST). *Probate.*

Lowndes County

Circuit & County Court PO Box 31, Columbus, MS 39703; 662-329-5900. Hours: 8AM-5PM (CST). *Felony, Civil.*

Civil Records: Access: Mail, in person. Both court and visitors may perform in person searches. Search fee: $10.00 per name. Required to search: name, years to search. Civil cases indexed by defendant, plaintiff. Civil records on computer from 2/94, on docket books from 1900s.
Criminal Records: Access: Mail, in person. Both court and visitors may perform in person searches. Search fee: $10.00 per name per year. Required to search: name, years to search, DOB; also helpful: SSN. Criminal records on computer since 11/93; prior on docket books.
General Information: Public Access terminal is available. No sealed, adoption, mental health, juvenile, sex or expunged cases released. Copy fee: $1.00 per page. Certification fee: $1.00. Fee payee: Clerk of Court. Personal checks accepted. Prepayment is required.

Justice Court 11 Airline Rd, Columbus, MS 39702; 662-329-5929; Fax: 662-245-4619. Hours: 8AM-5PM (CST). *Misdemeanor, Civil Actions Under $2,500, Eviction, Small Claims.*

Chancery Court PO Box 684, Columbus, MS 39703; 662-329-5800. Hours: 8AM-5PM *Probate.*

Madison County

Circuit & County Court PO Box 1626, Canton, MS 39046; 601-859-4365; Fax: 601-859-8555. Hours: 8AM-5PM (CST). *Felony, Civil.*

Civil Records: Access: Phone, fax, mail, in person. Both court and visitors may perform in person searches. No search fee. Required to search: name, years to search. Civil cases indexed by defendant, plaintiff. Civil records on computer since 1987, prior on docket books since 1950.
Criminal Records: Access: Mail, in person. Both court and visitors may perform in person searches. Search fee: $10.00 per name. Required to search: name, years to search. Criminal records on computer since 1992, prior on docket books since 1945.
General Information: Public Access terminal is available. No sealed, adoptions, mental health, juvenile, sex, or expunged records released. SASE requested. Turnaround time 1 week. Copy fee: $.25 per page. Certification fee: $1.00. Fee payee: Circuit Clerk. Personal checks accepted. Prepayment is required.

Justice Court 175 N Union, Canton, MS 39046; 601-859-6337; Fax: 601-859-5878. Hours: 8AM-5PM (CST). *Misdemeanor, Civil Actions Under $2,500, Eviction, Small Claims.*

Note: Request for history must be in writing with a $6.00 fee made out to Madison County Justice Court.

Chancery Court PO Box 404, Canton, MS 39046; 601-859-1177; Fax: 601-859-5875. Hours: 8AM-5PM (CST). *Probate.*

Marion County

Circuit Court 250 Broad St, Suite 1, Columbia, MS 39429; 601-736-8246. Hours: 8AM-5PM (CST). *Felony, Civil Actions Over $2,500.*

Civil Records: Access: Mail, in person, online. Both court and visitors may perform in person searches. Search fee: $10.00 per name. Required to search: name, years to search. Civil cases indexed by defendant, plaintiff. Civil records on docket books since 1800s. Online access to circuit court dockets is available by subscription at www.recordsusa.com/Mississippi/MarionCnMS.htm. Credit card, username and password is required; choose either monthly or per-use plan. Visit the web site for sign-up or call Lisa at 601-264-7701 for information.
Criminal Records: Access: Mail, in person, online. Both court and visitors may perform in person searches. Search fee: $10.00 per name. Required to search: name, years to search; also helpful: SSN. Criminal records on docket books since 1800s. Online access to criminal court dockets is the same as civil.
General Information: No sealed, adoptions, mental health, juvenile, sex, or expunged records released. SASE required. Turnaround time 1-2 days. Copy fee: $.50 per page. Certification fee: No cert fee. Fee payee: Circuit Clerk. Personal checks accepted. Prepayment is required.

Justice Court 500 Courthouse Square, Columbia, MS 39429; 601-736-2572; Fax: 601-736-2580. Hours: 8AM-5PM (CST). *Misdemeanor, Civil Actions Under $2,500, Eviction, Small Claims.*

Chancery Court 250 Broad St, Suite 2, Columbia, MS 39429; 601-736-2691; Fax: 601-736-1232. Hours: 8AM-5PM (CST). *Probate.*

Marshall County

Circuit Court PO Box 459, Holly Springs, MS 38635; 662-252-3434; Fax: 662-252-0004 & 252-5951. Hours: 8AM-5PM (CST). *Felony, Civil Actions Over $2,500.*

Civil Records: Access: Fax, mail, in person. Both court and visitors may perform in person searches. Search fee: $10.00 per name. Required to search: name, years to search. Civil cases indexed by defendant, plaintiff. Civil records on docket books since 1960s.
Criminal Records: Access: Mail, in person. Both court and visitors may perform in person searches. Search fee: $10.00 per name. Required to search: name, years to search; also helpful: DOB, SSN. Criminal records on docket books since 1960s.
General Information: No sealed or expunged records released. Turnaround time 1-2 days. Fax notes: No fee to fax results. Fax copy of search fee check. Copy fee: $.50 per page. Certification fee: $2.50. Fee payee: Circuit Court Clerk. Personal checks accepted. Prepayment is required.

Justice Court - North & South Districts PO Box 729, Holly Springs, MS 38635; 662-252-3585. Hours: 8AM-5PM (CST). *Misdemeanor, Civil Actions Under $2,500, Eviction, Small Claims.*

Chancery Court PO Box 219, Holly Springs, MS 38635; 662-252-4431; Fax: 662-252-0004. Hours: 8AM-5PM (CST). *Probate.*

Monroe County

Circuit Court PO Box 843, Aberdeen, MS 39730; 662-369-8695; Fax: 662-369-3684. Hours: 8AM-5PM (CST). *Felony, Civil Actions Over $2,500.*

Civil Records: Access: In person only. Visitors must perform in person searches for themselves. No search fee. Required to search: name, years to search; also helpful: address. Civil cases indexed by defendant, plaintiff. Civil records on docket books since 1821.
Criminal Records: Access: In person only. Visitors must perform in person searches for themselves. No search fee. Required to search: name, years to search, DOB; also helpful: address, SSN. Criminal records on docket books since 1821.
General Information: No sealed, adoptions, mental health, juvenile, sex, or expunged records released. Copy fee: $.50 per page. Certification fee: $3.00. Fee payee: Monroe County Circuit Clerk. Only cashiers checks and money orders accepted. Prepayment is required.

Justice Court - District 1, 2, 3 PO Box 518 (101 9th St), Amory, MS 38821; 662-256-8493; Fax: 662-256-7876. *Misdemeanor, Civil Actions Under $2,500, Eviction, Small Claims.*

Justice Court - District 2 PO Box 518, Amory, MS 38821; 662-256-8493. *Misdemeanor, Civil Actions Under $2,500, Eviction, Small Claims.*

Note: Aberdeen Justice Court Dist. 2 is closed; records now at Amory Justice Court 1 & 2.

Chancery Court PO Box 578, Aberdeen, MS 39730; 662-369-8143; Fax: 662-369-7928. Hours: 8AM-5PM (CST). *Probate.*

Montgomery County

Circuit Court PO Box 765, Winona, MS 38967; 662-283-4161; Fax: 662-283-2233. Hours: 8AM-5PM (CST). *Felony, Civil Actions Over $2,500.*

Civil Records: Access: Mail, in person. Both court and visitors may perform in person searches. Search fee: $10.00 per name. Required to search: name, years to search. Civil cases indexed by defendant, plaintiff. Civil records on docket books since early 1900s.

Criminal Records: Access: Mail, in person. Both court and visitors may perform in person searches. Search fee: $10.00 per name. Required to search: name, years to search. Criminal records on docket books since early 1900s.
General Information: No sealed or expunged records released. SASE required. Turnaround time 1-2 days. Copy fee: $.25 per page. Certification fee: $2.00. Fee payee: Circuit Clerk. Personal checks accepted. Prepayment is required.

Justice Court PO Box 229, Winona, MS 38967; 662-283-2290; Fax: 662-283-2233. Hours: 8AM-5PM (CST). *Misdemeanor, Civil Actions Under $2,500, Eviction, Small Claims.*

Chancery Court PO Box 71, Winona, MS 38967; 662-283-2333; Fax: 662-283-2233. Hours: 8AM-5PM (CST). *Probate.*

Neshoba County

Circuit Court 401 E Beacon St Suite 110, Philadelphia, MS 39350; 601-656-4781; Fax: 601-650-3997. Hours: 8AM-5PM (CST). *Felony, Civil Actions Over $2,500.*

Civil Records: Access: Mail, in person. Both court and visitors may perform in person searches. Search fee: $10.00 per name. Required to search: name, years to search. Civil cases indexed by defendant.
Criminal Records: Access: Mail, in person. Both court and visitors may perform in person searches. Search fee: $10.00 per name. Required to search: name, years to search, DOB; also helpful: SSN. Criminal records on docket books since 1877.
General Information: No sealed, adoptions, mental health, juvenile, sex, or expunged records released. Turnaround time 1 day. Copy fee: $.50 per page. Certification fee: $2.00. Fee payee: Circuit Clerk. Business checks accepted.

Justice Court 401 E Beacon St, Philadelphia, MS 39350; 601-656-5361/1101; Fax: 601-650-3280. *Misdemeanor, Civil Actions Under $2,500, Eviction, Small Claims.*

Chancery Court 401 Beacon St Suite 107, Philadelphia, MS 39350; 601-656-3581; Fax: 601-650-3280. Hours: 8AM-5PM (CST). *Probate.*

Newton County

Circuit Court PO Box 447, Decatur, MS 39327; 601-635-2368; Fax: 601-635-3210. Hours: 8AM-5PM (CST). *Felony, Civil Actions Over $2,500.*

Civil Records: Access: Phone, mail, in person. Both court and visitors may perform in person searches. Search fee: $10.00 per name. Required to search: name, years to search. Civil cases indexed by defendant, plaintiff. Civil records on docket books.
Criminal Records: Access: Mail, in person. Both court and visitors may perform in person searches. Search fee: $10.00 per name. Required to search: name, years to search, DOB; also helpful: SSN. Criminal records on docket books.
General Information: Public Access terminal is available. No sealed, adoptions, mental health, juvenile, sex, or expunged records released. SASE required. Turnaround time same day. Copy fee: $.50 per page. Certification fee: $1.50. Fee payee: Circuit Court. Personal checks accepted. Prepayment is required.

Justice Court PO Box 69, Decatur, MS 39327; 601-635-2740. Hours: 8AM-5PM (CST). *Misdemeanor, Civil Actions Under $2,500, Eviction, Small Claims.*

Chancery Clerk Office PO Box 68, Decatur, MS 39327; 601-635-2367. Hours: 8AM-5PM (CST). *Probate.*

Noxubee County

Circuit Court PO Box 431, Macon, MS 39341; 662-726-5737; Fax: 662-726-6041. Hours: 8AM-5PM (CST). *Felony, Civil Actions Over $2,500.*

Civil Records: Access: Mail, in person. Both court and visitors may perform in person searches. Search fee: $10.00 per name. Required to search: name, years to search. Civil cases indexed by defendant. Civil records on docket books since 1800s.

Criminal Records: Access: Mail, in person. Both court and visitors may perform in person searches. Search fee: $10.00 per name. Required to search: name, years to search; also helpful: SSN. Criminal records on docket books since 1800s.

General Information: No sealed, adoptions, mental health, juvenile, sex, or expunged records released. SASE required. Turnaround time 1 week. Copy fee: $.50 per page. Certification fee: $5.00. Fee payee: Circuit Clerk. Business checks accepted. Prepayment is required.

Justice Court - North & South Districts 507 S Jefferson, Macon, MS 39341; 662-726-5834; Fax: 662-726-2944. Hours: 8AM-5PM (CST). *Misdemeanor, Civil Actions Under $2,500, Eviction, Small Claims.*

Chancery Court PO Box 147, Macon, MS 39341; 662-726-4243; Fax: 662-726-2272. Hours: 8AM-5PM (CST). *Probate.*

Oktibbeha County

Circuit Court Courthouse, 101 E Main, Starkville, MS 39759; 662-323-1356. Hours: 8AM-5PM (CST). *Felony, Civil Actions Over $2,500.*

Civil Records: Access: Mail, fax, in person. Both court and visitors may perform in person searches. Search fee: $10.00 per name. Required to search: name, years to search; also helpful: address. Civil cases indexed by defendant, plaintiff. Civil records on docket books since 1938.

Criminal Records: Access: Mail, fax, in person. Both court and visitors may perform in person searches. Search fee: $10.00 per name. Required to search: name, years to search; also helpful: DOB, SSN. Criminal records on docket since 1950.

General Information: Public Access terminal is available. No sealed, adoptions, mental health, juvenile, sex, or expunged records released. Turnaround time 1 week. Copy fee: $1.00 per page. Certification fee: $1.50. Fee payee: Circuit Clerk. Personal checks accepted. Prepayment is required.

Justice Court - Districts 1-3 104 Felix Long Dr, Starkville, MS 39759; 662-324-3032; Fax: 662-338-1078. Hours: 8AM-5PM (CST). *Misdemeanor, Civil Actions Under $2,500, Eviction, Small Claims.*

Chancery Court Courthouse, 101 E Main, Starkville, MS 39759; 662-323-5834. Hours: 8AM-5PM (CST). *Probate.*

Panola County

Circuit Court - 1st District PO Box 130, Sardis, MS 38666; 662-487-2073; Fax: 662-487-3595. Hours: 8AM-5PM (CST). *Felony, Civil Actions Over $2,500.*

Civil Records: Access: Fax, mail, in person. Both court and visitors may perform in person searches. Search fee: $10.00 per name. Fee is for dual district search. Required to search: name, years to search. Civil cases indexed by defendant, plaintiff. Civil records on docket books since 1925.

Criminal Records: Access: Fax, mail, in person. Both court and visitors may perform in person searches. Search fee: $10.00 per name. Fee is for dual district search. Required to search: name, years to search, DOB;

also helpful: SSN. Criminal records on docket books since 1925.

General Information: No sealed, adoptions, mental health, juvenile, sex, or expunged records released. SASE required. Turnaround time varies. Fax notes: No fee to fax results. Fax copy of the search fee check. Copy fee: $.50 per page. Certification fee: $1.50. Fee payee: Circuit Clerk. Business checks accepted. Prepayment is required.

Circuit Court - 2nd District PO Box 346, Batesville, MS 38606; 662-563-6210; Fax: 662-563-8233. Hours: 8AM-5PM (CST). *Felony, Civil Actions Over $2,500.*

Civil Records: Access: Phone, fax, mail, in person. Both court and visitors may perform in person searches. Search fee: $10.00 per name. Fee is per district. Required to search: name, years to search. Civil cases indexed by defendant, plaintiff. Civil records on docket books since 1925.

Criminal Records: Access: Phone, fax, mail, in person. Both court and visitors may perform in person searches. Search fee: $10.00 per name. Fee is per district. Required to search: name, years to search, address, DOB; also helpful: SSN. Criminal records on docket books since 1925.

General Information: No sealed, adoptions, mental health, juvenile, sex, or expunged records released. Turnaround time same day. Fax notes: $1.00 per page. Copy fee: $.25 per page. Certification fee: $5.00. Fee payee: Circuit Clerk's Office. Personal checks accepted. Prepayment is required.

Justice Court PO Box 249, Sardis, MS 38666; 662-487-2080. Hours: 8AM-5PM (CST). *Misdemeanor, Civil Actions Under $2,500, Eviction, Small Claims.*

Note: This Justice Court houses all the Justices for Panola County.

Panola County Chancery Clerk 151 Public Square, Batesville, MS 38606; 662-563-6205; Fax: 662-563-8233. Hours: 8AM-5PM (CST). *Probate.*

Sardis Chancery Court PO Box 130, Sardis, MS 38666; 662-487-2070; Fax: 662-487-3595. Hours: 8AM-Noon, 1-5PM (CST). *Probate.*

Pearl River County

Circuit Court Courthouse, Poplarville, MS 39470; 601-795-3059; Fax: 601-795-3084. Hours: 8AM-5PM (CST). *Felony, Civil Actions Over $2,500.*

Civil Records: Access: Mail, fax, in person. Both court and visitors may perform in person searches. Search fee: $10.00 per name. Required to search: name, years to search. Civil cases indexed by defendant, plaintiff. Civil records on docket books since 1890.

Criminal Records: Access: Mail, fax, in person. Both court and visitors may perform in person searches. Search fee: $10.00 per name. Required to search: name, years to search. Criminal records on computer since late 1960s, prior on docket books since 1890.

General Information: No sealed, adoptions, mental health, juvenile, sex, or expunged records released. Turnaround time 1-2 days. Copy fee: $.50 per page. Certification fee: $2.50. Fee payee: Circuit Clerk. Personal checks accepted. Prepayment is required.

Justice Court - Northern, Southeastern & Southwestern Districts 204 Julia St, Poplarville, MS 39470; 601-795-8018; Fax: 601-795-3063. Hours: 8AM-5PM (CST). *Misdemeanor, Civil Actions Under $2,500, Eviction, Small Claims.*

Chancery Court PO Box 431, Poplarville, MS 39470; 601-795-2238; Fax: 601-795-3093. Hours: 8AM-5PM (CST). *Probate.*

Perry County

Circuit Court PO Box 198, New Augusta, MS 39462; 601-964-8663; Fax: 601-964-8740. Hours: 8AM-5PM (CST). *Felony, Civil Actions Over $2,500.*

Civil Records: Access: Mail, fax, in person. Both court and visitors may perform in person searches. Search fee: $10.00 per name. Fee is per 10 years searched. Required to search: name, years to search. Civil cases indexed by defendant, plaintiff. Civil records on docket books since 1962; on computer since.

Criminal Records: Access: Mail, fax, in person. Both court and visitors may perform in person searches. Search fee: $10.00 per name. Fee is per 10 years searched. Required to search: name, years to search, DOB; also helpful: SSN, sex, signed release. Criminal records on docket books since 1962; on computer since.

General Information: No sealed, adoptions, mental health, juvenile, sex, or expunged records released. Turnaround time 1-2 days. Copy fee: $.50 per page. Certification fee: $2.50. Fee payee: Circuit Clerk. Personal checks accepted. Prepayment is required.

Justice Court PO Box 455, New Augusta, MS 39462; 601-964-8366. Hours: 8AM-5PM (CST). *Misdemeanor, Civil Actions Under $2,500, Eviction, Small Claims.*

Justice Court - District 1 316 Forest St, Hattiesburg, MS 39401; 601-544-3136. Hours: 8AM-5PM (CST). *Misdemeanor, Civil Actions Under $2,500, Eviction, Small Claims.*

Chancery Court PO Box 198, New Augusta, MS 39462; 601-964-8398; Fax: 601-964-8764. Hours: 8AM-5PM (CST). *Probate.*

Pike County

Circuit & County Court PO Drawer 31, Magnolia, MS 39652; 601-783-2581; Fax: 601-783-4101. Hours: 8AM-5PM (CST). *Felony, Misdemeanor, Civil.*

Civil Records: Access: Fax, mail, in person. Both court and visitors may perform in person searches. Search fee: $6.00 per name. Required to search: name, years to search. Civil cases indexed by defendant, plaintiff. Civil records on docket books since 1950s; on computer back to 1984.

Criminal Records: Access: Fax, mail, in person. Both court and visitors may perform in person searches. Search fee: $6.00 per name. Required to search: name, years to search, DOB; also helpful: SSN. Criminal records on docket books since 1950s; on computer back to 1984.

General Information: Public Access terminal is available. No sealed, adoptions, mental health, juvenile, sex, or expunged records released. SASE required. Turnaround time 1-2 days. Copy fee: $.50 per page. Certification fee: $1.50. Fee payee: Circuit Clerk. Personal checks accepted. Prepayment is required.

Justice Court - Divisions 1-3 PO Box 509, Magnolia, MS 39652; 601-783-5333; Fax: 601-783-4181. Hours: 8AM-5PM (CST). *Misdemeanor, Civil Actions Under $2,500, Eviction, Small Claims.*

Chancery Court PO Box 309, Magnolia, MS 39652; 601-783-3362; Fax: 601-783-4101. Hours: 8AM-5PM (CST). *Probate.*

Pontotoc County

Circuit Court PO Box 428, Pontotoc, MS 38863; 662-489-3908. Hours: 8AM-5PM (CST). *Felony, Civil Actions Over $2,500.*

Civil Records: Access: Mail, in person. Both court and visitors may perform in person searches. Search fee: $5.00 per name. Required to search: name, years to

search. Civil cases indexed by defendant, plaintiff. Civil records on books from 1849.

Criminal Records: Access: Mail, in person. Both court and visitors may perform in person searches. Search fee: $5.00 per name. Required to search: name, years to search, DOB; also helpful: SSN. Criminal records on books from 1849.

General Information: No sealed, adoptions, mental health, juvenile, sex, or expunged records released. SASE required. Turnaround time 1 week. Copy fee: $.50 per page. Certification fee: No cert fee. Fee payee: Circuit Clerk. Prepayment is required.

Justice Court - East & West Districts 29 E Washington St, Pontotoc, MS 38863-2923; 662-489-3920; Fax: 662-489-3921. Hours: 8AM-5PM (CST). *Misdemeanor, Civil Actions Under $2,500, Eviction, Small Claims.*

Chancery Court 11 Washington, PO Box 209, Pontotoc, MS 38863; 662-489-3900; Fax: 662-489-3940. Hours: 8AM-5PM (CST). *Probate.*

Prentiss County

Circuit Court PO Box 727, 101 N Main St, Booneville, MS 38829; 662-728-4611; Fax: 662-728-2006. Hours: 8AM-5PM (CST). *Felony, Civil Actions Over $2,500.*

Civil Records: Access: Mail, in person. Both court and visitors may perform in person searches. Search fee: $10.00 per name. Required to search: name, years to search. Civil cases indexed by defendant, plaintiff. Civil records on docket books from 1880, only judgments are on computer.

Criminal Records: Access: Fax, mail, in person. Both court and visitors may perform in person searches. Search fee: $10.00 per name. Required to search: name, years to search; also helpful: DOB, SSN. Criminal records on docket books from 1880, only judgments are on computer. Prepaid account is required for fax access.

General Information: No sealed, adoptions, mental health, juvenile, sex, or expunged records released. SASE required. Turnaround time varies. Copy fee: $.50 per page. Certification fee: $2.00. Fee payee: Circuit Clerk. Personal checks accepted. Accounts available.

Prentiss County Justice Court 1901C East Chambers Dr, Booneville, MS 38829; 662-728-8696; Fax: 662-728-2009. Hours: 8AM-5PM (CST). *Misdemeanor, Civil Actions Under $2,500, Eviction, Small Claims.*

Chancery Court PO Box 477, Booneville, MS 38829; 662-728-8151; Fax: 662-728-2007. Hours: 8AM-5PM (CST). *Probate.*

Quitman County

Circuit Court Courthouse, Marks, MS 38646; 662-326-8003; Fax: 662-326-8004. Hours: 8AM-5PM (CST). *Felony, Civil Actions Over $2,500.*

Civil Records: Access: Fax, mail, in person. Both court and visitors may perform in person searches. Search fee: $10.00 per name. Required to search: name, years to search. Civil cases indexed by defendant, plaintiff. Civil records on books and files since 1890.

Criminal Records: Access: Fax, mail, in person. Both court and visitors may perform in person searches. Search fee: $10.00 per name. Required to search: name, years to search, DOB; also helpful: SSN. Criminal records on books and files since 1890.

General Information: No sealed, adoptions, mental health, juvenile, sex, or expunged records released. SASE not required. Turnaround time 2 days, phone turnaround time 10 minutes. Fax notes: No fax fee when $10.00 has been paid. Copy fee: $.50 per page. Certification fee: $1.50. Fee payee: Circuit Clerk. Business checks accepted. Prepayment is required.

Justice Court - Districts 1 & 2 PO Box 100, Marks, MS 38646; 662-326-2104; Fax: 662-326-2330. Hours: 8AM-5PM (CST). *Misdemeanor, Civil Actions Under $2,500, Eviction, Small Claims.*

Chancery Court 230 Chestnut St, Marks, MS 38646; 662-326-2661; Fax: 662-326-8004. Hours: 8AM-Noon, 1-5PM (CST). *Probate.*

Rankin County

Circuit & County Court PO Drawer 1599, Brandon, MS 39043; 601-825-1466. Hours: 8AM-5PM (CST). *Felony, Misdemeanor, Civil.*

www.rankincounty.org

Civil Records: Access: Mail, in person. Both court and visitors may perform in person searches. Search fee: $5.00 per name. Required to search: name, years to search. Civil cases indexed by defendant, plaintiff. Civil records on computer since 1990, prior on docket books.

Criminal Records: Access: Mail, in person. Both court and visitors may perform in person searches. Search fee: $5.00 per name. Required to search: name, years to search; also helpful: DOB, SSN. Criminal records on computer since 1990, prior on docket books.

General Information: Public Access terminal is available. No sealed or expunged records released. Turnaround time 1-2 days. Copy fee: $.50 per page. Certification fee: $1.50. Fee payee: Circuit Clerk. Personal checks accepted. Prepayment is required.

Justice Court - Districts 1-4 110 Paul Truitt Lane, Pearl, MS 39208; 601-939-1885; Fax: 601-939-2320. Hours: 8AM-5PM (CST). *Misdemeanor, Civil Actions Under $2,500, Eviction, Small Claims.*

Chancery Court 203 Town Sq, PO Box 700, Brandon, MS 39042; 601-825-1649; Fax: 601-824-2450. Hours: 8AM-5PM (CST). *Probate.*

www.rankincounty.org

Scott County

Circuit Court PO Box 371, Forest, MS 39074; 601-469-3601. Hours: 8AM-5PM (CST). *Felony, Civil Actions Over $2,500.*

Civil Records: Access: Mail, in person. Both court and visitors may perform in person searches. Search fee: $10.00 per name. Fee is for 7 year search. Required to search: name, years to search. Civil cases indexed by defendant, plaintiff. Civil records on docket books since 1865.

Criminal Records: Access: Mail, in person. Both court and visitors may perform in person searches. Search fee: $10.00 per name. Fee is for 7 year search. Required to search: name, years to search, DOB; also helpful: SSN. Criminal records on docket books since 1865.

General Information: No sealed, adoptions, mental health, juvenile, sex, or expunged records released. SASE required. Turnaround time 1 week. Copy fee: $.50 per page. Certification fee: $1.50. Fee payee: Circuit Clerk. Personal checks accepted. Prepayment is required.

Justice Court PO Box 371, Forest, MS 39074; 601-469-4555; Fax: 601-469-5193. Hours: 8AM-5PM (CST). *Misdemeanor, Civil Actions Under $2,500, Eviction, Small Claims.*

Chancery Court 100 Main St, PO Box 630, Forest, MS 39074; 601-469-1922; Fax: 601-469-5180. Hours: 8AM-5PM (CST). *Probate.*

Sharkey County

Circuit Court 400 Locust St, Rolling Fork, MS 39159; 662-873-2766; Fax: 662-873-6045. Hours: 8AM-Noon, 1-5PM (CST). *Felony, Civil Actions Over $2,500.*

Civil Records: Access: Mail, in person. Both court and visitors may perform in person searches. Search fee: $10.00 per name. Required to search: name, years to search. Civil cases indexed by defendant, plaintiff. Civil records on docket books since 1893.

Criminal Records: Access: Mail, in person. Both court and visitors may perform in person searches. Search fee: $10.00 per name. Required to search: name, years to search, DOB; also helpful: SSN. Criminal records on docket books since 1893.

General Information: No sealed, adoptions, mental health, juvenile, sex, or expunged records released. Turnaround time 1 week. Fax notes: Fee to fax results is $1.00 per page. Copy fee: $.50 per page. Certification fee: $2.00. Fee payee: Circuit Clerk. Business checks accepted. Prepayment is required.

Justice Court PO Box 218, Rolling Fork, MS 39159; 662-873-6140. Hours: 8AM-5PM (CST). *Misdemeanor, Civil Actions Under $2,500, Eviction, Small Claims.*

Chancery Court 400 Locust St, PO Box 218, Rolling Fork, MS 39159; 662-873-2755; Fax: 662-873-6045. Hours: 8AM-Noon,1-5PM (CST). *Probate.*

Simpson County

Circuit Court PO Box 307, Mendenhall, MS 39114; 601-847-2474; Fax: 601-847-4011. Hours: 8AM-5PM (CST). *Felony, Civil Actions Over $2,500.*

Civil Records: Access: Fax, mail, in person. Both court and visitors may perform in person searches. Search fee: $9.00 per name. Required to search: name, years to search. Civil cases indexed by defendant, plaintiff. Civil records on docket books since 1978.

Criminal Records: Access: Fax, mail, in person. Both court and visitors may perform in person searches. Search fee: $9.00 per name. Required to search: name, years to search; also helpful: DOB, SSN. Criminal records on docket books since 1978.

General Information: No sealed or expunged records released. Turnaround time 1-2 days. Fax notes: No fee to fax results. Copy fee: $.50 per page. Certification fee: $1.50. Fee payee: Circuit Clerk. Business checks accepted. Prepayment is required.

Justice Court 159 Court Ave, Mendenhall, MS 39114; 601-847-5848; Fax: 601-847-5856. Hours: 8AM-5PM (CST). *Misdemeanor, Civil Actions Under $2,500, Eviction, Small Claims.*

Chancery Court Chancery Building, PO Box 367, Mendenhall, MS 39114; 601-847-2626. Hours: 8AM-5PM (CST). *Probate.*

Smith County

Circuit Court PO Box 517, Raleigh, MS 39153; 601-782-4751; Fax: 601-782-4007. Hours: 8AM-5PM (CST). *Felony, Civil Actions Over $2,500.*

Civil Records: Access: Mail, in person. Both court and visitors may perform in person searches. Search fee: $10.00 per name. Required to search: name, years to search. Civil cases indexed by defendant, plaintiff. Civil records on docket books since 1912.

Criminal Records: Access: Mail, in person. Both court and visitors may perform in person searches. Search fee: $10.00 per name. Required to search: name, years to search, DOB; also helpful: SSN. Criminal records on docket books since 1912.

General Information: No sealed, adoptions, mental health, juvenile, sex, or expunged records released.

SASE required. Turnaround time 2 days. Fax notes: Fee to fax results is $.50 per page. Copy fee: $.50 per page. Certification fee: $5.00. Fee payee: Circuit Clerk. Personal checks accepted.

Justice Court PO Box 171, Raleigh, MS 39153; 601-782-4334; Fax: 601-782-4005. Hours: 8AM-5PM (CST). *Misdemeanor, Civil Actions Under $2,500, Eviction, Small Claims.*

Chancery Court 123 Main St, PO Box 39, Raleigh, MS 39153; 601-782-9811. Hours: 8AM-Noon, 1-5PM (CST). *Probate.*

Stone County

Circuit Court Courthouse, 323 Cavers Ave, Wiggins, MS 39577; 601-928-5246; Fax: 601-928-5248. Hours: 8AM-5PM (CST). *Felony, Civil Actions Over $2,500.*

Civil Records: Access: Fax, mail, in person. Both court and visitors may perform in person searches. Search fee: $10.00 per name. Required to search: name, years to search. Civil cases indexed by defendant, plaintiff. Civil records on docket books since 1945.
Criminal Records: Access: Fax, mail, in person. Both court and visitors may perform in person searches. Search fee: $10.00 per name. Required to search: name, years to search, DOB, notarized release; also helpful: SSN. Criminal records on docket books since 1945.
General Information: No sealed, adoptions, mental health, juvenile, sex, or expunged records released. Turnaround time same day. Fax notes: $3.00 for first page, $.50 each add'l. Copy fee: $.50 per page. Certification fee: $1.50. Fee payee: Circuit Clerk. Business checks accepted. Prepayment is required.

Justice Court 231 3rd Street, Wiggins, MS 39577; 601-928-4415; Fax: 601-928-2114. Hours: 8AM-5PM (CST). *Misdemeanor, Civil Actions Under $2,500, Eviction, Small Claims.*

Justice Court - West District 231 3rd St, Wiggins, MS 39577; 601-928-4415. Hours: 8AM-5PM (CST). *Misdemeanor, Civil Actions Under $2,500, Eviction, Small Claims.*

Chancery Court 323 E Cavers, PO Drawer 7, Wiggins, MS 39577; 601-928-5266; Fax: 601-928-5248. Hours: 8AM-5PM (CST). *Probate.*

Sunflower County

Circuit Court PO Box 576, Indianola, MS 38751; 662-887-1252; Fax: 662-887-7077. Hours: 8AM-5PM (CST). *Felony, Civil Actions Over $2,500.*

Civil Records: Access: Mail, in person. Both court and visitors may perform in person searches. Search fee: $10.00 per name. Fee is for 7 year search. Required to search: name, years to search. Civil cases indexed by defendant, plaintiff. Civil records on docket books since 1881; on computer since 2000.
Criminal Records: Access: Mail, in person. Both court and visitors may perform in person searches. Search fee: $10.00 per name. Fee is for 7 year search. Required to search: name, years to search, DOB; also helpful: SSN. Criminal records on docket books since 1913; on computer since 2000.
General Information: Public Access terminal is available. No sealed, adoptions, mental health, juvenile, sex, or expunged records released. Turnaround time 1-3 days. Fax notes: $1.00 per page. Copy fee: $.50 per page. Certification fee: $1.50. Fee payee: Circuit Clerk. Personal checks accepted. Prepayment is required.

Justice Court - Northern District PO Box 52, Ruleville, MS 38771; 662-756-2835. Hours: 8AM-Noon, 1-5PM (CST). *Misdemeanor, Civil Actions Under $2,500, Eviction, Small Claims.*

Justice Court - Southern District PO Box 487, Indianola, MS 38751; 662-887-6921. Hours: 8AM-5PM (CST). *Misdemeanor, Civil Actions Under $2,500, Eviction, Small Claims.*

Chancery Court 200 Main St, PO Box 988, Indianola, MS 38751; 662-887-4703; Fax: 662-887-7054. Hours: 8AM-5PM (CST). *Probate.*

Tallahatchie County

Charleston Circuit Court PO Box 86, Charleston, MS 38921; 662-647-8758; Fax: 662-647-8490. Hours: 8AM-5PM (CST). *Felony, Civil Actions Over $2,500.*

Civil Records: Access: Mail, in person. Both court and visitors may perform in person searches. Search fee: $10.00 per name. Required to search: name, years to search. Civil cases indexed by defendant, plaintiff. Civil records on books since 1920s.
Criminal Records: Access: Mail, in person. Both court and visitors may perform in person searches. Search fee: $10.00 per name. Required to search: name, years to search, DOB; also helpful: SSN. Criminal records on books since 1920s.
General Information: No sealed, adoptions, mental health, juvenile, sex, or expunged records released. SASE requested. Turnaround time 3 days. Copy fee: $2.00 per page. Certification fee: $3.00. Fee payee: Circuit Clerk. Personal checks accepted. Prepayment is required.

Charleston Justice Court PO Box 440, Charleston, MS 38921; 662-647-3477; Fax: 662-647-3478. Hours: 8AM-5PM (CST). *Misdemeanor, Civil Actions Under $2,500, Eviction, Small Claims.*

Note: Court is located upstairs of the Charleston Circuit Court; records are not comingled.

Sumner Justice Court PO Box 155, Sumner, MS 38957; 662-375-9452; Fax: 662-375-8200. Hours: 8AM-5PM (CST). *Misdemeanor, Civil Actions Under $2,500, Eviction, Small Claims.*

Chancery Court #1 Main St, PO Box 350, Charleston, MS 38921; 662-647-5551; Fax: 662-647-8490. Hours: 8AM-5PM (CST). *Probate.*

Chancery Court PO Box 180, Sumner, MS 38957; 662-375-8731; Fax: 662-375-7252. Hours: 8AM-Noon, 1-5PM (CST). *Probate.*

Tate County

Circuit Court 201 Ward St, Senatobia, MS 38668; 662-562-5211; Fax: 662-562-7486. Hours: 8AM-5PM (CST). *Felony, Civil Actions Over $2,500.*

Civil Records: Access: Mail, in person. Both court and visitors may perform in person searches. Search fee: $10.00 per name. Required to search: name, years to search. Civil cases indexed by defendant, plaintiff. Civil records on books since 1872.
Criminal Records: Access: Mail, in person. Both court and visitors may perform in person searches. Search fee: $10.00 per name. Required to search: name, years to search; also helpful: SSN. Criminal records on books since 1872.
General Information: No sealed, adoptions, mental health, juvenile, sex, or expunged records released. SASE requested. Turnaround time same day. Copy fee: $.50 for first page, $.25 each add'l. Certification fee: $1.50. Fee payee: Circuit Clerk. Personal checks accepted. Prepayment is required.

Justice Court 111 Court St, Senatobia, MS 38668; 662-562-7626. Hours: 8AM-5PM (CST). *Misdemeanor, Civil Actions Under $2,500, Eviction, Small Claims.*

Chancery Court 201 Ward St, Senatobia, MS 38668; 662-562-5661; Fax: 662-562-7486. Hours: 8AM-5PM (CST). *Probate.*

Tippah County

Circuit Court Courthouse, Ripley, MS 38663; 662-837-7370; Fax: 662-837-1030. Hours: 8AM-5PM (CST). *Felony, Civil Actions Over $2,500.*

Civil Records: Access: Phone, fax, mail, in person. Both court and visitors may perform in person searches. Search fee: $5.00 per name. Required to search: name, years to search. Civil cases indexed by defendant. Civil records on docket books since 1800s.
Criminal Records: Access: Phone, fax, mail, in person. Both court and visitors may perform in person searches. Search fee: $5.00 per name. Required to search: name, years to search, DOB; also helpful: SSN. Criminal records on docket books since 1800s.
General Information: No sealed, adoptions, mental health, juvenile, sex or expunged records released. SASE not required. Turnaround time 1 week, phone turnaround time 30 minutes. Fax notes: $1.00 per page. Copy fee: $.50 per page. Certification fee: No cert fee. Fee payee: Circuit Clerk. Personal checks accepted. All fees may be billed.

Justice Court Justice Court, 205-B Spring Ave, Ripley, MS 38663; 662-837-8842; Fax: 662-837-1398. Hours: 8AM-5PM (CST). *Misdemeanor, Civil Actions Under $2,500, Eviction, Small Claims.*

Chancery Court PO Box 99, Ripley, MS 38663; 662-837-7374; Fax: 662-837-1030. Hours: 8AM-5PM (CST). *Probate.*

Tishomingo County

Circuit Court 1008 Battleground Dr, Iuka, MS 38852; 662-423-7026; Fax: 662-423-1667. Hours: 8AM-5PM (CST). *Felony, Civil Actions Over $2,500.*

Civil Records: Access: Mail, in person. Both court and visitors may perform in person searches. Search fee: $10.00 per name. Required to search: name, years to search. Civil cases indexed by defendant, plaintiff. Civil records on computer back to 2000, in docket books since 1950s, others in storage.
Criminal Records: Access: Mail, in person. Both court and visitors may perform in person searches. Search fee: $10.00 per name. Required to search: name, years to search, DOB; also helpful: SSN, signed release. Criminal records on computer back to 2000, in docket books since 1950s, others in storage.
General Information: Public Access terminal is available. No sealed, adoptions, mental health, juvenile, sex, or expunged records released. SASE requested. Turnaround time 1-2 days. Copy fee: $.25 per page. Certification fee: No cert fee. Fee payee: Circuit Clerk. Business checks accepted. Prepayment is required.

Justice Court - Northern & Southern Districts 1008 Battleground Drive, Iuka, MS 38852; 662-423-7033; Fax: 662-423-7050. Hours: 8AM-5PM (CST). *Misdemeanor, Civil Actions Under $2,500, Eviction, Small Claims.*

Chancery Court 1008 Battleground Dr, Iuka, MS 38852; 662-423-7010; Fax: 662-423-7005. Hours: 8AM-5PM (CST). *Probate.*

Tunica County

Circuit Court PO Box 184, Tunica, MS 38676; 662-363-2842. Hours: 8AM-5PM (CST). *Felony, Civil Actions Over $2,500.*

Civil Records: Access: Mail, in person. Both court and visitors may perform in person searches. Search fee: $10.00 per name. Required to search: name, years to

search. Civil cases indexed by defendant, plaintiff. Civil records on docket books since 1959, archived prior.

Criminal Records: Access: Mail, in person. Both court and visitors may perform in person searches. Search fee: $10.00 per name. Required to search: name, years to search, DOB; also helpful: SSN. Criminal records on docket books since 1954.

General Information: No sealed, adoptions, mental health, juvenile, sex, or expunged records released. SASE requested. Turnaround time 1 week. Copy fee: $.50 per page. Add postage. Certification fee: $1.50. Fee payee: Circuit Clerk. Personal checks accepted. Prepayment is required.

Justice Court 5130 Old Moon Landing, Tunica, MS 38676; 662-363-2178; Fax: 662-363-4234. Hours: 8AM-5PM (CST). *Misdemeanor, Civil Actions Under $2,500, Eviction, Small Claims.*

Chancery Court PO Box 217, Tunica, MS 38676; 662-363-2451; Fax: 662-357-5934. Hours: 8AM-Noon, 1-5PM (CST). *Probate.*

Union County

Circuit Court PO Box 298, New Albany, MS 38652; 662-534-1910; Fax: 662-534-2059. Hours: 8AM-5PM (CST). *Felony, Civil Actions Over $2,500.*

Civil Records: Access: Fax, mail, in person. Both court and visitors may perform in person searches. Search fee: $10.00 per name. Includes certification fee. Required to search: name, years to search, address. Civil cases indexed by defendant, plaintiff. Civil records on docket books since early 1900s.

Criminal Records: Access: Fax, mail, in person. Both court and visitors may perform in person searches. Search fee: $10.00 per name. Fee includes certification. Required to search: name, years to search, DOB; also helpful: SSN. Criminal records on docket books since early 1900s.

General Information: No adoptions, mental health or juvenile records released. SASE requested. Turnaround time 1 week. Fax notes: No fee to fax results. Copy fee: $.50 per page. Certification fee: $5.00. Fee payee: Helen Randle or Rhonda Dowdy. Personal checks accepted. Prepayment is required.

Justice Court - East & West Posts PO Box 27, New Albany, MS 38652; 662-534-1951; Fax: 662-534-1935. Hours: 8AM-5PM (CST). *Misdemeanor, Civil Actions Under $2,500, Eviction, Small Claims.*

Chancery Court PO Box 847, New Albany, MS 38652; 662-534-1900; Fax: 662-534-1907. Hours: 8AM-5PM (CST). *Probate.*

Walthall County

Circuit Court 200 Ball Ave, Tylertown, MS 39667; 601-876-5677; Fax: 601-876-6688. Hours: 8AM-Noon; 1-5PM (CST). *Felony, Civil Actions Over $2,500.*

Civil Records: Access: Mail, in person. Both court and visitors may perform in person searches. Search fee: $10.00 per name. Required to search: name, years to search. Civil cases indexed by defendant, plaintiff. Civil records on docket books since 1914.

Criminal Records: Access: Mail, in person. Both court and visitors may perform in person searches. Search fee: $10.00 per name. Required to search: name, years to search; also helpful: SSN. Criminal records on docket books since 1914.

General Information: No sealed, adoptions, mental health, juvenile, sex, or expunged records released. Turnaround time 1-2 days. Copy fee: $.25 per page. Certification fee: $1.50 plus $.50 per page. Fee payee: Circuit Clerk. Personal checks accepted. Prepayment is required.

Justice Court - Districts 1 & 2 PO Box 507, Tylertown, MS 39667; 601-876-2311. Hours: 8AM-5PM (CST). *Misdemeanor, Civil Actions Under $2,500, Eviction, Small Claims.*

Chancery Court 200 Ball Ave, PO Box 351, Tylertown, MS 39667; 601-876-3553; Fax: 601-876-7788. Hours: 8AM-5PM (CST). *Probate.*

Warren County

Circuit & County Court PO Box 351, Vicksburg, MS 39181; 601-636-3961; Fax: 601-630-4100. Hours: 8AM-5PM (CST). *Felony, Misdemeanor, Civil.*

Civil Records: Access: Mail, in person. Both court and visitors may perform in person searches. Search fee: $10.00 per name. Required to search: name, years to search. Civil cases indexed by defendant, plaintiff. Civil records on books since 1970s.

Criminal Records: Access: Mail, in person. Both court and visitors may perform in person searches. Search fee: $10.00 per name. Required to search: name, years to search; also helpful: DOB, SSN. Criminal records on books since 1970s.

General Information: No sealed or expunged records released. SASE required. Turnaround time 1 day. Copy fee: $1.00 per page. Certification fee: $1.50. Fee payee: Circuit Clerk. Personal checks accepted. Prepayment is required.

Justice Court - Northern, Central & Southern Districts PO Box 1598, Vicksburg, MS 39181; 601-634-6402. Hours: 8AM-5PM (CST). *Misdemeanor, Civil Actions Under $2,500, Eviction, Small Claims.*

Chancery Court PO Box 351, Vicksburg, MS 39181; 601-636-4415; Fax: 601-630-8016. Hours: 8AM-5PM (CST). *Probate.*

Washington County

Circuit & County Court PO Box 1276, Greenville, MS 38702; 662-378-2747; Fax: 662-334-2698. Hours: 8AM-5PM (CST). *Felony, Misdemeanor, Civil.*

Civil Records: Access: Fax, mail, in person. Both court and visitors may perform in person searches. Search fee: $10.00 per name. Required to search: name, years to search. Civil cases indexed by defendant, plaintiff. Civil records on books since 1964.

Criminal Records: Access: Fax, mail, in person. Both court and visitors may perform in person searches. Search fee: $10.00 per name. Required to search: name, years to search; also helpful: DOB, SSN. Criminal records on books since 1964.

General Information: No sealed or expunged records released. SASE required. Turnaround time 5-10 days. Fax notes: No fee to fax results. Copy fee: $.50 per page. Certification fee: $3.00. Fee payee: Circuit Clerk. Business checks accepted. Prepayment is required.

Justice Court - Districts 1-3 905 W Alexander, Greenville, MS 38701; 662-332-0633. Hours: 8AM-5PM (CST). *Misdemeanor, Civil Actions Under $2,500, Eviction, Small Claims.*

Chancery Court PO Box 309, Greenville, MS 38702-0309; 662-332-1595; Fax: 662-334-2725. Hours: 8AM-5PM (CST). *Probate.*

Wayne County

Circuit Court PO Box 428, Waynesboro, MS 39367; 601-735-1171; Fax: 601-735-6261. Hours: 8AM-5PM (CST). *Felony, Civil Actions Over $2,500.*

Civil Records: Access: Phone, fax, mail, in person. Both court and visitors may perform in person searches. Search fee: $10.00 per name. Required to search: name,

years to search. Civil cases indexed by defendant, plaintiff. Civil records on docket books since 1971, others in storage.

Criminal Records: Access: Fax, mail, in person. Both court and visitors may perform in person searches. Search fee: $10.00 per name. Required to search: name, years to search; also helpful: DOB, SSN, signed release. Criminal records on docket books since 1971, others in storage.

General Information: No sealed or expunged records released. Turnaround time 1-2 days. Fax notes: Fee to fax results is $1.00 per page. Copy fee: $.50 per page. Certification fee: $1.50. Fee payee: Circuit Clerk. Business checks accepted.

Justice Court - Posts 1 & 2 810 Chickasawhay St, Suite C, Waynesboro, MS 39367; 601-735-3118; Fax: 601-735-6266. *Misdemeanor, Civil Actions Under $2,500, Eviction, Small Claims.*

Chancery Court Courthouse, 609 Azalea Dr, Waynesboro, MS 39367; 601-735-2873; Fax: 601-735-6248. Hours: 8AM-5PM (CST). *Probate.*

Webster County

Circuit Court PO Box 308, Walthall, MS 39771; 662-258-6287; Fax: 662-258-7686. Hours: 8AM-5PM (CST). *Felony, Civil Actions Over $2,500.*

Civil Records: Access: Phone, fax, mail, in person. Both court and visitors may perform in person searches. Search fee: $10.00 per name. Required to search: name, years to search. Civil cases indexed by defendant, plaintiff. Civil records on docket books since 1874.

Criminal Records: Access: Fax, mail, in person. Both court and visitors may perform in person searches. Search fee: $10.00 per name. Required to search: name, years to search, DOB; also helpful: SSN. Criminal records on docket books since 1874.

General Information: No sealed, adoptions, mental health, juvenile, sex, or expunged records released. Turnaround time 1-2 days. Fax notes: No fee to fax results. Copy fee: $.50 per page. Certification fee: $1.00. Fee payee: Circuit Clerk. Business checks accepted. Prepayment is required.

Justice Court - Districts 1 & 2 114 Hwy 9 N, Eupora, MS 39744; 662-258-2590; Fax: 662-258-3093. Hours: 8AM-5PM (CST). *Misdemeanor, Civil Actions Under $2,500, Eviction, Small Claims.*

Chancery Court PO Box 398, Walthall, MS 39771; 662-258-4131; Fax: 662-258-6657. Hours: 8AM-5PM (CST). *Probate.*

Wilkinson County

Circuit Court PO Box 327, Woodville, MS 39669; 601-888-6697; Fax: 601-888-6984. Hours: 8:00AM-5:00PM (CST). *Felony, Civil Actions Over $2,500.*

Civil Records: Access: Mail, in person. Both court and visitors may perform in person searches. Search fee: $10.00 per name. Required to search: name, years to search. Civil cases indexed by defendant, plaintiff. Civil records on docket books since 1940s.

Criminal Records: Access: Mail, in person. Both court and visitors may perform in person searches. Search fee: $10.00 per name. Required to search: name, years to search; also helpful: DOB, SSN. Criminal records on docket books since 1940s.

General Information: No sealed or expunged records released. Turnaround time 1-2 days. Copy fee: $.50 per page. Certification fee: $5.00. Fee payee: Circuit Clerk. Personal checks accepted. Prepayment is required.

Justice Court - East & West Districts PO Box 40, Woodville, MS 39669; 601-888-3538; Fax: 601-888-6776. Hours: 8AM-5PM (CST). *Misdemeanor, Civil Actions Under $2,500, Eviction, Small Claims.*

Chancery Court PO Box 516, Woodville, MS 39669; 601-888-4381; Fax: 601-888-6776. Hours: 8AM-5PM (CST). *Probate.*

Winston County

Circuit Court PO Drawer 785, Louisville, MS 39339; 662-773-3581; Fax: 662-773-8825. Hours: 8AM-5PM (CST). *Felony, Civil Actions Over $2,500.*

Civil Records: Access: Phone, fax, mail, in person. Both court and visitors may perform in person searches. Search fee: $10.00 per name. Required to search: name, years to search. Civil cases indexed by defendant, plaintiff. Civil records on docket books since early 1950s; on computer back to 1994.

Criminal Records: Access: Fax, mail, in person. Both court and visitors may perform in person searches. Search fee: $10.00 per name. Required to search: name, years to search, DOB; also helpful: SSN. Criminal records on docket books since early 1950s; on computer back to 1994.

General Information: Public Access terminal is available. No sealed, adoptions, mental health, juvenile or expunged records released. SASE requested. Turnaround time 14 days. Fax notes: $5.00 for first page, $1.00 each add'l. Copy fee: $1.00 per page. Certification fee: $1.50. Fee payee: Circuit Clerk. Personal checks accepted. Prepayment is required.

Justice Court PO Box 327, Louisville, MS 39339; 662-773-6016; Fax: 662-773-8817. Hours: 8AM-5PM (CST). *Misdemeanor, Civil Actions Under $2,500, Eviction, Small Claims.*

Chancery Court PO Drawer 69, Louisville, MS 39339; 662-773-3631; Fax: 662-773-8825. Hours: 8AM-5PM (CST). *Probate.*

Yalobusha County

Coffeeville Circuit Court PO Box 260, Coffeeville, MS 38922; 662-675-8187; Fax: 662-675-8004. Hours: 8AM-5PM (CST). *Felony, Civil Actions Over $2,500.*

Civil Records: Access: Phone, fax, mail, in person. Both court and visitors may perform in person searches. Search fee: $10.00 per name. May mail request with check or fax request with copy of check to be mailed. Required to search: name, years to search. Civil cases indexed by defendant, plaintiff. Civil records on docket books since 1930s.

Criminal Records: Access: Phone, fax, mail, in person. Both court and visitors may perform in person searches. Search fee: $10.00 per name. May mail request with check or fax request with copy of check to be mailed. Required to search: name, years to search; also helpful: DOB. Criminal records on docket books since 1930s.

General Information: No sealed, adoptions, mental health, juvenile, sex, or expunged records released. SASE requested. Turnaround time 1-2 days. Copy fee: $.25 per page. Certification fee: $10.00. Fee payee: Circuit Clerk. Personal checks accepted. Prepayment is required.

Water Valley Circuit Court PO Box 431, Water Valley, MS 38965; 662-473-1341; Fax: 662-473-5020. Hours: 8AM-5PM (CST). *Felony, Civil Actions Over $2,500.*

Civil Records: Access: Fax, mail, in person. Both court and visitors may perform in person searches. Search fee: $10.00 per name. Includes certification fee. Required to search: name, years to search. Civil cases indexed by defendant, plaintiff. Civil records on docket books since 1930s.

Criminal Records: Access: Fax, mail, in person. Both court and visitors may perform in person searches. Search fee: $10.00 per name. Fee includes certification. Required to search: name, years to search, DOB; also helpful: SSN. Criminal records on docket books since 1930s.

General Information: No sealed, adoptions, mental health, juvenile, sex, or expunged records released. Turnaround time 1 week. Fax notes: No fee to fax results. Copy fee: $.50 per page. Certification fee: $1.50. Fee payee: Circuit Clerk. Personal checks accepted.

Justice Court - District 1 PO Box 218, Coffeeville, MS 38922; 662-675-8115; Fax: 662-675-8452. Hours: 8AM-5PM (CST). *Misdemeanor, Civil Actions Under $2,500, Eviction, Small Claims.*

Justice Court - Division 2 PO Box 272, Water Valley, MS 38965; 662-473-4502. Hours: 8AM-5PM (CST). *Misdemeanor, Civil Actions Under $2,500, Eviction, Small Claims.*

Chancery Court PO Box 260, Coffeeville, MS 38922; 662-675-2716; Fax: 662-675-8004. Hours: 8AM-Noon, 1-5PM (CST). *Probate.*

Chancery Court PO Box 664, Water Valley, MS 38965; 662-473-2091; Fax: 662-473-5020. Hours: 8AM-5PM (CST). *Probate.*

Yazoo County

Circuit & County Court PO Box 108, Yazoo City, MS 39194; 662-746-1872. Hours: 8AM-5PM (CST). *Felony, Misdemeanor, Civil.*

Civil Records: Access: Mail, in person. Both court and visitors may perform in person searches. Search fee: $10.00 per name. Required to search: name, years to search. Civil cases indexed by defendant, plaintiff. Civil records for Civil Circuit on docket books since 1973; for Civil County on docket books since 1977.

Criminal Records: Access: Mail, in person. Both court and visitors may perform in person searches. Search fee: $10.00 per name. Required to search: name, years to search, DOB; also helpful: SSN. Criminal records for Criminal Circuit from 1975; Criminal County on docket books since 1975.

General Information: No sealed, adoptions, mental health, juvenile, sex, or expunged records released. SASE required. Turnaround time 1 day. Copy fee: $.50 per page. Certification fee: $1.00. Fee payee: Circuit Clerk. Business checks accepted. Prepayment is required.

Justice Court - Northern & Southern Districts PO Box 798, Yazoo City, MS 39194; 662-746-8181. Hours: 8AM-5PM (CST). *Misdemeanor, Civil Actions Under $2,500, Eviction, Small Claims.*

Chancery Court PO Box 68, Yazoo City, MS 39194; 662-746-2661. Hours: 8AM-5PM (CST). *Probate.*

Mississippi Recording Offices

ORGANIZATION   82 counties, 92 recording offices. The recording officers are Chancery Clerk and Clerk of Circuit Court (state tax liens). Ten counties have two separate recording offices - Bolivar, Carroll, Chickasaw, Craighead, Harrison, Hinds, Jasper, Jones, Panola, Tallahatchie, and Yalobusha. See the notes under each county for how to determine which office is appropriate to search. The entire state is in the Central Time Zone (CST).

REAL ESTATE RECORDS   A few counties will perform real estate searches. Copies usually cost $.50 per page and certification fees $1.00 per document. The Assessor maintains tax records.

UCC RECORDS   This was a dual filing state. Until 07/2001, financing statements were filed both at the state level and with the Chancery Clerk, except for consumer goods, farm related and real estate related filings, which were filed only with the Chancery Clerk. Now, only real estate related filings are filed at the county level. Nearly all counties will perform UCC searches. Use search request form UCC-11. Search fees are usually $5.00 per debtor name. Copy fees vary from $.25 to $2.00 per page.

TAX LIEN RECORDS   Federal tax liens on personal property of businesses are filed with the Secretary of State. Federal tax liens on personal property of individuals are filed with the county Chancery Clerk. State tax liens on personal property are filed with the county Clerk of Circuit Court. Refer to the County Court section for information about Mississippi Circuit Courts. State tax liens on real property are filed with the Chancery Clerk. Most Chancery Clerk offices will perform a federal tax lien search for a fee of $5.00 per name. Copy fees vary.

OTHER LIENS   Mechanics, lis pendens, judgment (Circuit Court), construction.

Adams County

Chancery Clerk, P.O. Box 1006, Natchez, MS 39121. Chancery Clerk, R/E and UCC Recording 601-446-6684; Fax 601-445-7913.
Will search UCC records. Will not search real estate records. **Other Phone Numbers:** Assessor 601-442-6732; Elections 601-446-6326.

Alcorn County

Chancery Clerk, P.O. Box 69, Corinth, MS 38835-0069. 662-286-7700; Fax 662-286-7706.
Will search UCC records. Will not search real estate records. **Other Phone Numbers:** Elections 662-286-7740.

Amite County

Chancery Clerk, P.O. Box 680, Liberty, MS 39645-0680. 601-657-8022; Fax 601-657-8288.
Will search UCC records. Will not search real estate records. **Other Phone Numbers:** Assessor 601-657-8973; Treasurer 601-657-8932; Elections 601-657-8932.

Attala County

Chancery Clerk, Chancery Court Bldg., 230 W. Washington St., Kosciusko, MS 39090. 662-289-2921; Fax 662-289-7662.
Will search UCC records. Will not search real estate records. **Other Phone Numbers:** Assessor 662-289-5731; Elections 662-289-1471.

Benton County

Chancery Clerk, P.O. Box 218, Ashland, MS 38603. 662-224-6300; Fax 662-224-6303.
Will search UCC records. Will not search real estate records. **Other Phone Numbers:** Assessor 662-224-6315; Elections 662-224-6310.

Bolivar County (1st District)

Chancery Clerk, P.O. Box 238, Rosedale, MS 38769-0238. 662-759-3762; Fax 662-759-3467.
Will search UCC records. Will not search real estate records. **Other Phone Numbers:** Assessor 662-843-

3826; Treasurer 662-843-2531; Elections 662-843-2061.

Bolivar County (2nd District)

Chancery Clerk, P.O. Box 789, Cleveland, MS 38732. 662-843-2071; Fax 662-846-2940.
Will search UCC records. Will not search real estate records. **Other Phone Numbers:** Assessor 662-843-3926; Treasurer 662-843-2071; Elections 662-843-2061.

Calhoun County

Chancery Clerk, P.O. Box 8, Pittsboro, MS 38951. Chancery Clerk, R/E and UCC Recording 662-412-3117 UCC Recording: 662-412-3121; Fax 662-412-3128.
Will search UCC records. This agency will not do a federal tax lien search. Will not search real estate records. **Other Phone Numbers:** Assessor 662-412-3140; Treasurer 662-412-3117; Appraiser/Auditor 662-412-3146; Elections 662-412-3101; Vital Records 662-412-3101.

Carroll County (1st District)

Chancery Clerk, P.O. Box 60, Carrollton, MS 38917. 662-237-9274; Fax 662-237-9642.
Will search UCC records. Will not search real estate records. **Other Phone Numbers:** Assessor 662-237-9217; Elections 662-464-5476.

Carroll County (2nd District)

Chancery Clerk, P.O. Box 6, Vaiden, MS 39176. 662-464-5476; Fax 662-464-7745.
The 2nd district is split by section, township and range. Will search UCC records. This agency will not do a federal tax lien search. Will not search real estate records. **Other Phone Numbers:** Elections 662-464-5476.

Chickasaw County (1st District)

Chancery Clerk, Courthouse, Houston, MS 38851. 662-456-2513; Fax 662-456-5295.
Will search UCC records. Will not search real estate records. **Other Phone Numbers:** Assessor 662-456-3327; Treasurer 662-456-3941; Elections 662-456-2331.

Chickasaw County (2nd District)

Chancery Clerk, 234 Main Street, Room 201, Okolona, MS 38860-1438. 662-447-2092; Fax 662-447-5024.
Will search UCC records. Will not search real estate records. **Other Phone Numbers:** Assessor 662-447-2242; Treasurer 662-456-2513; Elections 662-456-2331.

Choctaw County

Chancery Clerk, P.O. Box 250, Ackerman, MS 39735-0250. 662-285-6329; Fax 662-285-3444.
Will search UCC records. Will not search real estate records. **Other Phone Numbers:** Elections 662-285-6245.

Claiborne County

Chancery Clerk, P.O. Box 449, Port Gibson, MS 39150. Chancery Clerk, R/E and UCC Recording 601-437-4992; Fax 601-437-3731.
Will search UCC records. UCC search includes federal tax liens if requested. Will not search real estate records. **Other Phone Numbers:** Assessor 601-437-5591; Treasurer 601-437-4992; Appraiser/Auditor 601-437-5591; Elections 601-437-5841.

Clarke County

Chancery Clerk, P.O. Box 689, Quitman, MS 39355. Chancery Clerk, R/E and UCC Recording 601-776-2126; Fax 601-776-1001.
Will search UCC records. This agency will not do a federal tax lien search. Will not search real estate records. **Other Phone Numbers:** Assessor 601-776-6931; Treasurer 601-776-2126; Appraiser/Auditor 601-776-1021; Elections 601-776-3111.

Clay County

Chancery Clerk, P.O. Box 815, West Point, MS 39773. 662-494-3124.
Will search UCC records. UCC search does not include federal tax liens. Will not search real estate records. **Other Phone Numbers:** Treasurer 662-494-2724; Elections 662-494-3384.

Coahoma County

Chancery Clerk, P.O. Box 98, Clarksdale, MS 38614. 662-624-3000; Fax 662-624-3029.
Will search UCC records. Will not search real estate records. **Other Phone Numbers:** Assessor 662-234-3006; Elections 662-624-3014.

Copiah County

Chancery Clerk, P.O. Box 507, Hazlehurst, MS 39083-0507. 601-894-3021; Fax 601-894-3026.
Will search UCC records. **Other Phone Numbers:** Assessor 601-894-2721; Elections 601-894-1241.

Covington County

Chancery Clerk, P.O. Box 1679, Collins, MS 39428. 601-765-4242; Fax 601-765-5016.
Will search UCC records. UCC search includes federal tax liens. Will not search real estate records. **Other Phone Numbers:** Assessor 601-756-6402; Elections 601-765-6506.

De Soto County

Chancery Clerk, P.O. Box 949, Hernando, MS 38632. Chancery Clerk, R/E and UCC Recording 662-429-1318.
Will search UCC records. UCC search does not include federal tax liens. Will not search real estate records. **Other Phone Numbers:** Assessor 662-429-1335; Elections 662-429-1325.

Forrest County

Chancery Clerk, P.O. Box 951, Hattiesburg, MS 39401. 601-545-6014; Fax 601-545-6095.
Will search UCC records. Will not search real estate records. **Other Phone Numbers:** Assessor 601-582-8228; Elections 601-582-3213.

Franklin County

Chancery Clerk, P.O. Box 297, Meadville, MS 39653-0297. 601-384-2330; Fax 601-384-5864.
Will search UCC records. **Other Phone Numbers:** Elections 601-384-2320; Tax Collector 601-384-2359.

George County

Chancery Clerk, 355 Cox Street, Lucedale, MS 39452. Chancery Clerk, R/E and UCC Recording 601-947-4801; Fax 601-947-1300.
Will search UCC records. UCC search includes federal tax liens if requested. Will not search real estate records. **Other Phone Numbers:** Assessor 601-947-7541; Treasurer 601-947-3766; Appraiser/Auditor 601-947-7541; Elections 601-947-4881.

Greene County

Chancery Clerk, P.O. Box 610, Leakesville, MS 39451. 601-394-2377.
Will search UCC records. UCC search includes federal tax liens if requested. RE owner, mortgage, and property transfer searches available. **Other Phone Numbers:** Assessor 601-394-2377; Treasurer 601-394-2377; Elections 601-394-2379.

Grenada County

Chancery Clerk, P.O. Drawer 1208, Grenada, MS 38902-1208. 662-226-1821.
Will search UCC records. This agency will not do a federal tax lien search. Will not search real estate records. **Other Phone Numbers:** Treasurer 662-226-1741; Elections 662-226-1941; Tax Collector 662-226-1741.

Hancock County

Chancery Clerk, P.O. Box 429, Bay Saint Louis, MS 39520. 228-467-5404; Fax 228-467-3159.

Will search UCC records. Will not search real estate records. **Other Phone Numbers:** Assessor 228-467-5727; Treasurer 228-467-4425; Elections 228-467-5265; Tax Collector 228-467-4425.

Harrison County (1st District)

Chancery Clerk, P.O. Drawer CC, Gulfport, MS 39502. 228-865-4195 R/E Recording: 228-865-4036; Fax 228-868-1480.
Will search UCC records. Will not search real estate records. **Other Phone Numbers:** Assessor 228-865-4043; Treasurer 228-865-4040; Appraiser/Auditor 228-865-4044; Elections 228-865-4049; Vital Records 228-960-7400.

Harrison County (2nd District)

Chancery Clerk, P.O. Box 544, Biloxi, MS 39533. 228-435-8220; Fax 228-435-8292.
Will search UCC records. Will not search real estate records. **Other Phone Numbers:** Elections 228-865-4167.

Hinds County (1st District)

Chancery Clerk, P.O. Box 686, Jackson, MS 39205-0686. 601-968-6516 R/E Recording: 601-968-6508; Fax 601-973-5535. http://www.co.hinds.ms.us/pgs/elected/chanceryclerk.asp
Will search UCC records. Will not search real estate records. **Online Access:** Real Estate, Judgments. Online access to the county records database is available free at www.co.hinds.ms.us/pgs/apps/gindex.asp. **Other Phone Numbers:** Treasurer 601-968-6588; Elections 601-968-6628; Tax Collector 601-968-6588.

Hinds County (2nd District)

Chancery Clerk, P.O. Box 88, Raymond, MS 39154. 601-857-8055; http://www.co.hinds.ms.us
The 2nd District consists of all towns/cities outside the limits of Jackson, including Bolton, part of Clinton, Edwards, Learned, Raymond, part of Terry, and Utica. Will search UCC records. UCC search does not include federal tax liens. Will not search real estate records. **Online Access:** Real Estate, Assessor, Grantor/Grantee, Judgments. Online access to the county clerk database is available free at www.co.hinds.ms.us/pgs/apps/gindex.asp. Chose to search general index, landroll, judgments, acreage, subdivision, condominiums. **Other Phone Numbers:** Assessor 601-857-8787; Treasurer 601-857-5574; Elections 601-968-6628; Tax Collector 601-857-5574.

Holmes County

Chancery Clerk, P.O. Box 239, Lexington, MS 39095. 662-834-2508 R/E Recording: 662-834-0005 UCC Recording: 662-834-0005; Fax 662-834-3020.
Will search UCC records. Will not search real estate records. **Other Phone Numbers:** Assessor 662-834-2865; Treasurer 662-834-0005; Appraiser/Auditor 662-834-3737; Elections 662-834-2476; Vital Records 662-834-2476.

Humphreys County

Chancery Clerk, P.O. Box 547, Belzoni, MS 39038. 662-247-1740; Fax 662-247-0101.
Will search UCC records. UCC search includes federal tax liens if requested. Mortgage and property transfer searches available. **Other Phone Numbers:** Assessor 662-247-3174; Treasurer 662-247-2552; Elections 662-247-3065; Tax Collector 662-247-2552.

Issaquena County

Chancery Clerk, P.O. Box 27, Mayersville, MS 39113-0027. Chancery Clerk, R/E and UCC Recording 662-873-2761; Fax 662-873-2061.

Will search UCC records. **Other Phone Numbers:** Assessor 662-873-4665; Treasurer 662-873-2761; Elections 662-873-2761; Marriages/Divorces 662-873-2761.

Itawamba County

Chancery Clerk, P.O. Box 776, Fulton, MS 38843. Chancery Clerk, R/E and UCC Recording 662-862-3421; Fax 662-862-3421. bds290@network-one.com
Will search UCC records. Will not search real estate records. **Other Phone Numbers:** Assessor 662-862-4304; Appraiser/Auditor 662-862-7598; Elections 662-862-3511; Vital Records 662-862-3511.

Jackson County

Chancery Clerk, P.O. Box 998, Pascagoula, MS 39568. 228-769-3131; Fax 228-769-3135.
Will search UCC records. Will not search real estate records. **Other Phone Numbers:** Assessor 228-769-3070; Treasurer 228-769-3131; Elections 228-769-3040.

Jasper County (1st District)

Chancery Clerk, P.O. Box 38, Paulding, MS 39348-0038. 601-727-4941; Fax 601-727-4475.
Will search UCC records. This agency will not do a federal tax lien search. Will not search real estate records. **Other Phone Numbers:** Assessor 601-764-2813; Elections 601-764-2245.

Jasper County (2nd District)

Chancery Clerk, P.O. Box 1047, Bay Springs, MS 39422. 601-764-3026; Fax 601-764-3468.
Will search UCC records. Will not search real estate records. **Other Phone Numbers:** Assessor 601764-2813; Elections 601-764-2245.

Jefferson County

Chancery Clerk, P.O. Box 145, Fayette, MS 39069. 601-786-3021; Fax 601-786-6009.
Will search UCC records. Will not search real estate records. **Other Phone Numbers:** Assessor 601-786-3021; Elections 601-786-3422; Tax Collector 601-786-3781.

Jefferson Davis County

Chancery Clerk, P.O. Box 1137, Prentiss, MS 39474. 601-792-4204; Fax 601-792-2894.
Will search UCC records. Will not search real estate records. **Other Phone Numbers:** Assessor 601-792-4291; Treasurer 601-792-4204; Elections 601-792-4231.

Jones County (1st District)

Chancery Clerk, Court Street, Jones County Courthouse, Ellisville, MS 39437. 601-477-3307.
Will search UCC records. This agency will not do a federal tax lien search. Will not search real estate records. **Other Phone Numbers:** Assessor 601-477-3250; Elections 601-425-2556.

Jones County (2nd District)

Chancery Clerk, P.O. Box 1468, Laurel, MS 39441. 601-428-0527; Fax 601-428-3602.
Will search UCC records. Will not search real estate records. **Other Phone Numbers:** Elections 601-425-2556.

Kemper County

Chancery Clerk, P.O. Box 188, De Kalb, MS 39328. 601-743-2460; Fax 601-743-2789.
Will search UCC records. Will not search real estate records. **Other Phone Numbers:** Elections 601-743-2224.

Lafayette County

Chancery Clerk, P.O. Box 1240, Oxford, MS 38655. 662-234-2131.
Will search UCC records. This agency will not do a federal tax lien search. Will not search real estate records. **Other Phone Numbers:** Elections 662-234-4951.

Lamar County

Chancery Clerk, P.O. Box 247, Purvis, MS 39475. 601-794-8504; Fax 601-794-1049.
Will search UCC records. Will not search real estate records. **Other Phone Numbers:** Elections 601-794-8504.

Lauderdale County

Chancery Clerk, P.O. Box 1587, Meridian, MS 39302-1587. 601-482-9701.
Will search UCC records. UCC search includes federal tax liens if requested. Will not search real estate records. **Other Phone Numbers:** Assessor 601-482-9779; Treasurer 601-482-4701; Elections 601-482-9731.

Lawrence County

Chancery Clerk, P.O. Box 821, Monticello, MS 39654. 601-587-7162; Fax 601-587-0750.
Will search UCC records. Will not search real estate records. **Other Phone Numbers:** Treasurer 601-587-2211; Elections 601-587-4791; Tax Collector 601-587-2211.

Leake County

Chancery Clerk, P.O. Box 72, Carthage, MS 39051. 601-267-7371; Fax 601-267-6137.
Will search UCC records. Will not search real estate records. **Other Phone Numbers:** Assessor 601-267-3021; Treasurer 601-267-7371; Elections 601-267-8357.

Lee County

Chancery Clerk, P.O. Box 7127, Tupelo, MS 38802. 662-841-9100; Fax 662-680-6091.
Will search UCC records. Will not search real estate records. **Other Phone Numbers:** Assessor 662-841-9030; Treasurer 662-841-9100; Elections 662-841-9024.

Leflore County

Chancery Clerk, P.O. Box 250, Greenwood, MS 38935-0250. 662-455-7913; Fax 662-455-7965.
Will search UCC records. Will not search real estate records. **Other Phone Numbers:** Assessor 662-453-1041; Elections 662-453-1435.

Lincoln County

Chancery Clerk, P.O. Box 555, Brookhaven, MS 39602. 601-835-3416.
Will search UCC records. UCC search includes federal tax liens if requested. Will not search real estate records. **Other Phone Numbers:** Assessor 601-835-3428; Treasurer 601-835-3412; Elections 601-835-3435.

Lowndes County

Chancery Clerk, P.O. Box 684, Columbus, MS 39703. 662-329-5800 R/E Recording: 662-329-5809 or 5806 UCC Recording: 662-329-5807.
Will search UCC records. UCC search does not include federal tax liens. Will not search real estate records. **Other Phone Numbers:** Assessor 662-329-5700; Treasurer 662-329-5700; Appraiser/Auditor 662-329-5701; Elections 662-329-5900.

Madison County

Chancery Clerk, P.O. Box 404, Canton, MS 39046. 601-859-1177; http://mcatax.com
Will search UCC records. UCC search does not include federal tax liens. Will not search real estate records. **Online Access:** Real Estate, Tax Assessor Records. Records from the county Assessor office are available free online. At www.mcatax.com/mcasearch.asp, click on "Search The Database." Records include parcel number, address, legal description, value information, and tax district. **Other Phone Numbers:** Assessor 601-859-1921; Elections 601-352-2049.

Marion County

Chancery Clerk, 250 Broad Street, Suite 2, Columbia, MS 39429. 601-736-2691; Fax 601-736-1232.
Will search UCC records. **Other Phone Numbers:** Assessor 601-736-8256; Elections 601-736-8246.

Marshall County

Chancery Clerk, P.O. Box 219, Holly Springs, MS 38635. 662-252-4431; Fax 662-252-0004.
Will search UCC records. Will not search real estate records. **Other Phone Numbers:** Assessor 662-252-3661; Elections 662-252-3434.

Monroe County

Chancery Clerk, P.O. Box 578, Aberdeen, MS 39730. 662-369-8143; Fax 662-369-7928.
Will search UCC records. Will not search real estate records. **Other Phone Numbers:** Assessor 662-369-2033; Treasurer 662-369-8143; Elections 662-369-8695.

Montgomery County

Chancery Clerk, P.O. Box 71, Winona, MS 38967. 662-283-2333; Fax 662-283-2233.
Will search UCC records. Will not search real estate records. **Other Phone Numbers:** Assessor 662-283-2112; Elections 662-283-4161.

Neshoba County

Chancery Clerk, 401 Beacon Street, Suite 107, Philadelphia, MS 39350. 601-656-3581.
Will search UCC records. This agency will not do a federal tax lien search. Will not search real estate records. **Other Phone Numbers:** Elections 601-656-4781.

Newton County

Chancery Clerk, P.O. Box 68, Decatur, MS 39327. 601-635-2367; Fax 601-635-3210.
Will search UCC records. Will not search real estate records. **Other Phone Numbers:** Assessor 601-635-2367; Elections 601-635-2368.

Noxubee County

Chancery Clerk, P.O. Box 147, Macon, MS 39341. Chancery Clerk, R/E and UCC Recording 662-726-4243; Fax 662-726-2272.
Will search UCC records. UCC search does not include federal tax liens. Will not search real estate records. **Other Phone Numbers:** Assessor 662-726-4744; Elections 662-726-5737.

Oktibbeha County

Chancery Clerk, 101 East Main, Courthouse, Starkville, MS 39759. 662-323-5834.
Will search UCC records. This agency will not do a federal tax lien search. Will not search real estate records. **Other Phone Numbers:** Assessor 662-323-1273; Elections 662-323-1356.

Panola County (1st District)

Chancery Clerk, P.O. Box 130, Sardis, MS 38666. 662-487-2070; Fax 662-487-3595.
Will search UCC records. Will not search real estate records. **Other Phone Numbers:** Assessor 662-487-2093; Treasurer 662-487-6215; Tax Collector 662-487-6215.

Panola County (2nd District)

Chancery Clerk, 151 Public Square, Batesville, MS 38606. 662-563-6205; Fax 662-563-8233.
Will search UCC records. Will not search real estate records. **Other Phone Numbers:** Assessor 662-563-6270; Treasurer 662-563-6215; Elections 662-563-6210.

Pearl River County

Chancery Clerk, P.O. Box 431, Poplarville, MS 39470. 601-795-2237.
Will search UCC records. UCC search includes federal tax liens if requested. Will not search real estate records. **Other Phone Numbers:** Elections 601-795-4911.

Perry County

Chancery Clerk, P.O. Box 198, New Augusta, MS 39462. Chancery Clerk, R/E and UCC Recording 601-964-8398; Fax 601-964-8265.
Will search UCC records. **Other Phone Numbers:** Assessor 601-964-3398; Appraiser/Auditor 601-964-3400; Elections 601-964-8663.

Pike County

Chancery Clerk, P.O. Box 309, Magnolia, MS 39652. 601-783-3362; Fax 601-783-2001.
Will search UCC records. Will not search real estate records. **Other Phone Numbers:** Assessor 601-783-5511; Elections 601-783-2581.

Pontotoc County

Chancery Clerk, P.O. Box 209, Pontotoc, MS 38863. 662-489-3900.
Will search UCC records. UCC search does not include federal tax liens. Will not search real estate records. **Other Phone Numbers:** Assessor 662-489-3903; Treasurer 662-489-3904; Elections 662-489-3908; Tax Collector 662-489-3904.

Prentiss County

Chancery Clerk, P.O. Box 477, Booneville, MS 38829. 662-728-8151; Fax 662-728-2007.
Will search UCC records. Will not search real estate records. **Other Phone Numbers:** Assessor 662-728-5044; Elections 662-728-4611.

Quitman County

Chancery Clerk, Chestnut Street, Courthouse, Marks, MS 38646. Chancery Clerk, R/E and UCC Recording 662-326-2661; Fax 662-326-8004.
Will search UCC records. Will not search real estate records. **Other Phone Numbers:** Assessor 662-326-8928; Treasurer 662-326-2661; Appraiser/Auditor 662-326-8928; Elections 662-326-8003.

Rankin County

Chancery Clerk, P.O. Box 700, Brandon, MS 39043. 601-825-1469; Fax 601-824-7116. http://www.rankincounty.org
Will search UCC records. Will not search real estate records. **Online Access:** Real Estate, Tax Assessor Records. Records on the county Land Roll database are available free online at www.rankincounty.org/TA/interact_LandRoll.asp. **Other Phone Numbers:** Assessor 601-825-1470; Treasurer 601-825-1366; Elections 601-825-1466.

Scott County

Chancery Clerk, P.O. Box 630, Forest, MS 39074. 601-469-1922; Fax 601-469-5180.
Will not search real estate records. **Other Phone Numbers:** Elections 601-469-3601; Tax Collector 601-469-4051.

Sharkey County

Chancery Clerk, P.O. Box 218, Rolling Fork, MS 39159. 662-873-2755; Fax 662-873-6045.
Will search UCC records. Will not search real estate records. **Other Phone Numbers:** Elections 662-873-2755; Tax Collector 662-873-4317.

Simpson County

Chancery Clerk, P.O. Box 367, Mendenhall, MS 39114. 601-847-2626; Fax 601-847-7004.
Will search UCC records. Will not search real estate records. **Other Phone Numbers:** Elections 601-847-2474.

Smith County

Chancery Clerk, P.O. Box 39, Raleigh, MS 39153. 601-782-9811; Fax 601-782-4690.
Will search UCC records. Will not search real estate records. **Other Phone Numbers:** Assessor 601-782-9803; Treasurer 601-782-9811; Elections 601-782-4751.

Stone County

Chancery Clerk, P.O. Drawer 7, Wiggins, MS 39577. 601-928-5266; Fax 601-928-5248.
Will search UCC records. Will not search real estate records. **Other Phone Numbers:** Assessor 601-928-3121; Treasurer 601-928-5266; Elections 601-928-5246.

Sunflower County

Chancery Clerk, P.O. Box 988, Indianola, MS 38751-0988. Chancery Clerk, R/E and UCC Recording 662-887-4703; Fax 662-887-7054.
Will search UCC records. Will not search real estate records. **Other Phone Numbers:** Assessor 662-887-1454; Treasurer 662-887-4703; Appraiser/Auditor 662-887-1454; Elections 662-887-1252; Vital Records 662-887-1252.

Tallahatchie County (1st District)

Chancery Clerk, P.O. Box 350, Charleston, MS 38921. 662-647-5551.
Will search UCC records. This agency will not do a federal tax lien search. Will not search real estate records. **Other Phone Numbers:** Assessor 662-647-8922; Elections 662-647-8758.

Tallahatchie County (2nd District)

Chancery Clerk, P.O. Box 180, Sumner, MS 38957. 662-375-8731; Fax 662-375-7252.
Will search UCC records. UCC search does not include federal tax liens. Will not search real estate records.

Tate County

Chancery Clerk, 201 Ward Street, Senatobia, MS 38668. Chancery Clerk, R/E and UCC Recording 662-562-5661; Fax 662-560-6205.
Will search UCC records. Will not search real estate records. **Other Phone Numbers:** Assessor 662-562-6011; Elections 662-562-5211.

Tippah County

Chancery Clerk, P.O. Box 99, Ripley, MS 38663. 662-837-7374; Fax 662-837-1030.
Will search UCC records. Will not search real estate records. **Other Phone Numbers:** Assessor 662-837-9410; Elections 662-837-7370.

Tishomingo County

Chancery Clerk, 1008 Battleground Dr., Courthouse, Iuka, MS 38852. 662-423-7010; Fax 662-423-7005.
Will search UCC records. Will not search real estate records. **Other Phone Numbers:** Assessor 662-423-7048; Treasurer 662-423-7032; Elections 662-423-7026.

Tunica County

Chancery Clerk, P.O. Box 217, Tunica, MS 38676. 662-363-2451.
Will search UCC records. UCC search includes federal tax liens if requested. RE owner, mortgage, and property transfer searches available. **Other Phone Numbers:** Assessor 662-363-1266; Treasurer 662-363-1465; Elections 662-363-2842.

Union County

Chancery Clerk, P.O. Box 847, New Albany, MS 38652. Chancery Clerk, R/E and UCC Recording 662-534-1900; Fax 662-534-1907.
Will search UCC records. Will not search real estate records. **Other Phone Numbers:** Assessor 662-534-1972; Treasurer 662-534-1973; Elections 662-534-1910; Tax Collector 662-534-1973.

Walthall County

Chancery Clerk, P.O. Box 351, Tylertown, MS 39667. 601-876-3553; Fax 601-876-6026.
Will search UCC records. Will not search real estate records. **Other Phone Numbers:** Assessor 601-876-4349; Elections 601-876-5677.

Warren County

Chancery Clerk, P.O. Box 351, Vicksburg, MS 39181. Chancery Clerk, R/E and UCC Recording 601-636-4415; Fax 601-634-4815. http://www.co.warren.ms.us
Will search UCC records. Will not search real estate records. **Other Phone Numbers:** Assessor 601-638-6161; Treasurer 601-638-6181; Appraiser/Auditor 601-638-6161; Elections 601-636-3961; Tax Collector 601-638-6181.

Washington County

Chancery Clerk, P.O. Box 309, Greenville, MS 38702-0309. Chancery Clerk, R/E and UCC Recording 662-332-1595; Fax 662-334-2725.
Will search UCC records. UCC search includes federal tax liens if requested. Will not search real estate records.

Other Phone Numbers: Assessor 662-332-2651; Treasurer 662-332-2922; Appraiser/Auditor 662-332-2651; Elections 662-378-2747.

Wayne County

Chancery Clerk, Wayne Co. Courthouse, 609 Azalea Dr., Waynesboro, MS 39367. 601-735-2873; Fax 601-735-6224.
Will search UCC records. Will not search real estate records. **Other Phone Numbers:** Elections 601-735-1171.

Webster County

Chancery Clerk, P.O. Box 398, Walthall, MS 39771. 662-258-4131; Fax 662-258-6657.
Will search UCC records. Will not search real estate records. **Other Phone Numbers:** Assessor 662-258-6446; Elections 662-258-6287.

Wilkinson County

Chancery Clerk, P.O. Box 516, Woodville, MS 39669. 601-888-4381; Fax 601-888-6776.
Will search UCC records. Will not search real estate records. **Other Phone Numbers:** Assessor 601-888-4562; Treasurer 601-888-4562; Elections 601-888-6697.

Winston County

Chancery Clerk, P.O. Drawer 69, Louisville, MS 39339. 662-773-3631; Fax 662-773-8831.
Will search UCC records. Will not search real estate records. **Other Phone Numbers:** Assessor 662-773-3694; Treasurer 662-773-3631; Elections 662-773-3581.

Yalobusha County (1st District)

Chancery Clerk, P.O. Box 260, Coffeeville, MS 38922. 662-675-2716 R/E Recording: 662-675-2091 UCC Recording: 662-675-2091; Fax 662-675-8004.
Will search UCC records. Will not search real estate records. **Other Phone Numbers:** Assessor 662-473-1235; Treasurer 662-675-2091; Appraiser/Auditor 662-675-1235; Elections 662-675-1341.

Yalobusha County (2nd District)

Chancery Clerk, P.O. Box 664, Water Valley, MS 38965. Chancery Clerk, R/E and UCC Recording 662-473-2091; Fax 662-473-5020.
Will search UCC records. Will not search real estate records. **Other Phone Numbers:** Assessor 662-473-1235; Treasurer 662-473-2092; Appraiser/Auditor 662-473-1341; Elections 662-473-1341.

Yazoo County

Chancery Clerk, P.O. Box 68, Yazoo City, MS 39194. Chancery Clerk, R/E and UCC Recording 662-746-2661; Fax 662-746-3893.
Will search UCC records. UCC search includes federal tax liens if requested. RE record owner and mortgage searches available. **Other Phone Numbers:** Assessor 662-746-1583; Treasurer 662-746-2661; Appraiser/Auditor 662-746-1583; Elections 662-746-1872.

Mississippi County Locator

You will usually be able to find the city name in the City/County Cross Reference below. In that case, it is a simple matter to determine the county from the cross reference. However, only the official US Postal Service city names are included in this index. There are an additional 40,000 place names that people use in their addresses. Therefore, we have also included a ZIP/City Cross Reference immediately following the City/County Cross Reference.

If you know the ZIP Code but the city name does not appear in the City/County Cross Reference index, look up the ZIP Code in the ZIP/City Cross Reference, find the city name, then look up the city name in the City/County Cross Reference. For example, you want to know the county for an address of Menands, NY 12204. There is no "Menands" in the City/County Cross Reference. The ZIP/City Cross Reference shows that ZIP Codes 12201-12288 are for the city of Albany. Looking back in the City/County Cross Reference, Albany is in Albany County.

City/County Cross Reference

ABBEVILLE Lafayette
ABERDEEN Monroe
ACKERMAN Choctaw
ALGOMA Pontotoc
ALLIGATOR (38720) Coahoma(71), Bolivar(29)
AMORY Monroe
ANGUILLA (38721) Sharkey(98), Humphreys(2)
ARCOLA Washington
ARKABUTLA Tate
ARTESIA Lowndes
ASHLAND Benton
AVALON (38912) Carroll(50), Grenada(50)
AVON Washington
BAILEY (39320) Lauderdale(79), Kemper(21)
BALDWYN (38824) Lee(76), Prentiss(17), Union(4), Itawamba(3)
BANNER (38913) Calhoun(93), Lafayette(7)
BASSFIELD (39421) Jefferson Davis(76), Marion(24)
BATESVILLE Panola
BAY SAINT LOUIS Hancock
BAY SPRINGS (39422) Jasper(82), Smith(19)
BEAUMONT Perry
BECKER Monroe
BELDEN Lee
BELEN Quitman
BELLEFONTAINE Webster
BELMONT Tishomingo
BELZONI Humphreys
BENOIT Bolivar
BENTON Yazoo
BENTONIA Yazoo
BEULAH Bolivar
BIG CREEK Calhoun
BIGBEE VALLEY Noxubee
BILOXI (39532) Harrison(80), Jackson(20)
BILOXI Harrison
BLUE MOUNTAIN (38610) Tippah(90), Union(8), Benton(2)
BLUE SPRINGS Union
BOGUE CHITTO Lincoln
BOLTON Hinds
BOONEVILLE Prentiss
BOYLE Bolivar
BRANDON Rankin
BRAXTON (39044) Simpson(61), Rankin(39)
BROOKHAVEN Lincoln
BROOKLYN (39425) Forrest(54), Perry(46)
BROOKSVILLE Noxubee
BRUCE (38915) Calhoun(98), Lafayette(2)
BUCKATUNNA Wayne
BUDE Franklin
BURNSVILLE Tishomingo
BYHALIA (38611) Marshall(98), De Soto(2)
CALEDONIA (39740) Monroe(89), Montgomery(11)

CALHOUN CITY (38916) Calhoun(97), Webster(3)
CAMDEN (39045) Madison(96), Attala(4)
CANTON Madison
CARLISLE Claiborne
CARRIERE Pearl River
CARROLLTON Carroll
CARSON Jefferson Davis
CARTHAGE (39051) Leake(97), Neshoba(2), Attala(1)
CARY Sharkey
CASCILLA Tallahatchie
CEDARBLUFF Clay
CENTREVILLE (39631) Wilkinson(75), Amite(26)
CHARLESTON Tallahatchie
CHATAWA Pike
CHATHAM Washington
CHUNKY (39323) Newton(77), Lauderdale(23)
CHURCH HILL Jefferson
CLARA Wayne
CLARKSDALE Coahoma
CLEVELAND (38732) Bolivar(98), Sunflower(2)
CLEVELAND Bolivar
CLINTON Hinds
COAHOMA Coahoma
COFFEEVILLE (38922) Yalobusha(83), Grenada(17)
COILA Carroll
COLDWATER Tate
COLLINS Covington
COLLINSVILLE (39325) Lauderdale(70), Kemper(14), Newton(11), Neshoba(5)
COLUMBIA Marion
COLUMBUS Lowndes
COMO (38619) Panola(63), Lafayette(34), Tate(3)
CONEHATTA (39057) Newton(90), Scott(10)
CORINTH Alcorn
COURTLAND Panola
CRAWFORD (39743) Lowndes(70), Oktibbeha(29), Noxubee(1)
CRENSHAW (38621) Panola(96), Quitman(3)
CROSBY Amite
CROWDER Quitman
CRUGER (38924) Holmes(92), Carroll(5), Leflore(3)
CRYSTAL SPRINGS (39059) Copiah(97), Hinds(3)
D LO Simpson
DALEVILLE (39326) Lauderdale(66), Kemper(34)
DARLING Quitman
DE KALB Kemper
DECATUR Newton
DELTA CITY Sharkey
DENNIS Tishomingo
DERMA Calhoun
DIAMONDHEAD Hancock

DODDSVILLE (38736) Sunflower(74), Leflore(26)
DREW (38737) Sunflower(96), Tallahatchie(4)
DUBLIN Coahoma
DUCK HILL (38925) Montgomery(72), Grenada(28)
DUMAS (38625) Tippah(82), Union(18)
DUNCAN Bolivar
DUNDEE (38626) Coahoma(96), Tunica(4)
DURANT Holmes
EASTABUCHIE Jones
EBENEZER Holmes
ECRU Pontotoc
EDWARDS Hinds
ELLIOTT Grenada
ELLISVILLE Jones
ENID (38927) Tallahatchie(82), Panola(17), Yalobusha(1)
ENTERPRISE (39330) Clarke(85), Lauderdale(12), Jasper(3)
ESCATAWPA Jackson
ETHEL Attala
ETTA Union
EUPORA Webster
FALCON Quitman
FALKNER (38629) Tippah(95), Benton(5)
FARRELL Coahoma
FAYETTE Jefferson
FERNWOOD Pike
FITLER Issaquena
FLORA (39071) Madison(98), Hinds(2)
FLORENCE (39073) Rankin(93), Simpson(7)
FOREST (39074) Scott(98), Smith(3)
FORKVILLE Scott
FOXWORTH Marion
FRENCH CAMP Choctaw
FRIARS POINT Coahoma
FULTON Itawamba
GALLMAN Copiah
GATTMAN (38844) Alcorn(82), Monroe(18)
GAUTIER Jackson
GEORGETOWN (39078) Copiah(95), Simpson(5)
GLEN (38846) Alcorn(79), Tishomingo(21)
GLEN ALLAN Washington
GLENDORA Tallahatchie
GLOSTER Amite
GOLDEN (38847) Itawamba(96), Tishomingo(4)
GOODMAN (39079) Madison(87), Holmes(7), Attala(6)
GORE SPRINGS (38929) Grenada(88), Webster(8), Calhoun(4)
GRACE Issaquena
GREENVILLE Bolivar
GREENVILLE Washington
GREENWOOD Leflore
GREENWOOD SPRINGS Monroe
GRENADA Grenada
GULFPORT Harrison
GUNNISON Bolivar

GUNTOWN Lee
HAMILTON Monroe
HARPERVILLE Scott
HARRISTON Jefferson
HARRISVILLE Simpson
HATTIESBURG (39402) Lamar(54), Forrest(46)
HATTIESBURG Forrest
HAZLEHURST Copiah
HEIDELBERG (39439) Jasper(51), Clarke(38), Jones(11)
HERMANVILLE (39086) Claiborne(70), Copiah(30)
HERNANDO De Soto
HICKORY (39332) Newton(97), Jasper(4)
HICKORY FLAT (38633) Benton(63), Union(37)
HILLSBORO Scott
HOLCOMB (38940) Grenada(93), Carroll(4), Tallahatchie(3)
HOLLANDALE (38748) Washington(96), Sharkey(4)
HOLLY BLUFF Yazoo
HOLLY RIDGE Sunflower
HOLLY SPRINGS (38635) Marshall(94), Tate(4), Benton(3)
HOLLY SPRINGS Marshall
HORN LAKE De Soto
HOULKA Chickasaw
HOUSTON Chickasaw
HURLEY Jackson
INDEPENDENCE Tate
INDIANOLA Sunflower
INVERNESS (38753) Sunflower(93), Humphreys(7)
ISOLA (38754) Humphreys(97), Sunflower(4)
ITTA BENA Leflore
IUKA Tishomingo
JACKSON (39213) Hinds(94), Madison(6)
JACKSON Hinds
JACKSON Rankin
JAYESS (39641) Lawrence(86), Walthall(14)
JONESTOWN Coahoma
KILMICHAEL Montgomery
KILN Hancock
KOKOMO (39643) Marion(84), Walthall(16)
KOSCIUSKO (39090) Attala(95), Leake(4), Winston(1)
LAKE (39092) Newton(93), Scott(7)
LAKE CORMORANT De Soto
LAKESHORE Hancock
LAMAR (38642) Marshall(80), Benton(21)
LAMBERT (38643) Quitman(97), Coahoma(3)
LAUDERDALE (39335) Lauderdale(94), Kemper(6)
LAUREL (39440) Jones(97), Wayne(2)
LAUREL Jones
LAWRENCE (99999) Newton(98), Jasper(1)
LEAKESVILLE Greene

LELAND Washington
LENA (39094) Leake(56), Scott(37), Rankin(8)
LEXINGTON (39095) Holmes(84), Yazoo(15)
LIBERTY Amite
LITTLE ROCK Newton
LONG BEACH Harrison
LORMAN (39096) Jefferson(64), Claiborne(36)
LOUIN (39338) Jasper(78), Smith(22)
LOUISE Humphreys
LOUISVILLE Winston
LUCEDALE (39452) George(77), Jackson(20), Greene(3)
LUDLOW Scott
LULA Coahoma
LUMBERTON (39455) Lamar(45), Pearl River(44), Stone(9), Marion(1)
LYON (38645) Coahoma(96), Quitman(4)
MABEN Webster
MACON (39341) Noxubee(98), Winston(2)
MADDEN Leake
MADISON Madison
MAGEE (39111) Simpson(96), Smith(4)
MAGNOLIA Pike
MANTACHIE Itawamba
MANTEE Calhoun
MARIETTA (38856) Prentiss(93), Itawamba(7)
MARION Lauderdale
MARKS Quitman
MATHISTON Webster
MATTSON Coahoma
MAYERSVILLE Issaquena
MAYHEW Lowndes
MC ADAMS Attala
MC CALL CREEK (39647) Franklin(95), Lincoln(5)
MC CARLEY Carroll
MC COMB Pike
MC CONDY Chickasaw
MC COOL (39108) Attala(39), Winston(38), Choctaw(23)
MC HENRY Stone
MC LAIN (39456) Perry(53), Greene(45), George(2)
MC NEILL Pearl River
MEADVILLE (39653) Franklin(98), Amite(1), Jefferson(1)
MENDENHALL (39114) Simpson(97), Rankin(2)
MERIDIAN (39301) Lauderdale(92), Clarke(8)
MERIDIAN Lauderdale
MERIGOLD (38759) Sunflower(89), Bolivar(11)
METCALFE Washington
MICHIGAN CITY Benton
MIDNIGHT Humphreys
MINERAL WELLS De Soto
MINTER CITY Leflore
MISSISSIPPI STATE Oktibbeha
MIZE Smith
MONEY Leflore
MONTICELLO Lawrence
MONTPELIER Clay
MOOREVILLE Lee
MOORHEAD Sunflower
MORGAN CITY Leflore
MORGANTOWN Marion
MORTON (39117) Scott(93), Smith(5), Rankin(2)
MOSELLE Jones
MOSS Jasper
MOSS POINT Jackson
MOUND BAYOU Bolivar
MOUNT OLIVE (39119) Covington(63), Smith(15), Simpson(14), Jefferson Davis(8)
MOUNT PLEASANT Marshall

MYRTLE (38650) Union(96), Benton(2), Tippah(2)
NATCHEZ Adams
NEELY Greene
NESBIT De Soto
NETTLETON (38858) Monroe(83), Itawamba(14), Lee(3)
NEW ALBANY Union
NEW AUGUSTA Perry
NEW SITE Prentiss
NEWHEBRON (39140) Lawrence(70), Jefferson Davis(19), Simpson(11)
NEWTON Newton
NICHOLSON Pearl River
NITTA YUMA Sharkey
NORTH CARROLLTON Carroll
NOXAPATER (39346) Winston(92), Neshoba(8)
OAK VALE (39656) Jefferson Davis(81), Lawrence(19)
OAKLAND (38948) Yalobusha(69), Tallahatchie(31)
OCEAN SPRINGS Jackson
OKOLONA (38860) Chickasaw(94), Lee(5)
OLIVE BRANCH De Soto
OSYKA (39657) Pike(99), Amite(1)
OVETT (39464) Perry(97), Jones(3)
OXFORD Lafayette
PACE Bolivar
PACHUTA (39347) Jasper(59), Clarke(41)
PANTHER BURN Sharkey
PARCHMAN Sunflower
PARIS Lafayette
PASCAGOULA Jackson
PASS CHRISTIAN (39571) Harrison(76), Hancock(24)
PATTISON (39144) Claiborne(79), Jefferson(14), Copiah(8)
PAULDING Jasper
PEARLINGTON Hancock
PELAHATCHIE (39145) Rankin(97), Scott(3)
PERKINSTON (39573) Stone(63), Hancock(25), Pearl River(4), George(4), Jackson(4)
PETAL (39465) Forrest(92), Perry(8)
PHEBA (39755) Clay(77), Oktibbeha(23)
PHILADELPHIA (39350) Neshoba(95), Winston(3), Kemper(1)
PHILIPP Tallahatchie
PICAYUNE Pearl River
PICKENS (39146) Yazoo(66), Madison(31), Holmes(3)
PINEY WOODS Rankin
PINOLA Simpson
PITTSBORO Calhoun
PLANTERSVILLE Lee
PLEASANT GROVE Panola
POCAHONTAS Hinds
PONTOTOC Pontotoc
POPE Panola
POPLARVILLE (39470) Pearl River(98), Hancock(2)
PORT GIBSON Claiborne
PORTERVILLE (39352) Kemper(99), Quitman(1)
POTTS CAMP (38659) Marshall(93), Benton(7)
PRAIRIE (39756) Clay(94), Monroe(5)
PRAIRIE POINT Noxubee
PRENTISS (99999) Jefferson Davis(99), Covington(1)
PRESTON (39354) Kemper(72), Winston(24), Neshoba(4)
PUCKETT Rankin
PULASKI (39152) Scott(52), Smith(48)
PURVIS Lamar
QUITMAN Clarke
RALEIGH Smith
RANDOLPH (38864) Pontotoc(90), Calhoun(10)
RAYMOND Hinds

RED BANKS Marshall
REDWOOD (39156) Warren(96), Yazoo(5)
REFORM Choctaw
RENA LARA Coahoma
RICH Coahoma
RICHTON (39476) Perry(64), Greene(25), Wayne(12)
RIDGELAND Madison
RIENZI Alcorn
RIPLEY Tippah
ROBINSONVILLE (38664) De Soto(87), Tunica(13)
ROLLING FORK (39159) Sharkey(93), Issaquena(7)
ROME Sunflower
ROSE HILL Jasper
ROSEDALE Bolivar
ROXIE (39661) Franklin(75), Adams(20), Jefferson(5)
RULEVILLE Sunflower
RUTH (39662) Lincoln(68), Lawrence(32)
SALLIS (39160) Attala(97), Leake(3)
SALTILLO Lee
SANATORIUM Simpson
SANDERSVILLE Jones
SANDHILL Rankin
SANDY HOOK (39478) Marion(88), Walthall(13)
SARAH Panola
SARDIS Panola
SATARTIA (39162) Warren(89), Yazoo(11)
SAUCIER Harrison
SCHLATER Leflore
SCOBEY (38953) Grenada(40), Yalobusha(33), Tallahatchie(27)
SCOOBA Kemper
SCOTT Bolivar
SEBASTOPOL Scott
SEMINARY (39479) Covington(91), Jones(9)
SENATOBIA Tate
SHANNON (38868) Lee(89), Pontotoc(7), Chickasaw(3)
SHARON Madison
SHAW (38773) Bolivar(76), Sunflower(24)
SHELBY Bolivar
SHERARD Coahoma
SHERMAN Pontotoc
SHUBUTA (39360) Clarke(77), Wayne(23)
SHUQUALAK (39361) Noxubee(98), Kemper(2)
SIBLEY Adams
SIDON (38954) Leflore(83), Carroll(18)
SILVER CITY Humphreys
SILVER CREEK (39663) Lawrence(86), Jefferson Davis(14)
SKENE Bolivar
SLATE SPRING Calhoun
SLEDGE (38670) Quitman(50), Tunica(50)
SMITHDALE (39664) Amite(55), Franklin(32), Lincoln(12)
SMITHVILLE (38870) Monroe(96), Itawamba(4)
SONTAG (39665) Lawrence(83), Lincoln(17)
SOSO (39480) Jones(97), Smith(3)
SOUTHAVEN De Soto
STAR Rankin
STARKVILLE Oktibbeha
STATE LINE (39362) Wayne(64), Greene(36)
STEENS Lowndes
STEWART Montgomery
STONEVILLE Washington
STONEWALL Clarke
STRINGER Jasper
STURGIS (39769) Oktibbeha(91), Winston(9)
SUMMIT (39666) Pike(68), Lincoln(26), Amite(6)
SUMNER Tallahatchie
SUMRALL (39482) Lamar(93), Jefferson

Davis(4), Marion(3)
SUNFLOWER Sunflower
SWAN LAKE Tallahatchie
SWIFTOWN Leflore
TAYLOR Lafayette
TAYLORSVILLE (39168) Smith(71), Jones(21), Covington(8)
TCHULA Holmes
TERRY Hinds
THAXTON (38871) Pontotoc(85), Lafayette(11), Union(4)
THOMASTOWN Leake
THORNTON Holmes
TIE PLANT Grenada
TILLATOBA (38961) Yalobusha(63), Tallahatchie(37)
TINSLEY Yazoo
TIPLERSVILLE Tippah
TIPPO Tallahatchie
TISHOMINGO Tishomingo
TOCCOPOLA Lafayette
TOOMSUBA Lauderdale
TOUGALOO Hinds
TREBLOC Chickasaw
TREMONT Itawamba
TRIBBETT Washington
TULA Lafayette
TUNICA Tunica
TUPELO Lee
TUTWILER (38963) Coahoma(76), Tallahatchie(22), Sunflower(1)
TYLERTOWN Walthall
UNION (39365) Newton(64), Neshoba(36)
UNION CHURCH (99999) Jefferson(98), Franklin(1), Lincoln(1)
UNIVERSITY Lafayette
UTICA (39175) Hinds(85), Copiah(13), Claiborne(2)
VAIDEN (39176) Carroll(65), Attala(25), Montgomery(10)
VALLEY PARK Issaquena
VAN VLEET Chickasaw
VANCE Quitman
VARDAMAN (38878) Calhoun(98), Chickasaw(2)
VAUGHAN Yazoo
VERONA Lee
VICKSBURG Warren
VICTORIA Marshall
VOSSBURG (39366) Clarke(51), Jasper(49)
WALLS De Soto
WALNUT (38683) Tippah(89), Alcorn(9), Benton(2)
WALNUT GROVE (39189) Leake(80), Scott(20)
WALTHALL Webster
WASHINGTON Adams
WATER VALLEY (38965) Yalobusha(82), Lafayette(12), Calhoun(5), Panola(1)
WATERFORD Lafayette
WAVELAND Hancock
WAYNESBORO (39367) Wayne(98), Clarke(2)
WAYSIDE Washington
WEBB Tallahatchie
WEIR Choctaw
WESSON (39191) Copiah(57), Lincoln(41), Lawrence(2)
WEST (39192) Attala(53), Holmes(42), Carroll(5)
WEST POINT (39773) Clay(99), Monroe(1)
WHEELER Prentiss
WHITFIELD Rankin
WIGGINS (39577) Stone(88), Forrest(12)
WINONA (38967) Montgomery(95), Carroll(5)
WINSTONVILLE Bolivar
WINTERVILLE Washington
WOODLAND Chickasaw
WOODVILLE Wilkinson
YAZOO CITY Yazoo

ZIP/City Cross Reference

ZIP	City	ZIP	City	ZIP	City	ZIP	City
38601-38601	ABBEVILLE	38745-38745	GRACE	38914-38914	BIG CREEK	39092-39092	LAKE
38602-38602	ARKABUTLA	38746-38746	GUNNISON	38915-38915	BRUCE	39094-39094	LENA
38603-38603	ASHLAND	38748-38748	HOLLANDALE	38916-38916	CALHOUN CITY	39095-39095	LEXINGTON
38606-38606	BATESVILLE	38749-38749	HOLLY RIDGE	38917-38917	CARROLLTON	39096-39096	LORMAN
38609-38609	BELEN	38751-38751	INDIANOLA	38920-38920	CASCILLA	39097-39097	LOUISE
38610-38610	BLUE MOUNTAIN	38753-38753	INVERNESS	38921-38921	CHARLESTON	39098-39098	LUDLOW
38611-38611	BYHALIA	38754-38754	ISOLA	38922-38922	COFFEEVILLE	39107-39107	MC ADAMS
38614-38614	CLARKSDALE	38756-38756	LELAND	38923-38923	COILA	39108-39108	MC COOL
38617-38617	COAHOMA	38758-38758	MATTSON	38924-38924	CRUGER	39109-39109	MADDEN
38618-38618	COLDWATER	38759-38759	MERIGOLD	38925-38925	DUCK HILL	39110-39110	MADISON
38619-38619	COMO	38760-38760	METCALFE	38926-38926	ELLIOTT	39111-39111	MAGEE
38620-38620	COURTLAND	38761-38761	MOORHEAD	38927-38927	ENID	39112-39112	SANATORIUM
38621-38621	CRENSHAW	38762-38762	MOUND BAYOU	38928-38928	GLENDORA	39113-39113	MAYERSVILLE
38622-38622	CROWDER	38763-38763	NITTA YUMA	38929-38929	GORE SPRINGS	39114-39114	MENDENHALL
38623-38623	DARLING	38764-38764	PACE	38930-38935	GREENWOOD	39115-39115	MIDNIGHT
38625-38625	DUMAS	38765-38765	PANTHER BURN	38940-38940	HOLCOMB	39116-39116	MIZE
38626-38626	DUNDEE	38767-38767	RENA LARA	38941-38941	ITTA BENA	39117-39117	MORTON
38627-38627	ETTA	38768-38768	ROME	38943-38943	MC CARLEY	39119-39119	MOUNT OLIVE
38628-38628	FALCON	38769-38769	ROSEDALE	38944-38944	MINTER CITY	39120-39122	NATCHEZ
38629-38629	FALKNER	38771-38771	RULEVILLE	38945-38945	MONEY	39130-39130	MADISON
38630-38630	FARRELL	38772-38772	SCOTT	38946-38946	MORGAN CITY	39140-39140	NEWHEBRON
38631-38631	FRIARS POINT	38773-38773	SHAW	38947-38947	NORTH CARROLLTON	39144-39144	PATTISON
38632-38632	HERNANDO	38774-38774	SHELBY	38948-38948	OAKLAND	39145-39145	PELAHATCHIE
38633-38633	HICKORY FLAT	38776-38776	STONEVILLE	38949-38949	PARIS	39146-39146	PICKENS
38634-38635	HOLLY SPRINGS	38778-38778	SUNFLOWER	38950-38950	PHILIPP	39148-39148	PINEY WOODS
38637-38637	HORN LAKE	38780-38780	WAYSIDE	38951-38951	PITTSBORO	39149-39149	PINOLA
38638-38638	INDEPENDENCE	38781-38781	WINSTONVILLE	38952-38952	SCHLATER	39150-39150	PORT GIBSON
38639-38639	JONESTOWN	38782-38782	WINTERVILLE	38953-38953	SCOBEY	39151-39151	PUCKETT
38641-38641	LAKE CORMORANT	38801-38803	TUPELO	38954-38954	SIDON	39152-39152	PULASKI
38642-38642	LAMAR	38820-38820	ALGOMA	38955-38955	SLATE SPRING	39153-39153	RALEIGH
38643-38643	LAMBERT	38821-38821	AMORY	38957-38957	SUMNER	39154-39154	RAYMOND
38644-38644	LULA	38824-38824	BALDWYN	38958-38958	SWAN LAKE	39156-39156	REDWOOD
38645-38645	LYON	38825-38825	BECKER	38959-38959	SWIFTOWN	39157-39158	RIDGELAND
38646-38646	MARKS	38826-38826	BELDEN	38960-38960	TIE PLANT	39159-39159	ROLLING FORK
38647-38647	MICHIGAN CITY	38827-38827	BELMONT	38961-38961	TILLATOBA	39160-39160	SALLIS
38649-38649	MOUNT PLEASANT	38828-38828	BLUE SPRINGS	38962-38962	TIPPO	39161-39161	SANDHILL
38650-38650	MYRTLE	38829-38829	BOONEVILLE	38963-38963	TUTWILER	39162-39162	SATARTIA
38651-38651	NESBIT	38833-38833	BURNSVILLE	38964-38964	VANCE	39163-39163	SHARON
38652-38652	NEW ALBANY	38834-38835	CORINTH	38965-38965	WATER VALLEY	39165-39165	SIBLEY
38654-38654	OLIVE BRANCH	38838-38838	DENNIS	38966-38966	WEBB	39166-39166	SILVER CITY
38655-38655	OXFORD	38839-38839	DERMA	38967-38967	WINONA	39167-39167	STAR
38658-38658	POPE	38841-38841	ECRU	39038-39038	BELZONI	39168-39168	TAYLORSVILLE
38659-38659	POTTS CAMP	38843-38843	FULTON	39039-39039	BENTON	39169-39169	TCHULA
38661-38661	RED BANKS	38844-38844	GATTMAN	39040-39040	BENTONIA	39170-39170	TERRY
38663-38663	RIPLEY	38846-38846	GLEN	39041-39041	BOLTON	39171-39171	THOMASTOWN
38664-38664	ROBINSONVILLE	38847-38847	GOLDEN	39042-39043	BRANDON	39173-39173	TINSLEY
38665-38665	SARAH	38848-38848	GREENWOOD SPRINGS	39044-39044	BRAXTON	39174-39174	TOUGALOO
38666-38666	SARDIS	38849-38849	GUNTOWN	39045-39045	CAMDEN	39175-39175	UTICA
38668-38668	SENATOBIA	38850-38850	HOULKA	39046-39046	CANTON	39176-39176	VAIDEN
38669-38669	SHERARD	38851-38851	HOUSTON	39047-39047	BRANDON	39177-39177	VALLEY PARK
38670-38670	SLEDGE	38852-38852	IUKA	39051-39051	CARTHAGE	39179-39179	VAUGHAN
38671-38671	SOUTHAVEN	38854-38854	MC CONDY	39054-39054	CARY	39180-39182	VICKSBURG
38673-38673	TAYLOR	38855-38855	MANTACHIE	39056-39056	CLINTON	39189-39189	WALNUT GROVE
38674-38674	TIPLERSVILLE	38856-38856	MARIETTA	39057-39057	CONEHATTA	39190-39190	WASHINGTON
38675-38675	TULA	38857-38857	MOOREVILLE	39058-39058	CLINTON	39191-39191	WESSON
38676-38676	TUNICA	38858-38858	NETTLETON	39059-39059	CRYSTAL SPRINGS	39192-39192	WEST
38677-38677	UNIVERSITY	38859-38859	NEW SITE	39060-39060	CLINTON	39193-39193	WHITFIELD
38679-38679	VICTORIA	38860-38860	OKOLONA	39061-39061	DELTA CITY	39194-39194	YAZOO CITY
38680-38680	WALLS	38862-38862	PLANTERSVILLE	39062-39062	D LO	39200-39298	JACKSON
38683-38683	WALNUT	38863-38863	PONTOTOC	39063-39063	DURANT	39301-39309	MERIDIAN
38685-38685	WATERFORD	38864-38864	RANDOLPH	39066-39066	EDWARDS	39320-39320	BAILEY
38686-38686	WALLS	38865-38865	RIENZI	39067-39067	ETHEL	39322-39322	BUCKATUNNA
38701-38704	GREENVILLE	38866-38866	SALTILLO	39069-39069	FAYETTE	39323-39323	CHUNKY
38720-38720	ALLIGATOR	38868-38868	SHANNON	39071-39071	FLORA	39324-39324	CLARA
38721-38721	ANGUILLA	38869-38869	SHERMAN	39072-39072	POCAHONTAS	39325-39325	COLLINSVILLE
38722-38722	ARCOLA	38870-38870	SMITHVILLE	39073-39073	FLORENCE	39326-39326	DALEVILLE
38723-38723	AVON	38871-38871	THAXTON	39074-39074	FOREST	39327-39327	DECATUR
38725-38725	BENOIT	38873-38873	TISHOMINGO	39077-39077	GALLMAN	39328-39328	DE KALB
38726-38726	BEULAH	38874-38874	TOCCOPOLA*	39078-39078	GEORGETOWN	39330-39330	ENTERPRISE
38730-38730	BOYLE	38875-38875	TREBLOC	39079-39079	GOODMAN	39332-39332	HICKORY
38731-38731	CHATHAM	38876-38876	TREMONT	39080-39080	HARPERVILLE	39335-39335	LAUDERDALE
38732-38733	CLEVELAND	38877-38877	VAN VLEET	39081-39081	HARRISTON	39336-39336	LAWRENCE
38736-38736	DODDSVILLE	38878-38878	VARDAMAN	39082-39082	HARRISVILLE	39337-39337	LITTLE ROCK
38737-38737	DREW	38879-38879	VERONA	39083-39083	HAZLEHURST	39338-39338	LOUIN
38738-38738	PARCHMAN	38880-38880	WHEELER	39086-39086	HERMANVILLE	39339-39339	LOUISVILLE
38739-38739	DUBLIN	38901-38902	GRENADA	39087-39087	HILLSBORO	39341-39341	MACON
38740-38740	DUNCAN	38912-38912	AVALON	39088-39088	HOLLY BLUFF	39342-39342	MARION
38744-38744	GLEN ALLAN	38913-38913	BANNER	39090-39090	KOSCIUSKO	39345-39345	NEWTON

39346-39346 NOXAPATER	39456-39456 MC LAIN	39564-39566 OCEAN SPRINGS	39668-39668 UNION CHURCH
39347-39347 PACHUTA	39457-39457 MC NEILL	39567-39569 PASCAGOULA	39669-39669 WOODVILLE
39348-39348 PAULDING	39459-39459 MOSELLE	39571-39571 PASS CHRISTIAN	39701-39710 COLUMBUS
39350-39350 PHILADELPHIA	39460-39460 MOSS	39572-39572 PEARLINGTON	39730-39730 ABERDEEN
39352-39352 PORTERVILLE	39461-39461 NEELY	39573-39573 PERKINSTON	39735-39735 ACKERMAN
39354-39354 PRESTON	39462-39462 NEW AUGUSTA	39574-39574 SAUCIER	39736-39736 ARTESIA
39355-39355 QUITMAN	39463-39463 NICHOLSON	39576-39576 WAVELAND	39737-39737 BELLEFONTAINE
39356-39356 ROSE HILL	39464-39464 OVETT	39577-39577 WIGGINS	39739-39739 BROOKSVILLE
39358-39358 SCOOBA	39465-39465 PETAL	39581-39595 PASCAGOULA	39740-39740 CALEDONIA
39359-39359 SEBASTOPOL	39466-39466 PICAYUNE	39601-39603 BROOKHAVEN	39741-39741 CEDARBLUFF
39360-39360 SHUBUTA	39470-39470 POPLARVILLE	39629-39629 BOGUE CHITTO	39743-39743 CRAWFORD
39361-39361 SHUQUALAK	39474-39474 PRENTISS	39630-39630 BUDE	39744-39744 EUPORA
39362-39362 STATE LINE	39475-39475 PURVIS	39631-39631 CENTREVILLE	39745-39745 FRENCH CAMP
39363-39363 STONEWALL	39476-39476 RICHTON	39632-39632 CHATAWA	39746-39746 HAMILTON
39364-39364 TOOMSUBA	39477-39477 SANDERSVILLE	39633-39633 CROSBY	39747-39747 KILMICHAEL
39365-39365 UNION	39478-39478 SANDY HOOK	39635-39635 FERNWOOD	39750-39750 MABEN
39366-39366 VOSSBURG	39479-39479 SEMINARY	39638-39638 GLOSTER	39751-39751 MANTEE
39367-39367 WAYNESBORO	39480-39480 SOSO	39641-39641 JAYESS	39752-39752 MATHISTON
39400-39407 HATTIESBURG	39481-39481 STRINGER	39643-39643 KOKOMO	39753-39753 MAYHEW
39421-39421 BASSFIELD	39482-39482 SUMRALL	39645-39645 LIBERTY	39754-39754 MONTPELIER
39422-39422 BAY SPRINGS	39483-39483 FOXWORTH	39647-39647 MC CALL CREEK	39755-39755 PHEBA
39423-39423 BEAUMONT	39500-39507 GULFPORT	39648-39649 MC COMB	39756-39756 PRAIRIE
39425-39425 BROOKLYN	39520-39522 BAY SAINT LOUIS	39652-39652 MAGNOLIA	39759-39760 STARKVILLE
39426-39426 CARRIERE	39525-39525 DIAMONDHEAD	39653-39653 MEADVILLE	39762-39762 MISSISSIPPI STATE
39427-39427 CARSON	39529-39529 BAY SAINT LOUIS	39654-39654 MONTICELLO	39766-39766 STEENS
39428-39428 COLLINS	39530-39535 BILOXI	39656-39656 OAK VALE	39767-39767 STEWART
39429-39429 COLUMBIA	39552-39552 ESCATAWPA	39657-39657 OSYKA	39769-39769 STURGIS
39436-39436 EASTABUCHIE	39553-39553 GAUTIER	39661-39661 ROXIE	39771-39771 WALTHALL
39437-39437 ELLISVILLE	39555-39555 HURLEY	39662-39662 RUTH	39772-39772 WEIR
39439-39439 HEIDELBERG	39556-39556 KILN	39663-39663 SILVER CREEK	39773-39773 WEST POINT
39440-39442 LAUREL	39558-39558 LAKESHORE	39664-39664 SMITHDALE	39776-39776 WOODLAND
39451-39451 LEAKESVILLE	39560-39560 LONG BEACH	39665-39665 SONTAG	
39452-39452 LUCEDALE	39561-39561 MC HENRY	39666-39666 SUMMIT	
39455-39455 LUMBERTON	39562-39563 MOSS POINT	39667-39667 TYLERTOWN	

Missouri

General Help Numbers:

Governor's Office
PO Box 720
Jefferson City, MO 65102-0720
http://www.gov.state.mo.us

573-751-3222
Fax 573-751-1495
8AM-5PM

Attorney General's Office
PO Box 899
Jefferson City, MO 65102
http://www.ago.state.mo.us

573-751-3321
Fax 573-751-0774
8AM-5PM

State Court Administrator
2112 Industrial Drive - PO Box 104480
Jefferson City, MO 65110
http://www.osca.state.mo.us

573-751-4377
Fax 573-751-5540
8AM-5PM

State Archives
Archives Division
PO Box 1747
Jefferson City, MO 65102-1747
http://mosl.sos.state.mo.us
rec-man/arch.html

573-751-3280
Fax 573-526-7333
8-5 M-F
(till 9PM on Th);
8:30-3:30 SA

State Specifics:

Capital:

Jefferson City
Cole County

Time Zone:

CST

Number of Counties:

114

Population:

5,595,211

Web Site:

www.state.mo.us

State Agencies

Criminal Records

Missouri State Highway Patrol, Criminal Record & Identification Division, PO Box 568, Jefferson City, MO 65102-0568 (Courier: 1510 E Elm St, Jefferson City, MO 65102); 573-526-6153, 573-751-9382 (Fax), 8AM-5PM.

http://www.mshp.state.mo.us

Indexing & Storage: Records are available from 1970 on. It takes 5 weeks before new records are available for inquiry. Records are indexed on inhouse computer.

Searching: Only convictions are reported or arrests less than 31 days old are reported to the general public; however, certain entites are entitled to the complete record file. Youth service providers must have signature of the subject. Include the following in your request-full name, date of birth, sex, race, Social Security Number. A request form can be downloaded from the web site.

Access by: mail, in person.

Fee & Payment: The search fee is $5.00 per individual for a name search. Searches by fingerprint cost $14.00 each. Fee payee: State of Missouri. Prepayment required. Personal checks accepted. No credit cards accepted.

Mail search: Turnaround time: 3-4 weeks. No self addressed stamped envelope is required.

In person search: Turnaround time: while you wait for one search only.

Corporation Records
Fictitious Name
Limited Partnership Records
Assumed Name
Trademarks/Servicemarks
Limited Liability Company Records

Secretary of State, Corporation Services, PO Box 778, Jefferson City, MO 65102 (Courier: 600 W Main, Jefferson City, MO 65101); 573-751-4153, 573-751-5841 (Fax), 8AM-5PM.

http://mosl.sos.state.mo.us

Note: Trademarks and servicemarks are handled by the Commissions Division within Sec. of State and can be reached at 573-751-4756.

Indexing & Storage: Records are available from the 1800s. New records are available for inquiry immediately. Records are indexed on microfilm, inhouse computer, hard copy.

Searching: Include the following in your request-full name of business, specific records that you need copies of. In addition to the articles of incorporation, corporation records include the following information: Annual Reports, Officers, Directors, DBAs, Prior (merged) names, Inactive and Reserved names.

Access by: mail, phone, fax, in person, online.

Fee & Payment: An uncertified copy of a record is $.50 per page, a certified copy of a record is $10.00 certification fee plus $.50 per page. The fee for an officers and directors list is $10.00. A Good Standing is $10.00. A trademark or servicemark search is $5.00. Fee payee: Secretary of State. Prepayment required. They will invoice. Personal checks accepted. Credit cards accepted: MasterCard, Visa.

Mail search: Turnaround time: 2 to 3 days. No self addressed stamped envelope is required.

Phone search: No fee for telephone request. Status information is given over the phone at no charge.

Fax search: Same criteria as mail searching. Records are returned by mail.

In person search: Results are returned by mail.

Online search: Searching can be done from the Internet site. The corporate name, the agent name or the charter number is required to search. The site will indicate the currency of the data. Many business entity type searches are available.

Uniform Commercial Code

UCC Division, Secretary of State, PO Box 1159, Jefferson City, MO 65102 (Courier: 600 W Main St, Rm 302, Jefferson City, MO 65101); 573-751-2360, 573-522-2057 (Fax), 8AM-5PM.

http://mosl.sos.state.mo.us/bus-ser/ucc/index.html

Indexing & Storage: Records are available from 1965. Records are on microfiche from 7-1-80 to present.

Searching: Use search request form UCC-11. Please note that all tax liens are filed at the county level only. Include the following in your request-debtor name.

Access by: mail, phone, in person.

Fee & Payment: A UCC-11 search is $27.00 plus $1.00 per page for copies. UCC-3's are not listed on the summary; order copies to review them. Fee payee: Secretary of State. Prepayment required.

Personal checks accepted. Credit cards accepted: MasterCard, Visa.

Mail search: Turnaround time: 2 weeks. A self addressed stamped envelope is requested.

Phone search: General information is available without charge.

In person search: You may request information in person.

Other access: The agency will release information for bulk purchase, call for procedures and pricing.

Federal Tax Liens
State Tax Liens
Records not maintained by a state level agency.

Note: All tax liens are filed at the county level.

Sales Tax Registrations
Access to Records is Restricted

Department of Revenue, Sales Tax Administration Bureau, PO Box 840, Jefferson City, MO 65105-0840; 573-751-5860, 573-751-2836, 573-751-3696 (Fax), 7:45AM-4:45PM.

http://www.state.mo.us/dor/tax

Note: This agency will neither confirm nor supply any information. Confidential information is only released to owners or corporate officers registered with the Department. They suggest other requesters to check at the city level.

Birth Certificates

Department of Health, Bureau of Vital Records, PO Box 570, Jefferson City, MO 65102-0570 (Courier: 930 Wildwood, Jefferson City, MO 65109); 573-751-6387, 573-751-6400 (Message Number), 573-526-3846 (Fax), 8AM-5PM.

http://www.health.state.mo.us

Indexing & Storage: Records are available from 1910 on. New records are available for inquiry immediately. Records are indexed on microfiche, inhouse computer.

Searching: Records are only released to person of record or legal representative of immediate family member. Must have a signed release form from person of record or immediate family member for investigative purposes. Include the following in your request-full name, names of parents, mother's maiden name, date of birth, place of birth, relationship to person of record, reason for information request.

Access by: mail, phone, in person.

Fee & Payment: Search fee is $10.00 per 5 years searched. Fee is charged regardless if record is found. Emergency requests using a credit card pay an additional $4.95 fee. Fee payee: Missouri Department of Health. Prepayment required. Personal checks accepted. Credit cards accepted: MasterCard, Visa, AmEx, Discover.

Mail search: Turnaround time: 2 to 3 weeks. No self addressed stamped envelope is required.

Phone search: This service is only available for emergencies.

In person search: Turnaround time 10 minutes.

Death Records

Department of Health, Bureau of Vital Records, PO Box 570, Jefferson City, MO 65102-0570

(Courier: 930 Wildwood, Jefferson City, MO 65109); 573-751-6370, 573-751-6400 (Message Number), 573-526-3846 (Fax), 8AM-5PM.

http://www.health.state.mo.us

Indexing & Storage: Records are available from 1910 on. New records are available for inquiry immediately. Records are indexed on microfiche, inhouse computer.

Searching: Records are only released to legal representative of person of record or immediate family member. Must have a signed release form from immediate family member for investigative purposes. Include the following in your request-full name, date of death, place of death, relationship to person of record, reason for information request.

Access by: mail, in person.

Fee & Payment: The $10.00 search fee is for 5 years searched. Use of credit card is additional $4.95. Fee payee: Missouri Department of Health. Prepayment required. Personal checks accepted.

Mail search: Turnaround time: 2 to 3 weeks. No self addressed stamped envelope is required.

In person search: Turnaround time 10 minutes.

Expedited service: Expedited service is available for mail and phone searches. This is for emergency use only. The additional fee is $14.95 for regular mail (includes credit card use) or $25.45 for express shipping.

Marriage Certificates
Divorce Records

Department of Health, Bureau of Vital Records, PO Box 570, Jefferson City, MO 65102-0570 (Courier: 930 Wildwood, Jefferson City, MO 65109); 573-751-6382, 573-751-6400 (Message Number), 573-526-3846 (Fax), 8AM-5PM.

http://www.health.state.mo.us

Note: Actual marriage and divorce records are found at county of issue. This agency will issue a certificate of statement only.

Indexing & Storage: Records are available from July 1, 1948 to present on microfiche.

Searching: Include names, year of occurrence and county in your request.

Access by: mail, in person.

Fee & Payment: The fee is $10.00 for each 5 years searched. Use of credit card is additional $4.95. Fee payee: Missouri Department of Health. Prepayment required. Personal checks accepted.

Mail search: Turnaround time: 1 to 2 weeks. No self addressed stamped envelope is required.

In person search: The agency personnel do the searching.

Expedited service: Expedited service is available for fax searches. Add $14.95 for regular mail and $25.95 for overnight (includes credit card fee).

Workers' Compensation Records

Labor & Industrial Relations Department, Workers Compensation Division, PO Box 58, Jefferson City, MO 65102-0058 (Courier: 3315 W Truman Blvd, Jefferson City, MO 65101); 573-751-4231, 573-751-2012 (Fax), 8AM-4:30PM.

http://www.dolir.state.mo.us

Indexing & Storage: Records are available from 1945. Records are computerized since 1994. Records are indexed on inhouse computer.

Searching: Report of injury and medical records released only with a release form. All other records are open. Include the following in your request-claimant name, Social Security Number, date of accident.

Access by: mail, fax, in person.

Fee & Payment: The search fee is $5.00. Fee payee: Workers Compensation Division. Personal checks accepted. No credit cards accepted.

Mail search: Turnaround time: 1 to 2 days. No self addressed stamped envelope is required.

Fax search: The initial fax must include a written request for the search. Turnaround time is 1 to 2 days.

In person search: To search in person, you must be party to the case in question or possess written authorization.

Driver Records

Department of Revenue, Driver and Vehicle Services Bureau, PO Box 200, Jefferson City, MO 65105-0200 (Courier: Harry S Truman Bldg, 301 W High St, Room 470, Jefferson City, MO 65105); 573-751-4300, 573-526-4769 (Fax), 7:45AM-4:45PM.

http://www.dor.state.mo.us/mvdl/drivers

Note: Copies of tickets are available from the same address. Requests must be in writing, include the name, DOB, license number, and specific violation information. The cost is $3.75 per ticket.

Indexing & Storage: Records are available for 5 years for moving violations and suspensions, permanent for DWI's. Zero point violations are not shown on the record. Accidents are stored in the state computer, but are not shown on the driving record, unless suspension/revocation action taken.

Searching: The state complies with DPPA. Casual requesters can obtain records without personal information.

Access by: mail, phone, fax, in person, online.

Fee & Payment: The fee is $1.25 per record for walk-in or mail-in requests. The fee for online retrieval is $1.25 per record plus network line charges. Fee payee: Department of Revenue. Prepayment required. Cashier's check and money orders preferred. Personal checks accepted. No credit cards accepted.

Mail search: Turnaround time: 2 days. A self addressed stamped envelope is requested.

Phone search: Search costs $1.50 per page. Phone-in service is available for pre-approved, established accounts. Call the number above for more information.

Fax search: Fax ordering-retrieval is available. Same criteria as phone requesting with an additional $.50 fee.

In person search: You may request information in person.

Online search: Online access costs $1.25 per record. Online inquiries can be put in Missouri's "mailbox" any time of the day. These inquiries are then picked up at 2 AM the following morning, and the resulting MVR's are sent back to each customer's "mailbox" approximately two hours later.

Other access: The tape-to-tape process has been replaced by the online system. The entire license file can be purchased, with updates. Call 573-751-5579 for more information.

Vehicle Ownership
Vehicle Identification
Vessel Ownership
Vessel Registration

Department of Revenue, Division of Motor Vehicles, PO Box 100, Jefferson City, MO 65105-0100 (Courier: Harry S Truman Bldg, 301 W High St, Jefferson City, MO 65105); 573-526-3669, 573-751-7060 (Fax), 7:45AM-4:45PM.

http://www.dor.state.mo.us/mvdl/default.htm

Note: Lien information shows on the title records.

Indexing & Storage: Records are available from 1968 to present. Records are indexed on microfiche from 1968 to present, and microfilm from 1981 to present. Records include boats and mobile homes. All motorized boats 12 ft or longer must be titled and registered.

Searching: Ownership and vehicle information is available with no restrictions to access, if request is of a legal nature. Casual requesters must have consent of subject to obtain records with personal information. Current registration/title records are on computer. Records are purged from the computer files after 2 years of no activity. However, the records will remain on microfiche.

Access by: mail, phone, fax, in person.

Fee & Payment: The fee for a record search is $4.50 and a complete title history is $8.00. There is an additional $3.00 for certification. Fee payee: Department of Revenue. Prepayment required. Pre-approved accounts may be billed. Personal checks accepted. No credit cards accepted.

Mail search: Turnaround time: 2 to 4 weeks.

Phone search: The state offers a phone-in service for title verification and lien holder information ONLY for dealers and lienholders. The fee is $1.50 per record. For more information, call 573-526-3669.

Fax search: To have results returned by fax costs an additional $.50 per page.

In person search: You may request records in person.

Other access: Missouri has an extensive range of records and information available on magnetic tape, labels or paper. Besides offering license, vehicle, title, dealer, and marine records, specific public report data is also available.

Accident Reports

Missouri Highway Patrol, Traffic Division, PO Box 568, Jefferson City, MO 65102-0568 (Courier: 1510 E Elm St, Jefferson City, MO 65102); 573-526-6113, 573-751-9921 (Fax), 8AM-5PM.

http://www.mshp.state.mo.us

Indexing & Storage: Records are available for 5 years to present on computer. Records are available within 2 weeks. Records are indexed on an in-house computer. Records are on a document imaging system or microfilm from 1941.

Searching: Record requests must be in writing. Generally, these records are open to the public. The first 60 days after the accident, records are restricted to only family members or those involved or their representatives. Include the following in your request-full name, date of accident, location of accident, relationship of requester to the subject. There is no telephone searching, but you can call to determine if an accident is on file.

Access by: mail, in person.

Fee & Payment: At present, due to restrictions imposed by legislation, the $5.00 fee for reports has not been implemented.

Mail search: Turnaround time: 3 to 4 working days. A self addressed stamped envelope is requested.

In person search: Turnaround time is immediate.

Legislation Records

Legislative Library, 117A State Capitol, Jefferson City, MO 65101; 573-751-4633 (Bill Status Only), 8:30AM-4:30PM.

http://www.moga.state.mo.us

Note: Sessions are from January to May.

Indexing & Storage: Records are available from 1993 to present on computer, from 1909-1972 and 1985 to 2000 on microfiche, and from 1973 to 1984 in books. Records are indexed on microfiche, books (volumes).

Searching: Include the following in your request-bill number, year.

Access by: mail, phone, in person, online.

Mail search: Turnaround time: 1 week to 10 days. No self addressed stamped envelope is required. No fee for mail request.

Phone search: No fee for telephone request. If the requests involves much time/paper, it will be refused.

In person search: No fee for request.

Online search: The web site offers access to bills and statutes. One can search or track bills by key words, bill number, or sponsors.

Voter Registration
Access to Records is Restricted

Secretary of State, Division of Elections, PO Box 1767, Jefferson City, MO 65102; 573-751-2301, 573-526-3242 (Fax), 8AM-5PM.

http://mosl.sos.state.mo.us

Note: The state will neither permit individual look-ups nor sell the records for commercial purposes. Records are sold in various media formats for political purposes. Individual look-ups can be done at the county level by the County Clerks.

GED Certificates

GED Office, PO Box 480, Jefferson City, MO 65102; 573-751-3504, 8AM-4:30PM.

http://www.dese.state.mo.us/divvoced/ged

Indexing & Storage: It takes 3-4 weeks before new records are available for inquiry.

Searching: Include the following in your request-signed release, date of birth, Social Security Number. The year and location of the test are very helpful and should also be included in the request.

Access by: mail, in person.

Fee & Payment: The fee is $2.00 for either a verification or a transcript. Fee payee: Treasurer, State of Missouri. Prepayment required. Personal checks accepted.

Mail search: Turnaround time: same day. No self addressed stamped envelope is required.

In person search: $2.00 fee per request.

Hunting License Information
Fishing License Information

Conservation Department, Fiscal Services, PO Box 180, Jefferson City, MO 65102-0180 (Courier: 2901 W Truman Blvd, Jefferson City, MO 65102); 573-751-4115, 573-751-4864 (Fax), 8AM-5PM.

http://www.conservation.state.mo.us

Indexing & Storage: Records are available for since 3/1/96. Records are indexed on inhouse computer, hard copy.

Searching: Records are only released to the permitee. Otherwise, they are not released until the reason for the request is reviewed by the Department's General Counsel. Names and addresses may be released, if request is approved. Include the following in your request-full name. For older records, you will need the permittee's name, date of birth, and type of permit.

Access by: mail.

Fee & Payment: Prepayment required. Fee payee: Conservation Department. Price is based upon

type of service provided. Personal checks accepted. Credit cards accepted: MasterCard, Visa.

Mail search: No self addressed stamped envelope is required.

Other access: Mailing lists of the hunting and fishing permit vendors are available. The cost is about $100.

Missouri State Licensing Agencies

Licenses Searchable Online

Architect #02 .... http://showme.ded.state.mo.us/dynded/pronline.form1
Athletic Trainer #28 .... http://showme.ded.state.mo.us/dynded/pronline.form1
Attorney #40 .... www.mobar.org/directory/index.htm
Audiologist (Clinical) #16 .... http://showme.ded.state.mo.us/dynded/pronline.form1
Audiologist/Speech (Combined), Clinical #16 ... http://showme.ded.state.mo.us/dynded/pronline.form1
Barber/Barber Shop #03 .... http://showme.ded.state.mo.us/dynded/pronline.form1
Barber School/Instructor #03 .... http://showme.ded.state.mo.us/dynded/pronline.form1
Boxer #44 .... http://riversrun.ded.state.mo.us/cgi-bin/professionalregistration.pl
Chiropractor #04 .... http://showme.ded.state.mo.us/dynded/pronline.form1
Cosmetologist/ Cosmetology Shop #05 .... http://showme.ded.state.mo.us/dynded/pronline.form1
Cosmetology School/Instructor #05 .... http://showme.ded.state.mo.us/dynded/pronline.form1
Counselor, Professional #23 .... http://showme.ded.state.mo.us/dynded/pronline.form1
Dental Hygienist #17 .... http://showme.ded.state.mo.us/dynded/pronline.form1
Dentist #17 .... http://showme.ded.state.mo.us/dynded/pronline.form1
Drug Distribution #09 .... http://showme.ded.state.mo.us/dynded/pronline.form1
Embalmer #06 .... http://showme.ded.state.mo.us/dynded/pronline.form1
Engineer #02 .... http://showme.ded.state.mo.us/dynded/pronline.form1
Funeral Director #06 .... http://showme.ded.state.mo.us/dynded/pronline.form1
Funeral Establishment #06 .... http://showme.ded.state.mo.us/dynded/pronline.form1
Funeral Preneed Provider/Seller #06 .... http://showme.ded.state.mo.us/dynded/pronline.form1
Interpreter for the Deaf #46 .... http://showme.ded.state.mo.us/dynded/pronline.form1
Landfill #37 .... www.dnr.state.mo.us/deq/swmp/availpub.htm
Landscape Architect #26 .... http://showme.ded.state.mo.us/dynded/pronline.form1
Landscape Architect Corp./or/Partnership #26 .http://showme.ded.state.mo.us/dynded/pronline.form1
Manicurist #05 .... http://showme.ded.state.mo.us/dynded/pronline.form1
Medical Doctor #11 .... http://showme.ded.state.mo.us/dynded/pronline.form1
Nurse #07 .... http://showme.ded.state.mo.us/dynded/pronline.form1
Nurse, Professional #07 .... www.ecodev.state.mo.us/pr/nursingdown.html
Nurse-LPN #07 .... http://showme.ded.state.mo.us/dynded/pronline.form1
Occupational Therapist #41 .... http://showme.ded.state.mo.us/dynded/pronline.form1
Occupational Therapist Assistant #41 .... http://showme.ded.state.mo.us/dynded/pronline.form1
Optometrist #08 .... http://showme.ded.state.mo.us/dynded/pronline.form1
Osteopathic Physician #11 .... http://showme.ded.state.mo.us/dynded/pronline.form1
Pharmacist/Pharmacy Intern #09 .... http://showme.ded.state.mo.us/dynded/pronline.form1
Pharmacy #09 .... http://showme.ded.state.mo.us/dynded/pronline.form1
Pharmacy Technician #09 .... http://showme.ded.state.mo.us/dynded/pronline.form1
Physical Therapist #11 .... http://showme.ded.state.mo.us/dynded/pronline.form1
Physician Assistant #11 .... http://showme.ded.state.mo.us/dynded/pronline.form1
Podiatrist #10 .... http://showme.ded.state.mo.us/dynded/pronline.form1
Podiatrist Temporary #10 .... http://showme.ded.state.mo.us/dynded/pronline.form1
Podiatrist/Ankle #10 .... http://showme.ded.state.mo.us/dynded/pronline.form1
Psychologist #36 .... http://showme.ded.state.mo.us/dynded/pronline.form1
Public Accountant Partnership #01 .... http://riversrun.ded.state.mo.us/cgi-bin/professionalregistration.pl
Public Accountant-CPA #01 .... http://riversrun.ded.state.mo.us/cgi-bin/professionalregistration.pl
Real Estate Appraiser #14 .... http://showme.ded.state.mo.us/dynded/pronline.form1
Real Estate Broker/Sales Agent #35 .... http://showme.ded.state.mo.us/dynded/pronline.form1
Respiratory Care Practitioner #42 .... http://showme.ded.state.mo.us/dynded/pronline.form1
Social Worker, Clinical #15 .... http://showme.ded.state.mo.us/dynded/pronline.form1
Speech Pathologist/Audiologist #16 .... http://showme.ded.state.mo.us/dynded/pronline.form1
Surveyor #02 .... http://showme.ded.state.mo.us/dynded/pronline.form1
Transfer Station #37 .... www.dnr.state.mo.us/deq/swmp/tranlist.htm
Veterinarian #31 .... http://showme.ded.state.mo.us/dynded/pronline.form1
Veterinary Technician #31 .... http://showme.ded.state.mo.us/dynded/pronline.form1
Waste Tire End User #37 .... www.dnr.state.mo.us/deq/swmp/tireend.htm
Waste Tire Hauler #37 .... www.dnr.state.mo.us/deq/swmp/tirehaul.htm
Waste Tire Processor/Site #37 .... www.dnr.state.mo.us/deq/swmp/tireend.htm
Wrestler #44 .... http://riversrun.ded.state.mo.us/cgi-bin/professionalregistration.pl

Licensing Quick Finder

Architect #02	573-751-0047
Athletic Trainer #28	573-751-0171
Attorney #40	573-635-4128
Audiologist (Clinical) #16	573-751-0171
Audiologist/Speech (Combined), Clinical #16	573-751-0171
Barber #03	573-751-0805
Barber Instructor #03	573-751-0805
Barber School #03	573-751-0805
Barber Shop #03	573-751-0805
Boxer #44	573-751-0243
Cemetery, Endowed Care Cemetery#25	573-751-0849
Child Care Facility #29	573-751-2450
Chiropractor #04	573-751-2104
Cosmetologist #05	573-751-1052
Cosmetology Instructor #05	573-751-1052
Cosmetology School #05	573-751-1052
Cosmetology Shop #05	573-751-1052
Counselor, Professional #23	573-751-0018
Court Reporter #12	573-751-4144
Dental Hygienist #17	573-751-0040
Dental Specialist #17	573-751-0040
Dentist #17	573-751-0040
Drug Distribution #09	573-751-0091
Embalmer #06	573-751-0813
Emergency Medical Technician (Basic) #19	573-751-6356
Engineer #02	573-751-0047
Funeral Director #06	573-751-0813
Funeral Establishment #06	573-751-0813
Funeral Preneed Provider #06	573-751-0813
Funeral Preneed Seller #06	573-751-0813
Gaming Occupational License #30	573-526-4092

Gaming Property (Boat) #30	573-526-4092
Gaming Supply #30	573-526-4092
Geologist #47	573-526-7625
Horse Racing #30	573-526-4083
Insurance Agent/Broker #20	573-751-3518
Interpreter for the Deaf #46	573-526-7787
Investment Advisor #34	573-751-4136
Landfill #37	573-751-5401
Landfill Operator #37	573-751-5401
Landscape Architect #26	573-751-0039
Landscape Architect Corp./or/Partnership #26	573-751-0039
Liquor Control #21	573-751-2333
Manicurist #05	573-751-1052
Marriage & Family Therapist #43	573-751-0870
Martial Artist #44	573-751-0243
Medical Doctor #11	573-751-0108
Notary Public #33	573-751-2783
Nurse #07	573-751-0681
Nurse, Professional #07	573-751-0681
Nurse-LPN #07	573-751-0681
Nursing Home Administrator #32	573-751-3511
Occupational Therapist #41	573-751-0877
Occupational Therapist Assistant #41	573-751-0877
Optometrist #08	573-751-0814
Osteopathic Physician #11	573-751-0108
Pesticide Applicator #18	573-751-5504
Pesticide Dealer #18	573-751-5504
Pesticide Technician #18	573-751-9298
Pharmacist/Pharmacy Intern #09	573-751-0091
Pharmacy #09	573-751-0091
Pharmacy Technician #09	573-751-0091
Physical Therapist #11	573-751-0171

Physician Assistant #11	573-751-0171
Podiatrist #10	573-751-0873
Podiatrist Temporary #10	573-751-0873
Podiatrist/Ankle #10	573-751-0873
Prevention Specialist (Social Work) #39	573-751-9211
Psychologist #36	573-751-0099
Public Accountant Partnership #01	573-751-0012
Public Accountant-CPA #01	573-751-0012
Real Estate Appraiser #14	573-751-0038
Real Estate Broker #35	573-751-2628
Real Estate Sales Agent #35	573-751-2628
Respiratory Care Practitioner #42	573-522-2864
School Commissioner Assistant #24	573-526-4900
School Librarian #24	573-526-4900
Securities Agent #34	573-751-4136
Securities Broker/Dealer #34	573-751-4136
Social Worker, Clinical #15	573-751-0885
Speech Pathologist/Audiologist (Speech-Language Pathologist) #16	573-751-0171
Substance Abuse Associate in Training #39	573-751-9211
Substance Abuse Counselor #39	573-751-9211
Surveyor #02	573-751-0047
Transfer Station #37	573-751-5401
Veterinarian #31	573-751-0031
Veterinary Technician #31	573-751-0031
Waste Tire End User #37	573-751-5401
Waste Tire Hauler #37	573-751-5401
Waste Tire Processor/Site #37	573-751-5401
Waste Water System Operator #38	573-526-6627
Water Supply Operator #38	573-526-6627
Wrestler #44	573-751-0243

Licensing Agency Information

#01 Board of Accountancy, 3605 Missouri Blvd, Jefferson City, MO 65102-0613; 573-751-1052, Fax: 573-751-0890.
www.ecodev.state.mo.us/pr/account
Direct web site URL to search for licensees: http://riversrun.ded.state.mo.us/cgi-bin/professionalregistration.pl

#02 Engineers & Land Survey, 3605 Missouri Blvd, #380, Jefferson City, MO 65102; 573-751-0047, Fax: 573-751-8046.
www.ecodev.state.mo.us/pr/moapels
Direct web site URL to search for licensees: www.ecodev.state.mo.us/pr/ftp4.htm

#03 Board of Barber Examiners, 3605 Missouri Blvd, Jefferson City, MO 65102-1335; 573-751-0805, Fax: 573-751-8167.
www.ecodev.state.mo.us/pr/barber
Direct web site URL to search for licensees: www.ecodev.state.mo.us/pr/ftp4.htm The online search URL is used to download the list of active licensees. Adobe Acrobat Reader software ineeded to open the downloaded files. To obtain the Acrobat Reader software, visit www.ecodev.state.mo.us/download/instructions.htm.

#04 Board of Chiropractic Examiners, 3605 Missouri Blvd, Jefferson City, MO 65102-0672; 573-751-2104, Fax: 573-751-0735.
www.ecodev.state.mo.us/pr/chiro
Direct web site URL to search for licensees: www.ecodev.state.mo.us/pr/ftp4.htm

#05 Board of Cosmetology, 3605 Missouri Blvd, Jefferson City, MO 65102; 573-751-1052, Fax: 573-751-8167.
www.ecodev.state.mo.us/pr/cosmo

#06 Board of Embalmers & Funeral Directors, 3605 Missouri Blvd, Jefferson City, MO 65102-0625; 573-751-0813, Fax: 573-751-1155.
www.ecodev.state.mo.us/pr/embalm
Direct web site URL to search for licensees: www.ecodev.state.mo.us/pr/ftp4.htm

#07 Board of Nursing, 3605 Missouri Blvd, Jefferson City, MO 65102; 573-751-0681, Fax: 573-751-0075.
www.ecodev.state.mo.us/pr/nursing
Direct web site URL to search for licensees: www.ecodev.state.mo.us/pr/nursingdown.html

#08 Board of Optometry, PO Box 1335 (3605 Missouri Blvd), Jefferson City, MO 65102-0423; 573-751-0814, Fax: 573-751-0735.
www.ecodev.state.mo.us/pr/optom
Direct web site URL to search for licensees: www.ecodev.state.mo.us/pr/optometristdown.html. You can search online using alphabetical list.

#09 Board of Pharmacy, 3605 Missouri Blvd, Jefferson City, MO 65102; 573-751-0091, Fax: 573-526-3464.
www.ecodev.state.mo.us/pr/pharmacy
Direct web site URL to search for licensees: www.ecodev.state.mo.us/pr/pharmacy/phsearch.htm. You can search online using name, pharmacy name, street, city, ZIP Code, and disciplinary status.

#10 Board of Podiatric Medicine, 3605 Missouri Blvd, Jefferson City, MO 65102; 573-751-0873, Fax: 573-751-1155.
www.ecodev.state.mo.us/pr/podiatry
Direct web site URL to search for licensees: www.ecodev.state.mo.us/pr/ftp4.htm

#11 Board of Registration for Healing Arts, 3605 Missouri Blvd, Jefferson City, MO 65102; 573-751-0098, Fax: 573-751-3166.
www.ecodev.state.mo.us/pr/healarts
Direct web site URL to search for licensees: www.ecodev.state.mo.us/pr/healingdown.html

#14 Commission of Real Estate Appraisers, 3605 Missouri Blvd, Jefferson City, MO 65109; 573-751-0038, Fax: 573-526-3489.
www.ecodev.state.mo.us/pr/rea
Direct web site URL to search for licensees: www.ecodev.state.mo.us/pr/rea/search.htm. You can search online using license number, name, business name, city, ZIP Code, and classification.

#15 Division of Professional Registration, 3605 Missouri Blvd, Jefferson City, MO 65102; 573-751-0085, Fax: 573-751-7670.
www.ecodev.state.mo.us/pr/social
Direct web site URL to search for licensees: www.ecodev.state.mo.us/pr/ftp4.htm. You can search online using

www.state.mo.us/boards/cgi/boards.cgi?FUNCTI
ON=LIST.

#16 Committee of Speech Pathology &
Audiology, 3605 Missouri Blvd, Jefferson City,
MO 65102; 573-751-0098, Fax: 573-751-3166.
www.ecodev.state.mo.us/pr/healarts/
Direct web site URL to search for licensees:
www.ecodev.state.mo.us/pr/healingdown.html

#17 Dental Board, 3605 Missouri Blvd, Jefferson
City, MO 65102; 573-751-0040, Fax: 573-751-
8216.
www.ecodev.state.mo.us/pr/dental/
Direct web site URL to search for licensees:
www.ecodev.state.mo.us/pr/ftp4.htm

#18 Department of Agriculture, Division of Plant
Industries, 1616 Missouri Blvd, Jefferson City,
MO 65102; 573-751-2462, Fax: 573-751-0005.
www.mda.state.mo.us/d.htm

#19 Department of Health, PO Box 570 (912
Wildwood Dr), Jefferson City, MO 65102-0570;
573-751-6356, Fax: 573-526-4102.
www.health.state.mo.us

#20 Department of Insurance, PO Box 690,
Jefferson City, MO 65102-0690; 573-751-4126,
Fax: 573-526-3416.
www.insurance.state.mo.us

#21 Department of Public Safety, Truman Bldg,
Rm 870, Jefferson City, MO 65102-0837; 573-
751-5445, Fax: 573-526-4540.
www.mdlc.state.mo.us

#23 Division of Professional Regulation, PO Box
1335 (3605 Missouri Blvd), Jefferson City, MO
65102-1335; 573-751-0018, Fax: 573-526-3489.
www.ecodev.state.mo.us/pr/counselr/
Direct web site URL to search for licensees:
www.ecodev.state.mo.us/pr/counselorsdown.html

#24 Education, Elementary & Secondary
Instruction, 205 Jefferson St, Jefferson City, MO
65102-0480; 573-751-4234, Fax: 573-751-9434.
www.dese.state.mo.us

#25 Endowed Care Cemeteries, 3605 Missouri
Blvd, Jefferson City, MO 65102-1335; 573-751-
0849, Fax: 573-751-0878.
www.ecodev.state.mo.us/pr/endowed/

#26 Landscape Architectural Council, 3605
Missouri Blvd, Jefferson City, MO 65102-1339;
573-751-0039, Fax: 573-751-2831.
www.ecodev.state.mo.us/pr/landarch/

#29 Department of Health, 1715 South Ridge,
Jefferson City, MO 65109; 573-751-2450, Fax:
573-526-5345.
www.health.state.mo.us/AbouttheDepartment/Bof
CC.html

#30 Gaming Commission, 3417 Knipp Dr,
Jefferson City, MO 65109; 573-526-4080, Fax:
573-526-4080.
www.dps.state.mo.us/mgc/index.htm

#31 Veterinary Medical Board, 3605 Missouri
Blvd, Jefferson City, MO 65102-0633; 573-751-
0031, Fax: 573-751-3856.
www.ecodev.state.mo.us/pr/vet
Direct web site URL to search for licensees:
www.ecodev.state.mo.us/pr/ftp4.htm

#32 Board of Nursing Home Administrators, 615
Howerton Ct, Jefferson City, MO 65102; 573-751-
3511, Fax: 573-573-4314.

#33 Office of Secretary of State, PO Box 784,
Jefferson City, MO 65102; 573-751-0018, Fax:
573-526-3489.
http://mosl.sos.state.mo.us/

#34 Secretary of State, 600 W Main St #229,
Jefferson City, MO 65101; 573-751-4136, Fax:
573-526-3124.
http://mosl.sos.state.mo.us/sos-sec/sossec.html

#35 Real Estate Commission, PO Box 1339 (3605
Missouri Blvd), Jefferson City, MO 65102-1339;
573-751-2628, Fax: 573-751-2777.
www.ecodev.state.mo.us/pr/restate/default.htm
Direct web site URL to search for licensees:
www.ecodev.state.mo.us/pr/. You can search
online using downloadable lists

#36 Committee of Psychology, 3605 Missouri
Blvd, Jefferson City, MO 65102-1335; 573-751-
0099, Fax: 573-526-3489.
www.ecodev.state.mo.us/pr/psych/

#37 Department of Natural Resources, Div of
Environmental Quality, 1738 E Elm, PO Box 176,
Jefferson City, MO 65102-0176; 573-751-5401,
Fax: 573-526-3902.
www.dnr.state.mo.us

#38 Department of Natural Resources, PO Box
176 (1659 Elm St), Jefferson City, MO 65102;
573-526-6627, Fax: 573-526-5808.
www.dnr.state.mo.us/deq/tap/oprtrain.htm

#39 Abuse Counselors Certification Board, 1706 E
Elm, Jefferson City, MO 65102; 573-751-9211,
Fax: 573-526-3489.
www.modmh.state.mo.us/msaccb

#40 The Missouri Bar, PO Box 119 (326 Monroe
St), Jefferson City, MO 65102-0119; 573-635-
4128, Fax: 573-635-2811.
www.mobar.org
Direct web site URL to search for licensees:
www.mobar.org/directory/index.htm

#41 Division of Professional Registration, PO Box
1335 (3605 Missouri Blvd, 65109), Jefferson
City, MO 65102-1335; 573-751-0877, Fax: 573-
526-3489.
www.ecodev.state.mo.us/pr/octherap

#42 Board for Respiratory Care, 3605 Missouri
Blvd, Jefferson City, MO 65102-1335; 573-522-
5864, Fax: 573-526-4176.
www.ecodev.state.mo.us/pr/mbrc
Direct web site URL to search for licensees:
www.ecodev.state.mo.us/pr/ftp4.htm

#43 Committee of Marital & Family Therapists,
3605 Missouri Blvd, Jefferson City, MO 65102-
1335; 573-751-0870, Fax: 573-526-3489.
www.ecodev.state.mo.us/pr/mft

#44 Office of Athletics, 3605 Missouri Blvd,
Jefferson City, MO 65102-1335; 573-751-0243,
Fax: 573-751-5649.
www.ecodev.state.mo.us/pr/athletic
Direct web site URL to search for licensees:
http://riversrun.ded.state.mo.us/cgi-
bin/professionalregistration.pl

#46 Committee of Interpreters, PO Box 1335
(3605 Missouri Blvd), Jefferson City, MO 65102-
1335; 573-526-7787, Fax: 573-526-3489.
www.ecodev.state.mo.us/pr/inter/
Direct web site URL to search for licensees:
www.ecodev.state.mo.us/pr/ftp4.htm

#47 Board of Geologist Registration, 3605
Missouri Blvd, PO Box 1335, Jefferson City, MO
65102; 573-526-7625, Fax: 573-526-3489.
www.ecodev.state.mo.us/pr/geo

Missouri Federal Courts

The following list indicates the district and division name for each county in the state. If the bankruptcy court location is different from the district court, then the location of the bankruptcy court appears in parentheses.

County/Court Cross Reference

County	District	Division
Adair	Eastern	Hannibal (St Louis)
Andrew	Western	St Joseph (Kansas City - Western)
Atchison	Western	St Joseph (Kansas City - Western)
Audrain	Eastern	Hannibal (St Louis)
Barry	Western	Joplin-Southwestern (Kansas City)
Barton	Western	Joplin-Southwestern (Kansas City)
Bates	Western	Kansas City - Western
Benton	Western	Jefferson City-Central (Kansas City)
Bollinger	Eastern	Cape Girardeau (St Louis)
Boone	Western	Jefferson City-Central (Kansas City)
Buchanan	Western	St Joseph (Kansas City - Western)
Butler	Eastern	Cape Girardeau (St Louis)
Caldwell	Western	St Joseph (Kansas City - Western)
Callaway	Western	Jefferson City-Central (Kansas City)
Camden	Western	Jefferson City-Central (Kansas City)
Cape Girardeau	Eastern	Cape Girardeau (St Louis)
Carroll	Western	Kansas City - Western
Carter	Eastern	Cape Girardeau (St Louis)
Cass	Western	Kansas City - Western
Cedar	Western	Springfield-Southern (Kansas City)
Chariton	Eastern	Hannibal (St Louis)
Christian	Western	Springfield-Southern (Kansas City)
Clark	Eastern	Hannibal (St Louis)
Clay	Western	Kansas City - Western
Clinton	Western	St Joseph (Kansas City - Western)
Cole	Western	Jefferson City-Central (Kansas City)
Cooper	Western	Jefferson City-Central (Kansas City)
Crawford	Eastern	St Louis
Dade	Western	Springfield-Southern (Kansas City)
Dallas	Western	Springfield-Southern (Kansas City)
Daviess	Western	St Joseph (Kansas City - Western)
De Kalb	Western	St Joseph (Kansas City - Western)
Dent	Eastern	St Louis
Douglas	Western	Springfield-Southern ((Kansas City)
Dunklin	Eastern	Cape Girardeau (St Louis)
Franklin	Eastern	St Louis
Gasconade	Eastern	St Louis
Gentry	Western	St Joseph (Kansas City - Western)
Greene	Western	Springfield-Southern (Kansas City)
Grundy	Western	St Joseph (Kansas City - Western)
Harrison	Western	St Joseph (Kansas City - Western)
Henry	Western	Kansas City - Western
Hickory	Western	Jefferson City-Central (Kansas City)
Holt	Western	St Joseph (Kansas City - Western)
Howard	Western	Jefferson City-Central (Kansas City)
Howell	Western	Springfield-Southern (Kansas City)
Iron	Eastern	St Louis
Jackson	Western	Kansas City – Western
Jasper	Western	Joplin-Southwestern (Kansas City)
Jefferson	Eastern	St Louis
Johnson	Western	Kansas City - Western
Knox	Eastern	Hannibal (St Louis)
Laclede	Western	Springfield-Southern (Kansas City
Lafayette	Western	Kansas City - Western
Lawrence	Western	Joplin-Southwestern (Kansas City)
Lewis	Eastern	Hannibal (St Louis)
Lincoln	Eastern	St Louis
Linn	Eastern	Hannibal (St Louis)
Livingston	Western	St Joseph (Kansas City - Western)
Macon	Eastern	Hannibal (St Louis)
Madison	Eastern	Cape Girardeau (St Louis)
Maries	Eastern	St Louis
Marion	Eastern	Hannibal (St Louis)
McDonald	Western	Joplin-Southwestern (Kansas City)
Mercer	Western	St Joseph (Kansas City - Western)
Miller	Western	Jefferson City-Central (Kansas City)
Mississippi	Eastern	Cape Girardeau (St Louis)
Moniteau	Western	Jefferson City-Central (Kansas City)
Monroe	Eastern	Hannibal (St Louis)
Montgomery	Eastern	Hannibal (St Louis)
Morgan	Western	Jefferson City-Central (Kansas City)
New Madrid	Eastern	Cape Girardeau (St Louis)
Newton	Western	Joplin-Southwestern (Kansas City)
Nodaway	Western	St Joseph (Kansas City - Western)
Oregon	Western	Springfield-Southern (Kansas City)
Osage	Western	Jefferson City-Central (Kansas City)
Ozark	Western	Springfield-Southern (Kansas City)
Pemiscot	Eastern	Cape Girardeau (St Louis)
Perry	Eastern	Cape Girardeau (St Louis)
Pettis	Western	Jefferson City-Central (Kansas City)
Phelps	Eastern	St Louis
Pike	Eastern	Hannibal (St Louis)
Platte	Western	St Joseph (Kansas City - Western)
Polk	Western	Springfield-Southern (Kansas City)
Pulaski	Western	Springfield-Southern (Kansas City)
Putnam	Western	St Joseph (Kansas City - Western)
Ralls	Eastern	Hannibal (St Louis)
Randolph	Eastern	Hannibal (St Louis)
Ray	Western	Kansas City - Western)
Reynolds	Eastern	Cape Girardeau (St Louis)
Ripley	Eastern	Cape Girardeau (St Louis)
Saline	Western	Kansas City - Western
Schuyler	Eastern	Hannibal (St Louis)
Scotland	Eastern	Hannibal (St Louis)
Scott	Eastern	Cape Girardeau (St Louis)
Shannon	Eastern	Cape Girardeau (St Louis)
Shelby	Eastern	Hannibal (St Louis)
St. Charles	Eastern	St Louis
St. Clair	Western	Kansas City - Western
St. Francois	Eastern	St Louis

St. Louis ....Eastern...................St Louis

St. Louis City City..................Eastern...................St Louis

Ste. Genevieve ....Eastern...................St Louis

Stoddard ....Eastern...................Cape Girardeau (St Louis)

Stone ....Western.................Joplin-Southwestern (Kansas City)

Sullivan ....Western.................St Joseph (Kansas City - Western)

Taney ....Western.................Springfield-Southern (Kansas City)

Texas.....................................Western.................Springfield-Southern (Kansas City)

Vernon...................................Western.................Joplin-Southwestern (Kansas City)

Warren ....Eastern...................St Louis

Washington............................Eastern...................St Louis

Wayne ....Eastern...................Cape Girardeau (St Louis)

Webster.................................Western.................Springfield-Southern (Kansas City)

Worth ....Western.................St Joseph (Kansas City - Western)

Wright ....Western.................Springfield-Southern (Kansas City)

US District Court

Eastern District of Missouri

Cape Girardeau Division 339 Broadway, Room 240, Cape Girardeau, MO 63701 (Courier Address: Use mail address for courier delivery), 573-335-8538, Fax: 573-335-0379.

http://www.moed.uscourts.gov

Counties: Bollinger, Butler, Cape Girardeau, Carter, Dunklin, Madison, Mississippi, New Madrid, Pemiscot, Perry, Reynolds, Ripley, Scott, Shannon, Stoddard, Wayne.

Indexing/Storage: Cases are indexed by defendant and plaintiff as well as by case number. New cases are available in the index 1-2 days after filing date. Both computer and card indexes are maintained. Computerized records are available from January 1, 1992. Open records are located at this court.

Fee & Payment: The fee is $20.00 per item (one party name or case number). Payment may be made by money order, cashier check, personal check. Prepayment is required. Payee: Clerk, US District Court. Certification fee: $7.00 per document. Copy fee: $.50 per page.

Phone Search: Only docket information is available by phone.

Mail Search: A stamped self addressed envelope is not required.

In Person: In person searching is available.

PACER: Sign-up number is 800-676-6856. Access fee is $.60 per minute. Toll-free access: 800-533-8105. Local access: 314-244-7775. Case records are available back to 1992. Records are never purged. New records are available online after 4-5 days. PACER is available online at http://pacer.moed.uscourts.gov.

Hannibal Division 801 Broadway, Hannibal, MO 63401 (Courier Address: Use mail address for courier delivery), 573-221-0757.

http://www.moed.uscourts.gov

Counties: Adair, Audrain, Chariton, Clark, Knox, Lewis, Linn, Macon, Marion, Monroe, Montgomery, Pike, Ralls, Randolph, Schuyler, Scotland, Shelby.

Indexing/Storage: Cases are indexed by defendant and plaintiff as well as by case number. New cases are available in the index after filing date. Open records are located at the Division.

Fee & Payment: The fee is no charge per item (one party name or case number). Payment may be made by money order, cashier check. Business checks are not accepted. Personal checks are not accepted.

Phone Search: Searching is not available by phone.

Mail Search: A stamped self addressed envelope is not required.

In Person: In person searching is available.

PACER: Sign-up number is 800-676-6856. Access fee is $.60 per minute. Toll-free access: 800-533-8105. Local access: 314-244-7775. Case records are available back to 1992. Records are never purged. New records are available online after 4-5 days. PACER is available online at http://pacer.moed.uscourts.gov.

St Louis Division 111 S. 10th St, Ste 3.300, St Louis, MO 63102 (Courier Address: Use mail address for courier delivery), 314-244-7900, Fax: 314-244-7909.

http://www.moed.uscourts.gov

Counties: Crawford, Dent, Franklin, Gasconade, Iron, Jefferson, Lincoln, Maries, Phelps, St. Charles, Ste. Genevieve, St. Francois, St. Louis, Warren, Washington, City of St. Louis.

Indexing/Storage: Cases are indexed by defendant and plaintiff as well as by case number. New cases are available in the index immediately after filing date. A computer index is maintained. Open records are located at this court.

Fee & Payment: The fee is $20.00 per item (one party name or case number). Payment may be made by money order, cashier check, personal check. Prepayment is required. Payee: Clerk, US District Court. Certification fee: $7.00 per document. Copy fee: $.50 per page.

Phone Search: Only docket information is available by phone.

Mail Search: A stamped self addressed envelope is not required.

In Person: In person searching is available.

PACER: Sign-up number is 800-676-6856. Access fee is $.60 per minute. Toll-free access: 800-533-8105. Local access: 314-244-7775. Case records are available back to 1992. Records are never purged. New records are available online after 4-5 days. PACER is available online at http://pacer.moed.uscourts.gov.

US Bankruptcy Court

Eastern District of Missouri

St Louis Division 4th Floor, 110 S. 10th St, St Louis, MO 63102-2734 (Courier Address: Use mail address for courier delivery), 314-244-4500, Fax: 314-244-4990.

http://www.moeb.uscourts.gov

Counties: Adair, Audrain, Bollinger, Butler, Cape Girardeau, Carter, Chariton, Clark, Crawford, Dent, Dunklin, Franklin, Gasconade, Iron, Jefferson, Knox, Lewis, Lincoln, Linn, Macon, Madison, Maries, Marion, Mississippi, Monroe, Montgomery, New Madrid, Pemiscot,Perry, Phelps, Pike, Ralls, Randolph, Reynolds, Ripley, Schuyler, Scotland, Scott, Shannon, Shelby, St. Charles, St. Francois, St. Louis, St.Louis City, Ste. Genevieve, Stoddard, Warren, Washington, Wayne.

Indexing/Storage: Cases are indexed by debtor as well as by case number. New cases are available in the index 24 hours after filing date. A computer index is maintained. Open records are located at this court.

Fee & Payment: The fee is $20.00 per item (one party name or case number). Payment may be made by money order, cashier check, personal check. Prepayment is required. Payee: Clerk, US Bankruptcy Court. Certification fee: $7.00 per document. Copy fee: $.50 per page.

Phone Search: Docket information is available by phone. An automated voice case information service (VCIS) is available. Call VCIS at 888-223-6431 or 314-425-4054.

Mail Search: A stamped self addressed envelope is not required.

In Person: In person searching is available.

PACER: Sign-up number is 800-676-6856. Access fee is $.60 per minute. Toll-free access: 888-577-1668. Local access: 314-244-4998. Case records are available back to January 1991. Records are purged every six months. New civil records are available online after 1 day. PACER is available online at http://pacer.moeb.uscourts.gov.

Other Online Access: Search records on the Internet using RACER at http://racer.moeb.uscourts.gov/perl/bkplog.html. Access fee is 7 cents per page.

US District Court

Western District of Missouri

Jefferson City-Central Division 131 W High St, Jefferson City, MO 65101 (Courier Address: Use mail address for courier delivery), 573-636-4015, Fax: 573-636-3456.

http://www.mow.uscourts.gov

Counties: Benton, Boone, Callaway, Camden, Cole, Cooper, Hickory, Howard, Miller, Moniteau, Morgan, Osage, Pettis.

Indexing/Storage: Cases are indexed by defendant and plaintiff as well as by case number. New cases are available in the index 1-2 days after filing date. A computer index is maintained. Open records are located at this court.

Fee & Payment: The fee is $20.00 per item (one party name or case number). Payment may be made by money order, cashier check, personal check. Prepayment is required. Payee: Clerk, US District Court. Certification fee: $7.00 per document. Copy fee: $.50 per page.

Phone Search: Only docket information is available by phone.

Mail Search: Always enclose a stamped self addressed envelope.

In Person: In person searching is available.

PACER: Sign-up number is 800-676-6856. Access fee is. Case records are available back to May 1, 1989. Records are purged as deemed necessary. New records are available online after 1 day. PACER is available online at http://pacer.mowd.uscourts.gov.

Electronic Filing: Electronic filing information is available online at http://www.mow.uscourts.gov/cmecf.htm

Joplin-Southwestern Division c/o Kansas City Division, Charles Evans Whitttaker Courthouse, 400 E 9th St, Kansas City, MO 64106 (Courier Address: Use mail address for courier delivery), 816-512-5000, Fax: 816-512-5078.

Counties: Barry, Barton, Jasper, Lawrence, McDonald, Newton, Stone, Vernon.

Indexing/Storage: Cases are indexed by defendant and plaintiff as well as by case number. New cases are available in the index after filing date. Open records are located at the Division.

Fee & Payment: The fee is no charge per item (one party name or case number). Payment may be made by money order, cashier check. Business checks not accepted. Personal checks not accepted.

Phone Search: Searching is not available by phone.

Mail Search: A stamped self addressed envelope is not required.

In Person: In person searching is available.

PACER: Sign-up number is 800-676-6856. Access fee is. Case records are available back to May 1, 1989. Records are purged as deemed necessary. New records are available online after 1 day. PACER is available online at http://pacer.mowd.uscourts.gov.

Electronic Filing: Electronic filing information is available online at https://ecf.mowb.uscourts.gov/

Kansas City-Western Division Clerk of Court, 201 US Courthouse, Rm 1056, 400 E 9th St, Kansas City, MO 64106 (Courier Address: Use mail address for courier delivery), 816-512-5000, Fax: 816-512-5078.

Counties: Bates, Carroll, Cass, Clay, Henry, Jackson, Johnson, Lafayette, Ray, St. Clair, Saline.

Indexing/Storage: Cases are indexed by defendant and plaintiff as well as by case number. New cases are available in the index 1-2 days after filing date. Records are indexed on computer and microfiche. Open records are located at this court.

Fee & Payment: The fee is $20.00 per item (one party name or case number). Payment may be made by money order, cashier check, personal check. Prepayment is required. Payee: US District Court Clerk. Certification fee: $7.00 per document. Copy fee: $.50 per page.

Phone Search: Only docket information is available by phone.

Fax Search: Will accept fax requests.

Mail Search: A stamped self addressed envelope is not required.

In Person: In person searching is available.

PACER: Sign-up number is 800-676-6856. Access fee is. Case records are available back to May 1, 1989. Records are purged as deemed necessary. New records are available online after 1 day. PACER is available online at http://pacer.mowd.uscourts.gov.

Electronic Filing: Electronic filing information is available online at https://ecf.mowb.uscourts.gov/

Springfield-Southern Division 222 N John Q Hammons Pkwy, Suite 1400, Springfield, MO 65806 (Courier Address: Use mail address for courier delivery), 417-865-3869, Fax: 417-865-7719.

Counties: Cedar, Christian, Dade, Dallas, Douglas, Greene, Howell, Laclede, Oregon, Ozark, Polk, Pulaski, Taney, Texas, Webster, Wright.

Indexing/Storage: Cases are indexed by defendant and plaintiff as well as by case number. New cases are available in the index immediately after filing date. A computer index is maintained. Open records are located at this court.

Fee & Payment: The fee is $20.00 per item (one party name or case number). Payment may be made by money order, cashier check, personal check. Prepayment is required. Payee: Clerk, US District Court. Certification fee: $7.00 per document. Copy fee: $.50 per page.

Phone Search: Only docket information is available by phone.

Mail Search: Always enclose a stamped self addressed envelope.

In Person: In person searching is available.

PACER: Sign-up number is 800-676-6856. Access fee is. Case records are available back to May 1, 1989. Records are purged as deemed necessary. New records are available online after 1 day. PACER is available online at http://pacer.mowd.uscourts.gov.

Electronic Filing: Electronic filing information is available online at https://ecf.mowb.uscourts.gov/

St Joseph Division PO Box 387, 201 S 8th St, St Joseph, MO 64501 (Courier Address: Use mail address for courier delivery), Fax: 816-279-0177.

Counties: Andrew, Atchison, Buchanan, Caldwell, Clinton, Daviess, De Kalb, Gentry, Grundy, Harrison, Holt, Livingston, Mercer, Nodaway, Platte, Putnam, Sullivan, Worth.

Indexing/Storage: Cases are indexed by defendant and plaintiff as well as by case number. New cases are available in the index immediately after filing date. A computer index is maintained. Open records are located at this court.

Fee & Payment: The fee is $20.00 per item (one party name or case number). Payment may be made by money order, cashier check, personal check. Prepayment is required. Payee: Clerk, US District Court. Certification fee: $7.00 per document. Copy fee: $.50 per page.

Phone Search: Only docket information is available by phone.

Mail Search: A stamped self addressed envelope is not required.

In Person: In person searching is available.

PACER: Sign-up number is 800-676-6856. Access fee is. Case records are available back to May 1, 1989. Records are purged as deemed necessary. New records are available online after 1 day. PACER is available online at http://pacer.mowd.uscourts.gov.

Electronic Filing: Electronic filing information is available online at https://ecf.mowb.uscourts.gov/

US Bankruptcy Court

Western District of Missouri

Kansas City-Western Division Room 1510, 400 E 9th st, Kansas City, MO 64106 (Courier Address: Use mail address for courier delivery), 816-512-1800.

http://www.mow.uscourt.gov

Counties: Andrew, Atchison, Barry, Barton, Bates, Benton, Boone, Buchanan, Caldwell, Callaway, Camden, Carroll, Cass, Cedar, Christian, Clay, Clinton, Cole, Cooper, Dade, Dallas, Daviess, De Kalb, Douglas, Gentry, Greene, Grundy, Harrison, Henry, Hickory, Holt,Howard, Howell, Jackson, Jasper, Johnson, Laclede, Lafayette, Lawrence, Livingston, McDonald, Mercer, Miller, Moniteau, Morgan, Newton, Nodaway, Oregon, Osage, Ozark, Pettis, Platte, Polk, Pulaski, Putnam, Ray, Saline, St. Clair, Sullivan, Taney, Texas,Vernon, Webster, Worth, Wright.

Indexing/Storage: Cases are indexed by debtor and creditors as well as by case number. New cases are available in the index 24 hours after filing date. A computer index is maintained. Older records are indexed on microfiche. Open records are located at this court. District wide searches are available from June 1989 from this division.

Fee & Payment: The fee is $20.00 per item (one party name or case number). Payment may be made by money order, cashier check, personal check. Prepayment is required. Payee: Clerk, US Bankruptcy Court. Certification fee: $7.00 per document. Copy fee: $.50 per page. You are allowed to make your own copies. These copies cost $.10 per page. There is no search fee for in person searchers.

Phone Search: Use VCIS for docket information. In addition to numbers given, call 816-426-2913 for information on cases closed prior to October 1995. An automated voice case information service (VCIS) is available. Call VCIS at 888-205-2527 or 816-426-5822.

Mail Search: Always enclose a stamped self addressed envelope.

In Person: In person searching is available.

PACER: Sign-up number is 800-676-6856. Access fee is. New records are available online after. PACER is available online at http://pacer.mowb.uscourts.gov/bc/index.html.

Electronic Filing: Electronic filing information is available online at https://ecf.mowb.uscourts.gov

Missouri County Courts

Court	Jurisdiction	No. of Courts	How Organized
Circuit Courts*	General	115	45 Circuits
Associate Circuit Courts*	Limited	114	45 Circuits
Combined Courts*		7	
Probate Courts*	Probate	5	
Municipal Courts	Municipal	406	
Family Courts	Special	8	

* Profiled in this Sourcebook.

Court	CIVIL								
	Tort	Contract	Real Estate	Min. Claim	Max. Claim	Small Claims	Estate	Eviction	Domestic Relations
Circuit Courts*	X	X	X	$25,000	No Max				X
Associate Circuit Courts*	X	X	X	$0	$25,000	$3000		X	
Municipal Courts									
Probate Courts*							X		
Family Courts									X

Court	CRIMINAL				
	Felony	Misdemeanor	DWI/DUI	Preliminary Hearing	Juvenile
Circuit Courts*	X				X
Associate Circuit Courts*		X	X	X	
Probate Courts*					
Family Courts					X

ADMINISTRATION State Court Administrator, 2112 Industrial Dr., PO Box 104480, Jefferson City, MO, 65109; 573-751-4377, Fax: 573-751-5540. www.osca.state.mo.us

COURT STRUCTURE The Circuit Court is the court of general jurisdiction. There are 45 circuits comprised of 114 county circuit courts and one independent city court. There are also Associate Circuit Courts with limited jurisdiction and some counties have Combined Courts. Municipal Courts only have jurisdiction over traffic and ordinance violations.

ONLINE ACCESS Available at http://casenet.osca.state.mo.us/casenet is Casenet, a limited but growing online system. The system includes 27 counties (with 16 more projected) as well as the Eastern, Western, and Southern Appellate Courts, the Supreme Court, and Fine Collection Center. Cases can be searched case number, filing date, or litigant name.

ADDITIONAL INFORMATION While the Missouri State Statutes set the Civil Case limit at $25,000 for the Associate Courts, and over $25,000 for the Circuit Courts, a great many Missouri County Courts have adopted their own Local Court Rules regarding civil cases and the monetary limits. Presumably, Local Court's Rules are setup to allow the county to choose which court - Circuit or Associate - to send a case. This may depend on the court's case load, but generally, the cases are assigned more by "the nature of the case" and less by the monetary amount involved. Often, Local Court Rules are found where both the Circuit and the Associate Court are located in the same building, or share the same offices and perhaps the same phones. A solution for court record searches is to use this source to find a telephone number of a County's Court Clerk, and call to determine the court location of the case.

Adair County

Circuit Court PO Box 690, Kirksville, MO 63501; 660-665-2552; Fax: 660-665-3420. Hours: 8AM-5PM *Felony, Misdemeanor, Civil Actions Over $45,000.*

Civil Records: Access: Fax, mail, in person. Only the court performs in person searches; visitors may not. No search fee. Required to search: name, years to search. Civil cases indexed by defendant, plaintiff. Civil records on computer since 1991, prior on index cards.

Criminal Records: Access: In person only. Visitors must perform in person searches for themselves. No search fee. Required to search: name, years to search. Criminal records on computer since 1991, prior on index cards. All written requests referred to State Highway Patrol.

General Information: No juvenile, mental, expunged, sealed, dismissed or suspended records released. Turnaround time 2 weeks. Fax notes: $.50 per page. No fee for faxing results to 800 number. Copy fee: $.10 per page. Certification fee: $1.00. Fee payee: Circuit Clerk. Personal checks accepted. Prepayment is required.

Associate Circuit Court Courthouse, Kirksville, MO 63501; 660-665-3877; Fax: 660-785-3222. Hours: 8AM-5PM (CST). *Misdemeanor, Civil Actions Under $25,000, Eviction, Small Claims, Probate.*

Civil Records: Access: Phone, fax, mail, in person. Only the court performs in person searches; visitors may not. No search fee. Required to search: name, years to search. Civil cases indexed by defendant, plaintiff. Civil records on computer back to 1990; probate records on microfilm since 1840.

Criminal Records: Access: Phone, fax, mail, in person. Only the court performs in person searches; visitors may not. No search fee. Required to search: name, years to search, DOB, SSN. Criminal records on computer back to 1990; prior records in files. Signed release required for closed cases.

General Information: No juvenile, mental, expunged, sealed, dismissed or suspended imposition of case records released. SASE required. Turnaround time 1 day. Fax notes: $1.50 per page. Copy fee: $.25 per page. Certification fee: No cert fee. Fee payee: Associate Circuit Court. Personal checks accepted. Prepayment is required.

Andrew County

Circuit Court PO Box 208 Division I, Savannah, MO 64485; 816-324-4221; Fax: 816-324-5667. Hours: 8AM-5PM (CST). *Felony, Misdemeanor, Civil Actions Over $45,000.*

Civil Records: Access: Phone, fax, mail, in person, online. Both court and visitors may perform in person searches. No search fee. Required to search: name, years to search. Civil cases indexed by defendant, plaintiff. Civil records on index cards since 1976, archived since 1850. Participates in the free state online court record system at http://casenet.osca.state.mo.us/casenet.

Criminal Records: Access: In person, online. Visitors must perform in person searches for themselves. No search fee. Required to search: name, years to search; also helpful: DOB. Criminal records on computer since mid-1993. Online access to criminal records is the same as civil.

General Information: No juvenile, mental, expunged, sealed, dismissed or suspended imposition of sentence records released. Turnaround time 1-2 days. Copy fee: $.25 per page. Certification fee: $2.50. Fee payee: Andrew County Circuit Clerk. Personal checks accepted. Prepayment is required.

Associate Circuit Court PO Box 49, Savannah, MO 64485; 816-324-3921; Fax: 816-324-5667. Hours: 8AM-5PM (CST). *Misdemeanor, Civil Actions Under $45,000, Eviction, Small Claims, Probate.*

Civil Records: Access: Mail, in person, online. Both court and visitors may perform in person searches. No search fee. Required to search: name, years to search. Civil cases indexed by defendant, plaintiff. Civil records on card file, archived from 1950. Participates in the free state online court record system at http://casenet.osca.state.mo.us/casenet.

Criminal Records: Access: Mail, in person, online. Both court and visitors may perform in person searches. No search fee. Required to search: name, years to search. Criminal records on computer since mid-1993. Online access to criminal records is the same as civil.

General Information: No juvenile, mental, expunged, sealed, dismissed or suspended imposition of sentence records released. SASE required. Turnaround time varies. Copy fee: $.50 per page. Certification fee: $2.50 plus additional pages for $.50 each. Fee payee: Associate Circuit Court. Personal checks accepted. Prepayment is required.

Atchison County

Circuit Court PO Box 280, Rock Port, MO 64482; 660-744-2707; Fax: 660-744-5705. Hours: 8:30AM-4:30PM (CST). *Felony, Misdemeanor, Civil Actions Over $25,000.*

www.mocourts.org

Civil Records: Access: Mail, in person. Both court and visitors may perform in person searches. No search fee. Required to search: name, years to search. Civil cases indexed by defendant, plaintiff. Civil records on index books, and archived from 1845.

Criminal Records: Access: Mail, in person. Both court and visitors may perform in person searches. Search fee: $4.00 per name. Required to search: name, years to search. Criminal records on index books, and archived from 1845.

General Information: No juvenile, mental, expunged, sealed, dismissed or suspended imposition of sentence records released. Turnaround time 1 day. Copy fee: $1.00 per page. Certification fee: $1.00. Fee payee: Circuit Clerk. Personal checks accepted. Prepayment is required.

Associate Division PO Box 187, Rock Port, MO 64482; 660-744-2700; Fax: 660-744-5705. Hours: 8AM-4:30PM (CST). *Misdemeanor, Civil Actions Under $25,000, Eviction, Small Claims, Probate.*

Civil Records: Access: Fax, mail, in person. Both court and visitors may perform in person searches. Search fee: $4.00 per name. Required to search: name, years to search; also helpful: address. Civil cases indexed by defendant, plaintiff. Civil records on books and cardex system, archived since 1845.

Criminal Records: Access: Fax, mail, in person. Both court and visitors may perform in person searches. Search fee: $4.00 per name. Required to search: name, years to search; also helpful: address, DOB, SSN, offense. Criminal records on computer since mid 1980s; prior on books and cardex system.

General Information: No juvenile, mental, expunged, sealed, dismissed or suspended imposition of sentence records released. SASE required. Turnaround time 7 days. Fax notes: $2.00 per page. Copy fee: $1.00 per page. Certification fee: $1.50. Fee payee: Circuit Court Division II. Personal checks accepted. Prepayment is required.

Audrain County

Circuit Court Courthouse, 101 N Jefferson, Mexico, MO 65265; 573-473-5840; Fax: 573-581-3237. Hours: 8AM-5PM (CST). *Felony, Misdemeanor, Civil Actions Over $25,000.*

www.audrain-county.org

Civil Records: Access: In person only. Visitors must perform in person searches for themselves. No search fee. Required to search: name, years to search. Civil cases indexed by defendant, plaintiff. Civil records on computer since 8/92, prior on index cards, older records archived at Genealogy Club in Mexico, MO.

Criminal Records: Access: In person only. Visitors must perform in person searches for themselves. No search fee. Required to search: name, years to search; also SSN, case number. Criminal records on computer since 8/92, stored for 25 years on site then archived (back to 1800s).

General Information: Public Access terminal is available. No juvenile, mental, expunged, sealed, dismissed or suspended imposition of sentence records released. Fax notes: Fee to fax results is $5.00. Copy fee: $.25 per page. Certification fee: $1.50 for first 2 pages; $.25 each add'l. Fee payee: Circuit Clerk. Prepayment is required.

Associate Circuit Court Courthouse, 101 N Jefferson, Rm 205, Mexico, MO 65265; 573-473-5850; Probate phone: 573-473-5854; Fax: 573-581-3237. Hours: 8AM-5PM (CST). *Misdemeanor, Civil Actions Under $25,000, Eviction, Small Claims, Probate.*

Civil Records: Access: Mail, in person. Both court and visitors may perform in person searches. No search fee. Required to search: name, years to search. Civil cases indexed by defendant, plaintiff. Civil records on computer since 9/93, prior on cards, archived to 1800s.

Criminal Records: Access: Mail, in person. Only the court performs in person searches; visitors may not. No search fee. Required to search: name, years to search, DOB, SSN, signed release. Criminal records on computer since 9/93, prior on cards, archived to 1800s.

General Information: No juvenile, mental, expunged, sealed, dismissed or suspended imposition of sentence records released. Turnaround time 1 week. Copy fee: $.15 per page. Certification fee: $1.50 first page, $1.00 each additional. Fee payee: Circuit Court Division II. Only cashiers checks and money orders accepted. Prepayment is required.

Barry County

Circuit Court Barry County Courthouse, 700 Main, Ste 1, Cassville, MO 65625; 417-847-2361. Hours: 8AM-4PM (CST). *Felony, Misdemeanor, Civil Actions Over $25,000.*

Civil Records: Access: Mail, in person. Both court and visitors may perform in person searches. Search fee: $4.00 per name. Required to search: name, years to search. Civil cases indexed by defendant, plaintiff. Civil records on index cards, archived since mid-1800s.

Criminal Records: Access: Mail, in person. Both court and visitors may perform in person searches. Search fee: $4.00 per name. Required to search: name, years to search. Criminal records on index cards, archived since mid-1800s.

General Information: No juvenile, mental expunged, sealed, dismissed or suspended imposition of sentence records released. SASE required. Turnaround time 1-3 days. Copy fee: $.25 per page. Certification fee: $1.00. Fee payee: Circuit Clerk. Personal checks accepted. Prepayment is required.

Associate Circuit Court Barry County Courthouse, Suite 8, Cassville, MO 65625; Civil phone: 417-847-2127; Criminal phone: 417-847-6557. Hours: 7:30AM-4PM (CST). *Misdemeanor, Civil Actions Under $25,000, Eviction, Small Claims, Probate.*

Civil Records: Access: Mail, in person. Both court and visitors may perform in person searches. No search fee. Required to search: name, years to search. Civil cases indexed by defendant, plaintiff. Civil records on index cards since 1982; prior records on index books to mid 1800s.

Criminal Records: Access: Mail, in person. Both court and visitors may perform in person searches. No search fee. Required to search: name, years to search. Criminal records on computer since 1996; prior records on index books to mid 1800s.

General Information: No juvenile, mental, expunged, sealed, dismissed or suspended imposition of sentence records released. Turnaround time 1-3 days. Copy fee: $.50 per page. Certification fee: No cert fee. Fee payee: Barry County. Personal checks accepted. Prepayment is required.

Barton County

Circuit & Associate Court Courthouse, 1007 Broadway, Lamar, MO 64759; 417-682-2444/5754; Fax: 417-682-2960. Hours: 8AM-4:30PM *Felony, Misdemeanor, Civil, Eviction, Small Claims, Probate.*

Civil Records: Access: Mail, online, in person. Both court and visitors may perform in person searches. No search fee. Required to search: name, years to search; also helpful: address. Civil cases indexed by defendant, plaintiff. Civil records on computer since 1993; prior from 1865 on books or archived. Participates in the free state online court record system at http://casenet.osca.state.mo.us/casenet.

Criminal Records: Access: Mail, online, in person. Both court and visitors may perform in person searches. No search fee. Required to search: name, years to search; also helpful: address, DOB, SSN. Criminal records on computer since 1993; prior from 1865 on books or archived. Online access to criminal records is the same as civil.

General Information: No juvenile, mental, expunged, dismissed, or suspended imposition of sentence records released. SASE required. Turnaround time 1 week. Fax notes: Fee to fax is $2.00 per document. Copy fee: $1.00 per page. Certification fee: $1.50. Fee payee: Circuit Court. Personal checks accepted. Prepayment is required.

Bates County

Circuit Court Bates County Courthouse, Butler, MO 64730; 660-679-5171; Fax: 660-679-4446. Hours: 8AM-4:30PM (CST). *Felony, Misdemeanor, Civil Actions Over $25,000.*

Civil Records: Access: Fax, mail, in person. Both court and visitors may perform in person searches. No search fee. Required to search: name, years to search. Civil cases indexed by defendant, plaintiff. Civil records on computer since 9/1/92, prior on books since 1858.

Criminal Records: Access: Fax, mail, in person. Both court and visitors may perform in person searches. No search fee. Required to search: name, years to search. Criminal records on computer since 9/1/92, prior on books since 1858.

General Information: No juvenile, mental, expunged, dismissed, or suspended imposition of sentence records released. SASE required. Turnaround time varies. Fax notes: No fee to fax results. Copy fee: $.25 per page. Certification fee: $1.50. Fee payee: Circuit Court. Only cashiers checks and money orders accepted. Prepayment is required.

Associate Circuit Court Courthouse, Butler, MO 64730; 660-679-3311. Hours: 8:30AM-4PM (CST). *Misdemeanor, Civil Actions Under $25,000, Eviction, Small Claims, Probate.*

Civil Records: Access: Mail, in person. Both court and visitors may perform in person searches. No search fee. Required to search: name, years to search. Civil cases indexed by defendant, plaintiff. Civil records on index cards (unsure of starting date).

Criminal Records: Access: Mail, in person. Only the court performs in person searches; visitors may not. No search fee. Required to search: name, years to search, DOB; also helpful: SSN. Criminal records on computer since 1992, prior on index cards.

General Information: No juvenile, mental, expunged, dismissed, or suspended imposition of sentence records released. SASE required. Turnaround time 1 week. Copy fee: $.50 per page. Certification fee: $1.50. Fee payee: Associate Circuit Court. Only cashiers checks and money orders accepted.

Benton County

Circuit Court PO Box 37, Warsaw, MO 65355; 660-438-7712; Fax: 660-438-5755. Hours: 8AM-4:30PM (CST). *Felony, Misdemeanor, Civil Actions Over $25,000.*

www.positech.net/~dcourt

Civil Records: Access: In person only. Visitors must perform in person searches for themselves. No search fee. Required to search: name, years to search. Civil cases indexed by defendant, plaintiff. Civil records on computer since 1993, prior on index cards since 1800. Court dockets and judgments from the circuit clerk's web site are available free at http://208.154.254.51:5061.

Criminal Records: Access: In person only. Visitors must perform in person searches for themselves. No search fee. Required to search: name, years to search. Criminal records on computer since 1993, prior on index cards since 1800. The court will only indicate if subject is on probation or has open case. For criminal searches contact Jefferson City Highway Patrol.

General Information: No juvenile, mental, expunged, dismissed, or suspended imposition of sentence records released. Copy fee: $1.00 for first page, $.25 each add'l. Certification fee: $2.50. Fee payee: Clerk of Circuit Court. Personal checks accepted. Prepayment is required.

Associate Circuit Court PO Box 37, Warsaw, MO 65355-0037; 660-438-6231. Hours: 8AM-4:30PM (CST). *Misdemeanor, Civil Actions Under $25,000, Eviction, Small Claims, Probate.*

www.positech.net/~dcourt

Civil Records: Access: Mail, in person. Visitors must perform in person searches for themselves. No search fee. Required to search: name, years to search. Civil cases indexed by defendant, plaintiff. Civil records on computer since 1994, in case files and judgment index cards prior. Will do searches as time permits.

Criminal Records: Access: Mail, in person. Visitors must perform in person searches for themselves. No search fee. Required to search: name, years to search. Criminal records on computer since 1994. Will do searches only if time permits.

General Information: No juvenile, mental, expunged, dismissed, or suspended imposition of sentence records released. Copy fee: $.50 per page. Certification fee: $1.50. Fee payee: Associate Circuit Court. Personal checks accepted. Prepayment is required.

Bollinger County

Circuit Court PO Box 949, Marble Hill, MO 63764; 573-238-2710; Fax: 573-238-2773. Hours: 8AM-4PM (CST). *Felony, Misdemeanor, Civil Actions Over $25,000.*

Civil Records: Access: Mail, in person. Only the court performs in person searches; visitors may not. No search fee. Required to search: name, years to search. Civil cases indexed by defendant, plaintiff. Civil records on computer to 1990, prior on index cards 1976-1990.

Criminal Records: Access: Mail, in person. Only the court performs in person searches; visitors may not. No search fee. Required to search: name, years to search. Criminal records on computer since 1990, prior on index cards 1976-1990.

General Information: No juvenile, mental, expunged, dismissed, or suspended imposition of sentence records released. SASE required. Turnaround time 1 day to 1 week. Copy fee: $1.00 for first page, $.50 each add'l. Certification fee: $2.00. Fee payee: Circuit Clerk and Recorder's Office. Personal checks accepted. Prepayment is required.

Associate Circuit Court PO Box 1040, Marble Hill, MO 63764-1040; 573-238-2730; Fax: 573-238-4511. Hours: 8AM-4PM *Misdemeanor, Civil Actions Under $25,000, Eviction, Small Claims, Probate.*

Civil Records: Access: In person, online. Visitors must perform in person searches for themselves. No search fee. Required to search: name, years to search. Civil cases indexed by defendant, plaintiff. Civil records on computer back to 1995, prior on books, archived to 1890. Participates in the free state online Banner court record system at http://casenet.osca.state.mo.us/casenet.

Criminal Records: Access: In person, online. Visitors must perform in person searches for themselves. No search fee. Required to search: name, years to search. Criminal records on computer back to 1995, prior on books, archived to 1890. Online access to criminal records is the same as civil.

General Information: Public Access terminal is available. No juvenile, mental, expunged, dismissed, or suspended imposition of sentence records released. Copy fee: $1.00 per page. Certification fee: $1.50. Fee payee: Circuit Court Division IV. Personal checks accepted. Prepayment is required.

Boone County

Circuit and Associate Court 705 E Walnut, Columbia, MO 65201; 573-886-4000; Fax: 573-886-4044. Hours: 8AM-5PM (CST). *Felony, Misdemeanor, Civil, Eviction, Small Claims, Probate.*

Civil Records: Access: Phone, mail, online, in person. Both court and visitors may perform in person searches. No search fee. Required to search: name, years to search. Civil cases indexed by defendant, plaintiff. Civil records on computer for recent cases, others on books. Participates in the free state online court record system at http://casenet.osca.state.mo.us/casenet.

Criminal Records: Access: Online, in person. Visitors must perform in person searches for themselves. No search fee. Required to search: name, years to search, DOB. Criminal records on computer for recent cases, others on books. Online access to criminal records is the same as civil.

General Information: Public Access terminal is available. No juvenile, mental, paternity, expunged, dismissed, or suspended imposition of sentence records released. SASE required. Turnaround time varies. Copy fee: $.25 per page. Certification fee: $1.00. Fee payee: Boone County Circuit Clerk. Business checks accepted. Prepayment is required.

Buchanan County

Circuit & Associate Court 411 Jules St, Rm 331, St Joseph, MO 64501; 816-271-1462; Fax: 816-271-1538. Hours: 8AM-5PM (CST). *Felony, Misdemeanor, Civil, Eviction, Small Claims.*

Civil Records: Access: In person, online. Visitors must perform in person searches for themselves. No search fee. Required to search: name, years to search. Civil cases indexed by defendant, plaintiff. Civil records on computer since 2/92, on index cards since 1976, prior archived. Participates in the free state online court record system at http://casenet.osca.state.mo.us/casenet.

Criminal Records: Access: In person, online. Visitors must perform in person searches for themselves. No search fee. Required to search: name, years to search. Criminal records on computer since 2/92, on index cards since 1976, prior archived. Online access to criminal records is the same as civil. County Case.net records go back to 1992.

General Information: Public Access terminal is available. No juvenile, mental, expunged, dismissed, or suspended imposition of sentence records released. Copy fee: $.25 per page. Certification fee: $2.50. Fee payee: Buchanan Circuit Court. Personal checks accepted.

Probate Court Buchanan County Courthouse, 411 Jules St, Room 333, St Joseph, MO 64501; 816-271-1477; Fax: 816-271-1538. Hours: 8AM-5PM *Probate.*

Butler County

Circuit Court Courthouse, Poplar Bluff, MO 63901; 573-686-8082; Fax: 573-686-8094. 7:30AM-4PM *Felony, Misdemeanor, Civil Actions Over $45,000.*

Civil Records: Access: Fax, mail, in person. Both court and visitors may perform in person searches. Search fee: $1.00 per name per year. Required to search: name, years to search. Civil cases indexed by defendant, plaintiff. Civil records on computer since 9/91, prior on cards and books since 1865.

Criminal Records: Access: Fax, mail, in person. Both court and visitors may perform in person searches. Search fee: $1.00 per name per year. Required to search: name, years to search. Criminal records on computer since 9/91, prior on cards and books since 1865.

General Information: Public Access terminal is available. No juvenile, mental, expunged, dismissed, or suspended imposition of sentence records released. SASE not required. Turnaround time 1-2 days. Fax notes: $1.00 per page. Copy fee: $.25 per page. Certification fee: $2.50. Fee payee: Clerk of Circuit Court. Business checks accepted. Prepayment required.

Associate Circuit Court Courthouse, Poplar Bluff, MO 63901; 573-686-8087; Fax: 573-686-8093. Hours: 7:30AM-4PM *Misdemeanor, Civil Actions Under $45,000, Eviction, Small Claims, Probate.*

Civil Records: Access: Fax, mail, in person. Both court and visitors may perform in person searches. No search fee. Required to search: name, years to search. Civil cases indexed by defendant, plaintiff. Civil records on cards since 1976, and index books since 1800s; computer since.

Criminal Records: Access: Fax, mail, in person. Only the court performs in person searches; visitors may not. No search fee. Required to search: name, years to search, signed release. Criminal records on cards since 1976, and index books since 1800s, computer since.

General Information: No juvenile, mental, expunged, dismissed, or suspended imposition of sentence records released. SASE required. Turnaround time varies. Fax notes: Fee to fax results is $.25 per page. Copy fee: $.25 per page. Certification fee: $2.50. Fee payee: Circuit Court Division II. Business checks accepted. Prepayment is required.

Caldwell County

Circuit Court PO Box 86, Kingston, MO 64650; 816-586-2581; Fax: 816-586-2705. Hours: 8:30AM-4:30PM (CST). *Felony, Misdemeanor, Civil Actions Over $45,000.*

Civil Records: Access: Phone, mail, in person. Both court and visitors may perform in person searches. No search fee. Required to search: name, years to search. Civil cases indexed by defendant, plaintiff. Civil records archived since 1860; on computer back to 1995.

Criminal Records: Access: Phone, mail, in person. Both court and visitors may perform in person searches. No search fee. Required to search: name, years to search. Criminal records archived since 1860; on computer back to 1995.

General Information: No juvenile, mental, expunged, dismissed, or suspended imposition of sentence records released. SASE required. Turnaround time 3 days, phone turnaround time 1 day. Copy fee: $1.00 per page. Certification fee: $.50 per page. Fee payee: Circuit Clerk. Personal checks accepted. Prepayment required.

Associate Circuit Court PO Box 5, Kingston, MO 64650; 816-586-2771; Fax: 816-586-2333. Hours: 8AM-4:30PM (CST). *Misdemeanor, Civil Actions Under $45,000, Eviction, Small Claims, Probate.*

Civil Records: Access: In person only. Visitors must perform in person searches for themselves. No search fee. Required to search: name, years to search. Civil cases indexed by defendant, plaintiff. Civil records on computer since 1992; prior records on index cards back to 1970s.

Criminal Records: Access: In person only. Visitors must perform in person searches for themselves. No search fee. Required to search: name, years to search; also helpful: DOB, SSN. Criminal records on computer since 1992; prior records on index cards back to 1970s.

General Information: No juvenile, mental, expunged, dismissed, or suspended imposition of sentence records released. Copy fee: $.25 per page. Legal Size Copy Fee: $.50 per page. Certification fee: $1.50. Fee payee: Associate Circuit Court. Only cashiers checks and money orders accepted. Prepayment is required.

Callaway County

Circuit Court 10 E 5th St, Fulton, MO 65251; 573-642-0780; Fax: 573-642-0700. Hours: 8AM-5PM *Felony, Misdemeanor, Civil Actions Over $25,000.*

www.osca.state.mo.us

Civil Records: Access: Fax, mail, in person, online. Both court and visitors may perform in person searches. Court will only perform searches as time permits No search fee. Required to search: name, years to search. Civil cases indexed by defendant, plaintiff. Civil records on index books and cards since 1821. Participates in the free state online court record system at http://casenet.osca.state.mo.us/casenet.

Criminal Records: Access: In person, online. Visitors must perform in person searches for themselves. No search fee. Required to search: name, years to search; also helpful: DOB, SSN. Criminal records on computer since 1993, prior on index books and cards since 1821. Online access to criminal records is the same as civil.

General Information: Public Access terminal is available. No juvenile, mental, expunged, dismissed, or suspended imposition of sentence records released. SASE not required. Turnaround time 3 days. Fax notes: $.25 per page. Copy fee: $.25 per page. Certification fee: $1.00. Fee payee: Circuit Clerk. Business checks accepted. Attorney & Law Firm checks accepted.

Associate Circuit Court Courthouse, Fulton, MO 65251; 573-642-0777; Fax: 573-642-0700. Hours: 8AM-5PM (CST). *Misdemeanor, Civil Actions Under $25,000, Eviction, Small Claims, Probate.*

Civil Records: Access: Mail, in person, online. Both court and visitors may perform in person searches. No search fee. Required to search: name, years to search. Civil cases indexed by defendant, plaintiff. Civil records on computer since 1988, archived since 1821. Participates in the free state online court record system at http://casenet.osca.state.mo.us/casenet.

Criminal Records: Access: Mail, in person, online. Both court and visitors may perform in person searches. No search fee. Required to search: name, years to search; also helpful: DOB. Criminal records on computer since 1989, prior on index cards since 1979. Online access to criminal records is the same as civil.

General Information: No juvenile, mental, expunged, dismissed, or suspended imposition of sentence records released. SASE requested. Turnaround time 2 days. No copy fee. Certification fee: No cert fee.

Camden County

Circuit Court 1 Court Circle, Camdenton, MO 65020; 573-346-4440 X289; Fax: 573-346-5422. Hours: 8:30AM-4:30PM (CST). *Felony, Misdemeanor, Civil Actions Over $25,000.*

Civil Records: Access: Mail, in person. Both court and visitors may perform in person searches. No search fee. Required to search: name, years to search. Civil cases indexed by defendant, plaintiff. Civil records on computer since 1989, on index cards from 1965 to 1989, prior on index books since 1903.

Criminal Records: Access: Mail, in person. Both court and visitors may perform in person searches. No search fee. Required to search: name, years to search; also helpful: DOB, SSN. Criminal records on computer since 1989, on index cards from 1965 to 1989, prior on index books since 1903.

General Information: No juvenile, mental, expunged, dismissed, or suspended imposition of sentence records released. SASE required. Turnaround time 7 days. No copy fee. Certification fee: No cert fee. Only cashiers checks and money orders accepted.

Associate Circuit Court 1 Court Circle #8, Camdenton, MO 65020; 573-346-4440; Civil phone: X242; Criminal phone: X243; Fax: 573-346-5422. Hours: 8:00AM-5:00PM *Misdemeanor, Civil Actions Under $25,000, Eviction, Small Claims, Probate.*

Civil Records: Access: In person only. Visitors must perform in person searches for themselves. No search fee. Required to search: name, years to search. Civil cases indexed by defendant, plaintiff. Civil records on index cards since 1976; on computer back to 1989.

Criminal Records: Access: Mail, in person. Only the court performs in person searches; visitors may not. No search fee. Required to search: name, years to search, DOB; also helpful: SSN. Criminal records on computer back to 1989, prior on index cards since 1980.

General Information: Public Access terminal is available. No juvenile, mental, expunged, dismissed, or suspended imposition of sentence records released. SASE required. Turnaround time 1-2 weeks. No copy fee. Certification: No cert fee. Personal checks accepted.

Cape Girardeau County

Circuit & Associate Circuit Court - Civil Division 44 N Lorimier, PO Box 2047, Cape Girardeau, MO 63702; 573-335-8253; Fax: 573-331-2565. Hours: 8AM-4:30PM (CST). *Civil.*

Civil Records: Access: Mail, in person. Both court and visitors may perform in person searches. No search fee. Required to search: name, years to search. Civil cases indexed by defendant, plaintiff. Civil records on computer since 1994, prior on index cards since 10/75.

General Information: Public Access terminal is available. No juvenile, mental, expunged, dismissed, or suspended imposition of sentence, paternity, cases where one party on AFDC records released. SASE required. Turnaround time 1 week. Copy fee: $1.00 for first page, $.50 each add'l. Certification fee: $1.00. Fee payee: Circuit Clerk. Personal checks accepted. Prepayment is required.

Circuit Court - Criminal Division I & II 100
Court St, Jackson, MO 63755; 573-243-8446 (misdemeanors); Criminal phone: 573-243-1755 (felo.); Fax: 573-204-2367. Hours: 8AM-4:30PM (CST). *Felony, Misdemeanor.*

Criminal Records: Access: Mail, in person. Both court and visitors may perform in person searches. Search fee: $10.00 per name. Required to search: name, years to search. Criminal records on computer since 1991, prior on books.
General Information: No juvenile, mental, expunged, dismissed, or suspended imposition of sentence records released. SASE required. Turnaround time 1 week. Copy fee: $1.00 for first page, $.50 each add'l. Certification fee: $1.00. Fee payee: Circuit Clerk. Personal checks accepted. Prepayment is required.

Carroll County

Circuit Court PO Box 245, Carrollton, MO 64633; 660-542-1466; Fax: 660-542-1444. Hours: 8:30AM-4:30PM (CST). *Felony, Misdemeanor, Civil Actions Over $25,000.*

Civil Records: Access: Fax, mail, in person. Both court and visitors may perform in person searches. No search fee. Required to search: name, years to search. Civil cases indexed by defendant, plaintiff. Civil records on books since 1833.
Criminal Records: Access: Fax, mail, in person. Both court and visitors may perform in person searches. No search fee. Required to search: name, years to search. Criminal records on books since 1833.
General Information: No juvenile, mental, expunged, dismissed, or suspended imposition of sentence records released. SASE not required. Turnaround time varies. Fax notes: No fee to fax results. No copy fee. Certification fee: $2.00. Fee payee: Circuit Clerk. Personal checks accepted. Prepayment is required.

Associate Circuit Court Courthouse, 8 S Main, Suite 1, Carrollton, MO 64633; 660-542-1818; Fax: 660-542-1877. Hours: 8:30AM-4:30PM (CST). *Misdemeanor, Civil Actions Under $25,000, Eviction, Small Claims, Probate.*

Civil Records: Access: Mail, in person. Only the court performs in person searches; visitors may not. No search fee. Required to search: name, years to search, address. Civil cases indexed by defendant, plaintiff. Civil records on index cards since 1982.
Criminal Records: Access: Mail, in person. Only the court performs in person searches; visitors may not. No search fee. Required to search: name, years to search, address, DOB. Criminal records on index cards to 1982.
General Information: No juvenile, mental, expunged, dismissed, or suspended imposition of sentence records released. SASE required. Turnaround time 2-3 days. Copy fee: $.35 per page. Certification fee: $2.50. Fee payee: Associate Circuit Court. Only cashiers checks and money orders accepted. Prepayment is required.

Carter County

Circuit Court PO Box 578, Van Buren, MO 63965; 573-323-4513; Fax: 573-323-4885. Hours: 8AM-4PM (CST). *Felony, Misdemeanor, Civil Actions Over $45,000.*

Civil Records: Access: Phone, mail, in person, online. Only the court performs in person searches; visitors may not. No search fee. Required to search: name, years to search. Civil cases indexed by defendant, plaintiff. Civil records on computer since 1988, on index cards since 1988, archived since late-1800s. Participates in the free state online court record system at http://casenet.osca.state.mo.us/casenet.

Criminal Records: Access: Phone, mail, in person, online. Only the court performs in person searches; visitors may not. No search fee. Required to search: name, years to search. Criminal records on computer since 1988, on index cards since 1988, archived since late-1800s. Online access to criminal records is the same as civil.
General Information: No juvenile, mental, paternity, expunged, dismissed, or suspended imposition of sentence records released. SASE required. Turnaround time 1 day. Copy fee: $.25 per page. Certification fee: $1.00. Payee: Circuit Clerk. Personal checks accepted.

Associate Circuit Court PO Box 328, Van Buren, MO 63965; 573-323-4344; Fax: 573-323-8914. Hours: 8AM-4PM (CST). *Misdemeanor, Civil Actions Under $45,000, Eviction, Small Claims, Probate.*

Civil Records: Access: Phone, fax, mail, in person, online. Only the court performs in person searches; visitors may not. Search fee: $5.00 per name. Required to search: name, years to search. Civil cases indexed by defendant, plaintiff. Civil records on index since 1979, prior on docket sheets. Participates in the free state online court record system at http://casenet.osca.state.mo.us/casenet.
Criminal Records: Access: Phone, fax, mail, in person, online. Only the court performs in person searches; visitors may not. Search fee: $5.00 per name. Required to search: name, years to search. Criminal records on index since 1979, prior on docket sheets. Online access to criminal records is the same as civil.
General Information: No juvenile, mental, expunged, dismissed, or suspended imposition of sentence records released. SASE required. Turnaround time varies. Copy fee: $.25 per page. Certification fee: No cert fee. Fee payee: Circuit Court Division II. Personal checks accepted. Prepayment is required.

Cass County

Circuit Court 102 E Wall, Harrisonville, MO 64701; 816-380-5100 X1525; Fax: 816-380-5798. Hours: 8AM-4:30PM (CST). *Felony, Misdemeanor, Civil Actions Over $45,000.*

Civil Records: Access: Phone, mail, in person. Both court and visitors may perform in person searches. No search fee. Required to search: name, years to search. Civil cases indexed by defendant, plaintiff. Civil records on computer since 1992, on index cards since 1976, prior on judgment books since 1800s.
Criminal Records: Access: Phone, mail, in person. Both court and visitors may perform in person searches. No search fee. Required to search: name, years to search. Criminal records on computer since 1992, on index cards to 1976, prior on judgment books to 1800s.
General Information: Public Access terminal is available. No juvenile, mental, expunged, dismissed, or suspended imposition of sentence records released. SASE required. Turnaround time 1 week. Copy fee: $.50 per page. Certification fee: $1.50. Fee payee: Cass County Circuit Clerk. Personal checks accepted. Prepayment is required.

Associate Circuit Court PO Box 384, Harrisonville, MO 64701; 816-380-8100; Fax: 816-380-8195. Hours: 8AM-4:30PM (CST). *Misdemeanor, Civil Actions Under $25,000, Eviction, Small Claims, Probate.*

Civil Records: Access: Mail, in person. Visitors must perform in person searches for themselves. No search fee. Required to search: name, years to search. Civil cases indexed by defendant, plaintiff. Civil records go back to 1960s; on index cards since 1983; on computer back to 1995.
Criminal Records: Access: Mail, in person. Visitors must perform in person searches for themselves. No search fee. Required to search: name, years to search,

signed release. Criminal records go back to 1960s; on index cards since 1983; on computer back to 1995.
General Information: Public Access terminal is available. No juvenile, mental, expunged, dismissed, or suspended imposition of sentence records released. SASE required. Turnaround time varies. Fax notes: Will not fax out. Copy fee: $1.00 per page. Certification fee: $2.00. Fee payee: Division III. Business checks accepted. Prepayment is required.

Probate Court 102 E Wall St, Harrisonville, MO 64701; 816-380-8217; Fax: 816-380-8215. Hours: 8AM-4:30PM (CST). *Probate.*

Cedar County

Circuit Court PO Box 665, Stockton, MO 65785; 417-276-6700; Fax: 417-276-5001. Hours: 8AM-4:30PM (CST). *Felony, Misdemeanor, Civil Actions Over $45,000.*

Civil Records: Access: Fax, mail, in person, online. Both court and visitors may perform in person searches. No search fee. Required to search: name, years to search. Civil cases indexed by defendant, plaintiff. Civil records on index cards since 1979, prior on docket books. Participates in the free state online court record system at http://casenet.osca.state.mo.us/casenet.
Criminal Records: Access: Fax, mail, in person. Both court and visitors may perform in person searches. No search fee. Required to search: name, years to search. Criminal records on index cards since 1979, prior on docket books.
General Information: No juvenile, mental, expunged, dismissed, or suspended imposition of sentence records released. Turnaround time varies. Fax notes: $1.00 per page. Copy fee: $1.00 per page. Certification fee: $3.00. Fee payee: Cedar County. Personal checks accepted. Prepayment is required.

Associate Circuit Court PO Box 665, Stockton, MO 65785; 417-276-6700; Fax: 417-276-5001. Hours: 8AM-4:30PM (CST). *Misdemeanor, Civil Actions Under $45,000, Eviction, Small Claims, Probate.*

Civil Records: Access: Mail, in person, online. Both court and visitors may perform in person searches. No search fee. Required to search: name, years to search. Civil cases indexed by defendant, plaintiff. Civil records archived since 1830. Participates in the free state online court record system at http://casenet.osca.state.mo.us/casenet.
Criminal Records: Access: Mail, in person. Only the court performs in person searches; visitors may not. No search fee. Required to search: name, years to search; also helpful: DOB. Criminal records archived since 1830.
General Information: No juvenile, mental, expunged, dismissed, or suspended imposition of sentence records released. SASE required. Turnaround time varies. Copy fee: $.25 per page. Certification fee: $1.50 plus $1.00 per page. Fee payee: Associate Circuit Court. Only cashiers checks and money orders accepted. Prepayment is required.

Chariton County

Circuit Court PO Box 112, Keytesville, MO 65261; 660-288-3602; Fax: 660-288-3763. Hours: 8:30AM-4:30PM (CST). *Felony, Misdemeanor, Civil Actions Over $25,000.*

Civil Records: Access: Fax, mail, in person. Both court and visitors may perform in person searches. Search fee: $4.00 per name. Required to search: name, years to search. Civil cases indexed by defendant, plaintiff. Civil records on index books since 1975, prior on docket books to 1827.
Criminal Records: Access: Fax, mail, in person. Both court and visitors may perform in person searches. Search fee: $4.00 per name. Required to search: name, years to search; also helpful: DOB, SSN. Criminal

records on index books since 1975, prior on docket books to 1827.

General Information: No juvenile, mental, expunged, dismissed, or suspended imposition of sentence records released. SASE required. Turnaround time same day. Fax notes: Fee to fax results is $1.00 per page. Copy fee: $1.00 per page. Certification fee: $1.50. Fee payee: Chariton County Circuit Clerk. Personal checks accepted.

Associate Circuit Court 306 South Cherry, Keytesville, MO 65261; 660-288-3271; Fax: 660-288-1511. 8AM-4:30PM *Misdemeanor, Civil Actions Under $25,000, Eviction, Small Claims, Probate.*

Civil Records: Access: Phone, fax, mail, in person. Both court and visitors may perform in person searches. No search fee. Required to search: name, years to search. Civil cases indexed by defendant, plaintiff. Civil records indexed on cards by year from 1977.

Criminal Records: Access: Phone, fax, mail, in person. Both court and visitors may perform in person searches. No search fee. Required to search: name, years to search; also helpful: DOB, SSN. Criminal records indexed on cards by year from 1977.

General Information: No juvenile, mental, expunged, dismissed, or suspended imposition of sentence records released. SASE required. Turnaround time 1 week, phone turnaround time 2 days. Copy fee: $.25 per page. Certification fee: $1.50. Fee payee: Associate Circuit Court or Probate Court (depending on search). Personal checks accepted. Fees may be billed.

Christian County

Circuit Court PO Box 278, Ozark, MO 65721; 417-581-6372; Fax: 417-581-0391. Hours: 8AM-4:30PM *Felony, Misdemeanor, Civil Actions Over $45,000.*

Civil Records: Access: Mail, in person. Both court and visitors may perform in person searches. Search fee: $6.00 per name. Required to search: name, years to search. Civil cases indexed by defendant, plaintiff. Civil records on computer since 9/97, pending cases indexed in card files. Old case card files back to 1979.

Criminal Records: Access: Mail, in person. Both court and visitors may perform in person searches. Search fee: $6.00 per name. Required to search: name, years to search. Criminal records on computer since 9/97, pending cases indexed in card files. Old case card files back to 1979.

General Information: No juvenile, mental, expunged, dismissed, or suspended imposition or execution of sentence records released. SASE required. Turnaround time 1 week. Copy fee: $.50 per page. Certification fee: $1.00. Fee payee: Christian County Circuit Clerk. Personal checks accepted. Prepayment is required.

Associate Circuit Court - Civil Division 1
100 W Church St, Rm 203, Ozark, MO 65721-6901; 417-581-2425. Hours: 8AM-4:30PM (CST). *Civil Actions Under $45,000, Eviction, Small Claims.*

Civil Records: Access: Phone, mail, in person. Both court and visitors may perform in person searches. No search fee. Required to search: name, years to search. Civil cases indexed by defendant. Civil records on computer since 07/91.

General Information: No juvenile, mental, expunged or dismissed records released. SASE required. Turnaround time 5 days, phone turnaround time immediate. Copy fee: $.25 per page. Certification fee: $1.50. Fee payee: Associate Division I. Personal checks accepted. Prepayment is required.

Associate Circuit Court - Criminal Division 2
100 W Church St, Rm 105, Ozark, MO 65721-6901; 417-581-4523; Fax: 417-581-1443. Hours: 8AM-4:30PM (CST). *Misdemeanor, Probate.*

Criminal Records: Access: Mail, fax, in person. Only the court performs in person searches; visitors may not.

No search fee. Required to search: name, years to search. Criminal records on computer since 1984; prior on index cards. Will accept phone requests from attorneys and law enforcement officials.

General Information: No juvenile, mental, expunged or dismissed records released. SASE required. Turnaround time 5 days. Copy fee: $.30 per page. Certification fee: $1.50. Fee payee: Associate Division 2. Prepayment is required.

Clark County

Circuit Court 111 E Court, Kahoka, MO 63445; 660-727-3292; Fax: 660-727-1051. Hours: 8AM-4PM (CST). *Felony, Misdemeanor, Civil Actions Over $45,000.*

Civil Records: Access: Phone, fax, mail, in person. Only the court performs in person searches; visitors may not. No search fee. Required to search: name, years to search. Civil cases indexed by defendant, plaintiff. Civil records on books since 1991, prior archived since 1836.

Criminal Records: Access: Phone, fax, mail, in person. Only the court performs in person searches; visitors may not. No search fee. Required to search: name, years to search. Criminal records on books since 1991, prior archived since 1836.

General Information: No juvenile, mental, expunged, dismissed, or suspended imposition of sentence records released. SASE required. Turnaround time 4 days. Fax notes: Fee to fax results is $1.00 per page. Copy fee: $.50 per page. Certification fee: $3.00. Fee payee: Clerk of Circuit Court. Personal checks accepted. Prepayment is required.

Associate Circuit Court 113 W Court, Kahoka, MO 63445; 660-727-3628; Fax: 660-727-2544. Hours: 8AM-4PM (CST). *Misdemeanor, Civil Actions Under $45,000, Eviction, Small Claims, Probate.*

Civil Records: Access: Mail, in person. Only the court performs in person searches; visitors may not. No search fee. Required to search: name, years to search. Civil cases indexed by defendant, plaintiff. Civil records on index cards, archived since 1836.

Criminal Records: Access: Mail, in person. Only the court performs in person searches; visitors may not. No search fee. Required to search: name, years to search. Criminal records on computer since 1988, prior archived since 1836.

General Information: No juvenile, mental, expunged, dismissed, or suspended imposition of sentence records released. SASE required. Turnaround time 1-10 days. Copy fee: $.25 per page. Certification fee: $2.50. Fee payee: Associate Circuit Court. Personal checks accepted. Prepayment is required.

Clay County

Circuit Court PO Box 218, Liberty, MO 64069-0218; 816-792-7706; Fax: 816-792-7778. Hours: 8AM-5PM (CST). *Felony, Misdemeanor, Civil Actions Over $25,000.*

www.circuit7.net

Civil Records: Access: Fax, mail, in person, online. Both court and visitors may perform in person searches. No search fee. Required to search: name, years to search. Civil cases indexed by defendant, plaintiff. Civil records on computer since 1988; prior records on index. Online access to civil records on the 7th Judicial Circuit database are available free at www.circuit7.net/publicaccess/default.htm. Includes traffic.

Criminal Records: Access: In person, online. Visitors must perform in person searches for themselves. No search fee. Required to search: name, years to search, DOB. Criminal records on computer since 1988, prior on index cards. Online access to criminal records is the same as civil.

General Information: Public Access terminal is available. No juvenile, mental, expunged, dismissed, or suspended imposition of sentence records released. SASE required. Turnaround time 1-2 days. Copy fee: $.25 per page. Certification fee: $5.00. Fee payee: Clay County Circuit Clerk. Personal checks accepted.

Associate Circuit Court PO Box 218, Liberty, MO 64069-0218; 816-792-7706; Fax: 816-792-7778. Hours: 8AM-5PM (CST). *Misdemeanor, Civil Actions Under $25,000, Eviction, Small Claims, Probate.*

www.circuit7.net

Civil Records: Access: Mail, in person, online. Both court and visitors may perform in person searches. No search fee. Required to search: name, years to search. Civil cases indexed by defendant, plaintiff. Civil records on computer since 8/87, prior on microfilm. Online access to Circuit 7 records is available free at www.circuit7.net/publicaccess/default.htm. Click on public access and search by name.

Criminal Records: Access: Mail, in person, online. Both court and visitors may perform in person searches. No search fee. Required to search: name, years to search. Criminal records on computer since 8/87, prior on microfilm. Online access to criminal records is the same as civil.

General Information: Public Access terminal is available. No juvenile, mental, expunged, dismissed, or suspended imposition of sentence records released. SASE required. Turnaround time 7-10 days. Copy fee: $.25 per page. Certification fee: $5.00. Fee payee: Clay County Circuit Court. Personal checks accepted. Prepayment is required.

Clinton County

Circuit Court PO Box 275, Plattsburg, MO 64477; 816-539-3731; Fax: 816-539-3893. Hours: 8AM-5PM *Felony, Misdemeanor, Civil Actions Over $45,000.*

Civil Records: Access: In person only. Visitors must perform in person searches for themselves. No search fee. Required to search: name, years to search. Civil cases indexed by defendant, plaintiff. Civil records (Judgments) on computer to 1976, archived since 1833.

Criminal Records: Access: In person only. Visitors must perform in person searches for themselves. No search fee. Required to search: name, years to search. Criminal records (Judgments) on computer from 1976, archived since 1833.

General Information: Public Access terminal is available. No juvenile, mental, expunged, dismissed, or suspended imposition of sentence records released. Copy fee: $1.00 per page. Certification fee: $1.00. Fee payee: Circuit Clerk. Personal checks accepted. Prepayment is required.

Associate Circuit Court PO Box 383, Plattsburg, MO 64477; 816-539-3755; Fax: 816-539-3439. 8AM-4:30PM *Misdemeanor, Civil Actions Under $45,000, Eviction, Small Claims, Probate.*

Civil Records: Access: Fax, mail, in person. Only the court performs in person searches; visitors may not. No search fee. Required to search: name, years to search. Civil cases indexed by defendant, plaintiff. Civil records on computer since 1992, prior on index cards since 1940s. Letterhead required for mail searches.

Criminal Records: Access: Fax, mail, in person. Only the court performs in person searches; visitors may not. No search fee. Required to search: name, years to search, DOB; also helpful - SSN. Criminal records on computer since 1992, prior on index cards since 1940s. Letterhead required.

General Information: Public Access terminal is available. No juvenile, mental, expunged, dismissed, or suspended imposition of sentence records released. SASE required. Turnaround time 1 week. No copy fee. Certification fee: No cert fee. No personal checks accepted.

Cole County

Circuit Court PO Box 1870, Jefferson City, MO 65102-1870; 573-634-9151; Fax: 573-635-0796. Hours: 7:30AM-4:30PM (CST). *Felony, Misdemeanor, Civil Actions Over $25,000.*

Civil Records: Access: Fax, mail, in person, online. Both court and visitors may perform in person searches. No search fee. Required to search: name, years to search. Civil cases indexed by defendant, plaintiff. Civil records (pending) on computer, on books since 1820. Participates in the free state online court record system at http://casenet.osca.state.mo.us/casenet.

Criminal Records: Access: In person, online. Visitors must perform in person searches for themselves. No search fee. Required to search: name, years to search; also helpful: DOB, SSN. Criminal records on computer since 1989, prior on book since 1820. Online access to criminal records is the same as civil.

General Information: No juvenile, mental, expunged, dismissed, or suspended imposition of sentence records released. Other access to criminal records: the court prefers that requesters go to the state highway patrol. SASE requested. Turnaround time 2-5 days. Fax notes: Fee to fax results is $1.00 per page. Copy fee: $.25 per page. Certification fee: $1.00. Fee payee: Cole County Circuit Clerk. Personal checks accepted.

Associate Circuit Court PO Box 503, Jefferson City, MO 65102; 573-634-9171; Fax: 573-635-5376. Hours: 7:30AM-4:30PM (CST). *Misdemeanor, Civil Actions Under $25,000, Eviction, Small Claims, Probate.*

Civil Records: Access: Fax, mail, in person, online. Only the court performs in person searches; visitors may not. No search fee. Required to search: name, years to search. Civil cases indexed by defendant, plaintiff. Civil records on cards for past 10 years. Participates in the free state online court record system at http://casenet.osca.state.mo.us/casenet.

Criminal Records: Access: Fax, mail, in person, online. Only the court performs in person searches; visitors may not. No search fee. Required to search: name, years to search; also helpful: address, DOB, SSN. Criminal records on computer since 1990, prior on cards. Online access to criminal records is the same as civil.

General Information: No juvenile, mental, expunged, dismissed, or suspended imposition of sentence records released. SASE required. Turnaround time 1-2 days. Copy fee: $.25 per page. Certification fee: $1.00. Fee payee: Circuit Court Division III. Personal checks accepted. Prepayment is required.

Cooper County

Circuit Court 200 Main St, Rm 26, Boonville, MO 65233; 660-882-2232; Fax: 660-882-2043. Hours: 8:30AM-5:00PM (CST). *Felony, Misdemeanor, Civil Actions Over $25,000.*

Civil Records: Access: Mail, in person. No search fee. Required to search: name, years to search. Civil cases indexed by defendant, plaintiff. Civil records on cards since 1975, case files from 1819 forward.

Criminal Records: Access: Mail, in person. Only the court performs in person searches; visitors may not. No search fee. Required to search: name, years to search; also helpful: DOB, SSN. Criminal records on cards since 1975, case files from 1819 forward.

General Information: No juvenile, mental, expunged, dismissed, or suspended imposition of sentence records released. SASE required. Turnaround time 1-2 days, phone-can tell you if record is available and cost. Copy fee: $1.00 per page. Certification fee: $1.50. Fee payee: Circuit Clerk or Recorder of Deeds. Personal checks accepted. Prepayment is required.

Associate Circuit Court 200 Main, Rm 31, Boonville, MO 65233; 660-882-5604; Fax: 660-882-2043. Hours: 8:30AM-5PM (CST). *Misdemeanor, Civil Actions Under $25,000, Eviction, Small Claims, Probate.*

Civil Records: Access: Mail, in person. No search fee. Required to search: name, years to search. Civil cases indexed by defendant, plaintiff. Civil records on index cards for 10 years.

Criminal Records: Access: Mail, in person. Only the court performs in person searches; visitors may not. No search fee. Required to search: name, years to search, DOB; also helpful: SSN. Criminal records on computer since mid-1990s, on index cards from 1980-1990.

General Information: No juvenile, mental, expunged, dismissed, or suspended imposition of sentence records released. SASE required. Turnaround time 10 days. Copy fee: $1.00 per page. Certification fee: $1.50. Fee payee: Cooper County Associate Circuit Court. Prepayment is required.

Crawford County

Circuit Court PO Box 177, Steelville, MO 65565; 573-775-2866; Fax: 573-775-2452. Hours: 8AM-5PM (CST). *Felony, Misdemeanor, Civil Actions Over $25,000.*

Civil Records: Access: In person, online. Both court and visitors may perform in person searches. Search fee: $4.00 per name; court may not have time to perform searches. Required to search: name, years to search. Civil cases indexed by defendant, plaintiff. Civil records on computer from 03/02/92 for judgments only, archived from 1800s, some records on index cards and books. Participates in the free state online Banner court record system at http://casenet.osca.state.mo.us/casenet.

Criminal Records: Access: Mail, in person, online. Both court and visitors may perform in person searches. Search fee: $4.00 per name; court may not have time to perform searches. Required to search: name, years to search, offense, date of offense. Criminal records on computer since 03/02/92, prior on cards. Online access to criminal court records is the same as civil.

General Information: Public Access terminal is available. No juvenile, mental, expunged, dismissed, or suspended imposition of sentence records released. SASE required. Turnaround time 1-2 weeks. Copy fee: $.30 per page. Certification fee: $1.00. Fee payee: Crawford County Circuit Clerk. Personal checks accepted. Prepayment is required.

Associate Circuit Court PO Box B.C., Steelville, MO 65565; 573-775-2149; Fax: 573-775-4010. Hours: 8AM-5PM (CST). *Misdemeanor, Civil Actions Under $25,000, Eviction, Small Claims, Probate.*

Civil Records: Access: Phone, fax, mail, in person. Only the court performs in person searches; visitors may not. No search fee. Required to search: name, years to search. Civil cases indexed by defendant, plaintiff. Civil records kept since 1989, prior destroyed.

Criminal Records: Access: Phone, fax, mail, in person. Only the court performs in person searches; visitors may not. No search fee. Required to search: name, years to search. Criminal records kept since 1989, prior destroyed.

General Information: No sealed records released. SASE required. Turnaround time 2 weeks. Fax notes: No fee to fax results. Copy fee: $.30 per page. Certification fee: $2.50. Fee payee: Associate Circuit Court. Personal checks accepted. Prepayment is required.

Dade County

Circuit Court Courthouse, Greenfield, MO 65661; 417-637-2271; Fax: 417-637-5055. Hours: 8AM-4PM (CST). *Felony, Misdemeanor, Civil Actions Over $25,000.*

Civil Records: Access: Mail, in person, online. Only the court performs in person searches; visitors may not. No search fee. Required to search: name, years to search. Civil cases indexed by defendant, plaintiff. Civil records in index cards since 1982, prior on books; on computer back to 2000. Participates in the free state online court record system at http://casenet.osca.state.mo.us/casenet.

Criminal Records: Access: Mail, in person, online. Only the court performs in person searches; visitors may not. No search fee. Required to search: name, years to search; also helpful-DOB, SSN, signed release. Criminal records in index cards since 1982, prior on books; on computer back to 2000. Online access to criminal records is the same as civil.

General Information: Public Access terminal is available. No juvenile, mental, expunged, dismissed, or suspended imposition of sentence records released. SASE required. Turnaround time 2-3 days. Copy fee: $1.00 per page. Certification fee: $2.50. Fee payee: Dade County Circuit Clerk. Personal checks accepted. Prepayment is required.

Associate Circuit Court 300 W Water, Greenfield, MO 65661; 417-637-2741; Fax: 417-637-5055. Hours: 8AM-4PM (CST). *Misdemeanor, Civil Actions Under $25,000, Eviction, Small Claims, Probate.*

Civil Records: Access: Mail, fax, in person, online. Both court and visitors may perform in person searches. Search fee: $5.00. Required to search: name, years to search. Civil cases indexed by defendant, plaintiff. Civil records on index cards since 1943; on computer back to 2000. Participates in the free state online court record system at http://casenet.osca.state.mo.us/casenet.

Criminal Records: Access: Mail, fax, in person, online. Both court and visitors may perform in person searches. No search fee. Required to search: name, years to search, DOB; also helpful-SSN, signed release. Criminal records on index cards since 1943; on computer back to 2000. Online access to criminal records is the same as civil.

General Information: Public Access terminal is available. No juvenile, mental, expunged, dismissed, or suspended imposition of sentence records released. SASE required. Turnaround time next day, phone turnaround time varies. Copy fee: $.25 per page. Certification fee: $2.50. Fee payee: Associate Circuit Court. Personal checks accepted. Prepayment is required.

Dallas County

Circuit Court PO Box 373, Buffalo, MO 65622; 417-345-2243; Fax: 417-345-5539. Hours: 7:30AM-4PM (CST). *Felony, Misdemeanor, Civil Actions Over $45,000.*

www.positech.net/~dcourt

Civil Records: Access: Phone, fax, mail, in person. Both court and visitors may perform in person searches. No search fee. Required to search: name, years to search. Civil cases indexed by defendant, plaintiff. Civil records on computer to 1991, prior on book since 1951.

Criminal Records: Access: Phone, fax, mail, in person. Both court and visitors may perform in person searches. No search fee. Required to search: name, years to search; also helpful: DOB. Criminal records on computer since 1992, prior on book since 1951.

General Information: Public Access terminal is available. No juvenile, mental, expunged, dismissed, or suspended imposition of sentence records released.

SASE required. Turnaround time 1-2 days. Fax notes: Fee to fax is $1.00 per page. Copy fee: $.25 per page. Certification fee: $1.00. Fee payee: Circuit Clerk. Personal checks accepted. Prepayment is required.

Associate Circuit Court PO Box 1150, Buffalo, MO 65622; 417-345-7641; Fax: 417-345-5358. Hours: 8AM-4PM (CST). *Misdemeanor, Civil Actions Under $45,000, Eviction, Small Claims, Probate.*

www.positech.net/~dcourt

Civil Records: Access: Phone, mail, in person. Both court and visitors may perform in person searches. No search fee. Required to search: name, years to search. Civil cases indexed by defendant, plaintiff. Civil records on index cards since 1800s.

Criminal Records: Access: Phone, mail, in person. Both court and visitors may perform in person searches. No search fee. Required to search: name, years to search. Criminal records on computer since 1991, on index cards since 1800s.

General Information: No juvenile, mental, expunged, dismissed, or suspended imposition of sentence records released. SASE required. Turnaround time 1 day. Copy fee: $.25 per page. Certification fee: $1.00. Fee payee: Associate Circuit Court. Only cashiers checks and money orders accepted. Prepayment is required.

Daviess County

Circuit Court PO Box 337, Gallatin, MO 64640; 660-663-2932; Fax: 660-663-3376. Hours: 8AM-4:30PM (CST). *Felony, Misdemeanor, Civil Actions Over $45,000.*

Civil Records: Access: Phone, fax, mail, in person. Both court and visitors may perform in person searches. Search fee: $10.00 per name. Required to search: name, years to search. Civil cases indexed by defendant, plaintiff. Civil records on records books since 1837.

Criminal Records: Access: Phone, fax, mail, in person. Both court and visitors may perform in person searches. Search fee: $10.00 per name. Required to search: name, years to search, DOB. Criminal records on records books since 1837.

General Information: No juvenile, mental, expunged, dismissed, or suspended imposition of sentence records released. SASE required. Turnaround time 1 day, phone turnaround time immediate. Fax notes: $2.00 per page. Copy fee: $1.00 per page. Certification fee: $2.00. Fee payee: Daviess County Circuit Clerk. Business checks accepted. Prepayment is required.

Associate Division Circuit Court Courthouse, PO Box 233, Gallatin, MO 64640; 660-663-2532. Hours: 8AM-4:30PM (CST). *Misdemeanor, Civil Actions Under $45,000, Eviction, Small Claims, Probate.*

Civil Records: Access: Fax, mail, in person. Both court and visitors may perform in person searches. No search fee. Required to search: name, years to search. Civil cases indexed by defendant, plaintiff. Civil records index cards since 9/84, prior on judgment books.

Criminal Records: Access: Mail, in person. Both court and visitors may perform in person searches. No search fee. Required to search: name, years to search. Criminal records on index cards since 1979, prior on judgment books.

General Information: No juvenile, mental, expunged, dismissed, or suspended imposition of sentence records released. SASE required. Turnaround time 1-2 days. Copy fee: $1.00 per page. Certification fee: $1.50. Fee payee: Associate Division Court. Only cashiers checks and money orders accepted. Prepayment is required.

De Kalb County

Circuit Court PO Box 248, Maysville, MO 64469; 816-449-2602; Fax: 816-449-2440. Hours: 8:30AM-4:30PM (CST). *Felony, Civil Actions Over $45,000.*

Civil Records: Access: In person only. Visitors must perform in person searches for themselves. No search fee. Required to search: name, years to search. Civil cases indexed by defendant, plaintiff. Civil records on index cards since 1970.

Criminal Records: Access: In person only. Visitors must perform in person searches for themselves. No search fee. Required to search: name, years to search. Criminal records on index cards since 1970.

General Information: No juvenile or suspended imposition of sentence records released. Fax notes: Fee to fax results is $1.00 per page. Copy fee: $1.00 per page. Certification fee: $1.00. Fee payee: Clifton DeShon, Circuit Clerk. Personal checks accepted. Prepayment is required.

Associate Circuit Court PO Box 248, Maysville, MO 64469; 816-449-5400; Fax: 816-449-2440. Hours: 8:30AM-4:30PM (CST). *Misdemeanor, Civil Actions Under $45,000, Eviction, Small Claims, Probate.*

Civil Records: Access: Mail, in person. Only the court performs in person searches; visitors may not. No search fee. Required to search: name, years to search. Civil cases indexed by defendant, plaintiff. Civil records on index cards since 1960s.

Criminal Records: Access: Mail, in person. Only the court performs in person searches; visitors may not. No search fee. Required to search: name, years to search; DOB; also helpful-SSN, case number. Criminal records on index cards since 1980s.

General Information: No juvenile, mental, expunged, dismissed, or suspended imposition of sentence records released. SASE required. Turnaround time 5 days. Fax notes: Will not fax results. Copy fee: $1.00 per page. Certification fee: $2.50. Fee payee: Associate Circuit Court. Only cashiers checks and money orders accepted. Prepayment is required.

Dent County

Circuit Court 112 E 5th St, Salem, MO 65560; 573-729-3931; Fax: 573-729-9414. Hours: 8AM-4:30PM (CST). *Felony, Misdemeanor, Civil Actions Over $45,000.*

Civil Records: Access: Mail, fax, in person. Both court and visitors may perform in person searches. No search fee. Required to search: name, years to search. Civil cases indexed by defendant, plaintiff. Civil records on computer since 1993, on index cards since 1978.

Criminal Records: Access: Mail, fax, in person. Both court and visitors may perform in person searches. No search fee. Required to search: name, years to search. Criminal records on computer since 1993, on index cards since 1978.

General Information: Public Access terminal is available. No juvenile, mental, expunged, dismissed, or suspended imposition of sentence records released. SASE required. Turnaround time 3-4 days. Copy fee: $.25 per page. Certification fee: $2.00. Fee payee: Dent County Circuit Clerk. Prepayment is required.

Associate Circuit Court 112 E 5th St, Salem, MO 65560; 573-729-3134; Fax: 573-729-5146. Hours: 8AM-4:30PM (CST). *Misdemeanor, Civil Actions Under $25,000, Eviction, Small Claims, Probate.*

Civil Records: Access: Mail, fax, in person. Both court and visitors may perform in person searches. No search fee. Required to search: name, years to search. Civil cases indexed by defendant, plaintiff. Civil records on computer since 1985, prior on index cards.

Criminal Records: Access: Mail, fax, in person. Both court and visitors may perform in person searches. No

search fee. Required to search: name, years to search, DOB, signed release. Criminal records on computer since 1985, prior on index cards.

General Information: Public Access terminal is available. No juvenile, mental, expunged, dismissed, or suspended imposition of sentence records released. SASE required. Turnaround time 2-3 days. Copy fee: $.25 per page. Certification fee: $2.00. Fee payee: Associate Circuit Court or Probate Court. Business checks accepted. Prepayment is required.

Douglas County

Circuit Court PO Box 249, Ava, MO 65608; 417-683-4713; Fax: 417-683-2794. Hours: 8AM-4:30PM (CST). *Felony, Misdemeanor, Civil Actions Over $45,000.*

Civil Records: Access: Phone, mail, in person. Only the court performs in person searches; visitors may not. Search fee: $5.00 per name. Required to search: name, years to search. Civil cases indexed by defendant, plaintiff. Civil records on alpha cards since 1977.

Criminal Records: Access: Phone, mail, in person. Only the court performs in person searches; visitors may not. Search fee: $5.00 per name. Required to search: name, years to search; also helpful: DOB, SSN. Criminal records on alpha cards since 1977.

General Information: No juvenile, mental, expunged, dismissed, or suspended imposition of sentence records released. SASE required. Turnaround time 1 week. Copy fee: $.25 per page. Certification fee: $2.50. Fee payee: Circuit Clerk. Personal checks accepted. Copy fees may be billed.

Associate Circuit Court PO Box 276, Ava, MO 65608; 417-683-2114; Fax: 417-683-3121. Hours: 8AM-4:30PM (CST). *Misdemeanor, Civil Actions Under $25,000, Eviction, Small Claims, Probate.*

Civil Records: Access: Phone, mail, in person. Both court and visitors may perform in person searches. No search fee. Required to search: name, years to search. Civil cases indexed by defendant, plaintiff. Civil records on index cards.

Criminal Records: Access: Phone, mail, in person. Both court and visitors may perform in person searches. No search fee. Required to search: name, years to search; also helpful: SSN. Criminal records on index cards.

General Information: No juvenile, mental, expunged, dismissed, or suspended imposition of sentence records released. SASE required. Turnaround time 2-3 days. Copy fee: $.25 per page. Certification fee: $1.50. Fee payee: Associate Circuit Court. Personal checks accepted. Prepayment is required.

Dunklin County

Circuit Court Division I PO Box 567, Kennett, MO 63857; 573-888-2456; Fax: 573-888-0319. Hours: 8:30AM-4:30PM (CST). *Felony, Misdemeanor, Civil Actions Over $45,000.*

Note: Records may soon be available online over MO CaseNet.

Civil Records: Access: In person only. Visitors must perform in person searches for themselves. No search fee. Required to search: name, years to search. Civil cases indexed by defendant, plaintiff. Civil records on index cards.

Criminal Records: Access: Fax, mail, in person. Visitors must perform in person searches for themselves. No search fee. Required to search: name, years to search, DOB, SSN. Criminal records on computer back to 8/94.

General Information: Public Access terminal is available. No juvenile, mental, expunged or dismissed records released. SASE not required. Fax notes: $.50 per page. Copy fee: $.50 per page. Certification fee:

$2.00. Fee payee: Circuit Clerk. Personal checks accepted. Attorney's, courts and abstract companies.

Associate Circuit Court Courthouse Rm 103, Kennett, MO 63857; 573-888-3378; Probate phone: 573-888-3272; Fax: 573-888-0754. Hours: 8AM-4:30PM (CST). *Felony, Misdemeanor, Civil Actions Under $25,000, Eviction, Small Claims, Probate.*

Civil Records: Access: Mail, in person. Both court and visitors may perform in person searches. Search fee: $2.00 per name. Required to search: name, years to search, address. Civil cases indexed by defendant, plaintiff. Civil records on index cards.

Criminal Records: Access: Mail, in person. Both court and visitors may perform in person searches. Search fee: $2.00 per name. Required to search: name, years to search, DOB; also helpful: address, SSN. Criminal records on index cards.

General Information: Public Access terminal is available. No juvenile, mental, expunged, dismissed, or suspended imposition of sentence records released. Turnaround time 1-2 days. Copy fee: $.50 per page. Certification fee: $2.50. Fee payee: Circuit Court Div 2. Business checks accepted. Prepayment is required.

Franklin County

Circuit Court 300 E Main St, Rm 301, Union, MO 63084; 636-583-6300. Hours: 8AM-4:30PM (CST). *Felony, Civil Actions Over $45,000.*

Civil Records: Access: Mail, online, in person. Both court and visitors may perform in person searches. Search fee: $2.00 per name. Required to search: name, years to search. Civil cases indexed by defendant, plaintiff. Civil records on computer back to 1995; others filed as originals. Participates in the free state online court record system at http://casenet.osca.state.mo.us/casenet.

Criminal Records: Access: Mail, online, in person. Both court and visitors may perform in person searches. Search fee: $2.00 per name. Required to search: name, years to search, DOB. Criminal records on computer back to 1995; others filed as originals. Online access to criminal records is the same as civil.

General Information: Public Access terminal is available. No juvenile, mental, expunged, dismissed, or suspended imposition of sentence records released. SASE required. Turnaround time 1-5 days. Copy fee: $1.00 per page or $.25 do-it-yourself. Certification fee: $1.00. Fee payee: Circuit Clerk. Personal checks accepted. Prepayment is required.

Associate Circuit Court PO Box 526, Union, MO 63084; 636-583-6326. Hours: 8AM-4:30PM (CST). *Misdemeanor, Civil Actions Under $25,000, Eviction, Small Claims, Probate.*

Civil Records: Access: Online, in person. Both court and visitors may perform in person searches. No search fee. Required to search: name, years to search. Civil cases indexed by defendant, plaintiff. Civil records on computer (limited), on index cards since 1983. Participates in the free state online court record system at http://casenet.osca.state.mo.us/casenet.

Criminal Records: Access: Online, in person. Both court and visitors may perform in person searches. No search fee. Required to search: name, years to search. Criminal records on index cards since 1979. Online access to criminal records is the same as civil.

General Information: No juvenile, mental, expunged, dismissed, or suspended imposition of sentence records released. No copy fee. Certification fee: No cert fee.

Gasconade County

Circuit Court 119 E 1st St, Rm 6, Hermann, MO 65041-1182; 573-486-2632; Fax: 573-486-3693 & 486-8893. Hours: 8AM-4:30PM (CST). *Felony, Misdemeanor, Civil Actions Over $45,000.*

Civil Records: Access: Phone, fax, mail, in person, online. Both court and visitors may perform in person searches. No search fee. Required to search: name, years to search. Civil cases indexed by defendant, plaintiff. Civil records on index cards since 1976, prior on books stored in vault. Participates in the free state online court record system at http://casenet.osca.state.mo.us/casenet.

Criminal Records: Access: Phone, fax, mail, in person, online. Only the court performs in person searches; visitors may not. No search fee. Required to search: name, years to search; also helpful: DOB, SSN. Criminal records on index cards since 1976, prior on books stored in vault. Online access to criminal records is the same as civil.

General Information: No juvenile, mental, expunged, dismissed, or suspended imposition of sentence records released. SASE required. Turnaround time 3-4 days. Fax notes: $2.00 for first page, $1.00 each add'l. Copy fee: $1.00 per page. Certification fee: $1.00. Fee payee: Gasconade Circuit Court. Personal checks accepted.

Associate Circuit Court 119 E. 1st St. Rm 3, Hermann, MO 65041; 573-486-2321; Fax: 573-486-3693. Hours: 8AM-4:30PM (CST). *Misdemeanor, Civil Actions Under $25,000, Eviction, Small Claims, Probate.*

Civil Records: Access: Fax, mail, in person, online. Only the court performs in person searches; visitors may not. No search fee. Required to search: name, years to search. Civil cases indexed by defendant, plaintiff. Civil records on computer since 1988, prior on index cards since 1979. Participates in the free state online court record system at http://casenet.osca.state.mo.us/casenet.

Criminal Records: Access: Fax, mail, in person, online. Only the court performs in person searches; visitors may not. No search fee. Required to search: name, years to search. Criminal records on computer since 1988, prior on index cards since 1979. Online access to criminal records is the same as civil.

General Information: No juvenile, mental, expunged, dismissed, or suspended imposition of sentence records released. SASE required. Turnaround time varies. Copy fee: $1.00 per page. Certification fee: $2.50. Fee payee: Associate Circuit Court. Personal checks accepted. Will bill probate fees.

Gentry County

Circuit Court PO Box 27, Albany, MO 64402; 660-726-3618; Fax: 660-726-4102. Hours: 8AM-4:30PM *Felony, Misdemeanor, Civil Actions Over $25,000.*

Civil Records: Access: Mail, in person. Both court and visitors may perform in person searches. No search fee. Required to search: name, years to search. Civil cases indexed by defendant, plaintiff. Civil records archived since 1885.

Criminal Records: Access: Mail, in person. Both court and visitors may perform in person searches. No search fee. Required to search: name, years to search; also helpful: DOB, SSN. Criminal records archived since 1885.

General Information: No juvenile, mental, expunged, dismissed, or suspended imposition of sentence records released. SASE required. Turnaround time 5 working days. Copy fee: $1.00 per page. Certification fee: $2.00. Fee payee: Circuit Clerk. Personal checks accepted. Prepayment is required.

Associate Circuit Court 200 W Clay St, Albany, MO 64402; 660-726-3411; Fax: 660-726-4102. Hours: 8AM-4:30PM (CST). *Misdemeanor, Civil Actions Under $25,000, Eviction, Small Claims, Probate.*

Civil Records: Access: In person only. Visitors must perform in person searches for themselves. No search fee. Required to search: name, years to search. Civil cases indexed by defendant, plaintiff. Civil records on index cards.

Criminal Records: Access: In person only. Visitors must perform in person searches for themselves. No search fee. Required to search: name, years to search. Criminal records on index cards.

General Information: No juvenile, mental, expunged, dismissed, or suspended imposition of sentence records released. Copy fee: $1.00 per page. Certification fee: $1.50. Fee payee: Associate Circuit Court. Personal checks accepted. Prepayment is required.

Greene County

Circuit Court 1010 Booneville, Springfield, MO 65802; 417-868-4074. Hours: 8AM-5AM (CST). *Felony, Civil Actions Over $25,000.*

www.greenecountymo.org

Civil Records: Access: Mail, in person. Both court and visitors may perform in person searches. Search fee: $5.00 per name. Required to search: name, years to search. Civil cases indexed by defendant, plaintiff. Civil records on computer back to 7/89, prior on index cards.

Criminal Records: Access: Mail, in person. Both court and visitors may perform in person searches. Search fee: $5.00 per name. Required to search: name, years to search; also helpful: address, DOB, SSN. Criminal records on computer back to 7/89, prior on index cards.

General Information: Public Access terminal is available. No juvenile, mental, expunged, sealed, dismissed or suspended imposition of sentence records released. SASE required. Turnaround time 1 week. Copy fee: $.20 per page. Certification fee: $5.00. Fee payee: Circuit Clerk. Personal checks accepted. Prepayment is required.

Associate Circuit Court 1010 N Boonville, Springfield, MO 65802; 417-868-4110; Probate phone: 417-868-4027. Hours: 8AM-5PM (CST). *Misdemeanor, Civil Actions Under $25,000, Eviction, Small Claims, Probate.*

www.greenecountymo.org

Note: Probate is a separate court at the same address.

Civil Records: Access: Phone, mail, in person. Both court and visitors may perform in person searches. Search fee: $2.00 per name. Required to search: name, years to search. Civil cases indexed by defendant, plaintiff. Civil records on computer since mid-1989, prior on index cards.

Criminal Records: Access: Mail, in person. Both court and visitors may perform in person searches. Search fee: $2.00. Required to search: name, years to search; also helpful: SSN. Criminal records on computer since mid-1989, prior on index cards.

General Information: Public Access terminal is available. (Very limited.) No juvenile, mental, expunged, sealed, dismissed or suspended imposition of sentence records released. SASE required. Turnaround time 2 days; if certified, 1 week. Copy fee: $.10 per page. Certification fee: No cert fee. Fee payee: Associate Circuit Clerk. Business checks accepted. Prepayment is required.

Grundy County

Circuit Court Courthouse, 700 Main St, PO Box 196, Trenton, MO 64683; 660-359-6605; Fax: 660-359-6604. Hours: 8:30AM-4:30PM (CST). *Felony, Misdemeanor, Civil Actions Over $45,000.*

Civil Records: Access: Mail, in person, online. Both court and visitors may perform in person searches. No search fee. Required to search: name, years to search. Civil cases indexed by defendant, plaintiff. Civil records archived since 1841; on computer back to 2000. Participates in the free state online court record system at http://casenet.osca.state.mo.us/casenet.

Criminal Records: Access: In person, online. Visitors must perform in person searches for themselves. No search fee. Required to search: name, years to search. Criminal records archived since 1841; on computer back to 2000. Online access to criminal records is the same as civil.

General Information: Public Access terminal is available. No juvenile, Title 4D, child support, mental, expunged, dismissed, or suspended imposition of sentence cases. SASE requested. Turnaround time 1 day. Fax notes: Fee to fax results is $2.00 per document. Copy fee: $.25 per page. Certification fee: $2.00. Fee payee: Circuit Clerk. Personal checks accepted. Prepayment is required.

Associate Circuit Court PO Box 26, Trenton, MO 64683; 660-359-6606/6909. Hours: 8:30AM-4:30PM (CST). *Misdemeanor, Civil Actions Under $25,000, Eviction, Small Claims, Probate.*

Civil Records: Access: Mail, in person, online. Both court and visitors may perform in person searches. No search fee. Required to search: name, years to search. Civil cases indexed by defendant, plaintiff. Civil records on index cards, probate records archived. Participates in the free state online court record system at http://casenet.osca.state.mo.us/casenet.

Criminal Records: Access: Mail, in person, online. Both court and visitors may perform in person searches. No search fee. Required to search: name, years to search. Criminal records on index cards, probate records archived. Online access to criminal records is the same as civil.

General Information: No juvenile, mental, expunged, dismissed, or suspended imposition of sentence records released. SASE required. Turnaround time 1-2 days. Copy fee: $.25 per page. Certification fee: $2.50 plus $1.00 per page. Fee payee: Grundy County Circuit Court Division II. Business checks accepted. Prepayment is required.

Harrison County

Circuit Court PO Box 189, Bethany, MO 64424; 660-425-6425; Fax: 660-425-6390. Hours: 8AM-5PM (CST). *Felony, Misdemeanor, Civil Actions Over $45,000.*

Civil Records: Access: Mail, in person, online. Only the court performs in person searches; visitors may not. No search fee. Required to search: name, years to search. Civil cases indexed by defendant, plaintiff. Civil records on index cards since 1979, prior on index books. Participates in the free state online court record system at http://casenet.osca.state.mo.us/casenet.

Criminal Records: Access: Mail, in person, online. Only the court performs in person searches; visitors may not. No search fee. Required to search: name, years to search; also helpful: address, DOB, SSN. Criminal records on index cards since 1979, prior on index books. Online access to criminal records same as civil.

General Information: No juvenile, mental, expunged, dismissed, or suspended imposition of sentence records released. SASE required. Turnaround time varies. Copy fee: $.25 per page. Certification fee: $1.00. Fee payee: Harrison County Circuit Court. Personal checks accepted. Prepayment is required.

Associate Circuit Court Box 189, Bethany, MO 64424; 660-425-6432; Fax: 660-425-6390. Hours: 8AM-5PM (CST). *Misdemeanor, Civil Actions Under $45,000, Eviction, Small Claims, Probate.*

Civil Records: Access: Mail, in person, online. Only the court performs in person searches; visitors may not. No search fee. Required to search: name, years to search. Civil cases indexed by defendant, plaintiff. Civil records on index cards or archives. Participates in the free state online court record system at http://casenet.osca.state.mo.us/casenet.

Criminal Records: Access: Mail, in person, online. Only the court performs in person searches; visitors may not. No search fee. Required to search: name, years to search. Criminal records on index cards or archives. Online access to criminal records is the same as civil.

General Information: No juvenile, mental, expunged, dismissed, or suspended imposition of sentence records released. Turnaround time 7 days. Copy fee: $.25 per page. Certification fee: $1.00. Fee payee: Associate Circuit Court of Harrison County. Personal checks accepted. Prepayment is required.

Henry County

Circuit Court 100 W Franklin Rm 12, Clinton, MO 64735; 660-885-6963 X209; Fax: 660-885-8247. Hours: 8AM-4:30PM (CST). *Felony, Misdemeanor, Civil Actions Over $45,000.*

http://tacnet.missouri.org/~court27

Civil Records: Access: Mail, in person. Both court and visitors may perform in person searches. No search fee. Required to search: name, years to search. Civil cases indexed by defendant, plaintiff. Civil records on computer since 8/91, on index cards since 1979, archived since 1877. You can fax requests, but no results are faxed.

Criminal Records: Access: Mail, in person. Both court and visitors may perform in person searches. No search fee. Required to search: name, years to search. Criminal records on computer since 8/91, on index cards since 1979, archived since 1877.

General Information: No juvenile, mental, expunged, dismissed, or suspended imposition of sentence records released. SASE required. Turnaround time 2 days. Copy fee: $.25 per page. There is a $2.50 fee for records copied from big books. Certification fee: $1.50. Fee payee: Henry County Circuit Clerk. Personal checks accepted. Copy fees may be billed.

Associate Circuit Court Courthouse, Clinton, MO 64735; 660-885-6963 X205/207; Fax: 660-885-5387. 8AM-4:30PM *Misdemeanor, Civil Actions Under $25,000, Eviction, Small Claims, Probate.*

Civil Records: Access: Mail, in person. Both court and visitors may perform in person searches. No search fee. Required to search: name, years to search. Civil cases indexed by defendant, plaintiff. Civil records on index cards since 1979, prior on judgment books.

Criminal Records: Access: Mail, in person. Both court and visitors may perform in person searches. No search fee. Required to search: name, years to search. Criminal records on index cards since 1979, prior on judgment books.

General Information: No juvenile, mental, expunged, dismissed, or suspended imposition of sentence records released. SASE required. Turnaround time 5 days. Copy fee: $.25 per page. Certification fee: $1.50. Fee payee: Associate Circuit Court. Personal checks okay.

Hickory County

Circuit Court PO Box 101, Hermitage, MO 65668; 417-745-6421; Fax: 417-745-6670. Hours: 8AM-4:30PM (CST). *Felony, Misdemeanor, Civil Actions Over $45,000.*

www.positech.net/~dcourt

Civil Records: Access: Mail, in person. Both court and visitors may perform in person searches. No search fee. Required to search: name, years to search. Civil cases indexed by defendant, plaintiff. Civil records on computer since 1992, prior on index books since 1976.

Criminal Records: Access: Mail, in person. Both court and visitors may perform in person searches. No search fee. Required to search: name, years to search, signed release. Criminal records on computer since 1992, prior on index books since 1976.

General Information: No juvenile, mental, expunged, dismissed, or suspended imposition of sentence records released. SASE required. Turnaround time 1 week-10 days. Fax notes: Fee to fax results is 1.00 per page. Copy fee: $1.00 per page. Certification fee: $1.00. Fee payee: Hickory County Circuit Clerk. Personal checks accepted. Prepayment is required.

Associate Circuit Court PO Box 75, Hermitage, MO 65668; 417-745-6822; Fax: 417-745-6670. Hours: 8AM-4:30PM (CST). *Misdemeanor, Civil Actions Under $45,000, Eviction, Small Claims, Probate.*

www.positech.net/~dcourt

Civil Records: Access: Mail, in person. Both court and visitors may perform in person searches. No search fee. Required to search: name, years to search. Civil cases indexed by defendant, plaintiff. Civil records on index cards since 1980.

Criminal Records: Access: Mail, in person. Both court and visitors may perform in person searches. No search fee. Required to search: name, years to search, DOB. Criminal records on index cards since 1980.

General Information: No juvenile, mental, expunged, dismissed, or suspended imposition of sentence records released. SASE required. Turnaround time 2-3 days. No copy fee. Certification fee: No cert fee.

Holt County

Circuit Court PO Box 318, Oregon, MO 64473; 660-446-3301; Fax: 660-446-3328. Hours: 8AM-4:30PM (CST). *Felony, Misdemeanor, Civil Actions Over $45,000.*

Civil Records: Access: Phone, fax, mail, in person. Only the court performs in person searches; visitors may not. No search fee. Required to search: name, years to search. Civil cases indexed by defendant, plaintiff. Civil records on books.

Criminal Records: Access: Phone, fax, mail, in person. Only the court performs in person searches; visitors may not. No search fee. Required to search: name, years to search. Criminal records on books.

General Information: No juvenile, mental, expunged, dismissed, or suspended imposition of sentence records released. SASE required. Turnaround time varies. Fax notes: $2.00 per document. Copy fee: $1.00 per page. Certification fee: $1.50. Fee payee: Recorder. Personal checks accepted. Prepayment is required.

Associate Circuit Court PO Box 173, Oregon, MO 64473; 660-446-3380. Hours: 8:30AM-4:30PM (CST). *Misdemeanor, Civil Actions Under $45,000, Eviction, Small Claims, Probate.*

Civil Records: Access: Mail, in person. Both court and visitors may perform in person searches. No search fee. Required to search: name, years to search. Civil cases indexed by defendant, plaintiff. Civil records on computer since 1991, prior on index cards since 1979.

Criminal Records: Access: Mail, in person. Both court and visitors may perform in person searches. No search fee. Required to search: name, years to search. Criminal records on computer since 1991, prior on index cards since 1979.

General Information: No juvenile, mental, expunged, dismissed, or suspended imposition of sentence records released. SASE required. Turnaround time varies. Copy fee: $.25 per page. Certification fee: $1.50. Fee payee:

Associate Circuit Court. Personal checks accepted. Prepayment is required.

Howard County

Circuit Court 1 Courthouse Square, Fayette, MO 65248; 660-248-2194; Fax: 660-248-1075. Hours: 8:30AM-4:30PM (CST). *Felony, Misdemeanor, Civil Actions Over $30,000.*

Civil Records: Access: In person only. Visitors must perform in person searches for themselves. No search fee. Required to search: name, years to search. Civil cases indexed by defendant, plaintiff. Civil records on index cards; computer records go back to the 1970's.

Criminal Records: Access: In person only. Visitors must perform in person searches for themselves. No search fee. Required to search: name, years to search. Criminal records on index cards; computer records go back to the 1970's.

General Information: Public Access terminal is available. No juvenile, mental, expunged, dismissed, or suspended imposition of sentence records released. Copy fee: $.25 per page. Certification fee: $2.00. Fee payee: Circuit Clerk. Personal checks accepted. Prepayment is required.

Associate Circuit Court PO Box 370, Fayette, MO 65248; 660-248-3326; Fax: 660-248-1075. Hours: 8:30AM-4:30PM (CST). *Misdemeanor, Civil Actions Under $45,000, Eviction, Small Claims, Probate.*

Civil Records: Access: In person only. Visitors must perform in person searches for themselves. No search fee. Required to search: name, years to search. Civil cases indexed by defendant, plaintiff. Civil records go back to 1975.

Criminal Records: Access: In person only. Visitors must perform in person searches for themselves. No search fee. Required to search: name, years to search, DOB. Criminal records go back to 1975.

General Information: No juvenile, mental, expunged, dismissed, or suspended imposition of sentence records released. Copy fee: $.25 per page. Certification fee: $1.50. Fee payee: Associate Circuit Court. Personal checks accepted. Prepayment is required.

Howell County

Circuit Court PO Box 1011, West Plains, MO 65775; 417-256-3741; Fax: 417-256-4650. Hours: 8AM-5PM (CST). *Felony, Misdemeanor, Civil Actions Over $25,000.*

Civil Records: Access: Phone, fax, mail, in person, online. Both court and visitors may perform in person searches. No search fee. Required to search: name, years to search. Civil cases indexed by defendant, plaintiff. Civil records on index cards since 1977. Participates in the free state online court record system at http://casenet.osca.state.mo.us/casenet. Online records go back to 8/2000.

Criminal Records: Access: In person, online. Visitors must perform in person searches for themselves. No search fee. Required to search: name, years to search. Criminal records on index cards since 1977. Online access to criminal records is the same as civil. Written requests are referred to the State Highway Patrol.

General Information: No juvenile, mental, expunged, dismissed, or suspended imposition of sentence records released. SASE required. Turnaround time varies. Fax notes: $1.00 per page. Copy fee: $.10 per page. Certification fee: $1.50. Fee payee: Howell County Circuit Clerk. Personal checks accepted. Will bill fees to attorneys.

Associate Circuit Court 222 Courthouse, West Plains, MO 65775; 417-256-4050; Fax: 417-256-5826. Hours: 8AM-4:30PM *Misdemeanor, Civil Actions Under $45,000, Eviction, Small Claims, Probate.*

Civil Records: Access: Mail, in person, online. Both court and visitors may perform in person searches. No

search fee. Required to search: name, years to search. Civil cases indexed by defendant, plaintiff. Civil records on index cards since 1/1/79, prior on books. Participates in the free state online court record system at http://casenet.osca.state.mo.us/casenet.

Criminal Records: Access: Mail, in person, online. Both court and visitors may perform in person searches. No search fee. Required to search: name, years to search, DOB; also helpful: SSN. Criminal records on computer since early 1991, on index cards since 1/1/79, prior on books. Online access to criminal records is the same as civil.

General Information: No juvenile, mental, expunged, dismissed, or suspended imposition of sentence records released. SASE required. Turnaround time ASAP. Copy fee: $.10 per page. Certification fee: $1.50. Fee payee: Associate/Probate Court. Only cashiers checks and money orders accepted. Prepayment is required.

Iron County

Circuit Court PO Box 24, Ironton, MO 63650; 573-546-2811; Fax: 573-546-2166. Hours: 8AM-4PM (CST). *Felony, Civil Actions Over $45,000.*

Civil Records: Access: In person only. Visitors must perform in person searches for themselves. No search fee. Required to search: name, years to search. Civil cases indexed by defendant, plaintiff. Civil records on index cards since 1976, prior on books.

Criminal Records: Access: In person only. Visitors must perform in person searches for themselves. No search fee. Required to search: name, years to search. Criminal records on index cards to 1976, prior on books.

General Information: No juvenile, mental, expunged, dismissed, or suspended imposition of sentence records released. Copy fee: $1.00 per page. Certification fee: $2.00. Fee payee: Iron County Circuit Clerk. Personal checks accepted. Prepayment is required.

Associate Circuit Court PO Box 325, Ironton, MO 63650; 573-546-2511; Fax: 573-546-6006. Hours: 9AM-4PM (CST). *Misdemeanor, Civil Actions Under $45,000, Eviction, Small Claims, Probate.*

Civil Records: Access: Mail, in person. Both court and visitors may perform in person searches. No search fee. Required to search: name, years to search; also helpful: address. Civil cases indexed by defendant, plaintiff. Civil records on index cards since 1979; on computer back to 1997.

Criminal Records: Access: Fax, mail, in person. Only the court performs in person searches; visitors may not. No search fee. Required to search: name, years to search, DOB; also helpful: address, signed release. Criminal records on index cards since 1979; on computer back to 1997.

General Information: No juvenile, mental, expunged, dismissed, or suspended imposition of sentence records released. SASE required. Turnaround time 5 days. Copy fee: $.25 per page. Certification fee: $1.50 plus $1.00 per page. Fee payee: Associate Circuit Court. Personal checks accepted. Prepayment is required.

Jackson County

Circuit Court - Civil Division 415 E 12th, Kansas City, MO 64106; 816-881-3926; 881-3522; Probate phone: 816-881-3755. Hours: 8AM-5PM (CST). *Civil, Eviction, Small Claims, Probate.*

www.16thcircuit.org

Note: There is a combined computer system with the Independence civil court. The Probate Court also participates in the free state online court record system at http://casenet.osca.state.mo.us/casenet.

Civil Records: Access: Online, in person. Visitors must perform in person searches for themselves. No search fee. Required to search: name, years to search. Civil cases indexed by defendant, plaintiff. Civil records on

computer since 1973, some records on microfiche and books, older records archived off-site. Participates in the free state online court record system at http://casenet.osca.state.mo.us/casenet.

General Information: Public Access terminal is available. No juvenile, mental, expunged, dismissed, or suspended imposition of sentence records released. Copy fee: $.50 per page. Certification fee: $2.50. Fee payee: Court Administrator's Office. Business checks accepted. Prepayment is required.

Independence Circuit Court - Civil Annex

308 W Kansas, Independence, MO 64050; 816-881-4497; Probate phone: 816-881-4552; Fax: 816-881-4410. Hours: 8AM-5PM (CST). *Civil, Eviction, Small Claims, Probate.*

This court is on the same computer system as Kansas City for civil cases, but files maintained separately.

Civil Records: Access: Mail, online, in person. Both court and visitors may perform in person searches. No search fee. Required to search: name, years to search. Civil cases indexed by defendant, plaintiff. Civil records on computer since 1989. The court will not do background checks, except for attorneys. You must have case number if the court is to pull a record. Participates in the free state online court record system at http://casenet.osca.state.mo.us/casenet.

Criminal Records: Access: In person, mail. Only the court performs in person searches; visitors may not. No search fee. Required to search: name. Online access to criminal records is the same as civil. The court will not do background checks, except for attorneys and government offices. Otherwise, the requested must have the case number to request file copies.

General Information: Public Access terminal is available. No sealed records released. Turnaround time 1 day. Copy fee: $.50 per page. Certification fee: $2.50. Fee payee: District Court Clerk. Only cashiers checks and money orders accepted. Prepayment is required.

Circuit Court - Criminal Division 1315 Locust, Kansas City, MO 64106; 816-881-4350; Fax: 816-881-3420. Hours: 8AM-5PM (CST). *Felony, Misdemeanor.*

www.16thcircuit.org

Criminal Records: Access: In person, online. Only the court performs in person searches; visitors may not. No search fee. Required to search: name, years to search, DOB, signed release; also helpful: SSN. Criminal records on computer since 1968 for felonies, 1980 for misdemeanors. Participates in the free state online court record system at http://casenet.osca.state.mo.us/casenet. All background checks are sent to the Missouri Highway Patrol in Jefferson City. The court will only pull file copies if a case number is given.

General Information: No juvenile, mental, expunged, dismissed, or suspended imposition of sentence records released. Copy fee: $.50 per page. Certification fee: $3.00. Fee payee: Dept. of Civil or Criminal Records. Only cashiers checks and money orders accepted. Prepayment is required.

Jasper County

Circuit Court Courthouse, Rm 303, 302 S. Main St, Carthage, MO 64836; 417-358-0441; Fax: 417-358-0461. Hours: 8:00AM-5:00PM (CST). *Felony, Misdemeanor, Civil Actions Over $45,000.*

www.osca.state.mo.us/circuits/index.nsf

Civil Records: Access: Mail, in person, online. No search fee. Required to search: name, years to search. Civil cases indexed by defendant, plaintiff. Civil records on computer since 7/1/91, prior on cards since 1975. Participates in the free state online court record system at http://casenet.osca.state.mo.us/casenet. Online records go back to 7/2000.

Criminal Records: Access: Mail, in person, online. Only the court performs in person searches; visitors may not. No search fee. Required to search: name, years to search. Criminal records on computer since 7/1/91, prior on cards since 1975. Online access to criminal records is the same as civil.

General Information: Public Access terminal is available. No juvenile, mental, expunged, dismissed, or suspended imposition of sentence records released. SASE required. Turnaround time 1 week. Copy fee: $.25 per page. Certification fee: $1.50. Fee payee: Jasper County Circuit Clerk. Business checks accepted. Prepayment is required.

Joplin Circuit Court Courthouse, 3rd Fl, 601 S Pearl, Joplin, MO 64801; 417-625-4310; Fax: 417-625-7172. Hours: 8:00AM-5:00PM (CST). *Felony, Misdemeanor, Civil Actions Over $45,000.*

www.osca.state.mo.us/circuits/index.nsf

Civil Records: Access: Mail, fax, in person, online. Both the court and visitors may perform in person searches. No search fee. Required to search: name, years to search. Civil cases indexed by defendant, plaintiff. Civil records on computer since 7/1/91, prior on cards since 1975. Participates in the free state online court record system at http://casenet.osca.state.mo.us/casenet. Online records go back to 7/2000.

Criminal Records: Access: Mail, fax, in person, online. Both the court and visitors may perform in person searches. No search fee. Required to search: name, years to search. Criminal records on computer back to 1993, prior on cards back to 1975. Online access to criminal records is the same as civil.

General Information: Public Access terminal is available. No juvenile, mental, expunged, dismissed, or suspended imposition of sentence records released. SASE required. Turnaround time 1 week. Copy fee: $.25 per page. Certification fee: $1.50. Fee payee: Jasper County Circuit Clerk. No checks accepted. Prepayment is required.

Carthage Associate Circuit Court Courthouse, Rm 304, 302 S. Main St, Carthage, MO 64836; 417-358-0450; Fax: 417-358-0460. Hours: 8:30AM-Noon, 1-4:30PM (CST). *Misdemeanor, Civil Actions Under $45,000, Eviction, Small Claims, Probate.*

Civil Records: Access: In person, online. Visitors must conduct in person searches for themselves. Search fee: Court does not perform civil searches. Required to search: name, years to search. Civil cases indexed by defendant, plaintiff. Civil records on computer back to 1997, prior on cards back to 1979. Participates in the free state online Banner court record system at http://casenet.osca.state.mo.us/casenet. Online records go back to 7/2000. For mail or fax searches, court recommends Amer. Research at 417-358-6494.

Criminal Records: Access: In person, online. Visitors must conduct in person searches for themselves. Search fee: Court does not perform criminal searches. Required to search: name, years to search. Criminal records on computer back to 1997, prior on cards back to 1979. Online access to criminal records is the same as civil. For mail or fax searches, court recommends Amer. Research at 417-358-6494.

General Information: Public Access terminal is available. No juvenile, mental, expunged, dismissed, or suspended imposition of sentence records released. Copy fee: $.25 per page. Certification fee: $1.50.

Joplin Associate Circuit Court Courthouse, 2nd Fl, 601 S Pearl, Joplin, MO 64801; 417-625-4316; Fax: 417-625-4340. Hours: 8AM-5PM (CST). *Misdemeanor, Civil Actions Under $45,000, Eviction, Small Claims, Probate.*

Civil Records: Access: Mail, fax, in person, online. Both court and visitors may perform in person searches. No search fee. Required to search: name, years to search. Civil cases indexed by defendant, plaintiff. Civil

records on computer back to 1993, prior on cards back to mid-1970s. Participates in the free state online Banner court record system at http://casenet.osca.state.mo.us/casenet. Online records go back to 7/2000.

Criminal Records: Access: Mail, fax, in person, online. Both court and visitors may perform in person searches. No search fee. Required to search: name, years to search. Criminal records on computer back to 1993, prior on cards back to mid-1970s. Online access to criminal records is the same as civil.

General Information: Public Access terminal is available. No juvenile, mental, expunged, dismissed, or suspended imposition of sentence records released. SASE required. Turnaround time is 1-3 days. Fax notes: Will fax results, no fee. Copy fee: $.25 per page. Certification fee: $1.00.

Jefferson County

Circuit Court - Civil Division PO Box 100, Hillsboro, MO 63050; 636-797-5443; Fax: 636-797-5073. Hours: 8AM-5PM (CST). *Civil Actions Over $25,000.*

Civil Records: Access: Phone, fax, mail, in person. Both court and visitors may perform in person searches. No search fee. Required to search: name, years to search. Civil cases indexed by defendant, plaintiff. Civil records on computer since 10/90, prior on books since 1966.

General Information: Public Access terminal is available. No juvenile, mental, expunged, dismissed, or suspended imposition of sentence records released. SASE required. Copy fee: $1.00 per page. Certification fee: $.50. Fee payee: Circuit Clerk. Business checks accepted. Prepayment is required.

Circuit Court - Criminal Division PO Box 100, Hillsboro, MO 63050; 636-797-5370; Fax: 636-797-5073. Hours: 8AM-4:30PM (CST). *Felony, Misdemeanor.*

Criminal Records: Access: Mail, fax, in person. Only the court performs in person searches; visitors may not. Search fee: $10.00 per name. Required to search: name, years to search, signed release, DOB or SSN. Criminal records on computer since 1989, on index cards 1976 to 1988, prior on books or microfilm.

General Information: No juvenile, mental, expunged, dismissed, or suspended imposition of sentence records released. SASE required. Turnaround time 1 week. Copy fee: $1.00 per page. Certification fee: No cert fee. Fee payee: Circuit Clerk. Business checks accepted.

Associate Circuit Court PO Box 100, Hillsboro, MO 63050; 636-797-5362; Probate phone: 636-797-5450; Fax: 636-797-3804. Hours: 8:00AM-4:30PM (CST). *Civil Under $25,000, Eviction, Small Claims, Probate.*

Civil Records: Access: Fax, mail, in person. No search fee. Required to search: name, years to search. Civil cases indexed by defendant, plaintiff. Civil records on computer since 1990, prior on books.

General Information: Public Access terminal is available. No juvenile, mental, expunged, dismissed, or suspended imposition of sentence records released. SASE required. Turnaround time 3-5 days. Copy fee: $1.00 per page. Certification fee: $1.50. Fee payee: Circuit Clerk. Business checks accepted. Prepayment is required.

Johnson County

Circuit Court Courthouse, PO Box 436, Warrensburg, MO 64093; 660-747-6331; Fax: 660-747-7927. Hours: 8AM-4:30PM (CST). *Felony, Civil Actions Over $25,000.*

Civil Records: Access: In person only. Visitors must perform in person searches for themselves. No search fee. Required to search: name, years to search. Civil

cases indexed by defendant, plaintiff. Civil records on file since 1800s, microfilmed from 1950s to 1988.

Criminal Records: Access: In person only. Visitors must perform in person searches for themselves. No search fee. Required to search: name, years to search, DOB, SSN. Criminal records on file since 1800s, microfilmed through 1988.

General Information: Public Access terminal is available. No juvenile, adoptions, mental, expunged, dismissed, or suspended imposition of sentence records released. Copy fee: $.25 per page. Certification fee: $1.50. Fee payee: Circuit Clerk. Personal checks accepted.

Associate Circuit Court Johnson County Courthouse, 300 N Holden #304, Warrensburg, MO 64093; 660-747-2227. Hours: 8AM-4:30PM (CST). *Misdemeanor, Civil Actions Under $45,000, Eviction, Small Claims, Probate.*

Civil Records: Access: Mail, in person. Both court and visitors may perform in person searches. No search fee. Required to search: name, years to search. Civil cases indexed by defendant, plaintiff. Civil records on computer since 1994, prior on index since 1979.

Criminal Records: Access: Mail, in person. Both court and visitors may perform in person searches. No search fee. Required to search: name, years to search. Criminal records on computer since 1994, prior on index since 1979.

General Information: No juvenile, mental, expunged, dismissed, or suspended imposition of sentence records released. SASE required. Turnaround time varies. Copy fee: $.25 per page. Certification fee: $2.00. Fee payee: Associate Circuit Court. Personal checks accepted. Prepayment is required.

Knox County

Circuit Court PO Box 116, Edina, MO 63537; 660-397-2305; Fax: 660-397-3331. Hours: 8:30AM-4PM (CST). *Felony, Misdemeanor, Civil Actions Over $45,000.*

Civil Records: Access: Mail, in person. Both court and visitors may perform in person searches. No search fee. Required to search: name, years to search. Civil cases indexed by defendant, plaintiff. Civil records on microfiche since 3/83, archived since 1845, no computerization.

Criminal Records: Access: Mail, in person. Both court and visitors may perform in person searches. No search fee. Required to search: name, years to search. Criminal records on microfiche since 3/83, archived since 1845, no computerization.

General Information: No juvenile, mental, expunged, dismissed, or suspended imposition of sentence records released. SASE not required. Turnaround time same day. Copy fee: $1.00 per page. Certification fee: $2.00. Fee payee: Circuit Court. Personal checks accepted. Prepayment is required.

Associate Circuit Court PO Box 126, Edina, MO 63537; 660-397-3146; Fax: 660-397-3331. Hours: 8:30AM-4PM (CST). *Misdemeanor, Civil Actions Under $25,000, Eviction, Small Claims, Probate.*

Civil Records: Access: Mail, in person. Both court and visitors may perform in person searches. No search fee. Required to search: name, years to search. Civil cases indexed by defendant, plaintiff. Civil records on computer since 1993, prior on index cards.

Criminal Records: Access: Mail, in person. Both court and visitors may perform in person searches. No search fee. Required to search: name, years to search; also helpful: DOB, SSN. Criminal records on computer since 1993, prior on index cards.

General Information: No juvenile, mental, expunged, dismissed, or suspended imposition of sentence records released. SASE required. Turnaround time 2-3 days. Copy fee: $.25 per page. Certification fee: $1.50. Fee payee: Associate Circuit Court. Personal checks accepted. Prepayment is required.

Laclede County

Circuit Court 200 N Adams St, Lebanon, MO 65536; 417-532-2471; Fax: 417-532-3683. Hours: 8AM-4PM (CST). *Felony, Misdemeanor, Civil Actions Over $45,000.*

Civil Records: Access: Phone, fax, mail, in person. Both court and visitors may perform in person searches. No search fee. Required to search: name, years to search. Civil cases indexed by defendant, plaintiff. Civil records on cards since 1976, prior on books.

Criminal Records: Access: Phone, fax, mail, in person. Both court and visitors may perform in person searches. No search fee. Required to search: name, years to search; also helpful: SSN. Criminal records on cards since 1976, prior on books.

General Information: Public Access terminal is available. No juvenile, mental, expunged, dismissed, or suspended imposition of sentence records released. SASE required. Turnaround time 1-2 days. Fax notes: $3.00 for first page, $1.00 each add'l. Copy fee: $.25 per page. Certification fee: $1.50. Fee payee: Laclede County Circuit Clerk. Personal checks accepted. Copy fees may be billed.

Associate Circuit Court 200 N Adams St, Lebanon, MO 65536; 417-532-9196. Hours: 8AM-4PM (CST). *Misdemeanor, Civil Actions Under $45,000, Eviction, Small Claims, Probate.*

Civil Records: Access: Phone, mail, in person. Only the court performs in person searches; visitors may not. No search fee. Required to search: name, years to search. Civil cases indexed by defendant, plaintiff. Civil records on books since 1979.

Criminal Records: Access: Phone, mail, in person. Only the court performs in person searches; visitors may not. No search fee. Required to search: name, years to search. Criminal records on computer since 1991, prior on books since 1979.

General Information: No juvenile, mental, expunged, dismissed, or suspended imposition of sentence records released. Turnaround time 7-10 days. Copy fee: $.25 per page. Certification fee: $1.50. Fee payee: Circuit Court. Only cashiers checks and money orders accepted. Prepayment is required.

Lafayette County

Circuit Court PO Box 340, Lexington, MO 64067; 660-259-6101; Fax: 660-259-6148. Hours: 8AM-4:30PM (CST). *Felony, Misdemeanor, Civil Actions Over $5,000.*

Civil Records: Access: Mail, fax, in person. Only the court performs in person searches; visitors may not. No search fee. Required to search: name, years to search. Civil cases indexed by defendant, plaintiff. Civil records on books, archived since 1823; on computer back to 1987. All search requests must be in writing.

Criminal Records: Access: Mail, fax, in person. Only the court performs in person searches; visitors may not. No search fee. Required to search: name, years to search; also helpful-case number. Criminal records on books, archived since 1823; on computer back to 1987.

General Information: Public Access terminal is available. No juvenile, mental, expunged, dismissed, or suspended imposition of sentence records released. SASE required. Turnaround time 5 days. Fax notes: Fee to fax results is $1.00 per page. Copy fee: $.25 per page. Certification fee: $2.50. Fee payee: Circuit Clerk. Personal checks accepted. Copy fees & attorney of record may be billed.

Associate Circuit Court - Division III PO Box 236, Lexington, MO 64067; 660-259-6151; Fax: 660-259-4997. Hours: 8AM-4:30PM (CST). *Misdemeanor, Civil Actions Under $25,000, Eviction, Small Claims, Probate.*

Note: Most civil action cases are directed to the Circuit Court, regardless of limits.

Civil Records: Access: Mail, in person. Only the court performs in person searches; visitors may not. No search fee. Required to search: name, years to search. Civil cases indexed by defendant, plaintiff. Civil records on index cards since 1979, prior on record books.

Criminal Records: Access: Mail, in person. Only the court performs in person searches; visitors may not. No search fee. Required to search: name, years to search, address, DOB, SSN. Criminal records on index cards since 1979, prior on record books.

General Information: No juvenile, mental, expunged, dismissed, or suspended imposition of sentence records released. SASE required. Turnaround time 1-2 days. No copy fee. Certification fee: $2.50. Fee payee: Associate Circuit Court. Personal checks accepted. Prepayment is required.

Lawrence County

Circuit Court One Courthouse Square #201, Mt Vernon, MO 65712; 417-466-2471. Hours: 8AM-5PM (CST). *Felony, Misdemeanor, Civil Actions Over $25,000.*

Civil Records: Access: Mail, in person. Both court and visitors may perform in person searches. Search fee: $5.00 per name. Required to search: name, years to search. Civil cases indexed by defendant, plaintiff. Civil records on computer back to 1991, prior archived since 1890.

Criminal Records: Access: Mail, in person. Both court and visitors may perform in person searches. Search fee: $5.00 per name. Required to search: name, years to search, DOB; also helpful: SSN. Criminal records on computer back to 1991, prior archived since 1890.

General Information: Public Access terminal is available. No juvenile, mental, expunged, dismissed, or suspended imposition of sentence records released. SASE required. Turnaround time 1 week. Copy fee: $.25 per page. Certification fee: $2.00. Fee payee: Circuit Court. Business checks accepted. Prepayment is required.

Associate Circuit Court 1 Courthouse Sg, Mt Vernon, MO 65712; 417-466-2463. Hours: 8:30AM-5PM (CST). *Misdemeanor, Civil Actions Under $45,000, Eviction, Small Claims, Probate.*

Civil Records: Access: Mail, in person. Both court and visitors may perform in person searches. No search fee. Required to search: name, years to search. Civil cases indexed by defendant, plaintiff. Civil records on index cards since 1979, prior on books.

Criminal Records: Access: Mail, in person. Both court and visitors may perform in person searches. No search fee. Required to search: name, years to search; also helpful: DOB, SSN. Criminal records on index cards since 1979, prior on books.

General Information: No juvenile, mental, expunged, dismissed, or suspended imposition of sentence records released. SASE required. Turnaround time 2-3 days. Copy fee: $.35 per page. Certification fee: No cert fee. Fee payee: Associate Circuit Court. Personal checks accepted. Prepayment is required.

Lewis County

Circuit Court PO Box 97, Monticello, MO 63457; 573-767-5440; Fax: 573-767-5378. Hours: 8AM-Noon,1-4PM (CST). *Felony, Misdemeanor, Civil Actions Over $25,000.*

Civil Records: Access: In person only. Visitors must perform in person searches for themselves. No search

fee. Required to search: name, years to search. Civil cases indexed by defendant, plaintiff. Civil records on computer back to 1976 (judgments) and index books, archived since 1830s.

Criminal Records: Access: In person only. Visitors must perform in person searches for themselves. No search fee. Required to search: name, years to search. Criminal records on computer and index books, archived since 1830s.

General Information: No juvenile, mental, expunged, dismissed, or suspended imposition of sentence records released. Certification fee: $2.50.

Associate Circuit Court PO Box 36, Monticello, MO 63457; 573-767-5352; Fax: 573-767-5412. Hours: 8AM-4:30PM (CST). *Misdemeanor, Civil Actions Under $25,000, Eviction, Small Claims, Probate.*

Civil Records: Access: Fax, mail, in person. Only the court performs in person searches; visitors may not. No search fee. Required to search: name, years to search. Civil cases indexed by defendant, plaintiff. Civil records on computer back to 1987; on books back to 1979.

Criminal Records: Access: Fax, mail, in person. Only the court performs in person searches; visitors may not. No search fee. Required to search: name, years to search; also helpful: DOB, SSN, signed release. Criminal records on computer back to 1987; on books back to 1979.

General Information: No juvenile, mental, expunged, dismissed, or suspended imposition of sentence records released. Turnaround time 1-2 days. Copy fee: $.10 per page. Certification fee: No cert fee. May bill fees to businesses and attorneys.

Lincoln County

Circuit Court 201 Main St, Troy, MO 63379; 636-528-6300. Hours: 8:00AM-4:30PM (CST). *Felony, Misdemeanor, Civil Actions Over $45,000.*

Civil Records: Access: In person only. Visitors must perform in person searches for themselves. No search fee. Required to search: name, years to search. Civil cases indexed by defendant, plaintiff. Civil records on computer since 8/92, prior on index cards since 1978.

Criminal Records: Access: In person only. Visitors must perform in person searches for themselves. No search fee. Required to search: name, years to search. Criminal records on computer since 8/92, prior on index cards since 1978.

General Information: Public Access terminal is available. No juvenile, mental, expunged, dismissed, or suspended imposition of sentence records released. Copy fee: $.25 per page. Certification fee: $1.00. Fee payee: Lincoln County Circuit Clerk. Personal checks accepted. Prepayment is required.

Associate Circuit Court 201 Main St, Troy, MO 63379; 636-528-6300. Hours: 8AM-4:30PM (CST). *Misdemeanor, Civil Actions Under $25,000, Eviction, Small Claims, Probate.*

Civil Records: Access: Phone, in person. Visitors must perform in person searches for themselves. No search fee. Required to search: name, years to search. Civil cases indexed by defendant, plaintiff. Civil records on index cards, archived since 1820; computerized since.

Criminal Records: Access: Mail, in person. Only the court performs in person searches; visitors may not. No search fee. Required to search: name, years to search, DOB. Criminal records on computer since 1991; on books or cards back to 1820s.

General Information: Public Access terminal is available. No juvenile, mental, expunged or dismissed records released. SASE helpful. Turnaround time 1 week to 10 days. Probate up to 30 days. Copy fee: $.25 per page. Certification fee: $1.50 plus $.25 per page. Fee payee: Associate Circuit Court. Personal checks accepted. Prepayment is required.

Linn County

Linn County Circuit Court PO Box 84, Linneus, MO 64653-0084; 660-895-5212; Fax: 660-895-5277. Hours: 8AM-Noon,1-5PM (CST). *Felony, Misdemeanor, Civil Actions Over $45,000.*

Civil Records: Access: Fax, mail, in person. Only the court performs in person searches; visitors may not. No search fee. Required to search: name, years to search. Civil cases indexed by defendant, plaintiff. Civil records on books.

Criminal Records: Access: Fax, mail, in person. Only the court performs in person searches; visitors may not. No search fee. Required to search: name, years to search. Criminal records on books.

General Information: No juvenile, mental, expunged, dismissed, or suspended imposition of sentence records released. SASE required. Turnaround time 1 week, phone turnaround time 1-2 days. Fax notes: No fee to fax results. Copy fee: $.25 per page. Certification fee: $2.00. Fee payee: Linn County Circuit Court. Only cashiers checks and money orders accepted. Prepayment is required.

Associate Circuit Court Box 93, Linneus, MO 64653; 660-895-5419; Fax: 660-895-5533. Hours: 8AM-4:30PM (CST). *Misdemeanor, Civil Actions Under $25,000, Eviction, Small Claims, Probate.*

Civil Records: Access: Phone, mail, in person. Only the court performs in person searches; visitors may not. No search fee. Required to search: name, years to search. Civil cases indexed by defendant, plaintiff. Civil records on index cards since 1979.

Criminal Records: Access: Phone, mail, in person. Only the court performs in person searches; visitors may not. No search fee. Required to search: name, years to search. Criminal records on index cards since 1979.

General Information: No juvenile, mental, expunged, dismissed, or suspended imposition of sentence records released. SASE required. Copy fee: $.25 per page. Certification fee: $2.00. Fee payee: Associate Circuit Court. Personal checks accepted.

Livingston County

Circuit Court 700 Webster St, Chillicothe, MO 64601; 660-646-1718; Fax: 660-646-2734. Hours: 8:30AM-4:30PM (CST). *Felony, Misdemeanor, Civil Actions Over $45,000.*

Civil Records: Access: In person only. Visitors must perform in person searches for themselves. No search fee. Required to search: name, years to search. Civil cases indexed by defendant, plaintiff. Civil records on index cards since 1974, prior on record books.

Criminal Records: Access: In person only. Visitors must perform in person searches for themselves. No search fee. Required to search: name, years to search. Criminal records on index cards since 1974, prior on record books.

General Information: No juvenile, mental, expunged, dismissed, or suspended imposition of sentence records released. Copy fee: $.25 per page. Certification fee: $1.00. Fee payee: Livingston County Circuit Clerk. Personal checks accepted. Attorneys may bill copy fees.

Associate Circuit Court Livingston County Courthouse, Suite 8, Chillicothe, MO 64601; 660-646-3103; Fax: 660-646-8014. Hours: Public hours: 8:30AM-4:30PM; Office hours: 8AM-5PM (CST). *Misdemeanor, Civil Actions Under $25,000, Eviction, Small Claims, Probate.*

Civil Records: Access: Phone, fax, mail, in person. Both court and visitors may perform in person searches. No search fee. Required to search: name, years to search; also helpful: address. Civil cases indexed by defendant, plaintiff. Civil records on index cards and record books since 1975, prior on record books.

Criminal Records: Access: Phone, fax, mail, in person. Both court and visitors may perform in person searches. No search fee. Required to search: name, years to search, DOB. Criminal records on index cards and record books since 1975, prior on record books. Signed release required for closed records.

General Information: No juvenile, mental, expunged, dismissed, or suspended imposition of sentence records released. SASE required. Turnaround time 5 days. Fax notes: Call for fax fee. Copy fee: $1.00 per page. Certification fee: $1.50. Fee payee: Associate Circuit Court. Personal checks accepted.

Macon County

Circuit Court PO Box 382, Macon, MO 63552; 660-385-4631; Fax: 660-385-4235. Hours: 8:30AM-4PM (CST). *Felony, Misdemeanor, Civil Actions Over $45,000.*

Civil Records: Access: Fax, mail, in person. Both court and visitors may perform in person searches. No search fee. Required to search: name, years to search. Civil cases indexed by defendant, plaintiff. Civil records on computer since 1/1/91, on index cards from 1976-1990, prior on books.

Criminal Records: Access: Fax, mail, in person. Both court and visitors may perform in person searches. Search fee: $1.00 per name. Required to search: name, years to search. Criminal records on computer since 1/1/91, on index cards from 1976-1990, prior on books.

General Information: No juvenile, mental, expunged, dismissed, or suspended imposition of sentence records released. SASE required. Turnaround time 2-5 days. Fax notes: $2.50 for first page, $.50 each add'l. Copy fee: $.25 per page. Certification fee: $3.00. Fee payee: Clerk of Circuit Court. Personal checks accepted. Prepayment is required.

Associate Circuit Court PO Box 491, Macon, MO 63552; 660-385-3531; Fax: 660-385-3132. Hours: 8AM-4:30PM (CST). *Misdemeanor, Civil Actions Under $25,000, Eviction, Small Claims, Probate.*

Civil Records: Access: Fax, mail, in person. Both court and visitors may perform in person searches. No search fee. Required to search: name, years to search. Civil cases indexed by defendant, plaintiff. Civil records on index cards and books; on computer back to 1992.

Criminal Records: Access: In person only. Visitors must perform in person searches for themselves. No search fee. Required to search: name, years to search, DOB. Criminal records on computer since 1992, prior on index cards back to 1989. Court will refer phone and mail requests to the State Police, 573-526-6153.

General Information: No juvenile, mental, expunged, dismissed, or suspended imposition of sentence records released. SASE required. Turnaround time 2 weeks. Copy fee: $1.00 per page. Certification fee: $1.50. Fee payee: Circuit Court Division II or Probate Court. Prepayment is required.

Madison County

Circuit Court PO Box 470, Fredericktown, MO 63645-0470; 573-783-2102; Fax: 573-783-2715. Hours: 8AM-5PM (CST). *Felony, Misdemeanor, Civil Actions Over $45,000.*

Civil Records: Access: Mail, in person. Both court and visitors may perform in person searches. No search fee. Required to search: name, years to search. Civil cases indexed by defendant, plaintiff. Civil records on computer since 1991, prior on index cards from 1979-1991. Limit one name per mail request.

Criminal Records: Access: Mail, in person. Both court and visitors may perform in person searches. No search fee. Required to search: name, years to search. Criminal records on computer since 1991, prior on index cards from 1979-1991. Limit one name per mail request.

General Information: Public Access terminal is available. No juvenile, mental, expunged, dismissed, or suspended imposition of sentence records released. SASE required. Turnaround time up to 1 week. Copy fee: $.25 per page. Certification fee: $1.00. Fee payee: Madison County Circuit Clerk. Personal checks accepted. Prepayment is required.

Associate Circuit Court PO Box 521, Fredericktown, MO 63645; 573-783-3105; Fax: 573-783-5920. Hours: 8AM-5PM (CST). *Misdemeanor, Civil Actions Under $25,000, Small Claims, Probate, Traffic.*

Civil Records: Access: Phone, fax, mail, in person. Both court and visitors may perform in person searches. No search fee. Required to search: name, years to search. Civil cases indexed by defendant, plaintiff. Civil records on index cards since 1979, prior on judgment books.

Criminal Records: Access: Phone, fax, mail, in person. Both court and visitors may perform in person searches. No search fee. Required to search: name, years to search; also helpful: DOB, SSN. Criminal records on index cards since 1979, prior on judgment books.

General Information: No juvenile, mental, expunged, dismissed, or suspended imposition of sentence records released. SASE required. Turnaround time 1 week. Copy fee: $.25 per page. Certification fee: $2.50. Fee payee: Associate Circuit Court. Only cashiers checks and money orders accepted.

Maries County

Circuit Court PO Box 213, Vienna, MO 65582; 573-422-3338; Fax: 573-422-3976. Hours: 8AM-4PM (CST). *Felony, Misdemeanor, Civil Actions Over $25,000.*

Civil Records: Access: Fax, mail, in person. Both court and visitors may perform in person searches. No search fee. Required to search: name, years to search. Civil cases indexed by defendant, plaintiff. Civil records on books and files.

Criminal Records: Access: Fax, mail, in person. Both court and visitors may perform in person searches. No search fee. Required to search: name, years to search. Criminal records on books and files.

General Information: No juvenile, mental, expunged, dismissed, or suspended imposition of sentence records released. Turnaround time 1-3 days. Fax notes: $.25 per page. Copy fee: $.25 per page. Certification fee: $1.50. Fee payee: Maries County Circuit Clerk. Personal checks accepted.

Associate Circuit Court PO Box 490, Vienna, MO 65582; 573-422-3303; Fax: 573-422-3100. Hours: 8AM-4PM (CST). *Misdemeanor, Civil Actions Under $25,000, Eviction, Small Claims, Probate.*

Note: Most civil cases are directed to the Circuit Court, regardless of limit.

Civil Records: Access: Mail, fax, in person. Both court and visitors may perform in person searches. No search fee. Required to search: name, years to search. Civil cases indexed by defendant, plaintiff. Civil records on index cards since 1985, archived since 1855.

Criminal Records: Access: Mail, fax, in person. Only the court performs in person searches; visitors may not. No search fee. Required to search: name, years to search, DOB, signed release; also helpful-SSN. Criminal records on index cards since 1985, archived since 1855.

General Information: No juvenile, mental, expunged, dismissed, or suspended imposition of sentence records released. SASE required. Turnaround time 5 days. Copy fee: $.25 per page. Certification fee: $1.50. Fee payee: Sheriff of Maries County. Only cashiers checks and money orders accepted. Prepayment is required.

Marion County

Circuit Court PO Box 392, 100 S Main St, Palmyra, MO 63461; 573-769-2550; Fax: 573-769-6012. Hours: 8:30AM-5PM (CST). *Felony, Civil Actions Over $25,000.*

Civil Records: Access: In person only. Visitors must perform in person searches for themselves. No search fee. Required to search: name, years to search. Civil cases indexed by defendant, plaintiff. Civil records on index cards since 1977, prior on judgment books.

Criminal Records: Access: Fax, mail, in person. Both court and visitors may perform in person searches. No search fee. Required to search: name, years to search, DOB. Criminal records on index cards since 1977, prior on judgment books.

General Information: No juvenile, mental, expunged, dismissed, or suspended imposition of sentence records released. SASE required. Turnaround time 1-2 days. Fax notes: $1.00 per page. Copy fee: $1.00 per page. Certification fee: $2.00. Fee payee: Marion County Circuit Clerk of Division I. Business checks accepted. All fees may be billed.

Circuit Court (Twps of Miller & Mason only)

906 Broadway, Rm 105, Hannibal, MO 63401; 573-221-0198; Fax: 573-221-9328. Hours: 8AM-5PM (CST). *Felony, Misdemeanor, Civil Actions Over $45,000.*

Civil Records: Access: Fax, mail, in person. Both court and visitors may perform in person searches. Search fee: $.50 per name. Required to search: name, years to search. Civil cases indexed by defendant, plaintiff. Civil records on computer since 1991, prior on index cards.

Criminal Records: Access: Fax, mail, in person. Only the court performs in person searches; visitors may not. Search fee: $.50 per name. Required to search: name, years to search. Criminal records on computer.

General Information: No juvenile, mental, expunged, dismissed, or suspended imposition of sentence records released. SASE required. Turnaround time 1 week. Copy fee: $.50 per page. Certification fee: $5.00. Fee payee: Circuit Clerk District II. Personal checks accepted.

Hannibal Associate Circuit Court

906 Broadway, Hannibal, MO 63401; 573-221-0288. Hours: 8AM-5PM (CST). *Misdemeanor, Civil Actions Under $45,000, Eviction, Small Claims, Probate.*

Civil Records: Access: Mail, in person. Only the court performs in person searches; visitors may not. No search fee. Required to search: name, years to search. Civil cases indexed by defendant, plaintiff. Civil records on index cards since 1979, prior on judgment books.

Criminal Records: Access: Mail, in person. Only the court performs in person searches; visitors may not. No search fee. Required to search: name, years to search. Criminal records on computer since 3/93, on index cards since 1979, prior on judgment books.

General Information: No juvenile, mental, expunged, dismissed, or suspended imposition of sentence records released. SASE required. Turnaround time 2 days. No copy fee. Certification fee: No cert fee.

Palmyra Associate Circuit Court

PO Box 449, Palmyra, MO 63461; 573-769-2318; Fax: 573-769-4558. Hours: 8AM-Noon, 1-5PM (CST). *Misdemeanor, Civil Actions Under $45,000, Eviction, Small Claims, Probate.*

Civil Records: Access: Mail, in person. Only the court performs in person searches; visitors may not. No search fee. Required to search: name, years to search. Civil cases indexed by defendant, plaintiff. Civil records on index cards since 1979, prior on judgment books.

Criminal Records: Access: Mail, in person. Only the court performs in person searches; visitors may not. No search fee. Required to search: name, years to search;

also helpful: DOB. Criminal records on computer since 1994, on index cards from 1979-1994, prior on judgment books.

General Information: No juvenile, mental, expunged, dismissed, or suspended imposition of sentence records released. SASE required. Turnaround time varies. Copy fee: $.50 per page. Certification fee: No cert fee. Fee payee: Circuit Court. Personal checks accepted.

McDonald County

Circuit & Associate Court PO Box 157, Pineville, MO 64856; 417-223-7515; Fax: 417-223-4125. Hours: 8AM-4:30PM (CST). *Felony, Misdemeanor, Civil, Small Claims, Probate.*

Civil Records: Access: Fax, mail, in person. Only the court performs in person searches; visitors may not. No search fee. Required to search: name, years to search. Civil cases indexed by defendant, plaintiff. Civil records on computer since 1999, on index cards since 1979, prior on index cards.

Criminal Records: Access: fax, mail, in person. Only the court performs in person searches; visitors may not. No search fee. Required to search: name, years to search. Criminal records on computer since 1999, on index cards since 1979, prior on index cards.

General Information: Public Access terminal is available. No juvenile, mental, expunged, dismissed, paternity or suspended imposition of sentence records released. SASE required. Fax notes: No fee to fax results. Copy fee: $.25 per page. Certification fee: $1.50. Fee payee: McDonald County Circuit Clerk. Business checks accepted. Prepayment is required.

Mercer County

Circuit Court Courthouse, 802 East Main, Princeton, MO 64673; 660-748-4335; Fax: 660-748-3180. Hours: 8:30AM-4:30PM (CST). *Felony, Misdemeanor, Civil Actions Over $45,000.*

Civil Records: Access: Mail, in person, online. Both court and visitors may perform in person searches. No search fee. Required to search: name, years to search. Civil cases indexed by defendant, plaintiff. Civil records on computer since 1991, on index cards since 1977, prior on books. Participates in the free state online court record system at http://casenet.osca.state.mo.us/casenet. Online records go back to 3/2000.

Criminal Records: Access: Mail, in person, online. Both court and visitors may perform in person searches. No search fee. Required to search: name, years to search, address, DOB, SSN, signed release. Criminal records on computer since 1991, on index cards since 1977, prior on books. Online access to criminal records is the same as civil.

General Information: No juvenile, mental, expunged, dismissed, or suspended imposition of sentence records released. SASE required. Turnaround time 1 week. Copy fee: $.25 per page. Certification fee: $2.00. Fee payee: Mercer County Circuit Clerk. Personal checks accepted. Prepayment is required.

Associate Circuit Court

Courthouse, 802 E Main Street, Princeton, MO 64673; 660-748-4232; Fax: 660-748-3180. Hours: 8:30AM-4:30PM (CST). *Misdemeanor, Civil Actions Under $45,000, Eviction, Small Claims, Probate.*

Note: The court expects to have a public access terminal by the end of 2000.

Civil Records: Access: In person, online. Both court and visitors may perform in person searches. No search fee. Required to search: name, years to search. Civil cases indexed by defendant. Civil records on index. Participates in the free state online court record system at http://casenet.osca.state.mo.us/casenet. Online records go back to 3/2000.

Criminal Records: Access: In person, online. Both court and visitors may perform in person searches. No

search fee. Required to search: name, years to search; also helpful: DOB, SSN. Criminal records on index. Online access to criminal records is the same as civil.

General Information: Public Access terminal is available. No juvenile, mental, expunged, dismissed, or suspended imposition of sentence records released. Copy fee: $.25 per page. Certification fee: $1.50 plus $1.00 per page. Fee payee: Circuit Court Division II. Personal checks accepted. Prepayment is required.

Associate Circuit Court

Courthouse Rm 304, Carthage, MO 64836; 417-358-0450; Fax: 417-358-0460. Hours: 8:30AM-4:30PM (CST). *Misdemeanor, Civil Actions Under $45,000, Eviction, Small Claims, Probate.*

Civil Records: Access: In person, online. Visitors must perform in person searches for themselves. No search fee. Required to search: name, years to search. Civil cases indexed by defendant, plaintiff. Civil records on computer since 1990, prior on index cards since 1979. Participates in the free state online court record system at http://casenet.osca.state.mo.us/casenet.

Criminal Records: Access: In person, online. Visitors must perform in person searches for themselves. No search fee. Required to search: name, years to search. Criminal records on computer since 1990, prior on index cards since 1979. Online access to criminal records is the same as civil.

General Information: No juvenile, mental, expunged, dismissed, or suspended imposition of sentence records released. No copy fee. Certification fee: No cert fee.

Miller County

Circuit Court PO Box 11, Tuscumbia, MO 65082; 573-369-2303; Fax: 573-369-2910. Hours: 8AM-4:30PM (CST). *Felony, Misdemeanor, Civil Actions Over $45,000.*

Civil Records: Access: Phone, fax, mail, in person. Both court and visitors may perform in person searches. Search fee: $4.00 per name. Required to search: name, years to search. Civil cases indexed by defendant, plaintiff. Civil records on index cards since 1976, prior on books.

Criminal Records: Access: Phone, fax, mail, in person. Both court and visitors may perform in person searches. Search fee: $4.00 per name. Required to search: name, years to search. Criminal records on index cards since 1976, prior on books.

General Information: Public Access terminal is available. No juvenile, mental, expunged, dismissed, or suspended imposition of sentence records released. SASE required. Turnaround time 1 week. Fax notes: No fee to fax results; other fees must be pre-paid. Will fax to local & 800 numbers only. Copy fee: $.50 per page. Certification fee: $2.00. Fee payee: Miller County Circuit Court. Personal checks accepted. Prepayment is required.

Associate Circuit Court

Miller County Courthouse Annex, Tuscumbia, MO 65082; 573-369-2330. Hours: 8AM-4PM (CST). *Misdemeanor, Civil Actions Under $25,000, Eviction, Small Claims, Probate.*

Civil Records: Access: Mail, in person. Only the court performs in person searches; visitors may not. No search fee. Required to search: name, years to search. Civil cases indexed by defendant, plaintiff. Civil records on computer since 1/92, on microfiche since 1980, on cards since 1979, prior archived.

Criminal Records: Access: Mail, in person. Only the court performs in person searches; visitors may not. No search fee. Required to search: name, years to search. Criminal records on computer since 1979, on microfiche since 1980, prior archived.

General Information: No juvenile, mental, expunged, dismissed, or suspended imposition of sentence records released. SASE required. Turnaround time 1 week.

Copy fee: $1.00 per page. Certification fee: $1.50. Fee payee: Associate Circuit Court. Only cashiers checks and money orders accepted. Prepayment is required.

Mississippi County

Circuit & Associate Court PO Box 369, Charleston, MO 63834; 573-683-2146; Fax: 573-649-2284. Hours: 8:30AM-4:30PM (CST). *Felony, Misdemeanor, Civil, Small Claims, Eviction, Probate.*

Note: The courts consolidated on July 1, 1999.

Civil Records: Access: Fax, mail, in person. Both court and visitors may perform in person searches. No search fee. Required to search: name, years to search. Civil cases indexed by defendant, plaintiff. Civil records in case files since 1973.

Criminal Records: Access: Fax, mail, in person. Both court and visitors may perform in person searches. No search fee. Required to search: name, years to search, DOB. Criminal records in case files since 1948.

General Information: No juvenile, mental, expunged, dismissed, or suspended imposition of sentence records released. SASE helpful. Turnaround time 1-2 days. Fax notes: No fee to fax results. Copy fee: $.25 per page. Certification fee: $.50. Fee payee: Circuit Clerk. Personal checks accepted. Copy fees may be billed.

Moniteau County

Circuit Court 200 E Main, California, MO 65018; 573-796-2071; Fax: 573-796-2591. Hours: 8AM-4:30PM (CST). *Felony, Misdemeanor, Civil Actions Over $25,000, Small Claims.*

Civil Records: Access: Mail, in person. Both court and visitors may perform in person searches. No search fee. Required to search: name, years to search; also helpful: case number. Civil cases indexed by defendant, plaintiff. Civil records on computer since 1992, prior on index cards and books.

Criminal Records: Access: Mail, in person. Both court and visitors may perform in person searches. No search fee. Required to search: name, years to search; also helpful: case number. Criminal records on computer since 1992, prior on index cards and books.

General Information: No juvenile, mental, expunged, dismissed, or suspended imposition of sentence records released. SASE required. Turnaround time 2-3 days. Fax notes: Fee to fax results is $1.00 per page. Copy fee: $.30 per page. Certification fee: $1.00. Fee payee: Montineau County Circuit Court. Personal checks accepted. Prepayment is required.

Associate Circuit Court 200 E Main, California, MO 65018; 573-796-2814. Hours: 8AM-4:30PM (CST). *Misdemeanor, Civil Actions Under $45,000, Eviction, Small Claims, Probate.*

Civil Records: Access: Phone, mail, in person. Both court and visitors may perform in person searches. No search fee. Required to search: name, years to search. Civil cases indexed by defendant, plaintiff. Civil records on index cards since 1979, prior on index books from 1948 to 1979, archived before.

Criminal Records: Access: Phone, mail, in person. Both court and visitors may perform in person searches. No search fee. Required to search: name, years to search. Criminal records on index cards since 1979, prior on index books from 1948 to 1979, archived before.

General Information: No juvenile, mental, expunged, dismissed, or suspended imposition of sentence records released. Turnaround time 1 week, phone turnaround time immediate. Copy fee: $.25 per page. Certification fee: $1.50 first page, $1.00 each additional. Personal checks accepted.

Monroe County

Circuit Court PO Box 227, Paris, MO 65275; 660-327-5204; Fax: 660-327-5781. Hours: 8AM-4:30PM (CST). *Felony, Misdemeanor, Civil Actions Over $45,000.*

Civil Records: Access: Mail, in person. Both court and visitors may perform in person searches. Search fee: $8.00 per name. Required to search: name, years to search. Civil cases indexed by defendant, plaintiff. Civil records on computer since 1996; index cards since 1979, prior on index books.

Criminal Records: Access: Mail, in person. Both court and visitors may perform in person searches. Search fee: $8.00 per name. Required to search: name, years to search, SSN, signed release. Criminal records on computer since 1996, on index cards from 1979 to 1990.

General Information: No juvenile, mental, expunged, dismissed, or suspended imposition of sentence records released. SASE required. Turnaround time 1 week. Fax notes: Fee to fax results is $1.00 per page. Copy fee: $1.00 per page. Certification fee: $2.00. Fee payee: Monroe County Circuit Court. Personal checks accepted. Prepayment is required.

Associate Circuit Court Courthouse, 300 N Main, Paris, MO 65275; 660-327-5220; Fax: 660-327-5781. Hours: 8AM-4:30PM (CST). *Misdemeanor, Civil Actions Under $45,000, Eviction, Small Claims, Probate.*

Civil Records: Access: Mail, in person. Both court and visitors may perform in person searches. Search fee: $3.00 per name. $4.00 if extensive search. Required to search: name, years to search. Civil cases indexed by defendant, plaintiff. Civil records on index cards since 1979, prior on books.

Criminal Records: Access: Mail, in person. Both court and visitors may perform in person searches. Search fee: $3.00 per name. $4.00 if extensive search. Required to search: name, years to search. Criminal records on index cards since 1979, prior on books.

General Information: No juvenile, mental, expunged, dismissed, or suspended imposition of sentence records released. SASE required. Turnaround time 2 weeks. Copy fee: $1.00 per page. Certification fee: $1.50 first page, $1.00 each additional. Fee payee: Associate Circuit Court. Personal checks accepted. Prepayment is required.

Montgomery County

Circuit Court 211 E 3rd, Montgomery City, MO 63361; 573-564-3341; Fax: 573-564-3914. Hours: 8AM-4:30PM (CST). *Felony, Misdemeanor, Civil Actions Over $45,000.*

Civil Records: Access: Online, in person. Visitors must perform in person searches for themselves. No search fee. Required to search: name, years to search. Civil cases indexed by defendant, plaintiff. Civil records on computer since 1987 for judgments, on index cards since 1979, prior on books. Participates in the free state online court record system at http://casenet.osca.state.mo.us/casenet.

Criminal Records: Access: Online, in person. Visitors must perform in person searches for themselves. No search fee. Required to search: name, years to search. Criminal records on computer since 1987 for judgments, on index cards since 1979, prior on books. Online access to criminal records is the same as civil.

General Information: Public Access terminal is available. (Judgments only.) No juvenile, mental, expunged, dismissed, or suspended imposition of sentence records released. Copy fee: $.25 per page. Certification fee: $1.00 plus $.25 per page. Fee payee: Montgomery County Circuit Court. Personal checks accepted. Prepayment is required.

Associate Circuit Court 211 E 3rd St, Montgomery City, MO 63361; 573-564-3348. Hours: 8:00AM-4:30PM (CST). *Misdemeanor, Civil Actions Under $25,000, Eviction, Small Claims, Probate.*

Civil Records: Access: Online, in person. Visitors must perform in person searches for themselves. No search fee. Required to search: name, years to search. Civil cases indexed by defendant, plaintiff. Civil records on computer back to 1976, prior on index cards. Participates in the free state online court record system at http://casenet.osca.state.mo.us/casenet.

Criminal Records: Access: Online, in person. Visitors must perform in person searches for themselves. No search fee. Required to search: name, years to search, DOB. Criminal records on computer back to 1976, prior on index cards. Online access to criminal records is the same as civil.

General Information: Public Access terminal is available. (Public terminal limited to judgments.) No juvenile, mental, expunged, dismissed, or suspended imposition of sentence records released. Copy fee: $.25 per page. Certification fee: $1.50 per page. Fee payee: Montgomery Circuit Clerk's Office. Personal checks accepted. Prepayment is required.

Morgan County

Circuit Court 211 E Newton, Versailles, MO 65084; 573-378-4413; Fax: 573-378-5356. Hours: 8AM-5PM (CST). *Felony, Civil Actions Over $25,000.*

Civil Records: Access: Phone, mail, in person. Both court and visitors may perform in person searches. No search fee. Required to search: name, years to search. Civil cases indexed by defendant, plaintiff. Civil records on computer since 1992, on index cards since 1979, prior archived since mid-1800s.

Criminal Records: Access: Phone, mail, in person. Both court and visitors may perform in person searches. No search fee. Required to search: name, years to search. Criminal records on computer since 1992, on index cards since 1979, prior archived since mid-1800s.

General Information: No juvenile, mental, expunged, dismissed, or suspended imposition of sentence records released. SASE required. Turnaround time 1 week, phone turnaround time immediate. Copy fee: $.25 per page. Certification fee: $.50. Fee payee: Circuit Court. Personal checks accepted. Copy fees may be billed.

Associate Circuit Court 211 E Newton St, Versailles, MO 65084; 573-378-4235; Fax: 573-378-6847. Hours: 8:30AM-5PM (CST). *Misdemeanor, Civil Actions Under $25,000, Eviction, Small Claims, Probate.*

Civil Records: Access: Phone, mail, in person. Both court and visitors may perform in person searches. No search fee. Required to search: name, years to search. Civil cases indexed by defendant, plaintiff. Civil records on computer since 1991, prior on index.

Criminal Records: Access: Phone, mail, in person. Only the court performs in person searches; visitors may not. No search fee. Required to search: name, years to search; also helpful: address, DOB, SSN, singed release. Criminal records on computer since 1989, prior on index. Signed release required for some searches.

General Information: No juvenile, mental, expunged, dismissed, or suspended imposition of sentence records released. SASE required. Turnaround time 2-3 days. Copy fee: $1.00 per page. Certification fee: $1.50. Fee payee: Associate Circuit Court or Probate Court. Only cashiers checks and money orders accepted. Prepayment is required.

New Madrid County

Circuit Court County Courthouse, 450 Main Street, New Madrid, MO 63869; 573-748-2228. Hours: 8AM-4:30PM (CST). *Felony, Misdemeanor, Civil Actions Over $45,000.*

www.osca.state.mo.us

Civil Records: Access: Mail, in person. Both court and visitors may perform in person searches. No search fee. Required to search: name, years to search. Civil cases indexed by defendant, plaintiff. Civil records on Cott index since 1979, prior on books.

Criminal Records: Access: Mail, in person. Both court and visitors may perform in person searches. No search fee. Required to search: name, years to search. Criminal records on Cott index since 1979, prior on books.

General Information: No juvenile, mental, expunged, dismissed, or suspended imposition of sentence records released. SASE is required. Turnaround time 1 week. Copy fee: $1.00 per page. Certification fee: Certification fee is $5.00. Fee payee: Circuit Clerk. Business checks accepted. Prepayment is required.

Associate Circuit Court County Courthouse, New Madrid, MO 63869; 573-748-5556. Hours: 8AM-5PM (CST). *Misdemeanor, Civil Actions Under $25,000, Eviction, Small Claims, Probate.*

Civil Records: Access: Mail, in person. Only the court performs in person searches; visitors may not. No search fee. Required to search: name, years to search. Civil cases indexed by defendant, plaintiff. Probate records archived since 1803.

Criminal Records: Access: Mail, in person. Only the court performs in person searches; visitors may not. No search fee. Required to search: name, years to search. Criminal records archived since 1947; on computer since.

General Information: No juvenile, mental, expunged, dismissed, or suspended imposition of sentence records released. Turnaround time 1-2 weeks. No copy fee. Certification fee: No cert fee.

Newton County

Circuit Court PO Box 130, Neosho, MO 64850; 417-451-8257; Fax: 417-451-8298. Hours: 8:30AM-5PM (CST). *Felony, Misdemeanor, Civil Actions Over $25,000.*

Civil Records: Access: Phone, fax, mail, in person. Only the court performs in person searches; visitors may not. No search fee. Required to search: name, years to search. Civil cases indexed by defendant, plaintiff. Civil records on computer since 1991, prior on index cards and books.

Criminal Records: Access: Phone, fax, mail, in person. Only the court performs in person searches; visitors may not. No search fee. Required to search: name, years to search; also helpful: DOB, SSN. Criminal records on computer since 1991, prior on index cards and books.

General Information: No juvenile, mental, expunged, dismissed, or suspended imposition of sentence records released. SASE required. Turnaround time 1-2 days. Fax notes: $2.00 per page. Copy fee: $.25 per page. Certification fee: $1.00. Fee payee: Newton County Circuit Clerk. Business checks accepted. Copy fees may be billed.

Associate Circuit Court PO Box 170, Neosho, MO 64850; 417-451-8212; Fax: 417-451-8272. Hours: 8AM-5PM (CST). *Misdemeanor, Civil Actions Under $25,000, Eviction, Small Claims, Probate.*

Civil Records: Access: Phone, mail, in person. Both court and visitors may perform in person searches. No search fee. Required to search: name, years to search. Civil cases indexed by defendant, plaintiff. Civil records on computer since 1989, prior on index cards.

Criminal Records: Access: Phone, mail, in person. Both court and visitors may perform in person searches. No search fee. Required to search: name, years to search, DOB. Criminal records on computer since 1989, prior on index cards.

General Information: No juvenile, mental, expunged, dismissed, or suspended imposition of sentence records released. SASE required. Turnaround time 1 week. Copy fee: $.25 per page. Certification fee: $1.00. Fee payee: Associate Circuit Court-Division II. Business checks accepted. Prepayment is required.

Nodaway County

Circuit Court PO Box 218, Maryville, MO 64468; 660-582-5431; Fax: 660-582-5499. Hours: 8AM-4:30PM (CST). *Felony, Misdemeanor, Civil Actions Over $25,000.*

Civil Records: Access: Phone, fax, mail, in person. Both court and visitors may perform in person searches. Search fee: $5.00 per name. Required to search: name, years to search. Civil cases indexed by defendant, plaintiff. Civil records on computer back to 5/91, archived since 1845.

Criminal Records: Access: Fax, mail, in person. Both court and visitors may perform in person searches. No search fee. Required to search: name, years to search, DOB, SSN, signed release. Criminal records on computer back to 5/91, archived since 1845.

General Information: Public Access terminal is available. No juvenile, mental, expunged, dismissed, or suspended imposition of sentence records released. SASE required. Turnaround time same day. Fax notes: Fee to fax results is $1.00 per page. Copy fee: $1.00 per page. Certification fee: $1.00. Fee payee: Circuit Clerk. Personal checks accepted. Prepayment is required.

Associate Circuit Court Courthouse Annex, 303 N Market, Maryville, MO 64468; 660-582-2531; Fax: 660-582-2047. Hours: 8AM-4:30PM (CST). *Misdemeanor, Civil Actions Under $45,000, Eviction, Small Claims, Probate.*

Civil Records: Access: Mail, in person. Only the court performs in person searches; visitors may not. Search fee: $5.00. Required to search: name, years to search. Civil cases indexed by defendant, plaintiff. Civil records on computer since 1981, archived since 1845.

Criminal Records: Access: Mail, in person. Only the court performs in person searches; visitors may not. Search fee: $5.00. Required to search: name, years to search. Criminal records on computer since 1981, archived since 1845.

General Information: No juvenile, mental, expunged, dismissed, or suspended imposition of sentence records released. SASE required. Turnaround time 2 days. Copy fee: $.50 per page. Certification fee: $1.50. Fee payee: Circuit Court Associate Division. Business checks accepted. Prepayment is required.

Oregon County

Circuit Court PO Box 406, Alton, MO 65606; 417-778-7460; Fax: 417-778-6641. Hours: 8AM-4PM (CST). *Felony, Misdemeanor, Civil Actions Over $45,000.*

Civil Records: Access: Phone, fax, mail, in person, online. Both court and visitors may perform in person searches. No search fee. Required to search: name, years to search; also helpful: address. Civil cases indexed by defendant, plaintiff. Civil records on books. Participates in the free state online court record system at http://casenet.osca.state.mo.us/casenet.

Criminal Records: Access: Phone, fax, mail, in person, online. Both court and visitors may perform in person searches. No search fee. Required to search: name, years to search; also helpful: DOB, SSN. Criminal records on books. Online access to criminal records is the same as civil.

General Information: No juvenile, mental, expunged, dismissed, or suspended imposition of sentence records released. SASE required. Turnaround time 1-2 days. Fax notes: $1.00 for first page, $.50 each add'l. Copy fee: $.50 per page. Certification fee: $2.00. Fee payee: Circuit Court. Personal checks accepted. Prepayment is required.

Associate Circuit Court PO Box 211, Alton, MO 65606; 417-778-7461; Fax: 417-778-6209. Hours: 8:00AM-4:00PM (CST). *Misdemeanor, Civil Actions Under $45,000, Eviction, Small Claims, Probate.*

Civil Records: Access: Mail, in person, online. Both court and visitors may perform in person searches. No search fee. Required to search: name, years to search. Civil cases indexed by defendant, plaintiff. Civil records on index cards, archived since 1850. Participates in the free state online court record system at http://casenet.osca.state.mo.us/casenet.

Criminal Records: Access: Mail, in person, online. Both court and visitors may perform in person searches. No search fee. Required to search: name, years to search. Criminal records on computer since 3/11/92, prior on files. Online access to criminal records is the same as civil.

General Information: Public Access terminal is available. No juvenile, mental, expunged, dismissed, or suspended imposition of sentence records released. SASE not required. Turnaround time varies. Copy fee: $1.00 per page. Certification fee: $2.00. Fee payee: Associate Circuit Court. Business checks accepted. Prepayment is required.

Osage County

Circuit Court PO Box 825, Linn, MO 65051; 573-897-3114 573-897-2136 (Assoc Div). Hours: 8AM-4:30PM (CST). *Felony, Misdemeanor, Civil Actions Over $45,000.*

Civil Records: Access: Phone, mail, in person, online. Both court and visitors may perform in person searches. No search fee. Required to search: name, years to search. Civil cases indexed by defendant, plaintiff. Civil records on index cards and books. Participates in the free state online court record system at http://casenet.osca.state.mo.us/casenet.

Criminal Records: Access: Phone, mail, in person, online. Both court and visitors may perform in person searches. No search fee. Required to search: name, years to search, DOB; also helpful: SSN. Criminal records on index cards and books. Online access to criminal records is the same as civil.

General Information: Public Access terminal is available. No juvenile, mental, expunged, dismissed, or suspended imposition of sentence records released. SASE required. Turnaround time ASAP. Fax notes: Fee to fax results is $1.00 per page. Copy fee: $.50 per page. $1.00 minimum. Certification fee: $2.00. Fee payee: Circuit Clerk. Personal checks accepted. Prepayment is required.

Associate Circuit Court PO Box 470, Linn, MO 65051; 573-897-2136; Fax: 573-897-4741. Hours: 8AM-4:30PM (CST). *Misdemeanor, Civil Actions Under $25,000, Eviction, Small Claims, Probate.*

Civil Records: Access: Phone, mail, in person, online. Only the court performs in person searches; visitors may not. No search fee. Required to search: name, years to search. Civil cases indexed by defendant, plaintiff. Civil records on index cards. Participates in the free state online court record system at http://casenet.osca.state.mo.us/casenet.

Criminal Records: Access: Phone, mail, in person, online. Only the court performs in person searches; visitors may not. No search fee. Required to search: name, years to search, DOB; also helpful: SSN. Criminal records on index cards. Online access to criminal records is the same as civil.

General Information: No juvenile, mental, expunged, dismissed, or suspended imposition of sentence records released. SASE not required. Turnaround time 2 weeks. Copy fee: \$.25 per page. Certification fee: \$2.00. Fee payee: Osage County Circuit Court-Associate Division. Personal checks accepted. Prepayment is required.

Ozark County

Circuit Court PO Box 36, Gainesville, MO 65655; 417-679-4232; Fax: 417-679-4554. Hours: 8AM-Noon, 12:30-4:30PM (CST). *Felony, Misdemeanor, Civil Actions Over \$45,000.*

Civil Records: Access: Mail, in person. No search fee. Required to search: name, years to search. Civil cases indexed by defendant, plaintiff. Civil records on index cards since 1979, archived since 1841.

Criminal Records: Access: Mail, in person. Only the court performs in person searches; visitors may not. No search fee. Required to search: name, years to search, DOB; also helpful: SSN. Criminal records on index cards since 1979, archived since 1841.

General Information: No juvenile, mental, expunged, dismissed, or suspended imposition of sentence records released. SASE requested. Turnaround time 10 days-2 weeks. Copy fee: \$1.00 per page. Certification fee: \$1.50. Fee payee: Ozark County Circuit Court. Personal checks accepted. Prepayment is required.

Associate Circuit Court PO Box 278, Gainesville, MO 65655; 417-679-4611; Fax: 417-679-2099. Hours: 8AM-4:30PM (CST). *Misdemeanor, Civil Actions Under \$25,000, Eviction, Small Claims, Probate.*

Civil Records: Access: Fax, mail, in person. Only the court performs in person searches; visitors may not. No search fee. Required to search: name, years to search. Civil cases indexed by defendant, plaintiff. Civil records on case files.

Criminal Records: Access: Fax, mail, in person. Only the court performs in person searches; visitors may not. No search fee. Required to search: name, years to search, DOB, signed release; also helpful: SSN. Criminal records on computer since 1990.

General Information: No juvenile, mental, expunged, dismissed, or suspended imposition of sentence records released. SASE required. Turnaround time 2 weeks. Fax notes: \$1.00 per page. Copy fee: \$1.00 per page. Certification fee: \$1.50. Fee payee: Associate Circuit Court. Personal checks accepted. Prepayment is required.

Pemiscot County

Circuit Court County Courthouse, PO Box 34, Caruthersville, MO 63830; 573-333-0182. Hours: 7:30AM-4:30PM (CST). *Felony, Misdemeanor, Civil Actions Over \$45,000.*

Civil Records: Access: In person, online. Visitors must perform in person searches for themselves. No search fee. Required to search: name, years to search. Civil cases indexed by defendant, plaintiff. Civil records on index cards since 1979, prior on books. Participates in the free state online court record system at http://casenet.osca.state.mo.us/casenet.

Criminal Records: Access: In person, online. Visitors must perform in person searches for themselves. No search fee. Required to search: name, years to search. Criminal records on index cards since 1979, prior on books. Online access to criminal records is the same as civil.

General Information: Public Access terminal is available. No juvenile, mental, expunged, dismissed, or suspended imposition of sentence records released. Copy fee: \$.25 per page. Certification fee: No cert fee. Fee payee: Pemiscot County Treasurer. Personal checks accepted.

Associate Circuit Court County Courthouse, PO Drawer 228, Caruthersville, MO 63830; 573-333-2784. Hours: 7:30AM-4:30PM (CST). *Misdemeanor, Civil Actions Under \$45,000, Eviction, Small Claims, Probate.*

Civil Records: Access: Mail, in person. Both court and visitors may perform in person searches. No search fee. Required to search: name, years to search. Civil cases indexed by defendant, plaintiff. Civil records on index cards since 1979, prior on books.

Criminal Records: Access: Mail, in person. Both court and visitors may perform in person searches. No search fee. Required to search: name, years to search. Criminal records on computer since 5/90, on index cards from 1979-1990, prior on books.

General Information: No juvenile, mental, expunged, dismissed, or suspended imposition of sentence records released. SASE required. Turnaround time varies. Copy fee: \$1.00 per page. Certification fee: No cert fee. Fee payee: Pemiscot County Clerk. Only cashiers checks and money orders accepted. Prepayment is required.

Perry County

Circuit Court 15 W Saint Maries St #2, Perryville, MO 63775-1399; 573-547-6581; Fax: 573-547-9323. Hours: 8AM-5PM (CST). *Felony, Misdemeanor, Civil Actions Over \$25,000.*

Civil Records: Access: Fax, mail, in person. Visitors must perform in person searches for themselves. No search fee. Required to search: name, years to search. Civil cases indexed by defendant, plaintiff. Civil records on computer since 1994, prior on index cards.

Criminal Records: Access: Fax, mail, in person. Both court and visitors may perform in person searches. No search fee. Required to search: name, years to search. Criminal records on computer since 1993, prior on index cards.

General Information: Public Access terminal is available. No juvenile, mental, paternity (except final judgment), expunged, dismissed, or suspended imposition of sentence records released. SASE required. Turnaround time 3 days. Fax notes: No fee to fax results. Copy fee: \$1.00 for first page, \$.50 each add'l. Certification fee: \$1.00. Fee payee: Perry County Circuit Clerk. Personal checks accepted. Prepayment is required.

Associate Circuit Court 15 W Saint Maries, Suite 3, Perryville, MO 63775-1399; 573-547-7861; Fax: 573-547-9323. Hours: 8AM-5PM (CST). *Misdemeanor, Civil Actions Under \$25,000, Eviction, Small Claims, Probate.*

Civil Records: Access: Mail, in person. Only the court performs in person searches; visitors may not. No search fee. Required to search: name, years to search; also helpful: address. Civil cases indexed by defendant, plaintiff. Civil records on computer since 1994, prior on index cards.

Criminal Records: Access: Mail, in person. Only the court performs in person searches; visitors may not. No search fee. Required to search: name, years to search, DOB; also helpful: address, SSN. Criminal records on computer since 1994, prior on index cards.

General Information: Public Access terminal is available. No juvenile, mental, expunged, dismissed, or suspended imposition of sentence records released. SASE required. Turnaround time varies. Copy fee: \$.50 per page. Certification fee: \$1.50 plus \$1.00 per page. Fee payee: Circuit Court Division 6. Only cashiers checks and money orders accepted. Prepayment is required.

Pettis County

Circuit Court PO Box 804, Sedalia, MO 65302-0804; 660-826-0617; Fax: 660-827-8637. Hours: 8AM-5PM (CST). *Felony, Misdemeanor, Civil Actions Over \$45,000.*

Civil Records: Access: Phone, fax, mail, in person. Both court and visitors may perform in person searches. No search fee. Required to search: name, years to search. Civil cases indexed by defendant, plaintiff. Civil records on index books since 9/75, prior on judgment books.

Criminal Records: Access: Phone, fax, mail, in person. Both court and visitors may perform in person searches. No search fee. Required to search: name, years to search, DOB. Criminal records on computer since 1993, prior on index cards since 9/75.

General Information: Public Access terminal is available. No juvenile, mental, expunged, dismissed, or suspended imposition of sentence records released. SASE required. Turnaround time 1-2 days. Fax notes: \$2.50 for first page, \$1.50 each add'l. Copy fee: \$.15 per page. Certification fee: \$1.50. Fee payee: Pettis County Circuit Clerk. Personal checks accepted.

Associate Circuit Court 415 S Ohio, Sedalia, MO 65301; 660-826-4699; Probate phone: 660-826-0368; Fax: 660-827-8637. Hours: 8:30AM-5PM (CST). *Misdemeanor, Civil Actions Under \$45,000, Eviction, Small Claims, Probate.*

Civil Records: Access: Fax, mail, in person. Both court and visitors may perform in person searches. No search fee. Required to search: name, years to search. Civil cases indexed by defendant, plaintiff. Civil records on index cards since 1975, prior on judgment books.

Criminal Records: Access: Fax, mail, in person. Both court and visitors may perform in person searches. No search fee. Required to search: name, years to search. Criminal records on computer since 1993, on index cards from 1975-1993, prior on judgment books.

General Information: No juvenile, mental, expunged, dismissed, or suspended imposition of sentence records released. SASE required. Turnaround time 1-2 weeks. Copy fee: \$.15 per page. Certification fee: \$1.50 per page. Fee payee: Circuit Court Division 6. Only cashiers checks and money orders accepted.

Phelps County

Circuit & Associate Court 200 N Main St, Rolla, MO 65401; 573-364-1891 X200; Fax: 573-364-1419. Hours: 8AM-5PM (CST). *Felony, Misdemeanor, Civil, Small Claims, Eviction, Probate.*

Civil Records: Access: Fax, mail, in person. Only the court performs in person searches; visitors may not. No search fee. Required to search: name, years to search. Civil cases indexed by defendant, plaintiff. Civil records on computer since 1991; prior on books to 1957.

Criminal Records: Access: Fax, mail, in person. Only the court performs in person searches; visitors may not. No search fee. Required to search: name, years to search. Criminal records on computer since 1991, prior on books to 1957.

General Information: Public Access terminal is available. No juvenile, mental, expunged or dismissed records released. SASE required. Turnaround time 1 week. Fax notes: Fee to fax results is \$1.00 per page. Copy fee: \$.20 per page. Certification fee: \$1.00. Fee payee: Circuit Clerk. Personal checks accepted. no out-of-state checks accepted. Copy fees may be billed.

Pike County

Circuit Court 115 W Main, Bowling Green, MO 63334; 573-324-3112. Hours: 8AM-4:30PM (CST). *Felony, Misdemeanor, Civil Actions Over \$45,000.*

Civil Records: Access: Mail, in person. Both court and visitors may perform in person searches. No search fee.

Required to search: name, years to search; also helpful: address. Civil cases indexed by defendant, plaintiff. Civil records on index cards since 1977, prior on books. **Criminal Records:** Access: In person only. Visitors must perform in person searches for themselves. No search fee. Required to search: name, years to search; also helpful: DOB. Criminal records on index cards since 1977, prior on books. The Circuit Clerks will provide a from to mail requests to the State Patrol. **General Information:** Public Access terminal is available. No juvenile, mental, expunged, dismissed, or suspended imposition of sentence records released. SASE required. Turnaround time 1-2 days. Copy fee: $.25 per page. Certification fee: $1.00. Fee payee: Pike County Circuit Clerk. Personal checks accepted.

Associate Circuit Court 115 W Main, Bowling Green, MO 63334; 573-324-5582; Fax: 573-324-6297. Hours: 8AM-4:30PM (CST). *Misdemeanor, Civil Actions Under $25,000, Eviction, Small Claims, Probate.*

Civil Records: Access: Phone, mail, fax, in person. Both court and visitors may perform in person searches. No search fee. Required to search: name, years to search. Civil cases indexed by defendant, plaintiff. Civil records on index cards since 1979, archived since 1819. **Criminal Records:** Access: Phone, mail, fax, in person. Only the court performs in person searches; visitors may not. No search fee. Required to search: name, years to search; also helpful: DOB. Criminal records on index cards since 1979, archived since 1819. **General Information:** No juvenile, mental, expunged, dismissed records released. SASE required. Turnaround time 3-7 days. Copy fee: $.50 per page. Certification fee: $1.50. Fee payee: Associate Circuit or Probate Court. Business checks accepted. Prepayment is required.

Platte County

Circuit Court 328 Main St, #5, Platte City, MO 64079; 816-858-2232; Fax: 816-858-3392. Hours: 8AM-5PM (CST). *Felony, Misdemeanor, Civil Actions Over $45,000.*

Civil Records: Access: Mail, online, in person. Both court and visitors may perform in person searches. No search fee. Required to search: name, years to search. Civil cases indexed by defendant, plaintiff. Civil records on computer since 10/91. Participates in the free state online court record system at http://casenet.osca.state.mo.us/casenet. **Criminal Records:** Access: Mail, online, in person. Both court and visitors may perform in person searches. No search fee. Required to search: name, years to search, DOB; also helpful: SSN. Criminal records on computer since 10/91. Online access to criminal records is the same as civil. **General Information:** Public Access terminal is available. No juvenile, mental, expunged, dismissed, or suspended imposition of sentence records released. SASE required. Turnaround time 2-3 days. Copy fee: $.25 per page. Certification fee: $1.00. Fee payee: Platte County Circuit Clerk. Only cashiers checks and money orders accepted. Prepayment is required.

Associate Circuit Court 328 Main St, Box 5CH, Platte City, MO 64079; 816-858-2232; Fax: 816-858-3392. Hours: 8AM-5PM (CST). *Misdemeanor, Civil Actions Under $25,000, Eviction, Small Claims.*

Civil Records: Access: Mail, online, in person. Both court and visitors may perform in person searches. No search fee. Required to search: name, years to search. Civil cases indexed by defendant, plaintiff. Civil records on computer since 11/91, prior on index cards. Participates in the free state online court record system at http://casenet.osca.state.mo.us/casenet. **Criminal Records:** Access: Mail, online, in person. Both court and visitors may perform in person searches.

No search fee. Required to search: name, years to search, DOB; also helpful: SSN. Criminal records on computer since 11/91, prior on index cards. Online access to criminal records is the same as civil. **General Information:** Public Access terminal is available. No juvenile, mental, expunged, dismissed, or suspended imposition of sentence records released. SASE required. Turnaround time 1-3 days. Copy fee: $.25 per page. Certification fee: $1.00. Fee payee: Circuit Clerk. Only cashiers checks and money orders accepted. Prepayment is required.

Probate Court 415 Third St, #95, Platte City, MO 64079; 816-858-2232 X3438; Fax: 816-858-3392. Hours: 8AM-5PM (CST). *Probate.*

Polk County

Circuit Court 102 E Broadway, Rm 14, Bolivar, MO 65613; 417-326-4912; Fax: 417-326-4194. Hours: 8AM-5PM (CST). *Felony, Misdemeanor, Civil Actions Over $45,000.*

www.positech.net/~dcourt

Civil Records: Access: Fax, mail, in person. Both court and visitors may perform in person searches. Search fee: $5.00 per name. Required to search: name, years to search. Civil cases indexed by defendant, plaintiff. Civil records on computer since 1991, prior on card index since 1979. **Criminal Records:** Access: Fax, mail, in person. Only the court performs in person searches; visitors may not. Search fee: $5.00 per name. Required to search: name, years to search. Criminal records on computer since 1991, prior on card index since 1979. **General Information:** No juvenile, mental, expunged, dismissed, or suspended imposition of sentence records released. SASE required. Turnaround time 1 week. Fax notes: $3.00 for first page, $.25 each add'l. Copy fee: $.25 per page. Certification fee: $2.00. Fee payee: Circuit Clerk. Personal checks accepted.

Associate Circuit Court Courthouse, Rm 7, Bolivar, MO 65613; 417-326-4921; Fax: 417-326-5238. Hours: 8:00AM-5:00PM (CST). *Misdemeanor, Civil Actions Under $25,000, Eviction, Small Claims, Probate.*

www.positech.net/~dcourt

Civil Records: Access: Phone, fax, mail, in person. Only the court performs in person searches; visitors may not. No search fee. Required to search: name, years to search; also helpful: case number. Civil cases indexed by defendant, plaintiff. Civil records go back to 1980; on computer back to 1990. **Criminal Records:** Access: Phone, fax, mail, in person. Only the court performs in person searches; visitors may not. No search fee. Required to search: name, years to search; also helpful: case number, signed release. Criminal records go back to 1980; on computer back to 1990. **General Information:** No juvenile, mental, expunged, dismissed, or suspended imposition of sentence records released. SASE required. Turnaround time 1 week. Fax notes: Will not fax results. Copy fee: $.25 per page. Certification fee: $1.50. Fee payee: Associate Circuit Court. Only cashiers checks and money orders accepted. Prepayment is required.

Pulaski County

Circuit & Associate Circuit Courts 301 Historic Rt 66 E, Suite 202, Waynesville, MO 65583; 573-774-4755; Fax: 573-774-6967. Hours: 8AM-4:30PM (CST). *Felony, Misdemeanor, Civil, Eviction, Small Claims.*

Civil Records: Access: In person only. Visitors must perform in person searches for themselves. No search fee. Required to search: name, years to search; also helpful: address. Civil cases indexed by defendant,

plaintiff. Civil records on computer since 1990, prior on books since 1903. **Criminal Records:** Access: Fax, mail, in person. Both court and visitors may perform in person searches. No search fee. Required to search: name, years to search; also helpful: DOB, SSN. Criminal records on computer since 1990, prior on books since 1903. **General Information:** Public Access terminal is available. No juvenile, mental, paternity, expunged, dismissed, or suspended imposition of sentence records released. SASE requested. Turnaround time 1 day. Fax notes: No fee to fax results. Will only fax to 800 numbers. Copy fee: $.25 per page. Certification fee: $2.00. Fee payee: Circuit Clerk. Business checks accepted. Prepayment is required.

Probate Court 301 Historic 66 East, Suite 316, Waynesville, MO 65583; 573-774-4784; Fax: 573-774-6673. *Probate.*

Putnam County

Circuit Court Courthouse Rm 202, Unionville, MO 63565; 660-947-2071; Fax: 660-947-2320. Hours: 8AM-12; 1PM-5PM (CST). *Felony, Misdemeanor, Civil Actions Over $45,000.*

Civil Records: Access: Mail, in person, online. Both court and visitors may perform in person searches. No search fee. Required to search: name, years to search. Civil cases indexed by defendant, plaintiff. Civil records on index cards since late 1970s; on computer since. Participates in the free state online court record system at http://casenet.osca.state.mo.us/casenet. **Criminal Records:** Access: Mail, in person, online. Both court and visitors may perform in person searches. No search fee. Required to search: name, years to search. Criminal records on index cards since late 1970s; on computer since. Online access to criminal records is the same as civil. **General Information:** Public Access terminal is available. No juvenile, mental, expunged, dismissed, or suspended imposition of sentence records released. SASE required. Turnaround time same day. Fax notes: Fee to fax results is $1.00 for 1st page; $50 each add'l. Copy fee: $.25 per page. Certification fee: $1.00. Fee payee: Circuit Clerk. Business checks accepted. Prepayment is required.

Associate Circuit Court Courthouse Rm 101, Unionville, MO 63565; 660-947-2117; Fax: 660-947-7348. Hours: 9AM-5PM (CST). *Misdemeanor, Civil Actions Under $45,000, Eviction, Small Claims, Probate.*

Civil Records: Access: Mail, in person, online. Both court and visitors may perform in person searches. No search fee. Required to search: name, years to search. Civil cases indexed by defendant, plaintiff. Civil records on computer since 1994, prior on books. Participates in the free state online court record system at http://casenet.osca.state.mo.us/casenet. **Criminal Records:** Access: Mail, in person, online. Only the court performs in person searches; visitors may not. No search fee. Required to search: name, years to search. Criminal records on computer since 1994, prior on books. Online access to criminal records is the same as civil. **General Information:** No mental, expunged, dismissed, or suspended imposition of sentence records released. SASE required. Turnaround time 30-60 days. Copy fee: $1.00 per page. Certification fee: $1.50. Fee payee: Associate Circuit Court. Only cashiers checks and money orders accepted. Prepayment is required.

Ralls County

Circuit Court PO Box 444, New London, MO 63459; 573-985-5633. Hours: 8:30AM-4:30PM (CST). *Felony, Misdemeanor, Civil Actions Over $45,000.*

Civil Records: Access: Mail, in person. Only the court performs in person searches; visitors may not. No search fee. Required to search: name, years to search. Civil cases indexed by defendant, plaintiff. Civil records on index cards since 1976, prior on books.
Criminal Records: Access: Mail, in person. Only the court performs in person searches; visitors may not. No search fee. Required to search: name, years to search, signed release. Criminal records on index cards since 1976, prior on books.
General Information: No juvenile, mental, expunged, dismissed, or suspended imposition of sentence records released. SASE required. Turnaround time varies. Copy fee: $.25 per page. Certification fee: $1.00. Fee payee: Ralls County Circuit Clerk. Personal checks accepted. Prepayment is required.

Associate Circuit Court PO Box 466, New London, MO 63459; 573-985-5641; Fax: 573-985-3446. Hours: 8:00AM-4:30PM (CST). *Misdemeanor, Civil Actions Under $25,000, Eviction, Small Claims, Probate.*

Civil Records: Access: Phone, mail, fax, in person. Both court and visitors may perform in person searches. Search fee: $5.00 per name. Required to search: name, years to search. Civil cases indexed by defendant, plaintiff. Civil records on index cards since 1979, prior on record books.
Criminal Records: Access: Phone, mail, fax, in person. Both court and visitors may perform in person searches. Search fee: $5.00 per name. Required to search: name, years to search, signed release. Criminal records on index cards since 1979, prior on record books.
General Information: No juvenile, mental, expunged, dismissed, or suspended imposition of sentence records released. SASE required. Turnaround time 1-2 weeks, genealogy turnaround time varies. Copy fee: $.25 per page. Certification fee: $1.50. Fee payee: Associate Circuit Court. Personal checks accepted. Prepayment is required.

Randolph County

Circuit Court 223 N Williams, Moberly, MO 65270; 660-263-4474; Fax: 660-263-5966. Hours: 8AM-4:30PM (CST). *Felony, Misdemeanor, Civil Actions Over $45,000.*

Civil Records: Access: Fax, mail, in person. Both court and visitors may perform in person searches. No search fee. Required to search: name, years to search, address. Civil cases indexed by defendant, plaintiff. Civil records on index cards since 1975, prior on record books.
Criminal Records: Access: Fax, mail, in person. Both court and visitors may perform in person searches. No search fee. Required to search: name, years to search, address, DOB; also helpful: SSN. Criminal records on computer since 1994, prior on index books.
General Information: No juvenile, mental, expunged, dismissed, or suspended imposition of sentence records released. SASE required. Turnaround time 1 week. Fax notes: $4.00 per page. Copy fee: $1.00 per page. Certification fee: $1.50. Fee payee: Randolph County Circuit Clerk. Personal checks accepted.

Associate Circuit Court 223 N Williams, Moberly, MO 65270; 660-263-4450; Fax: 660-263-1007. Hours: 8AM-4:30PM (CST). *Misdemeanor, Civil Actions Under $45,000, Eviction, Small Claims, Probate.*

Civil Records: Access: Mail, in person. Both court and visitors may perform in person searches. No search fee. Required to search: name, years to search. Civil cases

indexed by defendant, plaintiff. Civil records on index cards since 1979, prior on books.
Criminal Records: Access: Mail, in person. Both court and visitors may perform in person searches. No search fee. Required to search: name, years to search. Criminal records on computer since 1994, prior on index cards and books.
General Information: No juvenile, mental, expunged, dismissed, or suspended imposition of sentence records released. SASE required. Turnaround time 3-5 days or up to 2 weeks if office busy. Copy fee: $.50 per page. Certification fee: $1.50. Fee payee: Associate Circuit Court. Personal checks accepted.

Ray County

Circuit Court PO Box 594, Richmond, MO 64085; 816-776-3377; Fax: 816-776-6016. Hours: 8AM-4PM (CST). *Felony, Misdemeanor, Civil Actions Over $45,000.*

www.osca.state.mo.us/circuits/index.nsf/County+/+Ray

Civil Records: Access: Phone, fax, mail, in person. Only the court performs in person searches; visitors may not. No search fee. Required to search: name, years to search. Civil cases indexed by defendant, plaintiff. Civil records on index cards since 1977, prior on judgment books.
Criminal Records: Access: Phone, fax, mail, in person. Only the court performs in person searches; visitors may not. No search fee. Required to search: name, years to search; also helpful: DOB, SSN. Criminal records on index cards since 1977, prior on judgment books.
General Information: No juvenile, mental, expunged, dismissed, or suspended imposition of sentence records released. SASE required. Turnaround time varies. Fax notes: Fee to fax results is $1.00 per page. Copy fee: $.25 per page. Certification fee: $2.50. Fee payee: Ray County Circuit Clerk. Business checks accepted. Prepayment is required.

Associate Circuit Court Ray County Courthouse, 100 W Main St, Richmond, MO 64085-1710; 816-776-2335; Fax: 816-776-2185. Hours: 8AM-4PM (CST). *Misdemeanor, Civil Actions Under $25,000, Eviction, Small Claims, Probate.*

Civil Records: Access: Fax, mail, in person. Only the court performs in person searches; visitors may not. No search fee. Required to search: name; also helpful: years to search. Civil cases indexed by defendant, plaintiff. Civil records on index cards since 1979, prior on books.
Criminal Records: Access: Fax, mail, in person. Only the court performs in person searches; visitors may not. No search fee. Required to search: name, DOB; also helpful: years to search, SSN. Criminal records on index cards since 1979, prior on books.
General Information: No juvenile, mental, expunged, dismissed, or suspended imposition of sentence records released. SASE required. Turnaround time varies. Fax notes: No fee to fax results. Copy fee: $.20 per page. Certification fee: $1.50. Fee payee: Associate Circuit Court. Business checks accepted. Prepayment is required.

Reynolds County

Circuit Court PO Box 76, Centerville, MO 63633; 573-648-2494 X44; Fax: 573-648-2296. Hours: 8AM-4PM (CST). *Felony, Civil Actions Over $45,000.*

Civil Records: Access: Phone, mail, in person, online. Both court and visitors may perform in person searches. No search fee. Required to search: name, years to search. Civil cases indexed by defendant, plaintiff. Civil records on cards and books, archived since 1872. Access to civil records is available free at http://casenet.osca.state.mo.us/casenet/. At the web site, select the judicial district, then search by name, case # or date.

Criminal Records: Access: Phone, mail, in person, online. Both court and visitors may perform in person searches. No search fee. Required to search: name, years to search, DOB; also helpful: SSN, sex, signed release. Criminal records on cards and books, archived since 1872. Online access to criminal records is the same as civil.
General Information: Public Access terminal is available. No juvenile, mental, expunged, dismissed, or suspended imposition of sentence records released. SASE required. Turnaround time 2 days. Fax notes: Fee to fax results is $2.00 per document plus $1.00 per page. Copy fee: $1.00 per page. Certification fee: $2.00. Fee payee: Randy L Cowin. Personal checks accepted. Prepayment is required.

Associate Circuit Court PO Box 39, Centerville, MO 63633; 573-648-2494 X41; Fax: 573-648-2296. Hours: 8AM-4PM (CST). *Misdemeanor, Civil Actions Under $45,000, Eviction, Small Claims, Probate.*

Civil Records: Access: Phone, mail, in person, online. Both court and visitors may perform in person searches. No search fee. Required to search: name, years to search. Civil cases indexed by defendant, plaintiff. Civil records on index cards and files (probate in books); on computer back to 2000. Participates in the free state online court record system at http://casenet.osca.state.mo.us/casenet.
Criminal Records: Access: Phone, mail, in person, online. Both court and visitors may perform in person searches. No search fee. Required to search: name, years to search. Criminal records on index cards and files back to early 1970's; on computer back to 2000. Online access to criminal records is the same as civil.
General Information: Public Access terminal is available. No juvenile, mental, expunged, dismissed, or suspended imposition of sentence records released. SASE not required. Turnaround time 1 day, phone turnaround time same day. Copy fee: $1.00 per page. Certification fee: $2.00. Fee payee: Associate Circuit Court. Personal checks accepted.

Ripley County

Circuit Court Courthouse, Doniphan, MO 63935; 573-996-2818; Fax: 573-996-7826. Hours: 8AM-4PM (CST). *Felony, Misdemeanor, Civil Actions Over $25,000.*

Civil Records: Access: Phone, fax, mail, in person. Both court and visitors may perform in person searches. Search fee: $5.00 per name. Required to search: name, years to search. Civil cases indexed by defendant, plaintiff. Civil records on cards and books since 1976, archived since 1850s.
Criminal Records: Access: Fax, mail, in person. Both court and visitors may perform in person searches. Search fee: $5.00 per name. Required to search: name, years to search, DOB. Criminal records on cards and books since 1976, archived since 1850s.
General Information: No juvenile, mental, expunged, dismissed, or suspended imposition of sentence records released. SASE required. Turnaround time same day. Copy fee: $3.00 per page. Certification fee: $2.00 if done by in-person searcher, otherwise certification is included in the search fee. Fee payee: Circuit Clerk. Personal checks accepted. Prepayment is required.

Associate Circuit Court 100 Court Sq, Courthouse, Doniphan, MO 63935; 573-996-2013; Fax: 573-996-5014. Hours: 8AM-4PM (CST). *Misdemeanor, Civil Actions Under $25,000, Eviction, Small Claims, Probate.*

Civil Records: Access: Phone, fax, mail, in person. Both court and visitors may perform in person searches. No search fee. Required to search: name, years to search. Civil cases indexed by defendant, plaintiff. Civil records on index cards since 1984, prior on books.

Criminal Records: Access: Phone, mail, in person. Both court and visitors may perform in person searches. No search fee. Required to search: name, years to search; also helpful: DOB, SSN. Criminal records on index cards since 1984, prior on books.

General Information: No juvenile, mental, expunged, dismissed, or suspended imposition of sentence records released. SASE required. Turnaround time 1 week. Copy fee: $.25 per page. Certification fee: $1.00. Fee payee: Circuit Court Division II. Only cashiers checks and money orders accepted.

Saline County

Circuit Court PO Box 597, Marshall, MO 65340; 660-886-2300. Hours: 8:00AM-4:30PM (CST). *Felony, Misdemeanor, Civil Actions Over $45,000.*

Civil Records: Access: Mail, in person. Both court and visitors may perform in person searches. No search fee. Required to search: name, years to search. Civil cases indexed by defendant, plaintiff. Civil records on index cards since 1974, prior on books since 1820.

Criminal Records: Access: Mail, in person. Both court and visitors may perform in person searches. No search fee. Required to search: name, years to search. Criminal records on index cards to 1974, prior on books to 1820.

General Information: No juvenile, mental, expunged, dismissed, or suspended imposition of sentence records released. SASE required. Turnaround time 1 week. Copy fee: $.25 per page. Certification fee: $1.50. Fee payee: Saline County Circuit Court. Personal checks accepted. Copy fees may be billed.

Associate Circuit Court PO Box 751, Marshall, MO 65340; 660-886-6988; Fax: 660-886-2919. Hours: 8AM-4:30PM (CST). *Misdemeanor, Civil Actions Under $25,000, Eviction, Small Claims.*

Civil Records: Access: Phone, mail, in person. Only the court performs in person searches; visitors may not. No search fee. Required to search: name, years to search. Civil cases indexed by defendant, plaintiff. Civil records on index cards since 1979, prior on books.

Criminal Records: Access: Phone, mail, in person. Only the court performs in person searches; visitors may not. No search fee. Required to search: name, years to search. Criminal records on computer since 1993, prior on cards and books.

General Information: No juvenile, mental, expunged, dismissed, or suspended imposition of sentence records released. SASE required. Turnaround time 1-2 days. No copy fee. Certification fee: No cert fee.

Schuyler County

Circuit Court PO Box 186, Lancaster, MO 63548; 660-457-3784; Fax: 660-457-3016. Hours: 8AM-4PM *Felony, Misdemeanor, Civil Actions Over $45,000.*

Civil Records: Access: Mail, in person. Both court and visitors may perform in person searches. Search fee: $14.00 per name. Required to search: name, years to search. Civil cases indexed by defendant, plaintiff. Civil records on index cards & books.

Criminal Records: Access: Mail, in person. Both court and visitors may perform in person searches. Search fee: $14.00 per name. Required to search: name, years to search. Criminal records on index cards & books.

General Information: No juvenile, mental, expunged, dismissed, or suspended imposition of sentence records released. SASE required. Turnaround time 1-2 days. Fax notes: Fee to fax is $2.00 plus $1.00 each page. Copy fee: $1.00 per page. Certification fee: $1.00. Fee payee: Schuyler County Circuit Clerk. Personal checks accepted. Prepayment is required.

Associate Circuit Court Box 158, Lancaster, MO 63548; 660-457-3755; Fax: 660-457-3016. Hours: 8:00AM-4PM (CST). *Misdemeanor, Civil Actions Under $45,000, Eviction, Small Claims, Probate.*

Civil Records: Access: Mail, fax, in person. Both court and visitors may perform in person searches. Search fee: $5.00 per name. Required to search: name, years to search. Civil cases indexed by defendant, plaintiff. Civil records on index cards since 1976; computerized records go back to 1992.

Criminal Records: Access: Mail, fax, in person. Both court and visitors may perform in person searches. Search fee: $5.00 per name. Required to search: name, years to search, SSN, DOB. Criminal records on computer since 5/92, prior on index cards.

General Information: No juvenile, mental, expunged, dismissed, or suspended imposition of sentence records released. SASE required. Turnaround time 4 days. Copy fee: $.25 per page. Certification fee: $1.50. Fee payee: Associate Circuit Court. Business checks accepted. Prepayment is required.

Scotland County

Circuit Court 117 S Market St #106, Memphis, MO 63555; 660-465-8605; Fax: 660-465-8673. Hours: 9AM-4PM (CST). *Felony, Misdemeanor, Civil Actions Over $45,000.*

Civil Records: Access: Mail, in person. Both court and visitors may perform in person searches. No search fee. Required to search: name, years to search. Civil cases indexed by defendant, plaintiff. Civil records on index cards since 1979, prior on books. Only judgments on computer.

Criminal Records: Access: Mail, in person. Both court and visitors may perform in person searches. No search fee. Required to search: name, years to search, DOB, signed release; also helpful: address. Criminal records on index cards since 1979, prior on books. Only judgments on computer.

General Information: No juvenile, mental, expunged, dismissed, or suspended imposition of sentence records released. SASE required. Turnaround time same day. Copy fee: $.25 per page. Certification fee: $2.50. Fee payee: Scotland County Circuit Clerk. Personal checks accepted. Prepayment is required.

Associate Circuit Court Courthouse, Rm 102, 117 S Market, Memphis, MO 63555; 660-465-2404; Fax: 660-465-8673. Hours: 8AM-4:30PM (CST). *Misdemeanor, Civil Actions Under $25,000, Eviction, Small Claims, Probate.*

Civil Records: Access: Phone, mail, fax, in person. Both court and visitors may perform in person searches. No search fee. Required to search: name, years to search. Civil cases indexed by defendant, plaintiff. Civil records on computer since 1986, prior on cards and books to 1841.

Criminal Records: Access: Phone, mail, in person. Both court and visitors may perform in person searches. No search fee. Required to search: name, years to search. Criminal records on computer since 1986, prior on cards and books to 1841.

General Information: No juvenile, mental, expunged, dismissed, or suspended imposition of sentence records released. SASE required. Turnaround time ASAP. Fax notes: Fee to fax results is 1.00 per page. Copy fee: $.25 per page. Certification fee: $1.50 plus $1.00 per page. Fee payee: Info provided on bill. Personal checks accepted.

Scott County

Circuit Court PO Box 277, Benton, MO 63736; 573-545-3596; Fax: 573-545-3597. Hours: 8:30AM-12, 1-5PM (CST). *Felony, Misdemeanor, Civil Actions Over $25,000.*

Civil Records: Access: In person only. Visitors must perform in person searches for themselves. No search fee. Required to search: name, years to search. Civil cases indexed by defendant, plaintiff. Civil records on computer since 1991, prior on index cards and books.

Criminal Records: Access: Mail, fax, in person. Both court and visitors may perform in person searches. No search fee. Required to search: name, years to search, DOB, SSN. Criminal records on computer since 1991, prior on index cards and books.

General Information: Public Access terminal is available. No juvenile, mental, expunged, dismissed, or suspended imposition of sentence records released. SASE required. Turnaround time 2 days-1 week. Copy fee: $1.00 for first page, $.25 each add'l. Certification fee: $3.00. Fee payee: Pam Glastetter, Circuit Clerk. Personal checks accepted. Prepayment is required.

Associate Circuit Court PO Box 249, Benton, MO 63736; 573-545-3576; Fax: 573-545-4231. Hours: 8AM-5PM (CST). *Misdemeanor, Civil Actions Under $45,000, Eviction, Small Claims, Probate.*

Civil Records: Access: Phone, mail, in person. No search fee. Required to search: name, years to search. Civil cases indexed by defendant, plaintiff. Civil records on index cards and books.

Criminal Records: Access: Phone, mail, in person. Visitors must perform in person searches for themselves. No search fee. Required to search: name, years to search. Criminal records on index cards and books.

General Information: No juvenile, mental, expunged, dismissed, or suspended imposition of sentence records released. SASE required. Turnaround time varies. No copy fee. Certification fee: No cert fee.

Shannon County

Circuit Court PO Box 148, Eminence, MO 65466; 573-226-3315; Fax: 573-226-5321. Hours: 8AM-4:30PM (CST). *Felony, Misdemeanor, Civil Actions Over $45,000.*

Civil Records: Access: Mail, in person, online. Only the court performs in person searches; visitors may not. No search fee. Required to search: name, years to search. Civil cases indexed by defendant, plaintiff. Civil records on index cards and books. Record index searchable on computer back to 1980. Participates in the free state online court record system at http://casenet.osca.state.mo.us/casenet.

Criminal Records: Access: Mail, in person, online. Only the court performs in person searches; visitors may not. No search fee. Required to search: name, years to search, offense. Criminal records on index cards and books. Record index searchable on computer back to 1980. Online access to criminal records is the same as civil.

General Information: Public Access terminal is available. No juvenile, mental, expunged, dismissed, or suspended imposition of sentence records released. SASE required. Turnaround time 1 week. Fax notes: Fee to fax results is $2.00 per page. Copy fee: $.25 per page. Certification fee: $2.00. Fee payee: Shannon County Circuit Clerk. Personal checks accepted. Prepayment is required.

Associate Circuit Court PO Box 845, Eminence, MO 65466-0845; 573-226-5515; Fax: 573-226-3239. Hours: 8AM-4:30PM (CST). *Misdemeanor, Civil Actions Under $45,000, Eviction, Small Claims, Probate.*

Civil Records: Access: Mail, fax, in person, online. Only the court performs in person searches; visitors may not. Search fee: $10.00 per name. Required to search: name, years to search. Civil cases indexed by defendant, plaintiff. Civil records on index cards since 1979, archived since 1881. Participates in the free state online court record system at http://casenet.osca.state.mo.us/casenet.

Criminal Records: Access: Mail, fax, in person, online. Only the court performs in person searches; visitors may not. Search fee: $10.00 per name. Required to search: name, years to search, DOB; also helpful:

SSN. Criminal records on computer since 1992; prior on index cards to 1979. Online access to criminal records is the same as civil.

General Information: No juvenile, mental, expunged, dismissed, or suspended imposition of sentence records released. SASE required. Turnaround time 1 week. Fax notes: Fee to fax results in $3.00 per page. Copy fee: $.25 per page. Certification fee: $3.00. Fee payee: Associate Circuit Court. Personal checks accepted. Prepayment is required.

Shelby County

Circuit Court PO Box 176, Shelbyville, MO 63469; 573-633-2151; Fax: 573-633-1004. Hours: 8AM-4:30PM (CST). *Felony, Misdemeanor, Civil Actions Over $45,000.*

Civil Records: Access: Mail, fax, in person. Both court and visitors may perform in person searches. No search fee. Required to search: name, years to search. Civil cases indexed by defendant, plaintiff. Civil records on index cards since 1975, prior on books since 1835.

Criminal Records: Access: Mail, fax, in person. Both court and visitors may perform in person searches. No search fee. Required to search: name, years to search. Criminal records on index cards since 1975, prior on books since 1835.

General Information: No juvenile, mental, expunged, dismissed, or suspended imposition of sentence records released. SASE required. Turnaround time 1 day. Fax notes: Fee to fax results in $3.00 per document. Copy fee: $.25 per page. Certification fee: $2.00. Fee payee: Shelby County Circuit Clerk. Personal checks accepted. Prepayment is required.

Associate Circuit Court PO Box 206, Shelbyville, MO 63469; 573-633-2251; Fax: 573-633-2142. Hours: 8AM-4:30PM (CST). *Misdemeanor, Civil Actions Under $25,000, Eviction, Small Claims, Probate.*

Civil Records: Access: Fax, mail, in person. Both court and visitors may perform in person searches. No search fee. Required to search: name, years to search. Civil cases indexed by defendant, plaintiff. Civil records on index cards, archived from 1845 to 1950.

Criminal Records: Access: Phone, fax, mail, in person. Both court and visitors may perform in person searches. No search fee. Required to search: name, years to search, DOB. Criminal records on index cards, archived from 1845 to 1950.

General Information: No juvenile, mental, expunged, dismissed, or suspended imposition of sentence records released. SASE not required. Turnaround time 2 weeks. Fax notes: No fee to fax results. Copy fee: $.25 per page. Certification fee: $1.50. Fee payee: Probate Court or Associate Circuit Court. Personal checks accepted.

St. Charles County

Circuit Court 300 N 2nd St, St. Charles, MO 63301; 636-949-7900 X3098; Fax: 636-949-7390. Hours: 8:30AM-5PM (CST). *Felony, Misdemeanor, Civil Actions Over $25,000.*

Civil Records: Access: Mail, online, in person. Both court and visitors may perform in person searches. No search fee. Required to search: name, years to search. Civil cases indexed by defendant, plaintiff. Civil records on index cards since 1971, prior on books; judgment records (A-M) on computer since 1987. Participates in the free state online court record system at http://casenet.osca.state.mo.us/casenet. Clerk refers all record requests to the Sheriff or Highway Patrol.

Criminal Records: Access: Online, in person. Visitors must perform in person searches for themselves. No search fee. Required to search: name, years to search; also helpful: DOB. Criminal records on index cards since 1971, prior on books; judgment records (A-M) on

computer since 1987. Online access to criminal records is the same as civil.

General Information: Public Access terminal is available. No juvenile, mental, expunged, dismissed, or suspended imposition of sentence records released. SASE required. Turnaround time varies. Copy fee: $.25 per page. Certification fee: $1.00. Fee payee: St. Charles Circuit Clerk. Personal checks accepted. Prepayment is required.

Associate Circuit Court 300 N 2nd, Suite 436, St. Charles, MO 63301; 636-949-3043. Hours: 8:30AM-5:00PM (CST). *Civil Actions Under $25,000, Eviction, Small Claims, Probate.*

Civil Records: Access: Online, in person. Visitors must perform in person searches for themselves. No search fee. Required to search: name, years to search. Civil cases indexed by defendant, plaintiff. Civil records on computer since 1988 (judgments only), prior on index cards and books. Participates in the free state online court record system at http://casenet.osca.state.mo.us casenet.

General Information: SASE required. Turnaround time varies. Copy fee: $.25 per page. Certification fee: No cert fee. Fee payee: Associate Circuit Court. Only cashiers checks and money orders accepted. Prepayment is required.

St. Clair County

Circuit & Associate Circuit Courts PO Box 493, Osceola, MO 64776; 417-646-2226; Fax: 417-646-2401. Hours: 8AM-4:30PM (CST). *Felony, Misdemeanor, Civil, Eviction, Small Claims, Probate.*

Civil Records: Access: Mail, in person. Both court and visitors may perform in person searches. Search fee: $2.00 per name. Required to search: name, years to search. Civil cases indexed by defendant, plaintiff. Civil records on computer since 1991 for judgments, on index cards since 1980, prior records on index books.

Criminal Records: Access: Mail, in person. Both court and visitors may perform in person searches. Search fee: $2.00 per name. Required to search: name, years to search, DOB. Criminal records on computer since 1991, on index cards since 1980, prior records on index books.

General Information: No juvenile, mental, expunged, dismissed, or suspended imposition of sentence records released. SASE required. Turnaround time 1-2 days. No copy fee. Certification fee: $1.50. Fee payee: St Clair County Circuit Clerk. Personal checks accepted. Prepayment is required.

St. Francois County

Circuit Court - Division I & II 1 N Washington, Rm 303, Farmington, MO 63640; 573-756-4551; Fax: 573-756-3733. Hours: 8AM-5PM (CST). *Felony, Misdemeanor, Civil Actions Over $25,000.*

Civil Records: Access: Fax, mail, in person. Both court and visitors may perform in person searches. No search fee. Required to search: name, years to search. Civil cases indexed by defendant, plaintiff. Civil records on computer since 6/90, on microfiche since 1970, archived since 1821.

Criminal Records: Access: Fax, mail, in person. Both court and visitors may perform in person searches. No search fee. Required to search: name, years to search; also helpful: DOB, SSN. Criminal records on computer since 3/1/93.

General Information: Public Access terminal is available. No juvenile, mental, expunged, dismissed, or suspended imposition of sentence records released. SASE required. Turnaround time 1-2 weeks. Copy fee: $.25 per page. Certification fee: $1.50. Fee payee: Clerk of Circuit Court. Business checks accepted.

Associate Circuit Court County Courthouse, 2nd Fl, 1 N. Washington, Rm 202, Farmington, MO 63640; 573-756-5755; Fax: 573-756-8173. Hours: 8AM-5PM (CST). *Misdemeanor, Civil Actions Under $25,000, Eviction, Small Claims, Probate.*

Civil Records: Access: Phone, mail, fax, in person. Only the court performs in person searches; visitors may not. No search fee. Required to search: name, years to search. Civil cases indexed by defendant, plaintiff. Civil records on index cards since 1979; on computer back to 1990.

Criminal Records: Access: Mail, fax, in person. Only the court performs in person searches; visitors may not. No search fee. Required to search: name, years to search. Criminal records on computer back to 1990; other records go back to 1980.

General Information: No juvenile, mental, expunged, dismissed, or suspended imposition of sentence records released. SASE not required. No copy fee. Certification fee: No cert fee. Business checks accepted.

St. Louis County

Circuit Court of St. Louis County 7900 Carondolet, Clayton, MO 63105-1766; 314-615-8029; Fax: 314-615-8739. Hours: 8AM-5PM (CST). *Felony, Misdemeanor, Civil.*

Civil Records: Access: Phone, fax, mail, in person. Both court and visitors may perform in person searches. No search fee. Required to search: name, years to search; also helpful: address. Civil cases indexed by defendant, plaintiff. Civil records on computer back to 1990, prior on index cards. Permanent records on microfiche since 1978, earlier in books. Case files archived for 25 years.

Criminal Records: Access: Phone, fax, mail, in person. Both court and visitors may perform in person searches. No search fee. Required to search: name, years to search, DOB; also helpful: address, SSN. Criminal records on computer back to 1990; prior on index cards. Permanent records on microfiche since 1978, earlier in books. Case files archived for 25 years.

General Information: Public Access terminal is available. No juvenile, paternity, mental, expunged, dismissed, or suspended imposition of sentence records released. SASE not required. Turnaround time up to 5 days. Copy fee: $.30 per page. Certification fee: $1.50 plus $.30 per page after first. Fee payee: Circuit Clerk. Personal checks accepted. Prepayment is required.

Associate Circuit - Civil Division 7900 Carondolet, Clayton, MO 63105; 314-615-8090; Probate phone: 314-615-2629; Fax: 314-615-2689. Hours: 8AM-5PM (CST). *Civil Actions Under $25,000, Eviction, Small Claims, Probate.*

Note: Probate records are available free on the state online court record system at http://casenet.osca. state.mo.us/ casenet.

Civil Records: Access: Phone, mail, in person. Both court and visitors may perform in person searches. No search fee. Required to search: name, years to search. Civil cases indexed by defendant, plaintiff. Civil records on computer since 1986, prior on cards.

General Information: Public Access terminal is available. No juvenile, mental, expunged, dismissed, paternity, suspended imposition of sentence records released. SASE required. Turnaround time 1 week. Copy fee: $.30 per page. Certification fee: $1.50. Fee payee: Circuit Clerk-Civil Division. Personal checks accepted. Prepayment is required.

Associate Circuit Court - Criminal Division 7900 Carondolet, Clayton, MO 63105; 314-615-2675; Fax: 314-615-2689. *Misdemeanor.*

Criminal Records: Access: Mail, fax, in person. Both court and visitors may perform in person searches. No search fee. Required to search: name, years to search,

DOB, offense, date of offense. Criminal records on computer back to 1990.

General Information: Public Access terminal is available. No juvenile, mental, expunged, dismissed, or suspended imposition of sentence records released. SASE required. Turnaround time varies. Copy fee: $.30 per page. Certification fee: $1.50. Fee payee: Circuit Clerk. Personal checks accepted. Prepayment required.

St. Louis City

Circuit & Associate Circuit Courts 10 N Tucker, Civil Courts Bldg, St Louis, MO 63101; 314-622-4405; Fax: 314-622-4537. Hours: 8:00AM-5:00PM (CST). *Civil, Eviction, Small Claims, Probate.*

Civil Records: Access: Mail, online, in person. No search fee. Required to search: name, years to search. Civil cases indexed by defendant, plaintiff. Civil records on computer since 1/80, on index cards since early 1800s. Remote access is through MoBar Net and is open only to attorneys. Call 314-535-1950 for more information.

General Information: Public Access terminal is available. No sealed or confidential records released. SASE required. Turnaround time usually 1 week. Copy fee: $.20 per page. Certification fee: $3.50. Fee payee: City of St. Louis Circuit Clerk. Only cashiers checks and money orders accepted. Prepayment is required.

City of St Louis Circuit Court 1320 Market, St Louis, MO 63103; 314-622-4582; Fax: 314-622-3202. Hours: 8AM-5PM (CST). *Felony, Misdemeanor, Probate.*

Note: The Probate Court participates in the free state online court record system at http://casenet.osca.state .mo.us/casenet.

Criminal Records: Access: In person only. Both court and visitors may perform in person searches. No search fee. Required to search: name, years to search, DOB, signed release; also helpful: address, SSN. Criminal records on computer since 1990 for misdemeanor; since 1992 for felony.

General Information: No juvenile, mental, expunged, dismissed, or suspended imposition of sentence records released. SASE required. Copy fee: $.50 per page. Certification fee: $3.50. Fee payee: City of St. Louis Circuit Clerk. Business checks accepted. Prepayment is required.

Ste. Genevieve County

Circuit Court 55 S 3rd, Rm 23, Ste Genevieve, MO 63670; 573-883-2705; Fax: 573-883-9351. Hours: 8AM-5PM (CST). *Felony, Misdemeanor, Civil Actions Over $25,000.*

Civil Records: Access: In person only. Visitors must perform in person searches for themselves. No search fee. Required to search: name, years to search. Civil cases indexed by defendant, plaintiff. Civil records on books since early 1800s, recent civil records computerized.

Criminal Records: Access: In person only. Visitors must perform in person searches for themselves. No search fee. Required to search: name, years to search. Criminal Record indexes on books, not computerized.

General Information: Public Access terminal is available. No juvenile, mental, expunged, paternity, dismissed, or suspended imposition of sentence records released. Copy fee: $1.00 per page. Certification fee: $1.50. Fee payee: St Genevieve County Circuit Clerk. Business checks accepted. Prepayment is required.

Associate Circuit Court 3rd and Market, Ste Genevieve, MO 63670; 573-883-2265; Fax: 573-883-9351. Hours: 8AM-5PM (CST). *Misdemeanor, Civil Actions Under $45,000, Eviction, Small Claims, Probate.*

Civil Records: Access: In person only. Visitors must perform in person searches for themselves. No search fee. Required to search: name, years to search. Civil cases indexed by defendant, plaintiff. Civil records on books.

Criminal Records: Access: In person only. Visitors must perform in person searches for themselves. No search fee. Required to search: name, years to search. Criminal records on books.

General Information: No juvenile, mental, expunged, dismissed, or suspended imposition of sentence records released. Copy fee: $1.00 per page. Certification fee: $2.50. Only cashiers checks and money orders accepted.

Stoddard County

Circuit Court PO Box 30, Bloomfield, MO 63825; 573-568-4640; Fax: 573-568-2271. Hours: 8:30AM-4:30PM (CST). *Felony, Misdemeanor, Civil Actions Over $45,000.*

Civil Records: Access: Fax, mail, in person. Both court and visitors may perform in person searches. No search fee. Required to search: name, years to search. Civil cases indexed by defendant, plaintiff. Civil records on computer since 1991, prior on cards and books.

Criminal Records: Access: Mail, in person. Both court and visitors may perform in person searches. No search fee. Required to search: name, years to search; also helpful: DOB, SSN. Criminal records on computer since 1991, prior on cards and books.

General Information: Public Access terminal is available. No juvenile, mental, expunged, dismissed, or suspended imposition of sentence records released. SASE required. Turnaround time 1 day. Copy fee: $.10 per page. Certification fee: $1.50. Fee payee: Stoddard County Circuit Clerk. Personal checks accepted.

Division III & Probate PO Box 518, Bloomfield, MO 63825; 573-568-2181; Fax: 573-568-3229. Hours: 7:30AM-4PM (CST). *Civil Actions Under $25,000, Eviction, Small Claims, Probate.*

Associate Circuit Court - Criminal Division II PO Box 218, Bloomfield, MO 63825; 573-568-4671; Fax: 573-568-2299. Hours: 8:30AM-4:30PM (CST). *Misdemeanor.*

Criminal Records: Access: In person only. Visitors must perform in person searches for themselves. No search fee. Required to search: name, years to search. Criminal records on index cards, traffic on computer since 1994.

General Information: No juvenile, mental, expunged, dismissed, or suspended imposition of sentence records released. No copy fee. Certification fee: No cert fee. Fee payee: Stoddard County. Personal checks accepted. Prepayment is required.

Stone County

Circuit Court PO Box 18, Galena, MO 65656; 417-357-6114; 417-357-6115 child support; Fax: 417-357-6163. Hours: 7:30AM-4PM (CST). *Felony, Misdemeanor, Civil Actions Over $25,000.*

Civil Records: Access: Phone, fax, mail, in person. Both court and visitors may perform in person searches. No search fee. Required to search: name, years to search. Civil cases indexed by defendant, plaintiff. Civil records on cards and books, archived since 1852.

Criminal Records: Access: Phone, fax, mail, in person. Both court and visitors may perform in person searches. No search fee. Required to search: name, years to search; also helpful: DOB, SSN. Criminal records on cards and books, archived since 1852.

General Information: No juvenile, mental, expunged, dismissed, or suspended imposition of sentence records released. SASE required. Turnaround time 1 week. Fax notes: $3.00 per page. Copy fee: $.25 per page.

Certification fee: $1.00. Fee payee: Circuit Court. Personal checks accepted.

Circuit Court - Division II & III PO Box 186, Galena, MO 65656; 417-357-6511; Fax: 417-357-6163. Hours: 7:30AM-4PM (CST). *Misdemeanor, Civil Actions, Eviction, Small Claims, Probate.*

Note: No collar limit on civil actions; prior to 2001, the civil action maximum limit was $25,000.

Civil Records: Access: Phone, fax, mail, in person. Both court and visitors may perform in person searches. No search fee. Required to search: name, years to search; also helpful: address. Civil cases indexed by defendant, plaintiff. Civil records on index cards since 1979, prior on log sheets.

Criminal Records: Access: Phone, fax, mail, in person. Both court and visitors may perform in person searches. No search fee. Required to search: name, years to search, signed release; also helpful: address, DOB, SSN. Criminal records on computer and microfiche.

General Information: No juvenile, mental, expunged, dismissed, or suspended imposition of sentence records released. SASE required. Turnaround time 2-3 weeks. Fax notes: $3.00 per page. Copy fee: $.25 per page. Certification fee: $2.50. Fee payee: Circuit Court Division II. Only cashiers checks and money orders accepted. Prepayment is required.

Sullivan County

Circuit Court Courthouse, 109 N Main, Milan, MO 63556-1358; 660-265-4717; Fax: 660-265-5071. Hours: 9:00AM-4:30PM (CST). *Felony, Misdemeanor, Civil Actions Over $45,000.*

www.circuit7.net

Civil Records: Access: In person only. Visitors must perform in person searches for themselves. No search fee. Required to search: name, years to search. Civil cases indexed by defendant, plaintiff. Civil records on index cards since 1979, prior on books.

Criminal Records: Access: In person only. Visitors must perform in person searches for themselves. No search fee. Required to search: name, years to search; also helpful: DOB, SSN. Criminal records on index cards since 1979, prior on books.

General Information: No juvenile, mental, expunged, dismissed, or suspended imposition of sentence records released. Copy fee: $.25 per page. Certification fee: $1.50. Fee payee: Consolidated Circuit Court of Sullivan County. Personal checks accepted. Prepayment is required.

Associate Circuit Court Courthouse, Milan, MO 63556; 660-265-3303; Fax: 660-265-5071. Hours: 9AM-4:30PM (CST). *Misdemeanor, Civil Actions Under $50,000, Eviction, Small Claims, Probate.*

Civil Records: Access: In person only. Both court and visitors may perform in person searches. No search fee. Required to search: name, years to search. Civil cases indexed by defendant, plaintiff. Civil records on index cards and books.

Criminal Records: Access: In person only. Both court and visitors may perform in person searches. No search fee. Required to search: name, years to search. Criminal records on computer since 5/93.

General Information: No juvenile, mental, expunged, dismissed, or suspended imposition of sentence records released. Certification fee: $1.50. Fee payee: Associate Circuit Court. Personal checks accepted. Prepayment is required.

Taney County

Circuit Court PO Box 335, Forsyth, MO 65653; 417-546-7230; Fax: 417-546-6133. Hours: 8AM-5PM *Felony, Misdemeanor, Civil Actions Over $45,000.*

Civil Records: Access: Mail, in person. Both court and visitors may perform in person searches. Search fee: $4.00 per name. Required to search: name, years to search. Civil cases indexed by defendant, plaintiff. Civil records on computer since 1/95, prior on index cards and books since 1885.

Criminal Records: Access: Mail, in person. Both court and visitors may perform in person searches. Search fee: $4.00 per name. Required to search: name, years to search, DOB; also helpful: SSN. Criminal records on computer since 1/95, prior on index cards and books since 1885.

General Information: Public Access terminal is available. No juvenile, mental, expunged, dismissed, or suspended imposition of sentence records released. SASE helpful. Copy fee: $.25 per page. Certification fee: $1.50. Fee payee: Circuit Clerk. Personal checks accepted. Prepayment is required.

Associate Circuit Court PO Box 129, Forsyth, MO 65653; 417-546-7212; Fax: 417-546-4513. Hours: 8AM-5PM (CST). *Misdemeanor, Civil Actions Under $25,000, Eviction, Small Claims, Probate.*

Civil Records: Access: Mail, in person. Only the court performs in person searches; visitors may not. Search fee: $4.00 per name. Required to search: name, years to search. Civil cases indexed by defendant, plaintiff. Civil records on computer since 1984, prior on cards and books.

Criminal Records: Access: Mail, in person. Only the court performs in person searches; visitors may not. Search fee: $4.00 per name. Required to search: name, years to search, DOB, SSN. Criminal records on computer since 1984, prior on cards and books.

General Information: No juvenile, mental, expunged, dismissed, or suspended imposition of sentence records released. SASE required. Turnaround time 2 days, more if busy. Copy fee: $.25 per page. Certification fee: $1.50. Fee payee: Associate Circuit Court. Personal checks accepted. Prepayment is required.

Texas County

Circuit Court 210 N Grand, Houston, MO 65483; 417-967-3742; Fax: 417-967-4220. Hours: 8AM-5PM *Felony, Misdemeanor, Civil Actions Over $45,000.*

Civil Records: Access: In person only. Both court and visitors may perform in person searches. No search fee. Required to search: name, years to search. Civil cases indexed by defendant, plaintiff. Civil records on index books since 1900s.

Criminal Records: Access: In person only. Both court and visitors may perform in person searches. No search fee. Required to search: name, years to search. Criminal records on index books since 1900s.

General Information: No juvenile, mental, expunged, dismissed, or suspended imposition of sentence records released. Copy fee: $1.00 per page. Certification fee: $2.00. Fee payee: Texas County Circuit Clerk. Personal checks accepted. Prepayment is required.

Associate Circuit Court County Courthouse, 210 N Grand, Rm 205, Houston, MO 65483; 417-967-3663; Fax: 417-967-4128. Hours: 8AM-noon; 1-5PM (CST). *Misdemeanor, Civil Actions Under $45,000, Eviction, Small Claims, Probate.*

Civil Records: Access: Phone, fax, mail, in person. Only the court performs in person searches; visitors may not. No search fee. Required to search: name, years to search. Civil cases indexed by defendant, plaintiff. Civil records on index cards since 1979, prior on cards and books.

Criminal Records: Access: Phone, fax, mail, in person. Only the court performs in person searches; visitors may not. No search fee. Required to search: name, years to search. Criminal records on index cards since 1979, prior on cards and books.

General Information: No juvenile, mental, expunged, dismissed, or suspended imposition of sentence records released. SASE required. Turnaround time 7-10 days, phone turnaround time immediate. Fax notes: $2.00 for first page, $.50 each add'l. Copy fee: $1.00 per page. Certification fee: $1.50. Fee payee: Associate Circuit Court. Business checks accepted.

Vernon County

Circuit Court Courthouse, 3rd Fl, Nevada, MO 64772; 417-448-2525; Fax: 417-448-2512. Hours: 8AM-4:30PM (CST). *Felony, Misdemeanor, Civil Actions Over $45,000.*

Civil Records: Access: Fax, mail, in person, online. Both court and visitors may perform in person searches. Search fee: $5.00 per name. Required to search: name, years to search. Civil cases indexed by defendant, plaintiff. Civil records on computer back to 7/94, prior on index cards (judgments only). Participates in the free state online court record system at http://casenet.osca.state.mo.us/casenet. Records go back to 9/2000.

Criminal Records: Access: Fax, mail, in person, online. Both court and visitors may perform in person searches. Search fee: $5.00 per name. Required to search: name, years to search; also helpful: DOB, SSN. Criminal records on computer back to 7/94. Online access to criminal records is the same as civil.

General Information: Public Access terminal is available. No juvenile, mental, expunged, dismissed, or suspended imposition of sentence records released. SASE required. Turnaround time varies. Fax notes: Will not fax results. Copy fee: $.20 per page. Certification fee: $1.50. Fee payee: Vernon County Circuit Clerk. Personal checks accepted. Prepayment is required.

Associate Circuit Court County Courthouse, Nevada, MO 64772; 417-448-2550; Fax: 417-448-2512. Hours: 8:30AM-4:30PM (CST). *Misdemeanor, Civil Actions Under $25,000, Eviction, Small Claims, Probate.*

Civil Records: Access: Fax, mail, in person, online. Both court and visitors may perform in person searches. Search fee: $5.00 per name. Required to search: name, years to search. Civil cases indexed by defendant, plaintiff. Civil records on computer since 1990, on index cards since 1979, prior on index books. Participates in the free state online court record system at http://casenet.osca.state.mo.us/casenet. Records go back to 9/2000.

Criminal Records: Access: Mail, in person, online. Both court and visitors may perform in person searches. Search fee: $5.00 per name. Required to search: name, years to search; also helpful: DOB, SSN. Criminal records on computer since 1990, on index cards since 1979, prior on index books. Online access to criminal records is the same as civil.

General Information: Public Access terminal is available. No juvenile, mental, expunged, dismissed, or suspended imposition of sentence records released. SASE required. Turnaround time 1-2 weeks. Fax notes: Will not fax results. Copy fee: $.20 per page. Certification fee: $1.50. Fee payee: Circuit Court. Personal checks accepted. Prepayment is required.

Warren County

Circuit Court 104 W Main, Warrenton, MO 63383; 636-456-3363; Fax: 636-456-2422. Hours: 8AM-4:30PM (CST). *Felony, Misdemeanor, Civil Actions Over $45,000.*

Civil Records: Access: Online, in person. Visitors must perform in person searches for themselves. No search fee. Required to search: name, years to search. Civil cases indexed by defendant, plaintiff. Civil records on index cards since 1976, prior on books. Participates in the free state online court record system at http://casenet.osca.state.mo.us/casenet.

Criminal Records: Access: Online, in person. Visitors must perform in person searches for themselves. No search fee. Required to search: name, years to search. Criminal records on index cards since 1976, prior on books. Online access to criminal records is the same as civil.

General Information: No juvenile, mental, expunged, dismissed, or suspended imposition of sentence records released. Copy fee: $.25 per page. Certification fee: $1.00. Fee payee: Warren County Circuit Clerk. Business checks accepted. Prepayment is required.

Associate Circuit Court Warren County Courthouse, 104 W Main, Warrenton, MO 63383; 636-456-3375; Fax: 636-456-2422. Hours: 8:30AM-4:30PM (CST). *Misdemeanor, Civil Actions Under $25,000, Eviction, Small Claims, Probate.*

http://casenet.asca.state.mo.us/casenet

Civil Records: Access: Phone, fax, mail, online, in person. Both court and visitors may perform in person searches. No search fee. Required to search: name, years to search. Civil cases indexed by defendant, plaintiff. Civil records on index cards since 1979, prior on books. Participates in the free state online court record system at http://casenet.osca.state.mo.us/casenet.

Criminal Records: Access: Phone, fax, mail, online, in person. Only the court performs in person searches; visitors may not. No search fee. Required to search: name, years to search; also helpful: DOB, SSN. Criminal records on computer since 2/92, on cards since 1979, prior on books. Online access to criminal records is the same as civil.

General Information: No juvenile, mental, expunged, dismissed, or suspended imposition of sentence records released. SASE not required. Turnaround time 1 week. Fax notes: $1.00 per page. Copy fee: $.25 per page. Certification fee: $1.50 plus $1.00 per page. Fee payee: Associate Circuit Clerk. Personal checks accepted. Prepayment is required.

Washington County

Circuit Court PO Box 216, Potosi, MO 63664; 573-438-4171; Fax: 573-438-7900. Hours: 8AM-5PM *Felony, Misdemeanor, Civil Actions Over $45,000.*

Civil Records: Access: Mail, in person. Both court and visitors may perform in person searches. No search fee. Required to search: name, years to search. Civil cases indexed by defendant, plaintiff. Civil records on index cards since 1976, prior on books.

Criminal Records: Access: Mail, in person. Both court and visitors may perform in person searches. No search fee. Required to search: name, years to search. Criminal records on index cards since 1976, prior on books.

General Information: No juvenile, mental, expunged, dismissed, or suspended imposition of sentence records released. SASE required. Turnaround time 1-2 days. Copy fee: $.50 per page. Certification fee: $2.00. Fee payee: Washington County Circuit Clerk. Personal checks accepted. Prepayment is required.

Associate Circuit Court 102 N Missouri St, Potosi, MO 63664; 573-438-3691; Fax: 573-438-7900. Hours: 8AM-5PM (CST). *Misdemeanor, Civil Actions Under $45,000, Eviction, Small Claims, Probate.*

Civil Records: Access: Phone, fax, mail, in person. Both court and visitors may perform in person searches. No search fee. Required to search: name, years to search. Civil cases indexed by defendant, plaintiff. Civil records on index cards since 1976.

Criminal Records: Access: Phone, fax, mail, in person. Both court and visitors may perform in person searches. No search fee. Required to search: name, years to search; also helpful: DOB, SSN. Criminal records on index cards since 1976.

General Information: No juvenile, mental, expunged, dismissed, or suspended imposition of sentence records released. SASE required. Turnaround time 1 week. Copy fee: $.50 per page. Certification fee: No cert fee. Fee payee: Associate Circuit Clerk. Personal checks accepted. Prepayment is required.

Wayne County

Circuit Court PO Box 78, Greenville, MO 63944; 573-224-3014; Fax: 573-224-3015. Hours: 8:30AM-4:30PM (CST). *Felony, Misdemeanor, Civil Actions Over $45,000.*

Civil Records: Access: Mail, in person. Both court and visitors may perform in person searches. Search fee: $14.00 per name. Required to search: name, years to search. Civil cases indexed by defendant, plaintiff. Civil records on index cards since 1978, prior on books.

Criminal Records: Access: Mail, in person. Both court and visitors may perform in person searches. Search fee: $14.00 per name. Required to search: name, years to search; also helpful: DOB. Criminal records on index cards since 1978, prior on books.

General Information: No juvenile, mental, expunged, dismissed, or suspended imposition of sentence records released. SASE required. Turnaround time 1 week. Copy fee: $.25 per page. Certification fee: $2.00. Fee payee: Wayne County Circuit Clerk. Personal checks accepted. Prepayment is required.

Associate Circuit Court PO Box 47, Greenville, MO 63944; 573-224-3052; Fax: 573-224-3225. Hours: 8:30AM-4:30PM (CST). *Misdemeanor, Civil Actions Under $45,000, Eviction, Small Claims, Probate.*

Civil Records: Access: Phone, fax, mail, in person. Both court and visitors may perform in person searches. No search fee. Required to search: name, years to search. Civil cases indexed by defendant, plaintiff. Civil records on index cards since 1979.

Criminal Records: Access: Phone, fax, mail, in person. Only the court performs in person searches; visitors may not. No search fee. Required to search: name, years to search, DOB; also helpful: SSN. Criminal records on computer since 1992, prior on index cards.

General Information: No juvenile, mental, expunged, dismissed, or suspended imposition of sentence records released. SASE required. Turnaround time 1 day. Fax notes: $.50 per page. Copy fee: $.25 per page. Certification fee: $1.50 per page. Fee payee: Associate Circuit Court. Personal checks accepted.

Webster County

Circuit Court PO Box 529, Marshfield, MO 65706; 417-859-2006; Fax: 417-468-3786. Hours: 8AM-5PM (CST). *Felony, Misdemeanor, Civil Actions Over $25,000.*

www.positech.net/~dcourt

Note: Records should be available online on MO CaseNet on 2/2002.

Civil Records: Access: Fax, mail, in person. Both court and visitors may perform in person searches. No search fee. Required to search: name, years to search. Civil cases indexed by defendant, plaintiff. Civil records on computer since 1976 (judgment index).

Criminal Records: Access: Fax, mail, in person. Only the court performs in person searches; visitors may not. No search fee. Required to search: name, years to search, DOB. Criminal records on computer since 1976 (judgment index).

General Information: Public Access terminal is available. (Judgments only.) No juvenile, mental, expunged, dismissed, or suspended imposition of sentence records released. SASE required. Turnaround time 1 day. Fax notes: $2.00 per page. Copy fee: $.15 per page. Certification fee: $2.00. Fee payee: Webster County Circuit Clerk. Personal checks accepted.

Associate Circuit Court Courthouse, Marshfield, MO 65706; 417-859-2041; Fax: 417-859-6265. Hours: 8AM-5PM (CST). *Misdemeanor, Civil Actions Under $45,000, Eviction, Small Claims, Probate.*

www.positech.net/~dcourt

Civil Records: Access: Phone, fax, mail, in person. Only the court performs in person searches; visitors may not. No search fee. Required to search: name, years to search. Civil cases indexed by defendant, plaintiff. Civil records on computer since 1992; prior records on index cards since 1980 & on books.

Criminal Records: Access: Mail, in person. Only the court performs in person searches; visitors may not. No search fee. Required to search: name, years to search; also helpful: DOB, SSN. Criminal records on computer since 1992.

General Information: No juvenile, mental, expunged, dismissed, or suspended imposition of sentence records released. SASE required. Turnaround time varies. Copy fee: $1.00 per page. Certification fee: $1.50. Fee payee: Associate Circuit Court. Only cashiers checks and money orders accepted. Prepayment is required.

Worth County

Circuit Court PO Box 340, Grant City, MO 64456; 660-564-2210; Fax: 660-564-2432. Hours: 8:30AM-4:30PM (CST). *Felony, Misdemeanor, Civil Actions Over $45,000.*

Civil Records: Access: Mail, in person. Both court and visitors may perform in person searches. No search fee. Required to search: name, years to search. Civil cases indexed by defendant, plaintiff. Civil records on computer since 1990, prior on index cards.

Criminal Records: Access: Mail, in person. Both court and visitors may perform in person searches. No search fee. Required to search: name, years to search. Criminal records on computer since 1990, prior on index cards.

General Information: Public Access terminal is available. No juvenile, mental, expunged, dismissed, or suspended imposition of sentence records released. SASE required. Turnaround time same day. Copy fee:

$.20 per page. Certification fee: $2.50. Fee payee: Worth County Circuit Clerk. Personal checks accepted. Prepayment is required.

Associate Circuit Court PO Box 428, Grant City, MO 64456; 660-564-2152; Fax: 660-564-2432. Hours: 9AM-4:30PM (CST). *Misdemeanor, Civil Actions Under $45,000, Eviction, Small Claims, Probate.*

Civil Records: Access: In person only. Visitors must perform in person searches for themselves. No search fee. Required to search: name, years to search. Civil cases indexed by defendant, plaintiff. Civil records on index cards since 1979, prior on index books.

Criminal Records: Access: Mail, in person. Both court and visitors may perform in person searches. No search fee. Required to search: name, years to search. Criminal records on index cards since 1979, prior on index books.

General Information: No juvenile, mental, expunged, dismissed, or suspended imposition of sentence records released. SASE required. Turnaround time varies. Copy fee: $1.00 per page. Certification fee: $2.50. Fee payee: Associate Circuit Court. Personal checks accepted. Prepayment is required.

Wright County

Circuit Court PO Box 39, Hartville, MO 65667; 417-741-7121; Fax: 417-741-7504. Hours: 8AM-4:30PM (CST). *Felony, Misdemeanor, Civil Actions Over $45,000.*

Civil Records: Access: Mail, in person. Both court and visitors may perform in person searches. No search fee. Required to search: name, years to search. Civil cases indexed by defendant, plaintiff. Civil records on index cards since 1979, prior on books.

Criminal Records: Access: Mail, in person. Both court and visitors may perform in person searches. No search fee. Required to search: name, years to search. Criminal records on index cards since 1979, prior on books.

General Information: No juvenile, mental, expunged, dismissed, or suspended imposition of sentence records released. SASE not required. Turnaround time 1 day. Copy fee: $.25 per page. Certification fee: $2.00. Fee payee: Wright County Circuit Clerk. Personal checks accepted. Prepayment is required.

Associate Circuit Court PO Box 58, Hartville, MO 65667; 417-741-6450; Fax: 417-741-7504. Hours: 8AM-4:30PM (CST). *Misdemeanor, Civil Actions Under $25,000, Eviction, Small Claims, Probate.*

Civil Records: Access: Phone, fax, mail, in person. Only the court performs in person searches; visitors may not. No search fee. Required to search: name, years to search. Civil cases indexed by defendant, plaintiff. Civil records on index cards since 1979, prior on books; on computer back to 1990.

Criminal Records: Access: Phone, fax, mail, in person. Only the court performs in person searches; visitors may not. No search fee. Required to search: name, years to search; also helpful: DOB, SSN. Criminal records on computer since 1989, prior on cards and books; on computer back to 1990.

General Information: No juvenile, mental, expunged, or dismissed records released. SASE required. Turnaround time 1 week. Fax notes: Fee to fax results is $1.00 per page. Copy fee: $.25 per page. Certification fee: $1.00. Fee payee: Associate Circuit Court. Only cashiers checks and money orders accepted.

Missouri Recording Offices

ORGANIZATION   114 counties and one independent city, 115 recording offices. The recording officer is. Recorder of Deeds. The City of St. Louis has its own recording office. See the City/County Locator section at the end of this chapter for ZIP Codes that cover both the city and county of St. Louis. The entire state is in the Central Time Zone (CST).

REAL ESTATE RECORDS   A few counties will perform real estate searches. Copy and certification fees vary.

UCC RECORDS   Missouri was a dual filing state. Until 07/2001, financing statements were filed both at the state level and with the Recorder of Deeds, except for consumer goods, farm related and real estate related filings, which were filed only with the Recorder. Now only real estate relating filings are filed at the county level. Most all counties will perform UCC searches. Use search request form UCC-11. Search fees are usually $14.00 per debtor name without copies and $28.00 with copies. Copies usually cost $.50 per page.

TAX LIEN RECORDS   All federal and state tax liens are filed with the county Recorder of Deeds. They are usually indexed together. Some counties will perform tax lien searches. Search and copy fees vary widely.

OTHER LIENS   Mechanics, judgment, child support.

Adair County

Recorder of Deeds, Courthouse, 106 W. Washington St., Kirksville, MO 63501. 660-665-3890; Fax 660-785-3212.
Will search UCC records. UCC search includes tax liens if requested. Will not search real estate records. **Other Phone Numbers:** Assessor 660-665-4423.

Andrew County

Recorder of Deeds, P.O Box 208, Savannah, MO 64485. Recorder of Deeds, R/E and UCC Recording 816-324-4221; Fax 816-324-5667.
Will search UCC records. This agency will not do a tax lien search. Will not search real estate records. **Other Phone Numbers:** Assessor 816-324-3023; Treasurer 816-324-3614; Elections 816-324-3624.

Atchison County

Recorder of Deeds, Box 280, Rock Port, MO 64482. 660-744-2707; Fax 660-744-5705.
Will search UCC records. Will not search real estate records. **Other Phone Numbers:** Assessor 660-744-2707; Treasurer 660-744-2800.

Audrain County

Recorder of Deeds, Room 105, Audrain County Courthouse, 101 N. Jefferson, Mexico, MO 65265. 573-473-5830; Fax 573-581-2380.
Will search UCC records. UCC search includes tax liens if requested. Will not search real estate records. **Other Phone Numbers:** Assessor 573-473-5827.

Barry County

Recorder of Deeds, Courthouse, Cassville, MO 65625. 417-847-2914.
Will search UCC records. UCC search includes tax liens. Will not search real estate records. **Other Phone Numbers:** Assessor 417-847-4589.

Barton County

Recorder of Deeds, Courthouse, Room 107, 1004 Gulf, Lamar, MO 64759. Recorder of Deeds, R/E and UCC Recording 417-682-2110.
Will search UCC records. This agency will not do a tax lien search. Will not search real estate records. **Other Phone Numbers:** Assessor 417-682-3553; Treasurer 417-682-5881; Elections 417-682-3529; Circuit Court 417-682-2444.

Bates County

Recorder of Deeds, Box 186, Butler, MO 64730. Recorder of Deeds, R/E and UCC Recording 660-679-3611.
Will search UCC records. Will not search tax liens. RE record owner and mortgage searches available. **Other Phone Numbers:** Assessor 660-679-3157; Treasurer 660-679-3341; Elections 660-679-3371.

Benton County

Recorder of Deeds, P.O. Box 37, Warsaw, MO 65355. 660-438-5732; Fax 660-438-3652.
Will search UCC records. Property transfer searches available. **Other Phone Numbers:** Assessor 660-438-5323; Treasurer 660-438-6313.

Bollinger County

Recorder of Deeds, Box 949, Marble Hill, MO 63764. 573-238-2710; Fax 573-238-2773.
Will search UCC records. This agency will not do a tax lien search. Will not search real estate records. **Other Phone Numbers:** Assessor 573-238-2914; Treasurer 573-238-2313.

Boone County

Recorder of Deeds, Boone County Gov't Center, 801 E. Walnut, Rm 132, Columbia, MO 65201-7728. Recorder of Deeds, R/E and UCC Recording 573-886-4345 UCC Recording: 573-886-4353; Fax 573-886-4359. http://www.showmeboone.com
Will search UCC records. This agency will not do a tax lien search. Will not search real estate records. **Online Access:** Real Estate, Liens, Vital Statistics, UCC. Online access to the County Recorder database is available free at http://www.showmeboone.com/RECORDER. **Other Phone Numbers:** Assessor 573-886-4270; Treasurer 573-886-4365; Appraiser/Auditor 573-886-4270; Elections 573-886-4295; Marriage License 573-886-4350.

Buchanan County

Recorder of Deeds, 411 Jules Streets, Courthouse, St. Joseph, MO 64501-1789. 816-271-1437; Fax 816-271-1582.
Will search UCC records. This agency will not do a tax lien search. Will not search real estate records. **Other Phone Numbers:** Assessor 816-271-1469; Treasurer 816-271-1432.

Butler County

Recorder of Deeds, 100 N. Main Street, Courthouse, Poplar Bluff, MO 63901. Recorder of Deeds, R/E and UCC Recording 573-686-8086.
Will search UCC records. Tax liens not included in UCC search. Will not search real estate records. **Other Phone Numbers:** Assessor 573-686-8084; Treasurer 573-686-8083; Appraiser/Auditor 573-686-8084; Elections 573-686-8050; Vital Records 573-686-8086.

Caldwell County

Recorder of Deeds, P.O. Box 86, Kingston, MO 64650. 816-586-3080; Fax 816-586-2705.
Will search UCC records. This agency will not do a tax lien search. Will not search real estate records. **Other Phone Numbers:** Assessor 816-586-5261.

Callaway County

Recorder of Deeds, PO Box 406, Fulton, MO 65251. 573-642-0787; Fax 573-642-7929.
Will search UCC records. This agency will not do a tax lien search. Will not search real estate records. **Other Phone Numbers:** Assessor 573-642-0766.

Camden County

Recorder of Deeds, 1 Court Circle, Camdenton, MO 65020. 573-346-4440 R/E Recording: 573-346-4440 x234 UCC Recording: 573-346-4440 x235; Fax 573-346-5422.
Will search UCC records. This agency will not do a tax lien search. Will not search real estate records. **Other Phone Numbers:** Assessor 573-346-4440 x224-6; Treasurer 573-346-4440 x215-6.

Cape Girardeau County

Recorder of Deeds, P.O. Box 248, Jackson, MO 63755. 573-243-8123; Fax 573-204-2477.
Will search UCC records. This agency will not do a tax lien search. Will not search real estate records. **Other Phone Numbers:** Assessor 573-243-2468; Treasurer 573-243-3720.

Carroll County

Recorder of Deeds, P.O. Box 245, Carrollton, MO 64633. 660-542-1466; Fax 660-542-1444.
Will search UCC records. UCC search includes tax liens if requested. Will not search real estate records.

Other Phone Numbers: Assessor 660-542-2184; Treasurer 660-542-1977.

Carter County

Recorder of Deeds, P.O. Box 578, Van Buren, MO 63965. Recorder of Deeds, R/E and UCC Recording 573-323-4513; Fax 573-323-4885.
Will search UCC records. Tax liens not included in UCC search. Will not search real estate records. **Other Phone Numbers:** Assessor 573-323-4709; Treasurer 573-323-8271; Elections 573-323-4527.

Cass County

Recorder of Deeds, 102 East Wall Street, Cass County Court House, Harrisonville, MO 64701. Recorder of Deeds, R/E and UCC Recording 816-380-8117 UCC Recording: 816-380-8118; Fax 816-380-8165. http://www.casscounty.com/cassfr.htm
Will search UCC records. UCC search includes tax liens if requested. Will not search real estate records. **Online Access:** Real Estate, Liens. Access to county online records via modem requires a $250 monthly fee plus $.10 per minute after 90 minutes usage. Records date back to 1990. Images are viewable and can be printed, $1.00 each. Prepaid fax accounts available. For information, contact Sandy Gregory at 816-380-8117. **Other Phone Numbers:** Assessor 816-380-8117; Treasurer 816-380-8117; Elections 816-380-8102.

Cedar County

Recorder of Deeds, P.O. Box 665, Stockton, MO 65785. 417-276-6700 x246; Fax 417-276-5001.
Will search UCC records. This agency will not do a tax lien search. Will not search real estate records. **Other Phone Numbers:** Assessor 417-276-4765; Treasurer 417-276-4413.

Chariton County

Recorder of Deeds, P.O. Box 112, Keytesville, MO 65261. 660-288-3602; Fax 660-288-3763.
Will search UCC records. Will not search real estate records. **Other Phone Numbers:** Assessor 660-288-3873; Treasurer 660-288-3789.

Christian County

Recorder of Deeds, P.O. Box 278, Ozark, MO 65721. 417-581-6372; Fax 417-581-0391.
Will search UCC records. UCC search includes tax liens if requested. Will not search real estate records. **Other Phone Numbers:** Assessor 417-581-2440.

Clark County

Recorder of Deeds, 111 East Court, Courthouse, Kahoka, MO 63445. Recorder of Deeds, R/E and UCC Recording 660-727-3292; Fax 660-727-1051.
Will search UCC records. This agency will not do a tax lien search. Will not search real estate records. **Other Phone Numbers:** Assessor 660-727-3023; Treasurer 660-727-3272; Elections 660-727-3283.

Clay County

Recorder of Deeds, P.O. Box 238, Liberty, MO 64069. 816-792-7641.
Will search UCC records. RE record owner and mortgage searches available. **Other Phone Numbers:** Assessor 816-792-7664; Treasurer 816-792-7649 x284.

Clinton County

Recorder of Deeds, P.O. Box 275, Plattsburg, MO 64477. 816-539-3719; Fax 816-539-3893.
Will search UCC records. This agency will not do a tax lien search. Will not search real estate records. **Other Phone Numbers:** Assessor 816-539-3716; Treasurer 816-539-3724; Elections 816-539-3713.

Cole County

Recorder of Deeds, P.O. Box 353, Jefferson City, MO 65102. 573-634-9115.
Will search UCC records. Tax liens not included in UCC search. RE owner, mortgage, and property transfer searches available. **Other Phone Numbers:** Assessor 573-634-9135; Treasurer 573-634-9121.

Cooper County

Recorder of Deeds, 200 Main Street, Courthouse - Room 26, Boonville, MO 65233-1276. 660-882-2232; Fax 660-882-2043.
Will search UCC records. UCC search includes tax liens if requested. Will not search real estate records. **Other Phone Numbers:** Assessor 660-882-2646.

Crawford County

Recorder of Deeds, P.O. Box 177, Steelville, MO 65565. 573-775-5048; Fax 573-775-3365.
Will search UCC records. RE record owner and mortgage searches available. **Other Phone Numbers:** Assessor 573-775-2065; Treasurer 573-775-2899.

Dade County

Recorder of Deeds, Courthouse, Greenfield, MO 65661. 417-637-5373; Fax 417-637-5055.
Will search UCC records. This agency will not do a tax lien search. Will not search real estate records. **Other Phone Numbers:** Assessor 417-637-2224; Treasurer 417-637-2732.

Dallas County

Recorder of Deeds, P.O. Box 373, Buffalo, MO 65622. Recorder of Deeds, R/E and UCC Recording 417-345-2242; Fax 417-345-5539.
Will search UCC records. This agency will not do a tax lien search. Will not search real estate records. **Other Phone Numbers:** Assessor 417-345-8774; Treasurer 417-345-2020; Elections 417-345-2632.

Daviess County

Recorder of Deeds, P.O. Box 337, Gallatin, MO 64640. 660-663-2932; Fax 660-663-3376.
Will search UCC records. UCC search includes tax liens if requested. Will not search real estate records. **Other Phone Numbers:** Assessor 660-663-3300; Treasurer 660-663-2432.

De Kalb County

Recorder of Deeds, P.O. Box 248, Maysville, MO 64469-0248. 816-449-2602; Fax 816-449-2440.
Will search UCC records. UCC search includes tax liens if requested. RE record owner and mortgage searches available. **Other Phone Numbers:** Assessor 816-449-2212; Treasurer 816-449-5810.

Dent County

Recorder of Deeds, 112 East 5th Street, Salem, MO 65560-1444. 573-729-3931; Fax 573-729-9414.
Will search UCC records. UCC search includes tax liens if requested. Will not search real estate records. **Other Phone Numbers:** Assessor 573-729-6010; Treasurer 573-729-8260.

Douglas County

Recorder of Deeds, P.O. Box 249, Ava, MO 65608. 417-683-4713; Fax 417-683-2794.
Will search UCC records. Tax liens not included in UCC search. RE owner, mortgage, and property transfer searches available. **Other Phone Numbers:** Assessor 417-683-2829; Treasurer 417-683-2183; Elections 417-683-4714.

Dunklin County

Recorder of Deeds, P.O. Box 389, Kennett, MO 63857. 573-888-3468.
Will search UCC records. This agency will not do a tax lien search. Will not search real estate records. **Other Phone Numbers:** Assessor 573-888-1409.

Franklin County

Recorder of Deeds, 300 E Main St #101, Union, MO 63084. Recorder of Deeds, R/E and UCC Recording 636-583-6367; Fax 636-583-7330. http://www.usmo.com/~fcrd
Will search UCC records. This agency will not do a tax lien search. Will not search real estate records. **Other Phone Numbers:** Assessor 636-583-6346; Treasurer 636-583-6392.

Gasconade County

Recorder of Deeds, 119 E.1st St., Room 6, Hermann, MO 65041-1182. Recorder of Deeds, R/E and UCC Recording 573-486-2632; Fax 573-486-3693.
Will search UCC records. Tax liens not included in UCC search. Will not search real estate records. **Other Phone Numbers:** Assessor 573-486-3100; Treasurer 573-486-2411; Appraiser/Auditor 573-486-3100; Elections 573-486-5427.

Gentry County

Recorder of Deeds, P.O. Box 27, Albany, MO 64402. 660-726-3618; Fax 660-726-4102.
Will search UCC records. This agency will not do a tax lien search. Will not search real estate records. **Other Phone Numbers:** Assessor 660-726-5289.

Greene County

Recorder of Deeds, 940 Boonville, Room 100, Springfield, MO 65802. 417-868-4068; Fax 417-868-4807.
Will search UCC records. UCC search includes tax liens if requested. Will not search real estate records. **Online Access:** Divorce. Records for divorces that occurred 1837 to 1920 in Greene County are available free online at http://userdb.rootsweb.com/divorces. **Other Phone Numbers:** Assessor 417-868-4101.

Grundy County

Recorder of Deeds, P.O. Box 196, Trenton, MO 64683. Recorder of Deeds, R/E and UCC Recording 660-359-5409; Fax 660-359-6604.
Will search UCC records. This agency will not do a tax lien search. Will not search real estate records. **Other Phone Numbers:** Assessor 660-359-2413; Treasurer 660-359-2171; Elections 660-359-6305.

Harrison County

Recorder of Deeds, P.O. Box 189, Bethany, MO 64424. Recorder of Deeds, R/E and UCC Recording 660-425-6425; Fax 660-425-3772.
Will not search UCC records. This agency will not do a tax lien search. Will not search real estate records. **Other Phone Numbers:** Assessor 660-425-2313; Treasurer 660-425-6442.

Henry County

Recorder of Deeds, 100 W. Franklin #4, Courthouse, Clinton, MO 64735. 660-885-6963 R/E Recording: 660-885-6963 x233 UCC Recording: 660-885-6963 x233; Fax 660-885-2264.
Will search UCC records. This agency will not do a tax lien search. Will not search real estate records. **Other Phone Numbers:** Assessor 660-885-6963 x203; Treasurer 660-885-6963 x236.

Hickory County

Recorder of Deeds, P.O. Box 101, Hermitage, MO 65668. 417-745-6421; Fax 417-745-6670.
Will search UCC records. UCC search includes tax liens if requested. Will not search real estate records. **Other Phone Numbers:** Assessor 417-745-6346; Treasurer 417-745-6310; Appraiser/Auditor 417-745-6957; Elections 417-745-6450.

Holt County

Recorder of Deeds, P.O. Box 318, Oregon, MO 64473. 660-446-3301.
Will search UCC records. UCC search includes tax liens if requested. Will not search real estate records. **Other Phone Numbers:** Assessor 660-446-3329; Treasurer 660-446-3397.

Howard County

Recorder of Deeds, 1 Courthouse Square, Fayette, MO 65248. Recorder of Deeds, R/E and UCC Recording 660-248-2194; Fax 660-248-1075.
Will search UCC records. UCC search includes tax liens if requested. RE owner, mortgage, and property transfer searches available. **Other Phone Numbers:** Assessor 660-248-3400; Treasurer 660-248-2196.

Howell County

Recorder of Deeds, P.O. Box 1011, West Plains, MO 65775. 417-256-3750.
Will search UCC records. Tax liens not included in UCC search. Will not search real estate records. **Other Phone Numbers:** Assessor 417-256-8284; Treasurer 417-256-4261.

Iron County

Recorder of Deeds, P.O. Box 24, Ironton, MO 63650. 573-546-2811; Fax 573-546-2166.
Will search UCC records. This agency will not do a tax lien search. Will not search real estate records. **Other Phone Numbers:** Assessor 573-546-7319; Treasurer 573-546-7611.

Jackson County (Kansas City)

Recorder of Deeds, 415 East 12th Street, Room 104, Kansas City, MO 64106. 816-881-3192 R/E Recording: 816-881-3048 UCC Recording: 816-881-3048; Fax 816-881-3719. http://www.co.jackson.mo.us
There is another office in Independence, which covers the western part of the county. However, it is not necessary to file there as the Kansas City office can search and record any UCC filings for the entire county. Will search UCC records. This agency will not do a tax lien search. RE record owner searches available. **Online Access:** Property, Tax Assessor. Records from the county tax assessor database are available free at the web site. Click on "Tax Search." Search by owner name, address, street, or neighborhood. Property owner records on the Kansas City Neighborhood Network are available free online at www.kcmo-net.org/cgi-bin/db2www/realform.d2w/report. **Other Phone Numbers:** Assessor 816-881-3187; Treasurer 816-881-3270; Appraiser/Auditor 816-881-3091; Elections 816-881-4820.

Jasper County

Recorder of Deeds, P.O. Box 387, Carthage, MO 64836-0387. 417-358-0432.
Will search UCC records. This agency will not do a tax lien search. Will not search real estate records. **Other Phone Numbers:** Assessor 417-358-0437; Treasurer 417-358-0448.

Jefferson County

Recorder of Deeds, P.O. Box 100, Hillsboro, MO 63050. Recorder of Deeds, R/E and UCC Recording 636-797-5414 UCC Recording: 636-797-5499; http://www.jeffcomo.org/
Will search UCC records. This agency will not do a tax lien search. Will not search real estate records. **Other Phone Numbers:** Assessor 636-797-5466; Treasurer 636-797-5368; Appraiser/Auditor 636-797-5474; Elections 636-797-5486; Birth & Death Records 636-789-3372.

Johnson County

Recorder of Deeds, P.O. Box 32, Warrensburg, MO 64093. 660-747-6811.
Will search UCC records. This agency will not do a tax lien search. Will not search real estate records. **Other Phone Numbers:** Assessor 660-747-9822; Treasurer 660-747-7411.

Knox County

Recorder of Deeds, P.O. Box 116, Edina, MO 63537. 660-397-2305; Fax 660-397-3331.
Will search UCC records. This agency will not do a tax lien search. Will not search real estate records. **Other Phone Numbers:** Assessor 660-397-2423; Treasurer 660-397-3364.

Laclede County

Recorder of Deeds, 200 N Adams, 200 North Adams, Lebanon, MO 65536-3046. Recorder of Deeds, R/E and UCC Recording 417-532-4011; Fax 417-532-3852. http://laclede.county.missouri.org/recorder/
Will search UCC records. UCC search includes tax liens if requested. Will not search real estate records. **Other Phone Numbers:** Assessor 417-532-7163; Treasurer 417-532-4741; Appraiser/Auditor 417-532-7163; Elections 417-532-5471; Vital Records 417-532-2134 (Birth); 4011 (Marriage); Collector 417-532-4301.

Lafayette County

Recorder of Deeds, P.O. Box 416, Lexington, MO 64067. 660-259-6178; Fax 660-259-2918.
Will search UCC records. This agency will not do a tax lien search. Will not search real estate records. **Other Phone Numbers:** Assessor 660-259-6158; Treasurer 660-259-3711.

Lawrence County

Recorder of Deeds, P.O. Box 449, Mount Vernon, MO 65712. 417-466-2670; Fax 417-466-4995.
Will search UCC records. This agency will not do a tax lien search. Will not search real estate records. **Other Phone Numbers:** Assessor 417-466-2831; Treasurer 417-466-2662.

Lewis County

Recorder of Deeds, P.O. Box 97, Monticello, MO 63457-0097. 573-767-5440; Fax 573-767-5378.
Will search UCC records. This agency will not do a tax lien search. Will not search real estate records. **Other Phone Numbers:** Assessor 573-767-5209.

Lincoln County

Recorder of Deeds, 201 Main Street, Troy, MO 63379. 636-528-6300; Fax 636-528-2665.
Will search UCC records. RE record owner and mortgage searches available. **Other Phone Numbers:** Assessor 636-528-0320.

Linn County

Recorder of Deeds, P.O. Box 151, Linneus, MO 64653. 660-895-5216; Fax 660-895-5533.
Will search UCC records. UCC search includes tax liens if requested. Will not search real estate records. **Other Phone Numbers:** Assessor 660-895-5387; Treasurer 660-895-5410.

Livingston County

Recorder of Deeds, Courthouse, Suite 6, 700 Webster St., Chillicothe, MO 64601. Recorder of Deeds, R/E and UCC Recording 660-646-0166.
Will search UCC records. This agency will not do a tax lien search. Will not search real estate records. **Other Phone Numbers:** Assessor 660-646-2027; Treasurer 660-646-3076; Elections 660-646-2293.

Macon County

Recorder of Deeds, P.O. Box 382, Macon, MO 63552. 660-385-2732; Fax 660-385-4235.
Will search UCC records. Will not search real estate records. **Other Phone Numbers:** Assessor 660-385-2416; Treasurer 660-385-2713.

Madison County

Recorder of Deeds, P.O. Box 470, Fredericktown, MO 63645-0470. 573-783-2102; Fax 573-783-2715.
Will search UCC records. This agency will not do a tax lien search. Will not search real estate records. **Other Phone Numbers:** Assessor 573-783-3325; Treasurer 573-783-3325.

Maries County

Recorder of Deeds, P.O. Box 213, Vienna, MO 65582. Recorder of Deeds, R/E and UCC Recording 573-422-3338; Fax 573-422-3269.
Will search UCC records. UCC search includes tax liens if requested. Will not search real estate records. **Other Phone Numbers:** Assessor 573-422-3540; Treasurer 573-422-3311; Elections 573-422-3388; Vital Records 573-422-3338; Collector 573-422-3343; Sheriff 573-422-3381;

Marion County

Recorder of Deeds, P.O. Box 392, Palmyra, MO 63461. 573-769-2550; Fax 573-769-6012.
Will search UCC records. This agency will not do a tax lien search. Will not search real estate records. **Other Phone Numbers:** Assessor 573-248-1514; Treasurer 573-769-2552; Elections 573-729-2549.

McDonald County

Recorder of Deeds, P.O. Box 157, Pineville, MO 64856. 417-223-7523; Fax 417-223-4125.
Will search UCC records. UCC search includes tax liens if requested. Will not search real estate records. **Other Phone Numbers:** Assessor 417-223-4361; Treasurer 417-223-4462.

Mercer County

Recorder of Deeds, Courthouse, Princeton, MO 64673. 660-748-4335; Fax 660-748-3180.
Will search UCC records. Tax liens not included in UCC search. Will not search real estate records. **Other Phone Numbers:** Assessor 660-748-3511; Treasurer 660-748-3435.

Miller County

Recorder of Deeds, P.O. Box 11, Tuscumbia, MO 65082. Recorder of Deeds, R/E and UCC Recording 573-369-2911; Fax 573-369-2910.
Will search UCC records. **Other Phone Numbers:** Assessor 573-369-2614; Treasurer 573-369-2214.

Mississippi County

County Recorder, PO Box 369, Charleston, MO 63834. 573-683-2146 R/E Recording: 573-683-2146 x226; Fax 573-683-7696.
Will search UCC records. **Other Phone Numbers:** Assessor 573-683-2146 x238; Treasurer 573-683-2146 x235; Elections 573-683-2146 x222.

Moniteau County

Circuit Clerk and Recorder, 200 East Main Street, California, MO 65018. 573-796-2071 R/E Recording: 573-796-4822 UCC Recording: 573-796-4822; Fax 573-796-2591.

Will search UCC records. Will not search real estate records. **Other Phone Numbers:** Assessor 573-796-4637; Treasurer 573-796-4608; Elections 573-796-4661; Vital Records 573-796-4671.

Monroe County

Recorder of Deeds, P.O. Box 227, Paris, MO 65275. 660-327-5204; Fax 660-327-5781.

Will search UCC records. Will not search real estate records. **Other Phone Numbers:** Assessor 660-327-5607; Treasurer 660-327-4711.

Montgomery County

Recorder of Deeds, 211 East 3rd Street, Montgomery City, MO 63361. Recorder of Deeds, R/E and UCC Recording 573-564-3157; Fax 573-564-3914.

Will search UCC records. **Other Phone Numbers:** Assessor 573-564-2445; Treasurer 573-564-2319; Elections 573-564-3357.

Morgan County

County Recorder, 100 Newton Street, Courthouse, Versailles, MO 65084. County Recorder, R/E and UCC Recording 573-378-4029; Fax 573-378-6431.

Will search UCC records. Will not search real estate records. **Other Phone Numbers:** Assessor 573-378-5459; Treasurer 573-378-4404; Elections 573-378-5436.

New Madrid County

Recorder of Deeds, P.O. Box 217, New Madrid, MO 63869. 573-748-5146.

Will search UCC records. Tax liens not included in UCC search. Will not search real estate records. **Other Phone Numbers:** Assessor 573-748-2387.

Newton County

Recorder of Deeds, P.O. Box 130, Neosho, MO 64850-0130. 417-451-8224; Fax 417-451-8273.

Will search UCC records. Will not search real estate records. **Other Phone Numbers:** Assessor 417-451-8228; Treasurer 417-451-8226.

Nodaway County

Recorder of Deeds, 305 N. Main, Room 104, Maryville, MO 64468. 660-582-5711; Fax 660-582-5282.

Will search UCC records. Will not search real estate records. **Other Phone Numbers:** Assessor 660-582-3372.

Oregon County

Recorder of Deeds, P.O. Box 406, Alton, MO 65606. 417-778-7460; Fax 417-778-7206.

Will search UCC records. Will not search real estate records. **Other Phone Numbers:** Assessor 417-778-7471; Treasurer 417-778-6303.

Osage County

Recorder of Deeds, P.O. Box 825, Linn, MO 65051-0825. Recorder of Deeds, R/E and UCC Recording 573-897-3114.

Will search UCC records. UCC search includes tax liens if requested. Will not search real estate records. **Other Phone Numbers:** Assessor 573-897-2217; Treasurer 573-897-3095; Elections 573-897-2139.

Ozark County

Circuit Clerk & Recorder, P.O. Box 36, Gainesville, MO 65655. Circuit Clerk & Recorder, R/E and UCC Recording 417-679-4232; Fax 417-679-4554.

Will search UCC records. Will not search tax liens. **Other Phone Numbers:** Assessor 417-679-4705; Treasurer 417-679-3553; Elections 417-679-3516.

Pemiscot County

Recorder of Deeds, Courthouse, 610 Ward Ave., Caruthersville, MO 63830. 573-333-2204.

Will search UCC records. UCC search includes tax liens if requested. Will not search real estate records. **Other Phone Numbers:** Assessor 573-333-1390; Treasurer 573-333-4171.

Perry County

Recorder of Deeds, 15 West Ste. Marie Street, Suite 1, Perryville, MO 63775. Recorder of Deeds, R/E and UCC Recording 573-547-1611; Fax 573-547-9323.

Will search UCC records. Will not search real estate records. **Other Phone Numbers:** Assessor 573-547-5211; Treasurer 573-547-4502; Elections 573-547-4242.

Pettis County

Recorder of Deeds, 415 South Ohio, Sedalia, MO 65301. 660-826-1136; Fax 660-827-8637.

Will search UCC records. Will not search real estate records. **Other Phone Numbers:** Assessor 660-827-6023; Treasurer 660-827-0486.

Phelps County

Recorder of Deeds, Courthouse, 200 N. Main, Rolla, MO 65401. 573-364-1891 R/E Recording: 573-364-1891 x210/211 UCC Recording: 573-364-1891 x210/211; Fax 573-364-1419.

Will search UCC records. Will not search real estate records. **Other Phone Numbers:** Assessor 573-364-1891 x140; Treasurer 573-364-1891 x130; Elections 573-364-1891 x100; Vital Records 573-364-1891 x490.

Pike County

Recorder of Deeds, 115 West Main Street, Bowling Green, MO 63334. 573-324-5567.

Will search UCC records. UCC search includes tax liens if requested. Will not search real estate records. **Other Phone Numbers:** Assessor 573-324-3261; Treasurer 573-324-2102; Appraiser/Auditor 573-528-5180; Elections 573-324-2412.

Platte County

Chief Deputy, 415 3rd St., Suite 70, Platte City, MO 64079. 816-858-3323 R/E Recording: 816-858-3326 UCC Recording: 816-858-3320; Fax 816-858-2379. http://www.co.platte.mo.us/recorder.html

Will search UCC records. Will not search real estate records. **Other Phone Numbers:** Assessor 816-858-3301; Treasurer 816-858-3318; Elections 816-858-4400.

Polk County

Recorder of Deeds, 102 E. Broadway, Courthouse, Bolivar, MO 65613-1502. Recorder of Deeds, R/E and UCC Recording 417-326-4924; Fax 417-326-6898.

Will search UCC records. Will not search real estate records. **Other Phone Numbers:** Assessor 417-326-4643; Treasurer 417-326-4913; Appraiser/Auditor 417-326-4346; Elections 417-326-4031; Vital Records 417-326-4031.

Pulaski County

Recorder of Deeds, 301 Historic Route 66, Courthouse Suite 202, Waynesville, MO 65583. 573-774-4760; Fax 573-774-6967.

Will search UCC records. This agency will not do a tax lien search. Will not search real estate records. **Other Phone Numbers:** Assessor 573-774-6609 x117; Treasurer 573-774-6609 x124.

Putnam County

Recorder of Deeds, Courthouse, Room 202, Unionville, MO 63565-1659. 660-947-2071; Fax 660-947-2320.

Will search UCC records. Will not search real estate records. **Other Phone Numbers:** Assessor 660-947-3900; Treasurer 660-947-2095; Elections 660-947-2674.

Ralls County

Recorder of Deeds, P.O. Box 444, New London, MO 63459-0444. 573-985-5631.

Will search UCC records. UCC search includes tax liens if requested. Will not search real estate records. **Other Phone Numbers:** Assessor 573-985-5671; Treasurer 573-985-7151.

Randolph County

Recorder of Deeds, 110 S. Main St., Courthouse, Huntsville, MO 65259. Recorder of Deeds, R/E and UCC Recording 660-277-4718; Fax 660-277-3246.

Will search UCC records. Will not search real estate records. **Other Phone Numbers:** Assessor 660-277-4716; Treasurer 660-277-4714; Elections 660-277-4717.

Ray County

Recorder of Deeds, P.O. Box 167, Richmond, MO 64085. 660-776-4500.

Will search UCC records. This agency will not do a tax lien search. Will not search real estate records. **Other Phone Numbers:** Assessor 660-776-2676; Treasurer 660-776-6140.

Reynolds County

Recorder of Deeds, P.O. Box 76, Centerville, MO 63633-0076. 573-648-2494; Fax 573-648-2296.

Will search UCC records. Will not search real estate records. **Other Phone Numbers:** Assessor 573-648-2494.

Ripley County

Recorder of Deeds, 100 Courthouse Square, Suite 3, Doniphan, MO 63935. 573-996-2818; Fax 573-966-5014.

Will search UCC records. Will not search real estate records. **Other Phone Numbers:** Assessor 573-996-7113.

Saline County

Recorder of Deeds, Courthouse, Room 206, Marshall, MO 65340. Recorder of Deeds, R/E and UCC Recording 660-886-2677; Fax 660-886-2603.

Will search UCC records. Will not search real estate records. **Other Phone Numbers:** Assessor 660-335-3111; Treasurer 660-886-3636.

Schuyler County

Recorder of Deeds, P.O. Box 186, Lancaster, MO 63548. 660-457-3784; Fax 660-457-3016.

Will search UCC records. **Other Phone Numbers:** Assessor 660-457-3211; Treasurer 660-457-3825.

Scotland County

Recorder of Deeds, 117 South Market St., Ste 106, Memphis, MO 63555-1449. 660-465-8605; Fax 660-465-8673.

Will search UCC records. UCC search includes tax liens if requested. Will search record owner and mortgages. **Other Phone Numbers:** Assessor 660-465-2269; Treasurer 660-465-2529.

Scott County

Recorder of Deeds, P.O. Box 78, Benton, MO 63736. 573-545-3551.
Will search UCC records. UCC search includes tax liens if requested. Will not search real estate records. **Other Phone Numbers:** Assessor 573-545-3535; Treasurer 573-545-3543.

Shannon County

Recorder of Deeds, P.O. Box 148, Eminence, MO 65466. 573-226-3315; Fax 573-226-5321.
Will search UCC records. Will not search real estate records. **Other Phone Numbers:** Assessor 573-226-5539; Treasurer 573-226-3614.

Shelby County

Recorder of Deeds, P.O. Box 176, Shelbyville, MO 63469. 573-633-2151; Fax 573-633-1004.
Will search UCC records. Will not search real estate records. **Other Phone Numbers:** Assessor 573-633-2521; Treasurer 573-633-2574.

St. Charles County

Recorder of Deeds, P.O. Box 99, St. Charles, MO 63302-0099. Recorder of Deeds, R/E and UCC Recording 636-949-7505 UCC Recording: 636-949-7508; Fax 636-949-7512. http://www.win.org
Will search UCC records. This agency will not do a tax lien search. Will not search real estate records. **Online Access:** Assessor. Records on the county Property Assessment database are available free online at www.win.org/library/library_office/assessment. **Other Phone Numbers:** Assessor 636-949-7425; Appraiser/Auditor 636-949-7431; Elections 636-949-7550; Vital Records 636-949-7558.

St. Clair County

Circuit Clerk / ex-officio, P.O. Box 493, Osceola, MO 64776-0493. 417-646-2226; Fax 417-646-2401.
Will search UCC records. Will not search real estate records. **Other Phone Numbers:** Assessor 417-646-2449; Treasurer 417-646-8068.

St. Francois County

Recorder of Deeds, Courthouse, Farmington, MO 63640. 573-756-2323.
Will search UCC records. This agency will not do a tax lien search. RE record owner searches available. **Other Phone Numbers:** Assessor 573-756-2509; Treasurer 573-756-3349.

St. Louis City

Recorder of Deeds, Tucker & Market Streets, City Hall Room 127, St. Louis, MO 63103. 314-622-4328; Fax 314-622-4175.
Will search UCC records. Will not search real estate records. **Other Phone Numbers:** Assessor 314-615-5124; Treasurer 314-622-2062.

St. Louis County

Recorder of Deeds, 41 S. Central Ave., 4th Floor, Clayton, MO 63105. 314-889-2185.
Will search UCC records. Will not search real estate records. **Other Phone Numbers:** Assessor 314-889-2235.

Ste. Genevieve County

Recorder of Deeds, 3rd Street, Court House, Ste. Genevieve, MO 63670. 573-883-2706; Fax 573-883-5312.
Will search UCC records. Will not search real estate records. **Other Phone Numbers:** Assessor 573-883-2333.

Stoddard County

Recorder of Deeds, P.O. Box 217, Bloomfield, MO 63825-0217. Recorder of Deeds, R/E and UCC Recording 573-568-3444; Fax 573-568-2545.
Will search UCC records. Will not search real estate records. **Other Phone Numbers:** Assessor 573-568-3163; Treasurer 573-568-3327.

Stone County

Recorder of Deeds, P.O. Box 18, Galena, MO 65656. 417-357-6362; Fax 417-357-8131.
Will search UCC records. **Other Phone Numbers:** Assessor 417-357-6141.

Sullivan County

Recorder of Deeds, Courthouse, Milan, MO 63556. 660-265-3630; Fax 660-265-5071.
Will search UCC records. Will not search real estate records. **Other Phone Numbers:** Assessor 660-265-4474; Treasurer 660-265-4514.

Taney County

Recorder of Deeds, P.O. Box 335, Forsyth, MO 65653. 417-546-7234.
Will search UCC records. UCC search includes tax liens if requested. Will not search real estate records. **Other Phone Numbers:** Assessor 417-546-4751; Treasurer 417-546-4584.

Texas County

Recorder of Deeds, 210 North Grand, P.O. Box 237, Houston, MO 65483. 417-967-3742; Fax 417-967-4220.
Will search UCC records. Will not search real estate records. **Other Phone Numbers:** Assessor 417-967-4709; Treasurer 417-967-2589.

Vernon County

Recorder of Deeds, Courthouse, Nevada, MO 64772. Recorder of Deeds, R/E and UCC Recording 417-448-2520; Fax 417-448-2524.
Will search UCC records. This agency will not do a tax lien search. Will not search real estate records. **Other Phone Numbers:** Assessor 417-448-2530; Treasurer 417-448-2510; Elections 417-448-2500.

Warren County

Recorder of Deeds, 104 West Boone's Lick Rd., Warrenton, MO 63383. 636-456-9800.
Will search UCC records. This agency will not do a tax lien search. Will not search real estate records. **Other Phone Numbers:** Assessor 636-456-8885; Treasurer 636-456-3389.

Washington County

Recorder of Deeds, P.O. Box 216, Potosi, MO 63664-0216. 573-438-5023; Fax 573-438-7900.
Will search UCC records. Will not search real estate records. **Other Phone Numbers:** Assessor 573-438-4992; Treasurer 573-438-2031.

Wayne County

Recorder of Deeds, P.O. Box 187A, Greenville, MO 63944. 573-224-3221; Fax 573-224-3225.
Will search UCC records. Will not search real estate records. **Other Phone Numbers:** Assessor 573-224-3221 x22; Treasurer 573-224-3221 x16.

Webster County

Circuit Clerk & Recorder, P.O. Box 529, Marshfield, MO 65706. 417-468-2173; Fax 417-468-3786.
Will search UCC records. Will not search real estate records. **Other Phone Numbers:** Assessor 417-859-2169; Treasurer 417-859-2683; Elections 417-468-2224.

Worth County

Recorder of Deeds, Box 340, Grant City, MO 64456. 660-564-2210; Fax 660-564-2432.
Will search UCC records. **Other Phone Numbers:** Assessor 660-564-2153; Treasurer 660-564-2154.

Wright County

Deputy, P.O. Box 39, Hartville, MO 65667. Deputy, R/E and UCC Recording 417-741-7322; Fax 417-741-7504.
Will search UCC records. Will not search real estate records. **Other Phone Numbers:** Assessor 417-741-6400; Treasurer 417-741-7225; Elections 417-741-6661; Vital Records 573-751-6400.

Missouri County Locator

You will usually be able to find the city name in the City/County Cross Reference below. In that case, it is a simple matter to determine the county from the cross reference. However, only the official US Postal Service city names are included in this index. There are an additional 40,000 place names that people use in their addresses. Therefore, we have also included a ZIP/City Cross Reference immediately following the City/County Cross Reference.

If you know the ZIP Code but the city name does not appear in the City/County Cross Reference index, look up the ZIP Code in the ZIP/City Cross Reference, find the city name, then look up the city name in the City/County Cross Reference. For example, you want to know the county for an address of Menands, NY 12204. There is no "Menands" in the City/County Cross Reference. The ZIP/City Cross Reference shows that ZIP Codes 12201-12288 are for the city of Albany. Looking back in the City/County Cross Reference, Albany is in Albany County.

City/County Cross Reference

ADRIAN (64720) Bates(99), Cass(1)
ADVANCE (63730) Stoddard(79), Cape Girardeau(16), Bollinger(4)
AGENCY Buchanan
ALBA Jasper
ALBANY Gentry
ALDRICH (65601) Polk(82), Dade(17)
ALEXANDRIA Clark
ALLENDALE Worth
ALLENTON St. Louis
ALMA Lafayette
ALTAMONT Daviess
ALTENBURG (63732) Cape Girardeau(82), Perry(18)
ALTON Oregon
AMAZONIA Andrew
AMITY De Kalb
AMORET Bates
AMSTERDAM Bates
ANABEL Macon
ANDERSON McDonald
ANNADA Pike
ANNAPOLIS (63620) Iron(60), Madison(33), Reynolds(8)
ANNISTON Mississippi
APPLETON CITY (64724) St. Clair(92), Bates(8)
ARBELA (63432) Scotland(88), Clark(12)
ARBYRD Dunklin
ARCADIA (63621) Iron(69), Madison(31)
ARCHIE (64725) Cass(94), Bates(6)
ARCOLA (65603) Dade(97), Cedar(3)
ARGYLE (65001) Maries(70), Osage(30)
ARMSTRONG (65230) Howard(97), Randolph(3)
ARNOLD Jefferson
ARROW ROCK Saline
ASBURY (64832) Barton(61), Jasper(39)
ASH GROVE (65604) Greene(61), Lawrence(38), Dade(2)
ASHBURN Pike
ASHLAND Boone
ATLANTA Macon
AUGUSTA St. Charles
AURORA (65605) Lawrence(91), Barry(9)
AUXVASSE Callaway
AVA (65608) Douglas(90), Taney(10)
AVALON Livingston
AVILLA Jasper
BAKERSFIELD (65609) Ozark(76), Howell(24)
BALLWIN St. Louis
BARING (63531) Knox(60), Scotland(40)
BARNARD (64423) Nodaway(99), Andrew(1)
BARNETT (65011) Morgan(93), Moniteau(7)
BARNHART Jefferson
BATES CITY (64011) Lafayette(51), Cass(41), Johnson(8)
BEAUFORT Franklin
BELGRADE Washington
BELL CITY (63735) Stoddard(94), Scott(6)

BELLE (65013) Maries(67), Osage(33)
BELLEVIEW (63623) Iron(97), Reynolds(3)
BELLFLOWER (63333) Montgomery(97), Lincoln(3)
BELTON Cass
BENDAVIS Texas
BENTON Scott
BENTON CITY Audrain
BERGER Franklin
BERNIE (63822) Stoddard(98), Dunklin(2)
BERTRAND (63823) Mississippi(95), Scott(5)
BETHANY Harrison
BETHEL Shelby
BEULAH (65436) Phelps(87), Texas(9), Pulaski(3)
BEVIER Macon
BILLINGS (65610) Christian(90), Stone(5), Greene(4), Lawrence(2)
BIRCH TREE (65438) Shannon(81), Oregon(19)
BISMARCK (63624) St. Francois(90), Washington(6), Iron(3)
BIXBY Iron
BLACK (63625) Reynolds(88), Iron(12)
BLACKBURN (65321) Saline(88), Lafayette(12)
BLACKWATER Cooper
BLACKWELL (63626) St. Francois(69), Washington(31)
BLAIRSTOWN Henry
BLAND (65014) Gasconade(85), Osage(11), Maries(3)
BLODGETT Scott
BLOOMFIELD Stoddard
BLOOMSDALE (63627) Ste. Genevieve(89), Jefferson(11)
BLUE EYE (65611) Stone(87), Taney(13)
BLUE SPRINGS Jackson
BLYTHEDALE Harrison
BOGARD Carroll
BOIS D ARC (65612) Greene(91), Lawrence(9)
BOLCKOW (64427) Andrew(94), Nodaway(6)
BOLIVAR Polk
BONNE TERRE (63628) St. Francois(96), Ste. Genevieve(2), Washington(1)
BONNOTS MILL Osage
BOONVILLE Cooper
BOSS (65440) Dent(57), Reynolds(33), Iron(10)
BOSWORTH Carroll
BOURBON (99999) Crawford(98), Washington(1)
BOWLING GREEN (63334) Pike(98), Lincoln(2)
BRADLEYVILLE (65614) Taney(92), Christian(8)
BRAGG CITY Pemiscot
BRAGGADOCIO Pemiscot
BRANDSVILLE Howell
BRANSON (65616) Taney(97), Stone(3)

BRANSON Taney
BRASHEAR (63533) Adair(98), Knox(2)
BRAYMER (64624) Caldwell(83), Ray(12), Carroll(4)
BRAZEAU Perry
BRECKENRIDGE (64625) Caldwell(84), Daviess(10), Livingston(6)
BRIAR Ripley
BRIDGETON St. Louis
BRIGHTON Polk
BRINKTOWN Maries
BRIXEY Ozark
BRONAUGH (64728) Vernon(72), Barton(28)
BROOKFIELD (64628) Linn(98), Chariton(2)
BROOKLINE STATION (65619) Greene(96), Christian(4)
BROSELEY Butler
BROWNING (64630) Linn(84), Sullivan(16)
BROWNWOOD Stoddard
BRUMLEY Miller
BRUNER (65620) Christian(98), Douglas(2)
BRUNSWICK Chariton
BUCKLIN (64631) Linn(84), Macon(16)
BUCKNER Jackson
BUCYRUS Texas
BUFFALO (65622) Dallas(97), Polk(3)
BUNCETON Cooper
BUNKER (63629) Reynolds(65), Dent(26), Shannon(9)
BURFORDVILLE Cape Girardeau
BURLINGTON JUNCTION (64428) Nodaway(95), Atchison(5)
BUTLER Bates
BUTTERFIELD Barry
CABOOL (65689) Howell(57), Texas(40), Douglas(3)
CADET Washington
CAINSVILLE (64632) Harrison(76), Mercer(24)
CAIRO Randolph
CALEDONIA Washington
CALHOUN Henry
CALIFORNIA (65018) Moniteau(95), Cooper(5)
CALLAO Macon
CAMDEN (64017) Ray(92), Lafayette(8)
CAMDEN POINT Platte
CAMDENTON Camden
CAMERON (64429) Clinton(69), De Kalb(26), Caldwell(3), Daviess(2)
CAMPBELL Dunklin
CANALOU New Madrid
CANTON (63435) Lewis(93), Clark(7)
CAPE FAIR Stone
CAPE GIRARDEAU Cape Girardeau
CAPLINGER MILLS Cedar
CARDWELL Dunklin
CARL JUNCTION Jasper
CARROLLTON Carroll
CARTERVILLE Jasper
CARTHAGE Jasper

CARUTHERSVILLE Pemiscot
CASCADE Wayne
CASSVILLE Barry
CATAWISSA (63015) Franklin(80), Jefferson(20)
CATRON (63833) New Madrid(67), Stoddard(33)
CAULFIELD (65626) Howell(72), Ozark(28)
CEDAR CITY Callaway
CEDAR HILL Jefferson
CEDARCREEK Taney
CENSUS BUREAU Boone
CENTER Ralls
CENTERTOWN (65023) Cole(89), Moniteau(11)
CENTERVIEW Johnson
CENTERVILLE Reynolds
CENTRALIA (65240) Boone(78), Audrain(20), Callaway(1)
CHADWICK (65629) Christian(98), Taney(2)
CHAFFEE (63740) Scott(95), Cape Girardeau(6)
CHAMOIS Osage
CHARLESTON (63834) Mississippi(95), Scott(5)
CHERRYVILLE Crawford
CHESTERFIELD St. Louis
CHESTNUTRIDGE Christian
CHILHOWEE (64733) Johnson(71), Henry(27), Jackson(3)
CHILLICOTHE Livingston
CHULA (64635) Livingston(61), Linn(29), Grundy(10)
CLARENCE (63437) Shelby(91), Macon(7), Monroe(2)
CLARK (65243) Boone(43), Audrain(31), Randolph(16), Howard(9), Monroe(2)
CLARKSBURG (65025) Cooper(50), Moniteau(50)
CLARKSDALE (64430) De Kalb(96), Andrew(4)
CLARKSVILLE Pike
CLARKTON (63837) Dunklin(98), New Madrid(2)
CLEARMONT (64431) Nodaway(99), Daviess(1)
CLEVELAND Cass
CLEVER Christian
CLIFTON HILL (65244) Randolph(96), Chariton(4)
CLIMAX SPRINGS (65324) Camden(98), Benton(2)
CLINTON (64735) Henry(99), Benton(1)
CLUBB Wayne
CLYDE Nodaway
COATSVILLE (63535) Schuyler(54), Putnam(22), Cole(14), Audrain(11)
COFFEY (64636) Daviess(89), Harrison(11)
COLE CAMP (65325) Benton(95), Pettis(4), Morgan(2)
COLLINS St. Clair

COLUMBIA (65202) Boone(98), Callaway(2)
COLUMBIA Boone
COMMERCE Scott
CONCEPTION Nodaway
CONCEPTION JUNCTION Nodaway
CONCORDIA (64020) Lafayette(89), Johnson(9), Saline(1)
CONRAN New Madrid
CONTEL CORPORATION St. Charles
CONWAY (65632) Laclede(72), Webster(14), Dallas(14)
COOK STATION (65449) Crawford(97), Phelps(3)
COOTER Pemiscot
CORDER Lafayette
CORNING Holt
COSBY Andrew
COTTLEVILLE St. Charles
COUCH Oregon
COWGILL (64637) Caldwell(86), Ray(14)
CRAIG Holt
CRANE (65633) Stone(88), Barry(12)
CREIGHTON (64739) Henry(78), Cass(22)
CROCKER (65452) Pulaski(97), Miller(3)
CROSS TIMBERS (65634) Hickory(94), Benton(5), Camden(2)
CRYSTAL CITY Jefferson
CUBA (65453) Crawford(99), Gasconade(1)
CURRYVILLE Pike
DADEVILLE Dade
DAISY Cape Girardeau
DALTON Chariton
DARLINGTON Gentry
DAVISVILLE Crawford
DAWN (64638) Livingston(71), Carroll(29)
DE KALB (64440) Howell(72), Buchanan(27), Platte(1)
DE SOTO Jefferson
DE WITT Carroll
DEARBORN Platte
DEEPWATER (64740) Henry(86), St. Clair(14)
DEERFIELD Vernon
DEERING Pemiscot
DEFIANCE St. Charles
DELTA Cape Girardeau
DENVER (64441) Worth(65), Gentry(35)
DES ARC (63636) Iron(68), Madison(26), Wayne(6)
DEVILS ELBOW (65457) Pulaski(90), Phelps(11)
DEXTER Stoddard
DIAMOND (64840) Newton(98), Jasper(3)
DIGGINS Webster
DITTMER Jefferson
DIXON (65459) Pulaski(83), Maries(10), Miller(5), Phelps(2)
DOE RUN St. Francois
DONIPHAN (63935) Ripley(98), Carter(1)
DORA (65637) Ozark(63), Howell(25), Douglas(12)
DOVER Lafayette
DOWNING (63536) Schuyler(67), Scotland(34)
DREXEL (64742) Cass(78), Bates(22)
DRURY (65638) Douglas(90), Ozark(11)
DUDLEY Stoddard
DUENWEG Jasper
DUKE (65461) Phelps(94), Pulaski(6)
DUNNEGAN (65640) Polk(90), Cedar(10)
DURHAM (63438) Marion(65), Lewis(35)
DUTCHTOWN Cape Girardeau
DUTZOW Warren
EAGLE ROCK Barry
EAGLEVILLE Harrison
EARTH CITY St. Louis
EAST LYNNE Cass
EAST PRAIRIE Mississippi
EASTON Buchanan

EDGAR SPRINGS (65462) Phelps(97), Dent(3)
EDGERTON (64444) Platte(93), Buchanan(7)
EDINA Knox
EDWARDS (65326) Benton(63), Camden(36), Hickory(1)
EL DORADO SPRINGS (64744) Cedar(86), Vernon(8), St. Clair(6)
ELDON (65026) Miller(96), Morgan(4)
ELDRIDGE (65463) Laclede(99), Dallas(1)
ELK CREEK Texas
ELKLAND (65644) Webster(51), Dallas(49)
ELLINGTON (63638) Reynolds(93), Shannon(5), Carter(2)
ELLSINORE (63937) Carter(83), Butler(16)
ELMER Macon
ELMO Nodaway
ELSBERRY (63343) Lincoln(97), Pike(4)
EMDEN (63439) Marion(52), Shelby(48)
EMINENCE Shannon
EMMA Lafayette
EOLIA (63344) Pike(60), Lincoln(40)
ESSEX Stoddard
ETHEL Macon
ETTERVILLE Miller
EUDORA Polk
EUGENE (65032) Cole(89), Miller(11)
EUNICE Texas
EUREKA (63025) St. Louis(67), Jefferson(33)
EVERTON (65646) Dade(62), Lawrence(38)
EWING (63440) Marion(51), Lewis(47), Shelby(2)
EXCELLO Macon
EXCELSIOR SPRINGS (64024) Clay(77), Ray(23)
EXETER (65647) Barry(78), Newton(20), McDonald(2)
FAGUS Butler
FAIR GROVE (65648) Greene(88), Dallas(8), Webster(2), Polk(2)
FAIR PLAY (65649) Polk(82), Cedar(18)
FAIRDEALING Ripley
FAIRFAX (64446) Atchison(90), Holt(10)
FAIRPORT De Kalb
FAIRVIEW (64842) Newton(98), Barry(2)
FALCON (65470) Wright(71), Laclede(29)
FARBER Audrain
FARLEY Platte
FARMINGTON (63640) St. Francois(97), Ste. Genevieve(3)
FARRAR Perry
FAUCETT Buchanan
FAYETTE Howard
FENTON (63026) St. Louis(52), Jefferson(49)
FENTON St. Louis
FESTUS (63028) Jefferson(94), Ste. Genevieve(6)
FILLMORE Andrew
FISK Butler
FLEMINGTON (65650) Polk(69), Hickory(31)
FLETCHER (63030) Jefferson(82), Washington(19)
FLINTHILL St. Charles
FLORENCE Morgan
FLORISSANT St. Louis
FOLEY Lincoln
FORDLAND (65652) Webster(82), Christian(14), Douglas(5)
FOREST CITY Holt
FORISTELL (63348) St. Charles(64), Warren(33), Lincoln(3)
FORSYTH (65653) Taney(98), Christian(2)
FORT LEONARD WOOD Pulaski
FORTESCUE Holt
FORTUNA (65034) Morgan(55), Moniteau(45)
FOSTER Bates

FRANKFORD (63441) Pike(98), Ralls(2)
FRANKLIN Howard
FREDERICKTOWN (63645) Madison(97), St. Francois(2), Ste. Genevieve(1)
FREEBURG Osage
FREEMAN Cass
FREISTATT Lawrence
FREMONT (63941) Carter(68), Oregon(24), Ripley(8)
FRENCH VILLAGE (63036) St. Francois(74), Ste. Genevieve(26)
FRIEDHEIM Cape Girardeau
FROHNA Perry
FULTON Callaway
GAINESVILLE Ozark
GALENA (65656) Stone(95), Barry(4), Christian(1)
GALLATIN Daviess
GALT (64641) Grundy(92), Sullivan(8)
GARDEN CITY Cass
GARRISON (65657) Christian(98), Taney(2)
GASCONADE Gasconade
GATEWOOD (63942) Ripley(80), Oregon(20)
GENTRY Gentry
GERALD Franklin
GIBBS Adair
GIBSON Dunklin
GIDEON (63848) New Madrid(65), Pemiscot(35)
GILLIAM Saline
GILMAN CITY (64642) Harrison(85), Grundy(8), Daviess(7)
GIPSY Bollinger
GLASGOW (65254) Howard(96), Chariton(4)
GLENALLEN Bollinger
GLENCOE St. Louis
GLENWOOD Schuyler
GLOVER Iron
GOBLER (63849) Pemiscot(65), Dunklin(35)
GOLDEN Barry
GOLDEN CITY (64748) Barton(54), Jasper(27), Dade(16), Lawrence(3)
GOODMAN (64843) McDonald(66), Newton(34)
GOODSON Polk
GORDONVILLE Cape Girardeau
GORIN (63543) Scotland(96), Knox(3), Clark(1)
GOWER (64454) Clinton(51), Buchanan(49)
GRAFF (65660) Wright(95), Texas(5)
GRAHAM (64455) Nodaway(89), Andrew(11)
GRAIN VALLEY Jackson
GRANBY Newton
GRANDIN (63943) Carter(81), Ripley(19)
GRANDVIEW Jackson
GRANGER Scotland
GRANT CITY (64456) Worth(98), Harrison(2)
GRASSY Bollinger
GRAVOIS MILLS (65037) Morgan(93), Camden(7)
GRAY SUMMIT Franklin
GRAYRIDGE Stoddard
GREEN CASTLE (63544) Sullivan(50), Adair(43), Putnam(7)
GREEN CITY Sullivan
GREEN RIDGE Pettis
GREENFIELD Dade
GREENTOP (63546) Adair(64), Schuyler(34), Scotland(3)
GREENVILLE Wayne
GREENWOOD (64034) Jackson(91), Cass(9)
GROVER St. Louis
GROVESPRING (65662) Wright(79), Laclede(20)

GRUBVILLE (63041) Franklin(76), Jefferson(24)
GUILFORD (64457) Nodaway(90), Andrew(10)
HALE (64643) Carroll(63), Livingston(37)
HALF WAY Polk
HALLSVILLE Boone
HALLTOWN Lawrence
HAMILTON (64644) Caldwell(97), Daviess(3)
HANNIBAL (63401) Marion(93), Ralls(7)
HARDENVILLE Ozark
HARDIN (64035) Ray(99), Carroll(1)
HARRIS (64645) Sullivan(73), Mercer(28)
HARRISBURG (65256) Boone(82), Howard(18)
HARRISONVILLE Cass
HARTSBURG (65039) Boone(86), Callaway(14)
HARTSHORN (65479) Texas(69), Shannon(31)
HARTVILLE Wright
HARVIELL (63945) Butler(92), Ripley(8)
HARWOOD (64750) Vernon(97), St. Clair(3)
HATFIELD (64458) Harrison(96), Worth(4)
HAWK POINT (63349) Lincoln(98), Warren(2)
HAYTI Pemiscot
HAZELWOOD St. Louis
HELENA Andrew
HEMATITE Jefferson
HENLEY (65040) Cole(97), Miller(3)
HENRIETTA Ray
HERCULANEUM Jefferson
HERMANN (65041) Gasconade(84), Montgomery(14), Warren(1)
HERMANN Montgomery
HERMITAGE Hickory
HIGBEE (65257) Randolph(60), Howard(41)
HIGGINSVILLE Lafayette
HIGH HILL Montgomery
HIGH POINT Moniteau
HIGH RIDGE (63049) Jefferson(98), St. Louis(2)
HIGHLANDVILLE (65669) Christian(94), Stone(6)
HILLSBORO Jefferson
HIRAM Wayne
HOLCOMB (63852) Dunklin(97), Pemiscot(3)
HOLDEN Johnson
HOLLAND (63853) Pemiscot(93), Dunklin(7)
HOLLIDAY Monroe
HOLLISTER Taney
HOLT (64048) Clay(92), Clinton(8)
HOLTS SUMMIT Callaway
HOPKINS Nodaway
HORNERSVILLE Dunklin
HORTON Vernon
HOUSE SPRINGS Jefferson
HOUSTON Texas
HOUSTONIA (65333) Pettis(98), Saline(2)
HUGGINS Texas
HUGHESVILLE Pettis
HUMANSVILLE (65674) Polk(73), Cedar(20), Hickory(4), St. Clair(3)
HUME (64752) Bates(73), Vernon(27)
HUMPHREYS (64646) Sullivan(77), Linn(23)
HUNNEWELL (63443) Marion(50), Shelby(32), Monroe(19)
HUNTSVILLE Randolph
HURDLAND (63547) Knox(90), Adair(10)
HURLEY Stone
IBERIA Miller
IMPERIAL Jefferson
INDEPENDENCE Jackson
IONIA (65335) Pettis(83), Benton(18)

IRONDALE (63648) Washington(60), St. Francois(40)
IRONTON (63650) Iron(78), St. Francois(19), Madison(3)
ISABELLA Ozark
JACKSON Cape Girardeau
JACKSONVILLE (65260) Macon(50), Randolph(43), Monroe(7)
JADWIN Dent
JAMESON Daviess
JAMESPORT (64648) Daviess(84), Grundy(11), Livingston(5)
JAMESTOWN (65046) Moniteau(98), Cooper(3)
JASPER (64755) Jasper(92), Barton(8)
JEFFERSON CITY Cole
JERICO SPRINGS (64756) Cedar(83), Dade(17)
JEROME Phelps
JONESBURG (63351) Montgomery(80), Warren(20)
JOPLIN (64804) Jasper(51), Newton(49)
JOPLIN Jasper
KAHOKA Clark
KAISER (65047) Miller(97), Camden(4)
KANSAS CITY (64147) Jackson(75), Cass(25)
KANSAS CITY (64164) Platte(98), Clay(2)
KANSAS CITY (64188) Clay(96), Jackson(4)
KANSAS CITY Clay
KANSAS CITY Jackson
KANSAS CITY Platte
KEARNEY Clay
KELSO Scott
KENNETT Dunklin
KEWANEE New Madrid
KEYTESVILLE Chariton
KIDDER (64649) Caldwell(83), Daviess(18)
KIMBERLING CITY Stone
KIMMSWICK Jefferson
KING CITY (64463) Gentry(84), De Kalb(12), Andrew(4)
KINGDOM CITY Callaway
KINGSTON Caldwell
KINGSVILLE (64061) Johnson(98), Jackson(2)
KIRBYVILLE Taney
KIRKSVILLE Adair
KISSEE MILLS Taney
KNOB LICK St. Francois
KNOB NOSTER (65336) Johnson(91), Pettis(9)
KNOX CITY (63446) Knox(93), Lewis(7)
KOELTZTOWN Osage
KOSHKONONG (65692) Howell(53), Oregon(47)
LA BELLE (63447) Lewis(93), Knox(7)
LA GRANGE Lewis
LA MONTE Pettis
LA PLATA (63549) Macon(96), Adair(4)
LA RUSSELL (64848) Lawrence(93), Jasper(7)
LABADIE Franklin
LACLEDE Linn
LADDONIA (63352) Audrain(98), Ralls(3)
LAKE OZARK (65049) Camden(73), Miller(27)
LAKE SAINT LOUIS St. Charles
LAKE SPRING Dent
LAMAR Barton
LAMPE Stone
LANAGAN McDonald
LANCASTER Schuyler
LAQUEY (65534) Pulaski(81), Laclede(19)
LAREDO Grundy
LATHAM Moniteau
LATHROP (64465) Clinton(88), Caldwell(12)
LATOUR (64760) Johnson(51), Cass(49)
LAURIE Morgan

LAWSON (64062) Ray(75), Clinton(18), Clay(7)
LEADWOOD St. Francois
LEASBURG Crawford
LEBANON Laclede
LECOMA (65540) Dent(81), Phelps(19)
LEES SUMMIT (64082) Jackson(89), Cass(11)
LEES SUMMIT Jackson
LEETON (64761) Johnson(93), Henry(7)
LENOX Dent
LENTNER (63450) Shelby(70), Monroe(30)
LEONARD (63451) Shelby(89), Knox(6), Macon(5)
LEOPOLD Bollinger
LESLIE Franklin
LESTERVILLE (63654) Reynolds(88), Iron(12)
LEVASY Jackson
LEWISTOWN Lewis
LEXINGTON Lafayette
LIBERAL Barton
LIBERTY Clay
LICKING (65542) Texas(99), Dent(1)
LIGUORI Jefferson
LILBOURN (63862) Bollinger(51), New Madrid(49)
LINCOLN Benton
LINN Osage
LINN CREEK Camden
LINNEUS Linn
LIVONIA Putnam
LOCK SPRINGS Daviess
LOCKWOOD (65682) Dade(86), Lawrence(13)
LODI Wayne
LOHMAN Cole
LONE JACK (64070) Jackson(96), Johnson(4)
LONEDELL Franklin
LONG LANE Dallas
LOOSE CREEK Osage
LOUISBURG (65685) Dallas(97), Polk(3)
LOUISIANA Pike
LOWNDES Wayne
LOWRY CITY St. Clair
LUCERNE Putnam
LUDLOW Livingston
LUEBBERING (63061) Franklin(96), Jefferson(4)
LURAY Clark
LYNCHBURG (65543) Laclede(88), Wright(11)
MACKS CREEK (65786) Camden(97), Dallas(4)
MACOMB (65702) Wright(80), Douglas(20)
MACON Macon
MADISON (65263) Monroe(94), Randolph(4), Audrain(2)
MAITLAND Holt
MALDEN (63863) Dunklin(98), New Madrid(2)
MALTA BEND Saline
MANSFIELD (65704) Wright(96), Douglas(4)
MAPAVILLE Jefferson
MARBLE HILL (63764) Bollinger(92), Cape Girardeau(8)
MARCELINE (64658) Linn(83), Chariton(17)
MARIONVILLE (65705) Lawrence(94), Stone(6)
MARQUAND (63655) Madison(78), Bollinger(21), Wayne(2)
MARSHALL (65340) Saline(97), Pettis(3)
MARSHFIELD Webster
MARSTON New Madrid
MARTHASVILLE (63357) Warren(94), St. Charles(6)
MARTINSBURG (65264) Audrain(70), Callaway(26), Montgomery(4)
MARTINSVILLE Harrison

MARYLAND HEIGHTS St. Louis
MARYVILLE Nodaway
MATTHEWS New Madrid
MAYSVILLE De Kalb
MAYVIEW Lafayette
MAYWOOD (63454) Marion(88), Lewis(12)
MC BRIDE Perry
MC CLURG (65701) Taney(82), Douglas(18)
MC FALL (64657) Gentry(55), Harrison(40), Daviess(5)
MC GEE Wayne
MC GIRK Moniteau
MEADVILLE Linn
MEMPHIS Scotland
MENDON Chariton
MENFRO Perry
MERCER Mercer
META (65058) Maries(68), Osage(17), Miller(8), Cole(7)
METZ Vernon
MEXICO Audrain
MIAMI Saline
MID MISSOURI Boone
MIDDLE BROOK (63656) Iron(82), Reynolds(18)
MIDDLETOWN (63359) Pike(50), Montgomery(38), Lincoln(7), Audrain(5)
MILAN Sullivan
MILFORD Barton
MILL SPRING Wayne
MILLER Lawrence
MILLERSVILLE (63766) Cape Girardeau(92), Bollinger(8)
MILO Vernon
MINDENMINES Barton
MINERAL POINT Washington
MISSOURI CITY Clay
MISSOURI STATE LOTTERY COMM Cole
MOBERLY Randolph
MOKANE Callaway
MONETT (65708) Barry(67), Lawrence(33)
MONROE CITY (63456) Monroe(48), Marion(44), Ralls(8)
MONTGOMERY CITY (63361) Montgomery(80), Callaway(20)
MONTICELLO Lewis
MONTIER Shannon
MONTREAL Camden
MONTROSE (64770) Henry(91), Bates(7), St. Clair(2)
MOODY Howell
MOORESVILLE Livingston
MORA (65345) Pettis(77), Morgan(13), Benton(11)
MOREHOUSE New Madrid
MORLEY Scott
MORRISON (65061) Gasconade(71), Osage(29)
MORRISVILLE Polk
MORSE MILL Jefferson
MOSBY Clay
MOSCOW MILLS Lincoln
MOUND CITY Holt
MOUNDVILLE Vernon
MOUNT MORIAH Harrison
MOUNT STERLING (65062) Gasconade(91), Osage(9)
MOUNT VERNON Lawrence
MOUNTAIN GROVE (65711) Wright(88), Texas(9), Douglas(3)
MOUNTAIN VIEW (65548) Howell(95), Shannon(2), Texas(1)
MYRTLE Oregon
NAPOLEON (64074) Lafayette(96), Jackson(4)
NAYLOR (63953) Ripley(96), Butler(4)
NECK CITY Jasper
NEELYVILLE (63954) Butler(92), Ripley(8)
NELSON (65347) Pettis(48), Saline(30), Cooper(22)
NEOSHO Newton

NEVADA Vernon
NEW BLOOMFIELD Callaway
NEW BOSTON (63557) Linn(71), Macon(27), Sullivan(1)
NEW CAMBRIA (63558) Macon(93), Chariton(7)
NEW FLORENCE (63363) Montgomery(98), Warren(2)
NEW FRANKLIN Howard
NEW HAMPTON (64471) Harrison(95), Gentry(5)
NEW HARTFORD Pike
NEW HAVEN (63068) Franklin(99), Gasconade(1)
NEW LONDON (63459) Ralls(86), Pike(14)
NEW MADRID New Madrid
NEW MELLE St. Charles
NEW OFFENBURG Ste. Genevieve
NEWARK Knox
NEWBURG (65550) Phelps(97), Pulaski(3)
NEWTONIA Newton
NEWTOWN (64667) Sullivan(61), Mercer(26), Putnam(14)
NIANGUA (65713) Webster(67), Wright(33)
NIXA (65714) Christian(94), Stone(6)
NOBLE Ozark
NOEL McDonald
NORBORNE (64668) Carroll(88), Ray(12)
NORWOOD (65717) Wright(89), Douglas(11)
NOVELTY Knox
NOVINGER (63559) Adair(95), Putnam(5)
O FALLON St. Charles
OAK GROVE (64075) Jackson(89), Lafayette(11)
OAK RIDGE Cape Girardeau
ODESSA (64076) Lafayette(97), Johnson(3)
OLD APPLETON (63770) Cape Girardeau(65), Perry(35)
OLD MONROE Lincoln
OLDFIELD (65720) Christian(85), Douglas(15)
OLEAN (65064) Miller(99), Cole(2)
OLNEY Lincoln
ORAN (63771) Scott(73), Stoddard(25), Cape Girardeau(2)
OREGON Holt
ORONOGO (64855) Jasper(94), Barton(6)
ORRICK (64077) Ray(82), Clay(18)
OSAGE BEACH Camden
OSBORN (64474) De Kalb(87), Clinton(13)
OSCEOLA (64776) St. Clair(97), Benton(3)
OTTERVILLE (65348) Cooper(86), Morgan(10), Pettis(4)
OWENSVILLE (65066) Gasconade(94), Crawford(6)
OXLY Ripley
OZARK Christian
PACIFIC (63069) Franklin(68), St. Louis(17), Jefferson(16)
PAINTON Stoddard
PALMYRA Marion
PARIS Monroe
PARK HILLS St. Francois
PARMA (63870) Stoddard(75), New Madrid(25)
PARNELL (64475) Nodaway(77), Worth(20), Gentry(3)
PASCOLA Pemiscot
PASSAIC Bates
PATTERSON Wayne
PATTON Bollinger
PATTONSBURG (64670) Daviess(66), De Kalb(22), Harrison(10), Gentry(1)
PAYNESVILLE Pike
PEACE VALLEY (65788) Howell(95), Oregon(5)
PECULIAR Cass
PERKINS Scott
PERRY (63462) Ralls(86), Monroe(14)
PERRYVILLE Perry

PEVELY Jefferson
PHILADELPHIA (63463) Marion(99), Shelby(1)
PHILLIPSBURG (65722) Laclede(94), Dallas(6)
PICKERING (64476) Daviess(71), Nodaway(29)
PIEDMONT Wayne
PIERCE CITY (65723) Lawrence(88), Newton(8), Barry(4)
PILOT GROVE Cooper
PILOT KNOB Iron
PINEVILLE McDonald
PITTSBURG Hickory
PLATO (65552) Texas(95), Pulaski(3), Laclede(2)
PLATTE CITY Platte
PLATTSBURG Clinton
PLEASANT HILL (64080) Cass(96), Jackson(4)
PLEASANT HOPE (65725) Greene(76), Polk(24)
PLEVNA (63464) Knox(81), Marion(19)
POCAHONTAS Cape Girardeau
POINT LOOKOUT Taney
POLK (65727) Polk(94), Hickory(6)
POLLOCK (63560) Sullivan(92), Putnam(9)
POLO (64671) Caldwell(68), Ray(32)
POMONA Howell
PONCE DE LEON (65728) Christian(65), Stone(35)
PONTIAC Ozark
POPLAR BLUFF Butler
PORTAGE DES SIOUX St. Charles
PORTAGEVILLE (63873) New Madrid(87), Pemiscot(13)
PORTLAND Callaway
POTOSI Washington
POTTERSVILLE (65790) Howell(89), Ozark(11)
POWELL McDonald
POWERSITE Taney
POWERSVILLE (64672) Putnam(93), Mercer(7)
PRAIRIE HOME Cooper
PRESTON (65732) Hickory(95), Dallas(5)
PRINCETON Mercer
PROTEM Taney
PURCELL Jasper
PURDIN Linn
PURDY Barry
PUXICO (63960) Stoddard(97), Bollinger(2)
QUEEN CITY Schuyler
QUINCY (65735) Hickory(73), Benton(16), St. Clair(11)
QUITMAN Nodaway
QULIN Butler
RACINE Newton
RAVENWOOD (64479) Nodaway(93), Gentry(7)
RAYMONDVILLE Texas
RAYMORE Cass
RAYVILLE Ray
REA Andrew
REDFORD Reynolds
REEDS Jasper
REEDS SPRING (65737) Stone(68), Taney(26), Christian(5)
RENICK Randolph
REPUBLIC (65738) Greene(87), Christian(13)
REVERE Clark
REYNOLDS Reynolds
RHINELAND (65069) Montgomery(80), Callaway(20)
RICH HILL (64779) Bates(94), Vernon(6)
RICHARDS Vernon
RICHLAND (65556) Pulaski(66), Laclede(25), Camden(8)
RICHMOND Ray
RICHWOODS (63071) Washington(93), Jefferson(7)

RIDGEDALE Taney
RIDGEWAY Harrison
RISCO New Madrid
RIVES Dunklin
ROACH Camden
ROBERTSVILLE (63072) Franklin(96), Jefferson(4)
ROBY Texas
ROCHEPORT (65279) Boone(85), Howard(15)
ROCK PORT Atchison
ROCKAWAY BEACH Taney
ROCKBRIDGE Ozark
ROCKVILLE (64780) Bates(56), St. Clair(44)
ROCKY COMFORT (64861) McDonald(83), Newton(13), Barry(4)
ROCKY MOUNT (65072) Morgan(92), Miller(8)
ROGERSVILLE (65742) Greene(54), Webster(37), Christian(9)
ROLLA Phelps
ROMBAUER Butler
ROSCOE St. Clair
ROSEBUD (63091) Gasconade(70), Franklin(30)
ROSENDALE Andrew
ROTHVILLE Chariton
RUETER Taney
RUSH HILL Audrain
RUSHVILLE (64484) Buchanan(57), Platte(43)
RUSSELLVILLE (65074) Cole(78), Moniteau(21), Miller(2)
RUTLEDGE (63563) Scotland(54), Knox(47)
SAGINAW Newton
SAINT ALBANS Franklin
SAINT ANN St. Louis
SAINT CATHERINE Linn
SAINT CHARLES St. Charles
SAINT CLAIR Franklin
SAINT ELIZABETH Miller
SAINT JAMES (65559) Phelps(98), Maries(2)
SAINT JOSEPH (64505) Buchanan(85), Andrew(15)
SAINT JOSEPH (64506) Buchanan(98), Andrew(2)
SAINT JOSEPH Buchanan
SAINT LOUIS (63105) St. Louis(91), St. Louis City(9)
SAINT LOUIS (63117) St. Louis(91), St. Louis City(9)
SAINT LOUIS (63119) St. Louis(97), St. Louis City(3)
SAINT LOUIS (63120) St. Louis City(89), St. Louis(11)
SAINT LOUIS (63123) St. Louis(97), St. Louis City(3)
SAINT LOUIS (63125) St. Louis(99), St. Louis City(1)
SAINT LOUIS (63130) St. Louis(97), St. Louis City(3)
SAINT LOUIS (63133) St. Louis(96), St. Louis City(4)
SAINT LOUIS (63136) St. Louis(96), St. Louis City(4)
SAINT LOUIS (63137) St. Louis(92), St. Louis City(8)
SAINT LOUIS (63143) St. Louis(88), St. Louis City(12)
SAINT LOUIS St. Louis
SAINT LOUIS St. Louis City
SAINT MARY (63673) Ste. Genevieve(89), Perry(11)
SAINT PATRICK Clark
SAINT PETERS St. Charles
SAINT THOMAS (65076) Cole(97), Osage(3)
SAINTE GENEVIEVE Ste. Genevieve
SALEM (65560) Dent(98), Shannon(1)

SALISBURY (65281) Chariton(98), Howard(2)
SANTA FE Monroe
SARCOXIE (64862) Jasper(85), Lawrence(10), Newton(6)
SAVANNAH Andrew
SAVERTON Ralls
SCHELL CITY (64783) Vernon(79), St. Clair(21)
SCOTT CITY Scott
SEDALIA Pettis
SEDGEWICKVILLE (63781) Bollinger(86), Perry(13), Cape Girardeau(1)
SELIGMAN Barry
SENATH Dunklin
SENECA (64865) Newton(97), McDonald(3)
SEYMOUR (65746) Webster(96), Douglas(2), Wright(2)
SHELBINA (63468) Shelby(89), Monroe(12)
SHELBYVILLE (63469) Shelby(99), Knox(1)
SHELDON (64784) Vernon(72), Barton(21), Jackson(4), Cedar(3)
SHELL KNOB (65747) Barry(65), Stone(35)
SHERIDAN (64486) Worth(81), Nodaway(19)
SHOOK Wayne
SIBLEY Jackson
SIKESTON (63801) Scott(92), New Madrid(7), Stoddard(1)
SILEX Lincoln
SILVA (63964) Wayne(80), Madison(20)
SKIDMORE (64487) Nodaway(76), Holt(17), Atchison(7)
SLATER Saline
SMITHTON (65350) Pettis(95), Morgan(5)
SMITHVILLE (64089) Clay(98), Platte(2)
SOLO Texas
SOUTH FORK Howell
SOUTH GREENFIELD (65752) Dade(68), Lawrence(32)
SOUTH WEST CITY McDonald
SPARTA (65753) Christian(99), Douglas(1)
SPICKARD (64679) Grundy(93), Mercer(7)
SPOKANE (65754) Christian(99), Stone(2)
SPRINGFIELD Greene
SQUIRES (65755) Douglas(51), Ozark(49)
STANBERRY (64489) Gentry(94), Nodaway(6)
STANTON Franklin
STARK CITY Newton
STEEDMAN Callaway
STEELE (63877) Pemiscot(98), Dunklin(2)
STEELVILLE (65565) Crawford(98), Washington(1)
STEFFENVILLE (63470) Lewis(94), Shelby(6)
STELLA (64867) Newton(80), McDonald(20)
STET Carroll
STEWARTSVILLE (64490) De Kalb(54), Clinton(42), Buchanan(4)
STOCKTON (65785) Cedar(97), St. Clair(2)
STOTTS CITY Lawrence
STOUTLAND (65567) Camden(68), Laclede(32)
STOUTSVILLE Monroe
STOVER (65078) Morgan(98), Benton(1)
STRAFFORD (65757) Greene(84), Webster(16)
STRASBURG Cass
STURDIVANT Bollinger
STURGEON (65284) Boone(95), Audrain(5)
SUCCESS Texas
SULLIVAN (63080) Franklin(84), Crawford(14), Washington(2)
SULPHUR SPRINGS Jefferson
SUMMERSVILLE (65571) Texas(84), Shannon(16)

SUMNER (64681) Chariton(87), Linn(13)
SUNRISE BEACH (65079) Camden(91), Morgan(9)
SWEDEBORG Pulaski
SWEET SPRINGS (65351) Saline(74), Pettis(24), Johnson(2)
SYRACUSE (65354) Morgan(87), Cooper(13)
TALLAPOOSA New Madrid
TANEYVILLE (65759) Taney(98), Christian(2)
TARKIO Atchison
TAYLOR (63471) Marion(98), Lewis(2)
TEBBETTS Callaway
TECUMSEH Ozark
TERESITA Shannon
THAYER Oregon
THEODOSIA (65761) Ozark(76), Taney(24)
THOMPSON Audrain
THORNFIELD Ozark
TIFF Washington
TIFF CITY McDonald
TINA Carroll
TIPTON (65081) Moniteau(85), Cooper(13), Morgan(2)
TRELOAR Warren
TRENTON Grundy
TRIMBLE Clinton
TRIPLETT Chariton
TROY Lincoln
TRUXTON (63381) Lincoln(62), Montgomery(25), Warren(13)
TUNAS Dallas
TURNERS Greene
TURNEY Clinton
TUSCUMBIA Miller
UDALL Ozark
ULMAN Miller
UNION Franklin
UNION STAR (64494) De Kalb(88), Andrew(12)
UNIONTOWN Perry
UNIONVILLE Putnam
URBANA (65767) Dallas(78), Hickory(20), Polk(2)
URICH (64788) Henry(90), Bates(11)
UTICA Livingston
VALLES MINES (63087) St. Francois(91), Jefferson(9)
VALLEY PARK St. Louis
VAN BUREN (63965) Carter(94), Reynolds(6)
VANDALIA (63382) Audrain(86), Pike(9), Ralls(5)
VANDUSER (63784) Scott(67), Carter(33)
VANZANT Douglas
VERONA (65769) Lawrence(73), Barry(27)
VERSAILLES Morgan
VIBURNUM Iron
VICHY Maries
VIENNA Maries
VILLA RIDGE Franklin
VISTA St. Clair
VULCAN (63675) Iron(91), Washington(6), Reynolds(3)
WACO Jasper
WAKENDA Carroll
WALDRON Platte
WALKER Vernon
WALNUT GROVE (65770) Greene(89), Polk(9), Dade(2)
WALNUT SHADE Taney
WAPPAPELLO (63966) Wayne(54), Butler(46)
WARDELL (63879) Pemiscot(96), New Madrid(4)
WARRENSBURG Johnson
WARRENTON (63383) Warren(98), Lincoln(2)
WARSAW (65355) Benton(99), Hickory(1)

WASHBURN (65772) Barry(86),
   McDonald(14)
WASHINGTON Franklin
WASOLA (65773) Ozark(99), Douglas(1)
WATSON Atchison
WAVERLY (64096) Lafayette(98), Saline(2)
WAYLAND Clark
WAYNESVILLE Pulaski
WEATHERBY (64497) De Kalb(82),
   Daviess(18)
WEAUBLEAU (65774) Hickory(87), St.
   Clair(14)
WEBB CITY Jasper
WELLINGTON Lafayette
WELLSVILLE (63384) Montgomery(89),
   Audrain(9), Callaway(2)

WENTWORTH (64873) Lawrence(80),
   Newton(20)
WENTZVILLE St. Charles
WESCO Crawford
WEST ALTON St. Charles
WEST PLAINS Howell
WESTBORO Atchison
WESTON Platte
WESTPHALIA Osage
WHEATLAND Hickory
WHEATON Barry
WHEELING (64688) Linn(55),
   Livingston(45)
WHITEMAN AIR FORCE BASE Johnson
WHITEOAK Dunklin
WHITESIDE Lincoln

WHITEWATER (63785) Cape
   Girardeau(99), Bollinger(1)
WILLARD (65781) Greene(99), Polk(2)
WILLIAMSBURG Callaway
WILLIAMSTOWN (63473) Lewis(56),
   Clark(44)
WILLIAMSVILLE (63967) Wayne(70),
   Butler(30)
WILLOW SPRINGS (65793) Howell(96),
   Texas(5)
WINDSOR (65360) Henry(56), Pettis(29),
   Johnson(10), Benton(5)
WINDYVILLE Dallas
WINFIELD Lincoln
WINIGAN (63566) Linn(90), Sullivan(10)
WINONA (65588) Shannon(93), Oregon(7)
WINSTON Daviess

WITTENBERG Perry
WOLF ISLAND Mississippi
WOOLDRIDGE (65287) Cooper(82),
   Moniteau(18)
WORTH (64499) Worth(94), Gentry(6)
WORTHINGTON (63567) Putnam(89),
   Morgan(12)
WRIGHT CITY (63390) Warren(88),
   Lincoln(12)
WYACONDA (63474) Clark(93),
   Scotland(5), Lewis(1)
WYATT Mississippi
YUKON Texas
ZALMA (63787) Bollinger(94), Wayne(6)
ZALMA Bollinger
ZANONI Ozark

ZIP/City Cross Reference

63001-63001 ALLENTON	63101-63199 SAINT LOUIS	63441-63441 FRANKFORD	63565-63565 UNIONVILLE
63005-63006 CHESTERFIELD	63301-63304 SAINT CHARLES	63442-63442 GRANGER	63566-63566 WINIGAN
63010-63010 ARNOLD	63330-63330 ANNADA	63443-63443 HUNNEWELL	63567-63567 WORTHINGTON
63011-63011 BALLWIN	63332-63332 AUGUSTA	63445-63445 KAHOKA	63601-63601 PARK HILLS
63012-63012 BARNHART	63333-63333 BELLFLOWER	63446-63446 KNOX CITY	63620-63620 ANNAPOLIS
63013-63013 BEAUFORT	63334-63334 BOWLING GREEN	63447-63447 LA BELLE	63621-63621 ARCADIA
63014-63014 BERGER	63336-63336 CLARKSVILLE	63448-63448 LA GRANGE	63622-63622 BELGRADE
63015-63015 CATAWISSA	63338-63338 COTTLEVILLE	63450-63450 LENTNER	63623-63623 BELLEVIEW
63016-63016 CEDAR HILL	63339-63339 CURRYVILLE	63451-63451 LEONARD	63624-63624 BISMARCK
63017-63017 CHESTERFIELD	63341-63341 DEFIANCE	63452-63452 LEWISTOWN	63625-63625 BLACK
63019-63019 CRYSTAL CITY	63342-63342 DUTZOW	63453-63453 LURAY	63626-63626 BLACKWELL
63020-63020 DE SOTO	63343-63343 ELSBERRY	63454-63454 MAYWOOD	63627-63627 BLOOMSDALE
63021-63022 BALLWIN	63344-63344 EOLIA	63456-63456 MONROE CITY	63628-63628 BONNE TERRE
63023-63023 DITTMER	63345-63345 FARBER	63457-63457 MONTICELLO	63629-63629 BUNKER
63024-63024 BALLWIN	63346-63346 FLINTHILL	63458-63458 NEWARK	63630-63630 CADET
63025-63025 EUREKA	63347-63347 FOLEY	63459-63459 NEW LONDON	63631-63631 CALEDONIA
63026-63026 FENTON	63348-63348 FORISTELL	63460-63460 NOVELTY	63632-63632 CASCADE
63028-63028 FESTUS	63349-63349 HAWK POINT	63461-63461 PALMYRA	63633-63633 CENTERVILLE
63030-63030 FLETCHER	63350-63350 HIGH HILL	63462-63462 PERRY	63636-63636 DES ARC
63031-63034 FLORISSANT	63351-63351 JONESBURG	63463-63463 PHILADELPHIA	63637-63637 DOE RUN
63036-63036 FRENCH VILLAGE	63352-63352 LADDONIA	63464-63464 PLEVNA	63638-63638 ELLINGTON
63037-63037 GERALD	63353-63353 LOUISIANA	63465-63465 REVERE	63640-63640 FARMINGTON
63038-63038 GLENCOE	63357-63357 MARTHASVILLE	63466-63466 SAINT PATRICK	63645-63645 FREDERICKTOWN
63039-63039 GRAY SUMMIT	63359-63359 MIDDLETOWN	63467-63467 SAVERTON	63646-63646 GLOVER
63040-63040 GROVER	63361-63361 MONTGOMERY CITY	63468-63468 SHELBINA	63648-63648 IRONDALE
63041-63041 GRUBVILLE	63362-63362 MOSCOW MILLS	63469-63469 SHELBYVILLE	63650-63650 IRONTON
63042-63042 HAZELWOOD	63363-63363 NEW FLORENCE	63470-63470 STEFFENVILLE	63651-63651 KNOB LICK
63043-63043 MARYLAND HEIGHTS	63364-63364 NEW HARTFORD	63471-63471 TAYLOR	63653-63653 LEADWOOD
63044-63044 BRIDGETON	63365-63365 NEW MELLE	63472-63472 WAYLAND	63654-63654 LESTERVILLE
63045-63045 EARTH CITY	63366-63366 O FALLON	63473-63473 WILLIAMSTOWN	63655-63655 MARQUAND
63047-63047 HEMATITE	63367-63367 LAKE SAINT LOUIS	63474-63474 WYACONDA	63656-63656 MIDDLE BROOK
63048-63048 HERCULANEUM	63369-63369 OLD MONROE	63501-63501 KIRKSVILLE	63660-63660 MINERAL POINT
63049-63049 HIGH RIDGE	63370-63370 OLNEY	63530-63530 ATLANTA	63661-63661 NEW OFFENBURG
63050-63050 HILLSBORO	63371-63371 PAYNESVILLE	63531-63531 BARING	63662-63662 PATTON
63051-63051 HOUSE SPRINGS	63373-63373 PORTAGE DES SIOUX	63532-63532 BEVIER	63663-63663 PILOT KNOB
63052-63052 IMPERIAL	63376-63376 SAINT PETERS	63533-63533 BRASHEAR	63664-63664 POTOSI
63053-63053 KIMMSWICK	63377-63377 SILEX	63534-63534 CALLAO	63665-63665 REDFORD
63055-63055 LABADIE	63378-63378 TRELOAR	63535-63535 COATSVILLE	63666-63666 REYNOLDS
63056-63056 LESLIE	63379-63379 TROY	63536-63536 DOWNING	63670-63670 SAINTE GENEVIEVE
63057-63057 LIGUORI	63381-63381 TRUXTON	63537-63537 EDINA	63673-63673 SAINT MARY
63060-63060 LONEDELL	63382-63382 VANDALIA	63538-63538 ELMER	63674-63674 TIFF
63061-63061 LUEBBERING	63383-63383 WARRENTON	63539-63539 ETHEL	63675-63675 VULCAN
63065-63065 MAPAVILLE	63384-63384 WELLSVILLE	63540-63540 GIBBS	63701-63705 CAPE GIRARDEAU
63066-63066 MORSE MILL	63385-63385 WENTZVILLE	63541-63541 GLENWOOD	63730-63730 ADVANCE
63068-63068 NEW HAVEN	63386-63386 WEST ALTON	63543-63543 GORIN	63732-63732 ALTENBURG
63069-63069 PACIFIC	63387-63387 WHITESIDE	63544-63544 GREEN CASTLE	63735-63735 BELL CITY
63070-63070 PEVELY	63388-63388 WILLIAMSBURG	63545-63545 GREEN CITY	63736-63736 BENTON
63071-63071 RICHWOODS	63389-63389 WINFIELD	63546-63546 GREENTOP	63737-63737 BRAZEAU
63072-63072 ROBERTSVILLE	63390-63390 WRIGHT CITY	63547-63547 HURDLAND	63738-63738 BROWNWOOD
63073-63073 SAINT ALBANS	63401-63401 HANNIBAL	63548-63548 LANCASTER	63739-63739 BURFORDVILLE
63074-63074 SAINT ANN	63430-63430 ALEXANDRIA	63549-63549 LA PLATA	63740-63740 CHAFFEE
63077-63077 SAINT CLAIR	63431-63431 ANABEL	63551-63551 LIVONIA	63742-63742 COMMERCE
63079-63079 STANTON	63432-63432 ARBELA	63552-63552 MACON	63743-63743 DAISY
63080-63080 SULLIVAN	63433-63433 ASHBURN	63555-63555 MEMPHIS	63744-63744 DELTA
63084-63084 UNION	63434-63434 BETHEL	63556-63556 MILAN	63745-63745 DUTCHTOWN
63087-63087 VALLES MINES	63435-63435 CANTON	63557-63557 NEW BOSTON	63746-63746 FARRAR
63088-63088 VALLEY PARK	63436-63436 CENTER	63558-63558 NEW CAMBRIA	63747-63747 FRIEDHEIM
63089-63089 VILLA RIDGE	63437-63437 CLARENCE	63559-63559 NOVINGER	63748-63748 FROHNA
63090-63090 WASHINGTON	63438-63438 DURHAM	63560-63560 POLLOCK	63750-63750 GIPSY
63091-63091 ROSEBUD	63439-63439 EMDEN	63561-63561 QUEEN CITY	63751-63751 GLENALLEN
63099-63099 FENTON	63440-63440 EWING	63563-63563 RUTLEDGE	63752-63752 GORDONVILLE

63753-63753 GRASSY	63940-63940 FISK	64423-64423 BARNARD	64637-64637 COWGILL
63755-63755 JACKSON	63941-63941 FREMONT	64424-64424 BETHANY	64638-64638 DAWN
63758-63758 KELSO	63942-63942 GATEWOOD	64426-64426 BLYTHEDALE	64639-64639 DE WITT
63760-63760 LEOPOLD	63943-63943 GRANDIN	64427-64427 BOLCKOW	64640-64640 GALLATIN
63763-63763 MC GEE	63944-63944 GREENVILLE	64428-64428 BURLINGTON JUNCTION	64641-64641 GALT
63764-63764 MARBLE HILL	63945-63945 HARVIELL	64429-64429 CAMERON	64642-64642 GILMAN CITY
63766-63766 MILLERSVILLE	63947-63947 HIRAM	64430-64430 CLARKSDALE	64643-64643 HALE
63767-63767 MORLEY	63950-63950 LODI	64431-64431 CLEARMONT	64644-64644 HAMILTON
63769-63769 OAK RIDGE	63951-63951 LOWNDES	64432-64432 CLYDE	64645-64645 HARRIS
63770-63770 OLD APPLETON	63952-63952 MILL SPRING	64433-64433 CONCEPTION	64646-64646 HUMPHREYS
63771-63771 ORAN	63953-63953 NAYLOR	64434-64434 CONCEPTION JUNCTION	64647-64647 JAMESON
63772-63772 PAINTON	63954-63954 NEELYVILLE	64436-64436 COSBY	64648-64648 JAMESPORT
63774-63774 PERKINS	63955-63955 OXLY	64437-64437 CRAIG	64649-64649 KIDDER
63775-63775 PERRYVILLE	63956-63956 PATTERSON	64438-64438 DARLINGTON	64650-64650 KINGSTON
63776-63776 MC BRIDE	63957-63957 PIEDMONT	64439-64439 DEARBORN	64651-64651 LACLEDE
63779-63779 POCAHONTAS	63960-63960 PUXICO	64440-64440 DE KALB	64652-64652 LAREDO
63780-63780 SCOTT CITY	63961-63961 QULIN	64441-64441 DENVER	64653-64653 LINNEUS
63781-63781 SEDGEWICKVILLE	63962-63962 ROMBAUER	64442-64442 EAGLEVILLE	64654-64654 LOCK SPRINGS
63782-63782 STURDIVANT	63963-63963 SHOOK	64443-64443 EASTON	64655-64655 LUCERNE
63783-63783 UNIONTOWN	63964-63964 SILVA	64444-64444 EDGERTON	64656-64656 LUDLOW
63784-63784 VANDUSER	63965-63965 VAN BUREN	64445-64445 ELMO	64657-64657 MC FALL
63785-63785 WHITEWATER	63966-63966 WAPPAPELLO	64446-64446 FAIRFAX	64658-64658 MARCELINE
63787-63787 ZALMA	63967-63967 WILLIAMSVILLE	64447-64447 FAIRPORT	64659-64659 MEADVILLE
63801-63801 SIKESTON	64001-64001 ALMA	64448-64448 FAUCETT	64660-64660 MENDON
63820-63820 ANNISTON	64011-64011 BATES CITY	64449-64449 FILLMORE	64661-64661 MERCER
63821-63821 ARBYRD	64012-64012 BELTON	64451-64451 FOREST CITY	64664-64664 MOORESVILLE
63822-63822 BERNIE	64013-64015 BLUE SPRINGS	64453-64453 GENTRY	64665-64665 MOUNT MORIAH
63823-63823 BERTRAND	64016-64016 BUCKNER	64454-64454 GOWER	64667-64667 NEWTOWN
63824-63824 BLODGETT	64017-64017 CAMDEN	64455-64455 GRAHAM	64668-64668 NORBORNE
63825-63825 BLOOMFIELD	64018-64018 CAMDEN POINT	64456-64456 GRANT CITY	64670-64670 PATTONSBURG
63826-63826 BRAGGADOCIO	64019-64019 CENTERVIEW	64457-64457 GUILFORD	64671-64671 POLO
63827-63827 BRAGG CITY	64020-64020 CONCORDIA	64458-64458 HATFIELD	64672-64672 POWERSVILLE
63828-63828 CANALOU	64021-64021 CORDER	64459-64459 HELENA	64673-64673 PRINCETON
63829-63829 CARDWELL	64022-64022 DOVER	64461-64461 HOPKINS	64674-64674 PURDIN
63830-63830 CARUTHERSVILLE	64024-64024 EXCELSIOR SPRINGS	64463-64463 KING CITY	64676-64676 ROTHVILLE
63833-63833 CATRON	64028-64028 FARLEY	64465-64465 LATHROP	64679-64679 SPICKARD
63834-63834 CHARLESTON	64029-64029 GRAIN VALLEY	64466-64466 MAITLAND	64680-64680 STET
63837-63837 CLARKTON	64030-64030 GRANDVIEW	64467-64467 MARTINSVILLE	64681-64681 SUMNER
63838-63838 CONRAN	64034-64034 GREENWOOD	64468-64468 MARYVILLE	64682-64682 TINA
63839-63839 COOTER	64035-64035 HARDIN	64469-64469 MAYSVILLE	64683-64683 TRENTON
63840-63840 DEERING	64036-64036 HENRIETTA	64470-64470 MOUND CITY	64686-64686 UTICA
63841-63841 DEXTER	64037-64037 HIGGINSVILLE	64471-64471 NEW HAMPTON	64687-64687 WAKENDA
63845-63845 EAST PRAIRIE	64040-64040 HOLDEN	64473-64473 OREGON	64688-64688 WHEELING
63846-63846 ESSEX	64048-64048 HOLT	64474-64474 OSBORN	64689-64689 WINSTON
63847-63847 GIBSON	64050-64058 INDEPENDENCE	64475-64475 PARNELL	64701-64701 HARRISONVILLE
63848-63848 GIDEON	64060-64060 KEARNEY	64476-64476 PICKERING	64720-64720 ADRIAN
63849-63849 GOBLER	64061-64061 KINGSVILLE	64477-64477 PLATTSBURG	64722-64722 AMORET
63850-63850 GRAYRIDGE	64062-64062 LAWSON	64478-64478 QUITMAN	64723-64723 AMSTERDAM
63851-63851 HAYTI	64063-64065 LEES SUMMIT	64479-64479 RAVENWOOD	64724-64724 APPLETON CITY
63852-63852 HOLCOMB	64066-64066 LEVASY	64480-64480 REA	64725-64725 ARCHIE
63853-63853 HOLLAND	64067-64067 LEXINGTON	64481-64481 RIDGEWAY	64726-64726 BLAIRSTOWN
63855-63855 HORNERSVILLE	64068-64069 LIBERTY	64482-64482 ROCK PORT	64728-64728 BRONAUGH
63857-63857 KENNETT	64070-64070 LONE JACK	64483-64483 ROSENDALE	64730-64730 BUTLER
63860-63860 KEWANEE	64071-64071 MAYVIEW	64484-64484 RUSHVILLE	64733-64733 CHILHOWEE
63862-63862 LILBOURN	64072-64072 MISSOURI CITY	64485-64485 SAVANNAH	64734-64734 CLEVELAND
63863-63863 MALDEN	64073-64073 MOSBY	64486-64486 SHERIDAN	64735-64735 CLINTON
63866-63866 MARSTON	64074-64074 NAPOLEON	64487-64487 SKIDMORE	64738-64738 COLLINS
63867-63867 MATTHEWS	64075-64075 OAK GROVE	64489-64489 STANBERRY	64739-64739 CREIGHTON
63868-63868 MOREHOUSE	64076-64076 ODESSA	64490-64490 STEWARTSVILLE	64740-64740 DEEPWATER
63869-63869 NEW MADRID	64077-64077 ORRICK	64491-64491 TARKIO	64741-64741 DEERFIELD
63870-63870 PARMA	64078-64078 PECULIAR	64492-64492 TRIMBLE	64742-64742 DREXEL
63871-63871 PASCOLA	64079-64079 PLATTE CITY	64493-64493 TURNEY	64743-64743 EAST LYNNE
63873-63873 PORTAGEVILLE	64080-64080 PLEASANT HILL	64494-64494 UNION STAR	64744-64744 EL DORADO SPRINGS
63874-63874 RISCO	64081-64082 LEES SUMMIT	64496-64496 WATSON	64745-64745 FOSTER
63875-63875 RIVES	64083-64083 RAYMORE	64497-64497 WEATHERBY	64746-64746 FREEMAN
63876-63876 SENATH	64084-64084 RAYVILLE	64498-64498 WESTBORO	64747-64747 GARDEN CITY
63877-63877 STEELE	64085-64085 RICHMOND	64499-64499 WORTH	64748-64748 GOLDEN CITY
63878-63878 TALLAPOOSA	64086-64086 LEES SUMMIT	64501-64508 SAINT JOSEPH	64750-64750 HARWOOD
63879-63879 WARDELL	64088-64088 SIBLEY	64601-64601 CHILLICOTHE	64751-64751 HORTON
63880-63880 WHITEOAK	64089-64089 SMITHVILLE	64620-64620 ALTAMONT	64752-64752 HUME
63881-63881 WOLF ISLAND	64090-64090 STRASBURG	64621-64621 AVALON	64755-64755 JASPER
63882-63882 WYATT	64092-64092 WALDRON	64622-64622 BOGARD	64756-64756 JERICO SPRINGS
63901-63902 POPLAR BLUFF	64093-64093 WARRENSBURG	64623-64623 BOSWORTH	64759-64759 LAMAR
63931-63931 BRIAR	64096-64096 WAVERLY	64624-64624 BRAYMER	64761-64761 LEETON
63932-63932 BROSELEY	64097-64097 WELLINGTON	64625-64625 BRECKENRIDGE	64762-64762 LIBERAL
63933-63933 CAMPBELL	64098-64098 WESTON	64628-64628 BROOKFIELD	64763-64763 LOWRY CITY
63934-63934 CLUBB	64101-64199 KANSAS CITY	64630-64630 BROWNING	64765-64765 METZ
63935-63935 DONIPHAN	64401-64401 AGENCY	64631-64631 BUCKLIN	64766-64766 MILFORD
63936-63936 DUDLEY	64402-64402 ALBANY	64632-64632 CAINSVILLE	64767-64767 MILO
63937-63937 ELLSINORE	64420-64420 ALLENDALE	64633-64633 CARROLLTON	64769-64769 MINDENMINES
63938-63938 FAGUS	64421-64421 AMAZONIA	64635-64635 CHULA	64770-64770 MONTROSE
63939-63939 FAIRDEALING	64422-64422 AMITY	64636-64636 COFFEY	64771-64771 MOUNDVILLE

64772-64772 NEVADA	65053-65053 LOHMAN	65329-65329 FLORENCE	65590-65590 LONG LANE
64776-64776 OSCEOLA	65054-65054 LOOSE CREEK	65330-65330 GILLIAM	65591-65591 MONTREAL
64777-64777 PASSAIC	65055-65055 MC GIRK	65332-65332 GREEN RIDGE	65601-65601 ALDRICH
64778-64778 RICHARDS	65058-65058 META	65333-65333 HOUSTONIA	65603-65603 ARCOLA
64779-64779 RICH HILL	65059-65059 MOKANE	65334-65334 HUGHESVILLE	65604-65604 ASH GROVE
64780-64780 ROCKVILLE	65061-65061 MORRISON	65335-65335 IONIA	65605-65605 AURORA
64781-64781 ROSCOE	65062-65062 MOUNT STERLING	65336-65336 KNOB NOSTER	65606-65606 ALTON
64783-64783 SCHELL CITY	65063-65063 NEW BLOOMFIELD	65337-65337 LA MONTE	65607-65607 CAPLINGER MILLS
64784-64784 SHELDON	65064-65064 OLEAN	65338-65338 LINCOLN	65608-65608 AVA
64788-64788 URICH	65065-65065 OSAGE BEACH	65339-65339 MALTA BEND	65609-65609 BAKERSFIELD
64789-64789 VISTA	65066-65066 OWENSVILLE	65340-65340 MARSHALL	65610-65610 BILLINGS
64790-64790 WALKER	65067-65067 PORTLAND	65344-65344 MIAMI	65611-65611 BLUE EYE
64801-64804 JOPLIN	65068-65068 PRAIRIE HOME	65345-65345 MORA	65612-65612 BOIS D ARC
64830-64830 ALBA	65069-65069 RHINELAND	65347-65347 NELSON	65613-65613 BOLIVAR
64831-64831 ANDERSON	65072-65072 ROCKY MOUNT	65348-65348 OTTERVILLE	65614-65614 BRADLEYVILLE
64832-64832 ASBURY	65074-65074 RUSSELLVILLE	65349-65349 SLATER	65615-65616 BRANSON
64833-64833 AVILLA	65075-65075 SAINT ELIZABETH	65350-65350 SMITHTON	65617-65617 BRIGHTON
64834-64834 CARL JUNCTION	65076-65076 SAINT THOMAS	65351-65351 SWEET SPRINGS	65618-65618 BRIXEY
64835-64835 CARTERVILLE	65077-65077 STEEDMAN	65354-65354 SYRACUSE	65619-65619 BROOKLINE STATION
64836-64836 CARTHAGE	65078-65078 STOVER	65355-65355 WARSAW	65620-65620 BRUNER
64840-64840 DIAMOND	65079-65079 SUNRISE BEACH	65360-65360 WINDSOR	65622-65622 BUFFALO
64841-64841 DUENWEG	65080-65080 TEBBETTS	65401-65409 ROLLA	65623-65623 BUTTERFIELD
64842-64842 FAIRVIEW	65081-65081 TIPTON	65433-65433 BENDAVIS	65624-65624 CAPE FAIR
64843-64843 GOODMAN	65082-65082 TUSCUMBIA	65436-65436 BEULAH	65625-65625 CASSVILLE
64844-64844 GRANBY	65083-65083 ULMAN	65438-65438 BIRCH TREE	65626-65626 CAULFIELD
64847-64847 LANAGAN	65084-65084 VERSAILLES	65439-65439 BIXBY	65627-65627 CEDARCREEK
64848-64848 LA RUSSELL	65085-65085 WESTPHALIA	65440-65440 BOSS	65629-65629 CHADWICK
64849-64849 NECK CITY	65101-65111 JEFFERSON CITY	65441-65441 BOURBON	65630-65630 CHESTNUTRIDGE
64850-64850 NEOSHO	65201-65218 COLUMBIA	65443-65443 BRINKTOWN	65631-65631 CLEVER
64853-64853 NEWTONIA	65230-65230 ARMSTRONG	65444-65444 BUCYRUS	65632-65632 CONWAY
64854-64854 NOEL	65231-65231 AUXVASSE	65446-65446 CHERRYVILLE	65633-65633 CRANE
64855-64855 ORONOGO	65232-65232 BENTON CITY	65449-65449 COOK STATION	65634-65634 CROSS TIMBERS
64856-64856 PINEVILLE	65233-65233 BOONVILLE	65452-65452 CROCKER	65635-65635 DADEVILLE
64857-64857 PURCELL	65236-65236 BRUNSWICK	65453-65453 CUBA	65636-65636 DIGGINS
64858-64858 RACINE	65237-65237 BUNCETON	65456-65456 DAVISVILLE	65637-65637 DORA
64859-64859 REEDS	65239-65239 CAIRO	65457-65457 DEVILS ELBOW	65638-65638 DRURY
64861-64861 ROCKY COMFORT	65240-65240 CENTRALIA	65459-65459 DIXON	65640-65640 DUNNEGAN
64862-64862 SARCOXIE	65243-65243 CLARK	65461-65461 DUKE	65641-65641 EAGLE ROCK
64863-64863 SOUTH WEST CITY	65244-65244 CLIFTON HILL	65462-65462 EDGAR SPRINGS	65644-65644 ELKLAND
64864-64864 SAGINAW	65246-65246 DALTON	65463-65463 ELDRIDGE	65645-65645 EUDORA
64865-64865 SENECA	65247-65247 EXCELLO	65464-65464 ELK CREEK	65646-65646 EVERTON
64866-64866 STARK CITY	65248-65248 FAYETTE	65466-65466 EMINENCE	65647-65647 EXETER
64867-64867 STELLA	65250-65250 FRANKLIN	65468-65468 EUNICE	65648-65648 FAIR GROVE
64868-64868 TIFF CITY	65251-65251 FULTON	65470-65470 FALCON	65649-65649 FAIR PLAY
64869-64869 WACO	65254-65254 GLASGOW	65473-65473 FORT LEONARD WOOD	65650-65650 FLEMINGTON
64870-64870 WEBB CITY	65255-65255 HALLSVILLE	65479-65479 HARTSHORN	65652-65652 FORDLAND
64873-64873 WENTWORTH	65256-65256 HARRISBURG	65483-65483 HOUSTON	65653-65653 FORSYTH
64874-64874 WHEATON	65257-65257 HIGBEE	65484-65484 HUGGINS	65654-65654 FREISTATT
64944-64999 KANSAS CITY	65258-65258 HOLLIDAY	65486-65486 IBERIA	65655-65655 GAINESVILLE
65001-65001 ARGYLE	65259-65259 HUNTSVILLE	65501-65501 JADWIN	65656-65656 GALENA
65010-65010 ASHLAND	65260-65260 JACKSONVILLE	65529-65529 JEROME	65657-65657 GARRISON
65011-65011 BARNETT	65261-65261 KEYTESVILLE	65532-65532 LAKE SPRING	65658-65658 GOLDEN
65013-65013 BELLE	65262-65262 KINGDOM CITY	65534-65534 LAQUEY	65659-65659 GOODSON
65014-65014 BLAND	65263-65263 MADISON	65535-65535 LEASBURG	65660-65660 GRAFF
65016-65016 BONNOTS MILL	65264-65264 MARTINSBURG	65536-65536 LEBANON	65661-65661 GREENFIELD
65017-65017 BRUMLEY	65265-65265 MEXICO	65540-65540 LECOMA	65662-65662 GROVESPRING
65018-65018 CALIFORNIA	65270-65270 MOBERLY	65541-65541 LENOX	65663-65663 HALF WAY
65020-65020 CAMDENTON	65274-65274 NEW FRANKLIN	65542-65542 LICKING	65664-65664 HALLTOWN
65022-65022 CEDAR CITY	65275-65275 PARIS	65543-65543 LYNCHBURG	65666-65666 HARDENVILLE
65023-65023 CENTERTOWN	65276-65276 PILOT GROVE	65546-65546 MONTIER	65667-65667 HARTVILLE
65024-65024 CHAMOIS	65278-65278 RENICK	65548-65548 MOUNTAIN VIEW	65668-65668 HERMITAGE
65025-65025 CLARKSBURG	65279-65279 ROCHEPORT	65550-65550 NEWBURG	65669-65669 HIGHLANDVILLE
65026-65026 ELDON	65280-65280 RUSH HILL	65552-65552 PLATO	65672-65673 HOLLISTER
65031-65031 ETTERVILLE	65281-65281 SALISBURY	65555-65555 RAYMONDVILLE	65674-65674 HUMANSVILLE
65032-65032 EUGENE	65282-65282 SANTA FE	65556-65556 RICHLAND	65675-65675 HURLEY
65034-65034 FORTUNA	65283-65283 STOUTSVILLE	65557-65557 ROBY	65676-65676 ISABELLA
65035-65035 FREEBURG	65284-65284 STURGEON	65559-65559 SAINT JAMES	65679-65679 KIRBYVILLE
65036-65036 GASCONADE	65285-65285 THOMPSON	65560-65560 SALEM	65680-65680 KISSEE MILLS
65037-65037 GRAVOIS MILLS	65286-65286 TRIPLETT	65564-65564 SOLO	65681-65681 LAMPE
65038-65038 LAURIE	65287-65287 WOOLDRIDGE	65565-65565 STEELVILLE	65682-65682 LOCKWOOD
65039-65039 HARTSBURG	65299-65299 MID MISSOURI	65566-65566 VIBURNUM	65685-65685 LOUISBURG
65040-65040 HENLEY	65301-65302 SEDALIA	65567-65567 STOUTLAND	65686-65686 KIMBERLING CITY
65041-65041 HERMANN	65305-65305 WHITEMAN AIR FORCE BASE	65570-65570 SUCCESS	65688-65688 BRANDSVILLE
65042-65042 HIGH POINT		65571-65571 SUMMERSVILLE	65689-65689 CABOOL
65043-65043 HOLTS SUMMIT	65320-65320 ARROW ROCK	65572-65572 SWEDEBORG	65690-65690 COUCH
65046-65046 JAMESTOWN	65321-65321 BLACKBURN	65573-65573 TERESITA	65692-65692 KOSHKONONG
65047-65047 KAISER	65322-65322 BLACKWATER	65580-65580 VICHY	65701-65701 MC CLURG
65048-65048 KOELTZTOWN	65323-65323 CALHOUN	65582-65582 VIENNA	65702-65702 MACOMB
65049-65049 LAKE OZARK	65324-65324 CLIMAX SPRINGS	65583-65583 WAYNESVILLE	65704-65704 MANSFIELD
65050-65050 LATHAM	65325-65325 COLE CAMP	65586-65586 WESCO	65705-65705 MARIONVILLE
65051-65051 LINN	65326-65326 EDWARDS	65588-65588 WINONA	65706-65706 MARSHFIELD
65052-65052 LINN CREEK	65327-65327 EMMA	65589-65589 YUKON	65707-65707 MILLER

65708-65708	MONETT	65730-65730	POWELL	65754-65754	SPOKANE
65710-65710	MORRISVILLE	65731-65731	POWERSITE	65755-65755	SQUIRES
65711-65711	MOUNTAIN GROVE	65732-65732	PRESTON	65756-65756	STOTTS CITY
65712-65712	MOUNT VERNON	65733-65733	PROTEM	65757-65757	STRAFFORD
65713-65713	NIANGUA	65734-65734	PURDY	65759-65759	TANEYVILLE
65714-65714	NIXA	65735-65735	QUINCY	65760-65760	TECUMSEH
65715-65715	NOBLE	65737-65737	REEDS SPRING	65761-65761	THEODOSIA
65717-65717	NORWOOD	65738-65738	REPUBLIC	65762-65762	THORNFIELD
65720-65720	OLDFIELD	65739-65739	RIDGEDALE	65764-65764	TUNAS
65721-65721	OZARK	65740-65740	ROCKAWAY BEACH	65765-65765	TURNERS
65722-65722	PHILLIPSBURG	65741-65741	ROCKBRIDGE	65766-65766	UDALL
65723-65723	PIERCE CITY	65742-65742	ROGERSVILLE	65767-65767	URBANA
65724-65724	PITTSBURG	65744-65744	RUETER	65768-65768	VANZANT
65725-65725	PLEASANT HOPE	65745-65745	SELIGMAN	65769-65769	VERONA
65726-65726	POINT LOOKOUT	65746-65746	SEYMOUR	65770-65770	WALNUT GROVE
65727-65727	POLK	65747-65747	SHELL KNOB	65771-65771	WALNUT SHADE
65728-65728	PONCE DE LEON	65752-65752	SOUTH GREENFIELD	65772-65772	WASHBURN
65729-65729	PONTIAC	65753-65753	SPARTA	65773-65773	WASOLA

65774-65774	WEAUBLEAU
65775-65775	WEST PLAINS
65776-65776	SOUTH FORK
65777-65777	MOODY
65778-65778	MYRTLE
65779-65779	WHEATLAND
65781-65781	WILLARD
65783-65783	WINDYVILLE
65784-65784	ZANONI
65785-65785	STOCKTON
65786-65786	MACKS CREEK
65787-65787	ROACH
65788-65788	PEACE VALLEY
65789-65789	POMONA
65790-65790	POTTERSVILLE
65791-65791	THAYER
65793-65793	WILLOW SPRINGS
65801-65899	SPRINGFIELD

Montana

General Help Numbers:

Governor's Office
PO Box 200801, State Capitol   406-444-3111
Helena, MT 59620-0801   Fax 406-444-5529
http://www.discoveringmontana.com/   8AM-5PM
gov2/css/default.asp

Attorney General's Office
PO Box 201401   406-444-2026
Helena, MT 59620   Fax 406-444-3549
http://www.doj.state.mt.us/ago/index.htm   8AM-5PM

State Court Administrator
PO Box 203002   406-444-2621
Helena, MT 59620-3002   Fax 406-444-0834
http://www.lawlibrary.state.mt.us   8AM-5PM

State Archives
Library/Archives Division   406-444-2694
PO Box 201201, 225 N Roberts St   Fax 406-444-2696
Helena, MT 59620-1201   8AM-5PM M-F;
http://www.his.state.mt.us   9AM-4:30PM
1st SA of each month

State Specifics:

Capital: Helena
Lewis and Clark County

Time Zone: MST

Number of Counties: 56

Population: 902,195

Web Site: www.discoveringmontana.com/css/default.asp

State Agencies

Criminal Records

Department of Justice, Criminal Records, PO Box 201403, Helena, MT 59620-1403; 406-444-3625, 406-444-0689 (Fax), 8AM-5PM.

http://www.doj.state.mt.us

Indexing & Storage: Records are available from 1950's on and are computerized. It takes four days before new records are available for inquiry.

Searching: All felonies, and misdemeanors (except traffic violations) for the past 5 years, are reported on convictions. Include the following in your request-name, date of birth, Social Security Number, any aliases. Place on request letterhead.

Access by: mail, in person.

Fee & Payment: The fee is $5.00 per individual for a name check, or $8.00 per individual for a fingerprint check. Fee payee: Montana Criminal

Records Prepayment required. Personal checks accepted. No credit cards accepted.

Mail search: Turnaround time: 5-10 days. A self addressed stamped envelope is requested.

In person search: Turnaround time is usually immediate, unless there is a record or "hit."

Corporation Records
Limited Liability Company Records
Fictitious Name
Limited Partnerships
Assumed Name
Trademarks/Servicemarks

Business Services Bureau, Secretary of State, PO Box 202801, Helena, MT 59620-2801 (Courier: State Capitol, Room 225, Helena, MT 59620); 406-444-3665, 406-444-3976 (Fax), 8AM-5PM.

http://sos.state.mt.us/css/index.asp

Indexing & Storage: Records are available from the 1860s. New records are available for inquiry immediately. Records are indexed on inhouse computer.

Searching: Include the following in your request-full name of business, specific records that you need copies of. In addition to the articles of incorporation, corporation records include the following information: Annual Reports, Officers, Directors, DBAs, Prior (merged) names, Inactive and Reserved names.

Access by: mail, phone, fax, in person, online.

Fee & Payment: There is no search fee, copies are $.50 each, certification is $2.00 per document. A computerized print-out is $1.00. Fee payee: Secretary of State. Prepayment required. Prepaid accounts may be established. Personal checks accepted. No credit cards accepted.

Mail search: Turnaround time: 2 weeks. A self addressed stamped envelope is requested.

Phone search: Limit of three requests per call.

Fax search: Fax requests are accepted for prepaid accounts at a cost of $3.00 for up to 10 pages and $.25 per additional page to fax back. Turnaround time is up to 10 business days.

Online search: Visit http://app.discoveringmontana.com/bes for free searches of MT business entities.

Other access: Lists of the new corporations per month are available.

Expedited service: Expedited service is available for mail, phone and in person searches. Turnaround time: 1 day. Add $20.00 per search.

Uniform Commercial Code
Federal Tax Liens

Business Services Bureau, Secretary of State, Rm 260, PO Box 202801, Helena, MT 59620-2801 (Courier: State Capital, 2nd Fl, Helena, MT 59620); 406-444-3665, 406-444-3976 (Fax), 8AM-5PM.

http://sos.state.mt.us/css/index.asp

Indexing & Storage: Records are available from 1965, indexed on computer and on microfiche. Terminated or expired financing statements are not available with the exception of notices of federal tax liens. It takes one day before new records are available for inquiry.

Searching: Use search request form UCC-11. The search includes notice of federal tax liens on businesses and individuals. All state tax liens are filed at the county level. Include the following in your request-debtor exact name and any fictitious names.

Access by: mail, fax, in person, online.

Fee & Payment: The search fee is $7.00 per debtor name, copies are $.50 per page. Fee payee: Secretary of State. Prepayment required. The state will accept prepaid accounts. Personal checks accepted. No credit cards accepted.

Mail search: Turnaround time: 3 to 5 days. A self addressed stamped envelope is requested.

Fax search: Same fees and turnaround time apply.

Online search: This web-based subscription service provides information about all active liens filed with the office. (It does not include lapsed and terminated liens.) To use the service, you need to establish a prepaid account with the Secretary of State's Office for a fee of $25 per month. Contact the Business Services Bureau, P.O. Box 202801, Helena MT 59620-2801, 406-444-3665 or visit the web site.

Other access: The agency offers farm bill filings lists on a monthly basis for $5.00 per product. A CD-Rom for Farm Products is available for $20.00.

Expedited service: Expedited service is available for fax searches. Turnaround time: 1 to 2 days. Add $20.00 per document.

State Tax Liens
Records not maintained by a state level agency.

Note: Records are at the county level.

Sales Tax Registrations
State does not impose sales tax.

Birth Certificates

Montana Department of Health, Vital Records, PO Box 4210, Helena, MT 59604 (Courier: 111 N Sanders, Rm 209, Helena, MT 59601); 406-444-4228 (Recording), 406-444-2685, 406-444-1803 (Fax), 8AM-5PM.

Indexing & Storage: Records are available from 1907 on. It takes 3 months before new records are available for inquiry.

Searching: Must be able to show direct and tangible interest of records. The decision if you can get copies of records will be up to the staff of the Vital Records department. Include the following in your request-full name, names of parents, mother's maiden name, date of birth, place of birth, relationship to person of record, reason for information request. Must include copy of guardianship papers, if you are guardian. All requesters must include photo ID and phone number.

Access by: mail, fax, in person.

Fee & Payment: The search fee is $10.00. Add $5.00 for using a credit card. The search fee is per 5 years searched. Fee payee: Montana Vital Records. Prepayment required. Personal checks accepted. Credit cards accepted: MasterCard, Visa, AmEx, Discover.

Mail search: Turnaround time: 10 days. No self addressed stamped envelope is required. Search costs $10.00 for each name in request.

Fax search: Must use credit card for additional $5.00.

In person search: Search costs $10.00 for each name in request. Turnaround time same day.

Expedited service: Expedited service is available for mail and phone searches. Turnaround time: overnight delivery. Add $11.00 per package for Fed Ex return or $11.75 per package for Express Mail return plus the $5.00 credit card fee and the $10.00 search fee.

Death Records

Montana Department of Health, Vital Records, PO Box 4210, Helena, MT 59604 (Courier: 111 N Sanders, Rm 209, Helena, MT 59601); 406-444-4228 (Recording), 406-444-2685, 406-444-1803 (Fax), 8AM-5PM.

Indexing & Storage: Records are available from 1907 on. It takes 3 months before new records are available for inquiry.

Searching: Records are open. Include the following in your request-full name, date of death, place of death, relationship to person of record, reason for information request. Requesters should include a copy of picture ID and phone number.

Access by: mail, fax, in person.

Fee & Payment: The search fee is $10.00. Add $5.00 for using a credit card. The search fee is per 5 years searched. Fee payee: Montana Vital Records. Prepayment required. Personal checks accepted. Credit cards accepted: MasterCard, Visa, AmEx, Discover.

Mail search: Turnaround time: 10 days. Search costs $10.00 for each name in request.

Fax search: Must use credit card.

In person search: Search costs $10.00 for each name in request. Turnaround time same day.

Expedited service: Expedited service is available for mail and phone searches. Turnaround time: overnight delivery. Add $11.00 per document for Fed Ex return and $11.75 per document for Express Mail return, plus the search and credit card fee.

Marriage Certificates
Divorce Records
Records not maintained by a state level agency.

Note: Marriage and divorce records are found at county of issue. The State is required by law to maintain an index of these records. The index is from 1943 to present. The State can direct you to the correct county for a fee of $10.00 per 5 years searched.

Workers' Compensation Records

Montana State Fund, PO Box 4759, Helena, MT 59604-4759 (Courier: 5 S. Last Chance Gulch, Helena, MT 59601); 406-444-6500, 406-444-7796 (Fax), 8AM-5PM.

http://www.montanastatefund.com

Indexing & Storage: Records are available from mid 1980's to 1995 on microfiche. Records 1996 forward are computerized.

Searching: Put request in writing, including reason for the request. They will determine whether the request is legitimate, unless you include a signed release form. Include the following in your request-claimant name, Social Security Number, date of accident, employer.

Access by: mail, fax, in person.

Fee & Payment: Copy fees are $.35 per page if from computer, $.50 per page if from microfiche.

There is no search fee. Fee payee: Montana State Fund. Personal checks accepted. No credit cards accepted.

Mail search: Turnaround time: 7 days. No self addressed stamped envelope is required.

Fax search: Same criteria as mail searches.

In person search: One may request information in person.

Driver Records

Motor Vehicle Division, Driver's Services, PO Box 201430, Helena, MT 59620-1430 (Courier: Records Unit, 303 N Roberts, Room 262, Helena, MT 59620); 406-444-4590, 406-444-1631 (Fax), 8AM-5PM.

http://www.doj.state.mt.us

Note: Copies of tickets are available from the same address; requests must be in writing.

Indexing & Storage: Records are available for lifetime. For suspensions the time varies according to violation-90 days to indefinite and 6 years for an unsatisfied judgment. Note this is availability; records are stored indefinitely. It takes 5 to 10 days before new records are available for inquiry.

Searching: Anyone may order a driving record; however, personal information including address, SSN, photo, and medical information is not released. Opt out is not necessary. The driver's full name, DOB, and/or license number is required.

Access by: mail, phone, fax, in person.

Fee & Payment: The fee is $4.00 per three year record history and $10.00 for a certified history. Fee payee: Motor Vehicle Division. Prepayment required. Billing or draw accounts available. Personal checks accepted. No credit cards accepted.

Mail search: Turnaround time: 3 days. Requests must be in writing, stating purpose and on letterhead.A self addressed stamped envelope is requested.

Phone search: Accounts must be pre-paid.

Fax search: Established pre-paid accounts may fax requests and receive results for an additional $2.00 per record.

In person search: Up to 5 records may be requested in person for immediate delivery at a Montana Driver Exam Station. There are 16 stations in the state that will provide driving records. ID must be provided.

Other access: Magnetic tape overnight batch retrieval is available for higher volume users.

Vehicle Ownership
Vehicle Identification
Vessel Ownership
Vessel Registration

Department of Justice, Title and Registration Bureau, 1032 Buckskin Drive, Deer Lodge, MT 59722; 406-846-6000, 406-846-6039 (Fax), 8AM-5PM.

http://www.doj.state.mt.us

Note: Lien information appears on the title record.

Indexing & Storage: Records are available from 1976 to present on microfiche. Watercraft data is available from 1988. It takes 5 to 10 days before new records are available for inquiry.

Searching: Casual requesters may not obtain records without consent of the subject. DPPA

requirements enforced. Items required for search could include full name, VIN, plate number, or title number.

Access by: mail, phone, fax, in person.

Fee & Payment: The fee is $6.00 per vehicle/vessel or name search. Fee payee: Title and Registration Bureau. Prepayment required. Personal checks accepted. No credit cards accepted.

Mail search: Turnaround time: 5 to 7 days. Requests must be in writing and signed; using letterhead or the state form is suggested.No self addressed stamped envelope is required.

Phone search: Phone-in accounts have to be pre-approved and must carry a "bank account" with the Bureau.

Fax search: Fee is $6.00 for the first page and a $1.00 for each additional page. Turnaround time is 5-7 days.

Other access: Bulk or batch ordering of registration information is available on tape, disk, or paper. The user must fill out a specific form, which gives the user the capability of customization. For further information, contact the Registrar at address above.

Accident Reports

Montana Highway Patrol, Accident Records, 2550 Prospect Ave, Helena, MT 59620-1419; 406-444-3278, 406-444-4169 (Fax), 8AM-5PM.

Note: Digital images are available with previous year's data.

Indexing & Storage: Records are available for 10 years to present. Computer indexing since 1991. Digital images are available starting with the year 1995. It takes 10 to 14 days after the accident before new records are available for inquiry.

Searching: Records are only released to persons involved in accident, or an attorney involved in the case. Insurance representatives must have signed authority. Witness statements are only released with a signed authorization from the witness. Include the following in your request-location of accident, date of accident, full name.

Access by: mail, phone, in person.

Fee & Payment: The fee is $2.00 per report. Fee payee: Montana Highway Patrol. Prepayment required. Personal checks accepted. No credit cards accepted.

Mail search: Turnaround time: 3 to 4 working days. Requests must be submitted in writing following guidelines mentioned above.No self addressed stamped envelope is required.

Phone search: The agency will only release names over the phone of people involved in crash.

In person search: Records will be released if proper authorization is shown.

Other access: Statistics, but not reports, are available.

Legislation Records

State Legislature of Montana, State Capitol, Rm 110, PO Box 201706, Helena, MT 59620-1706; 406-444-3064, 406-444-3036 (Fax), 8AM-5PM.

http://www.leg.state.mt.us

Indexing & Storage: Records are available from 1983 to present, on computer since 1997 and on microfiche 1987 to 1997.

Searching: Include the following in your request-bill number, year.

Access by: mail, phone, in person, online.

Fee & Payment: Copy fee is $.15 per page. Fee payee: Montana Legislative Services Division. Personal checks accepted. No credit cards accepted.

Mail search: Turnaround time: variable. No self addressed stamped envelope is required. No fee for mail request.

Phone search: No fee for telephone request.

In person search: No fee for request. No cash will be accepted.

Online search: Information is available on the Internet. Committee minutes for 1999 forward are available on the Internet. Exhibits from 1999 forward are available on CD-ROM.

Other access: Current session bills and resolutions are available on CD-ROM for $150; other products include the Montana Code, House and Senate Journals, and Annotations, among others.

Voter Registration

Secretary of State, Election Records, PO Box 202801, Helena, MT 59620; 406-444-4732, 406-444-3976 (Fax), 8AM-5PM.

http://www.state.mt.us/sos

Note: Searching by state personnel depends on the voter file system workload.

Indexing & Storage: Records are available from 1998 (new centralized system). Counties will update the state database 3 times during a 2 year election cycle. Therefore, it is suggested to also search at the county level.

Searching: The following data is not released: Social Security Numbers.

Access by: mail, phone, fax, in person.

Fee & Payment: There are no fees at this time.

Mail search: Turnaround time: 2 to 4 days. No self addressed stamped envelope is required.

Phone search: Records are available by phone.

Fax search: Fax searching available.

Other access: The state database can be purchased on disk or CD-ROM. Cost depends on sort parameters. For more information, contact Jelaine Graveley.

GED Certificates

Office of Public Instruction, GED Program, PO Box 202501, Helena, MT 59620-2501; 406-444-4438, 406-444-1373 (Fax), 7AM-4PM.

Indexing & Storage: It takes three weeks before new records are available for inquiry.

Searching: The agency will not issue duplicate diplomas. To search, submit the name, SSN and reason for request. The following are also helpful: a signed release, approximate year of test, date of birth, and city of test. Please include a self-addressed stamped envelope.

Access by: mail, phone, in person.

Fee & Payment: There is no fee for either a verification or transcript.

Mail search: Turnaround time 1 week.A self addressed stamped envelope is requested.

Phone search: Limited information is available by telephone.

In person search: No fee for request. Turnaround time same day.

Hunting License Information
Fishing License Information

Fish, Wildlife & Parks Department, Department of Fish & Wildlife, PO Box 200701, Helena, MT 59620-0701 (Courier: 1420 E 6th Ave, Helena, MT 59620); 406-444-2950, 406-444-4952 (Fax), 8AM-5PM.

http://fwp.state.mt.us

Indexing & Storage: Records are available from 1976 for the special resident and non-resident permits and the general permits go back for 5 years. Records are computerized for the current year, prior on microfiche. Records are indexed on inhouse computer, microfiche.

Searching: State law restricts distribution of license lists. The agency will only verify if a person has purchased a license. Include the following in your request-full name, date of birth, Social Security Number. The following data is not released: phone nor social security number

Access by: mail, phone, in person.

Fee & Payment: There is no search fee.

Mail search: Turnaround time: 1 week. A self addressed stamped envelope is requested.

Phone search: Records are available by phone.

Montana State Licensing Agencies

Licenses Searchable Online

Acupuncturist #33 .... www.discoveringmontana.com/dli/bsd/license/bsd_boards/med_board/board_page.htm
Appraiser, Real Estate #14 .... www.discoveringmontana.com/dli/bsd/license/license.htm
Architect #05 .... www.discoveringmontana.com/dli/bsd/license/license.htm
Athletic Event/Event Timekeeper #03 .... www.discoveringmontana.com/dli/bsd/license/license.htm
Audiologist #21 .... www.discoveringmontana.com/dli/bsd/license/license.htm
Barber/Barber Instructor #02 .... www.discoveringmontana.com/dli/bsd/license/BSD_boards/BAR_Board/Board_page.htm
Boxer/Boxing Professional #03 .... www.discoveringmontana.com/dli/bsd/license/license.htm
Boxing Manager/Promoter/Judge #03 ...... www.discoveringmontana.com/dli/bsd/license/license.htm
Cemetery #03 .... www.discoveringmontana.com/dli/bsd/license/license.htm
Chemical Dependency Counselor #19 ...... www.discoveringmontana.com/dli/bsd/license/license.htm
Chiropractor #03 .... www.discoveringmontana.com/dli/bsd/license/license.htm
Construction Blaster #18 .... www.discoveringmontana.com/dli/bsd/license/license.htm
Contractor, Public #36 .... http://app.discoveringmontana.com/bes/
Cosmetologist/Instructor/School #02 .... www.discoveringmontana.com/dli/bsd/license/BSD_boards/COS_Board/Board_page.htm
Crematory/Operator/Technician #03 .... www.discoveringmontana.com/dli/bsd/license/license.htm
Dental Hygienist #05 .... www.discoveringmontana.com/dli/bsd/license/license.htm
Dentist/Dental Assistant #05 .... www.discoveringmontana.com/dli/bsd/license/license.htm
Denturist #05 .... www.discoveringmontana.com/dli/bsd/license/license.htm
Drug Wholesaler #07 .... www.discoveringmontana.com/dli/bsd/license/license.htm
Drugs, Dangerous #07 .... www.discoveringmontana.com/dli/bsd/license/license.htm
Electrician #08 .... www.discoveringmontana.com/dli/bsd/license/license.htm
Electrologist #02 .... www.discoveringmontana.com/dli/bsd/license/BSD_boards/BAR_Board/Board_page.htm
Emergency Medical Technician #33 .... www.discoveringmontana.com/dli/bsd/license/bsd_boards/med_board/board_page.htm
Engineer #10 .... www.discoveringmontana.com/dli/bsd/license/bsd_boards/pel_board/board_page.htm
Esthetician #02 .... www.discoveringmontana.com/dli/bsd/license/BSD_boards/BAR_Board/Board_page.htm
Funeral Director #03 .... www.discoveringmontana.com/dli/bsd/license/license.htm
Hairstylist #21 .... www.discoveringmontana.com/dli/bsd/license/license.htm
Hearing Aid Dispenser #03 .... www.discoveringmontana.com/dli/bsd/license/license.htm
Land Surveyor #10 .... www.discoveringmontana.com/dli/bsd/license/bsd_boards/pel_board/board_page.htm
Landscape Architect #03 .... www.discoveringmontana.com/dli/bsd/license/license.htm
Lobbyist #23 .... www.lobbyist.net/Montana/MONLOB.htm
Manicurist #02 .... www.discoveringmontana.com/dli/bsd/license/BSD_boards/BAR_Board/Board_page.htm
Medical Doctor #33 .... www.discoveringmontana.com/dli/bsd/license/bsd_boards/med_board/board_page.htm
Midwife Nurse #32 .... www.discoveringmontana.com/dli/bsd/license/bsd_boards/nur_board/board_page.htm
Midwife, Direct Entry/Apprentice #01 ...... www.discoveringmontana.com/dli/bsd/license/bsd_boards/ahc_board/board_page.htm
Mortuary/Mortician #03 .... www.discoveringmontana.com/dli/bsd/license/license.htm
Naturopathic Physician #01 .... www.discoveringmontana.com/dli/bsd/license/bsd_boards/ahc_board/board_page.htm
Nurse Anesthetist #32 .... www.discoveringmontana.com/dli/bsd/license/bsd_boards/nur_board/board_page.htm
Nurse-RN-LPN #32 .... www.discoveringmontana.com/dli/bsd/license/bsd_boards/nur_board/board_page.htm
Nursing #32 .... www.discoveringmontana.com/dli/bsd/license/bsd_boards/nur_board/board_page.htm
Nutritionist #33 .... www.discoveringmontana.com/dli/bsd/license/bsd_boards/med_board/board_page.htm
Occupational Therapist #21 .... www.discoveringmontana.com/dli/bsd/license/license.htm
Optometrist #07 .... www.odfinder.org/LicSearch.asp
Osteopathic Physician #33 .... www.discoveringmontana.com/dli/bsd/license/bsd_boards/med_board/board_page.htm
Outfitter #06 .... www.discoveringmontana.com/dli/bsd/license/license.htm
Pharmacist #07 .... www.discoveringmontana.com/dli/bsd/license/license.htm
Physical Therapist #09 .... www.discoveringmontana.com/dli/bsd/license/license.htm
Physician Assistant #33 .... www.discoveringmontana.com/dli/bsd/license/bsd_boards/med_board/board_page.htm
Plumber #08 .... www.discoveringmontana.com/dli/bsd/license/license.htm
Podiatrist #33 .... www.discoveringmontana.com/dli/bsd/license/bsd_boards/med_board/board_page.htm

Prescriptive Authority (Nurse) #32............www.discoveringmontana.com/dli/bsd/license/bsd_boards/nur_board/board_page.htm
Private Investigator #09 ....www.discoveringmontana.com/dli/bsd/license/license.htm
Private Security Guard #09.....................www.discoveringmontana.com/dli/bsd/license/license.htm
Property Manager #15 ....www.discoveringmontana.com/dli/bsd/license/bsd_boards/rre_board/board_page.htm
Psychologist #11 ....www.discoveringmontana.com/dli/bsd/license/license.htm
Public Accountant #12 ....www.discoveringmontana.com/dli/bsd/license/license.htm
Radiologic Technologist #21 ....www.discoveringmontana.com/dli/bsd/license/license.htm
Real Estate Broker/Salesperson #15 ....www.discoveringmontana.com/dli/bsd/license/bsd_boards/rre_board/board_page.htm
Referee #03..www.discoveringmontana.com/dli/bsd/license/license.htm
Respiratory Care Practitioner #21 ....www.discoveringmontana.com/dli/bsd/license/license.htm
Sanitarian #21 ....www.discoveringmontana.com/dli/bsd/license/license.htm
Security Alarm Installer #09 ....www.discoveringmontana.com/dli/bsd/license/license.htm
Security Company #09............................www.discoveringmontana.com/dli/bsd/license/license.htm
Security Guard #21.................................www.discoveringmontana.com/dli/bsd/license/license.htm
Social Worker #21 ....www.discoveringmontana.com/dli/bsd/license/license.htm
Speech Pathologist #21 ....www.discoveringmontana.com/dli/bsd/license/license.htm
Surveyor #10 ....www.discoveringmontana.com/dli/bsd/license/bsd_boards/pel_board/board_page.htm
Timeshare Broker/Salesperson #15 ....www.discoveringmontana.com/dli/bsd/license/bsd_boards/rre_board/board_page.htm
Underground Storage Tank Inspector #42 www.deq.state.mt.us/rem/tsb/ess/enfLicensedComplianceInspectors.pdf
Underground Tank Installer/Remover #42 www.deq.state.mt.us/rem/tsb/ess/installation_closure.asp
Veterinarian #11 ....www.discoveringmontana.com/dli/bsd/license/license.htm
Wrestler #03...www.discoveringmontana.com/dli/bsd/license/license.htm

Licensing Quick Finder

Acupuncturist #33 406-841-2359
Adoption Agency #04 406-444-5916
Appraiser, Real Estate #14...................406-841-2386
Architect #05.......................................406-841-2390
Asbestos Abatement Contractor/Supervisor/Supplier
#25..406-444-3490
Asbestos Abatement Inspector/Worker #25.............
....406-444-3490
Asbestos Abatement Project Designer/Mgmt. Planner
#25..406-444-3490
Athletic Event/Event Timekeeper #03 ...406-841-2393
Attorney #16 406-444-3858
Audiologist #21 406-444-3091
Barber/Barber Instructor #02 406-841-2333
Boxer/Boxing Professional #03 406-841-2393
Boxing Manager/Promoter/Judge #03...406-841-2393
Calcutta, Gaming #28..........................406-444-1971
Card Contractor/Card Tournament #28 .406-444-1971
Card Dealer #28...................................406-444-1971
Card Table, Live #28 406-444-1971
Casino Night #28 406-444-1971
Cemetery #03 406-841-2393
Chemical Dependency Counselor #19 ..406-444-2827
Child Care Agency #04.........................406-444-1675
Chiropractor #03 406-841-2393
Construction Blaster #18 406-841-2351
Contractor, Public #36..........................406-444-7734
Cosmetologist/Cosmetology Instructor/School #02
....406-841-2333
Crematory/Crematory Operator/Technician #03 ....
....406-841-2393
Day Care Center #26 406-444-2012
Dental Hygienist #05............................406-841-2390
Dentist/Dental Assistant #05................406-841-2390
Denturist #05 406-841-2390
Dietitian #33..406-841-2359
Drug Wholesaler #07............................406-841-2356
Drugs, Dangerous #07.........................406-841-2356
Electrician #08 406-841-2328
Electrologist #02 406-841-2333
Emergency Medical Technician #33......406-444-3895

Engineer #10 406-841-2367
Esthetician #02 406-841-2333
Foster Care Home/Program #04 406-444-1675
Funeral Director #03............................406-841-2393
Fur/Hide Dealer #27............................406-444-4558
Gambling Machine, Video/Electronic #28 ....
....406-444-1971
Gambling Operator #28 406-444-1971
Gaming Mfg./Distributor #28 406-444-1971
Group Home, Youth #30.......................406-444-6587
Hairstylist #21 406-444-4288
Hearing Aid Dispenser #03..................406-841-2395
Horse Racing #22 406-444-4287
Insurance Adjuster #37........................406-444-2040
Insurance Advisor Representative #37..406-444-2040
Insurance Advisor/Solicitor #37............406-444-2040
Insurance Agent #37 406-444-2040
Jockey #22 406-444-4287
Land Surveyor #10...............................406-841-2367
Landscape Architect #03 406-841-2395
Lobbyist #23 406-444-2942
Lottery Retailer #23.............................406-444-5825
Manicurist #02 406-841-2333
Medical Doctor #33 406-841-2359
Midwife Nurse #32 406-444-2071
Midwife, Direct Entry/Apprentice #01 406-841-2394
Milk & Cream Weigher/Grader/Sampler/Tester #29
....406-444-5202
Mortuary/Mortician #03........................406-841-2393
Naturopathic Physician #01 406-841-2394
Notary Public #35.................................406-444-5379
Nurse Anesthetist #32..........................406-444-2071
Nurse-RN-LPN #32..............................406-444-2071
Nurseryman #20 406-444-5400
Nursing #32 406-444-2071
Nutritionist #33 406-841-2359
Occupational Therapist #21 406-444-3091
Optometrist #07 406-841-2395
Osteopathic Physician #33 406-841-2359
Outfitter #06..406-444-3738
Pesticide Applicator/Dealer #20 406-444-5400

Pharmacist #07 406-841-2356
Physical Therapist #09 406-841-2387
Physician Assistant #33.......................406-841-2359
Plumber #08 406-841-2328
Podiatrist #33 406-841-2359
Prescriptive Authority (Nurse) #32 406-444-2071
Private Investigator #09 406-841-2387
Private Security Guard #09...................406-841-2387
Property Manager #15..........................406-444-2961
Psychologist #11 406-841-2394
Public Accountant #12..........................406-841-2388
Radiologic Technologist #21 406-444-3091
Real Estate Broker/Salesperson #15 406-444-2961
Referee #03...406-841-2393
Respiratory Care Practitioner #21 406-444-3091
Sanitarian #21.....................................406-444-3091
School Guidance Counselor #34 406-444-3150
School Librarian #34 406-444-3150
School Principal #34.............................406-444-3150
School Superintendent #34 406-444-3150
Securities Broker/Salesperson #38 406-444-2040
Security Alarm Installer #09 406-841-2387
Security Company #09 406-841-2387
Security Guard #21 406-444-4288
Septic Tank Cleaner #25 406-444-4400
Shorthand Reporter #31 406-721-1143
Social Worker #21................................406-444-4288
Speech Pathologist #21........................406-444-3091
Surveyor #10 406-841-2367
Taxidermist #27 406-444-4558
Teacher #34...406-444-3150
Timeshare Broker/Salesperson #15 406-444-2961
Underground Storage Tank Inspector #42.................
....406-444-1420
Underground Storage Tank Installer/Remover #42.....
....406-444-1420
Veterinarian #11...................................406-841-2394
Water & Sewage Plant Operator #25 406-444-4400
Weather Modifier #40 406-444-6601
Well Driller #40....................................406-444-6601
Wrestler #03 406-841-2393

Licensing Agency Information

#01 Board of Alternative Health Care, PO Box 200513 (301 S Park, 4th Fl), Helena, MT 59620-0513; 406-841-2394, Fax: 406-841-2305. Direct web site URL to search for licensees: www.discoveringmontana.com/dli/bsd/license/bsd _boards/ahc_board/board_page.htm

#02 Board of Barbers & Cosmetologists, PO Box 200513 (301 S Park, 4th Fl), Helena, MT 59620-0513; 406-841-2333, Fax: 406-841-2305. www.discoveringmontana.com/dli/bsd/lisence/bus. index.htm
Direct web site URL to search for licensees: www.discoveringmontana.com/dli/bsd/license/bus _licensing_boards.htm

#03 Board: Chiropractor, Funerary, Hearing, Lanscape Architect, Athletic Events, PO Box 200513 (301 S Park, 4th Fl, #428), Helena, MT 59620-0513; 406-841-2393, Fax: 406-841-2305. http://commerce.state.mt.us/license/pol/index.htm
Direct web site URL to search for licensees: www.discoveringmontana.com/dli/bsd/license/lice nse.htm

#04 Department of Public Health Human Services, PO Box 8005 (1400 Boadway), Helena, MT 59604; 406-444-5900, Fax: 406-444-5956. www.dphhs.mt.gov

#05 Board: Dentistry, Architects, PO Box 200513 (301 S Park), Helena, MT 59620-0513; 406-841-2390, Fax: 406-841-2305. www.discoveringmontana.com/dli/bsd/
Direct web site URL to search for licensees: www.discoveringmontana.com/dli/bsd/license/lice nse.htm. Search online using name of person.

#06 Board of Outfitters, PO Box 200513 (301 S Park, 4th Fl), Helena, MT 59620-0513; 406-444-5983, Fax: 406-444-1667.
Direct web site URL to search for licensees: www.discoveringmontana.com/dli/bsd/license/lice nse.htm

#07 Board of Pharmacy & Optometry, PO Box 200513 (301 S Park, 4th Fl), Helena, MT 59620-0513; 406-841-2394, Fax: 406-841-2343. www.com.state.mt.us/license/POL
Direct web site URL to search for licensees: www.discoveringmontana.com/dli/bsd/license/lice nse.htm. You can search online using nationaol database by name, city or state.

#08 Plumbing and Electrical Board, PO Box 200513 (301 S Park, 4th Fl), Helena, MT 59620-0513; 406-841-2328, Fax: 406-841-2305.
Direct web site URL to search for licensees: www.discoveringmontana.com/dli/bsd/license/lice nse.htm

#09 Board of Private Security Patrol Officers & Invest, PO Box 200513 (301 S Park, 4th Fl), Helena, MT 59620-0513; 406-841-2387, Fax: 406-841-2305.
Direct web site URL to search for licensees: www.discoveringmontana.com/dli/bsd/license/lice nse.htm

#10 Board of Professional Engineers & Land Surveyors, PO Box 200513 (301 S Park, 4th Fl), Helena, MT 59620-0513; 406-841-2367, Fax: 406-841-2309. www.discoveringmontana.com/doa/aed/ aeinfo.html

Direct web site URL to search for licensees: www.discoveringmontana.com/dli/bsd/license/bsd _boards/pel_board/board_page.htm

#11 Veterinary Board, PO Box 200513 (301 S Park, 4th Fl), Helena, MT 59620-0513; 406-841-2394, Fax: 406-841-2305. www.discovering montana.com/dli/bsd/license/license.htm
Direct web site URL to search for licensees: www.discoveringmontana.com/dli/bsd/license/lice nse.htm

#12 Board of Public Accountants, 301 South Park (PO Box 200513), Helena, MT 59620-0513; 406-841-2388, Fax: 406-841-2309. www.com.state.mt.us/license/POL
Direct web site URL to search for licensees: www.discoveringmontana.com/dli/bsd/license/lice nse.htm

#14 Board of Real Estate Appraisers, PO Box 200513 (301 S Park Ave), Helena, MT 59620-0513; 406-841-2386, Fax: 406-841-2305. www.com.state.mt.us/LICENSE/pol/pol_boards/re a_board/board_page.htm
Direct web site URL to search for licensees: www.discoveringmontana.com/dli/bsd/license/lice nse.htm

#15 Board of Realty Regulation, PO Box 200513 (301 S. Park), Helena, MT 59620-0513; 406-444-2961, Fax: 406-841-2323. www.com.state.mt.us/LICENSE/pol/pol_boards/rr e_board/board_page.htm
Direct web site URL to search for licensees: www.discoveringmontana.com/dli/bsd/license/bsd _boards/rre_board/board_page.htm

#16 Clerk of Superior Court, 215 N Sanders, RM 323 Justice Bldg, Helena, MT 59620; 406-444-3858, Fax: 406-444-5705. www.montanabar.org

#18 Construction Blasters, PO Box 200513 (301 S Park), Helena, MT 59620-0513; 406-841-2351, Fax: 406-841-2309. www.com.mt.gov/license/pol/ licensing_boards.htm
Direct web site URL to search for licensees: www.discoveringmontana.com/dli/bsd/license/lice nse.htm

#19 Chemical Dependency Counselors Board, PO Box 200513 (301 S Park), Helena, MT 59620-0513; 406-444-2827, Fax: 406-841-2305. www.com.state.mt.us/license/POL/pol_boards/cdc _board/board_page.htm
Direct web site URL to search for licensees: www.discoveringmontana.com/dli/bsd/license/lice nse.htm

#20 Agriculture Dept., PO Box 200201, Helena, MT 59620; 406-444-5400, Fax: 406-444-7336.

#21 Department of Commerce, PO Box 200513 (301 South Park, 4th Fl), Helena, MT 59620-0513; 406-841-2300, Fax: 406-841-2305. www.com.state.mt.us/License/POL/index.htm

#22 Department of Commerce, PO Box 200512 (1424 9th Av), Helena, MT 59620-0512; 406-444-4287, Fax: 406-444-4305. www.com.mt.gov/license/horse/index.htm

#23 Department of Commerce, PO Box 200544, Helena, MT 59620-0544; 406-444-5825, Fax: 406-444-5830.

#25 Department of Environmental Quality, 1520 E 6th Ave, PO Box 200901, Helena, MT 59620-0901; 406-444-2544, Fax: 406-444-1374. www.deq.state.mt.us

#26 Department of Health & Human Services, PO Box 202953, Helena, MT 59620; 406-444-2012, Fax: 406-444-1742. www.dphhs.mt.gov

#27 Department of Fish, Wildlife & Parks, 1420 E 6th Ave, Helena, MT 59620-0701; 406-444-4558, Fax: 406-444-4952.

#28 Department of Justice, 2550 Prospect Ave, Helena, MT 59620-1424; 406-444-1971, Fax: 406-444-9157. www.doj.mt.gov

#29 Department of Livestock, PO 202001, Helena, MT 59620; 406-444-5202, Fax: 406-444-1929.

#30 Department of Public Health Human Services, 48 N Last Chance Gulch, Helena, MT 59620-4001; 406-444-6587, Fax: 406-444-5956. www.dphhs.mt.gov

#31 Jeffries Court Reporting Inc., 161 S Mt Ave #C, Missoula, MT 59801; 406-721-1143, Fax: 406-728-0888.

#32 Board of Nursing, PO Box 200513 (301 S Park), Helena, MT 59620-0513; 406-444-2071, Fax: 406-4841-2343. www.com.state.mt.us/License/POL/pol_boards/nu r_board/board_page.htm
Direct web site URL to search for licensees: www.discoveringmontana.com/dli/bsd/license/bsd _boards/nur_board/board_page.htm

#33 Board of Medical Examiners, PO Box 200513, Helena, MT 59620-0513; 406-444-4284, Fax: 406-841-2363.
Direct web site URL to search for licensees: www.discoveringmontana.com/dli/bsd/license/bsd _boards/med_board/board_page.htm

#35 Certification Division, PO Box 1043, Helena, MT 59620-2501; 406-444-3095, Fax: 406-444-2893. http://161.7.114.15/OPI/opi.html

#36 Public Contractors Licensing, PO Box 8011, Helena, MT 59604; 406-444-7734, Fax: 406-444-3465. http://sos.state.mt.us/css/index.asp
Direct web site URL to search for licensees: http://app.discoveringmontana.com/bes/. You can search online using name At State main site, click on Government Agencies, Then Labor & Industry, then Employer Information, then Construction Contractors and download the alphabetical list.

#37 Insurance Division, PO Box 4009, Helena, MT 59604-4009; 406-444-2040.

#38 Securities Division, PO Box 4009, Helena, MT 59604-4009; 406-444-2040, Fax: 406-444-5558. www.mt.gov/sao/lic.htm

#40 Dept. of Natural Resoruces & Conservation, PO Box 201601 (48 N Last Chance Gulch), Helena, MT 59620-1601; 406-444-6601, Fax: 406-444-0533.

#42 Department of Environmental Quality, 2209 Phoenix Ave, Helena, MT 59620-0901; 406-444-1420, Fax: 406-444-1901. www.deq.state.mt.us/rem
Direct web site URL to search for licensees: www.deq.state.mt.us/rem/tsb/ess/installation_closu re.asp. Search online using alphabetized lists

Montana Federal Courts

The following list indicates the district and division name for each county in the state. If the bankruptcy court location is different from the district court, then the location of the bankruptcy court appears in parentheses.

County/Court Cross Reference

Beaverhead	Butte	Meagher	Helena (Butte)
Big Horn	Billings (Butte)	Mineral	Missoula (Butte)
Blaine	Great Falls (Butte)	Missoula	Missoula (Butte)
Broadwater	Helena (Butte)	Musselshell	Billings (Butte)
Carbon	Billings (Butte)	Park	Billings (Butte)
Carter	Billings (Butte)	Petroleum	Billings (Butte)
Cascade	Great Falls (Butte)	Phillips	Billings (Butte)
Chouteau	Great Falls (Butte)	Pondera	Great Falls (Butte)
Custer	Billings (Butte)	Powder River	Billings (Butte)
Daniels	Billings (Butte)	Powell	Helena (Butte)
Dawson	Billings (Butte)	Prairie	Billings (Butte)
Deer Lodge	Butte	Ravalli	Missoula (Butte)
Fallon	Billings (Butte)	Richland	Billings (Butte)
Fergus	Great Falls (Butte)	Roosevelt	Billings (Butte)
Flathead	Missoula (Butte)	Rosebud	Billings (Butte)
Gallatin	Butte	Sanders	Missoula (Butte)
Garfield	Billings (Butte)	Sheridan	Billings (Butte)
Glacier	Great Falls (Butte)	Silver Bow	Butte
Golden Valley	Billings (Butte)	Stillwater	Billings (Butte)
Granite	Missoula (Butte)	Sweet Grass	Billings (Butte)
Hill	Great Falls (Butte)	Teton	Great Falls (Butte)
Jefferson	Helena (Butte)	Toole	Great Falls (Butte)
Judith Basin	Great Falls (Butte)	Treasure	Billings (Butte)
Lake	Missoula (Butte)	Valley	Billings (Butte)
Lewis and Clark	Helena (Butte)	Wheatland	Billings (Butte)
Liberty	Great Falls (Butte)	Wibaux	Billings (Butte)
Lincoln	Missoula (Butte)	Yellowstone	Billings (Butte)
Madison	Butte	Yellowstone Nat. Park (part)	Billings (Butte)
McCone	Billings (Butte)		

US District Court

District of Montana

Billings Division Clerk, Room 5405, Federal Bldg, 316 N 26th St, Billings, MT 59101 (Courier Address: Use mail address for courier delivery), 406-247-7000, Fax: 406-247-7008.

Counties: Big Horn, Carbon, Carter, Custer, Dawson, Fallon, Garfield, Golden Valley, McCone, Musselshell, Park, Petroleum, Powder River, Prairie, Richland, Rosebud, Stillwater, Sweet Grass, Treasure, Wheatland, Wibaux, Yellowstone, Yellowstone National Park.

Indexing/Storage: Cases are indexed by defendant and plaintiff as well as by case number. New cases are available in the index 1 week after filing date. A computer index is maintained. Open records are located at this court.

Fee & Payment: The fee is $25.00 per item (one party name or case number). Payment may be made by money order, cashier check, personal check. Prepayment is required. Payee: Clerk, US District Court. Certification fee: $7.00 per document. Copy fee: $.50 per page. You are allowed to make your own copies. These copies cost $.10 per page.

Phone Search: Only docket information is available by phone.

Fax Search: The fee is $15.00.

Mail Search: A stamped self addressed envelope is not required.

In Person: In person searching is available.

PACER: Sign-up number is 800-676-6856. Access fee is $.60 per minute. Toll-free access: 800-305-5235. Local access: 406-452-9851. Case records are available back to 1992. Records are never purged. New records are available online after 5 days.

Butte Division Room 303, Federal Bldg, Butte, MT 59701 (Courier Address: Use mail address for courier delivery), 406-782-0432, Fax: 406-782-0537.

Counties: Beaverhead, Deer Lodge, Gallatin, Madison, Silver Bow.

Indexing/Storage: Cases are indexed by defendant and plaintiff as well as by case number. New cases are available in the index 1 week after filing date. A computer index is maintained. Open records are located at this court.

Fee & Payment: The fee is $20.00 per item (one party name or case number). Payment may be made by money order, cashier check, personal check. Prepayment is required. Payee: Clerk, US District Court. Certification fee: $7.00 per document. Copy fee: $.50 per page. You are allowed to make your own copies. These copies cost $.10 per page.

Phone Search: Searching is not available by phone.

Fax Search: Will accept fax requests if search fee paid in advance.

Mail Search: A stamped self addressed envelope is not required.

In Person: In person searching is available.

PACER: Sign-up number is 800-676-6856. Access fee is $.60 per minute. Toll-free access: 800-305-5235. Local access: 406-452-9851. Case records are available back to 1992. Records are

never purged. New records are available online after 5 days.

Great Falls Division Clerk, PO Box 2186, Great Falls, MT 59403 (Courier Address: 215 1st Ave N, Great Falls, MT 59401), 406-727-1922, Fax: 406-727-7648.

Counties: Blaine, Cascade, Chouteau, Daniels, Fergus, Glacier, Hill, Judith Basin, Liberty, Phillips, Pondera, Roosevelt, Sheridan, Teton, Toole, Valley.

Indexing/Storage: Cases are indexed by defendant and plaintiff as well as by case number. New cases are available in the index immediately after filing date. A computer index is maintained. Open records are located at this court. District wide searches are available for all information from this division.

Fee & Payment: The fee is $20.00 per item (one party name or case number). Payment may be made by money order, cashier check, personal check. Prepayment required. Payee: Clerk, US District Court. Certification fee: $7.00 per document. Copy fee: $.50 per page.

Phone Search: Only docket information available by case number.

Mail Search: Always enclose a stamped self addressed envelope.

In Person: In person searching is available.

PACER: Sign-up number is 800-676-6856. Access fee is $.60 per minute. Toll-free access: 800-305-5235. Local access: 406-452-9851. Case records are available back to 1992. Records are never purged. New records are available online after 5 days.

Helena Division Federal Bldg, 301 S. Park Ave, Rm 542, Helena, MT 59626 (Courier Address: Room 542, 301 S Park Ave, Helena, MT 59626), 406-441-1355, Fax: 406-441-1357.

Counties: Broadwater, Jefferson, Lewis and Clark, Meagher, Powell.

Indexing/Storage: Cases are indexed by defendant and plaintiff as well as by case number. New cases are available in the index same day if possible after filing date. Both computer and card indexes are maintained. Open records are located at this court. Cases filed in the Missoula division prior to January 1997 are held here.

Fee & Payment: The fee is $20.00 per item (one party name or case number). Payment may be made by money order, cashier check, personal check. Prepayment is required. Payee: Clerk, US District Court. Certification fee: $7.00 per document. Copy fee: $.50 per page.

Phone Search: Information by phone is limited.

Mail Search: Always enclose a stamped self addressed envelope.

In Person: In person searching is available.

PACER: Sign-up number is 800-676-6856. Access fee is $.60 per minute. Toll-free access: 800-305-5235. Local access: 406-452-9851. Case records are available back to 1992. Records are never purged. New records are available online after 5 days.

Missoula Division Russell Smith Courthouse, PO Box 8537, Missoula, MT 59807 (Courier Address: 201 E Broadway, Missoula, MT 59802), 406-542-7260, Fax: 406-542-7272.

Counties: Flathead, Granite, Lake, Lincoln, Mineral, Missoula, Ravalli, Sanders.

Indexing/Storage: Cases are indexed by defendant and plaintiff as well as by case number. New cases are available in the index 1-2 days after filing date. A computer index is maintained. Open records are located at this court. Cases in this district originate here; after closing they are held here rather than being sent to a Federal Records Center.

Fee & Payment: The fee is $20.00 per item (one party name or case number). Payment may be made by money order, cashier check, personal check. Prepayment required except for attorneys. Court will fax results for a $5.00 fee. Payee: Clerk, US District Court. Certification fee: $7.00 per document. Copy fee: $.50 per page.

Phone Search: Docket information is available by phone.

Mail Search: A stamped self addressed envelope is not required.

In Person: In person searching is available.

PACER: Sign-up number is 800-676-6856. Access fee is $.60 per minute. Toll-free access: 800-305-5235. Local access: 406-452-9851. Case records are available back to 1992. Records are never purged. New records are available online after 5 days.

US Bankruptcy Court

District of Montana

Butte Division PO Box 689, Butte, MT 59703 (Courier Address: 303 Federal Bldg, 400 N Main St, Butte, MT 59703), 406-782-3354, Fax: 406-782-0537.

http://www.mtb.uscourts.gov

Counties: All counties in Montana.

Indexing/Storage: Cases are indexed by debtor as well as by case number. New cases are available in the index immediately after filing date. A computer index is maintained. Open records are located at this court.

Fee & Payment: The fee is $20.00 per item (one party name or case number). Payment may be made by money order, cashier check, personal check. Debtor's checks are not accepted. Payee: Clerk, US Bankruptcy Court. Certification fee: $7.00 per document. Copy fee: $.50 per page.

Phone Search: Only docket information is available by phone. An automated voice case information service (VCIS) is available. Call VCIS at 888-879-0071 or 406-782-1060.

Fax Search: Will accept fax searches. Will fax results at $1.00 per page.

Mail Search: A stamped self addressed envelope is not required.

In Person: In person searching is available.

PACER: Sign-up number is 800-676-6856. Access fee is $.60 per minute. Toll-free access: 800-716-4305. Local access: 406-782-1051. Use of PC Anywhere v4.0 suggested. Case records are available back to 1986. New civil records are available online after 1 day. PACER is available online at http://pacer.mtb.uscourts.gov.

Montana County Courts

Court	Jurisdiction	No. of Courts	How Organized
District Courts*	General	57	21 Districts
Limited Jurisdiction Courts*	Limited	64	56 Counties
City Courts	Limited	83	
Municipal Court	Municipal	1	
Water Courts	Special		4 Divisions
Workers' Compensation Court	Special	1	

* Profiled in this Sourcebook.

Court	CIVIL								
	Tort	Contract	Real Estate	Min. Claim	Max. Claim	Small Claims	Estate	Eviction	Domestic Relations
District Courts*	X	X	X	$5000-7000	No Max		X		X
Limited Jurisdiction Courts*	X	X	X	$0	$5000-7000	$3000		X	
City Courts	X	X	X	$0	$5000				
Municipal Court	X	X	X	$0	$5000	$3000			
Water Courts			X						
Workers' Comp. Court									

Court	CRIMINAL				
	Felony	Misdemeanor	DWI/DUI	Preliminary Hearing	Juvenile
District Courts*	X				X
Limited Jurisdiction Courts*		X	X		
City Courts		X	X		
Municipal Court		X	X		
Water Courts					
Workers' Comp. Court					

ADMINISTRATION Court Administrator, Justice Building, 215 N Sanders, Room 315 (PO Box 203002), Helena, MT, 59620; 406-444-2621, Fax: 406-444-0834.

COURT STRUCTURE The District Courts have no maximum amount for civil judgment cases. Most District Courts handle civil over $7,000; there are exceptions that handle a civil minimum as low as $5,000. Limited Jurisdiction Courts, which are also known as Justice Courts, may handle civil actions up to $7,000. The Small Claims limit is $3000.

Many Montana Justices of the Peace maintain case record indexes on their personal PCs, which does speed the retrieval process.

ONLINE ACCESS There is no statewide internal or external online computer system available. Those courts with computer systems use them for internal purposes only.

Beaverhead County

District Court Beaverhead County Courthouse, 2 S Pacific St, Dillon, MT 59725; 406-683-5831; Fax: 406-683-6473. Hours: 8AM-5PM (MST). *Felony, Civil Actions Over $7,000, Eviction, Probate.*

Civil Records: Access: Fax, mail, in person. Both court and visitors may perform in person searches. Search fee: $.50 per name per year. Maximum fee-$25.00. Required to search: name, years to search. Civil cases indexed by defendant, plaintiff. Civil records in books; on computer since 1997. For fax, send fax copy of check for fee.

Criminal Records: Access: Fax, mail, in person. Both court and visitors may perform in person searches. Search fee: $.50 per name per year. Maximum fee-$25.00. Required to search: name, years to search. Criminal records in books; on computer since 1997. For fax, send fax copy of check for fee.

General Information: Public Access terminal is available. No adoption, juvenile, sanity, paternity or dismissed criminal records released. SASE required. Turnaround time 1-2 days. Fax notes: $1.00 per page. Copy fee: $.50 per page. $.25 per page after first 5. Certification fee: $2.00. Fee payee: Clerk of Court. Personal checks accepted. Prepayment is required.

Beaverhead County Justice Court PO Box 107, Lima, MT 59739; 406-276-3741. Hours: 3:30-6PM (MST). *Misdemeanor, Civil Actions Under $7,000, Eviction, Small Claims.*

Dillon Justice Court 2 S Pacific, Cluster #16, Dillon, MT 59725; 406-683-2383; Fax: 406-683-5776. Hours: 8AM-Noon (MST). *Misdemeanor, Civil Actions Under $7,000, Eviction, Small Claims.*

Big Horn County

District Court 121 West 3rd St, Room 221, PO Box 908, Hardin, MT 59034; 406-665-9750; Fax: 406-665-9755. Hours: 8AM-5PM (MST). *Felony, Civil Actions Over $7,000, Probate.*

Civil Records: Access: Phone, fax, mail, in person. Both court and visitors may perform in person searches. Search fee: $.50 per name per year. Maximum fee-$25.00. Required to search: name, years to search; also helpful: address. Civil cases indexed by defendant, plaintiff. Civil records in books and on microfilm back to 1913; on computer back to 1979.

Criminal Records: Access: Fax, mail, in person. Both court and visitors may perform in person searches. Search fee: $.50 per name per year. Maximum fee-$25.00. Required to search: name, years to search, DOB; also helpful: address, SSN. Criminal records in books and on microfilm back to 1913; on computer back to 1979. Court order required for confidential information.

General Information: Public Access terminal is available. No adoption, sanity, pre-sentence, psychiatric evaluation, dependent & neglected, or confidential criminal justice records released. SASE required. Turnaround time same day. Fax notes: Fee to fax results is $1.00 per page. Copy fee: $.50 per page. $.25 per page after first 5. Certification fee: $2.00. Fee payee: Clerk of Court. Personal checks accepted. Prepayment is required. Will bill government agencies.

Limited Jurisdiction Court PO Box Drawer H, Hardin, MT 59034; 406-665-2275; Fax: 406-665-3101. Hours: 8AM-5PM (MST). *Misdemeanor, Civil Actions Under $7,000, Eviction, Small Claims.*

Blaine County

District Court PO Box 969, Chinook, MT 59523; 406-357-3230; Fax: 406-357-2199. Hours: 8AM-5PM (MST). *Felony, Civil Actions Over $5,000, Eviction, Probate.*

Civil Records: Access: Fax, mail, in person. Both court and visitors may perform in person searches. Search fee: $.50 per name per year. Maximum fee-$25.00. Required to search: name, years to search. Civil cases indexed by defendant, plaintiff. Civil records in books from 1912; on computer back to 1995.

Criminal Records: Access: Fax, mail, in person. Both court and visitors may perform in person searches. Search fee: $.50 per name per year. Maximum fee-$25.00. Required to search: name, years to search, signed release. Criminal records in books from 1912; on computer back to 1995.

General Information: No adoption, juvenile or sanity records released. SASE required. Turnaround time same day. Fax notes: Fee to fax results is $1.00 per page. Copy fee: $.50 per page. $.25 per page after first 5. Certification fee: $2.00. Fee payee: Clerk of Court. Personal checks accepted. Prepayment is required.

Chinook Justice Court PO Box 1266, Chinook, MT 59523; 406-357-2335. Hours: 8AM-3PM M,W,F; 9AM-3PM T,Th (MST). *Misdemeanor, Civil Actions Under $7,000, Eviction, Small Claims.*

Broadwater County

District Court 515 Broadway, Townsend, MT 59644; 406-266-9236; Fax: 406-266-4720. Hours: 8AM-Noon, 1-5PM (MST). *Felony, Civil Actions Over $7,000, Eviction, Probate.*

Civil Records: Access: Fax, mail, in person. Both court and visitors may perform in person searches. Search fee: $.50 per name per year. Maximum fee-$25.00. Required to search: name, years to search, DOB. Civil records on microfiche and archives back to 1897; on computer back to 1997.

Criminal Records: Access: Fax, mail, in person. Both court and visitors may perform in person searches. Search fee: $.50 per name per year. Maximum fee-$25.00. Required to search: name, years to search, DOB. Criminal records on microfiche and archives back to 1897; on computer back to 1997.

General Information: Public Access terminal is available. No adoption, juvenile or sanity records released. SASE required. Turnaround time same day. Copy fee: $.50 per page. $.25 per page after first 5. Certification fee: $2.00. Fee payee: Clerk of Court. Personal checks accepted. Prepayment is required.

Limited Jurisdiction Court 515 Broadway, Townsend, MT 59644; 406-266-9231; Fax: 406-266-4720. Hours: 8AM-5PM (MST). *Misdemeanor, Civil Actions Under $7,000, Eviction, Small Claims.*

Carbon County

District Court PO Box 948, Red Lodge, MT 59068; 406-446-1225; Fax: 406-446-1911. Hours: 8AM-5PM (MST). *Felony, Civil Actions, Probate.*

Note: Also, this court holds youth, adoption and sanity records.

Civil Records: Access: Phone, fax, mail, in person. Both court and visitors may perform in person searches. Search fee: $.50 per name per year. Maximum fee-$25.00. Required to search: name, years to search. Civil cases indexed by defendant, plaintiff. Civil records on docket books from 1895; on computer back to 1997.

Criminal Records: Access: Fax, mail, in person. Only the court performs in person searches; visitors may not. Search fee: $.50 per name per year. Maximum fee-$25.00. Required to search: name, years to search.

Criminal records on docket books from 1895; on computer back to 1997.

General Information: No adoption, juvenile or sanity records released. SASE required. Turnaround time 1-2 days. Fax notes: $1.00 per page. Will fax to 800 numbers no charge. Copy fee: $.50 per page. $.25 per page after first 5. Certification fee: $2.00. Fee payee: Clerk of Court. Personal checks accepted. Prepayment is required.

Carbon County Justice Court PO Box 2, Red Lodge, MT 59068; 406-446-1440; Fax: 406-446-1911. Hours: 8AM-5PM (MST). *Misdemeanor, Civil Actions Under $7,000, Eviction, Small Claims.*

Joliet City Court PO Box 210, Joliet, MT 59041; 406-962-3133; Fax: 406-962-9803. Hours: 8AM-1PM on 1st, 2nd &3rd Wed of month (MST). *Misdemeanor, Civil Actions Under $7,000.*

Carter County

District Court PO Box 322, Ekalaka, MT 59324; 406-775-8714; Fax: 406-775-8730. Hours: 8AM-5PM (MST). *Felony, Civil Actions Over $5,000, Eviction, Probate.*

Civil Records: Access: Phone, fax, mail, in person. Both court and visitors may perform in person searches. Search fee: $.50 per name per year. Maximum fee-$25.00. Required to search: name, years to search. Civil cases indexed by defendant, plaintiff. Civil records in books from 1917; computerized back to 1996.

Criminal Records: Access: Phone, fax, mail, in person. Only the court performs in person searches; visitors may not. Search fee: $.50 per name per year. Maximum fee-$25.00. Required to search: name, years to search, signed release; also helpful: SSN. Criminal records in books from 1917; computerized to 1996.

General Information: No adoption, juvenile or sanity records released. SASE required. Turnaround time 1-2 days, same to next day for phone requests. Fax notes: $1.00 per page. Copy fee: $.50 per page. $.25 per page after first 5. Certification fee: $2.00. Fee payee: Clerk of Court. Personal checks accepted. Prepayment is required.

Limited Jurisdiction Court PO Box 72, Ekalaka, MT 59324-0072; 406-775-8754; Fax: 406-775-8714. Hours: 8AM-5PM TH (MST). *Misdemeanor, Civil Actions Under $7,000, Eviction, Small Claims.*

Note: 1st & 3rd Thurs of month here, 2nd & 4th Thurs of month in Alzada (406-775-8749).

Cascade County

District Court County Courthouse, 415 2nd Ave North, Great Falls, MT 59401; 406-454-6780. Hours: 8AM-5PM (MST). *Felony, Civil Actions Over $5,000, Probate.*

Civil Records: Access: Mail, in person. Both court and visitors may perform in person searches. Search fee: $.50 per name per year. Maximum fee-$25.00. Required to search: name, years to search. Civil cases indexed by defendant, plaintiff. Civil records on computer from 1987; on docket books to 1889.

Criminal Records: Access: Mail, in person. Both court and visitors may perform in person searches. Search fee: $.50 per name per year. Maximum fee-$25.00. Required to search: name, years to search, DOB, SSN. Criminal records on computer from 1987; on docket books to 1889.

General Information: Public Access terminal is available. No adoption or sanity records released. SASE required. Turnaround time 1-2 days. Copy fee: $.50 per page. $.25 per page after first 5. Certification fee: $2.00. Fee payee: Clerk of Court. Business checks accepted. Prepayment is required.

Cascade Justice Court Cascade County Courthouse, 415 2nd Ave N, Great Falls, MT 59401; 406-454-6870; Fax: 406-454-6877. Hours: 8AM-5PM (MST). *Misdemeanor, Civil Actions Under $7,000, Eviction, Small Claims.*

Chouteau County

District Court PO Box 459, Ft Benton, MT 59442; 406-622-5024; Fax: 406-622-3028. Hours: 8AM-5PM (MST). *Felony, Civil Actions Over $5,000, Eviction, Probate.*

Civil Records: Access: Fax, mail, in person. Both court and visitors may perform in person searches. Search fee: $.50 per name per year. Maximum fee-$25.00. Required to search: name, years to search. Civil cases indexed by defendant, plaintiff. Civil records on books from 1886; on computer back to 1996.

Criminal Records: Access: Fax, mail, in person. Both court and visitors may perform in person searches. Search fee: $.50 per name per year. Maximum fee-$25.00. Required to search: name, years to search. Criminal records on books from 1886; on computer back to 1996.

General Information: Public Access terminal is available. No adoption, paternity, juvenile or sanity records released. SASE required. Turnaround time 1 day. Fax notes: $2.00 for first page, $1.00 each add'l. Copy fee: $.50 per page. $.25 per page after first 5. Certification fee: $2.00. Fee payee: Clerk of Court. Business checks accepted. Prepayment is required.

Big Sandy Justice Court PO Box 234, Big Sandy, MT 59520; 406-378-2203; Fax: 406-378-2378. Hours: 1-5PM Th (MST). *Misdemeanor, Civil Actions Under $7,000, Eviction, Small Claims.*

Ft Benton Justice Court PO Box 459, Ft Benton, MT 59442; 406-622-5502; Fax: 406-622-3815. Hours: 8AM-4PM M,T,W (MST). *Misdemeanor, Civil Actions Under $7,000, Eviction, Small Claims.*

Custer County

District Court 1010 Main, Miles City, MT 59301-3419; 406-233-3326; Fax: 406-233-3451. Hours: 8AM-5PM (MST). *Felony, Civil Actions Over $5,000, Eviction, Probate.*

Civil Records: Access: Mail, in person. Both court and visitors may perform in person searches. Search fee: $.50 per name per year. Maximum fee-$25.00. Required to search: name, years to search. Civil cases indexed by defendant, plaintiff. Civil records in books.

Criminal Records: Access: Mail, in person. Both court and visitors may perform in person searches. Search fee: $.50 per name per year. Maximum fee-$25.00. Required to search: name, years to search. Criminal records in books.

General Information: Public Access terminal is available. No dependent & neglected, juvenile or sanity records released. SASE required. Turnaround time 1-2 days. Copy fee: $.50 per page. $.25 per page after first 5. Certification fee: $2.00. Fee payee: Clerk of District Court. Personal checks accepted. Prepayment is required.

Limited Jurisdiction Court 1010 Main St, Miles City, MT 59301; 406-233-3408; Fax: 406-233-3452. Hours: 8AM-5PM (MST). *Misdemeanor, Civil Actions Under $7,000, Eviction, Small Claims.*

Daniels County

District Court PO Box 67, Scobey, MT 59263; 406-487-2651. Hours: 8AM-5PM (MST). *Felony, Civil Actions Over $5,000, Eviction, Probate.*

Civil Records: Access: Phone, mail, in person. Both court and visitors may perform in person searches. Search fee: $.50 per name per year. Maximum fee-

$25.00. Required to search: name, years to search. Civil cases indexed by defendant, plaintiff. Civil records on books since 1920; on computer back to 1986.

Criminal Records: Access: Mail, in person. Both court and visitors may perform in person searches. Search fee: $.50 per name per year. Maximum fee-$25.00. Required to search: name, years to search. Criminal records on books since 1920; on computer back to 1986.

General Information: No adoption, juvenile or sanity records released. SASE required. Turnaround time 1-2 days. Fax notes: Fee to fax results is $.50 per page. Copy fee: $.50 per document. Add $.25 per page after first 5. Certification fee: $2.00. Fee payee: Clerk of Court. Personal checks accepted. Prepayment is required.

Limited Jurisdiction Court Daniels County Courthouse, Scobey, MT 59263; 406-487-5432; Fax: 406-487-5432. Hours: 8AM-5PM (MST). *Misdemeanor, Civil Actions Under $7,000, Eviction, Small Claims.*

Dawson County

District Court 207 W Bell, Glendive, MT 59330; 406-377-3967; Fax: 406-377-7280. Hours: 8AM-5PM (MST). *Felony, Civil Actions Over $5,000, Eviction, Probate.*

Civil Records: Access: Mail, in person. Both court and visitors may perform in person searches. Search fee: $.50 per name per year. Maximum fee-$25.00. Required to search: name, years to search. Civil cases indexed by defendant, plaintiff. Civil records on computer from 1991, on card index prior.

Criminal Records: Access: Mail, in person. Only the court performs in person searches; visitors may not. Search fee: $.50 per name per year. Maximum fee-$25.00. Required to search: name, years to search, DOB, SSN. Criminal records on computer from 1991, on card index prior.

General Information: Public Access terminal is available. No adoption, juvenile, sanity or expunged records released. SASE required. Turnaround time same day. Copy fee: $.50 per page. $.25 per page after first 5. Certification fee: $2.00. Fee payee: Justice Court. Only cashiers checks and money orders accepted. Prepayment is required.

Limited Jurisdiction Court 207 W Towne, Glendive, MT 59330; 406-377-5425; Fax: 406-377-2022. Hours: 8AM-5PM (MST). *Misdemeanor, Civil Actions Under $7,000, Eviction, Small Claims.*

Deer Lodge County

District Court 800 S Main, Anaconda, MT 59711; 406-563-4040; Fax: 406-563-4077. Hours: 8AM-5PM (MST). *Felony, Civil Actions Over $5,000, Eviction, Probate.*

Civil Records: Access: Mail, in person. Only the court performs in person searches; visitors may not. Search fee: $.50 per name per year. Maximum fee-$25.00. Required to search: name, years to search. Civil cases indexed by defendant, plaintiff. Civil records in archives and index books; on computer back to 1996.

Criminal Records: Access: Mail, in person. Only the court performs in person searches; visitors may not. Search fee: $.50 per name per year. Maximum fee-$25.00. Required to search: name, years to search. Criminal records in archives and index books; on computer back to 1996.

General Information: Public Access terminal is available. No adoption, juvenile or sanity records released. SASE required. Turnaround time 2-3 days. Fax notes: Fee to fax results is $4.00 per document. Copy fee: $.50 per page. $.25 per page after first 5. Certification fee: $2.00. Fee payee: Clerk of Court. Personal checks accepted.

Limited Jurisdiction Court 800 S Main, Anaconda, MT 59711; 406-563-4025; Fax: 406-563-4028. Hours: 8AM-5PM (MST). *Misdemeanor, Civil Actions Under $7,000, Eviction, Small Claims.*

Fallon County

District Court PO Box 1521, Baker, MT 59313; 406-778-7114; Fax: 406-778-2815. Hours: 8AM-5PM (MST). *Felony, Civil Actions Over $5,000, Eviction, Probate.*

Civil Records: Access: Mail, in person. Both court and visitors may perform in person searches. Search fee: $.50 per name per year. Maximum fee-$25.00. Required to search: name, years to search, address. Civil cases indexed by defendant, plaintiff. Civil records in books.

Criminal Records: Access: Mail, in person. Both court and visitors may perform in person searches. Search fee: $.50 per name per year. Maximum fee-$25.00. Required to search: name, years to search. Criminal records in books.

General Information: Public Access terminal is available. No confidential records released. SASE required. Turnaround time same day. Fax notes: Fee to fax results is $1.00 per page. Copy fee: $.50 per page. $.25 per page after first 5. Certification fee: $2.00. Fee payee: Clerk of Court. Personal checks accepted. Prepayment is required.

Limited Jurisdiction Court Box 846, Baker, MT 59313; 406-778-7128; Fax: 406-778-7128. Hours: 11:00AM-4:00PM T,W,Th (MST). *Misdemeanor, Civil Actions Under $7,000, Eviction, Small Claims.*

Fergus County

District Court PO Box 1074, Lewistown, MT 59457; 406-538-5026; Fax: 406-538-6076. Hours: 8AM-5PM (MST). *Felony, Civil Actions Over $7,000, Eviction, Probate.*

Civil Records: Access: Phone, fax, mail, in person. Both court and visitors may perform in person searches. Search fee: $.50 per name per year. Maximum fee-$25.00. Required to search: name, years to search. Civil cases indexed by defendant, plaintiff. Civil records on docket books, microfiche.

Criminal Records: Access: Phone, fax, mail, in person. Both court and visitors may perform in person searches. Search fee: $.50 per name per year. Maximum fee-$25.00. Required to search: name, years to search. Criminal records on docket books, microfiche.

General Information: No adoption, juvenile, sanity or expunged records released. SASE required. Turnaround time 1 day. Fax notes: $1.00 per page. Copy fee: $.50 per page. $.25 per page after first 5. Certification fee: $2.00. Fee payee: Clerk of Court. Personal checks accepted. Prepayment is required.

Limited Jurisdiction Court 121 8th Ave South, Lewistown, MT 59457; 406-538-5418; Fax: 406-538-3860. Hours: 9AM-4PM (MST). *Misdemeanor, Civil Actions Under $7,000, Eviction, Small Claims.*

Flathead County

District Court 800 S Main (920 S. Main, 3rd Fl), Kalispell, MT 59901; 406-758-5660. Hours: 8AM-5PM (MST). *Felony, Civil Actions Over $5,000, Eviction, Probate.*

www.co.flathead.mt.us/clkcrt/index.html

Civil Records: Access: Phone, mail, in person. Both court and visitors may perform in person searches. Search fee: $.50 per name per year. Maximum fee-$25.00. Required to search: name, years to search. Civil cases indexed by defendant, plaintiff. Civil records on computer since 1/1/93.

Criminal Records: Access: Phone, mail, in person. Only the court performs in person searches; visitors may not. Search fee: $.50 per name per year. Maximum fee-$25.00. Required to search: name, years to search. Criminal records on computer since 1/1/93.

General Information: Public Access terminal is available. No adoption, dependent/neglected children or sanity records released. SASE required. Turnaround time 3 days. Fax notes: Fee to fax results is $.50 per page. Certification fee: $2.00. Fee payee: Clerk of Court. Personal checks accepted. Prepayment is required.

Limited Jurisdiction Court 800 S Main St, Kalispell, MT 59901; 406-758-5643; Fax: 406-758-5642. Hours: 8AM-5PM (MST). *Misdemeanor, Civil Actions Under $7,000, Eviction, Small Claims.*

www.co.flathead.mt.us/justice/index.html

Gallatin County

District Court 615 S 16th, Rm 302, Bozeman, MT 59715; 406-582-2165; Fax: 406-582-2176. Hours: 8AM-5PM (MST). *Felony, Civil Actions Over $7,000, Eviction, Probate.*

Civil Records: Access: Mail, in person. Both court and visitors may perform in person searches. Search fee: $.50 per name per year. Maximum fee-$25.00. Required to search: name, years to search. Civil cases indexed by defendant, plaintiff. Civil records on computer back to 1990; docket books back to 1860.

Criminal Records: Access: Mail, in person. Both court and visitors may perform in person searches. Search fee: $.50 per name per year. Maximum fee-$25.00. Required to search: name, years to search. Criminal records on computer back to 1990; docket books back to 1860.

General Information: Public Access terminal is available. No adoption, juvenile or sanity records released. SASE required. Turnaround time same day. Fax notes: Fee to fax results is $2.00 per page. Copy fee: $.50 per page. $.25 per page after first 5. Certification fee: $2.00. Fee payee: Clerk of Court. Personal checks accepted. Prepayment is required.

Belgrade Justice & City Court 91 E Central, Belgrade, MT 59714; 406-388-3774; Fax: 406-388-3779. Hours: 8AM-Noon M,W,F (MST). *Misdemeanor, Civil Actions Under $7,000, Eviction, Small Claims.*

Bozeman Justice Court 615 S 16th St, Bozeman, MT 59715; 406-582-2191; Fax: 406-582-2041. Hours: 8AM-5PM (MST). *Misdemeanor, Civil Actions Under $7,000, Eviction, Small Claims.*

Garfield County

District Court PO Box 8, Jordan, MT 59337; 406-557-6254; Fax: 406-557-2625. Hours: 8AM-5PM (MST). *Felony, Civil Actions Over $5,000, Eviction, Probate.*

Civil Records: Access: Phone, mail, in person. Both court and visitors may perform in person searches. Search fee: $.50 per name per year. Maximum fee-$25.00. Required to search: name, years to search. Civil cases indexed by plaintiff. Civil records in books from early 1900s. Some records lost due to fire in December, 1997.

Criminal Records: Access: Phone, mail, in person. Both court and visitors may perform in person searches. Search fee: $.50 per name per year. Maximum fee-$25.00. Required to search: name, years to search; also helpful: DOB. Criminal records in books from early 1900s. Some records lost due to fire in December, 1997.

General Information: No adoption, juvenile or sanity records released. SASE required. Turnaround time 1 week. Copy fee: $.50 per page. $.25 per page after first 5. Certification fee: $2.00. Fee payee: Clerk of Court. Personal checks accepted. Prepayment is required.

Limited Jurisdiction Court PO Box 482, Jordan, MT 59337; 406-557-2733; Fax: 406-557-2735. Hours: 8AM-5PM Wed (MST). *Misdemeanor, Civil Actions Under $7,000, Eviction, Small Claims.*

Glacier County

District Court 512 E Main St, Cut Bank, MT 59427; 406-873-5063 X36; Fax: 406-873-5627. Hours: 8AM-5PM (MST). *Felony, Civil Actions, Eviction, Probate.*

Civil Records: Access: Phone, fax, mail, in person. Both court and visitors may perform in person searches. Search fee: $.50 per name per year. Maximum fee-$25.00. Required to search: name, years to search. Civil cases indexed by defendant, plaintiff. Civil records in books from 1919; on computer since.

Criminal Records: Access: Fax, mail, in person. Both court and visitors may perform in person searches. Search fee: $.50 per name per year. Maximum fee-$25.00. Required to search: name, years to search; also helpful: DOB, SSN. Criminal records in books from 1919; on computer since. Written request required.

General Information: No adoption, juvenile, sanity or paternity records released without court order. SASE required. Turnaround time usually same day, 2-3 hours for phone requests, depending on workload. Fax notes: $1.00 per page. Copy fee: $.50 per page. $.25 per page after first 5. Certification fee: $2.00. Fee payee: Clerk of District Court. Personal checks accepted. Prepayment is required.

Limited Jurisdiction Court 512 E Main St, Cut Bank, MT 59427; 406-873-5063 X39; Fax: 406-873-4218. Hours: 8AM-Noon, 1-5PM (MST). *Misdemeanor, Civil Actions Under $7,000, Eviction, Small Claims.*

Golden Valley County

District Court PO Box 10, Ryegate, MT 59074; 406-568-2231; Fax: 406-568-2598. Hours: 8AM-5PM (MST). *Felony, Civil Actions Over $5,000, Eviction, Probate.*

Civil Records: Access: Fax, mail, in person. Search fee: $.50 per name per year. Maximum fee-$25.00. Required to search: name, years to search. Civil cases indexed by defendant, plaintiff. Civil records on books.

Criminal Records: Access: Fax, mail, in person. Only the court performs in person searches; visitors may not. Search fee: $.50 per name per year. Maximum fee-$25.00. Required to search: name, years to search. Criminal records on books.

General Information: No adoption, juvenile or sanity records released. SASE required. Turnaround time 2-3 days. Fax notes: $1.00 per page; no fee to a toll-free number. Copy fee: $.50 per page. $.25 per page after first 5. Certification fee: $2.00. Fee payee: Clerk of Court. Personal checks accepted. Prepayment is required.

Limited Jurisdiction Court PO Box 10, Ryegate, MT 59074; 406-568-2272; Fax: 406-568-2598. Hours: 10AM-2PM Tues (MST). *Misdemeanor, Civil Actions Under $7,000, Eviction, Small Claims.*

Granite County

District Court PO Box 399, Philipsburg, MT 59858-0399; 406-859-3712; Fax: 406-859-3817. Hours: 8AM-Noon, 1-5PM (MST). *Felony, Civil Actions Over $5,000, Eviction, Probate.*

Civil Records: Access: Phone, fax, mail, in person. Both court and visitors may perform in person searches. Search fee: $.50 per name per year. Maximum fee-$25.00. Sorequired to search: name, years to search. Civil cases indexed by defendant, plaintiff. Civil records on docket books since 1893.

Criminal Records: Access: Phone, fax, mail, in person. Both court and visitors may perform in person searches. Search fee: $.50 per name per year. Maximum fee-$25.00. Required to search: name, years to search. Criminal records on docket books since 1893.

General Information: No adoption, juvenile or sanity records released. SASE required. Turnaround time 1-4 days. Copy fee: $.50 per page. $.25 per page after first 5. Certification fee: $2.00. Fee payee: Clerk of Court. Personal checks accepted. Prepayment is required.

Drummond Justice Court PO Box 159, Drummond, MT 59832; 406-288-3446; Fax: 406-288-3050. Hours: 9AM-4PM M,W,F (MST). *Misdemeanor, Civil Actions Under $7,000, Eviction, Small Claims.*

Philipsburg Justice Court PO Box 356, Philipsburg, MT 59858; 406-859-3006; Fax: 406-859-3817. Hours: 11AM-Noon, 1-5PM M,W,F (MST). *Misdemeanor, Civil Actions Under $7,000, Eviction, Small Claims.*

Hill County

District Court Hill County Courthouse, Havre, MT 59501; 406-265-5481 X224; Fax: 406-265-1273. Hours: 8AM-5PM (MST). *Felony, Civil Actions Over $5,000, Eviction, Probate.*

http://co.hill.mt.us

Civil Records: Access: Phone, fax, mail, in person. Both court and visitors may perform in person searches. Search fee: $.50 per name per year. Maximum fee-$25.00. Required to search: name, years to search. Civil cases indexed by defendant, plaintiff. Civil records on computer since 1985; prior records on docket books. Maiden name helpful in searching.

Criminal Records: Access: Fax, mail, in person. Both court and visitors may perform in person searches. Search fee: $.50 per name per year. Maximum fee-$25.00. Required to search: name, years to search; also helpful: maiden name. Criminal records on computer since 1988; prior records on docket books.

General Information: Public Access terminal is available. No adoption, juvenile, paternity, sanity records released. SASE required. Turnaround time 2-3 days. Fax notes: $1.00 per page. Copy fee: $.50 per page. $.25 per page after first 5. Certification fee: $2.00. Fee payee: Clerk of Court. Business checks accepted. Prepayment is required.

Limited Jurisdiction Court Hill County Courthouse, Havre, MT 59501; 406-265-5481 X240; Fax: 406-265-5487. Hours: 8AM-4PM (MST). *Misdemeanor, Civil Actions Under $7,000, Eviction, Small Claims.*

http://co.hill.mt.us

Jefferson County

District Court PO Box H, Boulder, MT 59632; 406-225-4041 & 4042; Fax: 406-225-4149. Hours: 8AM-Noon, 1-5PM (MST). *Felony, Civil Actions Over $7,000, Eviction, Probate.*

Civil Records: Access: Mail, fax, in person. Both court and visitors may perform in person searches. Search fee: $.50 per name per year. Maximum fee-$25.00. Required to search: name, years to search. Civil cases indexed by defendant, plaintiff. Civil records on computer since 1992, on microfilm since 1925.

Criminal Records: Access: Mail, fax, in person. Both court and visitors may perform in person searches. Search fee: $.50 per name per year. Maximum fee-$25.00. Required to search: name, years to search. Criminal records on computer since 1992, on microfilm since 1925.

General Information: Public Access terminal is available. Juvenile, sanity or adoption records not released. SASE required. Turnaround time same day. Fax notes: Fee to fax results is $1.00 per page. Copy fee: $.50 per page. $.25 per page after first 5. Certification fee: $2.00. Fee payee: Clerk of Court. Personal checks accepted. Prepayment is required.

Limited Jurisdiction Court PO Box H, Boulder, MT 59632; 406-225-4055. Hours: 8AM-5PM (MST). *Misdemeanor, Civil Actions Under $7,000, Eviction, Small Claims.*

Judith Basin County

District Court PO Box 307, Stanford, MT 59479; 406-566-2277 X113; Fax: 406-566-2211. Hours: 8AM-5PM (MST). *Felony, Civil Actions Over $5,000, Eviction, Probate.*

Civil Records: Access: Phone, mail, in person. Both court and visitors may perform in person searches. Search fee: $.50 per name per year. Maximum fee-$25.00. Required to search: name, years to search. Civil cases indexed by defendant, plaintiff. Civil records on books.
Criminal Records: Access: Phone, mail, in person. Both court and visitors may perform in person searches. Search fee: $.50 per name per year. Maximum fee-$25.00. Required to search: name, years to search, signed release. Criminal records on books.
General Information: No adoption, sanity records released. SASE required. Turnaround time 10 days. Copy fee: $.50 per page. $.25 per page after first 5. Certification fee: $2.00. Fee payee: Clerk of Court. Business checks accepted. Prepayment is required.

Hobson Justice Court PO Box 276, Hobson, MT 59452; 406-423-5503. Hours: 4:30-9:30PM M-Th (MST). *Misdemeanor, Civil Actions Under $7,000, Eviction, Small Claims.*

Stanford Justice Court PO Box 339, Stanford, MT 59479; 406-566-2277 X117. Hours: 9AM-Noon M,W,F (MST). *Misdemeanor, Civil Actions Under $7,000, Eviction, Small Claims.*

Lake County

District Court Clerk of District Court Office, 106 4th Ave E, Polson, MT 59860; 406-883-7254; Fax: 406-883-7343. Hours: 8AM-5PM (MST). *Felony, Civil Actions Over $7,000, Probate.*

Civil Records: Access: Phone, fax, mail, in person. Both court and visitors may perform in person searches. Search fee: $.50 per name per year. Maximum fee-$25.00. Required to search: name, years to search. Civil cases indexed by defendant, plaintiff. Civil records on books since 1923; on computer since 1990.
Criminal Records: Access: Phone, fax, mail, in person. Both court and visitors may perform in person searches. Search fee: $.50 per name per year. Maximum fee-$25.00. Required to search: name, years to search, DOB, SSN. Criminal records on books since 1923; on computer since 1990.
General Information: Public Access terminal is available. No adoption, juvenile, sanity or expunged records released. SASE required. Turnaround time 3 days; 2 hours for phone requests. Fax notes: $1.00 per page. Copy fee: $.50 per page. $.25 per page after first 5. Certification fee: $2.00. Fee payee: Clerk of Court. Business checks accepted. Prepayment is required.

Limited Jurisdiction Court 106 4th Ave E, Polson, MT 59860; 406-883-7258; Fax: 406-883-7343. Hours: 8AM-5PM (MST). *Misdemeanor, Civil Actions Under $7,000, Eviction, Small Claims.*

Lewis and Clark County

District Court 228 Broadway, PO Box 158, Helena, MT 59624; 406-447-8216; Fax: 406-447-8275. Hours: 8AM-5PM (MST). *Felony, Civil Actions Over $5,000, Eviction, Probate, Small Claims.*

www.co.lewis-clark.mt.us

Civil Records: Access: Fax, mail, online, in person. Both court and visitors may perform in person searches. Search fee: $.50 per name per year. Maximum fee-$25.00. Required to search: name, years to search. Civil cases indexed by defendant, plaintiff. Civil records on computer since 9/90, microfilm prior to 01/89. Will accept e-mail record requests to jwright@co.lewis-clark.mt.us.
Criminal Records: Access: Fax, mail, online, in person. Both court and visitors may perform in person searches. Search fee: $.50 per name per year. Maximum fee-$25.00. Required to search: name, years to search. Criminal records on computer since 1/93, microfilm prior to 1/90. Will accept e-mail record requests to jwright@co.lewis-clark.mt.us.
General Information: Public Access terminal is available. No adoption, juvenile or sanity records released. SASE required. Turnaround time 2 days. Fax notes: $1.00 per page. Copy fee: $.50 per page. $.25 per page after first 5. Certification fee: $2.00. Fee payee: Clerk of Court. Personal checks accepted. Prepayment is required.

Limited Jurisdiction Court 228 Broadway, Helena, MT 59623; 406-447-8202; Fax: 406-447-8269. Hours: 8AM-5PM (MST). *Misdemeanor, Civil Actions Under $7,000, Eviction, Small Claims.*

Liberty County

District Court PO Box 549, Chester, MT 59522; 406-759-5615; Fax: 406-759-5996. Hours: 8AM-5PM (MST). *Felony, Civil Actions Over $5,000, Eviction, Probate.*

Civil Records: Access: Phone, mail, in person. Only the court performs in person searches; visitors may not. Search fee: $.50 per name per year. Maximum fee-$25.00. Required to search: name, years to search, address. Civil cases indexed by defendant, plaintiff. Civil records on books since 1920.
Criminal Records: Access: Phone, mail, in person. Both court and visitors may perform in person searches. Search fee: $.50 per name per year. Maximum fee-$25.00. Required to search: name, years to search, signed release. Criminal records on books since 1920.
General Information: No adoption, juvenile or sanity records released. SASE required. Turnaround time 2-3 days. Copy fee: $.50 per page. $.25 per page after first 5. Certification fee: $2.00. Fee payee: Clerk of Court. Personal checks accepted. Prepayment is required.

Limited Jurisdiction Court PO Box K, Chester, MT 59522; 406-759-5172; Fax: 406-759-5395. Hours: 9AM-5PM Tues (MST). *Misdemeanor, Civil Actions Under $7,000, Eviction, Small Claims.*

Lincoln County

District Court 512 California Ave, Libby, MT 59923; 406-293-7781; Fax: 406-293-9816. Hours: 8AM-5PM (MST). *Felony, Civil Actions Over $5,000, Eviction, Probate.*

Civil Records: Access: Mail, in person. Both court and visitors may perform in person searches. Search fee: $3.00 per name for ten year search; $.50 each add'l year with $25.00 maximum. Required to search: name, years to search. Civil cases indexed by defendant, plaintiff. Civil records on computer from 1991, prior on docket books.
Criminal Records: Access: Mail, in person. Both court and visitors may perform in person searches. Search

fee: $3.00 per name. Fee is for 10 year search. Maximum fee $25.00. Required to search: name, years to search, DOB. Criminal records on computer from 1991, prior on docket books.
General Information: No adoption, juvenile or sanity records released. SASE required. Turnaround time 1 week. Copy fee: $.50 per page. $.25 per page after first 5. Certification fee: $2.00. Fee payee: Clerk of Court. Personal checks accepted. Prepayment is required.

Eureka Justice Court #2 Highway 93 North, Eureka, MT 59917; 406-296-2622; Fax: 406-296-3829. Hours: 8AM-5M M-W (MST). *Misdemeanor, Civil Actions Under $7,000, Eviction, Small Claims.*

Libby Justice Court #1 418 Mineral Ave, Libby, MT 59923; 406-293-7781 X236; Fax: 406-293-5948. Hours: 8AM-5PM (MST). *Misdemeanor, Civil Actions Under $7,000, Eviction, Small Claims.*

Madison County

District Court PO Box 185, Virginia City, MT 59755; 406-843-4230; Fax: 406-843-5207. Hours: 8AM-5PM (MST). *Felony, Civil Actions Over $5,000, Eviction, Probate.*

Civil Records: Access: Phone, fax, mail, in person. Both court and visitors may perform in person searches. Search fee: $.50 per name per year. Maximum fee-$25.00. Required to search: name, years to search. Civil cases indexed by defendant, plaintiff. Civil records on books since 1864; on computer back to 1990.
Criminal Records: Access: Fax, mail, in person. Only the court performs in person searches; visitors may not. Search fee: $.50 per name per year. Maximum fee-$25.00. Required to search: name, years to search. Criminal records on books since 1864; on computer back to 1990.
General Information: Public Access terminal is available. No adoption, juvenile or sanity records released. SASE required. Turnaround time 1 week. Fax notes: Fee to fax results is $4.00 1st page, $1.00 each add'l. Copy fee: $.50 per page. $.25 per page after first 5. Certification fee: $2.00. Fee payee: Clerk of Court. Personal checks accepted. Prepayment is required.

Limited Jurisdiction Court PO Box 277, Virginia City, MT 59755; 406-843-4230; Fax: 406-843-5517. Hours: 8AM-5PM (MST). *Misdemeanor, Civil Actions Under $7,000, Eviction, Small Claims.*

McCone County

District Court PO Box 199, Circle, MT 59215; 406-485-3410; Fax: 406-485-3410. Hours: 8AM-5PM (MST). *Felony, Civil Actions Over $5,000, Eviction, Probate.*

Civil Records: Access: Mail, in person. Only the court performs in person searches; visitors may not. Search fee: $.50 per name per year. Maximum fee-$25.00. Required to search: name, years to search. Civil cases indexed by defendant, plaintiff. Civil records in books from 1919.
Criminal Records: Access: Mail, in person. Only the court performs in person searches; visitors may not. Search fee: $.50 per name per year. Maximum fee-$25.00. Required to search: name, years to search. Criminal records in books and microfilm since 1919.
General Information: No adoption, juvenile, sanity or mental health records released. SASE required. Turnaround time 1-2 days. Copy fee: $.50 per page. $.25 per page after first 5. Certification fee: $2.00. Fee payee: Clerk of Court. Personal checks accepted. Prepayment is required.

Limited Jurisdiction Court PO Box 24, Circle, MT 59215; 406-485-3548. Hours: 2-5PM Wed (MST). *Misdemeanor, Civil Actions Under $7,000, Eviction, Small Claims.*

Meagher County

District Court PO Box 443, White Sulphur Springs, MT 59645; 406-547-3612 Ext110; Fax: 406-547-3836. Hours: 8AM-5PM (MST). *Felony, Civil Actions Over $5,000, Eviction, Probate.*

Civil Records: Access: Phone, mail, fax, in person. Both court and visitors may perform in person searches. Search fee: $.50 per name per year. Maximum fee-$25.00. Required to search: name, years to search. Civil cases indexed by defendant, plaintiff. Civil records on docket books or microfiche to 1900; on computer back to 1996.

Criminal Records: Access: Phone, mail, fax, in person. Both court and visitors may perform in person searches. Search fee: $.50 per name per year. Maximum fee-$25.00. Required to search: name, years to search, DOB. Criminal records on docket books or microfiche to 1900; on computer back to 1996.

General Information: No adoption, juvenile or sanity records released. SASE required. Turnaround time 3 days. Copy fee: $.50 per page. $.25 per page after first 5. Certification fee: $2.00. Fee payee: Clerk of Court. Personal checks accepted.

Limited Jurisdiction Court Justice Court, W. Main St., White Sulphur Springs, MT 59645; 406-547-3954 X115; Fax: 406-547-3388. Hours: 8AM-5PM T-Th (MST). *Misdemeanor, Civil Actions Under $7,000, Eviction, Small Claims.*

Mineral County

District Court PO Box 129, Superior, MT 59872; 406-822-3538; Fax: 406-822-3579. Hours: 8AM-Noon,1-5PM (MST). *Felony, Civil Actions Over $5,000, Probate.*

Civil Records: Access: Phone, fax, mail, in person. Both court and visitors may perform in person searches. Search fee: $.50 per name per year. Maximum fee-$25.00. Required to search: name, years to search. Civil cases indexed by defendant, plaintiff. Civil records on docket books from 1914, on computer back to 1990.

Criminal Records: Access: Phone, fax, mail, in person. Only the court performs in person searches; visitors may not. Search fee: $.50 per name per year. Maximum fee-$25.00. Required to search: name, years to search. Criminal records on docket books from 1914, on computer back to 1990.

General Information: No adoption, sanity records released. SASE required. Turnaround time same day after payment received. Fax notes: Fee to fax results is $5.00 per document. Copy fee: $.50 per page. $.25 per page after first 5. Certification fee: $2.00. Fee payee: Clerk of Court. Personal checks accepted. Prepayment is required.

Limited Jurisdiction Court PO Box 658, Superior, MT 59872; 406-822-3550; Fax: 406-822-3579. Hours: 8AM-5PM (MST). *Misdemeanor, Civil Actions Under $7,000, Eviction, Small Claims.*

Missoula County

District Court 200 W Broadway, Missoula, MT 59802; 406-523-4780 X3523; Fax: 406-523-4899. Hours: 8AM-5PM (MST). *Felony, Civil Actions Over $5,000, Probate.*

Civil Records: Access: Fax, mail, in person. Both court and visitors may perform in person searches. Search fee: $.50 per name per year. Maximum fee-$25.00. Required to search: name, years to search. Civil cases indexed by defendant, plaintiff. Civil records on computer from 10/89, microfilm from 1970s, archived to late 1800s.

Criminal Records: Access: Fax, mail, in person. Both court and visitors may perform in person searches. Search fee: $.50 per name per year. Maximum fee-$25.00. Required to search: name, years to search.

Criminal records on computer from 10/89, microfilm from 1970s, archived to late 1800s.

General Information: Public Access terminal is available. No adoption, juvenile, sealed, expunged or pre-sentence psychiatric records released. SASE not required. Turnaround time up to 2 weeks. Fax notes: $2.00 per document. No fee if returning on toll free line. Copy fee: $.50 per page. $.25 per page after first 5. Certification fee: $2.00. Fee payee: Clerk of Court. Personal checks accepted. Credit cards accepted: Visa, MasterCard. Prepayment is required.

Limited Jurisdiction Court - Dept 1 200 W Broadway, Missoula County Courthouse, Missoula, MT 59802; 406-721-2703; Fax: 406-721-4043. Hours: 8AM-5PM (MST). *Misdemeanor, Civil Actions Under $7,000, Eviction, Small Claims.*

Musselshell County

District Court PO Box 357, Roundup, MT 59072; 406-323-1413; Fax: 406-323-1710. Hours: 8AM-5PM (MST). *Felony, Civil Actions Over $5,000, Eviction, Probate.*

Civil Records: Access: Mail, in person. Both court and visitors may perform in person searches. Search fee: $.50 per name per year. Maximum fee-$25.00. Required to search: name, years to search. Civil cases indexed by defendant, plaintiff. Civil records on docket books from 1911.

Criminal Records: Access: Mail, in person. Both court and visitors may perform in person searches. Search fee: $.50 per name per year. Maximum fee-$25.00. Required to search: name, years to search. Criminal records on docket books from 1911.

General Information: No adoption, (some) juvenile or sanity records released. SASE required. Turnaround time 2-3 days. Copy fee: $.50 per page. $.25 per page after first 5. Certification fee: $2.00. Fee payee: Clerk of Court. Personal checks accepted. Prepayment is required.

Limited Jurisdiction Court PO Box 660, Roundup, MT 59072; 406-323-1078; Fax: 406-323-3452. Hours: 9AM-Noon (MST). *Misdemeanor, Civil Actions Under $7,000, Eviction, Small Claims.*

Park County

District Court PO Box 437, Livingston, MT 59047; 406-222-4125; Fax: 406-222-4128. Hours: 8AM-5PM (MST). *Felony, Civil Actions Over $7,000, Eviction, Probate.*

Civil Records: Access: Fax, mail, in person. Both court and visitors may perform in person searches. Search fee: $.50 per name per year. Maximum fee-$25.00. Required to search: name, years to search. Civil cases indexed by defendant, plaintiff. Civil records on computer, microfiche, and docket books from 1889 to present.

Criminal Records: Access: Fax, mail, in person. Both court and visitors may perform in person searches. Search fee: $.50 per name per year. Maximum fee-$25.00. Required to search: name, years to search. Criminal records on computer, microfiche, and docket books from 1889 to present.

General Information: Public Access terminal is available. No adoption, juvenile or sanity records released. SASE not required. Turnaround time 1-2 days for all requests. Copy fee: $.50 per page. $.25 per page after first 5. Certification fee: $2.00. Fee payee: Clerk of Court. Personal checks accepted. Prepayment is required.

Limited Jurisdiction Court 414 E Callender, Livingston, MT 59047; 406-222-4169/4171; Fax: 406-222-4103. Hours: 8AM-5PM (MST). *Misdemeanor, Civil Actions Under $7,000, Eviction, Small Claims.*

Petroleum County

District Court PO Box 226, Winnett, MT 59087; 406-429-5311; Fax: 406-429-6328. Hours: 8AM-5PM (MST). *Felony, Civil Actions Over $5,000, Eviction, Probate.*

Civil Records: Access: Phone, mail, in person. Both court and visitors may perform in person searches. Search fee: $.50 per name per year. Maximum fee-$25.00. Required to search: name, years to search. Civil cases indexed by defendant, plaintiff. Civil records on docket books from 1924.

Criminal Records: Access: Phone, mail, in person. Only the court performs in person searches; visitors may not. Search fee: $.50 per name per year. Maximum fee-$25.00. Required to search: name, years to search. Criminal records on docket books from 1924.

General Information: No adoption, juvenile or sanity records released. SASE required. Turnaround time 1 day. Copy fee: $.50 per page. $.25 per page after first 5. Certification fee: $2.00. Fee payee: Clerk of Court. Personal checks accepted. Prepayment is required.

Limited Jurisdiction Court PO Box 223, Winnett, MT 59087; 406-429-5311; Fax: 406-429-6328. Hours: 9AM-Noon Th (MST). *Misdemeanor, Civil Actions Under $7,000, Eviction, Small Claims.*

Phillips County

District Court PO Box 530, Malta, MT 59538; 406-654-1023; Fax: 406-654-1023. Hours: 8AM-5PM (MST). *Felony, Civil Actions Over $5,000, Eviction, Probate.*

Civil Records: Access: Fax, mail, in person. Only the court performs in person searches; visitors may not. Search fee: $.50 per name per year. Maximum fee-$25.00. Required to search: name, years to search; also helpful: address. Civil cases indexed by defendant, plaintiff. Civil records on computer, books, microfilm back to 1915.

Criminal Records: Access: Mail, in person. Only the court performs in person searches; visitors may not. Search fee: $.50 per name per year. Maximum fee-$25.00. Required to search: name, years to search, signed release; also helpful: address. Criminal records on computer, books, microfilm back to 1915.

General Information: No adoption, juvenile or sanity records released. SASE required. Turnaround time 1-2 days. Fax notes: There is a $5.00 fee to return by fax, unless a toll free line is used. Copy fee: $.50 per page. $.25 per page after first 5. Certification fee: $2.00. Fee payee: Clerk of Court. Personal checks accepted. Prepayment is required.

Limited Jurisdiction Court PO Box 1396, Malta, MT 59538; 406-654-1118; Fax: 406-654-1213. Hours: 10AM-4PM M-Th (MST). *Misdemeanor, Civil Actions Under $7,000, Eviction, Small Claims.*

Pondera County

District Court 20 Fourth Ave SW, Conrad, MT 59425; 406-271-4026; Fax: 406-271-4081. Hours: 8AM-5PM (MST). *Felony, Civil Actions Over $5,000, Eviction, Probate.*

Civil Records: Access: Fax, mail, in person. Both court and visitors may perform in person searches. Search fee: $.50 per name per year. Maximum fee-$25.00. Required to search: name, years to search. Civil cases indexed by defendant, plaintiff. Civil records on docket books from 1919; on computer back to 1995.

Criminal Records: Access: Fax, mail, in person. Both court and visitors may perform in person searches. Search fee: $.50 per name per year. Maximum fee-$25.00. Required to search: name, years to search. Criminal records on docket books from 1919; on computer back to 1995.

General Information: No adoption or sanity records released. SASE required. Turnaround time 2-3 days. Fax notes: Fax fee: $.50 1st 5 pages, $.25 each additional page. $1.00 for cover page. Copy fee: $.50 per page. $.25 per page after first 5. Certification fee: $2.00. Fee payee: Clerk of Court. Personal checks accepted. Prepayment is required.

Limited Jurisdiction Court 20 Fourth Ave SW, Conrad, MT 59425; 406-278-4030; Fax: 406-278-4070. Hours: 9AM-4PM (MST). *Misdemeanor, Civil Actions Under $7,000, Eviction, Small Claims.*

Powder River County

District Court PO Box 239, Broadus, MT 59317; 406-436-2320; Fax: 406-436-2325. Hours: 8AM-Noon, 1-5PM (MST). *Felony, Civil Actions Over $5,000, Eviction, Probate.*

Civil Records: Access: Fax, mail, in person. Both court and visitors may perform in person searches. Search fee: $.50 per name per year. Maximum fee-$25.00. Required to search: name, years to search. Civil cases indexed by defendant, plaintiff. Civil records on computer since 1993, microfiche since 1974, and books since 1919.
Criminal Records: Access: Fax, mail, in person. Both court and visitors may perform in person searches. Search fee: $.50 per name per year. Maximum fee-$25.00. Required to search: name, years to search. Criminal records on computer since 1993, microfiche since 1974, and books since 1919.
General Information: Public Access terminal is available. No adoption, juvenile, sanity, dismissed criminal records released. SASE required. Turnaround time same day if pre-paid. Fax notes: Fee to fax is $.50 per page. Copy fee: $.50 per page. $.25 per page after first 5. Certification fee: $2.00. Fee payee: Clerk of Court. Only cashiers checks and money orders accepted. Prepayment is required.

Limited Jurisdiction Court PO Box 488, Broadus, MT 59317; 406-436-2503; Fax: 406-436-2866. Hours: 9AM-3:30PM M-Th (MST). *Misdemeanor, Civil Actions Under $7,000, Eviction, Small Claims.*

Powell County

District Court 409 Missouri Ave, Deer Lodge, MT 59722; 406-846-3680 X234/235; Fax: 406-846-2784. Hours: 8AM-5PM (MST). *Felony, Civil Actions Over $5,000, Eviction, Probate.*

Civil Records: Access: Mail, in person. Both court and visitors may perform in person searches. Search fee: $.50 per name per year. Maximum fee-$25.00. Required to search: name, years to search. Civil cases indexed by defendant, plaintiff. Civil records on docket books since turn of century, on computer since 1996.
Criminal Records: Access: Mail, in person. Both court and visitors may perform in person searches. Search fee: $.50 per name per year. Maximum fee-$25.00. Required to search: name, years to search, DOB, SSN. Criminal records on docket books since turn of century, on computer since 1996.
General Information: No adoption, juvenile or sanity records released. SASE required. Turnaround time 2-3 days, immediately over phone. Copy fee: $.50 per page. $.25 per page after first 5. Certification fee: $2.00. Fee payee: Clerk of Court. Personal checks accepted. Prepayment is required.

Limited Jurisdiction Court 409 Missouri, Powell County Courthouse, Deer Lodge, MT 59722; 406-846-3680 X40. Hours: 8AM-5PM (MST). *Misdemeanor, Civil Actions Under $7,000, Eviction, Small Claims.*

Prairie County

District Court PO Box 125, Terry, MT 59349; 406-635-5575. Hours: 8AM-5PM (MST). *Felony, Civil Actions Over $5,000, Eviction, Probate.*

Civil Records: Access: Mail, in person. Both court and visitors may perform in person searches. Search fee: $.50 per name. Maximum fee-$25.00. Required to search: name, years to search. Civil cases indexed by defendant, plaintiff. Civil records on books since 1915.
Criminal Records: Access: Mail, in person. Both court and visitors may perform in person searches. Search fee: $.50 per name. Maximum fee-$25.00. Required to search: name, years to search, DOB, SSN. Criminal records on books since 1915.
General Information: No adoption, juvenile or sanity records released. SASE required. Turnaround time 5 days. Copy fee: $.25 per page. Certification fee: $2.00. Fee payee: Clerk of Court. Personal checks accepted.

Limited Jurisdiction Court PO Box 40, Terry, MT 59349; 406-635-4466; Fax: 406-635-5580. Hours: 1-2PM (MST). *Misdemeanor, Civil Actions Under $7,000, Eviction, Small Claims.*

Ravalli County

District Court Ravalli County Courthouse, Box 5014, Hamilton, MT 59840; 406-375-6214; Fax: 406-375-6327. Hours: 8AM-5PM (MST). *Felony, Civil Actions Over $7,000, Probate.*

Civil Records: Access: Fax, mail, in person. Both court and visitors may perform in person searches. Search fee: $.50 per name per year. Maximum fee-$25.00. Required to search: name, years to search. Civil cases indexed by defendant, plaintiff. Civil records on microfiche (1989), docket books (1914).
Criminal Records: Access: Fax, mail, in person. Both court and visitors may perform in person searches. Search fee: $.50 per name per year. Maximum fee-$25.00. Required to search: name, years to search. Criminal records on microfiche (1989), docket books (1914).
General Information: Public Access terminal is available. No adoption, juvenile, psychological, medical or expunged records released. SASE required. Turnaround time 4-5 days. Fax notes: $1.00 per page. Copy fee: $.50 per page. $.25 per page after first 5. Certification fee: $2.00. Fee payee: Clerk of Court. Personal checks accepted. Prepayment is required.

Limited Jurisdiction Court Courthouse Box 5023, Hamilton, MT 59840; 406-375-6252; Fax: 406-375-6383. Hours: 8AM-5PM (MST). *Misdemeanor, Civil Actions Under $7,000, Eviction, Small Claims.*

Richland County

District Court 201 W Main, Sidney, MT 59270; 406-433-1709; Fax: 406-433-6945. Hours: 8AM-5PM (MST). *Felony, Civil Actions Over $5,000, Eviction, Probate.*

Civil Records: Access: Phone, fax, mail, in person. Both court and visitors may perform in person searches. Search fee: $.50 per name per year. Maximum fee-$25.00. Required to search: name, years to search. Civil cases indexed by defendant, plaintiff. Civil records in books since 1914; on computer back to 1997.
Criminal Records: Access: Phone, fax, mail, in person. Both court and visitors may perform in person searches. Search fee: $.50 per name per year. Maximum fee-$25.00. Required to search: name, years to search. Criminal records in books since 1914; on computer back to 1997.
General Information: No adoption, juvenile, paternity, sanity, dismissed or expunged records released. SASE required. Turnaround time 1-3 days. Fax notes: $1.00 per page. Copy fee: $.50 per page. $.25 per page after first 5. Certification fee: $2.00. Fee payee: Clerk of

Court. Personal checks accepted. Prepayment is required.

Limited Jurisdiction Court 123 W Main, Sidney, MT 59270; 406-433-2815; Fax: 406-433-6885. Hours: 8AM-5PM (MST). *Misdemeanor, Civil Actions Under $7,000, Eviction, Small Claims.*

Roosevelt County

District Court County Courthouse, Wolf Point, MT 59201; 406-653-6266; Fax: 406-653-6203. Hours: 8AM-5PM (MST). *Felony, Civil Actions Over $5,000, Eviction, Probate.*

Civil Records: Access: Fax, mail, in person. Only the court performs in person searches; visitors may not. Search fee: $.50 per name per year. Maximum fee-$25.00. Required to search: name, years to search. Civil cases indexed by defendant, plaintiff. Civil records on books and microfiche.
Criminal Records: Access: Fax, mail, in person. Only the court performs in person searches; visitors may not. Search fee: $.50 per name per year. Maximum fee-$25.00. Required to search: name, years to search; also helpful: DOB. Criminal records on books and microfiche.
General Information: No adoption, juvenile or sanity records released. SASE required. Turnaround time 2-3 days after receipt of payment. Fax notes: Fee to fax results is $3.00 per document. Copy fee: $.50 per page. $.25 per page after first 5. Certification fee: $2.00. Fee payee: Clerk of Court. Personal checks accepted. Prepayment is required.

Culbertson Justice Court Post #2 PO Box 421, Culbertson, MT 59218; 406-787-6607; Fax: 406-787-6607. Hours: 9AM-3PM M-Th (MST). *Misdemeanor, Civil Actions Under $7,000, Eviction, Small Claims.*

Wolf Point Justice Court Post #1 County Courthouse, 400 Second Ave. S., Wolf Point, MT 59201; 406-653-6261; Fax: 406-653-6203. Hours: 8AM-1PM M-Th; 8AM-Noon Fri. (MST). *Misdemeanor, Civil Actions Under $7,000, Eviction, Small Claims.*

Rosebud County

District Court PO Box 48, Forsyth, MT 59327; 406-356-7322; Fax: 406-356-7551. Hours: 8AM-5PM (MST). *Felony, Civil Actions Over $5,000, Eviction, Probate.*

Civil Records: Access: Fax, mail, in person. Only the court performs in person searches; visitors may not. Search fee: $.50 per name per year. Maximum fee-$25.00, written requests only. Required to search: name, years to search. Civil cases indexed by defendant, plaintiff. Civil records in books, on microfiche.
Criminal Records: Access: Mail, in person. Only the court performs in person searches; visitors may not. Search fee: $.50 per name per year. Maximum fee-$25.00, written requests only. Required to search: name, years to search, signed release. Criminal records in books, on microfiche.
General Information: No adoption, juvenile, sanity or sealed records released. SASE required. Turnaround time 2 days. Fax notes: No fee to fax results. Copy fee: $.50 per page. $.25 per page after first 5. Certification fee: $2.00. Fee payee: Clerk of Court. Personal checks accepted. Prepayment is required.

Limited Jurisdiction Court #1 Rosebud County Courthouse, PO Box 504, Forsyth, MT 59327; 406-356-2638; Fax: 406-356-7551. Hours: 8AM-5PM (MST). *Misdemeanor, Civil Actions Under $7,000, Eviction, Small Claims.*

Limited Jurisdiction Court #2 PO Box 575, Colstrip, MT 59323; 406-748-2934; Fax: 406-748-

4832. Hours: 8AM-5PM; Ashland 2nd & 4th Wed 1PM (MST). *Misdemeanor, Civil Actions Under $7,000, Eviction, Small Claims.*

Sanders County

District Court PO Box 519, Thompson Falls, MT 59873; 406-827-6962; Fax: 406-827-0094. Hours: 8AM-5PM (MST). *Felony, Civil Actions Over $5,000, Eviction, Probate.*

Civil Records: Access: Mail, in person. Both court and visitors may perform in person searches. Search fee: $.50 per name per year. Maximum fee-$25.00. Required to search: name, years to search. Civil cases indexed by defendant, plaintiff. Civil records on docket books since 1906, on computer since.

Criminal Records: Access: Mail, in person. Both court and visitors may perform in person searches. Search fee: $.50 per name per year. Maximum fee-$25.00. Required to search: name, years to search, DOB, SSN, signed release. Criminal records on docket books since 1906, on computer since.

General Information: Public Access terminal is available. No adoption, juvenile, sanity or pre-sentence investigation records released. SASE required. Turnaround time 1-4 days. Copy fee: $.50 per page. $.25 per page after first 5. Certification fee: $2.00. Fee payee: Clerk of Court. Personal checks accepted. Prepayment is required.

Limited Jurisdiction Court PO Box 519, Thompson Falls, MT 59873; 406-827-4318; Fax: 406-827-4388. Hours: 8AM-5PM (MST). *Misdemeanor, Civil Actions Under $7,000, Eviction, Small Claims.*

Sheridan County

District Court 100 W Laurel, Plentywood, MT 59254; 406-765-3404; Fax: 406-765-2602. Hours: 8AM-Noon, 1-5PM (MST). *Felony, Civil Actions Over $5,000, Eviction, Probate.*

Civil Records: Access: Phone, mail, in person. Both court and visitors may perform in person searches. Search fee: $.50 per name per year. Maximum fee-$25.00. Required to search: name, years to search. Civil cases indexed by defendant, plaintiff. Civil records on docket books since 1913.

Criminal Records: Access: Phone, mail, in person. Both court and visitors may perform in person searches. Search fee: $.50 per name per year. Maximum fee-$25.00. Required to search: name, years to search. Criminal records on docket books since 1913.

General Information: No adoption, juvenile or sanity records released. SASE required. Turnaround time 1-2 days. Copy fee: $.50 per page. $.25 per page after first 5. Certification fee: $2.00. Fee payee: Clerk of District Court. Personal checks accepted. Prepayment is required.

Limited Jurisdiction Court 100 W Laurel, Plentywood, MT 59254; 406-765-1700/2074. Hours: 8AM-5PM (MST). *Misdemeanor, Civil Actions Under $7,000, Eviction, Small Claims.*

Silver Bow County

District Court 155 W Granite St, Butte, MT 59701; 406-497-6350; Fax: 406-497-6358. Hours: 8AM-5PM (MST). *Felony, Civil Actions Over $5,000, Probate.*

Civil Records: Access: Fax, mail, in person. Search fee: $.50 per name per year. Maximum fee-$25.00. Required to search: name, years to search. Civil cases indexed by defendant, plaintiff. Civil records in original files since 1970, on microfilm back to 1881.

Criminal Records: Access: Fax, mail, in person. Only the court performs in person searches; visitors may not. Search fee: $.50 per name per year. Maximum fee-$25.00. Required to search: name, years to search.

Criminal records in original files since 1970, on microfilm back to 1881.

General Information: Public Access terminal is available. No adoption, juvenile or sanity records released. SASE required. Turnaround time 1-3 days, will not do phone searches. Fax notes: Fee to fax results is $1.00 per page. Copy fee: $.50 per page. $.25 per page after first 5. Certification fee: $2.00. Fee payee: Clerk of Court. Personal checks accepted. Prepayment is required.

Limited Jurisdiction Court #1 & #2 155 W Granite St, Silver Bow County Courthouse, Butte, MT 59701; 406-497-6391/6393. Hours: 8AM-5PM (MST). *Misdemeanor, Civil Actions Under $7,000, Small Claims.*

Note: There are two Justice Courts at this location. Both courts must be searched for records

Stillwater County

District Court PO Box 367, Columbus, MT 59019; 406-322-8030; Fax: 406-322-8048. Hours: 8AM-5PM (MST). *Felony, Civil Actions Over $5,000, Eviction, Probate.*

Civil Records: Access: Phone, mail, in person. Both court and visitors may perform in person searches. Search fee: $.50 per name per year. Maximum fee-$25.00. Required to search: name, years to search. Civil cases indexed by defendant, plaintiff. Civil records on docket books since 1913; on computer back to 1994.

Criminal Records: Access: Phone, mail, in person. Both court and visitors may perform in person searches. Search fee: $.50 per name per year. Maximum fee-$25.00. Required to search: name, years to search. Criminal records on docket books since 1913; on computer back to 1994.

General Information: No adoption, juvenile or sanity records released. SASE required. Turnaround time 1-2 days. Copy fee: $.50 per page. $.25 per page after first 5. Certification fee: $2.00. Fee payee: Clerk of Court. Personal checks accepted. Prepayment is required.

Limited Jurisdiction Court PO Box 77, Columbus, MT 59019; 406-322-8040; Fax: 406-322-5838. Hours: 9AM-5PM M-Th (MST). *Misdemeanor, Civil Actions Under $7,000, Eviction, Small Claims.*

Sweet Grass County

District Court PO Box 698, Big Timber, MT 59011; 406-932-5154; Fax: 406-932-5433. Hours: 8AM-Noon, 1-5PM (MST). *Felony, Civil Actions Over $5,000, Eviction, Probate.*

Civil Records: Access: Phone, mail, in person. Only the court performs in person searches; visitors may not. Search fee: $.50 per name per year. Maximum fee-$25.00. Required to search: name, years to search. Civil cases indexed by defendant, plaintiff. Civil records in books since 1895, on microfiche since 1972.

Criminal Records: Access: Phone, mail, in person. Only the court performs in person searches; visitors may not. Search fee: $.50 per name per year. Maximum fee-$25.00. Required to search: name, years to search. Criminal records in books since 1895, on microfiche since 1972.

General Information: No adoption, juvenile or sanity records released. SASE required. Turnaround time 1 day. Copy fee: $.50 per page. $.25 per page after first 5. Certification fee: $2.00. Fee payee: Clerk of Court. Personal checks accepted. Prepayment is required.

Limited Jurisdiction Court PO Box 1432, Big Timber, MT 59011; 406-932-5150; Fax: 406-932-5433. Hours: 8AM-5PM (MST). *Misdemeanor, Civil Actions Under $7,000, Eviction, Small Claims.*

Teton County

District Court PO Box 487, Choteau, MT 59422; 406-466-2909; Fax: 406-466-2138. Hours: 8AM-5PM (MST). *Felony, Civil Actions Over $5,000, Eviction, Probate.*

Civil Records: Access: Phone, fax, mail, in person. Only the court performs in person searches; visitors may not. Search fee: $.50 per name per year. Maximum fee-$25.00. Required to search: name, years to search. Civil cases indexed by defendant, plaintiff. Civil records on books from 1893; on computer back to 1995.

Criminal Records: Access: Phone, mail, in person. Only the court performs in person searches; visitors may not. Search fee: $.50 per name per year. Maximum fee-$25.00. Required to search: name, years to search. Criminal records on books from 1893; on computer back to 1995.

General Information: No adoption, juvenile or sanity records released. SASE required. Turnaround time 1 day. Fax notes: $1.00 per page. Copy fee: $.50 per page. $.25 per page after first 5. Certification fee: $2.00. Fee payee: Clerk of Court. Personal checks accepted. Prepayment is required.

Limited Jurisdiction Court PO Box 337, Choteau, MT 59422; 406-466-5611; Fax: 406-466-2138. Hours: 1-5PM (MST). *Misdemeanor, Civil Actions Under $7,000, Eviction, Small Claims.*

Toole County

District Court PO Box 850, Shelby, MT 59474; 406-434-2271; Fax: 406-434-7225. Hours: 8AM-5PM (MST). *Felony, Civil Actions Over $5,000, Probate.*

Civil Records: Access: Phone, fax, mail, in person. Both court and visitors may perform in person searches. Search fee: $.50 per name per year. Maximum fee-$25.00. Required to search: name, years to search. Civil cases indexed by defendant, plaintiff. Civil records in books from 1914; on computer since 1997.

Criminal Records: Access: Phone, fax, mail, in person. Both court and visitors may perform in person searches. Search fee: $.50 per name per year. Maximum fee-$25.00. Required to search: name, years to search, DOB, SSN. Criminal records in books from 1914; on computer since 1997.

General Information: No adoption, juvenile or sanity records released. SASE is required. Turnaround time same day as request received. Fax notes: $.50 per page. Copy fee: $.50 per page. $.25 per page after first 5. Certification fee: $2.00 per document. Fee payee: Clerk of Court. Personal checks accepted. Prepayment is required.

Limited Jurisdiction Court PO Box 748, Shelby, MT 59474; 406-434-2651. Hours: 8AM-4PM M,T,W,F; 8AM-5PM Th (MST). *Misdemeanor, Civil Actions Under $7,000, Eviction, Small Claims.*

Treasure County

District Court PO Box 392, Hysham, MT 59038; 406-342-5547; Fax: 406-342-5445. Hours: 8AM-5PM (MST). *Felony, Civil Actions Over $5,000, Eviction, Probate.*

Civil Records: Access: Fax, mail, in person. Both court and visitors may perform in person searches. Search fee: $.50 per name per year. Maximum fee-$25.00. Required to search: name, years to search; also helpful: address. Civil cases indexed by defendant, plaintiff. Civil records on books since 1919, on microfilm from 1985 to present; on computer back to 1996.

Criminal Records: Access: Fax, mail, in person. Both court and visitors may perform in person searches. Search fee: $.50 per name per year. Maximum fee-$25.00. Required to search: name, years to search, DOB; also helpful: address. Criminal records on books since 1919, on microfilm from 1985 to present; on computer back to 1996.

General Information: Public Access terminal is available. No adoption or sanity records released. SASE required. Turnaround time 1 week. Fax notes: Fee to fax results to $1.50 per page. Copy fee: $.50 per page. $.25 per page after first 5. Certification fee: $2.00. Fee payee: Clerk of Court. Personal checks accepted. Prepayment is required.

Limited Jurisdiction Court PO Box 267, Hysham, MT 59038; 406-342-5532; Fax: 406-342-5532. Hours: 9AM-Noon (MST). *Misdemeanor, Civil Actions Under $7,000, Eviction, Small Claims.*

Valley County

District Court 501 Court Sq #6, Glasgow, MT 59230; 406-228-8221 X67/68; Fax: 406-228-9027/4601. Hours: 8AM-5PM (MST). *Felony, Civil Actions Over $5,000, Eviction, Probate.*

Civil Records: Access: Phone, fax, mail, in person. Only the court performs in person searches; visitors may not. Search fee: $.50 per name per year. Maximum fee-$25.00. Required to search: name, years to search. Civil cases indexed by defendant, plaintiff. Civil records in books since 1893; on computer back to 1996.

Criminal Records: Access: Fax, mail, in person. Only the court performs in person searches; visitors may not. Search fee: $.50 per name per year. Maximum fee-$25.00. Required to search: name, years to search, signed release. Criminal records in books since 1893; on computer back to 1996.

General Information: No adoption, juvenile or sanity records released. SASE required. Turnaround time same day. Fax notes: Fee to fax results is $1.00 per page. Copy fee: $.50 per page. $.25 per page after first 5. Certification fee: $2.00. Fee payee: Clerk of Court. Business checks accepted. Prepayment is required.

Limited Jurisdiction Court 501 Court Sq #10, Glasgow, MT 59230; 406-228-8221 X71; Fax: 406-228-4601. Hours: 8AM-Noon (MST). *Misdemeanor, Civil Actions Under $7,000, Eviction, Small Claims.*

Wheatland County

District Court Box 227, Harlowton, MT 59036; 406-632-4893; Fax: 406-632-4873. Hours: 8AM-5PM (MST). *Felony, Civil Actions Over $5,000, Eviction, Probate.*

Civil Records: Access: Phone, mail, in person. Only the court performs in person searches; visitors may not. Search fee: $.50 per name per year. Maximum fee-$25.00. Required to search: name, years to search. Civil cases indexed by defendant, plaintiff. Civil records on docket books since 1917, probate on microfiche from 1984.

Criminal Records: Access: Phone, mail, in person. Only the court performs in person searches; visitors may not. Search fee: $.50 per name per year. Maximum fee-$25.00. Required to search: name, years to search. Criminal records on docket books since 1917, probate on microfiche from 1984.

General Information: No adoption, juvenile or sanity records released. SASE required. Turnaround time 2-3 days. Copy fee: $.50 per page. $.25 per page after first 5. Certification fee: $2.00. Fee payee: Clerk of Court. Personal checks accepted. Prepayment is required.

Limited Jurisdiction Court PO Box 618, Harlowton, MT 59036; 406-632-4821; Fax: 406-632-5654. Hours: 10AM-1PM T,Th (MST). *Misdemeanor, Civil Actions Under $7,000, Eviction, Small Claims.*

Wibaux County

District Court PO Box 292, Wibaux, MT 59353; 406-796-2484; Fax: 406-796-2484. Hours: 8AM-5PM, Closed 12-1 (MST). *Felony, Civil Actions Over $5,000, Eviction, Probate.*

Civil Records: Access: Phone, fax, mail, in person. Both court and visitors may perform in person searches. Search fee: $.50 per name per year. Maximum fee-$25.00. Required to search: name, years to search. Civil records on docket books since 1914, on computer since 01/97.

Criminal Records: Access: Phone, fax, mail, in person. Only the court performs in person searches; visitors may not. Search fee: $.50 per name per year. Maximum fee-$25.00. Required to search: name, years

to search. Criminal records on docket books since 1914, on computer since 01/97.

General Information: No adoption, juvenile or sanity records released. SASE required. Turnaround time 1 week. Fax notes: $2.00 for first page, $.50 each add'l. Copy fee: $.50 per page. $.25 per page after first 5. Certification fee: $2.00. Fee payee: Clerk of Court. Personal checks accepted. Prepayment is required.

Limited Jurisdiction Court PO Box 445, Wibaux, MT 59353; 406-796-2484. Hours: 1-5PM M&W, 8AM-Noon F (MST). *Misdemeanor, Civil Actions Under $7,000, Eviction, Small Claims.*

Yellowstone County

District Court PO Box 35030, Billings, MT 59107; 406-256-2860; Fax: 406-256-2995. Hours: 8AM-5PM (MST). *Felony, Civil Actions Over $7,000, Probate.*

www.co.yellowstone.mt.us/clerk_court

Civil Records: Access: Mail, in person. Both court and visitors may perform in person searches. Search fee: $.50 per name per year. Maximum fee-$25.00. Required to search: name, years to search. Civil cases indexed by defendant, plaintiff. Civil records in books, on microfilm.

Criminal Records: Access: Mail, in person. Both court and visitors may perform in person searches. Search fee: $.50 per name per year. Maximum fee-$25.00. Required to search: name, years to search. Criminal records in books, on microfilm.

General Information: Public Access terminal is available. No adoption, juvenile or sanity records released. SASE required. Turnaround time 1 day if record less than 10 years old. Copy fee: $.50 per page. $.25 per page after first 5. Certification fee: $2.00. Fee payee: Clerk of Court. Personal checks accepted. Prepayment is required.

Limited Jurisdiction Court PO Box 35032, Billings, MT 59107; 406-256-2895; Fax: 406-256-2898. Hours: 8AM-5PM (MST). *Misdemeanor, Civil Actions Under $7,000, Eviction, Small Claims.*

Montana Recording Offices

ORGANIZATION

57 counties, 56 recording offices. The recording officer is County Clerk and Recorder (Clerk of District Court for state tax liens). Yellowstone National Park is considered a county, but is not included as a filing location. The entire state is in the Mountain Time Zone (MST).

REAL ESTATE RECORDS

Many Montana counties will perform real estate searches. Search and copy fees vary. Certification usually costs $2.00 per document.

UCC RECORDS

Financing statements are filed at the state level, except for real estate related collateral, which are filed with the Clerk and Recorder. However, prior to 07/2001, consumer goods collateral were also filed at the county and these older records can be searched there. All counties will perform UCC searches. Use search request form UCC-11. Search fees are usually $7.00 per debtor name. Copy fees vary.

TAX LIEN RECORDS

Federal tax liens on personal property of businesses are filed with the Secretary of State. Other federal tax liens are filed with the county Clerk and Recorder. State tax liens are filed with the Clerk of District Court. Usually tax liens on personal property filed with the Clerk and Recorder are in the same index with UCC financing statements. Most counties will perform tax lien searches, some as part of a UCC search and others for a separate fee, usually $7.00 per name. Copy fees vary.

OTHER LIENS

Mechanics, thresherman, judgment, lis pendens, construction, logger.

STATEWIDE ONLINE INFO:

Search for a for a Montana property owner by name and county on the Montana Cadastral Mapping Project GIS mapping database at http://gis.doa.state.mt.us/.

Beaverhead County

Clerk and Recorder, 2 South Pacific, Dillon, MT 59725-2799. Clerk and Recorder, R/E and UCC Recording 406-683-2642; Fax 406-683-5776.
Will search UCC records. UCC search includes federal tax liens if requested. RE owner, mortgage, and property transfer searches available. **Other Phone Numbers:** Assessor 406-683-5612; Treasurer 406-683-5821; Appraiser/Auditor 406-683-4000; Elections 406-683-2642; Vital Records 406-683-2642.

Big Horn County

Clerk and Recorder, P.O. Box 908, Hardin, MT 59034. 406-665-1506; Fax 406-665-1608.
Will search UCC records. **Other Phone Numbers:** Assessor 406-665-1504; Treasurer 406-665-1505.

Blaine County

Clerk and Recorder, P.O. Box 278, Chinook, MT 59523-0278. Clerk and Recorder, R/E and UCC Recording 406-357-3240; Fax 406-357-2199.
Will search UCC records. Will not search real estate records. **Other Phone Numbers:** Assessor 406-357-3210; Treasurer 406-357-3280; Appraiser/Auditor 406-357-3210; Elections 406-357-3240; Vital Records 406-357-3240.

Broadwater County

Clerk and Recorder, 515 Broadway, Townsend, MT 59644. 406-266-3443; Fax 406-266-3674.
Will search UCC records. **Other Phone Numbers:** Assessor 406-266-3430; Treasurer 406-266-3445.

Carbon County

Clerk and Recorder, P.O. Box 887, Red Lodge, MT 59068. Clerk and Recorder, R/E and UCC Recording 406-446-1220; Fax 406-446-2640.
Will search UCC records. Will not search real estate records. **Other Phone Numbers:** Assessor 406-466-1223; Treasurer 406-446-1221; Appraiser/Auditor 406-446-1224; Elections 406-446-1595; Vital Records 406-446-1220.

Carter County

Clerk and Recorder, P.O. Box 315, Ekalaka, MT 59324-0315. 406-775-8749; Fax 406-775-8750.

Will search UCC records. Will not search real estate records. **Other Phone Numbers:** Assessor 406-775-8717; Treasurer 406-775-8735.

Cascade County

Clerk and Recorder, P.O. Box 2867, Great Falls, MT 59403-2867. 406-454-6800 R/E Recording: 406-454-6801 UCC Recording: 406-454-6801; Fax 406-454-6802. http://www.co.cascade.mt.us
Will search UCC records. **Other Phone Numbers:** Assessor 406-454-6744; Treasurer 406-454-6850; Appraiser/Auditor 406-454-7460; Elections 406-454-6803; Vital Records 406-454-6718.

Chouteau County

Clerk and Recorder, P.O. Box 459, Fort Benton, MT 59442-0459. 406-622-5151; Fax 406-622-3012.
Will search UCC records. UCC search includes federal tax liens if requested. RE owner, mortgage, and property transfer searches available. **Other Phone Numbers:** Assessor 406-622-5261; Treasurer 406-622-5032.

Custer County

Clerk and Recorder, 1010 Main Street, Miles City, MT 59301-1010. 406-233-3343; Fax 406-233-3452.
Will search UCC records. RE record owner searches available. **Other Phone Numbers:** Assessor 406-232-1295; Treasurer 406-233-3427.

Daniels County

Clerk and Recorder, P.O. Box 247, Scobey, MT 59263. 406-487-5561.
Will search UCC records. UCC search includes federal tax liens if requested. RE record owner and mortgage searches available. **Other Phone Numbers:** Assessor 406-487-2791; Treasurer 406-487-2671.

Dawson County

Clerk and Recorder, 207 West Bell, Glendive, MT 59330. Clerk and Recorder, R/E and UCC Recording 406-377-3058; Fax 406-377-2022.
Will search UCC records. **Other Phone Numbers:** Assessor 406-377-4256; Treasurer 406-377-3026; Appraiser/Auditor 406-377-4500; Elections 406-377-3058; Vital Records 406-377-3058.

Deer Lodge County

Clerk and Recorder, 800 South Main St., Courthouse, Anaconda, MT 59711-2999. 406-563-4060 R/E Recording: 406-563-4061 UCC Recording: 406-563-4061; Fax 406-563-4001.
Will search UCC records. Will do limited searches. Search fee is $6.00 per page (recordings.) **Other Phone Numbers:** Assessor 406-563-4045; Treasurer 406-563-4051; Appraiser/Auditor 406-563-4045; Elections 406-563-4060; Vital Records 406-563-4062.

Fallon County

Clerk and Recorder, P.O. Box 846, Baker, MT 59313-0846. 406-778-7105; Fax 406-778-3431.
Will search UCC records. **Other Phone Numbers:** Assessor 406-778-2883 x29; Treasurer 406-778-2883 x28.

Fergus County

Clerk and Recorder, 712 West Main, Lewistown, MT 59457. 406-538-5242; Fax 406-538-9023.
Will search UCC records. UCC search includes tax liens if requested. Will not search real estate records. **Other Phone Numbers:** Treasurer 406-538-9220.

Flathead County

Clerk and Recorder, 800 South Main, Courthouse, Kalispell, MT 59901-5400. 406-758-5532 R/E Recording: 406-758-5526 UCC Recording: 406-758-5526; Fax 406-758-5865. www.co.flathead.mt.us
Will search UCC records. UCC search includes federal tax liens if requested. Will not search real estate records. **Other Phone Numbers:** Assessor 406-758-5700; Treasurer 406-758-5680; Elections 406-758-5535; Vital Records 406-758-5526.

Gallatin County

Clerk and Recorder, 311 West Main, Rm 204, Room 204, Bozeman, MT 59715. Clerk and Recorder, R/E and UCC Recording 406-582-3050; Fax 406-582-3037.
Will search UCC records. UCC search does not include federal tax liens. RE record owner and mortgage searches available. **Other Phone Numbers:** Assessor 406-582-3400; Treasurer 406-582-3030; Appraiser/Auditor 406-582 3400; Elections 406-582-3060; Vital Records 406-582-3050.

Garfield County

Clerk and Recorder, P.O. Box 7, Jordan, MT 59337-0007. 406-557-2760; Fax 406-557-2625.
Will search UCC records. **Other Phone Numbers:** Assessor 406-557-6164; Treasurer 406-557-2233; Appraiser/Auditor 406-557-2772; Elections 406-557-2760.

Glacier County

Deputy Clerk, 512 East Main, Cut Bank, MT 59427. Deputy Clerk, R/E and UCC Recording 406-873-5063 x22; Fax 406-873-2125.
Will search UCC records. Will not search real estate records. **Other Phone Numbers:** Assessor 406-873-5063 x43; Treasurer 406-873-5063 x31; Appraiser/Auditor 406-873-5063 x45; Elections 406-873-5063 x17; Vital Records 406-873-5063 x22.

Golden Valley County

Clerk and Recorder, P.O. Box 10, Ryegate, MT 59074. 406-568-2231; Fax 406-568-2598.
Will search UCC records. Will not search real estate records. **Other Phone Numbers:** Assessor 406-586-2371; Treasurer 406-586-2342.

Granite County

Clerk and Recorder, P.O. Box 925, Philipsburg, MT 59858. Clerk and Recorder, R/E and UCC Recording 406-859-3771; Fax 406-859-3817.
Will search UCC records. Will not search real estate records. **Other Phone Numbers:** Assessor 406-859-3521; Treasurer 406-859-3831; Elections 406-859-3771; Vital Records 406-859-3771.

Hill County

Clerk and Recorder, 315 4th Street, Courthouse, Havre, MT 59501. 406-265-5481; Fax 406-265-2445. http://co.hill.mt.us
Will search UCC records. UCC search includes federal tax liens if requested. RE record owner searches available. **Other Phone Numbers:** Assessor 406-265-5481 x210; Treasurer 406-265-5481 x257.

Jefferson County

Clerk and Recorder, P.O. Box H, Boulder, MT 59632. Clerk and Recorder, R/E and UCC Recording 406-225-4020; Fax 406-225-4149. http://co.jefferson.mt.us
Will not search UCC records. **Other Phone Numbers:** Assessor 406-225-4001; Treasurer 406-225-4103; Appraiser/Auditor 406-225-4001; Elections 406-225-4018; Vital Records 406-225-4020.

Judith Basin County

Clerk and Recorder, P.O. Box 427, Stanford, MT 59479. Clerk and Recorder, R/E and UCC Recording 406-566-2277; Fax 406-566-2211.
Will search UCC records. **Other Phone Numbers:** Assessor 406-566-2291; Treasurer 406-566-2277; Elections 406-566-2277; Vital Records 406-566-2277.

Lake County

Clerk and Recorder, 106 4th Avenue East, Polson, MT 59860. 406-883-7210 R/E Recording: 406-883-7208; Fax 406-883-7283. http://www.lakecounty-mt.org/
Will search UCC records. UCC search includes federal tax liens if requested. Mortgage searches available. **Other Phone Numbers:** Assessor 406-883-7232; Treasurer 406-883-7224; Appraiser/Auditor 406-883-7227; Elections 406-883-7268; Vital Records 406-883-7208; Clerk of Court (tax liens) 406-883-7254.

Lewis and Clark County

Clerk and Recorder, P.O. Box 1721, Helena, MT 59624. Clerk and Recorder, R/E and UCC Recording 406-447-8337; Fax 406-457-8598. http://www.co.lewis-clark.mt.us
Will search UCC records. UCC search includes federal tax liens if requested. Mortgage and property transfer searches; fee is $6.00 per page. **Online Access:** Real Estate, Liens, Recording. Currently, the Records Department is in the processing of automating their recording and filing procedures. This automation will include document imaging. Available is the GIS map and parcel search at www.co.lewis-clark.mt.us/gis/atlas/index.html. **Other Phone Numbers:** Assessor 406-444-4000; Treasurer 406-447-8329; Elections 406-447-8338; Vital Records 406-447-8335.

Liberty County

Clerk and Recorder, P.O. Box 459, Chester, MT 59522-0459. Clerk and Recorder, R/E and UCC Recording 406-759-5365; Fax 406-759-5395.
Will search UCC records. **Other Phone Numbers:** Treasurer 406-759-5455; Appraiser/Auditor 406-759-5126; Elections 406-759-5365; Vital Records 406-759-5365.

Lincoln County

Recorder, 512 California Avenue, Libby, MT 59923. 406-293-7781 R/E Recording: 406-293-7781 x205 UCC Recording: 406-293-7781 x205; Fax 406-293-8577.
Will search UCC records. Will not search real estate records. **Other Phone Numbers:** Assessor 406-293-7781 x213; Treasurer 406-293-7781; Appraiser/Auditor 406-293-7781 x219; Elections 406-293-7781 x283; Vital Records 406-293-7781 x205.

Madison County

Clerk and Recorder, P.O. Box 366, Virginia City, MT 59755. 406-843-5392.
Will search UCC records. UCC search includes federal tax liens. RE record owner and property searches available. **Other Phone Numbers:** Assessor 406-843-5392 x15; Treasurer 406-843-5392 x24.

McCone County

Clerk and Recorder, P.O. Box 199, Circle, MT 59215-0199. Clerk and Recorder, R/E and UCC Recording 406-485-3505; Fax 406-485-2689.
Will search UCC records. UCC search includes federal tax liens if requested. RE owner, mortgage, and property transfer searches available. **Other Phone Numbers:** Assessor 406-485-3565; Treasurer 406-485-3590; Appraiser/Auditor 406-485-3432; Elections 406-485-3505; Vital Records 406-485-3505.

Meagher County

Deputy Clerk & Recording, P.O. Box 309, White Sulphur Springs, MT 59645. Deputy Clerk & Recording, R/E and UCC Recording 406-547-3612; Fax 406-547-3388.
Will search UCC records. **Other Phone Numbers:** Assessor 406-547-3653; Treasurer 406-547-3641; Appraiser/Auditor 406-547-3653; Elections 406-547-3612; Vital Records 406-547-3612.

Mineral County

Clerk and Recorder, P.O. Box 550, Superior, MT 59872-0550. 406-822-3520; Fax 406-822-3579.
Will search UCC records. **Other Phone Numbers:** Assessor 406-822-3540; Treasurer 406-822-3530; Elections 406-822-3520; Vital Records 406-822-3520.

Missoula County

Clerk and Recorder, 200 West Broadway, Missoula, MT 59802-4292. 406-523-4752; Fax 406-721-4043.
Will search UCC records. Will not search real estate records.

Musselshell County

Clerk and Recorder, 506 Main Street, Courthouse, Roundup, MT 59072. Clerk and Recorder, R/E and UCC Recording 406-323-1104; Fax 406-323-3303.
Will search UCC records. Will not search real estate records. **Other Phone Numbers:** Assessor 406-323-1513; Treasurer 406-323-2504; Appraiser/Auditor 406-323-1513; Elections 406-323-1104; Vital Records 406-323-1104.

Park County

Clerk and Recorder, P.O. Box 1037, Livingston, MT 59047. 406-222-4110; Fax 406-222-4199.
Will search UCC records. UCC search does not include federal tax liens. Will not search real estate records. **Other Phone Numbers:** Assessor 406-222-6120 x227; Treasurer 406-222-6120 x252.

Petroleum County

Clerk and Recorder, P.O. Box 226, Winnett, MT 59087. 406-429-5311; Fax 406-429-6328.
Will search UCC records. UCC search does not include federal tax liens. Mortgage searches available. **Other Phone Numbers:** Assessor 406-429-5531; Treasurer 406-429-5551.

Phillips County

Recorder, P.O. Box 360, Malta, MT 59538. 406-654-2423; Fax 406-654-2429.
Will search UCC records. **Other Phone Numbers:** Assessor 406-654-2123; Treasurer 406-654-1742.

Pondera County

Clerk and Recorder, 20 4th Avenue S.W., Conrad, MT 59425. 406-271-4000 R/E Recording: 406-271-4001; Fax 406-271-4070. http://ponderacountymontana.org
Will search UCC records. **Other Phone Numbers:** Assessor 406-271-4015; Treasurer 406-271-4015; Appraiser/Auditor 406-271-4012.

Powder River County

Clerk and Recorder, P.O. Box 270, Broadus, MT 59317-0270. 406-436-2361; Fax 406-436-2151.
Will search UCC records. UCC search does not include federal tax liens. Mortgage and property transfer searches available. **Other Phone Numbers:** Assessor 406-436-2407; Treasurer 406-436-2444.

Powell County

Clerk and Recorder, 409 Missouri Avenue, Deer Lodge, MT 59722. 406-846-3680; Fax 406-846-2784.
Will search UCC records. UCC search does not include federal tax liens. Mortgage and property transfer searches available. **Other Phone Numbers:** Assessor 406-846-3680 x230; Treasurer 406-846-3680 x226; Appraiser/Auditor 406-846-3680; Elections 406-846-3680 x223.

Prairie County

Clerk and Recorder, P.O. Box 125, Terry, MT 59349. 406-635-5575; Fax 406-635-5576.
Will search UCC records. **Other Phone Numbers:** Assessor 406-637-5560.

Ravalli County Clerk & Recorder

Clerk and Recorder, Courthouse Box 5002, Hamilton, MT 59840. Clerk and Recorder, R/E and UCC Recording 406-375-6212; Fax 406-375-6326.
Will search UCC records. Will search real estate records. Search per debtor name-$6.00 **Other Phone Numbers:** Assessor 406-375-6312; Treasurer 406-375-6300; Appraiser/Auditor 406-375-6312; Elections 406-375-6213; Vital Records 406-375-6212.

Richland County

Clerk and Recorder, 201 West Main Street, Sidney, MT 59270. 406-482-1708; Fax 406-482-3731.
Will search UCC records. **Other Phone Numbers:** Assessor 406-482-1203.

Roosevelt County

Clerk and Recorder, 400 Second Avenue South, Wolf Point, MT 59201. 406-653-6250; Fax 406-653-6289.
Will search UCC records. Will not search real estate records. **Other Phone Numbers:** Assessor 406-653-6256; Treasurer 406-653-6239; Appraiser/Auditor 406-653-6255.

Rosebud County

Clerk and Recorder, P.O. Box 47, Forsyth, MT 59327. 406-356-7318; Fax 406-356-7551.
Will search UCC records. **Other Phone Numbers:** Assessor 406-356-2516.

Sanders County

Clerk and Recorder, P.O. Box 519, Thompson Falls, MT 59873. Clerk and Recorder, R/E and UCC Recording 406-827-6922; Fax 406-827-4388.
Will search UCC records. **Other Phone Numbers:** Assessor 406-827-6922; Treasurer 406-827-6924; Appraiser/Auditor 406-827-6932; Elections 406-827-6922; Vital Records 406-827-6922.

Sheridan County

Clerk and Recorder, 100 West Laurel Avenue, Plentywood, MT 59254. Clerk and Recorder, R/E and UCC Recording 406-765-3403; Fax 406-765-2609.
http://www.co.sheridan.mt.us/
Will search UCC records. Will not search real estate records. **Other Phone Numbers:** Assessor 406-765-2291; Treasurer 406-765-3414; Appraiser/Auditor 406-765-2291; Elections 406-765-3403; Vital Records 406-765-3403.

Silver Bow County

Clerk and Recorder, P.O. Box 585, Butte, MT 59703. 406-723-8262; Fax 406-782-6637.
Will search UCC records. Will not search real estate records. **Other Phone Numbers:** Assessor 406-723-8262 x260; Treasurer 406-723-8262 x250.

Stillwater County

Clerk and Recorder, P.O. Box 149, Columbus, MT 59019. Clerk and Recorder, R/E and UCC Recording 406-322-8000; Fax 406-322-8007.
Will search UCC records. Mortgage searches available. **Other Phone Numbers:** Assessor 406-322-8015; Treasurer 406-322-8020; Appraiser/Auditor 406-322-8015; Elections 406-322-8000; Vital Records 406-322-8000.

Sweet Grass County

Clerk and Recorder, P.O. Box 460, Big Timber, MT 59011. 406-932-5152; Fax 406-932-4777.
Will search UCC records. Will not search real estate records. **Other Phone Numbers:** Assessor 406-932-5149; Treasurer 406-932-5151.

Teton County

Clerk and Recorder, P.O. Box 610, Choteau, MT 59422. Clerk and Recorder, R/E and UCC Recording 406-466-2693; Fax 406-466-2138. www.tetoncomt.org
Will search UCC records. Will search real estate records. Real estate search fee is $.50 per name per year per index (mortgage or deeds). **Other Phone Numbers:** Assessor 406-466-2908; Treasurer 406-466-2694; Appraiser/Auditor 406-466-2908; Elections 406-466-2907; Vital Records 406-466-2693.

Toole County

Clerk and Recorder, 226 1st Street South, Shelby, MT 59474. Clerk and Recorder, R/E and UCC Recording 406-434-2232; Fax 406-434-2467.
Will search UCC records. **Other Phone Numbers:** Assessor 406-434-2142; Treasurer 406-434-5501; Appraiser/Auditor 406-434-2142; Elections 406-434-2232; Vital Records 406-434-2232.

Treasure County

Clerk and Recorder, P.O. Box 392, Hysham, MT 59038. 406-342-5547; Fax 406-342-5445.
Will search UCC records. UCC search includes federal tax liens if requested. RE owner, mortgage, and property transfer searches available. **Other Phone Numbers:** Assessor 406-342-5540; Treasurer 406-342-5545.

Valley County

Clerk and Recorder, 501 Court Square, Box 2, Glasgow, MT 59230. 406-228-8221; Fax 406-228-9027.
Will search UCC records. **Other Phone Numbers:** Assessor 406-228-8221 x33; Treasurer 406-228-8221 x35.

Wheatland County

Clerk and Recorder, P.O. Box 1903, Harlowton, MT 59036. 406-632-4891; Fax 406-632-5654.
Will search UCC records. **Other Phone Numbers:** Assessor 406-632-4894; Treasurer 406-632-4892.

Wibaux County

Clerk and Recorder, P.O. Box 199, Wibaux, MT 59353-0199. Clerk and Recorder, R/E and UCC Recording 406-796-2481; Fax 406-796-2625.
Will search UCC records. **Other Phone Numbers:** Assessor 406-795-2483; Treasurer 406-795-2482; Elections 406-796-2481; Vital Records 406-796-2481.

Yellowstone County

Clerk and Recorder, P.O. Box 35001, Billings, MT 59107. Clerk and Recorder, R/E and UCC Recording 406-256-2785; Fax 406-256-2736.
http://www.co.yellowstone.mt.us/clerk
Will search UCC records. UCC search does not include federal tax liens. Property transfer searches available. **Online Access:** Assessor, Tax Records, Grantor/Grantee. Online access to the county clerk & recorder records are available free online at www.co.yellowstone.mt.us/clerk. Also, access to the tax assessor records is available free at www.co.yellowstone.mt.us/gis. **Other Phone Numbers:** Assessor 406-896-4000; Treasurer 406-256-2785; Elections 406-256-2743; Vital Records 406-256-2788.

Montana County Locator

You will usually be able to find the city name in the City/County Cross Reference below. In that case, it is a simple matter to determine the county from the cross reference. However, only the official US Postal Service city names are included in this index. There are an additional 40,000 place names that people use in their addresses. Therefore, we have also included a ZIP/City Cross Reference immediately following the City/County Cross Reference.

If you know the ZIP Code but the city name does not appear in the City/County Cross Reference index, look up the ZIP Code in the ZIP/City Cross Reference, find the city name, then look up the city name in the City/County Cross Reference. For example, you want to know the county for an address of Menands, NY 12204. There is no "Menands" in the City/County Cross Reference. The ZIP/City Cross Reference shows that ZIP Codes 12201-12288 are for the city of Albany. Looking back in the City/County Cross Reference, Albany is in Albany County.

City/County Cross Reference

ABSAROKEE Stillwater
ACTON Yellowstone
ALBERTON (59820) Missoula(54),
    Mineral(46)
ALDER Madison
ALZADA Carter
ANACONDA (59711) Deer Lodge(94),
    Granite(6)
ANGELA Rosebud
ANTELOPE Sheridan
ARLEE (59821) Lake(72), Missoula(27),
    Sanders(2)
ASHLAND Rosebud
AUGUSTA Lewis and Clark
AVON Powell
BABB Glacier
BAINVILLE Roosevelt
BAKER Fallon
BALLANTINE Yellowstone
BASIN Jefferson
BEARCREEK Carbon
BELFRY Carbon
BELGRADE Gallatin
BELT Cascade
BIDDLE Powder River
BIG ARM Lake
BIG SANDY Chouteau
BIG SKY Gallatin
BIG TIMBER Sweet Grass
BIGFORK (59911) Flathead(69), Lake(31)
BIGHORN Treasure
BILLINGS Yellowstone
BIRNEY Rosebud
BLACK EAGLE Cascade
BLOOMFIELD Dawson
BONNER Missoula
BOULDER Jefferson
BOX ELDER Hill
BOYD Carbon
BOYES Carter
BOZEMAN Gallatin
BRADY Pondera
BRIDGER Carbon
BROADUS Powder River
BROADVIEW (59015) Yellowstone(93),
    Stillwater(5), Musselshell(2)
BROCKTON Roosevelt
BROCKWAY McCone
BROWNING Glacier
BRUSETT Garfield
BUFFALO Fergus
BUSBY Big Horn
BUTTE Silver Bow
BYNUM Teton
CAMERON Madison
CANYON CREEK Lewis and Clark
CAPITOL Carter
CARDWELL (59721) Jefferson(50),
    Madison(50)
CARTER Chouteau
CASCADE Cascade
CAT CREEK Petroleum
CHARLO Lake

CHESTER Liberty
CHINOOK Blaine
CHOTEAU Teton
CIRCLE (59215) McCone(88), Dawson(12)
CLANCY Jefferson
CLINTON (59825) Missoula(82),
    Granite(18)
CLYDE PARK Park
COFFEE CREEK Fergus
COHAGEN Garfield
COLSTRIP Rosebud
COLUMBIA FALLS Flathead
COLUMBUS Stillwater
CONDON Missoula
CONNER Ravalli
CONRAD (59425) Pondera(98), Teton(2)
COOKE CITY Park
CORAM Flathead
CORVALLIS Ravalli
CORWIN SPRINGS Park
CRANE Richland
CROW AGENCY Big Horn
CULBERTSON Roosevelt
CUSTER Yellowstone
CUT BANK Glacier
DAGMAR (59219) Sheridan(99),
    Roosevelt(2)
DARBY Ravalli
DAYTON (59914) Flathead(75), Lake(25)
DE BORGIA Mineral
DECKER Big Horn
DEER LODGE Powell
DELL Beaverhead
DENTON Fergus
DILLON Beaverhead
DIVIDE Silver Bow
DIXON Sanders
DODSON (59524) Phillips(78), Blaine(22)
DRUMMOND Granite
DUPUYER Pondera
DUTTON Teton
EAST GLACIER PARK Glacier
EAST HELENA (59635) Lewis and
    Clark(97), Jefferson(3)
EDGAR Carbon
EKALAKA Carter
ELLISTON Powell
ELMO Lake
EMIGRANT Park
ENNIS Madison
ESSEX Flathead
ETHRIDGE Toole
EUREKA Lincoln
FAIRFIELD Teton
FAIRVIEW Richland
FALLON Prairie
FISHTAIL Stillwater
FLAXVILLE Daniels
FLORENCE (59833) Ravalli(62),
    Missoula(38)
FLOWEREE (59440) Cascade(84),
    Chouteau(16)
FORESTGROVE Fergus

FORSYTH Rosebud
FORT BENTON Chouteau
FORT HARRISON Lewis and Clark
FORT PECK Valley
FORT SHAW (59443) Cascade(92),
    Teton(8)
FORTINE Lincoln
FOUR BUTTES Daniels
FRAZER Valley
FRENCHTOWN Missoula
FROID (59226) Roosevelt(81),
    Sheridan(19)
FROMBERG Carbon
GALATA Toole
GALLATIN GATEWAY Gallatin
GARDINER Park
GARNEILL Fergus
GARRISON Powell
GARRYOWEN Big Horn
GERALDINE Chouteau
GEYSER Judith Basin
GILDFORD Hill
GLASGOW Valley
GLEN Beaverhead
GLENDIVE Dawson
GLENTANA Valley
GOLD CREEK Powell
GRANTSDALE Ravalli
GRASS RANGE Fergus
GREAT FALLS Cascade
GREENOUGH Missoula
GREYCLIFF Sweet Grass
HALL Granite
HAMILTON Ravalli
HAMMOND Carter
HARDIN Big Horn
HARLEM Blaine
HARLOWTON Wheatland
HARRISON Madison
HATHAWAY Rosebud
HAUGAN Mineral
HAVRE Hill
HAYS Blaine
HEART BUTTE Pondera
HELENA Lewis and Clark
HELMVILLE Powell
HERON Sanders
HIGHWOOD (59450) Chouteau(95),
    Cascade(5)
HILGER Fergus
HINGHAM Hill
HINSDALE Valley
HOBSON Judith Basin
HOGELAND Blaine
HOMESTEAD Roosevelt
HOT SPRINGS (59845) Sanders(77),
    Flathead(12), Lake(11)
HUNGRY HORSE Flathead
HUNTLEY Yellowstone
HUSON Missoula
HYSHAM Treasure
INGOMAR Rosebud
INVERNESS Hill

ISMAY Custer
JACKSON Beaverhead
JEFFERSON CITY Jefferson
JOLIET Carbon
JOPLIN Liberty
JORDAN Garfield
JUDITH GAP Wheatland
KALISPELL Flathead
KEVIN Toole
KILA Flathead
KINSEY Custer
KREMLIN Hill
LAKE MC DONALD Flathead
LAKESIDE (59922) Flathead(75), Lake(25)
LAMBERT Richland
LAME DEER Rosebud
LARSLAN Valley
LAUREL (59044) Yellowstone(98),
    Carbon(1)
LAVINA Golden Valley
LEDGER Pondera
LEWISTOWN Fergus
LIBBY Lincoln
LIMA Beaverhead
LINCOLN Lewis and Clark
LINDSAY Dawson
LIVINGSTON Park
LLOYD Blaine
LODGE GRASS Big Horn
LOLO Missoula
LOMA Chouteau
LONEPINE Sanders
LORING Phillips
LOTHAIR Toole
LUTHER Carbon
MALMSTROM A F B Cascade
MALTA Phillips
MANHATTAN Gallatin
MARION Flathead
MARTIN CITY Flathead
MARTINSDALE Meagher
MARYSVILLE Lewis and Clark
MC ALLISTER Madison
MC CABE Roosevelt
MC LEOD Sweet Grass
MEDICINE LAKE Sheridan
MELROSE Silver Bow
MELSTONE Musselshell
MELVILLE Sweet Grass
MILDRED Prairie
MILES CITY Custer
MILL IRON Carter
MILLTOWN Missoula
MISSOULA Missoula
MOCCASIN Judith Basin
MOLT (59057) Yellowstone(86),
    Stillwater(14)
MONARCH Cascade
MOORE Fergus
MOSBY Garfield
MUSSELSHELL Musselshell
NASHUA Valley
NEIHART Cascade

NIARADA (59852) Sanders(86), Flathead(14)
NORRIS Madison
NOXON Sanders
NYE Stillwater
OILMONT Toole
OLIVE Powder River
OLNEY Flathead
OPHEIM Valley
OTTER Powder River
OUTLOOK Sheridan
OVANDO Powell
PABLO Lake
PARADISE Sanders
PARK CITY Stillwater
PEERLESS Daniels
PENDROY Teton
PHILIPSBURG Granite
PINESDALE Ravalli
PLAINS Sanders
PLENTYWOOD Sheridan
PLEVNA Fallon
POLARIS Beaverhead
POLEBRIDGE Flathead
POLSON Lake
POMPEYS PILLAR Yellowstone
PONY Madison
POPLAR Roosevelt
POWDERVILLE Powder River
POWER (59468) Teton(82), Cascade(18)
PRAY Park
PROCTOR Lake
PRYOR Big Horn
RADERSBURG Broadwater
RAMSAY Silver Bow
RAPELJE Stillwater

RAVALLI Lake
RAYMOND Sheridan
RAYNESFORD Judith Basin
RED LODGE Carbon
REDSTONE Sheridan
REEDPOINT Stillwater
RESERVE (59258) Sheridan(94), Roosevelt(7)
REXFORD Lincoln
RICHEY Dawson
RICHLAND Valley
RINGLING Meagher
ROBERTS Carbon
ROLLINS (59931) Flathead(88), Lake(13)
RONAN Lake
ROSCOE Carbon
ROSEBUD Rosebud
ROUNDUP Musselshell
ROY Fergus
RUDYARD Hill
RYEGATE Golden Valley
SACO Phillips
SAINT IGNATIUS Lake
SAINT MARIE Valley
SAINT REGIS Mineral
SAINT XAVIER Big Horn
SALTESE Mineral
SAND COULEE Cascade
SAND SPRINGS Garfield
SANDERS Treasure
SANTA RITA Glacier
SAVAGE (59262) Richland(62), Dawson(38)
SCOBEY Daniels
SEELEY LAKE Missoula
SHAWMUT Wheatland

SHELBY Toole
SHEPHERD Yellowstone
SHERIDAN Madison
SIDNEY Richland
SILVER GATE Park
SILVER STAR Madison
SIMMS Cascade
SOMERS Flathead
SONNETTE Powder River
SPRINGDALE Park
STANFORD Judith Basin
STEVENSVILLE Ravalli
STOCKETT Cascade
STRYKER Lincoln
SULA Ravalli
SUMATRA Rosebud
SUN RIVER Cascade
SUNBURST Toole
SUPERIOR Mineral
SWEETGRASS Toole
TEIGEN Petroleum
TERRY Prairie
THOMPSON FALLS Sanders
THREE FORKS (59752) Gallatin(91), Broadwater(9)
TOSTON Broadwater
TOWNSEND Broadwater
TREGO Lincoln
TROUT CREEK Sanders
TROY Lincoln
TURNER Blaine
TWIN BRIDGES Madison
TWODOT Wheatland
ULM Cascade
VALIER Pondera
VANDALIA Valley

VAUGHN (59487) Cascade(93), Teton(7)
VICTOR Ravalli
VIDA McCone
VIRGINIA CITY Madison
VOLBORG Custer
WARMSPRINGS Deer Lodge
WEST GLACIER Flathead
WEST YELLOWSTONE Gallatin
WESTBY Sheridan
WHITE SULPHUR SPRINGS Meagher
WHITEFISH Flathead
WHITEHALL (59759) Jefferson(81), Madison(16), Silver Bow(2)
WHITETAIL Daniels
WHITEWATER Phillips
WHITLASH Liberty
WIBAUX Wibaux
WILLARD Fallon
WILLOW CREEK Gallatin
WILSALL Park
WINIFRED Fergus
WINNETT Petroleum
WINSTON Broadwater
WISDOM Beaverhead
WISE RIVER (59762) Beaverhead(52), Deer Lodge(48)
WOLF CREEK Lewis and Clark
WOLF POINT Roosevelt
WORDEN Yellowstone
WYOLA Big Horn
YELLOWTAIL Big Horn
ZORTMAN Phillips
ZURICH Blaine

ZIP/City Cross Reference

59001-59001	ABSAROKEE	59055-59055	MELVILLE	59222-59222	FLAXVILLE	59322-59322	COHAGEN
59002-59002	ACTON	59057-59057	MOLT	59223-59223	FORT PECK	59323-59323	COLSTRIP
59003-59003	ASHLAND	59058-59058	MOSBY	59225-59225	FRAZER	59324-59324	EKALAKA
59006-59006	BALLANTINE	59059-59059	MUSSELSHELL	59226-59226	FROID	59326-59326	FALLON
59007-59007	BEARCREEK	59061-59061	NYE	59230-59230	GLASGOW	59327-59327	FORSYTH
59008-59008	BELFRY	59062-59062	OTTER	59231-59231	SAINT MARIE	59330-59330	GLENDIVE
59010-59010	BIGHORN	59063-59063	PARK CITY	59240-59240	GLENTANA	59332-59332	HAMMOND
59011-59011	BIG TIMBER	59064-59064	POMPEYS PILLAR	59241-59241	HINSDALE	59333-59333	HATHAWAY
59012-59012	BIRNEY	59065-59065	PRAY	59242-59242	HOMESTEAD	59336-59336	ISMAY
59013-59013	BOYD	59066-59066	PRYOR	59243-59243	LAMBERT	59337-59337	JORDAN
59014-59014	BRIDGER	59067-59067	RAPELJE	59244-59244	LARSLAN	59338-59338	KINSEY
59015-59015	BROADVIEW	59068-59068	RED LODGE	59245-59245	MC CABE	59339-59339	LINDSAY
59016-59016	BUSBY	59069-59069	REEDPOINT	59247-59247	MEDICINE LAKE	59341-59341	MILDRED
59018-59018	CLYDE PARK	59070-59070	ROBERTS	59248-59248	NASHUA	59343-59343	OLIVE
59019-59019	COLUMBUS	59071-59071	ROSCOE	59250-59250	OPHEIM	59344-59344	PLEVNA
59020-59020	COOKE CITY	59072-59073	ROUNDUP	59252-59252	OUTLOOK	59345-59345	POWDERVILLE
59022-59022	CROW AGENCY	59074-59074	RYEGATE	59253-59253	PEERLESS	59347-59347	ROSEBUD
59024-59024	CUSTER	59075-59075	SAINT XAVIER	59254-59254	PLENTYWOOD	59348-59348	SONNETTE
59025-59025	DECKER	59076-59076	SANDERS	59255-59255	POPLAR	59349-59349	TERRY
59026-59026	EDGAR	59077-59077	SAND SPRINGS	59256-59256	RAYMOND	59351-59351	VOLBORG
59027-59027	EMIGRANT	59078-59078	SHAWMUT	59257-59257	REDSTONE	59353-59353	WIBAUX
59028-59028	FISHTAIL	59079-59079	SHEPHERD	59258-59258	RESERVE	59354-59354	WILLARD
59029-59029	FROMBERG	59081-59081	SILVER GATE	59259-59259	RICHEY	59401-59401	GREAT FALLS
59030-59030	GARDINER	59082-59082	SPRINGDALE	59260-59260	RICHLAND	59402-59402	MALMSTROM A F B
59031-59031	GARRYOWEN	59083-59083	SUMATRA	59261-59261	SACO	59403-59406	GREAT FALLS
59032-59032	GRASS RANGE	59084-59084	TEIGEN	59262-59262	SAVAGE	59410-59410	AUGUSTA
59033-59033	GREYCLIFF	59085-59085	TWODOT	59263-59263	SCOBEY	59411-59411	BABB
59034-59034	HARDIN	59086-59086	WILSALL	59270-59270	SIDNEY	59412-59412	BELT
59035-59035	YELLOWTAIL	59087-59087	WINNETT	59273-59273	VANDALIA	59414-59414	BLACK EAGLE
59036-59036	HARLOWTON	59088-59088	WORDEN	59274-59274	VIDA	59416-59416	BRADY
59037-59037	HUNTLEY	59089-59089	WYOLA	59275-59275	WESTBY	59417-59417	BROWNING
59038-59038	HYSHAM	59101-59117	BILLINGS	59276-59276	WHITETAIL	59418-59418	BUFFALO
59039-59039	INGOMAR	59201-59201	WOLF POINT	59301-59301	MILES CITY	59419-59419	BYNUM
59041-59041	JOLIET	59211-59211	ANTELOPE	59311-59311	ALZADA	59420-59420	CARTER
59043-59043	LAME DEER	59212-59212	BAINVILLE	59312-59312	ANGELA	59421-59421	CASCADE
59044-59044	LAUREL	59213-59213	BROCKTON	59313-59313	BAKER	59422-59422	CHOTEAU
59046-59046	LAVINA	59214-59214	BROCKWAY	59314-59314	BIDDLE	59424-59424	COFFEE CREEK
59047-59047	LIVINGSTON	59215-59215	CIRCLE	59315-59315	BLOOMFIELD	59425-59425	CONRAD
59050-59050	LODGE GRASS	59217-59217	CRANE	59316-59316	BOYES	59427-59427	CUT BANK
59052-59052	MC LEOD	59218-59218	CULBERTSON	59317-59317	BROADUS	59430-59430	DENTON
59053-59053	MARTINSDALE	59219-59219	DAGMAR	59318-59318	BRUSETT	59432-59432	DUPUYER
59054-59054	MELSTONE	59221-59221	FAIRVIEW	59319-59319	CAPITOL	59433-59433	DUTTON

59434-59434 EAST GLACIER PARK	59527-59527 HAYS	59732-59732 GLEN	59848-59848 LONEPINE
59435-59435 ETHRIDGE	59528-59528 HINGHAM	59733-59733 GOLD CREEK	59851-59851 MILLTOWN
59436-59436 FAIRFIELD	59529-59529 HOGELAND	59735-59735 HARRISON	59853-59853 NOXON
59440-59440 FLOWEREE	59530-59530 INVERNESS	59736-59736 JACKSON	59854-59854 OVANDO
59441-59441 FORESTGROVE	59531-59531 JOPLIN	59739-59739 LIMA	59855-59855 PABLO
59442-59442 FORT BENTON	59532-59532 KREMLIN	59740-59740 MC ALLISTER	59856-59856 PARADISE
59443-59443 FORT SHAW	59535-59535 LLOYD	59741-59741 MANHATTAN	59858-59858 PHILIPSBURG
59444-59444 GALATA	59537-59537 LORING	59743-59743 MELROSE	59859-59859 PLAINS
59445-59445 GARNEILL	59538-59538 MALTA	59745-59745 NORRIS	59860-59860 POLSON
59446-59446 GERALDINE	59540-59540 RUDYARD	59746-59746 POLARIS	59863-59863 RAVALLI
59447-59447 GEYSER	59542-59542 TURNER	59747-59747 PONY	59864-59864 RONAN
59448-59448 HEART BUTTE	59544-59544 WHITEWATER	59748-59748 RAMSAY	59865-59865 SAINT IGNATIUS
59450-59450 HIGHWOOD	59545-59545 WHITLASH	59749-59749 SHERIDAN	59866-59866 SAINT REGIS
59451-59451 HILGER	59546-59546 ZORTMAN	59750-59750 BUTTE	59867-59867 SALTESE
59452-59452 HOBSON	59547-59547 ZURICH	59751-59751 SILVER STAR	59868-59868 SEELEY LAKE
59453-59453 JUDITH GAP	59601-59626 HELENA	59752-59752 THREE FORKS	59870-59870 STEVENSVILLE
59454-59454 KEVIN	59631-59631 BASIN	59754-59754 TWIN BRIDGES	59871-59871 SULA
59456-59456 LEDGER	59632-59632 BOULDER	59755-59755 VIRGINIA CITY	59872-59872 SUPERIOR
59457-59457 LEWISTOWN	59633-59633 CANYON CREEK	59756-59756 WARMSPRINGS	59873-59873 THOMPSON FALLS
59460-59460 LOMA	59634-59634 CLANCY	59758-59758 WEST YELLOWSTONE	59874-59874 TROUT CREEK
59461-59461 LOTHAIR	59635-59635 EAST HELENA	59759-59759 WHITEHALL	59875-59875 VICTOR
59462-59462 MOCCASIN	59636-59636 FORT HARRISON	59760-59760 WILLOW CREEK	59901-59904 KALISPELL
59463-59463 MONARCH	59638-59638 JEFFERSON CITY	59761-59761 WISDOM	59910-59910 BIG ARM
59464-59464 MOORE	59639-59639 LINCOLN	59762-59762 WISE RIVER	59911-59911 BIGFORK
59465-59465 NEIHART	59640-59640 MARYSVILLE	59771-59773 BOZEMAN	59912-59912 COLUMBIA FALLS
59466-59466 OILMONT	59641-59641 RADERSBURG	59801-59812 MISSOULA	59913-59913 CORAM
59467-59467 PENDROY	59642-59642 RINGLING	59820-59820 ALBERTON	59914-59914 DAYTON
59468-59468 POWER	59643-59643 TOSTON	59821-59821 ARLEE	59915-59915 ELMO
59469-59469 RAYNESFORD	59644-59644 TOWNSEND	59823-59823 BONNER	59916-59916 ESSEX
59471-59471 ROY	59645-59645 WHITE SULPHUR	59824-59824 CHARLO	59917-59917 EUREKA
59472-59472 SAND COULEE	SPRINGS	59825-59825 CLINTON	59918-59918 FORTINE
59473-59473 SANTA RITA	59647-59647 WINSTON	59826-59826 CONDON	59919-59919 HUNGRY HORSE
59474-59474 SHELBY	59648-59648 WOLF CREEK	59827-59827 CONNER	59920-59920 KILA
59477-59477 SIMMS	59701-59707 BUTTE	59828-59828 CORVALLIS	59921-59921 LAKE MC DONALD
59479-59479 STANFORD	59710-59710 ALDER	59829-59829 DARBY	59922-59922 LAKESIDE
59480-59480 STOCKETT	59711-59711 ANACONDA	59830-59830 DE BORGIA	59923-59923 LIBBY
59482-59482 SUNBURST	59713-59713 AVON	59831-59831 DIXON	59925-59925 MARION
59483-59483 SUN RIVER	59714-59714 BELGRADE	59832-59832 DRUMMOND	59926-59926 MARTIN CITY
59484-59484 SWEETGRASS	59715-59715 BOZEMAN	59833-59833 FLORENCE	59927-59927 OLNEY
59485-59485 ULM	59716-59716 BIG SKY	59834-59834 FRENCHTOWN	59928-59928 POLEBRIDGE
59486-59486 VALIER	59717-59719 BOZEMAN	59835-59835 GRANTSDALE	59929-59929 PROCTOR
59487-59487 VAUGHN	59720-59720 CAMERON	59836-59836 GREENOUGH	59930-59930 REXFORD
59489-59489 WINIFRED	59721-59721 CARDWELL	59837-59837 HALL	59931-59931 ROLLINS
59501-59501 HAVRE	59722-59722 DEER LODGE	59840-59840 HAMILTON	59932-59932 SOMERS
59520-59520 BIG SANDY	59724-59724 DELL	59841-59841 PINESDALE	59933-59933 STRYKER
59521-59521 BOX ELDER	59725-59725 DILLON	59842-59842 HAUGAN	59934-59934 TREGO
59522-59522 CHESTER	59727-59727 DIVIDE	59843-59843 HELMVILLE	59935-59935 TROY
59523-59523 CHINOOK	59728-59728 ELLISTON	59844-59844 HERON	59936-59936 WEST GLACIER
59524-59524 DODSON	59729-59729 ENNIS	59845-59845 HOT SPRINGS	59937-59937 WHITEFISH
59525-59525 GILDFORD	59730-59730 GALLATIN GATEWAY	59846-59846 HUSON	
59526-59526 HARLEM	59731-59731 GARRISON	59847-59847 LOLO	

Nebraska

General Help Numbers:

Governor's Office
PO Box 94848   402-471-2244
Lincoln, NE 68509-4848   Fax 402-471-6031
http://gov.nol.org   8AM-5PM

Attorney General's Office
2115 State Capitol   402-471-2682
Lincoln, NE 68509   Fax 402-471-3297
http://www.nol.org/home/ago   8AM-5PM

State Court Administrator
PO Box 98910   402-471-3730
Lincoln, NE 68509-8910   Fax 402-471-2197
http://court.nol.org/AOC   8AM-4:30PM

State Archives
Archives   402-471-4771
PO Box 82554   Fax 402-471-8922
Lincoln, NE 68501-2554   9:30AM-4:30PM M-F;
     8-5 SA; 1:30PM-5PM SU
http://www.nebraskahistory.org

State Specifics:

Capital: Lincoln
     Lancaster County

Time Zone: CST*

* Nebraska's nineteen western-most counties are MST:

They are: Arthur, Banner, Box Butte, Chase, Cherry, Cheyenne, Dawes, Deuel, Dundy, Garden, Grant, Hooker, Keith, Kimball, Morrill, Perkins, Scotts. Bluff, Sheridan, Sioux.

Number of Counties: 93

Population: 1,711,263

Web Site: www.state.ne.us

State Agencies

Criminal Records

Nebraska State Patrol, CID, PO Box 94907, Lincoln, NE 68509-4907 (Courier: 1500 Nebraska Highway 2, Lincoln, NE 68502); 402-479-4924, 402-471-4545, 8AM-4PM.

http://www.nebraska-state-patrol.org

Note: Arrest records will not be released unless disposition is provided, except if an arrest without disposition is less than one year old.

Indexing & Storage: Records are available from 1937 to present. New records are available for inquiry immediately. Records are indexed on inhouse computer, fingerprint cards.

Searching: State keeps record of requesters and will inform the person of record if asked. Include the following in your request-full name, disposition, date of birth, Social Security Number, sex, race. The following data is not released: juvenile records.

Access by: mail, in person.

Fee & Payment: The search fee is $10.00 per name. Fee payee: Nebraska State Patrol.

Prepayment required. Personal checks accepted. No credit cards accepted.

Mail search: Turnaround time: 15 days. No self addressed stamped envelope is required.

In person search: They accept requests in person, but they will still mail back the report (unless it is the requester's own report).

Corporation Records
Limited Liability Company Records
Limited Partnerships
Trade Names
Trademarks/Servicemarks

Secretary of State, Corporation Commission, 1305 State Capitol Bldg, Lincoln, NE 68509; 402-471-4079, 402-471-3666 (Fax), 8AM-5PM.

http://www.nol.org.home/SOS

Indexing & Storage: Records are available from the beginning of state corporation filings. Records are indexed on microfilm, index cards.

Searching: Include the following in your request-full name of business. In addition to the articles of incorporation, corporation records include the following information: Reports, Officers, Directors, Prior (merged) names, Inactive and Reserved names and Occupation Tax records for the last 5 years.

Access by: mail, phone, fax, in person, online.

Fee & Payment: No search fee, copies are $1.00 per page. Fee payee: Secretary of State. They will send an invoice. Personal checks accepted. No credit cards accepted.

Mail search: Turnaround time: 2 days. No self addressed stamped envelope is required.

Phone search: Records are available by phone.

Fax search: Fax searching available.

Online search: The state has designated Nebrask@ Online (800-747-8177) to facilitate online retrieval of records. Access is through both a dial-up system and the Internet; however an account and payment is required. The state Internet site has general information only.

Other access: Nebrask@ Online has the capability of offering database purchases.

Uniform Commercial Code
Federal Tax Liens
State Tax Liens

UCC Division, Secretary of State, PO Box 95104, Lincoln, NE 68509 (Courier: 1301 State Capitol Bldg, Lincoln, NE 68509); 402-471-4080, 402-471-4429 (Fax), 7:30AM-5PM.

http://www.nol.org/home/SOS

Note: Effective July 1, 1999, all federal and state tax liens are filed at this agency. Previously filed tax liens must be searched at the county level (except federal tax liens in indivduals which have always been filed at the statelevel.)

Indexing & Storage: Records are available from 1981 to present, on both computer and microfiche.

Searching: Use search request form UCC-11. Include the following in your request-debtor name.

Access by: mail, fax, in person, online.

Fee & Payment: The search fee is $3.50 per debtor name. Copies are $.50 per page. Certification is an additional $4.00. Fee payee: Secretary of State. They will invoice fax requesters. Personal checks accepted. No credit cards accepted.

Mail search: Turnaround time: 1 day. A self addressed stamped envelope is requested.

Fax search: The fee is $5.00 per debtor. Use the National Search Form (UCC-11). Turnaround time is 4 hours or less.

In person search: Records are generally available with a short wait.

Online search: Access is outsourced to Nebrask@ Online at www.nol.org. The system is available 24 hours daily. There is an annual $50 fee but no further charges to view records. Call 800-747-8177 for more information.

Other access: Check with Nebrask@ Online for bulk purchase programs.

Sales Tax Registrations

Revenue Department, Revenue Operations Division, PO Box 94818, Lincoln, NE 68509-4818 (Courier: 301 Centennial Mall South, Lincoln, NE 68509); 402-471-5695, 402-471-5608 (Fax), 8AM-5PM.

http://www.nol.org/revenue

Indexing & Storage: Records are available from 1967. Records are indexed on computer.

Searching: This office will confirm that a business is registered and supply requester will name, address and date of license. Include the following in your request-business name. They will also search by tax permit number or by federal tax ID.

Access by: mail, phone.

Mail search: A self addressed stamped envelope is requested. No fee for mail request.

Phone search: No fee for telephone request.

Birth Certificates

NE Health & Human Services System, Vital Statistics Section, PO Box 95065, Lincoln, NE 68509-5065 (Courier: 301 Centennial Mall S, 3rd Floor, Lincoln, NE 68509); 402-471-2871, 8AM-5PM.

http://www.hhs.state.ne.us/ced/cedindex.htm

Note: Records may also be ordered at regional offices in Omaha, Kearney, North Platte, and Scottsbluff.

Indexing & Storage: Records are available from 1904 to present. Records are indexed by Soundex code, year and county. Records are indexed by computer since 1912, and can be found on microfiche from 1912 to 1977.

Searching: Non-family members must have a signed release from person of record or immediate family member for investigative purposes. If the birth certificate is more than 50 years old, a release form is not required. Closed records are not released. Include the following in your request-full name, date of birth, place of birth, names of parents, mother's maiden name, relationship to person of record, reason for information request. If adopted, indicate so. Expedited services are only available from 9AM to 3PM. The following data is not released: original records of adoption or sealed records.

Access by: mail, phone, in person, online.

Fee & Payment: The fee is $8.00 per record. Fee payee: Vital Records. Prepayment required. Credit cards may only be used for expedited searches by calling in. The file search fee is non-refundable if no records are found. Personal checks accepted. Credit cards accepted: MasterCard, Visa, AmEx, Discover.

Mail search: Turnaround time: 2 to 3 weeks. If the agency receives the request by overnight mail, they will mail it back within 2 to 3 days.A self addressed stamped envelope is requested.

Phone search: See expedited service.

In person search: Turnaround time is 20 to 30 minutes.

Online search: Records may be ordered online from the Internet site.

Death Records

Health and Human Services System, Vital Statistics Section, PO Box 95065, Lincoln, NE 68509-5065 (Courier: 301 Centennial Mall S, 3rd Floor, Lincoln, NE 68509); 402-471-2871, 8AM-5PM.

http://www.hhs.state.ne.us/ced/cedindex.htm

Note: If a certificate is more than 50 years in the past, release form is not required.

Indexing & Storage: Records are available from 1904 to present. Records are on microfilm from 1956-1997.

Searching: Must have a signed release from immediate family member for investigative purposes. Include the following in your request-full name, date of death, place of death, relationship to person of record, reason for information request. Expedited services are available from 9AM to 3 PM.

Access by: mail, phone, in person.

Fee & Payment: The fee is $7.00 per record. Fee payee: Vital Records. Prepayment required. Credit cards may only be used for phone expedited service. The file search fee is non-refundable if no records are found. Personal checks accepted. Credit cards accepted: MasterCard, Visa, AmEx, Discover.

Mail search: Turnaround time: 2 to 3 weeks. If the agency receives a search request by overnight mail, they will mail the response within 2 to 3 days.A self addressed stamped envelope is requested.

Phone search: See expedited service.

In person search: Turnaround time is 20 to 30 minutes.

Marriage Certificates

Health and Human Services System, Vital Statistics Section, PO Box 95065, Lincoln, NE 68509-5065 (Courier: 301 Centennial Mall S, 3rd Floor, Lincoln, NE 68509); 402-471-2871, 8AM-5PM.

http://www.hhs.state.ne.us/ced/cedindex.htm

Note: If a certificate is more than 50 years old, a release is not required.

Indexing & Storage: Records are available from 1909 to present. Records are indexed by Soundex code, year and county and are on microfilm from 1956 to present. Records are indexed on microfiche.

Searching: Must have a signed release from persons of record or immediate family member for investigative purposes. Include the following in your request-names of husband and wife, date of marriage, place or county of marriage, relationship to person of record, reason for information request, wife's maiden name. Expedited service is only available from 9AM to 3PM.

Access by: mail, phone, in person.

Fee & Payment: The fee is $7.00 per record. Fee payee: Vital Records. Prepayment required. Credit cards may only be used for phone expedited service. The file search fee is non-refundable if no records are found. Personal checks accepted. Credit cards accepted: MasterCard, Visa, AmEx, Discover.

Mail search: Turnaround time: 2 to 3 weeks. If this agency receives a search request by overnight mail, they will mail a response within 2 to 3 days.A self addressed stamped envelope is requested.

Phone search: See expedited service.

In person search: Turnaround time is 30 minutes.

Divorce Records

Health and Human Services System, Vital Statistics Section, PO Box 95065, Lincoln, NE 68509-5065 (Courier: 301 Centennial Mall S, 3rd Floor, Lincoln, NE 68509); 402-471-2871, 8AM-5PM.

http://www.hhs.state.ne.us/ced/cedindex.htm

Note: If a certificate is more than 50 years, a release is not required.

Indexing & Storage: Records are available from 1909 to present. Records are indexed by Soundex code, year and county and are on microfilm from 1956 to present.

Searching: Must have a signed release from person of record or immediate family member for investigative purposes. Include the following in your request-names of husband and wife, date of divorce, relationship to person of record, reason for information request. Must also have county where divorce was granted. Expedited service is only available from 9AM to 3PM.

Access by: mail, phone, in person.

Fee & Payment: Fee is $7.00 per record. Fee payee: Vital Records. Prepayment required. Credit cards may only be used for phone expedited service. The file search fee is non-refundable if no records are found. Personal checks accepted. Credit cards accepted: MasterCard, Visa, AmEx, Discover.

Mail search: Turnaround time: 2 to 3 weeks. If this agency receives a request by overnight mail, they will mail a response within 2-3 days.A self addressed stamped envelope is requested.

Phone search: See expedited service.

In person search: Turnaround time is 20-30 minutes.

Workers' Compensation Records

Workers' Compensation Court, PO Box 98908, Lincoln, NE 68509-8908 (Courier: State Capitol, 13th Floor, Lincoln, NE 68509); 402-471-6468, 800-599-5155 (In-state), 402-471-2700 (Fax), 8AM-5PM.

http://www.nol.org/workcomp

Indexing & Storage: Records are available from 1972 on. It takes 2 days before new records are available for inquiry. Records are indexed on microfilm, printout sheets (SS# & name only), computer.

Searching: Must have a release form for medical records. All other records are public record. Include the following in your request-claimant name, Social Security Number, date of birth, date of accident, docket number. A date of injury is required for searches going back more than 10 years.

Access by: mail, in person, online.

Fee & Payment: A search is $5.00 per name for 5 years searched. If 10 years, then $10.00; if older than 1991, then $15.00. The first 20 pages of file copied are free, then the fee is $25 per page. Microfilm copies are $.50 per page. Fee payee: Workers' Compensation Court. Prepayment required. Personal checks accepted. No credit cards accepted.

Mail search: Turnaround time: 2 to 3 days. No self addressed stamped envelope is required.

In person search: Appointments are required.

Online search: Access to orders and decisions is available from the web site.

Driver Records

Department of Motor Vehicles, Driver & Vehicle Records Division, PO Box 94789, Lincoln, NE 68509-4789 (Courier: 301 Centennial Mall, S, Lincoln, NE 68509); 402-471-4343, 8AM-5PM.

http://www.nol.org/home/dmv/driverec.htm

Note: It is suggested you obtain copies of tickets at the local courts.

Indexing & Storage: Records are available for 5 years for moving violations and suspensions; lifetime for DWIs. Accidents are reported on the record, but fault is not indicated. Surrendered licenses are purged one year after expiration date. It takes 30 days before new records are available for inquiry.

Searching: SSNs will not be released. The general public cannot get personal data. Approved requesters receive the driver's address. The driver's full name and DOB or license number are needed for ordering.

Access by: mail, in person, online.

Fee & Payment: The fee is $3.00 per record. Fee payee: Department of Motor Vehicles. Prepayment required. Personal checks accepted. No credit cards accepted.

Mail search: Turnaround time: 24 hours. A self addressed stamped envelope is requested.

In person search: Drivers can view records in-person for no fee. Up to 7 records can be ordered with immediate processing. Walk-in requesters are not charged for a no record found.

Online search: Nebraska outsources all online and tape record requests through Nebrask@ Online (800-747-8177). The system is interactive and open 24 hours a day, 7 days a week. Fee is $3.00 per record. There is an annual fee of $50.00 and a $.40 per minute connect fee or $.12 if through the Internet.

Vehicle Ownership
Vehicle Identification
Vessel Ownership

Department of Motor Vehicles, Driver & Vehicle Records Division, PO Box 94789, Lincoln, NE 68509-4789 (Courier: 301 Centennial Mall, S, Lincoln, NE 68509); 402-471-3918, 8AM-5PM.

http://www.nol.org/home/DMV

Indexing & Storage: Records are available from 1939. Boat ownership information is available from 1997. All motorized boats manufactured after 11/1/72 must be titled.

Searching: The general public cannot obtain personal data. Typical items required for search include; full name, VIN or plate number, and year and make.

Access by: mail, in person, online.

Fee & Payment: The fee is $1.00 per record. Lien information appears on the record. Fee payee: Department of Motor Vehicles. Prepayment required. Personal checks accepted. No credit cards accepted.

Mail search: Turnaround time: 7 to 10 days. A self addressed stamped envelope is requested.

In person search: Turnaround time is while you wait. "No record founds" are charged the full amount.

Online search: Electronic access is through Nebrask@ Online. There is a start-up fee and line charges are incurred in addition to the $1.00 per record fee. The system is open 24 hours a day, 7 days a week. Call 800-747-8177 for more information.

Other access: Bulk requesters must be authorized by state officials. Purpose of the request and subsequent usage are reviewed. For more information, call 402-471-3909.

Accident Reports

Department of Roads, Accident Records Bureau, Box 94669, Lincoln, NE 68509 (Courier: 1500 Nebraska Highway 2, Lincoln, NE 68502); 402-479-4645, 402-479-4325 (Fax), 8AM-5PM.

http://www.dor.state.ne.us

Indexing & Storage: Records are available from 1978 to 1994 on microfilm; however, fatal accidents are on microfilm since 1956. Records are computerized since 1988.

Searching: Individual driver's own reports are not released. Include the following in your request-full name, date of accident, county.

Access by: mail, phone, in person.

Fee & Payment: The fee is $6.00 per record. Fee payee: Accident Records Bureau. Prepayment required. Personal checks accepted. No credit cards accepted.

Mail search: Turnaround time: 1 week to 10 days. No self addressed stamped envelope is required.

Phone search: They will schedule requests by phone.

Other access: Records can be purchased in bulk from the computer database (1988 to present).

Vessel Registration
Records not maintained by a state level agency.

Note: All boats must be registered. Records are found at the county recorder offices.

Legislation Records

Clerk of Legislature Office, PO Box 94604, Lincoln, NE 68509-4604 (Courier: State Capitol, 1445 K Street, Room 2018, Lincoln, NE 68509); 402-471-2271, 402-471-2126 (Fax), 8AM-5PM.

http://www.unicam.state.ne.us

Indexing & Storage: Records are available from 1961 to present (floor debate). They can pull histories on bills back to 1937.

Searching: Include the following in your request-bill number.

Access by: mail, phone, fax, in person, online.

Fee & Payment: There is no charge for a copy of a bill. A legislative history of a bill costs $.15 per page. Fee payee: State of Nebraska. Prepayment required. Personal checks accepted. No credit cards accepted.

Mail search: Turnaround time: 3 to 5 days. Bill number and year required to perform mail searches.No self addressed stamped envelope is required.

Phone search: You may call for information.

Fax search: Fee is $1.00 per page. Turnaround time is same day if possible or 1-2 days.

In person search: You may request information in person.

Online search: The web site features the state statutes, legislative bills for the present session and a legislative journal. You can search by bill number or subject.

Voter Registration
Access to Records is Restricted

Secretary of State, Election Divisions, PO Box 94608, Lincoln, NE 68509; 402-471-2554, 402-471-3237 (Fax), 8AM-5PM.

http://www.nol.org/home/SOS

Note: Individual look-ups must be done at the county level. The state has developed a new statewide system. Current law dictates that the database can only be sold for political purposes, and not for commercial purposes. A CD can be purchased for $500.

GED Certificates

NE Dept of Education, Adult Education, PO Box 94987, Lincoln, NE 68509 (Courier: 301 Centennial Mall S, Lincoln, NE 68509); 402-471-2475, 402-471-8127 (Fax).

http://www.edneb.org/ADED/home.htm

Searching: To search, all of the following is required: a signed release, date of birth, all last names used, and Social Security Number. If known, the year and city of test are helpful.

Access by: mail, fax, in person.

Fee & Payment: There is no fee for verification. Copies of transcripts are $2.00. Fee payee: NE Dept of Education. Prepayment required. Money orders are accepted. Personal checks accepted. No credit cards accepted.

Mail search: Turnaround time: 1 to 2 days. No self addressed stamped envelope is required.

Fax search: Same criteria as mail searching.

In person search: Turnaround time is immediate in most instances.

Hunting License Information
Fishing License Information

Game & Parks Commission, PO Box 30370, Lincoln, NE 68503 (Courier: 2200 N 33rd St, Lincoln, NE 68503); 402-471-5455, 402-471-5528 (Fax), 8AM-5PM.

http://www.ngpc.state.ne.us

Note: Only permits for deer, antelope and turkey are available.

Indexing & Storage: Records are available from 1988 to present on microfiche. It takes 2 to 3 days before new records are available for inquiry. Records are indexed on microfiche.

Searching: All information on the face of the license is public information, except for release of SSNs. Include the following in your request-date of birth, name. Date of application helpful.

Access by: mail, phone, in person.

Fee & Payment: There is no search fee.

Mail search: Turnaround time: 1 to 2 days. No self addressed stamped envelope is required.

Phone search: Records are available by phone.

Other access: Database purchase of information is available.

Nebraska State Licensing Agencies

Licenses Searchable Online

Alcohol/Drug Testing #30 .... www.hhs.state.ne.us/lis/lis.asp
Architect #02 .... www.nol.org/home/NBOP/roster.html
Asbestos-related Occupation #30 .... www.hhs.state.ne.us/lis/lis.asp
Assisted Living Facility #30 .... www.nlc.state.ne.us/docs/pilot/pubs/h.html
Athletic Trainer #30 .... www.hhs.state.ne.us/lis/lis.asp
Attorney #32 .... www.nebar.com/directory/dir.asp
Bank #31 .... www.ndbf.org/banks.htm
Chiropractor #30 .... www.hhs.state.ne.us/lis/lis.asp
Collection Agency #26 .... www.nol.org/home/SOS/Collections/col-agn.htm
Cosmetology Salon/School #30 .... www.hhs.state.ne.us/lis/lis.asp
Credit Union #31 .... www.ndbf.org/culist.htm
Debt Management Agency #26 .... www.nol.org/home/SOS/Collections/debtlist.htm
Delayed Deposit Service #31 .... www.ndbf.org/ddslist.htm
Dental Hygienist #30 .... www.hhs.state.ne.us/lis/lis.asp
Dentist #30 .... www.hhs.state.ne.us/lis/lis.asp
Developmentally Disabled Center #30 .... www.nlc.state.ne.us/docs/pilot/pubs/h.html
Emergency Medical Care Facility/Clinic #30 .... www.hhs.state.ne.us/lis/lis.asp
Engineer #02 .... www.nol.org/home/NBOP/roster.html
Environmental Health Specialist #30 .... www.hhs.state.ne.us/lis/lis.asp
Exterminator #18 .... www.kellysolutions.com/ne/
Funeral Establishment #30 .... www.hhs.state.ne.us/lis/lis.asp
Health Clinic #30 .... www.hhs.state.ne.us/lis/lis.asp
Hearing Aid Dispenser/Fitter #30 .... www.hhs.state.ne.us/lis/lis.asp
Home Health Agency #30 .... www.nlc.state.ne.us/docs/pilot/pubs/h.html
Hospice #30 .... www.nlc.state.ne.us/docs/pilot/pubs/h.html
Hospital #30 .... www.nlc.state.ne.us/docs/pilot/pubs/h.html
Investigator, Plainclothes #26 .... www.nol.org/home/SOS/Privatedetectives/pilist.htm
Investment Advisor/Advisor Representative #11 www.ndbf.org/secsearch.htm
Liquor Vendor #19 .... www.nol.org/home/NLCC/nlccsearch.html
Lobbyist #08 .... www.lobbyist.net/Nebraska/NEBLOB.htm
Massage Therapy School #30 .... www.hhs.state.ne.us/lis/lis.asp
Mental Health Center #30 .... www.hhs.state.ne.us/lis/lis.asp
Nurse #30 .... www.hhs.state.ne.us/lis/lis.asp
Nursing Home #30 .... www.hhs.state.ne.us/lis/lis.asp
Nutrition Therapy, Medical #30 .... www.hhs.state.ne.us/lis/lis.asp
Occupational Therapist #30 .... www.hhs.state.ne.us/lis/lis.asp
Optometrist #30 .... www.hhs.state.ne.us/lis/lis.asp
Pesticide Applicator/Dealer #18 .... www.kellysolutions.com/ne/
Pharmacist/Pharmacy #30 .... www.hhs.state.ne.us/lis/lis.asp
Physical Therapist #30 .... www.hhs.state.ne.us/lis/lis.asp
Physician #30 .... www.hhs.state.ne.us/lis/lis.asp
Physician Assistant #30 .... www.hhs.state.ne.us/lis/lis.asp
Podiatrist #30 .... www.hhs.state.ne.us/lis/lis.asp
Polygraph Examiner, Private/Public #26 .... www.nol.org/home/SOS/Polygraph/polypri.htm
Private Detective #26 .... www.nol.org/home/SOS/Privatedetectives/pdlist.htm
Psychologist #30 .... www.hhs.state.ne.us/lis/lis.asp
Public Accountant-CPA #05 .... www.nol.org/home/BPA/license
Radiographer #30 .... www.hhs.state.ne.us/lis/lis.asp
Real Estate Appraiser #22 .... http://dbdec.nrc.state.ne.us/appraiser/docs/list.html
Respiratory Care #30 .... www.hhs.state.ne.us/lis/lis.asp
Securities Agent #11 .... www.ndbf.org/secsearch.htm
Securities Broker/Dealer #11 .... www.ndbf.org/secsearch.htm
Substance Abuse Treatment Center #30 .... www.nlc.state.ne.us/docs/pilot/pubs/h.html
Surveyor #03 .... www.sso.state.ne.us/bels/index.htm
Swimming Pool Operator #30 .... www.hhs.state.ne.us/lis/lis.asp
Veterinarian #30 .... www.hhs.state.ne.us/lis/lis.asp
Voice Stress Examiner (Polygraph) #26 .... www.nol.org/home/SOS/Polygraph/voice.htm
Water Operator #30 .... www.hhs.state.ne.us/lis/lis.asp

Licensing Quick Finder

Abstractor #04 402-471-2383
Aerial Applicator #10 402-471-2371
Air Conditioning/Heating Contractor #12402-441-7508
Alcohol/Drug Testing #30 402-471-2118
Amusement Ride Inspector #21 402-471-2031
Animal Technician #30 402-471-2118
Architect #02 402-471-2021
Asbestos-related Occupation #30 402-471-2299
Assisted Living Facility #30..................402-471-4970
Athletic Trainer #30 402-471-2299
Attorney #32 402-471-3731
Auctioneer #06...................................402-441-7437
Bank #31 402-471-2171
Barber #01 402-471-2051
Boiler & Pressure Vessel Inspector#16 .402-471-4721
Boxer #28 402-471-2009
Boxing Promoter #28...........................402-471-2009
Chauffeur #06 402-441-7437
Child Caring/Placing Agency #15..........402-471-9138
Chiropractor #30 402-471-2299
Collection Agency #26.........................402-471-2555
Contractor #21 402-595-3189
Contractor, Building #12 402-441-6456
Contractor, General #12.......................402-471-5729
Cosmetology Salon/School #30 402-471-2115
Credit Union #31.................................402-471-2171
Debt Management Agency #26..............402-471-2555
Delayed Deposit Service #31................402-471-2171
Dental Anesthesia Permit #30 402-471-2118
Dental Hygienist #30 402-471-2118
Dentist #30 402-471-2118
Developmentally Disabled Center#30 ...402-471-2115
Drug Distributor, Wholesale #30 402-471-2118
Drug Wholesale Facility #30 402-471-2115
Educational Interpreter Performance-Hearing Impaired
#09 402-471-3593
Educational Media Specialist/Librarian #13 ....
....402-471-0739
Electrician #29 402-471-3550
Electrologist #15 402-471-2117
Elevator Inspector/Inspection Manager #21.................
....402-471-8674
Embalmer #15 402-471-2115
Emergency Medical Care Facility/Clinic #30 ....
....402-471-2115

Employment Agency #21......................402-471-2230
Engineer #02 402-471-2021
Environmental Health Specialist #30.....402-471-2299
Esthetician #15 402-471-2117
Exterminator #18.................................402-471-2394
Farm Labor Contractor #21 402-471-2230
Fertilizer Professional/Business #18 402-471-2394
Fire Protection Sprinkler Contractor#12 402-441-6456
Foster/Group Home #15.......................402-471-9138
Funeral Director #15............................402-471-2115
Funeral Establishment #30 402-471-2115
Health Clinic #30 402-471-2115
Hearing Aid Dispenser/Fitter #30 402-471-2299
Hearing Assessment (EIPA) #09...........402-471-3593
Hearing Quality Assurance Screening Test #09 ....
....402-471-3593
Home Health Agency #30.....................402-471-2115
Hospice #30.......................................402-471-2115
Hospital #30.......................................402-471-2115
Insurance Agency/Agent/Broker #14.....402-471-4913
Insurance Company #14 402-471-4913
Insurance Consultant #14....................402-471-4913
Insurance Utilization Review Agent #14 402-471-4913
Interpreter for the Hearing Impaired (Nebraska
   Registry of Interpreters) #09 402-471-3593
Investigator, Plainclothes #26 402-471-2384
Investment Advisor/Advisor Representative #11.........
....402-471-3445
Jewelry Dealer, Secondhand #06 402-441-7437
Landscape Architect #23 402-471-2021
Law Enforcement Officer #20 308-385-6030
Liquor Vendor #19...............................402-471-2571
Lobbyist #08 402-471-2608
Local Anesthesia Certification #30 402-471-2118
Marriage & Family Therapist #15 402-471-9138
Massage Establishment #30.................402-471-2115
Massage Therapy School #30 402-471-2115
Mental Health Center #30.....................402-471-2115
Notary Public #27...............................402-471-2558
Nurse #30 402-471-2115
Nursing Education Program #30............402-471-2115
Nursing Home #30...............................402-471-2115
Nursing Home Administrator #15 402-471-2115
Nutrition Therapy, Medical #30 402-471-2115
Occupational Therapist #30 402-471-2299

Optometrist #30 402-471-2118
Osteopathic Physician #30 402-471-2118
Pawnbroker #06..................................402-441-7437
Pesticide Applicator/Dealer #18 402-471-2394
Pharmacist #30 402-471-2118
Pharmacy #30 402-471-2115
Pharmacy, Mail Order #30....................402-471-2115
Physical Therapist #30 402-471-2299
Physician #30 402-471-2118
Physician Assistant #30.......................402-471-2118
Plant Nursery/Nursery Professional #18 402-471-2394
Plumber Journeyman #07.....................402-466-5154
Podiatrist #30.....................................402-471-2118
Polygraph Examiner, Private #26...........402-471-4070
Polygraph Examiner, Public #26 402-471-4070
Private Detective #26 402-471-2384
Psychologist #30.................................402-471-4905
Public Accountant-CPA #05..................402-471-3595
Racing Event/Professional #24 402-471-4155
Radiographer #30 402-471-2118
Real Estate Appraiser #22 402-471-9015
Real Estate Broker #25 402-471-2004
Real Estate Salesperson #25 402-471-2004
Respiratory Care #30 402-471-2299
Sanitarian #17....................................402-471-0515
School Administrator/Supervisor #13 402-471-0739
School Nurse #13................................402-471-0739
Securities Agent #11 402-471-3445
Securities Broker/Dealer #11 402-471-3445
Skin Care Salon #30 402-471-2115
Social Worker #15...............................402-471-9138
Speech-Language Pathologist/Audiologist #15..........
....402-471-9138
Substance Abuse Treatment Ctr. #30 ...402-471-2115
Surveyor #03 402-471-2566
Swimming Pool Operator #30 402-471-2299
Taxi Driver #06...................................402-441-7437
Teacher #13.......................................402-471-0739
Veterinarian #30.................................402-471-2118
Veterinary Technician #15 402-471-2118
Voice Stress Examiner (Polygraph) #26 402-471-4070
Water Operator #30 402-471-2299
Water Treatment Plant Operator #17 402-471-0515
Well Driller/Pump Installer #17.............402-471-0515
Wrestler #28 402-471-2009

Licensing Agency Information

#01 Board of Barber Examiners, 301 Centennial Mall S, 6th Fl, Lincoln, NE 68509-4723; 402-471-2051.

#02 Board of Examiners for Engineers & Architects, PO Box 95165, 301 Centennial Mall S 6th Fl, Lincoln, NE 68509-4751; 402-471-2021, Fax: 402-471-0787.
www.nol.org/home/NBOP
Direct web site URL to search for licensees: www.nol.org/home/NBOP/roster.html

#03 Board of Examiners for Land Surveyors, 555 N Cotner Blvd, Lincoln, NE 68505; 402-471-2566, Fax: 402-471-3057.
Direct web site URL to search for licensees: www.sso/state.ne/us/bels/index.htm

#04 Board of Examiners or Abstractors, 301 Centennial Mall S, Lincoln, NE 68509-4944; 402-471-2383.

#05 Board of Public Accountancy, PO Box 94725, Lincoln, NE 68509-4725; 402-471-3595, Fax: 402-471-4484.
www.nol.org/home/BPA/

#06 City Clerk's Office, 555 S 10th St, Lincoln, NE 68508; 402-441-7437, Fax: 402-441-8325.
http://interlinc.ci.lincoln.ne.us

#07 City Codes Administration, 555 S 10th St, #203, Lincoln, NE 68508; 402-441-7785.

#08 Clerk of the Legislature, PO Box 94604, Lincoln, NE 68509-4604; 402-471-2608, Fax: 402-471-2126.
www.unicam.state.ne.us

#09 Commission for the Deaf & Hard of Hearing, 4600 Valley Rd #420, Lincoln, NE 68510-4844; 402-471-3593, Fax: 402-471-3067.
www.nol.org/home/NCDHH

#10 Department of Aeronautics, 3431 Aviation Rd #150 (68524), Lincoln, NE 68501; 402-471-2371, Fax: 402-471-2906.
www.nol.org/home/NDOA

#11 Department of Banking & Finance, PO Box 95006 (1200 "N" Street, Suite 311), Lincoln, NE 68509-5006; 402-471-3445.
www.ndbf.org/sec.htm
Direct web site URL to search for licensees: www.ndbf.org/secsearch.htm

#12 Department of Building & Safety, 555 S 10th St, Lincoln, NE 68508; 402-441-7791, Fax: 402-471-8214.
www.ci.lincoln.ne.us

#13 Department of Education, 301 Centennial Mall S 6th Fl, Lincoln, NE 68509-4987; 402-471-0739, Fax: 402-471-9735.
www.nde.state.ne.us/TCERT/TCERT.html

#14 Department of Insurance, 641 O St #400, Lincoln, NE 68508-3639; 402-471-2201, Fax: 402-471-6559.
www.nol.org/home/NDOI/

#15 Department of Health & Human Services, PO Box 95044 (301 Centennial Mall S, 5th Fl), Lincoln, NE 68509; 402-471-9138, Fax: 402-471-9435.
www.hhs.state.ne.us/reg/regindex.htm

#16 Division of Safety, PO Box 95024, Lincoln, NE 68509; 402-471-4721, Fax: 402-471-5039.
www.dol.state.ne.us/safety/boiler.htm

#17 Drinking Water & Environmental Sanitation Division, PO Box 95007 (301 Centennial Mall S), Lincoln, NE 68509; 402-471-2541, Fax: 402-471-6436.
www.hhs.state.ne.us

#18 Department of Agriculture, PO Box 94756 (301 Centennial Mall South), Lincoln, NE 68509; 402-471-2394, Fax: 402-471-6892.
www.kellysolutions.com/ne/
Direct web site URL to search for licensees: www.kellysolutions.com/ne/

#19 Liquor Control Commission, 301 Centennial Mall S, 5th Fl, Lincoln, NE 68509-5046; 402-471-2571, Fax: 402-471-2814.
www.nol.org/home/NLCC
Direct web site URL to search for licensees: www.nol.org/home/NLCC/nlccsearch.html

#20 Crime Commission, 3600 N Academy Rd, Grand Island, NE 68801; 308-385-6030, Fax: 308-385-6032.
www.nol.org/home/crimecom

#21 Department of Labor, State Capitol, #2300, Lincoln, NE 68509; 402-471-2230, Fax: 402-471-5039.
www.dol.state.ne.us

#22 Real Estate Appraiser Board, PO Box 95066, Lincoln, NE 68509-4963; 402-471-9015, Fax: 402-471-9017.
http://linux1.nrc.state.ne.us/appraiser/
Direct web site URL to search for licensees: http://dbdec.nrc.state.ne.us/appraiser/docs/list.html

#23 Board of Landscape Architects, PO Box 95165, Lincoln, NE 68509-5165; 402-471-2021, Fax: 402-471-0787.

#24 Racing Commission, 301 Centennial Mall S 4th Fl, Lincoln, NE 68509-5014; 402-471-4155, Fax: 402-471-2339.

#25 Real Estate Commission, 301 Centennial Mall S, 6th Fl, Lincoln, NE 68509-4667; 402-471-2004, Fax: 402-471-4492.
www.nol.org/home/NREC/index.htm

#26 Secretary of State, PO Box 94608, Lincoln, NE 68509-4608; 402-471-2554, Fax: 402-471-3237.
www.nol.org/home/SOS
Direct web site URL to search for licensees: www.nol.org/home/SOS/. You can search online using links to professions/board, then search alpha lists

#27 Secretary of State, Rm 1301 State Capitol Bldg, Lincoln, NE 68509-5104; 402-471-2558, Fax: 402-471-4429.
www.nol.org/home/SOS/Notary/notary.htm

#28 Athletic Commission, 301 Centennial Mall S, 3rd Fl, Lincoln, NE 68509-4743; 402-471-2009, Fax: 402-471-2009.

#29 Electrical Division, 800 S 13th St #109, Lincoln, NE 68509; 402-471-3550, Fax: 402-471-4297.

#30 NE Health & Human Svcs Regulation & Licensure, PO Box 94986, Lincoln, NE 68509-4986; 402-471-2115, Fax: 402-471-3577.
www.hhs.state.ne.us/crl/crlindex.htm
Direct web site URL to search for licensees: www.hhs.state.ne.us/lis/lis.asp. You can search online using name, license number, profession, and license type. When searching online, you must choose between "by name" (to search individual profession licenses) and "by facility" (to search business licenses).

#31 Department of Banking and Finance, PO Box 95006 (1200 "N" Street, Suite 311), Lincoln, NE 68509-5006; 402-471-2171.
www.ndbf.org/fin.htm
Direct web site URL to search for licensees: www.ndbf.org/finsearch.htm. You can search online using alphabetical lists

#32 Supreme Court, State Capitol, Rm 2413, Lincoln, NE 68509; 402-471-3731.

#38 Real Estate Commission, 4040 N. Lincoln, Ste. 100, Lincoln, NE 73105; 405-521-3387, Fax: 405-424-1534.

Nebraska Federal Courts

The following list indicates the district and division name for each county in the state.

County/Court Cross Reference

County	District	County	District
Adams	Lincoln	Jefferson	Lincoln
Antelope	Lincoln	Johnson	Lincoln
Arthur	North Platte	Kearney	Lincoln
Banner	North Platte	Keith	North Platte
Blaine	North Platte	Keya Paha	North Platte
Boone	Lincoln	Kimball	North Platte
Box Butte	North Platte	Knox	Omaha
Boyd	Lincoln	Lancaster	Lincoln
Brown	North Platte	Lincoln	North Platte
Buffalo	Lincoln	Logan	North Platte
Burt	Omaha	Loup	North Platte
Butler	Lincoln	Madison	Lincoln
Cass	Lincoln	McPherson	North Platte
Cedar	Omaha	Merrick	Lincoln
Chase	North Platte	Morrill	North Platte
Cherry	North Platte	Nance	Lincoln
Cheyenne	North Platte	Nemaha	Lincoln
Clay	Lincoln	Nuckolls	Lincoln
Colfax	Lincoln	Otoe	Lincoln
Cuming	Omaha	Pawnee	Lincoln
Custer	North Platte	Perkins	North Platte
Dakota	Omaha	Phelps	Lincoln
Dawes	North Platte	Pierce	Omaha
Dawson	North Platte	Platte	Lincoln
Deuel	North Platte	Polk	Lincoln
Dixon	Omaha	Red Willow	North Platte
Dodge	Omaha	Richardson	Lincoln
Douglas	Omaha	Rock	North Platte
Dundy	North Platte	Saline	Lincoln
Fillmore	Lincoln	Sarpy	Omaha
Franklin	Lincoln	Saunders	Lincoln
Frontier	North Platte	Scotts. Bluff	North Platte
Furnas	North Platte	Seward	Lincoln
Gage	Lincoln	Sheridan	North Platte
Garden	North Platte	Sherman	Lincoln
Garfield	North Platte	Sioux	North Platte
Gosper	North Platte	Stanton	Omaha
Grant	North Platte	Thayer	Lincoln
Greeley	Lincoln	Thomas	North Platte
Hall	Lincoln	Thurston	Omaha
Hamilton	Lincoln	Valley	North Platte
Harlan	Lincoln	Washington	Omaha
Hayes	North Platte	Wayne	Omaha
Hitchcock	North Platte	Webster	Lincoln
Holt	Lincoln	Wheeler	Lincoln
Hooker	North Platte	York	Lincoln
Howard	Lincoln		

US District Court

Lincoln Division PO Box 83468, Lincoln, NE 68501 (Courier Address: 593 Federal Bldg, 100 Centennial Mall N, Lincoln, NE 68508), 402-437-5225, Fax: 402-437-5651.

http://www.ned.uscourts.gov

Counties: Nebraska cases may be filed in any of the three courts at the option of the attorney, except that filings in the North Platte Division must be during trial session.

Indexing/Storage: Cases are indexed by defendant and plaintiff as well as by case number. New cases are available in the index 1-2 days after filing date. Both computer and card indexes are maintained. Open records are located at this court.

Fee & Payment: The fee is $20.00 per item (one party name or case number). Payment may be made by money order, cashier check, personal check. Prepayment is required. Payee: Clerk, US District Court. Certification fee: $7.00 per document. Copy fee: $.50 per page.

Phone Search: Only docket information available.

Mail Search: Always enclose a stamped self addressed envelope.

In Person: In person searching is available.

PACER: Sign-up number is 800-676-6856. Access fee is $.60 per minute. Toll-free access: 800-252-9724. Local access: 402-661-7399. Case records are available back to late 1990. Records are purged every year. New records are available online after 2 days. PACER is available online at http://pacer.ned.uscourts.gov.

North Platte Division c/o Lincoln Division, PO Box 83468, Lincoln, NE 68501 (Courier Address: 593 Federal Bldg, 100 Centennial Mall N, Lincoln), 402-437-5225, Fax: 402-437-5651.

http://www.ned.uscourts.gov

Counties: Nebraska cases may be filed in any of the three courts at the option of the attorney, except that filings in the North Platte Division must be during trial session. Some case records may be in Omaha Division and Lincoln Division.

Indexing/Storage: Cases are indexed by defendant and plaintiff as well as by case number. New cases are available in the index 1-2 days after filing date. Records can also be located at Omaha or Lincoln, depending on the judge assigned. Open records are located at the Division.

Fee & Payment: The fee is $20.00 per item (one party name or case number). Payment may be made by money order, cashier check, personal check. Payee: Clerk, US District Court. Copy fee: $.50 per page. You are allowed to make your own copies. These copies cost $.50 per page.

Phone Search: Searching not available by phone.

Mail Search: Always enclose a stamped self addressed envelope.

In Person: In person searching is available.

PACER: Sign-up number is 800-676-6856. Access fee is $.60 per minute. Toll-free access: 800-252-9724. Local access: 402-661-7399. Case records are available back to late 1990. Records are purged every year. New records are available online after 2 days. PACER is available online at http://pacer.ned.uscourts.gov.

Omaha Division 111 S 18th Plaza, Ste 1152, Omaha, NE 68102 (Courier Address: same), 402-661-7350, Fax: 402-661-7387.

http://www.ned.uscourts.gov

Counties: Nebraska cases may be filed in any of the three courts at the option of the attorney, except that filings in the North Platte Division must be during trial session.

Indexing/Storage: Cases are indexed by defendant and plaintiff as well as by case number. New cases are available in the index 1-2 days after filing date. Both computer and card indexes are maintained. Open records are located at this court.

Fee & Payment: The fee is $20.00 per item (one party name or case number). Payment may be made by money order, cashier check, personal check. Prepayment is required. Payee: Clerk, US District Court. Certification fee: $7.00 per document. Copy fee: $.50 per page.

Phone Search: Searching not available by phone.

Mail Search: Always enclose a stamped self addressed envelope.

In Person: In person searching is available.

PACER: Sign-up number is 800-676-6856. Access fee is $.60 per minute. Toll-free access: 800-252-9724. Local access: 402-661-7399. Case records are available back to late 1990. Records are purged every year. New records are available online after 2 days. PACER is available online at http://pacer.ned.uscourts.gov.

US Bankruptcy Court

Lincoln Division 460 Federal Bldg, 100 Centennial Mall N, Lincoln, NE 68508 (Courier: same), 402-437-5100, Fax: 402-437-5454.

http://www.neb.uscourts.gov

Counties: Adams, Antelope, Boone, Boyd, Buffalo, Butler, Cass, Clay, Colfax, Fillmore, Franklin, Gage, Greeley, Hall, Hamilton, Harlan, Holt, Howard, Jefferson, Johnson, Kearney, Lancaster, Madison, Merrick, Nance, Nemaha, Nuckolls, Otoe, Pawnee, Phelps, Platte,Polk, Richardson, Saline, Saunders, Seward, Sherman, Thayer, Webster, Wheeler, York. Cases from the North Platte Division may also be assigned here.

Indexing/Storage: Cases are indexed by as well as by case number. New cases are available in the index 1 day after filing date. All debtor names are indexed for files from 9/89 to the present. A computer index is maintained. Open records are located at this court. District wide searches are available from this division. This court maintains records for the main bankruptcy office in Omaha.

Fee & Payment: The fee is $20.00 per item (one party name or case number). Payment may be made by money order, cashier check, personal check. Prepayment is required. Debtor's checks are not accepted. Payee: Clerk, US Bankrutpcy Court. Certification fee: $7.00 per document. Copy fee: $.50 per page.

Phone Search: Debtor's name, case number, date filed, 341 information and date discharged and closed will be released. An automated voice case information service (VCIS) is available. Call VCIS at 800-829-0112 or 402-221-3757.

Mail Search: A stamped self addressed envelope is not required.

In Person: In person searching is available.

PACER: Sign-up number is 800-676-6856. Access fee is $.60 per minute. Toll-free access: 800-788-0656. Local access: 402-221-4882. Case records are available back to September 1989. Records are purged every six months. New civil

records are available online after 3 days. PACER is available online at http://pacer.neb.uscourts.gov.

North Platte Division c/o Omaha Division, 111 S 18th Plaza, Ste 1125, Omaha, NE 68102 (courier: same) 402-661-7444, Fax: 402-661-7492.

http://www.neb.uscourts.gov

Counties: Arthur, Banner, Blaine, Box Butte, Brown, Chase, Cherry, Cheyenne, Custer, Dawes, Dawson, Deuel, Dundy, Frontier, Furnas, Garden, Garfield, Gosper, Grant, Hayes, Hitchcock, Hooker, Keith, Keya Paha, Kimball, Lincoln, Logan, Loup, McPherson, Morrill,Perkins, Red Willow, Rock, Scotts Bluff, Sheridan, Sioux, Thomas, Valley. Cases may be randomly allocated to Omaha or Lincoln.

Indexing/Storage: Cases are indexed by as well as by case number. New cases are available in the index 1 day after filing date. Open records are located at the Division. Case records may also be in the Lincoln Division (Lancaster County).

Fee & Payment: The fee is no charge per item (one party name or case number). Payment may be made by money order, cashier check. Business checks not accepted. Personal checks not accepted.

Phone Search: An automated voice case information service (VCIS) is available. Call VCIS at 800-829-0112 or 402-221-3757.

Mail Search: A stamped self addressed envelope is not required.

In Person: In person searching is available.

PACER: Sign-up number is 800-676-6856. Access fee is $.60 per minute. Toll-free access: 800-788-0656. Local access: 402-221-4882. Case records are available back to September 1989. Records are purged every six months. New civil records are available online after 3 days. PACER is available online at http://pacer.neb.uscourts.gov.

Omaha Division 111 S. 18th Plaza, Ste 1125, Omaha, NE 68102 (Courier Address: same), 402-661-7444, Fax: 402-661-7492.

http://www.neb.uscourts.gov

Counties: Burt, Cedar, Cuming, Dakota, Dixon, Dodge, Douglas, Knox, Pierce, Sarpy, Stanton, Thurston, Washington, Wayne.

Indexing/Storage: Cases are indexed by debtor and creditors as well as by case number. New cases are available in the index 24 hours after filing date. A computer index is maintained. Open records are located at this court.

Fee & Payment: The fee is $20.00 per item (one party name or case number). Payment may be made by money order, cashier check, personal check. Prepayment is required. Payee: Clerk, US Bankruptcy Court. Certification fee: $7.00 per document. Copy fee: $.50 per page.

Phone Search: Only docket information is available by phone. An automated voice case information service (VCIS) is available. Call VCIS at 800-829-0112 or 402-221-3757.

Mail Search: Always enclose a stamped self addressed envelope.

In Person: In person searching is available.

PACER: Sign-up number is 800-676-6856. Access fee is $.60 per minute. Toll-free access: 800-788-0656. Local access: 402-221-4882. Case records are available back to September 1989. Records are purged every six months. New civil records are available online after 3 days. PACER is available online at http://pacer.neb.uscourts.gov.

Nebraska County Courts

Court	Jurisdiction	No. of Courts	How Organized
District Courts*	General	93	12 Districts
County Courts*	Limited	93	11 Districts
Juvenile Courts	Special	3	3 Counties
Workers' Compensation Court	Special	1	

* Profiled in this Sourcebook.

Court	CIVIL								
	Tort	Contract	Real Estate	Min. Claim	Max. Claim	Small Claims	Estate	Eviction	Domestic Relations
District Courts*	X	X	X	$15,000	No Max				X
County Courts*	X	X	X	$0	$15,000	$1800	X	X	X
Juvenile Courts									
Workers' Compensation Court									

Court	CRIMINAL				
	Felony	Misdemeanor	DWI/DUI	Preliminary Hearing	Juvenile
District Courts*	X				
County Courts*		X	X	X	X
Juvenile Courts					X
Workers' Compensation Court					

ADMINISTRATION
Court Administrator, PO Box 98910, Lincoln, NE, 68509-8910; 402-471-2643, Fax: 402-471-2197. http://court.nol.org/AOC

COURT STRUCTURE
The District Court is the court of general jurisdiction. The minimum on civil judgment matters for District Courts is $15,000, however, the State raised the County Court limit on civil matters from $15,000 to $45,000 as of Sept. 1, 2001. As it is less expensive to file civil cases in County Court than in District Court, civil cases in the $15,000 to $45,000 range are more likely to be found in County Court, if after Sept. 1, 2001.

The number of judicial districts went from 21 to the current 12 in July 1992. County Courts have juvenile jurisdiction in all but 3 counties. Douglas, Lancaster, and Sarpy counties have separate Juvenile Courts.

ONLINE ACCESS
Online access to District and County courts is being tested. For more information, call John Cariotto at 402-471-2643. Currently, Douglas county offers remote online access.

ADDITIONAL INFORMATION
Most Nebraska courts require the public to do their own in-person searches and will not respond to written search requests. The State Attorney General has recommended that courts not perform searches because of the time involved and concerns over possible legal liability.

📖 📖 📖 📖 📖 📖 📖

Adams County

District Court PO Box 9, Hastings, NE 68902; 402-461-7264; Fax: 402-461-7269. Hours: 8:30AM-5PM (CST). *Felony, Civil Actions Over $15,000.*

Civil Records: Access: In person only. Visitors must perform in person searches for themselves. No search fee. Required to search: name, years to search. Civil cases indexed by defendant, plaintiff. Civil records on microfiche from 1800s, 5 yrs on index cards, on docket books from 1800s.

Criminal Records: Access: In person only. Visitors must perform in person searches for themselves. No search fee. Required to search: name, years to search. Criminal records on microfiche from 1800s, 5 yrs on index cards, on docket books from 1800s.

General Information: No juvenile, search warrants or mental health records released. Copy fee: $.25 per page. Certification fee: $1.00.

County Court PO Box 95, Hastings, NE 68902-0095; 402-461-7143; Fax: 402-461-7144. Hours: 8AM-5PM (CST). *Misdemeanor, Civil Actions Under $45,000, Eviction, Small Claims, Probate.*

Civil Records: Access: In person only. Visitors must perform in person searches for themselves. No search fee. Required to search: name, years to search; also helpful: address. Civil cases indexed by defendant. Civil records on index cards and files from 1970s.

Criminal Records: Access: In person only. Visitors must perform in person searches for themselves. No search fee. Required to search: name, years to search; also helpful: DOB, SSN. Criminal records on index cards and files from 1970s.

General Information: Public Access terminal is available. No adoption or juvenile records released. Copy fee: $.25 per page. Certification fee: $1.00. Fee payee: Adams County Court. Business checks accepted. Prepayment required.

Antelope County

District Court PO Box 45, Neligh, NE 68756; 402-887-4508; Fax: 402-887-4870. Hours: 8:30AM-5PM (CST). *Felony, Civil Actions Over $15,000.*

Civil Records: Access: In person only. Visitors must perform in person searches for themselves. No search fee. Required to search: name, years to search. Civil cases indexed by defendant, plaintiff. Civil records on index books from 1872.

Criminal Records: Access: In person only. Visitors must perform in person searches for themselves. No search fee. Required to search: name, years to search. Criminal records on index books from 1872.

General Information: Public Access terminal is available. No juvenile, sealed, search warrants, or mental health record released. Fax notes: $1.00 per page. Copy fee: $.25 per page. Certification fee: $1.00. Fee payee: Clerk of District Court. Personal checks accepted.

Antelope County Court 501 Main, Neligh, NE 68756; 402-887-4650; Fax: 402-887-4160. Hours: 8:30AM-5PM (CST). *Misdemeanor, Civil Actions Under $45,000, Eviction, Small Claims, Probate.*

Civil Records: Access: In person only. Visitors must perform in person searches for themselves. No search fee. Required to search: name, years to search. Civil cases indexed by defendant, plaintiff. Civil records on computer from 1994, probate on microfiche from 1800s, civil and small claims indexed from 1983.

Criminal Records: Access: In person only. Visitors must perform in person searches for themselves. No search fee. Required to search: name, years to search, DOB, signed release; also helpful: SSN. Criminal index on computer from 1994, indexed from 1800s.

General Information: No adoption, or sealed records released. Copy fee: $.25 per page. Certification fee: $1.00 plus $.25 per page. Fee payee: Antelope County Court. Personal checks accepted. Prepayment required.

Arthur County

District & County Court PO Box 126, Arthur, NE 69121; 308-764-2203; Fax: 308-764-2216. Hours: 8AM-4PM (MST). *Felony, Misdemeanor, Civil, Eviction, Small Claims, Probate.*

Civil Records: Access: Phone, fax, mail, in person. Both court and visitors may perform in person searches. No search fee. Required to search: name, years to search. Civil cases indexed by defendant, plaintiff. Civil records on index books from 1987, on docket books from 1913.

Criminal Records: Access: Phone, fax, mail, in person. Both court and visitors may perform in person searches. No search fee. Required to search: name, years to search. Criminal records on index books from 1987, on docket books from 1913.

General Information: No search warrants, juvenile, adoption, mental health, or sealed records released. SASE required. Turnaround time 1-2 days. Fax notes: $1.00 per page. Incoming fax fee $.25. Copy fee: $.20 per page. Certification fee: $1.00. Fee payee: Arthur County Clerk. Personal checks accepted.

Banner County

District Court PO Box 67, Harrisburg, NE 69345; 308-436-5265; Fax: 308-436-4180. Hours: 8AM-5PM (MST). *Felony, Civil Actions Over $15,000.*

Civil Records: Access: Fax, mail, in person. Both court and visitors may perform in person searches. Search fee: $3.00 per name. Required to search: name, years to search; also helpful: address. Civil cases indexed by defendant, plaintiff. Civil records on docket books from 1800s.

Criminal Records: Access: Fax, mail, in person. Both court and visitors may perform in person searches. Search fee: $3.00 per name. Required to search: name, years to search, DOB; also helpful: address. Criminal records on docket books from 1800s.

General Information: No search warrants, mental health, or sealed records released. SASE required. Turnaround time 5-7 days. Fax notes: $1.00 per page. Copy fee: $.25 per page. Certification fee: $1.00. Fee payee: Banner County Clerk. Personal checks accepted. Prepayment required.

Banner County Court PO Box 67, Harrisburg, NE 69345; 308-436-5268. Hours: 8AM-Noon, 1-5PM (MST). *Misdemeanor, Civil Actions Under $45,000, Eviction, Small Claims, Probate.*

Civil Records: Access: Mail, in person. Both court and visitors may perform in person searches. No search fee. Required to search: name, years to search. Civil cases indexed by defendant, plaintiff. Civil records on register of action cards from 1992, prior on docket books, on computer from 12/2000.

Criminal Records: Access: Mail, in person. Both court and visitors may perform in person searches. No search fee. Required to search: name, years to search, signed release; also helpful: address, DOB. Criminal records on register of action cards from 1992, prior on docket books, on computer from 6/2000.

General Information: No adoption, sealed records released. SASE required. Turnaround time 4 days from receipt. Fax notes: $3.00 for first page, $1.00 each add'l. Copy fee: $.25 per page. Certification fee: $1.00. Fee payee: Banner County Court. Personal checks accepted.

Blaine County

District Court Lincoln Ave, Box 136, Brewster, NE 68821; 308-547-2222; Fax: 308-547-2228. Hours: 8AM-4PM (CST). *Felony, Civil Actions Over $15,000.* www.nol.org/home/DC8

Civil Records: Access: Fax, mail, in person. Only the court performs in person searches; visitors may not. No search fee. Required to search: name, years to search. Civil cases indexed by defendant, plaintiff. Civil records on index books from late 1800s.

Criminal Records: Access: Fax, mail, in person. Only the court performs in person searches; visitors may not. No search fee. Required to search: name, years to search, DOB. Criminal records on index books from late 1800s.

General Information: Public Access terminal is available. No search warrants, mental health, or sealed records released. SASE required. Turnaround time 1-2 days. Fax notes: $1.00 per page. Copy fee: $.25 per page. Certification fee: $1.50. Fee payee: Blaine County Clerk. Personal checks accepted. Prepayment required.

Blaine County Court Lincoln Ave, Box 123, Brewster, NE 68821; 308-547-2225; Fax: 308-547-2228. Hours: 8AM-4PM (CST). *Misdemeanor, Civil Actions Under $45,000, Eviction, Small Claims, Probate.*

Civil Records: Access: Phone, fax, mail, in person. Only the court performs in person searches; visitors may not. No search fee. Required to search: name, years to search; also helpful: address. Civil cases indexed by

defendant, plaintiff. Civil records on index books from 1960. on microfiche prior to 1960.

Criminal Records: Access: Phone, fax, mail, in person. Only the court performs in person searches; visitors may not. No search fee. Required to search: name, years to search; also helpful: address, DOB, SSN. Criminal records on index books from 1960. on microfiche prior to 1960.

General Information: No juvenile, adoption, or sealed records released. SASE required. Turnaround time 2 days. Fax notes: $1.00 per page. Copy fee: $.25 per page. Certification fee: $1.25. Fee payee: Blaine County Court. Personal checks accepted. Prepayment required.

Boone County

District Court 222 Fourth St, Albion, NE 68620; 402-395-2057; Fax: 402-395-6592. Hours: 8:30AM-5PM (CST). *Felony, Civil Actions Over $15,000.*

Civil Records: Access: Phone, fax, mail, in person. Both court and visitors may perform in person searches. No search fee. Required to search: name, years to search. Civil cases indexed by defendant, plaintiff. Civil records in general index and dockets from 1800s.

Criminal Records: Access: Phone, fax, mail, in person. Both court and visitors may perform in person searches. No search fee. Required to search: name, years to search; also helpful: DOB. Criminal records in general index and dockets from 1800s.

General Information: No search warrants, mental health, or sealed records released. SASE required. Turnaround time 2-3 days. Fax notes: $3.00 for first page, $1.00 each add'l. Copy fee: $.25 per page. Certification fee: $1.00. Fee payee: Clerk of District Court. Personal checks accepted. Prepayment required.

Boone County Court 222 S 4th St, Albion, NE 68620; 402-395-6184; Fax: 402-395-6592. Hours: 8AM-5PM (CST). *Misdemeanor, Civil Actions Under $45,000, Eviction, Small Claims, Probate.*

Civil Records: Access: Fax, mail, in person. Both court and visitors may perform in person searches. No search fee. Required to search: name, years to search. Civil cases indexed by defendant, plaintiff. Civil records on general index and docket books from late 1800s, probate on microfiche from 1970.

Criminal Records: Access: Fax, mail, in person. Both court and visitors may perform in person searches. No search fee. Required to search: name, years to search; also helpful: DOB. Criminal records on general index and docket books from late 1800s, probate on microfiche from 1970.

General Information: No adoption, or sealed records released. SASE required. Turnaround time 1-2 days. SASE required for large requests. Fax notes: No fee to fax results. Copy fee: $.25 per page. Certification fee: $1.00. Fee payee: Clerk of County Court. Personal checks accepted.

Box Butte County

District Court 515 Box Butte Suite 300, Alliance, NE 69301; 308-762-6293; Fax: 308-762-7703. Hours: 9AM-5PM (MST). *Felony, Civil Actions Over $15,000.*

Civil Records: Access: In person only. Visitors must perform in person searches for themselves. No search fee. Required to search: name, years to search. Civil cases indexed by defendant, plaintiff. Civil records on general index and docket books from late 1800s.

Criminal Records: Access: In person only. Visitors must perform in person searches for themselves. No search fee. Required to search: name, years to search. Criminal records on general index and docket books from late 1800s.

General Information: No search warrants, mental health, or sealed records released. Copy fee: $.25 per page. Certification fee: $1.00.

Box Butte County Court PO Box 613, Alliance, NE 69301; 308-762-6800; Fax: 308-762-6802. Hours: 8:30AM-5PM (MST). *Misdemeanor, Civil Actions Under $45,000, Eviction, Small Claims, Probate.*

Civil Records: Access: Phone, fax, mail, in person. Both court and visitors may perform in person searches. No search fee. Required to search: name, years to search. Civil cases indexed by defendant, plaintiff. Civil records on microfiche for 10 years, on index cards to docket books from late 1800s.

Criminal Records: Access: Phone, fax, mail, in person. Both court and visitors may perform in person searches. No search fee. Required to search: name, years to search, DOB. Criminal records on microfiche for 10 years, on index cards to docket books from late 1800s.

General Information: No juvenile, adoption, or sealed records released. SASE required. Turnaround time 5-10 days. Fax notes: No fee to fax results. Copy fee: $.25 per page. Certification fee: $1.00. Fee payee: Box Butte County Court. Personal checks accepted.

Boyd County

District Court PO Box 26, Butte, NE 68722; 402-775-2391; Fax: 402-775-2146. Hours: 8:15AM-Noon; 1-5PM (CST). *Felony, Civil Actions Over $15,000.*

Civil Records: Access: Mail, fax, in person. Both court and visitors may perform in person searches. Search fee: $3.00 per name. Required to search: name, years to search, address. Civil cases indexed by defendant, plaintiff. Civil records on general index and docket books from late 1800s.

Criminal Records: Access: Mail, fax, in person. Both court and visitors may perform in person searches. Search fee: $3.00 per name. Required to search: name, years to search, address. Criminal records on general index and docket books from late 1800s.

General Information: Public Access terminal is available. No search warrants, mental health, or sealed records released. SASE required. Turnaround time 3-4 days. Copy fee: $.25 per page. Certification fee: $1.50. Fee payee: Boyd County Clerk. Personal checks accepted. Prepayment required.

Boyd County Court PO Box 396, Butte, NE 68722; 402-775-2211; Fax: 402-775-2146. Hours: 8AM-5PM W,Th (CST). *Misdemeanor, Civil Actions Under $45,000, Eviction, Small Claims, Probate.*

Civil Records: Access: Phone, fax, mail, in person. Both court and visitors may perform in person searches. No search fee. Required to search: name, years to search; also helpful: address. Civil cases indexed by defendant, plaintiff. Civil records on general index and docket books from late 1800s.

Criminal Records: Access: Phone, fax, mail, in person. Both court and visitors may perform in person searches. No search fee. Required to search: name, years to search; also helpful: address, DOB, SSN. Criminal records on general index and docket books from late 1800s.

General Information: No adoption, juvenile, or sealed records released. SASE required. Turnaround time 2 weeks. Fax notes: $3.00 for first page, $1.00 each add'l. Copy fee: $.25 per page. Certification fee: $1.00. Fee payee: Boyd County Court. Personal checks accepted. Prepayment required.

Brown County

District Court 148 W Fourth St, Ainsworth, NE 69210; 402-387-2705; Fax: 402-387-0918. Hours: 8AM-5PM (CST). *Felony, Civil Actions Over $15,000.*

Civil Records: Access: Phone, fax, mail, in person. Both court and visitors may perform in person searches. No search fee. Required to search: name, years to search; also helpful: address. Civil cases indexed by defendant, plaintiff. Civil records on general index and docket books from late 1800s; on computer back to 2000.

Criminal Records: Access: Fax, mail, in person. Both court and visitors may perform in person searches. No search fee. Required to search: name, years to search, signed release; also helpful: address, DOB, SSN. Criminal records on general index and docket books from late 1800s; on computer back to 2000.

General Information: Public Access terminal is available. No search warrants, mental health, or sealed records released. SASE required. Turnaround time 3-4 days. Fax notes: Fee to fax results is $3.00 per page. Copy fee: $.25 per page. Certification fee: $3.00. Fee payee: Clerk of District Court, Brown County. Personal checks accepted.

Brown County Court 148 W Fourth St, Ainsworth, NE 69210; 402-387-2864; Fax: 402-387-0918. Hours: 8AM-5PM (CST). *Misdemeanor, Civil Actions Under $45,000, Eviction, Small Claims, Probate.*

Civil Records: Access: Phone, fax, mail, in person. Both court and visitors may perform in person searches. No search fee. Required to search: name, years to search. Civil cases indexed by defendant, plaintiff. Civil records in boxes in office since 1980; on computer since.

Criminal Records: Access: Phone, fax, mail, in person. Both court and visitors may perform in person searches. No search fee. Required to search: name, years to search, DOB. Criminal records in boxes in office since 1980; on computer since.

General Information: No adoption, juvenile, or sealed records released. SASE required. Copy fee: $.25 per page. Certification fee: $1.00. Fee payee: Brown County Court. Personal checks accepted. Prepayment required.

Buffalo County

District Court PO Box 520, Kearney, NE 68848; 308-236-1246; Fax: 308-233-3693. Hours: 8AM-5PM (CST). *Felony, Civil Actions Over $15,000.*

Civil Records: Access: Mail, in person. Both court and visitors may perform in person searches. No search fee. Required to search: name, years to search; also helpful: address. Civil cases indexed by defendant, plaintiff. Civil records on computer from 1993, on microfiche through 1991, on books from 1800s.

Criminal Records: Access: In person only. Visitors must perform in person searches for themselves. No search fee. Required to search: name, years to search; also helpful: DOB, SSN. Criminal records on computer from 1993, on microfiche through 1991, on books from 1800s.

General Information: Public Access terminal is available. No juvenile, mental health, search warrants or sealed records released. SASE required. Turnaround time 1 week. Copy fee: $.50 per page. Certification fee: $1.00. Fee payee: Clerk of District Court. Business checks accepted. Prepayment required.

Buffalo County Court PO Box 520, Kearney, NE 68848; 308-236-1228; Fax: 308-236-1243. Hours: 8AM-5PM (CST). *Misdemeanor, Civil Actions Under $45,000, Eviction, Small Claims, Probate.*

Civil Records: Access: In person only. Visitors must perform in person searches for themselves. No search fee. Required to search: name, years to search. Civil cases indexed by defendant, plaintiff. Civil records on computer from 4/94, on microfiche, general index, and docket books from late 1800s.

Criminal Records: Access: In person only. Visitors must perform in person searches for themselves. No search fee. Required to search: name, years to search. Criminal records on computer from 4/94, on microfiche, general index, and docket books from late 1800s.

General Information: Public Access terminal is available. No adoption, or sealed records released. Copy fee: $.25 per page. Certification fee: $1.00. Fee payee: County Court. Personal checks accepted. Prepayment required.

Burt County

District Court 111 N 13th St, Tekamah, NE 68061; 402-374-2905; Fax: 402-374-2906. Hours: 8AM-4:30PM (CST). *Felony, Civil Actions Over $15,000.*

Civil Records: Access: Mail, in person. Both court and visitors may perform in person searches. No search fee. Required to search: name, years to search. Civil cases indexed by defendant, plaintiff. Civil records on books from 1800s.

Criminal Records: Access: Mail, in person. Both court and visitors may perform in person searches. No search fee. Required to search: name, years to search; also helpful: DOB, SSN. Criminal records on books from 1800s.

General Information: No mental health records released. SASE required. Copy fee: $.50 per page. Certification fee: $2.00. Fee payee: Clerk of District Court. Personal checks accepted.

Burt County Court 111 N 13th St, PO Box 87, Tekamah, NE 68061; 402-374-2950; Fax: 402-374-2951. Hours: 8AM-4:30PM (CST). *Misdemeanor, Civil Actions Under $45,000, Eviction, Small Claims, Probate.*

Civil Records: Access: In person only. Visitors must perform in person searches for themselves. No search fee. Required to search: name, years to search, address. Civil cases indexed by defendant, plaintiff. Civil records on index cards.

Criminal Records: Access: In person only. Visitors must perform in person searches for themselves. No search fee. Required to search: name, years to search, address, DOB, SSN, signed release. Criminal records on index cards.

General Information: No adoption records released. Copy fee: $.25 per page. Certification fee: $1.25. Fee payee: County Court. Personal checks accepted. Prepayment required.

Butler County

District Court 451 5th St, David City, NE 68632-1666; 402-367-7460; Fax: 402-367-3249. Hours: 8:30AM-5PM (CST). *Felony, Civil Actions Over $15,000.*

Civil Records: Access: Phone, fax, mail, in person. Both court and visitors may perform in person searches. Search fee: $2.00 per name. Required to search: name, years to search. Civil cases indexed by defendant, plaintiff. Civil records on books.

Criminal Records: Access: Phone, fax, mail, in person. Both court and visitors may perform in person searches. Search fee: $2.00 per name. Required to search: name, years to search; also helpful: DOB, SSN. Criminal records on books.

General Information: No juvenile, mental health or protection order records released. SASE required. Turnaround time 1-2 days. Fax notes: No fee to fax results. Copy fee: $.10 per page. Certification fee: $1.50. Fee payee: District Court. Personal checks accepted.

Butler County Court 451 5th St, David City, NE 68632-1666; 402-367-7480; Fax: 402-367-3249. Hours: 8AM-Noon, 1-5PM (CST). *Misdemeanor, Civil Actions Under $45,000, Eviction, Small Claims, Probate.*

Civil Records: Access: In person only. Visitors must perform in person searches for themselves. No search fee. Required to search: name, years to search. Civil cases indexed by defendant, plaintiff. Civil records on computer since 1998, docket books from late 1800s, probate on microfiche. They can refer requestors to parties who perform searches at the court.

Criminal Records: Access: In person only. Visitors must perform in person searches for themselves. No search fee. Required to search: name, years to search; also helpful: DOB, SSN. Criminal records on computer since 1998, docket books from late 1800s, probate on microfiche. They can refer requestors to parties who perform searches at the court.

General Information: No adoption records released. Some juvenile requires signed release. Fax notes: $3.00 for first page, $1.00 each add'l. Copy fee: $.25 per page. Certification fee: $1.00. Fee payee: Butler County Court. Personal checks accepted.

Cass County

District Court Cass County Courthouse, 346 Main Street, Plattsmouth, NE 68048; 402-296-9339; Fax: 402-296-9345. Hours: 8AM-5PM (CST). *Felony, Civil Actions Over $15,000.*

Civil Records: Access: In person only. Visitors must perform in person searches for themselves. No search fee. Required to search: name, years to search. Civil cases indexed by defendant, plaintiff. Civil records on index books from 1860s, index on computer since 09/97.

Criminal Records: Access: In person only. Visitors must perform in person searches for themselves. No search fee. Required to search: name, years to search. Criminal records on index books from 1860s, index on computer since 09/97.

General Information: Public Access terminal is available. Copy fee: $.25 per page. Certification fee: $1.50. Fee payee: Clerk of District Court.

Cass County Court Cass County Courthouse, Plattsmouth, NE 68048; 402-296-9334. Hours: 8AM-5PM (CST). *Misdemeanor, Civil Actions Under $45,000, Eviction, Small Claims, Probate.*

Civil Records: Access: In person only. Visitors must perform in person searches for themselves. No search fee. Required to search: name, years to search. Civil cases indexed by defendant, plaintiff. Civil records on index cards for 5 years then sent to Capital for storage.

Criminal Records: Access: In person only. Visitors must perform in person searches for themselves. No search fee. Required to search: name, years to search. Criminal records on computer since 1/97.

General Information: Copy fee: $.25 per page. Certification fee: $1.00. Fee payee: Cass County Court. No personal checks accepted. Prepayment required.

Cedar County

District Court PO Box 796, Hartington, NE 68739-0796; 402-254-6957; Fax: 402-254-6954. Hours: 8AM-5PM (CST). *Felony, Civil Actions Over $15,000.*

Civil Records: Access: In person only. Visitors must perform in person searches for themselves. No search fee. Required to search: name, years to search. Civil cases indexed by defendant, plaintiff. Civil records in books from 1890.

Criminal Records: Access: In person only. Visitors must perform in person searches for themselves. No search fee. Required to search: name, years to search; also helpful: SSN. Criminal records in books from 1890.

General Information: No mental health records released. Copy fee: $.25 per page. Certification fee: $1.00. Fee payee: District Court. Prepayment required.

Cedar County Court P O Box 695, Hartington, NE 68739; 402-254-7441; Fax: 402-254-6954. Hours: 8AM-5PM (CST). *Misdemeanor, Civil Actions Under $45,000, Eviction, Small Claims, Probate.*

Civil Records: Access: In person only. Visitors must perform in person searches for themselves. No search fee. Required to search: name, years to search. Civil

cases indexed by defendant. Civil records on general index, docket books 15 years; some on microfiche.

Criminal Records: Access: In person only. Visitors must perform in person searches for themselves. No search fee. Required to search: name, years to search, offense; also helpful: DOB. Criminal records on general index, docket books for 18 years; some on microfiche.

General Information: No juvenile or judge sealed records released. Copy fee: $.25 per page. Certification fee: $1.00. Fee payee: Cedar County Court. Personal checks accepted. Prepayment required.

Chase County

District Court PO Box 1299, Imperial, NE 69033; 308-882-5266; Fax: 308-882-5390. Hours: 8AM-4PM (MST). *Felony, Civil Actions Over $15,000.*

Civil Records: Access: Phone, fax, mail, in person. Both court and visitors may perform in person searches. Search fee: $5.00 per name. Required to search: name, years to search. Civil cases indexed by defendant, plaintiff. Civil records general index, docket books from early 1900s.

Criminal Records: Access: Phone, fax, mail, in person. Both court and visitors may perform in person searches. Search fee: $5.00 per name. Required to search: name, years to search; also helpful: DOB, SSN. Criminal records general index, docket books from early 1900s.

General Information: No restrictions. SASE required. Turnaround time 5 days. Fax notes: $1.00 per page. Copy fee: $.25 per page. Certification fee: $1.50. Fee payee: Chase County Clerk. Personal checks accepted. Prepayment required.

Chase County Court PO Box 1299, Imperial, NE 69033; 308-882-4690; Fax: 308-882-5679. Hours: 7:30AM-4:30PM (MST). *Misdemeanor, Civil Actions Under $45,000, Eviction, Small Claims, Probate.*

Civil Records: Access: Phone, mail, in person. No search fee. Required to search: name, years to search. Civil records on general index, docket books from 1910; prior incomplete. Some probate on microfiche.

Criminal Records: Access: Phone, mail, in person. Both court and visitors may perform in person searches. No search fee. Required to search: name, years to search, DOB. Criminal records on general index, docket books from 1910; prior incomplete. Some probate on microfiche.

General Information: No adoption, juvenile. SASE required. Turnaround time 1 day. Copy fee: $.25 per page. Certification fee: $1.00. Fee payee: Chase County Court. Personal checks accepted. Prepayment required.

Cherry County

District Court 365 N Main St, Valentine, NE 69201; 402-376-1840; Fax: 402-376-3830. Hours: 8:30AM-4:30PM (MST). *Felony, Civil Actions Over $15,000.*

Civil Records: Access: In person only. Visitors must perform in person searches for themselves. No search fee. Required to search: name, years to search; also helpful: address. Civil cases indexed by defendant, plaintiff. Civil records on index books from late 1800s. Fax & mail access limited to partial search to confirm: if case was filed, case #, title & date of filing.

Criminal Records: Access: In person only. Visitors must perform in person searches for themselves. No search fee. Required to search: name, years to search. Criminal records on index books from late 1800s.

General Information: Public Access terminal is available. No juvenile records released. Copy fee: $.25 per page. Certification fee: $1.00. Fee payee: Clerk of District Court. Personal checks accepted.

Cherry County Court 365 N Main St, Valentine, NE 69201; 402-376-2590; Fax: 402-376-5942. Hours: 8AM-5PM (CST). *Misdemeanor, Civil Actions Under $45,000, Eviction, Small Claims, Probate.*

Civil Records: Access: In person only. Visitors must perform in person searches for themselves. No search fee. Required to search: name, years to search. Civil cases indexed by defendant. Civil records on docket card file from 1986, general index prior from late 1800s.

Criminal Records: Access: In person only. Visitors must perform in person searches for themselves. No search fee. Required to search: name, years to search, DOB. Criminal records on docket card file from 1986, general index prior from late 1800s; on computer since 8/2000.

General Information: No adoption records released. Juvenile released only to parties involved. Copy fee: $.25 per page. Certification fee: $1.25. Fee payee: Cherry County Court. Personal checks accepted.

Cheyenne County

District Court PO Box 217, Sidney, NE 69162; 308-254-2814; Fax: 308-254-4293. Hours: 8AM-Noon,1-5PM (MST). *Felony, Civil Actions Over $15,000.*

Civil Records: Access: In person only. Visitors must perform in person searches for themselves. No search fee. Required to search: name, years to search. Civil cases indexed by defendant, plaintiff. Civil records on general index, docket books going back to late 1800s, on computer since 09/98.

Criminal Records: Access: In person only. Visitors must perform in person searches for themselves. No search fee. Required to search: name, years to search; also helpful: DOB, SSN. Criminal records on general index, docket books going back to late 1800s, on computer since 09/98.

General Information: No mental health or search warrants released. Copy fee: $.25 per page. Certification fee: $2.00. Fee payee: Clerk of District Court. Personal checks accepted. All fees can be billed to attorneys.

Cheyenne County Court 1000 10th Ave, Sidney, NE 69162; 308-254-2929; Fax: 308-254-4641 permission to use required. Hours: 8AM-5PM (MST). *Misdemeanor, Civil Actions Under $45,000, Eviction, Small Claims, Probate.*

Civil Records: Access: Mail, in person. Both court and visitors may perform in person searches. No search fee. Required to search: name, years to search. Civil cases indexed by defendant, plaintiff. Civil records on index books from late 1800s. Fax access requires special permission.

Criminal Records: Access: Mail, in person. Both court and visitors may perform in person searches. No search fee. Required to search: name, years to search; also helpful: DOB. Criminal records on index books from late 1800s.

General Information: No adoption, juvenile, confidential records released. SASE required. Turnaround time within 1 week. Copy fee: $.25 per page. Certification fee: $1.00. Fee payee: Cheyenne County Court. Personal checks accepted. Prepayment required.

Clay County

District Court Clerk of The District Court, 111 W Fairfield St, Clay Center, NE 68933; 402-762-3595; Fax: 402-762-3604. Hours: 8:30AM-5PM (CST). *Felony, Civil Actions Over $15,000.*

Civil Records: Access: In person only. Visitors must perform in person searches for themselves. No search fee. Required to search: name; also helpful: years to search. Civil cases indexed by defendant, plaintiff. Civil records on index books from late 1800s, on microfiche from 1986.

Criminal Records: Access: In person only. Visitors must perform in person searches for themselves. No search fee. Required to search: name, DOB; also helpful: years to search, SSN. Criminal records on index books from late 1800s, on microfiche from 1986.

General Information: No mental health records released. Copy fee: $.25 per page. Certification fee: $1.00. Fee payee: Clerk of District Court. Personal checks accepted.

Clay County Court 111 W Fairfield St, Clay Center, NE 68933; 402-762-3651; Fax: 402-762-3250. Hours: 8:30AM-5PM (CST). *Misdemeanor, Civil Actions Under $45,000, Eviction, Small Claims, Probate.*

Civil Records: Access: In person only. Visitors must perform in person searches for themselves. No search fee. Required to search: name, years to search. Civil cases indexed by defendant. Civil records in index books from late 1800s.

Criminal Records: Access: In person only. Visitors must perform in person searches for themselves. No search fee. Required to search: name, years to search; also helpful: DOB, SSN. Criminal records in index books from late 1800s.

General Information: No adoption or juvenile records released. Copy fee: $.25 per page. Certification fee: $1.00. Fee payee: Clay County. Personal checks accepted.

Colfax County

District Court 411 E 11th St, PO Box 429, Schuyler, NE 68661; 402-352-8506; Fax: 402-352-2847. Hours: 8:30AM-5PM (CST). *Felony, Civil Actions Over $15,000.*

Civil Records: Access: In person only. Visitors must perform in person searches for themselves. No search fee. Required to search: name, years to search; also helpful: address. Civil cases indexed by defendant, plaintiff. Civil records on index books and general index from 1880.

Criminal Records: Access: In person only. Visitors must perform in person searches for themselves. No search fee. Required to search: name, years to search; also helpful: address, DOB, SSN. Criminal records on index books and general index from 1880.

General Information: Public Access terminal is available. No juvenile or mental health records released. Copy fee: $.25 per page. Certification fee: $2.00. Fee payee: Clerk of District Court. Business checks accepted. Will take personal check if local. Prepayment required.

Colfax County Court 411 E 11th St, Box 191, Schuyler, NE 68661; 402-352-8511; Fax: 402-352-8535. Hours: 8AM-5PM (CST). *Misdemeanor, Civil Actions Under $45,000, Eviction, Small Claims, Probate.*

Civil Records: Access: In person only. Visitors must perform in person searches for themselves. No search fee. Required to search: name, years to search. Civil cases indexed by defendant, plaintiff. Civil records on index books from 1880s.

Criminal Records: Access: In person only. Visitors must perform in person searches for themselves. No search fee. Required to search: name, years to search; also helpful: DOB, SSN. Criminal records on index books from 1880s.

General Information: No juvenile records released. Copy fee: $.25 per page. Certification fee: $1.00. Fee payee: Colfax County Court. Personal checks accepted. Prepayment required.

Cuming County

District Court 200 S Lincoln, Rm 200, West Point, NE 68788; 402-372-6004; Fax: 402-372-6017. Hours: 8:30AM-4:30PM (CST). *Felony, Civil Actions Over $15,000.*

Civil Records: Access: In person only. Visitors must perform in person searches for themselves. No search fee. Required to search: name, years to search. Civil cases indexed by defendant, plaintiff. Civil records in books from 1939.

Criminal Records: Access: In person only. Visitors must perform in person searches for themselves. No search fee. Required to search: name, years to search. Criminal records in books from 1939.

General Information: No mental health records released. Copy fee: $.25 per page. Certification fee: $1.00. No personal checks accepted.

Cuming County Court 200 S Lincoln, Rm 103, West Point, NE 68788; 402-372-6003; Fax: 402-372-6030. Hours: 8:30AM-4:30PM (CST). *Misdemeanor, Civil Actions Under $45,000, Eviction, Small Claims, Probate.*

Civil Records: Access: In person only. Visitors must perform in person searches for themselves. No search fee. Required to search: name, years to search. Civil cases indexed by defendant, plaintiff. Civil records on index cards, also on computer since April 2000.

Criminal Records: Access: In person only. Visitors must perform in person searches for themselves. No search fee. Required to search: name, years to search; also helpful: DOB, SSN. Criminal records on index cards, also on computer since April 2000.

General Information: No mental health records released. Copy fee: $.25 per page. Certification fee: $1.00. Personal checks accepted, ID required for payment by check. Prepayment required.

Custer County

District Court 431 S 10th Ave, Broken Bow, NE 68822; 308-872-2121; Fax: 308-872-5826. Hours: 9AM-5PM (CST). *Felony, Civil Actions Over $15,000.*

Civil Records: Access: Phone, fax, mail, in person. Both court and visitors may perform in person searches. No search fee. Required to search: name, years to search; also helpful: address. Civil cases indexed by defendant, plaintiff. Civil records on index books and docket books from late 1800s; on computer back to 4/1998.

Criminal Records: Access: Phone, fax, mail, in person. Both court and visitors may perform in person searches. No search fee. Required to search: name, years to search; also helpful: address, DOB, SSN. Criminal records on index books and docket books from late 1800s; on computer back to 4/1998.

General Information: Public Access terminal is available. No search warrants, mental health, or sealed records released, SASE required. Turnaround time 3-4 days. Fax notes: Fee to fax results is $3.00 per page. Copy fee: $.25 per page. Certification fee: $1.25. Fee payee: Clerk of District Court. Business checks accepted. Prepayment required.

Custer County Court 431 South 10th Ave, Broken Bow, NE 68822; 308-872-5761; Fax: 308-872-6052. Hours: 8AM-12 1-5PM (CST). *Misdemeanor, Civil Actions Under $45,000, Eviction, Small Claims, Probate.*

Civil Records: Access: In person only. Visitors must perform in person searches for themselves. No search fee. Required to search: name, years to search. Civil cases indexed by defendant, plaintiff. Civil records on computer back to 2000, on index books from 1988, probate from 1986, balance are archived.

Criminal Records: Access: In person only. Visitors must perform in person searches for themselves. No

search fee. Required to search: name, years to search. Criminal records on computer back to 2000, index books from 1988, probate from 1986, balance are archived.

General Information: No adoption or juvenile records released. Copy fee: $.25 per page. Certification fee: $1.00. Fee payee: Custer County Court. Personal checks accepted. Prepayment required.

Dakota County

District Court PO Box 66, Dakota City, NE 68731; 402-987-2114; Fax: 402-987-2117. Hours: 8AM-4:30PM (CST). *Felony, Civil Actions Over $15,000.*

Civil Records: Access: In person only. Visitors must perform in person searches for themselves. No search fee. Required to search: name, years to search. Civil cases indexed by defendant, plaintiff. Civil records on index books from 1985, prior records archived at NE State Historical Society, Lincoln, NE.

Criminal Records: Access: In person only. Visitors must perform in person searches for themselves. No search fee. Required to search: name, years to search. Criminal records on index books from 1985, prior records archived at NE State Historical Society, Lincoln, NE.

General Information: No juvenile or mental health records released. Copy fee: $.25 per page. Certification fee: $1.00. Fee payee: Clerk of District Court. Personal checks accepted.

Dakota County Court PO Box 385, Dakota City, NE 68731; 402-987-2145; Fax: 402-987-2185. Hours: 8AM-4:30PM (CST). *Misdemeanor, Civil Actions Under $45,000, Eviction, Small Claims, Probate.*

Civil Records: Access: In person only. Visitors must perform in person searches for themselves. No search fee. Required to search: name, years to search. Civil cases indexed by defendant, plaintiff. Civil records on index books from late 1800s.

Criminal Records: Access: In person only. Visitors must perform in person searches for themselves. No search fee. Required to search: name, years to search. Criminal records on index books from late 1800s.

General Information: Public Access terminal is available. No adoption or juvenile records released. Copy fee: $.25 per page. Certification fee: $1.00. Fee payee: Dakota County Court. Business checks accepted. Prepayment required.

Dawes County

District Court PO Box 630, Chadron, NE 69337; 308-432-0109; Fax: 308-432-0110. Hours: 8:30AM-4:30PM (MST). *Felony, Civil Actions Over $15,000.*

Civil Records: Access: In person only. Visitors must perform in person searches for themselves. No search fee. Required to search: name, years to search. Civil cases indexed by defendant, plaintiff. Civil records on general index, docket books from 1886.

Criminal Records: Access: In person only. Visitors must perform in person searches for themselves. No search fee. Required to search: name, years to search. Criminal records on general index, docket books from 1886.

General Information: No mental health records released. Copy fee: $.25 per page. Certification fee: $1.00. Fee payee: Clerk of District Court. Personal checks accepted.

Dawes County Court PO Box 806, Chadron, NE 69337; 308-432-0116; Fax: 308-432-0118. Hours: 7:30AM-4:30PM (MST). *Misdemeanor, Civil Actions Under $45,000, Eviction, Small Claims, Probate.*

Civil Records: Access: In person only. Visitors must perform in person searches for themselves. No search fee. Required to search: name, years to search. Civil cases indexed by defendant, plaintiff. Civil records on case cards, case files kept since 1892.

Criminal Records: Access: In person only. Visitors must perform in person searches for themselves. No search fee. Required to search: name, years to search, DOB; also helpful: address. Criminal records on case cards, case files kept since 1892.

General Information: Public Access terminal is available. No confidential records released. No copy fee. Certification fee: $1.00. Fee payee: Dawes County Court. Personal checks accepted. Prepayment required.

Dawson County

District Court PO Box 429, Lexington, NE 68850; 308-324-4261; Fax: 308-324-3374. Hours: 8AM-5PM (CST). *Felony, Civil Actions Over $15,000.*

Civil Records: Access: In person only. Visitors must perform in person searches for themselves. No search fee. Required to search: name, years to search. Civil cases indexed by defendant, plaintiff. Recent civil records on microfiche, some older records on microfilm, index books date to late 1800s.

Criminal Records: Access: In person only. Visitors must perform in person searches for themselves. No search fee. Required to search: name, years to search. Recent records on microfiche, some older records on microfilm, index books date to late 1800s.

General Information: No juvenile or mental health records released. Copy fee: $.25 per page. Certification fee: $1.00. Fee payee: Clerk of District Court. Personal checks accepted. Prepayment required.

Dawson County Court 700 N Washington St, Lexington, NE 68850; 308-324-5606. Hours: 8AM-5PM (CST). *Misdemeanor, Civil Actions Under $45,000, Eviction, Small Claims, Probate.*

Civil Records: Access: In person only. Visitors must perform in person searches for themselves. No search fee. Required to search: name, years to search; also helpful: address. Civil cases indexed by defendant, plaintiff. Civil records on books from late 1800s, docket books 15 years back; on computer since 1998.

Criminal Records: Access: In person only. Visitors must perform in person searches for themselves. No search fee. Required to search: name, years to search, offense, DOB; also helpful: address, SSN. Criminal records on books from late 1800s, docket books 15 years back; on computer since 1998.

General Information: Public Access terminal is available. No adoption or juvenile records released. Fax notes: Fee to fax is $3.00 plus $1.00 each add'l page. Copy fee: $.25 per page. Certification fee: $1.00. Fee payee: Dawson County Court. Personal checks accepted. Credit cards accepted: Visa, MasterCard. Prepayment required.

Deuel County

District Court PO Box 327, Chappell, NE 69129; 308-874-3308; Fax: 308-874-3472. Hours: 8AM-4PM (MST). *Felony, Civil Actions Over $15,000.*

Civil Records: Access: Phone, fax, mail, in person. Both court and visitors may perform in person searches. No search fee. Required to search: name; also helpful: years to search. Civil cases indexed by defendant, plaintiff. Civil records on general index and docket books form late 1800s.

Criminal Records: Access: Phone, fax, mail, in person. Both court and visitors may perform in person searches. No search fee. Required to search: name; also helpful: years to search, DOB, SSN. Criminal records on general index and docket books form late 1800s.

General Information: No mental health or service discharge records released. SASE required. Turnaround time 1 week. Fax notes: No fee to fax results. Copy fee: $.50 per page. Only $.25 if you make the copy. Certification fee: $1.00. Fee payee: Clerk of District Court. Personal checks accepted. Prepayment required.

Deuel County Court PO Box 514, Chappell, NE 69129; 308-874-2909; Fax: 308-874-2994. Hours: 8AM-4PM (MST). *Misdemeanor, Civil Actions Under $45,000, Eviction, Small Claims, Probate.*

Civil Records: Access: Mail, in person. Both court and visitors may perform in person searches. No search fee. Required to search: name, years to search. Civil cases indexed by defendant, plaintiff. Civil records on index cards.

Criminal Records: Access: Mail, in person. Both court and visitors may perform in person searches. No search fee. Required to search: name, years to search, DOB, signed release. Criminal records on index cards.

General Information: No juvenile records released. SASE required. Turnaround time 3-4 days. Copy fee: $.25 per page. Certification fee: $1.00. Fee payee: Deuel County Court. No personal checks accepted. Prepayment required.

Dixon County

District Court PO Box 395, Ponca, NE 68770; 402-755-2881; Fax: 402-755-2632. Hours: 8AM-Noon, 1-5PM (CST). *Felony, Civil Actions Over $15,000.*

Civil Records: Access: In person only. Visitors must perform in person searches for themselves. No search fee. Required to search: name, years to search. Civil cases indexed by defendant, plaintiff. Civil records on books from 1876; computerized records go back to 1999.

Criminal Records: Access: In person only. Visitors must perform in person searches for themselves. No search fee. Required to search: name, years to search, DOB. Criminal records on books from 1876; computerized records go back to 1999.

General Information: Public Access terminal is available. No mental health records released. Copy fee: $.25 per page. Certification fee: $1.00. Fee payee: Clerk of District Court. Personal checks accepted. Will bill copy fees.

Dixon County Court PO Box 497, Ponca, NE 68770; 402-755-2355; Fax: 402-755-2632. Hours: 8AM-4:30PM (CST). *Misdemeanor, Civil Actions Under $45,000, Eviction, Small Claims, Probate.*

Civil Records: Access: In person only. Visitors must perform in person searches for themselves. No search fee. Required to search: name, years to search. Civil cases indexed by defendant, plaintiff. Civil records in files, cards from 1987, prior in dockets from 1876.

Criminal Records: Access: In person only. Visitors must perform in person searches for themselves. No search fee. Required to search: name, years to search, DOB. Criminal records in files, cards from 1987, prior in dockets from 1876.

General Information: Public Access terminal is available. No adoption or juvenile records released. Copy fee: $.25 per page. Certification fee: $1.00. Fee payee: Dixon County Court. Personal checks accepted.

Dodge County

District Court PO Box 1237, Fremont, NE 68026; 402-727-2780; Fax: 402-727-2773. Hours: 8:30AM-4:30PM (CST). *Felony, Civil Actions Over $15,000.*

Civil Records: Access: In person only. Visitors must perform in person searches for themselves. No search fee. Required to search: name, years to search. Civil cases indexed by defendant, plaintiff. Civil records on general index, docket books from late 1800s.

Criminal Records: Access: In person only. Visitors must perform in person searches for themselves. No search fee. Required to search: name, years to search. Criminal records on general index, docket books from late 1800s.

General Information: No mental health records released. Copy fee: $.25 per page. Certification fee: $1.50. Fee payee: District Court. Personal checks accepted. Prepayment required.

Dodge County Court 428 N Broad St, Fremont, NE 68025; 402-727-2755; Fax: 402-727-2762. Hours: 8AM-5PM (CST). *Misdemeanor, Civil Actions Under $45,000, Eviction, Small Claims, Probate.*

Civil Records: Access: In person only. Visitors must perform in person searches for themselves. No search fee. Required to search: name, years to search. Civil cases indexed by defendant. Civil records on general index, docket books from early 1900s; on computer back to 1998. Probate on microfilm from early 1900s.

Criminal Records: Access: In person only. Visitors must perform in person searches for themselves. No search fee. Required to search: name, years to search; also helpful: DOB. Criminal records on general index, docket books from early 1900s; on computer back to 1998.

General Information: No adoption or juvenile records released. Fax notes: Fee to fax results is $3.00 for 1st page; $1.00 each add'l. Copy fee: $.25 per page. Certification fee: $1.00 per document plus $.25 per page. Fee payee: Dodge County Court. Prepayment required.

Douglas County

District Court 1701 Farnam, Hall of Justice, Rm 300, Omaha, NE 68183; 402-444-7018. Hours: 8:30AM-4:30PM (CST). *Felony, Civil Actions Over $15,000.*

Civil Records: Access: Mail, in person. Both court and visitors may perform in person searches. No search fee. Required to search: name, years to search; also helpful: address. Civil cases indexed by defendant, plaintiff. Civil records on computer from 1980, on books back to late 1800s.

Criminal Records: Access: Mail, in person. Visitors must perform in person searches for themselves. No search fee. Required to search: name, years to search; also helpful: address, DOB, SSN. Criminal records on computer from 1980, on books back to late 1800s.

General Information: Public Access terminal is available. No juvenile records released. SASE required. Turnaround time 1-2 days. Copy fee: $.50 per page. $1.00 minimum. Add $.50 postage fee. Certification fee: $3.50 for 1-5 pages, then $15.50 per page. Fee payee: Clerk of District Court. Personal checks accepted. Prepayment required.

Douglas County Court 1819 Farnam, #F03, Omaha, NE 68183; Civil phone: 402-444-5425; Criminal phone: 402-444-5387. Hours: 8AM-4:30PM (CST). *Misdemeanor, Civil Actions Under $45,000, Eviction, Small Claims, Probate.*

www.co.douglas.ne.us

Civil Records: Access: Mail, online, in person. Visitors must perform in person searches for themselves. No search fee. Required to search: name, years to search. Civil cases indexed by defendant, plaintiff. Civil records on computer from 1987 (small claims), from 1983 (civil). Civil records are purged after about 20 years. Access to the remote online system requires $25 per month for the first 250 transactions and $.10 per transaction thereafter. System can be searched by name or case number. Call John at 402-471-3049 for more information.

Criminal Records: Access: Mail, in person, online. Visitors must perform in person searches for themselves. No search fee. Required to search: name, years to search; also helpful: DOB. Criminal records on computer from 1987 (small claims), from 1983 (civil). Civil records are purged after about 20 years. Online access to criminal records is the same as civil.

General Information: Public Access terminal is available. SASE required. Copy fee: $.25 per page.

Certification fee: $1.00. Fee payee: Douglas County Court. Personal checks accepted. Prepayment required.

Dundy County

District Court PO Box 506, Benkelman, NE 69021; 308-423-2058. Hours: 8AM-5PM (MST). *Felony, Civil Actions Over $15,000.*

Civil Records: Access: Phone, mail, in person. Both court and visitors may perform in person searches. No search fee. Required to search: name, years to search; also helpful: address. Civil cases indexed by defendant, plaintiff. Civil records on index books from late 1800s.

Criminal Records: Access: Phone, mail, in person. Both court and visitors may perform in person searches. No search fee. Required to search: name, years to search; also helpful: address, DOB, SSN. Criminal records on index books from late 1800s.

General Information: No juvenile records released. SASE required. Turnaround time 1-2 days. Copy fee: $.50 per page. Certification fee: $1.00. Fee payee: Clerk of District Court. Personal checks accepted. Prepayment required.

Dundy County Court PO Box 377, Benkelman, NE 69021; 308-423-2374. Hours: 8AM-4:30PM (MST). *Misdemeanor, Civil Actions Under $45,000, Eviction, Small Claims, Probate.*

Civil Records: Access: Phone, mail, in person. Only the court performs in person searches; visitors may not. No search fee. Required to search: name, years to search. Civil cases indexed by defendant, plaintiff. Civil records on general index, docket books from late 1800s; some probate, civil on microfiche.

Criminal Records: Access: Phone, mail, in person. Only the court performs in person searches; visitors may not. No search fee. Required to search: name, years to search, DOB, signed release; also helpful: address. Criminal records on general index, docket books from late 1800s; some probate, civil on microfiche.

General Information: No adoption or juvenile records released. SASE required. Turnaround time 3-4 days. Copy fee: $.25 per page. Certification fee: $1.00. Fee payee: Dundy County Court. Business checks accepted. Prepayment required.

Fillmore County

District Court PO Box 147, Geneva, NE 68361-0147; 402-759-3811; Fax: 402-759-4440. Hours: 8AM-Noon, 1-5PM (CST). *Felony, Civil Actions Over $15,000.*

Civil Records: Access: Phone, fax, mail, in person. Both court and visitors may perform in person searches. No search fee. Required to search: name, years to search. Civil cases indexed by defendant, plaintiff. Civil records on index books to late 1800s, last 10 years on microfiche.

Criminal Records: Access: Phone, fax, mail, in person. Both court and visitors may perform in person searches. No search fee. Required to search: name, years to search. Criminal records on index books to late 1800s, last 10 years on microfiche.

General Information: Public Access terminal is available. No juvenile or mental health records released. SASE required. Turnaround time 1-5 days, 1 day for phone and FAX. Fax notes: $2.00 for first page, $1.00 each add'l. Copy fee: $.35 per page. Certification fee: $1.00. Fee payee: Clerk of District Court. Personal checks accepted. Will bill fax & copy fees.

Fillmore County Court PO Box 66, Geneva, NE 68361; 402-759-3514; Fax: 402-759-4440. Hours: 8AM-5PM (CST). *Misdemeanor, Civil Actions Under $45,000, Eviction, Small Claims, Probate.*

Civil Records: Access: Fax, mail, in person. Both court and visitors may perform in person searches. No search fee. Required to search: name, years to search. Civil cases indexed by defendant, plaintiff. Civil records on

general index, docket books from late 1800s; probate on microfiche.

Criminal Records: Access: Fax, mail, in person. Both court and visitors may perform in person searches. No search fee. Required to search: name, years to search. Criminal records on general index, docket books from late 1800s; probate on microfiche.

General Information: No adoption or juvenile records released. SASE required. Turnaround time 7-8 days. Fax notes: $2.00 for first page, $1.00 each add'l. Copy fee: $.25 per page. Certification fee: $1.25. Fee payee: County Court. Personal checks accepted. Prepayment required.

Franklin County

District Court PO Box 146, Franklin, NE 68939; 308-425-6202; Fax: 308-425-6093. Hours: 8:30AM-4:30PM (CST). *Felony, Civil Actions Over $15,000.*

Civil Records: Access: In person only. Visitors must perform in person searches for themselves. No search fee. Required to search: name, years to search. Civil cases indexed by defendant, plaintiff. Civil records on index books back to turn of century; on computer back to 2/2000.

Criminal Records: Access: In person only. Visitors must perform in person searches for themselves. No search fee. Required to search: name, years to search. Criminal records on index books back to turn of century; on computer back to 2/2000.

General Information: Public Access terminal is available. No adoption or juvenile records released. Copy fee: $.25 per page. Certification fee: $1.00. Fee payee: Clerk of District Court or County Clerk. Personal checks accepted. Prepayment required.

Franklin County Court PO Box 174, Franklin, NE 68939; 308-425-6288; Fax: 308-425-6289. Hours: 8:30AM-4:30PM M-F (CST). *Misdemeanor, Civil Actions Under $45,000, Eviction, Small Claims, Probate.*

Civil Records: Access: Mail, in person. Both court and visitors may perform in person searches. No search fee. Required to search: name, years to search. Civil cases indexed by defendant, plaintiff. Civil records on docket cards since 1988, prior on docket books.

Criminal Records: Access: Mail, in person. Both court and visitors may perform in person searches. No search fee. Required to search: name, years to search. Criminal records on docket cards since 1988, prior on docket books.

General Information: Public Access terminal is available. No juvenile, adoption records released. SASE required. Turnaround time 2 days. Copy fee: $.25 per page. Certification fee: $1.00. Fee payee: Franklin County Court. Personal checks accepted.

Frontier County

District Court PO Box 40, Stockville, NE 69042; 308-367-8641; Fax: 308-367-8730. Hours: 9AM-4:30PM (CST). *Felony, Civil Actions Over $15,000.*

Civil Records: Access: Mail, in person. Both court and visitors may perform in person searches. No search fee. Required to search: name, years to search. Civil cases indexed by defendant, plaintiff. Civil records on general index, docket books from late 1800s.

Criminal Records: Access: Mail, in person. Both court and visitors may perform in person searches. No search fee. Required to search: name, years to search, DOB, signed release. Criminal records on general index, docket books from late 1800s.

General Information: SASE required. Turnaround time 5 days. Copy fee: $.25 per page. Certification fee: $1.00. Fee payee: Clerk of District Court. Only cashiers checks and money orders accepted. Prepayment required.

Frontier County Court PO Box 38, Stockville, NE 69042; 308-367-8629; Fax: 308-367-8730. Hours: 9AM-4:30PM (CST). *Misdemeanor, Civil Actions Under $45,000, Eviction, Small Claims, Probate.*

Civil Records: Access: Fax, mail, in person. Only the court performs in person searches; visitors may not. No search fee. Required to search: name, years to search. Civil cases indexed by plaintiff. Civil records on general index, docket books from late 1800s, no computerization.

Criminal Records: Access: Fax, mail, in person. Only the court performs in person searches; visitors may not. No search fee. Required to search: name, years to search, DOB, signed release. Criminal records on general index, docket books from late 1800s, no computerization.

General Information: Public Access terminal is available. No adoption or juvenile records released. SASE required. Turnaround time 5 days. Fax notes: $3.00 per page. Copy fee: $.25 per page. Certification fee: $1.00. Fee payee: County Court. Only cashiers checks and money orders accepted. Prepayment required.

Furnas County

District Court PO Box 413, Beaver City, NE 68926; 308-268-4015; Fax: 308-268-2345. Hours: 10AM-Noon, 1-3PM (CST). *Felony, Civil Actions Over $15,000.*

Civil Records: Access: Mail, in person. Both court and visitors may perform in person searches. No search fee. Required to search: name, years to search. Civil cases indexed by defendant, plaintiff. Civil records in general index books and files from late 1800s.

Criminal Records: Access: Mail, in person. Both court and visitors may perform in person searches. No search fee. Required to search: name, years to search. Criminal records in general index books and files from late 1800s.

General Information: No mental health records released. SASE required. Turnaround time 3-4 days. Copy fee: $.25 per page. Certification fee: $1.00. Fee payee: Clerk of District Court. Personal checks accepted.

Furnas County Court 912 R St (PO Box 373), Beaver City, NE 68926; 308-268-4025. Hours: 8AM-4PM (CST). *Misdemeanor, Civil Actions Under $45,000, Eviction, Small Claims, Probate.*

Civil Records: Access: In person only. Visitors must perform in person searches for themselves. No search fee. Required to search: name, years to search. Civil cases indexed by defendant, plaintiff. Civil records on card system from 1984, docket books back to late 1800s.

Criminal Records: Access: In person only. Visitors must perform in person searches for themselves. No search fee. Required to search: name, years to search; also helpful: DOB. Criminal records on card system from 1984, docket books back to late 1800s.

General Information: No adoption, juvenile or sealed records released. Copy fee: $.25 per page. Certification fee: $1.00. Plus $.25 per page. Fee payee: County Court. Personal checks accepted.

Gage County

District Court PO Box 845, Beatrice, NE 68310; 402-223-1332; Fax: 402-223-1313. Hours: 8AM-5PM (CST). *Felony, Civil Actions Over $15,000.*

Civil Records: Access: Mail, fax, in person. Both court and visitors may perform in person searches. No search fee. Required to search: name, years to search. Civil cases indexed by defendant, plaintiff. Civil records on index books from late 1800s; on computer back to 1997.

Criminal Records: Access: Mail, fax, in person. Both court and visitors may perform in person searches. No search fee. Required to search: name, years to search, DOB. Criminal records on index books from late 1800s; on computer back to 1997.

General Information: Public Access terminal is available. No juvenile or mental health records released. SASE required. Turnaround time up to 7-10 days. Copy fee: $.25 per page. Certification fee: $1.00. Fee payee: Clerk of District Court. Personal checks accepted. Prepayment required.

Gage County Court PO Box 219, Beatrice, NE 68310; 402-223-1323. Hours: 8AM-5PM (CST). *Misdemeanor, Civil Actions Under $45,000, Eviction, Small Claims, Probate.*

Civil Records: Access: Mail, in person. Both court and visitors may perform in person searches. No search fee. Required to search: name, years to search. Civil cases indexed by defendant, plaintiff. Probate records from 1860, probate on microfiche. Contact court before faxing.

Criminal Records: Access: Mail, in person. Both court and visitors may perform in person searches. No search fee. Required to search: name, years to search; also helpful: DOB. Contact court before faxing.

General Information: No adoption or juvenile records released. SASE required. Turnaround time 1-3 weeks. Copy fee: $.25 per page. Certification fee: $1.00. Fee payee: Gage County Court. Personal checks accepted. Prepayment required.

Garden County

District Court PO Box 486, Oshkosh, NE 69154; 308-772-3924; Fax: 308-772-4143. Hours: 8AM-4PM (MST). *Felony, Civil Actions Over $15,000.*

Civil Records: Access: Fax, mail, in person. Both court and visitors may perform in person searches. No search fee. Required to search: name, years to search. Civil cases indexed by defendant, plaintiff. Civil records in files, docket books back to 1910; on computer back to 1998.

Criminal Records: Access: Fax, mail, in person. Both court and visitors may perform in person searches. No search fee. Required to search: name, years to search. Criminal records in files, docket books back to 1910; on computer back to 1998.

General Information: Public Access terminal is available. No confidential records released. SASE required. Turnaround time same day. Fax notes: $2.00 for first page, $1.00 each add'l. Copy fee: $.50 per page. Certification fee: $5.00. Fee payee: Clerk of District Court. Personal checks accepted. Prepayment required.

Garden County Court PO Box 465, Oshkosh, NE 69154; 308-772-3696. Hours: 8AM-4PM (MST). *Misdemeanor, Civil Actions Under $45,000, Eviction, Small Claims, Probate.*

Civil Records: Access: In person only. Visitors must perform in person searches for themselves. No search fee. Required to search: name, years to search. Civil cases indexed by defendant, plaintiff. Civil records on general index, docket books from 1910. Phone access limited to short searches.

Criminal Records: Access: In person only. Visitors must perform in person searches for themselves. No search fee. Required to search: name, years to search. Criminal records on general index, docket books from 1910.

General Information: No adoption or juvenile records released. Certification fee: $1.00. Fee payee: Garden County Court. Personal checks accepted. Prepayment required.

Garfield County

District Court PO Box 218, Burwell, NE 68823; 308-346-4161. Hours: 9AM-5PM (CST). *Felony, Civil Actions Over $15,000.*

Civil Records: Access: Mail, in person. Both court and visitors may perform in person searches. Search fee: $5.00. Required to search: name, years to search; also helpful: address. Civil cases indexed by defendant, plaintiff. Civil records on index books from 1885.

Criminal Records: Access: Mail, in person. Both court and visitors may perform in person searches. Search fee: $5.00. Required to search: name, years to search; also helpful: address, DOB, SSN. Criminal records on index books from 1885.

General Information: SASE required. Turnaround time 3-4 days. Copy fee: $.25 per page. Certification fee: $1.50. Fee payee: Clerk of District Court. Personal checks accepted. Prepayment required.

Garfield County Court PO Box 431, Burwell, NE 68823; 308-346-4123; Fax: 308-346-5064. Hours: 9AM-4PM (CST). *Misdemeanor, Civil Actions Under $45,000, Eviction, Small Claims, Probate.*

Civil Records: Access: Mail, in person. Both court and visitors may perform in person searches. No search fee. Required to search: name, years to search. Civil cases indexed by defendant. Civil records on index books, from 1885 (probate), 25 years for civil; on computer back to 2000.

Criminal Records: Access: Mail, in person. Both court and visitors may perform in person searches. No search fee. Required to search: name, years to search. Criminal record keeping back for 25 years; on computer back to 2000.

General Information: No juvenile records released. SASE required. Turnaround time within 5 days. Fax notes: $3.00 for first page, $1.00 each add'l. Copy fee: $.25 per page. Certification fee: $1.00. Fee payee: County Court. Personal checks accepted. Prepayment required.

Gosper County

District Court PO Box 136, Elwood, NE 68937; 308-785-2611. Hours: 8:30AM-4:30PM (CST). *Felony, Civil Actions Over $15,000.*

Civil Records: Access: In person only. Visitors must perform in person searches for themselves. No search fee. Required to search: name, years to search. Civil cases indexed by defendant, plaintiff. Civil records in general index books since late 1800s.

Criminal Records: Access: In person only. Visitors must perform in person searches for themselves. No search fee. Required to search: name, years to search; also helpful: DOB. Criminal records in general index books since late 1800s.

General Information: No juvenile records or search warrants released. Copy fee: $.25 per page. Certification fee: $1.00. Fee payee: Clerk of District Court. Personal checks accepted. Prepayment required.

Gosper County Court PO Box 55, Elwood, NE 68937; 308-785-2531; Fax: 308-785-2300 (call before faxing). Hours: 8:30AM-4:30PM (CST). *Misdemeanor, Civil Actions Under $45,000, Eviction, Small Claims, Probate.*

Civil Records: Access: In person only. Visitors must perform in person searches for themselves. No search fee. Required to search: name, years to search. Civil cases indexed by defendant, plaintiff. Civil records on index cards, docket books kept for 10 years (civil), to late 1800s (probate). Mail access limited to short searches.

Criminal Records: Access: In person only. Visitors must perform in person searches for themselves. No search fee. Required to search: name, years to search, DOB. Criminal record keeping back for 10 years.

General Information: No adoption or juvenile records released. Copy fee: $.25 per page. Certification fee: $1.00. Fee payee: Gosper County Court. Personal checks accepted. Out of state checks not accepted. Prepayment required.

Grant County

District Court PO Box 139, Hyannis, NE 69350; 308-458-2488; Fax: 308-458-2485. Hours: 8AM-4PM (MST). *Felony, Civil Actions Over $15,000.*

Civil Records: Access: Fax, mail, in person. Both court and visitors may perform in person searches. No search fee. Required to search: name, years to search. Civil cases indexed by defendant, plaintiff. Civil records on index books from 1888.

Criminal Records: Access: Fax, mail, in person. Both court and visitors may perform in person searches. No search fee. Required to search: name, years to search. Criminal records on index books from 1888.

General Information: No mental health records released. SASE required. Turnaround time 3-4 days. Fax notes: $.20 per page. Copy fee: $.20 per page. Certification fee: $1.50. Fee payee: Grant County Clerk. Personal checks accepted. Prepayment required.

Grant County Court PO Box 97, Hyannis, NE 69350; 308-458-2433; Fax: 308-458-2283 (Sheriff). Hours: 8AM-4PM (MST). *Misdemeanor, Civil Actions Under $45,000, Eviction, Small Claims, Probate.*

Civil Records: Access: Phone, mail, in person. Both court and visitors may perform in person searches. No search fee. Required to search: name, years to search; also helpful: address. Civil cases indexed by defendant, plaintiff. Civil records in files, docket books from 1888.

Criminal Records: Access: Phone, mail, in person. Both court and visitors may perform in person searches. No search fee. Required to search: name, years to search, DOB; also helpful: address, SSN. Criminal records in files, docket books from 1888.

General Information: No adoption records released. SASE not required. Turnaround time 7 days, limited phone searching immediate. Copy fee: $.20 per page. Certification fee: $1.50. Fee payee: Grant County Court. Personal checks accepted.

Greeley County

District Court PO Box 287, Greeley, NE 68842; 308-428-3625; Fax: 308-428-6500. Hours: 8AM-4PM (CST). *Felony, Civil Actions Over $15,000.*

Civil Records: Access: Mail, in person. Only the court performs in person searches; visitors may not. No search fee. Required to search: name, years to search, address. Civil cases indexed by defendant, plaintiff. Civil records on general index books from late 1800s.

Criminal Records: Access: Mail, in person. Only the court performs in person searches; visitors may not. No search fee. Required to search: name, years to search, DOB, signed release. Criminal records on general index books from late 1800s.

General Information: No mental health records released. SASE required. Turnaround time 1 day. Copy fee: $.25 per page. Certification fee: $1.50. Fee payee: Clerk of District Court. Only cashiers checks and money orders accepted. Prepayment required.

Greeley County Court PO Box 302, Greeley, NE 68842; 308-428-2705; Fax: 308-428-6500. Hours: 8AM-5PM (CST). *Misdemeanor, Civil Actions Under $45,000, Eviction, Small Claims, Probate.*

Civil Records: Access: In person only. Visitors must perform in person searches for themselves. No search fee. Required to search: name, years to search. Civil cases indexed by defendant, plaintiff. Civil records on index cards, kept from late 1800s.

Criminal Records: Access: In person only. Visitors must perform in person searches for themselves. No

search fee. Required to search: name, years to search. Criminal records on index cards, kept from late 1800s.

General Information: Public Access terminal is available. No adoption records released. Copy fee: $.25 per page. Certification fee: $1.00. Fee payee: County Court. Only cashiers checks and money orders accepted. Prepayment required.

Hall County

District Court PO Box 1926, Grand Island, NE 68802; 308-385-5144; Fax: 308-385-5110. Hours: 8AM-5PM (CST). *Felony, Civil Actions Over $15,000.*

Civil Records: Access: Mail, in person. Both court and visitors may perform in person searches. No search fee. Required to search: name, years to search. Civil cases indexed by defendant, plaintiff. Many records on computer since 1985, some on microfilm, original index books back to late 1800s.

Criminal Records: Access: Mail, in person. Both court and visitors may perform in person searches. No search fee. Required to search: name, years to search. Many records on computer since 1985, some on microfilm, original index books back to late 1800s.

General Information: Public Access terminal is available. No mental health records released. SASE required. Turnaround time 3-4 days. Copy fee: $.20 per page. Certification fee: $2.00. Fee payee: Clerk of District Court. Personal checks accepted. Prepayment required.

Hall County Court 111 W 1st Suite 1, Grand Island, NE 68801; 308-385-5135. Hours: 8AM-4:30PM (CST). *Misdemeanor, Civil Actions Under $45,000, Eviction, Small Claims, Probate.*

Civil Records: Access: In person only. Visitors must perform in person searches for themselves. No search fee. Required to search: name, years to search. Civil cases indexed by defendant. Civil records on index books, on computer after 1/24/00.

Criminal Records: Access: In person only. Visitors must perform in person searches for themselves. No search fee. Required to search: name, years to search, DOB. Criminal records on index books; on computer after 5/19/97.

General Information: Public Access terminal is available. No confidential records released. Copy fee: $.25 per page. Certification fee: $1.00. Fee payee: County Court. Personal checks accepted. Prepayment required.

Hamilton County

District Court PO Box 201, Aurora, NE 68818-0201; 402-694-3533; Fax: 402-694-2250. Hours: 8AM-5PM (CST). *Felony, Civil Actions Over $15,000.*

Civil Records: Access: In person only. Both court and visitors may perform in person searches. No search fee. Required to search: name, years to search. Civil cases indexed by defendant, plaintiff. Civil records on index books and files from late 1800s.

Criminal Records: Access: In person only. Both court and visitors may perform in person searches. No search fee. Required to search: name, years to search. Criminal records on index books and files from late 1800s.

General Information: No mental health board hearing records released. Copy fee: $.25 per page. Certification fee: $1.00. Fee payee: Clerk of District Court. Personal checks accepted. Prepayment required.

Hamilton County Court PO Box 323, Aurora, NE 68818; 402-694-6188; Fax: 402-694-2250. *Misdemeanor, Civil Actions Under $45,000, Eviction, Small Claims, Probate.*

Civil Records: Access: In person only. Visitors must perform in person searches for themselves. No search fee. Required to search: name, years to search. Civil cases indexed by defendant, plaintiff. Civil records

computerized since 1998, older on docket cards, probate on microfiche from late 1800s.

Criminal Records: Access: In person only. Visitors must perform in person searches for themselves. No search fee. Required to search: name, years to search. computerized since 1997.

General Information: Public Access terminal is available. No adoption records released. Copy fee: $.25 per page. Certification fee: $1.00. Fee payee: Hamilton County Court. Personal checks accepted. Credit cards accepted: Visa, MasterCard. Prepayment required.

Harlan County

District Court PO Box 698, Alma, NE 68920; 308-928-2173; Fax: 308-928-2592. Hours: 8:30AM-4:30PM (CST). *Felony, Civil Actions Over $15,000.*

Civil Records: Access: Phone, mail, in person. Both court and visitors may perform in person searches. Search fee: $5.00 per name. Required to search: name, years to search. Civil cases indexed by defendant, plaintiff. Civil records on books and in files from late 1800s, on computer since.

Criminal Records: Access: Phone, mail, in person. Both court and visitors may perform in person searches. Search fee: $5.00 per name. Required to search: name, years to search. Criminal records on books and in files from late 1800s; on computer since.

General Information: Public Access terminal is available. No juvenile records released. SASE not required. Turnaround time 1 day. Copy fee: $.25 per page. Certification fee: $3.00. Fee payee: Clerk of District Court. Personal checks accepted.

Harlan County Court PO Box 379, Alma, NE 68920; 308-928-2179; Fax: 308-928-2170. Hours: 8:30AM-4:30PM (CST). *Misdemeanor, Civil Actions Under $45,000, Eviction, Small Claims, Probate.*

Civil Records: Access: In person only. Visitors must perform in person searches for themselves. No search fee. Required to search: name, years to search; also helpful: address. Civil cases indexed by defendant. Civil records on index cards, back to late 1800s.

Criminal Records: Access: In person only. Visitors must perform in person searches for themselves. No search fee. Required to search: name, years to search; also helpful: address, DOB, SSN. Criminal records on index cards, computer terminal.

General Information: Public Access terminal is available. (CD-ROM legal research only.) No adoption records released. Limited access to juvenile records. Copy fee: $.25 per page. Certification fee: $1.00. Fee payee: Harlan County Court. Business checks accepted. Prepayment required.

Hayes County

District Court PO Box 370, Hayes Center, NE 69032; 308-286-3413; Fax: 308-286-3208. Hours: 8AM-4PM (CST). *Felony, Civil Actions Over $15,000.*

Civil Records: Access: Fax, mail, in person. Both court and visitors may perform in person searches. No search fee. Required to search: name; also helpful: years to search, address. Civil cases indexed by defendant, plaintiff. Civil records on index books back to late 1800s.

Criminal Records: Access: Fax, mail, in person. Both court and visitors may perform in person searches. No search fee. Required to search: name; also helpful: years to search, address, DOB, SSN. Criminal records on index books back to late 1800s.

General Information: No sealed records released. SASE required. Turnaround time 2 days. Copy fee: $.25 per page. Certification fee: $4.00. Fee payee: Clerk of District Court. Personal checks accepted. Prepayment required.

Hayes County Court PO Box 370, Hayes Center, NE 69032; 308-286-3315. Hours: 9AM-Noon, 1-4PM Tuesday (Clerk's hours) (CST). *Misdemeanor, Civil Actions Under $45,000, Eviction, Small Claims, Probate.*

Civil Records: Access: Phone, mail, in person. Both court and visitors may perform in person searches. No search fee. Required to search: name, years to search. Civil cases indexed by defendant, plaintiff. Civil records on general index books and files back to late 1800s; on computer back to mid-2000.

Criminal Records: Access: Phone, mail, in person. Both court and visitors may perform in person searches. No search fee. Required to search: name, years to search, DOB. Criminal records on general index books and files back to late 1800s; on computer back to mid-2000.

General Information: No juvenile or adoption records released. SASE required. Turnaround time 1 week. Copy fee: $.25 per page. Certification fee: $1.00. Fee payee: County Court. Personal checks accepted. Prepayment required.

Hitchcock County

District Court PO Box 248, Trenton, NE 69044; 308-334-5646; Fax: 308-334-5398. Hours: 8:30AM-4PM (CST). *Felony, Civil Actions Over $15,000.*

www.co.hitchcock.ne.us/court.html

Civil Records: Access: Phone, fax, mail, in person. Both court and visitors may perform in person searches. No search fee. Required to search: name, years to search. Civil cases indexed by defendant, plaintiff. Civil records on books from late 1800s; on computer back to 1999.

Criminal Records: Access: Phone, fax, mail, in person. Both court and visitors may perform in person searches. No search fee. Required to search: name, years to search. Criminal records on books from late 1800s; on computer back to 1999.

General Information: Public Access terminal is available. No sealed records released. SASE required. Turnaround time 2 days. Fax notes: $3.00 for first page, $1.50 each add'l. Copy fee: $.25 per page. Certification fee: $1.00. Fee payee: Clerk of District Court. Personal checks accepted. Prepayment required.

Hitchcock County Court PO Box 366, Trenton, NE 69044; 308-334-5383. Hours: 8:30AM-4PM (CST). *Misdemeanor, Civil Actions Under $45,000, Eviction, Small Claims, Probate.*

Civil Records: Access: Phone, mail, in person. Both court and visitors may perform in person searches. No search fee. Required to search: name, years to search. Civil cases indexed by defendant, plaintiff. Civil records on docket books, cards; on computer back to 2000. Probate records go back to late 1800s.

Criminal Records: Access: Phone, mail, in person. Both court and visitors may perform in person searches. No search fee. Required to search: name, years to search, DOB. Criminal records on docket books, cards; on computer back to 2000.

General Information: No adoption or juvenile records released. SASE required. Turnaround time 2 weeks, limited phone searching same day. Copy fee: $.25 per page. Certification fee: $1.00. Fee payee: County Court. Personal checks accepted. Prepayment required.

Holt County

District Court PO Box 755, O'Neill, NE 68763; 402-336-2840; Fax: 402-336-3601. Hours: 8AM-4:30PM (CST). *Felony, Civil Actions Over $15,000.*

Civil Records: Access: Phone, fax, mail, in person. Both court and visitors may perform in person searches. No search fee. Required to search: name, years to search; also helpful: address. Civil cases indexed by defendant, plaintiff. Civil records on docket books and general index books since late 1800s.

Criminal Records: Access: Phone, fax, mail, in person. Both court and visitors may perform in person searches. No search fee. Required to search: name, years to search, DOB. Criminal records on docket books and general index books since late 1800s.

General Information: Public Access terminal is available. No juvenile or mental health records released. SASE required. Turnaround time 1 week or less. Fax notes: $3.00 for first page, $1.00 each add'l. Copy fee: $.25 per page. Certification fee: $1.00. Fee payee: Clerk of District Court. Personal checks accepted.

Holt County Court 204 N 4th St, O'Neill, NE 68763; 402-336-1662; Fax: 402-336-1663. Hours: 8AM-4:30PM (CST). *Misdemeanor, Civil Actions Under $45,000, Eviction, Small Claims, Probate.*

Civil Records: Access: Mail, in person. Both court and visitors may perform in person searches. No search fee. Required to search: name, years to search. Civil cases indexed by defendant. Civil records in files for 15 years, probate kept longer.

Criminal Records: Access: Mail, in person. Both court and visitors may perform in person searches. No search fee. Required to search: name, years to search, DOB. Criminal records in files for 15 years, probate kept longer.

General Information: No adoption records released. SASE required. Turnaround time 1 week. Copy fee: $.25 per page. Certification fee: $1.25. Fee payee: Holt County Court. Personal checks accepted. Prepayment required.

Hooker County

District Court PO Box 184, Mullen, NE 69152; 308-546-2244; Fax: 308-546-2490. Hours: 8:30AM-Noon, 1-4:30PM (MST). *Felony, Civil Actions Over $15,000.*

Civil Records: Access: Phone, fax, mail, in person. Visitors must perform in person searches for themselves. No search fee. Required to search: name, years to search. Civil cases indexed by defendant, plaintiff. Civil records on index books since late 1800s.

Criminal Records: Access: Phone, fax, mail, in person. Visitors must perform in person searches for themselves. No search fee. Required to search: name, years to search. Criminal records on index books since late 1800s.

General Information: No mental health records released. SASE required. Turnaround time 3-4 days. Fax notes: $2.00 for first page, $1.00 each add'l. Copy fee: $1.00 per page. Certification fee: $1.50. Fee payee: Clerk of District Court. Personal checks accepted. Prepayment required.

Hooker County Court PO Box 184, Mullen, NE 69152; 308-546-2249; Fax: 308-546-2490 (Sheriff). Hours: 8:30AM-4:30PM (MST). *Misdemeanor, Civil Actions Under $45,000, Eviction, Small Claims, Probate.*

Civil Records: Access: Fax, mail, in person. Both court and visitors may perform in person searches. No search fee. Required to search: name, years to search. Civil cases indexed by defendant, plaintiff. Civil records on index cards and books from late 1800s.

Criminal Records: Access: Fax, mail, in person. Both court and visitors may perform in person searches. No search fee. Required to search: name, years to search; also helpful: DOB, SSN. Criminal records on index cards and books from late 1800s.

General Information: No adoption or juvenile records released. SASE required. Turnaround time 3-4 days. Fax notes: No fee to fax results. Copy fee: $.25 per page. Certification fee: $1.00. Fee payee: County Court. Business checks accepted. Prepayment required.

Howard County

District Court PO Box 25, St Paul, NE 68873; 308-754-4343; Fax: 308-754-4727. Hours: 8AM-5PM (CST). *Felony, Civil Actions Over $15,000.*

Civil Records: Access: In person only. Both court and visitors may perform in person searches. No search fee. Required to search: name, years to search. Civil cases indexed by defendant, plaintiff. Civil records on microfiche from 1986, books prior.

Criminal Records: Access: In person only. Both court and visitors may perform in person searches. No search fee. Required to search: name, years to search, DOB. Criminal records on microfiche from 1986, books prior.

General Information: Public Access terminal is available. No pending case records released. Copy fee: $.25 per page. Certification fee: $4.00. Fee payee: Clerk of District Court. Personal checks accepted. Prepayment required.

Howard County Court 612 Indian St Suite #6, St Paul, NE 68873; 308-754-4192. Hours: 8AM-5PM (CST). *Misdemeanor, Civil Actions Under $45,000, Eviction, Small Claims, Probate.*

Civil Records: Access: In person only. Visitors must perform in person searches for themselves. No search fee. Required to search: name, years to search. Civil cases indexed by defendant. Civil records on docket cards since 1982.

Criminal Records: Access: In person only. Visitors must perform in person searches for themselves. No search fee. Required to search: name, years to search; also helpful: DOB. Criminal records on docket cards since 1982.

General Information: Copy fee: $.25 per page. Certification fee: $1.00. Fee payee: Howard County Court. Business checks accepted. Prepayment required.

Jefferson County

District Court Jefferson County Courthouse, 411 Fourth Street, Fairbury, NE 68352; 402-729-2019; Fax: 402-729-2016. Hours: 9AM-5PM (CST). *Felony, Civil Actions Over $15,000.*

Civil Records: Access: Fax, mail, in person. Both court and visitors may perform in person searches. No search fee. Required to search: name, years to search. Civil cases indexed by defendant, plaintiff. Civil records on index books from 1870s; on computer to 1996.

Criminal Records: Access: In person only. Visitors must perform in person searches for themselves. No search fee. Required to search: name, years to search, DOB. Criminal records on index books from 1870s; on computer to 1996.

General Information: Public Access terminal is available. No mental health records released. SASE required. Turnaround time 1-2 days. Fax notes: Fee to fax results is $2.00 per document. Copy fee: $.20 per page. Certification fee: $1.00. Fee payee: Clerk of District Court. Personal checks accepted. Prepayment required.

Jefferson County Court 411 Fourth St, Fairbury, NE 68352; 402-729-2312. Hours: 8AM-Noon, 1-5PM (CST). *Misdemeanor, Civil Actions Under $45,000, Eviction, Small Claims, Probate.*

Civil Records: Access: Mail, in person. Both court and visitors may perform in person searches. No search fee. Required to search: name, years to search. Civil cases indexed by defendant, plaintiff. Civil records on cards from 1988, prior on docket books.

Criminal Records: Access: Mail, in person. Both court and visitors may perform in person searches. No search fee. Required to search: name, years to search, DOB, signed release. Criminal records from 1988, prior on docket books.

General Information: Public Access terminal is available. No adoption or sealed records released. SASE

required. Turnaround time varies. Fax notes: Will not fax results. Copy fee: $.25 per page. Certification fee: $1.00. Fee payee: County Court. Personal checks accepted. Prepayment required.

Johnson County

District Court PO Box 416, Tecumseh, NE 68450; 402-335-6301; Fax: 402-335-6311. Hours: 8AM-Noon, 1-4:30PM (CST). *Felony, Civil Actions Over $15,000.*

Civil Records: Access: In person only. Both court and visitors may perform in person searches. No search fee. Required to search: name, years to search. Civil cases indexed by defendant, plaintiff. Civil records on index and docket books from late 1800s, microfiche back 7 years.

Criminal Records: Access: In person only. Both court and visitors may perform in person searches. No search fee. Required to search: name, years to search. Criminal records on index and docket books from late 1800s, microfiche back 7 years.

General Information: Public Access terminal is available. No juvenile records released. Fax notes: Fee to fax results is $2.00 per document. Copy fee: $.50 per page. Certification fee: $1.50. Fee payee: Clerk of District Court. Personal checks accepted. Prepayment required.

Johnson County Court PO Box 285, Tecumseh, NE 68450; 402-335-3050; Fax: 402-335-3070. Hours: 8AM-4:30PM (CST). *Misdemeanor, Civil Actions Under $45,000, Eviction, Small Claims, Probate.*

Note: The court is in the process of computerizing their records.

Civil Records: Access: In person only. Visitors must perform in person searches for themselves. No search fee. Required to search: name, years to search; also helpful: address. Civil cases indexed by defendant, plaintiff. Civil records on index cards back 15 years, microfiche back to late 1800s for probate.

Criminal Records: Access: In person only. Visitors must perform in person searches for themselves. No search fee. Required to search: name, years to search, DOB, signed release; also helpful: address, SSN. Criminal records on index cards back 15 years, microfiche back to late 1800s for probate.

General Information: No adoption or juvenile records released. Copy fee: $.25 per page. Certification fee: $1.00. Fee payee: County Court. Personal checks accepted. Prepayment required.

Kearney County

District Court PO Box 208, Minden, NE 68959; 308-832-1742; Fax: 308-832-0636. Hours: 8:30AM-5PM (CST). *Felony, Civil Actions Over $15,000.*

Civil Records: Access: In person only. Visitors must perform in person searches for themselves. No search fee. Required to search: name, years to search. Civil cases indexed by defendant, plaintiff. All records on microfilm since 1800s; on computer back to 9/1998. Mail access available to attorneys only.

Criminal Records: Access: In person only. Visitors must perform in person searches for themselves. No search fee. Required to search: name, years to search. Criminal records on microfilm since 1800s; on computer back to 9/1998.

General Information: Public Access terminal is available. (For records since 09/98.) No mental health records released. Copy fee: $.25 per page. Certification fee: $1.50. Fee payee: Clerk of District Court. Personal checks accepted. Prepayment required.

Kearney County Court PO Box 377, Minden, NE 68959; 308-832-2719; Fax: 308-832-0636. Hours: 8:30AM-5PM (CST). *Misdemeanor, Civil Actions Under $45,000, Eviction, Small Claims, Probate.*

Civil Records: Access: In person only. Visitors must perform in person searches for themselves. No search fee. Required to search: name, years to search. Civil cases indexed by defendant. Civil records computerized since 10/99, rest on index cards, some probate on microfiche.

Criminal Records: Access: In person only. Visitors must perform in person searches for themselves. No search fee. Required to search: name, years to search. Criminal records computerized since 03/97.

General Information: Copy fee: $.25 per page. Certification fee: $1.00. Fee payee: Kearney County Court. Personal checks accepted. Prepayment required.

Keith County

District Court PO Box 686, Ogallala, NE 69153; 308-284-3849; Fax: 308-284-3978. Hours: 8AM-4PM (MST). *Felony, Civil Actions Over $15,000.*

Civil Records: Access: Fax, mail, in person. Both court and visitors may perform in person searches. No search fee. Required to search: name, years to search. Civil cases indexed by defendant, plaintiff. Civil records on index books from late 1800s; on computer back to 1975.

Criminal Records: Access: Fax, mail, in person. Both court and visitors may perform in person searches. No search fee. Required to search: name, years to search, DOB. Criminal records on index books from late 1800s; on computer back to 1975.

General Information: Public Access terminal is available. No juvenile or mental health records released. SASE not required. Turnaround time 2-3 days. Fax notes: No fee to fax results. Fee is charged if long distance. Copy fee: $.25 per page. Certification fee: $1.00. Fee payee: Clerk of District Court. Personal checks accepted.

Keith County Court PO Box 358, Ogallala, NE 69153; 308-284-3693; Fax: 308-284-6825. Hours: 8AM-5PM M-Th; 7AM-4PM F (MST). *Misdemeanor, Civil Actions Under $45,000, Eviction, Small Claims, Probate.*

Civil Records: Access: In person only. Visitors must perform in person searches for themselves. No search fee. Required to search: name, years to search. Civil cases indexed by defendant, plaintiff. Civil records on index cards, files.

Criminal Records: Access: In person only. Visitors must perform in person searches for themselves. No search fee. Required to search: name, years to search. Criminal records on index cards, files.

General Information: Public Access terminal is available. No adoption records released. Copy fee: $.25 per page. Certification fee: $1.00. Fee payee: County Court. Local checks only.

Keya Paha County

District Court PO Box 349, Springview, NE 68778; 402-497-3791; Fax: 402-497-3799. Hours: 8AM-5PM (CST). *Felony, Civil Actions Over $15,000.*

Civil Records: Access: Fax, mail, in person. Both court and visitors may perform in person searches. No search fee. Required to search: name, years to search. Civil cases indexed by defendant, plaintiff. Civil records on microfiche 7-9 years, on docket books since late 1800s.

Criminal Records: Access: Fax, mail, in person. Both court and visitors may perform in person searches. No search fee. Required to search: name, years to search. Criminal records on microfiche 7-9 years, on docket books since late 1800s.

General Information: No confidential records released. SASE required. Turnaround time 3-4 days.

Fax notes: $2.00 for first page, $1.00 each add'l. Copy fee: $.25 per page. Legal Size Copy Fee: $.30 per page. Certification fee: $4.00. Fee payee: Clerk of District Court. Personal checks accepted. Prepayment required.

Keya Paha County Court PO Box 275, Springview, NE 68778; 402-497-3021. Hours: 8AM-Noon M; 8AM-4:30PM Th,F (CST). *Misdemeanor, Civil Actions Under $45,000, Eviction, Small Claims, Probate.*

Civil Records: Access: In person only. Visitors must perform in person searches for themselves. No search fee. Required to search: name, years to search; also helpful: address. Civil cases indexed by defendant, plaintiff. Civil records in index books and files, many records on microfiche, back to late 1800s.

Criminal Records: Access: In person only. Visitors must perform in person searches for themselves. No search fee. Required to search: name, years to search; also helpful: address, DOB, SSN. Criminal records in index books and files, many records on microfiche, back to late 1800s.

General Information: No juvenile records released. Copy fee: $.25 per page. Certification fee: $1.25. Fee payee: County Clerk. Personal checks accepted.

Kimball County

District Court 114 E 3rd St, Kimball, NE 69145; 308-235-3591; Fax: 308-235-3654. Hours: 8AM-5PM M-Th, 8AM-4PM F (MST). *Felony, Civil Actions Over $15,000.*

Civil Records: Access: In person only. Visitors must perform in person searches for themselves. No search fee. Required to search: name, years to search. Civil cases indexed by defendant, plaintiff. Civil records on microfiche from 1960 forward, prior in books from early 1900s, computerized since 11/97.

Criminal Records: Access: In person only. Visitors must perform in person searches for themselves. No search fee. Required to search: name, years to search; also helpful: DOB. Criminal records on microfiche from 1960 forward, prior in books from early 1900s, computerized since 11/97.

General Information: Public Access terminal is available. No mental health records released. Fax notes: Fee to fax results is $1.00 per page. Copy fee: $1.00 per page. Certification fee: $1.50. Fee payee: Clerk of District Court. Personal checks accepted. Prepayment required.

Kimball County Court 114 E 3rd St, Kimball, NE 69145; 308-235-2831. Hours: 8AM-5PM (MST). *Misdemeanor, Civil Actions Under $45,000, Small Claims, Probate.*

Civil Records: Access: In person only. Visitors must perform in person searches for themselves. No search fee. Required to search: name, years to search. Civil cases indexed by defendant, plaintiff. Civil records on index cards and original files, also state computer.

Criminal Records: Access: In person only. Visitors must perform in person searches for themselves. No search fee. Required to search: name, years to search. Criminal records on index cards and original files.

General Information: Copy fee: The court reports that photocopying is not available. Certification fee: $1.25. Fee payee: County Court. Only cashiers checks and money orders accepted. Prepayment required.

Knox County

District Court PO Box 126, Center, NE 68724; 402-288-4484; Fax: 402-288-4275. Hours: 8:30AM-4:30PM (CST). *Felony, Civil Actions Over $15,000.*

Civil Records: Access: In person only. Visitors must perform in person searches for themselves. No search fee. Required to search: name, years to search. Civil cases indexed by defendant, plaintiff. Civil records on

index books from late 1800s; on computer back to 9/1998.

Criminal Records: Access: In person only. Visitors must perform in person searches for themselves. No search fee. Required to search: name, years to search; also helpful: DOB. Criminal records on index books from late 1800s; on computer back 10 9/1998.

General Information: Public Access terminal is available. No mental health records released. Copy fee: $.25 per page. Certification fee: $1.00. Fee payee: Clerk of District Court. Personal checks accepted.

Knox County Court PO Box 125, Center, NE 68724; 402-288-4277; Fax: 402-288-4275. Hours: 8:30AM-4:30PM (CST). *Misdemeanor, Civil Actions Under $45,000, Eviction, Small Claims, Probate.*

Civil Records: Access: In person only. Visitors must perform in person searches for themselves. No search fee. Required to search: name, years to search. Civil cases indexed by defendant, plaintiff. Civil records on index cards and general docket books from late 1800s; on computer from 10/2000.

Criminal Records: Access: In person only. Visitors must perform in person searches for themselves. No search fee. Required to search: name, years to search; also helpful: DOB. Criminal records on index cards and general docket books from late 1800s; on computer from 10/2000.

General Information: Public Access terminal is available. No adoption records released. Fax notes: Fee to fax results is $1.00 per page. Copy fee: $.25 per page. Certification fee: $1.00. Fee payee: County Court. Personal checks accepted. Prepayment required.

Lancaster County

District Court 575 S Tenth St, Lincoln, NE 68508-2810; 402-441-7328; Fax: 402-441-6190. Hours: 8AM-4:30PM (CST). *Felony, Civil Actions Over $15,000.*

www.ci.lincoln.ne.us/cnty/discrt/index.htm

Civil Records: Access: Phone, mail, in person. Both court and visitors may perform in person searches. No search fee. Required to search: name, years to search. Civil cases indexed by defendant, plaintiff. Civil records on computer from 1985, microfiche from 1900s, docket books from 1800s.

Criminal Records: Access: Phone, mail, in person. Both court and visitors may perform in person searches. No search fee. Required to search: name, years to search, DOB. Criminal records on computer from 1985, microfiche from 1900s, docket books from 1800s.

General Information: Public Access terminal is available. No juvenile, mental health or grand jury records released. SASE required. Turnaround time 1 week. Copy fee: $.25 per page. Certification fee: $1.00. Fee payee: Clerk of District Court. Personal checks accepted. Prepayment required.

Lancaster County Court 575 S 10th, Lincoln, NE 68508; 402-441-7291. Hours: 8AM-4:30PM (CST). *Misdemeanor, Civil Actions Under $45,000, Eviction, Small Claims, Probate.*

Civil Records: Access: In person only. Visitors must perform in person searches for themselves. No search fee. Required to search: name, years to search. Civil cases indexed by defendant, plaintiff. Civil records on index cards back to 1968, computerized since 11/98.

Criminal Records: Access: In person only. Visitors must perform in person searches for themselves. No search fee. Required to search: name, years to search; also helpful: DOB. Criminal records on computer since 2/95; prior records are available if the case number is known.

General Information: Public Access terminal is available. (Criminal only.) No adoption records released. Copy fee: $.25 per page. Certification fee: $1.00. Fee payee: County Court. Personal checks accepted. Credit cards accepted: Visa, MasterCard. $3.00 service charge. Prepayment required.

Lincoln County

District Court (301 N Jeffers Third Floor), PO Box 1616, North Platte, NE 69103-1616; 308-534-4350 X301 & X303. Hours: 8AM-5PM (CST). *Felony, Civil Actions Over $15,000.*

Civil Records: Access: In person only. Visitors must perform in person searches for themselves. No search fee. Required to search: name, years to search. Civil cases indexed by defendant, plaintiff. Civil records on computer back to 5/1997; books from 1866.
Criminal Records: Access: In person only. Visitors must perform in person searches for themselves. No search fee. Required to search: name, years to search. Criminal records on computer back to 5/1997; books from 1866.
General Information: Public Access terminal is available. No sealed, court ordered or mental health records released. Copy fee: $.25 per page. Certification fee: $1.00. Fee payee: Clerk of District Court. Personal checks accepted. Prepayment required.

Lincoln County Court PO Box 519, North Platte, NE 69103; 308-534-4350; Fax: 308-534-6468. Hours: 8AM-5PM (CST). *Misdemeanor, Civil Actions Under $45,000, Eviction, Small Claims, Probate.*

Civil Records: Access: In person only. Visitors must perform in person searches for themselves. No search fee. Required to search: name, years to search. Civil cases indexed by defendant, plaintiff. Civil records kept on index books back 20-25 years.
Criminal Records: Access: In person only. Visitors must perform in person searches for themselves. No search fee. Required to search: name, years to search, DOB. Criminal records on computer since 04/97; prior on books back 20 years.
General Information: Public Access terminal is available. No adoption records released. Copy fee: $.25 per page. Certification fee: $1.00. Fee payee: County Court. Personal checks accepted. Credit cards accepted: Visa, MasterCard, Discover. $3.00 service charge. Prepayment required.

Logan County

District Court PO Box 8, Stapleton, NE 69163; 308-636-2311. Hours: 8:30AM-4:30PM M-Th; 8:30AM-4PM F (CST). *Felony, Civil Actions Over $15,000.*

Civil Records: Access: Mail, in person. Both court and visitors may perform in person searches. No search fee. Required to search: name, years to search. Civil cases indexed by defendant, plaintiff. Civil records on docket books.
Criminal Records: Access: Mail, in person. Both court and visitors may perform in person searches. No search fee. Required to search: name, years to search. Criminal records on docket books.
General Information: Turnaround time same day. Copy fee: $.25 per page. Certification fee: $1.00. Fee payee: Clerk of the District Court. Personal checks accepted. Prepayment required.

Logan County Court PO Box 8, Stapleton, NE 69163; 308-636-2677. Hours: 8AM-Noon, 1-4:30PM M-Th; 8:30AM-Noon, 1-4PM F (CST). *Misdemeanor, Civil Actions Under $45,000, Eviction, Small Claims, Probate.*

Civil Records: Access: Fax, mail, in person. Both court and visitors may perform in person searches. No search fee. Required to search: name, years to search; also helpful: address. Civil cases indexed by defendant, plaintiff. Civil records on docket books since 1837.
Criminal Records: Access: Fax, mail, in person. Both court and visitors may perform in person searches. No search fee. Required to search: name, years to search,

signed release; also helpful: DOB. Criminal records on docket books since 1837.
General Information: Adoption and juvenile records are not released. SASE required. Turnaround time 3-4 days. Fax notes: Fee to fax results is $3.00 1st page, $1.00 each add'l. Copy fee: $.25 per page. Certification fee: $1.00. Fee payee: County Court. Personal checks accepted. Prepayment required.

Loup County

District Court PO Box 146, Taylor, NE 68879; 308-942-6035; Fax: 308-942-6015. Hours: 8:30AM-4:30PM M-Th, 8:30AM-Noon F (CST). *Felony, Civil Actions Over $15,000.*

Civil Records: Access: In person only. Visitors must perform in person searches for themselves. No search fee. Required to search: name, years to search. Civil cases indexed by defendant, plaintiff. Civil records in index books from late 1800s.
Criminal Records: Access: In person only. Visitors must perform in person searches for themselves. No search fee. Required to search: name, years to search; also helpful: address, DOB, SSN. Criminal records in index books from late 1800s.
General Information: No juvenile or adoption records released. Fax notes: Fee to fax results is $3.00 1st page; $1.00 each add'l. Copy fee: $.25 per page. Certification fee: $1.00. Fee payee: Clerk of District Court. Personal checks accepted. Prepayment required.

Loup County Court PO Box 146, Taylor, NE 68879; 308-942-6035; Fax: 308-942-6015. Hours: 8:30AM-4:30PM M-Th, 8:30AM-Noon F (CST). *Misdemeanor, Civil Actions Under $45,000, Eviction, Small Claims, Probate.*

Civil Records: Access: In person only. Visitors must perform in person searches for themselves. No search fee. Required to search: name, years to search. Civil cases indexed by defendant, plaintiff. Civil records on index books since late 1800s. Some records have been filmed and forwarded to state archives.
Criminal Records: Access: In person only. Visitors must perform in person searches for themselves. No search fee. Required to search: name, years to search. Criminal records on index books since late 1800s. Some records have been filmed and forwarded to state archives.
General Information: Fax notes: Fee to fax results is $3.00 1st page; $1.00 each add'l. Copy fee: $.25 per page. Certification fee: $1.00. Fee payee: County Court. Personal checks accepted. Prepayment required.

Madison County

District Court PO Box 249, Madison, NE 68748; 402-454-3311 X140; Fax: 402-454-6528. Hours: 8AM-5PM (CST). *Felony, Civil Actions Over $15,000.*

Civil Records: Access: In person only. Visitors must perform in person searches for themselves. No search fee. Required to search: name, years to search. Civil cases indexed by defendant, plaintiff. Civil records on microfiche from late 1970s, prior on docket books from 1800s.
Criminal Records: Access: In person only. Visitors must perform in person searches for themselves. No search fee. Required to search: name, years to search. Criminal records on microfiche from late 1970s, prior on docket books from 1800s.
General Information: Public Access terminal is available. No mental health records released. Copy fee: $.25 per page. Certification fee: $1.50. Fee payee: Clerk of District Court. Personal checks accepted.

Madison County Court PO Box 230, Madison, NE 68748; 402-454-3311 X73; Fax: 402-454-3438. Hours: 8:30AM-5PM (CST). *Misdemeanor, Civil Actions Under $45,000, Eviction, Small Claims, Probate.*

Civil Records: Access: In person only. Visitors must perform in person searches for themselves. No search fee. Required to search: name, years to search. Civil cases indexed by defendant, plaintiff. Civil records on computer since 1986, prior on docket book, cards.
Criminal Records: Access: In person only. Visitors must perform in person searches for themselves. No search fee. Required to search: name, years to search, DOB. Criminal records on computer from 1986.
General Information: Public Access terminal is available. No adoption records released. Copy fee: $.25 per page. Certification fee: $1.00. Fee payee: Madison County Court. Personal checks accepted. Prepayment required.

McPherson County

District Court PO Box 122, Tryon, NE 69167; 308-587-2363; Fax: 308-587-2363 (Call first). Hours: 8:30AM-4:30PM (CST). *Felony, Civil Actions Over $15,000.*

Civil Records: Access: Fax, mail, in person. Both court and visitors may perform in person searches. No search fee. Required to search: name, years to search; also helpful: address. Civil cases indexed by defendant, plaintiff. Civil records on index books since late 1800s.
Criminal Records: Access: Fax, mail, in person. Both court and visitors may perform in person searches. No search fee. Required to search: name, years to search; also helpful: address, DOB, SSN. Criminal records on index books since late 1800s.
General Information: No adoption records released. SASE required. Turnaround time 3-4 days. Fax notes: $2.00 for first page, $1.00 each add'l. Copy fee: $.50 per page. Certification fee: $1.50. Fee payee: Clerk of District Court. Business checks accepted. Prepayment required.

McPherson County Court PO Box 122, Tryon, NE 69167; 308-587-2363; Fax: 308-587-2363 (Call first). Hours: 8:30AM-Noon, 1-4:30PM (CST). *Misdemeanor, Civil Actions Under $45,000, Eviction, Small Claims, Probate.*

Civil Records: Access: Fax, mail, in person. Both court and visitors may perform in person searches. No search fee. Required to search: name, years to search; also helpful: address. Civil cases indexed by defendant, plaintiff. Civil records computerized since 06/99, rest on index cards, are not computerized.
Criminal Records: Access: Fax, mail, in person. Both court and visitors may perform in person searches. No search fee. Required to search: name, years to search, signed release; also helpful: address, DOB. Criminal records computerized since 08/98.
General Information: Adoption and juvenile records are not released. SASE required. Turnaround time 3-4 days. Fax notes: Fee to fax results is $3.00 1st page, $1.00 each add'l. Copy fee: $.25 per page. Certification fee: $1.00. Fee payee: County Court. Personal checks accepted. Prepayment required.

Merrick County

District Court PO Box 27, Central City, NE 68826; 308-946-2461; Fax: 308-946-3692. Hours: 8AM-5PM (CST). *Felony, Civil Actions Over $15,000.*

Civil Records: Access: In person only. Visitors must perform in person searches for themselves. No search fee. Required to search: name, years to search. Civil cases indexed by defendant, plaintiff. Civil records on index books from 1860; on computer back to 1994.
Criminal Records: Access: In person only. Visitors must perform in person searches for themselves. No

search fee. Required to search: name, years to search, signed release. Criminal records on index books from 1860; on computer back to 1994.

General Information: Public Access terminal is available. No probation or mental health records released. Copy fee: $.25 per page. Certification fee: $1.00. Fee payee: Clerk of District Court. Personal checks accepted.

Merrick County Court

Merrick County Court County Courthouse, PO Box 27, Central City, NE 68826; 308-946-2812. Hours: 8AM-5PM (CST). *Misdemeanor, Civil Actions Under $45,000, Eviction, Small Claims, Probate.*

Civil Records: Access: In person only. Visitors must perform in person searches for themselves. No search fee. Required to search: name, years to search. Civil cases indexed by defendant, plaintiff. Civil records on index books from 1860; on computer back to 1994.

Criminal Records: Access: In person only. Visitors must perform in person searches for themselves. No search fee. Required to search: name, years to search, DOB. Criminal records on index books from 1860; on computer back to 1994.

General Information: Public Access terminal is available. No financial affidavits or sealed records released. Copy fee: $.25 per page. Certification fee: $1.00. Fee payee: County Court. Personal checks accepted. Prepayment required.

Morrill County

District Court PO Box 824, Bridgeport, NE 69336; 308-262-1261; Fax: 308-262-1799. Hours: 8AM-Noon, 1-4:30PM (MST). *Felony, Civil Actions Over $15,000.*

Civil Records: Access: Phone, fax, mail, in person. Both court and visitors may perform in person searches. Search fee: $5.00 per hour. Required to search: name, years to search. Civil cases indexed by defendant, plaintiff. Civil records on microfilm, books dating back to late 1800s.

Criminal Records: Access: Phone, fax, mail, in person. Both court and visitors may perform in person searches. Search fee: $5.00 per hour. Required to search: name, years to search. Criminal records on microfilm, books dating back to late 1800s.

General Information: Public Access terminal is available. No mental health records released. SASE required. Turnaround time 2-3 days. Fax notes: $3.25 for first page, $.25 each add'l. Copy fee: $.25 per page. Certification fee: $1.00. Fee payee: Clerk of District Court. Personal checks accepted. Prepayment required.

Morrill County Court PO Box 418, Bridgeport, NE 69336; 308-262-0812. Hours: 8AM-4:30PM (MST). *Misdemeanor, Civil Actions Under $45,000, Eviction, Small Claims, Probate.*

Civil Records: Access: In person only. Visitors must perform in person searches for themselves. No search fee. Required to search: name, years to search. Civil cases indexed by defendant, plaintiff. Civil records on index books to 1908; probate on microfiche.

Criminal Records: Access: In person only. Visitors must perform in person searches for themselves. No search fee. Required to search: name, years to search. Criminal records on index books to 1908; probate on microfiche.

General Information: No adoption records released. No copy fee. Certification fee: $1.00. Fee payee: County Court. Personal checks accepted. Prepayment required.

Nance County

District Court PO Box 338, Fullerton, NE 68638; 308-536-2365; Fax: 308-536-2742. Hours: 8AM-5PM (CST). *Felony, Civil Actions Over $15,000.*

Civil Records: Access: Phone, fax, mail, in person. Both court and visitors may perform in person searches. No search fee. Required to search: name, years to

search; also helpful: address. Civil cases indexed by defendant, plaintiff. Civil records on index books from late 1800s.

Criminal Records: Access: Phone, fax, mail, in person. Both court and visitors may perform in person searches. No search fee. Required to search: name, years to search; also helpful: address, DOB, SSN. Criminal records on index books from late 1800s.

General Information: No mental health records released. SASE required. Turnaround time 2 days. Fax notes: $1.50 per page. Copy fee: $.25 per page. Certification fee: $1.00. Fee payee: Clerk of District Court. Personal checks accepted. Prepayment required.

Nance County Court PO Box 837, Fullerton, NE 68638; 308-536-2675; Fax: 308-536-2742. Hours: 8AM-5PM (CST). *Misdemeanor, Civil Actions Under $45,000, Eviction, Small Claims, Probate.*

Civil Records: Access: Mail, in person. Both court and visitors may perform in person searches. No search fee. Required to search: name, years to search; also helpful: address. Civil cases indexed by defendant, plaintiff. Civil records on index cards since late 1800s, probate on microfilm.

Criminal Records: Access: Mail, in person. Both court and visitors may perform in person searches. No search fee. Required to search: name, years to search; also helpful: address, DOB. Criminal records on index cards since late 1800s, probate on microfilm.

General Information: No juvenile, psychological reports or adoption records released. SASE required. Turnaround time 1-2 days. Copy fee: $.25 per page. Certification fee: $1.00. Fee payee: County Court. Personal checks accepted. Prepayment required.

Nemaha County

District Court 1824 N St, Auburn, NE 68305; 402-274-3616; Fax: 402-274-4478. Hours: 8AM-5PM (CST). *Felony, Civil Actions Over $15,000.*

Civil Records: Access: In person, mail. Both court and visitors may perform in person searches. Court will search on a time available basis No search fee. Required to search: name, years to search; also helpful: address. Civil cases indexed by defendant, plaintiff. Civil records on general index and docket books since the late 1800s; computerized records go back to 1998.

Criminal Records: Access: In person, mail. Both court and visitors may perform in person searches. Court will search on a time available basis. No search fee. Required to search: name, years to search; also helpful: address, DOB, SSN. Criminal records on general index and docket books since the late 1800s; computerized records go back to 1998.

General Information: Public Access terminal is available. No mental, juvenile records released. Copy fee: $.25 per page. Certification fee: $1.00. Fee payee: Clerk of District Court. Personal checks accepted. Prepayment required.

Nemaha County Court 1824 N St, Auburn, NE 68305; 402-274-3008; Fax: 402-274-4605. Hours: 8AM-Noon, 1-5PM (CST). *Misdemeanor, Civil Actions Under $45,000, Eviction, Small Claims, Probate.*

Note: This court also handles adoption, juvenile, and preliminary felony hearings.

Civil Records: Access: In person only. Visitors must perform in person searches for themselves. No search fee. Required to search: name, years to search. Civil cases indexed by defendant, plaintiff. Civil records on index books since late 1800s.

Criminal Records: Access: In person only. Visitors must perform in person searches for themselves. No search fee. Required to search: name, years to search; also helpful: DOB, SSN. Criminal records on index books since late 1800s.

General Information: No adoption records released. Copy fee: $.25 per page. Certification fee: $1.00. Fee payee: Clerk of County Court. Personal checks accepted.

Nuckolls County

District Court PO Box 362, Nelson, NE 68961; 402-225-4341; Fax: 402-225-2373. Hours: 8:30AM-4:30PM (CST). *Felony, Civil Actions Over $15,000.*

Civil Records: Access: In person only. Visitors must perform in person searches for themselves. No search fee. Required to search: name, years to search. Civil cases indexed by defendant, plaintiff. Civil records on index books since late 1800s. Search services not available to employment agencies.

Criminal Records: Access: In person. Visitors must perform in person searches for themselves. No search fee. Required to search: name, years to search. Criminal records on index books since late 1800s.

General Information: Copy fee: $.25 per page. Certification fee: $1.00. Fee payee: Clerk of District Court. Personal checks accepted. Prepayment required.

Nuckolls County Court PO Box 372, Nelson, NE 68961; 402-225-2371; Fax: 402-225-2373. Hours: 8AM-4:30PM (CST). *Misdemeanor, Civil Actions Under $45,000, Eviction, Small Claims, Probate.*

Civil Records: Access: In person only. Visitors must perform in person searches for themselves. No search fee. Required to search: name, years to search. Civil cases indexed by defendant, plaintiff. Civil records on index cards, probate on microfilm. Mail access limited to short searches.

Criminal Records: Access: In person only. Visitors must perform in person searches for themselves. No search fee. Required to search: name, years to search. Criminal records on index cards, probate on microfilm.

General Information: No adoption or juvenile records released. Copy fee: $.25 per page. Certification fee: $1.00. Fee payee: County Court. Personal checks accepted. Prepayment required.

Otoe County

District Court 1021 Central Ave, Rm 209, PO Box 726, Nebraska City, NE 68410; 402-873-9550. Hours: 8AM-Noon, 1-5PM (CST). *Felony, Civil Actions Over $15,000.*

Civil Records: Access: In person only. Visitors must perform in person searches for themselves. No search fee. Required to search: name, years to search, address. Civil cases indexed by defendant, plaintiff. Civil records on index books from late 1800s, computerized from 08/97.

Criminal Records: Access: In person only. Visitors must perform in person searches for themselves. No search fee. Required to search: name, years to search. Criminal records on index books from late 1800s, computerized from 08/97.

General Information: Public Access terminal is available. Copy fee: $1.00 per page. Certification fee: $1.00. Fee payee: Clerk of District Court. Personal checks accepted. Prepayment required.

Otoe County Court 1021 Central Ave, Rm 109, PO Box 487, Nebraska City, NE 68410-0487; 402-873-9575; Fax: 402-873-9030. Hours: 8AM-5PM (CST). *Misdemeanor, Civil Actions Under $45,000, Eviction, Small Claims, Probate.*

Civil Records: Access: Phone, fax, mail, in person. Only the court performs in person searches; visitors may not. No search fee. Required to search: name, years to search. Civil cases indexed by defendant, plaintiff.

Criminal Records: Access: Fax, mail, in person. Only the court performs in person searches; visitors may not. No search fee. Required to search: name, offense; also helpful: years to search, address, DOB. Criminal records indexed on cards.

General Information: Public Access terminal is available. No adoption records released without court order; juvenile records only released with signed release statement. SASE required. Turnaround time 2-3 days. Fax notes: $1.00 per page. Copy fee: $.25 per page. Certification fee: $1.00. Fee payee: County Court. Personal checks accepted. Prepayment required.

Pawnee County

District Court PO Box 431, Pawnee City, NE 68420; 402-852-2963. Hours: 8AM-4PM (CST). *Felony, Civil Actions Over $15,000.*

Civil Records: Access: Phone, mail, in person. Both court and visitors may perform in person searches. Search fee: $3.00 per name. Required to search: name, years to search. Civil cases indexed by defendant, plaintiff. Civil records on index books since late 1800s.
Criminal Records: Access: Phone, mail, in person. Both court and visitors may perform in person searches. Search fee: $3.00 per name. Required to search: name, years to search. Criminal records on index books since late 1800s.
General Information: No mental health records released. SASE required. Turnaround time 2 weeks, limited phone searches immediate. Copy fee: $.50 per page. Certification fee: $1.00. Fee payee: Clerk of District Court. Personal checks accepted.

Pawnee County Court PO Box 471, Pawnee City, NE 68420; 402-852-2388; Fax: 402-852-2388. Hours: 8AM-4:30PM (CST). *Misdemeanor, Civil Actions Under $45,000, Eviction, Small Claims, Probate.*

Note: Probate requests are accepted by mail.

Civil Records: Access: In person only. Visitors must perform in person searches for themselves. No search fee. Required to search: name, years to search; also helpful: address. Civil cases indexed by defendant, plaintiff. Civil records indexed on computer since late 1980s and books back to late 1800s.
Criminal Records: Access: In person only. Visitors must perform in person searches for themselves. No search fee. Required to search: name, years to search, DOB; also helpful: SSN. Criminal records indexed on computer since late 1980s and books back to late 1800s.
General Information: Public Access terminal is available. No adoption records released. Copy fee: $.25 per page. Certification fee: $1.00. Fee payee: County Court. Personal checks accepted. Prepayment required.

Perkins County

District Court PO Box 156, Grant, NE 69140; 308-352-4643; Fax: 308-352-2455. Hours: 8AM-4PM (MST). *Felony, Civil Actions Over $15,000.*

Civil Records: Access: Fax, mail, in person. Both court and visitors may perform in person searches. No search fee. Required to search: name, years to search. Civil cases indexed by defendant, plaintiff. Civil records on index books since late 1800s.
Criminal Records: Access: Fax, mail, in person. Both court and visitors may perform in person searches. No search fee. Required to search: name, years to search. Criminal records on index books since late 1800s.
General Information: All records public. SASE required. Turnaround time is 2-4 days. Fax notes: $3.00 per document. add'l fees if over 10 pages. Copy fee: $.50 per page. Certification fee: $1.50. Fee payee: Clerk of District Court. Personal checks accepted. All fees may billed.

Perkins County Court PO Box 222, Grant, NE 69140; 308-352-4415; Fax: 308-352-2455. Hours: 8AM-4PM (MST). *Misdemeanor, Civil Actions Under $45,000, Eviction, Small Claims, Probate.*

Civil Records: Access: Phone, fax, mail, in person. Both court and visitors may perform in person searches.

No search fee. Required to search: name, years to search. Civil cases indexed by defendant, plaintiff. Civil records on index cards from 1987, prior on books; probate on microfilm & hard copy.
Criminal Records: Access: Phone, fax, mail, in person. Both court and visitors may perform in person searches. No search fee. Required to search: name, years to search; also helpful: DOB, SSN. Criminal records on index cards from 1987, prior on books; probate on microfilm & hard copy.
General Information: No sealed records released. SASE required. Turnaround time 1-2 days. Copy fee: $.25 per page. Certification fee: $1.00. Fee payee: Perkins County Court. Personal checks accepted. Prepayment required.

Phelps County

District Court PO Box 462, Holdrege, NE 68949; 308-995-2281. Hours: 9AM-5PM (CST). *Felony, Civil Actions Over $15,000.*

Civil Records: Access: In person only. Visitors must perform in person searches for themselves. No search fee. Required to search: name, years to search. Civil cases indexed by defendant, plaintiff. Civil records on computer from 1981, on books prior for 50 years.
Criminal Records: Access: In person only. Visitors must perform in person searches for themselves. No search fee. Required to search: name, years to search; also helpful: DOB. Criminal records on computer from 1981, on books prior for 50 years.
General Information: No mental health, sealed records released. Copy fee: $.25 per page. Certification fee: $1.00. Fee payee: Clerk of District Court. Personal checks accepted.

Phelps County Court PO Box 255, Holdrege, NE 68949; 308-995-6561; Fax: 308-995-6562. Hours: 8AM-5PM (CST). *Misdemeanor, Civil Actions Under $45,000, Eviction, Small Claims, Probate.*

Civil Records: Access: In person only. Visitors must perform in person searches for themselves. No search fee. Required to search: name, years to search. Civil cases indexed by defendant, plaintiff. Civil records computerized since 1999, on index cards going back to late 1970s; probate on microfiche to late 1800s.
Criminal Records: Access: In person only. Visitors must perform in person searches for themselves. No search fee. Required to search: name, years to search, DOB, signed release. Criminal records computerized since 1998.
General Information: Public Access terminal is available. No adoption records released. Copy fee: $.25 per page. Certification fee: $1.25. Fee payee: County Court. Personal checks accepted. Prepayment required.

Pierce County

District Court 111 W Court St, Rm 12, Pierce, NE 68767; 402-329-4335; Fax: 402-329-6412. Hours: 8:30 AM-4:30PM (CST). *Felony, Civil Actions Over $15,000.*

Civil Records: Access: In person only. Visitors must perform in person searches for themselves. No search fee. Required to search: name, years to search. Civil cases indexed by defendant, plaintiff. Civil records on index books from 1870s; on computer back to 3/1999.
Criminal Records: Access: In person only. Visitors must perform in person searches for themselves. No search fee. Required to search: name, years to search; also helpful: address, DOB, SSN. Criminal records on index books from 1870s; on computer back to 3/1999.
General Information: Public Access terminal is available. No mental health records released. Copy fee: $.25 per page. Certification fee: $1.00. Fee payee: Clerk of District Court. Personal checks accepted.

Pierce County Court 111 W Court St, Rm 11, Pierce, NE 68767; 402-329-6245; Fax: 402-329-6412. Hours: 8:30AM-4:30PM (CST). *Misdemeanor, Civil Actions Under $45,000, Eviction, Small Claims, Probate.*

Civil Records: Access: In person only. Visitors must perform in person searches for themselves. No search fee. Required to search: name, years to search. Civil cases indexed by defendant, plaintiff. Civil records on index books back about 15 years.
Criminal Records: Access: In person only. Visitors must perform in person searches for themselves. No search fee. Required to search: name, years to search. Criminal records on index books back about 15 years.
General Information: Public Access terminal is available. No adoption records released. Copy fee: $.25 per page. Certification fee: $1.00. Fee payee: County Court. Personal checks accepted. Prepayment required.

Platte County

District Court PO Box 1188, Columbus, NE 68602-1188; 402-563-4906; Fax: 402-562-6718. Hours: 8:30AM-5PM (CST). *Felony, Civil Actions Over $15,000.*

Civil Records: Access: In person only. Visitors must perform in person searches for themselves. No search fee. Required to search: name, years to search. Civil cases indexed by defendant, plaintiff. Civil records filed as hard copies; also on computer after 8/1/97.
Criminal Records: Access: In person only. Visitors must perform in person searches for themselves. No search fee. Required to search: name, years to search, DOB. Criminal records filed as hard copies; also on computer after 8/1/97.
General Information: Public Access terminal is available. No juvenile or sealed records released. Copy fee: $.25 per page. Certification fee: $1.00. Fee payee: District Court. Only cashiers checks and money orders accepted.

Platte County Court PO Box 538, Columbus, NE 68602-0538; 402-563-4905; Fax: 402-562-8158. Hours: 8AM-5PM (CST). *Misdemeanor, Civil Actions Under $45,000, Eviction, Small Claims, Probate.*

Civil Records: Access: In person only. Visitors must perform in person searches for themselves. No search fee. Required to search: name, years to search. Civil cases indexed by defendant, plaintiff. Civil records on index books from 1980; on computer back to 1996.
Criminal Records: Access: In person only. Visitors must perform in person searches for themselves. No search fee. Required to search: name, years to search, DOB. Criminal records on index books from 1980; on computer back to 1996.
General Information: Public Access terminal is available. No adoption records released. Copy fee: $.25 per page. Certification fee: $1.00 for seal. Fee payee: Platte County Court. Personal checks accepted. Prepayment required.

Polk County

District Court PO Box 447, Osceola, NE 68651; 402-747-3487; Fax: 402-747-8299. Hours: 8AM-Noon,1-5PM (CST). *Felony, Civil Actions Over $15,000.*

Civil Records: Access: In person only. Visitors must perform in person searches for themselves. No search fee. Required to search: name, years to search. Civil cases indexed by defendant, plaintiff. Civil records on index books from 1871.
Criminal Records: Access: In person only. Visitors must perform in person searches for themselves. No search fee. Required to search: name, years to search, DOB, signed release. Criminal records on index books from 1871.

General Information: Copy fee: $.25 per page. Certification fee: $1.00. Fee payee: Clerk of District Court. Personal checks accepted. Prepayment required.

Polk County Court PO Box 506, Osceola, NE 68651; 402-747-5371; Fax: 402-747-2656. Hours: 8AM-5PM (CST). *Misdemeanor, Civil Actions Under $45,000, Eviction, Small Claims, Probate.*

Civil Records: Access: In person only. Visitors must perform in person searches for themselves. No search fee. Required to search: name, years to search. Civil cases indexed by defendant, plaintiff. Civil records on index cards back to late 1970s; probate records back to late 1800s.

Criminal Records: Access: In person only. Visitors must perform in person searches for themselves. No search fee. Required to search: name, years to search, DOB. Criminal records on index cards back to late 1970s; probate records back to late 1800s.

General Information: No adoption, juvenile records released. Copy fee: $.25 per page. Certification fee: $1.00. Fee payee: County Court. Personal checks accepted. Prepayment required.

Red Willow County

District Court 520 Norris Ave (PO Box 847), McCook, NE 69001; 308-345-4583; Fax: 308-345-7907. Hours: 8AM-4PM (CST). *Felony, Civil Actions Over $15,000.*

Civil Records: Access: Phone, fax, mail, in person, email. Both court and visitors may perform in person searches. No search fee. Required to search: name, years to search. Civil cases indexed by defendant, plaintiff. Civil records on index books since 1871, on microfiche since mid 1980s, recent records computerized.

Criminal Records: Access: Phone, fax, mail, in person., email. Both court and visitors may perform in person searches. No search fee. Required to search: name, years to search. Criminal records on index books since 1871, on microfiche since mid 1980s, recent records computerized.

General Information: Public Access terminal is available. SASE required. Turnaround time 2-4 days. Fax notes: $3.00 for first page, $1.00 each add'l. Copy fee: $.50 per page. Certification fee: $1.00. Fee payee: Clerk of District Court. Personal checks accepted. Prepayment required.

Red Willow County Court 502 Norris Ave (PO Box 199), McCook, NE 69001; 308-345-1904; Fax: 308-345-1503. Hours: 8AM-4PM (CST). *Misdemeanor, Civil Actions Under $45,000, Eviction, Small Claims, Probate.*

Civil Records: Access: Mail, fax, in person. Both court and visitors may perform in person searches. No search fee. Required to search: name, years to search. Civil cases indexed by defendant, plaintiff. Civil records on case files and docket cards since 1984, probate on microfilm since 1977; on computer back to 1998.

Criminal Records: Access: Mail, fax, in person. Both court and visitors may perform in person searches. No search fee. Required to search: name, years to search, DOB. Criminal records on books since 1984; on computer back to 1998.

General Information: No adoption, juvenile, convictions set aside on misdemeanor offense, sealed records released. SASE required. Turnaround time 2 days. Fax notes: Fee to fax results is $3.00 per document. Copy fee: $.25 per page. Certification fee: $1.00. Fee payee: County Court. Personal checks accepted.

Richardson County

District Court 1700 Stone St, Falls City, NE 68355; 402-245-2023; Fax: 402-245-3725. Hours: 8:30AM-5PM (CST). *Felony, Civil Actions Over $15,000.*

Civil Records: Access: In person only. Visitors must perform in person searches for themselves. No search fee. Required to search: name, years to search. Civil cases indexed by defendant, plaintiff. Civil records on microfiche and at state archives to 1930; on computer back to 1998.

Criminal Records: Access: In person only. Visitors must perform in person searches for themselves. No search fee. Required to search: name, years to search, DOB, signed release. Criminal records on microfiche and at state archives to 1930; on computer back to 1998.

General Information: Public Access terminal is available. No sealed records released. Copy fee: $.25 per page. Certification fee: $1.00. Fee payee: Clerk of District Court. Personal checks accepted. Prepayment required.

Richardson County Court 1700 Stone St Room 205, Falls City, NE 68355; 402-245-2812; Fax: 402-245-3352. Hours: 8AM-5PM (CST). *Misdemeanor, Civil Actions Under $45,000, Eviction, Small Claims, Probate.*

Civil Records: Access: In person only. Visitors must perform in person searches for themselves. No search fee. Required to search: name, years to search. Civil cases indexed by defendant, plaintiff. Civil records on index cards back to 1970s.

Criminal Records: Access: In person only. Visitors must perform in person searches for themselves. No search fee. Required to search: name, years to search; also helpful: DOB. Criminal records on index cards back to 1970s.

General Information: No adoption records released. Copy fee: $.25 per page. Certification fee: $1.00. Fee payee: County Court. Only cashiers checks and money orders accepted. Prepayment required.

Rock County

District Court PO Box 367, Bassett, NE 68714; 402-684-3933; Fax: 402-684-2741. Hours: 9AM-5PM (CST). *Felony, Civil Actions Over $15,000.*

Civil Records: Access: Phone, fax, mail, in person. Both court and visitors may perform in person searches. No search fee. Required to search: name, years to search. Civil cases indexed by defendant, plaintiff. Civil records on index books since 1800s.

Criminal Records: Access: Phone, fax, mail, in person. Both court and visitors may perform in person searches. No search fee. Required to search: name, years to search, DOB. Criminal records on index books since 1800s.

General Information: No juvenile or sealed records released. SASE required. Turnaround time 1-2 days. Copy fee: $.25 per page. Certification fee: $1.50. Fee payee: Clerk of District Court. Personal checks accepted. Prepayment required.

Rock County Court PO Box 249, Bassett, NE 68714; 402-684-3601; Fax: 402-684-2741. Hours: 8AM-5PM (CST). *Misdemeanor, Civil Actions Under $45,000, Eviction, Small Claims, Probate.*

Civil Records: Access: In person only. Visitors must perform in person searches for themselves. No search fee. Required to search: name, years to search. Civil cases indexed by defendant, plaintiff. Civil records on index books from 1800s, index cards from 1985; on computer back to 8/2000.

Criminal Records: Access: In person only. Visitors must perform in person searches for themselves. No search fee. Required to search: name, years to search, DOB. Criminal records on index books from 1800s, index cards from 1985; on computer back to 8/2000.

General Information: Fax notes: Fee to fax results is $3.00 plus $1.00 per page. Copy fee: $.25 per page. Certification fee: $1.00. Fee payee: County Court. Personal checks accepted. Prepayment required.

Saline County

District Court 215 S Court St, Wilber, NE 68465; 402-821-2823; Fax: 402-821-2132. Hours: 8AM-Noon, 1-5PM (CST). *Felony, Civil Actions Over $15,000.*

Civil Records: Access: In person only. Visitors must perform in person searches for themselves. No search fee. Required to search: name, years to search. Civil cases indexed by defendant, plaintiff. Civil records being entered on computer beginning 8/94, index in dockets books from 1800s.

Criminal Records: Access: In person only. Visitors must perform in person searches for themselves. No search fee. Required to search: name, years to search; also helpful: DOB. Criminal records being entered on computer beginning 8/94, index in dockets books from 1800s.

General Information: Public Access terminal is available. No sealed or mental health records released. Copy fee: $.25 per page. Certification fee: $1.00. Fee payee: Clerk of District Court. Personal checks accepted. Prepayment required.

Saline County Court PO Box 865, Wilber, NE 68465; 402-821-2131; Fax: 402-821-2132. Hours: 8AM-5PM (CST). *Misdemeanor, Civil Actions Under $45,000, Eviction, Small Claims, Probate.*

Civil Records: Access: Fax, mail, in person. Both court and visitors may perform in person searches. No search fee. Required to search: name, years to search. Civil cases indexed by defendant, plaintiff. Civil records on index books from 1860s.

Criminal Records: Access: Fax, mail, in person. Both court and visitors may perform in person searches. No search fee. Required to search: name, years to search. Criminal records on index books from 1860s.

General Information: Public Access terminal is available. (Available in District Court.) No juvenile or sealed records released. SASE required. Turnaround time 2-3 days. Fax notes: No fee to fax results. Copy fee: $.25 per page. Certification fee: $1.00. Fee payee: County Court. Personal checks accepted. Prepayment required.

Sarpy County

District Court 1210 Golden Gate Dr, Ste 3141, Papillion, NE 68046; 402-593-2267; Fax: 402-593-4403. Hours: 8AM-4:45PM (CST). *Felony, Civil Actions Over $15,000.*

Civil Records: Access: Phone, mail, in person. Both court and visitors may perform in person searches. No search fee. Required to search: name, years to search. Civil cases indexed by defendant, plaintiff. Civil records on computer from 1979 forward, on books prior.

Criminal Records: Access: Phone, mail, in person. Both court and visitors may perform in person searches. No search fee. Required to search: name, years to search. Criminal records on computer from 1979 forward, on books prior. For phone requests, will only verify from computer index.

General Information: Public Access terminal is available. No mental health or search warrant records released. SASE required. Turnaround time 1-2 days. Copy fee: $.75 for first page, $.25 each add'l. Certification fee: $1.00. Fee payee: Clerk of District Court. Only cashiers checks and money orders accepted. Prepayment required.

Sarpy County Court 1210 Golden Gate Dr, Ste 3142, Papillion, NE 68046; 402-593-5995. Hours: 8AM-4:45PM (CST). *Misdemeanor, Civil Actions Under $45,000, Eviction, Small Claims, Probate.*

Civil Records: Access: In person only. Visitors must perform in person searches for themselves. No search fee. Required to search: name, years to search. Civil cases indexed by defendant, plaintiff. Civil records on computer since 08/97; prior records on docket books and cards from 1800s.

Criminal Records: Access: In person only. Visitors must perform in person searches for themselves. No search fee. Required to search: name, years to search, DOB. Criminal records on computer since 08/97; prior records on docket books and cards from 1800s.

General Information: Public Access terminal is available. No adoption records released. Copy fee: $.25 per page. Certification fee: $1.00. Fee payee: County Court. Personal checks accepted.

Saunders County

District Court County Courthouse, 433 N Chestnut, Wahoo, NE 68066; 402-443-8113; Fax: 402-443-8170. Hours: 8AM-5PM (CST). *Felony, Civil Actions Over $15,000.*

Civil Records: Access: In person only. Visitors must perform in person searches for themselves. No search fee. Required to search: name, years to search. Civil cases indexed by defendant, plaintiff. Civil records on index books to late 1800s; on computer back to 1998.

Criminal Records: Access: In person only. Visitors must perform in person searches for themselves. No search fee. Required to search: name, years to search; also helpful: DOB, SSN. Criminal records on index books to late 1800s; on computer back to 1998.

General Information: Public Access terminal is available. No mental health records released. Copy fee: $.25 per page. Certification fee: $1.00. Fee payee: Clerk of District Court. Personal checks accepted.

Saunders County Court 433 N Chestnut, Wahoo, NE 68066; 402-443-8119; Fax: 402-443-5010. Hours: 8AM-5PM (CST). *Misdemeanor, Civil Actions Under $45,000, Eviction, Small Claims, Probate.*

Civil Records: Access: In person only. Visitors must perform in person searches for themselves. No search fee. Required to search: name, years to search. Civil cases indexed by defendant, plaintiff. Civil records on index books.

Criminal Records: Access: In person only. Visitors must perform in person searches for themselves. No search fee. Required to search: name, years to search. Criminal records on index books.

General Information: No adoption or sealed records released. Copy fee: $.25 per page. Certification fee: $1.00. Fee payee: County Court. Personal checks accepted. Prepayment required.

Scotts Bluff County

District Court 1725 10th St, PO Box 47, Gering, NE 69341-0047; 308-436-6641; Fax: 308-436-6759. Hours: 8AM-4:30PM (MST). *Felony, Civil Actions Over $15,000.*

Civil Records: Access: In person only. Visitors must perform in person searches for themselves. No search fee. Required to search: name, years to search. Civil cases indexed by defendant, plaintiff. Civil records on index books to 1800s; on computer back to 1997.

Criminal Records: Access: Phone, fax, mail, in person. Both court and visitors may perform in person searches. Search fee: $5.00 per name. Required to search: name, years to search; also helpful-DOB, SSN. Criminal records on index books to 1800s; on computer back to 1997.

General Information: Public Access terminal is available. No juvenile or mental health records released.

SASE required. Turnaround time 6 days or less. Copy fee: $.50 per page. Certification fee: $1.00. Fee payee: Clerk of District Court. Business checks accepted. Prepayment required.

Scotts Bluff County Court 1725 10th St, Gering, NE 69341; 308-436-6648. Hours: 8AM-5PM (MST). *Misdemeanor, Civil Actions Under $45,000, Eviction, Small Claims, Probate.*

Civil Records: Access: In person only. Visitors must perform in person searches for themselves. No search fee. Required to search: name, years to search. Civil cases indexed by defendant, plaintiff.

Criminal Records: Access: In person only. Visitors must perform in person searches for themselves. No search fee. Required to search: name, years to search, DOB.

General Information: No adoption records released. Fax notes: $3.00 per document. Copy fee: $.25 per page. Certification fee: $1.00. Fee payee: County Court. Personal checks accepted. Prepayment required.

Seward County

District Court PO Box 36, Seward, NE 68434; 402-643-4895. Hours: 8AM-5PM (CST). *Felony, Civil Actions Over $15,000.*

Civil Records: Access: In person only. Visitors must perform in person searches for themselves. No search fee. Required to search: name, years to search. Civil cases indexed by defendant, plaintiff. Civil records on index books since late 1800s.

Criminal Records: Access: In person only. Visitors must perform in person searches for themselves. No search fee. Required to search: name, years to search. Criminal records on index books since late 1800s.

General Information: Personal checks accepted.

Seward County Court PO Box 37, Seward, NE 68434; 402-643-3341; Fax: 402-643-2950. Hours: 8AM-5PM (CST). *Misdemeanor, Civil Actions Under $45,000, Eviction, Small Claims, Probate.*

Civil Records: Access: In person only. Visitors must perform in person searches for themselves. No search fee. Required to search: name, years to search. Civil cases indexed by defendant, plaintiff. Civil records on index books, cards.

Criminal Records: Access: In person only. Visitors must perform in person searches for themselves. No search fee. Required to search: name, years to search. Criminal records on index books, cards.

General Information: No adoption, juvenile or sealed records released. Copy fee: $.25 per page. Certification fee: $1.00. Fee payee: County Court. Personal checks accepted. Prepayment required.

Sheridan County

District Court PO Box 581, Rushville, NE 69360; 308-327-2123; Fax: 308-327-2712. Hours: 8:30AM-4:30PM (MST). *Felony, Civil Actions Over $10,000.*

Civil Records: Access: Mail, fax, in person. Both court and visitors may perform in person searches. Search fee: $5.00 per name. Required to search: name, years to search. Civil cases indexed by defendant, plaintiff. Civil records on index and docket books since 1800s.

Criminal Records: Access: Mail, fax, in person. Both court and visitors may perform in person searches. Search fee: $5.00 per name. Required to search: name, years to search, signed release; also helpful: DOB. Criminal records on index and docket books since 1800s.

General Information: Public Access terminal is available. No mental health, grand jury records released. SASE required. Turnaround time 1-2 days. Copy fee: $.25 per page. Certification fee: $1.00. Fee payee: Clerk of District Court. Personal checks accepted.

Sheridan County Court PO Box 430, Rushville, NE 69360; 308-327-2692; Fax: 308-327-2936. Hours: 8AM-4:30PM (MST). *Misdemeanor, Civil Actions Under $45,000, Eviction, Small Claims, Probate.*

Civil Records: Access: In person only. Visitors must perform in person searches for themselves. No search fee. Required to search: name, years to search. Civil cases indexed by defendant, plaintiff. Civil records on index books, on microfiche from 1920 forward; on computer back to 6/2000.

Criminal Records: Access: Fax, mail, in person. Visitors must perform in person searches for themselves. No search fee. Required to search: name, years to search. Criminal records on index books, on microfiche from 1920 forward; on computer back to 6/2000.

General Information: Public Access terminal is available. No adoption or confidential records released. SASE required. Turnaround time 1-2 days. Fax notes: No fee to fax results. Faxing available to 800 numbers only. Copy fee: $.25 per page. Certification fee: $1.00. Fee payee: Sheridan County Court. Personal checks accepted. Prepayment required.

Sherman County

District Court 630 O St, PO Box 456, Loup City, NE 68853; 308-745-1513; Fax: 308-745-1820. Hours: 8:30AM-4:30PM (CST). *Felony, Civil Actions Over $15,000.*

Civil Records: Access: Mail, in person. Both court and visitors may perform in person searches. Search fee: $10.00 per name. Required to search: name, years to search. Civil cases indexed by defendant, plaintiff. Civil records on index and docket books since late 1800s.

Criminal Records: Access: Mail, in person. Both court and visitors may perform in person searches. Search fee: $10.00 per name. Required to search: name, years to search. Criminal records on index and docket books since late 1800s.

General Information: No mental health records released. SASE required. Turnaround time 1-2 days. Copy fee: $.50 per page. Certification fee: $1.50. Fee payee: Clerk of District Court. Personal checks accepted.

Sherman County Court 630 O St, PO Box 55, Loup City, NE 68853; 308-745-1513 x102; Fax: 308-745-1510. Hours: 8:30AM-4:30PM (CST). *Misdemeanor, Civil Actions Under $45,000, Eviction, Small Claims, Probate.*

Civil Records: Access: Fax, mail, in person. Both court and visitors may perform in person searches. No search fee. Required to search: name, years to search. Civil cases indexed by defendant, plaintiff. Civil records on index books from late 1800s; most recent records are computerized. Newer names indexed by defendant only.

Criminal Records: Access: Fax, mail, in person. Both court and visitors may perform in person searches. No search fee. Required to search: name, years to search, DOB. Criminal records on index books from late 1800s; most recent records are computerized. Newer names indexed by defendant only.

General Information: Public Access terminal is available. (Terminal located in District Court Office) No adoption records released. SASE required. Turnaround time 1-2 weeks. Fax notes: Fee to fax results is $3.00 1st page; $1.00 each add'l. No copy fee. Certification fee: $1.00. Fee payee: Sherman County Court. Business checks accepted. Prepayment required.

Sioux County

District Court PO Box 158, Harrison, NE 69346; 308-668-2443; Fax: 308-668-2443. Hours: 8AM-4;30PM (MST). *Felony, Civil Actions Over $15,000.*

Civil Records: Access: Mail, in person. Only the court performs in person searches; visitors may not. No search fee. Required to search: name, years to search. Civil cases indexed by defendant, plaintiff. Civil records in index and docket books since 1800s.

Criminal Records: Access: Mail, in person. Only the court performs in person searches; visitors may not. No search fee. Required to search: name, years to search; also helpful: DOB, SSN. Criminal records in index and docket books since 1800s.

General Information: No adoption or sealed records released. SASE required. Turnaround time 3-4 days. Copy fee: $.50 per page. Certification fee: $1.00. Fee payee: Clerk of District Court. Personal checks accepted. Prepayment required.

Sioux County Court PO Box 477, Harrison, NE 69346; 308-668-2475. Hours: 8AM-Noon (MST). *Misdemeanor, Civil Actions Under $45,000, Eviction, Small Claims, Probate.*

Civil Records: Access: Phone, mail, in person. Only the court performs in person searches; visitors may not. No search fee. Required to search: name, years to search. Civil cases indexed by defendant, plaintiff. Civil records on index books from late 1800s. Prefer to take phone requests. Very few civil cases handled each year.

Criminal Records: Access: Phone, mail, in person. Only the court performs in person searches; visitors may not. No search fee. Required to search: name, years to search. Criminal records on index books from late 1800s.

General Information: No sealed, expunged, or adoption records released. SASE required. Turnaround time 3-4 days. Copy fee: $.25 per page. Certification fee: $1.00. Fee payee: County Court. Personal checks accepted. Prepayment required.

Stanton County

District Court PO Box 347, Stanton, NE 68779; 402-439-2222; Fax: 402-439-2200. Hours: 8:30AM-4:30PM (CST). *Felony, Civil Actions Over $15,000.*

Civil Records: Access: Fax, mail, in person. Both court and visitors may perform in person searches. Search fee: $1.00 per name. Required to search: name, years to search. Civil cases indexed by defendant, plaintiff. Civil records on books from 1867, on computer from December 1999.

Criminal Records: Access: Fax, mail, in person. Both court and visitors may perform in person searches. Search fee: $1.00 per name. Required to search: name, years to search; also helpful: address, DOB, SSN. Criminal records on books from 1867, on computer from December 1999.

General Information: Public Access terminal is available. No juvenile records released. SASE required. Turnaround time 1-2 days, limited phone data immediately. Fax notes: $2.50 for first page, $1.00 each add'l. Copy fee: $.50 per page. Certification fee: $1.50 per page. Fee payee: Clerk of District Court. Personal checks accepted. Prepayment required.

Stanton County Court 804 Ivy St, PO Box 536, Stanton, NE 68779; 402-439-2221; Fax: 402-439-2229. Hours: 8:30AM-4:30PM *Misdemeanor, Civil Actions Under $45,000, Eviction, Small Claims, Probate.*

Civil Records: Access: In person only. Visitors must perform in person searches for themselves. No search fee. Required to search: name, years to search. Civil cases indexed by defendant, plaintiff. Civil records on docket cards and books back to 1800s; probate on microfilm.

Criminal Records: Access: In person only. Visitors must perform in person searches for themselves. No search fee. Required to search: name, years to search, DOB. Criminal records on docket cards and books back to 1800s; probate on microfilm.

General Information: No adoption records released. Copy fee: $.25 per page. Certification fee: $1.25. Fee payee: Stanton County. Personal checks accepted. Prepayment required.

Thayer County

District Court PO Box 297, Hebron, NE 68370; 402-768-6116; Fax: 402-768-7232. Hours: 8AM-Noon, 12:30-4:30PM *Felony, Civil Actions Over $15,000.*

Civil Records: Access: In person only. Visitors must perform in person searches for themselves. No search fee. Required to search: name, years to search. Civil cases indexed by defendant, plaintiff. Civil records on books from 1900s.

Criminal Records: Access: Fax, mail, in person. Visitors must perform in person searches for themselves. No search fee. Required to search: name, years to search. Criminal records on books from 1900s.

General Information: No mental health or sealed records released. SASE required. Turnaround time 5 days. Copy fee: $.25 per page. Certification fee: $1.00. Fee payee: Clerk of District Court. Personal checks accepted.

Thayer County Court PO Box 94, Hebron, NE 68370; 402-768-6325; Fax: 402-768-7232. Hours: 8AM-5PM (CST). *Misdemeanor, Civil Actions Under $45,000, Eviction, Small Claims, Probate.*

Civil Records: Access: Mail, in person. Both court and visitors may perform in person searches. No search fee. Required to search: name, years to search, address. Civil cases indexed by defendant, plaintiff. Civil records on docket cards from 1871; probate on microfiche.

Criminal Records: Access: Mail, in person. Both court and visitors may perform in person searches. No search fee. Required to search: name, years to search, DOB. Criminal records on docket cards from 1871; probate on microfiche.

General Information: No adoption or juvenile records released. SASE required. Turnaround time within 2 weeks. Copy fee: $.25 per page. Certification fee: $1.00. Fee payee: County Court. Prepayment required.

Thomas County

District Court PO Box 226, Thedford, NE 69166; 308-645-2261; Fax: 308-645-2623. Hours: 8AM-Noon,1-4PM *Felony, Civil Actions Over $15,000.*

Civil Records: Access: Mail, fax, in person. Both court and visitors may perform in person searches. Search fee: $3.00 per name. Required to search: name, years to search. Civil cases indexed by defendant, plaintiff. Civil records indexed in books and in case files since 1800s; on computer back to 6/2000.

Criminal Records: Access: Fax, mail, in person. Both court and visitors may perform in person searches. Search fee: $3.00 per name. Required to search: name, years to search, DOB; also helpful- SSN, signed release. Criminal records indexed in books and in case files since 1800s; on computer back to 6/2000.

General Information: No sealed or juvenile records released. SASE required. Turnaround time 2 days. Fax notes: Fee to fax results is $1.00 per document and $.25 per page. Copy fee: $.25 per page. Certification fee: $4.00. Fee payee: Clerk of District Court. Personal checks accepted.

Thomas County Court PO Box 233, Thedford, NE 69166; 308-645-2266; Fax: 308-645-2623. Hours: 8AM-Noon, 1-4PM *Misdemeanor, Civil Actions Under $45,000, Eviction, Small Claims, Probate.*

Civil Records: Access: Fax, mail, in person. Both court and visitors may perform in person searches. No search

fee. Required to search: name, years to search. Civil cases indexed by defendant, plaintiff. Civil records on index cards and books from late 1800s.

Criminal Records: Access: Fax, mail, in person. Both court and visitors may perform in person searches. No search fee. Required to search: name, years to search, signed release. Criminal records on index cards and books from late 1800s.

General Information: No adoption or juvenile records released. SASE required. Turnaround time 2 days. Copy fee: $.25 per page. Certification fee: $1.00. Fee payee: County Court. Personal checks accepted. Prepayment required.

Thurston County

District Court PO Box 216, Pender, NE 68047; 402-385-3318; Fax: 402-385-2762. Hours: 8:30AM-5PM (CST). *Felony, Civil Actions Over $15,000.*

Civil Records: Access: In person only. Visitors must perform in person searches for themselves. No search fee. Required to search: name, years to search. Civil cases indexed by defendant, plaintiff. Civil records on index books from late 1800s; on computer to 1998.

Criminal Records: Access: In person only. Visitors must perform in person searches for themselves. No search fee. Required to search: name, years to search. Criminal records on index books from late 1800s; on computer back to 1998.

General Information: Public Access terminal is available. No mental health records released. Fax notes: Fee to fax results is $.25 per page. Copy fee: $.25 per page. Certification fee: $1.00. Fee payee: Clerk of District Court. No personal checks accepted. Prepayment required.

Thurston County Court County Courthouse, PO Box 129, Pender, NE 68047; 402-385-3136; Fax: 402-385-3143. Hours: 8:30AM-Noon,1-5PM (CST). *Misdemeanor, Civil Actions Under $45,000, Eviction, Small Claims, Probate.*

Civil Records: Access: In person only. Visitors must perform in person searches for themselves. No search fee. Required to search: name, years to search. Civil cases indexed by defendant, plaintiff. Civil records on books; probate on microfiche since 1800s; on computer back to 1/2000.

Criminal Records: Access: In person only. Visitors must perform in person searches for themselves. No search fee. Required to search: name, years to search. Criminal records on books per state requirement; on computer back to 1/2000.

General Information: Public Access terminal is available. No adoption or juvenile records released. Fax notes: Fee to fax results is $3.00 per document. Copy fee: $.25 per page. Certification fee: $1.00. Fee payee: County Court. Personal checks accepted. Out of state personal checks not accepted.

Valley County

District Court 125 S 15th St, Ord, NE 68862; 308-728-3700; Fax: 308-728-7725. Hours: 8AM-5PM (CST). *Felony, Civil Actions Over $15,000.*

Civil Records: Access: Fax, mail, in person. Both court and visitors may perform in person searches. Search fee: $5.00 per name. Required to search: name, years to search. Civil cases indexed by defendant, plaintiff. Civil records in general index books since late 1800s.

Criminal Records: Access: Fax, mail, in person. Both court and visitors may perform in person searches. Search fee: $5.00 per name. Required to search: name, years to search; also helpful: DOB, SSN. Criminal records in general index books since late 1800s. All requests must be in writing.

General Information: Public Access terminal is available. SASE required. Turnaround time 3-5 days. Fax notes: Will fax back to a toll-free number. Copy fee: $.10 per page. $.15 per page for legal size copy. Certification fee: $1.00. Fee payee: Valley County Clerk. Personal checks accepted. Prepayment required.

Valley County Court 125 S 15th St, Ord, NE 68862; 308-728-3831; Fax: 308-728-7725. Hours: 8AM-5PM (CST). *Misdemeanor, Civil Actions Under $45,000, Eviction, Small Claims, Probate.*

Civil Records: Access: Phone, fax, mail, in person. Both court and visitors may perform in person searches. No search fee. Required to search: name, years to search. Civil cases indexed by defendant, plaintiff. Civil records on books and in files since 1890s; probate on microfiche.

Criminal Records: Access: Phone, fax, mail, in person. Both court and visitors may perform in person searches. No search fee. Required to search: name, years to search. Criminal records on books and in files since 1890s; probate on microfiche.

General Information: No adoption records released. SASE required. Turnaround time 1 week. Fax notes: $3.00 for first page, $1.00 each add'l. Copy fee: $.25 per page. Certification fee: $1.25. Fee payee: Valley County Court. Personal checks accepted.

Washington County

District Court PO Box 431, Blair, NE 68008; 402-426-6899; Fax: 402-426-6898. Hours: 8AM-4:30PM (CST). *Felony, Civil Actions Over $15,000.*

Civil Records: Access: In person only. Visitors must perform in person searches for themselves. No search fee. Required to search: name, years to search. Civil cases indexed by defendant, plaintiff. Civil records in index books and files since 1930s, prior sent to capitol.

Criminal Records: Access: In person only. Visitors must perform in person searches for themselves. No search fee. Required to search: name, years to search, DOB. Criminal records on index books and in files since 1930s, prior sent to capitol.

General Information: No juvenile, mental health records released. Copy fee: $.25 per page. Certification fee: $1.00. Fee payee: Clerk of District Court. Personal checks accepted. Prepayment required.

Washington County Court 1555 Colfax St, Blair, NE 68008; 402-426-6833; Fax: 402-426-6840. Hours: 8AM-4:30PM *Misdemeanor, Civil Actions Under $45,000, Eviction, Small Claims, Probate.*

Civil Records: Access: In person only. Visitors must perform in person searches for themselves. No search fee. Required to search: name, years to search. Civil cases indexed by defendant, plaintiff. Civil records on index books, cards; probate on microfilm since 1800s.

Criminal Records: Access: In person only. Visitors must perform in person searches for themselves. No search fee. Required to search: name, years to search, DOB, SSN. Criminal records on index books, cards; probate on microfilm since 1800s.

General Information: No adoption records released. Copy fee: $.25 per page. Certification fee: $1.25. Fee payee: Washington County Court. Personal checks accepted. Prepayment required.

Wayne County

District Court 510 Pearl St, Wayne, NE 68787; 402-375-2260. Hours: 8:30AM-5PM (CST). *Felony, Civil Actions Over $15,000.*

Civil Records: Access: In person only. Visitors must perform in person searches for themselves. No search fee. Required to search: name, years to search. Civil cases indexed by defendant, plaintiff. Civil records on index books from late 1800s, computerized since 03/99.

Criminal Records: Access: In person only. Visitors must perform in person searches for themselves. No search fee. Required to search: name, years to search.

Criminal records on index books from late 1800s, computerized since 03/99.

General Information: No mental health records released. Copy fee: $.25 per page. $1.00 minimum. Certification fee: $1.00. Fee payee: Clerk of District Court. Only cashiers checks and money orders accepted. Prepayment required.

Wayne County Court 510 Pearl St, Wayne, NE 68787; 402-375-1622; Fax: 402-375-1622. Hours: 8:30AM-5PM (CST). *Misdemeanor, Civil Actions Under $45,000, Eviction, Small Claims, Probate.*

Civil Records: Access: In person only. Visitors must perform in person searches for themselves. No search fee. Required to search: name, years to search. Civil cases indexed by defendant, plaintiff. Civil records on index books, cards from late 1800s.

Criminal Records: Access: In person only. Visitors must perform in person searches for themselves. No search fee. Required to search: name, years to search. Criminal records on index books, cards from late 1800s.

General Information: No adoption records released. Copy fee: $.25 per page. Certification fee: $1.00. Fee payee: County Court. Personal checks accepted. Prepayment required.

Webster County

District Court 621 N Cedar, Red Cloud, NE 68970; 402-746-2716; Fax: 402-746-2710. Hours: 8:30AM-4:30PM (CST). *Felony, Civil Actions Over $15,000.*

Civil Records: Access: In person only. Visitors must perform in person searches for themselves. No search fee. Required to search: name, years to search. Civil cases indexed by defendant, plaintiff. Civil records indexed on microfiche; in files back to 1800s.

Criminal Records: Access: In person. Visitors must perform in person searches for themselves. No search fee. Required to search: name, years to search; also helpful: address, DOB, SSN. Criminal records indexed on microfiche; in files back to 1800s.

General Information: No mental health records released. Copy fee: $1.00 per page if by court, $.25 in person. Certification fee: $1.50. Fee payee: Clerk of District Court. Personal checks accepted. Prepayment required.

Webster County Court 621 N Cedar, Red Cloud, NE 68970; 402-746-2777; Fax: 402-746-2771. Hours: 8:30AM-4:30PM (CST). *Misdemeanor, Civil Actions Under $45,000, Eviction, Small Claims, Probate.*

Civil Records: Access: In person only. Visitors must perform in person searches for themselves. No search fee. Required to search: name, years to search; also helpful: address. Civil cases indexed by defendant. Civil records on index cards and books; probate on microfiche since late 1930.

Criminal Records: Access: In person only. Visitors must perform in person searches for themselves. No search fee. Required to search: name, years to search, DOB, SSN. Criminal records on index cards and books; probate on microfiche since late 1930.

General Information: No adoption or juvenile records released. Copy fee: $.25 per page. Sales tax is added to the fee. Certification fee: $1.00. Fee payee: County Court. Business checks accepted. Prepayment required.

Wheeler County

District Court PO Box 127, Bartlett, NE 68622; 308-654-3235; Fax: 308-654-3442. Hours: 9AM-Noon, 1-5PM (CST). *Felony, Civil Actions Over $15,000.*

Civil Records: Access: In person only. Visitors must perform in person searches for themselves. No search fee. Required to search: name, years to search. Civil cases indexed by defendant, plaintiff. Civil records on

index books from late 1800s. Mail access limited to short searches.

Criminal Records: Access: In person only. Visitors must perform in person searches for themselves. No search fee. Required to search: name, years to search. Criminal records on index books from late 1800s.

General Information: No juvenile or adoption records released. Copy fee: $.15 per page. Certification fee: $7.00. Fee payee: Clerk of District Court. Personal checks accepted.

Wheeler County Court PO Box 127, Bartlett, NE 68622; 308-654-3376; Fax: 308-654-3442. Hours: 9AM-4PM (CST). *Misdemeanor, Civil Actions Under $45,000, Eviction, Small Claims, Probate.*

Civil Records: Access: Mail, in person. Only the court performs in person searches; visitors may not. No search fee. Required to search: name, years to search. Civil cases indexed by defendant, plaintiff. Civil records on index books from late 1800s.

Criminal Records: Access: Mail, in person. Visitors must perform in person searches for themselves. No search fee. Required to search: name, years to search. Criminal records on index books from late 1800s.

General Information: No adoption records released. SASE required. Turnaround time 1-2 weeks. Copy fee: $.25 per page. Certification fee: $1.00. Fee payee: County Court. Personal checks accepted.

York County

District Court 510 Lincoln Ave, York, NE 68467; 402-362-4038; Fax: 402-362-2577. Hours: 8:30AM-5PM (CST). *Felony, Civil Actions Over $15,000.*

Note: The SSN does not show up in the computer index, but will show in the case files.

Civil Records: Access: In person only. Visitors must perform in person searches for themselves. No search fee. Required to search: name, years to search. Civil cases indexed by defendant, plaintiff. Civil records on index books and in files from 1875, most recent are computerized.

Criminal Records: Access: In person only. Visitors must perform in person searches for themselves. No search fee. Required to search: name, years to search. Criminal records on index books and in files from 1875, most recent are computerized.

General Information: Copy fee: $.25 per page. Certification fee: $1.00. Fee payee: Clerk of District Court. Personal checks accepted. Prepayment required.

York County Court 510 Lincoln Ave, York, NE 68467; 402-362-4925; Fax: 402-362-2577. Hours: 8AM-5PM (CST). *Misdemeanor, Civil Actions Under $45,000, Eviction, Small Claims, Probate.*

Civil Records: Access: In person only. Visitors must perform in person searches for themselves. No search fee. Required to search: name, years to search. Civil cases indexed by defendant, plaintiff. Civil records on docket cards, files from 1875.

Criminal Records: Access: In person only. Visitors must perform in person searches for themselves. No search fee. Required to search: name, years to search. Criminal records on docket cards, files from 1875.

General Information: Public Access terminal is available. No adoption or sealed records released. Copy fee: $.25 per page. Certification fee: $1.00. Fee payee: York County Court. Personal checks accepted. Credit cards accepted: Visa, MasterCard. $3.00 service charge.

Nebraska Recording Offices

ORGANIZATION

93 counties, 109 recording offices. The recording officers are County Clerk (UCC and some state tax liens) and Register of Deeds (real estate and most tax liens). Most counties have a combined Clerk/Register office, which are designated "County Clerk" in this section. Sixteen counties have separate offices for County Clerk and for Register of Deeds - Adams, Cass, Dakota, Dawson, Dodge, Douglas, Gage, Hall, Lancaster, Lincoln, Madison, Otoe, Platte, Sarpy, Saunders, and Scotts. Bluff. In combined offices, the Register of Deeds is frequently a different person from the County Clerk. 74 counties are in the Central Time Zone (CST) and 19 are in the Mountain Time Zone (MST).

REAL ESTATE RECORDS

Some Nebraska counties will perform real estate searches, including owner of record from the legal description of the property. Address search requests and make checks payable to the Register of Deeds, not the County Clerk. Fees vary.

UCC RECORDS

Financing statements are filed at the state level, and real estate related collateral are filed with the County Clerk. Previously, financing statements could be filed at any county. All non-real estate UCC filings are entered into a statewide database that is accessible from any county office. All but a few counties will perform UCC searches. Use search request form UCC-11. The UCC statute allows for telephone searching. Search fees are usually $3.50 per debtor name. Copy fees vary.

TAX LIEN RECORDS

All federal and some state tax liens are filed with the County Register of Deeds. Some state tax liens on personal property are filed with the County Clerk. Most counties will perform tax lien searches, some as part of a UCC search, and others for a separate fee, usually $3.50 per name in each index. Copy fees vary.

OTHER LIENS

Mechanics, artisans, judgment, motor vehicle, agricultural.

STATEWIDE ONLINE INFO:

Nebrask@online offers online access to Secretary of State's UCC database; registration and a usage fee is required. For information, visit www.nol.org/subinfo.html.

Adams County Clerk

County Clerk, P.O. Box 2067, Hastings, NE 68902. 402-461-7107; Fax 402-461-7185.
Will search UCC records. UCC search includes state tax liens if requested See Register of Deeds for real estate records. **Other Phone Numbers:** Assessor 402-461-7116.

Adams County Register of Deeds

County Clerk, P.O. Box 203, Hastings, NE 68902. County Clerk, R/E and UCC Recording 402-461-7148; Fax 402-461-7154. www.adamscounty.org
Will search UCC records. Will not search real estate records. **Other Phone Numbers:** Assessor 402-461-7116; Treasurer 402-461-7120; Elections 402-461-7165.

Antelope County

County Clerk, Courthouse, 501 Main St., Neligh, NE 68756. 402-887-4410; Fax 402-887-4719.
Will search UCC records. **Other Phone Numbers:** Assessor 402-887-4515; Treasurer 402-887-4247.

Arthur County

County Clerk, Box 126, Arthur, NE 69121-0126. 308-764-2203; Fax 308-764-2216.
Will search UCC records. **Other Phone Numbers:** Assessor 308-764-2203.

Banner County

County Clerk, P.O. Box 67, Harrisburg, NE 69345-0067. 308-436-5265; Fax 308-436-4180.
Will search UCC records. UCC search includes tax liens if requested. Will not search real estate records. **Other Phone Numbers:** Assessor 308-436-5265; Treasurer 308-436-5260.

Blaine County

County Clerk, P.O. Box 136, Brewster, NE 68821. County Clerk, R/E and UCC Recording 308-547-2222; Fax 308-547-2228.
Will search UCC records. **Other Phone Numbers:** Assessor 308-541-2222; Treasurer 308-547-2223; Elections 308-547-2222.

Boone County

County Clerk, 222 South 4th Street, Albion, NE 68620-1247. 402-395-2055; Fax 402-395-6592.
Will search UCC records. Will not search real estate records. **Other Phone Numbers:** Assessor 402-395-2045; Treasurer 402-395-2513.

Box Butte County

Box Butte County Clerk, Box 678, Alliance, NE 69301-0678. Box Butte County Clerk, R/E and UCC Recording 308-762-6565 UCC Recording: 402-471-4080 (Sec of State); Fax 308-762-2867.
The recording officers are County Clerk (state tax liens) Register of Deeds (real estate and most tax liens). Will search UCC records. Will not search real estate records. **Other Phone Numbers:** Assessor 308-762-6101; Treasurer 308-762-6975; Elections 308-762-6565; Vital Records 402-471-2871.

Boyd County

County Clerk, P.O. Box 26, Butte, NE 68722. 402-775-2391; Fax 402-775-2146.
Will search UCC records. **Other Phone Numbers:** Assessor 402-775-2311; Treasurer 402-775-2581.

Brown County

Brown County Clerk, Courthouse, 148 W. 4th St., Ainsworth, NE 69210. 402-387-2705; Fax 402-387-0918.
Will search UCC records. **Other Phone Numbers:** Assessor 402-387-1621; Treasurer 402-387-2650;

Elections 402-387-2705; Secretary of State (UCC) 402-471-2554.

Buffalo County

County Clerk, P.O. Box 1270, Kearney, NE 68848-1270. 308-236-1239; Fax 308-236-1291.
Will search UCC records. Will not search real estate records. **Other Phone Numbers:** Assessor 308-236-1205; Treasurer 308-236-1250.

Burt County

County Clerk, P.O. Box 87, Tekamah, NE 68061. 402-374-2955; Fax 402-374-2956.
Will search UCC records. Will not search real estate records. **Other Phone Numbers:** Assessor 402-374-2926; Treasurer 402-374-2911; Elections 402-374-2955.

Butler County

Deputy Clerk, P.O. Box 289, David City, NE 68632-0289. 402-367-7430 R/E Recording: 402-367-7431 UCC Recording: 402-471-4080; Fax 402-367-3329.
Will search UCC records. Will not search real estate records. **Other Phone Numbers:** Assessor 402-367-7420; Treasurer 402-367-7450; Elections 402-367-7430; Vital Records 402-471-2871.

Cass County Clerk

County Clerk, Courthouse, Room 202, 346 Main St., Plattsmouth, NE 68048-1964. 402-296-9300; Fax 402-296-9327.
Will search UCC records. This agency will not do a tax lien search. See Register of Deeds for real estate records. **Other Phone Numbers:** Assessor 402-296-9310.

Cass County Register of Deeds

County Clerk, County Courthouse, 346 Main St., Plattsmouth, NE 68048-1964. 402-296-9330; Fax 402-296-9331. www.cassne.org

Will search UCC records. Will search real estate records for one legal description. **Other Phone Numbers:** Assessor 402-296-9310; Treasurer 402-296-9320; Appraiser/Auditor 402-296-9310; Elections 402-296-9306.

Cedar County

County Clerk, P.O. Box 47, Hartington, NE 68739. County Clerk, R/E and UCC Recording 402-254-7411 UCC Recording: 402-471-2554; Fax 402-254-7410. Will search UCC records. Will not search real estate records. **Other Phone Numbers:** Assessor 402-254-7431; Treasurer 402-254-7421; Elections 402-254-7411; Vital Records 402-254-7411.

Chase County

County Clerk, Box 1299, Imperial, NE 69033-1299. 308-882-5266; Fax 308-882-5390. Will search UCC records. **Other Phone Numbers:** Assessor 308-882-5207; Treasurer 308-882-4756.

Cherry County

County Clerk, Box 120, Valentine, NE 69201-0120. County Clerk, R/E and UCC Recording 402-376-2771; Fax 402-376-3095. Will search UCC records. Will not search real estate records. **Other Phone Numbers:** Assessor 402-376-1630; Treasurer 402-376-1580; Elections 402-376-2771; Vital Records 402-471-2871.

Cheyenne County

County Clerk, P.O. Box 217, Sidney, NE 69162-0217. 308-254-2141; Fax 308-254-4293. Will search UCC records. Will not search real estate records. **Other Phone Numbers:** Assessor 308-254-2633; Treasurer 308-254-2733.

Clay County

County Clerk, 111 West Fairfield Street, Clay Center, NE 68933-1499. 402-762-3463; Fax 402-762-3250. Will search UCC records. Will not search real estate records. **Other Phone Numbers:** Assessor 402-762-3792; Treasurer 402-762-3505.

Colfax County

County Clerk, 411 East 11th Street, Schuyler, NE 68661. 402-352-8504; Fax 402-352-8515. http://www.co.colfax.ne.us
Will search UCC records. This agency will not do a tax lien search. RE record owner and mortgage searches available. **Other Phone Numbers:** Assessor 402-352-8500; Treasurer 402-352-2105.

Cuming County

County Clerk, Box 290, West Point, NE 68788. 402-372-6002; Fax 402-372-6013. Will search UCC records. Will not search real estate records. **Other Phone Numbers:** Assessor 402-372-6000; Treasurer 402-372-6011.

Custer County

County Clerk, 431 South 10th, Broken Bow, NE 68822. 308-872-5701. Will search UCC records. Tax liens not included in UCC search. RE record owner searches available. **Other Phone Numbers:** Assessor 308-872-2981; Treasurer 308-872-2921.

Dakota County Clerk

Register of Deeds, P.O. Box 39, Dakota City, NE 68731-0039. Register of Deeds, R/E and UCC Recording 402-987-2166 UCC Recording: 402-987-2126; Fax 402-494-9228. http://www.sscdc.net/county Will search county level UCC records. See Register of Deeds for real estate records. **Other Phone Numbers:**

Assessor 402-987-0264; Treasurer 402-987-2131; Elections 402-987-2126; Vital Records 402-471-2871.

Dakota County Register of Deeds

County Register of Deeds, P.O. Box 511, Dakota City, NE 68731. 402-987-2166. Will search UCC records, but only real estate related UCC filed here. This agency will not do a tax lien search. Will not search real estate records. **Other Phone Numbers:** Assessor 402-987-0264; Treasurer 402-987-2131.

Dawes County

County Clerk, 451 Main Street, Courthouse, Chadron, NE 69337-2698. County Clerk, R/E and UCC Recording 308-432-0100; Fax 308-432-5179. Will search UCC records. Tax liens not included in UCC search. Will not search real estate records. **Other Phone Numbers:** Assessor 308-432-0103; Treasurer 308-432-0105; Elections 308-432-0100.

Dawson County Clerk

County Clerk, P.O. Box 370, Lexington, NE 68850-0370. 308-324-2127 R/E Recording: 308-324-4271; Fax 308-324-6106. Will search UCC records. See Register of Deeds for real estate records. **Other Phone Numbers:** Assessor 308-324-3471; Treasurer 308-324-3241; Appraiser/Auditor 308-324-3471; Elections 308-324-6106; Vital Records 308-324-2127.

Dawson County Register of Deeds

County Register of Deeds, County Courthouse, 700 N. Washington, Lexington, NE 68850. 308-324-4271. Will search UCC records, but only real estate related UCC filed here. This agency will not do a tax lien search. Will not search real estate records. **Other Phone Numbers:** Assessor 308-324-3471; Treasurer 308-324-3241.

Deuel County

County Clerk, P.O. Box 327, Chappell, NE 69129. 308-874-3308; Fax 308-874-3472. Will search UCC records. **Other Phone Numbers:** Assessor 308-874-2608; Treasurer 308-874-3307.

Dixon County

County Clerk, Box 546, Ponca, NE 68770-0546. 402-755-2208; Fax 402-755-4276. Will search UCC records. UCC search includes tax liens if requested. Will not search real estate records. **Other Phone Numbers:** Assessor 402-755-2626; Treasurer 402-755-2701.

Dodge County Clerk

County Clerk, 435 North Park, Courthouse - Room 102, Fremont, NE 68025-4967. 402-727-2767; Fax 402-727-2764. Will search UCC records. See Register of Deeds for real estate records. **Other Phone Numbers:** Assessor 402-727-3911.

Dodge County Register of Deeds

County Register of Deeds, 435 North Park, Room 201, Fremont, NE 68025. 402-727-2735; Fax 402-727-2734. http://www.registerofdeeds.com
Will search UCC records, but only real estate related UCC filed here. This agency will not do a tax lien search. Will not search real estate records. **Online Access:** Real Estate. Online access to Register of Deeds mortgages database is available at the web site. Registration is required. The site is under development. **Other Phone Numbers:** Assessor 402-727-3911; Treasurer 402-727-2750.

Douglas County Clerk

County Clerk, 1819 Farnam St., Room H08, Omaha, NE 68183-0008. 402-444-6744; Fax 402-444-6456. Will search UCC records. See Register of Deeds for real estate records. **Online Access:** Assessor. Property tax records on the county assessor database are available free online at www.co.douglas.ne.us/dept.assessor/framevalinfo.htm. There is no name searching. **Other Phone Numbers:** Assessor 402-444-7060.

Douglas County Register of Deeds

County Clerk, 1819 Farnam, Room H09, Omaha, NE 68183. 402-444-7194; Fax 402-444-6693. Will search UCC records. Will not search real estate records. **Other Phone Numbers:** Assessor 402-444-7060; Treasurer 402-444-7272.

Dundy County

County Clerk, P.O. Box 506, Benkelman, NE 69021-0506. 308-423-2058. Will search UCC records. UCC search includes tax liens. Will not search real estate records. **Other Phone Numbers:** Assessor 308-423-2821; Treasurer 308-423-2346.

Fillmore County

Register of Deeds, P.O. Box 307, Geneva, NE 68361-0307. 402-759-4931; Fax 402-759-4307. http://www.fillmorecounty.org/government/gov1.html
The recording officers are County Clerk (Federal and state tax liens) and Register of Deeds (real estate and most tax liens). Will not search UCC records, but will search tax liens. **Other Phone Numbers:** Assessor 402-759-3613; Treasurer 402-759-3812; Elections 402-759-4931.

Franklin County

County Clerk, P.O. Box 146, Franklin, NE 68939. 308-425-6202; Fax 308-425-6289. Will search UCC records. Will not search real estate records. **Other Phone Numbers:** Assessor 308-425-6229; Treasurer 308-425-6265.

Frontier County

County Clerk, P.O. Box 40, Stockville, NE 69042-004. 308-367-8641; Fax 308-367-8730. Will search UCC records. UCC search includes tax liens if requested. RE owner, mortgage, and property transfer searches available. **Other Phone Numbers:** Assessor 308-367-8637; Treasurer 308-367-8631; Appraiser/Auditor 308-367-8637; Elections 308-367-8641.

Furnas County

County Clerk, P.O. Box 387, Beaver City, NE 68926. 308-268-4145. Will search UCC records. This agency will not do a tax lien search. Will not search real estate records. **Other Phone Numbers:** Assessor 308-268-3145; Treasurer 308-268-2195.

Gage County Clerk

County Clerk, P.O. Box 429, Beatrice, NE 68310-0429. 402-223-1300; Fax 402-223-1371. Will search UCC records. See Register of Deeds for real estate records. **Other Phone Numbers:** Assessor 402-223-1308.

Gage County Register of Deeds

County Register of Deeds, P.O. Box 337, Beatrice, NE 68310. 402-223-1361.

Will search UCC records, but only real estate related UCC filed here. This agency will not do a tax lien search. Will not search real estate records. **Other Phone Numbers:** Assessor 402-223-1308; Treasurer 402-223-1315.

Garden County

County Clerk, P.O. Box 486, Oshkosh, NE 69154. 308-772-3924; Fax 308-772-4143.
Will search UCC records. Will not search real estate records. **Other Phone Numbers:** Assessor 308-772-4464; Treasurer 308-772-3622.

Garfield County

County Clerk, Box 218, Burwell, NE 68823. 308-346-4161.
Will search UCC records. Tax liens not included in UCC search. Will not search real estate records. **Other Phone Numbers:** Assessor 308-346-4045; Treasurer 308-346-4125.

Gosper County

County Clerk, P.O. Box 136, Elwood, NE 68937-0136. 308-785-2611.
Will search UCC records. UCC search includes tax liens if requested. Will not search real estate records. **Other Phone Numbers:** Assessor 308-785-2250; Treasurer 308-785-2450.

Grant County

County Clerk, P.O. Box 139, Hyannis, NE 69350-0139. 308-458-2488; Fax 308-458-2485.
Will search UCC records. **Other Phone Numbers:** Assessor 308-458-2488; Treasurer 308-458-2422; Appraiser/Auditor 308-762-2474; Elections 308-458-2488; Marriages 308-458-2488.

Greeley County

County Clerk, P.O. Box 287, Greeley, NE 68842. 308-428-3625; Fax 308-428-6500.
Will search UCC records. Will not search real estate records. **Other Phone Numbers:** Assessor 308-428-5310; Treasurer 308-428-3535.

Hall County Clerk

County Clerk, P.O. Box 1692, Grand Island, NE 68802-1692. 308-385-5080; Fax 308-385-5094.
Will search UCC records. See Register of Deeds for real estate records. **Other Phone Numbers:** Assessor 308-385-5050.

Hall County Register of Deeds

County Register of Deeds, P.O. Box 1692, Grand Island, NE 68802-1692. County Register of Deeds, R/E and UCC Recording 308-385-5040; http://www.grand-island.com/
Will search UCC records, but only real estate related UCC filed here. This agency will not do a tax lien search. Will not search real estate records. **Other Phone Numbers:** Assessor 308-385-5050; Treasurer 308-385-5025.

Hamilton County

County Clerk, Register of Deeds, Courthouse, 1111 13th St. - Suite 1, Aurora, NE 68818-2017. County Clerk, Register of Deeds, R/E and UCC Recording 402-694-3443 UCC Recording: 402-471-2554; Fax 402-694-2396. http://www.co.hamilton.ne.us/
Will search UCC records. Will not search real estate records. **Other Phone Numbers:** Assessor 402-694-2757; Treasurer 402-694-2291; Elections 402-694-3443; Vital Records 402-471-2871.

Harlan County

County Clerk, P.O. Box 698, Alma, NE 68920-0698. 308-928-2173; Fax 308-928-2592.
Will search UCC records. Will not search real estate records. **Other Phone Numbers:** Assessor 308-928-2177; Treasurer 308-928-2171.

Hayes County

County Clerk, P.O. Box 370, Hayes Center, NE 69032-0370. 308-286-3413; Fax 308-286-3208.
Will search UCC records. This agency will not do a tax lien search. Will not search real estate records. **Other Phone Numbers:** Assessor 308-286-3399; Treasurer 308-286-3214.

Hitchcock County

County Clerk, P.O. Box 248, Trenton, NE 69044. 308-334-5646; Fax 308-334-5351.
Will search UCC records. Will not search real estate records. **Other Phone Numbers:** Assessor 308-334-5219; Treasurer 308-334-5544.

Holt County

County Clerk, P.O. Box 329, O'Neill, NE 68763-0329. 402-336-2250; Fax 402-336-2885.
Will search UCC records. Will not search real estate records. **Other Phone Numbers:** Assessor 402-336-1624; Treasurer 402-336-1291.

Hooker County

County Clerk, P.O. Box 184, Mullen, NE 69152. County Clerk, R/E and UCC Recording 308-546-2244; Fax 308-546-2490.
Will search UCC records. UCC search includes tax liens if requested. RE owner, mortgage, and property transfer searches available. **Other Phone Numbers:** Assessor 308-546-2244; Treasurer 308-546-2245; Elections 308-546-2244.

Howard County

County Clerk, P.O. Box 25, St. Paul, NE 68873. 308-754-4343; Fax 308-754-4725.
Will search UCC records. UCC search includes tax liens if requested. Will not search real estate records. **Other Phone Numbers:** Assessor 308-754-4261; Treasurer 308-754-4852; Elections 308-754-4343.

Jefferson County

County Clerk, 411 4th, Courthouse, Fairbury, NE 68352-1619. County Clerk, R/E and UCC Recording 402-729-5201 UCC Recording: 402-471-2554; Fax 402-729-2016.
The recording officers are County Clerk (some state tax liens) and Register of Deeds (real estate and most tax liens). Will search UCC records. Will search real estate records. **Other Phone Numbers:** Assessor 402-729-3103; Treasurer 402-729-2411; Elections 402-729-2323; Vital Records 402-471-2872.

Johnson County

County Clerk, P.O. Box 416, Tecumseh, NE 68450. County Clerk, R/E and UCC Recording 402-335-6300; Fax 402-335-6311.
Will search UCC records. UCC search includes tax liens. Will not search real estate records. **Other Phone Numbers:** Assessor 402-335-3845; Treasurer 402-335-6310; Elections 402-335-6300.

Kearney County

County Clerk, P.O. Box 339, Minden, NE 68959-0339. 308-832-2723; Fax 308-832-1748.
Will search UCC records. **Other Phone Numbers:** Assessor 308-832-2625; Treasurer 308-832-2730.

Keith County

County Clerk, P.O. Box 149, Ogallala, NE 69153. 308-284-4726; Fax 308-284-6277.
Will search UCC records. Will not search real estate records. **Other Phone Numbers:** Assessor 308-284-8040; Treasurer 308-284-3231.

Keya Paha County

County Clerk, P.O. Box 349, Springview, NE 68778. 402-497-3791; Fax 402-497-3799.
Will search UCC records. UCC search includes tax liens. Will not search real estate records. **Other Phone Numbers:** Assessor 402-497-3791; Treasurer 402-497-3891.

Kimball County

County Clerk, 114 East Third Street, Kimball, NE 69145-1296. 308-235-2241; Fax 308-235-3654.
Will search UCC records. Will not search real estate records. **Other Phone Numbers:** Assessor 308-235-2362; Treasurer 308-235-2242; Elections 308-235-2241.

Knox County Clerk

County Clerk, P.O. Box 166, Center, NE 68724-0166. County Clerk, R/E and UCC Recording 402-288-4424 UCC Recording: 402-288-4282; Fax 402-288-4424.
Will search UCC records. Will not search real estate records. **Other Phone Numbers:** Assessor 402-288-4255; Treasurer 402-288-4491.

Lancaster County Clerk

County Clerk, 555 South 10th Street, County-City Building, Lincoln, NE 68508-2867. 402-441-7482 R/E Recording: 402-441-7577; Fax 402-441-8728. http://interlinc.ci.lincoln.ne.us
Will search UCC records. This agency will do a state tax lien search only. See Register of Deeds for real estate records. **Online Access:** Assessor. Records on the county Assessor Property Information Search database are available free online at http://interlinc.ci.lincoln.ne.us/cnty/assess/property.htm. **Other Phone Numbers:** Assessor 402-441-7463; Treasurer 402-441-7425; Appraiser/Auditor 402-441-7463; Elections 402-441-7311; Vital Records 402-471-2872.

Lancaster County Register of Deeds

Register of Deeds, 555 South 10th Street, Lincoln, NE 68508. 402-441-7577; Fax 402-441-7012. http://www.ci.lincoln.ne.us/co_agenc.htm
Will search UCC records. Will search real estate records. **Online Access:** Real Estate, Liens, Grantor/Grantee, Assessor, Treasurer. Online access to the county on-line deeds search is available free at www.ci.lincoln.ne.us/cnty/deeds/deeds.htm. Also, access to the assessor database is available at www.ci.lincoln.ne.us/cnty/assess/property.htm.
Treasurer information is also here. Also, search property information free on the map server site at http://ims.ci.lincoln.ne.us/isa/parcel. **Other Phone Numbers:** Assessor 402-441-7643; Treasurer 402-441-7425; Vital Records 402-441-2871.

Lincoln County Clerk

County Clerk, Courthouse, Room 101, 301 North Jeffers, North Platte, NE 69101. 308-534-4350.
Will search UCC records. UCC search includes state tax liens. See Register of Deeds for real estate records. **Other Phone Numbers:** Assessor 308-534-4350.

Lincoln County Register of Deeds

County Clerk, 301 N. Jeffers, Room 103, North Platte, NE 69101-3931. 308-534-4350; Fax 308-534-5287.

Will search UCC records. Will not search real estate records. **Other Phone Numbers:** Assessor 308-534-4350; Treasurer 308-534-4350.

Logan County

County Clerk, P.O. Box 8, Stapleton, NE 69163. 308-636-2311.
Will search UCC records. UCC search includes tax liens if requested. Will not search real estate records. **Other Phone Numbers:** Assessor 308-636-2311; Treasurer 308-636-2441.

Loup County

County Clerk, P.O. Box 187, Taylor, NE 68879-0187. 308-942-3135; Fax 308-942-6015.
Will search UCC records. UCC search includes tax liens if requested. Will not search real estate records. **Other Phone Numbers:** Assessor 308-942-3135; Treasurer 308-942-3115.

Madison County Clerk

County Clerk, P.O. Box 290, Madison, NE 68748-0290. 402-454-3311 x137 R/E Recording: 402-454-3311 x124 UCC Recording: 402-454-3311 x136; Fax 402-454-6682.
Will search UCC records. See Register of Deeds for real estate records. **Other Phone Numbers:** Assessor 402-454-3311 x178; Treasurer 402-454-3311 x133; Appraiser/Auditor 402-454-3311; Elections 402-454-3311 x136.

Madison County Register of Deeds

County Register of Deeds, P.O. Box 229, Madison, NE 68748. 402-454-3311 R/E Recording: 402-454-3311 x124 UCC Recording: 402-454-3311 x124; Fax 402-454-6682.
Will search UCC records, but only real estate related UCC filed here. This agency will not do a tax lien search. Will not search real estate records. **Other Phone Numbers:** Assessor 402-454-3311 x178; Treasurer 402-454-3311 x133; Elections 402-454-3311 x136; Vital Records 402-471-2871.

McPherson County

County Clerk, P.O. Box 122, Tryon, NE 69167-0122. 308-587-2363; Fax 308-587-2363.
Will search UCC records. Will not search real estate records. **Other Phone Numbers:** Assessor 308-587-2363; Treasurer 308-587-2363.

Merrick County

County Clerk, P.O. Box 27, Central City, NE 68826. 308-946-2881; Fax 308-946-2332.
Will search pre-1999 UCC records. UCC search does not include tax liens Will not search real estate records. **Other Phone Numbers:** Assessor 308-946-2443; Treasurer 308-946-2171; Elections 308-946-2881.

Morrill County

County Clerk, P.O. Box 610, Bridgeport, NE 69336. County Clerk, R/E and UCC Recording 308-262-0860; Fax 308-262-1469.
Will search UCC records. Will not search real estate records. **Other Phone Numbers:** Assessor 308-262-1534; Treasurer 308-262-1177; Elections 308-262-0860.

Nance County

County Clerk, P.O. Box 338, Fullerton, NE 68638. 308-536-2331; Fax 308-536-2742.
Will search UCC records. Will not search real estate records. **Other Phone Numbers:** Assessor 308-536-2653; Treasurer 308-536-2165; Elections 308-536-2331.

Nemaha County

County Clerk, 1824 N Street, Courthouse, Auburn, NE 68305-2399. 402-274-4213; Fax 402-274-4389.
Will search UCC records. UCC search includes tax liens. Will not search real estate records. **Other Phone Numbers:** Assessor 402-274-3820; Treasurer 402-274-3319.

Nuckolls County

County Clerk, P.O. Box 366, Nelson, NE 68961-0366. County Clerk, R/E and UCC Recording 402-225-4361; Fax 402-225-4301.
Will search UCC records. **Other Phone Numbers:** Assessor 402-225-2401; Treasurer 402-225-4351; Elections 402-225-4361.

Otoe County Clerk

Register of Deeds, P.O. Box 249, Nebraska City, NE 68410-0249. 402-873-9505 R/E Recording: 402-873-9530; Fax 402-873-9506. http://www.co.otoe.ne.us/deeds.html
Will search UCC records. See Register of Deeds for real estate records. **Other Phone Numbers:** Assessor 402-873-9520; Treasurer 402-873-9510; Appraiser/Auditor 402-873-9522; Elections 402-873-9505; Vital Records 402-471-2872.

Otoe County Register of Deeds

County Register of Deeds, 1021 Central Ave., Room 203, Nebraska City, NE 68410. 402-873-9530; Fax 402-873-6130.
Will search UCC records, but only real estate related UCC filed here. This agency will not do a tax lien search. Will not search real estate records. **Other Phone Numbers:** Assessor 402-873-9520; Treasurer 402-873-3589.

Pawnee County

County Clerk, P.O. Box 431, Pawnee City, NE 68420. 402-852-2962; Fax 402-852-2963.
Will search UCC records. UCC search includes tax liens if requested. RE record owner and mortgage searches available. **Other Phone Numbers:** Assessor 402-852-2292; Treasurer 402-852-2380.

Perkins County

County Clerk, P.O. Box 156, Grant, NE 69140-0156. County Clerk, R/E and UCC Recording 308-352-4643; Fax 308-352-2455.
Will search UCC records. Will not search real estate records. **Other Phone Numbers:** Assessor 308-352-4938; Treasurer 308-352-4542; Elections 308-352-4643.

Phelps County

County Clerk, P.O. Box 404, Holdrege, NE 68949-0404. 308-995-4469; Fax 308-995-4368.
Will search UCC records. Will search real estate records but only from legal description. **Other Phone Numbers:** Assessor 308-995-4061; Treasurer 308-995-6115.

Pierce County

County Clerk, 111 West Court, Courthouse - Room 1, Pierce, NE 68767-1224. 402-329-4225; Fax 402-329-6439.
Will search UCC records. UCC search includes tax liens. Will not search real estate records. **Other Phone Numbers:** Assessor 402-329-4215; Treasurer 402-329-6335.

Platte County Clerk

County Clerk, 2610 14th Street, Columbus, NE 68601. 402-563-4904 R/E Recording: 402-563-4911; Fax 402-564-4614.

Will search UCC records. See Register of Deeds for real estate records. **Other Phone Numbers:** Assessor 402-563-4902; Treasurer 402-563-4913; Elections 402-563-4908.

Platte County Register of Deeds

County Register of Deeds, 2610 14th Street, Columbus, NE 68601. 402-563-4911.
Will search UCC records, but only real estate related UCC filed here. This agency will not do a tax lien search. Will not search real estate records. **Other Phone Numbers:** Assessor 402-563-4902; Treasurer 402-563-4913.

Polk County

County Clerk, P.O. Box 276, Osceola, NE 68651-0276. 402-747-5431; Fax 402-747-2656.
Will search UCC records. UCC search includes tax liens if requested. Will not search real estate records. **Other Phone Numbers:** Assessor 402-747-4491; Treasurer 402-747-5441; Vital Records 402-471-2871.

Red Willow County

County Clerk, 502 Norris Avenue, McCook, NE 69001. 308-345-1552; Fax 308-345-7307.
Will search UCC records. UCC search includes tax liens if requested. Will not search real estate records. **Other Phone Numbers:** Assessor 308-345-4388; Treasurer 308-345-6515.

Richardson County

County Clerk, Courthouse, 1700 Stone, Falls City, NE 68355. 402-245-2911; Fax 402-245-3725.
Will search UCC records. Will not search real estate records. **Other Phone Numbers:** Assessor 402-245-4012; Treasurer 402-245-3511.

Rock County

County Clerk, P.O. Box 367, Bassett, NE 68714. 402-684-3933.
Will search UCC records. UCC search includes tax liens. Will not search real estate records. **Other Phone Numbers:** Assessor 402-684-3831; Treasurer 402-684-3515.

Saline County

Real Estate-County Clerek, P.O. Box 865, Wilber, NE 68465. Real Estate-County Clerek, R/E and UCC Recording 402-821-2374 UCC Recording: 402-471-4080 (filed at State level); Fax 402-821-3381.
Will search UCC records. Will not search real estate records. **Other Phone Numbers:** Assessor 402-821-2588; Treasurer 402-821-2375; Elections 402-821-2374; Vital Records 402-471-2872 (State Bureau of Vital Statistics).

Sarpy County Clerk

County Clerk, 1210 Golden Gate Drive, Suite 1118, Papillion, NE 68046-2895. 402-593-2114; Fax 402-593-4360. http://www.sarpy.com
Will not search UCC records. See Register of Deeds for real estate records. **Online Access:** Real Estate. Records on the county Property Lookup database are available free online at www.sarpy.com/boe/capslookup.htm. **Other Phone Numbers:** Assessor 402-593-2121.

Sarpy County Register of Deeds

County Clerk, 1210 Golden Gate Drive #1109, Papillion, NE 68046. 402-593-2186; Fax 402-593-2338.
Will search UCC records. Will not search real estate records. **Other Phone Numbers:** Assessor 402-593-2121; Treasurer 402-436-6621.

Saunders County Clerk

County Clerk, P.O. Box 61, Wahoo, NE 68066-0187. 402-443-8101; Fax 402-443-5010.
Will search UCC records. UCC search includes state tax liens See Register of Deeds for real estate records. **Other Phone Numbers:** Assessor 402-443-5700.

Saunders County Register of Deeds

Register of Deeds, P.O. Box 184, Wahoo, NE 68066. Register of Deeds, R/E and UCC Recording 402-443-8111; Fax 402-443-5010.
Will search UCC records. Will not search real estate records. **Other Phone Numbers:** Assessor 402-443-5700; Treasurer 402-443-8129; Appraiser/Auditor 402-443-5702; Elections 402-443-8100.

Scotts Bluff County Clerk

County Clerk, 1825 10th Street, Administration Office Building, Gering, NE 69341. 308-436-6601; Fax 308-436-3178.
Will search UCC records. UCC search includes state tax liens See Register of Deeds for real estate records. **Other Phone Numbers:** Assessor 308-436-6627.

Scotts Bluff County Register of Deeds

County Register of Deeds, 1825 10th Street, Administration Office Building, Gering, NE 69341. County Register of Deeds, R/E and UCC Recording 308-436-6607; Fax 308-436-6609.
http://www.scottsbluffcounty.org
Will search UCC records, but only real estate related UCC filed here. This agency will not do a tax lien search. Will not search real estate records. **Other Phone Numbers:** Assessor 308-436-6627; Treasurer 308-436-6621.

Seward County

County Clerk, P.O. Box 190, Seward, NE 68434-0190. 402-643-2883; Fax 402-643-9243.
http://connectseward.org/www/docs/cgov
Will search UCC records. Will not search real estate records. **Other Phone Numbers:** Assessor 402-643-3311; Treasurer 402-643-4574; Elections 402-643-2883; Land or Marriage records 402-643-2883.

Sheridan County

County Clerk, P.O. Box 39, Rushville, NE 69360. County Clerk, R/E and UCC Recording 308-327-2633. Will search UCC records. UCC search includes tax liens if requested. Will not search real estate records. **Other Phone Numbers:** Assessor 308-327-2113; Treasurer 308-327-2362.

Sherman County

County Clerk, P.O. Box 456, Loup City, NE 68853-0456. 308-745-1513; Fax 308-745-1820.
Will search UCC records. **Other Phone Numbers:** Assessor 308-745-0113; Treasurer 308-745-1513.

Sioux County

County Clerk, P.O. Box 158, Harrison, NE 69346. 308-668-2443; Fax 308-668-2443.
Will search UCC records. Will not search real estate records. **Other Phone Numbers:** Assessor 308-668-2443; Treasurer 308-668-2422.

Stanton County

Register of Deeds, P.O. Box 347, Stanton, NE 68779-0347. Register of Deeds, R/E and UCC Recording 402-439-2222; Fax 402-439-2200.
Will search UCC records. Will not search real estate records. **Other Phone Numbers:** Assessor 402-439-2210; Treasurer 402-439-2223; Elections 402-439-2222.

Thayer County

County Clerk, P.O. Box 208, Hebron, NE 68370. 402-768-6126.
Will search UCC records. UCC search includes tax liens if requested. RE owner, mortgage, and property transfer searches available. **Other Phone Numbers:** Assessor 402-768-6417; Treasurer 402-768-6227.

Thomas County

County Clerk, P.O. Box 226, Thedford, NE 69166-0226. 308-645-2261; Fax 308-645-2623.
Will search UCC records. UCC search includes tax liens if requested. Will not search real estate records. **Other Phone Numbers:** Assessor 308-645-2261; Treasurer 308-645-2262.

Thurston County

County Clerk, P.O. Box G, Pender, NE 68047. 402-385-2343; Fax 402-385-3544.

Will search UCC records. Will not search real estate records. **Other Phone Numbers:** Assessor 402-385-2251; Treasurer 402-385-3058; Elections 402-385-2343.

Valley County

County Clerk, 125 South 15th, Ord, NE 68862-1499. 308-728-3700.
Will Search UCC records. UCC search includes tax liens. Will not search real estate records. **Other Phone Numbers:** Assessor 308-728-5081; Treasurer 308-728-5606.

Washington County

County Clerk, P.O. Box 466, Blair, NE 68008. 402-426-6822; Fax 402-426-6825.
Will search UCC records. **Other Phone Numbers:** Assessor 402-426-6800; Treasurer 402-426-6888.

Wayne County

County Clerk, P.O. Box 248, Wayne, NE 68787-0248. 402-375-2288; Fax 402-375-2288.
Will search UCC records. This agency will not do a tax lien search. Will not search real estate records. **Other Phone Numbers:** Assessor 402-375-1979; Treasurer 402-375-3885; Elections 402-375-2288.

Webster County

County Clerk, Webster County Clerk P.O. Box 250, Red Cloud, NE 68970. 402-746-2716; Fax 402-746-2710.
Will search UCC records. **Other Phone Numbers:** Assessor 402-746-2717; Treasurer 402-746-2877.

Wheeler County

County Clerk, P.O. Box 127, Bartlett, NE 68622. 308-654-3235; Fax 308-654-3442.
Will search UCC records. Will not search real estate records. **Other Phone Numbers:** Assessor 308-654-3235; Treasurer 308-654-3236.

York County

County Clerk, Courthouse, 510 Lincoln Ave., York, NE 68467. 402-362-7759; Fax 402-362-2651.
Will search UCC records. Will not search real estate records. **Other Phone Numbers:** Assessor 402-362-4926; Treasurer 402-362-4949.

Nebraska County Locator

You will usually be able to find the city name in the City/County Cross Reference below. In that case, it is a simple matter to determine the county from the cross reference. However, only the official US Postal Service city names are included in this index. There are an additional 40,000 place names that people use in their addresses. Therefore, we have also included a ZIP/City Cross Reference immediately following the City/County Cross Reference.

If you know the ZIP Code but the city name does not appear in the City/County Cross Reference index, look up the ZIP Code in the ZIP/City Cross Reference, find the city name, then look up the city name in the City/County Cross Reference. For example, you want to know the county for an address of Menands, NY 12204. There is no "Menands" in the City/County Cross Reference. The ZIP/City Cross Reference shows that ZIP Codes 12201-12288 are for the city of Albany. Looking back in the City/County Cross Reference, Albany is in Albany County.

City/County Cross Reference

ABIE Butler
ADAMS (68301) Gage(74), Lancaster(22), Otoe(4)
AINSWORTH Brown
ALBION Boone
ALDA Hall
ALEXANDRIA (68303) Thayer(92), Jefferson(8)
ALLEN Dixon
ALLIANCE (69301) Box Butte(97), Sioux(3)
ALMA Harlan
ALVO Cass
AMELIA Holt
AMES Dodge
AMHERST Buffalo
ANGORA Morrill
ANSELMO (68813) Custer(81), Blaine(11), Loup(8)
ANSLEY Custer
ARAPAHOE (68922) Furnas(62), Gosper(38)
ARCADIA (68815) Valley(63), Custer(19), Sherman(18)
ARCHER Merrick
ARLINGTON Washington
ARNOLD (69120) Custer(77), Logan(13), Lincoln(11)
ARTHUR Arthur
ASHBY Grant
ASHLAND (68003) Saunders(77), Cass(23)
ASHTON (68817) Sherman(91), Howard(9)
ATKINSON Holt
ATLANTA Phelps
AUBURN Nemaha
AURORA (68818) Hamilton(99), Clay(1)
AVOCA (68307) Cass(92), Otoe(8)
AXTELL (68924) Kearney(98), Phelps(2)
AYR Adams
BANCROFT Cuming
BARNESTON Gage
BARTLETT Wheeler
BARTLEY Red Willow
BASSETT (68714) Rock(97), Brown(3)
BATTLE CREEK Madison
BAYARD (69334) Morrill(62), Scotts. Bluff(36), Banner(1)
BEATRICE Gage
BEAVER CITY Furnas
BEAVER CROSSING (99999) Seward(99), York(1)
BEE (68314) Seward(97), Butler(3)
BEEMER Cuming
BELDEN Cedar
BELGRADE (68623) Nance(94), Boone(6)
BELLEVUE (68147) Sarpy(98), Douglas(2)
BELLEVUE Sarpy
BELLWOOD Butler
BELVIDERE Thayer
BENEDICT (68316) York(91), Polk(9)
BENKELMAN Dundy
BENNET (68317) Lancaster(98), Otoe(2)
BENNINGTON (68007) Douglas(91), Washington(9)

BERTRAND (68927) Phelps(62), Gosper(38)
BERWYN Custer
BIG SPRINGS (69122) Deuel(84), Keith(9), Perkins(4), Garden(3)
BINGHAM (69335) Sheridan(52), Garden(48)
BLADEN (68928) Webster(69), Adams(31)
BLAIR Washington
BLOOMFIELD Knox
BLOOMINGTON Franklin
BLUE HILL (68930) Webster(67), Adams(34)
BLUE SPRINGS Gage
BOELUS Howard
BOONE Boone
BOYS TOWN Douglas
BRADSHAW (68319) York(97), Hamilton(3)
BRADY Lincoln
BRAINARD (68626) Butler(96), Saunders(4)
BREWSTER Blaine
BRIDGEPORT Morrill
BRISTOW Boyd
BROADWATER Morrill
BROCK (68320) Nemaha(99), Otoe(1)
BROKEN BOW Custer
BROWNVILLE Nemaha
BRULE (69127) Keith(99), Perkins(1)
BRUNING (68322) Thayer(77), Fillmore(24)
BRUNO Butler
BRUNSWICK Antelope
BURCHARD Pawnee
BURR (68324) Otoe(96), Johnson(4)
BURWELL (68823) Garfield(66), Loup(17), Valley(11), Rock(4), Custer(2)
BUSHNELL Kimball
BUTTE Boyd
BYRON Thayer
CAIRO (68824) Hall(95), Howard(5)
CALLAWAY Custer
CAMBRIDGE (69022) Furnas(51), Frontier(29), Red Willow(15), Gosper(4)
CAMPBELL (68932) Franklin(76), Kearney(10), Webster(9), Adams(6)
CARLETON (68326) Thayer(99), Fillmore(2)
CARROLL (68723) Wayne(97), Chase(3)
CEDAR BLUFFS Saunders
CEDAR CREEK Cass
CEDAR RAPIDS (68627) Boone(90), Nance(9), Greeley(2)
CENTER Knox
CENTRAL CITY Merrick
CERESCO (68017) Saunders(81), Lancaster(19)
CHADRON Dawes
CHAMBERS (68725) Holt(93), Wheeler(5), Garfield(2)
CHAMPION Chase
CHAPMAN Merrick
CHAPPELL Deuel
CHESTER Thayer

CLARKS (68628) Merrick(83), Hamilton(9), Polk(8)
CLARKSON (68629) Colfax(84), Stanton(16)
CLATONIA Gage
CLAY CENTER Clay
CLEARWATER (68726) Antelope(89), Holt(11)
CODY Cherry
COLERIDGE Cedar
COLON Saunders
COLUMBUS (68601) Platte(95), Colfax(3), Polk(2), Butler(1)
COLUMBUS Platte
COMSTOCK (68828) Custer(71), Valley(29)
CONCORD Dixon
COOK (68329) Johnson(68), Otoe(31), Nemaha(1)
CORDOVA Seward
CORNLEA Platte
CORTLAND Gage
COTESFIELD (68829) Howard(90), Greeley(10)
COZAD Dawson
CRAB ORCHARD (68332) Johnson(96), Gage(4)
CRAIG (68019) Burt(94), Washington(4), Dodge(2)
CRAWFORD Dawes
CREIGHTON (68729) Knox(93), Antelope(7)
CRESTON (68631) Platte(88), Stanton(12)
CRETE (68333) Saline(94), Lancaster(6)
CROFTON (68730) Knox(53), Cedar(47)
CROOKSTON Cherry
CULBERTSON (69024) Hitchcock(83), Hayes(9), Red Willow(9)
CURTIS (69025) Frontier(94), Lincoln(5), Hitchcock(1)
DAKOTA CITY Dakota
DALTON Cheyenne
DANBURY Red Willow
DANNEBROG Howard
DAVENPORT (68335) Thayer(69), Nuckolls(27), Fillmore(3)
DAVEY Lancaster
DAVID CITY Butler
DAWSON Richardson
DAYKIN (68338) Jefferson(97), Saline(3)
DE WITT (68341) Saline(63), Gage(36)
DECATUR (68020) Burt(93), Thurston(7)
DENTON (68339) Lancaster(82), Seward(17), Saline(2)
DESHLER Thayer
DEWEESE (68934) Clay(62), Nuckolls(38)
DICKENS Lincoln
DILLER (68342) Jefferson(90), Gage(10)
DIX (69133) Kimball(97), Cheyenne(3)
DIXON (68732) Dixon(98), Cedar(2)
DODGE (68633) Dodge(65), Cuming(27), Colfax(9)
DONIPHAN (68832) Hall(74), Hamilton(26)

DORCHESTER (68343) Saline(92), Seward(8)
DOUGLAS Otoe
DU BOIS (68345) Pawnee(74), Richardson(27)
DUNBAR Otoe
DUNCAN Platte
DUNNING (68833) Blaine(81), Logan(12), Custer(7)
DWIGHT Butler
EAGLE (68347) Cass(71), Otoe(28)
EDDYVILLE (68834) Dawson(83), Custer(17)
EDGAR (68935) Clay(73), Nuckolls(28)
EDISON (68936) Furnas(60), Gosper(22), Greeley(18)
ELBA (68835) Howard(98), Greeley(2)
ELGIN (68636) Antelope(96), Wheeler(4)
ELK CREEK (68348) Johnson(77), Nemaha(13), Pawnee(10)
ELKHORN Douglas
ELLSWORTH Sheridan
ELM CREEK (68836) Buffalo(65), Phelps(18), Dawson(17)
ELMWOOD Cass
ELSIE Perkins
ELSMERE (69135) Cherry(53), Brown(47)
ELWOOD (68937) Gosper(77), Dawson(22)
ELYRIA Valley
EMERSON (68733) Dakota(55), Thurston(23), Dixon(22)
EMMET Holt
ENDERS (69027) Chase(93), Dundy(7)
ENDICOTT Jefferson
ERICSON (68637) Wheeler(80), Garfield(21)
EUSTIS (69028) Frontier(50), Dawson(36), Gosper(13)
EWING (68735) Holt(66), Antelope(17), Wheeler(17)
EXETER (68351) Fillmore(81), York(19)
FAIRBURY Jefferson
FAIRFIELD (68938) Clay(66), Franklin(33)
FAIRMONT (68354) Fillmore(90), York(10)
FALLS CITY Richardson
FARNAM Dawson
FARWELL Howard
FILLEY (68357) Gage(98), Johnson(2)
FIRTH (68358) Lancaster(68), Gage(32)
FORDYCE Cedar
FORT CALHOUN Washington
FOSTER Pierce
FRANKLIN Franklin
FREMONT (68025) Dodge(99), Saunders(1)
FREMONT Dodge
FRIEND (68359) Saline(92), Seward(8)
FULLERTON (68638) Nance(98), Merrick(2)
FUNK Phelps
GARLAND (68360) Seward(98), Lancaster(2)

GENEVA Fillmore
GENOA (68640) Nance(79), Platte(20), Merrick(2)
GERING Scotts. Bluff
GIBBON (68840) Kearney(65), Buffalo(35)
GILEAD Thayer
GILTNER Hamilton
GLENVIL (68941) Adams(74), Clay(26)
GOEHNER Seward
GORDON (69343) Sheridan(95), Cherry(5)
GOTHENBURG (69138) Dawson(95), Custer(3), Lincoln(2)
GRAFTON (68365) Fillmore(98), York(2)
GRAND ISLAND (68801) Hall(96), Merrick(5)
GRAND ISLAND Hall
GRANT Perkins
GREELEY Greeley
GREENWOOD (68366) Cass(96), Lancaster(3)
GRESHAM (68367) York(46), Seward(34), Polk(18), Butler(2)
GRETNA Sarpy
GUIDE ROCK (68942) Webster(83), Nuckolls(17)
GURLEY Cheyenne
HADAR Pierce
HAIGLER Dundy
HALLAM (68368) Lancaster(96), Gage(5)
HALSEY Thomas
HAMLET Hayes
HAMPTON (68843) Hamilton(97), York(3)
HARDY Nuckolls
HARRISBURG Banner
HARRISON Sioux
HARTINGTON Cedar
HARVARD (68944) Clay(86), Hamilton(14)
HASTINGS Adams
HAY SPRINGS (69347) Sheridan(66), Dawes(35)
HAYES CENTER Hayes
HAZARD (68844) Sherman(77), Buffalo(23)
HEARTWELL (68945) Kearney(95), Adams(5)
HEBRON Thayer
HEMINGFORD (69348) Box Butte(72), Dawes(26), Sioux(2)
HENDERSON (68371) York(58), Hamilton(42)
HENDLEY Furnas
HENRY Scotts. Bluff
HERMAN (68029) Washington(89), Burt(12)
HERSHEY Lincoln
HICKMAN Lancaster
HILDRETH (68947) Franklin(79), Kearney(21)
HOLBROOK (68948) Furnas(60), Gosper(35), Frontier(6)
HOLDREGE (68949) Phelps(99), Harlan(2)
HOLMESVILLE Gage
HOLSTEIN Adams
HOMER Dakota
HOOPER (68031) Dodge(91), Washington(8)
HORDVILLE Hamilton
HOSKINS (68740) Wayne(92), Stanton(8)
HOWELLS (68641) Cuming(48), Colfax(39), Stanton(12)
HUBBARD Dakota
HUBBELL Thayer
HUMBOLDT (68376) Richardson(90), Nemaha(8), Pawnee(2)
HUMPHREY (68642) Platte(89), Madison(12)
HUNTLEY Harlan
HYANNIS Grant
IMPERIAL (69033) Chase(94), Perkins(6)
INAVALE Webster
INDIANOLA (69034) Red Willow(89), Frontier(11)
INLAND Clay

INMAN Holt
ITHACA Saunders
JACKSON Dakota
JANSEN Jefferson
JOHNSON (68378) Nemaha(89), Johnson(7), Otoe(4)
JOHNSTOWN (69214) Brown(99), Cherry(1)
JULIAN Nemaha
JUNIATA Adams
KEARNEY Buffalo
KENESAW (68956) Adams(81), Buffalo(8), Kearney(6), Hall(6)
KENNARD Washington
KEYSTONE (69144) Keith(96), Arthur(4)
KILGORE Cherry
KIMBALL (69145) Kimball(98), Banner(2)
LAKESIDE Sheridan
LAMAR Chase
LAUREL (68745) Cedar(96), Dixon(2), Wayne(2)
LAVISTA (68128) Sarpy(98), Douglas(2)
LAWRENCE (68957) Nuckolls(59), Webster(34), Adams(7)
LEBANON Red Willow
LEIGH (68643) Colfax(62), Platte(22), Stanton(16)
LEMOYNE Keith
LESHARA Saunders
LEWELLEN (69147) Keith(79), Garden(21)
LEWISTON Pawnee
LEXINGTON (68850) Dawson(99), Gosper(1)
LIBERTY (68381) Gage(77), Pawnee(23)
LINCOLN Lancaster
LINDSAY (68644) Platte(81), Madison(20)
LINWOOD (68036) Butler(98), Saunders(2)
LISCO (69148) Garden(84), Morrill(16)
LITCHFIELD (68852) Sherman(90), Custer(10)
LODGEPOLE (69149) Cheyenne(92), Garden(7), Deuel(1)
LONG PINE Brown
LOOMIS (68958) Phelps(97), Webster(3)
LORTON Otoe
LOUISVILLE Cass
LOUP CITY Sherman
LYMAN Scotts. Bluff
LYNCH (68746) Boyd(71), Holt(30)
LYONS (68038) Burt(96), Cuming(4)
MACY Thurston
MADISON (68748) Madison(92), Stanton(7), Platte(1)
MADRID Perkins
MAGNET Cedar
MALCOLM Lancaster
MALMO Saunders
MANLEY Cass
MARQUETTE Hamilton
MARSLAND Dawes
MARTELL Lancaster
MASKELL Dixon
MASON CITY Custer
MAX Dundy
MAXWELL Lincoln
MAYWOOD (69038) Frontier(92), Lincoln(8)
MC COOK (69001) Red Willow(98), Frontier(2)
MC COOL JUNCTION (68401) York(99), Fillmore(1)
MCGREW Scotts. Bluff
MCLEAN (68747) Pierce(98), Cedar(2)
MEAD Saunders
MEADOW GROVE (68752) Madison(92), Pierce(7)
MELBETA Scotts. Bluff
MEMPHIS Saunders
MERNA Custer
MERRIMAN Cherry
MILFORD Seward
MILLER (68858) Buffalo(96), Custer(3)

MILLIGAN (68406) Fillmore(67), Saline(32), Adams(1)
MILLS Keya Paha
MINATARE Scotts. Bluff
MINDEN Kearney
MITCHELL (69357) Scotts. Bluff(97), Sioux(3)
MONROE Platte
MOOREFIELD (69039) Frontier(81), Lincoln(19)
MORRILL (69358) Scotts. Bluff(87), Sioux(13)
MORSE BLUFF Saunders
MULLEN Hooker
MURDOCK Cass
MURRAY Cass
NAPER (68755) Boyd(99), Keya Paha(1)
NAPONEE (68960) Franklin(82), Harlan(13), Webster(5)
NEBRASKA CITY Otoe
NEHAWKA (68413) Cass(99), Otoe(1)
NELIGH Antelope
NELSON Nuckolls
NEMAHA Nemaha
NENZEL Cherry
NEWCASTLE (68757) Dixon(97), Cedar(3)
NEWMAN GROVE (68758) Madison(66), Platte(20), Boone(14)
NEWPORT (68759) Rock(68), Keya Paha(32)
NICKERSON (68044) Washington(62), Dodge(38)
NIOBRARA Knox
NORFOLK (68701) Madison(95), Stanton(4)
NORFOLK Madison
NORMAN Kearney
NORTH BEND Dodge
NORTH LOUP (68859) Valley(97), Greeley(2), Sherman(2)
NORTH PLATTE Lincoln
OAK (68964) Nuckolls(94), Thayer(6)
OAKDALE Antelope
OAKLAND (68045) Burt(93), Cuming(6)
OBERT Cedar
OCONTO (68860) Custer(97), Dawson(3)
OCTAVIA Butler
ODELL Gage
ODESSA Buffalo
OFFUTT A F B Sarpy
OGALLALA Keith
OHIOWA (68416) Fillmore(91), Thayer(9)
OMAHA (68122) Douglas(93), Washington(8)
OMAHA (68136) Sarpy(96), Douglas(4)
OMAHA (68138) Sarpy(99), Douglas(1)
OMAHA (68142) Douglas(93), Washington(8)
OMAHA (68152) Douglas(92), Washington(8)
OMAHA (68157) Sarpy(98), Douglas(2)
OMAHA Douglas
ONEILL Holt
ONG (68452) Clay(85), Fillmore(15)
ORCHARD (68764) Antelope(59), Knox(31), Holt(9)
ORD Valley
ORLEANS Harlan
OSCEOLA Polk
OSHKOSH Garden
OSMOND Pierce
OTOE Otoe
OVERTON Dawson
OXFORD (68967) Furnas(60), Harlan(40)
PAGE Holt
PALISADE (69040) Hitchcock(66), Hayes(34)
PALMER (68864) Merrick(77), Nance(13), Howard(10)
PALMYRA (68418) Otoe(96), Cass(4)
PANAMA Lancaster
PAPILLION Sarpy

PARKS Dundy
PAWNEE CITY Pawnee
PAXTON Keith
PENDER (68047) Thurston(57), Cuming(36), Wayne(6)
PERU (68421) Nemaha(96), Otoe(4)
PETERSBURG (68652) Boone(97), Antelope(3)
PHILLIPS Hamilton
PICKRELL Gage
PIERCE Pierce
PILGER (68768) Stanton(85), Cuming(12), Wayne(4)
PLAINVIEW (68769) Pierce(76), Antelope(23), Knox(1)
PLATTE CENTER Platte
PLATTSMOUTH Cass
PLEASANT DALE (68423) Seward(89), Lancaster(11)
PLEASANTON (68866) Buffalo(99), Custer(1)
PLYMOUTH (99999) Jefferson(99), Gage(1)
POLK (68654) Polk(58), York(21), Hamilton(21)
PONCA (68770) Dixon(84), Dakota(16)
POTTER Cheyenne
PRAGUE Saunders
PRIMROSE (68655) Boone(93), Greeley(7)
PROSSER Adams
PURDUM (69157) Blaine(48), Cherry(35), Thomas(13), Brown(4)
RAGAN Harlan
RANDOLPH (68771) Cedar(65), Pierce(22), Wayne(13)
RAVENNA (68869) Buffalo(94), Sherman(6)
RAYMOND (68428) Lancaster(97), Seward(3)
RED CLOUD Webster
REPUBLICAN CITY Harlan
REYNOLDS Thayer
RICHFIELD Sarpy
RISING CITY (68658) Butler(93), Polk(7)
RIVERDALE Buffalo
RIVERTON Franklin
ROCA Lancaster
ROCKVILLE Sherman
ROGERS Colfax
ROSALIE (68055) Thurston(86), Cuming(12), Burt(2)
ROSE (68772) Rock(95), Loup(5)
ROSELAND Adams
ROYAL (68773) Antelope(94), Brown(6)
RULO Richardson
RUSHVILLE Sheridan
RUSKIN (68974) Nuckolls(89), Thayer(11)
SAINT EDWARD (68660) Boone(68), Platte(24), Nance(8)
SAINT HELENA Cedar
SAINT LIBORY (68872) Howard(80), Merrick(20)
SAINT MARY Johnson
SAINT PAUL Howard
SALEM Richardson
SARGENT (68874) Custer(96), Loup(3), Hall(1)
SARONVILLE (68975) Clay(67), Fillmore(33)
SCHUYLER Colfax
SCOTIA (68875) Greeley(97), Howard(3)
SCOTTSBLUFF Scotts. Bluff
SCRIBNER Dodge
SENECA (69161) Thomas(62), Cherry(38)
SEWARD Seward
SHELBY (68662) Polk(96), Butler(4)
SHELTON (68876) Hall(56), Buffalo(44)
SHICKLEY (68436) Fillmore(98), Clay(2)
SHUBERT (68437) Richardson(87), Nemaha(13)
SIDNEY Cheyenne

SILVER CREEK (68663) Merrick(52), Polk(25), Nance(23)
SMITHFIELD Gosper
SNYDER Dodge
SOUTH BEND Cass
SOUTH SIOUX CITY Dakota
SPALDING (68665) Greeley(78), Wheeler(23)
SPARKS Cherry
SPENCER (68777) Boyd(87), Holt(13)
SPRAGUE Lancaster
SPRINGFIELD Sarpy
SPRINGVIEW Keya Paha
ST COLUMBANS Sarpy
STAMFORD (68977) Harlan(68), Furnas(32)
STANTON Stanton
STAPLEHURST Seward
STAPLETON (69163) Logan(86), Lincoln(14)
STEELE CITY Jefferson
STEINAUER (68441) Pawnee(98), Johnson(2)
STELLA (68442) Richardson(80), Nemaha(20)
STERLING (68443) Johnson(98), Otoe(2)
STOCKVILLE Frontier
STRANG Fillmore
STRATTON (69043) Hitchcock(96), Dundy(4)
STROMSBURG (68666) Polk(97), York(3)

STUART Holt
SUMNER (68878) Dawson(95), Custer(5)
SUPERIOR Nuckolls
SURPRISE Butler
SUTHERLAND (69165) Lincoln(89), Keith(11)
SUTTON (68979) Clay(83), Fillmore(9), Hamilton(7), York(2)
SWANTON Saline
SYRACUSE Otoe
TABLE ROCK (68447) Pawnee(93), Johnson(3), Nemaha(3)
TALMAGE (68448) Otoe(71), Nemaha(18), Johnson(11)
TAYLOR Loup
TECUMSEH Johnson
TEKAMAH Burt
THEDFORD Thomas
THURSTON Thurston
TILDEN (68781) Antelope(49), Madison(44), Pierce(5), Boone(3)
TOBIAS (68453) Saline(77), Fillmore(15), Jefferson(7), Thayer(2)
TRENTON Hitchcock
TRUMBULL (68980) Clay(48), Adams(40), Hamilton(12)
TRYON McPherson
UEHLING Dodge
ULYSSES (68669) Butler(85), Seward(15)
UNADILLA (68454) Otoe(98), Cass(2)
UNION Cass

UPLAND (68981) Franklin(93), Kearney(7)
UTICA Seward
VALENTINE Cherry
VALLEY Douglas
VALPARAISO (68065) Saunders(55), Lancaster(37), Seward(7), Butler(2)
VENANGO (69168) Perkins(76), Chase(24)
VERDIGRE Knox
VERDON Richardson
VIRGINIA (68458) Gage(83), Pawnee(13), Johnson(5)
WACO (68460) York(97), Seward(3)
WAHOO Saunders
WAKEFIELD (68784) Dixon(64), Wayne(35), Thurston(2)
WALLACE (69169) Lincoln(73), Perkins(25), Hayes(3)
WALTHILL Thurston
WALTON (68461) Lancaster(96), Cass(3)
WASHINGTON Washington
WATERBURY (68785) Dixon(60), Dakota(40)
WATERLOO (68069) Douglas(98), Sarpy(2)
WAUNETA (69045) Chase(65), Dundy(30), Hitchcock(5)
WAUSA (68786) Knox(87), Cedar(9), Pierce(4)
WAVERLY (68462) Lancaster(98), Cass(2)
WAYNE (68787) Wayne(98), Dixon(2)
WEEPING WATER Cass

WEISSERT Custer
WELLFLEET Lincoln
WEST POINT Cuming
WESTERN (68464) Saline(95), Jefferson(5)
WESTERVILLE Custer
WESTON Saunders
WHITECLAY Sheridan
WHITMAN Grant
WHITNEY Dawes
WILBER Saline
WILCOX (68982) Kearney(37), Franklin(36), Harlan(27)
WILLOW ISLAND Dawson
WILSONVILLE (69046) Furnas(89), Red Willow(11)
WINNEBAGO (68071) Burt(77), Thurston(23)
WINNETOON Knox
WINSIDE Wayne
WINSLOW Dodge
WISNER (68791) Cuming(98), Wayne(2)
WOLBACH (68882) Greeley(68), Howard(27), Nance(4)
WOOD LAKE Cherry
WOOD RIVER Hall
WYMORE Gage
WYNOT (68792) Cedar(99), Dixon(1)
YORK York
YUTAN Saunders

ZIP/City Cross Reference

68001-68001	ABIE	68064-68064	VALLEY	68332-68332	CRAB ORCHARD	68404-68404	MARTELL
68002-68002	ARLINGTON	68065-68065	VALPARAISO	68333-68333	CRETE	68405-68405	MILFORD
68003-68003	ASHLAND	68066-68066	WAHOO	68335-68335	DAVENPORT	68406-68406	MILLIGAN
68004-68004	BANCROFT	68067-68067	WALTHILL	68336-68336	DAVEY	68407-68407	MURDOCK
68005-68005	BELLEVUE	68068-68068	WASHINGTON	68337-68337	DAWSON	68409-68409	MURRAY
68007-68007	BENNINGTON	68069-68069	WATERLOO	68338-68338	DAYKIN	68410-68410	NEBRASKA CITY
68008-68009	BLAIR	68070-68070	WESTON	68339-68339	DENTON	68413-68413	NEHAWKA
68010-68010	BOYS TOWN	68071-68071	WINNEBAGO	68340-68340	DESHLER	68414-68414	NEMAHA
68014-68014	BRUNO	68072-68072	WINSLOW	68341-68341	DE WITT	68415-68415	ODELL
68015-68015	CEDAR BLUFFS	68073-68073	YUTAN	68342-68342	DILLER	68416-68416	OHIOWA
68016-68016	CEDAR CREEK	68101-68112	OMAHA	68343-68343	DORCHESTER	68417-68417	OTOE
68017-68017	CERESCO	68113-68113	OFFUTT A F B	68344-68344	DOUGLAS	68418-68418	PALMYRA
68018-68018	COLON	68114-68122	OMAHA	68345-68345	DU BOIS	68419-68419	PANAMA
68019-68019	CRAIG	68123-68123	BELLEVUE	68346-68346	DUNBAR	68420-68420	PAWNEE CITY
68020-68020	DECATUR	68124-68127	OMAHA	68347-68347	EAGLE	68421-68421	PERU
68022-68022	ELKHORN	68128-68128	LAVISTA	68348-68348	ELK CREEK	68422-68422	PICKRELL
68023-68023	FORT CALHOUN	68130-68132	OMAHA	68349-68349	ELMWOOD	68423-68423	PLEASANT DALE
68025-68026	FREMONT	68133-68133	PAPILLION	68350-68350	ENDICOTT	68424-68424	PLYMOUTH
68028-68028	GRETNA	68134-68145	OMAHA	68351-68351	EXETER	68428-68428	RAYMOND
68029-68029	HERMAN	68147-68147	BELLEVUE	68352-68352	FAIRBURY	68429-68429	REYNOLDS
68030-68030	HOMER	68152-68198	OMAHA	68354-68354	FAIRMONT	68430-68430	ROCA
68031-68031	HOOPER	68301-68301	ADAMS	68355-68355	FALLS CITY	68431-68431	RULO
68033-68033	ITHACA	68303-68303	ALEXANDRIA	68357-68357	FILLEY	68433-68433	SALEM
68034-68034	KENNARD	68304-68304	ALVO	68358-68358	FIRTH	68434-68434	SEWARD
68035-68035	LESHARA	68305-68305	AUBURN	68359-68359	FRIEND	68436-68436	SHICKLEY
68036-68036	LINWOOD	68307-68307	AVOCA	68360-68360	GARLAND	68437-68437	SHUBERT
68037-68037	LOUISVILLE	68309-68309	BARNESTON	68361-68361	GENEVA	68438-68438	SPRAGUE
68038-68038	LYONS	68310-68310	BEATRICE	68362-68362	GILEAD	68439-68439	STAPLEHURST
68039-68039	MACY	68313-68313	BEAVER CROSSING	68364-68364	GOEHNER	68440-68440	STEELE CITY
68040-68040	MALMO	68314-68314	BEE	68365-68365	GRAFTON	68441-68441	STEINAUER
68041-68041	MEAD	68315-68315	BELVIDERE	68366-68366	GREENWOOD	68442-68442	STELLA
68042-68042	MEMPHIS	68316-68316	BENEDICT	68367-68367	GRESHAM	68443-68443	STERLING
68044-68044	NICKERSON	68317-68317	BENNET	68368-68368	HALLAM	68444-68444	STRANG
68045-68045	OAKLAND	68318-68318	BLUE SPRINGS	68370-68370	HEBRON	68445-68445	SWANTON
68046-68046	PAPILLION	68319-68319	BRADSHAW	68371-68371	HENDERSON	68446-68446	SYRACUSE
68047-68047	PENDER	68320-68320	BROCK	68372-68372	HICKMAN	68447-68447	TABLE ROCK
68048-68048	PLATTSMOUTH	68321-68321	BROWNVILLE	68374-68374	HOLMESVILLE	68448-68448	TALMAGE
68050-68050	PRAGUE	68322-68322	BRUNING	68375-68375	HUBBELL	68450-68450	TECUMSEH
68054-68054	RICHFIELD	68323-68323	BURCHARD	68376-68376	HUMBOLDT	68452-68452	ONG
68055-68055	ROSALIE	68324-68324	BURR	68377-68377	JANSEN	68453-68453	TOBIAS
68056-68056	ST COLUMBANS	68325-68325	BYRON	68378-68378	JOHNSON	68454-68454	UNADILLA
68057-68057	SCRIBNER	68326-68326	CARLETON	68380-68380	LEWISTON	68455-68455	UNION
68058-68058	SOUTH BEND	68327-68327	CHESTER	68381-68381	LIBERTY	68456-68456	UTICA
68059-68059	SPRINGFIELD	68328-68328	CLATONIA	68382-68382	LORTON	68457-68457	VERDON
68061-68061	TEKAMAH	68329-68329	COOK	68401-68401	MC COOL JUNCTION	68458-68458	VIRGINIA
68062-68062	THURSTON	68330-68330	CORDOVA	68402-68402	MALCOLM	68460-68460	WACO
68063-68063	UEHLING	68331-68331	CORTLAND	68403-68403	MANLEY	68461-68461	WALTON

ZIP Range	City	ZIP Range	City	ZIP Range	City	ZIP Range	City
68462-68462	WAVERLY	68745-68745	LAUREL	68856-68856	MERNA	69020-69020	BARTLEY
68463-68463	WEEPING WATER	68746-68746	LYNCH	68858-68858	MILLER	69021-69021	BENKELMAN
68464-68464	WESTERN	68747-68747	MCLEAN	68859-68859	NORTH LOUP	69022-69022	CAMBRIDGE
68465-68465	WILBER	68748-68748	MADISON	68860-68860	OCONTO	69023-69023	CHAMPION
68466-68466	WYMORE	68749-68749	MAGNET	68861-68861	ODESSA	69024-69024	CULBERTSON
68467-68467	YORK	68751-68751	MASKELL	68862-68862	ORD	69025-69025	CURTIS
68501-68588	LINCOLN	68752-68752	MEADOW GROVE	68863-68863	OVERTON	69026-69026	DANBURY
68601-68602	COLUMBUS	68753-68753	MILLS	68864-68864	PALMER	69027-69027	ENDERS
68620-68620	ALBION	68755-68755	NAPER	68865-68865	PHILLIPS	69028-69028	EUSTIS
68621-68621	AMES	68756-68756	NELIGH	68866-68866	PLEASANTON	69029-69029	FARNAM
68622-68622	BARTLETT	68757-68757	NEWCASTLE	68869-68869	RAVENNA	69030-69030	HAIGLER
68623-68623	BELGRADE	68758-68758	NEWMAN GROVE	68870-68870	RIVERDALE	69031-69031	HAMLET
68624-68624	BELLWOOD	68759-68759	NEWPORT	68871-68871	ROCKVILLE	69032-69032	HAYES CENTER
68626-68626	BRAINARD	68760-68760	NIOBRARA	68872-68872	SAINT LIBORY	69033-69033	IMPERIAL
68627-68627	CEDAR RAPIDS	68761-68761	OAKDALE	68873-68873	SAINT PAUL	69034-69034	INDIANOLA
68628-68628	CLARKS	68763-68763	ONEILL	68874-68874	SARGENT	69036-69036	LEBANON
68629-68629	CLARKSON	68764-68764	ORCHARD	68875-68875	SCOTIA	69037-69037	MAX
68631-68631	CRESTON	68765-68765	OSMOND	68876-68876	SHELTON	69038-69038	MAYWOOD
68632-68632	DAVID CITY	68766-68766	PAGE	68878-68878	SUMNER	69039-69039	MOOREFIELD
68633-68633	DODGE	68767-68767	PIERCE	68879-68879	TAYLOR	69040-69040	PALISADE
68634-68634	DUNCAN	68768-68768	PILGER	68880-68880	WEISSERT	69041-69041	PARKS
68635-68635	DWIGHT	68769-68769	PLAINVIEW	68881-68881	WESTERVILLE	69042-69042	STOCKVILLE
68636-68636	ELGIN	68770-68770	PONCA	68882-68882	WOLBACH	69043-69043	STRATTON
68637-68637	ERICSON	68771-68771	RANDOLPH	68883-68883	WOOD RIVER	69044-69044	TRENTON
68638-68638	FULLERTON	68772-68772	ROSE	68901-68902	HASTINGS	69045-69045	WAUNETA
68640-68640	GENOA	68773-68773	ROYAL	68920-68920	ALMA	69046-69046	WILSONVILLE
68641-68641	HOWELLS	68774-68774	SAINT HELENA	68922-68922	ARAPAHOE	69101-69103	NORTH PLATTE
68642-68642	HUMPHREY	68776-68776	SOUTH SIOUX CITY	68923-68923	ATLANTA	69120-69120	ARNOLD
68643-68643	LEIGH	68777-68777	SPENCER	68924-68924	AXTELL	69121-69121	ARTHUR
68644-68644	LINDSAY	68778-68778	SPRINGVIEW	68925-68925	AYR	69122-69122	BIG SPRINGS
68647-68647	MONROE	68779-68779	STANTON	68926-68926	BEAVER CITY	69123-69123	BRADY
68648-68648	MORSE BLUFF	68780-68780	STUART	68927-68927	BERTRAND	69125-69125	BROADWATER
68649-68649	NORTH BEND	68781-68781	TILDEN	68928-68928	BLADEN	69127-69127	BRULE
68651-68651	OSCEOLA	68783-68783	VERDIGRE	68929-68929	BLOOMINGTON	69128-69128	BUSHNELL
68652-68652	PETERSBURG	68784-68784	WAKEFIELD	68930-68930	BLUE HILL	69129-69129	CHAPPELL
68653-68653	PLATTE CENTER	68785-68785	WATERBURY	68932-68932	CAMPBELL	69130-69130	COZAD
68654-68654	POLK	68786-68786	WAUSA	68933-68933	CLAY CENTER	69131-69131	DALTON
68655-68655	PRIMROSE	68787-68787	WAYNE	68934-68934	DEWEESE	69132-69132	DICKENS
68658-68658	RISING CITY	68788-68788	WEST POINT	68935-68935	EDGAR	69133-69133	DIX
68659-68659	ROGERS	68789-68789	WINNETOON	68936-68936	EDISON	69134-69134	ELSIE
68660-68660	SAINT EDWARD	68790-68790	WINSIDE	68937-68937	ELWOOD	69135-69135	ELSMERE
68661-68661	SCHUYLER	68791-68791	WISNER	68938-68938	FAIRFIELD	69138-69138	GOTHENBURG
68662-68662	SHELBY	68792-68792	WYNOT	68939-68939	FRANKLIN	69140-69140	GRANT
68663-68663	SILVER CREEK	68801-68803	GRAND ISLAND	68940-68940	FUNK	69141-69141	GURLEY
68664-68664	SNYDER	68810-68810	ALDA	68941-68941	GLENVIL	69142-69142	HALSEY
68665-68665	SPALDING	68812-68812	AMHERST	68942-68942	GUIDE ROCK	69143-69143	HERSHEY
68666-68666	STROMSBURG	68813-68813	ANSELMO	68943-68943	HARDY	69144-69144	KEYSTONE
68667-68667	SURPRISE	68814-68814	ANSLEY	68944-68944	HARVARD	69145-69145	KIMBALL
68669-68669	ULYSSES	68815-68815	ARCADIA	68945-68945	HEARTWELL	69146-69146	LEMOYNE
68701-68702	NORFOLK	68816-68816	ARCHER	68946-68946	HENDLEY	69147-69147	LEWELLEN
68710-68710	ALLEN	68817-68817	ASHTON	68947-68947	HILDRETH	69148-69148	LISCO
68711-68711	AMELIA	68818-68818	AURORA	68948-68948	HOLBROOK	69149-69149	LODGEPOLE
68713-68713	ATKINSON	68819-68819	BERWYN	68949-68949	HOLDREGE	69150-69150	MADRID
68714-68714	BASSETT	68820-68820	BOELUS	68950-68950	HOLSTEIN	69151-69151	MAXWELL
68715-68715	BATTLE CREEK	68821-68821	BREWSTER	68952-68952	INAVALE	69152-69152	MULLEN
68716-68716	BEEMER	68822-68822	BROKEN BOW	68954-68954	INLAND	69153-69153	OGALLALA
68717-68717	BELDEN	68823-68823	BURWELL	68955-68955	JUNIATA	69154-69154	OSHKOSH
68718-68718	BLOOMFIELD	68824-68824	CAIRO	68956-68956	KENESAW	69155-69155	PAXTON
68719-68719	BRISTOW	68825-68825	CALLAWAY	68957-68957	LAWRENCE	69156-69156	POTTER
68720-68720	BRUNSWICK	68826-68826	CENTRAL CITY	68958-68958	LOOMIS	69157-69157	PURDUM
68722-68722	BUTTE	68827-68827	CHAPMAN	68959-68959	MINDEN	69160-69160	SIDNEY
68723-68723	CARROLL	68828-68828	COMSTOCK	68960-68960	NAPONEE	69161-69161	SENECA
68724-68724	CENTER	68831-68831	DANNEBROG	68961-68961	NELSON	69162-69162	SIDNEY
68725-68725	CHAMBERS	68832-68832	DONIPHAN	68963-68963	NORMAN	69163-69163	STAPLETON
68726-68726	CLEARWATER	68833-68833	DUNNING	68964-68964	OAK	69165-69165	SUTHERLAND
68727-68727	COLERIDGE	68834-68834	EDDYVILLE	68966-68966	ORLEANS	69166-69166	THEDFORD
68728-68728	CONCORD	68835-68835	ELBA	68967-68967	OXFORD	69167-69167	TRYON
68729-68729	CREIGHTON	68836-68836	ELM CREEK	68969-68969	RAGAN	69168-69168	VENANGO
68730-68730	CROFTON	68837-68837	ELYRIA	68970-68970	RED CLOUD	69169-69169	WALLACE
68731-68731	DAKOTA CITY	68838-68838	FARWELL	68971-68971	REPUBLICAN CITY	69170-69170	WELLFLEET
68732-68732	DIXON	68840-68840	GIBBON	68972-68972	RIVERTON	69171-69171	WILLOW ISLAND
68733-68733	EMERSON	68841-68841	GILTNER	68973-68973	ROSELAND	69190-69190	OSHKOSH
68734-68734	EMMET	68842-68842	GREELEY	68974-68974	RUSKIN	69201-69201	VALENTINE
68735-68735	EWING	68843-68843	HAMPTON	68975-68975	SARONVILLE	69210-69210	AINSWORTH
68736-68736	FORDYCE	68844-68844	HAZARD	68976-68976	SMITHFIELD	69211-69211	CODY
68737-68737	FOSTER	68846-68846	HORDVILLE	68977-68977	STAMFORD	69212-69212	CROOKSTON
68738-68738	HADAR	68847-68849	KEARNEY	68978-68978	SUPERIOR	69214-69214	JOHNSTOWN
68739-68739	HARTINGTON	68850-68850	LEXINGTON	68979-68979	SUTTON	69216-69216	KILGORE
68740-68740	HOSKINS	68852-68852	LITCHFIELD	68980-68980	TRUMBULL	69217-69217	LONG PINE
68741-68741	HUBBARD	68853-68853	LOUP CITY	68981-68981	UPLAND	69218-69218	MERRIMAN
68742-68742	INMAN	68854-68854	MARQUETTE	68982-68982	WILCOX	69219-69219	NENZEL
68743-68743	JACKSON	68855-68855	MASON CITY	69001-69001	MC COOK	69220-69220	SPARKS

69221-69221	WOOD LAKE	69339-69339	CRAWFORD	69349-69349	HENRY	69357-69357	MITCHELL
69301-69301	ALLIANCE	69340-69340	ELLSWORTH	69350-69350	HYANNIS	69358-69358	MORRILL
69331-69331	ANGORA	69341-69341	GERING	69351-69351	LAKESIDE	69360-69360	RUSHVILLE
69333-69333	ASHBY	69343-69343	GORDON	69352-69352	LYMAN	69361-69363	SCOTTSBLUFF
69334-69334	BAYARD	69345-69345	HARRISBURG	69353-69353	MCGREW	69365-69365	WHITECLAY
69335-69335	BINGHAM	69346-69346	HARRISON	69354-69354	MARSLAND	69366-69366	WHITMAN
69336-69336	BRIDGEPORT	69347-69347	HAY SPRINGS	69355-69355	MELBETA	69367-69367	WHITNEY
69337-69337	CHADRON	69348-69348	HEMINGFORD	69356-69356	MINATARE		

Nevada

General Help Numbers:

Governor's Office
Capitol Building   775-684-5670
Carson City, NV 89701   Fax 775-684-5683
http://gov.state.nv.us   8AM-5PM

Attorney General's Office
100 N Carson St   775-684-1100
Carson City, NV 89710   Fax 775-684-1108
http://ag.state.nv.us   8AM-5PM

State Court Administrator
Administrative Office of the Courts   775-684-1700
201 S Carson St, #250   Fax 775-684-1723
Carson City, NV 89701-4702   8AM-5PM
http://silver.state.nv.us/elec_judicial.htm

State Archives
100 N Stewart St   775-684-3360
Carson City, NV 89701-4285   Fax 775-684-3330
http://dmla.clan.lib.nv.us/docs/nsla   8AM-5PM M-F

State Specifics:

Capital:	Carson City
	Carson City County
Time Zone:	PST
Number of Counties:	17
Number of Filing Locations:	17
Population:	1,998,257
Web Site:	www.state.nv.us

State Agencies

Criminal Records

Nevada Highway Patrol, Record & ID Services, 808 W Nye Lane, Carson City, NV 89703; 775-687-1600, 775-687-1843 (Fax), 8AM-5PM.

http://nhp.state.nv.us

Indexing & Storage: Records are available from 1987 and are on computer.

Searching: This repository has maintains all "fingerprintable charges" meaning essentially all felony records and misdemeanor offenses like DUI and domestic violence. They will not release an arrest record without a disposition, unless a waiver is submitted. Include the following in your request-set of fingerprints, signed release, full name. DOB, SS#, sex and race are helpful. The following data is not released: sealed records or juvenile records.

Access by: mail, in person.

Fee & Payment: The search fee is $15.00 per individual. Fee payee: Nevada Highway Patrol. Prepayment required. Money order or cashier's check preferred. No credit cards accepted.

Mail search: Turnaround time: 10 days. No self addressed stamped envelope is required.

In person search: Records are still returned by mail.

Corporation Records
Limited Partnerships
Limited Liability Company Records
Limited Partnership Records

Secretary of State, Records, 101 N Carson, #3, Carson City, NV 89701-4786; 775-684-5708, 702-486-2880 (Las Vegas Ofc.:), 702-486-2888 (Las Vegas Ofc fax:), 775-684-5725 (Fax), 8AM-5PM.

http://www.sos.state.nv.us

Note: File are here, but records can also be looked up on computer at the Las Vegas office (555 E

Washington Ave., #2900, Las Vegas, NV 89101). To get forms, use their Document-on-Demand System 800-583-9486.

Indexing & Storage: Records are available since inception of laws. Old, inactive records are purged from computer and archived. New records are available for inquiry immediately. Records are indexed on microfiche, inhouse computer.

Searching: Fax searching is available only for state government agencies. Include the following in your request-full name of business, corporation file number. In addition to the articles of incorporation, corporation records include the following information: Annual Lists of Officers & Directors, Prior (merged) names, Inactive and Reserved names, and Resident Agent names.

Access by: mail, phone, in person, online.

Fee & Payment: The search fee is $20.00. The certification fee is $10.00. Copy fees are $1.00 per page. There are set fees for certain specific documents that range from $10.00 to $25.00. Fee payee: Secretary of State. Prepayment required. Personal checks accepted. Credit cards accepted: MasterCard, Visa.

Mail search: Turnaround time: 1 to 2 weeks. No self addressed stamped envelope is required.

Phone search: Staff will give status for corporations and partnerships, corporate officer names, and trademark information.

In person search: Information requests are available.

Online search: Online access is offered on the Internet site for no charge. You can search by corporate name, resident agent, corporate officers, or by file number.

Expedited service: Expedited service is available for mail, phone and in person searches. There is a $25.00 fee for overnight service of copies if 1 to 10 pages, and $50.00 if over 10 pages.

Assumed Name
Fictitious Name
Records not maintained by a state level agency.

Note: Records are at the county level.

Trademarks/Servicemarks

Secretary of State, Corporate Expedite Office, 555 E. Washington Ave, #2900, Las Vegas, NV 89101, 702-486-2885, 702-486-2888 (Fax), 8AM-5PM.

http://www.sos.state.nv.us

Note: Trademark files are kept here; however, they are on the same computer system as the Carson City office. They can do all of the same searches on corporate records as Carson City, except for making copies of actual documents in files.

Indexing & Storage: Records are available since inception.

Searching: The same search requirements apply here as in Carson City.

Access by: mail, phone, fax, in person.

Fee & Payment: Certified copies of trademarks are $10.00. Fee payee: NV Secretary of State. Prepayment required. Personal checks accepted. No credit cards accepted.

Mail search: Turnaround time: 1 to 2 weeks.

Phone search: Limited information is offered over the phone.

Fax search: Turnaround time is 1-2 weeks. Add $1.00 per page.

Uniform Commercial Code
Federal Tax Liens
State Tax Liens

UCC Department, Secretary of State, 200 N Carson St, Carson City, NV 89701-4069; 775-684-5708, 775-684-5630 (Fax), 8AM-5PM.

http://www.sos.state.nv.us

Note: At present, the only material about UCC on the web site is a form download. The agency plans a more extensive site in the future.

Indexing & Storage: Records are available from 1967 on both computer and microfilm.

Searching: As of 7/1/2001, use search request form UCC-11. Federal tax lien search must be requested separately. Tax liens on individuals are filed at the county level, on businesses here. With no state income tax, most state liens are on unemployment withholding. Include the following in your request-debtor name.

Access by: mail, fax, in person, online.

Fee & Payment: The fee for written request to search a debtor name is $20.00. Copies cost $1.00 per page. Fee payee: Secretary of State. Prepayment required. Personal checks accepted. Credit cards accepted: MasterCard, Visa.

Mail search: Turnaround time: 3 to 5 days. A self addressed stamped envelope is requested.

Fax search: See Expedited Services.

In person search: You may request information in person.

Online search: This is a PC dial-up system. The fee is $24.50 per hour or $10.75 per hour on an 800 number for unlimited access. There is a $50.00 minimum deposit. The system is up from 7 AM to 5 PM. Call 775-684-5704 and ask for Tom Horgan.

Expedited service: Expedited service is available for mail and fax searches. Turnaround time: 1 day. Add $25.00 per name.

Sales Tax Registrations
State does not impose sales tax.

Birth Certificates

Nevada Department of Health, Office of Vital Statistics, 505 E King St, Rm 102, Carson City, NV 89701-4749; 775-684-4242, 775-684-4280 (Message Phone), 775-684-4156 (Fax), 8AM-4PM.

Indexing & Storage: Records are available from 1911 to present. It takes 30 days of filing before new records are available for inquiry. Records are indexed on microfiche, index cards, inhouse computer, hard copy.

Searching: Birth and death records are considered confidential and not open to the general public. Include the following in your request-full name, names of parents, mother's maiden name, date of birth, place of birth, relationship to person of record, reason for information request. Parents' names are a must to get record.

Access by: mail, phone, fax, in person.

Fee & Payment: The fee for a verification only is $8.00. For a certified copy the fee is $11.00. If you

wish to purchase using a credit card, there is an additional $5.00 fee. Fee payee: Office of Vital Statistics. Prepayment required. Personal checks accepted. Credit cards accepted: MasterCard, Visa, AmEx, Discover.

Mail search: Turnaround time: 2 to 3 days. No self addressed stamped envelope is required.

Phone search: You must use a credit card.

Fax search: You must use a credit card.

In person search: Turnaround time 20 minutes.

Expedited service: Expedited service is available for mail, phone and fax searches. The overnight fee is $15.50. Use of credit card required.

Death Records

Nevada Department of Health, Office of Vital Statistics, 505 E King St, Rm 102, Carson City, NV 89701-4749; 775-684-4242, 775-684-4280 (Message Phone), 775-684-4156 (Fax), 8AM-4PM.

Indexing & Storage: Records are available from 1911 on. It takes 30 days of filing before new records are available for inquiry. Records are indexed on microfiche, index cards, inhouse computer, hard copy.

Searching: Records are considered confidential, need to state relationship. However, a verification printout with name, date, and location is available to the public. Include the following in your request-full name, date of death, place of death, relationship to person of record, reason for information request.

Access by: mail, phone, fax, in person.

Fee & Payment: The fee for a verification only is $8.00. A certified copy is $8.00. There is an additional $5.00 fee if using a credit card. Fee payee: Office of Vital Statistics. Prepayment required. Personal checks accepted. Credit cards accepted: MasterCard, Visa, AmEx, Discover.

Mail search: Turnaround time: 5 to 10 working days. No self addressed stamped envelope is required.

Phone search: Use of credit card required.

Fax search: Same search criteria.

In person search: Turnaround time is 20 minutes.

Expedited service: Expedited service is available for mail, phone and fax searches. Records are sent overnight at expense of requester, usually $15.50. A credit card is required.

Marriage Certificates
Divorce Records
Access to Records is Restricted

Nevada Department of Health, Office of Vital Statistics, 505 E King St, Rm 102, Carson City, NV 89701-4749; 775-684-4481.

Note: Marriage and Divorce records are found at county of issue. However, the agency has an index and will relate the county and date of the event. The fee is $8.00. Call (775) 684-4242.

Workers' Compensation Records

Employers Insurance Co of NV, Workers Compensation Records, 515 E Musser St, Carson City, NV 89714; 775-886-1000, 8AM-5PM.

http://www.employersinsco.com

Note: Effective 01/01/00, the state of Nevada privatized the business of workers' compensation insurance. The state agency formally named State Industrial Insurance System became a private company. This company holds the records from the state agency.

Indexing & Storage: Records are available from 1940's on. It takes 1 week before new records are available for inquiry. Records are indexed on microfilm, inhouse computer, file folders.

Searching: Must have a signed release form from claimant and you must specify what you want from the file. Older records are kept on microfilm, the records on the in-house computer are for general information only. Include the following in your request-claimant name, Social Security Number, claim number, date of accident.

Access by: mail, fax, in person.

Fee & Payment: Fee is $.20 per page if copies are over 20 pages. Fee payee: Employers Insurance CO of NV. Personal checks accepted. No credit cards accepted.

Mail search: Turnaround time: 30 days. A self addressed stamped envelope is requested.

Fax search: Same criteria as mail searches.

In person search: By going in person, you will only reduce the mail time.

Driver Records

Department of Motor Vehicles and Public Safety, Records Section, 555 Wright Way, Carson City, NV 89711-0250; 775-684-4590, 800-992-7945 (In-state), 8AM-5PM.

http://www.nevadadmv.state.nv.us/nvdl.htm

Note: Copies of citations may be obtained at the same address. There is no fee when requesting your own citation, otherwise the fee is $8.

Indexing & Storage: Records are available for 3 years. Non-moving violations are not listed on the driving record for non-CDL drivers. Nevada complies with the Driver's Privacy Protection Act, so personal information is available only to specific users. Records are computer indexed since 1980.

Searching: Authorized users may establish an account by completing the appropriate application. Call 775-684-4590 to request an application. The driver's license number, or name and DOB are needed for a request. The SSN is helpful for searching, but will not be released on the record. Accidents do not appear on the record.

Access by: mail, phone.

Fee & Payment: The fee is $5.00 per record. Fee payee: Nevada Department of Motor Vehicles. Prepayment required. Personal checks accepted. No credit cards accepted.

Mail search: Turnaround time: 10 days. Your request must be on department approved forms.No self addressed stamped envelope is required.

Phone search: Phone-in requesters must be pre-approved, are assigned a five-digit account number and can request up to five records at one time over the phone. Call 775-684-4590 for more information. There is an in-state toll free line at 800-992-7945.

Other access: Overnight magnetic tape requesting is available for high volume users.

Vehicle Ownership
Vehicle Identification

Department of Motor Vehicles and Public Safety, Motor Vehicle Record Section, 555 Wright Way, Carson City, NV 89711-0250; 775-684-4590, 775-684-4740 (Fax), 8AM-5PM.

http://www.nevadadmv.state.nv.us/nvreg.htm

Indexing & Storage: Records are available for the present on computer and on microfilm back to 1980.

Searching: Social Security Numbers, withdrawal action, accidents, and information connected to a license plate are not released to the general public. Nevada enacted its version of the Driver's Privacy Protection Act, restricting access to certain permissible users. Requesters must show a legal right to the information, otherwise, records are confidential. Forms are available at the web site.

Access by: mail, phone.

Fee & Payment: The cost is $5.00 per record. Fee payee: Nevada Department of Motor Vehicles. Prepayment required. Personal checks accepted. No credit cards accepted.

Mail search: Turnaround time: 10 days. Be sure to give as much specific information as possible. Your request must be on department-approved forms.No self addressed stamped envelope is required.

Phone search: Phone-in service is offered in the same manner as driving record requests.

Other access: Database is available for sale to permissible users under DPPA at costs varying from $500 to $2,500.

Accident Reports

Department of Motor Vehicles, Highway Patrol Division, 555 Wright Way, Carson City, NV 89711; 775-684-4870, 775-684-4879 (Fax), 8AM-5PM.

http://ps.state.nv.us/index.htm

Indexing & Storage: Records are available from 1995 to 1997 at this office. Records are computer indexed. Records are indexed on inhouse computer.

Searching: Requests must be in writing. You may use the department's form. Include the following in your request-full name, date of accident, location of accident, report number. For any accidents after 1997, the reports will be found at a regional office (Las Vegas 702-486-4100; Reno 775-688-2500; or Elko 775-738-8035) associated with where the accidents occurred. Call for further information.

Access by: mail, fax, in person.

Fee & Payment: The fee is $3.50 per report (up to 10 pages), and report(s) will not be mailed until payment has been received. Fee payee: Nevada Highway Patrol. Prepayment required. Personal checks accepted. No credit cards accepted.

Mail search: Turnaround time: 3 days. A self addressed stamped envelope is requested.

Fax search: Fax searching available.

In person search: Turnaround time is immediate if the record is on file.

Vessel Ownership
Vessel Registration

Division of Wildlife, Boat Registration, 1100 Valley Rd, Reno, NV 89512-2815; 775-688-1511, 8AM-5PM M-F.

http://nevadadivisionofwildlife.org

Indexing & Storage: Records are available from 1972 to the present and are indexed on computer. All boats must be registered.

Searching: To search, one of the following is required: hull ID #, boat #, or name. The following data is not released: Social Security Numbers.

Access by: mail, in person.

Fee & Payment: The fee is $5.00 per boat or person, which includes 1 computer print-out. Photocopies cost $1.00 per page. Fee payee: NDOW. Prepayment required. Cash is accepted from in person searchers only. No credit cards accepted.

Mail search: Turnaround time: 4 days. No self addressed stamped envelope is required.

In person search: Turnaround time can be immediate if search is not lengthy.

Other access: Information is available on magnetic tape, labels, and printed lists. Fees depend on media type, can be up to $750.

Legislation Records

Nevada Legislature, 401 S Carson St, Carson City, NV 89701-4747; 775-684-6827 (Bill Status Only), 775-684-6800 (Main Number), 775-684-6835 (Publications), 775-684-6600 (Fax), 8AM-5PM.

http://www.leg.state.nv.us

Note: If you want to order copies, call the publications number.

Indexing & Storage: Records are available from 1915 to present. Records are computer indexed from 1985 to present, and on microfiche from 1967 to present.

Searching: Include the following in your request-bill number, year.

Access by: mail, phone, fax, in person, online.

Fee & Payment: No charge for one or two bills. If you request more than two, the fee varies by page numbers requested, You may request any search by mail or telephone. The agency will determine fee, but will not release copies until paid. Fee payee: Legislative Council Bureau. Prepayment required. Personal checks accepted. Credit cards accepted: MasterCard, Visa.

Mail search: Turnaround time: 1 to 2 days. Information requests are available.No self addressed stamped envelope is required.

Phone search: You may request bills by phone.

Fax search: Turnaround time is generally in 1 to 2 days.

In person search: You may request bills in person.

Online search: Bills and bill status information is available via this agency's web site. Legislative bills, hearings, journals are searchable online for years 1997, 1999, and 2001.

Expedited service: Expedited service is available for mail and phone searches. You must provide an account number with a shipper.

Voter Registration
Records not maintained by a state level agency.

Note: Records are open to the public at the county level. All data is released except for SSNs.

GED Certificates
Department of Education, State GED Administration-Transcripts, 700 E 5th Street, Carson City, NV 89701; 775-687-9104, 775-687-9114 (Fax), 8AM-5PM.

http://www.nde.state.nv.us

Indexing & Storage: Records are available from 1954 to present, for GED. This agencies also holds many other education-based records including military, federal prison, etc.

Searching: Include the following in your request-signed release, date of birth, Social Security Number. There is a possibility that this office may not have the tests results, so it is important to also submit the location and year of the test.

Access by: mail, fax, in person.

Fee & Payment: There is no fee.

Mail search: Turnaround time: 7 to 10 days.

Fax search: Same criteria as mail searching.

In person search: Searching is available in person.

Hunting License Information
Fishing License Information
Division of Wildlife, 1100 Valley Rd, Reno, NV 89512-2817; 775-688-1500, 775-688-1509 (Fax), 8AM-5PM.

http://www.nevadadivisionofwildlife.org

Indexing & Storage: Records are available from 1976 to present on microfiche.

Searching: Include the following in your request-full name, date of birth, Social Security Number. The following data is not released: Social Security Numbers or telephone numbers.

Access by: mail.

Fee & Payment: The fee is $5.00 per name per year searched. Fee payee: NDOW Prepayment required with guaranteed funds. No credit cards accepted.

Mail search: Turnaround time: 3 to 4 working days. No self addressed stamped envelope is required.

Other access: The Division offers mailing lists, labels, magnetic tapes of hunting and fishing license holders for fees ranging from $150 to $365.

Nevada State Licensing Agencies

Licenses Searchable Online

Architect #02	http://nsbaidrd.state.nv.us
Carpentry Contractor #46	http://nscb.tecxprs.com
Chiropractor #03	www.state.nv.us/chirobd/home.htm
Dental Hygienist #04	www.nvdentalboard.org/databaseRDH.html
Dentist #04	www.nvdentalboard.org/databaseDDS.html
Engineer #19	http://nevada7.natinfo.net/boe/rost_home.htm
Floor & Carpet Layer #46	http://nscb.tecxprs.com
Glazier Contractor #46	http://nscb.tecxprs.com
Heating & Air Conditioning Mechanic #46	http://nscb.tecxprs.com
Insulation Installer Contractor #46	http://nscb.tecxprs.com
Interior Designer #02	http://nsbaidrd.state.nv.us
Lobbyist #27	www.lobbyistdirectory.com/Nevada/NEVLOB.htm
Optometrist #00	www.odfinder.org/LicSearch.asp
Painter #46	http://nscb.tecxprs.com
Painter/Paper Hanger #46	http://nscb.tecxprs.com
Plasterer/Drywall Installer #46	http://nscb.tecxprs.com
Plumber #46	http://nscb.tecxprs.com
Residential Designer #02	http://nsbaidrd.state.nv.us
Roofer #46	http://nscb.tecxprs.com
Surveyor #19	http://nevada7.natinfo.net/boe/rost_home.htm
Water Well Driller #30	http://ndwr.state.nv.us/Engineering/welldrill.htm
Well Driller/Monitor #30	http://ndwr.state.nv.us/Engineering/welldrill.htm

Licensing Quick Finder

Acupuncturist #14	702-486-7280
Adult Day Care #22	775-687-4475
Adult Group Care #22	775-687-4475
Aesthetician #38	702-486-6542
Alcohol & Drug Abuse Center #22	775-687-4475
Alcohol & Drug Abuse Counselor #22	775-687-4475
Ambulance Attendant #22	775-687-4475
Ambulance Permit #22	775-687-4475
Animal Technician #21	775-688-1788
Announcer, Athletic Event (Ring) #35	702-486-2575
Appraiser (MVD) #24	702-486-4009
Architect #02	702-486-7300
Athletic Promoter (Professional & Amateur) #35	702-486-2575
Attorney #44	702-382-2200
Audiologist #31	775-857-3500
Auditor #01	775-786-0231
Barber #45	702-456-4769
Blood Gas Technician/Technologist#22	775-687-4475
Boxer #35	702-486-2575
Bus Driver #25	775-684-4590
Carpentry Contractor #46	702-486-1100
Casino General Manager #36	775-687-6520
Cemetery #07	702-646-6860
Chiropractor #03	775-688-1919
Claims Adjuster #24	702-486-4009
Clinical Laboratory Technologist #22	775-687-4475
Cosmetologist #38	702-486-6542
Court Reporter, Certified #23	702-384-1663
Crematorium #07	702-646-6860
Dental Hygienist #04	702-486-7044
Dentist #04	702-486-7044
Director (Medical Laboratory) #22	775-687-4475

Driller, Rotary #29	775-687-3861
Drug Wholesalers/Distributor #16	775-850-1440
Electrologist #38	702-486-6542
Embalmer #07	702-646-6860
Emergency Care Center, Independent #22	775-687-4475
Emergency Medical Technician #22	775-687-4475
Engineer #19	775-688-1231
Environmental Health Specialist #42	775-328-2422
ESRD #22	775-687-4475
Euthanasia Technician #21	775-688-1788
Exempt Laboratory #22	775-687-4475
Financial Advisor (Investment Advisor) #40	702-486-2440
First Responder EMT #22	775-687-4475
Fishing Guide #26	775-688-1541
Floor & Carpet Layer #46	702-486-1100
Funeral Director #07	702-646-6860
Fur Dealer #26	775-688-1541
Gaming #36	775-687-6570
Gaming Device Mfg./Distributor #36	775-687-6570
Gaming License by Company #36	775-687-6570
Glazier Contractor #46	702-486-1100
Groundskeeper/Gardener #28	775-688-1182x243
Guard Dog Handler #39	775-684-1147
Hair Stylist (Designer) #38	702-486-6542
Health Clinic, Rural #22	775-687-4475
Hearing Aid Specialist #08	702-571-9000
Heating & Air Conditioning Mechanic #46	702-486-1100
Histotechnologist #22	775-687-4475
Histotogic Technician #22	775-687-4475
Home Health Agency #22	775-687-4475

Homeopathic Physician/Assistant #09	702-451-3332
Homeopathic Practitioner, Advanced #09	702-451-3332
Hospice #22	775-687-4475
Hospital #22	775-687-4475
IC Emergency Center #22	775-687-4475
Insulation Installer Contractor #46	702-486-1100
Insurance Agent #24	702-486-4009
Interior Designer #02	702-486-7300
Intermediate Care Facility for the Mentally Retarded #22	775-687-4475
Intermedical Care Facility #22	775-687-4475
Investment Advisor #40	702-486-2440
Kickboxer #35	702-486-2575
Laboratory (Medical) #22	775-687-4475
Laboratory Assistant/Blood Gas Assistant #22	775-687-4475
Laboratory Certification #22	775-687-4475
Laboratory Office Assistant #22	775-687-4475
Landscape Architect #10	775-626-0604
Lobbyist #27	775-684-6800
LPG-Liquefied Petroleum Dist./Technician #33	775-687-4890
Manicurist #38	702-486-6542
Marriage & Family Therapist #32	702-486-7388
Medical Doctor #11	775-688-2559
Medical Technician #22	775-687-4475
Mobile Home Dealer/Limited Dealer#34	702-486-4590
Mobile Home Installer/Mfg. #34	702-486-4590
Mobile Home Salesman #34	702-486-4590
Mobile Home Serviceman/Limited Serviceman #34	702-486-4590
Mobile/Manufactured Home Rebuilder #34	

...........................702-486-4590	
Notary Public #41...........................775-684-5749	
Nurse #16...........................775-850-1440	
Nursing Care (Skilled) Facility #22.........775-687-4475	
Nursing Facility #22...........................775-687-4475	
Nursing Home Administrator #49..........702-486-5445	
Nursing Pool Operator #22...................775-687-4475	
Occupational Therapist/Assistant #12...775-857-1700	
Optician #05...........................775-853-1421	
Optician Apprentice #05.....................775-853-1421	
Optometrist #00...........................775-883-8367	
Osteopathic Physician #15...................702-732-2147	
Osteopathic Physician Assistant #15....702-732-2147	
Painter #46...........................702-486-1100	
Painter/Paper Hanger #46...................702-486-1100	
Pathologist Assistant #22....................775-687-4475	
Patrol Company, Private #39................775-684-1147	
Patrol Man, Private #39......................775-684-1147	
Pest Control #28...........................775-688-1182x252	
Pesticide, Restricted Use #28.......775-688-1182x251	
Pharmacist/Pharmacy Technician #16..775-850-1440	
Pharmacy #16...........................775-850-1440	

Physical Therapist #17.....................702-876-5535	
Physical Therapist Assistant #17..........702-876-5535	
Physician Assistant #11......................775-688-2559	
Plasterer/Drywall Installer #46.............702-486-1100	
Plumber #46...........................702-486-1100	
Podiatrist #18...........................775-829-8066	
Polygraph Examiner #39.....................775-684-1147	
Private Investigator #39......................775-684-1147	
Process Server #39...........................775-684-1147	
Psychologist #20...........................775-688-1268	
Public Accountant-CPA #01.................775-786-0231	
Racing #37...........................775-687-6500	
Real Estate Broker #50......................702-486-4033	
Real Estate Salesperson #50...............702-486-4033	
Referee/Judge/Timekeeper #35............702-486-2575	
Rehabilitation Service #22...................775-687-4475	
Repossessor #39...........................775-684-1147	
Residential Designer #02.....................702-486-7300	
Roofer #46...........................702-486-1100	
Sanitarian, Public #42.........................775-328-2418	
School Administrator #47.....................702-486-6458	
School Counselor #47.........................702-486-6458	

School Librarian #47...........................702-486-6458	
School Program Administrator #47.......702-486-6458	
Scientific Collection Permit #26.............775-688-1541	
Securities Branch Office #40................702-486-2440	
Securities Broker/Dealer #40...............702-486-2440	
Securities Registration #40...................702-486-2440	
Securities Sales Representative #40.....702-486-2440	
Slot Route Operator #36......................775-687-6570	
Social Worker #06...........................702-688-2555	
Speech Pathologist/Audiologist #31......775-857-3500	
Supervisory Medical Technology, General #22...........	
...........................775-687-4475	
Surgical Center, Ambulatory #22..........775-687-4475	
Surveyor #19...........................775-688-1231	
Taxi Driver #48...........................702-486-6532	
Teacher #47...........................702-486-6458	
Veterinarian #21...........................775-688-1788	
Water Well Driller #30.........................775-687-3861	
Well Driller/Monitor #30......................775-687-3861	
Wrestler #35...........................702-486-2575	

Licensing Agency Information

#01 Board of Accountancy, 200 S Virginia St, #670, Reno, NV 89501; 775-786-0231, Fax: 775-786-0234.
www.state.nv.us/accountancy

#02 Interior & Residential Design, 2080 E Flamingo Rd, #225, Las Vegas, NV 89119; 702-486-7300, Fax: 702-486-7304.
http://nsbaidrd.state.nv.us/
Direct web site URL to search for licensees: http://nsbaidrd.state.nv.us/. You can search online using alphabetical lists

#03 Board of Chiropractic Examiners, 4600 Kietzke Ln, M, #245, Reno, NV 89502; 775-688-1919, Fax: 775-688-1920.
www.state.nv.us/chirobd/home.htm
Direct web site URL to search for licensees: www.state.nv.us/chirobd/home.htm. You can search online using name. Licensee data is available in PDF format.

#04 Board of Dental Examiners, 2295 Renaissance Dr, #B, Las Vegas, NV 89119-6171; 800-337-3926 or 702-486-7044, Fax: 702-486-7046.
www.nvdentalboard.org
Direct web site URL to search for licensees: www.nvdentalboard.org/DatabaseIndex.html. You can search online using search the alphabetical list

#05 Board of Dispensing Opticians, PO Box 19625, Reno, NV 89511-0868; 775-883-8367, Fax: 775-853-1408.
www.nvbdo.state.nv.us

#06 Board of Examiners for Social Workers, 4600 Kietzke Ln, Bldg C, Rm 121, Reno, NV 89502; 775-688-2555, Fax: 775-688-2557.

#07 Board of Funeral Directors & Embalmers, 4894 Lone Mt Rd PMB186, Las Vegas, NV 89130; 702-646-6860, Fax: 702-648-5858.
http://funeral.state.nv.us

#08 Board of Hearing Aid Specialists, PO Box 18068, Reno, NV 89511-0068; 702-571-9000.

#09 Board of Homeopathic Medical Examiners, 4475 S Pecos Rd, Las Vegas, NV 89121; 702-451-3332, Fax: 702-451-3332.
www.nvbhme.com

#10 Board of Landscape Architecture, PO Box 51780, Sparks, NV 89435; 775-626-0604, Fax: 775-626-0604.

#11 Board of Medical Examiners, 1105 Terminal Way, #301, Reno, NV 89510; 775-688-2559, Fax: 775-688-2321.
www.state.nv.us/medical/

#12 Board of Occupational Therapy, PO Box 70220, Reno, NV 89570-0220; 775-857-1700, Fax: 775-857-2121.
www.nvot.org

#14 Board of Oriental Medicine, 900 E Karen, Ste. B203, Las Vegas, NV 89109; 702-486-7280.
www.oriental_medicine.state.nv.us

#15 Board of Osteopathic Medicine, 2950 E Flamingo, #E-3, Las Vegas, NV 89121; 702-732-2147, Fax: 702-732-2079.
www.state.nv.us/osteo

#16 Board of Pharmacy, 555 Double Eagle Ct #1100, Reno, NV 89511-8991; 775-850-1440, Fax: 775-850-1444.
www.state.nv.us/pharmacy/

#17 Board of Physical Therapy Examiners, PO Box 81467, Las Vegas, NV 89180-1467; 702-876-5535, Fax: 702-876-2097.

#18 Board of Podiatry, PO Box 12215, Reno, NV 89510-2215; 775-829-8066, Fax: 775-829-8069.
http://podiatry.state.nv.us/

#19 Board of Professional Engineers & Land Surveyors, 1755 E Plumb Ln, #135, Reno, NV 89502; 775-688-1231, Fax: 775-688-2991.
www.state.nv.us/boe
Direct web site URL to search for licensees: http://nevada7.natinfo.net/boe/rost_home.htm. You can search online using name.

#20 Board of Psychological Examiners, PO Box 2286 (275 Hill St, #246), Reno, NV 89505-2286; 775-688-1268, Fax: 775-688-1272.

#21 Board of Veterinary Medical Examiners, 4600 Kietzke, Bldg O, #265, Reno, NV 89502; 775-688-1788, Fax: 775-688-1808.
www.state.nv.us/vet/

#22 Bureau of Licensure & Certification, 1550 College Parkway #158, Carson City, NV 89710; 775-687-4475, Fax: 775-687-6588.

#23 Certified Court Reporters Board, 3355 Spring Mountain Rd #2, Las Vegas, NV 89102-8631; 702-384-1663, Fax: 702-876-9249.

#24 Department of Business & Industry, 2501 E Sahara Ave, #302, Las Vegas, NV 89104; 702-486-4009, Fax: 702-486-4007.
www.doi.state.nv.us

#25 Department of Motor Vehicles & Public Safety, 555 Wright Way, Carson City, NV 89711-0250; 775-684-4590, Fax: 775-684-4740.
http://nevadadmv.state.nv.us

#26 Wildlife Commission, 1100 Valley Rd, Reno, NV 89520; 775-688-1530, Fax: 775-688-1551.
www.nevadadivisionofwildlife.org/nwc/index.htm

#27 Director of Legislative Counsel Bureau, 401 S Carson, Carson City, NV 89701-4747; 775-684-6800, Fax: 775-684-6600.
www.leg.state.nv.us/lcb/admin/lobbyist.htm

#28 Department of Agriculture, 350 Capitol Hill, Reno, NV 89502-2923; 775-688-1180, Fax: 775-688-1178.
www.state.nv.us/b&i/ad/chem/index.htm

#29 Division of Water Resources, 123 W Nye Lane, #246, Carson City, NV 89706; 775-687-4380, Fax: 775-687-6972.
http://ndwr.state.nv.us

#30 Division of Water Resources, 123 W Nye Ln, Capitol Complex Rm 246, Carson City, NV 89706-0818; 775-687-3861, Fax: 775-687-1393.
http://ndwr.state.nv.us
Direct web site URL to search for licensees: http://ndwr.state.nv.us/Engineering/welldrill.htm. You can search online using name, license number, or city.

#31 Examiners for Audiology & Speech Pathology, Redfield Bldg #152, Reno, NV 89557; 775-784-4887, Fax: 775-857-2121.
http://speech_pathology.state.nv.us

#32 Board of Examiners of Marriage & Family Therapists, PO Box 72758, Las Vegas, NV 89170; 702-486-7388, Fax: 702-434-7181.

#33 Liquefied Petroleum Gas Regulation Board, PO Box 338 (106 E Adams, Rm 216), Carson City, NV 89702; 775-687-4890, Fax: 775-687-3956.
www.state.nv.us/lpg

#34 Attn: Gisele Jordan, Licensing Officer, 2501 E Sahara Ave, #205, Las Vegas, NV 89104; 702-486-4135, Fax: 702-486-4309.

#35 Athletic Commission, 555 E Washington St #1500, Las Vegas, NV 89101; 702-486-2575, Fax: 702-486-2577.
www.state.nv.us/b&i/ac

#36 Tax & License Division, PO Box 8003, Carson City, NV 89702; 775-486-2000, Fax: 775-687-5817.
www.state.nv.us/gaming

#37 Gaming Control Board, PO Box 8003, Carson City, NV 89702; 775-687-6500.
www.state.nv.us/gaming

#38 Board of Cosmetology, 1785 E Sahara Ave, #255, Las Vegas, NV 89104; 702-486-6542, Fax: 702-369-8064.

#39 Office of the Attorney General, 100 N Carson St, Carson City, NV 89701; 775-684-1147, Fax: 775-684-1108.
http://aq.state.nv.us/pilb

#40 Office of the Secretary of State, 555 E Washington Av #5200, Las Vegas, NV 89101; 702-486-2440, Fax: 702-486-2452.
www.sos.state.nv.us/securities

#41 Office of the Secretary of State, 101 N Carson St, Carson City, NV 89710-4786; 775-684-5708, Fax: 775-684-5725.
http://sos.state.nv.us/notary/

#42 Environmental Health Services, PO Box 1130 (1001 E 9th St), Reno, NV 89520; 775-328-2434, Fax: 775-328-6176.

#44 State Bar of Nevada, 600 E Charleston Blvd, Las Vegas, NV 89104; 702-382-2200, Fax: 702-385-2878.
www.nvbar.org

#45 Barbers' Health & Sanitation Board, 4710 E Flamingo Rd, Las Vegas, NV 89121; 702-731-1966, Fax: 702-456-1948.

#46 Contractors' Board, 4220 S Maryland Pky, Bldg D, #800, Las Vegas, NV 89119; 702-486-1100, Fax: 702-486-1190.
www.state.nv.us/nscb

#47 Department of Education, 1820 E Sahara, #205, Las Vegas, NV 89104; 702-486-6458, Fax: 702-687-9101.
www.nde.state.nv.us/licensure/index.html

#48 Taxicab Authority, 1785 E Sahara Ave #200, Las Vegas, NV 89104; 702-486-6532, Fax: 702-486-7350.
www.state.nv.us/b&i/ta/

#49 Board of Examiners for Long Term Care Administrators, 6010 W Cheyenne Ave #970, Las Vegas, NV 89108; 702-486-5445.

Nevada Federal Courts

The following list indicates the district and division name for each county in the state. If the bankruptcy court location is different from the district court, then the location of the bankruptcy court appears in parentheses.

County/Court Cross Reference

Carson City	Reno	Lincoln	Las Vegas
Churchill	Reno	Lyon	Reno
Clark	Las Vegas	Mineral	Reno
Douglas	Reno	Nye	Las Vegas
Elko	Reno	Pershing	Reno
Esmeralda	Las Vegas	Storey	Reno
Eureka	Reno	Washoe	Reno
Humboldt	Reno	White Pine	Reno
Lander	Reno		

US District Court

District of Nevada

Las Vegas Division Room 4425, 300 Las Vegas Blvd S, Las Vegas, NV 89101 (Courier Address: Use mail address for courier delivery), 702-464-5400.

http://www.nvd.uscourts.gov

Counties: Clark, Esmeralda, Lincoln, Nye.

Indexing/Storage: Cases are indexed by defendant and plaintiff as well as by case number. New cases are available in the index 2 weeks after filing date. A computer index is maintained. Open records are located at this court.

Fee & Payment: The fee is $20.00 per item (one party name or case number). Payment may be made by money order, cashier check, personal check. Prepayment is required. Payee: Clerk, US District Court. Certification fee: $7.00 per document. Copy fee: $.50 per page.

Phone Search: Only docket information available by phone.

Mail Search: A stamped self addressed envelope is not required.

In Person: In person searching is available.

PACER: There is no PACER access to this court.

Reno Division Room 301, 400 S Virginia St, Reno, NV 89501 (Courier Address: Use mail address for courier delivery), 775-686-5800, Fax: 702-686-5851.

http://www.nvd.uscourts.gov

Counties: Carson City, Churchill, Douglas, Elko, Eureka, Humboldt, Lander, Lyon, Mineral, Pershing, Storey, Washoe, White Pine.

Indexing/Storage: Cases are indexed by defendant and plaintiff as well as by case number. New cases are available in the index 1-2 days after filing date. A computer index is maintained. Records are also indexed on microfiche. Open records are located at this court.

Fee & Payment: The fee is $20.00 per item (one party name or case number). Payment may be

made by money order, cashier check, personal check. Prepayment is required. Payee: Clerk, US District Court. Certification fee: $7.00 per document. Copy fee: $.50 per page.

Phone Search: Only docket information available by phone.

Fax Search: The cost for a fax search is $15.00 per name to be certified. Will fax results for $.50 per page prepaid.

Mail Search: A stamped self addressed envelope is not required.

In Person: In person searching is available.

PACER: There is no PACER access to this court.

US Bankruptcy Court

District of Nevada

Las Vegas Division Room 2130, 300 Las Vegas Blvd S, Las Vegas, NV 89101 (Courier Address: Use mail address for courier delivery), 702-388-6257.

http://www.nvb.uscourts.gov

Counties: Clark, Esmeralda, Lincoln, Nye.

Indexing/Storage: Cases are indexed by debtor as well as by case number. New cases are available in the index 24 hours after filing date. Both computer and card indexes are maintained. Open records are located at this court.

Fee & Payment: The fee is $20.00 per item (one party name or case number). Payment may be made by money order, cashier check, personal check. Debtor's checks are not accepted. Payee: Clerk, US Bankruptcy Court. Certification fee: $7.00 per document. Copy fee: $.50 per page. You are allowed to make your own copies. These copies cost $.25 per page.

Phone Search: An automated voice case information service (VCIS) is available. Call VCIS at 800-314-3436 or 702-388-6708.

Mail Search: Always enclose a stamped self addressed envelope.

In Person: In person searching is available.

PACER: Sign-up number is 800-676-6856. Access fee is. Case records are available back to September 1993. Records are purged every 16 months. New civil records are available online after 1 day. PACER is available online at http://pacer.nvd.uscourts.gov.

Other Online Access: Search records online using RACER. Currently the system is free and requires free registration. Access RACER via the court main web site, above.

Reno-Northern Division Room 1109, 300 Booth St, Reno, NV 89509 (Courier Address: Use mail address for courier delivery), 775-784-5559.

http://www.nvb.uscourts.gov

Counties: Carson City, Churchill, Douglas, Elko, Eureka, Humboldt, Lander, Lyon, Mineral, Pershing, Storey, Washoe, White Pine.

Indexing/Storage: Cases are indexed by debtor as well as by case number. New cases are available in the index 24 hours after filing date. A computer index is maintained. Open records are located at this court.

Fee & Payment: The fee is $20.00 per item (one party name or case number). Payment may be made by money order, cashier check, personal check. Debtor's checks are not accepted. Payee: Clerk, US Bankruptcy Court. Certification fee: $7.00 per document. Copy fee: $.50 per page.

Phone Search: An automated voice case information service (VCIS) is available. Call VCIS at 800-314-3436 or 702-388-6708.

Mail Search: Always enclose a stamped self addressed envelope.

In Person: In person searching is available.

PACER: Sign-up number is 800-676-6856. Access fee is. Case records are available back to September 1993. Records are purged every 16 months. New civil records are available online after 1 day. PACER is available online at http://pacer.nvb.uscourts.gov.

Other Online Access: Search records online using RACER. Currently the system is free and requires free registration. Access RACER via the court main web site, above.

Nevada County Courts

Court	Jurisdiction	No. of Courts	How Organized
District Courts*	General	17	9 Districts
Justice Courts*	Limited	45	56 Townships
Municipal Courts	Municipal	19	19 Incorporated Cities/Towns

* Profiled in this Sourcebook.

Court	Tort	Contract	Real Estate	Min. Claim	Max. Claim	Small Claims	Estate	Eviction	Domestic Relations
District Courts*	X	X	X	$7500	No Max		X		X
Justice Courts*	X	X	X	$0	$7500	$3500		X	
Municipal Courts	X	X	X	$0	$3500	$3500			

Court	Felony	Misdemeanor	DWI/DUI	Preliminary Hearing	Juvenile
District Courts*	X	X	X		X
Justice Courts*		X	X	X	
Municipal Courts					

ADMINISTRATION   Supreme Court of Nevada, Administrative Office of the Courts, Capitol Complex, 201 S Carson Street, Carson City, Nevada, 89701; 775-684-1700, Fax: 775-684-1723. http://silver.state.nv.us/elec_judicial.htm

COURT STRUCTURE   There are 17 District Courts within 9 judicial districts. The 45 Justice Courts are named for the township of jurisdiction. Note that, due to their small populations, some townships no longer have Justice Courts. Probate is handled by the District Courts.

ONLINE ACCESS   Some Nevada Courts have internal online computer systems, but only Clark County has online access available to the public. A statewide court automation system is being implemented.

ADDITIONAL INFORMATION   Many Nevada Justice Courts are small and have very few records. Their hours of operation vary widely and contact is difficult. It is recommended that requesters call ahead for information prior to submitting a written request or attempting an in-person retrieval.

Carson City

1st Judicial District Court 885 E Musser St #3031, Carson City, NV 89701-4775; 775-887-2082; Fax: 775-887-2177. Hours: 9AM-5PM (PST). *Felony, Gross Misdemeanor, Civil Actions Over $7,500, Probate.*

Note: The Justice Courts retain records for minor misdemeanors.

Civil Records: Access: Mail, in person. Only the court performs in person searches; visitors may not. Search fee: $1.00 per name per year. Required to search: name, years to search. Civil cases indexed by defendant, plaintiff. Civil records on computer from 1988, on microfiche and archives from beginning of court.

Criminal Records: Access: Mail, in person. Only the court performs in person searches; visitors may not. Search fee: $1.00 per name per year. Required to search: name, years to search. Criminal records on computer from 1988, on microfiche and archives from beginning of court.

General Information: No sealed or juvenile records released. SASE required. Turnaround time 2-7 days.

Copy fee: $1.00 per page. Certification fee: $5.00. Fee payee: Carson City. Personal checks accepted. Personal check accepted with check guarantee card only. Prepayment is required.

Justice Court Dept II 885 E Musser St, #7, Carson City, NV 89701; 775-887-2275; Fax: 775-887-2297. Hours: 8:30AM-5PM (PST). *Civil Actions Under $7,500, Eviction, Small Claims.*

Civil Records: Access: Mail, in person. Only the court performs in person searches; visitors may not. Search fee: $1.00 per name per year. Required to search: name, years to search. Civil cases indexed by defendant, plaintiff. Civil records on computer alpha index from 1991.

General Information: No sealed, sexual victims, juvenile records released. SASE required. Turnaround time 1 week. Copy fee: $.30 per page. Certification fee: $3.00. Fee payee: Carson City. Personal checks accepted. Prepayment is required.

Justice Court Dept I 885 E Musser St #2007, Carson City, NV 89701-4775; 775-887-2121; Fax: 775-

887-2297. Hours: 8:30AM-5PM (PST). *Felony, Gross Misdemeanor, Misdemeanor.*

Criminal Records: Access: Mail, in person. Only the court performs in person searches; visitors may not. Search fee: $1.00 per name per year. Required to search: name, years to search. Criminal records on computer alpha index from 1991.

General Information: No sealed, sexual victims, juvenile records released. SASE required. Turnaround time 1 week. Copy fee: $1.00 per page. Certification fee: $3.00. Fee payee: Carson City. Personal checks accepted. Prepayment is required.

Churchill County

3rd Judicial District Court 73 N Maine St, Ste B, Fallon, NV 89406; 775-423-6080; Fax: 775-423-8578. Hours: 8AM-Noon, 1-5PM (PST). *Felony, Gross Misdemeanor, Civil Actions Over $7,500, Probate.*

Civil Records: Access: Fax, mail, in person. Only the court performs in person searches; visitors may not. Search fee: $1.00 per name per year. Required to search: name, years to search. Civil cases indexed by defendant, plaintiff. Civil records on computer from 1990, prior on books, microfiche.

Criminal Records: Access: Fax, mail, in person. Only the court performs in person searches; visitors may not. Search fee: $1.00 per name per year. Required to search: name, years to search, DOB; also helpful: SSN. Criminal records on computer from 1990, prior on books, microfiche.

General Information: No juvenile, adoption or sealed records released. SASE required. Turnaround time 1-2 day. Fax notes: No fee to fax results. local or toll free numbers only. Copy fee: $1.00 per page. Certification fee: $5.00. Fee payee: Office of Court Clerk. Personal checks accepted. Prepayment is required.

Justice Court 71 N Maine St, Fallon, NV 89406; 775-423-2845; Fax: 775-423-0472. Hours: 8AM-5PM (PST). *Misdemeanor, Civil Actions Under $7,500, Eviction, Small Claims.*

Civil Records: Access: Mail, fax, in person. Both court and visitors may perform in person searches. Search fee: $1.00 per name per year. Required to search: name, years to search. Civil cases indexed by defendant, plaintiff. Civil records on computer from 1987, prior on microfiche.

Criminal Records: Access: Mail, fax, in person. Both court and visitors may perform in person searches. Search fee: $1.00 per name per year. Required to search: name, years to search, DOB. Criminal records on computer from 1987, prior on microfiche.

General Information: No sealed records released. SASE not required. Turnaround time 1 day. Copy fee: $.30 per page. Certification fee: $3.00. Fee payee: Justice Court. Personal checks accepted. Credit cards accepted: Visa, MasterCard. Prepayment is required.

Clark County

8th Judicial District Court 200 S 3rd (PO Box 551601), Las Vegas, NV 89155; 702-455-3156; Fax: 702-455-4929. Hours: 8AM-5PM (PST). *Felony, Gross Misdemeanor, Civil Actions Over $7,500, Probate.*

Civil Records: Access: Mail, online, in person. Only the court performs in person searches; visitors may not. Search fee: $1.00 per name per year. Fee is per case type. Required to search: name, years to search. Civil cases indexed by defendant, plaintiff. Civil records on computer from 11/90, prior records on microfilm to 1909. Records from the court are available free online at http://courtgate.coca.co.clark.nv.us:8490. Search by case number or party name. Probate also available.

Criminal Records: Access: Mail, online, in person. Only the court performs in person searches; visitors may not. Search fee: $1.00 per name per year. Fee is per case type. Required to search: name, years to search. Criminal records on computer from 11/90, prior records on microfilm to 1909. Online access to criminal records is the same as civil.

General Information: Public Access terminal is available. No sealed records released. SASE required. Turnaround time 10 working days. Copy fee: $1.00 per page. Certification fee: $3.00. Fee payee: County Clerk's Office. Personal checks accepted. Prepayment is required.

Boulder Township Justice Court 505 Avenue G, Boulder City, NV 89005; 702-455-8000; Fax: 702-455-8003. Hours: 7:30AM-5PM (PST). *Misdemeanor, Civil Actions Under $7,500, Eviction, Small Claims.*

Civil Records: Access: Fax, mail, in person. Both court and visitors may perform in person searches. Search fee: $1.00 per name per year. Required to search: name, years to search; also helpful: address. Civil cases indexed by defendant. Civil records on microfiche varies depending on subject.

Criminal Records: Access: Fax, mail, in person. Only the court performs in person searches; visitors may not. Search fee: $1.00 per name per year. Required to search: name, years to search, DOB, date of offense; also helpful: SSN. Criminal records on microfiche varies depending on subject.

General Information: No financial records released. SASE required. Turnaround time 1 week. Copy fee: $.30 per page. Certification fee: $3.00. Fee payee: Justice Court. Personal checks accepted. Prepayment is required.

Bunkerville Justice Court 190 W Virgin St, Bunkerville, NV 89007; 702-346-5711; Fax: 702-346-7212. Hours: 7AM-5PM M-Th (PST). *Misdemeanor, Civil Actions Under $7,500, Eviction, Small Claims.*

Civil Records: Access: Mail, in person. Only the court performs in person searches; visitors may not. Search fee: $1.00 per name per year. Required to search: name, years to search. Civil cases indexed by plaintiff. Civil records (citations) on computer from 1991, on docket books.

Criminal Records: Access: Mail, in person. Only the court performs in person searches; visitors may not. Search fee: $1.00 per name per year. Required to search: name, years to search, DOB; also helpful: SSN. Criminal records (citations) on computer from 1991, on docket books.

General Information: No sealed or confidential records released. SASE required. Turnaround time 2 weeks. Copy fee: $.30 per page. Certification fee: $3.00. Fee payee: Bunkerville Justice Court. Only cashiers checks and money orders accepted. Prepayment required.

Goodsprings Township Jean Justice Court 1 Main St (PO Box 19155), Jean, NV 89019; 702-874-1405; Fax: 702-874-1612. Hours: 7AM-5PM M-Th (PST). *Misdemeanor, Civil Actions Under $7,500, Eviction, Small Claims.*

Civil Records: Access: Phone, fax, mail, in person. Only the court performs in person searches; visitors may not. Search fee: $1.00 per name per year. Required to search: name, years to search. Civil cases indexed by defendant, plaintiff. Civil records on computer for 6 months, file reports from 1990.

Criminal Records: Access: Phone, fax, mail, in person. Only the court performs in person searches; visitors may not. Search fee: $1.00 per name per year. Required to search: name, years to search, DOB; also helpful: SSN. Criminal records on computer for 6 months, file reports from 1990.

General Information: No sealed records released. SASE required. Turnaround time within 2-3 days. Copy fee: $.25 per page. Certification fee: $2.00. Fee payee: Jean Justice Court. Business checks accepted.

Henderson Township Justice 243 Water St, Henderson, NV 89015; 702-455-7951; Fax: 702-455-7935. Hours: 7AM-6PM M-Th (PST). *Misdemeanor, Civil Actions Under $7,500, Eviction, Small Claims.*

www.co.clark.nv.us/hendersonjc/general_information.htm

Civil Records: Access: Mail, in person. Only the court performs in person searches; visitors may not. Search fee: $1.00 per name per year. Required to search: name, years to search. Civil cases indexed by defendant. Civil records on index cards and docket books. Evictions kept for 2 years; civil and small claims for 6 years.

Criminal Records: Access: Mail, in person. Only the court performs in person searches; visitors may not. Search fee: $1.00 per name per year. Required to search: name, years to search, DOB; also helpful: SSN. Criminal records on index cards and docket books. Evictions kept 2 years; civil/small claims for 6 years.

General Information: SASE required. Turnaround time 2 weeks. Fax notes: Fee to fax results is $.30 per page. Copy fee: $.30 per page. Certification fee: $3.00. Fee payee: Henderson Justice Court. Personal checks accepted. Prepayment is required.

Las Vegas Township Justice Court 200 S 3rd, 2nd Fl, PO Box 552511, Las Vegas, NV 89155-2511; 702-455-4435; Fax: 702-455-4529. Hours: 8AM-5PM (PST). *Misdemeanor, Civil Actions Under $7,500, Eviction, Small Claims.*

www.co.clark.nv.us/juscourt/welcome.htm

Note: Calendars are available online at the website.

Civil Records: Access: Phone, fax, mail, in person. Both court and visitors may perform in person searches. Search fee: $1.00 per name per year. Required to search: name, years to search. Civil cases indexed by defendant, plaintiff. Civil records on computer to 1994.

Criminal Records: Access: Phone, fax, mail, in person. Only the court performs in person searches; visitors may not. Search fee: $1.00 per name per year. Required to search: name, years to search, DOB; also helpful: SSN. Criminal records on computer to 1980.

General Information: No sealed, confidential or judge's notes records released. SASE required. Turnaround time 2 weeks. Copy fee: $.30 per page. Certification fee: $3.00. Fee payee: Justice Court, Las Vegas Township. Personal checks accepted. Prepayment is required.

Laughlin Township Justice Court 101 Civic Way #2, Laughlin, NV 89029; 702-298-4622; Fax: 702-298-7508. Hours: 8AM-5PM *Misdemeanor, Civil Actions Under $7,000, Eviction, Small Claims.*

Civil Records: Access: Fax, mail, in person. Search fee: $1.00 per name per year. Required to search: name, years to search. Civil cases indexed by defendant, plaintiff. Civil records on docket book by name and case number.

Criminal Records: Access: Fax, mail, in person. Only the court performs in person searches; visitors may not. Search fee: $1.00 per name per year. Required to search: name, years to search, DOB. Criminal records on computer from 1990, prior in files and must be cross referenced.

General Information: No sealed records released. SASE required. Turnaround time 2 weeks. Copy fee: $.30 per page. Certification fee: $3.00. Fee payee: Laughlin Justice Court. Personal checks accepted. Prepayment is required.

Mesquite Township Justice Court PO Box 1209 (51 E 1st North), Mesquite, NV 89024; 702-346-5298; Fax: 702-346-7319. Hours: 7AM-4PM (PST). *Felony, Misdemeanor, Civil Actions Under $7,500, Eviction, Small Claims.*

Civil Records: Access: Phone, fax, mail, in person. Only the court performs in person searches; visitors may not. Search fee: $1.00 per name per year. Required to search: name, years to search. Civil cases indexed by defendant. Civil records in files. None available prior to 1989.

Criminal Records: Access: Phone, fax, mail, in person. Only the court performs in person searches; visitors may not. Search fee: $1.00 per name per year. Required to search: name, years to search, DOB; also helpful: SSN. Criminal records in files. None available prior to 1989.

General Information: No sealed records released. SASE not required. Turnaround time approx 1-2 weeks. Copy fee: $.30 per page. Certification fee: $3.00. Fee payee: Mesquite Justice Court. Only cashiers checks and money orders accepted. Prepayment is required.

Moapa Township Justice Court 1340 E Com Hwy, PO Box 280, Moapa, NV 89025; 702-864-2333; Fax: 702-864-2585. Hours: 8AM-5PM M-Th (PST). *Misdemeanor, Civil Actions Under $7,500, Eviction, Small Claims.*

Civil Records: Access: Fax, mail, in person. Only the court performs in person searches; visitors may not. Search fee: $1.00 per name per year. Required to search: name, years to search. Civil cases indexed by defendant, plaintiff. Civil records on computer from 10/90, prior records on index cards and docket books. Archives flooded in 1980s.

Criminal Records: Access: Fax, mail, in person. Only the court performs in person searches; visitors may not. Search fee: $1.00 per name per year. Required to search: name, years to search; also helpful: DOB, SSN. Criminal records on computer from 10/90, prior records on index cards and docket books. Archives flooded in 1980s.

General Information: No sealed records released. SASE required. Turnaround time 1-5 days. Fax notes: No fee to fax results. Copy fee: $.25 per page. Certification fee: $3.00. Fee payee: Moapa Township Justice Court. Personal checks accepted. Prepayment is required.

Moapa Valley Township Justice Court 320 N Moapa Valley Blvd, Overton, NV 89040; 702-397-2840; Fax: 702-397-2842. Hours: 6:30AM-4:30PM M-Th (PST). *Misdemeanor, Civil Actions Under $7,500, Eviction, Small Claims.*

Civil Records: Access: Mail, in person. Only the court performs in person searches; visitors may not. Search fee: $1.00 per name per year. Required to search: name, years to search. Civil cases indexed by defendant, plaintiff. Civil records on computer from 1991, prior on docket books.

Criminal Records: Access: Mail, in person. Only the court performs in person searches; visitors may not. Search fee: $1.00 per name per year. Required to search: name, years to search, DOB; also helpful: SSN. Criminal records on computer from 1991, prior on docket books.

General Information: No sealed records released. SASE required. Turnaround time approx 1-2 weeks. Copy fee: $.25 per page. Certification fee: $3.00. Fee payee: Moapa Valley Justice Court. Personal checks accepted. Prepayment is required.

North Las Vegas Township Justice 2428 N Martin L King Blvd, N Las Vegas, NV 89032-3700; 702-455-7802; Civil phone: 702-455-7801; Fax: 702-455-7831. Hours: 7AM-5:45PM (PST). *Misdemeanor, Civil Actions Under $7,500, Eviction, Small Claims.*

Note: Judge must approve all search requests.

Civil Records: Access: Phone, in person. Visitors must perform in person searches for themselves. No search fee. Required to search: name, years to search. Civil cases indexed by defendant, plaintiff. Civil records on docket books, microfilm.

Criminal Records: Access: Phone, mail, in person. Only the court performs in person searches; visitors may not. Search fee: $1.00 per name per year. Required to search: name, years to search, DOB, SSN. Criminal records on docket books, microfilm.

General Information: SASE required. Turnaround time 1-10 days. Copy fee: $.30 per page. Certification fee: $3.00. Fee payee: Clark County Justice Court. Personal checks accepted. Personal check accepted with bank card. Prepayment is required.

Searchlight Township Justice Court PO Box 815, Searchlight, NV 89046; 702-297-1252; Fax: 702-297-1022. 7AM-5:30PM M-Th *Misdemeanor, Civil Actions Under $7,500, Eviction, Small Claims.*

Civil Records: Access: Fax, mail, in person. Only the court performs in person searches; visitors may not.

Search fee: $1.00 per name per year. Required to search: name, years to search. Civil cases indexed by defendant, plaintiff. Civil records on computer from 1988, prior to 1988 filed by case number.

Criminal Records: Access: Fax, mail, in person. Only the court performs in person searches; visitors may not. Search fee: $1.00 per name per year. Required to search: name, years to search, DOB; also helpful: SSN. Criminal records on computer from 1988, prior to 1988 filed by case number.

General Information: No sealed records released. SASE required. Turnaround time 1-2 weeks. Copy fee: $1.00 per page. Certification fee: $2.00. Fee payee: Searchlight Justice Court. Personal checks accepted. Prepayment is required.

Douglas County

9th Judicial District Court Box 218, Minden, NV 89423; 775-782-9820; Fax: 775-782-9954. Hours: 8AM-5PM (PST). *Felony, Civil Actions Over $7,500, Probate.*

http://cltr.co.douglas.nv.us/CourtClerk/courtideas/courtc lerkhome.htm

Note: Misdemeanors are handled by the East Fork Justice Court.

Civil Records: Access: Mail, in person. Only the court performs in person searches; visitors may not. Search fee: $1.00 per name per year. Required to search: name, years to search. Civil cases indexed by defendant, plaintiff. Civil records on index cards from 1962, docket books prior to 1962, archived from mid-1850s. On computer back to 1996.

Criminal Records: Access: Mail, in person. Only the court performs in person searches; visitors may not. Search fee: $1.00 per name per year. Required to search: name, years to search, DOB. Criminal records on index cards from 1962, docket books prior to 1962, archived from mid-1850s. On computer back to 1996.

General Information: No sealed records released. SASE required. Turnaround time 1 week. Copy fee: $1.00 per page. Certification fee: $3.00. Fee payee: Douglas County Court Clerk. Business checks accepted. Prepayment is required.

East Fork Justice Court PO Box 218, Minden, NV 89423; 775-782-9955; Fax: 775-782-9947. Hours: 8AM-5PM (PST). *Misdemeanor, Civil Actions Under $7,500, Eviction, Small Claims.*

Civil Records: Access: Mail, in person. Only the court performs in person searches; visitors may not. Search fee: $1.00 per name per year. Required to search: name, years to search, DOB or SSN. Civil cases indexed by defendant, plaintiff.

Criminal Records: Access: Mail, in person. Only the court performs in person searches; visitors may not. Search fee: $1.00 per name per year. Required to search: name, years to search, DOB or SSN.

General Information: No sealed records released. SASE required. Turnaround time 2-4 days. Copy fee: $.30 per page. Certification fee: $3.00. Fee payee: East Fork Justice Court. Only local personal or business checks accepted. Prepayment is required.

Tahoe Justice Court PO Box 7169, Stateline, NV 89449; 775-586-7200; Fax: 775-588-7203. Hours: 9AM-5PM (PST). *Misdemeanor, Civil Actions Under $7,500, Eviction, Small Claims.*

Civil Records: Access: Phone, mail, in person. Only the court performs in person searches; visitors may not. Search fee: $1.00 per name per year. Required to search: name, years to search. Civil cases indexed by defendant, plaintiff. Civil records on index cards from 1985, prior records on docket books to 1/1/81. Prior to 1/1/81, records destroyed, but are in docket books.

Criminal Records: Access: Phone, mail, in person. Only the court performs in person searches; visitors

may not. Search fee: $1.00 per name per year. Required to search: name, years to search, DOB. Criminal records prior to 1/1/81 records are destroyed, are in process of placing on computer.

General Information: No sealed records released. SASE required. Turnaround time 2 weeks. Copy fee: $.30 per page. Certification fee: $3.00 per page. Fee payee: Tahoe Justice Court. Credit cards accepted: Visa, MasterCard. Prepayment is required.

Elko County

4th Judicial District Court 571 Idaho St, 3rd Flr, Elko, NV 89801; 775-753-4600; Fax: 775-753-4610. Hours: 9AM-5PM (PST). *Felony, Gross Misdemeanor, Civil Actions Over $7,500, Probate.*

Civil Records: Access: Phone, mail, in person. Both court and visitors may perform in person searches. Search fee: $1.00 per name per year. Fee is for years prior to 10/01/91. Required to search: name, years to search. Civil cases indexed by defendant, plaintiff. Civil records on computer from 1991; prior on microfilm.

Criminal Records: Access: Phone, mail, in person. Both court and visitors may perform in person searches. Search fee: $1.00 per name per year. Fee is for years prior to 1980. Required to search: name, years to search. Criminal records on computer go back 10 years; prior primarily on microfilm (including probate).

General Information: No sealed records released. SASE required. Turnaround time 1 day. Fax notes: Fee to fax results is $1.00 per page. Copy fee: $1.00 per page. Certification fee: $3.00 if court prepares copies, $5.00 if you prepare copies. Fee payee: Elko County Clerk. Personal checks accepted. Prepayment is required.

Carlin Justice Court PO Box 789, Carlin, NV 89822; 775-754-6321; Fax: 775-754-6893. Hours: 8AM-5PM (PST). *Misdemeanor, Civil Actions Under $7,500, Eviction, Small Claims.*

Civil Records: Access: Mail, in person. Both court and visitors may perform in person searches. Search fee: $1.00 per name per year. Required to search: name, years to search. Civil cases indexed by defendant, plaintiff. Civil records on computer starting in 1994, prior are in books.

Criminal Records: Access: Mail, in person. Only the court performs in person searches; visitors may not. Search fee: $1.00 per name per year. Required to search: name, years to search, DOB, SSN. Criminal records on computer starting in 1994, prior are in books.

General Information: SASE required. Turnaround time 1 week. Copy fee: $.30 per page. Certification fee: $3.00. Fee payee: Carlin Court. Personal checks accepted. Prepayment is required.

Eastline Justice Court PO Box 2300, West Wendover, NV 89883; 775-664-2305; Fax: 775-664-2979. Hours: 9AM-4PM (PST). *Misdemeanor, Civil Actions Under $7,500, Eviction, Small Claims.*

Civil Records: Access: Mail, in person. Only the court performs in person searches; visitors may not. Search fee: $7.00 per name per year. Required to search: name, years to search. Civil cases indexed by defendant. Civil records on computer from 1992, prior on index, docket book.

Criminal Records: Access: Mail, in person. Only the court performs in person searches; visitors may not. Search fee: $1.00 per name per year. Required to search: name, years to search; also helpful: DOB. Criminal records on computer from 1992, prior on index, docket book.

General Information: No open case records released. SASE required. Turnaround time 1 week. Copy fee: $.30 per page. Certification fee: $3.00. Fee payee: Eastline Justice Court. Only cashiers checks and money orders accepted. Prepayment is required.

Elko Justice Court PO Box 176, Elko, NV 89803; 775-738-8403; Fax: 775-738-8416. Hours: 9AM-Noon, 1-5PM (PST). *Misdemeanor, Civil Actions Under $7,500, Eviction, Small Claims.*

Note: There is a small Justice Court located in Tecoma Township at PO Box 8, Montello, NV 89830, 775-776-2544.

Civil Records: Access: Fax, mail, in person. Both court and visitors may perform in person searches. Search fee: $1.00 per name per year. Fee is per court. Required to search: name, years to search. Civil cases indexed by defendant, plaintiff. Civil records on computer after 1994, on docket books after 1970s, prior in county archives.

Criminal Records: Access: Mail, in person. Both court and visitors may perform in person searches. Search fee: $1.00 per name per year. Fee is per court. Required to search: name, years to search; DOB or SSN also required. Criminal records on computer after 1994, on docket books after 1970s, prior in county archives.

General Information: No confidential evaluations or sealed records released. SASE required. Turnaround time 7-10 days. Copy fee: $.30 per page. Certification fee: $3.00. Fee payee: Elko Justice Court. Personal checks accepted. Prepayment is required.

Jackpot Justice Court PO Box 229, Jackpot, NV 89825; 775-755-2456; Fax: 775-755-2727. Hours: 9AM-Noon, 1-5PM (PST). *Misdemeanor, Civil Actions Under $7,500, Eviction, Small Claims.*

Civil Records: Access: Mail, in person. Only the court performs in person searches; visitors may not. Search fee: $1.00 per name per year. Required to search: name, years to search. Civil cases indexed by defendant. Civil records on docket books per year since 1978; on computer back to 1995.

Criminal Records: Access: Fax, mail, in person. Only the court performs in person searches; visitors may not. Search fee: $1.00 per name per year. Required to search: name, years to search, DOB. Criminal records on docket books per year since 1978; on computer back to 1995.

General Information: SASE required. Turnaround time 1 week. Fax notes: No fee to fax results. Copy fee: $.25 per page. Certification fee: $3.00. Fee payee: Jackpot Justice Court. Business checks accepted.

Jarbidge Justice Court PO Box 26001, Jarbidge, NV 89826-2001; 775-488-2331. *Misdemeanor, Civil Actions Under $7,500, Eviction, Small Claims.*

Note: This is "unincorporated ghost town." No criminal or civil cases in more than 20 years. Mostly marriages, fish and game violations. Only 40 year round residents.

Civil Records: Access: In person only. Visitors must perform in person searches for themselves. No search fee. Required to search: name, years to search.

Criminal Records: Access: In person only. Visitors must perform in person searches for themselves. No search fee. Required to search: name, years to search.

Mountain City Justice Court PO Box 116, Mountain City, NV 89831; 775-763-6699. *Misdemeanor, Civil Actions Under $7,500, Eviction, Small Claims.*

Note: New records held in Elko Justice Court; older ones may soon be transferred also. Limited cases heard here. Phone listed is sheriff's office. 49 people live here.

Civil Records: Access: Mail, in person. Both court and visitors may perform in person searches. No search fee. Required to search: name, years to search. Civil cases indexed by defendant.

Criminal Records: Access: Mail, in person. Both court and visitors may perform in person searches. No search fee. Required to search: name, years to search, DOB.

General Information: SASE required. Copy fee: $.25 per page. Certification fee: $2.00.

Wells Justice Municipal Court PO Box 297, Wells, NV 89835; 775-752-3726; Fax: 775-752-3363. Hours: 9AM-Noon,1-5PM (PST). *Misdemeanor, Civil Actions Under $7,500, Eviction, Small Claims.*

Civil Records: Access: Mail, in person. Only the court performs in person searches; visitors may not. Search fee: $1.00 per name per year. Required to search: name, years to search. Civil cases indexed by defendant, plaintiff. Civil records on computer from 1989, prior on docket books. In person access may require fee for clerical assistance.

Criminal Records: Access: Mail, in person. Only the court performs in person searches; visitors may not. Search fee: $1.00 per name per year. Required to search: name, years to search; also DOB or SSN. Criminal records on computer from 1989, prior on docket books. Same as civil.

General Information: No pending, confidential records released. SASE required. Turnaround time 2 weeks. Copy fee: $.30 per page. Certification fee: $3.00. Fee payee: Wells Justice Court. Personal checks accepted. Prepayment is required.

Esmeralda County

5th Judicial District Court PO Box 547, Goldfield, NV 89013; 775-485-6367; Fax: 775-485-6376. Hours: 8AM-5PM (PST). *Felony, Gross Misdemeanor, Civil Actions Over $7,500, Probate.*

Note: E-mail address is escdct@sierra.net.

Civil Records: Access: Fax, mail, in person, email. Both court and visitors may perform in person searches. Search fee: $1.00 per name per year. Required to search: name, years to search. Civil cases indexed by defendant, plaintiff. Civil records on docket books from 1800s.

Criminal Records: Access: Fax, mail, in person, e-mail. Both court and visitors may perform in person searches. Search fee: $1.00 per name per year. Required to search: name, years to search. Criminal records on docket books from 1800s.

General Information: No juvenile or pre-sentence records released. SASE required. Turnaround time 2 weeks. Fax notes: Fee to fax results is $1.00 per page. Copy fee: $1.00 per page. Certification fee: $3.00. Fee payee: Esmeralda County Clerk. Personal checks accepted. Credit cards accepted: Visa and MasterCard. Prepayment is required.

Esmeralda Justice Court PO Box 370, Goldfield, NV 89013; 775-485-6359; Fax: 775-485-3462. Hours: 8AM-5PM (PST). *Misdemeanor, Civil Actions Under $7,500, Eviction, Small Claims.*

Civil Records: Access: Phone, fax, mail, in person. Only the court performs in person searches; visitors may not. Search fee: $1.00 per name per year. Required to search: name, years to search. Civil cases indexed by plaintiff. Civil records on docket books for 6 years.

Criminal Records: Access: Phone, fax, mail, in person. Only the court performs in person searches; visitors may not. Search fee: $1.00 per name per year. Required to search: name, years to search. Criminal records on docket books for 6 years.

General Information: No sealed records released. SASE required. Turnaround time 1 day. Fax notes: $1.00 per page. Copy fee: $.30 per page. Certification fee: $3.00. Fee payee: Justice Court. Only cashiers checks and money orders accepted. Prepayment is required.

Eureka County

7th Judicial District Court PO Box 677, Eureka, NV 89316; 775-237-5262; Fax: 775-237-6015. Hours: 8AM-Noon, 1-5PM (PST). *Felony, Gross Misdemeanor, Civil Actions Over $7,500, Probate.*

Civil Records: Access: Phone, fax, mail, in person. Both court and visitors may perform in person searches. Search fee: $1.00 per name per year. Required to search: name, years to search. Civil cases indexed by defendant, plaintiff. Civil records archived from 1873. Public can search docket books.

Criminal Records: Access: Phone, fax, mail, in person. Both court and visitors may perform in person searches. Search fee: $1.00 per name per year. Required to search: name, years to search. Criminal records archived from 1873. Public can search docket books.

General Information: No juvenile, sealed records released. SASE required. Turnaround time 1 day. Copy fee: $1.00 per page. Certification fee: $3.00. Fee payee: Eureka County Clerk. Personal checks accepted. Prepayment is required.

Beowawe Justice Court PO Box 211338, Crescent Valley, NV 89821; 775-468-0244; Fax: 775-468-0323. 8AM-Noon, 1-5PM (PST). *Misdemeanor, Civil Actions Under $7,500, Eviction, Small Claims.*

Civil Records: Access: Mail, in person. Only the court performs in person searches; visitors may not. Search fee: $1.00 per name per year. Required to search: name, years to search. Civil cases indexed by plaintiff. Civil records on docket books.

Criminal Records: Access: Mail, in person. Only the court performs in person searches; visitors may not. Search fee: $1.00 per name per year. Required to search: name, years to search. Criminal records on docket books.

General Information: SASE required. Copy fee: $.30 per page. Certification fee: $3.00. Fee payee: Beowawe Justice Court. Only cashiers checks and money orders accepted. Prepayment is required.

Eureka Justice Court PO Box 496, Eureka, NV 89316; 775-237-5540; Fax: 775-237-6016. Hours: 8AM-Noon,1-5PM (PST). *Misdemeanor, Civil Actions Under $7,500, Eviction, Small Claims.*

Civil Records: Access: Phone, mail, in person. Only the court performs in person searches; visitors may not. No search fee. Required to search: name, years to search. Civil cases indexed by defendant, plaintiff. Civil records on computer since 1995; on docket books, archived from 1940.

Criminal Records: Access: Phone, mail, in person. Only the court performs in person searches; visitors may not. No search fee. Required to search: name, years to search. Criminal records on computer since 1995; on docket books, archived from 1940.

General Information: SASE required. Turnaround time 2 days. Copy fee: $.50 per page. Certification fee: $3.00. Fee payee: Eureka Justice Court. Only cashiers checks and money orders accepted. Prepayment is required.

Humboldt County

6th Judicial District Court 50 W Fifth St, Winnemucca, NV 89445; 775-623-6343; Fax: 775-623-6309. Hours: 8AM-5PM (PST). *Felony, Gross Misdemeanor, Civil Actions Over $7,500, Probate.*

Civil Records: Access: Phone, fax, mail, in person. Both court and visitors may perform in person searches. Search fee: $1.00 per name per year. Required to search: name, years to search. Civil cases indexed by defendant, plaintiff. Civil records on computer from 1984, on microfiche from 1900.

Criminal Records: Access: Phone, fax, mail, in person. Both court and visitors may perform in person searches. Search fee: $1.00 per name per year. Required to search: name, years to search. Criminal records on computer from 1984, on microfiche from 1900.

General Information: Public Access terminal is available. No adoption, sealed records released. SASE required. Turnaround time 1 day, immediate if on computer and requested by phone. Copy fee: $1.00 per page. Certification fee: $3.00. Fee payee: Humboldt County Clerk. Personal checks accepted. Prepayment is required.

Union Justice Court PO Box 1218, Winnemucca, NV 89446; 775-623-6377; Fax: 775-623-6439. Hours: 7AM-5PM (PST). *Misdemeanor, Civil Actions Under $7,500, Eviction, Small Claims.*

www.humboldt-county-nv.net/justice

Civil Records: Access: Fax, mail, in person. Only the court performs in person searches; visitors may not. Search fee: $1.00 per name per year; minimum of $7.00. Required to search: name, years to search; also helpful: address. Civil cases indexed by defendant, plaintiff. Civil records on computer from 1988, prior on docket books.

Criminal Records: Access: Fax, mail, in person. Only the court performs in person searches; visitors may not. Search fee: $1.00 per name per year; minimum of $7.00. Required to search: name, years to search; also helpful: address, DOB, SSN. Criminal records on computer from 1988.

General Information: SASE required. Turnaround time 1-2 days. Fax notes: No fee to fax results. Certification fee: $3.00. Fee payee: Justice Court. Personal checks accepted. Prepayment is required.

Lander County

6th Judicial District Court 315 S Humboldt, Battle Mountain, NV 89820; 775-635-5738; Fax: 775-635-5761. Hours: 8AM-5PM (PST). *Felony, Gross Misdemeanor, Civil Actions Over $7,500, Probate.*

Civil Records: Access: Phone, fax, mail, in person. Only the court performs in person searches; visitors may not. No search fee. Required to search: name, years to search. Civil cases indexed by defendant, plaintiff. Civil records on computer from 1992, on index from 1986-1990, on microfiche until 1985, prior records on docket books.

Criminal Records: Access: Phone, fax, mail, in person. Only the court performs in person searches; visitors may not. No search fee. Required to search: name, years to search. Criminal records on computer from 1992, on index from 1986-1990, on microfiche until 1985, prior records on docket books.

General Information: No juvenile, sealed records released. SASE required. Turnaround time 7 days. Fax notes: Fee to fax results is $1.00 per page. Copy fee: $1.00 per page. Certification fee: $5.00. Fee payee: Lander County Clerk. Personal checks accepted.

Argenta Justice Court 315 S Humboldt, Battle Mountain, NV 89820; 775-635-5151; Fax: 775-635-0604. Hours: 8AM-5PM (PST). *Misdemeanor, Civil Actions Under $7,500, Eviction, Small Claims.*

Civil Records: Access: Phone, fax, mail, in person. Only the court performs in person searches; visitors may not. Search fee: $1.00 per name per year. Required to search: name, years to search. Civil cases indexed by defendant, plaintiff. Civil records on computer from 1988, prior on docket books.

Criminal Records: Access: Phone, fax, mail, in person. Only the court performs in person searches; visitors may not. Search fee: $1.00 per name per year. Required to search: name, years to search; also helpful: DOB, SSN. Criminal records on computer from 1988, prior on docket books.

General Information: No unserved search warrant records released. SASE required. Turnaround time 1 day. Fax notes: $1.00 per page. Copy fee: $.50 per page. Certification fee: $3.00 per page. Fee payee: Argenta

Justice Court. Only cashiers checks and money orders accepted.

Austin Justice Court PO Box 100, Austin, NV 89310; 775-964-2380; Fax: 775-964-2327. Hours: 8AM-5PM M, 8AM-Noon T-Th (PST). *Misdemeanor, Civil Actions Under $7,500, Eviction, Small Claims.*

Note: No fees for requests from government agencies.

Civil Records: Access: Phone, mail, fax, in person. Only the court performs in person searches; visitors may not. No search fee. Required to search: name, years to search. Civil cases indexed by defendant, plaintiff. Civil records on docket books.

Criminal Records: Access: Phone, mail, fax, in person. Only the court performs in person searches; visitors may not. No search fee. Required to search: name, years to search. Criminal records on computer from 1988.

General Information: SASE required. Turnaround time 1 week. Copy fee: $.25 per page. Fee payee: Austin Justice Court. Prepayment is required.

Lincoln County

7th Judicial District Court PO Box 90, Pioche, NV 89043; 775-962-5390; Fax: 702-962-5180. Hours: 9AM-5PM (PST). *Felony, Gross Misdemeanor, Civil Actions Over $7,500, Probate.*

Civil Records: Access: Mail, in person. Both court and visitors may perform in person searches. Search fee: $1.00 per name per year. Required to search: name, years to search. Civil cases indexed by defendant, plaintiff. Civil records on docket books from 1876. Minimal recent records are computerized.

Criminal Records: Access: Mail, in person. Both court and visitors may perform in person searches. Search fee: $1.00 per name per year. Required to search: name, years to search. Criminal records on docket books from 1876. Minimal recent records are computerized.

General Information: No juvenile, sealed records released. SASE not required. Turnaround time 2-3 days. Fax notes: Fee to fax results is $1.00 per page. Copy fee: $1.00 per page. Certification fee: $5.00. Fee payee: Lincoln County Clerk. Personal checks accepted. Prepayment is required.

Meadow Valley Justice Court PO Box 36, Pioche, NV 89043; 775-962-5140; Fax: 775-962-5559. Hours: 9AM-5PM (PST). *Misdemeanor, Civil Actions Under $7,500, Eviction, Small Claims.*

Civil Records: Access: Phone, fax, mail, in person. Only the court performs in person searches; visitors may not. Search fee: $1.00 per name per year. Required to search: name, years to search. Civil cases indexed by defendant, plaintiff. Civil records archived from 1982 on docket books; on computer back to 2000.

Criminal Records: Access: Phone, fax, mail, in person. Only the court performs in person searches; visitors may not. Search fee: $1.00 per name per year. Required to search: name, years to search. Criminal records are all originals; they go back to 1982; on computer back to 2000.

General Information: Juvenile records are not released. SASE required. Turnaround time 1-5 days. Fax notes: $3.00 for first page, $1.00 each add'l. Copy fee: $1.00 per page. Certification fee: No cert fee. Fee payee: Meadow Valley Justice Court. Personal checks accepted. Prepayment is required.

Pahranagat Valley Justice Court PO Box 449, Alamo, NV 89001; 775-725-3357; Fax: 775-725-3566. Hours: 9AM-5PM (PST). *Misdemeanor, Civil Actions Under $7,500, Eviction, Small Claims.*

Civil Records: Access: Fax, mail, in person. Only the court performs in person searches; visitors may not. No search fee. Required to search: name, years to search. Civil cases indexed by defendant. Civil records on docket books to 1980; on computer back to 1997.

Criminal Records: Access: Fax, mail, in person. Only the court performs in person searches; visitors may not. No search fee. Required to search: name, years to search, DOB; also helpful: SSN, signed release. Criminal records on docket books to 1980; on computer back to 1997.

General Information: No personal notes released. SASE required. Turnaround time 1-3 days. Fax notes: No fee to fax results. Copy fee: $.25 per page. Certification fee: $2.00 per page. Fee payee: Pahranagat Valley Justice Court. Personal checks accepted. Prepayment is required.

Lyon County

3rd Judicial District Court PO Box 816, Yerington, NV 89447; 775-463-6503; Fax: 775-463-6575. Hours: 8AM-5PM (PST). *Felony, Gross Misdemeanor, Civil Actions Over $7,500, Probate.*

Civil Records: Access: Phone, mail, in person. Only the court performs in person searches; visitors may not. Search fee: $1.00 per name per year. Required to search: name, years to search. Civil cases indexed by defendant, plaintiff. Civil records on computer from 1989.

Criminal Records: Access: Phone, mail, in person. Only the court performs in person searches; visitors may not. Search fee: $1.00 per name per year. Required to search: name, years to search. Criminal records on computer from 1985.

General Information: No adoption, juvenile or sealed records released. SASE required. Turnaround time 1 week for mail requests, immediate for phone requests if on computer. Copy fee: $.25 per page. Certification fee: $3.00. Fee payee: Lyon County Clerk. Personal checks accepted. Prepayment is required.

Dayton Township Justice Court 235 Main St, Dayton, NV 89403; 775-246-6233; Fax: 775-246-6203. Hours: 8AM-5PM (PST). *Misdemeanor, Civil Actions Under $7,500, Eviction, Small Claims.*

Civil Records: Access: Phone, fax, mail, in person. Only the court performs in person searches; visitors may not. Search fee: $1.00 per name per year. Required to search: name, years to search. Civil cases indexed by defendant, plaintiff. Civil records on computer from 1991, prior on docket books by year.

Criminal Records: Access: Phone, fax, mail, in person. Only the court performs in person searches; visitors may not. Search fee: $1.00 per name per year. Required to search: name, years to search. Criminal records on computer from 1991, prior on docket books by year.

General Information: No sealed records released. SASE required. Turnaround time within 1 week. Copy fee: $.25 per page. Certification fee: $3.00. Fee payee: Dayton Township Justice Court. Personal checks accepted. Prepayment is required.

Fernley Justice Court 565 E Main St, Fernley, NV 89408; 775-575-3355; Fax: 775-575-3359. Hours: 8AM-5PM (PST). *Misdemeanor, Civil Actions Under $7,500, Eviction, Small Claims.*

Civil Records: Access: Phone, mail, in person. Only the court performs in person searches; visitors may not. Search fee: $1.00 per name per year. Required to search: name, years to search. Civil cases indexed by defendant, plaintiff. Civil records on computer from 1992, prior on docket books.

Criminal Records: Access: Phone, mail, in person. Only the court performs in person searches; visitors may not. Search fee: $1.00 per name per year. Required to search: name, years to search; also helpful: SSN. Criminal records on computer from 1992, prior on docket books.

General Information: No police reports or sealed records released. SASE required. Turnaround time 1 week. Copy fee: $.30 per page. Certification fee: $2.00.

Fee payee: Fernley Justice Court. Personal checks accepted. Out of state checks not accepted. Prepayment is required.

Mason Valley Justice Court 30 Nevin Way, Yerington, NV 89447; 775-463-6639; Fax: 775-463-6610. Hours: 8AM-5PM (PST). *Misdemeanor, Civil Actions Under $7,500, Eviction, Small Claims.*

Civil Records: Access: Phone, mail, in person. Only the court performs in person searches; visitors may not. Search fee: $1.00 per name per year. Required to search: name, years to search. Civil cases indexed by defendant, plaintiff. Civil records on computer from 1988, archives from 1900s.
Criminal Records: Access: Phone, mail, in person. Only the court performs in person searches; visitors may not. Search fee: $1.00 per name per year. Required to search: name, years to search; also helpful: DOB, SSN. Criminal records on computer from 1988, archives from 1900s.
General Information: No police, sheriff reports released. SASE required. Turnaround time 3 days, immediate for phone requests. Copy fee: $.25 per page. Certification fee: $3.00. Fee payee: Mason Valley Justice Court. Personal checks accepted. Prepayment is required.

Smith Valley Justice Court PO Box 141, Smith, NV 89430; 775-465-2313; Fax: 775-465-2153. Hours: 8AM-Noon Tues & Fri or by appointment (PST). *Misdemeanor, Civil Actions Under $10,000, Eviction, Small Claims.*

Civil Records: Access: Phone, fax, mail, in person. Only the court performs in person searches; visitors may not. No search fee. Required to search: name, years to search; also helpful: address. Civil cases indexed by defendant, plaintiff. Civil records on computer from 1994, prior in docket books.
Criminal Records: Access: Phone, mail, in person. Only the court performs in person searches; visitors may not. No search fee. Required to search: name, years to search; also helpful: address, DOB, SSN. Criminal records on computer from 1994, prior in docket books.
General Information: SASE required. Turnaround time 1-2 weeks. Copy fee: $.30 per page. Certification fee: $3.00. Fee payee: Smith Valley Justice Court. Personal checks accepted. Prepayment is required.

Mineral County

5th Judicial District Court PO Box 1450, Hawthorne, NV 89415; 775-945-2446; Fax: 775-945-0706. Hours: 8AM-5PM (PST). *Felony, Gross Misdemeanor, Civil Actions Over $7,500, Probate.*

Civil Records: Access: Phone, fax, mail, in person. Both court and visitors may perform in person searches. Search fee: $1.00 per name per year. Required to search: name, years to search. Civil cases indexed by defendant, plaintiff. Civil records on computer.
Criminal Records: Access: Phone, fax, mail, in person. Both court and visitors may perform in person searches. Search fee: $1.00 per name per year. Required to search: name, years to search. Criminal records on computer.
General Information: No juvenile records released. SASE required. Turnaround time 1 day. Fax notes: $1.50 per page. Copy fee: $1.00 per page. Certification fee: $3.00. Fee payee: Mineral County Clerk. Personal checks accepted. Prepayment is required.

Hawthorne Justice Court PO Box 1660, Hawthorne, NV 89415; 775-945-3859; Fax: 775-945-0700. Hours: 8AM-5PM (PST). *Misdemeanor, Civil Actions Under $7,500, Eviction, Small Claims.*

Note: This court holds records from Schurz Justice Court.

Civil Records: Access: Phone, mail, in person. Both court and visitors may perform in person searches. No search fee. Required to search: name, years to search. Civil cases indexed by defendant. Civil records on computer from 1994, prior on docket books.
Criminal Records: Access: Phone, mail, in person. Both court and visitors may perform in person searches. No search fee. Required to search: name, years to search. Criminal records on computer from 1992.
General Information: No pending case or sealed records released. SASE required. Turnaround time 1-5 days. Copy fee: $.25 per page. Legal Size Copy Fee: $1.00 per page. Certification fee: No cert fee. Fee payee: Hawthorne Justice Court. Personal checks accepted.

Mina Justice Court PO Box 415, Mina, NV 89422; 775-573-2547; Fax: 775-573-2663. Hours: 9AM-2PM Tues-Fri. (PST). *Misdemeanor, Civil Actions Under $7,500, Eviction, Small Claims.*

Civil Records: Access: Phone, mail, in person. Only the court performs in person searches; visitors may not. No search fee. Required to search: name, years to search. Civil cases indexed by plaintiff. Civil records on docket books.
Criminal Records: Access: Phone, mail, in person. Only the court performs in person searches; visitors may not. No search fee. Required to search: name, years to search; also helpful DOB, SSN. Criminal records on docket books.
General Information: No sealed records released. SASE required. Turnaround time 1 day. Copy fee: $.50 for first page, $.25 each add'l. Certification fee: No cert fee. Fee payee: Mina Justice Court. Personal checks accepted. Prepayment is required.

Schurz Justice Court c/o Hawthorne Justice Ct, Hawthorne, NV 89415.

Note: Schurz court closed 1/1/2001; record now housed at Hawthorne Justice Court (see above.)

Nye County

5th Judicial District Court PO Box 1031, Tonopah, NV 89049; 775-482-8131; Fax: 775-482-8133. Hours: 8AM-5PM (PST). *Felony, Gross Misdemeanor, Civil Actions Over $7,500, Probate.*

Civil Records: Access: Phone, fax, mail, in person. Search fee: $1.00 per name per year. Required to search: name, years to search. Civil records on computer from 1991, on docket books from 1800s, many are microfilmed.
Criminal Records: Access: Phone, fax, mail, in person. Only the court performs in person searches; visitors may not. Search fee: $1.00 per name per year. Required to search: name, years to search. Criminal records on computer from 1991, on docket books from 1800s, many are microfilmed.
General Information: Public Access terminal is available. No adoptions or juvenile records released. SASE required. Turnaround time 1 day. Fax notes: $2.00 for first page, $1.00 each add'l. Copy fee: $1.00 per page. Certification fee: $3.00. Fee payee: Nye County Clerk. Business checks accepted. In-state personal checks accepted. Prepayment is required. Payment required if more than $15.00.

Beatty Justice Court PO Box 805, Beatty, NV 89003; 775-553-2951; Fax: 775-553-2136. Hours: 8AM-5PM (PST). *Misdemeanor, Civil Actions Under $7,500, Eviction, Small Claims.*

Civil Records: Access: Phone, mail, in person. Only the court performs in person searches; visitors may not. Search fee: $1.00 per name per year. Computer printouts on all civil actions (no way to segregate small claims or evictions) is $.50 per page. Required to search: name, years to search. Civil cases indexed by defendant, plaintiff. Civil records on computer from 1991, archived from 1950s, some on docket books.

Criminal Records: Access: Phone, mail, in person. Only the court performs in person searches; visitors may not. Search fee: $1.00 per name per year. Required to search: name, years to search, DOB. Criminal records on computer from 1989.
General Information: No sealed, confidential records released. SASE required. Turnaround time 1 week for mail requests, same day for phone requests when possible. Copy fee: $.30 per page. Certification fee: $3.00. Fee payee: Beatty Justice Court. Personal checks accepted. Prepayment is required.

Gabbs Justice Court PO Box 1151, Gabbs, NV 89409; 775-285-2379; Fax: 775-285-4263. Hours: 9AM-4PM M-Th (PST). *Misdemeanor, Civil Actions Under $7,500, Eviction, Small Claims.*

Civil Records: Access: Phone, mail, in person. Only the court performs in person searches; visitors may not. Search fee: $1.00 per name per year. Required to search: name, years to search. Civil cases indexed by plaintiff. Civil records on computer from 1993, archived from 1950s, some on docket books.
Criminal Records: Access: Phone, mail, in person. Only the court performs in person searches; visitors may not. Search fee: $1.00 per name per year. Required to search: name, years to search, DOB, offense, date of offense; also helpful: SSN. Criminal records on computer from 1993, archived from 1950s, some on docket books.
General Information: No juvenile records released. SASE required. Turnaround time same day. Copy fee: $1.00 per page. Certification fee: No cert fee. Fee payee: Gabbs Justice Court. Personal checks accepted.

Tonopah Justice Court PO Box 1151, Tonopah, NV 89049; 775-482-8155. Hours: 8AM-Noon, 1-5PM (PST). *Misdemeanor, Civil Actions Under $7,500, Eviction, Small Claims.*

Civil Records: Access: Phone, mail, in person. Only the court performs in person searches; visitors may not. Search fee: $1.00 per name per year. Required to search: name, years to search. Civil cases indexed by plaintiff. Civil records on computer from 1992, on archives from 1950s, some on docket books.
Criminal Records: Access: Phone, mail, in person. Only the court performs in person searches; visitors may not. Search fee: $1.00 per name per year. Required to search: name, years to search, offense, date of offense; also helpful: DOB, SSN. Criminal records on computer from 1992, on archives from 1950s, some on docket books.
General Information: SASE required. Turnaround time 1-2 weeks. Copy fee: $.30 per page. Certification fee: $3.00 per certification. Fee payee: Tonopah Justice Court. Business checks accepted.

Pershing County

6th Judicial District Court PO Box 820, Lovelock, NV 89419; 775-273-2410; Fax: 775-273-2434. Hours: 9AM-5PM (PST). *Felony, Civil Actions Over $7,500, Probate.*

Note: Misdemeanors are handled by the Lake Justice Court.

Civil Records: Access: Phone, fax, mail, in person. Only the court performs in person searches; visitors may not. Search fee: $1.00 per name per year. Required to search: name, years to search. Civil cases indexed by defendant, plaintiff. Civil records on computer from 1992, microfilmed from 1919-1938, books from 1919.
Criminal Records: Access: Phone, fax, mail, in person. Only the court performs in person searches; visitors may not. Search fee: $1.00 per name per year. Required to search: name, years to search. Criminal records on computer from 1992, microfilmed from 1919-1938, books from 1919.
General Information: No adoption, juvenile or sealed records released. SASE required. Turnaround time 1-3

days. Fax notes: No fee to fax results. Copy fee: $1.00 per page. Certification fee: $3.00. Fee payee: Pershing County Clerk. Personal checks accepted. Prepayment is required.

Lake Township Justice Court
PO Box 8, Lovelock, NV 89419; 775-273-2753; Fax: 775-273-0416. Hours: 8AM-5PM (PST). *Misdemeanor, Civil Actions Under $7,500, Eviction, Small Claims.*

Civil Records: Access: Phone, mail, in person. Only the court performs in person searches; visitors may not. Search fee: $1.00 per name per year. Required to search: name, years to search; also helpful: address. Civil cases indexed by defendant, plaintiff. Civil records on computer from 1988, on docket books prior.

Criminal Records: Access: Phone, mail, in person. Only the court performs in person searches; visitors may not. Search fee: $1.00 per name per year. Required to search: name, years to search; also helpful: DOB. Criminal records on computer from 1988, on docket books prior.

General Information: Public Access terminal is available. No sealed, driver's history or highway patrol records released. SASE required. Turnaround time 2 days, 30 minutes for phone requests for records prior to 1988. Copy fee: $.25 per page. Certification fee: $3.00. Fee payee: Lake Township Justice Court. Personal checks accepted. For payment by check proof of ID required.

Storey County

1st Judicial District Court
PO Drawer D, Virginia City, NV 89440; 775-847-0969; Fax: 775-847-0949. Hours: 9AM-5PM (PST). *Felony, Gross Misdemeanor, Civil Actions Over $7,500, Probate.*

Civil Records: Access: Phone, mail, in person. Both court and visitors may perform in person searches. Search fee: $1.00 per name per year. Required to search: name, years to search. Civil cases indexed by defendant, plaintiff. Civil records on computer since 1992; prior years on books. Search by phone only if paid in advance.

Criminal Records: Access: Phone, mail, in person. Both court and visitors may perform in person searches. Search fee: $1.00 per name per year. Required to search: name, years to search; also helpful: DOB, SSN. Criminal records on computer since 1992; prior years on books. Search by phone only if pre-paid.

General Information: No juvenile or sealed records released. SASE required. Turnaround time 1 week, 5 minutes for phone requests when possible. Copy fee: $1.00 per page. Certification fee: $5.00. Fee payee: Storey County Clerk. Personal checks accepted. Prepayment is required.

Virginia City Justice Court
PO Box 674, Virginia City, NV 89440; 775-847-0962; Fax: 775-847-0915. Hours: 9AM-5PM (PST). *Misdemeanor, Civil Actions Under $7,500, Eviction, Small Claims.*

Civil Records: Access: Phone, mail, in person. Only the court performs in person searches; visitors may not. Search fee: $1.00 per name per year. Required to search: name, years to search. Civil cases indexed by

defendant, plaintiff. Civil records retained for 7 years, some on docket books.

Criminal Records: Access: Phone, mail, in person. Both court and visitors may perform in person searches. Search fee: $1.00 per name per year. Required to search: name, years to search, DOB; also helpful: SSN. Criminal records on computer since 1988.

General Information: SASE required. Turnaround time 1 week. Copy fee: $.25 per page. Certification fee: $3.00. Fee payee: Justice Court. Personal checks accepted. Prepayment is required.

Washoe County

2nd Judicial District Court
PO Box 30083, Reno, NV 89520; 775-328-3110; Fax: 775-328-3515. Hours: 8AM-5PM (PST). *Felony, Gross Misdemeanor, Civil Actions Over $7,500, Probate.*

Civil Records: Access: Phone, mail, fax, in person. Both court and visitors may perform in person searches. Search fee: $1.00 per name per year. Required to search: name, years to search. Civil cases indexed by defendant, plaintiff. Civil records on computer back to 1984, microfiche from 1983, archives from 1920. Phone access limited to computer records.

Criminal Records: Access: Phone, Mail, fax, in person. Both court and visitors may perform in person searches. Search fee: $1.00 per name per year. Required to search: name, years to search. Criminal records on computer back to 1984, microfiche from 1983, archives from 1920. Phone access limited to computer records.

General Information: No sealed or juvenile records released. SASE required. Turnaround time 2 weeks. Copy fee: $1.00 per page. Certification fee: $6.00. Fee payee: Washoe County Clerk. Business checks accepted. Prepayment is required.

Reno Justice Court
PO Box 30083, Reno, NV 89520; 775-325-6501; Criminal phone: 775-325-6500; Fax: 775-325-6510. Hours: 8AM-5PM (PST). *Misdemeanor, Civil Actions Under $7,500, Eviction, Small Claims.*

Civil Records: Access: Phone, mail, in person. Both court and visitors may perform in person searches. Search fee: $1.00 per name per year. Required to search: name, years to search. Civil cases indexed by defendant. Civil records archived from 1982, on docket books. For mail access call first. Court will send form to be filled out & returned with payment.

Criminal Records: Access: Phone, mail, in person. Only the court performs in person searches; visitors may not. Search fee: $1.00 per name per year. Required to search: name, years to search; also helpful: DOB, SSN, aliases. Criminal records archived from 1982, on docket books. Same as civil.

General Information: No sealed records released. SASE required. Turnaround time 2-5 days. Copy fee: $.25 per page. Certification fee: $3.00 per page. Fee payee: Reno Justice Court. Only cashiers checks and money orders accepted.

Sparks Justice Court
630 Greenbrae Dr, Sparks, NV 89431; 775-352-3000. Hours: 8AM-5PM (PST). *Misdemeanor, Civil Actions Under $7,500, Eviction, Small Claims.*

Civil Records: Access: Phone, mail, in person. Both court and visitors may perform in person searches. Search fee: $1.00 per name per year. Required to search: name, years to search. Civil cases indexed by defendant, plaintiff. Civil records on computer last 11 years, prior in books and on cards.

Criminal Records: Access: Phone, mail, in person. Both court and visitors may perform in person searches. Search fee: $1.00 per name per year. Required to search: name, years to search; also helpful: DOB, SSN. Criminal records on computer last 6 years, prior in books and on cards.

General Information: Public Access terminal is available. Turnaround time 1-3 days. Fax notes: Will fax results if prepayment received. Copy fee: $.30 per document. Certification fee: $3.00. Fee payee: Justice Court. Personal checks accepted. For payment by check guarantee card required. Prepayment is required.

White Pine County

Ely Justice Court
PO Box 396, Ely, NV 89301; 775-289-2678; Fax: 775-289-3392. Hours: 9AM-5PM (PST). *Misdemeanor, Civil Actions Under $7,500, Eviction, Small Claims.*

Civil Records: Access: Phone, fax, mail, in person. Only the court performs in person searches; visitors may not. Search fee: $1.00 per name per year. Required to search: name, years to search. Civil cases indexed by defendant, plaintiff. Civil records on computer from 1988, archived from 1899.

Criminal Records: Access: Phone, fax, mail, in person. Only the court performs in person searches; visitors may not. Search fee: $1.00 per name per year. Required to search: name, years to search; also helpful: DOB, SSN. Criminal records on computer from 1988, archived from 1899.

General Information: No sealed records released. SASE required. Turnaround time 1-5 days. Copy fee: $.30 per page. Certification fee: $3.00. Fee payee: Ely Justice Court. Only cashiers checks and money orders accepted. Prepayment is required.

Lund Justice Court
PO Box 87, Lund, NV 89317; 775-238-5400; Fax: 775-238-5400. Hours: 10AM-2:30PM M,W,F (PST). *Misdemeanor, Civil Actions Under $7,500, Eviction, Small Claims.*

Civil Records: Access: Mail, in person. Only the court performs in person searches; visitors may not. Search fee: $1.00 per name per year. Required to search: name, years to search. Civil records only kept in files, archives from 1899.

Criminal Records: Access: Mail, in person. Only the court performs in person searches; visitors may not. Search fee: $1.00 per name per year. Required to search: name, years to search, DOB; also helpful: SSN. Criminal records only kept in files, archives from 1899.

General Information: SASE required. Turnaround time 1 day. Copy fee: $.25 per page. Certification fee: $2.00. Fee payee: Lund Justice Court. Personal checks accepted. Prepayment is required.

Nevada Recording Offices

ORGANIZATION
16 counties and one independent city, 17 recording offices. The recording officer is County Recorder. Carson City has a separate filing office. The entire state is in the Pacific Time Zone (PST).

REAL ESTATE RECORDS
Most counties will not provide real estate searches. Copies cost $1.00 per page and certification fees are usually $4.00 per document.

UCC RECORDS
Financing statements are filed at the state level, except for real estate related collateral, which are filed with the County Recorder. However, prior to 07/2001, consumer goods and farm collateral were also filed at the County Recorder and these older records can be searched there. All recording offices will perform UCC searches. Search fees are $15.00 per debtor name using the approved UCC-3 request form and $20.00 using a non-standard form. Copies cost $1.00 per page.

TAX LIEN RECORDS
Federal tax liens on personal property of businesses are filed with the Secretary of State. Federal tax liens on personal property of individuals are filed with the County Recorder. Although not called state tax liens, employment withholding judgments have the same effect and are filed with the County Recorder. Most counties will provide tax lien searches for a fee of $15.00 per name - $20.00 if the standard UCC request form is not used.

OTHER LIENS
Mechanics

STATEWIDE ONLINE INFO:
Online access to Assessor, Treasurer, Recorder and other county databases requires registration with goverNet, 208-522-1225. Sliding monthly and per-hit fees apply. Counties online are Churchill, Clark, Elko, Esmeralda, Eureka, Lander, Mineral, Nye, Pershing, Storey, Washoe, and White Pine. System includes access to Secretary of State's Corporation, Partnership, UCC, Fictitious Name, and Federal Tax Lien records.

Carson City

City Recorder, 885 E. Musser St., Ste 1028, Carson City, NV 89701-4775. City Recorder, R/E and UCC Recording 775-887-2260 UCC Recording: 775-887-2260 city level or 775-687-4280 St level; Fax 775-887-2146.
Will search UCC records. UCC search includes federal tax liens if requested. Will not search real estate records. **Other Phone Numbers:** Assessor 775-887-2130; Treasurer 775-887-2092; Elections 775-887-2087; Vital Records 775-684-4242.

Churchill County

County Recorder, 155 N. Taylor, Suite 131, Fallon, NV 89406-2748. County Recorder, R/E and UCC Recording 775-423-6001; Fax 775-423-8933. http://www.churchillcounty.org
Will search UCC records. UCC search includes federal tax liens if requested. Will not search real estate records. **Online Access:** Assessor, Treasurer, Recording. Online access is available on goverNet, 208-522-1225; requires registration and fees; see beginning of this section. **Other Phone Numbers:** Assessor 775-423-6584; Treasurer 775-423-6028; Appraiser/Auditor 775-423-6584; Elections 775-423-6028; Vital Records 775-684-4280.

Clark County

County Recorder, P.O. Box 551510, Las Vegas, NV 89155-1510. 702-455-4336; Fax 702-455-5644. http://www.co.clark.nv.us/assessor/Disclaim.htm
Will search UCC records. Will not search real estate records. **Online Access:** Real Estate, Liens, Property Assessor, UCC, Fictitious Names, Vital Records, Marriage. Property records, assessor maps, manufactured housing and road documents on the county Assessor database are available free online at www.co.clark.nv.us/assessor/Disclaim.htm. Search by parcel number, owner name, address, map, book & page. Marriage records are available online at www.co.clark.nv.us/recorder/mar_srch.htm. Real estate, UCC and Vital records are available free online at www.co.clark.nv.us/recorder/recindex.htm. County fictitious names can be searched at http://sandgate.co.clark.nv.us:8498/clarkcounty/clerk/cl

erkSearch.html. **Other Phone Numbers:** Assessor 702-455-3891; Treasurer 702-455-4323.

Douglas County

County Recorder, P.O. Box 218, Minden, NV 89423. 775-782-9025 R/E Recording: 775-782-9027; Fax 775-783-6413. http://www.recorder.co.douglas.nv.us
Will search UCC records. Will not search real estate records. **Online Access:** Assessor, Real Estate. Property records on the Assessor's database are available free online at www.co.douglas.nv.us/databases/assessors. **Other Phone Numbers:** Assessor 775-782-9830; Treasurer 775-782-9022; Vital Records 775-782-9027.

Elko County

County Recorder, 571 Idaho St., Room 103, Elko, NV 89801-3770. County Recorder, R/E and UCC Recording 775-738-6526; Fax 775-738-3299. http://www.governet.net/nv/co/elk/dir.cfm
Will search UCC records. Will not search real estate records. **Online Access:** Assessor, Treasurer, Recording. Online access is available on goverNet, 208-522-1225; requires registration and fees; see beginning of this section. **Other Phone Numbers:** Assessor 775-738-3088; Treasurer 775-738-5694; Elections 775-738-4600; Marriages 775-738-6526.

Esmeralda County

County Recorder, P.O. Box 458, Goldfield, NV 89013. 775-485-6337; Fax 775-485-3524.
Will search UCC records. **Online Access:** Assessor, Treasurer, Recording. Online access is available on goverNet, 208-522-1225; requires registration and fees; see beginning of this section. **Other Phone Numbers:** Assessor 775-485-6380; Treasurer 775-485-6367.

Eureka County

County Recorder, P.O. Box 556, Eureka, NV 89316. County Recorder, R/E and UCC Recording 775-237-5263; Fax 775-237-5614.
Will search UCC records. Will not search real estate records. **Online Access:** Assessor, Treasurer, Recorder. Online access is available on goverNet, 208-522-1225; requires registration and fees; see beginning of this section. **Other Phone Numbers:** Assessor 775-237-

5270; Treasurer 775-237-5262; Appraiser/Auditor 775-237-5270; Elections 775-237-5262.

Humboldt County

County Recorder, 25 West 4th Street, Winnemucca, NV 89445. County Recorder, R/E and UCC Recording 775-623-6414 UCC Recording: 775-623-6412; Fax 775-623-6337. www.humboldt-county-nv.net
Will search UCC records. UCC search does not include federal tax liens. Will not search real estate records. **Other Phone Numbers:** Assessor 775-623-6310; Treasurer 775-623-6444; Appraiser/Auditor 775-623-6310; Elections 775-623-6343; Vital Records 775-623-6412; 775-623-6414.

Lander County

County Recorder, 315 South Humboldt, Battle Mountain, NV 89820. County Recorder, R/E and UCC Recording 775-635-5173; Fax 775-635-8272.
Will search UCC records. Federal tax liens not included in UCC search Will not search real estate records. **Other Phone Numbers:** Assessor 775-635-2610; Treasurer 775-635-5127.

Lincoln County

County Recorder, P.O. Box 218, Pioche, NV 89043. 775-962-5495; Fax 775-962-5180.
Will search UCC records. Will not search real estate records. **Other Phone Numbers:** Assessor 775-962-5890; Treasurer 775-962-5805.

Lyon County

County Recorder, P.O. Box 927, Yerington, NV 89447-0927. County Recorder, R/E and UCC Recording 775-463-6581; Fax 775-463-6585.
Will search UCC records. Will not search real estate records. **Other Phone Numbers:** Assessor 775-463-6524; Treasurer 775-463-6502; Appraiser/Auditor 775-463-6524; Elections 775-463-6502; Vital Records 775-463-6581.

Mineral County

County Recorder, P.O. Box 1447, Hawthorne, NV 89415-1447. 775-945-3676; Fax 775-945-1749.

Will search UCC records. Will not search real estate records. **Online Access:** Assessor, Treasurer, Recording. Online access is available on goverNet, 208-522-1225; requires registration and fees; see beginning of this section. **Other Phone Numbers:** Assessor 775-945-3684; Treasurer 775-945-2446.

Nye County

County Recorder, P.O. Box 1111, Tonopah, NV 89049-1111. 775-482-8116 R/E Recording: 775-482-8118; Fax 775-482-8111.
Will search UCC records. Will not search real estate records. **Online Access:** Assessor, Treasurer, Recording. Online access is available on goverNet, 208-522-1225; requires registration and fees. **Other Phone Numbers:** Assessor 775-482-8174; Treasurer 775-482-8194.

Pershing County

County Recorder, P.O. Box 736, Lovelock, NV 89419-0736. County Recorder, R/E and UCC Recording 775-273-2408; Fax 775-273-1039.
Will search UCC records. UCC search does not include federal tax liens. Will not search real estate records. **Online Access:** Assessor, Treasurer, Recording. Online access is available on goverNet, 208-522-1225; requires registration and fees; see beginning of this section.

Other Phone Numbers: Assessor 775-273-2369; Treasurer 775-273-2208.

Storey County

County Recorder, P.O. Box 493, Virginia City, NV 89440. 775-847-0967; Fax 775-847-1009.
Will search UCC records. UCC search does not include federal tax liens. Will not search real estate records. **Online Access:** Assessor, Treasurer, Recording. Online access is available on goverNet, 208-522-1225; requires registration and fees; see beginning of this section. **Other Phone Numbers:** Assessor 775-847-0961; Treasurer 775-847-0969; Elections 775-847-0969.

Washoe County

County Recorder, P.O. Box 11130, Reno, NV 89520-0027. 775-328-3661 R/E Recording: 775-328-2230.
Will search UCC records. UCC search does not include federal tax liens. Will not search real estate records. **Online Access:** Assessor, Treasurer, Recording. Online access is available on goverNet, 208-522-1225; requires registration and fees; see beginning of this section. **Other Phone Numbers:** Assessor 775-328-2277; Treasurer 775-328-2510.

White Pine County

County Recorder, P.O. Box 68, Ely, NV 89301. County Recorder, R/E and UCC Recording 775-289-4567; Fax 775-289-1541.
Will search UCC records. Will not search real estate records. **Other Phone Numbers:** Assessor 775-289-3016; Treasurer 775-289-4783.

Nevada County Locator

You will usually be able to find the city name in the City/County Cross Reference below. In that case, it is a simple matter to determine the county from the cross reference. However, only the official US Postal Service city names are included in this index. There are an additional 40,000 place names that people use in their addresses. Therefore, we have also included a ZIP/City Cross Reference immediately following the City/County Cross Reference.

If you know the ZIP Code but the city name does not appear in the City/County Cross Reference index, look up the ZIP Code in the ZIP/City Cross Reference, find the city name, then look up the city name in the City/County Cross Reference. For example, you want to know the county for an address of Menands, NY 12204. There is no "Menands" in the City/County Cross Reference. The ZIP/City Cross Reference shows that ZIP Codes 12201-12288 are for the city of Albany. Looking back in the City/County Cross Reference, Albany is in Albany County.

City/County Cross Reference

ALAMO Lincoln
AMARGOSA VALLEY Nye
AUSTIN Lander
BAKER White Pine
BATTLE MOUNTAIN Lander
BEATTY Nye
BLUE DIAMOND Clark
BOULDER CITY Clark
BUNKERVILLE Clark
CAL NEV ARI Clark
CALIENTE Lincoln
CARLIN Elko
CARSON CITY (89706) Carson City(88), Lyon(11)
CARSON CITY Carson City
CARSON CITY Douglas
CRESCENT VALLEY Eureka
CRYSTAL BAY Washoe
DAYTON (89403) Lyon(82), Storey(18)
DEETH Elko
DENIO Humboldt
DUCKWATER White Pine
DYER (89010) Esmeralda(95), Pershing(5)
EAST ELY White Pine
ELKO Elko
ELY White Pine
EMPIRE Washoe

EUREKA Eureka
FALLON Churchill
FERNLEY Lyon
GABBS Nye
GARDNERVILLE Douglas
GENOA Douglas
GERLACH Washoe
GLENBROOK Douglas
GOLCONDA Humboldt
GOLDFIELD Esmeralda
HALLECK Elko
HAWTHORNE Mineral
HENDERSON Clark
HIKO Lincoln
IMLAY Pershing
INCLINE VILLAGE Washoe
INDIAN SPRINGS Clark
JACKPOT Elko
JARBIDGE Elko
JEAN Clark
LAMOILLE Elko
LAS VEGAS Clark
LAUGHLIN Clark
LOGANDALE Clark
LOVELOCK Pershing
LUND White Pine
LUNING Mineral

MANHATTAN Nye
MC DERMITT Humboldt
MC GILL White Pine
MERCURY Nye
MESQUITE Clark
MINA Mineral
MINDEN Douglas
MOAPA Clark
MONTELLO Elko
MOUNTAIN CITY Elko
NELLIS AFB Clark
NIXON Washoe
NORTH LAS VEGAS Clark
OROVADA Humboldt
OVERTON Clark
OWYHEE Elko
PAHRUMP Nye
PANACA Lincoln
PARADISE VALLEY Humboldt
PIOCHE Lincoln
RENO (89511) Washoe(94), Storey(7)
RENO Washoe
ROUND MOUNTAIN Nye
RUBY VALLEY Elko
RUTH White Pine
SCHURZ Mineral
SEARCHLIGHT Clark

SILVER CITY Lyon
SILVER SPRINGS Lyon
SILVERPEAK Esmeralda
SMITH Lyon
SPARKS (89434) Washoe(97), Storey(3)
SPARKS Washoe
STATELINE Douglas
SUN VALLEY Washoe
THE LAKES Clark
TONOPAH (89049) Nye(98), Esmeralda(2)
TUSCARORA Elko
VALMY Humboldt
VERDI Washoe
VIRGINIA CITY Storey
WADSWORTH Washoe
WASHOE VALLEY Washoe
WELLINGTON Lyon
WELLS Elko
WEST WENDOVER Elko
WINNEMUCCA (89445) Humboldt(93), Pershing(7)
WINNEMUCCA Humboldt
YERINGTON Lyon
ZEPHYR COVE Douglas

ZIP/City Cross Reference

88901-88905	THE LAKES	89042-89042	PANACA	89408-89408	FERNLEY	89444-89444	WELLINGTON
89001-89001	ALAMO	89043-89043	PIOCHE	89409-89409	GABBS	89445-89446	WINNEMUCCA
89003-89003	BEATTY	89045-89045	ROUND MOUNTAIN	89410-89410	GARDNERVILLE	89447-89447	YERINGTON
89004-89004	BLUE DIAMOND	89046-89046	SEARCHLIGHT	89411-89411	GENOA	89448-89448	ZEPHYR COVE
89005-89006	BOULDER CITY	89047-89047	SILVERPEAK	89412-89412	GERLACH	89449-89449	STATELINE
89007-89007	BUNKERVILLE	89048-89048	PAHRUMP	89413-89413	GLENBROOK	89450-89452	INCLINE VILLAGE
89008-89008	CALIENTE	89049-89049	TONOPAH	89414-89414	GOLCONDA	89496-89496	FALLON
89009-89009	HENDERSON	89053-89053	HENDERSON	89415-89415	HAWTHORNE	89501-89599	RENO
89010-89010	DYER	89070-89070	INDIAN SPRINGS	89418-89418	IMLAY	89701-89703	CARSON CITY
89011-89012	HENDERSON	89101-89160	LAS VEGAS	89419-89419	LOVELOCK	89704-89704	WASHOE VALLEY
89013-89013	GOLDFIELD	89163-89163	THE LAKES	89420-89420	LUNING	89705-89721	CARSON CITY
89014-89016	HENDERSON	89164-89185	LAS VEGAS	89421-89421	MC DERMITT	89801-89803	ELKO
89017-89017	HIKO	89191-89191	NELLIS AFB	89422-89422	MINA	89820-89820	BATTLE MOUNTAIN
89018-89018	INDIAN SPRINGS	89193-89199	LAS VEGAS	89423-89423	MINDEN	89821-89821	CRESCENT VALLEY
89019-89019	JEAN	89301-89301	ELY	89424-89424	NIXON	89822-89822	CARLIN
89020-89020	AMARGOSA VALLEY	89310-89310	AUSTIN	89425-89425	OROVADA	89823-89823	DEETH
89021-89021	LOGANDALE	89311-89311	BAKER	89426-89426	PARADISE VALLEY	89824-89824	HALLECK
89022-89022	MANHATTAN	89314-89314	DUCKWATER	89427-89427	SCHURZ	89825-89825	JACKPOT
89023-89023	MERCURY	89315-89315	EAST ELY	89428-89428	SILVER CITY	89826-89826	JARBIDGE
89024-89024	MESQUITE	89316-89316	EUREKA	89429-89429	SILVER SPRINGS	89828-89828	LAMOILLE
89025-89025	MOAPA	89317-89317	LUND	89430-89430	SMITH	89830-89830	MONTELLO
89026-89026	JEAN	89318-89318	MC GILL	89431-89432	SPARKS	89831-89831	MOUNTAIN CITY
89027-89027	MESQUITE	89319-89319	RUTH	89433-89433	SUN VALLEY	89832-89832	OWYHEE
89028-89029	LAUGHLIN	89402-89402	CRYSTAL BAY	89434-89436	SPARKS	89833-89833	RUBY VALLEY
89030-89036	NORTH LAS VEGAS	89403-89403	DAYTON	89438-89438	VALMY	89834-89834	TUSCARORA
89039-89039	CAL NEV ARI	89404-89404	DENIO	89439-89439	VERDI	89835-89835	WELLS
89040-89040	OVERTON	89405-89405	EMPIRE	89440-89440	VIRGINIA CITY	89883-89883	WEST WENDOVER
89041-89041	PAHRUMP	89406-89407	FALLON	89442-89442	WADSWORTH		

New Hampshire

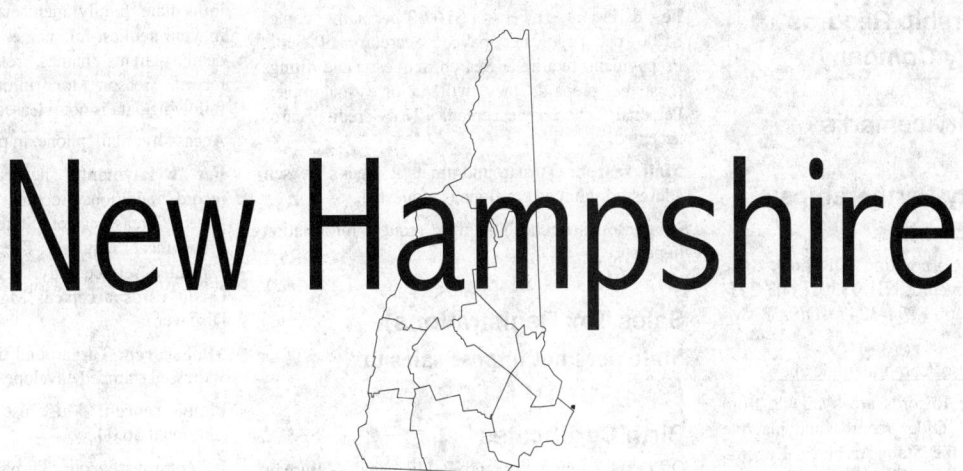

General Help Numbers:

Governor's Office
State House   603-271-2121
107 N Main St, Rm 204   Fax 603-271-5686
Concord, NH 03301-4990   8AM-5PM
http://www.state.nh.us/governor/index.html

Attorney General's Office
33 Capitol St   603-271-3658
Concord, NH 03301-6397   Fax 603-271-2110
http://webster.state.nh.us/nhdoj   8AM-5PM

State Court Administrator
2 Noble Dr   603-271-2521
Concord, NH 03301-6160   Fax 603-271-3977
http://www.state.nh.us/courts/aoc.htm   8AM-5PM

State Archives
Division of Records Management   603-271-2236
  & Archives
71 S Fruit St   Fax 603-271-2272
Concord, NH 03301   8AM-4:30PM
http://webster.state.nh.us/state

State Specifics:

Capital: Concord
     Merrimack County

Time Zone: EST

Number of Counties: 10

Population: 1,235,786

Web Site: www.state.nh.us

State Agencies

Criminal Records

State Police Headquarters, Criminal Records, James H. Hayes Bldg, 10 Hazen Dr, Concord, NH 03305; 603-271-2538, 8:15AM-4:15PM.

http://www.state.nh.us/nhsp/cr.html

Note: Sex offender data is available online at www.wmur.com/sexoffenders.

Indexing & Storage: Records are available from circa 1900. New records are available for inquiry immediately.

Searching: Requester must have "authorization in writing, duly signed and notarized, explicitly allowing the requester to receive such information." Also specify exactly what information is needed. Non-conviction information is not released. Include the following in your request-full name, date of birth, any aliases, sex, race.

Access by: mail, in person.

Fee & Payment: The search fee is $10.00 per name. Fee payee: NH State Police. Prepayment required. Personal checks accepted. No credit cards accepted.

Mail search: Turnaround time: 1 week. No self addressed stamped envelope is required.

In person search: Searching is available in person.

Corporation Records
Limited Partnership Records
Limited Liability Company Records
Trademarks/Servicemarks
Trade Names
Limited Liability Partnerships
Not For Profit Entities

Secretary of State, Corporation Division, State House, Room 204, Concord, NH 03301; 603-271-3246, 603-271-3244, 603-271-3247 (Fax), 8AM-4:30PM.

http://www.state.nh.us/sos/corporate/index.htm

Indexing & Storage: Records are available from inception of the laws. Older records and inactive records are stored at the State Archives. Records also include foreign partnerships, investment trusts and cooperatives. New records are available for inquiry immediately. Records are indexed on inhouse computer.

Searching: Include the following in your request-full name of business, specific records that you need copies of. In addition to the articles of incorporation, corporation records include the following information: Annual Reports, Officers, Directors, Prior (merged) names, Inactive and Reserved names.

Access by: mail, phone, fax, in person.

Fee & Payment: There is no charge for 20 pages or less. If more than 20 pages, the charge is $.50 per page for every page. Certification is $5.00 plus $1.00 per page. Note that they do not print computer screens, but take copies straight from files. Fee payee: Secretary of State. They will invoice for copy fees, but you must pay in advance for certificates of good standing. Fax accounts may be billed monthly. Personal checks accepted. No credit cards accepted.

Mail search: Turnaround time: 1 to 2 days. A self addressed stamped envelope is requested.

Phone search: No fee for telephone request. An information line, 603-271-3246, is open from 8 to 12 and 1 to 4. You can obtain name, address, incorporation date, and registered agent, check name availability, and request document copies.

Fax search: See expedited service information.

In person search: You may request information in person, the agency does the copying.

Other access: Corporation or trade name monthly hard copies are $20.00 each or $180.00 for a 1 year subscription. A list of new registrations is $350.00 per 6 months.

Uniform Commercial Code
Federal Tax Liens
State Tax Liens

UCC Division, Secretary of State, 25 Capitol St, State House Annex, 3rd Floor, Concord, NH 03301; 603-271-3276, 9AM-3:30PM (searches).

http://www.state.nh.us/sos/UCC

Indexing & Storage: Records are available for active filings only.

Searching: Use search request form UCC-11. In general, tax liens on businesses are filed here and on individuals at the town/county level. It is suggested to search both places. Include the following in your request-debtor name.

Access by: mail, in person.

Fee & Payment: Fees is $10.00 per name, copies $1.00 per page. Fee payee: Secretary of State. Prepayment required. Search requests and filings must be prepaid, they will invoice for copies. Personal checks accepted. No credit cards accepted.

Mail search: Turnaround time: 2 weeks. A self addressed stamped envelope is requested.

In person search: You may request information in person.

Sales Tax Registrations
State does not impose sales tax.

Birth Certificates

Office of Community and Public Health, Bureau of Vital Records, 6 Hazen Dr, Concord, NH 03301-6527; 603-271-4650, 603-271-4654 (Recording), 800-852-3345 x4651 (In-state), 603-271-3447 (Fax), 8:30AM-4PM.

http://www.dhhs.state.nh.us

Note: For genealogical purposes, birth records prior to 1901 may be released without restriction.

Indexing & Storage: Records are available from 1640 to present. Records are on computer since 1990, indexed since 1948. Records are indexed on microfiche, index cards, computer.

Searching: Must have a signed release from person of record or immediate family member or show proof of "tangible interest." Order forms are available at the web site. Include the following in your request-full name, names of parents, mother's maiden name, date of birth, place of birth, relationship to person of record, reason for information request.

Access by: mail, phone, in person.

Fee & Payment: The search fee is $12.00 per record and $8.00 for each additional copy of the same record. Fee payee: Treasurer of State of New Hampshire. Prepayment required. Credit cards accepted for expedited service only. Personal checks accepted. Credit cards accepted: MasterCard, Visa, AmEx, Discover.

Mail search: Turnaround time: 3 to 5 days. A self addressed stamped envelope is requested.

Phone search: Must use credit card for additional $6.00 fee.

In person search: Turnaround time while you wait.

Expedited service: Expedited service is available for mail and phone searches. Turnaround time: overnight delivery. Add $12.50 per package. Add regular fees and credit card fee.

Death Records

Office of Community and Public Health, Bureau of Vital Records, 6 Hazen Dr, Concord, NH 03301-6527; 603-271-4650, 603-271-4654 (Recording), 800-852-3345 x4651 (In-state), 603-271-3447 (Fax), 8:30AM-4PM.

http://www.dhhs.state.nh.us

Note: For genealogical purposes, death records prior to 1938 may be released without restriction.

Indexing & Storage: Records are available from 1640 to present. Records are computerized since 1990, indexed on computer since 1948. Records are indexed on microfiche, index cards, computer.

Searching: Must have a signed release form from immediate family member. Include the following in your request-full name, date of death, place of death, parents' names, relationship to person of record, reason for information request. The following data is not released: cause of death.

Access by: mail, phone, in person.

Fee & Payment: The search fee is $12.00 per record, additional copies are $8.00 each. Fee payee: Treasurer of State of New Hampshire. Prepayment required. Credit cards accepted for expedited service only. Personal checks accepted. Credit cards accepted: MasterCard, Visa, AmEx, Discover.

Mail search: Turnaround time: 3 to 5 days. A self addressed stamped envelope is requested.

Phone search: Must use a credit card for an additional $6.00 fee.

In person search: Turnaround time while you wait.

Expedited service: Expedited service is available for mail and phone searches. Turnaround time: overnight delivery. Add $12.50 per package. Add regular fees and credit card fee.

Marriage Certificates

Office of Community and Public Health, Bureau of Vital Records & Health Statistics, 6 Hazen Dr, Concord, NH 03301-6527; 603-271-4650, 603-271-4654 (Recording), 800-852-3345 x4651 (In-state), 603-271-3447 (Fax), 8:30AM-4PM.

http://www.dhhs.state.nh.us

Note: For genealogical purposes, marriage records prior to 1938 may be released without restriction.

Indexing & Storage: Records are available from 1640 to present. Records are computerized from 1990, indexed on computer since 1948. Records are indexed on microfiche, index cards.

Searching: Must have a signed release form from persons of record or immediate family member. Include the following in your request-names of husband and wife, date of marriage, place or county of marriage, relationship to person of record, reason for information request, wife's maiden name.

Access by: mail, phone, in person.

Fee & Payment: The search fee is $12.00 per record, each additional copy is $8.00. Fee payee: Treasurer of State of New Hampshire. Prepayment required. Credit cards accepted for expedited service only. Personal checks accepted. Credit cards accepted: MasterCard, Visa, AmEx, Discover.

Mail search: Turnaround time: 3 to 5 days. A self addressed stamped envelope is requested.

Phone search: Must use a credit card for an additional $6.00 fee.

In person search: Turnaround time while you wait.

Expedited service: Expedited service is available for mail and phone searches. Turnaround time: overnight delivery. Add $12.50 per package. Add regular search fee and credit card fee.

Divorce Records

Office of Community and Public Health, Bureau of Vital Records, 6 Hazen Dr, Concord, NH 03301-6527; 603-271-4650, 603-271-4654 (Recording), 800-852-3345 x4651 (In-state), 603-271-3447 (Fax), 8:30AM-4PM.

http://www.dhhs.state.nh.us

Note: For genealogical purposes, divorce records prior to 1938 may be released without restriction.

Indexing & Storage: Records are available from 1640 to present. Records are computerized since 1990, indexed on computer since 1948. Records are indexed on microfiche, index cards.

Searching: Must have a signed release from person of record or immediate family member. Include the following in your request-names of husband and wife, date of divorce, year divorce case began, case number (if known), relationship to person of record, reason for information request.

Access by: mail, phone, in person.

Fee & Payment: The search fee is $12.00 per record, additional copies are $8.00 each. Fee payee: Treasurer of State of New Hampshire. Prepayment required. Credit cards accepted for expedited service only. Personal checks accepted. Credit cards accepted: MasterCard, Visa, AmEx, Discover.

Mail search: Turnaround time: 3 to 5 days. A self addressed stamped envelope is requested.

Phone search: Must use a credit card for an additional $6.00 fee.

In person search: Turnaround time while you wait.

Expedited service: Expedited service is available for mail and phone searches. Turnaround time: overnight delivery. Add $12.50 per package. Add search fee and credit card fee.

Workers' Compensation Records

Labor Department, Workers Compensation Division, State Office Park S, 95 Pleasant St, Concord, NH 03301; 603-271-3174, 603-271-6149 (Fax), 8AM-4:30PM.

Indexing & Storage: Records are available from 1990 to present. Records prior to 1990 are kept at the State Archives. However, one must go through this office for records. It takes 1-2 weeks before new records are available for inquiry. Records are indexed on microfilm.

Searching: Must have an authorized release from claimant. Include the following in your request-claimant name, Social Security Number, date of accident, place of employment at time of accident.

Access by: mail, fax.

Fee & Payment: There is no search fee, copy fee is $.35 per page. Fee payee: Labor Department. Prepayment required. Personal checks accepted. No credit cards accepted.

Mail search: Turnaround time: 2 to 3 weeks. A self addressed stamped envelope is requested.

Fax search: Allow 1 week turnaround time.

Driver Records

Department of Motor Vehicles, Driving Records, 10 Hazen Dr, Concord, NH 03305; 603-271-2322, 8:15AM-4:15PM.

http://www.state.nh.us/dmv

Note: New Hampshire recommends going to the local courts for copies of tickets or to state Financial Responsibility agency.

Indexing & Storage: Records are available for 5 years for moving violations and 7 for DWIs. Surrendered license information remains on the system at least 5 years after the expiration date. The driver's address is on manually processed

records, but not on tape records. It takes 2 to 3 weeks normally before new records are available for inquiry.

Searching: Unless written, notarized authorization by subject is received, only specific business entities may receive records with personal information. Include the following in your request-full name, date of birth. The license number is not required for a search, but is suggested.

Access by: mail, in person, online.

Fee & Payment: Records are $7.00. If you wish the record certified records the fee is $10.00. Fee payee: Department of Safety. Prepayment required. Personal checks accepted. No credit cards accepted.

Mail search: Turnaround time: 2 days. Mail-in requests must include requester's name and address. Casual requesters must include the notarized authorization from the subject.A self addressed stamped envelope is requested.

In person search: Three requests can be processed while you wait.

Online search: Online access is offered for approved commercial accounts. The system is open 22 hours a day. Searches are by license number or by name and DOB. Fee is $7.00 per record. For more information, call Chuck DeGrace at 603 271-2314.

Other access: Overnight magnetic tape access is available for higher volume users. Minimum order is 50 requests. The state offers database sales of license information to approved requesters.

Vehicle Identification

Department of Safety, Bureau of Title, 10 Hazen Dr, Concord, NH 03305; 603-271-3111 (Bureau of Title), 8:15AM-4:15PM.

http://www.state.nh.us/safety/dmv.htm

Indexing & Storage: Records are available 11 years to present. It takes 2 weeks before new records are available for inquiry.

Searching: The state will only release to requesters authorized by statute or with a signed release. VIN must be submitted with each request.

Access by: mail, in person.

Fee & Payment: The fee is $20.00 for a title and lien history; $5.00 for a registration listing. Fee payee: Department of Safety. Prepayment required. Personal checks accepted. No credit cards accepted.

Mail search: Turnaround time: 2 to 5 days. A self addressed stamped envelope is requested.

In person search: Turnaround time while you wait.

Vehicle Ownership
Vessel Registration

Department of Safety, Registration, 10 Hazen Dr, Concord, NH 03305; 603-271-2251, 603-271-2333 (Boat Desk), 8:15AM-4:15PM.

Indexing & Storage: Records are available for current registration records only. All motorized boats and all sailboats over 14 ft must be registered. (Boats are not titled, liens on boats are at the Secretary of State).

Searching: Records are restricted to those authorized by statute. Authorization is stricter than the DPPA requirements. Include the following in

your request-owner's name, plate number or VIN is required to search.

Access by: mail, in person.

Fee & Payment: The fee is $5.00 per record. Fee payee: State of New Hampshire. Personal checks accepted. No credit cards accepted.

Mail search: Turnaround time: 3 to 5 days.

In person search: Turnaround time is immediate.

Other access: For authorized requesters, the entire database in available on microfiche or magnetic tape with quarterly updates. Also, customized selection is available on tape, microfiche or paper output. Call 603-271-2314 for more details.

Accident Reports

Department of Safety, Accident Reproduction Section, 10 Hazen Dr, Concord, NH 03305; 603-271-2128, 8:15AM-4:15PM.

Indexing & Storage: Records are available for 5 years. Records are indexed on computer. It takes 3 to 4 weeks before new records are available for inquiry.

Searching: Access is not open to the public due to Privacy Act, Chapter 295,260:14. This requires by law a notarized DSMV 505 Form to be filled out by the subject involved or by an insurance representative licensed to write auto policies in this state. Include the following in your request-full name, date of birth, date of accident, location of accident. It is suggested to include both operators' names in the request.

Access by: mail.

Fee & Payment: The fee is $1.00 per page. There is no charge for a "no record found." Requesters are notified of the fee for reports after the report has become available. Fee payee: Department of Safety. Prepayment required. Personal checks accepted. No credit cards accepted.

Mail search: Turnaround time: 3 to 4 weeks. A self addressed stamped envelope is requested.

Legislation Records

New Hampshire State Library, 20 Part St, Concord, NH 03301; 603-271-2239, 603-271-2205 (Fax), 8AM-4:30PM.

http://www.state.nh.us/gencourt/iegencourt.html

Indexing & Storage: Records are available from 1989 to present on computer. There are also bound House and Senate Journals from 1800's to present.

Searching: Bill number or key word required to search.

Access by: mail, phone, fax, in person, online.

Fee & Payment: There is no search fee, but there is a copy fee of $.20 per page, minimum $1.00. Fee payee: New Hampshire State Library. Personal checks accepted. No credit cards accepted.

Mail search: Turnaround time: 1 day. No self addressed stamped envelope is required.

Phone search: Will invoice.

Fax search: Fax charge is $.35 per page, minimum $1.00.

In person search: Searching is available in person.

Online search: Information can be viewed from the web site.

Voter Registration

Records not maintained by a state level agency.

Note: All records are kept by Town Clerks. Records are open.

GED Certificates

Department of Education, GED Testing, 101 Pleasant Street, Concord, NH 03301; 603-271-6699, 603-271-3454 (Fax), 7:30AM-4PM.

http://www.ed.state.nh.us

Indexing & Storage: Records are indexed on microfiche.

Searching: Include the following in your request-Social Security Number, date of birth, year of issue, name at the time. The date is needed since records are filed by year. For a copy of a transcript, include a signed release.

Access by: mail.

Fee & Payment: The fee is $3.00 for a transcript, there is no fee for a verification. Fee payee: State of New Hampshire. Prepayment required. No credit cards accepted.

Mail search: Turnaround time: 1 week. No self addressed stamped envelope is required.

Hunting License Information
Fishing License Information

Fish & Game Department, Licensing Department, Two Hazen Dr, Concord, NH 03301; 603-271-3421, 603-271-5829 (Fax), 8AM-4:30PM.

http://www.wildlife.state.nh.us

Indexing & Storage: Records are available for 3 years back to present. Records are indexed on computer. Records are indexed on inhouse computer.

Searching: Requests must be in writing on their form with payment in advance in order to be processed. Include the following in your request-full name, date of birth. The following data is not released: financial information.

Access by: mail, in person.

Fee & Payment: There is a $5.00 minimum fee; copies are $2.00 for the first page, $1.00 each additional. Fee payee: NH Fish & Game. Prepayment required. Turnaround time: 1 to 3 weeks. Personal checks accepted. No credit cards accepted.

Mail search: Turnaround time: 2 weeks. Request must be in writing with payment in advance.No self addressed stamped envelope is required.

In person search: Written request is require with payment in advance.

Other access: Mailing labels are available at a cost of $25.00 plus $.10 per label.

New Hampshire State Licensing Agencies

Licenses Searchable Online

Architect #34 .... www.state.nh.us/jtboard/arlist.htm

Bank #01 .... http://webster.state.nh.us/banking/banking.html

Credit Union #01 .... http://webster.state.nh.us/banking/banking.html

Engineer #34 .... www.state.nh.us/jtboard/pe.htm

Forester #34 .... www.state.nh.us/jtboard/forlist.htm

Lobbyist #30 .... www.lobbyist.net/NewHamps/NEWLOB.htm

Marital Mediator #36 .... www.state.nh.us/marital/mediators.html

Natural Scientist #34 .... www.state.nh.us/jtboard/ns.htm

Optometrist #23 .... www.odfinder.org/LicSearch.asp

Surveyor #34 .... www.state.nh.us/jtboard/lsis.htm

Licensing Quick Finder

Accessibility Lift Mechanic #28 603-271-2585	Engineer #34 603-271-2219	Pharmacist #27 603-271-2350
Acupuncturist #10 603-335-1425	Esthetician #04 603-271-3608	Pharmacy #27 603-271-2350
Alcohol/Drug Counselor #41 603-271-6112	Explosive Storage License #39 603-271-3575	Pharmacy Technicians #27 603-271-2350
Ambulance Attendent #22 603-271-7048	Explosives Competency License #39 603-271-3575	Physical Therapist #45 603-271-8389
Ambulance Service #22 603-271-7048	Fire Inspector #38 603-271-2661	Physical Therapist Assistant #45 603-271-8389
Architect #34 603-271-2219	Firefighter #38 603-271-2661	Physician #19 603-271-1203
Asbestos Abatement Worker #46 603-271-4609	Fireworks Competency License #39 603-271-3575	Physician Assitant #19 603-271-1203
Athletic Trainer #45 603-271-8389	Forester #34 603-271-2219	Plumber #09 603-271-3267
Attorney #43 603-271-2646	Foster Family Home #10 800-852-3345	Podiatrist #19 603-271-1203
Auctioneer #03 603-271-3242	Funeral Director #17 603-271-4648	Police Detective #49 603-271-2133
Audiologist #47 603-436-4010	Hearing Aid Dispenser/Fitter #25 603-271-5127	Police Officer #49 603-271-2133
Bail Bondsman #50 603-271-1463	Horse Trainer #48 603-271-2158	Private Detective #39 603-271-3575
Bank #01 603-271-3561	Insurance Adjuster #33 603-271-2261	Private Investigator #38 603-271-3575
Bank Holding Company #01 603-271-3561	Insurance Advisor/Consultant #33 603-271-2261	Psychologist #26 603-271-6762
Bank, Cooperative #01 603-271-3561	Insurance Agent #33 603-271-2261	Public Accountant-CPA #02 603-271-3286
Barber #04 603-271-3608	Insurance Broker #33 603-271-2261	Public Health Clinic #27 603-271-2350
Bingo/Lottery Operation #44 603-271-3391	Insurance Company #33 603-271-2261	Pump Installer #40 603-271-3139
Boiler Inspector #28 603-271-2585	Itinerant Vendor #30 603-271-3242	Real Estate Appraiser #31 603-271-6186
Boxing or Wrestling Contestant #30 603-271-3242	Liquor License #35 603-271-3755	Real Estate Broker #32 603-271-2701
Boxing or Wrestling Manager/Promoter #30	Loan Company, Small #01 603-271-3561	Real Estate Firm #32 603-271-2701
....603-271-3242	Loan Production Office #01 603-271-3561	Real Estate Salesperson #32 603-271-2701
Boxing or Wrestling Referee/Second/Timekeeper #30	Lobbyist #30 603-271-3242	Residential Care Facility, Children #21..603-271-4624
....603-271-3242	Manicurist #04 603-271-3608	Respiratory Care Practitioner #20 603-271-1203
Cash Dispensing (Non-Bank) Machine #01	Marital Mediator #36 603-271-6593	Respiratory Care Practitioner #45 603-271-8389
....603-271-3561	Marriage & Family Therapist #26 603-271-6762	Savings Bank #01 603-271-3561
Child Care Facility #21 603-271-4624	Mental Health Counselor, Clinical #26...603-271-6762	School Administrator #07 603-271-3871
Child Placing Agency #10 800-852-3345	Midwife #24 603-271-4667	Second Mortgage Home Loan Lender #01 ....
Chiropractor #14 603-271-4560	Mortgage (First) Banker, Non-Depository #01	603-271-3561
Concealed Weapons License, Non-Resident #39	603-271-3561	Securities Salesperson #50 603-271-1463
....603-271-3575	Mortgage (First) Broker #01 603-271-3561	Security Guard #39 603-271-3575
Corrections Officer #49 603-271-2133	Mortgage Servicer #01 603-271-3561	Shorthand Reporter #37 603-271-2030
Cosmetologist #04 603-271-3608	Motor Vehicle Retail Seller #01 603-271-3561	Social Worker #25 603-271-6762
Court Reporter #37 603-271-2030	Motor Vehicle Sales Finance Co. #01 ...603-271-3561	Social Worker, Clinical #26 603-271-6762
Credit Union #01 603-271-3561	Natural Scientist #34 603-271-2219	Speech Language Pathology #45 603-271-8389
Debt Adjuster #01 603-271-3561	Naturopath #10 603-271-5127	Speech-Language Pathologist #10 603-271-1203
Dental Hygienist #15 603-271-4561	Notary Public #42 603-271-3242	Surveyor #34 603-271-2219
Dentist #15 603-271-4561	Nurse #18 603-271-2323	Tattoo Establishment/Practitioner #13...603-271-4594
Dog Trainer #48 603-271-2158	Nursing Home Administrator #16 603-271-4728	Teacher #07 603-271-3871
Drug Wholesaler/Mfg. #27 603-271-2350	Occupational Therapist/Assistant #45 ...603-271-8389	Tobacco Law Enforcement #35 603-271-3755
Electrician-Master/Journeyman/Apprentice #29	Occupational Therapy Assistant #45 603-271-8389	Trust Company #01 603-271-3561
....603-271-3748	Ophthalmic Dispenser #10 603-271-5127	Veterinary Medicine #05 603-271-3706
Electrologist #12 603-271-5127	Optometrist #23 603-271-2428	Vocational Rehabilitation Providers#28 .603-271-3328
Elevator Inspector #28 603-271-2585	Pastoral Psychotherist #26 603-271-6762	Waste Water Treatment Plant Operator #40..............
Elevator Mechanic #28 603-271-2585	Pesticide Dealer/Sales #06 603-271-3550	603-271-3406
Embalmer #17 603-271-4648	Pesticide Disposal #06 603-271-3550	Water Distribution System Operator#40 603-271-3406
Energy Facility Construction #08...........603-271-3503	Pesticide Labeling #06 603-271-3550	Water Well Contractor #40 603-271-3139
Energy Facility Site #08.......................603-271-3503	Pesticide User #06 603-271-3550	

Licensing Agency Information

#01 Banking Department, 56 Old Suncook Rd, Concord, NH 03301-5127; 603-271-3561, Fax: 603-271-1090.
http://webster.state.nh.us/banking/

#02 Department of State, 57 Regional Dr, Concord, NH 03301-8506; 603-271-3286, Fax: 603-271-2856.
www.state.nh.us/accountancy/index.html

#03 Secretary of State, 107 N Main St., State House Rm 204, Concord, NH 03301; 603-271-3242, Fax: 603-271-6316.
www.webster.state.nh.us/soso

#04 Board of Barbering, Cosmetology & Esthetics, 2 Industrial Park Dr, Concord, NH 03301; 603-271-3608, Fax: 603-271-8889.
http://webster.state.nh.us/cosmet/

#05 Board of Veterinary Medicine, PO Box 2042 (25 Capitol St), Concord, NH 03302-2042; 603-271-3706, Fax: 604-271-1109.
www.state.nh.us/veterinary/index.html

#06 Department of Agriculture, 25 Capitol St 2nd Fl, Concord, NH 03301-2042; 603-271-3551, Fax: 603-271-1109.
www.state.nh.us/agric/peco.html

#07 Department of Education, 101 Pleansant St, State Office Park S, Concord, NH 03301-3860; 603-271-3494, Fax: 603-271-4134.
www.ed.state.nh.us

#08 Department of Environmental Services, 6 Hazen Dr. POB 95, Concord, NH 03301; 603-271-3503, Fax: 603-271-8013.
www.des.state.nh.us

#09 Plumbing Licensing Board, PO Box 1386, Concord, NH 03302-1386; 603-271-3267, Fax: 603-271-6656.
http://webster.state.nh.us/plumbing/

#10 Department of Health & Human Services, 129 Pleasant, Concord, NH 03301; 800-852-3345, Fax: 603-271-4729.
www.dhhs.state.nh.us/Index.nsf?Open

#12 Department of Health & Human Services, 129 Pleasant, Concord, NH 03301; 603-271-5127, Fax: 603-271-3745.
www.dhhs.state/nh.us/index.nsf?Open

#13 Department of Health & Human Services, 129 Pleasant, Concord, NH 03301; 603-271-4594, Fax: 603-271-4968.
www.dhhs.state.nh.us/index.nsf?Open

#14 Department of Health & Human Services, 125 Pleasant, Concord, NH 03301; 603-271-4560, Fax: 603-271-3745.
www.dhhs.state.nh.us/index.nsf?Open

#15 Department of Health & Human Services, 2 Industrial Park Dr, Concord, NH 03301-8520; 603-271-4561, Fax: 603-271-6702.
http://webster.state.nh.us/dental/

#16 Department of Health & Human Services, 2 Industrial Park Dr #8, Concord, NH 03301; 603-271-4728, Fax: 603-271-6702.

#17 Department of Health & Human Services, 6 Hazen Dr, Concord, NH 03301-6507; 603-271-4648, Fax: 603-271-3447.
http://webster.state.nh.us/funeral/

#18 Department of Health & Human Services, PO Box 3898, 78 Regional Dr, Bldg B, Concord, NH 03302-3898; 603-271-2323, Fax: 603-271-6282.
www.state.nh.us/nursing/nursing.htm

#19 Department of Health & Human Services, 2 Industrial Park Dr #8, Concord, NH 03301; 603-271-1203, Fax: 603-271-6702.
www.state.nh.us/podiatry/index.html

#20 Department of Health & Human Services, 2 Industrial Park Dr, Concord, NH 03301; 603-271-1203, Fax: 603-271-6702.
www.dhhs.state.nh.us/index.nsf?Open

#21 Department of Health & Human Services, 129 Pleasant St, Brown Bldg, Concord, NH 03301-3857; 603-271-4624, Fax: 603-271-4782.
www.dhhs.state.nh.us/Index.nsf?Open

#22 Department of Safety, 10 Hazen Dr, Concord, NH 03305-0003; 603-271-4568, Fax: 603-271-4567.
http://webster.state.nh.us/safety/ems/

#23 Department of Health & Human Services, 2 Industrial Park Dr. # 8, Concord, NH 03301; 603-271-2428, Fax: 603-271-6702.
http://webster.state.nh.us/optometry/
Direct web site URL to search for licensees: www.odfinder.org/LicSearch.asp. Search online using national database by name, city or state.

#24 Department of Health & Human Services, 129 Pleasant, Concord, NH 03301; 603-271-4667, Fax: 603-271-3827.
www.dhhs.state.nh.us/index.nsf?Open

#25 Department of Health & Human Services, 129 Pleasant, Concord, NH 03301; 603-271-4816, Fax: 603-271-4141.
www.dhhs.state.nh.us/index.nsf?Open

#26 Board of Mental Health Practices, 105 Pleasant St, Concord, NH 03301; 603-271-6762, Fax: 603-271-3950.
http://webster.state.nh.us/mhpb

#27 Department of Health & Human Services, 57 Regional Dr, Concord, NH 03301-8518; 603-271-2350, Fax: 603-271-2856.
www.state.nh.us/pharmacy

#28 Department of Labor, 95 Pleasant St, State Office Park S, Concord, NH 03301-3836; 603-271-3176, Fax: 603-271-2668.
www.state.nh.us/dol/index.htm

#29 Electricians' Licensing Board, 2 Industrial Park Dr, Concord, NH 03302-0646; 603-271-3748, Fax: 603-271-2257.
http://webster.state.nh.us/electrician/

#30 Department of State, 107 N Main #204, Concord, NH 03301; 603-271-3242.
www.state.nh.us/sos

#31 Real Estate Appraiser Board, 25 Capitol St, Rm 426, Concord, NH 03301-6312; 603-271-6186, Fax: 603-271-6513.
http://webster.state.nh.us/nhreab/

#32 Department of State, 25 Capitol St Rm 437, Concord, NH 03301; 603-271-2701, Fax: 603-271-1039.
www.state.nh.us/nhrec/license.html

#33 Insurance Department, 56 Old Suncook Rd, Concord, NH 03301-7131; 603-271-2261, Fax: 603-271-7029.
http://webster.state.nh.us/insurance/

#34 Joint Board of Licensure & Certification, 57 Regional Dr, Concord, NH 03301; 603-271-2219, Fax: 603-271-6990.
www.state.nh.us/jtboard/home.htm
Direct web site URL to search for licensees: www.state.nh.us/jtboard/home.htm

#35 Licensing & Enforcement, 10 Commercial St, Concord, NH 03301; 603-271-3755, Fax: 603-271-3758.
www.state.nh.us/liquor/index.html

#36 c/o Judicial Council, 25 Capitol St, Concord, NH 03301; 603-224-6593, Fax: 603-224-8388.
http://webster.state.nh.us/marital/
Direct web site URL to search for licensees: www.state.nh.us/marital/mediators.html. You can search online using member list

#37 Superior Court Center, 99 N State St, Concord, NH 03301; 603-271-2030, Fax: 603-271-2033.

#38 Department of Safety, 10 Hazen Dr, Concord, NH 03305-0002; 603-271-3575.
www.state.nh.us/safety/safety.htm

#39 State Police, 10 Hazen Dr, Concord, NH 03305; 603-271-3575.

#40 Department of Environmental Services, 6 Hazen Dr, Concord, NH 03302; 603-271-3139, Fax: 603-271-5171.
www.des.state.nh.us

#41 Office of Alcohol & Drug Abuse Prevention, 105 Pleasant St, Concord, NH 03301; 603-271-6112, Fax: 603-271-6116.

#42 Office of Secretary of State, 107 N Main St, State House Rm 204, Concord, NH 03301-4989; 603-271-3242, Fax: 603-271-6316.
www.webster.state.nh.us/sos

#43 Supreme Court, 1 Noble Dr, Concord, NH 03301; 603-271-2646, Fax: 603-271-6630.
www.state.nh.us/sos/electionsnew.htm

#44 Bingo/Lucky 7 Division, 14 Integra Dr, Concord, NH 03301-1208; 603-271-3391, Fax: 603-271-1160.
www.state.nh.us/lottery/nhlotto.htm

#45 Office of Allied Health Professions, 2 Industrial Park Dr, Concord, NH 03301-8520; 603-271-8389.

#46 Department of Health & Human Svcs, 6 Hazen Dr, Concord, NH 03301; 603-271-4609.

#47 Board of Hearing Care Providers, PO Box 418, Portsmouth, NH 03802-0418; 603-436-4010.

#48 Pari-Mutuel Commission, 244 N Main St 3rd Fl, Concord, NH 03301; 603-271-2158, Fax: 603-271-3381.
http://webster.state.nh.us/nhpmc/

#49 Police Standards & Training Council, 17 Fan Rd, Concord, NH 03301-7413; 603-271-2133.

#50 Department of State, State House Rm 204, Concord, NH 03301; 603-271-1463.

New Hampshire Federal Courts

The following list indicates the district and division name for each county in the state. If the bankruptcy court location is different from the district court, then the location of the bankruptcy court appears in parentheses.

County/Court Cross Reference

Belknap .... Concord (Manchester)

Carroll .... Concord (Manchester)

Cheshire .... Concord (Manchester)

Coos .... Concord (Manchester)

Grafton .... Concord (Manchester)

Hillsborough .... Concord (Manchester)

Merrimack .... Concord (Manchester)

Rockingham .... Concord (Manchester)

Strafford .... Concord (Manchester)

Sullivan .... Concord (Manchester)

US District Court

District of New Hampshire

Concord Division Warren B Rudman Courthouse, 55 Pleasant St, #110, Concord, NH 03301 (Courier Address: Use mail address for courier delivery), 603-225-1423.

http://www.nhd.uscourts.gov

Counties: Belknap, Carroll, Cheshire, Coos, Grafton, Hillsborough, Merrimack, Rockingham, Strafford, Sullivan.

Indexing/Storage: Cases are indexed by defendant and plaintiff as well as by case number. New cases are available in the index 24 hours after filing date. A computer index is maintained. Open records are located at this court.

Fee & Payment: The fee is $20.00 per item (one party name or case number). Payment may be made by money order, cashier check, business check. Personal checks are not accepted. Prepayment is required. Payee: Clerk, US District Court. Certification fee: $7.00 per document. Copy fee: $.50 per page. You are allowed to make your own copies. These copies cost $.10 per page. Public copiers are available.

Phone Search: Only docket information is available by phone.

Mail Search: A stamped self addressed envelope is not required.

In Person: In person searching is available.

PACER: Sign-up number is 800-676-6856. Access fee is $.60 per minute. Toll-free access: 800-361-7205. Local access: 603-226-7737. Case records are available back to 1980. Records are purged every two years. New records are available online after 1 day. PACER is available online at http://pacer.nhd.uscourts.gov.

US Bankruptcy Court

District of New Hampshire

Manchester Division Room 404, 275 Chestnut St, Manchester, NH 03101 (Courier Address: Use mail address for courier delivery), 603-222-2600, Fax: 603-666-7408.

http://www.nhb.uscourts.gov

Counties: Belknap, Carroll, Cheshire, Coos, Grafton, Hillsborough, Merrimack, Rockingham, Strafford, Sullivan.

Indexing/Storage: Cases are indexed by debtor as well as by case number. New cases are available in the index 24 hours after filing date. Both computer and card indexes are maintained. Open records are located at this court.

Fee & Payment: The fee is $20.00 per item (one party name or case number). Payment may be made by money order, cashier check, personal check, Visa or Mastercard. Prepayment is required. Debtor checks are not accepted. Payee: Clerk, US Bankruptcy Court. Certification fee: $7.00 per document. Copy fee: $.50 per page. You are allowed to make your own copies. These copies cost $.25 per page.

Phone Search: Only the case number, name, trustee, attorney for the debtor and deadlines will be released. An automated voice case information service (VCIS) is available. Call VCIS at 800-851-8954 or 603-666-7424.

Mail Search: A stamped self addressed envelope is not required.

In Person: In person searching is available.

PACER: Sign-up number is 800-676-6856. Access fee is $.60 per minute. Toll-free access: 800-610-9325. Local access: 603-666-7923. Case records are available back to 1989. Records are purged every six months. New civil records are available online after 2 days. PACER is available online at http://pacer.nhb.uscourts.gov.

New Hampshire County Courts

Court	Jurisdiction	No. of Courts	How Organized
Superior Courts*	General	11	10 Counties
District Courts*	Limited	36	40 Districts
Probate Courts*	Probate	10	10 Counties
Family Court	Special	8	

* Profiled in this Sourcebook.

						CIVIL			
Court	Tort	Contract	Real Estate	Min. Claim	Max. Claim	Small Claims	Estate	Eviction	Domestic Relations
Circuit Courts*	X	X	X	$1500	No Max				X
District Courts*	X	X	X	$0	$25,000	$2500		X	X
Probate Courts*							X		X
Family Courts									X

			CRIMINAL		
Court	Felony	Misdemeanor	DWI/DUI	Preliminary Hearing	Juvenile
Circuit Courts*	X				
District Courts*		X	X	X	X
Probate Courts*					
Family Courts					X

ADMINISTRATION Administrative Office of the Courts, Supreme Court Bldg, Noble Dr, Concord, NH, 03301; 603-271-2521, Fax: 603-271-3977. www.state.nh.us/courts/home.htm

COURT STRUCTURE The Superior Court is the court of General Jurisdiction. Felony cases include Class A misdemeanors.

The District Court upper civil limit was increased to $25,000 from $10,000 on 1/1/93. Filing a civil case in the monetary "overlap" area between the Superior Court minimum and the District Court maximum is at the discretion of the filer.

The municipal courts have been closed as the judges retire and the caseload and records are absorbed by the nearest District Court.

ONLINE ACCESS There is no remote online computer access available.

ADDITIONAL INFORMATION A statutory search fee has been implemented in the District Courts, as follows:

Computer search - $10.00 for up to 10 names in one request; $25.00 for 10 or more names in one request; $25.00 per hour for search time beyond one hour.

Manual search - $25.00 per hour.

If the search requires both types, the fee is the total for each.

Belknap County

Superior Court 64 Court St, Laconia, NH 03246; 603-524-3570. Hours: 8AM-4:30PM (EST). *Felony, Civil Actions Over $1,500.*

Civil Records: Access: Phone, mail, in person. Only the court performs in person searches; visitors may not. No search fee. Required to search: name, years to search. Civil cases indexed by defendant, plaintiff. Civil records on computer from 1/80, index cards from 1900, docket books from 1840.

Criminal Records: Access: Phone, mail, in person. Only the court performs in person searches; visitors may not. No search fee. Required to search: name, years

to search; also helpful: DOB, SSN. Criminal records on computer from 1/80, index cards from 1900, docket books from 1840.

General Information: No adoptions, sealed, juvenile, mental health, expunged, or dismissed records released. SASE not required. Turnaround time 1 week. Copy fee: $.50 per page. Certification fee: $5.00. Fee payee: Belknap County Superior Court. Business checks accepted. Prepayment is required.

Laconia District Court 26 Academy St, PO Box 1010, Laconia, NH 03247; 603-524-4128. Hours: 8AM-4PM (EST). *Misdemeanor, Civil Actions Under $25,000, Eviction, Small Claims.*

Civil Records: Access: Mail, in person. Only the court performs in person searches; visitors may not. Search fee: $25.00 for records before 5/2/92; $10.00 after 5/92. Required to search: name, years to search. Civil cases indexed by defendant, plaintiff. Civil records on computer from 5/92, index cards from 7/64.

Criminal Records: Access: Mail, in person. Only the court performs in person searches; visitors may not. Search fee: $25.00 for records before 5/2/92; $10.00

after 5/92. Required to search: name, years to search, DOB. Criminal records on computer from 5/92, index cards from 7/64.

General Information: No sealed, juvenile, mental health, expunged or dismissed records released. SASE required. Turnaround time 2 weeks. Copy fee: $.50 per page. Certification fee: $5.00. Fee payee: Laconia District Court. Personal checks accepted. Prepayment is required.

Probate Court 64 Court St, PO Box 1343, Laconia, NH 03247-1343; 603-524-0903. Hours: 8AM-4PM (EST). *Probate.*

Carroll County

Superior Court PO Box 433, Ossipee, NH 03864; 603-539-2201. Hours: 8AM-4:30PM (EST). *Felony, Civil Actions Over $1,500.*

Civil Records: Access: Mail, in person. Only the court performs in person searches; visitors may not. No search fee. Required to search: name, years to search. Civil cases indexed by defendant, plaintiff. Civil records on index cards from 1960, index books from 1840.

Criminal Records: Access: Mail, in person. Only the court performs in person searches; visitors may not. No search fee. Required to search: name, years to search; also helpful: DOB, SSN. Criminal records on index cards from 1960, index books from 1840.

General Information: No adoptions, sealed, juvenile, mental health, expunged or dismissed records released. SASE required. Turnaround time same day. Copy fee: $.50 per page. Certification fee: $5.00. Fee payee: Carroll County. Personal checks accepted. Prepayment is required.

Northern Carroll County District Court PO Box 940, Conway, NH 03818; 603-356-7710. Hours: 8:30AM-4:30PM (EST). *Misdemeanor, Civil Actions Under $25,000, Eviction, Small Claims.*

Civil Records: Access: Phone, mail, in person. Both court and visitors may perform in person searches. Search fee: $25.00 before 10/01/92; $10.00 after 10/01/92. Required to search: name, years to search. Civil cases indexed by defendant, plaintiff. Civil records on computer from 1993, on index cards from 1980, on index books from 1954.

Criminal Records: Access: Phone, mail, in person. Both court and visitors may perform in person searches. Search fee: $10.00 per name. Required to search: name, years to search; also helpful: DOB, SSN. Criminal records on computer from 1993, on index cards from 1980, on index books from 1954.

General Information: No adoptions, sealed, juvenile, mental health, expunged or dismissed records released. SASE required. Turnaround time 1 week. Copy fee: $.50 per page. Certification fee: $5.00 per page. Fee payee: District Court for Northern Carroll County. Personal checks accepted. Prepayment is required.

Southern Carroll County District Court PO Box 421, Ossipee, NH 03864; 603-539-4561. Hours: 8AM-4PM (EST). *Misdemeanor, Civil Actions Under $25,000, Eviction, Small Claims.*

Note: The former Wolfeboro District Court has been combined with this court.

Civil Records: Access: Mail, in person. Only the court performs in person searches; visitors may not. No search fee. Required to search: name, years to search. Civil cases indexed by defendant, plaintiff. Civil records on computer from 1992, on index cards from 1950s.

Criminal Records: Access: Mail, in person. Only the court performs in person searches; visitors may not. No search fee. Required to search: name, years to search; also helpful: DOB, SSN. Criminal records on computer from 1992, on index cards from 1950s.

General Information: No sealed, juvenile, mental health, expunged or dismissed records released. SASE

required. Turnaround time 2-3 days. Copy fee: $.50 per page. Certification fee: $5.00. Fee payee: South Carroll County District Court. Only cashiers checks and money orders accepted. Prepayment is required.

Probate Court PO Box 419, Ossipee, NH 03864; 603-539-4123; Fax: 603-539-4761. Hours: 8:30AM-4:30PM (phone is answered from 11:30 AM-4:30 PM (EST). *Probate.*

Cheshire County

Superior Court PO Box 444, Keene, NH 03431; 603-352-6902. Hours: 9AM-4PM (EST). *Felony, Civil Actions Over $1,500.*

Civil Records: Access: Mail, in person. Only the court performs in person searches; visitors may not. No search fee. Required to search: name, years to search. Civil cases indexed by defendant, plaintiff. Civil records on computer from 1993, on index cards from 1919; records prior to 1918 difficult to access; organized 1769.

Criminal Records: Access: Mail, in person. Only the court performs in person searches; visitors may not. No search fee. Required to search: name, years to search, DOB. Criminal records on computer from 1992.

General Information: No adoptions, sealed, juvenile, mental health, expunged or dismissed records released. SASE required. Turnaround time 2 weeks. Copy fee: $.50 per page. Certification fee: $5.00. Fee payee: Clerk of Superior Court. Personal checks accepted. Prepayment is required.

Jaffrey-Peterborough District Court 7 Knight St, PO Box 39, Jaffrey, NH 03452-0039; 603-532-8698. Hours: 8AM-4PM (EST). *Misdemeanor, Civil Actions Under $25,000, Eviction, Small Claims.*

Civil Records: Access: Mail, in person. Only the court performs in person searches; visitors may not. Search fee: $35.00 per name. Required to search: name, years to search. Civil cases indexed by defendant, plaintiff. Civil records on computer from 1993, on index cards from 1980, index books in back room.

Criminal Records: Access: Mail, in person. Only the court performs in person searches; visitors may not. Search fee: $35.00 per name. Required to search: name, years to search, DOB; also helpful: SSN. Criminal records on computer from 1993, on index cards from 1980, index books in back room.

General Information: No sealed, juvenile, mental health records released. SASE required. Turnaround time 3-4 weeks. Copy fee: $.50 per page. Certification fee: $5.00. Fee payee: Jaffrey-Peterborough District Court. Personal checks accepted. Prepayment required.

Keene District Court PO Box 364, Keene, NH 03431; 603-352-2559. Hours: 8AM-4PM (EST). *Misdemeanor, Civil Actions Under $25,000, Eviction, Small Claims.*

Civil Records: Access: Mail, in person. Only the court performs in person searches; visitors may not. Search fee: $10.00 electronic search (1992 to present), $25.00 if previous. Required to search: name, years to search. Civil cases indexed by defendant, plaintiff. Civil records on computer from 7/92, on index cards from 1980, docket books from 1968 to 1979.

Criminal Records: Access: Mail, in person. Only the court performs in person searches; visitors may not. Search fee: $10.00 computer search (1992 forward), $25.00 for previous years. Required to search: name, years to search; also helpful: DOB, SSN. Criminal records on computer from 7/92, on index cards from 1980, docket books from 1968 to 1979.

General Information: No sealed, juvenile, mental health or expunged records released. SASE required. Turnaround time 5-10 days. Copy fee: $.50 per page. There is no copy fee is document is certified. Certification fee: $5.00. Fee payee: Keene District Court. Personal checks accepted. Prepayment required.

Probate Court 12 Court St, Keene, NH 03431; 603-357-7786. Hours: 8AM-4:30PM (EST). *Probate.*

Coos County

Superior Court 55 School St #301, Lancaster, NH 03584; 603-788-4900. Hours: 8AM-4:15PM (EST). *Felony, Civil Actions Over $1,500.*

Civil Records: Access: Phone, mail, in person. Only the court performs in person searches; visitors may not. No search fee. Required to search: name, years to search. Civil cases indexed by defendant, plaintiff. Civil records on computer from 1994, on index cards from 1960, index books from 1887; courthouse burned in 1887, prior records lost (organized 1803).

Criminal Records: Access: Phone, mail, in person. Only the court performs in person searches; visitors may not. No search fee. Required to search: name, years to search, DOB. Criminal records on computer from 1992; prior records on index cards from 1960, index books from 1887.

General Information: No adoptions, sealed, juvenile, mental health, expunged or dismissed records released. SASE required. Turnaround time 2-3 days. Copy fee: $.50 per page. Certification fee: $5.00. Fee payee: Coos Superior Court. Personal checks accepted. Prepayment is required.

Berlin District Court 220 Main St, Berlin, NH 03570; 603-752-3160. Hours: 8AM-4PM (EST). *Misdemeanor, Civil Actions Under $25,000, Eviction, Small Claims.*

Civil Records: Access: Mail, in person. Only the court performs in person searches; visitors may not. Search fee: $25.00 per name before 1993; $10.00 per name after 1993. Required to search: name, years to search. Civil cases indexed by defendant, plaintiff. Civil records on index cards from 1980, index books from 1970, prior to 1970 archived in basement.

Criminal Records: Access: Mail, in person. Only the court performs in person searches; visitors may not. Search fee: $25.00 per name before 1993; $10.00 per name after 1993. Required to search: name, years to search; also helpful: DOB, SSN. Criminal records on index cards from 1980, index books from 1970, prior to 1970 archived in basement.

General Information: No sealed, juvenile, mental health, expunged or dismissed records released. SASE required. Turnaround time 1-2 weeks. Copy fee: $.50 per page. Certification fee: $5.00. Fee payee: Berlin District Court. Personal checks accepted. Credit cards accepted. Prepayment is required.

Colebrook District Court PO Box 5 - 10 Bridge St, Colebrook, NH 03576; 603-237-4229. Hours: 8AM-Noon,1-4PM (EST). *Misdemeanor, Civil Actions Under $25,000, Eviction, Small Claims.*

Civil Records: Access: Mail, in person. Only the court performs in person searches; visitors may not. Search fee: $10.00 for computer search 93 to present. $25.00 for manual search, prior to 93. Required to search: name, years to search. Civil cases indexed by defendant, plaintiff. Civil records on index cards from 1979, index books from 1964.

Criminal Records: Access: Mail, in person. Only the court performs in person searches; visitors may not. Search fee: $10.00 for computer search. $25.00 for manual search. Required to search: name, years to search, DOB. Criminal records on index cards from 1979, index books from 1964.

General Information: No sealed, juvenile, mental health or expunged records released. SASE required. Turnaround time same day. Copy fee: $.50 per page. Certification fee: $5.00 per page. Fee payee: Colebrook District Court. Personal checks accepted. Prepayment is required.

Gorham District Court PO Box 176, Gorham, NH 03581; 603-466-2454. 8AM-4PM *Misdemeanor, Civil Actions Under $25,000, Eviction, Small Claims.*

Civil Records: Access: Mail, in person. Only the court performs in person searches; visitors may not. Search fee: $25.00 per hour. Electronic searches are $10 for less than 10 names, $25 for 10-25 names, then the hourly kicks in. Required to search: name, years to search. Civil cases indexed by defendant, plaintiff. Civil records on computer from 1993, on index cards from 1980, index books from 1964.

Criminal Records: Access: Mail, in person. Only the court performs in person searches; visitors may not. Search fee: Same fees as civil. Required to search: name, years to search, DOB. Criminal records on computer from 1993, on index cards from 1980, index books from 1964.

General Information: No adoptions, sealed, juvenile, mental health, expunged or dismissed records released. SASE required. Turnaround time 3-4 days. Copy fee: $.50 per page. Certification fee: $10.00. Fee payee: Gorham District Court. Personal checks accepted. Prepayment is required.

Lancaster District Court 55 School St, Suite 201, Lancaster, NH 03584; 603-788-4485. Hours: 8:30AM-4PM (EST). *Misdemeanor, Civil Actions Under $25,000, Eviction, Small Claims.*

Civil Records: Access: Mail, in person. Only the court performs in person searches; visitors may not. Search fee: $25.00. Required to search: name, years to search; also helpful: address. Civil cases indexed by defendant, plaintiff. Civil records on index cards from 1981, index books for public review only.

Criminal Records: Access: Mail, in person. Only the court performs in person searches; visitors may not. Search fee: Fee is based on type of search, and is normally $10.00 per request. See state introduction. Required to search: name, years to search, DOB; also helpful: address. Criminal records on index cards from 1981, index books for public review only.

General Information: No adoptions, sealed, juvenile, mental health, expunged or dismissed records released. SASE required. Turnaround time 1 week. Copy fee: $.50 per page. Certification fee: $5.00 per page. Fee payee: Lancaster District Court. Personal checks accepted. Prepayment is required.

Probate Court 55 School St #104, Lancaster, NH 03584; 603-788-2001. Hours: 8AM-4PM *Probate.*

Grafton County

Superior Court RR1 Box 65, North Haverhill, NH 03774; 603-787-6961. Hours: 8AM-4:30PM (EST). *Felony, Civil Actions Over $1,500.*

Civil Records: Access: Mail, in person. Only the court performs in person searches; visitors may not. No search fee. Required to search: name, years to search. Civil cases indexed by defendant, plaintiff. Civil records on index cards from 1900, index books from 1950. All prior records are found at the Archives in Concord.

Criminal Records: Access: Mail, in person. Only the court performs in person searches; visitors may not. No search fee. Required to search: name, years to search; also helpful: DOB, SSN. Criminal records on index cards from 1900, index books from 1950. All prior records are found at the Archives in Concord.

General Information: No sealed records released. SASE required. Turnaround time 10 days. Copy fee: $.50 per page. Certification fee: $5.00 plus $.50 per add'l page. Fee payee: Grafton County Superior Court. Personal checks accepted. Prepayment is required.

Haverhill District Court Grafton County Courthouse, 3785 Dartmouth College Highway - Box 10, North Haverhill, NH 03774; 603-787-6626. Hours:

8:00AM-4:30PM (EST). *Misdemeanor, Civil Actions Under $25,000, Eviction, Small Claims.*

Civil Records: Access: Mail, in person. Only the court performs in person searches; visitors may not. Search fee: Electronic records search fee is $10.00 per name (less than 10 names); 10 or more names are $25.00 each search. Manual search fee is $25.00 per hour. Required to search: name, years to search. Civil cases indexed by defendant, plaintiff. Civil records on computer from 1993, on index cards to 1979, index books from 1950s.

Criminal Records: Access: Mail, in person. Only the court performs in person searches; visitors may not. Search fee: Same fees as civil. Required to search: name, years to search, DOB. Criminal records on computer from 1993, on index cards from 1979, index books from 1950s.

General Information: No adoptions, sealed, juvenile, mental health, expunged or dismissed records released. SASE required. Turnaround time 1-2 days. Copy fee: $.50 per page. Certification fee: $5.00. Fee payee: Haverhill District Court. Personal checks accepted. Prepayment is required.

Lebanon District Court 38 Centerra Parkway, Lebanon, NH 03766; 603-643-3555. Hours: 8AM-4PM (EST). *Misdemeanor, Civil Actions Under $25,000, Eviction, Small Claims.*

Civil Records: Access: Mail, in person. Only the court performs in person searches; visitors may not. Search fee: $10.00 for computer search (1993-present); $25 for index search (prior to 1993). Required to search: name, years to search. Civil cases indexed by defendant, plaintiff. Civil records on computer from 1993, on index cards from 1986, index books from 1960s.

Criminal Records: Access: Mail, in person. Only the court performs in person searches; visitors may not. Search fee: $10.00 for computer search (1993-present); $25 for index search (prior to 1993). Required to search: name, years to search, DOB. Criminal records on computer from 1993, on index cards from 1986, index books from 1960s.

General Information: No sealed, juvenile, mental health or expunged records released. SASE required. Turnaround time 5 days. Copy fee: $.50 per page. Certification fee: $1.00. Fee payee: Lebanon District Court. Personal checks accepted. Prepayment required.

Littleton District Court 134 Main St, Littleton, NH 03561; 603-444-7750. Hours: 8AM-4PM (EST). *Misdemeanor, Civil Actions Under $25,000, Eviction, Small Claims.*

Civil Records: Access: Mail, in person. Only the court performs in person searches; visitors may not. Search fee: $10.00 per name. Required to search: name, years to search. Civil cases indexed by defendant, plaintiff. Civil records on computer from 1/90, index cards from 1985, index books from 1950.

Criminal Records: Access: Mail, in person. Only the court performs in person searches; visitors may not. Search fee: $10.00 per name. Required to search: name, years to search; also helpful: DOB, SSN. Criminal records on computer from 1/90, index cards from 1985, index books from 1950.

General Information: No adoptions, sealed, juvenile, mental health, domestic violence, expunged or dismissed records released. SASE required. Turnaround time 3 weeks. Copy fee: $.50 per page. Certification fee: $5.00. Fee payee: Littleton District Court. Personal checks accepted. Prepayment is required.

Plymouth District Court 26 Green St, Plymouth, NH 03264; 603-536-3326. Hours: 8AM-4PM (EST). *Misdemeanor, Civil Actions Under $25,000, Eviction, Small Claims.*

Civil Records: Access: Mail, in person. Only the court performs in person searches; visitors may not. Search fee: $10.00 per name. If a complete search (from 1981)

is required, fee is $25.00. Required to search: name, years to search. Civil cases indexed by defendant, plaintiff. Civil records on computer from 1991, index cards from 1981. Request for an appointment must be made two weeks prior to in person searching.

Criminal Records: Access: Mail, in person. Only the court performs in person searches; visitors may not. Search fee: $10.00 per name. same fees as civil. Required to search: name, years to search; also helpful: DOB, SSN. Criminal records on computer from 1991, index cards from 1981. Request for an appointment must be made two weeks prior to in person searching.

General Information: No sealed, mental health, expunged or dismissed records released. SASE required. Turnaround time one week. Copy fee: $.50 per page. Certification fee: $5.00. Fee payee: Plymouth District Court. Personal checks accepted. Prepayment is required.

Probate Court 3785 Dartmouth College Hwy, Box 3, North Haverhill, NH 03774-9700; 603-787-6931. Hours: 8AM-4PM (EST). *Probate.*

Hillsborough

Superior Court - North District 300 Chestnut St Rm 127, Manchester, NH 03101; 603-424-9951. Hours: 8AM-4PM *Felony, Civil Actions Over $1,500.*

Civil Records: Access: Mail, in person. Only the court performs in person searches; visitors may not. No search fee. Required to search: name, years to search. Civil cases indexed by defendant, plaintiff. Civil records on computer from 5/85, index cards from 1980s, index books from 1900s; organized 1769.

Criminal Records: Access: Mail, in person. Only the court performs in person searches; visitors may not. No search fee. Required to search: name, years to search, DOB. Criminal records on computer from 5/85, index cards to 1980s, index books to 1900s; organized 1769.

General Information: No sealed, juvenile, mental health records released. SASE required. Turnaround time 3 days. Certification fee: $5.00. Fee payee: Hillsborough Superior Court-Northern District. Personal checks accepted.

Superior Court - Southern District 30 Spring St, Nashua, NH 03061; 603-883-6461. Hours: 8AM-4PM (EST). *Felony, Civil Actions Over $1,500.*

Civil Records: Access: Mail, in person. Only the court performs in person searches; visitors may not. No search fee. Required to search: name, years to search. Civil cases indexed by defendant, plaintiff. Civil records on computer to 3/92; overall records go back to 1992.

Criminal Records: Access: Mail, in person. Only the court performs in person searches; visitors may not. No search fee. Required to search: name, years to search; also helpful: DOB. Criminal records on computer back to 3/92; overall records go back to 1992.

General Information: No sealed, juvenile or annulled records released. Turnaround time 2-3 days. Copy fee: $.50 per page. Certification fee: $5.00. Fee payee: Superior Court. Personal checks accepted. Prepayment is required.

Goffstown District Court PO Box 129, Goffstown, NH 03045; 603-497-2597. Hours: 8AM-4PM (EST). *Misdemeanor, Civil Actions Under $25,000, Eviction, Small Claims.*

Civil Records: Access: Mail, in person. Only the court performs in person searches; visitors may not. Search fee: $10.00 fee for electronic search up to 10 names, $25.00 for 10+ names. Manual search is $25.00 per name. Required to search: name, years to search. Civil cases indexed by defendant, plaintiff. Civil records on computer from 3/92, kept in files prior.

Criminal Records: Access: Mail, in person. Only the court performs in person searches; visitors may not. Search fee: Same fees as civil. Required to search:

name, years to search, DOB; also helpful: SSN. Criminal records on computer to 3/92, in files prior.

General Information: No sealed, juvenile, mental health, expunged or dismissed records released. SASE required. Turnaround time 2 weeks. Copy fee: $.50 per page. Certification fee: $5.00. Fee payee: Goffstown District Court. Personal checks accepted. Prepayment is required.

Hillsborough District Court PO Box 763, Hillsborough, NH 03244; 603-464-5811. Hours: 8AM-4PM (EST). *Misdemeanor, Civil Actions Under $25,000, Eviction, Small Claims.*

Civil Records: Access: Mail, in person. Only the court performs in person searches; visitors may not. Search fee: Research fees will vary, call first. Required to search: name, years to search. Civil cases indexed by defendant, plaintiff. Civil records on computer from 1994, on index cards from 1980, index books from 1960. Appointment required for in person searching.

Criminal Records: Access: Mail, in person. Only the court performs in person searches; visitors may not. Search fee: Research fees will vary, call first. Required to search: name, years to search, DOB; also helpful: SSN. Criminal records on computer from 1994, on index cards from 1980, index books from 1960.

General Information: No adoptions, sealed, juvenile, mental health, expunged or dismissed records released. SASE required. Turnaround time 1 week. Copy fee: $.50 per page. Certification fee: $5.00. Fee payee: Hillsborough District Court. Personal checks accepted. Prepayment is required.

Manchester District Court PO Box 456, Manchester, NH 03105; 603-624-6510. Hours: 8AM-4PM (EST). *Misdemeanor, Civil Actions Under $25,000, Eviction, Small Claims.*

Civil Records: Access: Mail, in person. Only the court performs in person searches; visitors may not. Search fee: $10.00 per request up to 10 names or $25.00 per request over 10. Manual searches $25.00 per hour. Required to search: name, years to search, DOB; also helpful: address. Civil cases indexed by defendant, plaintiff. Civil records on computer from 6/92, on index cards from 1960.

Criminal Records: Access: Mail, in person. Only the court performs in person searches; visitors may not. Search fee: $10.00 per request up to 10 names or $25.00 per request over 10. Manual searches $25.00 per hour. Required to search: name, years to search, DOB; also helpful: address. Criminal records on computer from 6/92, on index cards from 1960.

General Information: No adoptions, sealed, juvenile, mental health, expunged or dismissed records released. SASE required. Turnaround time 2 weeks. Copy fee: $.50 per page. Certification fee: $1.00. Fee payee: Manchester District Court. Personal checks accepted.

Merrimack District Court PO Box 324, Merrimack, NH 03054-0324; 603-424-9916. Hours: 8AM-4PM (EST). *Misdemeanor, Civil Actions Under $25,000, Eviction, Small Claims.*

Civil Records: Access: Mail, in person. Only the court performs in person searches; visitors may not. Search fee: $25 per hour for manual searches. For electronic, $10 for up to first 9 names or $25 for first 25 names, then hour rate. Required to search: name, years to search. Civil cases indexed by defendant, plaintiff. Civil records on computer from 7/92, on index cards from 1970, index books in archives at Concord.

Criminal Records: Access: Mail, in person. Both court and visitors may perform in person searches. Search fee: Same fees as civil. Required to search: name, years to search; also helpful: DOB. Criminal records on computer from 7/92, on index cards from 1970, index books in archives at Concord.

General Information: No adoptions, sealed, juvenile, mental health, expunged or dismissed records released.

SASE required. Turnaround time 1-2 days. Copy fee: $.50 per page. Certification fee: $5.00. Fee payee: Merrimack District Court. Personal checks accepted. Prepayment is required.

Milford District Court PO Box 148, Amherst, NH 03031; 603-673-2900. Hours: 8AM-4PM (EST). *Misdemeanor, Civil Actions Under $25,000, Eviction, Small Claims.*

Civil Records: Access: Mail, in person. Only the court performs in person searches; visitors may not. Search fee: Searching via computer is $10.00 per name; lengthy manual searching is $25.00 per hour. Required to search: name, years to search. Civil cases indexed by defendant, plaintiff. Civil records on computer from 08/92, on index cards from 1950s, prior records may or may not be at old courthouse.

Criminal Records: Access: Mail, in person. Only the court performs in person searches; visitors may not. Search fee: Same as Civil. Required to search: name, years to search; also helpful: DOB, SSN. Criminal records on computer from 08/92, on index cards from 1950s, prior records may or may not be at old courthouse.

General Information: No adoptions, sealed, juvenile, mental health, expunged or dismissed records released. SASE required. Turnaround time 10 days. Copy fee: $.50 per page. Certification fee: $5.00. Fee payee: Milford District Court. Personal checks accepted. Prepayment is required.

Nashua District Court Walnut St Oval, Nashua, NH 03060; 603-880-3333. Hours: 8AM-4PM (EST). *Misdemeanor, Civil Actions Under $25,000, Eviction, Small Claims.*

Civil Records: Access: Mail, in person. Only the court performs in person searches; visitors may not. Search fee: $25.00 for records prior to 08/92; after are $10.00. Required to search: name, years to search. Civil cases indexed by defendant, plaintiff. Civil records on computer from 1993, index cards from 1982. All requests must be in writing.

Criminal Records: Access: Mail, in person. Only the court performs in person searches; visitors may not. Search fee: Same fees as civil. Required to search: name, years to search; also helpful: DOB, SSN. Criminal records on computer from August 1992, index cards from 1982. All requests must be in writing.

General Information: No adoptions, sealed, juvenile, mental health, expunged records released. SASE required. Turnaround time 10 days. Copy fee: $.50 per page. Certification fee: $5.00. Fee payee: Nashua District Court. Personal checks accepted. Prepayment is required.

Probate Court PO Box P, Nashua, NH 03061-6015; 603-882-1231; Fax: 603-882-1620. Hours: 8AM-4PM (EST). *Probate.*

Merrimack County

Superior Court PO Box 2880, Concord, NH 03302-2880; 603-225-5501. Hours: 8:30AM-4PM (EST). *Felony, Civil Actions Over $1,500.*

Civil Records: Access: Mail, in person. Only the court performs in person searches; visitors may not. No search fee. Required to search: name, years to search. Civil cases indexed by defendant, plaintiff. Civil records on computer from 1983, index cards from 1950, index books from 1800s; organized 1823.

Criminal Records: Access: Phone, mail, in person. Only the court performs in person searches; visitors may not. No search fee. Required to search: name, years to search, DOB; also helpful: SSN. Criminal records on computer since 1984.

General Information: No adoptions, sealed, juvenile, mental health, expunged or dismissed records released. SASE required. Turnaround time 2-3 days. Copy fee:

$.50 per page. Certification fee: $5.00. Fee payee: Merrimack Superior Court. Personal checks accepted. Prepayment is required.

Concord District Court 32 Clinton St, PO Box 3420, Concord, NH 03302-3420; 603-271-6400. Hours: 8AM-4PM; Drive-up hours: 8AM-4PM (EST). *Misdemeanor, Civil Actions Under $25,000, Eviction, Small Claims.*

Note: The former Pittsfield District Court has been combined with this court.

Civil Records: Access: Mail, in person. Only the court performs in person searches; visitors may not. Search fee: $10 for less than 10 electronic searches or $25 per hour. Required to search: name, years to search. Civil cases indexed by defendant, plaintiff. Civil records on computer from 1989, index cards from 1978, docket books from 1800.

Criminal Records: Access: Mail, in person. Only the court performs in person searches; visitors may not. Search fee: $10 for less than 10 electronic searches or $25 per hour. Required to search: name, years to search, DOB. Criminal records on computer from 1989, index cards from 1978, docket books from 1800.

General Information: No adoptions, sealed, juvenile, mental health, expunged or dismissed records released. SASE required. Turnaround time 10 days. Copy fee: $.50 per page. Certification fee: $1.00. Fee payee: Concord District Court. Personal checks accepted. Prepayment is required.

Franklin District Court 7 Hancock Terrace, Franklin, NH 03235; 603-934-3290. Hours: 8AM-4PM (EST). *Misdemeanor, Civil Actions Under $25,000, Eviction, Small Claims.*

Civil Records: Access: Mail, in person. Only the court performs in person searches; visitors may not. Search fee: $10.00 per name. Required to search: name, years to search. Civil cases indexed by plaintiff. Civil records on computer from 1/91, index cards from 1/80, index books from 1960s.

Criminal Records: Access: Mail, in person. Only the court performs in person searches; visitors may not. Search fee: $10.00 per name. Required to search: name, years to search; also helpful: DOB, SSN. Criminal records on computer from 1/91, index cards from 1/80, index books from 1960s.

General Information: No adoptions, sealed, juvenile, mental health, expunged or dismissed records released. SASE required. Turnaround time 2-3 days. No copy fee. Certification fee: $1.00 per page. Fee payee: Franklin District Court. Personal checks accepted. Prepayment is required.

Henniker District Court 2 Depot St, Henniker, NH 03242; 603-428-3214. Hours: 8AM-4PM (EST). *Misdemeanor, Civil Actions Under $25,000, Eviction, Small Claims.*

Civil Records: Access: Mail, in person. Only the court performs in person searches; visitors may not. Search fee: Searching via computer is $10.00 per name; lengthy manual searching is $25.00 per hour. Required to search: name, years to search. Civil cases indexed by defendant, plaintiff. Civil records on index cards from 1988, index books from 1960s; on computer to 1989.

Criminal Records: Access: Mail, in person. Only the court performs in person searches; visitors may not. Search fee: Same as Civil. Required to search: name, years to search, DOB; also helpful: SSN. Criminal records on index cards from 1988, index books from 1960s; on computer back to 1989.

General Information: No adoptions, sealed, juvenile, mental health, expunged or dismissed records released. SASE required. Turnaround time can take as long as 6 weeks. Copy fee: $.50 per page. Certification fee: $5.00. Fee payee: Henniker District Court. Personal checks accepted. Prepayment is required.

Hooksett District Court 101 Merrimack, Hooksett, NH 03106; 603-485-9901. Hours: 8AM-4PM (EST). *Misdemeanor, Civil Actions Under $25,000, Eviction, Small Claims.*

Civil Records: Access: Mail, in person. Only the court performs in person searches; visitors may not. Search fee: Fee for electronic searching is $10.00 per name if less than 10 names submitted; 10 or more names are $25.00 each. Manual research is charged at $25.00 per hour. Browse screens are $.50 per page (bilk case info). Required to search: name, years to search. Civil cases indexed by defendant, plaintiff. Civil records on computer from 1993, on index cards from 1980, index books from 1975. All requests must be in writing.

Criminal Records: Access: Mail, in person. Only the court performs in person searches; visitors may not. Search fee: Same fees as civil. Required to search: name, years to search; also helpful: DOB, SSN. Criminal records on computer from 1993, on index cards from 1980, index books from 1975.

General Information: No sealed, juvenile, mental health, expunged or dismissed records released. SASE required. Turnaround time 1-2 months. Copy fee: $.50 per page. Certification fee: $5.00. Fee payee: Hooksett District Court. Personal checks accepted. Prepayment is required.

New London District Court PO Box 1966, New London, NH 03257; 603-526-6519. Hours: 8:30AM-4PM (EST). *Misdemeanor, Civil Actions Under $25,000, Eviction, Small Claims.*

Civil Records: Access: Mail, in person. Only the court performs in person searches; visitors may not. Search fee: $10.00 for 1-10 names; 11-24 names is $25.00; 25+ names is $25.00 per hour. Required to search: name, years to search. Civil cases indexed by defendant, plaintiff. Civil records on computer from 1993, on index cards from 1980, index books from 1800s. An appointment is necessary before performing an in person search.

Criminal Records: Access: Mail, in person. Only the court performs in person searches; visitors may not. Search fee: Same fees as civil. Required to search: name, years to search; also helpful: DOB, SSN. Criminal records on computer from 1993, on index cards from 1980, index books from 1800s. An appointment is necessary before performing an in person search.

General Information: No adoptions, sealed, juvenile, mental health, expunged or dismissed records released. SASE required. Turnaround time 1-2 days. Copy fee: $.50 per page. Certification fee: $1.00. Fee payee: New London District Court. Personal checks accepted. Prepayment is required.

Probate Court 163 N Main St, Concord, NH 03301; 603-224-9589. 8AM-4:30PM (EST). *Probate.*

Rockingham County

Superior Court PO Box 1258, Kingston, NH 03848-1258; 603-642-5256. Hours: 8AM-4PM (EST). *Felony, Civil Actions Over $1,500.*

Civil Records: Access: In person only. Only the court performs in person searches; visitors may not. No search fee. Required to search: name, years to search. Civil cases indexed by defendant, plaintiff. Civil records on computer from 1988, index cards from 1920, organized 1769.

Criminal Records: Access: In person only. Only the court performs in person searches; visitors may not. No search fee. Required to search: name, years to search; also helpful: DOB, SSN. Criminal records on computer from 1988, index cards from 1920, organized 1769.

General Information: No sealed, juvenile, mental health, expunged, annulled records released. Copy fee: $.50 if court makes the copy, $.25 if visitor makes the copy. Certification fee: $5.00. Fee payee: Clerk

Superior Court. Personal checks accepted. Prepayment is required.

Auburn District Court 5 Priscilla Lane, Auburn, NH 03032; 603-624-2265; Criminal phone: 603-624-2084. Hours: 8AM-4PM (EST). *Misdemeanor, Civil Actions Under $25,000, Eviction, Small Claims.*

Civil Records: Access: Mail, in person. Only the court performs in person searches; visitors may not. Search fee: $25.00 per hour. Required to search: name, years to search; also helpful: address. Civil cases indexed by defendant, plaintiff. Civil records on computer from 5/92, index cards from 1980, index books from 1968.

Criminal Records: Access: Mail, in person. Only the court performs in person searches; visitors may not. Search fee: $25.00 per hour. Required to search: name, years to search, DOB, signed release. Criminal records on computer from 5/92, index cards from 1980, index books from 1968.

General Information: No adoptions, sealed, juvenile, mental health, expunged or dismissed records released. SASE required. Turnaround time 3 days. Copy fee: $.50 per page. Certification fee: $5.00. Fee payee: Auburn District Court. Personal checks accepted. Prepayment is required.

Derry District Court 10 Manning St, Derry, NH 03038; 603-434-4676. Hours: 8AM-4PM (EST). *Misdemeanor, Civil Actions Under $25,000, Eviction, Small Claims.*

Civil Records: Access: Phone, mail, in person. Only the court performs in person searches; visitors may not. Search fee: $10.00 fee applies for all computer searches for up to 10 names. If searching over 10 names in the computer, the fee is $25.00. For lengthy computer searches, the fee is $25.00 per hour. All index book searches are $25.00 per hour. Required to search: name, years to search. Civil cases indexed by defendant, plaintiff. Civil records on computer from 10/92, on index cards prior.

Criminal Records: Access: Phone, mail, in person. Only the court performs in person searches; visitors may not. Search fee: Same fees as civil. Required to search: name, years to search; also helpful: DOB, SSN. Criminal records on computer from 10/92, on index cards prior.

General Information: No adoptions, sealed, juvenile, mental health, expunged, dismissed or annulment records released. SASE required. Turnaround time 1 week. Copy fee: $.50 per page. Certification fee: $5.00. Fee payee: Derry District Court. Personal checks accepted. Prepayment is required.

Exeter District Court PO Box 394, Exeter, NH 03833; 603-772-2931. Hours: 8AM-4PM (EST). *Misdemeanor, Civil Actions Under $25,000, Eviction, Small Claims.*

Civil Records: Access: Mail, in person. Only the court performs in person searches; visitors may not. Search fee: $10.00. Required to search: name, years to search; also helpful: address. Civil cases indexed by defendant, plaintiff. Civil records on computer back to 1991.

Criminal Records: Access: Mail, in person. Both court and visitors may perform in person searches. Search fee: $10.00. Required to search: name, years to search, DOB. Criminal records on computer back to 1991.

General Information: No adoptions, sealed, juvenile, mental health, expunged or dismissed records released. SASE required. Turnaround time 3 days. Copy fee: $.50 per page. Certification fee: $5.00. Fee payee: Exeter District Court. Personal checks accepted. Prepayment is required.

Hampton District Court PO Box 10, Hampton, NH 03843-0010; 603-926-8117. Hours: 8AM-4PM (EST). *Misdemeanor, Civil Actions Under $25,000, Eviction, Small Claims.*

Civil Records: Access: Mail, in person. Only the court performs in person searches; visitors may not. Search fee: $10.00 fee applies for all computer searches for up to 10 names. If searching over 10 names in the computer, the fee is $25.00. For lengthy computer searches, the fee is $25.00 per hour. All index book searches are $25.00 per hour. Required to search: name, years to search. Civil cases indexed by defendant. Civil records on computer from 4/91, index cards from 1979, index books from 1900s.

Criminal Records: Access: Mail, in person. Only the court performs in person searches; visitors may not. Search fee: Same fees as civil. Required to search: name, years to search; also helpful: DOB, SSN. Criminal records on computer from 4/91, index cards from 1979, index books from 1900s.

General Information: No adoptions, sealed, juvenile, mental health, expunged or dismissed records released. SASE required. Turnaround time 1 week. No copy fee. Certification fee: $5.00. Fee payee: Hampton District Court. Personal checks accepted. Prepayment is required.

Plaistow District Court 14 Elm Street (PO Box 129), Plaistow, NH 03865; 603-382-4651; Fax: 603-382-4952. Hours: 8AM-4PM (EST). *Misdemeanor, Civil Actions Under $25,000, Eviction, Small Claims.*

Civil Records: Access: Mail, in person. Only the court performs in person searches; visitors may not. Search fee: $10.00 1-9 names; $25.00 10 or more names. $25.00 per hour manual search fee. Required to search: name, years to search. Civil cases indexed by defendant, plaintiff. Civil records on computer from 7/91, index cards from 1980, index books from 1960s.

Criminal Records: Access: Mail, in person. Only the court performs in person searches; visitors may not. Search fee: $10.00 1-9 names; $25.00 10 or more names. $25.00 per hour manual search fee. Required to search: name, years to search, DOB. Criminal records on computer from 7/91, index cards from 1980, index books from 1960s.

General Information: No adoptions, sealed, juvenile, mental health, expunged or dismissed records released. SASE required. Turnaround time 2-3 days. Copy fee: $.50 per page. Certification fee: $5.00. Fee payee: Plaistow District Court. Personal checks accepted. Prepayment is required.

Portsmouth District Court 111 Parrott Ave, Portsmouth, NH 03801; 603-431-2192. Hours: 8AM-4PM (EST). *Misdemeanor, Civil Actions Under $25,000, Eviction, Small Claims.*

Civil Records: Access: Mail, in person. Only the court performs in person searches; visitors may not. Search fee: $10.00 if computerized search (after 1992), otherwise $35.00. Required to search: name, years to search. Civil cases indexed by defendant, plaintiff. Civil records on computer from 04/92, docket cards from 1980, index books from 1960s.

Criminal Records: Access: Mail, in person. Only the court performs in person searches; visitors may not. Search fee: Same fees as civil. Required to search: name, years to search; also helpful: DOB, SSN. Criminal records on computer from 04/92, docket cards from 1980, index books from 1960s.

General Information: No adoptions, sealed, juvenile, mental health, expunged or dismissed records released. SASE required. Turnaround time 2-3 days. Copy fee: $.50 per page. Certification fee: $1.00 per page. Fee payee: Portsmouth District Court. Personal checks accepted. Prepayment is required.

Salem District Court 35 Geremonty Dr, Salem, NH 03079; 603-893-4483. Hours: 8AM-4PM (EST). *Misdemeanor, Civil Actions Under $25,000, Eviction, Small Claims.*

Civil Records: Access: Mail, in person. Search fee: Fee varies based on number of names per request. Required to search: name, years to search. Civil cases indexed by defendant, plaintiff. Civil records on computer from 4/92, docket cards from 1980, docket books from 1950. An appointment is necessary before performing an in person search.

Criminal Records: Access: Mail, in person. Only the court performs in person searches; visitors may not. Search fee: Fee varies based on number of names per request. Required to search: name, years to search, DOB. Criminal records on computer from 4/92, docket cards from 1980, docket books from 1950.

General Information: No adoptions, sealed, juvenile, mental health, expunged or dismissed records released. SASE required. Turnaround time 2-3 week. Copy fee: $.50 per page. Certification fee: $1.00. Fee payee: Salem District Court. Personal checks accepted. Prepayment is required.

Probate Court PO Box 789, Kingston, NH 03848; 603-642-7117. Hours: 8AM-4PM (EST). *Probate.*

Strafford County

Superior Court PO Box 799, Dover, NH 03821-0799; 603-742-3065. Hours: 8:30AM-4:30PM (EST). *Felony, Civil Actions Over $1,500.*

Civil Records: Access: Mail, in person. Only the court performs in person searches; visitors may not. No search fee. Required to search: name, years to search. Civil cases indexed by defendant, plaintiff. Civil records on computer from 3/89, index cards from 1970, index books from 1900s, organized 1769.

Criminal Records: Access: Mail, in person. Only the court performs in person searches; visitors may not. No search fee. Required to search: name, years to search; also helpful: DOB, SSN. Criminal records on computer from 3/89, index cards from 1970, index books from 1900s, organized 1769.

General Information: No sealed, juvenile, mental health, expunged or dismissed records released. SASE required. Turnaround time 1 week. Copy fee: $.50 per page. Certification fee: $5.00. Fee payee: Superior Court Clerk. Personal checks accepted. Prepayment is required.

Dover District Court 25 St Thomas St, Dover, NH 03820; 603-742-7202. Hours: 8AM-4PM (EST). *Misdemeanor, Civil Actions Under $20,000, Eviction, Small Claims.*

Civil Records: Access: Mail, in person. Only the court performs in person searches; visitors may not. Search fee: $10.00 per name. Required to search: name, years to search. Civil cases indexed by defendant, plaintiff. Civil records on computer from 1993, on index cards from 1980, index books from 1970.

Criminal Records: Access: Mail, in person. Only the court performs in person searches; visitors may not. Search fee: $10.00 per name. Required to search: name, years to search, DOB. Criminal records on computer from 1993, on index cards from 1980, index books from 1970.

General Information: No adoptions, sealed, juvenile, mental health, expunged or dismissed records released. SASE required. Turnaround time 1-2 days. Copy fee: $.50 per page. Certification fee: $5.00. Fee payee: Dover District Court. Personal checks accepted. Prepayment is required.

Durham District Court 1 Main Street, Durham, NH 03824; 603-868-2323. Hours: 8:30AM-4PM (EST). *Misdemeanor, Civil Actions Under $25,000, Eviction, Small Claims.*

Civil Records: Access: Mail, in person. Only the court performs in person searches; visitors may not. Search fee: Searching via computer is $10.00 per name;

lengthy manual searching is $25.00 per hour. Required to search: name, years to search. Civil cases indexed by defendant, plaintiff. Civil records on computer from 1/91, index cards from 1980, index books from 1945.

Criminal Records: Access: Mail, in person. Only the court performs in person searches; visitors may not. Search fee: Same as Civil. Required to search: name, years to search; also helpful: DOB, SSN. Criminal records on computer from 1/91, index cards from 1980, index books from 1945.

General Information: No adoptions, sealed, juvenile, mental health, expunged or dismissed records released. SASE required. Turnaround time 4 days. Copy fee: $.50 per page. Certification fee: $5.00. Fee payee: Durham District Court. Personal checks accepted. Prepayment is required.

Rochester District Court 76 N Main St, Rochester, NH 03867; 603-332-3516. Hours: 8AM-4PM (EST). *Misdemeanor, Felony PC's, Civil Actions Under $25,000, Eviction, Small Claims.*

Civil Records: Access: Mail, in person. Only the court performs in person searches; visitors may not. Search fee: If on computer, $10 for up to 10 names, $25.00 if over 10 names. If manual, then 25.00. Required to search: name, years to search. Civil cases indexed by defendant, plaintiff. Civil records on computer from 1989, index cards from 7/80, index books from 1960s.

Criminal Records: Access: Mail, in person. Only the court performs in person searches; visitors may not. Search fee: Same fees as civil. Required to search: name, years to search; also helpful: DOB. Criminal records on computer from 1989, index cards from 7/80, index books from 1960s.

General Information: No adoptions, sealed, juvenile, mental health, expunged records released. SASE required. Turnaround time 1 week. Copy fee: $.50 per page. Certification fee: $5.00 per page. Fee payee: Rochester District Court. Personal checks accepted. Prepayment is required.

Somersworth District Court 2 Pleasant St, Somersworth, NH 03878-2543; 603-692-5967; Fax: 603-692-5752. Hours: 8AM-4PM (EST). *Misdemeanor, Civil Actions Under $25,000, Eviction, Small Claims.*

Note: The first 3 Tuesdays of the month the court is open until 8:30PM.

Civil Records: Access: Phone, mail, in person. Only the court performs in person searches; visitors may not. Search fee: Fee is based on type of search. See state introduction. Required to search: name, years to search. Civil cases indexed by defendant, plaintiff. Civil records on computer from 1993, on index cards from 1981, index books from 1960s.

Criminal Records: Access: Phone, mail, in person. Only the court performs in person searches; visitors may not. Search fee: Fee is based on type of search. See state introduction. Required to search: name, years to search, DOB. Criminal records on computer from 1993, on index cards from 1981, index books from 1960s.

General Information: No adoptions, sealed, juvenile, mental health, expunged or dismissed records released. SASE required. Turnaround time 7-10 days. Copy fee: $.50 per page. No fee for computer printouts. Certification fee: $5.00. Fee payee: Somersworth District Court. Personal checks accepted. Credit cards accepted. Prepayment is required.

Probate Court PO Box 799, Dover, NH 03821-0799; 603-742-2550. Hours: 8AM-4:30PM (EST). *Probate.*

www.state.nh.us/courts/probate.htm

Sullivan County

Superior Court 22 Main St, Newport, NH 03773; 603-863-3450. Hours: 8AM-4:30PM (EST). *Felony, Civil Actions Over $1,500.*

Civil Records: Access: Mail, in person. Only the court performs in person searches; visitors may not. No search fee. Required to search: name, years to search. Civil cases indexed by defendant, plaintiff. Civil records on computer from 1992, on index cards from 1980s, index books from 1800s.

Criminal Records: Access: Mail, in person. Only the court performs in person searches; visitors may not. No search fee. Required to search: name, years to search, DOB. Criminal records on computer from 1992, on index cards from 1980s, index books from 1800s.

General Information: No adoptions, sealed, juvenile, mental health, expunged or dismissed records released. SASE required. Turnaround time 1 week. Copy fee: $.50 per page. Certification fee: $5.00. Fee payee: Sullivan County Superior Court. Personal checks accepted. Prepayment is required.

Claremont District Court PO Box 313, Claremont, NH 03743; 603-542-6064. Hours: 8AM-4PM (EST). *Misdemeanor, Civil Actions Under $25,000, Eviction, Small Claims.*

Civil Records: Access: Phone, mail, in person. Only the court performs in person searches; visitors may not. Search fee: $10.00 1992 to present. $35.00 prior to 1992. Required to search: name, years to search. Civil cases indexed by defendant, plaintiff. Civil records on computer from 10/92, on index cards from 1980, index books from 1960.

Criminal Records: Access: Phone, mail, in person. Only the court performs in person searches; visitors may not. Search fee: $10.00 1992 to present. $35.00 prior to 1992. Required to search: name, years to search, DOB. Criminal records on computer from 10/92, on index cards from 1980, index books from 1960.

General Information: No adoptions, sealed, juvenile, mental health, expunged or dismissed records released. SASE required. Turnaround time 1 week. Copy fee: $.50 per page. Certification fee: $5.00. Fee payee: Claremont District Court. Personal checks accepted. Prepayment is required.

Newport District Court PO Box 581, Newport, NH 03773; 603-863-1832. Hours: 8AM-4PM (EST). *Misdemeanor, Civil Actions Under $25,000, Eviction, Small Claims.*

Civil Records: Access: Phone, mail, fax, in person. Only the court performs in person searches; visitors may not. Search fee: $25.00 per hour. Required to search: name, years to search. Civil cases indexed by defendant, plaintiff. Civil records on computer from 1993, on index cards from 1980, index books from 1960s.

Criminal Records: Access: Phone, mail, fax, in person. Only the court performs in person searches; visitors may not. Search fee: $25.00 per hour. Required to search: name, years to search, DOB. Criminal records on computer from 1993, on index cards from 1980, index books from 1960s.

General Information: No adoptions, sealed, juvenile, mental health, expunged or dismissed records released. SASE required. Turnaround time 2-3 days. Copy fee: $.50 per page. Certification fee: $1.00. Fee payee: Newport District Court. Personal checks accepted. Prepayment is required.

Probate Court PO Box 417, Newport, NH 03773; 603-863-3150. Hours: 8AM-4:30PM (EST). *Probate.*

New Hampshire Recording Offices

ORGANIZATION
238 cities/towns and 10 counties, 10 recording offices and 242 UCC filing offices. The recording officers are Town/City Clerk (UCC) and Register of Deeds (real estate only). Each town/city profile indicates the county in which the town/city is located. Be careful to distinguish the following names that are identical for both a town/city and a county - Grafton, Hillsborough, Merrimack, Strafford, and Sullivan. Many towns are so small that their mailing addresses are within another town. The following unincorporated towns do not have a Town Clerk, so all liens are located at the corresponding county: Cambridge (Coos), Dicksville (Coos), Green's Grant (Coos), Hale's Location (Carroll), Millsfield (Coos), and Wentworth's Location (Coos). The entire state is in the Eastern Time Zone (EST).

REAL ESTATE RECORDS
Real estate transactions are recorded at the county level, and property taxes are handled at the town/city level. Local town real estate ownership and assessment records are usually located at the Selectman's Office. Each town/city profile indicates the county in which the town/city is located. Most counties will not perform real estate searches. Copy fees vary. Certification fees generally are $2.00 per document.

UCC RECORDS
This was a dual filing state until Revised Article 9. Previously, financing statements were filed at the state level and with the Town/City Clerk, except for consumer goods and farm related collateral, which were filed only with the Town/City Clerk, and real estate related collateral, which was and still is filed with the county Register of Deeds. Most recording offices will perform UCC searches. Use search request form UCC-11. Search fees are usually $5.00 per debtor name using the standard UCC-11 request form and $7.00 using a non-standard form. Copy fees are usually $.75 per page.

TAX LIEN RECORDS
Federal and state tax liens on personal property of businesses are filed with the Secretary of State. Other federal and state tax liens on personal property are filed with the Town/City Clerk. Federal and state tax liens on real property are filed with the county Register of Deeds. There is wide variation in indexing and searching practices among the recording offices. Where a search fee of $7.00 is indicated, it refers to a non-standard request form such as a letter.

OTHER LIENS
Condominium, town tax, mechanics, welfare.

Acworth Town

Town Clerk, Box 193, South Acworth, NH 03601. 603-835-6879.
Will search UCC records prior to 7/2001 and current liens only. This agency will not do a tax lien search. Real estate records located in Sullivan County.

Albany Town

Town Clerk, 19728 NH Route 16, Conway, NH 03818. 603-447-2877; Fax 603-447-2877.
Will search UCC records prior to 7/2001 and current liens only. Real estate records located in Carroll County. **Other Phone Numbers:** Assessor 603-586-4402.

Alexandria Town

Town Clerk, 44 Perkins Hill Road, Alexandria, NH 03222. 603-744-3288 R/E Recording: 603-787-6921; Fax 603-744-1079.
Will search UCC records. This agency will not do a tax lien search. Real estate records located in Grafton County. **Other Phone Numbers:** Assessor 603-744-3220.

Allenstown Town

Town Clerk, 16 School St, Allenstown, NH 03275. Town Clerk, R/E and UCC Recording 603-485-4276; Fax 603-485-8669. http://www.allenstown.org
Will search UCC records prior to 7/2001 and current liens only. Real estate records located in Merrimack County. **Other Phone Numbers:** Assessor 603-485-4276; Treasurer 603-485-4276; Elections 603-485-4276; Vital Records 603-485-4276.

Alstead Town

Town Clerk, Box 65, Alstead, NH 03602. 603-835-2242; Fax 603-835-2986.
Will search UCC records prior to 7/2001 and current liens only. Real estate records located in Cheshire County.

Alton Town

Town Clerk, Box 637, Alton, NH 03809. 603-875-2101 R/E Recording: 603-875-5095; Fax 603-875-3894.
Will search UCC records prior to 7/2001 and current liens only. Real estate records located in Belknap County. **Other Phone Numbers:** Assessor 603-875-2162; Treasurer 603-875-2161; Appraiser/Auditor 603-875-5095; Elections 603-875-2101; Vital Records 603-875-2101.

Amherst Town

Town Clerk, P.O. Box 960, Amherst, NH 03031. 603-673-6041; Fax 603-673-6794.
Will search UCC records prior to 7/2001 and current liens only. This agency will not do a tax lien search. Real estate records located in Hillsborough County. **Other Phone Numbers:** Assessor 603-673-6041; Treasurer 603-673-6041.

Andover Town

Town Clerk, P.O. Box 61, Andover, NH 03216. 603-735-5332; Fax 603-735-6975.
Will search UCC records. Real estate records located in Merrimack County. **Other Phone Numbers:** Assessor 603-735-5332; Treasurer 603-735-5516; Vital Records 603-735-5332.

Antrim Town

Town Clerk, P.O. Box 517, Antrim, NH 03440. 603-588-6785; Fax 603-588-2969.
Will search UCC records prior to 7/2001 and current liens only. Real estate records located in Hillsborough County.

Ashland Town

Town Clerk, P.O. Box 517, Ashland, NH 03217. 603-968-4432; Fax 603-968-3776.
Will search UCC records prior to 7/2001 and current liens only. Real estate records located in Grafton County.

Atkinson Town

Town Clerk, 21 Academy Avenue, Town Hall, Atkinson, NH 03811-2204. 603-362-4920; Fax 603-362-5305.
Will search UCC records prior to 7/2001 and current liens only. This agency will not do a tax lien search. Real estate records located in Rockingham County.

Auburn Town

Town Clerk, P.O. Box 309, Auburn, NH 03032-0309. 603-483-2281; Fax 603-483-0518.
Will search UCC records prior to 7/2001 and current liens only. Real estate records located in Rockingham County. **Other Phone Numbers:** Assessor 603-483-5052.

Barnstead Town

Town Clerk, P.O. Box 11, Center Barnstead, NH 03225. 603-269-4631; Fax 603-269-4072.
Will search UCC records prior to 7/2001 and current liens only. Real estate records located in Belknap County.

Barrington Town

Town Clerk, 41 Province Lane, Barrington, NH 03825. 603-664-5476; Fax 603-664-5179.
Will search UCC records prior to 7/2001 and current liens only. Real estate records located at Strafford County, Registrar of Deeds, Strafford County Courthouse, Dover, NH 03820. **Other Phone Numbers:** Assessor 603-664-9007; Elections 603-664-5476; Vital Records 603-664-5476; Tax Collector 603-664-2230.

Bartlett Town

Town Clerk, RFD 1 Box 50, Intervale, NH 03845. 603-356-2300 R/E Recording: 603-356-2950.
Will search UCC records. This agency will not do a tax lien search. Real estate records located in Carroll County. **Other Phone Numbers:** Assessor 603-356-2950; Treasurer 603-356-2950; Elections 603-356-2300; Vital Records 603-356-2300.

Bath Town

Town Clerk, P.O. Box 165, Bath, NH 03740. 603-747-2454.
Will search UCC records prior to 7/2001 and current liens only. UCC search includes tax liens if requested. Real estate records located in Grafton County. **Other Phone Numbers:** Treasurer 603-747-2454.

Bedford Town

Town Clerk, 24 North Amherst Road, Bedford, NH 03110. 603-472-3550; Fax 603-472-4573.
http://www.ci.bedford.nh.us
Will search UCC records prior to 7/2001 and current liens only. Real estate records located in Hillsborough County. **Other Phone Numbers:** Assessor 603-472-8104; Vital Records 603-472-3550.

Belknap County

Register of Deeds, P.O. Box 1343, Laconia, NH 03247-1343. Register of Deeds, R/E and UCC Recording 603-527-5420; Fax 603-527-5429.
Will search UCC records prior to 7/2001 and current liens only. Will not search real estate records.

Belmont Town

Town Clerk, P.O. Box 310, Belmont, NH 03220. 603-267-8302; Fax 603-267-8305.
Will search UCC records prior to 7/2001 and current liens only. Real estate records located at the Belknap County Register of Deeds office. **Other Phone Numbers:** Assessor 603-267-8300; Treasurer 603-267-8300; Appraiser/Auditor 603-267-8300; Elections 603-267-8302; Vital Records 603-267-8303.

Bennington Town

Town Clerk, 7 School Street, #101, Bennington, NH 03442. 603-588-2189; Fax 603-588-8005.
Will search UCC records prior to 7/2001 and current liens only. Real estate records located in Hillsborough County. **Other Phone Numbers:** Assessor 603-588-2189.

Benton Town

Town Clerk, 30 Ingerson Rd., Benton, NH 03785. 603-787-6541 R/E Recording: 603-787-6053; Fax 603-787-6883.
Will search UCC records prior to 7/2001 and current liens only. Real estate records located in Grafton County. **Other Phone Numbers:** Assessor 603-787-6053; Treasurer 603-787-6004; Appraiser/Auditor 603-787-6053; Elections 603-787-2129; Vital Records 603-787-6541.

Berlin City

City Clerk, 168 Main Street, City Hall, Berlin, NH 03570. 603-752-2340; Fax 603-752-8586.
Will search UCC records prior to 7/2001 and current liens only. Real estate records located in Coos County. **Other Phone Numbers:** Assessor 603-752-5245; Treasurer 603-752-1610.

Bethlehem Town

Town Clerk, P.O. Box 189, Bethlehem, NH 03574. 603-869-2293; Fax 603-869-2280.

Will search UCC records prior to 7/2001 and current liens only. This agency will not do a tax lien search. Real estate records located in Grafton County.

Boscawen Town

Town Clerk, 17 High Street, Boscawen, NH 03303. 603-796-2426; Fax 603-796-2316.
Will search UCC records prior to 7/2001 and current liens only. Real estate records located in Merrimack County. **Other Phone Numbers:** Assessor 603-796-2426; Treasurer 603-796-2343.

Bow Town

Town Clerk, 10 Grandview Road, Bow, NH 03304-3410. 603-225-2683.
Will search UCC records prior to 7/2001 and current liens only. This agency will not do a tax lien search. Real estate records located in Merrimack County.

Bradford Town

Town Clerk/Tax Collector, P.O. Box 607, Bradford, NH 03221-0607. 603-938-2288; Fax 603-938-5900.
Will search UCC records prior to 7/2001 and current liens only. Real estate records located in Merrimack County. **Other Phone Numbers:** Assessor 603-938-5900.

Brentwood Town

Town Clerk, 1 Dalton Road, Brentwood, NH 03833. 603-642-6400 x14; Fax 603-642-6310.
Will search UCC records prior to 7/2001 and current liens only. This agency will not do a tax lien search. Real estate records located in Rockingham County. **Other Phone Numbers:** Assessor 603-642-6400 x10; Treasurer 603-642-6400 x19; Elections 603-642-6400 x14; Vital Records 603-642-6400 x14.

Bridgewater Town

Town Clerk, P.O. Box 419, Plymouth, NH 03264. 603-968-7911; Fax 603-968-3506.
Will search UCC records prior to 7/2001 and current liens only. This agency will not do a tax lien search. Real estate records located in Grafton County.

Bristol Town

Town Clerk, 230 Lake Street, Suite A, Bristol, NH 03222-1120. 603-744-8478; Fax 603-744-2521.
Will search UCC records prior to 7/2001 and current liens only. Real estate records located in Grafton County. **Other Phone Numbers:** Assessor 603-744-3354.

Brookfield Town

Town Clerk, P.O. Box 756, Sanbornville, NH 03872. 603-522-3231; Fax 603-522-6245.
Will search UCC records prior to 7/2001 and current liens only. UCC search includes tax liens if requested. Real estate records located in Carroll County. **Other Phone Numbers:** Assessor 603-522-6018; Treasurer 603-522-6756; Appraiser/Auditor 603-522-6018.

Brookline Town

Town Clerk, P.O. Box 336, Brookline, NH 03033. 603-673-8933; Fax 603-673-8136.
Will search UCC records prior to 7/2001 and current liens only. UCC search includes tax liens. Real estate records located in Hillsborough County.

Campton Town

Town Clerk, P.O. Box 127, Campton, NH 03223. 603-726-3223; Fax 603-726-9817.
Will Search UCC records prior to 7/2001 and current liens only. Real estate records located in Grafton County.

Canaan Town

Town Clerk, P.O. Box 38, Canaan, NH 03741-0038. 603-523-7106; Fax 603-523-4526.
Will search UCC records prior to 7/2001 and current liens only. Real estate records located in Grafton County.

Candia Town

Town Clerk, 74 High Street, Candia, NH 03034-2713. 603-483-5573; Fax 603-483-0252.
Will search UCC records prior to 7/2001 and current liens only. Real estate records located in Rockingham County.

Canterbury Town

Town Clerk, P.O. Box 500, Canterbury, NH 03224. 603-783-9955.
Will search UCC records prior to 7/2001 and current liens only. UCC search includes tax liens. Real estate records located in Merrimack County.

Carroll County

Register of Deeds, P.O. Box 163, Ossipee, NH 03864-0163. 603-539-4872; Fax 603-539-5239.
Will search UCC records prior to 7/2001 and current liens only. Will not search real estate records.

Carroll Town

Town Clerk, P.O. Box 88, Twin Mountain, NH 03595-0088. 603-846-5494; Fax 603-846-5754.
Will search UCC records prior to 7/2001 and current liens only. Real estate records located in Carroll County. **Other Phone Numbers:** Assessor 603-846-5754.

Center Harbor Town

Town Clerk, P.O. Box 140, Center Harbor, NH 03226. 603-253-4561; Fax 603-253-8420.
Will search UCC records prior to 7/2001 and current liens only. Real estate records located in Belknap County.

Charlestown Town

Town Clerk, P.O. Box 834, Charlestown, NH 03603. 603-826-5821.
Will search UCC records prior to 7/2001 and current liens only. UCC search includes tax liens if requested. Real estate records located in Sullivan County. **Other Phone Numbers:** Assessor 603-826-4400.

Chatham Town

Town Clerk, 1717 Main Road, Chatham, NH 03813. 603-694-2043.
Will search UCC records prior to 7/2001 and current liens only. This agency will not do a tax lien search. Real estate records located in Carroll County. **Other Phone Numbers:** Treasurer 603-694-2321; Elections 603-694-2043; Vital Records 603-694-2043.

Cheshire County

Register of Deeds, 33 West Street, Keene, NH 03431. 603-352-0403; Fax 603-352-7678.
Will search UCC records prior to 7/2001 and current liens only. Will not search real estate records.

Chester Town

Town Clerk, P.O. Box 275, Chester, NH 03036. 603-887-3636.
Will search UCC records prior to 7/2001 and current liens only. UCC search includes tax liens if requested. Real estate records located in Rockingham County.

Chesterfield Town

Town Clerk, P.O. Box 64, Chesterfield, NH 03443-0064. 603-363-8071 R/E Recording: 603-363-4624; Fax 603-363-8047. www.nhchesterfield.com
Will search UCC records prior to 7/2001 and current liens only. UCC search includes tax liens if requested. Real estate records located in Cheshire County. **Other Phone Numbers:** Assessor 603-363-4624; Treasurer 603-363-4624; Appraiser/Auditor 603-363-4624; Elections 603-363-8071; Vital Records 603-363-8071.

Chichester Town

Town Clerk, 54 Main St., Chichester, NH 03234. 603-798-5808 R/E Recording: 603-798-5350; Fax 603-798-3170.
Will search UCC records prior to 7/2001 and current liens only. Real estate records located in Merrimack County. **Other Phone Numbers:** Assessor 603-798-5350; Appraiser/Auditor 603-798-5350; Elections 603-798-4808; Vital Records 603-798-4808.

Claremont City

City Clerk, City Hall - Finance Office, 58 Tremont Square, Claremont, NH 03743. 603-542-7001 UCC Recording: 603-542-7003; Fax 603-542-7014. www.claremontnh.com
Will search UCC records prior to 7/2001 and current liens only. Real estate records located in Sullivan County. **Other Phone Numbers:** Assessor 603-542-7008; Treasurer 603-542-7000; Elections 603-542-7003; Vital Records 603-542-7003.

Clarksville Town

Town Clerk, 408 NH Route 145, Clarksville, NH 03592. Town Clerk, R/E and UCC Recording 603-246-7751; Fax 603-246-3480.
The County Register of Deeds records real estate transactions, and the City Clerk records UCC filings. Will search UCC records prior to 7/2001 and current liens only. UCC search includes tax liens if requested. Real estate records located in Coos County. **Other Phone Numbers:** Assessor 603-417-2297; Treasurer 603-246-8896; Appraiser/Auditor 800-417-2297; Elections 603-246-7751; Vital Records 603-246-7751.

Colebrook Town

Assessor, 10 Bridge Street, Colebrook, NH 03576. 603-237-5200 R/E Recording: 603-237-4070; Fax 603-237-9852.
Will search UCC records prior to 7/2001 and current liens only. Real estate records located in Coos County. **Other Phone Numbers:** Assessor 603-237-4070; Treasurer 603-237-4142; Appraiser/Auditor 603-237-4142; Elections 603-237-5200; Vital Records 603-237-5200.

Columbia Town

Town Clerk, P.O. Box 157, Colebrook, NH 03576. 603-237-5255; Fax 603-237-8270.
Will search UCC records prior to 7/2001 and current liens only. Real estate records located in Coos County.

Concord City

City Clerk, 41 Green Street, Room 2, Concord, NH 03301-4255. 603-225-8500; Fax 603-228-2724.
Will search UCC records prior to 7/2001 and current liens only. Real estate records located in Merrimack County. **Online Access:** Assessor. Records on the city assessor database are available free online at http://140.239.211.227/ConcordNH/. Registration is required; no charge. **Other Phone Numbers:** Assessor 603-225-8550.

Conway Town

Town Clerk, Box 70, Center Conway, NH 03813-0070. 603-447-3822; Fax 603-447-1348.
Will search UCC records prior to 7/2001 and current liens only. Real estate records located in Carroll County.

Coos County

Register of Deeds, Coos County Courthouse, 55 School St, Suite 103, Lancaster, NH 03584. Register of Deeds, R/E and UCC Recording 603-788-2392; Fax 603-788-4291.
The County Register of Deeds records real estate and Real Estate/UCC transactions, and the Town/City Clerk records UCC filings. Will search UCC records prior to 7/2001 and current liens only. This agency will not do a tax lien search. Will not search real estate records.

Cornish Town

Town Clerk, P.O. Box 183, Cornish Flat, NH 03746. 603-675-5207; Fax 603-675-5605.
Will search UCC records prior to 7/2001 and current liens only. Real estate records located in Sullivan County.

Croydon Town

Town Clerk, 879 NHRT10, Newport, NH 03773. 603-863-7830; Fax 603-863-2601.
Will search UCC records prior to 7/2001 and current liens only. This agency will not do a tax lien search. Real estate records located in Sullivan County. **Other Phone Numbers:** Assessor 603-863-7830.

Dalton Town

Town Clerk, 741 Dalton Rd, Dalton, NH 03598. 603-837-2096; Fax 603-837-9642.
Will search UCC records prior to 7/2001 and current liens only. Real estate records located in Coos County. **Other Phone Numbers:** Treasurer 603-837-9802.

Danbury Town

Town Clerk, Box 4A High St., Danbury, NH 03230. 603-768-5448; Fax 603-768-3313.
Will search UCC records prior to 7/2001 and current liens only. This agency will not do a tax lien search. Real estate records located in Merrimack County.

Danville Town

Town Clerk, P.O. Box 11, Danville, NH 03819. 603-382-8253; Fax 603-382-3363.
Will search UCC records prior to 7/2001 and current liens only. Real estate records located in Rockingham County.

Deerfield Town

Town Clerk, P.O. Box 159, Deerfield, NH 03037. 603-463-8811; Fax 603-463-2820.
Will search UCC records prior to 7/2001 and current liens only. Real estate records located in Rockingham County. **Other Phone Numbers:** Assessor 603-463-8811.

Deering Town

Town Clerk, 762 Deering Center Rd., Deering, NH 03244. 603-464-6557; Fax 603-464-3804. http://www.deering.nh.us/
Will search UCC records prior to 7/2001 and current liens only. Real estate records located in Hillsborough County.

Derry Town

Town Clerk, 48 East Broadway, Derry, NH 03038. 603-432-6105; Fax 603-432-6131. http://derrytax.4nh.com
Will search UCC records prior to 7/2001 and current liens only. Real estate records located in Rockingham County. **Online Access:** Assessor. Records on the Derry Tax Assessment database are available free online at http://derrytax.4nh.com. **Other Phone Numbers:** Assessor 603-432-6104.

Dorchester Town

Town Clerk, 368 N Dorchester Rd, Dorecester, NH 03266. 603-786-9076 UCC Recording: 603-786-9476.
Will search UCC records prior to 7/2001 and current liens only. UCC search includes tax liens. Real estate records located in Grafton County. **Other Phone Numbers:** Assessor 603-523-7658; Treasurer 603-523-9658; Elections 603-786-9076; Vital Records 603-786-9076.

Dover City

City Clerk, 288 Central Avenue, City Hall, Dover, NH 03820. 603-743-6021; Fax 603-790-6322.
Will search UCC records prior to 7/2001 and current liens only. Real estate records located in Strafford County. **Other Phone Numbers:** Assessor 603-743-6014.

Dublin Town

Town Clerk, Box 62, Dublin, NH 03444. 603-563-8859; Fax 603-563-9221.
Will search UCC records prior to 7/2001 and current liens only. Real estate records located in Cheshire County.

Dummer Town

Town Clerk, 1420 East Side River Rd., Dummer, NH 03588. 603-449-3408; Fax 603-449-3349.
Will search UCC records prior to 7/2001 and current liens only. This agency will not do a tax lien search. Real estate records located in Coos County. **Other Phone Numbers:** Treasurer 603-449-3417; Elections 603-449-3442; Vital Records 603-449-3408.

Dunbarton Town

Town Clerk, 1011 School St., Dunbarton, NH 03045. 603-774-3547; Fax 603-774-5541.
Will search UCC records prior to 7/2001 and current liens only. Real estate records located in Merrimack County.

Durham Town

Town Clerk/Tax Collector, 15 Newmarket Road, Town Hall, Durham, NH 03824-2898. 603-868-5577; Fax 603-868-8033. http://www.ci.durham.nh.us/html/town_info.html
Will search UCC records prior to 7/2001 and current liens only. Real estate records located in Strafford County. **Other Phone Numbers:** Assessor 603-868-8065; Treasurer 603-868-8043.

East Kingston Town

Town Clerk, P.O. Box 249, East Kingston, NH 03827-0249. Town Clerk, R/E and UCC Recording 603-642-8794; Fax 603-642-8406.
Will search UCC records prior to 7/2001 and current liens only. Real estate records located in Rockingham County. **Other Phone Numbers:** Assessor 603-642-8406; Treasurer 603-642-8406; Appraiser/Auditor 603-642-8406; Elections 603-642-8794; Vital Records 603-642-8794.

Easton Town

Town Clerk, 381 Easton Valley Road, Easton, NH 03580. 603-823-5293; Fax 603-823-7780.
Will search UCC records prior to 7/2001 and current liens only. This agency will not do a tax lien search. Real estate records located in Grafton County.

Eaton Town

Town Clerk, Box 118, Eaton Center, NH 03832. 603-447-2840; Fax 603-447-2840.
Will search UCC records prior to 7/2001 and current liens only. Real estate records located in Carroll County.

Effingham Town

Town Clerk, P.O. Box 48, South Effingham, NH 03882. 603-539-7551; Fax 603-539-7799.
Will search UCC records prior to 7/2001 and current liens only. Real estate records located in Carroll County.

Ellsworth Town

Town Clerk, Ellsworth Pond Road, RR 1, Box 852, Plymouth, NH 03264-9608. 603-726-4748.
Will search UCC records prior to 7/2001 and current liens only. This agency will not do a tax lien search. Real estate records located in Grafton County. **Other Phone Numbers:** Treasurer 603-726-8668.

Enfield Town

Town Clerk, P.O. Box 373, Enfield, NH 03748-0373. 603-632-5001; Fax 603-632-5182. www.enfield.nh.us
Will search UCC records prior to 7/2001 and current liens only. This agency will not do a tax lien search. Real estate records located in Grafton County. **Other Phone Numbers:** Assessor 603-632-4201.

Epping Town

Town Clerk, 157 Main Street, Epping, NH 03042. 603-679-8288; Fax 603-679-3302.
Will search UCC records prior to 7/2001 and current liens only. Real estate records located in Rockingham County.

Epsom Town

Town Clerk, P.O. Box 10, Epsom, NH 03234. 603-736-4825; Fax 603-736-8539.
Will search UCC records prior to 7/2001 and current liens only. Real estate records located in Merrimack County.

Errol Town

Town Clerk, P.O. Box 100, Errol, NH 03579. 603-482-3351; Fax 603-482-3804.
Will search UCC records prior to 7/2001 and current liens only. Real estate records located in Coos County. **Other Phone Numbers:** Assessor 603-482-3351; Treasurer 603-482-3351.

Exeter Town

Town Clerk, 10 Front Street, Exeter, NH 03833-2792. 603-778-0591; Fax 603-772-4709.
Will search UCC records prior to 7/2001 and current liens only. **Other Phone Numbers:** Assessor 603-778-0591.

Farmington Town

Town Clerk, Main Street, Town Hall, Farmington, NH 03835. 603-755-3657; Fax 603-755-9128.
Will search UCC records prior to 7/2001 and current liens only. Real estate records located in Strafford County. **Other Phone Numbers:** Assessor 603-755-2208; Treasurer 603-755-3657; Elections 603-755-3657; Vital Records 603-755-3657.

Fitzwilliam Town

Town Clerk, P.O. Box 504, Fitzwilliam, NH 03447-0504. 603-585-7791; Fax 603-585-7744.
Will search UCC records prior to 7/2001 and current liens only. Real estate records located in Cheshire County.

Francestown Town

Town Clerk, P.O. Box 67, Francestown, NH 03043-0067. 603-547-6251; Fax 603-547-2818.
Will search UCC records prior to 7/2001 and current liens only. Real estate records located in Hillsborough County.

Franconia Town

Town Clerk, P.O. Box 900, Franconia, NH 03580. 603-823-5237; Fax 603-823-5581.
Will search UCC records prior to 7/2001 and current liens only. UCC search includes tax liens if requested. Real estate records located in Grafton County.

Franklin City

City Clerk, 316 Central Street, Franklin, NH 03235. 603-934-3109.
Will search UCC records prior to 7/2001 and current liens only. This agency will not do a tax lien search. Real estate records located in Merrimack County. **Other Phone Numbers:** Assessor 603-934-5449.

Freedom Town

Town Clerk, P.O. Box 457, Freedom, NH 03836. 603-539-6323 R/E Recording: 603-539-4872; Fax 603-539-8270.
Will search UCC records prior to 7/2001 and current liens only. Real estate records located in Carroll County. **Other Phone Numbers:** Assessor 603-539-6323; Treasurer 603-539-6323.

Fremont Town

Town Clerk, PO Box 120, Fremont, NH 03044. Town Clerk, R/E and UCC Recording 603-895-2226; Fax 603-895-3149.
Will search UCC records prior to 7/2001 and current liens only. Real estate records located in Rockingham County. **Other Phone Numbers:** Assessor 603-895-2226; Treasurer 603-895-6936; Elections 603-895-2226; Vital Records 603-895-2226.

Gilford Town

Town Clerk, 47 Cherry Valley Road, Town Hall, Gilford, NH 03246. 603-524-3286; Fax 603-528-1183.
Will search UCC records prior to 7/2001 and current liens only. Real estate records located in Belknap County. **Other Phone Numbers:** Assessor 603-524-3293.

Gilmanton Town

Town Clerk, P.O. Box 550, Gilmanton, NH 03237-0550. 603-267-6726; Fax 603-267-6701.
Will search UCC records prior to 7/2001 and current liens only. Real estate records located in Belknap County.

Gilsum Town

Town Clerk, P.O. Box 36, Gilsum, NH 03448. 603-357-0320; Fax 603-352-0845.
Will search UCC records prior to 7/2001 and current liens only. Real estate records located in Cheshire County.

Goffstown Town

Town Clerk, 16 Main Street, Goffstown, NH 03045. 603-497-3613 R/E Recording: 603-497-3611; Fax 603-497-8993. http://www.ci.goffstown.nh.us
Will search UCC records prior to 7/2001 and current liens only. Real estate records located in Hillsborough County. **Other Phone Numbers:** Assessor 603-497-3611; Treasurer 603-497-3615; Elections 603-497-3613; Vital Records 603-497-3617.

Gorham Town

Town Clerk, 20 Park Street, Gorham, NH 03581-1694. 603-466-2744; Fax 603-466-3100. www.gorhamnh.org
Will search UCC records prior to 7/2001 and current liens only. Real estate records located in Coos County. **Other Phone Numbers:** Assessor 603-466-3322; Vital Records 603-466-2744.

Goshen Town

Town Clerk, P.O. Box 58, Goshen, NH 03752. 603-863-5655.
Will search UCC records prior to 7/2001 and current liens only. This agency will not do a tax lien search. Real estate records located in Sullivan County.

Grafton County

Registry of Deeds, 3785 Dartmouth College Hwy, Box 2, North Haverhill, NH 03774-9700. Registry of Deeds, R/E and UCC Recording 603-787-6921; Fax 603-787-2363.
Wil not search UCC records. Will not search real estate records. **Online Access:** Real Estate, Liens. Access to the County dial-up service requires a $100 set up fee and $40 per month access fee. Two years of data are kept on system; prior years on CD. Lending agency information is available. A fax-back service is available in-state only. For further information, call 603-787-6921. **Other Phone Numbers:** Treasurer 603-787-6941; Elections 603-787-6941.

Grafton Town

Town Clerk, P.O. Box 297, Grafton, NH 03240. 603-523-7270 R/E Recording: 603-523-7700; Fax 603-523-4397.
Will search UCC records prior to 7/2001 and current liens only. Real estate records located in Grafton County. **Other Phone Numbers:** Treasurer 603-523-7700; Appraiser/Auditor 603-523-7700; Elections 603-523-7270; Vital Records 603-523-7270.

Grantham Town

Town Clerk, P.O. Box 135, Grantham, NH 03753-0135. 603-863-5608; Fax 603-863-4499.
Will search UCC records prior to 7/2001 and current liens only. This agency will not do a tax lien search. Real estate records located in Sullivan County. **Other Phone Numbers:** Assessor 603-863-5608; Treasurer 603-863-5608.

Greenfield Town

Town Clerk, P.O. Box 256, Greenfield, NH 03047. 603-547-2782; Fax 603-547-3004. http://green fieldnh.org
Will search UCC records prior to 7/2001 and current liens only. Real estate records located in Hillsborough County.

Greenland Town

Town Clerk, P.O. Box 100, Greenland, NH 03840-0100. Town Clerk, R/E and UCC Recording 603-431-7111; Fax 603-430-3761.
Will search UCC records prior to 7/2001 and current liens only. Real estate records located in Rockingham County. **Other Phone Numbers:** Assessor 603-431-7111; Treasurer 603-431-7111; Appraiser/Auditor 603-431-7111; Elections 603-431-7111; Vital Records 603-431-7111.

Greenville Town

Town Clerk, P.O. Box 354, Greenville, NH 03048-0354. 603-878-4155; Fax 603-878-4645.
Will search UCC records prior to 7/2001 and current liens only. Real estate records located in Hillsborough County. **Other Phone Numbers:** Assessor 603-878-2084.

Groton Town

Town Clerk, 63-1 N. Groton Rd, Groton, NH 03241. 603-744-8849.
Will search UCC records prior to 7/2001 and current liens only. This agency will not do a tax lien search. Real estate records located in Grafton County.

Hampstead Town

Town Clerk, P.O. Box 298, Hampstead, NH 03841. 603-329-6840; Fax 603-329-6628.
Will search UCC records prior to 7/2001 and current liens only. Real estate records located in Rockingham County.

Hampton Falls Town

Town Clerk, 1 Drinkwater Road, Town Hall, Hampton Falls, NH 03844. 603-926-4618 R/E Recording: 603-929-0828; Fax 603-926-1848.
Will search UCC records prior to 7/2001 and current liens only. Real estate records located in Rockingham County. **Other Phone Numbers:** Assessor 603-929-0828; Treasurer 603-929-3613; Elections 603-926-4618; Vital Records 603-926-4618; Town Hall: 603-926-7101.

Hampton Town

Town Clerk, 100 Winnacunnet Road, Hampton, NH 03842. 603-926-0406; Fax 603-929-5917.
Will search UCC records prior to 7/2001 and current liens only. Real estate records located in Rockingham County. **Other Phone Numbers:** Assessor 603-929-5923; Elections 603-926-0406; Vital Records 603-926-0406.

Hancock Town

Town Clerk, P.O. Box 6, Hancock, NH 03449. 603-525-4441; Fax 603-525-9327.
Will search UCC records prior to 7/2001 and current liens only. Real estate records located in Hillsborough County. **Other Phone Numbers:** Assessor 603-525-4441; Treasurer 603-525-4441.

Hanover Town

Town Clerk, P.O. Box 483, Hanover, NH 03755-0483. 603-643-4123; Fax 603-643-1720.
Will search UCC records prior to 7/2001 and current liens only. Real estate records located in Grafton County. **Other Phone Numbers:** Assessor 603-643-0703; Treasurer 603-643-4123.

Harrisville Town

Town Clerk, P.O. Box 284, Harrisville, NH 03450. 603-827-5546; Fax 603-827-2917.
Will search UCC records prior to 7/2001 and current liens only. Real estate records located in Cheshire County.

Hart's Location Town

Town Clerk, 5 Forest Rd, Hart's Location, NH 03812. 603-374-2436.
Will search UCC records prior to 7/2001 and current liens only. UCC search includes tax liens if requested. Real estate records located in Carroll County.

Haverhill Town

Town Clerk, 2975 Dartmouth College Hwy, N. Haverhill, NH 03774. 603-787-6200 R/E Recording: 603-787-6444; Fax 603-787-2226.
Will search UCC records prior to 7/2001 and current liens only. Real estate records located in Grafton County. **Other Phone Numbers:** Assessor 603-787-6444; Treasurer 603-747-2735.

Hebron Town

Town Clerk, HC 58, Box 286, East Hebron, NH 03232. 603-744-7999; Fax 603-744-7999.
Will search UCC records prior to 7/2001 and current liens only. This agency will not do a tax lien search. Real estate records located in Grafton County.

Henniker Town

Town Clerk, 2 Depot Hill Road, Henniker, NH 03242. 603-428-3240; Fax 603-428-4366.
Will search UCC records prior to 7/2001 and current liens only. Real estate records located in Merrimack County.

Hill Town

Town Clerk, P.O. Box 251, Hill, NH 03243. 603-934-3951; Fax 603-934-1094.
Will search UCC records prior to 7/2001 and current liens only. Real estate records located in Merrimack County.

Hillsborough County

Register of Deeds, P.O. Box 370, Nashua, NH 03061-0370. 603-882-6933; Fax 603-594-4137.
Will search UCC records prior to 7/2001 and current liens only. Will not search real estate records.

Hillsborough Town

Town Clerk, P.O. Box 1699, Hillsborough, NH 03244. 603-464-5571; Fax 603-464-4270.
Will search UCC records prior to 7/2001 and current liens only. Real estate records located in Hillsborough County.

Hinsdale Town

Town Clerk, 27 Spring Street, Hinsdale, NH 03451. 603-336-5719.
Will search UCC records prior to 7/2001 and current liens only. This agency will not do a tax lien search. Real estate records located in Cheshire County.

Holderness Town

Town Clerk, P.O. Box 203, Holderness, NH 03245. 603-968-7536; Fax 603-968-9954.
Will search UCC records prior to 7/2001 and current liens only. Real estate records located in Grafton County.

Hollis Town

Town Clerk, 7 Monument Square, Hollis, NH 03049-6568. 603-465-2064; Fax 603-465-3701.
Will search UCC records prior to 7/2001 and current liens only. Real estate records located in Hillsborough County.

Hooksett Town

Town Clerk, 16 North Main Street, Hooksett, NH 03106. 603-485-9534; Fax 603-485-4423.
Will search UCC records prior to 7/2001 and current liens only. Real estate records located in Merrimack County.

Hopkinton Town

Town Clerk, P.O. Box 169, Contoocook, NH 03229-0169. 603-746-3180; Fax 603-746-4011.
Will search UCC records prior to 7/2001 and current liens only. Real estate records located in Merrimack County. **Other Phone Numbers:** Assessor 603-746-3170; Treasurer 603-746-3180.

Hudson Town

Town Clerk, 12 School Street, Hudson, NH 03051-4294. 603-886-6003.

Will search UCC records prior to 7/2001 and current liens only. UCC search includes tax liens if requested. Real estate records located in Hillsborough County, Registry of Deeds, 19 Temple St., Nashua, NH 03060. **Other Phone Numbers:** Assessor 603-886-6024; Treasurer 603-886-6000.

Jackson Town

Town Clerk, P.O. Box 336, Jackson, NH 03846-0336. 603-383-6248; Fax 603-383-6980.
Will search UCC records prior to 7/2001 and current liens only. Real estate records located in Carroll County.

Jaffrey Town

Town Clerk, 10 Goodnow St., Jaffrey, NH 03452. 603-532-7861; Fax 603-532-7862.
Will search UCC records prior to 7/2001 and current liens only. Real estate records located in Cheshire County. **Other Phone Numbers:** Assessor 603-532-7445; Treasurer 603-532-7445.

Jefferson Town

Town Clerk, RFD #1 Box 162A, Jefferson, NH 03583. 603-586-4553; Fax 603-586-4553.
Will search UCC records prior to 7/2001 and current liens only. Real estate records located in Coos County. **Other Phone Numbers:** Assessor 603-586-4553; Treasurer 603-586-4400; Appraiser/Auditor 603-586-4553; Elections 603-586-4553.

Keene City

City Clerk, 3 Washington Street, Keene, NH 03431. 603-352-0133; Fax 603-357-9884.
Will search UCC records prior to 7/2001 and current liens only. Real estate records located in Cheshire County. **Other Phone Numbers:** Assessor 603-352-2125; Treasurer 603-357-9801.

Kensington Town

Town Hall, Town Hall, 95 Amesbury Rd., Rte 150, Kensington, NH 03833. Town Hall, R/E and UCC Recording 603-772-5423; Fax 603-772-6841. town.kensington.nh.us
Will search UCC records prior to 7/2001 and current liens only. Real estate records located in Rockingham County. **Other Phone Numbers:** Assessor 603-436-5916; Treasurer 603-772-5423; Elections 603-772-5423; Vital Records 603-772-5423.

Kingston Town

Town Clerk, P.O. Box 657, Kingston, NH 03848-0657. 603-642-3112; Fax 603-642-3204.
Will search UCC records prior to 7/2001 and current liens only. Real estate records located in Rockingham County. **Other Phone Numbers:** Treasurer 603-643-8195.

Laconia City

City Clerk, P.O. Box 489, Laconia, NH 03247. 603-527-1265 R/E Recording: 603-527-5420; Fax 603-524-1766. http://data.visionappraisal.com/LaconiaNH
Will search UCC records prior to 7/2001 and current liens only. Real estate records located in Belknap County. **Online Access:** Assessor. Property records on the Town assessor database are available free online at http://data.visionappraisal.com/LaconiaNH. Registration is required for full access; registration is free. **Other Phone Numbers:** Assessor 603-527-1268; Treasurer 603-524-3877; Elections 603-527-1265; Vital Records 603-527-1265; Tax Office 603-527-1269.

Lancaster Town

Town Clerk, 25 Main Street, Lancaster, NH 03584. 603-788-2306; Fax 603-788-2114.

Will search UCC records prior to 7/2001 and current liens only. Real estate records located in Coos County. **Other Phone Numbers:** Assessor 603-788-3391; Treasurer 603-788-3391.

Landaff Town

Town Clerk, P.O. Box 125, Landaff, NH 03585. 603-838-6220; Fax 603-838-6220.
Will search UCC records prior to 7/2001 and current liens only. UCC search includes tax liens. Real estate records located in Grafton County. **Other Phone Numbers:** Assessor 207-778-3881; Treasurer 603-835-2907.

Langdon Town

Town Clerk, Village Rd. Box 158A, Langdon Town Hall, Langdon, NH 03602. 603-835-2389; Fax 603-835-2389.
Will search UCC records prior to 7/2001 and current liens only. UCC search includes tax liens. Real estate records located in Sullivan County.

Lebanon City

City Clerk, 51 North Park Street, Lebanon, NH 03766. 603-448-3054; Fax 603-448-4891.
Will search UCC records prior to 7/2001 and current liens only. Real estate records located in Grafton County. **Online Access:** Assessor. Records from the city assessor database are available free online at http://140.239.211.227/LebanonNH. Registration is required; no charge. **Other Phone Numbers:** Assessor 603-448-1499.

Lee Town

Town Clerk, 7 Mast Road, Town Hall, Lee, NH 03824. 603-659-2964; Fax 603-659-7202.
Will search UCC records prior to 7/2001 and current liens only. Real estate records located in Strafford County. **Other Phone Numbers:** Treasurer 603-659-5414.

Lempster Town

Town Clerk, P.O. Box 33, East Lempster, NH 03605-0033. 603-863-3213; Fax 603-863-8105.
Will search UCC records prior to 7/2001 and current liens only. Real estate records located in Sullivan County. **Other Phone Numbers:** Treasurer 603-863-3213.

Lincoln Town

Town Clerk, P.O. Box 25, Lincoln, NH 03251. 603-745-8971; Fax 603-745-6743.
Will search UCC records prior to 7/2001 and current liens only. UCC search includes tax liens if requested. Real estate records located in Grafton County. **Other Phone Numbers:** Assessor 603-745-2757; Treasurer 603-745-8971.

Lisbon Town

Town Clerk, 21 School Street, Lisbon, NH 03585. 603-838-2862; Fax 603-838-6790.
Will search UCC records prior to 7/2001 and current liens only. Real estate records located in Grafton County. **Other Phone Numbers:** Assessor 603-838-6377.

Litchfield Town

Town Clerk, 2 Liberty Way, Suite 3, Litchfield, NH 03052. 603-424-4045.
Will search UCC records prior to 7/2001 and current liens only. This agency will not do a tax lien search. Real estate records located in Hillsborough County.

Littleton Town

Town Clerk, 26 Union Street, Littleton, NH 03561. 603-444-3995 x40; Fax 603-444-1715.
Will search UCC records prior to 7/2001 and current liens only. Real estate records located in Grafton County.

Londonderry Town

Town Clerk, 50 Nashua Rd., Suite 100, Londonderry, NH 03053. 603-432-1100 x133; Fax 603-432-1142.
Will search UCC records prior to 7/2001 and current liens only. Real estate records located in Rockingham County. **Other Phone Numbers:** Assessor 603-432-1120; Treasurer 603-432-1126.

Loudon Town

Town Clerk, P.O. Box 7837, Loudon, NH 03301. 603-798-4542 R/E Recording: 603-798-4541; Fax 603-798-4546.
Will search UCC records prior to 7/2001 and current liens only. Real estate records located in Merrimack County. **Other Phone Numbers:** Assessor 603-798-4541; Treasurer 603-798-4541; Elections 603-798-4542; Vital Records 603-798-4542.

Lyman Town

Town Clerk, 65 Parker Hill Rd, Lyman, NH 03585. 603-838-6113; Fax 603-838-6818.
Will search UCC records prior to 7/2001 and current liens only. Real estate records located in Grafton County. **Other Phone Numbers:** Assessor 603-838-5900; Treasurer 603-838-6689.

Lyme Town

Town Clerk, P.O. Box 342, Lyme, NH 03768. 603-795-2535 R/E Recording: 603-795-4639 (Selectmen's office); Fax 603-795-4637.
Will search UCC records. This agency will not do a tax lien search. Real estate records located in Grafton County. **Other Phone Numbers:** Assessor 603-795-4639 (Selectmen's office); Treasurer 603-795-4639 (Selectmen's office); Elections 603-795-2535; Vital Records 603-795-2535.

Lyndeborough Town

Town Clerk, P.O. Box 164, Lyndeborough, NH 03082. 603-654-9653.
Will search UCC records prior to 7/2001 and current liens only. UCC search includes tax liens if requested. Real estate records located in Hillsborough County.

Madbury Town

Town Clerk, 13 Town Hall Road, Madbury, NH 03820-9510. 603-742-5131; Fax 603-742-2505.
Will search UCC records prior to 7/2001 and current liens only. Real estate records located in Strafford County. **Other Phone Numbers:** Assessor 603-742-5131.

Madison Town

Town Clerk, P.O. Box 248, Madison, NH 03849. 603-367-9931 R/E Recording: 603-538-4872 UCC Recording: 603-367-3276; Fax 603-367-4547.
Will search UCC records prior to 7/2001 and current liens only. Real estate records located in Carroll County. **Other Phone Numbers:** Assessor 603-367-4332; Treasurer 603-367-4332; Elections 603-367-9931; Vital Records 603-367-9931.

Manchester City

City Clerk, One City Hall Plaza, Manchester, NH 03101. 603-624-6455 R/E Recording: 603-624-6520; Fax 603-624-6481.
Will search UCC records prior to 7/2001 and current liens only. UCC search includes tax liens. Real estate records located in Hillsborough County. **Other Phone Numbers:** Assessor 603-624-6520; Treasurer 603-624-6460; Elections 603-624-6455; Vital Records 603-624-6455.

Marlborough Town

Town Clerk, P.O. Box 487, Marlborough, NH 03455-0487. 603-876-4529 R/E Recording: 603-876-3751; Fax 603-876-3313.
Will search UCC records prior to 7/2001 and current liens only. Real estate records located in Cheshire County. **Other Phone Numbers:** Assessor 603-876-4529; Treasurer 603-876-3842; Appraiser/Auditor 603-876-3751; Elections 603-876-4529; Vital Records 603-876-4703.

Marlow Town

Tax Collector, P.O. Box 184, Marlow, NH 03456. 603-446-2245; Fax 603-446-3806. http://www.marlow-nh.com/
Will search UCC records prior to 7/2001 and current liens only. Real estate records located in Cheshire County. **Other Phone Numbers:** Treasurer 603-446-2245; Elections 603-446-2245; Vital Records 603-446-2245.

Mason Town

Town Clerk, 16 Darling Hill Rd., Mason, NH 03048-4717. Town Clerk, R/E and UCC Recording 603-878-2070; Fax 603-878-6146.
Will search UCC records prior to 7/2001 and current liens only. Real estate records located in Hillsborough County. **Other Phone Numbers:** Assessor 603-878-2070; Treasurer 603-878-2098; Appraiser/Auditor 603-878-2070; Elections 603-878-3801; Vital Records 603-878-2070.

Meredith Town

Town Clerk, 41 Main Street, Meredith, NH 03253-9704. 603-279-4538; Fax 603-279-1042.
Will search UCC records prior to 7/2001 and current liens only. Real estate records located in Belknap County.

Merrimack County Registry of Deeds

Register of Deeds, P.O. Box 248, Concord, NH 03302-0248. 603-228-0101; Fax 603-226-0868. http://www.nhdeeds.com
Will not search any records. Will not search real estate records. **Online Access:** real estate. Records on the county Registry of Deeds database are available free online at www.nhdeeds.com. **Other Phone Numbers:** Vital Records 603-271-4650 (State).

Merrimack Town

Town Clerk, P.O. Box 27, Merrimack, NH 03054. 603-424-3651; http://www.ci.merrimack.nh.us
Will search UCC records prior to 7/2001 and current liens only. UCC search includes tax liens if requested. Real estate records located in Hillsborough County Register of Deeds. **Other Phone Numbers:** Assessor 603-424-5136; Treasurer 603-424-3531.

Middleton Town

Town Clerk, Middleton Town Offices, 182 Kings Highway, Middleton, NH 03887. 603-473-2576; Fax 603-473-2577.
Will search UCC records prior to 7/2001 and current liens only. Real estate records located in Strafford County. **Other Phone Numbers:** Assessor 603-473-2261; Treasurer 603-473-2134.

Milan Town

Town Clerk, P.O. Box 158, Milan, NH 03588. 603-449-3461; Fax 603-449-2142.
Will search UCC records prior to 7/2001 and current liens only. Real estate records located in Coos County.

Milford Town

Town Clerk, 1 Union Square, Milford, NH 03055. 603-673-3403; Fax 603-673-2273.
Will search UCC records. Real estate records located in Hillsborough County. **Other Phone Numbers:** Assessor 603-672-0525; Treasurer 603-672-1061; Elections 603-673-3403; Vital Records 603-673-3403.

Milton Town

Town Clerk, P.O. Box 180, Milton, NH 03851-0180. 603-652-9414; Fax 603-652-4120. http://www. miltonnh-us.com
Will search UCC records prior to 7/2001 and current liens only. Real estate records located in Strafford County. **Other Phone Numbers:** Assessor 603-652-4501; Treasurer 603-652-4501; Elections 603-652-9414.

Monroe Town

Treasurer, P.O. Box 63, Monroe, NH 03771-0063. 603-638-2644; Fax 603-638-2021.
Will search UCC records. Real estate records located in Grafton County. **Other Phone Numbers:** Assessor 603-638-2644; Treasurer 603-638-2644; Appraiser/Auditor 603-638-2644; Vital Records 603-638-2644.

Mont Vernon Town

Town Clerk, Box 444, Mont Vernon, NH 03057. 603-673-9126; Fax 603-672-9021.
Will search UCC records prior to 7/2001 and current liens only. Real estate records located in Hillsborough County.

Moultonborough Town

Town Clerk, P.O. Box 15, Moultonborough, NH 03254. Town Clerk, R/E and UCC Recording 603-476-2347; Fax 603-476-5835.
Will search UCC records. Real estate records located in Carroll County. **Other Phone Numbers:** Assessor 603-476-2347; Treasurer 603-476-2347; Appraiser/Auditor 603-476-2347; Elections 603-476-2347; Vital Records 603-476-2347.

Nashua City

City Clerk, 229 Main Street, Nashua, NH 03061-2019. 603-589-3010.
Will search UCC records prior to 7/2001 and current liens only. Real estate records located in Hillsborough County. **Other Phone Numbers:** Assessor 603-594-3040.

Nelson Town

Town Clerk, HCR 33 Box 660, Nelson, NH 03457. 603-847-9043 R/E Recording: 603-847-0047; Fax 603-847-9043.
Will search UCC records prior to 7/2001 and current liens only. Real estate records located in Cheshire County. **Other Phone Numbers:** Assessor 603-847-9043; Treasurer 603-847-9043; Appraiser/Auditor 603-847-0047; Elections 603-847-9043; Vital Records 603-847-9043.

New Boston Town

Town Clerk, P.O. Box 250, New Boston, NH 03070-0250. 603-487-5571; Fax 603-487-2885.
Will search UCC records prior to 7/2001 and current liens only. This agency will not do a tax lien search. Real estate records located in Hillsborough County.

Other Phone Numbers: Assessor 603-487-5571; Treasurer 603-487-5571.

New Castle Town

Town Clerk, P.O. Box 367, New Castle, NH 03854-0367. 603-431-6710; Fax 603-431-7710.
Will search UCC records prior to 7/2001 and current liens only. Real estate records located in Rockingham County.

New Durham Town

Town Clerk, P.O. Box 207, New Durham, NH 03855. 603-859-2091; Fax 603-859-6644.
Will search UCC records prior to 7/2001 and current liens only. Real estate records located in Strafford County.

New Hampton Town

Town Clerk, P.O. Box 538, New Hampton, NH 03256. 603-744-8454; Fax 603-744-5106. http://www.new-hampton.nh.us
Will search UCC records prior to 7/2001 and current liens only. Real estate records located in Belknap County. **Other Phone Numbers:** Elections 603-744-8454; Vital Records 603-744-8454.

New Ipswich Town

Town Clerk, 661 Turnpike Rd., New Ipswich, NH 03071. 603-878-3567; Fax 603-878-3855.
Will search UCC records prior to 7/2001 and current liens only. Real estate records located in Hillsborough County. **Other Phone Numbers:** Assessor 603-878-2772; Treasurer 603-878-2772.

New London Town

Town Clerk, P.O. Box 314, New London, NH 03257-0314. 603-526-4046; Fax 603-526-9494.
Will search UCC records prior to 7/2001 and current liens only. Real estate records located in Merrimack County. **Other Phone Numbers:** Assessor 603-526-4821; Treasurer 603-526-4821; Elections 603-526-4046; Vital Records 603-526-4046.

Newbury Town

Town Clerk, P.O. Box 253, Newbury, NH 03255. 603-763-5326.
Will search UCC records prior to 7/2001 and current liens only. This agency will not do a tax lien search. Real estate records located in Merrimack County. **Other Phone Numbers:** Assessor 603-763-4940; Treasurer 603-763-4940.

Newfields Town

Town Clerk, P.O. Box 300, Newfields, NH 03856-0300. Town Clerk, R/E and UCC Recording 603-772-5070; Fax 603-772-9004.
Will search UCC records prior to 7/2001 and current liens only. Real estate records located in Rockingham County. **Other Phone Numbers:** Assessor 603-772-7047; Treasurer 603-772-7199; Elections 603-772-5070; Vital Records 603-772-5070.

Newington Town

Town Clerk, 205 Nimble Hill Road, Town Offices, Newington, NH 03801. 603-436-7640; Fax 603-436-7188.
Will search UCC records prior to 7/2001 and current liens only. Real estate records located in Rockingham County.

Newmarket Town

Town Clerk, 186 Main Street, Town Hall, Newmarket, NH 03857. 603-659-3073; Fax 603-659-8508.
Will search UCC records prior to 7/2001 and current liens only. Real estate records located in Rockingham

County. **Other Phone Numbers:** Assessor 603-659-3073.

Newport Town

Town Clerk, 15 Sunapee Street, Newport, NH 03773. 603-863-2224 R/E Recording: 603-863-6407; Fax 603-863-8008.
Will search UCC records prior to 7/2001 and current liens only. Real estate records located in Sullivan County. **Other Phone Numbers:** Assessor 603-863-6407; Treasurer 603-863-3000; Appraiser/Auditor 603-863-6407; Elections 603-863-2224; Vital Records 603-863-2224.

Newton Town

Tax Collector, Box 375, Newton, NH 03858-0375. Tax Collector, R/E and UCC Recording 603-382-4096; Fax 603-382-9140.
Will search UCC records prior to 7/2001 and current liens only. Real estate records located in Rockingham County. **Other Phone Numbers:** Assessor 603-382-4405; Treasurer 603-382-4405; Appraiser/Auditor 603-382-4405; Elections 603-382-4096; Vital Records 603-382-4096.

North Hampton Town

Town Clerk, P.O. Box 141, North Hampton, NH 03862-0141. 603-964-6029 R/E Recording: 603-964-8087; Fax 603-964-1514. http://www.north-hampton-nh.com
Will search UCC records prior to 7/2001 and current liens only. Real estate records located in Rockingham County. **Other Phone Numbers:** Assessor 603-964-8087; Treasurer 603-964-8087; Elections 603-964-6029; Vital Records 603-964-6029.

Northfield Town

Town Clerk, 21 Summer Street, Northfield, NH 03276. 603-286-4482; Fax 603-286-3328.
Will search UCC records. Real estate records located in Merrimack County. **Other Phone Numbers:** Assessor 603-286-7039; Elections 603-286-4482; Vital Records 603-286-4482.

Northumberland Town

Town Clerk, 2 State Street, Groveton, NH 03582. 603-636-1451; Fax 603-636-1450.
Will search UCC records prior to 7/2001 and current liens only. Real estate records located in Coos County.

Northwood Town

Town Clerk, P.O. Box 314, Northwood, NH 03261-0314. 603-942-5422; Fax 603-942-9107.
Will search UCC records. Real estate records located in Rockingham County. **Other Phone Numbers:** Assessor 603-942-5586; Vital Records 603-942-5422.

Nottingham Town

Town Clerk, P.O. Box 114, Nottingham, NH 03290. 603-679-1630; Fax 603-679-1013.
Will search UCC records prior to 7/2001 and current liens only. UCC search includes tax liens. Real estate records located in Rockingham County. **Other Phone Numbers:** Assessor 603-679-5022.

Orford Town

Town Clerk, Clerk's Office, RR 1 Box 243, Orford, NH 03777. 603-353-4404.
Will search UCC records prior to 7/2001 and current liens only. UCC search includes tax liens if requested. Real estate records located in Grafton County.

Ossipee Town

Town Clerk, P.O. Box 67, Center Ossipee, NH 03814. 603-539-2008 R/E Recording: 603-539-4872; Fax 603-539-4183.

Will search UCC records prior to 7/2001 and current liens only. Real estate records located in Carroll County. **Other Phone Numbers:** Assessor 603-539-4181; Treasurer 603-539-4181; Elections 603-539-2008; Vital Records 603-539-2008.

Pelham Town

Town Clerk, 6 Main Street, Town Hall, Pelham, NH 03076. 603-635-2040; Fax 603-635-6954.

Will search UCC records prior to 7/2001 and current liens only. Real estate records located in Rockingham County. **Other Phone Numbers:** Assessor 603-635-3317.

Pembroke Town

Town Clerk, 311 Pembroke Street, Pembroke, NH 03275. 603-485-4747; Fax 603-485-3967.

Will search UCC records prior to 7/2001 and current liens only. Real estate records located in Merrimack County.

Peterborough Town

Tax Collector, 1 Grove Street, Peterborough, NH 03458. 603-924-8010 R/E Recording: 603-924-8020; Fax 603-924-8001. http://www.townofpeterborough.com/

Will search UCC records prior to 7/2001 and current liens only. Real estate records located in Hillsborough County. **Other Phone Numbers:** Assessor 603-924-8000; Treasurer 603-924-7155; Elections 603-924-8010; Vital Records 603-924-8010.

Piermont Town

Town Clerk, P.O. Box 27, Piermont, NH 03779. 603-272-4840; Fax 603-272-4947.

Will search UCC records prior to 7/2001 and current liens only. Real estate records located in Grafton County.

Pittsburg Town

Town Clerk, RD 1, Box 581, Pittsburg, NH 03592. 603-538-6697; Fax 603-538-6697.

Will search UCC records prior to 7/2001 and current liens only. Real estate records located in Coos County.

Pittsfield Town

Town Clerk, Box 98, Pittsfield, NH 03263-0098. 603-435-6773; Fax 603-435-7922.

Will search UCC records prior to 7/2001 and current liens only. Real estate records located in Merrimack County. **Other Phone Numbers:** Assessor 603-435-6773.

Plainfield Town

Town Clerk, Town Clerk's Office, Box 380, Meriden, NH 03770. 603-469-3201; Fax 603-469-3642.

Will search UCC records prior to 7/2001 and current liens only. Real estate records located in Sullivan County. **Other Phone Numbers:** Assessor 603-469-3201; Elections 603-469-3201; Vital Records 603-469-3201.

Plaistow Town

Town Clerk, 145 Main Street, Town Hall, Suite 2, Plaistow, NH 03865. 603-382-8129; Fax 603-382-7183.

Will search UCC records prior to 7/2001 and current liens only. Real estate records located in Rockingham County. **Other Phone Numbers:** Assessor 603-382-8469; Treasurer 603-382-8469.

Plymouth Town

Town Clerk, 6 PO Square, Town Hall, Plymouth, NH 03264. 603-536-1732; Fax 603-536-0036.

Will search UCC records prior to 7/2001 and current liens only. Real estate records located in Grafton County.

Portsmouth City

City Clerk, P.O. Box 628, Portsmouth, NH 03802-0628. 603-431-2000; Fax 603-427-1526.

Will search UCC records prior to 7/2001 and current liens only. Real estate records located in Rockingham County. **Online Access:** Assessor. Records from the Portsmouth Assessed Property Values database are available free online at www.portsmouthnh.com/realestate/index.htm. **Other Phone Numbers:** Assessor 603-431-2000 x212; Treasurer 603-431-2000 x221.

Randolph Town

Town Clerk, RD 1, Town Hall, Randolph, NH 03570. 603-466-5771; Fax 603-466-9856.

Will search UCC records prior to 7/2001 and current liens only. This agency will not do a tax lien search. Real estate records located in Coos County.

Raymond Town

Town Clerk, Epping Street, Town Office Building, Raymond, NH 03077. 603-895-4735; Fax 603-895-0903.

Will search UCC records prior to 7/2001 and current liens only. Real estate records located in Rockingham County. **Online Access:** Assessor. Records on the Town assessor database are available free online at http://140.239.211.227/raymondNH. Registration is required, no charge.

Richmond Town

Town Clerk, 105 Old Homestead Hwy., Richmond, NH 03470. 603-239-6202.

Will search UCC records prior to 7/2001 and current liens only. Tax liens not included in UCC search. Real estate records located in Cheshire County. **Other Phone Numbers:** Assessor 603-239-4202; Elections 603-239-6202; Vital Records 603-239-6202.

Rindge Town

Town Clerk, P.O. Box 11, Rindge, NH 03461. Town Clerk, R/E and UCC Recording 603-899-3354; Fax 603-899-2101.

See Town Tax Collector for property tax liens. Will search UCC records prior to 7/2001 and current liens only. Separate federal and state tax lien search costs same as UCC search. Real estate records and property tax liens are found at the Town Tax Collector. **Other Phone Numbers:** Assessor 603-899-5181; Treasurer 603-899-5579; Elections 603-899-5539; Vital Records 603-899-3354.

Rochester City

City Clerk, 31 Wakefield Street, City Hall, Rochester, NH 03867-1917. 603-332-2130; Fax 603-335-7565.

Will search UCC records. Real estate records located in Strafford County. **Other Phone Numbers:** Assessor 603-332-5109; Treasurer 603-335-7502; Appraiser/Auditor 603-332-5109; Elections 603-332-2130; Vital Records 603-332-2130.

Rockingham County

Register of Deeds, P.O. Box 896, Kingston, NH 03848. 603-642-5526; Fax 603-642-8548.

For Assessor data, you must contact the Tax Assessor for each town within the county. Will search UCC records prior to 7/2001 and current liens only. Will not search real estate records.

Rollinsford Town

Town Clerk, P.O. Box 309, Rollinsford, NH 03869. 603-742-2510; Fax 603-740-0254.

Will search UCC records prior to 7/2001 and current liens only. Real estate records located in Strafford County.

Roxbury Town

Town Clerk, 404 Branch Rd., Roxbury, NH 03431. 603-352-4903.

Will search UCC records prior to 7/2001 and current liens only. This agency will not do a tax lien search. Real estate records located in Cheshire County.

Rumney Town

Town Clerk, 15 Quincy Bog Road, Rumney, NH 03266. 603-786-2237; Fax 603-786-2237.

Will search UCC records prior to 7/2001 and current liens only. Real estate records located in Grafton County.

Rye Town

Town Clerk, 10 Central Road, Rye, NH 03870. 603-964-8562; Fax 603-964-4132.

Will search UCC records prior to 7/2001 and current liens only. Real estate records located in Rockingham County. **Other Phone Numbers:** Assessor 603-964-5523.

Salem Town

Town Clerk, 33 Geremonty Drive, Municipal Building, Salem, NH 03079-3390. 603-890-2110 UCC Recording: 603-890-2116; Fax 603-898-1223. http://www.ci.salem.nh.us/

Will search UCC records prior to 7/2001 and current liens only. UCC search includes tax liens. Real estate records located in Rockingham County. **Online Access:** Assessor. Records from the Town database are available free online at http://data.visionappraisal.com/SalemNH/. Registration is required, no charge. **Other Phone Numbers:** Assessor 603-893-5731.

Salisbury Town

Town Clerk, RFD Box 180, Franklin Rd., Salisbury, NH 03268-0180. Town Clerk, R/E and UCC Recording 603-648-2473; Fax 603-648-6658.

Will search UCC records prior to 7/2001 and current liens only. Real estate records located in Merrimack County. **Other Phone Numbers:** Assessor 603-648-2473; Treasurer 603-648-2473; Appraiser/Auditor 603-648-2473; Elections 603-648-2473; Vital Records 603-648-2473.

Sanbornton Town

Town Clerk, P.O. Box 124, Sanbornton, NH 03269. 603-286-4034; Fax 603-286-9544.

Will search UCC records prior to 7/2001 and current liens only. Real estate records located in Belknap County. **Other Phone Numbers:** Assessor 603-286-8303.

Sandown Town

Town Clerk, 320 Main Street, Town Hall, Sandown, NH 03873-2627. 603-887-4870 R/E Recording: 603-887-3646; Fax 603-887-5163.

Will search UCC records prior to 7/2001 and current liens only. Real estate records located in Rockingham County. **Other Phone Numbers:** Assessor 603-887-3646; Treasurer 603-887-3646; Elections 603-887-4870; Vital Records 603-887-4870.

Sandwich Town

Town Clerk, P.O. Box 194, Center Sandwich, NH 03227. 603-284-7113; Fax 603-284-6819.

Will search UCC records prior to 7/2001 and current liens only. Real estate records located in Carroll County.

Seabrook Town

Town Clerk, P.O. Box 476, Seabrook, NH 03874. 603-474-3152; Fax 603-474-8007.
Will search UCC records prior to 7/2001 and current liens only. UCC search includes tax liens if requested. Real estate records located in Rockingham County.

Sharon Town

Town Clerk, 423 Route 123, Sharon, NH 03458. 603-924-9250; Fax 603-924-9250.
Will search UCC records prior to 7/2001 and current liens only. This agency will not do a tax lien search. Real estate records located in Hillsborough County. **Other Phone Numbers:** Assessor 603-924-9250.

Shelburne Town

Town Clerk, 881 North Road, Philbrook Farm Inn, Shelburne, NH 03581. 603-466-3831.
Will search UCC records prior to 7/2001 and current liens only. This agency will not do a tax lien search. Real estate records located in Coos County. **Other Phone Numbers:** Assessor 603-466-3926.

Somersworth City

City Clerk, 157 Main Street, Somersworth, NH 03878-3192. 603-692-4262; Fax 603-692-7338.
Will search UCC records prior to 7/2001 and current liens only. Real estate records located in Strafford County.

South Hampton Town

Town Clerk, 3 Hilldale Ave., South Hampton, NH 03827. 603-394-7696.
Will search UCC records prior to 7/2001 and current liens only. This agency will not do a tax lien search. Real estate records located in Rockingham County.

Springfield Town

Town Clerk, P.O. Box 22, Springfield, NH 03284. 603-763-4805; Fax 603-763-3336.
Will search UCC records prior to 7/2001 and current liens only. Real estate records located in Sullivan County.

Stark Town

Town Clerk, 1189 Stark Hwy., Groveton, NH 03582. Town Clerk, R/E and UCC Recording 603-636-2118; Fax 603-636-6199.
Will search UCC records prior to 7/2001 and current liens only. This agency will not do a tax lien search. Real estate records located in Coos County. **Other Phone Numbers:** Assessor 603-636-2118; Treasurer 603-636-2118; Appraiser/Auditor 603-636-2118; Elections 603-636-2118; Vital Records 603-636-2118.

Stewartstown Town

Town Clerk, P.O. Box 35, West Stewartstown, NH 03597-0035. 603-246-3329.
Will search UCC records prior to 7/2001 and current liens only. UCC search includes tax liens if requested. Real estate records located in Coos County.

Stoddard Town

Town Clerk, 2175 Route 9, Stoddard, NH 03464. 603-446-2203 R/E Recording: 603-847-3029; Fax 603-446-2203.
Will search UCC records prior to 7/2001 and current liens only. Real estate records located in Cheshire County. **Other Phone Numbers:** Assessor 603-446-3326; Treasurer 603-446-3442; Appraiser/Auditor 603-446-3326; Elections 603-446-3326; Vital Records 603-446-2203.

Strafford County

Register of Deeds, P.O. Box 799, Dover, NH 03820. 603-742-1741; Fax 603-749-5130.
Will search UCC records prior to 7/2001 and current liens only. Will not search real estate records. **Other Phone Numbers:** Assessor 603-743-6014; Treasurer 603-742-1458.

Strafford Town

Town Clerk, P.O. Box 169, Strafford, NH 03884-0169. 603-664-2192; Fax 603-664-7276.
Will search UCC records prior to 7/2001 and current liens only. Real estate records located in Strafford County.

Stratford Town

Town Clerk, P.O. Box 366, North Stratford, NH 03590. 603-922-5598; Fax 603-922-5533.
Will search UCC records prior to 7/2001 and current liens only. Real estate records located in Coos County.

Stratham Town

Town Clerk, 10 Bunker Hill Avenue, Stratham, NH 03885. 603-772-4741; Fax 603-775-0517. http://www.strathamnh.org
Will search UCC records prior to 7/2001 and current liens only. Real estate records located in Rockingham County. **Other Phone Numbers:** Assessor 603-772-4741.

Sugar Hill Town

Town Clerk, Box 574, Sugar Hill, NH 03585. 603-823-8516; Fax 603-823-8446.
Will search UCC records prior to 7/2001 and current liens only. Real estate records located in Grafton County.

Sullivan County

Register of Deeds, P.O. Box 448, Newport, NH 03773. Register of Deeds, R/E and UCC Recording 603-863-2110; Fax 603-863-0013.
Will search UCC records prior to 7/2001 and current liens only. Will not search real estate records. **Other Phone Numbers:** Assessor 603-863-2110; Treasurer 603-863-2110.

Sullivan Town

Town Clerk, 522 South Rd, Sullivan, NH 03445. 603-352-1495 R/E Recording: 603-352-0403.
Will search UCC records prior to 7/2001 and current liens only. This agency will not do a tax lien search. Real estate records located in Cheshire County, 33 West St, Keene, NH 03421. **Other Phone Numbers:** Assessor 603-847-9720; Treasurer 603-847-2340.

Sunapee Town

Town Clerk, P.O. Box 303, Sunapee, NH 03782-0303. 603-763-2449; Fax 603-763-4925.
Will search UCC records prior to 7/2001 and current liens only. This agency will not do a tax lien search. Real estate records located in Sullivan County.

Surry Town

Tx Collector, 1 Village Rd., Surry, NH 03431. 603-352-3075; Fax 603-357-4890.
Will search UCC records prior to 7/2001 and current liens only. Real estate records located in Cheshire County.

Sutton Town

Town Clerk, P.O. Box 554, South Sutton, NH 03273. 603-927-4575; Fax 603-927-4631.

Will search UCC records prior to 7/2001 and current liens only. Real estate records located in Merrimack County.

Swanzey Town

Town Clerk, P.O. Box 10009, Swanzey, NH 03446. 603-352-7411; Fax 603-352-6250.
Will search UCC records prior to 7/2001 and current liens only. Real estate records located in Cheshire County. **Other Phone Numbers:** Assessor 603-352-7411.

Tamworth Town

Town Clerk, P.O. Box 279, Tamworth, NH 03886. 603-323-7971; Fax 603-323-2347.
Will search UCC records prior to 7/2001 and current liens only. UCC search includes tax liens if requested. Real estate records located in Carroll County.

Temple Town

Town Clerk, Box 69, Temple, NH 03084. 603-878-3873; Fax 603-878-5067.
Will search UCC records prior to 7/2001 and current liens only. Real estate records located in Hillsborough County. **Other Phone Numbers:** Assessor 603-878-2536; Treasurer 603-878-3873.

Thornton Town

Town Clerk, P.O. Box 1436, Campton, NH 03223. 603-726-4232; Fax 603-726-2078.
Will search UCC records prior to 7/2001 and current liens only. Real estate records located in Grafton County. **Other Phone Numbers:** Assessor 603-726-3223; Treasurer 603-764-9450.

Tilton Town

Town Clerk, 257 Main Street, Tilton, NH 03276-1207. 603-286-4425; Fax 603-286-3519.
Will search UCC records prior to 7/2001 and current liens only. Real estate records located in Belknap County. **Other Phone Numbers:** Assessor 603-286-4521; Treasurer 603-286-4521.

Troy Town

Town Clerk, P.O. Box 249, Troy, NH 03465-0249. 603-242-3845; Fax 603-242-3430. www.town.troy.nh.us
Will search UCC records prior to 7/2001 and current liens only. This agency will not do a tax lien search. Real estate records located in Cheshire County. **Other Phone Numbers:** Assessor 603-242-7722; Vital Records 603-242-3845.

Tuftonboro Town

Town Clerk, P.O. Box 98, Center Tuftonboro, NH 03816. 603-569-4539; Fax 603-569-4328.
Will search UCC records prior to 7/2001 and current liens only. Real estate records located in Carroll County. **Other Phone Numbers:** Assessor 603-569-4539.

Unity Town

Town Clerk, HCR 66, Box 176A, Newport, NH 03773. 603-542-9665; Fax 603-542-9736.
Will search UCC records prior to 7/2001 and current liens only. Real estate records located in Sullivan County. **Other Phone Numbers:** Assessor 603-542-9665.

Wakefield Town

Town Clerk, 2 High St., Sanbornville, NH 03872. 603-522-6205 x306; Fax 603-522-6794.
Will search UCC records prior to 7/2001 and current liens only. Real estate records located in Carroll County. **Other Phone Numbers:** Assessor 603-522-6205.

Walpole Town

Town Clerk, P.O. Box 756, Walpole, NH 03608. 603-756-3514.
Drewsville and North Walpole are in the Town of Walpole. Will search UCC records prior to 7/2001 and current liens only. This agency will not do a tax lien search. Real estate records located in Cheshire County.

Warner Town

Town Clerk, P.O. Box 265, Warner, NH 03278-0265. 603-456-3362 R/E Recording: 603-228-0101; Fax 603-456-3647. http://www.warner.nh.us/departments.htm
Will search UCC records prior to 7/2001 and current liens only. Real estate records located in Merrimack County. **Other Phone Numbers:** Assessor 603-456-2298; Treasurer 603-456-2298; Appraiser/Auditor 603-456-2298; Elections 603-456-3362; Vital Records 603-456-3362.

Warren Town

Town Clerk, Rte. 25, RR 1 Box 2008, Warren, NH 03279. 603-764-9463; Fax 603-764-9315.
Will search UCC records prior to 7/2001 and current liens only. Real estate records located in Grafton County. **Other Phone Numbers:** Assessor 603-764-5780.

Washington Town

Town Clerk, P.O. Box 109, Washington, NH 03280-0109. 603-495-3667; Fax 603-495-3299.
Will search UCC records prior to 7/2001 and current liens only. Real estate records located in Sullivan County. **Other Phone Numbers:** Assessor 603-495-3074; Treasurer 603-495-3667.

Waterville Valley Town

Town Clerk, Box 500, Waterville Valley, NH 03215. 603-236-4730; Fax 603-236-2056.
Will search UCC records prior to 7/2001 and current liens only. This agency will not do a tax lien search. Real estate records located in Grafton County. **Other Phone Numbers:** Assessor 603-236-4730.

Weare Town

Town Clerk, P.O. Box 190, Weare, NH 03281-0190. 603-529-7575; Fax 603-529-4554. http://www.town.weare.nh.us
Will search UCC records prior to 7/2001 and current liens only. Real estate records located in Hillsborough County. **Other Phone Numbers:** Assessor 603-629-1515; Elections 603-529-7575; Vital Records 603-529-7575.

Webster Town

Town Clerk, 945 Battle St., Rte 127, Webster, NH 03303. 603-648-2538; Fax 603-648-2448.
Will search UCC records. This agency will not do a tax lien search. Real estate records located in Merrimack County.

Wentworth Town

Town Clerk, P.O. Box 2, Wentworth, NH 03282. 603-764-5244; Fax 603-764-9362.
Will search UCC records prior to 7/2001 and current liens only. Real estate records located in Grafton County.

Westmoreland Town

Town Clerk, 108 Pierce Lane, Westmoreland, NH 03467. 603-399-4471.
Will search UCC records prior to 7/2001 and current liens only. This agency will not do a tax lien search. Real estate records located in Cheshire County. **Other Phone Numbers:** Assessor 603-399-4471; Treasurer 603-399-4471.

Whitefield Town

Town Clerk, 7 Jefferson Road, Whitefield, NH 03598. 603-837-9871; Fax 603-837-3148.
Will search UCC records prior to 7/2001 and current liens only. Real estate records located in Grafton County. **Other Phone Numbers:** Assessor 603-837-2551; Treasurer 603-837-2551.

Wilmot Town

Town Clerk, P.O. Box 94, Wilmot, NH 03287. 603-526-9639; Fax 603-526-2523.
Will search UCC records prior to 7/2001 and current liens only. Real estate records located in Merrimack County.

Wilton Town

Town Clerk, P.O. Box 83, Wilton, NH 03086. 603-654-9451; Fax 603-654-6663.
Will search UCC records prior to 7/2001 and current liens only. Real estate records located in Hillsborough County. **Other Phone Numbers:** Assessor 603-654-9451.

Winchester Town

Town Clerk, P.O. Box 512, Winchester, NH 03470. 603-239-6233; Fax 603-239-4710.
Will search UCC records prior to 7/2001 and current liens only. Real estate records located in Cheshire County. **Other Phone Numbers:** Assessor 603-239-4951.

Windham Town

Town Clerk, 3 North Lowell Road, P.O. Box 120, Windham, NH 03087. 603-434-5075; Fax 603-425-6582.
Will search UCC records prior to 7/2001 and current liens only. Real estate records located in Rockingham County. **Other Phone Numbers:** Assessor 603-434-7530; Treasurer 603-432-7732.

Windsor Town

Town Clerk, HC 68, Box 378, Hillsborough, NH 03244. 603-478-3292.
Will search UCC records prior to 7/2001 and current liens only. Real estate records located in Hillsborough County.

Wolfeboro Town

Town Clerk, Box 1207, Wolfeboro, NH 03894. 603-569-5328; Fax 603-569-8167.
Will search UCC records prior to 7/2001 and current liens only. Real estate records located in Carroll County. **Other Phone Numbers:** Assessor 603-569-8152; Appraiser/Auditor 603-569-8152; Elections 603-569-5328; Vital Records 603-569-5328.

Woodstock Town

Town Clerk, Box 156, North Woodstock, NH 03262. 603-745-8752; Fax 603-745-2393.

Will search UCC records prior to 7/2001 and current liens only. Real estate records located in Grafton County. **Other Phone Numbers:** Assessor 603-745-8752; Treasurer 603-745-9085.

New Hampshire County Locator

You will usually be able to find the city name in the City/County Cross Reference below. In that case, it is a simple matter to determine the county from the cross reference. However, only the official US Postal Service city names are included in this index. There are an additional 40,000 place names that people use in their addresses. Therefore, we have also included a ZIP/City Cross Reference immediately following the City/County Cross Reference.

If you know the ZIP Code but the city name does not appear in the City/County Cross Reference index, look up the ZIP Code in the ZIP/City Cross Reference, find the city name, then look up the city name in the City/County Cross Reference. For example, you want to know the county for an address of Menands, NY 12204. There is no "Menands" in the City/County Cross Reference. The ZIP/City Cross Reference shows that ZIP Codes 12201-12288 are for the city of Albany. Looking back in the City/County Cross Reference, Albany is in Albany County.

City/County Cross Reference

ACWORTH Sullivan
ALSTEAD Cheshire
ALTON Belknap
ALTON BAY Belknap
AMHERST Hillsborough
ANDOVER Merrimack
ANTRIM Hillsborough
ASHLAND Grafton
ASHUELOT Cheshire
ATKINSON Rockingham
AUBURN Rockingham
BARNSTEAD Belknap
BARRINGTON Strafford
BARTLETT Carroll
BATH Grafton
BEDFORD Hillsborough
BELMONT Belknap
BENNINGTON Hillsborough
BERLIN Coos
BETHLEHEM Grafton
BOW Merrimack
BRADFORD Merrimack
BRETTON WOODS Coos
BRISTOL Grafton
BROOKLINE Hillsborough
CAMPTON Grafton
CANAAN Grafton
CANDIA Rockingham
CANTERBURY Merrimack
CENTER BARNSTEAD Belknap
CENTER CONWAY Carroll
CENTER HARBOR Belknap
CENTER OSSIPEE Carroll
CENTER SANDWICH Carroll
CENTER STRAFFORD Strafford
CENTER TUFTONBORO Carroll
CHARLESTOWN Sullivan
CHESTER Rockingham
CHESTERFIELD Cheshire
CHOCORUA Carroll
CLAREMONT Sullivan
COLEBROOK Coos
CONCORD Merrimack
CONTOOCOOK Merrimack
CONWAY Carroll
CORNISH Sullivan
CORNISH FLAT Sullivan
DANBURY Merrimack
DANVILLE Rockingham
DEERFIELD Rockingham
DERRY Rockingham
DOVER Strafford
DREWSVILLE Cheshire
DUBLIN Cheshire
DURHAM Strafford
EAST ANDOVER Merrimack
EAST CANDIA Rockingham
EAST DERRY Rockingham
EAST HAMPSTEAD Rockingham
EAST HEBRON Grafton
EAST KINGSTON Rockingham
EAST WAKEFIELD Carroll
EATON CENTER Carroll
ELKINS Merrimack

ENFIELD (03748) Grafton(98), Sullivan(2)
ENFIELD CENTER Grafton
EPPING Rockingham
EPSOM Merrimack
ERROL Coos
ETNA Grafton
EXETER Rockingham
FARMINGTON Strafford
FITZWILLIAM Cheshire
FRANCESTOWN Hillsborough
FRANCONIA Grafton
FRANKLIN Merrimack
FREEDOM Carroll
FREMONT Rockingham
GEORGES MILLS Sullivan
GILMANTON Belknap
GILMANTON IRON WORKS Belknap
GILSUM Cheshire
GLEN Carroll
GLENCLIFF Grafton
GOFFSTOWN (03045) Hillsborough(87), Merrimack(13)
GORHAM Coos
GOSHEN Sullivan
GRAFTON Grafton
GRANTHAM Sullivan
GREENFIELD Hillsborough
GREENLAND Rockingham
GREENVILLE Hillsborough
GROVETON Coos
GUILD Sullivan
HAMPSTEAD Rockingham
HAMPTON Rockingham
HAMPTON FALLS Rockingham
HANCOCK Hillsborough
HANOVER Grafton
HARRISVILLE Cheshire
HAVERHILL Grafton
HEBRON Grafton
HENNIKER (03242) Merrimack(98), Hillsborough(2)
HILL (03243) Merrimack(95), Grafton(5)
HILLSBORO (03244) Hillsborough(98), Sullivan(2)
HINSDALE Cheshire
HOLDERNESS Grafton
HOLLIS Hillsborough
HOOKSETT Merrimack
HUDSON Hillsborough
INTERVALE Carroll
JACKSON Carroll
JAFFREY Cheshire
JEFFERSON Coos
KEARSARGE Carroll
KEENE Cheshire
KINGSTON Rockingham
LACONIA Belknap
LANCASTER Coos
LEBANON Grafton
LEMPSTER Sullivan
LINCOLN Grafton
LISBON Grafton
LITCHFIELD Hillsborough
LITTLETON Grafton

LOCHMERE Belknap
LONDONDERRY Rockingham
LYME Grafton
LYME CENTER Grafton
LYNDEBOROUGH Hillsborough
MADISON Carroll
MANCHESTER Hillsborough
MARLBOROUGH Cheshire
MARLOW Cheshire
MEADOWS Coos
MELVIN VILLAGE Carroll
MEREDITH Belknap
MERIDEN Sullivan
MERRIMACK Hillsborough
MILAN Coos
MILFORD Hillsborough
MILTON Strafford
MILTON MILLS Strafford
MIRROR LAKE Carroll
MONROE Grafton
MONT VERNON Hillsborough
MOULTONBOROUGH Carroll
MOUNT SUNAPEE Merrimack
MOUNT WASHINGTON Coos
MUNSONVILLE Cheshire
NASHUA Hillsborough
NEW BOSTON Hillsborough
NEW CASTLE Rockingham
NEW DURHAM Strafford
NEW HAMPTON Belknap
NEW IPSWICH Hillsborough
NEW LONDON (03257) Merrimack(98), Sullivan(2)
NEWBURY Merrimack
NEWFIELDS Rockingham
NEWMARKET Rockingham
NEWPORT Sullivan
NEWTON Rockingham
NEWTON JUNCTION Rockingham
NORTH CONWAY Carroll
NORTH HAMPTON Rockingham
NORTH HAVERHILL Grafton
NORTH SALEM Rockingham
NORTH SANDWICH Carroll
NORTH STRATFORD Coos
NORTH SUTTON Merrimack
NORTH WALPOLE Cheshire
NORTH WOODSTOCK Grafton
NORTHWOOD Rockingham
NOTTINGHAM Rockingham
ORFORD Grafton
OSSIPEE Carroll
PELHAM Hillsborough
PETERBOROUGH Hillsborough
PIERMONT Grafton
PIKE Grafton
PITTSBURG Coos
PITTSFIELD Merrimack
PLAINFIELD Sullivan
PLAISTOW Rockingham
PLYMOUTH Grafton
PORTSMOUTH Rockingham
RAYMOND Rockingham
RINDGE Cheshire

ROCHESTER Strafford
ROLLINSFORD Strafford
RUMNEY Grafton
RYE Rockingham
RYE BEACH Rockingham
SALEM Rockingham
SALISBURY Merrimack
SANBORNTON Belknap
SANBORNVILLE Carroll
SANDOWN Rockingham
SEABROOK Rockingham
SILVER LAKE Carroll
SOMERSWORTH Strafford
SOUTH ACWORTH Sullivan
SOUTH EFFINGHAM Carroll
SOUTH NEWBURY Merrimack
SOUTH SUTTON Merrimack
SOUTH TAMWORTH Carroll
SPOFFORD Cheshire
SPRINGFIELD Sullivan
STINSON LAKE Grafton
STODDARD Cheshire
STRAFFORD Strafford
STRATHAM Rockingham
SULLIVAN Cheshire
SUNAPEE Sullivan
SUNCOOK Merrimack
SWANZEY Cheshire
TAMWORTH Carroll
TEMPLE Hillsborough
TILTON (03276) Belknap(59), Merrimack(41)
TROY Cheshire
TWIN MOUNTAIN Coos
UNION (03887) Strafford(74), Carroll(26)
WALPOLE Cheshire
WARNER Merrimack
WARREN Grafton
WASHINGTON Sullivan
WATERVILLE VALLEY Grafton
WEARE Hillsborough
WENTWORTH Grafton
WEST CHESTERFIELD Cheshire
WEST LEBANON Grafton
WEST NOTTINGHAM Rockingham
WEST OSSIPEE Carroll
WEST PETERBOROUGH Hillsborough
WEST STEWARTSTOWN Coos
WEST SWANZEY Cheshire
WESTMORELAND Cheshire
WHITEFIELD Coos
WILMOT Merrimack
WILTON Hillsborough
WINCHESTER Cheshire
WINDHAM Rockingham
WINNISQUAM Belknap
WOLFEBORO Carroll
WOLFEBORO FALLS Carroll
WONALANCET Carroll
WOODSTOCK Grafton
WOODSVILLE Grafton

ZIP/City Cross Reference

ZIP	City	ZIP	City	ZIP	City	ZIP	City
00210-00215	PORTSMOUTH	03244-03244	HILLSBORO	03470-03470	WINCHESTER	03812-03812	BARTLETT
03031-03031	AMHERST	03245-03245	HOLDERNESS	03561-03561	LITTLETON	03813-03813	CENTER CONWAY
03032-03032	AUBURN	03246-03247	LACONIA	03570-03570	BERLIN	03814-03814	CENTER OSSIPEE
03033-03033	BROOKLINE	03251-03251	LINCOLN	03574-03574	BETHLEHEM	03815-03815	CENTER STRAFFORD
03034-03034	CANDIA	03252-03252	LOCHMERE	03575-03575	BRETTON WOODS	03816-03816	CENTER TUFTONBORO
03036-03036	CHESTER	03253-03253	MEREDITH	03576-03576	COLEBROOK	03817-03817	CHOCORUA
03037-03037	DEERFIELD	03254-03254	MOULTONBOROUGH	03579-03579	ERROL	03818-03818	CONWAY
03038-03038	DERRY	03255-03255	NEWBURY	03580-03580	FRANCONIA	03819-03819	DANVILLE
03040-03040	EAST CANDIA	03256-03256	NEW HAMPTON	03581-03581	GORHAM	03820-03822	DOVER
03041-03041	EAST DERRY	03257-03257	NEW LONDON	03582-03582	GROVETON	03824-03824	DURHAM
03042-03042	EPPING	03259-03259	NORTH SANDWICH	03583-03583	JEFFERSON	03825-03825	BARRINGTON
03043-03043	FRANCESTOWN	03260-03260	NORTH SUTTON	03584-03584	LANCASTER	03826-03826	EAST HAMPSTEAD
03044-03044	FREMONT	03261-03261	NORTHWOOD	03585-03585	LISBON	03827-03827	EAST KINGSTON
03045-03045	GOFFSTOWN	03262-03262	NORTH WOODSTOCK	03587-03587	MEADOWS	03830-03830	EAST WAKEFIELD
03047-03047	GREENFIELD	03263-03263	PITTSFIELD	03588-03588	MILAN	03832-03832	EATON CENTER
03048-03048	GREENVILLE	03264-03264	PLYMOUTH	03589-03589	MOUNT WASHINGTON	03833-03833	EXETER
03049-03049	HOLLIS	03266-03266	RUMNEY	03590-03590	NORTH STRATFORD	03835-03835	FARMINGTON
03051-03051	HUDSON	03268-03268	SALISBURY	03592-03592	PITTSBURG	03836-03836	FREEDOM
03052-03052	LITCHFIELD	03269-03269	SANBORNTON	03595-03595	TWIN MOUNTAIN	03837-03837	GILMANTON IRON
03053-03053	LONDONDERRY	03272-03272	SOUTH NEWBURY	03597-03597	WEST STEWARTSTOWN		WORKS
03054-03054	MERRIMACK	03273-03273	SOUTH SUTTON	03598-03598	WHITEFIELD	03838-03838	GLEN
03055-03055	MILFORD	03274-03274	STINSON LAKE	03601-03601	ACWORTH	03839-03839	ROCHESTER
03057-03057	MONT VERNON	03275-03275	SUNCOOK	03602-03602	ALSTEAD	03840-03840	GREENLAND
03060-03063	NASHUA	03276-03276	TILTON	03603-03603	CHARLESTOWN	03841-03841	HAMPSTEAD
03070-03070	NEW BOSTON	03278-03278	WARNER	03604-03604	DREWSVILLE	03842-03843	HAMPTON
03071-03071	NEW IPSWICH	03279-03279	WARREN	03605-03605	LEMPSTER	03844-03844	HAMPTON FALLS
03073-03073	NORTH SALEM	03280-03280	WASHINGTON	03607-03607	SOUTH ACWORTH	03845-03845	INTERVALE
03076-03076	PELHAM	03281-03281	WEARE	03608-03608	WALPOLE	03846-03846	JACKSON
03077-03077	RAYMOND	03282-03282	WENTWORTH	03609-03609	NORTH WALPOLE	03847-03847	KEARSARGE
03079-03079	SALEM	03284-03284	SPRINGFIELD	03740-03740	BATH	03848-03848	KINGSTON
03082-03082	LYNDEBOROUGH	03287-03287	WILMOT	03741-03741	CANAAN	03849-03849	MADISON
03084-03084	TEMPLE	03289-03289	WINNISQUAM	03743-03743	CLAREMONT	03850-03850	MELVIN VILLAGE
03086-03086	WILTON	03290-03290	NOTTINGHAM	03745-03745	CORNISH	03851-03851	MILTON
03087-03087	WINDHAM	03291-03291	WEST NOTTINGHAM	03746-03746	CORNISH FLAT	03852-03852	MILTON MILLS
03101-03105	MANCHESTER	03293-03293	WOODSTOCK	03748-03748	ENFIELD	03853-03853	MIRROR LAKE
03106-03106	HOOKSETT	03301-03303	CONCORD	03749-03749	ENFIELD CENTER	03854-03854	NEW CASTLE
03107-03109	MANCHESTER	03304-03304	BOW	03750-03750	ETNA	03855-03855	NEW DURHAM
03110-03110	BEDFORD	03305-03305	CONCORD	03751-03751	GEORGES MILLS	03856-03856	NEWFIELDS
03111-03111	MANCHESTER	03431-03435	KEENE	03752-03752	GOSHEN	03857-03857	NEWMARKET
03215-03215	WATERVILLE VALLEY	03440-03440	ANTRIM	03753-03753	GRANTHAM	03858-03858	NEWTON
03216-03216	ANDOVER	03441-03441	ASHUELOT	03754-03754	GUILD	03859-03859	NEWTON JUNCTION
03217-03217	ASHLAND	03442-03442	BENNINGTON	03755-03755	HANOVER	03860-03860	NORTH CONWAY
03218-03218	BARNSTEAD	03443-03443	CHESTERFIELD	03756-03756	LEBANON	03862-03862	NORTH HAMPTON
03220-03220	BELMONT	03444-03444	DUBLIN	03765-03765	HAVERHILL	03864-03864	OSSIPEE
03221-03221	BRADFORD	03445-03445	SULLIVAN	03766-03766	LEBANON	03865-03865	PLAISTOW
03222-03222	BRISTOL	03446-03446	SWANZEY	03768-03768	LYME	03866-03868	ROCHESTER
03223-03223	CAMPTON	03447-03447	FITZWILLIAM	03769-03769	LYME CENTER	03869-03869	ROLLINSFORD
03224-03224	CANTERBURY	03448-03448	GILSUM	03770-03770	MERIDEN	03870-03870	RYE
03225-03225	CENTER BARNSTEAD	03449-03449	HANCOCK	03771-03771	MONROE	03871-03871	RYE BEACH
03226-03226	CENTER HARBOR	03450-03450	HARRISVILLE	03772-03772	MOUNT SUNAPEE	03872-03872	SANBORNVILLE
03227-03227	CENTER SANDWICH	03451-03451	HINSDALE	03773-03773	NEWPORT	03873-03873	SANDOWN
03229-03229	CONTOOCOOK	03452-03452	JAFFREY	03774-03774	NORTH HAVERHILL	03874-03874	SEABROOK
03230-03230	DANBURY	03455-03455	MARLBOROUGH	03777-03777	ORFORD	03875-03875	SILVER LAKE
03231-03231	EAST ANDOVER	03456-03456	MARLOW	03779-03779	PIERMONT	03878-03878	SOMERSWORTH
03232-03232	EAST HEBRON	03457-03457	MUNSONVILLE	03780-03780	PIKE	03882-03882	SOUTH EFFINGHAM
03233-03233	ELKINS	03458-03458	PETERBOROUGH	03781-03781	PLAINFIELD	03883-03883	SOUTH TAMWORTH
03234-03234	EPSOM	03461-03461	RINDGE	03782-03782	SUNAPEE	03884-03884	STRAFFORD
03235-03235	FRANKLIN	03462-03462	SPOFFORD	03784-03784	WEST LEBANON	03885-03885	STRATHAM
03237-03237	GILMANTON	03464-03464	STODDARD	03785-03785	WOODSVILLE	03886-03886	TAMWORTH
03238-03238	GLENCLIFF	03465-03465	TROY	03801-03804	PORTSMOUTH	03887-03887	UNION
03240-03240	GRAFTON	03466-03466	WEST CHESTERFIELD	03805-03805	ROLLINSFORD	03890-03890	WEST OSSIPEE
03241-03241	HEBRON	03467-03467	WESTMORELAND	03809-03809	ALTON	03894-03894	WOLFEBORO
03242-03242	HENNIKER	03468-03468	WEST PETERBOROUGH	03810-03810	ALTON BAY	03896-03896	WOLFEBORO FALLS
03243-03243	HILL	03469-03469	WEST SWANZEY	03811-03811	ATKINSON	03897-03897	WONALANCET

New Jersey

General Help Numbers:

Governor's Office
PO Box 001, 125 W State St   609-292-6000
Trenton, NJ 08625-0001   Fax 609-292-3454
http://www.state.nj.us/governor   8:30AM-4:30PM

Attorney General's Office
Law & Public Safety Department   609-292-8740
PO Box 080, 25 Market St   Fax 609-292-3508
Trenton, NJ 08625-0080   8:30AM-5PM
http://www.state.nj.us/lps

State Court Administrator
RJH Justice Complex   609-984-0275
PO Box 037, Courts Bldg, 7th Floor Fax 609-984-6968
Trenton, NJ 08625   8:30AM-4:30PM
http://www.judiciary.state.nj.us/admin.htm

State Archives
PO Box 307, 225 W. State Street, L2   609-292-6260
Trenton, NJ 08625-0307   Fax 609-396-2454
http://www.state.nj.us/state/   8:30AM-4:30PM TU-F
darm/archives.html

State Specifics:

Capital:	Trenton Mercer County
Time Zone:	EST
Number of Counties:	21
Population:	8,414,350
Web Site:	www.state.nj.us

State Agencies

Criminal Records

Division of State Police, Records and Identification Section, PO Box 7068, West Trenton, NJ 08628-0068; 609-882-2000 x2878, 609-530-5780 (Fax), 9AM-5PM.

http://www.state.nj.us/njsp

Note: For requesters not living in the state, it is advised to contact a NJ-based investigator to obtain the record.

Searching: Criminal records are not open to the public, but can be obtained by NJ employers, NJ volunteer organizations, NJ private investigators, NJ attorney firms, and the subject. Include the following in your request-date of birth, Social Security Number, set of fingerprints. The name must match exactly. All requesters, except attorney firms, must submit Form 212 B which must be signed by the subject. Attorney firms do not need the subject's signature.

Access by: mail, in person.

Fee & Payment: The fee is $15.00 for a name check and $25.00 for a full check with fingerprints. Fee payee: Division of State Police-SBI. Prepayment required. No credit cards accepted.

Mail search: Turnaround time: 5 to 10 working days.

In person search: Searching is available in person.

Corporation Records
Limited Liability Company Records
Fictitious Name
Limited Partnerships

Division of Revenue, Business Support Services Bureau, PO 308, Trenton, NJ 08625 (Courier: 225 W State St, 3rd Fl, Trenton, NJ 08608); 609-292-9292, 8:30AM-5:00PM.

http://www.state.nj.us/njbgs

Indexing & Storage: Records are available from inception of laws. New records are available for inquiry immediately. Records are indexed on inhouse computer.

Searching: Include the following in your request-full name of business. In addition to the articles of incorporation, corporation records include the following information: Annual Reports, Officers, Directors, Prior (merged) names, Inactive and Reserved names. Assumed names are located at the county level.

Access by: mail, phone, in person, online.

Fee & Payment: A status report is $5.00. Copies are $1.00 per page (except LLC, then $10.00 first and $2.00 each additional). There is a $25.00 ($15.00 if non-profit) fee to certify a document. A Good Standing is $25.00. Fee payee: Treasurer, State of NJ. Prepayment required. Ongoing requesters may set up a pre-paid account. Call 609-633-8255 for more information. Personal checks accepted. Credit cards accepted: MasterCard, Visa, Discover, AMEX

Mail search: Turnaround time: 2 to 3 weeks.

Phone search: This is considered expedited service.

In person search: You can look at 3 records per day for no fee. Copies can be provided. The turnaround time is over 1 week.

Online search: Records are available from the New Jersey Business Gateway Service (NJBGS) web site at www.state.nj.us/njbgs. There is no fee to browse the site to locate a name; however fees are involved for copies or status reports.

Expedited service: Expedited service is available for phone and in person searches. Turnaround time: 8.5 business hours. Add $10.00 per search. Records may be picked up the next day.

Trademarks/Servicemarks

Department of Treasury, Trademark Division, PO Box 453, Trenton, NJ 08625-0453 (Courier: 225 W State St, 3rd Floor, Trenton, NJ 08608); 609-633-8259, 8:30AM-5PM.

http://www.state.nj.us/njbgs/services.html

Indexing & Storage: Records are available from the inception of the Division. It takes 2 to 3 days before new records are available for inquiry. Records are indexed on computer.

Searching: Include the following in your request-trademark/servicemark name, name of owner, date of application. Information returned includes name and address of owner and date of filing.

Access by: mail, in person.

Fee & Payment: Search fee is $25.00 for up to 3 names (for name availability). Copies are $1.00 per page. A status is $5.00 per name searched. Fee payee: NJ State Treasurer. Prepayment required. Personal checks and credit cards are accepted.

Mail search: Turnaround time: 1 week. A self addressed stamped envelope is appreciated.

In person search: You can take the request in person, but they return the records by mail unless expedited service is requested.

Uniform Commercial Code

UCC Section, Secretary of State, PO 303, Trenton, NJ 08625 (Courier: 225 West State St, Trenton, NJ 08608); 609-292-9292, 8AM-5PM.

http://www.state.nj.us/njbgs

Note: The state plans to place the Index on the Internet in 2001. Fees will be involved.

Indexing & Storage: Records are indexed on inhouse computer.

Searching: Use search request form UCC-11. Federal tax liens are filed at the county level. State tax liens follow two rules: certificates of debt are filed in Superior Court at Trenton; a warrant of execution is filed at the county level. Include the following in your request-debtor name, address.

Access by: mail, fax, in person.

Fee & Payment: The fee is $25.00 for a search certificate per debtor name, $25.00 for certification of any document, copies are $1.00 per page. Fee payee: Secretary of State. Prepayment required. Regular requesters can set up a pre-paid account, call 609-530-6424. Personal checks accepted. Credit cards accepted: MasterCard, Visa.

Mail search: Turnaround time: 2 weeks. A self addressed stamped envelope is requested.

Fax search: You can order using a credit card; however, results will be mailed or available for pickup by a courier.

In person search: Information is mailed, unless you pay the $10.00 expedite fee for 24 hour service.

Expedited service: Expedited service is available for mail and phone searches. Turnaround time: same day if possible. Add $10.00 per name. This is not available for mail-in requests.

Federal Tax Liens
State Tax Liens
Records not maintained by a state level agency.

Note: Federal tax liens are filed with the county clerk or register of deeds. All state "docket judgment" liens are filed at the Superior Court in Trenton. "Certificates of Debt" are filed at the respective county superior court.

Sales Tax Registrations
Access to Records is Restricted

State of New Jersey, Division of Taxation - Taxpayer Services, PO Box 269, Trenton, NJ 08695-0269; 609-588-2200, 609-777-4319, 609-292-5995, 609-588-4191 (Fax), 8:30AM-4:30PM.

http://www.state.nj.us/treasury/taxation

Note: Sales tax information is considered confidential. The only way to verify if an entity has a license is to ask to look at the certificate at the place of business, per Joan Bench, Chief of Taxpayer Services Branch.

Birth Certificates

Department of Health, Bureau of Vital Statistics, PO Box 370, Trenton, NJ 08625-0370 (Courier: S Warren St, Room 504, Health & Agriculture Building, Trenton, NJ 08625); 609-292-4087, 609-633-2860 (Credit Card Requests), 609-392-4292 (Fax), 9AM-5PM.

http://www.state.nj.us/health/vital/vital.htm

Indexing & Storage: Records are available from 1878 to present. New records are available for inquiry immediately. Records are indexed on microfiche.

Searching: The general public is denied access to records. You must include the county in your request if it is regarding events before 1903. Include the following in your request-full name, names of parents, mother's maiden name, date of birth, place of birth.

Access by: mail, phone, fax, in person.

Fee & Payment: The fee is $4.00 per record. Add $2.00 per copy for additional copies. Add $1.00 per year for each additional year searched. The fee for using a credit card is $8.95. Fee payee: New Jersey Department of Health & Senior Services. Prepayment required. Personal checks accepted. Credit cards accepted: MasterCard, Visa, AmEx, Discover.

Mail search: Turnaround time: 3 to 4 weeks. No self addressed stamped envelope is required.

Phone search: Must use a credit card. The hours are 8AM to 3PM.

Fax search: Same criteria as phone searching.

In person search: Turnaround time 2 hours.

Expedited service: Expedited service is available for fax searches. Turnaround time: 2 to 3 days. Add fee of overnight carrier ($14.75) if used, plus credit card fee. Federal Express 5-7 day service available.

Death Records

Department of Health, Bureau of Vital Statistics, PO Box 370, Trenton, NJ 08625-0370 (Courier: S Warren St, Room 504, Health & Agriculture Building, Trenton, NJ 08625); 609-292-4087, 609-633-2860 (Credit Card Requests), 609-392-4292 (Fax), 9AM-4PM.

http://www.state.nj.us/health/vital/vital.htm

Indexing & Storage: Records are available from 1878 to present. It takes the 10th of the following month before new records are available for inquiry. Records are indexed on microfiche.

Searching: Cause of death, unless immediate family, is not released. Only those with a legal interest may obtain a record. Include the following in your request-full name, date of death, place of death, Social Security Number.

Access by: mail, phone, fax, in person.

Fee & Payment: The fee is $4.00 per record. Add $2.00 per copy for additional copies. Add $1.00 per year for each additional year searched. Add $8.95 if credit card is used. Fee payee: NJ Department of Health and Senior Services. Prepayment required. Personal checks accepted. Credit cards accepted: MasterCard, Visa, AmEx, Discover.

Mail search: Turnaround time: 1 month. No self addressed stamped envelope is required.

Phone search: Must use a credit card.

Fax search: Same criteria as phone, turnaround time is 10-15 days.

In person search: Turnaround time 2 hours.

Expedited service: Expedited service is available for mail, phone and fax searches. Turnaround time: 2 to 3 days. Add carrier fee of $14.75 plus the $8.95 credit card fee. Federal Express 5-7 day service available.

Marriage Certificates

Department of Health, Bureau of Vital Statistics, PO Box 370, Trenton, NJ 08625-0370 (Courier: S Warren St, Room 504, Health & Agriculture Building, Trenton, NJ 08625); 609-292-4087, 609-633-2860 (Credit Card Requests), 609-392-4292 (Fax), 8:45AM-5PM.

http://www.state.nj.us/health/vital/vital.htm

Indexing & Storage: Records are available from 1878 to present. New records are available for inquiry immediately. Records are indexed on microfiche.

Searching: The general public is denied access to the records. You must include the county in your request if it is regarding events before 1903. Include the following in your request-names of husband and wife, date of marriage, place or county of marriage.

Access by: mail, phone, fax, in person.

Fee & Payment: The fee is $4.00 per record. Add $2.00 per copy for additional copies. Add $1.00 per year for each additional year searched. The fee to use a credit card is $8.95. Fee payee: New Jersey Department of Health. Prepayment required. Personal checks accepted. Credit cards accepted: MasterCard, Visa, AmEx, Discover.

Mail search: Turnaround time: 3 to 4 weeks. No self addressed stamped envelope is required.

Phone search: Must use a credit card. The hours are from 8AM to 3PM.

Fax search: Same criteria as phone searches.

In person search: Turnaround time 2 hours.

Expedited service: Expedited service is available for fax searches. Turnaround time: 2 to 3 days. Add $14.75 carrier fees for overnight shipping and the $8.95 credit card fee. Federal Express 5-7 day service available.

Divorce Records

Clerk of Superior Court, Records Center, PO Box 967, Trenton, NJ 08625-0967 (Courier: Corner of Jerser & Tremont Streets, Building #2, Trenton, NJ 08625); 609-777-0092, 609-777-0094 (Fax), 8:30AM-4PM.

Indexing & Storage: Records are available until 9/89. Records after 1989 must be obtained from the Family Division Court in county of occurrence.

Searching: Also provide married name, unless maiden name was used during the marriage. Information on cases that are impounded is not released. Include the following in your request-names of husband and wife, date of divorce, year divorce case began, docket number (if known). No copies are made and no records are retrieved after 3:30PM. The following data is not released: adoption, impound cases.

Access by: mail, fax, in person.

Fee & Payment: There is no search fee, but there is a $10.00 certification fee. Fee payee: Clerk of Superior Court. Prepayment required. If you are not sure how many pages the results or your request will be, you may send a blank check with "Not to exceed $25.00" written in the memo.

Personal checks accepted. No credit cards accepted.

Mail search: Turnaround time: 2 to 3 weeks. Mail is the preferred request method. A self addressed stamped envelope is requested.

Fax search: Requesters must be pre-approved to fax, and only written information is faxed back. Attorneys with charge accounts with the Superior Court can receive copies, without the seal of the court, via fax.

In person search: Turnaround time: while you wait. The Clerk's Office recommends that you not come to the office in person except for emergency requests.

Workers' Compensation Records

Labor Department, Division of Workers Compensation, John Fitch Plaza, PO Box 381, Trenton, NJ 08625 (Courier: Labor Building, 6th Floor, John Fitch Plaza, Trenton, NJ 08625); 609-292-6026, 609-984-3924 (Fax), 8:30AM-4:30PM.

http://www.state.nj.us/labor/wc/Default.htm

Indexing & Storage: Records are available for 45 years, then are purged. New records are available for inquiry immediately. Records are indexed on inhouse computer.

Searching: First report of injury-accident is not available to the public. All other records are subject to NJSA 34:15-128 which prohibits the copying of records for resale. Use WC-147 if you want copies of a case. Include the following in your request-claimant name, Social Security Number, date of accident.

Access by: mail, in person.

Fee & Payment: There is no search fee. The copy fee is $.75 each for first 10 pages; $.50 each for next 10; and $.25 per page over 20. Fee payee: Division of Workers' Compensation. Prepayment required. Personal checks accepted. No credit cards accepted.

Mail search: Turnaround time: 4 to 6 weeks. If request is just to know if the person has a claim, the turnaround time is same day. A self addressed stamped envelope is requested.

In person search: Turnaround time is same day.

Driver Records

Motor Vehicle Services, Driver History Abstract Unit, PO Box 142, Trenton, NJ 08666; 609-292-6500, 888-486-3339 (In-state only), 609-292-7500 (Suspensions), 8AM-5PM.

http://www.state.nj.us/mvs

Note: Copies of tickets are not kept on file and must be obtained from the municipal courts.

Indexing & Storage: Records are available for five years for the public (complete history for attorneys). Non-moving violations are not reported on the record. Accidents are reported, but fault is not shown. The driver's address is provided on the record. It takes 3 days to 2 weeks normally before new records are available for inquiry.

Searching: Access of driving records is strict, release to casual requesters is prohibited. The driver's license number should be submitted with all requests. The full name, DOB, sex, and eye color are also helpful. The following data is not released: Social Security Numbers or medical records.

Access by: mail, in person, online.

Fee & Payment: The current fee is $10.00 for mail-in or walk-in requests, $2.00 for magnetic tape requests, and $2.00 per record using control cards (100 minimum purchase) Fee payee: Motor Vehicle Services. Prepayment required. Personal checks accepted. No credit cards accepted.

Mail search: Turnaround time: 2 weeks. Batches of 100 or more requested can be submitted on customized format cards at a cost of $2.00 per record. A self addressed stamped envelope is requested.

In person search: Driving records can obtained at any one of the four Regional Service Centers - Deptford, Wayne, Eatontown, and Trenton.

Online search: Fee is $4.00 per record. Access is limited to insurance, bus and trucking companies, parking authorities, and approved vendors. There is a minimum of 100 requests per quarter. For more information, call 609-984-7771.

Other access: Most high volume requesters use the magnetic tape method to obtain overnight records at $2.00 per request (minimum 500 requests) or purchase control cards at $2.00 (100 purchased at a time, used whenever).

Vehicle Ownership
Vehicle Identification
Vessel Ownership
Vessel Registration

Motor Vehicle Services, Certified Information Unit, PO Box 146, Trenton, NJ 08666; 609-292-6500, 888-486-3339 (In-state), 8AM-5PM.

http://www.state.nj.us/mvs

Note: Lien records must be ordered from Special Titles at Motor Vehicle Services, CN-017 (Zip is 08666-0017). Lien records are on the complete title history, or can be purchased at $5.00 for each lien history search.

Indexing & Storage: Records are available from 1986 for most records. All boats 12 ft and over must be titled and registered. All motorized boats and sailboats under 12 ft must be registered. It takes 3 days to 3 weeks normally before new records are available for inquiry.

Searching: SSNs and medical information are not currently released and more restrictions are forthcoming. Casual requesters cannot obtain records. A special request form is required for ownership searches. Also, this agency maintains records on mobile homes.

Access by: mail, online.

Fee & Payment: The fee is $8.00 per record non-certified and $10.00 certified and take 1-2 weeks to process. A lien history search is $5.00 for each lien. A complete title history costs $10.50 and can take as long as 12 weeks to obtain. Fee payee: Motor Vehicle Services. Prepayment required. Personal checks accepted. No credit cards accepted.

Mail search: Requests must be submitted on Form ISM/DO-11A for registration requests and on Form ISM/DO-22A for title record requests. A self addressed stamped envelope is requested.

Online search: Limited online access is available for insurance companies, bus and trucking companies, highway/parking authorities, and approved vendors for these businesses. Participation requires a minimum of 100 requests per calendar quarter at $4.00 per request. Call 609-684-7771 for more information.

Other access: Electronic file transfer is available for volume users at $4.00 per record. There is no program for massive/customized bulk look-ups. Each request is looked at on an individual basis. Records are not sold for commercial or political reasons.

Accident Reports

New Jersey State Police, Criminal Justice Records Bureau, PO Box 7068, West Trenton, NJ 08628-0068; 609-882-2000 x2234, 8AM-5PM.

http://www.state.nj.us/lps/njsp/index.html

Indexing & Storage: Records are available for 6 years. Records are computer indexed. It takes 2 weeks before new records are available for inquiry.

Searching: Fatal accident information is not available until it has been released from the County Prosecutor. Include the following in your request-location of accident, date of accident, driver's full name.

Access by: mail.

Fee & Payment: Fees: $10.00 for first 3 pages and $2.00 for each additional page with a maximum fee of $16.00. Fee payee: New Jersey State Police Department. Prepayment required. Personal checks accepted. No credit cards accepted.

Mail search: Turnaround time: 3 weeks. A self addressed stamped envelope is requested.

Legislation Records

New Jersey State Legislature, State House Annex, PO Box 068, Room B01, Trenton, NJ 08625-0068; 609-292-4840 (Bill Status Only), 609-292-6395

(Copy Room), 800-792-8630 (In State Only), 609-777-2440 (Fax), 8:30AM-5PM.

http://www.njleg.state.nj.us

Note: Older bills may be found at the State Law Library.

Indexing & Storage: Records are available from 1988 to present.

Searching: Include the following in your request-bill number and/or sponsor.

Access by: mail, phone, fax, in person, online.

Fee & Payment: There is no search fee.

Mail search: Turnaround time: same day. For mail searches, provide bill number with the year or sponsor with accurate bill description. No self addressed stamped envelope is required.

Phone search: Records are available by phone.

Fax search: Fax searching available.

In person search: For in person searches, please provide bill number with year or sponsor with accurate bill description.

Online search: The web site is a good source of information about bills. All statutes are online, also.

Voter Registration
Access to Records is Restricted

Dept of Law and Public Safety, Division of Elections, PO Box 304, Trenton, NJ 08625; 609-292-3760, 609-777-1280 (Fax), 8:30AM-5PM.

http://www.state.nj.us/state/election

Note: The Commissioner of Registration maintains these records, but they can only be access at the county level. While these county agencies may

permit individual look-ups, records in mass may be purchased only for political purposes.

GED Certificates

GED Testing Program, Dept. of Education - Bureau Adult Ed. & Literacy, PO Box 500, Trenton, NJ 08625-0500; 609-777-0577.

http://www.state.nj.us/njded/students/ged

Searching: GED Information Request Form is required and can be obtained by calling 609- 777-0577. To search, all of the following is required: a signed release, name, date/year of test, Social Security Number, and city of test. Records are not maintained for persons tested at federal correctional institutions.

Access by: mail.

Fee & Payment: The fee is $5.00 for a verification or a copy of the transcript. Fee payee: Commissioner of Education. Prepayment required. Money orders and business checks are accepted. No credit cards accepted.

Mail search: Turnaround time can take as long as 4 weeks.

Hunting License Information
Fishing License Information
Records not maintained by a state level agency.

Note: They do not have a central database. You must contact the vendor where the license was purchased.

New Jersey State Licensing Agencies

Licenses Searchable Online

Acupuncturist #01 .... www.state.nj.us/lps/ca/bme/acupdir.htm
Architect #06 .... www.state.nj.us/lps/ca/arch/archdir.htm
Chiropractor #08 .... www.state.nj.us/lps/ca/chiro/chirofrm.htm
Counselor, Professional #13 .... www.state.nj.us/lps/ca/marriage/pcdir.htm
Court Reporter #24 .... www.state.nj.us/lps/ca/short/shortdir.htm
Dentist/Dental Hygienist #10 .... www.state.nj.us/lps/ca/dentistry/dentdir.htm
Electrical Contractor #11 .... www.state.nj.us/lps/ca/electric/elecdir.htm
Embalmer #15 .... www.state.nj.us/lps/ca/mort/mortdir.htm
Engineer #20 .... www.state.nj.us/lps/ca/nonmed.htm
Funeral Practitioner #15 .... www.state.nj.us/lps/ca/mort/mortdir.htm
Hearing Aid Dispenser/Fitter #44 .... www.state.nj.us/lps/ca/hear/heardir.htm
Landscape Architect #06 .... www.state.nj.us/lps/ca/arch/archdir.htm
Marriage Counselor #13 .... www.state.nj.us/lps/ca/marriage/pcdir.htm
Mortician #57 .... www.state.nj.us/lps/ca/mort/mortdir.htm
Occupational Therapist/Therapist Assistant #08 ... www.state.nj.us/lps/ca/occup/otdir.htm
Optician/Optician Technician #51 .... www.state.nj.us/lps/ca/medical.htm#0848
Optometrist #17 .... www.state.nj.us/lps/ca/optometry/optomet.htm
Pharmacist #18 .... www.state.nj.us/lps/ca/pharm/pharmdir.htm
Physician #14 .... www.state.nj.us/lps/ca/bme/medfrm.htm
Plumber/Master Plumber #12 .... www.state.nj.us/lps/ca/plumber/plumdir.htm
Podiatrist #14 .... www.state.nj.us/lps/ca/bme/podfrm.htm
Psychologist #22 .... www.state.nj.us/lps/ca/psyfrm.htm
Respiratory Care Practitioner #54 .... www.state.nj.us/lps/ca/respcare/respdir.htm
Shorthand Reporter #24 .... www.state.nj.us/lps/ca/short/shortdir.htm
Speech-Language Pathologist/Audiologist #07 ..... www.state.nj.us/lps/ca/aud/auddir.htm
Surveyor #20 .... www.state.nj.us/lps/ca/nonmed.htm
Tree Expert #55 .... www.state.nj.us/dep/forestry/community/cte.html
Veterinarian #26 .... www.state.nj.us/lps/ca/vetmed/vetdir.htm

Licensing Quick Finder

Accountant, Municipal #05 973-504-6380
Acupuncturist #01 973-273-8090
Alcohol Abuse Counselor #03 732-390-5900
Alcohol/Drug Counselor #13 973-504-6069
Animal Control Officer #59 609-588-3121
Appraiser, General #23 973-504-6480
Appraiser, Residential #23 973-504-6480
Architect #06 973-504-6385
Asbestos Employee/Employer #33 609-633-3760
Asbestos Permit #33 609-633-3760
Athletic Trainer #04 609-292-4843
Attorney #49 609-984-7783
Automobile Dealer #42 609-292-4517
Barber #09 973-504-6400
Barber Shop/Manicure Shop #09 973-504-6400
Beautician #09 973-504-6400
Bio-Analytical Lab Director #14 609-292-4843
Boiler Operator #34 609-984-3001
Boxer #53 609-292-0317
Boxing Manager #28 609-292-0317
Building Inspector #45 609-984-7834
Casino #28 609-441-3555
Casino Employee #28 609-441-3015
Cemetery #46 973-504-6553
Cemetery Salesman #46 973-504-6553
Check Casher/Seller #38 609-292-5340
Chiropractor #08 973-504-6395

Club/Cabaret #37 609-984-3231
Construction Code Official #45 609-984-7834
Consulting Firm/Headquarter #40 973-504-6367
Cosmetologist-Hairstylist #09 973-504-6400
Counselor, Social Work #25 973-504-6495
Counselor, Professional (Marriage & Family)#13 ....
.... 973-504-6082
Court Reporter #24 973-504-6490
Crane Operator #34 609-984-3001
Dental Assistant #10 973-504-6405
Dentist/Dental Hygienist #10 973-504-6405
Director of Student Personnel Svc. #29 609-292-0739
Drug Abuse Counselor #03 732-390-5900
Educational Media Specialist/Librarian #29 ....
.... 609-292-0739
Elevator Inspector #45 609-984-7834
Electrical Contractor #11 973-504-6410
Embalmer #15 973-273-8090
Emergency Medical Svc. Provider #32 . 609-633-7777
Emergency Medical Technician #32 609-633-7777
Employment Agency #40 973-504-6367
Engineer #20 973-504-6460
Fire Protection Inspector #45 609-984-7834
Firefighter #58 609-633-6117
Funeral Practitioner #15 973-273-8090
Health Care Service Agency #40 973-504-6367
Hearing Aid Dispenser/Fitter #44 973-504-6331

Home Health Aide #16 973-504-6586
Home Repair Contractor/Salesperson #39 ....
.... 609-292-3420
Horse Racing #47 609-292-0613
Horse Racing Owner/Trainer #47 609-292-0613
Hotel/Motel #37 609-984-3231
Implant Inspector #45 609-984-7834
Insurance Agent #41 609-292-5360
Insurance Public Adjuster #41 609-292-5360
Investment Advisor #27 201-504-6200
Landscape Architect #06 973-504-6385
Lender, Consumer #39 609-292-5340
Librarian #29 609-292-2070
Liquor Control #37 609-984-3231
Liquor Distribution, Plenary Retail/Limited Retail #37
.... 609-984-3231
Liquor Rectifier/Blender #37 609-984-3231
Liquor Retail, Plenary/Seasonal #37 ... 609-984-3231
Liquor Sales, Retail/Limited/Plenary #37 609-984-3231
Liquor Transit, Plenary Retail #37 609-984-3231
Liquor Wholesale, Limited/Plenary #37 . 609-984-3231
Lobbyist #43 609-292-8700
Manicurist #09 973-504-6400
Marriage & Family Therapist #25 973-504-6495
Marriage Counselor #13 973-504-6415
Midwife #14 609-292-4843
Modeling & Talent Agency #40 973-504-6367

Mortgage Banker/Broker #27	201-504-6200
Mortician #57	973-504-6425
Mover/Warehouseman #02	973-504-6512
Notary Public #36	609-292-9292
Nurse, Advance Practice #16	973-504-6586
Nurse-RN-LPN #16	973-504-6586
Nursing Home Administrator #50	609-633-9051
Occupational Therapist/Therapist Assistant #08	973-504-6395
Optician/Optician Technician #51	973-504-6435
Optometrist #17	973-504-6440
Orthodontic Assistant, Limited Registered #10	973-504-6405
Orthopedist #14	609-292-4843
Orthotics & Prosthetics #52	973-504-6445
Paramedic #32	609-633-7777
Pesticide Applicator #31	609-530-4070
Pesticide Dealer #31	609-530-4070
Pesticide Operator #31	609-530-4070
Pharmacist #18	973-504-6450
Pharmacy #18	973-504-6450
Physical Therapist #19	973-504-6455
Physical Therapist Assistant #19	973-504-6455
Physician #14	609-292-4843
Planner, Professional #21	973-504-6465
Plumber/Master Plumber #12	973-504-6420
Podiatrist #14	609-292-4843
Private Detective #56	609-882-2000 X2680
Psychologist #22	973-504-6470
Public Accountant-CPA #05	973-504-6380
Pump Installer #30	609-777-1007
Real Estate Agent #48	609-292-8280
Real Estate Appraiser/Apprentice #23	973-504-6480
Real Estate Broker #48	609-292-8280
Real Estate Instructor #48	609-292-8280
Real Estate Salesperson #48	609-292-8280
Refrigeration Technician #34	609-984-3001
Respiratory Care Practitioner #54	973-504-6485
School Accountant #05	973-504-6380
School Principal/Admin./Supervisor #29	609-292-0739
School Counselor #29	609-292-0739
School, Accredited #29	609-292-0739
Second Mortgage Lender #39	609-292-5340
Securities Agent #27	201-504-6200
Securities Broker/Dealer #27	201-504-6200
Securities Issuer #27	201-504-6200
Shorthand Reporter #24	973-504-6490
Skin Care Specialist #09	973-504-6400
Social Worker #25	973-504-6495
Speech-Language Pathologist/Audiologist #07	973-504-6390
Stable Mate #47	609-292-0613
Surveyor #20	973-504-6460
Teacher #29	609-292-0739
Theater #37	609-984-3231
Tree Expert #55	609-292-2532
Veterinarian #26	973-504-6500
Waste Water System Operator #30	609-777-1007
Weighmaster #35	732-815-4845
Weights & Measures Mechanic #35	732-815-4845
Well Driller #30	609-777-1007
Wine Wholesaler/Winery #37	609-984-3231

Licensing Agency Information

#01 Board of Medical Examiners, PO Box 183, Trenton, NJ 08625-0183; 609-826-7100.
Direct web site URL to search for licensees: www.state.nj.us/lps/ca/bme/acupdir.htm. You can search online using name

#02 Office of Consumer Protection, 124 Halsey St, Newark, NJ 07101; 973-504-6442, Fax: 973-648-2807.
www.state.nj.us/lps/ca

#03 Alcohol-Other Drugs of Abuse Counselor Cert Board, 5A Aver Ct, East Brunswick, NJ 08816; 732-390-5900, Fax: 732-257-6070.
www.webspan.net/~certbd/

#04 Athletic Training Advisory Commission, Board of Medical Examiners, 140 E Front St, 2nd Fl, Trenton, NJ 08625-0183; 609-292-4843, Fax: 609-826-7117.
www.state.nj.us/lps/ca/medical.htm

#05 Board of Accountancy, PO Box 45000, Newark, NJ 07101; 973-504-6380, Fax: 973-648-2855.
www.state.nj.us/lps/ca/nonmed.htm#acc1

#06 Division of Consumer Affairs, 124 Halsey St, Newark, NJ 07102; 973-504-6385, Fax: 973-504-6458.
www.state.nj.us/lps/ca
Direct web site URL to search for licensees: www.state.nj.us/lps/ca/arch/archdir.htm

#07 Board of Audiology & Speech Language Pathology, 124 Halsey St (07102), Newark, NJ 07101; 973-504-6390, Fax: 973-648-3355.

#08 Division of Consumer Affairs, 124 Halsey St, Newark, NJ 07102; 973-504-6395, Fax: 973-648-3538.
www.state.nj.us/lps/ca
Direct web site URL to search for licensees: www.state.nj.us/lps/ca/director.htm

#09 Board of Cosmetology & Hairstyling, PO Box 45003, Newark, NJ 07101; 973-504-6400, Fax: 973-648-3536.

#10 Board of Dentistry, PO Box 45005, 124 Halsey St (07102), Newark, NJ 07101; 973-504-6405, Fax: 973-273-8075.
www.state.nj.us/lps/ca/dentistry There is an automated license verification line (need license

number) 973-273-8090 with fax back capability for written verifications.

#11 Division of Consumer Affairs, 124 Halsey St (07102), Newark, NJ 07101; 973-504-6410, Fax: 973-648-3355.
www.state.nj.us/lps/ca/boards/list1.htm
Direct web site URL to search for licensees: www.state.nj.us/lps/ca/electric/elecdir.htm. You can search online using name. Phone verifications are available at 973-273-8090.

#12 Board of Examiners of Master Plumbers, PO Box 45008 (124 Halsey St, 07102), Newark, NJ 07101; 973-504-6420.
www.state.nj.us/lps/ca/home.htm
Direct web site URL to search for licensees: www.state.nj.us/lps/ca/plumber/plumdir.htm. You can search online using name. Phone verifications are available at 973-273-8090.

#13 Board of Marriage & Family Therapy Examiners, 124 Halsey St (07102), 6th Fl, Newark, NJ 07101; 973-594-6415, Fax: 973-648-3536.
www.state.nj.us/lps/ca/boards.htm
Direct web site URL to search for licensees: www.state.nj.us/lps/ca/marriage/pcdir.htm. You can search online using last name. Also, use 973-273-8090 for the most current listings.

#14 Board of Medical Examiners, PO Box 183, Trenton, NJ 08625-0183; 609-292-4843, Fax: 609-984-3950.
www.state.nj.us./lps/ca/medical.htm Use these 3-digit codes when using the state verification system at 973-273-8090: 100=MD, 101=DO, 102=Podiatrist

#15 Division of Consumer Affairs, 124 Halsey St, Newark, NJ 07102; 973-504-6425, Fax: 973-648-3636.
www.state.nj.us/lps/ca
Direct web site URL to search for licensees: www.state.nj.us/lps/ca/mort/mortdir.htm. You can search online using name

#16 Board of Nursing, 124 Halsey St (07102), Newark, NJ 07101; 973-504-6586, Fax: 973-648-3481.
www.state.nj.us/lps/ca/home.htm

#17 Division of Consumer Affairs, 124 Halsey St (07102), Newark, NJ 07101; 973-504-6440, Fax: 973-645-3536.
www.state.nj.us/lps/ca/optometry/optomet.htm
Direct web site URL to search for licensees: www.state.nj.us/lps/ca/optometry/optomet.htm. You can search online using name

#18 Board of Pharmacy, PO Box 45013 (124 Halsey St, 07102), Newark, NJ 07101; 973-504-6450, Fax: 973-648-3355.
www.state.nj.us/lps/ca/medical.htm#pharm11
Direct web site URL to search for licensees: www.state.nj.us/lps/ca/pharm/pharmdir.htm. You can search online using last name. Also, use 973-273-8090 for the most current listings.

#19 Board of Physical Therapists, 124 Halsey St, Newark, NJ 07101; 973-504-6455, Fax: 973-648-3536.

#20 Board of Professional Engineers & Land Surveyors, 124 Halsey St (07102), Newark, NJ 07101; 973-504-6460, Fax: 973-648-3536.
www.state.nj.us/lps/ca/nonmed.htm
Direct web site URL to search for licensees: www.state.nj.us/lps/ca/nonmed.htm. You can search online using name.

#21 Board of Professional Planners, PO Box 45016 (124 Halsey St, 07102), Newark, NJ 07101; 973-504-6465, Fax: 973-648-3536.
www.state.nj.us/lps/ca/plan/planner.htm

#22 Division of Consumer Affairs, 124 Halsey St, Newark, NJ 07102; 973-504-6470.
www.state.nj.us/lps/ca
Direct web site URL to search for licensees: www.state.nj.us/lps/ca/psyfrm.htm. You can search online using name

#23 Division of Consumer Affairs, PO Box 45032 (124 Halsey St, 07102), Newark, NJ 07101; 973-504-6480, Fax: 973-648-3536.
www.state.nj.us/lps/ca

#24 Board of Shorthand Reporting, 124 Halsey St, Newark, NJ 07101; 973-504-6490, Fax: 973-648-3536.
www.state.nj.us/pls/ca/boards.htm
Direct web site URL to search for licensees: www.state.nj.us/lps/ca/short/shortdir.htm. You can search online using name. Also, you may call 973-273-8090 for up to date verifications.

#25 Board of Social Work Examiners, PO Box 45033, Newark, NJ 07101; 973-504-6495, Fax: 973-648-3536.

#26 Board of Veterinary Medical Examiners, PO Box 45033, Newark, NJ 07101; 973-504-6500, Fax: 973-648-3355.
www.state.nj.us/lps/ca/medical.htm
Direct web site URL to search for licensees: www.state.nj.us/lps/ca/vetmed/vetdir.htm.   You can search online using last name. Also, use 973-273-8090 for the most current listings.

#27 Bureau of Securities, PO Box 47029, 153 Halsey St 6th Fl, Newark, NJ 07101; 973-504-3600, Fax: 973-504-3601.
www.state.nj.us/lps/ca/bos.htm

#28 Casino Control Commission, Tennessee Ave & Boardwalk, Arcade Bldg, Atlantic City, NJ 08401; 609-441-3000, Fax: 609-441-3752.
www.state.nj.us/casinos

#29 Department of Education, PO Box 500, 100 Riverview Plaza, Trenton, NJ 08625-0500; 609-292-2045, Fax: 609-292-3768.

#30 Department of Environmental Protection, PO Box 402 (401 E State St, CN-402), Trenton, NJ 08625; 609-292-8046, Fax: 609-633-3727.
www.state.nj.us/dep/index.htm

#31 Department of Environmental Protection, PO Box 411, Trenton, NJ 08625-0411; 609-530-4070, Fax: 609-984-6555.
www.state.nj.us/dep/enforcement/pcp

#32 Office of Emergency Medicinal Svcs, Ofc. of Commissioner, 50 E State St CN-360, Trenton, NJ 08625; 609-633-7777, Fax: 609-633-7954.
www.state.nj.us/health/ems/hltems.htm   only disciplinary actions, fines, and enforcement actions are available online.

#33 Department of Community Affairs, PO Box 816, 101 S Broad St 4th Fl, Trenton, NJ 08625-0816; 609-633-3760, Fax: 609-984-7952.

#34 Division of Community Affairs, PO Box 814 (101 South Broad St), Trenton, NJ 08625-0814; 609-984-3001, Fax: 609-984-1577.

#35 Department of Law & Public Safety, 1261 Route 1 & 9 South, Avanel, NJ 07001; 732-815-4845, Fax: 732-382-5298.
www.state.nj.us/lps/index.html

#36 Department of Treasury, Division of Revenue, PO Box 452, West Trenton, NJ 08625; 609-292-9292, Fax: 609-984-6681.

www.state.nj.us/treasury/revenue/dcr/programs/notary.html

#37 Division of Alcoholic Beverage Control, 140 E Front St, CN087, Trenton, NJ 08625-0087; 609-984-3230, Fax: 609-633-6078.
www.state.nj.us/lps/abc/licbur.htm

#38 Division of Banking, 20 W State St CN-040, Trenton, NJ 08625; 609-292-5340, Fax: 609-292-5461.
www.nail.org/nj/NJHOME.PG.html

#39 Division of Banking, 20 W State St CN-040, Trenton, NJ 08625; 609-292-5340, Fax: 609-292-5461.
www.nail.org/nj/NJHOME.PG.html

#40 Division of Consumer Affairs, 124 Halsey St (07102), Newark, NJ 07101; 973-504-6200, Fax: 973-648-2807.
www.state.nj.us/lps/ca

#41 Division of Insurance, PO Box 327 (20 W. State St), Trenton, NJ 08625-0327; 609-292-5360, Fax: 609-984-5263.
www.njdobi.org

#42 Division of Motor Vehicles, 225 E State St, Trenton, NJ 08666; 609-292-4517, Fax: 609-292-5153.
www.state.nj.us/mvs

#43 Election Law Enforcement Commission, PO Box 185, CN-185 (28 W State St), Trenton, NJ 08625-0185; 609-292-8700, Fax: 609-633-9854.
www.elec.state.nj.us

#44 Hearing Aid Dispensers Examining Committee, PO Box 45038, Newark, NJ 07101; 973-504-6331, Fax: 973-648-3355.
www.state.nj.us/lps/ca/medical.htm
Direct web site URL to search for licensees: www.state.nj.us/lps/ca/hear/heardir.htm. You can search online using last name. Also, use 973-273-8090 for the most current listings.

#45 Department of Community Affairs, Bureau of Code Services, CN-816, Trenton, NJ 08625-0816; 609-984-7834, Fax: 609-984-7952.
www.state.nj.us/dca/codes/

#46 Cemetery Board, PO Box 45036, Newark, NJ 07101; 973-504-6553, Fax: 973-648-3536.
www.state.nj.us/lps/ca/nonmed.htm

#47 Racing Commission, POB 088 (140 Front St), Trenton, NJ 08625-0080; 609-292-0613, Fax: 609-599-1785.

#48 Division of Occupational Safety, 399 Washington St 5th Fl, Trenton, NJ 08625-0328; 609-292-8280, Fax: 609-292-0944.
www.naic.org/nj/NJHOMEPG.HTML
Direct web site URL to search for licensees: www.naic.org/nj/recdiscp.htm. You can search online using list for revoked licenses.

#49 State Bar Association, PO Box 973 (25 Market St, 8th Fl), Trenton, NJ 08625; 609-984-7783, Fax: 609-984-6859.
www.judiciary.state.nj.us

#50 Nursing Home Administrators Licensing Board, PO Box 367, 120 S Stockton, Trenton, NJ 08625-0367; 609-633-9051, Fax: 609-633-9087.
www.state.nj.us/health/

#51 Division of Consumer Affairs, 124 Halsey St, Newark, NJ 07102; 973-504-6435, Fax: 973-648-3355.
Direct web site URL to search for licensees: www.state.nj.us/lps/ca/medical.htm#0848

#52 Division of Consumer Affairs, 124 Halsey St., Newark, NJ 07102; 973-504-6445, Fax: 973-648-3536.
www.state.nj.us/lps/ca

#53 Athletic Control Board, 140 E Front St, CN-180, Trenton, NJ 08625-0180; 609-292-0317, Fax: 609-292-3756.

#54 Board of Respiratory Care, 122 Halsey St, Newark, NJ 07101; 973-504-6485, Fax: 973-648-3355.
www.state.nj.us/lps/ca/home.htm

#55 Forestry Service, 501 E State St CN-404, Trenton, NJ 08625-0404; 609-292-2532, Fax: 609-984-0378.
www.state.nj.us/dep/forestry/community/home.htm
Direct web site URL to search for licensees: www.state.nj.us/dep/forestry/community/cte.html

#56 State Police Department, River Rd, Trenton, NJ 08628; 609-882-2000 x2680, Fax: 609-637-9583.

#57 Board of Mortuary Science, PO Box 45009, Newark, NJ 07101; 973-504-6425.

#58 Department of Community Affairs, PO Box 809, Trenton, NJ 08625-0809; 609-633-6117.

#59 Department of Health & Senior Svcs, PO Box 369, Trenton, NJ 08625-0369; 609-588-3121.

New Jersey Federal Courts

The following list indicates the district and division name for each county in the state. If the bankruptcy court location is different from the district court, then the location of the bankruptcy court appears in parentheses.

County/Court Cross Reference

Atlantic	Camden	Middlesex	Newark (Trenton)
Bergen	Newark	Monmouth	Newark (Trenton)
Burlington	Camden	Morris	Newark
Camden	Camden	Ocean	Trenton
Cape May	Camden	Passaic	Newark
Cumberland	Camden	Salem	Camden
Essex	Newark	Somerset	Trenton
Gloucester	Camden	Sussex	Newark
Hudson	Newark	Union	Newark
Hunterdon	Trenton	Warren	Trenton
Mercer	Trenton		

US District Court

District of New Jersey

Camden Division Clerk, PO Box 2797, Camden, NJ 08101 (Courier Address: Room 1050, 4th & Cooper Sts, Camden, NJ 08101), 856-757-5021, Fax: 856-757-5370.

http://pacer.njd.uscourts.gov

Counties: Atlantic, Burlington, Camden, Cape May, Cumberland, Gloucester, Salem.

Indexing/Storage: Cases are indexed by defendant and plaintiff as well as by case number. New cases are available in the index 1-2 days after filing date. Both computer and card indexes are maintained. Records are also indexed on microfiche. Open records are located at this court. District wide searches are available for all information from this court.

Fee & Payment: The fee is $20.00 per item (one party name or case number). Payment may be made by money order, cashier check, personal check. Prepayment is required. Payee: Clerk, US District Court. Certification fee: $7.00 per document. Copy fee: $.50 per page.

Phone Search: Only docket information is available by phone.

Mail Search: Always enclose a stamped self addressed envelope.

In Person: In person searching is available.

PACER: Sign-up number is 800-676-6856. Access fee is $.60 per minute. Toll-free access: 888-297-9938. Local access: 609-989-0590. Case records are available back to May 1991. Records are never purged. New records are available online after 1 day. PACER is available online at http://pacer.njd.uscourts.gov.

Opinions Online: Court opinions are available online at http://lawlibrary.rutgers.edu/fed/search.html

Newark Division ML King, Jr Federal Bldg. & US Courthouse, 50 Walnut St, Room 4015, Newark, NJ 07101 (Courier Address: Use mail address for courier delivery), 973-645-3730.

http://pacer.njd.uscourts.gov

Counties: Bergen, Essex, Hudson, Middlesex, Monmouth, Morris, Passaic, Sussex, Union. Monmouth County was transferred from Trenton Division in late 1997; closed cases remain in Trenton.

Indexing/Storage: Cases are indexed by defendant and plaintiff as well as by case number. New cases are available in the index 1-3 days after filing date. Both computer and card indexes are maintained. Open records are located at this court.

Fee & Payment: The fee is $20.00 per item (one party name or case number). Payment may be made by money order, cashier check, business check. Personal checks are not accepted. Prepayment is required. Payee: Clerk, US District Court. Certification fee: $7.00 per document. Copy fee: $.50 per page.

Phone Search: Only docket information available by telephone.

Mail Search: Always enclose a stamped self addressed envelope.

In Person: In person searching is available.

PACER: Sign-up number is 800-676-6856. Access fee is $.60 per minute. Toll-free access: 888-297-9938. Local access: 609-989-0590. Case records are available back to May 1991. Records are never purged. New records are available online after 1 day. PACER is available online at http://pacer.njd.uscourts.gov.

Opinions Online: Court opinions are available online at http://lawlibrary.rutgers.edu/fed/search.html

Trenton Division Clerk, US District Court, Room 2020, 402 E State St, Trenton, NJ 08608 (Courier Address: Use mail address for courier delivery), 609-989-2065.

http://pacer.njd.uscourts.gov

Counties: Hunterdon, Mercer, Ocean, Somerset, Warren. Monmouth County was transferred to Newark and Camden Division in late 1997; closed Monmouth cases remain in Trenton.

Indexing/Storage: Cases are indexed by defendant and plaintiff as well as by case number. New cases are available in the index several days after filing date. A computer index is maintained. Records are also indexed on microfiche. Open records are located at this court. District wide searches are available for information from 1920 from this district. This court also maintained closed files for the Newark division until 1997.

Fee & Payment: The fee is $20.00 per item (one party name or case number). Payment may be made by money order, cashier check, personal check. Prepayment is required. Payee: Clerk, US District Court. Certification fee: $7.00 per document. Copy fee: $.50 per page.

Phone Search: Only docket information available by phone.

Mail Search: A stamped self addressed envelope is not required.

In Person: In person searching is available.

PACER: Sign-up number is 800-676-6856. Access fee is $.60 per minute. Toll-free access: 888-297-9938. Local access: 609-989-0590. Case records are available back to May 1991. Records are never purged. New records are available online after 1 day. PACER is available online at http://pacer.njd.uscourts.gov.

Opinions Online: Court opinions are available online at http://lawlibrary.rutgers.edu/fed/search.html

US Bankruptcy Court

District of New Jersey

Camden Division PO Box 2067, Camden, NJ 08101 (Courier Address: 401 Market St, 2nd Floor, Camden, NJ 08101), 856-757-5485.

http://www.njb.uscourts.gov

Counties: Atlantic, Burlington (partial), Camden, Cape May, Cumberland, Gloucester, Salem.

Indexing/Storage: Cases are indexed by debtor as well as by case number. New cases are available in the index immediately after filing date. A computer index is maintained. Open records are located at this court.

Fee & Payment: The fee is $20.00 per item (one party name or case number). Payment may be made by money order, cashier check, business check. Personal checks are not accepted. Prepayment is required. Payee: Clerk, US Bankruptcy Court. Certification fee: $7.00 per document. Copy fee: $.50 per page.

Phone Search: Only docket information available by phone. An automated voice case information service (VCIS) is available.

Mail Search: Always enclose a stamped self addressed envelope.

In Person: In person searching is available.

PACER: Sign-up number is 800-676-6856. Access fee is $.60 per minute. Toll-free access: 800-253-1597. Local access: 973-645-3555. Case records are available back to 1991. Records are purged every 6 months. New civil records are available online after 1 day. PACER is available online at http://pacer.njb.uscourts.gov.

Electronic Filing: Electronic filing information is available online at https://ecf.njb.uscourts.gov

Other Online Access: Search records on the Internet using RACER at http://racer.njb.uscourts.gov. Access fee is 7 cents per page.

Newark Division PO Box 1352, Newark, NJ 17101, Courier Address: ML King Jr Federal Bldg, 50 Walnut St, 3rd Fl, Newark, NJ 07102), 973-645-4764.

http://www.njb.uscourts.gov

Counties: Bergen, Essex, Hudson, Morris, Passaic, Sussex. Also Elizabeth, Springfield and Hillside townships in Union County.

Indexing/Storage: Cases are indexed by debtor as well as by case number. New cases are available in the index immediately after filing date. A computer index is maintained. Open records are located at this court.

Fee & Payment: The fee is $20.00 per item (one party name or case number). Payment may be made by money order, cashier check, business check. Personal checks are not accepted. Prepayment is required. All copywork requests should be referred to Lexplex Management Services, at 201-624-9171. Payee: Clerk, US Bankruptcy Court. Certification fee: $7.00 per document. Copy fee: $.50 per page.

Phone Search: An automated voice case information service (VCIS) is available.

Mail Search: Always enclose a stamped self addressed envelope.

In Person: In person searching is available.

PACER: Sign-up number is 800-676-6856. Access fee is $.60 per minute. Toll-free access: 800-253-1597. Local access: 973-645-3555. Case records are available back to 1991. Records are purged every 6 months. New civil records are available online after 1 day. PACER is available online at http://pacer.njb.uscourts.gov.

Electronic Filing: Electronic filing information is available online at https://ecf.njb.uscourts.gov/

Other Online Access: Search records on the Internet using RACER/PACER at http://racer.njb.uscourts.gov. Access fee is 7 cents per page.

Trenton Division Clerk of Court, 402 E State St, 1st Fl, Trenton, NJ 08608 (Courier Address: Use mail address for courier delivery), 609-989-2128.

http://www.njb.uscourts.gov

Counties: Burlington (partial), Hunterdon, Mercer, Middlesex, Monmouth, Ocean, Somerset, Warren, Union except the townships of Elizabeth, Hillside and Springfield.

Indexing/Storage: Cases are indexed by debtor as well as by case number. New cases are available in the index immediately after filing date. A computer index is maintained. Open records are located at this court.

Fee & Payment: The fee is $20.00 per item (one party name or case number). Payment may be made by money order, cashier check, business check. Personal checks are not accepted. Prepayment is required. Payee: Clerk, US Bankruptcy Court. Certification fee: $7.00 per document. Copy fee: $.50 per page.

Phone Search: An automated voice case information service (VCIS) is available.

Mail Search: Always enclose a stamped self addressed envelope.

In Person: In person searching is available.

PACER: Sign-up number is 800-676-6856. Access fee is $.60 per minute. Toll-free access: 800-253-1597. Local access: 973-645-3555. Case records are available back to 1991. Records are purged every 6 months. New civil records are available online after 1 day. PACER is available online at http://pacer.njb.uscourts.gov.

Electronic Filing: Electronic filing information is available online at https://ecf.njb.uscourts.gov

Other Online Access: Search records on the Internet using RACER at http://racer.njb.uscourts.gov. Access fee is 7 cents per page.

New Jersey County Courts

Court	Jurisdiction	No. of Courts	How Organized
Superior Courts*	General	21	21 Counties/15 Vicinages
Special Civil Part*	Limited	21	21 Counties
Municipal Courts	Municipal	535	
Tax Court	Special	1	

* Profiled in this Sourcebook.

Court	CIVIL								
	Tort	Contract	Real Estate	Min. Claim	Max. Claim	Small Claims	Estate	Eviction	Domestic Relations
Superior Courts*	X	X	X	$10,000	No Max		X		X
Special Civil Part*	X	X	X	$0	$10,000	$2000		X	
Municipal Courts									
Tax Court									

Court	CRIMINAL				
	Felony	Misdemeanor	DWI/DUI	Preliminary Hearing	Juvenile
Superior Courts*	X				X
Special Civil Part*					
Municipal Courts		X	X		
Tax Court					

ADMINISTRATION
Administrative Office of the Courts, RJH Justice Complex, Courts Bldg 7th Floor, CN 037, Trenton, NJ, 08625; 609-984-0275, Fax: 609-984-6968.

www.judiciary.state.nj.us

COURT STRUCTURE
Each Superior Court has 2 divisions; one for the Civil Division and another for the Criminal Division. Search requests should be addressed separately to each division.

The Special Civil Part of the Superior Court acts like a division of the court, and handles only the smaller civil claims. The small claims limit is $2,000. The Superior Court designation refers to the court where criminal cases and civil claims over $10,000 are heard. Probate is handled by Surrogates.

ONLINE ACCESS
Online computer access is available through the ACMS, AMIS, and FACTS systems.

ACMS (Automated Case Management System) contains data on all active civil cases statewide from the Law Division-Civil Part, Chancery Division-Equity Part, the Special Civil Part for 21 counties, and the Appellate Division.

AMIS (Archival Management Information System) contains closed case information.

FACTS (Family Automated Case Tracking System) contains information on dissolutions from all counties.

The fee is $1.00 per minute of use. For further information and/or an Inquiry System Guidebook containing hardware and software requirements and an enrollment form, write to: Superior Court Clerk's Office, Electronic Access Program, 25 Market St, CN971, Trenton NJ 08625, FAX 609-292-6564, or call 609-292-4987

ADDITIONAL INFORMATION
Effective 1/1/95, all court employees became state employees and each section is responsible for its own fees. Note that Cape May County offices are located in the city of Cape May Court House, and not in the city of Cape May.

Atlantic County

Superior Court - Criminal Division Criminal Courthouse, 5909 Main St, Mays Landing, NJ 08330; 609-625-7000; Fax: 609-645-5875. Hours: 8:30AM-4:30PM (EST). *Felony.*

www.judiciary.state.nj.us/atlantic/index.htm

Criminal Records: Access: Mail, fax, in person. Both court and visitors may perform in person searches. No search fee. Required to search: name, years to search, DOB; also helpful: SSN. Criminal records on computer from 1985, prior on docket books and index cards back to 1940.

General Information: Public Access terminal is available. No sealed, expunged, judges notes, PSI's, or mental illness records released. SASE required. Copy fee: $.75 per page. Certification fee: $5.00. Fee payee: Treasurer-State of New Jersey. No personal checks accepted. Prepayment is required.

Superior Court - Civil Division Civil Courthouse, Mays Landing, NJ 08330; 609-625-7000 X5251; Fax: 609-645-5875. Hours: 8:30AM-4:30PM (EST). *Civil Actions Over $10,000, Probate.*

www.judiciary.state.nj.us/atlantic/index.htm

Civil Records: Access: Mail, online, in person. No search fee. Required to search: name, years to search. Civil cases indexed by defendant, plaintiff. Civil records on computer from 9/84, on dockets from 1960, prior to 1960 archived. Prior to 1960 records are for public review only (in large books, difficult to find records). See state introduction for information on how to sign up for online access.

General Information: No sealed, expunged, judges notes, PSI's, or mental illness records released. SASE required. Turnaround time 1 day. Copy fee: $.25 per page. Certification fee: $5.00. Fee payee: Treasurer-State of New Jersey. No personal checks accepted. Prepayment is required.

Special Civil Part 1201 Bacharach Blvd., Atlantic City, NJ 08401; 609-345-6700 X3376; Fax: 609-343-2326. Hours: 8:30AM-4:30PM (EST). *Civil Actions Under $10,000, Eviction, Small Claims.*

www.judiciary.state.nj.us/atlantic/index.htm

Civil Records: Access: Mail, online, in person. Both court and visitors may perform in person searches. No search fee. Required to search: name, years to search. Civil cases indexed by defendant, plaintiff. Civil records on computer from 1985 (some from 1987), prior on index books. In order to review index books, call in advance for an appointment. See state introduction for information on how to sign up for online access.

General Information: Public Access terminal is available. No adoption, sealed, juvenile, expunged, dismissed, or mental health records released. SASE required. Turnaround time 1 week. Copy fee: $.75 per page. Certification fee: $5.00. Fee payee: Clerk, Special Civil Part. Personal checks accepted. Prepayment is required.

Bergen County

Superior Court - Criminal Division 10 Main St, Rm 134, Justice Center, Hackensack, NJ 07601; 201-646-3000; 646-2105 (records); Fax: 201-342-9083. Hours: 8:30AM-4:30PM (EST). *Felony.*

www.judiciary.state.nj.us/bergen/index.htm

Criminal Records: Access: Fax, mail, in person. Both court and visitors may perform in person searches. Search fee: $2.00 per name. Required to search: name, years to search, SSN, signed release; also helpful: address, DOB. Criminal records on computer from 1973.

General Information: No sealed, expunged, dismissed, judges notes, PSI's, or discovery packets

records released. SASE required. Turnaround time 1 week. Copy fee: $.25. No charge for single copy of criminal record. Certification fee: $5.00. Fee payee: Bergen County Clerk. Personal checks accepted. Prepayment is required.

Superior Court - Civil Division 10 Main St. Rm 119, Justice Center, Hackensack, NJ 07601; 201-646-2783/3011; Fax: 201-752-4031. Hours: 8:30AM-4:30PM (EST). *Civil Actions Over $10,000, Probate.*

www.judiciary.state.nj.us/bergen/index.htm

Civil Records: Access: Mail, online, in person. Only the court performs in person searches; visitors may not. No search fee. Required to search: name, years to search. Civil cases indexed by defendant, plaintiff. Civil records on computer for 2-5 years, on dockets from 1900s. See state introduction for information on how to sign up for online access.

General Information: No sealed, expunged, dismissed, judges notes, PSI's, or discovery packets records released. SASE required. Turnaround time 1 week. Copy fee: $.50 per page. Certification fee: $5.00. Fee payee: Bergen County Clerk. Personal checks accepted. Prepayment is required.

Special Civil Part 10 Main St. Rm 430, Justice Center, Hackensack, NJ 07601; 201-646-2289/2243. Hours: 8:30AM-5PM (EST). *Civil Actions Under $10,000, Eviction, Small Claims.*

www.judiciary.state.nj.us/bergen/index.htm

Civil Records: Access: Mail, online, in person. Both court and visitors may perform in person searches. No search fee. Required to search: name, years to search. Civil cases indexed by defendant, plaintiff. Civil records on computer from 1990, prior on index cards. See state introduction for information on how to sign up for online access.

General Information: No adoption, sealed, juvenile, expunged, dismissed, or mental illness records released. SASE required. Turnaround time varies from 2 days-3 weeks. Copy fee: $.50 per page. Certification fee: $5.00. Fee payee: Bergen County Special Civil Part. Personal checks accepted. Prepayment is required.

Burlington County

Superior Court - Criminal Division 49 Rancocas Rd, Mount Holly, NJ 08060; 609-518-2568. Hours: 8AM-5PM (EST). *Felony.*

www.judiciary.state.nj.us/burlington/index.htm

Criminal Records: Access: Mail, in person. Both court and visitors may perform in person searches. Search fee: $5.00 per name. Required to search: name, years to search; also helpful: DOB, SSN. Criminal records on computer from 1986, on docket books from 1954.

General Information: No sealed, expunged, judges notes, PSI's, or discovery packets released. SASE required. Turnaround time 10 days. Copy fee: $.75 per page for first ten pages; $.50 per page next ten; each add'l page $.25. Certification fee: $5.00. Fee payee: State of New Jersey. Personal checks accepted. Prepayment is required.

Superior Court - Civil Division 49 Rancocas Rd, Mount Holly, NJ 08060; 609-518-2622. Hours: 8AM-5PM (EST). *Civil Actions Over $10,000, Probate.*

www.judiciary.state.nj.us/burlington/index.htm

Civil Records: Access: Mail, online, in person. Both court and visitors may perform in person searches. No search fee. Required to search: name, years to search. Civil cases indexed by defendant, plaintiff. Local judgment records on computer since 1989, all others from 1954 to present. See state introduction for information on how to sign up for online access.

General Information: Public Access terminal is available. No sealed, expunged, judges notes, PSI's, or

discovery packets released. SASE required. Turnaround time 10 days. Copy fee: $.75 per page for first ten, $.50 per page for next ten pages, and $.25 per page thereafter. Certification fee: $5.00. Fee payee: State of New Jersey. Personal checks accepted. Prepayment is required.

Special Civil Part 49 Rancocas Rd., Mount Holly, NJ 08060; 609-518-2865; Fax: 609-518-2872. Hours: 8AM-5PM (EST). *Civil Actions Under $10,000, Eviction, Small Claims.*

www.judiciary.state.nj.us/burlington/index.htm

Civil Records: Access: Fax, mail, online, in person. Both court and visitors may perform in person searches. No search fee. Required to search: name, years to search. Civil cases indexed by defendant, plaintiff. Civil records on computer from 1985, microfilm from 1984, prior on index books by docket number. See state introduction for information on how to sign up for online access.

General Information: Public Access terminal is available. No adoption, sealed, juvenile, expunged, dismissed, or mental health records released. Turnaround time 1-2 weeks. Fax notes: No fee to fax results. Copy fee: $.75 per page. Fee is for first 10 pages; $.50 per page next 10; each add'l $.25. Certification fee: $5.00. Fee payee: State of New Jersey. Personal checks accepted.

Camden County

Superior Court - Criminal Division Hall of Justice, 101 S 5th St, Camden, NJ 08103; 856-225-7452. Hours: 8AM-4PM (EST). *Felony.*

www.judiciary.state.nj.us/camden/index.htm

Criminal Records: Access: Mail, in person. Only the court performs in person searches; visitors may not. Search fee: $7.00 per name. Required to search: name, years to search, DOB, SSN. Criminal records on computer from 1986, on docket books from 1970.

General Information: No sealed, expunged, dismissed, judges notes, PSI's or discovery packets records released. SASE required. Turnaround time 3 days. No copy fee. Certification fee: $1.50 per page. Fee payee: Clerk of Superior Court. Business checks accepted. Prepayment is required.

Superior Court - Civil Division Hall of Justice, 101 S 5th St, Camden, NJ 08103; 856-225-7494. Hours: 8AM-4PM (EST). *Civil Actions Over $10,000, Probate.*

www.judiciary.state.nj.us/camden/index.htm

Civil Records: Access: Mail, online, in person. Only the court performs in person searches; visitors may not. No search fee. Required to search: name, years to search. Civil cases indexed by defendant, plaintiff. Civil records on computer from 1987. See state introduction for information on how to sign up for online access.

General Information: No sealed, dismissed, judges notes, or discovery packets records released. SASE required. Turnaround time 3 days. Copy fee: $.75 per page. Fee is for first 10 pages; $.50 per page next 10; each add'l $.25. Certification fee: $5.00. Fee payee: Clerk of Superior Court. Personal checks accepted. Prepayment is required.

Special Civil Part Hall of Justice Complex, 101 S. 5th St., Camden, NJ 08103; 856-225-7433. Hours: 8:30AM-4:30PM (EST). *Civil Actions Under $10,000, Eviction, Small Claims.*

www.judiciary.state.nj.us/camden/index.htm

Civil Records: Access: Mail, online, in person. Both court and visitors may perform in person searches. No search fee. Required to search: name, years to search. Civil cases indexed by defendant, plaintiff. Civil records on computer from 1988. Prior records on docket books. See state introduction for information on how to sign up for online access. In person access is limited to one name.

General Information: No adoption, sealed, juvenile, expunged, restricted, or mental health records released. Turnaround time varies. Copy fee: $.75 per page for the first ten, $.50 per page for the next ten, and $.25 per page thereafter. Certification fee: $5.00. Fee payee: Clerk Special Civil Part. Personal checks accepted. Prepayment is required.

Cape May County

Superior Court - Criminal Division 9 N Main St, Superior Court, Cape May Court House, NJ 08210; 609-463-6550; Fax: 609-463-6458. Hours: 8:30AM-4:30PM (EST). *Felony.*

www.judiciary.state.nj.us/atlantic/index.htm

Criminal Records: Access: In person only. Visitors must perform in person searches for themselves. No search fee. Required to search: name, years to search, DOB; also helpful: SSN. Criminal records on computer from 1985; on index books back to 1950.

General Information: No sealed, expunged, dismissed, judges notes, PSI's, or discovery packets records released. Copy fee: $.75 per page. Certification fee: $5.00. Fee payee: State of New Jersey. Personal checks accepted. Prepayment is required.

Superior Court Civil/Equity Division-Law, DN-203, 9 N Main St, Cape May Court House, NJ 08210; 609-463-6508; Fax: 609-463-6465. Hours: 8:30AM-4:30PM (EST). *Civil Actions Over $10,000, Probate.*

www.judiciary.state.nj.us/atlantic/index.htm

Civil Records: Access: Mail, online, in person. Both court and visitors may perform in person searches. No search fee. Required to search: name, years to search. Civil cases indexed by defendant, plaintiff. Civil records on computer from 04/91, on index books and archived from 1900s. See state introduction for information on how to sign up for online access. A fee is charged for online access.

General Information: Public Access terminal is available. No sealed records released. SASE required. Turnaround time 1 week. Copy fee: pgs 1-10, $.75 per pg; pgs 11-20, $.50 per pg; over 20 pgs $.25 per pg. Certification fee: First copy free; $5.00 1st 5 pgs; $.75 per pg each add'l pg. $5.00 minimum charge. Fee payee: Clerk of Superior Court. Personal checks accepted. Prepayment is required.

Special Civil Part, DN-203, 9 N. Main St, Cape May Court House, NJ 08210; 609-463-6502; Fax: 609-463-6465. Hours: 8:30AM-4:30PM (EST). *Civil Actions Under $10,000, Eviction, Small Claims.*

www.judiciary.state.nj.us/atlantic/index.htm

Civil Records: Access: Mail, online, in person. Both court and visitors may perform in person searches. No search fee. Required to search: name, years to search; also helpful: address. Civil cases indexed by defendant, plaintiff. Civil records on computer from 4/1991, on index from 1973. See state introduction for information on how to sign up for online access. A fee is charged for remote online access.

General Information: Public Access terminal is available. No sealed records released. SASE required. Turnaround time 1 week. Copy fee: $.75 per page for the first ten pages, $.50 per page for the next ten, and $.25 per page thereafter. Certification fee: None if a party to the action; $5.00 if not. Fee payee: Clerk of the Special Civil Part. Personal checks accepted. Prepayment is required.

Cumberland County

Superior Court - Criminal Division PO Box 757, Bridgeton, NJ 08302; 856-453-4300; Fax: 856-451-7152. Hours: 8:30AM-4:30PM (EST). *Felony.*

www.judiciary.state.nj.us/gloucester/cum/index.htm

Criminal Records: Access: Mail, in person. Only the court performs in person searches; visitors may not. Search fee: $4.00 per name. Required to search: name, years to search, DOB, SSN, signed release; also helpful: address. Criminal records on computer from 1986, on index from 1900.

General Information: No sealed, expunged, dismissed, judges notes, PSI's, or discovery packets records released. SASE Required. Turnaround time 1 week. Copy fee: $.25 per page. Certification fee: $5.00. Fee payee: State of New Jersey, Misc Fund. Personal checks accepted. Prepayment is required.

Superior Court - Civil Division PO Box 757, Bridgeton, NJ 08302; 856-453-4300; Fax: 856-451-7152. Hours: 8:30AM-4:30PM (EST). *Civil Actions Over $10,000, Probate.*

www.judiciary.state.nj.us/gloucester/cum/index.htm

Civil Records: Access: Mail, online, in person. Search fee: $4.00 per name. Required to search: name, years to search. Civil records on computer from 1986, on index from 1900. See state introduction for information on how to sign up for online access.

General Information: No sealed, expunged, dismissed, judges notes, PSI's, or discovery packets records released. SASE Required. Turnaround time 1 week. Copy fee: $.25 per page. Certification fee: $5.00. Fee payee: State of New Jersey, Misc Fund. Personal checks accepted. Prepayment is required.

Special Civil Part PO Box 10, Bridgeton, NJ 08302; 856-453-4350. Hours: 8:30AM-4:30PM (EST). *Civil Actions Under $10,000, Eviction, Small Claims.*

www.judiciary.state.nj.us/gloucester/cum/index.htm

Civil Records: Access: Phone, mail, online, in person. Only the court performs in person searches; visitors may not. No search fee. Required to search: name, years to search. Civil cases indexed by defendant, plaintiff. Civil records on computer from 12/89, on docket books from 1949 to 11/89. See state introduction for information on how to sign up for online access. Phone access is limited to 1 or 2 searches.

General Information: Public Access terminal is available. No adoption, sealed, juvenile, expunged, dismissed, or mental illness records released. SASE requested. Turnaround time 1 week. Copy fee: $.75 per page for the first ten, $.50 per page for the next ten, and $.25 per page thereafter. Certification fee: No cert fee. Fee payee: Clerk, Special Civil Part. Personal checks accepted. Prepayment is required.

Essex County

Superior Court - Criminal Division 50 W Market St, Rm 610, Essex County Court Bldg, Newark, NJ 07102-1681; 973-623-5700; Fax: 973-623-5960. Hours: 8:30AM-4:30PM (EST). *Felony.*

www.judiciary.state.nj.us/essex/index.htm

Criminal Records: Access: Fax, mail, in person. Only the court performs in person searches; visitors may not. Search fee: $3.00 per name. Required to search: name, years to search, DOB, SSN, signed release. Criminal records on computer from 1985.

General Information: No sealed, expunged, dismissed, judges notes, PSI's, or discovery packets records released. SASE required. Turnaround time 1 week. Fax notes: $3.00 per page. Copy fee: $.25 per page. Certification fee: $5.00. Fee payee: State of New Jersey Judiciary. Business checks accepted. Prepayment is required.

Superior Court - Civil Division 465 Dr. Martin Luther King Blvd, Newark, NJ 07102-1681; 973-693-6460. Hours: 8:30AM-4:30PM (EST). *Civil Actions Over $10,000, Probate.*

www.judiciary.state.nj.us/essex/index.htm

Civil Records: Access: Mail, online, in person. Only the court performs in person searches; visitors may not. No search fee. Required to search: name, years to search. Civil cases indexed by defendant, plaintiff. Civil records on computer from 1984, on index from 1930. See state introduction for information on how to sign up for online access.

General Information: No sealed, expunged, dismissed, judges notes, PSI's, or discovery packets records released. SASE required. Turnaround time 1 week. Fax notes: $3.00 per page. Copy fee: $1.50 per page. Certification fee: $5.00. Fee payee: State of New Jersey Judiciary. Business checks accepted. Prepayment is required.

Special Civil Part 465 Martin Luther King Blvd, Newark, NJ 07102; 973-693-6494; 693-6458 (general info); Fax: 973-621-5914. Hours: 8:30AM-4:30PM (EST). *Civil Actions Under $10,000, Eviction, Small Claims.*

www.judiciary.state.nj.us/essex/index.htm

Civil Records: Access: Mail, online, in person. Both court and visitors may perform in person searches. No search fee. Required to search: name, years to search. Civil cases indexed by defendant, plaintiff. Civil records on computer from 1989 and archived prior. See state introduction for information on how to sign up for online access.

General Information: No adoption, sealed, juvenile, expunged, dismissed, or mental illness records released. SASE required. Turnaround time 7-10 days. Certification fee: No cert fee. Fee payee: Essex County Special Civil Part. Personal checks accepted. Prepayment is required.

Gloucester County

Superior Court - Criminal Division PO Box 187 (1 N Broad St), Woodbury, NJ 08096; 856-853-3531. Hours: 8:30AM-4:30 PM (EST). *Felony.*

www.judiciary.state.nj.us/gloucester/glo/index.htm

Criminal Records: Access: Mail, in person. Visitors must perform in person searches for themselves. Search fee: $4.00 per name. Required to search: name, years to search, DOB, SSN, signed release. Criminal records on computer from 1982, on index from 1955.

General Information: No sealed, expunged, dismissed, judges notes, PSI's, or discovery packets records released. SASE required. Turnaround time 1-3 days. Copy fee: $1.00 per page. Certification fee: $1.50. Fee payee: State of New Jersey, Miscellaneous. Personal checks accepted. Prepayment is required.

Superior Court - Civil Division 1 North Broad St, Woodbury, NJ 08096; 856-853-3250. Hours: 8:30AM-4:30 PM (EST). *Civil Actions Over $10,000, Probate.*

www.judiciary.state.nj.us/gloucester/glo/index.htm

Civil Records: Access: Mail, online, in person. Only the court performs in person searches; visitors may not. No search fee. Required to search: name, years to search. Civil cases indexed by defendant, plaintiff. Civil records on computer from 1988, prior records on county books. See state introduction for information on how to sign up for online access.

General Information: No sealed, expunged, dismissed, judges notes, PSI's, or discovery packets records released. SASE required. Turnaround time 1-2 days. Copy fee: $1.00 per page. Certification fee: $1.50. Fee payee: State of New Jersey. Personal checks accepted. Prepayment is required.

Special Civil Part Old Courthouse, 1 N Broad St., Woodbury, NJ 08096; 856-853-3392; Fax: 856-853-3416. Hours: 8:30AM-4:30PM (EST). *Civil Actions Under $10,000, Eviction, Small Claims.*

www.judiciary.state.nj.us/gloucester/glo/index.htm

Civil Records: Access: Mail, online, in person. No search fee. Required to search: name, years to search, address. Civil cases indexed by defendant, plaintiff. Civil records on computer from 08/89, on index books from 1900. See state introduction for information on how to sign up for online access.

General Information: SASE required. Copy fee: $.75 per page. Fee is for less after 10 pages. Certification fee: No cert fee. Fee payee: Clerk, Special Civil Part. Personal checks accepted. Prepayment is required.

Hudson County

Superior Court - Criminal Division 595 Newark Ave, Jersey City, NJ 07306; 201-795-6704. Hours: 8:30AM-4:30PM (EST). *Felony.*

www.judiciary.state.nj.us/hudson/index.htm

Criminal Records: Access: Mail, in person. Both court and visitors may perform in person searches. No search fee. Required to search: name, years to search, DOB, SSN. Criminal records on computer from 1985, on index books from 1900.

General Information: No sealed, expunged, dismissed, judges notes, PSI's, or discovery packets records released. Turnaround time 1 week. Copy fee: $.75 per page for the first ten pages, $.50 per page for the next ten pages, and $.25 per page thereafter. Certification fee: $5.00. An uncertified copy of a judgment of conviction is $1.50. Fee payee: Treasurer, State of New Jersey. Personal checks accepted. Prepayment is required.

Superior Court - Civil Division 583 Newark Ave, Jersey City, NJ 07306; 201-795-6723; 201-217-5163 (Records Rm). Hours: 8:30AM-4:30PM (EST). *Civil Actions Over $10,000, Probate.*

www.judiciary.state.nj.us/hudson/index.htm

Civil Records: Access: Mail, online, in person. Both court and visitors may perform in person searches. No search fee. Required to search: name, years to search. Civil cases indexed by defendant, plaintiff. Civil records on computer for three years, on index books from 1900. See state introduction for information on how to sign up for online access. Mail access is limited to one name.

General Information: No sealed, expunged, dismissed, judges notes, PSI's, or discovery packets records released. Turnaround time 1 week. Copy fee: $.35 per page. Certification fee: $5.00. Fee payee: Clerk of Superior Court. Personal checks accepted. Prepayment is required.

Special Civil Part 595 Newark Ave, Jersey City, NJ 07306; 201-795-6680. Hours: 8:30AM-4:30PM (EST). *Civil Actions Under $10,000, Eviction, Small Claims.*

www.judiciary.state.nj.us/hudson/index.htm

Civil Records: Access: Online, in person. Visitors must perform in person searches for themselves. No search fee. Required to search: name, years to search, address. Civil cases indexed by defendant, plaintiff. Civil records on index cards from 1993, prior on docket books. See state introduction for information on how to sign up for online access.

General Information: No adoptions, sealed, juvenile, expunged, dismissed, or mental illness released. Copy fee: $.75 per page. Certification fee: No cert fee. Fee payee: Clerk, Special Civil Part. Personal checks accepted. Prepayment is required.

Hunterdon County

Superior Court - Criminal Division 65 Park Ave, Flemington, NJ 08822; 908-806-4338; Fax: 908-806-4378. Hours: 8:30AM-4:30PM (EST). *Felony.*

www.judiciary.state.nj.us/somerset/index.htm

Criminal Records: Access: Fax, mail, in person. Both court and visitors may perform in person searches. Search fee: $6.00 per name. Required to search: name, years to search; also helpful: DOB, SSN. Criminal records on computer from 1987, prior on index books.

General Information: No sealed, expunged, dismissed, judges notes, PSI's, or discovery packets records released. SASE required. Turnaround time 1 week. Fax notes: Will fax results, no charge. Copy fee: $1.50 per page. Certification fee: $3.00. Fee payee: State of New Jersey. Personal checks accepted. Prepayment is required.

Superior Court - Civil Division Hunterdon County Justice Center, 65 Park Ave, Flemington, NJ 08822; 908-806-5123. Hours: 8:30AM-4:30PM (EST). *Civil Actions.*

www.judiciary.state.nj.us/somerset/index.htm

Civil Records: Access: Mail, online, in person. Both court and visitors may perform in person searches. No search fee. Required to search: name, years to search. Civil cases indexed by defendant, plaintiff. Civil records on computer for 5-8 years, on index from 1950. See state introduction for information on how to sign up for online access.

General Information: No sealed, expunged, dismissed, judges notes, PSI's, or discovery packets records released. SASE required. Turnaround time 1-2 weeks. Copy fee: $.75 per page 1st 10; $.50 for 2nd 10; $.25 each add'l. Certification fee: $5.00. Fee payee: State of New Jersey Judiciary. Personal checks accepted. Prepayment is required.

Special Civil Part County Justice Center, 65 Park Ave, 2nd Floor, Flemington, NJ 08822; 908-806-5123. Hours: 8:30AM-4:30PM (EST). *Civil Actions Under $10,000, Eviction, Small Claims.*

www.judiciary.state.nj.us/somerset/index.htm

Civil Records: Access: Phone, mail, online, in person. Only the court performs in person searches; visitors may not. No search fee. Required to search: name, years to search. Civil cases indexed by defendant, plaintiff. Civil records on computer from 1991, on index books from 1900. See state introduction for information on how to sign up for online access.

General Information: No protective order files records released. SASE required. Turnaround time 1-2 weeks. Copy fee: $.75 per page for the first ten, $.50 per page for the next ten, and $.25 per page thereafter. Certification fee: $5.00. Fee payee: Superior Court of New Jersey. Personal checks accepted. Prepayment is required.

Mercer County

Superior Court - Criminal Division 209 S. Broad, PO Box 8068, Trenton, NJ 08650-0068; 609-989-6462; Fax: 609-989-6975. Hours: 8:30AM-4:30PM; Search Hours: 9AM-3:30PM (EST). *Felony.*

www.judiciary.state.nj.us/mercer/index.htm

Criminal Records: Access: In person only. Visitors must perform in person searches for themselves. No search fee. Required to search: name, years to search, DOB, SSN. Criminal records on computer from 1985, on docket books from 1900s.

General Information: No sealed, expunged, judges notes, PSI's, or discovery packets records released. SASE required for Civil. Turnaround time up to 2 weeks. Copy fee: $.75 per page. $5.00 minimum. Fee less after 10 pages. Certification fee: $5.00. Fee payee:

Clerk of Superior Court. Personal checks accepted. Prepayment is required.

Superior Court - Civil Division 175 S Broad, PO Box 8068, Trenton, NJ 08650-0068; 609-989-6450; Fax: 609-278-5761. Hours: 8:30AM-4:30PM (EST). *Civil Actions Over $10,000, Probate.*

www.judiciary.state.nj.us/mercer/index.htm

Civil Records: Access: Fax, mail, online, in person. Only the court performs in person searches; visitors may not. No search fee. Required to search: name, years to search. Civil cases indexed by defendant, plaintiff. Civil records on computer for 3-5 years, archived from 1972, on microfiche from 1965, prior indexed from 1894. See state introduction for information on how to sign up for online access.

General Information: No sealed, expunged, dismissed, judges notes, PSI's, or discovery packets records released. SASE required for Civil. Turnaround time up to 2 weeks. Copy fee: $.75 per page. $5.00 minimum. Certification fee: $5.00. Fee payee: Clerk of Superior Court. Personal checks accepted. Prepayment is required.

Special Civil Part Box 8068, Trenton, NJ 08650; 609-989-6206; Fax: 609-278-2721. Hours: 8:30AM-4:30PM (EST). *Civil Actions Under $10,000, Eviction, Small Claims.*

www.judiciary.state.nj.us/mercer/index.htm

Civil Records: Access: Mail, online, in person. Only the court performs in person searches; visitors may not. No search fee. Required to search: name, years to search. Civil cases indexed by defendant, plaintiff. Civil records on computer from 1989, on index from 1984. See state introduction for information on how to sign up for online access.

General Information: Public Access terminal is available. No adoptions, sealed, juvenile, expunged, dismissed, or mental illness records released. Turnaround time 1 week. Copy fee: $.75 per page for the first ten pages, $.50 per page for the next ten, and $.25 per page thereafter. Certification fee: No cert fee. Fee payee: State of New Jersey. Only cashiers checks and money orders accepted.

Middlesex County

Superior Court - Criminal Division PO Box 2673 (1 JFK Sq), New Brunswick, NJ 08903; 732-981-3135. Hours: 8:30AM-4:30PM (EST). *Felony.*

www.judiciary.state.nj.us/middlesex/index.htm

Criminal Records: Access: Mail, in person. Both court and visitors may perform in person searches. Search fee: $4.00 per name. Required to search: name, years to search, DOB; also helpful: SSN, singed release. Criminal records on computer from 1981, prior on index books back to 1956.

General Information: No sealed, expunged, dismissed, judges notes, PSI's, on discovery packets records released. SASE required. Turnaround time up to 2 weeks. Copy fee: $.75 per page first 10, $.20 each next 10, Then $.25 per page. Certification fee: $6.00. Fee payee: State of New Jersey. Personal checks accepted. Prepayment is required.

Superior Court - Civil Division PO Box 2633 (1 JFK Sq), New Brunswick, NJ 08903; 732-981-3301. Hours: 8:30AM-4:30PM (EST). *Civil Actions Over $10,000, Probate.*

www.judiciary.state.nj.us/middlesex/index.htm

Civil Records: Access: Mail, online, in person. Search fee: $4.00 per name. Required to search: name, years to search. Civil cases indexed by defendant, plaintiff. Civil records on computer from 1990, on docket books from 1940. See state introduction for information on how to sign up for online access.

General Information: Public Access terminal is available. No sealed, expunged, dismissed, judges notes, PSI's, on discovery packets records released. SASE required. Turnaround time up to 1 week. Certification fee: $5.00. Fee payee: State of New Jersey, Clerk of Superior Court. Personal checks accepted. Prepayment is required.

Special Civil Part PO Box 1146 (1 JKF Sq), New Brunswick, NJ 08903; 732-981-3200. Hours: 8:30AM-4:30PM (EST). *Civil Actions Under $10,000, Eviction, Small Claims.*

www.judiciary.state.nj.us/middlesex/index.htm

Civil Records: Access: Phone, mail, online, in person. Both court and visitors may perform in person searches. No search fee. Required to search: name, years to search. Civil cases indexed by defendant, plaintiff. Civil records on computer from 1985, on docket books from 1960. See state introduction for information on how to sign up for online access.

General Information: Public Access terminal is available. No adoption, sealed, juvenile, expunged, dismissed, or mental health records released. Turnaround time 30 days. Certification fee: $5.00. Fee payee: Middlesex Special Civil Part. Personal checks accepted. Prepayment is required.

Monmouth County

Superior Court - Criminal Division 71 Monument Park, Rm 149, PO Box 1271, Freehold, NJ 07728-1271; 732-431-7880; Fax: 732-866-3565. Hours: 8:30AM-4:30PM (EST). *Felony.*

www.judiciary.state.nj.us/monmouth/index.htm

Criminal Records: Access: In person only. Visitors must perform in person searches for themselves. No search fee. Required to search: name, years to search. Criminal records on computer back to 1990, on index books from 1956.

General Information: Public Access terminal is available. (Information on civil cases only.) No sealed, expunged, dismissed, judges notes, PSI's, or discovery packets records released. Copy fee: $.75 per page. Fee is for first 10 pages; $.50 per page next 10; each add'l $.25. Certification fee: $5.00. Fee payee: State of New Jersey. Personal checks accepted. ID required for payment by personal check. Prepayment is required.

Superior Court - Civil Division PO Box 1255 (71 Monument Pk), Freehold, NJ 07728-1255; 732-431-8783. Hours: 8:30AM-4:30PM (EST). *Civil Actions Over $10,000, Probate.*

www.judiciary.state.nj.us/monmouth/index.htm

Civil Records: Access: Mail, online, in person. Visitors must perform in person searches for themselves. No search fee. Required to search: name, years to search. Civil cases indexed by defendant, plaintiff. Civil records on computer from 1990, on index books from 1956. See state introduction for information on how to sign up for online access.

General Information: Public Access terminal is available. (Information on civil cases only.) No sealed, expunged, dismissed, judges notes, PSI's, or discovery packets records released. Copy fee: $.25. Certification fee: $5.00. Fee payee: Clerk of Superior Court. Personal checks accepted. Prepayment is required.

Special Civil Part Courthouse, 71 Monument Pk., Freehold, NJ 07728; 732-577-6749. Hours: 8:30AM-4:30PM (EST). *Civil Actions Under $10,000, Eviction, Small Claims.*

www.judiciary.state.nj.us/monmouth/index.htm

Civil Records: Access: Mail, online, in person. Both court and visitors may perform in person searches. No search fee. Required to search: name, years to search. Civil cases indexed by defendant, plaintiff. Civil records on computer from 11/1/94, on index books from 1985,

prior in archives. See state introduction for information on how to sign up for online access.

General Information: Public Access terminal is available. SASE required. Turnaround time 1 day to weeks; longer if archived. Copy fee: $.75 per page. Fee is for first 10 pages; $.50 per page next 10; each add'l $.25. Certification fee: $5.00. Fee payee: Monmouth Special Civil Part. Personal checks accepted. Prepayment is required.

Morris County

Superior Court - Criminal Division PO Box 910 (Washington St), Morristown, NJ 07960-0910; 973-285-6119; Fax: 973-455-0615. Hours: 8:30AM-4:30PM (EST). *Felony.*

www.judiciary.state.nj.us/morris/index.htm

Criminal Records: Access: Fax, mail, in person. Both court and visitors may perform in person searches. No search fee. Required to search: name, years to search, DOB, SSN, signed release. Criminal records on computer from 1984, on index books from 1966.

General Information: Public Access terminal is available. No sealed, expunged, dismissed, judges notes, PSI's, or discovery packets records released. SASE required. Turnaround time 1 week. Copy fee: $.75 per page. Fee is for first 10 pages; $.50 per page next 10; each add'l $.25. Certification fee: $5.00. Fee payee: State of New Jersey. Personal checks accepted. Prepayment is required.

Superior Court - Civil Division PO Box 910 (Washington St), Morristown, NJ 07960-0910; 973-285-6165; Fax: 973-829-8413. Hours: 7:45AM-5PM (EST). *Civil Actions Over $10,000, Probate.*

www.judiciary.state.nj.us/morris/index.htm

Civil Records: Access: Online, in person. Visitors must perform in person searches for themselves. No search fee. Required to search: name, years to search; also helpful: address. Civil cases indexed by defendant, plaintiff. Civil records on computer from 1984, on index books from 1966. See state introduction for information on how to sign up for online access.

General Information: Public Access terminal is available. No sealed, expunged, dismissed, judges notes, PSI's, or discovery packets records released. Copy fee: $.25 per page. Certification fee: $5.00. Fee payee: State of New Jersey. Personal checks accepted. Prepayment is required.

Special Civil Part PO Box 910 (Court St), Morristown, NJ 07963-0910; 973-285-6150. Hours: 8:30AM-4:30PM (EST). *Civil Actions Under $10,000, Eviction, Small Claims.*

www.judiciary.state.nj.us/morris/index.htm

Civil Records: Access: Online, in person. Visitors must perform in person searches for themselves. No search fee. Required to search: name, years to search. Civil cases indexed by defendant, plaintiff. Civil records on computer from 8/1988, on index books from 1979. See state introduction for information on how to sign up for online access.

General Information: Public Access terminal is available. No adoptions, sealed, juvenile, expunged, dismissed, or mental illness records released. Turnaround time 1 week. Fax notes: Will not fax results. Copy fee: $.75 per page for first 10, $.50 per page for next 10, and $.25 per page thereafter. Public copier is $.25 per copy. Certification fee: $5.00. Fee payee: State of New Jersey. Personal checks accepted.

Ocean County

Superior Court - Criminal Division PO Box 2191, Justice Complex, Rm 220, Toms River, NJ 08754-2191; 732-929-2009. Hours: 8:30AM-4:30PM (EST). *Felony.*

www.judiciary.state.nj.us/ocean/index.htm

Criminal Records: Access: Mail, in person. Both court and visitors may perform in person searches. Search fee: $3.00 per name if court performs search. Required to search: name, years to search; also helpful: address, DOB, SSN. Criminal records on computer from 1990, on index books from 1920.

General Information: No sealed, expunged, judges notes, PSI's, or discovery packets records released. Turnaround time 1 week. Copy fee: $.75 per page, 11-20 pages $.50 per page, over 20 pages $.25 per page. Certification fee: $5.00. Fee payee: NJ State Treasurer. Personal checks accepted. Prepayment is required.

Superior Court - Civil Division 118 Washington, Toms River, NJ 08754; 732-929-2035. Hours: 8:30AM-4:30PM (EST). *Civil Actions Over $10,000, Probate.*

www.judiciary.state.nj.us/ocean/index.htm

Civil Records: Access: Mail, online, in person. Both court and visitors may perform in person searches. No search fee. Required to search: name, years to search. Civil cases indexed by defendant, plaintiff. Civil records on computer from 1989, on index books from 1920. See state introduction for information on how to sign up for online access.

General Information: Public Access terminal is available. Turnaround time 1 week. Copy fee: $.25. Certification fee: No cert fee. Fee payee: Superior Court Clerk. Personal checks accepted. Prepayment is required.

Special Civil Part Box 2191 (100 Washington St), Toms River, NJ 08754; 732-929-2016; Fax: 732-506-5398. Hours: 8AM-4:30PM (EST). *Civil Actions Under $10,000, Eviction, Small Claims.*

www.judiciary.state.nj.us/ocean/index.htm

Civil Records: Access: Fax, mail, online, in person. Both court and visitors may perform in person searches. No search fee. Required to search: name, years to search. Civil cases indexed by defendant, plaintiff. Civil records on computer from 1985, on index books from 1972, on microfilm prior. See state introduction for information on how to sign up for online access.

General Information: No adoptions, sealed, juvenile, expunged, dismissed, or mental illness records released. Turnaround time 1-2 days. Copy fee: $.75 per page first 10 pages; $.50 per page next 10; each add'l $.25. Certification fee: $5.00. Fee payee: Ocean County Special Civil Part. Personal checks accepted.

Passaic County

Superior Court - Criminal Division 77 Hamilton St., Paterson, NJ 07505-2108; 973-247-8403; Fax: 973-247-8401. Hours: 8:30AM-4:30PM *Felony.*

www.judiciary.state.nj.us/passaic/index.htm

Criminal Records: Access: Mail, in person. Both court and visitors may perform in person searches. Search fee: $5.00 per name. Required to search: name, years to search, DOB, SSN; also helpful: address. Criminal records on computer from 1986, on microfiche prior.

General Information: Public Access terminal is available. (Only criminal information can be accessed.) No sealed, expunged, dismissed, judges notes, PSI's, or discovery packets records released. Turnaround time 3-4 days. Copy fee: $.75 per page for the first 10 pages, $.50 per page for the second set of 10 pages, and $.25 per page thereafter. Certification fee: $5.00. Fee payee: Superior Court of New Jersey. Personal checks accepted. Prepayment is required.

Superior Court - Civil Division 77 Hamilton St., Paterson, NJ 07505-2108; 973-881-4078. Hours: 8:30AM-4:30PM (EST). *Civil Actions Over $10,000, Probate.*

www.judiciary.state.nj.us/passaic/index.htm

Civil Records: Access: Phone, mail, online, in person. Both court and visitors may perform in person searches. No search fee. Required to search: name, years to search. Civil cases indexed by defendant, plaintiff. Civil records on computer from 1986, on index books from 1979. See state introduction for information on how to sign up for online access. Phone access limited to short searches.

General Information: Public Access terminal is available. (Only criminal information can be accessed.) No sealed, expunged, dismissed, judges notes, PSI's, or discovery packets records released. Turnaround time up to 1 week. Copy fee: $.25 per page. Certification fee: $5.00. Fee payee: State of New Jersey or Clerk of Superior Court. Personal checks accepted. Prepayment is required.

Special Civil Part 71 Hamilton St., Paterson, NJ 07505; 973-247-8238. Hours: 8:30AM-4:30PM (EST). *Civil Actions Under $10,000, Eviction, Small Claims.*

www.judiciary.state.nj.us/passaic/index.htm

Civil Records: Access: Mail, online, in person. Both court and visitors may perform in person searches. No search fee. Required to search: name, years to search. Civil cases indexed by defendant, plaintiff. Civil records on computer from 1993, on index from 1980, prior archived. See state introduction for information on how to sign up for online access. Include phone # with written requests.

General Information: Public Access terminal is available. No adoptions, sealed, juvenile, expunged, dismissed, or mental illness records released. Turnaround time 2-3 days. Copy fee: $.75 per page. Fee is for first 10 pages; $.50 per page next 10; each add'l $.25. Certification fee: No cert fee. Fee payee: Passaic County Special Civil Part. Personal checks accepted. Prepayment is required.

Salem County

Superior Court - Criminal Division PO Box 78 (92 Market St), Salem, NJ 08079-1913; 856-935-7510. Hours: 8:30AM-4:30PM (EST). *Felony.*

www.judiciary.state.nj.us/gloucester/sal/index.htm

Criminal Records: Access: Mail, in person. Both court and visitors may perform in person searches. Search fee: $4.00 per name. Required to search: name, years to search, DOB, SSN. Criminal records on computer from 1987, indexed from 1953.

General Information: No sealed, expunged, dismissed, judges notes, PSI's, or discovery packets records released. SASE required. Turnaround time 3-4 days. Copy fee: $.25 per page. Certification fee: $5.00. Fee payee: State of New Jersey. Personal checks accepted. Prepayment is required.

Superior Court - Civil Division PO Box 29 (92 Market St), Salem, NJ 08079-1913; 856-935-7510 X8210; Probate phone: 856-935-7510 X8322; Fax: 856-935-6551. Hours: 8:30AM-4:30PM (EST). *Civil Under Over $10,000, Probate.*

www.judiciary.state.nj.us/gloucester/sal/index.htm

Note: Probate located at 92 Market Street in Salem

Civil Records: Access: Phone, fax, mail, online, in person. Only the court performs in person searches; visitors may not. No search fee. Required to search: name, years to search. Civil cases indexed by defendant, plaintiff. Civil records on computer from 1987, indexed from 1953. See state introduction for information on online access.

General Information: No sealed, expunged, dismissed, judges notes, PSI's, or discovery packets records released. SASE required. Turnaround time 1-2 days. Copy fee: $.25 per page. Certification fee: $5.00. Fee payee: Special Civil Part. Personal checks accepted. Prepayment is required.

Special Civil Part PO Box 29 (92 Market St), Salem, NJ 08079; 856-935-7510 x8214; Fax: 856-935-6551. Hours: 8:30AM-4:30PM (EST). *Civil Actions Under $10,000, Eviction, Small Claims.*

www.judiciary.state.nj.us/gloucester/sal/index.htm

Civil Records: Access: Phone, fax, mail, online, in person. Only the court performs in person searches; visitors may not. No search fee. Required to search: name, years to search. Civil cases indexed by defendant, plaintiff. Civil records on computer from 1990, on index from 1953. See state introduction for information on online access.

General Information: No adoptions, sealed, juvenile, expunged, dismissed, or mental illness records released. Turnaround time 1-2 days. Copy fee: $25per page. Certification fee: $5.00. Fee payee: Special Civil Part. Personal checks accepted. Prepayment is required.

Somerset County

Superior Court - Criminal Division PO Box 3000 (20 North Bridge St, 2nd Fl), Somerville, NJ 08876-1262; 908-231-7600. Hours: 8:30AM-4:30PM (EST). *Felony.*

www.judiciary.state.nj.us/somerset/index.htm

Criminal Records: Access: Phone, fax, mail, in person. Both court and visitors may perform in person searches. Search fee: $6.00 per name. Required to search: name, years to search, DOB; also helpful: SSN. Criminal records on computer back to 1981, prior on index books. Public access terminal does not include criminal records.

General Information: No sealed, expunged, judges notes, PSI's, or discovery packets records released. SASE required. Turnaround time 1-2 days. Copy fee: $1.50 per page. Certification fee: $3.00 plus $1.50 per page. Fee payee: State of New Jersey. Personal checks accepted. Prepayment is required.

Superior Court - Civil Division Somerset Cty Courthouse, Civil Division, PO Box 3000 (Bridge & Main St), Somerville, NJ 08876-1262; 908-231-7054. Hours: 8:30AM-4:30PM (EST). *Civil Actions Over $10,000, Probate.*

www.judiciary.state.nj.us/somerset/index.htm

Civil Records: Access: Phone, mail, online, in person. Both court and visitors may perform in person searches. No search fee. Required to search: name; also helpful: years to search. Civil cases indexed by defendant, plaintiff. Civil records on computer from 1990, prior on index books. See state introduction for information on how to sign up for online access.

General Information: Public Access terminal is available. (No information on civil, criminal only.) No sealed, expunged, dismissed, judges notes, PSI's, or discovery packets records released. SASE required. Turnaround time 1-2 days. Copy fee: $.75 per page. Fee after 1st 10 pages $.50 per pg up to 20pgs, then $.25 per pg. Certification fee: $5.00 per page. Fee payee: Superior Court of NJ. Personal checks accepted. Prepayment is required.

Special Civil Part Courthouse, Bridge and Main St, PO Box 3000, Somerville, NJ 08876-1262; 908-231-7014/7015. Hours: 8:30AM-4:30PM (EST). *Civil Actions Under $10,000, Eviction, Small Claims.*

www.judiciary.state.nj.us/somerset/index.htm

Civil Records: Access: Mail, online, in person. Both court and visitors may perform in person searches. No search fee. Required to search: name, years to search.

Civil cases indexed by defendant, plaintiff. Civil records on computer from 1990, prior on index books. See state introduction for information on how to sign up for online access. In person access requires an appointment.

General Information: Public Access terminal is available. (By appointment/For public at counter. Book help available only.) No adoptions, sealed, juvenile, expunged, dismissed, or mental illness records released. SASE required. Turnaround time varies, may be lengthy. Copy fee: $.75 per page for the first ten, $.50 per page for the next ten, and $.25 per page thereafter. Certification fee: No cert fee. Fee payee: Superior Court of New Jersey. Personal checks accepted. Prepayment is required.

Sussex County

Superior Court - Criminal Division 43-47 High St, Sussex Judicial Center, Newton, NJ 07860; 973-579-0696. 8:30AM-4:30PM (EST). *Felony.*

www.judiciary.state.nj.us/morris/index.htm

Criminal Records: Access: In person only. Visitors must perform in person searches for themselves. No search fee. Required to search: name, years to search, DOB, signed release; also helpful: SSN. Criminal records on computer from 1986, on docket books to 1950s.

General Information: No sealed, expunged, dismissed, judges notes, PSI's, or discovery packets records released. Turnaround time up to 1 week. Copy fee: $.75 per page. Fee is for first 10 pages; $.50 per page next 10; each add'l $.25. Certification fee: $6.00. Fee payee: State of New Jersey Judiciary. Only cashiers checks and money orders accepted. Prepayment is required.

Superior Court - Civil Division 43-47 High St, Sussex Judicial Center, Newton, NJ 07860; 973-579-0914/0915. Hours: 8:30AM-4:30PM (EST). *Civil Actions Over $10,000, Probate.*

www.judiciary.state.nj.us/morris/index.htm

Civil Records: Access: Phone, mail, online, in person. Only the court performs in person searches; visitors may not. No search fee. Required to search: name, years to search. Civil cases indexed by defendant, plaintiff. Civil records on computer from 1989, on microfiche by plaintiff prior to 1989, closed cases archived yearly and sent to Trenton. See state introduction for information on how to sign up for online access.

General Information: No sealed, expunged, dismissed, judges notes, PSI's, or discovery packets records released. Turnaround time up to 1 week. Copy fee: $.75 per page for the first ten pages, $.50 per page for the next ten, and $.25 per page thereafter. Certification fee: $5.00. Fee payee: Clerk of Superior Court. Personal checks accepted. Prepayment is required.

Special Civil Part 43-47 High St., Newton, NJ 07860; 973-579-0918. Hours: 8:30AM-4:30PM (EST). *Civil Actions Under $10,000, Eviction, Small Claims.*

www.judiciary.state.nj.us/morris/index.htm

Civil Records: Access: Phone, mail, online, in person. Both court and visitors may perform in person searches. No search fee. Required to search: name, years to search. Civil cases indexed by defendant, plaintiff. Civil records on computer from mid 1989, on index books from 1940. See state introduction for information on how to sign up for online access.

General Information: No adoptions, sealed, juvenile, expunged, dismissed, or mental illness records released. Turnaround time up to 2 weeks. Copy fee: $.75 per page for first 10 pages; $.50 per page next 10; each add'l $.25. Certification fee: $5.00. Fee payee: State of New Jersey Judiciary. Personal checks accepted. Prepayment is required.

Union County

Superior Court - Criminal Division County

Courthouse - New Annex, Rm 201, Elizabeth, NJ 07207; 908-659-3376; Fax: 908-659-3391. Hours: 8:30AM-4:30PM (EST). *Felony.*

www.judiciary.state.nj.us/union/index.htm

Criminal Records: Access: In person only. Visitors must perform in person searches for themselves. No search fee. Required to search: name, years to search; also helpful: DOB, SSN. Criminal records on computer from 1985 updated monthly, prior on index books from 1960. In person access available 9AM-3:30PM.

General Information: No sealed, expunged, dismissed, judges notes, PSI's, or discovery packets records released. Turnaround time is a minimum of 5 business days. Copy fee: $.75 per page. Fee is for first 10 pages; $.50 per page next 10; each add'l $.25. Certification fee: $5.00. Fee payee: State of New Jersey Judiciary. Business checks accepted. Prepayment is required.

Superior Court - Civil Division 2 Broad St,

Elizabeth, NJ 07207; 908-659-4176; Fax: 908-659-4185. Hours: 8:30AM-4:30PM (EST). *Civil Actions Over $10,000.*

www.judiciary.state.nj.us/union/index.htm

Civil Records: Access: Phone, mail, online, in person. Only the court performs in person searches; visitors may not. No search fee. Required to search: name, years to search. Civil cases indexed by defendant, plaintiff. Civil records on computer from 1988, prior records archived in Trenton NJ. See state introduction for information on how to sign up for online access.

General Information: Public Access terminal is available. No sealed, expunged, dismissed, judges notes, PSI's, or discovery packets records released. Turnaround time varies. Copy fee: $.75 per page for the first ten pages, $.50 per page for the next ten, and $.25 per page thereafter. Certification fee: $5.00. Fee payee: Clerk of Superior Court. Personal checks accepted. Prepayment is required.

Special Civil Part 2 Broad St, Elizabeth, NJ

07207; 908-659-3637/8. Hours: 8:30AM-4:30PM *Civil Actions Under $10,000, Eviction, Small Claims.*

www.judiciary.state.nj.us/union/index.htm

Civil Records: Access: Phone, mail, online, in person. Both court and visitors may perform in person searches. No search fee. Required to search: name, years to search. Civil cases indexed by defendant, plaintiff. Civil records on computer from 1993, on index books 1965, prior archived. See state introduction for information on how to sign up for online access. Phone access limited to info after 11/93.

General Information: No adoptions, sealed, juvenile, expunged, dismissed, or mental illness records released. Turnaround time varies. Copy fee: $.75 per page. Fee is for first 10 pages; $.50 per page next 10; each add'l $.25. Certification fee: $5.00. Fee payee: Special Civil Part. Personal checks accepted. Prepayment is required.

Warren County

Warren County Superior Court Criminal

Case Management Division, PO Box 900, Belvidere, NJ 07823; 908-475-6990; Fax: 908-475-6982. Hours: 8:30AM-4:30PM (EST). *Felony.*

www.judiciary.state.nj.us/somerset/index.htm

Criminal Records: Access: Phone, mail, fax, in person. Only the court performs in person searches; visitors may not. Search fee: $6.00 per name. Required to search: name, years to search, DOB; also helpful: SSN, signed release. Criminal records on computer back 10 years; prior on index cards to 1927.

General Information: No sealed, expunged, dismissed, judges notes, PSI's, or discovery packets records released. Turnaround time 2 days. Copy fee: $1.50 per page. Certification fee: $3.00. Fee payee: State of New Jersey Judiciary. Personal checks accepted. Prepayment is required.

Superior Court - Civil Division PO Box 900

(314 2nd St), Belvidere, NJ 07823; 908-475-6140. Hours: 8:30AM-4:30PM (EST). *Civil Actions Over $10,000, Probate.*

www.judiciary.state.nj.us/somerset/index.htm

Civil Records: Access: Mail, online, in person. Only the court performs in person searches; visitors may not. No search fee. Required to search: name, years to search. Civil cases indexed by defendant, plaintiff. Civil records on computer from 1990, prior on index cards. See state introduction for information on how to sign up for online access.

General Information: Public Access terminal is available. No sealed, expunged, dismissed, judges notes, PSI's, or discovery packets records released. Turnaround time 2 days. Copy fee: $.75 fee per page for first 10 pages; $.50 per page next 10; each add'l $.10. Certification fee: Certification is free for 1st page, next 5 pgs $5.00; each add'l pg $.75. Fee payee: Superior Court of New Jersey. Personal checks accepted. Prepayment is required.

Special Civil Part PO Box 900 (314 2nd St),

Belvidere, NJ 07823; 908-475-6140. Hours: 8:30AM-4:30PM (EST). *Civil Actions Under $10,000, Eviction, Small Claims.*

www.judiciary.state.nj.us/somerset/index.htm

Civil Records: Access: Mail, online, in person. Only the court performs in person searches; visitors may not. No search fee. Required to search: name, years to search. Civil cases indexed by defendant, plaintiff. Civil records on computer from 10/91, prior on index books from 1951. See state introduction for information on how to sign up for online access. In person access requires an appointment.

General Information: Public Access terminal is available. No adoptions, sealed, juvenile, expunged, dismissed, or mental illness records released. SASE required. Turnaround time 2-3 days. Copy fee: $.75 per page for the first ten pages, $.50 per page for the second ten pages, and $.25 per page thereafter. Certification fee: No cert fee. Fee payee: Clerk of Special Civil Part. Personal checks accepted. Prepayment is required.

New Jersey Recording Offices

ORGANIZATION 21 counties, 21 recording offices. The recording officer title varies depending upon the county. It is either Register of Deeds or County Clerk. The Clerk of Circuit Court records the equivalent of some state's tax liens. The entire state is in the Eastern Time Zone (EST).

REAL ESTATE RECORDS No counties will provide real estate searches. Copy and certification fees vary. Assessment and tax offices are at the municipal level.

UCC RECORDS Financing statements are filed at the state level, except for real estate related collateral, which are filed with the County Clerk. However, prior to 07/2001, consumer goods and farm collateral were also filed at the County Clerk and these older records can be searched there. About half of the recording offices will perform UCC searches. Use search request form UCC-11. Search fees are usually $25.00 per debtor name and copy fees vary.

TAX LIEN RECORDS All federal tax liens are filed with the County Clerk/Register of Deeds and are indexed separately from all other liens. State tax liens comprise two categories - certificates of debt are filed with the Clerk of Superior Court (some, called docketed judgments are filed specifically with the Trenton court), and warrants of execution are filed with the County Clerk/Register of Deeds. Few counties will provide tax lien searches. Refer to the County Court section for information about New Jersey Superior Courts.

OTHER LIENS Judgment, mechanics, bail bond.

STATEWIDE ONLINE INFO: A statewide database of property tax records can be accessed at http://taxrecords.com.

Atlantic County
County Clerk, 5901 Main Street, Courthouse-CN 2005, Mays Landing, NJ 08330-1797. 609-625-4011; Fax 609-625-4738. www.atlanticcountyclerk.org
Will search UCC records. Will not search real estate records. **Online Access:** Real Estate. Property records for communities along the Jersey Shore in Atlantic county are available free online at www.philly.com/packages/njshore/lookup.htm. Site is sponsored by the Philadelphia Inquirer. Search by clicking on community name, then search by owner name, owner's city/state, address, or property value range.

Bergen County
County Clerk, Justice Center Room 214, 10 Main St., Hackensack, NJ 07601-7000. 201-646-2291.
Will search UCC records. Tax liens not included in UCC search. Will not search real estate records. **Other Phone Numbers:** Assessor 201-646-3185; Treasurer 201-646-3237.

Burlington County
County Clerk, P.O. Box 6000, Mount Holly, NJ 08060. 609-265-5180; Fax 609-265-0696.
Will search UCC records. Will not search real estate records. **Other Phone Numbers:** Assessor 609-265-5056.

Camden County
County Clerk, Courthouse Room 102, 520 Market Street, Camden, NJ 08102-1375. County Clerk, R/E and UCC Recording 856-225-5300; Fax 856-225-7100.
Will search UCC records. This agency will not do a tax lien search. Computer index for all transactions after August 1988

Cape May County
County Clerk, P.O. Box 5000, Cape May Court House, NJ 08210-5000. County Clerk, R/E and UCC Recording 609-465-1010; Fax 609-465-8625. http://www.co.cape-may.nj.us/CLERKCMC.HTM
Will not search UCC records or tax liens Will not search real estate records. **Online Access:** Real Estate. Property records for communities along the Jersey Shore in Cape May county are available free online at www.philly.com/packages/njshore/lookup.htm. Site is sponsored by the Philadelphia Inquirer. Search by clicking on community name, then search by owner name, owner's city/state, address, or property value range. **Other Phone Numbers:** Elections 609-465-1013; Vital Records 609-465-1023.

Cumberland County
County Clerk, P.O. Box 716, Bridgeton, NJ 08302. 856-453-4864; Fax 856-455-1410.
Will search UCC records. Will not search real estate records.

Essex County
County Register of Deeds, 465 Martin Luther King Boulevard, Hall of Records, Room 130, Newark, NJ 07102. 973-621-4960; Fax 973-621-6114. http://www.essexregister.com
Will search UCC records. This agency will not do a tax lien search. Will not search real estate records. **Other Phone Numbers:** Assessor 973-673-2344; Treasurer 973-621-4997.

Gloucester County
County Clerk, P.O. Box 129, Woodbury, NJ 08096-0129. County Clerk, R/E and UCC Recording 856-853-3230; Fax 856-853-3327. http://www.co.gloucester.nj.us
Will search UCC records. This agency will not do a tax lien search. Will not search real estate records. **Online Access:** Real Estate, Recording. County Recorder records are accessible through a private online service at www.landaccess.com; Fees and registration are required. **Other Phone Numbers:** Assessor 856-384-6945; Treasurer 856-853-3353; Elections 856-853-3243; Tx Collector 856-853-6945.

Hudson County
County Clerk, 595 Newark Ave, Room 105, Jersey City, NJ 07306. 201-795-6571; Fax 201-795-5179.
Will search UCC records. Will not search real estate records.

Hunterdon County
County Clerk, 71 Main Street, Hall of Records, Flemington, NJ 08822. 908-788-1221; Fax 908-782-4068.
Will search UCC records. Will not search real estate records. **Other Phone Numbers:** Assessor 908-788-1173.

Mercer County
County Clerk, 209 South Broad Street, Courthouse, Room 100, Trenton, NJ 08650. 609-989-6466 R/E Recording: 609-989-6487 UCC Recording: 609-989-6487; Fax 609-989-1111. www.mercercounty.org
Will not search real estate records. **Other Phone Numbers:** Assessor 609-989-6704; Treasurer 609-989-6694; Elections 609-989-6495; Vital Records 609-292-4087.

Middlesex County
County Clerk, P.O. Box 1110, New Brunswick, NJ 08903. 732-745-3204.
Will search UCC records. This agency will not do a tax lien search. Will not search real estate records. **Other Phone Numbers:** Assessor 732-745-3000; Treasurer 732-754-3482.

Monmouth County
County Clerk, Hall of Records, Main Street, Room 102, Freehold, NJ 07728. 732-431-7321.
Will search UCC records. This agency will not do a tax lien search. Will not search real estate records.

Morris County
County Clerk, P.O. Box 315, Morristown, NJ 07963-0315. 973-285-6135; Fax 973-285-5231.
Will search UCC records. Will not search real estate records.

Ocean County
County Clerk, P.O. Box 2191, Toms River, NJ 08754. 732-929-2110; Fax 732-349-4336. http://www.oceancountyclerk.com
Will search UCC records. This agency will not do a tax lien search. Will not search real estate records. **Online Access:** Property Tax, Real Estate. Land records on the County Clerk database are available free online at www.oceancountyclerk.com/search.htm. Search by parties, document or instrument type, or township. Also, property records for communities along the Jersey Shore in Ocean County are available free online at www.philly.com/packages/njshore/lookup.htm. Site is sponsored by the Philadelphia Inquirer. Tax records for Ocean county are also available on the taxrecords.com web site at http://oc.taxrecords.com. Search by name, address or property description.

Passaic County

County Register of Deeds, 77 Hamilton Street, Courthouse, Paterson, NJ 07505. 973-881-4777.
Will search UCC records. This agency will not do a tax lien search. Will not search real estate records. **Other Phone Numbers:** Treasurer 201-881-4777 x931.

Salem County

County Clerk, 92 Market Street, Salem, NJ 08079-1911. 856-935-7510 x8218; Fax 856-935-8882.
Will search UCC records. Will not search real estate records. **Other Phone Numbers:** Assessor 856-935-9231; Treasurer 856-935–9036.

Somerset County

County Clerk, P.O. Box 3000, Somerville, NJ 08876. 908-231-7006.

Will search UCC records. This agency will not do a tax lien search. Will not search real estate records. **Other Phone Numbers:** Treasurer 908-231-7000 x7631.

Sussex County

County Clerk, 4 Park Place, Hall of Records, Newton, NJ 07860-1795. County Clerk, R/E and UCC Recording 973-579-0900; Fax 973-383-7493. http://www.sussexcountyclerk.com/recording.html
Will not search UCC records. Will not search real estate records. **Other Phone Numbers:** Assessor 973-579-0970; Treasurer 973-579-0330; Elections 973-579-0950.

Union County

County Clerk, 2 Broad Street, Courthouse, Room 115, Elizabeth, NJ 07207. County Clerk, R/E and UCC Recording 908-527-4787 UCC Recording: 908-527-

4794; Fax 908-558-2589. http://www.union countynj.org/constit/clerk/record.html
Will search UCC records. This agency will not do a tax lien search. Will not search real estate records. **Other Phone Numbers:** Elections 908-527-4996.

Warren County

County Clerk, 413 Second Street, Courthouse, Belvidere, NJ 07823-1500. County Clerk, R/E and UCC Recording 908-475-6211.
Will not search UCC records. This agency will not do a tax lien search. Will not search real estate records. **Other Phone Numbers:** Elections 908-475-6211.

New Jersey County Locator

You will usually be able to find the city name in the City/County Cross Reference below. In that case, it is a simple matter to determine the county from the cross reference. However, only the official US Postal Service city names are included in this index. There are an additional 40,000 place names that people use in their addresses. Therefore, we have also included a ZIP/City Cross Reference immediately following the City/County Cross Reference.

If you know the ZIP Code but the city name does not appear in the City/County Cross Reference index, look up the ZIP Code in the ZIP/City Cross Reference, find the city name, then look up the city name in the City/County Cross Reference. For example, you want to know the county for an address of Menands, NY 12204. There is no "Menands" in the City/County Cross Reference. The ZIP/City Cross Reference shows that ZIP Codes 12201-12288 are for the city of Albany. Looking back in the City/County Cross Reference, Albany is in Albany County.

City/County Cross Reference

ABSECON Atlantic
ADELPHIA Monmouth
ALLAMUCHY Warren
ALLENDALE Bergen
ALLENHURST Monmouth
ALLENTOWN (08501) Monmouth(65),
   Mercer(19), Burlington(16)
ALLENWOOD Monmouth
ALLOWAY Salem
ALPINE Bergen
ANDOVER Sussex
ANNANDALE Hunterdon
ASBURY (08802) Hunterdon(71),
   Warren(29)
ASBURY PARK Monmouth
ATCO (08004) Camden(85), Burlington(15)
ATLANTIC CITY Atlantic
ATLANTIC HIGHLANDS Monmouth
AUDUBON Camden
AUGUSTA Sussex
AVALON Cape May
AVENEL Middlesex
AVON BY THE SEA Monmouth
BAPTISTOWN Hunterdon
BARNEGAT Ocean
BARNEGAT LIGHT Ocean
BARRINGTON Camden
BASKING RIDGE Somerset
BAYONNE Hudson
BAYVILLE Ocean
BEACH HAVEN Ocean
BEACHWOOD Ocean
BEDMINSTER Somerset
BELFORD Monmouth
BELLE MEAD Somerset
BELLEVILLE Essex
BELLMAWR Camden
BELMAR Monmouth
BELVIDERE Warren
BERGENFIELD Bergen
BERKELEY HEIGHTS Union
BERLIN Camden
BERNARDSVILLE Somerset
BEVERLY Burlington
BIRMINGHAM Burlington
BLACKWOOD (08012) Camden(56),
   Gloucester(45)
BLAIRSTOWN Warren
BLAWENBURG Somerset
BLOOMFIELD Essex
BLOOMINGDALE Passaic
BLOOMSBURY (08804) Warren(94),
   Hunterdon(6)
BOGOTA Bergen
BOONTON Morris
BORDENTOWN Burlington
BOUND BROOK Somerset
BRADLEY BEACH Monmouth
BRANCHVILLE (07826) Sussex(92),
   Morris(9)
BRANCHVILLE Sussex
BRICK Ocean
BRIDGEPORT Gloucester
BRIDGETON (08302) Cumberland(94),
   Salem(6)
BRIDGEWATER Somerset

BRIELLE Monmouth
BRIGANTINE Atlantic
BROADWAY Warren
BROOKSIDE Morris
BROWNS MILLS Burlington
BUDD LAKE Morris
BUENA Atlantic
BURLINGTON Burlington
BUTLER Morris
BUTTZVILLE Warren
CALDWELL Essex
CALIFON (07830) Hunterdon(90),
   Morris(9), Warren(1)
CAMDEN Camden
CAPE MAY Cape May
CAPE MAY COURT HOUSE Cape May
CAPE MAY POINT Cape May
CARLSTADT Bergen
CARTERET Middlesex
CEDAR BROOK Camden
CEDAR GROVE Essex
CEDAR KNOLLS Morris
CEDARVILLE Cumberland
CHANGEWATER Warren
CHATHAM Morris
CHATSWORTH Burlington
CHERRY HILL Camden
CHESTER Morris
CLARK Union
CLARKSBORO Gloucester
CLARKSBURG (99999) Monmouth(99),
   Ocean(1)
CLAYTON Gloucester
CLEMENTON Camden
CLIFFSIDE PARK Bergen
CLIFFWOOD Monmouth
CLIFTON Passaic
CLINTON Hunterdon
CLOSTER Bergen
COLLINGSWOOD Camden
COLOGNE Atlantic
COLONIA Middlesex
COLTS NECK Monmouth
COLUMBIA Warren
COLUMBUS Burlington
COOKSTOWN Burlington
CRANBURY (08512) Middlesex(72),
   Mercer(29)
CRANBURY Middlesex
CRANFORD Union
CREAMRIDGE (08514) Monmouth(70),
   Ocean(30)
CRESSKILL Bergen
CROSSWICKS Burlington
DAYTON Middlesex
DEAL Monmouth
DEEPWATER Salem
DEERFIELD STREET Cumberland
DELAWARE Warren
DELMONT Cumberland
DEMAREST Bergen
DENNISVILLE Cape May
DENVILLE Morris
DIVIDING CREEK Cumberland
DORCHESTER Cumberland
DOROTHY Atlantic

DOVER Morris
DUMONT Bergen
DUNELLEN (08812) Somerset(52),
   Middlesex(48)
EAST BRUNSWICK Middlesex
EAST HANOVER Morris
EAST ORANGE Essex
EAST RUTHERFORD Bergen
EATONTOWN Monmouth
EDGEWATER Bergen
EDISON Middlesex
EGG HARBOR CITY (08215) Atlantic(99),
   Burlington(1)
EGG HARBOR TOWNSHIP Atlantic
ELIZABETH Union
ELMER Salem
ELMWOOD PARK Bergen
ELWOOD Atlantic
EMERSON Bergen
ENGLEWOOD Bergen
ENGLEWOOD CLIFFS Bergen
ENGLISHTOWN Monmouth
ESSEX FELLS Essex
ESTELL MANOR Atlantic
EWAN Gloucester
FAIR HAVEN Monmouth
FAIR LAWN Bergen
FAIRFIELD Essex
FAIRTON Cumberland
FAIRVIEW Bergen
FANWOOD Union
FAR HILLS (07931) Somerset(83),
   Morris(17)
FARMINGDALE Monmouth
FLAGTOWN Somerset
FLANDERS Morris
FLEMINGTON Hunterdon
FLORENCE Burlington
FLORHAM PARK Morris
FORDS Middlesex
FORKED RIVER Ocean
FORT LEE Bergen
FORT MONMOUTH Monmouth
FORTESCUE Cumberland
FRANKLIN Sussex
FRANKLIN LAKES Bergen
FRANKLIN PARK Somerset
FRANKLINVILLE Gloucester
FREEHOLD Monmouth
FRENCHTOWN Hunterdon
GARFIELD Bergen
GARWOOD Union
GIBBSBORO Camden
GIBBSTOWN Gloucester
GILLETTE Morris
GLADSTONE Somerset
GLASSBORO Gloucester
GLASSER Sussex
GLEN GARDNER Hunterdon
GLEN RIDGE Essex
GLEN ROCK Bergen
GLENDORA Camden
GLENWOOD Sussex
GLOUCESTER CITY Camden
GOSHEN Cape May
GREAT MEADOWS Warren

GREEN CREEK Cape May
GREEN VILLAGE Morris
GREENDELL Sussex
GREENWICH Cumberland
GRENLOCH Gloucester
HACKENSACK Bergen
HACKETTSTOWN (07840) Warren(83),
   Morris(17)
HADDON HEIGHTS Camden
HADDONFIELD Camden
HAINESPORT Burlington
HALEDON Passaic
HAMBURG Sussex
HAMMONTON (08037) Atlantic(83),
   Camden(18)
HAMPTON Hunterdon
HANCOCKS BRIDGE Salem
HARRINGTON PARK Bergen
HARRISON Hudson
HARRISONVILLE Gloucester
HASBROUCK HEIGHTS Bergen
HASKELL Passaic
HAWORTH Bergen
HAWTHORNE Passaic
HAZLET Monmouth
HEISLERVILLE Cumberland
HELMETTA Middlesex
HEWITT Passaic
HIBERNIA Morris
HIGH BRIDGE Hunterdon
HIGHLAND LAKES Sussex
HIGHLAND PARK Middlesex
HIGHLANDS Monmouth
HIGHTSTOWN (08520) Mercer(97),
   Middlesex(2), Monmouth(1)
HILLSDALE Bergen
HILLSIDE Union
HO HO KUS Bergen
HOBOKEN Hudson
HOLMDEL Monmouth
HOPATCONG Sussex
HOPE Warren
HOPEWELL (08525) Mercer(93),
   Hunterdon(7)
HOWELL Monmouth
IMLAYSTOWN Monmouth
IRONIA Morris
IRVINGTON Essex
ISELIN Middlesex
ISLAND HEIGHTS Ocean
JACKSON Ocean
JAMESBURG Middlesex
JERSEY CITY Hudson
JOBSTOWN Burlington
JOHNSONBURG Warren
JULIUSTOWN Burlington
KEANSBURG Monmouth
KEARNY Hudson
KEASBEY Middlesex
KENDALL PARK Middlesex
KENILWORTH Union
KENVIL Morris
KEYPORT (07735) Monmouth(92),
   Middlesex(8)
KINGSTON Somerset
KIRKWOOD VOORHEES Camden

LAFAYETTE Sussex
LAKE HIAWATHA Morris
LAKE HOPATCONG Morris
LAKEHURST Ocean
LAKEWOOD Ocean
LAMBERTVILLE (08530) Hunterdon(96),
   Mercer(4)
LANDING Morris
LANDISVILLE Atlantic
LANOKA HARBOR Ocean
LAVALLETTE Ocean
LAWNSIDE Camden
LAYTON Sussex
LEBANON Hunterdon
LEDGEWOOD Morris
LEEDS POINT Atlantic
LEESBURG Cumberland
LEONARDO Monmouth
LEONIA Bergen
LIBERTY CORNER Somerset
LINCOLN PARK Morris
LINCROFT Monmouth
LINDEN Union
LINWOOD Atlantic
LITTLE FALLS Passaic
LITTLE FERRY Bergen
LITTLE SILVER Monmouth
LITTLE YORK Hunterdon
LIVINGSTON Essex
LODI Bergen
LONG BRANCH Monmouth
LONG VALLEY Morris
LONGPORT Atlantic
LUMBERTON Burlington
LYNDHURST Bergen
LYONS Somerset
MADISON Morris
MAGNOLIA Camden
MAHWAH Bergen
MALAGA Gloucester
MANAHAWKIN Ocean
MANASQUAN Monmouth
MANTOLOKING Ocean
MANTUA Gloucester
MANVILLE Somerset
MAPLE SHADE Burlington
MAPLEWOOD Essex
MARGATE CITY Atlantic
MARLBORO Monmouth
MARLTON Burlington
MARMORA Cape May
MARTINSVILLE Somerset
MATAWAN (07747) Monmouth(82),
   Middlesex(18)
MAURICETOWN Cumberland
MAYS LANDING Atlantic
MAYWOOD Bergen
MC AFEE Sussex
MEDFORD Burlington
MENDHAM Morris
MERCHANTVILLE Camden
METUCHEN Middlesex
MICKLETON Gloucester
MIDDLESEX Middlesex
MIDDLETOWN Monmouth
MIDDLEVILLE Sussex
MIDLAND PARK Bergen
MILFORD Hunterdon
MILLBURN Essex
MILLINGTON Morris
MILLTOWN Middlesex
MILLVILLE Cumberland
MILMAY (08340) Cumberland(52),
   Atlantic(48)
MINE HILL Morris
MINOTOLA Atlantic
MIZPAH Atlantic
MONMOUTH BEACH Monmouth
MONMOUTH JUNCTION Middlesex
MONROEVILLE (08343) Gloucester(69),
   Salem(31)
MONTAGUE (07827) Sussex(98), Morris(2)

MONTCLAIR (07043) Essex(97),
   Passaic(3)
MONTCLAIR Essex
MONTVALE Bergen
MONTVILLE Morris
MOONACHIE Bergen
MOORESTOWN Burlington
MORGANVILLE Monmouth
MORRIS PLAINS Morris
MORRISTOWN Morris
MOUNT ARLINGTON Morris
MOUNT EPHRAIM Camden
MOUNT FREEDOM Morris
MOUNT HOLLY Burlington
MOUNT LAUREL Burlington
MOUNT ROYAL Gloucester
MOUNT TABOR Morris
MOUNTAIN LAKES Morris
MOUNTAINSIDE Union
MULLICA HILL Gloucester
MUSICAL HERITAGE Monmouth
NATIONAL PARK Gloucester
NAVESINK Monmouth
NEPTUNE Monmouth
NESHANIC STATION Somerset
NETCONG Morris
NEW BRUNSWICK Middlesex
NEW EGYPT Ocean
NEW GRETNA Burlington
NEW LISBON Burlington
NEW MILFORD Bergen
NEW PROVIDENCE Union
NEW VERNON Morris
NEWARK Essex
NEWFIELD (08344) Gloucester(72),
   Cumberland(15), Salem(10), Atlantic(3)
NEWFOUNDLAND Passaic
NEWPORT Cumberland
NEWTON Sussex
NEWTONVILLE Atlantic
NORMA Salem
NORMANDY BEACH Ocean
NORTH ARLINGTON Bergen
NORTH BERGEN Hudson
NORTH BRUNSWICK Middlesex
NORTHFIELD Atlantic
NORTHVALE Bergen
NORWOOD Bergen
NUTLEY Essex
OAK RIDGE (07438) Passaic(78),
   Morris(22)
OAKHURST Monmouth
OAKLAND Bergen
OAKLYN Camden
OCEAN CITY Cape May
OCEAN GATE Ocean
OCEAN GROVE Monmouth
OCEAN VIEW Cape May
OCEANPORT Monmouth
OCEANVILLE Atlantic
OGDENSBURG Sussex
OLD BRIDGE Middlesex
OLDWICK Hunterdon
ORADELL Bergen
ORANGE Essex
OXFORD Warren
PALISADES PARK Bergen
PALMYRA Burlington
PARAMUS Bergen
PARK RIDGE Bergen
PARLIN Middlesex
PARSIPPANY Morris
PASSAIC Passaic
PATERSON Passaic
PAULSBORO Gloucester
PEAPACK Somerset
PEDRICKTOWN Salem
PEMBERTON Burlington
PENNINGTON Mercer
PENNS GROVE Salem
PENNSAUKEN Camden
PENNSVILLE Salem

PEQUANNOCK Morris
PERRINEVILLE (08535) Monmouth(88),
   Ocean(12)
PERTH AMBOY Middlesex
PHILLIPSBURG Warren
PICATINNY ARSENAL Morris
PINE BEACH Ocean
PINE BROOK Morris
PISCATAWAY Middlesex
PITMAN Gloucester
PITTSTOWN Hunterdon
PLAINFIELD (07060) Union(55),
   Somerset(45)
PLAINFIELD (07062) Union(92),
   Somerset(8)
PLAINFIELD (07063) Union(71),
   Somerset(29)
PLAINFIELD Union
PLAINSBORO Middlesex
PLEASANTVILLE Atlantic
PLUCKEMIN Somerset
POINT PLEASANT BEACH Ocean
POMONA Atlantic
POMPTON LAKES Passaic
POMPTON PLAINS Morris
PORT ELIZABETH Cumberland
PORT MONMOUTH Monmouth
PORT MURRAY Warren
PORT NORRIS Cumberland
PORT READING Middlesex
PORT REPUBLIC Atlantic
POTTERSVILLE Hunterdon
PRINCETON (08540) Mercer(75),
   Middlesex(13), Somerset(12)
PRINCETON Mercer
PRINCETON JUNCTION Mercer
QUAKERTOWN Hunterdon
QUINTON Salem
RAHWAY Union
RAMSEY Bergen
RANCOCAS Burlington
RANDOLPH Morris
RARITAN Somerset
READINGTON Hunterdon
RED BANK Monmouth
RICHLAND Atlantic
RICHWOOD Gloucester
RIDGEFIELD Bergen
RIDGEFIELD PARK Bergen
RIDGEWOOD Bergen
RINGOES Hunterdon
RINGWOOD Passaic
RIO GRANDE Cape May
RIVER EDGE Bergen
RIVERDALE Morris
RIVERSIDE Burlington
RIVERTON Burlington
ROCHELLE PARK Bergen
ROCKAWAY Morris
ROCKY HILL Somerset
ROEBLING Burlington
ROOSEVELT Monmouth
ROSELAND Essex
ROSELLE Union
ROSELLE PARK Union
ROSEMONT Hunterdon
ROSENHAYN Cumberland
RUMSON Monmouth
RUNNEMEDE Camden
RUTHERFORD Bergen
SADDLE BROOK Bergen
SADDLE RIVER Bergen
SALEM Salem
SAYREVILLE Middlesex
SCHOOLEYS MOUNTAIN Morris
SCOTCH PLAINS Union
SEA GIRT Monmouth
SEA ISLE CITY Cape May
SEASIDE HEIGHTS Ocean
SEASIDE PARK Ocean
SECAUCUS Hudson
SERGEANTSVILLE Hunterdon

SEWAREN Middlesex
SEWELL Gloucester
SHILOH Cumberland
SHORT HILLS Essex
SHREWSBURY Monmouth
SICKLERVILLE (08081) Camden(97),
   Gloucester(4)
SKILLMAN (08558) Somerset(99),
   Mercer(1)
SOMERDALE Camden
SOMERS POINT Atlantic
SOMERSET Somerset
SOMERVILLE Somerset
SOUTH AMBOY Middlesex
SOUTH BOUND BROOK Somerset
SOUTH DENNIS Cape May
SOUTH HACKENSACK Bergen
SOUTH ORANGE Essex
SOUTH PLAINFIELD Middlesex
SOUTH RIVER Middlesex
SOUTH SEAVILLE Cape May
SPARTA Sussex
SPOTSWOOD Middlesex
SPRING LAKE Monmouth
SPRINGFIELD Union
STANHOPE Sussex
STANTON Hunterdon
STEWARTSVILLE Warren
STILLWATER Sussex
STIRLING Morris
STOCKHOLM (07460) Sussex(94),
   Morris(4), Passaic(2)
STOCKTON Hunterdon
STONE HARBOR Cape May
STRATFORD Camden
STRATHMERE Cape May
SUCCASUNNA Morris
SUMMIT Union
SUSSEX Sussex
SWARTSWOOD Sussex
SWEDESBORO (08085) Gloucester(97),
   Salem(3)
TEANECK Bergen
TENAFLY Bergen
TENNENT Monmouth
TETERBORO Bergen
THOROFARE Gloucester
THREE BRIDGES Hunterdon
TITUSVILLE Mercer
TOMS RIVER Ocean
TOTOWA Passaic
TOWACO Morris
TRANQUILITY Sussex
TRENTON (08620) Mercer(86),
   Burlington(14)
TRENTON (08691) Mercer(96),
   Monmouth(4)
TRENTON Burlington
TRENTON Mercer
TUCKAHOE Cape May
TUCKERTON (08087) Ocean(94),
   Burlington(6)
UNION Union
UNION CITY Hudson
VAUXHALL Union
VENTNOR CITY Atlantic
VERNON Sussex
VERONA Essex
VIENNA Warren
VILLAS Cape May
VINCENTOWN Burlington
VINELAND (08360) Cumberland(90),
   Atlantic(6), Gloucester(4)
VINELAND Cumberland
VOORHEES Camden
WALDWICK Bergen
WALLINGTON Bergen
WALLPACK CENTER Sussex
WANAQUE Passaic
WARETOWN Ocean
WARREN Somerset
WASHINGTON Warren

WATERFORD WORKS Camden	WESTFIELD Union	WICKATUNK Monmouth	WOODBINE (08270) Cape May(89),
WAYNE Passaic	WESTVILLE Gloucester	WILDWOOD Cape May	Atlantic(12)
WENONAH Gloucester	WESTWOOD Bergen	WILLIAMSTOWN (08094) Gloucester(89),	WOODBRIDGE Middlesex
WEST BERLIN Camden	WHARTON Morris	Atlantic(11)	WOODBURY Gloucester
WEST CREEK Ocean	WHIPPANY Morris	WILLINGBORO Burlington	WOODBURY HEIGHTS Gloucester
WEST LONG BRANCH Monmouth	WHITEHOUSE Hunterdon	WINDSOR Mercer	WOODSTOWN Salem
WEST MILFORD Passaic	WHITEHOUSE STATION Hunterdon	WINSLOW Camden	WRIGHTSTOWN Burlington
WEST NEW YORK Hudson	WHITESBORO Cape May	WOOD RIDGE Bergen	WYCKOFF Bergen
WEST ORANGE Essex	WHITING Ocean		ZAREPHATH Somerset

ZIP/City Cross Reference

07001-07001	AVENEL	07096-07096	SECAUCUS	07624-07624	CLOSTER	07758-07758	PORT MONMOUTH
07002-07002	BAYONNE	07097-07097	JERSEY CITY	07626-07626	CRESSKILL	07760-07760	RUMSON
07003-07003	BLOOMFIELD	07099-07099	KEARNY	07627-07627	DEMAREST	07762-07762	SPRING LAKE
07004-07004	FAIRFIELD	07101-07108	NEWARK	07628-07628	DUMONT	07763-07763	TENNENT
07005-07005	BOONTON	07109-07109	BELLEVILLE	07630-07630	EMERSON	07764-07764	WEST LONG BRANCH
07006-07007	CALDWELL	07110-07110	NUTLEY	07631-07631	ENGLEWOOD	07765-07765	WICKATUNK
07008-07008	CARTERET	07111-07111	IRVINGTON	07632-07632	ENGLEWOOD CLIFFS	07777-07777	HOLMDEL
07009-07009	CEDAR GROVE	07112-07199	NEWARK	07640-07640	HARRINGTON PARK	07799-07799	EATONTOWN
07010-07010	CLIFFSIDE PARK	07201-07202	ELIZABETH	07641-07641	HAWORTH	07801-07802	DOVER
07011-07015	CLIFTON	07203-07203	ROSELLE	07642-07642	HILLSDALE	07803-07803	MINE HILL
07016-07016	CRANFORD	07204-07204	ROSELLE PARK	07643-07643	LITTLE FERRY	07806-07806	PICATINNY ARSENAL
07017-07019	EAST ORANGE	07205-07205	HILLSIDE	07644-07644	LODI	07820-07820	ALLAMUCHY
07020-07020	EDGEWATER	07206-07216	ELIZABETH	07645-07645	MONTVALE	07821-07821	ANDOVER
07021-07021	ESSEX FELLS	07302-07399	JERSEY CITY	07646-07646	NEW MILFORD	07822-07822	AUGUSTA
07022-07022	FAIRVIEW	07401-07401	ALLENDALE	07647-07647	NORTHVALE	07823-07823	BELVIDERE
07023-07023	FANWOOD	07403-07403	BLOOMINGDALE	07648-07648	NORWOOD	07825-07825	BLAIRSTOWN
07024-07024	FORT LEE	07405-07405	BUTLER	07649-07649	ORADELL	07826-07826	BRANCHVILLE
07026-07026	GARFIELD	07407-07407	ELMWOOD PARK	07650-07650	PALISADES PARK	07827-07827	MONTAGUE
07027-07027	GARWOOD	07410-07410	FAIR LAWN	07652-07653	PARAMUS	07828-07828	BUDD LAKE
07028-07028	GLEN RIDGE	07416-07416	FRANKLIN	07656-07656	PARK RIDGE	07829-07829	BUTTZVILLE
07029-07029	HARRISON	07417-07417	FRANKLIN LAKES	07657-07657	RIDGEFIELD	07830-07830	CALIFON
07030-07030	HOBOKEN	07418-07418	GLENWOOD	07660-07660	RIDGEFIELD PARK	07831-07831	CHANGEWATER
07031-07031	NORTH ARLINGTON	07419-07419	HAMBURG	07661-07661	RIVER EDGE	07832-07832	COLUMBIA
07032-07032	KEARNY	07420-07420	HASKELL	07662-07662	ROCHELLE PARK	07833-07833	DELAWARE
07033-07033	KENILWORTH	07421-07421	HEWITT	07663-07663	SADDLE BROOK	07834-07834	DENVILLE
07034-07034	LAKE HIAWATHA	07422-07422	HIGHLAND LAKES	07666-07666	TEANECK	07836-07836	FLANDERS
07035-07035	LINCOLN PARK	07423-07423	HO HO KUS	07670-07670	TENAFLY	07837-07837	GLASSER
07036-07036	LINDEN	07424-07424	LITTLE FALLS	07675-07675	WESTWOOD	07838-07838	GREAT MEADOWS
07039-07039	LIVINGSTON	07428-07428	MC AFEE	07688-07688	TEANECK	07839-07839	GREENDELL
07040-07040	MAPLEWOOD	07430-07430	MAHWAH	07701-07701	RED BANK	07840-07840	HACKETTSTOWN
07041-07041	MILLBURN	07432-07432	MIDLAND PARK	07702-07702	SHREWSBURY	07842-07842	HIBERNIA
07042-07043	MONTCLAIR	07435-07435	NEWFOUNDLAND	07703-07703	FORT MONMOUTH	07843-07843	HOPATCONG
07044-07044	VERONA	07436-07436	OAKLAND	07704-07704	FAIR HAVEN	07844-07844	HOPE
07045-07045	MONTVILLE	07438-07438	OAK RIDGE	07709-07709	ALLENHURST	07845-07845	IRONIA
07046-07046	MOUNTAIN LAKES	07439-07439	OGDENSBURG	07710-07710	ADELPHIA	07846-07846	JOHNSONBURG
07047-07047	NORTH BERGEN	07440-07440	PEQUANNOCK	07711-07711	ALLENHURST	07847-07847	KENVIL
07050-07051	ORANGE	07442-07442	POMPTON LAKES	07712-07712	ASBURY PARK	07848-07848	LAFAYETTE
07052-07052	WEST ORANGE	07444-07444	POMPTON PLAINS	07715-07715	BELMAR	07849-07849	LAKE HOPATCONG
07054-07054	PARSIPPANY	07446-07446	RAMSEY	07716-07716	ATLANTIC HIGHLANDS	07850-07850	LANDING
07055-07055	PASSAIC	07450-07451	RIDGEWOOD	07717-07717	AVON BY THE SEA	07851-07851	LAYTON
07057-07057	WALLINGTON	07452-07452	GLEN ROCK	07718-07718	BELFORD	07852-07852	LEDGEWOOD
07058-07058	PINE BROOK	07456-07456	RINGWOOD	07719-07719	BELMAR	07853-07853	LONG VALLEY
07059-07059	WARREN	07457-07457	RIVERDALE	07720-07720	BRADLEY BEACH	07855-07855	MIDDLEVILLE
07060-07063	PLAINFIELD	07458-07458	SADDLE RIVER	07721-07721	CLIFFWOOD	07856-07856	MOUNT ARLINGTON
07064-07064	PORT READING	07460-07460	STOCKHOLM	07722-07722	COLTS NECK	07857-07857	NETCONG
07065-07065	RAHWAY	07461-07461	SUSSEX	07723-07723	DEAL	07860-07860	NEWTON
07066-07066	CLARK	07462-07462	VERNON	07724-07724	EATONTOWN	07863-07863	OXFORD
07067-07067	COLONIA	07463-07463	WALDWICK	07726-07726	ENGLISHTOWN	07865-07865	PORT MURRAY
07068-07068	ROSELAND	07465-07465	WANAQUE	07727-07727	FARMINGDALE	07866-07866	ROCKAWAY
07070-07070	RUTHERFORD	07470-07477	WAYNE	07728-07728	FREEHOLD	07869-07869	RANDOLPH
07071-07071	LYNDHURST	07480-07480	WEST MILFORD	07730-07730	HAZLET	07870-07870	SCHOOLEYS MOUNTAIN
07072-07072	CARLSTADT	07481-07481	WYCKOFF	07731-07731	HOWELL	07871-07871	SPARTA
07073-07073	EAST RUTHERFORD	07495-07498	MAHWAH	07732-07732	HIGHLANDS	07874-07874	STANHOPE
07074-07074	MOONACHIE	07501-07505	PATERSON	07733-07733	HOLMDEL	07875-07875	STILLWATER
07075-07075	WOOD RIDGE	07506-07507	HAWTHORNE	07734-07734	KEANSBURG	07876-07876	SUCCASUNNA
07076-07076	SCOTCH PLAINS	07508-07508	HALEDON	07735-07735	KEYPORT	07877-07877	SWARTSWOOD
07077-07077	SEWAREN	07509-07510	PATERSON	07737-07737	LEONARDO	07878-07878	MOUNT TABOR
07078-07078	SHORT HILLS	07511-07512	TOTOWA	07738-07738	LINCROFT	07879-07879	TRANQUILITY
07079-07079	SOUTH ORANGE	07513-07533	PATERSON	07739-07739	LITTLE SILVER	07880-07880	VIENNA
07080-07080	SOUTH PLAINFIELD	07538-07538	HALEDON	07740-07740	LONG BRANCH	07881-07881	WALLPACK CENTER
07081-07081	SPRINGFIELD	07543-07544	PATERSON	07746-07746	MARLBORO	07882-07882	WASHINGTON
07082-07082	TOWACO	07601-07602	HACKENSACK	07747-07747	MATAWAN	07885-07885	WHARTON
07083-07083	UNION	07603-07603	BOGOTA	07748-07748	MIDDLETOWN	07890-07890	BRANCHVILLE
07087-07087	UNION CITY	07604-07604	HASBROUCK HEIGHTS	07750-07750	MONMOUTH BEACH	07901-07902	SUMMIT
07088-07088	VAUXHALL	07605-07605	LEONIA	07751-07751	MORGANVILLE	07920-07920	BASKING RIDGE
07090-07091	WESTFIELD	07606-07606	SOUTH HACKENSACK	07752-07752	NAVESINK	07921-07921	BEDMINSTER
07092-07092	MOUNTAINSIDE	07607-07607	MAYWOOD	07753-07754	NEPTUNE	07922-07922	BERKELEY HEIGHTS
07093-07093	WEST NEW YORK	07608-07608	TETERBORO	07755-07755	OAKHURST	07924-07924	BERNARDSVILLE
07094-07094	SECAUCUS	07620-07620	ALPINE	07756-07756	OCEAN GROVE	07926-07926	BROOKSIDE
07095-07095	WOODBRIDGE	07621-07621	BERGENFIELD	07757-07757	OCEANPORT	07927-07927	CEDAR KNOLLS

ZIP Range	City	ZIP Range	City	ZIP Range	City	ZIP Range	City
07928-07928	CHATHAM	08068-08068	PEMBERTON	08316-08316	DORCHESTER	08735-08735	LAVALLETTE
07930-07930	CHESTER	08069-08069	PENNS GROVE	08317-08317	DOROTHY	08736-08736	MANASQUAN
07931-07931	FAR HILLS	08070-08070	PENNSVILLE	08318-08318	ELMER	08738-08738	MANTOLOKING
07932-07932	FLORHAM PARK	08071-08071	PITMAN	08319-08319	ESTELL MANOR	08739-08739	NORMANDY BEACH
07933-07933	GILLETTE	08072-08072	QUINTON	08320-08320	FAIRTON	08740-08740	OCEAN GATE
07934-07934	GLADSTONE	08073-08073	RANCOCAS	08321-08321	FORTESCUE	08741-08741	PINE BEACH
07935-07935	GREEN VILLAGE	08074-08074	RICHWOOD	08322-08322	FRANKLINVILLE	08742-08742	POINT PLEASANT
07936-07936	EAST HANOVER	08075-08075	RIVERSIDE	08323-08323	GREENWICH		BEACH
07938-07938	LIBERTY CORNER	08076-08077	RIVERTON	08324-08324	HEISLERVILLE	08750-08750	SEA GIRT
07939-07939	LYONS	08078-08078	RUNNEMEDE	08326-08326	LANDISVILLE	08751-08751	SEASIDE HEIGHTS
07940-07940	MADISON	08079-08079	SALEM	08327-08327	LEESBURG	08752-08752	SEASIDE PARK
07945-07945	MENDHAM	08080-08080	SEWELL	08328-08328	MALAGA	08753-08757	TOMS RIVER
07946-07946	MILLINGTON	08081-08081	SICKLERVILLE	08329-08329	MAURICETOWN	08758-08758	WARETOWN
07950-07950	MORRIS PLAINS	08083-08083	SOMERDALE	08330-08330	MAYS LANDING	08759-08759	WHITING
07960-07963	MORRISTOWN	08084-08084	STRATFORD	08332-08332	MILLVILLE	08801-08801	ANNANDALE
07970-07970	MOUNT FREEDOM	08085-08085	SWEDESBORO	08340-08340	MILMAY	08802-08802	ASBURY
07974-07974	NEW PROVIDENCE	08086-08086	THOROFARE	08341-08341	MINOTOLA	08803-08803	BAPTISTOWN
07976-07976	NEW VERNON	08087-08087	TUCKERTON	08342-08342	MIZPAH	08804-08804	BLOOMSBURY
07977-07977	PEAPACK	08088-08088	VINCENTOWN	08343-08343	MONROEVILLE	08805-08805	BOUND BROOK
07978-07978	PLUCKEMIN	08089-08089	WATERFORD WORKS	08344-08344	NEWFIELD	08807-08807	BRIDGEWATER
07979-07979	POTTERSVILLE	08090-08090	WENONAH	08345-08345	NEWPORT	08808-08808	BROADWAY
07980-07980	STIRLING	08091-08091	WEST BERLIN	08346-08346	NEWTONVILLE	08809-08809	CLINTON
07981-07999	WHIPPANY	08092-08092	WEST CREEK	08347-08347	NORMA	08810-08810	DAYTON
08001-08001	ALLOWAY	08093-08093	WESTVILLE	08348-08348	PORT ELIZABETH	08812-08812	DUNELLEN
08002-08003	CHERRY HILL	08094-08094	WILLIAMSTOWN	08349-08349	PORT NORRIS	08816-08816	EAST BRUNSWICK
08004-08004	ATCO	08095-08095	WINSLOW	08350-08350	RICHLAND	08817-08820	EDISON
08005-08005	BARNEGAT	08096-08096	WOODBURY	08352-08352	ROSENHAYN	08821-08821	FLAGTOWN
08006-08006	BARNEGAT LIGHT	08097-08097	WOODBURY HEIGHTS	08353-08353	SHILOH	08822-08822	FLEMINGTON
08007-08007	BARRINGTON	08098-08098	WOODSTOWN	08358-08358	CHERRY HILL	08823-08823	FRANKLIN PARK
08008-08008	BEACH HAVEN	08099-08099	BELLMAWR	08360-08362	VINELAND	08824-08824	KENDALL PARK
08009-08009	BERLIN	08101-08105	CAMDEN	08370-08370	RIVERSIDE	08825-08825	FRENCHTOWN
08010-08010	BEVERLY	08106-08106	AUDUBON	08401-08401	ATLANTIC CITY	08826-08826	GLEN GARDNER
08011-08011	BIRMINGHAM	08107-08107	OAKLYN	08402-08402	MARGATE CITY	08827-08827	HAMPTON
08012-08012	BLACKWOOD	08108-08108	COLLINGSWOOD	08403-08403	LONGPORT	08828-08828	HELMETTA
08014-08014	BRIDGEPORT	08109-08109	MERCHANTVILLE	08404-08405	ATLANTIC CITY	08829-08829	HIGH BRIDGE
08015-08015	BROWNS MILLS	08110-08110	PENNSAUKEN	08406-08406	VENTNOR CITY	08830-08830	ISELIN
08016-08016	BURLINGTON	08201-08201	ABSECON	08411-08411	ATLANTIC CITY	08831-08831	JAMESBURG
08018-08018	CEDAR BROOK	08202-08202	AVALON	08501-08501	ALLENTOWN	08832-08832	KEASBEY
08019-08019	CHATSWORTH	08203-08203	BRIGANTINE	08502-08502	BELLE MEAD	08833-08833	LEBANON
08020-08020	CLARKSBORO	08204-08204	CAPE MAY	08504-08504	BLAWENBURG	08834-08834	LITTLE YORK
08021-08021	CLEMENTON	08210-08210	CAPE MAY COURT	08505-08505	BORDENTOWN	08835-08835	MANVILLE
08022-08022	COLUMBUS		HOUSE	08510-08510	CLARKSBURG	08836-08836	MARTINSVILLE
08023-08023	DEEPWATER	08212-08212	CAPE MAY POINT	08511-08511	COOKSTOWN	08837-08837	EDISON
08025-08025	EWAN	08213-08213	COLOGNE	08512-08512	CRANBURY	08840-08840	METUCHEN
08026-08026	GIBBSBORO	08214-08214	DENNISVILLE	08514-08514	CREAMRIDGE	08846-08846	MIDDLESEX
08027-08027	GIBBSTOWN	08215-08215	EGG HARBOR CITY	08515-08515	CROSSWICKS	08848-08848	MILFORD
08028-08028	GLASSBORO	08217-08217	ELWOOD	08518-08518	FLORENCE	08850-08850	MILLTOWN
08029-08029	GLENDORA	08218-08218	GOSHEN	08520-08520	HIGHTSTOWN	08852-08852	MONMOUTH JUNCTION
08030-08030	GLOUCESTER CITY	08219-08219	GREEN CREEK	08525-08525	HOPEWELL	08853-08853	NESHANIC STATION
08031-08031	BELLMAWR	08220-08220	LEEDS POINT	08526-08526	IMLAYSTOWN	08854-08855	PISCATAWAY
08032-08032	GRENLOCH	08221-08222	LINWOOD	08527-08527	JACKSON	08857-08857	OLD BRIDGE
08033-08033	HADDONFIELD	08223-08223	MARMORA	08528-08528	KINGSTON	08858-08858	OLDWICK
08034-08034	CHERRY HILL	08224-08224	NEW GRETNA	08530-08530	LAMBERTVILLE	08859-08859	PARLIN
08035-08035	HADDON HEIGHTS	08225-08225	NORTHFIELD	08533-08533	NEW EGYPT	08861-08862	PERTH AMBOY
08036-08036	HAINESPORT	08226-08226	OCEAN CITY	08534-08534	PENNINGTON	08863-08863	FORDS
08037-08037	HAMMONTON	08227-08227	LINWOOD	08535-08535	PERRINEVILLE	08865-08865	PHILLIPSBURG
08038-08038	HANCOCKS BRIDGE	08230-08230	OCEAN VIEW	08536-08536	PLAINSBORO	08867-08867	PITTSTOWN
08039-08039	HARRISONVILLE	08231-08231	OCEANVILLE	08540-08544	PRINCETON	08868-08868	QUAKERTOWN
08041-08041	JOBSTOWN	08232-08233	PLEASANTVILLE	08550-08550	PRINCETON JUNCTION	08869-08869	RARITAN
08042-08042	JULIUSTOWN	08234-08234	EGG HARBOR	08551-08551	RINGOES	08870-08870	READINGTON
08043-08043	VOORHEES		TOWNSHIP	08553-08553	ROCKY HILL	08871-08872	SAYREVILLE
08045-08045	LAWNSIDE	08240-08240	POMONA	08554-08554	ROEBLING	08873-08875	SOMERSET
08046-08046	WILLINGBORO	08241-08241	PORT REPUBLIC	08555-08555	ROOSEVELT	08876-08876	SOMERVILLE
08048-08048	LUMBERTON	08242-08242	RIO GRANDE	08556-08556	ROSEMONT	08877-08877	SOUTH RIVER
08049-08049	MAGNOLIA	08243-08243	SEA ISLE CITY	08557-08557	SERGEANTSVILLE	08878-08879	SOUTH AMBOY
08050-08050	MANAHAWKIN	08244-08244	SOMERS POINT	08558-08558	SKILLMAN	08880-08880	SOUTH BOUND BROOK
08051-08051	MANTUA	08245-08245	SOUTH DENNIS	08559-08559	STOCKTON	08882-08882	SOUTH RIVER
08052-08052	MAPLE SHADE	08246-08246	SOUTH SEAVILLE	08560-08560	TITUSVILLE	08884-08884	SPOTSWOOD
08053-08053	MARLTON	08247-08247	STONE HARBOR	08561-08561	WINDSOR	08885-08885	STANTON
08054-08054	MOUNT LAUREL	08248-08248	STRATHMERE	08562-08562	WRIGHTSTOWN	08886-08886	STEWARTSVILLE
08055-08055	MEDFORD	08250-08250	TUCKAHOE	08570-08570	CRANBURY	08887-08887	THREE BRIDGES
08056-08056	MICKLETON	08251-08251	VILLAS	08601-08695	TRENTON	08888-08888	WHITEHOUSE
08057-08057	MOORESTOWN	08252-08252	WHITESBORO	08701-08701	LAKEWOOD	08889-08889	WHITEHOUSE STATION
08059-08059	MOUNT EPHRAIM	08260-08260	WILDWOOD	08720-08720	ALLENWOOD	08890-08890	ZAREPHATH
08060-08060	MOUNT HOLLY	08270-08270	WOODBINE	08721-08721	BAYVILLE	08896-08896	RARITAN
08061-08061	MOUNT ROYAL	08302-08302	BRIDGETON	08722-08722	BEACHWOOD	08899-08899	EDISON
08062-08062	MULLICA HILL	08310-08310	BUENA	08723-08724	BRICK	08901-08901	NEW BRUNSWICK
08063-08063	NATIONAL PARK	08311-08311	CEDARVILLE	08730-08730	BRIELLE	08902-08902	NORTH BRUNSWICK
08064-08064	NEW LISBON	08312-08312	CLAYTON	08731-08731	FORKED RIVER	08903-08903	NEW BRUNSWICK
08065-08065	PALMYRA	08313-08313	DEERFIELD STREET	08732-08732	ISLAND HEIGHTS	08904-08904	HIGHLAND PARK
08066-08066	PAULSBORO	08314-08314	DELMONT	08733-08733	LAKEHURST	08905-08989	NEW BRUNSWICK
08067-08067	PEDRICKTOWN	08315-08315	DIVIDING CREEK	08734-08734	LANOKA HARBOR		

New Mexico

General Help Numbers:

Governor's Office

State Capitol, Room 400   505-827-3000
Santa Fe, NM 87503   Fax 505-827-3026
http://www.governor.state.nm.us   8AM-5PM

Attorney General's Office

PO Drawer 1508   505-827-6000
Santa Fe, NM 87504-1508   Fax 505-827-5826
http://www.ago.state.nm.us   8AM-5PM

State Court Administrator

237 Don Gaspar, Rm 25   505-827-4800
Santa Fe, NM 87501   Fax 505-827-4246
http://www.nmcourts.com/aoc.htm   8AM-5PM

State Archives

1205 Camino Carols Rey   505-476-7908
Santa Fe, NM 87505   Fax 505-476-7909
http://www.state.nm.us/cpr   8AM-5PM

State Specifics:

Capital: Santa Fe
                            Santa Fe County

Time Zone: MST

Number of Counties: 33

Population: 1,819,046

Web Site: www.state.nm.us

State Agencies

Criminal Records

Department of Public Safety, Records Bureau, PO Box 1628, Santa Fe, NM 87504-1628 (Courier: 4491 Cerrillos Rd, Santa Fe, NM 87504); 505-827-9181, 505-827-3388 (Fax), 8AM-5PM.

Indexing & Storage: Records are available from 1935 on. It takes 2 to 4 weeks before new records are available for inquiry. Records are indexed on inhouse computer.

Searching: Must have a state notarized signed release from person of record authorizing the State of New Mexico to release records to requester. Except for law enforcement officials, specify which records you want. Juvenile records are not released. Include the following in your request-date of birth, Social Security Number, full name.

Access by: mail, in person.

Fee & Payment: The fee is $7.00 per individual. Fee payee: Department of Public Safety. Prepayment required. Must use cashiers check or money order. No credit cards accepted.

Mail search: Turnaround time: 1 to 2 weeks. A self addressed stamped envelope is requested.

In person search: Searching is available in person.

Corporation Records
Limited Liability Company Records

New Mexico Public Regulation Commission, Corporate Department, PO Box 1269, Santa Fe, NM 87504-1269 (Courier: 1120 Paseo de Peralta, Pera Bldg 4th Fl, Rm 413, Santa Fe, NM 87501); 505-827-4502 (Main Number), 800-947-4722 (In-state Only), 505-827-4510 (Good Standing), 505-827-4513 (Copy Request), 505-827-4387 (Fax), 8AM-12:00: 1PM-5PM.

http://www.nmprc.state.nm.us

Note: For Charter Requirement Information call 505-827-4511.

Indexing & Storage: Records are available for all entities. Records are indexed on microfilm.

Searching: Include the following in your request-full name of business. In addition to the articles of incorporation, corporation records include the following information: Annual Reports, Officers, Directors, Prior (merged) names, Inactive, Registered and Reserved names. The following data is not released: financial information.

Access by: mail, phone, fax, in person, online.

Fee & Payment: There is no charge for a computer printout. minimum fees are $10.00 for for-profit companies or domestic LLCs and a $5.00 for non-profit companies. Certification fee is $25.00, except for non-profits which is $10.00. Copies are $1.00 per page. Fee payee: Public Regulation Commission. Payment is due in 10 days. Personal checks accepted. No credit cards accepted.

Mail search: Turnaround time: 2 days. A self addressed stamped envelope is requested.

Phone search: Limited information is given over the phone.

Fax search: Information can be requested by fax, but is returned by mail in 3-5 days.

In person search: Call is to schedule viewing time for microfilm.

Online search: There is no charge to view records at the Internet site, www.nmprc.state.nm. us/ftq.htm. Records can be searched by company name or by director name.

Other access: The state makes the database available on electronic format using a 3480 tape cartridge.

Trademarks/Servicemarks
Trade Names

Secretary of State, Trademarks Division, State Capitol North, Santa Fe, NM 87503; 505-827-3600, 505-827-3611 (Fax), 8AM-5PM.

http://www.sos.state.nm.us

Note: Effective July 1, 1997, New Mexico no longer registers trade names. However, the agency will do searches for records on file.

Indexing & Storage: Records are available from 1980 to present. It takes 1 to 2 days before new records are available for inquiry. Records are indexed on inhouse computer.

Searching: Include the following in your request-trademark/servicemark name. Include your full name, address and telephone number.

Access by: mail, phone, fax, in person.

Fee & Payment: Prepayment required. Fee payee: Secretary of State. Personal checks accepted.

Mail search: Turnaround time: 2 to 3 days. No self addressed stamped envelope is required. No fee for mail request.

Phone search: They will do a computer search and will give you the information over the phone for no fee.

Fax search: There is no fee. Turnaround time: 24 hours.

In person search: No fee for request. Turnaround time is usually immediate.

Other access: Monthly listings are available at $.10 per trademark/service mark record.

Uniform Commercial Code

UCC Division, Secretary of State, State Capitol North, Santa Fe, NM 87503; 505-827-3610, 505-827-3611 (Fax), 8AM-5PM.

http://www.sos.state.nm.us/ucc/ucchome.htm

Note: This agency will not conduct in-person searches. You must come in yourself, hire a local search company, or conduct your search at the agency web site.

Indexing & Storage: Records are available from 1965. It takes 24 hours before new records are available for inquiry.

Searching: Please note that all tax liens are filed at the county level. The system does not give information on collateral.

Access by: in person, online.

Fee & Payment: Copies are S1.00 per page plus $3.00 if certification requested. Fee payee: Secretary of State. Prepayment required. Personal checks accepted. No credit cards accepted. No self addressed stamped envelope is required.

In person search: You may use their in-house computer by appointment only. Call 505-827-3614. You may view documents for free.

Online search: The web site permits searches and a form to use to order copies of filings. You can also request records via e-mail.

Federal Tax Liens
State Tax Liens
Records not maintained by a state level agency.

Note: Records are filed with the Clerk at the county level.

Sales Tax Registrations

Taxation & Revenue Department, Tax Administrative Services Division, PO Box 630, Santa Fe, NM 87504-0630 (Courier: Montoya Bldg, 1100 S St Francis Drive, Santa Fe, NM 87501); 505-827-0700, 505-827-0469 (Fax), 8AM-5PM.

http://www.state.nm.us/tax

Indexing & Storage: Records are available from 1988.

Searching: This agency will only confirm that a business is registered and active. They will provide no other information. The business name is required, the permit number and federal ID are optional.

Access by: mail, phone, in person.

Fee & Payment: There is no search fee, copies are $.05 per page

Mail search: Turnaround time: 6 to 12 weeks. A self addressed stamped envelope is requested.

Phone search: Records are available by phone.

In person search: Searching is available in person.

Birth Certificates

Department of Health, Bureau of Vital Records, PO Box 26111, Santa Fe, NM 87502 (Courier: 1105 South St Francis Dr, Santa Fe, NM 87502); 505-827-0121, 505-827-2338 (Information), 505-984-1048 (Fax), 8AM-5:00PM (Counter Service: 9AM-4PM).

http://www.health.state.nm.us

Note: All requesters must sign and date the request. It is a felony to obtain a record fraudulently.

Indexing & Storage: Records are available from 1920 on. New records are available for inquiry immediately. Records are indexed on microfiche, inhouse computer.

Searching: Records available only to immediate family members or those demonstrating legal tangible interest in the desired record. Sealed records (e.g. adoptions and paternity) are unavailable. Include the following in your request-full name, names of parents, mother's maiden name, date of birth, place of birth, relationship to person of record, reason for information request. Signature of requester and physical & mailing addresses are required.

Access by: mail, phone, fax, in person.

Fee & Payment: The search fee is $10.00 per record. There is an additional $10.00 fee if you order by phone or by fax for use of a credit card. Fee payee: NM Vital Records. Prepayment required. Personal checks accepted. Credit cards accepted: MasterCard, Visa, AmEx, Discover.

Mail search: Turnaround time: 3 weeks. No self addressed stamped envelope is required.

Phone search: Records are available by phone.

Fax search: Same criteria as phone searches.

In person search: Turnaround time is usually less than 1/2 hour.

Expedited service: Expedited service is available for phone searches. Turnaround time: 24 hours. Use of credit card required for additional fee and add fee for delivery service. (Call for fees.)

Death Records

Department of Health, Bureau of Vital Records, PO Box 26111, Santa Fe, NM 87502 (Courier: 1105 South St Francis Dr, Santa Fe, NM 87502); 505-827-0121, 505827-2338 (Information), 505-984-1048 (Fax), 8AM-5PM (Counter Service: 9AM-4PM).

http://www.health.state.nm.us

Indexing & Storage: Records are available from 1920 to present. New records are available for inquiry immediately. Records are indexed on microfiche, inhouse computer.

Searching: Only immediate family member or a person with tangible interest can receive record. Include the following in your request-full name, date of death, place of death, Social Security Number, relationship to person of record, reason for information request. Age at death and name of mortuary must also be included for search.

Access by: mail, phone, fax, in person.

Fee & Payment: The fee is $5.00 per record. An additional fee may be charged if required information is not submitted. Use of credit card is an additional $10.00. Fee payee: NM Vital Records. Prepayment required. Credit cards are only used for phone and fax ordering. Personal checks accepted. Credit cards accepted: MasterCard, Visa, AmEx, Discover.

Mail search: Turnaround time: 3 to 4 weeks. No self addressed stamped envelope is required.

Phone search: You must use a credit card.

Fax search: Same criteria as phone searches.

In person search: Turnaround time is usually 1 hour or less.

Expedited service: Expedited service is available for mail, phone and fax searches. Turnaround time: 24 hours. Use of credit card required. Delivery fee is $13.25 minimum.

Marriage Certificates
Divorce Records
Records not maintained by a state level agency.

Note: Marriage and Divorce records are found at county of issue.

Workers' Compensation Records
Access to Records is Restricted

Workers Compensation Administration, PO Box 27198, Albuquerque, NM 87125-7198 (Courier: 2410 Centre Ave, SE, Albuquerque, NM 87106); 505-841-6000, 800-255-7965 (In-State Toll Free), 505-841-6060 (Fax), 8AM-5PM.

http://www.state.nm.us/wca

Note: The subject must write the agency, provide proof of ID with a driver's license, and request the record, and pay a copy fee of $.25 per page. Most records are confidential but access is permitted for all parties to a case and other cases involving the same worker; positive ID is required.

Driver Records

Motor Vehicle Division, Driver Services Bureau, PO Box 1028, Santa Fe, NM 87504-1028 (Courier: Joseph M. Montoya Bldg, 1100 S St. Francis Dr, 2nd Floor, Santa Fe, NM 87504); 505-827-2234, 505-827-2267 (Fax), 8AM-5PM.

http://www.state.nm.us/tax/mvd

Note: Copies of tickets may be obtained from the same address. There is no fee.

Indexing & Storage: Records are available for 3 years for moving violations; 25 years DWIs. Accidents are not reported on the record and neither are violations less than 10 mph over the limit in 55 or 65 zones. The driver's address is included on the record. It takes 30 to 40 days before new records are available for inquiry.

Searching: The law lists 9 permissible user groups and permits release of records with written consent. Purchasers may not use the information for direct mail solicitation or resell the reports after usage. The full name, DOB and either the license number or Social Security Number is required when ordering. The following data is not released: Social Security Numbers, addresses or date of birth.

Access by: mail, in person, online.

Fee & Payment: There is no fee for mail or walk-in requests. Fee payee: Motor Vehicle Division. Prepayment required. Personal checks accepted. No credit cards accepted.

Mail search: Turnaround time: 3 to 5 days. No fee for manual search. A self addressed stamped envelope is requested.

In person search: No fee for manual search. Up to 2 requests can be processed while you wait, the rest must be in writing and left overnight.

Online search: New Mexico Technet is the state authorized vendor for access. The costs are $2.50 per record for interactive, $1.50 per record for batch, plus a $.25 per minute network fee. The system is open 24 hours a day, batch requesters must wait 24 hours. Call 505-345-6555 for more information.

Vehicle Ownership
Vehicle Identification
Vessel Ownership
Vessel Registration

Motor Vehicle Division, Vehicle Services Bureau, PO Box 1028, Santa Fe, NM 87504-1028 (Courier: Joseph M. Montoya Bldg, 1100 S St. Francis Dr, 2nd Floor, Santa Fe, NM 87504); 505-827-4636, 505-827-1004, 505-827-0395 (Fax), 8AM-5PM.

http://www.state.nm.us/tax/mvd

Indexing & Storage: Records are available for a minimum of 3 years on boats and 6 years on vehicles. All motorized boats, sailboats, and jet skis must be both titled and registered if over 10 ft, and only registered if 10 ft or less. It takes 30 days before new records are available for inquiry.

Searching: Authorized requesters are restricted to 9 user groups and must sign a contract that states purpose of request and subsequent use. Requesters may not use ownership and vehicle information to create a resalable database. The following data is not released: addresses, Social Security Numbers or date of birth.

Access by: mail, in person, online.

Fee & Payment: There are no fees for mail or in person requests. A vehicle history search (microfilm) goes back 6 years. Fee payee: Department of Motor Vehicles. Prepayment required. Personal checks accepted. No credit cards accepted.

Mail search: Turnaround time: 3 to 4 weeks. A self addressed stamped envelope is requested.

In person search: Up to ten requests will be processed while you wait.

Online search: Records are available, for authorized users, from the state's designated vendor New Mexico Technet. Cost is $2.50 per record plus a $.25 per minute network charge. There is a $35.00 set-up fee, also. Call 505-345-6555 for more information.

Other access: Bulk requests for vehicle or ownership information must be approved by the Director's office. Once a sale is made, further resale is prohibited.

Accident Reports

Department of Public Safety, Records, PO Box 1628, Santa Fe, NM 87504-1628 (Courier: New Mexico State Police Complex, 4491 Cerrillos Rd, Santa Fe, NM 87504); 505-827-9300, 505-827-3396 (Fax), 8AM-5PM.

http://www.dps.nm.org

Indexing & Storage: Records are available 1 year to present in-house (on computer) and up to 10 years archived (25 years for fatalities). It takes 15 days before new records are available for inquiry.

Searching: Arrest information is not released. Include the following in your request-full name, date of accident, county, location of accident.

Access by: mail, phone, in person.

Fee & Payment: The fee is $1.00 per page. There is no fee for a no record found. There is no fee charged for persons directly involved in the accident. Fee payee: Department of Public Safety. Prepayment required. Personal checks accepted. No credit cards accepted.

Mail search: Turnaround time: 2 weeks. A self addressed stamped envelope is requested.

Phone search: No fee for telephone request.

In person search: Turnaround time is immediate if incident one year or less old.

Legislation Records

Legislative Council Service, State Capitol Bldg, Room 411, Santa Fe, NM 87501; 505-986-4600, 505-986-4350 (Bill Room During Session Only), 505-986-4610 (Fax), 8AM-5PM.

http://legis.state.nm.us

Note: Signed laws of the current year can be obtained from the Secretary of State's Office at 505-827-3600. Searchers are encouraged to use the web.

Indexing & Storage: Records are available for current back five years, online. The current session meets starting the third Tuesday in January. Sessions are 60 days in odd-numbered years and 30 days in even-numbered years.

Searching: Submit bill number or topic to search. Records on computer.

Access by: mail, phone, in person, online.

Fee & Payment: Depending on the extent of the search, the agency may charge for copies. There is no search fee. Fee payee: New Mexico State Legislature. Personal checks accepted. No credit cards accepted.

Mail search: Turnaround time: variable.

Phone search: Limited searching is available during session.

In person search: You may request bills in person.

Online search: The Internet site is a complete source of information about bills and legislators. There are also links to other NM state agencies and NM statutes.

Other access: Subscription purchase for the complete file of current session is available. However, you must request your subscription by mid-session.

Voter Registration
Access to Records is Restricted

Secretary of State, Bureau of Elections, State Capitol Annex, Ste 300, Santa Fe, NM 87503; 505-827-3620, 505-827-4954 (Fax), 8AM-5PM.

Note: Individual look-ups must be done at the county level. This agency will sell its database, but for restricted purposes only (not for commercial purposes).

GED Certificates

Department of Education, GED Testing Program, 300 Don Gaspar, Rm 122, Santa Fe, NM 87501-

2786; 505-827-6702, 505-827-6616 (Fax), 8AM-5PM.

http://sde.state.nm.us

Indexing & Storage: Records are available from 1942 to present It takes 45 days before new records are available for inquiry.

Searching: The SSN, DOB, and year of test are needed for a verification. A signed release is needed for a copy of a transcript.

Access by: mail, fax, in person.

Fee & Payment: There are no fees.

Mail search: Turnaround time: 2 weeks. No self addressed stamped envelope is required.

Fax search: Same criteria as mail searching.

In person search: Searching is available in person.

Hunting License Information
Fishing License Information

NM Dept of Game & Fish, PO Box 25112, Santa Fe, NM 87504 (Courier: Villagra Bldg, 408 Galisto St, Santa Fe, NM 87501); 505-827-7911, 800-862-9310, 505-827-7915 (Fax), 8AM-12PM; 1PM-5PM.

http://www.gmfsh.state.nm.us

Indexing & Storage: Records are available for last season only. Records are indexed on hard copy.

Searching: Include the following in your request- name.

Access by: in person.

Fee & Payment: Fee is $60 per hours plus $.25 per copy. Fee payee: NM Dept of Fish & Game. Records are available by mail.

In person search: You may do the search yourself for no fee.

New Mexico State Licensing Agencies

Licenses Searchable Online

Architect #17 .... www.nmbea.org/People/Aroster.htm

Art Therapist #57 .... www.rld.state.nm.us/b&c/counseling/licensee_search.asp

Attorney #20 .... http:www.nmbar.org/cgi-bin/QQQ/search.pl

Clinical Nurse Specialist #19 .... www.state.nm.us/nursing/lookup.html

Contractor #13 .... http://66.87.10.169/pub/index.cfm

Engineer #44 .... www.state.nm.us/pepsboard/roster.htm

Hemodialysis Technician #19 .... www.state.nm.us/nursing/lookup.html

Journeyman #13 .... http://66.87.10.169/pub/index.cfm

Lobbyist #32 .... http://web.state.nm.us/LOBBY/LOB.htm

LPG-Liquefied Petroleum Gas Licensing #13 ... http://66.87.10.169/pub/index.cfm

LPN #19 .... www.state.nm.us/nursing/lookup.html

Marriage & Family Therapist #57 .... www.rld.state.nm.us/b&c/counseling/licensee_search.asp

Medical Doctor #36 .... www.docboard.org/nm/

Medication Aide #19 .... www.state.nm.us/nursing/lookup.html

Mental Health Counselor #57 .... www.rld.state.nm.us/b&c/counseling/licensee_search.asp

Nurse #19 .... www.state.nm.us/nursing/lookup.html

Nurse Anesthetist #19 .... www.state.nm.us/nursing/lookup.html

Nurse-RN #19 .... www.state.nm.us/nursing/lookup.html

Optometrist #40 .... www.odfinder.org/LicSearch.asp

Physician Assistant #36 .... www.docboard.org/nm/

Psychologist #37 .... www.rld.state.nm.us/b&c/psychology/lcnssrch.asp

Substance Abuse Counselor/Intern #57 .... www.rld.state.nm.us/b&c/counseling/licensee_search.asp

Surveyor #44 .... www.state.nm.us/pepsboard/roster.htm

Licensing Quick Finder

Acupuncturist #26 505-476-7081	Dental Hygienist #04 505-476-7125	Manicurist #02 505-476-7110
Animal Pregnancy Diagnosis #55 505-841-9112	Dentist #04 505-476-7125	Manufactured Housing Dealer #52 505-827-7070
Announcer, Athletic Event (Ring) #39 ... 505-827-7172	Dietitian/Nutritionist #08 505-476-7127	Manufactured Housing Installer/Repairman #52 ....
Architect #17 505-827-6375	Direct Disposer (Funerary) #12 505-476-7090	 505-827-7070
Art Therapist #57 505-827-7554	Electrologist #02 505-827-7550	Manufactured Housing Mfg. #52 505-827-7070
Artificial Inseminator #55 505-841-9112	Electrophysician #02 505-476-7110	Manufactured Housing Salesman #52 ... 505-827-7070
Athletic Promoter/Matchmaker #39 505-827-7172	Emergency Medical Technician #22 505-476-7000	Marriage & Family Therapist #57 505-476-7100
Athletic Trainer #39 505-827-7172	Endowed/Perpetual Care Cemetery #51 505-827-7100	Massage Instructor/Practitioner/School #05 ....
Attorney #20 505-271-9706	Engineer #44 505-827-7561	 505-476-7090
Audiologist #11 505-476-7098	Escrow Company #51 505-827-7100	Massage Therapist #05 505-476-7090
Bank #51 505-827-7100	Esthetician #02 505-476-7110	Mechanic #31 505-827-7030
Barber #02 505-476-7110	Fireworks Dist. Class C or Class B #54. 505-827-3761	Medical Doctor #36 505-827-6784
Boiler Operator Journeyman #33 505-884-5850	Fireworks Mfg. 1.4G #54 505-827-3761	Medical Researcher #41 505-841-9102
Booking Agent #39 505-827-7172	Fireworks Vendor (Retailer/Wholesaler) #54	Medical Wholesale Company #41 505-841-9102
Boxer #39 505-827-7172	 505-827-3761	Medication Aide #19 505-841-8340
Boxer Manager #39 505-827-7172	Funeral Director #12 505-476-7090	Mental Health Counselor #57 505-476-7100
Boxing Judge/Timekeeper #39 505-827-7172	Funeral Home #12 505-476-7090	Midwife #34 505-476-8586
Broker #52 505-827-7070	Gambling (Non-profit) #14 505-827-7088	Midwife (CNM) #34 505-476-8586
Chiropractor #03 505-827-7120	Hearing Aid Specialist #11 505-476-7098	Money Order Company #51 505-827-7100
Clinical Nurse Specialist #19 505-841-8340	Hemodialysis Technician #19 505-841-8340	Mortgage Company/Loan Broker #51 ... 505-827-7100
Collection Agency #51 505-827-7100	Insurance Agent #23 505-827-4349	Motor Vehicle Sales Finance Company #51 ....
Collection Agency Manager #51 505-827-7100	Interior Designer #25 505-476-7077	 505-827-7100
Consumer Credit Grantor #51 505-827-7100	Investment Advisor/Representative #32 505-827-7140	Notary Public #53 505-827-3605
Consumer Loan Company #51 505-827-7100	Journeyman #13 505-827-7030	Nuclear Medicine Technologist #38 505-827-1870
Contractor #13 505-827-7030	Landscape Architect #18 505-476-7077	Nurse #19 505-841-8340
Cosmetologist #02 505-476-7110	Liquor Distributor #14 505-827-7066	Nurse Anesthetist #19 505-841-8340
Credit Union #51 505-827-7100	Lobbyist #32 505-827-7140	Nurse-RN #19 505-841-8340
Crematory #12 505-476-7090	LPG-Liquefied Petroleum Gas Lic. #13 . 505-827-7030	Nursing Home Administrator #06 505-827-7121
Dental Assistant #04 505-476-7125	LPN #19 505-841-8340	Nutrition/Dietetic Counselor #04 505-476-7125

Occupational Therapist #27 505-476-7085	Polygraph Examiner #43 505-476-7080	Securities Division Agent #32 505-827-7140
Occupational Therapist Assistant #27 ...505-476-7085	Private Investigator #09 505-827-7080	Securities Sales Representative #32.....505-827-7140
Optometrist #40 505-827-7121	Psychologist #37 505-476-7077	Security Guard #43 505-476-7080
Osteopathic Physician #07 505-476-7120	Psychologist Associate #37 505-476-7077	Shorthand Reporter #16 505-841-6740
Patrol Operator, Private #43 505-476-7080	Public Accountant-CPA #35..................505-841-9108	Social Worker (LBSW) (LI) (LM) #10.....505-476-7100
Pest Management Consultant #21 505-646-2133	Racing #45 505-841-6400	Social Worker, Provisional #10 505-476-7100
Pesticide Applicator #21 505-646-2133	Radiation Therapy Technologist #38.....505-827-1870	Speech-Language Pathologist #11 505-476-7098
Pesticide Dealer #21 505-646-2133	Radiologic Technologist #38.................505-827-1870	Substance Abuse Counselor/Intern #57 505-476-7100
Pesticide Operator #21........................505-646-2133	Real Estate Agent #46 505-841-9120	Surveyor #44 505-827-7561
Pharmacist #41 505-841-9102	Real Estate Appraiser #49 505-476-7096	Teacher #24 505-827-6587
Pharmacy, Non-Residential #41 505-841-9102	Real Estate Broker #46 505-841-9120	Veterinarian/Veterinary Technician #55.505-841-9112
Physical Therapist #28 505-476-7085	Referee #39 505-827-7172	Veterinary Facility #55.........................505-841-9112
Physical Therapist Assistant #28 505-476-7085	Respiratory Care Therapist #56 505-476-7121	Waste Water System Operator #38.......505-827-2836
Physician #41 505-841-9102	School Administrator #24 505-827-6587	Wreslter #39 505-827-7172
Physician Assistant #36.......................505-827-6784	School Counselor #24 505-827-6587	
Podiatrist #42......................................505-827-7120	Securities Broker/Dealer #32 505-827-7140	

Licensing Agency Information

#01 Administrative Services Division, POB 25101, Santa Fe, NM 87504; 505-476-7100. www.state.nm.us/cgi-bin/intercept.pl?/rld/b&c/athletic%20trainers%20board.htm

#02 Administrative Services Division, PO Box 25101, 2055 S. Pacheco St, Santa Fe, NM 87504; 505-476-7110, Fax: 505-476-7118. www.rld.state.nm.us/b&c/barber_and_cosmetologist_board.htm

#03 Administrative Services Division, PO Box 25101, Santa Fe, NM 87504; 505-476-7120, Fax: 505-476-7095. www.rld.state.nm.us/b&c/chiropractic_examiners_board.htm

#04 Administrative Services Division, PO Box 25101, Santa Fe, NM 87504; 505-476-7125, Fax: 505-476-7095. www.rld.state.nm.us/b&c/dental/index.htm

#05 Administrative Services Division, PO Box 25101, Santa Fe, NM 87504; 505-476-7090, Fax: 505-476-7095. www.rld.state.nm.us/b&c/massage/index.htm

#06 Regulation and Licensing Department, PO Box 25101 (2055 Pacheco St, #400), Santa Fe, NM 87504; 505-476-7121, Fax: 505-827-7095. www.rld.state.nm.us/b&c/nhab/index.htm

#07 Administrative Services Division, 725 St Michael's Dr, Santa Fe, NM 87504; 505-476-7120, Fax: 505-476-7095. www.rld.state.nm.us/b&c/osteopathic_examiners_board.htm

#08 Administrative Services Division, 2055 S Pacheco #400, Santa Fe, NM 87504; 505-476-7127, Fax: 505-476-7095.

#09 Regulation & Licensing Department, 725 St Michael's Dr, Santa Fe, NM 87501; 505-476-7100. www.rld.state.nm.us/b&c/private_investigators_board.htm

#10 Regulation & Licensing Dept, PO Box 25101, Santa Fe, NM 87504; 505-476-7100, Fax: 505-827-7548. www.rld.state.nm.us/b&c/social_work_examiners_board.htm

#11 Dispensers Board, PO Box 25101 (2055 Pacheco St, #300), Santa Fe, NM 87504; 505-476-7100, Fax: 505-476-7094. www.rld.state.nm.us/b&c/speech/index.htm

#12 Regulation & Licensing Department, 2055 S Pacheco St #400, Santa Fe, NM 87505; 505-476-7090, Fax: 505-476-7095. www.rld.state.nm.us/b&c/thanato/

#13 Regulation & Licensing Department, 725 St. Michael's Dr, Sante Fe, NM 87505; 505-827-7030, Fax: 505-765-5670. http://rld.state.nm.us/cid Direct web site URL to search for licensees: http://66.87.10.169/pub/index.cfm.

#14 Alcohol & Gaming Division, 725 St. Michaels Dr, Santa Fe, NM 87505-7605; 505-827-7088, Fax: 505-827-7168. www.rld.state.nm.us/agd/index.htm

#16 Board Governing Recording of Judicial Proceedings, PO Box 25883, Albuquerque, NM 87125; 505-797-6000, Fax: 505-843-8765.

#17 Board of Examiners for Architects, PO Box 509, Santa Fe, NM 87504; 505-827-6375, Fax: 505-827-6373. www.nmbea.org Direct web site URL to search for licensees: www.nmbea.org/People/Aroster.htm. Search online using registration #, name, city, or state

#18 Board of Landscape Architects, 2055 South Pacheco #400 (PO Box 25101), Santa Fe, NM 87504; 505-476-7077, Fax: 505-476-7087.

#19 Board of Nursing, 4206-A Lousiana Blvd NE, Albuquerque, NM 87109; 505-841-8340, Fax: 505-841-8347. www.state.nm.us/nursing Direct web site URL to search for licensees: www.state.nm.us/nursing/lookup.html. You can search online using name, SSN, license #, or certificate number.

#20 Board of Bar Examiners, 9420 Indian School NE, Albuquerque, NM 87112; 505-271-9706, Fax: 505-271-9768. www.nmbar.org Direct web site URL to search for licensees: http:www.nmbar.org/cgi-bin/QQQ/search.pl

#21 Department of Agriculture, PO Box 30005, Las Cruces, NM 88003-8005; 505-646-2133, Fax: 505-646-5977. http://nmdaweb.nmsu.edu/AES/PEST/tconlic.htm

#22 Department of Health, PO Box 26110 (1190 S St. Francis Dr, Santa Fe, NM 87502; 505-476-7000, Fax: 505-476-7010.

www.health.state.nm.us/website.nsf/frames?ReadForm

#23 Department of Insurance, PO Drawer 1269 (Old Santa Fe Trail Bldg, 4th Fl), Santa Fe, NM 87501; 505-827-4349, Fax: 505-827-4734. www.nmprc.state.nu.us

#24 Education Department, 300 Don Gaspar, Education Bldg, Santa Fe, NM 87501-2786; 505-827-6587, Fax: 505-827-6696. www.sde.state.nm.us

#25 Board of Interior Design, 2055 South Pacheco St #400 (PO Box 25101), Santa Fe, NM 87504; 505-476-7077, Fax: 505-827-7087. www.rld.state.nm.us/b&c/interior_design_board.htm

#26 Regulation & Licensing Department, PO Box 25101 (2055 S Pacheco St #400), Santa Fe, NM 87505; 505-476-7081, Fax: 505-476-7095. www.rld.state.nm.us/b&c/acupunture_oriental_medicine-bd.htm

#27 Regulation & Licensing Department, 725 St Michael's Dr, Santa Fe, NM 87504; 505-476-7085, Fax: 505-476-7086. www.rld.state.nm.us/b&c/otb/index.htm

#28 Regulation & Licensing Department, 2055 S Pacheco #400, Santa Fe, NM 87505; 505-476-7085, Fax: 505-476-7086. www.rld.state.nm.us/b&c/ptb/index.htm

#31 Regulation and Licensing Dept., 725 St Michaels Dr, Santa Fe, NM 87503; 505-827-7030. www.rld.state.nm.us

#32 Securities Division, 725 St Michael's Dr, Santa Fe, NM 87505; 505-827-7140, Fax: 505-984-0617. www.rld.state.nm.us/sec/index.htm

#33 Boiler Operator Journeyman Licensing Board, 3311 Candelaria NE #C, Albuquerque, NM 87107; 505-884-5850, Fax: 505-883-7696.

#34 Maternal Health program, 525 Camino De Los Marquez #1, Santa Fe, NM 87501; 505-476-8586, Fax: 505-476-8620.

#35 Regulation & Licensing Department, 1650 University Blvd, #400A, Albuquerque, NM 87102; 505-841-9108, Fax: 505-841-9113. www.rld.state.nm.us/accountancy

#36 Board of Medical Examiners, 491 Old Sante Fe Trail, Lamy Bldg, 2nd Fl, Santa Fe, NM 87501; 505-827-5022, Fax: 505-827-7377.

www.nmbeme.org

#37 Board of Psychologist Examiners, PO Box 25101, 2055 South Pacheco St #400, Santa Fe, NM 87504; 505-476-7100, Fax: 505-827-7017. www.rld.state.nm.us/b&c/psychology
Direct web site URL to search for licensees: www.rld.state.nm.us/b&c/psychology. You can search online using name, city, state

#38 Environment Department, PO Box 26110, Santa Fe, NM 87505-6110; 505-827-1870, Fax: 505-827-1544.

#39 Regulation & Licensing Department, PO Box 25101, Santa Fe, NM 87504; 505-827-7124, Fax: 505-827-7095.
www.state.nm.us/cgi-bin/intercept.pl?/rld/b&c/athletic%20commission.htm

#40 Regulation and Licensing Department, PO Box 25101 (2055 South Pacheco Street), Santa Fe, NM 87504; 505-476-7121, Fax: 505-476-7095.
www.rld.state.nm.us/b&c/optometry/index.htm
Direct web site URL to search for licensees: www.odfinder.org/LicSearch.asp. Search online using national database by name, city or state.

#41 Administrative Services Division, 1650 University Blvd, Ste. 400B, Albuquerque, NM 87102; 505-841-9102, Fax: 505-841-9113.
www.state.nm.us/pharmacy

#42 Regulation & Licensing Department, PO Box 25101 (2055 S Pacheco St. #300), Santa Fe, NM 87504; 505-476-7120, Fax: 505-827-7095.

www.rld.state.nm.us/b&c/podiatry_board.htm

#43 Polygraph Examiners Bureau, PO Box 25101, Santa Fe, NM 87504; 505-476-7080, Fax: 505-476-7095.
www.rld.state.nm.us/b&c/otb/index.htm

#44 Professional Engineers & Surveyors Board, 1010 Marquez Pl, Santa Fe, NM 87501; 505-827-7561, Fax: 505-827-7566.
www.state.nm.us/pepsboard
Direct web site URL to search for licensees: www.state.nm.us/pepsboard/roster.htm. You can search online using name. When checked in 1999, the online search page was only current as of November 1998.

#45 Racing Commission, 300 San Mateo Blvd NE, #110, Albuquerque, NM 87198; 505-841-6400, Fax: 505-841-6400. www.state.nm.us/src

#46 Regulation & Licensing Department, 1650 University Blvd, #490, Albuquerque, NM 87102; 505-841-9120, Fax: 505-276-0725.
www.state.nm.us/nmrec

#48 Regulation & Licensing Department, PO Box 25101, Santa Fe, NM 87504; 505-827-7140, Fax: 505-984-0617.
www.rld.state.nm.us/sec/index.htm

#49 Regulation & Licensing Department, POB 25101 (2055 S. Pacheco St), Santa Fe, NM 87504; 505-476-7096, Fax: 505-827-7096.
www.rld.state.nm.us/b&c/real_estate_appraisers_board.htm

#51 Regulation & Licensing Department, PO Box 26110, Santa Fe, NM 87501; 505-827-7110, Fax: 505-827-7107.
www.state.nm.us/cgi-bin/intercept.pl?/rld/rld_fid.html

#52 Regulation & Licensing Department, 725 St Michael's Dr, Santa Fe, NM 87501; 505-827-7070, Fax: 505-827-7074.
www.rld.state.nm.us/mhd/index.htm

#53 Secretary of State, Notary Public, State Capitol North, Santa Fe, NM 87503; 505-827-3600, Fax: 505-827-3611.
www.sos.state.nm.us

#54 State Fire Marshal, PO Drawer 1269, Santa Fe, NM 87504; 505-827-3761, Fax: 505-827-3778.

#55 Veterinary Medicine Board, 1650 University Blvd NE, #400C, Albuquerque, NM 87102; 505-841-9112, Fax: 505-841-9113.
www.state.nm.us/vetbd

#56 Repiratory Care Advisory Board, PO Box 25101 (2055 Pacheco St, #400), Santa Fe, NM 87504; 505-476-7121, Fax: 505-476-7095.
www.rld.state.nm.us/b&c/rcb/index.htm

#57 Regulation & Licensing Department, 1599 St Francis Dr, PO Box 25101, Sante Fe, NM 87504; 505-476-7100.
www.rld.state.nm.us/b&c/counseling/index.htm
Direct web site URL to search for licensees: www.rld.state.nm.us/b&c/counseling/licensee_search.asp

New Mexico Federal Courts

The following list indicates the district and division name for each county in the state.

County/Court Cross Reference

Bernalillo	Albuquerque	McKinley	Albuquerque
Catron	Albuquerque	Mora	Albuquerque
Chaves	Albuquerque	Otero	Albuquerque
Cibola	Albuquerque	Quay	Albuquerque
Colfax	Albuquerque	Rio Arriba	Albuquerque
Curry	Albuquerque	Roosevelt	Albuquerque
De Baca	Albuquerque	San Juan	Albuquerque
Dona Ana	Albuquerque	San Miguel	Albuquerque
Eddy	Albuquerque	Sandoval	Albuquerque
Grant	Albuquerque	Santa Fe	Albuquerque
Guadalupe	Albuquerque	Sierra	Albuquerque
Harding	Albuquerque	Socorro	Albuquerque
Hidalgo	Albuquerque	Taos	Albuquerque
Lea	Albuquerque	Torrance	Albuquerque
Lincoln	Albuquerque	Union	Albuquerque
Los Alamos	Albuquerque	Valencia	Albuquerque
Luna	Albuquerque		

US District Court

Albuquerque Division 333 Lomas Blvd NW #270, Albuquerque, NM 87102-2274 (Courier Address: Use mail address for courier delivery), 505-348-2000, Fax: 505-348-2028.

http://www.nmcourt.fed.us/dcdocs

Counties: All counties in New Mexico. Cases may be assigned to any of its three divisions.

Indexing/Storage: Cases are indexed by defendant and plaintiff as well as by case number. New cases are available in the index 2 days after filing date. Inquirer's phone number and the years to search are required to search for a record. Records from 1990 to the present can be searched by the plaintiff's name. Prior records can be searched by defendant or case number. A computer index is maintained. Open records are located at this court.

Fee & Payment: The fee is $20.00 per item (one party name or case number). Payment may be made by money order, cashier check, personal check. Copies are made through a copy service only. They charge $.15 per page. Prepayment is required. Payee: Clerk, US District Court. Certification fee: $7.00 per document. Copy fee: $.35 per page.

Phone Search: Only docket information available by phone.

Mail Search: A stamped self addressed envelope is not required.

In Person: In person searching is available.

PACER: Sign-up number is. Access fee is. Case records are available back to 1990. Records are purged every six months. New records are available online after 2 weeks.

Electronic Filing: Electronic filing information is available online at http://www.nmcourt.fed.us/dcdocs (Click on ACE Filing)

US Bankruptcy Court

Albuquerque Division PO Box 546, Albuquerque, NM 87103-0546 (Courier Address: 3rd Floor, Room 316, 421 Gold Ave SW, Albuquerque, NM 87102), 505-348-2500, Fax: 505-348-2473.

http://www.nmcourt.fed.us/bkdocs/

Counties: All counties in New Mexico.

Indexing/Storage: Cases are indexed by debtor as well as by case number. New cases are available in the index 24 hours after filing date. Both computer and card indexes are maintained. Card indexes are maintained on cases filed prior to May 26, 1987. Cases filed after that date are indexed in the computer. Open records are located at this court.

Fee & Payment: The fee is $20.00 per item (one party name or case number). Payment may be made by money order, cashier check, personal check, Visa or Mastercard. Prepayment is required. Debtor's checks are not accepted. Payee: Clerk, US Bankruptcy Court. Certification fee: $7.00 per document. Copy fee: $.50 per page.

Phone Search: Index, docket and claim information will be released over the phone. An automated voice case information service (VCIS) is available. Call VCIS at 888-435-7822 or 505-248-6536.

Fax Search: The fee is $15.00 and must be prepaid.

Mail Search: Fee will be charged only when a case file search is required. Always enclose a stamped self addressed envelope.

In Person: In person searching is available.

PACER: Sign-up number is 800-676-6856. Access fee is $.60 per minute. Toll-free access: 888-821-8813. Local access: 505-348-2496. Case records are available back to July 1, 1991. New civil records are available online after 1 day.

New Mexico County Courts

Court	Jurisdiction	No. of Courts	How Organized
District Courts*	General	30	13 Districts
Magistrate Courts*	Limited	48	32 Magistrate Districts
Metropolitan Court of Bernalillo County*	Municipal	1	
Municipal Courts	Municipal	82	
Probate Courts	Probate	30	33 Counties

* Profiled in this Sourcebook.

Court	CIVIL								
	Tort	Contract	Real Estate	Min. Claim	Max. Claim	Small Claims	Estate	Eviction	Domestic Relations
District Courts*	X	X	X	$0	No Max		X		X
Magistrate Courts*	X	X	X	$0	$7500	$5000		X	
Metropolitan Court of Bernalillo County*	X	X	X	$0	$5000	$5000			
Municipal Courts									
Probate Courts*							X		

Court	CRIMINAL				
	Felony	Misdemeanor	DWI/DUI	Preliminary Hearing	Juvenile
District Courts*	X				X
Magistrate Courts*		X	X	X	
Metropolitan Court of Bernalillo County*		X	X	X	
Municipal Courts					
Probate Courts*					

ADMINISTRATION Administrative Office of the Courts, Supreme Court Building Room 25, Santa Fe, NM, 87503; 505-827-4800, Fax: 505-827-7549. www.nmcourts.com/aoc.htm

COURT STRUCTURE The 30 District Courts in 13 districts are the courts of general jurisdiction. Starting July 1, 2001, the Magistrate Courts will handle civil cases up to $10,000. Previously, the Magistrate Court limit was $7,500. The Bernalillo Metropolitan Court has jurisdiction in cases up to $5000.

ONLINE ACCESS The www.nmcourts.com web site offers free access to District and Magistrate Court case information. In general, records are available from June 1997 forward.

Also, a commercial online service is available for the Metropolitan Court of Bernalillo County. There is a $35.00 set up fee, a connect time fee based on usage. The system is available 24 hours a day. Call 505-345-6555 for more information.

ADDITIONAL INFORMATION There are some "shared" courts in New Mexico, with one county handling cases arising in another. Records are held at the location(s) indicated in the text.

All magistrate courts and the Bernalillo Metropolitan Court have public access terminals to access civil records only.

PROBATE COURTS County Clerks handle "informal" (uncontested) probate cases, and the District Courts handle "formal" (contested) probate cases.

Bernalillo County

2nd Judicial District Court PO Box 488, Albuquerque, NM 87103; 505-841-7425 (Administration); Civil phone: 505-841-6774; Criminal phone: 505-841-6789; Probate phone: 505-841-7687; Fax: 505-841-7446. Hours: 8AM-5PM (MST).

Felony, Civil.

www.cabq.gov/cjnet/dst2alb

Civil Records: Access: Mail, online, in person. Both court and visitors may perform in person searches. Search fee: $1.50 per name. Required to search: name, years to search. Civil cases indexed by defendant, plaintiff. Civil records on computer from 1984, prior on docket books/microfiche. Online access available through New Mexico Technet. There is a setup fee and an access fee. Records go back 7 years. Call 505-345-6555 for information.

Criminal Records: Access: Mail, online, in person. Both court and visitors may perform in person searches. Search fee: $1.50 per name. Required to search: name, years to search; also helpful: DOB, SSN. Criminal records on computer from 1979, prior on docket books/microfiche. Online access to criminal records is the same as civil.

General Information: No sequestered or juvenile records released. SASE required. Turnaround time up to 10 days. Copy fee: $.35 per page. Certification fee: $1.50. Fee payee: Clerk of the Court. Only cashiers checks and money orders accepted. Prepayment is required.

Metropolitan Court 401 Roma NW, Albuquerque, NM 87102; 505-841-8151/841-8142; Fax: 505-222-4800. Hours: 8AM-5PM (MST). *Misdemeanor, Civil Actions Under $10,000, Eviction, Small Claims.*

www.metrocourt.state.nm.us

Civil Records: Access: Phone, fax, mail, online, in person. Both court and visitors may perform in person searches. No search fee. Required to search: name, years to search. Civil cases indexed by defendant, plaintiff. Civil records on computer from 1987. Max. 5 years back except uncollected judgments which stay open 14 years from date of judgment. Access Metropolitan court civil records online at www.technet.nm.nte/menu/metro-ct.htm. There is a set up fee plus a per minute charge based on usage. For information or to obtain an account call 505-345-6555.

Criminal Records: Access: Phone, fax, mail, online, in person. Both court and visitors may perform in person searches. No search fee. Required to search: name, SSN; also helpful: DOB. Criminal records on computer from 1983. Online access to criminal records is available at www.metrocourt.state.nm.us.

General Information: Public Access terminal is available. (Only civil records are available.) No presentence reports, psychological evaluations, confidential records released. SASE required. Turnaround time 5-10 days. Copy fee: $.50 per page. Computer printouts are $1.00 per page. Certification fee: $1.50. Fee payee: Metro Court. Personal checks accepted. Credit cards accepted: Visa, AmEx. Prepayment is required.

County Clerk #1 Civic Plaza NW, 6th Fl, Albuquerque, NM 87102; 505-768-4247. Hours: 8AM-4:30PM (MST). *Probate.*

Catron County

7th Judicial District Court PO Drawer 1129, Socorro, NM 87801; 505-835-0050; Fax: 505-838-5217. Hours: 8AM-4PM (MST). *Felony, Civil.*

Note: This court is also responsible for Socorro County.

Civil Records: Access: Phone, fax, mail, online, in person. Both court and visitors may perform in person searches. No search fee. Required to search: name, years to search. Civil cases indexed by defendant, plaintiff. Civil records on microfiche and hard copies from 1925; on computer back to 1997. Access to court records from 1997 forward is available free online at www.nmcourts.com/disclaim.html.

Criminal Records: Access: Phone, fax, mail, online, in person. Both court and visitors may perform in person searches. No search fee. Required to search: name, years to search, DOB; also helpful-SSN, signed release. Criminal records on microfiche and hard copies from 1925; on computer back to 1997. Online access to criminal records is the same as civil.

General Information: Public Access terminal is available. No sequestered records released. SASE required. Turnaround time 1 day. Copy fee: $.35 per page. Certification fee: $2.50. Fee payee: District Court Clerk. Business checks accepted. Prepayment required.

Quemado Magistrate Court PO Box 283, Quemado, NM 87829; 505-773-4604; Fax: 505-773-4688. Hours: 8AM-5PM (MST). *Misdemeanor, Civil Actions Under $10,000, Eviction, Small Claims.*

Reserve Magistrate Court PO Box 447, Reserve, NM 87830; 505-533-6474; Fax: 505-533-6623. Hours: 8AM-5PM (MST). *Misdemeanor, Civil Actions Under $10,000, Eviction, Small Claims.*

County Clerk PO Box I, Socorro, NM 87801; 505-835-0423. Hours: 8AM-5PM (MST). *Probate.*

Chaves County

5th Judicial District Court Box 1776, Roswell, NM 88202; 505-622-2212; Fax: 505-624-9510. Hours: 8AM-Noon,1-5PM (MST). *Felony, Civil.*

www.fifthdistrictcourt.com

Civil Records: Access: Online, in person. Visitors must perform in person searches for themselves. No search fee. Required to search: name, years to search. Civil cases indexed by defendant, plaintiff. Civil records on computer from 1996, on microfiche and archived from 1891. Access to court records from 1997 forward is available free online at www.nmcourts.com/disclaim.html.

Criminal Records: Access: Online, in person. Visitors must perform in person searches for themselves. No search fee. Required to search: name, years to search, DOB, aliases. Criminal records on computer from 1996, on microfiche and archived from 1891. Online access to criminal records is the same as civil.

General Information: Public Access terminal is available. No sequestered records released. Copy fee: $.35 per page. Certification fee: $1.50. Fee payee: District Court Clerk. Only cashiers checks and money orders accepted. Prepayment is required.

Magistrate Court 200 E 4th St, Roswell, NM 88201; 505-624-6088; Fax: 505-624-6092. Hours: 8AM-4PM (MST). *Misdemeanor, Civil Actions Under $10,000, Eviction, Small Claims.*

www.nmcourts.com

County Clerk Box 820, Roswell, NM 88201; 505-624-6614; Fax: 505-624-6523. Hours: 7AM-5PM (MST). *Probate.*

Cibola County

13th Judicial District Court Box 758, Grants, NM 87020; 505-287-8831; Fax: 505-285-5755. Hours: 8AM-5PM (MST). *Felony, Civil, Probate.*

Civil Records: Access: Phone, fax, mail, online, in person. Both court and visitors may perform in person searches. Search fee: $5.00 for 2 names; 3-10 for 10 names; $20.00 over 20 names. Required to search: name, years to search. Civil cases indexed by defendant, plaintiff. Civil records on microfiche from 1981; prior to 1981 belong to Valencia County. Access to court records from 1997 forward is available free online at www.nmcourts.com/disclaim.html.

Criminal Records: Access: Phone, fax, mail, online, in person. Search fee: $5.00 for 2 names; 3-10 for 10 names; $20.00 over 20 names. Required to search: name, years to search. Criminal records on microfiche from 1981; prior to 1981 belong to Valencia County. Online access to criminal records is the same as civil.

General Information: Public Access terminal is available. No sequestered records released. Turnaround time 2-3 days. Fax notes: Will fax results: $2.50 in-state; $5.00 out-of-state unless toll-free # is provided. Copy fee: $.35 per page. Certification fee: $1.50. Fee payee: District Court Clerk. Business checks accepted. Prepayment is required.

Magistrate Court 515 W High, PO Box 130, Grants, NM 87020; 505-285-4605. Hours: 8AM-4PM (MST). *Misdemeanor, Civil Actions Under $10,000, Eviction, Small Claims.*

County Clerk 515 W. High, PO Box 19, Grants, NM 87020; 505-285-2535; Fax: 505-285-5434. Hours: 8AM-5PM (MST). *Probate.*

Colfax County

8th Judicial District Court Box 160, Raton, NM 87740; 505-445-5585; Fax: 505-445-2626. Hours: 8AM-4PM (MST). *Felony, Civil.*

Civil Records: Access: Phone, mail, online, in person. Both court and visitors may perform in person searches. No search fee. Required to search: name, years to search. Civil cases indexed by defendant, plaintiff. Civil records archived from 1912. Access to court records from 1997 forward is available free online at www.nmcourts.com/disclaim.html.

Criminal Records: Access: Phone, mail, online, in person. Both court and visitors may perform in person searches. No search fee. Required to search: name, years to search; also helpful: DOB, SSN. Criminal records archived from 1912. Online access to criminal records is the same as civil.

General Information: Public Access terminal is available. No adoption, mental, guardianship, children's cases (neglect & child in need of supervision) records released. SASE required. Turnaround time 1 week. Fax notes: Fee to fax results is $2.00 per page. Copy fee: $.35 per page. Certification fee: $1.50. Fee payee: District Court. Business checks accepted.

Cimarron Magistrate Court PO Drawer 367, Highway 21, Cimarron, NM 87714; 505-376-2634. *Misdemeanor, Civil Actions Under $10,000, Eviction, Small Claims.*

Raton Magistrate Court PO Box 68, Raton, NM 87740; 505-445-2220; Fax: 505-445-8966. Hours: 8AM-5PM (MST). *Misdemeanor, Civil Actions Under $10,000, Eviction, Small Claims.*

Springer Magistrate Court 300 Colbert Ave. PO Box 760, Springer, NM 87747; 505-483-2417; Fax: 505-483-0127. Hours: 8AM-Noon, 1-5PM (MST). *Misdemeanor, Civil Actions Under $10,000, Eviction, Small Claims.*

County Clerk PO Box 159, Raton, NM 87740; 505-445-5551; Fax: 505-445-4031. Hours: 8AM-5PM (MST). *Probate.*

Curry County

9th Judicial District Court Curry County Courthouse, 700 N Main, #11, Clovis, NM 88101; 505-762-9148; Fax: 505-763-5160. Hours: 8AM-4PM (MST). *Felony, Civil.*

Civil Records: Access: Online, in person. Visitors must perform in person searches for themselves. No search fee. Required to search: name, years to search, address. Civil cases indexed by defendant, plaintiff. Civil records on computer from 1986, on microfiche and archived from 1910. Access to court records from 1997 forward is available free online at www.nmcourts.com/ disclaim.html.
Criminal Records: Access: Online, in person. Visitors must perform in person searches for themselves. No search fee. Required to search: name, years to search; also helpful: SSN. Criminal records on computer from 1986, on microfiche and archived from 1910. Online access to criminal records is the same as civil.
General Information: No adoptions, insanity, sequestered, neglect or abuse released. Copy fee: $.35 per page. Certification fee: $1.50. Fee payee: 9th Judicial District Court. Only cashiers checks and money orders accepted. Prepayment is required.

Magistrate Court 900 Main St, Clovis, NM 88101; 505-762-3766; Fax: 505-769-1437. Hours: 8AM-4PM (MST). *Misdemeanor, Civil Actions Under $10,000, Eviction, Small Claims.*

De Baca County

10th Judicial District Court Box 910, Ft. Sumner, NM 88119; 505-355-2896; Fax: 505-355-2899. Hours: 8AM-4:30PM (MST). *Felony, Civil.*

Civil Records: Access: Phone, mail, online, in person. Only the court performs in person searches; visitors may not. No search fee. Required to search: name, years to search. Civil cases indexed by defendant, plaintiff. Civil records on index cards and docket books archived from 1917; on computer since 1997. Access to court records from 1997 forward is available free online at www.nmcourts.com/disclaim.html.
Criminal Records: Access: Phone, mail, online, in person. Only the court performs in person searches; visitors may not. No search fee. Required to search: name, years to search. Criminal records on index cards and docket books archived from 1917; on computer since 1997. Online access to criminal records is the same as civil.
General Information: No mental, adoptions, or juvenile released. SASE required. Turnaround time 2 days. Fax notes: Fee to fax results is $1.00 per page. Copy fee: $.35 per page. Certification fee: $1.50. Fee payee: District Court. Only cashiers checks and money orders accepted. Prepayment is required.

Magistrate Court Box 24, Ft Sumner, NM 88119; 505-355-7371; Fax: 505-355-7149. Hours: 8AM-5PM (MST). *Misdemeanor, Civil Actions Under $10,000, Eviction, Small Claims.*

County Clerk 514 Ave C, PO Box 347, Ft. Sumner, NM 88119; 505-355-2601; Fax: 505-355-2441. Hours: 8AM-Noon, 1-4:30PM (MST). *Probate.*

Dona Ana County

3rd Judicial District Court 201 W Picacho, Suite A, Las Cruces, NM 88005; 505-523-8200; Fax: 505-523-8290. Hours: 8AM-Noon, 1-5PM (MST). *Felony, Civil.*

Civil Records: Access: Mail, online, in person. Both court and visitors may perform in person searches. Search fee: $1.50 per name. Required to search: name, years to search. Civil cases indexed by defendant, plaintiff. Civil records on computer from 1986, on microfiche and archived from 1912. Access to court records from 1997 forward is available free online at www.nmcourts.com/disclaim.html.
Criminal Records: Access: Mail, online, in person. Both court and visitors may perform in person searches. Search fee: $1.50 per name. Required to search: name, years to search; also helpful: DOB, SSN. Criminal records on computer from 1986, on microfiche and archived from 1912. Online access to criminal records is the same as civil.
General Information: Public Access terminal is available. No adoption, mental health, or juvenile released. SASE required. Turnaround time 2-3 days. Copy fee: $.35 per page. Certification fee: $1.50. Fee payee: 3rd Judicial District. Only cashiers checks and money orders accepted. Prepayment is required.

Anthony Magistrate Court PO Box 1259, Anthony, NM 88021; 505-233-3147. Hours: 8AM-Noon, 1-5PM (MST). *Misdemeanor, Civil Actions Under $10,000, Eviction, Small Claims.*

Las Cruces Magistrate Court 151 N Church, Las Cruces, NM 88001; 505-524-2814; Fax: 505-525-2951. Hours: 8AM-Noon, 1-5PM (MST). *Misdemeanor, Civil Actions Under $10,000, Eviction, Small Claims.*

County Clerk 251 W Amador, Los Cruces, NM 88005; 505-647-7419; Fax: 505-647-7464. Hours: 8AM-5PM (MST). *Probate.*

Eddy County

5th Judicial District Court Box 1838, Carlsbad, NM 88221; 505-885-4740; Fax: 505-887-7095. Hours: 8AM-Noon, 1-5PM (MST). *Felony, Civil.*

www.fifthdistrictcourt.com

Civil Records: Access: Phone, mail, online, in person. Both court and visitors may perform in person searches. No search fee. Required to search: name, years to search. Civil cases indexed by defendant. Civil records on computer from 1986, microfiche from 1900s. Access to court records from 1997 forward is free online at www.nmcourts.com/disclaim.html, or via the court web site above.
Criminal Records: Access: Phone, mail, online, in person. Both court and visitors may perform in person searches. No search fee. Required to search: name, years to search. Criminal records on computer from 1986, microfiche from 1900s. Online access to criminal records is the same as civil.
General Information: Public Access terminal is available. No adoption, SS case w/children, or guardianship released. SASE required. Turnaround time 1 day. Copy fee: $.35 per page. Certification fee: $1.50. Fee payee: District Court Clerk. Only cashiers checks and money orders accepted. Law firm checks only. Prepayment is required.

Artesia Magistrate Court 611 Mahone Dr Ste A, Artesia, NM 88210; 505-746-2481; Fax: 505-746-6763. Hours: 8AM-4PM (MST). *Misdemeanor, Civil Actions Under $10,000, Eviction, Small Claims.*

www.nmcourts.com

Carlsbad Magistrate Court 302 N Main St, Carlsbad, NM 88220; 505-885-3218; Fax: 505-887-3460. Hours: 8AM-4PM (MST). *Felony, Misdemeanor, Civil Actions Under $10,000, Eviction, Small Claims.*

County Clerk Eddy County Probate Judge, Rm 100, PO Box 850, Carlsbad, NM 88221; 505-885-4008; Fax: 505-887-1039. Hours: 8AM-5PM *Probate.*

Grant County

6th Judicial District Court Box 2339, Silver City, NM 88062; 505-538-3250; Fax: 505-588-5439. Hours: 8AM-5PM (MST). *Felony, Civil.*

Civil Records: Access: Fax, mail, online, in person. Both court and visitors may perform in person searches. Search fee: $3.00 per name. Required to search: name, years to search. Civil cases indexed by defendant, plaintiff. Civil records on microfiche from 1912-1977, on books from 1977. Access to court records from 1997 forward is available free online at www.nmcourts.com/disclaim.html.
Criminal Records: Access: Fax, mail, online, in person. Both court and visitors may perform in person searches. Search fee: $3.00 per name. Required to search: name, years to search. Criminal records on microfiche from 1912-1977, on books from 1977. Online access to criminal records is the same as civil.
General Information: No adoptions or abuse records released. SASE required. Turnaround time 1 day. Fax notes: Fee to fax results is $2.50 per page. Copy fee: $.35 per page. Certification fee: $1.50. Fee payee: District Court Clerk. Only cashiers checks and money orders accepted. Prepayment is required.

Bayard Magistrate Court PO Box 125, Bayard, NM 88023; 505-537-3402; Fax: 505-537-7365. Hours: 8AM-5PM (MST). *Misdemeanor, Civil Actions Under $10,000, Eviction, Small Claims.*

Silver City Magistrate Court 1620 E Pine St, Silver City, NM 88061; 505-538-3811; Fax: 505-538-8079. Hours: 8AM-5PM; Public hours 9AM-4PM (MST). *Misdemeanor, Civil Actions Under $10,000, Eviction, Small Claims.*

www.nmcourts.com

County Clerk Box 898, Silver City, NM 88061; 505-538-2979; Fax: 505-538-8926. Hours: 8AM-5PM (MST). *Probate.*

Guadalupe County

4th Judicial District Court 420 Parker Ave Suite #5, Guadalupe County Courthouse, Santa Rosa, NM 88435; 505-472-3888; Fax: 505-472-3888. Hours: 8AM-5PM (MST). *Felony, Civil.*

Civil Records: Access: Online, in person. Visitors must perform in person searches for themselves. No search fee. Required to search: name, years to search. Civil cases indexed by defendant, plaintiff. Civil records on docket books from 1912. Access to court records from 1997 forward is available free online at www.nmcourts.com/disclaim.html.
Criminal Records: Access: Online, in person. Visitors must perform in person searches for themselves. No search fee. Required to search: name, years to search, DOB; also helpful: SSN. Criminal records on docket books from 1912. Online access to criminal records is the same as civil.
General Information: No adoption, insanity, juvenile, guardianship records released. Copy fee: $.35 per page. Certification fee: $1.50. Fee payee: District Court Clerk Office. Only cashiers checks and money orders accepted.

Santa Rosa Magistrate Court 603 Parker Ave, Santa Rosa, NM 88435; 505-472-3237. Hours: 8AM-Noon, 1-5PM (MST). *Misdemeanor, Civil Actions Under $10,000, Eviction, Small Claims.*

Vaughn Magistrate Court c/o Santa Rosa Justice Court, 602 Parker Av, Santa Rosa, NM 88435; 505-584-2345. 8AM-4PM (MST). *Misdemeanor, Civil Actions Under $10,000, Eviction, Small Claims.*

Note: The Vaugh court is only open the 2nd Wednesday of the month. It is located at 8th & Calle De Carill, Vaughn, NM 88353. Most records are at Santa Rosa (phone # given here).

County Clerk 420 Parker Ave, Courthouse, Santa Rosa, NM 88435; 505-472-3791; Fax: 505-472-3735. Hours: 8AM-5PM (MST). *Probate.*

Harding County

10th Judicial District Court Box 1002, Mosquero, NM 87733; 505-673-2252; Fax: 505-673-2252. Hours: 9AM-3PM M-W,F (MST). *Felony, Civil.*

Civil Records: Access: Phone, fax, mail, online, in person. No search fee. Required to search: name; also helpful: years to search. Civil cases indexed by defendant, plaintiff. Civil records on books from 1927, will have records available on microfiche. Access to court records from 1997 forward is available free online at www.nmcourts.com/disclaim.html.
Criminal Records: Access: Phone, fax, mail, online, in person. Visitors must perform in person searches for themselves. No search fee. Required to search: name, DOB, SSN; also helpful: years to search. Criminal records on books from 1927, will have records available on microfiche. Online access to criminal records is the same as civil.
General Information: No adoption records released. SASE required. Turnaround time 1 week. Fax notes: $2.00 for first page, $1.00 each add'l. Copy fee: $.35 per page. Certification fee: $1.50. Fee payee: District Court Clerk. Business checks accepted. Prepayment required.

Magistrate Court Box 9, Roy, NM 87743; 505-485-2549; Fax: 505-485-2407. Hours: 8AM-4:30PM (MST). *Misdemeanor, Civil Actions Under $10,000, Eviction, Small Claims.*

County Clerk County Clerk, Box 1002, Mosquero, NM 87733; 505-673-2301; Fax: 505-673-2922. Hours: 8AM-5PM (MST). *Probate.*

Hidalgo County

6th Judicial District Court PO Box 608, Lordsburg, NM 88045; 505-542-3411; Fax: 505-542-3481. Hours: 8AM-Noon, 1-5PM *Felony, Civil.*

Civil Records: Access: Phone, fax, mail, online, in person. Only the court performs in person searches; visitors may not. No search fee. Required to search: name, years to search. Civil cases indexed by defendant, plaintiff. Civil records on microfiche and archived from 1920. Access to court records from 1997 forward is available free online at www.nmcourts.com/disclaim.html.
Criminal Records: Access: Phone, fax, mail, online, in person. Only the court performs in person searches; visitors may not. No search fee. Required to search: name, years to search; also helpful: alias. Criminal records on microfiche and archived from 1920. Online access to criminal records is the same as civil.
General Information: No juvenile or adoption records released. SASE required. Turnaround time 3-5 days. Fax notes: Fee to fax results is $5.00 per document; will only fax back results to toll-free numbers. Copy fee: $.35 per page. Certification fee: $1.50. Fee payee: District Court Clerk. Business checks accepted. No personal checks. Prepayment is required.

Magistrate Court 420 Wabash Ave, Lordsburg, NM 88045; 505-542-3582. Hours: 8AM-5PM (MST). *Misdemeanor, Civil Actions Under $10,000, Eviction, Small Claims.*

www.nmcourts.com

County Clerk 300 S Shakespeare, Lordsburg, NM 88045; 505-542-9213; Fax: 505-542-3193. Hours: 9AM-Noon (MST). *Probate.*

Lea County

5th Judicial District Court 100 N. Main, Box 6C, Lovington, NM 88260; 505-396-8571; Fax: 505-396-2428. Hours: 8AM-5PM (MST). *Felony, Civil.*

www.fifthdistrictcourt.com

Civil Records: Access: Fax, mail, online, in person. Both court and visitors may perform in person searches. No search fee. Required to search: name, years to search. Civil cases indexed by defendant, plaintiff. Civil records on computer from 1990, on microfiche from 1912. Access to court records from 1997 forward is available free online at www.nmcourts.com/disclaim.html. Court refers search requests to a private researcher.
Criminal Records: Access: Fax, mail, online, in person. Both court and visitors may perform in person searches. No search fee. Required to search: name, years to search. Criminal records on computer from 1990, on microfiche from 1912. Online access to criminal records is the same as civil. Court refers searches to a private researcher.
General Information: Public Access terminal is available. No adoptions, mental, abuse records released. SASE required. Turnaround time 1-3 days. Copy fee: $.35 per page. Certification fee: $1.50. Fee payee: District Court Clerk. Only cashiers checks and money orders accepted. Prepayment is required.

Eunice Magistrate Court PO Box 240, Eunice, NM 88231; 505-394-3368; Fax: 505-394-3335. *Misdemeanor, Civil Actions Under $10,000, Eviction, Small Claims.*

Hobbs Magistrate Court 2110 N Alto Dr, Hobbs, NM 88240-3455; 505-397-3621; Fax: 505-393-9121. Hours: 8AM-4PM (MST). *Misdemeanor, Civil Actions Under $10,000, Eviction, Small Claims.*

www.nmcourts.com

Lovington Magistrate Court 100 W Central, Suite D, Lovington, NM 88260; 505-396-6677; Fax: 505-396-6163. Hours: 8AM-4PM (MST). *Misdemeanor, Civil Actions Under $10,000, Eviction, Small Claims.*

www.nmcourts.com

Tatum Magistrate Court PO Box 918, Tatum, NM 88267; 505-398-5300; Fax: 505-398-5310. Hours: 8AM-4PM (MST). *Misdemeanor, Civil Actions Under $10,000, Eviction, Small Claims.*

County Clerk Box 1507, Lovington, NM 88260; 505-396-8531; Fax: 505-396-3293. Hours: 8AM-5PM (MST). *Probate.*

Lincoln County

12th Judicial District Court Box 725, Carrizozo, NM 88301; 505-648-2432; Fax: 505-648-2581. Hours: 8AM-5PM (MST). *Felony, Civil.*

www.12thdistrict.com

Civil Records: Access: Online, in person. Visitors must perform in person searches for themselves. No search fee. Required to search: name, years to search. Civil cases indexed by defendant, plaintiff. Civil records on computer from 1991, docket books from 1960, microfiche to 1960. Access to court records from 1997

forward is available free online at www.nmcourts.com/disclaim.html. The court will refer searches to a private researcher.
Criminal Records: Access: Online, in person. Visitors must perform in person searches for themselves. No search fee. Required to search: name, years to search. Criminal records on computer from 1991, docket books from 1960, microfiche to 1960. Online access to criminal records is the same as civil. The court will refer all search requests to a private researcher.
General Information: Public Access terminal is available. No juvenile, adoption, or mental records released. Copy fee: $.35 per page. Certification fee: $1.50. Fee payee: District Court Clerk. Business checks accepted. Prepayment is required.

Ruidoso Magistrate Court 301 W Highway 70 #2, Ruidoso, NM 88345; 505-378-7022; Fax: 505-378-8508. Hours: 8AM-4PM (MST). *Misdemeanor, Civil Actions Under $10,000, Eviction, Small Claims.*

County Clerk PO Box 338, Carrizozo, NM 88301; 505-648-2394; Fax: 505-648-2576. Hours: 8AM-5PM (MST). *Probate.*

Note: This court will not do searches

Los Alamos County

1st Judicial District Court, NM.

http://firstdistrictcourt.com

Note: All civil and criminal cases handled by Santa Fe District Court

Magistrate Court 1319 Trinity Dr, Los Alamos, NM 87544; 505-662-2727; Fax: 505-661-6258. Hours: 8AM-5PM (MST). *Misdemeanor, Civil Actions Under $10,000, Eviction, Small Claims.*

County Clerk PO Box 30, Los Alamos, NM 87544; 505-662-8010; Fax: 505-662-8008. Hours: 8AM-5PM (MST). *Probate.*

Luna County

6th Judicial District Court Luna County Courthouse Room 40, Deming, NM 88030; 505-546-9611; Fax: 505-546-0971. Hours: 8AM-4PM (MST). *Felony, Civil.*

www.nmcourts.com

Civil Records: Access: Mail, online, in person. Both court and visitors may perform in person searches. Search fee: $5.00 per name. Required to search: name, years to search. Civil cases indexed by defendant, plaintiff. Civil records on microfiche from 1911; on computer back to 1997. Access to court records from 1997 forward is available free online at www.nmcourts.com/disclaim.html.
Criminal Records: Access: Mail, online, in person. Both court and visitors may perform in person searches. Search fee: $5.00 per name. Required to search: name, years to search. Criminal records on microfiche from 1911; on computer back to 1997. Online access to criminal records is the same as civil.
General Information: Public Access terminal is available. No adoptions, mental, sequestered or juvenile records released. SASE required. Turnaround time 5 days. Fax notes: Fee to fax results is $.35 per page. Copy fee: $.35 per page. Certification fee: $1.50. Only cashiers checks and money orders accepted. Prepayment is required.

Magistrate Court 912 S Silver St, Deming, NM 88030; 505-546-9321; Fax: 505-546-4896. Hours: 8AM-Noon, 1-5PM (MST). *Misdemeanor, Civil Actions Under $10,000, Eviction, Small Claims.*

www.nmcourts.com

County Clerk PO Box 1838, Deming, NM 88031; 505-546-0491; Fax: 505-546-4708. Hours: 8AM-5PM (MST). *Probate.*

McKinley County

11th Judicial District Court 201 W. Hill, Room 4, Gallup, NM 87301; 505-863-6816; Fax: 505-722-9172. Hours: 8AM-Noon, 1-5PM (MST). *Felony, Civil.*

Civil Records: Access: Phone, mail, online, in person. Both court and visitors may perform in person searches. No search fee. Required to search: name, years to search. Civil cases indexed by defendant, plaintiff. Civil records on computer from 1989, on microfiche from 1923. Access to court records from 1997 forward is free online at www.nmcourts.com/disclaim.html. One name only by phone.

Criminal Records: Access: Phone, mail, online, in person. Both court and visitors may perform in person searches. No search fee. Required to search: name, years to search, DOB; also helpful: SSN. Criminal records on computer from 1989, on microfiche from 1923. Online access to criminal records is the same as civil. Will search one name only by phone.

General Information: Public Access terminal is available. No adoption or juvenile records released. SASE required. Turnaround time 3-5 days. Fax notes: Fee to fax results is $5.00 per call. Copy fee: $.35 per page. Certification fee: $1.50. Fee payee: McKinley County District Court. No personal checks accepted. Prepayment is required.

Magistrate Court 285 S Boardman Dr, Gallup, NM 87301; 505-722-6636. Hours: 8AM-4PM (MST). *Misdemeanor, Civil Actions Under $10,000, Eviction, Small Claims.*

County Clerk PO Box 1268, Gallup, NM 87305; 505-863-6866; Fax: 505-863-1419. Hours: 8AM-5PM (MST). *Probate.*

Mora County

4th Judicial District Court PO Box 1540, Las Vegas, NM 87701; 505-425-7281; Fax: 505-425-6307. Hours: 8AM-Noon, 1-5PM (MST). *Felony, Civil.*

Civil Records: Access: Online, in person. Visitors must perform in person searches for themselves. No search fee. Required to search: name, years to search. Civil cases indexed by defendant. Civil records on microfiche from 1912, archived before 1912. Access to court records from 1997 forward is available free online at www.nmcourts.com/disclaim.html.

Criminal Records: Access: Online, in person. Visitors must perform in person searches for themselves. No search fee. Required to search: name, years to search. Criminal records on microfiche from 1912, archived before 1912. Online access to criminal records is the same as civil.

General Information: No adoptions, insanity, or juvenile records released. Copy fee: $.35 per page. Certification fee: $1.50. Fee payee: 4th Judicial District Court. Only cashiers checks and money orders accepted. Prepayment is required.

Magistrate Court 1927 7th Street, Las Vegas, NM 87701-4957; 505-425-5204. Hours: 8AM-4PM (closed for lunch) (MST). *Misdemeanor, Civil Actions Under $10,000, Eviction, Small Claims.*

Probate Court PO Box 36, Mora, NM 87732; 505-387-5702. Hours: 8AM-5PM (MST). *Probate.*

Otero County

12th Judicial District Court 1000 New York Ave, Rm 209, Alamogordo, NM 88310-6940; 505-437-7310; Fax: 505-434-8886. Hours: 8AM-5PM (MST). *Felony, Civil.*

Civil Records: Access: Online, in person. Visitors must perform in person searches for themselves. No search fee. Required to search: name, years to search. Civil cases indexed by defendant, plaintiff. Civil records on computer from 1991, on microfiche from 1926. Access to court records from 1997 forward is available free online at www.nmcourts.com/disclaim.html. Phone & mail access limited to 5 names each.

Criminal Records: Access: Online, in person. Visitors must perform in person searches for themselves. No search fee. Required to search: name, years to search. Criminal records on computer from 1991, on microfiche from 1926. Online access to criminal records is the same as civil. Phone & mail access limited to 5 names each. Only court performs searches prior to March 1986.

General Information: No sealed, adoption records released. Copy fee: $.35 per page. Certification fee: $1.50. Fee payee: District Court. Only cashiers checks and money orders accepted. Prepayment is required.

Magistrate Court 263 Robert H Bradley Dr, Alamogordo, NM 88310-8288; 505-437-9000 x256; Fax: 505-439-1365. Hours: 8AM-4PM (MST). *Misdemeanor, Civil Actions Under $10,000, Eviction, Small Claims.*

County Clerk 1000 New York Ave, Rm 108, Alamogordo, NM 88310-6932; 505-437-4942; Fax: 505-443-2922. Hours: 7:30AM-6PM (MST). *Probate.*

Quay County

10th Judicial District Court Box 1067, Tucumcari, NM 88401; 505-461-2764; Fax: 505-461-4498. Hours: 8AM-5PM (MST). *Felony, Civil.*

Note: May change to new area code 575 late in 2001.

Civil Records: Access: Phone, fax, mail, online, in person. Both court and visitors may perform in person searches. No search fee. Required to search: name, years to search. Civil cases indexed by defendant, plaintiff. Civil records on hard copy file from 1995 to present, microfiche 1912 to 1994, archived from 1911, on computer back to 1997. Access to court records from 1997 forward is available free online at www.nmcourts.com/disclaim.html.

Criminal Records: Access: Phone, fax, mail, online, in person. Both court and visitors may perform in person searches. No search fee. Required to search: name; also helpful: years to search, DOB, SSN. Criminal records on hard copy file from 1995 to present, microfiche 1912 to 1994, archived from 1911, on computer back to 1997. Online access to criminal records is the same as civil.

General Information: Public Access terminal is available. No adoptions, juvenile, insanity records released. SASE required. Turnaround time same day. Fax notes: $2.00 for first page, $1.00 each add'l. Copy fee: $.35 per page. Certification fee: $1.50. Fee payee: District Court Clerk. Only cashiers checks and money orders accepted.

Tucumcari Magistrate Court PO Box 1301, Tucumcari, NM 88401; 505-461-1700; Fax: 505-461-4522. Hours: 8AM-Noon, 1-5PM (MST). *Misdemeanor, Civil Actions Under $10,000, Eviction, Small Claims.*

Note: San Jon Magistrate Court (closed) records are found here.

County Clerk 3000 S Third St, PO Box 1225, Tucumcari, NM 88401; 505-461-0510; Fax: 505-461-0513. Hours: 8AM-5PM (MST). *Probate.*

Rio Arriba County

1st Judicial District Court, NM.

http://firstdistrictcourt.com

Note: All civil and criminal cases handled by Santa Fe District Court

Rio Arriba Magistrate Court - Division 1 PO Box 538, Chama, NM 87520; 505-756-2278. Hours: 8AM-Noon, 1-5PM (MST). *Misdemeanor, Civil Actions Under $10,000, Eviction, Small Claims.*

Rio Arriba Magistrate Court - Division 2 410 Paseo de Onate, Espanola, NM 87532; 505-753-2532. Hours: 8AM-4PM (MST). *Misdemeanor, Civil Actions Under $10,000, Eviction, Small Claims.*

County Clerk PO Box 158, Tierra Amarilla, NM 87575; 505-588-7724; Fax: 505-588-7418. Hours: 8AM-5PM (MST). *Probate.*

Roosevelt County

9th Judicial District Court 109 West 1st St, Suite 207, Portales, NM 88130; 505-356-4463; Fax: 505-359-2140. Hours: 8AM-4PM *Felony, Civil.*

Civil Records: Access: Online, in person. Visitors must perform in person searches for themselves. No search fee. Required to search: name, years to search. Civil cases indexed by defendant, plaintiff. Civil records on microfiche from 1912, archived before 1912. Access to court records from 1997 forward is available free online at www.nmcourts.com/disclaim.html.

Criminal Records: Access: Online, in person. Visitors must perform in person searches for themselves. No search fee. Required to search: name, years to search. Criminal records on microfiche from 1912, archived before 1912. Online access to criminal records is the same as civil.

General Information: No adoption, guardianship, insanity records released. Copy fee: $.35 per page. Certification fee: $1.50. Fee payee: 9th Judicial District Court. Only cashiers checks and money orders accepted. Prepayment is required.

Magistrate Court 42427 US Hwy 70, Portales, NM 88130; 505-356-8569; Fax: 505-359-6883. Hours: 8AM-4PM (MST). *Misdemeanor, Civil Actions Under $10,000, Eviction, Small Claims.*

www.nmcourts.com

County Clerk Roosevelt County Courthouse, 109 W First, Portales, NM 88130; 505-356-8562; Fax: 505-356-3560. Hours: 8AM-5PM (MST). *Probate.*

San Juan County

11th Judicial District Court 103 S. Oliver, Aztec, NM 87410; 505-334-6151; Fax: 505-334-1940. Hours: 8AM-Noon, 1-5PM (MST). *Felony, Civil.*

Civil Records: Access: Online, in person. Visitors must perform in person searches for themselves. No search fee. Required to search: name, years to search; also helpful: address. Civil cases indexed by defendant, plaintiff. Civil records on computer from 1982, on microfiche from 1900s, on cards from 1800s. Access to court records from 1997 forward is available free online at www.nmcourts.com/disclaim.html.

Criminal Records: Access: Online, in person. Visitors must perform in person searches for themselves. No search fee. Required to search: name, years to search, DOB; also helpful: address, SSN. Criminal records on computer from 1982, on microfiche from 1900s, on cards from 1800s. Online access to criminal records is the same as civil.

General Information: Public Access terminal is available. No adoptions, insanity, sealed, expunged records released. Copy fee: $.35 per page. Certification fee: $1.50 per page. Fee payee: Eleventh District Court. No personal or out-of-state checks accepted. Prepayment is required.

Aztec Magistrate Court 1810 W Aztec Blvd, Aztec, NM 87410; 505-334-9479; Fax: 505-334-2178. Hours: 8AM-Noon, 1-5PM (MST). *Misdemeanor, Civil Actions Under $10,000, Eviction, Small Claims.*

Farmington Magistrate Court 950 W Apache St, Farmington, NM 87401; 505-326-4338; Fax: 505-325-2618. Hours: 8AM-4PM (MST). *Misdemeanor, Civil Actions Under $10,000, Eviction, Small Claims.*
www.nmcourts.com

County Clerk PO Box 550, Aztec, NM 87410; 505-334-9471; Fax: 505-334-3635. Hours: 7AM-5:30PM (MST). *Probate.*

San Miguel County

4th Judicial District Court PO Box 1540, Las Vegas, NM 87701; 505-425-7281; Fax: 505-425-6307. Hours: 8AM-Noon, 1-5PM (MST). *Felony, Civil, Probate.*

Note: Also handles cases for Mora County.

Civil Records: Access: Phone, mail, online, in person. Visitors must perform in person searches for themselves. No search fee. Required to search: name, years to search. Civil cases indexed by defendant, plaintiff. Civil records on microfiche from 1912, archived before 1912. Access to court records from 1997 forward is available free online at www.nmcourts.com/disclaim.html.
Criminal Records: Access: Online, in person. Visitors must perform in person searches for themselves. No search fee. Required to search: name, years to search. Criminal records on microfiche from 1912, archived before 1912. Online access to criminal records is the same as civil.
General Information: No adoptions, insanity, juvenile records released. SASE required. Turnaround time 2 days. Copy fee: $.35 per page. Certification fee: $1.50. Fee payee: 4th Judicial District Court Clerk. Only cashiers checks and money orders accepted.

Magistrate Court 1927 7th St, Las Vegas, NM 87701-4957; 505-425-5204; Fax: 505-425-0422. Hours: 8AM-4PM (MST). *Misdemeanor, Civil Actions Under $10,000, Eviction, Small Claims.*

County Clerk San Miguel County Clerk, 500 W. National Av, Las Vegas, NM 87701; 505-425-9331; Fax: 505-454-7199. Hours: 8AM-Noon, 1-5PM (MST). *Probate.*

Sandoval County

13th Judicial District Court 110 Avenida De Justicia, Bernalillo, NM 87004; 505-867-2376. Hours: 8AM-Noon, 1-5PM (MST). *Felony, Civil.*

Civil Records: Access: Fax, mail, online, in person. Both court and visitors may perform in person searches. Search fee: $5.00 search fee. Required to search: name, years to search. Civil cases indexed by defendant, plaintiff. Civil records indexed on computer back to 11/96; prior on microfiche. Access to court records from 1997 forward is available free online at www.nmcourts.com/disclaim.html.
Criminal Records: Access: Fax, mail, online, in person. Both court and visitors may perform in person searches. Search fee: $5.00 for up to 2 names; 3-10 names $10.00; 11+ names $20.00. Required to search: name, years to search. Criminal records on computer back to 11/96. Online access to criminal records is the same as civil.
General Information: Public Access terminal is available. No sequestered, juvenile, probate or guardianship records released. Turnaround time 1-2 days. Fax notes: Fee to fax results is $2.50 per page. Copy fee: $.35 per page. Microfilm copies $.50 per page (1991 and prior). Certification fee: $1.50. Fee

payee: 13th Judicial District Court. Business checks accepted.

Bernalillo Magistrate Court PO Box 818, Bernalillo, NM 87004; 505-867-5202. Hours: 8AM-4PM (MST). *Misdemeanor, Civil Actions Under $10,000, Eviction, Small Claims.*

Cuba Magistrate Court 16B Cordova St, Cuba, NM 87013; 505-289-3519; Fax: 505-289-3013. Hours: 8AM-Noon, 1-5PM (MST). *Misdemeanor, Civil Actions Under $10,000, Eviction, Small Claims.*

County Clerk PO Box 40, Bernalillo, NM 87004; 505-867-7572; Fax: 505-771-8610. Hours: 8AM-5PM (MST). *Probate.*

Santa Fe County

1st Judicial District Court Box 2268, Santa Fe, NM 87504; 505-476-0189; Fax: 505-827-7998. Hours: 8AM-4PM (MST). *Felony, Civil.*

http://firstdistrictcourt.com

Note: Because this court also handles the counties of Los Alamos and Rio Arriba, you must indicate which county you are searching.

Civil Records: Access: Phone, mail, online, in person. Both court and visitors may perform in person searches. Search fee: $10.00 minimum if more than 5 names requested or to search docket books. Required to search: name, years to search. Civil cases indexed by defendant, plaintiff. Civil records on computer from 1986, older records on docket books. Access to court records from 1997 forward is available free online at www.nmcourts.com/disclaim.html.
General Information: Public Access terminal is available. No adoption, juvenile, mental or abuse records released. SASE required. Turnaround time 2 days. Copy fee: $.35 per page. Certification fee: $1.50. Fee payee: District Court. Business checks accepted. Prepayment is required.

Magistrate Court 2052 Galisteo St, Santa Fe, NM 87505; 505-476-0189; Fax: 505-984-0189. Hours: 8AM-4PM (MST). *Misdemeanor, Civil Actions Under $10,000, Eviction, Small Claims.*

Pojoaque Magistrate Court Rte 11, Box 21M, Pojoaque, NM 87501; 505-455-7938; Fax: 505-455-3053. Hours: 8AM-Noon,1-5PM (MST). *Misdemeanor, Civil Actions Under $10,000, Eviction, Small Claims.*

Note: Court is often closed though the clerk can be contacted at the Santa Fe Magistrate Court, 2052 Galisteo St, 505-476-0189.

County Clerk Box 276, Santa Fe, NM 87504; 505-986-6279; Fax: 505-986-6362. Hours: 8AM-5PM (MST). *Probate.*

Sierra County

7th Judicial District Court PO Box 3009, Truth or Consequences, NM 87901; 505-894-7167; Fax: 505-894-7168. Hours: 8AM-4PM (MST). *Felony, Civil.*

Civil Records: Access: Fax, mail, online, in person. Only the court performs in person searches; visitors may not. No search fee. Required to search: name, years to search, address. Civil cases indexed by defendant, plaintiff. Civil records on microfiche from 1920, archived before 1920. Access to court records from 1997 forward is available free online at www.nmcourts.com/disclaim.html.
Criminal Records: Access: Fax, mail, online, in person. Only the court performs in person searches; visitors may not. No search fee. Required to search: name, years to search, address, SSN. Criminal records on microfiche from 1920, archived before 1920. Online access to criminal records is the same as civil.

General Information: Public Access terminal is available. No adoptions, insanity, juvenile, guardianship records released. SASE required. Turnaround time 2 days. Copy fee: $.35 per page. Certification fee: $1.50. Fee payee: Sierra County District Court. Only cashiers checks and money orders accepted. Prepayment is required.

Magistrate Court 155 W Barton, Truth or Consequences, NM 87901; 505-894-3051; Fax: 505-894-0476. Hours: 8AM-4PM (MST). *Misdemeanor, Civil Actions Under $10,000, Eviction, Small Claims.*

County Clerk 311 Date St., Truth or Consequences, NM 87901; 505-894-2840; Probate phone: 505-894-4416; Fax: 505-894-2516. Hours: 8AM-5PM (MST). *Probate.*

Socorro County

7th Judicial District Court, NM.

Note: All civil and criminal cases are handled by Catron County District Court.

Magistrate Court 404 Park St, Socorro, NM 87801; 505-835-2500. Hours: 8AM-Noon, 1-5PM (MST). *Misdemeanor, Civil Actions Under $10,000, Eviction, Small Claims.*

County Clerk 200 Church St, Socorro, NM 87801; 505-835-0423; Fax: 505-835-1043. Hours: 8AM-5PM (MST). *Probate.*

Taos County

8th Judicial District Court 105 Albright St Ste H, Taos, NM 87571; 505-758-3173; Fax: 505-751-1281. Hours: 8AM-4PM (MST). *Felony, Civil.*

Civil Records: Access: Mail, fax, online, in person. Visitors must perform in person searches for themselves. No search fee. Required to search: name, years to search. Civil cases indexed by defendant, plaintiff. Civil records on computer since 1993, books since 1912, microfiche from 1912-1950. Access to court records from 1997 forward is available free online at www.nmcourts.com/disclaim.html.
Criminal Records: Access: Mail, fax, online, in person. Visitors must perform in person searches for themselves. No search fee. Required to search: name, years to search, DOB; also helpful: signed release, SSN. Criminal records on computer since 1993, books since 1912, microfiche from 1912-1950. Online access to criminal records is the same as civil.
General Information: Public Access terminal is available. No adoption, juvenile, abuse or sequestered case records released. SASE required. Turnaround time 2 days. Fax notes: Fee to fax results is $2.00 per page. Copy fee: $.35 per page. Certification fee: $1.50. Fee payee: District Court. Only cashiers checks and money orders accepted. Prepayment is required.

Questa Magistrate Court PO Box 586, Questa, NM 87556; 505-586-0761; Fax: 505-586-0428. Hours: 8AM-Noon,1-5PM (MST). *Misdemeanor, Civil Actions Under $10,000, Eviction, Small Claims.*

Taos Magistrate Court Box 1121 (920 Salazar Rd #B), Taos, NM 87571; 505-758-4030; Fax: 505-751-0983. Hours: 8AM-4PM (MST). *Misdemeanor, Civil Actions Under $10,000, Eviction, Small Claims.*

County Clerk 105 Albright, Suite D, Taos, NM 87551; 505-758-8266; Fax: 505-751-3391. Hours: 8AM-5PM (MST). *Probate.*

Torrance County

7th Judicial District Court County Courthouse, PO Box 78, Estancia, NM 87016; 505-384-2974; Fax: 505-384-2229. Hours: 8AM-4PM (MST). *Felony, Civil.*

www.nmcourts.com

Civil Records: Access: Mail, online, in person. Both court and visitors may perform in person searches. No search fee. Required to search: name, years to search. Civil cases indexed by defendant, plaintiff. Civil records on hard copy until filmed, microfiche from 1912; on computer back to 1997. Access to court records from 1997 forward is available free online at www.nmcourts.com/disclaim.html.

Criminal Records: Access: Mail, online, in person. Only the court performs in person searches; visitors may not. No search fee. Required to search: name, years to search; also helpful: SSN, DOB. Criminal records on hard copy until filmed, microfiche from 1912; on computer back to 1997. Online access to criminal records is the same as civil.

General Information: Public Access terminal is available. No juvenile, neglect, adoption, mental health records released. SASE required. Turnaround time 1 day. Copy fee: $.35 per page. Certification fee: $1.50. Fee payee: Seventh Judicial District Court. Only cashiers checks and money orders accepted. Prepayment is required.

Moriarty Magistrate Court PO Box 2027, Moriarty, NM 87035; 505-832-4476; Fax: 505-832-1563. Hours: 8AM-4PM (MST). *Misdemeanor, Civil Actions Under $10,000, Eviction, Small Claims.*

County Clerk PO Box 48, Estancia, NM 87016; 505-384-2221; Fax: 505-384-4080. Hours: 8AM-Noon, 1-5PM (MST). *Probate.*

Union County

8th Judicial District Court Box 310, Clayton, NM 88415; 505-374-9577; Fax: 505-374-2089. Hours: 8AM-Noon, 1-5PM (MST). *Felony, Civil.*

Civil Records: Access: Mail, online, in person. Both court and visitors may perform in person searches. No search fee. Required to search: name, years to search. Civil cases indexed by defendant, plaintiff. Civil records on cards from 1981. Access to court records from 1997 forward is available free online at www.nmcourts.com/disclaim.html.

Criminal Records: Access: Mail, online, in person. Both court and visitors may perform in person searches. No search fee. Required to search: name, years to search. Criminal records on docket sheets from 1981. Online access to criminal records is the same as civil.

General Information: No adoption, juvenile records released. SASE required. Turnaround time 1-2 days. Copy fee: $.35 per page. Certification fee: $1.50. Fee payee: Clerk of District Court. Only cashiers checks and money orders accepted. Prepayment is required.

Magistrate Court 836 Main Street, Clayton, NM 88415; 505-374-9472; Fax: 505-374-9368. Hours: 8AM-Noon, 1-5PM (MST). *Misdemeanor, Civil Actions Under $10,000, Eviction, Small Claims.*

County Clerk PO Box 430, Clayton, NM 88415; 505-374-9491; Fax: 505-374-2763. Hours: 9AM-Noon, 1-5PM (MST). *Probate.*

Valencia County

13th Judicial District Court Box 1089, Los Lunas, NM 87031; 505-865-4291; Fax: 505-865-8801. Hours: 8AM-5PM (MST). *Felony, Civil.*

Civil Records: Access: Fax, mail, online, in person. Both court and visitors may perform in person searches. Search fee: $5.00 for up to 2 names, $10.00 for 3-10 names. Required to search: name, years to search. Civil cases indexed by defendant, plaintiff. Civil records on microfiche from 1915. Access to court records from 1997 forward is available free online at www.nmcourts.com/disclaim.html.

Criminal Records: Access: Mail, online, in person. Both court and visitors may perform in person searches. Search fee: $5.00 fee for 2 names, $10.00 for 3-10 names. Required to search: name, years to search. Criminal records on microfiche from 1915. Online access to criminal records is the same as civil.

General Information: Public Access terminal is available. No adoptions or juvenile records released. SASE required. Turnaround time 2 days. Fax notes: Fax fees: $2.50 in-state; $5.00 out-of-state. Copy fee: $.35 per page. Certification fee: $1.50. Fee payee: 13th Judicial District Court. Only cashiers checks and money orders accepted.

Belen Magistrate Court 237 N Main St, Belen, NM 87002; 505-864-7509; Fax: 505-864-9532. Hours: 8AM-4PM (MST). *Misdemeanor, Civil Actions Under $10,000, Eviction, Small Claims.*

Los Lunas Magistrate Court 121 SE Don Diego, Los Lunas, NM 87031; 505-865-4637. Hours: 8AM-4PM (MST). *Misdemeanor, Civil Actions Under $10,000, Eviction, Small Claims.*

County Clerk PO Box 939, Los Lunas, NM 87031; 505-866-2073; Fax: 505-866-2023. Hours: 8AM-4:30PM (MST). *Probate.*

New Mexico Recording Offices

ORGANIZATION 33 counties, 33 recording offices. The recording officer is County Clerk. Most counties maintain a grantor/grantee index and a miscellaneous index. The entire state is in the Mountain Time Zone (MST).

REAL ESTATE RECORDS Most counties will not perform real estate searches. Copy and certification fees vary.

UCC RECORDS Financing statements are filed at the state level, except for real estate related collateral, which are filed with the County Clerk. However, prior to 07/2001, consumer goods and farm collateral were also filed at the County Clerk and these older records can be searched there. Only a few recording offices will perform UCC searches. Use search request form UCC-11. Search and copy fees vary, but search fee is usually $5.00.

TAX LIEN RECORDS All federal and state tax liens are filed with the County Clerk. Most counties will not provide tax lien searches.

OTHER LIENS Judgment, mechanics, lis pendens, contractors, hospital.

Bernalillo County

County Clerk, P.O. Box 542, Albuquerque, NM 87103-0542. 505-768-4141; Fax 505-768-4631. http://www.berncotreasurer.com
Will search UCC records. Tax liens not included in UCC search. RE record owner and mortgage searches available. **Online Access:** Real Estate. Records on the county Records Search page are available free online at www.berncotreasurer.com/ProcessSearch.asp?cmd=NewSearch. **Other Phone Numbers:** Assessor 505-768-4040.

Catron County

County Clerk, P.O. Box 197, Reserve, NM 87830-0197. County Clerk, R/E and UCC Recording 505-533-6400; Fax 505-533-6400.
Will not search UCC records. This agency will not do a tax lien search. Will not search R/E records. **Other Phone Numbers:** Assessor 505-533-6577; Treasurer 505-533-6384; Elections 505-533-6400.

Chaves County

County Clerk, Box 580, Roswell, NM 88202-0580. County Clerk, R/E and UCC Recording 505-624-6614; Fax 505-624-6523.
Will not search UCC records. This agency will not do a tax lien search. Will not search real estate records. **Other Phone Numbers:** Assessor 505-624-6603; Treasurer 505-624-6618; Appraiser/Auditor 505-624-6603; Elections 505-624-6614; Vital Records 505-827-0121.

Cibola County

County Clerk, P.O. Box 190, Grants, NM 87020. 505-287-9431; Fax 505-285-5434.
Will search UCC records. Will not search real estate records. **Other Phone Numbers:** Assessor 505-285-2527.

Colfax County

County Clerk, P.O. Box 159, Raton, NM 87740-0159. County Clerk, R/E and UCC Recording 505-445-5551; Fax 505-445-4031.
Will not search UCC records. Will not search real estate records. **Other Phone Numbers:** Assessor 505-445-2341; Treasurer 505-445-3171; Elections 505-445-5551; Vital Records 505-445-5551.

Curry County

County Clerk, P.O. Box 1168, Clovis, NM 88102-1168. County Clerk, R/E and UCC Recording 505-763-5591; Fax 505-763-4232. http://www.currycounty.org/clerk's.html

Will not search UCC records or tax liens. Will not search real estate records. **Other Phone Numbers:** Assessor 505-763-5731; Treasurer 505-763-3931; Appraiser/Auditor 505-763-5731; Elections 505-763-5591; Vital Records 505-827-0121.

De Baca County

County Clerk, P.O. Box 347, Fort Sumner, NM 88119. 505-355-2601; Fax 505-355-2441.
Will search UCC records. Will not search real estate records. **Other Phone Numbers:** Assessor 505-355-7448; Treasurer 505-355-7395; Elections 505-355-2601.

Dona Ana County

County Clerk, 251 West Amador, Room 103, Las Cruces, NM 88005-2893. 505-647-7421; Fax 505-647-7464. http://www.co.dona-ana.nm.us
Will search UCC records. Will not search real estate records. **Online Access:** Assessor, Liens, Real Estate. Records on the Real Property database are available free online at www.co.dona-ana.nm.us/newpages/assr/search.html. **Other Phone Numbers:** Assessor 505-647-7400.

Eddy County

County Clerk, 101 W. Greene St., Room 312, Carlsbad, NM 88220. County Clerk, R/E and UCC Recording 505-885-3383; Fax 505-234-1793.
Will search UCC records. Will not search real estate records. **Other Phone Numbers:** Assessor 505-885-3813; Treasurer 505-885-9313; Appraiser/Auditor 505-885-3813; Elections 505-885-3383; Vital Records 505-827-0121.

Grant County

County Clerk, P.O. Box 898, Silver City, NM 88062. 505-538-2979; Fax 505-538-8926.
Will search UCC records.

Guadalupe County

County Clerk, 420 Parker Avenue, Courthouse-Suite 1, Santa Rosa, NM 88435. 505-472-3791; Fax 505-472-3735.
Will search UCC records. **Other Phone Numbers:** Assessor 505-472-3738; Treasurer 505-472-3133.

Harding County

County Clerk, P.O. Box 1002, Mosquero, NM 87733-1002. County Clerk, R/E and UCC Recording 505-673-2301; Fax 505-673-2922.
Will not search UCC records. This agency will not do a tax lien search. Will not search R/E records. **Other**

Phone Numbers: Assessor 505-673-2926; Treasurer 505-673-2928; Appraiser/Auditor 505-673-2926; Elections 505-673-2301.

Hidalgo County

County Clerk, 300 Shakespeare Street, Lordsburg, NM 88045. 505-542-9213.
Will search UCC records. This agency will not do a tax lien search. Will not search real estate records. **Other Phone Numbers:** Assessor 505-542-3433; Treasurer 505-542-9313.

Lea County

County Clerk, P.O. Box 1507, Lovington, NM 88260. 505-396-8531; Fax 505-396-3293.
Will search UCC records. Will not search real estate records. **Other Phone Numbers:** Assessor 505-396-8527.

Lincoln County

County Clerk, P.O. Box 338, Carrizozo, NM 88301. County Clerk, R/E and UCC Recording 505-648-2394; Fax 505-648-2576.
Will not search UCC records. Will not search real estate records. **Other Phone Numbers:** Assessor 505-648-2306; Treasurer 505-648-2397; Appraiser/Auditor 505-648-2306; Elections 505-648-2331; Vital Records 505-648-2394; Manager 505-648-2385.

Los Alamos County

County Clerk, P.O. Box 30, Los Alamos, NM 87544. County Clerk, R/E and UCC Recording 505-662-8010; www.lac.losalamos.nm.us
Will not search UCC records. This agency will not do a tax lien search. Will not search real estate records. **Other Phone Numbers:** Assessor 505-662-8030; Treasurer 505-662-8070; Elections 505-662-8011; Vital Records 505-827-2338.

Luna County

County Clerk, P.O. Box 1838, Deming, NM 88031-1838. County Clerk, R/E and UCC Recording 505-546-0491; Fax 505-546-4708.
Will search UCC records. **Other Phone Numbers:** Assessor 505-546-0404; Treasurer 505-546-0401; Elections 505-546-0491; Vital Records 505-827-0121 (Santa Fe, NM).

McKinley County

County Clerk, P.O. Box 1268, Gallup, NM 87301. 505-863-6866.
Will search UCC records. This agency will not do a tax lien search. RE owner, mortgage, and property transfer

searches available. **Other Phone Numbers:** Assessor 505-863-3032; Treasurer 505-722-4459.

Mora County

County Clerk, P.O. Box 360, Mora, NM 87732-0360. 505-387-2448; Fax 505-387-9023.
Will search UCC records. **Other Phone Numbers:** Assessor 505-387-5029; Treasurer 505-387-2756; Elections 505-387-2448.

Otero County

County Clerk, 1000 New York Avenue, Room 108, Alamogordo, NM 88310-6932. County Clerk, R/E and UCC Recording 505-437-4942; Fax 505-443-2922.
Will search UCC records. This agency will not do a tax lien search. Will not search real estate records. **Other Phone Numbers:** Assessor 505-437-5310; Treasurer 505-437-2030; Elections 505-437-4942.

Quay County

County Clerk, P.O. Box 1225, Tucumcari, NM 88401-1225. 505-461-0510; Fax 505-461-0513.
Will search UCC records. **Other Phone Numbers:** Assessor 505-461-1760.

Rio Arriba County

County Clerk, P.O. Box 158, Tierra Amarilla, NM 87575. 505-588-7724.
Will search UCC records. This agency will not do a tax lien search. Will not search real estate records. **Other Phone Numbers:** Assessor 505-588-7726; Treasurer 505-588-7727.

Roosevelt County

County Clerk, 101 West First, Portales, NM 88130. 505-356-8562; Fax 505-356-8562.
Will search UCC records. Will not search real estate records. **Other Phone Numbers:** Assessor 505-356-6971; Treasurer 505-356-4081.

San Juan County

County Clerk and Recorder, P.O. Box 550, Aztec, NM 87410. County Clerk and Recorder, R/E and UCC Recording 505-334-9471; Fax 505-334-3635. http://www.co.san-juan.nm.us

This agency will not search UCC records. Will not search real estate records. **Online Access:** Real Estate, Assessor. Online access to county real estate tax data is available free at www.co.san-juan.nm.us/InfoSJC/ProfilePublicAccess.asp. **Other Phone Numbers:** Assessor 505-334-6157; Treasurer 505-334-9421; Appraiser/Auditor 505-334-6157; Elections 505-334-9471.

San Miguel County

County Clerk, Courthouse, Las Vegas, NM 87701. County Clerk, R/E & UCC Recording 505-425-9331; Fax 505-425-7019.
Will search UCC records. Will not search real estate records. **Other Phone Numbers:** Assessor 505-454-4980; Treasurer 505-425-9376; Elections 505-425-9331; Vital Records 505-425-9368.

Sandoval County

County Clerk, P.O. Box 40, Bernalillo, NM 87004. County Clerk, R/E and UCC Recording 505-867-7572; Fax 505-771-8610.
Will search UCC records. Will not search real estate records. **Other Phone Numbers:** Assessor 505-867-2355; Treasurer 505-867-2945; Appraiser/Auditor 505-867-7503; Elections 505-867-7577; Vital Records 505-841-4185.

Santa Fe County

County Clerk, P.O. Box 1985, Santa Fe, NM 87504-1985. 505-986-6280; Fax 505-995-2767.
Will search UCC records. **Other Phone Numbers:** Assessor 505-986-6308; Treasurer 505-986-6253.

Sierra County

County Clerk, 100 Date Street, Truth or Consequences, NM 87901. County Clerk, R/E and UCC Recording 505-894-2840; Fax 505-894-2516.
Will search UCC records. This agency will not do a tax lien search. Will not search real estate records. **Other Phone Numbers:** Assessor 505-894-2589; Treasurer 505-894-3524; Elections 505-894-2840; Vital Records 505-827-2338.

Socorro County

County Clerk, P.O. Box I, Socorro, NM 87801. 505-835-3263 R/E Recording: 505-835-0423 UCC Recording: 505-835-0589; Fax 505-835-1043.
Will search UCC records. Will not search real estate records. **Other Phone Numbers:** Assessor 505-835-0714; Treasurer 505-835-1701; Appraiser/Auditor 505-835-0714; Elections 505-835-0423; Vital Records 505-835-0423.

Taos County

County Clerk, 105 Albright Street, Suite D, Taos, NM 87571-. County Clerk, R/E and UCC Recording 505-751-8654; Fax 505-751-8637.
Will search UCC records. Will not search real estate records. **Other Phone Numbers:** Assessor 505-751-8651; Treasurer 505-751-8672; Appraiser/Auditor 505-751-8554; Elections 505-751-8657.

Torrance County

County Clerk, P.O. Box 48, Estancia, NM 87016. 505-384-2221; Fax 505-384-4080.
Will search UCC records. Will not search real estate records.

Union County

County Clerk, P.O. Box 430, Clayton, NM 88415. County Clerk, R/E and UCC Recording 505-374-9491; Fax 505-374-2763.
Will search UCC records. Will not search real estate records. **Other Phone Numbers:** Assessor 505-374-9441; Treasurer 505-374-2331; Appraiser/Auditor 505-374-9441; Elections 505-374-9491.

Valencia County

County Clerk, P.O. Box 969, Los Lunas, NM 87031. County Clerk, R/E and UCC Recording 505-866-2073; Fax 505-866-2023.
Will search UCC records. **Other Phone Numbers:** Assessor 505-866-2065; Treasurer 505-866-2090; Elections 505-866-2080; Vital Records 505-841-4100.

New Mexico County Locator

You will usually be able to find the city name in the City/County Cross Reference below. In that case, it is a simple matter to determine the county from the cross reference. However, only the official US Postal Service city names are included in this index. There are an additional 40,000 place names that people use in their addresses. Therefore, we have also included a ZIP/City Cross Reference immediately following the City/County Cross Reference.

If you know the ZIP Code but the city name does not appear in the City/County Cross Reference index, look up the ZIP Code in the ZIP/City Cross Reference, find the city name, then look up the city name in the City/County Cross Reference. For example, you want to know the county for an address of Menands, NY 12204. There is no "Menands" in the City/County Cross Reference. The ZIP/City Cross Reference shows that ZIP Codes 12201-12288 are for the city of Albany. Looking back in the City/County Cross Reference, Albany is in Albany County.

City/County Cross Reference

ABIQUIU Rio Arriba
ALAMOGORDO Otero
ALBUQUERQUE (87114) Bernalillo(99), Sandoval(1)
ALBUQUERQUE Bernalillo
ALCALDE Rio Arriba
ALGODONES Sandoval
ALTO Lincoln
AMALIA Taos
AMISTAD Union
ANGEL FIRE Colfax
ANIMAS Hidalgo
ANTHONY (88021) Dona Ana(87), Otero(13)
ANTON CHICO Guadalupe
ARAGON Catron
ARENAS VALLEY Grant
ARREY Sierra
ARROYO HONDO Taos
ARROYO SECO Taos
ARTESIA Eddy
AZTEC San Juan
BARD Quay
BAYARD Grant
BELEN Valencia
BELL RANCH San Miguel
BELLVIEW Curry
BENT Otero
BERINO Dona Ana
BERNALILLO Sandoval
BINGHAM Socorro
BLANCO San Juan
BLOOMFIELD San Juan
BLUEWATER Cibola
BOSQUE (87006) Socorro(87), Valencia(13)
BOSQUE FARMS (87068) Bernalillo(99), Valencia(2)
BRIMHALL McKinley
BROADVIEW (88112) Curry(92), Quay(8)
BUCKHORN Grant
BUENA VISTA Mora
BUEYEROS Harding
CABALLO Sierra
CANJILON Rio Arriba
CANNON AFB Curry
CANONES Rio Arriba
CAPITAN Lincoln
CAPROCK Lea
CAPULIN Union
CARLSBAD Eddy
CARRIZOZO (88301) Lincoln(77), Torrance(23)
CARSON Taos
CASA BLANCA Cibola
CAUSEY Roosevelt
CEBOLLA Rio Arriba
CEDAR CREST Bernalillo
CEDARVALE Torrance
CERRILLOS Santa Fe
CERRO Taos
CHACON Mora
CHAMA Rio Arriba
CHAMBERINO Dona Ana
CHAMISAL Taos
CHIMAYO Rio Arriba
CHURCH ROCK McKinley

CIMARRON Colfax
CLAUNCH Socorro
CLAYTON Union
CLEVELAND Mora
CLIFF Grant
CLINES CORNERS Torrance
CLOUDCROFT Otero
CLOVIS Curry
COCHITI LAKE Sandoval
COCHITI PUEBLO Sandoval
COLUMBUS Luna
CONCHAS DAM San Miguel
CONTINENTAL DIVIDE McKinley
CORDOVA Rio Arriba
CORONA Lincoln
CORRALES Sandoval
COSTILLA Taos
COUNSELOR Sandoval
COYOTE Rio Arriba
CROSSROADS Lea
CROWNPOINT McKinley
CUBA Sandoval
CUBERO Cibola
CUCHILLO Sierra
CUERVO Guadalupe
DATIL Catron
DEMING Luna
DERRY Sierra
DES MOINES Union
DEXTER Chaves
DIXON Rio Arriba
DONA ANA Dona Ana
DORA Roosevelt
DULCE Rio Arriba
DURAN Torrance
EAGLE NEST Colfax
EDGEWOOD Santa Fe
EL PRADO Taos
EL RITO Rio Arriba
ELEPHANT BUTTE Sierra
ELIDA (88116) Roosevelt(97), Chaves(4)
EMBUDO Rio Arriba
ENCINO Torrance
ESPANOLA Rio Arriba
ESTANCIA Torrance
EUNICE Lea
FAIRACRES Dona Ana
FARMINGTON San Juan
FAYWOOD Grant
FENCE LAKE Cibola
FLORA VISTA San Juan
FLOYD (88118) Roosevelt(94), Curry(6)
FLYING H Chaves
FOLSOM Union
FORT BAYARD Grant
FORT STANTON Lincoln
FORT SUMNER De Baca
FORT WINGATE McKinley
FRUITLAND San Juan
GALLINA Rio Arriba
GALLUP McKinley
GALLUP San Juan
GAMERCO McKinley
GARFIELD Dona Ana
GARITA San Miguel
GILA Grant
GLADSTONE Union

GLENCOE Lincoln
GLENRIO Quay
GLENWOOD Catron
GLORIETA Santa Fe
GONZALES RANCH San Miguel
GRADY (88120) Quay(82), Curry(18)
GRANTS Cibola
GRENVILLE Union
GUADALUPITA Mora
HACHITA Grant
HAGERMAN Chaves
HANOVER Grant
HATCH Dona Ana
HERNANDEZ Rio Arriba
HIGH ROLLS MOUNTAIN PARK Otero
HILLSBORO Sierra
HOBBS Lea
HOLLOMAN AIR FORCE BASE Otero
HOLMAN Mora
HONDO Lincoln
HOPE (88250) Chaves(61), Eddy(40)
HOUSE Quay
HURLEY Grant
ILFELD San Miguel
ISLETA Bernalillo
JAL Lea
JAMESTOWN (87347) McKinley(80), Valencia(20)
JARALES Valencia
JEMEZ PUEBLO Sandoval
JEMEZ SPRINGS Sandoval
KENNA Roosevelt
KIRTLAND San Juan
KIRTLAND AFB Bernalillo
LA JARA Sandoval
LA JOYA Socorro
LA LOMA Guadalupe
LA LUZ Otero
LA MADERA Rio Arriba
LA MESA Dona Ana
LA PLATA San Juan
LAGUNA Cibola
LAKE ARTHUR (88253) Chaves(97), Eddy(3)
LAKEWOOD Eddy
LAMY Santa Fe
LAS CRUCES Dona Ana
LAS TABLAS Rio Arriba
LAS VEGAS San Miguel
LEDOUX Mora
LEMITAR Socorro
LINCOLN Lincoln
LINDRITH Rio Arriba
LINGO Roosevelt
LLANO Taos
LOCO HILLS Eddy
LOGAN Quay
LORDSBURG Hidalgo
LOS ALAMOS Los Alamos
LOS LUNAS Valencia
LOS OJOS Rio Arriba
LOVING Eddy
LOVINGTON Lea
LUMBERTON Rio Arriba
LUNA Catron
MAGDALENA Socorro
MALAGA Eddy

MALJAMAR Lea
MAXWELL Colfax
MAYHILL (88339) Otero(81), Chaves(19)
MC ALISTER Quay
MC DONALD Lea
MC INTOSH Torrance
MEDANALES Rio Arriba
MELROSE (88124) Curry(79), Quay(13), Roosevelt(8)
MENTMORE McKinley
MESCALERO Otero
MESILLA Dona Ana
MESILLA PARK Dona Ana
MESQUITE Dona Ana
MEXICAN SPRINGS McKinley
MIAMI Colfax
MILAN Cibola
MILLS Harding
MILNESAND Roosevelt
MIMBRES Grant
MONTEZUMA San Miguel
MONTICELLO Sierra
MONUMENT Lea
MORA Mora
MORIARTY Torrance
MOSQUERO Harding
MOUNT DORA Union
MOUNTAINAIR Torrance
MULE CREEK Grant
NAGEEZI San Juan
NARA VISA Quay
NAVAJO (87328) McKinley(79), San Juan(21)
NAVAJO DAM San Juan
NEW LAGUNA Cibola
NEWCOMB San Juan
NEWKIRK Guadalupe
NOGAL Lincoln
OCATE Mora
OIL CENTER Lea
OJO CALIENTE Taos
OJO FELIZ Mora
OJO SARCO Rio Arriba
ORGAN Dona Ana
OROGRANDE Otero
PAGUATE Cibola
PECOS San Miguel
PENA BLANCA Sandoval
PENASCO Taos
PEP Roosevelt
PERALTA (87042) Valencia(93), Bernalillo(7)
PETACA Rio Arriba
PICACHO Lincoln
PIE TOWN Catron
PINEHILL Cibola
PINON (88344) Chaves(87), Otero(13)
PINOS ALTOS Grant
PLACITAS Sandoval
PLAYAS Hidalgo
POLVADERA Socorro
PONDEROSA Sandoval
PORTALES Roosevelt
PREWITT McKinley
PUEBLO OF ACOMA Valencia
QUAY Quay
QUEMADO Catron

QUESTA Taos
RADIUM SPRINGS Dona Ana
RAINSVILLE Mora
RAMAH (87321) Cibola(54), McKinley(46)
RANCHOS DE TAOS Taos
RATON Colfax
RED RIVER Taos
REDROCK Grant
REGINA Sandoval
REHOBOTH McKinley
RESERVE Catron
RIBERA San Miguel
RINCON Dona Ana
RIO RANCHO Bernalillo
RIO RANCHO Sandoval
ROCIADA (87742) Mora(63), San Miguel(38)
RODARTE Taos
RODEO Hidalgo
ROGERS Roosevelt
ROSWELL Chaves
ROWE San Miguel
ROY Harding
RUIDOSO Lincoln
RUIDOSO DOWNS Lincoln
RUTHERON Rio Arriba
SACRAMENTO Otero
SAINT VRAIN Curry
SALEM Dona Ana
SAN ACACIA Socorro

SAN ANTONIO Socorro
SAN CRISTOBAL Taos
SAN FIDEL Cibola
SAN JON Quay
SAN JOSE San Miguel
SAN JUAN PUEBLO Rio Arriba
SAN MATEO Cibola
SAN MIGUEL Dona Ana
SAN PATRICIO Lincoln
SAN RAFAEL Cibola
SAN YSIDRO Sandoval
SANDIA PARK (87047) Bernalillo(52), Santa Fe(48)
SANOSTEE (87461) San Juan(83), McKinley(17)
SANTA CLARA Grant
SANTA CRUZ Santa Fe
SANTA FE Santa Fe
SANTA ROSA Guadalupe
SANTA TERESA Dona Ana
SANTO DOMINGO PUEBLO Sandoval
SAPELLO San Miguel
SEBOYETA Cibola
SEDAN Union
SENA San Miguel
SENECA Union
SERAFINA San Miguel
SHEEP SPRINGS San Juan
SHIPROCK San Juan
SILVER CITY Grant

SMITH LAKE McKinley
SOCORRO Socorro
SOLANO Harding
SPRINGER Colfax
STANLEY Santa Fe
STEAD Union
SUNLAND PARK Dona Ana
SUNSPOT Otero
TAIBAN (88134) Roosevelt(42), De Baca(37), Quay(21)
TAJIQUE Torrance
TAOS Taos
TAOS SKI VALLEY Taos
TATUM Lea
TERERRO San Miguel
TESUQUE Santa Fe
TEXICO Curry
THOREAU McKinley
TIERRA AMARILLA Rio Arriba
TIJERAS Bernalillo
TIMBERON Otero
TINNIE Lincoln
TOHATCHI (87325) McKinley(93), San Juan(7)
TOME Valencia
TORREON Torrance
TRAMPAS Taos
TREMENTINA San Miguel
TRES PIEDRAS Taos
TRUCHAS Rio Arriba

TRUTH OR CONSEQUENCES Sierra
TUCUMCARI Quay
TULAROSA Otero
TYRONE Grant
UTE PARK Colfax
VADITO Taos
VADO Dona Ana
VALDEZ Taos
VALLECITOS Rio Arriba
VALMORA Mora
VANADIUM Grant
VANDERWAGEN McKinley
VAUGHN Guadalupe
VEGUITA Socorro
VELARDE Rio Arriba
VILLANUEVA San Miguel
WAGON MOUND Mora
WATERFLOW San Juan
WATROUS Mora
WEED Otero
WHITE SANDS MISSILE RANGE Dona Ana
WHITES CITY Eddy
WILLARD Torrance
WILLIAMSBURG Sierra
WINSTON Sierra
YATAHEY McKinley
YESO De Baca
YOUNGSVILLE Rio Arriba
ZUNI McKinley

ZIP/City Cross Reference

ZIP Range	City
87001-87001	ALGODONES
87002-87002	BELEN
87004-87004	BERNALILLO
87005-87005	BLUEWATER
87006-87006	BOSQUE
87007-87007	CASA BLANCA
87008-87008	CEDAR CREST
87009-87009	CEDARVALE
87010-87010	CERRILLOS
87011-87011	CLAUNCH
87012-87012	COYOTE
87013-87013	CUBA
87014-87014	CUBERO
87015-87015	EDGEWOOD
87016-87016	ESTANCIA
87017-87017	GALLINA
87018-87018	COUNSELOR
87020-87020	GRANTS
87021-87021	MILAN
87022-87022	ISLETA
87023-87023	JARALES
87024-87024	JEMEZ PUEBLO
87025-87025	JEMEZ SPRINGS
87026-87026	LAGUNA
87027-87027	LA JARA
87028-87028	LA JOYA
87029-87029	LINDRITH
87031-87031	LOS LUNAS
87032-87032	MC INTOSH
87034-87034	PUEBLO OF ACOMA
87035-87035	MORIARTY
87036-87036	MOUNTAINAIR
87037-87037	NAGEEZI
87038-87038	NEW LAGUNA
87040-87040	PAGUATE
87041-87041	PENA BLANCA
87042-87042	PERALTA
87043-87043	PLACITAS
87044-87044	PONDEROSA
87045-87045	PREWITT
87046-87046	REGINA
87047-87047	SANDIA PARK
87048-87048	CORRALES
87049-87049	SAN FIDEL
87051-87051	SAN RAFAEL
87052-87052	SANTO DOMINGO PUEBLO
87053-87053	SAN YSIDRO
87056-87056	STANLEY
87057-87057	TAJIQUE
87059-87059	TIJERAS
87060-87060	TOME
87061-87061	TORREON
87062-87062	VEGUITA
87063-87063	WILLARD
87064-87064	YOUNGSVILLE
87068-87068	BOSQUE FARMS
87070-87070	CLINES CORNERS
87072-87072	COCHITI PUEBLO
87083-87083	COCHITI LAKE
87101-87116	ALBUQUERQUE
87117-87117	KIRTLAND AFB
87118-87123	ALBUQUERQUE
87124-87124	RIO RANCHO
87125-87158	ALBUQUERQUE
87174-87174	RIO RANCHO
87176-87201	ALBUQUERQUE
87300-87305	GALLUP
87310-87310	BRIMHALL
87311-87311	CHURCH ROCK
87312-87312	CONTINENTAL DIVIDE
87313-87313	CROWNPOINT
87315-87315	FENCE LAKE
87316-87316	FORT WINGATE
87317-87317	GAMERCO
87319-87319	MENTMORE
87320-87320	MEXICAN SPRINGS
87321-87321	RAMAH
87322-87322	REHOBOTH
87323-87323	THOREAU
87325-87325	TOHATCHI
87326-87326	VANDERWAGEN
87327-87327	ZUNI
87328-87328	NAVAJO
87347-87347	JAMESTOWN
87357-87357	PINEHILL
87364-87364	SHEEP SPRINGS
87365-87365	SMITH LAKE
87375-87375	YATAHEY
87401-87402	FARMINGTON
87410-87410	AZTEC
87412-87412	BLANCO
87413-87413	BLOOMFIELD
87415-87415	FLORA VISTA
87416-87416	FRUITLAND
87417-87417	KIRTLAND
87418-87418	LA PLATA
87419-87419	NAVAJO DAM
87420-87420	SHIPROCK
87421-87421	WATERFLOW
87455-87455	NEWCOMB
87461-87461	SANOSTEE
87499-87499	FARMINGTON
87500-87509	SANTA FE
87510-87510	ABIQUIU
87511-87511	ALCALDE
87512-87512	AMALIA
87513-87513	ARROYO HONDO
87514-87514	ARROYO SECO
87515-87515	CANJILON
87516-87516	CANONES
87517-87517	CARSON
87518-87518	CEBOLLA
87519-87519	CERRO
87520-87520	CHAMA
87521-87521	CHAMISAL
87522-87522	CHIMAYO
87523-87523	CORDOVA
87524-87524	COSTILLA
87525-87525	TAOS SKI VALLEY
87527-87527	DIXON
87528-87528	DULCE
87529-87529	EL PRADO
87530-87530	EL RITO
87531-87531	EMBUDO
87532-87533	ESPANOLA
87535-87535	GLORIETA
87537-87537	HERNANDEZ
87538-87538	ILFELD
87539-87539	LA MADERA
87540-87540	LAMY
87543-87543	LLANO
87544-87545	LOS ALAMOS
87548-87548	MEDANALES
87549-87549	OJO CALIENTE
87551-87551	LOS OJOS
87552-87552	PECOS
87553-87553	PENASCO
87554-87554	PETACA
87556-87556	QUESTA
87557-87557	RANCHOS DE TAOS
87558-87558	RED RIVER
87560-87560	RIBERA
87562-87562	ROWE
87564-87564	SAN CRISTOBAL
87565-87565	SAN JOSE
87566-87566	SAN JUAN PUEBLO
87567-87567	SANTA CRUZ
87569-87569	SERAFINA
87571-87571	TAOS
87573-87573	TERERRO
87574-87574	TESUQUE
87575-87575	TIERRA AMARILLA
87576-87576	TRAMPAS
87577-87577	TRES PIEDRAS
87578-87578	TRUCHAS
87579-87579	VADITO
87580-87580	VALDEZ
87581-87581	VALLECITOS
87582-87582	VELARDE
87583-87583	VILLANUEVA
87592-87594	SANTA FE
87701-87701	LAS VEGAS
87710-87710	ANGEL FIRE
87711-87711	ANTON CHICO
87712-87712	BUENA VISTA
87713-87713	CHACON
87714-87714	CIMARRON
87715-87715	CLEVELAND
87718-87718	EAGLE NEST
87722-87722	GUADALUPITA
87723-87723	HOLMAN
87724-87724	LA LOMA
87728-87728	MAXWELL
87729-87729	MIAMI
87730-87730	MILLS
87731-87731	MONTEZUMA
87732-87732	MORA
87733-87733	MOSQUERO
87734-87734	OCATE
87735-87735	OJO FELIZ
87736-87736	RAINSVILLE
87740-87740	RATON
87742-87742	ROCIADA
87743-87743	ROY
87745-87745	SAPELLO
87746-87746	SOLANO
87747-87747	SPRINGER
87749-87749	UTE PARK
87750-87750	VALMORA
87752-87752	WAGON MOUND
87753-87753	WATROUS
87801-87801	SOCORRO
87820-87820	ARAGON
87821-87821	DATIL
87823-87823	LEMITAR
87824-87824	LUNA
87825-87825	MAGDALENA
87827-87827	PIE TOWN
87828-87828	POLVADERA
87829-87829	QUEMADO
87830-87830	RESERVE
87831-87831	SAN ACACIA
87832-87832	SAN ANTONIO

Zip Range	Place	Zip Range	Place	Zip Range	Place	Zip Range	Place
87901-87901	TRUTH OR CONSEQUENCES	88043-88043	HURLEY	88201-88202	ROSWELL	88341-88341	NOGAL
87930-87930	ARREY	88044-88044	LA MESA	88210-88211	ARTESIA	88342-88342	OROGRANDE
87931-87931	CABALLO	88045-88045	LORDSBURG	88213-88213	CAPROCK	88343-88343	PICACHO
87933-87933	DERRY	88046-88046	MESILLA	88220-88221	CARLSBAD	88344-88344	PINON
87935-87935	ELEPHANT BUTTE	88047-88047	MESILLA PARK	88230-88230	DEXTER	88345-88345	RUIDOSO
87936-87936	GARFIELD	88048-88048	MESQUITE	88231-88231	EUNICE	88346-88346	RUIDOSO DOWNS
87937-87937	HATCH	88049-88049	MIMBRES	88232-88232	HAGERMAN	88347-88347	SACRAMENTO
87939-87939	MONTICELLO	88051-88051	MULE CREEK	88240-88244	HOBBS	88348-88348	SAN PATRICIO
87940-87940	RINCON	88052-88052	ORGAN	88250-88250	HOPE	88349-88349	SUNSPOT
87941-87941	SALEM	88053-88053	PINOS ALTOS	88252-88252	JAL	88350-88350	TIMBERON
87942-87942	WILLIAMSBURG	88054-88054	RADIUM SPRINGS	88253-88253	LAKE ARTHUR	88351-88351	TINNIE
87943-87943	WINSTON	88055-88055	REDROCK	88254-88254	LAKEWOOD	88352-88352	TULAROSA
88001-88001	LAS CRUCES	88056-88056	RODEO	88255-88255	LOCO HILLS	88353-88353	VAUGHN
88002-88002	WHITE SANDS MISSILE RANGE	88058-88058	SAN MIGUEL	88256-88256	LOVING	88354-88354	WEED
		88061-88062	SILVER CITY	88260-88260	LOVINGTON	88355-88355	RUIDOSO
88003-88006	LAS CRUCES	88063-88063	SUNLAND PARK	88262-88262	MC DONALD	88401-88401	TUCUMCARI
88008-88008	SANTA TERESA	88065-88065	TYRONE	88263-88263	MALAGA	88410-88410	AMISTAD
88009-88009	PLAYAS	88072-88072	VADO	88264-88264	MALJAMAR	88411-88411	BARD
88011-88012	LAS CRUCES	88101-88102	CLOVIS	88265-88265	MONUMENT	88414-88414	CAPULIN
88020-88020	ANIMAS	88103-88103	CANNON AFB	88267-88267	TATUM	88415-88415	CLAYTON
88021-88021	ANTHONY	88112-88112	BROADVIEW	88268-88268	WHITES CITY	88416-88416	CONCHAS DAM
88022-88022	ARENAS VALLEY	88113-88113	CAUSEY	88301-88301	CARRIZOZO	88417-88417	CUERVO
88023-88023	BAYARD	88114-88114	CROSSROADS	88310-88311	ALAMOGORDO	88418-88418	DES MOINES
88024-88024	BERINO	88115-88115	DORA	88312-88312	ALTO	88419-88419	FOLSOM
88025-88025	BUCKHORN	88116-88116	ELIDA	88314-88314	BENT	88421-88421	GARITA
88026-88026	SANTA CLARA	88118-88118	FLOYD	88316-88316	CAPITAN	88422-88422	GLADSTONE
88027-88027	CHAMBERINO	88119-88119	FORT SUMNER	88317-88317	CLOUDCROFT	88424-88424	GRENVILLE
88028-88028	CLIFF	88120-88120	GRADY	88318-88318	CORONA	88426-88426	LOGAN
88029-88029	COLUMBUS	88121-88121	HOUSE	88321-88321	ENCINO	88427-88427	MC ALISTER
88030-88031	DEMING	88122-88122	KENNA	88323-88323	FORT STANTON	88429-88429	MOUNT DORA
88032-88032	DONA ANA	88123-88123	LINGO	88324-88324	GLENCOE	88430-88430	NARA VISA
88033-88033	FAIRACRES	88124-88124	MELROSE	88325-88325	HIGH ROLLS MOUNTAIN PARK	88431-88431	NEWKIRK
88034-88034	FAYWOOD	88125-88125	MILNESAND			88433-88433	QUAY
88036-88036	FORT BAYARD	88126-88126	PEP	88330-88330	HOLLOMAN AIR FORCE BASE	88434-88434	SAN JON
88038-88038	GILA	88130-88130	PORTALES			88435-88435	SANTA ROSA
88039-88039	GLENWOOD	88132-88132	ROGERS	88336-88336	HONDO	88436-88436	SEDAN
88040-88040	HACHITA	88133-88133	SAINT VRAIN	88337-88337	LA LUZ	88437-88437	SENECA
88041-88041	HANOVER	88134-88134	TAIBAN	88338-88338	LINCOLN	88439-88439	TREMENTINA
88042-88042	HILLSBORO	88135-88135	TEXICO	88339-88339	MAYHILL	88441-88441	BELL RANCH
		88136-88136	YESO	88340-88340	MESCALERO		

New York

General Help Numbers:

Governor's Office
Executive Chamber, State Capitol   518-474-8390
Albany, NY 12224
http://www.state.ny.us/governor   9AM-5PM

Attorney General's Office
State Capitol   518-474-7330
Albany, NY 12224-0341   Fax 518-473-9909
http://www.oag.state.ny.us   9AM-5:30PM

State Court Administrator
Empire State Plaza   518-473-1196
Agency Bldg #4, Suite 2001   Fax 518-473-6860
Albany, NY 12223   9AM-5PM
http://www.courts.state.ny.us

State Court Administrator-NYC
New York City Office   212-428-2100
25 Beaver St   Fax 212-428-2190
New York, NY 10004   9AM-5PM
http://www.courts.state.ny.us

State Archives
Empire State Plaza   518-474-8955
Cultural Education Center Rm 11D40   Fax 518-473-9985
Albany, NY 12230   9AM-5PM
http://www.sara.nysed.gov

State Specifics:

Capital: Albany, Albany County

Time Zone: EST

Number of Counties: 62

Population: 18,976,457

Web Site: www.state.ny.us

State Agencies

Criminal Records
Access to Records is Restricted
Division of Criminal Justice Services, 4 Tower Place, Albany, NY 12203; 518-457-6043, 518-457-6550 (Fax), 8AM-5PM.

http://www.criminaljustice.state.ny.us
Note: The sex offender registry level 3 can be searched at http://www.criminaljustice.state.ny.us/nsor/index.htm. Records are released by court order, subpoena or to person of record only. The public must search other counties at the county court level.

Corporation Records
Limited Partnership Records
Limited Liability Company Records
Limited Liability Partnerships

Division of Corporations, Department of State, 41 State St, Albany, NY 12231; 518-473-2492 (General Information), 900-835-2677 (Corporate Searches), 518-474-1418 (Fax), 8AM-4:30PM.

http://www.dos.state.ny.us

Note: Information available includes date of incorporation, subsequent filings, status, principle business location, registered agent, service of process address, number and type of stock shares entitled to issue, and biennial statements w/addresses.

Indexing & Storage: Records are available from inception. Information on active entities is automated. Records on entities inactive prior to 1978 are not automated and require additional research. New records are available for inquiry immediately.

Searching: All data is considered public information. Include the following in your request-full name of business.

Access by: mail, phone, in person, online.

Fee & Payment: There is no fee for basic information up to 5 names. Over 5 names, the fee is $5.00 per name. For documents, the certification fee is $10.00, $25.00 if SOS seal is required. The fee is $5.00 for every name availability checked. Fee payee: New York Department of State. Payments must be by check, money order, credit card or drawdown account.

Mail search: Turnaround time: 1 week. A self addressed stamped envelope is requested.

Phone search: Call 1-900-TEL-CORP. You may search up to 5 names per call for a flat rate charge of $4.00 per call.

In person search: The general public may obtain copies of documents and certificates under seal while they wait ONLY if expedited fees are paid.

Online search: A commercial account can be set up for direct access. Fee is $.75 per transaction through a drawdown account. There is an extensive amount of information available including historical information. Also, the Division's corporate and business entity database may be accessed via the Internet without charge. Historical information is not available, nor is it real time. The Internet files are updated weekly.

Other access: You may submit an e-mail search request at corporations@dos.state.ny.us.

Trademarks/Servicemarks

Department of State, Miscellaneous Records, 41 State St, Albany, NY 12231; 518-474-4770, 518-473-0730 (Fax), 8:30AM-4:30PM.

http://dos.state.ny.us

Indexing & Storage: Records are available for past 10 years. It takes 1 to 2 days before new records are available for inquiry.

Searching: Searches are only done on registered marks, not on pending marks. You need to provide written description of design or features of the mark.

Access by: mail, phone, fax, in person.

Fee & Payment: The first two requests by mail, fax, or phone are free. Additional requests cost $5.00 per search. Fee payee: New York Department of State. Prepayment required. Payments of more than $500.00 must be certified check or money order; personal checks accepted for amounts less than $500.00 Personal checks accepted. No credit cards accepted.

Mail search: Turnaround time: 2 to 3 days. A self addressed stamped envelope is requested.

Phone search: Limited verification information is available.

Fax search: Turnaround time is 2-3 days. There is a $.50 fee per page to return results by fax.

In person search: No fee for request. You can request 1 search in person.

Other access: New marks can be photocopied and sent out on a regular monthly basis. Fees are determined by numbers of marks.

Uniform Commercial Code
Federal Tax Liens
State Tax Liens

UCC Division, Department of State, 41 State Street, Albany, NY 12231; 518-474-4763, 8AM-4:30PM.

http://www.dos.state.ny.us/corp/uccfaq.html

Indexing & Storage: Records are available from 1964. Records are computerized from 1/96. Records are indexed on computer, microfilm.

Searching: Use search request form UCC-11. Federal tax liens on businesses will be included. Lists of state tax liens (warrants) are available, but must be searched separately on premises. Federal tax liens on individuals are filed at the county level. Include the following in your request-debtor name. It is suggested for written requests that the form be 5" x 8" or use a UCC-11.

Access by: mail, in person.

Fee & Payment: UCC search is $7.00 per debtor name, one name per form. Individual debtor names should list addresses. The copy fee is $1.50 per page. You can search state tax liens, in person, at no charge. Fee payee: Secretary of State. Prepayment required. All checks over $5.00 must be certified. No credit cards accepted.

Mail search: Turnaround time: 2 days. No self addressed stamped envelope is required.

In person search: You may request information in person.

Other access: The state offers its database for sale on microfilm.

Sales Tax Registrations

Sales Tax Registration Bureau, WA Harriman Campus, Building 8, Rm 408, Albany, NY 12227; 518-457-0259, 518-457-0453 (Fax), 7AM-5PM.

Indexing & Storage: Records are available for current records only. Records are computerized since 1970.

Searching: This agency will confirm that a business is registered and release the legal name and physical address. Include the following in your request-business name. They will also search by tax permit number or federal tax number.

Access by: mail, phone, fax, in person.

Mail search: Turnaround time: 2 to 3 weeks. A self addressed stamped envelope is requested. No fee for mail request.

Phone search: No fee for telephone request.

Fax search: Fax searching available.

In person search: No fee for request.

Birth Certificates

Vital Records Section, Certification Unit, PO Box 2602, Albany, NY 12220-2602; 518-474-3038, 518-474-3077, 877-854-4481 (Searching), 877-854-4607 (Fax), 8:30AM-4:30PM.

http://www.health.state.ny.us

Note: For records from New York City information, see that profile.

Indexing & Storage: Records are available from 1881 on. New records are available for inquiry immediately. Records are indexed on microfiche, inhouse computer.

Searching: May only obtain your own or a dependent child's records, without notarized release. They will not return records to a PO Box or an "in care of." Include the following in your request-full name, names of parents, mother's maiden name, date of birth, place of birth, relationship to person of record, reason for information request. Requester must show or include valid identification.

Access by: mail, phone, fax, in person.

Fee & Payment: The fee is $15.00 per name per record for a 3-year search. Fee payee: New York State Department of Health. Prepayment required. Personal checks accepted. Credit cards accepted: MasterCard, Visa, AmEx, Discover.

Mail search: Turnaround time: 2 to 3 months. Turnaround time will be 2 weeks if you send your request by Express Mail.A self addressed stamped envelope is requested.

Phone search: Use of a credit card is required, there is an additional $8.95 fee. Turnaround time is 1 week.

Fax search: Same criteria as phone searches.

In person search: Results are still returned by mail.

Expedited service: Expedited service is available for mail, phone and fax searches. Add $8.95 for use of credit card and $11.00 for express delivery.

Death Records

Vital Records Section, Certification Unit, 733 Broadway, Albany, NY 12237-0023; 518-474-3038, 518-474-3077, 518-474-9168 (Fax), 8:30AM-4:30PM.

http://www.health.state.ny.us

Note: For New York City, see the separate entry.

Indexing & Storage: Records are available from 1880 on. New records are available for inquiry immediately. Records are indexed on microfiche, inhouse computer.

Searching: You must show cause why record is needed on letterhead, if not member of the immediate family. Include the following in your request-full name, date of death, place of death, relationship to person of record, reason for information request.

Access by: mail, in person.

Fee & Payment: The fee is $15.00 per record. Use of credit card adds $5.00. Fee payee: New

York State Department of Health. Prepayment required. Personal checks accepted. Credit cards accepted: MasterCard, Visa, AmEx, Discover.

Mail search: Turnaround time: 2 to 3 months. If request is sent by express mail, turnaround time shortened to 2 weeks.A self addressed stamped envelope is requested.

In person search: Turnaround time shortened by mail time only.

Expedited service: Expedited service is available for mail, phone and fax searches. Use of credit card is required, add $10.50 for overnight delivery.

Marriage Certificates

Vital Records Section, Certification Unit, 733 Broadway, Albany, NY 12237-0023; 518-474-3038, 518-474-3077, 8:30AM-4:30PM.

http://www.health.state.ny.us

Note: For New York City information, see the separate entry.

Indexing & Storage: Records are available from 1881 on. New records are available for inquiry immediately. Records are indexed on microfiche, inhouse computer.

Searching: Must have a notarized release form from persons of record or immediate family member for investigative purposes. Include the following in your request-names of husband and wife, date of marriage, place or county of marriage, relationship to person of record, reason for information request, wife's maiden name.

Access by: mail, in person.

Fee & Payment: The fee is $5.00 per record (for 1-3 years, additional years cost more). Also, there is a $5.00 fee to use a credit card. Fee payee: New York State Department of Health. Prepayment required. Personal checks accepted. Credit cards accepted: MasterCard, Visa, AmEx, Discover.

Mail search: Turnaround time: 2 to 3 months. Turnaround time is 2 weeks if request is sent by overnight express mail.A self addressed stamped envelope is requested.

In person search: Turnaround time shortened by mail time only.

Expedited service: Expedited service is available for mail, phone and fax searches. Add credit card fee and express delivery fee ($10.50).

Divorce Records

Vital Records Section, Certification Unit, 733 Broadway, Albany, NY 12237-0023; 518-474-3038, 518-474-3077, 8:30AM-4:30PM.

http://www.health.state.ny.us

Note: For New York City information, see the separate entry.

Indexing & Storage: Records are available from 1963 on. New records are available for inquiry immediately. Records are indexed on microfiche, inhouse computer.

Searching: If you are not a party to the divorce you must have a court order to obtain records or show legal cause. Include the following in your request-names of husband and wife, date of divorce, place of divorce, relationship to person of record, reason for information request.

Access by: mail, in person.

Fee & Payment: The fee is $15.00 for searching 1994 to present; $25.00 for 1975-1994; $35 for

search from 1963-1994. Add $5.00 for use of credit card. Fee payee: New York State Department of Health. Prepayment required. Personal checks accepted. Credit cards accepted: MasterCard, Visa, AmEx, Discover.

Mail search: Turnaround time: 2 to 3 months. A self addressed stamped envelope is requested.

In person search: Turnaround time shortened by mail time only.

Expedited service: Expedited service is available for mail, phone and fax searches. Plus $5.00 for using a credit card and $10.50 for express delivery.

Birth Certificate-New York City
Death Records-New York City

Department of Health, Bureau of Vital Records, 125 Worth St, Rm 133, New York, NY 10013; 212-788-4520, 212-442-1999, 212-962-6105 (Fax), 9AM-4PM.

http://www.ci.nyc.ny.us/html/doh/html/vr/vr.html

Indexing & Storage: Records are available from 1910 to present for birth and from 1949 forward for death. For prior records, call Municipal Archives at 212-566-5292. It takes 2 months before new records are available for inquiry. Records are indexed on microfiche, inhouse computer.

Searching: Must have a notarized signed release form from immediate family member. Include a copy of your photo ID. Include the following in your request-full name, date of birth, date of death, place of birth, place of death, reason for information request, name of the hospital. Parents' names are also required, mother's maiden name for birth.

Access by: mail, phone, fax, in person.

Fee & Payment: The fee is $15.00 per record plus $5.00 if using a credit card. Only those parties appearing on the birth record may order via a credit card. All other parties must order by mail or in-person and show cause or reason for the request. Fee payee: Department of Health. Prepayment required. Personal checks accepted. Credit cards accepted: MasterCard, Visa, AmEx, Discover.

Mail search: Allow 3-4 weeks for a birth record and 8-10 weeks for a death record.A self addressed stamped envelope is requested.

Phone search: Birth only. Use of credit card is required. Turnaround time is 5-7 days.

Fax search: Same criteria as phone searching.

In person search: Turnaround time is usually while you wait.

Expedited service: Expedited service is available for fax searches. Turnaround time: 1 to 2 days. Add $11.00 for delivery service. The $15.00 search fee and $5.00 credit card fee must also be included.

Marriage Certificate-New York City

City Clerk's Office, Department of Records & Information Services, 1 Centre Street, Rm 252, New York, NY 10007; 212-669-8898, 8AM-4PM M-F.

Note: Records from 1866-1929 can be obtained from the Municipal Archives at 212-788-8580. Records from 1995 forward can be obtained from the City Clerk's Borough Office. Call this office for further information.

Indexing & Storage: Records are available from 1930 to present.

Searching: Current records are not public information and are only available to the parties involved or their authorization or to legal representatives for litigation purposes.

Access by: mail, in person.

Fee & Payment: Search fee of $15.00 includes certification. Each additional year searched is add'l $1.00. Additional copies same search are $10.00 each. Fee payee: City Clerk. Prepayment required. No personal checks accepted, except attorneys.

Mail search: Turnaround time: 6-8 weeks.

In person search: Searching is available in person.

Divorce Records-New York City

New York County Clerk's Office, Division of Old Records, 60 Centre Street, Rm 141, New York City, NY 10007; 212-374-4376, 9AM-3PM, M-F.

Note: Records of divorces from 1979 to 1991 can be found at 31 Chambers St, Room 703. This is open Tuesdays and Thursdays from 9-1 and 2-5. Call for specific details.

Indexing & Storage: Records are available from 1955 to 1970 on index cards, computerized since 1971.

Searching: Manhattan records are limited by statute to parties or attorneys of record or with notarized authorization by party involved.

Access by: mail, in person.

Fee & Payment: Fee is $8.00 for the search and a certified copy. Fee payee: New York County Clerk. Prepayment required. On site requests require cash; mail requests require postal money order or certified check. No credit cards accepted.

Mail search: Turnaround time: 2 weeks.

In person search: You may make copies at $.25 per page. Go to basement, either room 103 or room 141 and bring identification.

Workers' Compensation Records

NY Workers' Compensation Board, Director of Claims Office, 180 Livingston St, Room 400, Brooklyn, NY 11248; 718-802-6621, 718-834-2116 (Fax), 9AM-5PM.

http://www.wcb.state.ny.us

Note: File copies of records are not released for employment purposes, even with a signed release.

Indexing & Storage: Records are available for up to 18 years after the case is closed. Older records are destroyed. New records are available for inquiry immediately. Records are indexed on inhouse computer.

Searching: Must have a notarized release from claimant naming requesting party and stating the purpose for which information is going to be used to access case files. Include the following in your request-claimant name, Social Security Number, claim number, date of accident.

Access by: mail, in person.

Fee & Payment: There is a $10.00 "mailing and handling fee" but no search fee. Copies are $.25 each. Fee payee: Workers' Compensation Board. Prepayment required. Personal checks accepted. No credit cards accepted.

Mail search: Turnaround time: 2 weeks. No self addressed stamped envelope is required.

In person search: Turnaround time is while you wait.

Driver Records

Department of Motor Vehicles, MV-15 Processing, 6 Empire State Plaza, Room 430, Albany, NY 12228; 518-473-5595, 800-225-5368 (In-state), 8AM-5PM.

http://www.nydmv.state.ny.us

Note: Copies of tickets may be purchased from the same address for a fee of $6.00 per ticket.

Indexing & Storage: Records are available for 3 years in addition to the current year for moving violations, 10 years for DWIs, and indefinitely for open (4 years for closed) suspensions. Most non-moving violations are not shown on record. It takes a few days after conviction before new records are available for inquiry. Records are normally destroyed after 5 years from expiration.

Searching: New York restricts the release of personal information on driving records to casual requesters. The driver's license number (ID#), name, and DOB are required when ordering a record.

Access by: mail, phone, in person, online.

Fee & Payment: The fee is $5.00 per record search, $4.00 if online or by tape. Fee payee: Department of Motor Vehicles. Prepayment required. Escrow accounts can be set up for high volume users. Personal checks accepted. No credit cards accepted.

Mail search: Turnaround time: 4 to 6 weeks. Form MV-15 is required when ordering. A self addressed stamped envelope is requested.

Phone search: Only drivers wishing to obtain their own record may call. The DL# or name, DOB and sex are required when ordered. Payment by a credit card is required and an additional $5.00 is charged.

In person search: Records can be ordered from most any county-operated motor vehicle office and at the state offices in Albany. A photo ID of the requester and use of Form MV-14C is required.

Online search: NY has implemented a "Dial-In Inquiry" system which enables customers to obtain data online 24 hours a day. The DL# or name, DOB and sex are required to retrieve. If the DOB and sex are not entered, the system defaults to a limited group of 5 records. The fee is $5.00 per record. For more information, call 518-474-4293.

Other access: Tape-to-tape ordering is available. For more information call (518) 474-0606.

Vehicle Ownership
Vehicle Identification
Vessel Ownership
Vessel Registration

Department of Motor Vehicles, MV-15 Processing, 6 Empire State Plaza, Room 430, Albany, NY 12228; 518-474-0710, 518-474-8510, 8AM-5PM.

http://www.nydmv.state.ny.us

Indexing & Storage: Records are available for a minimum of 4 years on computer. All motorized vessels must be registered, titles are not issued. New records are available for inquiry immediately.

Searching: Generally, vehicle and ownership information is available. However, accessed is restricted in adherence to the Drivers' Privacy Protection Act and casual requesters cannot obtain records.

Access by: mail, in person, online.

Fee & Payment: Mail requests are $5.00 per record, online inquiries are $4.00 per record. Fee payee: Commissioner of Motor Vehicles. Prepayment required. For information regarding deposit accounts, call 518-474-4293. Personal checks accepted. No credit cards accepted.

Mail search: Turnaround time: 4 to 6 weeks. A self addressed stamped envelope is requested.

In person search: Results are returned by mail.

Online search: New York offers plate, VIN and ownership data through the same network discussed in the Driving Records Section. The system is interactive and open 24 hours a day, with the exception of 10 hours on Sunday. The fee is $5.00 per record. Call 518-474-4293 for more information.

Other access: New York also offers a tape to diskette search of registration information at $4.00 per record. There is no bulk list retrieval offered at lesser prices; however, a contracted vendor may sell data. Call 518-474-0606 for more information.

Accident Reports

DMV Certified Document Center, Accident Report Section, Empire State Plaza, Swan St Bldg, Albany, NY 12228; 518-474-0710, 8AM-4:30PM.

http://www.nysdmv.com

Indexing & Storage: Records are available for 4 years to present. It takes 120 days after date of accident before new records are available for inquiry. Records are indexed on inhouse computer.

Searching: Records are open to the public, but request must be in writing. Use of Form MV-198C is suggested. Release of records is restricted based on the Drivers' Privacy Protection Act. Include the following in your request-date of accident, location of accident, full name. Provide driver's address, if known.

Access by: mail, in person.

Fee & Payment: Fees: $5.00 per search and $15.00 per accident report. Express mail is given priority. Fee payee: Commissioner of Motor Vehicle. Prepayment required. Personal checks accepted. No credit cards accepted.

Mail search: Turnaround time: 4 to 6 weeks. No self addressed stamped envelope is required.

In person search: Turnaround time is next day pickup.

Legislation Records

NY Senate Document Room, State Capitol, State Street Rm 317, Albany, NY 12247, 518-455-2312 (Senate Document Room), 518-455-3216, 9AM-5PM.

http://www.senate.state.ny.us

Note: Prior session bills may be found at the State Library, 518-474-5355.

Indexing & Storage: Records are available for current session and back to 1995. Records are indexed on computer.

Searching: Include the following in your request-bill number. The law section number or description can be helpful.

Access by: mail, phone, in person, online.

Fee & Payment: There is no search fee.

Mail search: Turnaround time: same day. No self addressed stamped envelope is required.

Phone search: Records are available by phone.

In person search: Research materials are available if bill number is not known.

Online search: Both the Senate - www.senate.state.ny.us - and the Assembly - www.assembly.state.ny.us - have web sites to search for a bill or specific bill text. A much more complete system is the LRS online system. This offers complete state statutes, agency rules and regulations, bill text, bill status, summaries, and more. For more information, call Barbara Lett at 800-356-6566.

Voter Registration
Records not maintained by a state level agency.

Note: Records may only be viewed or purchased at the county level. Purchases are restricted for political purposes only.

GED Certificates

NY State Education Dept, GED Testing, PO Box 7348, Albany, NY 12224-0348; 518-474-5906, 518-474-3041 (Fax), 10AM-12PM, 1PM-3PM M-F.

http://www.nysed.gov/Programs.html

Searching: To search, all of the following is required: full name, SSN, and date of birth. If the subject was tested prior to 1985, include the address, year of test, and location.

Access by: mail, phone.

Fee & Payment: There is no fee for verification. Copies of transcripts are $4.00 each. Copies of diplomas are $10.00 each. Fee payee: NY State Education Dept. Prepayment required. Money orders are accepted. No credit cards accepted.

Mail search: Turnaround time is 3 to 4 weeks. No self addressed stamped envelope is required.

Phone search: Automated phone verifications can be accomplished for records that are from 1985 to the present.

Hunting License Information
Fishing License Information
Records not maintained by a state level agency.

Note: They do not have a central database. Only vendors have the names and addresses.

New York State Licensing Agencies

Licenses Searchable Online

Acupuncturist/Acupuncturist Assistant #19........www.op.nysed.gov/opsearches.htm#nme
Apartment Information Vendor #10 ....http://wdb.dos.state.ny.us/lcns_public/lcns_wdb.status_check_lcns.show
Apartment Sharing Manager #10 ....http://wdb.dos.state.ny.us/lcns_public/lcns_wdb.status_check_lcns.show
Appearance Enhancement Business #10 ....http://wdb.dos.state.ny.us/lcns_public/lcns_wdb.status_check_lcns.show
Architect #19 ....www.op.nysed.gov/opsearches.htm#nme
Armored Car/Car Carrier #10...........................http://wdb.dos.state.ny.us/lcns_public/lcns_wdb.status_check_lcns.show
Athletic Trainer #19..www.op.nysed.gov/opsearches.htm#nme
Attorney #18 ....www.courts.state.ny.us/webdb/wdbcgi.exe/apps/INTERNETDB.attyreghome.show
Audiologist #19...www.op.nysed.gov/opsearches.htm#nme
Bail Enforcement Agent #10..............................http://wdb.dos.state.ny.us/lcns_public/lcns_wdb.status_check_lcns.show
Barber #10..http://wdb.dos.state.ny.us/lcns_public/lcns_wdb.status_check_lcns.show
Chiropractor #19...www.op.nysed.gov/opsearches.htm#nme
Court Reporter #19 ....www.op.nysed.gov/opsearches.htm#nme
Dental Hygienist #19...www.op.nysed.gov/opsearches.htm#nme
Dentist/Dental Assistant #19.............................www.op.nysed.gov/opsearches.htm#nme
Dietitian #19 ....www.op.nysed.gov/opsearches.htm#nme
Dispatch Facility (Alarm/Security/Fire) #10........http://wdb.dos.state.ny.us/lcns_public/lcns_wdb.status_check_lcns.show
Engineer #19 ....www.op.nysed.gov/opsearches.htm#nme
Guard Dog Agency #10......................................http://wdb.dos.state.ny.us/lcns_public/lcns_wdb.status_check_lcns.show
Guard/Patrol Agency #10...................................http://wdb.dos.state.ny.us/lcns_public/lcns_wdb.status_check_lcns.show
Hearing Aid Dealer #10.....................................http://wdb.dos.state.ny.us/lcns_public/lcns_wdb.status_check_lcns.show
HMO #12..www.ins.state.ny.us/tocol4.htm
Insurance Company #12.....................................www.ins.state.ny.us/tocol4.htm
Interior Designer #19 ....www.op.nysed.gov/opsearches.htm#nme
Landscape Architect #19...................................www.op.nysed.gov/opsearches.htm#nme
Lobbyist #16...www.nylobby.state.ny.us/lobbysearch.html
Massage Therapist #19.....................................www.op.nysed.gov/opsearches.htm#nme
Medical Doctor #19...www.op.nysed.gov/opsearches.htm#nme
Midwife #19 ....www.op.nysed.gov/opsearches.htm#nme
Notary Public #10 ....http://wdb.dos.state.ny.us/lcns_public/lcns_wdb.status_check_lcns.show
Nurse #19...www.op.nysed.gov/opsearches.htm#nme
Nurse-LPN/RPN #19...www.op.nysed.gov/opsearches.htm#nme
Nutritionist #19 ....www.op.nysed.gov/opsearches.htm#nme
Occupational Therapist/Assistant #19 ....www.op.nysed.gov/opsearches.htm#nme
Ophthalmic Dispenser #19................................www.op.nysed.gov/opsearches.htm#nme
Optometrist #19..www.op.nysed.gov/opsearches.htm#nme
Pharmacist #19 ....www.op.nysed.gov/opsearches.htm#nme
Physical Therapist/Assistant #19 ....www.op.nysed.gov/opsearches.htm#nme
Physician/Physician Assistant #19....................www.op.nysed.gov/opsearches.htm#nme
Physicians' Specialist Assistant #19..................www.op.nysed.gov/opsearches.htm#nme
Podiatrist #19 ....www.op.nysed.gov/opsearches.htm#nme
Private Investigator #10 ....http://wdb.dos.state.ny.us/lcns_public/lcns_wdb.status_check_lcns.show
Psychiatrist #19..www.ptofview.com/nyspa/search/
Psychologist #19 ....www.op.nysed.gov/opsearches.htm#nme
Public Accountant-CPA #19...............................www.op.nysed.gov/opsearches.htm#nme
Real Estate Salesperson/Broker/Appraiser #10 .http://wdb.dos.state.ny.us/lcns_public/lcns_wdb.status_check_lcns.show
Respiratory Therapist/Therapy Technician #19..www.op.nysed.gov/opsearches.htm#nme
Security & Fire Alarm Installer #10....................http://wdb.dos.state.ny.us/lcns_public/lcns_wdb.status_check_lcns.show
Security Guard #10..http://wdb.dos.state.ny.us/lcns_public/lcns_wdb.status_check_lcns.show
Social Worker #19 ....www.op.nysed.gov/opsearches.htm#nme
Speech Pathologist/Audiologist #19 ....www.op.nysed.gov/opsearches.htm#nme
Surveyor #19..www.op.nysed.gov/opsearches.htm#nme
Teacher #17 ....www.highered.nysed.gov/tcert/ocvsintro.htm
Telemarketer Business #10...............................http://wdb.dos.state.ny.us/lcns_public/lcns_wdb.status_check_lcns.show
Veterinarian #19 ....www.op.nysed.gov/opsearches.htm#nme

Licensing Quick Finder

Acupuncturist/Acupuncturist Assit. #19 .518-474-3817
Apartment Information Vendor #10 518-474-4429
Apartment Manager/Vendor/Agent #10 .518-474-4429
Apartment Sharing Manager #10 518-474-4429
Appearance Enhancement Business #10...................
....518-474-4429
Architect #19 518-474-3817
Armored Car/Car Carrier #10...............518-474-4429
Asbestos Handler #09 518-457-2735
Athletic Trainer #19 518-474-3817
Attorney #18 212-428-2800
Audiologist #19 518-474-3817
Bail Bond Agent #12.............................518-474-6630
Bail Enforcement Agent #10 518-474-4429
Barber #10 518-474-4429
Blaster #09 518-457-2735
Boiler Inspector #08 518-457-2722
Casino Employee #15 ....518-453-8460 X2
Charitable Gaming #15.................518-453-8460 X2
Chiropractor #19 518-474-3817
Collection Agency #11..........................702-687-4259
Commercial Applicator #02....................518-402-8748
Cosmetologist #10 518-474-4429
Court Reporter #19 518-474-3817
Crane Operator #09 518-457-2735
Dental Hygienist #19 518-474-3817
Dentist/Dental Assistant #19.................518-474-3817
Dietitian #19...518-474-3817
Dispatch Facility (Alarm/Security/Fire) #10................
....518-474-4429
Emergency Medical Technician-Paramedic #07 ....
....518-402-0985
Engineer #19 518-474-3817
Esthetics Specialist #10........................518-474-4429
Fishing Guide #03 518-457-9311
Franchise Sales #01.............................212-416-8222
Funeral Home/Director #06 518-402-0785

Games of Chance Registration #10 518-474-4429
Guard Dog Agency #10 518-474-4429
Guard/Patrol Agency #10 518-474-4429
Guide #03 518-457-9311
Hair Styling, Natural #10.......................518-474-4429
Health Club #10 518-474-4429
Hearing Aid Dealer #10 518-474-4429
Hiking Guide #03 518-457-9311
HMO #12 518-474-6630
Hunting Guide #03................................518-457-9311
Insurance Agent/Consultant/Broker #12 518-474-6630
Insurance Appraiser #12 518-474-6630
Insurance Company #12 518-474-6630
Interior Designer #19.............................518-474-3817
Investment Advisor #01.........................212-416-8222
Landscape Architect #19 518-474-3817
Laser Operator, Mobile #09 518-457-2735
Lobbyist #16 518-474-7126
Massage Therapist #19 518-474-3817
Medical Doctor #19 518-474-3817
Midwife #19 518-474-3817
Nail Technology #10..............................518-474-4429
Notary Public #10.................................518-474-4429
Nurse #19...518-474-3817
Nurse-LPN/RPN#19..............................518-474-3817
Nurses' Aide #05..................................518-474-3817
Nursing Home Administrator #05 518-474-3817
Nutritionist #19 518-474-3817
Occupational Therapist/Assistant #19 ...518-474-3817
Off-Track Betting #15 ....518-453-8460 X2
Ophthalmic Dispenser #19 518-474-3817
Optometrist #19 518-474-3817
Pesticide Applicator #02 518-402-8748
Pesticide Distributor #02.......................518-402-8748
Pesticide Distributor, Restricted #02 518-402-8748
Pet Cemetery #10 518-474-4429
Pharmacist #19 518-474-3817

Physical Therapist/Assistant #19 518-474-3817
Physician #19 518-474-3817
Physician Assistant #19........................518-474-3817
Physicians' Specialist Assistant #19......518-474-3817
Podiatrist #19 518-474-3817
Private Investigator #10.........................518-474-4429
Psychologist #19 518-474-3817
Public Accountant-CPA #19..................518-474-3817
Racetrack #15...........................518-453-8460 X2
Racing #15 ....518-453-8460 X2
Radiologic Technologist #14 518-402-7580
Radiotherapy Technologist #14 518-402-7580
Rafting Guide, Whitewater #03 518-457-9311
Real Estate Salesperson/Broker/Appraiser #10 ....
....518-474-4429
Respiratory Therapist/Therapy Technician #19 ....
....518-474-3817
School Administrator/Supervisor #17 518-474-3901
School Counselor #17 518-474-3901
School Media Specialist #17 518-474-3901
Securities Broker/Dealer #01 212-416-8222
Securities Salesperson #01 212-416-8222
Security & Fire Alarm Installer #10........518-474-4429
Security Guard #10 518-474-4429
Short Hand Reporter #19.......................518-474-3817
Social Worker #19 518-474-3817
Speech Pathologist/Audiologist #19......518-474-3817
Surveyor #19 518-474-3817
Teacher #17..518-474-3901
Telemarketer Business #10 518-474-4429
Theatrical Syndication #01 212-416-8222
Upholster & Bedding Industry #10.........518-474-4429
Veterinarian #19....................................518-474-3817
Veterinary Technician #19 518-474-3901
Waste Water Treatment Plant Operator #04..............
....518-457-5968
Water Treatment Plant Operator #13 518-458-6755

Licensing Agency Information

#01 Bureau of Investor Protection & Securities, 120 Broadway, 23rd Floor, New York, NY 10271; 212-416-8222, Fax: 212-416-8816. www.oag.state.ny.us

#02 Department of Environmental Conservation, 625 Broadway, Albany, NY 12233-7254; 518-402-8748, Fax: 518-485-8366. www.dec.state.ny.us

#03 Department of Environmental Conservation, 50 Wolf Rd Rm 440C, Albany, NY 12233-2560; 518-457-5740, Fax: 518-485-8458. www.dec.state.ny.us/website/protection/rangers/frguid6.html

#04 Department of Environmental Conservation, Division of Water, 50 Wolf Rd Rm 340, Albany, NY 12233-3506; 518-457-5968, Fax: 518-457-7038. www.dec.state.ny.us

#05 Board of Examiners of Nursing Home Administrators, 161 Delaware Av, Delmar, NY 10254; 518-478-1060.

#06 Department of Health, 433 River St #303, Troy, NY 12180-2299; 518-402-0785, Fax: 518-402-0784.

#07 Department of Health, 433 River St, Troy, NY 12180; 518-402-0996, Fax: 518-402-0985. www.health.state.ny.us

#08 Department of Labor, Bldg 12, Rm 165, Albany, NY 12240-0102; 518-457-2722, Fax: 518-485-9077.

#09 Department of Labor, State Campus, Bldg 12 Rm 133, Albany, NY 12240; 518-457-2735, Fax: 518-457-8452.

#10 Department of State, 84 Holland Ave, Albany, NY 12208-3490; 518-474-4429, Fax: 518-473-6648. www.dos.state.ny.us/lcns/licensing.html
Direct web site URL to search for licensees: http://wdb.dos.state.ny.us/lcns_public/lcns_wdb.status_check_lcns.show

#12 Insurance Department, Empire State Plaza, Bldg 1, Albany, NY 12257; 518-474-6630. www.ins.state.ny.us

#13 Department of Health, 150 Broadway #8, Albany, NY 12204-2719; 518-458-6731, Fax: 518-458-6732. www.health.state.ny.us

#14 Department of Health, Bureau of Environmental Radiation Protection, 547 River St, Troy, NY 12180-2216; 518-402-7580, Fax: 518-402-7554.

#15 Racing & Wagering Board, 1 Watervliet Av Extension #2, Albany, NY 12206; 518-453-8460 x2, Fax: 518-453-8492. www.racing.state.ny.us

#16 Temporary Commission on Lobbying, Agency Bldg #2, 17th Fl, Albany, NY 12223-1254; 518-474-7126, Fax: 518-473-6492. www.nylobby.state.ny.us
Direct web site URL to search for licensees: www.nylobby.state.ny.us/lobbysearch.html. You can search online using lobbyist, client, business nature, city, income level, and expense level.

#17 Office of Teaching, Education Bldg, Albany, NY 12234; 518-474-3901, Fax: 518-473-0271. www.highered.nysed.gov/tcert/
Direct web site URL to search for licensees: www.highered.nysed.gov/tcert/ocvsintro.htm. Search online using school district, name, or map.

#18 Unified Court System, PO Box 2806, Church Street Station, New York, NY 10008; 212-428-2800, Fax: 212-428-2804. www.courts.state.ny.us
Direct web site URL to search for licensees: www.courts.state.ny.us/webdb/wdbcgi.exe/apps/INTERNETDB.attyreghome.show. You can search online using name.

#19 Education Department, State Education Bldg, 2nd Fl, Albany, NY 12234; 518-474-3817 attendant available 9-11:45AM and 12:45-4:30PM ESTTDD 518-473-1426 wwwnysedgov/dpls/opnmehtml. Direct web site URL to search for licensees: www.op.nysed.gov/opsearches.htm#nme. You can search online using name and license number.

New York Federal Courts

The following list indicates the district and division name for each county in the state. If the bankruptcy court location is different from the district court, then the location of the bankruptcy court appears in parentheses.

County/Court Cross Reference

County	District	Division
Albany	Northern	Albany
Allegany	Western	Buffalo
Bronx	Southern	New York City
Broome	Northern	Binghamton (Utica)
Cattaraugus	Western	Buffalo
Cayuga	Northern	Syracuse (Utica)
Chautauqua	Western	Buffalo
Chemung	Western	Rochester
Chenango	Northern	Binghamton (Utica)
Clinton	Northern	Albany
Columbia	Northern (Southern)	Albany (Poughkeepsie)
Cortland	Northern	Syracuse (Utica)
Delaware	Northern	Binghamton (Utica)
Dutchess	Southern	White Plains (Poughkeepsie)
Erie	Western	Buffalo
Essex	Northern	Albany
Franklin	Northern	Binghamton (Albany)
Fulton	Northern	Syracuse (Albany)
Genesee	Western	Buffalo
Greene	Northern (Southern)	Albany (Poughkeepsie)
Hamilton	Northern	Syracuse (Utica)
Herkimer	Northern	Syracuse (Utica)
Jefferson	Northern	Binghamton (Albany)
Kings	Eastern	Brooklyn
Lewis	Northern	Binghamton (Utica)
Livingston	Western	Rochester
Madison	Northern	Syracuse (Utica)
Monroe	Western	Rochester
Montgomery	Northern	Syracuse (Albany)
Nassau	Eastern	Brooklyn (Westbury)
New York	Southern	New York City
Niagara	Western	Buffalo
Oneida	Northern	Utica
Onondaga	Northern	Syracuse (Utica)
Ontario	Western	Rochester
Orange	Southern	White Plains (Poughkeepsie)
Orleans	Western	Buffalo
Oswego	Northern	Syracuse (Utica)
Otsego	Northern	Binghamton (Utica)
Putnam	Southern	White Plains (Poughkeepsie)
Queens	Eastern	Brooklyn
Rensselaer	Northern	Albany
Richmond	Eastern	Brooklyn
Rockland	Southern	White Plains
Saratoga	Northern	Albany
Schenectady	Northern	Albany
Schoharie	Northern	Albany
Schuyler	Western	Rochester
Seneca	Western	Rochester
St. Lawrence	Northern	Binghamton (Albany)
Steuben	Western	Rochester
Suffolk	Eastern	Central Islip
Sullivan	Southern	White Plains (Poughkeepsie)
Tioga	Northern	Binghamton (Utica)
Tompkins	Northern	Syracuse (Utica)
Ulster	Northern (Southern)	Albany (Poughkeepsie)
Warren	Northern	Albany
Washington	Northern	Albany
Wayne	Western	Rochester
Westchester	Southern	White Plains
Wyoming	Western	Buffalo
Yates	Western	Rochester

US District Court

Eastern District of New York

Brooklyn Division Brooklyn Courthouse, 225 Cadman Plaza E, Room 130, Brooklyn, NY 11201 (Courier Address: Use mail address for courier delivery), 718-260-2600.

http://www.nyed.uscourts.gov

Counties: Kings, Queens, Richmond. Cases from Nassau and Suffolk may also be heard here.

Indexing/Storage: Cases are indexed by defendant and plaintiff as well as by case number. New cases are available in the index 2 days after filing date. A computer index is maintained. Open records are located at this court.

Fee & Payment: The fee is $20.00 per item (one party name or case number). Payment may be made by money order, cashier check, personal check. Prepayment is required. Payee: Clerk, US District Court. Certification fee: $7.00 per document. Copy fee: $.50 per page. You are allowed to make your own copies. These copies cost $.25 per page.

Phone Search: Searching is not available by phone.

Mail Search: A stamped self addressed envelope is not required.

In Person: In person searching is available.

PACER: Sign-up number is 800-676-6856. Access fee is $.60 per minute. Toll-free access: 888-331-4965. Local access: 718-246-2494. Case records are available back to January 1, 1990. Records are never purged. New records are available online after 1 day. PACER is available online at http://pacer.nyed.uscourts.gov.

Electronic Filing: Only law firms and practitioners may file cases electronically. Anyone can search online; however only cases filed electronically are included in the search. Electronic filing information is available online at http://ecf.nyed.uscourts.gov

Central Islip Division 100 Federal Plaza, Central Islip, NY 17722-4438 (Courier Address: Use mail address for courier delivery), 613-712-6000.

http://www.nyed.uscourts.gov

Counties: Nassau, Suffolk.

Indexing/Storage: Cases are indexed by defendant and plaintiff as well as by case number. New cases are available in the index 2 days after filing date. Both computer and card indexes are maintained. Indexes and files are available here from 1987 on. Open records are located at this court.

Fee & Payment: The fee is $20.00 per item (one party name or case number). Payment may be made by money order, cashier check, personal check. Prepayment is required. Payee: Clerk, US District Court. Certification fee: $7.00 per document. Copy fee: $.50 per page. You are allowed to make your own copies. These copies cost $.25 per page.

Phone Search: Some limited docket information is available by phone.

Fax Search: Fax requests may only be made for a few names at most. Regular fees apply to fax requests.

Mail Search: Always enclose a stamped self addressed envelope.

In Person: In person searching is available.

PACER: Sign-up number is 800-676-6856. Access fee is $.60 per minute. Toll-free access: 888-331-4965. Local access: 718-250-4420. Case records are available back to January 1, 1990. Records are never purged. New records are available online after 1 day. PACER is available online at http://pacer.nyed.uscourts.gov.

Electronic Filing: Only law firms and practitioners may file cases electronically. Anyone can search online; however only cases filed electronically are included in the search. Electronic filing information is available online at http://ecf.nyed.uscourts.gov

Hauppauge Division No Longer Available - See Central Islip, NY.

US Bankruptcy Court

Eastern District of New York

Brooklyn Division 75 Clinton St, Brooklyn, NY 11201 (Courier Address: Use mail address for courier delivery), 718-330-2188.

http://www.nyeb.uscourts.gov

Counties: Kings, Queens, Richmond. Kings and Queens County Chapter 11 cases may also be assigned to Westbury. Other Queens County cases may be assigned to Westbury Division. Nassau County Chapter 11 cases may be assigned here.

Indexing/Storage: Cases are indexed by debtor as well as by case number. New cases are available in the index 1 day after filing date. Older cases are indexed on microfiche. A computer index is maintained. Open records are located at this court.

Fee & Payment: The fee is $20.00 per item (one party name or case number). Payment may be made by money order, cashier check, business check. Personal checks are not accepted. Prepayment is required. Payee: Clerk, US Bankruptcy Court. Certification fee: $7.00 per document. Copy fee: $.50 per page. You are allowed to make your own copies. These copies cost $.10 per page.

Phone Search: Only docket information is available by phone.

Mail Search: A stamped self addressed envelope is not required.

In Person: In person searching is available.

PACER: Sign-up number is 800-676-6856. Access fee is $.60 per minute. Toll-free access: 800-263-7790. Local access: 718-488-7012. Case records are available back to 1991. Records are

purged every year. New civil records are available online after 3 days. PACER is available online at http://pacer.nyeb.uscourts.gov.

Electronic Filing: Electronic filing information is available online at https://ecf.nyeb.uscourts.gov

Central Islip Division Long Island Federal Courthouse, 290 Federal Plaza, Central Islip, NY 11722 (Courier Address: Use mail address for courier delivery), 613-712-6200.

http://www.nyeb.uscourts.gov

Counties: .

Indexing/Storage: Cases are indexed by debtor as well as by case number. New cases are available in the index 1-2 days after filing date. A computer index is maintained. Open records are located at this court.

Fee & Payment: The fee is $20.00 per item (one party name or case number). Payment may be made by money order, cashier check, personal check. Prepayment is required. Debtor's checks are not accepted. Enclose a FedEx package for expedited service. Payee: Clerk, US Bankruptcy Court. Certification fee: $7.00 per document. Copy fee: $.50 per page. You are allowed to make your own copies. These copies cost $.10 per page.

Phone Search: Basic docket information only available by phone.

Mail Search: A stamped self addressed envelope is not required.

In Person: In person searching is available.

PACER: Sign-up number is 800-676-6856. Access fee is $.60 per minute. Toll-free access: 800-263-7790. Local access: 718-488-7012. Case records are available back to 1991. Records are purged every year. New civil records are available online after 3 days. PACER is available online at http://pacer.nyeb.uscourts.gov.

Electronic Filing: Electronic filing information is available online at https://ecf.nyeb.uscourts.gov

Hauppauge Division No Longer Available - See Central Islip, NY.

Westbury Division 1635 Privado Rd, Westbury, NY 11590 (Courier Address: Use mail address for courier delivery), 516-832-8801.

http://www.nyeb.uscourts.gov

Counties: Nassau. Chapter 11 cases for Nassau County may also be assigned to the Brooklyn or Hauppauge Divisions. Kings and Suffolk County Chapter 11 cases may be assigned here. Any Queens County cases may be assigned here. Non-Chapter 11 cases from western Suffolk County may also be assigned here.

Indexing/Storage: Cases are indexed by debtor as well as by case number. New cases are available in the index 48 hours after filing date. Both computer and card indexes are maintained. Open records are located at this court.

Fee & Payment: The fee is $20.00 per item (one party name or case number). Payment may be made by money order, cashier check, personal check. Prepayment is required. Payee: Clerk, US Bankruptcy Court. Certification fee: $7.00 per document. Copy fee: $.50 per page. You are allowed to make your own copies. These copies cost $.10 per page.

Phone Search: Docket information is available by phone. An automated voice case information service (VCIS) is available. Call VCIS at 800-252-2537 or 718-852-5726.

Mail Search: Always enclose a stamped self addressed envelope.

In Person: In person searching is available.

PACER: Sign-up number is 800-676-6856. Access fee is $.60 per minute. Toll-free access: 800-263-7790. Local access: 718-488-7012. Case records are available back to 1991. Records are purged every year. New civil records are available online after 3 days. PACER is available online at http://pacer.nyeb.uscourts.gov.

Electronic Filing: Electronic filing information is available online at https://ecf.nyeb.uscourts.gov

US District Court

Northern District of New York

Albany Division 445 Broadway, Room 222, James T Foley Courthouse, Albany, NY 12207-2924 (Courier Address: Use mail address for courier delivery), 518-257-1800.

http://www.nynd.uscourts.gov

Counties: Albany, Clinton, Columbia, Essex, Greene, Rensselaer, Saratoga, Schenectady, Schoharie, Ulster, Warren, Washington.

Indexing/Storage: Cases are indexed by defendant and plaintiff as well as by case number. New cases are available in the index 1 day after filing date. Case indexes are available on computer terminal in any of the divisions in the Northern District. Both computer and card indexes are maintained. Open records are located at this court.

Fee & Payment: The fee is $20.00 per item (one party name or case number). Payment may be made by money order, cashier check, personal check. Prepayment is required. Payee: Clerk, US District Court. Certification fee: $7.00 per document. Copy fee: $.50 per page.

Phone Search: Searching is not available by phone.

Mail Search: A stamped self addressed envelope is not required.

In Person: In person searching is available.

PACER: Sign-up number is 800-676-6856. Access fee is $.60 per minute. Toll-free access: 800-480-7525. Local access: 315-234-8663. Case records are available back to June 1991. New records are available online after 2 days.

Binghamton Division 15 Henry St, Binghamton, NY 13901 (Courier Address: Use mail address for courier delivery), 607-773-2893.

http://www.nynd.uscourts.gov

Counties: Broome, Chenango, Delaware, Franklin, Jefferson, Lewis, Otsego, St. Lawrence, Tioga.

Indexing/Storage: Cases are indexed by defendant and plaintiff as well as by case number. New cases are available in the index 1 day after filing date. A computer index is maintained. Open records are located at this court.

Fee & Payment: The fee is $20.00 per item (one party name or case number). Payment may be made by money order, cashier check, personal check. Prepayment is required. Payee: Clerk, US District Court. Certification fee: $7.00 per document. Copy fee: $.50 per page.

Phone Search: Searching is not available by phone. Only docket information is available by phone.

Mail Search: Always enclose a stamped self addressed envelope.

In Person: In person searching is available.

PACER: Sign-up number is 800-676-6856. Access fee is $.60 per minute. Toll-free access: 800-480-7525. Local access: 315-234-8663. Case records are available back to June 1991. New records are available online after 2 days.

Syracuse Division PO Box 7367, Syracuse, NY 13261-7367 (Courier Address: 100 S Clinton St, Syracuse, NY 13261-7367), 315-234-8500.

http://www.nynd.uscourts.gov

Counties: Cayuga, Cortland, Fulton, Hamilton, Herkimer, Madison, Montgomery, Onondaga, Oswego, Tompkins.

Indexing/Storage: Cases are indexed by defendant and plaintiff as well as by case number. New cases are available in the index 1 day after filing date. A computer index is maintained. Open records are located at this court.

Fee & Payment: The fee is $20.00 per item (one party name or case number). Payment may be made by money order, cashier check, personal check. Prepayment is required. Credit cards accepted in person only. Payee: Clerk, US District Court. Certification fee: $7.00 per document. Copy fee: $.50 per page.

Phone Search: Searching is not available by phone. Only docket information is available by phone.

Mail Search: Always enclose a stamped self addressed envelope.

In Person: In person searching is available.

PACER: Sign-up number is 800-676-6856. Access fee is $.60 per minute. Toll-free access: 800-480-7525. Local access: 315-234-8663. Case records are available back to June 1991. New records are available online after 2 days.

Utica Division Alexander Pirnie Bldg, 10 Broad St, Utica, NY 13501 (Courier Address: Use mail address for courier delivery), 315-793-8151.

http://www.nynd.uscourts.gov

Counties: Oneida.

Indexing/Storage: Cases are indexed by defendant and plaintiff as well as by case number. New cases are available in the index 1 day after filing date. Indexes are on computer starting in 1991 and on cards prior to that. Open records are located at this court. Closed case records from the other three Northern district courts were assembled here before going to the New York Federal Records Center. Starting in 1995, Albany and Binghamton and Syracuse are no longer sending their records to Utica.

Fee & Payment: The fee is $20.00 per item (one party name or case number). Payment may be made by money order, cashier check, business check. Personal checks are not accepted. Prepayment is required. Payee: Clerk, US District Court. Certification fee: $7.00 per document. Copy fee: $.50 per page.

Phone Search: Information from the computer for 1991 forward is available by phone.

Mail Search: A stamped self addressed envelope is not required.

In Person: In person searching is available.

PACER: Sign-up number is 800-676-6856. Access fee is $.60 per minute. Toll-free access: 800-480-7525. Local access: 315-234-8663. Case

records are available back to June 1991. New records are available online after 2 days.

US Bankruptcy Court

Northern District of New York

Albany Division James T Foley Courthouse, 445 Broadway #330, Albany, NY 12207 (Courier Address: Use mail address for courier delivery), 518-257-1661.

http://www.nynb.uscourts.gov

Counties: Albany, Clinton, Essex, Franklin, Fulton, Jefferson, Montgomery, Rensselaer, Saratoga, Schenectady, Schoharie, St. Lawrence, Warren, Washington.

Indexing/Storage: Cases are indexed by debtor as well as by case number. New cases are available in the index 48 hours after filing date. Both computer and card indexes are maintained. Open records are located at this court. As of January 1, 1995, Jefferson and St. Lawrence Counties moved to Albany Division from Utica, while Broome, Chenango, Delaware, Otsego, Tioga and Tompkins Counties moved to Utica Division from Albany.

Fee & Payment: The fee is $20.00 per item (one party name or case number). Payment may be made by money order, cashier check. Business checks are not accepted, Visa or Mastercard. Personal checks are not accepted. Prepayment is required. Credit cards are only accepted from in-person searchers. Payee: Clerk, US Bankruptcy Court. Certification fee: $7.00 per document. Copy fee: $.25 per page.

Phone Search: Only docket information is available by phone. An automated voice case information service (VCIS) is available. Call VCIS at 800-206-1952 or.

Mail Search: If a case number is not known, the turnaround time may be as long as 5 days after the request is received. Always enclose a stamped self addressed envelope.

In Person: In person searching is available.

PACER: Sign-up number is 800-676-6856. Access fee is $.60 per minute. Toll-free access: 800-390-8432. Local access: 518-257-1669. Case records are available back to 1992. New civil records are available online after 48 hours. PACER is available online at http://pacer.nynb.uscourts.gov.

Utica Division Room 230, 10 Broad St, Utica, NY 13501 (Courier Address: Use mail address for courier delivery), 315-793-8101, Fax: 315-793-8128.

http://www.nynb.uscourts.gov

Counties: Broome, Cayuga, Chenango, Cortland, Delaware, Hamilton, Herkimer, Lewis, Madison, Oneida, Onondaga, Otsego, Oswego, Tioga, Tompkins.

Indexing/Storage: Cases are indexed by debtor as well as by case number. New cases are available in the index 24 hours after filing date. Both computer and card indexes are maintained. Open records are located at this court. As of January 1, 1995, Jefferson and St. Lawrence Counties moved to Albany Division from Utica, while Broome, Chenango, Delaware, Otsego, Tioga and Tompkins Counties moved to Utica Division from Albany.

Fee & Payment: The fee is $20.00 per item (one party name or case number). Payment may be made by money order, cashier check, personal check. Debtor's checks are not accepted. Payee: Clerk, US Bankruptcy Court. Certification fee: $7.00 per document. Copy fee: $.50 per page.

Phone Search: Only docket information is available by phone. An automated voice case information service (VCIS) is available. Call VCIS at 800-206-1952 or.

Mail Search: A stamped self addressed envelope is not required.

In Person: In person searching is available.

PACER: Sign-up number is 800-676-6856. Access fee is $.60 per minute. Toll-free access: 800-390-8432. Local access: 518-257-1669. Case records are available back to 1992. New civil records are available online after 48 hours. PACER is available online at http://pacer.nynb.uscourts.gov.

US District Court

Southern District of New York

New York City Division 500 Pearl St, New York, NY 10007 (Courier Address: Use mail address for courier delivery), 212-805-0136.

http://www.nysd.uscourts.gov

Counties: Bronx, New York. Some cases from the counties in the White Plains Division are also assigned to the New York Division.

Indexing/Storage: Cases are indexed by defendant and plaintiff as well as by case number. New cases are available in the index 2 days after filing date. A computer index is maintained. Open records are located at this court.

Fee & Payment: The fee is $20.00 per item (one party name or case number). Payment may be made by money order, cashier check. Business checks are not accepted. Personal checks are not accepted. Prepayment is required. Payee: Clerk of Court, S.D.N.Y. Certification fee: $7.00 per document. Copy fee: $.50 per page. You are allowed to make your own copies. These copies cost Not Applicable per page.

Phone Search: Searching is not available by phone. Only docket information is available by phone.

Mail Search: Always enclose a stamped self addressed envelope.

In Person: In person searching is available.

PACER: Sign-up number is 800-676-6856. Access fee is $.60 per minute. Local access: 212-805-6373. Case records are available back to early 1990. Records are purged every six months. New records are available online after 1 day.

Opinions Online: Selected rulings are searchable online using CourtWeb. To download and view copies of rulings you must have Adobe Acrobat Reader. Court opinions are available online at http://www.nysd.uscourts.gov/courtweb

White Plains Division 300 Quarropas St, White Plains, NY 10601 (Courier Address: Use mail address for courier delivery), 914-390-4000.

http://www.nysd.uscourts.gov

Counties: Dutchess, Orange, Putnam, Rockland, Sullivan, Westchester. Some cases may be assigned to New York Division.

Indexing/Storage: Cases are indexed by defendant and plaintiff as well as by case number. New cases are available in the index 2 days after filing date. A computer index is maintained. Indexes have been automated since 1983. Open records are located at this court.

Fee & Payment: The fee is $20.00 per item (one party name or case number). Payment may be made by money order, cashier check. Business checks are not accepted. Personal checks are not accepted. Prepayment is required. Attorney checks are accepted. Payee: Clerk of Court, S.D.N.Y. Certification fee: $7.00 per document. Copy fee: $.50 per page. You are allowed to make your own copies. These copies cost $.15 per page.

Phone Search: Searching is not available by phone.

Mail Search: Always enclose a stamped self addressed envelope.

In Person: In person searching is available.

PACER: Sign-up number is 800-676-6856. Access fee is $.60 per minute. Local access: 212-805-6373. Case records are available back to early 1990. Records are purged every six months. New records are available online after 1 day.

Opinions Online: Selected rulings are searchable online using CourtWeb. To download and view copies of rulings you must have Adobe Acrobat Reader. Court opinions are available online at http://www.nysd.uscourts.gov/courtweb

US Bankruptcy Court

Southern District of New York

New York City Division Room 534, 1 Bowling Green, New York, NY 10004-1408 (Courier Address: Use mail address for courier delivery), 212-668-2870.

http://www.nysb.uscourts.gov

Counties: Bronx, New York.

Indexing/Storage: Cases are indexed by debtor as well as by case number. New cases are available in the index 1-3 days after filing date. Both computer and card indexes are maintained. Open records are located at this court.

Fee & Payment: The fee is $20.00 per item (one party name or case number). Payment may be made by money order, cashier check, business check. Personal checks are not accepted. Prepayment is required. Payee: Clerk, US Bankruptcy Court. Certification fee: $7.00 per document. Copy fee: $.50 per page. You are allowed to make your own copies. These copies cost $.25 per page.

Phone Search: Over the phone, this court will only provide whether a case is pending. A copy service is available at 212-480-0737 if you have the case number. An automated voice case information service (VCIS) is available.

Mail Search: A stamped self addressed envelope is not required.

In Person: In person searching is available.

PACER: Sign-up number is 800-676-6856. Access fee is $.60 per minute. Local access: 212-668-2896, 212-668-2897, 212-668-2898. Case records are available back to June 1991. Records are purged every six months. New civil records are available online after 2 days. PACER is available online at https://ecf.nysb.uscourts.gov/cgi-bin/login.pl.

Electronic Filing: Electronic filing information is available online at http://ecf.nysb.uscourts.gov

Poughkeepsie Division 176 Church St, Poughkeepsie, NY 12601 (Courier Address: Use mail address for courier delivery), 845-452-4200, Fax: 845-452-8375.

http://www.nysb.uscourts.gov

Counties: Columbia, Dutchess, Greene, Orange, Putnam, Sullivan, Ulster.

Indexing/Storage: Cases are indexed by debtor as well as by case number. New cases are available in the index 1-3 days after filing date. Both computer and card indexes are maintained. Open records are located at this court.

Fee & Payment: The fee is $20.00 per item (one party name or case number). Payment may be made by money order, cashier check, business check. Personal checks are not accepted. Prepayment is required. Payee: Clerk, US Bankruptcy Court. Certification fee: $7.00 per document. Copy fee: $.50 per page. You are allowed to make your own copies. These copies cost $.15 per page.

Phone Search: Over the phone, this court will only reveal whether the case is pending. An automated voice case information service (VCIS) is available.

Mail Search: A stamped self addressed envelope is not required.

In Person: In person searching is available.

PACER: Sign-up number is 800-676-6856. Access fee is $.60 per minute. Local access: 212-668-2896, 212-668-2897, 212-668-2898. Case records are available back to June 1991. Records are purged every six months. New civil records are available online after 2 days. PACER is available online at https://ecf.nysb.uscourts.gov/cgi-bin/login.pl.

Electronic Filing: Electronic filing information is available online at http://ecf.nysb.uscourts.gov

White Plains Division 300 Quarropas St, White Plains, NY 10601 (Courier Address: Use mail address for courier delivery), 914-390-4060.

http://www.nysb.uscourts.gov

Counties: Rockland, Westchester.

Indexing/Storage: Cases are indexed by debtor as well as by case number. New cases are available in the index 1-3 days after filing date. Both computer and card indexes are maintained. Records are also indexed on microfiche. Open records are located at this court. District wide searches are available for cases from 1991 from this court.

Fee & Payment: The fee is $20.00 per item (one party name or case number). Payment may be made by money order, business check. Personal checks are not accepted. Prepayment is required. Checks and credit cards are not accepted from debtors. Payee: Clerk, US Bankruptcy Court. Certification fee: $7.00 per document. Copy fee: $.50 per page. You are allowed to make your own copies. These copies cost $.15 per page. Visa and MasterCard are only accepted for in person searches.

Phone Search: Over the phone, this court will only reveal whether the case is pending. An automated voice case information service (VCIS) is available.

Mail Search: Always enclose a stamped self addressed envelope.

In Person: In person searching is available.

PACER: Sign-up number is 800-676-6856. Access fee is $.60 per minute. Local access: 212-668-2896, 212-668-2897, 212-668-2898. Case records are available back to June 1991. Records are purged every six months. New civil records are available online after 2 days. PACER is available online at https://ecf.nysb.uscourts.gov/cgi-bin/login.pl.

Electronic Filing: Electronic filing information is available online at http://ecf.nysb.uscourts.gov

US District Court

Western District of New York

Buffalo Division Room 304, 68 Court St, Buffalo, NY 14202 (Courier Address: Use mail address for courier delivery), 716-551-4211, Fax: 716-551-4850.

http://www.nywd.uscourts.gov

Counties: Allegany, Cattaraugus, Chautauqua, Erie, Genesee, Niagara, Orleans, Wyoming. Prior to 1982, this division included what is now the Rochester Division.

Indexing/Storage: Cases are indexed by defendant and plaintiff as well as by case number. New cases are available in the index 2 days after filing date. A computer index is maintained. Open records are located at this court.

Fee & Payment: The fee is $20.00 per item (one party name or case number). Payment may be made by money order, cashier check, personal check. Prepayment is required. Payee: Clerk, US District Court. Certification fee: $7.00 per document. Copy fee: $.50 per page.

Phone Search: Searching is not available by phone.

Mail Search: A stamped self addressed envelope is not required.

In Person: In person searching is available.

PACER: Sign-up number is 800-676-6856. Access fee is $.60 per minute. Toll-free access: 877-233-5848. Local access: 716-551-3333. Case records are available back to 1992. Records are never purged. New civil records are available online after 1 day. New criminal records are available online after 2 days. PACER is available online at http://pacer.nywd.uscourts.gov.

Rochester Division Room 2120, 100 State St, Rochester, NY 14614 (Courier Address: Use mail address for courier delivery), 716-263-6263, Fax: 716-263-3178.

http://www.nywd.uscourts.gov

Counties: Chemung, Livingston, Monroe, Ontario, Schuyler, Seneca, Steuben, Wayne, Yates.

Indexing/Storage: Cases are indexed by defendant and plaintiff as well as by case number. New cases are available in the index 1 day after filing date. A computer index is maintained. Open records are located at this court. This division was established in 1981. Cases closed from 1996 to present are also held here. Earlier case records and indexes are held in the Buffalo Division (Erie County).

Fee & Payment: The fee is $20.00 per item (one party name or case number). Payment may be made by money order, cashier check, personal check. Prepayment is required. Payee: Clerk, US District Court. Certification fee: $7.00 per document. Copy fee: $.50 per page.

Phone Search: Simple docket information available by phone.

Fax Search: Fees for fax requests depend on the nature of the search. Call for more information. Will fax results. Call for instructions.

Mail Search: Mail searches including years prior to 1982 will be forwarded to the Buffalo Division. A stamped self addressed envelope is not required.

In Person: In person searching is available.

PACER: Sign-up number is 800-676-6856. Access fee is $.60 per minute. Toll-free access: 877-233-5848. Local access: 716-551-3333. Case records are available back to 1992. Records are never purged. New civil records are available online after 1 day. New criminal records are available online after 2 days. PACER is available online at http://pacer.nywd.uscourts.gov.

US Bankruptcy Court

Western District of New York

Buffalo Division Olympic Towers, 300 Pearl St #250, Buffalo, NY 14202-2501 (Courier Address: Use mail address for courier delivery), 716-551-4130.

http://www.nywb.uscourts.gov

Counties: Allegany, Cattaraugus, Chautauqua, Erie, Genesee, Niagara, Orleans, Wyoming.

Indexing/Storage: Cases are indexed by debtor as well as by case number. New cases are available in the index 24 hours after filing date. Both computer and card indexes are maintained. Open records are located at this court.

Fee & Payment: The fee is $20.00 per item (one party name or case number). Payment may be made by money order, cashier check, business check. Personal checks are not accepted. Prepayment is required. Payee: Clerk, US Bankruptcy Court. Certification fee: $7.00 per document. Copy fee: $.50 per page.

Phone Search: Only docket information is available by phone. An automated voice case information service (VCIS) is available. Call VCIS at 800-776-9578 or 716-551-5311.

Mail Search: Always enclose a stamped self addressed envelope.

In Person: In person searching is available.

PACER: Sign-up number is 800-676-6856. Access fee is $.60 per minute. Toll-free access: 800-450-8052. Local access: 716-551-3152. Case records are available back to August 1987. Records are never purged. New civil records are available online after 1 day. PACER is available online at http://pacer.nywb.uscourts.gov.

Rochester Division Room 1220, 100 State St, Rochester, NY 14614 (Courier Address: Use mail address for courier delivery), 716-263-3148.

http://www.nywb.uscourts.gov

Counties: Chemung, Livingston, Monroe, Ontario, Schuyler, Seneca, Steuben, Wayne, Yates.

Indexing/Storage: Cases are indexed by debtor as well as by case number. New cases are available in the index 24 hours after filing date. A computer index is maintained. Records are also indexed on microfiche. Open records are located at this court. District wide searches are available for information from August 1, 1987 from this division.

Fee & Payment: The fee is $20.00 per item (one party name or case number). Payment may be made by money order, cashier check, business check. Personal checks are not accepted. Prepayment is required. The SASE should be large enough to hold all copies and have sufficient postage to send them. Payee: Clerk, US Bankruptcy Court. Certification fee: $7.00 per document. Copy fee: $.50 per page.

Phone Search: Only docket information is available by phone. An automated voice case information service (VCIS) is available. Call VCIS at 800-776-9578 or 716-551-5311.

Mail Search: Always enclose a stamped self addressed envelope.

In Person: In person searching is available.

PACER: Sign-up number is 800-676-6856. Access fee is $.60 per minute. Toll-free access: 800-450-8052. Local access: 716-551-3152. Case records are available back to August 1987. Records are never purged. New civil records are available online after 1 day. PACER is available online at http://pacer.nywb.uscourts.gov.

New York County Courts

Court	Jurisdiction	No. of Courts	How Organized
Supreme Courts*	General	11	12 Districts
County Courts*	General	2	57 Counties
Combined Courts*	General	57	
City Courts*	Limited	61	61 Cities
District Courts*	Limited	10	Nassau, Suffolk
Civil /Criminal Courts of the City of New York*	Municipal	6	
Town and Village Justice Courts	Municipal	1269	
Surrogates' Courts*	Probate	62	62 Counties and Boroughs
Court of Claims	Limited	1	
Family Courts	Special	62	62 Counties and Boroughs

* Profiled in this Sourcebook.

Court	CIVIL								
	Tort	Contract	Real Estate	Min. Claim	Max. Claim	Small Claims	Estate	Eviction	Domestic Relations
Supreme Courts*	X	X	X	$25,000	No Max				X
County Courts*	X	X	X	$0	$25,000				
City Courts*	X	X	X	$0	$15,000	$3000		X	
District Courts*	X	X	X	$0	$15,000	$3000		X	
Civil /Criminal Courts of the City of New York*	X	X	X	$0	$25,000	$3000		X	
Town and Village Justice Courts	X	X	X	$0	$3000	$3000			
Surrogates' Courts*							X		X
Court of Claims	X	X	X	$0	No Max				
Family Courts									X

Court	CRIMINAL				
	Felony	Misdemeanor	DWI/DUI	Preliminary Hearing	Juvenile
Supreme Courts*	X				
County Courts*				X	
City Courts*	X	X	X	X	
District Courts*		X	X	X	
Civil /Criminal Courts of the City of New York*		X	X	X	
Town and Village Justice Courts		X	X	X	
Surrogates' Courts*					
Court of Claims					
Family Courts					X

ADMINISTRATION   Office of Administration, Empire State Plaza, Agency Plaza #4, Suite 2001, Albany, NY, 12223; 518-473-1196, Fax: 518-473-6860. www.courts.state.ny.us

COURT STRUCTURE   New York State has two sites for Administration; in addition to the Albany address above, there is a New York City office at this address: Office of Administration, 25 Beaver St, New York NY 10004, and telephone: 212-428-2100.

"Supreme Courts" are the highest trial courts in the state, equivalent to Circuit or District Courts in other states; they are not appeals courts. Many New York City courts are indexed by plaintiff only.

Records for Supreme and County Courts are maintained by County Clerks. In most counties, the address for the clerk is the same as the court. Exceptions are noted in the court profiles.

In at least 20 New York Counties, Misdemeanor records are only available at city, town or village courts. This is also true of small claims and eviction records. Town and Village Courts are be listed at the end of each county section.

CRIMINAL COURTS   The New York State Office of Court Administration-OCA (address below) will perform an electronic search for criminal history information from a database of criminal case records from the boroughs and counties of Bronx, Dutchess, Erie, Kings, Nassau, New York, Orange, Putnam, Queens, Richmond, Rockland, Suffolk and Westchester. The request must include complete name and date of birth, and, for mail requests, be accompanied by two (2) self addressed stamped return envelopes. The fee, payable by check, is $16.00 per name per county. Mail and in person requests go to

> Office of Court Administration (OCA)
> Criminal History Search
> 25 Beaver St, 8th Floor
> New York, NY 10004

You may obtain copies of any case dispositions found from the applicable county court.

ONLINE ACCESS   Civil case information from the 13 largest counties is available through DataCase, a database index of civil case information publicly available at terminals located at Supreme and County Courts. In addition to the civil case index, DataCase also includes judgment docket and lien information, New York County Clerk system data, and the New York State attorney registration file. Remote access is also available at a fee of $1.00 per minute. Call 800-494-8981 for more remote access information.

ADDITIONAL INFORMATION   Supreme and County Court records are generally maintained in the County Clerk's Office, which outside of New York City may index civil cases by defendant, whereas the court itself maintains only a plaintiff index.

Fees for Supreme and County Courts are generally as follows: $5.00 per 2 year search per name for a manual search, and $16.00 per name for a computer or OCA search; $.50 per page (minimum $1.00) for copies; and $4.00 for certification. City Courts charge $5.00 for certification. Effective 4-1-95, no New York courts accept credit cards for any transaction.

📖 📖 📖 📖 📖 📖 📖

Albany County

Supreme & County Court Courthouse Rm 128, 16 Eagle St, Albany, NY 12207; 518-487-5118; Fax: 518-487-5099. Hours: 9AM-5PM (EST). *Felony, Civil.* www.albanycounty.com/clerk

Civil Records: Access: Mail, in person. Both court and visitors may perform in person searches. Search fee: $5.00 per name. Fee is for each two years requested. Required to search: name, years to search. Civil cases indexed by defendant, plaintiff. Civil records on computer from 1981, prior in books.

Criminal Records: Access: Mail, in person. Both court and visitors may perform in person searches. Search fee: $5.00 per name. Fee is per two years requested. Required to search: name, years to search, DOB, Criminal records on computer from 1981, prior in books. Search requests must be in writing.

General Information: Public Access terminal is available. No sealed, expunged, adoption, sex offense, juvenile, mental health or divorce records released. SASE appreciated. Turnaround time 1-3 days. Copy fee: $.50 per page. Certification fee: $4.00. Fee payee: County Clerk. Personal checks accepted. Prepayment is required.

Albany City Court - Civil Part City Hall Rm 209, Albany, NY 12207; 518-434-5115; Fax: 518-434-5034. Hours: 8:30AM-5PM (EST). *Civil Actions Under $15,000, Eviction, Small Claims.*

Civil Records: Access: Mail, in person. Only the court performs in person searches; visitors may not. Search fee: $16.00 per name. Required to search: name, years to search. Civil cases indexed by plaintiff. Civil records on computer from 1993, prior in books.

General Information: No code enforcement records released. SASE required. Turnaround time varies. Copy fee: $1.00 for first page, $.50 each add'l. Certification fee: $5.00. Fee payee: Albany City Court. Business checks accepted.

Albany City Court - Misdemeanors Morton & Broad St, Albany, NY 12202; 518-462-6714; Fax: 518-447-8778. Hours: 8AM-4PM *Misdemeanor.*

Criminal Records: Access: Phone, mail, in person. Only the court performs in person searches; visitors may not. Search fee: $5.00 per name. Required to search: name, years to search, DOB, SSN, signed release. Criminal records on computer since mid-'93, on index cards prior.

General Information: No sealed, expunged, adoption, sex offense, juvenile, or mental health records released without a signed release from the party. SASE required. Turnaround time 5 Days. Copy fee: $.50 per page. Certification fee: $4.00. Fee payee: Albany City Court Criminal Part. Business checks accepted. Prepayment is required.

Cohoes City Court 97 Mohawk St, PO Box 678, Cohoes, NY 12047-0678; Civil phone: 518-233-2133; Criminal phone: 518-233-2134. Hours: 8AM-4PM (EST). *Misdemeanor, Civil Actions Under $15,000, Eviction, Small Claims.*

Civil Records: Access: Mail, in person. Only the court performs in person searches; visitors may not. Search fee: $16.00 per name. Required to search: name, years to search. Civil cases indexed by defendant, plaintiff. Civil records on computer to 1/95, prior in books./cards.

Criminal Records: Access: Mail, in person. Only the court performs in person searches; visitors may not. Search fee: $16.00 per name by computer; $5 per name plus $5 for each consecutive 2 year period searched manually. Required to search: name, years to search, DOB; also helpful: SSN. Criminal records on computer from 1/95, prior in books, on cards.

General Information: No sealed or expunged records released. SASE required. Turnaround time 2 weeks. Copy fee: $.25 per page. Certification fee: $5.00. Fee payee: City Court. Only cashiers checks and money orders accepted. Prepayment is required.

Watervliet City Court 15th & Broadway, Watervliet, NY 12189; 518-270-3803; Fax: 518-270-3812. Hours: 8AM-3PM (EST). *Misdemeanor, Civil Actions Under $15,000, Eviction, Small Claims.*

Civil Records: Access: Phone, fax, mail, in person. Only the court performs in person searches; visitors may not. Search fee: $5.00 per name. Required to search: name, years to search. Civil cases indexed by plaintiff. Civil records on computer from 1991, prior on index cards back to 1975.
Criminal Records: Access: Mail, in person. Only the court performs in person searches; visitors may not. Search fee: $5.00 per name. Required to search: name, years to search, DOB. Criminal records on computer from 1991, prior on index cards back to 1975.
General Information: SASE required. Turnaround time 1-2 weeks. Fax notes: Fee to fax results is $5.00 per document. Copy fee: $5.00 per page. Certification fee: $5.00. Fee payee: City Court. Business checks accepted. Prepayment is required.

Surrogate Court Courthouse, 16 Eagle St, Albany, NY 12207; 518-487-5393. Hours: 9AM-5PM (EST). *Probate.*

Note: Search fee is $25.00 for up to 25 year search, $70 over.

Town/Village Courts; *Misdemeanor, Civil Actions Under $3,000, Small Claims:* Menands Village, 518-434-3992; New Scotland Town, 518-475-0493; Bethlehem Town, 518-439-8717; Guilderland Town, 518-356-1980; Rensselaerville Town, 518-239-4225; Voorheesville Village, 518-765-5524; Ravena Village, 518-756-2313; Knox Town, 518-872-2551; Westerlo Town, 518-797-3239; Berne Town, 518-872-1448; Altamont Village, 518-861-8554; Colonie Town, 518-783-2714; Green Island Town, 518-273-0661; Coeymans Town, 518-756-8480.

Allegany County

Supreme & County Court 7 Court Street, Belmont, NY 14813; 716-268-5813; Fax: 716-268-7090. Hours: 9AM-5PM (EST). *Felony, Civil.*

Note: Misdemeanor records are maintained by city, town and village courts.
Civil Records: Access: Phone, mail, in person. Only the court performs in person searches; visitors may not. No search fee. Required to search: name, years to search. Civil cases indexed by defendant. Civil records with the County Court books, all in books, no computer.
Criminal Records: Access: Fax, mail, in person. Only the court performs in person searches; visitors may not. Search fee: $5.00 for each 2 year period. Required to search: name, years to search, DOB. Criminal records with the Supreme Court, no computer, all in books.
General Information: No youth offender or sealed records released. SASE required. Turnaround time 7-10 days. Fax notes: No fee to fax results. Will fax to toll free numbers only. Copy fee: $1.00 per page. Fee payee: Joseph Presutti, County Clerk. Personal checks accepted. Prepayment is required.

Surrogate Court Courthouse, 7 Court St, Belmont, NY 14813; 716-268-5815; Fax: 716-268-7090. Hours: 9AM-5PM Sept-May; 8:30AM-4PM June-Aug (EST). *Probate.*

Town/Village Courts; *Misdemeanor, Civil Actions Under $3,000, Small Claims:* Wellsville Village, 716-593-5609; Burns Town, 607-545-8998; Rushford Town, 716-437-2206; Cuba Town, 716-968-1690; Caneadea Town, 716-365-8240; Bolivar Village, 716-928-

2234; Scio Town, 716-593-5777; West Almond Town, 607-276-6680; Wellsville Town, 716-593-1750; Independence Town; Centerville Town; Alfred Town, 607-587-8524; Alfred Village, 607-587-9142; Almond Town, 607-276-6665; Allen Town; Alma Town, 716-593-4021; Clarksville Town; Angelica Village Court; New Hudson Town, 716-968-3288; Canaseraga Village, 607-545-0963; Angelica Town, 716-466-7928; Andover Village, 607-478-8455; Belfast Town, 716-365-2623; Andover Town, 607-478-8446; Friendship Town, 716-973-7566; Belmont Village, 716-268-5305; Wirt Town, 716-928-2130; Bolivar Town, 716-928-1860; Genesee Town, 716-928-1384; Amity Town, 716-268-5305; Richburg Village Court; Granger Town, 716-567-4575; Willing Town.

Bronx County

Supreme Court - Civil Division 851 Grand Concourse, Bronx, NY 10451; 718-590-3641; Fax: 718-590-8122. Hours: 9AM-5PM (EST). *Civil Actions Over $25,000.*

Civil Records: Access: Mail, in person. Both court and visitors may perform in person searches. Search fee: $5.00 per name. Fee is for each 2 years searched. Required to search: name, years to search. Civil cases indexed by defendant, plaintiff. Civil records on computer since 1995; prior records on microfilm.
General Information: Public Access terminal is available. No marriage or divorce records released. SASE required. Turnaround time 7-10 days. Copy fee: $.75 per page. Certification fee: $5.00. Fee payee: Bronx County Clerk. Only cashiers checks and money orders accepted. Prepayment is required.

Supreme Court - Criminal Division 851 Grand Concourse, Rm 123, Bronx, NY 10451; 718-590-3803. Hours: 9AM-5PM (EST). *Felony.*

Criminal Records: Access: Mail, in person. Only the court performs in person searches; visitors may not. Search fee: $16.00 per name. Fee is per county searched. Required to search: name, years to search, DOB. Criminal records on computer back to 1977, prior on microfiche.
General Information: No sealed, expunged, juvenile or sex offense records released. SASE required. Copy fee: $.75 per page. Certification fee: $8.00. Fee payee: Bronx County Clerk. Only cashiers checks and money orders accepted. Prepayment is required.

Civil Court of the City of New York - Bronx Branch 851 Grand Concourse, Bronx, NY 10451; 718-590-3601. Hours: 9AM-5PM (EST). *Civil Actions Under $25,000, Eviction, Small Claims.*

Civil Records: Access: In person only. Visitors must perform in person searches for themselves. No search fee. Required to search: name, years to search. Civil cases indexed by defendant, plaintiff. Civil records in books, on file cards. Records archived after five years, requiring 3-5 days to requisition.
General Information: Copy fee: $.25 per page. Certification fee: $5.00. Fee payee: County Clerk. Business checks accepted.

Supreme Court - Criminal Div.ision - Misdemeanors Central Clerk's Office, 215 W 161st St, Bronx, NY 10451; 718-590-2853. Hours: 9AM-5PM (EST). *Misdemeanor.*

Criminal Records: Access: Mail, in person. Only the court performs in person searches; visitors may not. Search fee: None reported. Required to search: name, years to search, DOB. Some criminal records on computer back to 1976, prior on microfiche.
General Information: No sealed, expunged, juvenile or sex offense records released. SASE required. Certification fee: $5.00. Fee payee: Bronx Central Clerk's Office. Only cashiers checks and money orders accepted. Prepayment is required.

Surrogate Court 851 Grand Concourse, Bronx, NY 10451; 718-590-4515; Fax: 718-537-5158. Hours: 9AM-5PM (EST). *Probate.*

Broome County

Supreme & County Court PO Box 2062, Binghamton, NY 13902; 607-778-2448/2451; Fax: 607-778-6426. Hours: 9AM-5PM (EST). *Felony, Civil.*

Civil Records: Access: Fax, mail, in person. Both court and visitors may perform in person searches. Search fee: $5.00 per name. Fee is per 2 years searched. Required to search: name, years to search. Civil cases indexed by defendant, plaintiff. Civil records on computer from 1985, prior in books.
Criminal Records: Access: Fax, mail, in person. Both court and visitors may perform in person searches. Search fee: $5.00 per name. Fee is per 2 years searched, 10 year maximum. Required to search: name, years to search, DOB. Criminal records on computer from 1985, prior in books.
General Information: Public Access terminal is available. No sealed or youthful offender records released. SASE required. Turnaround time 3-5 days. Fax notes: $1.00 per page. Copy fee: $.50 per page. $1.00 minimum. Certification fee: $4.00. Fee payee: County Clerk. Personal checks accepted. No personal checks over $1000.00. Prepayment is required.

Binghamton City Court Governmental Plaza, Binghamton, NY 13901; 607-772-7006; Fax: 607-772-7041. Hours: 9AM-5PM (EST). *Misdemeanor, Civil Actions Under $15,000, Eviction, Small Claims.*

Civil Records: Access: Phone, mail, in person. Both court and visitors may perform in person searches. No search fee. Required to search: name, years to search. Civil cases indexed by defendant. Civil records on computer from 1990, prior in books, index cards. In person searching only for 04/21/99 forward.
Criminal Records: Access: Mail, in person. Only the court performs in person searches; visitors may not. Search fee: $5.00 fee per each 2 years for a manual search prior to 1990; electronic search $16.00 (pending or disposed) 1990 to present. Required to search: name, years to search, DOB. Criminal records on computer from 1990.
General Information: Public Access terminal is available. (Civil only, since 1996.) No sealed records released. SASE required. Turnaround time 1-2 weeks. Copy fee: $.50 per page. $1.00 minimum. Certification fee: $5.00. per certificate. Fee payee: Binghamton City Court. Only cashiers checks and money orders accepted. Prepayment is required.

Surrogate Court Courthouse, 92 Court St, Rm 109, Binghamton, NY 13901; 607-778-2111; Fax: 607-778-2308. Hours: 9AM-5PM (EST). *Probate.*

Note: $25 search fee

Town/Village Courts; *Misdemeanor, Civil Actions Under $3,000, Small Claims:* Dickinson Town, 607-723-9403; Fenton Town, 607-648-4801; Triangle Town, 607-692-4332; Windsor Town, 607-655-1973; Union Town, 607-754-2102; Johnson City Village, 607-798-0002; Endicott Village, 607-757-2483; Conklin Town, 607-775-5244; Colesville Town, 607-693-1172; Barker Town, 607-648-6961; Chenango Town, 607-722-4191; Maine Town, 607-862-3427; Binghampton Town, 607-772-0357; Kirkwood Town, 607-775-2653; Nanticoke Town, 607-692-4041; Deposit Village, 607-467-4240; Vestal Town, 607-748-1514; Sanford Town, 607-467-3157; Lisle Town, 607-849-6969.

Cattaraugus County

Supreme & County Court 303 Court St, Little Valley, NY 14755; 716-938-9111; Fax: 716-938-6413. Hours: 9AM-5PM (EST). *Felony, Civil.*

Note: Misdemeanor records are maintained by city, town and village courts.

Civil Records: Access: Mail, in person. Both court and visitors may perform in person searches. Search fee: $5.00 per name. Fee is per 2 years searched. Required to search: name, years to search. Civil cases indexed by defendant, plaintiff. Civil records on computer from 1989, prior in books, index cards from 1900.

Criminal Records: Access: Phone, mail, in person. Both court and visitors may perform in person searches. Search fee: $5.00 per name. Fee is per 2 years searched. Required to search: name, years to search, DOB. Criminal records on computer from 1989, prior in books, index cards from 1900.

General Information: No sealed or youthful offender records released. SASE not required. Turnaround time 2-3 days. Copy fee: $1.00 per page. Certification fee: $4.00. Fee payee: County Clerk. Business checks accepted. Prepayment is required.

Olean City Court PO Box 631, Olean, NY 14760; 716-376-5620; Fax: 716-376-5623. Hours: 8:30AM-4:30PM (EST). *Misdemeanor, Civil Actions Under $15,000, Eviction, Small Claims.*

Civil Records: Access: Mail, in person. Only the court performs in person searches; visitors may not. Search fee: $5.00 per name. Required to search: name, years to search. Civil cases indexed by defendant. Civil records on docket books.

Criminal Records: Access: Mail, in person. Only the court performs in person searches; visitors may not. Search fee: $5.00 per name. Required to search: name, years to search, DOB. Criminal records on computer from 1990, prior in books.

General Information: No sealed or youthful offender records released. SASE required. Turnaround time 2 days. Certification fee: $5.00. Fee payee: City Court. Business checks accepted. Prepayment is required.

Salamanca City Court Municipal Center, 225 Wildwood, Salamanca, NY 14779; 716-945-4153. Hours: 8AM-4PM (EST). *Misdemeanor, Civil Actions Under $15,000, Eviction, Small Claims.*

Civil Records: Access: Mail, in person. Only the court performs in person searches; visitors may not. Search fee: $5.00 per name. Required to search: name, years to search. Civil cases indexed by defendant. Civil records on dockets from 1930s; on computer back to 1995.

Criminal Records: Access: Mail, in person. Only the court performs in person searches; visitors may not. Search fee: $5.00 per name. Required to search: name, years to search, DOB, SSN. Criminal records on dockets from 1930s; on computer back to 1995.

General Information: No sealed records released. SASE required. Turnaround time 1-2 weeks. Certification fee: $5.00. Fee payee: Salamanca City Court. No personal checks accepted. Prepayment is required.

Surrogate Court 303 Court St, Little Valley, NY 14755; 716-938-9111; Fax: 716-938-6983. Hours: 9AM-5PM (EST). *Probate.*

Note: Public can search, but if court has to search there is a fee

Town/Village Courts; *Misdemeanor, Civil Actions Under $3,000, Small Claims:* Farmersville Town, 716-676-3030; Little Valley Town; Humphrey Town; Conewango Town, 716-358-6386; South Dayton Village, 716-988-3833; Machias Town, 716-353-8207; South Valley Town, 716-354-5854; Ellicottville Town, 716-699-2240; Ashford Town; Mansfield Town; Carrollton Town, 716-925-8508; Ischua Town, 716-

557-2236; Lyndon Town, 716-676-9928; Randolph Town, 716-358-2591; Dayton Town, 716-532-3758; Perrysburg Town, 716-532-4090; Persia Town, 716-532-4042; Great Valley Town, 716-945-4200; Cold-spring Town, 716-354-5752; Red House Town; Napoli Town, 716-938-9418; Salamanca Town; Allegany Town, 716-373-3670; East Otto Town; Olean Town, 716-373-0582; New Albion Town, 716-257-3661; Portville Town, 716-933-6658; Portville Village, 716-933-8407; Freedom Town, 716-492-0961; Otto Town, 716-257-3111; Fraklinville Town, 716-676-3077; Allegany Village, 716-373-1460; Cattaraugus Village, 716-257-3661; Ellicottville Village, 716-699-4636; Yorkshire Town, 716-492-1640; Hinsdale Town.

Cayuga County

Supreme & County Court 160 Genesee St, Auburn, NY 13021-3424; 315-253-1271; Fax: 315-253-1586. Hours: 9AM-5PM Sept-June; 8AM-4PM July-Aug (EST). *Felony, Misdemeanor, Civil.*

Note: The court is located at 154 Genesee Street.

Civil Records: Access: Mail, in person. Both court and visitors may perform in person searches. Search fee: $5.00 per name. Required to search: name, years to search. Civil cases indexed by defendant, plaintiff. Civil records on computer from 1986, prior in books.

Criminal Records: Access: Mail, in person. Both court and visitors may perform in person searches. Search fee: $16.00 per name. Required to search: name, years to search, DOB. Criminal records names are computerized since 1930.

General Information: Public Access terminal is available. No sealed records released. SASE required. Turnaround time 1 day. Copy fee: $.50 per page. Certification fee: $4.00 plus $.50 per page after first 8. Fee payee: County Clerk. Personal checks accepted. Prepayment is required.

Auburn City Court 153 Genesee St, Auburn, NY 13021-3434; 315-253-1570; Fax: 315-253-1085. Hours: 8AM-4PM (EST). *Misdemeanor, Civil Actions Under $15,000, Eviction, Small Claims.*

Civil Records: Access: Mail, in person. Only the court performs in person searches; visitors may not. Search fee: Electronic search is $16.00, extra years are $5.00. Required to search: name, years to search. Civil cases indexed by defendant. Civil records on computer from 1986.

Criminal Records: Access: Mail, in person. Only the court performs in person searches; visitors may not. Search fee: Electronic search is $16.00, extra years are $5.00 per 2 years. Required to search: name, years to search, DOB. Criminal records on computer from 1986.

General Information: No sealed, expunged, adoption, sex offense, juvenile or mental health records released. SASE required. Turnaround time 3 days. Certification fee: $5.00. Fee payee: City Court. Only cashiers checks and money orders accepted. Prepayment is required.

Surrogate Court Courthouse, 154 Genesee St, Auburn, NY 13021-3471; 315-255-4316; Fax: 315-255-4322. Hours: 8:30AM-4:30PM; Summer hours 8AM-4:00PM (EST). *Probate.*

www.courts.state.ny.us/www/jd7/cayuga_surrogate.htm

Town/Village Courts; *Misdemeanor, Civil Actions Under $3,000, Small Claims:* Owasco Town, 315-253-9021; Fleming Town, 315-252-8988; Brutus Town, 315-834-6618; Sterling Town, 315-865-5087; Genoa Town; Locke Town, 315-497-1932; Summerhill Town; Conquest Town, 315-776-5288; Throop Town, 315-252-7373; Ledyard Town, 315-364-8169; Port Byron Village Court; Victory Town, 315-626-6817; Sempronius Town, 315-497-0549; Montezuma Town, 315-776-8822; Moravia Town, 315-497-1972; Springport Town; Sennett Town, 315-253-7748; Meridian Village, 315-626-6230; Weedsport Village, 315-834-6634;

Niles Town, 315-497-0066; Ira Town, 315-626-2154; Mentz Town, 315-776-8692; Moravia Village, 315-497-1820; Cato Town, 315-626-6230; Venice Town, 315-364-8936; Cato Village, 315-626-2397; Aurelius Town, 315-255-0065; Scipio Town, 315-364-7754.

Chautauqua County

Supreme & County Court - Civil PO Box 170, Mayville, NY 14757; 716-753-4331. Hours: 9AM-5PM/Summer 8:30AM-4:30PM (EST). *Civil.*

Civil Records: Access: Mail, in person. Only the court performs in person searches; visitors may not. No search fee. Required to search: name, years to search. Civil cases indexed by plaintiff. Civil records in docket books or cards; on computer back to 8/1/1997.

General Information: No sealed records released. SASE required. Turnaround time 1-2 days. Copy fee: $4.00. Add $1.00 per page after first 4. Certification fee: No cert fee. Fee payee: Chautauqua County Clerk. Personal checks accepted. Prepayment is required.

Supreme & County Court - Criminal Courthouse, PO Box 292, Mayville, NY 14757; 716-753-4266; Fax: 716-753-4993. Hours: 9AM-5PM/Summer 8:30AM-4:30PM (EST). *Felony.*

Note: Misdemeanor records are maintained by city, town and village courts.

Criminal Records: Access: Mail, in person. Only the court performs in person searches; visitors may not. Search fee: $16.00 per name. Also, a Certificate of Conviction can be ordered for $5.00. Required to search: name, years to search, DOB, signed release. Criminal records on computer from 1/1987. Be advised that all requests without a DOB will be returned.

General Information: No sealed records released. SASE required. Turnaround time 1-2 days. Copy fee: $4.00. Add $1.00 per page after first 4. Certification fee: No cert fee. Fee payee: County Clerk. Prepayment is required.

Dunkirk City Court City Hall, 342 Central Ave, Dunkirk, NY 14048; 716-366-2055; Fax: 716-366-3622. Hours: 9AM-5PM (EST). *Misdemeanor, Civil Actions Under $15,000, Eviction, Small Claims.*

Civil Records: Access: Mail, fax, in person. Only the court performs in person searches; visitors may not. Search fee: $16.00 per name. Required to search: name, years to search. Civil cases indexed by defendant. Civil records on computer back to 1990, prior in books.

Criminal Records: Access: Mail, fax, in person. Only the court performs in person searches; visitors may not. Search fee: $16.00 per name. Required to search: name, years to search, DOB. Criminal records on computer back to 1990, prior in books.

General Information: No sealed, expunged, adoption, sex offense, juvenile or mental health records released. SASE required. Turnaround time 1 week. Copy fee: $.50 per page. Certification fee: $5.00. Fee payee: Dunkirk City Court. Only cashiers checks and money orders accepted. Prepayment is required.

Jamestown City Court City Hall, Jamestown, NY 14701; 716-483-7561/7562; Fax: 716-483-7519. Hours: 9AM-5PM (EST). *Misdemeanor, Civil Actions Under $15,000, Eviction, Small Claims.*

Civil Records: Access: Fax, mail, in person. Both court and visitors may perform in person searches. No search fee. Required to search: name, years to search. Civil cases indexed by defendant. Civil records on computer back to 1989, prior in books.

Criminal Records: Access: Fax, mail, in person. Only the court performs in person searches; visitors may not. Search fee: $5.00 per name. Fee is for 2 year search, or $16.00 for automated search. Required to search: name, years to search, DOB, signed release; also helpful: address, SSN. Criminal records on computer back to 1989, prior in books.

General Information: No sealed records released. SASE required. Turnaround time 1 week. Copy fee: $1.00 per page. Certification fee: $5.00. Fee payee: City Court. Business checks accepted. Prepayment is required.

Surrogate Court Gerace Office Bldg, Rm 231 (PO Box C), 3 N Erie St, Mayville, NY 14757; 716-753-4339; Fax: 716-753-4600. Hours: 9AM-5PM (EST). *Probate.*

Town/Village Courts; *Misdemeanor, Civil Actions Under $3,000, Small Claims:* Silver Creek Village, 716-934-3558; Portland Town, 716-792-4111; Sherman Town, 716-761-6770; Sheridan Town, 716-672-2600; Mina Town, 716-769-7555; Pomfret Town, 716-672-6867; Ellery Town, 716-386-2521; Stockton Town, 716-595-2259; Poland Town, 716-267-2912; Ripley Town, 716-736-7575; North Harmony Town, 716-789-3445; Busti Town, 716-763-4695; Arkwright Town, 716-679-4445; Clymer Town, 716-355-6331; Dunkirk Town, 716-366-3945; Ellicott Town, 716-665-5319; Brocton Village Court; Ellington Town, 716-287-2026; Hanover Town, 716-934-4770; Kiantone Town, 716-488-0383; Gerry Town, 716-985-5323; Cherry Creek Town, 716-296-5721; French Creek Town, 716-355-8801; Chautauqua Town, 716-753-5245; Harmony Town; Charlotte Town; Carroll Town, 716-569-5365; Westfield Town, 716-326-3211; Westfield Village, 716-326-4961; Villenova Town, 716-988-3678; Fredonia Village, 716-679-2312.

Chemung County

Supreme & County Court - Civil 210 Lake St, Elmira, NY 14901; 607-737-2920; Fax: 607-737-2897. Hours: 8:30AM-4:30PM (EST). *Civil.*

www.chemungcounty.com

Civil Records: Access: Mail, in person. Only the court performs in person searches; visitors may not. Search fee: $5.00 per name. Fee is per 2 years searched. Required to search: name, years to search. Civil cases indexed by defendant, plaintiff. Civil records on computer from 1994, prior in books.
General Information: Public Access terminal is available. (For land records only from 1991 forward.) No sealed, divorce or adoption records released. SASE required. Turnaround time 4-6 weeks. Copy fee: $.50 per page. $1.00 minimum. Certification fee: $4.00 plus $1.00 per page after first 4. Fee payee: County Clerk. Personal checks accepted. Prepayment is required.

Supreme & County Court - Criminal PO Box 588, Elmira, NY 14902-0588; 607-737-2844. Hours: 8:30AM-4:30PM (EST). *Felony.*

Criminal Records: Access: Mail, in person. Only the court performs in person searches; visitors may not. Search fee: $5.00 for every 2 years searched or $20.00 for a seven year search. Searches with both maiden and married names are considered two searches. Required to search: name, years to search, DOB, SSN. Criminal records in docket books back to 1979.
General Information: No sealed, divorce or adoption records released. SASE required. Turnaround time 4-6 weeks. Copy fee: $.50 per page. Certification fee: $5.00. Fee payee: County Clerk. Personal checks accepted. Prepayment is required.

Elmira City Court 317 E Church St, Elmira, NY 14901-2790; 607-737-5681; Fax: 607-737-5820. Hours: 8AM-4PM (EST). *Misdemeanor, Civil Actions Under $15,000, Eviction, Small Claims.*

Civil Records: Access: Mail, in person. Both court and visitors may perform in person searches. Search fee: $16.00 per name. Required to search: name, years to search. Civil cases indexed by defendant. Civil records on computer since 1997; prior records on index cards.
Criminal Records: Access: Mail, in person. Only the court performs in person searches; visitors may not.

Search fee: $16.00 per name. Required to search: name, years to search, DOB; also helpful: SSN. Criminal records on computer from 1987.
General Information: Public Access terminal is available. (Civil only.) No sealed records released. SASE required. Turnaround time 3-5 days. Copy fee: $1.00 per page. Certification fee: $5.00. Fee payee: Elmira City Court. Personal checks accepted. Prepayment is required.

Surrogate Court 224 Lake St, Elmira, NY 14901; 607-737-2946/2819; Fax: 607-737-2874. Hours: 9AM-5PM (EST). *Probate.*

Town/Village Courts; *Misdemeanor, Civil Actions Under $3,000, Small Claims:* Chemung Town, 607-529-3322; Catlin Town, 607-739-5598; Horseheads Village, 607-739-0158; Baldwin Town; Van Etten Town, 607-589-4435; Erin Town, 607-739-8681; Elmira Town, 607-734-5971; Big Flats Town, 607-562-3516; Ashland Town, 607-732-0723; Wellsburg Village, 607-733-8211; Elmira Heights Village, 607-734-9693; Horseheads Town, 607-739-2113; Veteran Town, 607-739-1476; Southport Town, 607-734-1548; Millport Village.

Chenango County

Supreme & County Court County Office Bldg, Norwich, NY 13815-1676; 607-337-1450. Hours: 8:30AM-5PM (EST). *Felony, Civil.*

Civil Records: Access: Mail, in person. Both court and visitors may perform in person searches. Search fee: $5.00 per name. Fee is per 2 years searched. Required to search: name, years to search. Civil cases indexed by defendant, plaintiff. Civil records on computer from 1994, prior in books since 1880.
Criminal Records: Access: Mail, in person. Both court and visitors may perform in person searches. Search fee: $5.00 per name. Fee is per 2 years searched. Required to search: name, years to search, DOB. Criminal records in docket books.
General Information: Public Access terminal is available. No sealed, expunged, adoption, sex offense, juvenile or mental health records released. SASE required. Turnaround time 2 days. Copy fee: $.50 per page. $1.00 minimum. Certification fee: Certification fee is $1.00 per pg, $4.00 minimum. Fee payee: County Clerk. Personal checks accepted. Prepayment required.

Norwich City Court 1 Court Plaza, Norwich, NY 13815; 607-334-1224; Fax: 607-334-8494. Hours: 8:30AM-4:30PM (EST). *Misdemeanor, Civil Actions Under $15,000, Eviction, Small Claims.*

Civil Records: Access: Fax, mail, in person. Both court and visitors may perform in person searches. Search fee: $16.00 per name. Required to search: name, years to search. Civil cases indexed by defendant. Civil records on computer from 1990, prior in books.
Criminal Records: Access: Fax, mail, in person. Both court and visitors may perform in person searches. Search fee: $16.00 per name 1990-present; $5.00 if prior to 1990. Required to search: name, years to search, DOB, signed release. Criminal records on computer from 1990, prior in books.
General Information: No sealed, expunged, adoption, sex offense, juvenile or mental health records released. SASE required. Turnaround time 1 week. Certification fee: $5.00. Fee payee: City Court. Business checks accepted. Prepayment is required.

Surrogate Court County Office Bldg, 5 Court St, Norwich, NY 13815; 607-337-1822/1827; Fax: 607-337-1834. Hours: 9AM-Noon, 1-5PM (EST). *Probate.*

Town/Village Courts; *Misdemeanor, Civil Actions Under $3,000, Small Claims:* Smithville Town, 607-656-7969; Bainbridge Village, 607-967-7465; Pitcher Town; Coventry Town, 607-656-8602; Pharsalia Town, 607-647-5203; New Berlin Village, 607-847-6249;

Bainbridge Town, 607-967-7465; Earlville Village, 315-691-6020; Otselic Town, 315-653-7201; Norwich Town, 607-334-6359; Guilford Town, 607-895-6818; North Norwich Town, 607-334-9224; Sherburne Village, 607-674-4827; Oxford Village, 607-843-9772; Greene Town, 607-656-4333; New Berlin Town, 607-847-8909; Smyrna Town; Sherburne Town, 607-674-4827; Columbus Town; Sherburne Village, 607-674-4827; Greene Village Court; Oxford Town, 607-843-9772; German Town; Lincklaen Town, 315-852-6128; Afton Village Court; Plymouth Town; Preston Town, 607-336-1013; Afton Town.

Clinton County

Supreme & County Court County Government Center, 137 Margaret St, Plattsburgh, NY 12901; 518-565-4715; Fax: 518-565-4708. Hours: 9AM-5PM (EST). *Felony, Civil.*

Civil Records: Access: In person only. Visitors must perform in person searches for themselves. No search fee. Required to search: name, years to search. Civil cases indexed by defendant. Civil records in docket books.
Criminal Records: Access: Mail, in person. Both court and visitors may perform in person searches. Search fee: $16.00 per name. Required to search: name, years to search, DOB. Criminal records on computer from 1986, prior in docket books.
General Information: No sealed or sex case records released. SASE required. Turnaround time 3-4 days. Copy fee: $.50 per page. Certification fee: Certification $4.00 up to 4 pages, then $1.00 per additional page. Fee payee: County Clerk. Personal checks accepted. Prepayment is required.

Plattsburg City Court 41 City Hall Pl, Plattsburgh, NY 12901; 518-563-7870; Fax: 518-563-3124. Hours: 8AM-4PM (EST). *Misdemeanor, Civil Actions Under $15,000, Eviction, Small Claims.*

Civil Records: Access: Mail, in person. Only the court performs in person searches; visitors may not. Search fee: $16.00 for computerized search. Required to search: name, years to search. Civil cases indexed by defendant. Civil records on computer back to 1986, prior in books.
Criminal Records: Access: Mail, in person. Only the court performs in person searches; visitors may not. Search fee: $16.00 per name. Required to search: name, years to search, DOB, signed release. Criminal records on computer back to 1986, prior in books.
General Information: No sealed records released. SASE required. Turnaround time same day. Copy fee: $1.00 per page. Certification fee: $5.00. Fee payee: City Court. Only cashiers checks and money orders accepted. Prepayment is required.

Surrogate Court 137 Margaret St, Plattsburgh, NY 12901-2933; 518-565-4630; Fax: 518-565-4769. Hours: 9AM-5PM (EST). *Probate.*

Town/Village Courts; *Misdemeanor, Civil Actions Under $3,000, Small Claims:* Plattsburgh Town, 518-563-8100; Saranac Town, 518-293-6666; Champlain Village Court; Dannemora Village, 518-492-7000; Black Brook Town, 518-647-5412; Beekmantown Town, 518-563-9930; AuSable Town, 518-834-9052; Peru Town, 518-643-2745; Dannemora Town, 518-492-7541; Champlain Town, 518-298-2043; Ellenburg Town, 518-594-7708; Chazy Town, 518-846-8600; Clinton Town, 518-497-6133; Altona Town; Mooers Town; Schuyler Falls Town, 518-563-1129; Rouses Point Village, 518-297-6648.

Columbia County

Supreme & County Court 560 Warren Street, Hudson, NY 12534; 518-828-3339; Fax: 518-828-5299. Hours: 9AM-5PM (EST). *Felony, Civil.*

Note: Supreme and County courts are actually located at 401 Union in Hudson, but records for both courts are located at the County Clerk's Office as listed above.

Civil Records: Access: Mail, in person. Both court and visitors may perform in person searches. Search fee: $5.00 per name. Fee is per 2 years searched. Required to search: name, years to search. Civil cases indexed by defendant. Civil records on computer from 1993, prior on cards to 1985.

Criminal Records: Access: Mail, in person. Both court and visitors may perform in person searches. Search fee: $5.00 per name. Required to search: name, years to search, DOB. Criminal records on computer from 1993, prior on cards to 1985.

General Information: Public Access terminal is available. No sealed records released. SASE required. Turnaround time 1 week. Copy fee: $.25 per page. Certification fee: $4.00. Fee payee: County Clerk. Personal checks accepted. Prepayment is required.

Hudson City Court 429 Warren St, Hudson, NY 12534; 518-828-3100; Fax: 518-828-3628. Hours: 8AM-4PM (EST). *Misdemeanor, Civil Actions Under $15,000, Eviction, Small Claims.*

Civil Records: Access: Fax, mail, in person. Only the court performs in person searches; visitors may not. Search fee: $5.00 per name, per every two years; $16.00 if prior to 1991. Required to search: name, years to search; also helpful: address. Civil cases indexed by defendant, plaintiff. Civil records on computer from 1991, prior in books.

Criminal Records: Access: Fax, mail, in person. Only the court performs in person searches; visitors may not. Search fee: $5.00 per name, per every two years; $16.00 if prior to 1991. Required to search: name, years to search, DOB. Criminal records on computer from 1991, prior in books.

General Information: No sealed, expunged, adoption, sex offense, juvenile or mental health records released. SASE required. Turnaround time 1 week. Copy fee: $.50 per page. Certification fee: $5.00. Fee payee: Hudson City Court. Business checks accepted. Prepayment is required.

Surrogate Court Courthouse, 401 Union St, Hudson, NY 12534; 518-828-0414; Fax: 518-828-1603. Hours: 9AM-5PM (EST). *Probate.*

Town/Village Courts; *Misdemeanor, Civil Actions Under $3,000, Small Claims:* New Lebanon Town, 518-794-9456; Stuyvesant Town; Stockport Town, 518-828-9389; Chatham Town; Claverack Town, 518-672-4468; Hillsdale Town, 518-325-5073; Chatham Village, 518-392-9476; Ancram Town, 518-329-6512; Valatie Village, 518-758-9838; Canaan Town, 518-781-4455; Ghent Town, 518-392-4644; Philmont Village, 518-672-7032; Taghkanic Town, 518-329-3030; Germantown Town, 518-537-6687; Greenport Town, 518-828-4656; Clermont Town, 518-537-6868; Austerlitz Town, 518-392-3260; Gallatin Town, 518-329-3030; Livingston Town, 518-851-7201; Kinderhook Town, 518-784-2506; Kinderhook Village Court; Copake Town, 518-329-1234.

Cortland County

Supreme & County Court 46 Greenbush St, Ste 301, Cortland, NY 13045; Civil phone: 607-753-5021; Criminal phone: 607-753-5010; Fax: 607-756-3409. Hours: 9AM-5PM (EST). *Felony, Civil.*

Civil Records: Access: Mail, in person. Both court and visitors may perform in person searches. Search fee: $5.00 per name. per 2 year search. Required to search:

name, years to search. Civil cases indexed by defendant, plaintiff. Civil records on computer from 5/94, prior in books.

Criminal Records: Access: Mail, in person. Only the court performs in person searches; visitors may not. Search fee: $5.00 per name. Per 2 year search. Required to search: name, years to search, DOB. Criminal records on computer from 1986, prior in books.

General Information: No sealed or youthful offender records released. SASE required. Turnaround time 1 day. Copy fee: $.50 per page. Certification fee: $1.00. Minimum $4.00. Fee payee: County Clerk. Personal checks accepted. Prepayment is required.

Cortland City Court 25 Court St, Cortland, NY 13045; 607-753-1811; Fax: 607-753-9932. Hours: 8:30AM-4:30PM (EST). *Misdemeanor, Civil Actions Under $15,000, Eviction, Small Claims.*

Civil Records: Access: Mail, in person. Only the court performs in person searches; visitors may not. Search fee: $5.00 per name per 2 years. Required to search: name, years to search. Civil cases indexed by defendant. Civil records on computer from 1991, prior in books.

Criminal Records: Access: Mail, in person. Only the court performs in person searches; visitors may not. Search fee: $5.00 per name per 2 years. $16.00 for electronic search. Required to search: name, years to search, DOB. Criminal records on computer from 1991, prior in books.

General Information: No sealed records released. SASE required. Turnaround time 10 days. Copy fee: $.50 per page. Certification fee: $5.00. Fee payee: City Court. Only cashiers checks and money orders accepted. Prepayment is required.

Surrogate Court 46 Greenbush St, Ste 301, Cortland, NY 13045; 607-753-5355. Hours: 9AM-5PM (EST). *Probate.*

Town/Village Courts; *Misdemeanor, Civil Actions Under $3,000, Small Claims:* Cuyler Town; Taylor Town, 607-863-3716; Preble Town, 607-749-2377; Truxton Town, 607-842-6291; Lapeer Town, 607-849-3808; Freetown Town, 607-849-6372; Virgil Town, 607-835-6587; Solon Town; Cortlandville Town, 607-756-2352; Cincinnatus Town, 607-863-4220; Marathon Village, 607-849-6966; Marathon Town; Homer Village, 607-749-2326; Homer Town, 607-749-2326; Willet Town, 607-863-3265; Scott Town, 607-749-2902; Harford Town.

Delaware County

Supreme & County Court 3 Court St, Delhi, NY 13753; 607-746-2131; Fax: 607-746-3253. Hours: 9AM-5PM (EST). *Felony, Civil.*

Note: Misdemeanor records are maintained by city, town and village courts.

Civil Records: Access: Mail, in person. Both court and visitors may perform in person searches. Search fee: $5.00 per name. Required to search: name, years to search. Civil cases indexed by defendant, plaintiff. Civil records in books.

Criminal Records: Access: Mail, in person. Both court and visitors may perform in person searches. Search fee: $5.00 per name. Required to search: name, years to search, DOB. Criminal records in books.

General Information: No sealed records released. SASE required. Turnaround time 2 days. Copy fee: $.50 per page. Certification fee: Certification $4.00 for up to 4 pages, then $1.00 per page. Fee payee: County Clerk. Personal checks accepted. Prepayment is required.

Surrogate Court 3 Court St, Delhi, NY 13753; 607-746-2126; Fax: 607-746-3253. *Probate.*

Town/Village Courts; *Misdemeanor, Civil Actions Under $3,000, Small Claims:* Davenport Town; Delhi

Town, 607-746-7278; Colchester Town, 845-498-5575; Delhi Village, 607-746-7161; Deposit Town, 607-467-3208; Roxbury Town, 607-588-7507; Fleischmanns Village, 845-254-5514; Hancock Town, 607-637-3651; Walton Village Court; Sidney Village, 845-561-2307; Sidney Town, 845-561-2309; Middletown Town, 845-586-2575; Harpersfield Town, 607-652-5060; Meredith Town, 607-746-2341; Masonville Town; Walton Town, 607-865-5182; Hancock Village, 607-637-5341; Stamford Town, 607-538-9421; Stamford Village, 607-652-6671; Tompkins Town, 607-865-4979; Bovina Town; Andes Town, 845-676-3550; Kortright Town; Hamden Town, 607-746-6660.

Dutchess County

Supreme & County Court 22 Market St, Poughkeepsie, NY 12601-3203; 845-486-2125. Hours: 9AM-5PM (EST). *Felony, Civil.*

Civil Records: Access: In person only. Visitors must perform in person searches for themselves. No search fee. Required to search: name, years to search. Civil cases indexed by defendant, plaintiff. Civil records on computer from 1986, prior in books.

Criminal Records: Access: Mail, in person. Both court and visitors may perform in person searches. Search fee: $5.00 per name. Fee is per 2 years or part thereof (convictions only). Required to search: name, years to search, aliases. Criminal records on computer from 1987.

General Information: Public Access terminal is available. No sealed or youthful offender records released. SASE required. Turnaround time 2 weeks. Copy fee: $5.00 per document. Certification fee: $4.00 plus $.50 per page after first 8 in person. $6.00 per document by mail. $5.00 for assumed name, if in person. Fee payee: Dutchess County Clerk. Personal checks accepted. Prepayment is required.

Beacon City Court One Municipal Plaza, #2, Beacon, NY 12508; 845-838-5030; Fax: 845-838-5041. Hours: 8AM-4PM (EST). *Misdemeanor, Civil Actions Under $15,000, Eviction, Small Claims.*

Civil Records: Access: Mail, in person. Both court and visitors may perform in person searches. Search fee: $16.00 per name. Required to search: name, years to search. Civil cases indexed by defendant, plaintiff. Civil records on computer from 1996, prior in books/cards.

Criminal Records: Access: Mail, in person. Only the court performs in person searches; visitors may not. Search fee: $16.00 per name. Required to search: name, years to search, DOB, SSN, signed release. Criminal records computerized since 1990.

General Information: No sealed or youthful offender records released. SASE required. Turnaround time 3-4 days. Copy fee: $.75 per page. Certification fee: $5.00. Fee payee: City Court of Beacon. Only cashiers checks and money orders accepted. Prepayment is required.

Poughkeepsie City Court Civic Center Plaza, PO Box 300, Poughkeepsie, NY 12602; 845-451-4091; Fax: 845-485-6795. Hours: 8AM-4PM (EST). *Misdemeanor, Civil Actions Under $15,000, Eviction, Small Claims.*

Civil Records: Access: Mail, in person. Both court and visitors may perform in person searches. Search fee: $16.00 per name. $5.00 for certificate of disposition. Required to search: name, years to search. Civil cases indexed by defendant. Civil records on computer from 1993.

Criminal Records: Access: Mail, in person. Both court and visitors may perform in person searches. Search fee: $16.00 per name. $5.00 per certified disposition. Required to search: name, years to search, DOB, signed release. Criminal records on computer from 1990.

General Information: No sealed, expunged, adoption, sex offense, juvenile or mental health records released. SASE required. Turnaround time 1 week. Copy fee:

$.50 per page. Certification fee: $5.00. Fee payee: Poughkeepsie City Court. Only cashiers checks and money orders accepted. Prepayment is required.

Surrogate Court 10 Market St, Poughkeepsie, NY 12601; 845-486-2235; Fax: 845-486-2234. Hours: 9AM-5PM (EST). *Probate.*

Town/Village Courts; *Misdemeanor, Civil Actions Under $3,000, Small Claims:* Beekman Town, 845-724-5581; Pine Plains Town, 518-398-7194; Milan Town, 914-758-6960; LaGrange Town, 845-452-1837; Pleasant Valley Town, 845-635-2856; Red Hook Town, 845-758-5851; Rhinebeck Town, 845-876-7303; Stanford Town, 845-868-2269; Red Hook Village, 845-758-4113; Poughkeepsie Town, 845-485-3695; Amenia Town, 845-373-7017; Dover Town; Union Vale Town, 845-724-5600; Rhinebeck Village, 845-876-4119; Pawling Village, 845-855-5602; North East Town, 518-789-3080; Millbrook Village, 845-677-8277; Wappinger Town, 845-297-6070; East Fishkill Town, 845-226-4229; Wappingers Falls Village, 845-297-6777; Washington Town, 845-677-6366; Hyde Park Town, 845-229-2606; Tivoli Village, 845-757-2021; Clinton Town, 845-266-5988; Fishkill Village, 914-879-2103; Fishkill Town, 845-831-7800; Pawling Town, 845-855-3516.

Erie County

Supreme & County Court 25 Delaware Ave, Buffalo, NY 14202; Civil phone: 716-858-7766; Criminal phone: 716-858-7877; Fax: 716-858-6550. Hours: 9AM-5PM (EST). *Felony, Civil.*

Civil Records: Access: Mail, in person. Both court and visitors may perform in person searches. Search fee: $5.00 per name. Fee is per 2 years searched. Required to search: name, years to search. Civil cases indexed by defendant. Civil records on computer from 1994, prior in books. Plaintiffs indexed starting in 1994.
Criminal Records: Access: Mail, in person. Both court and visitors may perform in person searches. Search fee: $5.00 per name. Fee is per 2 years searched. Required to search: name, years to search. Criminal records on computer from 1994, prior in books. Plaintiffs indexed starting in 1994.
General Information: Public Access terminal is available. No sealed records released. SASE required. Turnaround time 3-4 days. Copy fee: $1.00 per page. Certification fee: $4.00. Fee payee: County Clerk. Personal checks accepted. Prepayment is required.

Buffalo City Court 50 Delaware Ave, Buffalo, NY 14202; 716-847-8200; Fax: 716-847-8257. Hours: 9AM-5PM (EST). *Misdemeanor, Civil Actions Under $15,000, Eviction, Small Claims.*

Civil Records: Access: Mail, fax, in person. Both court and visitors may perform in person searches. Search fee: $5.00 per name. Required to search: name, years to search. Civil cases indexed by defendant, plaintiff. Criminal records on computer back to 1983, prior in books back to 1974.
Criminal Records: Access: In person only. Only the court performs in person searches; visitors may not. Search fee: $5.00 per disposition. Required to search: name, DOB, date of offense. Criminal records on computer back to 1983, prior in books back to 1974. Will perform a disposition search. No general searches are done; searches are directed to OCA in NYC.
General Information: No sealed or youthful offender records released. SASE required. Turnaround time 3 days. Copy fee: $1.00 per page. Certification fee: $5.00. Fee payee: City Court. Business checks accepted. Prepayment is required.

Lackawanna City Court 714 Ridge Rd, Rm 225, Lackawanna, NY 14218; 716-827-6486; Fax: 716-827-1874. Hours: 8:30AM-4:30PM (EST). *Misdemeanor, Civil Actions Under $15,000, Eviction, Small Claims.*

Civil Records: Access: Mail, in person. Both court and visitors may perform in person searches. Search fee: $16.00 per name. Required to search: name; also helpful: years to search. Civil cases indexed by defendant. Civil records on computer from 1994, prior on docket books. Mail access available to government agencies only.
Criminal Records: Access: Mail, in person. Only the court performs in person searches; visitors may not. Search fee: $16.00 per name. Required to search: name; also helpful: years to search, DOB. Criminal records on computer from 1994, prior on docket books. Mail access available to government agencies only.
General Information: No sealed or youthful offender records released. SASE required. Turnaround time 2-3 days. Copy fee: $1.00 per page. Certification fee: $5.00. Fee payee: City Court. Only cashiers checks and money orders accepted. Prepayment is required.

Tonawanda City Court 200 Niagara St, Tonawanda, NY 14150; 716-693-3484; Fax: 716-693-1612. Hours: 9AM-4PM (EST). *Misdemeanor, Civil Actions Under $15,000, Eviction, Small Claims.*

Civil Records: Access: Mail, in person. Only the court performs in person searches; visitors may not. Search fee: $5.00 per name. Required to search: name, years to search. Civil cases indexed by defendant, plaintiff. Civil records on computer since 1997, prior on index cards, in books.
Criminal Records: Access: Mail, in person. Only the court performs in person searches; visitors may not. Search fee: $5.00 per name. Required to search: name, years to search, DOB, SSN, signed release. Criminal records on computer since 1997, prior on index cards, in books.
General Information: No sealed records released. SASE not required. Turnaround time 3-5 days. Copy fee: $1.00 per page. Certification fee: $5.00. Fee payee: City Court of Tonawanda. Business checks accepted. Prepayment is required.

Surrogate Court 92 Franklin St, Buffalo, NY 14202; 716-854-7867; Fax: 716-853-3741. Hours: 9AM-5PM (EST). *Probate.*

Town/Village Courts; *Misdemeanor, Civil Actions Under $3,000, Small Claims:* Brant Town, 716-549-0300; Hamburg Town, 716-649-6111; East Aurora Village, 716-652-5275; Lancaster Town, 716-683-1814; Lancaster Village, 716-683-6780; Elma Town, 716-652-1855; Orchard Park Town, 716-662-6415; Depew Village, 716-683-0978; Hamburg Village, 716-649-7204; Orchard Park Village, 716-662-6415; Clarence Town, 716-741-2802; North Collins Town, 716-337-3712; Marilla Town, 716-652-5350; Kenmore Village Court; Evans Town, 716-549-3707; Farnham Village Court; Holland Town, 716-457-3022; Grand Island Town, 716-773-9650; Cheektowaga Town, 716-686-3437; Newstead Town, 716-542-4575; Eden Town, 716-992-3559; Boston Town, 716-941-6115; Blasdell Village, 716-822-7118; West Seneca Town, 716-674-5600; Amherst Town, 716-689-4200; Angola Village Court; Concord Town, 716-592-9898; Wales Town, 716-652-3320; Collins Town, 716-532-4887; Colden Town, 716-941-5012; Tonawanda Town, 716-876-5536; Sardinia Town, 716-496-8900; Alden Town, 716-937-3411; Williamsville Village, 716-632-0450; Akron Village, 716-542-9636; Alden Village, 716-937-9057; Aurora Town, 716-652-5275.

Essex County

Supreme & County Courts Essex County Government Center, Court St, PO Box 217, Elizabethtown, NY 12932; Civil phone: 518-873-3600; Criminal phone: 518-873-3370; Fax: 518-873-3376. Hours: 8:30AM-5PM (EST). *Felony, Civil.*

Note: Misdemeanor records are maintained by city, town and village courts.

Civil Records: Access: Mail, in person. Both court and visitors may perform in person searches. No search fee. Required to search: name, years to search. Civil cases indexed by defendant, plaintiff. Civil records on computer from 11/93, prior in books.
Criminal Records: Access: Mail, in person. Both court and visitors may perform in person searches. Search fee: Two types of searches available-manual since 1956 at $5.00 per name per each two years, and computer at $16.00 per name. Call for copy of special form to compute fee and submit with payment. Required to search: name, years to search, DOB. Criminal records on computer from 1950s, prior in books.
General Information: No sealed or youthful offender records released. SASE required. Turnaround time same day. Copy fee: $.50 per page. Certification fee: $1.00. Minimum $4.00. Fee payee: Essex County Clerk. Personal checks accepted. Prepayment required.

Surrogate Court 100 Court St, PO Box 505, Elizabethtown, NY 12932; 518-873-3384. Hours: 9AM-5PM (EST). *Probate.*

Town/Village Courts; *Misdemeanor, Civil Actions Under $3,000, Small Claims:* North Elba Town, 518-523-9516; Lewis Town, 518-873-6777; Chesterfield Town, 518-834-9211; St Armand Town; Elizabethtown Town, 518-873-6555; Minerva Town, 518-251-2869; Moriah Town; Ticonderoga Town, 518-585-7141; Newcomb Town, 518-582-2010; Schroon Town, 518-532-0659; Crown Point Town, 518-597-4144; North Hudson Town; Westport Town, 518-962-4882; Lake Placid Village, 518-523-2004; Keene Town, 518-576-4444; Essex Town, 518-963-4287; Jay Town; Wilmington Town, 518-946-2105; Willsboro Town, 518-963-8933.

Franklin County

Supreme & County Court 63 W Main St, Malone, NY 12953-1817; 518-481-1748. Hours: 9AM-5PM (EST). *Felony, Civil, Misdemeanor, Evition, Small Claims.*

Civil Records: Access: Mail, in person. Both court and visitors may perform in person searches. Search fee: $5.00 per name per year. Fee is per name per 2 years. Required to search: name, years to search. Civil cases indexed by defendant. Civil records on computer from 1990, prior in file folders in Clerk's office.
Criminal Records: Access: Mail, in person. Both court and visitors may perform in person searches. Search fee: $5.00 per name per year. Fee is per 2 years. Computer search by court: $16.00. Required to search: name, years to search, DOB. Criminal records on computer from 1992.
General Information: No sealed or youthful offender records released. SASE required. Turnaround time 1 week. Copy fee: $.50 per page. Certification fee: $4.00. Fee payee: County Clerk. Personal checks accepted.

Surrogate Court Courthouse, 63 W Main St, Malone, NY 12953-1817; 518-481-1736 & 1737. Hours: 9AM-5PM Sept-May; 8AM-4PM June-Aug (EST). *Probate.*

Town/Village Courts; *Misdemeanor, Civil Actions Under $3,000, Small Claims:* Bombay Town, 518-358-9939; Franklin Town; Santa Clara Town, 518-891-1919; Brandon Town; Saranac Lake Village, 518-891-4423; Fort Covington Town; Chateaugay Town, 518-

497-6931; Westville Town, 518-358-4180; Tupper Lake Village, 518-359-9161; Harrietstown Town, 518-891-4500; Malone Village, 518-483-5210; Waverly Town, 518-856-9482; Moira Town, 518-529-6080; Altamont Town, 518-359-9278; Burke Town, 518-483-5497; Malone Town, 518-481-6634; Constable Town, 518-481-6113; Duane Town, 518-483-0386; Brighton Town, 518-327-3202; Dickinson Town, 518-856-9339; Bangor Town; Bellmont Town.

Fulton County

Supreme & County Court 223 West Main St, County Bldg, Johnstown, NY 12095; 518-736-5539; Fax: 518-762-5078. 9AM-5PM (EST). *Felony, Civil.*

Civil Records: Access: Phone, mail, fax, in person. Both court and visitors may perform in person searches. Search fee: $16.00 per name. Fee is $5.00 for in person searching, if record found. Required to search: name, years to search. Civil cases indexed by defendant, plaintiff. Civil records in file folders; back to 1977.
Criminal Records: Access: Phone, mail, fax, in person. Only the court performs in person searches; visitors may not. Search fee: $16.00 per name. Fee is $5.00 for in person searching, if record is found. Required to search: name, years to search, DOB. Criminal records in file folders; back to 1977.
General Information: No sealed, expunged, adoption, sex offense, juvenile or mental health records released. SASE required. Turnaround time 1 week. Copy fee: $1.00 per page. $.15 per page self service. Certification fee: $4.00. Fee payee: County Clerk. Business checks accepted. Prepayment is required.

Gloversville City Court City Hall, Frontage Rd, Gloversville, NY 12078; 518-773-4527; Fax: 518-773-4599. Hours: 8AM-4PM (EST). *Misdemeanor, Civil Actions Under $15,000, Eviction, Small Claims.*

Civil Records: Access: Mail, in person. Only the court performs in person searches; visitors may not. Search fee: $16.00 per name. Required to search: name, years to search. Civil cases indexed by plaintiff. Civil records in books; on computer since.
Criminal Records: Access: Mail, in person. Only the court performs in person searches; visitors may not. Search fee: $16.00 per name. Required to search: name, years to search, DOB. Criminal records in books, on computer since.
General Information: No sealed, youthful offender records released. SASE required. Turnaround time 2 weeks. Copy fee: $.50. There is a $1.00 minimum. Certification fee: $5.00. Fee payee: Gloversville City Court. Only cashiers checks and money orders accepted. Prepayment is required.

Johnstown City Court City Hall, 33-41 E Main St, Johnstown, NY 12095; 518-762-0007; Fax: 518-762-2720. Hours: 8AM-4PM (EST). *Misdemeanor, Civil Actions Under $15,000, Eviction, Small Claims.*

Civil Records: Access: Mail, in person. Only the court performs in person searches; visitors may not. Search fee: $16.00 per name. Required to search: name, years to search. Civil cases indexed by plaintiff. Civil records in file folders.
Criminal Records: Access: Mail, in person. Only the court performs in person searches; visitors may not. Search fee: $16.00 per name. Required to search: name, years to search, DOB. Criminal records on computer from 1986.
General Information: No sealed or youthful offender records released. SASE required. Turnaround time 1 month. Copy fee: $.50 per page. Certification fee: $5.00. Fee payee: City Court. Only cashiers checks and money orders accepted. Prepayment is required.

Surrogate Court 223 West Main St, Johnstown, NY 12095; 518-762-0685; Fax: 518-762-6372. Hours: 8AM-5PM (8AM-4PM July-August) (EST). *Probate.*

Town/Village Courts; *Misdemeanor, Civil Actions Under $3,000, Small Claims:* Caroga Town, 518-835-4211; Oppenheim Town, 518-568-7503; Broadalbin Village, 518-883-3353; Mayfield Town, 518-661-5225; Bleeker Town, 518-725-3684; Broadalbin Town, 518-883-5131; Stratford Town, 315-429-8612; Ephratah Town, 518-568-7560; Perth Town, 518-843-6977; Northampton Town, 518-863-4875; Johnstown Town, 518-762-7070.

Genesee County

Supreme & County Court PO Box 379 (1 W Main St.), Batavia, NY 14021-0379; 716-344-2550 X2242; Civil phone: x2310 for court info; Fax: 716-344-8521. Hours: 8:30AM-5PM (EST). *Felony, Civil.*

Note: 2002 Area Code will be 585. All records maintained at County Clerk's office, PO Box 379, Batavia, NY 14021.

Civil Records: Access: Mail, in person. Both court and visitors may perform in person searches. Search fee: $5.00 per five year period. Required to search: name, years to search; also helpful: address. Civil cases indexed by defendant, plaintiff; indexed by defendant only prior to 1995. Civil records in books from 1802; on computer back to 1995.
Criminal Records: Access: Fax, mail, in person. Both court and visitors may perform in person searches. Search fee: $5.00 per five year period. Required to search: name, years to search, DOB; also helpful: SSN. Criminal records in books from 1802; on computer back to 1995.
General Information: Public Access terminal is available. No sealed, expunged, adoption, sex offense, juvenile or mental health records released. SASE required. Turnaround time 1-3 days. Fax notes: Fee to fax results is $5.00 per document; no charge if to a toll free number. Copy fee: $1.00 for first page, $.50 each add'l. Certification fee: $4.00 plus $.50 per page in excess of 8 pages. Fee payee: County Clerk. Personal checks accepted. Prepayment is required.

Batavia City Court Genesee County Courts Facility, 1 W Main St, Batavia, NY 14020; 716-344-2550 X2416, 2417, 2418; Fax: 716-344-8556. Hours: 9AM-5PM (EST). *Misdemeanor, Civil Actions Under $15,000, Eviction, Small Claims.*

Civil Records: Access: Fax, mail, in person. Both court and visitors may perform in person searches. Search fee: $5.00 per name. Required to search: name, years to search. Civil cases indexed by plaintiff. Civil records on computer from 1993, in books from 1970.
Criminal Records: Access: Fax, mail, in person. Only the court performs in person searches; visitors may not. Search fee: $16.00 per name. Required to search: name, years to search, DOB. Criminal records on computer from 1993, in books from 1970.
General Information: No sealed, expunged, sex offense or mental health records released. SASE required. Turnaround time 1-3 days. Copy fee: $.50 per page. Certification fee: $5.00. Fee payee: City Court. Only cashiers checks and money orders accepted. Prepayment is required.

Surrogate Court 1 West Main St, Batavia, NY 14020; 716-344-2550 X237; Fax: 716-344-8517. Hours: 9AM-5PM (EST). *Probate.*

Note: $25.00 search fee

Town/Village Courts; *Misdemeanor, Civil Actions Under $3,000, Small Claims:* Darien Town, 716-547-2274; Oakfield Town, 716-948-5835; Bethany Town, 716-343-3325; Elba Town, 716-757-9200; Alabama Town; Oakfield Village, 716-948-9588; Bergen Town, 716-494-1121; Corfu Village, 716-599-3327; Stafford

Town, 716-344-4020; LeRoy Town, 716-768-6910; Pembroke Town, 716-591-4892; Batavia Town, 716-343-1729; Byron Town, 716-548-7123; Alexander Town, 716-591-0908; Pavilion Town, 716-584-3850.

Greene County

Supreme & County Court Courthouse, 320 Main St, Catskill, NY 12414; 518-943-2230; Fax: 518-943-7763. Hours: 9AM-5PM (EST). *Felony, Misdemeanor, Civil.*

Civil Records: Access: Phone, fax, mail, in person. Both court and visitors may perform in person searches. No search fee. Required to search: name, years to search. Civil cases indexed by defendant, plaintiff. Civil records in file folder, computerized since 06/13/97.
Criminal Records: Access: Fax, mail, in person. Only the court performs in person searches; visitors may not. Search fee: $17.50 per name. Required to search: name, years to search, DOB. Criminal records on index cards. Address requests to the County Clerk's office.
General Information: Public Access terminal is available. No sealed or youthful offender records released. SASE required. Turnaround time 1 week. Fax notes: $1.00 per document. Copy fee: $1.00 per page. Certification fee: $5.00. Fee payee: County Clerk. Personal checks accepted. Prepayment is required.

Surrogate Court Courthouse, 320 Main St, Catskill, NY 12414; 518-943-2484; Fax: 518-943-4372. Hours: 9AM-5PM (EST). *Probate.*

Town/Village Courts; *Misdemeanor, Civil Actions Under $3,000, Small Claims:* Windham Town, 518-734-3431; Durham Town, 518-239-6122; Coxsackie Village, 518-731-2225; New Baltimore Town, 518-756-2079; Coxsackie Town, 518-731-6934; Greenville Town, 518-966-4873; Halcott Town, 518-254-5132; Hunter Village, 518-263-4288; Athens Town, 518-945-3360; Catskill Village, 518-943-9544; Prattsville Town, 518-299-3125; Lexington Town, 518-989-6303; Tannersville Village, 518-589-7168; Catskill Town, 518-943-2142; Hunter Town, 518-589-6150; Athens Village Court; Cairo Town, 518-622-3388; Ashland Town, 518-734-3636; Jewett Town.

Hamilton County

Supreme & County Court Hamilton County Clerk, PO Box 204, Route 8, Lake Pleasant, NY 12108; 518-548-7111. 8:30AM-4:30PM (EST). *Felony, Civil.*

Note: Misdemeanor records are maintained by city, town and village courts.

Civil Records: Access: Mail, in person. Both court and visitors may perform in person searches. No search fee. Required to search: name, years to search. Civil cases indexed by defendant. Civil records in books.
Criminal Records: Access: Mail, in person. Only the court performs in person searches; visitors may not. Search fee: $5.00 per name. Fee is per two years searched. Required to search: name, years to search, DOB. Criminal records in books. Request must be in writing.
General Information: No sealed or youthful offender records released. SASE not required. Turnaround time 2-3 days. Fax notes: Fee to fax results is $1.00 per document. Copy fee: $.50 per page. $1.00 minimum. Certification fee: $1.00 per page; $4.00 minimum. Fee payee: Hamilton County Clerk. Personal checks accepted. Prepayment is required.

Surrogate Court Hamilton County Ofc. Bldg, White Birch Lane, Indian Lake, NY 12842; 518-648-5411; Fax: 518-648-6286. Hours: 8:30AM-4:30PM (EST). *Probate.*

Town/Village Courts; *Misdemeanor, Civil Actions Under $3,000, Small Claims:* Lake Pleasant Town, 518-548-3625; Long Lake Town; Benson Town, 518-863-8510; Inlet Town, 315-357-6121; Arietta Town, 518-548-6203; Hope Town, 518-924-2662; Wells Town, 518-924-9285; Hamilton Village, 315-824-3508; Morehouse Town; Indian Lake Town, 518-648-6226.

Herkimer County

Supreme & County Court 301 N Washington Street, Herkimer County Office Bldg, Herkimer, NY 13350-1993; 315-867-1209; Fax: 315-866-1802. Hours: 9AM-5PM Sept-May; 8:30AM-4PM June-Aug (EST). *Felony, Civil.*

Note: Misdemeanor records are maintained by city, town and village courts.

Civil Records: Access: Phone, mail, in person. Only the court performs in person searches; visitors may not. Search fee: $5.00 per name. Search is per 2 year period. Required to search: name, years to search. Civil cases indexed by defendant, plaintiff. Civil records on index books since 1800s.

Criminal Records: Access: Phone, mail, in person. Only the court performs in person searches; visitors may not. Search fee: $5.00 per name. Required to search: name, years to search, DOB. Criminal records on index books since 1800s.

General Information: No sealed, expunged, adoption, sex offense, juvenile or mental health records released. SASE required. Turnaround time varies. Copy fee: $1.00 for first page, $.50 each add'l. Certification fee: $1.00 per page, $4.00 minimum. Fee payee: County Clerk. Personal checks accepted. Prepayment is required.

Little Falls City Court 659 E Main St, Little Falls, NY 13365; 315-823-1690; Fax: 315-823-1623. Hours: 8:30AM-4:30PM (EST). *Misdemeanor, Civil Actions Under $15,000, Eviction, Small Claims.*

Civil Records: Access: Mail, in person. Search fee: $5.00 per name. Required to search: name, years to search. Civil cases indexed by defendant. Civil records in books, files.

Criminal Records: Access: Mail, in person. Only the court performs in person searches; visitors may not. Search fee: $5.00 per name. Required to search: name, years to search, DOB. Criminal records in books, files.

General Information: No sealed, expunged, adoption, sex offense, juvenile or mental health records released. SASE required. Turnaround time 1 week. Certification fee: $5.00. Fee payee: City Court. Only cashiers checks and money orders accepted. Prepayment is required.

Surrogate Court 301 N Washington St #5548, Herkimer, NY 13350; 315-867-1170. Hours: 9AM-5PM Sept-May; 8:30AM-4PM June-Aug (EST). *Probate.*

Town/Village Courts; *Misdemeanor, Civil Actions Under $3,000, Small Claims:* Ilion Village, 315-894-4175; Litchfield Town; Newport Town; Newport Village, 315-845-8938; Schuyler Town, 315-733-1093; Webb Town, 315-369-3321; German Flatts Town, 315-866-3571; Winfield Town, 315-822-4555; Frankfort Town, 315-895-7267; Salisbury Town, 315-429-8581; Little Falls Town, 315-823-3390; Herkimer Village, 315-866-0604; Mohawk Village, 315-866-4312; Manheim Town, 315-429-9631; Columbia Town, 315-866-1309; Fairfield Town, 315-891-7645; Russia Town, 315-826-3432; Ohio Town, 315-826-7912; Herkimer Town, 315-866-1280; Warren Town; Cold Brook Village, 315-826-3772; Norway Town, 315-845-8272; Poland Village, 315-826-3422; Frankfort Village, 315-894-8513; Danube Town; Stark Town, 315-858-2091; Middleville Village.

Jefferson County

Supreme & County Court Jefferson County Clerk's Office-Court Records, 175 Arsenal St, County Building, Watertown, NY 13601-3783; 315-785-3200; Fax: 315-785-5048. Hours: 9AM-5PM Sept-June; 8:30AM-4PM July-Aug (EST). *Felony, Civil.*

www.sunyjefferson.edu/jc

Civil Records: Access: In person only. Visitors must perform in person searches for themselves. No search fee. Required to search: name, years to search. Civil cases indexed by defendant, plaintiff. Civil records on computer from 1992 (by first defendant name only); prior in books from 1805.

Criminal Records: Access: Mail, in person. Both court and visitors may perform in person searches. Search fee: $5.00 per name. Fee is per 2 years searched. Required to search: name, years to search, DOB, signed release. Criminal records on computer from 1992 (by first defendant name only); prior in books from 1805.

General Information: Public Access terminal is available. No sealed, expunged, adoption, sex offense, juvenile or mental health records released. SASE required. Turnaround time 1 week. Copy fee: $.50 per page. The minimum copy fee is $1.00. Certification fee: $4.00. Plus $1.00 per page. Fee payee: County Clerk of Jefferson County. Personal checks accepted. Prepayment is required.

Watertown City Court Municipal Bldg, 245 Washington St, Watertown, NY 13601; 315-785-7785; Fax: 315-785-7818. Hours: 9AM-5PM (EST). *Misdemeanor, Civil Actions Under $15,000, Eviction, Small Claims.*

Civil Records: Access: Mail, in person. Only the court performs in person searches; visitors may not. Search fee: $5.00 per name. Fee is per name & docket. Required to search: name, years to search. Civil cases indexed by defendant. Civil records in docket books.

Criminal Records: Access: Mail, in person. Only the court performs in person searches; visitors may not. Search fee: $16.00 per name. Required to search: name, years to search, DOB. Criminal records in docket books.

General Information: No sealed records released. SASE required. Turnaround time same day. Copy fee: $.50 per page. Certification fee: $5.00. Fee payee: City Court. Only cashiers checks and money orders accepted. Prepayment is required.

Surrogate Court County Office Bldg, 7th Flr, 175 Arsenal St, Watertown, NY 13601-2562; 315-785-3019; Fax: 315-785-5194. Hours: 9AM-5PM Sept-May; 8:30AM-4PM June-Aug (EST). *Probate.*

Town/Village Courts; *Misdemeanor, Civil Actions Under $3,000, Small Claims:* Lyme Town, 315-649-2791; Clayton Town; Orleans Town, 315-482-9210; Champion Town, 315-788-1912; Alexandria Bay Village, 315-482-4786; West Carthage Village, 315-493-6345; Ellisburg Town, 315-846-5116; Adams Village Court; Alexandria Town, 315-482-9519; Clayton Village, 315-686-2427; Pamelia Town, 315-785-9794; Dexter Village Court; Sackets Harbor Village, 315-646-3548; Evans Mills Village, 315-629-4052; Henderson Town, 315-938-5614; Cape Vincent Town, 315-654-2471; Worth Town; Brownville Town, 315-788-7889; Carthage Village, 315-493-2890; Brownville Village, 315-782-7650; Watertown Town; Hounsfield Town, 315-646-2030; Rutland Town, 315-688-4249; Antwerp Town, 315-659-2432; Adams Town, 315-583-5085; Wilna Town, 315-493-2771; Glen Park Village, 315-788-7889; LeRay Town, 315-629-4052; Rodman Town, 315-232-4029; Philadelphia Town, 315-642-3421; Philadelphia Village, 315-642-3452; Theresa Town, 315-628-5758; Chaumont Village Court; Lorraine Town, 315-232-2548.

Kings County

Supreme Court - Civil Division 360 Adams St, Brooklyn, NY 11201; 718-643-5894; Fax: 718-643-8187. Hours: 9AM-5PM (EST). *Civil Actions Over $25,000.*

www.courts.state.ny.us/courtguides/Guide_24.pdf

Civil Records: Access: In person only. Visitors must perform in person searches for themselves. No search fee. Required to search: name, years to search; also helpful-index number. Civil cases indexed by defendant. Civil records on computer back to 1993; in books, on microfiche back to 1900's. Picture ID required.

General Information: Public Access terminal is available. No sealed, expunged, adoption, sex offense, juvenile or mental health records released. Copy fee: $.75 per page. Certification fee: $8.00. Fee payee: County Clerk. Only cashiers checks and money orders accepted. Prepayment is required.

Supreme Court - Criminal 120 Schermerhorn St, Brooklyn, NY 11210; 718-428-2810; Fax: 718-417-5856. Hours: 9:30AM-4:30PM (EST). *Felony, Misdemeanor.*

www.courts.state.ny.us/courtguides/Guide_24.pdf

Criminal Records: Access: In person only. Only the court performs in person searches; visitors may not. Search fee: $16.00 per name. Fee is per county. Required to search: name, DOB, signed release. Criminal records on computer from 1976, prior on index.

General Information: No sealed, sex offense or youthful offender records released. SASE required. Turnaround time 1-3 days. Copy fee: Included in search fee. Certification fee: Included in search fee. Fee payee: Office of Court Administration. Personal checks accepted. Prepayment is required.

Civil Court of the City of New York - Kings Branch 141 Livingston St, Brooklyn, NY 11201; 718-643-5069/643-8133 Clerk. Hours: 9AM-5PM (EST). *Civil Actions Under $25,000, Eviction, Small Claims.*

www.courts.state.ny.us/courtguides/Guide_24.pdf

Civil Records: Access: In person only. Visitors must perform in person searches for themselves. No search fee. Required to search: name, years to search. Civil cases indexed by plaintiff. Civil records on computer from 1987 for small claims, 1990 for tenant/landlord, and from January 1998 for civil.

General Information: Public Access terminal is available. (Landlord & Tenant, civil, and small claims since 1998.) All records public. Copy fee: $.15 public copying machine fee. Certification fee: $5.00. Fee payee: NYC Civil Court. Only cashiers checks and money orders accepted. Prepayment is required.

Surrogate Court 2 Johnson St, Brooklyn, NY 11201; 718-643-5262. 9AM-5PM (EST). *Probate.*

www.courts.state.ny.us/courtguides/Guide_24.pdf

Lewis County

Supreme & County Court Courthouse, PO Box 232, Lowville, NY 13367; 315-376-5333; Fax: 315-376-3768. Hours: 8:30AM-4:30PM (EST). *Felony, Civil.*

Note: Misdemeanor records are maintained by city, town and village courts.

Civil Records: Access: Mail, in person. Both court and visitors may perform in person searches. Search fee: $10.00 per name. Required to search: name, years to search. Civil cases indexed by defendant. Civil records on index cards from 1935.

Criminal Records: Access: Mail, in person. Both court and visitors may perform in person searches. Search

fee: $10.00 per name. Required to search: name, years to search. Criminal records on index cards from 1935.

General Information: No sealed, youthful offender or sex abuse case records released. SASE required. Turnaround time 2 days. Copy fee: $.50 per page. Certification fee: $4.00. Fee payee: County Clerk. Personal checks accepted. Prepayment is required.

Surrogate Court Courthouse, 7660 State St, Lowville, NY 13367; 315-376-5344; Fax: 315-376-4145. Hours: 8:30AM-4:30PM (EST). *Probate.*

Note: Fee is $25 for under 25 years to $70 for over 70 years

Town/Village Courts; *Misdemeanor, Civil Actions Under $3,000, Small Claims:* Lyonsdale Town; Lewis Town; Turin Town, 315-348-6403; Denmark Town; Watson Town, 315-376-3866; Pinckney Town; Lowville Village Court; Lowville Town, 315-376-8070; Diana Town, 315-543-2628; New Bremen Town, 315-376-3752; Leyden Town, 315-348-6215; Osceola Town, 315-599-8869; Port Leyden Village, 315-348-6215; Martinsburg Town, 315-376-2299; Croghan Town, 315-346-1212; West Turin Town, 315-348-8971; Greig Town.

Livingston County

Supreme & County Court 6 Court St, Rm 201, Geneseo, NY 14454; 716-243-7010. Hours: 8:30AM-4:30PM Oct-May; 8AM-4PM June-Sept (EST). *Felony, Civil.*

Civil Records: Access: Mail, in person. Both court and visitors may perform in person searches. Search fee: $2.50 per name per year. Required to search: name, years to search. Civil cases indexed by defendant, plaintiff. Civil records on computer since 1996. Plaintiff index available only on computer searches.

Criminal Records: Access: Mail, in person. Both court and visitors may perform in person searches. Search fee: $2.50 per name per year. Required to search: name, years to search. Criminal records on computer since 1996. Plaintiff index available only on computer.

General Information: Public Access terminal is available. No sealed or youthful offender records released. SASE required. Turnaround time same day. Copy fee: $.50 per page. Certification fee: $4.00 plus $.50 per page after first 4. Fee payee: County Clerk. Personal checks accepted. Prepayment is required.

Surrogate Court 2 Court St, Geneseo, NY 14454; 716-243-7095; Fax: 716-243-7583. Hours: 9AM-5PM (EST). *Probate.*

Town/Village Courts; *Misdemeanor, Civil Actions Under $3,000, Small Claims:* Groveland Town, 716-243-3782; Avon Village, 716-226-3660; Springwater Town, 716-669-2635; Avon Town, 716-226-2130; Leicester Town, 716-382-9419; North Dansville Town, 716-335-1460; Geneseo Town, 716-243-4530; Lima Town, 716-582-1011; Portage Town; West Sparta Town, 716-335-2443; Caledonia Town, 716-538-4927; York Town, 716-243-0666; Ossian Town, 716-335-8040; Geneseo Village, 716-243-4530; Sparta Town; Nunda Town, 716-468-2215; Nunda Village, 716-468-5739; Mount Morris Village, 716-658-3249; Dansville Village, 716-335-2460; Conesus Town, 716-346-3130; Caledonia Village, 716-538-4800; Mount Morris Town, 716-658-2333; Livonia Town, 716-346-3710.

Madison County

Supreme & County Court County Office Bldg, PO Box 668, Wampsville, NY 13163; 315-366-2261; Fax: 315-366-2615. 9AM-5PM (EST). *Felony, Civil.*

Note: Misdemeanor records are maintained by city, town and village courts.

Civil Records: Access: Mail, in person. Both court and visitors may perform in person searches. Search fee:

$5.00 per name. Fee is per 5 years searched. Required to search: name, years to search. Civil cases indexed by defendant. Judgment records on computer from 1997, prior in books.

Criminal Records: Access: Mail, in person. Both court and visitors may perform in person searches. Search fee: $5.00 per name. Per 5 years. Required to search: name, years to search, DOB. Criminal records on computer to 1989, previous years in books.

General Information: No sealed, expunged, adoption, sex offense, juvenile or mental health records released. SASE required. Turnaround time 2 days. Copy fee: $1.00 for first page, $.50 each add'l. Certification fee: $1.00. Minimum $4.00. Fee payee: County Clerk. Personal checks accepted. Prepayment is required.

Oneida City Court 109 N Main St, Oneida, NY 13421; 315-363-1310; Fax: 315-363-3230. Hours: 8:30AM-4:30PM (EST). *Misdemeanor, Civil Actions Under $15,000, Eviction, Small Claims.*

Civil Records: Access: Mail, in person. Only the court performs in person searches; visitors may not. Search fee: $5.00 per name. Fee is for search prior to 1990, other years $16.00 per name. Required to search: name, years to search. Civil cases indexed by plaintiff. Civil records on computer to 1990, prior in books to 1950s.

Criminal Records: Access: Mail, in person. Only the court performs in person searches; visitors may not. Search fee: $16 fee is for 1989 forward; searches prior to 1989 are $5.00 per name. Required to search: name, years to search, DOB. Criminal records on computer back to 1989; prior in books back to 1950s.

General Information: No sealed, expunged, sex offense, mental health or youthful offender records released. SASE required. Turnaround time 1-2 days. Copy fee: $.50 per page. Certification fee: $5.00. Fee payee: City Court. Personal checks accepted. Prepayment is required.

Surrogate Court County Courthouse, North Court st, Wampsville, NY 13163; 315-366-2392; Fax: 315-366-2539. Hours: 9AM-5PM (EST). *Probate.*

Town/Village Courts; *Misdemeanor, Civil Actions Under $3,000, Small Claims:* Lenox Town; Georgetown Town, 315-837-4795; Lebanon Town, 315-837-4835; Chittenango Village Court; Wampsville Village, 315-363-5810; DeRuyter Village, 315-852-9650; Smithfield Town; Lincoln Town, 315-697-7018; Hamilton Town, 315-824-3508; Sullivan Town, 315-687-3347; Stockbridge Town, 315-495-3333; Brookfield Town; Morrisville Village, 315-684-9111; Nelson Town, 315-655-8582; Canastota Village, 315-697-9410; Cazenovia Village, 315-655-4011; Cazenovia Town; Fenner Town, 315-655-2705; Madison Town, 315-893-7544; Madison Village Court; Eaton Town, 315-684-9111.

Monroe County

Supreme & County Court County Office Bldg, County Clerk's Office, 39 Main Street West, Rochester, NY 14614; 716-428-5151; Fax: 716-428-4698. Hours: 9AM-5PM (EST). *Felony, Civil.*

www.clerk.co.monroe.ny.us

Civil Records: Access: Fax, mail, online, in person. Both court and visitors may perform in person searches. Search fee: $5.00 per name. Fee is per 2 years searched. Required to search: name, years to search. Civil cases indexed by defendant. Civil records on computer since 6/93, prior in books. Online access to felony, civil, and divorce records are available free online at www.clerk.co.monroe.ny.us. Records go back to 6/1993, although earlier film images are being added. Also, access to the remote online system requires $.50 per minute of usage. Fax back is available for $.50 per page. Call Tom Fiorilli 716-428-5151 for more information.

Criminal Records: Access: Fax, mail, online, in person. Both court and visitors may perform in person searches. Search fee: $5.00 per name. Fee is per 2 years searched. Required to search: name, years to search, DOB. Criminal records on computer since 6/93, prior in books. Online access to criminal records is the same as civil.

General Information: Public Access terminal is available. No sealed, divorce records, confidential files released. SASE required. Turnaround time 2 weeks. Copy fee: $.50 per page. $1.00 minimum. Call Tom Fiorilli for more information. Certification fee: $4.00 plus $1.00 per page after first 4. Fee payee: County Clerk. Personal checks accepted. Prepayment required.

Rochester City Court Hall of Justice, Rochester, NY 14614; Civil phone: 716-428-2444; Criminal phone: 716-428-2447; Fax: 716-428-2588 (Civil) 428-2732 (Criminal). Hours: 9AM-5PM (EST). *Misdemeanor, Civil Actions Under $15,000, Eviction, Small Claims.*

Civil Records: Access: Phone, fax, mail, in person. Both court and visitors may perform in person searches. Search fee: $16.00 per name. Required to search: name, years to search. Civil cases indexed by defendant, plaintiff. Civil records on computer from 1983, prior in books from 1973.

Criminal Records: Access: Phone, fax, mail, in person. Both court and visitors may perform in person searches. Search fee: $16.00 per name. Required to search: name, years to search, DOB, SSN, signed release. Criminal records on computer since 1986, prior on books from 1973. Certificate of disposition $5.00.

General Information: Public Access terminal is available. No sealed, expunged, probation reports, adoption, sex offense, juvenile or mental health records released. SASE required. Turnaround time 1 week. Copy fee: $1.00 per page. Certification fee: $5.00. Only cashiers checks and money orders accepted. Prepayment is required.

Surrogate Court Hall of Justice, Rm 541, 99 Exchange Blvd, Rochester, NY 14614; 716-428-5200; Fax: 716-428-2650. Hours: 9AM-4PM (EST). *Probate.*

Town/Village Courts; *Misdemeanor, Civil Actions Under $3,000, Small Claims:* Parma Town, 716-392-9470; Penfield Town, 716-377-8623; Pittsford Town, 716-248-6238; Sweden Town, 716-637-9157; Perinton Town, 716-377-3388; Rush Town, 716-533-1130; Irondequoit Town, 716-336-6040; Brighton Town, 716-473-8849; Hamlin Town, 716-964-8641; East Rochester Town, 716-385-2576; Chili Town, 716-889-1999; Greece Town, 716-227-3155; Ogden Town, 716-352-3498; Henrietta Town, 716-359-2640; Riga Town; Clarkson Town, 716-637-1134; Gates Town, 716-247-6106; Mendon Town, 716-624-6064; Webster Town, 716-872-1000; Honeoye Falls Village, 716-624-1711; Wheatland Town, 716-889-3074; Fairport Village, 716-223-0316.

Montgomery County

Supreme & County Court Montgomery County Office Bldg, PO Box 1500, Fonda, NY 12068; Civil phone: 518-853-8113; Criminal phone: 518-853-4516; Fax: 518-853-3596 (Criminal). Hours: 9AM-5PM; 8:30AM-4PM (civil) (EST). *Felony, Misdemeanor, Civil.*

Note: Court keeps record of its own Misdemeanor cases only; also search city, town and village courts.

Civil Records: Access: Mail, in person. Both court and visitors may perform in person searches. Search fee: $5.00 per name. Fee is per 2 years searched. Required to search: name, years to search, address. Civil cases indexed by defendant, plaintiff. Civil records in books and on index cards back to 1965; on computer back to 1992. Public access terminal available for Civil records.

Criminal Records: Access: Mail, in person. Both court and visitors may perform in person searches. Search fee: $16.00 per name. Required to search: name, years to search, DOB; also helpful-SSN. Criminal records on computer back to 1992; file index back to 1965. Public access terminal not available for Criminal records.

General Information: No sealed or youthful offender records released. SASE required. Turnaround time 1 week. Copy fee: $1.00 per page. Certification fee: $4.00 plus $1.00 per page after first. Fee payee: County Clerk. Personal checks accepted. Prepayment is required.

Amsterdam City Court Public Safety Bldg, Rm 208, One Guy Park Ave Ext, Amsterdam, NY 12010; 518-842-9510; Fax: 518-843-8474. Hours: 8AM-4PM (EST). *Misdemeanor, Civil Actions Under $15,000, Eviction, Small Claims.*

Civil Records: Access: Mail, in person. Only the court performs in person searches; visitors may not. Search fee: $16.00 per name. Required to search: name, years to search. Civil cases indexed by defendant. Civil records on computer since 1995, on index cards.

Criminal Records: Access: Mail, in person. Only the court performs in person searches; visitors may not. Search fee: $16.00 per name. Required to search: name, years to search, DOB. Criminal records on computer from 11/93, prior on index cards.

General Information: No sealed, expunged, adoption, sex offense, juvenile or mental health records released. Turnaround time 1 week. Copy fee: $.25 per page. Certification fee: $10.00. Fee payee: City Court. Only cashiers checks and money orders accepted. Prepayment is required.

Surrogate Court 58 Broadway, Fonda, NY 12068; 518-853-8108; Fax: 518-853-8148. Hours: 9AM-5PM (EST). *Probate.*

Note: Court also handles administration of estates, guardianships and adoptions.

Town/Village Courts; *Misdemeanor, Civil Actions Under $3,000, Small Claims:* Glen Town, 518-853-4825; Amsterdam Town, 518-842-7961; Charleston Town, 518-922-6771; Florida Town, 518-843-6468; Mohawk Town, 518-853-3031; Canajoharie Village, 518-673-5116; Palatine Town; Minden Town, 518-568-2728; Canajoharie Town, 518-673-3013; St Johnsville Village, 518-568-2226; St Johnsville Town, 518-568-2662.

Nassau County

Supreme Court Supreme Court Bldg, Supreme Court Dr, Mineola, NY 11501; 516-571-1660; Civil phone: 516-571-2906. Hours: 9AM-5PM (EST). *Civil Actions Over $15,000.*

Note: All records are maintained at the County Clerk's Office, 240 Old County Rd, Mineola, NY, 11501, 516-571-2664/2272.

Civil Records: Access: Mail, in person. Both court and visitors may perform in person searches. Search fee: $5.00 per name. Fee is for archived cases only. Required to search: name, years to search. Civil cases indexed by defendant, plaintiff. Civil records on computer from 1992, prior in books.

General Information: Public Access terminal is available. No sealed, expunged, adoption, sex offense, juvenile or mental health records released. SASE required. Turnaround time 3 weeks for cases prior to 1996. Copy fee: $.25 per page. Certification fee: $4.00. Includes up to 4 pages, then $1.00 per page additional. Includes copy fees. Fee payee: Nassau County Clerk's Office. Personal checks accepted. Prepayment is required.

County Court 262 Old Country Rd, Mineola, NY 11501; 516-571-2800; Fax: 516-571-2160. Hours: 9AM-5PM (EST). *Felony.*

Criminal Records: Access: Mail, in person. Only the court performs in person searches; visitors may not. Search fee: $16.00 per name. Searches 1982-present done at OCA. Required to search: name, years to search, DOB. Criminal records on computer from 1982, prior in archives or on microfilm.

General Information: No sealed, expunged, sex offense, juvenile, or mental health records released. Turnaround time 3 weeks. Copy fee: $.50 per page. $1.00 minimum. Certification fee: $4.00. Fee payee: Clerk of Court. Only cashiers checks and money orders accepted. Prepayment is required.

District Court - 1st & 2nd Districts 99 Main St, Hempstead, NY 11550; 516-572-2355. Hours: 9AM-5PM (EST). *Misdemeanors, Civil Actions Under $15,000, Eviction, Small Claims.*

Note: Records for 2nd District are separate prior to 1980. 1st District handles Misdemeanor case records.

Civil Records: Access: Mail, in person. Both court and visitors may perform in person searches. Search fee: $16.00 per name. Required to search: name, years to search. Civil cases indexed by defendant, plaintiff. Civil records on computer back to 1980, prior in books back to 1960.

Criminal Records: Access: Mail, in person. Both court and visitors may perform in person searches. Search fee: $16.00 per name. Required to search: name, years to search, DOB. Criminal records on computer back to 1980, prior in books back to 1960.

General Information: No sealed records released. SASE required. Turnaround time 5-10 days. Copy fee: $1.00. Add $.50 per page after 2. Certification fee: $5.00. Fee payee: Clerk of Court. Only cashiers checks and money orders accepted. Prepayment is required.

District Court - 3rd District 435 Middle Neck, Great Neck, NY 11023; 516-571-8400/8402; Fax: 516-571-8403. Hours: 9AM-5PM (EST). *Civil Actions Under $15,000, Eviction, Small Claims.*

Civil Records: Access: Mail, in person. Only the court performs in person searches; visitors may not. Search fee: $16.00 per name. Required to search: name, years to search. Civil cases indexed by defendant, plaintiff. Civil records on computer from 1989, prior in books.

General Information: No sealed, expunged, adoption, sex offense, juvenile or mental health records released. SASE required. Turnaround time 1 week. Copy fee: $1.00 for first page, $.50 each add'l. Certification fee: $5.00. Fee payee: Clerk of Court. Only cashiers checks and money orders accepted. Prepayment is required.

District Court - 4th District 87 Bethpage Rd, Hicksville, NY 11801; 516-571-7090. Hours: 9AM-5PM (EST). *Civil Actions Under $15,000, Eviction, Small Claims.*

Civil Records: Access: Mail, in person. Only the court performs in person searches; visitors may not. Search fee: $16.00 per name. Required to search: name, years to search. Civil cases indexed by defendant. Civil records on computer from 1989, prior in books.

General Information: SASE required. Turnaround time 1 week. Copy fee: $1.00. Add $.50 per page after first 2. Certification fee: $5.00. Fee payee: Clerk of District Court. Only cashiers checks and money orders accepted. Prepayment is required.

Glen Cove City Court 13 Glen St, Glen Cove, NY 11542-2704; 516-676-0109; Fax: 516-676-1570. Hours: 9AM-5PM (EST). *Misdemeanor, Civil Actions Under $15,000, Eviction, Small Claims.*

Civil Records: Access: Mail, fax, in person. Only the court performs in person searches; visitors may not.

Search fee: $16.00 per name. Required to search: name, years to search.

Criminal Records: Access: Mail, fax, in person. Only the court performs in person searches; visitors may not. Search fee: $16.00 per name. Required to search: name, years to search, DOB. Same record keeping as civil.

General Information: No sealed, expunged, adoption, sex offense, juvenile or mental health records released. SASE required. Turnaround time 3-5 days. Copy fee: Varies. Certification fee: $5.00. Fee payee: Glen Cove City Court. Only cashiers checks and money orders accepted. Prepayment is required.

Long Beach City Court 1 West Chester St, Long Beach, NY 11561; 516-431-1000; Fax: 516-889-3511. Hours: 9AM-5PM (EST). *Misdemeanor, Civil Actions Under $15,000, Eviction, Small Claims.*

Civil Records: Access: Mail, in person. Only the court performs in person searches; visitors may not. Search fee: $16.00. Required to search: name, years to search.

Criminal Records: Access: Mail, in person. Only the court performs in person searches; visitors may not. Search fee: $16.00 per name. Required to search: name, years to search, DOB. Criminal records on computer from 1986.

General Information: No sealed, expunged, adoption, sex offense, juvenile or mental health records released. Copy fee: $1.00 for first page, $.50 each add'l. Certification fee: $5.00. Fee payee: City Court of Long Beach. Only cashiers checks and money orders accepted. Prepayment is required.

Surrogate Court 262 Old Country Rd, Mineola, NY 11501; 516-571-2082; Fax: 516-571-3864. Hours: 9AM-5PM (EST). *Probate.*

Town/Village Courts; *Misdemeanor, Civil Actions Under $3,000, Small Claims:* Floral Park Village, 516-326-6325; Kings Point Village, 516-482-7872; Thomaston Village Court; Roslyn Harbor Village, 516-621-0368; Old Westbury Village, 516-626-0800; Kensington Village, 516-482-4409; Roslyn Estates Village, 516-621-3541; Great Neck Village, 516-487-0775; Upper Brookville Village, 516-676-5619; Flower Hill Village Court; Plandome Manor Village Court; Lattington Village, 516-922-0767; Laurel Hollow Village, 516-692-8826; Lake Success Village, 516-482-7430; Plandome Heights Village, 516-365-0501; North Hills Village Court; Old Brookville Village Court; East Hills Village, 516-621-4251; Plandome Village Court; Rockville Centre Village, 516-678-9233; Williston Park Village, 516-248-5150; Bayville Village, 516-628-1410; Great Neck Estates Village, 516-482-6430; Great Neck Plaza Village, 516-482-4500; Lawrence Village, 516-239-9166; Sands Point Village, 516-883-3100; Sea Cliff Village, 516-671-0328; Freeport Village, 516-378-8687; Garden City Village, 516-742-5800; Bellerose Village, 516-358-2962; Malverne Village Court; Stewart Manor Village, 516-352-6240; Hempstead Village, 516-489-3400; Mill Neck Village, 516-922-6722; Cedarhurst Village, 516-295-5522; Centre Island Village, 516-922-0606; Manorhaven Village Court; South Floral Park Village, 516-353-8047; Cove Neck Village, 516-624-9600; Russell Gardens Village Court; Woodsburgh Village Court; Matinecock Village, 516-922-8198; Oyster Bay Cove Village, 516-681-9271; Sadd'le Rock Village Court; Roslyn Village, 516-621-1961; New Hyde Park Village, 516-354-6330; Farmingdale Village, 516-293-2292; East Rockaway Village Court; Mineola Village, 516-746-0754; Massapequa Park Village Court; Valley Stream Village Court; Westbury Village, 516-334-1700; Muttontown Village, 516-364-2240; Lynbrook Village, 516-599-0416; Munsey Park Village, 516-365-7790; Brookville Village, 516-922-2983; Atlantic Beach Village, 516-371-4552.

New York County

Supreme Court - Civil Division County Clerk, 60 Centre St, Room 103, New York City, NY 10007; 212-374-4704/374-8339. Hours: 9AM-3PM (EST). *Civil Actions.*

Civil Records: Access: Mail, in person. Both court and visitors may perform in person searches. Search fee: $5.00 per name. Fee is per 2 years searched. Required to search: name, years to search. Civil cases indexed by defendant, plaintiff. Civil records on computer from 1993, prior in books.
General Information: SASE required. Turnaround time 1 month. Certification fee: $8.00 per document. Fee payee: County Clerk. Only cashiers checks and money orders accepted. Prepayment is required.

Supreme Court - Criminal Division 100 Centre St, Room 1000, New York, NY 10013; 212-374-4984. 9AM-5PM (EST). *Felony, Misdemeanor.*

Criminal Records: Access: In person only. Visitors must perform in person searches for themselves. Search fee: If written: $16.00 for an electronic search, or $5.00 for a 5 year manual search. Required to search: name, years to search, DOB. Criminal records on computer from 1977, prior records archived. Written requests must be directed to OAS, Criminal History Searches, Ofc. Court Admin., 25 Beaver St. NY, NY.
General Information: No sealed, expunged, adoption, sex offense, juvenile or mental health records released. SASE required. Turnaround time 1-2 days. Fax notes: Will not fax results. Copy fee: $.15 per page self-serve. Certification fee: $8.00 per document; $10.00 for certificate of disposition. Fee payee: Office of Court Administration. No personal checks accepted. Prepayment is required.

Civil Court of the City of New York 111 Centre St, New York, NY 10013; 212-374-7915; Fax: 212-374-5709. Hours: 9AM-5PM (EST). *Civil Actions Under $25,000, Eviction, Small Claims.*

Civil Records: Access: Mail, in person. Visitors must perform in person searches for themselves. No search fee. Required to search: name, years to search; also helpful: address. Civil cases indexed by plaintiff. Landlord/Tenant records on computer from 1984, civil from 1994, prior in books. Records are archived after 3 years; search by defendant available only from 6/94 on.
General Information: Public Access terminal is available. (Available for cases since 1994.) no sealed records released. SASE required. No copy fee. Certification fee: $5.00. Fee payee: Clerk of Civil Court. Only cashiers checks and money orders accepted. Attorney's and certified checks accepted. Prepayment is required.

Surrogate Court 31 Chambers St, New York City, NY 10007; 212-374-8233, 9AM-5PM (EST). *Probate.*

Niagara County

Supreme Court 775 3rd St, Niagara Falls, NY 14302; 716-278-1800; Fax: 716-278-1809. Hours: 9AM-5PM (EST). *Felony, Civil Actions Over $25,000.*

Note: All records are maintained at County Clerk's Office, 75 Hawley St, Lockport, NY 14094 (716-439-7030).

Civil Records: Access: Mail, in person. Both court and visitors may perform in person searches. No search fee. Required to search: name, years to search. Civil cases indexed by defendant. Civil records in index books back to 1950, computerized since 1997.
Criminal Records: Access: Mail, in person. Only the court performs in person searches; visitors may not. Search fee: $5.00 per name. per every 2 years searched. Required to search: name, years to search, DOB. Criminal records in index books back to 1950, computerized since 1997.

General Information: No sealed or youthful offender records released. SASE not required. Turnaround time 3 days. Copy fee: $1.00 per page. Certification fee: $4.00. Fee payee: County Clerk. Personal checks accepted. Prepayment is required.

County Court Courthouse, 175 Hawley St, Lockport, NY 14094; 716-439-7022; Fax: 716-439-4023. Hours: 9AM-5PM (EST). *Felony, Civil Actions Under $25,000.*

Civil Records: Access: Fax, mail, in person. Only the court performs in person searches; visitors may not. Search fee: $5.00 per name. Fee is per two years searched. Required to search: name, years to search. Civil cases indexed by defendant, plaintiff. Civil records on computer since 1/96; prior records in books.
Criminal Records: Access: Fax, mail, in person. Both court and visitors may perform in person searches. Search fee: $5.00 per name. Fee is per two years searched. Required to search: name, years to search, DOB. Criminal records on computer since 1/96; prior records in books.
General Information: No sealed, youthful offender or sex abuse case records released. SASE required. Turnaround time 1 day. Fax notes: $1.00 per page. Copy fee: $1.00 per page. Certification fee: $4.00. Fee payee: County Clerk. Business checks accepted. Prepayment is required.

Lockport City Court Municipal Bldg, One Locks Plaza, Lockport, NY 14094; Civil phone: 716-439-6660; Criminal phone: 716-439-6671; Fax: 716-439-6684. Hours: 8AM-4:30PM (EST). *Misdemeanor, Civil Actions Under $15,000, Eviction, Small Claims.*

Civil Records: Access: Phone, fax, mail, in person. Both court and visitors may perform in person searches. Search fee: $16.00 per name. Required to search: name, years to search. Civil cases indexed by defendant. Civil records on computer from 1988, prior in books from 1900s.
Criminal Records: Access: Phone, fax, mail, in person. Both court and visitors may perform in person searches. Search fee: $16.00 per name. Required to search: name, years to search, DOB. Criminal records in books from 1988 forward.
General Information: No sealed, expunged, adoption, sex offense, juvenile or mental health records released. SASE required. Turnaround time 1 week. Copy fee: $1.00 per page. Certification fee: $5.00. Fee payee: City Court of Lockport. Only cashiers checks and money orders accepted. Prepayment is required.

Niagara Falls City Court PO Box 1586, Niagara Falls, NY 14302-2725; Civil phone: 716-278-9860; Criminal phone: 716-278-9800; Fax: 716-278-9809. Hours: 8:30AM-4:30PM (EST). *Misdemeanor, Civil Actions Under $15,000, Eviction, Small Claims.*

Civil Records: Access: Mail, in person. Both court and visitors may perform in person searches. Search fee: $5.00 per name for 2 years; computer search is $16.00. Required to search: name, years to search. Civil cases indexed by defendant. Civil records on microfilm from 1985, in books since 1970.
Criminal Records: Access: Mail, in person. Both court and visitors may perform in person searches. Search fee: $5.00 per name for 2 years; computer search is $16.00. Required to search: name, years to search, DOB. Criminal records in books from 1970.
General Information: No sealed, expunged, adoption, sex offense, juvenile or mental health records released. SASE required. Turnaround time 3-4 days. Copy fee: $1.00 per page. Certification fee: Certificate of Disposition is $5.00. Fee payee: City Court of Niagara Falls. Prepayment is required.

North Tonawanda City Court City Hall, North Tonawanda, NY 14120-5446; 716-693-1010; Fax: 716-743-1754. Hours: 8AM-5PM (EST). *Misdemeanor, Civil Actions Under $15,000, Eviction, Small Claims.*

Civil Records: Access: Mail, in person. Only the court performs in person searches; visitors may not. Search fee: $16.00 for an electronic search plus $5.00 per name to certify. Required to search: name, years to search. Civil cases indexed by defendant. Civil records on computer from 1993, prior in books.
Criminal Records: Access: Mail, in person. Only the court performs in person searches; visitors may not. Search fee: Fees same as civil. Required to search: name, years to search, DOB, signed release. Criminal records on computer from 1986, prior in books.
General Information: No sealed, expunged, adoption, sex offense, juvenile or mental health records released. SASE requested. Turnaround time 2 days. Copy fee: $1.00 per page. Certification fee: $5.00. Fee payee: City Court. Only cashiers checks and money orders accepted. Prepayment is required.

Surrogate Court Niagara County Courthouse, 175 Hawley St, Lockport, NY 14094; 716-439-7130; Fax: 716-439-7157. Hours: 9AM-5PM (EST). *Probate.*

Town/Village Courts; *Misdemeanor, Civil Actions Under $3,000, Small Claims:* Hartland Town, 716-735-7239; Wilson Town, 716-751-0549; Wheatfield Town, 716-694-6793; Porter Town, 716-745-7036; Lewiston Town, 716-754-8213; Niagara Town, 716-297-2150; Cambria Town, 716-433-7664; Newfane Town, 716-778-9292; Lockport Town, 716-439-9528; Barker Village, 716-795-9193; Royalton Town, 716-772-2588; Pendleton Town, 716-625-8833; Somerset Town, 716-795-9193.

Oneida County

Supreme & County Court 800 Park Ave, Utica, NY 13501; 315-798-5790. Hours: 9AM-5PM (EST). *Felony, Civil.*

Civil Records: Access: Phone, mail, in person. Both court and visitors may perform in person searches. Search fee: $5.00 per name. Fee is for 10 year search. Required to search: name, years to search. Civil cases indexed by defendant, plaintiff. Civil records on computer from 1992, prior in books by plaintiff only.
Criminal Records: Access: Mail, in person. Both court and visitors may perform in person searches. Search fee: $5.00 per name. Fee is for 10 year search. Required to search: name, years to search, SSN, signed release. Criminal records on computer from 1992, prior in books by plaintiff only.
General Information: Public Access terminal is available. No sealed, expunged, adoption, sex offense, juvenile or mental health records released. SASE required. Turnaround time 1 week. Copy fee: $1.00 per page. Certification fee: $4.00. Fee payee: County Clerk. Personal checks accepted. Prepayment is required.

Rome City Court 301 N James St, Rome, NY 13440; 315-337-6440; Fax: 315-338-0343. Hours: 9AM-5PM (EST). *Misdemeanor, Civil Actions Under $15,000, Eviction, Small Claims.*

Civil Records: Access: Mail, in person. Only the court performs in person searches; visitors may not. Search fee: $5.00 per name. Required to search: name, years to search. Civil cases indexed by defendant, plaintiff. Civil records in books and some on computer.
Criminal Records: Access: Mail, in person. Only the court performs in person searches; visitors may not. Search fee: $16.00 for electronic automated search or $5.00 for manual search per 2 years. Required to search: name, years to search, DOB.
Most records are computerized.
General Information: No sealed or youthful offender records released. SASE required. Turnaround time 5-7

days. Copy fee: $.50 per page. $1.00 minimum. Certification fee: $5.00. Fee payee: Rome City Court. Only cashiers checks and money orders accepted. Prepayment is required.

Sherrill City Court 373 Sherrill Rd, Sherrill, NY 13461; 315-363-0996; Fax: 315-363-1176. Hours: 8AM-4PM (EST). *Misdemeanor, Civil Actions Under $15,000, Eviction, Small Claims.*

Civil Records: Access: Mail, in person. Only the court performs in person searches; visitors may not. Search fee: $5.00 per name. Required to search: name, years to search. Civil cases indexed by defendant, plaintiff. Civil records in books since 1800s.

Criminal Records: Access: Mail, in person. Only the court performs in person searches; visitors may not. Search fee: $5.00 per name. Required to search: name, years to search; also helpful: DOB. Criminal records in books since 1800s.

General Information: No sealed, expunged, adoption, sex offense, juvenile or mental health records released. SASE required. Turnaround time 1-2 days. Copy fee: $.50 per page. Certification fee: $5.00. Fee payee: Sherrill City Court. Personal checks accepted. Prepayment is required.

Utica City Court 411 Oriskany St West, Utica, NY 13502; Civil phone: 315-724-8157; Criminal phone: 315-724-8227; Fax: 315-724-0762 (criminal)/792-8038 (civil). Hours: 9AM-5PM (EST). *Misdemeanor, Civil Actions Under $15,000, Eviction, Small Claims.*

Civil Records: Access: Mail, in person. Both court and visitors may perform in person searches. Search fee: $5.00 per name. Required to search: name, years to search, address. Civil cases indexed by defendant. Civil records in books from 1900s.

Criminal Records: Access: Mail, in person. Only the court performs in person searches; visitors may not. Search fee: Computer criminal history search $16.00, manual 2 year search is $5.00. Required to search: name, years to search, address, DOB, signed release. Criminal records in books from 1900s.

General Information: No sealed, expunged, adoption, sex offense, juvenile or mental health records released. SASE required. Turnaround time 1-2 days. Copy fee: $.50 per page. $1.00 minimum. Certification fee: $5.00. Fee payee: City Court of Utica. Only cashiers checks and money orders accepted. Prepayment is required.

Surrogate Court 200 Elizabeth St, Utica, NY 13501; 315-798-5866. Hours: 9AM-5PM Sept-May; 8:30AM-4PM June-Aug (EST). *Probate.*

Town/Village Courts; *Misdemeanor, Civil Actions Under $3,000, Small Claims:* Florence Town; Boonville Town, 315-942-3416; Marcy Town; Vernon Village, 315-829-2691; Ava Town, 315-942-6542; Whitestown Town, 315-736-1251; Whitesboro Village, 315-736-4353; Bridgewater Town, 315-822-6808; Vienna Town, 315-245-2191; Remsen Village Court; New York Mills Village, 315-736-7811; Verona Town, 315-363-4394; Marshall Town, 315-841-8515; New Hartford Village, 315-732-5924; Westmoreland Town, 315-853-4333; New Hartford Town, 315-732-5924; Western Town, 315-827-4928; Clinton Village Court; Augusta Town, 315-843-4811; Camden Town, 315-245-0817; Waterville Village, 315-841-8007; Deerfield Town, 315-724-0605; Remsen Town, 315-831-5330; Lee Town, 315-336-1585; Kirkland Town, 315-853-5082; Orinsky Village, 315-736-3512; Annsville Town, 315-336-1295; Sylvan Beach Village, 315-762-4240; Boonville Village, 315-942-3438; Floyd Town, 315-865-4256; Forestport Town, 315-392-2801; Paris Town, 315-839-5400; Trenton Town, 315-896-4510; Vernon Town, 315-829-3211; Sangerfield Town, 315-841-8631.

Onondaga County

Supreme & County Court 401 Montgomery St Room 200, Syracuse, NY 13202; 315-435-2226. Hours: 8AM-5PM (EST). *Felony, Civil.*

Civil Records: Access: Mail, in person. Both court and visitors may perform in person searches. Search fee: $5.00 per name. Fee is per name & per 2 years searched. Required to search: name, years to search. Civil cases indexed by defendant, plaintiff. Civil records on computer from 1989, prior in books.

Criminal Records: Access: Mail, in person. Both court and visitors may perform in person searches. Search fee: $5.00 per name. Fee is per 2 years searched. Required to search: name, years to search; also helpful: DOB. Criminal records on computer from 1990, prior in books.

General Information: Public Access terminal is available. No sealed, divorce, judgment or sexual abuse records released. SASE required. Turnaround time 2-3 days. Copy fee: $.50 per page. $1.00 minimum. Certification fee: Fee is $1.00 per page with a $4.00 minimum. Fee payee: County Clerk. Personal checks accepted. $60.00 limit for personal checks. Prepayment is required.

Syracuse City Court 511 State St, Syracuse, NY 13202-2179; Civil phone: 315-477-2782; Criminal phone: 315-477-2760; Fax: 315-426-8454 Civil; 472-2963 Criminal. Hours: 9AM-4PM (EST). *Misdemeanor, Civil Actions Under $15,000, Eviction, Small Claims.*

Note: Criminal records are in Room 115, Civil in Room 107. Small claims(Rm 107) phone is 315-477-2784; their fax is 315-426-8454.

Civil Records: Access: Phone, fax, mail, in person. Both court and visitors may perform in person searches. Search fee: $16.00 per name. Required to search: name, years to search; also helpful: address. Civil cases indexed by defendant, plaintiff. Civil records on computer from 1993, from 1980-93 on fiche or microfilm.

Criminal Records: Access: Phone, fax, mail, in person. Both court and visitors may perform in person searches. Search fee: 7 year search is $16.00 per name. Fee is for certificate of conviction or of disposition. Required to search: name, years to search, DOB; also helpful: offense. Criminal records from 1960 to present are on either computer, dockets or manual books.

General Information: No sealed, expunged, adoption, sex offense, juvenile or mental health records released. SASE required. Turnaround time 1-2 weeks. Copy fee: $.50 per page. $1.00 minimum. Certification fee: $5.00 cert fee is for civil only; criminal records are certified as part of search fee. Fee payee: Syracuse City Court. Only cashiers checks and money orders accepted. Attorney checks only. Prepayment is required.

Surrogate Court Onondaga Courthouse, Rm 209, 401 Montgomery St, Syracuse, NY 13202; 315-671-2100; Fax: 315-671-1162. Hours: 8:30AM-5PM (EST). *Probate.*

Town/Village Courts; *Misdemeanor, Civil Actions Under $3,000, Small Claims:* Geddes Town, 315-468-3613; Baldwinsville Village, 315-635-6355; East Syracuse Village, 315-437-6456; LaFayette Town, 315-677-9350; Spafford Town; Cicero Town, 315-699-8478; Skaneateles Town, 315-685-5880; Fayetteville Village, 315-637-8070; Minoa Village, 315-656-2203; Marcellus Town, 315-673-1773; Tully Town, 315-696-5884; Otisco Town; Elbridge Town, 315-689-7380; Liverpool Village, 315-457-5379; North Syracuse Village, 315-458-4695; Lysander Town, 315-638-1308; Van Buren Town, 315-635-3523; Pompey Town, 315-682-9877; Jordan Village, 315-689-7350; Solvay Village, 315-468-1608; DeWitt Town, 315-446-9180; Onondaga Town, 315-469-1674; Clay Town, 315-652-3800;

Manlius Town, 315-637-3251; Fabius Town, 315-696-8725; Manlius Village, 315-682-7245; Camillus Town, 315-487-7066; Salina Town, 315-457-5379.

Ontario County

Supreme & County Court 27 N Main St, Rm 130, Canandaigua, NY 14424-1447; 716-396-4239; Fax: 716-396-4576. 9AM-5PM (EST). *Felony, Civil.*

Note: Records are maintained at County Clerk's office, 20 Ontario, Municipal Bldg, NY 14424, 716-396-4205.

Civil Records: Access: Phone, fax, mail, in person. Only the court performs in person searches; visitors may not. Search fee: $5.00. Required to search: name, years to search. Civil cases indexed by defendant, plaintiff. Civil records on computer from 1986, prior in books.

Criminal Records: Access: Phone, fax, mail, in person. Only the court performs in person searches; visitors may not. Search fee: $5.00. Required to search: name, years to search, DOB. Criminal records on computer from 1986, prior in books.

General Information: No sealed, youthful offender, sex abuse, sex crime, marriage or incompetence records released. SASE required. Turnaround time 1 week. Copy fee: $.50 per page. Certification fee: $4.00. Fee payee: County Clerk. Personal checks accepted. Prepayment is required.

Canandaigua City Court 2 N Main St, Canandaigua, NY 14424-1448; 716-396-5011; Fax: 716-396-5012. Hours: 8AM-4PM (EST). *Misdemeanor, Civil Actions Under $15,000, Eviction, Small Claims.*

Civil Records: Access: Mail, in person. Only the court performs in person searches; visitors may not. Search fee: $5.00 per two years searched. Required to search: name, years to search. Civil cases indexed by defendant, plaintiff. Civil records on computer from 1986, prior in books from 1960.

Criminal Records: Access: Mail, in person. Only the court performs in person searches; visitors may not. Search fee: $5.00 per two years searched. Required to search: name, years to search, DOB. Criminal records on computer from 1986, prior in books from 1960.

General Information: No sealed, expunged, adoption, sex offense, juvenile or mental health records released. SASE required. Turnaround time 1 week. Copy fee: $.50 per page. Certification fee: No cert fee. Fee payee: Canandaigua City Court. Only cashiers checks and money orders accepted. Prepayment is required.

Geneva City Court 255 Exchange Street, Geneva, NY 14456; 315-789-6560; Fax: 315-781-2802. Hours: 8AM-4PM (EST). *Misdemeanor, Civil Actions Under $15,000, Eviction, Small Claims.*

Civil Records: Access: Phone, mail, in person. Only the court performs in person searches; visitors may not. No search fee. Required to search: name, years to search. Civil cases indexed by plaintiff. Civil records on computer from 1992, prior in books.

Criminal Records: Access: Mail, in person. Only the court performs in person searches; visitors may not. Search fee: None, however there is a $5.00 fee for a certificate of conviction. Required to search: name, years to search, DOB. Criminal records on computer from 1992, prior in books.

General Information: No youthful offender records released. SASE required. Turnaround time 1 month. Copy fee: $1.00 per page. Certification fee: $5.00. Fee payee: City Court. Only cashiers checks and money orders accepted. Prepayment is required.

Surrogate Court 27 N Main St, Canandaigua, NY 14424-1447; 716-396-4055. Hours: 9AM-5PM (EST). *Probate.*

Town/Village Courts; *Misdemeanor, Civil Actions Under $3,000, Small Claims:* Geneva Town, 315-789-3922; Naples Town, 716-374-2500; Bristol Town, 716-229-2400; West Bloomfield Town, 716-624-2914; Seneca Town, 716-526-4780; Shortsville Village, 716-289-3010; East Bloomfield Town, 716-657-7248; Clifton Springs Village, 315-462-3048; Phelps Town, 315-548-2090; Gorham Town, 716-526-6298; Richmond Town; Canadice Town, 716-367-2560; Victor Town, 716-924-5262; Canandaigua Town, 716-394-9040; South Bristol Town, 716-374-6341; Hopewell Town, 716-394-0036; Manchester Town, 716-289-6846; Farmington Town, 315-986-4774.

Orange County

Supreme & County Court 255 Main St, Goshen, NY 10924; 845-291-2690; Civil phone: 845-291-3076; Criminal phone: 845-291-3083; Fax: 845-291-2595. Hours: 9AM-5PM (EST). *Felony, Civil.*

Note: Misdemeanor records are maintained by city, town and village courts.

Civil Records: Access: Mail, in person. Both court and visitors may perform in person searches. Search fee: $2.50 per name; $5.00 per 2 years. Required to search: name, years to search. Civil cases indexed by defendant, plaintiff. Civil records on computer from 1993; prior indexed only by plaintiff.

Criminal Records: Access: Mail, in person. Both court and visitors may perform in person searches. Search fee: $2.50 per name; $5.00 per 2 years. Required to search: name, years to search, DOB. Criminal records on computer since 1993; prior on index Rolodex cards.

General Information: Public Access terminal is available. No sealed records released. SASE required. Turnaround time 2 weeks. Copy fee: $.50 per page. Minimum $1.00. Certification fee: $1.00 per page, $4.00 minimum. Fee payee: County Clerk. Business checks accepted. Prepayment is required.

Middletown City Court 2 James St, Middletown, NY 10940; 845-346-4050; Fax: 845-343-5737. Hours: 8AM-4PM (EST). *Misdemeanor, Civil Actions Under $15,000, Eviction, Small Claims.*

Civil Records: Access: Mail, in person. Only the court performs in person searches; visitors may not. Search fee: $16.00 per name. Prior to 1986 is $5.00 per name per 2 year search. Required to search: name, years to search. Civil cases indexed by defendant, plaintiff. Civil records on computer from 1986, prior on cards.

Criminal Records: Access: Mail, in person. Only the court performs in person searches; visitors may not. Search fee: $16.00 per name. Prior to 1986 $5.00 per name per 2 year search. Required to search: name, years to search, DOB; also helpful: SSN, date of offense. Criminal records on computer to 1986, prior on cards.

General Information: No sealed or youthful offender records released. SASE required. Turnaround time 2-3 weeks. Copy fee: $.50 per page. $1.00 minimum. Certification fee: $5.00. Fee payee: City Court of Middletown. Only cashiers checks and money orders accepted. Prepayment is required.

Newburgh City Court 57 Broadway, Newburgh, NY 12550; 845-565-3208. Hours: 8AM-4PM (EST). *Misdemeanor, Civil Actions Under $15,000, Eviction, Small Claims.*

Civil Records: Access: Mail, in person. Only the court performs in person searches; visitors may not. Search fee: $5.00 per name. $16.00 for computer search. Required to search: name, years to search. Civil cases indexed by defendant. Civil records on computer from 1997, prior in books or on cards.

Criminal Records: Access: Mail, in person. Only the court performs in person searches; visitors may not. Search fee: $5.00 per name. $16.00 for computer

search. Required to search: name, years to search, DOB. Criminal records on computer from 1986.

General Information: No sealed, youthful offender or sex abuse victim records released. SASE required. Turnaround time 3-5 days. Copy fee: $1.00 per page. Certification fee: $5.00. Fee payee: Newburgh City Court. Only cashiers checks and money orders accepted. Prepayment is required.

Port Jervis City Court 14-18 Hammond St, Port Jervis, NY 12771-2495; 845-858-4034; Fax: 845-856-2767. Hours: 9AM-5PM (EST). *Misdemeanor, Civil Actions Under $15,000, Eviction, Small Claims.*

Civil Records: Access: Mail, in person. Both court and visitors may perform in person searches. Search fee: $16.00 per name. Fee is computer search. Required to search: name, years to search. Civil cases indexed by defendant. Civil records on dockets from 1974.

Criminal Records: Access: Mail, in person. Both court and visitors may perform in person searches. Search fee: $16.00 per name. A certified disposition or conviction is $5.00. Required to search: name, years to search, DOB. Criminal records on dockets from 1974.

General Information: No sealed, expunged, adoption, sex offense, juvenile or mental health records released. SASE required. Turnaround time 1 week. Copy fee: $1.00 for first page, $.50 each add'l. Certification fee: $5.00. Fee payee: City Court. Only cashiers checks and money orders accepted. Prepayment is required.

Surrogate Court 30 Park Place, Surrogate's Courthouse, Goshen, NY 10924; 845-291-2193; Fax: 845-291-2300. Hours: 9AM-5PM; Vault closes at 4PM (EST). *Probate.*

Town/Village Courts; *Misdemeanor, Civil Actions Under $3,000, Small Claims:* Warwick Town, 845-986-1128; Maybrook Village, 845-427-2717; Florida Village, 845-651-4940; Tuxedo Park Village, 845-351-4745; Cornwall Town, 845-534-8717; Unionville Village Court; New Windsor Town, 845-563-4682; Warwick Village, 845-986-7044; Greenville Town, 845-856-5064/8890; Wallkill Town, 845-692-5811; Hamptonburgh Town, 845-427-5432; Goshen Village, 845-294-5826; Goshen Town, 845-294-6477; Greenwood Lake Village, 845-477-9218; Newburgh Town, 845-564-0960; Walden Village, 845-778-1632; Crawford Town, 845-744-1435; Blooming Grove Town, 845-496-7631; Minisink Town, 845-726-3700; Wawayanda Town, 845-355-1313; Highlands Town, 845-446-8666; Monroe Town, 845-783-9733; Montgomery Town, 845-457-2620; Montgomery Village, 845-457-9037; Chester Village, 845-469-2388; Tuxedo Town, 845-351-5655; Chester Town, 845-469-9541; Deerpark Town, 845-856-2928; Harriman Village, 845-782-6143; Mount Hope Town, 845-386-5303; Woodbury Town, 845-928-2311; Washingtonville Village, 914-419-9797; Otisville Village, 845-386-1004.

Orleans County

Supreme & County Court Courthouse, Albion, NY 14411-9998; 716-589-5458; Criminal phone: 716-589-5489; Fax: 716-589-1632. Hours: 9AM-5PM (EST). *Felony, Civil, Misdemeaner, Small Claims.*

Civil Records: Access: Mail, in person. Both court and visitors may perform in person searches. Search fee: $5.00 per name. Fee is for 2 year search. Required to search: name, years to search. Civil cases indexed by defendant. Civil records in books.

Criminal Records: Access: Phone, mail, in person. Only the court performs in person searches; visitors may not. No search fee. Required to search: name, years to search, DOB. Criminal records in books.

General Information: No sealed or divorce records released. SASE required. Turnaround time 1 week. Copy fee: $1.00 per page. Certification fee: $4.00 plus $1.00 per page after first 4. Fee payee: County Clerk. Personal checks accepted. Prepayment is required.

Surrogate Court 3 S Main St, Albion, NY 14411; 716-589-4457; Fax: 716-589-0632. Hours: 9AM-5PM (EST). *Probate.*

Town/Village Courts; *Misdemeanor, Civil Actions Under $3,000, Small Claims:* Barre Town, 716-589-5100; Carlton Town, 716-682-3356; Murray Town, 716-638-6727; Shelby Town, 716-798-3120; Yates Town, 716-765-9603; Albion Village, 716-589-2335; Ridgeway Town, 716-798-0730; Albion Town, 716-589-7048; Clarendon Town, 716-638-6371; Medina Village, 716-798-4875; Kendall Town, 716-659-8540; Gaines Town, 716-589-4525.

Oswego County

Supreme & County Court 46 E Bridge St, Oswego, NY 13126; 315-349-3277, 315-349-8616 (Clk); Fax: 315-349-8513. Hours: 9AM-5PM (EST). *Felony, Civil.*

Civil Records: Access: Mail, in person. Both court and visitors may perform in person searches. Search fee: $5.00 per name. Required to search: name, years to search. Civil cases indexed by defendant. Civil records on computer from 1/90, prior in books.

Criminal Records: Access: Mail, in person. Only the court performs in person searches; visitors may not. Search fee: $5.00 per name. Required to search: name, years to search, DOB, signed release. Criminal records on computer from 1976, prior in docket books.

General Information: No sealed, youthful offender or divorce records released. SASE required. Turnaround time 2-3 days. Copy fee: $.50 per page. Certification fee: $4.00. Fee payee: County Clerk. Personal checks accepted. Prepayment is required.

Fulton City Court 141 S 1st St, Fulton, NY 13069; 315-593-8400; Fax: 315-592-3415. Hours: 9AM-4PM; Summer 8:30AM-4PM (EST). *Misdemeanor, Civil Actions Under $15,000, Eviction, Small Claims.*

Civil Records: Access: Mail, in person. Only the court performs in person searches; visitors may not. No search fee. Required to search: name, years to search. Civil cases indexed by defendant. Civil records on dockets from 1991.

Criminal Records: Access: Mail, in person. Only the court performs in person searches; visitors may not. Search fee: $16.00 per name. Fee is for computer search. $5.00 for manual search per 2 years searched. Required to search: name, years to search, DOB. Criminal records on dockets from 1987.

General Information: No sealed, expunged, adoption, sex offense, juvenile or mental health records released. SASE not required. Turnaround time 1 week. Copy fee: $.50 per page. Certification fee: $5.00. Fee payee: Fulton City Court. Only cashiers checks and money orders accepted. Prepayment is required.

Oswego City Court Conway Municipal Building, 20 West Oneida St, Oswego, NY 13126; 315-343-0415; Fax: 315-343-0531. Hours: 8:30AM-5PM (EST). *Misdemeanor, Civil Actions Under $15,000, Eviction, Small Claims.*

Civil Records: Access: Mail, in person. Only the court performs in person searches; visitors may not. No search fee. Required to search: name, years to search. Civil cases indexed by defendant. Civil records on computer from 1987, prior in books.

Criminal Records: Access: Mail, in person. Only the court performs in person searches; visitors may not. No search fee. Required to search: name, years to search, DOB. Criminal records on computer from 1987, prior in books.

General Information: No sealed or youthful offender records released. SASE required. Turnaround time 3-4 days. Copy fee: $.50 per page. Certification fee: $5.00 plus $.50 per page after first. Fee payee: Oswego City

Court. Only cashiers checks and money orders accepted. Prepayment is required.

Surrogate Court Courthouse, 25 E Oneida St, Oswego, NY 13126; 315-349-3295. Hours: 9AM-5PM Sept-May; 8:30AM-3:30 PM June-Aug (EST). *Probate.*

Town/Village Courts; *Misdemeanor, Civil Actions Under $3,000, Small Claims:* Palermo Town, 315-593-2333; Sandy Creek Town, 315-387-5456; Pulaski Village, 315-298-2526; Orwell Town, 315-298-5563; Oswego Town, 315-343-7249; Boylston Town; Parish Town, 315-625-7362; Granby Town, 315-598-2958; Amboy Town, 315-964-1165; Constantia Town, 315-623-7713; Redfield Town, 315-599-7786; Cleveland Village, 315-675-8611; West Monroe Town, 315-668-8314; Mexico Town, 315-963-3785; New Haven Town, 315-963-3900; Scriba Town, 315-343-3250; Albion Town, 315-298-6325; Volney Town, 315-598-7082; Hannibal Town, 315-564-6037; Williamstown Town; Minetto Town, 315-343-2393; Richland Town, 315-298-5174; Schroeppel Town, 315-695-6177; Hastings Town, 315-676-4317.

Otsego County

Supreme & County Court 197 Main St, Cooperstown, NY 13326; 607-547-4364; Fax: 607-547-7567. Hours: 9AM-5PM (EST). *Felony, Civil.*

Note: Misdemeanor records are maintained by city, town and village courts.

Civil Records: Access: Mail, in person. Both court and visitors may perform in person searches. Search fee: $5.00 per name. Required to search: name, years to search. Civil cases indexed by defendant. Civil records on computer back to 1997; prior in books.

Criminal Records: Access: Mail, in person. Both court and visitors may perform in person searches. Search fee: $5.00 per name. Required to search: name, years to search, address, DOB. Criminal records on computer back to 1997; prior in books.

General Information: Public Access terminal is available. No sealed, expunged, adoption, sex offense, juvenile or mental health records released. SASE required. Turnaround time 1-2 days. Copy fee: $1.00 per page. Certification fee: $4.00. Fee payee: County Clerk. Business checks accepted. Prepayment is required.

Oneonta City Court 81 Main St, Oneonta, NY 13820; 607-432-4480; Fax: 607-432-2328. Hours: 8AM-4PM (EST). *Misdemeanor, Civil Actions Under $15,000, Eviction, Small Claims.*

Civil Records: Access: Mail, in person. Only the court performs in person searches; visitors may not. Search fee: $16.00 per name. Will do computer-only search for $5.00 per name. Required to search: name, years to search. Civil cases indexed by defendant. Civil records on computer from 1987, prior in books.

Criminal Records: Access: Mail, in person. Only the court performs in person searches; visitors may not. Search fee: $16.00 per name. Will do computer-only search for $5.00 per name. Required to search: name, years to search, DOB. Criminal records on computer from 1987, prior in books.

General Information: No sealed or youthful offender records released. SASE required. Turnaround time 1 day. Copy fee: $.50 per page. $1.00 minimum. Certification fee: $5.00. Fee payee: Oneonta City Court. Only cashiers checks and money orders accepted. Prefer certified funds. Prepayment is required.

Surrogate Court Surrogate's Office, 197 Main St, Cooperstown, NY 13326; 607-547-4338; Fax: 607-547-7566. Hours: 9AM-5PM (EST). *Probate.*

Town/Village Courts; *Misdemeanor, Civil Actions Under $3,000, Small Claims:* Cherry Valley Village,

607-264-3791; Morris Village, 607-263-5944; Otego Town, 607-988-2698; Cherry Valley Town, 607-264-8491; Otsego Town, 607-547-5689; Worcester Town, 607-397-8182; Unadilla Town, 607-369-7458; Edmeston Town, 607-965-9823; Hartwick Town, 607-293-6614; Roseboom Town, 607-264-3293; Plainfield Town; Milford Town, 607-286-7773; Laurens Village Court; Laurens Town, 607-433-2816; Middlefield Town, 607-547-8800; Pittsfield Town, 607-847-6524; Morris Town, 607-263-5944; Cooperstown Village, 607-547-9597; Burlington Town; Decatur Town, 607-397-9116; Richfield Springs Village Court; Springfield Town, 315-858-1508; Exeter Town, 315-858-0937; New Lisbon Town, 607-965-8627; Richfield Town, 315-858-2830; Oneonta Town, 607-432-0124; Maryland Town, 607-738-9495; Westford Town, 607-397-9210; Butternuts Town, 607-783-2758.

Putnam County

Supreme & County Court 40 Gleneida Ave, Carmel, NY 10512; 845-225-3641 X307; Fax: 845-228-0231. Hours: 9AM-5PM (EST). *Felony, Civil.*

www.putnamcountyny.com

Civil Records: Access: Mail, in person. Both court and visitors may perform in person searches. Search fee: $5.00 per name. Fee is per 2 years searched. Required to search: name, years to search. Civil cases indexed by defendant, plaintiff. Civil records on computer from 4/93, prior in books.

Criminal Records: Access: Mail, in person. Both court and visitors may perform in person searches. Search fee: $5.00 per name. Fee is per 2 years searched. Required to search: name, years to search, DOB. Criminal records computerized since 1983.

General Information: Public Access terminal is available. No sealed or youthful offender records released. SASE required. Turnaround time 2 days. Copy fee: $1.00 per page. Certification fee: $4.00. Fee payee: County Clerk. Personal checks accepted. Prepayment is required.

Surrogate Court 44 Gleneida Ave, Carmel, NY 10512; 845-225-3641 X295; Fax: 845-228-5761. Hours: 9AM-5PM (EST). *Probate.*

Town/Village Courts; *Misdemeanor, Civil Actions Under $3,000, Small Claims:* Cold Spring Village, 845-265-9070; Southeast Town, 845-279-8939; Kent Town, 845-225-1606; Philipstown Town, 845-265-2951; Nelsonville Village Court; Brewster Village, 845-279-4020; Putnam Valley Town, 845-526-3050; Carmel Town, 845-628-1500; Patterson Town, 845-878-6500.

Queens County

Supreme Court - Civil Division 88-11 Sutphin Blvd, Jamaica, NY 11435; 718-520-3136; Fax: 718-520-4731. Hours: 9AM-5PM, no cashier transactions after 4:45PM (EST). *Civil Actions Over $25,000.*

Civil Records: Access: Mail, in person. Both court and visitors may perform in person searches. Search fee: $10.00 per name. Fee is for first two years. Add $5.00 per additional 2 years. Required to search: name, years to search, address. Civil cases indexed by plaintiff. Civil records on computer from 1992, prior in books.

General Information: No marriage or incompetence records released. Identification required to review confidential matrimonial case records. SASE required. Turnaround time 1 week. Certification fee: $8.00. Fee payee: County Clerk. Only cashiers checks and money orders accepted. Prepayment is required.

Supreme Court - Criminal Division 125-01 Queens Blvd, Kew Gardens, NY 11415; 718-520-3494. Hours: 9:30AM-4:30PM (EST). *Felony, Misdemeanor.*

Criminal Records: Access: Mail, in person. Only the court performs in person searches; visitors may not. Search fee: $16.00 per name. Required to search: name, years to search, SSN, signed release. Criminal records on computer from 1990, prior in books.

General Information: No sealed or youthful offender records released. SASE required. Turnaround time 1-2 days. Copy fee: $.15 per page. Certification fee: $4.00. Based on $1.00 per page with 4 page minimum. Fee payee: County Clerk. Personal checks accepted. Prepayment is required.

Civil Court of the City of New York - Queens Branch 89-17 Sutphin Blvd, Jamaica, NY 11435; 718-262-7100. Hours: 9AM-5PM (EST). *Civil Actions Under $25,000, Eviction, Small Claims.*

Civil Records: Access: In person only. Visitors must perform in person searches for themselves. No search fee. Required to search: name, years to search. Civil cases indexed by plaintiff. Civil records on computer from 1996, prior in books.

General Information: Public Access terminal is available. (Civil only.) No sealed, youthful offender or sex victim records released. SASE required. Turnaround time 3-5 days; 7-10 for older records. Copy fee: $.25 per page. Certification fee: $5.00. Fee payee: Civil Court. Only cashiers checks and money orders accepted. Prepayment is required.

Surrogate Court 88-11 Sutphin Blvd, Jamaica, NY 11435; 718-520-3132. Hours: 9AM-5PM (EST). *Probate.*

Rensselaer County

Supreme & County Court 105 3rd Street, Troy, NY 12180; 518-270-4080; Fax: 518-271-7998. Hours: 9AM-5PM (EST). *Felony, Civil.*

www.rensco.com

Civil Records: Access: In person only. Visitors must perform in person searches for themselves. No search fee. Required to search: name, years to search. Civil cases indexed by plaintiff pre-1996; by defendant & plaintiff after 1996. Civil records on computer back to 1990s; prior in books to 1970s.

Criminal Records: Access: Mail, in person. Only the court performs in person searches; visitors may not. Search fee: $5.00 per name. Fee is per 2 years searched. Required to search: name, years to search, DOB. Criminal records on computer back to 1990s; prior in books to 1970s.

General Information: No sealed, open/pending cases, youthful offender records released. SASE required. Turnaround time 1 week. Copy fee: $1.00 per page. Certification fee: $4.00 plus $.50 per page after first 8. Fee payee: County Clerk. Personal checks accepted. Prepayment is required.

Rensselaer City Court City Hall, Rensselaer, NY 12144; 518-462-6751; Fax: 518-462-3307. Hours: 8AM-3:30PM (EST). *Misdemeanor, Civil Actions Under $15,000, Eviction, Small Claims.*

Civil Records: Access: In person only. Visitors must perform in person searches for themselves. No search fee. Required to search: name, years to search. Civil cases indexed by defendant. Civil records in books.

Criminal Records: Access: In person only. Visitors must perform in person searches for themselves. No search fee. Required to search: name, years to search, DOB, signed release. Criminal records in books. Court will only confirm convictions.

General Information: No sealed, expunged, adoption, sex offense, juvenile or mental health records released.

Copy fee: $.50 per page. Certification fee: $5.00. Fee payee: Rensselaer City Court. Only cashiers checks and money orders accepted. Prepayment is required.

Troy City Court 51 State St, 2nd Fl, Troy, NY 12180; 518-271-1602; Fax: 518-274-2816. Hours: 9AM-3:30PM (EST). *Misdemeanor.*

Criminal Records: Access: Mail, in person. Only the court performs in person searches; visitors may not. Search fee: $16.00 per name. Required to search: name, years to search, DOB, aliases, offense. Criminal records on computer from 1989, prior in books.
General Information: No sealed records released. SASE required. Turnaround time 1 week. No copy fee. Certification fee: $5.00. Fee payee: City Court. Personal checks accepted.

Surrogate Court County Courthouse, 72 Second St, Troy, NY 12180; 518-270-3724. Hours: 9AM-5PM (EST). *Probate.*

Town Courts; *Misdemeanor, Civil Actions Under $3,000, Small Claims:* East Greenbush Town, 518-477-5412; Petersburg Town, 518-658-3777; Nassau Village, 518-766-3044; Berlin Town, 518-650-2020; Poestenkill Town, 518-283-5100; Brunswick Town, 518-279-3461; Sand Lake Town, 518-674-3033; Schaghticoke Town, 518-753-6915; Schodack Town, 518-477-9390; Pittstown Town; North Greenbush Town; Stephentown Town, 518-733-5636; Castleton-on-Hudson Village, 518-732-2211; Hoosick Town, 518-686-4571; Hoosick Falls Village, 518-686-7900; Nassau Town, 518-766-2813; Grafton Town, 518-279-3565.

Richmond County

Supreme Court - Civil Division 130 Stuyvesant Pl, Staten Island, NY 10301; 718-390-5389 Court Desk; Civil phone: 718-390-5352. Hours: 9AM-5PM (EST). *Civil Actions Over $25,000.*

Civil Records: Access: In person only. Visitors must perform in person searches for themselves. No search fee. Required to search: name, years to search. Civil cases indexed by plaintiff. Civil records go back to 1990; on computer back to 1993.
General Information: Public Access terminal is available. No matrimonial records released. Fax notes: Will not fax results. Copy fee: $.25. Certification fee: $8.00. Fee payee: Richmond County Clerk. Only cashiers checks and money orders accepted. Prepayment is required.

Supreme Court - Criminal Division 18 Richmond Terrace, Rm 110, Staten Island, NY 10301; 718-390-5280. Hours: 9AM-5PM, Closed 1-2PM (EST). *Felony, Misdemeanors.*

Criminal Records: Access: In person only. Visitors must perform in person searches for themselves. Search fee: Court does not perform searches. Electronic searches referred to 202-428-2940, $16.00 per county. Required to search: name, years to search, DOB. Criminal records on computer back to 1975, prior archived.
General Information: No sealed or youthful offender records released. SASE required. Turnaround time 1-2 days. Certification fee: $10.00. Fee payee: NY State Office of Court Administration. Only cashiers checks and money orders accepted. Prepayment is required.

Civil Court of the City of New York - Richmond Branch 927 Castleton Ave, Staten Island, NY 10310; 718-390-5417-5419. Hours: 9AM-4:30PM (EST). *Civil Actions Under $25,000, Eviction, Small Claims.*

Civil Records: Access: Mail, in person. Both court and visitors may perform in person searches. No search fee. Required to search: name. Civil cases indexed by plaintiff. Civil records on computer since 1999; prior on books.

General Information: Public Access terminal is available. No sealed records released. SASE required. Turnaround time 3-5 days. Copy fee: $.25 per page. Certification fee: $5.00. Fee payee: Clerk Civil Court. Only cashiers checks and money orders accepted. Prepayment is required.

Surrogate Court 18 Richmond Terrace, Rm 201, Staten Island, NY 10301; 718-390-5400. Hours: 9AM-5PM (EST). *Probate.*

Rockland County

Supreme & County Court 27 New Hempstead Rd, New City, NY 10956; 845-638-5070; Fax: 845-638-5647. Hours: 7AM-6PM (EST). *Felony, Civil.*

www.rocklandcountyclerk.com

Note: Court may have a misdemeanor record if you provide the index number. Misdemeanor records are maintained by city, town and village courts.

Civil Records: Access: Mail, online, in person. Both court and visitors may perform in person searches. Search fee: $5.00 per name. Fee is per each 2 years searched. Required to search: name, years to search. Civil cases indexed by defendant, plaintiff. Civil records on computer from 1982. Online access is the county clerk's expanding list of court records is available free at the web site. Click on "Index to all records." System includes criminal index since 1982 plus civil judgments, real estate records, tax warrants. Call Paul Pipearto at 845-638-5221 for more information.
Criminal Records: Access: Mail, online, in person. Both court and visitors may perform in person searches. Search fee: $5.00 per name. Fee is per each 2 years searched. Required to search: name, years to search. Criminal records on computer from 1982. Online access to criminal records is the same as civil.
General Information: Public Access terminal is available. No retention records released. SASE required. Turnaround time 10 days. Fax notes: Fee to fax results is $1.00 per page. Copy fee: $1.00 per page. Certification fee: $4.00. Fee payee: County Clerk. Personal checks accepted. Prepayment is required.

Stony Point 73 Central Dr, Stony Point, NY 10980; 845-786-2506. *Misdemeanor, Civil Actions Under $3,000, Small Claims.*

Civil Records: Access: In person only. Both court and visitors may perform in person searches. No search fee. Required to search: name.
Criminal Records: Access: In person only. Both court and visitors may perform in person searches. No search fee. Required to search: name.

Surrogate Court 18 New Hempstead Rd, New City, NY 10956; 845-638-5330; Fax: 845-638-5632. Hours: 9AM-5PM (EST). *Probate.*

Town/Village Courts; *Misdemeanor, Civil Actions Under $3,000, Small Claims:* Orangetown Town, 845-359-5100; New Hempstead Village, 845-354-8101; Chestnut Ridge Village, 845-425-3108; Clarkstown Town, 845-639-2165; Ramapo Town, 845-357-5100; Spring Valley Village, 845-352-1100; Piermont Village, 845-359-0345; Sloatsburg Village, 845-753-2727; South Nyack Village, 845-358-5078; New Square Village Court; Grand View-on-Hudson Village, 845-358-2919; Suffern Village, 845-357-6424; Wesley Hills Village, 845-354-0404; Haverstraw Town, 845-354-7800; Upper Nyack Village, 845-358-0084; Stony Point, 845-786-2506; Haverstraw Village, 914-490-0303; Hillburn Village, 845-357-2036; Nyack Village, 845-358-4464; West Haverstraw Village.

Saratoga County

Supreme & County Court 40 McMaster St, Ballston Spa, NY 12020; 518-885-2213; Fax: 518-884-4726. Hours: 9AM-5PM (EST). *Felony, Civil.*

Note: Misdemeanor records are maintained by city, town and village courts.

Civil Records: Access: Mail, in person. Both court and visitors may perform in person searches. Search fee: $5.00 per name. Fee is per 2 years searched. Required to search: name, years to search; also helpful: address. Civil cases indexed by defendant, plaintiff. Civil records on computer from 03/88, prior in books.
Criminal Records: Access: Mail, in person. Both court and visitors may perform in person searches. Search fee: $16.00 per name. Fee is per 10 years searched. Required to search: name, years to search, DOB; also helpful: address. Criminal records not computerized here, on books.
General Information: Public Access terminal is available. No youthful offender or divorce records released. SASE required. Turnaround time 3-4 days. Copy fee: $1.00 per page. Certification fee: $4.00 per page, $4.00 minimum. Fee payee: County Clerk. Personal checks accepted. Prepayment is required.

Mechanicville City Court 36 N Main St, Mechanicville, NY 12118; 518-664-9876; Fax: 518-664-8606. Hours: 8AM-4PM (EST). *Misdemeanor, Civil Actions Under $15,000, Eviction, Small Claims.*

Civil Records: Access: Mail, in person. Both court and visitors may perform in person searches. Search fee: $16.00 per name. Required to search: name, years to search. Civil cases indexed by defendant. Civil records on computer since 1/97; prior records on cards.
Criminal Records: Access: Mail, in person. Only the court performs in person searches; visitors may not. Search fee: Manual search: $5.00 per 2 year period. Computer search: $16.00 per name. Required to search: name, years to search, DOB. Criminal records on computer from 9/93.
General Information: No sealed, expunged, adoption, sex offense, juvenile or mental health records released. SASE required. Turnaround time 1 day. Copy fee: $.50 per page; $1.00 minimum. Certification fee: $5.00. Fee payee: City Court. Personal checks accepted. Prepayment is required.

Saratoga Springs City Court City Hall, 474 Broadway, Saratoga Springs, NY 12866; 518-587-3550 x600. Hours: 9AM-4PM (EST). *Misdemeanor, Civil Actions Under $15,000, Eviction, Small Claims.*

Civil Records: Access: Mail, in person. Only the court performs in person searches; visitors may not. Search fee: $5.00 per name per 2 years or $16.00 computer search back to 10/94. Required to search: name, years to search. Civil cases indexed by defendant. Civil records on computer back to 10/94; prior records on index cards.
Criminal Records: Access: Mail, in person. Only the court performs in person searches; visitors may not. Search fee: $16.00 per name. For search prior to 1994 fee is $5.00 per 2 years searched. Required to search: name, years to search, DOB, notarized release. Criminal records on computer back to 08/93.
General Information: Sealed files not released. SASE required. Turnaround time 5-10 days. Certification fee: $5.00. Fee payee: City Court. Only cashiers checks and money orders accepted. Prepayment is required.

Surrogate Court 30 McMaster St, Bldg 3, Ballston Spa, NY 12020; 518-884-4722. Hours: 9AM-5PM (EST). *Probate.*

Town/Village Courts; *Misdemeanor, Civil Actions Under $3,000, Small Claims:* Day Town, 518-696-3789; Ballston Town, 518-885-8559; Galway Village, 518-882-6070; Milton Town, 518-885-9267; Clifton

Park Town, 518-371-6668; Ballston Spa Village Court; Edinburg Town, 518-863-2034; Galway Town, 518-882-6070; Moreau Town, 518-793-3188; Waterford Town, 518-237-6788; Providence Town; Hadley Town, 518-696-4379; Stillwater Village, 518-664-5392; Saratoga Town, 518-695-3644; Stillwater Town; Greenfield Town, 518-893-7432; Wilton Town, 518-587-1980; Northumberland Town, 518-792-9179; Halfmoon Town, 518-371-1592; Malta Town, 518-899-2687; Corinth Town, 518-654-6991; Charlton Town, 518-384-0152

Schenectady County

Supreme & County Court 612 State St, Schenectady, NY 12305; 518-388-4322; Civil phone: 518-388-4220; Criminal phone: 518-388-4323; Fax: 518-388-4520. Hours: 9AM-5PM (EST). *Felony, Civil.*

Civil Records: Access: Mail, in person. Only the court performs in person searches; visitors may not. Search fee: $5.00 per name. Fee is per 2 years searched. Required to search: name, years to search. Civil cases indexed by plaintiff. Civil records on computer from 1989, prior on index cards.

Criminal Records: Access: Mail, in person. Both court and visitors may perform in person searches. Search fee: Automated computer search $16.00 per name. Required to search: name, years to search, DOB. Criminal records on computer from 1989, prior on index cards. Notarized, signed release required to access sealed records.

General Information: No sealed, youthful offenders, infant compromise or divorce records released. SASE required. Turnaround time 4 days. Copy fee: $.50 per page. Certification fee: $4.00. Fee payee: County Clerk. Personal checks accepted. Prepayment is required.

Schenectady City Court Jay St, City Hall, Schenectady, NY 12305; Civil phone: 518-382-5077; Criminal phone: 518-382-5239; Fax: 518-382-5080/5241. Hours: 8AM-4PM (EST). *Misdemeanor, Civil Actions Under $15,000, Eviction, Small Claims.*

Civil Records: Access: Mail, in person. Only the court performs in person searches; visitors may not. Search fee: $5.00 per name. Fee is for 5 year search. $16.00 for computer search. Required to search: name, years to search. Civil cases indexed by defendant. Civil records on computer from 1981, prior in books.

Criminal Records: Access: Fax, mail, in person. Only the court performs in person searches; visitors may not. Search fee: $5.00 per name. Fee is for 5 year search. $16.00 for computer search. Required to search: name, years to search, DOB, signed release. Criminal records on computer from 1981, prior in books.

General Information: No sealed or youthful offender records released. SASE required. Turnaround time 2 weeks. Copy fee: $.50 per page. Certification fee: Included in search fee. Fee payee: City Court. Only cashiers checks and money orders accepted. Prepayment is required.

Surrogate Court 612 State St, Schenectady, NY 12305; 518-388-4293. 9AM-5PM (EST). *Probate.*

Town/Village Courts; *Misdemeanor, Civil Actions Under $3,000, Small Claims:* Scotia Village, 518-374-2099; Rotterdam Town, 518-356-2038; Princetown Town, 518-864-5256; Glenville Town, 518-382-3851; Niskayuna Town, 518-386-4560; Duanesburg Town, 518-895-8922.

Schoharie County

Supreme & County Court PO Box 669, Schoharie, NY 12157; 518-295-8316; Fax: 518-295-8338. Hours: 8:30AM-5PM (EST). *Felony, Civil, Misdemeanor, Eviction, Small Claims.*

Civil Records: Access: Fax, mail, in person. Both court and visitors may perform in person searches. Search

fee: $5.00 per name. Fee is per 2 years searched. Required to search: name, years to search. Civil cases indexed by defendant, plaintiff. Civil records on computer from 1994, prior in books.

Criminal Records: Access: Fax, mail, in person. Both court and visitors may perform in person searches. Search fee: $5.00 per name. Fee is per 2 years searched. Required to search: name, years to search. Criminal records in books.

General Information: No sealed criminal or divorce records released. SASE required. Turnaround time same day. Fax notes: $1.00 per page unless toll free line used. Copy fee: $.50 per page. Certification fee: $4.00. Fee payee: County Clerk. Personal checks accepted. Prepayment is required.

Surrogate Court Courthouse, 300 Main St, Schoharie, NY 12157; 518-295-8387. Hours: 9AM-5PM (EST). *Probate.*

Town/Village Courts; *Misdemeanor, Civil Actions Under $3,000, Small Claims:* Blenheim Town, 518-827-6157; Richmondville Town, 518-294-2851; Schoharie Town; Schoharie Village Court; Sharon Town, 518-284-3419; Cobleskill Town, 518-234-7886; Summit Town; Conesville Town, 607-588-7211; Wright Town, 518-872-1931; Cobleskill Village, 518-234-9886; Seward Town; Gilboa Town, 607-588-7526; Esperance Town, 518-875-6109; Jefferson Town, 607-652-2109; Carlisle Town, 518-868-4167; Middleburgh Town, 518-827-5100; Middleburgh Village, 518-827-5143; Broome Town, 518-827-5074; Fulton Town, 518-827-6300.

Schuyler County

Supreme & County Court Courthouse, Watkins Glen, NY 14891; Civil phone: 607-535-8133; Criminal phone: 607-535-7760; Fax: 607-535-8130. Hours: 9AM-5PM (EST). *Felony, Civil, Misdemeanor, Eviction, Small Claims.*

Civil Records: Access: Mail, in person. Both court and visitors may perform in person searches. Search fee: $5.00 per name. Required to search: name, years to search. Civil cases indexed by defendant. Civil records are indexed in books.

Criminal Records: Access: Mail, in person. Only the court performs in person searches; visitors may not. Search fee: $5.00 per name. Required to search: name, years to search, DOB. Criminal records are indexed in books.

General Information: No sealed or youthful offender records released. SASE required. Turnaround time 2-3 days. Copy fee: $.50 per page. Certification fee: $4.00. Fee payee: County Clerk. Personal checks accepted. Prepayment is required.

Surrogate Court County Courthouse, 105 Ninth St, Watkins Glen, NY 14891; 607-535-7144. Hours: 9AM-5PM (EST). *Probate.*

Town/Village Courts; *Misdemeanor, Civil Actions Under $3,000, Small Claims:* Montour Falls Village, 607-535-7362; Dix Town, 607-535-7973; Tyrone Town; Watkins Glen Village, 607-535-9717; Hector Town, 607-546-5286; Odessa Village Court; Montour Town, 607-535-7362; Orange Town; Reading Town; Catharine Town; Cayuta Town.

Seneca County

Supreme & County Court 1 DiPronio Dr, Waterloo, NY 13165-1396; 315-539-1771; Fax: 315-539-3789. Hours: 8:30AM-5PM (EST). *Felony, Civil.*

Note: Misdemeanor records are maintained by city, town and village courts.

Civil Records: Access: Fax, mail, in person. Both court and visitors may perform in person searches. Search fee: $10.00 per name. Required to search: name, years to search. Civil cases indexed by defendant. Civil

records on computer since March 1, 1997; prior records in books.

Criminal Records: Access: Fax, mail, in person. Both court and visitors may perform in person searches. Search fee: $10.00 per name. Required to search: name, years to search, signed release. Criminal records on computer since March 1, 1997; prior records in books.

General Information: Public Access terminal is available. No divorce records released. SASE required. Turnaround time 1 week. No copy fee. Certification fee: $4.00. Fee payee: Seneca County Clerk. Personal checks accepted. Prepayment is required.

Surrogate Court 48 W Williams St, Waterloo, NY 13165; 315-539-7531; Fax: 315-539-7929. Hours: 9AM-5PM (EST). *Probate.*

Town/Village Courts; *Misdemeanor, Civil Actions Under $3,000, Small Claims:* Waterloo Town, 315-539-3213; Covert Town, 607-387-6802; Junius Town; Seneca Falls Village, 315-568-2343; Seneca Falls Town; Waterloo Village, 315-539-2512; Varick Town; Fayette Town; Ovid Town, 607-869-5560; Lodi Town; Tyre Town; Romulus Town, 607-869-9650.

St. Lawrence County

Supreme & County Court 48 Court St, Canton, NY 13617-1199; 315-379-2237; Fax: 315-379-2302. Hours: 8:30AM-4:30PM (Thurs. til 7PM) (EST). *Felony, Civil.*

Note: Misdemeanor records are maintained by city, town and village courts.

Civil Records: Access: Fax, mail, in person. Both court and visitors may perform in person searches. Search fee: $5.00 per name. Required to search: name, years to search. Civil cases indexed by defendant, plaintiff. Civil records on computer since 1990, prior in books.

Criminal Records: Access: Fax, mail, in person. Both court and visitors may perform in person searches. Search fee: $5.00 per name. Required to search: name, years to search, DOB. Criminal records on computer since 1985, prior in books.

General Information: Public Access terminal is available. No sealed or divorce records released. SASE required. Turnaround time 2-3 days. Fax notes: $4.00 per document. No fee for 800 numbers. Copy fee: $.50 per page. Certification fee: $4.00. Fee payee: County Clerk. Personal checks accepted.

Ogdensburg City Court 330 Ford St, Ogdensburg, NY 13669; 315-393-3941; Fax: 315-393-6839. Hours: 8AM-4PM (EST). *Misdemeanor, Civil Actions Under $15,000, Eviction, Small Claims.*

Civil Records: Access: Mail, in person. Only the court performs in person searches; visitors may not. No search fee. Required to search: name, years to search. Civil cases indexed by defendant. Civil records on computer since 1995; prior records in books.

Criminal Records: Access: Mail, in person. Only the court performs in person searches; visitors may not. Search fee: $16.00 for computer search, manual search is $5.00 for every 2 years. Required to search: name, years to search, DOB. Criminal records on computer from 1994.

General Information: No youthful offender records released. SASE required. Turnaround time 1 week. Certification fee: $5.00. Fee payee: City Court. Business checks accepted. Prepayment is required.

Surrogate Court 48 Court St, Surrogate Bldg, Canton, NY 13617; 315-379-2217/9427. Hours: 9AM-5PM Sept-June; 8AM-4PM July-Aug (EST). *Probate.*

Town/Village Courts; *Misdemeanor, Civil Actions Under $3,000, Small Claims:* Canton Village, 315-379-9844; Waddington Town, 315-388-5629; Canton Town, 315-379-9844; Clare Town, 315-386-1970; Colton Town; Stockholm Town, 315-389-5171; Hopkinton Town, 315-328-4187; Hermon Town, 315-397-3606; Lawrence Town, 315-389-4487; DePeyster Town, 315-344-7259; Fowler Town, 315-287-0045; Parishville Town, 315-265-2131; Piercefield Town, 518-359-9660; Brasher Town, 315-769-5374; Pierrepont Town, 315-386-8311; Pitcairn Town, 315-543-2111; Norfolk Town, 315-384-4721; Morristown Town, 315-375-6510; Potsdam Town, 315-265-4318; Potsdam Village, 315-265-5890; Edwards Town, 315-562-8113; Clifton Town, 315-848-2915; Massena Village, 315-769-5431; Hammond Town, 315-324-5321; DeKalb Town; Rossie Town; Massena Town, 315-769-5431; Madrid Town, 315-322-5760; Macomb Town; Russell Town, 315-347-2162; Lisbon Town, 315-393-0489; Louisville Town, 315-764-1424; Fine Town; Gouverneur Town, 315-287-4623; Gouverneur Village, 315-287-0850; Oswegatchie Town, 315-344-2400.

Steuben County

Supreme & County Court 3 E Pulteney Square, Bath, NY 14810; 607-776-9631. Hours: 9AM-5PM (EST). *Felony, Civil.*

Note: Misdemeanor records are maintained by city, town and village courts.

Civil Records: Access: Phone, mail, in person. Both court and visitors may perform in person searches. No search fee. Required to search: name, years to search. Civil cases indexed by defendant. Civil records on computer to 1984, in book from 1931, prior archived.

Criminal Records: Access: Phone, mail, in person. Only the court performs in person searches; visitors may not. No search fee. Required to search: name, years to search, DOB, SSN, signed release. Criminal records on computer from 1984, in book from 1931, prior archived.

General Information: No sealed, expunged, adoption, sex offense, juvenile or mental health records released. SASE required. Turnaround time 1 day. Copy fee: $.25 per page. Certification fee: $4.00. Fee payee: County Clerk. Personal checks accepted. Prepayment is required.

Corning City Court 12 Civic Center Plaza, Corning, NY 14830-2884; 607-936-4111; Fax: 607-936-0519. Hours: 8AM-4PM (EST). *Misdemeanor, Civil Actions Under $15,000, Eviction, Small Claims.*

Civil Records: Access: Mail, in person. Only the court performs in person searches; visitors may not. Search fee: $16.00 for 7 year search. Required to search: name, years to search. Civil cases indexed by defendant. Civil records on computer from 1986, prior in books. Request must be in writing.

Criminal Records: Access: Mail, in person. Only the court performs in person searches; visitors may not. Search fee: $16.00 per 7 year search. Required to search: name, years to search, DOB; also helpful: date of offense. Criminal records on computer from 1986, prior in books. Request must be in writing.

General Information: No sealed or youthful offender records released. SASE required. Turnaround time 1 week. Copy fee: $5.00 per document. Certification fee: $5.00. Fee payee: Corning City Court. Business checks accepted. Prepayment is required.

Hornell City Court PO Box 627 (82 Main St.), Hornell, NY 14843-0627; 607-324-7531; Fax: 607-324-6325. Hours: 8AM-3:30PM (EST). *Misdemeanor, Civil Actions Under $15,000, Eviction, Small Claims.*

Civil Records: Access: Fax, mail, in person. Only the court performs in person searches; visitors may not. Search fee: $16.00 for 6-year search. Required to search: name, years to search. Civil cases indexed by defendant, plaintiff. Civil records on computer from 1985, prior in books, folders and index cards.

Criminal Records: Access: Fax, mail, in person. Only the court performs in person searches; visitors may not. Search fee: $16.00 for 6-year search. Required to search: name, years to search, DOB; also helpful: SSN. Criminal records on computer from 1985, prior in books, folders and index cards.

General Information: No sealed or sexual offense records released. SASE required. Turnaround time 2 days. Copy fee: $.50 per page. Certification fee: $5.00. Fee payee: Hornell City Court. Only cashiers checks and money orders accepted. Prepayment is required.

Surrogate Court 13 E Pulteney Square, Bath, NY 14810-1598; 607-776-7126. Hours: 9AM-5PM (EST). *Probate.*

Town/Village Courts; *Misdemeanor, Civil Actions Under $3,000, Small Claims:* Addison Town, 607-359-3615; Caton Town, 607-524-6303; Arkport Village, 607-295-8207; Canisteo Village, 607-698-4378; Canisteo Town; Cameron Town; Avoca Town, 607-566-2093; Avoca Village, 607-566-2093; Bath Town, 607-776-3192; Bath Village, 607-776-4666; Bradford Town, 607-583-4270; Campbell Town, 607-527-8244; Prattsburgh Town, 607-522-3761; Tuscarora Town, 607-359-2360; Troupsburg Town, 607-525-6403; Erwin Town, 607-936-3122; Thurston Town, 607-776-9448; Fremont Town, 607-324-7786; Rathbone Town; Urbana Town, 607-569-3369; Pulteney Town, 607-868-3913; Greenwood Town, 607-225-4558; Hartsville Town, 607-698-2672; Hornby Town, 607-962-0683; Hornellsville Town, 607-295-7768; Howard Town, 607-566-2554; Jasper Town, 607-792-3338; Cohocton Town, 607-384-5252; Lindley Town, 607-523-8816; Hammondsport Village Court; Wayland Village, 716-728-5156; Dansville Town, 607-295-7223; West Union Town; Cohocton Village Court; Wayland Town, 716-728-5660; Corning Town, 607-936-9062; Wayne Town, 607-292-3450; Woodhull Town, 607-458-5178; Wheeler Town.

Suffolk County

Supreme & County Court 310 Centre Dr, Attn: Court Actions, Riverhead, NY 11901; 631-852-3793. Hours: 9AM-5PM (EST). *Felony, Civil.*

www.co.suffolk.ny.us/clerk

Civil Records: Access: Mail, in person. Both court and visitors may perform in person searches. Search fee: $5.00 per name. Fee is per 2 years searched. Required to search: name, years to search. Civil cases indexed by defendant, plaintiff. Civil records on computer back to 04/84; prior in books.

Criminal Records: Access: Mail, in person. Both court and visitors may perform in person searches. Search fee: $5.00 per name. Fee is per 2 years searched prior to 1985; $16.00 for 1985 to present. Required to search: name, years to search, DOB. Criminal records on computer back to 1984.

General Information: Public Access terminal is available. No sealed or divorce records released. SASE required. Turnaround time 7-10 days. Fax notes: Will not fax results. Copy fee: $1.00 per page. Certification fee: $.50 per page, $4.00 minimum. Fee payee: County Clerk. Personal checks accepted. Prepayment required.

Suffolk District Court 400 Carleton Ave, Central Islip, NY 11722; 631-853-7500 (All District Courts). Hours: 9AM-5PM (EST). *Misdemeanor, Civil Actions Under $15,000, Eviction, Small Claims.*

Civil Records: Access: Mail, in person. Both court and visitors may perform in person searches. Search fee: $16.00 per name. Required to search: name, years to search. Civil cases indexed by plaintiff. Civil records on computer from 1991, prior in books.

Criminal Records: Access: Mail, in person. Both court and visitors may perform in person searches. Search fee: $16.00 per name. Required to search: name, years to search, DOB. Criminal records on computer from 1991, prior in books.

General Information: Public Access terminal is available. No sealed or youthful offender records released. SASE required. Turnaround time 3-5 days. Copy fee: $1.00 per page. Certification fee: $5.00. Fee payee: District Court Clerk. Only cashiers checks and money orders accepted. Prepayment is required.

1st & 5th District Courts 3105-1 Veterans Memorial Hwy, Ronkonkoma, NY 11779-7614; 631-854-9676 (1st); 9673 (5th). Hours: 9AM-5PM (EST). *Civil Actions Under $15,000, Eviction, Small Claims.*

Civil Records: Access: Mail, in person. Only the court performs in person searches; visitors may not. Search fee: $16.00 per name. Required to search: name, years to search. Civil cases indexed by defendant. Civil records on computer from 1990, prior in books.

Criminal Records: Access: Mail, in person. Only the court performs in person searches; visitors may not. Search fee: $16.00 per name. Required to search: name, years to search, DOB. Criminal records on computer from 1990, prior in books.

General Information: No sealed or youthful offender records released. SASE required. Turnaround time 2 weeks. Copy fee: $1.00 for first page, $.50 each add'l. Certification fee: $5.00. Fee payee: Clerk of the Court. Only cashiers checks and money orders accepted. Prepayment is required.

2nd District Court 375 Cormac Rd, Deer Park, NY 11702; 631-854-1950. Hours: 9AM-Noon, 1-5PM (EST). *Misdemeanor, Civil Actions Under $15,000, Eviction, Small Claims.*

Civil Records: Access: Mail, in person. Only the court performs in person searches; visitors may not. Search fee: $16.00 per name. Required to search: name, years to search. Civil cases indexed by plaintiff. Civil records on computer from 1989, prior in books, on cards.

Criminal Records: Access: Mail, in person. Only the court performs in person searches; visitors may not. Search fee: $16.00 per name. Required to search: name, years to search, DOB, SSN, signed release. Criminal records on computer from 1989, prior in books, on cards.

General Information: No sealed or youthful offender records released. SASE required. Turnaround time 1 week. Copy fee: $.50 per page. Certification fee: Included in search fee. Fee payee: County Clerk. Only cashiers checks and money orders accepted. Prepayment is required.

3rd District Court 1850 New York Ave, Huntington Station, NY 11746; 631-854-4545. Hours: 9AM-4:30PM (EST). *Misdemeanor, Civil Actions Under $15,000, Eviction, Small Claims.*

Civil Records: Access: Mail, in person. Only the court performs in person searches; visitors may not. Search fee: $16.00 per name. Required to search: name, years to search. Civil cases indexed by defendant. Civil records on computer from 1988, prior in books, on microfilm.

Criminal Records: Access: Mail, in person. Only the court performs in person searches; visitors may not. Search fee: $16.00 per name. Required to search: name, years to search, DOB, SSN, signed release. Criminal records on computer from 1988, prior in books, on microfilm.

General Information: No sealed records released. SASE required. Turnaround time 2 weeks. Certification fee: Included in search fee. Fee payee: Clerk of the Court. Business checks accepted. Attorney checks accepted. Prepayment is required.

4th District Court North County Complex Bldg C158, Hauppauge, NY 11787; Civil phone: 631-853-5400; Criminal phone: 631-853-5357. Hours: 9AM-5PM (EST). *Misdemeanor, Civil Actions Under $15,000, Eviction, Small Claims.*

Civil Records: Access: Mail, in person. Only the court performs in person searches; visitors may not. Search fee: $16.00 per name. Required to search: name, years to search. Civil cases indexed by defendant, plaintiff. Civil records on computer from 1987, prior in books.
Criminal Records: Access: Mail, in person. Only the court performs in person searches; visitors may not. Search fee: $16.00 per name. Required to search: name, years to search, DOB. Criminal records on computer from 1987, prior in books. Criminal searches limited to township searches. All others must be done through 1st District Court, 631-853-4530; 400 Carleton Ave, Central Islip, NY 11722.
General Information: No sealed records released. SASE required. Turnaround time 1-2 weeks. Copy fee: $.50 per page. Certification fee: $5.00. Fee payee: Clerk of Court. Only cashiers checks and money orders accepted. Prepayment is required.

6th District Court 150 W Main St, Patchogue, NY 11772; 631-854-1440. Hours: 9AM-5PM (EST). *Misdemeanor, Civil Actions Under $15,000, Eviction, Small Claims.*

Civil Records: Access: Mail, in person. Only the court performs in person searches; visitors may not. Search fee: $16.00 per name. Required to search: name, years to search. Civil records on computer from 1989, prior on microfilm.
Criminal Records: Access: Mail, in person. Only the court performs in person searches; visitors may not. Search fee: $16.00 per name. Required to search: name, years to search. Criminal records on computer from 1989, prior on microfilm.
General Information: No sealed or youthful offender records released. SASE required. Copy fee: $1.00 for first page, $.50 each add'l. Certification fee: $5.00. Fee payee: Clerk of Court. Only cashiers checks and money orders accepted. Prepayment is required.

Shoreham Village Justice PO Box 812, Shoreham, NY 11786. *Misdemeanor, Civil Actions Under $3,000, Small Claims.*

Civil Records: Access: In person only. Only the court performs in person searches; visitors may not. No search fee. Required to search: name.
Criminal Records: Access: In person only. Only the court performs in person searches; visitors may not. No search fee. Required to search: name.

Village of the Branch Court PO Box 725, Smithtown, NY 11787. *Misdemeanor, Civil Actions Under $3,000, Small Claims.*

Civil Records: Access: In person only. Both court and visitors may perform in person searches. No search fee. Required to search: name.
Criminal Records: Access: In person only. Both court and visitors may perform in person searches. No search fee. Required to search: name.

Surrogate Court 320 Centre Dr, Riverhead, NY 11901; 631-852-1745; Fax: 631-852-1777. Hours: 9AM-5PM (EST). *Probate.*

Town/Village Courts; *Misdemeanor, Civil Actions Under $3,000, Small Claims:* Hewlett Bay Park Village Court; Poquott Village Court; Port Jefferson Village, 631-473-8287; East Hampton Town, 631-324-4134; Belle Terre Village, 631-928-5785; Westhampton Beach Village Court; Quogue Village, 631-653-4498; Bellport Village, 516-475-2753; Patchogue Village, 631-475-2753; Old Field Village, 631-941-9412; Islandia Village, 631-348-0470; Ocean Beach Village, 631-583-5940; Northport Village, 631-261-7500;

Lindenhurst Village, 631-957-7509; Brightwaters Village, 631-665-1281; Lake Grove Village, 631-585-2008; Lloyd Harbor Village Court; Huntington Bay Village Court; Shoreham Village Justice; Asharoken Village, 631-261-8677; Amityville Village, 631-691-3303; Village of the Branch Court; Riverhead Town, 631-727-3200; Greenport Village, 631-477-0853; Harbor Village, 631-584-5550; Saltaire Village, 631-583-5566; Babylon Village Court; Shelter Island Town, 631-749-8989; Southold Town, 631-765-1852; Nissequogue Village, 631-862-8576; Southampton Town, 631-283-6000.

Sullivan County

Supreme & County Court County Courthouse, 414 Broadway, Monticello, NY 12701; 845-794-4066. Hours: 9AM-5PM (EST). *Felony, Civil, Misdemeanor, Eviction, Small Claims.*

Note: Civil records maintained at County Clerk's office, Sullivan Gov't Center, 100 North St, Monticello, NY 12701.

Civil Records: Access: Phone, mail, in person. Both court and visitors may perform in person searches. Search fee: $16.00 per name for 10 years with additional $5.00 for every 2 years prior. Required to search: name, years to search. Civil cases indexed by plaintiff. Civil records on computer from 1992, prior in books from 1800s.
Criminal Records: Access: Mail, in person. Only the court performs in person searches; visitors may not. Search fee: $16.00 per name. Required to search: name, years to search, DOB. Criminal records on computer from 1989.
General Information: No sealed, expunged, adoption, sex offense, juvenile or mental health records released. SASE not required. Turnaround time 1-2 weeks. Copy fee: $.50 per page. Certification fee: $4.00. Fee payee: County Clerk for civil; to Court Clerk for criminal. Personal checks accepted. Prepayment is required.

Surrogate Court County Government Center, 100 North St, Monticello, NY 12701; 845-794-3000 X3450/3451; Fax: 845-794-0310. Hours: 9AM-5PM (EST). *Probate.*

Town Courts; *Misdemeanor, Civil Actions Under $3,000, Small Claims:* Callicoon Town, 845-482-5390; Lumberland Town, 845-858-8548; Thompson Town, 845-794-7130; Fallsburg Town, 845-434-4574; Mamakating Town, 845-888-4712; Monticello Village Court; Neversink Town, 845-985-7685; Jeffersonville Village, 845-482-4275; Forestburgh Town, 845-794-0679; Fremont Town; Woodridge Village, 845-434-7444; Bloomingburg Village Court; Bethel Town, 845-583-7420; Highland Town, 845-557-8132; Tusten Town, 845-252-3310; Cochecton Town; Rockland Town, 845-439-3464; Delaware Town, 845-887-5250; Liberty Village, 845-292-0290; Liberty Town, 845-292-6980; Wurtsboro Village, 845-888-4712.

Tioga County

Supreme & County Court PO Box 307, Owego, NY 13827; 607-687-0544; Fax: 607-687-3240. Hours: 9AM-5PM (EST). *Felony, Civil, Misdemeanor, Eviction, Small Claims.*

Civil Records: Access: In person only. Visitors must perform in person searches for themselves. No search fee. Required to search: name, years to search. Civil cases indexed by defendant. Civil records in books. Visitor can search in County Clerk's Office.
Criminal Records: Access: Mail, in person. Both court and visitors may perform in person searches. Search fee: $5.00 per name. No fee for in person searches. Required to search: name, years to search, DOB. Criminal records in books.

General Information: No sealed, expunged, adoption, sex offense, juvenile or mental health records released. SASE required. Turnaround time varies. Copy fee: $.50 per page. Certification fee: $4.00. Fee payee: County Clerk. Personal checks accepted.

Surrogate Court County Court Annex Bldg, 20 Court St, Owego, NY 13827; 607-687-1303. Hours: 9AM-5PM (EST). *Probate.*

Town/Village Courts; *Misdemeanor, Civil Actions Under $3,000, Small Claims:* Newark Valley Town, 607-642-8746; Waverly Village, 607-565-4771; Tioga Town, 607-687-9577; Nichols Town, 607-699-3981; Spencer Village, 607-589-4310; Spencer Town; Owego Village Court; Berkshire Town, 607-657-2705; Richford Town; Barton Town, 607-565-8609; Owego Town, 607-687-2822; Candor Town, 607-659-3175; Candor Village, 607-659-3175.

Tompkins County

Supreme & County Court 320 N Tioga St, Ithaca, NY 14850; 607-274-5431; Fax: 607-274-5445. Hours: 9AM-5PM (EST). *Felony, Civil.*

Civil Records: Access: Fax, mail, in person. Both court and visitors may perform in person searches. Search fee: $5.00 per name. Fee is per 2 years searched. Required to search: name, years to search. Civil cases indexed by defendant, plaintiff. Civil records in books. Fax requests must be pre-paid.
Criminal Records: Access: Fax, mail, in person. Only the court performs in person searches; visitors may not. Search fee: $5.00 per name. Fee is per 2 years searched. Required to search: name, years to search, signed release; also helpful: DOB, SSN. Criminal records in books. Fax requests must be pre-paid.
General Information: No sealed, expunged, adoption, sex offense, juvenile or mental health records released. SASE required. Turnaround time 1-2 days. Copy fee: $1.00 for first page, $.50 each add'l. Certification fee: $4.00. Fee payee: County Clerk. Personal checks accepted. Prepayment is required.

Ithaca City Court 118 E Clinton St, Ithaca, NY 14850; 607-273-2263. Hours: 8AM-4PM (EST). *Misdemeanor, Civil Actions Under $15,000, Eviction, Small Claims.*

www.courts.state.ny.us/ithaca/city

Civil Records: Access: Mail, in person. Only the court performs in person searches; visitors may not. Search fee: $16.00 per name. For records prior to 1996, fee is $5.00 per each 2 year period searched. Required to search: name, years to search. Civil cases indexed by defendant. Civil records on computer since 1996; prior records in books.
Criminal Records: Access: Mail, in person. Only the court performs in person searches; visitors may not. Search fee: $16.00 per name. For records prior to 1990, fee is $5.00 per each 2 year period searched. Required to search: name, years to search, DOB. Criminal records on computer from 1990, prior in books.
General Information: No sealed, youthful offender records released. SASE required. Turnaround time 1 week. Copy fee: $.50 per page. $1.00 minimum. Certification fee: $5.00. Fee payee: City Court. Only cashiers checks and money orders accepted. Prepayment is required.

Surrogate Court 320 N Tioga St, Ithaca, NY 14850; 607-277-0622; Fax: 607-256-2572. Hours: 9AM-5PM (EST). *Probate.*

Town/Village Courts; *Misdemeanor, Civil Actions Under $3,000, Small Claims:* Groton Village, 607-898-3711; Danby Town, 607-277-4788; Dryden Town, 607-844-8621; Ulysses Town, 607-387-5411; Enfield Town, 607-272-6490; Freeville Village, 607-844-8470; Groton Town, 607-898-5273; Cayuga Heights Village,

607-257-3944; Caroline Town, 607-539-7796; Ithaca Town, 607-273-1721; Newfield Town, 607-564-9571; Lansing Town, 607-533-4776.

Ulster County

Supreme & County Court PO Box 1800, Kingston, NY 12401; 845-340-3288; Fax: 845-340-3299. Hours: 9AM-5PM (EST). *Felony, Civil.*

Civil Records: Access: Phone, mail, online, in person. Both court and visitors may perform in person searches. Search fee: $5.00 per name. Fee is per name & per 2 years searched. Required to search: name, years to search. Civil cases indexed by defendant, plaintiff. Civil records on computer from 1987, in books from 1920s, prior archived. Access to the remote online system requires a minimum $25 per month fee, 12 months required to signup. Search by name or case number. Call Valerie Harris 845-334-5367 for more information.

Criminal Records: Access: Phone, mail, online, in person. Both court and visitors may perform in person searches. Search fee: $5.00 per name. Fee is per 2 years searched. Required to search: name, years to search. Criminal records on computer from 1987, in books from 1920s, prior archived. Online access to criminal records is the same as civil.

General Information: Public Access terminal is available. No sealed, expunged, adoption, sex offense, juvenile or mental health records released. SASE not required. Turnaround time 5 days. Copy fee: $.50 per page. Certification fee: $4.00. Fee payee: County Clerk. Personal checks accepted. Prepayment is required.

Kingston City Court 1 Garraghan Dr, Kingston, NY 12401; 845-338-2974. Hours: 8AM-4PM (EST). *Misdemeanor, Civil Actions Under $15,000, Eviction, Small Claims.*

Civil Records: Access: Mail, in person. Only the court performs in person searches; visitors may not. Search fee: $5.00 per name. Fee is per case. Required to search: name, years to search. Civil cases indexed by plaintiff. Civil records on computer from 1995, prior in books. Request must be in writing.

Criminal Records: Access: Mail, in person. Only the court performs in person searches; visitors may not. Search fee: $5.00 per name. Fee is per 2 years searched. Required to search: name, years to search; also helpful: DOB. Criminal records on computer from 1995, prior in books. Request must be in writing.

General Information: No sealed or youthful offender records released. SASE required. Turnaround time 1 week. Copy fee: $1.00 per page. Certification fee: $5.00. Fee payee: City Court. Personal checks accepted. Prepayment is required.

Surrogate Court 244 Fair St, Kingston, NY 12401; 845-340-3348; Fax: 845-340-3352. Hours: 9AM-5PM (EST). *Probate.*

Town/Village Courts; *Misdemeanor, Civil Actions Under $3,000, Small Claims:* Wawarsing Town, 845-647-4770; Olive Town, 845-657-2912; Saugerties Town, 845-246-9989; Lloyd Town, 845-691-7544; Esopus Town, 845-331-5776; Ellenville Village, 845-647-5107; Gardiner Town, 845-255-9675; Saugerties Village, 845-246-4979; Rosendale Town, 845-658-3686; New Paltz Town, 845-255-0043; Ulster Town, 845-382-1737; Plattekill Town, 845-883-5805; Marlborough Town, 845-795-2256; Woodstock Town, 845-679-6345; Shawangunk Town, 845-895-2111; Rochester Town, 845-626-2522; Marbletown Town, 845-687-4324; Hurley Town; Shandaken Town, 845-688-5005; Hardenburgh Town; Kingston Town, 845-336-8853; Denning Town, 845-985-2411.

Warren County

Supreme & County Court - Civil Rt US 9, Lake George, NY 12845; 518-761-6426; Fax: 518-761-6253. Hours: 9AM-5PM (EST). *Civil.*

Civil Records: Access: Phone, mail, in person. Both court and visitors may perform in person searches. Search fee: $5.00 for each two years. Computer search back to 1989 is $16.00. Required to search: name, years to search. Civil cases indexed by plaintiff. Civil records on computer from 1986, prior on index from 1813.

General Information: No adoption, juvenile or mental health records released. SASE required. Turnaround time same day. Copy fee: $.50 per page. Certification fee: $4.00. Fee payee: Warren County Clerk. Personal checks accepted. Prepayment is required.

Supreme & County Court - Criminal Rt US 9, Lake George, NY 12845; 518-761-6430/6431; Fax: 518-761-6253. Hours: 9AM-5PM (EST). *Felony.*

Criminal Records: Access: Fax, mail, in person. Both court and visitors may perform in person searches. Search fee: $5.00 per 2 year search per name, information starts with 1929. Computer search: $16.00 per name, information starts with 1989. Required to search: name, years to search, DOB, SSN, signed release. Criminal records on computer from 1986, prior on index from 1929.

General Information: No adoption, juvenile or mental health records released. SASE required. Turnaround time same day. Copy fee: $.50 per page. Certification fee: $4.00. Fee payee: Warren County Clerk. Personal checks accepted. Prepayment is required.

Glens Falls City Court 42 Ridge St, Glens Falls, NY 12801; 518-798-4714; Fax: 518-798-0137. Hours: 8:30AM-4:30PM (EST). *Misdemeanor, Civil Actions Under $15,000, Eviction, Small Claims.*

Civil Records: Access: Mail, in person. Only the court performs in person searches; visitors may not. Search fee: $16.00 per name. Fee is for computer search. No fee for manual search. Required to search: name, years to search. Civil cases indexed by defendant, plaintiff. Civil records on computer to 1988, prior on microfilm.

Criminal Records: Access: Mail, in person. Only the court performs in person searches; visitors may not. Search fee: $16.00 per name. Fee prior to 1988 is $5.00 for each consecutive 2 yr search. Required to search: name, years to search, DOB; also helpful: SSN. Criminal records on computer from 1990, prior on microfilm.

General Information: No sealed records released. SASE required. Turnaround time 1 week. Copy fee: $.50 per page. There is a $1.00 minimum. Certification fee: $5.00. Fee payee: City Court. Only cashiers checks and money orders accepted. Prepayment is required.

Surrogate Court 1340 State Route 9, County Municipal Ctr, Lake George, NY 12845; 518-761-6514; Fax: 518-761-6465. Hours: 9AM-5PM (EST). *Probate.*

Town/Village Courts; *Misdemeanor, Civil Actions Under $3,000, Small Claims:* Warrensburg Town, 518-623-9776; Chester Town, 518-494-3133; Bolton Town, 518-644-2202; Horicon Town, 518-494-7958; Johnsburg Town, 518-251-3011; Lake Luzerne Town, 518-696-2711; Hague Town, 518-543-6161; Thurman Town, 518-623-9649; Lake George Town, 518-668-5420; Stony Creek Town, 518-696-3575; Queensbury Town, 518-745-5571.

Washington County

Supreme & County Court 383 Broadway, Fort Edward, NY 12828; Civil phone: 518-746-2170; Criminal phone: 518-746-2520. Hours: 8:30AM-4:30PM (EST). *Felony, Civil.*

Note: Misdemeanor records are maintained by city, town and village courts.

Civil Records: Access: In person only. Visitors must perform in person searches for themselves. No search fee. Required to search: name, years to search. Civil cases indexed by defendant. Civil records on books from 1800s.

Criminal Records: Access: Mail, in person. Both court and visitors may perform in person searches. Search fee: $16.00 per name. Required to search: name, years to search. Criminal records on books from 1800s.

General Information: No sealed or youthful offender records released. SASE required. Turnaround time 1-2 days. Copy fee: $1.00 per page. Certification fee: $4.00. Fee payee: County Clerk. Business checks accepted. Prepayment is required.

Surrogate Court 383 Broadway, Fort Edward, NY 12828; 518-746-2546; Fax: 518-746-2547. Hours: 8:30AM-4:30PM (EST). *Probate.*

Town/Village Courts; *Misdemeanor, Civil Actions Under $3,000, Small Claims:* Hebron Town, 518-854-9300; Granville Town, 518-642-1500; Salem Village, 518-854-9215; Hartford Town, 518-632-5255; Salem Town, 518-854-9215; Greenwich Village Court; Hampton Town, 518-282-9830; Putnam Town, 518-547-8317; Cambridge Town, 518-677-8936; Granville Village, 518-642-9386; Easton Town, 518-692-2678; Whitehall Village, 518-499-0772; Whitehall Town, 518-499-0772; White Creek Town, 518-677-8545; Dresden Town, 518-499-2040; Fort Edward Village, 518-747-6563; Kingsbury Town, 518-747-9436; Jackson Town; Fort Ann Town, 518-639-8929; Argyle Town, 518-638-8681; Greenwich Town; Cambridge Village, 518-677-2414; Fort Edward Town, 518-747-4023; Hudson Falls Village, 518-747-3292.

Wayne County

Supreme & County Court 9 Pearl St, PO Box 608, Lyons, NY 14489-0608; 315-946-7470; Fax: 315-946-5978. Hours: 9AM-5PM (EST). *Felony, Civil, Misdemeanor, Eviction, Small Claims.*

Civil Records: Access: Phone, fax, mail, in person. Both court and visitors may perform in person searches. Search fee: $5.00 per name. Per every 2 years. Required to search: name, years to search. Civil cases indexed by defendant, plaintiff. Civil records on computer from 1985, prior in books.

Criminal Records: Access: Fax, mail, in person. Both court and visitors may perform in person searches. Search fee: $5.00 per name certified back to 1979. $5.00 per name for every 2 years certified search. Required to search: name, years to search, DOB, sex. Criminal records on computer from 1979.

General Information: Public Access terminal is available. No matrimonial records released. SASE requested. Turnaround time 5-7 days. Fax notes: $1.50 for first page, $1.00 each add'l. Fax fees: Long distance within Wayne County $2.00 1st page, $1.00 each additional page; long distance outside Wayne County $3.00 1st page, $1.00 each additional page; no fax charge for 800 number. Copy fee: $.50 per page. $1.00 minimum. Certification fee: $4.00 plus $1.00 per page after first 4. Fee payee: County Clerk. Personal checks accepted. Prepayment is required.

Surrogate Court 34 Broad St, Hall of Justice, Lyons, NY 14489; 315-946-5430; Fax: 315-946-5433. Hours: 9AM-4PM (EST). *Probate.*

Town/Village Courts; *Misdemeanor, Civil Actions Under $3,000, Small Claims:* Rose Town, 315-587-4418; Clyde Village, 315-923-9375; Wolcott Village, 315-594-9501; Wolcott Town, 315-594-8257; Williamson Town, 315-589-8250; Macedon Village Court; Walworth Town; Galen Town, 315-923-9375; Savannah Town, 315-365-2811; Sodus Point Village, 315-483-6217; Arcadia Town, 315-331-2744; Sodus Town, 315-483-6807; Huron Town, 315-594-8074; Butler Town, 315-594-2719; Macedon Town, 315-986-9108; Palmyra Town, 315-597-5431; Ontario Town, 315-524-6511; Palmyra Village, 315-597-6757; Lyons Village, 315-946-4565; Newark Village, 315-331-7666; Lyons Town, 315-946-4565.

Westchester County

Supreme & County Court 110 Dr Martin L King Blvd, White Plains, NY 10601; 914-285-3070; Fax: 914-285-3172. Hours: 8AM-5:45PM (EST). *Felony, Civil, Misdemeanor, Eviction, Small Claims.*

www.westchesterclerk.com

Civil Records: Access: Mail, in person. Both court and visitors may perform in person searches. Search fee: $5.00 per name. Fee is per 2 years searched. Required to search: name, years to search. Civil cases indexed by defendant, plaintiff. Civil records on computer from 1986, prior in books from 1847.

Criminal Records: Access: Mail, in person. Both court and visitors may perform in person searches. Search fee: $5.00 per name. Fee is per 2 years searched. Required to search: name, years to search. Criminal records on computer to 1986, prior in books from 1847.

General Information: Public Access terminal is available. No sealed, expunged, adoption, sex offense, juvenile or mental health records released. SASE required. Turnaround time 1 week. Copy fee: $.50 per page. Certification fee: $4.00. The fee covers up to 8 pages, each add'l page is $.50. Fee payee: County Clerk. Personal checks accepted. Prepayment is required.

Mt Vernon City Court Municipal Bldg, Roosevelt Square, Mt Vernon, NY 10550-2019; 914-665-2400; Fax: 914-699-1230. Hours: 8:30AM-4:30PM (EST). *Misdemeanor, Civil Actions Under $15,000, Eviction, Small Claims.*

Civil Records: Access: Mail, in person. Only the court performs in person searches; visitors may not. Search fee: $16.00 per name. Required to search: name, years to search; also helpful: address. Civil cases indexed by defendant, plaintiff. Civil records on computer since 1986, prior in books.

Criminal Records: Access: Mail, in person. Only the court performs in person searches; visitors may not. Search fee: $16.00 per name. Required to search: name, years to search; also helpful: DOB. Criminal records on computer since 1986, prior in books.

General Information: No sealed records released. SASE required. Turnaround time 2 weeks. Copy fee: $1.00 per page. Certification fee: $5.00. Fee payee: City Court. Only cashiers checks and money orders accepted. Prepayment is required.

Peekskill City Court 2 Nelson Ave, Peekskill, NY 10566; 914-737-3405. Hours: 9AM-5PM (EST). *Misdemeanor, Civil Actions Under $15,000, Eviction, Small Claims.*

Civil Records: Access: Mail, in person. Only the court performs in person searches; visitors may not. Search fee: $5.00 per name per 2-years searched. Required to search: name, years to search. Civil cases indexed by plaintiff. Civil records on computer back to 1994, prior in books. Request must be in writing.

Criminal Records: Access: Mail, in person. Only the court performs in person searches; visitors may not. Search fee: $16.00 per name. Required to search: name, years to search, DOB, signed release. Criminal records on computer back to 1989, prior on cards. Request must be in writing.

General Information: No sealed records released. SASE required. Turnaround time 3-5 days. Copy fee: $.50 per page. Certification fee: $5.00. Fee payee: Peekskill City Court. Only cashiers checks and money orders accepted. Prepayment is required.

Rye City Court 21 McCullough Place, Rye, NY 10580; 914-967-1599; Fax: 914-967-3308. Hours: 8:30AM-4:30PM (EST). *Misdemeanor, Civil Actions Under $15,000, Eviction, Small Claims.*

Civil Records: Access: Mail, in person. Only the court performs in person searches; visitors may not. Search fee: $5.00 per name. Required to search: name, years to search. Civil cases indexed by plaintiff. Civil records on computer from 1994, prior on index cards.

Criminal Records: Access: Mail, in person. Only the court performs in person searches; visitors may not. Search fee: $21.00 per name. Required to search: name, years to search, DOB. Criminal records on computer from 1986.

General Information: No sealed records released. SASE required. Turnaround time 1 month. Copy fee: $.50 per page. Certification fee: $5.00. Fee payee: City Court. Only cashiers checks and money orders accepted. Prepayment is required.

White Plains City Court 77 S Lexington Ave, White Plains, NY 10601; 914-422-6050; Fax: 914-422-6058. Hours: 8:30AM-4:30PM (EST). *Misdemeanor, Civil Actions Under $15,000, Eviction, Small Claims.*

Civil Records: Access: Mail, in person. Only the court performs in person searches; visitors may not. Search fee: $21.00 per name. Required to search: name, years to search. Civil cases indexed by defendant. Civil records on docket cards.

Criminal Records: Access: Mail, in person. Only the court performs in person searches; visitors may not. Search fee: $21.00 per name. Add $16.00 for printout. Required to search: name, years to search, DOB. Criminal records on computer from 1988, prior on cards.

General Information: No sealed, youthful offender or sex case records released. SASE required. Turnaround time 2 weeks. Copy fee: $.25 per page. Certification fee: Included in search fee. Fee payee: City Court. Only cashiers checks and money orders accepted. Prepayment is required.

Yonkers City Court 100 S Broadway, Yonkers, NY 10701; 914-377-6352; Fax: 914-377-6395. Hours: 9AM-5PM (EST). *Misdemeanor, Civil Actions Under $15,000, Eviction, Small Claims.*

Civil Records: Access: Mail, in person. Only the court performs in person searches; visitors may not. Search fee: $16.00 per name. Required to search: name, years to search. Civil cases indexed by plaintiff. Civil records on computer since 01/95.

Criminal Records: Access: Mail, in person. Only the court performs in person searches; visitors may not. Search fee: $16.00 per name. Required to search: name, years to search, DOB, signed release; also helpful: date of offense. Criminal records on computer since 1993; prior records on index cards.

General Information: No sealed records released. SASE not required. Turnaround time 2-3 weeks. Copy fee: $.50 per page. Certification fee: Included in search fee. Fee payee: City Court. Only cashiers checks and money orders accepted. Prepayment is required.

Surrogate Court 140 Grand St, 8th Floor, White Plains, NY 10601; 914-285-3712; Fax: 914-285-3728. Hours: 9AM-5PM (EST). *Probate.*

Town/Village Courts; *Misdemeanor, Civil Actions Under $3,000, Small Claims:* Greenburgh Town, 914-682-5377; Elmsford Village, 914-592-8949; Tuckahoe Village, 914-961-4787; North Castle Town, 914-273-8627; North Salem Town, 914-669-9691; Irvington Village, 914-591-9505; Tarrytown Village, 914-631-5115; Ardsley Village, 914-693-1703; Ossining Town, 914-762-8562; North Tarrytown Village, 914-631-2783; Eastchester Town, 914-771-3354; New Castle Town, 914-238-4771; Bronxville Village, 914-337-2454; Mount Pleasant Town, 914-742-2354; Dobbs Ferry Village, 914-693-6161; Mount Kisco Town, 914-241-0500; Larchmont Village, 914-834-1826; Cronton-on-Hudson Village, 914-271-6266; Buchanan Village, 914-737-1033; Mamaroneck Village, 914-777-7710; Mamaroneck Town, 914-381-7875; Cortlandt Town, 914-734-1090; Yorktown Town, 914-962-6216; Rye Town, 914-939-3305; Scarsdale Town; Scarsdale Village, 914-723-5734; Pleasantville Village, 914-769-2027; Port Chester Village Court; Ossining Village, 914-941-3067; Hastings-on-Hudson Village, 914-478-3403; Pelham Town, 914-738-2205; Somers Town, 914-277-8225; Pound Ridge Town, 914-764-5511; Harrison Town, 914-835-2000; Bedford Town, 914-666-6965; Lewisboro Town, 914-763-5417; Briarcliff Manor Village, 914-941-4800.

Wyoming County

Supreme & County Court 147 N Main St, Warsaw, NY 14569; 716-786-2253; 786-8810-County Clerk; Fax: 716-786-3703. Hours: 9AM-5PM (EST). *Felony, Civil, Misdemeanor, Eviction, Small Claims.*

Note: All records maintained at County Clerk's office.

Civil Records: Access: Phone, fax, mail, in person. Only the court performs in person searches; visitors may not. Search fee: $5.00 per name. Required to search: name, years to search. Civil cases indexed by defendant. Civil records on computer back to 2/14/2001; prior on books.

Criminal Records: Access: Phone, fax, mail, in person. Only the court performs in person searches; visitors may not. Search fee: $5.00 per name. Required to search: name, years to search, DOB. Criminal records in books.

General Information: No sealed, divorce or sexual abuse records released. SASE required. Turnaround time 2-3 days. Fax notes: $.50 per page. Copy fee: $.50 per page. Certification fee: $4.00. Fee payee: County Clerk. Personal checks accepted. Prepayment required.

Surrogate Court 147 N Main St, Warsaw, NY 14569; 716-786-3148; Fax: 716-786-3800. Hours: 9AM-5PM (EST). *Probate.*

Town Courts; *Misdemeanor, Civil Actions Under $3,000, Small Claims:* Middlebury Town, 716-495-6300; Eagle Town, 716-322-7667; Bennington Town, 716-591-2157; Covington Town, 716-584-3565; Warsaw Village, 716-786-3361; Warsaw Town, 716-786-3361; Arcade Town, 716-492-1340; Pike Town, 716-493-5140; Wethersfield Town; Attica Town; Java Town, 716-457-3022; Perry Town, 716-237-2216; Sheldon Town, 716-535-7644; Genesee Falls Town; Castile Town, 716-493-5875; Gainesville; Orangeville Town, 716-786-2883; Attica Village, 716-591-0881; Arcade Village, 716-492-4479; Perry Village, 716-237-2216; Silver Springs Village, 716-493-2500.

Yates County

Supreme & County Court 110 Court St, Penn Yan, NY 14527-1191; 315-536-5120; Fax: 315-536-5545. Hours: 9AM-5PM (EST). *Felony, Civil, Misdemeanor, Eviction, Small Claims.*

Civil Records: Access: Phone, mail, fax, in person. Both court and visitors may perform in person searches. Search fee: $10.00 per name. Required to search: name, years to search. Civil cases indexed by defendant, plaintiff. Civil records on computer from 1988, prior in books.

Criminal Records: Access: Mail, fax, in person. Both court and visitors may perform in person searches. Search fee: $10.00 per name. Required to search: name, years to search. Criminal records on computer back to 1988; records also on book index.

General Information: Public Access terminal is available. No divorce records outside parties involved, sealed records released. SASE required. Turnaround time 2-3 days. Fax notes: Will not fax results. Copy fee: $.50 per page. Certification fee: $1.00 per page. Fee payee: Yates County Clerk. Personal checks accepted. Prepayment is required.

Surrogate Court 108 Court St, Penn Yan, NY 14527; 315-536-5130; Fax: 315-536-5190. Hours: 9AM-5PM (EST). *Probate.*

Town/Village Courts; *Misdemeanor, Civil Actions Under $3,000, Small Claims:* Starkey Town; Barrington Town; Rushville Village Court; Middlesex Town, 716-554-3607; Jerusalem Town; Italy Town; Potter Town, 716-554-6758; Torrey Town; Penn Yan Village, 315-536-7243; Benton Town, 315-536-2320; Dundee Village, 607-243-5551; Milo Town, 315-536-8911.

New York Recording Offices

ORGANIZATION	62 counties, 62 recording offices. The recording officers are County Clerk (New York City Register in the counties of Bronx, Kings, New York, and Queens). The entire state is in the Eastern Time Zone (EST).
REAL ESTATE RECORDS	Some counties will perform real estate searches. Certified copy fees are usually $1.00 per page with a $4.00 minimum. Tax records are located at the Treasurer's Office.
UCC RECORDS	This was a dual filing state. Financing statements were filed both at the state level and with the County Clerk, except for consumer goods, cooperatives (as in cooperative apartments), farm related and real estate related collateral, which were filed only with the County Clerk. Effective 07/2001, only real estate related collateral is filed at the county, but searches may still be done on all the records prior to 07/2001. All counties will perform UCC searches. Use search request form UCC-11. Search fees are usually $7.00 per debtor name using the approved UCC-11 request form and sometimes $12.00 using a non-New York form. Copies usually cost $1.50 per page.
TAX LIEN RECORDS	Federal tax liens on personal property of businesses are filed with the Secretary of State. Other federal tax liens are filed with the County Clerk. State tax liens are filed with the County Clerk, with a master list - called state tax warrants - available at the Secretary of State's office. Federal tax liens are usually indexed with UCC Records. State tax liens are usually indexed with other miscellaneous liens and judgments. Some counties include federal tax liens as part of a UCC search, and others will search tax liens for a separate fee. Search fees and copy fees vary.
OTHER LIENS	Judgment, mechanics, welfare, hospital, matrimonial, wage assignment, lis pendens.
STATEWIDE ONLINE INFO:	There are a handful of counties and towns offering free Internet access to assessor records, and the number is growing.

Albany County

County Clerk, County Courthouse, Room 128, Albany, NY 12207. County Clerk, R/E and UCC Recording 518-487-5120; Fax 518-487-5099. http://www.albanycounty.com/departments
Will search UCC records. **Online Access:** Naturalizations. Online access to the clerk's naturalization records from 1821-1991 are available free online at www.albanycounty.com/online/online.asp. Records are being added by volunteers. **Other Phone Numbers:** Assessor 518-487-5350; Treasurer 518-447-7070; Elections 518-487-5060; Vital Records 518-434-5045.

Allegany County

County Clerk, 7 Court St., 7 Court St., Belmont, NY 14813-0087. 716-268-9270; Fax 716-268-9659. http://www.alleganyco.com
Will search UCC records. UCC-11 search includes federal tax liens if requested. Will not search real estate records. **Other Phone Numbers:** Assessor 716-268-9381; Treasurer 716-268-9282.

Bronx County

City Register, 1932 Arthur Avenue, Bronx, NY 10457. 718-579-6827.
Will search UCC records. This agency will not do a tax lien search. Will not search real estate records. **Online Access:** Real Estate, Liens, Tax Assessor Records. Two options are available. Access to Bronx County online records - including Boroughs of Brooklyn, Queens, Staten Island, Bronx, Manhattan - requires a $250 monthly fee and $5 per transaction fee. Records are kept 2-5 years. For information, contact Richard Reskin at 718-935-6523. Also, property assessment rolls from NYC's Dept. of Finance are available free online at www.ci.nyc.ny.us/html/dof/html/asmt.html. Search by borough, block and lot number. Tax reports are also available, with enrollment required.

Broome County

County Clerk, P.O. Box 2062, Binghamton, NY 13902-2062. 607-778-2451; Fax 607-778-2243.

Will search UCC records. **Other Phone Numbers:** Assessor 607-778-2169; Treasurer 607-778-2161.

Cattaraugus County

County Clerk, 303 Court Street, Little Valley, NY 14755. 716-938-9111 x297; Fax 716-938-6009.
Will search UCC records. Will not search real estate records. **Online Access:** Real Estate, Tax Assessor Records. Records on the City of Olean assessor database are available free online at www.cityofolean.com/Assessor/main.htm. **Other Phone Numbers:** Assessor 716-938-9111; Treasurer 716-938-9111.

Cayuga County

County Clerk, 160 Genesee Street, Auburn, NY 13021. County Clerk, R/E and UCC Recording 315-253-1271; Fax 315-253-1653.
Will search UCC records. Will not search real estate records. **Other Phone Numbers:** Assessor 315-253-1270; Treasurer 315-253-1211; Elections 315-253-1285; Vital Records 315-255-4100.

Chautauqua County

County Clerk, P.O. Box 170, Mayville, NY 14757-0170. 716-753-4980; Fax 716-753-4310.
Will search UCC records. Will not search real estate records. **Other Phone Numbers:** Assessor 716-661-7223.

Chemung County

County Clerk, P.O. Box 588, Elmira, NY 14902-0588. 607-737-2920; Fax 607-737-2897.
Will search UCC records. Will not search real estate records.

Chenango County

County Clerk, 5 Court Street, Norwich, NY 13815. 607-337-1452.
Will search UCC records. UCC search includes tax liens. Will not search real estate records. **Other Phone Numbers:** Assessor 607-337-1822; Treasurer 607-337-1822.

Clinton County

County Clerk, 137 Margaret Street, Government Center, Plattsburgh, NY 12901-2974. 518-565-4700; Fax 518-565-4780.
Will search UCC records. UCC search includes tax liens if requested. Will not search real estate records. **Other Phone Numbers:** Assessor 518-565-4760; Treasurer 518-565-4730.

Columbia County

County Clerk, 560 Warren St., Hudson, NY 12534. County Clerk, R/E and UCC Recording 518-828-3339; Fax 518-828-5299.
Will search UCC records. Will not search real estate records. **Other Phone Numbers:** Assessor 518-828-7334; Treasurer 518-828-0513; Elections 518-828-3115.

Cortland County

County Clerk, 46 Greenbush St Suite 101, 46 Greenbush St., Cortland, NY 13045-3702. 607-753-5021 R/E Recording: 607-758-5021 UCC Recording: 607-758-5021; Fax 607-758-5500. www2.cortland-co.org
Will search UCC records. Fees are $13.00 plus $3.00 per page; $.50 extra for references on prior instruments. **Other Phone Numbers:** Assessor 607-753-5040 (Real Property); Treasurer 607-753-5070; Elections 607-753-5032; Vital Records 607-756-6521.

Delaware County

County Clerk, P.O. Box 426, Delhi, NY 13753. County Clerk, R/E and UCC Recording 607-746-2123; Fax 607-746-6924.
Will search UCC records. Will not search real estate records. **Other Phone Numbers:** Assessor 607-746-3747; Treasurer 607-746-2121; Elections 607-746-2315.

Dutchess County

County Clerk, 22 Market Street, Poughkeepsie, NY 12601. County Clerk, R/E and UCC Recording 845-

486-2120 UCC Recording: 845-486-2125; Fax 845-486-2138. http://www.dutchessny.gov
Will search UCC records. This agency will not do a tax lien search. Will not search real estate records. **Other Phone Numbers:** Assessor 845-431-2140; Treasurer 845-431-2025; Elections 845-486-2480.

Erie County

County Clerk, 25 Delaware Avenue, County Hall, Buffalo, NY 14202. 716-858-6724; Fax 716-858-6550. Will search UCC records. **Other Phone Numbers:** Assessor 716-858-8322; Treasurer 716-858-3236.

Essex County

County Clerk, P.O. Box 247, Elizabethtown, NY 12932. County Clerk, R/E and UCC Recording 518-873-3600; Fax 518-873-3548.
Will search UCC records. UCC search includes tax liens if requested. RE owner, mortgage, and property transfer searches available. **Other Phone Numbers:** Assessor 518-873-3390; Treasurer 518-873-3310; Elections 518-873-3474.

Franklin County

County Clerk, P.O. Box 70, Malone, NY 12953. County Clerk, R/E and UCC Recording 518-481-1681; Fax 518-483-9143.
Will search UCC records. Will not search real estate records. **Other Phone Numbers:** Assessor 518-481-1502; Treasurer 518-481-1516; Elections 518-481-1662; Vital Records 518-481-1671.

Fulton County

Clerk, P.O. Box 485, Johnstown, NY 12095. Clerk, R/E and UCC Recording 518-736-5555; Fax 518-762-3839. Will search UCC records. Will not search real estate records. **Other Phone Numbers:** Assessor 518-736-5510; Treasurer 518-736-5580; Elections 518-736-5526.

Genesee County

County Clerk, P.O. Box 379, Batavia, NY 14021-0379. 716-344-2550 x2245 R/E Recording: 716-344-2550 x2242 UCC Recording: 716-344-2550 x2243; Fax 716-344-8521. www.co.genesee.ny.us
Will search UCC records. Will not search real estate records. **Other Phone Numbers:** Assessor 716-344-2550 x2219; Treasurer 716-344-2550 x2210; Elections 716-344-2550 x2206.

Greene County

County Clerk, P.O. Box 446, Catskill, NY 12414. 518-943-2050; Fax 518-943-2146.
Will search UCC records. This agency will not do a tax lien search. Will not search real estate records. **Other Phone Numbers:** Assessor 518-943-6977; Treasurer 518-943-4152.

Hamilton County

County Clerk, P.O. Box 204, Rte. 8, Lake Pleasant, NY 12108. 518-548-7111.
Will search UCC records. This agency will not do a tax lien search. Will not search real estate records. **Other Phone Numbers:** Assessor 518-548-5531; Treasurer 518-548-7911.

Herkimer County

County Clerk, 109 Mary Street, Suite 1111, Herkimer, NY 13350. 315-867-1137; Fax 315-866-4396.
Will search UCC records. Will not search real estate records. **Other Phone Numbers:** Treasurer 315-867-1153.

Jefferson County

County Clerk, 175 Arsenal Street, Watertown, NY 13601-2555. County Clerk, R/E and UCC Recording 315-785-3081; Fax 315-785-5048.
Will search UCC records. **Other Phone Numbers:** Assessor 315-785-3074; Treasurer 315-785-3055; Elections 315-785-5119.

Kings County

County Clerk, Municipal Building, 1st Floor, Room 2, 210 Joralemon Street, Brooklyn, NY 11201. 718-802-3589; Fax 718-802-3745.
Will search UCC records. Will not search real estate records. **Online Access:** Real Estate, Liens, Tax Assessor Records. There are two options. The fee service supports the Boroughs of Brooklyn, Queens, Staten Island, Bronx, and Manhattan. There is a $250 monthly fee and a $5.00 fee per transaction. Records are kept 2-5 years. Search by name, grantor/grantee, and address. For information, contact Richard Reskin at 718-935-6523. Also, property assessment rolls from NYC's Dept. of Finance are available free online at www.ci.nyc.ny.us/html/dof/html/asmt.html. Search by borough, block and lot number. Tax reports are also available, with enrollment required. **Other Phone Numbers:** Assessor 718-802-3560; Treasurer 718-669-2746.

Lewis County

County Clerk, PO Box 232, Lowville, NY 13367-0232. County Clerk, R/E and UCC Recording 315-376-5333; Fax 315-376-3768.
Will search UCC records. UCC search includes federal tax liens Will not search real estate records. **Other Phone Numbers:** Assessor 315-376-5356; Treasurer 315-376-5326; Elections 315-376-5329.

Livingston County

County Clerk, Government Center, 6 Court St., Room 201, Geneseo, NY 14454-1043. 716-243-7010.
Will search UCC records. This agency will not do a tax lien search. Will not search real estate records. **Other Phone Numbers:** Assessor 716-243-7192; Treasurer 716-243-7050.

Madison County

County Clerk, P.O. Box 668, Wampsville, NY 13163. County Clerk, R/E and UCC Recording 315-366-2261 UCC Recording: 315-366-2262; Fax 315-366-2615. Will search UCC records. **Other Phone Numbers:** Assessor 315-366-2346; Treasurer 315-366-2371; Elections 315-366-2371.

Monroe County

County Clerk, 39 West Main Street, Rochester, NY 14614. County Clerk, R/E and UCC Recording 716-428-5151; Fax 716-428-5447. http://www.clerk.co.monroe.ny.us/
Will search UCC records. **Online Access:** Land Records, Judgments, UCCs, Liens, Court Records. Online access to the county clerk database are available online at http://www.clerk.co.monroe.ny.us. Includes mortgages, deeds, court records; free registration. Land records back to 1984. Liens, judgments, UCCS back to 5/1989. Court records - civil, felony, divorce - back to June, 1993. Earlier microfilm images are being added as time permits. **Other Phone Numbers:** Assessor 716-428-5290; Treasurer 716-428-5290; Elections 716-428-4550; Vital Records 716-274-6141.

Montgomery County

County Clerk, P.O. Box 1500, Fonda, NY 12068-1500. 518-853-8115.
Will search UCC records. UCC search includes only federal tax liens if requested Will not search real estate

records. **Other Phone Numbers:** Assessor 518-853-3996; Treasurer 518-853-8175.

Nassau County

County Clerk, 240 Old Country Road, Mineola, NY 11501. 516-571-2667; Fax 516-742-4099.
Will search UCC records. **Other Phone Numbers:** Assessor 516-571-2490; Treasurer 516-571-5021.

New York County

City Register, 31 Chambers Street, Room 202, New York, NY 10007. 212-788-8529; Fax 212-788-8521.
Will search UCC records. This agency will not do a tax lien search. Will not search real estate records. **Online Access:** Real Estate, Liens, Tax Assessor Records. Two options are available. Access to New York County online records - including Boroughs of Brooklyn, Queens, Staten Island, Bronx, Manhattan - requires a $250 monthly fee and $5 per transaction fee. Records are kept 2-5 years. For information, contact Richard Reskin at 718-935-6523. Also, property assessment rolls from NYC's Dept. of Finance are available free online at www.ci.nyc.ny.us/html/dof/html/asmt.html. Search by borough, block and lot number. Tax reports are also available, with enrollment required. **Other Phone Numbers:** Assessor 212-669-2387; Treasurer 212-669-3913.

Niagara County

County Clerk, P.O. Box 461, Lockport, NY 14095. 716-439-7029; Fax 716-439-7066.
Will search UCC records. UCC search includes tax liens if requested. RE record owner and mortgage searches available. **Other Phone Numbers:** Assessor 716-439-7031; Treasurer 716-439-7031.

Oneida County

County Clerk, 800 Park Avenue, Utica, NY 13501. 315-798-5792;   Fax   315-798-6440. http://www.oneidacounty.org/index1.htm
Will search UCC records. UCC search includes only federal tax liens, if requested RE record owner and mortgage searches available. **Other Phone Numbers:** Assessor 315-798-5750; Treasurer 315-798-5750; Elections 315-798-5763; Vital Records 315-798-5833.

Onondaga County

County Clerk, 401 Montgomery St., Room 200, Syracuse, NY 13202. 315-435-8200; Fax 315-435-3455.
Will search UCC records. **Other Phone Numbers:** Treasurer 315-435-2426.

Ontario County

County Clerk, Ontario County Municipal Bldg., 20 Ontario St., Canandaigua, NY 14424. County Clerk, R/E and UCC Recording 716-396-4200; Fax 716-393-2951. www.co.ontario.ny.us
Will search UCC records. **Other Phone Numbers:** Assessor 716-396-4396; Treasurer 716-396-4432; Elections 716-396-4005.

Orange County

County Clerk, 255-275 Main Street, Goshen, NY 10924. 845-291-2690 R/E Recording: 845-291-3062 UCC Recording: 845-291-3062; Fax 845-291-2691. http://www.co.orange.ny.us
Will search UCC records. UCC search includes tax liens if requested. RE owner, mortgage, and property transfer searches available. **Other Phone Numbers:** Assessor 845-291-2480; Treasurer 845-291-2485; Elections 845-291-2444.

Orleans County

County Clerk, 3 South Main Street, Courthouse Square, Albion, NY 14411-1498. County Clerk, R/E and UCC Recording 716-589-5334; Fax 716-589-0181.
Will search UCC records. **Other Phone Numbers:** Assessor 716-589-5400; Treasurer 716-589-5353; Elections 716-589-7004.

Oswego County

County Clerk, 46 East Bridge Street, Oswego, NY 13126. 315-349-8385; Fax 315-343-8383.
Will search UCC records. **Other Phone Numbers:** Assessor 315-349-8315; Treasurer 315-349-8393.

Otsego County

County Clerk, P.O. Box 710, Cooperstown, NY 13326-0710. 607-547-4278; Fax 607-547-7544.
Will search UCC records. Will not search real estate records.

Putnam County

County Clerk, 40 Gleneida Ave., Carmel, NY 10512. 845-225-3641; Fax 845-228-0231.
Will search UCC records. UCC search includes tax liens if requested. RE record owner and mortgage searches available. A $1.00 "processing fee" per title was been added in 2000. **Online Access:** Real Estate, Recording. County Recorder records are accessible through a private online service at www.landaccess.com; Fees and registration are required. **Other Phone Numbers:** Assessor 845-225-3641 x310; Treasurer 845-225-3641 x321.

Queens County

City Register, 144-06 94th Ave., Jamaica, NY 11435. 718-298-7000.
Will search UCC records. This agency will not do a tax lien search. Will not search real estate records. **Online Access:** Real Estate, Liens, Tax Assessor Records. Two options are available. Access to Queens County online records - including Boroughs of Brooklyn, Queens, Staten Island, Bronx, Manhattan - requires a $250 monthly fee and $5 per transaction fee. Records are kept 2-5 years. For information, contact Richard Reskin at 718-935-6523. Also, property assessment rolls from NYC's Dept. of Finance are available free online at www.ci.nyc.ny.us/html/dof/html/asmt.html. Search by borough, block and lot number. Tax reports are also available, with enrollment required. **Other Phone Numbers:** Assessor 718-658-4626.

Rensselaer County

County Clerk, Courthouse, Congress & 2nd Street, Troy, NY 12180. 518-270-4080.
Will search UCC records. This agency will not do a tax lien search. Will search deeds and mortgages with name and year. **Other Phone Numbers:** Assessor 518-270-2751; Treasurer 518-270-2751.

Richmond County

County Clerk, 18 Richmond Terrace, County Courthouse, Staten Island, NY 10301-1990. 718-390-5386.
Will search UCC records. This agency will not do a tax lien search. Will not search real estate records. **Online Access:** Real Estate, Liens, Tax Assessor Records. Two options are available. Access to Richmond-Staten Is. online records - including Boroughs of Brooklyn, Queens, Staten Island, Bronx, Manhattan - requires a $250 monthly fee and $5 per transaction fee. Records are kept 2-5 years. For further information, contact Richard Reskin at 718-935-6523. Property assessment rolls from NYC's Dept. of Finance are available free online at www.ci.nyc.ny.us/html/dof/html/asmt.html. Search by borough, block and lot number. Tax reports are also available, with enrollment required. **Other Phone Numbers:** Assessor 718-390-5292.

Rockland County

County Clerk, 27 New Hempstead Road, New City, NY 10956. 845-638-5354 R/E Recording: 845-638-5069; Fax 845-638-5647. http://www.rockland countyclerk.com
Will search UCC records. Tax liens not included in UCC search. RE owner, mortgage, and property transfer searches available. **Online Access:** Real Estate, Liens, Court Records. Online access is the clerk's expanding list of recordings, land records, and court records is available at the web site. Click on "Index to all records." System includes criminal index since 1982 plus civil judgments, real estate records, tax warrants. Images back to 6/96 are viewable, and more are being added. Call Paul Pipearto at 845-638-5221 for more information. **Other Phone Numbers:** Assessor 845-638-5131; Elections 845-638-5712.

Saratoga County

County Clerk, 40 McMaster Street, Ballston Spa, NY 12020. 518-885-2213; Fax 518-884-4726.
Will search UCC records. UCC search includes tax liens if requested. RE record owner and mortgage searches available. **Other Phone Numbers:** Assessor 518-885-5381 x455; Treasurer 518-885-5381 x281.

Schenectady County

County Clerk, 620 State Street, Schenectady, NY 12305-2114. 518-388-4220; Fax 518-388-4224. http://www.scpl.org
Will search UCC records. **Online Access:** Real Estate, Tax Assessor Records. Records for approximately 2/5 of the county property assessments are available free online on the library database at www.scpl.org/assessments. **Other Phone Numbers:** Assessor 518-388-4247; Treasurer 518-388-4262.

Schoharie County

County Clerk, P.O. Box 549, Schoharie, NY 12157. County Clerk, R/E and UCC Recording 518-295-8316; Fax 518-295-8338.
Will search UCC records. Will not search real estate records. **Other Phone Numbers:** Assessor 518-295-7141; Treasurer 518-295-8386.

Schuyler County

County Clerk, 105 Ninth Street Unit 8, County Office Building, Watkins Glen, NY 14891. 607-535-8133.
Will search UCC records. This agency will not do a tax lien search. Will not search real estate records. **Other Phone Numbers:** Assessor 607-535-8118; Treasurer 607-535-8181.

Seneca County

County Clerk, 1 DiPronio Drive, Waterloo, NY 13165. 315-539-1771 R/E Recording: 315-539-1770 UCC Recording: 315-539-1772; Fax 315-539-3789.
Will search UCC records. Will not search real estate records. **Other Phone Numbers:** Assessor 315-539-1720; Treasurer 315-539-1738; Appraiser/Auditor 315-539-1718; Elections 315-539-1762; Vital Records 315-539-1765.

St. Lawrence County

County Clerk, 48 Court Street, Canton, NY 13617-1198. County Clerk, R/E and UCC Recording 315-379-2237; Fax 315-379-2302. http://www.co.st-lawrence.ny.us/CoTOC2.htm
Will search UCC records. This agency will not do a tax lien search. Will not search real estate records. **Other Phone Numbers:** Assessor 315-379-2272; Treasurer 315-379-2234; Appraiser/Auditor 315-379-2272; Elections 315-379-2202.

Steuben County

County Clerk, 3 East Pulteney Square, County Office Building, Bath, NY 14810. 607-776-9631 x3210; Fax 607-776-7158.
Will search UCC records. **Online Access:** Tax Assessor Records. Access to Town of Erwin Real Property Assessment Roll is available free online at www.pennynet.org/erwin/er95tax.htm. **Other Phone Numbers:** Assessor 607-324-3074; Treasurer 607-324-7421.

Suffolk County

Clerk's Office, 310 Center Drive, Riverhead, NY 11901-3392. 631-852-2038 R/E Recording: 631-852-2043; Fax 631-852-2004.
Will search UCC records. Will not search real estate records. **Other Phone Numbers:** Assessor 631-852-1551; Treasurer 631-852-1500.

Sullivan County

County Clerk, P.O. Box 5012, Monticello, NY 12701. 845-794-3000 x3152.
Will search UCC records. This agency will not do a tax lien search. Will not search real estate records. **Other Phone Numbers:** Assessor 845-794-3000 x5014; Treasurer 845-794-3000.

Tioga County

County Clerk, P.O. Box 307, Owego, NY 13827. County Clerk, R/E and UCC Recording 607-687-8660; Fax 607-687-4612.
Will search UCC records. Will not search real estate records. **Other Phone Numbers:** Assessor 607-687-8661; Treasurer 607-687-8670; Elections 607-687-8261.

Tompkins County

County Clerk, 320 North Tioga Street, Ithaca, NY 14850-4284. 607-274-5432; http://www.co.tompkins.ny.us/assessment
Will search UCC records. UCC search includes federal tax liens RE owner, mortgage, and property transfer searches available. **Online Access:** Tax Assessor Records. 1999 records on the county Division of Assessment database are available free online at a mirror site: http://rd2020.hypermart.net/tentative.html. (this URL may change in 2001 - see the main assessor page.). **Other Phone Numbers:** Assessor 607-274-5517.

Ulster County

County Clerk, P.O. Box 1800, Kingston, NY 12402-0800. County Clerk, R/E and UCC Recording 845-340-3288; Fax 845-340-3299. http://www.co.ulster.ny.us
Will search UCC records. Tax liens not included in UCC search. RE owner, mortgage, and property transfer searches available. **Online Access:** Real Estate, Liens, Property Tax, Voter Registration, Court Records. Two options exist. Access to county online records requires a $33.33 or $44.55 monthly fee and a commitment to one year of service. Land Records date back to 1984. Includes county court records back to 7/1987. Lending agency information is available. For information, contact Valerie Harris at 914-340-5300. Also, the Ulster County Parcel Viewer at http://www.maphost.com/ulster provides free access to tax parcel information. Search by GIS map, parcel ID number, street name, or other criteria. **Other Phone Numbers:** Assessor 845-340-3431; Treasurer 845-340-3431; Elections 845-340-5470.

Warren County

County Clerk, Municipal Center, 1340 State Route 9, Lake George, NY 12845. 518-761-6426; Fax 518-761-6551.

Will search UCC records. Will not search real estate records. **Other Phone Numbers:** Assessor 518-761-6465.

Washington County

County Clerk, 383 Broadway, Bldg A, Fort Edward, NY 12828. County Clerk, R/E and UCC Recording 518-746-2170; Fax 518-746-2166.

Will search UCC records. This agency will not do a tax lien search. Will not search real estate records. **Other Phone Numbers:** Assessor 518-746-2130 (Real Property Tax); Treasurer 518-746-2220; Elections 518-746-2180.

Wayne County

County Clerk, P.O. Box 608, Lyons, NY 14489-0608. County Clerk, R/E and UCC Recording 315-946-7470; Fax 315-946-5978. http://www.co.wayne.ny.us

Will search UCC records. **Other Phone Numbers:** Assessor 315-946-5916; Treasurer 315-946-7443; Elections 315-946-7400.

Westchester County

County Clerk, 110 Dr. Martin Luther King Jr. Blvd., White Plains, NY 10601. 914-995-3098; Fax 914-995-3172.

Will search UCC records. Will not search real estate records. **Other Phone Numbers:** Assessor 914-422-1223.

Wyoming County

County Clerk, P.O. Box 70, Warsaw, NY 14569-0070. 716-786-8810; Fax 716-786-3703.

Will search UCC records. Tax liens not included in UCC search. RE owner, mortgage, and property transfer searches available. **Online Access:** Real Estate, Recording. County Recorder records are accessible through a private online service at www.landaccess.com; Fees and registration are required. **Other Phone Numbers:** Assessor 716-786-8828; Treasurer 716-786-8800.

Yates County

County Clerk, 110 Court Street, Penn Yan, NY 14527. County Clerk, R/E and UCC Recording 315-536-5120; Fax 315-536-5545.

Will search UCC records. Will not search real estate records. **Other Phone Numbers:** Assessor 315-536-5165; Treasurer 315-536-5192; Elections 315-536-5135.

New York County Locator

You will usually be able to find the city name in the City/County Cross Reference below. In that case, it is a simple matter to determine the county from the cross reference. However, only the official US Postal Service city names are included in this index. There are an additional 40,000 place names that people use in their addresses. Therefore, we have also included a ZIP/City Cross Reference immediately following the City/County Cross Reference.

If you know the ZIP Code but the city name does not appear in the City/County Cross Reference index, look up the ZIP Code in the ZIP/City Cross Reference, find the city name, then look up the city name in the City/County Cross Reference. For example, you want to know the county for an address of Menands, NY 12204. There is no "Menands" in the City/County Cross Reference. The ZIP/City Cross Reference shows that ZIP Codes 12201-12288 are for the city of Albany. Looking back in the City/County Cross Reference, Albany is in Albany County.

City/County Cross Reference

ACCORD Ulster
ACRA Greene
ADAMS Jefferson
ADAMS BASIN Monroe
ADAMS CENTER Jefferson
ADDISON Steuben
ADIRONDACK Warren
AFTON (13730) Broome(51),
   Chenango(49)
AKRON (14001) Erie(92), Niagara(4),
   Genesee(4)
ALABAMA Genesee
ALBANY Albany
ALBERTSON Nassau
ALBION Orleans
ALCOVE Albany
ALDEN (14004) Erie(93), Wyoming(6),
   Genesee(2)
ALDER CREEK Oneida
ALEXANDER Genesee
ALEXANDRIA BAY Jefferson
ALFRED Allegany
ALFRED STATION (14803) Allegany(89),
   Steuben(11)
ALLEGANY Cattaraugus
ALLENTOWN Allegany
ALMA Allegany
ALMOND Allegany
ALPINE Schuyler
ALPLAUS Schenectady
ALTAMONT Albany
ALTMAR Oswego
ALTON Wayne
ALTONA Clinton
AMAGANSETT Suffolk
AMAWALK Westchester
AMENIA Dutchess
AMITYVILLE Suffolk
AMSTERDAM (12010) Montgomery(94),
   Schenectady(4), Fulton(1)
ANCRAM Columbia
ANCRAMDALE Columbia
ANDES Delaware
ANDOVER (14806) Allegany(84),
   Steuben(16)
ANGELICA Allegany
ANGOLA Erie
ANNANDALE ON HUDSON Dutchess
ANTWERP (13608) Jefferson(88), St.
   Lawrence(12)
APALACHIN Tioga
APO
APPLETON Niagara
APULIA STATION Onondaga
AQUEBOGUE Suffolk
ARCADE (14009) Wyoming(90),
   Cattaraugus(10)
ARDEN Orange
ARDSLEY Westchester
ARDSLEY ON HUDSON Westchester
ARGYLE Washington
ARKPORT (14807) Steuben(79),
   Allegany(21)

ARKVILLE (12406) Delaware(65),
   Ulster(36)
ARMONK Westchester
ASHLAND Greene
ASHVILLE Chautauqua
ATHENS Greene
ATHOL Warren
ATHOL SPRINGS Erie
ATLANTA Steuben
ATLANTIC BEACH Nassau
ATTICA (14011) Wyoming(91), Genesee(9)
AU SABLE FORKS (12912) Clinton(96),
   Essex(4)
AUBURN Cayuga
AURIESVILLE Montgomery
AURORA Cayuga
AUSTERLITZ Columbia
AVA Oneida
AVERILL PARK Rensselaer
AVOCA Steuben
AVON Livingston
BABYLON Suffolk
BAINBRIDGE (13733) Chenango(97),
   Delaware(2), Otsego(2)
BAKERS MILLS Warren
BALDWIN Nassau
BALDWIN PLACE (10505)
   Westchester(71), Putnam(29)
BALDWINSVILLE Onondaga
BALLSTON LAKE Saratoga
BALLSTON SPA Saratoga
BALMAT St. Lawrence
BANGALL Dutchess
BANGOR Franklin
BARKER (14012) Niagara(95), Orleans(5)
BARNEVELD Oneida
BARRYTOWN Dutchess
BARRYVILLE Sullivan
BARTON Tioga
BASOM Genesee
BATAVIA Genesee
BATH Steuben
BAY SHORE Suffolk
BAYPORT Suffolk
BAYVILLE Nassau
BEACON Dutchess
BEAR MOUNTAIN Rockland
BEARSVILLE Ulster
BEAVER DAMS (14812) Schuyler(44),
   Chemung(33), Steuben(23)
BEAVER FALLS Lewis
BEDFORD Westchester
BEDFORD HILLS Westchester
BELFAST Allegany
BELLEVILLE Jefferson
BELLMORE Nassau
BELLONA Yates
BELLPORT Suffolk
BELLVALE Orange
BELMONT Allegany
BEMUS POINT Chautauqua
BERGEN (14416) Genesee(90),
   Monroe(10)

BERKSHIRE (13736) Tioga(89),
   Tompkins(6), Broome(5)
BERLIN Rensselaer
BERNE (12023) Albany(94), Schoharie(6)
BERNHARDS BAY Oswego
BETHEL Sullivan
BETHPAGE Nassau
BIBLE SCHOOL PARK Broome
BIG FLATS (14814) Chemung(86),
   Steuben(14)
BIG INDIAN Ulster
BILLINGS Dutchess
BINGHAMTON Broome
BLACK CREEK Allegany
BLACK RIVER Jefferson
BLAUVELT Rockland
BLISS (14024) Wyoming(90), Allegany(10)
BLODGETT MILLS Cortland
BLOOMFIELD Ontario
BLOOMING GROVE Orange
BLOOMINGBURG (12721) Sullivan(92),
   Orange(8)
BLOOMINGDALE (12913) Essex(75),
   Franklin(26)
BLOOMINGTON Ulster
BLOOMVILLE Delaware
BLOSSVALE Oneida
BLUE MOUNTAIN LAKE Hamilton
BLUE POINT Suffolk
BOHEMIA Suffolk
BOICEVILLE Ulster
BOLIVAR Allegany
BOLTON LANDING Warren
BOMBAY (12914) Franklin(96), St.
   Lawrence(4)
BOONVILLE (13309) Oneida(95), Lewis(5)
BOSTON Erie
BOUCKVILLE Madison
BOUQUET Essex
BOVINA CENTER Delaware
BOWMANSVILLE Erie
BRADFORD (14815) Schuyler(66),
   Steuben(34)
BRAINARD Rensselaer
BRAINARDSVILLE Franklin
BRANCHPORT (14418) Yates(91),
   Steuben(10)
BRANT Erie
BRANT LAKE Warren
BRANTINGHAM Lewis
BRASHER FALLS St. Lawrence
BREESPORT Chemung
BRENTWOOD Suffolk
BREWERTON Onondaga
BREWSTER (10509) Putnam(98),
   Westchester(2)
BRIARCLIFF MANOR Westchester
BRIDGEHAMPTON Suffolk
BRIDGEPORT (13030) Onondaga(79),
   Madison(21)
BRIDGEWATER Oneida
BRIER HILL St. Lawrence
BRIGHTWATERS Suffolk

BROADALBIN (12025) Fulton(97),
   Saratoga(3)
BROCKPORT Monroe
BROCTON Chautauqua
BRONX Bronx
BRONX New York
BRONXVILLE Westchester
BROOKFIELD Madison
BROOKHAVEN Suffolk
BROOKLYN Kings
BROOKTONDALE (14817) Tompkins(94),
   Tioga(6)
BROOKVIEW Rensselaer
BROWNVILLE Jefferson
BRUSHTON Franklin
BUCHANAN Westchester
BUFFALO Erie
BULLVILLE Orange
BURDETT Schuyler
BURKE Franklin
BURLINGHAM Sullivan
BURLINGTON FLATS Otsego
BURNT HILLS (12027) Saratoga(81),
   Schenectady(19)
BURT Niagara
BUSKIRK (12028) Rensselaer(94),
   Washington(6)
BYRON (14422) Genesee(98), Orleans(2)
CADYVILLE Clinton
CAIRO Greene
CALCIUM Jefferson
CALEDONIA (14423) Livingston(98),
   Monroe(2)
CALLICOON Sullivan
CALLICOON CENTER Sullivan
CALVERTON Suffolk
CAMBRIDGE Washington
CAMDEN (13316) Oneida(98), Lewis(1)
CAMERON Steuben
CAMERON MILLS Steuben
CAMILLUS Onondaga
CAMPBELL Steuben
CAMPBELL HALL Orange
CANAAN Columbia
CANAJOHARIE Montgomery
CANANDAIGUA Ontario
CANASERAGA (14822) Allegany(88),
   Livingston(12)
CANASTOTA Madison
CANDOR Tioga
CANEADEA Allegany
CANISTEO Steuben
CANTON St. Lawrence
CAPE VINCENT Jefferson
CARLE PLACE Nassau
CARLISLE Schoharie
CARMEL Putnam
CAROGA LAKE Fulton
CARTHAGE (13619) Jefferson(81), St.
   Lawrence(11), Lewis(8)
CASSADAGA Chautauqua
CASSVILLE Oneida
CASTILE Wyoming

CASTLE CREEK Broome
CASTLE POINT Dutchess
CASTLETON ON HUDSON Rensselaer
CASTORLAND Lewis
CATO Cayuga
CATSKILL Greene
CATTARAUGUS Cattaraugus
CAYUGA Cayuga
CAYUTA (14824) Schuyler(70),
     Chemung(30)
CAZENOVIA (13035) Madison(96),
     Onondaga(4)
CEDARHURST Nassau
CELORON Chautauqua
CEMENTON Greene
CENTER MORICHES Suffolk
CENTEREACH Suffolk
CENTERPORT Suffolk
CENTERVILLE Allegany
CENTRAL BRIDGE Schoharie
CENTRAL ISLIP Suffolk
CENTRAL SQUARE Oswego
CENTRAL VALLEY Orange
CERES Allegany
CHADWICKS Oneida
CHAFFEE (14030) Erie(77),
     Cattaraugus(18), Wyoming(5)
CHAMPLAIN Clinton
CHAPPAQUA Westchester
CHARLOTTEVILLE (12036) Schoharie(77),
     Otsego(23)
CHASE MILLS St. Lawrence
CHATEAUGAY Franklin
CHATHAM Columbia
CHAUMONT Jefferson
CHAUTAUQUA Chautauqua
CHAZY Clinton
CHELSEA Dutchess
CHEMUNG Chemung
CHENANGO BRIDGE Broome
CHENANGO FORKS (13746) Broome(73),
     Chenango(27)
CHERRY CREEK Chautauqua
CHERRY PLAIN Rensselaer
CHERRY VALLEY Otsego
CHESTER Orange
CHESTERTOWN Warren
CHICHESTER Ulster
CHILDWOLD St. Lawrence
CHIPPEWA BAY St. Lawrence
CHITTENANGO Madison
CHURCHVILLE Monroe
CHURUBUSCO Clinton
CICERO Onondaga
CINCINNATUS (13040) Cortland(97),
     Chenango(3)
CIRCLEVILLE Orange
CLARENCE Erie
CLARENCE CENTER (14032) Erie(98),
     Niagara(2)
CLARENDON Orleans
CLARK MILLS Oneida
CLARKSON Monroe
CLARKSVILLE Albany
CLARYVILLE (12725) Ulster(60),
     Sullivan(41)
CLAVERACK Columbia
CLAY Onondaga
CLAYTON Jefferson
CLAYVILLE (13322) Herkimer(81),
     Oneida(19)
CLEMONS Washington
CLEVELAND (13042) Oswego(92),
     Oneida(8)
CLEVERDALE Warren
CLIFTON PARK Saratoga
CLIFTON SPRINGS Ontario
CLIMAX Greene
CLINTON Oneida
CLINTON CORNERS Dutchess
CLINTONDALE Ulster
CLOCKVILLE Madison

CLYDE (14433) Wayne(95), Seneca(5)
CLYMER Chautauqua
COBLESKILL Schoharie
COCHECTON (12726) Sullivan(99),
     Delaware(2)
COCHECTON CENTER Sullivan
COEYMANS Albany
COEYMANS HOLLOW (12046)
     Albany(98), Greene(2)
COHOCTON Steuben
COHOES Albany
COLD BROOK Herkimer
COLD SPRING Putnam
COLD SPRING HARBOR Suffolk
COLDEN Erie
COLLIERSVILLE Otsego
COLLINS Erie
COLLINS CENTER Erie
COLTON St. Lawrence
COLUMBIAVILLE Columbia
COMMACK Suffolk
COMSTOCK Washington
CONESUS Livingston
CONEWANGO VALLEY (14726)
     Cattaraugus(89), Chautauqua(11)
CONGERS Rockland
CONKLIN Broome
CONNELLY Ulster
CONSTABLE Franklin
CONSTABLEVILLE Lewis
CONSTANTIA Oswego
COOPERS PLAINS Steuben
COOPERSTOWN Otsego
COPAKE Columbia
COPAKE FALLS Columbia
COPENHAGEN (13626) Lewis(90),
     Jefferson(10)
COPIAGUE Suffolk
CORAM Suffolk
CORBETTSVILLE Broome
CORFU (14036) Genesee(98), Erie(2)
CORINTH Saratoga
CORNING (14830) Steuben(99),
     Chemung(1)
CORNING Steuben
CORNWALL Orange
CORNWALL ON HUDSON Orange
CORNWALLVILLE Greene
CORTLAND (13045) Cortland(97),
     Tompkins(2), Cayuga(1)
COSSAYUNA Washington
COTTEKILL Ulster
COWLESVILLE (14037) Wyoming(77),
     Erie(23)
COXSACKIE Greene
CRAGSMOOR Ulster
CRANBERRY LAKE St. Lawrence
CRARYVILLE Columbia
CRITTENDEN Erie
CROGHAN Lewis
CROMPOND Westchester
CROPSEYVILLE Rensselaer
CROSS RIVER Westchester
CROTON FALLS Westchester
CROTON ON HUDSON Westchester
CROWN POINT Essex
CUBA (14727) Allegany(80),
     Cattaraugus(20)
CUDDEBACKVILLE Orange
CUTCHOGUE Suffolk
CUYLER (13050) Cortland(96),
     Onondaga(5)
DALE Wyoming
DALTON (14836) Livingston(60),
     Allegany(41)
DANNEMORA Clinton
DANSVILLE (14437) Livingston(91),
     Steuben(9)
DARIEN CENTER (14040) Genesee(87),
     Wyoming(13)
DAVENPORT (13750) Delaware(98),
     Otsego(2)

DAVENPORT CENTER Delaware
DAYTON Cattaraugus
DE KALB JUNCTION St. Lawrence
DE LANCEY Delaware
DE PEYSTER St. Lawrence
DE RUYTER (13052) Madison(70),
     Chenango(27), Onondaga(3)
DEANSBORO Oneida
DEER PARK Suffolk
DEER RIVER Lewis
DEFERIET Jefferson
DELANSON (12053) Schenectady(81),
     Albany(16), Schoharie(3)
DELEVAN Cattaraugus
DELHI Delaware
DELMAR Albany
DELPHI FALLS Onondaga
DENMARK Lewis
DENVER Delaware
DEPAUVILLE Jefferson
DEPEW Erie
DEPOSIT (13754) Broome(58),
     Delaware(42)
DERBY Erie
DEWITTVILLE Chautauqua
DEXTER Jefferson
DIAMOND POINT Warren
DICKINSON CENTER (12930)
     Franklin(95), St. Lawrence(5)
DOBBS FERRY Westchester
DOLGEVILLE (13329) Herkimer(87),
     Fulton(13)
DORMANSVILLE Albany
DOVER PLAINS Dutchess
DOWNSVILLE Delaware
DRESDEN Yates
DRYDEN (13053) Tompkins(83),
     Cortland(17)
DUANESBURG Schenectady
DUNDEE (14837) Yates(76), Schuyler(22),
     Steuben(2)
DUNKIRK Chautauqua
DURHAM Greene
DURHAMVILLE Oneida
EAGLE BAY Herkimer
EAGLE BRIDGE (12057) Rensselaer(80),
     Washington(20)
EAGLE HARBOR Orleans
EARLTON Greene
EARLVILLE (13332) Chenango(52),
     Madison(48)
EAST AMHERST Erie
EAST AURORA Erie
EAST BERNE Albany
EAST BETHANY (14054) Genesee(91),
     Wyoming(9)
EAST BLOOMFIELD Ontario
EAST BRANCH Delaware
EAST CHATHAM Columbia
EAST CONCORD Erie
EAST DURHAM Greene
EAST FREETOWN Cortland
EAST GREENBUSH Rensselaer
EAST GREENWICH Washington
EAST HAMPTON Suffolk
EAST HOMER Cortland
EAST ISLIP Suffolk
EAST JEWETT Greene
EAST MARION Suffolk
EAST MEADOW Nassau
EAST MEREDITH Delaware
EAST MORICHES Suffolk
EAST NASSAU (12062) Columbia(87),
     Rensselaer(13)
EAST NORTHPORT Suffolk
EAST NORWICH Nassau
EAST OTTO Cattaraugus
EAST PALMYRA Wayne
EAST PEMBROKE Genesee
EAST PHARSALIA Chenango
EAST QUOGUE Suffolk
EAST RANDOLPH Cattaraugus

EAST ROCHESTER Monroe
EAST ROCKAWAY Nassau
EAST SCHODACK Rensselaer
EAST SETAUKET Suffolk
EAST SPRINGFIELD Otsego
EAST SYRACUSE Onondaga
EAST WILLIAMSON Wayne
EAST WORCESTER Otsego
EASTCHESTER Westchester
EASTPORT Suffolk
EATON Madison
EDEN Erie
EDMESTON Otsego
EDWARDS St. Lawrence
ELBA (14058) Genesee(95), Orleans(5)
ELBRIDGE (13060) Onondaga(97),
     Cayuga(3)
ELDRED Sullivan
ELIZABETHTOWN Essex
ELIZAVILLE Columbia
ELKA PARK Greene
ELLENBURG Clinton
ELLENBURG CENTER Clinton
ELLENBURG DEPOT Clinton
ELLENVILLE Ulster
ELLICOTTVILLE Cattaraugus
ELLINGTON Chautauqua
ELLISBURG Jefferson
ELMA Erie
ELMIRA Chemung
ELMONT Nassau
ELMSFORD Westchester
ENDICOTT (13760) Broome(88), Tioga(12)
ENDICOTT Broome
ENDWELL Broome
ERIEVILLE Madison
ERIN Chemung
ESOPUS Ulster
ESPERANCE (12066) Montgomery(85),
     Schoharie(12), Schenectady(3)
ESSEX Essex
ETNA Tompkins
EVANS MILLS Jefferson
FABIUS Onondaga
FAIR HAVEN (13064) Oswego(94),
     Onondaga(6)
FAIRFIELD Herkimer
FAIRPORT Monroe
FALCONER Chautauqua
FALLSBURG Sullivan
FANCHER Orleans
FAR ROCKAWAY Queens
FARMERSVILLE STATION (14060)
     Allegany(55), Cattaraugus(45)
FARMINGDALE (11735) Nassau(72),
     Suffolk(28)
FARMINGDALE Nassau
FARMINGTON Ontario
FARMINGVILLE Suffolk
FARNHAM Erie
FAYETTE Seneca
FAYETTEVILLE Onondaga
FELTS MILLS Jefferson
FERNDALE Sullivan
FEURA BUSH Albany
FILLMORE Allegany
FINDLEY LAKE Chautauqua
FINE St. Lawrence
FISHERS Ontario
FISHERS ISLAND Suffolk
FISHERS LANDING Jefferson
FISHKILL Dutchess
FISHS EDDY Delaware
FLEISCHMANNS (12430) Delaware(78),
     Greene(22)
FLORAL PARK Nassau
FLORAL PARK Queens
FLORIDA Orange
FLUSHING Queens
FLY CREEK Otsego
FONDA (12068) Montgomery(98), Fulton(2)
FORESTBURGH Sullivan

FORESTPORT (13338) Oneida(97), Herkimer(3)
FORESTVILLE Chautauqua
FORT ANN Washington
FORT COVINGTON Franklin
FORT DRUM Jefferson
FORT EDWARD (12828) Washington(77), Saratoga(23)
FORT HUNTER Montgomery
FORT JACKSON St. Lawrence
FORT JOHNSON (12070) Montgomery(84), Fulton(16)
FORT MONTGOMERY Orange
FORT PLAIN (13339) Montgomery(72), Herkimer(17), Fulton(11)
FPO
FRANKFORT Herkimer
FRANKLIN Delaware
FRANKLIN SPRINGS Oneida
FRANKLIN SQUARE Nassau
FRANKLINVILLE (14737) Cattaraugus(99), Allegany(1)
FREDONIA Chautauqua
FREEDOM (14065) Cattaraugus(54), Allegany(46)
FREEHOLD Greene
FREEPORT Nassau
FREEVILLE Tompkins
FREMONT CENTER Sullivan
FREWSBURG (14738) Chautauqua(91), Cattaraugus(9)
FRIENDSHIP Allegany
FULTON Oswego
FULTONHAM Schoharie
FULTONVILLE Montgomery
GABRIELS Franklin
GAINESVILLE Wyoming
GALLUPVILLE Schoharie
GALWAY Saratoga
GANSEVOORT Saratoga
GARDEN CITY Nassau
GARDINER Ulster
GARNERVILLE Rockland
GARRATTSVILLE Otsego
GARRISON Putnam
GASPORT Niagara
GENESEO Livingston
GENEVA (14456) Ontario(94), Seneca(6)
GENOA Cayuga
GEORGETOWN (13072) Madison(89), Chenango(12)
GEORGETOWN Chenango
GERMANTOWN Columbia
GERRY Chautauqua
GETZVILLE Erie
GHENT Columbia
GILBERTSVILLE Otsego
GILBOA Schoharie
GLASCO Ulster
GLEN AUBREY Broome
GLEN COVE Nassau
GLEN HEAD Nassau
GLEN OAKS Queens
GLEN SPEY Sullivan
GLEN WILD Sullivan
GLENFIELD Lewis
GLENFORD Ulster
GLENHAM Dutchess
GLENMONT Albany
GLENS FALLS Warren
GLENWOOD Erie
GLENWOOD LANDING Nassau
GLOVERSVILLE Fulton
GODEFFROY Orange
GOLDENS BRIDGE Westchester
GORHAM Ontario
GOSHEN Orange
GOUVERNEUR St. Lawrence
GOWANDA (14070) Cattaraugus(59), Erie(42)
GRAFTON Rensselaer

GRAHAMSVILLE (12740) Sullivan(87), Ulster(13)
GRAND GORGE Delaware
GRAND ISLAND Erie
GRANITE SPRINGS Westchester
GRANVILLE Washington
GREAT BEND Jefferson
GREAT NECK Nassau
GREAT RIVER Suffolk
GREAT VALLEY Cattaraugus
GREENE (13778) Chenango(82), Broome(18)
GREENFIELD CENTER Saratoga
GREENFIELD PARK Ulster
GREENHURST Chautauqua
GREENLAWN Suffolk
GREENPORT Suffolk
GREENVALE Nassau
GREENVILLE (12083) Greene(81), Albany(19)
GREENWICH Washington
GREENWOOD Steuben
GREENWOOD LAKE Orange
GREIG Lewis
GROTON (13073) Tompkins(99), Cayuga(1)
GROVELAND Livingston
GUILDERLAND Albany
GUILDERLAND CENTER Albany
GUILFORD Chenango
HADLEY (12835) Saratoga(98), Warren(2)
HAGAMAN (12086) Montgomery(95), Fulton(3), Saratoga(2)
HAGUE (99999) Warren(99), Essex(1)
HAILESBORO St. Lawrence
HAINES FALLS Greene
HALCOTTSVILLE Delaware
HALL Ontario
HAMBURG Erie
HAMDEN Delaware
HAMILTON Madison
HAMLIN (14464) Monroe(97), Orleans(3)
HAMMOND St. Lawrence
HAMMONDSPORT (14840) Steuben(97), Schuyler(3)
HAMPTON Washington
HAMPTON BAYS Suffolk
HANCOCK Delaware
HANKINS Sullivan
HANNACROIX (12087) Greene(94), Albany(6)
HANNAWA FALLS St. Lawrence
HANNIBAL Oswego
HARFORD Cortland
HARPERSFIELD Delaware
HARPURSVILLE (13787) Broome(89), Chenango(12)
HARRIMAN Orange
HARRIS Sullivan
HARRISON Westchester
HARRISVILLE (13648) St. Lawrence(65), Lewis(35)
HARTFORD Washington
HARTSDALE Westchester
HARTWICK Otsego
HARTWICK SEMINARY Otsego
HASTINGS Oswego
HASTINGS ON HUDSON Westchester
HAUPPAUGE Suffolk
HAVERSTRAW Rockland
HAWTHORNE Westchester
HECTOR Schuyler
HELENA St. Lawrence
HELMUTH Erie
HEMLOCK (14466) Ontario(60), Livingston(40)
HEMPSTEAD Nassau
HENDERSON Jefferson
HENDERSON HARBOR Jefferson
HENRIETTA Monroe
HENSONVILLE Greene
HERKIMER Herkimer

HERMON St. Lawrence
HEUVELTON St. Lawrence
HEWLETT Nassau
HICKSVILLE Nassau
HIGH FALLS Ulster
HIGHLAND Ulster
HIGHLAND FALLS Orange
HIGHLAND LAKE Sullivan
HIGHLAND MILLS Orange
HIGHMOUNT Ulster
HILLBURN Rockland
HILLSDALE Columbia
HILTON Monroe
HIMROD Yates
HINCKLEY Oneida
HINSDALE Cattaraugus
HOBART Delaware
HOFFMEISTER Hamilton
HOGANSBURG Franklin
HOLBROOK Suffolk
HOLLAND Erie
HOLLAND PATENT Oneida
HOLLEY (14470) Orleans(97), Monroe(3)
HOLLOWVILLE Columbia
HOLMES (12531) Dutchess(74), Putnam(26)
HOLTSVILLE Suffolk
HOMER Cortland
HONEOYE Ontario
HONEOYE FALLS (14472) Monroe(91), Livingston(7), Ontario(3)
HOOSICK Rensselaer
HOOSICK FALLS Rensselaer
HOPEWELL JUNCTION (12533) Dutchess(99), Putnam(1)
HOPKINTON St. Lawrence
HORNELL Steuben
HORSEHEADS Chemung
HORTONVILLE Sullivan
HOUGHTON Allegany
HOWELLS Orange
HOWES CAVE Schoharie
HUBBARDSVILLE Madison
HUDSON Columbia
HUDSON FALLS Washington
HUGHSONVILLE Dutchess
HUGUENOT Orange
HULETTS LANDING Washington
HUME Allegany
HUNT (14846) Livingston(77), Allegany(23)
HUNTER Greene
HUNTINGTON Suffolk
HUNTINGTON STATION Suffolk
HURLEY Ulster
HURLEYVILLE Sullivan
HYDE PARK Dutchess
ILION Herkimer
INDIAN LAKE Hamilton
INDUSTRY Monroe
INLET Hamilton
INTERLAKEN Seneca
INWOOD Nassau
INWOOD Queens
IONIA (14475) Ontario(90), Monroe(11)
IRVING (14081) Chautauqua(54), Erie(44), Cattaraugus(2)
IRVINGTON Westchester
ISLAND PARK Nassau
ISLIP Suffolk
ISLIP TERRACE Suffolk
ITHACA Tompkins
JACKSONVILLE Tompkins
JAMAICA Queens
JAMESPORT Suffolk
JAMESTOWN Chautauqua
JAMESVILLE Onondaga
JASPER Steuben
JAVA CENTER Wyoming
JAVA VILLAGE Wyoming
JAY Essex
JEFFERSON (12093) Schoharie(73), Delaware(27)

JEFFERSON VALLEY Westchester
JEFFERSONVILLE Sullivan
JERICHO Nassau
JEWETT Greene
JOHNSBURG Warren
JOHNSON Orange
JOHNSON CITY Broome
JOHNSONVILLE (12094) Rensselaer(99), Washington(1)
JOHNSTOWN (12095) Fulton(99), Montgomery(2)
JORDAN Onondaga
JORDANVILLE (13361) Herkimer(98), Otsego(2)
KANONA Steuben
KATONAH Westchester
KATTSKILL BAY (12844) Warren(78), Washington(22)
KAUNEONGA LAKE Sullivan
KEENE Essex
KEENE VALLEY Essex
KEESEVILLE (12944) Clinton(85), Essex(15)
KEESEVILLE Clinton
KENDALL (14476) Orleans(96), Monroe(4)
KENNEDY (14747) Chautauqua(89), Cattaraugus(11)
KENOZA LAKE Sullivan
KENT Orleans
KERHONKSON Ulster
KEUKA PARK Yates
KIAMESHA LAKE Sullivan
KILL BUCK Cattaraugus
KILLAWOG Broome
KINDERHOOK Columbia
KING FERRY Cayuga
KINGS PARK Suffolk
KINGSTON Ulster
KIRKVILLE (13082) Onondaga(53), Madison(47)
KIRKWOOD Broome
KNAPP CREEK Cattaraugus
KNOWLESVILLE Orleans
KNOX Albany
KNOXBORO Oneida
LA FARGEVILLE Jefferson
LA FAYETTE Onondaga
LACONA Oswego
LAGRANGEVILLE Dutchess
LAKE CLEAR Franklin
LAKE GEORGE Warren
LAKE GROVE Suffolk
LAKE HILL Ulster
LAKE HUNTINGTON Sullivan
LAKE KATRINE Ulster
LAKE LUZERNE Warren
LAKE PEEKSKILL Putnam
LAKE PLACID Essex
LAKE PLEASANT Hamilton
LAKE VIEW Erie
LAKEMONT Yates
LAKEVILLE Livingston
LAKEWOOD Chautauqua
LANCASTER Erie
LANESVILLE Greene
LANSING Tompkins
LARCHMONT Westchester
LATHAM Albany
LAUREL Suffolk
LAURENS Otsego
LAWRENCE Nassau
LAWRENCEVILLE St. Lawrence
LAWTONS Erie
LAWYERSVILLE Schoharie
LE ROY (14482) Genesee(96), Livingston(3)
LEBANON Madison
LEBANON SPRINGS Columbia
LEE CENTER Oneida
LEEDS Greene
LEICESTER (14481) Livingston(99), Wyoming(1)

LEON Cattaraugus
LEONARDSVILLE Madison
LEVITTOWN Nassau
LEW BEACH (12753) Ulster(58), Sullivan(38), Delaware(4)
LEWIS Essex
LEWISTON Niagara
LEXINGTON Greene
LIBERTY Sullivan
LILY DALE Chautauqua
LIMA (14485) Livingston(95), Ontario(5)
LIMERICK Jefferson
LIMESTONE Cattaraugus
LINCOLNDALE Westchester
LINDENHURST Suffolk
LINDLEY Steuben
LINWOOD Genesee
LISBON St. Lawrence
LISLE Broome
LITTLE FALLS Herkimer
LITTLE GENESEE Allegany
LITTLE VALLEY Cattaraugus
LITTLE YORK Cortland
LIVERPOOL Onondaga
LIVINGSTON Columbia
LIVINGSTON MANOR (12758) Sullivan(93), Ulster(7)
LIVONIA (14487) Livingston(92), Ontario(8)
LIVONIA CENTER Livingston
LOCH SHELDRAKE Sullivan
LOCKE (13092) Tompkins(64), Cayuga(36)
LOCKPORT Niagara
LOCKWOOD (14859) Tioga(60), Chemung(40)
LOCUST VALLEY Nassau
LODI Seneca
LONG BEACH Nassau
LONG EDDY (12760) Sullivan(63), Delaware(37)
LONG ISLAND CITY Queens
LONG LAKE Hamilton
LORRAINE Jefferson
LOWMAN Chemung
LOWVILLE Lewis
LYCOMING Oswego
LYNBROOK Nassau
LYNDONVILLE (14098) Orleans(98), Niagara(2)
LYON MOUNTAIN (12952) Clinton(98), Essex(2)
LYON MOUNTAIN (12955) Clinton(98), Franklin(3)
LYONS (14489) Wayne(95), Ontario(3), Seneca(2)
LYONS FALLS Lewis
LYSANDER Onondaga
MACEDON (14502) Wayne(97), Monroe(3)
MACHIAS Cattaraugus
MADISON (13402) Madison(80), Oneida(20)
MADRID St. Lawrence
MAHOPAC (10541) Putnam(99), Westchester(1)
MAHOPAC FALLS Putnam
MAINE Broome
MALDEN BRIDGE Columbia
MALDEN ON HUDSON Ulster
MALLORY Oswego
MALONE Franklin
MALVERNE Nassau
MAMARONECK Westchester
MANCHESTER Ontario
MANHASSET Nassau
MANLIUS Onondaga
MANNSVILLE (13661) Jefferson(98), Oswego(2)
MANORVILLE Suffolk
MAPLE SPRINGS Chautauqua
MAPLE VIEW Oswego
MAPLECREST Greene
MARATHON (13803) Cortland(92), Broome(8)

MARCELLUS Onondaga
MARCY Oneida
MARGARETVILLE Delaware
MARIETTA Onondaga
MARILLA Erie
MARION Wayne
MARLBORO (12542) Ulster(94), Orange(6)
MARTINSBURG Lewis
MARTVILLE (13111) Cayuga(88), Oswego(12)
MARYKNOLL Westchester
MARYLAND Otsego
MASONVILLE Delaware
MASSAPEQUA Nassau
MASSAPEQUA PARK Nassau
MASSENA St. Lawrence
MASTIC Suffolk
MASTIC BEACH Suffolk
MATTITUCK Suffolk
MATTYDALE Onondaga
MAYBROOK Orange
MAYFIELD Fulton
MAYVILLE Chautauqua
MC CONNELLSVILLE Oneida
MC DONOUGH Chenango
MC GRAW Cortland
MC LEAN Tompkins
MECHANICVILLE (12118) Saratoga(97), Rensselaer(3)
MECKLENBURG Schuyler
MEDFORD Suffolk
MEDINA Orleans
MEDUSA Albany
MELLENVILLE Columbia
MELROSE Rensselaer
MELVILLE Suffolk
MEMPHIS Onondaga
MENDON Monroe
MERIDALE Delaware
MERIDIAN Cayuga
MERRICK Nassau
MEXICO Oswego
MID HUDSON Orange
MID ISLAND Suffolk
MIDDLE FALLS Washington
MIDDLE GRANVILLE Washington
MIDDLE GROVE Saratoga
MIDDLE ISLAND Suffolk
MIDDLEBURGH (12122) Albany(54), Schoharie(47)
MIDDLEPORT (14105) Niagara(94), Orleans(4), Genesee(2)
MIDDLESEX Yates
MIDDLETOWN Orange
MIDDLEVILLE Herkimer
MILFORD Otsego
MILL NECK Nassau
MILLBROOK Dutchess
MILLER PLACE Suffolk
MILLERTON (12546) Dutchess(91), Columbia(9)
MILLPORT (14864) Chemung(81), Schuyler(19)
MILLWOOD Westchester
MILTON Ulster
MINEOLA Nassau
MINERVA Essex
MINETTO Oswego
MINEVILLE Essex
MINOA Onondaga
MODEL CITY Niagara
MODENA Ulster
MOHAWK Herkimer
MOHEGAN LAKE Westchester
MOIRA Franklin
MONGAUP VALLEY Sullivan
MONROE Orange
MONSEY Rockland
MONTAUK Suffolk
MONTEZUMA Cayuga
MONTGOMERY Orange
MONTICELLO Sullivan

MONTOUR FALLS Schuyler
MONTROSE Westchester
MOOERS Clinton
MOOERS FORKS Clinton
MORAVIA Cayuga
MORIAH Essex
MORIAH CENTER Essex
MORICHES Suffolk
MORRIS Otsego
MORRISONVILLE Clinton
MORRISTOWN St. Lawrence
MORRISVILLE Madison
MORTON Orleans
MOTTVILLE Onondaga
MOUNT KISCO Westchester
MOUNT MARION Ulster
MOUNT MORRIS Livingston
MOUNT SINAI Suffolk
MOUNT TREMPER Ulster
MOUNT UPTON (13809) Chenango(72), Otsego(28)
MOUNT VERNON Westchester
MOUNT VISION Otsego
MOUNTAIN DALE Sullivan
MOUNTAINVILLE Orange
MUMFORD Monroe
MUNNSVILLE Madison
NANUET Rockland
NAPANOCH Ulster
NAPLES (14512) Ontario(74), Yates(22), Steuben(4)
NARROWSBURG Sullivan
NASSAU Rensselaer
NATURAL BRIDGE (13665) Jefferson(64), Lewis(36)
NEDROW Onondaga
NELLISTON Montgomery
NESCONSET Suffolk
NEVERSINK Sullivan
NEW BALTIMORE Greene
NEW BERLIN Chenango
NEW CITY Rockland
NEW HAMPTON Orange
NEW HARTFORD Oneida
NEW HAVEN Oswego
NEW HYDE PARK Nassau
NEW KINGSTON Delaware
NEW LEBANON Columbia
NEW LISBON Otsego
NEW MILFORD Orange
NEW PALTZ Ulster
NEW ROCHELLE Westchester
NEW RUSSIA Essex
NEW SUFFOLK Suffolk
NEW WINDSOR Orange
NEW WOODSTOCK (13122) Onondaga(59), Madison(41)
NEW YORK New York
NEW YORK MILLS Oneida
NEWARK (14513) Wayne(98), Ontario(2)
NEWARK VALLEY (13811) Tioga(94), Broome(6)
NEWBURGH Orange
NEWCOMB Essex
NEWFANE Niagara
NEWFIELD Tompkins
NEWPORT Herkimer
NEWTON FALLS St. Lawrence
NEWTONVILLE Albany
NIAGARA FALLS Niagara
NIAGARA UNIVERSITY Niagara
NICHOLS Tioga
NICHOLVILLE St. Lawrence
NINEVEH (13813) Broome(86), Chenango(14)
NIOBE Chautauqua
NIVERVILLE Columbia
NORFOLK St. Lawrence
NORTH BABYLON Suffolk
NORTH BANGOR Franklin
NORTH BAY Oneida
NORTH BLENHEIM Schoharie

NORTH BOSTON Erie
NORTH BRANCH Sullivan
NORTH BROOKFIELD Madison
NORTH CHATHAM Columbia
NORTH CHILI Monroe
NORTH CLYMER Chautauqua
NORTH COHOCTON Steuben
NORTH COLLINS Erie
NORTH CREEK Warren
NORTH EVANS Erie
NORTH GRANVILLE Washington
NORTH GREECE Monroe
NORTH HOOSICK Rensselaer
NORTH HUDSON Essex
NORTH JAVA Wyoming
NORTH LAWRENCE (12967) St. Lawrence(98), Franklin(2)
NORTH NORWICH Chenango
NORTH PITCHER Chenango
NORTH RIVER Warren
NORTH ROSE Wayne
NORTH SALEM Westchester
NORTH TONAWANDA Niagara
NORTHPORT Suffolk
NORTHVILLE Fulton
NORTON HILL Greene
NORWICH Chenango
NORWOOD St. Lawrence
NUNDA Livingston
NYACK Rockland
OAK HILL Greene
OAKDALE Suffolk
OAKFIELD (99999) Genesee(99), Orleans(1)
OAKS CORNERS Ontario
OBERNBURG Sullivan
OCEAN BEACH Suffolk
OCEANSIDE Nassau
ODESSA Schuyler
OGDENSBURG St. Lawrence
OLCOTT Niagara
OLD BETHPAGE Nassau
OLD CHATHAM Columbia
OLD FORGE Herkimer
OLD WESTBURY Nassau
OLEAN Cattaraugus
OLIVEBRIDGE Ulster
OLIVEREA Ulster
OLMSTEDVILLE (12857) Essex(92), Warren(9)
ONCHIOTA Franklin
ONEIDA (13421) Madison(90), Oneida(10)
ONEONTA (13820) Otsego(90), Delaware(10)
ONTARIO (14519) Wayne(96), Monroe(4)
ONTARIO CENTER Wayne
ORAN Onondaga
ORANGEBURG Rockland
ORCHARD PARK Erie
ORIENT Suffolk
ORISKANY Oneida
ORISKANY FALLS Oneida
ORWELL Oswego
OSSINING Westchester
OSWEGATCHIE St. Lawrence
OSWEGO Oswego
OTEGO (13825) Otsego(98), Delaware(2)
OTISVILLE Orange
OTTO Cattaraugus
OUAQUAGA Broome
OVID Seneca
OWASCO Cayuga
OWEGO Tioga
OWLS HEAD Franklin
OXBOW Jefferson
OXFORD Chenango
OYSTER BAY Nassau
PAINTED POST (14870) Steuben(97), Schuyler(3)
PALATINE BRIDGE Montgomery
PALENVILLE Greene
PALISADES Rockland

PALMYRA (14522) Wayne(90), Ontario(10)
PANAMA Chautauqua
PARADOX Essex
PARIS Oneida
PARISH Oswego
PARISHVILLE St. Lawrence
PARKSVILLE Sullivan
PATCHOGUE Suffolk
PATTERSON (12563) Putnam(99), Dutchess(1)
PATTERSONVILLE Schenectady
PAUL SMITHS Franklin
PAVILION (14525) Genesee(60), Wyoming(34), Livingston(6)
PAWLING Dutchess
PEARL RIVER Rockland
PECONIC Suffolk
PEEKSKILL Westchester
PELHAM Westchester
PENFIELD Monroe
PENN YAN Yates
PENNELLVILLE Oswego
PERKINSVILLE Steuben
PERRY Wyoming
PERRYSBURG Cattaraugus
PERRYVILLE Madison
PERU Clinton
PETERBORO Madison
PETERSBURG Rensselaer
PHELPS (14532) Ontario(95), Seneca(5)
PHILADELPHIA Jefferson
PHILLIPSPORT Sullivan
PHILMONT Columbia
PHOENICIA Ulster
PHOENIX (13135) Oswego(91), Onondaga(9)
PIERCEFIELD St. Lawrence
PIERMONT Rockland
PIERREPONT MANOR Jefferson
PIFFARD Livingston
PIKE Wyoming
PINE BUSH (12566) Ulster(58), Orange(40), Sullivan(2)
PINE CITY (14871) Chemung(85), Steuben(16)
PINE HILL (12465) Ulster(94), Delaware(6)
PINE ISLAND Orange
PINE PLAINS (12567) Dutchess(88), Columbia(13)
PINE VALLEY Chemung
PISECO Hamilton
PITCHER (13136) Chenango(98), Cortland(2)
PITTSFORD Monroe
PLAINVIEW Nassau
PLAINVILLE Onondaga
PLATTEKILL Ulster
PLATTSBURGH Clinton
PLEASANT VALLEY Dutchess
PLEASANTVILLE Westchester
PLESSIS Jefferson
PLYMOUTH Chenango
POESTENKILL Rensselaer
POINT LOOKOUT Nassau
POLAND (13431) Herkimer(77), Oneida(23)
POMONA Rockland
POMPEY Onondaga
POND EDDY Sullivan
POOLVILLE Madison
POPLAR RIDGE Cayuga
PORT BYRON Cayuga
PORT CHESTER Westchester
PORT CRANE Broome
PORT EWEN Ulster
PORT GIBSON Ontario
PORT HENRY Essex
PORT JEFFERSON Suffolk
PORT JEFFERSON STATION Suffolk
PORT JERVIS Orange
PORT KENT Essex
PORT LEYDEN Lewis

PORT WASHINGTON Nassau
PORTAGEVILLE (14536) Wyoming(73), Allegany(27)
PORTER CORNERS Saratoga
PORTLAND Chautauqua
PORTLANDVILLE Otsego
PORTVILLE (14770) Cattaraugus(76), Allegany(24)
POTSDAM St. Lawrence
POTTERSVILLE Warren
POUGHKEEPSIE Dutchess
POUGHQUAG Dutchess
POUND RIDGE Westchester
PRATTS HOLLOW Madison
PRATTSBURGH (14873) Steuben(99), Yates(1)
PRATTSVILLE (12468) Greene(97), Delaware(3)
PREBLE (13141) Cortland(57), Onondaga(43)
PRESTON HOLLOW (12469) Albany(87), Schoharie(11), Greene(2)
PROSPECT Oneida
PULASKI Oswego
PULTENEY Steuben
PULTNEYVILLE Wayne
PURCHASE Westchester
PURDYS Westchester
PURLING Greene
PUTNAM STATION (12861) Washington(95), Essex(5)
PUTNAM VALLEY (10579) Putnam(99), Westchester(1)
PYRITES St. Lawrence
QUAKER STREET Schenectady
QUEENSBURY Warren
QUOGUE Suffolk
RAINBOW LAKE Franklin
RANDOLPH Cattaraugus
RANSOMVILLE Niagara
RAQUETTE LAKE Hamilton
RAVENA (12143) Albany(99), Greene(2)
RAY BROOK Essex
RAYMONDVILLE St. Lawrence
READING CENTER Schuyler
RED CREEK (13143) Wayne(96), Cayuga(3)
RED HOOK (12571) Dutchess(96), Columbia(4)
REDFIELD (13437) Oswego(98), Lewis(2)
REDFORD Clinton
REDWOOD (13679) Jefferson(95), St. Lawrence(5)
REMSEN (13438) Oneida(97), Herkimer(3)
REMSENBURG Suffolk
RENSSELAER Rensselaer
RENSSELAER FALLS St. Lawrence
RENSSELAERVILLE Albany
RETSOF Livingston
REXFORD (12148) Saratoga(96), Schenectady(4)
REXVILLE (14877) Steuben(98), Allegany(2)
RHINEBECK Dutchess
RHINECLIFF Dutchess
RICHBURG Allegany
RICHFIELD SPRINGS (13439) Otsego(86), Herkimer(14)
RICHFORD (13835) Tioga(56), Broome(31), Cortland(13)
RICHLAND Oswego
RICHMONDVILLE (12149) Schoharie(94), Otsego(6)
RICHVILLE St. Lawrence
RIDGE Suffolk
RIFTON Ulster
RIPARIUS Warren
RIPLEY Chautauqua
RIVERHEAD Suffolk
ROCHESTER Monroe
ROCK CITY FALLS Saratoga
ROCK HILL Sullivan

ROCK STREAM (14878) Schuyler(71), Yates(29)
ROCK TAVERN Orange
ROCKLAND M P C Rockland
ROCKVILLE CENTRE Nassau
ROCKY POINT Suffolk
RODMAN (13682) Jefferson(96), Lewis(4)
RODMAN Lewis
ROME Oneida
ROMULUS Seneca
RONKONKOMA Suffolk
ROOSEVELT Nassau
ROOSEVELTOWN St. Lawrence
ROSCOE (12776) Sullivan(71), Delaware(29)
ROSE Wayne
ROSEBOOM Otsego
ROSENDALE Ulster
ROSLYN Nassau
ROSLYN HEIGHTS Nassau
ROSSBURG Allegany
ROTTERDAM JUNCTION Schenectady
ROUND LAKE Saratoga
ROUND TOP Greene
ROUSES POINT Clinton
ROXBURY Delaware
RUBY Ulster
RUSH Monroe
RUSHFORD Allegany
RUSHVILLE (14544) Yates(55), Ontario(45)
RUSSELL St. Lawrence
RYE Westchester
SABAEL Hamilton
SACKETS HARBOR Jefferson
SAG HARBOR Suffolk
SAGAPONACK Suffolk
SAINT BONAVENTURE Cattaraugus
SAINT JAMES Suffolk
SAINT JOHNSVILLE (13452) Montgomery(91), Fulton(9)
SAINT REGIS FALLS (12980) Franklin(94), St. Lawrence(6)
SALAMANCA Cattaraugus
SALEM (12865) Washington(95), Albany(5)
SALISBURY CENTER Herkimer
SALISBURY MILLS Orange
SALT POINT Dutchess
SANBORN Niagara
SAND LAKE Rensselaer
SANDUSKY Cattaraugus
SANDY CREEK Oswego
SANGERFIELD Oneida
SARANAC Clinton
SARANAC LAKE (12983) Franklin(79), Essex(21)
SARANAC LAKE Franklin
SARATOGA SPRINGS Saratoga
SARDINIA Erie
SAUGERTIES Ulster
SAUQUOIT (13456) Oneida(97), Herkimer(3)
SAVANNAH Wayne
SAVONA Steuben
SAYVILLE Suffolk
SCARSDALE Westchester
SCHAGHTICOKE (12154) Rensselaer(95), Washington(5)
SCHENECTADY (12302) Schenectady(98), Saratoga(2)
SCHENECTADY (12303) Schenectady(69), Albany(31)
SCHENECTADY (12304) Schenectady(89), Albany(11)
SCHENECTADY (12309) Schenectady(93), Albany(7)
SCHENECTADY Schenectady
SCHENEVUS (12155) Otsego(86), Delaware(14)
SCHODACK LANDING (12156) Rensselaer(90), Columbia(10)
SCHOHARIE Schoharie

SCHROON LAKE (12870) Essex(92), Warren(8)
SCHUYLER FALLS Clinton
SCHUYLER LAKE Otsego
SCHUYLERVILLE Saratoga
SCIO Allegany
SCIPIO CENTER Cayuga
SCOTTSBURG Livingston
SCOTTSVILLE Monroe
SEA CLIFF Nassau
SEAFORD Nassau
SELDEN Suffolk
SELKIRK Albany
SENECA CASTLE Ontario
SENECA FALLS Seneca
SENNETT Cayuga
SEVERANCE Essex
SHANDAKEN (12480) Ulster(96), Greene(4)
SHARON SPRINGS (13459) Schoharie(93), Montgomery(5), Otsego(2)
SHEDS Madison
SHELTER ISLAND Suffolk
SHELTER ISLAND HEIGHTS Suffolk
SHENOROCK Westchester
SHERBURNE (13460) Chenango(99), Madison(1)
SHERIDAN Chautauqua
SHERMAN Chautauqua
SHERRILL Oneida
SHINHOPPLE Delaware
SHIRLEY Suffolk
SHOKAN Ulster
SHOREHAM Suffolk
SHORTSVILLE Ontario
SHRUB OAK Westchester
SHUSHAN Washington
SIDNEY (13838) Delaware(96), Otsego(4)
SIDNEY CENTER Delaware
SILVER BAY Warren
SILVER CREEK Chautauqua
SILVER LAKE Wyoming
SILVER SPRINGS Wyoming
SINCLAIRVILLE Chautauqua
SKANEATELES (13152) Onondaga(93), Cayuga(7)
SKANEATELES FALLS Onondaga
SLATE HILL Orange
SLATERVILLE SPRINGS Tompkins
SLINGERLANDS Albany
SLOANSVILLE Schoharie
SLOATSBURG Rockland
SMALLWOOD Sullivan
SMITHBORO Tioga
SMITHTOWN Suffolk
SMITHVILLE FLATS (13841) Cortland(53), Chenango(40), Broome(7)
SMYRNA Chenango
SODUS Wayne
SODUS CENTER Wayne
SODUS POINT Wayne
SOLSVILLE Madison
SOMERS Westchester
SONYEA Livingston
SOUND BEACH Suffolk
SOUTH BETHLEHEM Albany
SOUTH BUTLER Wayne
SOUTH BYRON Genesee
SOUTH CAIRO Greene
SOUTH COLTON St. Lawrence
SOUTH DAYTON (14138) Cattaraugus(63), Chautauqua(37)
SOUTH EDMESTON Otsego
SOUTH FALLSBURG Sullivan
SOUTH GLENS FALLS Saratoga
SOUTH JAMESPORT Suffolk
SOUTH KORTRIGHT Delaware
SOUTH LIMA Livingston
SOUTH NEW BERLIN (13843) Chenango(66), Otsego(34)
SOUTH OTSELIC Chenango

SOUTH PLYMOUTH Chenango
SOUTH RUTLAND Jefferson
SOUTH SALEM Westchester
SOUTH SCHODACK Rensselaer
SOUTH WALES Erie
SOUTH WESTERLO Albany
SOUTHAMPTON Suffolk
SOUTHFIELDS Orange
SOUTHOLD Suffolk
SPARKILL Rockland
SPARROW BUSH (12780) Orange(89),
   Sullivan(11)
SPECULATOR Hamilton
SPENCER (14883) Tioga(79),
   Tompkins(21)
SPENCERPORT Monroe
SPENCERTOWN Columbia
SPEONK Suffolk
SPRAKERS Montgomery
SPRING BROOK Erie
SPRING GLEN Ulster
SPRING VALLEY Rockland
SPRINGFIELD CENTER Otsego
SPRINGVILLE (14141) Erie(94),
   Cattaraugus(6)
SPRINGWATER (14560) Ontario(51),
   Livingston(49)
STAATSBURG Dutchess
STAFFORD Genesee
STAMFORD (12167) Delaware(74),
   Schoharie(26)
STANFORDVILLE Dutchess
STANLEY (14561) Ontario(95), Yates(6)
STAR LAKE St. Lawrence
STATEN ISLAND Richmond
STEAMBURG Cattaraugus
STELLA NIAGARA Niagara
STEPHENTOWN Rensselaer
STERLING Cayuga
STERLING FOREST Orange
STILLWATER Saratoga
STITTVILLE Oneida
STOCKTON Chautauqua
STONE RIDGE Ulster
STONY BROOK Suffolk
STONY CREEK Warren
STONY POINT Rockland
STORMVILLE (12582) Dutchess(98),
   Putnam(2)
STOTTVILLE Columbia
STOW Chautauqua
STRATFORD (13470) Fulton(97),
   Herkimer(3)
STRYKERSVILLE (14145) Wyoming(92),
   Erie(8)
STUYVESANT Columbia
STUYVESANT FALLS Columbia
SUFFERN Rockland
SUGAR LOAF Orange
SUMMIT Schoharie
SUMMITVILLE Sullivan
SUNDOWN Ulster
SURPRISE Greene
SWAIN Allegany
SWAN LAKE Sullivan
SYLVAN BEACH Oneida
SYOSSET Nassau
SYRACUSE Onondaga
TABERG Oneida
TALLMAN Rockland
TANNERSVILLE Greene
TAPPAN Rockland
TARRYTOWN Westchester
THENDARA Herkimer

THERESA Jefferson
THIELLS Rockland
THOMPSON RIDGE Orange
THOMPSONVILLE Sullivan
THORNWOOD Westchester
THOUSAND ISLAND PARK Jefferson
THREE MILE BAY Jefferson
TICONDEROGA Essex
TILLSON Ulster
TIOGA CENTER Tioga
TIVOLI (12583) Dutchess(62),
   Columbia(39)
TOMKINS COVE Rockland
TONAWANDA Erie
TREADWELL Delaware
TRIBES HILL Montgomery
TROUPSBURG Steuben
TROUT CREEK Delaware
TROY Albany
TROY Rensselaer
TRUMANSBURG (14886) Tompkins(62),
   Schuyler(26), Seneca(12)
TRUXTON Cortland
TUCKAHOE Westchester
TULLY (13159) Onondaga(71),
   Cortland(29)
TUNNEL Broome
TUPPER LAKE (12986) Franklin(97), St.
   Lawrence(3)
TURIN Lewis
TUXEDO PARK Orange
TYRONE Schuyler
ULSTER PARK Ulster
UNADILLA (13849) Otsego(81),
   Delaware(19)
UNION HILL Wayne
UNION SPRINGS Cayuga
UNIONDALE Nassau
UNIONVILLE Orange
UPPER JAY Essex
UPTON Suffolk
UTICA (13501) Oneida(99), Herkimer(1)
UTICA Oneida
VAILS GATE Orange
VALATIE Columbia
VALHALLA Westchester
VALLEY COTTAGE Rockland
VALLEY FALLS (12185) Rensselaer(96),
   Washington(4)
VALLEY STREAM Nassau
VALOIS (14888) Schuyler(83), Seneca(17)
VAN BUREN POINT Chautauqua
VAN ETTEN (14889) Chemung(89),
   Schuyler(6), Tioga(5)
VAN HORNESVILLE (13475)
   Herkimer(65), Otsego(35)
VARYSBURG Wyoming
VERBANK Dutchess
VERMONTVILLE Franklin
VERNON Oneida
VERNON CENTER Oneida
VERONA Oneida
VERONA BEACH Oneida
VERPLANCK Westchester
VERSAILLES Cattaraugus
VESTAL Broome
VICTOR (14564) Ontario(97), Monroe(3)
VICTORY MILLS Saratoga
VOORHEESVILLE Albany
WACCABUC Westchester
WADDINGTON St. Lawrence
WADHAMS Essex
WADING RIVER Suffolk
WAINSCOTT Suffolk

WALDEN Orange
WALES CENTER Erie
WALKER VALLEY Ulster
WALLKILL (12589) Ulster(77), Orange(23)
WALTON Delaware
WALWORTH Wayne
WAMPSVILLE Madison
WANAKENA St. Lawrence
WANTAGH Nassau
WAPPINGERS FALLS Dutchess
WARNERS Onondaga
WARNERVILLE Schoharie
WARRENSBURG Warren
WARSAW Wyoming
WARWICK Orange
WASHINGTON MILLS Oneida
WASHINGTONVILLE Orange
WASSAIC Dutchess
WATER MILL Suffolk
WATERFORD Saratoga
WATERLOO Seneca
WATERPORT Orleans
WATERTOWN Jefferson
WATERVILLE (13480) Oneida(98),
   Madison(2)
WATERVLIET Albany
WATKINS GLEN Schuyler
WAVERLY (14892) Tioga(92), Chemung(8)
WAWARSING Ulster
WAYLAND (14572) Steuben(79),
   Livingston(21)
WAYNE Schuyler
WEBSTER Monroe
WEBSTER CROSSING Livingston
WEEDSPORT Cayuga
WELLESLEY ISLAND Jefferson
WELLS Hamilton
WELLS BRIDGE (13859) Otsego(95),
   Delaware(5)
WELLSBURG Chemung
WELLSVILLE Allegany
WEST BABYLON Suffolk
WEST BLOOMFIELD Ontario
WEST BURLINGTON Otsego
WEST CAMP Ulster
WEST CHAZY Clinton
WEST CLARKSVILLE Allegany
WEST COPAKE Columbia
WEST COXSACKIE Greene
WEST DANBY Tompkins
WEST DAVENPORT Delaware
WEST EATON Madison
WEST EDMESTON (13485) Madison(63),
   Otsego(34), Chenango(3)
WEST EXETER Otsego
WEST FALLS Erie
WEST FULTON Schoharie
WEST HARRISON Westchester
WEST HAVERSTRAW Rockland
WEST HEMPSTEAD Nassau
WEST HENRIETTA Monroe
WEST HURLEY Ulster
WEST ISLIP Suffolk
WEST KILL Greene
WEST LEBANON Columbia
WEST LEYDEN (13489) Lewis(98),
   Oneida(2)
WEST MONROE Oswego
WEST NYACK Rockland
WEST ONEONTA Otsego
WEST PARK Ulster
WEST POINT Orange
WEST SAND LAKE Rensselaer
WEST SAYVILLE Suffolk

WEST SHOKAN Ulster
WEST STOCKHOLM St. Lawrence
WEST VALLEY Cattaraugus
WEST WINFIELD (13491) Herkimer(87),
   Otsego(9), Oneida(3)
WESTBROOKVILLE Sullivan
WESTBURY Nassau
WESTDALE (13483) Oneida(97),
   Oswego(3)
WESTERLO Albany
WESTERN Oneida
WESTERNVILLE Oneida
WESTFIELD Chautauqua
WESTFORD Otsego
WESTHAMPTON Suffolk
WESTHAMPTON BEACH Suffolk
WESTMORELAND Oneida
WESTONS MILLS Cattaraugus
WESTPORT Essex
WESTTOWN Orange
WEVERTOWN Warren
WHIPPLEVILLE Franklin
WHITE LAKE Sullivan
WHITE PLAINS Westchester
WHITE SULPHUR SPRINGS Sullivan
WHITEHALL Washington
WHITESBORO Oneida
WHITESVILLE (14897) Allegany(95),
   Steuben(5)
WHITNEY POINT (99999) Broome(99),
   Cortland(1)
WILLARD Seneca
WILLET (13863) Cortland(97), Broome(1),
   Chenango(1)
WILLIAMSON Wayne
WILLIAMSTOWN Oswego
WILLISTON PARK Nassau
WILLOW Ulster
WILLSBORO Essex
WILLSEYVILLE (13864) Tioga(70),
   Tompkins(30)
WILMINGTON (12997) Essex(87),
   Saratoga(13)
WILSON Niagara
WINDHAM Greene
WINDSOR Broome
WINGDALE Dutchess
WINTHROP St. Lawrence
WITHERBEE Essex
WOLCOTT Wayne
WOODBOURNE (12788) Sullivan(98),
   Ulster(2)
WOODBURY Nassau
WOODGATE Oneida
WOODHULL Steuben
WOODMERE Nassau
WOODRIDGE Sullivan
WOODSTOCK Ulster
WOODVILLE Jefferson
WORCESTER Otsego
WURTSBORO Sullivan
WYANDANCH Suffolk
WYNANTSKILL Rensselaer
WYOMING (14591) Wyoming(88),
   Genesee(13)
YAPHANK Suffolk
YONKERS Westchester
YORK Livingston
YORKSHIRE Cattaraugus
YORKTOWN HEIGHTS Westchester
YORKVILLE Oneida
YOUNGSTOWN Niagara
YOUNGSVILLE Sullivan
YULAN Sullivan

ZIP/City Cross Reference

00401-00401	PLEASANTVILLE	
00501-00544	HOLTSVILLE	
06390-06390	FISHERS ISLAND	
10001-10292	NEW YORK	
10301-10314	STATEN ISLAND	
10451-10499	BRONX	
10501-10501	AMAWALK	
10502-10502	ARDSLEY	
10503-10503	ARDSLEY ON HUDSON	
10504-10504	ARMONK	
10505-10505	BALDWIN PLACE	
10506-10506	BEDFORD	
10507-10507	BEDFORD HILLS	
10509-10509	BREWSTER	
10510-10510	BRIARCLIFF MANOR	
10511-10511	BUCHANAN	
10512-10512	CARMEL	
10514-10514	CHAPPAQUA	
10516-10516	COLD SPRING	
10517-10517	CROMPOND	

Zip	Place	Zip	Place	Zip	Place	Zip	Place
10518-10518	CROSS RIVER	10933-10933	JOHNSON	11569-11569	POINT LOOKOUT	11775-11775	MELVILLE
10519-10519	CROTON FALLS	10940-10943	MIDDLETOWN	11570-11571	ROCKVILLE CENTRE	11776-11776	PORT JEFFERSON STATION
10520-10521	CROTON ON HUDSON	10950-10950	MONROE	11572-11572	OCEANSIDE		
10522-10522	DOBBS FERRY	10951-10951	ROCKLAND M P C	11575-11575	ROOSEVELT	11777-11777	PORT JEFFERSON
10523-10523	ELMSFORD	10952-10952	MONSEY	11576-11576	ROSLYN	11778-11778	ROCKY POINT
10524-10524	GARRISON	10953-10953	MOUNTAINVILLE	11577-11577	ROSLYN HEIGHTS	11779-11779	RONKONKOMA
10526-10526	GOLDENS BRIDGE	10954-10954	NANUET	11579-11579	SEA CLIFF	11780-11780	SAINT JAMES
10527-10527	GRANITE SPRINGS	10956-10956	NEW CITY	11580-11583	VALLEY STREAM	11782-11782	SAYVILLE
10528-10528	HARRISON	10958-10958	NEW HAMPTON	11588-11588	UNIONDALE	11783-11783	SEAFORD
10530-10530	HARTSDALE	10959-10959	NEW MILFORD	11590-11590	WESTBURY	11784-11784	SELDEN
10532-10532	HAWTHORNE	10960-10960	NYACK	11592-11592	ROCKVILLE CENTRE	11786-11786	SHOREHAM
10533-10533	IRVINGTON	10962-10962	ORANGEBURG	11593-11595	WESTBURY	11787-11787	SMITHTOWN
10535-10535	JEFFERSON VALLEY	10963-10963	OTISVILLE	11596-11596	WILLISTON PARK	11788-11788	HAUPPAUGE
10536-10536	KATONAH	10964-10964	PALISADES	11597-11597	WESTBURY	11789-11789	SOUND BEACH
10537-10537	LAKE PEEKSKILL	10965-10965	PEARL RIVER	11598-11598	WOODMERE	11790-11790	STONY BROOK
10538-10538	LARCHMONT	10968-10968	PIERMONT	11599-11599	GARDEN CITY	11791-11791	SYOSSET
10540-10540	LINCOLNDALE	10969-10969	PINE ISLAND	11690-11695	FAR ROCKAWAY	11792-11792	WADING RIVER
10541-10541	MAHOPAC	10970-10970	POMONA	11696-11696	INWOOD	11793-11793	WANTAGH
10542-10542	MAHOPAC FALLS	10973-10973	SLATE HILL	11697-11697	FAR ROCKAWAY	11794-11794	STONY BROOK
10543-10543	MAMARONECK	10974-10974	SLOATSBURG	11701-11701	AMITYVILLE	11795-11795	WEST ISLIP
10545-10545	MARYKNOLL	10975-10975	SOUTHFIELDS	11702-11702	BABYLON	11796-11796	WEST SAYVILLE
10546-10546	MILLWOOD	10976-10976	SPARKILL	11703-11703	NORTH BABYLON	11797-11797	WOODBURY
10547-10547	MOHEGAN LAKE	10977-10977	SPRING VALLEY	11704-11704	WEST BABYLON	11798-11798	WYANDANCH
10548-10548	MONTROSE	10979-10979	STERLING FOREST	11705-11705	BAYPORT	11801-11802	HICKSVILLE
10549-10549	MOUNT KISCO	10980-10980	STONY POINT	11706-11706	BAY SHORE	11803-11803	PLAINVIEW
10550-10559	MOUNT VERNON	10981-10981	SUGAR LOAF	11707-11707	WEST BABYLON	11804-11804	OLD BETHPAGE
10560-10560	NORTH SALEM	10982-10982	TALLMAN	11708-11708	AMITYVILLE	11805-11805	MID ISLAND
10562-10562	OSSINING	10983-10983	TAPPAN	11709-11709	BAYVILLE	11815-11819	HICKSVILLE
10566-10566	PEEKSKILL	10984-10984	THIELLS	11710-11710	BELLMORE	11853-11853	JERICHO
10570-10572	PLEASANTVILLE	10985-10985	THOMPSON RIDGE	11713-11713	BELLPORT	11854-11855	HICKSVILLE
10573-10573	PORT CHESTER	10986-10986	TOMKINS COVE	11714-11714	BETHPAGE	11901-11901	RIVERHEAD
10576-10576	POUND RIDGE	10987-10987	TUXEDO PARK	11715-11715	BLUE POINT	11930-11930	AMAGANSETT
10577-10577	PURCHASE	10988-10988	UNIONVILLE	11716-11716	BOHEMIA	11931-11931	AQUEBOGUE
10578-10578	PURDYS	10989-10989	VALLEY COTTAGE	11717-11717	BRENTWOOD	11932-11932	BRIDGEHAMPTON
10579-10579	PUTNAM VALLEY	10990-10990	WARWICK	11718-11718	BRIGHTWATERS	11933-11933	CALVERTON
10580-10581	RYE	10992-10992	WASHINGTONVILLE	11719-11719	BROOKHAVEN	11934-11934	CENTER MORICHES
10583-10583	SCARSDALE	10993-10993	WEST HAVERSTRAW	11720-11720	CENTEREACH	11935-11935	CUTCHOGUE
10587-10587	SHENOROCK	10994-10995	WEST NYACK	11721-11721	CENTERPORT	11937-11937	EAST HAMPTON
10588-10588	SHRUB OAK	10996-10997	WEST POINT	11722-11722	CENTRAL ISLIP	11939-11939	EAST MARION
10589-10589	SOMERS	10998-10998	WESTTOWN	11724-11724	COLD SPRING HARBOR	11940-11940	EAST MORICHES
10590-10590	SOUTH SALEM	11001-11002	FLORAL PARK	11725-11725	COMMACK	11941-11941	EASTPORT
10591-10592	TARRYTOWN	11003-11003	ELMONT	11726-11726	COPIAGUE	11942-11942	EAST QUOGUE
10594-10594	THORNWOOD	11004-11004	GLEN OAKS	11727-11727	CORAM	11944-11944	GREENPORT
10595-10595	VALHALLA	11005-11005	FLORAL PARK	11729-11729	DEER PARK	11946-11946	HAMPTON BAYS
10596-10596	VERPLANCK	11010-11010	FRANKLIN SQUARE	11730-11730	EAST ISLIP	11947-11947	JAMESPORT
10597-10597	WACCABUC	11020-11027	GREAT NECK	11731-11731	EAST NORTHPORT	11948-11948	LAUREL
10598-10598	YORKTOWN HEIGHTS	11030-11030	MANHASSET	11732-11732	EAST NORWICH	11949-11949	MANORVILLE
10601-10603	WHITE PLAINS	11040-11044	NEW HYDE PARK	11733-11733	EAST SETAUKET	11950-11950	MASTIC
10604-10604	WEST HARRISON	11050-11055	PORT WASHINGTON	11735-11737	FARMINGDALE	11951-11951	MASTIC BEACH
10605-10650	WHITE PLAINS	11096-11096	INWOOD	11738-11738	FARMINGVILLE	11952-11952	MATTITUCK
10701-10705	YONKERS	11099-11099	NEW HYDE PARK	11739-11739	GREAT RIVER	11953-11953	MIDDLE ISLAND
10706-10706	HASTINGS ON HUDSON	11101-11120	LONG ISLAND CITY	11740-11740	GREENLAWN	11954-11954	MONTAUK
10707-10707	TUCKAHOE	11201-11256	BROOKLYN	11741-11741	HOLBROOK	11955-11955	MORICHES
10708-10708	BRONXVILLE	11351-11399	FLUSHING	11742-11742	HOLTSVILLE	11956-11956	NEW SUFFOLK
10709-10709	EASTCHESTER	11402-11499	JAMAICA	11743-11743	HUNTINGTON	11957-11957	ORIENT
10710-10710	YONKERS	11501-11501	MINEOLA	11745-11745	SMITHTOWN	11958-11958	PECONIC
10801-10802	NEW ROCHELLE	11507-11507	ALBERTSON	11746-11746	HUNTINGTON STATION	11959-11959	QUOGUE
10803-10803	PELHAM	11509-11509	ATLANTIC BEACH	11747-11747	MELVILLE	11960-11960	REMSENBURG
10804-10805	NEW ROCHELLE	11510-11510	BALDWIN	11749-11749	FARMINGVILLE	11961-11961	RIDGE
10901-10901	SUFFERN	11514-11514	CARLE PLACE	11750-11750	HUNTINGTON STATION	11962-11962	SAGAPONACK
10910-10910	ARDEN	11516-11516	CEDARHURST	11751-11751	ISLIP	11963-11963	SAG HARBOR
10911-10911	BEAR MOUNTAIN	11518-11518	EAST ROCKAWAY	11752-11752	ISLIP TERRACE	11964-11964	SHELTER ISLAND
10912-10912	BELLVALE	11520-11520	FREEPORT	11753-11753	JERICHO	11965-11965	SHELTER ISLAND HEIGHTS
10913-10913	BLAUVELT	11530-11536	GARDEN CITY	11754-11754	KINGS PARK		
10914-10914	BLOOMING GROVE	11542-11542	GLEN COVE	11755-11755	LAKE GROVE	11967-11967	SHIRLEY
10915-10915	BULLVILLE	11545-11545	GLEN HEAD	11756-11756	LEVITTOWN	11968-11969	SOUTHAMPTON
10916-10916	CAMPBELL HALL	11547-11547	GLENWOOD LANDING	11757-11757	LINDENHURST	11970-11970	SOUTH JAMESPORT
10917-10917	CENTRAL VALLEY	11548-11548	GREENVALE	11758-11758	MASSAPEQUA	11971-11971	SOUTHOLD
10918-10918	CHESTER	11549-11551	HEMPSTEAD	11760-11760	HAUPPAUGE	11972-11972	SPEONK
10919-10919	CIRCLEVILLE	11552-11552	WEST HEMPSTEAD	11762-11762	MASSAPEQUA PARK	11973-11973	UPTON
10920-10920	CONGERS	11553-11553	UNIONDALE	11763-11763	MEDFORD	11975-11975	WAINSCOTT
10921-10921	FLORIDA	11554-11554	EAST MEADOW	11764-11764	MILLER PLACE	11976-11976	WATER MILL
10922-10922	FORT MONTGOMERY	11555-11556	UNIONDALE	11765-11765	MILL NECK	11977-11977	WESTHAMPTON
10923-10923	GARNERVILLE	11557-11557	HEWLETT	11766-11766	MOUNT SINAI	11978-11978	WESTHAMPTON BEACH
10924-10924	GOSHEN	11558-11558	ISLAND PARK	11767-11767	NESCONSET	11980-11980	YAPHANK
10925-10925	GREENWOOD LAKE	11559-11559	LAWRENCE	11768-11768	NORTHPORT	12007-12007	ALCOVE
10926-10926	HARRIMAN	11560-11560	LOCUST VALLEY	11769-11769	OAKDALE	12008-12008	ALPLAUS
10927-10927	HAVERSTRAW	11561-11561	LONG BEACH	11770-11770	OCEAN BEACH	12009-12009	ALTAMONT
10928-10928	HIGHLAND FALLS	11563-11564	LYNBROOK	11771-11771	OYSTER BAY	12010-12010	AMSTERDAM
10930-10930	HIGHLAND MILLS	11565-11565	MALVERNE	11772-11772	PATCHOGUE	12015-12015	ATHENS
10931-10931	HILLBURN	11566-11566	MERRICK	11773-11773	SYOSSET	12016-12016	AURIESVILLE
10932-10932	HOWELLS	11568-11568	OLD WESTBURY	11774-11774	FARMINGDALE	12017-12017	AUSTERLITZ

12018-12018	AVERILL PARK	12132-12132	NORTH CHATHAM	12434-12434	GRAND GORGE	12530-12530	HOLLOWVILLE
12019-12019	BALLSTON LAKE	12133-12133	NORTH HOOSICK	12435-12435	GREENFIELD PARK	12531-12531	HOLMES
12020-12020	BALLSTON SPA	12134-12134	NORTHVILLE	12436-12436	HAINES FALLS	12533-12533	HOPEWELL JUNCTION
12022-12022	BERLIN	12136-12136	OLD CHATHAM	12438-12438	HALCOTTSVILLE	12534-12534	HUDSON
12023-12023	BERNE	12137-12137	PATTERSONVILLE	12439-12439	HENSONVILLE	12537-12537	HUGHSONVILLE
12024-12024	BRAINARD	12138-12138	PETERSBURG	12440-12440	HIGH FALLS	12538-12538	HYDE PARK
12025-12025	BROADALBIN	12139-12139	PISECO	12441-12441	HIGHMOUNT	12540-12540	LAGRANGEVILLE
12027-12027	BURNT HILLS	12140-12140	POESTENKILL	12442-12442	HUNTER	12541-12541	LIVINGSTON
12028-12028	BUSKIRK	12141-12141	QUAKER STREET	12443-12443	HURLEY	12542-12542	MARLBORO
12029-12029	CANAAN	12143-12143	RAVENA	12444-12444	JEWETT	12543-12543	MAYBROOK
12031-12031	CARLISLE	12144-12144	RENSSELAER	12446-12446	KERHONKSON	12544-12544	MELLENVILLE
12032-12032	CAROGA LAKE	12147-12147	RENSSELAERVILLE	12448-12448	LAKE HILL	12545-12545	MILLBROOK
12033-12033	CASTLETON ON	12148-12148	REXFORD	12449-12449	LAKE KATRINE	12546-12546	MILLERTON
	HUDSON	12149-12149	RICHMONDVILLE	12450-12450	LANESVILLE	12547-12547	MILTON
12035-12035	CENTRAL BRIDGE	12150-12150	ROTTERDAM JUNCTION	12451-12451	LEEDS	12548-12548	MODENA
12036-12036	CHARLOTTEVILLE	12151-12151	ROUND LAKE	12452-12452	LEXINGTON	12549-12549	MONTGOMERY
12037-12037	CHATHAM	12153-12153	SAND LAKE	12453-12453	MALDEN ON HUDSON	12550-12552	NEWBURGH
12040-12040	CHERRY PLAIN	12154-12154	SCHAGHTICOKE	12454-12454	MAPLECREST	12553-12553	NEW WINDSOR
12041-12041	CLARKSVILLE	12155-12155	SCHENEVUS	12455-12455	MARGARETVILLE	12555-12555	MID HUDSON
12042-12042	CLIMAX	12156-12156	SCHODACK LANDING	12456-12456	MOUNT MARION	12561-12561	NEW PALTZ
12043-12043	COBLESKILL	12157-12157	SCHOHARIE	12457-12457	MOUNT TREMPER	12563-12563	PATTERSON
12045-12045	COEYMANS	12158-12158	SELKIRK	12458-12458	NAPANOCH	12564-12564	PAWLING
12046-12046	COEYMANS HOLLOW	12159-12159	SLINGERLANDS	12459-12459	NEW KINGSTON	12565-12565	PHILMONT
12047-12047	COHOES	12160-12160	SLOANSVILLE	12460-12460	OAK HILL	12566-12566	PINE BUSH
12050-12050	COLUMBIAVILLE	12161-12161	SOUTH BETHLEHEM	12461-12461	OLIVEBRIDGE	12567-12567	PINE PLAINS
12051-12051	COXSACKIE	12162-12162	SOUTH SCHODACK	12463-12463	PALENVILLE	12568-12568	PLATTEKILL
12052-12052	CROPSEYVILLE	12164-12164	SPECULATOR	12464-12464	PHOENICIA	12569-12569	PLEASANT VALLEY
12053-12053	DELANSON	12165-12165	SPENCERTOWN	12465-12465	PINE HILL	12570-12570	POUGHQUAG
12054-12054	DELMAR	12166-12166	SPRAKERS	12466-12466	PORT EWEN	12571-12571	RED HOOK
12055-12055	DORMANSVILLE	12167-12167	STAMFORD	12468-12468	PRATTSVILLE	12572-12572	RHINEBECK
12056-12056	DUANESBURG	12168-12169	STEPHENTOWN	12469-12469	PRESTON HOLLOW	12574-12574	RHINECLIFF
12057-12057	EAGLE BRIDGE	12170-12170	STILLWATER	12470-12470	PURLING	12575-12575	ROCK TAVERN
12058-12058	EARLTON	12172-12172	STOTTVILLE	12471-12471	RIFTON	12577-12577	SALISBURY MILLS
12059-12059	EAST BERNE	12173-12173	STUYVESANT	12472-12472	ROSENDALE	12578-12578	SALT POINT
12060-12060	EAST CHATHAM	12174-12174	STUYVESANT FALLS	12473-12473	ROUND TOP	12580-12580	STAATSBURG
12061-12061	EAST GREENBUSH	12175-12175	SUMMIT	12474-12474	ROXBURY	12581-12581	STANFORDVILLE
12062-12062	EAST NASSAU	12176-12176	SURPRISE	12475-12475	RUBY	12582-12582	STORMVILLE
12063-12063	EAST SCHODACK	12177-12177	TRIBES HILL	12477-12477	SAUGERTIES	12583-12583	TIVOLI
12064-12064	EAST WORCESTER	12179-12183	TROY	12480-12480	SHANDAKEN	12584-12584	VAILS GATE
12065-12065	CLIFTON PARK	12184-12184	VALATIE	12481-12481	SHOKAN	12585-12585	VERBANK
12066-12066	ESPERANCE	12185-12185	VALLEY FALLS	12482-12482	SOUTH CAIRO	12586-12586	WALDEN
12067-12067	FEURA BUSH	12186-12186	VOORHEESVILLE	12483-12483	SPRING GLEN	12588-12588	WALKER VALLEY
12068-12068	FONDA	12187-12187	WARNERVILLE	12484-12484	STONE RIDGE	12589-12589	WALLKILL
12069-12069	FORT HUNTER	12188-12188	WATERFORD	12485-12485	TANNERSVILLE	12590-12590	WAPPINGERS FALLS
12070-12070	FORT JOHNSON	12189-12189	WATERVLIET	12486-12486	TILLSON	12592-12592	WASSAIC
12071-12071	FULTONHAM	12190-12190	WELLS	12487-12487	ULSTER PARK	12593-12593	WEST COPAKE
12072-12072	FULTONVILLE	12192-12192	WEST COXSACKIE	12489-12489	WAWARSING	12594-12594	WINGDALE
12073-12073	GALLUPVILLE	12193-12193	WESTERLO	12490-12490	WEST CAMP	12601-12604	POUGHKEEPSIE
12074-12074	GALWAY	12194-12194	WEST FULTON	12491-12491	WEST HURLEY	12701-12701	MONTICELLO
12075-12075	GHENT	12195-12195	WEST LEBANON	12492-12492	WEST KILL	12719-12719	BARRYVILLE
12076-12076	GILBOA	12196-12196	WEST SAND LAKE	12493-12493	WEST PARK	12720-12720	BETHEL
12077-12077	GLENMONT	12197-12197	WORCESTER	12494-12494	WEST SHOKAN	12721-12721	BLOOMINGBURG
12078-12078	GLOVERSVILLE	12198-12198	WYNANTSKILL	12495-12495	WILLOW	12722-12722	BURLINGHAM
12082-12082	GRAFTON	12201-12208	ALBANY	12496-12496	WINDHAM	12723-12723	CALLICOON
12083-12083	GREENVILLE	12301-12345	SCHENECTADY	12498-12498	WOODSTOCK	12724-12724	CALLICOON CENTER
12084-12084	GUILDERLAND	12401-12402	KINGSTON	12501-12501	AMENIA	12725-12725	CLARYVILLE
12085-12085	GUILDERLAND CENTER	12404-12404	ACCORD	12502-12502	ANCRAM	12726-12726	COCHECTON
12086-12086	HAGAMAN	12405-12405	ACRA	12503-12503	ANCRAMDALE	12727-12727	COCHECTON CENTER
12087-12087	HANNACROIX	12406-12406	ARKVILLE	12504-12504	ANNANDALE ON	12729-12729	CUDDEBACKVILLE
12089-12089	HOOSICK	12407-12407	ASHLAND		HUDSON	12732-12732	ELDRED
12090-12090	HOOSICK FALLS	12409-12409	BEARSVILLE	12506-12506	BANGALL	12733-12733	FALLSBURG
12092-12092	HOWES CAVE	12410-12410	BIG INDIAN	12507-12507	BARRYTOWN	12734-12734	FERNDALE
12093-12093	JEFFERSON	12411-12411	BLOOMINGTON	12508-12508	BEACON	12736-12736	FREMONT CENTER
12094-12094	JOHNSONVILLE	12412-12412	BOICEVILLE	12510-12510	BILLINGS	12737-12737	GLEN SPEY
12095-12095	JOHNSTOWN	12413-12413	CAIRO	12511-12511	CASTLE POINT	12738-12738	GLEN WILD
12106-12106	KINDERHOOK	12414-12414	CATSKILL	12512-12512	CHELSEA	12739-12739	GODEFFROY
12107-12107	KNOX	12416-12416	CHICHESTER	12513-12513	CLAVERACK	12740-12740	GRAHAMSVILLE
12108-12108	LAKE PLEASANT	12417-12417	CONNELLY	12514-12514	CLINTON CORNERS	12741-12741	HANKINS
12110-12111	LATHAM	12418-12418	CORNWALLVILLE	12515-12515	CLINTONDALE	12742-12742	HARRIS
12115-12115	MALDEN BRIDGE	12419-12419	COTTEKILL	12516-12516	COPAKE	12743-12743	HIGHLAND LAKE
12116-12116	MARYLAND	12420-12420	CRAGSMOOR	12517-12517	COPAKE FALLS	12745-12745	HORTONVILLE
12117-12117	MAYFIELD	12421-12421	DENVER	12518-12518	CORNWALL	12746-12746	HUGUENOT
12118-12118	MECHANICVILLE	12422-12422	DURHAM	12520-12520	CORNWALL ON HUDSON	12747-12747	HURLEYVILLE
12120-12120	MEDUSA	12423-12423	EAST DURHAM	12521-12521	CRARYVILLE	12748-12748	JEFFERSONVILLE
12121-12121	MELROSE	12424-12424	EAST JEWETT	12522-12522	DOVER PLAINS	12749-12749	KAUNEONGA LAKE
12122-12122	MIDDLEBURGH	12427-12427	ELKA PARK	12523-12523	ELIZAVILLE	12750-12750	KENOZA LAKE
12123-12123	NASSAU	12428-12428	ELLENVILLE	12524-12524	FISHKILL	12751-12751	KIAMESHA LAKE
12124-12124	NEW BALTIMORE	12429-12429	ESOPUS	12525-12525	GARDINER	12752-12752	LAKE HUNTINGTON
12125-12125	NEW LEBANON	12430-12430	FLEISCHMANNS	12526-12526	GERMANTOWN	12754-12754	LIBERTY
12128-12128	NEWTONVILLE	12431-12431	FREEHOLD	12527-12527	GLENHAM	12758-12758	LIVINGSTON MANOR
12130-12130	NIVERVILLE	12432-12432	GLASCO	12528-12528	HIGHLAND	12759-12759	LOCH SHELDRAKE
12131-12131	NORTH BLENHEIM	12433-12433	GLENFORD	12529-12529	HILLSDALE	12760-12760	LONG EDDY

Zip	Place	Zip	Place	Zip	Place	Zip	Place
12762-12762	MONGAUP VALLEY	12865-12865	SALEM	12993-12993	WESTPORT	13134-13134	PETERBORO
12763-12763	MOUNTAIN DALE	12866-12866	SARATOGA SPRINGS	12995-12995	WHIPPLEVILLE	13135-13135	PHOENIX
12764-12764	NARROWSBURG	12870-12870	SCHROON LAKE	12996-12996	WILLSBORO	13136-13136	PITCHER
12765-12765	NEVERSINK	12871-12871	SCHUYLERVILLE	12997-12997	WILMINGTON	13137-13137	PLAINVILLE
12766-12766	NORTH BRANCH	12872-12872	SEVERANCE	12998-12998	WITHERBEE	13138-13138	POMPEY
12767-12767	OBERNBURG	12873-12873	SHUSHAN	13020-13020	APULIA STATION	13139-13139	POPLAR RIDGE
12768-12768	PARKSVILLE	12874-12874	SILVER BAY	13021-13024	AUBURN	13140-13140	PORT BYRON
12769-12769	PHILLIPSPORT	12878-12878	STONY CREEK	13026-13026	AURORA	13141-13141	PREBLE
12770-12770	POND EDDY	12879-12879	NEWCOMB	13027-13027	BALDWINSVILLE	13142-13142	PULASKI
12771-12771	PORT JERVIS	12883-12883	TICONDEROGA	13028-13028	BERNHARDS BAY	13143-13143	RED CREEK
12775-12775	ROCK HILL	12884-12884	VICTORY MILLS	13029-13029	BREWERTON	13144-13144	RICHLAND
12776-12776	ROSCOE	12885-12885	WARRENSBURG	13030-13030	BRIDGEPORT	13145-13145	SANDY CREEK
12777-12777	FORESTBURGH	12886-12886	WEVERTOWN	13031-13031	CAMILLUS	13146-13146	SAVANNAH
12778-12778	SMALLWOOD	12887-12887	WHITEHALL	13032-13032	CANASTOTA	13147-13147	SCIPIO CENTER
12779-12779	SOUTH FALLSBURG	12901-12903	PLATTSBURGH	13033-13033	CATO	13148-13148	SENECA FALLS
12780-12780	SPARROW BUSH	12910-12910	ALTONA	13034-13034	CAYUGA	13152-13152	SKANEATELES
12781-12781	SUMMITVILLE	12911-12911	KEESEVILLE	13035-13035	CAZENOVIA	13153-13153	SKANEATELES FALLS
12782-12782	SUNDOWN	12912-12912	AU SABLE FORKS	13036-13036	CENTRAL SQUARE	13154-13154	SOUTH BUTLER
12783-12783	SWAN LAKE	12913-12913	BLOOMINGDALE	13037-13037	CHITTENANGO	13155-13155	SOUTH OTSELIC
12784-12784	THOMPSONVILLE	12914-12914	BOMBAY	13039-13039	CICERO	13156-13156	STERLING
12785-12785	WESTBROOKVILLE	12915-12915	BRAINARDSVILLE	13040-13040	CINCINNATUS	13157-13157	SYLVAN BEACH
12786-12786	WHITE LAKE	12916-12916	BRUSHTON	13041-13041	CLAY	13158-13158	TRUXTON
12787-12787	WHITE SULPHUR SPRINGS	12917-12917	BURKE	13042-13042	CLEVELAND	13159-13159	TULLY
		12918-12918	CADYVILLE	13043-13043	CLOCKVILLE	13160-13160	UNION SPRINGS
12788-12788	WOODBOURNE	12919-12919	CHAMPLAIN	13044-13044	CONSTANTIA	13162-13162	VERONA BEACH
12789-12789	WOODRIDGE	12920-12920	CHATEAUGAY	13045-13045	CORTLAND	13163-13163	WAMPSVILLE
12790-12790	WURTSBORO	12921-12921	CHAZY	13051-13051	DELPHI FALLS	13164-13164	WARNERS
12791-12791	YOUNGSVILLE	12922-12922	CHILDWOLD	13052-13052	DE RUYTER	13165-13165	WATERLOO
12792-12792	YULAN	12923-12923	CHURUBUSCO	13053-13053	DRYDEN	13166-13166	WEEDSPORT
12801-12801	GLENS FALLS	12924-12924	KEESEVILLE	13054-13054	DURHAMVILLE	13167-13167	WEST MONROE
12803-12803	SOUTH GLENS FALLS	12926-12926	CONSTABLE	13056-13056	EAST HOMER	13201-13210	SYRACUSE
12804-12804	QUEENSBURY	12927-12927	CRANBERRY LAKE	13057-13057	EAST SYRACUSE	13211-13211	MATTYDALE
12808-12808	ADIRONDACK	12928-12928	CROWN POINT	13060-13060	ELBRIDGE	13212-13290	SYRACUSE
12809-12809	ARGYLE	12929-12929	DANNEMORA	13061-13061	ERIEVILLE	13301-13301	ALDER CREEK
12810-12810	ATHOL	12930-12930	DICKINSON CENTER	13062-13062	ETNA	13302-13302	ALTMAR
12811-12811	BAKERS MILLS	12932-12932	ELIZABETHTOWN	13063-13063	FABIUS	13303-13303	AVA
12812-12812	BLUE MOUNTAIN LAKE	12933-12933	ELLENBURG	13064-13064	FAIR HAVEN	13304-13304	BARNEVELD
12814-12814	BOLTON LANDING	12934-12934	ELLENBURG CENTER	13065-13065	FAYETTE	13305-13305	BEAVER FALLS
12815-12815	BRANT LAKE	12935-12935	ELLENBURG DEPOT	13066-13066	FAYETTEVILLE	13308-13308	BLOSSVALE
12816-12816	CAMBRIDGE	12936-12936	ESSEX	13068-13068	FREEVILLE	13309-13309	BOONVILLE
12817-12817	CHESTERTOWN	12937-12937	FORT COVINGTON	13069-13069	FULTON	13310-13310	BOUCKVILLE
12819-12819	CLEMONS	12939-12939	GABRIELS	13071-13071	GENOA	13312-13312	BRANTINGHAM
12820-12820	CLEVERDALE	12941-12941	JAY	13072-13072	GEORGETOWN	13313-13313	BRIDGEWATER
12821-12821	COMSTOCK	12942-12942	KEENE	13073-13073	GROTON	13314-13314	BROOKFIELD
12822-12822	CORINTH	12943-12943	KEENE VALLEY	13074-13074	HANNIBAL	13315-13315	BURLINGTON FLATS
12823-12823	COSSAYUNA	12944-12944	KEESEVILLE	13076-13076	HASTINGS	13316-13316	CAMDEN
12824-12824	DIAMOND POINT	12945-12945	LAKE CLEAR	13077-13077	HOMER	13317-13317	CANAJOHARIE
12827-12827	FORT ANN	12946-12946	LAKE PLACID	13078-13078	JAMESVILLE	13318-13318	CASSVILLE
12828-12828	FORT EDWARD	12949-12949	LAWRENCEVILLE	13080-13080	JORDAN	13319-13319	CHADWICKS
12831-12831	GANSEVOORT	12950-12950	LEWIS	13081-13081	KING FERRY	13320-13320	CHERRY VALLEY
12832-12832	GRANVILLE	12952-12952	LYON MOUNTAIN	13082-13082	KIRKVILLE	13321-13321	CLARK MILLS
12833-12833	GREENFIELD CENTER	12953-12953	MALONE	13083-13083	LACONA	13322-13322	CLAYVILLE
12834-12834	GREENWICH	12955-12955	LYON MOUNTAIN	13084-13084	LA FAYETTE	13323-13323	CLINTON
12835-12835	HADLEY	12956-12956	MINEVILLE	13087-13087	LITTLE YORK	13324-13324	COLD BROOK
12836-12836	HAGUE	12957-12957	MOIRA	13088-13088	LIVERPOOL	13325-13325	CONSTABLEVILLE
12837-12837	HAMPTON	12958-12958	MOOERS	13092-13092	LOCKE	13326-13326	COOPERSTOWN
12838-12838	HARTFORD	12959-12959	MOOERS FORKS	13093-13093	LYCOMING	13327-13327	CROGHAN
12839-12839	HUDSON FALLS	12960-12960	MORIAH	13101-13101	MC GRAW	13328-13328	DEANSBORO
12841-12841	HULETTS LANDING	12961-12961	MORIAH CENTER	13102-13102	MC LEAN	13329-13329	DOLGEVILLE
12842-12842	INDIAN LAKE	12962-12962	MORRISONVILLE	13103-13103	MALLORY	13331-13331	EAGLE BAY
12843-12843	JOHNSBURG	12964-12964	NEW RUSSIA	13104-13104	MANLIUS	13332-13332	EARLVILLE
12844-12844	KATTSKILL BAY	12965-12965	NICHOLVILLE	13107-13107	MAPLE VIEW	13333-13333	EAST SPRINGFIELD
12845-12845	LAKE GEORGE	12966-12966	NORTH BANGOR	13108-13108	MARCELLUS	13334-13334	EATON
12846-12846	LAKE LUZERNE	12967-12967	NORTH LAWRENCE	13110-13110	MARIETTA	13335-13335	EDMESTON
12847-12847	LONG LAKE	12969-12969	OWLS HEAD	13111-13111	MARTVILLE	13337-13337	FLY CREEK
12848-12848	MIDDLE FALLS	12970-12970	PAUL SMITHS	13112-13112	MEMPHIS	13338-13338	FORESTPORT
12849-12849	MIDDLE GRANVILLE	12972-12972	PERU	13113-13113	MERIDIAN	13339-13339	FORT PLAIN
12850-12850	MIDDLE GROVE	12973-12973	PIERCEFIELD	13114-13114	MEXICO	13340-13340	FRANKFORT
12851-12851	MINERVA	12974-12974	PORT HENRY	13115-13115	MINETTO	13341-13341	FRANKLIN SPRINGS
12852-12852	NEWCOMB	12975-12975	PORT KENT	13116-13116	MINOA	13342-13342	GARRATTSVILLE
12853-12853	NORTH CREEK	12976-12976	RAINBOW LAKE	13117-13117	MONTEZUMA	13343-13343	GLENFIELD
12854-12854	NORTH GRANVILLE	12977-12977	RAY BROOK	13118-13118	MORAVIA	13345-13345	GREIG
12855-12855	NORTH HUDSON	12978-12978	REDFORD	13119-13119	MOTTVILLE	13346-13346	HAMILTON
12856-12856	NORTH RIVER	12979-12979	ROUSES POINT	13120-13120	NEDROW	13348-13348	HARTWICK
12857-12857	OLMSTEDVILLE	12980-12980	SAINT REGIS FALLS	13121-13121	NEW HAVEN	13350-13350	HERKIMER
12858-12858	PARADOX	12981-12981	SARANAC	13122-13122	NEW WOODSTOCK	13352-13352	HINCKLEY
12859-12859	PORTER CORNERS	12983-12983	SARANAC LAKE	13123-13123	NORTH BAY	13353-13353	HOFFMEISTER
12860-12860	POTTERSVILLE	12985-12985	SCHUYLER FALLS	13124-13124	NORTH PITCHER	13354-13354	HOLLAND PATENT
12861-12861	PUTNAM STATION	12986-12986	TUPPER LAKE	13126-13126	OSWEGO	13355-13355	HUBBARDSVILLE
12862-12862	RIPARIUS	12987-12987	UPPER JAY	13129-13129	GEORGETOWN	13357-13357	ILION
12863-12863	ROCK CITY FALLS	12989-12989	VERMONTVILLE	13131-13131	PARISH	13360-13360	INLET
12864-12864	SABAEL	12992-12992	WEST CHAZY	13132-13132	PENNELLVILLE	13361-13361	JORDANVILLE

ZIP	Place	ZIP	Place	ZIP	Place	ZIP	Place
13362-13362	KNOXBORO	13613-13613	BRASHER FALLS	13731-13731	ANDES	13856-13856	WALTON
13363-13363	LEE CENTER	13614-13614	BRIER HILL	13732-13732	APALACHIN	13859-13859	WELLS BRIDGE
13364-13364	LEONARDSVILLE	13615-13615	BROWNVILLE	13733-13733	BAINBRIDGE	13860-13860	WEST DAVENPORT
13365-13365	LITTLE FALLS	13616-13616	CALCIUM	13734-13734	BARTON	13861-13861	WEST ONEONTA
13367-13367	LOWVILLE	13617-13617	CANTON	13736-13736	BERKSHIRE	13862-13862	WHITNEY POINT
13368-13368	LYONS FALLS	13618-13618	CAPE VINCENT	13737-13737	BIBLE SCHOOL PARK	13863-13863	WILLET
13401-13401	MC CONNELLSVILLE	13619-13619	CARTHAGE	13738-13738	BLODGETT MILLS	13864-13864	WILLSEYVILLE
13402-13402	MADISON	13620-13620	CASTORLAND	13739-13739	BLOOMVILLE	13865-13865	WINDSOR
13403-13403	MARCY	13621-13621	CHASE MILLS	13740-13740	BOVINA CENTER	13901-13905	BINGHAMTON
13404-13404	MARTINSBURG	13622-13622	CHAUMONT	13743-13743	CANDOR	14001-14001	AKRON
13406-13406	MIDDLEVILLE	13623-13623	CHIPPEWA BAY	13744-13744	CASTLE CREEK	14003-14003	ALABAMA
13407-13407	MOHAWK	13624-13624	CLAYTON	13745-13745	CHENANGO BRIDGE	14004-14004	ALDEN
13408-13408	MORRISVILLE	13625-13625	COLTON	13746-13746	CHENANGO FORKS	14005-14005	ALEXANDER
13409-13409	MUNNSVILLE	13626-13626	COPENHAGEN	13747-13747	COLLIERSVILLE	14006-14006	ANGOLA
13410-13410	NELLISTON	13627-13627	DEER RIVER	13748-13748	CONKLIN	14008-14008	APPLETON
13411-13411	NEW BERLIN	13628-13628	DEFERIET	13749-13749	CORBETTSVILLE	14009-14009	ARCADE
13413-13413	NEW HARTFORD	13630-13630	DE KALB JUNCTION	13750-13750	DAVENPORT	14010-14010	ATHOL SPRINGS
13415-13415	NEW LISBON	13631-13631	DENMARK	13751-13751	DAVENPORT CENTER	14011-14011	ATTICA
13416-13416	NEWPORT	13632-13632	DEPAUVILLE	13752-13752	DE LANCEY	14012-14012	BARKER
13417-13417	NEW YORK MILLS	13633-13633	DE PEYSTER	13753-13753	DELHI	14013-14013	BASOM
13418-13418	NORTH BROOKFIELD	13634-13634	DEXTER	13754-13754	DEPOSIT	14020-14021	BATAVIA
13420-13420	OLD FORGE	13635-13635	EDWARDS	13755-13755	DOWNSVILLE	14024-14024	BLISS
13421-13421	ONEIDA	13636-13636	ELLISBURG	13756-13756	EAST BRANCH	14025-14025	BOSTON
13424-13424	ORISKANY	13637-13637	EVANS MILLS	13757-13757	EAST MEREDITH	14026-14026	BOWMANSVILLE
13425-13425	ORISKANY FALLS	13638-13638	FELTS MILLS	13758-13758	EAST PHARSALIA	14027-14027	BRANT
13426-13426	ORWELL	13639-13639	FINE	13760-13761	ENDICOTT	14028-14028	BURT
13428-13428	PALATINE BRIDGE	13640-13640	WELLESLEY ISLAND	13762-13762	ENDWELL	14029-14029	CENTERVILLE
13431-13431	POLAND	13641-13641	FISHERS LANDING	13763-13763	ENDICOTT	14030-14030	CHAFFEE
13433-13433	PORT LEYDEN	13642-13642	GOUVERNEUR	13774-13774	FISHS EDDY	14031-14031	CLARENCE
13435-13435	PROSPECT	13643-13643	GREAT BEND	13775-13775	FRANKLIN	14032-14032	CLARENCE CENTER
13436-13436	RAQUETTE LAKE	13645-13645	HAILESBORO	13776-13776	GILBERTSVILLE	14033-14033	COLDEN
13437-13437	REDFIELD	13646-13646	HAMMOND	13777-13777	GLEN AUBREY	14034-14034	COLLINS
13438-13438	REMSEN	13647-13647	HANNAWA FALLS	13778-13778	GREENE	14035-14035	COLLINS CENTER
13439-13439	RICHFIELD SPRINGS	13648-13648	HARRISVILLE	13780-13780	GUILFORD	14036-14036	CORFU
13440-13449	ROME	13649-13649	HELENA	13782-13782	HAMDEN	14037-14037	COWLESVILLE
13450-13450	ROSEBOOM	13650-13650	HENDERSON	13783-13783	HANCOCK	14038-14038	CRITTENDEN
13452-13452	SAINT JOHNSVILLE	13651-13651	HENDERSON HARBOR	13784-13784	HARFORD	14039-14039	DALE
13454-13454	SALISBURY CENTER	13652-13652	HERMON	13786-13786	HARPERSFIELD	14040-14040	DARIEN CENTER
13455-13455	SANGERFIELD	13654-13654	HEUVELTON	13787-13787	HARPURSVILLE	14041-14041	DAYTON
13456-13456	SAUQUOIT	13655-13655	HOGANSBURG	13788-13788	HOBART	14042-14042	DELEVAN
13457-13457	SCHUYLER LAKE	13656-13656	LA FARGEVILLE	13790-13790	JOHNSON CITY	14043-14043	DEPEW
13459-13459	SHARON SPRINGS	13657-13657	LIMERICK	13794-13794	KILLAWOG	14047-14047	DERBY
13460-13460	SHERBURNE	13658-13658	LISBON	13795-13795	KIRKWOOD	14048-14048	DUNKIRK
13461-13461	SHERRILL	13659-13659	LORRAINE	13796-13796	LAURENS	14051-14051	EAST AMHERST
13464-13464	SMYRNA	13660-13660	MADRID	13797-13797	LISLE	14052-14052	EAST AURORA
13465-13465	SOLSVILLE	13661-13661	MANNSVILLE	13801-13801	MC DONOUGH	14054-14054	EAST BETHANY
13468-13468	SPRINGFIELD CENTER	13662-13662	MASSENA	13802-13802	MAINE	14055-14055	EAST CONCORD
13469-13469	STITTVILLE	13664-13664	MORRISTOWN	13803-13803	MARATHON	14056-14056	EAST PEMBROKE
13470-13470	STRATFORD	13665-13665	NATURAL BRIDGE	13804-13804	MASONVILLE	14057-14057	EDEN
13471-13471	TABERG	13666-13666	NEWTON FALLS	13806-13806	MERIDALE	14058-14058	ELBA
13472-13472	THENDARA	13667-13667	NORFOLK	13807-13807	MILFORD	14059-14059	ELMA
13473-13473	TURIN	13668-13668	NORWOOD	13808-13808	MORRIS	14060-14060	FARMERSVILLE STATION
13475-13475	VAN HORNESVILLE	13669-13669	OGDENSBURG	13809-13809	MOUNT UPTON		
13476-13476	VERNON	13670-13670	OSWEGATCHIE	13810-13810	MOUNT VISION	14061-14061	FARNHAM
13477-13477	VERNON CENTER	13671-13671	OXBOW	13811-13811	NEWARK VALLEY	14062-14062	FORESTVILLE
13478-13478	VERONA	13672-13672	PARISHVILLE	13812-13812	NICHOLS	14063-14063	FREDONIA
13479-13479	WASHINGTON MILLS	13673-13673	PHILADELPHIA	13813-13813	NINEVEH	14065-14065	FREEDOM
13480-13480	WATERVILLE	13674-13674	PIERREPONT MANOR	13814-13814	NORTH NORWICH	14066-14066	GAINESVILLE
13482-13482	WEST BURLINGTON	13675-13675	PLESSIS	13815-13815	NORWICH	14067-14067	GASPORT
13483-13483	WESTDALE	13676-13676	POTSDAM	13820-13820	ONEONTA	14068-14068	GETZVILLE
13484-13484	WEST EATON	13677-13677	PYRITES	13825-13825	OTEGO	14069-14069	GLENWOOD
13485-13485	WEST EDMESTON	13678-13678	RAYMONDVILLE	13826-13826	OUAQUAGA	14070-14070	GOWANDA
13486-13486	WESTERNVILLE	13679-13679	REDWOOD	13827-13827	OWEGO	14072-14072	GRAND ISLAND
13488-13488	WESTFORD	13680-13680	RENSSELAER FALLS	13830-13830	OXFORD	14075-14075	HAMBURG
13489-13489	WEST LEYDEN	13681-13681	RICHVILLE	13832-13832	PLYMOUTH	14080-14080	HOLLAND
13490-13490	WESTMORELAND	13682-13682	RODMAN	13833-13833	PORT CRANE	14081-14081	IRVING
13491-13491	WEST WINFIELD	13683-13683	ROOSEVELTOWN	13834-13834	PORTLANDVILLE	14082-14082	JAVA CENTER
13492-13492	WHITESBORO	13684-13684	RUSSELL	13835-13835	RICHFORD	14083-14083	JAVA VILLAGE
13493-13493	WILLIAMSTOWN	13685-13685	SACKETS HARBOR	13837-13837	SHINHOPPLE	14085-14085	LAKE VIEW
13494-13494	WOODGATE	13687-13687	SOUTH COLTON	13838-13838	SIDNEY	14086-14086	LANCASTER
13495-13495	YORKVILLE	13688-13688	SOUTH RUTLAND	13839-13839	SIDNEY CENTER	14091-14091	LAWTONS
13501-13599	UTICA	13690-13690	STAR LAKE	13840-13840	SMITHBORO	14092-14092	LEWISTON
13601-13601	WATERTOWN	13691-13691	THERESA	13841-13841	SMITHVILLE FLATS	14094-14095	LOCKPORT
13602-13602	FORT DRUM	13692-13692	THOUSAND ISLAND	13842-13842	SOUTH KORTRIGHT	14098-14098	LYNDONVILLE
13603-13603	WATERTOWN		PARK	13843-13843	SOUTH NEW BERLIN	14101-14101	MACHIAS
13605-13605	ADAMS	13693-13693	THREE MILE BAY	13844-13844	SOUTH PLYMOUTH	14102-14102	MARILLA
13606-13606	ADAMS CENTER	13694-13694	WADDINGTON	13845-13845	TIOGA CENTER	14103-14103	MEDINA
13607-13607	ALEXANDRIA BAY	13695-13695	WANAKENA	13846-13846	TREADWELL	14105-14105	MIDDLEPORT
13608-13608	ANTWERP	13696-13696	WEST STOCKHOLM	13847-13847	TROUT CREEK	14107-14107	MODEL CITY
13610-13610	RODMAN	13697-13697	WINTHROP	13848-13848	TUNNEL	14108-14108	NEWFANE
13611-13611	BELLEVILLE	13699-13699	POTSDAM	13849-13849	UNADILLA	14109-14109	NIAGARA UNIVERSITY
13612-13612	BLACK RIVER	13730-13730	AFTON	13850-13851	VESTAL	14110-14110	NORTH BOSTON

ZIP Range	Place	ZIP Range	Place	ZIP Range	Place	ZIP Range	Place
14111-14111	NORTH COLLINS	14475-14475	IONIA	14592-14592	YORK	14805-14805	ALPINE
14112-14112	NORTH EVANS	14476-14476	KENDALL	14601-14694	ROCHESTER	14806-14806	ANDOVER
14113-14113	NORTH JAVA	14477-14477	KENT	14701-14704	JAMESTOWN	14807-14807	ARKPORT
14120-14120	NORTH TONAWANDA	14478-14478	KEUKA PARK	14706-14706	ALLEGANY	14808-14808	ATLANTA
14125-14125	OAKFIELD	14479-14479	KNOWLESVILLE	14707-14707	ALLENTOWN	14809-14809	AVOCA
14126-14126	OLCOTT	14480-14480	LAKEVILLE	14708-14708	ALMA	14810-14810	BATH
14127-14127	ORCHARD PARK	14481-14481	LEICESTER	14709-14709	ANGELICA	14812-14812	BEAVER DAMS
14129-14129	PERRYSBURG	14482-14482	LE ROY	14710-14710	ASHVILLE	14813-14813	BELMONT
14130-14130	PIKE	14485-14485	LIMA	14711-14711	BELFAST	14814-14814	BIG FLATS
14131-14131	RANSOMVILLE	14486-14486	LINWOOD	14712-14712	BEMUS POINT	14815-14815	BRADFORD
14132-14132	SANBORN	14487-14487	LIVONIA	14714-14714	BLACK CREEK	14816-14816	BREESPORT
14133-14133	SANDUSKY	14488-14488	LIVONIA CENTER	14715-14715	BOLIVAR	14817-14817	BROOKTONDALE
14134-14134	SARDINIA	14489-14489	LYONS	14716-14716	BROCTON	14818-14818	BURDETT
14135-14135	SHERIDAN	14502-14502	MACEDON	14717-14717	CANEADEA	14819-14819	CAMERON
14136-14136	SILVER CREEK	14504-14504	MANCHESTER	14718-14718	CASSADAGA	14820-14820	CAMERON MILLS
14138-14138	SOUTH DAYTON	14505-14505	MARION	14719-14719	CATTARAUGUS	14821-14821	CAMPBELL
14139-14139	SOUTH WALES	14506-14506	MENDON	14720-14720	CELORON	14822-14822	CANASERAGA
14140-14140	SPRING BROOK	14507-14507	MIDDLESEX	14721-14721	CERES	14823-14823	CANISTEO
14141-14141	SPRINGVILLE	14508-14508	MORTON	14722-14722	CHAUTAUQUA	14824-14824	CAYUTA
14143-14143	STAFFORD	14510-14510	MOUNT MORRIS	14723-14723	CHERRY CREEK	14825-14825	CHEMUNG
14144-14144	STELLA NIAGARA	14511-14511	MUMFORD	14724-14724	CLYMER	14826-14826	COHOCTON
14145-14145	STRYKERSVILLE	14512-14512	NAPLES	14726-14726	CONEWANGO VALLEY	14827-14827	COOPERS PLAINS
14150-14151	TONAWANDA	14513-14513	NEWARK	14727-14727	CUBA	14830-14831	CORNING
14166-14166	VAN BUREN POINT	14514-14514	NORTH CHILI	14728-14728	DEWITTVILLE	14836-14836	DALTON
14167-14167	VARYSBURG	14515-14515	NORTH GREECE	14729-14729	EAST OTTO	14837-14837	DUNDEE
14168-14168	VERSAILLES	14516-14516	NORTH ROSE	14730-14730	EAST RANDOLPH	14838-14838	ERIN
14169-14169	WALES CENTER	14517-14517	NUNDA	14731-14731	ELLICOTTVILLE	14839-14839	GREENWOOD
14170-14170	WEST FALLS	14518-14518	OAKS CORNERS	14732-14732	ELLINGTON	14840-14840	HAMMONDSPORT
14171-14171	WEST VALLEY	14519-14519	ONTARIO	14733-14733	FALCONER	14841-14841	HECTOR
14172-14172	WILSON	14520-14520	ONTARIO CENTER	14735-14735	FILLMORE	14842-14842	HIMROD
14173-14173	YORKSHIRE	14521-14521	OVID	14736-14736	FINDLEY LAKE	14843-14843	HORNELL
14174-14174	YOUNGSTOWN	14522-14522	PALMYRA	14737-14737	FRANKLINVILLE	14844-14845	HORSEHEADS
14201-14280	BUFFALO	14525-14525	PAVILION	14738-14738	FREWSBURG	14846-14846	HUNT
14301-14305	NIAGARA FALLS	14526-14526	PENFIELD	14739-14739	FRIENDSHIP	14847-14847	INTERLAKEN
14410-14410	ADAMS BASIN	14527-14527	PENN YAN	14740-14740	GERRY	14850-14853	ITHACA
14411-14411	ALBION	14529-14529	PERKINSVILLE	14741-14741	GREAT VALLEY	14854-14854	JACKSONVILLE
14413-14413	ALTON	14530-14530	PERRY	14742-14742	GREENHURST	14855-14855	JASPER
14414-14414	AVON	14532-14532	PHELPS	14743-14743	HINSDALE	14856-14856	KANONA
14415-14415	BELLONA	14533-14533	PIFFARD	14744-14744	HOUGHTON	14857-14857	LAKEMONT
14416-14416	BERGEN	14534-14534	PITTSFORD	14745-14745	HUME	14858-14858	LINDLEY
14418-14418	BRANCHPORT	14536-14536	PORTAGEVILLE	14747-14747	KENNEDY	14859-14859	LOCKWOOD
14420-14420	BROCKPORT	14537-14537	PORT GIBSON	14748-14748	KILL BUCK	14860-14860	LODI
14422-14422	BYRON	14538-14538	PULTNEYVILLE	14750-14750	LAKEWOOD	14861-14861	LOWMAN
14423-14423	CALEDONIA	14539-14539	RETSOF	14751-14751	LEON	14863-14863	MECKLENBURG
14424-14424	CANANDAIGUA	14541-14541	ROMULUS	14752-14752	LILY DALE	14864-14864	MILLPORT
14425-14425	FARMINGTON	14542-14542	ROSE	14753-14753	LIMESTONE	14865-14865	MONTOUR FALLS
14427-14427	CASTILE	14543-14543	RUSH	14754-14754	LITTLE GENESEE	14867-14867	NEWFIELD
14428-14428	CHURCHVILLE	14544-14544	RUSHVILLE	14755-14755	LITTLE VALLEY	14869-14869	ODESSA
14429-14429	CLARENDON	14545-14545	SCOTTSBURG	14756-14756	MAPLE SPRINGS	14870-14870	PAINTED POST
14430-14430	CLARKSON	14546-14546	SCOTTSVILLE	14757-14757	MAYVILLE	14871-14871	PINE CITY
14432-14432	CLIFTON SPRINGS	14547-14547	SENECA CASTLE	14758-14758	NIOBE	14872-14872	PINE VALLEY
14433-14433	CLYDE	14548-14548	SHORTSVILLE	14759-14759	NORTH CLYMER	14873-14873	PRATTSBURGH
14435-14435	CONESUS	14549-14549	SILVER LAKE	14760-14760	OLEAN	14874-14874	PULTENEY
14437-14437	DANSVILLE	14550-14550	SILVER SPRINGS	14766-14766	OTTO	14876-14876	READING CENTER
14441-14441	DRESDEN	14551-14551	SODUS	14767-14767	PANAMA	14877-14877	REXVILLE
14443-14443	EAST BLOOMFIELD	14555-14555	SODUS POINT	14769-14769	PORTLAND	14878-14878	ROCK STREAM
14444-14444	EAST PALMYRA	14556-14556	SONYEA	14770-14770	PORTVILLE	14879-14879	SAVONA
14445-14445	EAST ROCHESTER	14557-14557	SOUTH BYRON	14772-14772	RANDOLPH	14880-14880	SCIO
14449-14449	EAST WILLIAMSON	14558-14558	SOUTH LIMA	14774-14774	RICHBURG	14881-14881	SLATERVILLE SPRINGS
14450-14450	FAIRPORT	14559-14559	SPENCERPORT	14775-14775	RIPLEY	14882-14882	LANSING
14452-14452	FANCHER	14560-14560	SPRINGWATER	14776-14776	ROSSBURG	14883-14883	SPENCER
14453-14453	FISHERS	14561-14561	STANLEY	14777-14777	RUSHFORD	14884-14884	SWAIN
14454-14454	GENESEO	14563-14563	UNION HILL	14778-14778	SAINT BONAVENTURE	14885-14885	TROUPSBURG
14456-14456	GENEVA	14564-14564	VICTOR	14779-14779	SALAMANCA	14886-14886	TRUMANSBURG
14461-14461	GORHAM	14568-14568	WALWORTH	14781-14781	SHERMAN	14887-14887	TYRONE
14462-14462	GROVELAND	14569-14569	WARSAW	14782-14782	SINCLAIRVILLE	14888-14888	VALOIS
14463-14463	HALL	14571-14571	WATERPORT	14783-14783	STEAMBURG	14889-14889	VAN ETTEN
14464-14464	HAMLIN	14572-14572	WAYLAND	14784-14784	STOCKTON	14891-14891	WATKINS GLEN
14466-14466	HEMLOCK	14580-14580	WEBSTER	14785-14785	STOW	14892-14892	WAVERLY
14467-14467	HENRIETTA	14584-14584	WEBSTER CROSSING	14786-14786	WEST CLARKSVILLE	14893-14893	WAYNE
14468-14468	HILTON	14585-14585	WEST BLOOMFIELD	14787-14787	WESTFIELD	14894-14894	WELLSBURG
14469-14469	BLOOMFIELD	14586-14586	WEST HENRIETTA	14788-14788	WESTONS MILLS	14895-14895	WELLSVILLE
14470-14470	HOLLEY	14588-14588	WILLARD	14801-14801	ADDISON	14897-14897	WHITESVILLE
14471-14471	HONEOYE	14589-14589	WILLIAMSON	14802-14802	ALFRED	14898-14898	WOODHULL
14472-14472	HONEOYE FALLS	14590-14590	WOLCOTT	14803-14803	ALFRED STATION	14901-14975	ELMIRA
14474-14474	INDUSTRY	14591-14591	WYOMING	14804-14804	ALMOND		

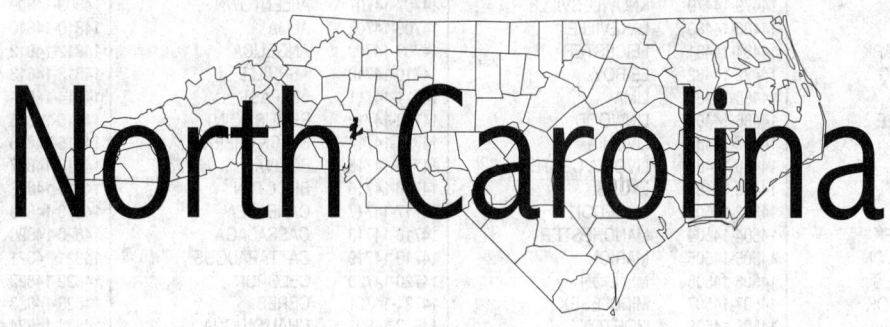

North Carolina

General Help Numbers:

Governor's Office
20301 Mail Service Center   919-733-4240
Raleigh, NC 27699-0301   Fax 919-715-3175
http://www.governor.state.nc.us   8AM-6PM

Attorney General's Office
Justice Department   919-716-6400
PO Box 629   Fax 919-716-6750
Raleigh, NC 27602-0629   8AM-5PM
http://www.jus.state.nc.us

State Court Administrator
2 E Morgan St, Justice Bldg, 4th Floor   919-733-7107
Raleigh, NC 27602   Fax 919-715-5779
http://www.aoc.state.nc.us/www/   8AM-5PM
public/html/aoc.htm

State Archives
Archives & History Division   919-733-3952
109 E Jones St   Fax 919-733-1354
Raleigh, NC 27601-2807   8AM-5:30PM TU-F, 9-5 SA
http://www.ah.dcr.state.nc.us

State Specifics:

Capital: Raleigh
Wake County

Time Zone: EST

Number of Counties: 100

Population: 8,049,313

Web Site: www.ncgov.com

State Agencies

Criminal Records
Access to Records is Restricted

State Bureau of Investigation, Identification Section, 407 N Blount St, Raleigh, NC 27601-1009; 919-662-4500 x300, 919-662-4380 (Fax), 7:30AM-5PM.

Note: Employers or screening companies are denied access unless subject is in the health or child care business. Contact agency for proper paperwork. Sex offender data is at http://sbi.jus.state.nc.us/cgi-bin/hsrun.hse/SOR/SOR/SOR.htx;start=HS_SORSearchFrames.

Record access is limited to criminal justice and other government agencies authorized by law.

Corporation Records
Limited Partnerships
Limited Liability Company Records
Trademarks/Servicemarks

Secretary of State, Corporations Section, PO Box 29622, Raleigh, NC 27626-0622 (Courier: 2 S Salisbury, Raleigh, NC 27603); 919-807-2251 (Corporations), 919-807-2164 (Trademarks), 919-807-2039 (Fax), 8AM-5PM.

http://www.secretary.state.nc.us

Note: DBAs, Fictitious Names and Assumed Name records are found at the county Register of Deeds offices.

Indexing & Storage: Records are available from 1800's on. Most information is available on the computer database and on the agency's website. New records are available for inquiry immediately.

Searching: Information is open to the public. Include the following in your request-full name of business. Information contained in filings includes officers' names and addresses; registered agent; principal office; date of incorporation; and nature of the business.

Access by: mail, phone, fax, in person, online.

Fee & Payment: There is no search fee. Copies are $1.00 per page. Certification is $5.00. Fee payee: Secretary of State. Prepayment required. They will invoice except for in person searching. Personal checks accepted. No credit cards accepted.

Mail search: Expect 6-10 day turnaround time for corporation documents, 2-3 day turnaround time for trademark documents.

Phone search: There is no fee to do simple searches over the phone.

Fax search: They will invoice.

In person search: Turnaround time is immediate. There is a public access terminal to view records.

Online search: Access is currently available through a dial-up system. There is an initial registration fee of $185 and a charge of $.02 each time the "enter key" is pushed. To register, call Bonnie Elek at (919) 807-2196. Also, the web site offers a free search of status and registered agent by corporation name. The trademark database is not available online.

Other access: The state makes database information available for purchase, contact Bonnie Elek at number above.

Uniform Commercial Code
Federal Tax Liens

UCC Division, Secretary of State, Raleigh, NC 27626-0622 (Courier: 2 South Salisbury St, Raleigh, NC 27603-5909); 919-807-2111, 919-807-2120 (Fax), 7:30AM-5PM.

http://www.secretary.state.nc.us/UCC

Indexing & Storage: Records are available from 1967. Records are computerized since 1985.

Searching: Use search request form UCC-11. The search includes federal tax liens on businesses since 1985 if you request (add $5.00). You may search federal tax liens separately. Federal tax liens on individuals and all state tax liens are filed at Superior Courts. Include the following in your request-debtor name. Name will be searched as submitted; name variation printouts will be given.

Access by: mail, in person, online.

Fee & Payment: As of Sept. 1, 2000, the search fee is $30.00 per debtor name. Copies are $1.00 per page if done by the staff or $.25 if done by yourself in person. Certification is $6.25 for the first page and $1.00 for each additional. Fee payee: Secretary of State. Prepayment required. Prepayment is required. Underpayment requests will be rejected. Personal checks accepted. No credit cards accepted.

Mail search: Turnaround time: 3 days. A self addressed stamped envelope is requested.

In person search: Searching is available in person.

Online search: Free access is available at http://ucc.secstate.state.nc.us. Search by ID number or debtor name. The state is preparing to offer a FTP system for ongoing commercial requesters. Call 919-807-2196 for more information.

Other access: The UCC or tax lien database can be purchased on microfilm. Updates can be purchased on either a weekly or monthly basis. For a packet, call 919-807-2196.

State Tax Liens
Records not maintained by a state level agency.

Note: Tax lien data is found at the county level.

Sales Tax Registrations
Access to Records is Restricted

Revenue Department, Sales & Use Tax Division, PO Box 25000, Raleigh, NC 27640 (Courier: 501 N Wilmington Street, Raleigh, NC 27604); 919-733-3661, 919-715-6086 (Fax), 8AM-5PM.

http://www.dor.state.us/dor

Note: This agency refuses to release any information about registrants, but will validate a number if presented with one.

Birth Certificates

Center for health Statistics, Vital Records Branch, 1903 Mail Service Center, Raleigh, NC 27699-1903 (Courier: 225 N McDowell St, Raleigh, NC 27603); 919-733-3526, 800-669-8310 (Credit Card Orders), 919-829-1359 (Fax), 8AM-4PM.

http://www.schs.state.nc.us/SCHS

Note: Anyone can order an non-certified copy of a record. Only family members can order a certified copy. The fee is the same.

Indexing & Storage: Records are available from 1913 to present. Prior to 1913, the state did not keep records of births. It takes 90 days after birth before new records are available for inquiry. Records indexed on microfiche, inhouse computer.

Searching: Investigative searches are permitted, but only non-certified copies are provided. Otherwise, requester must state relationship to subject and why record is needed. Include the following in your request-full name, names of parents, mother's maiden name, date of birth, place of birth. The following data is not released: adoption records or medical records.

Access by: mail, phone, fax, in person.

Fee & Payment: Search fee is $10.00 per 5 years searched. Add $5.00 for using a credit card. Add $5.00 per copy for additional copies. Fee payee: North Carolina Vital Records. Prepayment required. Credit cards accepted for expedited service only. Personal checks accepted. Credit cards accepted: MasterCard, Visa.

Mail search: Turnaround time: 2 weeks. No self addressed stamped envelope is required.

Phone search: See expedited service.

Fax search: See expedited service.

In person search: Turnaround time is 30 minutes.

Expedited service: Expedited service is available for credit card searches. Turnaround time: overnight delivery. Total fee is $42.95 and includes overnight delivery.

Death Records

Dept of Environment, Health & Natural Resources, Vital Records Section, 1903 Mail Service Center, Raleigh, NC 27699-1903 (Courier: 225 N McDowell St, Raleigh, NC 27603); 919-733-3526, 919-829-1359 (Fax), 8AM-4PM.

http://www.schs.state.nc.us/SCHS

Note: Non-certified records may be obtained by the public; certified copies can only be purchased by family members. The fee is the same for either record.

Indexing & Storage: Records are available from 1930 to present. It takes 90 days after death before new records are available for inquiry. Records are indexed on microfiche, inhouse computer.

Searching: Investigative searches are permitted, but only non-certified copies are provided. Include the following in your request-full name, date of death, place of death. Social Security Number is helpful.

Access by: mail, phone, fax, in person.

Fee & Payment: The search fee is $10.00 for each 5 years searched. Add $5.00 for using a credit card. Add $5.00 per copy for additional copies. Fee payee: North Carolina Vital Records. Prepayment required. Credit cards accepted for fax and phone service only. Personal checks accepted. Credit cards accepted: MasterCard, Visa, AmEx, Discover.

Mail search: Turnaround time: 2 weeks. No self addressed stamped envelope is required.

Phone search: See expedited service.

Fax search: See expedited service.

In person search: Turnaround time 30 minutes.

Expedited service: Expedited service is available for fax searches. Total fee is $42.95 and includes overnight delivery.

Marriage Certificates

Dept of Environment, Health & Natural Resources, Vital Records Section, 1903 Mail Service Center, Raleigh, NC 27699-1903 (Courier: 225 N McDowell St, Raleigh, NC 27603); 919-733-3526, 919-829-1359 (Fax), 8AM-4PM.

http://www.schs.state.nc.us/SCHS

Note: Non-certified copies may be purchased by the public. Certified copies can be obtained by family members. The fee is the same for either report.

Indexing & Storage: Records are available from 1962 to present. New records are available for inquiry immediately. Records are indexed on microfiche, inhouse computer.

Searching: Investigative searches are permitted, but only non-certified copies are provided. Include the following in your request-names of husband and wife, date of marriage, place or county of marriage.

Access by: mail, phone, fax, in person.

Fee & Payment: The search fee is $10.00 for each 5 years searched. Add $5.00 for using a credit card. Add $5.00 per copy for additional copies. Fee payee: North Carolina Vital Records. Prepayment required. Personal checks accepted. Credit cards accepted: MasterCard, Visa, AmEx, Discover.

Mail search: Turnaround time: 2 weeks. No self addressed stamped envelope is required.

Phone search: See expedited service.

Fax search: See expedited service.

In person search: Turnaround time 30 minutes.

Expedited service: Expedited service is available for fax searches. Total fee is $42.95 and includes overnight delivery.

Divorce Records

Dept of Environment, Health & Natural Resources, Vital Records Section, 1903 Mail Service Center, Raleigh, NC 27699-1903 (Courier: 225 N McDowell St, Raleigh, NC 27603); 919-733-3526, 919-829-1359 (Fax), 8AM-4PM.

http://www.schs.state.nc.us/SCHS

Note: Non-certified copies are available to the public, certified copies to family members. The fee is the same for either report.

Indexing & Storage: Records are available from 1958 to present. New records are available for inquiry immediately. Records are indexed on microfiche, inhouse computer.

Searching: Investigative searches are permitted, but only non-certified copies are provided. Include the following in your request-names of husband and wife, date of divorce, place of divorce, case number (if known).

Access by: mail, phone, in person.

Fee & Payment: The search fee is $10.00 for each 5 years searched. Add $5.00 for using a credit card. Add $5.00 per copy for additional copies. Fee payee: North Carolina Vital Records. Prepayment required. Personal checks accepted. Credit cards accepted: MasterCard, Visa, AmEx, Discover.

Mail search: Turnaround time: 2 weeks. No self addressed stamped envelope is required.

Phone search: See expedited service.

In person search: Turnaround time is 30 minutes.

Expedited service: Expedited service is available for fax searches. Total fee is $42.95 and includes overnight delivery.

Workers' Compensation Records

NC Industrial Commission, 4340 Mail Service Center, Raleigh, NC 27699-4340; 919-807-2500, 8AM-5PM.

http://www.comp.state.nc.us

Indexing & Storage: Records are available from 1980.

Searching: Searches require a signed release or statement of purpose of request on letterhead. Only parties to claim will be allowed access. Records may not be used for pre-employment screening.

Access by: mail, in person.

Fee & Payment: There is no search fee. There is no copy fee unless the file is over 20 pages, then the fee is $1.00 per page (over 20). Fee payee: NC Industrial Commission. Personal checks accepted. No credit cards accepted.

Mail search: Turnaround time: 2 to 3 days.

In person search: Generally turnaround time is immediate, unless the case is closed and records must be researched.

Driver Records

Division of Motor Vehicles, Driver's License Section, 1100 New Bern Ave, Raleigh, NC 27697; 919-715-7000, 8AM-5PM.

http://www.dmv.dot.state.nc.us

Note: Copies of tickets may be purchased from the same address for a fee of $5.00 per ticket.

Indexing & Storage: Records are available for 5 years or more for moving violations, 10 years or more for DWIs and suspensions. Records of

surrendered licenses are kept for one year after the expiration date. North Carolina utilizes two point systems-one for the DMV, one for insurance purposes. It takes 30 days or less before new records are available for inquiry.

Searching: Large volume users are pre-approved and must file a certificate with the state. Form DL-DPPA-1 is required. Casual requesters can obtain records, but no personal information is released. Include the following in your request-driver's license number, full name, date of birth. Some search modes will look at the driver's license number first, then the name and DOB as a secondary search. Online requesters must have the license number to search. The following data is not released: medical information.

Access by: mail, in person, online.

Fee & Payment: The current fee is $5.00 per record. Certified records are an additional $2.00. Fee payee: Division of Motor Vehicles. Prepayment required. Personal checks accepted. No credit cards accepted.

Mail search: Turnaround time: 7 business days. No self addressed stamped envelope is required.

In person search: Up to 2 requests will be processed across the counter; the rest are available the next day.

Online search: To qualify for online availability, a client must be an insurance agent or insurance company support organization. The mode is interactive and is open from 7 AM to 10 PM. The DL# and name are needed when ordering. Records are $5.00 each. A minimum $500 security deposit is required.

Other access: Magnetic tape for high volume batch users is available. Requests must be pre-paid.

Vehicle Ownership
Vehicle Identification

Division of Motor Vehicles, Registration/Correspondence Unit, 1100 New Bern Ave, Rm 100, Raleigh, NC 27697-0001; 919-715-7000, 8AM-5PM.

http://www.dmv.dot.state.nc.us

Indexing & Storage: Records are available from their first records for title records (on microfilm). Computer records are purged periodically according to plate activity. Records are maintained for mobile homes and boat trailers, also.

Searching: State complies with DPPA. Casual requesters receive records without personal information. Effective 01/01/00, only vehicle owners who have opted in, will be placed on marketing list requests. Include the following in your request-vehicle description, name, signed release.

Access by: mail, in person.

Fee & Payment: The fee is $1.00 per record (includes lien data) or $5.00 for a certified record. Fee payee: Department of Motor Vehicles. Prepayment required. Personal checks accepted. No credit cards accepted.

Mail search: Turnaround time: 3 days. The use of Form MVR-605A is helpful. The requests require the requester's signature.A self addressed stamped envelope is requested.

In person search: Turnaround time is while you wait if you have the correct authorization.

Other access: North Carolina offers a bulk retrieval of ownership and registration information on magnetic tape. A written request specifying the purpose and details of the request is required. For more information, call 913-250-4230.

Accident Reports

Division of Motor Vehicles, Traffic Records Section, 1100 New Bern Ave, Annex Bldg Rm 112, Raleigh, NC 27697; 919-733-7250, 919-733-9605 (Fax), 8AM-5PM.

http://www.dmv.dot.state.nc.us/trafficrecords/faq

Indexing & Storage: Records are available from 1986 to present on computer, from 1990 to present on microfiche. Hard copies are available from 1992.

Searching: Records are not released on minor drivers. Using Form TR-67A, the requester should submit at least one of the names of the participants, the county of occurrence, date of occurrence, and the exception under which he/she qualifies to receive personal information in accordance with DPPA.

Access by: mail, fax, in person.

Fee & Payment: The fee is $4.00 for a certified copy or no cost for a non-certified copy. Fee payee: Division of Motor Vehicles. Prepayment required. Charge accounts are not required to pre-pay. Personal checks accepted. No credit cards accepted.

Mail search: Turnaround time: 3 days. A self addressed stamped envelope is requested.

Fax search: Results may be returned by fax for a charge of $2.00 per report. This is only for ongoing requesters and a deposit is required.

In person search: Turnaround time is immediate if the record is available.

Other access: Bulk file purchase is available.

Vessel Ownership
Vessel Registration

North Carolina Wildlife Resources Commission, Transaction Management, 1709 Mail Service Center, Raleigh, NC 27699-1709; 800-628-3773, 919-662-4379 (Fax), 8AM-5PM.

http://www.state.nc.us/Wildlife

Indexing & Storage: Records are available from 1970 and are computerized. This is an optional title state. Lien information will show if the vessel is titled. All motorized boats and sailboats over 14 ft must be registered. New records are available for inquiry immediately.

Searching: Include the following in your request-Name, signed release. Submit the name or registration number or hull number.

Access by: mail, fax.

Fee & Payment: There is no search fee.

Mail search: Turnaround time: 1 to 2 weeks. No self addressed stamped envelope is required.

Fax search: Turnaround time is several days.

Other access: The agency sells a CD-ROM disk with registration information for $10.00 per disk.

Legislation Records

North Carolina General Assembly, State Legislative Bldg, 16 W. Jones Street, 1st Fl, Raleigh, NC 27603; 919-733-7779 (Bill Numbers), 919-733-3270 (Archives), 919-733-5648 (Order Desk), 8:30AM-5:30PM.

http://www.ncleg.net

Note: To get a copy of a bill, you must have a bill number first.

Indexing & Storage: Records are available for current and prior sessions only. Records are computer indexed since 1985, and are indexed on microfiche from 1969 to 1984.

Searching: Can search by 10 fields including bill number and subject.

Access by: mail, phone, in person, online.

Fee & Payment: There is no search fee, but copies are $.20 each. Fee payee: North Carolina General Assembly. Prepayment required. Money is only needed for the copy machine. Personal checks accepted. No credit cards accepted.

Mail search: Turnaround time: variable. No self addressed stamped envelope is required.

Phone search: Searches by phone are limited to between 5 and 8 bills depending on workload.

In person search: Turnaround time is immediate.

Online search: The Internet site has copies of bills, status, and state statutes.

Other access: This agency will mail lists of bills on computer printouts.

Voter Registration
Access to Records is Restricted

State Board of Elections, PO Box 27255, Raleigh, NC 27611-7255; 919-733-7173, 919-715-0135 (Fax), 8AM-5PM.

http://www.sboe.state.nc.us

Note: There is no statewide system, although one may be in place sometime in 2002. Records are open to the public and currently must be accessed at the county level through the County Director of Elections.

GED Certificates

Department of Community Colleges, GED Office, 5024 Mail Service Center, Raleigh, NC 27699-5024; 919-733-7051 x744, 919-715-5351 (Fax), 8AM-4PM.

http://www.ncccs.cc.nc.us

Indexing & Storage: Records are available from the 1940s, from 09/78 on microfilm.

Searching: Include the following in your request-signed release, Social Security Number, date of birth. The year of the test is helpful.

Access by: mail, phone, in person.

Fee & Payment: The fee for a transcript copy is $3.00, there is no fee for merely a verification or a duplicate diploma. Fee payee: GED Office. Prepayment required. Personal checks accepted. No credit cards accepted.

Mail search: Turnaround time: 1 week.

Phone search: Only records after 09/78 can be verified by phone.

In person search: No fee for request.

Hunting License Information
Fishing License Information
Access to Records is Restricted

Wildlife Resource Commission, Archdale Bldg, 512 N Salisbury Street, Raleigh, NC 27604-0118; 919-662-4370, 919-662-4381 (Fax), 8AM-5PM.

http://www.state.nc.us/wildlife

Note: They only maintain a database of lifetime license holders and consider the information to be confidential and not available to the general public.

North Carolina State Licensing Agencies

Licenses Searchable Online

Anesthetist Nurse #08 .... www.docboard.org/nc/df/ncsearch.htm

Architect #03 .... www.ncbarch.org/cgi-ncbarch/ncbarch_licdb/ncbarch/architects/query_form

Banking Division #17 .... www.banking.state.nc.us/banks.htm

Charitable/Sponsor Organization #52 .... www.secretary.state.nc.us/sls/sponsors.asp

Check Casher #17 .... www.banking.state.nc.us/checkcas.htm

Chiropractor #41 .... www.ncchiroboard.org/public/licensed_chiros.html

Clinical Nurse Specialist #08 .... www.docboard.org/nc/df/ncsearch.htm

Consumer Financer #17 .... www.banking.state.nc.us/cf.htm

Contractor, General #32 .... www.nclbgc.org/

Electrical Contractor/Inspector #06 .... www.ncbeec.org/LicSearch.asp

Engineer #48 .... www.member-base.com/ncbels/public/searchdb.asp

Fire Sprinkler Contractor/Inspector #31 ..... www.nclicensing.org/OnlineReg.htm

Fund Raiser Consultants/Solicitor #52 ...... www.secretary.state.nc.us/sls/solicitors.asp

Heating Contractor #31 .... www.nclicensing.org/OnlineReg.htm

Lobbyist #51 .... www.secretary.state.nc.us/lobbyists/Lsearch.asp

Medical Doctor/Physician #47 .... www.docboard.org/nc/df/ncsearch.htm

Midwife Nurse #08 .... www.docboard.org/nc/df/ncsearch.htm

Mortgage Division #17 .... www.banking.state.nc.us/mbb.htm

Nurse Practitioner #08 .... www.docboard.org/nc/df/ncsearch.htm

Nurse-LPN #08 .... www.docboard.org/nc/df/ncsearch.htm

Occupational Therapist #09 .... www.ncbot.org/fpdb/otimport.html

Occupational Therapist Assistant #09 .... www.ncbot.org/fpdb/otimport.html

Optometrist #18 .... www.ncoptometry.org/verify/index.asp

Osteopathic Physician #47 .... www.docboard.org/nc/df/ncsearch.htm

Pharmacist #11 .... www.ncbop.org/names1.asp

Physician Assistant #47 .... www.docboard.org/nc/df/ncsearch.htm

Plumber #31 .... www.nclicensing.org/OnlineReg.htm

Public Accountant-CPA #37 .... www.cpaboard.state.nc.us

Real Estate Broker/Dealer/Firm #39 .... http://ndsips01.sips.state.nc.us/NCREC/search.asp

Surveyor #48 .... www.member-base.com/ncbels/public/searchdb.asp

Licensing Quick Finder

Acupuncturist #40 919-773-0530	Beauty Shop/Salon #55 919-733-4117	Dental Hygienist #42 919-781-4901
Alarm Installer #01 919-875-3611	Bingo Operation #21 919-733-3029	Dentist #42 919-781-4901
Alarm System Business #01 919-875-3611	Boiler/Pressure Vessel Inspector #24 ... 919-807-2760	DME (Rx Device) #11 919-942-4454
Alcoholic Beverage Control #20 919-779-0700	Bondsman - Professional/Surety #23 919-733-2200	EDM #21 919-733-2285
Ambulance Attendant #21 919-733-2285	Building Inspector #23 919-733-3901	Electrical Contractor/Inspector #06 919-733-9042
Amusement Device #24 919-807-2770	Cemetery #19 919-981-2536	Electrologist #35 336-574-1414
Anesthetist Nurse #08 919-782-3211	Cemetery Salesperson #19 919-981-2536	Electrologist Instructor #35 336-574-1414
Architect #03 919-733-9544	Charitable/Sponsor Organization #52 ... 919-807-2214	Elevator Inspector #24 919-807-2770
Armed Security Guard #53 919-875-3611	Check Casher #17 919-733-3016	Embalmer #07 919-733-9380
Athletic Agent #51 919-807-2156	Chiropractor #41 704-782-0111	Emergency Medical Service #21 919-733-2285
Attorney #45 919-828-4886	Clinical Nurse Specialist #08 919-782-3211	Emergency Medical Technician #21 919-733-2285
Auction Company #02 919-981-5066	Consumer Financer #17 919-733-3016	Engineer #48 919-781-9499
Auctioneer/Auctioneer Apprentice #02 .. 919-981-5066	Contractor, General #32 919-571-4183	Esthetician Instructor/Apprentice/Practitioner #55 ....
Bail Bond Runner #23 919-733-2200	Cosmetologist Instructor/Apprentice/Practitioner #55	 919-733-4117
Bank #27 919-508-5973	 919-733-4117	Family Therapist #57 336-794-3891
Banking Division #17 919-733-3016	Counselor #13 919-515-2244	Fire Sprinkler Contractor/Inspector #31 . 919-875-3612
Barber Inspector #04 919-715-1159	Crematory #07 919-733-9380	Firearms Trainer #53 919-875-3611
Barber Instructor #04 919-715-1159	Day Care Administrator #21 919-622-4499	Fund Raiser Consultants/Solicitor #52 .. 919-807-2214
Barber/Barber Apprentice #04 919-715-1159	Day Care Center Teacher #21 919-622-4499	Funeral Director #07 919-733-9380

Funeral Home/Chapel #07	919-733-9380	
Funeral Pre-Need Seller #07	919-733-9380	
Funeral Service #07	919-733-9380	
Geologist #46	919-850-9669	
Guard Dog Service #53	919-875-3611	
Hearing Aid Dispenser/Fitter #43	919-981-5105	
Heating Contractor #31	919-875-3612	
Hospital #21	919-733-7461	
Insurance Agent #23	919-733-7487	
Insurance Company #23	919-733-7487	
Investment Advisor #27	919-733-3924	
Investment Representative #26	919-733-3924	
Jailer #56	919-716-6460	
Landscape Architect #44	919-850-9088	
Librarian, Public #28	919-733-2570	
Lobbyist #51	919-807-2156	
Manicurist #54	919-850-2793	
Manicurist Instructor/Apprentice #55	919-733-4117	
Marriage & Family Therapist #33	336-724-1288	
Medical Doctor/Physician #47	919-326-1100	
Medical Program Director #21	919-715-1872	
Medical Responder #21	919-733-2285	
Midwife Nurse #08	919-782-3211	
Mortgage Division #17	919-733-3016	
Notary Public #58	919-733-3406	
Nurse Practitioner #08	919-782-3211	
Nurse-LPN #08	919-782-3211	
Nursing Home #21	919-733-7461	
Nursing Home Administrator #05	919-571-4164	
Occupational Therapist #09	919-832-1380	
Occupational Therapist Assistant #09	919-832-1380	
Optician #10	919-733-9321	
Optometrist #18	919-285-3160	
Osteopathic Physician #47	919-326-1100	
Paramedic #21	919-733-2285	
Pesticide Applicator #16	919-733-3556	
Pesticide Consultant #16	919-733-3556	
Pesticide Dealer #16	919-733-3556	
Pharmacist #11	919-942-4454	
Pharmacy/Physician Pharmacy #11	919-942-4454	
Physical Therapist #49	919-490-6393	
Physician Assistant #47	919-326-1100	
Plumber #31	919-875-3612	
Podiatrist #12	919-468-8055	
Polygraph Examiner #53	919-875-3611	
Private Investigator #53	919-875-3611	
Psychological Associate #36	828-262-2258	
Psychologist #36	828-262-2258	
Public Accountant-CPA #37	919-733-4222	
Real Estate Broker/Dealer/Firm #39	919-733-9580	
Sanitarian #14	919-212-2000	
Shorthand Reporter #29	919-733-2927	
Social Worker #15	336-625-1679	
Solicitor #21	919-733-4510	
Solid Waste Facility Operator #34	919-733-0379	
Speech Pathologist/Audiologist #30	336-272-1828	
Surveyor #48	919-781-9499	
Taxidermist #25	919-733-4984	
Veterinarian #50	919-733-7689	
Veterinary Technician #50	919-733-7689	
Waste Water Treatment Plant Operator #34	919-733-0379	

Licensing Agency Information

#01 Alarm Systems Licensing Board, 1631 Midtown Pl #104, Raleigh, NC 27609; 919-875-3611, Fax: 919-875-3609.
www.jus.state.nc.us/justice/pps/aslmain.htm

#02 Auctioneer Licensing Board, 1001 Navajo Dr #105, Raleigh, NC 27609-7318; 919-981-5066, Fax: 919-981-5069.
www.ncalb.org

#03 Board of Architecture, 127 Hargett St #304, Raleigh, NC 27601; 919-733-9544, Fax: 919-733-1272.
www.ncbarch.org
Direct web site URL to search for licensees: www.ncbarch.org/cgi-ncbarch/ncbarch_licdb/ncbarch/architects/query_form. You can search online using personal name, firm name, license number, license status, city, state and ZIP Code. Or, at the main website, click on "Directory." You can also search for architect license applicants as well as licensed firms.

#04 Board of Barber Examiners, 2321 Crabtree Blvd #110, Raleigh, NC 27604-2260; 919-715-1159, Fax: 919-715-4669.

#05 Board of Examiners for Nursing Home Administrators, 3733 National Drive #228, Raleigh, NC 27612; 919-571-4164, Fax: 919-571-4166.

#06 Division of Enviornmental Health, PO Box 18727 (1299 Front St.), Raleigh, NC 27619; 919-733-9042, Fax: 919-733-6105.
www.ncbeec.org
Direct web site URL to search for licensees: www.ncbeec.org/LicSearch.asp. You can search online using license number, qualifier's name, licensee's name, city, state, ZIP Code and license class.

#07 Board of Mortuary Science, 2123 Crabtree Blvd #100, Raleigh, NC 27604; 919-733-9380, Fax: 919-733-8271.
www.ncbms.org

#08 Board of Nursing, PO Box 2129 (3724 National Dr.), Raleigh, NC 27602; 919-782-3211, Fax: 919-781-9461.
www.ncbon.com

Direct web site URL to search for licensees: www.docboard.org/nc/df/ncsearch.htm. You can search online using name.

#09 Board of Occupational Therapy, PO Box 2280, Raleigh, NC 27602; 919-832-1380, Fax: 919-833-1059.
www.ncbot.org
Direct web site URL to search for licensees: www.ncbot.org/fpdb/otimport.html

#10 Board of Opticians, PO Box 25336, Raleigh, NC 27611-5336; 919-733-9321, Fax: 919-733-0040.

#11 Board of Pharmacy, PO Box 459 (104 C Carrboro Plaza), Carrboro, NC 27510-0459; 919-942-4454, Fax: 919-967-5757.
www.ncbop.org
Direct web site URL to search for licensees: www.ncbop.org/names1.asp

#12 Board of Podiatry Examiners, PO Box 3914, Cary, NC 27519-3914; 919-468-8055, Fax: 919-468-4209.

#13 Board of Registered Practicing Counselors, 893 Hwy 70 W #202, Garner, NC 27529; 919-661-0820, Fax: 919-779-5642.
www.ncblpc.org

#14 Board of Sanitarian Examiners, 5025 Harbour Towne Dr, Raleigh, NC 27604; 919-212-2000, Fax: 919-212-2000.

#15 Certification Board for Social Workers, PO Box 1043, Asheboro, NC 27204; 336-625-1679, Fax: 336-625-1680.
www.nccbsw.org

#16 Department of Agriculture, PO Box 27647, Raleigh, NC 27611; 919-733-3556, Fax: 919-733-9796.
www.agr.state.nc.us
Direct web site URL to search for licensees: www.agr.state.nc.us/license.htm

#17 Department of Commerce, 4309 Mail Service Center (702 Oberlin Rd #400), Raleigh, NC 27699; 919-733-3016, Fax: 919-733-6918.
www.banking.state.nc.us
Direct web site URL to search for licensees: www.banking.state.nc.us

#18 Board of Examiners in Optometry, 109 N. Graham Street, Wallace, NC 28466; 910-285-3160, Fax: 910-285-4546.
www.ncoptometry.org
Direct web site URL to search for licensees: www.ncoptometry.org/verify/index.asp. You can search online using national database by name, city or state.

#19 Department of Commerce, 1000 Navaho Dr GL-2, Raleigh, NC 27609; 919-981-2536, Fax: 919-981-2538.

#20 Department of Commerce, 4307 Mail Service Center, Raleigh, NC 27699-4307; 919-779-0700, Fax: 919-662-3583.
www.ncabc.com

#21 Department of Health & Human Services, 2702 Mail Service Center (701 Barbour Drive), Raleigh, NC 27699-2707; 919-733-2285, Fax: 919-733-7021.
www.dhhs.state.nc.us/

#23 Department of Insurance, PO Box 26387, 430 N Salisbury St, Raleigh, NC 27611; 919-733-7487.
www.ncdoi.com

#24 Department of Labor, 4 W Edenton St, Labor Bldg, Raleigh, NC 27601-1092; 919-733-7166, Fax: 919-733-6197.
www.dol.state.nc.us

#25 Department of Natural Resources & Environment, 512 N Salisbury St, Raleigh, NC 27604-1188; 919-733-4984.
www.enr.state..nc.us

#26 Department of State, 300 N Salisbury #404, Raleigh, NC 27603; 919-733-3924, Fax: 919-821-0818.
www.secstate.state.nc.us/

#27 Department of State Treasurer, PO Box 29622 (300 N Salisbury St), Raleigh, NC 27626; 919-733-3924, Fax: 919-733-6918.
www.sosnc.com

#28 Division of State Library, 109 E Jones St, Raleigh, NC 27601-2807; 919-733-2570, Fax: 919-733-8714.
http://web.dcr.state.nc.us/divisions/library.html

#29 Examiners for Court Reporting Standards & Testing, PO Box 2448 (2 E Morgan St), Raleigh, NC 27602; 919-733-7107, Fax: 919-715-5779.

#30 Examiners for Speech Pathologists & Audiologists, PO Box 16885, Greensboro, NC 27416-0885; 336-272-1828, Fax: 336-272-4353.

#31 Board of Examiners of Plumbing, Heating & Fire Sprinkler Contractors, 3801 Wake Forest Rd #201, Raleigh, NC 27609; 919-875-3612, Fax: 919-875-3616.
www.nclicensing.org
Direct web site URL to search for licensees: www.nclicensing.org/OnlineReg.htm. You can search online using personal name, business name, and license number.

#32 Licensing Board for General Contractors, PO Box 17187, Raleigh, NC 27619; 919-571-4183, Fax: 919-571-4703.
www.nclbgc.org
Direct web site URL to search for licensees: www.nclbgc.org/lic-fr.html

#33 Marital & Family Therapy Certification Board, 1001 S Marshall St #5, Winston-Salem, NC 27101-5893; 336-724-1288, Fax: 336-777-3601.

#34 Water Treatment Facility Operators, 1635 Mail Service Center, Raleigh, NC 27699-1635; 919-733-0379, Fax: 919-715-2726.

#35 Board of Electrolysis Examiners, PO Box 13626, Greensboro, NC 27415-3626; 336-574-1414, Fax: 336-574-1414.

#36 Psychology Board, 895 State Farm Road #101, Boone, NC 28607; 828-262-2258, Fax: 828-265-8611.

#37 Board of CPA Examiners, PO Box 12827 (1101 Oberlin Rd, #104), Raleigh, NC 27605-2827; 919-733-4222.
www.cpaboard.state.nc.us
Direct web site URL to search for licensees: www.cpaboard.state.nc.us

#39 Real Estate Commission, 1313 Navaho Dr, Raleigh, NC 27609-7460; 919-875-3700, Fax: 919-877-4222.
www.ncrec.state.nc.us

Direct web site URL to search for licensees: http://ndsips01.sips.state.nc.us/NCREC/search.asp. You can search online using agent name, firm name, city, county, speciality and board name.

#40 Acupuncture Licensing Board, 893 US Highway 70 West, Garner, NC 27529; 919-773-0530, Fax: 919-779-5642.
www.covecreek.org

#41 Board of Chiropractic Examiners, 174 Church St N, Concord, NC 28025; 704-782-0111.
www.ncchiroboard.org
Direct web site URL to search for licensees: www.ncchiroboard.org/public/licensed_chiros.html

#42 Board of Dental Examiners, PO Box 32270 (37 National Dr, Spe. 221), Raleigh, NC 27622-2270; 919-781-4901, Fax: 919-571-4197.
www.ncdentalboard.org

#43 Board of Hearing Aid Dealers & Fitters, 3733 Benson Drive, Raleigh, NC 27609; 919-981-5105, Fax: 919-981-5045.
www.nchalb.org

#44 Board of Landscape Architecture, 3733 Benson Dr (27609), Raleigh, NC 27609; 919-850-9088, Fax: 919-872-1598.

#45 Board of Law Examiners, PO Box 2946 (208 Fayetteville St Mall), Raleigh, NC 27602; 919-828-4886, Fax: 919-828-2251.
www.ncble.org

#46 Board of Licensing Geologists, PO Box 41225 (3733 Benson Dr), Raleigh, NC 27629; 919-850-9669, Fax: 919-872-1598.

#47 Board of Medical Examiners, PO Box 20007 (1201 Front St, 27609), Raleigh, NC 27619; 919-326-1100, Fax: 919-326-1130.
www.docboard.org
Direct web site URL to search for licensees: www.docboard.org/nc/df/ncsearch.htm. You can search online using name

#48 Board of Registration for Prof Engineers & Land Surveyors, 310 W Mill Brook Rd, Raleigh, NC 27609; 919-841-4000, Fax: 919-841-4012.
www.ncbels.org
Direct web site URL to search for licensees: www.member-

base.com/ncbels/public/searchdb.asp. You can search online using name, license number, city, state, ZIP Code, county and status.

#49 Examining Committee of Physical Therapy, 18 W Colony Pl #120, Durham, NC 27705; 919-490-6393, Fax: 919-490-5106.
www.ncptboard.org
Direct web site URL to search for licensees: www.ncptboard.org/search.asp. You can search online using name or license number

#50 Veterinary Medical Board, PO Box 12587, Raleigh, NC 27605; 919-733-7689.

#51 Secretary of State, 2 N Salisbury St (PO Box 29622), Raleigh, NC 27626-0622; 919-807-2156, Fax: 919-807-2160.
www.secstate.state.nc.us/
Direct web site URL to search for licensees: www.secretary.state.nc.us/lobbyists/Lsearch.asp. You can search online using lobbyist name, principal, and year

#52 Secretary of State, PO Box 29622, Raleigh, NC 27626-0525; 919-807-2214, Fax: 919-807-2220.
www.secretary.state.nc.us/sls/default.asp
Direct web site URL to search for licensees: www.secretary.state.nc.us/sls/default.asp

#53 Private Protective Svcs Board, 1631 Midtown Pl #104, Raleigh, NC 27609; 919-875-3611, Fax: 919-875-3609.

#55 Board of Cosmetic Arts Examiners, 1201 Front St., #110, Raleigh, NC 27609; 919-733-4117, Fax: 919-733-4127.
www.cosmetology.state.nc.us

#56 Department of Justice, PO Drawer 629, Raleigh, NC 27602; 919-716-6460.

#57 Marital & Family Therapy Licensure Board, 3000 Bethesda Pl #503, Winston-Salem, NC 27103; 336-794-3891.

#58 Secretary of State, PO Box 29622, Raleigh, NC 27626-0622; 919-807-2131.
www.sosnc.com

North Carolina Federal Courts

The following list indicates the district and division name for each county in the state. If the bankruptcy court location is different from the district court, then the location of the bankruptcy court appears in parentheses.

County/Court Cross Reference

County	District	Division
Alamance	Middle	Greensboro
Alexander	Western	Statesville (Charlotte)
Alleghany	Western	Statesville (Charlotte)
Anson	Western	Charlotte
Ashe	Western	Statesville (Charlotte)
Avery	Western	Asheville (Charlotte)
Beaufort	Eastern	Greenville-Eastern (Wilson)
Bertie	Eastern	Elizabeth City (Wilson)
Bladen	Eastern	Wilmington (Wilson)
Brunswick	Eastern	Wilmington (Wilson)
Buncombe	Western	Asheville (Charlotte)
Burke	Western	Shelby (Charlotte)
Cabarrus	Middle	Greensboro
Caldwell	Western	Statesville (Charlotte)
Camden	Eastern	Elizabeth City (Wilson)
Carteret	Eastern	Greenville-Eastern (Wilson)
Caswell	Middle	Greensboro
Catawba	Western	Statesville (Charlotte)
Chatham	Middle	Greensboro
Cherokee	Western	Bryson City (Charlotte)
Chowan	Eastern	Elizabeth City (Wilson)
Clay	Western	Bryson City (Charlotte)
Cleveland	Western	Shelby (Charlotte)
Columbus	Eastern	Wilmington (Wilson)
Craven	Eastern	Greenville-Eastern (Wilson)
Cumberland	Eastern	Greenville-Eastern (Wilson)
Currituck	Eastern	Elizabeth City (Wilson)
Dare	Eastern	Elizabeth City (Wilson)
Davidson	Middle	Greensboro (Winston-Salem)
Davie	Middle	Greensboro
Duplin	Eastern	Wilmington (Wilson)
Durham	Middle	Greensboro
Edgecombe	Eastern	Raleigh (Wilson)
Forsyth	Middle	Greensboro (Winston-Salem)
Franklin	Eastern	Raleigh
Gaston	Western	Charlotte
Gates	Eastern	Elizabeth City (Wilson)
Graham	Western	Bryson City (Charlotte)
Granville	Eastern	Raleigh
Greene	Eastern	Greenville-Eastern (Wilson)
Guilford	Middle	Greensboro
Halifax	Eastern	Greenville-Eastern (Wilson)
Harnett	Eastern	Raleigh
Haywood	Western	Asheville (Charlotte)
Henderson	Western	Asheville (Charlotte)
Hertford	Eastern	Elizabeth City (Wilson)
Hoke	Middle	Greensboro
Hyde	Eastern	Greenville-Eastern (Wilson)
Iredell	Western	Statesville (Charlotte)
Jackson	Western	Bryson City (Charlotte)
Johnston	Eastern	Raleigh
Jones	Eastern	Greenville-Eastern (Wilson)
Lee	Middle	Greensboro
Lenoir	Eastern	Greenville-Eastern (Wilson)
Lincoln	Western	Statesville (Charlotte)
Macon	Western	Bryson City (Charlotte)
Madison	Western	Asheville (Charlotte)
Martin	Eastern	Greenville-Eastern (Wilson)
McDowell	Western	Shelby (Charlotte)
Mecklenburg	Western	Charlotte
Mitchell	Western	Asheville (Charlotte)
Montgomery	Middle	Greensboro
Moore	Middle	Greensboro
Nash	Eastern	Raleigh (Wilson)
New Hanover	Eastern	Wilmington (Wilson)
Northampton	Eastern	Elizabeth City (Wilson)
Onslow	Eastern	Wilmington (Wilson)
Orange	Middle	Greensboro
Pamlico	Eastern	Greenville-Eastern (Wilson)
Pasquotank	Eastern	Elizabeth City (Wilson)
Pender	Eastern	Wilmington (Wilson)
Perquimans	Eastern	Elizabeth City (Wilson)
Person	Middle	Greensboro
Pitt	Eastern	Greenville-Eastern (Wilson)
Polk	Western	Shelby (Charlotte)
Randolph	Middle	Greensboro
Richmond	Middle	Greensboro
Robeson	Eastern	Wilmington (Wilson)
Rockingham	Middle	Greensboro
Rowan	Middle	Greensboro
Rutherford	Western	Shelby (Charlotte)
Sampson	Eastern	Wilmington (Wilson)
Scotland	Middle	Greensboro
Stanly	Middle	Greensboro
Stokes	Middle	Greensboro (Winston-Salem)
Surry	Middle	Greensboro (Winston-Salem)
Swain	Western	Bryson City (Charlotte)
Transylvania	Western	Asheville (Charlotte)
Tyrrell	Eastern	Elizabeth City (Wilson)
Union	Western	Charlotte
Vance	Eastern	Raleigh
Wake	Eastern	Raleigh
Warren	Eastern	Raleigh
Washington	Eastern	Elizabeth City (Wilson)
Watauga	Western	Statesville (Charlotte)
Wayne	Eastern	Raleigh (Wilson)
Wilkes	Western	Statesville (Charlotte)
Wilson	Eastern	Raleigh (Wilson)
Yadkin	Middle	Greensboro (Winston-Salem)
Yancey	Western	Asheville (Charlotte)

US District Court

Eastern District of North Carolina

Elizabeth City Division
c/o Raleigh Division, PO Box 25670, Raleigh, NC 27611 (Courier Address: Room 574, 310 New Bern Ave, Raleigh, NC 27601), 919-856-4370.

http://www.nced.uscourts.gov

Counties: Bertie, Camden, Chowan, Currituck, Dare, Gates, Hertford, Northampton, Pasquotank, Perquimans, Tyrrell, Washington.

Indexing/Storage: Cases are indexed by as well as by case number. New cases are available in the index after filing date. Open records are located at the Division.

Fee & Payment: The fee is $20.00 per item (one party name or case number). Payment may be made by money order, cashier check, personal check.

Mail Search: A stamped self addressed envelope is not required.

Phone Search: Searching is not available by phone.

In Person: In person searching is available.

PACER: Sign-up number is 800-676-6856. Access fee is $.60 per minute. Toll-free access: 800-995-0313. Local access: 919-856-4768. Case records are available back to 1989. Records are purged when deemed necessary. New records are available online after 3 days.

Greenville-Eastern Division
Room 209, 201 S Evans St, Greenville, NC 27858-1137 (Courier Address: Use mail address for courier delivery), 252-830-6009, Fax: 919-830-2793.

http://www.nced.uscourts.gov

Counties: Beaufort, Carteret, Craven, Edgecombe, Greene, Halifax, Hyde, Jones, Lenoir, Martin, Pamlico, Pitt.

Indexing/Storage: Cases are indexed by defendant and plaintiff as well as by case number. New cases are available in the index same day if possible after filing date. A computer index is maintained. Open records are located at this court. Civil records are retained for 2 years. All criminal records after 1979 are forwarded to Raleigh.

Fee & Payment: The fee is $20.00 per item (one party name or case number). Payment may be made by money order, cashier check, business check. In state personal checks are also accepted. Prepayment is required. Payee: Clerk, US District Court. Certification fee: $7.00 per document. Copy fee: $.50 per page. You are allowed to make your own copies. These copies cost $.50 per page.

Phone Search: Only limited docket information is available by phone.

Mail Search: Always enclose a stamped self addressed envelope.

In Person: In person searching is available.

PACER: Sign-up number is 800-676-6856. Access fee is $.60 per minute. Toll-free access: 800-995-0313. Local access: 919-856-4768. Case records are available back to 1989. Records are purged when deemed necessary. New records are available online after 3 days.

Raleigh Division
Clerk's Office, PO Box 25670, Raleigh, NC 27611 (Courier Address: Room 574, 310 New Bern Ave, Raleigh, NC 27601), 919-856-4370, Fax: 919-856-4160.

http://www.nced.uscourts.gov

Counties: Cumberland, Franklin, Granville, Harnett, Johnston, Nash, Vance, Wake, Warren, Wayne, Wilson.

Indexing/Storage: Cases are indexed by defendant and plaintiff as well as by case number. New cases are available in the index 1 day after filing date. Records from a former office in Fayetteville that handled Cumberland and Harnett counties are maintained here. Both computer and card indexes are maintained. Open records are located at this court. District wide searches are available after 1979 for criminal records through this court.

Fee & Payment: The fee is $20.00 per item (one party name or case number). Payment may be made by money order, cashier check, business check. In state personal checks are also accepted. Prepayment is required. Payee: Clerk, US District Court. Certification fee: $7.00 per document. Copy fee: $.50 per page.

Phone Search: Only docket information is available by phone.

Mail Search: A stamped self addressed envelope is not required.

In Person: In person searching is available.

PACER: Sign-up number is 800-676-6856. Access fee is $.60 per minute. Toll-free access: 800-995-0313. Local access: 919-856-4768. Case records are available back to 1989. Records are purged when deemed necessary. New records are available online after 3 days.

Wilmington Division
PO Box 338, Wilmington, NC 28402 (Courier Address: Room 239, 2 Princess St, Wilmington, NC 28401), 910-815-4663, Fax: 910-815-4518.

http://www.nced.uscourts.gov

Counties: Bladen, Brunswick, Columbus, Duplin, New Hanover, Onslow, Pender, Robeson, Sampson.

Indexing/Storage: Cases are indexed by defendant and plaintiff as well as by case number. New cases are available in the index 1 day after filing date. Both computer and card indexes are maintained. Open records are located at this court. Closed civil records are retained for 2 years. All criminal records after 1979 are located in Raleigh.

Fee & Payment: The fee is $20.00 per item (one party name or case number). Payment may be made by money order, cashier check, personal check. Prepayment is required. Payee: Clerk, US District Court. Certification fee: $7.00 per document. Copy fee: $.50 per page. You are allowed to make your own copies. These copies cost $.50 per page.

Phone Search: Phone searches are only available for information from 1992 to the present.

Mail Search: A stamped self addressed envelope is not required.

In Person: In person searching is available.

PACER: Sign-up number is 800-676-6856. Access fee is $.60 per minute. Toll-free access: 800-995-0313. Local access: 919-856-4768. Case records are available back to 1989. Records are purged when deemed necessary. New records are available online after 3 days.

US Bankruptcy Court

Eastern District of North Carolina

Raleigh Division
PO Box 1441, Raleigh, NC 27602 (Courier Address: Room 209, Century Station Bldg, 300 Fayetteville St Mall, Raleigh, NC 27602), 919-856-4752.

http://www.nceb.uscourts.gov

Counties: Franklin, Granville, Harnett, Johnston, Vance, Wake, Warren.

Indexing/Storage: Cases are indexed by debtor as well as by case number. New cases are available in the index 1 day after filing date. A computer index is maintained. Open records are located here.

Fee & Payment: The fee is $20.00 per item (one party name or case number). Payment may be made by money order, cashier check, business check, Visa or Mastercard. Personal checks are not accepted. Credit cards are accepted from companies only. Prepayment is required. Payee: Clerk, US Bankruptcy Court. Certification fee: $7.00 per document. Copy fee: $.50 per page. You are allowed to make your own copies. These copies cost $.25 per page.

Phone Search: An automated voice case information service (VCIS) is available. Call VCIS at 888-513-9765 or 252-234-7655.

Mail Search: Always enclose a stamped self addressed envelope.

In Person: In person searching is available.

PACER: Sign-up number is. Access fee is. New records are available online after.

Other Online Access: Search records on the Internet using RACER at http://pacer.nceb.uscourts.gov. There is no fee.

Wilson Division
PO Drawer 2807, Wilson, NC 27894-2807 (Courier Address: The Thomas Milton Moore Bldg, 1760 Parkwood Blvd, Wilson, NC 27894), 252-237-0248.

http://www.nceb.uscourts.gov

Counties: Beaufort, Bertie, Bladen, Brunswick, Camden, Carteret, Chowan, Columbus, Craven, Cumberland, Currituck, Dare, Duplin, Edgecombe, Gates, Greene, Halifax, Hertford, Hyde, Jones, Lenoir, Martin, Nash, New Hanover, Northampton, Onslow, Pamlico, Pasquotank, Pender, Perquimans, Pitt, Robeson, Sampson, Tyrrell, Washington, Wayne, Wilson.

Indexing/Storage: Cases are indexed by debtor as well as by case number. New cases are available in the index 1 day after filing date. A computer index is maintained. Open records are located at this court.

Fee & Payment: The fee is $20.00 per item (one party name or case number). Payment may be made by money order, cashier check, business check, Visa or Mastercard. Personal checks are not accepted. Prepayment is required. Payee: Clerk, US Bankruptcy Court. Certification fee: $7.00 per document. Copy fee: $.50 per page. You are allowed to make your own copies. These copies cost $.25 per page.

Phone Search: Only major dates such as the 341 date, discharge date and entry date will be released. An automated voice case information service (VCIS) is available. Call VCIS at 888-513-9765 or 252-234-7655.

Mail Search: Always enclose a stamped self addressed envelope.

In Person: In person searching is available.

PACER: Sign-up number is. Access fee is. New records are available online after.

Other Online Access: Search records on the Internet using RACER at http://pacer.nceb.uscourts.gov. There is no fee.

US District Court

Middle District of North Carolina

Greensboro Division Clerk's Office, PO Box 2708, Greensboro, NC 27402 (Courier Address: Room 311, 324 W Market St, Greensboro, NC 27401), 336-332-6000.

http://www.ncmd.uscourts.gov

Counties: Alamance, Cabarrus, Caswell, Chatham, Davidson, Davie, Durham, Forsyth, Guilford, Hoke, Lee, Montgomery, Moore, Orange, Person, Randolph, Richmond, Rockingham, Rowan, Scotland, Stanly, Stokes, Surry, Yadkin.

Indexing/Storage: Cases are indexed by defendant and plaintiff as well as by case number. New cases are available in the index 1 day after filing date. Both computer and card indexes are maintained. Open records are located at this court. All other divisions in this district have been abolished as of July 1997.

Fee & Payment: The fee is $20.00 per item (one party name or case number). Payment may be made by money order, cashier check, business check. In state personal checks are also accepted. Prepayment is required. Payee: Clerk, US District Court. Certification fee: $7.00 per document. Copy fee: $.50 per page.

Phone Search: Searching is not available by phone. Only docket information is available by case number over the phone.

Mail Search: A stamped self addressed envelope is not required.

In Person: In person searching is available.

PACER: Sign-up number is 800-676-6856. Access fee is $.60 per minute. Toll-free access: 800-372-8820. Local access: 336-332-6010. Case records are available back to September 1991. Records are never purged. New records are available online after 2 days. PACER is available online at http://pacer.ncmd.uscourts.gov.

US Bankruptcy Court

Middle District of North Carolina

Greensboro Division PO Box 26100, Greensboro, NC 27420-6100 (Courier Address: 101 S Edgeworth St, Greensboro, NC 27401), 336-333-5647.

http://www.ncmb.uscourts.gov

Counties: Alamance, Cabarrus, Caswell, Chatham, Davidson, Davie, Durham, Guilford, Hoke, Lee, Montgomery, Moore, Orange, Person, Randolph, Richmond, Rockingham, Rowan, Scotland, Stanly.

Indexing/Storage: Cases are indexed by debtor as well as by case number. New cases are available in the index 1-2 days after filing date. A computer index is maintained. Only pre-BANCAP cases (cases filed prior to 7/17/89) are indexed on a separate computer program. Open records are

located at this court. District wide searches are available for information on cases filed after July 17, 1989 from this division on their VCIS system.

Fee & Payment: The fee is $20.00 per item (one party name or case number). Payment may be made by money order, cashier check, personal check. Prepayment is required. Debtor's checks are not accepted. Payee: Clerk, US Bankruptcy Court. Certification fee: $7.00 per document. Copy fee: $.50 per page.

Phone Search: Only the name of the debtor, case number, date filed, trustee and attorney for the debtor will be released over the phone. An automated voice case information service (VCIS) is available. Call VCIS at 888-319-0455 or 336-333-5532.

Mail Search: Always enclose a stamped self addressed envelope.

In Person: In person searching is available.

PACER: Sign-up number is 800-676-6856. Access fee is $.60 per minute. Toll-free access: 800-417-3571. Local access: 336-333-5389. Case records are available back to 1992. Records are purged every two years. New civil records are available online after 1 day. PACER is available online at http://pacer.ncmb.uscourts.gov.

Winston-Salem Division 226 S Liberty St, Winston-Salem, NC 27101 (Courier Address: Use mail address for courier delivery), 336-631-5340.

http://www.ncmb.uscourts.gov

Counties: Forsyth, Stokes, Surry, Yadkin.

Indexing/Storage: Cases are indexed by debtor as well as by case number. New cases are available in the index 2 days after filing date. Both computer and card indexes are maintained. Open records are located at this court.

Fee & Payment: The fee is $20.00 per item (one party name or case number). Payment may be made by money order, cashier check, personal check. Prepayment is required. Debtor's checks are not accepted. Payee: Clerk, US Bankruptcy Court. Certification fee: $7.00 per document. Copy fee: $.50 per page.

Phone Search: Basic docket information only is available by phone. An automated voice case information service (VCIS) is available. Call VCIS at 888-319-0455 or 336-333-5532.

Mail Search: Always enclose a stamped self addressed envelope.

In Person: In person searching is available.

PACER: Sign-up number is 800-676-6856. Access fee is $.60 per minute. Toll-free access: 800-417-3571. Local access: 336-333-5389. Case records are available back to 1992. Records are purged every two years. New civil records are available online after 1 day. PACER is available online at http://pacer.ncmb.uscourts.gov.

US District Court

Western District of North Carolina

Asheville Division Clerk of the Court, Room 309, US Courthouse Bldg, 100 Otis St, Asheville, NC 28801-2611 (Courier Address: Use mail address for courier delivery), 828-771-7200, Fax: 828-271-4343.

http://www.ncwd.uscourts.gov

Counties: Avery, Buncombe, Haywood, Henderson, Madison, Mitchell, Transylvania, Yancey.

Indexing/Storage: Cases are indexed by defendant and plaintiff as well as by case number. New cases are available in the index 1 day after filing date. Both computer and card indexes are maintained. Not all records are entered on the in house automated system. Open records are located at this court. This office also handles records for the Bryson City and Shelby Divisions.

Fee & Payment: The fee is $20.00 per item (one party name or case number). Payment may be made by money order, cashier check, personal check. Prepayment is required. Payee: Clerk, US District Court. Certification fee: $7.00 per document. Copy fee: $.50 per page. You are allowed to make your own copies. These copies cost $.50 per page.

Phone Search: Only docket information is available by phone.

Mail Search: Always enclose a stamped self addressed envelope.

In Person: In person searching is available.

PACER: Sign-up number is 800-676-6856. Access fee is. Case records are available back to 1991. New records are available online after 2 days. WebPACER is available online at http://www.ncwd.uscourts.gov/index.html.

Bryson City Division c/o Asheville Division, Clerk of the Court, Room 309, US Courthouse, 100 Otis St, Asheville, NC 28801-2611 (Courier Address: Use mail address for courier delivery), 828-771-7200.

http://www.ncwd.uscourts.gov

Counties: Cherokee, Clay, Graham, Jackson, Macon, Swain.

Indexing/Storage: Cases are indexed by as well as by case number. New cases are available in the index after filing date. Open records are located at the Division.

Fee & Payment: The fee is no charge per item (one party name or case number). Payment may be made by money order, cashier check. Business checks are not accepted. Personal checks are not accepted.

Mail Search: Always enclose a stamped self addressed envelope.

Phone Search: Searching is not available by phone.

In Person: In person searching is available.

PACER: Sign-up number is 800-676-6856. Access fee is. Case records are available back to 1991. New records are available online after 2 days. WebPACER is available online at http://www.ncwd.uscourts.gov/index.html.

Charlotte Division Clerk, Room 210, 401 W Trade St, Charlotte, NC 28202 (Courier Address: Use mail address for courier delivery), 704-350-7400.

http://www.ncwd.uscourts.gov

Counties: Anson, Gaston, Mecklenburg, Union.

Indexing/Storage: Cases are indexed by defendant and plaintiff as well as by case number. New cases are available in the index 1-2 days after filing date. A computer index is maintained. Open records are located at this court. District wide searches are available for records from 1950 forward from this court.

Fee & Payment: The fee is $20.00 per item (one party name or case number). Payment may be made by money order, cashier check, personal check. Prepayment is required. Payee: Clerk, US District Court. Certification fee: $7.00 per document. Copy fee: $.50 per page.

Phone Search: Searching is not available by phone. Only docket information is available by phone.

Mail Search: A stamped self addressed envelope is not required.

In Person: In person searching is available.

PACER: Sign-up number is 800-676-6856. Access fee is. Case records are available back to 1991. New records are available online after 2 days. WebPACER is available online at http://www.ncwd.uscourts.gov/index.html.

Electronic Filing: Electronic filing information is available online at https://ecf.ncwb.uscourts.gov

Other Online Access: Search records on the ECF/PACER system at https://ecf.ncwb.uscourts.gov/cgi-bin/login.pl. Access fee is 7 cents per page.

Shelby Division c/o Asheville Division, Clerk of the Court, Room 309, US Courthouse, 100 Otis St, Asheville, NC 28801-2611 (Courier Address: Use mail address for courier delivery), 828-771-7200.

http://www.ncwd.uscourts.gov

Counties: Burke, Cleveland, McDowell, Polk, Rutherford.

Indexing/Storage: Cases are indexed by as well as by case number. New cases are available in the index after filing date. Open records are located at the Division.

Fee & Payment: The fee is no charge per item (one party name or case number). Payment may be made by money order, cashier check. Business checks are not accepted. Personal checks are not accepted.

Phone Search: Searching is not available by phone.

Mail Search: Always enclose a stamped self addressed envelope.

In Person: In person searching is available.

PACER: Sign-up number is 800-676-6856. Access fee is. Case records are available back to 1991. New records are available online after 2 days. WebPACER is available online at http://www.ncwd.uscourts.gov/index.html.

Statesville Division PO Box 466, Statesville, NC 28687 (Courier Address: Room 205, 200 W Broad St, Statesville, NC 28687), 704-883-1000.

http://www.ncwd.uscourts.gov

Counties: Alexander, Alleghany, Ashe, Caldwell, Catawba, Iredell, Lincoln, Watauga, Wilkes.

Indexing/Storage: Cases are indexed by defendant and plaintiff as well as by case number. New cases are available in the index 2 days after filing date. Both computer and card indexes are maintained. Open records are located at this court.

Fee & Payment: The fee is $20.00 per item (one party name or case number). Payment may be made by money order, cashier check, personal check. Prepayment is required. Payee: Clerk, US District Court. Certification fee: $7.00 per document. Copy fee: $.50 per page. You are allowed to make your own copies. These copies cost Not Applicable per page.

Phone Search: Only docket information is available by phone.

Mail Search: A stamped self addressed envelope is not required.

In Person: In person searching is available.

PACER: Sign-up number is 800-676-6856. Access fee is. Case records are available back to 1991. New records are available online after 2 days. WebPACER is available online at http://www.ncwd.uscourts.gov/index.html.

US Bankruptcy Court

Western District of North Carolina

Charlotte Division P.O. Box 34189, Charlotte, NC 28234-4189 (Courier Address: 401 W Trade St, Charlotte, NC 28202), 704-350-7500.

http://www.ncwb.uscourts.gov

Counties: Alexander, Alleghany, Anson, Ashe, Avery, Buncombe, Burke, Caldwell, Catawba, Cherokee, Clay, Cleveland, Gaston, Graham, Haywood, Henderson, Iredell, Jackson, Lincoln, Macon, Madison, McDowell, Mecklenburg, Mitchell, Polk, Rutherford, Swain, Transylvania, Union, Watauga, Wilkes, Yancey.

Indexing/Storage: Cases are indexed by debtor as well as by case number. New cases are available in the index 1-2 days after filing date. A computer index is maintained. Open records are located at this court.

Fee & Payment: The fee is $20.00 per item (one party name or case number). Payment may be made by money order, cashier check, business check. Personal checks are not accepted. Prepayment is required. Debtor's checks are not accepted. Payee: Clerk, US Bankruptcy Court. Certification fee: $7.00 per document. Copy fee: $.50 per page.

Phone Search: Only docket information available by telephone. An automated voice case information service (VCIS) is available. Call VCIS at 800-884-9868 or 704-350-7505.

Mail Search: Always enclose a stamped self addressed envelope.

In Person: In person searching is available.

PACER: Sign-up number is 800-676-6856. Access fee is $.60 per minute. Toll-free access: 800-324-5614. Local access: 704-344-6121, 704-344-6122, 705-344-6123, 705-344-6124. Case records are available back to 1992. Records are purged every 2 years. New civil records are available online after 1 day.

Electronic Filing: Electronic filing information is available online at https://ecf.ncwb.uscourts.gov

Other Online Access: Search records on the ECF/PACER system at https://ecf.ncwb.uscourts.gov/cgi-bin/login.pl. Access fee is 7 cents per page.

North Carolina County Courts

Court	Jurisdiction	No. of Courts	How Organized
Superior Courts*	General	0	34 Districts
District Courts*	Limited	0	34 Districts
Combined Courts*		100	

* Profiled in this Sourcebook.

Court	CIVIL								
	Tort	Contract	Real Estate	Min. Claim	Max. Claim	Small Claims	Es-tate	Eviction	Domestic Relations
Superior Courts*	X	X	X	$10,000	No Max				X
District Courts*	X	X	X	$0	$10,000	3000		X	X

Court	CRIMINAL				
	Felony	Misdemeanor	DWI/DUI	Preliminary Hearing	Juvenile
Superior Courts*	X				
District Courts*		X	X	X	X

ADMINISTRATION Administrative Office of the Courts, Justice Bldg, 2 E Morgan St, Raleigh, NC, 27602; 919-733-7107, Fax: 919-715-5779. www.aoc.state.nc.us

COURT STRUCTURE The Superior Court is the court of general jurisdiction, the District Court is limited. The counties combine the courts, thus searching is done through one court, not two, within the county.

ONLINE ACCESS Access active North Carolina criminal calendars on a county or statewide basis at www.aoc.state.nc.us/www/public/html/calendars.html. Historical information is not available.

ADDITIONAL INFORMATION Many courts recommend that civil searches be done in person or by a retriever and that only criminal searches be requested in writing (for a $5.00 search fee). Many courts have archived their records prior to 1968 in the Raleigh State Archives, 919-733-5722.

PROBATE COURTS Probate is handled by County Clerks.

Alamance County

Superior - District Court - Criminal 212 West Elm St, Suite 105, Graham, NC 27253; 336-570-6867. Hours: 8AM-5PM *Felony, Misdemeanor.*

www.aoc.state.nc.us/www/public/courts/alamance.html

Criminal Records: Access: Mail, online, in person. Both court and visitors may perform in person searches. Search fee: $5.00 per name. Required to search: name, years to search, DOB; also helpful: address, SSN. Criminal records on computer since 1985, on index cards back to 1975. Search the active Criminal Calendar by defendant name at the web site.
General Information: Public Access terminal is available. No sealed cases, sex offenders, or dismissed records released. Turnaround time 1 week. Copy fee: $1.00 for first page, $.25 each add'l. Certification fee: $2.00. Fee payee: Clerk of Superior Court. Only cashiers checks and money orders accepted. Prepayment is required.

Superior-District Court - Civil 1 Court Square, Graham, NC 27253; 336-438-1002. Hours: 8AM-5PM (EST). *Civil, Eviction, Small Claims, Probate.*

Civil Records: Access: In person only. Visitors must perform in person searches for themselves. No search fee. Required to search: name, years to search. Civil cases indexed by defendant, plaintiff. Civil records computerized since 1985, prior indexed on books.
General Information: Public Access terminal is available. No adoptions, sealed cases, juvenile, sex offenders, or mental records released. Copy fee: $1.00 for first page, $.25 each add'l. Certification fee: $2.00.

Alexander County

Superior - District Court PO Box 100, Taylorsville, NC 28681; 828-632-2215; Fax: 828-632-3550. Hours: 8AM-5PM (EST). *Felony, Misdemeanor, Civil, Eviction, Small Claims, Probate.*

www.aoc.state.nc.us/www/public/courts/alexander.htm

Civil Records: Access: Mail, in person. Both court and visitors may perform in person searches. Search fee: $5.00 per name. Required to search: name, years to search, address. Civil cases indexed by defendant, plaintiff. Civil records on computer since 10/1989, prior on books.
Criminal Records: Access: Mail, online, in person. Both court and visitors may perform in person searches. Search fee: $5.00 per name. Required to search: name, years to search, address, DOB, SSN. Criminal records on computer since 10/1989, prior on books. Search the active Criminal Calendar by defendant name at the web site.

General Information: Public Access terminal is available. No adoptions, sealed cases, juvenile, sex offenders, mental, expunged records released. SASE required. Turnaround time 1-3 days. Copy fee: $.25 per page. Certification fee: $2.00. Fee payee: Clerk of Superior Court. Business checks accepted. Prepayment is required.

Alleghany County

Superior - District Court PO Box 61, Sparta, NC 28675; 336-372-8949; Fax: 336-372-4899. Hours: 8AM-5PM (EST). *Felony, Misdemeanor, Civil, Eviction, Small Claims, Probate.*

www.aoc.state.nc.us/www/public/courts/alleghany.html

Civil Records: Access: Fax, mail, in person. Both court and visitors may perform in person searches. Search fee: $5.00 per name. Required to search: name, years to search; also helpful: address. Civil cases indexed by defendant, plaintiff. Civil records on computer from 11/1988, index books prior.
Criminal Records: Access: Fax, mail, online, in person. Only the court performs in person searches; visitors may not. Search fee: $5.00 per name. Required to search: name, years to search, DOB; also helpful: address, SSN. Criminal records on computer from 11/1988, index books prior. Search the active Criminal Calendar by defendant name at the web site.

General Information: No adoptions, sealed cases, juvenile, sex offenders, mental or expunged records released. SASE required. Turnaround time 2 days. Fax notes: $4.00 per page. Copy fee: $1.00 for first page, $.25 each add'l. Certification fee: $2.00. Fee payee: Clerk of Superior Court. Business checks accepted. Prepayment is required.

Anson County

Superior - District Court PO Box 1064 (114 N Greene St), Wadesboro, NC 28170; 704-694-2314; Fax: 704-695-1161. Hours: 8AM-5PM (EST). *Felony, Misdemeanor, Civil, Eviction, Small Claims, Probate.*

www.aoc.state.nc.us/www/public/courts/anson.htm

Civil Records: Access: Mail, in person. Visitors must perform in person searches for themselves. Search fee: $5.00 per name. Required to search: name, years to search. Civil cases indexed by defendant, plaintiff. Civil records on computer since Oct. 1989, in books prior.

Criminal Records: Access: Mail, online, in person. Only the court performs in person searches; visitors may not. Search fee: $5.00 per name. Required to search: name, years to search, DOB; also helpful: SSN. Criminal records on computer since 10/89, on microfilm 1982-89, in books prior. Search the active Criminal Calendar by defendant name at the web site.

General Information: Public Access terminal is available. (Estates & Special Proceedings only.) No adoptions, sealed cases, juvenile, mental, or expunged records released. SASE required. Turnaround time 2-5 days. Copy fee: $1.00 for first page, $.25 each add'l. Certification fee: $2.00. Fee payee: Clerk of Superior Court. Business checks accepted. Prepayment required.

Ashe County

Superior - District Court 150 Government Circle #3100, Jefferson, NC 28640-9378; 336-246-5641; Fax: 336-246-4276. Hours: 8AM-5PM *Felony, Misdemeanor, Civil, Eviction, Small Claims, Probate.*

www.aoc.state.nc.us/www/public/courts/ashe.html

Civil Records: Access: Mail, in person. Both court and visitors may perform in person searches. Search fee: $5.00 per name. Required to search: name, years to search. Civil cases indexed by defendant, plaintiff. Civil records on computer from 12/89, on index books back to 1900s.

Criminal Records: Access: Mail, online, in person. Both court and visitors may perform in person searches. Search fee: $5.00 per name. Required to search: name, years to search. Criminal records on computer from 12/89, on index books back to 1900s. Online access to the Criminal Calendar by defendant name is available at the web site. Court will search records after 1988; visitors or researchers must search themselves for records prior to 1988.

General Information: Public Access terminal is available. No adoptions, sealed cases, juvenile, sex offenders, mental or expunged records released. Turnaround time 1-3 days. Copy fee: $1.00 for first page, $.25 each add'l. Certification fee: $2.00. Fee payee: Clerk of Superior Court. Only cashiers checks and money orders accepted.

Avery County

Superior-District Court PO Box 115, Newland, NC 28657; 828-733-2900; Fax: 828-733-8410. Hours: 8AM-4:30PM (EST). *Felony, Misdemeanor, Civil, Eviction, Small Claims, Probate.*

www.aoc.state.nc.us/www/public/courts/avery.htm

Civil Records: Access: Mail, in person. Only the court performs in person searches; visitors may not. Search fee: $5.00 per name. Required to search: name, years to search; also helpful: address. Civil cases indexed by defendant, plaintiff. Civil records on computer since 1988, on index books to 1912.

Criminal Records: Access: Mail, online, in person. Only the court performs in person searches; visitors may not. Search fee: $5.00 per name. Required to search: name, years to search; also helpful: address. Criminal records on computer from 11/88; on cards and books back to 1968. Search the active Criminal Calendar by defendant name at the web site.

General Information: No adoptions, sealed cases, juvenile, sex offenders, mental or expunged records released. Turnaround time 2-3 days. Copy fee: $.25 per page. Certification fee: $2.00. Fee payee: Clerk of Superior Court. Only cashiers checks and money orders accepted. Will bill copy fees.

Beaufort County

Superior - District Court PO Box 1403, Washington, NC 27889; 919-946-5184. Hours: 8:30AM-5:30PM (EST). *Felony, Misdemeanor, Civil, Eviction, Small Claims, Probate.*

www.aoc.state.nc.us/www/public/courts/beaufort.html

Civil Records: Access: In person only. Visitors must perform in person searches for themselves. No search fee. Required to search: name, years to search, address. Civil cases indexed by defendant, plaintiff. Civil records on computer since 6/87, docket books to 1800s.

Criminal Records: Access: Mail, online, in person. Both court and visitors may perform in person searches. Search fee: $5.00 per name. Required to search: name, years to search, address, DOB, SSN. Criminal records on computer since 6/87, docket books to 1800s. Search the active Criminal Calendar by defendant name at the web site.

General Information: Public Access terminal is available. No adoptions, sealed cases, juvenile, sex offenders, mental or expunged records released. Turnaround time 5 days. Copy fee: $1.00 for first page, $.25 each add'l. Certification fee: $2.00. Fee payee: Clerk of Superior Court. Business checks accepted.

Bertie County

Superior - District Court PO Box 370, Windsor, NC 27983; 252-794-3039; Fax: 252-794-2482. Hours: 8AM-5PM (EST). *Felony, Misdemeanor, Civil, Eviction, Small Claims, Probate.*

www.aoc.state.nc.us/www/public/courts/bertie.html

Civil Records: Access: In person only. Visitors must perform in person searches for themselves. No search fee. Required to search: name, years to search. Civil cases indexed by defendant, plaintiff. Civil records on computer from 11/96, prior on books to 1968.

Criminal Records: Access: Mail, fax, online, in person. Both court and visitors may perform in person searches. Search fee: $5.00 per name. Required to search: name, years to search, DOB; also helpful: address, SSN. Criminal records on computer from 3/89, prior on books to 1968. Search the active Criminal Calendar by defendant name at the web site.

General Information: Public Access terminal is available. No adoptions, sealed cases, juvenile, mental, expunged records released. SASE requested. Turnaround time 1-2 days. Fax notes: Fee to fax results is $1.00 first page; $.25 each add'l. Copy fee: $1.00 for first page, $.25 each add'l. Certification fee: Court will not certify any in-person searches, otherwise $2.00. Fee payee: Clerk of Superior Court. Only cashiers checks and money orders accepted. Prepayment is required.

Bladen County

Superior - District Court PO Box 2619, Elizabethtown, NC 28337; 910-862-2143. Hours: 8:30AM-5PM (EST). *Felony, Misdemeanor, Civil, Eviction, Small Claims, Probate.*

www.aoc.state.nc.us/www/public/courts/bladen.html

Civil Records: Access: In person only. Visitors must perform in person searches for themselves. No search

fee. Required to search: name, years to search. Civil cases indexed by defendant, plaintiff. Civil records on computer since 1989, prior on judgment books to 1896.

Criminal Records: Access: Mail, online, in person. Both court and visitors may perform in person searches. Search fee: $5.00 per name. Required to search: name, years to search, DOB. Criminal records on computer from 5/89, on books to 1968. Search the active Criminal Calendar by defendant name at the web site.

General Information: Public Access terminal is available. No adoptions, sealed cases, juvenile, sex offenders, mental or expunged records released. Turnaround time 5 days. Copy fee: $1.00 for first page, $.25 each add'l. Certification fee: $2.00. Fee payee: Clerk of Superior Court. Only cashiers checks and money orders accepted. Prepayment is required.

Brunswick County

Superior - District Court PO Box 127, Bolivia, NC 28422; 910-253-8502; Fax: 910-253-7652. Hours: 8:30AM-5:00PM (EST). *Felony, Misdemeanor, Civil, Eviction, Small Claims, Probate.*

www.aoc.state.nc.us/www/public/courts/brunswick.html

Civil Records: Access: In person only. Visitors must perform in person searches for themselves. No search fee. Required to search: name, years to search. Civil cases indexed by defendant, plaintiff. Civil records on computer since 1989, prior on books to 1968.

Criminal Records: Access: Mail, online, in person. Both court and visitors may perform in person searches. Search fee: $5.00 per name. Required to search: name, years to search. Criminal records on computer since 1989, prior on books to 1968. Search the active Criminal Calendar by defendant name at the web site.

General Information: No adoptions, sealed cases, juvenile, mental or expunged records. Turnaround time 1-2 days. Copy fee: $1.00 for first page, $.25 each add'l. Certification fee: $2.00. Fee payee: Clerk of Court. Business checks accepted. Prepayment is required.

Buncombe County

Superior - District Court 60 Court Plaza, Asheville, NC 28801-3519; 828-232-2605; Fax: 828-251-6257. Hours: 8:30AM-5PM (EST). *Felony, Misdemeanor, Civil, Eviction, Small Claims, Probate.*

www.aoc.state.nc.us/www/public/courts/buncombe.html

Civil Records: Access: Mail, fax, in person. Both court and visitors may perform in person searches. Search fee: $5.00 per name. Required to search: name, years to search. Civil cases indexed by defendant, plaintiff. Civil records on computer since 1/89; on books or dockets to 1832; judgment books in archives.

Criminal Records: Access: Mail, fax, online, in person. Both court and visitors may perform in person searches. Search fee: $5.00 per name. Required to search: name, years to search, DOB. Criminal records on computer since 1/89; on books or dockets to 1832; judgment books in archives. Search the active Criminal Calendar by defendant name at the web site.

General Information: Public Access terminal is available. No adoptions, sealed cases, juvenile, sex offenders, mental or expunged records required. SASE required. Turnaround time 1 week. Fax notes: Fee to fax results is $1.00 1st page; $.25 each add'l. Copy fee: $1.00 for first page, $.25 each add'l. Certification fee: $2.00. Fee payee: Clerk of Court. Only cashiers checks and money orders accepted. Prepayment is required.

Burke County

Superior - District Court PO Box 796, Morganton, NC 28680; 828-432-2800; Fax: 828-438-5460. Hours: 8AM-5PM (EST). *Felony, Misdemeanor, Civil, Eviction, Small Claims, Probate.*

www.aoc.state.nc.us/www/public/courts/burke.html

Civil Records: Access: Fax, mail, in person. Both court and visitors may perform in person searches. Search fee: $5.00 per name. Required to search: name, years to search; also helpful: address. Civil cases indexed by defendant, plaintiff. Civil records on computer since 10/88, on index books to 1890s.

Criminal Records: Access: Fax, mail, online, in person. Both court and visitors may perform in person searches. Search fee: $5.00 per name. Required to search: name, years to search, DOB; also helpful: address, SSN. Criminal records on computer since 6/86, on cards or books back to 1900s. Search the active Criminal Calendar by defendant name at the web site.

General Information: Public Access terminal is available. No adoptions, sealed cases, juvenile, sex offenders, mental or expunged records released. SASE required. Turnaround time 1-2 days. Fax notes: Fee to fax results is $3.00 per document. Copy fee: $1.00 for first page, $.25 each add'l. Certification fee: $5.00. Fee payee: Clerk of Court. Business checks accepted. Prepayment is required.

Cabarrus County

Superior - District Court PO Box 70, Concord, NC 28026-0070; 704-786-4137 (Estates & Special Proceed); Civil phone: 704-786-4201; Criminal phone: 704-786-4138. Hours: 8:30AM-5PM (EST). *Felony, Misdemeanor, Civil, Eviction, Small Claims, Probate.*

www.aoc.state.nc.us/www/public/courts/cabarrus.htm

Civil Records: Access: In person only. Visitors must perform in person searches for themselves. No search fee. Required to search: name, years to search; also helpful: address. Civil cases indexed by defendant, plaintiff. Civil records on computer to 1/89, prior on books.

Criminal Records: Access: Mail, online, in person. Both court and visitors may perform in person searches. Search fee: $5.00 per name. Required to search: name; also helpful: address, DOB, SSN, maiden name. Criminal records computerized since 01/85. Search the active Criminal Calendar by defendant name at the web site.

General Information: Public Access terminal is available. No adoptions, sealed cases, juvenile, sex offenders, mental or expunged records released. Turnaround time 2-3 days. Copy fee: $1.00 for first page, $.25 each add'l. Certification fee: $2.00. Fee payee: Clerk of Superior Court. Only cashiers checks and money orders accepted. Prepayment is required.

Caldwell County

Superior - District Court PO Box 1376, Lenoir, NC 28645; 828-757-1373; Fax: 828-757-1479. Hours: 8AM-5PM (EST). *Felony, Misdemeanor, Civil, Eviction, Small Claims, Probate.*

www.aoc.state.nc.us/www/public/courts/caldwell.html

Civil Records: Access: Mail, in person. Both court and visitors may perform in person searches. Search fee: $5.00 per name. Required to search: name, years to search. Civil cases indexed by defendant, plaintiff. Civil records on computer to 11/88, prior on books to 1849.

Criminal Records: Access: Mail, online, in person. Both court and visitors may perform in person searches. Search fee: $5.00 per name. Required to search: name. Criminal records on computer from 8/86, prior in books to 1966. Search the active Criminal Calendar by defendant name at the web site.

General Information: Public Access terminal is available. No adoptions, sealed cases, juvenile, sex offenders, mental or expunged records released. Turnaround time 1-2 days. Fax notes: Fee to fax results is $1.00 1st page; $.25 each add'l. Copy fee: $1.00 for first page, $.25 each add'l. Certification fee: $2.00; $.500 for criminal. Fee payee: Clerk of Superior Court. Only cashiers checks and money orders accepted. Prepayment is required.

Camden County

Superior - District Court PO Box 219, Camden, NC 27921; 252-331-4871; Fax: 252-331-4827. Hours: 8AM-5PM (EST). *Felony, Misdemeanor, Civil, Eviction, Small Claims, Probate.*

www.aoc.state.nc.us/www/public/courts/camden.html

Civil Records: Access: In person only. Visitors must perform in person searches for themselves. Search fee: $5.00 per name. Required to search: name, years to search. Civil cases indexed by defendant, plaintiff. Civil records on computer since Nov. 27 1989, prior on index books to 1966.

Criminal Records: Access: Mail, online, in person. Both court and visitors may perform in person searches. Search fee: $5.00 per name. Required to search: name, years to search, DOB. Criminal records on computer since Nov. 27 1989, prior on index books to 1966. Search the active Criminal Calendar by defendant name at the web site.

General Information: Public Access terminal is available. No adoptions, sealed cases, juvenile, sex offenders, mental or expunged records released. Turnaround time 1-2 days. Copy fee: $1.00 for first page, $.25 each add'l. Certification fee: $2.00 if you do search, otherwise is included in search fee. Fee payee: Clerk of Superior Court. Business checks accepted. Prepayment is required.

Carteret County

Superior-District Court - Carteret County Courthouse Square, Beaufort, NC 28516; 252-728-8500; Fax: 252-728-6502. Hours: 8AM-5PM (EST). *Felony, Misdemeanor, Civil, Eviction, Small Claims, Probate.*

www.aoc.state.nc.us/www/public/courts/carteret.html

Civil Records: Access: In person only. Visitors must perform in person searches for themselves. No search fee. Required to search: name, years to search. Civil cases indexed by defendant, plaintiff. Civil records on computer back to 1988, prior on books to 1800s.

Criminal Records: Access: Mail, fax, online, in person. Both court and visitors may perform in person searches. Search fee: $5.00 per name. Required to search: name, years to search; also helpful: address, DOB, SSN. Criminal records on computer back to 1/87, prior on cards and books to 1800s. Search the active Criminal Calendar by defendant name at the web site.

General Information: Public Access terminal is available. No adoptions, sealed cases, juvenile, sex offenders, mental or expunged records released. Turnaround time 1-2 days. Copy fee: $1.00 for first page, $.25 each add'l. Certification fee: $2.00. Fee payee: Clerk of Superior Court. Business checks accepted. Prepayment is required.

Caswell County

Superior-District Court PO Drawer 790, Yanceyville, NC 27379; 336-694-4171; Fax: 336-694-7338. Hours: 8AM-5PM (EST). *Felony, Misdemeanor, Civil, Eviction, Small Claims, Probate.*

www.aoc.state.nc.us/www/public/courts/caswell.html

Civil Records: Access: In person only. Visitors must perform in person searches for themselves. No search fee. Required to search: name, years to search. Civil cases indexed by defendant, plaintiff. Civil records on computer from 3/89 to present, on index books back to 1970, prior records in civil summons book.

Criminal Records: Access: Mail, online, in person. Both court and visitors may perform in person searches. Search fee: $5.00 per name. Required to search: name, years to search, DOB; also helpful: address. Criminal records on computer since 5/88, prior on books and cards. Search the active Criminal Calendar by defendant name at the web site.

General Information: Public Access terminal is available. No adoptions, sealed cases, juvenile, mental or expunged records released. SASE helpful. Turnaround time 1-2 days. Copy fee: $1.00 for first page, $.25 each add'l. Certification fee: $2.00. Fee payee: Clerk of Superior Court. Business checks accepted. Prepayment is required.

Catawba County

Superior-District Court PO Box 790, Newton, NC 28658; 828-466-6100. Hours: 8AM-5PM *Felony, Misdemeanor, Civil, Eviction, Small Claims, Probate.*

www.aoc.state.nc.us/www/public/courts/catawba.html

Civil Records: Access: In person only. Visitors must perform in person searches for themselves. No search fee. Required to search: name, years to search. Civil cases indexed by defendant, plaintiff. Civil records on computer since 3/1988, prior on books.

Criminal Records: Access: Mail, online, in person. Both court and visitors may perform in person searches. Search fee: $5.00 per name. Required to search: name, years to search, DOB. Criminal records on computer since 4/85, on books to 1966, archived prior. Search the active Criminal Calendar by defendant name at the web site.

General Information: Public Access terminal is available. No adoptions, sealed cases, juvenile, sex offenders, mental or expunged records released. SASE required. Turnaround time 5 days. Copy fee: $1.00 for first page, $.25 each add'l. Certification fee: $2.00. Fee payee: Clerk of Court. Only cashiers checks and money orders accepted. Prepayment is required.

Chatham County

Superior-District Court PO Box 369, Pittsboro, NC 27312; 919-542-3240; Fax: 919-542-1402. Hours: 8AM-5PM (EST). *Felony, Misdemeanor, Civil, Eviction, Small Claims, Probate.*

www.aoc.state.nc.us/www/public/courts/chatham.html

Civil Records: Access: Phone, mail, in person. Both court and visitors may perform in person searches. Search fee: $5.00 per name. Required to search: name, years to search. Civil cases indexed by defendant, plaintiff. Civil records on computer since 4/89, prior on books, archived 1968 back in Raleigh.

Criminal Records: Access: Mail, online, in person. Both court and visitors may perform in person searches. Search fee: $5.00 per name. Required to search: name, years to search; also helpful: address, DOB, SSN. Criminal records on computer since 7/87, prior on books or cards to 1968. Search the active Criminal Calendar by defendant name at the web site.

General Information: Public Access terminal is available. No adoptions, sealed cases, juvenile, sex offenders, mental or expunged records released. Turnaround time 1 day. Copy fee: $1.00 for first page, $.25 each add'l. Certification fee: $2.00. Fee payee: Clerk of Superior Court. Personal checks accepted. Prepayment is required.

Cherokee County

Superior-District Court 75 Peachtree St, Rm 201, Murphy, NC 28906; 828-837-2522. Hours: 8AM-5PM (EST). *Felony, Misdemeanor, Civil, Eviction, Small Claims, Probate.*

www.aoc.state.nc.us/www/public/courts/cherokee.html

Civil Records: Access: Mail, in person. Both court and visitors may perform in person searches. Search fee: $5.00 per name. Required to search: name, years to search, address. Civil cases indexed by defendant, plaintiff. Civil records on computer since 5/89, on index books to 1867.

Criminal Records: Access: Mail, online, in person. Only the court performs in person searches; visitors may not. Search fee: $5.00 per name. Required to search: name, years to search, DOB. Criminal records on computer since 5/89, index cards to 1985, index books to 1966. Search the active Criminal Calendar by defendant name at the web site. There is no public access terminal for searching criminal records.

General Information: Public Access terminal is available. No adoptions, sealed cases, juvenile or mental records released. SASE required. Turnaround time 1-2 days. Fax notes: Fee to fax results is $1.00 1st page, $.25 each add'l. Copy fee: $1.00 for first page, $.25 each add'l. Certification fee: $4.00. Fee payee: Clerk of Superior Court. No personal checks accepted.

Chowan County

Superior-District Court N.C. Courier Box 106319, PO Box 588, Edenton, NC 27932; 252-482-2323; Fax: 252-482-2190. Hours: 9AM-5PM (EST). *Felony, Misdemeanor, Civil, Eviction, Small Claims, Probate.*

www.aoc.state.nc.us/www/public/courts/chowan.html

Civil Records: Access: In person only. Visitors must perform in person searches for themselves. No search fee. Required to search: name, years to search; also helpful: address. Civil cases indexed by defendant, plaintiff. Civil records on computer since 1990, prior on books to 1800s.

Criminal Records: Access: Mail, online, in person. Both court and visitors may perform in person searches. Search fee: $5.00 per name. Required to search: name, years to search, DOB; also helpful: address, SSN. Criminal records on computer from 1/90, prior as civil. Search the active Criminal Calendar by defendant name at the web site.

General Information: Public Access terminal is available. No adoptions, sealed cases, juvenile, sex offenders, mental or expunged records released. SASE required. Turnaround time 3-5 days. Copy fee: $1.00 for first page, $.25 each add'l. Certification fee: $2.00. Fee payee: Clerk of Superior Court. Only cashiers checks and money orders accepted. Prepayment is required.

Clay County

Superior-District Court PO Box 506, Hayesville, NC 28904; 828-389-8334; Fax: 828-389-3329. Hours: 8AM-5PM (EST). *Felony, Misdemeanor, Civil, Eviction, Small Claims, Probate.*

www.aoc.state.nc.us/www/public/courts/clay.html

Civil Records: Access: Fax, mail, in person. Only the court performs in person searches; visitors may not. Search fee: $5.00 per name. Required to search: name, years to search; also helpful: address. Civil cases indexed by defendant, plaintiff. Civil records on computer since 1989, on books since 1888.

Criminal Records: Access: Fax, mail, online, in person. Only the court performs in person searches; visitors may not. Search fee: $5.00 per name. Required to search: name, years to search, DOB; also helpful: address, SSN. Criminal records on computer back to 1989, on books since 1888. Search the active Criminal Calendar by defendant name at the web site.

General Information: Public Access terminal is available. (Civil only.) No adoptions, sealed cases, juvenile, sex offenders, mental or expunged records released. Turnaround time 1-2 days. Fax notes: Fee to fax results is $.25 per page. Copy fee: $1.00 for first page, $.25 each add'l. Certification fee: $1.00. Fee payee: Clerk of Court. Business checks accepted. Prepayment is required.

Cleveland County

Superior-District Court 100 Justice Place, Shelby, NC 28150; 704-484-4851; Fax: 704-480-5487. Hours: 8AM-5PM (EST). *Felony, Misdemeanor, Civil, Eviction, Small Claims, Probate.*

www.aoc.state.nc.us/www/public/courts/cleveland.html

Civil Records: Access: In person only. Visitors must perform in person searches for themselves. No search fee. Required to search: name, years to search; also helpful: address. Civil cases indexed by defendant, plaintiff. Civil records on computer since 1988, books to 1968, archived prior.

Criminal Records: Access: Fax, mail, online, in person. Both court and visitors may perform in person searches. Search fee: $5.00 per name. Required to search: name, years to search, DOB; also helpful: address, SSN. Criminal records on computer since 6/86, on books to 1972, archived prior. Search the active Criminal Calendar by defendant name at the web site.

General Information: Public Access terminal is available. No adoptions, sealed cases, juvenile, sex offenders, mental or expunged records released. SASE requested. Turnaround time 1-2 days. Fax notes: $1.00 for first page, $.25 each add'l. Copy fee: $1.00 for first page, $.25 each add'l. Certification fee: $2.00. Fee payee: Clerk of Superior Court. No out-of-state checks accepted. Prepayment is required.

Columbus County

Superior-District Court PO Box 1587, Whiteville, NC 28472; 910-641-3000; Fax: 910-641-3027. Hours: 8AM-5PM (EST). *Felony, Misdemeanor, Civil, Eviction, Small Claims, Probate.*

www.aoc.state.nc.us/www/public/courts/columbus.html

Civil Records: Access: Mail, fax, online, in person. Visitors must perform in person searches for themselves. No search fee. Required to search: name, years to search; also helpful: address. Civil cases indexed by defendant, plaintiff. Civil records on computer from 5/89, prior on books to 1968.

Criminal Records: Access: Mail, fax, online, in person. Both court and visitors may perform in person searches. Search fee: $5.00 per name. Required to search: name, years to search, DOB; also helpful: address, SSN. Criminal records on computer from 6/87, prior on books or cards to 1968. Search the active Criminal Calendar by defendant name at the web site.

General Information: Public Access terminal is available. No adoptions, sealed, juvenile, sex offender, mental, expunged or dismissed. SASE required. Turnaround time 2-5 days. Fax notes: Do not fax. Copy fee: $1.00 per page. Certification fee: $2.00 per copy. Fee payee: Clerk of Superior Court. Only cashiers checks and money orders accepted. Prepayment is required.

Craven County

Superior-District Court PO Box 1187, New Bern, NC 28563; 252-514-4774; Fax: 252-514-4891. Hours: 8AM-5PM (EST). *Felony, Misdemeanor, Civil, Eviction, Small Claims, Probate.*

www.aoc.state.nc.us/www/public/courts/craven.htm

Civil Records: Access: Mail, in person. Both court and visitors may perform in person searches. Search fee: $5.00 per name. Required to search: name, years to search; also helpful: address. Civil cases indexed by defendant, plaintiff. Civil records on computer from 10/88, prior to 1968 are archived.

Criminal Records: Access: Mail, online, in person. Both court and visitors may perform in person searches. Search fee: $5.00 per name. Required to search: name, years to search, DOB; also helpful: address, SSN. Criminal records on computer since 1/87, prior on books and cards to 1968. Search the active Criminal Calendar by defendant name at the web site.

General Information: Public Access terminal is available. No adoptions, sealed cases, juvenile, sex offenders, mental, expunged, or dismissed. SASE required. Turnaround time 1-2 days. Copy fee: $1.00 for first page, $.25 each add'l. Certification fee: $2.00. Fee payee: Clerk of Superior Court. Only cashiers checks and money orders accepted. Prepayment is required.

Cumberland County

Superior-District Court PO Box 363, Fayetteville, NC 28302; Civil phone: 910-678-2909; Criminal phone: 910-678-2906. Hours: 8:30AM-5PM (EST). *Felony, Misdemeanor, Civil, Eviction, Small Claims, Probate.*

www.aoc.state.nc.us/data/district12

Civil Records: Access: Mail, in person. Both court and visitors may perform in person searches. Search fee: $5.00 per name. Required to search: name, years to search; also helpful: address. Civil cases indexed by defendant, plaintiff. Civil records on computer since 1988, books back to 1956.

Criminal Records: Access: Mail, online, in person. Both court and visitors may perform in person searches. Search fee: $5.00 per name. Required to search: name, years to search; also helpful: address, DOB, SSN. Criminal records on computer since 5/82, books and cards to 1920s. Search the active Criminal Calendar by defendant name at the web site.

General Information: Public Access terminal is available. No adoptions, sealed cases, juvenile, sex offenders, mental or expunged records released. Turnaround time 2 weeks. Copy fee: $2.00 per page. Certification fee: Included in search fee, unless in-person then $2.00. Fee payee: Clerk of Superior Court. Business checks accepted. Prepayment is required.

Currituck County

Superior-District Court PO Box 175, Currituck, NC 27929; 252-232-2010; Fax: 252-232-3722. Hours: 8AM-5PM (EST). *Felony, Misdemeanor, Civil, Eviction, Small Claims, Probate.*

www.aoc.state.nc.us/www/public/courts/currituck/html

Civil Records: Access: Fax, mail, in person. Both court and visitors may perform in person searches. Search fee: $5.00 per name. Required to search: name, years to search. Civil cases indexed by defendant, plaintiff. Civil records on computer back to 11/27/89, books to 1968, prior archived.

Criminal Records: Access: Fax, mail, online, in person. Both court and visitors may perform in person searches. Search fee: $5.00 per name. Required to search: name, years to search, DOB; also helpful-SSN, signed release. Criminal records on computer back to 11/27/89, books to 1968, prior archived. Search the active Criminal Calendar by defendant name at the web site.

General Information: Public Access terminal is available. No adoptions, sealed cases, juvenile, sex offenders, mental or expunged records released. Copy fee: $1.00 for first page, $.25 each add'l. Certification fee: $2.00. Fee payee: Clerk of Superior Court. Only cashiers checks and money orders accepted. Prepayment is required.

Dare County

Superior-District Court PO Box 1849, Manteo, NC 27954; 252-473-2950; Fax: 252-473-1620. Hours: 8:30AM-5PM (EST). *Felony, Misdemeanor, Civil, Eviction, Small Claims, Probate.*

www.aoc.state.nc.us/www/public/courts/dare.htm

Civil Records: Access: Mail, in person. Both court and visitors may perform in person searches. Search fee: $5.00 per name. Required to search: name, years to search; also helpful: address. Civil cases indexed by defendant, plaintiff. Civil records on computer since 1985, on books to 1968.

Criminal Records: Access: Mail, online, in person. Both court and visitors may perform in person searches. Search fee: $5.00 per name. Required to search: name, years to search, DOB; also helpful: SSN. Criminal records on computer since 1987, on books and cards to 1968. Search the active Criminal Calendar by defendant name at the web site.

General Information: Public Access terminal is available. No adoptions, sealed cases, juvenile, sex offenders, mental or expunged records released. Turnaround time 2 days. Copy fee: $1.00 for first page, $.25 each add'l. Certification fee: $2.00. Fee payee: Superior District Court. Business checks accepted. Out of state business checks not accepted. Prepayment required.

Davidson County

Superior - District Court PO Box 1064, Lexington, NC 27293-1064; 336-249-0351; Fax: 336-249-6951. Hours: 8AM-5PM (EST). *Felony, Misdemeanor, Civil, Eviction, Small Claims, Probate.*

www.aoc.state.nc.us/www/public/courts/davidson.html

Civil Records: Access: In person only. Visitors must perform in person searches for themselves. No search fee. Required to search: name, years to search; also helpful: address. Civil cases indexed by defendant, plaintiff. Civil records on computer since 5/16/88, prior on books.

Criminal Records: Access: Mail, online, in person. Both court and visitors may perform in person searches. Search fee: $5.00 per name. Required to search: name, years to search; also helpful: address, DOB, SSN. Criminal records on computer since 10/85, on books and cards to 1952. Search the active Criminal Calendar by defendant name at the web site.

General Information: Public Access terminal is available. No adoptions, sealed cases, juvenile, sex offenders, mental or expunged records released. SASE requested. Turnaround time 2-3 days. Copy fee: $1.00 for first page, $.25 each add'l. Certification fee: $2.00. Fee payee: Clerk of Superior Court. Business checks accepted. Prepayment is required.

Davie County

Superior - District Court 140 S Main St, Mocksville, NC 27028; Civil phone: 336-751-3507; Criminal phone: 336-751-3508; Fax: 336-751-4720. Hours: 8:30AM-5PM (EST). *Felony, Misdemeanor, Civil, Eviction, Small Claims, Probate.*

www.aoc.state.nc.us/www/public/courts/davie.html

Civil Records: Access: Mail, in person. Both court and visitors may perform in person searches. Search fee: $5.00 per name. Required to search: name, years to search. Civil cases indexed by defendant, plaintiff. Civil records on computer back to 10/89; on books to 1970.

Criminal Records: Access: Mail, online, in person. Both court and visitors may perform in person searches. Search fee: $5.00 per name. Required to search: name, years to search, DOB, signed release. Criminal records on computer back to 10/89; on books to 1970. Search the active Criminal Calendar by defendant name at the web site.

General Information: Public Access terminal is available. No adoptions, sealed cases, juvenile, sex offenders, mental or expunged records released. SASE required. Turnaround time 5 days. Copy fee: $1.00 for first page, $.25 each add'l. Certification fee: $2.00. Fee payee: Clerk of Superior Court. Personal checks accepted. Prepayment is required.

Duplin County

Superior-District Court PO Box 189, Kenansville, NC 28349; Civil phone: 910-296-1686; Criminal phone: 910-296-0110; Fax: 910-296-2310. Hours: 8AM-5PM (EST). *Felony, Misdemeanor, Civil, Eviction, Small Claims, Probate.*

www.aoc.state.nc.us/www/public/courts/duplin.htm

Civil Records: Access: Phone, fax, mail, in person. Both court and visitors may perform in person searches. Search fee: $5.00 per name. Required to search: name, years to search. Civil cases indexed by defendant,

plaintiff. Civil records on computer since 1989, prior on books to early 1900s.

Criminal Records: Access: Phone, fax, mail, online, in person. Only the court performs in person searches; visitors may not. Search fee: $5.00 per name. Required to search: name, years to search, DOB. Criminal records on computer since 5/88, on cards and books to 1927. Search the active Criminal Calendar by defendant name at the web site.

General Information: Public Access terminal is available. No adoptions, sealed cases, juvenile, sex offenders, mental or expunged records released. Turnaround time 1-2 days. Copy fee: $1.00 for first page, $.25 each add'l. Certification fee: $2.00. Fee payee: Clerk of Superior Court. Personal checks accepted. Prepayment is required.

Durham County

Superior-District Court 201 E Main St, Durham, NC 27702; Civil phone: 919-560-6823; Criminal phone: 919-560-6821. Hours: 8:30AM-5PM (EST). *Felony, Misdemeanor, Civil, Eviction, Small Claims, Probate.*

www.aoc.state.nc.us/www/public/courts/durham.htm

Civil Records: Access: In person only. Visitors must perform in person searches for themselves. No search fee. Required to search: name, years to search; also helpful: address. Civil cases indexed by defendant, plaintiff. Civil records on computer since 1/88, on books to late 1800s.

Criminal Records: Access: Mail, online, in person. Both court and visitors may perform in person searches. Search fee: $5.00 per name. Required to search: name, years to search, DOB; also helpful: address. Criminal records on microfiche since 1982, prior on books to 1979. Search the active Criminal Calendar by defendant name at the web site.

General Information: Public Access terminal is available. No adoptions, sealed cases, juvenile, sex offenders, mental or expunged records released. SASE required. Turnaround time 3-4 days. Copy fee: $1.00 for first page, $.25 each add'l. Certification fee: Certification is $2.00 for civil, but is included in search fee for criminal. Fee payee: Clerk of Superior Court. Only cashiers checks and money orders accepted. Prepayment is required.

Edgecombe County

Superior-District Court PO Drawer 9, Tarboro, NC 27886; Civil phone: 919-823-6161; Criminal phone: 919-823-2056; Fax: 919-823-1278. Hours: 8AM-5PM (EST). *Felony, Misdemeanor, Civil, Eviction, Small Claims, Probate.*

www.aoc.state.nc.us/www/public/courts/edgecombe.htm

Civil Records: Access: In person only. Visitors must perform in person searches for themselves. No search fee. Required to search: name, years to search, address. Civil cases indexed by defendant, plaintiff. Civil records on computer since 1988, prior on books to 1945, files to 1968.

Criminal Records: Access: Mail, online, in person. Both court and visitors may perform in person searches. Search fee: $5.00 per name. Required to search: name, years to search, DOB, SSN; also helpful: address. Criminal records on computer since 4/87, on books and cards to 1900s. Search the active Criminal Calendar by defendant name at the web site.

General Information: Public Access terminal is available. No adoptions, sealed cases, juvenile, sex offenders, mental or expunged records required. Turnaround time 1-2 days. Copy fee: $1.00 for first page, $.25 each add'l. Certification fee: $2.00. Fee payee: Clerk of Superior Court. Business checks accepted.

Forsyth County

Superior-District Court PO Box 20099, Winston Salem, NC 27120-0099; 336-761-2250; Civil phone: 336-761-2340; Criminal phone: 336-761-2366; Fax: 336-761-2018. Hours: 8AM-5PM (EST). *Felony, Misdemeanor, Civil, Eviction, Small Claims, Probate.*

www.aoc.state.nc.us/www/public/courts/forsyth.html

Civil Records: Access: Mail, in person. Both court and visitors may perform in person searches. Search fee: $5.00 per name. Required to search: name, years to search. Civil cases indexed by defendant, plaintiff. Civil records on computer since 4/1988, prior on books to 1968, on microfiche prior.

Criminal Records: Access: Mail, online, in person. Both court and visitors may perform in person searches. Search fee: $5.00 per name. Required to search: name, years to search, DOB. Criminal records on computer since 10/1983, prior on books to 1968, on microfiche prior. Search the active Criminal Calendar by defendant name at the web site.

General Information: Public Access terminal is available. No adoptions, sealed cases, juvenile, sex offenders, mental or expunged records released. SASE required. Turnaround time 1-2 days. Copy fee: $1.00 for first page, $.25 each add'l. Certification fee: $2.00. Fee payee: Clerk of Superior Court. Business checks accepted. Prepayment is required.

Franklin County

Superior-District Court 102 S Main St, Louisburg, NC 27549; 919-496-5104; Fax: 919-496-0407. Hours: 8:30AM-5PM (EST). *Felony, Misdemeanor, Civil, Eviction, Small Claims, Probate.*

www.aoc.state.nc.us/www/public/courts/franklin.html

Civil Records: Access: Fax, mail, in person. Both court and visitors may perform in person searches. Search fee: $5.00 per name. Required to search: name, years to search; also helpful: address. Civil cases indexed by defendant, plaintiff. Civil records on computer since June 1989, prior on books.

Criminal Records: Access: Fax, mail, in person. Both court and visitors may perform in person searches. Search fee: $5.00 per name. Required to search: name, years to search, DOB; also helpful: address. Criminal records on computer since 1980, on index books back to 1968. Search the active Criminal Calendar by defendant name at the web site.

General Information: Public Access terminal is available. No adoptions, sealed cases, juvenile, mental or expunged records released. SASE requested. Turnaround time 1-2 days. Copy fee: $1.00 for first page, $.25 each add'l. Certification fee: $2.00. Fee payee: Clerk of Superior Court. Personal checks accepted. Prepayment is required.

Gaston County

Superior-District Court PO Box 340, Gastonia, NC 28053; 704-852-3100. Hours: 8AM-5PM (EST). *Felony, Misdemeanor, Civil, Eviction, Small Claims, Probate.*

www.aoc.state.nc.us/www/public/courts/gaston.htm

Civil Records: Access: In person only. Visitors must perform in person searches for themselves. No search fee. Required to search: name, years to search; also helpful: address. Civil cases indexed by defendant, plaintiff. Civil records on computer since 1988, prior on books to 1891.

Criminal Records: Access: Mail, online, in person. Both court and visitors may perform in person searches. Search fee: $5.00 per name. Required to search: name, address, DOB; also helpful: years to search, SSN. Criminal records on criminal to 1/83, on books and cards to 1973. Search the active Criminal Calendar by defendant name at the web site.

General Information: Public Access terminal is available. No adoptions, sealed cases, juvenile, mental or expunged records released. Turnaround time 1-2 days. Copy fee: $.25 per page. Certification fee: $2.00. Fee payee: Clerk of Superior Court. Only cashiers checks and money orders accepted. No out of state checks. Prepayment is required.

Gates County

Superior-District Court PO Box 31, Gatesville, NC 27938; 252-357-1365; Fax: 252-357-1047. Hours: 8AM-5PM (EST). *Felony, Misdemeanor, Civil, Eviction, Small Claims, Probate.*

www.aoc.state.nc.us/www/public/courts/gates.html

Civil Records: Access: In person only. Visitors must perform in person searches for themselves. No search fee. Required to search: name, years to search; also helpful: address. Civil cases indexed by defendant, plaintiff. Civil records on computer since 1990, prior on books to 1966.
Criminal Records: Access: Mail, online, in person. Only the court performs in person searches; visitors may not. Search fee: $5.00 per name. Required to search: name, years to search, DOB; also helpful: address, SSN. Criminal records on computer since 1990, prior on books to 1966. Search the active Criminal Calendar by defendant name at the web site.
General Information: Public Access terminal is available. (Civil only.) No adoptions, sealed cases, juvenile, sex offenders, mental or expunged records released. Turnaround time 1-2 days. Copy fee: $1.00 for first page, $.25 each add'l. Certification fee: Included in search fee. Fee payee: Clerk of Superior Court. Business checks accepted. Prepayment is required.

Graham County

Superior-District Court PO Box 1179, Robbinsville, NC 28771; 828-479-7986; Civil phone: X7974; Criminal phone: X7975; Fax: 828-479-6417. Hours: 8AM-5PM M-Th; 8AM-4:30PM Fri *Felony, Misdemeanor, Civil, Eviction, Small Claims, Probate.*

www.aoc.state.nc.us/www/public/courts/graham.html

Civil Records: Access: In person only. Visitors must perform in person searches for themselves. No search fee. Required to search: name, years to search. Civil cases indexed by defendant, plaintiff. Civil records on computer since 1989, on books since 1920s.
Criminal Records: Access: Mail, online, in person. Both court and visitors may perform in person searches. Search fee: $5.00 per name. Required to search: name, years to search; also helpful: address, DOB, SSN. Criminal records on computer since 1984, on books to 1920s. Search the active Criminal Calendar by defendant name at the web site.
General Information: Public Access terminal is available. No adoptions, sealed cases, juvenile, sex offenders, mental or expunged records released. SASE required. Turnaround time 3-5 days. Copy fee: $1.00 for first page, $.25 each add'l. Certification fee: $2.00. Fee payee: Clerk of Superior Court. Only cashiers checks and money orders accepted. Prepayment is required.

Granville County

Superior-District Court Courthouse, 101 Main Street, Oxford, NC 27565; 919-693-2649; Fax: 919-693-8944. *Felony, Misdemeanor, Civil, Eviction, Small Claims, Probate.*

www.aoc.state.nc.us/www/public/courts/granville.html

Civil Records: Access: Phone, mail, in person. No search fee. Required to search: name, years to search; also helpful: address. Civil cases indexed by defendant, plaintiff. Civil records on computer since June 12, 1989, on books to 1968, prior files destroyed.
Criminal Records: Access: Mail, online, in person. Both court and visitors may perform in person searches.

Search fee: $5.00 per name. Required to search: name, years to search, DOB; also helpful: address. Criminal records on computer since Feb. 29, 1988, prior on books on cards to 1968. Search the active Criminal Calendar by defendant name at the web site.
General Information: Public Access terminal is available. No adoptions, sealed cases, juvenile, mental or expunged records released. SASE would be helpful. Turnaround time 1 day. Copy fee: $1.00 for first page, $.25 each add'l. Certification fee: $2.00. Fee payee: Clerk of Superior Court. Personal checks accepted. Prepayment is required.

Greene County

Superior-District Court PO Box 675, Snow Hill, NC 28580; 252-747-3505. 8AM-5PM (EST). *Felony, Misdemeanor, Civil, Eviction, Small Claims, Probate.*

www.aoc.state.nc.us/www/public/courts/greene.htm

Civil Records: Access: In person only. Visitors must perform in person searches for themselves. No search fee. Required to search: name, years to search; also helpful: address. Civil cases indexed by defendant, plaintiff. Civil records on computer since Oct. 1989, prior on books to 1865.
Criminal Records: Access: Mail, online, in person. Both court and visitors may perform in person searches. Search fee: $5.00 per name. Required to search: name, years to search; also helpful: address, DOB, SSN. Criminal records on computer since Oct. 1989, prior on books to 1865. Search the active Criminal Calendar by defendant name at the web site.
General Information: Public Access terminal is available. No adoptions, sealed cases, juvenile, sex offenders, mental or expunged records released. Turnaround time 1-2 days. Copy fee: $1.00 for first page, $.25 each add'l. Certification fee: Included in search fee, unless in-person then $2.00. Fee payee: Clerk of Superior Court. Business checks accepted. Prepayment is required.

Guilford County

Superior-District Court 201 S Eugene, PO Box 3008, Greensboro, NC 27402; Civil phone: 336-574-4305; Criminal phone: 336-574-4307. Hours: 8:30AM-5PM (EST). *Felony, Misdemeanor, Civil, Eviction, Small Claims, Probate.*

www.aoc.state.nc.us/www/public/courts/guilford.html

Civil Records: Access: In person only. Visitors must perform in person searches for themselves. No search fee. Required to search: name, years to search; also helpful: address. Civil cases indexed by defendant, plaintiff. Civil records on computer since 9/88, on books to late 1800s.
Criminal Records: Access: Mail, online, in person. Both court and visitors may perform in person searches. Search fee: $5.00 per name. Required to search: name, years to search, DOB; also helpful: address, full name. Criminal records on computer since 5/83, on cards and books to late 1800s. Search the active Criminal Calendar by defendant name at the web site.
General Information: Public Access terminal is available. No adoptions, sealed cases, juvenile, sex offenders, mental or expunged records released. SASE required. Turnaround time 1 week. Copy fee: $1.00 for first page, $.25 each add'l. Certification fee: $2.00. Fee payee: Clerk of Superior Court. Business checks accepted. Prepayment is required.

Halifax County

Superior-District Court PO Box 66, Halifax, NC 27839; 252-583-5061; Fax: 252-583-1005. Hours: 8:30AM-5PM (EST). *Felony, Misdemeanor, Civil, Eviction, Small Claims, Probate.*

www.aoc.state.nc.us/www/data/halifax/index.html

Civil Records: Access: In person only. Visitors must perform in person searches for themselves. No search fee. Required to search: name, years to search; also helpful: address. Civil cases indexed by defendant, plaintiff. Civil records on computer since 1988, on books to 1968, prior archived.
Criminal Records: Access: Mail, online, in person. Both court and visitors may perform in person searches. Search fee: $5.00 per name. Required to search: name, years to search; also helpful: address, DOB, SSN. Criminal records on computer since 1988, on books to 1968, prior archived. Search the active Criminal Calendar by defendant name at the web site.
General Information: Public Access terminal is available. (Civil only.) No adoptions, sealed cases, juvenile, sex offenders, mental or expunged records released. Turnaround time 1-2 days. Copy fee: $1.00 for first page, $.25 each add'l. Certification fee: $2.00. Fee payee: Clerk of Superior Court. Business checks accepted. Prepayment is required.

Harnett County

Superior-District Court PO Box 849, Lillington, NC 27546; 910-893-5164; Civil phone: 910-893-4961; Criminal phone: 910-893-5692; Probate phone: 910-893-5046; Fax: 910-893-3683. Hours: 8:15AM-5:15PM (EST). *Felony, Misdemeanor, Civil, Eviction, Small Claims, Probate.*

www.aoc.state.nc.us/www/public/courts/harnett.html

Civil Records: Access: In person only. Visitors must perform in person searches for themselves. No search fee. Required to search: name, years to search; also helpful: address. Civil cases indexed by defendant, plaintiff. Civil records on computer since April 17, 1989, prior on books from 1938.
Criminal Records: Access: Mail, online, in person. Both court and visitors may perform in person searches. Search fee: $5.00 per name. Required to search: name, years to search; also helpful: address, DOB, SSN. Criminal records on computer since 5/87, on books from 1968. Search the active Criminal Calendar by defendant name at the web site.
General Information: Public Access terminal is available. No adoptions, sealed cases, juvenile, mental or expunged records released. SASE required. Turnaround time 1 week-10 days. Copy fee: $1.00 for first page, $.25 each add'l. Certification fee: $2.00. Fee payee: Clerk of Superior Court. Only cashiers checks and money orders accepted. Prepayment is required.

Haywood County

Superior-District Court 215 N. Main, Waynesville, NC 28786; 828-456-3540; Fax: 828-456-4937. Hours: 8:30AM-5PM (EST). *Felony, Misdemeanor, Civil, Eviction, Small Claims, Probate.*

www.aoc.state.nc.us/www/public/courts/haywood.html

Civil Records: Access: In person only. Visitors must perform in person searches for themselves. No search fee. Required to search: name, years to search; also helpful: address. Civil cases indexed by defendant, plaintiff. Civil records on computer since Oct. 13, 1988, prior on books to 1955.
Criminal Records: Access: Mail, online, in person. Both court and visitors may perform in person searches. Search fee: $5.00 per name. Required to search: name, years to search, DOB; also helpful: address, SSN. Criminal records on computer from 5/87, on books or cards from 1800s. Search the active Criminal Calendar by defendant name at the web site.
General Information: Public Access terminal is available. No adoptions, sealed cases, juvenile, sex offenders, mental or expunged records released. Turnaround time 1-2 days. Copy fee: $1.00 for first page, $.25 each add'l. Certification fee: Included in search fee, unless do it yourself, then $1.00 first page and $.25 each additional. Fee payee: Clerk of Superior

Court. Only cashiers checks and money orders accepted. Prepayment is required.

Henderson County

Superior-District Court PO Box 965, Hendersonville, NC 28793; Civil phone: 828-697-4851; Criminal phone: 828-697-4859. Hours: 8:30AM-5PM (EST). *Felony, Misdemeanor, Civil, Eviction, Small Claims, Probate.*

www.aoc.state.nc.us/www/public/courts/henderson.html

Civil Records: Access: Mail, in person. Both court and visitors may perform in person searches. Search fee: $5.00 per name. Required to search: name, years to search; also helpful: address. Civil cases indexed by defendant, plaintiff. Civil records on computer back to 1988, prior on books to 1968.

Criminal Records: Access: Mail, online, in person. Both court and visitors may perform in person searches. Search fee: $5.00 per name. Required to search: name, years to search, DOB; also helpful: address, SSN. Criminal records on computer back to 09/89, prior on books to 1968. Search the active Criminal Calendar by defendant name at the web site.

General Information: Public Access terminal is available. No adoptions, sealed cases, juvenile, sex offenders, mental or expunged records released. SASE not required. Turnaround time 1 week. Copy fee: $.25 per page. Certification fee: $2.00. Fee payee: Clerk of Superior Court. Personal checks accepted. Prepayment is required.

Hertford County

Superior-District Court PO Box 86, Winton, NC 27986; 252-358-7845; Fax: 252-358-0793. Hours: 8AM-5PM (EST). *Felony, Misdemeanor, Civil, Eviction, Small Claims, Probate.*

www.aoc.state.nc.us/www/public/courts/hertford.html

Civil Records: Access: In person only. Visitors must perform in person searches for themselves. No search fee. Required to search: name, years to search; also helpful: address. Civil cases indexed by defendant, plaintiff. Civil records on computer back to 4/1989, prior on index cards and judgment books to 1968.

Criminal Records: Access: Mail, online, in person. Both court and visitors may perform in person searches. Search fee: $5.00 per name. Required to search: name, years to search, DOB; also helpful: address, SSN. Criminal records on computer back to 4/1989, prior on index cards or judgment books to 1968. Search the active Criminal Calendar by defendant name at the web site.

General Information: Public Access terminal is available. No adoptions, sealed cases, juvenile, sex offenders, mental or expunged records released. Turnaround time 1-2 days. Copy fee: $1.00 for first page, $.25 each add'l. Certification fee: Included in search fee, unless do it yourself then $2.00. Fee payee: Clerk of Superior Court. Only cashiers checks and money orders accepted. Local personal checks accepted. Prepayment is required.

Hoke County

Superior-District Court PO Drawer 1569, Raeford, NC 28376; 910-875-3728; Fax: 910-904-1708. Hours: 8:30AM-5PM (EST). *Felony, Misdemeanor, Civil, Eviction, Small Claims, Probate.*

www.aoc.state.nc.us/www/public/courts/hoke.html

Civil Records: Access: In person only. Visitors must perform in person searches for themselves. No search fee. Required to search: name, years to search; also helpful: address. Civil cases indexed by defendant, plaintiff. Civil records on computer since 10/89, on books to 1967.

Criminal Records: Access: Mail, online, in person. Only the court performs in person searches; visitors

may not. Search fee: $5.00 per name. Required to search: name, years to search, DOB; also helpful: address, SSN. Criminal records on computer since 10/89, on books to 1967. Search the active Criminal Calendar by defendant name at the web site.

General Information: Public Access terminal is available. No adoptions, sealed cases, juvenile, mental or expunged records released. SASE required. Turnaround time 1-2 days. Copy fee: $1.00 for first page, $.25 each add'l. Certification fee: $2.00. Fee payee: Clerk of Superior Court. Business checks accepted. Prepayment is required.

Hyde County

Superior-District Court PO Box 337, Swanquarter, NC 27885; 252-926-4101; Fax: 252-926-1002. Hours: 8:30AM-5:30PM (EST). *Felony, Misdemeanor, Civil, Eviction, Small Claims, Probate.*

www.aoc.state.nc.us/www/public/courts/hyde.html

Note: Phone requesting only for general inquires.

Civil Records: Access: Phone, mail, in person. Both court and visitors may perform in person searches. Search fee: $5.00 per name. Required to search: name, years to search. Civil cases indexed by defendant, plaintiff. Civil records on computer since 7/89, on books to 1968; estate & special proceedings to 1996.

Criminal Records: Access: Phone, mail, online, in person. Only the court performs in person searches; visitors may not. Search fee: $5.00 per name. Required to search: name, years to search, DOB; also helpful-signed release. Criminal records on computer since 7/89, on books to 1968. Search the active Criminal Calendar by defendant name at the web site.

General Information: Public Access terminal is available. (Civil only.) No adoptions, sealed cases, juvenile, sex offenders, mental or expunged records released. SASE required. Turnaround time 2 days, phone searches 15 minutes. Fax notes: Fee to fax results is $1.00 1st page, $.25 each add'l. Copy fee: $1.00 for first page, $.25 each add'l. Certification fee: $2.00. Fee payee: Clerk of Superior Court. Only cashiers checks and money orders accepted. Prepayment is required.

Iredell County

Superior-District Court PO Box 186, Statesville, NC 28687; Civil phone: 704-878-4306; Criminal phone: 704-878-4204; Fax: 704-878-3261. Hours: 8AM-5PM (EST). *Felony, Misdemeanor, Civil, Eviction, Small Claims, Probate.*

www.aoc.state.nc.us/www/public/courts/iredell.htm

Civil Records: Access: Mail, in person. Both court and visitors may perform in person searches. Search fee: $5.00 per name. Required to search: name, years to search. Civil cases indexed by defendant, plaintiff. Civil records on computer since 1986, in books since, 1786, on microfiche since 1939.

Criminal Records: Access: Mail, online, in person. Both court and visitors may perform in person searches. Search fee: $5.00 per name. Required to search: name, years to search, DOB. Criminal records on computer since 9/85, prior on books and cards to 1970. Search the active Criminal Calendar by defendant name at the web site.

General Information: Public Access terminal is available. No adoptions, sealed cases, juvenile, sex offenders, mental or expunged records released. SASE required. Turnaround time 2 days. Copy fee: $1.00 for first page, $.25 each add'l. Certification fee: $2.00. Fee payee: Clerk of Superior Court. Only cashiers checks and money orders accepted. Prepayment is required.

Jackson County

Superior-District Court 401 Grindstaff Cove Rd, Sylva, NC 28779; 828-586-7512; Fax: 828-586-9009. Hours: 8:30AM-5PM (EST). *Felony, Misdemeanor, Civil, Eviction, Small Claims, Probate.*

www.aoc.state.nc.us/www/public/courts/jackson.html

Civil Records: Access: In person only. Visitors must perform in person searches for themselves. No search fee. Required to search: name, years to search; also helpful: address. Civil cases indexed by defendant, plaintiff. Civil records on computer since May 29, 1989, prior on books from 1966.

Criminal Records: Access: Mail, online, in person. Both court and visitors may perform in person searches. Search fee: $5.00 per name. Required to search: name, years to search, DOB; also helpful: address, SSN. Criminal records on computer since May 29, 1989, prior on books from 1966. Search the active Criminal Calendar by defendant name at the web site.

General Information: Public Access terminal is available. (Civil only.) No adoptions, sealed cases, juvenile, mental or expunged records released. SASE required. Turnaround time 1-2 days. Copy fee: $1.00 for first page, $.25 each add'l. Certification fee: $2.00. Fee payee: Clerk of Superior Court. Only cashiers checks and M.O.s accepted. Prepayment is required.

Johnston County

Superior-District Court PO Box 297, Smith-field, NC 27577; 919-934-3192; Fax: 919-934-5857. Hours: 8AM-5PM (EST). *Felony, Misdemeanor, Civil, Eviction, Small Claims, Probate.*

www.aoc.state.nc.us/www/public/courts/johnston.html

Civil Records: Access: In person only. Visitors must perform in person searches for themselves. No search fee. Required to search: name, years to search; also helpful: address. Civil cases indexed by defendant, plaintiff. Civil records on computer since 1989, prior on books to 1930s.

Criminal Records: Access: Mail, online, in person. Both court and visitors may perform in person searches. Search fee: $5.00 per name. Required to search: name, DOB; also helpful: years to search, address, SSN. Criminal records on computer from 5/86, prior on books and cards to 1968. Search the active Criminal Calendar by defendant name at the web site.

General Information: Public Access terminal is available. No adoptions, sealed cases, juvenile, sex offenders, mental or expunged records released. SASE requested. Turnaround time 1-2 days. Copy fee: $1.00 for first page, $.25 each add'l. Certification fee: $2.00. Fee payee: Clerk of Superior Court. Business checks accepted. Prepayment is required.

Jones County

Superior-District Court PO Box 280, Trenton, NC 28585; 252-448-7351; Fax: 252-448-1607. Hours: 8AM-5PM (EST). *Felony, Misdemeanor, Civil, Eviction, Small Claims, Probate.*

www.aoc.state.nc.us/www/public/courts/jones.html

Civil Records: Access: Mail, in person. Both court and visitors may perform in person searches. Search fee: $5.00 per name. Required to search: name, years to search. Civil cases indexed by defendant, plaintiff. Civil records on computer since 1989, prior on microfilm.

Criminal Records: Access: Mail, online, in person. Both court and visitors may perform in person searches. Search fee: $5.00 per name. Required to search: name, years to search, DOB. Criminal records on computer since 1989, prior on microfilm. Search the active Criminal Calendar by defendant name at the web site.

General Information: Public Access terminal is available. No adoptions, sealed cases, juvenile, sex offenders, mental or expunged records released. SASE required. Turnaround time 5 days. Copy fee: $1.00 for first page, $.25 each add'l. Certification fee: $2.00. Fee payee: Clerk of Court. Only cashiers checks and money orders accepted. Prepayment is required.

Lee County

Superior-District Court PO Box 4209, Sanford, NC 27331; 919-708-4400; Fax: 919-775-3483. Hours: 8AM-5PM (EST). *Felony, Misdemeanor, Civil, Eviction, Small Claims, Probate.*

www.aoc.state.nc.us/www/public/courts/lee.html

Civil Records: Access: Mail, in person. Both court and visitors may perform in person searches. Search fee: $5.00 per name. Required to search: name, years to search; also helpful: address. Civil cases indexed by defendant, plaintiff. Civil records on computer since 1989, prior on books to 1967.

Criminal Records: Access: Mail, online, in person. Both court and visitors may perform in person searches. Search fee: $5.00 per name. Required to search: name, years to search, DOB. Criminal records on computer since 1989, prior on books to 1967. Search the active Criminal Calendar by defendant name at the web site.

General Information: Public Access terminal is available. No adoptions, sealed cases, juvenile, sex offenders, mental or expunged records released. Turnaround time 1-3 days. Copy fee: $1.00 for first page, $.25 each add'l. Certification fee: $2.00. Fee payee: Clerk of Superior Court. Only cashiers checks and money orders accepted. Prepayment is required.

Lenoir County

Superior-District Court PO Box 68, Kinston, NC 28502-0068; 252-527-6231; Fax: 252-527-9154. Hours: 8AM-5PM (EST). *Felony, Misdemeanor, Civil, Eviction, Small Claims, Probate.*

www.aoc.state.nc.us/www/public/courts/lenoir.htm

Civil Records: Access: In person only. Both court and visitors may perform in person searches. No search fee. Required to search: name, years to search; also helpful: address. Civil cases indexed by defendant, plaintiff. Civil records on computer since Oct. 24, 1988, prior on books to 1900s, prior destroyed due to fire.

Criminal Records: Access: Mail, online, in person. Both court and visitors may perform in person searches. Search fee: $5.00 per name. Required to search: name, years to search, DOB; also helpful: address. Criminal records on computer since 8/86, prior records on books and cards to 1925. Search the active Criminal Calendar by defendant name at the web site.

General Information: Public Access terminal is available. No adoptions, sealed cases, juvenile, sex offenders, mental or expunged records released. SASE required. Turnaround time 1-2 days. Copy fee: $1.00 for first page, $.25 each add'l. Certification fee: Included in search fee, unless do it yourself then $2.00. Fee payee: Clerk of Superior Court. Only cashiers checks and money orders accepted. Prepayment is required.

Lincoln County

Superior-District Court PO Box 8, Lincolnton, NC 28093; 704-736-8566; Fax: 704-736-8718. Hours: 8AM-5PM (EST). *Felony, Misdemeanor, Civil, Eviction, Small Claims, Probate.*

www.aoc.state.nc.us/www/public/courts/lincoln.htm

Civil Records: Access: In person only. Visitors must perform in person searches for themselves. No search fee. Required to search: name, years to search. Civil cases indexed by defendant, plaintiff. Civil records on computer since 1988, in books since 1920s, on microfiche since 1988.

Criminal Records: Access: Mail, online, in person. Both court and visitors may perform in person searches. Search fee: $5.00 per name. Required to search: name, years to search, DOB. Criminal records on computer

since 1986, prior on books and cards to 1968. Search the active Criminal Calendar by defendant name at the web site.

General Information: Public Access terminal is available. No adoptions, sealed cases, juvenile, sex offenders, mental or expunged records released. SASE required. Turnaround time 2 days to 1 week. Copy fee: $1.00 for first page, $.25 each add'l. Certification fee: $2.00. Fee payee: Clerk of Court. Business checks accepted. Prepayment is required.

Macon County

Superior-District Court PO Box 288, Franklin, NC 28744; 828-349-2000; Fax: 828-369-2515. Hours: 8:30AM-5PM (EST). *Felony, Misdemeanor, Civil, Eviction, Small Claims, Probate.*

www.aoc.state.nc.us/www/public/courts/macon.html

Civil Records: Access: In person only. Visitors must perform in person searches for themselves. No search fee. Required to search: name, years to search; also helpful: address. Civil cases indexed by defendant, plaintiff. Civil records on computer since May 1989, prior on books to 1968.

Criminal Records: Access: Mail, online, in person. Only the court performs in person searches; visitors may not. Search fee: $5.00 per name. Required to search: name, DOB; also helpful: years to search, address. Criminal records on computer since May 1989, prior on books to 1968. Search the active Criminal Calendar by defendant name at the web site.

General Information: Public Access terminal is available. (Civil only.) No adoptions, sealed cases, juvenile, sex offenders, mental or expunged records released. Turnaround time 1-2 days. Copy fee: $.25 per page. Certification fee: $2.00. Fee payee: Clerk of Superior Court. Local personal checks accepted. Prepayment is required.

Madison County

Superior-District Court PO Box 217, Marshall, NC 28753; 828-649-2531; Fax: 828-649-2829. Hours: 8AM-5PM (EST). *Felony, Misdemeanor, Civil, Eviction, Small Claims, Probate.*

www.aoc.state.nc.us/www/public/courts/madison.htm

Civil Records: Access: In person only. Visitors must perform in person searches for themselves. No search fee. Required to search: name, years to search; also helpful: address. Civil cases indexed by defendant, plaintiff. Civil records on computer back to 10/88, prior on books to 1968.

Criminal Records: Access: Mail, online, in person. Only the court performs in person searches; visitors may not. Search fee: $5.00 per name. Required to search: name, DOB; also helpful: years to search. Criminal records on computer since 10/88, prior on books to 1968. Search the active Criminal Calendar by defendant name at the web site.

General Information: Public Access terminal is available. No adoptions, sealed cases, juvenile, sex offenders, mental, expunged, or dismissed records released. Turnaround time 1-2 days. Copy fee: $1.00 for first page, $.25 each add'l. Certification fee: $2.00. Fee payee: Clerk of Superior Court. Only cashiers checks and money orders accepted. Prepayment is required.

Martin County

Superior-District Court PO Box 807, Williamston, NC 27892; 252-792-2515; Fax: 252-792-6668. Hours: 8AM-5PM (EST). *Felony, Misdemeanor, Civil, Eviction, Small Claims, Probate.*

www.aoc.state.nc.us/www/public/courts/martin.html

Civil Records: Access: Mail, in person. Both court and visitors may perform in person searches. Search fee: $5.00 per name. Required to search: name, years to search, address. Civil cases indexed by defendant,

plaintiff. Civil records on computer since 1989, in books since 1968.

Criminal Records: Access: Mail, online, in person. Both court and visitors may perform in person searches. Search fee: $5.00 per name. Required to search: name, years to search, address, DOB; also helpful: SSN. Criminal records on computer since 1989, in books since 1968. Search the active Criminal Calendar by defendant name at the web site.

General Information: Public Access terminal is available. No adoptions, sealed cases, juvenile, mental or expunged records released. SASE required. Turnaround time 1 week. Copy fee: $1.00 for first page, $.25 each add'l. Certification fee: $2.00. Fee payee: Clerk of Court. Only cashiers checks and money orders accepted. Prepayment is required.

McDowell County

Superior-District Court 21 S Main St, Marion, NC 28752; 828-652-7717; Fax: 828-659-2641. Hours: 8:30AM-5PM (EST). *Felony, Misdemeanor, Civil, Eviction, Small Claims, Probate.*

www.aoc.state.nc.us/www/public/courts/mcdowell.html

Civil Records: Access: Mail, in person. Both court and visitors may perform in person searches. No search fee. Required to search: name, years to search; also helpful: address. Civil cases indexed by defendant, plaintiff. Civil records on computer since 11/88, prior on books to 1930.

Criminal Records: Access: Mail, online, in person. Both court and visitors may perform in person searches. Search fee: $5.00 per name. Required to search: name, DOB; also helpful: years to search, address, SSN. Criminal records on computer since Oct. 1987, prior on books to 1968. Search the active Criminal Calendar by defendant name at the web site.

General Information: Public Access terminal is available. No adoptions, sealed cases, juvenile, sex offenders, mental or expunged records released. SASE required. Turnaround time 1-2 days. Copy fee: $1.00 for first page, $.25 each add'l. Certification fee: $3.00. Fee payee: Clerk of Superior Court. Business checks accepted. Prepayment is required.

Mecklenburg County

Superior-District Court 800 E 4th St, PO Box 37971, Charlotte, NC 28237; Civil phone: 704-347-7814; Criminal phone: 704-347-7809. Hours: 8AM-5PM (EST). *Felony, Misdemeanor, Civil, Eviction, Small Claims, Probate.*

www.aoc.state.nc.us/www/public/courts/mecklenburg.htm

Civil Records: Access: In person only. Visitors must perform in person searches for themselves. No search fee. Required to search: name. Civil cases indexed by defendant, plaintiff. Civil records on computer since April 1988, prior on books to 1940s.

Criminal Records: Access: Mail, online, in person. Both court and visitors may perform in person searches. Search fee: $5.00 per name. Required to search: name, years to search, address, DOB; also helpful: SSN. Criminal records on computer from 1/83, prior on cards and books to 1930s. Search the active Criminal Calendar by defendant name at the web site.

General Information: Public Access terminal is available. No adoptions, sealed cases, juvenile, sex offenders, mental or expunged records released. SASE requested. Turnaround time 1-2 days. Copy fee: $1.00 for first page, $.25 each add'l. Certification fee: $2.00. Fee payee: Clerk of Superior Court. Only cashiers checks and money orders accepted.

Mitchell County

Superior-District Court PO Box 402, Bakersville, NC 28705; 828-688-2161; Fax: 828-688-2168. Hours: 8:30AM-5PM (EST). *Felony, Misdemeanor, Civil, Eviction, Small Claims, Probate.*

www.clerkofcourt.org

Civil Records: Access: Mail, in person. Both court and visitors may perform in person searches. Search fee: $5.00 per name. Required to search: name, years to search; also helpful: address. Civil cases indexed by defendant, plaintiff. Civil records on computer since 1988, prior on books since 1968.

Criminal Records: Access: Mail, online, in person. Only the court performs in person searches; visitors may not. Search fee: $5.00 per name. Required to search: name, years to search, DOB, SSN; also helpful: address. Criminal records on computer since 1988, prior on books since 1968. Search the active Criminal Calendar by defendant name at www.aoc.state.nc.us/www/public/courts/mitchell.htm.

General Information: Public Access terminal is available. (Civil only.) No adoptions, sealed cases, juvenile, sex offenders, mental or expunged records released. SASE required. Turnaround time 1-2 days. Copy fee: $1.00 for first page, $.25 each add'l. Certification fee: $2.00. Fee payee: Superior-District Court. Business checks accepted. Prepayment required.

Montgomery County

Superior - District Court PO Box 527, Troy, NC 27371; 910-576-4211; Fax: 910-576-5020. Hours: 8AM-5PM (EST). *Felony, Misdemeanor, Civil, Eviction, Small Claims, Probate.*

www.aoc.state.nc.us/www/public/courts/montgomery.html

Civil Records: Access: In person only. Visitors must perform in person searches for themselves. No search fee. Required to search: name, years to search. Civil cases indexed by defendant, plaintiff. Civil records on computer since April 1989, on books to 170, archived in Raleigh to 1843, prior records destroyed in fire.

Criminal Records: Access: Phone, fax, mail, online, in person. Both court and visitors may perform in person searches. Search fee: $5.00 per name. Required to search: name, years to search, address, DOB, signed release. Criminal records on computer since April 1989, on books to 170, archived in Raleigh to 1843, prior records destroyed in fire. Search the active Criminal Calendar by defendant name at the web site.

General Information: Public Access terminal is available. No adoptions, sealed cases, juvenile, sex offenders, mental or expunged records released. Turnaround time 1-2 days. Copy fee: $.25 per page. Certification fee: $2.00. Fee payee: Clerk of Superior Court. Only cashiers checks and money orders accepted. Prepayment is required.

Moore County

Superior-District Court PO Box 936, Carthage, NC 28327; 910-947-2396; Fax: 910-947-1444. Hours: 8AM-5PM (EST). *Felony, Misdemeanor, Civil, Eviction, Small Claims, Probate.*

www.aoc.state.nc.us/www/public/courts/moore.html

Civil Records: Access: Mail, in person. Both court and visitors may perform in person searches. Search fee: $5.00 per name. Required to search: name, years to search. Civil cases indexed by defendant, plaintiff. Civil records on computer since March 1989, prior on books to 1968, older records in basement.

Criminal Records: Access: Mail, online, in person. Only the court performs in person searches; visitors may not. Search fee: $5.00 per name. Required to search: name, years to search, DOB, signed release; also helpful: address, SSN. Criminal records on computer since March 1989, prior on books to 1968, older records in basement. Search the active Criminal Calendar by defendant name at the web site.

General Information: Public Access terminal is available. No adoptions, sealed cases, juvenile, sex offenders, mental or expunged records released. Turnaround time 2-4 days. Copy fee: $1.00 for first page, $.25 each add'l. Certification fee: $2.00. Fee payee: Clerk of Superior Court. Only cashiers checks and money orders accepted. Prepayment is required.

Nash County

Superior-District Court PO Box 759, Nashville, NC 27856; Civil phone: 252-459-4081; Criminal phone: 252-459-4085; Fax: 252-459-6050. Hours: 8AM-5PM (EST). *Felony, Misdemeanor, Civil, Eviction, Small Claims, Probate.*

www.aoc.state.nc.us/www/public/courts/nash.html

Civil Records: Access: Mail, in person. Both court and visitors may perform in person searches. No search fee. Required to search: name, years to search; also helpful: address. Civil cases indexed by defendant, plaintiff. Civil records on computer since 6/88, prior in books to 1988.

Criminal Records: Access: Mail, online, in person. Both court and visitors may perform in person searches. Search fee: $5.00 per name. Required to search: name, years to search, DOB; also helpful: address. Criminal records on computer since 5/80, prior on books and cards dating back to late 1800s. Search the active Criminal Calendar by defendant name at the web site.

General Information: Public Access terminal is available. (Criminal & Civil.) No adoptions, sealed cases, juvenile, mental or expunged records released. SASE required. Turnaround time 1 week. Copy fee: $1.00 for first page, $.25 each add'l. Certification fee: $2.00. Fee payee: Rachel M Joyner, CSC. Only cashiers checks and money orders accepted. Prepayment required.

New Hanover County

Superior-District Court PO Box 2023, Wilmington, NC 28402; 910-341-4430; Criminal phone: 910-341-4440; Fax: 910-251-2676. Hours: 8AM-5PM (EST). *Felony, Misdemeanor, Civil, Eviction, Small Claims, Probate.*

www.aoc.state.nc.us/www/public/courts/new_hanover.html

Civil Records: Access: In person only. Visitors must perform in person searches for themselves. No search fee. Required to search: name, years to search; also helpful: address. Civil cases indexed by defendant, plaintiff. Civil records on computer since 1988, on books to late 1800s.

Criminal Records: Access: Mail, online, in person. Both court and visitors may perform in person searches. Search fee: $5.00 per name. Required to search: name, years to search, DOB; also helpful: address, SSN. Criminal records on computer since 11/83, prior on books and files to late 1800s. Search the active Criminal Calendar by defendant name at the web site.

General Information: Public Access terminal is available. No adoptions, sealed cases, juvenile, sex offenders, mental or expunged records released. SASE required. Turnaround time 1-2 days. Copy fee: $1.00 for first page, $.25 each add'l. Certification fee: $2.50. Fee payee: Clerk of Superior Court. Only cashiers checks and money orders accepted. Prepayment is required.

Northampton County

Superior-District Court PO Box 217, Jackson, NC 27845; 252-534-1631; Fax: 252-534-1308. Hours: 8:30AM-5PM (EST). *Felony, Misdemeanor, Civil, Eviction, Small Claims, Probate.*

www.aoc.state.nc.us/www/public/courts/northampton.html

Onslow County

Superior-District Court 625 Court St, Jacksonville, NC 28540; 910-455-4458. Hours: 8AM-5PM (EST). *Felony, Misdemeanor, Civil, Eviction, Small Claims, Probate.*

www.aoc.state.nc.us/www/public/courts/onslow.htm

Civil Records: Access: In person only. Visitors must perform in person searches for themselves. No search fee. Required to search: name, years to search; also helpful: address. Civil cases indexed by defendant, plaintiff. Civil records on computer since 1988, prior on books to 1920s.

Criminal Records: Access: Mail, online, in person. Both court and visitors may perform in person searches. Search fee: $5.00 per name. Required to search: name, years to search, DOB; also helpful: address, SSN. Criminal records on computer since 2/83, prior on books to 1920s. Search the active Criminal Calendar by defendant name at the web site.

General Information: Public Access terminal is available. No adoptions, sealed cases, juvenile, sex offenders, mental or expunged records released. Turnaround time 1-2 days. Copy fee: $1.00 for first page, $.25 each add'l. Certification fee: $2.00. Fee payee: Clerk of Superior Court. Business checks accepted. Prepayment is required.

Orange County

Superior-District Court 106 E Margaret Lane, Hillsborough, NC 27278; 919-245-2210; Criminal phone: 919-245-2200; Fax: 919-644-3043. Hours: 8AM-5PM (EST). *Felony, Misdemeanor, Civil, Eviction, Small Claims, Probate.*

www.aoc.state.nc.us/www/public/courts/orange.htm

Civil Records: Access: Mail, in person. Both court and visitors may perform in person searches. Search fee: $5.00 per name. Required to search: name, years to search; also helpful: address. Civil cases indexed by defendant, plaintiff. Civil records on computer since May 1989, prior on books to early 1800s.

Criminal Records: Access: Mail, online, in person. Both court and visitors may perform in person searches. Search fee: $5.00 per name. Required to search: name, years to search, DOB; also helpful: address, SSN, race, sex. computer records go to 3/87. Search the active Criminal Calendar by defendant name at the web site.

General Information: Public Access terminal is available. No adoptions, sealed cases, juvenile, sex offenders, mental or expunged records released. SASE required. Turnaround time 1-3 days. Copy fee: $1.00 for first page, $.25 each add'l. Certification fee: $2.00. Fee payee: Clerk of Superior Court. Business checks accepted. Prepayment is required.

(Nash County General Information continued:) in basement. Search the active Criminal Calendar by defendant name at the web site.

General Information: Public Access terminal is available. No adoptions, sealed cases, juvenile, sex offenders, mental or expunged records released. Turnaround time 2-4 days. Copy fee: $1.00 for first page, $.25 each add'l. Certification fee: $2.00. Fee payee: Clerk of Superior Court. Only cashiers checks and money orders accepted. Prepayment is required.

(Onslow County Civil Records continued:) **Civil Records:** Access: Mail, in person. Search fee: $5.00 per name. Required to search: name, years to search; also helpful: address. Civil cases indexed by defendant, plaintiff. Civil records on computer back to 1989, prior on books to 1968.

Criminal Records: Access: Mail, online, in person. Both court and visitors may perform in person searches. Search fee: $5.00 per name. Required to search: name, years to search, DOB; also helpful: address, SSN. Criminal records on computer back to 1989, prior on books to 1968. Search the active Criminal Calendar by defendant name at the web site.

General Information: Public Access terminal is available. No adoptions, sealed cases, juvenile, sex offenders, mental or expunged records released. Turnaround time is 3-10 days. Copy fee: $1.00 for first page, $.25 each add'l. Certification fee: $2.50. Fee payee: Clerk of Superior Court. Business checks accepted. Prepayment is required.

Pamlico County

Superior-District Court PO Box 38, Bayboro, NC 28515; 252-745-6000; Fax: 252-745-6018. Hours: 8AM-5PM (EST). *Felony, Misdemeanor, Civil, Eviction, Small Claims, Probate.*

www.aoc.state.nc.us/www/public/courts/pamlico.html

Civil Records: Access: Mail, in person. Both court and visitors may perform in person searches. Search fee: $5.00 per name. Required to search: name, years to search, address. Civil cases indexed by defendant, plaintiff. Civil records on computer since 9/84, prior on books to 1968.

Criminal Records: Access: Mail, online, in person. Only the court performs in person searches; visitors may not. Search fee: $5.00 per name. Required to search: name, years to search, DOB. Criminal records on computer since 9/84, prior on books to 1968. Search the active Criminal Calendar by defendant name at the web site.

General Information: Public Access terminal is available. No adoptions, sealed cases, juvenile, sex offenders, mental or expunged records released. SASE required. Turnaround time 1-2 days. Copy fee: $1.00 for first page, $.25 each add'l. Certification fee: $2.00. Fee payee: Clerk of Court. Only cashiers checks and money orders accepted. Prepayment is required.

Pasquotank County

Superior-District Court PO Box 449, Elizabeth City, NC 27907-0449; 252-331-4751. Hours: 8AM-5PM (EST). *Felony, Misdemeanor, Civil, Eviction, Small Claims, Probate.*

www.aoc.state.nc.us/www/public/courts/pasquotank.html

Civil Records: Access: In person only. Visitors must perform in person searches for themselves. No search fee. Required to search: name, years to search; also helpful: address. Civil cases indexed by defendant, plaintiff. Civil records on computer since March 6, 1989, books prior to 1800s (some in Raleigh).

Criminal Records: Access: Mail, online, in person. Both court and visitors may perform in person searches. Search fee: $5.00 per name. Required to search: name, years to search, DOB; also helpful: address, SSN, race, sex. Criminal records on computer since 4/88, prior on books and microfiche. Search the active Criminal Calendar by defendant name at the web site.

General Information: Public Access terminal is available. No adoptions, sealed cases, juvenile, sex offenders, mental or expunged records released. Turnaround time 2 days. Copy fee: $1.00 for first page, $.25 each add'l. Certification fee: Included in search fee, court must do search. Fee payee: Clerk of Superior Court. Business checks accepted. Prepayment required.

Pender County

Superior-District Court PO Box 308, Burgaw, NC 28425; 910-259-1229; Fax: 910-259-1292. Hours: 8AM-5PM (EST). *Felony, Misdemeanor, Civil, Eviction, Small Claims, Probate.*

www.aoc.state.nc.us/www/public/courts/pender.html

Civil Records: Access: In person only. Visitors must perform in person searches for themselves. No search fee. Required to search: name, years to search; also helpful: address. Civil cases indexed by defendant, plaintiff. Civil records on computer since 9/89, prior in books from 1968.

Criminal Records: Access: Fax, mail, online, in person. Only the court performs in person searches; visitors may not. Search fee: $5.00 per name. Required to search: name, years to search, DOB; also helpful: address, SSN. Criminal records on computer since 9/89, prior in books from 1968. Search the active Criminal Calendar by defendant name at the web site.

General Information: Public Access terminal is available. No adoptions, sealed cases, juvenile, sex offenders, mental or expunged records released. Turnaround time 1 week. Fax notes: $1.00 for first page, $.25 each add'l. Copy fee: $1.00 for first page, $.25 each add'l. Certification fee: Included in search fee, unless do it yourself then $2.00. Fee payee: Clerk of Superior Court. Business checks accepted. Prepayment is required.

Perquimans County

Superior-District Court PO Box 33, Hertford, NC 27944; 252-426-1505. Hours: 8AM-5PM (EST). *Felony, Misdemeanor, Civil, Eviction, Small Claims, Probate.*

www.aoc.state.nc.us/www/public/courts/perquimans.html

Civil Records: Access: In person only. Visitors must perform in person searches for themselves. No search fee. Required to search: name, years to search. Civil cases indexed by defendant, plaintiff. Civil records on computer since 1989, prior in books to 1966, rest archived and must be searched in person only.

Criminal Records: Access: Mail, online, in person. Both court and visitors may perform in person searches. Search fee: $5.00 per name. Required to search: name, years to search, DOB. Criminal records on computer since 1989, prior in books to 1966, rest archived and must be searched in person only. Search the active Criminal Calendar by defendant name at the web site.

General Information: No adoptions, sealed cases, juvenile, sex offenders, mental or expunged records released. Turnaround time 1-2 days. Copy fee: $1.00 for first page, $.25 each add'l. Certification fee: $2.00. Fee payee: Clerk of Superior Court. Only cashiers checks and money orders accepted. Prepayment is required.

Person County

Superior-District Court 105 S Main St, Roxboro, NC 27573; Civil phone: 336-597-0554; Criminal phone: 336-597-0556; Fax: 336-597-0568. Hours: 8:30AM-5PM (EST). *Felony, Misdemeanor, Civil, Eviction, Small Claims, Probate.*

www.aoc.state.nc.us/www/public/courts/person.html

Civil Records: Access: In person only. Both court and visitors may perform in person searches. No search fee. Required to search: name, years to search. Civil cases indexed by defendant, plaintiff. Civil records on microfiche since 4/89, prior in index books to 1968.

Criminal Records: Access: Mail, online, in person. Both court and visitors may perform in person searches. Search fee: $5.00 per name. Required to search: name, years to search, DOB. Criminal records on computer since 3/88, index cards and books prior to 1968. Search the active Criminal Calendar by defendant name at the web site.

General Information: Public Access terminal is available. No adoptions, sealed cases, juvenile, sex offenders, mental or expunged records released. SASE required. Turnaround time 1-2 days. Copy fee: $1.00 for first page, $.25 each add'l. Certification fee: Included in search fee, unless do it yourself then $2.00. Fee payee: Clerk of Superior Court. Business checks accepted.

Pitt County

Superior - District Court PO Box 6067, Greenville, NC 27835; 252-695-7100; Civil phone: 252-695-7150; Criminal phone: 252-695-7117; Fax: 252-830-3144. Hours: 8AM-5PM (EST). *Felony, Misdemeanor, Civil, Eviction, Small Claims, Probate.*

www.aoc.state.nc.us/www/public/courts/pitt.htm

Civil Records: Access: In person only. Visitors must perform in person searches for themselves. No search fee. Required to search: name, years to search; also helpful: address. Civil cases indexed by defendant, plaintiff. Civil records on computer back to 1988, on books to 1968.

Criminal Records: Access: Mail, online, in person. Both court and visitors may perform in person searches. Search fee: $5.00 per name. Required to search: name, years to search, DOB; also helpful: address, SSN. Criminal records on computer back to 2/85, on books and cards to early 1900s. Search the active Criminal Calendar by defendant name at the web site.

General Information: Public Access terminal is available. No adoptions, sealed cases, juvenile, sex offenders, mental or expunged records released. Turnaround time 1-2 days. Copy fee: $1.00 for first page, $.25 each add'l. Certification fee: $5.00. Fee payee: Clerk of Court. Business checks accepted. Prepayment is required.

Polk County

Superior-District Court PO Box 38, Columbus, NC 28722; 828-894-8231; Fax: 828-894-5752. Hours: 8AM-5PM (EST). *Felony, Misdemeanor, Civil, Eviction, Small Claims, Probate.*

www.aoc.state.nc.us/www/public/courts/polk.html

Civil Records: Access: Mail, in person. Both court and visitors may perform in person searches. Search fee: $5.00 per name. Required to search: name, years to search. Civil cases indexed by defendant, plaintiff. Civil records on computer since 5/89, prior on books to 1968.

Criminal Records: Access: Mail, online, in person. Only the court performs in person searches; visitors may not. Search fee: $5.00 per name. Required to search: name, years to search, DOB. Criminal records on computer since 5/89, prior on books to 1968. Search the active Criminal Calendar by defendant name at the web site.

General Information: No adoptions, sealed cases, juvenile, sex offenders, mental, expunged or dismissed records released. SASE required. Turnaround time 1-2 days. Copy fee: $1.00 for first page, $.25 each add'l. Certification fee: $2.00. Fee payee: Clerk of Superior Court. Business checks accepted. Prepayment required.

Randolph County

Superior-District Court PO Box 1925, Asheboro, NC 27204-1925; Civil phone: 336-318-6750; Criminal phone: 336-318-6710; Fax: 336-318-6709. Hours: 8AM-5PM (EST). *Felony, Misdemeanor, Civil, Eviction, Small Claims, Probate.*

www.aoc.state.nc.us/www/public/courts/randolph.htm

Civil Records: Access: In person only. Visitors must perform in person searches for themselves. No search fee. Required to search: name, years to search. Civil cases indexed by defendant, plaintiff. Civil records on computer since 02/89, prior on books to 1800s.

Criminal Records: Access: Mail, online, in person. Only the court performs in person searches; visitors may not. Search fee: $5.00 per name. Required to search: name, years to search, address, DOB. Criminal records on computer since 06/85, prior on books and cards from 1970 to 1981. Microfilm from 1981 to 06/85. Search the active Criminal Calendar by defendant name at the web site.

General Information: Public Access terminal is available. (Civil only.) No adoptions, sealed cases, juvenile, sex offenders, mental or expunged records released. SASE required. Turnaround time 1-2 days. Copy fee: $1.00 for first page, $.25 each add'l. Certification fee: $2.00. Fee payee: Clerk of Superior Court. Only cashiers checks and money orders accepted. Prepayment is required.

Richmond County

Superior-District Court 114 E Franklin St #103, Rockingham, NC 28379; Civil phone: 910-997-9102; Criminal phone: 910-997-9101; Fax: 910-997-9126. Hours: 8AM-5PM (EST). *Felony, Misdemeanor, Civil, Eviction, Small Claims, Probate.*

www.aoc.state.nc.us/www/public/courts/richmond.htm

Civil Records: Access: In person only. Visitors must perform in person searches for themselves. No search fee. Required to search: name, years to search; also helpful: address. Civil cases indexed by defendant, plaintiff. Civil records on computer since 4/89, prior on books since 1968.

Criminal Records: Access: Mail, online, in person. Both court and visitors may perform in person searches. Search fee: $5.00 per name. Required to search: name, years to search, DOB; also helpful: address, SSN. Criminal records on computer since 1977, cards to 1977, books to 1940, prior archived. Search the active Criminal Calendar by defendant name at the web site.

General Information: Public Access terminal is available. No adoptions, sealed cases, juvenile, sex offenders, mental or expunged records released. SASE required. Turnaround time 1-2 days. Copy fee: $1.00 for first page, $.25 each add'l. Certification fee: $2.00. Fee payee: Clerk of Superior Court. Business checks accepted. Prepayment is required.

Robeson County

Superior-District Court PO Box 1084, Lumberton, NC 28358; 910-737-5035; Civil phone: 910-671-3372; Criminal phone: 910-671-3395; Fax: 910-618-5598. Hours: 8:30AM-5PM (EST). *Felony, Misdemeanor, Civil, Eviction, Small Claims, Probate.*

www.aoc.state.nc.us/www/public/courts/robeson.html

Civil Records: Access: In person only. Visitors must perform in person searches for themselves. No search fee. Required to search: name, years to search; also helpful: address. Civil cases indexed by defendant, plaintiff. Civil records on computer since 1988, prior on books since 1966.

Criminal Records: Access: Mail, online, in person. Both court and visitors may perform in person searches. Search fee: $5.00 per name. Required to search: name, years to search; also helpful: address, DOB. Criminal records on computer since 1983, index books prior. Search the active Criminal Calendar by defendant name at the web site.

General Information: Public Access terminal is available. No sealed cases, juvenile, sex offenders, mental or expunged records released. SASE required. Turnaround time 1-2 days. Copy fee: $1.00 for first page, $.25 each add'l. Certification fee: $2.00; Exemplification is $5.00. Fee payee: Clerk of Superior Court. Business checks accepted. Prepayment required.

Rockingham County

Superior-District Court PO Box 127, Wentworth, NC 27375; 336-342-8700. Hours: 8AM-5PM (EST). *Felony, Misdemeanor, Civil, Eviction, Small Claims, Probate.*

www.aoc.state.nc.us/www/public/courts/rockingham.html

Civil Records: Access: In person only. Both court and visitors may perform in person searches. No search fee. Required to search: name, years to search. Civil cases indexed by defendant, plaintiff. Civil records on computer since 2/89, prior on books.

Criminal Records: Access: Mail, online, in person. Both court and visitors may perform in person searches. No search fee. Required to search: name, years to search, DOB. Criminal records on computer since 5/85, prior on cards and books. Search the active Criminal Calendar by defendant name at the web site.

General Information: Public Access terminal is available. No adoptions, sealed cases, juvenile, sex

offenders, mental or expunged records released. Turnaround time 1-2 days. Copy fee: $1.00 for first page, $.25 each add'l. Certification fee: $2.00. Fee payee: Clerk of Superior Court. Only cashiers checks and money orders accepted. Prepayment is required.

Rowan County

Superior-District Court PO Box 4599, 210 N Main St, Salisbury, NC 28144; 704-639-7505. Hours: 8AM-5PM (EST). *Felony, Misdemeanor, Civil, Eviction, Small Claims, Probate.*

www.aoc.state.nc.us/www/public/courts/rowan.html

Civil Records: Access: In person only. Both court and visitors may perform in person searches. No search fee. Required to search: name, years to search; also helpful: address. Civil cases indexed by defendant, plaintiff. Civil records on computer since 1989, prior on books to 1800s.

Criminal Records: Access: Mail, online, in person. Both court and visitors may perform in person searches. Search fee: $5.00 per name. Required to search: name, DOB; also helpful: years to search, address, SSN. Criminal records on computer from 5/85, prior on books and cards to 1970. Search the active Criminal Calendar by defendant name at the web site.

General Information: No adoptions, sealed cases, juvenile, sex offenders, mental or expunged records released. Turnaround time 1-3 days. Copy fee: $1.00 for first page, $.25 each add'l. Certification fee: Included in search fee, unless do it yourself then $2.00. Fee payee: Clerk of Superior Court. Business checks accepted. Prepayment is required.

Rutherford County

Superior-District Court PO Box 630, Rutherfordton, NC 28139; Civil phone: 828-286-9136; Criminal phone: 828-286-3243; Fax: 828-286-4322. Hours: 8:30AM-5PM (EST). *Felony, Misdemeanor, Civil, Eviction, Small Claims, Probate.*

www.aoc.state.nc.us/www/public/courts/rutherford.htm

Civil Records: Access: In person only. Visitors must perform in person searches for themselves. No search fee. Required to search: name, years to search; also helpful: address. Civil cases indexed by defendant, plaintiff. Civil records on computer Oct. 1988, prior on books, some records to 1700s.

Criminal Records: Access: Mail, online, in person. Both court and visitors may perform in person searches. Search fee: $5.00 per name. Required to search: name, years to search, DOB; also helpful: address, SSN. Criminal records on computer since 6/87, prior on microfiche and books dating to 1800s. Search the active Criminal Calendar by defendant name at the web site.

General Information: Public Access terminal is available. No adoptions, sealed cases, juvenile, sex offenders, mental or expunged records released. Turnaround time 1-2 days. Copy fee: $1.00 for first page, $.25 each add'l. Certification fee: $2.00. Fee payee: Clerk of Superior Court. Business checks accepted. Prepayment is required.

Sampson County

Superior - District Court Courthouse, Clinton, NC 28328; 910-592-5191; Civil phone: 910-592-5192; Criminal phone: 910-592-6981; Fax: 910-592-5502. Hours: 8AM-5PM (EST). *Felony, Misdemeanor, Civil, Eviction, Small Claims, Probate.*

www.aoc.state.nc.us/www/public/courts/sampson.html

Civil Records: Access: In person only. Visitors must perform in person searches for themselves. No search fee. Required to search: name, years to search; also helpful: address. Civil cases indexed by defendant, plaintiff. Civil records on computer since 1989, prior on books.

Criminal Records: Access: Phone, mail, in person. Only the court performs in person searches; visitors may not. Search fee: $5.00 per name. Required to search: name, years to search, DOB; also helpful: address, SSN. Criminal records on computer since 7/87, prior on books. Search the active Criminal Calendar by defendant name at the web site.

General Information: Public Access terminal is available. No adoptions, sealed cases, juvenile, sex offenders, mental or expunged records released. SASE requested. Turnaround time 1-2 days. Copy fee: $1.00 for first page, $.25 each add'l. Certification fee: $2.00. Fee payee: Clerk of Superior Court. Personal checks accepted. Prepayment is required.

Scotland County

Superior-District Court PO Box 769, Laurinburg, NC 28353; 910-277-3240. Hours: 8:30AM-5PM (EST). *Felony, Misdemeanor, Civil, Eviction, Small Claims, Probate.*

www.aoc.state.nc.us/www/public/courts/scotland.html

Civil Records: Access: Mail, in person. Both court and visitors may perform in person searches. Search fee: $5.00 per name. Required to search: name, years to search. Civil cases indexed by defendant, plaintiff. Civil records on computer since 1988, in books since 1966, on microfiche since 1984.

Criminal Records: Access: Mail, online, in person. Only the court performs in person searches; visitors may not. Search fee: $5.00 per name. Required to search: name, years to search, DOB. Criminal records on computer since 1988, in books since 1966, on microfiche since 1984. Search the active Criminal Calendar by defendant name at the web site.

General Information: Public Access terminal is available. No adoptions, sealed cases, juvenile, sex offenders, mental or expunged records released. SASE required. Turnaround time 1-2 days. Copy fee: $1.00 for first page, $.25 each add'l. Certification fee: $2.00. Fee payee: Clerk of Court. Only cashiers checks and money orders accepted. Prepayment is required.

Stanly County

Superior-District Court PO Box 668, Albemarle, NC 28002-0668; 704-982-2161; Fax: 704-982-8107. Hours: 8:30AM-5PM (EST). *Felony, Misdemeanor, Civil, Eviction, Small Claims, Probate.*

www.aoc.state.nc.us/www/public/courts/stanly.htm

Civil Records: Access: In person only. Visitors must perform in person searches for themselves. No search fee. Required to search: name, years to search; also helpful: address. Civil cases indexed by defendant, plaintiff. Civil records on computer since 1989, books to 1968.

Criminal Records: Access: Mail, online, in person. Both court and visitors may perform in person searches. Search fee: $5.00 per name. Required to search: name, years to search, DOB; also helpful: address, SSN. Criminal records on computer since 1989, books to 1968. Search the active Criminal Calendar by defendant name at the web site.

General Information: Public Access terminal is available. No adoptions, sealed cases, juvenile, sex offenders, mental or expunged records released. SASE required. Turnaround time 1-2 days. Copy fee: $1.00 for first page, $.25 each add'l. Certification fee: $2.00. Fee payee: Clerk of Superior Court. Only cashiers checks and money orders accepted. Prepayment is required.

Stokes County

Superior-District Court PO Box 256, Danbury, NC 27016; 336-593-2416. Hours: 8AM-5PM *Felony, Misdemeanor, Civil, Eviction, Small Claims, Probate.*

www.aoc.state.nc.us/www/public/courts/stokes.html

Civil Records: Access: In person only. Visitors must perform in person searches for themselves. No search fee. Required to search: name, years to search; also helpful: address. Civil cases indexed by defendant, plaintiff. Civil records on computer since 1988, prior on books to early 1900s. Civil background checks not performed.

Criminal Records: Access: Mail, online, in person. Both court and visitors may perform in person searches. Search fee: $5.00 per name. Required to search: name, years to search; also helpful: address, DOB. Criminal records on computer since 1988, prior on books to early 1900s. Search the active Criminal Calendar by defendant name at the web site.

General Information: Public Access terminal is available. No adoptions, sealed cases, juvenile, sex offenders, mental or expunged records released. SASE required. Turnaround time 1 week. Copy fee: $1.00 for first page, $.25 each add'l. Certification fee: Included in search fee, unless do it yourself then $2.00. Fee payee: Clerk of Superior Court. Only cashiers checks and money orders accepted. Prepayment is required.

Surry County

Superior-District Court PO Box 345, Dobson, NC 27017; 336-386-8131; Fax: 336-386-9879. Hours: 8AM-5PM (EST). *Felony, Misdemeanor, Civil, Eviction, Small Claims, Probate.*

www.aoc.state.nc.us/www/public/courts/surry.html

Civil Records: Access: In person only. Visitors must perform in person searches for themselves. No search fee. Required to search: name, years to search; also helpful: address. Civil cases indexed by defendant, plaintiff. Civil records on computer since 10/88, on books to 1970, must know township for prior.

Criminal Records: Access: Mail, online, in person. Both court and visitors may perform in person searches. Search fee: $5.00 per name. Required to search: name, years to search, DOB. Criminal records on computer since 10/88, on books to 1970, must know township for prior. Search the active Criminal Calendar by defendant name at the web site.

General Information: Public Access terminal is available. No adoptions, sealed cases, juvenile, sex offenders, mental or expunged records released. SASE required. Turnaround time 1-2 days. Copy fee: $1.00 for first page, $.25 each add'l. Certification fee: $2.00. Fee payee: Clerk of Superior Court. Business checks accepted. Prepayment is required.

Swain County

Superior-District Court PO Box 1397, Bryson City, NC 28713; 828-488-2288; Fax: 828-488-9360. Hours: 8:30AM-5PM (EST). *Felony, Misdemeanor, Civil, Eviction, Small Claims, Probate.*

www.aoc.state.nc.us/www/public/courts/swain.html

Civil Records: Access: Mail, in person. Both court and visitors may perform in person searches. Search fee: $5.00 per name. Required to search: name, years to search. Civil cases indexed by defendant, plaintiff. Civil records on computer since 5/1989, prior on books to 1966.

Criminal Records: Access: Mail, online, in person. Only the court performs in person searches; visitors may not. Search fee: $5.00 per name. Required to search: name, years to search, DOB; also helpful-SSN, signed release. Criminal records on computer back to 1987, prior on books to 1966. Search the active Criminal Calendar by defendant name at the web site.

General Information: Public Access terminal is available. (Civil only.) No adoptions, sealed cases, juvenile, sex offenders, mental or expunged records released. SASE requested. Turnaround time 1-2 days. Copy fee: $1.00 for first page, $.25 each add'l. Certification fee: $2.00. Fee payee: Clerk of Superior

Court. Only cashiers checks and money orders accepted. Prepayment is required.

Transylvania County

Superior-District Court 12 E Main St, Brevard, NC 28712; 828-884-3120; Fax: 828-883-2161. Hours: 8AM-5PM (EST). *Felony, Misdemeanor, Civil, Eviction, Small Claims, Probate.*

www.aoc.state.nc.us/www/public/courts/transylvania.html

Civil Records: Access: In person only. Visitors must perform in person searches for themselves. No search fee. Required to search: name, years to search; also helpful: address. Civil cases indexed by defendant, plaintiff. Civil records on computer from 6/89, on books 1968-1989.

Criminal Records: Access: Mail, online, in person. Visitors may perform in person searches for themselves. Search fee: $5.00 per name. Fee is for certified record check. Required to search: name, years to search, DOB; also helpful: address, SSN. Criminal records on computer from 6/89, on books 1968-1989. Search the active Criminal Calendar by defendant name at the web site.

General Information: No adoptions, sealed cases, juvenile, mental or expunged records released. SASE required. Turnaround time 1-3 days. Copy fee: $1.00 for first page, $.25 each add'l. Certification fee: $2.00. Fee payee: Clerk of Superior Court. Personal checks accepted. Prepayment is required.

Tyrrell County

Superior - District Court PO Box 406, Columbia, NC 27925; 252-796-6281; Fax: 252-796-0008. Hours: 8:30AM-5PM (EST). *Felony, Misdemeanor, Civil, Eviction, Small Claims, Probate.*

www.aoc.state.nc.us/www/public/courts/tyrrell.html

Civil Records: Access: In person only. Visitors must perform in person searches for themselves. No search fee. Required to search: name, years to search; also helpful: address. Civil cases indexed by defendant, plaintiff. Civil records on computer since 10/89, prior on books to 1968.

Criminal Records: Access: Mail, online, in person. Both court and visitors may perform in person searches. Search fee: $5.00 per name. Required to search: name, years to search, DOB; also helpful: address, SSN. Criminal records on computer since 10/89, prior on books to 1968. Search the active Criminal Calendar by defendant name at the web site.

General Information: Public Access terminal is available. No adoptions, sealed cases, juvenile, sex offenders, mental records expunged. Turnaround time 1-2 days. Copy fee: $1.00 for first page, $.25 each add'l. Certification fee: $2.00. Fee payee: Clerk of Superior Court. Business checks accepted. Prepayment required.

Union County

Superior-District Court PO Box 5038, Monroe, NC 28111; 704-283-4313. Hours: 8AM-5PM (EST). *Felony, Misdemeanor, Civil, Eviction, Small Claims, Probate.*

www.aoc.state.nc.us/www/public/courts/union.htm

Civil Records: Access: In person only. Visitors must perform in person searches for themselves. No search fee. Required to search: name, years to search; also helpful: address. Civil cases indexed by defendant, plaintiff. Civil records on computer since 1987, prior on books to 1968.

Criminal Records: Access: Mail, online, in person. Both court and visitors may perform in person searches. Search fee: $5.00 per name. Required to search: name, years to search; also helpful: address, DOB, SSN. Criminal record on computer since 1987; prior on

books to 1968. Search the active Criminal Calendar by defendant name at the web site.

General Information: Public Access terminal is available. No adoptions, sealed cases, juvenile, sex offenders, mental or expunged records released. Turnaround time 1-2 days. Copy fee: $1.00 for first page, $.25 each add'l. Certification fee: Included in copy fee or search fee. Fee payee: Clerk of Superior Court. Only cashiers checks and money orders accepted. Local business checks only. Prepayment is required.

Vance County

Superior-District Court 122 Young St, Henderson, NC 27536; 919-492-0031. Hours: 8AM-5PM (EST). *Felony, Misdemeanor, Civil, Eviction, Small Claims, Probate.*

www.aoc.state.nc.us/www/public/courts/vance.html

Civil Records: Access: In person only. Visitors must perform in person searches for themselves. No search fee. Required to search: name, years to search; also helpful: address. Civil cases indexed by defendant, plaintiff. Civil records on computer since 1989, prior on books to 1881.

Criminal Records: Access: Mail, online, in person. Both court and visitors may perform in person searches. Search fee: $5.00 per name. Required to search: name, years to search, address, DOB; also helpful: SSN. Criminal records on computer to 12/80, prior on books and cards to 1881. Search the active Criminal Calendar by defendant name at the web site.

General Information: Public Access terminal is available. No adoptions, sealed cases, juvenile, sex offenders, mental or expunged records released. Turnaround time 1-2 days. Copy fee: $1.00 for first page, $.25 each add'l. Certification fee: Included in search fee, unless do it yourself then $2.00. Fee payee: Clerk of Superior Court. Business checks accepted. Prepayment is required.

Wake County

Superior - District Court PO Box 351, Raleigh, NC 27602; 919-755-4105; Civil phone: 919-755-4108; Criminal phone: 919-755-4112. Hours: 8:30AM-5:00PM (EST). *Felony, Misdemeanor, Civil, Eviction, Small Claims, Probate.*

www.aoc.state.nc.us/www/public/courts/wake.htm

Civil Records: Access: In person only. Visitors must perform in person searches for themselves. No search fee. Required to search: name, years to search. Civil cases indexed by defendant, plaintiff. Civil records on computer since 1988, prior on books to 1920s.

Criminal Records: Access: Mail, online, in person. Both court and visitors may perform in person searches. Search fee: $5.00 per name. Required to search: name, years to search. Criminal records on computer from 5/82, prior on books and cards from 1968. Search the active Criminal Calendar by defendant name at the web site.

General Information: Public Access terminal is available. No adoptions, sealed cases, juvenile, sex offenders, mental or expunged records released. Turnaround time 1-2 days. Copy fee: $1.00 for first page, $.25 each add'l. Certification fee: $2.00. Fee payee: Clerk of Superior Court. Business checks accepted.

Warren County

Superior-District Court PO Box 709, Warrenton, NC 27589; 252-257-3261; Fax: 252-257-5529. Hours: 8:30AM-5PM (EST). *Felony, Misdemeanor, Civil, Eviction, Small Claims, Probate.*

www.aoc.state.nc.us/www/public/courts/warren.htm

Civil Records: Access: In person only. Visitors must perform in person searches for themselves. No search fee. Required to search: name, years to search. Civil

cases indexed by defendant, plaintiff. Civil records on computer since 1989, prior on books to 1968.

Criminal Records: Access: Mail, online, in person. Both court and visitors may perform in person searches. Search fee: $5.00 per name. Required to search: name, years to search, DOB. Criminal records on computer from 5/81, prior on books as civil. Search the active Criminal Calendar by defendant name at the web site.

General Information: No adoptions, sealed cases, juvenile, sex offenders, mental or expunged records released. Turnaround time 1-2 days. Copy fee: $1.00 for first page, $.25 each add'l. Certification fee: $2.00. Fee payee: Clerk of Superior Court. Business checks accepted. Prepayment is required.

Washington County

Superior-District Court PO Box 901, Plymouth, NC 27962; 252-793-3013; Fax: 252-793-1081. Hours: 8AM-5PM (EST). *Felony, Misdemeanor, Civil, Eviction, Small Claims, Probate.*

www.aoc.state.nc.us/www/public/courts/washington.html

Civil Records: Access: In person only. Visitors must perform in person searches for themselves. No search fee. Required to search: name, years to search. Civil cases indexed by defendant, plaintiff. Civil records on computer back to 12/89, prior on books.

Criminal Records: Access: Mail, online, in person. Both court and visitors may perform in person searches. Search fee: $5.00 per name. Required to search: name, years to search; also helpful: address, DOB, SSN. Criminal records on computer back to 12/89, prior on books. Search the active Criminal Calendar by defendant name at the web site.

General Information: Public Access terminal is available. No adoptions, sealed, juvenile, mental health, expunged or dismissed records released. SASE required. Turnaround time 2-3 days. Copy fee: $1.00 for first page, $.25 each add'l. Certification fee: $2.00. Fee payee: Clerk of Court. Business checks accepted. Prepayment is required.

Watauga County

Superior-District Court Courthouse Suite 13, 842 West King St, Boone, NC 28607-3525; 828-265-5364; Fax: 828-262-5753. Hours: 8AM-5PM (EST). *Felony, Misdemeanor, Civil, Eviction, Small Claims, Probate.*

www.aoc.state.nc.us/www/public/courts/watauga.htm

Civil Records: Access: Mail, in person. Both court and visitors may perform in person searches. Search fee: $5.00 per name. Required to search: name, years to search. Civil cases indexed by defendant, plaintiff. Civil records on computer since 12/5/88, on books to 1872, prior destroyed by fire.

Criminal Records: Access: Mail, online, in person. Both court and visitors may perform in person searches. Search fee: $5.00 per name. Required to search: name, years to search, DOB, SSN. Criminal records on computer from 11/88, prior on cards and books to 1968. Search the active Criminal Calendar by defendant name at the web site.

General Information: Public Access terminal is available. No adoptions, sealed, juvenile, sex offenders, mental, expunged or dismissed records released. SASE requested. Turnaround time 1-2 days. Copy fee: $1.00 for first page, $.25 each add'l. Certification fee: $2.00. Fee payee: Clerk of Court. Only cashiers checks and money orders accepted.

Wayne County

Superior-District Court PO Box 267, Goldsboro, NC 27530; Civil phone: 919-731-7919; Criminal phone: 919-731-7910; Fax: 919-731-2037. Hours: 8AM-5PM (EST). *Felony, Misdemeanor, Civil, Eviction, Small Claims, Probate.*

www.aoc.state.nc.us/www/public/courts/wayne.htm

Civil Records: Access: In person only. Visitors must perform in person searches for themselves. No search fee. Required to search: name, years to search; also helpful: address. Civil cases indexed by defendant, plaintiff. Civil records on computer since 7-18-88, on books since 1968, open to public prior. The court will not do a search unless book and page number or a year of judgment given.

Criminal Records: Access: Mail, online, in person. Both court and visitors may perform in person searches. Search fee: $5.00 per name. Required to search: name, years to search, DOB; also helpful: address, SSN, aliases. Criminal records on computer since 7-18-88, on books since 1968, open to public prior. Search the active Criminal Calendar by defendant name at the web site.

General Information: Public Access terminal is available. No adoptions, sealed, juvenile, sex offenders, mental, expunged or dismissed. SASE requested. Turnaround time 1-2 days. Copy fee: $1.00 for first page, $.25 each add'l. Certification fee: $2.00. Fee payee: Clerk of Superior Court. Business checks accepted. Prepayment is required.

Wilkes County

Superior-District Court 500 Courthouse Drive, #1115, Wilkesboro, NC 28697; Civil phone: 336-667-1201; Criminal phone: 336-667-5266; Fax: 336-667-1985. Hours: 8AM-5PM (EST). *Felony, Misdemeanor, Civil, Eviction, Small Claims, Probate.*

www.aoc.state.nc.us/www/public/courts/wilkes.htm

Civil Records: Access: In person only. Visitors must perform in person searches for themselves. No search fee. Required to search: name, years to search. Civil cases indexed by defendant, plaintiff. Civil records on computer since 12/88, prior on books to early 1900s.

Criminal Records: Access: Mail, online, in person. Only the court performs in person searches; visitors may not. Search fee: $5.00 per name. Required to search: name, years to search, DOB; also helpful: address. Criminal records on computer since 12/88, prior on books to early 1900s. Search the active Criminal Calendar by defendant name at the web site.

General Information: Public Access terminal is available. No adoptions, sealed cases, juvenile, sex offenders, mental or expunged records released. SASE requested. Turnaround time 1-2 days. Copy fee: $1.00 for first page, $.25 each add'l. Certification fee: $2.00. Fee payee: Clerk of Superior Court. Only cashiers checks and money orders accepted. Prepayment required.

Wilson County

Superior-District Court PO Box 1608, Wilson, NC 27894; 252-291-7500; Fax: 252-291-8049 (Criminal) 291-8635 (Civil). Hours: 9AM-5PM (EST). *Felony, Misdemeanor, Civil, Eviction, Small Claims, Probate.*

www.aoc.state.nc.us/www/public/courts/wilson.html

Civil Records: Access: In person only. Visitors must perform in person searches for themselves. No search fee. Required to search: name, years to search; also helpful: address. Civil cases indexed by defendant,

plaintiff. Civil records on computer since 8/88, prior on books to 1968, public viewing from 1915 to 1968.

Criminal Records: Access: Mail, fax, online, in person. Both court and visitors may perform in person searches. Search fee: $5.00 per name. Required to search: name, years to search, DOB; also helpful: address, SSN. Criminal records on computer since 5/86, Index cards to 9/76, books to 1918. Search the active Criminal Calendar by defendant name at the web site.

General Information: Public Access terminal is available. No adoptions, sealed cases, juvenile, sex offenders, mental, or expunged records released. SASE requested. Turnaround time 2-4 days. Copy fee: $1.00 for first page, $.25 each add'l. Certification fee: $2.00. Fee payee: Clerk of Court. Only cashiers checks and money orders accepted. In-state personal checks accepted. Prepayment is required.

Yadkin County

Superior-District Court PO Box 95, Yadkinville, NC 27055; 336-679-8838; Fax: 336-679-4378. Hours: 8AM-5PM (EST). *Felony, Misdemeanor, Civil, Eviction, Small Claims, Probate.*

www.aoc.state.nc.us/www/public/courts/yadkin.htm

Civil Records: Access: In person only. Visitors must perform in person searches for themselves. No search fee. Required to search: name, years to search; also helpful: address. Civil cases indexed by defendant, plaintiff. Civil records on computer since 8/89, prior on books to 1970.

Criminal Records: Access: Mail, online, in person. Both court and visitors may perform in person searches. Search fee: $5.00 per name. Required to search: name, years to search, DOB; also helpful: address. Criminal records on computer since 8/89, prior on books to 1970. Search the active Criminal Calendar by defendant name at the web site.

General Information: Public Access terminal is available. No adoptions, sealed cases, juvenile, sex offenders, mental or expunged records released. SASE required. Turnaround time 1-2 days. Copy fee: $1.00 for first page, $.25 each add'l. Certification fee: $2.00. Fee payee: Clerk of Superior Court. Business checks accepted. Prepayment is required.

Yancey County

Superior-District Court 110 Town Square, Burnsville, NC 28714; 828-682-2122. Hours: 8:30AM-5PM (EST). *Felony, Misdemeanor, Civil, Eviction, Small Claims, Probate.*

www.aoc.state.nc.us/www/public/courts/yancey.htm

Civil Records: Access: In person only. Visitors must perform in person searches for themselves. No search fee. Required to search: name, years to search; also helpful: address. Civil cases indexed by defendant, plaintiff. Civil records on computer since 1988, prior on books.

Criminal Records: Access: Mail, online, in person. Only the court performs in person searches; visitors may not. Search fee: $5.00 per name. Required to search: name, years to search, DOB; also helpful: address, SSN. Criminal records on computer since 1988, prior on books. Search the active Criminal Calendar by defendant name at the web site.

General Information: Public Access terminal is available. (Civil only.) No adoptions, sealed cases, juvenile, sex offenders, mental, expunged or dismissed records released. Turnaround time depends on ease of access, can take up to 2 weeks. Copy fee: $1.00 for first page, $.25 each add'l. Certification fee: $2.00. Fee payee: Clerk of Superior Court. Business checks accepted. Prepayment is required.

North Carolina Recording Offices

ORGANIZATION 100 counties, 100 recording offices. The recording officers are Register of Deeds and Clerk of Superior Court (tax liens). The entire state is in the Eastern Time Zone (EST).

REAL ESTATE RECORDS Counties will not perform real estate searches. Copy fees are usually $1.00 per page. Certification usually costs $3.00 for the first page and $1.00 for each additional page of a document.

UCC RECORDS This was a dual filing state. Financing statements are were both at the state level and with the Register of Deeds, except for consumer goods, farm related and real estate related collateral. As of 7/1/2001, only real estate related collateral is filed at the county level. All counties will perform UCC searches on the records recorded prior to 7/1/2001. Use search request form UCC-11. Search fees were raised in 2001 to $30.00 per debtor name. Copies usually cost $1.00 per page.

TAX LIEN RECORDS Federal tax liens on personal property of businesses are filed with the Secretary of State. Other federal and all state tax liens are filed with the county Clerk of Superior Court, not with the Register of Deeds. (Oddly, even tax liens on real property are also filed with the Clerk of Superior Court, not with the Register of Deeds.) Refer to the County Court Records section for information about North Carolina Superior Courts.

OTHER LIENS Judgment, mechanics (all at Clerk of Superior Court).

STATEWIDE ONLINE INFO: A growing number of counties offer free access to assessor and real estate records via the web.

Alamance County

Register of Deeds, P.O. Box 837, Graham, NC 27253. 336-570-6565 R/E Recording: 336-228-1312.
Will search UCC records prior to 7/2001 and current fixture (land) files. No tax liens filed here. Will not search real estate records. **Other Phone Numbers:** Assessor 336-228-1318; Treasurer 336-570-1318.

Alexander County

Register of Deeds, 201 First Street SW, Suite 1, Taylorsville, NC 28681-2504. 828-632-3152 R/E Recording: 704-632-3152; Fax 828-632-1119.
Will search UCC records prior to 7/2001 and current fixture (land) files. No tax liens filed here. Will not search real estate records.

Alleghany County

Register of Deeds, P.O. Box 186, Sparta, NC 28675. 336-372-4342; Fax 336-372-2061. http://www.allcorod.com
Will search UCC records prior to 7/2001 and current fixture (land) files. No tax liens filed here. **Online Access:** Real Estate, Grantor/Grantee. Online access to the Register of Deeds database are available free at www.allcorod.com/cgi-bin/viewer/date.sh. Records go back to 12/1988. Also, search for property information on a GIS mapping site at www.webgis.net/Alleghany. **Other Phone Numbers:** Assessor 336-372-8291; Treasurer 336-372-4179; Appraiser/Auditor 336-372-8291; Elections 336-372-4557; Vital Records 336-372-4342.

Anson County

Register of Deeds, P.O. Box 352, Wadesboro, NC 28170-0352. Register of Deeds, R/E and UCC Recording 704-694-3212 UCC Recording: 704-694-7594; Fax 704-694-6135. http://www.co.anson.nc.us/servicesf0.htm
Will search UCC records prior to 7/2001 and current fixture (land) files. No tax liens filed here. Will not search real estate records. **Online Access:** Assessor, Real Estate. Records on the county Online Tax Inquiry System are available free online at www.co.anson.nc.us/pubcgi/taxinq. **Other Phone Numbers:** Assessor 704-694-2918; Treasurer 704-694-6219; Appraiser/Auditor 704-694-3072; Elections 704-694-7593.

Ashe County

Register of Deeds, 150 Government Circle, #2300, Jefferson, NC 28640. Register of Deeds, R/E and UCC Recording 336-219-2540; Fax 336-219-2564.
Will search UCC records prior to 7/2001 and current fixture (land) files. No tax liens filed here. Will not search real estate records. **Online Access:** Assessor, Real Estate. Online access to records on the county Tax Parcel Information System are available free at www.webgis.net/ashe. **Other Phone Numbers:** Assessor 336-219-2554; Treasurer 336-219-2560; Appraiser/Auditor 336-219-2554; Elections 336-219-2570; Vital Records 336-219-2540.

Avery County

Register of Deeds, P.O. Box 87, Newland, NC 28657. 828-733-8260; Fax 828-733-8261.
Will search UCC records prior to 7/2001 and current fixture (land) files. No tax liens filed here. Will not search real estate records. **Other Phone Numbers:** Assessor 828-733-8216; Treasurer 828-732-8200.

Beaufort County

Register of Deeds, P.O. Box 514, Washington, NC 27889. Register of Deeds, R/E and UCC Recording 252-946-2323.
Will search UCC records prior to 7/2001 and current fixture (land) files. No tax liens filed here. Will not search real estate records. **Other Phone Numbers:** Vital Records 252-946-2323.

Bertie County

Register of Deeds, P.O. Box 340, Windsor, NC 27983. 252-794-5309; Fax 252-794-5327.
Will search UCC records prior to 7/2001 and current fixture (land) files. No tax liens filed here. Will not search real estate records. **Other Phone Numbers:** Assessor 252-794-5310.

Bladen County

Register of Deeds, P.O. Box 247, Elizabethtown, NC 28337. Register of Deeds, R/E and UCC Recording 910-862-6710; Fax 910-862-6716.
Will search UCC records prior to 7/2001 and current fixture (land) files. No tax liens filed here. Will not search real estate records. **Other Phone Numbers:** Assessor 910-862-6748.

Brunswick County

Register of Deeds, P.O. Box 87, Bolivia, NC 28422-0087. 910-253-2690 R/E Recording: 910-253-4371; Fax 910-253-2703.
Will search UCC records prior to 7/2001 and current fixture (land) files. No tax liens filed here. Will not search real estate records. **Other Phone Numbers:** Assessor 910-253-4351; Treasurer 910-253-4331.

Buncombe County

Register of Deeds, 60 Court Plaza, Room 110, Asheville, NC 28801-3563. 828-250-4300 R/E Recording: 828-250-4305 UCC Recording: 828-250-4302; Fax 828-255-5829. http://www.buncombecounty.org
Will search UCC records prior to 7/2001 and current fixture (land) files. No tax liens filed here. Will not search real estate records. **Online Access:** Assessor, Real Estate. Online access to property information is available free on the gis mapping site at http://199.90.58.245/property. Click on "Search methods" and search by owner name. Also, records from the county assessor are available free online from a private company at www.propex.com/main_taxrecds.htm. http://199.90.58.245/property/. **Other Phone Numbers:** Assessor 828-250-4940; Appraiser/Auditor 828-250-4900; Elections 828-250-4200; Vital Records 828-250-4301.

Burke County

Register of Deeds, P.O. Box 936, Morganton, NC 28680. Register of Deeds, R/E and UCC Recording 828-438-5450 UCC Recording: 828-438-5456; Fax 828-438-5463. http://www.co.burke.nc.us
Will search UCC records prior to 7/2001 and current fixture (land) files. No tax liens filed here. Will not search real estate records. **Online Access:** Real Estate, Assessor. Online access to the property information is available free on the gis mapping site at http://www.webgis.net/burke. **Other Phone Numbers:** Assessor 828-438-5444; Treasurer 828-438-5446; Appraiser/Auditor 828-438-5403; Elections 828-433-1703; Vital Records 828-438-5453; Liens/Judgments 828-432-2804.

Cabarrus County

Register of Deeds, P.O. Box 707, Concord, NC 28026. 704-788-8112; Fax 704-788-9898. http://www.co. cabarrus.nc.us
Will search UCC records prior to 7/2001 and current fixture (land) files. No tax liens filed here. Will not search real estate records. **Online Access:** Assessor, Real Estate. Records on the county GIS map server database are available free online at www.co.cabarrus.nc.us/pages/gis/applications.htm. Click on the county map to enter, then search at the bottom of the query page. **Other Phone Numbers:** Assessor 704-788-8166.

Caldwell County

Register of Deeds, 905 West Avenue N.W., County Office Building, Lenoir, NC 28645. 828-757-1399 R/E Recording: 704-757-1310; Fax 828-757-1294.
Will search UCC records prior to 7/2001 and current fixture (land) files. No tax liens filed here. Will not search real estate records. **Online Access:** Assessor, Real Estate. Records on the county GIS map server site are available free online at http://maps.co. caldwell.nc.us. Click on "Start Spatial-data Explorer" then find query field at bottom of next page.

Camden County

Register of Deeds, P.O. Box 190, Camden, NC 27921. 252-335-4077 R/E Recording: 919-335-4077.
Will search UCC records prior to 7/2001 and current fixture (land) files. No tax liens filed here. RE record owner searches available.

Carteret County

Register of Deeds, Courthouse Square, Beaufort, NC 28516-1898. Register of Deeds, R/E and UCC Recording 252-728-8474; Fax 252-728-7693.
Will search UCC records prior to 7/2001 and current fixture (land) files. No tax liens filed here. Will not search real estate records. **Other Phone Numbers:** Vital Records 252-728-8474.

Caswell County

Register of Deeds, P.O. Box 98, Yanceyville, NC 27379. 336-694-4197 R/E Recording: 336-694-4193; Fax 336-694-1405.
Will search UCC records prior to 7/2001 and current fixture (land) files. No tax liens filed here. Will not search real estate records.

Catawba County

Register of Deeds, P.O. Box 65, Newton, NC 28658-0065. 828-465-1573; http://www.co.catawba.nc.us
Will search UCC records prior to 7/2001 and current fixture (land) files. No tax liens filed here. Will not search real estate records. **Online Access:** Assessor, Real Estate. Records on the Catawba County Geographic Information System database are available free online at www.gis.catawba.nc.us/maps/public.htm. Click on map area; zoom in to find the parcel on the map, or search using query fields. **Other Phone Numbers:** Assessor 828-465-8421.

Chatham County

Register of Deeds, P.O. Box 756, Pittsboro, NC 27312. 919-542-8235 R/E Recording: 919-542-2588.
Will search UCC records prior to 7/2001 and current fixture (land) files. No tax liens filed here. Will not search real estate records. **Other Phone Numbers:** Assessor 919-542-8250.

Cherokee County

Register of Deeds, 53 Peachtree St, Murphy, NC 28906. Register of Deeds, R/E and UCC Recording 828-837-2613; Fax 828-837-8414.

Will search UCC records prior to 7/2001 and current fixture (land) files. No tax liens filed here. Will not search real estate records. **Other Phone Numbers:** Assessor 828-837-6626; Elections 828-837-6670.

Chowan County

Register of Deeds, P.O. Box 487, Edenton, NC 27932-0487. 252-482-2619 R/E Recording: 919-482-2619.
Will search UCC records prior to 7/2001 and current fixture (land) files. No tax liens filed here. Will not search real estate records.

Clay County

Register of Deeds, P.O. Box 118, Hayesville, NC 28904. 828-389-0087 R/E Recording: 828-389-8231; Fax 828-389-9749.
Will search UCC records prior to 7/2001 and current fixture (land) files. No tax liens filed here. Will not search real estate records. **Other Phone Numbers:** Assessor 828-389-6301.

Cleveland County

Register of Deeds, P.O. Box 1210, Shelby, NC 28151-1210. 704-484-4834 R/E Recording: 704-484-4800; Fax 704-484-4909. http://www.clevelandcounty.com
Will search UCC records prior to 7/2001 and current fixture (land) files. No tax liens filed here. Will not search real estate records. **Online Access:** Real Estate, Assessor. Online access to proeprty information on a gis mapping site is available free at www.webgis.net/Cleveland. **Other Phone Numbers:** Assessor 704-484-4847; Treasurer 704-484-4807.

Columbus County

Register of Deeds, P.O. Box 1086, Whiteville, NC 28472-1086. 910-640-6625 R/E Recording: 919-642-5700; Fax 910-640-2547.
Will search UCC records prior to 7/2001 and current fixture (land) files. No tax liens filed here. Will not search real estate records.

Craven County

Register of Deeds, 226 Pollack St, New Bern, NC 28560. Register of Deeds, R/E and UCC Recording 252-636-6617; Fax 252-636-1937.
Will search UCC records prior to 7/2001 and current fixture (land) files. No tax liens filed here. Will not search real estate records. **Online Access:** Assessor, Real Estate. Records on the County Assessor database are available free online at http://gismaps.craven ounty.com/taxinfo.htm. **Other Phone Numbers:** Assessor 252-636-6605; Treasurer 252-636-6603; Appraiser/Auditor 252-636-6640; Elections 252-636-6610; Vital Records 252-636-6617.

Cumberland County

Register of Deeds, P.O. 2039, Fayetteville, NC 28302-2039. 910-678-7718 R/E Recording: 910-678-7783; Fax 910-323-1456. http://www.ccrod.org
Will search UCC records prior to 7/2001 and current fixture (land) files. No tax liens filed here. Will not search real estate records. **Other Phone Numbers:** Assessor 910-678-7506; Appraiser/Auditor 910-678-7507; Elections 910-678-7733; Vital Records 910-678-7767.

Currituck County

Register of Deeds, P.O. Box 71, Currituck, NC 27929. 252-232-3297; Fax 252-232-3906.
Will search UCC records prior to 7/2001 and current fixture (land) files. No tax liens filed here. Will not search real estate records. **Other Phone Numbers:** Assessor 252-232-3005.

Dare County

Register of Deeds, P.O. Box 70, Manteo, NC 27954. 252-473-3438 R/E Recording: 252-473-1101; http://www.co.dare.nc.us
Will search UCC records prior to 7/2001 and current fixture (land) files. No tax liens filed here. Will not search real estate records. **Online Access:** Assessor, Real Estate. Records on the county Property Inquiry database are available free online at www.co.dare.nc.us/interactive/setup.htm. **Other Phone Numbers:** Assessor 252-473-1101; Treasurer 252-473-1101; Appraiser/Auditor 252-473-1101; Elections 252-473-1101.

Davidson County

Register of Deeds, P.O. Box 464, Lexington, NC 27293-0464. 336-242-2150 R/E Recording: 704-249-7011; Fax 336-238-2318. http://www.co.davidson.nc.us
Will search UCC records prior to 7/2001 and current fixture (land) files. No tax liens filed here. Will not search real estate records. **Online Access:** Assessor, Real Estate. Records on the county Tax Department database are available free online at www.co.davidson.nc.us/asp/taxsearch.asp.

Davie County

Register of Deeds, 123 South Main Street, Mocksville, NC 27028. 336-634-2513.
Will search UCC records prior to 7/2001 and current fixture (land) files. No tax liens filed here. Will not search real estate records. **Other Phone Numbers:** Assessor 336-634-3416.

Duplin County

Register of Deeds, P.O. Box 970, Kenansville, NC 28349. Register of Deeds, R/E and UCC Recording 910-296-2108; Fax 910-296-2344. http://www.duplin county.org
Will search UCC records prior to 7/2001 and current fixture (land) files. No tax liens filed here. Will not search real estate records. **Other Phone Numbers:** Assessor 910-296-2110; Appraiser/Auditor 910-296-2110; Elections 910-296-2170; Vital Records 910-296-2108.

Durham County

Register of Deeds, P.O. Box 1107, Durham, NC 27702. 919-560-0494 R/E Recording: 919-560-0480; Fax 919-560-0497. http://199.72.142.253
Will search UCC records prior to 7/2001 and current fixture (land) files. No tax liens filed here. Will not search real estate records. **Online Access:** Property Records. Property records are available on the GIS map server; however, there is no name searching. **Other Phone Numbers:** Assessor 919-560-0300.

Edgecombe County

Register of Deeds, P.O. Box 386, Tarboro, NC 27886. 252-641-7924; Fax 252-641-1771.
Will search UCC records prior to 7/2001 and current fixture (land) files. No tax liens filed here. Will not search real estate records. **Other Phone Numbers:** Assessor 252-641-7855; Treasurer 252-641-7834.

Forsyth County

Register of Deeds, P.O. Box 20639, Winston-Salem, NC 27120-0639. 336-727-2903; Fax 336-727-2341.
Will search UCC records prior to 7/2001 and current fixture (land) files. No tax liens filed here. Will not search real estate records. **Online Access:** Real Estate. Online access to the county Geo-Data Exploer database is available free online at http://maps.co.forsyth.nc.us. Address and Parcel ID searching only. Includes Board of Adjustment and building permit records. Also, Register of Deed records are available on CD-ROM.

Other Phone Numbers: Assessor 336-727-2513; Treasurer 336-727-2655.

Franklin County

Register of Deeds, P.O. Box 545, Louisburg, NC 27549-0545. Register of Deeds, R/E and UCC Recording 919-496-3500; Fax 919-496-1457. http://www.co.franklin.nc.us
Will search UCC records prior to 7/2001 and current fixture (land) files. No tax liens filed here. Will not search real estate records. **Online Access:** Real Property. Online access to the county spatial data explorer database is available free at http://www.co.franklin.nc.us/docs/frame_tax.htm.
Search the gis map or click on "text search" for name searching. **Other Phone Numbers:** Assessor 919-496-1497; Elections 919-496-3710.

Gaston County

Register of Deeds, P.O. Box 1578, Gastonia, NC 28053. 704-862-7681 R/E Recording: 704-866-3181; Fax 704-862-7519.
Will search UCC records prior to 7/2001 and current fixture (land) files. No tax liens filed here. Will not search real estate records.

Gates County

Register of Deeds, P.O. Box 471, Gatesville, NC 27938-0471. Register of Deeds, R/E and UCC Recording 252-357-0850; Fax 252-357-0850.
Will search UCC records prior to 7/2001 and current fixture (land) files. No tax liens filed here. Will not search real estate records. **Other Phone Numbers:** Assessor 252-357-1360; Treasurer 252-357-1240; Appraiser/Auditor 252-357-1360; Elections 252-357-1780; Vital Records 252-357-0850.

Graham County

Register of Deeds, P.O. Box 406, Robbinsville, NC 28771-0406. Register of Deeds, R/E and UCC Recording 828-479-7971; Fax 828-479-7988.
Will search UCC records prior to 7/2001 and current fixture (land) files. No tax liens filed here. Will not search real estate records. **Other Phone Numbers:** Assessor 828-479-7965; Treasurer 828-479-7962; Appraiser/Auditor 828-479-7963; Elections 828-479-7969; Vital Records 828-479-7971.

Granville County

Register of Deeds, P.O. Box 427, Oxford, NC 27565. Register of Deeds, R/E and UCC Recording 919-693-6314; Fax 919-603-1345.
Will search UCC records prior to 7/2001 and current fixture (land) files. No tax liens filed here. Will not search real estate records. **Other Phone Numbers:** Assessor 919-693-4181; Vital Records 919-693-2515.

Greene County

Register of Deeds, P.O. Box 86, Snow Hill, NC 28580. 252-747-3620 R/E Recording: 919-747-3620.
Will search UCC records prior to 7/2001 and current fixture (land) files. No tax liens filed here. Will not search real estate records.

Guilford County

Register of Deeds, P.O. Box 1467, High Point, NC 27261-1467. Register of Deeds, R/E and UCC Recording 336-884-7931; http://www.co.guilford.nc.us/
Will search UCC records prior to 7/2001 and current fixture (land) files. No tax liens filed here. Will not search real estate records. **Online Access:** Recorder, Assessor, Property, UCC, Vital Statistics. Online access to the county tax department database is available http://www.co.guilford.nc.us/egov/index.html. **Other Phone Numbers:** Assessor 336-884-7911; Treasurer

336-884-7911; Appraiser/Auditor 336-884-7895; Elections 336-884-7931; Vital Records 336-373-7556.

Halifax County

Register of Deeds, P.O. Box 67, Halifax, NC 27839-0067. Register of Deeds, R/E and UCC Recording 252-583-2101; Fax 252-583-1273. http://www.halifaxnc.com/halinav.html
Will search UCC records prior to 7/2001 and current fixture (land) files. No tax liens filed here. Will not search real estate records. **Other Phone Numbers:** Assessor 252-583-2121; Treasurer 252-583-3771; Appraiser/Auditor 252-583-2121; Elections 252-583-4391; Vital Records 252-583-2101.

Harnett County

Register of Deeds, P.O. Box 279, Lillington, NC 27546. Register of Deeds, R/E and UCC Recording 910-893-7540; Fax 910-814-3841. http://www.harnett.org/departments/rod.html
Will search UCC records prior to 7/2001 and current fixture (land) files. No tax liens filed here. Will not search real estate records. **Online Access:** Real Estate, Grantor/Grantee. County real estate and property tax information is available free online at http://152.34.178.4/nc32. **Other Phone Numbers:** Vital Records 910-893-7542.

Haywood County

Register of Deeds, Courthouse, 215 N. Main St., Waynesville, NC 28786. Register of Deeds, R/E and UCC Recording 828-452-6635; Fax 828-452-6762.
Will search UCC records prior to 7/2001 and current fixture (land) files. No tax liens filed here. Will not search real estate records. **Online Access:** Real Estate. Records on the Land Records Search database are available free online at www.undersys.com/haywood/haywood.html. Search will result in a map showing the parcel and owner, parcel number, and deed book & page information. **Other Phone Numbers:** Assessor 828-452-6635; Treasurer 828-452-6635.

Henderson County

Register of Deeds, Suite 129, 200 N. Grove St., Hendersonville, NC 28792. 704-697-4901 R/E Recording: 919-438-4155.
Will search UCC records prior to 7/2001 and current fixture (land) files. No tax liens filed here. Will not search real estate records.

Hertford County

Register of Deeds, P.O. Box 36, Winton, NC 27986. 252-358-7850 R/E Recording: 252-358-7805; Fax 252-358-7806.
Will search UCC records prior to 7/2001 and current fixture (land) files. No tax liens filed here. Will not search real estate records. **Other Phone Numbers:** Assessor 252-358-7810; Treasurer 252-358-7815; Elections 252-358-7812; Vital Records 252-358-7850.

Hoke County

Register of Deeds, 304 N. Main St., Raeford, NC 28376. Register of Deeds, R/E and UCC Recording 910-875-2035 UCC Recording: 910-875-0235; Fax 910-875-9515.
Will search UCC records prior to 7/2001 and current fixture (land) files. No tax liens filed here. Will not search real estate records. **Other Phone Numbers:** Assessor 910-875-8751; Appraiser/Auditor 910-875-8751; Elections 910-875-8751; Vital Records 910-875-2035.

Hyde County

Register of Deeds, P.O. Box 294, Swanquarter, NC 27885. 252-926-3011; Fax 252-926-3082.
Will search UCC records. No tax liens filed here. Will not search real estate records. **Other Phone Numbers:** Assessor 252-926-5151; Treasurer 252-926-4101.

Iredell County

Register of Deeds, P.O. Box 904, Statesville, NC 28687. 704-872-7468; Fax 704-878-3055.
Will search UCC records prior to 7/2001 and current fixture (land) files. No tax liens filed here. Will not search real estate records. **Other Phone Numbers:** Assessor 704-872-3021.

Jackson County

Register of Deeds, 401 Grindstaff Cove Rd., Sylva, NC 28779. 828-586-7530 R/E Recording: 828-586-4055; Fax 828-586-6879.
Will search UCC records prior to 7/2001 and current fixture (land) files. No tax liens filed here. Will not search real estate records. **Other Phone Numbers:** Assessor 828-586-4055.

Johnston County

Register of Deeds, Box 118, Smithfield, NC 27577. 919-989-5164 R/E Recording: 919-989-5160.
Will search UCC records prior to 7/2001 and current fixture (land) files. No tax liens filed here. Will not search real estate records.

Jones County

Register of Deeds, P.O. Box 189, Trenton, NC 28585-0189. 252-448-2551; Fax 252-448-1357.
Will search UCC records prior to 7/2001 and current fixture (land) files. No tax liens filed here. Will not search real estate records. **Other Phone Numbers:** Assessor 252-448-2546.

Lee County

Register of Deeds, P.O. Box 2040, Sanford, NC 27331-2040. 919-774-4821; Fax 919-774-5063.
Will search UCC records prior to 7/2001 and current fixture (land) files. No tax liens filed here. Will not search real estate records.

Lenoir County

Register of Deeds, P.O. Box 3289, Kinston, NC 28502. 252-559-6420 R/E Recording: 252-523-2390; Fax 252-523-6139.
Will search UCC records prior to 7/2001 and current fixture (land) files. No tax liens filed here. Will not search real estate records. **Other Phone Numbers:** Assessor 252-527-7174; Treasurer 252-527-7174.

Lincoln County

Register of Deeds, P.O. Box 218, Lincolnton, NC 28093-0218. 704-736-8530 R/E Recording: 704-736-8535 UCC Recording: 704-736-8533; Fax 704-732-9049.
Will search UCC records prior to 7/2001 and current fixture (land) files. No tax liens filed here. Will not search real estate records. **Other Phone Numbers:** Assessor 704-736-8540; Elections 704-736-8480; Vital Records 704-736-8530.

Macon County

Register of Deeds, 5 West Main Street, Franklin, NC 28734. 828-349-2095 R/E Recording: 828-524-6421; Fax 828-369-6382.
Will search UCC records prior to 7/2001 and current fixture (land) files. No tax liens filed here. Will not search real estate records. **Other Phone Numbers:** Assessor 828-524-6421.

Madison County

Register of Deeds, P.O. Box 66, Marshall, NC 28753. Register of Deeds, R/E and UCC Recording 828-649-3131.
Will search UCC records. No tax liens filed here. Will not search real estate records. **Other Phone Numbers:** Assessor 828-649-3014; Treasurer 828-649-2521; Appraiser/Auditor 828-649-3014; Elections 828-649-3731; Vital Records 828-649-3131.

Martin County

Register of Deeds, P.O. Box 348, Williamston, NC 27892. 252-792-1683 R/E Recording: 252-792-1901; Fax 252-792-1684.
Will search UCC records. No tax liens filed here. Will not search real estate records. **Other Phone Numbers:** Assessor 252-792-1031; Elections 252-792-5845; Vital Records 252-792-1683.

McDowell County

Register of Deeds, 21 South Main Street, Courthouse, Marion, NC 28752-3992. 828-652-4727; Fax 828-652-4727.
Will search UCC records prior to 7/2001 and current fixture (land) files. No tax liens filed here. Will not search real estate records. **Other Phone Numbers:** Assessor 828-652-7121; Treasurer 828-652-7121; Elections 828-652-7121; Vital Records 828-652-4727.

Mecklenburg County

Register of Deeds, 720 East 4th Street, Ste. 103, Charlotte, NC 28202. 704-336-2443; Fax 704-336-7699. http://meckrod.hartic.com
Will search UCC records prior to 7/2001 and current fixture (land) files. No tax liens filed here. Will not search real estate records. **Online Access:** Assessor, Real Estate, Grantor/Grantee, Vital Records. Property Records on the GIS map server are available free online at http://maps.co.mecklenburg.nc.us/taxgis/disclaimer.htm . Also, birth, death, marriage, recordings, and grantor/grantee indices are available free at http://meckrod.hartic.com/default.asp.

Mitchell County

Register of Deeds, P.O. Box 82, Bakersville, NC 28705-0082. 828-688-2139; Fax 828-688-3666.
Will search UCC records prior to 7/2001 and current fixture (land) files. No tax liens filed here. Will not search real estate records. **Other Phone Numbers:** Assessor 828-688-2139.

Montgomery County

Register of Deeds, P.O. Box 695, Troy, NC 27371-0695. 910-576-4271 R/E Recording: 919-576-4271; Fax 910-576-2209.
Will search UCC records prior to 7/2001 and current fixture (land) files. Search UCC records filed after 7/2001 at the Sec. of State's office only. No tax liens filed here. Will not search real estate records.

Moore County

Register of Deeds, P.O. Box 1210, Carthage, NC 28327. 910-947-6370 R/E Recording: 910-947-6372 UCC Recording: 910-947-6372; Fax 910-947-6396. http://www.co.moore.nc.us
Will search UCC records prior to 7/2001 and current fixture (land) files. No tax liens filed here. **Online Access:** Real Estate, Liens, Grantor/Grantee, Vital Statistics, DD214, Property Tax. Online access to the recorder's Online Public Records (OPR) database is available free at http://rod.co.moore.nc.us/nc32. Also, access to county Tax Information System (TIS) data is available free online to registrants and subject to approval at www.co.moore.nc.us/property/TIS/Taxpayer%20Infor mation%20Login.htm. For information, contact Kay Ingram at 910-947-6306. **Other Phone Numbers:** Treasurer 910-947-6310; Appraiser/Auditor 910-947-6412; Elections 910-947-3868; Vital Records 910-947-6370.

Nash County

Register of Deeds, P.O. Box 974, Nashville, NC 27856. 252-459-9836 R/E Recording: 252-459-4141 UCC Recording: 252-459-9825; Fax 252-459-9889.
Will search UCC records prior to 7/2001 and current fixture (land) files. No tax liens filed here. Will not search real estate records. **Other Phone Numbers:** Assessor 252-459- 9824; Vital Records 252-459-9839.

New Hanover County

Register of Deeds, 316 Princess Street, Room 216, Wilmington, NC 28401. 910-341-4530 R/E Recording: 919-341-4530; Fax 910-341-4169.
Will search UCC records prior to 7/2001 and current fixture (land) files. No tax liens filed here. Will not search real estate records. **Other Phone Numbers:** Vital Records 910-341-4547.

Northampton County

Register of Deeds, P.O. Box 128, Jackson, NC 27845. 252-534-2511 R/E Recording: 919-534-2511.
Will search UCC records prior to 7/2001 and current fixture (land) files. No tax liens filed here. Will not search real estate records.

Onslow County

Register of Deeds, 109 Old Bridge Street, Jacksonville, NC 28540. 910-347-3451 R/E Recording: 919-347-3451.
Will search UCC records prior to 7/2001 and current fixture (land) files. No tax liens filed here. Will not search real estate records.

Orange County

Register of Deeds, P.O. Box 8181, Hillsborough, NC 27278-8181. 919-732-8181; Fax 919-644-3015.
Will search UCC records prior to 7/2001 and current fixture (land) files. No tax liens filed here. Will not search real estate records.

Pamlico County

Register of Deeds, P.O. Box 433, Bayboro, NC 28515. 252-745-4421.
Will search UCC records prior to 7/2001 and current fixture (land) files. No tax liens filed here. Will not search real estate records. **Other Phone Numbers:** Assessor 252-745-4125 x33.

Pasquotank County

Register of Deeds, P.O. Box 154, Elizabeth City, NC 27907-0154. Register of Deeds, R/E and UCC Recording 252-335-4367; Fax 252-335-5106.
Will search UCC records. No tax liens filed here. Will not search real estate records. **Other Phone Numbers:** Assessor 252-338-5169; Treasurer 252-335-4580; Elections 252-335-1739; Vital Records 252-335-4367.

Pender County

Register of Deeds, P.O. Box 43, Burgaw, NC 28425. 910-259-1225; Fax 910-259-1299.
Will search UCC records prior to 7/2001 and current fixture (land) files. No tax liens filed here. Will not search real estate records. **Other Phone Numbers:** Assessor 910-259-1225; Elections 910-259-1225; Vital Records 910-259-1458.

Perquimans County

Register of Deeds, P.O. Box 74, Hertford, NC 27944. 252-426-5660 R/E Recording: 252-426-8484; Fax 252-426-7443.
Will search UCC records prior to 7/2001 and current fixture (land) files. No tax liens filed here. Will not search real estate records. **Other Phone Numbers:** Assessor 252-426-5564.

Person County

Register of Deeds, Courthouse Square, Roxboro, NC 27573. Register of Deeds, R/E and UCC Recording 336-597-1733;
http://www.personcounty.net/sections.php
Will search UCC records prior to 7/2001 and current fixture (land) files. No tax liens filed here. Will not search real estate records. **Other Phone Numbers:** Assessor 336-597-1712; Elections 336-597-1727; Vital Records 336-597-1727; Deed Vault 336-597-1729.

Pitt County

Register of Deeds, P.O. Box 35, Greenville, NC 27835-0035. Register of Deeds, R/E and UCC Recording 252-830-4128.
Will search UCC records. No tax liens filed here. Will not search real estate records. **Other Phone Numbers:** Assessor 252-830-4128; Treasurer 252-830-4128; Appraiser/Auditor 252-830-4128; Elections 252-830-4128; Vital Records 252-830-4128.

Polk County

Register of Deeds, P.O. Box 308, Columbus, NC 28722. 828-894-8450 R/E Recording: 704-894-8450; Fax 828-894-5781.
Will search UCC records prior to 7/2001 and current fixture (land) files. No tax liens filed here. Will not search real estate records. **Other Phone Numbers:** Assessor 828-894-8500; Treasurer 828-894-8500.

Randolph County

Register of Deeds, P.O. Box 4066, Asheboro, NC 27204. Register of Deeds, R/E and UCC Recording 336-318-6960; http://www.co.randolph.nc.us
Will search UCC records prior to 7/2001 and current fixture (land) files. No tax liens filed here. Will not search real estate records. **Online Access:** Real Property. Online access to the gouncty GIS database is available free at www.co.randolph.nc.us/gis.htm. In the "Search functions" on the map page, click on "parcel owner.". **Other Phone Numbers:** Vital Records 336-318-6960.

Richmond County

Register of Deeds, 114 E Franklin St., Suite 101, Rockingham, NC 28379-3601. 910-997-8250 R/E Recording: 910-997-5041; Fax 910-997-8499.
Will search UCC records prior to 7/2001 and current fixture (land) files. No tax liens filed here. Will not search real estate records. **Online Access:** Property. Online access to County property records is available via a subscription service; registration and fees are required. For information, call 334-344-3333. **Other Phone Numbers:** Assessor 910-997-8274.

Robeson County

Register of Deeds, Box 22 Courthouse-Room 102, Lumberton, NC 28358. 910-671-3046 R/E Recording: 910-671-3043; Fax 910-671-3041.
Will search UCC records prior to 7/2001 and current fixture (land) files. No tax liens filed here. Will not search real estate records. **Other Phone Numbers:** Assessor 910-671-3060; Elections 910-671-3080; Vital Records 910-671-4045.

Rockingham County

Register of Deeds, P.O. Box 56, Wentworth, NC 27375-0056. 336-342-8820 R/E Recording: 919-342-8820.

Will search UCC records prior to 7/2001 and current fixture (land) files. No tax liens filed here. Will not search real estate records.

Rowan County

Register of Deeds, P.O. Box 2568, Salisbury, NC 28145. 704-638-3102; http://www.co.rowan.nc.us/rod

Will search UCC records prior to 7/2001 and current fixture (land) files. No tax liens filed here. Will not search real estate records. **Online Access:** Real Estate, Recording. Online access to the Register of Dees land records database is available free at http://rod.co.rowan.nc.us. Records go back to 1975; financing statements back to 1993; images back to 6/2000. **Other Phone Numbers:** Assessor 704-633-4601; Treasurer 704-633-3871.

Rutherford County

Register of Deeds, P.O. Box 551, Rutherfordton, NC 28139. 828-287-6155 R/E Recording: 704-287-6155; Fax 828-287-6470.

Will search UCC records prior to 7/2001 and current fixture (land) files. No tax liens filed here. Will not search real estate records.

Sampson County

Register of Deeds, P.O. Box 256, Clinton, NC 28329. Register of Deeds, R/E and UCC Recording 910-592-8026; Fax 910-592-1803.

Will search UCC records prior to 7/2001 and current fixture (land) files. No tax liens filed here. Will not search real estate records. **Other Phone Numbers:** Vital Records 910-592-8026.

Scotland County

Register of Deeds, P.O. Box 769, Laurinburg, NC 28353. 910-277-2575 R/E Recording: 910-277-2400; Fax 910-277-3133.

Will search UCC records prior to 7/2001 and current fixture (land) files. No tax liens filed here. Will not search real estate records. **Other Phone Numbers:** Assessor 910-277-3270.

Stanly County

Register of Deeds, P.O. Box 97, Albemarle, NC 28002-0097. 704-986-3640 R/E Recording: 704-983-7200; http://www.co.stanly.nc.us

Will search UCC records prior to 7/2001 and current fixture (land) files. No tax liens filed here. Will not search real estate records. **Online Access:** Real Estate, Assessor. Online access to the county Property database is available free on the gis mapping site at www.webgis.net/stanly. Provides parcel ID and tax numbers, owner, address, year, land and building values.

Stokes County

Register of Deeds, P.O. Box 67, Danbury, NC 27016. Register of Deeds, R/E and UCC Recording 336-593-2811; Fax 336-593-9360.

Will search UCC records prior to 7/2001 and current fixture (land) files. No tax liens filed here. Will not search real estate records. **Other Phone Numbers:** Assessor 336-593-2811; Appraiser/Auditor 336-593-2811; Elections 336-593-2811; Vital Records 336-593-2811.

Surry County

Register of Deeds, P.O. Box 303, Dobson, NC 27017-0303. 336-401-8150 R/E Recording: 336-386-9201; Fax 336-401-8151.

Will search UCC records prior to 7/2001 and current fixture (land) files. No tax liens filed here. Will not search real estate records. **Other Phone Numbers:** Treasurer 336-386-9230.

Swain County

Register of Deeds, P.O. Box 1183, Bryson City, NC 28713. 828-488-9273; Fax 828-488-6947.

Will search UCC records prior to 7/2001 and current fixture (land) files. No tax liens filed here. Will not search real estate records. **Other Phone Numbers:** Assessor 828-488-9273 x223; Elections 828-488-6177; Vital Records 828-488-9273 x205.

Transylvania County

Register of Deeds, 12 East Main Street, Courthouse, Brevard, NC 28712. Register of Deeds, R/E and UCC Recording 828-884-3162.

Will search UCC records. No tax liens filed here. Will not search real estate records. **Other Phone Numbers:** Assessor 828-884-3197; Treasurer 828-884-3104; Appraiser/Auditor 828-884-3200; Elections 828-884-3114; Vital Records 828-884-3162.

Tyrrell County

Register of Deeds, P.O. Box 449, Columbia, NC 27925. 252-796-2901 R/E Recording: 252-796-1371; Fax 252-796-0148.

Will search UCC records prior to 7/2001 and current fixture (land) files. No tax liens filed here. Will not search real estate records. **Other Phone Numbers:** Assessor 252-796-1371.

Union County

Register of Deeds, P.O. Box 248, Monroe, NC 28111-0248. Register of Deeds, R/E and UCC Recording 704-283-3727 UCC Recording: 704-283-3610; Fax 704-283-3569.

Will search UCC records prior to 7/2001 and current fixture (land) files. No tax liens filed here. Will not search real estate records. **Other Phone Numbers:** Vital Records 704-283-3610; Land Records 704-283-3728.

Vance County

Register of Deeds, 122 Young Street, Courthouse, Suite F, Henderson, NC 27536. 252-438-4155 R/E Recording: 919-438-4155.

Will search UCC records prior to 7/2001 and current fixture (land) files. No tax liens filed here. Will not search real estate records.

Wake County

Register of Deeds, P.O. Box 1897, Raleigh, NC 27602. 919-856-5460.

Will search UCC records prior to 7/2001 and current fixture (land) files. No tax liens filed here. Will not search real estate records. **Online Access:** Real Estate, Assessor. Records from the County Department of Revenue are downloadable by township for free at http://web.co.wake.nc.us/revenue/realdata2.html. Also, Online access to Town of Cary property information is available free at a gis mapping site at http://www.webgis.net/cary. **Other Phone Numbers:** Assessor 919-856-6600; Treasurer 919-856-6600.

Warren County

Register of Deeds, P.O. Box 506, Warrenton, NC 27589. 252-257-3265; Fax 252-257-1524.

Will search UCC records prior to 7/2001 and current fixture (land) files. No tax liens filed here. Will not search real estate records. **Other Phone Numbers:** Assessor 252-257-4158; Treasurer 252-257-3337.

Washington County

Register of Deeds, P.O. Box 1007, Plymouth, NC 27962. 252-793-2325 R/E Recording: 919-793-5823; Fax 252-793-6982.

Will search UCC records prior to 7/2001 and current fixture (land) files. No tax liens filed here. Will not search real estate records. **Other Phone Numbers:** Assessor 252-793-1176.

Watauga County

Register of Deeds, 842 West King St., Suite 9, Boone, NC 28607-3585. 828-265-8052 R/E Recording: 828-265-1300; Fax 828-265-7632.

Will search UCC records prior to 7/2001 and current fixture (land) files. No tax liens filed here. Will not search real estate records. **Other Phone Numbers:** Assessor 828-265-8036; Elections 828-265-8061; Vital Records 828-265-8052.

Wayne County

Register of Deeds, P.O. Box 267, Goldsboro, NC 27533-0267. 919-731-1449.

Will search UCC records prior to 7/2001 and current fixture (land) files. No tax liens filed here. Will not search real estate records. **Other Phone Numbers:** Assessor 919-731-1461.

Wilkes County

Register of Deeds, 500 Courthouse Dr, Ste. 1000, 500 Courthouse Dr., Wilkesboro, NC 28697. Register of Deeds, R/E and UCC Recording 336-651-7351.

Will search UCC records prior to 7/2001 and current fixture (land) files. No tax liens filed here. Will not search real estate records. **Other Phone Numbers:** Vital Records 336-651-7351.

Wilson County

Register of Deeds, P.O. Box 1728, Wilson, NC 27893. 252-399-2935 R/E Recording: 252-237-6600; Fax 252-399-2942. http://www.wilson-co.com

Will search UCC records prior to 7/2001 and current fixture (land) files. No tax liens filed here. Will not search real estate records. **Online Access:** Assessor, Real Estate, Voter Records. Records on the county Tax Administrator database are available free online at www.wilson-co.com/wctax.html. Records on the county registered voter database are available at www.wilson-co.com/wcbe_search.cfm. **Other Phone Numbers:** Treasurer 252-399-2902.

Yadkin County

Register of Deeds, P.O. Box 211, Yadkinville, NC 27055. 336-679-4225 R/E Recording: 919-679-4225; Fax 336-679-2703.

Will search UCC records prior to 7/2001 and current fixture (land) files. No tax liens filed here. Will not search real estate records.

Yancey County

Register of Deeds, Courthouse, Room #4, Burnsville, NC 28714. 828-682-2174 R/E Recording: 704-682-2174; Fax 828-682-4520.

Will search UCC records. No tax liens filed here. Will not search real estate records.

North Carolina County Locator

You will usually be able to find the city name in the City/County Cross Reference below. In that case, it is a simple matter to determine the county from the cross reference. However, only the official US Postal Service city names are included in this index. There are an additional 40,000 place names that people use in their addresses. Therefore, we have also included a ZIP/City Cross Reference immediately following the City/County Cross Reference.

If you know the ZIP Code but the city name does not appear in the City/County Cross Reference index, look up the ZIP Code in the ZIP/City Cross Reference, find the city name, then look up the city name in the City/County Cross Reference. For example, you want to know the county for an address of Menands, NY 12204. There is no "Menands" in the City/County Cross Reference. The ZIP/City Cross Reference shows that ZIP Codes 12201-12288 are for the city of Albany. Looking back in the City/County Cross Reference, Albany is in Albany County.

City/County Cross Reference

ABERDEEN (28315) Moore(76), Hoke(24)
ADVANCE Davie
AHOSKIE Hertford
ALAMANCE Alamance
ALBEMARLE Stanly
ALBERTSON Duplin
ALEXANDER Buncombe
ALEXIS (28006) Gaston(94), Lincoln(6)
ALLIANCE Pamlico
ALMOND Swain
ALTAMAHAW Alamance
ANDREWS Cherokee
ANGIER (27501) Harnett(73), Johnston(27)
ANSONVILLE Anson
APEX (27502) Wake(88), Chatham(12)
AQUONE Macon
ARAPAHOE Pamlico
ARARAT Surry
ARDEN (28704) Buncombe(95), Swain(3),
   Henderson(2)
ASH Brunswick
ASHEBORO Randolph
ASHEVILLE (28803) Buncombe(98),
   Mecklenburg(2)
ASHEVILLE Buncombe
ATKINSON Pender
ATLANTIC Carteret
ATLANTIC BEACH Carteret
AULANDER (27805) Bertie(60),
   Hertford(40)
AURORA Beaufort
AUTRYVILLE (28318) Sampson(94),
   Cumberland(6)
AVON Dare
AYDEN (28513) Pitt(98), Greene(2)
AYDLETT Currituck
BADIN Stanly
BAHAMA Durham
BAILEY (27807) Nash(76), Wilson(24)
BAKERSVILLE Mitchell
BALSAM Jackson
BALSAM GROVE Transylvania
BANNER ELK (28604) Watauga(54),
   Avery(46)
BARBER Rowan
BARCO Currituck
BARIUM SPRINGS Iredell
BARNARDSVILLE (28709) Henderson(91),
   Buncombe(10)
BARNESVILLE Robeson
BAT CAVE Henderson
BATH Beaufort
BATTLEBORO (27809) Nash(50),
   Edgecombe(50)
BAYBORO Pamlico
BEAR CREEK Chatham
BEAUFORT Carteret
BELEWS CREEK (27009) Forsyth(97),
   Stokes(3)
BELHAVEN (27810) Beaufort(98), Hyde(2)
BELLARTHUR Pitt
BELMONT Gaston

BELVIDERE (27919) Perquimans(83),
   Chowan(11), Gates(6)
BENNETT (27208) Chatham(58),
   Randolph(37), Moore(5)
BENSON Johnston
BESSEMER CITY Gaston
BETHANIA Forsyth
BETHEL (27812) Pitt(95), Edgecombe(6)
BEULAVILLE (28518) Duplin(90),
   Onslow(11)
BISCOE (27209) Montgomery(79),
   Moore(21)
BLACK CREEK Wilson
BLACK MOUNTAIN Buncombe
BLADENBORO Bladen
BLANCH Caswell
BLOUNTS CREEK Beaufort
BLOWING ROCK Watauga
BOILING SPRINGS Cleveland
BOLIVIA Brunswick
BOLTON (28423) Columbus(95), Bladen(5)
BONLEE Chatham
BOOMER (28606) Wilkes(95), Caldwell(5)
BOONE Watauga
BOONVILLE Yadkin
BOSTIC Rutherford
BRASSTOWN (28902) Clay(93),
   Cherokee(7)
BREVARD Transylvania
BRIDGETON Craven
BROADWAY (27505) Harnett(60), Lee(40)
BROWNS SUMMIT (27214) Guilford(89),
   Rockingham(11)
BRUNSWICK Columbus
BRYSON CITY Swain
BUIES CREEK Harnett
BULLOCK Granville
BUNN Franklin
BUNNLEVEL Harnett
BURGAW Pender
BURLINGTON (27217) Alamance(92),
   Caswell(8)
BURLINGTON Alamance
BURNSVILLE Yancey
BUTNER Granville
BUTTERS Bladen
BUXTON Dare
BYNUM Chatham
CALABASH Brunswick
CALYPSO Duplin
CAMDEN Camden
CAMERON (28326) Harnett(48),
   Moore(42), Lee(10)
CAMP LEJEUNE Onslow
CANDLER Buncombe
CANDOR Montgomery
CANTON Haywood
CAROLEEN Rutherford
CAROLINA BEACH New Hanover
CARRBORO Orange
CARTHAGE Moore
CARY Wake

CASAR (28020) Cleveland(91),
   Rutherford(9)
CASHIERS Jackson
CASTALIA (27816) Nash(72), Franklin(28)
CASTLE HAYNE New Hanover
CATAWBA Catawba
CEDAR FALLS Randolph
CEDAR GROVE Orange
CEDAR ISLAND Carteret
CEDAR MOUNTAIN Transylvania
CERRO GORDO Columbus
CHADBOURN Columbus
CHAPEL HILL (27514) Orange(77),
   Chatham(16), Durham(7)
CHAPEL HILL (27516) Orange(86),
   Chatham(14)
CHAPEL HILL Orange
CHARLOTTE (28215) Mecklenburg(91),
   Cabarrus(9)
CHARLOTTE Mecklenburg
CHEROKEE Swain
CHERRY POINT Craven
CHERRYVILLE (28021) Gaston(85),
   Lincoln(12), Cleveland(4)
CHIMNEY ROCK Rutherford
CHINA GROVE Rowan
CHINQUAPIN (28521) Duplin(95),
   Onslow(5)
CHOCOWINITY Beaufort
CLAREMONT Catawba
CLARENDON Columbus
CLARKTON (28433) Bladen(70),
   Columbus(31)
CLAYTON (27520) Johnston(97), Wake(3)
CLEMMONS (27012) Forsyth(73),
   Davidson(27)
CLEVELAND Rowan
CLIFFSIDE Rutherford
CLIMAX (27233) Randolph(67),
   Guilford(33)
CLINTON Sampson
CLYDE Haywood
COATS Harnett
COFIELD Hertford
COINJOCK Currituck
COLERAIN Bertie
COLFAX Guilford
COLLETTSVILLE (28611) Caldwell(92),
   Avery(8)
COLUMBIA Tyrrell
COLUMBUS Polk
COMFORT Jones
COMO Hertford
CONCORD Cabarrus
CONETOE Edgecombe
CONNELLYS SPRINGS Burke
CONOVER Catawba
CONWAY Northampton
COOLEEMEE Davie
CORAPEAKE Gates
CORDOVA Richmond
CORNELIUS Mecklenburg
COROLLA Currituck

COUNCIL Bladen
COVE CITY Craven
CRAMERTON Gaston
CRANBERRY Avery
CREEDMOOR (27522) Granville(87),
   Wake(13)
CRESTON Ashe
CRESWELL (27928) Washington(96),
   Tyrrell(4)
CROSSNORE Avery
CROUSE (28033) Lincoln(95), Gaston(5)
CRUMPLER Ashe
CULBERSON Cherokee
CULLOWHEE Jackson
CUMBERLAND Cumberland
CUMNOCK Lee
CURRIE Pender
CURRITUCK Currituck
DALLAS Gaston
DANA Henderson
DANBURY Stokes
DAVIDSON (28036) Mecklenburg(68),
   Cabarrus(32)
DAVIS Carteret
DEEP GAP (28618) Watauga(97),
   Wilkes(3)
DEEP RUN (28525) Lenoir(89), Duplin(11)
DELCO Columbus
DENTON (27239) Davidson(76),
   Randolph(24)
DENVER (28037) Lincoln(89), Catawba(11)
DILLSBORO Jackson
DOBSON Surry
DOVER (28526) Craven(91), Jones(7),
   Lenoir(2)
DREXEL Burke
DUBLIN Bladen
DUDLEY Wayne
DUNN (28334) Harnett(51), Sampson(40),
   Johnston(9)
DUNN Harnett
DURANTS NECK Perquimans
DURHAM (27705) Durham(81), Orange(19)
DURHAM (27707) Durham(98), Orange(2)
DURHAM Durham
EAGLE ROCK Wake
EAGLE SPRINGS Moore
EARL Cleveland
EAST BEND Yadkin
EAST FLAT ROCK Henderson
EAST SPENCER Rowan
EDEN Rockingham
EDENTON Chowan
EDNEYVILLE Henderson
EDWARD Beaufort
EFLAND Orange
ELIZABETH CITY Pasquotank
ELIZABETHTOWN Bladen
ELK PARK Avery
ELKIN (28621) Surry(88), Wilkes(12)
ELLENBORO (28040) Rutherford(75),
   Hoke(17), Cleveland(8)

ELLERBE (28338) Richmond(97),
    Cumberland(3)
ELM CITY (27822) Wilson(88), Nash(9),
    Edgecombe(3)
ELON COLLEGE (27244) Alamance(95),
    Guilford(4)
EMERALD ISLE Carteret
ENFIELD Halifax
ENGELHARD Hyde
ENKA Buncombe
ENNICE Alleghany
ERNUL Craven
ERWIN Harnett
ETHER Montgomery
ETOWAH Henderson
EURE Gates
EVERETTS Martin
EVERGREEN Columbus
FAIR BLUFF Columbus
FAIRFIELD (27826) Hyde(67), Tyrrell(33)
FAIRMONT Robeson
FAIRVIEW Buncombe
FAISON (28341) Sampson(78), Duplin(22)
FAITH Rowan
FALCON Cumberland
FALKLAND Pitt
FALLSTON Cleveland
FARMVILLE Pitt
FAYETTEVILLE (28301) Cumberland(98),
    Bladen(2)
FAYETTEVILLE (28304) Cumberland(98),
    Hoke(2)
FAYETTEVILLE (28306) Cumberland(97),
    Bladen(2), Hoke(2)
FAYETTEVILLE Cumberland
FERGUSON Wilkes
FLAT ROCK Henderson
FLEETWOOD Ashe
FLETCHER (28732) Buncombe(94),
    Henderson(6)
FONTANA DAM (28733) Graham(83),
    Macon(17)
FOREST CITY Rutherford
FORT BRAGG Cumberland
FOUNTAIN (27829) Wilson(70), Pitt(22),
    Edgecombe(8)
FOUR OAKS (27524) Johnston(99),
    Wayne(2)
FRANKLIN Macon
FRANKLINTON (27525) Franklin(77),
    Granville(23)
FRANKLINVILLE Randolph
FREMONT (27830) Wayne(96), Wilson(4)
FRISCO Dare
FUQUAY VARINA (27526) Wake(78),
    Harnett(23)
GARLAND (28441) Sampson(58),
    Bladen(42)
GARNER (27529) Wake(82), Johnston(18)
GARYSBURG Northampton
GASTON Northampton
GASTONIA Gaston
GATES Gates
GATESVILLE Gates
GERMANTON (27019) Stokes(70),
    Forsyth(30)
GERTON Henderson
GIBSON Scotland
GIBSONVILLE (27249) Guilford(57),
    Alamance(33), Caswell(10)
GLADE VALLEY Alleghany
GLEN ALPINE Burke
GLENDALE SPRINGS Ashe
GLENDON Moore
GLENVILLE (28736) Jackson(98),
    Buncombe(2)
GLENWOOD McDowell
GLOUCESTER Carteret
GODWIN (28344) Sampson(94),
    Cumberland(6)
GOLD HILL (28071) Rowan(92), Stanly(6),
    Cabarrus(2)

GOLDSBORO Wayne
GOLDSTON Chatham
GRAHAM Alamance
GRANDY Currituck
GRANITE FALLS Caldwell
GRANITE QUARRY Rowan
GRANTSBORO Pamlico
GRASSY CREEK Ashe
GRAYSON Ashe
GREENMOUNTAIN Yancey
GREENSBORO Guilford
GREENVILLE Pitt
GRIFTON (28530) Pitt(38), Craven(31),
    Lenoir(29), Greene(2)
GRIMESLAND (27837) Pitt(93), Beaufort(7)
GROVER Cleveland
GULF Chatham
GUMBERRY Northampton
HALIFAX Halifax
HALLSBORO Columbus
HAMILTON Martin
HAMLET Richmond
HAMPSTEAD Pender
HAMPTONVILLE (27020) Yadkin(81),
    Wilkes(20)
HARBINGER Currituck
HARKERS ISLAND Carteret
HARMONY (28634) Iredell(93), Davie(8)
HARRELLS (28444) Sampson(51),
    Bladen(47), Duplin(2)
HARRELLSVILLE Hertford
HARRIS Rutherford
HARRISBURG (28075) Cabarrus(98),
    Mecklenburg(2)
HASSELL Martin
HATTERAS Dare
HAVELOCK Craven
HAW RIVER Alamance
HAYESVILLE Clay
HAYS Wilkes
HAZELWOOD Haywood
HENDERSON (27536) Vance(97),
    Franklin(2)
HENDERSONVILLE Henderson
HENRICO (27842) Northampton(92),
    Warren(8)
HENRIETTA Rutherford
HERTFORD Perquimans
HICKORY (28601) Catawba(99),
    Caldwell(1)
HICKORY Catawba
HIDDENITE (28636) Alexander(96),
    Iredell(4)
HIGH POINT (27260) Guilford(99),
    Randolph(1)
HIGH POINT (27262) Guilford(93),
    Davidson(7)
HIGH POINT (27263) Randolph(61),
    Guilford(39)
HIGH POINT (27265) Guilford(77),
    Davidson(22), Forsyth(2)
HIGH POINT Guilford
HIGH SHOALS Gaston
HIGHFALLS Moore
HIGHLANDS Macon
HILDEBRAN Burke
HILLSBOROUGH (27278) Orange(96),
    Durham(4)
HOBBSVILLE (27946) Gates(94),
    Chowan(4), Perquimans(2)
HOBGOOD (27843) Halifax(81),
    Edgecombe(17), Martin(2)
HOBUCKEN Pamlico
HOFFMAN (28347) Richmond(92),
    Moore(8)
HOLLISTER Halifax
HOLLY RIDGE (28445) Onslow(58),
    Pender(41)
HOLLY SPRINGS Wake
HOOKERTON (28538) Greene(74),
    Lenoir(26)
HOPE MILLS Cumberland

HORSE SHOE Henderson
HOT SPRINGS Madison
HUBERT Onslow
HUDSON Caldwell
HUNTERSVILLE (28078) Mecklenburg(96),
    Cabarrus(3)
HUNTERSVILLE Mecklenburg
HURDLE MILLS (27541) Orange(54),
    Person(46)
HUSK Ashe
ICARD Burke
INDIAN TRAIL Union
INGOLD Sampson
IRON STATION Lincoln
IVANHOE (28447) Sampson(36),
    Pender(33), Bladen(32)
JACKSON Northampton
JACKSON SPRINGS (27281) Moore(59),
    Montgomery(41)
JACKSONVILLE Onslow
JAMESTOWN Guilford
JAMESVILLE Martin
JARVISBURG Currituck
JEFFERSON Ashe
JONAS RIDGE Burke
JONESVILLE Yadkin
JULIAN (27283) Guilford(84), Randolph(16)
KANNAPOLIS (28081) Cabarrus(63),
    Rowan(37)
KANNAPOLIS (28083) Cabarrus(73),
    Rowan(27)
KANNAPOLIS Cabarrus
KELFORD Bertie
KELLY Bladen
KENANSVILLE Duplin
KENLY (27542) Wilson(61), Johnston(39)
KERNERSVILLE (27284) Forsyth(93),
    Guilford(5), Davidson(2)
KERNERSVILLE Forsyth
KILL DEVIL HILLS Dare
KING Stokes
KINGS MOUNTAIN Cleveland
KINSTON Lenoir
KIPLING Harnett
KITTRELL (27544) Vance(80),
    Granville(13), Franklin(7)
KITTY HAWK Dare
KNIGHTDALE Wake
KNOTTS ISLAND Currituck
KURE BEACH New Hanover
LA GRANGE (28551) Lenoir(69),
    Wayne(28), Greene(3)
LAKE JUNALUSKA Haywood
LAKE LURE Rutherford
LAKE TOXAWAY Transylvania
LAKE WACCAMAW Columbus
LAKEVIEW Moore
LANDIS Rowan
LANSING Ashe
LASKER Northampton
LATTIMORE Cleveland
LAUREL HILL Scotland
LAUREL SPRINGS (28644) Ashe(88),
    Alleghany(12)
LAURINBURG Scotland
LAWNDALE Cleveland
LAWSONVILLE Stokes
LEASBURG Caswell
LEICESTER Buncombe
LELAND Brunswick
LEMON SPRINGS Lee
LENOIR (28645) Caldwell(98), Wilkes(2)
LENOIR Caldwell
LEWISTON WOODVILLE Bertie
LEWISVILLE Forsyth
LEXINGTON Davidson
LIBERTY (27298) Randolph(63),
    Alamance(27), Guilford(10), Catawba(1)
LILESVILLE Anson
LILLINGTON Harnett
LINCOLNTON Lincoln

LINDEN (28356) Cumberland(94),
    Harnett(6)
LINVILLE Avery
LINVILLE FALLS Burke
LINWOOD Davidson
LITTLE SWITZERLAND McDowell
LITTLETON (27850) Halifax(84),
    Warren(15)
LOCUST Stanly
LONGISLAND Catawba
LONGWOOD Brunswick
LOUISBURG Franklin
LOWELL Gaston
LOWGAP Surry
LOWLAND Pamlico
LUCAMA Wilson
LUMBER BRIDGE (28357) Hoke(55),
    Robeson(46)
LUMBERTON Robeson
LYNN Polk
MACCLESFIELD (27852) Wilson(49),
    Edgecombe(48), Pitt(3)
MACON Warren
MADISON (27025) Rockingham(92),
    Stokes(8)
MAGGIE VALLEY Haywood
MAGNOLIA (28453) Duplin(71),
    Sampson(29)
MAIDEN (28650) Catawba(99), Lincoln(1)
MAMERS Harnett
MANNS HARBOR Dare
MANSON (27553) Vance(98), Warren(2)
MANTEO Dare
MAPLE Currituck
MAPLE HILL (28454) Pender(80),
    Onslow(20)
MARBLE Cherokee
MARGARETTSVILLE Northampton
MARIETTA Robeson
MARION (28752) McDowell(99),
    Rutherford(1)
MARS HILL (28754) Madison(88),
    Yancey(12)
MARSHALL Madison
MARSHALLBERG Carteret
MARSHVILLE Union
MARSTON (28363) Scotland(52),
    Richmond(48)
MATTHEWS (28105) Mecklenburg(76),
    Union(24)
MATTHEWS Mecklenburg
MAURY Greene
MAXTON (28364) Robeson(85),
    Scotland(15)
MAYODAN Rockingham
MAYSVILLE (28555) Onslow(86),
    Jones(14)
MC ADENVILLE Gaston
MC FARLAN Anson
MC GRADY Wilkes
MC LEANSVILLE Guilford
MCCAIN Hoke
MCCUTCHEON FIELD Onslow
MEBANE (27302) Alamance(56),
    Orange(28), Caswell(16)
MERRITT Pamlico
MERRY HILL Bertie
MICAVILLE Yancey
MICRO Johnston
MIDDLEBURG Vance
MIDDLESEX (27557) Johnston(64),
    Nash(34), Wilson(1)
MIDLAND (28107) Cabarrus(94),
    Mecklenburg(5), Stanly(1)
MIDWAY PARK Onslow
MILL SPRING Polk
MILLERS CREEK Wilkes
MILTON Caswell
MILWAUKEE Northampton
MINERAL SPRINGS Union
MINNEAPOLIS Avery
MISENHEIMER Stanly

MOCKSVILLE Davie
MONCURE Chatham
MONROE Union
MONTREAT Avery
MONTREAT Buncombe
MOORESBORO (28114) Cleveland(51), Rutherford(49)
MOORESVILLE (28115) Iredell(94), Rowan(4), Mecklenburg(1)
MORAVIAN FALLS (28654) Wilkes(97), Alexander(3)
MOREHEAD CITY Carteret
MORGANTON Burke
MORRISVILLE (27560) Wake(97), Durham(3)
MORVEN Anson
MOUNT AIRY Surry
MOUNT GILEAD (27306) Montgomery(55), Richmond(45)
MOUNT HOLLY Gaston
MOUNT MOURNE Iredell
MOUNT OLIVE (28365) Wayne(66), Duplin(29), Sampson(5)
MOUNT PLEASANT (28124) Cabarrus(98), Stanly(2)
MOUNT ULLA (28125) Rowan(95), Iredell(5)
MOUNTAIN HOME Henderson
MOYOCK Currituck
MURFREESBORO (27855) Hertford(96), Northampton(4)
MURPHY Cherokee
NAGS HEAD Dare
NAKINA Columbus
NAPLES Henderson
NASHVILLE Nash
NEBO (28761) McDowell(99), Polk(1)
NEW BERN (28560) Craven(90), Pamlico(10)
NEW BERN (28562) Craven(97), Jones(3)
NEW BERN Craven
NEW HILL (27562) Wake(64), Chatham(33), Harnett(3)
NEW LONDON (28127) Stanly(87), Montgomery(11)
NEWELL Mecklenburg
NEWLAND (28657) Avery(87), Burke(13)
NEWPORT Carteret
NEWTON Catawba
NEWTON GROVE (28366) Sampson(82), Johnston(19)
NORLINA Warren
NORMAN Richmond
NORTH WILKESBORO Wilkes
NORTHSIDE Granville
NORWOOD Stanly
OAK CITY Martin
OAK ISLAND Brunswick
OAK RIDGE Guilford
OAKBORO Stanly
OCEAN ISLE BEACH Brunswick
OCRACOKE Hyde
OLD FORT McDowell
OLIN Iredell
OLIVIA Harnett
ORIENTAL Pamlico
ORRUM Robeson
OTTO Macon
OXFORD (27565) Granville(92), Vance(6), Person(1)
PALMYRA Halifax
PANTEGO Beaufort
PARKTON (28371) Robeson(72), Cumberland(27)
PARMELE Martin
PATTERSON Caldwell
PAW CREEK Mecklenburg
PEACHLAND (28133) Anson(76), Union(24)
PELHAM (27311) Caswell(96), Rockingham(4)
PEMBROKE Robeson

PENDLETON Northampton
PENLAND Mitchell
PENROSE Transylvania
PFAFFTOWN Forsyth
PIKEVILLE (27863) Wayne(65), Greene(35)
PILOT MOUNTAIN (27041) Surry(90), Stokes(10)
PINE HALL Stokes
PINE LEVEL Johnston
PINEBLUFF Moore
PINEHURST Moore
PINEOLA Avery
PINETOPS Edgecombe
PINETOWN Beaufort
PINEVILLE Mecklenburg
PINEY CREEK Alleghany
PINK HILL (28572) Duplin(92), Jones(5), Lenoir(2)
PINNACLE (27043) Stokes(58), Surry(42)
PISGAH FOREST Transylvania
PITTSBORO Chatham
PLEASANT GARDEN (27313) Guilford(53), Randolph(47)
PLEASANT HILL Northampton
PLUMTREE Avery
PLYMOUTH Washington
POINT HARBOR Currituck
POLKTON Anson
POLKVILLE Cleveland
POLLOCKSVILLE (28573) Jones(98), Craven(2)
POPE A F B Cumberland
POPLAR BRANCH Currituck
POTECASI Northampton
POWELLS POINT Currituck
POWELLSVILLE Bertie
PRINCETON (27569) Johnston(96), Wayne(4)
PROCTORVILLE Robeson
PROSPECT HILL Caswell
PROVIDENCE Caswell
PURLEAR Wilkes
RAEFORD Hoke
RALEIGH (27603) Wake(99), Johnston(2)
RALEIGH (27613) Wake(97), Durham(3)
RALEIGH Wake
RAMSEUR Randolph
RANDLEMAN (27317) Randolph(99), Guilford(1)
RED OAK Nash
RED SPRINGS (28377) Robeson(62), Hoke(38)
REIDSVILLE (27320) Rockingham(89), Caswell(11)
REIDSVILLE Rockingham
REX Robeson
RHODHISS (28667) Caldwell(93), Burke(7)
RICH SQUARE Northampton
RICHFIELD (28137) Rowan(53), Stanly(47)
RICHLANDS (28574) Onslow(95), Duplin(4), Jones(1)
RIDGECREST Buncombe
RIDGEWAY Warren
RIEGELWOOD (28456) Columbus(60), Bladen(30), Brunswick(10)
ROANOKE RAPIDS Halifax
ROARING GAP Alleghany
ROARING RIVER Wilkes
ROBBINS (27325) Moore(99), Randolph(1)
ROBBINSVILLE Graham
ROBERSONVILLE (27871) Pitt(83), Martin(17)
ROCKINGHAM Richmond
ROCKWELL (28138) Rowan(94), Cabarrus(6)
ROCKY MOUNT (27803) Nash(88), Wilson(12)
ROCKY MOUNT Edgecombe
ROCKY MOUNT Nash
ROCKY POINT Pender
RODANTHE Dare

RODUCO Gates
ROLESVILLE Wake
RONDA Wilkes
ROPER Washington
ROSE HILL (28458) Duplin(74), Sampson(27)
ROSEBORO (28382) Sampson(93), Cumberland(7)
ROSMAN Transylvania
ROUGEMONT (27572) Orange(43), Durham(35), Person(17), Granville(6)
ROWLAND Robeson
ROXBORO Person
ROXOBEL Bertie
RUFFIN Rockingham
RURAL HALL (27045) Forsyth(97), Stokes(3)
RURAL HALL Forsyth
RUTHERFORD COLLEGE Burke
RUTHERFORDTON (28139) Rutherford(98), Polk(2)
SAINT PAULS (28384) Robeson(88), Bladen(10), Cumberland(2)
SALEMBURG Sampson
SALISBURY Rowan
SALTER PATH Carteret
SALUDA (28773) Polk(95), Macon(5)
SALVO Dare
SANDY RIDGE Stokes
SANFORD (27330) Lee(91), Chatham(6), Harnett(2)
SANFORD Lee
SAPPHIRE (28774) Jackson(54), Transylvania(46)
SARATOGA Wilson
SAXAPAHAW Alamance
SCALY MOUNTAIN Macon
SCOTLAND NECK Halifax
SCOTTS Iredell
SCOTTVILLE Ashe
SCRANTON Hyde
SEABOARD (27876) Northampton(83), Pitt(17)
SEAGROVE (27341) Randolph(68), Moore(23), Montgomery(9)
SEALEVEL Carteret
SEDALIA Guilford
SELMA Johnston
SEMORA (27343) Person(99), Caswell(1)
SEVEN SPRINGS (28578) Wayne(71), Lenoir(16), Duplin(14)
SEVERN Northampton
SHALLOTTE Brunswick
SHANNON (28386) Robeson(56), Hoke(44)
SHARPSBURG (27878) Nash(96), Edgecombe(5)
SHAWBORO (27973) Currituck(69), Camden(31)
SHELBY Cleveland
SHERRILLS FORD (28673) Catawba(97), Lincoln(3)
SHILOH Camden
SILER CITY (27344) Chatham(97), Randolph(3)
SILOAM Surry
SIMPSON Pitt
SIMS (27880) Wilson(94), Nash(7)
SKYLAND Buncombe
SMITHFIELD Johnston
SMYRNA Carteret
SNEADS FERRY Onslow
SNOW CAMP (27349) Alamance(69), Chatham(32)
SNOW HILL (28580) Greene(99), Lenoir(1)
SOPHIA Randolph
SOUTH BRUNSWICK Brunswick
SOUTH MILLS Camden
SOUTHERN PINES Moore
SOUTHMONT Davidson
SOUTHPORT Brunswick
SPARTA Alleghany

SPEED Edgecombe
SPENCER Rowan
SPINDALE Rutherford
SPRING HOPE Nash
SPRING LAKE (28390) Cumberland(54), Harnett(47)
SPRUCE PINE Mitchell
STACY Carteret
STALEY (27355) Randolph(71), Chatham(29)
STANFIELD Stanly
STANLEY (28164) Gaston(82), Lincoln(18)
STANTONSBURG (27883) Wilson(66), Wayne(20), Greene(14)
STAR (27356) Montgomery(86), Moore(14)
STATE ROAD (28676) Wilkes(59), Surry(41)
STATESVILLE Iredell
STEDMAN Cumberland
STELLA (28582) Onslow(52), Carteret(48)
STEM Granville
STOKES Pitt
STOKESDALE (27357) Rockingham(80), Guilford(21)
STONEVILLE Rockingham
STONEWALL Pamlico
STONY POINT (28678) Alexander(98), Iredell(2)
STOVALL Granville
STUMPY POINT Dare
SUGAR GROVE Watauga
SUMMERFIELD (27358) Guilford(60), Rockingham(40)
SUNBURY Gates
SUNSET BEACH Brunswick
SUPPLY Brunswick
SWANNANOA Buncombe
SWANQUARTER Hyde
SWANSBORO (28584) Carteret(60), Onslow(40)
SWEPSONVILLE Alamance
SYLVA Jackson
TABOR CITY Columbus
TAPOCO Graham
TAR HEEL Bladen
TARAWA TERRACE Onslow
TARBORO Edgecombe
TAYLORSVILLE Alexander
TEACHEY Duplin
TERRELL Catawba
THOMASVILLE (27360) Davidson(95), Randolph(5)
THOMASVILLE Davidson
THURMOND (28683) Wilkes(86), Surry(14)
TILLERY Halifax
TIMBERLAKE (27583) Person(96), Orange(4)
TOAST Surry
TOBACCOVILLE (27050) Forsyth(84), Stokes(16)
TODD (28684) Watauga(55), Ashe(45)
TOPTON (28781) Macon(58), Cherokee(42)
TOWNSVILLE Vance
TRAPHILL Wilkes
TRENTON Jones
TRINITY Randolph
TRIPLETT Watauga
TROUTMAN Iredell
TROY (27371) Montgomery(75), Randolph(25)
TRYON Polk
TUCKASEGEE Jackson
TURKEY Sampson
TURNERSBURG Iredell
TUXEDO Henderson
TYNER (27980) Chowan(99), Perquimans(1)
UNION GROVE Iredell
UNION MILLS (28167) Rutherford(98), McDowell(2)
VALDESE Burke

VALE (28168) Lincoln(72), Catawba(28)
VALLE CRUCIS Watauga
VANCEBORO (28586) Craven(85), Pitt(9), Beaufort(7)
VANDEMERE Pamlico
VASS Moore
VAUGHAN Warren
VILAS Watauga
WACO Cleveland
WADE Cumberland
WADESBORO Anson
WAGRAM Scotland
WAKE FOREST (27587) Wake(94), Granville(4), Franklin(3)
WAKE FOREST Wake
WAKULLA Robeson
WALKERTOWN Forsyth
WALLACE (28466) Duplin(77), Pender(21), Sampson(2)
WALLBURG Davidson
WALNUT COVE (27052) Stokes(92), Forsyth(8)
WALSTONBURG (27888) Greene(72), Wilson(23), Pitt(6)
WANCHESE Dare

WARNE Clay
WARRENSVILLE Ashe
WARRENTON (27589) Warren(91), Franklin(9)
WARSAW Duplin
WASHINGTON (27889) Beaufort(97), Pitt(3)
WATHA Pender
WAVES Dare
WAXHAW Union
WAYNESVILLE Haywood
WEAVERVILLE (28787) Buncombe(94), Madison(6)
WEBSTER Jackson
WELCOME Davidson
WELDON Halifax
WENDELL (27591) Wake(87), Johnston(13)
WENTWORTH Rockingham
WEST END Moore
WEST JEFFERSON Ashe
WESTFIELD (27053) Stokes(97), Surry(3)
WHITAKERS (27891) Nash(85), Edgecombe(12), Halifax(2)

WHITE OAK (28399) Bladen(99), Cumberland(1)
WHITE PLAINS Surry
WHITEHEAD Alleghany
WHITEVILLE Columbus
WHITSETT Guilford
WHITTIER Jackson
WILBAR Wilkes
WILKESBORO Wilkes
WILLARD (28478) Pender(90), Sampson(10)
WILLIAMSTON Martin
WILLISTON Carteret
WILLOW SPRING (27592) Wake(60), Johnston(40)
WILMINGTON (28401) New Hanover(99), Pender(1)
WILMINGTON (28405) New Hanover(96), Pender(4)
WILMINGTON Brunswick
WILMINGTON New Hanover
WILSON (27896) Wilson(82), Nash(18)
WILSON Wilson
WILSONS MILLS Johnston
WINDSOR Bertie

WINFALL Perquimans
WINGATE Union
WINNABOW Brunswick
WINSTON SALEM (27107) Forsyth(75), Davidson(25)
WINSTON SALEM (27127) Forsyth(91), Davidson(9)
WINSTON SALEM Forsyth
WINSTON-SALEM Forsyth
WINTERVILLE Pitt
WINTON Hertford
WISE Warren
WOODLAND (27897) Northampton(81), Hertford(19)
WOODLEAF Rowan
WRIGHTSVILLE BEACH New Hanover
YADKINVILLE Yadkin
YANCEYVILLE Caswell
YOUNGSVILLE (27596) Franklin(88), Wake(9), Granville(3)
ZEBULON (27597) Wake(76), Franklin(19), Johnston(3), Nash(3)
ZIONVILLE (28698) Watauga(94), Ashe(6)
ZIRCONIA Henderson

ZIP/City Cross Reference

ZIP	City	ZIP	City	ZIP	City	ZIP	City
27006-27006	ADVANCE	27233-27233	CLIMAX	27357-27357	STOKESDALE	27563-27563	NORLINA
27007-27007	ARARAT	27235-27235	COLFAX	27358-27358	SUMMERFIELD	27564-27564	NORTHSIDE
27009-27009	BELEWS CREEK	27237-27237	CUMNOCK	27359-27359	SWEPSONVILLE	27565-27565	OXFORD
27010-27010	BETHANIA	27239-27239	DENTON	27360-27361	THOMASVILLE	27568-27568	PINE LEVEL
27011-27011	BOONVILLE	27242-27242	EAGLE SPRINGS	27370-27370	TRINITY	27569-27569	PRINCETON
27012-27012	CLEMMONS	27243-27243	EFLAND	27371-27371	TROY	27570-27570	RIDGEWAY
27013-27013	CLEVELAND	27244-27244	ELON COLLEGE	27373-27373	WALLBURG	27571-27571	ROLESVILLE
27014-27014	COOLEEMEE	27247-27247	ETHER	27374-27374	WELCOME	27572-27572	ROUGEMONT
27016-27016	DANBURY	27248-27248	FRANKLINVILLE	27375-27375	WENTWORTH	27573-27573	ROXBORO
27017-27017	DOBSON	27249-27249	GIBSONVILLE	27376-27376	WEST END	27576-27576	SELMA
27018-27018	EAST BEND	27251-27251	GLENDON	27377-27377	WHITSETT	27577-27577	SMITHFIELD
27019-27019	GERMANTON	27252-27252	GOLDSTON	27379-27379	YANCEYVILLE	27581-27581	STEM
27020-27020	HAMPTONVILLE	27253-27253	GRAHAM	27401-27499	GREENSBORO	27582-27582	STOVALL
27021-27021	KING	27256-27256	GULF	27501-27501	ANGIER	27583-27583	TIMBERLAKE
27022-27022	LAWSONVILLE	27258-27258	HAW RIVER	27502-27502	APEX	27584-27584	TOWNSVILLE
27023-27023	LEWISVILLE	27259-27259	HIGHFALLS	27503-27503	BAHAMA	27586-27586	VAUGHAN
27024-27024	LOWGAP	27260-27265	HIGH POINT	27504-27504	BENSON	27587-27588	WAKE FOREST
27025-27025	MADISON	27278-27278	HILLSBOROUGH	27505-27505	BROADWAY	27589-27589	WARRENTON
27027-27027	MAYODAN	27281-27281	JACKSON SPRINGS	27506-27506	BUIES CREEK	27591-27591	WENDELL
27028-27028	MOCKSVILLE	27282-27282	JAMESTOWN	27507-27507	BULLOCK	27592-27592	WILLOW SPRING
27030-27030	MOUNT AIRY	27283-27283	JULIAN	27508-27508	BUNN	27593-27593	WILSONS MILLS
27031-27031	WHITE PLAINS	27284-27285	KERNERSVILLE	27509-27509	BUTNER	27594-27594	WISE
27040-27040	PFAFFTOWN	27288-27289	EDEN	27510-27510	CARRBORO	27596-27596	YOUNGSVILLE
27041-27041	PILOT MOUNTAIN	27291-27291	LEASBURG	27511-27513	CARY	27597-27597	ZEBULON
27042-27042	PINE HALL	27292-27295	LEXINGTON	27514-27516	CHAPEL HILL	27599-27599	CHAPEL HILL
27043-27043	PINNACLE	27298-27298	LIBERTY	27518-27519	CARY	27601-27699	RALEIGH
27045-27045	RURAL HALL	27299-27299	LINWOOD	27520-27520	CLAYTON	27701-27722	DURHAM
27046-27046	SANDY RIDGE	27301-27301	MC LEANSVILLE	27521-27521	COATS	27801-27804	ROCKY MOUNT
27047-27047	SILOAM	27302-27302	MEBANE	27522-27522	CREEDMOOR	27805-27805	AULANDER
27048-27048	STONEVILLE	27305-27305	MILTON	27523-27523	EAGLE ROCK	27806-27806	AURORA
27049-27049	TOAST	27306-27306	MOUNT GILEAD	27524-27524	FOUR OAKS	27807-27807	BAILEY
27050-27050	TOBACCOVILLE	27310-27310	OAK RIDGE	27525-27525	FRANKLINTON	27808-27808	BATH
27051-27051	WALKERTOWN	27311-27311	PELHAM	27526-27526	FUQUAY VARINA	27809-27809	BATTLEBORO
27052-27052	WALNUT COVE	27312-27312	PITTSBORO	27529-27529	GARNER	27810-27810	BELHAVEN
27053-27053	WESTFIELD	27313-27313	PLEASANT GARDEN	27530-27534	GOLDSBORO	27811-27811	BELLARTHUR
27054-27054	WOODLEAF	27314-27314	PROSPECT HILL	27536-27536	HENDERSON	27812-27812	BETHEL
27055-27055	YADKINVILLE	27315-27315	PROVIDENCE	27540-27540	HOLLY SPRINGS	27813-27813	BLACK CREEK
27094-27099	RURAL HALL	27316-27316	RAMSEUR	27541-27541	HURDLE MILLS	27814-27814	BLOUNTS CREEK
27101-27199	WINSTON SALEM	27317-27317	RANDLEMAN	27542-27542	KENLY	27816-27816	CASTALIA
27201-27201	ALAMANCE	27320-27323	REIDSVILLE	27543-27543	KIPLING	27817-27817	CHOCOWINITY
27202-27202	ALTAMAHAW	27325-27325	ROBBINS	27544-27544	KITTRELL	27818-27818	COMO
27203-27204	ASHEBORO	27326-27326	RUFFIN	27545-27545	KNIGHTDALE	27819-27819	CONETOE
27207-27207	BEAR CREEK	27330-27331	SANFORD	27546-27546	LILLINGTON	27820-27820	CONWAY
27208-27208	BENNETT	27340-27340	SAXAPAHAW	27549-27549	LOUISBURG	27821-27821	EDWARD
27209-27209	BISCOE	27341-27341	SEAGROVE	27551-27551	MACON	27822-27822	ELM CITY
27212-27212	BLANCH	27342-27342	SEDALIA	27552-27552	MAMERS	27823-27823	ENFIELD
27213-27213	BONLEE	27343-27343	SEMORA	27553-27553	MANSON	27824-27824	ENGELHARD
27214-27214	BROWNS SUMMIT	27344-27344	SILER CITY	27555-27555	MICRO	27825-27825	EVERETTS
27215-27220	BURLINGTON	27349-27349	SNOW CAMP	27556-27556	MIDDLEBURG	27826-27826	FAIRFIELD
27228-27228	BYNUM	27350-27350	SOPHIA	27557-27557	MIDDLESEX	27827-27827	FALKLAND
27229-27229	CANDOR	27351-27351	SOUTHMONT	27559-27559	MONCURE	27828-27828	FARMVILLE
27230-27230	CEDAR FALLS	27355-27355	STALEY	27560-27560	MORRISVILLE	27829-27829	FOUNTAIN
27231-27231	CEDAR GROVE	27356-27356	STAR	27562-27562	NEW HILL	27830-27830	FREMONT

27831-27831	GARYSBURG	27938-27938	GATESVILLE	28091-28091	LILESVILLE	28357-28357	LUMBER BRIDGE
27832-27832	GASTON	27939-27939	GRANDY	28092-28093	LINCOLNTON	28358-28359	LUMBERTON
27833-27836	GREENVILLE	27941-27941	HARBINGER	28097-28097	LOCUST	28361-28361	MCCAIN
27837-27837	GRIMESLAND	27942-27942	HARRELLSVILLE	28098-28098	LOWELL	28362-28362	MARIETTA
27838-27838	GUMBERRY	27943-27943	HATTERAS	28101-28101	MC ADENVILLE	28363-28363	MARSTON
27839-27839	HALIFAX	27944-27944	HERTFORD	28102-28102	MC FARLAN	28364-28364	MAXTON
27840-27840	HAMILTON	27946-27946	HOBBSVILLE	28103-28103	MARSHVILLE	28365-28365	MOUNT OLIVE
27841-27841	HASSELL	27947-27947	JARVISBURG	28105-28106	MATTHEWS	28366-28366	NEWTON GROVE
27842-27842	HENRICO	27948-27948	KILL DEVIL HILLS	28107-28107	MIDLAND	28367-28367	NORMAN
27843-27843	HOBGOOD	27949-27949	KITTY HAWK	28108-28108	MINERAL SPRINGS	28368-28368	OLIVIA
27844-27844	HOLLISTER	27950-27950	KNOTTS ISLAND	28109-28109	MISENHEIMER	28369-28369	ORRUM
27845-27845	JACKSON	27953-27953	MANNS HARBOR	28110-28112	MONROE	28370-28370	PINEHURST
27846-27846	JAMESVILLE	27954-27954	MANTEO	28114-28114	MOORESBORO	28371-28371	PARKTON
27847-27847	KELFORD	27956-27956	MAPLE	28115-28115	MOORESVILLE	28372-28372	PEMBROKE
27848-27848	LASKER	27957-27957	MERRY HILL	28119-28119	MORVEN	28373-28373	PINEBLUFF
27849-27849	LEWISTON WOODVILLE	27958-27958	MOYOCK	28120-28120	MOUNT HOLLY	28374-28374	PINEHURST
27850-27850	LITTLETON	27959-27959	NAGS HEAD	28123-28123	MOUNT MOURNE	28375-28375	PROCTORVILLE
27851-27851	LUCAMA	27960-27960	OCRACOKE	28124-28124	MOUNT PLEASANT	28376-28376	RAEFORD
27852-27852	MACCLESFIELD	27962-27962	PLYMOUTH	28125-28125	MOUNT ULLA	28377-28377	RED SPRINGS
27853-27853	MARGARETTSVILLE	27964-27964	POINT HARBOR	28126-28126	NEWELL	28378-28378	REX
27854-27854	MILWAUKEE	27965-27965	POPLAR BRANCH	28127-28127	NEW LONDON	28379-28380	ROCKINGHAM
27855-27855	MURFREESBORO	27966-27966	POWELLS POINT	28128-28128	NORWOOD	28382-28382	ROSEBORO
27856-27856	NASHVILLE	27967-27967	POWELLSVILLE	28129-28129	OAKBORO	28383-28383	ROWLAND
27857-27857	OAK CITY	27968-27968	RODANTHE	28130-28130	PAW CREEK	28384-28384	SAINT PAULS
27858-27858	GREENVILLE	27969-27969	RODUCO	28133-28133	PEACHLAND	28385-28385	SALEMBURG
27859-27859	PALMYRA	27970-27970	ROPER	28134-28134	PINEVILLE	28386-28386	SHANNON
27860-27860	PANTEGO	27972-27972	SALVO	28135-28135	POLKTON	28387-28388	SOUTHERN PINES
27861-27861	PARMELE	27973-27973	SHAWBORO	28136-28136	POLKVILLE	28390-28390	SPRING LAKE
27862-27862	PENDLETON	27974-27974	SHILOH	28137-28137	RICHFIELD	28391-28391	STEDMAN
27863-27863	PIKEVILLE	27976-27976	SOUTH MILLS	28138-28138	ROCKWELL	28392-28392	TAR HEEL
27864-27864	PINETOPS	27978-27978	STUMPY POINT	28139-28139	RUTHERFORDTON	28393-28393	TURKEY
27865-27865	PINETOWN	27979-27979	SUNBURY	28144-28147	SALISBURY	28394-28394	VASS
27866-27866	PLEASANT HILL	27980-27980	TYNER	28150-28152	SHELBY	28395-28395	WADE
27867-27867	POTECASI	27981-27981	WANCHESE	28159-28159	SPENCER	28396-28396	WAGRAM
27868-27868	RED OAK	27982-27982	WAVES	28160-28160	SPINDALE	28398-28398	WARSAW
27869-27869	RICH SQUARE	27983-27983	WINDSOR	28163-28163	STANFIELD	28399-28399	WHITE OAK
27870-27870	ROANOKE RAPIDS	27985-27985	WINFALL	28164-28164	STANLEY	28401-28412	WILMINGTON
27871-27871	ROBERSONVILLE	27986-27986	WINTON	28166-28166	TROUTMAN	28420-28420	ASH
27872-27872	ROXOBEL	28001-28002	ALBEMARLE	28167-28167	UNION MILLS	28421-28421	ATKINSON
27873-27873	SARATOGA	28006-28006	ALEXIS	28168-28168	VALE	28422-28422	BOLIVIA
27874-27874	SCOTLAND NECK	28007-28007	ANSONVILLE	28169-28169	WACO	28423-28423	BOLTON
27875-27875	SCRANTON	28009-28009	BADIN	28170-28170	WADESBORO	28424-28424	BRUNSWICK
27876-27876	SEABOARD	28010-28010	BARIUM SPRINGS	28173-28173	WAXHAW	28425-28425	BURGAW
27877-27877	SEVERN	28012-28012	BELMONT	28174-28174	WINGATE	28428-28428	CAROLINA BEACH
27878-27878	SHARPSBURG	28016-28016	BESSEMER CITY	28201-28299	CHARLOTTE	28429-28429	CASTLE HAYNE
27879-27879	SIMPSON	28017-28017	BOILING SPRINGS	28301-28306	FAYETTEVILLE	28430-28430	CERRO GORDO
27880-27880	SIMS	28018-28018	BOSTIC	28307-28307	FORT BRAGG	28431-28431	CHADBOURN
27881-27881	SPEED	28019-28019	CAROLEEN	28308-28308	POPE A F B	28432-28432	CLARENDON
27882-27882	SPRING HOPE	28020-28020	CASAR	28309-28309	FAYETTEVILLE	28433-28433	CLARKTON
27883-27883	STANTONSBURG	28021-28021	CHERRYVILLE	28310-28310	FORT BRAGG	28434-28434	COUNCIL
27884-27884	STOKES	28023-28023	CHINA GROVE	28311-28314	FAYETTEVILLE	28435-28435	CURRIE
27885-27885	SWANQUARTER	28024-28024	CLIFFSIDE	28315-28315	ABERDEEN	28436-28436	DELCO
27886-27886	TARBORO	28025-28027	CONCORD	28318-28318	AUTRYVILLE	28438-28438	EVERGREEN
27887-27887	TILLERY	28031-28031	CORNELIUS	28319-28319	BARNESVILLE	28439-28439	FAIR BLUFF
27888-27888	WALSTONBURG	28032-28032	CRAMERTON	28320-28320	BLADENBORO	28441-28441	GARLAND
27889-27889	WASHINGTON	28033-28033	CROUSE	28323-28323	BUNNLEVEL	28442-28442	HALLSBORO
27890-27890	WELDON	28034-28034	DALLAS	28325-28325	CALYPSO	28443-28443	HAMPSTEAD
27891-27891	WHITAKERS	28036-28036	DAVIDSON	28326-28326	CAMERON	28444-28444	HARRELLS
27892-27892	WILLIAMSTON	28037-28037	DENVER	28327-28327	CARTHAGE	28445-28445	HOLLY RIDGE
27893-27896	WILSON	28038-28038	EARL	28328-28329	CLINTON	28446-28446	INGOLD
27897-27897	WOODLAND	28039-28039	EAST SPENCER	28330-28330	CORDOVA	28447-28447	IVANHOE
27906-27909	ELIZABETH CITY	28040-28040	ELLENBORO	28331-28331	CUMBERLAND	28448-28448	KELLY
27910-27910	AHOSKIE	28041-28041	FAITH	28332-28332	DUBLIN	28449-28449	KURE BEACH
27915-27915	AVON	28042-28042	FALLSTON	28333-28333	DUDLEY	28450-28450	LAKE WACCAMAW
27916-27916	AYDLETT	28043-28043	FOREST CITY	28334-28335	DUNN	28451-28451	LELAND
27917-27917	BARCO	28051-28056	GASTONIA	28337-28337	ELIZABETHTOWN	28452-28452	LONGWOOD
27919-27919	BELVIDERE	28070-28070	HUNTERSVILLE	28338-28338	ELLERBE	28453-28453	MAGNOLIA
27920-27920	BUXTON	28071-28071	GOLD HILL	28339-28339	ERWIN	28454-28454	MAPLE HILL
27921-27921	CAMDEN	28072-28072	GRANITE QUARRY	28340-28340	FAIRMONT	28455-28455	NAKINA
27922-27922	COFIELD	28073-28073	GROVER	28341-28341	FAISON	28456-28456	RIEGELWOOD
27923-27923	COINJOCK	28074-28074	HARRIS	28342-28342	FALCON	28457-28457	ROCKY POINT
27924-27924	COLERAIN	28075-28075	HARRISBURG	28343-28343	GIBSON	28458-28458	ROSE HILL
27925-27925	COLUMBIA	28076-28076	HENRIETTA	28344-28344	GODWIN	28459-28459	SHALLOTTE
27926-27926	CORAPEAKE	28077-28077	HIGH SHOALS	28345-28345	HAMLET	28460-28460	SNEADS FERRY
27927-27927	COROLLA	28078-28078	HUNTERSVILLE	28347-28347	HOFFMAN	28461-28461	SOUTHPORT
27928-27928	CRESWELL	28079-28079	INDIAN TRAIL	28348-28348	HOPE MILLS	28462-28462	SUPPLY
27929-27929	CURRITUCK	28080-28080	IRON STATION	28349-28349	KENANSVILLE	28463-28463	TABOR CITY
27930-27930	DURANTS NECK	28081-28083	KANNAPOLIS	28350-28350	LAKEVIEW	28464-28464	TEACHEY
27932-27932	EDENTON	28086-28086	KINGS MOUNTAIN	28351-28351	LAUREL HILL	28465-28465	OAK ISLAND
27935-27935	EURE	28088-28088	LANDIS	28352-28353	LAURINBURG	28466-28466	WALLACE
27936-27936	FRISCO	28089-28089	LATTIMORE	28355-28355	LEMON SPRINGS	28467-28467	CALABASH
27937-27937	GATES	28090-28090	LAWNDALE	28356-28356	LINDEN	28468-28468	SUNSET BEACH

28469-28469	OCEAN ISLE BEACH	28584-28584	SWANSBORO	28665-28665	PURLEAR	28734-28734	FRANKLIN
28470-28470	SOUTH BRUNSWICK	28585-28585	TRENTON	28666-28666	ICARD	28735-28735	GERTON
28471-28471	WATHA	28586-28586	VANCEBORO	28667-28667	RHODHISS	28736-28736	GLENVILLE
28472-28472	WHITEVILLE	28587-28587	VANDEMERE	28668-28668	ROARING GAP	28737-28737	GLENWOOD
28478-28478	WILLARD	28589-28589	WILLISTON	28669-28669	ROARING RIVER	28738-28738	HAZELWOOD
28479-28479	WINNABOW	28590-28590	WINTERVILLE	28670-28670	RONDA	28739-28739	HENDERSONVILLE
28480-28480	WRIGHTSVILLE BEACH	28594-28594	EMERALD ISLE	28671-28671	RUTHERFORD COLLEGE	28740-28740	GREENMOUNTAIN
28501-28504	KINSTON	28601-28603	HICKORY	28672-28672	SCOTTVILLE	28741-28741	HIGHLANDS
28508-28508	ALBERTSON	28604-28604	BANNER ELK	28673-28673	SHERRILLS FORD	28742-28742	HORSE SHOE
28509-28509	ALLIANCE	28605-28605	BLOWING ROCK	28674-28674	NORTH WILKESBORO	28743-28743	HOT SPRINGS
28510-28510	ARAPAHOE	28606-28606	BOOMER	28675-28675	SPARTA	28744-28744	FRANKLIN
28511-28511	ATLANTIC	28607-28608	BOONE	28676-28676	STATE ROAD	28745-28745	LAKE JUNALUSKA
28512-28512	ATLANTIC BEACH	28609-28609	CATAWBA	28677-28677	STATESVILLE	28746-28746	LAKE LURE
28513-28513	AYDEN	28610-28610	CLAREMONT	28678-28678	STONY POINT	28747-28747	LAKE TOXAWAY
28515-28515	BAYBORO	28611-28611	COLLETTSVILLE	28679-28679	SUGAR GROVE	28748-28748	LEICESTER
28516-28516	BEAUFORT	28612-28612	CONNELLYS SPRINGS	28680-28680	MORGANTON	28749-28749	LITTLE SWITZERLAND
28518-28518	BEULAVILLE	28613-28613	CONOVER	28681-28681	TAYLORSVILLE	28750-28750	LYNN
28519-28519	BRIDGETON	28615-28615	CRESTON	28682-28682	TERRELL	28751-28751	MAGGIE VALLEY
28520-28520	CEDAR ISLAND	28616-28616	CROSSNORE	28683-28683	THURMOND	28752-28752	MARION
28521-28521	CHINQUAPIN	28617-28617	CRUMPLER	28684-28684	TODD	28753-28753	MARSHALL
28522-28522	COMFORT	28618-28618	DEEP GAP	28685-28685	TRAPHILL	28754-28754	MARS HILL
28523-28523	COVE CITY	28619-28619	DREXEL	28687-28687	STATESVILLE	28755-28755	MICAVILLE
28524-28524	DAVIS	28621-28621	ELKIN	28688-28688	TURNERSBURG	28756-28756	MILL SPRING
28525-28525	DEEP RUN	28622-28622	ELK PARK	28689-28689	UNION GROVE	28757-28757	MONTREAT
28526-28526	DOVER	28623-28623	ENNICE	28690-28690	VALDESE	28758-28758	MOUNTAIN HOME
28527-28527	ERNUL	28624-28624	FERGUSON	28691-28691	VALLE CRUCIS	28760-28760	NAPLES
28528-28528	GLOUCESTER	28625-28625	STATESVILLE	28692-28692	VILAS	28761-28761	NEBO
28529-28529	GRANTSBORO	28626-28626	FLEETWOOD	28693-28693	WARRENSVILLE	28762-28762	OLD FORT
28530-28530	GRIFTON	28627-28627	GLADE VALLEY	28694-28694	WEST JEFFERSON	28763-28763	OTTO
28531-28531	HARKERS ISLAND	28628-28628	GLEN ALPINE	28697-28697	WILKESBORO	28765-28765	PENLAND
28532-28532	HAVELOCK	28629-28629	GLENDALE SPRINGS	28698-28698	ZIONVILLE	28766-28766	PENROSE
28533-28533	CHERRY POINT	28630-28630	GRANITE FALLS	28699-28699	SCOTTS	28768-28768	PISGAH FOREST
28537-28537	HOBUCKEN	28631-28631	GRASSY CREEK	28701-28701	ALEXANDER	28770-28770	RIDGECREST
28538-28538	HOOKERTON	28633-28633	LENOIR	28702-28702	ALMOND	28771-28771	ROBBINSVILLE
28539-28539	HUBERT	28634-28634	HARMONY	28704-28704	ARDEN	28772-28772	ROSMAN
28540-28541	JACKSONVILLE	28635-28635	HAYS	28705-28705	BAKERSVILLE	28773-28773	SALUDA
28542-28542	CAMP LEJEUNE	28636-28636	HIDDENITE	28707-28707	BALSAM	28774-28774	SAPPHIRE
28543-28543	TARAWA TERRACE	28637-28637	HILDEBRAN	28708-28708	BALSAM GROVE	28775-28775	SCALY MOUNTAIN
28544-28544	MIDWAY PARK	28638-28638	HUDSON	28709-28709	BARNARDSVILLE	28776-28776	SKYLAND
28545-28545	MCCUTCHEON FIELD	28640-28640	JEFFERSON	28710-28710	BAT CAVE	28777-28777	SPRUCE PINE
28546-28546	JACKSONVILLE	28641-28641	JONAS RIDGE	28711-28711	BLACK MOUNTAIN	28778-28778	SWANNANOA
28547-28547	CAMP LEJEUNE	28642-28642	JONESVILLE	28712-28712	BREVARD	28779-28779	SYLVA
28551-28551	LA GRANGE	28643-28643	LANSING	28713-28713	BRYSON CITY	28781-28781	TOPTON
28552-28552	LOWLAND	28644-28644	LAUREL SPRINGS	28714-28714	BURNSVILLE	28782-28782	TRYON
28553-28553	MARSHALLBERG	28645-28645	LENOIR	28715-28715	CANDLER	28783-28783	TUCKASEGEE
28554-28554	MAURY	28646-28646	LINVILLE	28716-28716	CANTON	28784-28784	TUXEDO
28555-28555	MAYSVILLE	28647-28647	LINVILLE FALLS	28717-28717	CASHIERS	28786-28786	WAYNESVILLE
28556-28556	MERRITT	28649-28649	MC GRADY	28718-28718	CEDAR MOUNTAIN	28787-28787	WEAVERVILLE
28557-28557	MOREHEAD CITY	28650-28650	MAIDEN	28719-28719	CHEROKEE	28788-28788	WEBSTER
28560-28564	NEW BERN	28651-28651	MILLERS CREEK	28720-28720	CHIMNEY ROCK	28789-28789	WHITTIER
28570-28570	NEWPORT	28652-28652	MINNEAPOLIS	28721-28721	CLYDE	28790-28790	ZIRCONIA
28571-28571	ORIENTAL	28653-28653	MONTEZUMA	28722-28722	COLUMBUS	28791-28793	HENDERSONVILLE
28572-28572	PINK HILL	28654-28654	MORAVIAN FALLS	28723-28723	CULLOWHEE	28801-28816	ASHEVILLE
28573-28573	POLLOCKSVILLE	28655-28655	MORGANTON	28724-28724	DANA	28901-28901	ANDREWS
28574-28574	RICHLANDS	28656-28656	NORTH WILKESBORO	28725-28725	DILLSBORO	28902-28902	BRASSTOWN
28575-28575	SALTER PATH	28657-28657	NEWLAND	28726-28726	EAST FLAT ROCK	28903-28903	CULBERSON
28577-28577	SEALEVEL	28658-28658	NEWTON	28727-28727	EDNEYVILLE	28904-28904	HAYESVILLE
28578-28578	SEVEN SPRINGS	28659-28659	NORTH WILKESBORO	28728-28728	ENKA	28905-28905	MARBLE
28579-28579	SMYRNA	28660-28660	OLIN	28729-28729	ETOWAH	28906-28906	MURPHY
28580-28580	SNOW HILL	28661-28661	PATTERSON	28730-28730	FAIRVIEW	28909-28909	WARNE
28581-28581	STACY	28662-28662	PINEOLA	28731-28731	FLAT ROCK		
28582-28582	STELLA	28663-28663	PINEY CREEK	28732-28732	FLETCHER		
28583-28583	STONEWALL	28664-28664	PLUMTREE	28733-28733	FONTANA DAM		

North Dakota

General Help Numbers:

Governor's Office
State Capitol   701-328-2200
600 E Boulevard Ave, 1st Floor   Fax 701-328-2205
Bismarck, ND 58505-0001   8AM-5PM
http://www.governor.state.nd.us

Attorney General's Office
State Capitol - Dept 125   701-328-2210
600 E Boulevard Ave   Fax 701-328-3535
Bismarck, ND 58505-0040   8AM-5PM
http://www.ag.state.nd.us

State Court Administrator
North Dakota Supreme Court   701-328-4216
600 E Blvd Ave, Dept 180   Fax 701-328-4480
Bismarck, ND 58505-0530   8AM-5PM
http://www.court.state.nd.us

State Archives
State Archives &   701-328-2666
  Historical Research Library   Fax 701-328-3710
N Dakota Heritage Center, 612 E Blvd Ave   8AM-5PM
Bismarck, ND 58505-0830
http://www.state.nd.us/hist/sal.htm

State Specifics:

Capital: Bismark
                 Burleigh County

Time Zone: CST

Number of Counties: 53

Population: 642,200

Web Site: http://discovernd.com

State Agencies

Criminal Records

Bureau of Criminal Investigation, PO Box 1054, Bismarck, ND 58502-1054 (Courier: 4205 N State St, Bismarck, ND 58501); 701-328-5500, 701-328-5510 (Fax), 8AM-5PM.

http://www.state.nd.us/ndag

Indexing & Storage: Records are available from 1930 to present. New records are available for inquiry immediately. Records are indexed on computer.

Searching: Must have a signed release from person of record or a current address. Subject will be notified of the request. Only convictions will be released. Charges that are dismissed or sealed are not released. Include the following in your request- name, date of birth, Social Security Number.

Access by: mail, in person.

Fee & Payment: The search fee is $20.00 per name. Fee payee: ND Attorney General.

Prepayment required. Personal checks accepted. No credit cards accepted.

Mail search: Turnaround time: 3 to 5 days. No self addressed stamped envelope is required.

In person search: Turnaround time while you wait.

Corporation Records
Limited Liability Company Records
Limited Partnership Records
Trademarks/Servicemarks
Fictitious Name
Assumed Name

Secretary of State, Business Information/ Registration, 600 E Boulevard Ave, Dept 108, Bismarck, ND 58505-0500; 701-328-4284, 800-352-0867, 701-328-2992 (Fax), 8AM-5PM.

http://www.state.nd.us/sec

Indexing & Storage: Records are available from 1890's on. Records are computerized since 1989. Records inactive prior to 1989 are maintained by state archives, and may take as long as two weeks to search. Records are indexed on index cards, inhouse computer.

Searching: Include the following in your request-full name of business. In addition to the articles of incorporation, corporation records include the following information: Annual Reports, Officers, Directors, DBAs, Prior (merged) names, Inactive names, and Reserved names. The following data is not released: financial information.

Access by: mail, phone, fax, in person, online.

Fee & Payment: There is a search fee of $5.00 if a written confirmation is required or if data must be retrieved from the archives. Copies cost $1.00 for each 4 pages or fraction thereof. Certification is an additional $15.00. Fee payee: Secretary of State. Prepayment required. Personal checks accepted. Credit cards accepted: MasterCard, Visa, Discover.

Mail search: Turnaround time: 3 to 5 days. No self addressed stamped envelope is required.

Phone search: There is no fee for verbal confirmation on an active record, otherwise there is a $5.00 fee.

Fax search: Same fees as phone searching. Turnaround time is 1-3 days if written confirmation required. Add $1.00 per page for fax results.

In person search: No fee on active records, $5.00 fee on inactive records or if in archives. Turnaround time is while you wait.

Online search: The Secretary of State's registered business database may be viewed at the Internet for no charge. Records include corporations, limited liability companies, limited partnerships, limited liability partnerships, limited liability limited partnerships, partnership fictitious names, trade names, trademarks, and real estate investment trusts. The database includes all active records and those records inactivated within the past twelve months. Access by the first few words of a business name, by any significant word in a business name, or by the System ID number assigned to the record.

Other access: The state provides a database purchase program. Costs are $35.00 per database and processing fees vary for type of media.

Uniform Commercial Code
Federal Tax Liens
State Tax Liens

UCC Division, Secretary of State, 600 E Boulevard Ave Dept 108, Bismarck, ND 58505-

0500; 701-328-3662, 701-328-4214 (Fax), 8AM-5PM.

http://www.state.nd.us/sec

Note: The state has a Central Indexing System which allows UCC and tax lien searches at this office or at any of the county Register of Deeds (53).

Indexing & Storage: Records are available from 1966. Records are computerized on index statewide since 1992. Records are indexed on inhouse computer.

Searching: Use search request form UCC-11. Include the following in your request-debtor name.

Access by: mail, phone, fax, in person, online.

Fee & Payment: The search fee is $7.00 for the first 5 entries and $2.00 for each additional 5 entries or fraction thereof. A copy request with certificate is $7.00 for first 3 copies and $2.00 for each additional. All tax liens will show on the record request. Fee payee: Secretary of State. Will invoice, if requested. Monthly billing is offered to ongoing requesters. Personal checks accepted. Credit cards accepted: MasterCard, Visa.

Mail search: Turnaround time: 1 day. A self addressed stamped envelope is requested.

Phone search: General information is available without charge.

Fax search: There is an additional fee of $3.00 (maximum 20 pages). Please allow 20 minutes to 1 hour.

In person search: You may request information in person.

Online search: There is a limited free publ;ic search and a commercial system for professionals. Sign-up for access to the Central Indexing System includes an annual subscription $120 fee and a one-time $50.00 registration fee. The $7.00 fee applies, but documents will not be certified. Searches include UCC-11 information listing and farm product searches.

Sales Tax Registrations

State Tax Commission, Sales & Special Tax Division, State Capitol, 600 E Boulevard Ave, Bismarck, ND 58505-0599; 701-328-3470, 701-328-3700 (Fax), 8AM-5PM.

http://www.state.nd.us/taxdpt

Indexing & Storage: Records are available from 1995 to present. Records are computer indexed from 1995 to present.

Searching: This agency will only confirm if a business is registered and active. They will provide no other information as it is confidential. Include the following in your request-business name. They will also search by tax permit number or owner name.

Access by: mail, phone, fax.

Mail search: Turnaround time: 7 to 10 days. A self addressed stamped envelope is requested. No fee for mail request.

Phone search: No fee for telephone request.

Fax search: There is no fee.

Birth Certificates

ND Department of Health, Vital Records, State Capitol, 600 E Blvd, Dept 301, Bismarck, ND 58505-0200; 701-328-2360, 701-328-1850 (Fax), 7:30AM-5PM.

http://www.health.state.nd.us/ndhd/admin/vital

Indexing & Storage: Records are available from 1870 on. New records are available for inquiry immediately. Records are indexed on inhouse computer.

Searching: Must have a signed release from person of record if it is an out-of-wedlock birth. If under 18, parent or legal guardian signature needed. Include the following in your request-full name, names of parents, mother's maiden name, date of birth, place of birth, relationship to person of record, reason for information request.

Access by: mail, fax, in person, online.

Fee & Payment: The fee is $7.00 per name. Add $4.00 per name for second copies. Fee payee: North Dakota Department of Health. Prepayment required. Personal checks accepted. Credit cards accepted: MasterCard, Visa, AmEx, Discover.

Mail search: Turnaround time: 3 to 4 days. No self addressed stamped envelope is required.

Fax search: Use of credit card required. Turnaround time is same day if received by 10AM and request is marked for FedEx or UPS.

In person search: Turnaround time is less than 15 minutes.

Online search: Records may be ordered online from the Internet site, $7.00 per name.

Expedited service: Expedited service is available for fax or online searches. Turnaround time: overnight delivery. Expedited service options are available using a credit card and additional $15.00 fee for shipping.

Death Records

ND Department of Health, Vital Records, State Capitol, 600 E Blvd, Dept 301, Bismarck, ND 58505-0200; 701-328-2360, 701-328-1850 (Fax), 7:30AM-5PM.

http://www.health.state.nd.us/ndhd/admin/vital

Indexing & Storage: Records are available from 1881 on. Early records are few. New records are available for inquiry immediately. Records are indexed on inhouse computer.

Searching: Cause of death not shown on copy of Death Certificate if not a family member. Include the following in your request-full name, date of death, place of death, relationship to person of record, reason for information request.

Access by: mail, fax, in person, online.

Fee & Payment: The fee is $5.00 per name. Add $2.00 per name for second copies. Fee payee: North Dakota Department of Health. Prepayment required. Personal checks accepted. Credit cards accepted: MasterCard, Visa, AmEx, Discover.

Mail search: Turnaround time: 2 to 3 days. A self addressed stamped envelope is requested.

Fax search: This is considered expedited service. Turnaround time is same day if received by 10AM noon and request is marked for FedEx or UPS.

In person search: Turnaround time is 10 to 15 minutes.

Online search: Records may be ordered from the Internet site, $7.00 per name.

Expedited service: Expedited service is available for fax searches. Turnaround time: overnight delivery. Expedited service options are available using a credit card and for additional $15.00 fee indicated for shipping.

Marriage Certificates

ND Department of Health, Vital Records, State Capitol, 600 E Blvd, Dept 301, Bismarck, ND 58505-0200; 701-328-2360, 701-328-1850 (Fax), 7:30AM-5PM.

http://www.health.state.nd.us/ndhd/admin/vital

Indexing & Storage: Records are available from July 1, 1925 to present. New records are available for inquiry immediately. Records are indexed on inhouse computer.

Searching: Include the following in your request-names of husband and wife, date of marriage, place or county of marriage, relationship to person of record, reason for information request, wife's maiden name.

Access by: mail, fax, in person, online.

Fee & Payment: The fee is $5.00 per name. Add $2.00 per name for second copies. Add $5.00 if credit card used. Fee payee: North Dakota Department of Health. Prepayment required. Personal checks accepted. Credit cards accepted: MasterCard, Visa, AmEx, Discover.

Mail search: Turnaround time: 3 to 4 days. No self addressed stamped envelope is required.

Fax search: Turnaround time is same day if received by 10 AM and request is being returned by FedEx or UPS.

In person search: Turnaround time is 10 to 15 minutes.

Online search: Records may be ordered over the Internet, $7.00 per name.

Expedited service: Expedited service is available for fax or online searches. Turnaround time: overnight delivery. Expedited service options are available using a credit card ($5.00 additional fee) and an additional $15.00 fee.

Divorce Records

Access to Records is Restricted

ND Department of Health, Vital Records, State Capitol, 600 E Blvd, Dept 301, Bismarck, ND 58505-0200; 701-328-2360.

Note: The State has an index to direct people to which county has the records. The index contains records from July 1, 1949 to present. Call or e-mail to vitalrec@state.nd.us.

Workers' Compensation Records

ND Workers Compensation, 500 E Front Ave, Bismarck, ND 58504-5685; 701-328-3800, 800-777-5033, 701-328-3820 (Fax), 8AM-5PM.

http://www.ndworkerscomp.com

Indexing & Storage: Records are available from 1919 but more reliable information is from 1975 on. It takes 24 hours before new records are available for inquiry. Records are indexed on inhouse computer.

Searching: Must have a signed release from person of record stating exactly what information is requested. Include the following in your request-claimant name, Social Security Number, date of birth. Also, a signed release by the subject is required, unless the requester is involved within the case.

Access by: mail.

Fee & Payment: Copies are $.35 per page. There is no search fee, unless file needs to be retrieved from off-site, then $5.00 is charged. Fee payee:

Worker's Compensation Bureau. Prepayment required. Personal checks accepted.

Mail search: Turnaround time: 5 days. A self addressed stamped envelope is requested.

Driver Records

Department of Transportation, Driver License & Traffic Safety Division, 608 E Boulevard Ave, Bismarck, ND 58505-0780; 701-328-2603, 701-328-2435 (Fax), 8AM-5PM.

http://www.state.nd.us/dot

Note: Copies of tickets must be obtained from the local courts.

Indexing & Storage: Records are available for 3 years for moving violations, DWI and suspensions. Records available to the public will show neither violations less than 2 points nor accidents. The record will not show the driver's address to casual requesters without consent. It takes 1 day before new records are available for inquiry.

Searching: The Division sends an additional copy of the abstract to the driver whose record was requested, accompanied by a statement identifying the requester. The driver's license number, name, and DOB are required when ordering, but "two out of three" may produce a "hit."

Access by: mail, in person, online.

Fee & Payment: The fee is $3.00 per record. Fee payee: Driver License & Traffic Safety. Prepayment required. Personal checks accepted. Credit cards accepted: MasterCard, Visa.

Mail search: Turnaround time: 3 days. A self addressed stamped envelope is requested.

In person search: Up to eight requests will be processed while you wait.

Online search: The system is interactive and is open 24 hours daily. Fee is $3.00 per record, requester must be approved. For more information, call 701-328-4790.

Other access: Magnetic tape ordering is available for high volume users. Bulk requests of mailing list data (names, DOBs and addresses, except opt outs) are charged a rate of $9.00 per thousand names, minimum $250.00 for approved vendors.

Vehicle Ownership
Vehicle Identification

Department of Transportation, Records Section/Motor Vehicle Div., 608 E Boulevard Ave, Bismarck, ND 58505-0780; 701-328-2725, 701-328-4156 (TTY:), 701-328-3500 (Fax), 8AM-4:50PM.

http://www.state.nd.us/dot

Note: Records on mobile homes are also maintained by this agency.

Indexing & Storage: Records are available from 1911 for license plate numbers. It takes 10 to 14 days before new records are available for inquiry.

Searching: Records are available with the prior authorization. Personal information is not released to casual requesters without consent. A written request or use of Form SFN-2963 is required. The following data is not released: Social Security Numbers or medical records.

Access by: mail, in person.

Fee & Payment: The fee is $3.00 per record (includes lien data). There is a fee for a no record found. Fee payee: Motor Vehicle Division.

Prepayment required. Personal checks accepted. Credit cards accepted: MasterCard, Visa.

Mail search: Turnaround time: 3 days. A self addressed stamped envelope is requested.

In person search: The state may limit the number of requests processed immediately, if busy.

Other access: North Dakota offers bulk or batch retrieval of VIN or ownership information of vehicles. The requester must explain purpose and intent; however, there are no restrictions placed upon requests of a legal nature. Customized or special runs are available.

Accident Reports

Driver License & Traffic Safety Division, CRASH Records Section, 608 E Boulevard Ave, Bismarck, ND 58505-0780; 701-328-4397, 701-328-2601, 701-328-2435 (Fax), 8AM-5PM.

http://www.state.nd.us/dot

Indexing & Storage: Records are available from 1994. Records are computer indexed since 1993.

Searching: The front page which includes drivers, witnesses, and insurance information, can be ordered by anyone with a written request. The investigating officer's report is also only to parties involved or their legal representative or insurer. Include the following in your request-date of accident, location of accident, full name of at least one driver, reason for information request.

Access by: mail, in person.

Fee & Payment: Fee is $3.00 for front page record (drivers, witnesses, etc.). Add $5.00 to receive the investigating officer's report. Fee payee: Driver License & Traffic Safety Division. Prepayment required. Personal checks accepted. Credit cards accepted: MasterCard, Visa.

Mail search: Turnaround time: 5 days. A self addressed stamped envelope is requested.

In person search: Turnaround time while you wait.

Other access: Each request is reviewed. Cost is $9.00 per thousand records.

Vessel Ownership
Vessel Registration

North Dakota Game & Fish Department, 100 N Bismarck Expressway, Bismarck, ND 58501; 701-328-6335, 701-328-6352 (Fax), 8AM-5PM.

http://www.state.nd.us/gnf

Note: Liens are filed at same locations as UCCs.

Indexing & Storage: Records are available from 1975 to present. Records are computer indexed for the last five years. All motorized boat must be registered. No titles are issued.

Searching: To search, one of the following is required: hull ID #, registration #, decal #, or name.

Access by: mail, phone, fax, in person, online.

Fee & Payment: There is no fee for 1-2 names.

Mail search: Turnaround time: 1 day. No self addressed stamped envelope is required.

Phone search: Records are available by phone.

Fax search: Results can be faxed, mailed, or phoned.

In person search: Turnaround time is usually immediate.

Online search: There is a free public inquiry system on the home page. One can also search lottery hunting permit applications.

Other access: A printed list is available of all registered vessels.

Legislation Records

North Dakota Legislative Council, State Capitol, 600 E Boulevard Ave, Bismarck, ND 58505; 701-328-2916, 701-328-2900 (Secretary of State), 701-328-2992 (Sec of State fax), 8AM-5PM.

http://www.state.nd.us/lr

Note: Copies of "enrolled bills" are found at the Secretary of State's office (as well as online); search fee is $1.00 for each 4 pages. The legislature meets every odd year.

Indexing & Storage: Records are available from 1889 on. Records are on microfiche from 1969 to 2001, and computerized from 1997 forward. Records are indexed on inhouse computer, hard copy.

Searching: Include the following in your request-bill number.

Access by: mail, phone, fax, in person, online.

Fee & Payment: Fees is $1.00 for each 4 pages (through Sec of State). Fee payee: Secretary of State. Prepayment required. Personal checks accepted. Credit cards accepted: MasterCard, Visa, Discover.

Mail search: Turnaround time: 1 to 2 days. No self addressed stamped envelope is required.

Phone search: You may call for information.

Fax search: Fax to Secretary of State.

In person search: You may request information in person.

Online search: Their Internet site offers an extensive array of legislative information at no charge, including proposed and enacted legislation since 1997. Also, one may e-mail requests for information.

Voter Registration

Records not maintained by a state level agency.

Note: Records are maintained at the county level by the County Auditors. Records are open to the public.

GED Certificates

Department of Public Instruction, GED Testing, 600 E Blvd Ave, Bismarck, ND 58505-0440; 701-328-2393, 701-328-4770 (Fax), 8AM-4:30PM.

http://www.dpi.state.nd.us

Searching: A verification will only verify that a test was taken, but not if the subject passed the test. Include the following in your request-signed release, Social Security Number, date of birth.

Access by: mail, fax, in person, online.

Fee & Payment: There is no fee for a verification and a $2.00 fee for a copy of a transcript. Fee payee: Dept of Public Instruction. Prepayment required. Personal checks accepted. No credit cards accepted.

Mail search: Turnaround time: 1 week. No self addressed stamped envelope is required.

Fax search: Used only for verification.

In person search: Picture ID required.

Online search: One may request records via e-mail at JMarcell@mail.dpi.state.nd.us. There is no fee, unless a transcript is ordered.

Hunting License Information
Fishing License Information

ND Game & Fish Department, 100 N Bismarck Expressway, Bismarck, ND 58501-5095; 701-328-6300, 701-328-6335 (Licensing), 701-328-6352 (Fax), 8AM-5PM.

http://www.state.nd.us/gnf

Indexing & Storage: Records are available from 1992 on computer. Big Game Lottery Permits are only available for the current season. Records are indexed on inhouse computer.

Searching: Include the following in your request-full name, date of birth, Social Security Number. This agency also registers boats.

Access by: mail, fax, in person, online.

Fee & Payment: There is no search fee.

Mail search: Turnaround time: 1 to 3 days. A self addressed stamped envelope is requested.

Fax search: Same criteria as mail searches.

In person search: You can go in and access their records. They also make the boat registrations available.

Online search: One can search to see if a person has been chosen (lottery) for a specific hunt or passed hunter safety.

Other access: They sell mailing lists. Call Paul Schadewald at 701-328-6328 for more information.

North Dakota State Licensing Agencies

Licenses Searchable Online

Asbestos Abatement Contractor/Worker #27.............. www.health.state.nd.us/ndhd/environ/ee/rad/asb/

Asbestos Abatement Inspector/Monitor/Supervisor #27www.health.state.nd.us/ndhd/environ/ee/rad/asb/

Asbestos Abatement Project Planner/Designer #27..... www.health.state.nd.us/ndhd/environ/ee/rad/asb/

Attorney #41 .... www.court.state.nd.us/court/lawyers/index/frameset.htm

Bank #20 .... www.state.nd.us/dfi/Bank List.htm

Charitable Solicitation #39 .... www.state.nd.us/sec/charitableorganizationsearch.htm

Collection Agency #20 .... www.state.nd.us/dfi/Collection Agencies.htm

Consumer Finance Company #20 .... www.state.nd.us/dfi/Finance Companies.htm

Contractor/General Contractor #39 .... www.state.nd.us/sec/contractorsearch.htm

Credit Union #20... www.state.nd.us/dfi/Credit Union List.htm

Livestock Auction Market #19 .... www.agdepartment.com/Services.html

Livestock Dealer/Agent #19.................................... www.agdepartment.com/Services.html

Lobbyist #39... www.state.nd.us/sec/RegLobbyists/lobbyistregmnu.htm

Medical Doctor #47... www.docboard.org/nd/

Money Broker Firm #20 .... www.state.nd.us/dfi/Money Brokers.htm

Optometrist #49... http://home.ctctel.com/ndsbopt/ods.htm

Pesticide Applicator/Dealer #19 .... www.ag.ndsu.nodak.edu/aginfo/pesticid/cert_info.htm

Physician Assistant #47... www.docboard.org/nd/

Public Accountant-CPA #42 .... www.state.nd.us/ndsba/

Public Accounting Firm #42 .... www.state.nd.us/ndsba/

Trust Company #20.. www.state.nd.us/dfi/Trust Companies.htm

Licensing Quick Finder

Abstractor/Abstractor Company #01 701-947-2446
Addiction Counselor #04 701-255-1439
Adoption Service #22 701-328-4805
Aerial Applicator #30 701-328-9650
Aircraft Dealer #30 701-328-9650
Aircraft Registration #30 701-328-9650
Alcoholic Beverage Control #3............... 701-328-2329
Amusement Device, Coin-Operated #3 . 701-328-2329
Architect #43.. 701-223-3184
Asbestos Abatement Contractor #27..... 701-328-5188
Asbestos Abatement Inspector/Monitor/Supervisor #27
.... 701-328-5188
Asbestos Abatement Project Planner/Designer #27....
.... 701-328-5188
Asbestos Worker #27 701-328-5188
Athletic Trainer #05 701-857-5286
Attorney #41 701-328-4201
Auction Clerk #34................................. 701-328-4097
Auctioneer #34..................................... 701-328-4097
Bank #20 701-328-9933
Barber #06... 701-523-3327
Barber Shop #06................................... 701-523-3327
Boxer/Boxing Professional #38.............. 701-328-3665
Broker, Corporate #28 701-328-3548
Charitable Solicitation #39 701-328-3665
Check Seller #20 701-328-9933
Chiropractor #07 701-352-1690
Coal Mine, Surface #34 701-328-4096
Collection Agency #20........................... 701-328-9933
Consumer Finance Company #20......... 701-328-9933
Contractor/General Contractor #39 701-328-3665
Cosmetologist/Cosmetologist Instructor #08..............
.... 701-224-9800
Counselor, Professional #09................. 701-667-5969
Credit Union #20.................................. 701-328-9933
Crematorium #44 701-662-2511

Day Care Service #22 701-328-4809
Debt Collector #20................................ 701-328-9933
Dental Assistant #10............................ 701-224-1815
Dental Hygienist #10............................ 701-224-1815
Dentist #10.. 701-224-1815
Dietitian/Nutritionist #11...................... 701-746-9171
Drug Mfg., Wholesale #14 701-328-9535
Electrician #25 701-328-9522
Electrician Apprentice #25.................... 701-328-9522
Embalmer #44...................................... 701-662-2511
Employment Agency (Permanent Placing) #23..........
.... 701-328-2660
Engineer #36.. 701-258-0786
Engineer/Land Surveyor #36 701-258-0786
Esthetician #08 701-224-9800
Fireworks, Wholesale #03 701-328-2329
Fishing Guide #26................................. 701-328-6300
Foster Care Program #22 701-328-3587
Fund Raiser, Professional #39............... 701-328-3665
Funeral Director #44............................. 701-662-2511
Funeral Home #44 701-662-2511
Gaming #03 701-328-2329
Gaming Distributor/Manufacturer #03 ... 701-328-2329
Grain Buyer #34 701-328-4097
Grain Warehouse #34 701-328-4097
Hearing Aid Dealer/Fitter #45 701-237-9977
Hunting Guide #26................................ 701-328-6300
Hunting/Fishing Guide Combo #26 701-328-6300
Insurance Agency/Agent #28................ 701-328-3548
Insurance Broker #28 701-328-3548
Investment Advisor #40 701-328-2910
Kickboxer #38 701-328-3665
Laboratory Clinician #53....................... 701-224-1815
Land Surveyor #36................................ 701-258-0786
Livestock Auction Market #19 701-328-4756
Livestock Dealer/Agent #19.................. 701-328-4756

Lobbyist #39 701-328-3665
Manicurist #08 701-224-9800
Massage Therapist #46......................... 701-255-1525
Medical Doctor #47............................... 701-328-6500
Money Broker Firm #20 701-328-9933
Mortician #44 701-662-2511
Notary Public #39................................. 701-328-2901
Nurse Assistant #31.............................. 701-328-9780
Nurse-LPN/RN #31 701-328-9777
Nursing Home Administrator #13 701-222-4867
Nutritionist #11.................................... 701-746-9171
Occupational Therapist #48 701-250-0847
Oil & Gas Broker #40 701-328-2910
Oil & Gas Wellhead Welder #40 701-328-2910
Optometrist #49 701-225-9333
Osteopathic Physician #47 701-328-6500
Pesticide Applicator/Dealer #19 701-231-7180
Pharmacist/Pharmacy #14.................... 701-328-9535
Physical Therapist/Assistant #51 701-352-0125
Physician Assistant #47........................ 701-328-6500
Plumber Journeyman/Apprentice/Master #32............
.... 701-328-9977
Podiatrist #15....................................... 701-258-8120
Polygraph Examiner #03 701-328-2329
Private Investigation Agency #33........... 701-222-3063
Private Investigator #33......................... 701-222-3063
Psychologist #16.................................. 701-777-2044
Public Accountant-CPA #42................... 701-775-7100
Public Accounting Firm #42 701-775-7100
Racing #03 701-328-4633
Real Estate Agent/Broker #35 701-328-9749
Respiratory Care Practitioner #37 701-222-1564
School Counselor/Designate #24............ 701-328-2260
School Media Specialist #24.................. 701-328-2260
School Principal/Assistant #24............... 701-328-2260
School Superintendent/Assistant #24.... 701-328-2260

Securities Agent/Dealer #40 701-328-2910	Taxidermist #26 701-328-6300	Waste Water System Operator #21.......701-328-6628
Security Employee #33.........................701-222-2063	Teacher #24 701-328-2260	Water Conditioning Contractor/Installer #32 ....
Security Provider/Company #33 701-222-3063	Telecommunications Personnel #34 701-328-4076	701-328-9977
Sewer & Water Contractor/Installer #32 701-328-9977	Tobacco, Retail/Wholesale #03 701-328-2329	Water Distribution System Operator #21 701-328-6628
Social Worker #18................................701-222-0255	Transient Merchant #03........................701-328-2329	Water Well Driller #50 701-328-2754
Soil Classifier #17...............................701-225-3381	Trust Company #20...............................701-328-9933	Water Well Pump & Pitless Unit #50 701-328-2754
Speech-Language Pathologist/Audiologist #12..........	Veterinarian #29...................................701-328-9540	Weather Modifier #02 701-328-2788
....701-777-4421	Veterinary Technician #29 701-328-9540	Well Contractor, Monitoring #50...........701-328-2754

Licensing Agency Information

#01 Abstractors Board of Examiners, PO Box 551, New Rockford, ND 58356; 701-947-2446, Fax: 701-947-2443.

#02 Atmospheric Resource Board, Water Commission, 900 E Boulevard Ave, Bismarck, ND 58505; 701-328-4940, Fax: 701-328-4749. http://water.swc.state.nd.us

#03 Attorney General's Office, 600 E Boulevard Ave, Dept 125, Bismarck, ND 58505-0240; 701-328-2210, Fax: 701-328-3535. www.ag.state.nd.us/buslic/bli.html

#04 Board of Addiction Counseling Examiners, PO Box 975, Bismarck, ND 58502-0975; 701-255-1439, Fax: 701-224-9824.

#05 Board of Athletic Trainers, PO Box 5020, Minot, ND 58702; 701-857-5286, Fax: 701-857-5694.

#06 Board of Barber Examiners, PO Box 885, Bowman, ND 58623; 701-523-3327, Fax: 701-574-3126.

#07 c/o Jerry Blanchard, PO Box 185, Grafton, ND 58237; 701-352-1690, Fax: 701-352-2258.

#08 Board of Cosmetology, PO Box 2177, Bismarck, ND 58502; 701-224-9800, Fax: 701-222-8756.

#09 Board of Counselor Examiners, 2112 10th Av SE, Mandan, ND 58554-5066; 701-667-5969. www.sendit.nodak.edu/ndbce/

#10 Board of Dental Examiners, PO Box 7246, Bismarck, ND 58507-7246; 701-224-1815, Fax: 701-224-9824. www.nddentalboard.org

#11 Board of Dietetic Practice, PO Box 6142, Grand Forks, ND 58206-6142; 701-777-2539, Fax: 701-777-3268.

#12 Board of Examiners in Audiology/Speech Pathology, 720 4th St N, Fargo, ND 58122; 701-777-4421, Fax: 701-777-4365.

#13 Board of Examiners in Nursing Home Administrators, 1900 N 11th St, Bismarck, ND 58501-1914; 701-222-4867, Fax: 701-223-0977.

#14 Board of Pharmacy, PO Box 1354, Bismarck, ND 58502-1354; 701-328-9535, Fax: 701-258-9312.

#15 Dr. Hofsommer, 2631 12th Ave S, Fargo, ND 58103-2354; 701-258-8120.

#16 University of North Dakota - Psychology Department, PO Box 8380, Grand Forks, ND 58202-8380; 701-777-2044, Fax: 701-777-3454. www.health.state.nd.us/gov/boards/boards.htm

#17 Board of Registry for Professional Soil Classifier, 2493 4th Ave W, Dickinson, ND 58601; 701-225-3381.

#18 Board of Social Worker Examiners, PO Box 914, Bismarck, ND 58502-0914; 701-224-1815, Fax: 701-224-9824. www.aptnd.com/ndbswe

#19 Department of Agriculture, 600 E Boulevard Ave,Dept 602, Bismarck, ND 58505-0020; 701-328-2231, Fax: 701-328-4567. www.state.nd.us/agr Direct web site URL to search for licensees: www.state.nd.us/agr. You can search online using name

#20 Department of Banking & Financial Institutions, 2000 Schaefer St #G, Bismarck, ND 58501-1204; 701-328-9933, Fax: 701-328-9955. www.state.nd.us/dfi

#21 Department of Health, 1200 Missouri Av, Bismarck, ND 58506-5520; 701-328-6628, Fax: 701-328-6206.

#22 Department of Human Services, 600 E Boulevard Ave, Bismarck, ND 58505-0250; 701-328-2310, Fax: 701-328-2359.

#23 Department of Labor, 600 E Blvd Ave, Dept 406, Bismarck, ND 58505-0340; 701-328-2660, Fax: 701-328-2031. www.state.nd.us/labor

#24 Department of Public Instruction, 600 E Boulevard Ave, 1st Fl-Judicial Wing, Bismarck, ND 58505-0440; 701-328-2260, Fax: 701-328-2461. www.dpi.state.ns.us

#25 Electrical Board, PO Box 857, Bismarck, ND 58502; 701-328-9522, Fax: 701-328-9524.

#26 Game & Fish Department, 100 N Bismarck Exprwy, Bismarck, ND 58501-5095; 701-328-6300, Fax: 701-328-6352. www.state.nd.us/gnf/

#27 Department of Health, PO Box 5520 (1200 Missouri Ave), Bismarck, ND 58506-5520; 701-328-5188, Fax: 701-328-5200. www.health.state.nd.us/ndhd/environ/ee/rad/asb/ Direct web site URL to search for licensees: www.health.state.nd.us/ndhd/environ/ee/rad/asb/. You can search online using alphabetical list

#28 Insurance Department, 600 E Boulevard Ave, Capitol Bldg, 1st Fl, Bismarck, ND 58505-0320; 701-328-2440, Fax: 701-328-4880. www.state.nd.us/ndins/prodinfo/license.html

#29 Veterinarian Examining Board, PO Box 5001, Bismarck, ND 58502-5001; 701-328-9540, Fax: 701-224-0435.

#30 Aeronautics Commission, PO Box 5020, Bismarck, ND 58502-5020; 701-328-9650, Fax: 701-328-9656. www.state.nd.us/ndaero

#31 Board of Nursing, 919 S 7th St #504, Bismarck, ND 58504-5881; 701-328-9777, Fax: 701-328-9785. www.ndbon.org

#32 Plumbing Board, 204 W Thayer Av, Bismarck, ND 58501; 701-328-9977, Fax: 701-328-9979.

#33 Private Investigation & Security Board, 513 E Bismarck Expy, #5, Bismarck, ND 58504-6577; 701-222-3063, Fax: 701-222-3063.

#34 Public Service Commission, 600 E Boulevard Ave, Dept 408, Bismarck, ND 58505-0480; 701-328-4097, Fax: 701-328-2410. www.psc.state.nd.us

#35 Real Estate Commission, PO Box 727, Bismarck, ND 58502-0727; 701-328-9749, Fax: 701-328-9750.

#36 Registration for Prof. Engineers & Land Surveyors, PO Box 1357, Bismarck, ND 58502-1357; 701-258-0786, Fax: 701-258-7471.

#37 Respiratory Care Examining Board, PO Box 2223, Bismarck, ND 58502; 701-222-1564, Fax: 701-255-9149.

#38 Secretary of State, 600 E Blvd Ave, Dept 108, Bismarck, ND 58505-0040; 701-328-2900, Fax: 701-328-1690. www.state.nd.us/sec

#39 Secretary of State, 600 East Blvd Av, Dept 108, Bismarck, ND 58505-0500; 701-328-3665, Fax: 701-328-1690. www.state.nd.us/sec/ Direct web site URL to search for licensees: www.state.nd.us/sec/administrativelicencing.htm. You can search online using name, license number, business name.

#40 Securities Commissioner, 600 E Blvd Ave, Dept 414, State Capitol, 5th Fl, Bismarck, ND 58505-0510; 701-328-2910, Fax: 701-255-3113. www.state.nd.us/securities

#41 Bar Board, 600 E Boulevard Ave, Dept. 180, Bismarck, ND 58505-0530; 701-328-4201, Fax: 701-328-4480. www.court.state.nd.us Direct web site URL to search for licensees: www.court.state.nd.us/court/lawyers/index/frames et.htm. You can search online using alphabetical list or name finder

#42 Board of Accountancy, 2701 S Columbia Rd, Grand Forks, ND 58201-6029; 800-532-5904, Fax: 701-775-7430.

www.state.nd.us/ndsba
Direct web site URL to search for licensees: www.state.nd.us/ndsba. You can search online using first or last name and city

#43 Board of Architects, 419 E Brandon Dr, Bismarck, ND 58501-0410; 701-223-3184, Fax: 701-223-8154.

#44 Board of Funeral Service, PO Box 633, Devil's Lake, ND 58201; 701-662-2511, Fax: 701-662-2501.

#45 Board of Examiners for Hearing Instrument Dispensers, 825 25th St SW, Fargo, ND 58103; 701-237-9977.

#46 Richard Radspinner, 104 Georgia, Bismarck, ND 58504; 701-255-1525.

#47 Board of Medical Examiners, 418 E. Broadway #12, Bismarck, ND 58501; 701-328-6500, Fax: 701-328-6505.
www.ndbomex.com
Direct web site URL to search for licensees: www.sdofnd.com/cart/ndbomex/Search%20Page.a sp. You can search online using last name or license #

#48 Board of Occupational Therapy Practice, PO Box 4005, Bismarck, ND 58502-4005; 701-250-0847, Fax: 701-224-9824.
www.aptnd.com/ndsbot

#49 Board of Optometry, 341 1st St E, Dickinson, ND 58601; 701-483-9141, Fax: 701-483-9501.
http://home.ctctel.com/ndsbopt
Direct web site URL to search for licensees: http://home.ctctel.com/ndsbopt/ods.htm. You can search online using alphabetical list.

#50 Board of Water Well Contractors, 900 E Boulevard Ave, Bismarck, ND 58505; 701-328-2754, Fax: 701-328-3696.

#51 Examining Committee of Physical Therapists, PO Box 69, Grafton, ND 58237; 701-352-0125, Fax: 701-352-3093.

#53 Board of Clinical Laboratory Practice, PO Box 4103, Bismarck, ND 58502-4103; 701-224-1815, Fax: 701-224-9824.

North Dakota Federal Courts

The following list indicates the district and division name for each county in the state. If the bankruptcy court location is different from the district court, then the location of the bankruptcy court appears in parentheses.

County/Court Cross Reference

County	Court
Adams	Bismarck-Southwestern (Fargo)
Barnes	Fargo-Southeastern (Fargo)
Benson	Grand Forks-Northeastern (Fargo)
Billings	Bismarck-Southwestern (Fargo)
Bottineau	Minot-Northwestern (Fargo)
Bowman	Bismarck-Southwestern (Fargo)
Burke	Minot-Northwestern (Fargo)
Burleigh	Bismarck-Southwestern (Fargo)
Cass	Fargo-Southeastern (Fargo)
Cavalier	Grand Forks-Northeastern (Fargo)
Dickey	Fargo-Southeastern (Fargo)
Divide	Minot-Northwestern (Fargo)
Dunn	Bismarck-Southwestern (Fargo)
Eddy	Fargo-Southeastern (Fargo)
Emmons	Bismarck-Southwestern (Fargo)
Foster	Fargo-Southeastern (Fargo)
Golden Valley	Bismarck-Southwestern (Fargo)
Grand Forks	Grand Forks-Northeastern (Fargo)
Grant	Bismarck-Southwestern (Fargo)
Griggs	Fargo-Southeastern (Fargo)
Hettinger	Bismarck-Southwestern (Fargo)
Kidder	Bismarck-Southwestern (Fargo)
La Moure	Fargo-Southeastern (Fargo)
Logan	Bismarck-Southwestern (Fargo)
McHenry	Minot-Northwestern (Fargo)
McIntosh	Bismarck-Southwestern (Fargo)
McKenzie	Minot-Northwestern (Fargo)
McLean	Bismarck-Southwestern (Fargo)
Mercer	Bismarck-Southwestern (Fargo)
Morton	Bismarck-Southwestern (Fargo)
Mountrail	Minot-Northwestern (Fargo)
Nelson	Grand Forks-Northeastern (Fargo)
Oliver	Bismarck-Southwestern (Fargo)
Pembina	Grand Forks-Northeastern (Fargo)
Pierce	Minot-Northwestern (Fargo)
Ramsey	Grand Forks-Northeastern (Fargo)
Ransom	Fargo-Southeastern (Fargo)
Renville	Minot-Northwestern (Fargo)
Richland	Fargo-Southeastern (Fargo)
Rolette	Minot-Northwestern (Fargo)
Sargent	Fargo-Southeastern (Fargo)
Sheridan	Minot-Northwestern (Fargo)
Sioux	Bismarck-Southwestern (Fargo)
Slope	Bismarck-Southwestern (Fargo)
Stark	Bismarck-Southwestern (Fargo)
Steele	Fargo-Southeastern (Fargo)
Stutsman	Fargo-Southeastern (Fargo)
Towner	Grand Forks-Northeastern (Fargo)
Traill	Grand Forks-Northeastern (Fargo)
Walsh	Grand Forks-Northeastern (Fargo)
Ward	Minot-Northwestern (Fargo)
Wells	Minot-Northwestern (Fargo)
Williams	Minot-Northwestern (Fargo)

US District Court

District of North Dakota

Bismarck-Southwestern Division PO

Box 1193, Bismarck, ND 58502 (Courier Address: 220 E Rosser Ave, Room 476, Bismarck, ND 58501), 701-530-2300, Fax: 701-530-2312.

http://www.ndd.uscourts.gov

Counties: Adams, Billings, Bowman, Burleigh, Dunn, Emmons, Golden Valley, Grant, Hettinger, Kidder, Logan, McIntosh, McLean, Mercer, Morton, Oliver, Sioux, Slope, Stark.

Indexing/Storage: Cases are indexed by defendant and plaintiff as well as by case number. New cases are available in the index 24 hours after filing date. A computer index is maintained. Records are on computer and stored as hard copy records. Open records are located at this court.

Fee & Payment: The fee is $20.00 per item (one party name or case number). Payment may be made by money order, cashier check, in-state business check. In state personal checks are also accepted. Court will bill for copies. Payee: Clerk, US District Court. Certification fee: $7.00 per document. Copy fee: $.50 per page.

Phone Search: Only docket information is available by phone.

Mail Search: A stamped self addressed envelope is not required.

In Person: In person searching is available.

PACER: Sign-up number is 800-676-6856. Access fee is $.60 per minute. Toll-free access: 800-407-4453. Local access: 701-530-2367. Case records are available back to October 1990. Records are never purged. New records are available online after 1 day.

Fargo-Southeastern Division PO Box

870, Fargo, ND 58107 (Courier Address: 655 1st Ave N, Fargo, ND 58102), 701-297-7000, Fax: 701-297-7005.

http://www.ndd.uscourts.gov

Counties: Barnes, Cass, Dickey, Eddy, Foster, Griggs, La Moure, Ransom, Richland, Sargent, Steele, Stutsman. Rolette County cases prior to 1995 may be located here.

Indexing/Storage: Cases are indexed by defendant and plaintiff as well as by case number. New cases are available in the index 1 day after filing date. Both computer and card indexes are maintained. Civil cases prior to 10/90 are on index cards as well as all criminal records. Current records are on computer and stored as hard copy records. Open records are located at this court.

Fee & Payment: The fee is $20.00 per item (one party name or case number). Payment may be made by money order, cashier check, in-state business check. In state personal checks are also accepted. Prepayment is required. Payee: Clerk,

US District Court. Certification fee: $7.00 per document. Copy fee: $.50 per page.

Phone Search: Only docket information is available by phone.

Fax Search: Will accept fax search request, but results are held until payment received. Will fax results at $.50 per page paid in advance.

Mail Search: A stamped self addressed envelope is not required.

In Person: In person searching is available.

PACER: Sign-up number is 800-676-6856. Access fee is $.60 per minute. Toll-free access: 800-407-4453. Local access: 701-530-2367. Case records are available back to October 1990. Records are never purged. New records are available online after 1 day.

Grand Forks-Northeastern Division c/o

Fargo-Southeastern Division, 102 N 4th St, Grand Forks, ND 58201 (Courier Address: 655 1st Ave N, Fargo, ND 58102), 701-772-0511, Fax: 701-746-7544.

http://www.ndd.uscourts.gov

Counties: Benson, Cavalier, Grand Forks, Nelson, Pembina, Ramsey, Towner, Traill, Walsh.

Indexing/Storage: Cases are indexed by as well as by case number. New cases are available in the index after filing date. Open records are located at the Division.

Fee & Payment: The fee is no charge per item (one party name or case number). Payment may be made by money order, cashier check. Business checks are not accepted. Personal checks are not accepted.

Phone Search: Searching is not available by phone.

Mail Search: A stamped self addressed envelope is not required.

In Person: In person searching is available.

PACER: Sign-up number is 800-676-6856. Access fee is $.60 per minute. Toll-free access: 800-407-4453. Local access: 701-530-2367. Case records are available back to October 1990. Records are never purged. New records are available online after 1 day.

Minot-Northwestern Division c/o

Bismarck Division, PO Box 1193, Bismarck, ND 58502 (Courier Address: 100 1st St SW, Minot, ND 58701), 701-839-6251, Fax: 701-838-3267.

http://www.ndd.uscourts.gov

Counties: Bottineau, Burke, Divide, McHenry, McKenzie, Mountrail, Pierce, Renville, Rolette, Sheridan, Ward, Wells, Williams. Case records from Rolette County prior to 1995 may be located in Fargo-Southeastern Division.

Indexing/Storage: Cases are indexed by as well as by case number. New cases are available in the index after filing date. Open records are located at the Division.

Fee & Payment: The fee is no charge per item (one party name or case number). Payment may be made by money order, cashier check. Business checks are not accepted. Personal checks are not accepted.

Phone Search: Searching is not available by phone.

Mail Search: A stamped self addressed envelope is not required.

In Person: In person searching is available.

PACER: Sign-up number is 800-676-6856. Access fee is $.60 per minute. Toll-free access: 800-407-4453. Local access: 701-530-2367. Case records are available back to October 1990. Records are never purged. New records are available online after 1 day.

US Bankruptcy Court

District of North Dakota

Fargo Division 655 1st Ave N #210, Fargo,

ND 58102-4932 (Courier Address: Room 236, Federal Bldg & US Courthouse, Fargo, ND 58102), 701-297-7104.

http://www.ndb.uscourts.gov

Counties: All counties in North Dakota.

Indexing/Storage: Cases are indexed by debtor as well as by case number. New cases are available in the index 1 day after filing date. A computer index is maintained. Open records are located at this court.

Fee & Payment: The fee is $20.00 per item (one party name or case number). Payment may be made by money order, cashier check, business check. Personal checks are not accepted. Prepayment is required. Exemplification costs $10.00 per document. The court will FAX in an emergency for $.50 per page sending or receiving. Payee: Clerk, US Bankruptcy Court. Certification fee: $7.00 per document. Copy fee: $.50 per page.

Phone Search: Only docket information available by telephone. An automated voice case information service (VCIS) is available.

Mail Search: A stamped self addressed envelope is not required.

In Person: In person searching is available.

PACER: Sign-up number is 800-676-6856. Access fee is $.60 per minute. Toll-free access: 800-810-4092. Local access: 701-297-7164. Case records are available back to 1990. New civil records are available online after 1 day. PACER is available online at http://pacer.okwd.uscourts.gov.

Other Online Access: Search records on the Internet using RACER at https://racer.ndb.uscourts.gov/perl/bkplog.html. Access fee is 7 cents per page.

North Dakota County Courts

Court	Jurisdiction	No. of Courts	How Organized
District Courts*	General	53	7 Judicial Districts
Municipal Courts	Municipal	76	76 Cities

* Profiled in this Sourcebook.

CIVIL									
Court	Tort	Contract	Real Estate	Min. Claim	Max. Claim	Small Claims	Estate	Eviction	Domestic Relations
District Courts*	X	X	X	$0	No Max	$5000	X	X	X
Municipal Courts									

CRIMINAL					
Court	Felony	Misdemeanor	DWI/DUI	Preliminary Hearing	Juvenile
District Courts*	X	X	X	X	X
Municipal Courts			X		

ADMINISTRATION   State Court Administrator, North Dakota Judiciary, 600 E Blvd, 1st Floor Judicial Wing, Dept. 180, Bismarck, ND, 58505-0530; 701-328-4216, Fax: 701-328-2092. www.ndcourts.com or www.court.state.nd.us

COURT STRUCTURE   In 1995, the County Courts merged with the District Courts statewide. County court records are maintained by the 53 District Court Clerks in the seven judicial districts. We recommend stating "include all County Court cases" in search requests. There are 76 Municipal Courts that handle traffic cases.

ONLINE ACCESS   A statewide computer system for internal purposes is in operation in most counties. You may now search North Dakota Supreme Court dockets and opinions at www.ndcourts.com. Search by docket number, party name, or anything else that may appear in the text. Records are from 1991 forward. Email notification of new opinions is also available.

ADDITIONAL INFORMATION   In the summer of 1997, the standard search fee in District Courts increased to $10.00 per name, and the certification fee increased to $10.00 per document. Copy fees remain at $.50 per page, but many courts charge only $.25.

📖 📖 📖 📖 📖 📖 📖

Adams County

Southwest Judicial District Court 602 Adams Ave, PO Box 469, Hettinger, ND 58639; 701-567-2460; Fax: 701-567-2910. Hours: 8:30AM-5PM (MST). *Felony, Misdemeanor, Civil, Eviction, Small Claims, Probate.*

Civil Records: Access: Fax, mail, in person. Both court and visitors may perform in person searches. Search fee: $10.00 per name. Required to search: name, years to search; also helpful: address. Civil cases indexed by defendant, plaintiff. Civil records on index cards from 1990, on docket books in vault from 1900s.

Criminal Records: Access: Fax, mail, in person. Both court and visitors may perform in person searches. Search fee: $10.00 per name. Required to search: name, years to search, DOB; also helpful: address. Criminal records on index cards from 1990, on docket books in vault from 1900s.

General Information: No adoptions, sealed, juvenile, mental health, expunged, DV or dismissed records released. SASE required. Turnaround time 1-2 days. Fax notes: Fee to fax results is $3.00 1st 2 pages, $.50 each add'l. Copy fee: $.25 per page. Certification fee:

$10.00. Fee payee: Clerk of District Court. Personal checks accepted. Prepayment is required.

Barnes County

Southeast Judicial District Court PO Box 774, Valley City, ND 58072; 701-845-8512; Fax: 701-845-1341. Hours: 8AM-5PM (CST). *Felony, Misdemeanor, Civil, Eviction, Small Claims, Probate.*

Civil Records: Access: Fax, mail, in person. Only the court performs in person searches; visitors may not. Search fee: $10.00 per name. Required to search: name, years to search; also helpful: address. Civil cases indexed by defendant, plaintiff. Civil records on index books from early 1900s; on computer back to 1996.

Criminal Records: Access: Fax, mail, in person. Only the court performs in person searches; visitors may not. Search fee: $10.00 per name. Required to search: name, years to search; also helpful: address, DOB, SSN. Criminal records on index books from early 1900s; on computer back to 1996.

General Information: No adoptions, paternity, sealed, juvenile, mental health, expunged or dismissed records released. SASE required. Turnaround time 1-2 days. Fax notes: $10.00 per document. Copy fee: $.25 per

page. Certification fee: $10.00. $5.00 for second copy. Fee payee: Clerk of District Court. Personal checks accepted. Prepayment is required.

Benson County

Northeast Judicial District Court PO Box 213, Minnewaukan, ND 58351; 701-473-5345; Fax: 701-473-5571. Hours: 8:30AM-4:30PM (CST). *Felony, Misdemeanor, Civil, Eviction, Small Claims, Probate.*

Civil Records: Access: Fax, mail, in person. Only the court performs in person searches; visitors may not. Search fee: $10.00 per name. Fee is for written confirmation. Required to search: name, years to search; also helpful: address. Civil cases indexed by defendant, plaintiff. Civil records on docket books and index books from early 1900s, on index cards from 6/10/91.

Criminal Records: Access: Fax, mail, in person. Only the court performs in person searches; visitors may not. Search fee: $10.00 per name. Fee is for written confirmation. Required to search: name, years to search, DOB, signed release; also helpful: address. Criminal records on docket books and index books from early

1900s, on index cards from 6/10/91. Signed release required for juvenile cases.

General Information: No adoptions, sealed, juvenile, mental health, expunged or dismissed records released. SASE not required. Turnaround time 5 days. Fax notes: $1.00 per page. Copy fee: $1.00 per page. Certification fee: $10.00. Fee payee: Benson County Court. Personal checks accepted. Prepayment is required.

Billings County

Southwest Judicial District Court PO Box 138, Medora, ND 58645; 701-623-4492; Fax: 701-623-4896. Hours: 9AM-Noon, 1-5PM (MST). *Felony, Misdemeanor, Civil, Eviction, Small Claims, Probate.*

Civil Records: Access: Fax, mail, in person. Both court and visitors may perform in person searches. Search fee: $10.00 per name. Required to search: name, years to search; also helpful: address. Civil cases indexed by defendant, plaintiff. Civil records on index cards from 1986, on index books from 1800s.

Criminal Records: Access: Fax, mail, in person. Both court and visitors may perform in person searches. Search fee: $10.00 per name. Required to search: name, years to search; also helpful: address, DOB, SSN. Criminal records in books.

General Information: No adoptions, sealed, juvenile, mental health, expunged or dismissed records released. SASE required. Turnaround time 2-3 days. Fax notes: Fax fee $2.00 1st 4 pages, $.50 each additional page. Copy fee: $.25 per page. Certification fee: $10.00 plus $5.00 each add'l page. Fee payee: Clerk of District Court. Personal checks accepted. Prepayment is required.

Bottineau County

Northeast Judicial District Court 314 W 5th St, Bottineau, ND 58318; 701-228-3983; Fax: 701-228-2336. *Felony, Misdemeanor, Civil, Eviction, Small Claims, Probate.*

Civil Records: Access: Fax, mail, in person. Only the court performs in person searches; visitors may not. Search fee: $10.00 per name. Required to search: name, years to search; also helpful: address. Civil cases indexed by defendant, plaintiff. Civil records on index cards from 1987, on docket books from 1972.

Criminal Records: Access: Fax, mail, in person. Only the court performs in person searches; visitors may not. Search fee: $10.00 per name. Required to search: name, years to search; also helpful: address, DOB, SSN. Criminal records on docket books from 1885.

General Information: No adoptions, paternity, sealed, juvenile, mental health, expunged or dismissed records released. SASE required. Turnaround time 1 day. Fax notes: $4.00 for first page, $2.00 each add'l. Copy fee: $.20 per page. Certification fee: $10.00. Fee payee: Clerk of the Court. Personal checks accepted. Prepayment is required.

Bowman County

Southwest Judicial District Court PO Box 379, Bowman, ND 58623; 701-523-3450; Fax: 701-523-5443. Hours: 8:30AM-Noon, 1-5PM (MST). *Felony, Misdemeanor, Civil, Eviction, Small Claims, Probate.*

Civil Records: Access: Mail, in person. Both court and visitors may perform in person searches. Search fee: $10.00 per name. Required to search: name, years to search; also helpful: address. Civil cases indexed by defendant, plaintiff. Civil records on microfiche from 1978, on dockets from 1907.

Criminal Records: Access: Mail, in person. Both court and visitors may perform in person searches. Search fee: $10.00 per name. Required to search: name, years to search, DOB; also helpful: address. Criminal records on microfiche from 1978, on dockets from 1907.

General Information: No adoptions, sealed, juvenile, mental health, expunged or dismissed records released. SASE required. Turnaround time 1-2 days. Copy fee: $1.00 per page. Certification fee: $10.00. Fee payee: Clerk of Court. Personal checks accepted. Prepayment is required.

Burke County

Northwest Judicial District Court PO Box 219, Bowbells, ND 58721; 701-377-2718; Fax: 701-377-2020. Hours: 8:30AM-Noon, 1-5 PM (CST). *Felony, Misdemeanor, Civil, Eviction, Small Claims, Probate.*

Civil Records: Access: Mail, in person. Both court and visitors may perform in person searches. Search fee: $10.00 if a written reply is required. Required to search: name, years to search; also helpful: address. Civil cases indexed by defendant, plaintiff. Civil records for county civil, probate, and district from 1910, county criminal and small claims from 1980.

Criminal Records: Access: Mail, in person. Both court and visitors may perform in person searches. Search fee: $10.00 if a written reply is required. Required to search: name, years to search; also helpful: address, DOB, SSN. Criminal records for county civil, probate, and district from 1910, county criminal and small claims from 1980.

General Information: No adoptions, sealed, juvenile, mental health, expunged or dismissed records released. SASE not required. Turnaround time 1-3 days. Fax notes: Fee to fax results is $2.00 per page. Copy fee: $.50 per page. Certification fee: $10.00. Fee payee: Clerk of Court. Personal checks accepted. Prepayment is required.

Burleigh County

South Central Judicial District Court PO Box 1055, Bismarck, ND 58502; 701-222-6690; Criminal phone: Fax: 701-222-6758; Fax: 701-221-3756. Hours: 8AM-5PM (CST). *Felony, Misdemeanor, Civil, Eviction, Small Claims, Probate.*

Civil Records: Access: Mail, in person. Both court and visitors may perform in person searches. Search fee: $10.00 per name. Required to search: name; also helpful: years to search. Civil cases indexed by defendant, plaintiff. Civil records on computer from 1/91 in books from early 1900s.

Criminal Records: Access: Mail, in person. Both court and visitors may perform in person searches. Search fee: $10.00 per name. Required to search: name; also helpful: years to search, address, DOB, SSN. Criminal records on computer from 1/91 in books from early 1900s.

General Information: Public Access terminal is available. No adoptions, sealed, juvenile, mental health, expunged or dismissed records released. SASE required. Turnaround time 1-2 days. Copy fee: $.20 per page. Certification fee: $10.00 plus $5.00 each add'l copy of same document, if needed. Fee payee: Clerk of Court. Personal checks accepted. Prepayment is required.

Cass County

East Central Judicial District Court 211 South 9th St, Fargo, ND 58108; 701-241-5645; Fax: 701-241-5636. Hours: 8AM-5PM (CST). *Felony, Misdemeanor, Civil, Eviction, Small Claims, Probate.*

Civil Records: Access: Mail, in person. Only the court performs in person searches; visitors may not. Search fee: $10.00 per name. Required to search: name, years to search; also helpful: address. Civil cases indexed by defendant, plaintiff. Civil records on computer from 1988, on index books from late 1800s.

Criminal Records: Access: Mail, in person. Only the court performs in person searches; visitors may not. Search fee: $10.00 per name. Required to search: name,

years to search; also helpful: address, DOB, SSN. Criminal records on computer from 1988, on index cards from 1980.

General Information: No adoptions, sealed, juvenile, mental health, expunged or dismissed records released. SASE required. Turnaround time 3-5 days. Copy fee: $.25 per page. $1.00 minimum. Certification fee: $10.00. Fee payee: Clerk of District Court. Personal checks accepted. Prepayment is required.

Cavalier County

Northeast Judicial District Court 901 Third St, Langdon, ND 58249; 701-256-2124; Fax: 701-256-2124. Hours: 8:30AM-4:30PM (CST). *Felony, Misdemeanor, Civil, Eviction, Small Claims, Probate.*

Civil Records: Access: Fax, mail, in person. Only the court performs in person searches; visitors may not. Search fee: $10.00 per name. Required to search: name, years to search; also helpful: address. Civil cases indexed by defendant, plaintiff. Civil records going on computer, prior stored.

Criminal Records: Access: Fax, mail, in person. Only the court performs in person searches; visitors may not. Search fee: $10.00 per name. Required to search: name, years to search; also helpful: address, DOB, SSN. Criminal records for District Court on index books from 1937, for County Court on index books from 1983, prior stored.

General Information: No adoptions, sealed, juvenile, mental health, expunged or dismissed records released. SASE required. Turnaround time 1 week. Fax notes: No fee to fax results. Copy fee: $.25 per page. Certification fee: $10.00. Fee payee: Clerk of Court. Personal checks accepted. Prepayment is required.

Dickey County

Southeast Judicial District Court PO Box 336, Ellendale, ND 58436; 701-349-3249 X4; Fax: 701-349-3560. Hours: 9AM-Noon, 1-5PM (CST). *Felony, Misdemeanor, Civil, Eviction, Small Claims, Probate.*

Civil Records: Access: Mail, in person. Only the court performs in person searches; visitors may not. Search fee: $10.00 per name. Required to search: name, years to search; also helpful: address. Civil cases indexed by defendant, plaintiff. Civil records on index books from 1983; on computer back to 1997. Probate from 1800s. Old district court records have no index and are very hard to find.

Criminal Records: Access: Mail, in person. Only the court performs in person searches; visitors may not. Search fee: $10.00 per name. Required to search: name, years to search, DOB; also helpful: address, SSN. Criminal records on index books from 1983, on computer back to 1997. Old district court records have no index and are very hard to find.

General Information: No adoptions, sealed, juvenile, mental health, expunged or dismissed records released. SASE not required. Turnaround time 1-2 days. Copy fee: $.25 per page. Certification fee: $10.00. Fee payee: Clerk of Court. Personal checks accepted. Prepayment is required.

Divide County

Northwest Judicial District Court PO Box 68, Crosby, ND 58730; 701-965-6831; Fax: 701-965-6943. Hours: 8:30AM-Noon, 1-5PM (CST). *Felony, Misdemeanor, Civil, Eviction, Small Claims, Probate.*

Civil Records: Access: Fax, mail, in person. Only the court performs in person searches; visitors may not. Search fee: $10.00 per name. Required to search: name, years to search; also helpful: address. Civil cases indexed by defendant, plaintiff. Civil records on index books from 1910. Visitor can check for judgments.

Criminal Records: Access: Fax, mail, in person. Only the court performs in person searches; visitors may not.

Search fee: $10.00 per name. Required to search: name, years to search; also helpful: address, DOB, SSN. Criminal records on index books from 1910.

General Information: No adoptions, sealed, juvenile, mental health, expunged or dismissed records released. SASE required. Turnaround time 1-2 days. Fax notes: $3.00 for first page, $1.00 each add'l. There is also a charge of $1.00 per incoming fax page. Copy fee: $.25 per page. $1.00 minimum. Certification fee: Included in search fee. Fee payee: Clerk of District Court. Personal checks accepted. Prepayment is required.

Dunn County

District Court PO Box 136, Manning, ND 58642-0136; 701-573-4447; Fax: 701-573-4444. Hours: 8AM-Noon, 12:30-4:30PM (MST). *Felony, Misdemeanor, Civil, Small Claims, Probate.*

Civil Records: Access: Fax, mail, in person. Only the court performs in person searches; visitors may not. Search fee: $10.00 per name. Required to search: name, years to search; also helpful: address. Civil cases indexed by defendant, plaintiff. Civil records on plaintiff/defendant index cards from 1988, on docket books from 1900s, on computer since 01/97. Fax requests must fax copy of the check to be mailed.

Criminal Records: Access: Fax, mail, in person. Only the court performs in person searches; visitors may not. Search fee: $10.00 per name. Required to search: name, years to search, DOB; also helpful: address, SSN. Criminal records on plaintiff/defendant index cards from 1988, on docket books from 1900s, on computer since 01/97. Fax requesters must fax copy of the check, which can be mailed.

General Information: Public Access terminal is available. Adoptions, paternity, juvenile, mental health, deferred impositions, and termination of parental rights are restricted access files. SASE not required. Turnaround time 2 days. Fax notes: $2.00 plus $1.00 each page. Copy fee: $2.00 plus $.50 each page (mailed copies). Certification fee: $10.00. Fee payee: Dunn County Clerk of Court. Personal checks accepted. In state personal checks accepted. Prepayment is required.

Eddy County

Southeast Judicial District Court 524 Central Ave, New Rockford, ND 58356; 701-947-2813; Fax: 701-947-2067. Hours: 8AM-4PM (CST). *Felony, Misdemeanor, Civil, Eviction, Small Claims, Probate.*

Civil Records: Access: Fax, mail, in person. Only the court performs in person searches; visitors may not. Search fee: $10.00 per name. Required to search: name, years to search; also helpful: address. Civil cases indexed by defendant, plaintiff. Civil records on index cards from 4/92, on index books from early 1900s. All requests must be in writing.

Criminal Records: Access: Fax, mail, in person. Only the court performs in person searches; visitors may not. Search fee: $10.00 per name. Required to search: name, years to search; also helpful: address, DOB, SSN. Criminal records on index cards from 4/92, on index books from early 1900s. All requests must be in writing.

General Information: No adoptions, sealed, juvenile, mental health, expunged or dismissed records released. SASE required. Turnaround time 1-2 days. Fax notes: Fax fee $4.00 1st 3 pages, $1.00 each additional page. Copy fee: $1.00 per document. Certification fee: $10.00. Fee payee: Eddy County District Court. Personal checks accepted.

Emmons County

South Central Judicial District Court PO Box 905, Linton, ND 58552; 701-254-4812; Fax: 701-254-4012. Hours: 8:30AM-Noon, 1-5PM (CST). *Felony, Misdemeanor, Civil, Eviction, Small Claims, Probate.*

Civil Records: Access: Fax, mail, in person. Only the court performs in person searches; visitors may not. Search fee: $10.00 per name. Required to search: name, years to search; also helpful: address. Civil cases indexed by defendant, plaintiff. Civil records on index cards from 1988, on index books from 1914, on computer back to 1995.

Criminal Records: Access: Fax, mail, in person. Only the court performs in person searches; visitors may not. Search fee: $10.00 per name. Required to search: name, years to search, DOB; also helpful: address, SSN. Criminal records on index books back to 1983; on computer back to 1995.

General Information: No adoptions, sealed, juvenile, mental health, expunged or dismissed records released. SASE required. Turnaround time 1-2 days. Fax notes: Fee to fax results is $3.00 1st page, $1.00 each add'l. Copy fee: $.20 per page. Certification fee: $10.00. Fee payee: Clerk of Courts. Personal checks accepted. Prepayment is required.

Foster County

Southeast Judicial District Court PO Box 257, Carrington, ND 58421; 701-652-1001; Fax: 701-652-2173. Hours: 8:30AM-4:30PM (CST). *Felony, Misdemeanor, Civil, Eviction, Small Claims, Probate.*

Civil Records: Access: Mail, in person. Both court and visitors may perform in person searches. Search fee: $10.00 per name if court performs search. Required to search: name, years to search; also helpful: address. Civil cases indexed by defendant, plaintiff. Civil records on index books from early 1900s.

Criminal Records: Access: Mail, in person. Both court and visitors may perform in person searches. Search fee: $10.00 per name if court performs search. Required to search: name, years to search, DOB; also helpful: address. Criminal records on index books from early 1900s.

General Information: No adoptions, sealed, juvenile, mental health, expunged or dismissed records released. SASE required. Turnaround time 1-2 days. Fax notes: $3.00 per document. Copy fee: $1.00 per page. Certification fee: $10.00. Fee payee: Clerk of Courts. Personal checks accepted. Prepayment is required.

Golden Valley County

Southwest Judicial District Court PO Box 9, Beach, ND 58621-0009; 701-872-4352; Fax: 701-872-4383. Hours: 8-Noon, 1-4PM (MST). *Felony, Misdemeanor, Civil, Eviction, Small Claims, Probate.*

Civil Records: Access: Fax, mail, in person. Only the court performs in person searches; visitors may not. Search fee: $10.00 per name. Required to search: name, years to search; also helpful: address. Civil cases indexed by defendant, plaintiff. Civil records on index cards from 1987, on index books from 1913 to 1960. From 1960 to 1987, records are hard to find; there is no indexing and files are filed by number. Fax request must include copy of check.

Criminal Records: Access: Fax, mail, in person. Only the court performs in person searches; visitors may not. Search fee: $10.00 per name. Required to search: name, years to search, DOB; also helpful: address, SSN. Criminal records on index cards from 1987, on index books from 1913 to 1960. From 1960 to 1987, records are hard to find; there is no indexing and files are filed by number. Fax request must include copy of check.

General Information: No adoptions, sealed, juvenile, mental health, expunged or dismissed records released.

SASE required. Turnaround time 3-4 days. Fax notes: $1.00 per page. Copy fee: $.50 per page. Certification fee: $10.00. Fee payee: Clerk of Court. Personal checks accepted. Prepayment is required.

Grand Forks County

Northeast Central Judicial District Court PO Box 5939, Grand Forks, ND 58206-5939; 701-780-8214; Fax: 701-780-8217. Hours: 8AM-5PM (CST). *Felony, Misdemeanor, Civil, Eviction, Small Claims, Probate.*

Civil Records: Access: Mail, in person. Only the court performs in person searches; visitors may not. Search fee: $10.00 per name. Required to search: name, years to search; also helpful: address. Civil cases indexed by defendant, plaintiff. Civil records on computer from 10/91, on index books from early 1900s.

Criminal Records: Access: Mail, in person. Only the court performs in person searches; visitors may not. Search fee: $10.00 per name. Required to search: name, years to search, DOB, signed release; also helpful: address, SSN. Criminal records on computer from 10/91, on index books from early 1900s.

General Information: Public Access terminal is available. No adoptions, sealed, juvenile, mental health, expunged or dismissed records released. SASE required. Turnaround time 1-2 days. Fax notes: Fee to receive fax is $5.00. Fee to fax results is $1.00 per page, $3.00 minimum. Copy fee: $.25 per page; $1.00 minimum. Certification fee: $10.00. Fee payee: Clerk of District Court. Personal checks accepted. Prepayment is required.

Grant County

South Central Judicial District Court PO Box 258, Carson, ND 58529; 701-622-3615; Fax: 701-622-3717. Hours: 8AM-Noon, 12:30-4PM (MST). *Felony, Misdemeanor, Civil, Eviction, Small Claims, Probate.*

Civil Records: Access: Fax, mail, in person. Both court and visitors may perform in person searches. Search fee: $10.00 per name. Required to search: name, years to search; also helpful: address. Civil cases indexed by defendant, plaintiff. Civil records on index cards from 1990, on docket books in vault from 1900s.

Criminal Records: Access: Fax, mail, in person. Both court and visitors may perform in person searches. Search fee: $10.00 per name. Required to search: name, years to search; also helpful: address, DOB, SSN. Criminal records on index cards from 1990, on docket books in vault from 1900s.

General Information: No adoptions, sealed, juvenile, mental health, expunged or dismissed records released. SASE not required. Turnaround time 1 day. Fax notes: $3.00 per document. Copy fee: $.25 per page. Certification fee: $10.00. Fee payee: Clerk of Grant County Court. Personal checks accepted. Prepayment is required.

Griggs County

Southeast Judicial District Court PO Box 326, Cooperstown, ND 58425; 701-797-2772; Fax: 701-797-3587. Hours: 8AM-Noon, 1-4:30PM (CST). *Felony, Misdemeanor, Civil, Eviction, Small Claims, Probate.*

Civil Records: Access: Fax, mail, in person. Both court and visitors may perform in person searches. Search fee: $10.00 per name. Required to search: name, years to search; also helpful: address. Civil cases indexed by defendant, plaintiff. Civil records on docket books from 1890 for District and 1983 for County. Phone access discouraged.

Criminal Records: Access: Fax, mail, in person. Both court and visitors may perform in person searches. Search fee: $10.00 per name. Required to search: name, years to search; also helpful: address, DOB, SSN.

Criminal records on docket books from 1890 for District and 1983 for County. Phone access discouraged.

General Information: No adoptions, sealed, juvenile, mental health, expunged or dismissed records released. SASE required. Turnaround time 1-2 days. Fax notes: $1.00 per page. Incoming fax, $1.00 1st page, $.50 each additional page. Free for attorneys. Copy fee: $.25 per page. Certification fee: $10.00. Fee payee: Clerk of Courts. Personal checks accepted. Prepayment is required.

Hettinger County

Southwest Judicial District Court PO Box 668, Mott, ND 58646; 701-824-2645; Fax: 701-824-2717. Hours: 8AM-Noon, 1-4:30PM (MST). *Felony, Misdemeanor, Civil, Eviction, Small Claims, Probate.*

Civil Records: Access: Fax, mail, in person. Only the court performs in person searches; visitors may not. Search fee: $10.00 per name. Required to search: name, years to search; also helpful: address. Civil cases indexed by defendant, plaintiff. Civil records on index cards from 1987, on index books from 1908.

Criminal Records: Access: Fax, mail, in person. Only the court performs in person searches; visitors may not. Search fee: $10.00 per name. Required to search: name, years to search, DOB; also helpful: address. Criminal records on index cards from 1987, on index books from 1908.

General Information: No adoptions, sealed, juvenile, mental health, expunged or dismissed records released. SASE required. Turnaround time 1 day. Fax notes: $3.00 per document. Fee is for up to 20 pages. Copy fee: $.50 per page. Certification fee: $10.00. Fee payee: Hettinger Court Clerk. Personal checks accepted. Prepayment is required.

Kidder County

District Court PO Box 66, Steele, ND 58482; 701-475-2632; Fax: 701-475-2202. Hours: 9AM-5PM (CST). *Felony, Misdemeanor, Civil, Eviction, Small Claims, Probate.*

Civil Records: Access: Fax, mail, in person. Only the court performs in person searches; visitors may not. Search fee: $10.00 per name. Required to search: name, years to search; also helpful: address. Civil cases indexed by defendant, plaintiff. Civil records on index book from 1900s, on computer since 1990.

Criminal Records: Access: Mail, in person. Both court and visitors may perform in person searches. Search fee: $10.00 per name. Required to search: name, years to search, DOB; also helpful: address. Records on index book from 1900s, on computer since 1990.

General Information: Public Access terminal is available. No adoptions, sealed, juvenile, mental health, expunged or dismissed records released. SASE required. Turnaround time 1-2 days. Fax notes: Fee to fax is $3.00 per document. Copy fee: $1.00 per page. Certification fee: $10.00. Fee payee: Clerk of Court. Personal checks accepted. Prepayment is required.

La Moure County

Southeast Judicial District Court PO Box 128, LaMoure, ND 58458; 701-883-5193; Fax: 701-883-5304. Hours: 9AM-Noon, 1-5PM (CST). *Felony, Misdemeanor, Civil, Eviction, Small Claims, Probate.*

Civil Records: Access: Fax, mail, in person. Both court and visitors may perform in person searches. Search fee: $10.00 per name. Required to search: name, years to search; also helpful: address. Civil cases indexed by defendant, plaintiff. Civil records on docket books from 1800s.

Criminal Records: Access: Fax, mail, in person. Both court and visitors may perform in person searches. Search fee: $10.00 per name. Required to search: name,

years to search, DOB; also helpful: address. Criminal records on docket books from 1800s.

General Information: No adoptions, sealed, juvenile, mental health, expunged or dismissed records released. SASE required. Turnaround time 1 day. Fax notes: Will not fax results. Copy fee: $.25 for first page, $.10 each add'l. Certification fee: $10.00. Fee payee: Clerk of Court. Personal checks accepted. Prepayment is required.

Logan County

South Central Judicial District Court PO Box 6, Napoleon, ND 58561; 701-754-2751; Fax: 701-754-2270. Hours: 8:30AM-4:30PM (CST). *Felony, Misdemeanor, Civil, Eviction, Small Claims, Probate.*

Civil Records: Access: Fax, mail, in person. Both court and visitors may perform in person searches. Search fee: $10.00 per name. Required to search: name, years to search; also helpful: address. Civil cases indexed by defendant, plaintiff. Civil records on index books from 1884.

Criminal Records: Access: Fax, mail, in person. Both court and visitors may perform in person searches. Search fee: $10.00 per name. Required to search: name, years to search, DOB; also helpful: address. Criminal records on index books from 1884.

General Information: No adoptions, sealed, juvenile, mental health, expunged or dismissed records released. SASE required. Turnaround time 1-2 days. Fax notes: Fee to fax is $3.00 for first page, $1.00 each add'l. Copy fee: $1.00 per page. Certification fee: $10.00. Fee payee: Clerk of Court. Business checks accepted. Prepayment is required.

McHenry County

Northeast Judicial District Court PO Box 117, Towner, ND 58788; 701-537-5729; Fax: 701-537-5969. Hours: 8AM-4:30PM (CST). *Felony, Misdemeanor, Civil, Eviction, Small Claims, Probate.*

Civil Records: Access: Fax, mail, in person. Both court and visitors may perform in person searches. Search fee: $10.00 per name. Required to search: name, years to search; also helpful: address. Civil cases indexed by defendant, plaintiff. Civil records on index cards from 1991, on index books from 1905.

Criminal Records: Access: Fax, mail, in person. Both court and visitors may perform in person searches. Search fee: $10.00 per name. Required to search: name, years to search; also helpful: address, DOB, SSN. Criminal records on index cards from 1991, on index books from 1905.

General Information: No adoptions, sealed, juvenile, mental health, expunged or dismissed records released. SASE required. Turnaround time 1-2 days. Fax notes: $1.00 for first page, $.25 each add'l. Copy fee: $.25 per page. Certification fee: $10.00. Fee payee: Clerk of Courts. Personal checks accepted. Prepayment is required.

McIntosh County

South Central Judicial District Court PO Box 179, Ashley, ND 58413; 701-288-3450; Fax: 701-288-3671. Hours: 8AM-4:30PM (CST). *Felony, Misdemeanor, Civil, Eviction, Small Claims, Probate.*

Civil Records: Access: Fax, mail, in person. Visitors must perform in person searches for themselves. Search fee: $10.00 per name. Required to search: name, years to search; also helpful: address. Civil cases indexed by defendant, plaintiff. Civil records on index cards from 1987, on index books from 1930s.

Criminal Records: Access: Fax, mail, in person. Both court and visitors may perform in person searches. Search fee: $10.00 per name. Required to search: name, years to search, DOB; also helpful: address. Criminal records on index cards from 1987, on index books from 1930s.

General Information: No adoptions, sealed, juvenile, mental health, expunged or dismissed records released. SASE not required. Turnaround time 1-2 days. Copy fee: $.25 per page. Certification fee: $10.00. Fee payee: Clerk of Court. Only cashiers checks and money orders accepted. Prepayment is required.

McKenzie County

Northwest District Court PO Box 524, Watford City, ND 58854; 701-842-3452; Fax: 701-842-3916. Hours: 8:30AM-Noon, 1-5PM (CST). *Felony, Misdemeanor, Civil, Eviction, Small Claims, Probate.*

Civil Records: Access: Mail, in person. Both court and visitors may perform in person searches. Search fee: $10.00 per name. Required to search: name, years to search; also helpful: address. Civil cases indexed by defendant, plaintiff. Civil records on computer back to 01/96.

Criminal Records: Access: Mail, in person. Only the court performs in person searches; visitors may not. Search fee: $10.00 per name. Required to search: name, years to search, DOB; also helpful: address. Criminal records on computer back to 12/87; on books back to 1908.

General Information: No adoptions, juvenile, mental health, expunged or dismissed records released. SASE required. Turnaround time 1-2 days. Fax notes: $2.00 per page. Copy fee: $.25 per page. Certification fee: $10.00. Fee payee: Clerk of Court, McKenzie County. Personal checks accepted. Prepayment is required.

McLean County

South Central Judicial District Court PO Box 1108, Washburn, ND 58577; 701-462-8541; Fax: 701-462-8212. Hours: 8AM-Noon, 12:30-4:30PM (CST). *Felony, Misdemeanor, Civil, Eviction, Small Claims, Probate.*

Civil Records: Access: Mail, in person. Both court and visitors may perform in person searches. Search fee: $10.00 per name. Required to search: name, years to search; also helpful: address. Civil cases indexed by defendant, plaintiff. Civil records on index books from early 1900s; on computer back to 1996.

Criminal Records: Access: Mail, in person. Both court and visitors may perform in person searches. Search fee: $10.00 per name. Required to search: name, years to search, DOB; also helpful: address, SSN. Criminal records on index cards from 1983, on index books from early 1900s; on computer back to 1996.

General Information: No adoptions, sealed, juvenile, mental health, expunged or deferred imposition dismissed records released. SASE required. Turnaround time 1-2 days. Copy fee: $.25 per page. Certification fee: $10.00. Fee payee: Clerk of Courts. Personal checks accepted. Prepayment is required.

Mercer County

District Court PO Box 39, Stanton, ND 58571; 701-745-3262; Fax: 701-745-3710. Hours: 8AM-4PM (MST). *Felony, Misdemeanor, Civil, Eviction, Small Claims, Probate.*

Civil Records: Access: Fax, mail, in person. Both court and visitors may perform in person searches. Search fee: $10.00 per name. Required to search: name, years to search; also helpful: address. Civil cases indexed by defendant, plaintiff. Civil records on index cards from 1979, on index books from 1889.

Criminal Records: Access: Fax, mail, in person. Both court and visitors may perform in person searches. Search fee: $10.00 per name. Required to search: name, years to search, signed release; also helpful: address, DOB, SSN. Criminal records on index cards from 1979, on index books from 1889.

General Information: Public Access terminal is available. No adoptions, sealed, juvenile, mental health, expunged or dismissed records released. SASE required. Turnaround time 1-2 days. Fax notes: $5.00 per document. Copy fee: $.25 per page. Certification fee: $10.00. Fee payee: Mercer County Clerk of Court. Personal checks accepted. Prepayment is required.

Morton County

South Central Judicial District Court 210
2nd Ave NW, Mandan, ND 58554; 701-667-3358. Hours: 8AM-5PM (MST). *Felony, Misdemeanor, Civil, Eviction, Small Claims, Probate.*

Civil Records: Access: Mail, in person. Only the court performs in person searches; visitors may not. Search fee: $10.00 per name. Fee is for written search request. Required to search: name, years to search; also helpful: address. Civil cases indexed by defendant, plaintiff. Civil records on computer from 10/91, on index books from 1800s.
Criminal Records: Access: Mail, in person. Only the court performs in person searches; visitors may not. Search fee: $10.00 per name. Fee is for written search request. Required to search: name, years to search, DOB; also helpful: address. Criminal records on computer from 10/91, on index books from 1800s.
General Information: No adoptions, sealed, juvenile, mental health, expunged or dismissed records released. SASE required. Turnaround time 1-2 days. Copy fee: $5.00 per document. Certification fee: $10.00. Fee payee: Clerk of District Court. Personal checks accepted. Prepayment is required.

Mountrail County

Northwest Judicial District Court PO Box
69, Stanley, ND 58784; 701-628-2915; Fax: 701-628-3975. Hours: 8:30AM-4:30PM (CST). *Felony, Misdemeanor, Civil, Eviction, Small Claims, Probate.*

Civil Records: Access: Mail, in person. Only the court performs in person searches; visitors may not. Search fee: $10.00 per name. Fee is for written search. Required to search: name, years to search; also helpful: address. Civil cases indexed by defendant, plaintiff. Civil records on index books from 1909; on computer back to 1998.
Criminal Records: Access: Mail, in person. Only the court performs in person searches; visitors may not. Search fee: $10.00 per name. Fee is for written search. Required to search: name, years to search, DOB. Criminal records on index books from 1909; on computer back to 1998.
General Information: No adoptions, sealed, juvenile, mental health, expunged or dismissed records released. SASE not required. Turnaround time 1-2 days. Fax notes: No fee to fax results. Copy fee: $.25 per page. Certification fee: $10.00. Fee payee: Clerk of District Court. Personal checks accepted. Prepayment is required.

Nelson County

Northeast Central Judicial District Court
PO Box 565, Lakota, ND 58344; 701-247-2462; Fax: 701-247-2412. Hours: 8:30AM-5PM (CST). *Felony, Misdemeanor, Civil, Eviction, Small Claims, Probate.*

Note: Will accept e-mail record requests at rstevens@pioneer.state.nd.us.

Civil Records: Access: Fax, mail, in person. Both court and visitors may perform in person searches. Search fee: $10.00 per name. Required to search: name, years to search; also helpful: address. Civil cases indexed by defendant, plaintiff. Civil records on index books from 1883.
Criminal Records: Access: Fax, mail, in person. Only the court performs in person searches; visitors may not. Search fee: $10.00 per name. Required to search: name, years to search, DOB; also helpful: address, SSN. Criminal records on index books from 1883.
General Information: No adoptions, sealed, juvenile, mental health, expunged or dismissed records released.

SASE required. Turnaround time 1-2 days. Fax notes: $3.00 per document. Copy fee: $1.00 per page. Certification fee: $10.00. Fee payee: Clerk of Courts. Personal checks accepted. Prepayment is required.

Oliver County

South Central Judicial District Court Box
125, Center, ND 58530; 701-794-8777; Fax: 701-794-3476. Hours: 8AM-4PM (CST). *Felony, Misdemeanor, Civil, Eviction, Small Claims, Probate.*

Civil Records: Access: Fax, mail, in person. Only the court performs in person searches; visitors may not. Search fee: $10.00 per name. Required to search: name, years to search; also helpful: address. Civil cases indexed by defendant. Civil records on docket books from 1980s.
Criminal Records: Access: Fax, mail, in person. Only the court performs in person searches; visitors may not. Search fee: $10.00 per name. Required to search: name, years to search, DOB; also helpful: address. Criminal records on docket books from 1980s.
General Information: No adoptions, sealed, juvenile, mental health, expunged or dismissed records released. SASE required. Turnaround time 1-2 days. Fax notes: $1.00 for first page, $.50 each add'l. Copy fee: $.25 per page. Certification fee: $10.00. Fee payee: Clerk of Court. Personal checks accepted. Prepayment is required.

Pembina County

Pembina County District Court 301 Dakota
St West #6, Cavalier, ND 58220-4100; 701-265-4275; Fax: 701-265-4876. Hours: 8:30AM-5PM (CST). *Felony, Misdemeanor, Civil, Eviction, Small Claims, Probate.*

Civil Records: Access: Fax, mail, in person. Only the court performs in person searches; visitors may not. Search fee: $10.00 per name. Required to search: name, years to search; also helpful: address, DOB, SSN. Civil cases indexed by defendant, plaintiff. Civil records on index books from 1880s.
Criminal Records: Access: Fax, mail, in person. Only the court performs in person searches; visitors may not. Search fee: $10.00 per name. Required to search: name, years to search, DOB; also helpful: address, SSN. Felony records kept for 21 years, misdemeanor for 15 years.
General Information: No adoptions, sealed, juvenile, mental health, expunged or dismissed records released. SASE not required. Turnaround time 1-2 days. Fax notes: $5.00 per document. Copy fee: $.25 per page. Certification fee: $10.00. Fee payee: Pembina County Clerk of Court. Personal checks accepted. Prepayment is required.

Pierce County

Northeast Judicial District Court 240 SE
2nd St, Rugby, ND 58368; 701-776-6161; Fax: 701-776-5707. Hours: 9AM-5PM (CST). *Felony, Misdemeanor, Civil, Eviction, Small Claims, Probate.*

Civil Records: Access: Fax, mail, in person. Only the court performs in person searches; visitors may not. Search fee: $10.00 per name. Required to search: name, years to search; also helpful: address. Civil cases indexed by defendant, plaintiff. Civil records on computer from 1986, on index books and docket books from early 1900s.
Criminal Records: Access: Fax, mail, in person. Only the court performs in person searches; visitors may not. Search fee: $10.00 per name. Required to search: name, years to search, DOB; also helpful: address, SSN. Criminal records on computer from 1986, on index books and docket books from early 1900s.
General Information: No adoptions, sealed, juvenile, mental health, expunged or dismissed records released. SASE required. Turnaround time 1-2 days. Fax notes:

$5.00 per document. Copy fee: $.25 per page. Certification fee: $10.00. Fee payee: Clerk of Courts. Personal checks accepted. Prepayment is required.

Ramsey County

District Court 524 4th Ave #4, Devils Lake, ND
58301; 701-662-7066; Fax: 701-662-7063. Hours: 8AM-5PM (CST). *Felony, Misdemeanor, Civil, Eviction, Small Claims, Probate.*

Civil Records: Access: Fax, mail, in person. Only the court performs in person searches; visitors may not. Search fee: $10.00 per name. Required to search: name; also helpful: years to search. Civil cases indexed by defendant, plaintiff. Civil records on index cards from 1985, on index books from early 1900s.
Criminal Records: Access: Fax, mail, in person. Only the court performs in person searches; visitors may not. Search fee: $10.00 per name. Required to search: name; also helpful: years to search, address, DOB, SSN. Criminal records on index cards from 1985, on index books from early 1900s.
General Information: No adoptions, sealed, juvenile, mental health, expunged or dismissed records released. SASE required. Turnaround time 1-2 days. Fax notes: No fee to fax results. Fax only available to businesses. Copy fee: $.50 per page. Certification fee: $10.00. Fee payee: Clerk of Courts. Personal checks accepted. Prepayment is required.

Ransom County

Southeast Judicial District Court PO Box
626, Lisbon, ND 58054; 701-683-5823 X120; Fax: 701-683-5826. Hours: 8:30AM-5PM (CST). *Felony, Misdemeanor, Civil, Eviction, Small Claims, Probate.*

Civil Records: Access: Fax, mail, in person. Both court and visitors may perform in person searches. Search fee: $10.00 per name. Required to search: name, years to search; also helpful: address. Civil cases indexed by defendant, plaintiff. Civil records on docket books.
Criminal Records: Access: Fax, mail, in person. Both court and visitors may perform in person searches. Search fee: $10.00 per name. Required to search: name, years to search, DOB; also helpful: address. Criminal records on index books.
General Information: No adoptions, sealed, juvenile, mental health, expunged or dismissed records released. SASE required. Turnaround time 3-4 days. Fax notes: No fee to fax results. Copy fee: $.20 per page. Certification fee: $10.00. Fee payee: Clerk of Court. Personal checks accepted. Prepayment is required.

Renville County

Northeast Judicial District Court PO Box
68, Mohall, ND 58761; 701-756-6398; Fax: 701-756-6398. Hours: 9AM-4:30PM (CST). *Felony, Misdemeanor, Civil, Eviction, Small Claims, Probate.*

Civil Records: Access: Fax, mail, in person. Both court and visitors may perform in person searches. Search fee: $10.00 per name. Required to search: name, years to search; also helpful: address. Civil cases indexed by defendant, plaintiff. Civil records on index books from 1910.
Criminal Records: Access: Fax, mail, in person. Both court and visitors may perform in person searches. Search fee: $10.00 per name. Required to search: name, years to search, DOB; also helpful: address. Criminal records on computer from 1/88, on index books from 1910 but not reliable before 1940.
General Information: No adoptions, sealed, juvenile, mental health, expunged or dismissed records released. SASE required. Turnaround time 1-2 days. Fax notes: $3.00 for first page, $1.00 each add'l. Copy fee: $1.00 per page. Certification fee: $10.00. Fee payee: Clerk of Courts. Personal checks accepted. Prepayment is required.

Richland County

Southeast Judicial District Court 418 2nd Ave North, Wahpeton, ND 58074; 701-642-7818; Fax: 701-671-1512. Hours: 8AM-5PM (CST). *Felony, Misdemeanor, Civil, Eviction, Small Claims, Probate.*

Civil Records: Access: Mail, in person. Only the court performs in person searches; visitors may not. Search fee: $10.00 per name. Required to search: name, years to search; also helpful: address. Civil cases indexed by defendant. Civil records on index cards from 1985, on docket books from late 1800s, but not very accurate. Plaintiff and defendant names required to search.
Criminal Records: Access: Mail, in person. Only the court performs in person searches; visitors may not. Search fee: $10.00 per name. Required to search: name, years to search, DOB, SSN; also helpful: address. Criminal records on docket books from late 1800s but not very accurate.
General Information: No adoptions, sealed, juvenile, mental health, expunged or dismissed records released. SASE required. Turnaround time 1-2 days. Copy fee: $.25 per page. Certification fee: $10.00. Fee payee: Clerk of District Court. Personal checks accepted. Prepayment is required.

Rolette County

Northeast Judicial District Court PO Box 460, Rolla, ND 58367; 701-477-3816; Fax: 701-477-5770. Hours: 8:30AM-4:30PM (CST). *Felony, Misdemeanor, Civil, Eviction, Small Claims, Probate.*

Civil Records: Access: Fax, mail, in person. Both court and visitors may perform in person searches. Search fee: $10.00 per name. Required to search: name, years to search; also helpful: address. Civil cases indexed by defendant, plaintiff.
Criminal Records: Access: Fax, mail, in person. Both court and visitors may perform in person searches. Search fee: $10.00 per name. Required to search: name, years to search; also helpful: address, DOB, SSN. Criminal records on dockets from 1970. Prior to 1970, records hard to find and not very accurate.
General Information: No adoptions, sealed, juvenile, mental health, expunged or dismissed records released. SASE required. Turnaround time 1-2 days. Fax notes: $5.00 per document. Copy fee: $.50 per page. Certification fee: $10.00. Fee payee: Clerk of Court. Business checks accepted. Prepayment is required.

Sargent County

Southeast Judicial District Court 355 Main St (PO Box 176), Forman, ND 58032; 701-724-6241 X215-216; Fax: 701-724-6244. Hours: 9AM-Noon, 12:30-4:30PM (CST). *Felony, Misdemeanor, Civil, Eviction, Small Claims, Probate.*

Civil Records: Access: Fax, mail, in person. Both court and visitors may perform in person searches. Search fee: $10.00 per name. Required to search: name, years to search; also helpful: address. Civil cases indexed by defendant. Civil records on books from early 1800s.
Criminal Records: Access: Fax, mail, in person. Both court and visitors may perform in person searches. Search fee: $10.00 per name. Required to search: name, years to search, DOB; also helpful: address. Criminal records on books from early 1800s.
General Information: No adoptions, sealed, juvenile, mental health, expunged or dismissed records released. SASE not required. Turnaround time 1-2 days. Fax notes: $3.00 for first page, $1.00 each add'l. Copy fee: $.10 per page. Certification fee: $10.00. Fee payee: Clerk of Court. Personal checks accepted. Prepayment is required.

Sheridan County

South Central Judicial District Court PO Box 636, McClusky, ND 58463; 701-363-2207; Fax: 701-363-2953. Hours: 9AM-Noon, 1-5PM (CST). *Felony, Misdemeanor, Civil, Eviction, Small Claims, Probate.*

Civil Records: Access: Mail, in person. Both court and visitors may perform in person searches. Search fee: $5.00 per name. Required to search: name, years to search; also helpful: address. Civil cases indexed by defendant, plaintiff. Civil records on index books from 1909.
Criminal Records: Access: Mail, in person. Both court and visitors may perform in person searches. Search fee: $5.00 per name. Required to search: name, years to search, signed release; also helpful: address, DOB, SSN. Criminal records on index books from 1909.
General Information: No adoptions, sealed, juvenile, mental health, expunged or dismissed records released. SASE not required. Turnaround time 1-2 days. Copy fee: $.25 per page. Certification fee: $10.00. Fee payee: Clerk of District Court. Business checks accepted. Prepayment is required.

Sioux County

South Central Judicial District Court Box L, Fort Yates, ND 58538; 701-854-3853; Fax: 701-854-3854. Hours: 9AM-5PM (CST). *Felony, Misdemeanor, Civil, Eviction, Small Claims, Probate.*

Civil Records: Access: Fax, mail, in person. Both court and visitors may perform in person searches. Search fee: $10.00 per name per year. Required to search: name, years to search; also helpful: address. Civil cases indexed by defendant, plaintiff. Civil records on index books from 1914.
Criminal Records: Access: Mail, in person. Both court and visitors may perform in person searches. Search fee: $10.00 per name per year. Required to search: name, years to search; also helpful: address, DOB, SSN. Criminal records on index books from 1914.
General Information: No adoptions, sealed, juvenile, mental health, expunged or dismissed records released. SASE required. Turnaround time 1-2 days. Fax notes: Fee to fax results is $3.00 per document. Copy fee: $.50 per page. Certification fee: $10.00. Fee payee: Clerk of Court. Personal checks accepted. All fees may be billed.

Slope County

Southwest Judicial District Court PO Box JJ, Amidon, ND 58620; 701-879-6275; Fax: 701-879-6278. Hours: 9AM-5PM (MST). *Felony, Misdemeanor, Civil, Eviction, Small Claims, Probate.*

Civil Records: Access: Fax, mail, in person. Both court and visitors may perform in person searches. Search fee: $10.00 per name. Required to search: name, years to search; also helpful: address. Civil cases indexed by defendant, plaintiff. Civil records on index cards from 1989.
Criminal Records: Access: Fax, mail, in person. Both court and visitors may perform in person searches. Search fee: $10.00 per name. Required to search: name, years to search, DOB; also helpful: address. Criminal records on index books from 1915.
General Information: No adoptions, sealed, juvenile, mental health, expunged or dismissed records released. SASE required. Turnaround time 1-2 days. Fax notes: $3.00 per document. Copy fee: $.25 per page. Certification fee: $10.00. Fee payee: Clerk of Court. Personal checks accepted. Prepayment is required.

Stark County

District Court 51 Third St #106, Dickinson, ND 58602; 701-264-7637; Fax: 701-264-7640. Hours: 7AM-5PM (MST). *Felony, Misdemeanor, Civil, Eviction, Small Claims, Probate.*

Civil Records: Access: Mail, in person. Both court and visitors may perform in person searches. Search fee: $10.00 per name. Required to search: name, years to search. Civil cases indexed by defendant, plaintiff. Civil records on computer since 1/92, index cards since 1800s.
Criminal Records: Access: Mail, in person. Both court and visitors may perform in person searches. Search fee: $10.00 per name. Required to search: name, years to search, DOB; also helpful: SSN. Criminal records on computer since 1/92, index cards since 1800s.
General Information: Public Access terminal is available. No adoptions, sealed, juvenile, mental health, expunged or dismissed records. SASE required. Turnaround time 1-2 days. Copy fee: $.25 per page; $1.00 minimum. Certification fee: $10.00. Fee payee: Clerk of Court. Personal checks accepted. Prepayment is required.

Steele County

East Central Judicial District Court PO Box 296, Finley, ND 58230; 701-524-2152; Fax: 701-524-1325. Hours: 8AM-Noon; 1-4:30PM (CST). *Felony, Misdemeanor, Civil, Eviction, Small Claims, Probate.*

Civil Records: Access: Mail, in person. Only the court performs in person searches; visitors may not. Search fee: $10.00 per name. Required to search: name, years to search; also helpful: address. Civil cases indexed by defendant, plaintiff. Civil records on docket books from approx 1894.
Criminal Records: Access: Mail, in person. Only the court performs in person searches; visitors may not. Search fee: $10.00 per name. Required to search: name, years to search, DOB, signed release; also helpful: address. Criminal records on docket books from approx 1894.
General Information: No adoptions, sealed, juvenile, mental health, expunged or dismissed records released. SASE required. Turnaround time 1-2 days. Copy fee: $1.00 per page. Certification fee: $10.00. Fee payee: Clerk of Court. Business checks accepted. Prepayment is required.

Stutsman County

Southeast Judicial District Court 511 2nd Ave SE, Jamestown, ND 58401; 701-252-9042; Fax: 701-251-1006. Hours: 8AM-5PM (CST). *Felony, Misdemeanor, Civil, Eviction, Small Claims, Probate.*

Civil Records: Access: Mail, in person. Only the court performs in person searches; visitors may not. Search fee: $10.00 per name. Required to search: name, years to search; also helpful: address. Civil records on computer back to 1/87, on index books from 1800s.
Criminal Records: Access: Mail, in person. Only the court performs in person searches; visitors may not. Search fee: $10.00 per name. Required to search: name, years to search, DOB; also helpful: address. Criminal records on computer back to 1/96, on index books from 1800s.
General Information: No adoptions, sealed, juvenile, mental health, expunged or dismissed records released. SASE required. Turnaround time 1-2 days. Fax notes: Fee to fax results is $3.00 per document. Copy fee: $.25 per page. Certification fee: $10.00. Fee payee: Clerk of Court. Personal checks accepted. Prepayment is required.

Towner County

Northeast Judicial District Court Box 517, Cando, ND 58324; 701-968-4340 Ext 3; Fax: 701-968-4344. Hours: 8:30AM-5PM (CST). *Felony, Misdemeanor, Civil, Eviction, Small Claims, Probate.*

Civil Records: Access: Fax, mail, in person. Only the court performs in person searches; visitors may not. Search fee: $10.00 per name. Required to search: name, years to search; also helpful: address. Civil cases indexed by defendant, plaintiff. Civil records on index books from 1800s.

Criminal Records: Access: Fax, mail, in person. Only the court performs in person searches; visitors may not. Search fee: $10.00 per name. Required to search: name, years to search; also helpful: address, DOB, SSN. Criminal records on index books from 1800s.

General Information: No adoptions, sealed, juvenile, mental health, expunged or dismissed records released. SASE required. Turnaround time 1-2 days. Fax notes: $3.00 per document. Copy fee: $.50 per page. Certification fee: $10.00 plus $5.00 per copy. Fee payee: Clerk of District Court. Personal checks accepted. Prepayment is required.

Traill County

East Central Judicial District Court PO Box 805, Hillsboro, ND 58045; 701-436-4454; Fax: 701-436-5124. Hours: 8AM-4:30PM (CST). *Felony, Misdemeanor, Civil, Eviction, Small Claims, Probate.*

Civil Records: Access: Phone, fax, mail, in person. Only the court performs in person searches; visitors may not. Search fee: $10.00 per name. Required to search: name, years to search; also helpful: address. Civil cases indexed by defendant, plaintiff. Civil records on index books from 1800s.

Criminal Records: Access: Phone, fax, mail, in person. Only the court performs in person searches; visitors may not. Search fee: $10.00 per name. Required to search: name, years to search; also helpful: address, DOB, SSN. Criminal records on index books from 1800s.

General Information: No adoptions, sealed, juvenile, mental health, expunged or dismissed records released. SASE required. Turnaround time 1-2 days. Fax notes: $1.00 per page. Copy fee: $.25 per page. Certification fee: $10.00. Fee payee: Clerk of Court. Personal checks accepted. Prepayment is required.

Walsh County

Northeast Judicial District Court 600 Cooper Ave, Grafton, ND 58237; 701-352-0350; Fax: 701-352-4466. Hours: 8:30AM-5PM (CST). *Felony, Misdemeanor, Civil, Eviction, Small Claims, Probate.*

Civil Records: Access: Mail, in person. Both court and visitors may perform in person searches. Search fee: $10.00 per name. Required to search: name, years to search; also helpful: address. Civil cases indexed by defendant, plaintiff. Civil records on index books from early 1900s; on computer from 11/97.

Criminal Records: Access: Mail, in person. Only the court performs in person searches; visitors may not. Search fee: $10.00 per name. Required to search: name, years to search, DOB; also helpful: address, SSN. Criminal records on index books from early 1900s; on computer from 11/97.

General Information: No adoptions, sealed, juvenile, mental health, expunged or dismissed records released. SASE required. Turnaround time 5-10 days. Fax notes: Fee to fax results is $5.00 per document. Copy fee: $.25 per page; $1.00 minimum. Certification fee: $10.00, then $5.00 each add'l. Fee payee: Clerk of Court. Personal checks accepted. Prepayment is required.

Ward County

Northwest Judicial District Court PO Box 5005, Minot, ND 58702-5005; 701-857-6460; Fax: 701-857-6468. Hours: 8AM-4:30PM (CST). *Felony, Misdemeanor, Civil, Eviction, Small Claims, Probate.*

Civil Records: Access: Mail, in person. Both court and visitors may perform in person searches. Search fee: $10.00 per name. Required to search: name, years to search; also helpful: address. Civil cases indexed by defendant, plaintiff. Civil records on index cards from 1990, on index books from 1800s; computerized records go back to 1994.

Criminal Records: Access: Mail, in person. Both court and visitors may perform in person searches. Search fee: $10.00 per name. Required to search: name, years to search; also helpful: address, DOB, SSN. Criminal records on index cards from 1990, on index books from 1800s; computerized records go back to 1994.

General Information: Public Access terminal is available. No adoptions, sealed, juvenile, mental health, expunged or dismissed records released. SASE not required. Turnaround time 5 days. Copy fee: $.25 per page (minimum $1.00). Certification fee: $10.00. Fee payee: Clerk of District Court. Business checks accepted. Prepayment is required.

Wells County

Southeast Judicial District Court PO Box 596, Fessenden, ND 58438; 701-547-3122; Fax: 701-547-3719. Hours: 8AM-4:30PM (CST). *Felony, Misdemeanor, Civil, Eviction, Small Claims, Probate.*

Civil Records: Access: Mail, in person. Only the court performs in person searches; visitors may not. Search fee: $10.00 per name. Required to search: name, years to search; also helpful: address. Civil cases indexed by defendant, plaintiff. Civil records on index books.

Criminal Records: Access: Mail, in person. Only the court performs in person searches; visitors may not. Search fee: $10.00 per name. Required to search: name, years to search; also helpful: address, DOB, SSN. Criminal records on index books from 1980.

General Information: No adoptions, sealed, juvenile, mental health, expunged or dismissed records released. SASE required. Turnaround time 1-2 days. Copy fee: $1.00 per document. Certification fee: $10.00. Fee payee: District Court. Personal checks accepted. Prepayment is required.

Williams County

Northwest Judicial District Court PO Box 2047, Williston, ND 58802; 701-572-1720; Fax: 701-572-1760. Hours: 8AM-5PM (CST). *Felony, Misdemeanor, Civil, Eviction, Small Claims, Probate.*

Civil Records: Access: Mail, in person. Both court and visitors may perform in person searches. Search fee: $10.00 per name. Required to search: name, years to search; also helpful: address. Civil cases indexed by defendant, plaintiff. Civil records computerized since 1/98, on index cards from 1/92, on index books from 1899.

Criminal Records: Access: Mail, in person. Both court and visitors may perform in person searches. Search fee: $10.00 per name. Required to search: name, years to search; also helpful: address, DOB, SSN. Criminal records computerized since 1/98, on index cards from 1/92, on index books from 1899.

General Information: No adoptions, sealed, juvenile, mental health, expunged or dismissed records released. SASE required. Turnaround time 1-2 days. Copy fee: $2.00 fee for $.25 per page with $1 minimum. Certification fee: $10.00. Fee payee: Clerk of Court. Personal checks accepted. Prepayment is required.

North Dakota Recording Offices

ORGANIZATION
53 counties, 53 recording offices. The recording officer is the Register of Deeds. The entire state is in the Central Time Zone (CST).

REAL ESTATE RECORDS
Some counties will perform real estate searches by name or by legal description. Copy fees are usually $1.00 per page. Certified copies usually cost $5.00 for the first page and $2.00 for each additional page. Copies may be faxed.

UCC RECORDS
Since 07/1/2001, all financing statements must be filed at the state level, except for real estate related collateral, which are filed only with the Register of Deeds. Previously, the state was a dual filing state and record could be filed at either place. The good news is that all counties access a statewide computer database of filings and will perform UCC searches. Use search request form UCC-11. Various search options are available, including by federal tax identification number or Social Security number The search with copies costs $7.00 per debtor name, including three pages of copies and $1.00 per additional page. Copies may be faxed for an additional fee of $3.00.

TAX LIEN RECORDS
Federal tax liens on personal property of businesses are filed with the Secretary of State. Other federal and all state tax liens are filed with the county Register of Deeds. All counties will perform tax lien searches. Some counties automatically include business federal tax liens as part of a UCC search because they appear on the statewide database. (Be careful - federal tax liens on individuals may only be in the county lien books, not on the statewide system.) Separate searches are usually available at $5.00-7.00 per name. Copy fees vary. Copies may be faxed.

OTHER LIENS
Mechanics, judgment, hospital, repair, egg cutter.

STATEWIDE ONLINE INFO:
The North Dakota Recorders Information Network (NDRIN) is a electronic central repository for ten participating counties. Burleigh, Cass, Dunn, McLean, Stark and Ward currently offer internet access. Other counties participating in the system are McKenzie, Richland, Walsh, and Williams. There is a $200 set-up fee and a choice of two monthly plans: $500 per month for unlimited access, or $100 with $1.00 charge per image printed. Register or request information via the web site at www.ndrin.com.

Adams County

Register of Deeds, P.O. Box 469, Hettinger, ND 58639-0469. 701-567-2460; Fax 701-567-2910.
Will search UCC records. **Other Phone Numbers:** Assessor 701-567-2900; Treasurer 701-567-2537; Elections 701-567-4363.

Barnes County

Register of Deeds, P.O. Box 684, Valley City, ND 58072. 701-845-8506; Fax 701-845-8538.
Will search UCC records. Will not search real estate records. **Other Phone Numbers:** Assessor 701-845-8515; Treasurer 701-845-8505; Elections 701-845-8500.

Benson County

Register of Deeds, P.O. Box 193, Minnewaukan, ND 58351. 701-473-5332; Fax 701-473-5571.
Will search UCC records. Will not search real estate records. **Other Phone Numbers:** Assessor 701-473-5340; Treasurer 701-473-5458; Elections 701-473-5340.

Billings County

Register of Deeds, P.O. Box 138, Medora, ND 58645-0138. 701-623-4491; Fax 701-623-4896.
Will search UCC records. Will not search real estate records. **Other Phone Numbers:** Assessor 701-623-4810; Treasurer 701-623-4484; Elections 701-623-4377.

Bottineau County

Register of Deeds, 314 West 5th Street, Bottineau, ND 58318-1265. 701-228-2786; Fax 701-228-3658.
Will search UCC records. Will not search real estate records. **Other Phone Numbers:** Treasurer 701-228-2035; Elections 701-228-2225.

Bowman County

Register of Deeds, P.O. Box 379, Bowman, ND 58623. Register of Deeds, R/E and UCC Recording 701-523-3450; Fax 701-523-5443.
Will search UCC records. **Other Phone Numbers:** Assessor 701-523-3129; Treasurer 701-523-3665; Appraiser/Auditor 701-523-3129; Elections 701-523-3130; Vital Records 701-328-2360; Auditor 701-523-3130.

Burke County

Register of Deeds, P.O. Box 219, Bowbells, ND 58721-0219. Register of Deeds, R/E and UCC Recording 701-377-2818; Fax 701-377-2020.
Will search UCC records. **Other Phone Numbers:** Assessor 701-377-2661; Treasurer 701-377-2917; Appraiser/Auditor 701-377-2661; Elections 701-377-2861; Vital Records 701-377-2718.

Burleigh County

Register of Deeds, P.O. Box 5518, Bismarck, ND 58506-5518. Register of Deeds, R/E and UCC Recording 701-222-6749; Fax 701-222-6717. http://www.ndrin.com/
Will search UCC records. Will not search real estate records. **Online Access:** Real Estate. Online access the recorder's land records are available by subscription to NDRIN's central repository at www.ndrin.com. See section introduction. **Other Phone Numbers:** Assessor 701-222-6691; Treasurer 701-222-6696; Appraiser/Auditor 701-222-6691; Elections 701-222-6718; Vital Records 701-222-2360.

Cass County

Register of Deeds, P.O. Box 2806, Fargo, ND 58108-2806. 701-241-5620; Fax 701-241-5621.
Will search UCC records. Will not search real estate records. **Online Access:** Real Estate. Online access the recorder's land records are available by subscription to NDRIN's central repository at www.ndrin.com. See section introduction. **Other Phone Numbers:** Assessor 701-241-5611; Treasurer 701-241-5611; Elections 701-241-5601.

Cavalier County

Register of Deeds, 901 3rd Street, Langdon, ND 58249. Register of Deeds, R/E and UCC Recording 701-256-2136; Fax 701-256-2566.
Will search UCC records. Will not search real estate records. **Other Phone Numbers:** Assessor 701-256-3826; Treasurer 701-256-2549; Elections 701-256-2229; Vital Records 701-256-2124.

Dickey County

Register of Deeds, P.O. Box 148, Ellendale, ND 58436. 701-349-3029; Fax 701-349-4639.
Will search UCC records. Will not search real estate records. **Other Phone Numbers:** Elections 701-349-3249.

Divide County

Register of Deeds, P.O. Box 68, Crosby, ND 58730. 701-965-6661; Fax 701-965-6943.
Will search UCC records. Will not search real estate records. **Other Phone Numbers:** Assessor 701-965-6351; Treasurer 701-965-6312; Elections 701-965-6351.

Dunn County

Register of Deeds, P.O. Box 106, Manning, ND 58642-0106. Register of Deeds, R/E and UCC Recording 701-573-4443; Fax 701-573-4444. www.ndrin.com
Will search UCC records. Will not search real estate records. **Online Access:** Real Estate. Online access the recorder's land records are available by subscription to NDRIN's central repository at www.ndrin.com. See section introduction. **Other Phone Numbers:** Assessor

701-573-4445; Treasurer 701-573-4446; Elections 701-573-4448 (Auditor); Vital Records 701-328-2360.

Eddy County

Register of Deeds, 524 Central Avenue, New Rockford, ND 58356-1698. 701-947-2813; Fax 701-947-2067. Will search UCC records. **Other Phone Numbers:** Assessor 701-947-5220; Treasurer 701-947-5315; Elections 701-947-2434.

Emmons County

Register of Deeds, P.O. Box 905, Linton, ND 58552. 701-254-4812; Fax 701-254-4012. Will search UCC records. **Other Phone Numbers:** Assessor 701-254-4417; Treasurer 701-254-4802; Elections 701-254-4807.

Foster County

Register of Deeds, P.O. Box 257, Carrington, ND 58421. 701-652-2491; Fax 701-652-2173. Will search UCC records. **Other Phone Numbers:** Assessor 701-652-2441; Treasurer 701-652-2323; Elections 701-652-2441.

Golden Valley County

Register of Deeds, P.O. Box 130, Beach, ND 58621-0130. 701-872-3713 R/E Recording: 701-872-4352; Fax 701-872-4383. Will search UCC records. **Other Phone Numbers:** Assessor 701-872-4672; Treasurer 701-872-4411; Elections 701-872-4331.

Grand Forks County

Register of Deeds, P.O. Box 5066, Grand Forks, ND 58206. 701-780-8261 R/E Recording: 701-780-8200; Fax 701-780-8212. Will search UCC records. Will not search real estate records. **Other Phone Numbers:** Assessor 701-780-8261; Treasurer 701-780-8295; Elections 701-780-8200.

Grant County

Register of Deeds, P.O. Box 258, Carson, ND 58529. 701-622-3544; Fax 701-622-3717. Will search UCC records. **Other Phone Numbers:** Assessor 701-622-3275; Treasurer 701-622-3422; Elections 701-622-3275.

Griggs County

Register of Deeds, P.O. Box 237, Cooperstown, ND 58425. 701-797-2771; Fax 701-797-3587. Will search UCC records. Will not search real estate records. **Other Phone Numbers:** Assessor 701-797-3211; Treasurer 701-797-2411; Elections 701-797-3117.

Hettinger County

Register of Deeds, P.O. Box 668, Mott, ND 58646. Register of Deeds, R/E and UCC Recording 701-824-2545; Fax 701-824-2717. Will search UCC records. **Other Phone Numbers:** Assessor 701-824-2515; Treasurer 701-824-2655; Appraiser/Auditor 701-824-2515; Elections 701-824-2515; Vital Records 701-824-2545.

Kidder County

Register of Deeds, P.O. Box 66, Steele, ND 58482. Register of Deeds, R/E and UCC Recording 701-475-2632; Fax 701-475-2202. Will search UCC records. **Other Phone Numbers:** Assessor 701-475-2632; Treasurer 701-475-2632; Elections 701-475-2632.

La Moure County

Register of Deeds, P.O. Box 128, La Moure, ND 58458-0128. 701-883-5304 R/E Recording: 701-883-5301; Fax 701-883-5304. Will search UCC records. **Other Phone Numbers:** Assessor 701-883-5301; Treasurer 701-883-5103; Elections 701-883-5301.

Logan County

Register of Deeds, P.O. Box 6, Napoleon, ND 58561-0006. 701-754-2751; Fax 701-754-2270. Will search UCC records. UCC search includes federal tax liens if requested RE record owner and mortgage searches available. **Other Phone Numbers:** Assessor 701-754-2239; Treasurer 701-754-2286; Elections 701-754-2425.

McHenry County

Register of Deeds, P.O. Box 149, Towner, ND 58788. Register of Deeds, R/E and UCC Recording 701-537-5634; Fax 701-537-5969. www.state.nd.us Will search UCC records. Will not search real estate records. **Other Phone Numbers:** Assessor 701-537-5359; Treasurer 701-537-5731; Elections 701-537-5724; Vital Records 701-537-5729.

McIntosh County

Register of Deeds, P.O. Box 179, Ashley, ND 58413. 701-288-3589; Fax 701-288-3671. Will search UCC records. **Other Phone Numbers:** Assessor 701-288-3347; Treasurer 701-288-3342; Elections 701-288-3347.

McKenzie County

Register of Deeds, P.O. Box 523, Watford City, ND 58854. 701-842-3453 R/E Recording: 701-842-3616; Fax 701-842-3902. http://www.4eyes.net/county.htm Participates in the ND Recorders Information Network, www.ndrin.com. Will search UCC records. Will not search real estate records. **Other Phone Numbers:** Assessor 701-842-6852; Treasurer 701-842-3457; Appraiser/Auditor 701-842-6852; Elections 701-842-3616; Vital Records 701-842-3452.

McLean County

Register of Deeds, P.O. Box 1108, Washburn, ND 58577-1108. 701-462-8541 x225/6 R/E Recording: 701-462-8541 X226, x225 UCC Recording: 701-462-8541; Fax 701-462-3633. Will search UCC records. **Online Access:** Real Estate. Online access the recorder's land records are available by subscription to NDRIN's central repository at www.ndrin.com. See section introduction. **Other Phone Numbers:** Assessor 701-462-8541; Treasurer 701-462-8541 x223; Elections 701-462-8541 x216; Vital Records 701-462-8541 x228.

Mercer County

Register of Deeds, P.O. Box 39, Stanton, ND 58571. 701-745-3272; Fax 701-745-3364. Will search UCC records. Will not search real estate records. **Other Phone Numbers:** Elections 701-745-3292.

Morton County

Register of Deeds, 210 2nd Avenue, Mandan, ND 58554. 701-667-3305 R/E Recording: 701-667-3300; Fax 701-667-3453. Will search UCC records. Will not search real estate records. **Other Phone Numbers:** Assessor 701-667-3300; Treasurer 701-667-3310; Elections 701-667-3300.

Mountrail County

Register of Deeds, P.O. Box 69, Stanley, ND 58784. Register of Deeds, R/E and UCC Recording 701-628-2945; Fax 701-628-3975. Will search UCC records. Will not search real estate records. **Other Phone Numbers:** Assessor 701-826-2425; Treasurer 701-628-2935; Elections 701-628-2145.

Nelson County

Register of Deeds, P.O. Box 565, Lakota, ND 58344. 701-247-2433; Fax 701-247-2412. Will search UCC records. **Other Phone Numbers:** Assessor 701-247-2453; Treasurer 701-247-2840; Elections 701-247-2463.

Oliver County

Register of Deeds, P.O. Box 125, Center, ND 58530-0125. 701-794-8777; Fax 701-794-3476. Will search UCC records. **Other Phone Numbers:** Assessor 701-794-8721; Treasurer 701-794-8737; Elections 701-794-8721.

Pembina County

Register of Deeds, 301 Dakota Street W. 10, Cavalier, ND 58220. Register of Deeds, R/E and UCC Recording 701-265-4373; Fax 701-265-4876. Will search UCC records. Will not search real estate records. **Other Phone Numbers:** Assessor 701-265-4697; Treasurer 701-265-4465; Elections 701-265-4231.

Pierce County

Register of Deeds, 240 S.E. 2nd Street, Rugby, ND 58368. 701-776-5206; Fax 701-776-5707. Will search UCC records. Will not search real estate records. **Other Phone Numbers:** Assessor 701-776-5225; Treasurer 701-776-6841; Elections 701-776-5225.

Ramsey County

Register of Deeds, 524 4th Avenue #30, Devils Lake, ND 58301. 701-662-7018 R/E Recording: 701-62-7018; Fax 701-662-7093. Will search UCC records. Will not search real estate records. **Other Phone Numbers:** Assessor 701-662-7018; Treasurer 701-662-7021; Elections 701-62-7007.

Ransom County

Register of Deeds, P.O. Box 666, Lisbon, ND 58054-0666. 701-683-5823 R/E Recording: 701-683-5823 x115; Fax 701-683-5827. Will search UCC records. **Other Phone Numbers:** Assessor 701-683-5823 x144; Treasurer 701-683-5823 x118; Elections 701-683-5823 x113; Vital Records 701-683-5823 x 120.

Renville County

Register of Deeds, P.O. Box 68, Mohall, ND 58761-0068. Register of Deeds, R/E and UCC Recording 701-756-6398; Fax 701-756-6398. www.renvillecounty.org Will search UCC records. UCC search includes federal tax liens Will not search real estate records. **Other Phone Numbers:** Assessor 701-756-6368; Treasurer 701-756-6304; Appraiser/Auditor 701-756-6368; Elections 701-756-6301; Vital Records 701-756-6398.

Richland County

Register of Deeds, 418 2nd Avenue North, Courthouse, Wahpeton, ND 58075-4400. Register of Deeds, R/E and UCC Recording 701-642-7800; Fax 701-642-7820. Participates in the ND Recorders Information Network, www.ndrin.com. Will search UCC records. **Other Phone Numbers:** Assessor 701-642-7805; Treasurer

701-642-7705; Elections 701-642-7700; Vital Records 701-642-7800.

Rolette County

Register of Deeds, P.O. Box 276, Rolla, ND 58367. 701-477-3166; Fax 701-477-5770.

Will search UCC records. Will not search real estate records. **Other Phone Numbers:** Assessor 701-477-5665; Treasurer 701-477-3207; Elections 701-477-5665.

Sargent County

Register of Deeds, P.O. Box 176, Forman, ND 58032-0176. 701-724-6241; Fax 701-724-6244.

Will search UCC records. Will not search real estate records. **Other Phone Numbers:** Assessor 701-724-6241 x15; Treasurer 701-724-6241 x13,14; Elections 701-724-6241.

Sheridan County

Register of Deeds, P.O. Box 409, McClusky, ND 58463-0668. 701-363-2207 UCC Recording: 603-895-2226; Fax 701-363-2953.

Will search UCC records. **Other Phone Numbers:** Assessor 701-363-2201; Treasurer 701-363-2206; Elections 701-363-2205; Vital Records 603-895-2207.

Sioux County

Register of Deeds, P.O. Box L, Fort Yates, ND 58538. 701-854-3853; Fax 701-854-3854.

Will search UCC records. **Other Phone Numbers:** Assessor 701-854-3424; Elections 701-854-3481.

Slope County

Register of Deeds, P.O. Box JJ, Amidon, ND 58620-0445. 701-879-6275 R/E Recording: 701-879-6276; Fax 701-879-6278.

Will search UCC records. Will not search real estate records. **Other Phone Numbers:** Assessor 701-879-6276; Treasurer 701-879-6271; Elections 701-879-6276.

Stark County

Register of Deeds, P.O. Box 130, Dickinson, ND 58601. 701-264-7645; Fax 701-264-7628.

Will search UCC records. Will not search real estate records. **Online Access:** Real Estate. Online access the recorder's land records are available by subscription to NDRIN's central repository at www.ndrin.com. See section introduction. **Other Phone Numbers:** Assessor 701-264-7671; Elections 701-264-7630.

Steele County

Register of Deeds, P.O. Box 296, Finley, ND 58230. 701-524-2152 R/E Recording: 701-524-2790; Fax 701-524-1325.

Will search UCC records. Will not search real estate records. **Other Phone Numbers:** Assessor 701-524-2110; Treasurer 701-524-2890; Elections 701-524-2110.

Stutsman County

Register of Deeds, 511 2nd Avenue S.E., Courthouse, Jamestown, ND 58401. 701-252-9034 R/E Recording: 701-252-9035; Fax 701-251-1603.

Will search UCC records. Will not search real estate records. **Other Phone Numbers:** Assessor 701-252-9032; Treasurer 701-252-9036; Elections 701-252-9035.

Towner County

Register of Deeds, P.O. Box 517, Cando, ND 58324. 701-968-4343 R/E Recording: 701-968-4340 x5 UCC Recording: 701-968-4340 x5; Fax 701-968-4344.

Will search UCC records. Will not search real estate records. **Other Phone Numbers:** Assessor 701-968-4352; Treasurer 701-968-4347; Elections 701-968-4340.

Traill County

Register of Deeds, P.O. Box 399, Hillsboro, ND 58045. Register of Deeds, R/E and UCC Recording 701-436-4457; Fax 701-436-4457.

Will search UCC records. **Other Phone Numbers:** Assessor 701-436-5950; Treasurer 701-436-4459; Elections 701-436-4458; Vital Records 701-436-4454.

Walsh County

Register of Deeds, 600 Cooper Avenue, Courthouse, Grafton, ND 58237. 701-352-2380; Fax 701-352-3340. Participates in the ND Recorders Information Network, www.ndrin.com. Will search UCC records. **Other Phone Numbers:** Assessor 701-352-2851; Treasurer 701-352-2541; Elections 701-352-2851.

Ward County

Register of Deeds, 315 S.E. Third Street, Courthouse, Minot, ND 58705-5005. 701-857-6410 R/E Recording: 701-857-6420; Fax 701-857-6414.

Will search UCC records. Will not search real estate records. **Online Access:** Real Estate. Online access the recorder's land records are available by subscription to NDRIN's central repository at www.ndrin.com. See section introduction. **Other Phone Numbers:** Assessor 701-857-6430; Elections 701-857-6420.

Wells County

Register of Deeds, P.O. Box 125, Fessenden, ND 58438-0125. Register of Deeds, R/E and UCC Recording 701-547-3141; Fax 701-547-3719.

Will search UCC records. Will search real estate records; fee is $25.00 per hour after the first hour. **Other Phone Numbers:** Assessor 701-547-3220; Treasurer 701-547-3161; Elections 701-547-3521; Vital Records 701-547-3122.

Williams County

Register of Deeds, P.O. Box 2047, Williston, ND 58802-2047. 701-572-1740; Fax 701-572-1759. Participates in the ND Recorders Information Network, www.ndrin.com.

Will search UCC records. **Other Phone Numbers:** Assessor 701-572-1745; Treasurer 701-572-1737; Elections 701-572-1700.

North Dakota County Locator

You will usually be able to find the city name in the City/County Cross Reference below. In that case, it is a simple matter to determine the county from the cross reference. However, only the official US Postal Service city names are included in this index. There are an additional 40,000 place names that people use in their addresses. Therefore, we have also included a ZIP/City Cross Reference immediately following the City/County Cross Reference.

If you know the ZIP Code but the city name does not appear in the City/County Cross Reference index, look up the ZIP Code in the ZIP/City Cross Reference, find the city name, then look up the city name in the City/County Cross Reference. For example, you want to know the county for an address of Menands, NY 12204. There is no "Menands" in the City/County Cross Reference. The ZIP/City Cross Reference shows that ZIP Codes 12201-12288 are for the city of Albany. Looking back in the City/County Cross Reference, Albany is in Albany County.

City/County Cross Reference

ABERCROMBIE Richland
ABSARAKA Cass
ADAMS Walsh
AGATE Rolette
ALAMO (58830) Williams(77), Divide(23)
ALEXANDER McKenzie
ALFRED La Moure
ALICE Cass
ALMONT (58520) Morton(72), Grant(28)
ALSEN Cavalier
AMBROSE Divide
AMENIA Cass
AMIDON Slope
ANAMOOSE (58710) McHenry(55), Sheridan(26), Pierce(18)
ANETA (58212) Nelson(70), Griggs(20), Grand Forks(8), Steele(3)
ANTLER Bottineau
ARDOCH (58213) Walsh(66), Grand Forks(34)
ARENA (58412) Burleigh(99), Kidder(1)
ARGUSVILLE Cass
ARNEGARD McKenzie
ARTHUR Cass
ARVILLA Grand Forks
ASHLEY (58413) McIntosh(93), Dickey(7)
AYR Cass
BALDWIN Burleigh
BALFOUR McHenry
BALTA Pierce
BANTRY McHenry
BARNEY Richland
BARTON Pierce
BATHGATE Pembina
BEACH (58621) Golden Valley(99), McKenzie(1)
BELCOURT Rolette
BELFIELD (58622) Stark(64), Billings(36)
BENEDICT (58716) McLean(79), Ward(21)
BERLIN (58415) La Moure(98), Dickey(2)
BERTHOLD (58718) Ward(73), Mountrail(25), Renville(2)
BEULAH (58523) Mercer(98), Oliver(2)
BINFORD (58416) Griggs(96), Nelson(4)
BISBEE (58317) Towner(85), Rolette(8), Pierce(7)
BISMARCK Burleigh
BLAISDELL Mountrail
BLANCHARD Traill
BOTTINEAU Bottineau
BOWBELLS (58721) Burke(95), Ward(5)
BOWBELLS Burke
BOWDON (58418) Wells(98), Kidder(2)
BOWMAN (58623) Bowman(95), Slope(5)
BRADDOCK (58524) Emmons(74), Burleigh(14), Kidder(12)
BREMEN Wells
BRINSMADE Benson
BROCKET (58321) Nelson(38), Walsh(37), Ramsey(26)
BUCHANAN Stutsman
BUFFALO Cass
BURLINGTON Ward
BUTTE (58723) McLean(92), Sheridan(8)

BUXTON Traill
CALEDONIA Traill
CALVIN (58323) Cavalier(82), Towner(18)
CANDO Towner
CANNON BALL Sioux
CARPIO (58725) Ward(52), Renville(48)
CARRINGTON (58421) Foster(95), Stutsman(2), Wells(2), Eddy(1)
CARSON Grant
CARTWRIGHT McKenzie
CASSELTON Cass
CATHAY Wells
CAVALIER Pembina
CAYUGA Sargent
CENTER Oliver
CHAFFEE Cass
CHASELEY (58423) Wells(93), Kidder(7)
CHRISTINE (58015) Richland(98), Cass(2)
CHURCHS FERRY (58325) Ramsey(57), Benson(43)
CLEVELAND Stutsman
CLIFFORD (58016) Traill(66), Steele(34)
COGSWELL Sargent
COLEHARBOR McLean
COLFAX Richland
COLUMBUS Burke
COOPERSTOWN (99999) Griggs(99), Steele(1)
COURTENAY (58426) Stutsman(98), Foster(2)
CRARY Ramsey
CROSBY Divide
CRYSTAL Pembina
CRYSTAL SPRINGS Kidder
CUMMINGS Traill
DAHLEN (58224) Nelson(93), Walsh(7)
DAVENPORT Cass
DAWSON Kidder
DAZEY (58429) Barnes(98), Griggs(2)
DEERING (58731) McHenry(96), Ward(4)
DENHOFF Sheridan
DES LACS Ward
DEVILS LAKE Ramsey
DICKEY La Moure
DICKINSON (58601) Stark(98), Dunn(2)
DICKINSON Stark
DODGE (58625) Dunn(75), Mercer(25)
DONNYBROOK (58734) Ward(46), Mountrail(38), Renville(15)
DOUGLAS (58735) Ward(51), McLean(49)
DOYON Ramsey
DRAKE (58736) McHenry(86), Sheridan(14)
DRAYTON (58225) Pembina(77), Walsh(23)
DRISCOLL (58532) Burleigh(83), Kidder(17)
DUNN CENTER Dunn
DUNSEITH (58329) Rolette(82), Bottineau(18)
ECKELSON Barnes
EDGELEY (58433) La Moure(90), Dickey(10)

EDINBURG (58227) Walsh(65), Pembina(31), Cavalier(4)
EDMORE (58330) Ramsey(89), Walsh(9), Cavalier(3)
EGELAND Towner
ELGIN Grant
ELLENDALE Dickey
EMERADO Grand Forks
ENDERLIN (58027) Ransom(75), Cass(19), Barnes(6)
EPPING Williams
ERIE Cass
ESMOND (58332) Benson(75), Pierce(25)
FAIRDALE (58229) Walsh(90), Cavalier(9)
FAIRFIELD Billings
FAIRMOUNT Richland
FARGO Cass
FESSENDEN Wells
FINGAL (58031) Barnes(61), Cass(39)
FINLEY Steele
FLASHER (58535) Morton(81), Grant(19)
FLAXTON Burke
FORBES Dickey
FORDVILLE (58231) Walsh(79), Grand Forks(21)
FOREST RIVER (58233) Walsh(92), Grand Forks(8)
FORMAN Sargent
FORT RANSOM (58033) Ransom(98), La Moure(2)
FORT RICE Morton
FORT TOTTEN Benson
FORT YATES Sioux
FORTUNA Divide
FOXHOLM Ward
FREDONIA (58440) Logan(71), McIntosh(29)
FULLERTON Dickey
GACKLE (58442) Logan(85), Stutsman(15)
GALESBURG (58035) Traill(56), Cass(29), Steele(15)
GARDENA Bottineau
GARDNER Cass
GARRISON McLean
GILBY Grand Forks
GLADSTONE (58630) Stark(87), Dunn(13)
GLASSTON Pembina
GLEN ULLIN (58631) Morton(82), Grant(12), Mercer(5), Oliver(1)
GLENBURN (58740) Renville(68), Ward(28), McHenry(2), Bottineau(2)
GLENFIELD (58443) Foster(99), Griggs(1)
GOLDEN VALLEY Mercer
GOLVA Golden Valley
GOODRICH (58444) Sheridan(96), Burleigh(4)
GRACE CITY (58445) Foster(85), Eddy(16)
GRAFTON Walsh
GRAND FORKS Grand Forks
GRAND FORKS AFB Grand Forks
GRANDIN (58038) Cass(74), Traill(26)
GRANVILLE McHenry
GRASSY BUTTE (58634) McKenzie(92), Billings(8)

GREAT BEND Richland
GRENORA (58845) Williams(82), Divide(18)
GUELPH Dickey
GWINNER Sargent
HAGUE Emmons
HALLIDAY (58636) Dunn(97), Mercer(3)
HAMBERG Wells
HAMILTON Pembina
HAMPDEN (58338) Ramsey(70), Cavalier(30)
HANKINSON Richland
HANNAFORD (58448) Griggs(98), Barnes(2)
HANNAH Cavalier
HANSBORO Towner
HARVEY (58341) Wells(87), Pierce(11)
HARWOOD Cass
HATTON (58240) Traill(72), Steele(17), Grand Forks(11)
HAVANA Sargent
HAZELTON Emmons
HAZEN (58545) Mercer(95), Oliver(5)
HEATON (58450) Wells(87), Kidder(13)
HEBRON (58638) Morton(77), Mercer(9), Stark(9), Dunn(4), Grant(2)
HEIMDAL Wells
HENSEL Pembina
HENSLER Oliver
HETTINGER Adams
HILLSBORO Traill
HOOPLE (58243) Walsh(92), Pembina(8)
HOPE (58046) Steele(80), Barnes(16), Cass(4)
HORACE Cass
HUNTER (58048) Cass(96), Traill(5)
HURDSFIELD (58451) Wells(97), Sheridan(4)
INKSTER (58244) Grand Forks(94), Walsh(6)
JAMESTOWN Stutsman
JESSIE Griggs
JOLIETTE Pembina
JUD (58454) La Moure(80), Stutsman(20)
KARLSRUHE McHenry
KATHRYN (58049) Barnes(77), Ransom(17), La Moure(6)
KEENE McKenzie
KENMARE (58746) Ward(77), Burke(13), Renville(11)
KENSAL (58455) Stutsman(73), Foster(27)
KIEF (58747) Sheridan(82), McHenry(18)
KILLDEER (58640) Dunn(99), McKenzie(2)
KINDRED (58051) Cass(79), Richland(22)
KINTYRE (58549) Emmons(66), Logan(32), Kidder(2)
KNOX Benson
KRAMER (58748) Bottineau(93), McHenry(7)
KULM (58456) La Moure(77), Dickey(17), McIntosh(7)
LAKOTA (58344) Nelson(98), Ramsey(2)
LAMOURE (58458) La Moure(99), Dickey(1)

LANGDON Cavalier
LANKIN Walsh
LANSFORD (58750) Bottineau(61), Renville(40)
LARIMORE Grand Forks
LAWTON (58345) Walsh(60), Ramsey(40)
LEEDS (58346) Benson(93), Towner(6), Pierce(2)
LEFOR Stark
LEHR (58460) McIntosh(55), Logan(45)
LEITH Grant
LEONARD (58052) Cass(80), Richland(16), Ransom(4)
LIDGERWOOD (58053) Richland(86), Sargent(14)
LIGNITE Burke
LINTON Emmons
LISBON Ransom
LITCHVILLE (58461) Barnes(75), La Moure(26)
LUVERNE (58056) Barnes(59), Steele(30), Griggs(11)
MADDOCK (58348) Benson(86), Wells(14)
MAIDA Cavalier
MAKOTI (58756) Ward(79), Mountrail(17), McLean(4)
MANDAN Morton
MANDAREE (58757) McKenzie(53), Dunn(48)
MANFRED Wells
MANNING (58642) Dunn(85), Billings(15)
MANTADOR Richland
MANVEL Grand Forks
MAPLETON Cass
MARION (58466) La Moure(77), Barnes(21), Stutsman(2)
MARMARTH (58643) Slope(68), Bowman(32)
MARSHALL Dunn
MARTIN (58758) Sheridan(66), Wells(17), Pierce(17)
MAX (58759) Ward(57), McLean(43)
MAXBASS Bottineau
MAYVILLE Traill
MCCANNA Grand Forks
MCCLUSKY Sheridan
MCGREGOR (58755) Williams(71), Divide(16), Burke(13)
MCHENRY (58464) Foster(51), Eddy(46), Griggs(2)
MCKENZIE Burleigh
MCLEOD (58057) Richland(73), Ransom(27)
MCVILLE Nelson
MEDINA (58467) Stutsman(96), Kidder(4)
MEDORA (58645) Billings(92), Golden Valley(8)
MEKINOCK Grand Forks
MENOKEN Burleigh
MERCER (58559) McLean(87), Sheridan(13)
MERRICOURT Dickey
MICHIGAN Nelson

MILNOR (58060) Sargent(81), Ransom(19)
MILTON (58260) Cavalier(88), Walsh(12)
MINNEWAUKAN (58351) Benson(91), Ramsey(9)
MINOT Ward
MINOT AFB Ward
MINTO Walsh
MOFFIT (58560) Burleigh(81), Emmons(19)
MOHALL (58761) Renville(71), Bottineau(29)
MONANGO Dickey
MONTPELIER (58472) Stutsman(66), La Moure(34)
MOORETON Richland
MOTT (58646) Hettinger(98), Adams(2)
MOUNTAIN (58262) Pembina(94), Cavalier(6)
MUNICH (58352) Cavalier(96), Towner(4)
MYLO Rolette
NAPOLEON Logan
NECHE Pembina
NEKOMA Cavalier
NEW ENGLAND (58647) Hettinger(74), Slope(18), Stark(8)
NEW LEIPZIG (58562) Grant(91), Hettinger(8), Adams(1)
NEW ROCKFORD (58356) Eddy(94), Wells(4), Foster(2)
NEW SALEM (58563) Morton(82), Oliver(17)
NEW TOWN (58763) Mountrail(90), McKenzie(10)
NEWBURG (58762) Bottineau(80), McHenry(20)
NIAGARA (58266) Grand Forks(75), Nelson(26)
NOME (58062) Barnes(80), Ransom(20)
NOONAN Divide
NORTHWOOD (58267) Grand Forks(99), Steele(1)
NORWICH (58768) McHenry(55), Ward(45)
OAKES (58474) Dickey(97), Sargent(3)
OBERON Benson
ORISKA Barnes
ORRIN Pierce
OSNABROCK Cavalier
OVERLY Bottineau
PAGE (58064) Cass(89), Barnes(9), Steele(2)
PALERMO Mountrail
PARK RIVER Walsh
PARSHALL (58770) Mountrail(82), McLean(18)
PEKIN Nelson
PEMBINA Pembina
PENN Ramsey
PERTH (58363) Towner(80), Rolette(20)
PETERSBURG Nelson
PETTIBONE (58475) Kidder(90), Stutsman(10)
PILLSBURY Barnes
PINGREE Stutsman

PISEK Walsh
PLAZA (58771) Mountrail(78), Ward(20), McLean(3)
PORTAL Burke
PORTLAND (58274) Traill(85), Steele(15)
POWERS LAKE (58773) Burke(73), Mountrail(28)
RALEIGH Grant
RAY Williams
REEDER (58649) Adams(62), Hettinger(29)
REGAN Burleigh
REGENT (58650) Hettinger(96), Adams(5)
REYNOLDS (58275) Grand Forks(67), Traill(33)
RHAME (58651) Bowman(63), Slope(37)
RICHARDTON (58652) Stark(93), Dunn(7)
RIVERDALE McLean
ROBINSON Kidder
ROCKLAKE Towner
ROGERS Barnes
ROLETTE (58366) Rolette(96), Pierce(4)
ROLLA (58367) Rolette(94), Towner(6)
ROSEGLEN McLean
ROSS Mountrail
RUGBY (58368) Pierce(96), McHenry(3), Benson(1)
RUSO (58778) McLean(95), McHenry(5)
RUTLAND Sargent
RYDER (58779) McLean(57), Ward(44)
SAINT ANTHONY Morton
SAINT JOHN Rolette
SAINT MICHAEL Benson
SAINT THOMAS Pembina
SANBORN Barnes
SARLES (58372) Cavalier(65), Towner(35)
SAWYER Ward
SCRANTON (58653) Bowman(88), Slope(12)
SELFRIDGE (58568) Sioux(98), Grant(2)
SELZ Pierce
SENTINEL BUTTE (58654) Golden Valley(56), Slope(45)
SHARON Steele
SHELDON (58068) Ransom(99), Cass(1)
SHERWOOD (58782) Renville(96), Bottineau(5)
SHEYENNE (58374) Eddy(69), Benson(19), Wells(12)
SHIELDS Grant
SOLEN (58570) Morton(79), Sioux(21)
SOURIS Bottineau
SOUTH HEART Stark
SPIRITWOOD (58481) Stutsman(53), Barnes(47)
STANLEY (58784) Mountrail(94), Burke(6)
STANTON (58571) Mercer(74), Oliver(26)
STARKWEATHER (58377) Ramsey(83), Cavalier(9), Towner(7)
STEELE Kidder
STERLING Burleigh
STIRUM (58069) Sargent(95), Ransom(5)
STRASBURG Emmons

STREETER (58483) Stutsman(71), Logan(23), Kidder(7)
SURREY Ward
SUTTON (58484) Griggs(63), Foster(37)
SYKESTON (58486) Wells(94), Stutsman(6)
TAPPEN Kidder
TAYLOR (58656) Stark(90), Dunn(11)
THOMPSON Grand Forks
TIOGA (58852) Williams(90), Mountrail(11)
TOKIO Benson
TOLLEY (58787) Renville(98), Ward(2)
TOLNA (58380) Nelson(47), Eddy(45), Benson(8)
TOWER CITY (58071) Cass(81), Barnes(20)
TOWNER (58788) McHenry(95), Pierce(5)
TRENTON Williams
TROTTERS Golden Valley
TURTLE LAKE McLean
TUTTLE Kidder
UNDERWOOD McLean
UNION Cavalier
UPHAM (58789) McHenry(93), Bottineau(7)
VALLEY CITY Barnes
VELVA (58790) McHenry(91), Ward(9)
VENTURIA McIntosh
VERONA (58490) La Moure(87), Ransom(13)
VOLTAIRE McHenry
WAHPETON Richland
WALCOTT Richland
WALES Cavalier
WALHALLA (58282) Pembina(91), Cavalier(9)
WARWICK (58381) Eddy(74), Benson(26)
WASHBURN McLean
WATFORD CITY McKenzie
WEBSTER Ramsey
WEST FARGO Cass
WESTHOPE Bottineau
WHEATLAND Cass
WHITE EARTH (58794) Mountrail(99), Williams(2)
WILDROSE (58795) Williams(70), Divide(30)
WILLISTON Williams
WILLOW CITY (58384) Bottineau(61), Pierce(22), McHenry(11), Rolette(6)
WILTON (58579) McLean(53), Burleigh(48)
WIMBLEDON (58492) Barnes(81), Stutsman(13), Griggs(5)
WING Burleigh
WISHEK (58495) McIntosh(85), Logan(15)
WOLFORD (58385) Pierce(94), Rolette(6)
WOODWORTH Stutsman
WYNDMERE Richland
YORK (58386) Benson(54), Pierce(46)
YPSILANTI (58497) Stutsman(94), Barnes(6)
ZAHL (58856) Williams(84), Divide(16)
ZAP Mercer
ZEELAND McIntosh

ZIP/City Cross Reference

58001-58001	ABERCROMBIE	58018-58018	COLFAX	58043-58043	HAVANA	58061-58061	MOORETON
58002-58002	ABSARAKA	58021-58021	DAVENPORT	58045-58045	HILLSBORO	58062-58062	NOME
58004-58004	AMENIA	58027-58027	ENDERLIN	58046-58046	HOPE	58063-58063	ORISKA
58005-58005	ARGUSVILLE	58029-58029	ERIE	58047-58047	HORACE	58064-58064	PAGE
58006-58006	ARTHUR	58030-58030	FAIRMOUNT	58048-58048	HUNTER	58065-58065	PILLSBURY
58007-58007	AYR	58031-58031	FINGAL	58049-58049	KATHRYN	58067-58067	RUTLAND
58008-58008	BARNEY	58032-58032	FORMAN	58051-58051	KINDRED	58068-58068	SHELDON
58009-58009	BLANCHARD	58033-58033	FORT RANSOM	58052-58052	LEONARD	58069-58069	STIRUM
58011-58011	BUFFALO	58035-58035	GALESBURG	58053-58053	LIDGERWOOD	58071-58071	TOWER CITY
58012-58012	CASSELTON	58036-58036	GARDNER	58054-58054	LISBON	58072-58072	VALLEY CITY
58013-58013	CAYUGA	58038-58038	GRANDIN	58056-58056	LUVERNE	58074-58076	WAHPETON
58014-58014	CHAFFEE	58039-58039	GREAT BEND	58057-58057	MCLEOD	58077-58077	WALCOTT
58015-58015	CHRISTINE	58040-58040	GWINNER	58058-58058	MANTADOR	58078-58078	WEST FARGO
58016-58016	CLIFFORD	58041-58041	HANKINSON	58059-58059	MAPLETON	58079-58079	WHEATLAND
58017-58017	COGSWELL	58042-58042	HARWOOD	58060-58060	MILNOR	58081-58081	WYNDMERE

Zip	Place	Zip	Place	Zip	Place	Zip	Place
58102-58126	FARGO	58344-58344	LAKOTA	58486-58486	SYKESTON	58655-58655	SOUTH HEART
58201-58203	GRAND FORKS	58345-58345	LAWTON	58487-58487	TAPPEN	58656-58656	TAYLOR
58204-58205	GRAND FORKS AFB	58346-58346	LEEDS	58488-58488	TUTTLE	58701-58703	MINOT
58206-58208	GRAND FORKS	58348-58348	MADDOCK	58489-58489	VENTURIA	58704-58705	MINOT AFB
58210-58210	ADAMS	58351-58351	MINNEWAUKAN	58490-58490	VERONA	58707-58707	MINOT
58212-58212	ANETA	58352-58352	MUNICH	58492-58492	WIMBLEDON	58710-58710	ANAMOOSE
58213-58213	ARDOCH	58353-58353	MYLO	58494-58494	WING	58711-58711	ANTLER
58214-58214	ARVILLA	58355-58355	NEKOMA	58495-58495	WISHEK	58712-58712	BALFOUR
58216-58216	BATHGATE	58356-58356	NEW ROCKFORD	58496-58496	WOODWORTH	58713-58713	BANTRY
58218-58218	BUXTON	58357-58357	OBERON	58497-58497	YPSILANTI	58716-58716	BENEDICT
58219-58219	CALEDONIA	58359-58359	ORRIN	58501-58507	BISMARCK	58718-58718	BERTHOLD
58220-58220	CAVALIER	58361-58361	PEKIN	58520-58520	ALMONT	58721-58721	BOWBELLS
58222-58222	CRYSTAL	58362-58362	PENN	58521-58521	BALDWIN	58722-58722	BURLINGTON
58223-58223	CUMMINGS	58363-58363	PERTH	58523-58523	BEULAH	58723-58723	BUTTE
58224-58224	DAHLEN	58365-58365	ROCKLAKE	58524-58524	BRADDOCK	58725-58725	CARPIO
58225-58225	DRAYTON	58366-58366	ROLETTE	58528-58528	CANNON BALL	58727-58727	COLUMBUS
58227-58227	EDINBURG	58367-58367	ROLLA	58529-58529	CARSON	58730-58730	CROSBY
58228-58228	EMERADO	58368-58368	RUGBY	58530-58530	CENTER	58731-58731	DEERING
58229-58229	FAIRDALE	58369-58369	SAINT JOHN	58531-58531	COLEHARBOR	58733-58733	DES LACS
58230-58230	FINLEY	58370-58370	SAINT MICHAEL	58532-58532	DRISCOLL	58734-58734	DONNYBROOK
58231-58231	FORDVILLE	58372-58372	SARLES	58533-58533	ELGIN	58735-58735	DOUGLAS
58233-58233	FOREST RIVER	58374-58374	SHEYENNE	58535-58535	FLASHER	58736-58736	DRAKE
58235-58235	GILBY	58377-58377	STARKWEATHER	58538-58538	FORT YATES	58737-58737	FLAXTON
58236-58236	GLASSTON	58379-58379	TOKIO	58540-58540	GARRISON	58740-58740	GLENBURN
58237-58237	GRAFTON	58380-58380	TOLNA	58541-58541	GOLDEN VALLEY	58741-58741	GRANVILLE
58238-58238	HAMILTON	58381-58381	WARWICK	58542-58542	HAGUE	58744-58744	KARLSRUHE
58239-58239	HANNAH	58382-58382	WEBSTER	58544-58544	HAZELTON	58746-58746	KENMARE
58240-58240	HATTON	58384-58384	WILLOW CITY	58545-58545	HAZEN	58747-58747	KIEF
58241-58241	HENSEL	58385-58385	WOLFORD	58549-58549	KINTYRE	58748-58748	KRAMER
58243-58243	HOOPLE	58386-58386	YORK	58552-58552	LINTON	58750-58750	LANSFORD
58244-58244	INKSTER	58401-58405	JAMESTOWN	58553-58553	MCKENZIE	58752-58752	LIGNITE
58249-58249	LANGDON	58413-58413	ASHLEY	58554-58554	MANDAN	58755-58755	MCGREGOR
58250-58250	LANKIN	58415-58415	BERLIN	58558-58558	MENOKEN	58756-58756	MAKOTI
58251-58251	LARIMORE	58416-58416	BINFORD	58559-58559	MERCER	58757-58757	MANDAREE
58254-58254	MCVILLE	58418-58418	BOWDON	58560-58560	MOFFIT	58758-58758	MARTIN
58255-58255	MAIDA	58420-58420	BUCHANAN	58561-58561	NAPOLEON	58759-58759	MAX
58256-58256	MANVEL	58421-58421	CARRINGTON	58562-58562	NEW LEIPZIG	58760-58760	MAXBASS
58257-58257	MAYVILLE	58422-58422	CATHAY	58563-58563	NEW SALEM	58761-58761	MOHALL
58258-58258	MEKINOCK	58423-58423	CHASELEY	58564-58564	RALEIGH	58762-58762	NEWBURG
58259-58259	MICHIGAN	58424-58424	CLEVELAND	58565-58565	RIVERDALE	58763-58763	NEW TOWN
58260-58260	MILTON	58425-58425	COOPERSTOWN	58566-58566	SAINT ANTHONY	58765-58765	NOONAN
58261-58261	MINTO	58426-58426	COURTENAY	58568-58568	SELFRIDGE	58768-58768	NORWICH
58262-58262	MOUNTAIN	58428-58428	DAWSON	58569-58569	SHIELDS	58769-58769	PALERMO
58265-58265	NECHE	58429-58429	DAZEY	58570-58570	SOLEN	58770-58770	PARSHALL
58266-58266	NIAGARA	58430-58430	DENHOFF	58571-58571	STANTON	58771-58771	PLAZA
58267-58267	NORTHWOOD	58431-58431	DICKEY	58572-58572	STERLING	58772-58772	PORTAL
58269-58269	OSNABROCK	58432-58432	ECKELSON	58573-58573	STRASBURG	58773-58773	POWERS LAKE
58270-58270	PARK RIVER	58433-58433	EDGELEY	58575-58575	TURTLE LAKE	58775-58775	ROSEGLEN
58271-58271	PEMBINA	58436-58436	ELLENDALE	58576-58576	UNDERWOOD	58776-58776	ROSS
58272-58272	PETERSBURG	58438-58438	FESSENDEN	58577-58577	WASHBURN	58778-58778	RUSO
58273-58273	PISEK	58439-58439	FORBES	58579-58579	WILTON	58779-58779	RYDER
58274-58274	PORTLAND	58440-58440	FREDONIA	58580-58580	ZAP	58781-58781	SAWYER
58275-58275	REYNOLDS	58441-58441	FULLERTON	58581-58581	ZEELAND	58782-58782	SHERWOOD
58276-58276	SAINT THOMAS	58442-58442	GACKLE	58601-58602	DICKINSON	58783-58783	SOURIS
58277-58277	SHARON	58443-58443	GLENFIELD	58620-58620	AMIDON	58784-58784	STANLEY
58278-58278	THOMPSON	58444-58444	GOODRICH	58621-58621	BEACH	58785-58785	SURREY
58281-58281	WALES	58445-58445	GRACE CITY	58622-58622	BELFIELD	58787-58787	TOLLEY
58282-58282	WALHALLA	58448-58448	HANNAFORD	58623-58623	BOWMAN	58788-58788	TOWNER
58301-58301	DEVILS LAKE	58451-58451	HURDSFIELD	58625-58625	DODGE	58789-58789	UPHAM
58310-58310	AGATE	58452-58452	JESSIE	58626-58626	DUNN CENTER	58790-58790	VELVA
58311-58311	ALSEN	58454-58454	JUD	58627-58627	FAIRFIELD	58792-58792	VOLTAIRE
58313-58313	BALTA	58455-58455	KENSAL	58630-58630	GLADSTONE	58793-58793	WESTHOPE
58316-58316	BELCOURT	58456-58456	KULM	58631-58631	GLEN ULLIN	58794-58794	WHITE EARTH
58317-58317	BISBEE	58458-58458	LAMOURE	58632-58632	GOLVA	58795-58795	WILDROSE
58318-58318	BOTTINEAU	58460-58460	LEHR	58634-58634	GRASSY BUTTE	58801-58802	WILLISTON
58319-58319	BREMEN	58461-58461	LITCHVILLE	58636-56636	HALLIDAY	58830-58830	ALAMO
58320-58320	BRINSMADE	58463-58463	MCCLUSKY	58638-58638	HEBRON	58831-58831	ALEXANDER
58321-58321	BROCKET	58464-58464	MCHENRY	58639-58639	HETTINGER	58833-58833	AMBROSE
58323-58323	CALVIN	58466-58466	MARION	58640-58640	KILLDEER	58835-58835	ARNEGARD
58324-58324	CANDO	58467-58467	MEDINA	58641-58641	LEFOR	58838-58838	CARTWRIGHT
58325-58325	CHURCHS FERRY	58472-58472	MONTPELIER	58642-58642	MANNING	58843-58843	EPPING
58327-58327	CRARY	58474-58474	OAKES	58643-58643	MARMARTH	58844-58844	FORTUNA
58329-58329	DUNSEITH	58475-58475	PETTIBONE	58644-58644	MARSHALL	58845-58845	GRENORA
58330-58330	EDMORE	58476-58476	PINGREE	58645-58645	MEDORA	58847-58847	KEENE
58331-58331	EGELAND	58477-58477	REGAN	58646-58646	MOTT	58849-58849	RAY
58332-58332	ESMOND	58478-58478	ROBINSON	58647-58647	NEW ENGLAND	58852-58852	TIOGA
58335-58335	FORT TOTTEN	58479-58479	ROGERS	58649-58649	REEDER	58853-58853	TRENTON
58337-58337	HAMBERG	58480-58480	SANBORN	58650-58650	REGENT	58854-58854	WATFORD CITY
58338-58338	HAMPDEN	58481-58481	SPIRITWOOD	58651-58651	RHAME	58856-58856	ZAHL
58339-58339	HANSBORO	58482-58482	STEELE	58652-58652	RICHARDTON		
58341-58341	HARVEY	58483-58483	STREETER	58653-58653	SCRANTON		
58343-58343	KNOX	58484-58484	SUTTON	58654-58654	SENTINEL BUTTE		

General Help Numbers:

Governor's Office

77 S High St, 30th Floor   614-466-3555
Columbus, OH 43215   Fax 614-466-9354
http://www.state.oh.us/gov   8AM-5PM

Attorney General's Office

State Office Tower   614-466-4320
30 E Broad St, 17th Floor   Fax 614-644-6135
Columbus, OH 43215-3428   8AM-5PM
http://www.ag.state.oh.us

State Court Administrator

Supreme Court of Ohio   614-466-2653
30 E Broad St, 3rd Floor   Fax 614-752-8736
Columbus, OH 43266-0419   8AM-5PM
http://www.sconet.state.oh.us

State Archives

Archives/Library   614-297-2300
1982 Velma Ave   Fax 614-297-2546
Columbus, OH 43211-2497   9AM-5PM TH-SA: 10-5 SU
http://www.ohiohistory.org/ar_tools.html

State Specifics:

Capital: Columbus
    Franklin County

Time Zone: EST

Number of Counties: 88

Population: 11,353,140

Web Site: www.state.oh.us

State Agencies

Criminal Records

Ohio Bureau of Investigation, Civilian Background Section, PO Box 365, London, OH 43140 (Courier: 1560 State Rte 56, London, OH 43140); 740-845-2000 (General Info), 740-845-2375 (Civilian Background Cks), 740-845-2633 (Fax), 8AM-4:45PM.

http://www.ag.state.oh.us/bci/bcii.htm

Note: The state has an innovative system over the web for electronic transfer of fingerprints.

Indexing & Storage: Records are available from 1921 on. Records from 1972 on are computerized.

Searching: Must have a signed, witnessed release from person of record. Must also have a full set of

fingerprints with the release form. They will not release arrests without dispositions. Information required is the FP card, waiver, name, DOB and SSN.

Access by: mail.

Fee & Payment: The search fee is $15.00 per record. Fee payee: Treasurer - State of Ohio. Prepayment required. No credit cards accepted.

Mail search: Turnaround time: 30 days. No self addressed stamped envelope is required.

Corporation Records
Fictitious Name
Limited Partnership Records
Assumed Name
Trademarks/Servicemarks
Limited Liability Company Records

Secretary of State, Attn: Customer Service, 30 E Broad St, 14th Floor, Columbus, OH 43266-0418; 877-767-3453, 614-466-3910, 614-466-3899 (Fax), 8AM-5PM.

http://www.state.oh.us/sos

Note: Information regarding officers is available from the Department of Taxation at 614-438-5339.

Indexing & Storage: Records are available from the 1800's. New records are available for inquiry immediately. Records are indexed on microfilm, index cards, inhouse computer.

Searching: Include the following in your request-full name of business. In addition to the articles of incorporation, corporation records include the following information: Annual Reports, Prior (merged) names, Inactive and Reserved names.

Access by: mail, phone, fax, in person, online.

Fee & Payment: There is no search fee or a fee for certification of a document. Copy fees are no charges up to 34 pages, $1.05 for the 35th, and $.03 per copy thereafter. Good Standings are $5.00 each. There is no fee for a corporate printout or limited information. Fee payee: Secretary of State. Prepayment required. Personal checks accepted. No credit cards accepted.

Mail search: Turnaround time: 3 to 5 days. No self addressed stamped envelope is required.

Phone search: They will release limited information over the phone.

Fax search: No fee, turnaround time is 3-5 days.

In person search: There is no fee to look at records.

Online search: The agency has a free Internet search available for a number of business and corporation records, also includes UCC and campaign finance.

Other access: The state makes the database available for purchase, call for details.

Expedited service: Expedited service is available for mail and phone searches. Turnaround time: 1 day. Add $10.00 per page.

Uniform Commercial Code

UCC Division, 14th Floor, Secretary of State, 30 E Broad St, State Office Tower, Columbus, OH 43215; 877-767-3453, 614-466-3126, 614-466-2892 (Fax), 8AM-5PM.

http://www.state.oh.us/sos

Indexing & Storage: Records are available for only current or active filings. Records are indexed on inhouse computer.

Searching: Use search form UCC-11. All tax liens are filed at the county level. Include the following

in your request-debtor name. Be sure to include the words "any and all addresses" in your search request.

Access by: mail, phone, in person, online.

Fee & Payment: The search fee is $9.00 per debtor name plus $1.00 for each filing listed. Copy charges are: first 34 pages free, page 35 is $1.05, and each additional page is $.03. There is no search fee if the file # and date of recording is given. Fee payee: Secretary of State. Prepayment required. Personal checks accepted. No credit cards accepted.

Mail search: Turnaround time: 2 weeks.

Phone search: Calls are limited to 10 filings, 3 debtor names per call. There is no charge for verbal information.

In person search: Searching is available in person.

Online search: The Internet site offers free online access to records.

Other access: The complete database is available on magnetic tape on a $335 per week basis.

Expedited service: Expedited service is available for mail and phone searches. Turnaround time: 3 to 5 days. Add $10.00 per debtor name.

Federal Tax Liens
State Tax Liens
Records not maintained by a state level agency.

Note: Records are not housed by a state agency. You must secure from the local county recorder offices.

Sales Tax Registrations
Access to Records is Restricted

Taxation Department, Sale & Use Tax Division, 30 E Broad St, 20th Floor, Columbus, OH 43215; 614-466-7351, 888-405-4039, 614-466-4977 (Fax), 8AM-5PM M-F.

http://www.state.oh.us/tax

Note: This agency refuses to release any information about registrants.

Birth Certificates

Ohio Department of Health, Bureau of Vital Statistics, PO Box 15098, Columbus, OH 43215-0098 (Courier: 35 E Chestnut, 6th Floor, Columbus, OH 43215); 614-466-2531, 614-466-6604 (Fax), 7:45AM-4:30PM.

http://www.odh.state.oh.us/Birth/birthmain.htm

Indexing & Storage: Records are available from 1908 to present. Records are indexed using microfiche and books. It takes 6 months before new records are available for inquiry.

Searching: Include the following in your request-full name, names of parents, mother's maiden name, date of birth, place of birth.

Access by: mail, in person.

Fee & Payment: The fee is $3.00 per name covering a ten year search. If a certified copy is needed, the fee is $9.00. Uncertified copies are $.03 per page plus postage. Fee payee: Treasurer, State of Ohio Prepayment required. Credit card use only for expedited service. Personal checks

accepted. Credit cards accepted: MasterCard, Visa, AmEx, Discover.

Mail search: Turnaround time: 4 to 6 weeks. No self addressed stamped envelope is required.

In person search: Turnaround time 7 to 10 days.

Expedited service: Expedited service is available for fax searches at (877) 553-2439. Turnaround time: 5 days.

Death Records

Ohio Department of Health, Bureau of Vital Statistics, PO Box 15098, Columbus, OH 43215-0098 (Courier: 35 E Chestnut, 6th Floor, Columbus, OH 43215); 614-466-2531, 614-466-6604 (Fax), 7:45AM-4:30PM.

http://www.odh.state.oh.us/Birth/birthmain.htm

Indexing & Storage: Records are available from 1945 to present. Death records from 1908 to 1944 are found at Ohio Historical Society, 1982 Velma Ave, Columbus, OH 43211. Records prior to 1908 are located at the county level.

Searching: Requests must be in writing. Include the following in your request-full name, date of death, place of death.

Access by: mail, fax, in person, online.

Fee & Payment: The fee is $9.00 for a certified copy. The search includes a ten year period. There is an additional $3.00 for each 10 years searched. Uncertified copies are $.03 per page plus postage. Fee payee: Treasurer, State of Ohio. Prepayment required. Credit cards only accepted for expedited service. Personal checks accepted. Credit cards accepted: MasterCard, Visa, AmEx, Discover.

Mail search: Turnaround time: 4 to 6 weeks. No self addressed stamped envelope is required.

Fax search: See expedited service below.

In person search: Turnaround time is 7 to 10 days.

Online search: The Ohio Historical Society Death Certificate Index Searchable Database at www.ohiohistory.org/dindex/search.cfm permits searching by name, county, index. Data is available from 1913 to 1937 only.

Expedited service: Expedited service is available from 800-255-2414 Turnaround time: 5 days. This is available from VitalChek. The fee is $26.75 which includes use of credit card and express delivery.

Marriage Certificates
Divorce Records
Access to Records is Restricted

Bureau of Viatl Statistics., PO Box 15098, Columbus, OH 43215-0098 (Courier: 35 E Chestnut, 6th Floor, Columbus, OH 43215).

http://www.odh.state.oh.us/Birth/birthmain.htm

Note: Marriage and Divorce records are found at county of issue. However, marriage or divorce abstracts (basic information, but not copies of actual documents) are available through the state. Instructions at found at the website.

Workers' Compensation Records

Bureau of Workers Compensation, Customer Assistance, 30 W Spring St, Fl 10, Columbus, OH 43215-2241; 800-644-6292, 614-752-4732 (Fax), 7:30AM-5:30PM.

http://www.ohiobwc.com

Indexing & Storage: Records are available for the past 10 years. Records are indexed on inhouse computer. Records are normally destroyed after 10 years if records are inactive.

Searching: All information is public except injured worker medical report and information pertaining to the employer's financial condition. Include the following in your request-claimant name, Social Security Number. Claim number is helpful. All requests must be in writing.

Access by: mail, phone, fax, in person.

Fee & Payment: There is no search fee, copy fee is $.25 per page. Fee payee: Ohio Bureau of Workers Compensation. Prepayment required. Personal checks accepted. No credit cards accepted.

Mail search: Turnaround time: 1 week. A self addressed stamped envelope is requested.

Phone search: They will provide the information immediately unless file is lengthy or excessive.

Fax search: Service is available with a 24 hour turnaround time.

In person search: Call for location of records before going in because there are 22 different office locations.

Other access: Bulk data is released to approved accounts; however, the legal department must approve requesters. The agency has general information available on a web site.

Driver Records

Department of Public Safety, Bureau of Motor Vehicles, 1970 W Broad St, Columbus, OH 43223-1102; 614-752-7600, 8AM-5:30PM M-T-W; 8AM-4:30PM TH-F.

http://www.ohio.gov/odps

Note: Copies of tickets are available from the Bureau of Motor Vehicles, Transcript Records, PO Box 16520, Columbus 43266-0020. The fee is $1.00 per page.

Indexing & Storage: Records are available for 5 years for moving violations, DWI's and suspensions. Records are purged from public view after 7 years; insurance laws require 36 months of availability. It takes 2 to 5 weeks before new records are available for inquiry.

Searching: SSNs are not released unless provided by requester (except government agency requesters). Bulk requesters must sign "Agreement for the Sale of Information." Casual requesters cannot obtain records without consent. Include the following in your request-driver's license number, full name, date of birth, Social Security Number. Driver's address is included as part of the search report for permissible requesters, except for requests received from California. The following data is not released: mental health records.

Access by: mail, phone, in person, online.

Fee & Payment: The fee is $2.00 per record for non-CDL (commercial drivers) and $3.00 per record for CDL. You can purchase a license status record for $2.00. Fee payee: Treasurer, State of Ohio. Prepayment required. Personal checks accepted. No credit cards accepted.

Mail search: Turnaround time: 1 to 3 days. A self addressed stamped envelope is requested.

Phone search: Pre-approved accounts may order by phone. There is a $100.00 deposit.

In person search: Up to eight records will be processed while you wait.

Online search: The system is called "Defender System" and is suggested for requesters who order 100 or more motor vehicle reports per day in batch mode. Turnaround is in 4-8 hours. The DL# or SSN and name are needed when ordering. Fee is $2.00 per record. For more information, call 614-752-7692.

Other access: Overnight magnetic tape service is available for larger accounts.

Vehicle Ownership
Vehicle Identification

Bureau of Motor Vehicles, Motor Vehicle Title Records, 1970 W Broad St, Columbus, OH 43223-1102; 614-752-7671, 614-752-8929 (Fax), 7:30AM-4:45PM.

http://www.state.oh.us/odps/division/bmv/bmv/html

Indexing & Storage: Records are available for the current year plus four. It takes 1 to 2 days normally before new records are available for inquiry.

Searching: Bulk requesters must sign an "Agreement for the Sale of Information." The Social Security Number will not be provided unless included on request. Casual requesters cannot obtain records without consent. Lien information is not recorded on vehicle registration records in Ohio. The following data is not released: Social Security Numbers.

Access by: mail, in person, online.

Fee & Payment: The fee is $2.00 or each record searched. Fee payee: Treasurer, State of Ohio. Prepayment required. Personal checks accepted. No credit cards accepted.

Mail search: Turnaround time: 1 to 3 days. A self addressed stamped envelope is requested.

In person search: There may be a limit on the number of requests processed immediately, most are not available until the next day.

Online search: Ohio offers online access through AAMVAnet. All requesters must comply with a contractual agreement prior to release of data, which complies with DPPA regulations. Fee is $2.00 per record. Call 614-752-7692 for more information.

Accident Reports

Department of Public Safety, Central Records Unit, PO Box 182074, Columbus, OH 43218-2074; 614-752-1593, 614-644-9749 (Fax), 8AM-4:45PM.

Indexing & Storage: Records are available for 5 years to present. Records are indexed on computer. It takes 2 to 5 weeks before new records are available for inquiry.

Searching: Include the following in your request-full name, date of accident. Submitting the driver's license number or SSN is very helpful. The following data is not released: Social Security Numbers.

Access by: mail, in person.

Fee & Payment: The fee is $3.00 per record. There is a charge for a no record found. Fee payee: Department of Public Safety. Prepayment required. Personal checks accepted. No credit cards accepted.

Mail search: Turnaround time: 2 to 3 days.

In person search: Turnaround time is immediate if the record is on file.

Vessel Ownership
Vessel Registration

Natural Resources Department, Division of Watercraft, 4435 Fountain Square Dr Bldg A, Columbus, OH 43224-1300; 614-265-6480, 614-267-8883 (Fax), 8AM-5PM.

http://www.dnr.state.oh.us/odnr/watercraft

Indexing & Storage: Records are available from 1960 to the present. Records are indexed on computer for the last 3 years. Any boat operated on public waters must be registered. All boats 14 ft or longer or having a 10+ hp motor must be titled.

Searching: To search, one of the following is required: name, hull ID #, registration #, or serial #. The following data is not released: Social Security Numbers.

Access by: mail, phone, fax, in person.

Fee & Payment: There is no search fee for registration records. There is a $2.00 fee for a title search. Fee payee: Division of Watercraft. Prepayment required. Personal checks accepted. No credit cards accepted.

Mail search: Turnaround time: 2 to 4 days. No self addressed stamped envelope is required.

Phone search: There is a limit of five names per call for registration information.

Fax search: Same criteria as mail searching.

In person search: Searching is available in person.

Legislation Records

Ohio House of Representatives, 77 S High Street, Columbus, OH 43266 (Courier: Ohio Senate, State House, Columbus, OH 43215); 614-466-8842 (In-State Only), 614-466-9745 (Out-of-State), 614-466-3357 (Clerk's Office), 614-644-8744 (Fax), 8:30AM-5PM.

http://www.legislature.state.oh.us

Note: Note the two addresses for the different bodies.

Indexing & Storage: Records are available from 1888 to present on microfiche and are computerized since 1990. Bills for the years 1888-1990 are available on microfilm at many libraries in Ohio.

Searching: Include the following in your request-bill number.

Access by: mail, phone, fax, in person, online.

Fee & Payment: There is no search fee.

Mail search: Turnaround time: 1 to 2 days.

Phone search: Records are available by phone.

Fax search: Records are available by fax.

In person search: Searching is available in person.

Online search: The Internet site offers access to bill text, status, and enactment.

Other access: E-mail requests are accepted.

Voter Registration

Secretary of State, Elections Division, 180 E Broad St, 15th Fl, Columbus, OH 43215; 614-466-2585, 614-752-4360 (Fax), 8AM-5PM.

http://www.state.oh.us/sos

Indexing & Storage: Records are available for 6 years.

Searching: The state suggests that all individual requests be done at the county Board of Elections.

Access by: mail, in person.

Fee & Payment: There is no fee. Fee payee: Secretary of State. Prepayment required. No credit cards accepted.

Mail search: Turnaround time: 1 week to 10 days. No self addressed stamped envelope is required.

In person search: The state is not prepared to handle look-ups, but will assist as necessary.

Other access: Records may be purchased in a variety of formats. Lists are arranged in alpha order within precinct, unless otherwise indicated. For further information, contact Audrey Hatchett at (614) 466-8895.

GED Certificates

Department of Education, State GED Office, 25 S Front St, 1st Fl, Columbus, OH 43215-4104; 614-466-1577, 614-752-9445 (Fax), 8-4:45.

http://www.ode.ohio.gov/www/ae/ae_ged.html

Indexing & Storage: Records are available from 1984 to present. Priro records are on microfilm.

Searching: Include the following in your request- date of birth, Social Security Number, signed release, approx date of test. DOB is helpful.

Access by: fax, in person.

Fee & Payment: There is no fee for a verification, a $5.00 fee for a copy of a transcript. Fee payee: OH Dept of Education. Prepayment required. No credit cards accepted. No self addressed stamped envelope is required.

Fax search: Same criteria as mail searching.

In person search: Searching is available in person.

Hunting License Information
Fishing License Information
Records not maintained by a state level agency.

Note: They do not have a central database. Only vendors have the names and addresses **which are kept for one year.**

Ohio State Licensing Agencies

Licenses Searchable Online

Accounting Firm #01... www.state.oh.us/acc/search.html
Acupuncturist #28.. www.state.oh.us/scripts/med/license/Query.stm
Anesthesiologist Assistant #28............................ www.state.oh.us/scripts/med/license/Query.stm
Architect #02 .... www.state.oh.us/scripts/arc/query.asp
Athletic Trainer #29.. www.state.oh.us/scripts/pyt/query.asp
Barber School #26 .... www.state.oh.us/brb/barbsch.htm
Chiropractor #09.. http://156.63.245.111/index.html
Clinical Nurse Specialist #06................................ www.state.oh.us/scripts/nur/query.asp
Coil Cleaner (Liquor/Beverage) #27 .... www.state.oh.us/com/liquor/liquor13.htm
Cosmetic Therapist #28.. www.state.oh.us/scripts/med/license/Query.stm
Counselor #11 .... www.state.oh.us/scripts/csw/query.asp
Dental Assistant Radiologist #33.......................... www.state.oh.us/scripts/den/query.stm
Dental Hygienist #33... www.state.oh.us/scripts/den/query.stm
Dentist #33 .... www.state.oh.us/scripts/den/query.stm
Engineer #23 .... www.peps.state.oh.us/index.html
Executive Agency Lobbyist/Lobbyist Employer #30 ..... www.jlec-olig.state.oh.us/agent_search_form.cfm
Insurance Agent #20... www.ohioinsurance.gov/ConsumServ/ocs/agentloc.htm
Landscape Architect #02....................................... www.state.oh.us/scripts/arc/query.asp
Legislative Agent/Agent Employer #30 .... www.jlec-olig.state.oh.us/agent_search_form.cfm
Liquor Distributor/License #27............................... www.state.oh.us/com/liquor/liquor15.htm
Lottery Retailer #35 .... www.ohiolottery.com/frameset/games/retailer.html
Massage Therapist #28... www.state.oh.us/scripts/med/license/Query.stm
Mechanotherapist #28... www.state.oh.us/scripts/med/license/Query.stm
Medical Doctor #28... www.state.oh.us/scripts/med/license/Query.stm
Midwife Nurse #06 .... www.state.oh.us/scripts/nur/query.asp
Naprapath #28.. www.state.oh.us/scripts/med/license/Query.stm
Nurse Anesthetist #06... www.state.oh.us/scripts/nur/query.asp
Nurse Practitioner #06 .... www.state.oh.us/scripts/nur/query.asp
Nurse-RN/LPN #06 .... www.state.oh.us/scripts/nur/query.asp
Occupational Therapist/Assistant #29 .... www.state.oh.us/scripts/pyt/query.asp
Optometrist #37... www.state.oh.us/scripts/opt/query.asp
Optometrist, Diagnostic/Therapeutic #37 .... www.state.oh.us/scripts/opt/query.asp
Osteopathic Physician #28.................................... www.state.oh.us/scripts/med/license/Query.stm
Pharmacist #07 .... www.ohio.gov/pharmacy/
Physical Therapist/Assistant #29 .... www.state.oh.us/scripts/pyt/query.asp
Physician Assistant #28.. www.state.oh.us/scripts/med/license/Query.stm
Podiatrist #28 .... www.state.oh.us/scripts/med/license/Query.stm
Polygraph Examiner #46.. http://polygraph.org/states/oape/directory.htm
Psychologist #36 .... www2.state.oh.us/psy/query.asp
Public Accountant-CPA #01 .... www.state.oh.us/acc/search.html
Real Estate Sales Agent #15................................. www.ohiorealtors.org/search/locate.html
Respiratory Therapist/Student #42........................ www.state.oh.us/scripts/rsp/query.asp
School Psychologist #36.. www2.state.oh.us/psy/query.asp
Social Worker #11 .... www.state.oh.us/scripts/csw/query.asp
Surveyor #23 .... www.peps.state.oh.us/index.html
Teacher/Teacher's Aide #43.................................. www.ode.state.oh.us/tp/certifact.htm

Licensing Quick Finder

Accounting Firm #01 614-466-4135
Acupuncturist #28 614-644-3934
Adoption Agency #19 614-466-9274
Adult Care Home #18...........................614-466-7713
Airline Liquor Permit #27 614-644-2360
Anesthesiologist Assistant #28 614-644-3934
Architect #02......................................614-466-2316
Athletic Trainer #29 614-466-3774
Attorney #44.......................................614-466-1553
Auctioneer #15....................................614-466-4130
Audiologist/Audiologist Aide #08 614-466-3145
Backflow Prevention Assembly Inspector #34 ....
....614-644-2223
Bank #17...614-728-8400
Barber #26 614-466-5003
Barber InstructorSchool#26 614-466-5003
Barber Shop #26..................................614-466-5003
Bedding/Furniture Dealer/Dist. #38 614-644-2233
Bedding/Furniture Mfg. #38 614-644-2233
Bedding/Furniture Renovator #38 614-644-2233
Boiler Inspector #34 614-644-2223
Boiler Operator #34 614-644-2223
Boxer #32 330-742-5120
Boxing Event #32.................................330-742-5120
Boxing Physician #32 330-742-5120
Boxing Professional #32.......................330-742-5120
Boxing Promoter/Matchmaker #32........330-742-5120
Building Inspector #03..........................614-644-2613
Building Official #03.............................614-644-2613
Cemetery #15 216-787-3100
Check Cashing Service #17..................614-728-8400
Check Lending Service #17 614-728-8400
Child Day Care Facility #19 614-466-9274
Children's Residential Center #19 614-466-9274
Children's Services Agency #19............614-466-9274
Chiropractor #09 614-644-7032
Clinical Nurse Specialist #06 614-952-3980
Coil Cleaner (Liquor/Beverage) #27 614-644-2360
Consumer Finance Company #17...........614-728-8400
Cosmetic Therapist #28.......................614-466-3934
Cosmetologist/Managing Cosmetologist #04 ....
....614-644-3834
Cosmetology Instructor #04 614-644-3834
Counselor #11.....................................614-466-0912
Credit Service Organization #17 614-466-2221
Credit Union #73 ....614-466-2221or728-8400
Crematory #05 614-466-4252
Dairy Farm #12 614-466-5550
Dental Assistant Radiologist #33...........614-466-2580
Dental Hygienist #33 614-466-2580
Dentist #33 614-466-2580
Dietitian #31 614-466-3291
Drug Wholesaler/Distributor #07 614-466-4143
Electrical Safety Inspector #03..............614-644-2613
Electrical Safety Trainee #03 614-644-2613
Elevator Inspector #38.........................614-644-2233
Embalmer/Embalming Facility #05........614-466-4252
Emergency Medical Technician #22......614-466-9447
Emergency Medical Technician Instructor #22 ....

....614-466-9447
Engineer #23 614-466-3650
Esthetician/Managing Esthetician #04...614-644-3834
Executive Agency Lobbyist/Lobbyist Employer #30
....614-728-5100
Explosives #34.....................................614-752-7126
Family Foster Home #19 614-466-9274
Fire Alarm & Detection Inspector #34....614-644-7126
Fire Extinguisher (Portable) Inspector #34 ....
....614-644-7126
Fire Extinguisher Equipment Inspector #34................
....614-644-7126
Firefighter/Firefighter Instructor #22....614-466-9447
Fireworks Exhibitor/Assistant #34 614-752-7126
Fireworks Exhibitor #34 614-752-7126
Fishing Guide #21 419-625-8062
Foreign Real Estate Property #15.........614-466-4100
Funeral Director #05.............................614-466-4252
Funeral Home #05................................614-466-4252
Group Home Operator #19....................614-466-9274
Health Care Facility #18 614-466-7713
Hearing Aid Dealer/Fitter #25 614-466-5215
Horse Racing Facility/Owner #41..........614-466-2757
Hotel/Motel #34...................................614-752-7126
Independent Living Arranger #19 614-466-9274
Insurance Agent #20............................614-644-2665
Insurance Broker, Non-Resident #20 614-644-2665
Insurance Solicitor #20 614-644-2665
Investment Advisor #16........................614-644-7381
Investment Advisor Representative #16 614-644-7381
Landscape Architect #02......................614-466-2316
Legislative Agent/Agent Employer #30..614-728-5100
Liquor Distributor #27 614-644-2360
Liquor License #27...............................614-644-2360
Lottery Retailer #35.............................216-787-3200
Manicuring/Esthetician Instructor #04 ...614-644-3834
Manicurist/Managing Manicurist #04.....614-644-3834
Massage Therapist #28........................614-466-3934
Mechanical Inspector #03.....................614-644-2613
Mechanotherapist #28 614-644-3934
Medical Doctor #28 614-466-3934
Midwife Nurse #06...............................614-952-3980
Milk Hauler #12 614-466-5550
Milk Processor/Producer/Plant #12.......614-466-5550
Milk Tester/Sampler #12.......................614-466-5550
Mortgage Broker #17............................614-728-8400
Mortgage Broker, Real Estate #13 614-466-2221
Mortgage Loan Act #13 614-466-2221
Naprapath #28 614-644-3934
Notary Public #10.................................614-466-2566
Nurse Anesthetist #06 614-952-3980
Nurse Practitioner #06 614-952-3980
Nurse-RN/LPN #06...............................614-952-3980
Nursing Home #18 614-466-7713
Nursing Home Administrator #18 614-466-5114
Occupational Therapist/Assistant #29 ...614-466-3774
Ocularist/Ocularist Apprentice #39........614-466-9707
Optical Dispenser #39 614-466-9707
Optician/ Optician Apprentice #39.........614-466-9707

Optometrist #37 614-466-5115
Optometrist, diagnostic/therapeutic #37 614-466-5115
Osteopathic Physician #28 614-466-3934
Pawnbroker #17...................................614-728-8400
Pesticide Applicator #40 614-728-6987
Pesticide Dealer #40............................614-728-6987
Pesticide Operator #40.........................614-728-6987
Pharmacist #07....................................614-466-4143
Pharmacy Company #07.......................614-466-4143
Pharmacy Dispensary #07....................614-466-4143
Physical Therapist/Assistant #29 614-466-3774
Physician Assistant #28........................614-466-3934
Plan Examiner #03...............................614-644-2613
Podiatrist #28 614-644-3934
Polygraph Examiner #46 614-645-4174
Precious Metals Dealer #17..................614-728-8400
Pressure Piping Inspector #34 614-644-2223
Private Investigator #15........................614-466-4130
Psychologist #36..................................614-466-8808
Public Accountant-CPA #01..................614-752-8248
Public Adjuster #20 614-644-2665
Racetrack Personnel #41 614-466-2757
Racing Permit #41................................614-466-2757
Real Estate Appraiser #15....................216-787-3100
Real Estate Broker #15........................614-466-4100
Real Estate Sales Agent #15................614-466-4100
Residential Care Facility #18 614-466-7713
Residential Parenting Organization #19 614-466-9274
Respiratory Therapist/Student #42........614-752-9218
Savings & Loan Association #17............614-728-8400
Savings Bank #17 614-728-8400
School Administrator/Principal #43 614-466-3593
School Counselor #43 614-466-3593
School Psychologist #36 614-466-8808
Scientific Collection Permit #21.............614-265-6666
Securities Dealer/Salesperson #16........614-644-7381
Security Guard #15 614-466-4130
Social Worker #11................................614-466-0912
Solid Waste Facility Operator #24.........614-644-2621
Speech Pathologist Aide #08 614-466-3145
Speech Pathologist/Audiologist #08......614-466-3145
Sprinkler Equipment Inspector #34 614-644-7126
Sprinkler Inspector #03........................614-644-2613
Sprinkler, Fire Alarm, & Hazardous Designer #03.......
....614-644-2613
Steam Engineer #34.............................614-644-2223
Steam, Stationary #34..........................614-644-2223
Surveyor #23 614-466-3650
Teacher/Teacher's Aide #43 614-466-3593
Travel Agent #34..................................614-644-2223
Tour Promoter #34 614-644-2223
Treasurer & Business Manager #43.......614-466-3593
Underground Storage Tank #34.............614-752-7938
Underground Tank Inspector #34...........614-752-7921
Underground Tank Installer #34.............614-752-7921
Veterinarian #45...................................614-644-5281
Veterinary Technician #45 614-644-5281
Water Supply Equipment Inspector #34 614-644-2223

Licensing Agency Information

#01 Accountancy Board of Ohio, 77 S High St, 18th Fl, Columbus, OH 43266-0301; 614-466-4135, Fax: 614-466-2628.
www.state.oh.us/acc
Direct web site URL to search for licensees: www.state.oh.us/acc/search.html. You can search online using name or license #

#02 Architects Board of Ohio, 77 S High St, 16th Fl, Columbus, OH 43266-0303; 614-466-2316, Fax: 614-644-9048.
www.state.oh.us/arc

Direct web site URL to search for licensees: www.state.oh.us/scripts/arc/query.asp. You can search online using name and license number.

#03 Board of Building Standards, 6606 Tussing Rd, Reynoldsburg, OH 43068-9009; 614-644-2613, Fax: 614-644-3147.
www.com.state.oh.us/dic/Default.htm

#04 Board of Cosmetology, 1010 Sland Mall, Columbus, OH 43207-4041; 614-466-3834, Fax: 614-644-6880.

www.state.oh.us/cos An online search system is planned. Once available, the web address will be www.state.oh.us/cos/licensedb.htm.

#05 Board of Embalmers & Funeral Directors of Ohio, 77 S High St, 16th Fl, Columbus, OH 43266; 614-466-4252, Fax: 614-728-6825.
www.state.oh.us/fun

#06 Board of Nursing, 17 S High St #400, Columbus, OH 43215; 614-466-3947, Fax: 614-466-0388.
www.state.oh.us/nvr

Direct web site URL to search for licensees: www.state.oh.us/nvr. You can search online using SSN, license number.

#07 Board of Pharmacy, 77 S High St, 17th Fl, Columbus, OH 43266-0320; 614-466-4143, Fax: 614-752-4836.
www.ohio.gov/pharmacy

#08 Board of Speech Pathology & Audiology, 77 S High St, 16th Fl, Columbus, OH 43266-0324; 614-466-3145, Fax: 614-995-2286.

#09 Chiropractic Board, 77 S High St, 16th Fl, Columbus, OH 43266-0542; 614-644-7032, Fax: 614-752-2539.
www.state.oh.us/chr/
Direct web site URL to search for licensees: http://156.63.245.111/index.html. You can search online using name, license #, city, state, zip No Online searches

#10 Commission Clerk, 77 S High St, 19th Fl, Columbus, OH 43215; 614-466-2566.

#11 Counselor & Social Worker Board, 77 S High St, 16th Fl, Columbus, OH 43266-0340; 614-466-0912, Fax: 614-728-7790.
www.state.oh.us/csw
Direct web site URL to search for licensees: www.state.oh.us/scripts/csw/query.asp. You can search online using name and license number.

#12 Department of Agriculture, 8995 E Main St, Reynoldsburg, OH 43068-3399; 614-466-5550, Fax: 614-728-2652.
www.state.oh.us/agr/

#15 Department of Commerce, 77 S High St, 20th Fl, Columbus, OH 43266-0547; 614-466-4130, Fax: 614-466-0584.
www.com.state.oh.us/real

#16 Department of Commerce, 77 S High St, 22nd Fl, Columbus, OH 43215-0548; 614-644-7381, Fax: 614-466-3316.
www.securities.state.oh.us

#17 Department of Commerce, 77 S High St, 21st Fl, Columbus, OH 43266-0121; 614-466-2221, Fax: 614-466-1631.
www.com.state.oh.us/dfi/default.htm

#18 Department of Health, 246 N High St, Columbus, OH 43266-0118; 614-466-5114, Fax: 614-466-0271.
www.odh.state.oh.us

#19 Office For Children & Families, 255 E Main, 3rd Fl, Columbus, OH 43215; 614-466-9274, Fax: 614-728-9682; 614-752-2580.
www.oh.state.us/odhs/oapl

#20 Department of Insurance, 2100 Stella Ct, Columbus, OH 43215-1067; 614-644-2665, Fax: 614-644-3475.
www.ohioinsurance.gov

#21 Department of Natural Resources, 1840 Belcher Dr, Columbus, OH 43224; 614-265-7040, Fax: 614-262-1143.
www.dnr.state.oh.us

#22 Department of Public Safety, PO Box 182073, Columbus, OH 43218-2073; 614-466-9447, Fax: 614-466-9461.
www.state.oh.us/odps

#23 Engineers & Surveyors Board, 77 S High St, 16th Fl, Columbus, OH 43266-0314; 614-466-3650, Fax: 614-728-3059.
www.peps.state.oh.us/index.html
Direct web site URL to search for licensees: www.peps.state.oh.us/sbdefault.htm. You can search online using name, company name, license number and county.

#24 Hazardous Waste Facility Board, 122 S Front St, Columbus, OH 43215; 614-644-3020, Fax: 614-728-5315.
www.epa.state.oh.us/dsiwm

#25 Hearing Aid Dealers & Fitters Board, 246 N High St, Columbus, OH 43266-0118; 614-466-5215, Fax: 614-466-0271.

#26 Licensing Boards, 77 S High St, 16th Fl, Columbus, OH 43266-0304; 614-466-5003, Fax: 614-644-8112.
www.state.oh.us/brb

#27 Division of Liquor Control, 6606 Tussing Rd, Reynoldsburg, OH 43068-9005; 614-644-2360, Fax: 614-644-2480.
www.state.oh.us/com/liquor/liquor.htm

#28 Medical Board of Ohio, 77 S High St, 17th Fl, Columbus, OH 43266-0315; 614-466-3934, Fax: 614-728-5946.
www.state.oh.us/med/
Direct web site URL to search for licensees: www.state.oh.us/scripts/med/license/Query.stm. You can search online using name and license number.

#29 OTPTAT - Occupational Therapy - Physical Therapy Board, 77 S High St, 16th Fl, Columbus, OH 43266-0317; 614-466-3774, Fax: 614-644-8112.
www.state.oh.us/pyt
Direct web site URL to search for licensees: www.state.oh.us/scripts/pyt/query.asp

#30 Office of Legislative Inspector General, 50 W Broad St, #1308, Columbus, OH 43215-3365; 614-728-5100, Fax: 614-728-5074.
www.jlec-olig.state.oh.us
Direct web site URL to search for licensees: www.jlec-olig.state.oh.us/agent_search_form.cfm. You can search online using name.

#31 Board of Dietetics, 77 S High St, 18th Fl, Columbus, OH 43266-0337; 614-466-3291, Fax: 614-728-0723.
www.state.oh.us/obd

#32 Boxing Commission, 2545 Belmont Ave, Union Square Plaza, Youngstown, OH 44505; 330-742-5120, Fax: 330-742-2571.

#33 Dental Board, 77 S High St, 18th Fl, Columbus, OH 43266-0306; 614-466-2580, Fax: 614-752-8995.
www.state.oh.us/den
Direct web site URL to search for licensees: www.state.oh.us/scripts/den/query.stm. You can search online using name, license number, and SSN.

#34 Ohio Department of Commerce, 6606 Tussing Rd, Reynoldsburg, OH 43068-9009; 614-644-2223, Fax: 614-644-2428.

#35 Lottery Commission, 615 W Superior Ave, NW Frank J. Lausche Bldg, Cleveland, OH 44113; 216-787-3200, Fax: 216-787-3718.
www.ohiolottery.com
Direct web site URL to search for licensees: www.ohiolottery.com/frameset/games/retailer.htm l. You can search online using name, city, ZIP Code, and county.

#36 Board of Psychology, 77 S High St, 18th Fl, Columbus, OH 43266-0321; 614-466-8808, Fax: 614-728-7081.
www.state.oh.us/psy
Direct web site URL to search for licensees: www2.state.oh.us/psy/query.asp. You can search online using licensee name or license number. If "SP" is part of a license number, that indicates a "school psychologist."

#37 Board of Optometry, 77 S High St, 16th Fl, Columbus, OH 43266-0318; 614-466-5115, Fax: 614-644-3937.
www.state.oh.us/opt
Direct web site URL to search for licensees: www.state.oh.us/scripts/opt/query.asp. You can search online using name.

#38 Operations & Maintenance, 6606 Tussing Rd, Reynoldsburg, OH 43068-9009; 614-644-2233, Fax: 614-644-2428.
www.state.oh.us/com/fin/index.htm

#39 Optical Dispensers Board, 77 S High St, 16th Fl, Columbus, OH 43266-0328; 614-466-9707, Fax: 614-995-5392.
www.state.oh.us/odb

#40 Pesticide Regulations, 8995 E Main St, Reynoldsburg, OH 43068-3399; 614-728-6200, Fax: 614-728-4235.
www.state.oh.us/agr

#41 Racing Commission, 77 S High St, 18th Fl, Columbus, OH 43266-0416; 614-466-2757, Fax: 614-466-1900.

#42 Respiratory Care Board, 77 S High St, 16th Fl, Columbus, OH 43266-0777; 614-752-9218, Fax: 614-728-8691.
www.state.oh.us/rsp/
Direct web site URL to search for licensees: www.state.oh.us/scripts/rsp/query.asp. You can search online using name

#43 Department of Education, 25 S Front St, Columbus, OH 43215; 614-466-3593, Fax: 614-466-1999.
www.ode.state.oh.us/tp/ctp/candl.htm
Direct web site URL to search for licensees: www.ode.state.oh.us/tp/certifact.htm. You can search online using identification number, partial name. ID Number is required.

#44 Supreme Court, 30 E Broad St, Columbus, OH 43266-0419; 614-644-1553, Fax: 614-728-0930.

#45 Veterinary Medical Board, 77 S High St, 16th Fl, Columbus, OH 43266-0116; 614-644-5281, Fax: 614-644-9038.

#46 Association of Polygraph Examiners, 120 Marconi Blvd. 7th Fl, Columbus, OH 43215; 614-645-4174.
http://polygraph.org/states/oape/index.htm
Direct web site URL to search for licensees: http://polygraph.org/states/oape/directory.htm

Ohio Federal Courts

The following list indicates the district and division name for each county in the state. If the bankruptcy court location is different from the district court, then the location of the bankruptcy court appears in parentheses.

County/Court Cross Reference

County	District	Division
Adams	Southern	Cincinnati
Allen	Northern	Toledo
Ashland	Northern	Cleveland (Canton)
Ashtabula	Northern	Cleveland (Youngstown)
Athens	Southern	Columbus
Auglaize	Northern	Toledo
Belmont	Southern	Columbus
Brown	Southern	Cincinnati
Butler	Southern	Cincinnati (Dayton)
Carroll	Northern	Akron (Canton)
Champaign	Southern	Dayton
Clark	Southern	Dayton
Clermont	Southern	Cincinnati
Clinton	Southern	Cincinnati (Dayton)
Columbiana	Northern	Youngstown
Coshocton	Southern	Columbus
Crawford	Northern	Cleveland (Canton)
Cuyahoga	Northern	Cleveland
Darke	Southern	Dayton
Defiance	Northern	Toledo
Delaware	Southern	Columbus
Erie	Northern	Toledo
Fairfield	Southern	Columbus
Fayette	Southern	Columbus
Franklin	Southern	Columbus
Fulton	Northern	Toledo
Gallia	Southern	Columbus
Geauga	Northern	Cleveland
Greene	Southern	Dayton
Guernsey	Southern	Columbus
Hamilton	Southern	Cincinnati
Hancock	Northern	Toledo
Hardin	Northern	Toledo
Harrison	Southern	Columbus
Henry	Northern	Toledo
Highland	Southern	Cincinnati
Hocking	Southern	Columbus
Holmes	Northern	Akron (Canton)
Huron	Northern	Toledo
Jackson	Southern	Columbus
Jefferson	Southern	Columbus
Knox	Southern	Columbus
Lake	Northern	Cleveland
Lawrence	Southern	Cincinnati
Licking	Southern	Columbus
Logan	Southern	Columbus
Lorain	Northern	Cleveland
Lucas	Northern	Toledo
Madison	Southern	Columbus
Mahoning	Northern	Youngstown
Marion	Northern	Toledo
Medina	Northern	Cleveland (Akron)
Meigs	Southern	Columbus
Mercer	Northern	Toledo
Miami	Southern	Dayton
Monroe	Southern	Columbus
Montgomery	Southern	Dayton
Morgan	Southern	Columbus
Morrow	Southern	Columbus
Muskingum	Southern	Columbus
Noble	Southern	Columbus
Ottawa	Northern	Toledo
Paulding	Northern	Toledo
Perry	Southern	Columbus
Pickaway	Southern	Columbus
Pike	Southern	Columbus
Portage	Northern	Akron
Preble	Southern	Dayton
Putnam	Northern	Toledo
Richland	Northern	Cleveland (Canton)
Ross	Southern	Columbus
Sandusky	Northern	Toledo
Scioto	Southern	Cincinnati
Seneca	Northern	Toledo
Shelby	Southern	Dayton
Stark	Northern	Akron (Canton)
Summit	Northern	Akron
Trumbull	Northern	Youngstown
Tuscarawas	Northern	Akron (Canton)
Union	Southern	Columbus
Van Wert	Northern	Toledo
Vinton	Southern	Columbus
Warren	Southern	Cincinnati (Dayton)
Washington	Southern	Columbus
Wayne	Northern	Akron (Canton)
Williams	Northern	Toledo
Wood	Northern	Toledo
Wyandot	Northern	Toledo

US District Court

Northern District of Ohio

Akron Division 568 Federal Bldg, 2 S Main St, Akron, OH 44308 (Courier Address: Use mail address for courier delivery), 330-375-5705.

http://www.ohnd.uscourts.gov

Counties: Carroll, Holmes, Portage, Stark, Summit, Tuscarawas, Wayne. Cases filed prior to 1995 for counties in the Youngstown Division may be located here.

Indexing/Storage: Cases are indexed by defendant and plaintiff as well as by case number. New cases are available in the index immediately after filing date. A computer index is maintained. Open records are located at this court. Open cases may be located in another division in this district, depending on the judge assigned.

Fee & Payment: The fee is $20.00 per item (one party name or case number). Payment may be made by money order, cashier check, personal check. Prepayment is required. Payee: Clerk, US District Court. Certification fee: $7.00 per document. Copy fee: $.50 per page.

Phone Search: Only docket information is available by phone.

Mail Search: Always enclose a stamped self addressed envelope.

In Person: In person searching is available.

PACER: Sign-up number is 800-676-6856. Access fee is $.60 per minute. Toll-free access: 800-673-4409. Local access: 216-522-3669. Many cases prior to the indicated dates are also online. Case records are available back to January 1, 1990. Records are never purged. New records are available online after 1 day. PACER is available online at http://pacer.ohnd.uscourts.gov.

Electronic Filing: Electronic filing information is available online at http://ecf.ohnd.uscourts.gov

Cleveland Division 201 Superior Ave, NE, Cleveland, OH 44114 (Courier Address: Use mail address for courier delivery), 216-522-4355, Fax: 216-522-2140.

Counties: Ashland, Ashtabula, Crawford, Cuyahoga, Geauga, Lake, Lorain, Medina, Richland. Cases prior to July 1995 for the counties of Ashland, Crawford, Medina and Richland are located in the Akron Division. Cases filed prior to 1995 from the counties in the Youngstown Division may be located here.

Indexing/Storage: Cases are indexed by defendant and plaintiff as well as by case number. New cases are available in the index immediately after filing date. A computer index is maintained. Open records are located at this court. Open cases may be located in other divisions in this district, depending on the judge assigned.

Fee & Payment: The fee is $20.00 per item (one party name or case number). Payment may be made by money order, cashier check, personal check. Prepayment is required. Payee: Clerk, US District Court. Certification fee: $7.00 per document. Copy fee: $.50 per page. You are allowed to make your own copies. These copies cost $.25 per page.

Phone Search: Only docket information is available by phone.

Mail Search: A stamped self addressed envelope is not required.

In Person: In person searching is available.

PACER: Sign-up number is 800-676-6856. Access fee is $.60 per minute. Toll-free access: 800-673-4409. Local access: 216-522-3669. Many cases prior to the indicated dates are also online. Case records are available back to January 1, 1990. Records are never purged. New records are available online after 1 day. PACER is available online at http://pacer.ohnd.uscourts.gov.

Electronic Filing: Electronic filing information is available online at http://ecf.ohnd.uscourts.gov

Toledo Division 114 US Courthouse, 1716 Spielbusch, Toledo, OH 43624 (Courier Address: Use mail address for courier delivery), 419-259-6412.

http://www.ohnd.uscourts.gov

Counties: Allen, Auglaize, Defiance, Erie, Fulton, Hancock, Hardin, Henry, Huron, Lucas, Marion, Mercer, Ottawa, Paulding, Putnam, Sandusky, Seneca, Van Wert, Williams, Wood, Wyandot.

Indexing/Storage: Cases are indexed by defendant and plaintiff as well as by case number. New cases are available in the index 1 day after filing date. A computer index is maintained. Open records are located at this court.

Fee & Payment: The fee is $20.00 per item (one party name or case number). Payment may be made by money order, cashier check, personal check. Prepayment is required. Payee: Clerk, US District Court. Certification fee: $7.00 per document. Copy fee: $.50 per page.

Phone Search: Only docket information is available by phone.

Mail Search: Always enclose a stamped self addressed envelope.

In Person: In person searching is available.

PACER: Sign-up number is 800-676-6856. Access fee is $.60 per minute. Toll-free access: 800-673-4409. Local access: 216-522-3669. Many cases prior to the indicated dates are also online. Case records are available back to January 1, 1990. Records are never purged. New records are available online after 1 day. PACER is available online at http://pacer.ohnd.uscourts.gov.

Electronic Filing: Electronic filing information is available online at http://ecf.ohnd.uscourts.gov

Youngstown Division 337 Federal Bldg, 125 Market St, Youngstown, OH 44503-1787 (Courier Address: Use mail address for courier delivery), 330-746-1906, Fax: 330-746-2027.

http://www.ohnd.uscourts.gov

Counties: Columbiana, Mahoning, Trumbull. This division was reactivated in the middle of 1995. Older cases will be found in Akron or Cleveland.

Indexing/Storage: Cases are indexed by defendant and plaintiff as well as by case number. New cases are available in the index immediately after filing date. A computer index is maintained. Open records are located at this court. Open cases may also be located in other divisions in this district, depending upon the judge assigned.

Fee & Payment: The fee is $20.00 per item (one party name or case number). Payment may be made by money order, cashier check, personal check. Prepayment is required. Payee: Clerk, US District Court. Certification fee: $7.00 per document. Copy fee: $.50 per page.

Phone Search: Only docket information is available by phone.

Fax Search: Prepayment is required for all fax requests.

Mail Search: Always enclose a stamped self addressed envelope.

In Person: In person searching is available.

PACER: Sign-up number is 800-676-6856. Access fee is $.60 per minute. Toll-free access: 800-673-4409. Local access: 216-522-3669. Many cases prior to the indicated dates are also online. Case records are available back to January 1, 1990. Records are never purged. New records are available online after 1 day. PACER is available online at http://pacer.ohnd.uscourts.gov.

Electronic Filing: Electronic filing information is available online at http://ecf.ohnd.uscourts.gov

US Bankruptcy Court

Northern District of Ohio

Akron Division 455 Federal Bldg, 2 S Main, Akron, OH 44308 (Courier Address: Use mail address for courier delivery), 330-375-5840.

http://www.ohnb.uscourts.gov

Counties: Medina, Portage, Summit.

Indexing/Storage: Cases are indexed by debtor as well as by case number. New cases are available in the index 1-2 days after filing date. Both computer and card indexes are maintained. Open records are located at this court. Case records closed before 1993 were sent to the Chicago Federal Records Center. In Spring 1995, the 1994 closed cases were sent to Dayton.

Fee & Payment: The fee is $20.00 per item (one party name or case number). Payment may be made by money order, cashier check, personal check, Visa or Mastercard. Prepayment is required. Payee: Clerk, US Bankruptcy Court. Certification fee: $7.00 per document. Copy fee: $.50 per page. You are allowed to make your own copies. These copies cost $.25 per page.

Phone Search: An automated voice case information service (VCIS) is available. Call VCIS at 800-898-6899 or 330-489-4731.

Mail Search: Always enclose a stamped self addressed envelope.

In Person: In person searching is available.

PACER: Sign-up number is 800-676-6856. Access fee is $.60 per minute. Toll-free access: 800-579-5735. Local access: 330-489-4779. Case records are available back to January 1985. Records are purged only up to September 1990. New civil records are available online after 2 days. PACER is available online at http://pacer.ohnb.uscourts.gov.

Electronic Filing: Electronic filing information is available online at https://ecf.ohnb.uscourts.gov

Canton Division Frank T Bow Federal Bldg, 201 Cleveland Ave SW, Canton, OH 44702 (Courier Address: Use mail address for courier delivery), 330-489-4426, Fax: 330-489-4434.

http://www.ohnb.uscourts.gov

Counties: Ashland, Carroll, Crawford, Holmes, Richland, Stark, Tuscarawas, Wayne.

Indexing/Storage: Cases are indexed by debtor as well as by case number. New cases are available in the index 48 hours after filing date. A computer index is maintained. Records are indexed on computer from 1985 to the present. Records are indexed on index cards from 1982 to 1984, and also journalized in books from 1984 to 1990. Open records are located at this court. Prior to 1995, closed case records were sent to the Chicago Federal Records Center.

Fee & Payment: The fee is $20.00 per item (one party name or case number). Payment may be made by money order, cashier check, personal check, Visa or Mastercard. Prepayment is required. Debtor's checks are not accepted. Payee: Clerk, US Bankruptcy Court. Certification fee: $7.00 per document. Copy fee: $.50 per page. You are allowed to make your own copies. These copies cost $.25 per page.

Phone Search: An automated voice case information service (VCIS) is available. Call VCIS at 800-898-6899 or 330-489-4731.

Fax Search: Will accept fax search request, but will not process until fee is received.

Mail Search: Always enclose a stamped self addressed envelope.

In Person: In person searching is available.

PACER: Sign-up number is 800-676-6856. Access fee is $.60 per minute. Toll-free access: 800-579-5735. Local access: 330-489-4779. Case records are available back to January 1985. Records are purged only up to September 1990. New civil records are available online after 2 days. PACER is available online at http://pacer.ohnb.uscourts.gov.

Electronic Filing: Electronic filing information is available online at https://ecf.ohnb.uscourts.gov

Cleveland Division Key Tower, Room 3001, 127 Public Square, Cleveland, OH 44114 (Courier Address: Use mail address for courier delivery), 216-522-4373.

http://www.ohnb.uscourts.gov

Counties: Cuyahoga, Geauga, Lake, Lorain.

Indexing/Storage: Cases are indexed by debtor as well as by case number. New cases are available in the index 2 days after filing date. Both computer and card indexes are maintained. Records are also indexed on microfiche. Open records are located at this court. Prior to 1995, closed case records were sent to the Chicago Federal Records Center.

Fee & Payment: The fee is $20.00 per item (one party name or case number). Payment may be made by money order, personal check. Debtor's checks are not accepted. Payee: Clerk, US Bankruptcy Court. Certification fee: $7.00 per document. Copy fee: $.50 per page.

Phone Search: An automated voice case information service (VCIS) is available. Call VCIS at 800-898-6899 or 330-489-4731.

Mail Search: Always enclose a stamped self addressed envelope.

In Person: In person searching is available.

PACER: Sign-up number is 800-676-6856. Access fee is $.60 per minute. Toll-free access: 800-579-5735. Local access: 330-489-4779. Case records are available back to January 1985. Records are purged only up to September 1990. New civil records are available online after 2 days. PACER is available online at http://pacer.ohnb.uscourts.gov.

Electronic Filing: Electronic filing information is available online at https://ecf.ohnb.uscourts.gov

Toledo Division Room 411, 1716 Spielbusch Ave, Toledo, OH 43624 (Courier Address: Use mail address for courier delivery), 419-259-6440.

http://www.ohnb.uscourts.gov

Counties: Allen, Auglaize, Defiance, Erie, Fulton, Hancock, Hardin, Henry, Huron, Lucas, Marion, Mercer, Ottawa, Paulding, Putnam, Sandusky, Seneca, Van Wert, Williams, Wood, Wyandot.

Indexing/Storage: Cases are indexed by debtor as well as by case number. New cases are available in the index 24 hours after filing date. A computer index is maintained. Open records are located at this court. Prior to 1995, closed case records were sent to the Chicago Federal Records Center.

Fee & Payment: The fee is $20.00 per item (one party name or case number). Payment may be made by money order, cashier check, business check, Visa or Mastercard. Personal checks are not accepted. Prepayment is required. Payee: Clerk, US Bankruptcy Court. Certification fee: $7.00 per document. Copy fee: $.50 per page.

Phone Search: An automated voice case information service (VCIS) is available. Call VCIS at 800-898-6899 or 330-489-4731.

Mail Search: Always enclose a stamped self addressed envelope.

In Person: In person searching is available.

PACER: Sign-up number is 800-676-6856. Access fee is $.60 per minute. Toll-free access: 800-579-5735. Local access: 330-489-4779. Case records are available back to January 1985. Records are purged only up to September 1990. New civil records are available online after 2 days. PACER is available online at http://pacer.ohnb.uscourts.gov.

Electronic Filing: Electronic filing information is available online at https://ecf.ohnb.uscourts.gov

Youngstown Division PO Box 147, Youngstown, OH 44501 (Courier Address: 125 Market St, #210, Youngstown, OH 44503), 330-746-7027.

http://www.ohnb.uscourts.gov

Counties: Ashtabula, Columbiana, Mahoning, Trumbull.

Indexing/Storage: Cases are indexed by debtor and creditors as well as by case number. New cases are available in the index 24 hours after filing date. A card index is maintained. Open records are located at this court. Prior to 1995, closed cases were sent to the Chicago Federal Records Center. Now case records are sent to the Dayton Federal Records Center every few years.

Fee & Payment: The fee is $20.00 per item (one party name or case number). Payment may be made by money order, cashier check, business check, Visa or Mastercard. Personal checks are not accepted. Prepayment is required. Payee: Clerk, US Bankruptcy Court. Certification fee: $7.00 per document. Copy fee: $.50 per page.

Phone Search: An automated voice case information service (VCIS) is available. Call VCIS at 800-898-6899 or 330-489-4731.

Mail Search: A stamped self addressed envelope is not required.

In Person: In person searching is available.

PACER: Sign-up number is 800-676-6856. Access fee is $.60 per minute. Toll-free access: 800-579-5735. Local access: 330-489-4779. Case records are available back to January 1985. Records are purged only up to September 1990. New civil records are available online after 2 days. PACER is available online at http://pacer.ohnb.uscourts.gov.

Electronic Filing: Electronic filing information is available online at https://ecf.ohnb.uscourts.gov

US District Court

Southern District of Ohio

Cincinnati Division Clerk, US District Court, 324 Potter Stewart Courthouse, 100 E 5th St, Cincinnati, OH 45202 (Courier Address: Use mail address for courier delivery), 513-564-7500, Fax: 513-564-7505.

http://www.ohsd.uscourts.gov

Counties: Adams, Brown, Butler, Clermont, Clinton, Hamilton, Highland, Lawrence, Scioto, Warren.

Indexing/Storage: Cases are indexed by defendant and plaintiff as well as by case number. New cases are available in the index immediately after filing date. A computer index is maintained. Open records are located at this court.

Fee & Payment: The fee is $20.00 per item (one party name or case number). Payment may be made by money order, cashier check, personal check. Prepayment is required. Give FedEx account number for expedited copy delivery. Payee: Clerk, US District Court. Certification fee: $7.00 per document. Copy fee: $.50 per page.

Phone Search: Only docket information is available by phone.

Mail Search: A stamped self addressed envelope is not required.

In Person: In person searching is available.

PACER: Sign-up number is 800-676-6856. Access fee is $1.00 per minute. Toll-free access: 800-710-4939. Local access: 614-469-6990. Case records are available back to June January 1994. Records are never purged. New records are available online after 1 day. PACER is available online at http://pacer.ohsd.uscourts.gov.

Columbus Division Office of the clerk, Room 260, 85 Marconi Blvd, Columbus, OH 43215 (Courier Address: Use mail address for courier delivery), 614-719-3000, Fax: 614-469-5953.

http://www.ohsd.uscourts.gov

Counties: Athens, Belmont, Coshocton, Delaware, Fairfield, Fayette, Franklin, Gallia, Guernsey, Harrison, Hocking, Jackson, Jefferson, Knox, Licking, Logan, Madison, Meigs, Monroe, Morgan, Morrow, Muskingum, Noble, Perry, Pickaway, Pike, Ross, Union, Vinton,Washington.

Indexing/Storage: Cases are indexed by defendant and plaintiff as well as by case number. New cases are available in the index 1-2 days after filing date. Both computer and card indexes are maintained. Records are also indexed on microfiche back to 1982. Open records are located at this court. District wide searches are available from this division.

Fee & Payment: The fee is $20.00 per item (one party name or case number). Payment may be made by money order, cashier check, business check. Personal checks are not accepted. Prepayment is required. Payee: Clerk, US District Court. Certification fee: $7.00 per document. Copy fee: $.50 per page.

Phone Search: Only docket information is available by phone.

Mail Search: Always enclose a stamped self addressed envelope.

In Person: In person searching is available.

PACER: Sign-up number is 800-676-6856. Access fee is $1.00 per minute. Toll-free access: 800-710-4939. Local access: 614-469-6990. Case records are available back to June January 1994. Records are never purged. New records are available online after 1 day. PACER is available online at http://pacer.ohsd.uscourts.gov.

Dayton Division Federal Bldg, 200 W 2nd, Room 712, Dayton, OH 45402 (Courier Address: Use mail address for courier delivery), 937-512-1400.

http://www.ohsd.uscourts.gov

Counties: Champaign, Clark, Darke, Greene, Miami, Montgomery, Preble, Shelby.

Indexing/Storage: Cases are indexed by defendant and plaintiff as well as by case number. New cases are available in the index 1 day after filing date. Both computer and card indexes are maintained. Records are also indexed on microfiche. The computer is only valid for cases that were open and pending from 1/90 to present. A view box is available to the public for cases filed for the present day that have not been entered into the computer. Open records are located at this court.

Fee & Payment: The fee is $20.00 per item (one party name or case number). Payment may be made by money order, cashier check, business check. Personal checks are not accepted. Prepayment is required. The Clerk's office will not respond to telephone requests that involve copywork. The searcher must provide a wide envelope for return of documents or, if documents are bulky, the searcher must provide access for bulk mailing. Payee: Clerk, US District Court. Certification fee: $7.00 per document. Copy fee: $.50 per page.

Phone Search: Over the phone, this court will only reveal whether a case has been filed.

Mail Search: Always enclose a stamped self addressed envelope.

In Person: In person searching is available.

PACER: Sign-up number is 800-676-6856. Access fee is $1.00 per minute. Toll-free access: 800-710-4939. Local access: 614-469-6990. Case records are available back to June January 1994. Records are never purged. New records are available online after 1 day. PACER is available online at http://pacer.ohsd.uscourts.gov.

US Bankruptcy Court

Southern District of Ohio

Cincinnati Division Atrium Two, Suite 800, 221 E Fourth St, Cincinnati, OH 45202 (Courier Address: Use mail address for courier delivery), 513-684-2572.

http://www.ohsb.uscourts.gov

Counties: Adams, Brown, Clermont, Hamilton, Highland, Lawrence, Scioto and a part of Butler.

Indexing/Storage: Cases are indexed by debtor as well as by case number. New cases are available in the index 2 days after filing date. A computer index is maintained. Open records are located at this court. Prior to 1993, closed case records were sent to the Chicago Federal Records Center.

Fee & Payment: The fee is $20.00 per item (one party name or case number). Payment may be made by money order, cashier check. Business checks are not accepted, Visa or Mastercard. Personal checks are not accepted. Credit cards are accepted only from law firms. Debtor checks are not accepted. Payee: Clerk, US Bankruptcy Court. Certification fee: $7.00 per document. Copy fee: $.50 per page.

Phone Search: Only docket information is available by phone. An automated voice case information service (VCIS) is available. Call VCIS at 800-726-1004 or 937-225-2544.

Mail Search: Always enclose a stamped self addressed envelope.

In Person: In person searching is available.

PACER: Sign-up number is 800-676-6856. Access fee is $.60 per minute. Toll-free access: 800-793-7003. Local access: 937-225-7561. Case records are available back to 1990. Records are purged every six months. New civil records are available online after 1 day. PACER is available online at http://pacer.ohsb.uscourts.gov.

Columbus Division 170 N High St, Columbus, OH 43215 (Courier Address: Use mail address for courier delivery), 614-469-6638.

http://www.ohsb.uscourts.gov

Counties: Athens, Belmont, Coshocton, Delaware, Fairfield, Fayette, Franklin, Gallia, Guernsey, Harrison, Hocking, Jackson, Jefferson, Knox, Licking, Logan, Madison, Meigs, Monroe, Morgan, Morrow, Muskingum, Noble, Perry, Pickaway, Pike, Ross, Union, Vinton,Washington.

Indexing/Storage: Cases are indexed by as well as by case number. New cases are available in the index 1 day after filing date. A computer index is maintained. Open records are located at this court. Prior to 1993, closed cases were sent to the Chicago Federal Records Facility.

Fee & Payment: The fee is $20.00 per item (one party name or case number). Payment may be made by money order, cashier check, business check. Personal checks are not accepted. Debtor's checks are not accepted. Payee: Clerk, US Bankruptcy Court. Certification fee: $7.00 per document. Copy fee: $.50 per page.

Phone Search: An automated voice case information service (VCIS) is available. Call VCIS at 800-726-1006 or 513-225-2562.

Mail Search: A stamped self addressed envelope is not required.

In Person: In person searching is available.

PACER: Sign-up number is 800-676-6856. Access fee is $.60 per minute. Toll-free access: 800-793-7003. Local access: 937-225-7561. Case records are available back to 1990. Records are purged every six months. New civil records are available online after 1 day. PACER is available online at http://pacer.ohsb.uscourts.gov.

Dayton Division 120 W 3rd St, Dayton, OH 45402 (Courier Address: Use mail address for courier delivery), 937-225-2516.

http://www.ohsb.uscourts.gov

Counties: Butler, Champaign, Clark, Clinton, Darke, Greene, Miami, Montgomery, Preble, Shelby, Warren; parts of Butler County are handled by Cincinnati Division.

Indexing/Storage: Cases are indexed by debtor as well as by case number. New cases are available in the index 1 day after filing date. Both computer and card indexes are maintained. Open records are located at this court. Cases closed before June 1991 were sent to the Chicago Federal Records Facility.

Fee & Payment: The fee is $20.00 per item (one party name or case number). Payment may be made by money order, cashier check, in-state business check. Personal checks are not accepted. Debtor's checks are not accepted. Payee: Clerk, US Bankruptcy Court. Certification fee: $7.00 per document. Copy fee: $.50 per page.

Phone Search: Only docket information is available by phone. An automated voice case information service (VCIS) is available. Call VCIS at 800-726-1004 or 937-225-2544.

Mail Search: Always enclose a stamped self addressed envelope.

In Person: In person searching is available.

PACER: Sign-up number is 800-676-6856. Access fee is $.60 per minute. Toll-free access: 800-793-7003. Local access: 937-225-7561. Case records are available back to 1990. Records are purged every six months. New civil records are available online after 1 day. PACER is available online at http://pacer.ohsb.uscourts.gov.

Ohio County Courts

Court	Jurisdiction	No. of Courts	How Organized
Court of Common Pleas*	General	88	county
County Courts*	Limited	47	
Municipal Courts*	Municipal	118	
Mayors Courts	Municipal	400	
Court of Claims	Special	1	

* Profiled in this Sourcebook.

Court	CIVIL								
	Tort	Contract	Real Estate	Min. Claim	Max. Claim	Small Claims	Estate	Eviction	Domestic Relations
Court of Common Pleas*	X	X	X	$3000/ $10,000	No Max		X		X
County Courts*	X	X	X	$0	$15,000	$3000		X	
Municipal Courts*	X	X	X	$0	$15,000	$3000		X	
Mayors Courts									
Court of Claims					No Max				

Court	CRIMINAL				
	Felony	Misdemeanor	DWI/DUI	Preliminary Hearing	Juvenile
Court of Common Pleas*	X		Juvenile		X
County Courts*		X	X	X	
Municipal Courts*		X	X	X	
Mayors Courts		X	X		
Court of Claims					

ADMINISTRATION   Administrative Director, Supreme Court of Ohio, 30 E Broad St, 3rd Fl, Columbus, OH, 43266-0419; 614-466-2653, Fax: 614-752-8736. www.sconet.state.oh.us

COURT STRUCTURE   The Court of Common Pleas is the general jurisdiction court and County Courts have limited jurisdiction. Effective July 1, 1997, the dollar limits for civil cases in County and Municipal Courts were raised as follows: County Court - from $3,000 to $15,000; Municipal Court - from $10,000 to $15,000. In addition the small claims limit was raised from $2,000 to $3,000.

Effective in 2001, Ohio Common Pleas Courts may name their own civil action limits, though most of these courts have yet to make changes. In effect, these Common Pleas courts may take any civil cases. However, civil maximum limits for Ohio's County Courts and Municipal Courts remains the same: $15,000.

ONLINE ACCESS   There is no statewide computer system, but a number of counties offer online access.

PROBATE COURTS   Probate courts are separate from the Court of Common Pleas, but Probate Court phone numbers are given with that court in each county.

Adams County

Common Pleas Court 110 W Main, Rm 207, West Union, OH 45693; 937-544-2344; Probate phone: 937-544-2368; Fax: 937-544-8911. Hours: 8:30AM-4PM *Felony, Civil Actions Over $3,000, Probate.*

Civil Records: Access: In person only. Visitors must perform in person searches for themselves. No search fee. Required to search: name, years to search. Civil cases indexed by defendant, plaintiff. Civil records on computer from April, 93, prior in books, archived from 1910.

Criminal Records: Access: Mail, in person. Visitors must perform in person searches for themselves. No search fee. Required to search: name, years to search, signed release; also helpful: DOB, SSN. Criminal records on computer from April, 93, prior in books, archived from 1910.

General Information: Public Access terminal is available. Copy fee: $.25 per page. Certification fee: $1.00. Fee payee: Clerk of Court. Personal checks accepted. Prepayment is required.

County Court 110 W Main, Rm 25, West Union, OH 45693; 937-544-2011; Fax: 937-544-8911. Hours: 8AM-4PM (EST). *Misdemeanor, Civil Actions Under $15,000, Small Claims.*

Civil Records: Access: Mail, in person. Both court and visitors may perform in person searches. Search fee: $10.00 per name. Required to search: name, years to search. Civil cases indexed by defendant, plaintiff. Civil records on computer from April, 93, index from 1958, prior on dockets and microfilm.

Criminal Records: Access: Mail, in person. Both court and visitors may perform in person searches. Search fee: $10.00 per name. Required to search: name, years to search; also helpful: SSN. Criminal records on computer from April, 93, index from 1958, prior on dockets and microfilm.

General Information: Public Access terminal is available. SASE required. Turnaround time 1-2 days. Copy fee: $.50 per page. Certification fee: $1.00. Fee payee: Adams County Court. Business checks accepted. Prepayment is required.

Allen County

Common Pleas Court PO Box 1243, Lima, OH 45802; 419-228-3700; Fax: 419-222-8427. Hours: 8AM-4:30PM (EST). *Felony, Civil Actions Over $15,000, Probate.*

Note: Probate is a separate court.

Civil Records: Access: Fax, mail, in person. Both court and visitors may perform in person searches. No search fee. Required to search: name; also helpful: years to search, address. Civil cases indexed by defendant, plaintiff. Civil records on computer back to 1986; in books and archived prior.

Criminal Records: Access: Fax, mail, in person. Both court and visitors may perform in person searches. No search fee. Required to search: name, years to search; also helpful: address, DOB, SSN. Criminal records on computer back to 1986; in books and archived prior.

General Information: Public Access terminal is available. No secret indictment records released. SASE required. Turnaround time 1-2 days. Fax notes: $3.00 for first page, $1.00 each add'l. Copy fee: $1.00 for first page, $.25 each add'l. Certification fee: $3.00. Fee payee: Clerk of Court. Personal checks accepted. Prepayment is required.

Lima Municipal Court 109 N Union St (PO Box 1529), Lima, OH 45802; 419-221-5275; Civil phone: 419-221-5250; Fax: 419-998-5526. Hours: 8AM-5PM (EST). *Misdemeanor, Civil Actions Under $15,000, Eviction, Small Claims.*

www.limamunicipalcourt.org

Civil Records: Access: Phone, fax, mail, in person, email. Both court and visitors may perform in person searches. No search fee. Required to search: name, years to search; also helpful: address. Civil cases indexed by defendant, plaintiff. Civil records on computer from April, 90, microfilm from 1975, books and archived prior.

Criminal Records: Access: Phone, fax, mail, in person, email. Both court and visitors may perform in person searches. No search fee. Required to search: name, years to search; also helpful: address, DOB, SSN. Criminal records on computer from April, 90, microfilm from 1975, books and archived prior.

General Information: Public Access terminal is available. SASE required. Turnaround time same day. Fax notes: Fee to fax results is $.25 per page. Copy fee: $.25 per page. Certification fee: $2.00. Fee payee: Clerk of Court. Business checks accepted. Credit cards accepted: Visa, MasterCard. Prepayment is required.

Ashland County

Common Pleas Court 142 W 2nd St, Ashland, OH 44805; 419-289-0000; Probate phone: 419-282-4332. Hours: 8AM-4PM (EST). *Felony, Civil Actions Over $10,000, Probate.*

Note: Probate court is a separate court at the same address.

Civil Records: Access: In person only. Visitors must perform in person searches for themselves. No search fee. Required to search: name, years to search. Civil cases indexed by defendant, plaintiff. Civil records in books and index from 1800s.

Criminal Records: Access: Mail, in person. Both court and visitors may perform in person searches. Search fee: $10.00 per name. Required to search: name, years to search, DOB; also helpful: SSN. Criminal records in books and index from 1800s.

General Information: Public Access terminal is available. SASE not required. Turnaround time 1-2 days. Copy fee: $.10 per page. Certification fee: $1.00. Fee payee: Clerk of Court. Personal checks accepted. Prepayment is required.

Ashland Municipal Court 1209 E Main St, Ashland, OH 44805; 419-289-8137; Fax: 419-289-8545. Hours: 8AM-5PM (EST). *Misdemeanor, Civil Actions Under $15,000, Eviction, Small Claims.*

www.ashland-ohio.com

Civil Records: Access: Phone, mail, fax, in person, email. Both court and visitors may perform in person searches. No search fee. Required to search: name, years to search. Civil cases indexed by defendant, plaintiff. Civil records on docket books from 1952.

Criminal Records: Access: Phone, mail, fax, in person, email. Both court and visitors may perform in person searches. No search fee. Required to search: name, years to search, SSN. Criminal records on docket books from 1952.

General Information: Public Access terminal is available. SASE required. Turnaround time 1-3 days. Fax notes: Fee to fax results is $1.00 per page. Copy fee: $1.00 per page. Certification fee: $1.00. Fee payee: Municipal Court. Personal checks accepted. Prepayment is required.

Ashtabula County

Common Pleas Court 25 W Jefferson St, Jefferson, OH 44047; 440-576-3637; Probate phone: 440-576-3451; Fax: 440-576-2819. Hours: 8AM-4:30PM (EST). *Felony, Civil Actions Over $10,000, Probate.*

Civil Records: Access: In person only. Visitors must perform in person searches for themselves. No search fee. Required to search: name, years to search; also helpful: address. Civil cases indexed by defendant, plaintiff. Civil records on computer back to 5/93, in books back to the 1800s.

Criminal Records: Access: In person only. Visitors must perform in person searches for themselves. No search fee. Required to search: name, years to search; also helpful: address, DOB, SSN. Criminal records on computer back to 5/93, in books back to the 1800s.

General Information: Public Access terminal is available. No expungments released. Copy fee: $.50 per page. Certification fee: $1.00. Fee payee: Clerk of Court. Personal checks accepted. Prepayment required.

County Court Eastern Division 25 W Jefferson St, Jefferson, OH 44047; 440-576-3617. Hours: 8AM-4:30PM (EST). *Misdemeanor, Civil Actions Under $15,000, Eviction, Small Claims.*

Civil Records: Access: Mail, fax, in person. Both court and visitors may perform in person searches. No search fee. Required to search: name, years to search. Civil cases indexed by defendant, plaintiff. Civil records on computer since 01/09/95; in books back to 1960s.

Criminal Records: Access: Mail, fax, in person. Both court and visitors may perform in person searches. No search fee. Required to search: name, years to search, DOB or SSN. Criminal records on computer since 01/09/95; in books back to 1960s.

General Information: Public Access terminal is available. SASE required. Turnaround time 1-2 days. Fax notes: Fee to fax results is $.50 per page. Copy fee: $.50 per page. Certification fee: $1.50. Fee payee: Eastern County Court. Only cashiers checks and money orders accepted. Prepayment is required.

County Court Western Division 117 W Main St, Geneva, OH 44041; 440-466-1184; Fax: 440-466-7171. Hours: 8AM-4:30PM (EST). *Misdemeanor, Civil Actions Under $15,000, Small Claims.*

Civil Records: Access: In person only. Visitors must perform in person searches for themselves. No search fee. Required to search: name, years to search. Civil cases indexed by defendant, plaintiff. Civil records on computer since 1995; prior records on docket books.

Criminal Records: Access: In person only. Visitors must perform in person searches for themselves. No search fee. Required to search: name, years to search, DOB, SSN, signed release. Criminal records on computer since 1995; prior records on docket books.

General Information: Public Access terminal is available. No confidential records released. Copy fee: $.50 per page. Certification fee: $.50 per page. Fee payee: Western County Court. Only cashiers checks and money orders accepted. Prepayment is required.

Ashtabula Municipal Court 110 W 44th St, Ashtabula, OH 44004; 440-992-7110; Fax: 440-998-5786. Hours: 8AM-4:30PM (EST). *Misdemeanor, Civil Actions Under $15,000, Eviction, Small Claims.*

Note: 440-992-7109 gives a directory.

Civil Records: Access: In person only. Visitors must perform in person searches for themselves. No search fee. Required to search: name, years to search. Civil cases indexed by defendant, plaintiff. Civil records on computer from 1988, books back to 1971.

Criminal Records: Access: In person only. Visitors must perform in person searches for themselves. No search fee. Required to search: name, years to search, DOB, SSN, signed release. Criminal records on computer from 1988, books back to 1971.

General Information: Public Access terminal is available. No expunged records released. Copy fee: $.10 per page. Certification fee: $5.00. Fee payee: Municipal Court. Personal checks accepted. Prepayment is required.

1128

The Sourcebook to Public Record Information

County Courts - Ohio

Athens County

Common Pleas Court PO Box 290, Athens, OH 45701-0290; 740-592-3242; Probate phone: 740-592-3251. Hours: 8AM-4PM (EST). *Felony, Civil Actions Over $10,000, Probate.*

www.athenscountycpcourt.org

Civil Records: Access: In person, online. Visitors must perform in person searches for themselves. No search fee. Required to search: name, years to search; also helpful: address. Civil cases indexed by defendant, plaintiff. Civil records on computer back to 1/92; prior in books. Online access to the CP court records is available free at the web site.

Criminal Records: Access: In person, online. Visitors must perform in person searches for themselves. No search fee. Required to search: name, years to search; also helpful: address, DOB, SSN. Criminal records on computer back to 1/92; prior in books.

General Information: Public Access terminal is available. Copy fee: $1.00 per page. Certification fee: $1.00. Fee payee: Clerk of Court. Business checks accepted. Prepayment is required.

Athens Municipal Court City Hall, 8 East Washington St, Athens, OH 45701; 740-592-3328; Fax: 740-592-3331. Hours: 8AM-4PM (EST). *Misdemeanor, Civil Actions Under $15,000, Eviction, Small Claims.*

Civil Records: Access: In person only. Visitors must perform in person searches for themselves. No search fee. Required to search: name, years to search; also helpful: address. Civil cases indexed by defendant, plaintiff. Civil records on computer back to 1994, prior in books.

Criminal Records: Access: In person only. Visitors must perform in person searches for themselves. No search fee. Required to search: name, years to search; also helpful: address, DOB, SSN. Criminal records on computer back to 7/1993, prior in books.

General Information: Public Access terminal is available. No expunged or sealed records released. Copy fee: $.50 per page; self serve copies: $.05. Certification fee: $1.00. Fee payee: ACMC. Personal checks accepted. Credit cards accepted: Visa, MasterCard. Prepayment is required.

Auglaize County

Common Pleas Court PO Box 409, Wapakoneta, OH 45895; 419-738-4219; Probate phone: 419-738-7710. Hours: 8AM-4:30PM (EST). *Felony, Civil Actions Over $10,000, Probate.*

Civil Records: Access: In person only. Visitors must perform in person searches for themselves. No search fee. Required to search: name, years to search; also helpful: address. Civil cases indexed by defendant, plaintiff. Civil records on dockets from 1860, computerized since 02/00.

Criminal Records: Access: In person only. Visitors must perform in person searches for themselves. No search fee. Required to search: name, years to search; also helpful: address, DOB, SSN. Criminal records on dockets from 1860, computerized since 02/00.

General Information: Public Access terminal is available. Copy fee: $.50 per page. Certification fee: $1.00. Fee payee: Clerk of Court. Personal checks accepted. Prepayment is required.

Auglaize County Municipal Court PO Box 409, Wapakoneta, OH 45895; 419-738-2923. Hours: 8AM-4:30PM (EST). *Misdemeanor, Civil Actions Under $15,000, Eviction, Small Claims.*

Civil Records: Access: In person only. Visitors must perform in person searches for themselves. No search fee. Required to search: name, years to search; also helpful: address. Civil cases indexed by defendant,

plaintiff. Civil records on computer from April, 1994, docket back to 1976.

Criminal Records: Access: In person only. Visitors must perform in person searches for themselves. No search fee. Required to search: name, years to search, signed release; also helpful: address, DOB, SSN. Criminal records on computer from October, 1993, docket back to 1976.

General Information: Public Access terminal is available. No records released. Copy fee: $.50 per page. Certification fee: $1.00. Fee payee: Clerk of Court. Personal checks accepted. Prepayment is required.

Belmont County

Common Pleas Court Main St, Courthouse, St Clairsville, OH 43950; 740-695-2121; Probate phone: 740-695-2121 X202. Hours: 8:30AM-4:30PM (EST). *Felony, Civil Actions Over $3,000, Probate.*

Civil Records: Access: Mail, in person. Both court and visitors may perform in person searches. Search fee: $3.00 per name. Required to search: name, years to search. Civil cases indexed by defendant, plaintiff. Civil records in books, archived from 1896; computerized from 1995.

Criminal Records: Access: Mail, in person. Both court and visitors may perform in person searches. Search fee: $3.00 per name. Required to search: name, years to search. Criminal records in books, archived from 1896; computerized from 1995.

General Information: Public Access terminal is available. No secret criminal records released. SASE required. Turnaround time 1 day. Copy fee: $1.00 per page. Certification fee: $5.00. Fee payee: Clerk of Court. Personal checks accepted. Prepayment required.

County Court Eastern Division 400 W 26th St, Bellaire, OH 43906; 740-676-4490. Hours: 8AM-4PM (EST). *Misdemeanor, Civil Actions Under $15,000, Small Claims.*

Civil Records: Access: Mail, in person. Both court and visitors may perform in person searches. No search fee. Required to search: name, years to search. Civil cases indexed by defendant, plaintiff. Civil records on computer from September, 94, books back to 1950s. Mail access available to attorneys only.

Criminal Records: Access: Mail, in person. Both court and visitors may perform in person searches. No search fee. Required to search: name, years to search; also helpful: DOB, SSN. Criminal records on computer from September, 94, books back to 1950s.

General Information: Public Access terminal is available. No sealed or confidential records released. SASE required. Copy fee: $1.00 per page. Certification fee: No cert fee. Fee payee: Eastern Division. Only cashiers checks and money orders accepted. Prepayment is required.

County Court Northern Division PO Box 40, Martins Ferry, OH 43935; 740-633-3147; Fax: 740-633-6631. Hours: 8AM-4PM (EST). *Misdemeanor, Civil Actions Under $15,000, Small Claims.*

Civil Records: Access: Mail, in person. Both court and visitors may perform in person searches. No search fee. Required to search: name, years to search. Civil cases indexed by defendant, plaintiff. Civil records on computer from June, 1994, books back to 1950s.

Criminal Records: Access: Mail, in person. Both court and visitors may perform in person searches. No search fee. Required to search: name, years to search, DOB; also helpful: SSN, sex, signed release. Criminal records on computer from June, 1994, books back to 1950s.

General Information: Public Access terminal is available. SASE not required. Turnaround time 5-7 days. No copy fee. Certification fee: No cert fee. Fee payee: Clerk of Court, Northern Division. Only cashiers checks and money orders accepted. Prepayment required.

County Court Western Division 147 W Main St, St Clairsville, OH 43950; 740-695-2875; Fax: 740-695-7285. Hours: 8AM-4PM (EST). *Misdemeanor, Civil Actions Under $15,000, Small Claims.*

Civil Records: Access: Fax, mail, in person. Both court and visitors may perform in person searches. No search fee. Required to search: name, years to search, address. Civil cases indexed by defendant, plaintiff. Civil records on computer from 1994, books back to 1950s.

Criminal Records: Access: Fax, mail, in person. Both court and visitors may perform in person searches. No search fee. Required to search: name, years to search, address, DOB, SSN. Criminal records on computer from 1994, books back to 1950s.

General Information: Public Access terminal is available. Pending case information not released. SASE required. Turnaround time 1 week. Fax notes: No fee to fax results. Copy fee: $1.00 per page. Certification fee: $1.00. Fee payee: Western Division Court. Only cashiers checks and money orders accepted. Prepayment is required.

Brown County

Common Pleas Court 101 S Main, Georgetown, OH 45121; 937-378-3100; Probate phone: 937-378-6549. Hours: 7:30AM-4:30PM (EST). *Felony, Civil Actions Over $3,000, Probate.*

Civil Records: Access: Mail, in person. Both court and visitors may perform in person searches. No search fee. Required to search: name, years to search; also helpful: address. Civil cases indexed by defendant, plaintiff. Civil records on computer since 1995, in books back to 1860s.

Criminal Records: Access: Mail, in person. Both court and visitors may perform in person searches. No search fee. Required to search: name, years to search; also helpful: address, DOB, SSN. Criminal records on computer since 1995, in books back to 1860s.

General Information: Public Access terminal is available. No criminal expungment records released. SASE required. Turnaround time same day. Copy fee: $.25 per page. Certification fee: $1.00. Fee payee: Clerk of Court. Personal checks accepted. Prepayment is required.

County Court 770 Mount Orab Pike, Georgetown, OH 45121; 937-378-6358; Fax: 937-378-2462. Hours: 7:30AM-4:30PM M-F; 9AM-Noon S (EST). *Misdemeanor, Civil Actions Under $15,000, Eviction, Small Claims.*

www.browncountycourt.org

Civil Records: Access: Mail, in person. Both court and visitors may perform in person searches. No search fee. Required to search: name, years to search. Civil cases indexed by defendant, plaintiff. Civil records in books back to 1958, computerized since 1995.

Criminal Records: Access: Mail, in person. Both court and visitors may perform in person searches. No search fee. Required to search: name, years to search, DOB; also helpful: SSN. Criminal records in books back to 1958, computerized since 1995.

General Information: Public Access terminal is available. SASE required. Copy fee: $.25. Certification fee: No cert fee. Fee payee: Brown County Court. Only cashiers checks and money orders accepted. Prepayment is required.

Butler County

Common Pleas Court 101 High St, Hamilton, OH 45011; 513-887-3996; Probate phone: 513-887-3296; Fax: 513-887-3089. Hours: 8:30AM-4:30PM (EST). *Felony, Civil Actions Over $3,000, Probate.*

www.butlercountyclerk.org

Civil Records: Access: Online, in person. Visitors must perform in person searches for themselves. No search fee. Required to search: name, years to search. Civil cases indexed by defendant, plaintiff. Civil records on computer from 1988, prior in books. Online access to County Clerk of Courts records is available free at http://38.155.160.5/pa/pa.urd/pamw6500.display. Search by name, dates, or case number and type. Online access to Probate Court records is available free at www.butlercountyprobatecourt.org. Search the Estate or Guardianship databases.

Criminal Records: Access: Online, in person. Visitors must perform in person searches for themselves. No search fee. Required to search: name, years to search, DOB; also helpful: SSN. Criminal records on computer from 1988, prior in books. Online access to criminal records is the same as civil.

General Information: Public Access terminal is available. Copy fee: $.25 per page. Certification fee: $2.00. Fee payee: Clerk of Court. Personal checks accepted.

County Court Area #1 118 West High, Oxford, OH 45056; 513-523-4748; Fax: 513-523-4737. Hours: 8:30AM-4:30PM (EST). *Misdemeanor, Civil Actions Under $15,000, Small Claims.*

Civil Records: Access: Phone, mail, in person. Both court and visitors may perform in person searches. No search fee. Required to search: name, years to search. Civil cases indexed by defendant, plaintiff. Civil records on index back to 1983.

Criminal Records: Access: Phone, mail, in person. Both court and visitors may perform in person searches. No search fee. Required to search: name, years to search, DOB. Criminal records on index back to 1983.

General Information: No sealed records released. SASE required. Turnaround time 1-5 days. No copy fee. Certification fee: No cert fee.

County Court Area #2 Butler County Courthouse, 101 High St, 1st Fl, Hamilton, OH 45011; 513-887-3459. Hours: 8AM-5PM (EST). *Misdemeanor, Civil Actions Under $15,000, Small Claims.*

Civil Records: Access: Phone, in person. Visitors must perform in person searches for themselves. No search fee. Required to search: name, years to search. Civil cases indexed by defendant, plaintiff. Civil records on computer from 1993, books back to 1983.

Criminal Records: Access: Phone, in person. Visitors must perform in person searches for themselves. No search fee. Required to search: name, years to search. Criminal records on computer from 1993, books back to 1983.

General Information: Public Access terminal is available. No sealed records released. No copy fee. Certification fee: No cert fee. Only cashiers checks and money orders accepted. Prepayment is required.

County Court Area #3 9113 Cincinnati, Dayton Rd, West Chester, OH 45069; 513-867-5070; Fax: 513-777-0558. Hours: 8:AM-5PM (EST). *Misdemeanor, Civil Actions Under $15,000, Small Claims.*

Civil Records: Access: Mail, in person. Both court and visitors may perform in person searches. No search fee. Required to search: name, years to search. Civil cases indexed by defendant, plaintiff. Civil records on computer from 1993, books back to 1983.

Criminal Records: Access: Mail, in person. Both court and visitors may perform in person searches. No search fee. Required to search: name, years to search. Criminal records on computer from 1993, books back to 1983.

General Information: SASE required. Turnaround time 2-3 days. No copy fee. Certification fee: $1.00. Fee payee: Area #3 Court. Personal checks accepted. Prepayment is required.

Carroll County

Common Pleas Court PO Box 367, Carrollton, OH 44615; 330-627-4886; Probate phone: 330-627-2323; Fax: 330-627-6734. Hours: 8AM-4PM (EST). *Felony, Civil Actions Over $15,000, Probate.*

Note: Probate Court address is 199 Public Sq, Courthouse, Carrollton, OH.

Civil Records: Access: In person only. Visitors must perform in person searches for themselves. No search fee. Required to search: name, years to search. Civil cases indexed by defendant, plaintiff. Civil records in books back to 1900s.

Criminal Records: Access: In person only. Visitors must perform in person searches for themselves. No search fee. Required to search: name, years to search; also helpful: DOB, SSN. Criminal records in books back to 1900s.

General Information: Copy fee: $.05 per page. Certification fee: $1.00. Fee payee: Clerk of Court. Personal checks accepted. Prepayment is required.

County Court Courthouse, 3rd Fl, Carrollton, OH 44615; 330-627-5049; Fax: 330-627-3662. Hours: 8AM-4PM (EST). *Misdemeanor, Civil Actions Under $15,000, Small Claims.*

Civil Records: Access: In person only. Visitors must perform in person searches for themselves. No search fee. Required to search: name, years to search. Civil cases indexed by defendant, plaintiff. Civil records in books from 1958; on computer since.

Criminal Records: Access: In person only. Visitors must perform in person searches for themselves. No search fee. Required to search: name, years to search, DOB; also helpful: SSN. Criminal records in books from 1958; on computer since.

General Information: No confidential records released. Copy fee: $.25 per page. Certification fee: $2.00. Fee payee: Carroll County Court. Personal checks accepted. Prepayment is required.

Champaign County

Common Pleas Court 200 N Main St, Urbana, OH 43078; 937-653-2746; Probate phone: 937-652-2108. Hours: 8AM-4PM (EST). *Felony, Civil Actions Over $10,000, Probate.*

Note: Probate is separate court at phone number given.

Civil Records: Access: Phone, mail, in person. Visitors must perform in person searches for themselves. No search fee. Required to search: name, years to search. Civil cases indexed by defendant, plaintiff. Civil records on computer from 06/92, books back to late 1800'. Will only do phone or mail searches with a case number.

Criminal Records: Access: Phone, mail, in person. Visitors must perform in person searches for themselves. No search fee. Required to search: name, years to search, DOB, SSN, signed release. Criminal records on computer from 06/92, books back to late 1800'. Will only do mail or phone searches with a case number.

General Information: Public Access terminal is available. All records are public. SASE required. Copy fee: $.25 per page. Certification fee: $5.00. Fee payee: Clerk of Court. Personal checks accepted. Personal checks over $10.00 not accepted. Prepayment required.

Champaign County Municipal Court PO Box 85, Urbana, OH 43078; 937-653-7376. Hours: 8AM-4PM (EST). *Misdemeanor, Civil Actions Under $15,000, Eviction, Small Claims.*

Civil Records: Access: Mail, in person. Both court and visitors may perform in person searches. No search fee. Required to search: name, years to search. Civil cases indexed by defendant, plaintiff. Civil records on computer from June, 93, books back to late 1800s.

Criminal Records: Access: Mail, in person. Both court and visitors may perform in person searches. No search fee. Required to search: name, years to search; also helpful: DOB, SSN. Criminal records on computer from June, 93, books back to late 1800s.

General Information: No sealed records released. SASE required. Turnaround time 2-3 days. Copy fee: $.25 per page. Certification fee: $2.50. Fee payee: Municipal Court. Only cashiers checks and money orders accepted. Prepayment is required.

Clark County

Common Pleas Court 101 N Limestone St, Springfield, OH 45502; 937-328-2458; 937-328-4648 (Domestic); Probate phone: 937-328-2434; Fax: 937-328-2436. Hours: 8AM-4:30PM (EST). *Felony, Civil Actions Over $10,000, Probate.*

Note: Probate Court and records are at the same address, separate office and phone.

Civil Records: Access: In person only. Visitors must perform in person searches for themselves. No search fee. Required to search: name, years to search. Civil cases indexed by defendant. Civil records in index books.

Criminal Records: Access: In person only. Visitors must perform in person searches for themselves. No search fee. Required to search: name, years to search. Criminal records in index books.

General Information: Public Access terminal is available. Fax notes: Fee to fax results is $1.00 per page. Copy fee: $1.00 per page. Certification fee: $.25. Fee payee: Clerk of Court. Business checks accepted. Prepayment is required.

Clark County Municipal Court 50 E Columbia St, Springfield, OH 45502; 937-328-3700. Hours: 8AM-5PM (EST). *Misdemeanor, Civil Actions Under $15,000, Eviction, Small Claims.*

www.clerkofcourts.municipal.co.clark.ob.us

Civil Records: Access: Mail, in person. Both court and visitors may perform in person searches. No search fee. Required to search: name, years to search. Civil cases indexed by defendant, plaintiff. Civil records on computer from 1991.

Criminal Records: Access: Mail, in person. Both court and visitors may perform in person searches. No search fee. Required to search: name, years to search; also helpful: DOB, SSN. Criminal records on computer since 3/90.

General Information: Public Access terminal is available. SASE required. Turnaround time 2-3 days. Copy fee: $.50 per page. Certification fee: $2.00. Fee payee: Clerk of Court. Personal checks not accepted. Prepayment is required.

Clermont County

Common Pleas Court 270 Main St, Batavia, OH 45103; 513-732-7130; Probate phone: 513-732-7243; Fax: 513-732-7050. Hours: 8:30AM-4:30PM (EST). *Felony, Civil Actions Over $10,000, Probate.*

Civil Records: Access: In person only. Visitors must perform in person searches for themselves. No search fee. Required to search: name, years to search; also helpful: address. Civil cases indexed by defendant, plaintiff. Civil records on computer from 1987, some on microfiche from 1920s, index books from 1959.

Criminal Records: Access: In person only. Visitors must perform in person searches for themselves. No search fee. Required to search: name, years to search, DOB; also helpful: address, SSN. Criminal records on computer from 1987, some on microfiche from 1920s, index books from 1959. The clerk refers criminal record requests to the Sheriff (513-732-7500) who will do searches for $5.00 per name.

General Information: Public Access terminal is available. Copy fee: $.10 per page. Certification fee:

$1.00 per page. Fee payee: Clerk of Court. Business checks accepted. Prepayment is required.

Clermont County Municipal Court
289 Main St, Batavia, OH 45103; Civil phone: 513-732-7292; Criminal phone: 513-732-7290. Hours: 8AM-4PM (EST). *Misdemeanor, Civil Actions Under $15,000, Eviction, Small Claims.*

Civil Records: Access: Mail, in person. Visitors must perform in person searches for themselves. No search fee. Required to search: name, years to search. Civil cases indexed by defendant, plaintiff. Civil records in books and microfiche from 1965, docket books back to 1800s.

Criminal Records: Access: Mail, in person. Visitors must perform in person searches for themselves. No search fee. Required to search: name, years to search, DOB; also helpful: SSN. Criminal records in books and microfiche from 1965, docket books back to 1800s.

General Information: SASE required. Copy fee: $.25 per page. Certification fee: $1.00. Fee payee: Clerk of Court. Only cashiers checks and money orders accepted. Prepayment is required.

Clinton County

Common Pleas Court
46 S South St, Wilmington, OH 45177; 937-382-2316; Probate phone: 937-382-2280; Fax: 937-383-3455. Hours: 7:30AM-4:30PM (EST). *Felony, Civil Actions Over $15,000, Probate.*

Note: Probate fax is 937-383-1158; hours are 8AM-4:30PM.

Civil Records: Access: Fax, mail, in person. Both court and visitors may perform in person searches. No search fee. Required to search: name, years to search; also helpful: address. Civil cases indexed by defendant, plaintiff. Civil records on computer since 1995; prior in books back to 1810.

Criminal Records: Access: Mail, in person. Both court and visitors may perform in person searches. Search fee: $5.00 per name. Required to search: name, years to search, DOD, SSN; also helpful: address. Criminal records on computer since 1995; prior in books back to 1810.

General Information: Public Access terminal is available. No confidential records released. SASE required. Turnaround time 1 week. Copy fee: $.25 per page. Certification fee: $1.00. Fee payee: Clerk of Court. Personal checks accepted. Prepayment required.

Clinton County Municipal Court
69 N South St, PO Box 71, Wilmington, OH 45177; 937-382-8985; Fax: 937-383-0130. Hours: 8AM-3:30PM (EST). *Misdemeanor, Civil Actions Under $15,000, Eviction, Small Claims.*

Civil Records: Access: Phone, mail, in person. Both court and visitors may perform in person searches. No search fee. Required to search: name, years to search. Civil cases indexed by defendant, plaintiff. Civil records in books from 1960; computerized records go back to 1995.

Criminal Records: Access: Phone, mail, in person. Both court and visitors may perform in person searches. No search fee. Required to search: name, years to search, DOB; also helpful: SSN. Criminal records in books from 1960; computerized records go back to 1995.

General Information: SASE required. Turnaround time 1 day. Copy fee: $.25 per page after 10 pages. Certification fee: No cert fee. Fee payee: Clerk of Court. Only cashiers checks and money orders accepted.

Columbiana County

Common Pleas Court
105 S Market St, Lisbon, OH 44432; 330-424-7777; Fax: 330-424-3960. Hours: 8AM-4PM (EST). *Felony, Civil Actions Over $10,000, Probate.*

Civil Records: Access: In person only. Visitors must perform in person searches for themselves. No search fee. Required to search: name, years to search; also helpful: address. Civil cases indexed by defendant, plaintiff. Civil records on computer since 1993; prior in books from 1968, archived back to 1800s.

Criminal Records: Access: In person only. Visitors must perform in person searches for themselves. No search fee. Required to search: name, years to search, DOB; also helpful: address, SSN. Criminal records on computer since 1993; prior in books from 1968, archived back to 1800s.

General Information: Public Access terminal is available. No secret indictment records released. Copy fee: $.50 per page. Certification fee: $1.00. Fee payee: Clerk of Court. Personal checks accepted. Prepayment is required.

County Court Eastern Area
31 North Market St, East Palestine, OH 44413; 330-426-3774; Fax: 330-426-6328. Hours: 8AM-12, 1PM-4PM (EST). *Misdemeanor, Civil Actions Under $15,000, Small Claims.*

Civil Records: Access: Mail, in person. Both court and visitors may perform in person searches. No search fee. Required to search: name, years to search. Civil cases indexed by defendant, plaintiff. Civil records in books from 1950s, archived from 1800s, recent records computerized.

Criminal Records: Access: Mail, in person. Both court and visitors may perform in person searches. No search fee. Required to search: name, years to search. Criminal records in books from 1950s, archived from 1800s, recent records computerized.

General Information: Public Access terminal is available. SASE required. Turnaround time 1 day. Copy fee: $.25 per page. Certification fee: $1.00. Fee payee: Clerk of Court. Only cashiers checks and money orders accepted. Prepayment is required.

County Court Northwest Area
130 Penn Ave, Salem, OH 44460; 330-332-0297. Hours: 8AM-4PM (EST). *Misdemeanor, Civil Actions Under $15,000, Small Claims.*

Civil Records: Access: Mail, in person. Both court and visitors may perform in person searches. No search fee. Required to search: name, years to search. Civil cases indexed by defendant, plaintiff. Civil records in books from 1950s, archived from 1800s, computerized since 11/94.

Criminal Records: Access: Mail, in person. Both court and visitors may perform in person searches. No search fee. Required to search: name, years to search; also helpful: DOB. Criminal records in books from 1950s, archived from 1800s, computerized since 11/94.

General Information: Public Access terminal is available. SASE required. Turnaround time 2-3 days. Copy fee: $.25 per page. Certification fee: $1.00. Fee payee: Northwest Area Court. Only cashiers checks and money orders accepted. Prepayment is required.

County Court Southwest Area
41 N Park Ave, Lisbon, OH 44432; 330-424-5326; Fax: 330-424-6658. Hours: 8AM-4PM (EST). *Misdemeanor, Civil Actions Under $15,000, Small Claims.*

Civil Records: Access: In person only. Visitors must perform in person searches for themselves. No search fee. Required to search: name, years to search. Civil cases indexed by defendant, plaintiff. Civil records in books from 1950s, archived back to 1800s.

Criminal Records: Access: In person only. Both court and visitors may perform in person searches. No search fee. Required to search: name, years to search; also helpful: DOB, SSN. Criminal records in books from 1950s, archived back to 1800s.

General Information: Public Access terminal is available. No expungment records released. Copy fee: $.50 per page. Certification fee: $1.00. Fee payee: Southwest Court. Only cashiers checks and money orders accepted. Prepayment is required.

East Liverpool Municipal Court
126 W 6th St, East Liverpool, OH 43920; 330-385-5151; Fax: 330-385-1566. Hours: 8AM-4PM (EST). *Misdemeanor, Civil Actions Under $15,000, Eviction, Small Claims.*

www.eastliverpool.com/court.html

Civil Records: Access: Phone, fax, mail, in person. Both court and visitors may perform in person searches. No search fee. Required to search: name, years to search. Civil cases indexed by defendant, plaintiff. Civil records in books from 1968, archived back to 1800s, computerized since 11/92.

Criminal Records: Access: Phone, fax, mail, in person. Both court and visitors may perform in person searches. No search fee. Required to search: name, years to search, signed release; also helpful: DOB, SSN. Criminal records in books from 1968, archived back to 1800s, computerized since 11/92.

General Information: Public Access terminal is available. No expungment records released. SASE required. Turnaround time 1-2 days. Fax notes: No fee to fax results. Copy fee: $.25 per page. Certification fee: $3.00. Fee payee: East Liverpool Municipal Court. No business or personal checks. Prepayment is required.

Coshocton County

Common Pleas Court
318 Main St, Coshocton, OH 43812; 740-622-1456; Probate phone: 740-622-1837. Hours: 8AM-4PM (EST). *Felony, Civil Actions Over $10,000, Probate.*

Civil Records: Access: Mail, in person. Both court and visitors may perform in person searches. No search fee. Required to search: name, years to search. Civil cases indexed by defendant, plaintiff. Civil records in books, microfilm back to 1985, archived back to 1800s; on computer back to 1998.

Criminal Records: Access: Mail, in person. Both court and visitors may perform in person searches. No search fee. Required to search: name, years to search, DOB; also helpful: SSN. Criminal records in books, microfilm back to 1985, archived back to 1800s; on computer back to 1998.

General Information: Public Access terminal is available. No expunged records released. SASE not required. Turnaround time 2 days. Fax notes: Will not fax back results. Copy fee: $.25 per page. Certification fee: $1.00. Fee payee: Clerk of Court. Personal checks accepted. Prepayment is required.

Coshocton Municipal Court
760 Chesnut St, Coshocton, OH 43812; 740-622-2871; Fax: 740-623-5928. Hours: 8AM-4:30PM M-W,F; 8AM-Noon Th (EST). *Misdemeanor, Civil Actions Under $15,000, Eviction, Small Claims.*

www.coshoctonmunicipalcourt.com

Civil Records: Access: Phone, fax, mail, in person, online. Both court and visitors may perform in person searches. No search fee. Required to search: name, years to search. Civil cases indexed by defendant, plaintiff. Civil records on computer from 1989, books back to 1952. Online access to civil records is available at the web site. Search by name, case number, attorney, date.

Criminal Records: Access: Phone, fax, mail, in person, online. Both court and visitors may perform in person searches. No search fee. Required to search:

name, years to search; also helpful: DOB, SSN. Criminal records on computer from 1989, books back to 1952. Online access to criminal records is the same as civil. Search by name, attorney, citation or case number.
General Information: Public Access terminal is available. No expunged records released. SASE required. Turnaround time same day. Fax notes: No fee to fax results. Copy fee: $.50 per page. Certification fee: $5.00. Fee payee: Clerk of Court. Personal checks accepted. Prepayment is required.

Crawford County

Common Pleas Court PO Box 470, Bucyrus, OH 44820; 419-562-2766; Probate phone: 419-562-8891; Fax: 419-562-8011. Hours: 8:30AM-4:30PM (EST). *Felony, Civil Actions Over $3,000, Probate.*

Civil Records: Access: Mail, in person. Both court and visitors may perform in person searches. Search fee: $5.00 per name. Required to search: name, years to search; also helpful: address. Civil cases indexed by defendant, plaintiff. Civil records on computer from 1990, some on microfiche and index books from 1800s.
Criminal Records: Access: Mail, in person. Both court and visitors may perform in person searches. Search fee: $5.00 per name. Required to search: name, years to search, notarized release; also helpful: address, DOB, SSN. Criminal records on computer from 1990, some on microfiche and index books from 1800s.
General Information: Public Access terminal is available. No divorce investigations. SASE required. Turnaround time 1-2 days. Certification fee: $1.00. Fee payee: Clerk of Court. Personal checks accepted. Prepayment is required.

Crawford County Municipal Court PO Box 550, Bucyrus, OH 44820; 419-562-2731. Hours: 8:30AM-4:30PM (EST). *Misdemeanor, Civil Actions Under $15,000, Eviction, Small Claims.*

Civil Records: Access: Mail, in person. Both court and visitors may perform in person searches. No search fee. Required to search: name, years to search. Civil cases indexed by defendant, plaintiff. Civil records in books back to 1978.
Criminal Records: Access: Mail, in person. Both court and visitors may perform in person searches. No search fee. Required to search: name, years to search. Criminal records in books back to 1978.
General Information: Public Access terminal is available. No counseling report records released. SASE not required. Turnaround time within 1 week. Copy fee: $.10 per page. Certification fee: $2.00. Business checks accepted. Crawford county business checks accepted. Prepayment is required.

Crawford County Municipal Court Eastern Division 301 Harding Way East, Galion, OH 44833; 419-468-6819; Fax: 419-468-6828. Hours: 8:30AM-4:30PM (EST). *Misdemeanor, Civil Actions Under $15,000, Eviction, Small Claims.*

Civil Records: Access: Mail, in person. Both court and visitors may perform in person searches. No search fee. Required to search: name, years to search. Civil cases indexed by defendant, plaintiff. Civil records in books back to 1800s.
Criminal Records: Access: Mail, in person. Both court and visitors may perform in person searches. No search fee. Required to search: name, years to search, DOB, SSN, signed release. Criminal records in books back to 1800s.
General Information: SASE required. Turnaround time 2-3 days. Copy fee: $.25 per page. Certification fee: $3.00. Fee payee: Municipal Court. Only cashiers checks and money orders accepted. Prepayment required.

Cuyahoga County
Common Pleas Court - General Division
1200 Ontario St, Cleveland, OH 44113; 216-443-8560; Civil phone: 216-443-7966; Criminal phone: 216-443-7985; Probate phone: 216-443-8764; Fax: 216-443-5424. Hours: 8:30AM-4:30PM (EST). *Felony, Civil Actions Over $10,000, Probate.*

www.cuyahoga.oh.us
Note: Probate is a separate division with separate records and personnel.
Civil Records: Access: Phone, mail, in person. Both court and visitors may perform in person searches. No search fee. Required to search: name, years to search; also helpful: address. Civil cases indexed by defendant, plaintiff. Civil records on index and dockets from 1968, archived from 1800s. Address mail requests to Gerald Fuerst, 1st Floor, Index Dept.
Criminal Records: Access: In person only. Visitors must perform in person searches for themselves. No search fee. Required to search: name, years to search; also helpful: address, DOB, SSN. Criminal records on index and dockets from 1968, archived from 1800s. Address mail requests to Criminal Dept, 2nd Floor.
General Information: Public Access terminal is available. No expungments or sealed records released. SASE required. Copy fee: $.25 per page. Certification fee: $1.00 per page. Fee payee: Clerk of Court. Business checks accepted. Prepayment is required.

Cleveland Municipal Court - Civil Division
1200 Ontario St, Cleveland, OH 44113; 216-664-4870; Fax: 216-664-4065. Hours: 8AM-3:50PM (EST). *Civil Actions Under $15,000, Eviction, Small Claims.*

Civil Records: Access: Fax, mail, in person. Both court and visitors may perform in person searches. No search fee. Required to search: name, years to search; also helpful: address. Civil cases indexed by defendant, plaintiff. Civil records on computer from 1988, docket books and index from 1950s, prior archived.
General Information: Public Access terminal is available. SASE required. Turnaround time 2 days. Copy fee: $.25 per page. Certification fee: $1.00. Fee payee: Municipal Court. Personal checks accepted. Prepayment is required.

Cleveland Municipal Court - Criminal Division
1200 Ontario St, Cleveland, OH 44113; 216-664-4790. Hours: 8AM-3:50PM *Misdemeanor.*

Criminal Records: Access: Mail, in person. Both court and visitors may perform in person searches. No search fee. Required to search: name, years to search, DOB, SSN, signed release. Criminal records on computer since 1988, on books to 1950s, archived prior.
General Information: No adoption or juvenile records released. SASE required. Turnaround time 3-4 days. Copy fee: $.25 per page. Certification fee: $3.00. Fee payee: Municipal Court. Personal checks accepted. Prepayment is required.

Bedford Municipal Court 65 Columbus Rd, Bedford, OH 44146; 440-232-3420; Fax: 440-232-2510. Hours: 8:30AM-4:30PM (EST). *Misdemeanor, Civil Actions Under $15,000, Eviction, Small Claims.*

Civil Records: Access: Fax, mail, in person. Both court and visitors may perform in person searches. No search fee. Required to search: name, years to search. Civil cases indexed by defendant, plaintiff. Civil records on computer from 1985, docket books and index from 1970s, prior archived.
Criminal Records: Access: Fax, mail, in person. Both court and visitors may perform in person searches. No search fee. Required to search: name, years to search, signed release. Criminal records on computer from 1985, docket books and index from 1970s, prior archived.
General Information: SASE required. Turnaround time 3 days. Fax notes: No fee to fax results. Copy fee: $.50 per page. Certification fee: $2.00. Fee payee: Municipal Court. Only cashiers checks and money orders accepted. Prepayment is required.

Berea Municipal Court 11 Berea Commons, Berea, OH 44017; 440-826-5860; Fax: 440-891-3387. Hours: 8AM-4:30PM (EST). *Misdemeanor, Civil Actions Under $15,000, Eviction, Small Claims.*

Civil Records: Access: Mail, fax, in person. Both court and visitors may perform in person searches. No search fee. Required to search: name, years to search. Civil cases indexed by defendant, plaintiff. Civil records on computer back to 1991, prior in books and archived.
Criminal Records: Access: Fax, mail, in person. Both court and visitors may perform in person searches. Search fee: $5.00 per name. Required to search: name, years to search; also helpful: address, DOB, SSN. Criminal records on computer back to 1991, prior in books and archived.
General Information: No probation records released. SASE required. Turnaround time 1 week-10 days. Fax notes: No fee to fax results. Copy fee: $1.00 per page. Certification fee: $5.00. Fee payee: Berea Municipal Court. Personal checks accepted. Credit cards accepted: Visa, MasterCard. Prepayment is required.

Cleveland Heights Municipal Court 40 Severance Circle, Cleveland Heights, OH 44118; 216-291-4901; Fax: 216-291-2459. Hours: 8AM-5PM (EST). *Misdemeanor, Civil Actions Under $15,000, Eviction, Small Claims.*

www.clevelandheightscourt.com
Civil Records: Access: Online, in person. Visitors must perform in person searches for themselves. No search fee. Required to search: name, years to search; also helpful: address. Civil cases indexed by defendant, plaintiff. Civil records on computer from 1990, prior in books to 1970s. Civil (to $15,000) or misdemeanor docket records for Municipal Court are available on the web site. Search by name or case number.
Criminal Records: Access: Online, in person. Visitors must perform in person searches for themselves. No search fee. Required to search: name, years to search; also helpful: address, DOB, SSN. Criminal records on computer from 1990, prior in books to 1970s. Online access to criminal records is the same as civil.
General Information: Public Access terminal is available. No expungments or search warrant records released. Copy fee: $.10 per page. Certification fee: $3.00. Fee payee: Municipal Court. Personal checks accepted. Credit cards accepted: Visa, MasterCard. Visa, MC in person only. Prepayment is required.

East Cleveland Municipal Court 14340 Euclid Ave, East Cleveland, OH 44112; 216-681-2021/2022. Hours: 8:30AM-4:30PM *Misdemeanor, Civil Actions Under $15,000, Eviction, Small Claims.*

Civil Records: Access: In person only. Visitors must perform in person searches for themselves. No search fee. Required to search: name, years to search. Civil cases indexed by defendant, plaintiff. Civil records on computer from 1989, docket books and index from 1950s, prior archived.
Criminal Records: Access: Mail, in person. Visitors must perform in person searches for themselves. No search fee. Required to search: name, years to search, DOB, SSN, signed release; also helpful: address. Criminal records on computer from 1989, docket books and index from 1950s, prior archived. Address mail requests to Police Record Room.
General Information: SASE required. Turnaround time 1-2 weeks. Copy fee: $1.00 per page. Certification

fee: $3.00. Fee payee: Municipal Court. Personal checks accepted. Prepayment is required.

Euclid Municipal Court
555 E 222 St, Euclid, OH 44123-2099; 216-289-2888. Hours: 8:30AM-4:30PM (EST). *Misdemeanor, Civil Actions Under $15,000, Eviction, Small Claims.*

Civil Records: Access: Mail, in person. Both court and visitors may perform in person searches. Search fee: $5.00 per name. Required to search: name, years to search. Civil cases indexed by defendant, plaintiff. Civil records on computer from 1995, docket books and index from 1950s, prior archived.

Criminal Records: Access: Mail, in person. Both court and visitors may perform in person searches. Search fee: $5.00 per name. Required to search: name, years to search, DOB; also helpful: address, SSN. Criminal records on computer from 1995, docket books and index from 1950s, prior archived.

General Information: No expunged records released. SASE required. Turnaround time 1 week. Copy fee: $1.00 per page. Certification fee: $5.00. Fee payee: Municipal Court. Personal checks accepted. Prepayment is required.

Garfield Heights Municipal Court
5555 Turney Rd, Garfield Heights, OH 44125; 216-475-1900. Hours: 8:30AM-4:30PM (EST). *Misdemeanor, Civil Actions Under $15,000, Eviction, Small Claims.*

www.garfieldhts.org/court

Civil Records: Access: Phone, mail, in person, online. Both court and visitors may perform in person searches. No search fee. Required to search: name, years to search; also helpful: address. Civil cases indexed by defendant, plaintiff. Civil records on computer from 11/91, docket books and index from 1950s, prior archived. Phone access depends on age of case. Online access is limited to current dockets; search by name, date or case number at http://docket.garfieldhts.org/.

Criminal Records: Access: Phone, mail, in person, online. Both court and visitors may perform in person searches. No search fee. Required to search: name, years to search, DOB; also helpful: address, SSN, signed release. Criminal records on computer from 11/91, docket books and index from 1950s, prior archived. Online access to criminal records is the same as civil.

General Information: Public Access terminal is available. No expunged records released. SASE required. Turnaround time 2 weeks. Copy fee: $1.00 per page. Certification fee: $2.00. Fee payee: Municipal Court. Personal checks accepted. Prepayment required.

Lakewood Municipal Court
12650 Detroit Ave, Lakewood, OH 44107; 216-529-6700; Fax: 216-529-7687. Hours: 8AM-5PM (EST). *Misdemeanor, Civil Actions Under $15,000, Eviction, Small Claims.*

Civil Records: Access: Fax, mail, in person. Both court and visitors may perform in person searches. No search fee. Required to search: name, years to search; also helpful: address. Civil cases indexed by defendant, plaintiff. Civil records on computer from 1983, prior in books.

Criminal Records: Access: Fax, mail, in person. Both court and visitors may perform in person searches. No search fee. Required to search: name, years to search; also helpful: address, DOB, SSN. Criminal records on computer since 1983, prior in books.

General Information: Public Access terminal is available. No confidential records released. SASE required. Turnaround time 1 week. Fax notes: No fee to fax results. Local faxing only. Copy fee: $.25 per page. Certification fee: $3.00. Fee payee: Municipal Court. Personal checks accepted. Prepayment is required.

Lyndhurst Municipal Court
5301 Mayfield Rd, Lyndhurst, OH 44124; 216-461-6500. Hours: 8:30AM-5PM (EST). *Misdemeanor, Civil Actions Under $15,000, Eviction, Small Claims.*

Civil Records: Access: Mail, in person. Both court and visitors may perform in person searches. No search fee. Required to search: name, years to search; also helpful: address. Civil cases indexed by defendant, plaintiff. Civil records on computer from 1991, prior in books.

Criminal Records: Access: Mail, in person. Both court and visitors may perform in person searches. No search fee. Required to search: name, years to search, signed release; also helpful: address, DOB, SSN. Criminal records on computer from 1991, prior in books.

General Information: SASE required. Turnaround time 1 week. Copy fee: $1.00 per page. Certification fee: $2.00 per page. Fee payee: Municipal Court. Personal checks accepted. Prepayment is required.

Parma Municipal Court
5555 Powers Blvd, Parma, OH 44125; 440-887-7400; Fax: 440-887-7485. Hours: 8:30AM-4:30PM (EST). *Misdemeanor, Civil Actions Under $15,000, Eviction, Small Claims.*

Note: The court is making changes to block the SSN from appearing on record requests.

Civil Records: Access: Phone, fax, mail, in person. Both court and visitors may perform in person searches. No search fee. Required to search: name, years to search; also helpful: address. Civil cases indexed by defendant, plaintiff. Civil records on computer from 1993, prior in books.

Criminal Records: Access: Phone, fax, mail, in person. Both court and visitors may perform in person searches. No search fee. Required to search: name, years to search, DOB; also helpful: address, SSN. Criminal records on computer from 1993, prior in books.

General Information: SASE required. Turnaround time up to 1 week. Copy fee: $.50 per page. Certification fee: $1.00. Fee payee: Municipal Court. Personal checks accepted. Prepayment is required.

Rocky River Municipal Court
21012 Hilliard Blvd, Rocky River, OH 44116; 440-333-0066; Fax: 440-356-5613. Hours: 8:30AM-4:30PM *Misdemeanor, Civil Actions Under $15,000, Eviction, Small Claims.*

Civil Records: Access: Phone, fax, mail, in person. Both court and visitors may perform in person searches. No search fee. Required to search: name, years to search. Civil cases indexed by defendant, plaintiff. Civil records on computer from 1987, prior in books to 1958.

Criminal Records: Access: Phone, fax, mail, in person. Both court and visitors may perform in person searches. No search fee. Required to search: name, years to search, DOB. Criminal records on computer back to 1987, prior in books to 1958.

General Information: Public Access terminal is available. SASE required. Turnaround time 2 days. Copy fee: $.10 per page. Certification fee: $5.00. Fee payee: Municipal Court. Personal checks accepted. Prepayment is required.

Shaker Heights Municipal Court
3355 Lee Rd, Shaker Heights, OH 44120; 216-491-1300; Fax: 216-491-1314. 8:30AM-5PM (EST). *Misdemeanor, Civil Actions Under $15,000, Eviction, Small Claims.*

Civil Records: Access: Mail, fax, in person. Both court and visitors may perform in person searches. No search fee. Required to search: name, years to search; also helpful: address. Civil cases indexed by defendant, plaintiff. Civil records on computer from 06/86, prior in books.

Criminal Records: Access: Phone, fax, mail, in person. Both court and visitors may perform in person searches. Search fee: None, however complete dockets are $10.00. Required to search: name, years to search, DOB or SSN. Criminal records on computer from 06/86, prior in books. Phone access limited to gov't agencies.

General Information: Public Access terminal is available. No medical or LEADS print-out records released. SASE required. Turnaround time 2 days. Fax notes: Fee to fax results is $.50 per page. Copy fee: $.50 per page. Certification fee: $5.00. Fee payee: Shaker Heights Municipal Court. Personal checks accepted. Credit cards accepted: Visa, MasterCard. Visa, MC accepted in person only. Prepayment is required.

South Euclid Municipal Court
1349 S Green Rd, South Euclid, OH 44121; 216-381-2880; Fax: 216-381-1195. Hours: 8:30AM-5PM (EST). *Misdemeanor, Civil Actions Under $15,000, Eviction, Small Claims.*

Civil Records: Access: Mail, in person. Both court and visitors may perform in person searches. No search fee. Required to search: name, years to search; also helpful: address. Civil cases indexed by defendant, plaintiff. Civil records on computer since 10/97; prior in docket books.

Criminal Records: Access: Mail, in person. Both court and visitors may perform in person searches. No search fee. Required to search: name, years to search; also helpful: address, DOB, SSN. Criminal records on computer since 10/97; prior in docket books.

General Information: Public Access terminal is available. SASE required. Turnaround time 1 week. Copy fee: No charge until at least 10 pages, then $.10 per copy. Certification fee: $1.00 per page. Fee payee: Clerk of Court, South Euclid Municipal Court. Personal checks accepted. Prepayment is required.

Darke County

Common Pleas Court
Courthouse, Greenville, OH 45331; 937-547-7325; Probate phone: 937-547-7345; Fax: 937-547-7305. Hours: 8:30AM-4:30PM (EST). *Felony, Civil Actions Over $3,000, Probate.*

Note: Probate is a separate court located at 300 Garst Ave at the number given.

Civil Records: Access: Mail, in person. Both court and visitors may perform in person searches. Search fee: $5.00 per name. Required to search: name, years to search. Civil cases indexed by defendant, plaintiff. Civil records in books to 1832, on microfiche from 1940s.

Criminal Records: Access: Mail, in person. Both court and visitors may perform in person searches. Search fee: $5.00 per name. Required to search: name, years to search. Criminal records in books to 1832, on microfiche from 1940s.

General Information: Public Access terminal is available. No secret indictment records released. SASE required. Turnaround time 1-2 days. Copy fee: $.25 per page. Certification fee: $1.00. Fee payee: Clerk of Court. Business checks accepted. Prepayment required.

County Court
Courthouse, Greenville, OH 45331-1990; 937-547-7340; Fax: 937-547-7378. Hours: 8:30AM-4:30PM (EST). *Misdemeanor, Civil Actions Under $15,000, Small Claims.*

Civil Records: Access: Mail, in person. Both court and visitors may perform in person searches. Search fee: $5.00 per name. Required to search: name, years to search. Civil cases indexed by defendant, plaintiff. Civil records in books since 1959.

Criminal Records: Access: Mail, in person. Both court and visitors may perform in person searches. Search fee: $5.00 per name. Required to search: name, years to search, DOB; also helpful: SSN. Criminal records in books since 1959.

General Information: Public Access terminal is available. No sealed or confidential records released. SASE required. Turnaround time 1 week. Copy fee: $.25 per page. Certification fee: $1.00. Fee payee: Clerk of Court, Darke County. Only cashiers checks and money orders accepted. Credit cards accepted: Visa, MasterCard. Prepayment is required.

Defiance County

Common Pleas Court PO Box 716, Defiance, OH 43512; 419-782-1936; Probate phone: 419-782-4181. Hours: 8:30AM-4:30PM (EST). *Felony, Civil Actions Over $10,000, Probate.*

Civil Records: Access: Fax, mail, in person. Visitors must perform in person searches for themselves. No search fee. Required to search: name, years to search; also helpful: address. Civil records indexed by defendant, plaintiff. Civil Records on computer since 1995. Most recent records are kept here, usually up to 10 years.
Criminal Records: Access: Fax, mail, in person. Visitors must perform in person searches for themselves. No search fee. Required to search: name, years to search; also helpful: address, DOB, SSN. Criminal records on computer since 1995; prior records on docket books.
General Information: Public Access terminal is available. SASE required. Fax notes: $3.00 for first page, $1.00 each add'l. Copy fee: $.25 per page. Certification fee: $1.00. Fee payee: Clerk of Court. Personal checks accepted. Prepayment is required.

Defiance Municipal Court 324 Perry St, Defiance, OH 43512; 419-782-5756; Civil phone: 419-782-4092; Fax: 419-782-2018. Hours: 8AM-5PM (EST). *Misdemeanor, Civil Actions Under $15,000, Eviction, Small Claims.*

Civil Records: Access: Mail, in person. Both court and visitors may perform in person searches. Search fee: $8.00 per name. Fee only for records prior to 1989. Required to search: name, years to search; also helpful: DOB, SSN, address. Civil cases indexed by defendant, plaintiff. Civil records on computer from 10/89, prior in books to 1958.
Criminal Records: Access: Mail, in person. Both court and visitors may perform in person searches. Search fee: $8.00 per name. Fee only for records prior to 1989. Required to search: name, years to search; also helpful: address, DOB, SSN. Criminal records on computer from 10/89, prior in books to 1958.
General Information: Public Access terminal is available. No confidential records released. SASE required. Turnaround time 14 days. Copy fee: $.50 per page. Certification fee: $1.00. Fee payee: Municipal Court. Personal checks accepted. Credit cards accepted. Prepayment is required.

Delaware County

Common Pleas Court 91 N Sandusky, Delaware, OH 43015; 740-833-2500; Probate phone: 740-833-2680; Fax: 740-833-2499. Hours: 8:30AM-4:30PM (EST). *Felony, Civil Actions Over $10,000, Probate.*

www.co.delaware.oh.us/clerk/index.htm

Civil Records: Access: Mail, in person. Both court and visitors may perform in person searches. No search fee. Required to search: name, years to search; also helpful: address. Civil cases indexed by defendant, plaintiff. Civil records on computer from 1992, prior books go back to 1800s.
Criminal Records: Access: Mail, in person. Both court and visitors may perform in person searches. No search fee. Required to search: name, years to search, DOB; also helpful: address, SSN. Criminal records on computer from 1992, prior books go back to 1800s.
General Information: Public Access terminal is available. No grand jury proceedings or expungment records released. SASE required. Turnaround time 1-2 days. Copy fee: $.25 per page. Certification fee: $1.00. Fee payee: Clerk of Court. Personal checks accepted. Prepayment is required.

Delaware Municipal Court 70 N Union St, Delaware, OH 43015; 740-363-1555/548-6707; Fax: 740-368-1583. Hours: 8AM-4:30PM (EST). *Misdemeanor, Civil Actions Under $15,000, Eviction, Small Claims.*

www.municipalcourt.org

Civil Records: Access: Phone, mail, in person. Both court and visitors may perform in person searches. Search fee: $5.00 per name. Fee is per 5 years searched. Required to search: name, years to search. Civil cases indexed by defendant, plaintiff. Civil records on computer from 1990, prior in books.
Criminal Records: Access: Phone, mail, in person. Both court and visitors may perform in person searches. No search fee. Required to search: name, years to search, DOB; also helpful: SSN. Criminal records on computer from 1992, prior in books.
General Information: No assessment results or probation records released. SASE required. Turnaround time 1-2 weeks. Copy fee: $.05 per page. Certification fee: $1.00. Fee payee: Delaware Municipal Court. Personal checks accepted. Delaware County checks accepted. Prepayment is required.

Erie County

Common Pleas Court 323 Columbus Ave, Sandusky, OH 44870; 419-627-7705; Probate phone: 419-627-7759; Fax: 419-627-6873. Hours: 8AM-4PM M-Th/8AM-5PM F (EST). *Felony, Civil Actions Over $10,000, Probate.*

Civil Records: Access: In person only. Visitors must perform in person searches for themselves. No search fee. Required to search: name, years to search. Civil cases indexed by defendant, plaintiff. Civil records on books.
Criminal Records: Access: In person only. Visitors must perform in person searches for themselves. No search fee. Required to search: name, years to search, DOB, SSN, signed release. Criminal records on books.
General Information: Passports and expungments not released. Copy fee: $.25 per page. Certification fee: $5.00. Fee payee: Clerk of Court. Personal checks accepted. Prepayment is required.

Erie County Court 150 W Mason Rd, Milan, OH 44846; 419-499-4689; Fax: 419-499-3300. Hours: 8AM-4PM (EST). *Misdemeanor, Civil Actions Under $15,000, Small Claims.*

Civil Records: Access: Phone, mail, in person. Both court and visitors may perform in person searches. No search fee. Required to search: name, years to search; also helpful: address. Civil cases indexed by defendant, plaintiff. Civil records on computer back to 1990, microfiche back to 1982, index books from 1950s.
Criminal Records: Access: Phone, mail, in person. Both court and visitors may perform in person searches. No search fee. Required to search: name, years to search; also helpful: address, DOB. Criminal records on computer back to 1990, microfiche back to 1982, index books from 1950s.
General Information: Public Access terminal is available. No sealed records released. SASE required. Turnaround time 3-4 days. Copy fee: $.05 per page. Certification fee: No cert fee. Fee payee: County Court. Business checks accepted. Prepayment required.

Sandusky Municipal Court 222 Meigs St, Sandusky, OH 44870; 419-627-5926; Civil phone: 419-627-5917; Criminal phone: 419-627-5975; Fax: 419-627-5950. Hours: 7AM-4PM (EST). *Misdemeanor, Civil Actions Under $15,000, Eviction, Small Claims.*

Civil Records: Access: Phone, fax, mail, in person. Both court and visitors may perform in person searches. No search fee. Required to search: name, years to search; also helpful: case number. Civil cases indexed

by defendant, plaintiff. Civil records on computer from 1987, prior in books.
Criminal Records: Access: Phone, fax, mail, in person. Both court and visitors may perform in person searches. No search fee. Required to search: name, years to search, DOB; also helpful: SSN, case number. Criminal records on computer from 1987, prior in books.
General Information: Public Access terminal is available. No pending, (some) crimes of violence records, or expunged records released. SASE requested. Turnaround time 3-4 days. Copy fee: $.25 per page. Certification fee: $4.00. Fee payee: Sandusky Municipal Court.

Vermilion Municipal Court 687 Delatur St, Vermilion, OH 44089; 440-967-6543; Fax: 440-967-1467. Hours: 8AM-4PM (EST). *Misdemeanor, Civil Actions Under $15,000, Eviction, Small Claims.*

Civil Records: Access: Fax, mail, in person. Both court and visitors may perform in person searches. No search fee. Required to search: name, years to search. Civil cases indexed by defendant, plaintiff. Civil records on computer from 1992, prior in books.
Criminal Records: Access: Fax, mail, in person. Both court and visitors may perform in person searches. No search fee. Required to search: name, years to search, DOB; also helpful: SSN. Criminal records on computer from 1992, prior in books.
General Information: Public Access terminal is available. SASE required. Turnaround time 1-5 days. Copy fee: $1.00 per page. The fee is for a computer printout. Certification fee: $2.00. Fee payee: Vermilion Municipal Court. Only cashiers checks and money orders accepted. Credit cards accepted: Visa, MasterCard. Prepayment is required.

Fairfield County

Common Pleas Court 224 E Main, Clerk's Office, Lancaster, OH 43130-0370; 740-687-7030; Probate phone: 740-687-7093. Hours: 8AM-4PM (EST). *Felony, Civil Actions Over $10,000, Probate.*

Note: Probate Court is separate from this court, at the same address and at the Probate phone number above.

Civil Records: Access: Phone, mail, in person. Visitors must perform in person searches for themselves. No search fee. Required to search: name, years to search; also helpful: address. Civil cases indexed by defendant, plaintiff. Civil records on computer from 10/93, in books to 1970, prior archived to 1800s.
Criminal Records: Access: Phone, mail, in person. Visitors must perform in person searches for themselves. No search fee. Required to search: name, years to search; also helpful: address, DOB, SSN. Criminal records on computer from 10/93, in books to 1970, prior archived to 1800s.
General Information: Public Access terminal is available. No adoption or juvenile records released. SASE required. Turnaround time 1 week. Copy fee: $.50 per page. Certification fee: $5.00. Fee payee: Clerk of Court. Personal checks accepted. Credit cards accepted: Visa. Credit cards not accepted over the phone. Prepayment is required.

Fairfield County Municipal Court PO Box 2390, Lancaster, OH 43130; 740-687-6621. Hours: 8AM-4PM (EST). *Misdemeanor, Civil Actions Under $15,000, Eviction, Small Claims.*

Civil Records: Access: Mail, in person. Both court and visitors may perform in person searches. No search fee. Required to search: name, years to search. Civil cases indexed by defendant, plaintiff. Civil records on computer from 1990, prior in books.
Criminal Records: Access: Mail, in person. Both court and visitors may perform in person searches. No search fee. Required to search: name, years to search. Criminal records on computer from 1989, prior in books.

General Information: Public Access terminal is available. SASE required. Turnaround time 2 days. No copy fee. Certification fee: $1.00. Fee payee: Fairfiled County Court. Personal checks accepted. Prepayment is required.

Fayette County

Common Pleas Court 110 E Court St, Washington Court House, OH 43160; 740-335-6371; Probate phone: 740-335-0640. Hours: 9AM-4PM (EST). *Felony, Civil Actions Over $10,000, Probate.*

www.fayette-co-oh.com/

Note: Probate is a separate court at number given.

Civil Records: Access: Mail, in person. Both court and visitors may perform in person searches. Search fee: $3.00 per name. Required to search: name, years to search. Civil cases indexed by defendant, plaintiff. Civil records on computer from 1992, prior in books to 1800s.

Criminal Records: Access: Mail, in person. Both court and visitors may perform in person searches. Search fee: $3.00 per name. Required to search: name, years to search, DOB, SSN. Criminal records on computer from 1992, prior in books to 1800s.

General Information: Public Access terminal is available. No records released. SASE required. Turnaround time varies. Fax notes: Fee to fax results is $1.00 per page. Copy fee: $1.00 per page. Certification fee: $1.00. Fee payee: Clerk of Court. Personal checks accepted. Prepayment is required.

Municipal Court Washington Courthouse, 119 N Main St, Washington Court House, OH 43160; 740-636-2350; Fax: 740-636-2359. Hours: 8AM-4PM (EST). *Misdemeanor, Civil Actions Under $15,000, Eviction, Small Claims.*

Civil Records: Access: Mail, in person. Both court and visitors may perform in person searches. No search fee. Required to search: name, years to search. Civil cases indexed by defendant, plaintiff. Civil records on computer from 1990, prior in books to 1950s.

Criminal Records: Access: Mail, in person. Both court and visitors may perform in person searches. No search fee. Required to search: name, years to search, DOB; also helpful: SSN. Criminal records on computer from 1990, prior in books to 1950s.

General Information: Public Access terminal is available. No records protected by the privacy act released. SASE required. Turnaround time 1 week. No copy fee. Certification fee: $5.00. Fee payee: Clerk of Court. Only cashiers checks and money orders accepted. Prepayment is required.

Franklin County

Common Pleas Court 369 S High St, Columbus, OH 43215-6311; Civil phone: 614-462-3621; Criminal phone: 614-462-3650; Probate phone: 614-462-3894; Fax: 614-462-4325 Civil; 614-462-6661 Crim. Hours: 8AM-5PM (EST). *Felony, Civil Actions Over $15,000, Probate.*

www.franklincountyclerk.com

Civil Records: Access: Online, in person. Visitors must perform in person searches for themselves. No search fee. Required to search: name, years to search. Civil cases indexed by defendant, plaintiff. Access records via the web site. Java-enable web browser required. Online access to probate court records is available free at www.co.franklin.oh.us/probate/ProbateSearch.html; search marriage records at www.co.franklin.oh.us/probate/PBMLSearch.html.

Criminal Records: Access: Mail, in person. Both court and visitors may perform in person searches. Search fee: $4.00 per name. Required to search: name, years to search.

General Information: Public Access terminal is available. No psych, adoption or estate tax records released. SASE required. Turnaround time to 7 days. Copy fee: First 20 pages free, then $.25 per page. Certification fee: $1.00 per page. Fee payee: Franklin County Probate Court (Civil); Clerk of Court (Criminal). Only cashiers checks and money orders accepted. Prepayment is required.

Franklin County Municipal Court - Civil Division 375 S High St, 3rd Flr, Columbus, OH 43215; 614-645-7220; Civil phone: 614-645-8161; Fax: 614-645-6919. Hours: 8AM-5PM (EST). *Civil Actions Under $15,000, Eviction, Small Claims.*

www.fcmcclerk.com

Civil Records: Access: Phone, fax, mail, online, in person. Both court and visitors may perform in person searches. No search fee. Required to search: name, years to search. Civil cases indexed by defendant, plaintiff. Civil records on computer from 1992, prior in books to 1970s. Records from the Clerk of Court Courtview 2000 database are available free online at www.fcmcclerk.com/pa/pa.htm. Search by name, SSN, dates, ticket, DL or case numbers.

General Information: Public Access terminal is available. No sealed or expunged records released. SASE required. Turnaround time 2-3 days. Copy fee: First 20 copies are free, then $.05 each. Certification fee: $1.00. Fee payee: Franklin County Municipal Court. Personal checks accepted. Credit cards accepted: Visa, MasterCard, Discover. Prepayment is required.

Franklin County Municipal Court - Criminal Division 375 S High St, 2nd Fl, Columbus, OH 43215; 614-645-8186. Hours: Open 24 hours a day (EST). *Misdemeanor.*

www.fcmcclerk.com

Criminal Records: Access: Phone, mail, online, in person. Both court and visitors may perform in person searches. No search fee. Required to search: name, years to search; also helpful: DOB, SSN. Criminal records go back to 1987; on computer back to 1992. Criminal and traffic records from the Clerk of Court Courtview 2000 database are available free online at www.fcmcclerk.com/pa/pa.htm. Search by name, SSN, dates, ticket, DL or case numbers.

General Information: Public Access terminal is available. No sealed or expunged records released. SASE required. Turnaround time 2 days. Copy fee: $.25 per page. Certification fee: $1.00. Fee payee: Franklin County Municipal Court. Personal checks accepted. Credit cards accepted: Visa, MasterCard. Prepayment is required.

Fulton County

Common Pleas Court 210 S Fulton, Wauseon, OH 43567; 419-337-9230; Probate phone: 419-337-9242. Hours: 8:30AM-4:30PM (EST). *Felony, Civil Actions Over $3,000, Probate.*

Civil Records: Access: In person only. Visitors must perform in person searches for themselves. No search fee. Required to search: name, years to search. Civil cases indexed by defendant, plaintiff. Civil records on computer from 9/88, prior in books to 1968, archived to 1800s.

Criminal Records: Access: In person only. Visitors must perform in person searches for themselves. No search fee. Required to search: name, years to search, DOB; also helpful: SSN. Criminal records on computer from 9/88, prior in books to 1968, archived to 1800s.

General Information: Copy fee: $.25 per page. Certification fee: $1.00 per page. Fee payee: Mary Gype Clerk of Court. Personal checks accepted. Prepayment is required.

County Court Eastern District 128 N Main St, Swanton, OH 43558; 419-826-5636; Fax: 419-825-3324. Hours: 8:30AM-4:30PM (EST). *Misdemeanor, Civil Actions Under $15,000, Small Claims.*

www.fultoncountyoh.com/courts.htm

Civil Records: Access: Mail, in person. Both court and visitors may perform in person searches. No search fee. Required to search: name, years to search. Civil cases indexed by defendant, plaintiff. Civil records on computer from 1988, prior in books.

Criminal Records: Access: Mail, in person. Both court and visitors may perform in person searches. No search fee. Required to search: name, years to search, DOB. Criminal records on computer from 1988, prior in books.

General Information: No pending case records released. SASE required. Turnaround time 2 weeks. Copy fee: None, but must supply own paper for copies. Certification fee: No cert fee. Only cashiers checks and money orders accepted.

County Court Western District 224 S Fulton St, Wauseon, OH 43567; 419-337-9212; Fax: 419-337-9286. Hours: 8:30AM-4:30PM (EST). *Misdemeanor, Civil Actions Under $15,000, Small Claims.*

Civil Records: Access: Mail, in person. Both court and visitors may perform in person searches. No search fee. Required to search: name, years to search. Civil cases indexed by defendant, plaintiff. Civil records on computer from 1989, prior in books. In-person searchers should call first; Tuesdays are court day and computers in use.

Criminal Records: Access: Mail, in person. Both court and visitors may perform in person searches. No search fee. Required to search: name, years to search, DOB; also helpful: SSN. Criminal records on computer after 1988, indexed by name and DOB. In-person searchers should call first; be aware Tuesdays are busy and hard to get on computer to search.

General Information: Public Access terminal is available. No pending case records released. SASE required. Turnaround time 2-3 days. Copy fee: $.10 per page. Certification fee: $1.00. Fee payee: County Court Western District. Personal checks accepted.

Gallia County

Common Pleas Court - Gallia County Courthouse 18 Locust St, Rm 1290, Gallipolis, OH 45631-1290; 740-446-4612 x223; Probate phone: 740-446-4612 x240; Fax: 740-441-2094. Hours: 8AM-4PM (EST). *Felony, Civil Actions Over $10,000, Probate.*

Civil Records: Access: In person only. Visitors must perform in person searches for themselves. No search fee. Required to search: name, years to search. Civil cases indexed by defendant, plaintiff. Civil records on computer from 7/91, in books to 1968, archived to 1800s. Will fax copies for $1.00 per page if pre-paid.

Criminal Records: Access: In person only. Visitors must perform in person searches for themselves. No search fee. Required to search: name, years to search. Criminal records on computer from 7/91, in books to 1968, archived to 1800s. Will fax copies for $1.00 per page if pre-paid.

General Information: Public Access terminal is available. No records released. Copy fee: $.25 per page. Certification fee: $1.00. Fee payee: Clerk of Court. Personal checks accepted. Prepayment is required.

Gallipolis Municipal Court 518 2nd Ave, Gallipolis, OH 45631; 740-446-9400; Fax: 740-446-2070. Hours: 9AM-4:30PM (EST). *Misdemeanor, Civil Actions Under $15,000, Eviction, Small Claims.*

Civil Records: Access: Phone, mail, in person. Both court and visitors may perform in person searches. No search fee. Required to search: name, years to search; also helpful: address. Civil cases indexed by defendant, plaintiff. Civil records on computer from 8/93, prior in books.

Criminal Records: Access: Phone, mail, in person. Both court and visitors may perform in person searches. No search fee. Required to search: name, years to search; also helpful: address, DOB, SSN. Criminal records on computer from 8/93, prior in books.

General Information: Public Access terminal is available. No expunged records released. SASE required. Turnaround time 1 week. Copy fee: $.25 per page. Certification fee: $1.00. Fee payee: Municipal Court. Personal checks accepted. Prepayment required.

Geauga County

Common Pleas Court 100 Short Court, Chardon, OH 44024; 440-285-2222 X2380; Probate phone: 440-285-2222 X2000; Fax: 440-286-2127. Hours: 8AM-4:30PM (EST). *Felony, Civil Actions Over $10,000, Probate.*

www.co.geauga.oh.us

Civil Records: Access: In person only. Visitors must perform in person searches for themselves. No search fee. Required to search: name, years to search. Civil cases indexed by defendant, plaintiff. Civil records on computer from 1990, in books from 1968, prior archived.

Criminal Records: Access: In person only. Visitors must perform in person searches for themselves. No search fee. Required to search: name, years to search. Criminal records on computer from 1990, in books from 1968, prior archived.

General Information: Public Access terminal is available. no sealed records released. Copy fee: $.25 per page. Certification fee: $1.00. Fee payee: Clerk of Court. Personal checks accepted. Prepayment required.

Chardon Municipal Court 111 Water St, Chardon, OH 44024; 440-286-2670/2684; Fax: 440-286-2679. Hours: 8AM-4:30PM (EST). *Misdemeanor, Civil Actions Under $15,000, Eviction, Small Claims.*

Civil Records: Access: Mail, in person. Both court and visitors may perform in person searches. No search fee. Required to search: name, years to search; also helpful: address. Civil cases indexed by defendant, plaintiff. Civil records on computer from 1990, prior in books.

Criminal Records: Access: Mail, in person. Both court and visitors may perform in person searches. No search fee. Required to search: name, years to search; also helpful: address, DOB, SSN. Criminal records on computer from 1990, prior in books.

General Information: Public Access terminal is available. (Available 8AM-11:30AM, 1:30-4:30PM. Two hour maximum.) No expunged records released. SASE required. Turnaround time 2-4 days. Copy fee: $.25 per page. Certification fee: $1.50. Fee payee: Chardon Municipal Court. Personal checks accepted. Credit cards accepted: Visa, MasterCard. Accepted for criminal only. Prepayment is required.

Greene County

Common Pleas Court 45 N Detroit St (PO Box 156), Xenia, OH 45385; 937-562-5292; Probate phone: 937-376-5280; Fax: 937-562-5309. Hours: 8AM-4PM (EST). *Felony, Civil Actions Over $10,000, Probate.*

www.co.greene.oh.us/clerk.htm

Civil Records: Access: In person, online. Visitors must perform in person searches for themselves. No search fee. Required to search: name, years to search. Civil cases indexed by defendant, plaintiff. Civil records on computer from 1982, prior in books and on microfiche. Online access to clerk of court records is available free at http://198.30.12.229/pa/pa.htm. Search by name or case number.

Criminal Records: Access: In person, online. Visitors must perform in person searches for themselves. No search fee. Required to search: name, years to search;

also helpful: DOB, SSN, case number. Criminal records on computer from 1982, prior in books and on microfiche. Online access to criminal records is the same as civil.

General Information: Public Access terminal is available. No sealed records released. Fax notes: Fee to fax results is $1.00 per page. Copy fee: $.25 per page. Certification fee: $1.00 per page. Fee payee: Clerk of Court. Personal checks accepted. Credit cards accepted: Visa, MasterCard. Prepayment is required.

Fairborn Municipal Court 44 W Hebble Ave, Fairborn, OH 45324; Civil phone: 937-754-3044; Criminal phone: 937-754-3040; Fax: 937-879-4422. Hours: 7:30AM-4:30PM (EST). *Misdemeanor, Civil Actions Under $20,000, Eviction, Small Claims.*

Civil Records: Access: Mail, in person. Both court and visitors may perform in person searches. No search fee. Required to search: name, years to search; also helpful: address. Civil cases indexed by defendant, plaintiff. Civil records on computer from mid 1990, prior in books.

Criminal Records: Access: Mail, in person. Both court and visitors may perform in person searches. No search fee. Required to search: name, years to search, SSN; also helpful: address, DOB. Criminal records on computer from mid 1990, prior in books.

General Information: Public Access terminal is available. SASE required. Turnaround time 1 week. Copy fee: $.25 per page. Certification fee: $2.00. Fee payee: Municipal Court. Personal checks accepted. Prepayment is required.

Xenia Municipal Court 101 N Detroit, Xenia, OH 45385; 937-376-7294; 376-7297 (Civil Clerk); Fax: 937-376-7288. Hours: 8AM-4:30PM (EST). *Misdemeanor, Civil Actions Under $15,000, Eviction, Small Claims.*

Civil Records: Access: Fax, mail, in person. Both court and visitors may perform in person searches. No search fee. Required to search: name, years to search; also helpful: address. Civil cases indexed by defendant, plaintiff. Civil records on computer from 1994, prior in books to 1960s.

Criminal Records: Access: Fax, mail, in person. Both court and visitors may perform in person searches. No search fee. Required to search: name, years to search; also helpful: address, DOB, SSN. Criminal records on computer from 1994, prior in books to 1960s.

General Information: Public Access terminal is available. No search warrant records released. SASE required. Fax notes: No fee to fax results. Copy fee: $.10 per page. Certification fee: $2.00. Fee payee: Municipal Court. Business checks accepted. Credit cards accepted: Visa, MasterCard. Visa, MC. Prepayment is required.

Guernsey County

Common Pleas Court 801 E Wheeling Ave D-300, Cambridge, OH 43725; 740-432-9230; Probate phone: 740-432-9262; Fax: 740-432-7807. Hours: 8:30AM-4PM (EST). *Felony, Civil Actions Over $10,000, Probate.*

Note: Probate is a separate division with separate records and personnel.

Civil Records: Access: In person only. Visitors must perform in person searches for themselves. No search fee. Required to search: name, years to search. Civil cases indexed by defendant, plaintiff. Civil records on computer from 1990, prior in books, archived to 1800s.

Criminal Records: Access: In person only. Visitors must perform in person searches for themselves. No search fee. Required to search: name, years to search, DOB, SSN, signed release. Criminal records on computer from 1990, prior in books, archived to 1800s.

General Information: Public Access terminal is available. No expunged records released. Copy fee:

$.25 per page. Certification fee: $5.00. Fee payee: Clerk of Court. Personal checks accepted. Prepayment required.

Cambridge Municipal Court 134 Southgate Parkway, Cambridge, OH 43725; 740-439-5585 x40; Fax: 740-439-5666. Hours: 8:30AM-4:30PM (EST). *Misdemeanor, Civil Actions Under $15,000, Eviction, Small Claims.*

Civil Records: Access: Phone, mail, in person. Both court and visitors may perform in person searches. No search fee. Required to search: name, years to search; also helpful: address. Civil cases indexed by defendant, plaintiff. Civil records on computer from 1988, prior in books.

Criminal Records: Access: Mail, in person. Visitors must perform in person searches for themselves. No search fee. Required to search: name, years to search, DOB, SSN; also helpful: address. Criminal records on computer from 1988, prior in books.

General Information: Public Access terminal is available. No confidential records released. SASE required. Turnaround time 3-5 days. Copy fee: $1.00 per page. Certification fee: $2.00. Fee payee: Cambridge Municipal Court. Personal checks accepted. Credit cards accepted: Visa, MasterCard. Prepayment is required.

Hamilton County

Common Pleas Court 1000 Main St, Room 315, Cincinnati, OH 45202; Civil phone: 513-946-5635; Criminal phone: 513-946-5671; Probate phone: 513-946-3580; Fax: 513-632-7216. Hours: 8AM-4PM (EST). *Felony, Civil Actions Over $10,000, Probate.*

www.courtclerk.org

Note: Probate is separate court at telephone number given.

Civil Records: Access: Phone, fax, mail, online, in person. Both court and visitors may perform in person searches. No search fee. Required to search: name, years to search. Civil cases indexed by defendant, plaintiff. Civil records indexed on computer since 1960s, prior in books and files. Records from the court clerk are available free online at the web site. Civil index goes back to 1991.

Criminal Records: Access: Fax, mail, online, in person. Both court and visitors may perform in person searches. No search fee. Required to search: name, years to search, signed release; also helpful: DOB, SSN. Criminal records indexed on computer since 1960s, prior in books and files. Online access to criminal records is the same as civil. Criminal index goes back to 1986.

General Information: Public Access terminal is available. Criminal histories not released. SASE required. Turnaround time 2-3 days. Copy fee: Fees vary by storage media of original. Certification fee: $1.00. Fee payee: Clerk of Court. Personal checks accepted. Credit cards accepted. Prepayment required.

Hamilton County Municipal Court - Civil 1000 Main St, Cincinnati, OH 45202; 513-632-8891; Fax: 513-632-7325. Hours: 8AM-4PM (EST). *Civil Actions Under $15,000, Eviction, Small Claims.*

www.courtclerk.org

Civil Records: Access: Phone, fax, mail, online, in person. Both court and visitors may perform in person searches. No search fee. Required to search: name; also helpful: years to search. Civil cases indexed by defendant, plaintiff. Civil records on computer from 1989, prior in books. Records from the court clerk are available free online at the web site.

General Information: Public Access terminal is available. No expungement records released. Turnaround time 5 days. Fax notes: No fee to fax results. Copy fee: $.25 per page. $4.00 for docket sheet (civil). Certification fee: $5.00. Fee payee: Clerk of Courts. Personal checks accepted. Credit cards accepted: Visa, MasterCard. Prepayment is required.

Hamilton County Municipal Court - Criminal
1000 Sycamore St #111, Cincinnati, OH 45202; 513-632-8891; Fax: 513-632-7325. Hours: 8AM-4PM (EST). *Misdemeanors.*

www.courtclerk.org

Criminal Records: Access: Fax, mail, in person. Visitors must perform in person searches for themselves. No search fee. Required to search: name, years to search, DOB; also helpful: SSN. Criminal records on computer back to 2000, prior on microfiche back to 1973.
General Information: Public Access terminal is available. Turnaround time 2-3 days. Copy fee: $.10 per page. Fee payee: Clerk of Courts. Personal checks accepted. Credit cards accepted: Visa, MasterCard. Prepayment is required.

Hancock County

Common Pleas Court 300 S Main St, Findlay, OH 45840; 419-424-7037; Probate phone: 419-424-7079. Hours: 8:30AM-4:30PM (EST). *Felony, Civil Actions Over $10,000, Probate.*

Civil Records: Access: Mail, in person. Both court and visitors may perform in person searches. Search fee: $10.00 per name. Required to search: name, years to search. Civil cases indexed by defendant, plaintiff. Civil records on computer from 1985, microfiche from 1974, dockets archived to 1800s.
Criminal Records: Access: Mail, in person. Both court and visitors may perform in person searches. Search fee: $10.00 per name. Required to search: name, years to search. Criminal records on computer from 1985, microfiche from 1974, dockets archived to 1800s.
General Information: Public Access terminal is available. No home investigations, medical records released. SASE required. Turnaround time 1-2 days. Copy fee: $1.00 for first page, $.25 each add'l. Certification fee: $1.00. Fee payee: Clerk of Court. Personal checks accepted. Prepayment is required.

Findlay Municipal Court PO Box 826, Findlay, OH 45839; 419-424-7141; Fax: 419-424-7803. Hours: 8AM-5PM (EST). *Misdemeanor, Civil Actions Under $15,000, Eviction, Small Claims.*

Civil Records: Access: Mail, in person. Both court and visitors may perform in person searches. Search fee: $2.00 per name. Required to search: name, years to search. Civil cases indexed by defendant, plaintiff. Civil records on computer from 1984.
Criminal Records: Access: Mail, in person. Both court and visitors may perform in person searches. Search fee: $2.00 per name. Required to search: name, years to search, DOB, SSN. Criminal records on computer from 1984.
General Information: Public Access terminal is available. SASE required. Copy fee: $.25 per page. Certification fee: $1.00. Fee payee: Findlay Municipal Court. Only cashiers checks and money orders accepted. Local (Hancock County) personal checks accepted. Credit cards accepted: Visa, MasterCard. Prepayment is required.

Hardin County

Common Pleas Court Courthouse, Ste 310, Kenton, OH 43326; 419-674-2278; Probate phone: 419-674-2230; Fax: 419-674-2273. Hours: 8:30AM-4PM M-Th; 8:30AM-6PM F (EST). *Felony, Civil Actions Over $10,000, Probate.*

Civil Records: Access: Mail, in person. Both court and visitors may perform in person searches. No search fee. Required to search: name, years to search. Civil cases

indexed by defendant, plaintiff. Current records on computer as of 1/95.
Criminal Records: Access: Mail, in person. Both court and visitors may perform in person searches. No search fee. Required to search: name, years to search, DOB, signed release; also helpful: SSN. Current records on computer as of 1/95.
General Information: Public Access terminal is available. SASE required. Turnaround time 2-4 days. Copy fee: $.25 per page. Certified copies $1.00 per page. Certification fee: $1.00. Fee payee: Clerk of Court. No personal checks accepted. Prepayment is required.

Hardin County Municipal Court PO Box 250, Kenton, OH 43326; 419-674-4362; Fax: 419-674-4096. Hours: 8:30AM-4PM (EST). *Misdemeanor, Civil Actions Under $15,000, Eviction, Small Claims.*

Civil Records: Access: Mail, in person. Both court and visitors may perform in person searches. Search fee: $5.00. Required to search: name, years to search. Civil cases indexed by defendant, plaintiff. Civil records on computer since 1989, prior on books.
Criminal Records: Access: Mail, in person. Both court and visitors may perform in person searches. Search fee: $5.00. Required to search: name, years to search; also helpful: SSN. Criminal records on computer since 1989, prior on books.
General Information: Public Access terminal is available. SASE required. Turnaround time 1-2 days. Copy fee: $.25 per page. Certification fee: $2.00. Fee payee: Hardin County Municipal Court. Business checks accepted. Prepayment is required.

Harrison County

Common Pleas Court 100 W Market, Cadiz, OH 43907; 740-942-8863; Fax: 740-942-4693. Hours: 8:30AM-4:30PM (EST). *Felony, Civil Actions Over $3,000, Probate.*

Civil Records: Access: Phone, fax, mail, in person. Both court and visitors may perform in person searches. No search fee. Required to search: name, years to search; also helpful: address. Civil cases indexed by defendant, plaintiff. Civil records on computer since 1994, in books back to 1800s.
Criminal Records: Access: In person only. Visitors must perform in person searches for themselves. No search fee. Required to search: name, years to search; also helpful: address, DOB, SSN. Criminal records on computer since 1994, in books back to 1800s.
General Information: Public Access terminal is available. No secret records released. SASE required. Turnaround time 1-2 days. Fax notes: $1.00 per page. Copy fee: $1.00 per page. Certification fee: $1.00. Fee payee: Clerk of Court. Personal checks accepted. Prepayment is required.

Harrison County Court Courthouse, 100 W Market St, Cadiz, OH 43907; 740-942-8865; Fax: 740-942-4693. 8:00AM-4:30PM (EST). *Misdemeanor, Civil Actions Under $15,000, Small Claims.*

Civil Records: Access: In person only. Visitors must perform in person searches for themselves. No search fee. Required to search: name, years to search. Civil cases indexed by defendant, plaintiff. Civil records in books; on computer back to 2/2000 (older records being added).
Criminal Records: Access: In person only. Visitors must perform in person searches for themselves. No search fee. Required to search: name, years to search, DOB; also helpful: SSN. Criminal records in books; on computer back to 2/2000 (older records being added).
General Information: Public Access terminal is available. Copy fee: $.25 per page. Certification fee: $1.00. Fee payee: Harrison County Court. Only cashiers checks and money orders accepted. Prepayment is required.

Henry County

Common Pleas Court PO Box 71, Napoleon, OH 43545; 419-592-5886; Probate phone: 419-592-7771; Fax: 419-592-4575. Hours: 8:30AM-4:30PM (EST). *Felony, Civil Actions Over $10,000, Probate.*

Note: Probate Court's address is PO Box 70, fax is 419-592-7000.

Civil Records: Access: Fax, mail, in person. Both court and visitors may perform in person searches. No search fee. Required to search: name, years to search. Civil cases indexed by defendant, plaintiff. Civil records on computer from 10/94, prior in books.
Criminal Records: Access: Fax, mail, in person. Both court and visitors may perform in person searches. No search fee. Required to search: name, years to search. Criminal records on computer from 10/94, prior in books.
General Information: No adoption or mental records released. SASE required. Fax notes: $3.00 for first page, $1.00 each add'l. Copy fee: $1.00 per page. Certification fee: $1.00. Fee payee: Clerk of Court. Personal checks accepted. Prepayment is required.

Napoleon Municipal Court PO Box 502, Napoleon, OH 43545; 419-592-2851; Fax: 419-592-1805. Hours: 8AM-5PM (EST). *Misdemeanor, Civil Actions Under $15,000, Eviction, Small Claims.*

Civil Records: Access: Phone, fax, mail, in person. Both court and visitors may perform in person searches. No search fee. Required to search: name, years to search. Civil cases indexed by defendant, plaintiff. Civil records on computer from 1990, prior in books.
Criminal Records: Access: Phone, fax, mail, in person. Both court and visitors may perform in person searches. No search fee. Required to search: name, years to search, DOB; also helpful: SSN. Criminal records on computer from 1990, prior in books.
General Information: No alcohol treatment records released. SASE required. Turnaround time 1-2 days. Copy fee: $.75 per page. Certification fee: $1.00. Fee payee: Clerk of Court. Personal checks accepted. Credit cards accepted: Visa, MasterCard.

Highland County

Common Pleas Court PO Box 821, Hillsboro, OH 45133; 937-393-9957; Probate phone: 937-393-9981; Fax: 937-393-6878. Hours: 8AM-4:30PM (EST). *Felony, Civil Actions Over $10,000, Probate.*

Note: Probate is a separate court.

Civil Records: Access: Mail, fax, in person. Both court and visitors may perform in person searches. No search fee. Required to search: name, years to search; also helpful: address. Civil cases indexed by defendant, plaintiff. Civil records in books since 1800s; on computer since 1990.
Criminal Records: Access: Mail, fax, in person. Both court and visitors may perform in person searches. No search fee. Required to search: name, years to search, DOB, signed release; also helpful: SSN. Criminal records in books since 1800s; on computer since 1990.
General Information: Public Access terminal is available. no sealed records released. SASE required. Turnaround time same day. Copy fee: $.10 per page. Certification fee: $1.00 per page. Fee payee: Clerk of Court. Personal checks accepted.

Hillsboro County Municipal Court 108 Governor Trimble Pl, Hillsboro, OH 45133; 937-393-3022; Fax: 937-393-3273. Hours: 7AM-3:30PM M,T,Th,F; 7AM-Noon W (EST). *Misdemeanor, Civil Actions Under $15,000, Eviction, Small Claims.*

Civil Records: Access: Phone, fax, mail, in person. Only the court performs in person searches; visitors may not. No search fee. Required to search: name, years to search. Civil cases indexed by defendant, plaintiff. Civil records on computer from 1991, prior in books.

Criminal Records: Access: Phone, fax, mail, in person. Only the court performs in person searches; visitors may not. No search fee. Required to search: name, years to search. Criminal records on computer from 1991, prior in books.

General Information: No expunged records released. Turnaround time 1-2 days. Fax notes: No fee to fax results. local or toll free calls only. Copy fee: $.25 per page. Certification fee: No cert fee. Fee payee: Hillsboro Municipal Court. Personal checks accepted. Prepayment is required.

Hocking County

Common Pleas Court PO Box 108, Logan, OH 43138; 740-385-2616; Probate phone: 740-385-3022; Fax: 740-385-1822. Hours: 8:30AM-4PM (EST). *Felony, Civil Actions Over $10,000, Probate.*

Note: Probate is a separate court at the number given.

Civil Records: Access: Phone, fax, mail, in person. Both court and visitors may perform in person searches. No search fee. Required to search: name, years to search; also helpful: address. Civil cases indexed by defendant. Civil records on computer since 1996, in books to late 1800s.

Criminal Records: Access: Phone, fax, mail, in person. Both court and visitors may perform in person searches. No search fee. Required to search: name, years to search; also helpful: address, DOB, SSN. Criminal records date back to 1980 on docket books.

General Information: Public Access terminal is available. No secret records released. SASE required. Turnaround time 1-2 days. Fax notes: $1.00 per page. Copy fee: $1.00 per page. Certification fee: $1.00. Fee payee: Clerk of Court. Business checks accepted. Prepayment is required.

Hocking County Municipal Court 1 E Main St (PO Box 950), Logan, OH 43138-1278; 740-385-2250. Hours: 8:30AM-4PM (EST). *Misdemeanor, Civil Actions Under $15,000, Eviction, Small Claims.*

Civil Records: Access: Mail, in person. Both court and visitors may perform in person searches. No search fee. Required to search: name, years to search. Civil cases indexed by defendant, plaintiff. Civil records on computer from 1989, prior in books.

Criminal Records: Access: Mail, in person. Both court and visitors may perform in person searches. No search fee. Required to search: name, years to search, DOB, SSN, signed release. Criminal records on computer from 1989, prior in books.

General Information: SASE required. Turnaround time 1-2 days. Copy fee: $.50 per page. Certification fee: $1.00. Fee payee: Municipal Court. Personal checks accepted.

Holmes County

Common Pleas Court 1 E Jackson St #301, Millersburg, OH 44654; 330-674-1876; Probate phone: 330-674-5841; Fax: 330-674-0289. Hours: 8:30AM-4:30PM *Felony, Civil Actions Over $10,000, Probate.*

Note: Juvenile and probate court at Suite 201.

Civil Records: Access: Fax, mail, in person. Both court and visitors may perform in person searches. Search fee: $5.00 per name. Required to search: name, years to search; also helpful: address. Civil cases indexed by defendant, plaintiff. Civil records on computer from 6/30/94, prior in books to 1850.

Criminal Records: Access: Fax, mail, in person. Both court and visitors may perform in person searches. Search fee: $5.00 per name. Required to search: name, years to search; also helpful: address, DOB, SSN. Criminal records on computer from 6/30/94, prior in books to 1850.

General Information: Public Access terminal is available. No court order, expunged records released. SASE required. Turnaround time 1-2 days. Fax notes: Fee to fax results is $1.00 per page. Copy fee: $1.00 per page. Certification fee: $1.00. Fee payee: Clerk of Court. Personal checks accepted. Prepayment required.

County Court 1 E Jackson St, Ste 101, Millersburg, OH 44654; 330-674-4901; Fax: 330-674-5514. Hours: 8:30AM-4:30PM (EST). *Misdemeanor, Civil Actions Under $15,000, Small Claims.*

Civil Records: Access: Phone, fax, mail, in person. Both court and visitors may perform in person searches. Search fee: $1.00 per name. Required to search: name, years to search. Civil cases indexed by defendant, plaintiff. Civil records in books going back to 1813. Phone & fax access limited to 1 name.

Criminal Records: Access: Phone, fax, mail, in person. Both court and visitors may perform in person searches. Search fee: $1.00 per name. Required to search: name, years to search. Criminal records in books going back to 1813. Same as civil.

General Information: Public Access terminal is available. No search warrant records released. SASE required. Turnaround time 2-5 days. Copy fee: $.25 per page. Certification fee: $1.00 per page. Fee payee: Holmes County Court. Personal checks accepted. Prepayment is required.

Huron County

Common Pleas Court 2 E Main St, Norwalk, OH 44857; 419-668-5113; Probate phone: 419-668-4383. Hours: 8AM-4:30PM (EST). *Felony, Civil Actions Over $10,000, Probate.*

www.huroncountyclerk.com

Note: Probate is separate court at phone number given.

Civil Records: Access: Mail, in person. Both court and visitors may perform in person searches. Search fee: $1.00 per name. Required to search: name, years to search; also helpful: address. Civil cases indexed by defendant, plaintiff. Civil records on computer from 1989, prior in books and on microfiche.

Criminal Records: Access: Mail, in person. Both court and visitors may perform in person searches. Search fee: $1.00 per name. Required to search: name, years to search, offense, date of offense; also helpful: address, DOB, SSN. Criminal records on computer since 1989, records from 1985 to present in actual files, 1930 to 1985 on microfiche.

General Information: Public Access terminal is available. No secret records released. SASE required. Turnaround time 2 days. Fax notes: No fee to fax results. Copy fee: $.25 per page. Certification fee: $1.00. Fee payee: Clerk of Court. Personal checks accepted. Prepayment is required.

Bellevue Municipal Court 117 N Sandusky, PO Box 305, Bellevue, OH 44811; 419-483-5880; Fax: 419-484-8060. 8:30AM-4:30PM (EST). *Misdemeanor, Civil Actions Under $15,000, Eviction, Small Claims.*

Civil Records: Access: Phone, mail, in person. Both court and visitors may perform in person searches. No search fee. Required to search: name, years to search. Civil cases indexed by defendant, plaintiff. Civil records on index from 1988, prior in books. Will only do phone searching if not busy.

Criminal Records: Access: Phone, mail, in person. Both court and visitors may perform in person searches. No search fee. Required to search: name, years to search, DOB; also helpful: SSN. Criminal records on computer from 8/93. Court searches back to 8/93 only. Use an abstractor to go back further.

General Information: SASE required. Turnaround time 3-7 days. Certification fee: $1.00. Fee payee: Bellevue Municipal Court. Only cashiers checks and money orders accepted.

Norwalk Municipal Court 45 N Linwood, Norwalk, OH 44857; 419-663-6750; Fax: 419-663-6749. Hours: 8:30AM-4:30PM (EST). *Misdemeanor, Civil Actions Under $15,000, Eviction, Small Claims.*

Civil Records: Access: Fax, mail, in person. Both court and visitors may perform in person searches. Search fee: $1.00 per name. Required to search: name, years to search; also helpful: address. Civil cases indexed by defendant, plaintiff. Civil records on computer from 7/88; prior on docket books.

Criminal Records: Access: Fax, mail, in person. Both court and visitors may perform in person searches. Search fee: $1.00 per name. Required to search: name, years to search, DOB, SSN; also helpful: address. Criminal records on computer from 7/88, prior on docket books.

General Information: Public Access terminal is available. SASE is required. Turnaround time 2-7 days. Fax notes: Fee to fax results is $1.00 per page. Copy fee: $.05 per page. Certification fee: $1.00 per page. Fee payee: Municipal Court. Personal checks accepted. Prepayment is required.

Jackson County

Common Pleas Court 226 Main St, Jackson, OH 45640; 740-286-2006; Probate phone: 740-286-1401; Fax: 740-286-4061. Hours: 8AM-4PM (EST). *Felony, Civil Actions Over $10,000, Probate.*

Civil Records: Access: Mail, in person. Both court and visitors may perform in person searches. No search fee. Required to search: name, years to search; also helpful: address. Civil cases indexed by defendant, plaintiff. Civil records in books from late 1800s, computerized since 06/20/97.

Criminal Records: Access: Mail, in person. Both court and visitors may perform in person searches. Search fee: Searches only performed in emergency situations. Required to search: name, years to search; also helpful: address, DOB, SSN. Criminal records on books from 1980, computerized since 06/20/97.

General Information: No juvenile or search warrant record released. SASE required. Turnaround time varies. Copy fee: $.50 per page. Certification fee: $1.00. Fee payee: Clerk of Court. Personal checks accepted. Prepayment is required.

Jackson County Municipal Court 350 Portsmouth St #101, Jackson, OH 45640-1764; 740-286-2718; Fax: 740-286-0679. Hours: 8AM-4PM (EST). *Misdemeanor, Civil Actions Under $15,000, Eviction, Small Claims.*

Civil Records: Access: In person only. Visitors must perform in person searches for themselves. No search fee. Required to search: name, years to search. Civil cases indexed by defendant, plaintiff. Civil records in books readily available for 8-10 years, prior archived.

Criminal Records: Access: In person only. Visitors must perform in person searches for themselves. No search fee. Required to search: name, years to search, DOB, SSN. Criminal records in books readily available for 8-10 years, prior archived.

General Information: Public Access terminal is available. No victim records released. Copy fee: $.50 per page. Certification fee: No cert fee. Fee payee: Clerk of Municipal Court. Only cashiers checks and money orders accepted. Prepayment is required.

Jefferson County

Common Pleas Court 301 Market St (PO Box 1326), Steubenville, OH 43952; 740-283-8583. Hours: 8:30AM-4:30PM (EST). *Felony, Civil Actions Over $500, Probate.*

www.uov.net/jeffcodp/court1.htm

Note: Probate is at PO Box 649 and can be reached at 740-283-8653.

Civil Records: Access: In person only. Visitors must perform in person searches for themselves. No search fee. Required to search: name, years to search. Civil cases indexed by defendant, plaintiff. Civil records on books for 10 years or so, prior archived.

Criminal Records: Access: Mail, in person. Both court and visitors may perform in person searches. Search fee: $5.00 per name. Required to search: name, years to search, DOB, offense, date of offense. Criminal records on books for 10 years or so, prior archived.

General Information: Public Access terminal is available. No sealed records released. SASE required. Turnaround time 1-2 days. Copy fee: $.25 per page. Certification fee: $1.00 per page. Fee payee: Jefferson County Clerk of Courts. Business checks accepted. Prepayment is required.

County Court #1 1007 Franklin Ave, Toronto, OH 43964; 740-537-2020. Hours: 8:30AM-4:30PM (EST). *Misdemeanor, Civil Actions Under $15,000, Small Claims.*

www.uov.net/jeffcodp/court1.htm

Civil Records: Access: Mail, in person. Both court and visitors may perform in person searches. Search fee: $5.00 per name. Required to search: name, years to search. Civil cases indexed by defendant, plaintiff. Civil records in books, dating from 1813.

Criminal Records: Access: Mail, in person. Both court and visitors may perform in person searches. Search fee: $5.00 per name. Required to search: name, years to search, DOB, also helpful: SSN, sex, signed release. Criminal records in books, dating from 1813.

General Information: Public Access terminal is available. All records are public. SASE required. Turnaround time 1-2 days. No copy fee. Certification fee: No cert fee. Fee payee: Jefferson County Court #1. Only cashiers checks and money orders accepted.

County Court #2 PO Box 2207, Wintersville, OH 43953; 740-264-7644. Hours: 8:30AM-4PM (EST). *Misdemeanor, Civil Actions Under $15,000, Small Claims.*

www.uov.net/jeffcodp/court1.htm

Civil Records: Access: Mail, in person. Both court and visitors may perform in person searches. Search fee: $5.00 per name. Required to search: name, years to search. Civil cases indexed by defendant, plaintiff. Civil records on computer back to 1998; in books from 1950s, prior archived.

Criminal Records: Access: Mail, in person. Both court and visitors may perform in person searches. Search fee: $5.00 per name. Required to search: name, years to search, DOB or SSN. Criminal records on computer back to 1998; in books from 1950s, prior archived.

General Information: SASE required. Turnaround time 1-2 days. Copy fee: $.25 per page. Certification fee: $1.00 per page. Fee payee: County Court #2. Only cashiers checks and money orders accepted. Prepayment is required.

County Court #3 PO Box 495, Dillonvale, OH 43917; 740-769-2903. Hours: 8AM-4PM (EST). *Misdemeanor, Civil Actions Under $15,000, Small Claims.*

www.uov.net/jeffcodp/court1.htm

Civil Records: Access: Mail, in person. Both court and visitors may perform in person searches. No search fee. Required to search: name, years to search. Civil cases indexed by defendant, plaintiff. Civil records on computer from 1998, prior on microfiche.

Criminal Records: Access: Mail, in person. Both court and visitors may perform in person searches. No search fee. Required to search: name, years to search, DOB; also helpful: SSN. Criminal records on computer from 1998, prior on microfiche.

General Information: SASE required. Turnaround time 1-2 days. Copy fee: $1.00 per page. Certification

fee: $1.00. Fee payee: County Court #3. Only cashiers checks and money orders accepted. Prepayment is required.

Steubenville Municipal Court 123 S 3rd St, Steubenville, OH 43952; 740-283-6020; Fax: 740-283-6167. Hours: 8:30AM-4PM (EST). *Misdemeanor, Civil Actions Under $15,000, Eviction, Small Claims.*

www.uov.net/jeffcodp/court1.htm

Civil Records: Access: Mail, in person. Both court and visitors may perform in person searches. No search fee. Required to search: name, years to search; also helpful: address. Civil cases indexed by defendant, plaintiff. Civil records on computer from 1991, prior in books.

Criminal Records: Access: Mail, in person. Both court and visitors may perform in person searches. No search fee. Required to search: name, years to search; also helpful: address, DOB, SSN. Criminal records on computer from 1991, prior in books.

General Information: Public Access terminal is available. No expunged records released. SASE required. Turnaround time 1-5 days. Copy fee: $1.00 per page. Certification fee: $2.00. Fee payee: Steubenville Municipal Court. Only cashiers checks and money orders accepted. Prepayment is required.

Knox County

Common Pleas Court 117 E High St #201, Mt Vernon, OH 43050; 740-393-6788; Probate phone: 740-393-6797. Hours: 8AM-4PM (EST). *Felony, Civil Actions Over $10,000.*

www.knoxcountyclerk.org

Civil Records: Access: Online, in person. Visitors must perform in person searches for themselves. No search fee. Required to search: name, years to search. Civil cases indexed by defendant, plaintiff. Civil records on computer since 9/86, on microfilm from 1960, prior archived. Search court index, dockets, calendars free online at www.knoxcountycpcourt.org. Search by name or case number.

Criminal Records: Access: Online, in person. Visitors must perform in person searches for themselves. No search fee. Required to search: name, years to search, DOB, SSN, signed release. Criminal records on computer since 9/86, on microfilm from 1960, prior archived. Online access to criminal records is the same as civil.

General Information: Public Access terminal is available. Copy fee: $.25 per page. Certification fee: $1.00. Fee payee: Common Pleas Court. Personal checks accepted.

Mount Vernon Municipal Court 5 North Gay St, Mount Vernon, OH 43050; 740-393-9510; Fax: 740-393-5349. Hours: 8AM-4PM (EST). *Misdemeanor, Civil Actions Under $15,000, Eviction, Small Claims.*

Civil Records: Access: Phone, fax, mail, in person. Both court and visitors may perform in person searches. No search fee. Required to search: name, years to search. Civil cases indexed by defendant, plaintiff. Civil records on computer from 06/89, prior in books.

Criminal Records: Access: Phone, fax, mail, in person. Both court and visitors may perform in person searches. No search fee. Required to search: name, years to search. Criminal records on computer from 06/89, prior in books.

General Information: SASE required. Turnaround time 1 week. No copy fee. Certification fee: No cert fee. Personal checks accepted. Credit cards accepted in some cases.

Probate Court 111 E High St, Mt Vernon, OH 43050; 740-393-6796; Fax: 740-393-6832. Hours: 8AM-4PM, 8AM-6PM Tues. (EST). *Probate.*

Lake County

Common Pleas Court PO Box 490, Painesville, OH 44077; 440-350-2658; Probate phone: 440-350-2624. Hours: 8AM-4:30PM (EST). *Felony, Civil Actions Over $10,000, Probate.*

www.lakecountyohio.org/clerk

Civil Records: Access: In person, online. Visitors must perform in person searches for themselves. No search fee. Required to search: name, years to search; also helpful: address. Civil cases indexed by defendant, plaintiff. Civil records on computer from 1990, microfilm from 1960, prior archived. Online access to court records, docket sheets, and quick index are available free at http://web2.lakecountyohio.org/clerk/search.htm. Includes domestic and appeals cases.

Criminal Records: Access: In person, online. Visitors must perform in person searches for themselves. No search fee. Required to search: name, years to search; also helpful: address, DOB, SSN. Criminal records on computer from 1990, microfilm from 1960, prior archived. Online access to criminal records is the same as civil.

General Information: Public Access terminal is available. No adoption or juvenile records released. Copy fee: $.25 per page. Certification fee: $1.00. Fee payee: Clerk of Court. Business checks accepted. Prepayment is required.

Mentor Municipal Court 8500 Civic Center Blvd, Mentor, OH 44060-2418; Civil phone: 440-974-5744; Criminal phone: 440-974-5745; Fax: 440-974-5742. Hours: 8:30AM-4:30 PM (EST). *Misdemeanor, Civil Actions Under $15,000, Eviction, Small Claims.*

Civil Records: Access: In person only. Visitors must perform in person searches for themselves. No search fee. Required to search: name. Civil cases indexed by defendant, plaintiff. Civil records go back to 1972; on computer back to 11/1995.

Criminal Records: Access: In person only. Visitors must perform in person searches for themselves. No search fee. Required to search: name, years to search; also helpful: DOB. Criminal records go back to 1972; on computer back to 11/1995.

General Information: Public Access terminal is available. Copy fee: $1.00 per page. Certification fee: $1.00. Fee payee: Mentor Municipal Court. Only cashiers checks and money orders accepted. Prepayment is required.

Painesville Municipal Court 7 Richmond St (PO Box 601), Painesville, OH 44077; 440-639-4990; Fax: 440-352-0028 (criminal & traffic). Hours: 8AM-4:30PM (EST). *Misdemeanor, Civil Actions Under $15,000, Eviction, Small Claims.*

Note: Civil & Probation Fax# 440-639-4932.

Civil Records: Access: Fax, mail, in person. Both court and visitors may perform in person searches. No search fee. Required to search: name, years to search; also helpful: address. Civil cases indexed by defendant, plaintiff. Civil records on computer from 7/90 (all divisions), prior on books or archived.

Criminal Records: Access: Fax, mail, in person. Both court and visitors may perform in person searches. No search fee. Required to search: name, years to search, address; also helpful: DOB, SSN. Criminal records on computer from 7/90 (all divisions), prior on books or archived.

General Information: Public Access terminal is available. SASE not required. Turnaround time 1 week. Fax notes: Fax fee: local $1.00 per page; long distance $2.00 per page. Copy fee: $1.00 per page. $.20 per page after first 5. Certification fee: $2.00 plus $1.00 per page after first. Fee payee: Municipal Court. Personal checks accepted. Credit cards accepted: Visa, MasterCard. Prepayment is required.

Willoughby Municipal Court One Public Square, Willoughby, OH 44094-7888; Civil phone: 440-953-4170; Criminal phone: 440-953-4150; Fax: 440-953-4149. Hours: 7:30AM-4:30 PM (EST). *Misdemeanor, Civil Actions Under $15,000, Eviction, Small Claims.*

Civil Records: Access: Mail, in person. Both court and visitors may perform in person searches. No search fee. Required to search: name, years to search. Civil cases indexed by defendant. Civil records on docket books since 1960, computerized since 1986.

Criminal Records: Access: Mail, in person. Both court and visitors may perform in person searches. No search fee. Required to search: name; also helpful: DOB, SSN. Criminal records in docket books since 1960, computerized since 1986.

General Information: Public Access terminal is available. Turnaround time 2-3 days. Certification fee: $2.00 per page. Fee payee: Willoughby Municipal Court. Personal checks accepted. Prepayment required.

Lawrence County

Common Pleas Court Clerk of the Courts, PO Box 208, Ironton, OH 45638; 740-533-4355/4329; Probate phone: 740-533-4340. Hours: 8:30AM-4PM (EST). *Felony, Civil Actions, Probate.*

www.lawrencecountyclkofcrt.org

Note: Probate is a separate court at the same address.

Civil Records: Access: Mail, in person, online. Both court and visitors may perform in person searches. No search fee. Required to search: name, years to search; also helpful: address. Civil cases indexed by defendant, plaintiff. Civil records on computer back to 6/88, prior in books going back to 1800s. Online access to civil records is available free at the web site.

Criminal Records: Access: In person, online. Visitors must perform in person searches for themselves. No search fee. Required to search: name, years to search; also helpful: address, DOB, SSN. Criminal records on computer back to 1/88, prior in books going back to 1800s. Online access to criminal records is the same as civil.

General Information: Public Access terminal is available. SASE required. Turnaround time 1 week. Copy fee: $.25 per page. Certification fee: $1.00. Fee payee: Clerk of Court. Personal checks accepted.

Lawrence County Municipal Court PO Box 126, Chesapeake, OH 45619; 740-867-3128/3127; Fax: 740-867-3547. Hours: 8:30AM-4PM *Misdemeanor, Civil Actions Under $15,000, Eviction, Small Claims.*

Civil Records: Access: Phone, fax, mail, in person. Both court and visitors may perform in person searches. Search fee: $5.00 per name. Required to search: name, years to search. Civil cases indexed by defendant, plaintiff. Civil records on computer from 1991.

Criminal Records: Access: Phone, fax, mail, in person. Both court and visitors may perform in person searches. Search fee: $5.00 per name. Required to search: name, years to search, DOB; also helpful: SSN. Criminal records on computer from 1991.

General Information: All records public. SASE required. Turnaround time 7-10 days. Copy fee: $.10 per page. Certification fee: $2.00. Fee payee: Lawrence County Municipal Court. Personal checks accepted. Prepayment is required.

Ironton Municipal Court PO Box 237, Ironton, OH 45638; 740-532-3062; Fax: 740-533-6088. Hours: 8:30AM-4PM (EST). *Misdemeanor, Civil Actions Under $15,000, Eviction, Small Claims.*

Civil Records: Access: Mail, in person. Both court and visitors may perform in person searches. No search fee. Required to search: name, years to search; also helpful: address. Civil cases indexed by defendant, plaintiff. Civil records on computer from 7/89, prior in books.

Criminal Records: Access: Mail, in person. Both court and visitors may perform in person searches. No search fee. Required to search: name, years to search; also helpful: address, DOB, SSN, singed release. Criminal records on computer from 7/89, prior in books.

General Information: Public Access terminal is available. SASE required. Turnaround time 1-2 weeks. Copy fee: $.00 per page. Certification fee: $1.00 per page. Fee payee: Municipal Court. Prepayment is required.

Licking County

Common Pleas Court PO Box 4370, Newark, OH 43058-4370; 740-349-6171; Probate phone: 740-349-6141; Fax: 740-349-6945. Hours: 8AM-4:30PM (EST). *Felony, Civil Actions Over $10,000, Probate.*

Note: Probate court has a separate clerk at the same address.

Civil Records: Access: In person only. Visitors must perform in person searches for themselves. No search fee. Required to search: name, years to search; also helpful: address. Civil cases indexed by defendant, plaintiff. Civil records on computer from 1992, prior in books.

Criminal Records: Access: In person only. Visitors must perform in person searches for themselves. No search fee. Required to search: name, years to search, DOB; also helpful: address, SSN. Criminal records on computer from 1992, prior in books.

General Information: Public Access terminal is available. No sealed records released. Copy fee: $.05 per page. Certification fee: $1.00. Fee payee: Clerk of Court. Business checks accepted. Prepayment is required.

Licking County Municipal Court 40 W Main St, Newark, OH 43055; 740-349-6627. Hours: 8AM-4:30PM (EST). *Misdemeanor, Civil Actions Under $15,000, Eviction, Small Claims.*

Civil Records: Access: Phone, fax, mail, in person. Both court and visitors may perform in person searches. No search fee. Required to search: name, years to search. Civil cases indexed by defendant, plaintiff. Civil records on computer from 1990, prior in books.

Criminal Records: Access: Phone, fax, mail, in person. Both court and visitors may perform in person searches. No search fee. Required to search: name, years to search. Criminal records on computer from 1990, prior in books.

General Information: Public Access terminal is available. No sealed records released. SASE required. Turnaround time 2-3 days. Copy fee: $.25 per page. Certification fee: $2.00. Fee payee: Licking County Municipal Court. Personal checks accepted. Prepayment is required.

Logan County

Common Pleas Court 101 S Main St Rm 18, Bellefontaine, OH 43311-2097; 937-599-7260. Hours: 8:30AM-4:30PM (EST). *Felony, Civil Actions Over $10,000.*

Civil Records: Access: In person only. Visitors must perform in person searches for themselves. No search fee. Required to search: name, years to search; also helpful: address. Civil cases indexed by defendant, plaintiff. Civil records on computer from 6/88, prior in books.

Criminal Records: Access: In person only. Visitors must perform in person searches for themselves. No search fee. Required to search: name, years to search, DOB; also helpful: address, SSN. Criminal records on computer from 6/88, prior in books.

General Information: Public Access terminal is available. All records public. Fax notes: Fee to fax results is $2.00 per page. Copy fee: $.25 per page after first 25 pages. Certification fee: $1.00 per page. Fee

payee: Clerk of Court. Only cashiers checks and money orders accepted. Prepayment is required.

Bellefontaine Municipal Court 226 W Columbus Ave, Bellefontaine, OH 43311; 937-599-6127. Hours: 8AM-4:30PM (EST). *Misdemeanor, Civil Actions Under $15,000, Eviction, Small Claims.*

Civil Records: Access: In person only. Visitors must perform in person searches for themselves. No search fee. Required to search: name, years to search. Civil cases indexed by defendant, plaintiff. Civil records on computer from 1986, prior in books.

Criminal Records: Access: In person only. Visitors must perform in person searches for themselves. No search fee. Required to search: name, years to search, DOB, SSN, signed release; also helpful: address. Criminal records on computer from 1986, prior in books.

General Information: Public Access terminal is available. All records are public. Copy fee: $.25 per page. Certification fee: $1.00. Fee payee: Bellefontaine Municipal Court. Personal checks accepted. Local checks accepted. Credit cards accepted: Visa, MasterCard. Accepted for traffic & criminal only. Prepayment is required.

Lorain County

Common Pleas Court 226 Middle Ave, Elyria, OH 44035; 440-329-5536; Probate phone: 440-329-5175; Fax: 440-329-5404. Hours: 8AM-4:30PM (EST). *Felony, Civil Actions Over $10,000, Probate.*

www.loraincountycpcourt.org

Civil Records: Access: Mail, online, in person. Both court and visitors may perform in person searches. No search fee. Required to search: name, years to search. Civil cases indexed by defendant, plaintiff. Civil records on computer from 1988, prior in books archived to 1800s. some records on microfiche to 1960. The web site offers free access to indices and dockets for civil and domestic relationship cases. Court will not do index searching, but they will pull specified records.

Criminal Records: Access: Mail, online, in person. Both court and visitors may perform in person searches. No search fee. Required to search: name, years to search. Criminal records on computer from 1988, prior in books archived to 1800s. some records on microfiche to 1960. Online access to criminal records is the same as civil. Court will not do index searching, but they will pull specified records.

General Information: Public Access terminal is available. No juvenile records released. SASE required. Turnaround time 1-2 days. Copy fee: $.10 per page. Certification fee: $1.00. Fee payee: Clerk of Court. Personal checks accepted. Prepayment is required.

Avon Lake Municipal Court 32855 Walker Rd, Avon Lake, OH 44012; 440-930-4103. Hours: 8:30AM-4:30PM (EST). *Misdemeanor, Civil Actions Under $15,000, Eviction, Small Claims.*

Note: The court upgraded their computer system for 2000 and refrains from disclosing the SSN publicly.

Civil Records: Access: Phone, mail, in person. Only the court performs in person searches; visitors may not. No search fee. Required to search: name, years to search. Civil cases indexed by defendant, plaintiff. Civil records on computer from 7/92, prior in books.

Criminal Records: Access: Phone, mail, in person. Only the court performs in person searches; visitors may not. No search fee. Required to search: name, years to search, DOB; also helpful: SSN. Criminal records on computer from 7/92, prior in books.

General Information: No non-public records released. SASE required. Turnaround time 1-2 days. Fax notes: Fee to fax results is $3.00 per document. Copy fee: $.50 per page. Certification fee: $1.00. Fee payee: Avon Lake Municipal Court. Personal checks accepted. Prepayment is required.

Elyria Municipal Court 328 Broad St (PO Box 1498), Elyria, OH 44036; 440-323-5743; Criminal phone: 440-323-1328; Fax: 440-323-0785. Hours: 8AM-4:30PM (EST). *Misdemeanor, Civil Actions Under $15,000, Eviction, Small Claims.*

www.elyriamunicourt.org

Civil Records: Access: Fax, mail, online, in person. Both court and visitors may perform in person searches. No search fee. Required to search: name, years to search; also helpful: address. Civil cases indexed by defendant, plaintiff. Civil records in books to 1956, computer from 1991. Search by e-mail to civil@elyriamunicourt.org.

Criminal Records: Access: Fax, mail, in person. Both court and visitors may perform in person searches. No search fee. Required to search: name, years to search; also helpful: address, DOB, SSN. Criminal records in books to 1956, computer from 1991. Search by e-mail to crtr@elyriamunicourt.org.

General Information: All records are public. SASE required. Turnaround time 5 days. Fax notes: Will not fax results. No copy fee. Certification fee: No cert fee. Personal checks accepted.

Lorain Municipal Court 100 W Erie Ave, Lorain, OH 44052; 440-244-2286. Hours: 8:30AM-4:30PM (EST). *Misdemeanor, Civil Actions Under $15,000, Eviction, Small Claims.*

www.lorainmunicourt.org

Civil Records: Access: Online, in person. Visitors must perform in person searches for themselves. No search fee. Required to search: name, years to search; also helpful: address. Civil cases indexed by defendant, plaintiff. Civil records in books. Online access to municipal court records is available free at www.lorainmunicourt.org/search.shtml. Search by name, date, case number, driver license number or attorney.

Criminal Records: Access: Online, in person. Visitors must perform in person searches for themselves. No search fee. Required to search: name, years to search; also helpful: address, DOB, SSN. Criminal records in books. Online access to criminal records is the same as civil.

General Information: Public Access terminal is available. Copy fee: $1.00 per page. Certification fee: $2.00. Fee payee: Municipal Court. Personal checks accepted. Prepayment is required.

Oberlin Municipal Court 85 S Main St, Oberlin, OH 44074; 440-775-1751; Fax: 440-775-0619. Hours: 8AM-4PM (EST). *Misdemeanor, Civil Actions Under $15,000, Eviction, Small Claims.*

Civil Records: Access: In person only. Visitors must perform in person searches for themselves. No search fee. Required to search: name, years to search; also helpful: address. Civil cases indexed by defendant, plaintiff. Civil records on computer from 1991, prior in books.

Criminal Records: Access: In person only. Visitors must perform in person searches for themselves. No search fee. Required to search: name, years to search; also helpful: address, DOB, SSN. Criminal records on computer from 1991, prior in books.

General Information: Public Access terminal is available. Copy fee: $.10 per page. Certification fee: $1.00. Fee payee: Oberlin Municipal Court. Business checks accepted. Credit cards accepted: Visa, MasterCard. Prepayment is required.

Vermilion Municipal Court 687 Decatour St, Vermilion, OH 44089-1152; 440-967-6543; Fax: 440-967-1467. Hours: 8AM-4PM (EST). *Misdemeanor, Civil Actions Under $15,000, Eviction, Small Claims.*

www.vermilionmunicipalcourt.org

Civil Records: Access: Fax, mail, in person, online. Both court and visitors may perform in person searches.

No search fee. Required to search: name, years to search; also helpful: address. Civil cases indexed by defendant, plaintiff. Civil records on computer since late 1991, indexed in books since 1966. Online access to municipal court records is available at the web site.

Criminal Records: Access: Fax, mail, in person, online. Both court and visitors may perform in person searches. No search fee. Required to search: name, years to search; also helpful: SSN. Criminal records on computer since late 1991, indexed in books since 1966. Online access to criminal records is the same as civil.

General Information: Public Access terminal is available. no addresses, victim info or confidential report records released. Fax notes: No fee to fax results. Copy fee: $.10 per page. Certification fee: $2.00. Fee payee: Municipal Court. Personal checks accepted. Credit cards accepted: Visa, MasterCard. Prepayment is required.

Lucas County

Common Pleas Court 700 Adams, Courthouse, Toledo, OH 43624; 419-213-4483 & 4484; Fax: 419-213-4487. Hours: 8AM-4:45PM (EST). *Felony, Civil Actions Over $10,000, Probate.*

Civil Records: Access: Fax, mail, in person. Both court and visitors may perform in person searches. Search fee: $2.00 per name. Required to search: name, years to search. Civil cases indexed by defendant, plaintiff. Civil records computer from 1987, prior in books and on film.

Criminal Records: Access: Fax, mail, in person. Both court and visitors may perform in person searches. Search fee: $5.00 per name. Required to search: name, years to search; also helpful: DOB, SSN, sex. Criminal records computer from 1987, prior on books and film.

General Information: Public Access terminal is available. No expunged records released. SASE not required. Turnaround time 3 days. Fax notes: $1.00 per page. Add $3.00 transmittal fee. Copy fee: $.25 per page. Certification fee: $3.00. Fee payee: Clerk of Court. Only cashiers checks and money orders accepted. Prepayment is required.

Maumee Municipal Court 400 Conant St, Maumee, OH 43537-3397; Civil phone: 419-897-7145; Criminal phone: 419-897-7136; Fax: 419-897-7129. Hours: 8AM-4:30PM (EST). *Misdemeanor, Civil Actions Under $15,000, Eviction, Small Claims.*

www.maumee.org/court/court.htm

Note: The court expects to provide Internet access to records sometime in 2000.

Civil Records: Access: Phone, fax, mail, in person, online. Both court and visitors may perform in person searches. No search fee. Required to search: name; also helpful: years to search. Civil cases indexed by defendant, plaintiff. Civil records in docket books since 1964, on computer since 1987. Online access to the interactive web court system database is available free at www.maumee.org/court/courtsystem/index.html.

Criminal Records: Access: Phone, fax, mail, in person, online. Both court and visitors may perform in person searches. No search fee. Required to search: name, years to search, DOB; also helpful: SSN. Criminal records in docket books since 1964, on computer since 1987. Online access to criminal records is the same as civil.

General Information: Turnaround time 1 week. Fax notes: $3.00 per page. Copy fee: $.25 per page. Certification fee: $1.50. Fee payee: Maumee Municipal Court. Personal checks accepted. Credit cards accepted: Visa, MasterCard. Credit cards not accepted for phone orders. Prepayment is required.

Oregon Municipal Court 5330 Seaman Rd, Oregon, OH 43616; Civil phone: 419-698-7008; Criminal phone: 419-698-7173; Fax: 419-698-7013. Hours: 8:30AM-4:30PM (EST). *Misdemeanor, Civil Actions Under $15,000, Eviction, Small Claims, Traffic.*

www.ci.oregon.oh.us/ctydpt/court/court.htm

Civil Records: Access: Phone, fax, mail, in person, email. Both court and visitors may perform in person searches. No search fee. Required to search: name, years to search. Civil cases indexed by defendant, plaintiff. Civil records on books since 1960, computerized since 1989.

Criminal Records: Access: Phone, fax, mail, in person, email. Both court and visitors may perform in person searches. No search fee. Required to search: name, years to search; also helpful: DOB, SSN. Criminal records on books since 1960, computerized since 1989.

General Information: Turnaround time 1-2 days. Fax notes: No fee to fax results. Must be local call. Copy fee: $.50 for first page, $.10 each add'l. Certification fee: $2.50 per page. Fee payee: Oregon Municipal Court. Personal checks accepted. Credit cards accepted for criminal records only: Visa, MasterCard. For in person searching only. Prepayment is required.

Sylvania Municipal Court 6700 Monroe St, Sylvania, OH 43560-1995; 419-885-8975; Fax: 419-885-8987. Hours: 7:30AM-4PM (EST). *Misdemeanor, Civil Actions Under $15,000, Eviction, Small Claims.*

www.sylvaniacourt.com

Civil Records: Access: Fax, mail, in person. Both court and visitors may perform in person searches. No search fee. Required to search: name, years to search. Civil cases indexed by defendant, plaintiff. Civil records on books since 1964, computerized since 1987.

Criminal Records: Access: Fax, mail, in person. Both court and visitors may perform in person searches. No search fee. Required to search: name, years to search, DOB, SSN. Criminal records on books since 1964, computerized since 1987.

General Information: Public Access terminal is available. Turnaround time 1 week. Fax notes: No fee to fax results. Local calls only. Copy fee: $.10 per page. Certification fee: $2.00 per page. Fee payee: Clerk of Court. Business checks accepted. Prepayment required.

Toledo Municipal Court 555 N Erie St, Toledo, OH 43624-1391; 419-245-1926 (Small Claims); Civil phone: 419-245-1927; Criminal phone: 419-936-3650; Fax: 419-245-1801. Hours: 8AM-4:30PM civil; 6AM-6PM M-F, 6-11:30AM Sat crim & traffic (EST). *Misdemeanor, Civil Actions Under $15,000, Eviction, Small Claims.*

www.tmc-clerk.com

The daily docket is available online at the web site.

Civil Records: Access: Mail, fax, in person. Both court and visitors may perform in person searches. No search fee. Required to search: name, years to search; also helpful: address. Civil cases indexed by defendant. Civil records on computer to 1985, prior in books since 1969.

Criminal Records: Access: Mail, fax, in person. Both court and visitors may perform in person searches. No search fee. Required to search: name, years to search, DOB; also helpful: address, SSN. Criminal records on computer from 1985, prior in books since 1969. Have either date of birth or SSN to request a search.

General Information: Public Access terminal is available. (Civil only.) No expunged records released. SASE required. Turnaround time 1 day with a case number; 5 days without a case number. Copy fee: $.25 per page. Certification fee: $6.00. Fee payee: Toledo Municipal Court. Personal checks accepted. Credit cards accepted: Visa, MasterCard. Prepayment is required.

Madison County

Common Pleas Court PO Box 557, London, OH 43140; 740-852-9776; Probate phone: 740-852-0756. Hours: 8AM-4PM (EST). *Felony, Civil Actions Over $10,000, Probate.*

Civil Records: Access: In person only. Visitors must perform in person searches for themselves. No search fee. Required to search: name, years to search. Civil cases indexed by defendant, plaintiff. Civil records in books since 1981.

Criminal Records: Access: In person only. Visitors must perform in person searches for themselves. No search fee. Required to search: name, years to search; also helpful: address, DOB, SSN. Criminal records in books since 1981.

General Information: No secret indictment records released. Copy fee: $.25 per page. Certification fee: No cert fee. Fee payee: Clerk of Court. Personal checks accepted. Prepayment is required.

Madison County Municipal Court Main & High St, PO Box 646, London, OH 43140; 740-852-1669; Fax: 740-852-0812. Hours: 8AM-4PM (EST). *Misdemeanor, Civil Actions Under $15,000, Eviction, Small Claims.*

Civil Records: Access: Phone, fax, mail, in person. Both court and visitors may perform in person searches. No search fee. Required to search: name, years to search. Civil cases indexed by defendant, plaintiff. Civil records on computer from 1989, prior in books indexed from 1958.

Criminal Records: Access: Phone, fax, mail, in person. Both court and visitors may perform in person searches. No search fee. Required to search: name, years to search, DOB; also helpful: SSN. Criminal records on computer from 1989, prior in books indexed from 1958.

General Information: Public Access terminal is available. No probation records released. SASE required. Turnaround time up to 2 weeks. Fax notes: No fee to fax results. Copy fee: $.25 per page. Certification fee: $1.00. Fee payee: Madison County Municipal Court. Only cashiers checks and money orders accepted. Prepayment is required.

Mahoning County

Common Pleas Court 120 Market St, Youngstown, OH 44503; 330-740-2310; Probate phone: 330-740-2312; Fax: 330-740-2105. Hours: 8AM-4PM (EST). *Felony, Civil Actions Over $15,000, Probate.*

Civil Records: Access: In person only. Visitors must perform in person searches for themselves. No search fee. Required to search: name, years to search; also helpful: address. Civil cases indexed by defendant, plaintiff. Civil records on computer from 1989, prior in books indexed from 1946.

Criminal Records: Access: Phone, fax, mail, in person. Both court and visitors may perform in person searches. No search fee. Required to search: name, years to search; also helpful: address, DOB, SSN. Criminal records on computer from 1989, prior in books indexed from 1946.

General Information: Public Access terminal is available. No secret indictment records released. SASE required. Turnaround time 1 week. Fax notes: $2.00 for first page, $1.00 each add'l. Copy fee: $.10 per page. Certification fee: $1.00. Fee payee: Clerk of Court. Personal checks accepted. Prepayment is required.

County Court #2 127 Boardman Canfield Rd, Boardman, OH 44512; 330-726-5546; Fax: 330-740-2035. Hours: 8:30AM-4PM (EST). *Misdemeanor, Civil Actions Under $15,000, Small Claims.*

Civil Records: Access: Mail, in person. Both court and visitors may perform in person searches. No search fee. Required to search: name, years to search. Civil cases indexed by defendant, plaintiff. Civil records in books and dockets from 1960.

Criminal Records: Access: Mail, in person. Both court and visitors may perform in person searches. No search fee. Required to search: name, years to search, DOB; also helpful: SSN. Criminal records in books and dockets from 1960. Court will not perform party names searches for in-person requesters.

General Information: Public Access terminal is available. Expunged records are not released. SASE required. Turnaround time 5-10 days. Copy fee: $.25 per page. Certification fee: $1.00. Fee payee: County Court #2. Personal checks accepted. Prepayment is required.

County Court #3 605 E Ohio Ave, Sebring, OH 44672; 330-938-9873; Fax: 330-938-6518. Hours: 8:30AM-4PM (EST). *Misdemeanor, Civil Actions Under $15,000, Small Claims.*

Civil Records: Access: Mail, in person. Both court and visitors may perform in person searches. No search fee. Required to search: name, years to search. Civil cases indexed by defendant, plaintiff. Civil records in books from 1990; on computer back to 8/95.

Criminal Records: Access: Mail, in person. Both court and visitors may perform in person searches. No search fee. Required to search: name, years to search, DOB; also helpful: SSN. Criminal records in books from 1990; on computer back to 8/95.

General Information: Public Access terminal is available. No expunged records released. SASE required. Turnaround time 1 week. Copy fee: $.10 per page. Certification fee: $1.00 per page. Fee payee: Mahoning County Court #3. Personal checks accepted. Prepayment is required.

County Court #4 6000 Mahoning Ave, Youngstown, OH 44515-2288; 330-740-2001; Fax: 330-740-2036. Hours: 8:30AM-4PM (EST). *Misdemeanor, Civil Actions Under $15,000, Small Claims.*

Civil Records: Access: Phone, fax, mail, in person. Both court and visitors may perform in person searches. No search fee. Required to search: name, years to search. Civil cases indexed by defendant, plaintiff. Civil records in books from the 1940s, on microfiche recent. Phone, fax and mail access limited to out of town requests.

Criminal Records: Access: Phone, fax, mail, in person. Both court and visitors may perform in person searches. No search fee. Required to search: name, years to search, DOB, SSN, signed release. Criminal records in books from the 1940s, on microfiche recent.

General Information: Public Access terminal is available. No expunged records released. SASE required. Turnaround time same day. Fax notes: $2.00 for first page, $.50 each add'l. Copy fee: $.10 per page. Certification fee: $1.00. Fee payee: County Court #4. Personal checks accepted. Prepayment is required.

County Court #5 72 N Broad St, Canfield, OH 44406; 330-533-3643; Fax: 330-740-2034. Hours: 8:30AM-4PM (EST). *Misdemeanor, Civil Actions Under $15,000, Small Claims.*

Civil Records: Access: Fax, mail, in person. Both court and visitors may perform in person searches. Search fee: $5.00 per name. Fee includes certification. Required to search: name, years to search; also helpful: address. Civil cases indexed by defendant, plaintiff. Civil records on computer since 1995; prior records in books from 1994.

Criminal Records: Access: Fax, mail, in person. Both court and visitors may perform in person searches. Search fee: $5.00 per name. Fee includes certification. Required to search: name, years to search; also helpful: DOB, SSN. Criminal records on computer since 1995; prior records in books from 1994.

General Information: Public Access terminal is available. No LEADS printout records released. SASE required. Turnaround time 1-2 days. Fax notes: $2.00 for first page, $1.00 each add'l. Copy fee: $.10 per page. Certification fee: $1.00. Fee payee: County Court #5. Only cashiers checks and money orders accepted. Prepayment is required.

Youngstown Municipal Court - Civil Records PO Box 6047, Youngstown, OH 44501-6047; 330-742-8863; Fax: 330-742-8786. Hours: 8AM-4PM (EST). *Civil Actions Under $15,000, Eviction, Small Claims.*

Civil Records: Access: Phone, fax, mail, in person. Both court and visitors may perform in person searches. No search fee. Required to search: name, years to search; also helpful: address. Civil cases indexed by defendant, plaintiff. Civil records in books since 1974; on computer since.

General Information: Public Access terminal is available. All records are public. SASE required. Turnaround time 1-2 days. Copy fee: $.10 per page. Certification fee: $1.00. Fee payee: Municipal Court. Personal checks accepted. Prepayment is required.

Youngstown Municipal Court - Criminal Records 26 S Phelps St, Youngstown, OH 44503; 330-742-8860; Fax: 330-742-8786. Hours: 8AM-4PM (EST). *Misdemeanor.*

Criminal Records: Access: Fax, mail, in person. Both court and visitors may perform in person searches. No search fee. Required to search: name, years to search, DOB; also helpful: SSN. Criminal records kept available since 1981 on docket books, microfiche; also on computer since.

General Information: No records released. SASE required. Turnaround time 1 day. Copy fee: $.10 per page. Certification fee: $1.00. Fee payee: Municipal Court. Only cashiers checks and money orders accepted. Prepayment is required.

Campbell Municipal Court 351 Tenney Ave, Campbell, OH 44405; 330-755-2165; Fax: 330-750-3058. Hours: 8AM-4PM (EST). *Misdemeanor, Civil Actions Under $15,000, Eviction, Small Claims.*

Civil Records: Access: Phone, fax, mail, in person. Only the court performs in person searches; visitors may not. No search fee. Required to search: name, years to search. Civil cases indexed by defendant, plaintiff. Civil records in books from 1950s. Mail & fax access limited to short searches.

Criminal Records: Access: Fax, mail, in person. Only the court performs in person searches; visitors may not. No search fee. Required to search: name, years to search; also helpful: DOB, SSN. Criminal records in books from 1950s.

General Information: No sealed records released. SASE required. Turnaround time depends on workload. Fax notes: Will fax results to police agencies only. Copy fee: $.50 per page. Certification fee: $10.00. Fee payee: Campbell Municipal Court. Only cashiers checks and money orders accepted. Prepayment is required.

Struthers Municipal Court 6 Elm St, Struthers, OH 44471; 330-755-1800; Fax: 330-755-2790. Hours: 8AM-4PM; Public access only on Tuesday and Thursday (EST). *Misdemeanor, Civil Actions Under $15,000, Eviction, Small Claims.*

Civil Records: Access: Mail, in person. Both court and visitors may perform in person searches. No search fee. Required to search: name, years to search. Civil cases indexed by defendant, plaintiff. Civil records in books last 20 years; on computer since 1996.

Criminal Records: Access: Mail, in person. Both court and visitors may perform in person searches. No search fee. Required to search: name, years to search; also helpful: SSN, DOB, signed release. Criminal records in books last 20 years; on computer since 1996.

General Information: Public Access terminal is available. (Terminal only available Tuesdays and Thursdays.) No pending case records released. SASE required. Turnaround time 2-3 days. No copy fee. Certification fee: $10.00. Fee payee: Municipal Court. Only cashiers checks and money orders accepted. Prepayment is required.

Marion County

Common Pleas Court 100 N Main St, Marion, OH 43301-1823; 740-387-8128; Probate phone: 740-387-7614; Fax: 740-383-1190. Hours: 8:30AM-4:30PM (EST). *Felony, Civil Actions Over $10,000.*

Civil Records: Access: Mail, in person. Both court and visitors may perform in person searches. No search fee. Required to search: name, years to search. Civil cases indexed by defendant, plaintiff. Civil records on computer from 1991, prior in books since 1886.

Criminal Records: Access: Mail, in person. Visitors must perform in person searches for themselves. No search fee. Required to search: name, years to search; also helpful: DOB, SSN. Criminal records on computer from 1991, prior in books since 1886.

General Information: Public Access terminal is available. No sealed, expunged records released. SASE required. Turnaround time 1-3 days. Fax notes: Fee to fax is $2.00 per transmission and $1.00 per page. Copy fee: $.25 per page. Certification fee: $1.00. Fee payee: Marion County Clerk of Courts. Personal checks accepted. Prepayment is required.

Marion Municipal Court 233 W Center St, Marion, OH 43302-0326; 740-387-2020; Fax: 740-382-5274. Hours: 8:30AM-4:30PM (EST). *Misdemeanor, Civil Actions Under $15,000, Eviction, Small Claims.*

Civil Records: Access: In person only. Visitors must perform in person searches for themselves. No search fee. Required to search: name, years to search. Civil cases indexed by defendant, plaintiff. Civil records on computer since 1995.

Criminal Records: Access: Mail, in person. Both court and visitors may perform in person searches. No search fee. Required to search: name, years to search; also helpful: DOB, SSN. Criminal records on computer from 1986, prior in books.

General Information: SASE required. Turnaround time 7 days. Copy fee: $.25 per page. Certification fee: $5.00. Fee payee: Municipal Court. Only cashiers checks and money orders accepted. Prepayment is required.

Medina County

Common Pleas Court 93 Public Square, Medina, OH 44256; 330-725-9720; Probate phone: 330-725-9703. Hours: 8AM-4:30PM (EST). *Felony, Civil Actions Over $10,000, Probate.*

Civil Records: Access: Mail, in person. No search fee. Required to search: name, years to search. Civil cases indexed by defendant, plaintiff. Civil records on computer from 10/92, in books to early 1960s, prior archived.

Criminal Records: Access: Mail, in person. Both court and visitors may perform in person searches. No search fee. Required to search: name, years to search. Criminal records on computer from 10/92, in books to early 1960s, prior archived.

General Information: Public Access terminal is available. SASE required. Turnaround time 1-2 days. Copy fee: $.25 per page. Certification fee: $1.00. Fee payee: Clerk of Court. Personal checks accepted. Prepayment is required.

Medina Municipal Court 135 N Elmwood, Medina, OH 44256; 330-723-3287; Fax: 330-225-1108. Hours: 8AM-4:30PM (EST). *Misdemeanor, Civil Actions Under $15,000, Eviction, Small Claims.*

www.medinamunicipalcourt.org

Civil Records: Access: Mail, online, in person. Both court and visitors may perform in person searches. No search fee. Required to search: name, years to search. Civil cases indexed by defendant, plaintiff. Civil records on computer from 1986, prior in books. Access to the online system requires Procomm Plus. There are no fees. Search by either name or case number. The computer access number is 330-723-4337. For more information, call Rich Armstrong at ext. 230.

Criminal Records: Access: Mail, online, in person. Visitors must perform in person searches for themselves. No search fee. Required to search: name, years to search; also helpful: address, DOB, SSN. Criminal records on computer from 1986, prior in books. Online access to criminal records is the same as civil.

General Information: Public Access terminal is available. No expunged records released. SASE required. Copy fee: $.50 per page. Certification fee: $1.50. Fee payee: Municipal Court. Personal checks accepted. Credit cards accepted: Visa, MasterCard for criminal and traffic records only.

Wadsworth Municipal Court 120 Maple St, Wadsworth, OH 44281-1825; 330-335-1596; Fax: 330-335-2723. Hours: 8AM-4PM (EST). *Misdemeanor, Civil Actions Under $15,000, Eviction, Small Claims.*

Civil Records: Access: Fax, mail, in person. Both court and visitors may perform in person searches. No search fee. Required to search: name, years to search. Civil cases indexed by defendant, plaintiff. Civil records on computer from 3/90, prior in books.

Criminal Records: Access: Fax, mail, in person. Both court and visitors may perform in person searches. No search fee. Required to search: name, years to search; also helpful: address, DOB, SSN. Criminal records on computer from 3/90, prior in books.

General Information: Public Access terminal is available. No search warrant records released. SASE required. Turnaround time to 1 week. Fax notes: No fee to fax results. Local faxing only. Copy fee: $.25 per page. Certification fee: $1.00. Fee payee: Wadsworth Municipal Court. Personal checks accepted. Prepayment is required.

Meigs County

Common Pleas Court PO Box 151, Pomeroy, OH 45769; 740-992-5290; Probate phone: 740-992-3096; Fax: 740-992-4429. Hours: 8:30AM-4:30PM (EST). *Felony, Civil Actions Over $3,000, Probate.*

Note: Probate fax is 740-992-6727.

Civil Records: Access: In person only. Visitors must perform in person searches for themselves. No search fee. Required to search: name, years to search; also helpful: address. Civil cases indexed by defendant, plaintiff. Civil records on computer since 1996, in books to 1800s.

Criminal Records: Access: In person only. Visitors must perform in person searches for themselves. No search fee. Required to search: name, years to search, DOB; also helpful: address, SSN. Criminal records on computer since 1996, in books to 1800s.

General Information: Public Access terminal is available. No secret records released. Copy fee: $.25 per page. Certification fee: $1.00. Fee payee: Clerk of Court. Personal checks accepted. Prepayment is required.

Meigs County Court 2ns Street Courthouse, Pomeroy, OH 45769; 740-992-2279; Fax: 740-992-4570. Hours: 8:30AM-4:30PM (EST). *Misdemeanor, Civil Actions Under $15,000, Small Claims.*

Civil Records: Access: In person only. Visitors must perform in person searches for themselves. No search fee. Required to search: name, years to search. Civil cases indexed by defendant, plaintiff. Civil records on computer from 8/90, prior in docket books. Phone access limited to records from 1990 to present.

Criminal Records: Access: In person only. Visitors must perform in person searches for themselves. No search fee. Required to search: name, years to search, DOB, SSN, signed release. Criminal records on computer from 8/90, prior in docket books. Same as civil.

General Information: No sealed records released. Copy fee: $.10 per page. Certification fee: $2.00. Fee payee: Meigs County Court. Personal checks accepted. Out of state checks not accepted.

Mercer County

Common Pleas Court 101 N Main St, Rm 205, PO Box 28, Celina, OH 45822; 419-586-6461; Probate phone: 419-586-2418; Fax: 419-586-5826. Hours: 8:30AM-4PM (EST). *Felony, Civil Actions Over $10,000, Probate.*

Civil Records: Access: In person only. Visitors must perform in person searches for themselves. No search fee. Required to search: name, years to search; also helpful: address. Civil cases indexed by defendant, plaintiff. Civil records on computer back to 1997, microfiche up to and including 1985, prior in books.

Criminal Records: Access: In person only. Visitors must perform in person searches for themselves. No search fee. Required to search: name, years to search; also helpful: address, DOB, SSN. Criminal records on computer back to 1997, microfiche up to and including 1985, prior in books.

General Information: Public Access terminal is available. No juvenile or sealed records released. Copy fee: $.25 per page. Certification fee: $1.00. Fee payee: Clerk of Court. Personal checks accepted. Prepayment is required.

Celina Municipal Court PO Box 362, Celina, OH 45822; 419-586-6491; Fax: 419-586-4735. Hours: 8AM-5PM (EST). *Misdemeanor, Civil Actions Under $15,000, Eviction, Small Claims.*

Civil Records: Access: Phone, fax, mail, in person. Both court and visitors may perform in person searches. No search fee. Required to search: name, years to search; also helpful: address. Civil cases indexed by defendant, plaintiff. Civil records on computer from 1990, prior in books.

Criminal Records: Access: Phone, fax, mail, in person. Both court and visitors may perform in person searches. No search fee. Required to search: name, years to search; also helpful: address, DOB, SSN. Criminal records are on computer since 1989, prior found in books and files.

General Information: Public Access terminal is available. No confidential information released. SASE required. Turnaround time 2-3 days. Copy fee: $.05 per page. Certification fee: $1.00. Fee payee: Municipal Court. Personal checks accepted. Prepayment is required.

Miami County

Common Pleas Court & Court of Appeals Safety Bldg, 201 West Main St, 3rd Flr, Troy, OH 45373; 937-332-6855; Probate phone: 937-332-6832; Fax: 937-332-7069. Hours: 8AM-4PM (EST). *Felony, Civil Actions Over $10,000, Probate.*

Note: Probate is a separate division at the phone number given above.

Civil Records: Access: Fax, mail, in person. Both court and visitors may perform in person searches. Search fee: $5.00 per name. Required to search: name, years to search; also helpful: address. Civil cases indexed by defendant, plaintiff. Civil records in books for past 30 years, prior are archived; on computer since 1984.

Criminal Records: Access: Fax, mail, in person. Both court and visitors may perform in person searches. Search fee: $5.00 per name. Required to search: name, years to search, DOB, SSN; also helpful: address. Criminal records in books for past 30 years, prior are archived; on computer since 1984.

General Information: Public Access terminal is available. No expunged or sealed records released. Turnaround time 1-2 days. Fax notes: $1.00 per document. Copy fee: $.25 per page. Certification fee: $1.00. Fee payee: Miami County Clerk of Courts. Personal checks accepted. Prepayment is required.

Miami County Municipal Court 201 West Main St, Troy, OH 45373; 937-332-6920; Fax: 937-332-6932. Hours: 8AM-4PM (EST). *Misdemeanor, Civil Actions Under $15,000, Eviction, Small Claims.*

Note: If the SSN is not provided by the party doing the search, the court personnel will mask the SSN before providing copies.

Civil Records: Access: Mail, in person. Both court and visitors may perform in person searches. Search fee: $5.00 per name. Required to search: name, years to search. Civil cases indexed by defendant, plaintiff. Civil records on computer from 12/89, prior in books.

Criminal Records: Access: Mail, in person. Both court and visitors may perform in person searches. Search fee: $5.00 per name. Required to search: name, years to search; also helpful: SSN. Criminal records on computer since 1986, prior in books.

General Information: Public Access terminal is available. No search warrant records released. SASE required. Turnaround time 2-3 days. Fax notes: Fee to fax result is $1.00 per document. Copy fee: $1.00 per page. Certification fee: $2.00. Fee payee: Municipal Court. Credit cards accepted: Visa, MasterCard. Prepayment is required.

Monroe County

Common Pleas Court 101 N Main St Rm 26, Woodsfield, OH 43793; 740-472-0761; Probate phone: 740-472-1654; Fax: 740-472-2518/2549. 8:30AM-4:30PM *Felony, Civil Actions Over $3,000, Probate.*

Civil Records: Access: In person only. Visitors must perform in person searches for themselves. No search fee. Required to search: name, years to search; also helpful: address. Civil cases indexed by defendant, plaintiff. Civil records in books since 1851.

Criminal Records: Access: Mail, fax, in person. Both court and visitors may perform in person searches. Search fee: $2.00 per name. Will only search one name at a time. Required to search: name, years to search; also helpful: address, DOB, SSN. Criminal records in books since 1851. The court will not do party names searches for in-person requesters.

General Information: No secret indictment records released. SASE required. Turnaround time 3 days. Fax notes: Fee to fax results is $2.00 per page. Copy fee: $.25 per page. Certification fee: $1.00. Fee payee: Clerk of Court. Personal checks accepted. Prepayment is required.

County Court 101 N Main St, Rm 35, Woodsfield, OH 43793; 740-472-5181. Hours: 9AM-4:30PM (EST). *Misdemeanor, Civil Actions Under $15,000, Small Claims.*

Civil Records: Access: Phone, mail, in person. Both court and visitors may perform in person searches. No search fee. Required to search: name, years to search. Civil cases indexed by defendant, plaintiff. Civil records in books, indexed back to 1950; on computer back to 8/1999.

Criminal Records: Access: Phone, mail, in person. Both court and visitors may perform in person searches. No search fee. Required to search: name, years to search. Criminal records in books, indexed back to 1950; on computer back to 1999.

General Information: SASE required. Turnaround time 1-2 days. No copy fee. Certification fee: No cert fee. Personal checks accepted.

Montgomery County

Common Pleas Court 41 N Perry St, Dayton, OH 45422; 937-225-4512; Criminal phone: 937-225-4536; Probate phone: 937-225-4640; Fax: 937-496-7389/7220. Hours: 8:30AM-4:30PM (EST). *Felony, Civil Actions Over $10,000, Probate.*

www.clerk.co.montgomery.oh.us

Civil Records: Access: Fax, mail, in person, online. Both court and visitors may perform in person searches. No search fee. Required to search: name, years to search; also helpful: address. Civil cases indexed by defendant, plaintiff. Civil records on computer from 1970s, prior in books. Online access to the Courts county-wide PRO system is available free at www.clerk.co.montgomery.oh.us/pro/index.cfm. Address mail requests to Montgomery County Clerk of Court "Civil Records."

Criminal Records: Access: In person, online. Visitors must perform in person searches for themselves. No search fee. Required to search: name, years to search; also helpful: address, DOB, SSN. Criminal records on computer from 1970s, prior in books. Online access to criminal and traffic records is the same as civil.

General Information: Public Access terminal is available. No sealed records released. SASE required. Turnaround time 1 week. Copy fee: $.10 per page. Certification fee: $1.00 per page. Fee payee: Clerk of Court. Personal checks accepted. Credit cards accepted: Visa, MasterCard. Prepayment is required.

County Court - Area 1 195 S Clayton Rd, New Lebanon, OH 45345-9601; 937-687-9099; Fax: 937-687-7119. Hours: Noon-7PM M,W; 8AM-4PM T,Th,F (EST). *Misdemeanor, Civil Actions Under $15,000, Small Claims.*

http://areacourts.dnaco.net

Civil Records: Access: Mail, in person, online. Both court and visitors may perform in person searches. No search fee. Required to search: name, years to search. Civil cases indexed by defendant, plaintiff. Civil records on computer from 2/92, prior in books, Archives 937-225-6366. Search county-wide records online at www.clerk.co.montgomery.oh.us/clerk/pro/index.cfm. Also, online access to area civil and traffic records is available free at http://areacourts.dnaco.net/areaone. Click on "Public records online.".

Criminal Records: Access: Mail, in person, online. Both court and visitors may perform in person searches. No search fee. Required to search: name, years to search; also helpful: SSN. Criminal records on computer from 2/92, prior in books, Archives 937-225-6366. Online access to criminal records is the same as civil.

General Information: Public Access terminal is available. No medical, PSI report or LEADS print-out records released. SASE required. Turnaround time 2-3 days. Copy fee: $.75 per page. Certification fee: $1.00.

Fee payee: First District Court, Montgomery County. Only cashiers checks and money orders accepted. Prepayment is required.

County Court - Area 2 6111 Taylorsville Rd, Huber Heights, OH 45424; 937-496-7231; Fax: 937-496-7236. Hours: 8AM-4PM M & F; 8AM-3PM W; Noon-7PM T-Th (EST). *Misdemeanor, Civil Actions Under $15,000, Small Claims.*

http://areacourts.dnaco.net

Civil Records: Access: Phone, fax, mail, in person, online, e-mail. Both court and visitors may perform in person searches. No search fee. Required to search: name, years to search; also helpful: address. Civil cases indexed by defendant, plaintiff. Civil records on computer from 1992, prior in books back to 1974. Search county-wide records online at www.clerk.co.montgomery.oh.us/clerk/pro/index.cfm. Also, online access to area civil and traffic records is available free at http://areacourts.dnaco.net/areatwo/. Click on "Public records online.".

Criminal Records: Access: Phone, fax, mail, in person, online, e-mail. Both court and visitors may perform in person searches. No search fee. Required to search: name, years to search; also helpful: address, DOB, SSN. Criminal records on computer from 1992, prior in books back to 1974. Online access to criminal records is the same as civil.

General Information: Public Access terminal is available. No confidential, forensic evaluation or medical records released. SASE required. Turnaround time 2-7 days. Fax notes: No fee to fax results. Copy fee: $.25 per page. Certification fee: $1.00. Fee is for civil only. No fee for criminal. Fee payee: Second District Court. Business checks accepted. Prepayment is required.

Dayton Municipal Court - Civil Division 301 W 3rd St, PO Box 968, Dayton, OH 45402-0968; 937-333-4471; Fax: 937-333-4468. Hours: 8AM-4:30PM (EST). *Civil Actions Under $15,000, Eviction, Small Claims.*

Civil Records: Access: Phone, mail, in person. Both court and visitors may perform in person searches. No search fee. Required to search: name, years to search; also helpful: address. Civil cases indexed by defendant, plaintiff. Civil records on computer from 1990, prior in books to 1971.

General Information: Public Access terminal is available. No expunged case records released. SASE required. Turnaround time 2-3 days. Copy fee: $.25 per page. Certification fee: No cert fee. Fee payee: Clerk of Court. Personal checks accepted. Prepayment is required.

Dayton Municipal Court - Criminal Division 301 W 3rd St, Rm 331, Dayton, OH 45402; 937-333-4315; Fax: 937-333-4490. Hours: 8AM-4:30PM (EST). *Misdemeanor.*

Criminal Records: Access: In person only. Visitors must perform in person searches for themselves. No search fee. Required to search: name, years to search, DOB; also helpful: address, SSN, signed release. Criminal records on computer from 1992, prior in books. Phone access limited.

General Information: Public Access terminal is available. All records are public. SASE required. Copy fee: $.25 per page. Certification fee: No cert fee. Fee payee: Dayton Municipal Court. Personal checks accepted. Credit cards accepted: Visa, MasterCard. Prepayment is required.

Dayton Municipal Court - Traffic Division 301 W 3rd St, PO Box 968, Dayton, OH 45402; 937-333-4313; Fax: 937-333-7558. Hours: 8AM-4:30PM (EST). *Misdemeanor.*

www.cityofdayton.org/courts

Note: Difficult to provide case information prior to 1995

Criminal Records: Access: Phone, mail, in person. Both court and visitors may perform in person searches. No search fee. Required to search: name, years to search; also helpful: address, DOB, SSN. Criminal records on index books.

General Information: SASE required. Turnaround time 1 week. Copy fee: $.25 per page. Certification fee: No cert fee. Fee payee: Municipal Court. Personal checks accepted. Prepayment is required.

Kettering Municipal Court 3600 Shroyer Rd, Kettering, OH 45429; 937-296-2461; Fax: 937-296-3284 for Judge's office only. Hours: 8:30AM-4:30PM (EST). *Misdemeanor, Civil Actions Under $15,000, Eviction, Small Claims.*

www.ketteringcourt.org

Civil Records: Access: Phone, mail, in person. Both court and visitors may perform in person searches. No search fee. Required to search: name, years to search. Civil cases indexed by defendant, plaintiff. Civil records on computer from 1989, prior in books.

Criminal Records: Access: Phone, mail, in person. Both court and visitors may perform in person searches. No search fee. Required to search: name, years to search, DOB; also helpful: SSN. Criminal records on computer from 1988.

General Information: No expungment records released. SASE required. Turnaround time 1-5 days. Copy fee: $.05 per page. Certification fee: $2.50 per page. Fee payee: Kettering Municipal Court. Business checks accepted. Attorney's check accepted. Credit cards accepted: Visa, MasterCard. Prepayment is required.

Miamisburg Municipal Court 10 N First St, Miamisburg, OH 45342; 937-866-2203; Fax: 937-866-0135. Hours: 8AM-4PM (EST). *Misdemeanor, Civil Actions Under $15,000, Eviction, Small Claims.*

Civil Records: Access: Mail, in person. Both court and visitors may perform in person searches. No search fee. Required to search: name, years to search; also helpful: address. Civil cases indexed by defendant, plaintiff. Civil records on computer from 1988, prior in books.

Criminal Records: Access: Mail, in person. Both court and visitors may perform in person searches. No search fee. Required to search: name, years to search; also helpful: address, DOB, SSN. Criminal records on computer from 1988, prior in books.

General Information: No police reports, search warrants with no returns records released. SASE required. Turnaround time 1-2 weeks. Copy fee: $.25 per page. Certification fee: No cert fee. Fee payee: Clerk of Court. Personal checks accepted. Prepayment is required.

Oakwood Municipal Court 30 Park Ave, Dayton, OH 45419; 937-293-3058. Hours: 8:30AM-4PM (EST). *Misdemeanor, Civil Actions Under $15,000, Eviction, Small Claims.*

Civil Records: Access: Mail, in person. Only the court performs in person searches; visitors may not. No search fee. Required to search: name, years to search; also helpful: address. Civil cases indexed by defendant, plaintiff. Civil records in books since 1976.

Criminal Records: Access: Mail, in person. Only the court performs in person searches; visitors may not. No search fee. Required to search: name, years to search; also helpful: address, DOB, SSN. Criminal records in books since 1976. Address mail search requests to the Police Records Section.

General Information: No sealed, expunged or confidential records released. SASE required. Turnaround time 1-2 weeks. Copy fee: $.25 per page. Certification fee: $1.00. Fee payee: City of Oakwood.

Personal checks accepted. Local checks accepted. Prepayment is required.

Vandalia Municipal Court PO Box 429, Justice Center, 2nd Floor, Vandalia, OH 45377; 937-898-3996; Fax: 937-898-6648. Hours: 8AM-4PM *Misdemeanor, Civil Actions Under $15,000, Eviction, Small Claims.*

Civil Records: Access: Phone, fax, mail, in person. Both court and visitors may perform in person searches. No search fee. Required to search: name, years to search. Civil cases indexed by defendant, plaintiff. Civil records on computer from 1986, prior in books.

Criminal Records: Access: Phone, fax, mail, in person. Both court and visitors may perform in person searches. No search fee. Required to search: name, years to search, DOB, SSN. Criminal records on computer from 1986, prior in books.

General Information: Public Access terminal is available. No medical, psychological reports or domestic violence report records released. SASE required. Copy fee: $1.00 per page. Certification fee: No cert fee. Fee payee: Clerk of Court. Business checks accepted. Credit cards accepted. Prepayment is required.

Morgan County

Common Pleas Court 19 E Main St, McConnelsville, OH 43756; 740-962-4752, 740-962-3371 (clerk); Probate phone: 740-962-2861; Fax: 740-962-4589. Hours: 8AM-4PM M-Th; 8AM-5PM F (EST). *Felony, Civil Actions Over $3,000, Probate.*

Civil Records: Access: Mail, in person. Visitors must perform in person searches for themselves. Search fee: $2.00 per name. Required to search: name, years to search; also helpful: address. Civil cases indexed by defendant, plaintiff. Civil records in books, some back to 1850.

Criminal Records: Access: Mail, in person. Both court and visitors may perform in person searches. Search fee: $2.00 per name. Required to search: name, years to search; also helpful: address, DOB, SSN. Criminal records in books, some back to 1850.

General Information: No secret indictment records released. SASE required. Turnaround time 1-3 days. No copy fee. Certification fee: $1.00 per page. Fee payee: Clerk of Court. Personal checks accepted. Prepayment is required.

Morgan County Court 37 E Main St, McConnelsville, OH 43756; 740-962-4031; Fax: 740-962-2895. Hours: 8AM-4PM (EST). *Misdemeanor, Civil Actions Under $15,000, Small Claims.*

Civil Records: Access: Phone, fax, mail, in person. Both court and visitors may perform in person searches. No search fee. Required to search: name, years to search. Civil cases indexed by defendant, plaintiff. Civil records in books from 1958.

Criminal Records: Access: Phone, fax, mail, in person. Both court and visitors may perform in person searches. No search fee. Required to search: name, years to search, DOB; also helpful: SSN. Criminal records in books from 1958.

General Information: SASE required. Turnaround time 1-2 days. Fax notes: No fee to fax results. Copy fee: $.25 per page. Certification fee: $1.00. Fee payee: Morgan County Court. Personal checks accepted. Prepayment is required.

Morrow County

Common Pleas Court 48 E High St, Mount Gilead, OH 43338; 419-947-2085; Probate phone: 419-947-5575; Fax: 419-947-5421. Hours: 8AM-4PM (EST). *Felony, Civil Actions Over $3,000, Probate.*

Civil Records: Access: Phone, fax, mail, in person. Both court and visitors may perform in person searches. No search fee. Required to search: name, years to

search; also helpful: address. Civil cases indexed by defendant, plaintiff. Civil records in books from 1960.

Criminal Records: Access: Phone, fax, mail, in person. Both court and visitors may perform in person searches. No search fee. Required to search: name, years to search; also helpful: address, DOB, SSN. Criminal records in books from 1960.

General Information: SASE required. Turnaround time 1 day. Copy fee: $1.00 per page. Certification fee: $1.00. Fee payee: Clerk of Court. Personal checks accepted. Prepayment is required.

County Court 48 E High St, Mount Gilead, OH 43338; 419-947-5045; Fax: 419-947-1860. Hours: 7:30AM-5PM (EST). *Misdemeanor, Civil Actions Under $15,000, Small Claims.*

Civil Records: Access: Mail, in person. Both court and visitors may perform in person searches. No search fee. Required to search: name, years to search; also helpful-DOB or SSN. Civil cases indexed by defendant, plaintiff. Civil records on computer back to 1997, indexed on books from 1970s, archived from 1800s.

Criminal Records: Access: Mail, in person. Both court and visitors may perform in person searches. No search fee. Required to search: name, years to search, DOB or SSN. Criminal records on computer since 1987, indexed on books from 1970s, archived from 1800s.

General Information: No confidential records released. Turnaround time 1-2 days. No copy fee. Certification fee: No cert fee.

Muskingum County

Common Pleas Court 401 Main St, Zanesville, OH 43701; 740-455-7104; Probate phone: 740-455-7113. Hours: 8:30AM-4:30PM (EST). *Felony, Civil Actions, Probate.*

Note: As of 1/1/2001, there is no dollar limit on civil actions; prior, the civil action minimum was $15,000.

Civil Records: Access: Mail, in person. Both court and visitors may perform in person searches. No search fee. Required to search: name, years to search; also helpful: address. Civil cases indexed by defendant, plaintiff. Civil records in original files back to 1800s.

Criminal Records: Access: Mail, in person. Both court and visitors may perform in person searches. No search fee. Required to search: name, years to search, DOB; also helpful: address, SSN. Criminal records on docket books to 1960, original files back to 1800s.

General Information: Public Access terminal is available. No grand jury records released. SASE required. Turnaround time 2 weeks. Copy fee: $.25 per page. Certification fee: $1.00 per page. Fee payee: Clerk of Court. Personal checks accepted. Prepayment is required.

County Court 27 N 5th St, Zanesville, OH 43701; 740-455-7138; Fax: 740-455-7157. Hours: 8:30AM-4PM (EST). *Misdemeanor, Civil Actions Under $15,000, Small Claims.*

Civil Records: Access: Fax, mail, in person. Both court and visitors may perform in person searches. No search fee. Required to search: name, years to search; also helpful: address. Civil cases indexed by defendant, plaintiff. Civil records in books from 1958; on computer back to 1995.

Criminal Records: Access: Fax, mail, in person. Both court and visitors may perform in person searches. No search fee. Required to search: name, years to search, DOB; also helpful: address, SSN. Criminal records in books from 1958; on computer back to 1995.

General Information: Public Access terminal is available. No expunged records released. SASE required. Turnaround time up to 1 week. Fax notes: No fee to fax results. Fax available in emergency only. Copy fee: There is a $1.00 fee for certified copies, but no fee for uncertified. Certification fee: $1.00. Fee payee: Muskingum County Clerk. Personal checks accepted.

Zanesville Municipal Court

PO Box 566, Zanesville, OH 43702; 740-454-3269; Fax: 740-455-0739. Hours: 9AM-4:30PM (EST). *Misdemeanor, Civil Actions Under $15,000, Eviction, Small Claims.*

Civil Records: Access: Mail, in person. Both court and visitors may perform in person searches. No search fee. Required to search: name, years to search; also helpful: address. Civil cases indexed by defendant, plaintiff. Civil records on computer since 1987.

Criminal Records: Access: Mail, in person. Both court and visitors may perform in person searches. No search fee. Required to search: name, years to search; also helpful: address, DOB, SSN. Criminal records on computer since 1993.

General Information: Public Access terminal is available. SASE required. Turnaround time 1 week. Copy fee: $1.00 per page. Certification fee: $1.00. Fee payee: Municipal Court. Personal checks accepted. Prepayment is required.

Noble County

Common Pleas Court

350 Courthouse, Caldwell, OH 43724; 740-732-4408; Probate phone: 740-732-5047; Fax: 740-732-5702. Hours: 8-11:30AM,12:30-4PM M-W; 8-Midnight Th; 8-11:30AM, 12:30-6PM F (EST). *Felony, Civil Actions Over $3,000, Probate.*

Note: Probate office is separate from this court.

Civil Records: Access: Phone, fax, mail, in person. Both court and visitors may perform in person searches. No search fee. Required to search: name, years to search; also helpful: address. Civil cases indexed by defendant, plaintiff. Civil records in books, archived back to 1800s. Recent civil records are computerized.

Criminal Records: Access: Phone, fax, mail, in person. Both court and visitors may perform in person searches. Required to search: name, years to search; also helpful: address, DOB, SSN. Criminal records in books, archived back to 1800s. Recent civil records are computerized.

General Information: No sealed records released. SASE required. Turnaround time 1-2 days. Fax notes: No fee to fax results. Copy fee: $.50 per page. Certification fee: $1.00. Fee payee: Clerk of Court. Personal checks accepted. Will bill all court rule copies.

Noble County Court

100 Courthouse, Caldwell, OH 43724; 740-732-5795; Fax: 740-732-1435. Hours: 8:30AM-4PM M-W,F; 8:30-11:30AM Th (EST). *Misdemeanor, Civil Actions Under $15,000, Small Claims.*

Civil Records: Access: Phone, fax, mail, in person. No search fee. Required to search: name, years to search. Civil cases indexed by defendant, plaintiff. Civil records in books since 1960.

Criminal Records: Access: Fax, mail, in person. Both court and visitors may perform in person searches. No search fee. Required to search: name, years to search, DOB; also helpful- SSN, signed release. Criminal records in books since 1960.

General Information: SASE required. Turnaround time up to 1 week. Copy fee: $.50 per page. Certification fee: $5.00. Fee payee: County Court. Only cashiers checks and money orders accepted. Prepayment is required.

Ottawa County

Common Pleas Court

315 Madison St, 3rd Fl, Port Clinton, OH 43452; 419-734-6755 (General Division); Probate phone: 419-734-6830. Hours: 8:30AM-4:30PM (EST). *Felony, Civil Actions Over $10,000, Probate.*

www.ottawacocpcourt.com

Note: Probate is a separate court at 315 Madison St.

Civil Records: Access: In person only. Visitors must perform in person searches for themselves. No search fee. Required to search: name, years to search; also helpful: address. Civil cases indexed by defendant, plaintiff. Civil records on computer from 8/89, prior in books.

Criminal Records: Access: In person only. Visitors must perform in person searches for themselves. No search fee. Required to search: name, years to search; also helpful: address, DOB, SSN. Criminal records on computer from 8/89, prior in books.

General Information: Public Access terminal is available. No sealed records released. Copy fee: $1.00 per page. Certification fee: $1.00. Fee payee: Clerk of Courts. Personal checks accepted. Prepayment is required.

Ottawa County Municipal Court

1860 East Perry St, Port Clinton, OH 43452; 419-734-4143; Fax: 419-732-2862. Hours: 8:30AM-4:30PM (EST). *Misdemeanor, Civil Actions Under $15,000, Eviction, Small Claims.*

Civil Records: Access: In person only. Visitors must perform in person searches for themselves. No search fee. Required to search: name, years to search; also helpful: address. Civil cases indexed by defendant, plaintiff. Civil records on computer from 1989, prior in books.

Criminal Records: Access: In person only. Visitors must perform in person searches for themselves. No search fee. Required to search: name, years to search, DOB; also helpful: address, SSN. Criminal records on computer from 1989, prior in books.

General Information: Public Access terminal is available. No sealed records released. Copy fee: $.25 per page. Certification fee: $3.00. Fee payee: Municipal Court. Only cashiers checks and money orders accepted. Prepayment is required.

Paulding County

Common Pleas Court

115 N Williams St Rm 104, Paulding, OH 45879; 419-399-8210; Probate phone: 419-339-8256; Fax: 419-399-8248. Hours: 8AM-4PM (EST). *Felony, Civil Actions Over $3,000, Probate.*

Civil Records: Access: Fax, mail, in person. Both court and visitors may perform in person searches. Search fee: $5.00 per name. Required to search: name, years to search. Civil cases indexed by defendant, plaintiff. Civil records in books, archived from 1800s.

Criminal Records: Access: Fax, mail, in person. Both court and visitors may perform in person searches. Search fee: $5.00 per name. Required to search: name, years to search; also helpful: address, DOB, SSN. Criminal records in books, archived from 1800s.

General Information: No mental, adoption records released. SASE required. Turnaround time same day. Fax notes: No fee to fax results. Copy fee: $.25 per page. Certification fee: $1.00. Fee payee: Clerk of Court. Personal checks accepted. Prepayment is required.

County Court

201 E Carolina St, Suite 2, Paulding, OH 45879; 419-399-5370; Fax: 419-399-3421. Hours: 8AM-4PM (EST). *Misdemeanor, Civil Actions Under $15,000, Small Claims.*

Civil Records: Access: Fax, mail, in person. Both court and visitors may perform in person searches. Search fee: $5.00 per name. Required to search: name, years to search; also helpful: address. Civil cases indexed by defendant, plaintiff. Civil records in books since 1985.

Criminal Records: Access: Fax, mail, in person. Both court and visitors may perform in person searches. Search fee: $5.00 per name. Required to search: name, years to search; also helpful: address, DOB, SSN. Criminal records in books since 1985.

General Information: SASE required. Turnaround time 2-4 days. Fax notes: No fee to fax results. Copy fee: $.50 per page. Certification fee: $2.00. Fee payee: County Court. Personal checks accepted. Prepayment is required.

Perry County

Common Pleas Court

PO Box 67, New Lexington, OH 43764; 740-342-1022; Probate phone: 740-342-1493. Hours: 8AM-4PM (EST). *Felony, Civil Actions Over $3,000, Probate.*

Civil Records: Access: In person only. Visitors must perform in person searches for themselves. No search fee. Required to search: name, years to search; also helpful: address. Civil cases indexed by defendant, plaintiff. Civil records on computer since 3/96, in case files prior, indexed from 1940.

Criminal Records: Access: In person only. Visitors must perform in person searches for themselves. No search fee. Required to search: name, years to search; also helpful: address, DOB, SSN. Criminal records on computer since 3/96, in case files prior, indexed from 1940.

General Information: Public Access terminal is available. Copy fee: $1.00 per page. Certification fee: All copies with fee paid are considered certified. Fee payee: Clerk of Court. Personal checks accepted. Prepayment is required.

Perry County Court

PO Box 207, New Lexington, OH 43764-0207; 740-342-3156; Fax: 740-342-2189. Hours: 8:30AM-4:30PM M,W,F (EST). *Misdemeanor, Civil Actions Under $15,000, Small Claims.*

Civil Records: Access: In person only. Visitors must perform in person searches for themselves. No search fee. Required to search: name, years to search. Civil cases indexed by defendant, plaintiff. Civil records in books 10 to 12 years, computerized since 04/97.

Criminal Records: Access: In person only. Visitors must perform in person searches for themselves. No search fee. Required to search: name, years to search, DOB, SSN, signed release. Criminal records in books 10 to 12 years, computerized since 04/97.

General Information: Public Access terminal is available. All records are public. Copy fee: $.10 per page. Certification fee: $1.00. Fee payee: Perry County Court. Personal checks accepted. Prepayment required.

Pickaway County

Common Pleas Court

County Courthouse, 207 Court Street PO Box 270, Circleville, OH 43113; 740-474-5231; Probate phone: 740-474-3950. Hours: 8AM-4PM *Felony, Civil Actions Over $10,000, Probate.*

Civil Records: Access: Mail, in person. Both court and visitors may perform in person searches. No search fee. Required to search: name, years to search; also helpful: address. Civil cases indexed by defendant. Civil records on computer back to 1988, indexed to 1940s, archived from 1800s.

Criminal Records: Access: Mail, in person. Both court and visitors may perform in person searches. No search fee. Required to search: name, years to search; also helpful: address, DOB, SSN. Criminal records on computer back to 1988, indexed to 1940s, archived from 1800s.

General Information: Public Access terminal is available. SASE required. Turnaround time 2-3 days. Copy fee: $.25 per page. Certification fee: $1.00 per page. Fee payee: Clerk of Court. Prepayment required.

Circleville Municipal Court

PO Box 128, Circleville, OH 43113; 740-474-3171; Fax: 740-477-8291. Hours: 8AM-4PM (EST). *Misdemeanor, Civil Actions Under $15,000, Eviction, Small Claims.*

Civil Records: Access: Phone, fax, mail, in person. Both court and visitors may perform in person searches.

No search fee. Required to search: name, years to search. Civil cases indexed by defendant, plaintiff. Civil records on computer from 1989, prior in books.

Criminal Records: Access: Phone, fax, mail, in person. Both court and visitors may perform in person searches. No search fee. Required to search: name, years to search; also helpful: SSN. Criminal records on computer from 1989, prior in books.

General Information: Public Access terminal is available. No warrant records released. SASE required. Turnaround time 1-2 days. Copy fee: \$.50 per page. Certification fee: No cert fee. Fee payee: Circleville Municipal Court. Personal checks accepted. Credit cards accepted: Visa, MasterCard. Prepayment is required.

Pike County

Common Pleas Court 100 East 2nd St, Waverly, OH 45690; 740-947-2715; Probate phone: 740-947-2560; Fax: 740-947-1729. Hours: 8:30AM-4PM (EST). *Felony, Civil Actions Over \$15,000, Probate.*

Note: Probate is a separate court at the number given.

Civil Records: Access: Mail, in person. Visitors must perform in person searches for themselves. No search fee. Required to search: name, years to search; also helpful: address. Civil cases indexed by defendant, plaintiff. Civil records in books going back to 1815.

Criminal Records: Access: Main, in person. Visitors must perform in person searches for themselves. No search fee. Required to search: name, years to search; also helpful: address, DOB, SSN. Criminal records in books going back to 1815.

General Information: No grand jury secret indictment records released. SASE is required. Copy fee: \$.25 per page. Certification fee: \$1.00. Fee payee: Clerk of Court. Personal checks accepted. Prepayment is required.

Pike County Court 106 N Market St, Waverly, OH 45690; Criminal phone: 740-947-4003. Hours: 8:30AM-4PM (EST). *Misdemeanor, Civil Actions Under \$15,000, Small Claims.*

Civil Records: Access: Phone, fax, mail, in person. Both court and visitors may perform in person searches. No search fee. Required to search: name, years to search. Civil cases indexed by defendant, plaintiff. Civil records in books indexed to 1958 1960.

Criminal Records: Access: Phone, fax, mail, in person. Both court and visitors may perform in person searches. No search fee. Required to search: name, years to search. Criminal records in books indexed to 1958 1960.

General Information: Public Access terminal is available. No sealed or expunged records released. SASE required. Turnaround time 1 week. Copy fee: \$1.00 per page. Certification fee: No cert fee. Fee payee: Pike County Court. Personal checks accepted. Prepayment is required.

Portage County

Common Pleas Court PO Box 1035, Ravenna, OH 44266; 330-297-3644; Probate phone: 330-297-3870; Fax: 330-297-4554. Hours: 8AM-4PM (EST). *Felony, Civil Actions Over \$10,000, Probate.*

Note: Probate Court address is 241 S Chestnut, Ravenna, OH 44266.

Civil Records: Access: In person only. Visitors must perform in person searches for themselves. No search fee. Required to search: name, years to search; also helpful: address. Civil cases indexed by defendant, plaintiff. Civil records on computer from 1991, prior in books.

Criminal Records: Access: In person only. Visitors must perform in person searches for themselves. No search fee. Required to search: name, years to search;

also helpful: address, DOB, SSN. Criminal records on computer from 1991, prior in books.

General Information: Public Access terminal is available. Copy fee: \$.25 per page. Certification fee: \$1.00. Fee payee: Clerk of Court. Personal checks accepted. Monthly accounts available.

Portage County Municipal Court PO Box 958, Ravenna, OH 44266; Civil phone: 330-297-3635; Criminal phone: 330-297-3639; Fax: 330-297-3526. Hours: 8AM-4PM (EST). *Misdemeanor, Civil Actions Under \$15,000, Eviction, Small Claims.*

Civil Records: Access: In person only. Visitors must perform in person searches for themselves. No search fee. Required to search: name, years to search; also helpful: address. Civil cases indexed by defendant, plaintiff. Civil records on computer from 1992.

Criminal Records: Access: In person only. Visitors must perform in person searches for themselves. No search fee. Required to search: name, years to search; also helpful: address, DOB, SSN. Criminal records on computer from 1992.

General Information: Public Access terminal is available. No records released. Copy fee: \$.25 per page. Certification fee: \$1.00. Fee payee: Municipal Court. Personal checks accepted.

Portage Municipal Court - Kent Branch 214 S Water, Kent, OH 44240; 330-678-9170/9101; Fax: 330-677-9944. Hours: 8AM-4PM (EST). *Misdemeanor, Civil Actions Under \$15,000, Eviction, Small Claims.*

Civil Records: Access: In person only. Search fee: \$1.00 per name. Required to search: name, years to search; also helpful: address. Civil cases indexed by defendant, plaintiff. Civil records on computer from 1992, prior in books.

Criminal Records: Access: In person only. Both court and visitors may perform in person searches. Search fee: \$1.00 per name per year. Required to search: name, years to search; also helpful: address, DOB, SSN. Criminal records on computer from 1992, prior in books.

General Information: Public Access terminal is available. No expunged records released. Copy fee: \$.25 per page. Certification fee: \$1.00. Fee payee: Portage County Municipal Court. Personal checks accepted. Credit cards accepted: Visa, MasterCard. Accepted for criminal only, and only if "in person". Prepayment is required.

Preble County

Common Pleas Court 101 E Main, 3rd Fl, Eaton, OH 45320; 937-456-8160; 456-8165 (common pleas); Probate phone: 937-456-8138; Fax: 937-456-9548. Hours: 8AM-4:30PM (EST). *Felony, Civil, Probate.*

Note: Probate office is separate from this court.

Civil Records: Access: In person only. Visitors must perform in person searches for themselves. No search fee. Required to search: name, years to search; also helpful: address. Civil cases indexed by defendant, plaintiff. Civil records on computer from 11/89, prior in books indexed to 1940s.

Criminal Records: Access: Mail, in person. Both court and visitors may perform in person searches. Search fee: \$3.00 per name. Required to search: name, years to search; also helpful: address, DOB, SSN. Criminal records on computer from 11/89, prior in books indexed to 1940s.

General Information: Public Access terminal is available. No secret records released. SASE required. Turnaround time 1 day. Copy fee: \$1.00 per page. Certification fee: \$1.00. Fee payee: Clerk of Court. Personal checks accepted. Prepayment is required.

Eaton Municipal Court PO Box 65 (101 E Main St), Eaton, OH 45320; 937-456-4941/6204; Fax: 937-456-4685. Hours: 8AM-Noon, 1-4:30PM (EST). *Misdemeanor, Civil Actions Under \$15,000, Eviction, Small Claims.*

www.eatonmunicipalcourt.com

Civil Records: Access: Mail, in person. Both court and visitors may perform in person searches. No search fee. Required to search: name, years to search. Civil cases indexed by defendant, plaintiff. Civil records on computer from 1989, prior in books indexed to 1959.

Criminal Records: Access: Mail, in person. Both court and visitors may perform in person searches. No search fee. Required to search: name, years to search; also helpful: SSN. Criminal records on computer from 1989, prior in books indexed to 1959.

General Information: Public Access terminal is available. No driving records released. SASE required. Turnaround time 1 week. Copy fee: \$1.00 per page. Certification fee: \$1.00. Fee payee: Eaton Municipal Court. Personal checks accepted. Credit cards accepted: Visa, MasterCard.

Putnam County

Common Pleas Court 245 E Main, Rm 301, Ottawa, OH 45875; 419-523-3110; Probate phone: 419-523-3012; Fax: 419-523-5284. Hours: 8:30AM-4:30PM (EST). *Felony, Civil Actions Over \$3,000, Probate.*

Note: Probate is a separate court at number given.

Civil Records: Access: Fax, mail, in person. Both court and visitors may perform in person searches. Search fee: \$10.00 per name. Required to search: name, years to search. Civil cases indexed by defendant, plaintiff. Civil records on computer from 1990, indexed on docket books back to 1800s.

Criminal Records: Access: Fax, mail, in person. Both court and visitors may perform in person searches. Search fee: \$10.00 per name. Required to search: name, years to search; also helpful: address, DOB, SSN. Criminal records on computer from 1990, indexed on docket books back to 1800s.

General Information: Public Access terminal is available. No sealed records released. SASE required. Turnaround time 1-4 days. Fax notes: No fee to fax results. Copy fee: \$.50 per page. Certification fee: \$1.00. Fee payee: Clerk of Court. Personal checks accepted. Putnam County personal checks accepted. Prepayment is required. Prepayment not required under \$5.00.

Putnam County Court 245 E Main, Rm 303, Ottawa, OH 45875; 419-523-3110; Fax: 419-523-5284. Hours: 8:30AM-4:30PM (EST). *Misdemeanor, Civil Actions Under \$15,000, Small Claims.*

Civil Records: Access: Mail, in person. Both court and visitors may perform in person searches. Search fee: \$10.00 per name. Required to search: name, years to search. Civil cases indexed by defendant, plaintiff. Civil records on computer from 1992, prior in books.

Criminal Records: Access: Mail, in person. Both court and visitors may perform in person searches. Search fee: \$10.00 per name. Required to search: name, years to search. Criminal records on computer from 1992, prior in books.

General Information: Public Access terminal is available. SASE required. Turnaround time to 4 days. Copy fee: \$.50 per page. Certification fee: \$4.00. Fee payee: Clerk of Court. Only cashiers checks and money orders accepted. Prepayment is required.

Richland County

Common Pleas Court 50 Park Ave E, 2nd Floor, PO Box 127, Mansfield, OH 44901; 419-774-5549; Probate phone: 419-755-5583. Hours: 8AM-4PM (EST). *Felony, Civil Actions Over $10,000, Probate.*

Civil Records: Access: In person only. Visitors must perform in person searches for themselves. No search fee. Required to search: name, years to search; also helpful: address. Civil cases indexed by defendant, plaintiff. Civil records on computer from 1989, prior in books and on microfiche to 1960.

Criminal Records: Access: In person only. Visitors must perform in person searches for themselves. No search fee. Required to search: name, years to search, DOB, SSN, signed release; also helpful: address. Criminal records on computer from 1991, prior in books and on microfiche to 1960.

General Information: Public Access terminal is available. No sealed records released. Copy fee: $.25 per page. Certification fee: $5.00. Fee payee: Clerk of Court. Personal checks accepted. Prepayment required.

Mansfield Municipal Court PO Box 1228, Mansfield, OH 44901; 419-755-9617; Fax: 419-755-9647. Hours: 8AM-4PM (EST). *Misdemeanor, Civil Actions Under $15,000, Eviction, Small Claims.*

Civil Records: Access: Phone, fax, mail, in person. Both court and visitors may perform in person searches. No search fee. Required to search: name, years to search; also helpful: address. Civil cases indexed by defendant, plaintiff. Civil records on computer from 1990, prior in books. Phone & fax access limited to short searches.

Criminal Records: Access: Phone, fax, mail, in person. Both court and visitors may perform in person searches. No search fee. Required to search: name, years to search; also helpful: address, DOB, SSN. Criminal records on computer from 1990, prior in books. Same as civil.

General Information: Public Access terminal is available. No lead print out records released. SASE required. Turnaround time several 2-3 days. Fax notes: No fee to fax results. Copy fee: $.50 per page. Certification fee: No cert fee. Fee payee: Clerk of Court or Mansfield Municipal Court. Personal checks accepted. Prepayment is required.

Ross County

Common Pleas Court County Courthouse, 2 N Paint St, Ste A, Chillicothe, OH 45601; 740-702-3010; Probate phone: 740-774-1179; Fax: 740-702-3018. Hours: 8AM-4PM (EST). *Felony, Civil Actions Over $10,000, Probate.*

Civil Records: Access: In person only. Both court and visitors may perform in person searches. No search fee. Required to search: name, years to search; also helpful: address. Civil cases indexed by defendant, plaintiff. Civil records on computer from 1989, prior in books to 1800s.

Criminal Records: Access: In person only. Both court and visitors may perform in person searches. No search fee. Required to search: name, years to search; also helpful: address, DOB, SSN. Criminal records on computer from 1989, prior in books to 1800s.

General Information: Public Access terminal is available. No secret indictment records released. Copy fee: $1.00 per page. Certification fee: $1.00. Fee payee: Clerk of Court. Personal checks accepted. Prepayment is required.

Chillicothe Municipal Court 26 S Paint St, Chillicothe, OH 45601; 740-773-3515; Fax: 740-774-1101. Hours: 7:30AM-4:30PM (EST). *Misdemeanor, Civil Actions Under $15,000, Eviction, Small Claims.*

Civil Records: Access: Mail, in person. Both court and visitors may perform in person searches. No search fee.

Required to search: name, years to search; also helpful: address. Civil cases indexed by defendant, plaintiff. Civil records on computer from 6/93, prior in books.

Criminal Records: Access: Mail, in person. Both court and visitors may perform in person searches. No search fee. Required to search: name, years to search, DOB, SSN; also helpful: address. Criminal records on computer from 6/93, prior in books.

General Information: Public Access terminal is available. No confidential records released. SASE required. Turnaround time 10 days. Copy fee: $.25 per page. Certification fee: $1.00 per page. Fee payee: Municipal Court. Business checks accepted. Prepayment is required.

Sandusky County

Common Pleas Court 100 N Park Ave, Fremont, OH 43420; 419-334-6161/6163; Probate phone: 419-334-6217; Fax: 419-334-6164. Hours: 8AM-4:30PM (EST). *Felony, Civil Actions Over $3,000, Probate.*

Civil Records: Access: In person only. Visitors must perform in person searches for themselves. No search fee. Required to search: name, years to search; also helpful: address. Civil cases indexed by defendant, plaintiff. Civil records on computer from 1988, prior in books to 1800s.

Criminal Records: Access: In person only. Visitors must perform in person searches for themselves. No search fee. Required to search: name, years to search; also helpful: address, DOB, SSN. Criminal records on computer from 1988, prior in books to 1800s.

General Information: Public Access terminal is available. No search warrant records released. Copy fee: $.10 per page. Certification fee: $1.00. Fee payee: Clerk of Court. Personal checks accepted. Prepayment is required.

County Court #1 847 E McPherson Hwy (PO Box 267), Clyde, OH 43410; 419-547-0915; Fax: 419-547-9198. Hours: 8AM-4:30PM (EST). *Misdemeanor, Civil Actions Under $15,000, Small Claims.*

www.sandusky-county.org/NEW/countycourts.asp

Civil Records: Access: Phone, fax, mail, in person. Both court and visitors may perform in person searches. No search fee. Required to search: name, years to search; also helpful: address. Civil cases indexed by defendant, plaintiff. Civil records on computer from 1988, prior in books.

Criminal Records: Access: Phone, fax, mail, in person. Both court and visitors may perform in person searches. No search fee. Required to search: name, years to search, DOB, SSN; also helpful: address. Criminal records on computer from 1988, prior in books.

General Information: SASE required. Turnaround time 2-3 days. Fax notes: No fee to fax results to toll-free number. Copy fee: $.25 per page. Certification fee: $1.00. Fee payee: County Court. Personal checks accepted. Credit cards accepted: Visa, MasterCard. Prepayment is required.

County Court #2 215 W Main St, Woodville, OH 43469; 419-849-3961; Fax: 419-849-3932. Hours: 8AM-4:30PM (EST). *Misdemeanor, Civil Actions Under $15,000, Small Claims.*

www.sandusky-county.org/NEW/countycourts.asp

Civil Records: Access: Phone, fax, mail, in person. Both court and visitors may perform in person searches. No search fee. Required to search: name, years to search; also helpful: address. Civil cases indexed by defendant, plaintiff. Civil records on computer from 1990.

Criminal Records: Access: Phone, fax, mail, in person. Both court and visitors may perform in person searches. No search fee. Required to search: name, years to search, DOB, SSN, signed release; also helpful:

address. Criminal records on computer from 1989, indexed prior.

General Information: Public Access terminal is available. No confidential records released. SASE required. Turnaround time 10 days, by phone 3 hours. Fax notes: $5.00 per document. Copy fee: $.10 per page. Certification fee: $1.00. Fee payee: County Court. Personal checks accepted. Credit cards accepted: Visa, MasterCard. Prepayment is required.

Fremont Municipal Court PO Box 886, Fremont, OH 43420-0071; 419-332-1579; Fax: 419-332-1570. Hours: 8AM-4:30PM (EST). *Misdemeanor, Civil Actions Under $15,000, Eviction, Small Claims.*

www.sandusky-county.org/NEW/countycourts.asp

Civil Records: Access: Fax, mail, in person. Both court and visitors may perform in person searches. No search fee. Required to search: name, years to search. Civil cases indexed by defendant, plaintiff. Civil records in books from 1960, computerized since 1992.

Criminal Records: Access: Fax, mail, in person. Both court and visitors may perform in person searches. No search fee. Required to search: name, years to search; also helpful: DOB, SSN. Criminal records in books from 1960, computerized since 1992.

General Information: Public Access terminal is available. Turnaround time 2 days. Fax notes: No fee to fax results. Local calls only. Copy fee: $.25 per page. Certification fee: No cert fee. Fee payee: Fremont Municipal Court. Only cashiers checks and money orders accepted. Prepayment is required.

Scioto County

Common Pleas Court 602 7th St, Portsmouth, OH 45662; 740-355-8226; Probate phone: 740-355-8243. Hours: 8AM-4:30PM (EST). *Felony, Civil Actions Over $10,000, Probate.*

www.sciotocountycpcourt.org

Note: Probate is a separate office at the same address.

Civil Records: Access: In person, online. Visitors must perform in person searches for themselves. No search fee. Required to search: name, years to search; also helpful: address. Civil cases indexed by defendant, plaintiff. Civil records on computer from 1986, dockets to 1800s. Online access to civil records is available free at www.sciotocountycpcourt.org/search.htm. Search by court calendar, quick index, general index or docket sheet.

Criminal Records: Access: In person, online. Visitors must perform in person searches for themselves. No search fee. Required to search: name, years to search; also helpful: address, DOB, SSN. Criminal records on computer from 1986, dockets to 1800s. Online access to criminal records is the same as civil.

General Information: Public Access terminal is available. No sealed or secret records released. Fax notes: Fee to fax results is $1.00 per page. Copy fee: $1.00 per page. Certification fee: $1.00 per page. Fee payee: Clerk of Court. Personal checks accepted. Prepayment is required.

Portsmouth Municipal Court 728 2nd St, Portsmouth, OH 45662; 740-354-3283; Fax: 740-353-6645. Hours: 8AM-4PM (EST). *Misdemeanor, Civil Actions Under $15,000, Eviction, Small Claims.*

Civil Records: Access: Phone, fax, mail, in person. Both court and visitors may perform in person searches. Search fee: No fee for computer records search 1989 forward. Required to search: name, years to search. Civil cases indexed by defendant, plaintiff. Civil records on computer from 1989, prior on cards.

Criminal Records: Access: Phone, fax, mail, in person. Both court and visitors may perform in person searches. Search fee: $20.00 per name if search includes years prior to 1989. No fee for computer records search 1989 forward. Required to search: name, years to search, DOB, SSN, signed release. Criminal records on computer from 1989, prior on cards.

General Information: Public Access terminal is available. No competency hearing, protection order records released. SASE required. Turnaround time 2-3 days; older records up to 2 weeks. Fax notes: No fee to fax results. Copy fee: No search fee. Certification fee: $1.00 per page. Fee payee: Portsmouth Municipal Court. Prepayment is required.

Seneca County

Common Pleas Court 103 S Washington St, Tiffin, OH 44883; 419-447-0671; Probate phone: 419-447-3121; Fax: 419-443-7919. Hours: 8:30AM-4:30PM *Felony, Civil Actions Over $10,000, Probate.*

Civil Records: Access: Phone, fax, mail, in person. Both court and visitors may perform in person searches. No search fee. Required to search: name, years to search; also helpful: address. Civil cases indexed by defendant, plaintiff. Civil records on computer from 1/93, prior in books to 1900s, archived to 1800s.

Criminal Records: Access: Phone, fax, mail, in person. Both court and visitors may perform in person searches. No search fee. Required to search: name, years to search, SSN, date of offense. Criminal records on computer from 1/93, prior in books to 1900s, archived to 1800s.

General Information: Public Access terminal is available. No sealed records released. SASE required. Turnaround time 1 week. Fax notes: Fee to fax results is $2.00 per transmission. Copy fee: $.25 per page. Certification fee: $1.00. Fee payee: Clerk of Court. Personal checks accepted. Prepayment is required.

Fostoria Municipal Court PO Box 985, Fostoria, OH 44830; 419-435-8139; Fax: 419-435-1150. Hours: 8:30AM-5PM (EST). *Misdemeanor, Civil Actions Under $15,000, Eviction, Small Claims.*

Civil Records: Access: Phone, fax, mail, in person. Both court and visitors may perform in person searches. No search fee. Required to search: name, years to search. Civil cases indexed by defendant, plaintiff. Civil records computerized since 1987.

Criminal Records: Access: Phone, fax, mail, in person. Both court and visitors may perform in person searches. No search fee. Required to search: name, years to search; also helpful: SSN. Criminal records computerized since 1987.

General Information: Public Access terminal is available. Turnaround time 1-2 days. Fax notes: No fee if faxed to local or toll free number. Copy fee: $.10 per page. Certification fee: $5.00 first page and $.10 each additional. Fee payee: Fostoria Municipal Court. Personal checks accepted. Prepayment is required.

Tiffin Municipal Court PO Box 694, Tiffin, OH 44883; 419-448-5412; Civil phone: 419-448-5418; Criminal phone: 419-448-5411; Fax: 419-448-5419. Hours: 8:30AM-4:30PM (EST). *Misdemeanor, Civil Actions Under $15,000, Eviction, Small Claims.*

Civil Records: Access: Fax, mail, in person. Both court and visitors may perform in person searches. No search fee. Required to search: name, years to search; also helpful: address. Civil cases indexed by defendant, plaintiff. Civil records on computer from 8/90, prior in books.

Criminal Records: Access: Fax, mail, in person. Both court and visitors may perform in person searches. No search fee. Required to search: name, years to search, DOB, SSN, signed release; also helpful: address. Criminal records on computer from 8/90, prior in books.

General Information: Public Access terminal is available. (Fee to fax results is $.05 per page.) No expunged records released. SASE required. Turnaround time 3 days. Fax notes: $.25 per page. Copy fee: $.05 per page. Certification fee: $1.00. Fee payee: Municipal

Court. Personal checks accepted. Prepayment is required.

Shelby County

Common Pleas Court PO Box 809, Sidney, OH 45365; 937-498-7221; Fax: 937-498-7824. Hours: 8:30AM-4:30PM M-Th; 8:30AM-6PM F (EST). *Felony, Civil Actions Over $10,000, Probate.*

www.co.shelby.oh.us/ClerkCourts/LegalDept.asp

Civil Records: Access: Fax, mail, in person. Both court and visitors may perform in person searches. No search fee. Required to search: name, years to search; also helpful: address. Civil cases indexed by defendant, plaintiff. Civil records on computer from 1987, on indexes from 1819.

Criminal Records: Access: Mail, in person. Visitors must perform in person searches for themselves. No search fee. Required to search: name, years to search; also helpful: address, DOB, SSN. Criminal records on computer from 1987, on indexes from 1819.

General Information: Public Access terminal is available. No grand jury tapes released. SASE required. Turnaround time 5 days. Fax notes: $3.00 per document. Copy fee: $.25 per page. Certification fee: $4.00. Fee payee: Shelby County Clerk of Courts. Personal checks accepted. Prepayment is required.

Sidney Municipal Court 201 W Poplar, Sidney, OH 45365; 937-498-0011; Fax: 937-498-8179. Hours: 8AM-4:30PM (EST). *Misdemeanor, Civil Actions Under $15,000, Eviction, Small Claims.*

Note: Send mail requests to the address above; phone and in person searches are made at the court at 110 W Court St.

Civil Records: Access: Phone, fax, mail, in person. Both court and visitors may perform in person searches. No search fee. Required to search: name, years to search. Civil cases indexed by defendant, plaintiff. Civil records on computer from 1988; prior on books to 1958.

Criminal Records: Access: Phone, fax, mail, in person. Both court and visitors may perform in person searches. No search fee. Required to search: name, years to search; also helpful: address, DOB, SSN. Criminal records on computer from 1988; prior on books to 1958.

General Information: Public Access terminal is available. Confidential and probation records are not released. SASE not required. Turnaround time 2 days. Copy fee: $.10 per page. Certification fee: $1.00 per page. Fee payee: Municipal Court. Personal checks accepted. Prepayment is required.

Stark County

Common Pleas Court - Civil Division PO Box 21160, Canton, OH 44701; 330-451-7795; Fax: 330-451-7853. Hours: 8:30AM-4:30PM (EST). *Civil Actions Over $15,000, Probate.*

www.starkclerk.org

Civil Records: Access: Phone, fax, mail, in person, online. Both court and visitors may perform in person searches. No search fee. Required to search: name, years to search. Civil cases indexed by defendant, plaintiff. Civil records on computer from 1985, prior in books form 1940s. Online access to the county online case docket database is available free at www.starkclerk.org/docket/index.html.

General Information: Public Access terminal is available. No sealed records released. SASE required. Turnaround time up to 1 week. Fax notes: Fee to fax is $2.00 for 1st page, $1.00 each add'l. Copy fee: $.10 per page. Certification fee: $1.00. Fee payee: Clerk of Court. Personal checks accepted. Prepayment is required.

Common Pleas Court - Criminal Division
PO Box 21160, Canton, OH 44701-1160; 330-451-7929; Fax: 330-451-7853. Hours: 8:30AM-4:30PM (EST). *Felony.*

www.starkclerk.org

Criminal Records: Access: Mail, in person, online. Both court and visitors may perform in person searches. No search fee. Required to search: name, years to search, DOB, SSN. Criminal records on computer from 1985, prior in books to 1940s. Online access to the county online case docket database is available free at www.starkclerk.org/docket/index.html. Search by name.

General Information: Public Access terminal is available. No secret, expungement records released. SASE required. Turnaround time up to 2 weeks. Copy fee: $.10 per page. Certification fee: $1.00. Fee payee: Clerk of Courts. Personal checks accepted.

Canton Municipal Court 218 Cleveland Ave SW, PO Box 24218, Canton, OH 44702-4218; 330-489-3203; Fax: 330-489-3075 (civil) 489-3372 (criminal). Hours: 8AM-4:30PM (EST). *Misdemeanor, Civil Actions Under $15,000, Eviction, Small Claims.*

www.cantoncourt.org

Civil Records: Access: Phone, fax, mail, in person. Both court and visitors may perform in person searches. No search fee. Required to search: name, years to search. Civil cases indexed by defendant, plaintiff. Civil records on computer from 1991, prior in books to 1928.

Criminal Records: Access: Phone, fax, mail, in person. Both court and visitors may perform in person searches. No search fee. Required to search: name, years to search; also helpful: DOB, SSN. Criminal records on computer from 1986, books to 1928.

General Information: Public Access terminal is available. No sealed records released. SASE required. Turnaround time 1-2 days. Fax notes: No fee to fax results. Copy fee: $.25 per page. Certification fee: No cert fee. Fee payee: Municipal Court. Personal checks accepted. Prepayment is required.

Massillon Municipal Court Two James Duncan Plaza, Massillion, OH 44646-6690; Civil phone: 330-830-1731; Criminal phone: 330-830-1732; Fax: 330-830-3648. Hours: 8:30AM-4:30PM (EST). *Misdemeanor, Civil Actions Under $15,000, Eviction, Small Claims.*

Civil Records: Access: Fax, mail, in person. Both court and visitors may perform in person searches. No search fee. Required to search: name. Civil cases indexed by defendant, plaintiff. Civil records on docket books from 1986, some records computerized.

Criminal Records: Access: Fax, mail, in person. Both court and visitors may perform in person searches. No search fee. Required to search: name, years to search; also helpful: DOB, SSN. computerized since 1991.

General Information: Public Access terminal is available. (Criminal only.) Turnaround time 1 week. Fax notes: No fee to fax results. Copy fee: $.05 per page. Certification fee: $2.00 per page. Fee payee: Massillion Clerk of Court. Personal checks accepted. Prepayment is required.

Summit County

Common Pleas Court 209 S High St, Akron, OH 44308; 330-643-2201 (Divorce); Civil phone: 330-643-2217; Criminal phone: 330-643-2282; Probate phone: 330-643-2350; Fax: 330-643-7772. Hours: 9:30AM-4:15PM (EST). *Felony, Civil Actions Over $10,000, Probate.*

Note: Probate is a separate court at the number given.

Civil Records: Access: Mail, in person. Both court and visitors may perform in person searches. No search fee. Required to search: name, years to search. Civil cases

indexed by defendant, plaintiff. Civil records on computer from 1982, prior in books, some microfiche.

Criminal Records: Access: Mail, in person. Both court and visitors may perform in person searches. Search fee: $2.00 per name. Required to search: name, years to search, DOB; also helpful: SSN. Criminal records on computer from 1982, prior in books, some microfiche.

General Information: No secret indictment records released. SASE required. Turnaround time 1 week. Copy fee: $.05 per page. Certification fee: $1.00 per page. Fee payee: Clerk of Court. Only cashiers checks and money orders accepted. Prepayment is required.

Akron Municipal Court 217 S High St, Rm 837, Akron, OH 44308; Civil phone: 330-375-2920; Criminal phone: 330-375-2570; Fax: 330-375-2427. Hours: 8AM-4:30PM (EST). *Misdemeanor, Civil Actions Under $15,000, Eviction, Small Claims.*

Civil Records: Access: Mail, in person. Both court and visitors may perform in person searches. No search fee. Required to search: name, years to search. Civil cases indexed by defendant, plaintiff. Civil records on computer from 1988, prior in books to 1975.

Criminal Records: Access: Mail, in person. Both court and visitors may perform in person searches. No search fee. Required to search: name, years to search; also helpful: address, DOB, SSN. Criminal records on computer from 1988, prior in books to 1975.

General Information: Public Access terminal is available. No sealed records released. SASE required. Turnaround time to 1 week. Copy fee: $.25 per page. Certification fee: $1.00. Fee payee: Municipal Court. Personal checks accepted. Prepayment is required.

Barberton Municipal Court Municipal Bldg, 576 W Park Ave, Barberton, OH 44203-2584; 330-753-2261; Fax: 330-848-6779. Hours: 8AM-5PM (civ); Crim/traffic to 8PM (EST). *Misdemeanor, Civil Actions Under $15,000, Eviction, Small Claims.*

Civil Records: Access: Phone, fax, mail, in person. Both court and visitors may perform in person searches. No search fee. Required to search: name, years to search. Civil cases indexed by defendant, plaintiff. Civil records computerized since 1994.

Criminal Records: Access: Phone, fax, mail, in person. Both court and visitors may perform in person searches. No search fee. Required to search: name, years to search; also helpful: DOB, SSN. Criminal records computerized since 1994.

General Information: Public Access terminal is available. Turnaround time 1 week. Fax notes: No fee to fax results. Copy fee: $.10 per page. Certification fee: $1.00 per page. Fee payee: Barberton Municipal Court. Personal checks accepted. Prepayment is required.

Cuyahoga Falls Municipal Court 2310 Second St, Cuyahoga Falls, OH 44221; 330-971-8280; Civil phone: 330-971-8108; Criminal phone: 330-971-8109; Fax: 330-928-7722. Hours: 8AM-8PM (Criminal), 8AM-4:30PM (Civil) *Misdemeanor, Civil Actions Under $15,000, Eviction, Small Claims.*

www.cfmunicourt.com

Civil Records: Access: Phone, mail, in person. Both court and visitors may perform in person searches. No search fee. Required to search: name, years to search. Civil cases indexed by defendant, plaintiff. Civil records indexed back to 1954. Current court docket information is available free online on the web site.

Criminal Records: Access: Phone, mail, in person. Both court and visitors may perform in person searches. No search fee. Required to search: name; also helpful: SSN. Criminal records indexed back to 1954. Current court docket information is available free online on the web site.

General Information: Public Access terminal is available. Turnaround time 1 week. Copy fee: $.05 per page. Certification fee: $1.00 per page. Fee payee:

Cuyahoga Falls Municipal Court. Business checks accepted. Prepayment is required.

Trumbull County

Common Pleas Court 160 High St, Warren, OH 44481; 330-675-2557; Probate phone: 330-675-2521. Hours: 8:30AM-4:30PM (EST). *Felony, Civil Actions Over $10,000, Probate.*

www.clerk.co.trumbull.oh.us

Civil Records: Access: Phone, mail, in person, online. Both court and visitors may perform in person searches. Search fee: $5.00 per name. Required to search: name, years to search. Civil cases indexed by defendant, plaintiff. Civil records indexed in books from 1977, archived from 1800s; on computer back to 5/96. Online access to court records is available free at www.clerk.co.trumbull.oh.us/search/search.htm. Records go back to May, 1996.

Criminal Records: Access: Mail, in person, online. Both court and visitors may perform in person searches. Search fee: $5.00 per name. Required to search: name, years to search, DOB, SSN, signed release. Criminal records indexed in books from 1977, archived from 1800s; on computer back to 5/96. Online access to criminal records is the same as civil.

General Information: Public Access terminal is available. No secret or sealed records released. SASE required. Turnaround time 1 week. Copy fee: $.10 per page. Certification fee: $1.00 per page. Fee payee: Clerk of Court. Business checks accepted. Prepayment is required.

Trumbull County Court Central 180 N Mecca St, Cortland, OH 44410; 330-637-5023; Fax: 330-637-5021. Hours: 8AM-4PM (EST). *Misdemeanor, Civil Actions Under $15,000, Eviction, Small Claims.*

Civil Records: Access: Phone, fax, mail, in person. Both court and visitors may perform in person searches. No search fee. Required to search: name, years to search.

Criminal Records: Access: Phone, fax, mail, in person. Both court and visitors may perform in person searches. No search fee. Required to search: name, years to search; also helpful: DOB, SSN. Same record keeping as civil.

General Information: Public Access terminal is available. Turnaround time is 1-2 days. Fax notes: No fee to fax results. Local calls only. Copy fee: $.25 per page. Certification fee: $2.00 per page. Fee payee: Trumbull County Court Central. Personal checks accepted. Credit cards accepted: Visa, MasterCard. In person only. Prepayment is required.

Trumbull County Court East 7130 Brookwood Dr, Brookfield, OH 44403; 330-448-1726; Fax: 330-448-6310. Hours: 8:30AM-4:30PM (EST). *Misdemeanor, Civil Under $15,000, Eviction, Small Claims.*

Civil Records: Access: Phone, fax, mail, in person. Both court and visitors may perform in person searches. No search fee. Required to search: name, years to search.

Criminal Records: Access: Phone, fax, mail, in person. Both court and visitors may perform in person searches. No search fee. Required to search: name, years to search; also helpful: DOB, SSN. Criminal Records in docket books since 1990, computerized since 1994.

General Information: Public Access terminal is available. Turnaround time 1-2 days. Fax notes: No fee to fax results. Local calls only. Copy fee: $.25 per page. Certification fee: No cert fee. Fee payee: Trumbull County Court East. Personal checks accepted. Credit cards accepted: Visa, MasterCard. Prepayment is required.

Girard Municipal Court City Hall, 100 N Market St, Girard, OH 44420-2559; Civil phone: 330-545-3177; Criminal phone: 330-545-0069; Fax: 330-545-7045. Hours: 8AM-4PM (EST). *Misdemeanor, Civil Actions Under $15,000, Eviction, Small Claims.*

Note: Traffic Records at 330-545-3049.

Civil Records: Access: Fax, mail, in person. Both court and visitors may perform in person searches. No search fee. Required to search: name, years to search. Civil cases indexed by defendant, plaintiff. Civil records on books since 1964, computerized since 09/96.

Criminal Records: Access: Fax, mail, in person. Both court and visitors may perform in person searches. No search fee. Required to search: name, years to search; also helpful: DOB, SSN. Criminal records on books since 1964, computerized since 09/96.

General Information: Public Access terminal is available. Turnaround time 1 week. Fax notes: No fee to fax results. Copy fee: $1.00 per page 1st 10; $.10 per page each add'l. Certification fee: $10.00 per page. Fee payee: Girard Municipal Court. Business checks accepted. Prepayment is required.

Newton Falls Municipal Court 19 N Canal St, Newton Falls, OH 44444-1302; 330-872-0302; Fax: 330-872-3899. Hours: 8AM-4:30PM (EST). *Misdemeanor, Civil Actions Under $15,000, Eviction, Small Claims.*

Civil Records: Access: Fax, mail, in person. Both court and visitors may perform in person searches. No search fee. Required to search: name, years to search. Civil cases indexed by defendant, plaintiff. Civil records in books since 1970, computerized since 1992.

Criminal Records: Access: Fax, mail, in person. Both court and visitors may perform in person searches. No search fee. Required to search: name, years to search; also helpful: DOB, SSN. Criminal records in books since 1970, computerized since 1992.

General Information: Fax notes: No fee to fax results. Local calls only. Copy fee: $.10 per page. Certification fee: $2.50. Fee payee: Newton Falls Municipal Court. Only cashiers checks and money orders accepted. Prepayment is required.

Niles Municipal Court 15 East St, Niles, OH 44446-5051; 330-652-5863; Fax: 330-544-9025. Hours: 8AM-4PM (EST). *Misdemeanor, Civil Actions Under $15,000, Eviction, Small Claims.*

Civil Records: Access: Fax, mail, in person. Both court and visitors may perform in person searches. Search fee: $10.00 per name. Required to search: name, years to search. Civil cases indexed by defendant, plaintiff. Civil records on computer since 10/96, in books since 1990, in storage from 1930.

Criminal Records: Access: Fax, mail, in person. Both court and visitors may perform in person searches. Search fee: $10.00 per name. Required to search: name, years to search; also helpful: DOB, SSN. Criminal records on computer since 10/96, in books since 1990, in storage from 1930.

General Information: Public Access terminal is available. Turnaround time will vary. Fax notes: No fee to fax results. Local calls only. Copy fee: $.25 per page. Certification fee: $1.00 per page. Fee payee: Niles Municipal Court. Only cashiers checks and money orders accepted. Prepayment is required.

Warren Municipal Court 141 South St SE (PO Box 1550), Warren, OH 44482; Civil phone: 330-841-2527; Criminal phone: 330-841-2666; Fax: 330-841-2760. Hours: 8AM-4:30PM (EST). *Misdemeanor, Civil Actions Under $15,000, Eviction, Small Claims.*

Civil Records: Access: Fax, mail, in person. Both court and visitors may perform in person searches. No search fee. Required to search: name, years to search; also helpful: address. Civil cases indexed by defendant, plaintiff. Civil records on computer since 1995; prior in books to 1978.

Criminal Records: Access: Fax, mail, in person. Both court and visitors may perform in person searches. No search fee. Required to search: name, years to search, DOB, SSN, signed release; also helpful: address. Criminal records on computer since 1995; prior in books to 1978.

General Information: Public Access terminal is available. No open case records released. SASE required. Turnaround time to 1-5 days. Fax notes: No fee to fax results. Copy fee: $.25 per page. Certification fee: $1.00. Is per page and includes copy fee. Fee payee: Warren Municipal Court. Personal checks accepted. Credit cards accepted: Visa, MasterCard. Prepayment is required.

Tuscarawas County

Common Pleas Court 125 E High (PO Box 628), New Philadelphia, OH 44663; 330-364-8811 X243; Fax: 330-343-4682. Hours: 8AM-4:30PM (EST). *Felony, Civil Actions Over $15,000, Probate.*

www.co.tuscarawas.oh.us

Note: Probate is a separate court at 101 E High Ave.

Civil Records: Access: In person only. Visitors must perform in person searches for themselves. No search fee. Required to search: name, years to search; also helpful: address. Civil cases indexed by defendant, plaintiff. Civil records on computer from 1987, prior in books to 1808, archived prior.

Criminal Records: Access: In person only. Visitors must perform in person searches for themselves. No search fee. Required to search: name, years to search; also helpful: address, DOB, SSN. Criminal records on computer from 1987, prior in books to 1808, archived prior.

General Information: Public Access terminal is available. Fax notes: Fee to fax results is $2.00 per document plus $1.00 per page. Copy fee: $.10 per page. Certification fee: $1.00 per page. Fee payee: Clerk of Court. Personal checks accepted. Credit cards accepted: Visa, MasterCard. Visa, MC. Prepayment is required.

County Court 220 E 3rd, Uhrichsville, OH 44683; 740-922-4795; Fax: 740-922-7020. Hours: 8AM-4:30PM (EST). *Misdemeanor, Civil Actions Under $15,000, Small Claims.*

Note: Probation Office phone: 740-922-3653 & 922-4360. Probation Office hours: 8AM-4:30PM.

Civil Records: Access: Fax, mail, in person. Both court and visitors may perform in person searches. No search fee. Required to search: name, years to search. Civil cases indexed by defendant, plaintiff. Civil records on computer from 2/94, prior in books.

Criminal Records: Access: Fax, mail, in person. Both court and visitors may perform in person searches. No search fee. Required to search: name, years to search, DOB; also helpful: SSN. Criminal records on computer from 2/94, prior in books.

General Information: Public Access terminal is available. No confidential records released. SASE required. Turnaround time 1-2 days. Fax notes: No fee to fax results. Local faxing only. Copy fee: $1.00 per page. Certification fee: No cert fee. Fee payee: Tuscarawas County Court. Personal checks accepted. Tuscarawas County personal checks accepted. Prepayment is required.

New Philadelphia Municipal Court 166 E High Ave, New Philadelphia, OH 44663; 330-364-4491; Fax: 330-364-6885. Hours: 8AM-4PM (EST). *Misdemeanor, Civil Actions Under $15,000, Eviction, Small Claims.*

Civil Records: Access: Mail, in person. Only the court performs in person searches; visitors may not. No search fee. Required to search: name, years to search.

Civil cases indexed by defendant, plaintiff. Civil records on computer from 4/91, prior in books to 1976.

Criminal Records: Access: In person only. Visitors must perform in person searches for themselves. No search fee. Required to search: name, years to search. Criminal records on computer from 4/91, prior in books to 1976.

General Information: Public Access terminal is available. SASE required. Turnaround time 1-2 days. Copy fee: $.25 per page after first 10 free. Certification fee: $1.00 per page. Fee payee: Municipal Court. Personal checks accepted. Credit cards accepted: Visa, MasterCard. Prepayment is required.

Union County

Common Pleas Court County Courthouse, Clerk of Courts, 215 W 5th, PO Box 605, Marysville, OH 43040; 937-645-3006; Fax: 937-645-3162. Hours: 8:30AM-4PM (EST). *Felony, Civil Actions Over $10,000, Probate.*

www.co.union.oh.us

Civil Records: Access: In person only. Visitors must perform in person searches for themselves. No search fee. Required to search: name, years to search; also helpful: address. Civil cases indexed by defendant, plaintiff. Civil records on computer from 1990, prior in books back to 1800s.

Criminal Records: Access: Mail, in person. Both court and visitors may perform in person searches. Search fee: $5.00 per name. Required to search: name, years to search; also helpful: address, DOB, SSN. Criminal records on computer from 1990, prior in books back to 1800s.

General Information: Public Access terminal is available. Turnaround time 2 days. Fax notes: Fee to fax is $2.00 1st pg; $1.00 each add'l pg. Copy fee: $.50 per page. Certification fee: $1.00. Fee payee: Clerk of Court. Only cashiers checks and money orders accepted. Prepayment is required.

Marysville Municipal Court 125 East 6th Street, Marysville, OH 43040; 937-644-9102; Fax: 937-644-1228. Hours: 8AM-4PM (EST). *Misdemeanor, Civil Actions Under $15,000, Eviction, Small Claims.*

www.munict.ci.marysville.oh.us

Civil Records: Access: Phone, fax, mail, in person. Both court and visitors may perform in person searches. No search fee. Required to search: name, years to search. Civil cases indexed by defendant, plaintiff. Civil records on computer from 1989, prior on microfilm.

Criminal Records: Access: Phone, fax, mail, in person. Both court and visitors may perform in person searches. No search fee. Required to search: name, years to search; also helpful: SSN. Criminal records on computer from 1989, prior on microfilm.

General Information: Public Access terminal is available. No probation records released. SASE required. Turnaround time 1-2 days. Fax notes: No fee to fax results. No copy fee. Certification fee: No cert fee. No out-of-town checks accepted. Union County personal checks accepted. Credit cards accepted: Visa, MasterCard.

Van Wert County

Common Pleas Court PO Box 366 (305 Courthouse), 121 E Main St, Van Wert, OH 45891; 419-238-1022; Probate phone: 419-238-0027; Fax: 419-238-4760. Hours: 8AM-4PM (EST). *Felony, Civil Actions Over $10,000, Probate.*

www.vwcommonpleas.org

Civil Records: Access: In person only. Visitors must perform in person searches for themselves. No search fee. Required to search: name, years to search. Civil cases indexed by defendant, plaintiff. Some early records on microfiche, have docket books and files,

indexed on computer since 05/98. Court calendar available online.

Criminal Records: Access: In person only. Visitors must perform in person searches for themselves. No search fee. Required to search: name, years to search; also helpful: address, DOB, SSN. Some early years on microfiche, have docket books and files, indexed on computer since 05/98. Court calendar available online.

General Information: Public Access terminal is available. (Records available from 05/98.) All records public. Copy fee: $.15 per page. Certification fee: $1.00. Fee payee: Clerk of Court. Personal checks accepted. Prepayment is required.

Van Wert Municipal Court 124 S Market, Van Wert, OH 45891; 419-238-5767. Hours: 8AM-4PM (EST). *Misdemeanor, Civil Actions Under $15,000, Eviction, Small Claims.*

Civil Records: Access: Mail, in person. Both court and visitors may perform in person searches. No search fee. Required to search: name, years to search. Civil cases indexed by defendant, plaintiff. Civil records on computer from 1989.

Criminal Records: Access: Mail, in person. Both court and visitors may perform in person searches. No search fee. Required to search: name, years to search; also helpful: SSN. Criminal records on computer from 1989.

General Information: Public Access terminal is available. SASE required. Turnaround time 1-2 days. Fax notes: Fee to fax results is $1.00 per page. Copy fee: $1.00 per page. Certification fee: $1.00. Fee payee: Municipal Court. Personal checks accepted. Prepayment is required.

Vinton County

Common Pleas Court County Courthouse, 100 E Main St, McArthur, OH 45651; 740-596-3001; Probate phone: 740-596-3438; Fax: 740-596-9611. Hours: 8:30AM-4PM M-F (EST). *Felony, Civil Actions Over $3,000, Probate.*

Civil Records: Access: Mail, in person. Both court and visitors may perform in person searches. No search fee. Required to search: name, years to search. Civil cases indexed by defendant, plaintiff. Civil records in books since 1850.

Criminal Records: Access: Mail, in person. Both court and visitors may perform in person searches. No search fee. Required to search: name, years to search; also helpful: DOB, SSN. Criminal records in books since 1850.

General Information: No sealed records released. SASE required. Turnaround time 2-3 days. Copy fee: $.25 per page. Certification fee: $2.00. Fee payee: Clerk of Court. Personal checks accepted. Prepayment is required.

Vinton County Court County Courthouse, McArthur, OH 45651; 740-596-5000; Fax: 740-596-9721. Hours: 8:30AM-4PM (EST). *Misdemeanor, Civil Actions Under $15,000, Small Claims.*

Civil Records: Access: Phone, mail, in person. Both court and visitors may perform in person searches. No search fee. Required to search: name, years to search. Civil cases indexed by defendant, plaintiff. Civil records in books from 1980s, archived from 1800s.

Criminal Records: Access: Phone, mail, in person. Both court and visitors may perform in person searches. No search fee. Required to search: name, years to search, DOB; also helpful: SSN. Criminal records in books from 1980s, archived from 1800s.

General Information: SASE required. Turnaround time 1-2 days. No copy fee. Certification fee: No cert fee. Only cashiers checks and money orders accepted.

Warren County

Common Pleas Court PO Box 238, Lebanon, OH 45036; 513-695-1120; Probate phone: 513-695-1180; Fax: 513-695-2965. Hours: 8:30AM-4:30PM (EST). *Felony, Civil Actions Over $3,000, Probate.*

Civil Records: Access: Phone, mail, in person. Both court and visitors may perform in person searches. Search fee: $4.00 per name. Required to search: name, years to search. Civil cases indexed by defendant, plaintiff. Civil records on computer from 1974, archived from 1850.

Criminal Records: Access: Mail, in person. Both court and visitors may perform in person searches. Search fee: $4.00 per name. Required to search: name, years to search, DOB; also helpful: SSN. Criminal records on computer from 1974, archived from 1850.

General Information: Public Access terminal is available. SASE required. Turnaround time 1-4 days. Copy fee: $.20 per page. Certification fee: $1.00. Fee payee: Clerk of Court. Personal checks accepted. Prepayment is required.

County Court 550 Justice Dr, Lebanon, OH 45036; 513-695-1370. Hours: 8AM-4:30PM (EST). *Misdemeanor, Civil Actions Under $15,000, Small Claims under $3000.*

www.co.warren.oh.us/countycourt

Civil Records: Access: Phone, mail, in person. Both court and visitors may perform in person searches. No search fee. Required to search: name, years to search; also helpful: address. Civil cases indexed by defendant, plaintiff. Civil records on computer from 1990, prior in books. No in person searches Tuesdays or Thursdays.

Criminal Records: Access: Phone, mail, in person. Both court and visitors may perform in person searches. No search fee. Required to search: name, years to search, DOB; also helpful: SSN, address. Criminal records on computer from 1990, prior in books. No in person searches on Tuesdays or Thursdays.

General Information: Public Access terminal is available. SASE required. Turnaround time 1-2 weeks. Copy fee: $.05 per page. Certification fee: No cert fee. Warren County checks accepted. Credit cards accepted: Visa, MasterCard. Prepayment is required.

Franklin Municipal Court 35 E 4th Street, Franklin, OH 45006-2484; 513-746-2858; Fax: 513-743-7751. Hours: 8:30AM-5PM (EST). *Misdemeanor, Civil Actions Under $15,000, Eviction, Small Claims.*

Civil Records: Access: Phone, fax, mail, in person. Both court and visitors may perform in person searches. No search fee. Required to search: name, years to search. Civil cases indexed by defendant, plaintiff. Civil records in books since 1955, on computer back to 1990.

Criminal Records: Access: Phone, fax, mail, in person. Both court and visitors may perform in person searches. No search fee. Required to search: name, years to search, signed release; also helpful: DOB, SSN. Criminal records in books since 1955, on computer back to 1990.

General Information: Turnaround time 1-2 days. Fax notes: Fee to fax results is $10.00 per document. Copy fee: $.50 per page. Certification fee: $1.00. Fee payee: Franklin Municipal Court. Personal checks accepted. Credit cards accepted: Visa, MasterCard. In person only. Prepayment is required.

Lebanon Muncipal Court City Building, Lebanon, OH 45036-1777; 513-932-7210; Fax: 513-933-7212. Hours: 8AM-4PM (EST). *Misdemeanor, Civil Actions, Eviction, Small Claims.*

Civil Records: Access: Fax, mail, in person. Both court and visitors may perform in person searches. No search fee. Required to search: name, years to search. Civil cases indexed by defendant, plaintiff. Civil records on books since 1956, computerized since 1990.

Criminal Records: Access: Fax, mail, in person. Both court and visitors may perform in person searches. No search fee. Required to search: name, years to search; also helpful: DOB, SSN. Criminal records on books since 1956, computerized since 1990.

General Information: Public Access terminal is available. Turnaround time 2 days. Fax notes: No fee to fax results. Local calls only. Copy fee: $.50 per page. Certification fee: No cert fee. Personal checks accepted. Credit cards accepted: Visa, MasterCard. Only for criminal record searching, not civil.

Mason Municipal Court 200 W Main St, Mason, OH 45040-1620; 513-398-7901; Fax: 513-459-8085. Hours: 7:30AM-4PM (EST). *Misdemeanor, Civil Actions Under $15,000, Eviction, Small Claims.*

Civil Records: Access: Phone, fax, mail, in person. Both court and visitors may perform in person searches. Search fee: $25.00 per name. Required to search: name, years to search. Civil cases indexed by defendant, plaintiff. Civil records in docket books since 1985, computerized since 1988.

Criminal Records: Access: Phone, fax, mail, in person. Both court and visitors may perform in person searches. Search fee: $25.00 per name. Required to search: name, years to search; also helpful: SSN. Criminal records in docket books since 1985, computerized since 1988.

General Information: Turnaround time 1-2 weeks. Fax notes: No fee to fax results. Local calls only. Copy fee: $1.00 per page. Certification fee: $3.00 per page. Fee payee: Mason Municipal Court. Only cashiers checks and money orders accepted. Credit cards accepted: Visa, MasterCard. In person criminal searching only. Prepayment is required.

Washington County

Common Pleas Court 205 Putnam St, Marietta, OH 45750; 740-373-6623; Probate phone: 740-373-6623. Hours: 8AM-4:15PM (EST). *Felony, Civil Actions Over $10,000, Probate.*

Civil Records: Access: In person only. Visitors must perform in person searches for themselves. No search fee. Required to search: name, years to search. Civil cases indexed by defendant, plaintiff. Civil records on computer since 1985, microfilm to 1977, index in books prior.

Criminal Records: Access: In person only. Visitors must perform in person searches for themselves. No search fee. Required to search: name, years to search. Criminal records on computer since 1985, microfilm to 1977, index in books prior.

General Information: Public Access terminal is available. No sealed, expunged records released. Copy fee: $.25 per page. Certification fee: $1.00. Fee payee: Clerk of Court. Personal checks accepted.

Marietta Municipal Court PO Box 615, Marietta, OH 45750; 740-373-4474; Fax: 740-373-2547. Hours: 8AM-5PM (EST). *Misdemeanor, Civil Actions Under $15,000, Eviction, Small Claims.*

www.mariettacourt.com

Civil Records: Access: Mail, in person, online. Both court and visitors may perform in person searches. No search fee. Required to search: name, years to search. Civil cases indexed by defendant, plaintiff. Civil records on computer from 11/91, prior in books. Online access to courts records is to be available free at the web site.

Criminal Records: Access: Mail, in person, online. Both court and visitors may perform in person searches. No search fee. Required to search: name, years to search. Criminal records on computer from 11/91, prior in books back to 1975. Online access to criminal records is the same as civil.

General Information: Public Access terminal is available. SASE required. Turnaround time 1 week. Fax notes: Fee to fax results is $.25 per page. Copy fee: $.25

per page. Certification fee: $1.50. Fee payee: Municipal Court. Personal checks accepted. Prepayment is required.

Wayne County

Common Pleas Court PO Box 507, Wooster, OH 44691; 330-287-5590; Probate phone: 330-287-5575; Fax: 330-287-5416. Hours: 8AM-4:30PM (EST). *Felony, Civil Actions Over $15,000, Probate.*

http://waynecountyclerkofcourts.org/

Note: Probate is a separate court at number given.

Civil Records: Access: Phone, mail, in person. Visitors must perform in person searches for themselves. No search fee. Required to search: name, years to search. Civil cases indexed by defendant, plaintiff. Civil records on computer since 1995, in books to 1800s. No name searches are performed by mail.

Criminal Records: Access: Phone, mail, in person. Visitors must perform in person searches for themselves. No search fee. Required to search: name, years to search. Criminal records on computer since 1995, in books to 1800s.

General Information: Public Access terminal is available. No grand jury indictment records released. Copy fee: $.05 per page. Certification fee: $2.00. Fee payee: Clerk of Court. Personal checks accepted.

Wayne County Municipal Court 538 N Market St, Wooster, OH 44691; 330-287-5650; Fax: 330-263-4043. Hours: 8AM-4:30PM (EST). *Misdemeanor, Civil Actions Under $15,000, Eviction, Small Claims.*

Civil Records: Access: In person only. Visitors must perform in person searches for themselves. No search fee. Required to search: name, years to search. Civil cases indexed by defendant, plaintiff. Civil records are partly on computer from 9/94, in books from 1975.

Criminal Records: Access: In person only. Visitors must perform in person searches for themselves. No search fee. Required to search: name, years to search, offense, date of offense. Criminal records are partly on computer from 9/94, in books from 1975.

General Information: Public Access terminal is available. Copy fee: $.10 per page. Certification fee: $1.00. Fee payee: Wayne County Municipal Court. In state personal checks accepted. Prepayment is required.

Williams County

Common Pleas Court 1 Courthouse Square, Clerk of Court of Common Pleas, Bryan, OH 43506; 419-636-1551; Probate phone: 419-636-1548; Fax: 419-636-7877. Hours: 8:30AM-4:30PM (EST). *Felony, Civil Actions Over $10,000, Probate.*

Note: Probate Court is at the same address, different phone number.

Civil Records: Access: Phone, fax, mail, in person. Both court and visitors may perform in person searches. No search fee. Required to search: name, years to search. Civil cases indexed by defendant, plaintiff. Civil records on computer from 1988, prior in books archived from 1930.

Criminal Records: Access: Mail, in person. Both court and visitors may perform in person searches. No search fee. Required to search: name, years to search. Criminal records on computer from 1988, prior in books archived from 1930.

General Information: Public Access terminal is available. No expunged records released. SASE required. Turnaround time 1-2 days. Copy fee: $.50 per page. Certification fee: $1.00 per page. Fee payee: Clerk of Court. Personal checks accepted. Prepayment is required.

Bryan Municipal Court 1399 E High, PO Box 546, Bryan, OH 43506; 419-636-6939; Fax: 419-636-3417. Hours: 8:30AM-4:30PM (EST). *Misdemeanor, Civil Actions Under $15,000, Eviction, Small Claims.*

Civil Records: Access: Fax, mail, in person. Both court and visitors may perform in person searches. Search fee: $1.00 per name. Required to search: name, years to search. Civil cases indexed by defendant, plaintiff. Civil records on computer from 1988, prior in books to 1966, indexed prior.

Criminal Records: Access: Fax, mail, in person. Both court and visitors may perform in person searches. Search fee: $1.00 per name. Required to search: name, years to search, DOB; also helpful: SSN. Criminal records on computer from 1988, prior in books to 1966, indexed prior.

General Information: Public Access terminal is available. SASE required. Turnaround time 5 days. Fax notes: $2.00. Certification fee: $2.00. Fee payee: Municipal Court. Personal checks accepted. Credit cards accepted: Visa, MasterCard. Prepayment is required.

Wood County

Common Pleas Court Courthouse Square, Bowling Green, OH 43402; 419-354-9280; Probate phone: 419-354-9230; Fax: 419-354-9241. Hours: 8:30AM-4:30PM (EST). *Felony, Civil Actions Over $10,000, Probate.*

Note: Probate record searching and copy fees are different than those listed for civil and criminal records.

Civil Records: Access: Phone, fax, mail, in person. Both court and visitors may perform in person searches. Search fee: $3.00 per name. Required to search: name, years to search. Civil cases indexed by defendant, plaintiff. Civil records on computer from 7/90, in books and on microfilm from 1980, docket books, journals & microfilm back to 1800s.

Criminal Records: Access: Phone, mail, in person. Both court and visitors may perform in person searches. Search fee: $3.00 per name. Required to search: name, years to search; also helpful: SSN. Criminal records on computer from 7/90, in books and on microfilm from 1980, docket books, journals & microfilm back to 1800s.

General Information: Public Access terminal is available. No adoption commitment, parental rights, juvenile, mental illness records released. SASE required. Turnaround time same day. Fax notes: No fee to fax results. Copy fee: $.25 per page first 25 pages, $.10 thereafter. Certification fee: $1.00. Fee payee:

Clerk of Court. Business checks accepted. Personal checks accepted for amounts under 420.00. Prepayment is required.

Bowling Green Municipal Court PO Box 326, Bowling Green, OH 43402; 419-352-5263; Fax: 419-352-9407. Hours: 8:30AM-4:30PM (EST). *Misdemeanor, Civil Actions Under $15,000, Eviction, Small Claims.*

Civil Records: Access: Phone, fax, mail, in person. Both court and visitors may perform in person searches. No search fee. Required to search: name, years to search. Civil cases indexed by defendant, plaintiff. Civil records on computer from 1988.

Criminal Records: Access: Phone, fax, mail, in person. Both court and visitors may perform in person searches. No search fee. Required to search: name, years to search, DOB; also helpful: SSN. Criminal records on computer from 1988.

General Information: Public Access terminal is available. SASE required. Turnaround time 3 days. Fax notes: No fee to fax results. Local faxing only. Copy fee: $.50 per page. Certification fee: No cert fee. Fee payee: Municipal Court. Personal checks accepted. Credit cards accepted: Visa, MasterCard.

Perrysburg Municipal Court 300 Walnut, Perrysburg, OH 43551; 419-872-7900; Fax: 419-872-7905. Hours: 8AM-4:30PM (8AM-7PM Tues.) (EST). *Misdemeanor, Civil Actions Under $15,000, Eviction, Small Claims.*

www.ci.perrysburg.oh.us

Civil Records: Access: Phone, fax, mail, online, in person. Both court and visitors may perform in person searches. Search fee: $3.00 per name. Fee is $15.00 to look in closed, stored files. Required to search: name, years to search; also helpful: address. Civil cases indexed by defendant, plaintiff. Civil records on computer from 1989, prior in books to 1982, archived from 1972. Records from the Perrysburg Muni. Court are available free by remote online. Civil and criminal indexes go back to 1988. Contact Judy Daquano at 419-872-7906 for information.

Criminal Records: Access: Phone, fax, mail, online, in person. Both court and visitors may perform in person searches. Search fee: $3.00 per name. Fee is $15.00 to look in closed, stored files. Required to search: name, years to search; also helpful: DOB, SSN. Criminal records on computer from 1989, prior in books to 1982, archived from 1972. Online access to criminal records is the same as civil.

General Information: Public Access terminal is available. No expunged records released. SASE required. Turnaround time 2 days. Fax notes: $5.00 per document. Copy fee: $.10 per page. Certification fee: $3.00. Fee payee: Municipal Court. Personal checks accepted. Credit cards accepted: Visa, MasterCard. Not accepted over the phone. Prepayment is required.

Wyandot County

Common Pleas Court 109 S Sandusky Ave, Upper Sandusky, OH 43351; 419-294-1432; Probate phone: 419-294-2302. Hours: 8:30AM-4:30PM (EST). *Felony, Civil Actions Over $10,000, Probate.*

Civil Records: Access: Fax, mail, in person. No search fee. Required to search: name, years to search. Civil cases indexed by defendant, plaintiff. Civil records on computer from 1990, prior in books from late 1800s.

Criminal Records: Access: Fax, mail, in person. Both court and visitors may perform in person searches. No search fee. Required to search: name, years to search; also helpful: SSN. Criminal records on computer from 1990, prior in books from late 1800s.

General Information: Public Access terminal is available. SASE required. Turnaround time 1-2 days. Fax notes: $1.00 per page. Copy fee: $.25 per page. Certification fee: $1.00 per page. Fee payee: Clerk of Court. Personal checks accepted. Prepayment required.

Upper Sandusky Municipal Court 119 N 7th St, Upper Sandusky, OH 43351; 419-294-3809; Fax: 419-09-0474. Hours: 8AM-4:30PM (EST). *Misdemeanor, Civil Actions Under $15,000, Eviction, Small Claims.*

Civil Records: Access: Mail, in person. Both court and visitors may perform in person searches. Search fee: $10.00 per name. Required to search: name, years to search. Civil cases indexed by defendant, plaintiff. Civil records on computer from 5/90, prior in books.

Criminal Records: Access: Mail, in person. Both court and visitors may perform in person searches. Search fee: $10.00 per name. Required to search: name, years to search; also helpful: SSN. Criminal records on computer from 5/90, prior in books.

General Information: Public Access terminal is available. No sealed records released. SASE required. Turnaround time 1-2 days. Copy fee: $.50 per page. Certification fee: $1.00. Fee payee: Upper Sandusky. Personal checks accepted. Credit cards accepted: Visa, MasterCard. Not accepted over the phone. Prepayment is required.

Ohio Recording Offices

ORGANIZATION 88 counties, 88 recording offices. The recording officer is County Recorder and Clerk of Common Pleas Court (state tax liens). The entire state is in the Eastern Time Zone (EST).

REAL ESTATE RECORDS Counties will not perform real estate searches. Copy fees are usually $1.00 per page. Certification usually costs $.50 per document. Tax records are located at the Auditor's Office.

UCC RECORDS This was a dual filing state. Financing statements were filed both at the state level and with the County Recorder, except for consumer goods, farm related and real estate related collateral, which were filed only with the County Recorder. As of 0701/2001, only real estate related collateral is filed at the county level. All counties will perform UCC searches. Use search request form UCC-11. Search fees are usually $9.00 per debtor name. Copies usually cost $1.00 per page.

TAX LIEN RECORDS All federal tax liens are filed with the County Recorder. All state tax liens are filed with the Clerk of Common Pleas Court. Refer to County Court section for information about Ohio courts. Federal tax liens are filed in the "Official Records" of each county. Most counties will not perform a federal tax lien search.

OTHER LIENS Mechanics, workers compensation, judgment.

STATEWIDE ONLINE INFO: A growing number of Ohio counties offer online access, via the Internet, to assessor and real estate data.

Adams County
County Recorder, 110 West Main, Courthouse, West Union, OH 45693. 937-544-2513; Fax 937-544-5051. Will search UCC records. Will not search real estate records.

Allen County
County Recorder, P.O. Box 1243, Lima, OH 45802. 419-223-8517.
Will search UCC records. This agency will not do a federal tax lien search. Will not search real estate records.

Ashland County
County Recorder, Courthouse, 142 W. 2nd St., Ashland, OH 44805-2193. 419-282-4238; Fax 419-281-5715.
Will search UCC records. This agency will not do a federal tax lien search. Will not search real estate records. **Online Access:** Real Estate, Auditor. Property records on the county Auditor's database are available free online at www.ashlandcoauditor.org/ashland208/landrover.asp. **Other Phone Numbers:** Treasurer 419-282-4229; Appraiser/Auditor 419-282-4330; Elections 419-181-3172; Vital Records 419-282-4226.

Ashtabula County
County Recorder, 25 West Jefferson Street, Jefferson, OH 44047. County Recorder, R/E and UCC Recording 440-576-3762; Fax 440-576-3231. http://www.co.ashtabula.oh.us
Will search UCC records. Will not search real estate records. Can give specific information - filed date, deed volume/page, etc. - over phone. **Online Access:** Real Estate, Auditor. Property records on the county Auditor's database are available free online at http://216.28.192.48/ashtabula208/LandRover.asp.
Other Phone Numbers: Treasurer 440-576-3727; Appraiser/Auditor 440-576-3789; Elections 440-576-6915; Vital Records 440-576-3627; Auditor 440-576-3783.

Athens County
County Recorder, 15 South Court, Rm 236, 15 South Court, Athens, OH 45701. 740-592-3228; Fax 740-592-3229.
Will search UCC records. Will not search real estate records. **Other Phone Numbers:** Treasurer 740-592-3731; Auditor 740-592-3223.

Auglaize County
County Recorder, Courthouse, Suite 101, 201 S. Willipie St., Wapakoneta, OH 45895-1972. 419-738-4318; Fax 419-738-4115.
Will search UCC records. Will not search real estate records. **Other Phone Numbers:** Treasurer 419-738-2110; Auditor 419-738-2511.

Belmont County
County Recorder, Courthouse, Room 105, 101 Main St., St. Clairsville, OH 43950. 740-699-2140.
Will search UCC records. This agency will not do a tax lien search. Mortgage searches available. **Other Phone Numbers:** Treasurer 740-695-2120 x211; Auditor 740-695-2120 x257.

Brown County
County Recorder, P.O. Box 149, Georgetown, OH 45121. 937-378-6478; Fax 937-378-2848.
Will search UCC records. Will not search real estate records. **Other Phone Numbers:** Treasurer 937-378-6705; Auditor 937-378-6398.

Butler County
County Recorder, 130 High Street, Hamilton, OH 45011. 513-887-3191 R/E Recording: 513-887-3192; Fax 513-887-3198. http://www.butlercountyohio.org/recorder
Will search UCC records. This agency will not do a federal tax lien search. Will not search real estate records. **Online Access:** Probate, Voter Records. County voter records are available at www.butlercountyohio.org/elections. County probate records are available at www.butlercountyohio.org/probate/estate.cfm. **Other Phone Numbers:** Treasurer 513-887-3181; Appraiser/Auditor 513-887-3147; Elections 513-887-3700; Vital Records 513-863-1770; Auditor 513-887-3295.

Carroll County
County Recorder, P.O. Box 550, Carrollton, OH 44615-0550. 330-627-4545; Fax 330-627-4295. http://www.ohiorecorders.com
Will search UCC records. This agency will not do a tax lien search. Will not search real estate records. **Other Phone Numbers:** Assessor 330-327-2250; Treasurer 330-627-4221; Appraiser/Auditor 330-627-2250; Elections 330-627-2610.

Champaign County
County Recorder, 200 North Main Street, Urbana, OH 43078-1679. 937-652-2263; Fax 937-652-1515.
Will search UCC records. **Other Phone Numbers:** ; Auditor 937-652-2264.

Clark County
County Recorder, P.O. Box 1406, Springfield, OH 45501. County Recorder, R/E and UCC Recording 937-328-2445; Fax 937-328-4620.
Will search UCC records. **Other Phone Numbers:** Treasurer 937-328-2432; Auditor 937-328-2423.

Clermont County
County Recorder, 101 E. Main Street, Batavia, OH 45103-2958. 513-732-7236; Fax 513-732-7891.
Will search UCC records. Mortgage searches available. **Online Access:** Property Records. Records from the county Property database are available free online at http://clermont.akanda.com. **Other Phone Numbers:** Treasurer 513-732-7254; Auditor 513-732-7150.

Clinton County
County Recorder, 46 S. South Street, Courthouse, Wilmington, OH 45177. 937-382-2067; Fax 937-383-6653.
Will search UCC records. This agency will not do a federal tax lien search. Will not search real estate records. **Other Phone Numbers:** Treasurer 937-382-2224; Elections 937-382-3537; Vital Records 937-382-3829; Auditor 937-382-2250.

Columbiana County
County Recorder, County Courthouse, Room 104, 105 South Market St., Lisbon, OH 44432. 330-424-9517 x641; Fax 330-424-5067. http://www.columbianacntyauditor.org

Will search UCC records. Will not search real estate records. **Online Access:** Real Estate, Auditor. Property records on the county Auditor's database are available free online at www.columbianacntyauditor.org/columbv208/LandRover.asp.

Coshocton County

County Recorder, P.O. Box 817, Coshocton, OH 43812. County Recorder, R/E and UCC Recording 740-622-2817; Fax 740-622-0190.
Will search UCC records. Will not search real estate records. **Other Phone Numbers:** Treasurer 740-622-2713; Elections 740-622-1117; Auditor 740-622-1243.

Crawford County

County Recorder, P.O. Box 788, Bucyrus, OH 44820-0788. County Recorder, R/E and UCC Recording 419-562-6961; Fax 419-562-6061.
Will search UCC records. Will not search real estate records. **Other Phone Numbers:** Treasurer 419-562-7861; Appraiser/Auditor 419-562-7941; Elections 419-562-8721.

Cuyahoga County

County Recorder, 1219 Ontario Street, Room 220, Cleveland, OH 44113. 216-443-7314; Fax 216-443-8193.
http://www.cuyahoga.oh.us/auditor/approg/Default.asp
Will search UCC records. This agency will not do a federal tax lien search. Will not search real estate records. **Online Access:** Auditor/Assessor. Online access to the County Auditor Property Information database is available free at the web site. **Other Phone Numbers:** Appraiser/Auditor 216-443-7092.

Darke County

County Recorder, 504 South Broadway, Courthouse, Greenville, OH 45331. 937-547-7390.
Will search UCC records. This agency will not do a federal tax lien search. Will not search real estate records. **Online Access:** Real Estate. Property records on the Darke County database are available free online at www.darkecountyrealestate.org. County Recorder records are accessible through a private online service at www.landaccess.com; Fees and registration are required. **Other Phone Numbers:** Treasurer 937-547-7365; Auditor 937-547-7310.

Defiance County

County Recorder, 221 Clinton Street, Courthouse, Defiance, OH 43512. 419-782-4741; Fax 419-782-3421.
Will search UCC records. This agency will not do a federal tax lien search. Will not search real estate records.

Delaware County

County Recorder, 91 North Sandusky Street, Courthouse, Delaware, OH 43015. 740-368-1835; Fax 740-833-2459. http://www.co.delaware.oh.us
Will search UCC records. This agency will not do a federal tax lien search. Will not search real estate records. **Online Access:** Real Estate, Auditor. The Delaware Appraisal Land Information System Project (DALIS) maps with County Auditor records are available free online. At main site, click on "GIS mapping" in the lefthand menu bar, then select a search method. Once parcel is identified on the map, click on "identify" then on parcel map to get parcel information, values, sales, and building information. Also, access to auditor's property information is available free at www.delawarecountyauditor.org/delaware208/LandRover.asp. **Other Phone Numbers:** Treasurer 740-833-2460; Auditor 740-833-2460.

Erie County

County Recorder, Erie County Office Bldg, Room 225, 247 Columbus Ave., Sandusky, OH 44870-2635. 419-627-7686; Fax 419-627-6639.
Will search UCC records. UCC search does not include federal tax liens. Will not search real estate records. **Other Phone Numbers:** Treasurer 419-627-7201; Appraiser/Auditor 419-627-7746; Auditor 419-627-7741.

Fairfield County

County Recorder, P.O. Box 2420, Lancaster, OH 43130-5420. 740-687-7100; Fax 740-687-7104.
Will search UCC records. This agency will not do a federal tax lien search. Will not search real estate records. **Other Phone Numbers:** Treasurer 740-687-7094; Auditor 740-687-7090.

Fayette County

County Recorder, 110 East Court Street, Courthouse Building, Washington Court House, OH 43160-1393. 740-335-1770; Fax 740-333-3530.
Will search UCC records. Will not search real estate records.

Franklin County

County Recorder, 373 S. High Street, 18th Floor, Columbus, OH 43215-6307. County Recorder, R/E and UCC Recording 614-462-3930 UCC Recording: 614-462-3937; Fax 614-462-4312. www.ohiorecorders.com
Will search UCC records. Will not search real estate records. **Online Access:** Property, Auditor, Unclaimed Funds, Marriage. **Other Phone Numbers:** Appraiser/Auditor 614-462-463; Auditor 614-462-3894.

Fulton County

County Recorder, 152 S Fulton St #175, 210 S. Fulton St., Wauseon, OH 43567. County Recorder, R/E and UCC Recording 419-337-9232; Fax 419-337-9282. http://www.fultoncountyoh.com
Will search UCC records. This agency will not do a federal tax lien search. Will not search real estate records. **Other Phone Numbers:** Treasurer 419-337-9200; Auditor 419-337-9200.

Gallia County

County Recorder, 18 Locust Street, Room 1265, Gallipolis, OH 45631-1265. 740-446-4612 x248 R/E Recording: 740-446-4612 UCC Recording: 740-446-4612; Fax 740-446-4804. http://galliaauditor.ddti.net
Will search UCC records. Will not search real estate records. **Online Access:** Property, Real Estate. Property records on the county auditor real estate database are available free online at http://galliaauditor.ddti.net. Click on "attributes" for property information; click on "sales" to search by real estate attributes. **Other Phone Numbers:** Treasurer 740-446-6004; Auditor 740-446-4612.

Geauga County

County Recorder, 231 Main Street, Ste. 1C, Courthouse Annex, Chardon, OH 44024-1235. County Recorder, R/E and UCC Recording 440-285-2222 x3680.
Will search UCC records. This agency will not do a federal tax lien search. Will not search real estate records. **Other Phone Numbers:** Assessor 440-285-2222 x3450; Treasurer 440-285-2222 x3850; Appraiser/Auditor 440-285-2222 x4490; Elections 440-285-2222 x4020; Vital Records 440-285-2222 x6407.

Greene County

County Recorder, P.O. Box 100, Xenia, OH 45385-0100. 937-376-5270 R/E Recording: 937-562-5270

UCC Recording: 937-562-5275; Fax 937-376-5386. http://www.co.greene.oh.us/recorder.htm
Will search UCC records. This agency will not do a federal tax lien search. Will not search real estate records. **Online Access:** Real Estate, Auditor. Records on the county Internet Map Server are available free online at www.co.greene.oh.us/gismapserver.htm. Click on "Click here to enter. Server Site #1". Data includes owner, address, valuation, taxes, sales data, and parcel ID number. **Other Phone Numbers:** Treasurer 937-376-5065; Appraiser/Auditor 937-562-5278; Elections 937-562-5261; Vital Records 937-562-5686; Auditor 937-376-5065.

Guernsey County

County Recorder, Courthouse D-202, Wheeling Avenue, Cambridge, OH 43725. County Recorder, R/E and UCC Recording 740-432-9275.
Will search UCC records. This agency will not do a federal tax lien search. Will not search real estate records. **Other Phone Numbers:** Assessor 740-432-9243; Treasurer 740-432-9278; Appraiser/Auditor 740-432-9243; Elections 740-432-2680; Vital Records 740-432-3577.

Hamilton County

County Recorder, 138 East Court Street, Room 101-A, Cincinnati, OH 45202. 513-946-4588; Fax 513-946-4577. http://www.hcro.org
Will search UCC records. UCC search does not include federal tax liens. RE record owner and mortgage searches available. **Online Access:** Real Estate, Liens. Access to county online records requires a $100 escrow account, plus $1 per connection and $.30 per minute. Records date back to 6/1988. Lending agency information is available. For information, contact Vicky Jones at 513-946-4571. **Other Phone Numbers:** Treasurer 513-632-8380; Auditor 513-632-8585.

Hancock County

County Recorder, 300 South Main Street, Courthouse, Findlay, OH 45840. County Recorder, R/E and UCC Recording 419-424-7091; Fax 419-424-7828.
Will search UCC records. **Other Phone Numbers:** Treasurer 419-424-7213; Appraiser/Auditor 419-424-7015; Elections 419-422-3245; Vital Records 419-424-7869; Auditor 419-424-7083.

Hardin County

County Recorder, One Courthouse Square, Suite 220, Kenton, OH 43326. County Recorder, R/E and UCC Recording 419-674-2250; Fax 419-675-2802. http://www.co.hardin.oh.us
Will search UCC records. This agency will not do a federal tax lien search. Will not search real estate records. **Online Access:** Property. Property records from the county database are available at the web site. Click on "Real Estate Internet Inquiry.". **Other Phone Numbers:** Treasurer 419-674-2246; Appraiser/Auditor 419-674-2211; Auditor 419-674-2239.

Harrison County

County Recorder, 100 West Market Street, Courthouse, Cadiz, OH 43907. County Recorder, R/E and UCC Recording 740-942-8869; Fax 740-942-4693.
Will search UCC records. This agency will not do a federal tax lien search. Will not search real estate records. **Other Phone Numbers:** Treasurer 740-942-8864; Elections 740-942-8866; Vital Records 740-942-8868; Auditor 740-942-8861; Engineer 740-942-8867;

Henry County

County Recorder, Courthouse, Room 202, 660 North Perry St., Napoleon, OH 43545-1747. 419-592-1766; Fax 419-592-1652. http://www.ohiorecorders.com

Will search UCC records. This agency will not do a federal tax lien search. Will not search real estate records. **Other Phone Numbers:** Assessor 419-492-1956; Treasurer 419-592-1851; Elections 419-592-7956; Vital Records 419-599-5545.

Highland County

County Recorder, P.O. Box 804, Hillsboro, OH 45133. County Recorder, R/E and UCC Recording 937-393-9954; Fax 937-393-5855. www.ohiorecorders.com Will search UCC records. This agency will not do a federal tax lien search. Will not search real estate records. **Other Phone Numbers:** Assessor 937-393-1915; Treasurer 937-393-9951; Appraiser/Auditor 937-393-1915; Elections 937-393-9961; Vital Records 937-393-1941.

Hocking County

County Recorder, P.O. Box 949, Logan, OH 43138-0949. County Recorder, R/E and UCC Recording 740-385-2031; Fax 740-385-0377. Will search UCC records. Will not search real estate records. **Other Phone Numbers:** Assessor 740-385-2127; Treasurer 740-385-3517; Appraiser/Auditor 740-385-2127; Elections 740-385-0203; Vital Records 740-385-3030.

Holmes County

County Recorder, P.O. Box 213, Millersburg, OH 44654. 330-674-5916. Will search UCC records. This agency will not do a federal tax lien search. Will not search real estate records. **Other Phone Numbers:** Treasurer 330-674-1896; Auditor 330-674-1896.

Huron County

County Recorder, P.O. Box 354, Norwalk, OH 44857. 419-668-1916; Fax 419-663-4052. Will search UCC records. Will not search real estate records.

Jackson County

County Recorder, 226 E. Main St., Courthouse, Suite 1, Jackson, OH 45640. County Recorder, R/E and UCC Recording 740-286-1919. Will search UCC records. This agency will not do a federal tax lien search. Will not search real estate records. **Other Phone Numbers:** Treasurer 740-286-2402; Elections 740-286-2905; Auditor 740-286-4231.

Jefferson County

County Recorder, Jefferson County Recorder 301 Market St., Steubenville, OH 43952. 740-283-8566. Will search UCC records. UCC search includes federal tax liens if requested. Will not search real estate records. **Other Phone Numbers:** Treasurer 614-283-8511; Auditor 614-283-8511.

Knox County

County Recorder, 106 East High Street, Mount Vernon, OH 43050. 740-393-6755; http://www.knoxcounty auditor.org Will search UCC records. This agency will not do a federal tax lien search. Will not search real estate records. **Online Access:** Property. Records on the county auditor database are available free online at www.knoxcountyauditor.org/knox208/LandRover.asp.

Lake County

County Recorder, P.O. Box 490, Painesville, OH 44077-0490. County Recorder, R/E and UCC Recording 440-350-2510 UCC Recording: 440-350-2511; Fax 440-350-5940. http://www.lakecounty recorder.org

Will search UCC records. Will not search tax liens. Will not search real estate records. **Online Access:** Real Estate, Auditor, Recordings, Liens. Online access to the Recorder's Document Index database is available free at http://web2.lakecountyohio.org/recorders/search/index.asp. Records go back to 1986. Also, access to the treasurer and auditor's real estate databases is available free at www.lake.iviewauditor.com. Click on "by attibute.". **Other Phone Numbers:** Treasurer 440-350-2517; Appraiser/Auditor 440-350-2528; Elections 440-350-2700; Vital Records 440-350-2549; Auditor 440-350-2528.

Lawrence County

County Recorder, P.O. Box 77, Ironton, OH 45638. County Recorder, R/E and UCC Recording 740-533-4314; Fax 740-533-4411. Will search UCC records. Will not search real estate records. **Online Access:** Real Estate, Liens. Access to County Recorder records requires a $600-700 set-up fee, plus a $75. monthly fee. Mortgage records date back to 1988 and deeds to 1984. Only federal tax liens are online; state liens are kept by the Clerk of Court. UCC liens date back to 1989. Call 740-533-4314 for more information.

Licking County

County Recorder, P.O. Box 548, Newark, OH 43058-0548. 740-349-6061; Fax 740-349-1415. Will search UCC records. This agency will not do a federal tax lien search. Will not search real estate records.

Logan County Recorder

County Recorder, 100 South Madriver, Suite A, Suite A, Bellefontaine, OH 43311-2075. 937-599-7201; Fax 937-599-7287. Will search UCC records. Will not search real estate records. **Online Access:** Real Estate, Auditor. Records on the County Auditor's database are available free online at www2.co.logan.oh.us/logan208/LandRover.asp. **Other Phone Numbers:** Treasurer 937-599-7223; Elections 937-599-7255; Auditor 937-599-7213.

Lorain County

County Recorder, 226 Middle Avenue, Elyria, OH 44035-5643. County Recorder, R/E and UCC Recording 440-329-5148 UCC Recording: 440-329-5138; Fax 440-329-5477. http://www.lorain county.com/government/ Will search UCC records. Will not search real estate records. **Online Access:** Real Estate, Liens, Auditor. Online access to the county assessor database is available free at www.loraincounty.com/ recorder/register. Free registration is required. Also, records on the County Auditor's database are available free online at www.loraincountyauditor.org/lorain208/LandRover.asp.

Lucas County

County Recorder, 1 Government Center #700, Jackson Street, Toledo, OH 43604. 419-213-4400; Fax 419-213-4284. http://ww.co.lucas.oh.us Will search UCC records. UCC search includes federal tax liens if requested. Will not search real estate records. **Online Access:** Real Estate, Auditor. Property records on the County Auditor's Real Estate Information System (AREIS) database are available free online at http://www.co.lucas.oh.us/Real_Estate. User ID is required; registration is free. **Other Phone Numbers:** Treasurer 419-213-4303; Vital Records 419-213-4100; Auditor 419-213-4424.

Madison County

County Recorder, Courthouse, Room 40, 1 N. Main St., London, OH 43140. County Recorder, R/E and UCC Recording 740-852-1854; Fax 740-845-1776. http://www.co.madison.oh.us/elected.htm Will search UCC records. This agency will not do a federal tax lien search. Will not search real estate records. **Online Access:** Real Estate, Auditor. Records on the County Auditor's database are available free online at www.co.madison.oh.us/auditor/iViewW3/iViewW3.asp. Also, County Recorder records are accessible through a private online service at www.landaccess.com; Fees and registration are required. **Other Phone Numbers:** Treasurer 740-852-1936; Auditor 740-852-9717.

Mahoning County

County Recorder, P.O. Box 928, Youngstown, OH 44501. 330-740-2345; Fax 330-740-2006. http://www.mahoningcountyauditor.org Will search UCC records. **Online Access:** Real Estate, Auditor. Property records on the County Auditor's database are available free online at www.mahoningcountyauditor.org/maho208/LandRover.asp. **Other Phone Numbers:** Treasurer 330-740-2460; Auditor 330-740-2010.

Marion County

County Recorder, 171 E. Center St., Marion, OH 43302-3089. County Recorder, R/E and UCC Recording 740-387-4521; http://www.co.marion.oh.us Will search UCC records. This agency will not do a tax lien search. Will not search real estate records. **Online Access:** Real Estate, Auditor. Online access to the county auditor real estate database is available free at www.co.marion.oh.us. Click on "Real Estate Inquiry.". **Other Phone Numbers:** Assessor 740-387-4811; Treasurer 740-387-7345; Appraiser/Auditor 740-387-4811; Elections 740-387-4058; Auditor 740-387-7345.

Medina County

County Recorder, County Administration Bldg, 144 N. Broadway, Medina, OH 44256-2295. County Recorder, R/E and UCC Recording 330-725-9782 UCC Recording: 330-725-9783; http://www.recorder.co.medina.oh.us Will search UCC records. This agency will not do a federal tax lien search. Will not search real estate records. **Online Access:** Real Estate, Auditor. Online access to indexes 1983 to present on the County Recorder database is available free at the web site. Click on "Indexes" and use "View" as user name and password. Also, online access to property records on the Medina County Auditor database are available free online at www.medinacountyauditor.org - "Public Records.". **Other Phone Numbers:** Assessor 330-725-9754.

Meigs County

County Recorder, 100 East Second Street, Courthouse, Pomeroy, OH 45769. 740-992-3806; Fax 740-992-2867. Will search UCC records. This agency will not do a federal tax lien search. Will not search real estate records. **Other Phone Numbers:** Treasurer 740-992-2004; Auditor 740-992-5290.

Mercer County

County Recorder, 101 North Main Street, Courthouse Square-Room 203, Celina, OH 45822. 419-586-4232; Fax 419-586-3541. http://www.mercercountyohio.org Will search UCC records. This agency will not do a federal tax lien search. Will not search real estate records. **Online Access:** Real Estate, Auditor. RProperty records on the County Auditor - Real Estate

Department database are available free online at www.mercercountyohio.org/auditor/RealEstate/PcardInq/category.htm. **Other Phone Numbers:** Treasurer 419-586-2259; Appraiser/Auditor 419-586-6402; Elections 419-586-2215; Auditor 419-586-2259.

Miami County

County Recorder, P.O. Box 653, Troy, OH 45373. 937-332-6893 R/E Recording: 937-332-6912; Fax 937-332-6806.
Will search UCC records. This agency will not do a federal tax lien search. Will not search real estate records. **Other Phone Numbers:** Treasurer 937-332-6929; Appraiser/Auditor 937-332-6964; Elections 937-332-6926; Auditor 937-332-6964.

Monroe County

County Recorder, P.O. Box 152, Woodsfield, OH 43793-0152. 740-472-5264.
Will search UCC records. This agency will not do a federal tax lien search. Will not search real estate records. **Other Phone Numbers:** Treasurer 740-472-1521; Auditor 740-472-0873.

Montgomery County

County Recorder, P.O. Box 972, Dayton, OH 45422. 937-225-4282; Fax 937-225-5980. http://www.mctreas.org
Will search UCC records. Will not search real estate records. **Online Access:** Property. Property records on the county treasurer real estate tax information database are available free online at www.mctreas.org. **Other Phone Numbers:** Appraiser/Auditor 937-225-4002.

Morgan County

County Recorder, 19 East Main Street, McConnelsville, OH 43756. 740-962-4051; Fax 740-962-3364.
Will search UCC records. Will not search real estate records. **Other Phone Numbers:** Treasurer 740-962-4475; Elections 740-962-3116; Vital Records 740-962-4572; Auditor 740-962-4475.

Morrow County

County Recorder, 48 East High Street, Mount Gilead, OH 43338. 419-947-3060; Fax 419-947-3709.
Will search UCC records. Will not search real estate records. **Other Phone Numbers:** Treasurer 419-947-6070; Auditor 419-947-4060.

Muskingum County

County Recorder, P.O. Box 2333, Zanesville, OH 43702-2333. County Recorder, R/E and UCC Recording 740-455-7107; Fax 740-455-7943. http://www.muskingumcountyauditor.org
Will search UCC records. Will not search real estate records. **Online Access:** Real Estate, Assessor. Records on the county assesor database are available free online at www.muskingumcountyauditor.org/realestate/LandRover.asp. **Other Phone Numbers:** Treasurer 740-455-7118; Auditor 740-455-7109.

Noble County

County Recorder, 260 Courthouse, Room 2E, Caldwell, OH 43724. County Recorder, R/E and UCC Recording 740-732-4319.
Will search UCC records. This agency will not do a tax lien search. Will not search real estate records. **Other Phone Numbers:** Treasurer 740-732-2457; Elections 740-732-2057; Vital Records 740-732-5047.

Ottawa County

County Recorder, 315 Madison Street, Room 204, Port Clinton, OH 43452. 419-734-6730 R/E Recording: 419-734-6735 UCC Recording: 419-734-6735; Fax 419-734-6919.

Will search UCC records. Will not search tax liens. Will not search real estate records. **Other Phone Numbers:** Treasurer 419-734-6750; Appraiser/Auditor 419-734-6740; Vital Records 419-734-6800.

Paulding County

County Recorder, 115 N Williams St, 115 N. Williams St., Paulding, OH 45879. County Recorder, R/E and UCC Recording 419-399-8275; Fax 419-399-2862.
Will search UCC records. Will not search real estate records. **Other Phone Numbers:** Assessor 419-399-8205; Treasurer 419-399-8280; Appraiser/Auditor 419-399-8205; Elections 419-399-8230; Vital Records 419-399-3921.

Perry County

County Recorder, P.O. Box 147, New Lexington, OH 43764. 740-342-2494.
Will search UCC records. This agency will not do a federal tax lien search. Will not search real estate records. **Other Phone Numbers:** Treasurer 614-342-2074; Auditor 614-342-2074.

Pickaway County

County Recorder, 207 South Court Street, Circleville, OH 43113. 740-474-5826; Fax 740-477-6361.
Will search UCC records. Will not search real estate records. **Other Phone Numbers:** Treasurer 740-474-2370; Auditor 740-474-4765.

Pike County

County Recorder, Courthouse, 100 E. 2nd St., Waverly, OH 45690. 740-947-2622; Fax 740-947-7997.
Will search UCC records. Will not search real estate records. **Other Phone Numbers:** Treasurer 614-947-2713; Auditor 614-947-2713.

Portage County

County Recorder, 449 South Meridian Street, Ravenna, OH 44266. 330-297-3554; Fax 330-297-7349.
Will search UCC records. Will not search real estate records. **Other Phone Numbers:** Treasurer 330-297-3586; Auditor 330-297-3569.

Preble County

County Recorder, P.O. Box 371, Eaton, OH 45320-0371. 937-456-8173.
Will search UCC records. This agency will not do a federal tax lien search. Will not search real estate records. **Online Access:** Real Estate, Auditor. Property records on the County Auditor's database are available free online at www.preblecountyauditor.org/preble208/LandRover.asp. **Other Phone Numbers:** Assessor 937-456-8148.

Putnam County

County Recorder, 245 East Main Street, Courthouse - Suite 202, Ottawa, OH 45875-1959. 419-523-6490; Fax 419-523-4403.
Will search UCC records. Will not search real estate records. **Other Phone Numbers:** ; Auditor 419-523-6686.

Richland County

County Recorder, 50 Park Avenue East, Mansfield, OH 44902. County Recorder, R/E and UCC Recording 419-774-5599 UCC Recording: 419-774-5601; Fax 419-774-5603.
Will search UCC records. UCC search includes federal tax liens if requested. Will not search real estate records. **Online Access:** Real Estate, Auditor. Property records from the County Auditor database are available free online at www.richlandcountyauditor.org. Also, County Recorder records are accessible through a private online service at www.landaccess.com; Fees and registration

are required. **Other Phone Numbers:** Assessor 419-774-5502; Treasurer 419-774-5522; Appraiser/Auditor 419-774-5503; Elections 419-774-5530; Vital Records 419-774-5586.

Ross County

County Recorder, P.O. Box 6162, Chillicothe, OH 45601. 740-702-3000; Fax 740-702-3006.
Will search UCC records. This agency will not do a federal tax lien search. Will not search real estate records. **Other Phone Numbers:** Treasurer 614-774-7370; Auditor 614-774-7370.

Sandusky County

County Recorder, 100 N. Park Ave., Courthouse, Fremont, OH 43420-2477. 419-334-6226.
Will search UCC records. This agency will not do a federal tax lien search. Mortgage searches available. **Other Phone Numbers:** Treasurer 419-334-6233; Auditor 419-334-6123.

Scioto County

County Recorder, 602 7th Street, Rm 110, Room 110, Portsmouth, OH 45662-3950. County Recorder, R/E and UCC Recording 740-355-8304; Fax 740-353-7358.
Will search UCC records. Will not search real estate records. **Other Phone Numbers:** Assessor 740-355-8264; Treasurer 740-355-8296; Appraiser/Auditor 740-355-8264; Elections 740-355-8217.

Seneca County

County Recorder, 109 South Washington Street, Box 667, Room 7, Tiffin, OH 44883. 419-447-4434.
Will search UCC records. This agency will not do a federal tax lien search. Will not search real estate records.

Shelby County

County Recorder, 129 East Court Street, Shelby County Annex, Sidney, OH 45365. County Recorder, R/E and UCC Recording 937-498-7270; Fax 937-498-7272.
Will search UCC records. Will not search real estate records. **Other Phone Numbers:** Treasurer 937-498-7281; Appraiser/Auditor 937-498-7202; Elections 937-498-7208 or 7209; Vital Records 937-498-7249 (Birth & Death Certificates); Probate (Wills) 937-498-7263; Clerk of Courts-Divorce & judgments 937-498-7221;

Stark County

County Recorder, 110 Central Plaza South, Suite 170, Canton, OH 44702-1409. 330-451-7440 R/E Recording: 330-451-7443 x4464 UCC Recording: 330-451-7443 x7933; www.recorder.co.stark.oh.us
Will search UCC records. This agency will not do a federal tax lien search. Will not search real estate records. **Online Access:** Online searches can be maid on www.recorder.co.stark.oh.us. **Other Phone Numbers:** Treasurer 330-451-7814; Appraiser/Auditor 330-451-7814.

Summit County

Auditor, 175 South Main Street, Akron, OH 44308-1355. 330-643-2720 R/E Recording: 330-643-2719 UCC Recording: 330-643-2719; http://summitoh.net/
Will search UCC records. This agency will not do a federal tax lien search. Will not search real estate records. **Online Access:** Real Estate, Auditor, Property Tax. Tax map information from the County Auditor is available free online at http://scids.summitoh.net/taxmapsinternet, also property appraisal and tax information at www.summitoh.net:85/summit/pawsmain.html. Access to the full document images database requires registration, password and one-time $150.00 fee. Call Summit County Data Center, Help Desk at 330-643-2698 for information and sign-up.

Other Phone Numbers: Treasurer 330-643-2587; Appraiser/Auditor 330-643-2638; Auditor 330-643-2630.

Trumbull County

County Recorder, 160 High Street NW, Warren, OH 44481. County Recorder, R/E and UCC Recording 330-675-2401 UCC Recording: 330-675-2798; Fax 330-675-2404.
Will search UCC records. This agency will not do a federal tax lien search. Will not search real estate records. **Online Access:** Auditor/Assessor. Records on the County Auditor Real Estate web site are available free online at www.co.auditor.trumbull.oh.us/ trumv208/LandRover.asp. Click on "Press here to start. property search" to enter the database query page. **Other Phone Numbers:** Treasurer 330-675-2736; Appraiser/Auditor 330-675-2420; Elections 330-675-4050; Auditor 330-675-2401 x216.

Tuscarawas County

County Recorder, 125 East High Avenue, New Philadelphia, OH 44663. 330-365-3284; http://www.co.tuscarawas.oh.us
Will search UCC records. This agency will not do a federal tax lien search. Will not search real estate records. **Online Access:** Real Estate. County real estate records are available free online at www.co.tuscarawas.oh.us/Auditor/realsearch.htm Also, the county list of Unclaimed Funds may be searched at www.co.tuscarawas.oh.us/Auditor/Unclaimed%20Fun ds.htm. **Other Phone Numbers:** Treasurer 330-365-3254; Appraiser/Auditor 330-365-3220; Auditor 330-364-8811 x220.

Union County

County Recorder, 233 West Sixth St., Marysville, OH 43040. 937-645-3032; Fax 937-642-3397.
Will search UCC records. This agency will not do a federal tax lien search. Will not search real estate records. **Other Phone Numbers:** Treasurer 937-645-3029; Auditor 937-645-3155.

Van Wert County

County Recorder, 121 East Main Street, Courthouse - Room 206, Van Wert, OH 45891-1729. County Recorder, R/E and UCC Recording 419-238-2558; Fax 419-238-5410.
Will search UCC records. This agency will not do a federal tax lien search. Will not search real estate records. **Other Phone Numbers:** Treasurer 419-238-5177; Elections 419-238-4192; Vital Records 419-238-0808; Auditor 419-238-0843.

Vinton County

County Recorder, P.O. Box 11, McArthur, OH 45651. 740-596-4314; Fax 740-596-2265.
Will search UCC records. This agency will not do a federal tax lien search. Will not search real estate records. **Other Phone Numbers:** Treasurer 740-596-5690; Elections 740-596-5855; Vital Records 740-596-5480; Auditor 740-596-5445.

Warren County

County Recorder, 320 East Silver Street, Lebanon, OH 45036-1887. 513-695-1382; Fax 513-695-2949. www.co.warren.oh.us
Will search UCC records. Will not search real estate records. **Online Access:** Real Estate, Auditor. Online access to the county auditor database is available free at www.co.warren.oh.us/auditor/index.htm. Click on Warren County Property Information Search at the bottom of this web page. **Other Phone Numbers:** Treasurer 513-933-1300; Auditor 513-933-1239.

Washington County

County Recorder, 205 Putnam Street, Courthouse, Marietta, OH 45750. 740-373-6623; Fax 740-373-9643.
Will search UCC records. Will not search real estate records. **Other Phone Numbers:** Treasurer 740-373-6623 x256; Auditor 740-373-6623 x263.

Wayne County

County Recorder, 428 West Liberty Street, Wooster, OH 44691-5097. County Recorder, R/E and UCC Recording 330-287-5460; Fax 330-287-5685. www.ohiorecorders.com
Will search UCC records. This agency will not do a federal tax lien search. Will not search real estate records. **Other Phone Numbers:** Treasurer 330-287-5450; Appraiser/Auditor 330-287-5430; Elections 330-287-5480; Auditor 330-287-5430.

Williams County

County Recorder, 1 Courthouse Square, Bryan, OH 43506. 419-636-3259.
Will search UCC records. This agency will not do a federal tax lien search. Will not search real estate records. **Other Phone Numbers:** ; Auditor 419-636-5639.

Wood County

County Recorder, 1 Courthouse Square, Bowling Green, OH 43402-2427. County Recorder, R/E and UCC Recording 419-354-9140.
Will search UCC records. This agency will not do a tax lien search. Will not search real estate records. **Other Phone Numbers:** Assessor 419-354-9150; Treasurer 419-354-9130; Appraiser/Auditor 419-354-9150; Elections 419-354-9120; Vital Records 419-354-9130.

Wyandot County

County Recorder, Courthouse, 109 S. Sandusky Ave., Upper Sandusky, OH 43351. 419-294-1442 R/E Recording: 419-294-1531; Fax 419-294-6405. http://www.co.wyandot.oh.us/
Will search UCC records. Will not search real estate records. **Online Access:** Real Estate, Auditor. Online access to the Auditor's real estate database is available free at www.co.wyandot.oh.us/auditor/default.html. Click on "Real estate Internet Inquiry.". **Other Phone Numbers:** Assessor 419-294-1531; Treasurer 419-294-2131; Elections 419-294-1226; Vital Records 419-294-2302.

Ohio County Locator

You will usually be able to find the city name in the City/County Cross Reference below. In that case, it is a simple matter to determine the county from the cross reference. However, only the official US Postal Service city names are included in this index. There are an additional 40,000 place names that people use in their addresses. Therefore, we have also included a ZIP/City Cross Reference immediately following the City/County Cross Reference.

If you know the ZIP Code but the city name does not appear in the City/County Cross Reference index, look up the ZIP Code in the ZIP/City Cross Reference, find the city name, then look up the city name in the City/County Cross Reference. For example, you want to know the county for an address of Menands, NY 12204. There is no "Menands" in the City/County Cross Reference. The ZIP/City Cross Reference shows that ZIP Codes 12201-12288 are for the city of Albany. Looking back in the City/County Cross Reference, Albany is in Albany County.

City/County Cross Reference

ABERDEEN Brown
ADA (45810) Hardin(95), Hancock(3), Allen(2)
ADAMSVILLE Muskingum
ADDYSTON Hamilton
ADELPHI Ross
ADENA (43901) Jefferson(74), Harrison(16), Belmont(10)
ADRIAN Seneca
AKRON Summit
ALBANY (45710) Athens(54), Vinton(26), Meigs(20)
ALEXANDRIA Licking
ALGER (45812) Hardin(95), Allen(3), Paulding(2)
ALLEDONIA Belmont
ALLIANCE (44601) Stark(90), Mahoning(7), Columbiana(3)
ALPHA Greene
ALVADA (44802) Seneca(57), Hancock(42), Wyandot(1)
ALVORDTON Williams
AMANDA (43102) Fairfield(90), Hocking(9), Pickaway(2)
AMELIA Clermont
AMESVILLE (45711) Athens(90), Washington(8), Morgan(2)
AMHERST Lorain
AMLIN Franklin
AMSDEN Seneca
AMSTERDAM (43903) Carroll(77), Jefferson(24)
ANDOVER Ashtabula
ANNA Shelby
ANSONIA Darke
ANTWERP (45813) Paulding(99), Defiance(1)
APPLE CREEK Wayne
ARCADIA Hancock
ARCANUM (45304) Darke(86), Miami(13)
ARCHBOLD (43502) Fulton(91), Henry(9)
ARLINGTON Hancock
ASHLAND Ashland
ASHLEY (43003) Delaware(56), Morrow(44)
ASHTABULA Ashtabula
ASHVILLE Pickaway
ATHENS Athens
ATTICA (44807) Seneca(86), Huron(14)
ATWATER (44201) Portage(97), Stark(3)
AUGUSTA Carroll
AURORA (44202) Portage(86), Summit(11), Geauga(2)
AUSTINBURG Ashtabula
AVA Noble
AVON Lorain
AVON LAKE Lorain
B F GOODRICH CO Summit
BAINBRIDGE (45612) Ross(65), Pike(21), Highland(14)
BAKERSVILLE Coshocton
BALTIC (43804) Holmes(57), Tuscarawas(25), Coshocton(18)
BALTIMORE Fairfield
BANNOCK Belmont

BARBERTON Summit
BARLOW Washington
BARNESVILLE Belmont
BARTLETT Washington
BARTON Belmont
BASCOM Seneca
BATAVIA Clermont
BATH Summit
BAY VILLAGE Cuyahoga
BEACH CITY (44608) Stark(72), Tuscarawas(29)
BEACHWOOD Cuyahoga
BEALLSVILLE (43716) Monroe(75), Belmont(26)
BEAVER (45613) Pike(82), Jackson(18)
BEAVERDAM Allen
BEDFORD Cuyahoga
BELLAIRE Belmont
BELLBROOK Greene
BELLE CENTER (43310) Logan(74), Hardin(26)
BELLE VALLEY Noble
BELLEFONTAINE Logan
BELLEVUE (44811) Huron(43), Sandusky(41), Seneca(11), Erie(6)
BELLVILLE (44813) Richland(85), Knox(8), Morrow(7)
BELMONT Belmont
BELMORE Putnam
BELOIT (44609) Mahoning(60), Columbiana(40)
BELPRE Washington
BENTON RIDGE Hancock
BENTONVILLE Adams
BEREA Cuyahoga
BERGHOLZ (43908) Carroll(53), Jefferson(47)
BERKEY (43504) Lucas(94), Fulton(6)
BERLIN Holmes
BERLIN CENTER Mahoning
BERLIN HEIGHTS Erie
BETHEL Clermont
BETHESDA Belmont
BETTSVILLE Seneca
BEVERLY (45715) Washington(63), Morgan(29), Noble(8)
BIDWELL Gallia
BIG PRAIRIE (44611) Holmes(94), Wayne(6)
BIRMINGHAM Erie
BLACKLICK Franklin
BLADENSBURG Knox
BLAINE Belmont
BLAKESLEE Williams
BLANCHESTER Clinton
BLISSFIELD Coshocton
BLOOMDALE (44817) Wood(93), Hancock(7)
BLOOMINGBURG Fayette
BLOOMINGDALE (43910) Jefferson(97), Harrison(3)
BLOOMVILLE (44818) Seneca(62), Crawford(38)
BLUE CREEK (45616) Adams(84), Scioto(16)

BLUE ROCK (43720) Muskingum(91), Morgan(9)
BLUFFTON (45817) Allen(85), Hancock(14), Putnam(1)
BOLIVAR (44612) Tuscarawas(94), Stark(6)
BOTKINS (45306) Shelby(94), Auglaize(6)
BOURNEVILLE Ross
BOWERSTON (44695) Harrison(54), Carroll(46)
BOWERSVILLE Greene
BOWLING GREEN Wood
BRADFORD (45308) Darke(54), Miami(46)
BRADNER (43406) Wood(90), Sandusky(10)
BRADY LAKE Portage
BRECKSVILLE (44141) Cuyahoga(93), Summit(7)
BREMEN (43107) Fairfield(92), Hocking(5), Perry(3)
BREWSTER Stark
BRICE Franklin
BRIDGEPORT Belmont
BRILLIANT Jefferson
BRINKHAVEN (43006) Coshocton(39), Holmes(39), Knox(22)
BRISTOLVILLE Trumbull
BROADVIEW HEIGHTS Cuyahoga
BROADWAY Union
BROOKFIELD Trumbull
BROOKPARK Cuyahoga
BROOKVILLE (45309) Montgomery(99), Darke(1)
BROWNSVILLE Licking
BRUNSWICK Medina
BRYAN (43506) Williams(97), Defiance(3)
BUCHTEL Athens
BUCKEYE LAKE Licking
BUCKLAND Auglaize
BUCYRUS Crawford
BUFFALO Guernsey
BUFORD Highland
BURBANK (44214) Wayne(83), Medina(17)
BURGHILL Trumbull
BURGOON (43407) Sandusky(98), Seneca(2)
BURKETTSVILLE Mercer
BURTON Geauga
BUTLER (44822) Richland(61), Knox(38)
BYESVILLE Guernsey
CABLE Champaign
CADIZ Harrison
CAIRO Allen
CALDWELL (43724) Noble(98), Morgan(2)
CALEDONIA (43314) Marion(84), Morrow(10), Crawford(6)
CAMBRIDGE Guernsey
CAMDEN Preble
CAMERON Monroe
CAMP DENNISON Hamilton
CAMPBELL Mahoning
CANAL FULTON (44614) Stark(97), Summit(2), Wayne(1)
CANAL WINCHESTER (43110) Fairfield(55), Franklin(44)

CANFIELD Mahoning
CANTON (44720) Stark(93), Summit(8)
CANTON (44730) Stark(99), Carroll(1)
CANTON Stark
CARBON HILL Hocking
CARBONDALE Athens
CARDINGTON (43315) Morrow(93), Marion(7)
CAREY (43316) Wyandot(82), Seneca(16), Hancock(3)
CARROLL Fairfield
CARROLLTON Carroll
CASSTOWN (45312) Miami(98), Champaign(2)
CASTALIA (44824) Erie(98), Sandusky(3)
CATAWBA Clark
CECIL (45821) Paulding(93), Defiance(7)
CEDARVILLE (45314) Greene(97), Clark(3)
CELINA Mercer
CENTERBURG (43011) Knox(57), Morrow(17), Delaware(13), Licking(12)
CHAGRIN FALLS (44022) Cuyahoga(78), Geauga(22)
CHAGRIN FALLS Geauga
CHANDLERSVILLE Muskingum
CHARDON (44024) Geauga(98), Lake(2)
CHARM Holmes
CHATFIELD Crawford
CHAUNCEY Athens
CHERRY FORK Adams
CHESAPEAKE Lawrence
CHESHIRE (45620) Gallia(97), Meigs(3)
CHESTER Meigs
CHESTERHILL (43728) Morgan(92), Athens(8)
CHESTERLAND Geauga
CHESTERVILLE Morrow
CHICKASAW Mercer
CHILLICOTHE Ross
CHILO Clermont
CHIPPEWA LAKE Medina
CHRISTIANSBURG Champaign
CINCINNATI (45241) Hamilton(75), Butler(22), Warren(3)
CINCINNATI (45244) Hamilton(60), Clermont(40)
CINCINNATI (45246) Hamilton(94), Butler(6)
CINCINNATI (45249) Hamilton(97), Warren(3)
CINCINNATI (45255) Hamilton(71), Clermont(29)
CINCINNATI Brown
CINCINNATI Clermont
CINCINNATI Hamilton
CIRCLEVILLE Pickaway
CLARINGTON Monroe
CLARKSBURG (43115) Ross(79), Pickaway(21)
CLARKSVILLE Clinton
CLAY CENTER Ottawa
CLAYTON Montgomery
CLEVELAND Cuyahoga
CLEVES Hamilton

CLIFTON Greene
CLINTON (44216) Summit(88), Stark(11)
CLOVERDALE (45827) Putnam(87), Paulding(13)
CLYDE (43410) Sandusky(97), Seneca(4)
COAL RUN Washington
COALTON Jackson
COLDWATER Mercer
COLERAIN Belmont
COLLEGE CORNER Butler
COLLINS (44826) Huron(85), Erie(16)
COLLINSVILLE Butler
COLTON Henry
COLUMBIA STATION Lorain
COLUMBIANA (44408) Columbiana(87), Mahoning(13)
COLUMBUS Delaware
COLUMBUS Franklin
COLUMBUS GROVE (45830) Putnam(80), Allen(20)
COMMERCIAL POINT Pickaway
CONESVILLE (43811) Coshocton(99), Muskingum(1)
CONNEAUT Ashtabula
CONOVER (45317) Miami(50), Champaign(40), Shelby(10)
CONTINENTAL (45831) Putnam(96), Defiance(2), Paulding(2)
CONVOY (45832) Van Wert(98), Paulding(2)
COOLVILLE (45723) Athens(83), Meigs(14), Washington(3)
CORNING (43730) Perry(98), Morgan(3)
CORTLAND Trumbull
COSHOCTON Coshocton
COVINGTON (45318) Miami(96), Shelby(4)
CREOLA (45622) Vinton(98), Hocking(2)
CRESTLINE (44827) Crawford(99), Richland(1)
CRESTON (44217) Wayne(91), Medina(9)
CROOKSVILLE (43731) Perry(86), Morgan(14)
CROTON (99999) Licking(99), Delaware(1)
CROWN CITY (45623) Gallia(86), Lawrence(14)
CUBA Clinton
CUMBERLAND (43732) Guernsey(74), Noble(17), Muskingum(7), Morgan(2)
CURTICE (43412) Lucas(62), Ottawa(38)
CUSTAR (43511) Wood(77), Henry(23)
CUTLER (45724) Washington(96), Athens(4)
CUYAHOGA FALLS Summit
CYGNET Wood
CYNTHIANA Pike
DALTON (44618) Wayne(92), Stark(8)
DAMASCUS Mahoning
DANVILLE Knox
DAYTON (45424) Montgomery(97), Greene(3)
DAYTON (45431) Montgomery(59), Greene(41)
DAYTON (45432) Greene(52), Montgomery(48)
DAYTON (45433) Greene(97), Montgomery(3)
DAYTON (45434) Greene(99), Montgomery(1)
DAYTON (45440) Montgomery(60), Greene(40)
DAYTON (45458) Montgomery(95), Warren(5)
DAYTON (45459) Montgomery(99), Greene(1)
DAYTON Greene
DAYTON Montgomery
DE GRAFF (43318) Logan(77), Champaign(23)
DECATUR Brown
DEERFIELD Portage
DEERSVILLE Harrison

DEFIANCE (43512) Defiance(96), Paulding(4)
DELAWARE Delaware
DELLROY Carroll
DELPHOS (45833) Allen(56), Van Wert(40), Putnam(4)
DELTA Fulton
DENNISON (44621) Tuscarawas(91), Harrison(8), Carroll(1)
DERBY Pickaway
DERWENT Guernsey
DESHLER (43516) Henry(81), Wood(13), Putnam(4), Hancock(2)
DEXTER CITY Noble
DIAMOND (44412) Portage(77), Mahoning(23)
DILLONVALE (43917) Jefferson(77), Belmont(23)
DOLA Hardin
DONNELSVILLE Clark
DORSET Ashtabula
DOVER Tuscarawas
DOYLESTOWN (99999) Wayne(99), Medina(1)
DRESDEN (43821) Muskingum(85), Coshocton(15)
DUBLIN (43016) Franklin(97), Delaware(2)
DUBLIN (43017) Franklin(87), Delaware(13)
DUNBRIDGE Wood
DUNCAN FALLS Muskingum
DUNDEE (44624) Tuscarawas(57), Holmes(29), Wayne(12), Stark(1)
DUNKIRK (45836) Hardin(99), Hancock(1)
DUPONT Putnam
EAST CLARIDON Geauga
EAST FULTONHAM Muskingum
EAST LIBERTY (43319) Logan(97), Union(3)
EAST LIVERPOOL Columbiana
EAST PALESTINE Columbiana
EAST ROCHESTER (44625) Columbiana(81), Carroll(20)
EAST SPARTA (44626) Stark(95), Tuscarawas(5)
EAST SPRINGFIELD Jefferson
EASTLAKE Lake
EATON Preble
EDGERTON (43517) Williams(80), Defiance(20)
EDISON Morrow
EDON Williams
ELDORADO Preble
ELGIN Van Wert
ELKTON Columbiana
ELLSWORTH Mahoning
ELMORE (43416) Ottawa(89), Sandusky(11)
ELYRIA Lorain
EMPIRE Jefferson
ENGLEWOOD (45322) Montgomery(97), Miami(3)
ENON Clark
ETNA Licking
EUCLID Cuyahoga
EVANSPORT Defiance
FAIRBORN Greene
FAIRFIELD Butler
FAIRPOINT Belmont
FAIRVIEW Guernsey
FARMDALE Trumbull
FARMER Defiance
FARMERSVILLE Montgomery
FAYETTE (43521) Fulton(97), Williams(3)
FAYETTEVILLE (45118) Brown(98), Clermont(2)
FEESBURG Brown
FELICITY Clermont
FINDLAY Hancock
FLAT ROCK Seneca
FLEMING Washington
FLETCHER (45326) Miami(99), Shelby(1)

FLUSHING (43977) Belmont(77), Harrison(23)
FOREST (45843) Hardin(63), Wyandot(19), Hancock(17)
FORT JENNINGS (45844) Putnam(91), Allen(5), Van Wert(4)
FORT LORAMIE (45845) Shelby(94), Auglaize(5), Mercer(1)
FORT RECOVERY (45846) Mercer(88), Darke(12)
FORT SENECA Seneca
FOSTORIA (44830) Seneca(66), Hancock(18), Wood(17)
FOWLER Trumbull
FRANKFORT Ross
FRANKLIN Warren
FRANKLIN FURNACE (45629) Scioto(94), Lawrence(6)
FRAZEYSBURG (43822) Muskingum(60), Licking(21), Coshocton(11), Knox(8)
FREDERICKSBURG (44627) Wayne(66), Holmes(35)
FREDERICKTOWN (43019) Knox(82), Morrow(16), Richland(2)
FREEPORT (43973) Guernsey(52), Harrison(47), Tuscarawas(1)
FREMONT Sandusky
FRESNO (43824) Coshocton(92), Tuscarawas(8)
FRIENDSHIP Scioto
FULTON Morrow
FULTONHAM Muskingum
GALENA Delaware
GALION (44833) Crawford(87), Morrow(9), Richland(4)
GALLIPOLIS Gallia
GALLOWAY (43119) Franklin(94), Madison(6)
GAMBIER Knox
GARRETTSVILLE (44231) Portage(88), Geauga(10), Trumbull(2)
GATES MILLS Cuyahoga
GENEVA (44041) Ashtabula(99), Lake(2)
GENOA (43430) Ottawa(96), Wood(3)
GEORGETOWN Brown
GERMANTOWN (45327) Montgomery(95), Preble(4), Butler(1)
GETTYSBURG Darke
GIBSONBURG (43431) Sandusky(98), Wood(2)
GIRARD Trumbull
GLANDORF Putnam
GLENCOE Belmont
GLENFORD (43739) Perry(64), Licking(36)
GLENMONT (44628) Holmes(63), Knox(37)
GLOUSTER (45732) Athens(89), Morgan(6), Perry(5), Hocking(1)
GNADENHUTTEN Tuscarawas
GOMER Allen
GORDON Darke
GOSHEN Clermont
GRAFTON Lorain
GRAND RAPIDS (43522) Wood(54), Lucas(37), Henry(9)
GRAND RIVER Lake
GRANVILLE Licking
GRATIOT Licking
GRATIS Preble
GRAYSVILLE (45734) Monroe(76), Washington(24)
GRAYTOWN Ottawa
GREEN Summit
GREEN CAMP Marion
GREEN SPRINGS (44836) Seneca(64), Sandusky(36)
GREENFIELD Highland
GREENFORD Mahoning
GREENTOWN Stark
GREENVILLE Darke
GREENWICH (44837) Huron(77), Richland(12), Ashland(10)

GRELTON Henry
GROVE CITY Franklin
GROVEPORT (43125) Franklin(97), Pickaway(3)
GROVEPORT Franklin
GROVER HILL (45849) Paulding(65), Van Wert(33), Putnam(2)
GUYSVILLE (45735) Athens(98), Meigs(2)
GYPSUM Ottawa
HALLSVILLE Ross
HAMDEN Vinton
HAMERSVILLE Brown
HAMILTON Butler
HAMLER Henry
HAMMONDSVILLE (43930) Jefferson(54), Columbiana(46)
HANNIBAL Monroe
HANOVERTON Columbiana
HARBOR VIEW Lucas
HARLEM SPRINGS Carroll
HARPSTER (43323) Wyandot(97), Marion(3)
HARRISBURG Franklin
HARRISON Hamilton
HARRISVILLE Harrison
HARROD (45850) Allen(68), Hardin(22), Auglaize(10)
HARTFORD Trumbull
HARTVILLE (44632) Stark(95), Portage(5)
HARVEYSBURG Warren
HASKINS Wood
HAVERHILL Scioto
HAVILAND Paulding
HAYDENVILLE Hocking
HAYESVILLE Ashland
HEBRON Licking
HELENA Sandusky
HICKSVILLE (43526) Defiance(97), Paulding(4)
HIGGINSPORT Brown
HIGHLAND Highland
HILLIARD Franklin
HILLSBORO Highland
HINCKLEY Medina
HIRAM (44234) Portage(64), Geauga(36)
HOCKINGPORT Athens
HOLGATE (43527) Henry(90), Defiance(11)
HOLLAND Lucas
HOLLANSBURG Darke
HOLLOWAY Belmont
HOLMESVILLE Holmes
HOMER Licking
HOMERVILLE (44235) Medina(98), Ashland(2)
HOMEWORTH (44634) Columbiana(79), Stark(21)
HOOVEN Hamilton
HOPEDALE (43976) Harrison(98), Jefferson(2)
HOPEWELL (43746) Muskingum(88), Licking(12)
HOUSTON Shelby
HOWARD Knox
HOYTVILLE Wood
HUBBARD Trumbull
HUDSON (99999) Summit(99), Portage(1)
HUNTSBURG (44046) Geauga(99), Ashtabula(1)
HUNTSVILLE Logan
HURON Erie
IBERIA Morrow
INDEPENDENCE Cuyahoga
IRONDALE (43932) Jefferson(59), Columbiana(41)
IRONTON (45638) Lawrence(95), Scioto(5)
IRWIN (43029) Union(75), Madison(26)
ISLE SAINT GEORGE Ottawa
JACKSON Jackson
JACKSON Monroe
JACKSON CENTER (45334) Shelby(90), Auglaize(5), Logan(5)

JACKSONTOWN Licking
JACKSONVILLE Athens
JACOBSBURG Belmont
JAMESTOWN (45335) Greene(97), Fayette(2)
JASPER Pike
JEFFERSON Ashtabula
JEFFERSONVILLE Fayette
JENERA Hancock
JEROMESVILLE (44840) Ashland(98), Wayne(2)
JERRY CITY Wood
JERUSALEM (43747) Monroe(64), Belmont(36)
JEWELL Defiance
JEWETT (43986) Harrison(93), Carroll(7)
JOHNSTOWN (43031) Licking(98), Delaware(2)
JUNCTION CITY Perry
KALIDA Putnam
KANSAS (44841) Seneca(72), Sandusky(28)
KEENE Coshocton
KELLEYS ISLAND Erie
KENSINGTON (44427) Columbiana(54), Carroll(46)
KENT (44240) Portage(99), Summit(1)
KENT Portage
KENTON Hardin
KERR Gallia
KETTLERSVILLE Shelby
KIDRON Wayne
KILBOURNE Delaware
KILLBUCK (44637) Holmes(87), Coshocton(13)
KIMBOLTON (43749) Guernsey(93), Coshocton(5), Tuscarawas(2)
KINGS MILLS Warren
KINGSTON (45644) Ross(62), Pickaway(38)
KINGSVILLE Ashtabula
KINSMAN (44428) Trumbull(97), Ashtabula(4)
KIPLING Guernsey
KIPTON Lorain
KIRBY Wyandot
KIRKERSVILLE Licking
KITTS HILL Lawrence
KUNKLE Williams
LA RUE (43332) Marion(94), Hardin(4), Wyandot(2)
LACARNE Ottawa
LAFAYETTE Allen
LAFFERTY Belmont
LAGRANGE Lorain
LAINGS Monroe
LAKE MILTON (99999) Mahoning(99), Portage(1)
LAKEMORE Summit
LAKESIDE MARBLEHEAD Ottawa
LAKEVIEW (43331) Logan(95), Auglaize(5)
LAKEVILLE (44638) Holmes(73), Ashland(18), Wayne(9)
LAKEWOOD Cuyahoga
LANCASTER Fairfield
LANGSVILLE Meigs
LANSING Belmont
LATHAM Pike
LATTY Paulding
LAURA (45337) Miami(77), Darke(24)
LAURELVILLE (43135) Hocking(71), Pickaway(13), Ross(12), Vinton(4)
LEAVITTSBURG Trumbull
LEBANON Warren
LEES CREEK Clinton
LEESBURG (45135) Highland(99), Fayette(1)
LEESVILLE Carroll
LEETONIA Columbiana
LEIPSIC (45856) Putnam(97), Henry(2)
LEMOYNE Wood
LEWIS CENTER Delaware

LEWISBURG (45338) Preble(98), Montgomery(2)
LEWISTOWN Logan
LEWISVILLE Monroe
LIBERTY CENTER (43532) Henry(90), Fulton(7), Lucas(4)
LIMA (45806) Allen(95), Auglaize(6)
LIMA Allen
LIMAVILLE Stark
LINDSEY (43442) Sandusky(95), Ottawa(5)
LISBON Columbiana
LITCHFIELD (44253) Medina(81), Lorain(19)
LITHOPOLIS Fairfield
LITTLE HOCKING (45742) Washington(94), Athens(6)
LOCKBOURNE (43137) Franklin(58), Pickaway(42)
LODI Medina
LOGAN (43138) Hocking(98), Perry(2)
LONDON (99999) Madison(99), Franklin(1)
LONDONDERRY (45647) Ross(58), Vinton(42)
LONG BOTTOM Meigs
LORAIN Lorain
LORE CITY Guernsey
LOUDONVILLE (44842) Ashland(91), Holmes(9)
LOUISVILLE Stark
LOVELAND (45140) Clermont(91), Hamilton(4), Van Wert(3), Warren(1)
LOWELL (45744) Washington(80), Noble(18), Morgan(2)
LOWELLVILLE Mahoning
LOWER SALEM (45745) Noble(55), Monroe(26), Washington(20)
LUCAS (44843) Richland(94), Ashland(6)
LUCASVILLE (45648) Scioto(67), Pike(33)
LUCASVILLE Scioto
LUCKEY (43443) Wood(97), Sandusky(3)
LUDLOW FALLS Miami
LYNCHBURG (45142) Highland(90), Clinton(10)
LYNX Adams
LYONS Fulton
MACEDONIA Summit
MACKSBURG (45746) Washington(67), Noble(33)
MADISON Lake
MAGNETIC SPRINGS Union
MAGNOLIA (44643) Stark(43), Tuscarawas(38), Carroll(20)
MAINEVILLE (45039) Warren(98), Hamilton(2)
MALAGA Monroe
MALINTA Henry
MALTA Morgan
MALVERN Carroll
MANCHESTER Adams
MANSFIELD (44903) Richland(98), Morrow(1)
MANSFIELD (44904) Richland(89), Morrow(12)
MANSFIELD Richland
MANTUA (44255) Portage(88), Geauga(12)
MAPLE HEIGHTS Cuyahoga
MAPLEWOOD Shelby
MARATHON Clermont
MARENGO (43334) Morrow(96), Delaware(4)
MARIA STEIN (45860) Mercer(98), Darke(2)
MARIETTA Washington
MARION Marion
MARK CENTER Defiance
MARSHALLVILLE (44645) Wayne(97), Stark(3)
MARTEL Marion
MARTIN (43445) Ottawa(63), Lucas(37)
MARTINS FERRY Belmont
MARTINSBURG Knox
MARTINSVILLE Clinton

MARYSVILLE Union
MASON Warren
MASSILLON Stark
MASURY Trumbull
MAUMEE Lucas
MAXIMO Stark
MAYNARD Belmont
MC ARTHUR Vinton
MC CLURE (43534) Henry(98), Wood(2)
MC COMB (45858) Hancock(98), Putnam(2)
MC CONNELSVILLE (43756) Morgan(99), Muskingum(1)
MC CUTCHENVILLE (44844) Wyandot(60), Seneca(40)
MC DERMOTT Scioto
MC DONALD (44437) Trumbull(98), Mahoning(3)
MC GUFFEY Hardin
MECHANICSBURG (43044) Champaign(82), Clark(12), Madison(6)
MECHANICSTOWN Carroll
MEDINA Medina
MEDWAY Clark
MELMORE Seneca
MELROSE Paulding
MENDON (45862) Mercer(92), Auglaize(8)
MENTOR Lake
MESOPOTAMIA Trumbull
METAMORA Fulton
MIAMISBURG (99999) Montgomery(99), Warren(1)
MIAMITOWN Hamilton
MIAMIVILLE Clermont
MIDDLE BASS Ottawa
MIDDLE POINT Van Wert
MIDDLEBRANCH Stark
MIDDLEBURG Logan
MIDDLEFIELD (44062) Geauga(80), Trumbull(17), Ashtabula(3)
MIDDLEPORT Meigs
MIDDLETOWN Butler
MIDLAND Clinton
MIDVALE Tuscarawas
MILAN (44846) Erie(94), Huron(6)
MILFORD Clermont
MILFORD CENTER (43045) Union(96), Champaign(4)
MILLBURY (43447) Wood(85), Ottawa(16)
MILLEDGEVILLE Fayette
MILLER CITY Putnam
MILLERSBURG (44654) Holmes(97), Coshocton(3)
MILLERSPORT (43046) Fairfield(92), Licking(8)
MILLFIELD Athens
MILTON CENTER Wood
MINERAL CITY (44656) Tuscarawas(97), Carroll(3)
MINERAL RIDGE (44440) Trumbull(82), Mahoning(18)
MINERVA (44657) Stark(52), Carroll(34), Columbiana(14)
MINFORD Scioto
MINGO Champaign
MINGO JUNCTION Jefferson
MINSTER (45865) Auglaize(77), Shelby(22)
MOGADORE (44260) Portage(70), Summit(25), Stark(6)
MONCLOVA Lucas
MONROE Butler
MONROEVILLE (44847) Huron(67), Erie(33)
MONTEZUMA Mercer
MONTPELIER Williams
MONTVILLE (44064) Geauga(98), Ashtabula(2)
MORRAL (43337) Marion(83), Wyandot(17)
MORRISTOWN Belmont
MORROW Warren
MOSCOW Clermont

MOUNT BLANCHARD (45867) Hancock(93), Wyandot(7)
MOUNT CORY (45868) Hancock(95), Putnam(5)
MOUNT EATON Wayne
MOUNT GILEAD Morrow
MOUNT HOPE Holmes
MOUNT LIBERTY Knox
MOUNT ORAB Brown
MOUNT PERRY (43760) Perry(57), Muskingum(39), Licking(5)
MOUNT PLEASANT Jefferson
MOUNT SAINT JOSEPH Hamilton
MOUNT STERLING (43143) Madison(76), Pickaway(16), Fayette(8)
MOUNT VERNON Knox
MOUNT VICTORY (43340) Hardin(87), Union(13)
MOWRYSTOWN Highland
MOXAHALA Perry
MUNROE FALLS Summit
MURRAY CITY Hocking
NANKIN Ashland
NAPOLEON (43545) Henry(98), Defiance(1)
NASHPORT (43830) Muskingum(87), Licking(13)
NASHVILLE Holmes
NAVARRE (44662) Stark(97), Wayne(3)
NEAPOLIS Lucas
NEFFS Belmont
NEGLEY Columbiana
NELSONVILLE (45764) Athens(88), Hocking(12)
NEVADA (44849) Wyandot(79), Crawford(20)
NEVILLE Clermont
NEW ALBANY (43054) Franklin(82), Delaware(18)
NEW ATHENS Harrison
NEW BAVARIA (43548) Henry(95), Defiance(3), Putnam(2)
NEW BLOOMINGTON Marion
NEW BREMEN (45869) Auglaize(92), Mercer(5), Shelby(3)
NEW CARLISLE (45344) Clark(83), Miami(13), Montgomery(4)
NEW CONCORD (43762) Muskingum(83), Guernsey(17)
NEW HAMPSHIRE Auglaize
NEW HAVEN Huron
NEW HOLLAND (43145) Pickaway(63), Fayette(37)
NEW KNOXVILLE (45871) Auglaize(84), Shelby(16)
NEW LEBANON Montgomery
NEW LEXINGTON Perry
NEW LONDON (44851) Huron(83), Lorain(11), Ashland(5)
NEW MADISON Darke
NEW MARSHFIELD (45766) Athens(87), Vinton(13)
NEW MATAMORAS (45767) Washington(54), Monroe(46)
NEW MIDDLETOWN Mahoning
NEW PARIS Preble
NEW PHILADELPHIA Tuscarawas
NEW PLYMOUTH (45654) Vinton(78), Hocking(22)
NEW RICHMOND Clermont
NEW RIEGEL Seneca
NEW RUMLEY Harrison
NEW SPRINGFIELD (44443) Mahoning(95), Columbiana(5)
NEW STRAITSVILLE (43766) Perry(84), Hocking(16)
NEW VIENNA (45159) Clinton(96), Highland(4)
NEW WASHINGTON (44854) Crawford(92), Seneca(6), Huron(2)
NEW WATERFORD Columbiana
NEW WESTON Darke

NEWARK Licking
NEWBURY Geauga
NEWCOMERSTOWN (43832) Tuscarawas(86), Coshocton(13), Guernsey(2)
NEWPORT Washington
NEWTON FALLS (44444) Trumbull(93), Portage(5), Mahoning(2)
NEWTONSVILLE Clermont
NEY Defiance
NILES Trumbull
NORTH BALTIMORE (45872) Wood(98), Hancock(2)
NORTH BEND Hamilton
NORTH BENTON (44449) Portage(51), Mahoning(49)
NORTH BLOOMFIELD Trumbull
NORTH FAIRFIELD Huron
NORTH GEORGETOWN Columbiana
NORTH HAMPTON Clark
NORTH JACKSON Mahoning
NORTH KINGSVILLE Ashtabula
NORTH LAWRENCE (44666) Stark(84), Wayne(16)
NORTH LEWISBURG (43060) Champaign(42), Union(40), Logan(18)
NORTH LIMA Mahoning
NORTH OLMSTED Cuyahoga
NORTH RIDGEVILLE Lorain
NORTH ROBINSON Crawford
NORTH ROYALTON Cuyahoga
NORTH STAR Darke
NORTHFIELD Summit
NORTHWOOD Wood
NORWALK (44857) Huron(98), Erie(2)
NORWICH Muskingum
NOVA (44859) Ashland(96), Lorain(4)
NOVELTY Geauga
OAK HARBOR (43449) Ottawa(98), Sandusky(2)
OAK HILL (45656) Jackson(88), Gallia(8), Lawrence(4)
OAKWOOD Paulding
OBERLIN Lorain
OCEOLA Crawford
OHIO CITY Van Wert
OKEANA Butler
OKOLONA Henry
OLD FORT Seneca
OLD WASHINGTON Guernsey
OLMSTED FALLS Cuyahoga
ONTARIO Richland
ORANGEVILLE Trumbull
OREGON Lucas
OREGONIA Warren
ORIENT (43146) Pickaway(74), Franklin(25), Madison(1)
ORRVILLE Wayne
ORWELL (44076) Ashtabula(91), Trumbull(9)
OSGOOD Darke
OSTRANDER (43061) Delaware(80), Union(20)
OTTAWA Putnam
OTTOVILLE Putnam
OTWAY (45657) Scioto(80), Adams(18), Pike(2)
OVERPECK Butler
OWENSVILLE Clermont
OXFORD Butler
PAINESVILLE Lake
PALESTINE Darke
PANDORA (45877) Putnam(94), Allen(5)
PARIS Stark
PARKMAN Geauga
PATASKALA (99999) Licking(98), Franklin(1)
PATRIOT Gallia
PAULDING Paulding
PAYNE Paulding
PEDRO Lawrence

PEEBLES (45660) Adams(88), Pike(10), Highland(2)
PEMBERTON Shelby
PEMBERVILLE Wood
PENINSULA Summit
PERRY Lake
PERRYSBURG Wood
PERRYSVILLE (44864) Ashland(59), Richland(41)
PETERSBURG (44454) Mahoning(86), Columbiana(14)
PETTISVILLE Fulton
PHILLIPSBURG Montgomery
PHILO Muskingum
PICKERINGTON (43147) Fairfield(92), Franklin(7), Licking(1)
PIEDMONT (43983) Belmont(74), Guernsey(23), Harrison(3)
PIERPONT Ashtabula
PIKETON Pike
PINEY FORK Jefferson
PIONEER Williams
PIQUA (45356) Miami(96), Shelby(4)
PITSBURG Darke
PLAIN CITY (43064) Madison(52), Union(46), Franklin(1)
PLAINFIELD Coshocton
PLEASANT CITY (43772) Guernsey(58), Noble(42)
PLEASANT HILL Miami
PLEASANT PLAIN Warren
PLEASANTVILLE (43148) Fairfield(90), Perry(10)
PLYMOUTH (44865) Huron(50), Richland(47), Crawford(4)
POLK Ashland
POMEROY Meigs
PORT CLINTON Ottawa
PORT JEFFERSON Shelby
PORT WASHINGTON (43837) Tuscarawas(96), Guernsey(4)
PORT WILLIAM Clinton
PORTAGE Wood
PORTLAND Meigs
PORTSMOUTH Scioto
POTSDAM Miami
POWELL (43065) Delaware(69), Franklin(32)
POWHATAN POINT (43942) Belmont(93), Monroe(7)
PROCTORVILLE Lawrence
PROSPECT (43342) Marion(89), Delaware(8), Union(3)
PUT IN BAY Ottawa
QUAKER CITY (43773) Guernsey(56), Noble(39), Belmont(3), Monroe(2)
QUINCY (43343) Logan(77), Champaign(13), Shelby(10)
RACINE Meigs
RADCLIFF Vinton
RADNOR Delaware
RANDOLPH Portage
RARDEN (45671) Scioto(66), Pike(21), Adams(9), Fairfield(5)
RAVENNA Portage
RAWSON Hancock
RAY (45672) Vinton(80), Jackson(17), Ross(2)
RAYLAND (43943) Jefferson(95), Belmont(5)
RAYMOND Union
REEDSVILLE Meigs
REESVILLE Clinton
RENO Washington
REPUBLIC Seneca
REYNOLDSBURG (43068) Franklin(85), Licking(13), Fairfield(2)
REYNOLDSBURG Franklin
RICHFIELD Summit
RICHMOND Jefferson
RICHMOND DALE Ross

RICHWOOD (43344) Union(75), Marion(22), Delaware(3)
RIDGEVILLE CORNERS Henry
RIDGEWAY (43345) Logan(50), Hardin(48), Union(2)
RIO GRANDE Gallia
RIPLEY Brown
RISINGSUN (43457) Wood(71), Sandusky(23), Seneca(6)
RITTMAN (44270) Wayne(95), Medina(6)
ROBERTSVILLE Stark
ROCK CAMP Lawrence
ROCK CREEK Ashtabula
ROCKBRIDGE Hocking
ROCKFORD (45882) Mercer(96), Van Wert(4)
ROCKY RIDGE Ottawa
ROCKY RIVER Cuyahoga
ROGERS Columbiana
ROME Ashtabula
ROOTSTOWN Portage
ROSEVILLE (43777) Muskingum(69), Perry(31)
ROSEWOOD Champaign
ROSS Butler
ROSSBURG Darke
ROSSFORD Wood
ROUNDHEAD Hardin
RUDOLPH Wood
RUSHSYLVANIA (43347) Logan(93), Hardin(7)
RUSHVILLE (43150) Fairfield(70), Perry(30)
RUSSELLS POINT Logan
RUSSELLVILLE Brown
RUSSIA (45363) Shelby(96), Darke(4)
RUTLAND Meigs
SABINA Clinton
SAINT CLAIRSVILLE Belmont
SAINT HENRY (45883) Mercer(99), Darke(1)
SAINT JOHNS Auglaize
SAINT LOUISVILLE Licking
SAINT MARYS Auglaize
SAINT PARIS Champaign
SALEM (44460) Columbiana(90), Mahoning(11)
SALESVILLE (43778) Guernsey(96), Noble(4)
SALINEVILLE (43945) Columbiana(69), Carroll(21), Jefferson(10)
SANDUSKY Erie
SANDYVILLE Tuscarawas
SARAHSVILLE Noble
SARDINIA Brown
SARDIS Monroe
SAVANNAH Ashland
SCIO (43988) Harrison(72), Carroll(28)
SCIOTO FURNACE Scioto
SCOTT (45886) Van Wert(55), Paulding(45)
SCOTTOWN (45678) Lawrence(79), Gallia(21)
SEAMAN (45679) Adams(93), Highland(7)
SEBRING Mahoning
SEDALIA Madison
SENECAVILLE (43780) Guernsey(69), Noble(31)
SEVEN MILE Butler
SEVILLE Medina
SHADE (45776) Meigs(51), Athens(49)
SHADYSIDE Belmont
SHANDON Butler
SHARON CENTER Medina
SHARPSBURG Athens
SHAUCK Morrow
SHAWNEE Perry
SHEFFIELD LAKE Lorain
SHELBY (44875) Richland(97), Crawford(3)
SHERRODSVILLE (44675) Carroll(71), Tuscarawas(29)

SHERWOOD (43556) Defiance(98), Paulding(2)
SHILOH (44878) Richland(91), Huron(5), Ashland(3)
SHORT CREEK Harrison
SHREVE (44676) Wayne(81), Holmes(19)
SIDNEY Shelby
SINKING SPRING Highland
SMITHFIELD Jefferson
SMITHVILLE Wayne
SOLON Cuyahoga
SOMERDALE Tuscarawas
SOMERSET Perry
SOMERVILLE Butler
SOUTH BLOOMINGVILLE (43152) Hocking(83), Vinton(17)
SOUTH CHARLESTON (45368) Clark(98), Greene(1)
SOUTH LEBANON Warren
SOUTH POINT Lawrence
SOUTH SALEM Ross
SOUTH SOLON (43153) Madison(74), Fayette(14), Clark(7), Greene(6)
SOUTH VIENNA (45369) Clark(96), Madison(5)
SOUTH WEBSTER Scioto
SOUTHINGTON (44470) Trumbull(99), Portage(1)
SPARTA Morrow
SPENCER (44275) Medina(95), Lorain(5)
SPENCERVILLE (45887) Allen(76), Auglaize(15), Van Wert(7), Mercer(2)
SPRING HILL NURSERIES Miami
SPRING VALLEY (45370) Greene(98), Montgomery(2)
SPRINGBORO Warren
SPRINGFIELD (45502) Clark(98), Champaign(2)
SPRINGFIELD Clark
STAFFORD Monroe
STERLING Wayne
STEUBENVILLE Jefferson
STEWART Athens
STEWARTSVILLE Belmont
STILLWATER Tuscarawas
STOCKDALE Pike
STOCKPORT (43787) Morgan(96), Washington(4)
STOCKPORT Morgan
STONE CREEK (43840) Coshocton(65), Tuscarawas(35)
STONY RIDGE Wood
STOUT (45684) Scioto(68), Adams(32)
STOUTSVILLE (43154) Fairfield(89), Pickaway(11)
STOW Summit
STRASBURG Tuscarawas
STRATTON Jefferson
STREETSBORO Portage
STRONGSVILLE Cuyahoga
STRUTHERS Mahoning
STRYKER (43557) Williams(80), Henry(14), Fulton(6)
SUGAR GROVE (43155) Fairfield(73), Hocking(28)
SUGARCREEK (44681) Tuscarawas(78), Holmes(22)
SULLIVAN (44880) Ashland(84), Lorain(13), Medina(3)
SULPHUR SPRINGS Crawford
SUMMERFIELD (43788) Noble(79), Monroe(21)
SUMMIT STATION Licking
SUMMITVILLE Columbiana
SUNBURY (43074) Delaware(97), Licking(2)
SWANTON (43558) Fulton(70), Lucas(30)
SYCAMORE (44882) Wyandot(64), Crawford(31), Seneca(5)
SYCAMORE VALLEY Monroe
SYLVANIA Lucas
SYRACUSE Meigs

TALLMADGE (44278) Summit(97), Portage(3)
TARLTON Pickaway
TERRACE PARK Hamilton
THE PLAINS Athens
THOMPSON (44086) Geauga(79), Lake(16), Ashtabula(5)
THORNVILLE (43076) Perry(45), Licking(31), Fairfield(25)
THURMAN (45685) Gallia(74), Jackson(26)
THURSTON Fairfield
TIFFIN Seneca
TILTONSVILLE Jefferson
TIPP CITY Miami
TIPPECANOE (44699) Harrison(73), Tuscarawas(25), Guernsey(2)
TIRO Crawford
TOLEDO (43605) Lucas(98), Wood(2)
TOLEDO Lucas
TOLEDO Wood
TONTOGANY Wood
TORCH Athens
TORONTO Jefferson
TREMONT CITY Clark
TRENTON Butler
TRIMBLE Athens
TRINWAY Muskingum
TROY Miami
TUPPERS PLAINS Meigs
TUSCARAWAS Tuscarawas
TWINSBURG Summit
UHRICHSVILLE (44683) Tuscarawas(92), Harrison(8)
UNION CITY Darke
UNION FURNACE Hocking
UNIONPORT Jefferson
UNIONTOWN (44685) Stark(53), Summit(47)
UNIONVILLE Ashtabula
UNIONVILLE CENTER Union
UNIOPOLIS Auglaize
UPPER SANDUSKY Wyandot
URBANA Champaign
UTICA (43080) Licking(70), Knox(30)
VALLEY CITY (44280) Medina(95), Lorain(6)

VAN BUREN (45889) Hancock(97), Wood(3)
VAN WERT Van Wert
VANDALIA Montgomery
VANLUE Hancock
VAUGHNSVILLE Putnam
VENEDOCIA (45894) Van Wert(94), Mercer(5), Allen(1)
VERMILION (44089) Erie(58), Lorain(42)
VERONA Preble
VERSAILLES Darke
VICKERY (43464) Sandusky(78), Erie(22)
VIENNA Trumbull
VINCENT Washington
VINTON (45686) Gallia(94), Vinton(5), Meigs(2)
WADSWORTH Medina
WAKEFIELD Pike
WAKEMAN (44889) Huron(68), Erie(20), Lorain(13)
WALBRIDGE Wood
WALDO (43356) Marion(77), Delaware(17), Morrow(7)
WALHONDING (43843) Coshocton(66), Knox(34)
WALNUT CREEK Holmes
WAPAKONETA (45895) Auglaize(98), Logan(1)
WARNOCK Belmont
WARREN (99999) Trumbull(99), Mahoning(1)
WARSAW (43844) Coshocton(95), Knox(5)
WASHINGTON COURT HOUSE (43160) Fayette(99), Ross(1)
WASHINGTONVILLE Columbiana
WATERFORD (45786) Washington(74), Morgan(26)
WATERLOO (45688) Lawrence(95), Gallia(5)
WATERTOWN Washington
WATERVILLE Lucas
WAUSEON (43567) Fulton(99), Henry(1)
WAVERLY (45690) Pike(92), Ross(8)
WAYLAND Portage
WAYNE Wood
WAYNESBURG (44688) Stark(89), Carroll(11)

WAYNESFIELD (45896) Auglaize(79), Hardin(15), Allen(6)
WAYNESVILLE Warren
WELLINGTON Lorain
WELLSTON Jackson
WELLSVILLE Columbiana
WEST ALEXANDRIA (45381) Preble(96), Montgomery(4)
WEST CHESTER Butler
WEST ELKTON Preble
WEST FARMINGTON (44491) Trumbull(85), Geauga(14), Portage(1)
WEST JEFFERSON Madison
WEST LAFAYETTE Coshocton
WEST LIBERTY (43357) Logan(76), Champaign(24)
WEST MANCHESTER (45382) Preble(78), Darke(22)
WEST MANSFIELD (43358) Logan(59), Union(41)
WEST MILLGROVE Wood
WEST MILTON Miami
WEST POINT Columbiana
WEST PORTSMOUTH Scioto
WEST RUSHVILLE Fairfield
WEST SALEM (44287) Wayne(58), Ashland(35), Medina(7)
WEST UNION Adams
WEST UNITY (43570) Williams(95), Fulton(6)
WESTERVILLE (43081) Franklin(97), Delaware(3)
WESTERVILLE Delaware
WESTERVILLE Franklin
WESTFIELD CENTER Medina
WESTLAKE Cuyahoga
WESTON Wood
WESTVILLE Champaign
WHARTON Wyandot
WHEELERSBURG Scioto
WHIPPLE Washington
WHITE COTTAGE Muskingum
WHITEHOUSE Lucas
WICKLIFFE Lake
WILBERFORCE Greene
WILKESVILLE Vinton
WILLARD Huron

WILLIAMSBURG Clermont
WILLIAMSFIELD Ashtabula
WILLIAMSPORT (43164) Pickaway(94), Ross(6)
WILLIAMSTOWN Hancock
WILLISTON Ottawa
WILLOUGHBY Lake
WILLOW WOOD Lawrence
WILLSHIRE (45898) Van Wert(66), Mercer(34)
WILMINGTON Clinton
WILMOT (44689) Holmes(61), Stark(39)
WINCHESTER (45697) Adams(61), Brown(26), Highland(13)
WINDHAM (44288) Portage(99), Trumbull(1)
WINDSOR (44099) Ashtabula(89), Geauga(11)
WINESBURG Holmes
WINGETT RUN Monroe
WINONA Columbiana
WINTERSVILLE Jefferson
WOLF RUN Jefferson
WOODSFIELD Monroe
WOODSTOCK (43084) Champaign(90), Union(10)
WOODVILLE (43469) Sandusky(94), Ottawa(5), Wood(1)
WOOSTER Wayne
WREN Van Wert
XENIA Greene
YELLOW SPRINGS (45387) Greene(97), Clark(3)
YORKSHIRE (45388) Darke(94), Shelby(3), Mercer(2)
YORKVILLE (43971) Jefferson(62), Belmont(39)
YOUNGSTOWN (44504) Mahoning(96), Trumbull(4)
YOUNGSTOWN (44505) Mahoning(66), Trumbull(34)
YOUNGSTOWN Mahoning
ZALESKI Vinton
ZANESFIELD Logan
ZANESVILLE Muskingum
ZOAR Tuscarawas

ZIP/City Cross Reference

43001-43001 ALEXANDRIA	43040-43041 MARYSVILLE	43099-43099 BLACKLICK	43147-43147 PICKERINGTON
43002-43002 AMLIN	43044-43044 MECHANICSBURG	43101-43101 ADELPHI	43148-43148 PLEASANTVILLE
43003-43003 ASHLEY	43045-43045 MILFORD CENTER	43102-43102 AMANDA	43149-43149 ROCKBRIDGE
43004-43004 BLACKLICK	43046-43046 MILLERSPORT	43103-43103 ASHVILLE	43150-43150 RUSHVILLE
43005-43005 BLADENSBURG	43047-43047 MINGO	43105-43105 BALTIMORE	43151-43151 SEDALIA
43006-43006 BRINKHAVEN	43048-43048 MOUNT LIBERTY	43106-43106 BLOOMINGBURG	43152-43152 SOUTH BLOOMINGVILLE
43007-43007 BROADWAY	43050-43050 MOUNT VERNON	43107-43107 BREMEN	43153-43153 SOUTH SOLON
43008-43008 BUCKEYE LAKE	43054-43054 NEW ALBANY	43109-43109 BRICE	43154-43154 STOUTSVILLE
43009-43009 CABLE	43055-43058 NEWARK	43110-43110 CANAL WINCHESTER	43155-43155 SUGAR GROVE
43010-43010 CATAWBA	43060-43060 NORTH LEWISBURG	43111-43111 CARBON HILL	43156-43156 TARLTON
43011-43011 CENTERBURG	43061-43061 OSTRANDER	43112-43112 CARROLL	43157-43157 THURSTON
43013-43013 CROTON	43062-43062 PATASKALA	43113-43113 CIRCLEVILLE	43158-43158 UNION FURNACE
43014-43014 DANVILLE	43064-43064 PLAIN CITY	43115-43115 CLARKSBURG	43160-43160 WASHINGTON COURT
43015-43015 DELAWARE	43065-43065 POWELL	43116-43116 COMMERCIAL POINT	HOUSE
43016-43017 DUBLIN	43066-43066 RADNOR	43117-43117 DERBY	43162-43162 WEST JEFFERSON
43018-43018 ETNA	43067-43067 RAYMOND	43119-43119 GALLOWAY	43163-43163 WEST RUSHVILLE
43019-43019 FREDERICKTOWN	43068-43068 REYNOLDSBURG	43123-43123 GROVE CITY	43164-43164 WILLIAMSPORT
43021-43021 GALENA	43070-43070 ROSEWOOD	43125-43125 GROVEPORT	43199-43199 GROVEPORT
43022-43022 GAMBIER	43071-43071 SAINT LOUISVILLE	43126-43126 HARRISBURG	43201-43299 COLUMBUS
43023-43023 GRANVILLE	43072-43072 SAINT PARIS	43127-43127 HAYDENVILLE	43301-43307 MARION
43025-43025 HEBRON	43073-43073 SUMMIT STATION	43128-43128 JEFFERSONVILLE	43310-43310 BELLE CENTER
43026-43026 HILLIARD	43074-43074 SUNBURY	43130-43130 LANCASTER	43311-43311 BELLEFONTAINE
43027-43027 HOMER	43076-43076 THORNVILLE	43135-43135 LAURELVILLE	43314-43314 CALEDONIA
43028-43028 HOWARD	43077-43077 UNIONVILLE CENTER	43136-43136 LITHOPOLIS	43315-43315 CARDINGTON
43029-43029 IRWIN	43078-43078 URBANA	43137-43137 LOCKBOURNE	43316-43316 CAREY
43030-43030 JACKSONTOWN	43080-43080 UTICA	43138-43138 LOGAN	43317-43317 CHESTERVILLE
43031-43031 JOHNSTOWN	43081-43082 WESTERVILLE	43140-43140 LONDON	43318-43318 DE GRAFF
43032-43032 KILBOURNE	43083-43083 WESTVILLE	43142-43142 MILLEDGEVILLE	43319-43319 EAST LIBERTY
43033-43033 KIRKERSVILLE	43084-43084 WOODSTOCK	43143-43143 MOUNT STERLING	43320-43320 EDISON
43035-43035 LEWIS CENTER	43085-43085 COLUMBUS	43144-43144 MURRAY CITY	43321-43321 FULTON
43036-43036 MAGNETIC SPRINGS	43086-43086 WESTERVILLE	43145-43145 NEW HOLLAND	43322-43322 GREEN CAMP
43037-43037 MARTINSBURG	43093-43093 NEWARK	43146-43146 ORIENT	43323-43323 HARPSTER

ZIP Range	City	ZIP Range	City	ZIP Range	City	ZIP Range	City
43324-43324	HUNTSVILLE	43517-43517	EDGERTON	43755-43755	LORE CITY	43947-43947	SHADYSIDE
43325-43325	IBERIA	43518-43518	EDON	43756-43756	MC CONNELSVILLE	43948-43948	SMITHFIELD
43326-43326	KENTON	43519-43519	EVANSPORT	43757-43757	MALAGA	43950-43950	SAINT CLAIRSVILLE
43330-43330	KIRBY	43520-43520	FARMER	43758-43758	MALTA	43951-43951	LAFFERTY
43331-43331	LAKEVIEW	43521-43521	FAYETTE	43759-43759	MORRISTOWN	43952-43952	STEUBENVILLE
43332-43332	LA RUE	43522-43522	GRAND RAPIDS	43760-43760	MOUNT PERRY	43953-43953	WINTERSVILLE
43333-43333	LEWISTOWN	43523-43523	GRELTON	43761-43761	MOXAHALA	43960-43960	STEWARTSVILLE
43334-43334	MARENGO	43524-43524	HAMLER	43762-43762	NEW CONCORD	43961-43961	STRATTON
43335-43335	MARTEL	43525-43525	HASKINS	43764-43764	NEW LEXINGTON	43962-43962	SUMMITVILLE
43336-43336	MIDDLEBURG	43526-43526	HICKSVILLE	43766-43766	NEW STRAITSVILLE	43963-43963	TILTONSVILLE
43337-43337	MORRAL	43527-43527	HOLGATE	43767-43767	NORWICH	43964-43964	TORONTO
43338-43338	MOUNT GILEAD	43528-43528	HOLLAND	43768-43768	OLD WASHINGTON	43966-43966	UNIONPORT
43340-43340	MOUNT VICTORY	43529-43529	HOYTVILLE	43771-43771	PHILO	43967-43967	WARNOCK
43341-43341	NEW BLOOMINGTON	43530-43530	JEWELL	43772-43772	PLEASANT CITY	43968-43968	WELLSVILLE
43342-43342	PROSPECT	43531-43531	KUNKLE	43773-43773	QUAKER CITY	43970-43970	WOLF RUN
43343-43343	QUINCY	43532-43532	LIBERTY CENTER	43777-43777	ROSEVILLE	43971-43971	YORKVILLE
43344-43344	RICHWOOD	43533-43533	LYONS	43778-43778	SALESVILLE	43972-43972	BANNOCK
43345-43345	RIDGEWAY	43534-43534	MC CLURE	43779-43779	SARAHSVILLE	43973-43973	FREEPORT
43346-43346	ROUNDHEAD	43535-43535	MALINTA	43780-43780	SENECAVILLE	43974-43974	HARRISVILLE
43347-43347	RUSHSYLVANIA	43536-43536	MARK CENTER	43782-43782	SHAWNEE	43976-43976	HOPEDALE
43348-43348	RUSSELLS POINT	43537-43537	MAUMEE	43783-43783	SOMERSET	43977-43977	FLUSHING
43349-43349	SHAUCK	43540-43540	METAMORA	43786-43786	STAFFORD	43981-43981	NEW ATHENS
43350-43350	SPARTA	43541-43541	MILTON CENTER	43787-43787	STOCKPORT	43983-43983	PIEDMONT
43351-43351	UPPER SANDUSKY	43542-43542	MONCLOVA	43788-43788	SUMMERFIELD	43984-43984	NEW RUMLEY
43356-43356	WALDO	43543-43543	MONTPELIER	43789-43789	SYCAMORE VALLEY	43985-43985	HOLLOWAY
43357-43357	WEST LIBERTY	43545-43545	NAPOLEON	43791-43791	WHITE COTTAGE	43986-43986	JEWETT
43358-43358	WEST MANSFIELD	43547-43547	NEAPOLIS	43793-43793	WOODSFIELD	43988-43988	SCIO
43359-43359	WHARTON	43548-43548	NEW BAVARIA	43802-43802	ADAMSVILLE	43989-43989	SHORT CREEK
43360-43360	ZANESFIELD	43549-43549	NEY	43803-43803	BAKERSVILLE	44001-44001	AMHERST
43402-43403	BOWLING GREEN	43550-43550	OKOLONA	43804-43804	BALTIC	44003-44003	ANDOVER
43406-43406	BRADNER	43551-43552	PERRYSBURG	43805-43805	BLISSFIELD	44004-44005	ASHTABULA
43407-43407	BURGOON	43553-43553	PETTISVILLE	43811-43811	CONESVILLE	44010-44010	AUSTINBURG
43408-43408	CLAY CENTER	43554-43554	PIONEER	43812-43812	COSHOCTON	44011-44011	AVON
43410-43410	CLYDE	43555-43555	RIDGEVILLE CORNERS	43821-43821	DRESDEN	44012-44012	AVON LAKE
43412-43412	CURTICE	43556-43556	SHERWOOD	43822-43822	FRAZEYSBURG	44017-44017	BEREA
43413-43413	CYGNET	43557-43557	STRYKER	43824-43824	FRESNO	44021-44021	BURTON
43414-43414	DUNBRIDGE	43558-43558	SWANTON	43828-43828	KEENE	44022-44023	CHAGRIN FALLS
43416-43416	ELMORE	43560-43560	SYLVANIA	43830-43830	NASHPORT	44024-44024	CHARDON
43420-43420	FREMONT	43565-43565	TONTOGANY	43832-43832	NEWCOMERSTOWN	44026-44026	CHESTERLAND
43430-43430	GENOA	43566-43566	WATERVILLE	43836-43836	PLAINFIELD	44028-44028	COLUMBIA STATION
43431-43431	GIBSONBURG	43567-43567	WAUSEON	43837-43837	PORT WASHINGTON	44030-44030	CONNEAUT
43432-43432	GRAYTOWN	43569-43569	WESTON	43840-43840	STONE CREEK	44032-44032	DORSET
43433-43433	GYPSUM	43570-43570	WEST UNITY	43842-43842	TRINWAY	44033-44033	EAST CLARIDON
43434-43434	HARBOR VIEW	43571-43571	WHITEHOUSE	43843-43843	WALHONDING	44035-44036	ELYRIA
43435-43435	HELENA	43601-43615	TOLEDO	43844-43844	WARSAW	44039-44039	NORTH RIDGEVILLE
43436-43436	ISLE SAINT GEORGE	43616-43616	OREGON	43845-43845	WEST LAFAYETTE	44040-44040	GATES MILLS
43437-43437	JERRY CITY	43617-43617	TOLEDO	43901-43901	ADENA	44041-44041	GENEVA
43438-43438	KELLEYS ISLAND	43618-43618	OREGON	43902-43902	ALLEDONIA	44044-44044	GRAFTON
43439-43439	LACARNE	43619-43619	NORTHWOOD	43903-43903	AMSTERDAM	44045-44045	GRAND RIVER
43440-43440	LAKESIDE MARBLEHEAD	43620-43699	TOLEDO	43905-43905	BARTON	44046-44046	HUNTSBURG
43441-43441	LEMOYNE	43701-43702	ZANESVILLE	43906-43906	BELLAIRE	44047-44047	JEFFERSON
43442-43442	LINDSEY	43711-43711	AVA	43907-43907	CADIZ	44048-44048	KINGSVILLE
43443-43443	LUCKEY	43713-43713	BARNESVILLE	43908-43908	BERGHOLZ	44049-44049	KIPTON
43445-43445	MARTIN	43716-43716	BEALLSVILLE	43909-43909	BLAINE	44050-44050	LAGRANGE
43446-43446	MIDDLE BASS	43717-43717	BELLE VALLEY	43910-43910	BLOOMINGDALE	44052-44053	LORAIN
43447-43447	MILLBURY	43718-43718	BELMONT	43912-43912	BRIDGEPORT	44054-44054	SHEFFIELD LAKE
43449-43449	OAK HARBOR	43719-43719	BETHESDA	43913-43913	BRILLIANT	44055-44055	LORAIN
43450-43450	PEMBERVILLE	43720-43720	BLUE ROCK	43914-43914	CAMERON	44056-44056	MACEDONIA
43451-43451	PORTAGE	43721-43721	BROWNSVILLE	43915-43915	CLARINGTON	44057-44057	MADISON
43452-43452	PORT CLINTON	43722-43722	BUFFALO	43916-43916	COLERAIN	44060-44061	MENTOR
43456-43456	PUT IN BAY	43723-43723	BYESVILLE	43917-43917	DILLONVALE	44062-44062	MIDDLEFIELD
43457-43457	RISINGSUN	43724-43724	CALDWELL	43920-43920	EAST LIVERPOOL	44064-44064	MONTVILLE
43458-43458	ROCKY RIDGE	43725-43725	CAMBRIDGE	43925-43925	EAST SPRINGFIELD	44065-44065	NEWBURY
43460-43460	ROSSFORD	43727-43727	CHANDLERSVILLE	43926-43926	EMPIRE	44067-44067	NORTHFIELD
43462-43462	RUDOLPH	43728-43728	CHESTERHILL	43927-43927	FAIRPOINT	44068-44068	NORTH KINGSVILLE
43463-43463	STONY RIDGE	43730-43730	CORNING	43928-43928	GLENCOE	44070-44070	NORTH OLMSTED
43464-43464	VICKERY	43731-43731	CROOKSVILLE	43930-43930	HAMMONDSVILLE	44072-44073	NOVELTY
43465-43465	WALBRIDGE	43732-43732	CUMBERLAND	43931-43931	HANNIBAL	44074-44074	OBERLIN
43466-43466	WAYNE	43733-43733	DERWENT	43932-43932	IRONDALE	44076-44076	ORWELL
43467-43467	WEST MILLGROVE	43734-43734	DUNCAN FALLS	43933-43933	JACOBSBURG	44077-44077	PAINESVILLE
43468-43468	WILLISTON	43735-43735	EAST FULTONHAM	43934-43934	LANSING	44080-44080	PARKMAN
43469-43469	WOODVILLE	43736-43736	FAIRVIEW	43935-43935	MARTINS FERRY	44081-44081	PERRY
43501-43501	ALVORDTON	43738-43738	FULTONHAM	43937-43937	MAYNARD	44082-44082	PIERPONT
43502-43502	ARCHBOLD	43739-43739	GLENFORD	43938-43938	MINGO JUNCTION	44084-44084	ROCK CREEK
43504-43504	BERKEY	43740-43740	GRATIOT	43939-43939	MOUNT PLEASANT	44085-44085	ROME
43505-43505	BLAKESLEE	43746-43746	HOPEWELL	43940-43940	NEFFS	44086-44086	THOMPSON
43506-43506	BRYAN	43747-43747	JERUSALEM	43941-43941	PINEY FORK	44087-44087	TWINSBURG
43510-43510	COLTON	43748-43748	JUNCTION CITY	43942-43942	POWHATAN POINT	44088-44088	UNIONVILLE
43511-43511	CUSTAR	43749-43749	KIMBOLTON	43943-43943	RAYLAND	44089-44089	VERMILION
43512-43512	DEFIANCE	43750-43750	KIPLING	43944-43944	RICHMOND	44090-44090	WELLINGTON
43515-43515	DELTA	43752-43752	LAINGS	43945-43945	SALINEVILLE	44092-44092	WICKLIFFE
43516-43516	DESHLER	43754-43754	LEWISVILLE	43946-43946	SARDIS	44093-44093	WILLIAMSFIELD

ZIP	City	ZIP	City	ZIP	City	ZIP	City
44094-44094	WILLOUGHBY	44408-44408	COLUMBIANA	44643-44643	MAGNOLIA	44853-44853	NEW RIEGEL
44095-44095	EASTLAKE	44410-44410	CORTLAND	44644-44644	MALVERN	44854-44854	NEW WASHINGTON
44096-44096	WILLOUGHBY	44411-44411	DEERFIELD	44645-44645	MARSHALLVILLE	44855-44855	NORTH FAIRFIELD
44099-44099	WINDSOR	44412-44412	DIAMOND	44646-44648	MASSILLON	44856-44856	NORTH ROBINSON
44101-44106	CLEVELAND	44413-44413	EAST PALESTINE	44650-44650	MAXIMO	44857-44857	NORWALK
44107-44107	LAKEWOOD	44415-44415	ELKTON	44651-44651	MECHANICSTOWN	44859-44859	NOVA
44108-44115	CLEVELAND	44416-44416	ELLSWORTH	44652-44652	MIDDLEBRANCH	44860-44860	OCEOLA
44116-44116	ROCKY RIVER	44417-44417	FARMDALE	44653-44653	MIDVALE	44861-44861	OLD FORT
44117-44117	EUCLID	44418-44418	FOWLER	44654-44654	MILLERSBURG	44862-44862	ONTARIO
44118-44121	CLEVELAND	44420-44420	GIRARD	44656-44656	MINERAL CITY	44864-44864	PERRYSVILLE
44122-44122	BEACHWOOD	44422-44422	GREENFORD	44657-44657	MINERVA	44865-44865	PLYMOUTH
44123-44123	EUCLID	44423-44423	HANOVERTON	44659-44659	MOUNT EATON	44866-44866	POLK
44124-44130	CLEVELAND	44424-44424	HARTFORD	44660-44660	MOUNT HOPE	44867-44867	REPUBLIC
44131-44131	INDEPENDENCE	44425-44425	HUBBARD	44661-44661	NASHVILLE	44870-44871	SANDUSKY
44132-44132	EUCLID	44427-44427	KENSINGTON	44662-44662	NAVARRE	44874-44874	SAVANNAH
44133-44133	NORTH ROYALTON	44428-44428	KINSMAN	44663-44663	NEW PHILADELPHIA	44875-44875	SHELBY
44134-44135	CLEVELAND	44429-44429	LAKE MILTON	44665-44665	NORTH GEORGETOWN	44878-44878	SHILOH
44136-44136	STRONGSVILLE	44430-44430	LEAVITTSBURG	44666-44666	NORTH LAWRENCE	44880-44880	SULLIVAN
44137-44137	MAPLE HEIGHTS	44431-44431	LEETONIA	44667-44667	ORRVILLE	44881-44881	SULPHUR SPRINGS
44138-44138	OLMSTED FALLS	44432-44432	LISBON	44669-44669	PARIS	44882-44882	SYCAMORE
44139-44139	SOLON	44436-44436	LOWELLVILLE	44670-44670	ROBERTSVILLE	44883-44883	TIFFIN
44140-44140	BAY VILLAGE	44437-44437	MC DONALD	44671-44671	SANDYVILLE	44887-44887	TIRO
44141-44141	BRECKSVILLE	44438-44438	MASURY	44672-44672	SEBRING	44888-44888	WILLARD
44142-44142	BROOKPARK	44439-44439	MESOPOTAMIA	44675-44675	SHERRODSVILLE	44889-44889	WAKEMAN
44143-44144	CLEVELAND	44440-44440	MINERAL RIDGE	44676-44676	SHREVE	44890-44890	WILLARD
44145-44145	WESTLAKE	44441-44441	NEGLEY	44677-44677	SMITHVILLE	44901-44999	MANSFIELD
44146-44146	BEDFORD	44442-44442	NEW MIDDLETOWN	44678-44678	SOMERDALE	45001-45001	ADDYSTON
44147-44147	BROADVIEW HEIGHTS	44443-44443	NEW SPRINGFIELD	44679-44679	STILLWATER	45002-45002	CLEVES
44177-44199	CLEVELAND	44444-44444	NEWTON FALLS	44680-44680	STRASBURG	45003-45003	COLLEGE CORNER
44201-44201	ATWATER	44445-44445	NEW WATERFORD	44681-44681	SUGARCREEK	45004-45004	COLLINSVILLE
44202-44202	AURORA	44446-44446	NILES	44682-44682	TUSCARAWAS	45005-45005	FRANKLIN
44203-44203	BARBERTON	44449-44449	NORTH BENTON	44683-44683	UHRICHSVILLE	45011-45013	HAMILTON
44210-44210	BATH	44450-44450	NORTH BLOOMFIELD	44685-44685	UNIONTOWN	45014-45014	FAIRFIELD
44211-44211	BRADY LAKE	44451-44451	NORTH JACKSON	44687-44687	WALNUT CREEK	45015-45015	HAMILTON
44212-44212	BRUNSWICK	44452-44452	NORTH LIMA	44688-44688	WAYNESBURG	45018-45018	FAIRFIELD
44214-44214	BURBANK	44453-44453	ORANGEVILLE	44689-44689	WILMOT	45020-45026	HAMILTON
44215-44215	CHIPPEWA LAKE	44454-44454	PETERSBURG	44690-44690	WINESBURG	45030-45030	HARRISON
44216-44216	CLINTON	44455-44455	ROGERS	44691-44691	WOOSTER	45032-45032	HARVEYSBURG
44217-44217	CRESTON	44460-44460	SALEM	44693-44693	DEERSVILLE	45033-45033	HOOVEN
44221-44223	CUYAHOGA FALLS	44470-44470	SOUTHINGTON	44695-44695	BOWERSTON	45034-45034	KINGS MILLS
44224-44224	STOW	44471-44471	STRUTHERS	44697-44697	ZOAR	45036-45036	LEBANON
44230-44230	DOYLESTOWN	44473-44473	VIENNA	44699-44699	TIPPECANOE	45039-45039	MAINEVILLE
44231-44231	GARRETTSVILLE	44481-44488	WARREN	44701-44799	CANTON	45040-45040	MASON
44232-44232	GREEN	44490-44490	WASHINGTONVILLE	44801-44801	ADRIAN	45041-45041	MIAMITOWN
44233-44233	HINCKLEY	44491-44491	WEST FARMINGTON	44802-44802	ALVADA	45042-45044	MIDDLETOWN
44234-44234	HIRAM	44492-44492	WEST POINT	44803-44803	AMSDEN	45050-45050	MONROE
44235-44235	HOMERVILLE	44493-44493	WINONA	44804-44804	ARCADIA	45051-45051	MOUNT SAINT JOSEPH
44236-44238	HUDSON	44501-44599	YOUNGSTOWN	44805-44805	ASHLAND	45052-45052	NORTH BEND
44240-44240	KENT	44601-44601	ALLIANCE	44807-44807	ATTICA	45053-45053	OKEANA
44241-44241	STREETSBORO	44606-44606	APPLE CREEK	44809-44809	BASCOM	45054-45054	OREGONIA
44242-44243	KENT	44607-44607	AUGUSTA	44811-44811	BELLEVUE	45055-45055	OVERPECK
44250-44250	LAKEMORE	44608-44608	BEACH CITY	44813-44813	BELLVILLE	45056-45056	OXFORD
44251-44251	WESTFIELD CENTER	44609-44609	BELOIT	44814-44814	BERLIN HEIGHTS	45061-45061	ROSS
44253-44253	LITCHFIELD	44610-44610	BERLIN	44815-44815	BETTSVILLE	45062-45062	SEVEN MILE
44254-44254	LODI	44611-44611	BIG PRAIRIE	44816-44816	BIRMINGHAM	45063-45063	SHANDON
44255-44255	MANTUA	44612-44612	BOLIVAR	44817-44817	BLOOMDALE	45064-45064	SOMERVILLE
44256-44258	MEDINA	44613-44613	BREWSTER	44818-44818	BLOOMVILLE	45065-45065	SOUTH LEBANON
44260-44260	MOGADORE	44614-44614	CANAL FULTON	44820-44820	BUCYRUS	45066-45066	SPRINGBORO
44262-44262	MUNROE FALLS	44615-44615	CARROLLTON	44822-44822	BUTLER	45067-45067	TRENTON
44264-44264	PENINSULA	44617-44617	CHARM	44824-44824	CASTALIA	45068-45068	WAYNESVILLE
44265-44265	RANDOLPH	44618-44618	DALTON	44825-44825	CHATFIELD	45069-45069	WEST CHESTER
44266-44266	RAVENNA	44619-44619	DAMASCUS	44826-44826	COLLINS	45070-45070	WEST ELKTON
44270-44270	RITTMAN	44620-44620	DELLROY	44827-44827	CRESTLINE	45071-45071	WEST CHESTER
44272-44272	ROOTSTOWN	44621-44621	DENNISON	44828-44828	FLAT ROCK	45073-45099	MONROE
44273-44273	SEVILLE	44622-44622	DOVER	44830-44830	FOSTORIA	45101-45101	ABERDEEN
44274-44274	SHARON CENTER	44624-44624	DUNDEE	44833-44833	GALION	45102-45102	AMELIA
44275-44275	SPENCER	44625-44625	EAST ROCHESTER	44836-44836	GREEN SPRINGS	45103-45103	BATAVIA
44276-44276	STERLING	44626-44626	EAST SPARTA	44837-44837	GREENWICH	45105-45105	BENTONVILLE
44278-44278	TALLMADGE	44627-44627	FREDERICKSBURG	44838-44838	HAYESVILLE	45106-45106	BETHEL
44280-44280	VALLEY CITY	44628-44628	GLENMONT	44839-44839	HURON	45107-45107	BLANCHESTER
44281-44282	WADSWORTH	44629-44629	GNADENHUTTEN	44840-44840	JEROMESVILLE	45110-45110	BUFORD
44285-44285	WAYLAND	44630-44630	GREENTOWN	44841-44841	KANSAS	45111-45111	CAMP DENNISON
44286-44286	RICHFIELD	44631-44631	HARLEM SPRINGS	44842-44842	LOUDONVILLE	45112-45112	CHILO
44287-44287	WEST SALEM	44632-44632	HARTVILLE	44843-44843	LUCAS	45113-45113	CLARKSVILLE
44288-44288	WINDHAM	44633-44633	HOLMESVILLE	44844-44844	MC CUTCHENVILLE	45114-45114	CUBA
44301-44399	AKRON	44634-44634	HOMEWORTH	44845-44845	MELMORE	45115-45115	DECATUR
44401-44401	BERLIN CENTER	44636-44636	KIDRON	44846-44846	MILAN	45118-45118	FAYETTEVILLE
44402-44402	BRISTOLVILLE	44637-44637	KILLBUCK	44847-44847	MONROEVILLE	45119-45119	FEESBURG
44403-44403	BROOKFIELD	44638-44638	LAKEVILLE	44848-44848	NANKIN	45120-45120	FELICITY
44404-44404	BURGHILL	44639-44639	LEESVILLE	44849-44849	NEVADA	45121-45121	GEORGETOWN
44405-44405	CAMPBELL	44640-44640	LIMAVILLE	44850-44850	NEW HAVEN	45122-45122	GOSHEN
44406-44406	CANFIELD	44641-44641	LOUISVILLE	44851-44851	NEW LONDON	45123-45123	GREENFIELD

ZIP	City	ZIP	City	ZIP	City	ZIP	City
45130-45130	HAMERSVILLE	45347-45347	NEW PARIS	45672-45672	RAY	45809-45809	GOMER
45131-45131	HIGGINSPORT	45348-45348	NEW WESTON	45673-45673	RICHMOND DALE	45810-45810	ADA
45132-45132	HIGHLAND	45349-45349	NORTH HAMPTON	45674-45674	RIO GRANDE	45812-45812	ALGER
45133-45133	HILLSBORO	45350-45350	NORTH STAR	45675-45675	ROCK CAMP	45813-45813	ANTWERP
45135-45135	LEESBURG	45351-45351	OSGOOD	45677-45677	SCIOTO FURNACE	45814-45814	ARLINGTON
45138-45138	LEES CREEK	45352-45352	PALESTINE	45678-45678	SCOTTOWN	45815-45815	BELMORE
45140-45140	LOVELAND	45353-45353	PEMBERTON	45679-45679	SEAMAN	45816-45816	BENTON RIDGE
45142-45142	LYNCHBURG	45354-45354	PHILLIPSBURG	45680-45680	SOUTH POINT	45817-45817	BLUFFTON
45144-45144	MANCHESTER	45356-45356	PIQUA	45681-45681	SOUTH SALEM	45819-45819	BUCKLAND
45145-45145	MARATHON	45358-45358	PITSBURG	45682-45682	SOUTH WEBSTER	45820-45820	CAIRO
45146-45146	MARTINSVILLE	45359-45359	PLEASANT HILL	45683-45683	STOCKDALE	45821-45821	CECIL
45147-45147	MIAMIVILLE	45360-45360	PORT JEFFERSON	45684-45684	STOUT	45822-45822	CELINA
45148-45148	MIDLAND	45361-45361	POTSDAM	45685-45685	THURMAN	45826-45826	CHICKASAW
45150-45150	MILFORD	45362-45362	ROSSBURG	45686-45686	VINTON	45827-45827	CLOVERDALE
45152-45152	MORROW	45363-45363	RUSSIA	45687-45687	WAKEFIELD	45828-45828	COLDWATER
45153-45153	MOSCOW	45365-45367	SIDNEY	45688-45688	WATERLOO	45830-45830	COLUMBUS GROVE
45154-45154	MOUNT ORAB	45368-45368	SOUTH CHARLESTON	45690-45690	WAVERLY	45831-45831	CONTINENTAL
45155-45155	MOWRYSTOWN	45369-45369	SOUTH VIENNA	45692-45692	WELLSTON	45832-45832	CONVOY
45156-45156	NEVILLE	45370-45370	SPRING VALLEY	45693-45693	WEST UNION	45833-45833	DELPHOS
45157-45157	NEW RICHMOND	45371-45371	TIPP CITY	45694-45694	WHEELERSBURG	45835-45835	DOLA
45158-45158	NEWTONSVILLE	45372-45372	TREMONT CITY	45695-45695	WILKESVILLE	45836-45836	DUNKIRK
45159-45159	NEW VIENNA	45373-45374	TROY	45696-45696	WILLOW WOOD	45837-45837	DUPONT
45160-45160	OWENSVILLE	45377-45377	VANDALIA	45697-45697	WINCHESTER	45838-45838	ELGIN
45162-45162	PLEASANT PLAIN	45378-45378	VERONA	45698-45698	ZALESKI	45839-45840	FINDLAY
45164-45164	PORT WILLIAM	45380-45380	VERSAILLES	45699-45699	LUCASVILLE	45841-45841	JENERA
45165-45165	GREENFIELD	45381-45381	WEST ALEXANDRIA	45701-45701	ATHENS	45843-45843	FOREST
45166-45166	REESVILLE	45382-45382	WEST MANCHESTER	45710-45710	ALBANY	45844-45844	FORT JENNINGS
45167-45167	RIPLEY	45383-45383	WEST MILTON	45711-45711	AMESVILLE	45845-45845	FORT LORAMIE
45168-45168	RUSSELLVILLE	45384-45384	WILBERFORCE	45712-45712	BARLOW	45846-45846	FORT RECOVERY
45169-45169	SABINA	45385-45385	XENIA	45713-45713	BARTLETT	45848-45848	GLANDORF
45171-45171	SARDINIA	45387-45387	YELLOW SPRINGS	45714-45714	BELPRE	45849-45849	GROVER HILL
45172-45172	SINKING SPRING	45388-45388	YORKSHIRE	45715-45715	BEVERLY	45850-45850	HARROD
45174-45174	TERRACE PARK	45389-45389	CHRISTIANSBURG	45716-45716	BUCHTEL	45851-45851	HAVILAND
45176-45176	WILLIAMSBURG	45390-45390	UNION CITY	45717-45717	CARBONDALE	45853-45853	KALIDA
45177-45177	WILMINGTON	45401-45490	DAYTON	45719-45719	CHAUNCEY	45854-45854	LAFAYETTE
45201-45299	CINCINNATI	45501-45506	SPRINGFIELD	45720-45720	CHESTER	45855-45855	LATTY
45301-45301	ALPHA	45601-45601	CHILLICOTHE	45721-45721	COAL RUN	45856-45856	LEIPSIC
45302-45302	ANNA	45612-45612	BAINBRIDGE	45723-45723	COOLVILLE	45858-45858	MC COMB
45303-45303	ANSONIA	45613-45613	BEAVER	45724-45724	CUTLER	45859-45859	MC GUFFEY
45304-45304	ARCANUM	45614-45614	BIDWELL	45727-45727	DEXTER CITY	45860-45860	MARIA STEIN
45305-45305	BELLBROOK	45616-45616	BLUE CREEK	45729-45729	FLEMING	45861-45861	MELROSE
45306-45306	BOTKINS	45617-45617	BOURNEVILLE	45732-45732	GLOUSTER	45862-45862	MENDON
45307-45307	BOWERSVILLE	45618-45618	CHERRY FORK	45734-45734	GRAYSVILLE	45863-45863	MIDDLE POINT
45308-45308	BRADFORD	45619-45619	CHESAPEAKE	45735-45735	GUYSVILLE	45864-45864	MILLER CITY
45309-45309	BROOKVILLE	45620-45620	CHESHIRE	45739-45739	HOCKINGPORT	45865-45865	MINSTER
45310-45310	BURKETTSVILLE	45621-45621	COALTON	45740-45740	JACKSONVILLE	45866-45866	MONTEZUMA
45311-45311	CAMDEN	45622-45622	CREOLA	45741-45741	LANGSVILLE	45867-45867	MOUNT BLANCHARD
45312-45312	CASSTOWN	45623-45623	CROWN CITY	45742-45742	LITTLE HOCKING	45868-45868	MOUNT CORY
45314-45314	CEDARVILLE	45624-45624	CYNTHIANA	45743-45743	LONG BOTTOM	45869-45869	NEW BREMEN
45315-45315	CLAYTON	45628-45628	FRANKFORT	45744-45744	LOWELL	45870-45870	NEW HAMPSHIRE
45316-45316	CLIFTON	45629-45629	FRANKLIN FURNACE	45745-45745	LOWER SALEM	45871-45871	NEW KNOXVILLE
45317-45317	CONOVER	45630-45630	FRIENDSHIP	45746-45746	MACKSBURG	45872-45872	NORTH BALTIMORE
45318-45318	COVINGTON	45631-45631	GALLIPOLIS	45750-45750	MARIETTA	45873-45873	OAKWOOD
45319-45319	DONNELSVILLE	45633-45633	HALLSVILLE	45760-45760	MIDDLEPORT	45874-45874	OHIO CITY
45320-45320	EATON	45634-45634	HAMDEN	45761-45761	MILLFIELD	45875-45875	OTTAWA
45321-45321	ELDORADO	45636-45636	HAVERHILL	45764-45764	NELSONVILLE	45876-45876	OTTOVILLE
45322-45322	ENGLEWOOD	45638-45638	IRONTON	45766-45766	NEW MARSHFIELD	45877-45877	PANDORA
45323-45323	ENON	45640-45640	JACKSON	45767-45767	NEW MATAMORAS	45879-45879	PAULDING
45324-45324	FAIRBORN	45642-45642	JASPER	45768-45768	NEWPORT	45880-45880	PAYNE
45325-45325	FARMERSVILLE	45643-45643	KERR	45769-45769	POMEROY	45881-45881	RAWSON
45326-45326	FLETCHER	45644-45644	KINGSTON	45770-45770	PORTLAND	45882-45882	ROCKFORD
45327-45327	GERMANTOWN	45645-45645	KITTS HILL	45771-45771	RACINE	45883-45883	SAINT HENRY
45328-45328	GETTYSBURG	45646-45646	LATHAM	45772-45772	REEDSVILLE	45884-45884	SAINT JOHNS
45329-45329	GORDON	45647-45647	LONDONDERRY	45773-45773	RENO	45885-45885	SAINT MARYS
45330-45330	GRATIS	45648-45648	LUCASVILLE	45775-45775	RUTLAND	45886-45886	SCOTT
45331-45331	GREENVILLE	45650-45650	LYNX	45776-45776	SHADE	45887-45887	SPENCERVILLE
45332-45332	HOLLANSBURG	45651-45651	MC ARTHUR	45777-45777	SHARPSBURG	45888-45888	UNIOPOLIS
45333-45333	HOUSTON	45652-45652	MC DERMOTT	45778-45778	STEWART	45889-45889	VAN BUREN
45334-45334	JACKSON CENTER	45653-45653	MINFORD	45779-45779	SYRACUSE	45890-45890	VANLUE
45335-45335	JAMESTOWN	45654-45654	NEW PLYMOUTH	45780-45780	THE PLAINS	45891-45891	VAN WERT
45336-45336	KETTLERSVILLE	45656-45656	OAK HILL	45781-45781	TORCH	45893-45893	VAUGHNSVILLE
45337-45337	LAURA	45657-45657	OTWAY	45782-45782	TRIMBLE	45894-45894	VENEDOCIA
45338-45338	LEWISBURG	45658-45658	PATRIOT	45783-45783	TUPPERS PLAINS	45895-45895	WAPAKONETA
45339-45339	LUDLOW FALLS	45659-45659	PEDRO	45784-45784	VINCENT	45896-45896	WAYNESFIELD
45340-45340	MAPLEWOOD	45660-45660	PEEBLES	45786-45786	WATERFORD	45897-45897	WILLIAMSTOWN
45341-45341	MEDWAY	45661-45661	PIKETON	45787-45787	WATERTOWN	45898-45898	WILLSHIRE
45342-45343	MIAMISBURG	45662-45662	PORTSMOUTH	45788-45788	WHIPPLE	45899-45899	WREN
45344-45344	NEW CARLISLE	45663-45663	WEST PORTSMOUTH	45789-45789	WINGETT RUN	45944-45999	CINCINNATI
45345-45345	NEW LEBANON	45669-45669	PROCTORVILLE	45801-45807	LIMA		
45346-45346	NEW MADISON	45671-45671	RARDEN	45808-45808	BEAVERDAM		

Oklahoma

General Help Numbers:

Governor's Office
State Capitol, Suite 212
Oklahoma City, OK 73105
http://www.state.ok.us/~governor

405-521-2342
Fax 405-521-3317
8AM-5PM

Attorney General's Office
2300 N Lincoln, #112
Oklahoma City, OK 73105
http://www.oag.state.ok.us/
explorer.index.html

405-521-3921
Fax 405-521-6246
8:30AM-5PM

State Court Administrator
1915 N Stiles, #305
Oklahoma City, OK 73105
http://www.oscn.net

405-521-2450
Fax 405-521-6815
8AM-5PM

State Archives
Archives & Records Mgt Divisions
200 NE 18th
Oklahoma City, OK 73105-3298
http://www.odl.state.ok.us

405-522-3577
Fax 405-525-7804
8AM-5PM

State Specifics:

Capital:

Oklahoma City
Oklahoma County

Time Zone:

CST

Number of Counties:

77

Population:

3,450,654

Web Site:

www.state.ok.us

State Agencies

Criminal Records

OK State Bureau of Investigation, Criminal History Reporting; 6600 N Harvey, Oklahoma City, OK 73116; 405-848-6724, 8AM-5PM.

http://www.osbi.state.ok.us

Note: A record check request form is available at the web site. Sex offender data is available online at www.kwtv.com/crime/sex_offenders/sex-offenders-map.htm.

Indexing & Storage: Records are available from 1925 on.

Searching: Arrests with or without dispositions are available if the party was fingerprinted. Computer searches include arrests without dispositions. A DOB or approximate age is mandatory. A SSN, sex or race are helpful and provide a better search, but not required.

Access by: mail, fax, in person.

Fee & Payment: The fee for a computer name search is $15.00. The fee for a fingerprint search is $19.00. Copies are $.25 per page. Fee payee: O.S.B.I. Prepayment required. Credit cards accepted: MasterCard, Visa.

Mail search: Turnaround time: 2 weeks. A self addressed stamped envelope is requested.

Fax search: Use of credit card required.

In person search: Name requests take 20 minutes, fingerprint searches take up to ten days to process.

Corporation Records
Limited Liability Company Records
Limited Partnerships
Trademarks/Servicemarks
Limited Liability Partnerships

Secretary of State, 2300 N Lincoln Blvd, Rm 101, Oklahoma City, OK 73105-4897; 405-521-3911, 900-825-2424 (Corporate Records), 405-521-3771 (Fax), 8AM-5PM.

http://www.sos.state.ok.us

Note: Officers are available from the Franchise Tax Dept. of the Oklahoma Tax Commission, 405-521-3161.

Indexing & Storage: Records are available from late 1800's on. Older records are kept at the State Archives. More recent records are maintained on a mainframe. New records are available for inquiry immediately.

Searching: The search includes correct name, status, date of registration, service agent and address, state of domicile, authorized shares and par value, amendments, name changes, mergers, and trade names. The records do not include owner. Include the following in your request-full name of business. Records include:corporations, limited partnerships, limited liability companies, limited liability partnerships, certificate of partnership fictitious name for general partnerships and trade names.

Access by: mail, phone, fax, in person.

Fee & Payment: The search fee is $5.00. Copies are provided by the Certification Dept at $1.00 per page. Fee payee: Secretary of State. Prepayment required. Personal checks accepted. The Discover Card is accepted.

Mail search: Turnaround time: 1 to 2 days. A self addressed stamped envelope is requested.

Phone search: They will give an immediate verbal verification only. Dial 1-900-555-2424. The fee is $5.00 per call and you are allowed up to 3 record searches per call.

Fax search: Turnaround time 1 to 2 days.

In person search: There is no fee to search records on a public access terminal.

Other access: A copy of the corporation database is available on cartridges or on magnetic tape for $500.

Uniform Commercial Code

UCC Recorder, Oklahoma County Clerk, 320 R.S. Kerr Ave, County Office Bldg, Rm 105, Oklahoma City, OK 73102; 405-713-1521, 405-713-1810 (Fax), 8AM-5PM.

http://www.oklahomacounty.org/countyclerk

Note: This county agency is the central filing agency for the state.

Indexing & Storage: Records are available for since 2/91 on UCC, 10 years on tax liens on computer. Records are on microfiche from 1977 to present. It takes 2 to 3 days before new records are available for inquiry.

Searching: Use search request form UCC-4. Include the following in your request-debtor name.

Access by: mail, in person, online.

Fee & Payment: The search fee is $5.00 per debtor name, the copy fee is $1.00 per page. Fee payee: Oklahoma County Clerk. Prepayment required. Personal checks accepted. No credit cards accepted, but may 07/01.

Mail search: Turnaround time: 2 days.

In person search: Searching is available in person.

Online search: Records of all UCC financing statements may be viewed free on the Internet at www.oklahomacounty.org/coclerk/default.htm. Neither certified searches nor record requests are accepted at the web.

Other access: The entire database is available on microfilm or computer tapes, prices start at $500.

Federal Tax Liens
State Tax Liens
Records not maintained by a state level agency.

Note: All state tax liens and federal tax liens are filed at the local level. Federal tax liens on businesses are filed with the Clerk of Oklahoma County.

Sales Tax Registrations

Taxpayer Assistance, 2501 N Lincoln Blvd, Oklahoma City, OK 73194; 405-521-3160, 405-521-3826 (Fax), 7:30AM-4:30PM.

http://www.oktax.state.ok.us

Indexing & Storage: Records are available for the most recent 10 years on computer, microfilmed back to the 1970's.

Searching: This agency will provide any information found on the face of the permit-business name, address, tax permit number, and SIC code. Payment history is not released. Include the following in your request-business name. They will also search by owner name, federal tax ID, or by tax permit number.

Access by: mail, phone, in person.

Fee & Payment: No search fees, but there is a copy fee of $.25 per page. Fee payee: Oklahoma Tax Commission. Prepayment required. If the card is used, there is an additional fee equal to 1.35% of the purchase. Personal checks accepted. No credit cards accepted.

Mail search: Turnaround time: within 2 weeks. A self addressed stamped envelope is requested.

Phone search: Records are available by phone.

In person search: Copies cost $.25 per page.

Other access: Current permit holders are permitted to purchase the database on microfiche or on 3.5 inch floppies. The annual subscription is $150.00 and is updated monthly.

Birth Certificates

State Department of Health, Vital Records Service, PO Box 53551, Oklahoma City, OK 73152-3551 (Courier: 1000 NE 10th St, Oklahoma City, OK 73117); 405-271-4040, 405-271-1646 (Order Line), 405-232-3311 (Fax), 8:30AM-4PM.

http://www.health.state.ok.us/program/vital/brec.html

Indexing & Storage: Records are available from 1908 on. Records are computerized since 1945. New records are available for inquiry immediately. Records are indexed on inhouse computer, microfiche.

Searching: Must have a signed release from person of record or immediate family member. Include the following in your request-full name, names of parents, mother's maiden name, date of birth, place of birth, reason for information request. Also, daytime phone number.

Access by: mail, in person.

Fee & Payment: Fee is $5.00, add extra $5.00 for use of credit card. Fee payee: Oklahoma State Health Department. Prepayment required. Personal checks accepted. Credit cards accepted: MasterCard, Visa.

Mail search: Turnaround time: 2 weeks. A self addressed stamped envelope is requested.

In person search: Turnaround time is while you wait.

Expedited service: Expedited service is available for fax searches. Add 15.50 for express delivery. Use of credit card required.

Death Records

State Department of Health, Vital Records Service, PO Box 53551, Oklahoma City, OK 73152-3551 (Courier: 1000 NE 10th St, Oklahoma City, OK 73117), 405-271-4040, 405-271-1646 (Order Line), 405-232-3311 (Fax), 8:30AM-4PM.

http://www.health.state.ok.us/program/vital/brec.html

Indexing & Storage: Records are available from October 1908 on. Records are computerized since 1951. New records are available for inquiry immediately. Records are indexed on microfiche, inhouse computer.

Searching: Records are open to the public, Include the following in your request-full name, date of death, place of death. Also, daytime phone number.

Access by: mail, phone, fax, in person.

Fee & Payment: Fee is $10. per record. Add $5.00 if credit card used. Fee payee: Oklahoma State Health Department. Prepayment required. Personal checks accepted. No credit cards accepted.

Mail search: Turnaround time: 1 to 2 weeks. A self addressed stamped envelope is requested.

Phone search: Credit card required.

Fax search: Credit card required.

In person search: Turnaround time is while you wait.

Expedited service: Expedited service is available for fax searches. Add $15.50 for express delivery. Use of credit card required.

Marriage Certificates
Divorce Records
Records not maintained by a state level agency.

Note: Marriage and Divorce records are found at county level. The record should be requested from the county courthouse in the county where the marriage or divorce was filed or granted.

Workers' Compensation Records

Workers Compensation Court, 1915 N Stiles, Oklahoma City, OK 73105-4918; 405-522-8600, 405-522-8640 (Records Dept), 800-269-5353 (Enforcement), 405-552-8647 (Fax), 8AM-5PM.

Indexing & Storage: Records are available for last 7 years on computer. Index to case files are on print-outs and cards since the 1930's.

Searching: Claims information is considered public record. Anyone having a correct case number can access and review files. There are 2 searches involved-1st to get case number, and then to do search. The request must be on their form. Pending cases are available. Include the following in your request-claimant name, Social Security Number, claim number, date of birth, date of accident. If you do not have the claim number, send a written request (Attn: Prior Claims) with all other data, and they will notify you of the case number so copies can be pulled. Then, with case number, you can request copies, and you must use their form.

Access by: mail, phone, in person.

Fee & Payment: There is no search fee to get the case number. The copy fee is $1.00 for the first page and $.50 each additional page if done by staff; $.25 if by searcher. Fee payee: Workers' Compensation Court. Prepayment required. In-state businesses can set up charge accounts; payment due within 30 days. Personal checks accepted. No credit cards accepted.

Mail search: Turnaround time: 5 days. If payment not included, party will be billed and funds must be received before documents are mailed. A self addressed stamped envelope is requested.

Phone search: The only information provided is the case number. Requesters must provide name or SSN, and date of injury.

In person search: One may search on the in-house computer in the basement level and also request and review a file. Files are pulled for the public from 8:15AM to 4:15PM.

Driver Records

MVR Desk, Records Management Division, PO Box 11415, Oklahoma City, OK 73136 (Courier: 3600 Martin Luther King Blvd, Rm 206, Oklahoma City, OK 73111); 405-425-2262, 8AM-4:45PM.

http://www.dps.state.ok.us/dls

Note: Copies of tickets may be obtained for $3.00 per page from the address listed above. Most tickets are two pages. For certification of copies, add $3.00.

Indexing & Storage: Records are available for 3 years for moving violations, DWIs and suspensions. All violations, except speeding less than ten mph over the limit, appear on the driving record. Accidents are reported if there is a conviction of citation. It takes 2-6 months before new records are available for inquiry.

Searching: Information is available for law enforcement purposes. Anyone else requesting an MVR for another person is required to submit a consent to release records form signed by both parties. Ask for a State of Oklahoma Records Request Form. Include the following in your request-full name and date of birth, or driver's license number. The following data is not released: medical records, Social Security Numbers, addresses or personal information (height, weight, sex, eye color, etc.).

Access by: mail, in person.

Fee & Payment: The fee is $10.00 per driving record. There is a full fee for a no record found. Fee payee: Department of Public Safety. Prepayment required. Personal checks accepted. No credit cards accepted.

Mail search: Turnaround time: 1 week to 10 days. Oklahoma offers a monthly billing system for high volume requesters. A self addressed stamped envelope is requested.

In person search: Records may be requested at any Oklahoma Tag Agency statewide. Up to ten requests may be processed in one day or less. Many MV offices across the state will sell records.

Other access: Magnetic tape ordering is available for high volume users. Call 405-425-2222.

Vehicle Ownership
Vehicle Identification
Vessel Ownership
Vessel Registration

Oklahoma Tax Commission, Motor Vehicle Division, Attn: Research, 2501 N Lincoln Blvd, Oklahoma City, OK 73194; 405-521-3221, 7:30AM-4:30PM.

http://www.oktax.state.ok.us/mvhome.html

Indexing & Storage: Records are available for 3 years (registration records); the state keeps title records internally for 20 years. All watercraft must be titled and registered. All motors in excess of 10 HP must be titled. Lien information appears on title records. It takes 2 up to 5 weeks before new records are available for inquiry.

Searching: Records are not released to casual requesters. Approved requesters must use the Vehicle Information Request Form. Name searches are not performed. The title number, VIN or current plate number is needed for a search.

Access by: mail, in person.

Fee & Payment: The fee for VIN and plate look-ups is $1.00 per report. Certification is an additional $1.00 per page. If lien information is desired, it must be specified on the request. A title history search entails a $1.00 fee per page. Microfilm record is $7.50. Fee payee: Oklahoma Tax Commission, MVD. Prepayment required. Personal checks accepted. No credit cards accepted.

Mail search: Turnaround time: 7 to 10 days.

In person search: Turnaround time is while you wait, depending on the workload.

Other access: Oklahoma does not offer bulk delivery of vehicle and ownership information except for purposes such as vehicle recall.

Accident Reports

Department of Public Safety, Records Management Division, PO Box 11415, Oklahoma City, OK 73136 (Courier: 3600 Martin Luther King Blvd, Room 206, Oklahoma City, OK 73111); 405-425-2192, 405-425-2046 (Fax), 8AM-4:45PM.

http://www.dps.state.ok.us

Note: This agency refers to these reports as Collision Reports.

Indexing & Storage: Records are available for 3 years to present. It takes 10 to 14 days before new records are available for inquiry. Records are indexed on inhouse computer.

Searching: Include the following in your request-date of accident, location of accident, full name, county.

Access by: mail, phone, in person.

Fee & Payment: The fee is $7.00 for an uncertified copy and $10.00 for a certified copy. There is no charge for a no record found. Fee payee: Department of Public Safety. Prepayment required. Personal checks accepted. No credit cards accepted.

Mail search: Turnaround time: 24 hours. A self addressed stamped envelope is requested.

Phone search: No fee for telephone request. This agency will reveal whether there is an accident over the phone. No other information will be revealed over the phone.

In person search: Normal turnaround time is while you wait.

Legislation Records

Oklahoma Legislature, State Capitol, Bill Status Info-Rm B-30, Copies-Rm 310, Oklahoma City, OK 73105; 405-521-5642 (Bill Status Only), 405-521-5515 (Bill Distribution), 405-528-2546 (Bills in Progress), 405-521-5507 (Fax), 8:30AM-4:30PM.

http://www.lsb.state.ok.us

Note: For prior session bills, you may call the State Law Library at 405-521-2502, ext. 280.

Indexing & Storage: Records are available for current session only. Records are indexed on inhouse computer.

Searching: Include the following in your request-bill number.

Access by: mail, phone, in person, online.

Fee & Payment: There is no search fee.

Mail search: Turnaround time: same day. No self addressed stamped envelope is required.

Phone search: Turnaround time is same day.

In person search: Turnaround time is same day.

Online search: The web page provides a variety of legislative information including searching by topic or bill number.

Voter Registration

State Election Board, State Capitol-Rm B6, Box 53156, Oklahoma City, OK 73152; 405-521-2391, 405-521-6457 (Fax), 8AM-5PM.

http://www.state.ok.us/~elections

Indexing & Storage: Records are available for 4 years. It takes 7 to 10 days before new records are available for inquiry.

Searching: Records are open to the public and can be accessed at both the state and county levels. The following data is not released: phone numbers.

Access by: mail, phone, in person.

Fee & Payment: There is no fee for look-ups. Fee payee: OK State Board of Elections. Only certified funds or cashier's checks are accepted for database sales. No credit cards accepted.

Mail search: Turnaround time: 2 to 5 days. No self addressed stamped envelope is required.

Phone search: Limited information is given, depending on staff availability.

In person search: Searching is available in person.

Other access: A statewide database can be purchased on tape for a fee of $150. Large counties are available on tape for $50-75, and smaller counties or precincts are available on disk for $10-35. Data is in ACSII format.

GED Certificates

State Dept of Education, Lifelong Learning, 2500 N Lincoln Blvd, Oklahoma City, OK 73105; 405-521-3321, 405-521-6205 (Fax).

http://sde.state.ok.us

Searching: To search, all of the following is required: name, approximate year of test, date of birth, and Social Security Number.

Access by: mail, phone, fax, in person.

Fee & Payment: There is no fee for a verification. There is a $5.00 fee to obtain a transcript or a duplicate certification. Fee payee: State Dept of Education. Prepayment required. Money orders and business checks are accepted. No credit cards accepted.

Mail search: Turnaround time: 1 to 2 days. No self addressed stamped envelope is required.

Phone search: This is for verification only.

Fax search: Same criteria as mail searching.

In person search: Turnaround time is typically 30 minutes for verification.

Hunting License Information
Fishing License Information
Records not maintained by a state level agency.

Note: They do not have a central database. Vendors do not have names and addresses either. However, a list of license vendors can be obtained for $150.00.

Oklahoma State Licensing Agencies

Licenses Searchable Online

Accounting Firm #15..www.state.ok.us/~oab/firms.html

Athletic Trainer/Apprentice #08 ....http://medbd.netplus.net/physrch.html

Bank #35...www.state.ok.us/~osbd/

Consumer Finance Company #20.....................www.okdocc.state.ok.us/introSL.htm

Credit Services Organization #20......................www.okdocc.state.ok.us/introCSO.htm

Credit Union #35..www.state.ok.us/~osbd/

Dental Hygienist #29..www.state.ok.us/~dentist/

Dentist/ Dental Assistant #29 ....www.state.ok.us/~dentist/

Dietitian/Provisional Licensed Dietitian #08 ....http://medbd.netplus.net/physrch.html

Electrologist #08..http://medbd.netplus.net/physrch.html

Engineer #13...www.okpels.org/rosters.htm

Health Spa #20..www.okdocc.state.ok.us/introSpa.htm

Lobbyist #42..www.state.ok.us/~ethics/lobbyist.html

Medical Doctor #08..http://medbd.netplus.net/physrch.html

Money Order Agent #35.....................................www.state.ok.us/~osbd/

Mortgage Banker #20...www.okdocc.state.ok.us/introMB.htm

Occupational Therapist/Assistant #08 ....http://medbd.netplus.net/physrch.html

Optometrist #07...www.odfinder.org/LicSearch.asp

Osteopathic Physician #10................................www.docboard.org/ok/df/oksearch.htm

Pawnbroker #20...www.okdocc.state.ok.us/introPB.htm

Perfusionist #08...http://medbd.netplus.net/physrch.html

Physical Therapist/Assistant #08 ....http://medbd.netplus.net/physrch.html

Physician Assistant #08.....................................http://medbd.netplus.net/physrch.html

Podiatrist #12 ....http://medbd.netplus.net/physrch.html

Precious Metals & Gem Dealer #20...................www.okdocc.state.ok.us/introPMD.htm

Private Investigator #19 ....www.opia.com/searches/search.html

Private Investigator Agency #19.........................www.opia.com/searches/search.html

Public Accountant-CPA #15...............................www.state.ok.us/~oab/twotier.html

Rent to Own Dealer #20.....................................www.okdocc.state.ok.us/introRTO.htm

Respiratory Care Practitioner #08 ....http://medbd.netplus.net/physrch.html

Savings & Loan Association #35.......................www.state.ok.us/~osbd/

Surveyor #13 ....www.okpels.org/rosters.htm

Trust Company #35 ....www.state.ok.us/~osbd/

Licensing Quick Finder

Accounting Firm #15 405-521-2397	Facial Operator #04 405-521-2441	Osteopathic Physician #10 405-528-8625
Airport Development Project #27 405-521-2377	Firearm Permit for Retired Police Officer #19	Pawnbroker #20 405-521-3653
Alarm Company/Employee #37 405-271-5217	405-425-2760	Perfusionist #08 405-848-6841
Alcohol & Drug Influence Tester #17 405-425-2460	Forester #16 405-522-6147	Pharmacy/Pharmacist #11 405-521-3815
Animal Technician #18 405-843-0843	Funeral Director #05...............405-525-0158	Physical Therapist/Assistant #08 405-848-6841
Architect #23.................405-751-6512	Ground Water & Observation Water Well Driller #39	Physician Assistant #08...........405-848-6841
Asbestos Abatement Worker #44.........405-528-1500	405-530-8800	Placement Agency #21.............405-521-3561
Athletic Trainer/Apprentice #08 405-848-6841	Health Spa #20 405-521-3653	Plumbing Contractor/Inspector #36.......405-271-5217
Attorney #28 405-524-2365	Hearing Aid Dealer/Fitter #37 405-271-5217	Podiatrist #12...............405-848-6841
Audiologist #06 405-840-2774	Horse Groom #31...............405-943-6472	Police Officer #19................405-425-2755
Bail Bondsman #32 405-521-6610	Horse Racing #31 405-943-6472	Polygraph Examiner/Intern #40.......405-425-2778
Bank #35 405-521-2783	Horse Trainer #31..............405-943-6472	Polygraph Operator #19................405-425-2778
Barber Instructor #37..............405-271-5217	Insurance Adjuster #32................405-521-3961	Precious Metals & Gem Dealer #20 405-521-3653
Barber Shop #37..................405-271-5217	Insurance Agent/Representative #32 405-521-3961	Private Investigator #19...............405-425-2775
Barber/Barber Apprentice #37 405-271-5217	Insurance Consultant #32...................405-521-3961	Private Investigator Agency #19 405-425-2775
Beauty School #04 405-521-2441	Investment Adviser #34 405-280-7780	Psychologist #14...............405-271-6118
Beauty Shop/Salon #04 405-521-2441	Investment Adviser Representative #34 405-280-7780	Public Accountant-CPA #15...............405-521-2397
Blacksmith #31.................405-943-6472	Jockey #31 405-943-6472	Pump Installer #39.................405-530-8800
Building Inspector #37..............405-271-5217	Jockey Agent #31.................405-943-6472	Real Estate Appraiser #33 405-521-6636
Burglar Alarm Salesman #37 405-271-5217	Journeyman #36 405-271-5217	Real Estate Broker #38 405-521-3387
Burglar Alarm Service/Installer #37 405-271-5217	Landscape Architect #23 405-751-6512	Real Estate Salesperson #38 405-521-3387
Cemetery #35 405-521-2783	Liquor Industry #01 405-521-3484	Rent to Own Dealer #20 405-521-3653
Children & Youth Agency, Private/Public #21	Lobbyist #42 405-521-3451	Respiratory Care Practitioner #08 405-848-6841
...............405-521-3561	LPG-Liquefied Petroleum Dealer/Mfg./Manager #25	Sanitarian/Environmental Specialist #37 405-271-5217
Chiropractor #03 405-528-5505	405-521-2458	Savings & Loan Association #35...........405-521-2783
Consumer Finance Company #20.....405-521-3653	LPG-Liquefied Petroleum System Installer #25	School Accreditation #41...............405-521-3301
Cosmetology Instructor #04 405-521-2441	405-521-2458	School Transportation #41...................405-521-3301
Cosmetology Student & Apprentice #4 ..405-521-2441	Manicurist #04 405-521-2441	Securities Agent #34 405-280-7780
Counselor LPC/LM&T #43.................405-271-6030	Mechanical Contractor #36...................405-271-5217	Securities Broker/Dealer #34 405-280-7780
Credit Services Organization #20..........405-521-3653	Mechanical Inspector #36.....................405-271-5217	Security Guard/Guard Agency #19 405-425-2775
Credit Union #35 405-521-2783	Medical Doctor #08 405-848-6841	Shorthand Reporter #09 405-521-2450
Dental Assistant #29 405-848-1364	Midwife Nurse #30 405-962-1800	Social Worker #24.................405-946-7230
Dental Hygienist #29 405-848-1364	Mining Operation #22 405-521-3859	Speech Pathologist #06...........405-840-2774
Dentist #29 405-848-1364	Money Order Agent #35 405-521-2783	Surveyor #13 405-521-2874
Dietitian/Provisional Licensed Dietitian #08	Mortgage Banker #20...............405-521-3653	Teacher #41...............405-521-3301
...............405-848-6841	Notary Public #26...............405-521-2516	Trust Company #35...............405-521-2783
Electrical Contractor #37 405-271-5217	Nurse #30 405-962-1800	Veterinarian #18...............405-843-0843
Electrical Inspector #37 405-271-5217	Nurse Anesthetist #30 405-962-1800	Veterinary Technician #18...................405-843-0843
Electrician-Journeyman #37 405-271-5217	Nurse Specialist, Clinical #30 405-962-1800	Waste Water Operator #45...................405-271-5205
Electrologist #08 405-848-6841	Nurse-LPN/RN#30 405-962-1800	Well Driller/Monitor #39 405-530-8800
Embalmer #05 405-525-0158	Nursing Home Administrator #02 405-521-0991	
Emergency Medical Technician #37......405-271-4240	Occupational Therapist/Assistant #08 ...405-848-6841	
Engineer #13 405-521-2874	Optometrist #07 405-733-7836	

Licensing Agency Information

#01 Alcoholic Beverage Laws Enforcement Commission, 4545 N Lincoln Blvd, #270, Oklahoma City, OK 73105; 405-521-3484, Fax: 405-521-6578.
www.able.state.ok.us

#02 Board for Nursing Home Administrators, 3033 N Walnut, #100E, Oklahoma City, OK 73105; 405-521-0991, Fax: 405-528-3483.

#03 Board of Chiropractic Examiners, 310 NE 28th St, #205, Oklahoma City, OK 73105; 405-524-6223, Fax: 405-522-6830.
www.state.ok.us/~chiro/obce.htm

#04 Board of Cosmetology, 2200 Classen Blvd, #1530, Oklahoma City, OK 73106; 405-521-2441, Fax: 405-528-8310.
www.state.ok.us/~cosmo

#05 Board of Embalmers & Funeral Directors, 4545 N Lincoln Blvd, #175, Oklahoma City, OK 73105; 405-525-0158, Fax: 405-557-1844.
www.state.ok.us/~embalm

#06 Board of Examiners for Speech Pathology/Audiology, 1140 NW 63rd, #305 (PO Box 53592), Oklahoma City, OK 73152-3592; 405-840-2774, Fax: 405-843-3489.

#07 Board of Examiners in Optometry, 6912 E Reno Ave #302, Midwest City, OK 73110-2162; 405-733-7836, Fax: 405-741-3060.
www.state.ok.us/~optomerty
Direct web site URL to search for licensees: www.odfinder.org/LicSearch.asp. You can search online using national database by name, city or state.

#08 Board of Medical Licensure & Supervision, 5104 N Francis, #C, Oklahoma City, OK 73118-0256; 405-848-6841, Fax: 405-848-8240.
www.osbmls.state.ok.us
Direct web site URL to search for licensees: http://medbd.netplus.net/physrch.html. You can search online using name, county, license # and specialty.

#09 Board of Official Shorthand Reporters, 1915 N Stiles, Rm 305, Oklahoma City, OK 73105; 405-521-2450, Fax: 405-521-3815.
www.oscn.net

#10 Board of Osteopathic Examiners, 4848 N Lincoln, #100, Oklahoma City, OK 73105; 405-528-8625, Fax: 405-557-0653.
www.docboard.org/ok/ok.htm

#11 Board of Pharmacy, 4545 N Lincoln Blvd, North Terrace, #112, Oklahoma City, OK 73105-3488; 405-521-3815, Fax: 405-521-3758.
www.state.ok.us/~pharmacy web site offers forms, rules and general information; online record searching is under consideration.

#12 Board of Podiatry, 5104 N Francis, #C, Oklahoma City, OK 73154-0256; 405-848-6841, Fax: 405-848-8240.
www.obbmis.state.ok.us
Direct web site URL to search for licensees: http://medbd.netplus.net/physrch.html. You can search online using name, profession, county, license number

#13 Board of Professional Engineers & Land Surveyors, 201 NE 27th St, Rm 120, Oklahoma City, OK 73105; 405-521-2874, Fax: 405-523-3135.
www.okpels.org
Direct web site URL to search for licensees: www.okpels.org/rosters.htm. You can search online using company, name, and registration number.

#14 Board of Psychologists Examiners, 201 NE 38th Terr #C, Oklahoma City, OK 73105; 405-271-6118, Fax: 405-271-6137.

#15 Board of Public Accountancy, 4545 N Lincoln Blvd, #165, Oklahoma City, OK 73105; 405-521-2397, Fax: 405-521-3118.
www.state.ok.us/~oab

#16 Board of Registration for Foresters, 2800 N Lincoln Blvd, Agriculture Bldg, Oklahoma City, OK 73105-4298; 405-522-6147, Fax: 405-522-4583.

#17 Board of Tests for Alcohol & Drug Influence, PO Box 11415, Oklahoma City, OK 73136-0415; 405-425-2460, Fax: 405-425-2490.
www.dps.state.ok.us/btadi

#18 Board of Veterinary Medical Examiners, 5104 N Francis, #F, Oklahoma City, OK 73154; 405-843-0843, Fax: 405-840-4501.
www.telephath.com/vetmedex

#19 Council on Law Enforcement Education & Training, 3530 N Martin Luther King Ave, Oklahoma City, OK 73136-0476; 405-425-2750, Fax: 405-425-2773.
www.cleet.state.ok.us

#20 Department of Consumer Credit, 4545 N Lincoln Blvd, #104, Oklahoma City, OK 73105; 405-521-3653, Fax: 405-521-6740.
www.state.ok.us/~okdcc
Direct web site URL to search for licensees: www.okdocc.state.ok.us/

#21 Department of Human Services, PO Box 25352, Oklahoma City, OK 73126; 405-521-3561, Fax: 405-522-2564.
www.okdhs.org/childcare/

#22 Department of Mines, 4040 N Lincoln, #107, Oklahoma City, OK 73105; 405-521-3859, Fax: 405-427-9646.

#23 Licensed Architects & Landscape Architects, 11212 N May, #110, Oklahoma City, OK 73120; 405-751-6512, Fax: 405-755-6391.
www.boardofarch.state.ok.us

#24 Licensed Social Workers Registration Board, 3535 NW 58th St, #765, Oklahoma City, OK 73112; 405-946-7230, Fax: 405-942-1070.
www.state.ok.us/~osblsw

#25 Liquefied Petroleum Gas Board, 2101 N Lincoln Blvd, Jim Thorpe Bldg, Rm B-45, Oklahoma City, OK 73105-4990; 405-521-2458, Fax: 405-521-6037.

#26 Office of Secretary of State, PO Box 53390, Oklahoma City, OK 73152-3390; 405-521-2516, Fax: 405-522-3555.
www.sos.state.ok.us

#27 Aeronautics Commission, 200 NE 21st, B-7 1st Fl, Oklahoma City, OK 73105; 405-521-2377, Fax: 405-521-2379.
www.okladot.state.ok.us/hqdiv/aerot.htm

#28 Bar Association, 1901 Lincoln Blvd, Oklahoma City, OK 73105; 405-524-2365, Fax: 405-524-7001.
www.okbar.org

#29 Board of Dentistry, 6501 N Broadway, #220, Oklahoma City, OK 73116; 405-848-1364, Fax: 405-848-3279.
Direct web site URL to search for licensees: www.state.ok.us/~dentist

#30 Board of Nursing, 2915 N Classen Blvd, #524, Oklahoma City, OK 73106; 405-962-1800, Fax: 405-962-1821.

#31 Horse Racing Commission, Shepherd Mall 2614 Villa Prom, Oklahoma City, OK 73107; 405-943-6472, Fax: 405-943-6474.
www.state.ok.us/~ohrc

#32 Insurance Department, PO Box 53408, Oklahoma City, OK 73152-3408; 405-521-3916, Fax: 405-522-3642.
www.oid.state.ok.us/index.html

#33 Real Estate Appraiser Board, PO Box 53408, Oklahoma City, OK 73152-3408; 405-521-6636, Fax: 405-521-6635.
www.oid.state.ok.us/agentbrokers/index.html

#34 Securities Commission, 120 N Robinson, 1st National Center #860, Oklahoma City, OK 73102; 405-280-7700, Fax: 405-280-7742.
www.securities.state.ok.us

#35 Banking Department, 4545 N Lincoln Blvd, #164, Oklahoma City, OK 73105-3427; 405-521-2782, Fax: 405-525-9701.
www.state.ok.us/~osbd
Direct web site URL to search for licensees: www.state.ok.us/~osbd

#37 Department of Health, 1000 NE 10th St, Oklahoma City, OK 73117-1299; 405-271-5217, Fax: 405-271-5254.
www.health.state.ok.us

#39 Water Resources Board, 3800 N Classen Blvd, Oklahoma City, OK 73118; 405-530-8800, Fax: 405-530-8900.
www.state.ok.us/~owrb

#40 Polygraph Examiners Board, PO Box 11476, Oklahoma City, OK 73136-0476; 405-425-2778, Fax: 405-425-7314.

#41 Department of Education, 2500 N Lincoln Blvd, Oklahoma City, OK 73105-4599; 405-521-3301, Fax: 405-521-6205.
www.sde.state.ok.us

#42 Ethics Commission, 2300 N Lincoln Blvd, RM B5, Oklahoma City, OK 73105-4812; 405-521-3451, Fax: 405-521-4905.
www.state.ok.us/~ethics

#43 Department of Health, 1000 NE 10th, Oklahoma City, OK 73117-1299; 405-271-6030, Fax: 405-271-1918.
www.health.state.ok.us

#44 Department of Labor, 4001 N Lincoln Blvd, Oklahoma City, OK 73105-5212; 405-528-1500.

#45 Department of Environmental Quality, 1000 NE 10th St, Oklahoma City, OK 73117-1212; 405-271-5205.

Oklahoma Federal Courts

The following list indicates the district and division name for each county in the state. If the bankruptcy court location is different from the district court, then the location of the bankruptcy court appears in parentheses.

County/Court Cross Reference

County	District	Division
Adair	Eastern	Muskogee (Okmulgee)
Alfalfa	Western	Oklahoma City
Atoka	Eastern	Muskogee (Okmulgee)
Beaver	Western	Oklahoma City
Beckham	Western	Oklahoma City
Blaine	Western	Oklahoma City
Bryan	Eastern	Muskogee (Okmulgee)
Caddo	Western	Oklahoma City
Canadian	Western	Oklahoma City
Carter	Eastern	Muskogee (Okmulgee)
Cherokee	Eastern	Muskogee (Okmulgee)
Choctaw	Eastern	Muskogee (Okmulgee)
Cimarron	Western	Oklahoma City
Cleveland	Western	Oklahoma City
Coal	Eastern	Muskogee (Okmulgee)
Comanche	Western	Oklahoma City
Cotton	Western	Oklahoma City
Craig	Northern	Tulsa
Creek	Northern	Tulsa
Custer	Western	Oklahoma City
Delaware	Northern	Tulsa
Dewey	Western	Oklahoma City
Ellis	Western	Oklahoma City
Garfield	Western	Oklahoma City
Garvin	Western	Oklahoma City
Grady	Western	Oklahoma City
Grant	Western	Oklahoma City
Greer	Western	Oklahoma City
Harmon	Western	Oklahoma City
Harper	Western	Oklahoma City
Haskell	Eastern	Muskogee (Okmulgee)
Hughes	Eastern	Muskogee (Okmulgee)
Jackson	Western	Oklahoma City
Jefferson	Western	Oklahoma City
Johnston	Eastern	Muskogee (Okmulgee)
Kay	Western	Oklahoma City
Kingfisher	Western	Oklahoma City
Kiowa	Western	Oklahoma City
Latimer	Eastern	Muskogee (Okmulgee)
Le Flore	Eastern	Muskogee (Okmulgee)
Lincoln	Western	Oklahoma City
Logan	Western	Oklahoma City
Love	Eastern	Muskogee (Okmulgee)
Major	Western	Oklahoma City
Marshall	Eastern	Muskogee (Okmulgee)
Mayes	Northern	Tulsa
McClain	Western	Oklahoma City
McCurtain	Eastern	Muskogee (Okmulgee)
McIntosh	Eastern	Muskogee (Okmulgee)
Murray	Eastern	Muskogee (Okmulgee)
Muskogee	Eastern	Muskogee (Okmulgee)
Noble	Western	Oklahoma City
Nowata	Northern	Tulsa
Okfuskee	Eastern	Muskogee (Okmulgee)
Oklahoma	Western	Oklahoma City
Okmulgee	Northern (Eastern)	Tulsa (Okmulgee)
Osage	Northern	Tulsa
Ottawa	Northern	Tulsa
Pawnee	Northern	Tulsa
Payne	Western	Oklahoma City
Pittsburg	Eastern	Muskogee (Okmulgee)
Pontotoc	Eastern	Muskogee (Okmulgee)
Pottawatomie	Western	Oklahoma City
Pushmataha	Eastern	Muskogee (Okmulgee)
Roger Mills	Western	Oklahoma City
Rogers	Northern	Tulsa
Seminole	Eastern	Muskogee (Okmulgee)
Sequoyah	Eastern	Muskogee (Okmulgee)
Stephens	Western	Oklahoma City
Texas	Western	Oklahoma City
Tillman	Western	Oklahoma City
Tulsa	Northern	Tulsa
Wagoner	Eastern	Muskogee (Okmulgee)
Washington	Northern	Tulsa
Washita	Western	Oklahoma City
Woods	Western	Oklahoma City
Woodward	Western	Oklahoma City

US District Court

Eastern District of Oklahoma

Muskogee Division Clerk, PO Box 607, Muskogee, OK 74401 (Courier Address: 101 N 5th, Muskogee, OK 74401), 918-687-2471, Fax: 918-687-2400.

http://www.oked.uscourts.gov

Counties: Adair, Atoka, Bryan, Carter, Cherokee, Choctaw, Coal, Haskell, Hughes, Johnston, Latimer, Le Flore, Love, McCurtain, McIntosh, Marshall, Murray, Muskogee, Okfuskee, Pittsburg, Pontotoc, Pushmataha, Seminole, Sequoyah, Wagoner.

Indexing/Storage: Cases are indexed by defendant and plaintiff as well as by case number. New cases are available in the index 1 day after filing date. Both computer and card indexes are maintained. Open records are located at this court.

Fee & Payment: The fee is $20.00 per item (one party name or case number). Payment may be made by money order, cashier check. Business checks are not accepted. Personal checks are not accepted. Will bill law firms. Payee: Clerk, US District Court. Certification fee: $7.00 per document. Copy fee: $.50 per page. You are allowed to make your own copies. These copies cost $.50 per page.

Phone Search: Only docket information is available by phone.

Mail Search: A stamped self addressed envelope is not required.

In Person: In person searching is available.

PACER: Sign-up number is 800-676-6856. Access fee is $.60 per minute. Toll-free access: 866-863-3767. Local: 918-687-2625. Case records are available back to 1996. Records are never purged. Records are available online after 1 day.

US Bankruptcy Court

Eastern District of Oklahoma

Okmulgee Division PO Box 1347, Okmulgee, OK 74447 (Courier Address: PO &

Federal Bldg, 111 4th St, Room 229, Okmulgee, OK 74447), 918-758-0126, Fax: 918-756-9248.

http://www.okeb.uscourts.gov

Counties: Adair, Atoka, Bryan, Carter, Cherokee, Choctaw, Coal, Haskell, Hughes, Johnston, Latimer, Le Flore, Love, Marshall, McCurtain, McIntosh, Murray, Muskogee, Okfuskee, Okmulgee, Pittsburg, Pontotoc, Pushmataha, Seminole, Sequoyah, Wagoner.

Indexing/Storage: Cases are indexed by debtor as well as by case number. New cases are available in the index immediately after filing date. A computer index is maintained. Open records are located at this court.

Fee & Payment: The fee is $20.00 per item (one party name or case number). Payment may be made by money order, cashier check, personal check. Prepayment is required. Debtor's checks are not accepted. Payee: Clerk, US Bankruptcy Court. Certification fee: $7.00 per document. Copy fee: $.50 per page.

Phone Search: Only docket information available by phone. An automated voice case information service (VCIS) is available.

Fax Search: The fee is $15.00 per name or item searched. The fee is $2.00 per page.

Mail Search: Always enclose a stamped self addressed envelope.

In Person: In person searching is available.

PACER: Sign-up number is 800-676-6856. Access fee is $.60 per minute. Toll-free access: 877-377-1220. Local access: 918-756-4812. Case records are available back to 1986. Records are purged every six months. New civil records are available online after 1 day. PACER is available online at http://pacer.okeb.uscourts.gov.

US District Court

Northern District of Oklahoma

Tulsa Division 411 US Courthouse, 333 W 4th St, Tulsa, OK 74103 (Courier Address: same), 918-699-4700, Fax: 918-699-4756.

www.oknd.uscourts.gov

Counties: Craig, Creek, Delaware, Mayes, Nowata, Okmulgee, Osage, Ottawa, Pawnee, Rogers, Tulsa, Washington.

Indexing/Storage: Cases are indexed by defendant and plaintiff as well as by case number. New cases are available in the index immediately after filing date. A computer index is maintained. Open records are located at this court.

Fee & Payment: The fee is $20.00 per item (one party name or case number). Payment may be made by money order, cashier check, personal check, Visa, Mastercard. Credit cards are only accepted from in-person searchers. Prepayment is required. Payee: Clerk, US District Court. Certification fee: $7.00 per document. Copy fee: $.50 per page. You are allowed to make your own copies. These copies cost $.50 per page.

Phone Search: Only docket information is available by phone.

Mail Search: Always enclose a stamped self addressed envelope.

In Person: In person searching is available.

PACER: Sign-up number is 800-676-6856. Access fee is $.60 per minute. Toll-free access: 888-881-0574. Local access: 918-699-4742. Case

records are available back to 1992. New records are available online after 1 day. PACER is available online at http://pacer.oknd.uscourts.gov.

Other Online Access: Search records on the Internet using RACER at www.oknd.uscourts.gov/perl/bkplog.html. Access fee is 7 cents per page.

US Bankruptcy Court

Northern District of Oklahoma

Tulsa Division 224 S. Boulder, Tulsa, OK 74103 (Courier Address: Use mail address for courier delivery), 918-699-4000, Fax: 918-699-4051.

http://www.oknb.uscourts.gov

Counties: Craig, Creek, Delaware, Mayes, Nowata, Osage, Ottawa, Pawnee, Rogers, Tulsa, Washington.

Indexing/Storage: Cases are indexed by debtor as well as by case number. New cases are available in the index same day if possible after filing date. Both computer and card indexes are maintained. Open records are located at this court. District wide searches are available from this court.

Fee & Payment: The fee is $20.00 per item (one party name or case number). Payment may be made by money order, cashier check, personal check. Prepayment is required. Debtor's checks are not accepted. Payee: Clerk, US Bankruptcy Court. Certification fee: $7.00 per document. Copy fee: $.50 per page. You are allowed to make your own copies. These copies cost $.15 per page.

Phone Search: Only docket information is available by phone, and only if it takes a minimum amount of time.

Fax Search: The fees are the same as for mail searches. Prepayment is required. There is no fee for the fax, but copy fees must be prepaid.

Mail Search: A stamped self addressed envelope is not required.

In Person: In person searching is available.

PACER: Sign-up number is 800-676-6856. Access fee is $.60 per minute. Toll-free access: 800-790-0860. Local access: 918-699-4033. Case records are available back to 1990. Records are never purged. New civil records are available online after 1 day.

Other Online Access: Search records on the Internet using RACER at www.oknb.uscourts.gov/perl/bkplog.html. Access fee is 7 cents per page.

US District Court

Western District of Oklahoma

Oklahoma City Division Clerk, Room 1210, 200 NW 4th St, Oklahoma City, OK 73102 (Courier Address: Use mail address for courier delivery), 405-609-5000, Fax: 405-609-5099.

http://www.okwd.uscourts.gov

Counties: Alfalfa, Beaver, Beckham, Blaine, Caddo, Canadian, Cimarron, Cleveland, Comanche, Cotton, Custer, Dewey, Ellis, Garfield, Garvin, Grady, Grant, Greer, Harmon, Harper, Jackson, Jefferson, Kay, Kingfisher, Kiowa, Lincoln, Logan, McClain, Major, Noble,Oklahoma, Payne, Pottawatomie, Roger

Mills, Stephens, Texas, Tillman, Washita, Woods, Woodward.

Indexing/Storage: Cases are indexed by defendant and plaintiff as well as by case number. New cases are available in the index immediately after filing date. A computer index is maintained. Records are also indexed on microfiche. Open records are located at this court. District wide searches are available for records from 1907 from this court.

Fee & Payment: The fee is $20.00 per item (one party name or case number). Payment may be made by money order, cashier check, personal check. Will bill in some circumstances. Payee: Clerk, US District Court. Certification fee: $7.00 per document. Copy fee: $.50 per page.

Phone Search: Information relating to docket entries will be given over the phone.

Mail Search: A stamped self addressed envelope is not required.

In Person: In person searching is available.

PACER: Sign-up number is 800-676-6856. Access fee is $.60 per minute. Toll-free access: 888-699-7068. Local access: 405-231-4531. Case records are available back to 1991. Records are never purged. New records are available online after 2 days. PACER is available online at http://pacer.okwd.uscourts.gov.

US Bankruptcy Court

Western District of Oklahoma

Oklahoma City Division 1st Floor, Old Post Office Bldg, 215 Dean A McGee Ave, Oklahoma City, OK 73102 (Courier Address: Use mail address for courier delivery), 405-609-5700, Fax: 405-609-5752.

Counties: Alfalfa, Beaver, Beckham, Blaine, Caddo, Canadian, Cimarron, Cleveland, Comanche, Cotton, Custer, Dewey, Ellis, Garfield, Garvin, Grady, Grant, Greer, Harmon, Harper, Jackson, Jefferson, Kay, Kingfisher, Kiowa, Lincoln, Logan, Major, McClain, Noble,Oklahoma, Payne, Pottawatomie, Roger Mills, Stephens, Texas, Tillman, Washita, Woods, Woodward.

Indexing/Storage: Cases are indexed by debtor as well as by case number. New cases are available in the index 24 hours after filing date. Cases are also indexed by social security number. A computer index is maintained. Open records are located at this court.

Fee & Payment: The fee is $20.00 per item (one party name or case number). Payment may be made by money order, cashier check, personal check. Debtor's checks are not accepted. Payee: Clerk, US Bankruptcy Court. Certification fee: $7.00 per document. Copy fee: $.50 per page.

Phone Search: Docket information is available by phone. An automated voice case information service (VCIS) is available. Call VCIS at 800-872-1348 or 405-231-4768.

Mail Search: Always enclose a stamped self addressed envelope.

In Person: In person searching is available.

PACER: Sign-up number is 800-676-6856. Access fee is $.60 per minute. Local access: 405-231-5064, 405-231-5065. Case records are available back to May 1, 1992. Records are purged every six months. New civil records are available online after 1 day.

Oklahoma County Courts

Court	Jurisdiction	No. of Courts	How Organized
District Courts*	General	80	26 Districts
Municipal Courts of Record	Municipal	2	
Municipal Courts Not of Record	Municipal	340	
Workers' Compensation Court	Special	1	

* Profiled in this Sourcebook.

Court	CIVIL								
	Tort	Contract	Real Estate	Min. Claim	Max. Claim	Small Claims	Estate	Eviction	Domestic Relations
District Courts*	X	X	X	$0	No Max	$45000	X	X	X
Municipal Courts of Record									
Municipal Courts Not of Record									
Workers' Compensation Court									

Court	CRIMINAL				
	Felony	Misdemeanor	DWI/DUI	Preliminary Hearing	Juvenile
District Courts*	X	X	X	X	X
Municipal Courts of Record			X		
Municipal Courts Not of Record			X		
Workers' Compensation Court					

ADMINISTRATION   Administrative Director of Courts, 1915 N Stiles #305, Oklahoma City, OK, 73105; 405-521-2450, Fax: 405-521-6815. www.oscn.net

COURT STRUCTURE   There are 80 District Courts in 26 judicial districts. Cities with populations in excess of 200,000 (Oklahoma City and Tulsa) have municipal criminal courts of record. Cities with less than 200,000 do not have such courts.

The small claims limit was raised from $3000 to $4500 in 1998.

ONLINE ACCESS   Free Internet access is available for eight District Courts and all Appellate courts at www.oscn.net. Both civil and criminal records are available. The counties are Canadian, Cleveland, Comanche, Garfield, Oklahoma, Payne, Rogers, and Tulsa.

One can search the Oklahoma Supreme Court Network by single cite or multiple cite (no name searches) from the Internet site.

Case information is available in bulk form for downloading to computer. For information, call the Administrative Director of Courts, 405-521-2450.

Adair County

15th Judicial District Court PO Box 426 (220 W Division), Stilwell, OK 74960; 918-696-7633. Hours: 8AM-4:30PM (CST). *Felony, Misdemeanor, Civil, Eviction, Small Claims, Probate.*

Civil Records: Access: Phone, fax, mail, in person. Both court and visitors may perform in person searches. Search fee: $5.00 per name. Fee is for 7 year search. Required to search: name, years to search. Civil cases indexed by defendant, plaintiff. Civil records archived.

Criminal Records: Access: Phone, fax, mail, in person. Both court and visitors may perform in person searches. Search fee: $5.00 per name. Fee is for 7 year search. Required to search: name, years to search, DOB; also helpful: SSN. Criminal records archived.

General Information: No juvenile, mental health or guardianship records released. SASE required. Turnaround time 1 day. Copy fee: $1.00 for first page, $.50 each add'l. Certification fee: $.50 per page. Fee payee: Adair County Court Clerk. Personal checks accepted. Prepayment is required.

Alfalfa County

4th Judicial District Court County Courthouse, 300 S Grand, Cherokee, OK 73728; 580-596-3523. Hours: 8:30AM-4:30PM *Felony, Misdemeanor, Civil, Eviction, Small Claims, Probate.*

Civil Records: Access: Mail, in person. Both court and visitors may perform in person searches. Search fee: $5.00 per name. Required to search: name, years to search. Civil cases indexed by defendant, plaintiff. Civil records archived to 1907; on computer back to 1998.

Criminal Records: Access: Mail, in person. Both court and visitors may perform in person searches. Search fee: $5.00 per name. Required to search: name, years to search. Criminal records archived to 1907; on computer back to 1998.

General Information: No confidential or guardianship records not released. SASE required. Turnaround time 1 day. Fax notes: Fee to fax results is $4.00 per page; $2.00 each add'l. Copy fee: $1.00 for first page, $.50 each add'l. Certification fee: $.50 per page. Fee payee: Court Clerk. Only cashiers checks and money orders accepted. Prepayment is required.

Atoka County

25th Judicial District Court 200 E. Court St, Atoka, OK 74525; 580-889-3565. Hours: 8:30AM-4:30PM (CST). *Felony, Misdemeanor, Civil, Eviction, Small Claims, Probate.*

Civil Records: Access: Mail, in person. Both court and visitors may perform in person searches. Search fee: $5.00 per name. Required to search: name, years to search. Civil cases indexed by defendant, plaintiff. Civil records on computer back to 1998; prior on books.

Criminal Records: Access: Mail, in person. Both court and visitors may perform in person searches. Search fee: $5.00 per name. Required to search: name, years to search, DOB or SSN. Criminal records on books from 1920; on computer back to 1998.

General Information: Public Access terminal is available. No adoption, mental health or juvenile records released. SASE required. Turnaround time 1-2 days. Copy fee: $1.00 for first page, $.50 each add'l. Certification fee: $.50. Fee payee: Court Clerk. Personal checks accepted. Prepayment is required.

Beaver County

1st Judicial District Court PO Box 237, Beaver, OK 73932; 580-625-3191. Hours: 9AM-Noon, 1-5PM (CST). *Felony, Misdemeanor, Civil, Eviction, Small Claims, Probate.*

Civil Records: Access: Mail, in person. Both court and visitors may perform in person searches. Search fee:

$5.00 per name. Required to search: name, years to search. Civil cases indexed by defendant, plaintiff. Civil records on microfiche and archives from late 1800s.

Criminal Records: Access: Mail, in person. Both court and visitors may perform in person searches. Search fee: $5.00 per name. Required to search: name, years to search. Criminal records on microfiche and archives from late 1800s.

General Information: No adoption, mental health or juvenile records released. SASE required. Turnaround time 1-3 days. Copy fee: $1.00 for first page, $.50 each add'l. Certification fee: $.50. Fee payee: Court Clerk. Personal checks accepted. Prepayment is required.

Beckham County

2nd Judicial District Court PO Box 520, Sayre, OK 73662; 580-928-3330; Fax: 580-928-9278. Hours: 9AM-5PM (CST). *Felony, Misdemeanor, Civil, Eviction, Small Claims, Probate.*

Civil Records: Access: Fax, mail, in person. Both court and visitors may perform in person searches. Search fee: $5.00 per name. Required to search: name, years to search. Civil cases indexed by defendant, plaintiff. Civil records on microfiche; on computer back to 1997.

Criminal Records: Access: Fax, mail, in person. Both court and visitors may perform in person searches. Search fee: $5.00 per name. Required to search: name, years to search. Criminal records on microfiche; on computer back to 1997.

General Information: Public Access terminal is available. No juvenile, adoption or expunged records released. SASE required. Turnaround time 2 weeks. Fax notes: Fee to fax results is $1.00 per page. Copy fee: $1.00 for first page, $.50 each add'l. Certification fee: $.50. Fee payee: Court clerk. Personal checks accepted. Prepayment is required.

Blaine County

4th Judicial District Court 212 N. Weigle, Watonga, OK 73772; 580-623-5970. Hours: 8AM-4PM (CST). *Felony, Misdemeanor, Civil, Eviction, Small Claims, Probate.*

Civil Records: Access: Mail, in person. Both court and visitors may perform in person searches. Search fee: $5.00 per name. Required to search: name, years to search. Civil cases indexed by defendant, plaintiff. Civil records archived from 1900; on computer back to 1998.

Criminal Records: Access: Mail, in person. Both court and visitors may perform in person searches. Search fee: $5.00 per name. Required to search: name, years to search. Criminal records archived from 1900; on computer back to 1998.

General Information: Public Access terminal is available. No juvenile or expunged records released. SASE required. Turnaround time 7-10 days. Copy fee: $1.00 for first page, $.50 each add'l. Certification fee: $.50. Fee payee: Court Clerk. Personal checks accepted. Prepayment is required.

Bryan County

19th Judicial District Court Courthouse 3rd Fl, Durant, OK 74701; 580-924-1446. Hours: 8:00AM-12:00PM,1:00PM-5:00PM (CST). *Felony, Misdemeanor, Civil, Eviction, Small Claims, Probate.*

Civil Records: Access: Phone, mail, in person. Both court and visitors may perform in person searches. Search fee: $5.00 per name. Required to search: name, years to search. Civil cases indexed by defendant, plaintiff. Civil records archived from 1907.

Criminal Records: Access: Phone, mail, in person. Both court and visitors may perform in person searches. Search fee: $5.00 per name. Required to search: name, years to search; also helpful: DOB, SSN. Criminal records archived from 1907.

General Information: Public Access terminal is available. No juvenile, mental health or adoption

records released. SASE required. Turnaround time 2 days. Copy fee: $1.00 for first page, $.50 each add'l. Certification fee: $.50. Fee payee: Bryan County Court Clerk. Only cashiers checks and money orders accepted. Prepayment is required.

Caddo County

6th Judicial District Court PO Box 10, Anadarko, OK 73005; 405-247-3393. Hours: 8:30AM-4:30PM (CST). *Felony, Misdemeanor, Civil, Eviction, Small Claims, Probate.*

Civil Records: Access: Mail, in person. Both court and visitors may perform in person searches. Search fee: $10.00 per hour. Required to search: name, years to search. Civil cases indexed by defendant, plaintiff. Civil records on computer since 1997; prior on docket books to 1901.

Criminal Records: Access: Mail, in person. Both court and visitors may perform in person searches. Search fee: $10.00 per hour. Required to search: name, years to search. Criminal records on computer since 1997, prior on docket books to 1901.

General Information: Public Access terminal is available. No adoption, mental health, juvenile, and some guardianship records released. SASE would be helpful. Turnaround time 1 week. Copy fee: $1.00 for first page, $.50 each add'l. Certification fee: $.50. Fee payee: Court Clerk. No foreign checks accepted. Prepayment is required.

Canadian County

26th Judicial District Court PO Box 730, El Reno, OK 73036; 405-262-1070 X172. Hours: 8AM-4:30PM (CST). *Felony, Misdemeanor, Civil, Eviction, Small Claims, Probate.*

Civil Records: Access: Mail, online, in person. Both court and visitors may perform in person searches. Search fee: $5.00 per name. Required to search: name, years to search. Civil cases indexed by defendant, plaintiff. Civil records on computer back to 1993, archived from 1907. Online access to court dockets is available free online at www.oscn.net/applications/oscn/casesearch.asp. Dockets go back to 3/1983.

Criminal Records: Access: Mail, online, in person. Both court and visitors may perform in person searches. Search fee: $5.00 per name. Required to search: name, years to search, DOB or SSN. Criminal records on computer back to 1993, archived from 1907. Online access to criminal dockets is same as civil.

General Information: Public Access terminal is available. No expunged criminal cases, juvenile, adoption, confidential portion of guardianship records released. Copy fee: $1.00 for first page, $.50 each add'l. Certification fee: $.50 per page. Fee payee: Court Clerk. Personal checks accepted. Prepayment is required.

Carter County

20th Judicial District Court PO Box 37, Court Clerk, Ardmore, OK 73402; 580-223-5253. Hours: 8AM-Noon, 1-5PM (CST). *Felony, Misdemeanor, Civil, Eviction, Small Claims, Probate.*

www.brightok.net/chickasaw/ardmore/county/crtclerk.html

Civil Records: Access: Mail, in person. Both court and visitors may perform in person searches. Search fee: $5.00 per name. Required to search: name, years to search. Civil cases indexed by defendant, plaintiff. Civil records archived from 1907; on computer back to 1997.

Criminal Records: Access: Mail, in person. Both court and visitors may perform in person searches. Search fee: $5.00 per name. Required to search: name, years to search. Criminal records archived from 1907; on computer back to 1997.

General Information: Public Access terminal is available. No juvenile, mental health, or adoption records released. SASE required. Turnaround time 2 weeks. Fax notes: Will not fax results. Copy fee: $1.00 for first page, $.50 each add'l. Certification fee: $.50. Fee payee: Carter County Court Clerk. Personal checks accepted. Prepayment is required.

Cherokee County

15th Judicial District Court 213 W. Delaware, Rm 302, Tahlequah, OK 74464; 918-456-0691; Fax: 918-458-6587. Hours: 8AM-4:30PM (CST). *Felony, Misdemeanor, Civil, Eviction, Small Claims, Probate.*

Civil Records: Access: Phone, mail, in person. Both court and visitors may perform in person searches. Search fee: $5.00 per name. Required to search: name, years to search. Civil cases indexed by defendant, plaintiff. Civil records on microfiche from 1907 (civil, probate, vital).

Criminal Records: Access: Phone, mail, in person. Both court and visitors may perform in person searches. Search fee: $5.00 per name. Required to search: name, years to search, DOB. Criminal records kept form 1969.

General Information: Public Access terminal is available. No juvenile, adoption or mental health released. SASE required. Turnaround time 1-2 days. Copy fee: $1.00 for first page, $.50 each add'l. Certification fee: $.50 per page. Fee payee: Court Clerk. Personal checks accepted. Prepayment is required.

Choctaw County

17th Judicial District Court 300 E. Duke, Hugo, OK 74743; 580-326-7554 & 7555. Hours: 8AM-4PM (CST). *Felony, Misdemeanor, Civil, Eviction, Small Claims, Probate.*

Civil Records: Access: Phone, fax, mail, in person. Both court and visitors may perform in person searches. Search fee: $10.00 per name. Required to search: name, years to search. Civil cases indexed by defendant, plaintiff. Civil records archived from 1907.

Criminal Records: Access: Phone, fax, mail, in person. Both court and visitors may perform in person searches. Search fee: $10.00 per name. Required to search: name, years to search, DOB. Criminal records archived from 1907.

General Information: No juvenile, adoption, guardianship, wills or expunged records released. SASE required. Turnaround time 1 day. Fax notes: $7.50 per page. Copy fee: $1.00 for first page, $.50 each add'l. Certification fee: $.50. Fee payee: Court Clerk. Personal checks accepted. Prepayment is required.

Cimarron County

1st Judicial District Court PO Box 788, Boise City, OK 73933; 580-544-2221. Hours: 9AM-Noon,1-5PM (CST). *Felony, Misdemeanor, Civil, Eviction, Small Claims, Probate.*

Civil Records: Access: Phone, mail, in person. Only the court performs in person searches; visitors may not. Search fee: $2.00 every 15 minutes after the first 15 minutes. Required to search: name, years to search. Civil cases indexed by defendant, plaintiff. Civil records archived from 1907.

Criminal Records: Access: Phone, mail, in person. Only the court performs in person searches; visitors may not. Search fee: $2.00 every 15 minutes after first 15 minutes. Required to search: name, years to search. Criminal records archived from 1907.

General Information: No juvenile, adoption or mental health records released. SASE requested. Turnaround time 1 day. Copy fee: $1.00 for first page, $.50 each add'l. Certification fee: $.50. Fee payee: Court Clerk. Personal checks accepted. Prepayment is required.

Cleveland County

21st Judicial District Court - Civil Branch 200 S. Peters, Norman, OK 73069; 405-321-6402. Hours: 8AM-5PM (CST). *Civil, Eviction, Small Claims, Probate.*

Civil Records: Access: Mail, online, in person. Both court and visitors may perform in person searches. No search fee. Required to search: name, years to search. Civil cases indexed by defendant, plaintiff. Civil records on computer from 1989, on microfiche from 1800s, archived since 1970. Online access to court dockets is available free online at www.oscn.net/applications/oscn/casesearch.asp. Dockets go back to 1/1989.

General Information: Public Access terminal is available. No expunged, sealed records released. SASE required. Turnaround time 7-10 days. Copy fee: $1.00 for first page, $.50 each add'l. Certification fee: $.50. Fee payee: Court Clerk. Personal checks accepted. Prepayment is required.

21st Judicial District Court - Criminal 200 S. Peters, Norman, OK 73069; 405-321-6402. Hours: 8AM-5PM (CST). *Felony, Misdemeanor.*

Criminal Records: Access: Mail, online, in person. Both court and visitors may perform in person searches. No search fee. Required to search: name, years to search. Criminal records on computer from 1989, on microfiche from 1800s. Online access to criminal dockets is same as civil.

General Information: Public Access terminal is available. No juvenile, adoption, or guardianship records released. Turnaround time 7-10 days. Copy fee: $1.00 for first page, $.50 each add'l. Certification fee: $.50. Fee payee: Cleveland County Court Clerk. Personal checks accepted. Local personal checks accepted. Prepayment is required.

Coal County

25th Judicial District Court 4 N Main #9, Coalgate, OK 74538; 580-927-2281. Hours: 8AM-5PM (CST). *Felony, Misdemeanor, Civil, Eviction, Small Claims, Probate.*

Civil Records: Access: In person only. Visitors must perform in person searches for themselves. No search fee. Required to search: name, years to search. Civil cases indexed by defendant, plaintiff. Civil records archived since 1907; computerized back to 1999.

Criminal Records: Access: In person only. Visitors must perform in person searches for themselves. No search fee. Required to search: name, years to search. Criminal records archived since 1907; computerized back to 1999.

General Information: No juvenile, adoption, mental health, guardianship, wills or expunged records released. Fax notes: No fee to fax results. Copy fee: $1.00 for first page, $.50 each add'l. Certification fee: $1.00. Fee payee: Court Clerk. Personal checks accepted. Prepayment is required.

Comanche County

5th Judicial District Court 315 SW 5th Street, Rm 504, Lawton, OK 73501-4390; 580-355-4017. Hours: 8AM-5PM (CST). *Felony, Misdemeanor, Civil, Eviction, Small Claims, Probate.*

Civil Records: Access: Phone, mail, online, in person. Only the court performs in person searches; visitors may not. Search fee: $10.00 per name. Required to search: name, years to search; also helpful: address. Civil cases indexed by defendant, plaintiff. Civil records on computer from 8/88, prior in books to 1901. Online access to court dockets is available free online at www.oscn.net/applications/oscn/casesearch.asp. Dockets go back to 8/1988.

Criminal Records: Access: Mail, online, in person. Only the court performs in person searches; visitors

may not. Search fee: $10.00 per name. Required to search: name, years to search; also helpful: address, DOB, SSN. Criminal records on computer from 8/88, prior in books to 1901. Online access to criminal dockets is same as civil.

General Information: No juvenile, mental health, adoption or some probate records released. SASE required. Turnaround time 1 day. Fax notes: Fee to fax results is $1.00 per page. Copy fee: $1.00 for first page, $.50 each add'l. Certification fee: No certification fee. Fee payee: District Court Clerk. Business checks accepted. Prepayment is required.

Cotton County

5th Judicial District Court 301 N. Broadway, Walters, OK 73572; 580-875-3029. Hours: 8AM-4:30PM (CST). *Felony, Misdemeanor, Civil, Eviction, Small Claims, Probate.*

Civil Records: Access: Mail, fax, in person. Both court and visitors may perform in person searches. Search fee: $5.00 per name. Required to search: name, years to search. Civil cases indexed by defendant, plaintiff. Civil records archived from 1912; computerized back to 1997.

Criminal Records: Access: Mail, fax, in person. Both court and visitors may perform in person searches. Search fee: $5.00 per name. Required to search: name, years to search, DOB. Criminal records archived from 1912; computerized back to 1997.

General Information: Public Access terminal is available. No adoption, juvenile, and some guardianship records released. SASE not required. Turnaround time 2 day. Fax notes: No fee to fax results. Copy fee: $1.00 for first page, $.50 each add'l. Certification fee: $.50. Fee payee: Court Clerk. Personal checks accepted. Prepayment is required.

Craig County

12th Judicial District Court 301 W. Canadian, Vinita, OK 74301; 918-256-6451. Hours: 8:30AM-4:30PM (CST). *Felony, Misdemeanor, Civil, Eviction, Small Claims, Probate.*

Note: SSNs are released to the public on criminal case matters, but not for civil cases.

Civil Records: Access: Mail, in person. Both court and visitors may perform in person searches. Search fee: $5.00 per name. Required to search: name, years to search. Civil cases indexed by defendant, plaintiff. Civil records on microfilm from 1902; on computer since 4/97.

Criminal Records: Access: Mail, in person. Both court and visitors may perform in person searches. Search fee: $5.00 per name. Required to search: name, years to search; also helpful: SSN, DOB, sex. Criminal records on microfilm from 1902; on computer since 4/97.

General Information: Public Access terminal is available. No mental or juvenile records released. SASE required. Turnaround time 1-3 days. Copy fee: $1.00 for first page, $.50 each add'l. Certification fee: $.50. Fee payee: Court Clerk. Personal checks accepted. Prepayment is required.

Creek County

24th Judicial District Court 222 E Dewey, #201, Sapulpa, OK 74067; 918-227-2525; Fax: 918-227-5030. Hours: 8AM-5PM (CST). *Felony, Misdemeanor, Civil, Eviction, Small Claims, Probate.*

Civil Records: Access: In person only. Visitors must perform in person searches for themselves. No search fee. Required to search: name, years to search; also helpful: address. Civil cases indexed by defendant, plaintiff. Civil records on docket books and files. They go back "many years, no exact date known".

Criminal Records: Access: In person only. Visitors must perform in person searches for themselves. No search fee. Required to search: name, years to search;

also helpful: address, DOB, SSN. Criminal records on docket books and files. They go back "many years, no exact date known".

General Information: No juvenile, mental health, or adoption records released. Copy fee: $1.00 for first page, $.50 each add'l. Certification fee: $.50. Fee payee: Creek County Court Clerk. Personal checks accepted. Prepayment is required.

Custer County

2nd Judicial District Court Box D, Arapaho, OK 73620; 580-323-3233; Fax: 580-331-1121. Hours: 8AM-4PM (CST). *Felony, Misdemeanor, Civil, Eviction, Small Claims, Probate.*

Civil Records: Access: In person only. Visitors must perform in person searches for themselves Search fee: Court will not perform civil searches, but may assist. Required to search: name, years to search; also helpful: address. Civil cases indexed by defendant, plaintiff. Civil records on computer since 01/95; prior records on tract books, all original files.

Criminal Records: Access: Mail, in person. Both court and visitors may perform in person searches. Search fee: $5.00 per name. Required to search: name, years to search; also helpful: DOB, SSN. Criminal records on computer since 01/95; prior records on tract books, all original files.

General Information: Public Access terminal is available. No adoptions, juvenile, or mental records released. SASE requested. Turnaround time 2-3 days. Copy fee: $1.00 for first page, $.50 each add'l. Certification fee: $.50. Fee payee: Court Clerk. Personal checks accepted. Prepayment is required.

Delaware County

13th Judicial District Court Box 407, Jay, OK 74346; 918-253-4420. Hours: 8:30AM-4:30PM (CST). *Felony, Misdemeanor, Civil, Eviction, Small Claims, Probate.*

Civil Records: Access: Mail, in person. Both court and visitors may perform in person searches. Search fee: $5.00 per name. Required to search: name, years to search. Civil cases indexed by defendant, plaintiff. Civil records on computer since 1996 and on microfilm from 1913.

Criminal Records: Access: Mail, in person. Both court and visitors may perform in person searches. Search fee: $5.00 per name. Required to search: name, years to search; also helpful: DOB, SSN. Criminal records on computer since 1991.

General Information: Public Access terminal is available. No juvenile, adoption, guardianship or search warrant records released. SASE requested. Turnaround time 1-2 weeks. Copy fee: $1.00 for first page, $.50 each add'l. Certification fee: $.50. Fee payee: Delaware County Court Clerk. Business checks accepted. Prepayment is required.

Dewey County

4th Judicial District Court Box 278, Taloga, OK 73667; 580-328-5521. Hours: 8AM-4PM (CST). *Felony, Misdemeanor, Civil, Eviction, Small Claims, Probate.*

Civil Records: Access: Mail, in person. Both court and visitors may perform in person searches. No search fee. Required to search: name, years to search. Civil cases indexed by defendant, plaintiff. Civil records archived from late 1800s, recent records computerized. All requests must be in writing.

Criminal Records: Access: Mail, in person. Both court and visitors may perform in person searches. No search fee. Required to search: name, years to search; also helpful: SSN. Criminal records archived from late 1800s, recent records computerized. All requests must be in writing.

General Information: No expunged, adoption, mental, guardianship, juvenile records released. SASE requested. Turnaround time 2 days. Copy fee: $1.00 for first page, $.50 each add'l. Certification fee: $.50. Fee payee: Dewey County Court Clerk. Personal checks accepted. Prepayment is required.

Ellis County

2nd Judicial District Court Box 217, Arnett, OK 73832; 580-885-7255. Hours: 8:30AM-4:30PM (CST). *Felony, Misdemeanor, Civil, Eviction, Small Claims, Probate.*

Civil Records: Access: Phone, mail, in person. Both court and visitors may perform in person searches. No search fee. Required to search: name, years to search. Civil cases indexed by defendant, plaintiff. Civil records on docket books from 1900.

Criminal Records: Access: Phone, mail, in person. Both court and visitors may perform in person searches. Search fee: $5.00 per name. Required to search: name, years to search; also helpful: SSN. Criminal records on docket books from 1900.

General Information: No expunged records released. SASE required. Turnaround time 1 day. Copy fee: $1.00 for first page, $.50 each add'l. Certification fee: $.50. Fee payee: Ellis County Court Clerk. Personal checks accepted. Prepayment is required.

Garfield County

4th Judicial District Court 114 W Broadway, Enid, OK 73701-4024; 580-237-0232. Hours: 8AM-4:30PM (CST). *Felony, Misdemeanor, Civil, Eviction, Small Claims, Probate.*

Civil Records: Access: Mail, online, in person. Both court and visitors may perform in person searches. Search fee: $5.00 per name. Required to search: name, years to search. Civil cases indexed by defendant, plaintiff. Civil records on computer from 3-89, on microfiche from 1893. Online access to court dockets is available free online at www.oscn.net/applications/oscn/casesearch.asp. Dockets go back to 3/1989.

Criminal Records: Access: Mail, online, in person. Both court and visitors may perform in person searches. Search fee: $5.00 per name. Required to search: name, years to search, SSN. Criminal records on computer from 3-89, on microfiche from 1893. Online access to criminal dockets is same as civil.

General Information: Public Access terminal is available. No juvenile, mental health, or adoption records released. SASE required. Turnaround time 1 day. Copy fee: $1.00 for first page, $.50 each add'l. Certification fee: $.50. Fee payee: Court Clerk. Personal checks accepted. Prepayment is required.

Garvin County

21st Judicial District Court PO Box 239, Pauls Valley, OK 73075; 405-238-5596. Hours: 8:30AM-4:30PM (CST). *Felony, Misdemeanor, Civil, Eviction, Small Claims, Probate.*

Civil Records: Access: Mail, online, in person. Both court and visitors may perform in person searches. Search fee: $10.00 per name. $7.00 mailing fee if SASE not enclosed. Required to search: name, years to search. Civil cases indexed by defendant, plaintiff. Civil records on computer since 1994, docket books from 1907. Civil case information is available free online at www.idocket.com.

Criminal Records: Access: Mail, online, in person. Both court and visitors may perform in person searches. Search fee: $10.00 per name. $7.00 mailing fee if SASE not enclosed. Required to search: name, years to search; also helpful: SSN, DOB. Criminal records on computer since 1994, docket books from 1907. Online access to criminal dockets is same as civil.

General Information: Public Access terminal is available. No juvenile, adoption or guardianship

released. SASE required. Turnaround time 1 day. Copy fee: $1.00 for first page, $.50 each add'l. Certification fee: $.50 per page. Fee payee: Garvin County Court Clerk. Only cashiers checks and money orders accepted. Prepayment is required.

Grady County

6th Judicial District Court PO Box 605, 328 Choctaw St, Chickasha, OK 73023; 405-224-7446. Hours: 8AM-4:30PM (CST). *Felony, Misdemeanor, Civil, Eviction, Small Claims, Probate.*

Civil Records: Access: In person only. Visitors must perform in person searches for themselves. No search fee. Required to search: name, years to search. Civil cases indexed by defendant, plaintiff. Civil records on microfiche from 1982, archived from 1907.

Criminal Records: Access: In person only. Visitors must perform in person searches for themselves. No search fee. Required to search: name, years to search; also helpful: address, DOB, SSN. Criminal records on microfiche from 1982, archived from 1907.

General Information: Public Access terminal is available. No juvenile, adoption, guardianship or mental health records released. Copy fee: $1.00 for first page, $.50 each add'l. Certification fee: $.50 per document. Fee payee: Court Clerk. Personal checks accepted. Prepayment is required.

Grant County

4th Judicial District Court 112 E Guthrie, Medford, OK 73759; 580-395-2828. Hours: 8AM-4:30PM (CST). *Felony, Misdemeanor, Civil, Eviction, Small Claims, Probate.*

Civil Records: Access: Mail, in person. Both court and visitors may perform in person searches. Search fee: $5.00 per name. Required to search: name, years to search. Civil cases indexed by defendant, plaintiff. Civil records archived from 1893, in books since 1898.

Criminal Records: Access: Mail, in person. Both court and visitors may perform in person searches. Search fee: $5.00 per name. Required to search: name, years to search; also helpful: SSN. Criminal records archived from 1893, in books since 1898.

General Information: No juvenile, adoption, mental health, some guardianship or wills released. SASE helpful. Turnaround time 1-3 days. Copy fee: $1.00 for first page, $.50 each add'l. Certification fee: $.50 per page. Fee payee: Court Clerk. Personal checks accepted. No out of state personal checks accepted. Prepayment is required.

Greer County

2nd Judicial District Court PO Box 216, Mangum, OK 73554; 580-782-3665. Hours: 8:30AM-4:30PM (CST). *Felony, Misdemeanor, Civil, Eviction, Small Claims, Probate.*

Civil Records: Access: Mail, in person. Both court and visitors may perform in person searches. Search fee: $5.00 per name. Fee is per 15 minutes. Required to search: name, years to search. Civil cases indexed by defendant, plaintiff. Civil records on docket books from 1901; on computer back to 1997.

Criminal Records: Access: Mail, in person. Both court and visitors may perform in person searches. Search fee: $5.00 per name. Fee is per 15 minutes. Required to search: name, years to search, DOB; also helpful: SSN. Criminal records on docket books from 1901; on computer back to 1997.

General Information: Public Access terminal is available. No juvenile, mental health, adoption or guardianship records released. SASE required. Turnaround time 1-2 days. Fax notes: Fee to fax results is $1.00 per document. Copy fee: $1.00 for first page, $.50 each add'l. Certification fee: $.50. Fee payee: Court Clerk. Personal checks accepted. Prepayment is required.

Harmon County

2nd Judicial District Court 114 W. Hollis, Hollis, OK 73550; 580-688-3617; Fax: 580-688-2900. Hours: 8AM-5PM (CST). *Felony, Misdemeanor, Civil, Eviction, Small Claims, Probate.*

Civil Records: Access: Mail, fax, in person. Both court and visitors may perform in person searches. Search fee: $5.00 per name. Required to search: name, years to search. Civil cases indexed by defendant, plaintiff. Civil records on docket books from 1909; on computer since.

Criminal Records: Access: Mail, fax, in person. Both court and visitors may perform in person searches. Search fee: $5.00 per name. Required to search: name, years to search; also helpful: DOB, SSN, sex. Criminal records on docket books from 1909; on computer since.

General Information: No juvenile, adoption, mental health, or guardianship records released. SASE requested. Turnaround time 1-2 days. Fax notes: Will fax results if provided pre-payment or proof of payment such as facsimile of check, etc. Copy fee: $1.00 for first page, $.50 each add'l. Certification fee: $.50 per page. Fee payee: Harmon County Court Clerk. Personal checks accepted. Prepayment is required.

Harper County

1st Judicial District Court Box 347, Buffalo, OK 73834; 580-735-2010. Hours: 8AM-4PM (CST). *Felony, Misdemeanor, Civil, Eviction, Small Claims, Probate.*

Civil Records: Access: Mail, in person. Both court and visitors may perform in person searches. Search fee: $5.00 per name. Required to search: name, years to search. Civil cases indexed by defendant, plaintiff. Civil records on docket books from 1907.

Criminal Records: Access: Mail, in person. Both court and visitors may perform in person searches. Search fee: $5.00 per name. Required to search: name, years to search. Criminal records on docket books from 1907.

General Information: No adoption, juvenile, conservatorship, mental health, guardianship, or expunged records released. SASE requested. Turnaround time 3 or 4 days. Copy fee: $1.00 for first page, $.50 each add'l. Certification fee: $.50 per page. Fee payee: Harper County Court Clerk. Personal checks accepted. Prepayment is required.

Haskell County

16th Judicial District Court 202 E. Main, Stigler, OK 74462; 918-967-3323; Fax: 918-967-2819. Hours: 8AM-4:30PM (CST). *Felony, Misdemeanor, Civil, Eviction, Small Claims, Probate.*

Civil Records: Access: Phone, fax, mail, in person. Both court and visitors may perform in person searches. Search fee: $5.00. Required to search: name, years to search. Civil cases indexed by defendant, plaintiff. Civil records archived from 1907, they are in the process of placing files on microfiche starting with 1994.

Criminal Records: Access: Phone, fax, mail, in person. Both court and visitors may perform in person searches. Search fee: $5.00. Required to search: name, years to search; also helpful: SSN. Criminal records archived from 1907, they are in the process of placing files on microfiche starting with 1994.

General Information: Public Access terminal is available. No juvenile, adoption or mental health records released. SASE required. Turnaround time 1 week. Copy fee: $1.00 for first page, $.50 each add'l. Certification fee: $2.00. Fee payee: Haskell County Court Clerk. Personal checks accepted.

Hughes County

22nd Judicial District Court 200 N Broadway, Box 32, Holdenville, OK 74848; 405-379-3384. Hours: 8AM-4:30PM (CST). *Felony, Misdemeanor, Civil, Eviction, Small Claims, Probate.*

Civil Records: Access: Mail, in person. Both court and visitors may perform in person searches. Search fee: $5.00 per name. Required to search: name, years to search. Civil cases indexed by defendant, plaintiff. Civil records archived from 1907.

Criminal Records: Access: Mail, in person. Both court and visitors may perform in person searches. Search fee: $5.00 per name. Required to search: name, years to search; also helpful: SSN. Criminal records archived from 1907.

General Information: No juvenile or adoption records released. SASE required. Turnaround time 2 days. Copy fee: $1.00 for first page, $.50 each add'l. Certification fee: $.50. Fee payee: Hughes County Court Clerk. Personal checks accepted. Prepayment is required.

Jackson County

3rd Judicial District Court PO Box 616, 101 N. Main, Rm. 303, Jackson County Courthouse, Altus, OK 73522; 580-482-0448. Hours: 8AM-4PM *Felony, Misdemeanor, Civil, Eviction, Small Claims, Probate.*

Civil Records: Access: Mail, in person. Both court and visitors may perform in person searches. Search fee: $5.00 per name. Required to search: name, years to search. Civil cases indexed by defendant, plaintiff. Civil records archived from early 1900.

Criminal Records: Access: Mail, in person. Both court and visitors may perform in person searches. Search fee: $5.00 per name. Required to search: name, years to search; also helpful: SSN. Criminal records archived from early 1900.

General Information: No adoption, juvenile, mental health, or guardianship records released. SASE required. Turnaround time 3-4 days. Copy fee: $1.00 for first page, $.50 each add'l. Certification fee: $.50. Fee payee: Jackson County Court Clerk. Business checks accepted. Prepayment is required.

Jefferson County

5th Judicial District Court 220 N. Main, Waurika, OK 73573; 580-228-2961. Hours: 8AM-4PM (CST). *Felony, Misdemeanor, Civil, Eviction, Small Claims, Probate.*

Civil Records: Access: Mail, in person. Both court and visitors may perform in person searches. Search fee: $5.00 per name per year. Required to search: name, years to search, DOB or SSN. Civil cases indexed by defendant, plaintiff. Civil records on docket books from 1907; on computer since.

Criminal Records: Access: Mail, in person. Both court and visitors may perform in person searches. Search fee: $5.00 per name per year. Required to search: name, years to search, DOB; also helpful: SSN. Criminal records on docket books from 1907; on computer since.

General Information: Public Access terminal is available. No juvenile, adoption or guardianship records released. SASE required. Turnaround time 1 week. Copy fee: $1.00 for first page, $.50 each add'l. Certification fee: $.50. Fee payee: Court Clerk. Personal checks accepted. Prepayment is required.

Johnston County

20th Judicial District Court 403 W Main, Suite 201, Tishomingo, OK 73460; 580-371-3281. Hours: 8:30AM-4:30PM (CST). *Felony, Misdemeanor, Civil, Eviction, Small Claims, Probate.*

Civil Records: Access: Phone, mail, in person. Both court and visitors may perform in person searches. Search fee: $5.00 per name. Required to search: name,

years to search. Civil cases indexed by defendant, plaintiff. Civil records on docket books from 1907; on computer back to 1997. All requests must be in writing.

Criminal Records: Access: Mail, in person. Both court and visitors may perform in person searches. Search fee: $5.00 per name. Required to search: name, years to search; also helpful: DOB, SSN. Criminal records on docket books from 1907; on computer back to 1997. All requests must be in writing.

General Information: Public Access terminal is available. No juvenile or mental health records released. SASE required. Turnaround time 2 days. Copy fee: $1.00 for first page, $.50 each add'l. Certification fee: $.50. Fee payee: Court. Personal checks accepted. Prepayment is required.

Kay County

8th Judicial District Court Box 428, Newkirk, OK 74647; 580-362-3350. Hours: 8:00AM-4:30PM (CST). *Felony, Misdemeanor, Civil, Eviction, Small Claims, Probate.*

Civil Records: Access: Phone, mail, in person. Both court and visitors may perform in person searches. Search fee: $5.00 per name. Required to search: name, years to search. Civil cases indexed by defendant, plaintiff. Civil records on microfiche and original records.

Criminal Records: Access: Phone, mail, in person. Both court and visitors may perform in person searches. Search fee: $5.00 per name. Required to search: name, years to search; also helpful: DOB, SSN. Criminal records on microfiche and original records.

General Information: No juvenile, adoption, mental health, or sealed records released. Turnaround time 1 day. Copy fee: $1.00 for first page, $.50 each add'l. Certification fee: $.50. Fee payee: Kay County Court Clerk. Personal checks accepted. Prepayment required.

Kingfisher County

4th Judicial District Court Box 328, Kingfisher, OK 73750; 405-375-3813. Hours: 8:00AM-4:30PM (CST). *Felony, Misdemeanor, Civil, Eviction, Small Claims, Probate.*

Civil Records: Access: Phone, mail, in person. Both court and visitors may perform in person searches. Search fee: $5.00. Required to search: name, years to search. Civil cases indexed by defendant, plaintiff. Civil records archived from 1900.

Criminal Records: Access: Mail, in person. Both court and visitors may perform in person searches. Search fee: $5.00. Required to search: name, years to search; also helpful: SSN. Criminal records archived from 1900.

General Information: Public Access terminal is available. No juvenile, mental or guardianship records released. Turnaround time 1-2 days. Copy fee: $1.00 for first page, $.50 each add'l. Certification fee: $.50. Fee payee: Yvonne Dow, Court Clerk. Personal checks accepted. Prepayment is required.

Kiowa County

3rd Judicial District Court Box 854, Hobart, OK 73651; 580-726-5125. Hours: 9AM-5PM (CST). *Felony, Misdemeanor, Civil, Eviction, Small Claims, Probate.*

Civil Records: Access: Phone, mail, in person. Both court and visitors may perform in person searches. Search fee: $5.00 per name. Required to search: name, years to search. Civil cases indexed by defendant, plaintiff. Civil records archived from 1900.

Criminal Records: Access: Phone, mail, in person. Both court and visitors may perform in person searches. Search fee: $5.00 per name. Required to search: name, years to search; also helpful: SSN. Criminal records archived from 1900.

General Information: No juvenile or adoptions records released. SASE required. Turnaround time 1-2 days. Copy fee: $1.00 for first page, $.50 each add'l. Certification fee: $.50. Fee payee: Court Clerk. Only cashiers checks and money orders accepted. Prepayment is required.

Latimer County

16th Judicial District Court 109 N. Central, Rm 200, Wilburton, OK 74578; 918-465-2011. Hours: 8AM-4:30PM (CST). *Felony, Misdemeanor, Civil, Eviction, Small Claims, Probate.*

Civil Records: Access: Phone, mail, in person. Both court and visitors may perform in person searches. Search fee: $5.00 per name. Required to search: name, years to search. Civil cases indexed by defendant, plaintiff. Civil records in original files from 1907, court is in the process of placing indexes on computer.

Criminal Records: Access: Phone, mail, in person. Both court and visitors may perform in person searches. Search fee: $5.00 per name. Required to search: name, years to search; also helpful: DOB, SSN. Criminal records in original files from 1907, court is in the process of placing indexes on computer.

General Information: Public Access terminal is available. No guardianship or juvenile records released. SASE not required. Turnaround time 2 days. Copy fee: $1.00 for first page, $.50 each add'l. Certification fee: $.50. Fee payee: Latimer County Court Clerk. Personal checks accepted. Will bill search fee to law firms.

Le Flore County

16th Judicial District Court PO Box 688, Poteau, OK 74953; 918-647-3181. Hours: 8AM-4:30PM (CST). *Felony, Misdemeanor, Civil, Eviction, Small Claims, Probate.*

Civil Records: Access: Mail, in person. Both court and visitors may perform in person searches. Search fee: $5.00 per name. Required to search: name, years to search. Civil cases indexed by defendant, plaintiff. Civil records on computer since July 1, 1997; prior records archived since 1904 in files and books.

Criminal Records: Access: Mail, in person. Both court and visitors may perform in person searches. Search fee: $5.00 per name. Required to search: name, years to search; also helpful: SSN. Criminal records on computer since July 1, 1997; prior records archived since 1904 in files and books.

General Information: No juvenile, adoptions, mental health or guardian records released. SASE required. Turnaround time 1 week. Copy fee: $1.00 for first page, $.50 each add'l. Certification fee: $.50. Fee payee: Court Clerk. Personal checks accepted.

Lincoln County

23rd Judicial District Court PO Box 307, Chandler, OK 74834; 405-258-1309. Hours: 8AM-4:30PM (CST). *Felony, Misdemeanor, Civil, Eviction, Small Claims, Probate.*

Civil Records: Access: Mail, in person. Both court and visitors may perform in person searches. Search fee: $5.00 per name. Required to search: name, years to search. Civil cases indexed by defendant, plaintiff. Civil records archived since 1891.

Criminal Records: Access: Mail, in person. Both court and visitors may perform in person searches. Search fee: $5.00 per name. Required to search: name, years to search, DOB, signed release; also helpful: SSN. Criminal records archived since 1891.

General Information: Public Access terminal is available. No juvenile, adoption or guardianship records released. SASE required. Turnaround time can take 30 days or more. Record searching is a low priority. Copy fee: $1.00 for first page, $.50 each add'l. Certification fee: $3.00. Fee payee: Court Clerk. Personal checks accepted. Prepayment is required.

Logan County

9th Judicial District Court 301 E. Harrison, Rm 201, Guthrie, OK 73044; 405-282-0123. Hours: 8:30AM-4:30PM (CST). *Felony, Misdemeanor, Civil, Eviction, Small Claims, Probate.*

Civil Records: Access: Mail, in person. Both court and visitors may perform in person searches. Search fee: $5.00 per name. Required to search: name, years to search. Civil cases indexed by defendant, plaintiff. Civil records on microfiche from 1889.

Criminal Records: Access: Mail, in person. Both court and visitors may perform in person searches. Search fee: $5.00 per name. Required to search: name, years to search; also helpful: SSN. Criminal records on microfiche from 1889.

General Information: No juvenile, mental health or adoption records released. SASE required. Turnaround time 2 days. Copy fee: $1.00 for first page, $.50 each add'l. Certification fee: $.50. Fee payee: Court Clerk. Personal checks accepted. Prepayment is required.

Love County

20th Judicial District Court 405 W. Main, Marietta, OK 73448; 580-276-2235. Hours: 8AM-4:30PM (CST). *Felony, Misdemeanor, Civil, Eviction, Small Claims, Probate.*

Civil Records: Access: Mail, in person. Both court and visitors may perform in person searches. Search fee: $5.00 per name. Required to search: name, years to search. Civil cases indexed by defendant, plaintiff. Civil records on docket books from 1907.

Criminal Records: Access: Mail, in person. Both court and visitors may perform in person searches. Search fee: $5.00 per name. Required to search: name, years to search; also helpful: DOB, SSN. Criminal records on docket books from 1907.

General Information: No juvenile or adoptions records released. SASE required. Turnaround time 1-2 days. Copy fee: $1.00 for first page, $.50 each add'l. Certification fee: $.50. Fee payee: Court Clerk. Only cashiers checks and money orders accepted. Prepayment is required.

Major County

4th Judicial District Court 500 E Broadway, Fairview, OK 73737; 580-227-4690 X204. Hours: 8:30AM-4:30PM (CST). *Felony, Misdemeanor, Civil, Eviction, Small Claims, Probate.*

Civil Records: Access: Phone, fax, mail, in person. Both court and visitors may perform in person searches. Search fee: $5.00 per name. Fee is per book. Required to search: name, years to search. Civil cases indexed by defendant, plaintiff. Civil records on docket books from 1907, on microfiche to 1970, on computer to 1997.

Criminal Records: Access: Phone, fax, mail, in person. Both court and visitors may perform in person searches. Search fee: $5.00 per name. Fee is per book. Required to search: name, years to search, DOB; also helpful: SSN. Criminal records on docket books from 1907, on microfiche to 1970; on computer to 1997.

General Information: No juvenile, adoptions or mental records released. SASE required. Turnaround time 3 days. Copy fee: $1.00 for first page, $.50 each add'l. Certification fee: $.50. Fee payee: Court Clerk. Personal checks accepted. Attorney's or firms with previous credit paid.

Marshall County

20th Judicial District Court Box 58, Madill, OK 73446; 580-795-3278 X240. Hours: 8:30AM-5PM (CST). *Felony, Misdemeanor, Civil, Eviction, Small Claims, Probate.*

Civil Records: Access: Phone, mail, in person. Both court and visitors may perform in person searches. Search fee: $5.00. Required to search: name, years to

search. Civil cases indexed by defendant, plaintiff. Civil records on docket books from 1907.

Criminal Records: Access: Phone, mail, in person. Both court and visitors may perform in person searches. Search fee: $5.00. Required to search: name, years to search, DOB, SSN, signed release. Criminal records on docket books from 1907.

General Information: Public Access terminal is available. No juvenile, adoptions, mental health or guardianship records released. SASE required. Turnaround time 3 days. Copy fee: $1.00 for first page, $.50 each add'l. Certification fee: $3.00. Fee payee: Court Clerk. Personal checks accepted.

Mayes County

12th Judicial District Court Box 867, Pryor, OK 74362; 918-825-0133. Hours: 9AM-5PM (CST). *Felony, Misdemeanor, Civil, Eviction, Small Claims, Probate.*

Civil Records: Access: Phone, mail, in person. Both court and visitors may perform in person searches. Search fee: $1.00 per name per year. Search fee is payable to employee doing research after hours. Required to search: name, years to search. Civil cases indexed by defendant, plaintiff. Civil records archived from 1907 on microfilm.

Criminal Records: Access: Phone, mail, in person. Both court and visitors may perform in person searches. Search fee: $1.00 per name per year. Search fee is payable to employee doing research after hours. Required to search: name, years to search; also helpful: DOB, SSN. Criminal records archived from 1907 on microfilm.

General Information: Public Access terminal is available. No mental, adoption, most juvenile, and some reports in guardianship records not released. SASE required. Turnaround time 1 week. Copy fee: $1.00 for first page, $.50 each add'l. Certification fee: $.50. Fee payee: Clerk of Court. Personal checks accepted. Prepayment is required.

McClain County

21st Judicial District Court 121 N. 2nd Rm 231, Purcell, OK 73080; 405-527-3221. Hours: 8AM-4:30PM (CST). *Felony, Misdemeanor, Civil, Eviction, Small Claims, Probate.*

Civil Records: Access: Mail, in person. Both court and visitors may perform in person searches. Search fee: $10.00 per name. Required to search: name, years to search. Civil cases indexed by defendant, plaintiff. Civil records on docket books and cards from 1907, computerized since 01/97.

Criminal Records: Access: Mail, in person. Both court and visitors may perform in person searches. Search fee: $10.00 per name. Required to search: name, years to search; also helpful: DOB, SSN. Criminal records kept in individual docket files.

General Information: Public Access terminal is available. No adoptions, mental health or juvenile records released. SASE required. Turnaround time 2 days. Copy fee: $1.00 for first page, $.50 each add'l. Certification fee: $.50. Fee payee: Court Clerk. Personal checks accepted. Prepayment is required.

McCurtain County

17th Judicial District Court Box 1378, Idabel, OK 74745; 580-286-3693; Fax: 580-286-7095. Hours: 8AM-4PM (CST). *Felony, Misdemeanor, Civil, Eviction, Small Claims, Probate.*

Civil Records: Access: Phone, fax, mail, in person. Both court and visitors may perform in person searches. Search fee: $5.00 per name. Required to search: name, years to search. Civil cases indexed by defendant, plaintiff. Civil records on docket books from 1907.

Criminal Records: Access: Phone, fax, mail, in person. Both court and visitors may perform in person searches. Search fee: $5.00. Required to search: name, years to search; also helpful: SSN. Criminal records on docket books from 1907.

General Information: Public Access terminal is available. No adoptions, guardianship or juvenile records released. SASE required. Turnaround time 1 day. Copy fee: $2.00 per page. Certification fee: No certification fee. Fee payee: Court Clerk. Personal checks accepted. Prepayment is required.

McIntosh County

18th Judicial District Court Box 426, Eufaula, OK 74432; 918-689-2282. Hours: 8AM-4PM (CST). *Felony, Misdemeanor, Civil, Eviction, Small Claims, Probate.*

Civil Records: Access: Mail, in person. Both court and visitors may perform in person searches. Search fee: $5.00 per name. Required to search: name, years to search. Civil cases indexed by defendant, plaintiff. Civil records on microfilm since 1907; computerized back to 1996.

Criminal Records: Access: Mail, in person. Both court and visitors may perform in person searches. Search fee: $5.00 per name. Required to search: name, years to search; also helpful: SSN, DOB. Criminal records on microfilm since 1947; computerized back to 1996.

General Information: Public Access terminal is available. No adoptions, mental health, guardianship or juvenile records released. SASE required. Turnaround time 3 days. Fax notes: Do not fax. Copy fee: $1.00 for first page, $.50 each add'l. Certification fee: $.50 per instrument. Fee payee: Court. No personal checks accepted; must be cashier's check or money order. Prepayment is required.

Murray County

20th Judicial District Court Box 578, Sulphur, OK 73086; 580-622-3223. Hours: 8AM-4:30PM, closed for lunch (CST). *Felony, Misdemeanor, Civil, Eviction, Small Claims, Probate.*

Civil Records: Access: Phone, mail, in person. Both court and visitors may perform in person searches. Search fee: $5.00 per name. Required to search: name, years to search; also helpful: DOB. Civil cases indexed by defendant, plaintiff. Civil records on docket books from 1907, from 1973 back records are on microfilm; computerized back to 1997.

Criminal Records: Access: Phone, mail, in person. Both court and visitors may perform in person searches. Search fee: $5.00 per name. Required to search: name, years to search; also helpful: SSN, DOB. Criminal records on docket books from 1907, from 1973 back records are on microfilm; computerized back to 1997.

General Information: Public Access terminal is available. (For records since 1997.) No mental health, guardianship, juvenile or adoption records released. SASE required. Turnaround time 2 days, immediate if easily accessible. Fax notes: Do not fax. Copy fee: $1.00 for first page, $.50 each add'l. Certification fee: $5.00. Fee payee: Murray County Court Clerk. Personal checks accepted. Prepayment is required.

Muskogee County

15th Judicial District Court Box 1350, Muskogee, OK 74402; 918-682-7873. Hours: 8AM-4:30PM (CST). *Felony, Misdemeanor, Civil, Eviction, Small Claims, Probate.*

Civil Records: Access: Mail, in person. Both court and visitors may perform in person searches. Search fee: $10.00 per name. Required to search: name, years to search. Civil cases indexed by defendant, plaintiff. Civil records on docket books from 1907.

Criminal Records: Access: Mail, in person. Both court and visitors may perform in person searches. Search fee: $10.00 per name. Required to search: name, years

to search, DOB; also helpful: SSN. Criminal records on docket books from 1907.

General Information: No adoptions, mental health, guardianship or juvenile records released. SASE required. Turnaround time 2-3 days. Copy fee: $1.00 for first page, $.50 each add'l. Certification fee: $.50. Fee payee: Court Clerk. Personal checks accepted. Prepayment is required.

Noble County

8th Judicial District Court 300 Courthouse Dr, Box 14, Perry, OK 73077; 580-336-5187. Hours: 8AM-4:30PM (CST). *Felony, Misdemeanor, Civil, Eviction, Small Claims, Probate.*

Civil Records: Access: Mail, in person. Both court and visitors may perform in person searches. Search fee: $5.00 per name. Required to search: name, years to search. Civil cases indexed by defendant, plaintiff. Civil records on microfiche from 1893; computerized back to 1997.

Criminal Records: Access: Mail, in person. Both court and visitors may perform in person searches. Search fee: $5.00 per name. Required to search: name, years to search, DOB; also helpful: address, SSN. Criminal records on microfiche from 1893; computerized back to 1997.

General Information: Public Access terminal is available. No adoptions, mental health, guardianship or juvenile records released. SASE appreciated. Turnaround time 1 day. Copy fee: $1.00 for first page, $.50 each add'l. Certification fee: $.50. Fee payee: Noble County Court Clerk. Personal checks accepted. Prepayment is required.

Nowata County

11th Judicial District Court 229 N. Maple, Nowata, OK 74048; 918-273-0127. Hours: 8AM-4:30PM (CST). *Felony, Misdemeanor, Civil, Eviction, Small Claims, Probate.*

Civil Records: Access: Mail, in person. Both court and visitors may perform in person searches. Search fee: $5.00 per name. Required to search: name, years to search. Civil cases indexed by defendant, plaintiff. Civil records on docket books from 1907; on computer since 1998.

Criminal Records: Access: Mail, in person. Both court and visitors may perform in person searches. Search fee: $5.00 per name. Required to search: name, years to search; also helpful: SSN. Criminal records on docket books from 1907; on computer since 1998.

General Information: No adoptions, mental health, guardianship or juvenile records released. SASE requested. Turnaround time 1 day. Copy fee: $1.00 for first page, $.50 each add'l. Certification fee: $.50 per page. Fee payee: Court Clerk. Personal checks accepted. Prepayment is required.

Okfuskee County

24th Judicial District Court Box 30, Okemah, OK 74859; 918-623-0525. Hours: 8:30AM-4:30PM (CST). *Felony, Misdemeanor, Civil, Eviction, Small Claims, Probate.*

Civil Records: Access: Mail, in person. Both court and visitors may perform in person searches. Search fee: $5.00 per name. Required to search: name, years to search. Civil cases indexed by defendant, plaintiff. Civil records in files and docket books from 1907.

Criminal Records: Access: Mail, in person. Both court and visitors may perform in person searches. Search fee: $5.00 per name. Required to search: name, years to search; also helpful: SSN. Criminal records in files and docket books from 1907.

General Information: No adoptions, mental health, guardianship or juvenile released. SASE required. Turnaround time 3 day. Copy fee: $1.00 for first page, $.50 each add'l. Certification fee: $.50 per page. Fee

payee: Court Clerk. Personal checks accepted. Prepayment is required.

Oklahoma County

District Court 320 Robert S. Kerr St, Rm 409, Oklahoma City, OK 73102; 405-713-1705. Hours: 8AM-5PM (CST). *Felony, Misdemeanor, Civil, Eviction, Small Claims, Probate.*

Civil Records: Access: Mail, online, in person. Both court and visitors may perform in person searches. Search fee: Lengthy searches are $5.00 per half hour, otherwise no search fee. Required to search: name, years to search. Civil cases indexed by defendant, plaintiff. Civil records on microfiche from 1980, prior archived. Online access to court dockets is available free online at www.oscn.net/applications/oscn/casesearch. asp. Civil dockets go back to 12/1984.

Criminal Records: Access: Mail, online, in person. Both court and visitors may perform in person searches. Search fee: Lengthy searches $5.00 per half hour; commercial purpose searches: $25.00. Required to search: name, years to search, DOB; also helpful: SSN. Criminal records on microfiche from 1980, prior archived. Online access to criminal dockets is same as civil. Criminal dockets go back to 9/1988.

General Information: Public Access terminal is available. No juvenile, sealed, or expunged records released. SASE required. Turnaround time 5-10 days. Copy fee: $1.00 for first page, $.50 each add'l. Certification fee: $.50. Fee payee: District Court Clerk. Personal checks accepted. Prepayment is required.

Okmulgee County

24th Judicial District Court - Henryetta Branch 114 S 4th, Henryetta, OK 74437; 918-652-7142. Hours: 8:30AM-4:30PM (CST). *Felony, Misdemeanor, Civil, Eviction, Small Claims, Probate.*

Note: You must search both courts in this county, records are not co-mingled.

Civil Records: Access: Phone, mail, in person. Both court and visitors may perform in person searches. Search fee: $5.00 per name. Required to search: name, years to search. Civil cases indexed by defendant, plaintiff. Civil records on microfiche from 1970.

Criminal Records: Access: Phone, mail, in person. Both court and visitors may perform in person searches. Search fee: $5.00 per name. Required to search: name, years to search; also helpful: SSN. Criminal records on microfiche from 1970.

General Information: No expunged or guardianship records released. SASE required. Turnaround time 1-2 days, limited phone searching immediate. Copy fee: $1.00 for first page, $.50 each add'l. Certification fee: $5.00. Fee payee: Court Clerk. Business checks accepted. Prepayment is required.

24th Judicial District Court - Okmulgee Branch 314 W 7th, Okmulgee, OK 74447; 918-756-3042. Hours: 8AM-4:30PM *Felony, Misdemeanor, Civil, Eviction, Small Claims, Probate.*

Civil Records: Access: Phone, mail, in person. Both court and visitors may perform in person searches. Search fee: $5.00 per name. Required to search: name, years to search. Civil cases indexed by defendant, plaintiff. Civil records on microfiche from 1986, archived from 1907.

Criminal Records: Access: Phone, mail, in person. Both court and visitors may perform in person searches. Search fee: $5.00 per name. Required to search: name, years to search; also helpful: SSN. Criminal records on microfiche from 1986, archived from 1907.

General Information: Public Access terminal is available. No juvenile, mental health, adoption or guardianship records released. SASE requested. Turnaround time 1-2 days. Copy fee: $1.00 for first page, $.50 each add'l. Certification fee: $.50. Fee payee:

Linda Beaver Court Clerk. Business checks accepted. Prepayment is required.

Osage County

10th Judicial District Court County Courthouse, 600 Grandview, Pawhuska, OK 74056; 918-287-4104. Hours: 9AM-5PM (CST). *Felony, Misdemeanor, Civil, Eviction, Small Claims, Probate, Divorce.*

Civil Records: Access: Mail, in person. Both court and visitors may perform in person searches. Search fee: $5.00 per name. Required to search: name, years to search; also helpful: address. Civil cases indexed by defendant, plaintiff. Civil records archived from 1969.

Criminal Records: Access: Mail, in person. Both court and visitors may perform in person searches. Search fee: $5.00 per name. Required to search: name, years to search; also helpful: address. Criminal records archived from 1969.

General Information: Public Access terminal is available. No juvenile or adoption records released. SASE required. Turnaround time 2 days. Copy fee: $1.00 for first page, $.50 each add'l. Certification fee: $.50. Fee payee: Court Clerk. Only cashiers checks and money orders accepted. Prepayment is required.

Ottawa County

13th Judicial District Court 102 E Central Ave, Suite 300, Miami, OK 74354; 918-542-2801. Hours: 9:00AM-5:00PM (CST). *Felony, Misdemeanor, Civil, Eviction, Small Claims, Probate.*

Civil Records: Access: Phone, mail, in person. Both court and visitors may perform in person searches. Search fee: $5.00 per name. Required to search: name, years to search. Civil cases indexed by defendant, plaintiff. Civil records on docket books or cards from 1907, recent records computerized.

Criminal Records: Access: Mail, in person. Both court and visitors may perform in person searches. Search fee: $5.00. Required to search: name, years to search; also helpful: SSN. Criminal records on docket books or cards from 1907, recent records computerized.

General Information: Public Access terminal is available. No juvenile, mental health, adoption or guardianship records released. SASE required. Turnaround time 1-2 days. Copy fee: $1.00 for first page, $.50 each add'l. Certification fee: $.50. Fee payee: Clerk of Court. Business checks accepted.

Pawnee County

14th Judicial District Court Courthouse, 500 Harrison St, Pawnee, OK 74058; 918-762-2547. Hours: 8AM-4:30PM (CST). *Felony, Misdemeanor, Civil, Eviction, Small Claims, Probate.*

Civil Records: Access: Mail, in person. Both court and visitors may perform in person searches. Search fee: $5.00. Required to search: name, years to search. Civil cases indexed by defendant, plaintiff. Civil records on docket sheets.

Criminal Records: Access: Mail, in person. Both court and visitors may perform in person searches. Search fee: $5.00. Required to search: name, years to search; also helpful: SSN. Criminal records on docket sheets.

General Information: Public Access terminal is available. No sealed records released. SASE required. Turnaround time 1-3 days. Copy fee: $1.00 for first page, $.50 each add'l. Certification fee: $.50. Fee payee: Court Clerk. Personal checks accepted. Prepayment is required.

Payne County

9th Judicial District Court 606 S. Husband Rm 308, Stillwater, OK 74074; 405-372-4774. Hours: 8AM-5PM (CST). *Felony, Misdemeanor, Civil, Eviction, Small Claims, Probate.*

Civil Records: Access: Mail, online, in person. Both court and visitors may perform in person searches. Search fee: $10.00 per name. Fee is for 7 year search. Required to search: name, years to search. Civil cases indexed by defendant, plaintiff. Civil records on docket books from late 1800s, as of 1994 on computer. Online access to court dockets is available free online at www.oscn.net/applications/oscn/casesearch.asp. Dockets go back to 1/1994.

Criminal Records: Access: Mail, online, in person. Both court and visitors may perform in person searches. Search fee: $10.00 per name. Fee is for 7 year search. Required to search: name, years to search, DOB, SSN, signed release. Criminal records on docket books from late 1800s, as of 1994 on computer. Online access to criminal dockets is same as civil.

General Information: Public Access terminal is available. No sealed records, juveniles or adoption records released. SASE required. Turnaround time 2 days. Copy fee: $1.00 for first page, $.50 each add'l. Certification fee: $3.00. Fee payee: Clerk of Court. Personal checks accepted. Prepayment is required.

Pittsburg County

18th Judicial District Court Box 460, McAlester, OK 74502; 918-423-4859. Hours: 8AM-5PM (CST). *Felony, Misdemeanor, Civil, Eviction, Small Claims, Probate.*

Civil Records: Access: Mail, in person. Both court and visitors may perform in person searches. Search fee: $5.00 per name. Required to search: name, years to search. Civil cases indexed by defendant, plaintiff. Civil records on microfiche since 1907; on computer since.

Criminal Records: Access: Mail, in person. Both court and visitors may perform in person searches. Search fee: $5.00 per name. Required to search: name, years to search. Criminal records on microfiche since 1907; on computer since.

General Information: No juvenile, adoptions, mental health or guardianship records released. SASE required. Turnaround time 1-2 days. Copy fee: $1.00 for first page, $.50 each add'l. Certification fee: $.50. Fee payee: Court Clerk. Prepayment is required.

Pontotoc County

22nd Judicial District Court Box 427, Ada, OK 74820; 580-332-5763; Fax: 580-436-5613. Hours: 8AM-5PM (CST). *Felony, Misdemeanor, Civil, Eviction, Small Claims, Probate.*

Civil Records: Access: Mail, in person. Both court and visitors may perform in person searches. Search fee: $5.00 per name. Required to search: name, years to search. Civil cases indexed by defendant, plaintiff. Civil records on card index from 1907.

Criminal Records: Access: Mail, in person. Both court and visitors may perform in person searches. Search fee: $5.00 per name. Required to search: name, years to search; also helpful: DOB, SSN. Criminal records on card index from 1907.

General Information: No juvenile, adoptions, mental health or guardianship records released. SASE required. Turnaround time 2 days. Copy fee: $1.00 for first page, $.50 each add'l. Certification fee: $.50. Fee payee: Clerk of Court. Personal checks accepted. Must prepay if out of state. Will bill marriage license fees.

Pottawatomie County

23rd Judicial District Court 325 N. Broadway, Shawnee, OK 74801; 405-273-3624. Hours: 8:30AM-Noon, 1-5 PM (CST). *Felony, Misdemeanor, Civil, Eviction, Small Claims, Probate.*

Civil Records: Access: Mail, in person. Both court and visitors may perform in person searches. Search fee: $5.00 per name. Required to search: name, years to search. Civil cases indexed by defendant, plaintiff. Civil records on computer from 07/97; prior records on book of names from 1892.

Criminal Records: Access: Mail, in person. Both court and visitors may perform in person searches. Search fee: $5.00 per name. Required to search: name, years to search; also helpful: SSN. Criminal records on computer from 07/97; prior records on book of names from 1892.

General Information: No juvenile, adoptions, mental health or guardianship records released. SASE requested. Turnaround time 2 weeks or less. Copy fee: $1.00 for first page, $.50 each add'l. Certification fee: $.50. Fee payee: Court Clerk. Personal checks accepted. Prepayment is required.

Pushmataha County

17th Judicial District Court Push County Courthouse, Antlers, OK 74523; 580-298-2274. Hours: 8AM-4:30PM (CST). *Felony, Misdemeanor, Civil, Eviction, Small Claims, Probate.*

Civil Records: Access: Mail, in person. Both court and visitors may perform in person searches. Search fee: $5.00 per name. Required to search: name, years to search. Civil cases indexed by defendant, plaintiff. Civil records on docket book from 1907.

Criminal Records: Access: Mail, in person. Both court and visitors may perform in person searches. Search fee: $5.00 per name. Required to search: name, years to search; also helpful: SSN. Criminal records on docket book from 1907.

General Information: No juvenile or adoption records released. SASE required. Turnaround time 1 day. Copy fee: $1.00 for first page, $.50 each add'l. Certification fee: $.50. Fee payee: Court Clerk. Personal checks accepted. Prepayment is required.

Roger Mills County

2nd Judicial District Court Box 409, Cheyenne, OK 73628; 580-497-3361. Hours: 8AM-Noon, 1-4:30PM (CST). *Felony, Misdemeanor, Civil, Eviction, Small Claims, Probate.*

Civil Records: Access: Phone, mail, in person. Both court and visitors may perform in person searches. No search fee. Required to search: name, years to search. Civil cases indexed by defendant, plaintiff. Civil records on computer since 1992, in books since 1893.

Criminal Records: Access: Phone, mail, in person. Both court and visitors may perform in person searches. No search fee. Required to search: name, years to search, DOB; also helpful: SSN. Criminal records on computer since 1992, in books since 1893.

General Information: Public Access terminal is available. No adoption, juvenile, mental health or guardianship records released. SASE required. Turnaround time 1 day. Copy fee: $1.00 for first page, $.50 each add'l. Certification fee: $.50. Fee payee: Court Clerk. Personal checks accepted. Prepayment required.

Rogers County

12th Judicial District Court Box 839, 219 S Missouri, Claremore, OK 74018; 918-341-5711. Hours: 8AM-4:30PM (CST). *Felony, Misdemeanor, Civil, Eviction, Small Claims, Probate.*

Civil Records: Access: Phone, mail, online, in person. Both court and visitors may perform in person searches. Search fee: None, but phone and mail requests require case number. Required to search: name, years to search. Civil cases indexed by defendant, plaintiff. Civil records in card index for last 7 years, some computerized. Online access to court dockets is available free online at www.oscn.net/applications/oscn/casesearch.asp. Dockets go back to 7/1997.

Criminal Records: Access: Phone, mail, online, in person. Both court and visitors may perform in person searches. Search fee: None, but phone and mail requests require case number. Required to search: name, years to search, DOB; also helpful: SSN. Criminal records on card index for last 7 years, some computerized. Online access to criminal dockets is same as civil.

General Information: Public Access terminal is available. No juvenile or adoption records released. SASE required. Turnaround time 1 day. Copy fee: $1.00 for first page, $.50 each add'l. Certification fee: $.50. Fee payee: Court Clerk. Personal checks accepted. Prepayment is required.

Seminole County

22nd Judicial District Court - Seminole Branch Box 1320, 401 Main St, Seminole, OK 74868; 405-382-3424. Hours: 8AM-Noon, 1-4PM (CST). *Civil, Small Claims, Probate.*

Note: Criminal records are now maintained at 22nd Judicial District Court, PO Box 130, Wewoka, OK, 405-257-6236.

Civil Records: Access: Phone, mail, in person. Only the court performs in person searches; visitors may not. Search fee: $5.00 per name. Required to search: name, years to search. Civil cases indexed by defendant, plaintiff. Civil records on index cards from 1931, probate from 1969.

General Information: SASE required. Turnaround time 1 to 2 days. Copy fee: $1.00 for first page, $.50 each add'l. Certification fee: $.50. Fee payee: Court Clerk. Only cashiers checks and money orders accepted. Prepayment is required.

22nd Judicial District Court - Wewoka Branch Box 130, Wewoka, OK 74884; 405-257-6236. Hours: 8AM-4PM *Felony, Misdemeanor, Civil, Eviction, Small Claims, Probate.*

Civil Records: Access: Mail, in person. Both court and visitors may perform in person searches. Search fee: $5.00 per name. Required to search: name, years to search. Civil cases indexed by defendant, plaintiff. Civil records indexed on computer since 1995; prior records on books to 1909.

Criminal Records: Access: Mail, in person. Both court and visitors may perform in person searches. Search fee: $5.00 per name. Required to search: name, years to search; also helpful: SSN. Criminal records indexed on computer since 1995; prior records on books to 1909. They maintain the criminal records for the Seminole Branch in Seminole, OK.

General Information: Public Access terminal is available. No juvenile or adoption records released. SASE required. Turnaround time 1 day. Copy fee: $1.00 for first page, $.50 each add'l. Certification fee: $.50. Fee payee: Court Clerk. Personal checks accepted. Prepayment is required.

Sequoyah County

15th Judicial District Court 120 E Chickasaw, Sallisaw, OK 74955; 918-775-4411. Hours: 8AM-4PM (CST). *Felony, Misdemeanor, Civil, Eviction, Small Claims, Probate.*

Civil Records: Access: Mail, in person. Both court and visitors may perform in person searches. Search fee: $5.00 per name. Required to search: name, years to search. Civil cases indexed by defendant, plaintiff. Civil records in files and dockets from 1907; on computer back to 1997.

Criminal Records: Access: Phone, mail, in person. Both court and visitors may perform in person searches. Search fee: $5.00 per name. Required to search: name, years to search; also helpful: SSN. Some criminal records on computer back to 1997, prior in files and dockets.

General Information: Public Access terminal is available. No juvenile, adoptions, mental health or guardianship records released. SASE required. Turnaround time 1 week. Copy fee: $1.00 for first page, $.50 each add'l. Certification fee: $1.00. Fee payee: Court Clerk. Personal checks accepted. Will bill mail requests.

Stephens County

5th Judicial District Court 101 S 11th Rm 301, Duncan, OK 73533; 580-478-2000. Hours: 8:30AM-4:30PM (CST). *Felony, Misdemeanor, Civil, Eviction, Small Claims, Probate.*

Civil Records: Access: Mail, in person. Both court and visitors may perform in person searches. Search fee: $5.00 per name. Required to search: name, years to search. Civil cases indexed by defendant, plaintiff. Civil records on computer from 10/95; prior records on docket books from 1907.

Criminal Records: Access: Mail, in person. Both court and visitors may perform in person searches. Search fee: $5.00 per name. Required to search: name, years to search; also helpful: address, DOB, SSN. Criminal records on computer from 10/95; prior records on docket books from 1907.

General Information: Public Access terminal is available. No juvenile, adoptions, mental health or guardianship records released. SASE required. Turnaround time 1 day. Copy fee: $1.00 for first page, $.50 each add'l. Certification fee: $.50. Fee payee: Stephens County 5th Judicial Court. Personal checks accepted. Prepayment is required.

Texas County

1st Judicial District Court Box 1081, Guymon, OK 73942; 580-338-3003. Hours: 9AM-5PM (CST). *Felony, Misdemeanor, Civil, Eviction, Small Claims, Probate.*

Civil Records: Access: Mail, in person. Both court and visitors may perform in person searches. Search fee: $5.00 per name. Required to search: name, years to search. Civil cases indexed by defendant, plaintiff. Civil records on microfiche from 1976, archived prior, computerized since 03/95.

Criminal Records: Access: Mail, in person. Both court and visitors may perform in person searches. Search fee: $5.00 per name. Required to search: name, years to search; also helpful: SSN. Criminal records on microfiche from 1976, archived prior, computerized since 03/95.

General Information: Public Access terminal is available. No juvenile, adoptions, mental health or guardianship records released. SASE required. Turnaround time 5 days, 1 day for phone. Copy fee: $1.00 for first page, $.50 each add'l. Certification fee: $.50. Fee payee: Court Clerk. Personal checks accepted. Prepayment is required.

Tillman County

3rd Judicial District Court Box 116, Frederick, OK 73542; 580-335-3023. Hours: 8AM-4PM (CST). *Felony, Misdemeanor, Civil, Eviction, Small Claims, Probate.*

Civil Records: Access: Mail, in person. Both court and visitors may perform in person searches. Search fee: $5.00 per name. Required to search: name, years to search. Civil cases indexed by defendant, plaintiff. Civil records on docket books from 1907; on computer back to 1998.

Criminal Records: Access: Mail, in person. Both court and visitors may perform in person searches. Search fee: $5.00 per name. Required to search: name, years to search, DOB; also helpful: SSN. Criminal records on docket books from 1907; on computer back to 1998.

General Information: No expunged records released. SASE required. Turnaround time 1 day. Copy fee: $1.00 for first page, $.50 each add'l. Copy charge is only if the person does their own search in person. Certification fee: $1.00. Fee payee: District Court. Business checks accepted. Will bill law firms.

Tulsa County

14th Judicial District Court 500 S. Denver, Tulsa, OK 74103-3832; 918-596-5000. Hours: 8:30AM-5PM (CST). *Felony, Misdemeanor, Civil, Eviction, Small Claims, Probate.*

Civil Records: Access: Mail, online, in person. Both court and visitors may perform in person searches. Search fee: $5.00 per name. Required to search: name, years to search. Civil cases indexed by defendant, plaintiff. Civil records on computer from 1984, on microfiche from 1907, archived from 1907. Online access to court dockets is available free online at www.oscn.net/applications/oscn/casesearch.asp. Civil dockets go back to 10/1984.

Criminal Records: Access: Mail, online, in person. Both court and visitors may perform in person searches. Search fee: $5.00 per name. Required to search: name, years to search; also helpful: SSN. Criminal records on computer from 1984, on microfiche from 1907, archived from 1907. Online access to criminal dockets is same as civil. Criminal dockets go back to 1/1988.

General Information: Public Access terminal is available. No juvenile, adoption or guardianship records released. SASE required. Turnaround time 1 week. Copy fee: $1.00 for first page, $.50 each add'l. Certification fee: $.50. Fee payee: Court Clerk. Will accept attorney personal checks. Prepayment required.

Wagoner County

15th Judicial District Court Box 249, Wagoner, OK 74477; 918-485-4508. Hours: 8:00AM-4:30PM (CST). *Felony, Misdemeanor, Civil, Eviction, Small Claims, Probate.*

Civil Records: Access: Mail, in person. Both court and visitors may perform in person searches. Search fee: $5.00 per name. Required to search: name, years to search. Civil cases indexed by defendant, plaintiff. Civil records on docket books from 1980; on computer back to 1997.

Criminal Records: Access: Mail, in person. Both court and visitors may perform in person searches. Search fee: $5.00 per name if assisted. Required to search: name, years to search; also helpful: SSN. Criminal records are in files and dockets back to 1907; on computer back to 1997.

General Information: Public Access terminal is available. No juvenile, mental health, adoption or guardianship records released. SASE required. Turnaround time 1-2 days for civil, longer for criminal. Copy fee: $1.00 for first page, $.50 each add'l. Certification fee: $.50. Fee payee: Court Clerk. Personal checks accepted. Prepayment is required.

Washington County

11th Judicial District Court 420 S Johnstone, Rm 212, Bartlesville, OK 74003; 918-337-2870; Fax: 918-337-2897. Hours: 8AM-5PM (CST). *Felony, Misdemeanor, Civil, Eviction, Small Claims, Probate.*

Civil Records: Access: Phone, mail, in person. Both court and visitors may perform in person searches. Search fee: $5.00 per name. Required to search: name, years to search. Civil cases indexed by defendant, plaintiff. Civil records on microfiche from 1988, on docket books from 1907.

Criminal Records: Access: Phone, mail, in person. Both court and visitors may perform in person searches. Search fee: $5.00 per name. Required to search: name, years to search, signed release; also helpful: DOB, SSN. Criminal records on microfiche from 1988, on docket books from 1907.

General Information: Public Access terminal is available. No juvenile, mental health, adoption or guardianship records released. Turnaround time 1-3 days. Copy fee: $1.00 for first page, $.50 each add'l. Certification fee: $3.00. Fee payee: Court Clerk. Personal checks accepted. Prepayment is required.

Washita County

3rd Judicial District Court Box 397, Cordell, OK 73632,; 580-832-3836. Hours: 8AM-4PM (CST). *Felony, Misdemeanor, Civil, Small Claims, Probate.*

Civil Records: Access: Mail, in person. Both court and visitors may perform in person searches. Search fee: $5.00 per name. Required to search: name, years to search. Civil cases indexed by defendant, plaintiff. Civil records on computer since 1998; prior records on microfiche from 1980s & on docket books from 1892.

Criminal Records: Access: Mail, in person. Both court and visitors may perform in person searches. Search fee: $5.00 per name. Required to search: name, years to search; also helpful: DOB, SSN, aliases. Criminal records on computer since 1998; prior records on microfiche from 1980s & on docket books from 1892.

General Information: Public Access terminal is available. No juvenile, mental health, adoption or guardianship records released. SASE required. Turnaround time same day. Copy fee: $1.00 for first page, $.50 each add'l. Certification fee: $.50. Fee payee: Court Clerk. Personal checks accepted. Prepayment is required.

Woods County

4th Judicial District Court Box 924, Alva, OK 73717; 580-327-3119. Hours: 9AM-5PM (CST). *Felony, Misdemeanor, Civil, Eviction, Small Claims, Probate.*

Civil Records: Access: Mail, in person. Both court and visitors may perform in person searches. Search fee: $5.00 per name. Required to search: name, years to search. Civil cases indexed by defendant, plaintiff. Civil records on docket books from 1890.

Criminal Records: Access: Mail, in person. Both court and visitors may perform in person searches. Search fee: $5.00 per name. Required to search: name, years to search. Criminal records on computer since 1987, on dockets and cards from 1890s.

General Information: No juvenile, mental health, adoption or guardianship records released. SASE required. Turnaround time 2 days. Copy fee: $1.00 for first page, $.50 each add'l. Certification fee: $.50. Fee payee: Clerk of Court. Personal checks accepted. Prepayment is required.

Woodward County

4th Judicial District Court 1600 Main, Woodward, OK 73801; 580-256-3413. Hours: 9AM-5PM (CST). *Felony, Misdemeanor, Civil, Eviction, Small Claims, Probate.*

Civil Records: Access: Mail, in person. Both court and visitors may perform in person searches. Search fee: $5.00 per name. Required to search: name, years to search. Civil cases indexed by defendant, plaintiff. Civil records on docket books from 1890, on microfiche from 1989; on computer from 1997.

Criminal Records: Access: Mail, in person. Both court and visitors may perform in person searches. Search fee: $5.00 per name. Required to search: name, years to search; also helpful: DOB, SSN. Criminal records on docket books from 1890, on microfiche from 1989; on computer from 1997.

General Information: Public Access terminal is available. No mental, juvenile, adoption, guardianship records released. SASE required. Turnaround time 1-2 days unless older cases found. Fax notes: Fee to fax results is 1.00 per document. Copy fee: $1.00 for first page, $.50 each add'l. Certification fee: $.50 per page. $5.00 for whole file. Fee payee: Court Clerk. Personal checks accepted. Prepayment is required.

Oklahoma Recording Offices

ORGANIZATION	77 counties, 77 recording offices. The recording officer is County Clerk. The entire state is in the Central Time Zone (CST).
REAL ESTATE RECORDS	Many counties will perform real estate searches by legal description. Copy fees are usually $1.00 per page. Certification usually costs $1.00 per document.
UCC RECORDS	Financing statements are filed centrally with the County Clerk of Oklahoma County. Prior to 7/2001, consumer goods, farm related, and real estate related collateral were dual filed with the local County Clerk as well as the County Clerk of Oklahoma County. Now only real estate related collateral is filed at the local level. All counties will perform UCC searches. Use search request form UCC-4. Search fees are usually $5.00 per debtor name for a written request and $3.00 per name by telephone. Copies usually cost $1.00 per page.
TAX LIEN RECORDS	Federal tax liens on personal property of businesses are filed with the County Clerk of Oklahoma County, which is the central filing office for the state. Other federal and all state tax liens are filed with the County Clerk. Usually state and federal tax liens on personal property are filed in separate indexes. Some counties will perform tax lien searches. Search fees vary.
OTHER LIENS	Judgment, mechanics, physicians, hospital.

Adair County

County Clerk, P.O. Box 169, Stilwell, OK 74960. 918-696-7198; Fax 918-696-2603.
Will search UCC records. Will not search real estate records. **Other Phone Numbers:** Assessor 918-696-2012; Treasurer 918-696-7551; Elections 918-696-7221.

Alfalfa County

County Clerk, 300 South Grand, Cherokee, OK 73728. 580-596-3158.
Will search UCC records. This agency will not do a tax lien search. Will not search real estate records. **Other Phone Numbers:** Assessor 580-596-2145; Treasurer 580-596-3148; Elections 580-596-2718.

Atoka County

County Clerk, 200 East Court Street, Atoka, OK 74525. 580-889-5157; Fax 580-889-5063.
Will search UCC records. UCC search includes tax liens if requested. Will not search real estate records. **Other Phone Numbers:** Assessor 580-889-6036; Treasurer 580-889-5283.

Beaver County

County Clerk, P.O. Box 338, Beaver, OK 73932-0338. 580-625-3141 R/E Recording: 580-625-3418; Fax 580-625-3430.
Will search UCC records. Will not search real estate records. **Other Phone Numbers:** Assessor 580-625-3116; Treasurer 580-625-3161.

Beckham County

County Clerk, P.O. Box 428, Sayre, OK 73662-0428. 580-928-3383.
Will search UCC records. This agency will not do a tax lien search. Will not search real estate records. **Other Phone Numbers:** Assessor 580-928-3329; Treasurer 580-928-2589.

Blaine County

County Clerk, P.O. Box 138, Watonga, OK 73772. County Clerk, R/E and UCC Recording 580-623-5890; Fax 580-623-5009.
Will not search UCC records. Will not search real estate records. **Other Phone Numbers:** Assessor 580-623-5123; Treasurer 580-623-5007; Elections 580-623-5518.

Bryan County

County Clerk, P.O. Box 1789, Durant, OK 74702. County Clerk, R/E and UCC Recording 580-924-2202; Fax 580-924-2289.
Will search UCC records. **Other Phone Numbers:** Assessor 580-924-2166; Treasurer 580-924-0748; Appraiser/Auditor 580-924-2166; Elections 580-924-3228.

Caddo County

County Clerk, P.O. Box 68, Anadarko, OK 73005. County Clerk, R/E and UCC Recording 405-247-6609; Fax 405-247-6510.
Will search UCC records. Will not search real estate records. **Other Phone Numbers:** Assessor 405-247-2477; Treasurer 405-247-5151; Vital Records 405-271-4040; Real Estate 405-247-6510.

Canadian County

County Clerk, P.O. Box 458, El Reno, OK 73036. 405-262-1070; Fax 405-422-2411.
Will search UCC records. Will not search real estate records. **Other Phone Numbers:** Assessor 405-262-1070 x269; Treasurer 405-262-1070 x250.

Carter County

County Clerk, P.O. Box 1236, Ardmore, OK 73402. County Clerk, R/E and UCC Recording 580-223-8162.
Will search UCC records. Will not search real estate records. **Other Phone Numbers:** Assessor 580-223-9594; Treasurer 580-223-9467.

Cherokee County

County Clerk, 213 West Delaware, Room 200, Tahlequah, OK 74464. County Clerk, R/E and UCC Recording 918-456-3171 UCC Recording: 918-458-6512; Fax 918-458-6508.
Will search UCC records. UCC search includes tax liens if requested. Will not search real estate records. **Other Phone Numbers:** Assessor 918-456-3201; Treasurer 918-456-3321; Elections 918-456-2261.

Choctaw County

County Clerk, Courthouse, 300 E. Duke, Hugo, OK 74743. County Clerk, R/E and UCC Recording 580-326-3778; Fax 580-326-6787.
Will search UCC records. **Other Phone Numbers:** Assessor 405-326-2356; Treasurer 405-326-6142; Elections 405-326-5164; Vital Records 405-271-4040.

Cimarron County

County Clerk, P.O. Box 145, Boise City, OK 73933. County Clerk, R/E and UCC Recording 580-544-2251; Fax 580-544-2251.
Will search UCC records. Will not search real estate records. **Other Phone Numbers:** Assessor 580-544-2701; Treasurer 580-544-2261; Elections 580-544-3377.

Cleveland County

County Clerk, 201 South Jones, Room 204, Norman, OK 73069-6099. County Clerk, R/E and UCC Recording 405-366-0240 UCC Recording: 405-366-0234; Fax 405-366-0229. www.okclev.cogov.net
Will search UCC records. Will not search real estate records. **Other Phone Numbers:** Assessor 405-366-0230; Treasurer 405-366-0217; Elections 405-26-0120; Vital Records 405-271-4040.

Coal County

County Clerk, 4 North Main, Ste. 1, Suite 1, Coalgate, OK 74538. County Clerk, R/E and UCC Recording 580-927-2103; Fax 580-927-4003.
Will search UCC records. This agency will not do a tax lien search. Will not search real estate records. **Other Phone Numbers:** Assessor 580-927-3123; Treasurer 580-927-3121; Elections 580-927-3456; Vital Records 580-927-2281.

Comanche County

County Clerk, 315 SW 5th, Room 304, Lawton, OK 73501-4347. 580-355-5214.
Will search UCC records. UCC search does not include tax liens Will not search real estate records. **Other Phone Numbers:** Assessor 580-355-1052; Treasurer 580-355-5763.

Cotton County

County Clerk, 301 North Broadway, Walters, OK 73572. County Clerk, R/E and UCC Recording 580-875-3026; Fax 580-875-3756.
Will search UCC records. Will not search real estate records. **Other Phone Numbers:** Assessor 580-875-3289; Treasurer 580-875-3264; Elections 580-875-3403.

Craig County

County Clerk, P.O. Box 397, Vinita, OK 74301. 918-256-2507; Fax 918-256-3617.

Will search UCC records. Will not search real estate records. **Other Phone Numbers:** Assessor 918-256-3640; Treasurer 918-256-2286; Elections 918-256-7559.

Creek County

County Clerk, 317 E. Lee, First Floor, Sapulpa, OK 74066. 918-227-6306 R/E Recording: 918-227-4084. Will search UCC records. This agency will not do a tax lien search. Will not search real estate records. **Other Phone Numbers:** Assessor 918-224-4508; Treasurer 918-227-4501.

Custer County

County Clerk, P.O. Box 300, Arapaho, OK 73620. County Clerk, R/E and UCC Recording 580-323-1221; Fax 580-323-4421.
Will search UCC records. Will not search real estate records. **Other Phone Numbers:** Assessor 580-323-3271; Treasurer 580-323-2292; Elections 580-323-2291; Vital Records 580-323-4040.

Delaware County

County Clerk, P.O. Box 309, Jay, OK 74346. 918-253-4520; Fax 918-253-8352.
Will search UCC records. Will not search real estate records. **Other Phone Numbers:** Assessor 918-328-5561.

Dewey County

County Clerk, P.O. Box 368, Taloga, OK 73667. 580-328-5361.
Will search UCC records. UCC search includes tax liens if requested. RE owner, mortgage, and property transfer searches available. **Other Phone Numbers:** Assessor 580-885-7975; Treasurer 580-328-5501.

Ellis County

County Clerk, P.O. Box 197, Arnett, OK 73832. 580-885-7301; Fax 580-885-7258.
Will search UCC records. Will not search real estate records. **Other Phone Numbers:** Assessor 580-885-7975; Treasurer 580-885-7620.

Garfield County

County Clerk, P.O. Box 1664, Enid, OK 73702-1664. County Clerk, R/E and UCC Recording 580-237-0226; Fax 580-249-5951.
Will search UCC records. Will not search real estate records. **Other Phone Numbers:** Assessor 580-237-0220; Treasurer 580-237-0246; Elections 580-237-6016; Court Clerk 580-237-0232.

Garvin County

County Clerk, P.O. Box 926, Pauls Valley, OK 73075. 405-238-2772; Fax 405-238-6283.
Will search UCC records. Will not search real estate records. **Other Phone Numbers:** Assessor 405-238-2409; Treasurer 405-238-7301.

Grady County

County Clerk, P.O. Box 1009, Chickasha, OK 73023. 405-224-7388; Fax 405-222-4506. http://www.gradycounty.net
Will search UCC records. Will not search real estate records. **Other Phone Numbers:** Assessor 405-224-4361; Treasurer 405-224-5337; Elections 405-224-1430; Vital Records 405-271-4040.

Grant County

County Clerk, P.O. Box 167, Medford, OK 73759-0167. County Clerk, R/E and UCC Recording 580-395-2274.
Will search UCC records. UCC search includes tax liens if requested. Lien searches performed by phone

only, and if requested with UCC Will not search real estate records. **Other Phone Numbers:** Assessor 580-395-2844; Treasurer 580-395-2284; Elections 580-395-2862.

Greer County

County Clerk, P.O. Box 207, Mangum, OK 73554. County Clerk, R/E and UCC Recording 580-782-3664; Fax 580-782-3803.
Will search UCC records. **Other Phone Numbers:** Assessor 580-782-2740; Treasurer 580-782-5515; Appraiser/Auditor 580-782-2454; Elections 580-782-2307; Vital Records 405-271-4040.

Harmon County

County Clerk, Courthouse, 14 W. Hollis, Hollis, OK 73550. 580-688-3658.
Will search UCC records. Property transfer searches available. **Other Phone Numbers:** Assessor 580-882-2529; Treasurer 580-882-3566.

Harper County

County Clerk, P.O. Box 369, Buffalo, OK 73834. 580-735-2012.
Will search UCC records. UCC search includes tax liens if requested. Will not search real estate records. **Other Phone Numbers:** Assessor 580-735-2343; Treasurer 580-735-2442.

Haskell County

County Clerk, 202 East Main, Courthouse, Stigler, OK 74462. County Clerk, R/E and UCC Recording 918-967-2884; Fax 918-967-2885.
Will search UCC records. Will not search real estate records. **Other Phone Numbers:** Assessor 918-967-2611; Treasurer 918-967-2441; Appraiser/Auditor 918-967-8792.

Hughes County

County Clerk, 200 North Broadway ST. #5, Holdenville, OK 74848-3400. 405-379-5487; Fax 405-379-6890.
Will search UCC records. UCC search includes tax liens if requested. Will not search real estate records. **Other Phone Numbers:** Assessor 405-379-3862; Treasurer 405-379-5371; Elections 405-379-2174.

Jackson County

County Clerk, P.O. Box 515, Altus, OK 73522. County Clerk, R/E and UCC Recording 580-482-4070.
Will search UCC records. UCC search includes tax liens if requested. RE owner, mortgage, and property transfer searches available. Legal description of property required **Other Phone Numbers:** Assessor 580-482-0787; Treasurer 580-482-4371; Elections 580-482-2370; Vital Records 580-482-4070.

Jefferson County

County Clerk, 220 North Main, Courthouse - Room 103, Waurika, OK 73573. County Clerk, R/E and UCC Recording 580-228-2029; Fax 580-228-3418.
Will search UCC records. Will not search real estate records. **Other Phone Numbers:** Assessor 580-228-2377; Treasurer 580-228-2967.

Johnston County

County Clerk, 414 West Main, Room 101, Tishomingo, OK 73460. County Clerk, R/E and UCC Recording 580-371-3184.
Will search UCC records. UCC search includes tax liens if requested. $3.00 per name for uncertified verbal search RE owner, mortgage, and property transfer searches available. **Other Phone Numbers:** Assessor 580-371-3645; Treasurer 580-371-3082; Elections 580-371-3670.

Kay County

County Clerk, P.O. Box 450, Newkirk, OK 74647-0450. County Clerk, R/E and UCC Recording 580-362-2537; Fax 580-362-3300.
Will search UCC records. Real estate lands records search by mail or phone is free. **Other Phone Numbers:** Assessor 580-362-2566; Treasurer 580-362-2523; Elections 580-362-2130.

Kingfisher County

County Clerk, 101 South Main, Room #3, Kingfisher, OK 73750. 405-375-3887; Fax 405-375-6033.
Will search UCC records. **Other Phone Numbers:** Assessor 405-375-3884.

Kiowa County

County Clerk, P.O. Box 73, Hobart, OK 73651-0073. 580-726-5286; Fax 580-726-6033.
Will search UCC records. **Other Phone Numbers:** Assessor 580-726-2150; Treasurer 580-726-2362.

Latimer County

County Clerk, 109 North Central, Room 103, Wilburton, OK 74578. 918-465-3543; Fax 918-465-4001.
Will search UCC records. **Other Phone Numbers:** Assessor 918-465-3031; Treasurer 918-465-3450.

Le Flore County

County Clerk, P.O. Box 218, Poteau, OK 74953-0218. 918-647-5738; Fax 918-647-8930.
Will search UCC records. **Other Phone Numbers:** Assessor 918-647-3652; Treasurer 918-647-3525.

Lincoln County

County Clerk, P.O. Box 126, Chandler, OK 74834-0126. County Clerk, R/E and UCC Recording 405-258-1264.
Will search UCC records. Tax liens not included in UCC search. Property transfer searches available. **Other Phone Numbers:** Assessor 405-258-1209; Treasurer 405-258-1491; Elections 405-258-1349.

Logan County

County Clerk, 301 East Harrison, Suite 102, Guthrie, OK 73044-4999. County Clerk, R/E and UCC Recording 405-282-0266; Fax 405-282-0267.
Will search UCC records prior to 7/1/2001. UCC search includes tax liens if requested. **Other Phone Numbers:** Assessor 405-282-3509; Treasurer 405-282-3150; Elections 405-282-1900; Vital Records 405-271-4040.

Love County

County Clerk, 405 West Main, Room 203, Marietta, OK 73448. 580-276-3059.
Will search UCC records. UCC search includes tax liens if requested. Will not search real estate records. **Other Phone Numbers:** Assessor 580-276-3059; Treasurer 580-276-2360.

Major County

County Clerk, P.O. Box 379, Fairview, OK 73737-0379. 580-227-4732 R/E Recording: 580-227-3918 UCC Recording: 580-227-3918; Fax 580-227-2736.
Will search UCC records. This agency will not do a tax lien search. Will not search real estate records. **Other Phone Numbers:** Assessor 580-227-4821; Treasurer 580-227-4782.

Marshall County

County Clerk, Marshall County Courthouse, Room 101, Madill, OK 73446. County Clerk, R/E and UCC Recording 580-795-3220; Fax 580-795-7596.

Will search UCC records. UCC search includes tax liens if requested. Re record owner searches available. Legal description and name required. **Other Phone Numbers:** Assessor 580-795-2398; Treasurer 580-792-2463; Appraiser/Auditor 580-795-2398; Elections 580-795-5460.

Mayes County

County Clerk, P.O. Box 97, Pryor, OK 74362. County Clerk, R/E and UCC Recording 918-825-2426; Fax 918-825-3803.
Will search UCC records. Will not search real estate records. **Other Phone Numbers:** Assessor 918-825-0625; Treasurer 918-825-0160; Appraiser/Auditor 918-825-0625; Elections 918-825-1826.

McClain County

County Clerk, P.O. Box 629, Purcell, OK 73080-0629, 405-527-3360.
Will search UCC records. This agency will not do a tax lien search. RE owner, mortgage, and property transfer searches available. **Other Phone Numbers:** Assessor 405-527-3250; Treasurer 405-527-3261.

McCurtain County

County Clerk, P.O. Box 1078, Idabel, OK 74745. County Clerk, R/E and UCC Recording 580-286-2370.
Will search UCC records. UCC search includes tax liens. Will not search real estate records. **Other Phone Numbers:** Assessor 580-286-5272; Treasurer 580-286-5128; Elections 580-286-7405.

McIntosh County

County Clerk, P.O. Box 110, Eufaula, OK 74432-0110. 918-689-5419; Fax 918-689-3385.
Will search UCC records. Will not search real estate records. **Other Phone Numbers:** Assessor 918-689-5419; Treasurer 918-689-2491.

Murray County

County Clerk, P.O. Box 442, Sulphur, OK 73086. County Clerk, R/E and UCC Recording 580-622-3920; Fax 580-622-6209.
Will search UCC records. Will not search real estate records. **Other Phone Numbers:** Assessor 580-622-3433; Treasurer 580-622-5622; Elections 580-622-3920.

Muskogee County

County Clerk, P.O. Box 1008, Muskogee, OK 74401. 918-682-7781.
Will search UCC records. Tax liens not included in UCC search. Will not search real estate records. **Other Phone Numbers:** Assessor 918-682-8781; Treasurer 918-682-0811.

Noble County

County Clerk, 300 Courthouse Dr, Box 11, Courthouse, Box 11, Room 201, Perry, OK 73077. County Clerk, R/E and UCC Recording 580-336-2141; Fax 580-336-2481.
Will search UCC records. Will not search real estate records. **Other Phone Numbers:** Assessor 580-336-2185; Treasurer 580-336-2026; Elections 580-336-3527.

Nowata County

County Clerk, 229 North Maple, Nowata, OK 74048. County Clerk, R/E and UCC Recording 918-273-2480; Fax 918-273-2481.
Will search UCC records. This agency will not do a tax lien search. Will not search real estate records. **Other Phone Numbers:** Assessor 918-273-0581; Treasurer 918-273-3562; Elections 918-273-0710; Vital Records 918-273-0127.

Okfuskee County

County Clerk, P.O. Box 108, Okemah, OK 74859-0108. County Clerk, R/E and UCC Recording 918-623-1724; Fax 918-623-0739.
Will search UCC records. Will not search real estate records. **Other Phone Numbers:** Assessor 918-623-1535; Treasurer 918-623-1494.

Oklahoma County

County Clerk, 320 Robert S. Kerr Avenue, Courthouse - Room 107, Oklahoma City, OK 73102. 405-278-1538 R/E Recording: 405-713-1540 UCC Recording: 405-713-1522; Fax 405-278-2241.
http://www.oklahomacounty.org
Will search UCC records. Will not search real estate records. **Online Access:** Real Estate, Assessor, Grantor/Grantee, UCC. Assessor and property information on the county assessor database are available free online at www.oklahomacounty.org/assessor/disclaim.htm. Real estate, UCC, grantor/grantee records on the county clerk database are available free online at www.oklahomacounty.org/coclerk. **Other Phone Numbers:** Assessor 405-278-3838; Treasurer 405-713-1300; Appraiser/Auditor 405-713-1200; Elections 405-713-1515.

Okmulgee County

County Clerk, P.O. Box 904, Okmulgee, OK 74447-0904. County Clerk, R/E and UCC Recording 918-756-0788; Fax 918-758-1261.
Will search UCC records. Will search real estate records @ $5.00 per search. If extensive, an hourly rate will be charged. **Other Phone Numbers:** Assessor 918-758-1205; Treasurer 918-756-3848; Elections 918-756-2365.

Osage County

County Clerk, P.O. Box 87, Pawhuska, OK 74056. County Clerk, R/E and UCC Recording 918-287-3136; Fax 918-287-4979.
Will search UCC records. This agency will not do a tax lien search. Will not search real estate records. **Other Phone Numbers:** Assessor 918-287-3448; Treasurer 918-287-3101; Appraiser/Auditor 918-287-3448; Elections 918-287-3036.

Ottawa County

County Clerk, 102 E. Central, Suite 203, Miami, OK 74354-7043. County Clerk, R/E and UCC Recording 918-542-3332; Fax 918-542-8260.
Will search UCC records. This agency will not do a tax lien search. Will not search real estate records. **Other Phone Numbers:** Assessor 918-542-9418; Treasurer 918-542-8232; Elections 918-542-2893; Vital Records 918-571-2600.

Pawnee County

County Clerk, Courthouse, Room 202, 500 Harrison St., Pawnee, OK 74058. County Clerk, R/E and UCC Recording 918-762-2732.
Will search UCC records. Tax liens included in UCC search. Will not search real estate records. **Other Phone Numbers:** Assessor 918-762-2402; Treasurer 918-762-2418; Elections 918-762-2125.

Payne County

County Clerk, P.O. Box 7, Stillwater, OK 74076-0007. 405-747-8310.
Will search UCC records. This agency will not do a tax lien search. Will not search real estate records. **Other Phone Numbers:** Assessor 405-742-8300; Treasurer 405-747-9411.

Pittsburg County

County Clerk, P.O. Box 3304, McAlester, OK 74502. 918-423-6865; Fax 918-423-7304.
Will search UCC records. **Other Phone Numbers:** Assessor 918-423-4726; Treasurer 918-423-6895.

Pontotoc County

County Clerk, P.O. Box 1425, Ada, OK 74820. County Clerk, R/E and UCC Recording 580-332-1425; Fax 580-332-9509.
Will search UCC records. Will not search real estate records. **Other Phone Numbers:** Assessor 580-332-0317; Treasurer 580-332-0183; Vital Records 405-271-5600.

Pottawatomie County

County Clerk, P.O. Box 576, Shawnee, OK 74802. 405-273-8222; Fax 405-275-6898.
Will search UCC records. **Other Phone Numbers:** Assessor 405-275-4740; Treasurer 405-273-0213.

Pushmataha County

County Clerk, 302 SW 'B', Antlers, OK 74523. County Clerk, R/E and UCC Recording 580-298-3626; Fax 580-298-3626.
Will search UCC records. This agency will not do a tax lien search. Will not search real estate records. **Other Phone Numbers:** Assessor 580-298-3503; Treasurer 580-298-2580; Appraiser/Auditor 580-298-3504; Elections 580-298-3292.

Roger Mills County

County Clerk, P.O. Box 708, Cheyenne, OK 73628. 580-497-3395; Fax 580-497-3488.
Will search UCC records. This agency will not do a tax lien search. Will not search real estate records. **Other Phone Numbers:** Assessor 580-497-3350; Treasurer 580-497-3349.

Rogers County

County Clerk, P.O. Box 1210, Claremore, OK 74018. 918-341-1860 R/E Recording: 918-341-2518 UCC Recording: 918-341-2518; Fax 918-341-4529.
Will search UCC records. This agency will not do a tax lien search. Will not search real estate records. **Other Phone Numbers:** Assessor 918-341-3290; Treasurer 918-341-3159.

Seminole County

County Clerk, P.O. Box 1180, Wewoka, OK 74884. 405-257-2501; Fax 405-257-6422.
Will search UCC records. Will not search real estate records. **Other Phone Numbers:** Assessor 405-257-3371; Treasurer 405-257-6262.

Sequoyah County

County Clerk, 120 East Chickasaw, Sallisaw, OK 74955. 918-775-4516; Fax 918-775-1218.
Will search UCC records. Will not search real estate records. **Other Phone Numbers:** Assessor 918-775-2062.

Stephens County

County Clerk, 101 S. 11th St., Room 203, Duncan, OK 73533-4758. 580-255-0977; Fax 580-255-0991.
Will search UCC records. Will not search real estate records. **Other Phone Numbers:** Assessor 580-255-1542; Treasurer 580-255-0728.

Texas County

County Clerk, P.O. Box 197, Guymon, OK 73942-0197. County Clerk, R/E and UCC Recording 580-338-3141.

Will search UCC records. This agency will not do a tax lien search. Will not search real estate records. **Other Phone Numbers:** Assessor 580-338-3060; Treasurer 580-338-7050; Elections 580-338-7644; Vital Records 405-271-4040.

Tillman County

County Clerk, P.O. Box 992, Frederick, OK 73542. County Clerk, R/E and UCC Recording 580-335-3421; Fax 580-335-3795. www.oklahomacounty.org/countyclerk
Will search UCC records. Will not search real estate records. **Other Phone Numbers:** Assessor 580-335-3424; Treasurer 580-335-3425; Elections 580-335-2287; Vital Records 405-271-4040.

Tulsa County

County Clerk, 500 South Denver Avenue, County Admin. Bldg.-Room 112, Tulsa, OK 74103-3832. 918-596-5801; Fax 918-596-5867.
Will search UCC records. Will not search real estate records. **Other Phone Numbers:** Assessor 918-596-5828; Treasurer 918-596-5030.

Wagoner County

County Clerk, P.O. Box 156, Wagoner, OK 74477. County Clerk, R/E and UCC Recording 918-485-2216; Fax 918-485-8677.
Will search UCC records. Will not search real estate records. **Other Phone Numbers:** Assessor 918-485-2367; Treasurer 918-485-2149; Elections 918-485-2142.

Washington County

County Clerk, 420 South Johnstone, Room 102, Bartlesville, OK 74003. 918-337-2840; Fax 918-337-2894.
Will search UCC records. Will not search real estate records. **Other Phone Numbers:** Assessor 918-337-2830.

Washita County

County Clerk, P.O. Box 380, Cordell, OK 73632. 580-832-3548.
Will search UCC records. This agency will not do a tax lien search. Will not search real estate records. **Other Phone Numbers:** Assessor 580-832-2468; Treasurer 580-832-2667.

Woods County

County Clerk, P.O. Box 386, Alva, OK 73717-0386. 580-327-0998 R/E Recording: 580-327-6228; Fax 580-327-6230.
Will search UCC records. UCC search includes tax liens if requested. RE owner, mortgage, and property transfer searches available. **Other Phone Numbers:** Assessor 580-327-3118; Treasurer 580-327-0308; Elections 580-327-1452.

Woodward County

County Clerk, 1600 Main St, Ste. 8, Woodward, OK 73801-3051. 580-254-6800.
Will search UCC records. This agency will not do a tax lien search. Will not search real estate records. **Other Phone Numbers:** Assessor 580-254-5061; Treasurer 580-254-7404.

Oklahoma County Locator

You will usually be able to find the city name in the City/County Cross Reference below. In that case, it is a simple matter to determine the county from the cross reference. However, only the official US Postal Service city names are included in this index. There are an additional 40,000 place names that people use in their addresses. Therefore, we have also included a ZIP/City Cross Reference immediately following the City/County Cross Reference.

If you know the ZIP Code but the city name does not appear in the City/County Cross Reference index, look up the ZIP Code in the ZIP/City Cross Reference, find the city name, then look up the city name in the City/County Cross Reference. For example, you want to know the county for an address of Menands, NY 12204. There is no "Menands" in the City/County Cross Reference. The ZIP/City Cross Reference shows that ZIP Codes 12201-12288 are for the city of Albany. Looking back in the City/County Cross Reference, Albany is in Albany County.

City/County Cross Reference

ACHILLE Bryan
ADA Pontotoc
ADAIR Mayes
ADAMS Texas
ADDINGTON Jefferson
AFTON (74331) Delaware(72), Ottawa(26), Craig(2)
AGRA (74824) Lincoln(84), Payne(16)
ALBANY Bryan
ALBERT Caddo
ALBION Pushmataha
ALDERSON Pittsburg
ALEX (73002) Grady(89), McClain(12)
ALINE (73716) Alfalfa(57), Woods(36), Major(7)
ALLEN (74825) Pontotoc(69), Hughes(27), Coal(4)
ALTUS Jackson
ALTUS AFB Jackson
ALVA Woods
AMBER Grady
AMES (73718) Major(89), Garfield(9), Kingfisher(2)
AMORITA Alfalfa
ANADARKO Caddo
ANTLERS Pushmataha
APACHE (73006) Caddo(66), Comanche(34)
ARAPAHO Custer
ARCADIA (73007) Oklahoma(64), Logan(36)
ARDMORE Carter
ARKOMA Le Flore
ARNETT (73832) Ellis(90), Woodward(11)
ASHER Pottawatomie
ATOKA Atoka
ATWOOD Hughes
AVANT Osage
BACHE Pittsburg
BALKO Beaver
BARNSDALL Osage
BARTLESVILLE (74003) Washington(90), Osage(10)
BARTLESVILLE Washington
BATTIEST McCurtain
BEAVER Beaver
BEGGS Okmulgee
BENNINGTON Bryan
BESSIE Washita
BETHANY Oklahoma
BETHEL McCurtain
BIG CABIN (74332) Craig(51), Mayes(27), Rogers(21)
BILLINGS (74630) Noble(85), Garfield(15)
BINGER Caddo
BISON Garfield
BIXBY Tulsa
BLACKWELL Kay
BLAIR Jackson
BLANCHARD (73010) McClain(54), Grady(46)
BLANCO Pittsburg
BLOCKER Pittsburg

BLUEJACKET (74333) Ottawa(56), Craig(44)
BOISE CITY Cimarron
BOKCHITO Bryan
BOKOSHE Le Flore
BOLEY Okfuskee
BOSWELL (74727) Choctaw(84), Bryan(10), Atoka(6)
BOWLEGS Seminole
BOWRING Osage
BOYNTON (74422) Muskogee(65), Okmulgee(36)
BRADLEY Grady
BRAGGS Muskogee
BRAMAN Kay
BRAY (73012) McClain(50), Stephens(50)
BRISTOW Creek
BROKEN ARROW (74014) Wagoner(99), Tulsa(1)
BROKEN ARROW Tulsa
BROKEN BOW McCurtain
BROMIDE Johnston
BUFFALO Harper
BUNCH (74931) Adair(67), Cherokee(25), Sequoyah(9)
BURBANK Osage
BURLINGTON Alfalfa
BURNEYVILLE Love
BURNS FLAT Washita
BUTLER Custer
BYARS (74831) McClain(89), Pontotoc(9), Garvin(2)
BYRON Alfalfa
CACHE Comanche
CADDO (74729) Bryan(58), Atoka(42)
CALERA Bryan
CALUMET Canadian
CALVIN Hughes
CAMARGO Dewey
CAMERON Le Flore
CANADIAN Pittsburg
CANEY Atoka
CANTON (73724) Blaine(61), Dewey(39)
CANUTE Washita
CAPRON (73725) Woods(80), Alfalfa(20)
CARDIN Ottawa
CARMEN (73726) Alfalfa(78), Woods(22)
CARNEGIE (73015) Caddo(90), Washita(10)
CARNEY Lincoln
CARRIER Garfield
CARTER Beckham
CARTWRIGHT Bryan
CASHION (73016) Kingfisher(59), Logan(38), Canadian(4)
CASTLE Okfuskee
CATOOSA Rogers
CEMENT (73017) Grady(50), Caddo(46), Comanche(4)
CENTRAHOMA Coal
CHANDLER Lincoln
CHATTANOOGA Comanche
CHECOTAH McIntosh

CHELSEA (74016) Rogers(85), Mayes(7), Nowata(5), Craig(3)
CHEROKEE Alfalfa
CHESTER (73838) Major(90), Woodward(10)
CHEYENNE Roger Mills
CHICKASHA Grady
CHOCTAW Oklahoma
CHOUTEAU (74337) Mayes(90), Wagoner(10)
CLAREMORE Rogers
CLARITA Coal
CLAYTON (74536) Pushmataha(97), Latimer(2), Pittsburg(2)
CLEARVIEW Okfuskee
CLEO SPRINGS (73729) Major(84), Woods(13), Alfalfa(2)
CLEVELAND Pawnee
CLINTON (73601) Custer(98), Washita(3)
COALGATE Coal
COLBERT Bryan
COLCORD Delaware
COLEMAN Johnston
COLLINSVILLE (74021) Tulsa(76), Rogers(20), Washington(4)
COLONY (73021) Washita(66), Caddo(34)
COMANCHE Stephens
COMMERCE Ottawa
CONCHO Canadian
CONNERVILLE Johnston
COOKSON Cherokee
COPAN (74022) Washington(95), Osage(5)
CORDELL Washita
CORN Washita
COUNCIL HILL (74428) McIntosh(59), Muskogee(41)
COUNTYLINE Stephens
COVINGTON Garfield
COWETA Wagoner
COYLE (73027) Logan(66), Payne(34)
CRAWFORD Roger Mills
CRESCENT (73028) Logan(89), Kingfisher(11)
CROMWELL Seminole
CROWDER Pittsburg
CUSHING (74023) Payne(93), Lincoln(7)
CUSTER CITY Custer
CYRIL Caddo
DACOMA (73731) Woods(95), Alfalfa(6)
DAISY (74540) Pushmataha(55), Atoka(46)
DAVENPORT Lincoln
DAVIDSON Tillman
DAVIS (73030) Murray(98), Garvin(3)
DEER CREEK Grant
DELAWARE Nowata
DEPEW (74028) Creek(99), Lincoln(1)
DEVOL (73531) Cotton(99), McClain(1)
DEWAR Okmulgee
DEWEY Washington
DIBBLE McClain
DILL CITY Washita
DISNEY Mayes
DOUGHERTY Murray

DOUGLAS Garfield
DOVER Kingfisher
DRUMMOND (73735) Garfield(95), Major(5)
DRUMRIGHT (74030) Creek(98), Payne(2)
DUKE Jackson
DUNCAN Stephens
DURANT Bryan
DURHAM Roger Mills
DUSTIN (74839) Hughes(65), Okfuskee(24), McIntosh(11)
EAGLETOWN McCurtain
EAKLY Caddo
EARLSBORO (74840) Seminole(52), Pottawatomie(48)
EDMOND (73003) Oklahoma(87), Logan(13)
EDMOND (73034) Oklahoma(82), Logan(18)
EDMOND Oklahoma
EL RENO Canadian
ELDORADO (73537) Jackson(91), Harmon(9)
ELGIN Comanche
ELK CITY (73644) Beckham(98), Washita(2)
ELK CITY Beckham
ELMER Jackson
ELMORE CITY Garvin
ENID Garfield
ERICK Beckham
EUCHA Delaware
EUFAULA (74432) McIntosh(92), Pittsburg(8)
FAIRFAX Osage
FAIRLAND Ottawa
FAIRMONT Garfield
FAIRVIEW Major
FANSHAWE Le Flore
FARGO (73840) Ellis(65), Woodward(35)
FAXON Comanche
FAY (73646) Blaine(44), Dewey(41), Custer(15)
FELT Cimarron
FINLEY Pushmataha
FITTSTOWN Johnston
FITTSTOWN Pontotoc
FITZHUGH Pontotoc
FLETCHER Comanche
FORGAN Beaver
FORT COBB Caddo
FORT GIBSON (74434) Muskogee(85), Cherokee(8), Wagoner(7)
FORT SILL Comanche
FORT SUPPLY Woodward
FORT TOWSON (74735) Choctaw(73), Pushmataha(27)
FOSS (73647) Washita(84), Custer(16)
FOSTER (73039) Stephens(69), Garvin(31)
FOX Carter
FOYIL Rogers
FRANCIS Pontotoc
FREDERICK Tillman

FREEDOM (73842) Woods(64), Woodward(26), Harper(10)
GAGE (73843) Ellis(96), Beaver(4)
GANS Sequoyah
GARBER Garfield
GARVIN McCurtain
GATE (73844) Beaver(65), Harper(35)
GEARY (73040) Blaine(77), Canadian(23)
GENE AUTRY Carter
GERONIMO Comanche
GLENCOE (74032) Payne(76), Pawnee(15), Noble(8)
GLENPOOL (74033) Tulsa(98), Creek(2)
GOLDEN McCurtain
GOLTRY (73739) Alfalfa(78), Garfield(22)
GOODWELL Texas
GORE (74435) Sequoyah(88), Muskogee(12)
GOTEBO (73041) Kiowa(73), Washita(28)
GOULD Harmon
GOWEN Latimer
GRACEMONT Caddo
GRAHAM Carter
GRANDFIELD Tillman
GRANITE Greer
GRANT Choctaw
GREENFIELD Blaine
GROVE (74344) Delaware(98), Ottawa(1)
GROVE Delaware
GUTHRIE Logan
GUYMON Texas
HAILEYVILLE Pittsburg
HALLETT Pawnee
HAMMON (73650) Roger Mills(76), Custer(24)
HANNA McIntosh
HARDESTY Texas
HARRAH (73045) Oklahoma(70), Lincoln(26), Pottawatomie(4)
HARTSHORNE (74547) Pittsburg(98), Latimer(2)
HASKELL (74436) Muskogee(72), Wagoner(23), Okmulgee(5)
HASTINGS (73548) Stephens(43), Jefferson(30), Cotton(27)
HAWORTH McCurtain
HAYWOOD Pittsburg
HEADRICK Jackson
HEALDTON Carter
HEAVENER Le Flore
HELENA Alfalfa
HENDRIX Bryan
HENNEPIN (73046) Carter(57), Garvin(36), Murray(7)
HENNESSEY (73742) Kingfisher(97), Garfield(3)
HENRYETTA (74437) Okmulgee(99), McIntosh(1)
HILLSDALE Garfield
HINTON (73047) Caddo(73), Canadian(27)
HITCHCOCK (73744) Blaine(92), Kingfisher(8)
HITCHITA McIntosh
HOBART Kiowa
HODGEN Le Flore
HOLDENVILLE (74848) Hughes(98), Seminole(2)
HOLLIS Harmon
HOLLISTER Tillman
HOMINY Osage
HONOBIA (74549) Le Flore(89), Pushmataha(11)
HOOKER Texas
HOPETON Woods
HOWE Le Flore
HOYT Haskell
HUGO Choctaw
HULBERT Cherokee
HUNTER (74640) Garfield(79), Grant(21)
HYDRO (73048) Caddo(52), Custer(30), Blaine(18)
IDABEL McCurtain

INDIAHOMA Comanche
INDIANOLA Pittsburg
INOLA (74036) Rogers(89), Mayes(7), Wagoner(5)
ISABELLA Major
JAY Delaware
JENKS Tulsa
JENNINGS (74038) Pawnee(58), Creek(42)
JET Alfalfa
JONES Oklahoma
KANSAS (74347) Delaware(56), Adair(43)
KAW CITY Kay
KELLYVILLE Creek
KEMP Bryan
KENEFIC (74748) Johnston(59), Atoka(23), Bryan(18)
KENTON Cimarron
KEOTA (74941) Haskell(72), Le Flore(28)
KETCHUM Mayes
KEYES Cimarron
KIEFER Creek
KINGFISHER Kingfisher
KINGSTON Marshall
KINTA Haskell
KIOWA (74553) Pittsburg(70), Atoka(30)
KNOWLES Beaver
KONAWA (74849) Seminole(86), Pottawatomie(14)
KREBS Pittsburg
KREMLIN Garfield
LAHOMA (73754) Garfield(76), Major(22), Alfalfa(2)
LAMAR Hughes
LAMONT (74643) Grant(92), Kay(8)
LANE Atoka
LANGLEY Mayes
LANGSTON Logan
LAVERNE Harper
LAWTON Comanche
LEBANON Marshall
LEEDEY (73654) Dewey(58), Roger Mills(29), Custer(12)
LEFLORE Le Flore
LEHIGH Atoka
LENAPAH Nowata
LEON Love
LEONARD Tulsa
LEQUIRE Haskell
LEXINGTON Cleveland
LINDSAY (73052) Garvin(92), McClain(6), Stephens(1), Grady(1)
LOCO Stephens
LOCUST GROVE (74352) Mayes(77), Sequoyah(10), Wagoner(8), Cherokee(5)
LOGAN Beaver
LONE GROVE Carter
LONE WOLF Kiowa
LONGDALE (73755) Blaine(61), Major(33), Dewey(6)
LOOKEBA Caddo
LOVELAND Tillman
LOYAL Kingfisher
LUCIEN (73757) Garfield(57), Noble(39), McClain(4)
LUTHER (73054) Oklahoma(79), Lincoln(12), Logan(10)
MACOMB Pottawatomie
MADILL Marshall
MANCHESTER (73758) Grant(81), Alfalfa(19)
MANGUM Greer
MANITOU Tillman
MANNFORD (74044) Creek(66), Pawnee(34)
MANNSVILLE Johnston
MARAMEC (74045) Pawnee(97), Payne(4)
MARBLE CITY Sequoyah
MARIETTA Love
MARLAND (74644) Noble(98), Pawnee(2)
MARLOW (73055) Stephens(91), Grady(6), Comanche(3)

MARSHALL (73056) Logan(51), Garfield(40), Kingfisher(9)
MARTHA Jackson
MAUD (74854) Pottawatomie(53), Seminole(47)
MAY Harper
MAYFIELD McClain
MAYSVILLE (73057) Garvin(71), McClain(29)
MAZIE Mayes
MC LOUD (74851) Pottawatomie(76), Lincoln(14), Cleveland(10)
MCALESTER Pittsburg
MCCURTAIN (74944) Haskell(76), Le Flore(24)
MEAD Bryan
MEDFORD Grant
MEDICINE PARK Comanche
MEEKER (74855) Lincoln(88), Pottawatomie(12)
MEERS Comanche
MENO (73760) Major(99), Alfalfa(1)
MERIDIAN Logan
MIAMI Ottawa
MILBURN Johnston
MILFAY Creek
MILL CREEK (74856) Johnston(77), Murray(23)
MILLERTON McCurtain
MINCO (73059) Grady(67), Caddo(29), Canadian(5)
MOFFETT Sequoyah
MONROE Le Flore
MOODYS Cherokee
MOORELAND Woodward
MORRIS Okmulgee
MORRISON (73061) Noble(84), Pawnee(17)
MOUNDS (74047) Creek(41), Tulsa(40), Okmulgee(19)
MOUNTAIN PARK (73559) Kiowa(99), McClain(1)
MOUNTAIN VIEW (73062) Kiowa(99), Comanche(1)
MOYERS Pushmataha
MULDROW Sequoyah
MULHALL (73063) Logan(77), Payne(23)
MUSE Le Flore
MUSKOGEE Muskogee
MUSTANG Canadian
MUTUAL Woodward
NARDIN (74646) Kay(91), Grant(10)
NASH (73761) Grant(93), Garfield(7)
NASHOBA Pushmataha
NEWALLA (74857) Cleveland(69), Oklahoma(30), Pottawatomie(1)
NEWCASTLE McClain
NEWKIRK Kay
NICOMA PARK Oklahoma
NINNEKAH Grady
NOBLE Cleveland
NORMAN (73072) Cleveland(95), McClain(5)
NORMAN Cleveland
NORTH MIAMI Ottawa
NOWATA Nowata
OAKHURST Tulsa
OAKS (74359) Delaware(75), Cherokee(25)
OAKWOOD (73658) Dewey(90), Blaine(10)
OCHELATA Washington
OILTON Creek
OKARCHE (73762) Kingfisher(70), Canadian(30)
OKAY Wagoner
OKEENE (73763) Blaine(95), Major(5)
OKEMAH (74859) Okfuskee(94), Seminole(6)
OKLAHOMA CITY (73159) Oklahoma(94), Canadian(6)
OKLAHOMA CITY (73169) Oklahoma(88), Cleveland(12)

OKLAHOMA CITY (73173) Cleveland(98), Oklahoma(2)
OKLAHOMA CITY Cleveland
OKLAHOMA CITY Oklahoma
OKMULGEE Okmulgee
OKTAHA Muskogee
OLUSTEE Jackson
OMEGA (73764) Blaine(57), Kingfisher(43)
OOLOGAH Rogers
ORLANDO (73073) Noble(38), Logan(32), Payne(22), Garfield(8)
OSAGE Osage
OSCAR Jefferson
OVERBROOK Love
OWASSO (74055) Tulsa(74), Rogers(26)
PADEN Okfuskee
PANAMA Le Flore
PANOLA Latimer
PAOLI (73074) Garvin(80), McClain(20)
PARK HILL Cherokee
PAULS VALLEY Garvin
PAWHUSKA Osage
PAWNEE Pawnee
PEGGS (74452) Cherokee(73), Mayes(27)
PERKINS (74059) Payne(92), Lincoln(7)
PERNELL Garvin
PERRY Noble
PHAROAH Okfuskee
PICHER Ottawa
PICKENS McCurtain
PIEDMONT (73078) Canadian(99), Oklahoma(1)
PITTSBURG (74560) Pittsburg(90), Atoka(10)
PLATTER Bryan
POCASSET (73079) Grady(84), Caddo(15)
POCOLA Le Flore
PONCA CITY (74604) Kay(66), Osage(34)
PONCA CITY Kay
POND CREEK Grant
PORTER Wagoner
PORUM (74455) Muskogee(83), McIntosh(17)
POTEAU Le Flore
PRAGUE (74864) Lincoln(74), Pottawatomie(26)
PRESTON Okmulgee
PROCTOR Adair
PRUE Osage
PRYOR Mayes
PURCELL McClain
PUTNAM (73659) Dewey(96), Custer(2), McClain(2)
QUAPAW Ottawa
QUINTON (74561) Pittsburg(65), Haskell(35)
RALSTON (74650) Osage(60), Pawnee(40)
RAMONA Washington
RANDLETT Cotton
RATLIFF CITY Carter
RATTAN Pushmataha
RAVIA (73455) Johnston(83), Murray(17)
RED OAK Latimer
RED ROCK (74651) Noble(96), Pawnee(4)
REDBIRD Wagoner
RENTIESVILLE McIntosh
REYDON Roger Mills
RINGLING Jefferson
RINGOLD (74754) McCurtain(68), Pushmataha(30), Choctaw(2)
RINGWOOD Major
RIPLEY Payne
ROCKY (73661) Washita(98), Kiowa(2)
ROFF (74865) Pontotoc(66), Murray(26), Garvin(8)
ROLAND Sequoyah
ROOSEVELT (73564) Kiowa(96), Comanche(3)
ROSE (74364) Delaware(43), Cherokee(29), Mayes(28)
ROSSTON (73855) Harper(98), Roger Mills(2)

RUFE McCurtain
RUSH SPRINGS Grady
RYAN Jefferson
S COFFEYVILLE (74072) Nowata(95), Craig(5)
SAINT LOUIS (74866) Pottawatomie(75), Pontotoc(25)
SALINA (74365) Mayes(88), Delaware(12)
SALLISAW Sequoyah
SAND SPRINGS (74063) Tulsa(84), Osage(14), Creek(2)
SAPULPA (74066) Creek(98), Tulsa(2)
SAPULPA Creek
SASAKWA (74867) Seminole(94), Hughes(5)
SAVANNA Pittsburg
SAWYER Choctaw
SAYRE (73662) Beckham(97), Roger Mills(3)
SCHULTER Okmulgee
SEILING (73663) Dewey(89), Major(6), Woodward(5)
SEMINOLE Seminole
SENTINEL Washita
SHADY POINT Le Flore
SHAMROCK Creek
SHARON Woodward
SHATTUCK Ellis
SHAWNEE Pottawatomie
SHIDLER (74652) Osage(96), Kay(4)
SKIATOOK (74070) Osage(52), Tulsa(41), Washington(8)
SLICK Creek
SMITHVILLE (74957) McCurtain(55), Le Flore(45)
SNOW Pushmataha
SNYDER (73566) Kiowa(99), Tillman(1)
SOPER Choctaw
SOUTHARD (73770) Blaine(86), Roger Mills(14)
SPARKS Lincoln
SPAVINAW (74366) Mayes(85), Delaware(15)

SPENCER Oklahoma
SPENCERVILLE (74760) Choctaw(62), Pushmataha(39)
SPERRY (74073) Tulsa(72), Osage(28)
SPIRO Le Flore
SPRINGER (73458) Carter(99), Grady(1)
STERLING (73567) Comanche(89), McClain(11)
STIDHAM McIntosh
STIGLER (74462) Haskell(98), Pittsburg(2)
STILLWATER Payne
STILWELL Adair
STONEWALL (74871) Pontotoc(83), Coal(10), Johnston(8)
STRANG (74367) Mayes(99), Pontotoc(1)
STRATFORD (74872) Garvin(78), Pontotoc(19), McClain(3)
STRINGTOWN Atoka
STROUD (74079) Lincoln(94), Okfuskee(3), Creek(2)
STUART (74570) Hughes(51), Pittsburg(47), Coal(1)
SULPHUR Murray
SWEETWATER Roger Mills
SWINK Choctaw
TAFT Muskogee
TAHLEQUAH Cherokee
TALALA (74080) Rogers(70), Washington(30)
TALIHINA (74571) Latimer(54), Le Flore(41), Pushmataha(5)
TALOGA Dewey
TATUMS Carter
TECUMSEH Pottawatomie
TEMPLE Cotton
TERLTON (74081) Pawnee(88), Creek(13)
TERRAL Jefferson
TEXHOMA (73949) Cimarron(55), Texas(45)
TEXOLA Beckham
THACKERVILLE Love
THOMAS (73669) Custer(95), Blaine(3), Dewey(3)

TIPTON Tillman
TISHOMINGO Johnston
TONKAWA (74653) Kay(99), Noble(1)
TRYON Lincoln
TULLAHASSEE Wagoner
TULSA (74106) Tulsa(92), Osage(8)
TULSA (74108) Tulsa(88), Wagoner(12)
TULSA (74116) Tulsa(59), Rogers(41)
TULSA (74126) Tulsa(91), Osage(9)
TULSA (74127) Tulsa(65), Osage(35)
TULSA (74132) Tulsa(63), Creek(37)
TULSA Creek
TULSA Tulsa
TUPELO Coal
TURPIN (73950) Beaver(82), Texas(18)
TUSKAHOMA (74574) Pushmataha(51), Latimer(49)
TUSSY Carter
TUTTLE Grady
TWIN OAKS Delaware
TYRONE Texas
UNION CITY Canadian
VALLIANT (74764) McCurtain(89), Choctaw(11)
VELMA Stephens
VERA Washington
VERDEN (73092) Grady(72), Caddo(28)
VERNON McIntosh
VIAN Sequoyah
VICI (73859) Dewey(76), Woodward(21), Ellis(3)
VINITA (74301) Craig(91), Mayes(8)
VINSON Harmon
WAGONER Wagoner
WAINWRIGHT Muskogee
WAKITA Grant
WALTERS Cotton
WANETTE (74878) Pottawatomie(84), Cleveland(16)
WANN (74083) Nowata(76), Washington(24)
WAPANUCKA Johnston

WARDVILLE (74576) Atoka(51), Pittsburg(49)
WARNER (74469) Muskogee(95), McIntosh(5)
WASHINGTON McClain
WASHITA Caddo
WATONGA Blaine
WATSON McCurtain
WATTS (74964) Adair(87), Delaware(13)
WAUKOMIS Garfield
WAURIKA Jefferson
WAYNE McClain
WAYNOKA (73860) Woods(91), Major(10)
WEATHERFORD (73096) Custer(97), Washita(2)
WEBBERS FALLS Muskogee
WELCH Craig
WELEETKA (74880) Okfuskee(89), Okmulgee(11)
WELLING Cherokee
WELLSTON (74881) Lincoln(90), Logan(6), Beckham(3)
WELTY Okfuskee
WESTVILLE Adair
WETUMKA (74883) Hughes(95), Okfuskee(5)
WEWOKA Seminole
WHEATLAND Oklahoma
WHITEFIELD Haskell
WHITESBORO Le Flore
WILBURTON Latimer
WILLOW (73673) Greer(80), Beckham(20)
WILSON (73463) Carter(96), Love(4)
WISTER (74966) Le Flore(90), Latimer(11)
WOODWARD Woodward
WRIGHT CITY McCurtain
WYANDOTTE (74370) Ottawa(92), Delaware(8)
WYNNEWOOD Garvin
WYNONA Osage
YALE (74085) Payne(98), Pawnee(1)
YUKON Canadian

ZIP/City Cross Reference

ZIP	City	ZIP	City	ZIP	City	ZIP	City
73001-73001	ALBERT	73038-73038	FORT COBB	73077-73077	PERRY	73443-73443	LONE GROVE
73002-73002	ALEX	73039-73039	FOSTER	73078-73078	PIEDMONT	73446-73446	MADILL
73003-73003	EDMOND	73040-73040	GEARY	73079-73079	POCASSET	73447-73447	MANNSVILLE
73004-73004	AMBER	73041-73041	GOTEBO	73080-73080	PURCELL	73448-73448	MARIETTA
73005-73005	ANADARKO	73042-73042	GRACEMONT	73081-73081	RATLIFF CITY	73449-73449	MEAD
73006-73006	APACHE	73043-73043	GREENFIELD	73082-73082	RUSH SPRINGS	73450-73450	MILBURN
73007-73007	ARCADIA	73044-73044	GUTHRIE	73083-73083	EDMOND	73453-73453	OVERBROOK
73008-73008	BETHANY	73045-73045	HARRAH	73084-73084	SPENCER	73455-73455	RAVIA
73009-73009	BINGER	73046-73046	HENNEPIN	73085-73085	YUKON	73456-73456	RINGLING
73010-73010	BLANCHARD	73047-73047	HINTON	73086-73086	SULPHUR	73458-73458	SPRINGER
73011-73011	BRADLEY	73048-73048	HYDRO	73087-73087	TATUMS	73459-73459	THACKERVILLE
73012-73012	BRAY	73049-73049	JONES	73088-73088	TUSSY	73460-73460	TISHOMINGO
73013-73013	EDMOND	73050-73050	LANGSTON	73089-73089	TUTTLE	73461-73461	WAPANUCKA
73014-73014	CALUMET	73051-73051	LEXINGTON	73090-73090	UNION CITY	73463-73463	WILSON
73015-73015	CARNEGIE	73052-73052	LINDSAY	73091-73091	VELMA	73501-73502	LAWTON
73016-73016	CASHION	73053-73053	LOOKEBA	73092-73092	VERDEN	73503-73503	FORT SILL
73017-73017	CEMENT	73054-73054	LUTHER	73093-73093	WASHINGTON	73505-73507	LAWTON
73018-73018	CHICKASHA	73055-73055	MARLOW	73094-73094	WASHITA	73520-73520	ADDINGTON
73019-73019	NORMAN	73056-73056	MARSHALL	73095-73095	WAYNE	73521-73522	ALTUS
73020-73020	CHOCTAW	73057-73057	MAYSVILLE	73096-73096	WEATHERFORD	73523-73523	ALTUS AFB
73021-73021	COLONY	73058-73058	MERIDIAN	73097-73097	WHEATLAND	73526-73526	BLAIR
73022-73022	CONCHO	73059-73059	MINCO	73098-73098	WYNNEWOOD	73527-73527	CACHE
73023-73023	CHICKASHA	73061-73061	MORRISON	73099-73099	YUKON	73528-73528	CHATTANOOGA
73024-73024	CORN	73062-73062	MOUNTAIN VIEW	73101-73199	OKLAHOMA CITY	73529-73529	COMANCHE
73025-73025	COUNTYLINE	73063-73063	MULHALL	73401-73403	ARDMORE	73530-73530	DAVIDSON
73027-73027	COYLE	73064-73064	MUSTANG	73430-73430	BURNEYVILLE	73531-73531	DEVOL
73028-73028	CRESCENT	73065-73065	NEWCASTLE	73432-73432	COLEMAN	73532-73532	DUKE
73029-73029	CYRIL	73066-73066	NICOMA PARK	73435-73435	FOX	73533-73536	DUNCAN
73030-73030	DAVIS	73067-73067	NINNEKAH	73436-73436	GENE AUTRY	73537-73537	ELDORADO
73031-73031	DIBBLE	73068-73068	NOBLE	73437-73437	GRAHAM	73538-73538	ELGIN
73032-73032	DOUGHERTY	73069-73069	NORMAN	73438-73438	HEALDTON	73539-73539	ELMER
73033-73033	EAKLY	73073-73073	ORLANDO	73439-73439	KINGSTON	73540-73540	FAXON
73034-73034	EDMOND	73074-73074	PAOLI	73440-73440	LEBANON	73541-73541	FLETCHER
73035-73035	ELMORE CITY	73075-73075	PAULS VALLEY	73441-73441	LEON	73542-73542	FREDERICK
73036-73036	EL RENO	73076-73076	PERNELL	73442-73442	LOCO	73543-73543	GERONIMO

Zip	Name	Zip	Name	Zip	Name	Zip	Name
73544-73544	GOULD	73737-73737	FAIRVIEW	74030-74030	DRUMRIGHT	74425-74425	CANADIAN
73546-73546	GRANDFIELD	73738-73738	GARBER	74031-74031	FOYIL	74426-74426	CHECOTAH
73547-73547	GRANITE	73739-73739	GOLTRY	74032-74032	GLENCOE	74427-74427	COOKSON
73548-73548	HASTINGS	73741-73741	HELENA	74033-74033	GLENPOOL	74428-74428	COUNCIL HILL
73549-73549	HEADRICK	73742-73742	HENNESSEY	74034-74034	HALLETT	74429-74429	COWETA
73550-73550	HOLLIS	73743-73743	HILLSDALE	74035-74035	HOMINY	74430-74430	CROWDER
73551-73551	HOLLISTER	73744-73744	HITCHCOCK	74036-74036	INOLA	74431-74431	DEWAR
73552-73552	INDIAHOMA	73746-73746	HOPETON	74037-74037	JENKS	74432-74432	EUFAULA
73553-73553	LOVELAND	73747-73747	ISABELLA	74038-74038	JENNINGS	74434-74434	FORT GIBSON
73554-73554	MANGUM	73749-73749	JET	74039-74039	KELLYVILLE	74435-74435	GORE
73555-73555	MANITOU	73750-73750	KINGFISHER	74041-74041	KIEFER	74436-74436	HASKELL
73556-73556	MARTHA	73753-73753	KREMLIN	74042-74042	LENAPAH	74437-74437	HENRYETTA
73557-73557	MEDICINE PARK	73754-73754	LAHOMA	74043-74043	LEONARD	74438-74438	HITCHITA
73558-73558	MEERS	73755-73755	LONGDALE	74044-74044	MANNFORD	74440-74440	HOYT
73559-73559	MOUNTAIN PARK	73756-73756	LOYAL	74045-74045	MARAMEC	74441-74441	HULBERT
73560-73560	OLUSTEE	73757-73757	LUCIEN	74046-74046	MILFAY	74442-74442	INDIANOLA
73561-73561	OSCAR	73758-73758	MANCHESTER	74047-74047	MOUNDS	74444-74444	MOODYS
73562-73562	RANDLETT	73759-73759	MEDFORD	74048-74048	NOWATA	74445-74445	MORRIS
73564-73564	ROOSEVELT	73760-73760	MENO	74050-74050	OAKHURST	74446-74446	OKAY
73565-73565	RYAN	73761-73761	NASH	74051-74051	OCHELATA	74447-74447	OKMULGEE
73566-73566	SNYDER	73762-73762	OKARCHE	74052-74052	OILTON	74450-74450	OKTAHA
73567-73567	STERLING	73763-73763	OKEENE	74053-74053	OOLOGAH	74451-74451	PARK HILL
73568-73568	TEMPLE	73764-73764	OMEGA	74054-74054	OSAGE	74452-74452	PEGGS
73569-73569	TERRAL	73766-73766	POND CREEK	74055-74055	OWASSO	74454-74454	PORTER
73570-73570	TIPTON	73768-73768	RINGWOOD	74056-74056	PAWHUSKA	74455-74455	PORUM
73571-73571	VINSON	73770-73770	SOUTHARD	74058-74058	PAWNEE	74456-74456	PRESTON
73572-73572	WALTERS	73771-73771	WAKITA	74059-74059	PERKINS	74457-74457	PROCTOR
73573-73573	WAURIKA	73772-73772	WATONGA	74060-74060	PRUE	74458-74458	REDBIRD
73575-73575	DUNCAN	73773-73773	WAUKOMIS	74061-74061	RAMONA	74459-74459	RENTIESVILLE
73601-73601	CLINTON	73801-73802	WOODWARD	74062-74062	RIPLEY	74460-74460	SCHULTER
73620-73620	ARAPAHO	73832-73832	ARNETT	74063-74063	SAND SPRINGS	74461-74461	STIDHAM
73622-73622	BESSIE	73834-73834	BUFFALO	74066-74067	SAPULPA	74462-74462	STIGLER
73624-73624	BURNS FLAT	73835-73835	CAMARGO	74068-74068	SHAMROCK	74463-74463	TAFT
73625-73625	BUTLER	73838-73838	CHESTER	74070-74070	SKIATOOK	74464-74465	TAHLEQUAH
73626-73626	CANUTE	73840-73840	FARGO	74071-74071	SLICK	74466-74466	TULLAHASSEE
73627-73627	CARTER	73841-73841	FORT SUPPLY	74072-74072	S COFFEYVILLE	74467-74467	WAGONER
73628-73628	CHEYENNE	73842-73842	FREEDOM	74073-74073	SPERRY	74468-74468	WAINWRIGHT
73632-73632	CORDELL	73843-73843	GAGE	74074-74078	STILLWATER	74469-74469	WARNER
73638-73638	CRAWFORD	73844-73844	GATE	74079-74079	STROUD	74470-74470	WEBBERS FALLS
73639-73639	CUSTER CITY	73847-73847	KNOWLES	74080-74080	TALALA	74471-74471	WELLING
73641-73641	DILL CITY	73848-73848	LAVERNE	74081-74081	TERLTON	74472-74472	WHITEFIELD
73642-73642	DURHAM	73851-73851	MAY	74082-74082	VERA	74477-74477	WAGONER
73644-73644	ELK CITY	73852-73852	MOORELAND	74083-74083	WANN	74501-74502	MCALESTER
73645-73645	ERICK	73853-73853	MUTUAL	74084-74084	WYNONA	74521-74521	ALBION
73646-73646	FAY	73855-73855	ROSSTON	74085-74085	YALE	74522-74522	ALDERSON
73647-73647	FOSS	73857-73857	SHARON	74101-74194	TULSA	74523-74523	ANTLERS
73648-73648	ELK CITY	73858-73858	SHATTUCK	74301-74301	VINITA	74525-74525	ATOKA
73650-73650	HAMMON	73859-73859	VICI	74330-74330	ADAIR	74528-74528	BLANCO
73651-73651	HOBART	73860-73860	WAYNOKA	74331-74331	AFTON	74529-74529	BLOCKER
73654-73654	LEEDEY	73901-73901	ADAMS	74332-74332	BIG CABIN	74530-74530	BROMIDE
73655-73655	LONE WOLF	73931-73931	BALKO	74333-74333	BLUEJACKET	74531-74531	CALVIN
73656-73656	MAYFIELD	73932-73932	BEAVER	74335-74335	CARDIN	74533-74533	CANEY
73658-73658	OAKWOOD	73933-73933	BOISE CITY	74337-74337	CHOUTEAU	74534-74534	CENTRAHOMA
73659-73659	PUTNAM	73937-73937	FELT	74338-74338	COLCORD	74535-74535	CLARITA
73660-73660	REYDON	73938-73938	FORGAN	74339-74339	COMMERCE	74536-74536	CLAYTON
73661-73661	ROCKY	73939-73939	GOODWELL	74340-74340	DISNEY	74538-74538	COALGATE
73662-73662	SAYRE	73942-73942	GUYMON	74342-74342	EUCHA	74540-74540	DAISY
73663-73663	SEILING	73944-73944	HARDESTY	74343-74343	FAIRLAND	74542-74542	ATOKA
73664-73664	SENTINEL	73945-73945	HOOKER	74344-74345	GROVE	74543-74543	FINLEY
73666-73666	SWEETWATER	73946-73946	KENTON	74346-74346	JAY	74545-74545	GOWEN
73667-73667	TALOGA	73947-73947	KEYES	74347-74347	KANSAS	74546-74546	HAILEYVILLE
73668-73668	TEXOLA	73949-73949	TEXHOMA	74349-74349	KETCHUM	74547-74547	HARTSHORNE
73669-73669	THOMAS	73950-73950	TURPIN	74350-74350	LANGLEY	74549-74549	HONOBIA
73673-73673	WILLOW	73951-73951	TYRONE	74352-74352	LOCUST GROVE	74552-74552	KINTA
73701-73706	ENID	74001-74001	AVANT	74353-74353	MAZIE	74553-74553	KIOWA
73716-73716	ALINE	74002-74002	BARNSDALL	74354-74355	MIAMI	74554-74554	KREBS
73717-73717	ALVA	74003-74006	BARTLESVILLE	74358-74358	NORTH MIAMI	74555-74555	LANE
73718-73718	AMES	74008-74008	BIXBY	74359-74359	OAKS	74556-74556	LEHIGH
73719-73719	AMORITA	74009-74009	BOWRING	74360-74360	PICHER	74557-74557	MOYERS
73720-73720	BISON	74010-74010	BRISTOW	74361-74362	PRYOR	74558-74558	NASHOBA
73722-73722	BURLINGTON	74011-74014	BROKEN ARROW	74363-74363	QUAPAW	74559-74559	PANOLA
73724-73724	CANTON	74015-74015	CATOOSA	74364-74364	ROSE	74560-74560	PITTSBURG
73726-73726	CARMEN	74016-74016	CHELSEA	74365-74365	SALINA	74561-74561	QUINTON
73727-73727	CARRIER	74017-74018	CLAREMORE	74366-74366	SPAVINAW	74562-74562	RATTAN
73728-73728	CHEROKEE	74020-74020	CLEVELAND	74367-74367	STRANG	74563-74563	RED OAK
73729-73729	CLEO SPRINGS	74021-74021	COLLINSVILLE	74368-74368	TWIN OAKS	74565-74565	SAVANNA
73730-73730	COVINGTON	74022-74022	COPAN	74369-74369	WELCH	74567-74567	SNOW
73731-73731	DACOMA	74023-74023	CUSHING	74370-74370	WYANDOTTE	74569-74569	STRINGTOWN
73733-73733	DOUGLAS	74026-74026	DAVENPORT	74401-74403	MUSKOGEE	74570-74570	STUART
73734-73734	DOVER	74027-74027	DELAWARE	74421-74421	BEGGS	74571-74571	TALIHINA
73735-73735	DRUMMOND	74028-74028	DEPEW	74422-74422	BOYNTON	74572-74572	TUPELO
73736-73736	FAIRMONT	74029-74029	DEWEY	74423-74423	BRAGGS	74574-74574	TUSKAHOMA

74576-74576	WARDVILLE	74735-74735	FORT TOWSON	74836-74836	CONNERVILLE	74901-74901	ARKOMA
74577-74577	WHITESBORO	74736-74736	GARVIN	74837-74837	CROMWELL	74902-74902	POCOLA
74578-74578	WILBURTON	74737-74737	GOLDEN	74839-74839	DUSTIN	74930-74930	BOKOSHE
74601-74604	PONCA CITY	74738-74738	GRANT	74840-74840	EARLSBORO	74931-74931	BUNCH
74630-74630	BILLINGS	74740-74740	HAWORTH	74842-74842	FITTSTOWN	74932-74932	CAMERON
74631-74631	BLACKWELL	74741-74741	HENDRIX	74843-74843	FITZHUGH	74935-74935	FANSHAWE
74632-74632	BRAMAN	74743-74743	HUGO	74844-74844	FRANCIS	74936-74936	GANS
74633-74633	BURBANK	74745-74745	IDABEL	74845-74845	HANNA	74937-74937	HEAVENER
74636-74636	DEER CREEK	74747-74747	KEMP	74848-74848	HOLDENVILLE	74939-74939	HODGEN
74637-74637	FAIRFAX	74748-74748	KENEFIC	74849-74849	KONAWA	74940-74940	HOWE
74640-74640	HUNTER	74750-74750	MILLERTON	74850-74850	LAMAR	74941-74941	KEOTA
74641-74641	KAW CITY	74752-74752	PICKENS	74851-74851	MC LOUD	74942-74942	LEFLORE
74643-74643	LAMONT	74753-74753	PLATTER	74852-74852	MACOMB	74943-74943	LEQUIRE
74644-74644	MARLAND	74754-74754	RINGOLD	74854-74854	MAUD	74944-74944	MCCURTAIN
74646-74646	NARDIN	74755-74755	RUFE	74855-74855	MEEKER	74945-74945	MARBLE CITY
74647-74647	NEWKIRK	74756-74756	SAWYER	74856-74856	MILL CREEK	74946-74946	MOFFETT
74650-74650	RALSTON	74759-74759	SOPER	74857-74857	NEWALLA	74947-74947	MONROE
74651-74651	RED ROCK	74760-74760	SPENCERVILLE	74859-74859	OKEMAH	74948-74948	MULDROW
74652-74652	SHIDLER	74761-74761	SWINK	74860-74860	PADEN	74949-74949	MUSE
74653-74653	TONKAWA	74764-74764	VALLIANT	74864-74864	PRAGUE	74951-74951	PANAMA
74701-74702	DURANT	74766-74766	WRIGHT CITY	74865-74865	ROFF	74953-74953	POTEAU
74720-74720	ACHILLE	74801-74802	SHAWNEE	74866-74866	SAINT LOUIS	74954-74954	ROLAND
74721-74721	ALBANY	74818-74818	SEMINOLE	74867-74867	SASAKWA	74955-74955	SALLISAW
74722-74722	BATTIEST	74820-74821	ADA	74868-74868	SEMINOLE	74956-74956	SHADY POINT
74723-74723	BENNINGTON	74824-74824	AGRA	74869-74869	SPARKS	74957-74957	SMITHVILLE
74724-74724	BETHEL	74825-74825	ALLEN	74871-74871	STONEWALL	74959-74959	SPIRO
74726-74726	BOKCHITO	74826-74826	ASHER	74872-74872	STRATFORD	74960-74960	STILWELL
74727-74727	BOSWELL	74827-74827	ATWOOD	74873-74873	TECUMSEH	74962-74962	VIAN
74728-74728	BROKEN BOW	74829-74829	BOLEY	74875-74875	TRYON	74963-74963	WATSON
74729-74729	CADDO	74830-74830	BOWLEGS	74878-74878	WANETTE	74964-74964	WATTS
74730-74730	CALERA	74831-74831	BYARS	74880-74880	WELEETKA	74965-74965	WESTVILLE
74731-74731	CARTWRIGHT	74832-74832	CARNEY	74881-74881	WELLSTON	74966-74966	WISTER
74733-74733	COLBERT	74833-74833	CASTLE	74883-74883	WETUMKA		
74734-74734	EAGLETOWN	74834-74834	CHANDLER	74884-74884	WEWOKA		

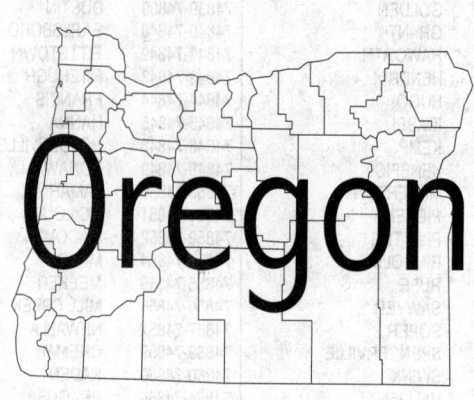

General Help Numbers:

Governor's Office

State Capitol Bldg.   503-378-4582
900 Court St NE   Fax 503-378-4863
Salem, OR 97301-4047   8AM-5PM
http://www.governor.state.or.us

Attorney General's Office

Department of Justice   503-378-4400
1162 Court St NE   Fax 503-378-4017
Salem, OR 97310   8AM-5PM
http://www.doj.state.or.us

State Court Administrator

Supreme Court Bldg, 1163 State St   503-986-5500
Salem, OR 97310   Fax 503-986-5503
http://www.ojd.state.or.us/osca   8AM-5PM

State Archives

Archives Division   503-373-0701
800 Summer St NE   Fax 503-373-0953
Salem, OR 97301   8AM-4:45PM
http://arcweb.sos.state.or.us

State Specifics:

Capital: Salem
                    Marion County

Time Zone: PST

Number of Counties: 36

Population: 3,421,399

Web Site: www.state.or.us

State Agencies

Criminal Records

Oregon State Police, Unit 11, Identification Services Section, PO Box 4395, Portland, OR 97208-4395 (Courier: 3772 Portland Rd NE, Bldg C, Salem, OR 97303); 503-378-3070, 503-378-2121 (Fax), 8AM-5PM.

http://www.osp.state.or.us

Indexing & Storage: Records are available from 1941 on and are computerized. Records are indexed on inhouse computer.

Searching: Information will include all convictions and all arrests within the past year

without disposition. Include the following in your request-name, date of birth. Submitting the SSN is helpful, but not required. If record exists, person of record will be notified of the request and the record will not be released for 14 additional days.

Access by: mail, fax, online.

Fee & Payment: Fee is $15.00 per individual name. If someone is submitting a search on oneself, the fee is $12.00 and fingerprints are required. $5.00 fee to notarize. Fee payee: Oregon State Police. Prepayment required. Personal checks accepted. No credit cards accepted.

Mail search: Clean records are returned in 7-10 days, records with activity take 3 weeks to return.A self addressed stamped envelope is requested.

Fax search: Requesters must be pre-approved.

Online search: A web based site is available for requesting and receiving criminal records. Use of this site is ONLY for high vol. requesters who must be pre-approved. Results are posted as "No Record" or "In Process" which means a record will be mailed in 14 days. Use the "open records" link to get into the proper site. Fee is $12.00 per record.

Call 503-373-1808, ext 230 to receive the application, or visit the web site.

Corporation Records
Limited Partnership Records
Trademarks/Servicemarks
Fictitious Name
Assumed Name
Limited Liability Company Records

Corporation Division, Public Service Building, 255 Capital St NE, #151, Salem, OR 97310-1327; 503-986-2200, 503-378-4381 (Fax), 8AM-5PM.

http://www.sos.state.or.us/corporation/corphp.htm

Indexing & Storage: Records are available on the computer screen for 10 years after inactive. Assumed names are only available for 5 years after inactive. The records prior to 20 years ago are stored in the State Archives back to the 1800's for corporations only. New records are available for inquiry immediately. Records are indexed on microfilm, inhouse computer.

Searching: All information is public record. Include the following in your request-full name of business. In addition to the articles of incorporation, corporation records include the following information: Annual Reports, Prior (merged) names, Articles of Amendment.

Access by: mail, phone, fax, in person, online.

Fee & Payment: There is no search fee. Copies cost $5.00 per business name or $15.00 if certified, otherwise there is a $1.00 fee per business name for a computer printout. A Good Standing certificate is $10.00. Fee payee: Corporation Division. Prepayment required. Personal checks accepted. Credit cards accepted: MasterCard, Visa.

Mail search: Turnaround time: 7 to 10 days. A self addressed stamped envelope is requested.

Phone search: There is a limit of 3 searches per phone call.

Fax search: Requesters must use a credit card, turnaround time is 5 days or less.

In person search: Turnaround time while you wait.

Online search: There is free, limited access at the web site for business registry information. A commercial dial-up system is alos available. Call 503-229-5133 for details. In addition, the complete database can be purchased with monthly updates via e-mail, call 503-986-2343.

Other access: A subscription service for new business lists and tapes of the database are available for $15.00 per month or $150.00 for an annual subscription. Call 503-986-2343 for more information.

Expedited service: Expedited service is available for phone and in person searches. Turnaround time: 1 day. They will ship overnight if you supply your shipper's account number. Fax requests are expedited only if phoned in first.

Uniform Commercial Code
Federal Tax Liens
State Tax Liens

UCC Division, Secretary of State, 255 Capitol St NE, Suite 151, Salem, OR 97310-1327; 503-986-2200, 503-373-1166 (Fax), 8AM-5PM.

http://www.sos.state.or.us/corporation/ucc/ucc.htm

Note: State tax liens on personal property are filed here; state tax liens on real property are filed at the county level.

Indexing & Storage: Records are available on microfiche. It takes 2 to 3 days before new records are available for inquiry.

Searching: Use search request form UCC-11. The search includes tax liens filed here. Include the following in your request-debtor name.

Access by: mail, phone, fax, in person, online.

Fee & Payment: The search fee is $10.00 per name. The copy fee is $5.00 per copy per name. The $5.00 copy fee is charged, whether or not copies are found. Microfilm service is $20.00 per reel. Special research projects are $20.00 per hour. Fee payee: Secretary of State. Prepayment required. Personal checks accepted. Credit cards accepted: MasterCard, Visa.

Mail search: Turnaround time: 1 to 4 days.

Phone search: Limited information is available.

Fax search: A credit card is required. Results are mailed.

In person search: Searching is available in person.

Online search: UCC index information can be obtained for free from the web site. You can search by debtor name or by lien number. You can also download forms from here.

Other access: Monthly UCC information can be on diskette or e-mail. Prices start at $15.00 per month or $150.00 annually. For more information, call Program Services at 503-986-2343.

Sales Tax Registrations
State does not impose sales tax.

Birth Certificates

Oregon State Health Division, Vital Records, PO Box 14050, Portland, OR 97293-0050 (Courier: 800 NE Oregon St, #205, Portland, OR 97232); 503-731-4095 (Recorded Message), 503-731-4108, 503-234-8417 (Fax), 8AM-4:30PM.

http://www.ohd.hr.state.or.us/chs/welcome.htm

Indexing & Storage: Records are available from July 1903 to present. There are some delayed filed records with DOBs from 1885 to 1902. There are no indexes available. Birth indexes prior to 1902 available at the State Archives. It takes 2 to 4 weeks before new records are available for inquiry.

Searching: Investigative searches must have a signed, notarized release form from person of record or immediate family member, unless record over 100 years old. Records only available to legal guardians & legal representatives with proof of such Include the following in your request-full name, names of parents, mother's maiden name, date of birth, place of birth, relationship to person of record. Must request "long form" if time of birth, hospital or physician's names is needed. The following data is not released: original records of adoption.

Access by: mail, phone, fax, in person.

Fee & Payment: The search fee is $15.00. Add $12 for each additional copy. Fee payee: Oregon Health Division. Prepayment required. Personal checks accepted. Credit cards accepted: MasterCard, Visa, AmEx, Discover.

Mail search: Turnaround time: 2 to 3 weeks. Express mail requests are handled immediately.No self addressed stamped envelope is required.

Phone search: Fax and phone orders are billed to credit cards and processed the next day. There is an additional $10.00 service fee.

Fax search: Same criteria as phone searching.

In person search: Turnaround time is under 20 minutes.

Expedited service: Expedited service is available for fax and phone searches. Turnaround time: overnight delivery. Orders are charged to credit cards. Fee depends on delivery service.

Death Records

Oregon State Health Division, Vital Records, PO Box 14050, Portland, OR 97293-0050 (Courier: 800 NE Oregon St, #205, Portland, OR 97232); 503-731-4095 (Recorded Message), 503-731-4108, 503-234-8417 (Fax), 8AM-4:30PM.

http://www.ohd.hr.state.or.us/chs/welcome.htm

Indexing & Storage: Records are available from July 1903 to present. It takes 2 to 4 weeks before new records are available for inquiry.

Searching: Investigative searches must have a signed, notarized release from immediate family member or legal representative or person with a personal property right. After 50 years, a record becomes public record and there are no restrictions. Include the following in your request-full name, date of death, place of death, relationship to person of record, reason for information request. The name of the spouse is helpful. The date of birth is helpful for common names.

Access by: mail, phone, fax, in person.

Fee & Payment: The search fee is $15.00 and additional copies are $12.00 each. Fee payee: Oregon Health Division. Prepayment required. Personal checks accepted. Credit cards accepted: MasterCard, Visa, AmEx, Discover.

Mail search: Turnaround time: 2 to 3 weeks. Express mail requests are processed immediately.No self addressed stamped envelope is required.

Phone search: Phone and fax orders require use of a credit card and an additional $10.00 service fee. Turnaround time is generally in 24 hours.

Fax search: Same criteria as phone searching.

In person search: Turnaround time is within 20 minutes.

Other access: Indexes are available at many state libraries.

Expedited service: Expedited service is available for fax and phone searches. Turnaround time: overnight delivery. Carrier chosen to return documents determines fees. Use of credit card is required.

Marriage Certificates

Oregon State Health Division, Vital Records, PO Box 14050, Portland, OR 97293-0050 (Courier: 800 NE Oregon St, #205, Portland, OR 97232); 503-731-4095 (Recorded Message), 503-731-4108, 503-234-8417 (Fax), 8AM-4:30PM.

http://www.ohd.hr.state.or.us/chs/welcome.htm

Indexing & Storage: Records are available from 1906 to 1925 and 1946 to 1960 on microfilm, from

1961 to 1996 on microfiche. It takes 4 to 8 weeks before new records are available for inquiry.

Searching: Records less than 50 years old are only available to family members, legal representatives or those with a personal or property right. Include the following in your request-names of husband and wife, date of marriage, place or county of marriage. Include daytime phone number and as many identifiers as possible.

Access by: mail, phone, fax, in person.

Fee & Payment: The search fee is $15.00, additional copies $12.00 per record. Fee payee: Oregon Health Division. Prepayment required. Personal checks accepted. Credit cards accepted: MasterCard, Visa, AmEx, Discover.

Mail search: Turnaround time: 2 to 3 weeks. If request is expressed, it will be answered ASAP.No self addressed stamped envelope is required.

Phone search: There is an additional $10.00 quick service search fee per telephone or fax order. Use of a credit card is required.

Fax search: Results are sent by mail. Turnaround time is next working day.

In person search: Turnaround time is usually within 20 minutes.

Other access: Many state libraries offer record indexes.

Expedited service: Expedited service is available for mail, phone and fax searches. Turnaround time: overnight delivery. Additional fees will be added, depending on carrier. For mail requests, enclose a prepaid, self-addressed envelope for overnight carrier.

Divorce Records

Oregon State Health Division, Vital Records, Suite 205, PO Box 14050, Portland, OR 97293-0050 (Courier: 800 NE Oregon St, #205, Portland, OR 97232); 503-731-4095 (Recorded Message), 502-731-4108, 503-234-8417 (Fax), 8AM-4:30PM.

http://www.ohd.hr.state.or.us/chs/welcome.htm

Indexing & Storage: Records are available from 1961 to 1996 on microfiche and 1906 to 1924 and 1945 to 1960 on microfilm. Only certificates of divorce are issued; copies of decrees must be obtained at the county level. It takes 4 to 8 weeks before new records are available for inquiry.

Searching: Records less than 50 years old are only available to family members, legal representatives and those with a personal or property right. Include the following in your request-date of divorce. Also include names of husband and wife, and reason for request.

Access by: mail, phone, fax, in person.

Fee & Payment: The search fee is $15.00, additional copies are $12.00 each. Fee payee: Oregon Health Division. Prepayment required. Using personal checks (with guarantee card) may delay processing by 2 weeks. For a mail request, enclose a prepaid, self-addressed envelope for overnight carrier. Personal checks accepted. Credit cards accepted: MasterCard, Visa, AmEx, Discover.

Mail search: Turnaround time: 2 to 3 weeks. Send request by overnight delivery and it will be processed ASAP.No self addressed stamped envelope is required.

Phone search: There is an additional $10.00 service fee for ordering by fax or phone and you must use a credit card.

Fax search: Results are sent by mail. Turnaround time next working day.

In person search: Turnaround time is usually within 20 minutes.

Other access: Indexes are available in many state libraries.

Expedited service: Expedited service is available for fax and phone searches. Turnaround time: overnight delivery.

Workers' Compensation Records

Department of Consumer & Business Srvs, Workers Compensation Division, 350 Winter Street NE Rm 27, Salem, OR 97301-3879; 503-947-7818, 503-947-7993 (TTY), 503-945-7630 (Fax), 8AM-5PM M-F.

http://www.oregonwcd.org

Indexing & Storage: Records are available from June 1980 on. Records from 1966 to June 1980 are in the State Archives. New records are available for inquiry immediately. Records are indexed on inhouse computer.

Searching: Per ORS 192.502(18), claims records are exempt from public disclosure. Access to records is at the discretion of the Director. In general, those with a legitimate business purpose are granted access. Include the following in your request-claimant name, Social Security Number, claim number. The web site features rules, bulletins, forms, and publications.

Access by: mail, fax, in person.

Fee & Payment: The Department has the authority to charge for staff time and resources for any record request. Records releases only after disclosure requirements are met. Fee payee: DCBS. Prepayment required. Personal checks accepted. No credit cards accepted.

Mail search: Turnaround time: 1 to 5 days. No self addressed stamped envelope is required.

Fax search: Fax requests are accepted if disclosure requirements are met. Completed report may be mailed back.

In person search: Completed report may need to be mailed back. Turnaround time: 1 to 5 days.

Driver Records

Driver and Motor Vehicle Services, Record Services, 1905 Lana Ave, NE, Salem, OR 97314; 503-945-5000, 8AM-5PM.

http://www.odot.state.or.us/dmv

Indexing & Storage: Records are available for 3 or 5 years; major conviction 10 years for moving violations; 3 or 10 years for DUIs; 3 or 5 years after reinstatement for suspensions. Note: Both 3 year and 5 year records are offered. It takes 2-3 weeks normally before new records are available for inquiry.

Searching: Oregon differentiates between "employment" and "non-employment" records. Include the following in your request-full name, date of birth, driver's license number. A driver's license report is available which lists the driver's name, address, date of birth, license number, issue and expiration dates, original business date, restrictions, status, and, if applicable, the ID card expiration date. The following data is not released: medical information.

Access by: mail, phone, fax.

Fee & Payment: Fees: $1.50 for a 3 year non-employment driving record; $2.00 for a 3 year employment driving record; $3.00 for 5 year combination of both records; $1.50 per record for a driver license information report. There is a charge of $1.50 for no record found. Fee payee: DMV Services. Prepayment required. Personal checks accepted. No credit cards accepted.

Mail search: Turnaround time: 1 day from receipt. No self addressed stamped envelope is required.

Phone search: Oregon offers "DAVE" (DMV's Interactive Voice Response System) which reads information from computer files in a human sounding voice. A variety of records are available on DAVE 24 hours a day. Call 503-945-7950 for more information.

Fax search: Records are available by fax.

Other access: Magnetic tape ordering is available for high volume batch requesters. The agency will sell its DL file to commercial vendors and has an automated "flag program" for customers with re-occurring name lists. Call 503-945-7950 for more information.

Vehicle Ownership
Vehicle Identification

Driver and Motor Vehicle Services, Record Services Unit, 1905 Lana Ave, NE, Salem, OR 97314; 503-945-5000, 503-945-5425 (Fax), 8AM-5PM.

http://www.odot.state.or.us/dmv

Indexing & Storage: Records are available from 1963 to present. Early records are on microfilm. It takes 2-3 weeks from issue before new records are available for inquiry.

Searching: Title and registration ownership records are open to the public, for a fee. By law, only certain entities may receive full records. Casual requesters cannot obtain records with personal information including address, telephone, license number, etc. DOB is helpful. The following data is not released: medical information.

Access by: mail, phone.

Fee & Payment: Vehicle record prints are $4.00, information given orally is $2.50 (to account holders). A complete vehicle title history is $22.50. An insurance information search is $10.00. Generally, $2.50 is charged if no record is found. Fee payee: Driver & Motor Services (DMV). Prepayment required. Personal checks accepted. No credit cards accepted.

Mail search: Turnaround time: 1 day. A self addressed stamped envelope is requested.

Phone search: The automated system called "DAVE" is open 24 hours a day. An account is necessary. Call 503-945-7950 for more information.

Other access: Oregon offers an extensive program to obtain bulk ownership and vehicle information on magnetic tape or paper. Many customized selections are available. Call 503-945-7950 for more information.

Accident Reports

Motor Vehicle Division, Accident Reports & Information, 1905 Lana Ave, NE, Salem, OR 97314; 503-945-5098, 503-945-5267 (Fax), 8AM-5PM.

Indexing & Storage: Records are available for 5 years to present. It takes 2-4 weeks before new records are available for inquiry.

Searching: The report is provided without personal information unless the requester qualifies for personal information under OR law. Qualified requesters include legal representatives, involved insurance companies and those involved with property damage or injury. Include the following in your request-full name, date of accident, location of accident.

Access by: mail, fax, in person.

Fee & Payment: The fee is $8.50 for the police accident report. There is a $1.50 charge for a "no record found." Fee payee: MVD Services. Prepayment required. Personal checks accepted. No credit cards accepted.

Mail search: Turnaround time: 3 to 5 days. No self addressed stamped envelope is required.

Fax search: Same fees and turnaround time (3-5 days).

In person search: Turnaround time will vary, record may not be available same day.

Other access: Bulk release of police accident reports is available for sale. Records are unsorted and include all counties.

Vessel Ownership
Vessel Registration

Oregon State Marine Board, PO Box 14145, Salem, OR 97309 (Courier: 435 Commercial St NE, #400, Salem, OR 97301); 503-378-8587, 503-378-4597 (Fax), 8AM-5PM M-F.

http://www.boatoregon.com

Indexing & Storage: Records are available from 1959 to present for titles. Records are indexed on computer for the last 3 years. Records are on microfiche from the 1970s to the present. Titles and registrations are issued on all motorized boats and sailboats over 12 ft. It takes about one day before new records are available for inquiry.

Searching: Extremely large boats which move along the OR-WA-CA border for 60 days or more are registered with the US Coast Guard. Call (800) 799-8362 for more information. To search, one of the following is required: name, Oregon #, or hull ID #. Requests can be made via e-mail, from the web site,

Access by: mail, phone, fax, in person.

Fee & Payment: There is no fee for 1 search. Fees for lists are dependent on the time involved. Fee payee: State Marine Board. Prepayment required. Personal checks accepted. No credit cards accepted.

Mail search: Turnaround time: 7 to 10 days. No self addressed stamped envelope is required.

Phone search: Limited registration information is released over the phone.

Fax search: Records are available by fax.

In person search: If the search is lengthy, the results will be sent by mail.

Other access: The DPPA opt out provision is in effect if mailing lists are requested. Records are available on CD starting at $165 and on labels starting at $250.

Legislation Records

Oregon Legislative Assembly, State Capitol-Information Services, State Capitol, Rm 49, Salem, OR 97310; 503-986-1180 (Current Bill Information), 503-373-0701 (Archives), 503-373-1527 (Fax), 8AM-5PM.

http://www.leg.state.or.us

Note: Older passed bills are located at the State Archives, 503-373-0701.

Indexing & Storage: Records are available for current session only. Records are indexed on inhouse computer.

Searching: Include the following in your request-bill number, year.

Access by: mail, phone, fax, in person, online.

Fee & Payment: There are no fees for copies of current bills. Copies of bills from Archives are $.25 per page copy fee and other charges depending on the search requirement.

Mail search: Turnaround time: same day. No self addressed stamped envelope is required.

Phone search: Records are available by phone.

Fax search: Fax searching available.

In person search: Searching is available in person.

Online search: Text and histories of measures can be found at the Internet site for no charge.

Voter Registration
Records not maintained by a state level agency.

Note: Records are maintained at the county level and cannot be purchased for commercial reasons.

GED Certificates

Dept of Community Colleges/ Workforce Development, GED Program, 255 Capitol St NE,

Salem, OR 97310; 503-378-8648 x369, 503-378-8434 (Fax), 8AM-5PM M-F.

http://www.odccwd.state.or.us

Searching: To verify, the following is a required: name, date/year of test, DOB, and Social Security Number. If a copy of a transcript is requested, include the above plus a signed release.

Access by: mail, phone, fax, in person.

Fee & Payment: There is no fee for verification. Copies of transcripts are $5.00 each. Fee payee: State of Oregon Prepayment required. Money orders are accepted. Personal checks accepted. No credit cards accepted.

Mail search: Turnaround time is 10-12 days.No self addressed stamped envelope is required. No fee for mail request.

Phone search: No fee for telephone request.

Fax search: You may request a verification of transcript by fax.

In person search: Turnaround time is typically 5 minutes.

Hunting License Information
Fishing License Information

Fish & Wildlife Department, Licensing Division, PO Box 59, Portland, OR 97207 (Courier: 2501 SW 1st Ave, Portland, OR 97201); 503-872-5275, 503-872-5261 (Fax), 8AM-5PM.

http://www.dfw.state.or.us

Indexing & Storage: Records are available from 1994 on computer.

Searching: Include the following in your request-full name, Social Security Number. Fishing licenses and hunting licenses are in the same building in different divisions. The following data is not released: phone numbers or Social Security Numbers.

Access by: mail, phone, fax, in person.

Fee & Payment: The fee for a search is $5.00. The record is certified. Fee payee: O.D.F.W. Prepayment required. Personal checks accepted. Credit cards accepted: MasterCard, Visa.

Mail search: Turnaround time: 1 to 3 days. No self addressed stamped envelope is required.

Phone search: Records are available by phone.

Fax search: Same fees and turnaround time as phone requests.

In person search: Records are usually returned by mail.

Other access: The state will release bulk lists for a fee. Call Patty Wehlan at 503-872-5267 x5617.

Oregon State Licensing Agencies

Licenses Searchable Online

Architect #06	www.architect-board.state.or.us/A-B.htm
Architectural Firm #06	www.architect-board.state.or.us/ARFirms.htm
Audiologist #58	http://bspa.ohd.hr.state.or.us
Bakery #23	www.oda.state.or.us/cgi/fm/food_safety/Search.html
Bank #26	www.cbs.state.or.us/external/dfcs/banking/regagent.htm
Building Official #19	www.cbs.state.or.us/external/imd/database/bcd/licensing/index.html
Check & Money Order Seller #26	www.oregondfcs.org/e_commerce/m_tran/m_tran.htm
Chiropractor/Chiropractic Assistant #08	www.obce.state.or.us
Christmas Tree Grower #25	www.oda.state.or.us/cgi/fm/nursery/Search.html
Collection Agency #26	www.oregondfcs.org/ca/ca.htm
Construction Contractor/Subcontractor #21	www.ccb.state.or.us/newq_start.htm
Consumer Finance Company #26	www.cbs.state.or.us/external/dfcs/cf/cfdatabase/search_main.htm
Credit Service Organization #26	www.oregondfcs.org/cso/cso.htm
Credit Union #26	www.cbs.state.or.us/external/dfcs/cu/cuagents.htm
Dairy #23	www.oda.state.or.us/cgi/fm/food_safety/Search.html
Debt Consolidation Agency #26	www.cbs.state.or.us/external/dfcs/dca/lic_dca.htm
Electrical Installation #19	www.cbs.state.or.us/external/imd/database/bcd/licensing/index.html
Florist #25	www.oda.state.or.us/cgi/fm/nursery/Search.html
Food Establishment, Retail #23	www.oda.state.or.us/cgi/fm/food_safety/Search.html
Food Exporter #23	www.oda.state.or.us/cgi/fm/food_safety/Search.html
Food Processing/Storage Facility #23	www.oda.state.or.us/cgi/fm/food_safety/Search.html
Geologist #12	www.open.org/~osbge/registrants.htm
Geologist, Engineering #12	www.open.org/~osbge/registrants.htm
Greenhouse Grower/herbaceous plants #25	www.oda.state.or.us/cgi/fm/nursery/Search.html
Inspector #19	www.cbs.state.or.us/external/imd/database/bcd/licensing/index.html
Inspector, Structural/Mechanical #19	www.cbs.state.or.us/external/imd/database/bcd/licensing/index.html
Insurance Agent/Adjuster/Consultant #26	www.cbs.state.or.us/external/imd/database/inslic/main.htm
Insurance Agency #26	www.cbs.state.or.us/external/imd/database/inslic/agency_main.htm
Insurance Company #26	www.cbs.state.or.us/external/imd/database/inslic/comp_main.htm
Investment Advisor #26	www.cbs.state.or.us/external/imd/database/lear/adviser_search_main.htm
Landscape Business #21	www.ccb.state.or.us/lcbmenu.htm
Landscaper #25	www.oda.state.or.us/cgi/fm/nursery/Search.html
Lobbyist #40	www.lobbyist.net/Oregon/ORELOB.htm
Manufactured Housing Construction #19	www.cbs.state.or.us/external/imd/database/bcd/licensing/index.html
Massage Therapist #38	http://pws.prserv.net/usinet.bholzma/LMTList.html
Medical Doctor/Surgeon #29	www.docboard.org/or/df/search.htm
Money Transmitter #26	www.oregondfcs.org/e_commerce/m_tran/m_tran.htm
Mortgage Banker/Broker/Lender #26	www.cbs.state.or.us/external/imd/database/lear/search_main.htm
Nursery Dealer #25	www.oda.state.or.us/cgi/fm/nursery/Search.html
Nursery Stock/Native Plants Collector #25	www.oda.state.or.us/cgi/fm/nursery/Search.html
Optometrist #14	www.obo.state.or.us/doctorinfo.htm
Osteopathic Physician #29	www.docboard.org/or/df/search.htm
Pawnbroker #26	www.cbs.state.or.us/external/dfcs/pawn/pawnshop.htm
Plans Examiner #19	www.cbs.state.or.us/external/imd/database/bcd/licensing/index.html
Plumber #19	www.cbs.state.or.us/external/imd/database/bcd/licensing/index.html
Psychologist/ Psychologist Associate #16	www.obpe.state.or.us/licensee_applicant.htm
Public Accountant-CPA #05	www.boa.state.or.us/search.htm
Pump Installation Contractor (Limited) #21	www.cbs.state.or.us/external/imd/database/bcd/licensing/index.html
Real Estate Appraiser #04	www.oda.state.or.us/aclb/search.html
Sign Contractor (Limited) #21	www.cbs.state.or.us/external/imd/database/bcd/licensing/index.html
Speech Language Pathologist #58	http://bspa.ohd.hr.state.or.us
Trust Company #26	www.cbs.state.or.us/external/dfcs/banking/regagent.htm
Veterinarian #54	www.oda.state.or.us/cgi/fm/vet_book/Search.html

Licensing Quick Finder

Acupuncturist #33 503-229-5770	Architectural Firm #06 503-378-4270	Body Piercer #57 503-378-8667
Aircraft Landing Area #03 503-378-4880	Athletic Trainer #57 503-378-8667	Boilermaker #19 503-373-1268
Aircraft Registration #03 503-378-4880	Attorney #43 503-620-0222	Boxer #44 503-378-8739
Airport #03 503-378-4880	Audiologist #58 503-731-4050	Brand Recording (Livestock) #22 503-986-4681
Amusement Ride Inspector #19 503-378-4133	Auditor, Municipal #05 503-378-4181	Brewery #41 503-872-5124
Animal Euthanasia Technician #54 503-731-4051	Bakery #23 503-986-4720	Building Official #19 503-373-1248
Animal Health Technician #54 503-731-4051	Bank #26 503-378-4387	Cemetery #52 .... 503-731-4040 x26
Architect #06 503-378-4270	Barber #07 503-378-8667	Check & Money Order Seller #26 503-378-4387

Chiropractor/Chiropractic Assistant #08 503-378-5816
Christmas Tree Grower #25 503-986-4644
Collection Agency #26 503-378-4387
Construction Contractor #21 .... 503-378-4621 x4900
Construction Subcontractor #21 .. 503-378-4621 x4900
Consumer Finance Company #26 503-378-4387
Corrections Officer #18 503-378-2100
Cosmetologist #57 503-378-8667
Counselor #28 503-378-5499
Credit Service Organization #26 503-378-4387
Credit Union #26 503-378-4387
Crematorium #52 .... 503-731-4040 x26
Dairy #23 503-986-4720
Debt Consolidation Agency #26 503-378-4387
Dental Hygienist #55 503-229-5520
Dental Specialist #55 503-229-5520
Dentist #55 503-229-5520
Denture Technologist #57 503-378-8667
Denturist #09 503-378-8667
Diagnostic Radiologic Technologist #39 503-731-4088
Dietitian #11 503-731-4085
Dog Racing #42 503-731-4052
Drug Mfg. #15 503-731-4032
Drug Outlet, Over-the-Counter #15 503-731-4032
Drug Wholesaler #15 503-731-4032
Electrical Installation #19 503-373-1268
Electrician #19 503-373-1268
Electrologist #01 503-378-8667
Electrology Facility #01 503-378-8667
Electrology Instructor/School #01 503-378-8667
Embalmer/Apprentice #52 .... 503-731-4040 x26
EMD #18 503-378-2100
Engineer #10 503-362-2666
Escrow Agent/Agency #46 503-378-4170
Facial Technician/Technologist #57 503-378-8667
Farm Labor Contractor #21 503-731-4200
Firefighter #18 503-378-2100
Florist #25 503-986-4644
Food Establishment, Retail #23 503-986-4720
Food Exporter #23 503-986-4720
Food Processing Facility #23 503-986-4720
Food Storage Facility #23 503-986-4720
Forest Labor Contractor #21 503-731-4200
Funeral Establishment #52 .... 503-731-4040 x26
Funeral Preneed Seller #52 .... 503-731-4040 x26
Funeral Service Practitioner/Apprentice #52 ....
.... 503-731-4040 x26
Geologist #12 503-566-2837
Geologist, Engineering #12 503-566-2837
Greenhouse Grower of Herbaceous Plants #25 ....
.... 503-986-4644
Hair Salon #07 503-378-8667
Hair Stylist (Designer) #57 503-378-8667

Hairdresser #07 503-378-8667
Hearing Aid Dealer #02 503-378-8667
Hearing Aid Dispenser #02 503-378-8667
Heliport #03 503-378-4880
Home Inspector #21 .... 503-378-4621 x4900
Horse Racing #42 503-731-4052
Immediate Disposition Co. #52 ...... 503-731-4040 x26
Inspector #19 503-373-1248
Inspector, Structural/Mechanical #19 ... 503-373-1248
Insurance Adjuster #26 503-378-4387
Insurance Agency #26 503-378-4387
Insurance Agent #26 503-378-4387
Insurance Company #26 503-378-4387
Insurance Consultant #26 503-378-4387
Investment Advisor #26 503-378-4140
Landscape Architect #50 503-589-0093
Landscape Business #21 503-378-4621
Landscaper #25 503-986-4644
Liquor Control #41 503-872-5000
Liquor Salesman/Agent #41 503-872-5123
Liquor, Wide Shipper #41 503-872-5124
Lobbyist #40 503-378-5105
Manicurist/Nail Technician #07 503-378-8667
Manufactured Housing Construct. #19 .. 503-373-1248
Marriage & Family Therapist #28 503-378-5499
Massage Therapist #38 503-365-8657
Medical Doctor/Surgeon #29 503-229-5770
Medical Examiner #51 503-280-6061
Midwife #57 503-378-8667
Money Transmitter #26 503-378-4387
Mortgage Banker/Broker/Lender #26 ... 503-378-4387
Nail Technician #07 503-378-8667
Naturopathic Physician #34 503-731-4045
Notary Public #37 503-986-2200
Nurse #13 503-731-3459
Nurse-LPN #13 503-731-3459
Nursery Dealer #25 503-986-4644
Nursery Stock/Collectors of Native Plants #25 ....
.... 503-986-4644
Nursing Assistant #13 503-731-3459
Nursing Home Administrator #35 503-731-4046
Occupational Therapist #36 503-731-4048
Occupational Therapist Assistant #36 ... 503-731-4048
Optometrist #14 503-373-7721
Osteopathic Physician #29 503-229-5770
Parole/Probation Officer #18 503-378-2100
Pathology, Oral Endorsement #09 503-378-8667
Pawnbroker #26 503-378-4387
Permanent Color Technician #57 503-378-8667
Pharmacist #15 503-731-4032
Pharmacy #15 503-731-4032
Physical Therapist #45 503-731-4047
Physical Therapist/Assistant #45 503-731-4047

Physician Assistant #30 503-229-5770
Pilot #03 503-378-4880
Plans Examiner #19 503-373-1248
Plumber #19 503-373-7479
Podiatrist #31 502-229-5770
Police Officer #18 503-378-2100
Polygraph Examiner #18 503-378-2100
Private Security Officer #18 503-378-2100
Property Manager #46 503-378-4170
Psychologist #16 503-378-4154
Psychologist Associate #16 503-378-4154
Public Accountant-CPA #05 503-378-4181
Pump Installation Contractor (Limited) #21 ....
.... 503-731-4072
Radiologic Technologist (Limited Permit) #39 ....
.... 503-731-4088
Radiologic Therapy Technologist #39 ... 503-731-4088
Real Estate Appraiser #04 503-373-1505
Real Estate Branch Office #46 503-378-4170
Real Estate Broker #46 503-378-4170
Real Estate Salesperson #46 503-378-4170
Respiratory Care Practitioner #32 503-378-8667x4330
Respiratory Care Therapist #57 503-378-8667
Sanitarian #47 503-378-8667
Sanitarian/Sanitarian Trainee #57 503-378-8667
Savings & Loan Association #26 503-378-4387
School Admin./Superintendent#53 503-378-6813
School Counselor #53 503-378-6813
School Supervisor #53 503-378-6813
Securities Broker/Dealer #26 503-378-4140
Securities Salesperson #26 503-378-4387
Shorthand Reporter #59 503-986-5695
Sign Contractor (Limited) #21 503-731-4072
Social Worker, Clinical #48 503-378-5735
Special Qualifications Corporation #26 .. 503-378-4387
Speech Language Pathologist #58 503-731-4050
Surveyor #10 503-362-2666
Tattoo Artist #57 503-378-8667
Tax Consultant/Preparer #17 503-378-4034
Teacher #53 503-378-6813
Telecommunicator #18 503-378-2100
Travel Agent #26 503-378-4387
Trust Company #26 503-378-4387
Veterinarian #54 503-731-4051
Veterinary Technician #54 503-731-4051
Waste Water Treatment System Operator #61 ....
.... 503-229-5696
Water Rights Examiner #10 503-362-2666
Water Well Constructor #60 503-378-8455
Winery #41 503-872-5124
Wrestler #44 503-378-8739

Licensing Agency Information

#02 Advisory Council on Hearing Aids, 700 Summer St, #320, Salem, OR 97301-1287; 503-378-8667, Fax: 503-585-9114.
www.hdlp.hr.state.or.us/hdhome.htm

#03 Department of Aviation, 3040 25th S SE, Salem, OR 97310; 503-378-4880, Fax: 503-373-1688. www.aviation.state.or.us

#04 Appraiser Certification & Licensure Board, 350 Winter St NE, Rm 21, Salem, OR 97310; 503-373-1505, Fax: 503-378-6576.
www.cbs.state.or.us/external/aclb
Direct web site URL to search for licensees: www.oda.state.or.us/aclb/search.html. You can search online using name, city, ZIP Code, date issued, license type, and company name.

#05 Board of Accountancy, 3218 Pringle Rd SE, #110, Salem, OR 97302-6307; 503-378-4181, Fax: 503-378-3575.
www.boa.state.or.us/boa.html

#06 Board of Architect Examiners, 750 Front St NE #260, Salem, OR 97301; 503-378-4270, Fax: 503-378-6091.
www.architect-board.state.or.us
Direct web site URL to search for licensees: www.architect-board.state.or.us. You can search online using last name.

#07 Board of Barbers & Hairdressers, 700 Summer St NE #320, Salem, OR 97301-1287; 503-378-8667, Fax: 503-585-9004.
www.hdlp.hr.state.or.us/bhhome.htm

#08 Board of Chiropractic Examiners, 3218 Pringle Rd SE, #150, Salem, OR 97302-6311; 503-378-5816, Fax: 503-362-1260.
www.obce.state.or.us

#09 Board of Denture Technology, 700 Summer St, #320, Salem, OR 97301-1287; 503-378-8667, Fax: 503-585-9114.
www.hdlp.hr.state.or.us/dthome.htm

#10 Board of Examiners for Engineer & Land Surveyors, 728 Hawthorne Ave NE, Salem, OR 97301; 503-362-2666, Fax: 503-362-5454.
www.osbeels.org
Direct web site URL to search for licensees: www.osbeels.org

#11 Board of Examiners of Licensed Dieticians, 800 NE Oregon, #407, Portland, OR 97232; 503-731-4085, Fax: 503-731-4207.
www.bld.state.or.us

#12 Board of Geologist Examiners, 707 13th St SE #275, Salem, OR 97301; 503-566-2837, Fax: 503-362-6393. www.osbge.org
Direct web site URL to search for licensees: www.open.org/~osbge/registrants.htm. You can search online using the "Registrant" tab.

#13 Board of Nursing, 800 NE Oregon St, #465, Portland, OR 97232-2162; 503-731-4745, Fax: 503-731-4755. www.osbn.state.or.us

#14 Board of Optometry, 3218 Pringle Rd SE, #270, Salem, OR 97310-6306; 503-373-7721, Fax: 503-378-3616.
www.obo.state.or.us
Direct web site URL to search for licensees: www.obo.state.or.us/doctorinfo.htm. You can search online using national database by name, city or state.

#15 Board of Pharmacy, 800 NE Oregon St, State Office Bldg, #9, Rm 425, Portland, OR 97232; 503-731-4032, Fax: 503-731-4067.
www.pharmacy.state.or.us

#16 Board of Psychologist Examiners, 3218 Pringle Road, #130, Salem, OR 97301-6309; 503-378-4154, Fax: 503-378-3575.
www.obpe.state.or.us
Direct web site URL to search for licensees: www.obpe.state.or.us/licensee_applicant.htm. You can search online using name, license #, or city

#17 Board of Tax Service Examiners, 3218 Pringle Road, #120, Salem, OR 97302; 503-378-4034, Fax: 503-378-3575.
www.open.org/~ortaxbrd

#18 Department of Public Safety Standards & Training, 550 N Monmouth Ave, Monmouth, OR 97361; 503-378-2100, Fax: 503-838-8907.
www.OregonVOS.net/dpsst/

#19 Department of Consumer & Business Svcs, PO Box 14470, Salem, OR 97309-0404; 503-378-4133, Fax: 503-378-2322.
www.oregonbcd.org
Direct web site URL to search for licensees: www.cbs.state.or.us/external/imd/database/bcd/licensing/index.html. You can search online using license number, name, city, and county.

#21 Construction & Landscape Contractors Boards, 700 Summer St NE #300, Salem, OR 97309-5052; 503-378-4621 x4900, Fax: 503-373-2007.
www.ccb.state.or.us 24-Hour Contractor Inquiry Line - 503-378-4610 or 888-366-5635.

#22 Department of Agriculture, 635 Capitol St NE, Salem, OR 97310-0110; 503-986-4681, Fax: 503-986-4734.
www.oda.state.or.us/livestock_Health_ID/livestock_id/livestock_main.html

#23 Department of Agriculture, 635 Capitol St NE, Salem, OR 97301; 503-986-4720, Fax: 503-986-4729.
www.oda.state.or.us/Food_Safety/FSDINFO.html
Direct web site URL to search for licensees: www.oda.state.or.us/cgi/fm/food_safety/Search.html

#25 Department of Agriculture, 635 Capitol St NE, Salem, OR 97310-0110; 503-986-4644, Fax: 503-986-4786.
www.oda.state.or.us
Direct web site URL to search for licensees: www.oda.state.or.us/cgi/fm/nursery/Search.html. You can search online using name, city, county, license number and species grown.

#26 Department of Consumer & Business Svcs, 350 Winter St, Labor & Industries Bldg, Rm 410, Salem, OR 97301-3881; 503-378-4140, Fax: 503-947-7862.
www.oregondfcs.org
Direct web site URL to search for licensees: www.oregondfcs.org. You can search online using alphabetical lists

#28 Licensed Professional Counselors & Therapists, 3218 Pringle Rd SE, #160, Salem, OR 97302-6312; 503-378-5499.
www.oblpct.state.or.us

#29 Medical Boards, 1500 SW 1st Ave, Crown Plaza Bldg, #620, Portland, OR 97201-5826; 503-229-5770, Fax: 503-229-6543.
www.bme.state.or.us
Direct web site URL to search for licensees: www.docboard.org/or/df/search.htm. You can search online using name and city.

#32 Respiratory Therapist Licensing Board, 700 summer St NE #320, Salem, OR 97310; 503-378-8667 x4330, Fax: 503-229-6543.
www.hdlp.hr.state.or.us/rthome.htm

#34 Naturopathic Board of Examiners, 800 NE Oregon, #407, Portland, OR 97232; 503-731-4045, Fax: 503-731-4207.
www.state.or.us/agencies.ns/83300/00060/index.html

#35 Nursing Home Board, 800 NE Oregon, #407, Portland, OR 97232; 503-731-4046, Fax: 503-731-4207.
www.state.or.us/agencies.ns

#36 Occupational Therapy Licensing, 800 NE Oregon, #407, Portland, OR 97232; 503-731-4048, Fax: 503-731-4207.
www.otlb.state.or.us

#37 Office of Secretary of State, 255 Capitol St NE, #151, Salem, OR 97310; 503-986-2200, Fax: 503-986-2300.
www.sos.state.or.us/corporation/notary/notary.htm

#38 Board of Massage Technicians, 3218 Pringle Rd SE #250, Salem, OR 97302; 503-365-8657, Fax: 503-378-3575.
www.oregonmassage.org
Direct web site URL to search for licensees: http://pws.prserv.net/usinet.bholzma/LMTList.html. You can search online using alphabetical list

#39 Board of Radiologic Technology, 800 NE Oregon, #407, Portland, OR 97232; 503-731-4088, Fax: 503-731-4207.
www.obrt.state.or.us

#40 Government Standards & Practices Commission, 100 High St SE, #220, Salem, OR 97310; 503-378-5105, Fax: 503-373-1456.
www.gspc.state.or.us

#41 Liquor Control Commission, 9079 SE McLoughlin Blvd, Portland, OR 97222-7355; 503-872-5000, Fax: 503-872-5018.
www.olcc.state.or.us

#42 Racing Commission, 800 NE Oregon, #11, Portland, OR 97232; 503-731-4052, Fax: 503-731-4053.
www.oregonvos.net/~orc/

#43 State Bar Association, PO Box 1689, Lake Oswego, OR 97035-0899; 503-620-0222, Fax: 503-684-1366.
www.osbar.org

#44 Boxing & Wrestling Commission, 4660 Portland Rd NE, Salem, OR 97305; 503-378-8739, Fax: 503-304-9157.

#45 Physical Therapist Licensing Board, 800 NE Oregon St, #407, Portland, OR 97232-2162; 503-731-4047, Fax: 503-731-4207.
www.ptboard.state.or.us

#46 Real Estate Agency, 1177 Center St NE, Salem, OR 97310-2503; 503-378-4170, Fax: 503-378-2491.
www.rea.state.or.us

#47 Sanitarians Registration Board, 700 Summer St NE, #320, Salem, OR 97301-1287; 503-378-8667, Fax: 503-585-9114.
www.hdlp.hr.state.or.us/snhome.htm

#48 Board of Clinical Social Workers, 3218 Pringle Rd SE, #240, Salem, OR 97302-6310; 503-378-5735, Fax: 503-378-3575.
http://bcsw.state.or.us

#50 Landscape Architect Board, 3295 Triangle Dr SE #114, Salem, OR 97302; 503-589-0093, Fax: 503-589-0545.

#52 Mortuary & Cemetery Board, 800 NE Oregon, #430, Portland, OR 97232-2162; 503-731-4040 X26, Fax: 503-731-4494.

#53 Teacher Standards & Practices Commission, 255 Capital St NE, Public Service Bldg, #105, Salem, OR 97310-1332; 503-378-6813, Fax: 503-378-4448.
www.ode.state.or.us/tspc

#54 Veterinary Medical Board, 800 NE Oregon, #407, Portland, OR 97232; 503-731-4051, Fax: 503-731-4207.
Direct web site URL to search for licensees: www.oda.state.or.us/cgi/fm/vet_book/Search.html. You can search online using name, clinic name, city, county, and practice type for veterinarians

#55 Board of Dentistry, 1515 SW 5th #400, Portland, OR 97201; 503-229-5520.

#57 Health Licensing Offc, 700 Summer St NE #320, Salem, OR 97310-1287; 503-378-8667, Fax: 503-585-9114.
www.hlo.state.or.us

#58 Board of Examiners for Speech-Language Pathology & Audiology, 800 NE Oregon St #21, State Office Bldg, Portland, OR 97232; 503-731-4050, Fax: 503-731-4207.
http://bspa.ohd.hr.state.or.us

#59 Judicial Department, 1163 State St, Salem, OR 97310-0260; 503-986-5695.

#60 Department of Water Resources, 158 12th St NE, Commerce Bldg, Salem, OR 97310; 503-378-8455.

#61 Department of Environmental Quality, 811 SW 6th Ave, Portland, OR 97304; 503-229-5696.

Oregon Federal Courts

The following list indicates the district and division name for each county in the state. If the bankruptcy court location is different from the district court, then the location of the bankruptcy court appears in parentheses.

County/Court Cross Reference

Baker	Portland	Lake	Medford (Eugene)
Benton	Eugene	Lane	Eugene
Clackamas	Portland	Lincoln	Eugene
Clatsop	Portland	Linn	Eugene
Columbia	Portland	Malheur	Portland
Coos	Eugene	Marion	Eugene
Crook	Portland	Morrow	Portland
Curry	Medford (Eugene)	Multnomah	Portland
Deschutes	Eugene (Portland)	Polk	Portland (Eugene)
Douglas	Eugene	Sherman	Portland
Gilliam	Portland	Tillamook	Portland
Grant	Portland	Umatilla	Portland
Harney	Portland	Union	Portland
Hood River	Portland	Wallowa	Portland
Jackson	Medford (Eugene)	Wasco	Portland
Jefferson	Portland	Washington	Portland
Josephine	Medford (Eugene)	Wheeler	Portland
Klamath	Medford (Eugene)	Yamhill	Portland

US District Court

District of Oregon

Eugene Division 100 Federal Bldg, 211 E 7th Ave, Eugene, OR 97401 (Courier Address: Use mail address for courier delivery), 541-465-6423, Fax: 541-465-6344.

http://www.ord.uscourts.gov

Counties: Benton, Coos, Deschutes, Douglas, Lane, Lincoln, Linn, Marion.

Indexing/Storage: Cases are indexed by defendant and plaintiff as well as by case number. New cases are available in the index immediately after filing date. A computer index is maintained. Records are also indexed on microfiche for criminal records older than 1986. Open records are located at this court. District wide searches are available from this division.

Fee & Payment: The fee is $20.00 per item (one party name or case number). Payment may be made by money order, cashier check, personal check, Visa, Mastercard. Prepayment is required. Payee: Clerk, US District Court. Certification fee: $7.00 per document. Copy fee: $.50 per page.

Phone Search: Only docket information is available by phone.

Mail Search: A stamped self addressed envelope is not required.

In Person: In person searching is available.

PACER: Sign-up number is 800-676-6856. Access fee is $.60 per minute. Local access: 503-326-8904. Case records are available back to September 1988. Records are never purged. New records are available online after 1 day. PACER is available online at http://pacer.ord.uscourts.gov.

Electronic Filing: Electronic filing information is available online at https://ecf.ord.uscourts.gov.

Other Online Access: Logon to ECF/PACER at https://ecf.ord.uscourts.gov/cgi-bin/login.pl. Access fee is 7 cents per page.

Medford Division 201 James A Redden US Courthouse, 310 W 6th St, Medford, OR 97501 (Courier Address: Use mail address for courier delivery), 541-776-3926, Fax: 541-776-3925.

http://www.ord.uscourts.gov

Counties: Curry, Jackson, Josephine, Klamath, Lake. Court set up in April 1994; Cases prior to that time were tried in Eugene.

Indexing/Storage: Cases are indexed by defendant and plaintiff as well as by case number. New cases are available in the index 1 day after filing date. A computer index is maintained. Open records are located at this court.

Fee & Payment: The fee is $20.00 per item (one party name or case number). Payment may be made by money order, cashier check, personal check, Visa, Mastercard. Prepayment is required.

Payee: Clerk, USDC. Certification fee: $7.00 per document. Copy fee: $.50 per page.

Phone Search: Only docket information is available by phone.

Fax Search: Will accept fax search request with $15.00 fee. Will fax docket listings at no extra charge.

Mail Search: A stamped self addressed envelope is not required.

In Person: In person searching is available.

PACER: Sign-up number is 800-676-6856. Access fee is $.60 per minute. Local access: 503-326-8903. Case records are available back to September 1988. Records are never purged. New records are available online after 1 day. PACER is available online at http://pacer.ord.uscourts.gov.

Electronic Filing: Electronic filing information is available online at https://ecf.ord.uscourts.gov

Other Online Access: Logon to ECF/PACER at https://ecf.ord.uscourts.gov/cgi-bin/login.pl. Access fee is 7 cents per page.

Portland Division Clerk, 740 US Courthouse, 1000 SW 3rd Ave, Portland, OR 97204-2902 (Courier Address: Use mail address for courier delivery), 503-326-8000, Fax: 503-326-8010.

http://www.ord.uscourts.gov

Counties: Baker, Clackamas, Clatsop, Columbia, Crook, Gilliam, Grant, Harney, Hood River, Jefferson, Malheur, Morrow, Multnomah, Polk,

Sherman, Tillamook, Umatilla, Union, Wallowa, Wasco, Washinton, Wheeler, Yamhill.

Indexing/Storage: Cases are indexed by defendant and plaintiff as well as by case number. New cases are available in the index 24 hours after filing date. A computer index is maintained. Records are also indexed on microfiche. Open records are located at this court. District wide searches are available from this court. All civil cases after 8/88 and all criminal cases after 3/91 are maintained in this division for the other divisions.

Fee & Payment: The fee is $20.00 per item (one party name or case number). Payment may be made by money order, cashier check, personal check. Prepayment is required. Payee: Clerk, USDC. Certification fee: $7.00 per document. Copy fee: $.50 per page. You are allowed to make your own copies. These copies cost $.15 per page.

Phone Search: If the case number is known, docket information will be released over the phone.

Fax Search: Will accept fax to determine fee for a search.

Mail Search: A stamped self addressed envelope is not required.

In Person: In person searching is available.

PACER: Sign-up number is 800-676-6856. Access fee is $.60 per minute. Local access: 503-326-8903. Case records are available back to September 1988. Records are never purged. New records are available online after 1 day. PACER is available online at http://pacer.ord.uscourts.gov.

Electronic Filing: Electronic filing information is available online at https://ecf.ord.uscourts.gov

Other Online Access: Logon to ECF/PACER at https://ecf.ord.uscourts.gov/cgi-bin/login.pl. Access fee is 7 cents per page.

US Bankruptcy Court

District of Oregon

Eugene Division PO Box 1335, Eugene, OR 97440 (Courier Address: 151 W 7th St, #300, Eugene, OR 97401), 541-465-6448.

http://www.orb.uscourts.gov

Counties: Benton, Coos, Curry, Deschutes, Douglas, Jackson, Josephine, Klamath, Lake, Lane, Lincoln, Linn, Marion.

Indexing/Storage: Cases are indexed by debtor as well as by case number. New cases are available in the index 1 day after filing date. Both computer and card indexes are maintained. Open records are located at this court.

Fee & Payment: The fee is $20.00 per item (one party name or case number). Payment may be made by money order, cashier check, personal check. Prepayment is required. Payee: Clerk, US Bankruptcy Court. Certification fee: $7.00 per document. Copy fee: $.50 per page. You are allowed to make your own copies. These copies cost $.15 per page.

Phone Search: Only docket information available by telephone. An automated voice case information service (VCIS) is available. Call VCIS at 800-726-2227 or 503-326-2249.

Mail Search: A stamped self addressed envelope is not required.

In Person: In person searching is available.

PACER: Sign-up number is 800-676-6856. Access fee is $.60 per minute. Toll-free access: 800-610-9315. Local access: 503-326-5650. Case records are available back to 1989. Records are purged every six months. New civil records are available online after 1 day. PACER is available online at http://pacer.orb.uscourts.gov.

Portland Division 1001 SW 5th Ave, #700, Portland, OR 97204 (Courier Address: Use mail address for courier delivery), 503-326-2231.

http://www.orb.uscourts.gov

Counties: Baker, Clackamas, Clatsop, Columbia, Crook, Gilliam, Grant, Harney, Hood River, Jefferson, Malheur, Morrow, Multnomah, Polk, Sherman, Tillamook, Umatilla, Union, Wallowa, Wasco, Washington, Wheeler, Yamhill.

Indexing/Storage: Cases are indexed by debtor as well as by case number. New cases are available in the index 1 day after filing date. Both computer and card indexes are maintained. Open records are located at this court.

Fee & Payment: The fee is $20.00 per item (one party name or case number). Payment may be made by money order, cashier check, personal check. Prepayment is required. Payee: Clerk, US Bankruptcy Court. Certification fee: $7.00 per document. Copy fee: $.50 per page. You are allowed to make your own copies. These copies cost $.15 per page.

Phone Search: Only docket information is available by phone. An automated voice case information service (VCIS) is available. Call VCIS at 800-726-2227 or 503-326-2249.

Mail Search: Always enclose a stamped self addressed envelope.

In Person: In person searching is available.

PACER: Sign-up number is 800-676-6856. Access fee is $.60 per minute. Toll-free access: 800-610-9315. Local access: 503-326-5650. Case records are available back to 1989. Records are purged every six months. New civil records are available online after 1 day. PACER is available online at http://pacer.orb.uscourts.gov.

Oregon County Courts

Court	Jurisdiction	No. of Courts	How Organized
Circuit Courts*	General	38	26 Districts
County Courts*	Probate	6	6 Counties
Justice Courts	Municipal	35	
Municipal Courts	Municipal	112	
Tax Court	Special	1	

* Profiled in this Sourcebook.

Court	CIVIL								
	Tort	Contract	Real Estate	Min. Claim	Max. Claim	Small Claims	Estate	Eviction	Domestic Relations
Circuit Courts*	X	X	X	$0	No Max	$2500	X	X	X
County Courts*							X		X
Justice Courts	X	X	X	$200	$2500	$2500			
Municipal Courts									
Tax Court									

Court	CRIMINAL				
	Felony	Misdemeanor	DWI/DUI	Preliminary Hearing	Juvenile
Circuit Courts*	X	X	X	X	X
County Courts*					X
Justice Courts		X	X	X	
Municipal Courts		X	X		
Tax Court					

ADMINISTRATION   Court Administrator, Supreme Court Building, 1163 State St, Salem, OR, 97310; 503-986-5500, Fax: 503-986-5503. www.ojd.state.or.us

COURT STRUCTURE   Effective January 15, 1998, the District and Circuit Courts were combined into "Circuit Courts." At the same time, 3 new judicial districts were created by splitting existing ones.

ONLINE ACCESS   Online computer access is available through the Oregon Judicial Information Network (OJIN). OJIN Online includes almost all cases filed in the Oregon state courts. Generally, the OJIN database contains criminal, civil, small claims, probate, and some, but not all, juvenile records. However, it does not contain any records from municipal nor county courts. There is a one-time setup fee of $295.00, plus a monthly usage charge (minimum $10.00) based on transaction type, type of job, shift, and number of units/pages (which averages $10-13 per hour). For further information and/or a registration packet, write to: Oregon Judicial System, Information Systems Division, ATTN: Technical Support, 1163 State Street, Salem OR 97310, or call 800-858-9658.

ADDITIONAL INFORMATION   Many Oregon courts indicated that in person searches would markedly improve request turnaround time as court offices are understaffed or spread very thin. Most Circuit Courts that have records on computer do have a public access terminal that will speed up in-person or retriever searches. Most records offices close from Noon to 1PM Oregon time for lunch. No staff is available during that period.

PROBATE COURTS   Probate is handled by the Circuit Court except in 6 counties (Gilliam, Grant, Harney, Malheur, Sherman, and Wheeler) where Probate in handled by County Courts.

Baker County

Circuit Court 1995 3rd St, #220, Baker City, OR 97814; 541-523-6305; Fax: 541-523-9738. Hours: 8AM-Noon, 1-4PM (PST). *Felony, Misdemeanor, Civil, Probate.*

Civil Records: Access: Phone, fax, mail, in person. Both court and visitors may perform in person searches. No search fee. Required to search: name, years to search. Civil cases indexed by defendant, plaintiff. Civil records on computer from 1987, archives back to 1899. Index available remotely online on the statewide OJIN system, call 800-858-9658 for information.

Criminal Records: Access: Phone, fax, mail, in person. Both court and visitors may perform in person searches. No search fee. Required to search: name, years to search. Criminal records on computer from 1987, archives back to 1899. Online access to criminal records is the same as civil.

General Information: Public Access terminal is available. No adoption, mental, juvenile or sealed records released. SASE required. Turnaround time 10 days. Fax notes: Fee to fax results is $5.00 minimum per document. Copy fee: $.25 per page. Certification fee: $3.75. Fee payee: State of Oregon. Personal checks accepted. Prepayment is required.

Benton County

Circuit Court Box 1870 (120 NW Fourth Street), Corvallis, OR 97339; 541-766-6828; Fax: 541-766-6028. Hours: 8AM-Noon,1-5PM (PST). *Felony, Misdemeanor, Civil, Eviction, Small Claims, Probate.* www.ojd.state.or.us/benton

Civil Records: Access: Phone, mail, online, in person. Both court and visitors may perform in person searches. No search fee. Required to search: name, years to search; also helpful: address. Civil cases indexed by defendant, plaintiff. Civil records on computer from 1987, archives back to the 1900s. Index available remotely online on the statewide OJIN system, call 800-858-9658 for information.

Criminal Records: Access: Phone, mail, online, in person. Both court and visitors may perform in person searches. No search fee. Required to search: name, years to search, DOB, offense; also helpful: address, SSN. Criminal records on computer from 1987, archives back to the 1900s. Online access to criminal records is the same as civil.

General Information: Public Access terminal is available. No adoption, juvenile, sealed by judge, expunged, mental health records released. SASE not required. Turnaround time up to 1 week. Copy fee: $.25 per page. Certification fee: $3.75. Fee payee: State of Oregon. Personal checks accepted. Prepayment is required.

Clackamas County

Circuit Court 807 Main St, Oregon City, OR 97045; 503-655-8447. Hours: 8:30AM-5PM (PST). *Felony, Misdemeanor, Civil, Eviction, Small Claims, Probate.*

Civil Records: Access: Mail, online, in person. Both court and visitors may perform in person searches. No search fee. Required to search: name, years to search. Civil cases indexed by defendant, plaintiff. Civil records on computer from 1986, index back to 1980. Index available remotely online on the statewide OJIN system, call 800-858-9658 for information.

Criminal Records: Access: Mail, online, in person. Both court and visitors may perform in person searches. No search fee. Required to search: name, years to search, DOB. Criminal records on computer from 1986, index back to 1980. Online access to criminal records is the same as civil.

General Information: Public Access terminal is available. No adoption, juvenile, sealed by judge,

expunged, mental health records released. SASE required. Turnaround time 4-6 weeks. Copy fee: $.25 per page. Certification fee: $3.75. Fee payee: State of Oregon. Personal checks accepted. Credit cards accepted: Visa, MasterCard. Prepayment is required.

Clatsop County

Circuit Court Box 835, Astoria, OR 97103; 503-325-8583; Fax: 503-325-9300. Hours: 8AM-Noon, 1-5PM *Felony, Civil Actions Over $10,000, Probate.*

Civil Records: Access: Phone, mail, online, in person. Both court and visitors may perform in person searches. No search fee. Required to search: name, years to search. Civil cases indexed by defendant, plaintiff. Civil records on computer from 1986, archives back to 1900. Index available remotely online on the statewide OJIN system, call 800-858-9658 for information.

Criminal Records: Access: Phone, mail, online, in person. Both court and visitors may perform in person searches. No search fee. Required to search: name, years to search, DOB. Criminal records on computer from 1987, archives back to 1900. Online access to criminal records is the same as civil.

General Information: Public Access terminal is available. No adoption, juvenile, sealed by judge, expunged, paternity or mental health records released. SASE required. Turnaround time 1 week. Copy fee: $.25 per page. Certification fee: $3.75. Fee payee: Clatsop County Circuit Court. Personal checks accepted. Prepayment is required.

Circuit Court Box 659, Astoria, OR 97103; 503-325-8536; Fax: 503-325-9300. Hours: 8AM-5PM (PST). *Misdemeanor.*

Criminal Records: Access: Mail, online, in person. Both court and visitors may perform in person searches. No search fee. Required to search: name, years to search. Criminal records on computer from 1987, archives back to 1900. Online access to criminal records is the same as civil.

General Information: Public Access terminal is available. No adoptions, juvenile, sealed by Judge, expunged, paternity or mental health records released. SASE required. Turnaround time 3-5 days. Copy fee: $.25 per page. Certification fee: $3.75. Fee payee: Circuit Court. Personal checks accepted. Prepayment is required.

Columbia County

Circuit Court Columbia County Courthouse, 244 Strand St, St. Helens, OR 97051; 503-397-2327; Fax: 503-397-3226. Hours: 8:30AM-5PM (PST). *Felony, Misdemeanor, Civil, Eviction, Small Claims, Probate.*

Civil Records: Access: Mail, fax, online, in person. Both court and visitors may perform in person searches. No search fee. Required to search: name, years to search; also helpful: address. Civil cases indexed by defendant, plaintiff. Civil records on computer from September, 1987, archives back to 1900. Index available remotely online on the statewide OJIN system, call 800-858-9658 for information.

Criminal Records: Access: Mail, fax, online, in person. Both court and visitors may perform in person searches. No search fee. Required to search: name, years to search, DOB; also helpful: address, SSN. Criminal records on computer from September, 1987, archives back to 1900. Online access to criminal records is the same as civil.

General Information: Public Access terminal is available. No adoptions, juvenile, sealed by Judge, expunged, mental health records released. SASE required. Turnaround time 4-5 days. Copy fee: $.25 per page. Certification fee: $3.75. Fee payee: State of Oregon. Personal checks accepted. Prepayment is required.

Coos County

Circuit Court Courthouse, Coquille, OR 97423; 541-396-3121; Civil phone: X343; Criminal phone: X251; Fax: 541-396-3456. Hours: 8AM-Noon,1-5PM (PST). *Felony, Misdemeanor, Civil, Eviction, Small Claims, Probate.*

Civil Records: Access: Phone, mail, online, in person. Both court and visitors may perform in person searches. No search fee. Required to search: name, years to search; also helpful: address. Civil cases indexed by defendant, plaintiff. Civil records on computer from 1987, archives back to 1800. Index available remotely online on the statewide OJIN system, call 800-858-9658 for information.

Criminal Records: Access: Phone, mail, online, in person. Both court and visitors may perform in person searches. No search fee. Required to search: name, years to search, DOB; also helpful: address, SSN. Criminal records on computer from 1987, archives back to 1800. Online access to criminal records is the same as civil.

General Information: Public Access terminal is available. No adoptions, sealed by Judge, expunged, paternity or mental health records released. SASE required. Turnaround time 1-2 days. Copy fee: $.25 per page. Certification fee: $3.75. Fee payee: State Courts. Personal checks accepted. Credit cards accepted: Visa, MasterCard. Visa, MC. Not accepted for filing fees. Prepayment is required.

Crook County

Circuit Court Crook County Courthouse, 300 NE Third St, Prineville, OR 97754; 541-447-6541. Hours: 8AM-5PM (PST). *Felony, Misdemeanor, Civil, Eviction, Small Claims, Probate.*

Civil Records: Access: Phone, mail, in person. Both court and visitors may perform in person searches. No search fee. Required to search: name, years to search; also helpful: address. Civil cases indexed by defendant, plaintiff. Civil records on computer from 1986, microfiche from 1907, archives from 1907. Index available remotely online on the statewide OJIN system, call 800-858-9658 for information.

Criminal Records: Access: Phone, mail, in person. Both court and visitors may perform in person searches. No search fee. Required to search: name, years to search, DOB; also helpful: address, SSN. Criminal records on computer from 1986, microfiche from 1907, archives from 1907. Online access to criminal records is the same as civil.

General Information: No adoptions, juvenile, sealed by Judge, expunged, paternity or mental health records released. SASE required. Turnaround time 2-4 days. Copy fee: $.25 per page. Certification fee: $3.75. Fee payee: State of Oregon. Personal checks accepted. Prepayment is required.

Curry County

Circuit Court Box 810, Gold Beach, OR 97444; 541-247-4511. Hours: 8AM-5PM (PST). *Felony, Misdemeanor, Civil, Eviction, Small Claims, Probate.*

Civil Records: Access: Phone, mail, online, in person. Both court and visitors may perform in person searches. No search fee. Required to search: name, years to search; also helpful: address. Civil cases indexed by defendant, plaintiff. Civil records on computer from 1987, archives back to 1891. Index available remotely online on the statewide OJIN system, call 800-858-9658 for information.

Criminal Records: Access: Phone, mail, online, in person. Both court and visitors may perform in person searches. No search fee. Required to search: name, years to search, DOB; also helpful: address, SSN. Criminal records on computer from 1987, archives back to 1891. Online access to criminal records is the same as civil.

General Information: Public Access terminal is available. No adoptions, sealed by Judge, expunged, paternity or mental health records released. SASE required. Turnaround time 1-2 days from receipt of payment. Copy fee: $.25 per page. Add postage if SASE not enclosed. Certification fee: $3.75 for 1st page and $.25 for each add'l page. Fee payee: State Courts. Personal checks accepted. Credit card accepted: Visa, MC. Prepayment is required.

Deschutes County

Deschutes County Courts 1100 NW Bond, Bend, OR 97701; 541-388-5300. Hours: 8AM-5PM (PST). *Felony, Misdemeanor, Civil, Eviction, Small Claims, Probate.*

www.empnet.com/deschutes-court

Civil Records: Access: Phone, mail, online, in person. Both court and visitors may perform in person searches. No search fee. Required to search: name, years to search. Civil cases indexed by defendant, plaintiff. Civil records on computer from 9/87, books from 1976, archived from 1916 on microfiche. Index available remotely online on the statewide OJIN system, call 800-858-9658 for information.

Criminal Records: Access: Phone, mail, online, in person. Both court and visitors may perform in person searches. No search fee. Required to search: name, years to search. Criminal records on computer from 9/87, books from 1976, archived from 1916 on microfiche. Criminal Index is available remotely online for records from 07/86 forward. see civil section.

General Information: Public Access terminal is available. No adoptions, juvenile, sealed by Judge, expunged, mental health records released. SASE required. Turnaround time 3-5 days. Copy fee: $.25 per page. Certification fee: $3.75. Fee payee: State of Oregon. Personal checks accepted. Prepayment is required.

Douglas County

Circuit Court 1036 S E Douglas Rm 202, Roseburg, OR 97470; 541-957-2470; Fax: 541-957-2462. Hours: 8AM-5PM (PST). *Felony, Misdemeanor, Civil, Eviction, Small Claims, Probate.*

Civil Records: Access: Phone, mail, online, in person. Both court and visitors may perform in person searches. No search fee. Required to search: name, years to search. Civil cases indexed by defendant, plaintiff. Civil records on computer from Oct 1987, microfiche from 1974 (district) 1962 (circuit), archived from 1910. Index available remotely online on the statewide OJIN system, call 800-858-9658 for information.

Criminal Records: Access: Phone, mail, online, in person. Both court and visitors may perform in person searches. No search fee. Required to search: name, years to search, DOB. Criminal records on computer from Oct 1987, microfiche from 1974 (district) 1962 (circuit), archived from 1910. Online access to criminal records is the same as civil.

General Information: Public Access terminal is available. No adoptions, juvenile, sealed by Judge, expunged or mental health records released. SASE required. Turnaround time 5-10 days. Copy fee: $.25 per page. Certification fee: $3.75. Fee payee: Oregon Judicial Department. Personal checks accepted. Prepayment is required.

Gilliam County

Circuit Court Box 622, Condon, OR 97823; 541-384-3572; Fax: 541-384-2166. Hours: 1-5PM (PST). *Felony, Misdemeanor, Civil.*

Civil Records: Access: Phone, mail, online, in person. Both court and visitors may perform in person searches. No search fee. Required to search: name, years to

search. Civil cases indexed by defendant, plaintiff. Civil records on computer from 1989, index cards back to 1800s. Index available remotely online on the statewide OJIN system, call 800-858-9658 for information.

Criminal Records: Access: Phone, mail, online, in person. Both court and visitors may perform in person searches. No search fee. Required to search: name, years to search; also helpful: DOB. Criminal records on computer from 1989, index cards back to 1800s. Online access to criminal records is the same as civil.

General Information: Public Access terminal is available. No adoptions, juvenile, sealed by Judge, expunged, mental health records released. SASE required. Turnaround time 1-2 days. Copy fee: $.25 per page. Certification fee: $3.75. Fee payee: Gilliam Circuit Court. Personal checks accepted. Prepayment is required.

County Court 221 S Oregon, PO Box 427, Condon, OR 97823; 541-384-2311; Fax: 541-384-2166. Hours: 8:30AM-Noon, 1-5PM (PST). *Probate.*

Grant County

Circuit Court Box 159 (205 S. Humbolt Street), Canyon City, OR 97820; 541-575-1438; Fax: 541-575-2165. Hours: 8AM-Noon, 1-5PM (PST). *Felony, Misdemeanor, Civil.*

www.ojd.state.or.us/grant

Civil Records: Access: Mail, online, in person. Only the court performs in person searches; visitors may not. No search fee. Required to search: name, years to search. Civil cases indexed by defendant, plaintiff. Civil records on computer from 1987, microfiche from 1950-1965, archives back to 1880. Index available remotely online on the statewide OJIN system, call 800-858-9658 for information.

Criminal Records: Access: Mail, online, in person. Only the court performs in person searches; visitors may not. No search fee. Required to search: name, years to search. Criminal records on computer from 1987, microfiche from 1950-1965, archives back to 1880. Online access to criminal records is the same as civil.

General Information: No adoptions, juvenile, sealed by Judge, expunged, mental health records released. SASE required. Turnaround time 3-5 days. Copy fee: $.25 per page. Certification fee: $3.75. Fee payee: Grant County Circuit Court. Personal checks accepted. Prepayment is required.

County Court 201 Humbolt St #290, Canyon City, OR 97820-6186; 541-575-1675; Fax: 541-575-2248. Hours: 8AM-5PM (PST). *Probate.*

Harney County

Circuit Court 450 N. Buena Vista, Burns, OR 97720; 541-573-5207; Fax: 541-573-5715. Hours: 8AM-5PM (PST). *Felony, Misdemeanor, Civil.*

www.ojd.state.or.us/harney

Civil Records: Access: Phone, fax, mail, online, in person. Both court and visitors may perform in person searches. No search fee. Required to search: name, years to search. Civil cases indexed by defendant, plaintiff. Civil records on computer from 1988, microfiche from 1970-1979, archives back to 1880. Index available remotely online on the statewide OJIN system, call 800-858-9658 for information.

Criminal Records: Access: Phone, fax, mail, online, in person. Both court and visitors may perform in person searches. No search fee. Required to search: name, years to search. Criminal records on computer from 1988, microfiche from 1970-1979, archives back to 1880. Online access to criminal records is the same as civil.

General Information: Public Access terminal is available. No adoptions, juvenile, sealed by Judge, expunged, paternity or mental health records released.

SASE required. Turnaround time 1-2 days. Fax notes: $2.00 for first page, $1.00 each add'l. Copy fee: $.25 per page. Certification fee: $3.75. Fee payee: Harney Circuit Court. Personal checks accepted. Prepayment is required.

County Court 450 N Buena Vista Ave, Burns, OR 97720-1518; 541-573-6641; Fax: 541-573-8370. Hours: 8:30AM-Noon, 1-5PM (PST). *Probate.*

Hood River County

Circuit Court 309 State St., Hood River, OR 97031; 541-386-1862; Fax: 541-386-3465. Hours: 8AM-Noon, 1-5PM (PST). *Felony, Misdemeanor, Civil, Eviction, Small Claims, Probate.*

Civil Records: Access: Phone, fax, mail, online, in person. Both court and visitors may perform in person searches. No search fee. Required to search: name, years to search. Civil cases indexed by defendant, plaintiff. Civil records on computer from 1989, docket books from 1950. Index available remotely online on the statewide OJIN system, call 800-858-9658 for information.

Criminal Records: Access: Phone, fax, mail, online, in person. Both court and visitors may perform in person searches. No search fee. Required to search: name, years to search, DOB. Criminal records on computer from 1989, docket books from 1950. Online access to criminal records is the same as civil.

General Information: Public Access terminal is available. No adoptions, juvenile, sealed by Judge, expunged, paternity or mental health records released. Turnaround time 1-2 days. Copy fee: $.25 per page. Certification fee: $3.75. Fee payee: Hood River Trial Courts. Personal checks accepted. Credit cards accepted. Prepayment is required.

Jackson County

Circuit Court 100 S. Oakdale, Medford, OR 97501; 541-776-7171; Fax: 541-776-7057. Hours: 8AM-5PM (PST). *Felony, Misdemeanor, Civil Actions, Eviction, Small Claims, Probate.*

Civil Records: Access: Phone, mail, online, in person. Both court and visitors may perform in person searches. No search fee. Required to search: name, years to search. Civil cases indexed by defendant, plaintiff. Civil records on computer from 1988, prior records on docket books and microfilm. Index available remotely online on the statewide OJIN system, call 800-858-9658 for information.

Criminal Records: Access: Phone, mail, online, in person. Both court and visitors may perform in person searches. No search fee. Required to search: name, years to search, DOB. Criminal records on computer from 1988, prior records on docket books and microfilm. Online access to criminal records is the same as civil.

General Information: Public Access terminal is available. No adoptions, juvenile, sealed by Judge, expunged, mental health records released. SASE required. Turnaround time 1 week. Copy fee: $.25 per page. Certification fee: $3.75. Fee payee: Jackson County Courts. Personal checks accepted. Credit cards accepted. Prepayment is required.

Jefferson County

Circuit Court 75 SE C St., Madras, OR 97741-1750; 541-475-3317; Fax: 541-475-3421. Hours: 8AM-5PM (PST). *Felony, Misdemeanor, Civil, Eviction, Small Claims, Probate.*

Civil Records: Access: Mail, online, in person. Both court and visitors may perform in person searches. No search fee. Required to search: name, years to search. Civil cases indexed by defendant, plaintiff. Civil records on computer from Oct 1986, archives from 1916-1986.

Index available remotely online on the statewide OJIN system, call 800-858-9658 for information.

Criminal Records: Access: Mail, online, in person. Both court and visitors may perform in person searches. No search fee. Required to search: name, years to search, DOB. Criminal records on computer from Oct 1986, archives from 1916-1986. Online access to criminal records is the same as civil.

General Information: Public Access terminal is available. No adoptions, juvenile, sealed by Judge, expunged, mental health records released. SASE required. Turnaround time 1-2 weeks. Copy fee: $.25 per page. Certification fee: $3.75. Fee payee: State of Oregon. Personal checks accepted.

Josephine County

Circuit Court Josephine County Courthouse, Rm 254, 500 NW 6th St, Grants Pass, OR 97526; 541-476-2309; Fax: 541-471-2079. Hours: 8AM-5PM (PST). *Felony, Misdemeanor, Civil, Eviction, Small Claims, Probate.*

Civil Records: Access: Fax, mail, online, in person. Both court and visitors may perform in person searches. No search fee. Required to search: name, years to search. Civil cases indexed by defendant, plaintiff. Civil records on computer from 1987, microfilm prior to 1980, archives from 1920, index books. Index available remotely online on the statewide OJIN system, call 800-858-9658 for information.

Criminal Records: Access: Fax, mail, online, in person. Both court and visitors may perform in person searches. No search fee. Required to search: name, years to search, DOB. Criminal records on computer from 1987, microfilm prior to 1980, archives from 1920, index books. Online access to criminal records is the same as civil.

General Information: Public Access terminal is available. No adoptions, juvenile, sealed by Judge, expunged, mental health records released. SASE required. Turnaround time 10-15 working days. Fax notes: No fee to fax results. Copy fee: $.25 per page. Certification fee: $3.75. Fee payee: Josephine County Court. Personal checks accepted. Credit cards accepted: Visa, MasterCard. Prepayment is required.

Klamath County

Circuit Court 316 Main Street, Klamath Falls, OR 97601; 541-883-5503; Fax: 541-882-6109. Hours: 8AM-5PM (PST). *Felony, Misdemeanor, Civil, Eviction, Small Claims, Probate.*

http://klamath-court.ojd.state.or.us

Civil Records: Access: Mail, fax, online, in person. Both court and visitors may perform in person searches. Search fee: $7.50 if requested by mail. Required to search: name, years to search. Civil cases indexed by defendant, plaintiff. Civil records on computer from 1988, microfiche from 1940-1980. Index available remotely online on the statewide OJIN system, call 800-858-9658 for information.

Criminal Records: Access: Mail, fax, online, in person. Both court and visitors may perform in person searches. Search fee: $7.50 if requested by mail. Required to search: name, years to search. Criminal records on computer from 1988, microfiche from 1940-1980. Online access to criminal records is the same as civil.

General Information: Public Access terminal is available. No adoptions, juvenile, sealed by Judge, expunged, paternity or mental health records released. SASE required. Turnaround time 2 weeks. Fax notes: Fee to fax results is $1.00 per page. Copy fee: $.25 per page. Certification fee: $3.75. Fee payee: Klamath County Circuit Court. No personal checks accepted. Credit cards accepted: Visa, MasterCard. Prepayment is required.

Lake County

Circuit Court 513 Center St., Lakeview, OR 97630; 541-947-6051; Fax: 541-947-3724. Hours: 8AM-5PM (PST). *Felony, Misdemeanor, Civil, Eviction, Small Claims, Probate.*

Civil Records: Access: Mail, online, in person. Both court and visitors may perform in person searches. No search fee. Required to search: name, years to search. Civil cases indexed by defendant, plaintiff. Civil records on computer from 1988, index cards prior. Index available remotely online on the statewide OJIN system, call 800-858-9658 for information.

Criminal Records: Access: Mail, online, in person. Both court and visitors may perform in person searches. No search fee. Required to search: name, years to search. Criminal records on computer from 1988, index cards prior. Online access to criminal records is the same as civil.

General Information: Public Access terminal is available. No adoptions, juvenile, sealed by Judge, expunged or mental health records released. SASE required. Turnaround time 1 week. Fax notes: Will fax back only if local and prepaid. Copy fee: $.25 per page. Certification fee: $3.75. Fee payee: Lake County Circuit Court. Personal checks accepted. Prepayment is required.

Lane County

Circuit Court 125 E. 8th Ave., Eugene, OR 97401; 541-682-4020. Hours: 8AM-5PM (PST). *Felony, Misdemeanor, Civil, Eviction, Small Claims, Probate.*

Civil Records: Access: Online, in person. Visitors must perform in person searches for themselves. No search fee. Required to search: name, years to search. Civil cases indexed by defendant, plaintiff. Civil records on computer from 1983, index books prior. Index available remotely online on the statewide OJIN system, call 800-858-9658 for information.

Criminal Records: Access: Online, in person. Visitors must perform in person searches for themselves. No search fee. Required to search: name, years to search. Criminal records on computer from 1983, index books prior. Online access to criminal records is the same as civil.

General Information: Public Access terminal is available. No adoptions, juvenile, sealed by Judge, expunged, mental health records released. Copy fee: $.25 per page. Certification fee: $3.75 plus $.25 per page. Fee payee: Lane County Circuit Court or Lane County Courts. Personal checks accepted. Credit cards accepted. Accepted in person only. Prepayment is required.

Lincoln County

Lincoln County Courts PO Box 100, Newport, OR 97365; 541-265-4236; Fax: 541-265-7561. Hours: 8AM-5PM (PST). *Felony, Misdemeanor, Civil, Eviction, Small Claims, Probate.*

Civil Records: Access: Mail, online, in person. Visitors must perform in person searches for themselves. No search fee. Required to search: name. Civil cases indexed by defendant, plaintiff. Civil records on computer from 2/88, archives back to 1893, prior to 1988, years to search must be specified. Index available remotely online on the statewide OJIN system, call 800-858-9658 for information.

Criminal Records: Access: Mail, online, in person. Visitors must perform in person searches for themselves. No search fee. Required to search: name, years to search. Criminal records on computer from 2/88, archives back to 1893, prior to 1988, years to search must be specified. Online access to criminal records is the same as civil.

General Information: Public Access terminal is available. No adoptions, sealed by Judge, expunged, or

mental health records released. SASE required. Turnaround time 1 week. Copy fee: $.25 per page. Certification fee: $3.75. Fee payee: State of Oregon. Personal checks accepted. Credit cards accepted: Visa, MasterCard. $1.00 minimum charge. Prepayment is required.

Linn County

Circuit Court PO Box 1749, Albany, OR 97321; 541-967-3845. Hours: 8AM-5PM (PST). *Felony, Misdemeanor, Civil, Eviction, Small Claims, Probate.*

www.ojd.state.or.us/linn-circuit

Civil Records: Access: Mail, online, in person. Both court and visitors may perform in person searches. No search fee. Required to search: name, years to search. Civil cases indexed by defendant, plaintiff. Civil records on computer from June 1987, archives back to 1863. Index available remotely online on the statewide OJIN system, call 800-858-9658 for information.

Criminal Records: Access: Mail, online, in person. Both court and visitors may perform in person searches. No search fee. Required to search: name, years to search, DOB. Criminal records on computer from June 1987, archives back to 1863. Online access to criminal records is the same as civil.

General Information: Public Access terminal is available. No adoptions, juvenile, sealed by judge, expunged, paternity or mental health records released. SASE required. Turnaround time 5-10 days. Copy fee: $.25 per page. Certification fee: $3.75. Fee payee: Linn County Courts. Personal checks accepted. Prepayment is required.

Malheur County

Circuit Court 251 B St West, Vale, OR 97918; 541-473-5171; Fax: 541-473-2213. Hours: 8AM-5PM; 9AM-Noon, 1-4PM (Record Inquiry) (MST). *Felony, Misdemeanor, Civil, Eviction, Small Claims.*

Civil Records: Access: Mail, online, in person. Both court and visitors may perform in person searches. Search fee: No fee, unless access needed to archived records. Required to search: name, years to search. Civil cases indexed by defendant, plaintiff. Civil records on computer from July 1988, archived from 1887. Index available remotely online on the statewide OJIN system, call 800-858-9658 for information.

Criminal Records: Access: Mail, online, in person. Both court and visitors may perform in person searches. Search fee: None fee unless archived records needed. Required to search: name, years to search, DOB. Criminal records on computer from July 1988, archived from 1887. Online access to criminal records is the same as civil.

General Information: Public Access terminal is available. No adoptions, juvenile, sealed by Judge, expunged, mental health records released. SASE requested. Turnaround time 2 weeks minimum. Fax notes: Fee to fax results is $1.00 per page. Copy fee: $.25 per page. Certification fee: $3.75. Fee payee: Trial Court Clerk. Personal checks accepted. Credit cards accepted: Visa, MasterCard. Accepted for filing fees only. Prepayment is required.

County Court 251 B St W #5, Vale, OR 97918; 541-473-5123; Fax: 541-473-5523. Hours: 8AM-Noon, 1-4:30PM (MST). *Probate.*

www.malheurco.org

Marion County

Circuit Court PO Box 12864 (100 High St NE), Salem, OR 97309; 503-588-5101; Fax: 503-373-4360. Hours: 8AM-5PM (PST). *Felony, Misdemeanor, Civil, Eviction, Small Claims, Probate.*

http://marion-court.ojd.state.or.us

Civil Records: Access: Mail, online, in person. Both court and visitors may perform in person searches. No search fee. Required to search: name, years to search. Civil cases indexed by defendant, plaintiff. Civil records on computer from 1986, prior to 1986 on microfiche. Index available remotely online on the statewide OJIN system, call 800-858-9658 for information.

Criminal Records: Access: Mail, online, in person. Both court and visitors may perform in person searches. No search fee. Required to search: name, years to search, signed release; also helpful: DOB, SSN. Criminal records on computer from 1986, prior to 1986 on microfiche. Online access to criminal records is the same as civil.

General Information: Public Access terminal is available. No adoptions, juvenile, sealed by Judge, expunged, paternity or mental health records released. SASE required. Turnaround time 1-2 days. Copy fee: $.25 per page. Certification fee: $3.00. Fee payee: State of Oregon. Personal checks accepted. Prepayment is required.

Morrow County

Circuit Court PO Box 609, Heppner, OR 97836; 541-676-5264; Fax: 541-676-9902. Hours: 8AM-Noon, 1-4:45PM (PST). *Felony, Misdemeanor, Civil, Eviction, Small Claims, Probate.*

Civil Records: Access: Phone, fax, mail, online, in person. Both court and visitors may perform in person searches. No search fee. Required to search: name, years to search. Civil cases indexed by defendant, plaintiff. Civil records on computer from 1987, archives back to 1940, index cards, docket books by case #. Index available remotely online on the statewide OJIN system, call 800-858-9658 for information.

Criminal Records: Access: Phone, fax, mail, online, in person. Both court and visitors may perform in person searches. No search fee. Required to search: name, years to search, DOB. Criminal records on computer from 1987, archives back to 1940, index cards, docket books by case #. Online access to criminal records is the same as civil.

General Information: Public Access terminal is available. No adoptions, juvenile, sealed by Judge, expunged, paternity or mental health records released. SASE required. Turnaround time 1-3 days. Fax notes: No fee to fax results. Copy fee: $.25 per page. Certification fee: $3.75. Fee payee: Circuit Court. Personal checks accepted. Prepayment is required.

Multnomah County

Circuit Court 1021 SW 4th Ave, Rm 131, Portland, OR 97204; 503-248-3003. Hours: 8AM-4:30PM (PST). *Felony, Misdemeanor, Civil Actions Over $10,000, Probate.*

Civil Records: Access: Mail, online, in person. Both court and visitors may perform in person searches. No search fee. Required to search: name, years to search. Civil cases indexed by defendant, plaintiff. Civil records on computer from 1988, microfiche, index books, docket books back to 1857. Index available remotely online on the statewide OJIN system, call 800-858-9658 for information.

Criminal Records: Access: Mail, online, in person. Both court and visitors may perform in person searches. No search fee. Required to search: name, years to search; also helpful: DOB. Criminal records on computer from 1988, microfiche, index books, docket books back to 1857. Online access to criminal records is the same as civil.

General Information: Public Access terminal is available. No adoptions, juvenile, sealed by Judge, expunged or mental health records released. SASE required. Turnaround time 4-5 days. Copy fee: $.25 per page. Certification fee: $3.75. Fee payee: State of

Oregon. Personal checks accepted. Prepayment is required.

Circuit Court - Civil Division 1021 SW 4th Ave, Rm 210, Portland, OR 97204; 503-988-3022. Hours: 8:30AM-5PM (Tele: 8-10AM; 1-3PM) (PST). *Civil Actions Under $10,000, Eviction, Small Claims.*

www.ojd.state.or.us/multnomah

Civil Records: Access: Phone, mail, online, in person. Both court and visitors may perform in person searches. Some limitations may apply. No search fee. Required to search: name, years to search. Civil cases indexed by defendant, plaintiff. Civil records on computer from 1988, microfiche 1984-1988, docket cards by case # and yr. Index available remotely online on the statewide OJIN system, call 800-858-9658 for information.

General Information: Public Access terminal is available. No adoptions, juvenile, sealed by Judge, expunged, paternity or mental health records released. SASE required. Turnaround time 5 days. Copy fee: $.25 per page. Certification fee: $3.75. Fee payee: State of Oregon. Personal checks accepted. Prepayment is required.

Polk County

Circuit Court Polk County Courthouse, Rm 301, 850 Main St, Dallas, OR 97338; Civil phone: 503-623-3154; Criminal phone: 503-831-1778; Fax: 503-623-6614. Hours: 8AM-Noon, 1-5PM (PST). *Felony, Misdemeanor, Civil, Eviction, Small Claims, Probate.*

Note: Fax for criminal is 503-831-1779.

Civil Records: Access: Phone, fax, mail, online, in person. Both court and visitors may perform in person searches. No search fee. Required to search: name, years to search. Civil cases indexed by defendant, plaintiff. Civil records on computer from 1985, microfilm, archives from 1969 (District) back to 1800s (Circuit). Index available remotely online on the statewide OJIN system, call 800-858-9658 for information.

Criminal Records: Access: Phone, fax, mail, online, in person. Both court and visitors may perform in person searches. No search fee. Required to search: name, years to search, DOB; also helpful: SSN. Criminal records on computer from 1985, microfilm, archives from 1969 (District) back to 1800s (Circuit). Online access to criminal records is the same as civil.

General Information: Public Access terminal is available. No adoptions, juvenile, sealed by Judge, expunged, mental health records released. SASE required. Turnaround time 2 weeks. Fax notes: No fee to fax results. Copy fee: $.25 per page. Certification fee: $3.75. Fee payee: Trial Court Administrator. Personal checks accepted. Credit cards accepted: Visa, MasterCard. Credit cards accepted in person only. Prepayment is required.

Sherman County

Circuit Court PO Box 402, Moro, OR 97039; 541-565-3650. Hours: 1-5PM (PST). *Felony, Misdemeanor, Civil.*

Civil Records: Access: Phone, mail, online, in person. Both court and visitors may perform in person searches. No search fee. Required to search: name, years to search. Civil cases indexed by defendant, plaintiff. Civil records on computer from 1992, microfiche up to 1987, index books, judgment docket books. Index available remotely online on the statewide OJIN system, call 800-858-9658 for information.

Criminal Records: Access: Phone, mail, online, in person. Both court and visitors may perform in person searches. No search fee. Required to search: name, years to search, DOB. Criminal record on computer from 1992, microfiche up to 1987, index books, judgment docket books. Online access to criminal records is the same as civil.

General Information: Public Access terminal is available. No adoptions, juvenile, sealed by Judge, expunged, paternity or mental health records released. SASE required. Turnaround time 2-5 days. Fax notes: Will not fax results. Copy fee: $.25 per page. Certification fee: $3.75. Fee payee: Sherman County Circuit Court. Personal checks accepted. Prepayment is required.

County Court PO Box 365, Moro, OR 97039; 541-565-3606; Fax: 541-565-3312. Hours: 8AM-5PM (PST). *Probate.*

Tillamook County

Circuit Court 201 Laurel Ave, Tillamook, OR 97141; 503-842-8014; Fax: 503-842-2597. Hours: 8AM-5PM (PST). *Felony, Misdemeanor, Civil, Eviction, Small Claims, Probate.*

Civil Records: Access: Mail, fax, online, in person. Both court and visitors may perform in person searches. No search fee. Required to search: name, years to search. Civil cases indexed by defendant, plaintiff. Civil records on computer from 1987, prior on case files. Index available remotely online on the statewide OJIN system, call 800-858-9658 for information.

Criminal Records: Access: Mail, fax, online, in person. Both court and visitors may perform in person searches. No search fee. Required to search: name, years to search. Criminal records on computer from 1987, prior on case files. Online access to criminal records is the same as civil.

General Information: Public Access terminal is available. No adoptions, juvenile, sealed by Judge, expunged, paternity or mental health records released. SASE required. Turnaround time 2-3 days. Copy fee: $.25 per page. Certification fee: $3.75. Fee payee: Trial Court Administrator. Personal checks accepted. Credit cards accepted. Prepayment is required.

Umatilla County

Circuit Court PO Box 1307, Pendleton, OR 97801; 541-278-0341; Fax: 541-278-2071. Hours: 8AM-5PM (PST). *Felony, Misdemeanor, Civil, Eviction, Small Claims, Probate.*

Civil Records: Access: Mail, online, in person. Both court and visitors may perform in person searches. No search fee. Required to search: name, years to search. Civil cases indexed by defendant, plaintiff. Civil records on computer from 11/86, microfiche, index card, docket books. Index available remotely online on the statewide OJIN system, call 800-858-9658 for information.

Criminal Records: Access: Mail, online, in person. Both court and visitors may perform in person searches. No search fee. Required to search: name, years to search. Criminal records on computer from 11/86, microfiche, index card, docket books. Online access to criminal records is the same as civil.

General Information: Public Access terminal is available. No adoptions, juvenile, sealed by Judge, expunged, paternity or mental health records released. SASE required. Turnaround time 1-3 weeks. Copy fee: $.25 per page. Certification fee: $3.75. Fee payee: Trial Court Administrator. Personal checks accepted. Credit cards accepted. Prepayment is required.

Union County

Circuit Court 1008 K Ave, La Grande, OR 97850; 541-962-9500; Fax: 541-963-0444. Hours: 8AM-Noon, 1-5PM (PST). *Felony, Misdemeanor, Civil, Eviction, Small Claims, Probate.*

Civil Records: Access: Mail, fax, online, in person. Both court and visitors may perform in person searches. No search fee. Required to search: name, years to search. Civil cases indexed by defendant, plaintiff. Civil records on computer from 1986, archives back to 1800s, on ledger books/docket books. Index available remotely online on the statewide OJIN system, call 800-858-9658 for information.

Criminal Records: Access: Mail, fax, online, in person. Both court and visitors may perform in person searches. No search fee. Required to search: name, years to search, DOB. Criminal records on computer from 1986, archives back to 1800s, on ledger books/docket books. Online access to criminal records is the same as civil.

General Information: Public Access terminal is available. No adoptions, juvenile, sealed by Judge, expunged, paternity or mental health records released. SASE required. Turnaround time 1-2 weeks. Copy fee: $.25 per page. Certification fee: $3.75. Fee payee: Circuit Court. Personal checks accepted. Credit cards accepted: Visa, MasterCard. Prepayment is required.

Wallowa County

Circuit Court 101 S River St, Rm 204, Enterprise, OR 97828; 541-426-4991; Fax: 541-426-4992. Hours: 8AM-5PM (PST). *Felony, Misdemeanor, Civil, Eviction, Small Claims, Probate.*

Civil Records: Access: Phone, mail, online, in person. Both court and visitors may perform in person searches. No search fee. Required to search: name, years to search. Civil cases indexed by defendant, plaintiff. Civil records on computer from 1987, prior on docket books. Index available remotely online on the statewide OJIN system, call 800-858-9658 for information.

Criminal Records: Access: Phone, mail, online, in person. Both court and visitors may perform in person searches. No search fee. Required to search: name, years to search. Criminal records on computer from 1987, prior on docket books. Online access to criminal records is the same as civil.

General Information: Public Access terminal is available. No adoptions, juvenile, sealed by Judge, expunged, paternity or mental health records released. SASE required. Turnaround time 1-3 days. Copy fee: $.25 per page. Certification fee: $3.75. Fee payee: Circuit Court. Personal checks accepted. Copy fees will be billed.

Wasco County

Circuit Court PO Box 1400, The Dalles, OR 97058-1400; 541-296-3154; Fax: 541-298-5611. 8AM-Noon,1-5PM (PST). *Felony, Misdemeanor, Civil, Eviction, Small Claims, Probate.*

Civil Records: Access: Mail, online, in person. Both court and visitors may perform in person searches. No search fee. Required to search: name, years to search. Civil cases indexed by defendant, plaintiff. Civil records

on computer from 1989, prior records in docket books by case # and year back to 1900s. Index available remotely online on the statewide OJIN system, call 800-858-9658 for information.

Criminal Records: Access: Mail, online, in person. Both court and visitors may perform in person searches. No search fee. Required to search: name, years to search. Criminal records on computer from 1989, prior records in docket books by case # and year back to 1900s. Online access to criminal records is the same as civil.

General Information: Public Access terminal is available. No adoptions, juvenile, sealed by Judge, expunged, paternity or mental health records released. SASE required. Turnaround time 2-3 days. Copy fee: $.25 per page. Certification fee: $3.75. Fee payee: Trial Court Administrator. Personal checks accepted. Credit cards accepted: Visa, MasterCard. Prepayment is required.

Washington County

Circuit Court 150 N 1st, Hillsboro, OR 97124; 503-846-8888 x2302 (civ) x6060 (crim); Fax: 503-846-6087. Hours: 8-11:30AM, 12:30-3PM (PST). *Felony, Misdemeanor, Civil, Eviction, Small Claims, Probate.*

Civil Records: Access: Phone, mail, online, in person. Both court and visitors may perform in person searches. No search fee. Required to search: name, years to search. Civil cases indexed by defendant, plaintiff. Civil records on computer from 1982, prior on docket books. Index available remotely online on the statewide OJIN system, call 800-858-9658 for information.

Criminal Records: Access: Phone, mail, online, in person. Both court and visitors may perform in person searches. No search fee. Required to search: name, years to search, DOB. Criminal records on computer from 1982, prior on docket books. Online access to criminal records is the same as civil.

General Information: Public Access terminal is available. No adoptions, juvenile, sealed by Judge, expunged, paternity or mental health records released. Turnaround time 2-5 days. Copy fee: $.25 per page. Certification fee: $3.75. Fee payee: State of Oregon. Personal checks accepted. Prepayment is required.

Wheeler County

Circuit Court PO Box 308, Fossil, OR 97830; 541-763-2541; Fax: 541-763-2026. Hours: 8:30AM-11:30AM (PST). *Felony, Misdemeanor, Civil.*

Civil Records: Access: Phone, mail, online, in person. Both court and visitors may perform in person searches. No search fee. Required to search: name, years to

search. Civil cases indexed by defendant. Civil records on computer from 1989, docket books by case # and yr. Index available remotely online on the statewide OJIN system, call 800-858-9658 for information.

Criminal Records: Access: Phone, mail, online, in person. Both court and visitors may perform in person searches. No search fee. Required to search: name, years to search, DOB. Criminal records on computer from 1989, docket books by case # and yr. Online access to criminal records is the same as civil.

General Information: Public Access terminal is available. No adoptions, juvenile, sealed by Judge, expunged, paternity or mental health records released. SASE required. Turnaround time 1 week. Copy fee: $.25 per page. Certification fee: $3.75. Fee payee: Wheeler Circuit Court. Personal checks accepted. Prepayment is required.

County Court PO Box 327 (701 Adams, Rm 204), Fossil, OR 97830; 541-763-2400; Fax: 541-763-2026. Hours: 9-5PM (PST). *Probate.*

Yamhill County

Circuit Court 535 NE Fifth, McMinnville, OR 97128; 503-434-7530; Fax: 503-472-5805. Hours: 8AM-Noon, 1-5PM (PST). *Felony, Misdemeanor, Civil, Eviction, Small Claims, Probate.*

Civil Records: Access: Mail, online, in person. Both court and visitors may perform in person searches. No search fee. Required to search: name, years to search. Civil cases indexed by defendant, plaintiff. Civil records on computer from 1987, microfiche (10 yrs Dist, unlimited Circuit), archives back to 1900s, docket books by case # and yr. Index available remotely online on the statewide OJIN system, call 800-858-9658 for information.

Criminal Records: Access: Mail, online, in person. Both court and visitors may perform in person searches. No search fee. Required to search: name, years to search, DOB. Criminal records on computer from 1987, microfiche (10 yrs Dist, unlimited Circuit), archives back to 1900s, docket books by case # and yr. Online access to criminal records is the same as civil.

General Information: Public Access terminal is available. No adoptions, juvenile, sealed by Judge, expunged or mental health records released. SASE requested. Turnaround time 1-7 days. Copy fee: $.25 per page. Certification fee: $3.75. Fee payee: Trial Court. Personal checks accepted. Two party, payroll checks not accepted. Credit cards accepted: Visa, MasterCard. Prepayment is required.

Oregon Recording Offices

ORGANIZATION	36 counties, 36 recording offices. The recording officer is County Clerk. 35 counties are in the Pacific Time Zone (PST) and one is in the Mountain Time Zone (MST).
REAL ESTATE RECORDS	Some counties will not perform real estate searches. Search fees vary. Many counties will search all liens together for $12.50 per name. Copy fees are usually $.25 per page. Certification usually costs $3.75 per document. The Assessor keeps tax and ownership records.
UCC RECORDS	Financing statements are filed at the state level, except for real estate related collateral. Many county clerks will not perform UCC searches.
TAX LIEN RECORDS	All federal and state tax liens on personal property are filed with the Secretary of State. Other federal and state tax liens are filed with the County Clerk. Most counties will perform tax lien searches and include both with a UCC search for an extra $7.50 per name. Search fees vary widely.
OTHER LIENS	County tax, public utility, construction, judgment, hospital.

Baker County

County Clerk, 1995 Third Street, Suite 150, Baker, OR 97814-3398. County Clerk, R/E and UCC Recording 541-523-8207; Fax 541-523-8240. http://www.baker county.org
Will search UCC records. **Other Phone Numbers:** Assessor 541-523-8203; Treasurer 541-523-8233; Appraiser/Auditor 541-523-8203; Elections 541-523-8207; Vital Records 541-731-4095.

Benton County

County Clerk, 120 NW 4th Street, Room 4, Corvallis, OR 97330. 541-766-6831; Fax 541-754-2870. http://www.co.benton.or.us
Will search UCC records. **Online Access:** Real Estate. The County is developing a Geographic Information System Internet site for viewing property information at www.co.benton.or.us/irm/gis/GISpage.htm. A law enforcement case system may soon offer open case data. **Other Phone Numbers:** Assessor 541-757-6878.

Clackamas County

County Clerk, 104 11th Street, Room 104, Oregon City, OR 97045. County Clerk, R/E and UCC Recording 503-655-8551; http://www.co.clackamas.or.us/clerk
Will not search UCC records. Agency will not search Real Estate records. **Other Phone Numbers:** Assessor 503-655-8671; Treasurer 503-655-8915; Elections 503-655-8510; Vital Records 503-731-4095.

Clatsop County

County Clerk, P.O. Box 178, Astoria, OR 97103-0178. County Clerk, R/E and UCC Recording 503-325-8511; Fax 503-325-9307. http://www.co.clatsop.or.us/ contact.htm
Will search UCC records. **Other Phone Numbers:** Assessor 503-325-8522; Treasurer 503-325-8565; Appraiser/Auditor 503-325-8522; Elections 503-325-8511; Vital Records 503-325-8511.

Columbia County

County Clerk, Courthouse, St. Helens, OR 97051-2041. County Clerk, R/E and UCC Recording 503-397-3796; Fax 503-397-7266.
Will search UCC records. Will not search real estate records. **Other Phone Numbers:** Assessor 503-397-7210; Treasurer 503-397-0344; Appraiser/Auditor 503-397-2240; Elections 503-397-7214 & 3796; Vital Records 503-397-3796.

Coos County

County Clerk, Courthouse, 250 N. Baxter, Coquille, OR 97423-1899. 541-396-3121 R/E Recording: 541-396-3121 x223 UCC Recording: 541-396-3121 x223; Fax 541-396-6551.

Will search UCC records. This agency will not do a tax lien search. Will not search real estate records. **Other Phone Numbers:** Assessor 541-396-3121 x274; Treasurer 541-396-3121 x333; Appraiser/Auditor 541-396-3121 x274; Elections 541-396-3121 x301.

Crook County

County Clerk, 300 East Third, Prineville, OR 97754. 541-447-6553; Fax 541-447-1051.
Will search UCC records. Will search R/E records. **Other Phone Numbers:** Assessor 541-447-4133; Treasurer 541-447-6554; Elections 541-447-6553.

Curry County

County Clerk, P.O. Box 746, Gold Beach, OR 97444. County Clerk, R/E and UCC Recording 541-247-7011 x209; Fax 541-247-6440. http://www.co.curry.or.us
Will search UCC records. **Other Phone Numbers:** Assessor 541-247-7011; Treasurer 541-247-7011; Appraiser/Auditor 541-247-7011 x230; Elections 541-247-7011 x223.

Deschutes County

County Clerk, 1340 NW Wall St., Bend, OR 97701. County Clerk, R/E and UCC Recording 541-388-6549; Fax 541-389-6830. http://recordings.co.deschutes.or.us
Will search UCC records. Will not search real estate records. **Online Access:** Real Estate, Tax Assessor Records. To access records on the Deschutes County "Assessor Inquiry System" web site, click on DIAL on the menu bar. Tax information, assessment, appraisal details, ownership, sales information, transaction histories, account histories, land use records, and lot numbers are available for no fee. **Other Phone Numbers:** Assessor 541-388-6508; Treasurer 541-388-6535; Elections 541-388-6546.

Douglas County

County Clerk, P.O. Box 10, Roseburg, OR 97470. 541-440-4322; Fax 541-440-4408.
Will search UCC records. **Other Phone Numbers:** Assessor 541-440-4222; Treasurer 541-440-3311.

Gilliam County

County Clerk, P.O. Box 427, Condon, OR 97823. County Clerk, R/E and UCC Recording 541-384-2311; Fax 541-384-2166.
Will search UCC records. This agency will not do a tax lien search. Will not search real estate records. **Other Phone Numbers:** Assessor 541-384-3781; Treasurer 541-384-6321; Appraiser/Auditor 541-384-3781; Elections 541-384-2311; Vital Records 541-384-2311.

Grant County

County Clerk, 201 South Humbolt, Suite 290, Canyon City, OR 97820. County Clerk, R/E and UCC Recording 541-575-1675; Fax 541-575-2248.
Will search UCC records. **Other Phone Numbers:** Assessor 541-575-0107; Treasurer 541-575-1798; Appraiser/Auditor 541-575-0107; Elections 541-575-1675.

Harney County

County Clerk, 450 North Buena Vista, Burns, OR 97720. 541-573-6641 R/E Recording: 541-573-6411 UCC Recording: 541-573-6411; Fax 541-573-8370.
Will not search UCC records. **Other Phone Numbers:** Assessor 541-573-8367; Treasurer 541-573-6541; Appraiser/Auditor 541-573-8368; Elections 541-573-6411.

Hood River County

County Clerk, 309 State Street, Hood River, OR 97031-2093. County Clerk, R/E and UCC Recording 541-386-1442; Fax 541-386-9392.
Will not search UCC records. Will Not search real estate records. **Other Phone Numbers:** Assessor 541-386-3970; Elections 541-386-1442.

Jackson County

County Clerk, 10 South Oakdale, Room 216A, Medford, OR 97501. 541-774-6151.
Will search UCC records. Tax liens included with UCC search for total fee of $12.50. Will not search real estate records. **Other Phone Numbers:** Assessor 541-776-7077.

Jefferson County

County Clerk, 75 S.E. C Street, Madras, OR 97741. County Clerk, R/E and UCC Recording 541-475-4451; Fax 541-475-4454.
Will search UCC records. **Other Phone Numbers:** Assessor 541-475-2443; Treasurer 541-475-4458; Appraiser/Auditor 541-475-2443; Elections 541-475-4451.

Josephine County

County Clerk, P.O. Box 69, Grants Pass, OR 97528. 541-474-5240; Fax 541-476-5246.
Will search UCC records. Will not search real estate records. **Other Phone Numbers:** Assessor 541-474-5260; Treasurer 541-474-5235.

Klamath County

County Clerk, 305 Main St., Klamath Falls, OR 97601. 541-883-5134; Fax 541-885-6757.
Will not search UCC records. This agency will do a federal tax lien search only. Mortgage searches

available. **Other Phone Numbers:** Assessor 541-883-5111.

Lake County

County Clerk, 513 Center Street, Lakeview, OR 97630-1539. 541-947-6006; Fax 541-947-6015.
Will search UCC records. tax lines included in UCC search if requested for $12.50 total fee. RE owner, mortgage, and property transfer searches available. **Other Phone Numbers:** Assessor 541-947-6000.

Lane County

County Clerk, 125 East 8th Avenue, Eugene, OR 97401. 541-682-3654.
Will search UCC records. Tax liens not included in UCC search. Will not search real estate records. **Online Access:** Assessor, Real Estate. Property records on the County Tax Map site are available at www.co.lane.or.us/taxmap/TaxMapSelect.asp. **Other Phone Numbers:** Assessor 541-687-4321.

Lincoln County

County Clerk, 225 West Olive Street, Room 201, Newport, OR 97365-3869. 541-265-4121; Fax 541-265-4950.
Will search UCC records. UCC search includes tax liens if requested. Will not search real estate records. **Other Phone Numbers:** Assessor 541-265-4102.

Linn County

County Clerk, P.O. Box 100, Albany, OR 97321. 541-967-3829; Fax 541-926-5109. http://www.co.linn.or.us
Will search UCC records. **Online Access:** Assessor, Real Estate. Records on the County Property Records database are available free online at the web site. **Other Phone Numbers:** Assessor 541-967-3808.

Malheur County

County Clerk, 251 B Street West, Ste 4, Vale, OR 97918. 541-473-5151; Fax 541-473-5523.
Will search UCC records. Will not search real estate records. **Other Phone Numbers:** Assessor 541-473-5117.

Marion County

County Clerk, 100 High Street NE, Room 1331, Salem, OR 97301. 503-588-5225; Fax 503-588-5237.
Will search UCC records. Will not search real estate records. **Other Phone Numbers:** Assessor 503-588-5236.

Morrow County

Chief Deputy Clerk, P.O. Box 338, Heppner, OR 97836. 541-676-9061 R/E Recording: 541-676-5604 UCC Recording: 541-676-5604; Fax 541-676-9876. http://www.rootsweb.com/~ormorrow/MorrowCounty Courthouse.htm
Will search UCC records. Will not search real estate records. **Other Phone Numbers:** Assessor 541-676-5607; Treasurer 541-676-5630; Appraiser/Auditor 541-676-9061; Elections 541-676-9061; Vital Records 541-676-5603.

Multnomah County

County Clerk, P.O. Box 5007, Portland, OR 97208-5007. 503-248-3034; http://metromap.metro-region.org/public
Will search UCC records. This agency will not do a tax lien search. Will not search real estate records. **Online Access:** Real Property. Records on the County Metromap database are available free online at the web site. No name searching. **Other Phone Numbers:** Assessor 503-248-3226.

Polk County

County Clerk, Courthouse, 850 Main St., Dallas, OR 97338-3179. County Clerk, R/E and UCC Recording 503-623-9217; Fax 503-623-0717.
Will not search UCC records. Will not search real estate records. **Other Phone Numbers:** Assessor 503-623-8391; Treasurer 503-623-9264; Appraiser/Auditor 503-623-8391; Elections 503-623-9217; Vital Records 503-731-0495 (Portland).

Sherman County

Deputy Clerk, P.O. Box 365, Moro, OR 97039. Deputy Clerk, R/E and UCC Recording 541-565-3606; Fax 541-565-3312.
Will search UCC records. Will search real estate for $25.00 per hour **Other Phone Numbers:** Assessor 541-565-3505; Treasurer 541-565-3553; Appraiser/Auditor 541-565-3605; Elections 541-565-3606.

Tillamook County

County Clerk, 201 Laurel Avenue, Tillamook, OR 97141. County Clerk, R/E and UCC Recording 503-842-3402; Fax 503-842-1599. http://www.co.tillamook.or.us/gov/clerk/default.htm
Will search UCC records. **Online Access:** Assessor, Real Estate. Assessment and taxation records on the County Property database are available free online at www.co.tillamook.or.us/Documents/Search/query.asp. **Other Phone Numbers:** Assessor 503-842-3400/3424; Treasurer 503-842-3425; Appraiser/Auditor 503-842-3400/3424; Elections 503-842-3402; Vital Records 503-731-4095.

Umatilla County

County Clerk, P.O. Box 1227, Pendleton, OR 97801-1227. 541-278-6236; Fax 541-278-5463.
Will search UCC records. Will not search real estate records. **Other Phone Numbers:** Assessor 541-276-7111 x214.

Union County

County Clerk, 1001 4th St., Suite "D", La Grande, OR 97850. 541-963-1006; Fax 541-963-1013.
Will search UCC records. Will not search real estate records. **Other Phone Numbers:** Assessor 541-963-1001.

Wallowa County

County Clerk, 101 S. River, ROom 100 Door 16, Enterprise, OR 97828. County Clerk, R/E and UCC Recording 541-426-4543 x15; Fax 541-426-5901.

Will search UCC records. Will not search real estate records. **Other Phone Numbers:** Assessor 541-426-4543; Treasurer 541-426-4543 x14; Appraiser/Auditor 541-426-4543 x36; Elections 541-426-4543 x15; State 503-731-4095.

Wasco County

County Clerk, 511 Washington St., Courthouse, The Dalles, OR 97058-2237. County Clerk, R/E and UCC Recording 541-296-6159; Fax 541-298-3607.
Will not search UCC records. Will not search real estate records. **Other Phone Numbers:** Assessor 541-296-5477; Treasurer 541-296-3327; Appraiser/Auditor 541-296-5477; Elections 541-296-6159; Vital Records 541-296-6159.

Washington County

County Clerk, 155 N. First Ave., Mail Stop 9, Hillsboro, OR 97124. County Clerk, R/E and UCC Recording 503-846-8752; http://www.co.washington.or.us
Will search UCC records. UCC search includes tax liens if requested. Will not search real estate records. **Online Access:** Real Estate. Records on County GIS Intermap database are available free online at www.co.washington.or.us/gisaps/cfdocs/gisweb/par_2.htm. General Recording Office information is available at www.co.washington.or.us/deptmts/at/recordng/record.htm. **Other Phone Numbers:** Assessor 503-846-8741; Appraiser/Auditor 503-846-8826; Elections 503-846-8670; Vital Records 503-846-3538.

Wheeler County

County Clerk, P.O. Box 327, Fossil, OR 97830-0327. 541-763-2400; Fax 541-763-2026.
Will search UCC records. Will not search real estate records. **Other Phone Numbers:** Assessor 541-763-4266; Treasurer 541-763-2078; Appraiser/Auditor 541-763-4266; Elections 541-763-2400; Vital Records 541-763-2400.

Yamhill County

County Clerk, 535 NE 5th Street, Rm 119, McMinnville, OR 97128-4593. 503-434-7518; Fax 503-434-7520. http://www.co.yamhill.or.us/clerk
Will not search UCC records. Will not search real estate records. **Other Phone Numbers:** Assessor 503-434-7521; Treasurer 503-434-7533; Appraiser/Auditor 503-434-7521; Vital Records 503-434-7523.

Oregon County Locator

You will usually be able to find the city name in the City/County Cross Reference below. In that case, it is a simple matter to determine the county from the cross reference. However, only the official US Postal Service city names are included in this index. There are an additional 40,000 place names that people use in their addresses. Therefore, we have also included a ZIP/City Cross Reference immediately following the City/County Cross Reference.

If you know the ZIP Code but the city name does not appear in the City/County Cross Reference index, look up the ZIP Code in the ZIP/City Cross Reference, find the city name, then look up the city name in the City/County Cross Reference. For example, you want to know the county for an address of Menands, NY 12204. There is no "Menands" in the City/County Cross Reference. The ZIP/City Cross Reference shows that ZIP Codes 12201-12288 are for the city of Albany. Looking back in the City/County Cross Reference, Albany is in Albany County.

City/County Cross Reference

ADAMS Umatilla
ADEL Lake
ADRIAN Malheur
AGNESS Curry
ALBANY (97321) Linn(87), Benton(13)
ALLEGANY Coos
ALSEA (97324) Benton(92), Lincoln(9)
ALVADORE Lane
AMITY (97101) Yamhill(83), Polk(17)
ANTELOPE Wasco
ARCH CAPE Clatsop
ARLINGTON Gilliam
AROCK Malheur
ASHLAND Jackson
ASHWOOD Jefferson
ASTORIA Clatsop
ATHENA Umatilla
AUMSVILLE Marion
AURORA (97002) Marion(84),
  Clackamas(16)
AZALEA Douglas
BAKER CITY Baker
BANDON Coos
BANKS Washington
BATES Grant
BAY CITY Tillamook
BEATTY (97621) Klamath(89), Lake(11)
BEAVER Tillamook
BEAVERCREEK Clackamas
BEAVERTON Washington
BEND Deschutes
BLACHLY Lane
BLODGETT (97326) Lincoln(59),
  Benton(41)
BLUE RIVER Lane
BLY (97622) Klamath(83), Lake(17)
BOARDMAN Morrow
BONANZA Klamath
BORING Clackamas
BRIDAL VEIL Multnomah
BRIDGEPORT Baker
BRIGHTWOOD Clackamas
BROADBENT Coos
BROGAN Malheur
BROOKINGS Curry
BROTHERS Deschutes
BROWNSVILLE Linn
BURNS Harney
BUTTE FALLS Jackson
BUXTON Washington
CAMAS VALLEY Douglas
CAMP SHERMAN Jefferson
CANBY Clackamas
CANNON BEACH Clatsop
CANYON CITY Grant
CANYONVILLE Douglas
CARLTON Yamhill
CASCADE LOCKS (97014) Hood
  River(80), Multnomah(20)
CASCADIA Linn
CAVE JUNCTION Josephine
CAYUSE Umatilla
CENTRAL POINT Jackson

CHEMULT Klamath
CHESHIRE Lane
CHILOQUIN Klamath
CHRISTMAS VALLEY Lake
CLACKAMAS Clackamas
CLATSKANIE (97016) Columbia(92),
  Clatsop(8)
CLOVERDALE Tillamook
COLTON Clackamas
COLUMBIA CITY Columbia
CONDON Gilliam
COOS BAY Coos
COQUILLE Coos
CORBETT Multnomah
CORNELIUS Washington
CORVALLIS (97333) Benton(92), Linn(8)
CORVALLIS Benton
COTTAGE GROVE Lane
COVE Union
CRABTREE Linn
CRANE Harney
CRATER LAKE Klamath
CRAWFORDSVILLE Linn
CRESCENT Klamath
CRESCENT LAKE Klamath
CRESWELL Lane
CULP CREEK Lane
CULVER Jefferson
CURTIN Douglas
DAIRY Klamath
DALLAS Polk
DAYS CREEK Douglas
DAYTON Yamhill
DAYVILLE Grant
DEADWOOD Lane
DEER ISLAND Columbia
DEPOE BAY Lincoln
DETROIT Marion
DEXTER Lane
DIAMOND Harney
DILLARD Douglas
DONALD Marion
DORENA Lane
DRAIN Douglas
DREWSEY Harney
DUFUR Wasco
DUNDEE Yamhill
DURKEE Baker
EAGLE CREEK Clackamas
EAGLE POINT Jackson
ECHO Umatilla
EDDYVILLE Lincoln
ELGIN Union
ELKTON Douglas
ELMIRA Lane
ENTERPRISE Wallowa
ESTACADA Clackamas
EUGENE Lane
FAIRVIEW Multnomah
FALL CREEK Lane
FALLS CITY Polk
FIELDS Harney
FLORENCE Lane

FOREST GROVE Washington
FORT KLAMATH (97626) Klamath(75),
  Lake(25)
FORT ROCK Lake
FOSSIL Wheeler
FOSTER Linn
FOX Grant
FRENCHGLEN Harney
GALES CREEK Washington
GARDINER Douglas
GARIBALDI Tillamook
GASTON (97119) Washington(76),
  Yamhill(24)
GATES (97346) Marion(68), Linn(32)
GERVAIS Marion
GILCHRIST Klamath
GLADSTONE Clackamas
GLENDALE Douglas
GLENEDEN BEACH Lincoln
GLIDE Douglas
GOLD BEACH Curry
GOLD HILL Jackson
GOVERNMENT CAMP Clackamas
GRAND RONDE (97347) Polk(64),
  Yamhill(34), Tillamook(2)
GRANTS PASS Josephine
GRASS VALLEY (97029) Wasco(67),
  Sherman(33)
GREENLEAF Lane
GRESHAM (97080) Multnomah(95),
  Clackamas(5)
GRESHAM Multnomah
HAINES Baker
HALFWAY Baker
HALSEY Linn
HAMMOND Clatsop
HARPER Malheur
HARRISBURG (97446) Linn(99), Lane(1)
HEBO Tillamook
HELIX Umatilla
HEPPNER Morrow
HEREFORD Baker
HERMISTON Umatilla
HILLSBORO (97123) Washington(96),
  Yamhill(4)
HILLSBORO (97124) Washington(94),
  Multnomah(6)
HINES Harney
HOOD RIVER Hood River
HUBBARD (97032) Marion(88),
  Clackamas(12)
HUNTINGTON (97907) Baker(54),
  Malheur(47)
IDANHA (97350) Marion(67), Linn(33)
IDLEYLD PARK Douglas
IMBLER Union
IMNAHA Wallowa
INDEPENDENCE Polk
IONE Morrow
IRONSIDE Malheur
IRRIGON Morrow
JACKSONVILLE Jackson
JAMIESON Malheur

JEFFERSON Marion
JOHN DAY Grant
JORDAN VALLEY Malheur
JOSEPH Wallowa
JUNCTION CITY (97448) Lane(99),
  Benton(1)
JUNTURA Malheur
KEIZER Marion
KENO (97627) Klamath(95), Lake(5)
KENT Sherman
KERBY Josephine
KIMBERLY Grant
KLAMATH FALLS Klamath
LA GRANDE Union
LA PINE (97739) Deschutes(93),
  Klamath(7)
LAFAYETTE Yamhill
LAKE OSWEGO (97034) Clackamas(99),
  Multnomah(1)
LAKE OSWEGO (97035) Clackamas(92),
  Multnomah(6), Washington(2)
LAKESIDE Coos
LAKEVIEW Lake
LANGLOIS Curry
LAWEN Harney
LEBANON Linn
LEXINGTON Morrow
LINCOLN CITY Lincoln
LOGSDEN Lincoln
LONG CREEK Grant
LORANE Lane
LOSTINE Wallowa
LOWELL Lane
LYONS (97358) Linn(75), Marion(25)
MADRAS Jefferson
MALIN Klamath
MANNING Washington
MANZANITA Tillamook
MAPLETON Lane
MARCOLA Lane
MARION Marion
MARYLHURST Clackamas
MAUPIN Wasco
MCMINNVILLE Yamhill
MEACHAM Umatilla
MEDFORD Jackson
MEHAMA Marion
MERLIN Josephine
MERRILL Klamath
MIDLAND Klamath
MIKKALO Gilliam
MILL CITY (97360) Linn(85), Marion(15)
MILTON FREEWATER Umatilla
MITCHELL Wheeler
MOLALLA Clackamas
MONMOUTH (97361) Polk(98), Benton(2)
MONROE Benton
MONUMENT Grant
MORO (97039) Wasco(54), Sherman(46)
MOSIER Wasco
MOUNT ANGEL (97362) Marion(95),
  Clackamas(5)
MOUNT HOOD PARKDALE Hood River

MOUNT VERNON Grant
MULINO Clackamas
MURPHY Josephine
MYRTLE CREEK Douglas
MYRTLE POINT Coos
NEHALEM (97131) Tillamook(97), Clatsop(4)
NEOTSU Lincoln
NESKOWIN Tillamook
NETARTS Tillamook
NEW PINE CREEK (97635) Lake(50), Morrow(50)
NEWBERG (97132) Yamhill(98), Washington(1)
NEWPORT Lincoln
NORTH BEND Coos
NORTH PLAINS Washington
NORTH POWDER (97867) Union(87), Baker(13)
NORWAY Coos
NOTI Lane
NYSSA Malheur
O BRIEN Josephine
OAKLAND Douglas
OAKRIDGE Lane
OCEANSIDE Tillamook
ODELL Hood River
ONTARIO Malheur
OPHIR Curry
OREGON CITY Clackamas
OTIS (97368) Lincoln(74), Tillamook(26)
OTTER ROCK Lincoln
OXBOW Baker
PACIFIC CITY Tillamook
PAISLEY Lake
PAULINA Crook
PENDLETON Umatilla
PHILOMATH Benton
PHOENIX Jackson
PILOT ROCK Umatilla
PLEASANT HILL Lane
PLUSH Lake
PORT ORFORD Curry
PORTLAND (97206) Multnomah(94), Clackamas(6)

PORTLAND (97219) Multnomah(97), Clackamas(2)
PORTLAND (97229) Washington(83), Multnomah(17)
PORTLAND (97231) Multnomah(90), Washington(7), Columbia(4)
PORTLAND (97236) Multnomah(82), Clackamas(18)
PORTLAND (97266) Multnomah(76), Clackamas(24)
PORTLAND Clackamas
PORTLAND Multnomah
PORTLAND Washington
POST Crook
POWELL BUTTE Crook
POWERS Coos
PRAIRIE CITY Grant
PRINCETON Harney
PRINEVILLE Crook
PROSPECT Jackson
RAINIER Columbia
REDMOND Deschutes
REEDSPORT Douglas
REMOTE Coos
RHODODENDRON Clackamas
RICHLAND Baker
RICKREALL Polk
RIDDLE Douglas
RILEY Harney
RITTER Grant
RIVERSIDE Malheur
ROCKAWAY BEACH Tillamook
ROGUE RIVER Jackson
ROSE LODGE Lincoln
ROSEBURG Douglas
RUFUS Sherman
SAGINAW Lane
SAINT BENEDICT Marion
SAINT HELENS Columbia
SAINT PAUL Marion
SALEM (97304) Polk(98), Yamhill(2)
SALEM Marion
SANDY Clackamas
SCAPPOOSE (97056) Columbia(99), Multnomah(1)
SCIO Linn

SCOTTS MILLS (97375) Marion(94), Clackamas(6)
SCOTTSBURG Douglas
SEAL ROCK Lincoln
SEASIDE Clatsop
SELMA Josephine
SENECA Grant
SHADY COVE Jackson
SHANIKO Wasco
SHEDD Linn
SHERIDAN (97378) Yamhill(85), Polk(15)
SHERWOOD (97140) Washington(71), Clackamas(24), Yamhill(5)
SILETZ Lincoln
SILVER LAKE Lake
SILVERTON Marion
SISTERS (97759) Deschutes(94), Jefferson(6)
SIXES Curry
SOUTH BEACH Lincoln
SPRAGUE RIVER Klamath
SPRAY Wheeler
SPRINGFIELD Lane
STANFIELD Umatilla
STAYTON (97383) Marion(96), Linn(4)
SUBLIMITY Marion
SUMMER LAKE Lake
SUMMERVILLE Union
SUMPTER Baker
SUTHERLIN Douglas
SWEET HOME Linn
SWISSHOME Lane
TALENT Jackson
TANGENT Linn
TENMILE Douglas
TERREBONNE Deschutes
THE DALLES Wasco
THURSTON Lane
TIDEWATER (97390) Lincoln(91), Lane(9)
TILLAMOOK Tillamook
TILLER Douglas
TIMBER Washington
TOLEDO Lincoln
TOLOVANA PARK Clatsop
TRAIL Jackson
TROUTDALE Multnomah

TUALATIN (97062) Washington(85), Clackamas(15)
TURNER Marion
TYGH VALLEY Wasco
UKIAH Umatilla
UMATILLA Umatilla
UMPQUA Douglas
UNION Union
UNITY Baker
VALE Malheur
VENETA Lane
VERNONIA Columbia
VIDA Lane
WALDPORT Lincoln
WALLOWA Wallowa
WALTERVILLE Lane
WALTON Lane
WARM SPRINGS Jefferson
WARREN Columbia
WARRENTON Clatsop
WASCO (97065) Wasco(76), Sherman(24)
WEDDERBURN Curry
WELCHES Clackamas
WEST LINN Clackamas
WESTFALL Malheur
WESTFIR Lane
WESTLAKE Lane
WESTON Umatilla
WHEELER Tillamook
WHITE CITY Jackson
WILBUR Douglas
WILDERVILLE Josephine
WILLAMINA (97396) Yamhill(55), Polk(46)
WILLIAMS Josephine
WILSONVILLE (97070) Clackamas(95), Washington(5)
WINCHESTER Douglas
WINSTON Douglas
WOLF CREEK Josephine
WOODBURN (97071) Marion(97), Clackamas(3)
YACHATS Lincoln
YAMHILL Yamhill
YONCALLA Douglas

ZIP/City Cross Reference

97001-97001 ANTELOPE	97040-97040 MOSIER	97108-97108 BEAVER	97146-97146 WARRENTON
97002-97002 AURORA	97041-97041 MOUNT HOOD PARKDALE	97109-97109 BUXTON	97147-97147 WHEELER
97004-97004 BEAVERCREEK		97110-97110 CANNON BEACH	97148-97148 YAMHILL
97005-97008 BEAVERTON	97042-97042 MULINO	97111-97111 CARLTON	97149-97149 NESKOWIN
97009-97009 BORING	97044-97044 ODELL	97112-97112 CLOVERDALE	97201-97299 PORTLAND
97010-97010 BRIDAL VEIL	97045-97045 OREGON CITY	97113-97113 CORNELIUS	97301-97306 SALEM
97011-97011 BRIGHTWOOD	97048-97048 RAINIER	97114-97114 DAYTON	97307-97307 KEIZER
97013-97013 CANBY	97049-97049 RHODODENDRON	97115-97115 DUNDEE	97308-97314 SALEM
97014-97014 CASCADE LOCKS	97050-97050 RUFUS	97116-97116 FOREST GROVE	97321-97321 ALBANY
97015-97015 CLACKAMAS	97051-97051 SAINT HELENS	97117-97117 GALES CREEK	97324-97324 ALSEA
97016-97016 CLATSKANIE	97053-97053 WARREN	97118-97118 GARIBALDI	97325-97325 AUMSVILLE
97017-97017 COLTON	97054-97054 DEER ISLAND	97119-97119 GASTON	97326-97326 BLODGETT
97018-97018 COLUMBIA CITY	97055-97055 SANDY	97121-97121 HAMMOND	97327-97327 BROWNSVILLE
97019-97019 CORBETT	97056-97056 SCAPPOOSE	97122-97122 HEBO	97329-97329 CASCADIA
97020-97020 DONALD	97057-97057 SHANIKO	97123-97124 HILLSBORO	97330-97333 CORVALLIS
97021-97021 DUFUR	97058-97058 THE DALLES	97125-97125 MANNING	97335-97335 CRABTREE
97022-97022 EAGLE CREEK	97060-97060 TROUTDALE	97127-97127 LAFAYETTE	97336-97336 CRAWFORDSVILLE
97023-97023 ESTACADA	97062-97062 TUALATIN	97128-97128 MCMINNVILLE	97338-97338 DALLAS
97024-97024 FAIRVIEW	97063-97063 TYGH VALLEY	97130-97130 MANZANITA	97339-97339 CORVALLIS
97026-97026 GERVAIS	97064-97064 VERNONIA	97131-97131 NEHALEM	97341-97341 DEPOE BAY
97027-97027 GLADSTONE	97065-97065 WASCO	97132-97132 NEWBERG	97342-97342 DETROIT
97028-97028 GOVERNMENT CAMP	97067-97067 WELCHES	97133-97133 NORTH PLAINS	97343-97343 EDDYVILLE
97029-97029 GRASS VALLEY	97068-97068 WEST LINN	97134-97134 OCEANSIDE	97344-97344 FALLS CITY
97030-97030 GRESHAM	97070-97070 WILSONVILLE	97135-97135 PACIFIC CITY	97345-97345 FOSTER
97031-97031 HOOD RIVER	97071-97071 WOODBURN	97136-97136 ROCKAWAY BEACH	97346-97346 GATES
97032-97032 HUBBARD	97075-97078 BEAVERTON	97137-97137 SAINT PAUL	97347-97347 GRAND RONDE
97033-97033 KENT	97080-97080 GRESHAM	97138-97138 SEASIDE	97348-97348 HALSEY
97034-97035 LAKE OSWEGO	97101-97101 AMITY	97140-97140 SHERWOOD	97350-97350 IDANHA
97036-97036 MARYLHURST	97102-97102 ARCH CAPE	97141-97141 TILLAMOOK	97351-97351 INDEPENDENCE
97037-97037 MAUPIN	97103-97103 ASTORIA	97143-97143 NETARTS	97352-97352 JEFFERSON
97038-97038 MOLALLA	97106-97106 BANKS	97144-97144 TIMBER	97355-97355 LEBANON
97039-97039 MORO	97107-97107 BAY CITY	97145-97145 TOLOVANA PARK	97357-97357 LOGSDEN

ZIP Range	City	ZIP Range	City	ZIP Range	City	ZIP Range	City
97358-97358	LYONS	97442-97442	GLENDALE	97535-97535	PHOENIX	97819-97819	BRIDGEPORT
97359-97359	MARION	97443-97443	GLIDE	97536-97536	PROSPECT	97820-97820	CANYON CITY
97360-97360	MILL CITY	97444-97444	GOLD BEACH	97537-97537	ROGUE RIVER	97821-97821	CAYUSE
97361-97361	MONMOUTH	97446-97446	HARRISBURG	97538-97538	SELMA	97823-97823	CONDON
97362-97362	MOUNT ANGEL	97447-97447	IDLEYLD PARK	97539-97539	SHADY COVE	97824-97824	COVE
97364-97364	NEOTSU	97448-97448	JUNCTION CITY	97540-97540	TALENT	97825-97825	DAYVILLE
97365-97365	NEWPORT	97449-97449	LAKESIDE	97541-97541	TRAIL	97826-97826	ECHO
97366-97366	SOUTH BEACH	97450-97450	LANGLOIS	97543-97543	WILDERVILLE	97827-97827	ELGIN
97367-97367	LINCOLN CITY	97451-97451	LORANE	97544-97544	WILLIAMS	97828-97828	ENTERPRISE
97368-97368	OTIS	97452-97452	LOWELL	97601-97603	KLAMATH FALLS	97830-97830	FOSSIL
97369-97369	OTTER ROCK	97453-97453	MAPLETON	97604-97604	CRATER LAKE	97831-97831	FOX
97370-97370	PHILOMATH	97454-97454	MARCOLA	97620-97620	ADEL	97833-97833	HAINES
97371-97371	RICKREALL	97455-97455	PLEASANT HILL	97621-97621	BEATTY	97834-97834	HALFWAY
97372-97372	ROSE LODGE	97456-97456	MONROE	97622-97622	BLY	97835-97835	HELIX
97373-97373	SAINT BENEDICT	97457-97457	MYRTLE CREEK	97623-97623	BONANZA	97836-97836	HEPPNER
97374-97374	SCIO	97458-97458	MYRTLE POINT	97624-97624	CHILOQUIN	97837-97837	HEREFORD
97375-97375	SCOTTS MILLS	97459-97459	NORTH BEND	97625-97625	DAIRY	97838-97838	HERMISTON
97376-97376	SEAL ROCK	97460-97460	NORWAY	97626-97626	FORT KLAMATH	97839-97839	LEXINGTON
97377-97377	SHEDD	97461-97461	NOTI	97627-97627	KENO	97840-97840	OXBOW
97378-97378	SHERIDAN	97462-97462	OAKLAND	97630-97630	LAKEVIEW	97841-97841	IMBLER
97380-97380	SILETZ	97463-97463	OAKRIDGE	97632-97632	MALIN	97842-97842	IMNAHA
97381-97381	SILVERTON	97464-97464	OPHIR	97633-97633	MERRILL	97843-97843	IONE
97383-97383	STAYTON	97465-97465	PORT ORFORD	97634-97634	MIDLAND	97844-97844	IRRIGON
97384-97384	MEHAMA	97466-97466	POWERS	97635-97635	NEW PINE CREEK	97845-97845	JOHN DAY
97385-97385	SUBLIMITY	97467-97467	REEDSPORT	97636-97636	PAISLEY	97846-97846	JOSEPH
97386-97386	SWEET HOME	97468-97468	REMOTE	97637-97637	PLUSH	97848-97848	KIMBERLY
97388-97388	GLENEDEN BEACH	97469-97469	RIDDLE	97638-97638	SILVER LAKE	97850-97850	LA GRANDE
97389-97389	TANGENT	97470-97470	ROSEBURG	97639-97639	SPRAGUE RIVER	97856-97856	LONG CREEK
97390-97390	TIDEWATER	97472-97472	SAGINAW	97640-97640	SUMMER LAKE	97857-97857	LOSTINE
97391-97391	TOLEDO	97473-97473	SCOTTSBURG	97641-97641	CHRISTMAS VALLEY	97859-97859	MEACHAM
97392-97392	TURNER	97476-97476	SIXES	97701-97709	BEND	97861-97861	MIKKALO
97394-97394	WALDPORT	97477-97478	SPRINGFIELD	97710-97710	FIELDS	97862-97862	MILTON FREEWATER
97396-97396	WILLAMINA	97479-97479	SUTHERLIN	97711-97711	ASHWOOD	97864-97864	MONUMENT
97401-97405	EUGENE	97480-97480	SWISSHOME	97712-97712	BROTHERS	97865-97865	MOUNT VERNON
97406-97406	AGNESS	97481-97481	TENMILE	97720-97720	BURNS	97867-97867	NORTH POWDER
97407-97407	ALLEGANY	97482-97482	THURSTON	97721-97721	PRINCETON	97868-97868	PILOT ROCK
97408-97408	EUGENE	97484-97484	TILLER	97722-97722	DIAMOND	97869-97869	PRAIRIE CITY
97409-97409	ALVADORE	97486-97486	UMPQUA	97730-97730	CAMP SHERMAN	97870-97870	RICHLAND
97410-97410	AZALEA	97487-97487	VENETA	97731-97731	CHEMULT	97872-97872	RITTER
97411-97411	BANDON	97488-97488	VIDA	97732-97732	CRANE	97873-97873	SENECA
97412-97412	BLACHLY	97489-97489	WALTERVILLE	97733-97733	CRESCENT	97874-97874	SPRAY
97413-97413	BLUE RIVER	97490-97490	WALTON	97734-97734	CULVER	97875-97875	STANFIELD
97414-97414	BROADBENT	97491-97491	WEDDERBURN	97735-97735	FORT ROCK	97876-97876	SUMMERVILLE
97415-97415	BROOKINGS	97492-97492	WESTFIR	97736-97736	FRENCHGLEN	97877-97877	SUMPTER
97416-97416	CAMAS VALLEY	97493-97493	WESTLAKE	97737-97737	GILCHRIST	97880-97880	UKIAH
97417-97417	CANYONVILLE	97494-97494	WILBUR	97738-97738	HINES	97882-97882	UMATILLA
97419-97419	CHESHIRE	97495-97495	WINCHESTER	97739-97739	LA PINE	97883-97883	UNION
97420-97420	COOS BAY	97496-97496	WINSTON	97740-97740	LAWEN	97884-97884	UNITY
97423-97423	COQUILLE	97497-97497	WOLF CREEK	97741-97741	MADRAS	97885-97885	WALLOWA
97424-97424	COTTAGE GROVE	97498-97498	YACHATS	97750-97750	MITCHELL	97886-97886	WESTON
97425-97425	CRESCENT LAKE	97499-97499	YONCALLA	97751-97751	PAULINA	97901-97901	ADRIAN
97426-97426	CRESWELL	97501-97501	MEDFORD	97752-97752	POST	97902-97902	AROCK
97427-97427	CULP CREEK	97502-97502	CENTRAL POINT	97753-97753	POWELL BUTTE	97903-97903	BROGAN
97428-97428	CURTIN	97503-97503	WHITE CITY	97754-97754	PRINEVILLE	97904-97904	DREWSEY
97429-97429	DAYS CREEK	97504-97504	MEDFORD	97756-97756	REDMOND	97905-97905	DURKEE
97430-97430	DEADWOOD	97520-97520	ASHLAND	97758-97758	RILEY	97906-97906	HARPER
97431-97431	DEXTER	97522-97522	BUTTE FALLS	97759-97759	SISTERS	97907-97907	HUNTINGTON
97432-97432	DILLARD	97523-97523	CAVE JUNCTION	97760-97760	TERREBONNE	97908-97908	IRONSIDE
97434-97434	DORENA	97524-97524	EAGLE POINT	97761-97761	WARM SPRINGS	97909-97909	JAMIESON
97435-97435	DRAIN	97525-97525	GOLD HILL	97801-97801	PENDLETON	97910-97910	JORDAN VALLEY
97436-97436	ELKTON	97526-97528	GRANTS PASS	97810-97810	ADAMS	97911-97911	JUNTURA
97437-97437	ELMIRA	97530-97530	JACKSONVILLE	97812-97812	ARLINGTON	97913-97913	NYSSA
97438-97438	FALL CREEK	97531-97531	KERBY	97813-97813	ATHENA	97914-97914	ONTARIO
97439-97439	FLORENCE	97532-97532	MERLIN	97814-97814	BAKER CITY	97917-97917	RIVERSIDE
97440-97440	EUGENE	97533-97533	MURPHY	97817-97817	BATES	97918-97918	VALE
97441-97441	GARDINER	97534-97534	O BRIEN	97818-97818	BOARDMAN	97920-97920	WESTFALL

Pennsylvania

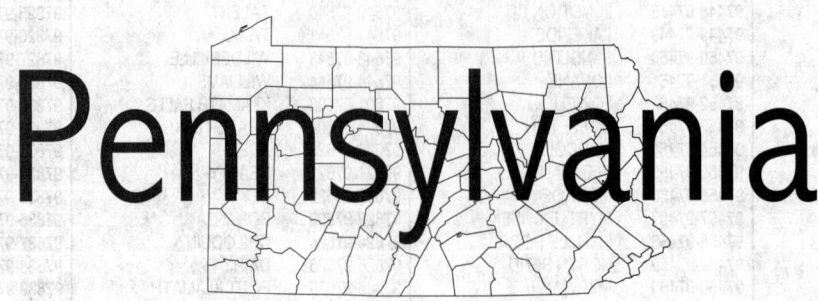

General Help Numbers:

Governor's Office
225 Main Capitol Bldg
Harrisburg, PA 17120
http://www.state.pa.us/PA_Exec/
Governor/organization.html

717-787-2500
Fax 717-772-8284
9AM-4:30PM

Attorney General's Office
Strawberry Square, 16th Floor
Harrisburg, PA 17120
http://www.attorneygeneral.gov

717-787-3391
Fax 717-787-1190
8AM-5PM

State Court Administrator
PO Box 229
Mechanicsburg, PA 17055
http://www.courts.state.pa.us

717-795-2000
Fax 717-795-2050
9AM-5PM

State Archives
Bureau of Archives & History
350 North St
Harrisburg, PA 17120
http://www.phmc.state.pa.us

717-783-3281
Fax 717-787-4822
9AM-4PM TU-F

State Specifics:

Capital:	Harrisburg
	Dauphin County
Time Zone:	EST
Number of Counties:	67
Population:	12,281,054
Web Site:	www.state.pa.us

State Agencies

Criminal Records

State Police Central Repository, 1800 Elmerton Ave, Harrisburg, PA 17110-9758; 717-783-9944, 717-783-9973, 717-705-8840 (Fax), 8:15AM-4:15PM.

http://www.pwp.state.pa.us

Indexing & Storage: Records are available from the 1920s. Records are available for all convictions. Arrests without dispositions are released if the charges are less than 3 years old. New records are available for inquiry immediately. Records are indexed on fingerprint cards. Records are normally destroyed after 70 years of age and there has been no criminal activity for 10 years, or

3 years after individual is confirmed deceased by fingerprints.

Searching: Must make request on Request Form SP4-164 or the request will be returned. Information will include felony and misdemeanor convictions and open cases less than 3 years old. Include the following in your request-full name, date of birth, Social Security Number, sex, race, any aliases. A release is not required.

Access by: mail.

Fee & Payment: Fee is $10.00 per name search. Fee payee: Commonwealth of Pennsylvania. Prepayment required. No personal checks accepted. No credit cards accepted.

Mail search: Turnaround time: 2-3 weeks. Turnaround can be 6 weeks if a record has a hit. No self addressed stamped envelope is required.

Corporation Records
Limited Partnership Records
Trademarks/Servicemarks
Fictitious Name
Assumed Name
Limited Liability Company Records
Limited Liability Partnerships

Corporation Bureau, Department of State, PO Box 8722, Harrisburg, PA 17105-8722 (Courier: 308 North Office Bldg, Harrisburg, PA 17120); 717-787-1057, 717-783-2244 (Fax), 8AM-5PM.

http://corps.state.pa.us/corps.htm

Indexing & Storage: Records are available from 1700's on. Records are indexed on computer since the 1800's.

Searching: Include the following in your request-full name of business. Corporation records include: Articles of Incorporation, Officers, Directors, DBAs, Prior (merged) names, Withdrawn and Reserved (120 days) names. Annual Reports on for-profit corporations are not required by the Department of State.

Access by: mail, phone, fax, in person, online.

Fee & Payment: The search fee is $12.00, copies are $2.00 per page. Fee payee: Department of State. Prepayment required. Ongoing requesters should open a customer deposit account. Personal checks accepted. No credit cards accepted.

Mail search: Turnaround time: 3 to 5 days. No self addressed stamped envelope is required.

Phone search: No fee for telephone request. They will provide basic information only.

Fax search: You must have an account to have materials returned by fax, same fees as above.

In person search: There are 3 computer terminals available for public use.

Online search: There is free general searching by entity name or number from the web site. Searching by name provides a list of entities whose name starts with the search name entered. Users can click on any one entity in the list displayed to get more detailed information regarding that entity.

Other access: Business lists, UCC on microfilm, and financing statements are available in bulk for $.25 per name.

Expedited service: Expedited service is available for mail and phone searches. Add $52.00 per transaction. If ordered before 1 PM, the record will be available by 5 PM.

Uniform Commercial Code

UCC Division, Department of State, PO Box 8721, Harrisburg, PA 17105-8721 (Courier: North Office Bldg, Rm 308, Harrisburg, PA 17120); 717-787-1057, 717-783-2244 (Fax), 8AM-5PM.

http://www.dos.state.pa.us/corp.htm

Indexing & Storage: Records are available from 1964 to present on microfiche and computer.

Searching: Use search request form UCC-11. All federal and state tax liens are filed at the Prothonotary of each county. Include the following in your request-debtor name.

Access by: mail, fax, in person, online.

Fee & Payment: The search fee is $12.00 per debtor name, copies cost $2.00 per page. In addition, the agency charges $1.00 per financing statement and statement of assignment reported on an information only listing. Fee payee: Pennsylvania Department of State. Prepayment required. Deposit accounts are accepted. Personal checks accepted. No credit cards accepted.

Mail search: Turnaround time: 3 to 5 days. A self addressed stamped envelope is requested.

Fax search: There is an additional $2.00 per page fee if returned by fax. A customer deposit account is required.

In person search: If the search is conducted by the customer, there is no $12.00 search fee.

Online search: The web site allows a search of UCC-1 financing statements filed with the Corporation Bureau by debtor name. This search displays a list of financing statements for which the debtor name starts with the search name entered. Users can refine the search further by entering a city and/or state for the search. The site also allows a search of financing statement records filed with the Corporation Bureau by financing statement number.

Other access: Daily computer tapes and copies of microfilm are available. Call the number above for details.

Federal Tax Liens
State Tax Liens
Records not maintained by a state level agency.

Note: All federal and state tax liens are filed at the Prothonotary of each county.

Sales Tax Registrations

Revenue Department, Sales Tax Division, Dept 280905, Harrisburg, PA 17128-0905; 717-783-9360, 717-783-5274 (Fax), 7:30AM-5PM.

http://www.revenue.state.pa.us

Indexing & Storage: Records are available from 1971 to present.

Searching: This agency will only confirm that a business is registered. They will provide no other information. They will only search with a tax permit number.

Access by: mail, phone, fax.

Fee & Payment: There is no search fee.

Mail search: Turnaround time: 2 to 7 days. A self addressed stamped envelope is requested.

Phone search: Records are available by phone.

Fax search: Same criteria as mail searches.

Birth Certificates

PA Department of Health, Division of Vital Records, PO Box 1528, New Castle, PA 16103-1528 (Courier: 101 S Mercer St, Room 401, New Castle, PA 16101); 724-656-3100 (Message Phone), 724-652-8951 (Fax), 8AM-4PM.

http://www.health.state.pa.us/vitalrecords

Indexing & Storage: Records are available from 1906 to present.

Searching: Must have a signed release form from person of record or immediate family member. Include the following in your request-full name, names of parents, mother's maiden name, date of birth, place of birth, relationship to person of record, reason for information request. Must include daytime phone number.

Access by: mail, phone, fax, in person.

Fee & Payment: The fee is $4.00 per record. Fee payee: Vital Records. Prepayment required. Personal checks accepted. Credit cards not accepted for mail requests. Credit cards accepted: MasterCard, Visa, AmEx, Discover.

Mail search: Turnaround time: 3 weeks. Credit cards not accepted for mail requests.A self addressed stamped envelope is requested.

Phone search: Phone requests accepted with a credit card for an additional $7.00 fee. Turnaround time is 2-4 days.

Fax search: Credit card is required for an additional $7.00. Results are mailed in 2-3 days.

In person search: Turnaround time is 1 hour.

Expedited service: Expedited service is available for phone and fax searches. Turnaround time: 2 to 3 days. Add fees for express delivery, use of credit card required.

Death Records

Department of Health, Division of Vital Records, PO Box 1528, New Castle, PA 16103-1528 (Courier: 101 S Mercer St, Room 401, New Castle, PA 16101); 724-656-3100 (Message Phone), 724-652-8951 (Fax), 8AM-4PM.

http://www.health.state.pa.us/vitalrecords

Indexing & Storage: Records are available from 1906 to present.

Searching: Must have a signed release form from immediate family member. Include the following in your request-full name, date of death, place of death, relationship to person of record, reason for information request. SSN helpful, if known. Include daytime phone number.

Access by: mail, phone, fax, in person.

Fee & Payment: The fee is $3.00 per record. Fee payee: Vital Records. Prepayment required. Personal checks accepted. Credit cards accepted: MasterCard, Visa, AmEx, Discover.

Mail search: Turnaround time: 3 to 4 weeks. A self addressed stamped envelope is requested.

Phone search: Phone service available with a credit card for an additional $7.00 fee. Turnaround time is 3 days.

Fax search: There is an additional $7.00 fee to use a credit card. Turnaround time is 3 days.

In person search: Turnaround time 1 hour.

Expedited service: Expedited service is available for mail, phone and fax searches. Turnaround time: 2 to 3 days. Add cost of express delivery, credit card required.

Marriage Certificates
Divorce Records
Records not maintained by a state level agency.

Note: Marriage and divorce records are found at county or Prothonotary of issue.

Workers' Compensation Records

Bureau of Workers' Compensation, Physical Records Section, 1171 S Cameron St, Rm 103, Harrisburg, PA 17104-2501; 717-772-4447, 7:30AM-4PM.

http://www.dli.state.pa.us/bwc

Indexing & Storage: Records are available for past 2 to 10 years. Records are indexed on inhouse computer.

Searching: Only the party to the record is allowed full access without a subpoena or a signed release. They will indicate whether they have a record for a person, but will not give any other information to the public. Include the following in your request-claimant name, year, date of accident, Social Security Number.

Access by: mail.

Fee & Payment: No fees involved for simple requests.

Mail search: Turnaround time: 30 days. No self addressed stamped envelope is required.

Driver Records

Department of Transportation, Driver Record Services, PO Box 68695, Harrisburg, PA 17106-8695 (Courier: 1101 S Front Street, Harrisburg, PA 17104); 717-391-6190, 800-932-4600 (In-state only), 7:30AM-4:30PM.

http://www.dmv.state.pa.us

Note: Copies of tickets may be purchased from this location for a fee of $5.00 each.

Indexing & Storage: Records are available for minimum of 3 calendar years for moving violations and departmental actions, minimum of 7 years for DWIs, and indefinite for suspensions. Accidents are reported on record as involvement only. The driver's address appears on the record. It takes 60 days from receipt before new records are available for inquiry.

Searching: Casual requesters submit Form DL-503. Large volume requesters must sign an agreement stating the individual authorizations are on file. There is no opt out. The state is in the process of authorizing all customers of MVR provider companies. Include the following in your request-driver's license number, full name, date of birth.

Access by: mail, in person, online.

Fee & Payment: The fee is $5.00 for each record. A 10 year employment record for commercial drivers is available. Fee payee: Department of Transportation. Prepayment required. Personal checks accepted. No credit cards accepted.

Mail search: Turnaround time: 5 to 7 days. No self addressed stamped envelope is required.

In person search: The state will process one record request while you wait, additional requests are mailed back to the requester.

Online search: The online system is available to high volume requesters only. Fee is $5.00 per record. Call 717-787-7154 for more information. The sale of records over the Internet is strictly forbidden.

Vehicle Ownership
Vehicle Identification

Department of Transportation, Vehicle Record Services, PO Box 68691, Harrisburg, PA 17106-8691 (Courier: 1101 South Front St, Harrisburg, PA 17104); 717-391-6190, 800-932-6000 (In-state), 7:30AM-4:30PM.

http://www.dmv.state.pa.us

Note: This agency also holds records for unattached mobile homes.

Searching: The requester must submit Form DL-135. The state does not authorize the bulk delivery or commercial use of ownership & vehicle information.

Access by: mail.

Fee & Payment: The fee is $5.00 per transaction. Title history may have more than one transaction per vehicle. You can call first to determine the number. There is an additional $5.00 for certification. Fee payee: Department of Transportation. Prepayment required. Personal checks accepted. No credit cards accepted.

Mail search: Turnaround time: 7 to 10 days. You can order a record in person, but results will be mailed.No self addressed stamped envelope is required.

Other access: Bulk information is not sold for commercial purposes. Certain statistical type user requests will be honored.

Accident Reports

State Police Headquarters, Accident Records Unit, 1800 Elmerton Ave, Harrisburg, PA 17110; 717-783-5516, 8AM-5PM.

http://www.psp.state.pa.us

Note: Order form is available at the Web site.

Indexing & Storage: Records are available for 5 years to present. It takes 60 days before new records are available for inquiry. Records are indexed on inhouse computer.

Searching: Only those involved, their attorney or insurer may request a copy of the accident report. Include the following in your request-full name, date of accident, State Police incident number. The following data is not released: medical information or expunged records.

Access by: mail.

Fee & Payment: Reports are $8.00 per record. Fee payee: Commonwealth of Pennsylvania. Prepayment required. Personal checks accepted. No credit cards accepted.

Mail search: Turnaround time: 6 weeks or more.

Vessel Ownership
Vessel Registration
Access to Records is Restricted

Fish and Boat Commission, Licensing & Registration Section, PO Box 68900, Harrisburg, PA 17106-8900; 717-705-7940.

http://www.fish.state.pa.us

Note: Boat registration and ownership information is not open to the public. Liens are filed at UCC filing locations.

Legislation Records

Pennsylvania General Assembly, Legislative Reference Bureau, Main Capitol Bldg, Room 641, Harrisburg, PA 17120; 717-787-2342 (History Room), 717-787-5320 (House Bills), 717-787-6732 (Senate Bills), House-8:30AM-4:30PM/Senate-8:30AM-5PM.

http://www.legis.state.pa.us

Note: Call the History Room first to get the bill number, print number, and status.

Indexing & Storage: Records are available from 1981 forward. Records indexed on inhouse computer.

Searching: Include the following in your request-the topic of bill (bill number is not required).

Access by: mail, phone, in person, online.

Fee & Payment: There is no search fee.

Mail search: Turnaround time: 2 days. No self addressed stamped envelope is required.

Phone search: Limited information is released.

In person search: Searching is available in person.

Online search: Free access to bill text is available at the Electronic Bill Room found at the web page by selecting "Session Information."

Voter Registration
Records not maintained by a state level agency.

Note: Records are kept at the county level and cannot be sold for commercial purposes.

GED Certificates

Commonwealth Diploma Program, GED Testing, 333 Market St 12th Fl, Harrisburg, PA 17126-0333; 717-787-6747, 8:30AM-4:30PM.

http://www.paadulted.org

Searching: For all requests the following is required: a signed release, name, approximate year of test, date of birth, Social Security Number, test city, and phone number where you can be reached.

Access by: mail.

Fee & Payment: Verifications and copies of transcripts are $3.00 each. The fee is non-refundable. Fee payee: Commonwealth of PA. Prepayment required. Cashier's checks and money orders are accepted. No credit cards or personal checks accepted.

Mail search: Turnaround time: 3 to 4 weeks. No self addressed stamped envelope is required.

Hunting License Information
Records not maintained by a state level agency.

Note: Hunting license information is not released to the public.

Fishing License Information
Access to Records is Restricted

Fish & Boat Commission, Fishing License Division, PO Box 67000, Harrisburg, PA 17106 (Courier: 3532 Walnut St, Harrisburg, PA 17106); 717-657-4518 (Fishing License Division), 717-787-4250 (Hunting License Division), 717-657-4549 (Fax), 8AM-4PM.

Pennsylvania State Licensing Agencies

Licenses Searchable Online

Athletic Agent #22 .... www.dos.state.pa.us/sac/agents.html

Bank #04 .... www.banking.state.pa.us/PA_Exec/Banking/organiz.htm#exambureau

Credit Union #04 .... www.banking.state.pa.us/PA_Exec/Banking/resource/cufrm.pdf

Education Specialist #06 .... http://tcp.ed.state.pa.us/tcsmainJS.asp

Insurance Company #11 .... www.insurance.state.pa.us/html/licensed.html

Lobbyist #17 .... www.lobbyist.net/Pennsylv/PENLOB.htm

Optometrist #20 .... www.odfinder.org/LicSearch.asp

Savings Association #04 .... www.banking.state.pa.us/PA_Exec/Banking/organiz.htm#exambureau

Trust Company #04 .... www.banking.state.pa.us/PA_Exec/Banking/organiz.htm#exambureau

Licensing Quick Finder

Acupuncturist #20 717-783-1400	Hearing Aid Apprentice, Temporary #7 .717-783-8078	Pesticide Applicator/Technician #2 717-787-5231 ext2
Ambulance Service #08.......................717-787-8740	Hearing Aid Dealer #07 717-783-8078	Pesticide Dealer #02 .... 717-787-5231 ext2
Amphetamine Program #20 717-787-2568	Hearing Aid Fitter/Apprentice#07 717-783-8078	Pharmacist #20 717-783-7156
Animal Health Technician #23 717-783-7134	Horse Racing #03 717-783-8726	Physical Therapist/Assistant #20 717-783-7134
Appraiser, Residential #20...................717-783-4866	Installment Loan Seller #04 717-787-3717	Physician Assistant #20........................717-787-2381
Architect #20.......................................717-783-3397	Installment Seller #04 717-787-3717	Podiatrist #20 717-783-4858
Athletic Agent #22...............................717-787-5720	Insurance Agent #11 717-787-3840	Pre-Hospital RN #08 717-787-8740
Athletic Event Manager #22.................717-787-5720	Insurance Broker/Supervisor #11..........717-787-3840	Private Investigator #15........................717-255-2692
Athletic Event Ring Announcer/Timekeeper #22.........	Insurance Company #11 717-787-2735	Private School Staff #06 717-783-8228
....717-787-5720	Investment Adviser #16 717-783-4211	Psychologist #23..................................717-783-7134
Athletic Physician #22 717-787-5720	Kickboxer #22 717-787-5720	Public Accountant Corporation #20 717-783-1404
Athletic Trainer #22 717-787-5720	Laboratory, Medical #10 610-363-8500	Public Accountant-CPA #20...................717-783-1404
Attorney #01 717-731-7073	Landscape Architect #20 717-772-8528	Public Accounting Partnership #20 717-783-1404
Auctioneer #20....................................717-783-3397	Liquor Dist./Retailer/Wholesaler #14 717-783-8250	Radiation Therapy Technician #20...717-783-4858
Auctioneer, Real Estate #20 717-783-3658	Lobbyist #17 717-787-5920	Radiologic Technologist #20..................717-783-4858
Bank #04 717-787-3717	Manicurist #20 717-783-7130	Real Estate Appraiser #20 717-783-4866
Barber #20 717-783-3402	Medical Doctor #20 717-787-2381	Real Estate Broker/Salesperson#20 717-783-3658
Boat Registration #13..........................717-705-7940	Midwife #20 717-783-1400	Referee #22 717-787-5720
Boxer #22 717-787-5720	Money Transmitter #04..........................717-787-3717	Respiratory Care Practitioner #20 717-783-4858
Boxing Judge/Promoter/Second #22.....717-787-5720	Mortgage (Accelerated) Payment Provider #04	Sales Finance Company #04 717-787-3717
Check Casher #04 717-787-3717	717-787-3717	Savings Association #04 717-787-3717
Child Day Care Facility #12 717-787-8691	Mortgage (First) Broker/Banker #04 717-787-3717	School Administrator #06.......................717-787-2967
Chiropractor #20 717-783-7155	Mortgage (First) Limited Broker #04.......717-787-3717	School Intermediate Unit Director #06...717-787-2967
Consumer Discount Company #04 717-787-3717	Mortgage (First) Loan Corresp. #04 717-787-3717	School Superintendent #06 717-787-2967
Cosmetologist/Cosmetician #20...........717-783-7130	Mortgage (Secondary) Lender #04 717-787-3717	School Supervisor #06 717-787-2967
Credit Services Loan Broker #04 717-787-3717	Mortgage (Secondary) Loan Broker/Agent #04..........	Securities Agent #16 717-783-4212
Credit Union #04..................................717-787-3717	717-787-3717	Securities Broker/Dealer #16 717-783-4213
Debt Collector-Repossessor #04 717-787-3717	Notary Public #21..................................717-787-5280	Social Worker #20 717-783-1389
Dental Assistant, Expd. Function #18....717-783-7162	Nuclear Medicine Technologist #20 ...717-787-4858	Speech Pathologist/Audiologist #20 717-783-1389
Dental Hygienist #18 717-783-7162	Nurse #20 717-783-7142	Surveyor #20 717-783-7049
Dentist #18 717-783-7162	Nursing Home #09 610-594-8041	Tablefunder, Wholesale #04 717-787-3717
Education Specialist #06 717-787-2967	Nursing Home Administrator #20 717-783-7155	Teacher #05..717-787-2967
Emergency Medical Technician #08......717-787-8740	Occupational Therapist/Assistant #20 ...717-783-1389	Trust Company #04................................717-787-3717
Engineer #20 717-783-7049	Optometrist #20 717-783-7155	Vehicle Dealer #19...............................717-783-1697
First Responder EMT #08.....................717-787-8740	Osteopathic Physician #20 717-783-4858	Vehicle Salesperson #19......................717-783-1697
Funeral Director #20.............................717-783-3397	Osteopathic Physician Assistant #20 717-783-4858	Veterinarian #20....................................717-783-7134
Geologist #20.......................................717-783-7049	Paramedic #08......................................717-787-8740	Veterinary Technician #20 717-783-7134
Harness Racing #03.............................717-787-5789	Pawnbroker #04 717-787-3717	Wrestling Promoter #22........................717-787-5720
Health Professional #08 717-787-8740	Pest Management Consultant #2.. 717-787-5231 ext2	

Licensing Agency Information

#01 Administration Office of PA Courts, PO Box 46, Camphill, PA 17001-0046; 717-731-7073, Fax: 717-731-7080.

#02 Department of Agriculture, 2301 N Cameron St, Harrisburg, PA 17110-9408; 717-772-5231, Fax: 717-783-3275.
http://sites.state.pa.us/PA_Exec/Agriculture/bureaus/plant_industry/index.html

#03 Department of Agriculture, 2301 N Cameron St, Agriculture Office Bldg, Harrisburg, PA 17110-9408; 717-787-5196, Fax: 717-787-2271.
www.pda.state.pa.us

#04 Department of Banking, 333 Market St, 16th Fl, Harrisburg, PA 17111-2290; 717-787-3717, Fax: 717-787-8773.
www.banking.state.pa.us/

#06 Department of Education, 333 Market St, 3rd Fl, Harrisburg, PA 17126-0333; 717-787-2967, Fax: 717-783-6736.
www.pde.psu.edu
Direct web site URL to search for licensees: http://tcp.ed.state.pa.us/tcsmainJS.asp. You can search online using SSN

#07 Department of Health, 132 Kline Plaza, Harrisburg, PA 17104; 717-783-8078, Fax: 717-787-3188.
www.state.pa.us

#08 Department of Health, PO Box 90 (7th & Forster), Harrisburg, PA 17108; 717-787-8740, Fax: 717-772-0910.
www.webserver.health.state.pa.us/health/site

#09 Department of Health, 110 Pickering Way, Lionville, PA 19353; 610-594-8041, Fax: 610-436-3346.
www.health.state.pa.us/qa/ltc

#10 Department of Health-Bureau of Labs, PO Box 500, Exton, PA 19341-0500; 610-363-8500, Fax: 610-436-3346.
www.health.state.pa.us/HPA/labinvst.htm

#11 Department of Insurance, 1300 Strawberry Sq, Harrisburg, PA 17120; 717-787-2735, Fax: 717-787-8557.
www.insurance.state.pa.us
Direct web site URL to search for licensees: www.insurance.state.pa.us/html/licensed.html. You can search online using alphabetical list for insurance companies

#12 Department of Public Welfare, 1401 N Market St, Harrisburg, PA 17105; 717-787-8691, Fax: 717-787-1529.
www.dpw.state.pa.us/ocyf/dpwocyf.asp

#13 Fish & Boat Commission, 1601 Elmerton Ave, Harrisburg, PA 17110-9299; 717-705-7940, Fax: 717-705-7931.
www.fish.state.pa.us

#14 Liquor Control Board, PO Box 8940 (Capitol & Forester St), Harrisburg, PA 17105-8940; 717-783-8250, Fax: 717-772-2165.
wwww.lcb.state.pa.us

#16 Securities Commission, 1010 N 7th St, Eastgate-2nd Fl, Harrisburg, PA 17102-1410; 717-787-8061, Fax: 717-783-5122.
www.psc.state.pa.us/

#17 State Ethics Commission, 309 Finance Bldg, PO Box 11470, Harrisburg, PA 17108-1470; 717-783-1610.
www.ethics.state.pa.us

#18 Department of State, PO Box 2649, Harrisburg, PA 17105-2649; 717-783-7162, Fax: 717-787-7769.
www.dos.state.pa.us/bpoa/denbd/mainpage.htm

#19 Bureau of Professional & Occupational Affairs, 124 Pine St, Transportation & Safety Bldg, 6th Fl, Harrisburg, PA 17101; 717-783-1697, Fax: 717-787-0250.
www.dos.state.pa.us/bpoa/vehbd.htm For verifications, call or contact the Board via e-mail at vehicle@pados.dos.state.pa.us.

#20 State Department, 124 Pine St, Harrisburg, PA 17105-2649; 717-787-8503, Fax: 717-787-7769.
www.dos.state.pa.us/sitemap.html

#21 State Department, North Office Bldg, Rm 304, Harrisburg, PA 17120; 717-787-5280, Fax: 717-787-2854.
www.dos.state.pa.us

#22 Department of State, 116 Pine St, 3rd Fl, Harrisburg, PA 17101; 717-787-5720, Fax: 717-783-0824.
www.dos.state.pa.us/sac/sac.html

#23 Department of State, 116 Pine St, Harrisburg, PA 17101; 717-783-7134.

Pennsylvania Federal Courts

The following list indicates the district and division name for each county in the state. If the bankruptcy court location is different from the district court, then the location of the bankruptcy court appears in parentheses.

County/Court Cross Reference

County	District	Division
Adams	Middle	Harrisburg
Allegheny	Western	Pittsburgh
Armstrong	Western	Pittsburgh
Beaver	Western	Pittsburgh
Bedford	Western	Johnstown (Pittsburgh)
Berks	Eastern	Allentown/Reading (Reading)
Blair	Western	Johnstown (Pittsburgh)
Bradford	Middle	Scranton (Wilkes-Barre)
Bucks	Eastern	Philadelphia
Butler	Western	Pittsburgh
Cambria	Western	Johnstown (Pittsburgh)
Cameron	Middle	Williamsport (Wilkes-Barre)
Carbon	Middle	Scranton (Wilkes-Barre)
Centre	Middle	Williamsport (Harrisburg)
Chester	Eastern	Philadelphia
Clarion	Western	Pittsburgh (Erie)
Clearfield	Western	Johnstown (Pittsburgh)
Clinton	Middle	Williamsport (Wilkes-Barre)
Columbia	Middle	Williamsport (Wilkes-Barre)
Crawford	Western	Erie
Cumberland	Middle	Harrisburg
Dauphin	Middle	Harrisburg
Delaware	Eastern	Philadelphia
Elk	Western	Erie
Erie	Western	Erie
Fayette	Western	Pittsburgh
Forest	Western	Erie
Franklin	Middle	Harrisburg
Fulton	Middle	Harrisburg
Greene	Western	Pittsburgh
Huntingdon	Middle	Harrisburg
Indiana	Western	Pittsburgh
Jefferson	Western	Pittsburgh (Erie)
Juniata	Middle	Harrisburg
Lackawanna	Middle	Scranton (Wilkes-Barre)
Lancaster	Eastern	Allentown/Reading (Reading)
Lawrence	Western	Pittsburgh
Lebanon	Middle	Harrisburg
Lehigh	Eastern	Allentown/Reading (Reading)
Luzerne	Middle	Scranton (Wilkes-Barre)
Lycoming	Middle	Williamsport (Wilkes-Barre)
McKean	Western	Erie
Mercer	Western	Pittsburgh (Erie)
Mifflin	Middle	Harrisburg
Monroe	Middle	Scranton (Wilkes-Barre)
Montgomery	Eastern	Philadelphia
Montour	Middle	Williamsport (Harrisburg)
Northampton	Eastern	Allentown/Reading (Reading)
Northumberland	Middle	Williamsport (Harrisburg)
Perry	Middle	Williamsport (Harrisburg)
Philadelphia	Eastern	Philadelphia
Pike	Middle	Scranton (Wilkes-Barre)
Potter	Middle	Williamsport (Wilkes-Barre)
Schuylkill	Eastern	Allentown/Reading (Reading)
Snyder	Middle	Williamsport (Harrisburg)
Somerset	Western	Johnstown (Pittsburgh)
Sullivan	Middle	Williamsport (Wilkes-Barre)
Susquehanna	Middle	Scranton (Wilkes-Barre)
Tioga	Middle	Williamsport (Wilkes-Barre)
Union	Middle	Williamsport (Harrisburg)
Venango	Western	Erie
Warren	Western	Erie
Washington	Western	Pittsburgh
Wayne	Middle	Scranton (Wilkes-Barre)
Westmoreland	Western	Pittsburgh
Wyoming	Middle	Scranton (Wilkes-Barre)
York	Middle	Harrisburg

US District Court

Eastern District of Pennsylvania

Allentown/Reading Division c/o Philadelphia Division, Room 2609, US Courthouse, 601 Market St, Philadelphia, PA 19106-1797 (Courier Address: Use mail address), 215-597-7704, Fax: 215-597-6390.

http://www.paed.uscourts.gov

Counties: Berks, Lancaster, Lehigh, Northampton, Schuylkill.

Indexing/Storage: Cases are indexed by as well as by case number. New cases are available in the index after filing date. Open records are located at the Division.

Fee & Payment: The fee is no charge per item (one party name or case number). Payment may be made by money order, cashier check. Business checks are not accepted. Personal checks are not accepted.

Phone Search: Searching not available by phone.

Mail Search: Always enclose a stamped self addressed envelope.

In Person: In person searching is available.

PACER: Sign-up number is 215-597-5710. Access fee is $.60 per minute. Toll-free access: 800-458-2993. Local access: 215-597-0258. Case records are available back to July 1, 1990. Records are never purged. New records are available online after 1 day. PACER is available online at http://pacer.paed.uscourts.gov.

Opinions Online: Court opinions are available online at http://www.paed.uscourts.gov/contents.shtml

Other Online Access: Online access is available free at http://www.paed.uscourts.gov/us04000.shtml. No fee to search.

Philadelphia Division Room 2609, US Courthouse, 601 Market St, Philadelphia, PA 19106-1797 (Courier Address: Use mail address), 215-597-7704, Fax: 215-597-6390.

http://www.paed.uscourts.gov

Counties: Bucks, Chester, Delaware, Montgomery, Philadelphia.

Indexing/Storage: Cases are indexed by defendant and plaintiff as well as by case number. New cases are available in the index immediately after filing date. A computer index is maintained. The computer index is from 1990 on. Records are also indexed on microfiche. Indexes by judgment and by nature of suit are also available. Open records are located at this court. District wide searches are available from this division.

Fee & Payment: The fee is $20.00 per item (one party name or case number). Payment may be made by money order, cashier check, personal check, Visa, Mastercard. Payee: Clerk, US District Court. Certification fee: $7.00 per document. Copy fee: $.50 per page.

Phone Search: Docket information available by phone if case number is known.

Fax Search: Will accept fax searches at $15.00 per name. Will fax docket listing at $.50 per page.

Mail Search: Always enclose a stamped self addressed envelope.

In Person: In person searching is available.

PACER: Sign-up number is 215-597-5710. Access fee is $.60 per minute. Toll-free access: 800-458-2993. Local access: 215-597-0258. Case records are available back to July 1, 1990. Records are never purged. New records are available online after 1 day. PACER is available online at http://pacer.paed.uscourts.gov.

Opinions Online: Court opinions are available online at http://www.paed.uscourts.gov/contents.shtml

Other Online Access: Online access is available free at http://www.paed.uscourts.gov/us04000.shtml. No fee to search.

US Bankruptcy Court

Eastern District of Pennsylvania

Philadelphia Division 4th Floor, 900 Market St, Philadelphia, PA 19107 (Courier Address: Use mail address for courier delivery), 215-408-2800.

http://www.paeb.uscourts.gov

Counties: Bucks, Chester, Delaware, Montgomery, Philadelphia.

Indexing/Storage: Cases are indexed by debtor and creditors as well as by case number. New cases are available in the index 1 day after filing date. A card index is maintained. A microfiche index is also maintained. Open records are located at this court.

Fee & Payment: The fee is $20.00 per item (one party name or case number). Payment may be made by money order, cashier check, business check, Visa or Mastercard. Personal checks are not accepted. Prepayment is required. Payee: Clerk, US Bankruptcy Court. Certification fee: $7.00 per document. Copy fee: $.50 per page. You are allowed to make your own copies. These copies cost $.25 per page. In person searchers may not search the card index.

Phone Search: An automated voice case information service (VCIS) is available. Call VCIS at 888-584-5853 or 215-597-2244.

Mail Search: Always enclose a stamped self addressed envelope.

In Person: In person searching is available.

PACER: Sign-up number is 800-676-6856. Access fee is $.60 per minute. Toll-free access: 888-381-2921. Local access: 215-597-3501. Case records are available back to 1988. Records are purged every 6 months. New civil records are available online after 1 day. PACER is available online at http://pacer.paeb.uscourts.gov.

Reading Division Suite 300, The Madison, 400 Washington St, Reading, PA 19601 (Courier Address: Use mail address for courier delivery), 610-320-5255.

http://www.paeb.uscourts.gov

Counties: Berks, Lancaster, Lehigh, Northampton, Schuylkill.

Indexing/Storage: Cases are indexed by debtor as well as by case number. New cases are available in the index 1 day after filing date. Both computer and card indexes are maintained. Open records are located at this court.

Fee & Payment: The fee is $20.00 per item (one party name or case number). Payment may be made by money order, cashier check, business check, Visa or Mastercard. Personal checks are not accepted. Prepayment is required. Payee: Clerk, US Bankruptcy Court. Certification fee: $7.00 per document. Copy fee: $.50 per page.

Phone Search: Only docket information is available by phone. An automated voice case information service (VCIS) is available. Call VCIS at 888-584-5853 or 215-597-2244.

Mail Search: Always enclose a stamped self addressed envelope.

In Person: In person searching is available.

PACER: Sign-up number is 800-676-6856. Access fee is $.60 per minute. Toll-free access: 888-381-2921. Local access: 215-597-3501. Case records are available back to 1988. Records are purged every 6 months. New civil records are available online after 1 day. PACER is available online at http://pacer.paeb.uscourts.gov.

US District Court

Middle District of Pennsylvania

Harrisburg Division PO Box 983, Harrisburg, PA 17108-0983 (Courier Address: US Courthouse & Federal Bldg, 228 Walnut St, Harrisburg, PA 17108), 717-221-3920, Fax: 717-221-3959.

http://www.pamd.uscourts.gov

Counties: Adams, Cumberland, Dauphin, Franklin, Fulton, Huntingdon, Juniata, Lebanon, Mifflin, York.

Indexing/Storage: Cases are indexed by defendant and plaintiff as well as by case number. New cases are available in the index immediately after filing date. Both computer and card indexes are maintained. Open records are located at this court.

Fee & Payment: The fee is $20.00 per item (one party name or case number). Payment may be made by money order, cashier check, personal check, American Express, Visa, Mastercard. Prepayment is required. Payee: Clerk, US District Court. Certification fee: $7.00 per document. Copy fee: $.50 per page.

Phone Search: Searching is not available by phone. Only accession numbers for a specific case are available by phone.

Fax Search: Will accept fax search requests for $25.00. The fee is $1.00 per page.

Mail Search: A stamped self addressed envelope is not required.

In Person: In person searching is available.

PACER: Sign-up number is 800-676-6856. Access fee is $.60 per minute. Toll-free access: 800-658-8381. Local access: 570-347-8286. Case records are available back to May 1989. Records are never purged. New records are available online after 1 day. PACER is available online at http://pacer.pamd.uscourts.gov.

Other Online Access: Search records on the Internet using RACER at https://racer.pamd.uscourts.gov/perl/bkplog.html. Access fee is 7 cents per page.

Scranton Division Clerk's Office, William J Nealon Fedearl Bldg & US Courthouse, PO Box 1148, Scranton, PA 18501 (Courier Address: 235 N Washington Ave, Room 101, Scranton, PA 18503), 570-207-5680, Fax: 717-207-5689.

http://www.pamd.uscourts.gov

Counties: Bradford, Carbon, Lackawanna, Luzerne, Monroe, Pike, Susquehanna, Wayne, Wyoming.

Indexing/Storage: Cases are indexed by defendant and plaintiff as well as by case number. New cases are available in the index 1 day after filing date. A computer index is maintained. Records are also indexed on microfiche. Records are stored on an in-house computer from 1989. Open records are located at this court. District wide searches are available for information from 1901 from this court.

Fee & Payment: The fee is $20.00 per item (one party name or case number). Payment may be made by money order, cashier check, personal check, Visa, Mastercard. Prepayment is required. Payee: Clerk, US District Court. Certification fee: $7.00 per document. Copy fee: $.50 per page.

Phone Search: Only minimal docket information will be released over the phone.

Fax Search: Will accept fax search with credit card number.

Mail Search: A stamped self addressed envelope is not required.

In Person: In person searching is available.

PACER: Sign-up number is 800-676-6856. Access fee is $.60 per minute. Toll-free access: 800-658-8381. Local access: 570-347-8286. Case records are available back to May 1989. Records are never purged. New records are available online after 1 day. PACER is available online at http://pacer.pamd.uscourts.gov.

Other Online Access: Search records on the Internet using RACER at https://racer.pamd.uscourts.gov/perl/bkplog.html. Access fee is 7 cents per page.

Williamsport Division
PO Box 608, Williamsport, PA 17703 (Courier Address: Federal Bldg, ROom 402, 240 W 3rd St, Williamsport, PA 17701), 570-323-6380, Fax: 717-323-0636.

http://www.pamd.uscourts.gov

Counties: Cameron, Centre, Clinton, Columbia, Lycoming, Montour, Northumberland, Perry, Potter, Snyder, Sullivan, Tioga, Union.

Indexing/Storage: Cases are indexed by defendant and plaintiff as well as by case number. New cases are available in the index immediately after filing date. A computer index is maintained. Open records are located at this court.

Fee & Payment: The fee is $20.00 per item (one party name or case number). Payment may be made by money order, cashier check, personal check, Visa, Mastercard. Prepayment is required. Payee: Clerk, US District Court. Certification fee: $7.00 per document. Copy fee: $.50 per page.

Phone Search: Only docket information is available by phone.

Fax Search: Fax requests require the original signature and prepayment.

Mail Search: Always enclose a stamped self addressed envelope.

In Person: In person searching is available.

PACER: Sign-up number is 800-676-6856. Access fee is $.60 per minute. Toll-free access: 800-658-8381. Local access: 570-347-8286. Case records are available back to May 1989. Records are never purged. New records are available online after 1 day. PACER is available online at http://pacer.pamd.uscourts.gov.

Other Online Access: Search records on the Internet using RACER at https://racer.pamd.uscourts.gov/perl/bkplog.html. Access fee is 7 cents per page.

US Bankruptcy Court
Middle District of Pennsylvania

Harrisburg Division
PO Box 908, Harrisburg, PA 17108 (Courier Address: 228 Walnut St, 3rd Floor, Harrisburg, PA 17101), 717-901-2800.

http://www.pamd.uscourts.gov

Counties: Adams, Centre, Cumberland, Dauphin, Franklin, Fulton, Huntingdon, Juniata, Lebanon, Mifflin, Montour, Northumberland, Perry, Schuylkill, Snyder, Union, York.

Indexing/Storage: Cases are indexed by debtor as well as by case number. New cases are available in the index 1 day after filing date. A computer index is maintained. Open records are located at this court.

Fee & Payment: The fee is $20.00 per item (one party name or case number). Payment may be made by money order, cashier check, personal check. Prepayment is required. Debtor's checks are not accepted. Payee: Clerk, US Bankruptcy Court. Certification fee: $7.00 per document. Copy fee: $.50 per page.

Phone Search: Only docket information is available by phone.

Mail Search: Always enclose a stamped self addressed envelope.

In Person: In person searching is available.

PACER: Sign-up number is 800-676-6856. Access fee is $.60 per minute. Toll-free access: 800-882-6899. Local access: 570-901-2835. Case records are available back to August 1986. Records are never purged. New civil records are available online after 1 day. PACER is available online at http://pacer.pamb.uscourts.gov.

Wilkes-Barre Division
Clerk's Office, Max Rosen US Courthouse, 197 S Main St, Wilkes-Barre, PA 18701 (Courier Address: Use mail address for courier delivery), 570-826-6450.

http://www.paeb.uscourts.gov

Counties: Bradford, Cameron, Carbon, Clinton, Columbia, Lackawanna, Luzerne, Lycoming, Monroe, Pike, Potter, Schuylkill, Sullivan, Susquehanna, Tioga, Wayne, Wyoming.

Indexing/Storage: Cases are indexed by debtor as well as by case number. New cases are available in the index 1-3 days after filing date. A computer index is maintained. Open records are located at this court.

Fee & Payment: The fee is $20.00 per item (one party name or case number). Payment may be made by money order, cashier check, personal check. Debtor's checks are not accepted. Make checks payable to the Clerk for services other than copy services; for copies, make checks payable to Louise Cannon Copy Service. Payee: Clerk, US Bankruptcy Court. Certification fee: $7.00 per document. Copy fee: $.50 per page. You are allowed to make your own copies. These copies cost Not Applicable per page.

Phone Search: Phone searches can be done if the name, social security number, or case number is provided. Only docket information will be released.

Mail Search: Always enclose a stamped self addressed envelope.

In Person: In person searching is available.

PACER: Sign-up number is 800-676-6856. Access fee is $.60 per minute. Toll-free access: 800-640-3037. Local access: 570-821-4033. Use of PC Anywhere v4.0 suggested. Case records are available back to 1987. New civil records are available online after 1 day. PACER is available online at http://pacer.pamb.uscourts.gov.

US District Court
Western District of Pennsylvania

Erie Division
PO Box 1820, Erie, PA 16507 (Courier Address: 102 US Courthouse, 617 State St, Erie, PA 16501), 814-453-4829.

http://www.pawd.uscourts.gov

Counties: Crawford, Elk, Erie, Forest, McKean, Venango, Warren.

Indexing/Storage: Cases are indexed by defendant and plaintiff as well as by case number. New cases are available in the index 1 day after filing date. The court prefers that you perform searches through the Pittsburgh Division. Both computer and card indexes are maintained. Open records are located at this court.

Fee & Payment: The fee is $20.00 per item (one party name or case number). Payment may be made by money order, cashier check, personal check, Visa, Mastercard. Prepayment is required. Payee: Clerk, US District Court. Certification fee: $7.00 per document. Copy fee: $.50 per page.

Phone Search: Only the number, caption and attorneys' names will be released over the phone.

Mail Search: Always enclose a stamped self addressed envelope.

In Person: In person searching is available.

PACER: Sign-up number is 800-676-6856. Access fee is $.60 per minute. Toll-free access: 800-770-4745. Local access: 412-208-7588. Case records are available back to 1989. Records are never purged. New records are available online after 1 day. PACER is available online at http://pacer.pawd.uscourts.gov.

Johnstown Division
Penn Traffic Bldg, Room 208, 319 Washington St, Johnstown, PA 15901 (Courier Address: Use mail address for courier delivery), 814-533-4504, Fax: 814-533-4519.

http://www.pawd.uscourts.gov

Counties: Bedford, Blair, Cambria, Clearfield, Somerset.

Indexing/Storage: Cases are indexed by defendant and plaintiff as well as by case number. New cases are available in the index 1 day after filing date. Both computer and card indexes are maintained. On computer since June 1992. Card index from 1989 to 1992. Open records are located at this court.

Fee & Payment: The fee is $20.00 per item (one party name or case number). Payment may be made by money order, cashier check, personal check, Visa. Prepayment is required. Payee: Clerk, US District Court. Certification fee: $7.00 per document. Copy fee: $.50 per page.

Phone Search: Only the number, caption and attorneys' names will be released over the phone.

Mail Search: A stamped self addressed envelope is not required.

In Person: In person searching is available.

PACER: Sign-up number is 800-676-6856. Access fee is $.60 per minute. Toll-free access: 800-770-4745. Local access: 412-208-7588. Case records are available back to 1989. Records are never purged. New records are available online after 1 day. PACER is available online at http://pacer.pawd.uscourts.gov.

Pittsburgh Division US Post Office & Courthouse, Room 829, 7th Ave & Grant St, Pittsburgh, PA 15219 (Courier Address: Use mail address for courier delivery), 412-644-3527.

http://www.pawd.uscourts.gov

Counties: Allegheny, Armstrong, Beaver, Butler, Clarion, Fayette, Greene, Indiana, Jefferson, Lawrence, Mercer, Washington, Westmoreland.

Indexing/Storage: Cases are indexed by defendant and plaintiff as well as by case number. New cases are available in the index 2 days after filing date. Both computer and card indexes are maintained. Open records are located at this court. The Erie and Johnstown Divisions send complete paper copies of case records to Pittsburgh, so that all case records for the District are available here.

Fee & Payment: The fee is $20.00 per item (one party name or case number). Payment may be made by money order, cashier check, personal check, Visa, Mastercard. Prepayment is required. Payee: Clerk, US District Court. Certification fee: $7.00 per document. Copy fee: $.50 per page.

Phone Search: Only docket information is available by phone.

Mail Search: Always enclose a stamped self addressed envelope.

In Person: In person searching is available.

PACER: Sign-up number is 800-676-6856. Access fee is $.60 per minute. Toll-free access: 800-770-4745. Local access: 412-208-7588. Case records are available back to 1989. Records are

never purged. New records are available online after 1 day. PACER is available online at http://pacer.pawd.uscourts.gov.

US Bankruptcy Court

Western District of Pennsylvania

Erie Division 717 State St, #501, Erie, PA 16501 (Courier Address: Use mail address for courier delivery), 814-453-7580.

http://www.pawb.uscourts.gov

Counties: Clarion, Crawford, Elk, Erie, Forest, Jefferson, McKean, Mercer, Venango, Warren.

Indexing/Storage: Cases are indexed by debtor as well as by case number. New cases are available in the index 1 day after filing date. A computer index is maintained. Open records are located at this court.

Fee & Payment: The fee is $20.00 per item (one party name or case number). Payment may be made by money order, cashier check, personal check. Prepayment is required. Payee: Clerk, US Bankruptcy Court. Certification fee: $7.00 per document. Copy fee: $.50 per page.

Phone Search: Docket information is available by phone. An automated voice case information service (VCIS) is available.

Mail Search: Always enclose a stamped self addressed envelope.

In Person: In person searching is available.

PACER: Sign-up number is 800-676-6856. Access fee is $.60 per minute. Toll-free access: 800-795-2829. Local access: 412-355-2588. Case records are available back to 1991. Records are purged every six months. New civil records are

available online after 1 day. PACER is available online at http://pacer.pawb.uscourts.gov.

Pittsburgh Division 600 Grant St #5414, Pittsburgh, PA 15219-2801 (Courier Address: Use mail address for courier delivery), 412-644-2700.

http://www.pawb.uscourts.gov

Counties: Allegheny, Armstrong, Beaver, Bedford, Blair, Butler, Cambria, Clearfield, Fayette, Greene, Indiana, Lawrence, Somerset, Washington, Westmoreland.

Indexing/Storage: Cases are indexed by debtor as well as by case number. New cases are available in the index 1 day after filing date. A computer index is maintained. Records are also indexed on microfiche. Open records are located at this court. District wide searches are available for information from 1986 from this division.

Fee & Payment: The fee is $20.00 per item (one party name or case number). Payment may be made by money order, personal check. Prepayment is required. Debtor's checks are not accepted. Payee: Clerk, US Bankruptcy Court. Certification fee: $7.00 per document. Copy fee: $.50 per page.

Phone Search: Docket information is available by phone. An automated voice case information service (VCIS) is available.

Mail Search: Always enclose a stamped self addressed envelope.

In Person: In person searching is available.

PACER: Sign-up number is 800-676-6856. Access fee is $.60 per minute. Toll-free access: 800-795-2829. Local access: 412-355-2588. Case records are available back to 1991. Records are purged every six months. New civil records are available online after 1 day. PACER is available online at http://pacer.pawb.uscourts.gov.

Pennsylvania County Courts

Court	Jurisdiction	No. of Courts	How Organized
Court of Common Pleas*	General	103	60 Districts
Philadelphia Municipal Court*	Municipal	1	1st District
Philadelphia Traffic Court	Municipal	1	1st District
Pittsburgh Magistrates Court	Municipal	1	Pittsburgh
Register of Wills*	Probate	67	
District Justice Courts	Limited	549	

* Profiled in this Sourcebook.

Court	CIVIL								
	Tort	Contract	Real Estate	Min. Claim	Max. Claim	Small Claims	Estate	Eviction	Domestic Relations
Court of Common Pleas*	X	X	X	$0	No Max			X	X
Philadelphia Municipal Court*	X	X	X	$0	$10,000	$5000		X	X
Philadelphia Traffic Court									
Pittsburgh City Magistrates Court			X	$0	No Max				
Register of Wills*							X		
Magisteruial District Courts	X	X	X	$0	$8000	$8000			

Court	CRIMINAL				
	Felony	Misdemeanor	DWI/DUI	Preliminary Hearing	Juvenile
Court of Common Pleas*	X	X	X	X	X
Philadelphia Municipal Court*	X	X	X	X	
Philadelphia Traffic Court					
Pittsburgh City Magistrates Court		X	X	X	
Register of Wills*					
Magisteruial District Courts		X	X	X	

ADMINISTRATION   Administrative Office of Pennsylvania Courts, PO Box 719, Mechanicsburg, PA, 17055; 717-795-2000, Fax: 717-795-2050. www.courts.state.pa.us

COURT STRUCTURE   The Courts of Common Pleas are the general trial courts, with jurisdiction over both civil and criminal matters and appellate jurisdiction over matters disposed of by the special courts. The civil records clerk of the Court of Common Pleas is called the Prothonotary.

Small claims cases are, usually, handled by the Magistrates and Magisterial District Courts (formerly known as District Justice Courts). These Magisterial Courts, which are designated as "special courts," also handle civil cases up to $8,000. However, all small claims and civil actions are recorded through the Prothonotary Section (civil) of the Court of Common Pleas, which then holds the records. It is not necessary to check with each Magisterial District Court, but rather to check with the Prothonotary for the county.

ONLINE ACCESS

The state's Magisterial District Courts are served by a statewide, automated case management system; online access to the case management system is not available. However, public access to statutorily authorized information is available from the Special Courts, filing offices of Appellate Courts, and from the AOPC. The courts are considering ways to implement a unified, statewide system in the criminal division of the Courts of Common Pleas.

The Infocon County Access System provides direct dial-up access to court record information for 15 counties - Armstrong, Bedford, Blair, Butler, Clarion, Clinton, Erie, Franklin, Huntingdon, Juaniata, Lawrence, Mercer, Mifflin, Pike, and Potter. Set up entails a $25.00 base set-up fee plus $25.00 per county. The monthly usage fee minimum is $25.00, plus time charges. For Information, call Infocon at 814-472-6066.

ADDITIONAL INFORMATION

Fees vary widely among jurisdictions. Many courts will not conduct searches due to a lack of personnel or, if they do search, turnaround time may be excessively lengthy. Many courts have public access terminals for in-person searches.

PROBATE COURTS

Probate is handled by the Register of Wills.

Adams County

Court of Common Pleas - Civil 111-117 Baltimore St Rm 104, Gettysburg, PA 17325; 717-334-6781 X285. 8AM-4:30PM (EST). *Civil, Eviction.*

Civil Records: Access: Mail, in person. Both court and visitors may perform in person searches. No search fee. Required to search: name, years to search. Civil cases indexed by defendant, plaintiff. Civil records on computer from 1988, some microfiche (dates unsure), on index from 1800s.
General Information: Public Access terminal is available. No mental health, sealed records released. SASE required. Turnaround time 1-2 days. Copy fee: $.25 per page. Certification fee: $3.00 plus $1.00 per page. Fee payee: Prothonotary. Personal checks accepted. Prepayment is required.

Court of Common Pleas - Criminal 111-117 Baltimore St, Gettysburg, PA 17325; 717-337-9806. Hours: 8AM-4:30PM (EST). *Felony, Misdemeanor.*

Criminal Records: Access: Mail, in person. Both court and visitors may perform in person searches. Search fee: $8.00 per name. Required to search: name, years to search, DOB. Criminal records on computer since 1985, on microfiche since 1974, previous records on microfilm.
General Information: Public Access terminal is available. No juvenile records released. SASE required. Turnaround time 1 day. Copy fee: $.25 per page. Certification fee: $8.00. Fee payee: Clerk of Courts. Personal checks accepted. No third party checks. Prepayment is required.

Register of Wills 111-117 Baltimore St Rm 102, Gettysburg, PA 17325; 717-337-9826; Fax: 717-334-1758. Hours: 8AM-4:30PM (EST). *Probate.*

Allegheny County

Court of Common Pleas - Civil City Bldg, 414 Grant St, First Floor, Pittsburgh, PA 15219; 412-350-4200; Fax: 412-350-5260. Hours: 8:30AM-4:30PM (EST). *Civil.*

www.county.allegheny.pa.us

Civil Records: Access: Mail, in person, online. Both court and visitors may perform in person searches. Search fee: $25.00 per name. Required to search: name, years to search. Civil cases indexed by defendant, plaintiff. Civil records archived from 1700s; on computer since. Online access to prothonotary civil records is available free at http://prothonotary.county.allegheny.pa.us/allegheny/welcome.htm. Search by case number.
General Information: Public Access terminal is available. No juvenile records released. SASE required. Turnaround time 10 days. Copy fee: $.50 per page.

Certification fee: $8.00. Fee payee: Prothonotary of Allegheny County. Business checks accepted. Prepayment is required. Business accounts may set up a draw down account.

Court of Common Pleas - Criminal 220 Courthouse, 436 Grant Street, Pittsburgh, PA 15219; 412-350-5322. Hours: 8:30AM-4:30PM (EST). *Felony, Misdemeanor.*

Criminal Records: Access: Mail, in person. Both court and visitors may perform in person searches. Search fee: $15.00 per name. Required to search: name, years to search, DOB; also helpful: SSN. Criminal records on files, microfilm back to 1800s; on computer since.
General Information: All records public. SASE required. Turnaround time 2 days. Copy fee: $.50 per page. Certification fee: $10.00. Fee payee: Clerk of Courts. Personal checks accepted. Prepayment required.

Register of Wills 414 Grant St, City Bldg, PIttsburgh, PA 15219; 412-350-4183. Hours: 8:30AM-4:30PM (EST). *Probate.*

www.info.co.alleghany.pa.us

Armstrong County

Court of Common Pleas - Civil 500 E Market St, Kittanning, PA 16201; 724-548-3251; Fax: 724-548-3236. Hours: 8AM-4:30PM (EST). *Civil, Eviction.*

www.geocities.com/acprothonotary

Civil Records: Access: Online, in person. Visitors must perform in person searches for themselves. No search fee. Required to search: name, years to search. Civil cases indexed by defendant, plaintiff. Civil records on files, microfiche since 1930; on computer since. Online access is available through a private company. For information, call Infocon at 814-472-6066.
General Information: Public Access terminal is available. No juvenile, civil commitment records released. Copy fee: $1.00 per page. Certification fee: $3.00. Fee payee: Prothonotary. Personal checks accepted. Prepayment is required.

Court of Common Pleas - Criminal 500 Market St, Kittanning, PA 16201; 724-548-3252. Hours: 8AM-4:30PM (EST). *Felony, Misdemeanor.*

www.geocities.com/acprothonotary

Criminal Records: Access: Mail, online, in person. Both court and visitors may perform in person searches. Search fee: $10.00 per name. Required to search: name, years to search; also helpful: DOB, SSN. Criminal records in card file from early 1900s; on computer since. Online access is available through a private company. For information, call Infocon at 814-472-6066.
General Information: Public Access terminal is available. No juvenile or mental health records released. SASE required. Turnaround time same day. Copy fee:

$1.00 per page. Certification fee: $5.00 first page; $1.00 each add'l. Fee payee: Clerk of Courts. Personal checks accepted. Prepayment is required.

Register of Wills 500 Market St, Kittanning, PA 16201; 724-548-3256; Fax: 724-548-3236. Hours: 8AM-4:30PM (EST). *Probate.*

Beaver County

Court of Common Pleas - Civil Beaver County Courthouse, 810 3rd St, Beaver, PA 15009; 724-728-5700. Hours: 8:30AM-4:30PM (EST). *Civil, Eviction.*

www.co.beaver.pa.us/prothonotary

Civil Records: Access: In person, mail. Both court and visitors may perform in person searches. No search fee. Required to search: name, years to search. Civil cases indexed by defendant, plaintiff. Civil records on computer since 1995.
General Information: Public Access terminal is available. No sealed records released. Turnaround time 1 week. Copy fee: $.25 per page. Certification fee: $5.00. Fee payee: Prothonotary. Personal checks accepted. Prepayment is required.

Court of Common Pleas - Criminal Beaver County Courthouse, 810 3rd St, Beaver, PA 15009; 724-728-5700; Fax: 724-728-8853. Hours: 8:30AM-4:30PM (EST). *Felony, Misdemeanor.*

www.co.beaver.pa.us

Criminal Records: Access: Fax, mail, in person. Both court and visitors may perform in person searches. Search fee: $16.00 per name. Required to search: name, years to search; also helpful: DOB, SSN. Criminal records on computer back to 1973, on microfiche since 1802.
General Information: Public Access terminal is available. Records sealed by court order not released. SASE required. Turnaround time 1 week. Fax notes: Fee to fax results is $1.00 per page. Copy fee: $.50 per page. Certification fee: $5.00. Fee payee: Clerk of Courts Office. Personal checks accepted. Prepayment is required.

Register of Wills Beaver County Courthouse, 3rd St, Beaver, PA 15009; 724-728-5700; Fax: 724-728-9810. Hours: 8:30AM-4:30PM (EST). *Probate.*

Bedford County

Court of Common Pleas - Criminal/Civil Bedford County Courthouse, Bedford, PA 15522; 814-623-4833; Fax: 814-623-4831. Hours: 8:30AM-4:30PM (EST). *Felony, Misdemeanor, Civil, Eviction.*

Civil Records: Access: Mail, online, in person. Both court and visitors may perform in person searches. Search fee: $12.00 per name. Required to search: name, years to search. Civil cases indexed by defendant, plaintiff. Civil records on file from late 1700s. Online access is available through a private company. For information, call Infocon at 814-472-6066.

Criminal Records: Access: Mail, online, in person. Both court and visitors may perform in person searches. Search fee: $10.00 per name. Required to search: name, years to search, DOB. Criminal records on file from late 1700s. Online access to criminal records is the same as civil.

General Information: No sex related or juvenile records released. SASE required. Turnaround time 2 weeks. Copy fee: $.50 per page. Certification fee: $3.00. Fee payee: Prothonotary of Beford County. Personal checks accepted. Prepayment is required.

Register of Wills 200 S Juliana St, Bedford, PA 15522; 814-623-4836; Fax: 814-624-0488. Hours: 8:30AM-4:30PM (EST). *Probate.*

Berks County

Court of Common Pleas - Civil 2nd Floor, 633 Court St, Reading, PA 19601; 610-478-6970; Fax: 610-478-6969. 8AM-4PM (EST). *Civil, Eviction.*

Civil Records: Access: Fax, mail, online, in person. Both court and visitors may perform in person searches. No search fee. Required to search: name, years to search. Civil cases indexed by defendant, plaintiff. Civil records partially on microfiche, on manual index files from 1750. Mail access limited to docket information only. The Registry of Wills has a free searchable website at www.berksregofwills.com which includes marriage, estate, birth and death records for the county. The estate and marriage records are current.

General Information: Public Access terminal is available. No mental, sealed records released. SASE required. Turnaround time 1-2 days. Fax notes: $5.00 for first page, $1.00 each add'l. For emergency use only. Copy fee: $.50 per page. Certification fee: $3.75. Fee payee: Prothonotary. Personal checks accepted. Prepayment is required.

Court of Common Pleas - Criminal 4th Floor, 633 Court St, Reading, PA 19601; 610-478-6550; Fax: 610-478-6570. Hours: 8AM-5PM (EST). *Felony, Misdemeanor.*

Criminal Records: Access: In person only. Visitors must perform in person searches for themselves. No search fee. Required to search: name, years to search; also helpful: DOB, SSN. Criminal records on computer from 1992, in files from 1989, prior archived.

General Information: Public Access terminal is available. No juvenile records released. Copy fee: $.25 per page. Add $1.00 for each page after first 10. Certification fee: $5.00. Fee payee: Berks County Clerk of Courts. Only cashiers checks and money orders accepted. Credit cards accepted for payments on criminal cases only.

Register of Wills 633 Court St 2nd Floor, Reading, PA 19601; 610-478-6600; Fax: 610-478-6251. Hours: 8AM-5PM (EST). *Probate.*
www.berksregofwills.com

Blair County

Court of Common Pleas - Criminal/Civil 423 Allegheny Street #144, Hollidaysburg, PA 16648; 814-693-3080. Hours: 8AM-4:30PM (EST). *Felony, Misdemeanor, Civil, Eviction.*

Civil Records: Access: Online, in person. Visitors must perform in person searches for themselves. No search fee. Required to search: name, years to search. Civil cases indexed by defendant, plaintiff. Civil records on computer from 1989, on index books from 1846 to 1989. Online access is available through a private company. For information, call Infocon, 814-472-6066.

Criminal Records: Access: Mail, online, in person. Both court and visitors may perform in person searches. Search fee: $10.00 per name. Required to search: name, years to search, DOB; also helpful: SSN. Criminal records on computer from 1989, on index books from 1846 to 1989. Online access is available through a private company. For information, call Infocon at 814-472-6066.

General Information: Public Access terminal is available. No adoption records released. SASE required. Turnaround time 2 days. Copy fee: $.50 per page. Certification fee: $5.00. Fee payee: Blair County Prothonotary. Personal checks accepted. Prepayment is required.

Register of Wills 423 Allegheny #145, Hollidaysburg, PA 16648-2022; 814-693-3095. Hours: 8AM-4PM (EST). *Probate.*

Bradford County

Court of Common Pleas - Criminal/Civil Courthouse, 301 Main St, Towanda, PA 18848; 570-265-1705. Hours: 9AM-5PM (EST). *Felony, Misdemeanor, Civil, Eviction.*

Civil Records: Access: Mail, in person. Both court and visitors may perform in person searches. Search fee: $5.00 per name. Required to search: name, years to search. Civil cases indexed by defendant, plaintiff. Civil records on computer from 1986, on microfiche from mid 1800s, archived from mid-1940s.

Criminal Records: Access: Mail, in person. Both court and visitors may perform in person searches. Search fee: $8.00 per name. Required to search: name, years to search, DOB. Criminal records on computer from 1986, on microfiche from mid 1800s, archived from mid-1940s.

General Information: Public Access terminal is available. SASE required. Turnaround time 1-2 days. Copy fee: $.25 per page. Certification fee: $3.00. $5.00 for criminal records. Fee payee: Prothonotary. Personal checks accepted. Prepayment is required.

Register of Wills 301 Main St., Towanda, PA 18848; 570-265-1702. 9AM-5PM (EST). *Probate.*

Bucks County

Court of Common Pleas - Civil 55 E Court St, Doylestown, PA 18901; 215-348-6191. Hours: 8:15AM-4:15PM (EST). *Civil, Eviction.*
www.buckscounty.org

Civil Records: Access: Online, in person. Visitors must perform in person searches for themselves. No search fee. Required to search: name, years to search. Civil cases indexed by defendant, plaintiff. Civil records on computer back to 1980, prior on dockets. Access to the remote online system requires a Sprint ID ($24). The per minute fee is $.60 with a 2 minute minimum. Contact John Morris at 215-348-6579 for more information.

General Information: Public Access terminal is available. No mental, sealed records released. Copy fee: $.25 per page. Certification fee: $4.50. Fee payee: Prothonotary. Personal checks accepted. Prepayment is required.

Court of Common Pleas - Criminal Bucks County Courthouse, Doylestown, PA 18901; 215-348-6389; Fax: 215-348-6740. Hours: 8AM-4:30PM (EST). *Felony, Misdemeanor.*

Criminal Records: Access: Mail, online, in person. Both court and visitors may perform in person searches. Search fee: $10.00 per name. Required to search: name, years to search, DOB. Criminal records on computer from 1980, some records on microfiche, on card index from 1932 to 1979. Access to the criminal online system requires a Sprint ID ($24). The per minute fee is $.60 with a 2 minute minimum. Search by name or case

number. Contact Jack Morris at 215-348-6579 for more information.

General Information: Public Access terminal is available. No sealed, juvenile or mental records released. SASE required. Turnaround time same day. Fax notes: Fee to fax results is $1.50 per page. No copy fee. Certification fee: $7.50. Fee payee: Clerk of Courts Criminal Division. Personal checks accepted.

Register of Wills Bucks County Courthouse, Doylestown, PA 18901; 215-348-6265; Fax: 215-348-6156. Hours: 8:15AM-4:15PM M-F; 8:15AM-7:30PM 1st & 3rd Wed of month (EST). *Probate.*

Butler County

Court of Common Pleas - Civil Butler County Courthouse, PO Box 1208, Butler, PA 16001-1208; 724-284-5214. Hours: 8:30AM-4:30PM (EST). *Civil, Eviction.*

Civil Records: Access: Online, in person. Visitors must perform in person searches for themselves. No search fee. Required to search: name, years to search. Civil cases indexed by defendant, plaintiff. Civil records on computer from 1993, prior on docket books. Online access is available through a private company. For information, call Infocon at 814-472-6066.

General Information: Public Access terminal is available. No mental records released. Copy fee: $.25 per page. Certification fee: $3.00. Fee payee: Prothonotary. Personal checks accepted. Prepayment is required.

Court of Common Pleas - Criminal Butler County Courthouse, PO Box 1208, Butler, PA 16003-1208; 724-284-5233; Fax: 724-284-5244. Hours: 8:30AM-4:30PM (EST). *Felony, Misdemeanor.*

Criminal Records: Access: Mail, online, in person. Both court and visitors may perform in person searches. Search fee: $16.00 per name. Required to search: name, DOB; also helpful: years to search, SSN. Original records in office for 10 years. Computerized from 1988 to present, prior in Russell Index. Online access is available through a private company. For information, call Infocon at 814-472-6066.

General Information: Public Access terminal is available. No mental, sealed, juvenile (16 & under) victim records released. SASE required. Turnaround time 1-2 days. Copy fee: $.50 per page. Certification fee: $8.00 per page. Fee payee: Clerk of Courts. Personal checks accepted. Prepayment is required.

Register of Wills Butler County Courthouse, PO Box 1208, Butler, PA 16003-1208; 724-284-5348; Fax: 724-284-5278. 8:30AM-4:30PM (EST). *Probate.*

Cambria County

Court of Common Pleas - Civil 200 S Center St, Ebensburg, PA 15931; 814-472-1636; Fax: 814-472-5632. Hours: 9AM-4PM (EST). *Civil, Eviction.*

Civil Records: Access: Phone, mail, fax, in person. Both court and visitors may perform in person searches. No search fee. Required to search: name, years to search. Civil cases indexed by defendant, plaintiff. Civil records on computer from 1/1/94, prior on dockets from 1800s.

General Information: Public Access terminal is available. No divorce or mental records released. SASE requested. Fax notes: Fee to fax results is $1.00 per page. Copy fee: $.25 per page. Certification fee: $3.00. Fee payee: Prothonotary. Personal checks accepted. Prepayment is required.

Court of Common Pleas - Criminal Cambria County Courthouse S Center St, Ebensburg, PA 15931; 814-472-1540. Hours: 9AM-4PM (EST). *Felony, Misdemeanor.*

Criminal Records: Access: Mail, in person. Only the court performs in person searches; visitors may not. Search fee: $4.00 per name. Required to search: name, years to search, DOB; also helpful: SSN. Criminal conviction records are computerized, indexed from 1800s.

General Information: No sealed or child victim records released. Turnaround time 3 days. Copy fee: $.50 per page. Certification fee: $8.00. Fee payee: Clerk of Court. Personal checks accepted. Third party checks not accepted. Prepayment is required.

Register of Wills 200 S Center St, Ebensburg, PA 15931; 814-472-5440 X1440; Fax: 814-472-0762. Hours: 9AM-4PM (EST). *Probate.*

Cameron County

Court of Common Pleas - Civil Cameron County Courthouse, East 5th St, Emporium, PA 15834; 814-486-3355; Fax: 814-468-0464. Hours: 8:30AM-4:30PM (EST). *Civil, Eviction.*

Civil Records: Access: Phone, fax, mail, in person. Both court and visitors may perform in person searches. Search fee: $15.00 per name. Required to search: name, years to search. Civil cases indexed by defendant, plaintiff. Civil records on computer from 1988, archived from 1860 to present.

General Information: Public Access terminal is available. No adoption, military discharge records released. SASE required. Turnaround time same day. Fax notes: $1.00 per page. Copy fee: $.50 per page. Certification fee: $5.00. Fee payee: Prothonotary. Personal checks accepted. Credit cards accepted: Visa, MasterCard. Will bill fees with prior permission form Clerk.

Court of Common Pleas - Criminal 20 East 5th St, Emporium, PA 15834; 814-486-3349; Fax: 814-486-0464. Hours: 8:30AM-4PM (EST). *Felony, Misdemeanor.*

Criminal Records: Access: Phone, fax, mail, in person. Both court and visitors may perform in person searches. Search fee: $15.00 per name. Required to search: name, years to search; also helpful: address, DOB, SSN. Criminal records archived from 1860.

General Information: No juvenile, mental health records released. SASE required. Turnaround time same day. Fax notes: $1.00 per page. Copy fee: $.50 per page. Certification fee: $5.00. Fee payee: Clerk of Court. Personal checks accepted. Credit cards accepted: Visa, MasterCard. Prepayment is required.

Register of Wills Cameron County Courthouse, East 5th St., Emporium, PA 15834; 814-486-3355; Fax: 814-486-0464. Hours: 8:30AM-4PM (EST). *Probate.*

Carbon County

Court of Common Pleas - Civil PO Box 130, Courthouse, Jim Thorpe, PA 18229; 570-325-2481; Fax: 570-325-8047. Hours: 8:30AM-4:30PM (EST). *Civil, Eviction.*

www.aopc.org/counties/carbon

Civil Records: Access: In person only. Visitors must perform in person searches for themselves. No search fee. Required to search: name. Civil cases indexed by defendant, plaintiff. Civil records on computer from 1/84, financing statements from 1/87, on microfiche from 1/84, prior archived.

General Information: Public Access terminal is available. No abuse, mental health records released. Copy fee: $1.00 per page. Certification fee: $7.50. Fee payee: Prothonotary of Carbon County. Personal checks accepted. Prepayment is required.

Court of Common Pleas - Criminal County Courthouse, Jim Thorpe, PA 18229; 570-325-3637; Fax: 570-325-5705. Hours: 8:30AM-4PM (EST). *Felony, Misdemeanor.*

Criminal Records: Access: Phone, mail, in person. Only the court performs in person searches; visitors may not. No search fee. Required to search: name, years to search, DOB; also helpful: SSN. Criminal records on computer from 1973, on microfiche from 1800.

General Information: No juvenile, mental health records released. SASE required. Turnaround time 1 day. Certification fee: $5.00. Fee payee: Clerk of Courts Carbon County. Personal checks accepted.

Register of Wills PO Box 286, Jim Thorpe, PA 18229; 570-325-2261; Fax: 570-325-5098. Hours: 8:30AM-4:30PM (EST). *Probate.*

Centre County

Court of Common Pleas - Criminal/Civil Centre County Courthouse, Bellefonte, PA 16823; 814-355-6796. Hours: 8:30AM-5PM (EST). *Felony, Misdemeanor, Civil, Eviction.*

http://countrystore.org/webpages/county/223.htm

Civil Records: Access: Mail, in person. Both court and visitors may perform in person searches. Search fee: $7.00 per name. Required to search: name, years to search, DOB. Civil cases indexed by defendant, plaintiff. Civil records on computer from 7-1-94, on card files and docket books from 1986, on microfiche and archived from 1800 to 1986.

Criminal Records: Access: Mail, in person. Both court and visitors may perform in person searches. Search fee: $7.00 per name. Required to search: name, years to search, DOB. Criminal records on computer from 7-1-94, on card files and docket books from 1986, on microfiche and archived from 1800 to 1986.

General Information: Public Access terminal is available. No sex related, juvenile, mental records released. SASE helpful. Turnaround time 3-5 days. Fax notes: Do not fax. Copy fee: $.50 per page. Certification fee: $4.00. Fee payee: Clerk of Court. Personal checks accepted. Prepayment is required.

Register of Wills Willowbank Office Bldg, 414 Holmes Ave #2, Bellefonte, PA 16823; 814-355-6724. Hours: 8:30AM-5PM (EST). *Probate.*

www.countrystore.org/county/224.htm

Chester County

Court of Common Pleas - Civil 2 North High St, Ste 130, West Chester, PA 19380; 610-344-6300. Hours: 8:30AM-4:30PM (EST). *Civil, Eviction.*

www.chesco.org

Civil Records: Access: Online, in person. Visitors must perform in person searches for themselves. No search fee. Required to search: name, years to search. Civil cases indexed by defendant, plaintiff. Civil records on dockets from 1985 to present, on microfiche from 1981 to 1984, archived from 1700s. Internet access to county records including court records requires a sign-up and credit card payment. Application fee is $50. There is a $10.00 per month minimum (no charge for no activity); and $.10 each transaction beyond 100. Sign-up and/or logon at http://epin.chesco.org.

General Information: Public Access terminal is available. No sealed records released. Copy fee: $.25 per page. Certification fee: $3.00. Fee payee: Prothonotary. Business checks accepted. Prepayment is required.

Court of Common Pleas - Criminal 2 North High St #160, West Chester, PA 19380; 610-344-6135. Hours: 8:30AM-4:30PM *Felony, Misdemeanor.*

www.chesco.org

Criminal Records: Access: Mail, online, in person. Both court and visitors may perform in person searches. Search fee: $10.00 per name. Required to search: name, years to search; also helpful: DOB. Criminal records on computer and microfiche from mid-70s, archived from the 1700s. Internet access to county records including criminal records requires a sign-up and credit card payment. Application fee is $50. There is a $10.00 per month minimum (no charge for no activity); and $.10 each transaction beyond 100. Sign-up and/or logon at http://epin.chesco.org.

General Information: Public Access terminal is available. No juvenile records released. Turnaround time 1 day. Copy fee: $1.00 per page. Certification fee: $5.00. Fee payee: Clerk of Courts. Business checks accepted. Prepayment is required.

Register of Wills 2 North High St, Suite 109, West Chester, PA 19380-3073; 610-344-6335; Fax: 610-344-6218. Hours: 8:30AM-4:30PM (EST). *Probate.*

Note: Internet access to probate records requires a sign-up and payment. Sign-up and/or logon at http://epin.chesco.org.

Clarion County

Court of Common Pleas - Civil Clarion County Courthouse, Main St, Clarion, PA 16214; 814-226-1119; Fax: 814-226-8069. Hours: 8:30AM-4:30PM (EST). *Civil, Eviction.*

Civil Records: Access: Phone, fax, mail, online, in person. Both court and visitors may perform in person searches. Search fee: $10.00 per name. Required to search: name, years to search. Civil cases indexed by defendant, plaintiff. Civil records on computer from mid-1990s, on dockets from 1800s. Online access is available through a private company. For information, call Infocon at 814-472-6066.

General Information: Public Access terminal is available. No juvenile, mental health records released. Fax notes: No fee to fax results. No copy fee. Certification fee: $5.00. Fee payee: Prothonotary. Personal checks accepted. Prepayment is required.

Court of Common Pleas - Criminal Clarion County Courthouse, Main St, Clarion, PA 16214; 814-226-4000; Fax: 814-226-8069. Hours: 8AM-4:30PM (EST). *Felony, Misdemeanor.*

Criminal Records: Access: Phone, fax, mail, online, in person. Both court and visitors may perform in person searches. Search fee: $10.00 per name. Required to search: name, years to search, DOB. Criminal records on computer and microfiche from 1990, on docket books from 1800s. Online access is available through a private company. For information, call Infocon at 814-472-6066.

General Information: Public Access terminal is available. No juvenile, mental health records released. Turnaround time same day. Fax notes: No fee to fax results. Copy fee: $.50 per page. Certification fee: $5.00. Payee: Clerk of Court. Personal checks accepted.

Register of Wills Clarion County Courthouse, Corner of 5th & Main, Clarion, PA 16214; 814-226-4000 X2500; Fax: 814-226-8069. Hours: 8:30AM-4:30PM (EST). *Probate.*

Clearfield County

Court of Common Pleas - Criminal/Civil PO Box 549 (1 N 2nd St), Clearfield, PA 16830; 814-765-2641 X1330; Fax: 814-765-7659. Hours: 8:30AM-4PM (EST). *Felony, Misdemeanor, Civil, Eviction.*

Civil Records: Access: Mail, in person. Both court and visitors may perform in person searches. Search fee: $7.00 per name, 5-years search. Required to search: name, years to search; also helpful: address. Civil cases indexed by defendant, plaintiff. Civil records indexed

(Russell System) on dockets from 1820s; on computer back to 11/01.

Criminal Records: Access: Mail, in person. Both court and visitors may perform in person searches. Search fee: $7.00 per name, 5-year search. Required to search: name, years to search, address, DOB, SSN, signed release. Criminal records indexed (Russell System) on dockets from 1820s; on computer back to 11/01.

General Information: Public Access terminal is available. No juvenile, sealed or mental health records released. SASE required. Turnaround time 2 days. Copy fee: $.25 per page. Certification fee: $1.50. Fee payee: Prothonotary. Personal checks accepted. Prepayment is required.

Register of Wills & Clerk of Orphans Court PO Box 361, Clearfield, PA 16830; 814-765-2641 X1351; Fax: 814-765-6089. Hours: 8:30AM-4PM (EST). *Probate.*

Clinton County

Court of Common Pleas - Criminal/Civil 230 E Water St, Lock Haven, PA 17745; 570-893-4007. Hours: 8AM-5PM M, T, Th, F; 8AM-12:30PM Wed (EST). *Felony, Misdemeanor, Civil, Eviction.*

Civil Records: Access: Online, in person. Visitors must perform in person searches for themselves. No search fee. Required to search: name, years to search. Civil cases indexed by defendant, plaintiff. Civil records on computer from 1992, on files from 1839. Online access is available through a private company. For information, call Infocon at 814-472-6066.

Criminal Records: Access: Online, in person. Visitors must perform in person searches for themselves. No search fee. Required to search: name, years to search, DOB, SSN, signed release. Criminal records on computer from 1992, on files from 1839. Online access is available through a private company. For information, call Infocon at 814-472-6066.

General Information: Public Access terminal is available. No sealed, mental health or minor victim abuse cases records released. Copy fee: $.50 per page. Certification fee: $4.50. Fee payee: Clerk of Court or Prothonotary. Personal checks accepted. Will bill Federal Liens fees.

Register of Wills PO Box 943, Lock Haven, PA 17745; 570-893-4010. Hours: 8:30AM-5PM M,T,Th,F; 8AM-12:30PM Wed (EST). *Probate.*

Columbia County

Court of Common Pleas - Criminal/Civil PO Box 380, Bloomsburg, PA 17815; 570-389-5600. Hours: 8AM-4:30PM (EST). *Felony, Misdemeanor, Civil, Eviction.*

Civil Records: Access: In person only. Both court and visitors may perform in person searches. Search fee: $10.00 per name. Required to search: name, years to search. Civil cases indexed by defendant, plaintiff. Civil records on computer to 1992, on microfiche from 1814 to present, on dockets from 1814.

Criminal Records: Access: Mail, in person. Both court and visitors may perform in person searches. Search fee: $10.00 per name. Required to search: name, years to search; also helpful: DOB. Criminal records on computer to 1992, on microfiche from 1814 to present, on dockets from 1814.

General Information: Public Access terminal is available. No juvenile, adoption, mental health petition or OAPSA records released. SASE required. Turnaround time same day. Copy fee: $.50 per page. Certification fee: $4.00. Fee payee: Prothonotary or Clerk of Court. Personal checks accepted. Prepayment is required.

Register of Wills 35 W Main St, PO Box 380, Bloomsburg, PA 17815; 570-389-5635; Fax: 570-389-5636. Hours: 8AM-4:30PM (EST). *Probate.*

Crawford County

Court of Common Pleas - Civil Crawford County Courthouse, Meadville, PA 16335; 814-333-7324. Hours: 8:30AM-4:30PM (EST). *Civil, Eviction.*

Civil Records: Access: Mail, in person. Both court and visitors may perform in person searches. Search fee: $7.50 per name. Required to search: name, years to search. Civil cases indexed by defendant, plaintiff. Civil records on dockets from 1800s.

General Information: No mental health, sealed records released. SASE required. Turnaround time 3 days. Copy fee: $.75 per page. Docket copy $1.50 per page. Certification fee: $1.50. Fee payee: Prothonotary Crawford County. Personal checks accepted. Checks accepted with ID. Prepayment is required.

Court of Common Pleas - Criminal Crawford County Courthouse, Meadville, PA 16335; 814-333-7442; Fax: 814-337-7349. Hours: 8:30AM-4:30PM (EST). *Felony, Misdemeanor.*

Criminal Records: Access: Mail, in person. Both court and visitors may perform in person searches. Search fee: $10.00 per name. Required to search: name, years to search, signed release; also helpful: DOB. Criminal records on microfiche from 1974, on dockets from 1914, archived from 1880s.

General Information: No juvenile records released. SASE required. Turnaround time 10-14 days. Copy fee: $1.00 per page. Certification fee: $5.00 per page. Fee payee: Clerk of Courts. Personal checks accepted. Prepayment is required.

Register of Wills 903 Diamond Park, Meadville, PA 16335; 814-333-7337; Fax: 814-337-5296. Hours: 8:30AM-4:30PM (EST). *Probate.*

Cumberland County

Court of Common Pleas - Civil Cumberland County Courthouse, Rm 100, One Courthouse Square, Carlisle, PA 17013-3387; 717-240-6195; Fax: 717-240-6573. Hours: 8AM-4:30PM (EST). *Civil, Eviction.*

www.ccpa.net/Courts

Civil Records: Access: In person only. Visitors must perform in person searches for themselves. No search fee. Required to search: name, years to search; also helpful: address. Civil cases indexed by defendant, plaintiff. Civil records on computer from 1994, on microfiche from 1966-1986, on dockets from 1800s.

General Information: Public Access terminal is available. No mental health records released. Copy fee: $.50 per page. Certification fee: No certification fee. Fee payee: Office of Prothonotary. Business checks accepted. No third party checks accepted. Prepayment is required.

Court of Common Pleas - Criminal Cumberland County Courthouse, East Wing, 1 Courthouse Sq, Carlisle, PA 17013-3387; 717-240-6250; Fax: 717-240-6571. Hours: 8AM-4:30PM (EST). *Felony, Misdemeanor.*

www.ccpa.net/Courts

Criminal Records: Access: Mail, in person. Both court and visitors may perform in person searches. Search fee: $15.00 per name. Required to search: name, years to search, DOB or SSN. Criminal records on computer from 1994, on files from 1976, archived from 1800s.

General Information: Public Access terminal is available. No juvenile records released (Including any case with a juvenile as the victim). SASE required. Turnaround time same day. Copy fee: $1.00 per page. Certification fee: $1.00 per page. Fee payee: Clerk of Courts. Personal checks accepted. Prepayment required.

Register of Wills Cumberland County Courthouse, Rm 102, 1 Courthouse Sq, Carlisle, PA 17013; 717-240-6345; Fax: 717-240-6490. Hours: 8AM-4:30PM (EST). *Probate.*

Dauphin County

Court of Common Pleas - Civil PO Box 945, Harrisburg, PA 17108; 717-255-2698. Hours: 8:30AM-5PM (EST). *Civil, Eviction.*

Civil Records: Access: Mail, in person. Both court and visitors may perform in person searches. Search fee: $10.00 per name. Fee is per 5 years searched. Required to search: name, years to search. Civil cases indexed by defendant, plaintiff. Civil records on microfiche and dockets from 1970s, archived from 1700s.

General Information: Public Access terminal is available. No mental health released. SASE required. Turnaround time 1 day. Copy fee: $.75 per page. Certification fee: $10.00. Fee payee: Dauphin County Prothonotary. Business checks accepted. Prepayment is required.

Court of Common Pleas - Criminal Front & Market St, Harrisburg, PA 17101; 717-255-2692; Fax: 717-255-2694. Hours: 8:30AM-5PM (EST). *Felony, Misdemeanor.*

Criminal Records: Access: Mail, in person. Both court and visitors may perform in person searches. Search fee: $20.00 per name. Required to search: name, years to search; also helpful: DOB, SSN. Criminal records on dockets and computer from 1950, archived from 1700s.

General Information: Public Access terminal is available. No juvenile, mental records released. SASE not required. Turnaround time 1 week. Copy fee: $.50 per page. Certification fee: $5.00. Fee payee: Clerk of Court. Business checks accepted. Prepayment required.

Register of Wills PO Box 1295, Harrisburg, PA 17101; 717-255-2657; Fax: 717-255-2749. Hours: 8:30AM-5PM (EST). *Probate.*

www.dauphinc.org

Delaware County

Court of Common Pleas - Criminal/Civil 201 W Front St, Media, PA 19063; 610-891-4370. 8:30AM-4:30PM (EST). *Felony, Misdemeanor, Civil, Eviction.*

www.co.delaware.pa.us

Civil Records: Access: Online, in person. Visitors must perform in person searches for themselves. No search fee. Required to search: name, years to search. Civil cases indexed by defendant, plaintiff. Civil records on computer from early 1990, on card file from 1920s, archived from 1800s. Online access to court civil records is available free at www2.co.delaware.pa.us/pa/default.htm. For more information, call 610-891-4675. Search online by name or document type.

Criminal Records: Access: Mail, in person. Both court and visitors may perform in person searches. No search fee. Required to search: name, years to search; also helpful: DOB, SSN. Criminal records on computer from late 1970s, prior on files. No online access to criminal records.

General Information: Public Access terminal is available. No juvenile, mental health records released. SASE required. Turnaround time 1-3 days. Copy fee: $1.00 per page. Certification fee: $4.50 first page and $1.00 thereafter. Fee payee: Office of Judical Support. Business checks accepted. Prepayment required.

Register of Wills Delaware County Courthouse, 201 W Front St, Media, PA 19063; 610-891-4400; Fax: 610-891-4812. Hours: 8:30AM-4:30PM (EST). *Probate.*

www.co.delaware.pa.us

Elk County

Court of Common Pleas - Criminal/Civil

PO Box 237, Ridgway, PA 15853; 814-776-5344; Fax: 814-776-5305. Hours: 8:30AM-4PM (EST). *Felony, Misdemeanor, Civil, Eviction.*

Civil Records: Access: Phone, mail, in person. Both court and visitors may perform in person searches. Search fee: $7.50 per name. Required to search: name, years to search. Civil cases indexed by defendant, plaintiff. Civil records on dockets from 1843, computerized recently.

Criminal Records: Access: Phone, mail, in person. Both court and visitors may perform in person searches. Search fee: $10.00 per name. Required to search: name, years to search, DOB. Criminal records on dockets from 1843, computerized recently.

General Information: No mental health or juvenile records released. SASE not required. Turnaround time 1 day. Copy fee: $.50 per page. Certification fee: $4.50. Fee payee: Elk County Prothonotary. Personal checks accepted. Prepayment is required.

Register of Wills PO Box 314, Ridgway, PA 15853; 814-776-5349; Fax: 814-776-5379. Hours: 8:30AM-4PM (EST). *Probate.*

Erie County

Court of Common Pleas - Civil

Erie County Courthouse, 140 West 6th St., Erie, PA 16501; 814-451-6076. Hours: 8:30AM-4:30PM (EST). *Civil, Eviction.*

www.eriecountygov.org/cor

Civil Records: Access: Mail, online, in person. Both court and visitors may perform in person searches. No search fee. Required to search: name, years to search. Civil cases indexed by defendant, plaintiff. Civil records on computer from 1992, on dockets from 1971, on microfilm/microfiche from 1800s. Online access is available through a private company. For information, call Infocon at 814-472-6066.

General Information: Public Access terminal is available. No sealed records released. SASE required. Turnaround time less than one week. Copy fee: $.50 per page. Computer page $1.00 per page. Certification fee: $3.00. Fee payee: Prothonotary. Personal checks accepted. Prepayment is required.

Court of Common Pleas - Criminal

Erie County Courthouse, 140 West 6th St, Erie, PA 16501; 814-451-6229; Fax: 814-451-6420. Hours: 8:30AM-4:30PM (EST). *Felony, Misdemeanor.*

Criminal Records: Access: Mail, online, in person. Both court and visitors may perform in person searches. Search fee: $10.00 per name. Required to search: name, years to search, DOB. Criminal records on computer from 1992, on docket index from 1951, on files from 1800s. Online access is available through a private company. For information, call Infocon at 814-472-6066.

General Information: Public Access terminal is available. No juvenile or ARD records released. SASE not required. Turnaround time 1 week. Copy fee: $.10 per page. Certification fee: No certification fee. Fee payee: Clerk of Courts. Personal checks accepted. Prepayment is required.

Register of Wills Erie County Courthouse 140 W 6th St, Erie, PA 16501; 814-451-6260. Hours: 8:30AM-4:30PM (EST). *Probate.*

Fayette County

Court of Common Pleas - Civil

61 East Main St, Uniontown, PA 15401; 724-430-1272; Fax: 724-430-4555. Hours: 8AM-4:30PM (EST). *Civil, Eviction.*

Civil Records: Access: Mail, in person. Both court and visitors may perform in person searches. Search fee:

$5.00 per name. Required to search: name, years to search. Civil cases indexed by defendant, plaintiff. Civil records on computer from 1992, archived from 1700s.

General Information: No mental records released. SASE not required. Turnaround time 2 weeks. Copy fee: $.50 per page. Certification fee: $10.00. Fee payee: Prothonotary. Personal checks accepted. Prepayment is required.

Court of Common Pleas - Criminal

61 East Main St, Uniontown, PA 15401; 724-430-1253; Fax: 724-438-8410. Hours: 8AM-4:30PM (EST). *Felony, Misdemeanor.*

Criminal Records: Access: Fax, mail, in person. Both court and visitors may perform in person searches. Search fee: $15.00 for 5-year search; $30.00 for 5-yr. plus. Required to search: name, years to search, DOB; also helpful: SSN. Criminal records on computer from 1993, on files from 1800s.

General Information: Public Access terminal is available. No sex related or juvenile records released. SASE not required. Turnaround time 5-10 days. Fax notes: $3.00 per document. Copy fee: $.50 per page. Certification fee: $16.50. Fee payee: Clerk of Courts. Personal checks accepted. Prepayment is required.

Register of Wills 61 East Main St, Uniontown, PA 15401; 724-430-1206. Hours: 8AM-4:30PM (EST). *Probate.*

Forest County

Court of Common Pleas - Criminal/Civil

Forest County Courthouse, PO Box 423, Tionesta, PA 16353; 814-755-3526; Fax: 814-755-8837. Hours: 9AM-4PM (EST). *Felony, Misdemeanor, Civil, Eviction, Probate.*

Note: Includes the Register of Wills.

Civil Records: Access: Mail, fax, in person. Both court and visitors may perform in person searches. No search fee. Required to search: name, years to search. Civil cases indexed by defendant, plaintiff. Civil records on dockets since 1995, archived from 1857.

Criminal Records: Access: Mail, fax, in person. Both court and visitors may perform in person searches. Search fee: $10.00 per name. Required to search: name, years to search; also helpful: DOB, SSN. Criminal records on dockets since 1995, archived from 1857.

General Information: Public Access terminal is available. No adoption records released. SASE required. Turnaround time same day. Fax notes: Fee to fax results is $4.00 per document. Copy fee: $2.00 per page. Certification fee: $2.00. Fee payee: Annette M Kiefer. Personal checks accepted. Prepayment is required.

Franklin County

Court of Common Pleas - Civil

157 Lincoln Way East, Chambersburg, PA 17201; 717-261-3858; Fax: 717-264-6772. Hours: 8:30AM-4:30PM (EST). *Civil, Eviction.*

Civil Records: Access: In person only. Visitors must perform in person searches for themselves. No search fee. Required to search: name, years to search. Civil cases indexed by defendant, plaintiff. Civil records on file from 1985; on computer since.

General Information: No mental records released. Fax notes: Fee to fax results is $1.00 per page. Copy fee: $1.00 per page. Certification fee: $3.00. Fee payee: Prothonotary or Linda L Beard. Personal checks accepted. Prepayment is required.

Court of Common Pleas - Criminal

157 Lincoln Way East, Chambersburg, PA 17201; 717-261-3805; Fax: 717-261-3896. Hours: 8:30AM-4:30PM (EST). *Felony, Misdemeanor.*

Criminal Records: Access: Mail, in person. Both court and visitors may perform in person searches. Search fee: $10.00 per name. Required to search: name, years

to search, DOB. Criminal records on files for 50 years, archived from 1800s.

General Information: Public Access terminal is available. No juvenile records released. SASE requested. Turnaround time same day. Copy fee: $.25 per page. Certification fee: $5.00. Fee payee: Clerk of Courts. Personal checks accepted. Prepayment is required.

Register of Wills 157 Lincoln Way East, Chambersburg, PA 17201; 717-261-3872; Fax: 717-267-3438. Hours: 8:30AM-4:30PM (EST). *Probate.*

Fulton County

Court of Common Pleas - Criminal/Civil

Fulton County Courthouse, 201 N 2nd St, McConnellsburg, PA 17233; 717-485-4212; Fax: 717-485-5568 Attn: Court of Common Pleas. Hours: 8:30AM-4:30PM (EST). *Felony, Misdemeanor, Civil, Eviction.*

Civil Records: Access: In person only. Visitors must perform in person searches for themselves. No search fee. Required to search: name, years to search. Civil cases indexed by defendant, plaintiff. Civil records on docket index from 1850s; on computer back to 1999.

Criminal Records: Access: Mail, in person. Both court and visitors may perform in person searches. Search fee: $5.00 per name. Required to search: name, years to search. Criminal records on docket index from 1850s; on computer back to 1994.

General Information: Public Access terminal is available. No juvenile, adoption records released. SASE required. Turnaround time 3-5 days. Fax notes: $5.00 per document. Copy fee: $.25 per page. Certification fee: $5.00. Fee payee: Prothonotary. Personal checks accepted. Prepayment is required.

Register of Wills 201 N 2nd St, McConnellsburg, PA 17233; 717-485-4212; Fax: 717-485-5568. Hours: 8:30AM-4:30PM (EST). *Probate.*

Greene County

Court of Common Pleas

Greene County Courthouse, Room 105, Waynesburg, PA 15370; 724-852-5289. 8:30AM-4:30PM (EST). *Civil, Eviction.*

Civil Records: Access: Mail, in person. Visitors must perform in person searches for themselves. No search fee. Required to search: name, years to search. Civil cases indexed by defendant, plaintiff. Civil records on index from 1948.

General Information: Public Access terminal is available. No mental health records released. SASE required. Turnaround time 1 week. Copy fee: $.50 per page. Certification fee: $6.00. Fee payee: Prothonotary. Personal checks accepted. Prepayment is required.

Court of Common Pleas - Criminal

Greene County Courthouse, Waynesburg, PA 15370; 724-852-5281; Fax: 724-852-5316. Hours: 8:30AM-4:30PM (EST). *Felony, Misdemeanor.*

Criminal Records: Access: Mail, in person. Both court and visitors may perform in person searches. Search fee: $10.00 per name. Required to search: name, years to search, DOB, signed release; also helpful: SSN. Criminal records on index books from 1940s, on computer since 1996.

General Information: Public Access terminal is available. (Limited number of cases only.) No juvenile, adoption records released. SASE required. Turnaround time same day. Fax notes: Fee to fax results is $2.00 1st page; $1.00 each add'l page. Copy fee: $.50 per page. Certification fee: $8.00. Fee payee: Clerk of Courts. Personal checks accepted. Prepayment is required.

Register of Wills Greene County Courthouse, 10 E High St, Waynesburg, PA 15370; 724-852-5283. Hours: 8:30AM-4PM (EST). *Probate.*

Huntingdon County

Court of Common Pleas - Criminal/Civil

PO Box 39, Courthouse, Huntingdon, PA 16652; 814-643-1610; Fax: 814-643-4172. Hours: 8:30AM-4:30PM (EST). *Felony, Misdemeanor, Civil, Eviction.*

Civil Records: Access: Phone, mail, fax, in person. Both court and visitors may perform in person searches. No search fee. Required to search: name, years to search; also helpful: address. Civil cases indexed by defendant, plaintiff. Civil records on computer from 08/03/92, on dockets from 1700s. Online access is available through a private company. For information, call Infocon at 814-472-6066.

Criminal Records: Access: Phone, mail, fax, in person. Both court and visitors may perform in person searches. No search fee. Required to search: name, years to search; also helpful: DOB, SSN. Criminal records on computer from 08/03/92, on dockets from 1700s. Online access is available through a private company. For information, call Infocon at 814-472-6066.

General Information: Public Access terminal is available. No juvenile records released. SASE required. Turnaround time 1-2 days. Copy fee: $.25 per page. Certification fee: $4.50. Fee payee: Kay Coons, Prothonotary. Personal checks accepted. Prepayment is required.

Register of Wills Courthouse, 223 Penn St, Huntingdon, PA 16652; 814-643-2740. Hours: 8:30AM-4:30PM (EST). *Probate.*

Indiana County

Court of Common Pleas - Criminal/Civil

County Courthouse, 825 Philadelphia St, Indiana, PA 15701; 724-465-3855/3858; Fax: 724-465-3968. Hours: 8AM-4PM (EST). *Felony, Misdemeanor, Civil, Eviction.*

Civil Records: Access: Fax, mail, in person. Both court and visitors may perform in person searches. Search fee: $10.00 per name. Will not conduct judgment searches. Required to search: name, years to search. Civil cases indexed by defendant, plaintiff. Civil records on computer from 1994, prior on index files.

Criminal Records: Access: Fax, mail, in person. Both court and visitors may perform in person searches. Search fee: $10.00 per name. Required to search: name, years to search, DOB, signed release. Criminal records on computer from 1994, prior on index files.

General Information: Public Access terminal is available. No juvenile, commitment records released. Turnaround time same day. Fax notes: $.25 per page. Copy fee: $.25 per page. Certification fee: $3.00. Fee payee: Clerk of Court or Prothonotary. Personal checks accepted. Prepayment is required.

Register of Wills County Courthouse, 825 Philadelphia St, Indiana, PA 15701; 724-465-3860; Fax: 724-465-3863. 8AM-4:30PM (EST). *Probate.*

Jefferson County

Court of Common Pleas - Criminal/Civil

Courthouse, 200 Main St, Brookville, PA 15825; 814-849-1606 X225; Fax: 814-849-1607. Hours: 8:30AM-4:30PM (EST). *Felony, Misdemeanor, Civil, Eviction.*

Civil Records: Access: Mail, in person. Both court and visitors may perform in person searches. Search fee: $5.00 per name. Required to search: name, years to search. Civil cases indexed by defendant, plaintiff. Civil records on computer from 1987, all incoming records microfilmed, records from 1823 on microfilm.

Criminal Records: Access: Mail, in person. Both court and visitors may perform in person searches. Search fee: $5.00 per name. Required to search: name, years to search, DOB; also helpful: SSN. Criminal records on computer from 1987, all incoming records microfilmed, records from 1823 on microfilm.

General Information: Public Access terminal is available. No juvenile, mental health, records released, including criminal cases with a minor as a victim. SASE required. Turnaround time 2 days. Copy fee: $.50 per page. Certification fee: $1.00. Fee payee: Clerk of Courts. Personal checks accepted. Prepayment is required.

Register of Wills Jefferson County Courthouse, 200 Main St, Brookville, PA 15825; 814-849-1610; Fax: 814-849-1612. Hours: 8:30AM-4:30PM (EST). *Probate.*

Juniata County

Court of Common Pleas - Criminal/Civil

Juniata County Courthouse, Mifflintown, PA 17059; 717-436-7715; Fax: 717-436-7734. Hours: 8AM-4:30PM (EST). *Felony, Misdemeanor, Civil, Eviction.*

Civil Records: Access: Mail, in person. Both court and visitors may perform in person searches. Search fee: $5.00 per name. Required to search: name, years to search. Civil cases indexed by defendant, plaintiff. Civil records on computer from 1993, on dockets from 1969, archived from 1700s.

Criminal Records: Access: Phone, mail, in person. Both court and visitors may perform in person searches. Search fee: $5.00 per name. Required to search: name, years to search, DOB. Criminal records on computer from 1993, on dockets from 1969, archived from 1700s.

General Information: Public Access terminal is available. No juvenile records released. SASE required. Turnaround time 1 week. Copy fee: $.50 per page. Certification fee: $1.00 per page. Fee payee: Prothonotary or Clerk of Courts. Personal checks accepted. Prepayment is required.

Register of Wills Juniata County Courthouse, PO Box 68, Mifflintown, PA 17059; 717-436-7709; Fax: 717-436-7756. Hours: 8AM-4:30PM M-F, 8AM-12PM Wed (June-Sept) (EST). *Probate.*

Lackawanna County

Court of Common Pleas - Civil

Clerk of Judicial Records, PO Box 133, Scranton, PA 18503; 570-963-6724; Civil phone: 717-963-6723. Hours: 9AM-4PM (EST). *Civil, Eviction.*

Civil Records: Access: In person only. Visitors must perform in person searches for themselves. Search fee: No civil searches performed by court - but exceptions are made. Required to search: name, years to search. Civil cases indexed by defendant, plaintiff. Civil records computerized since 09/95, dockets from 1920s, archived from 1800s. Case number is required.

General Information: Public Access terminal is available. No juvenile records released. Fax notes: Will not fax results. Copy fee: $.25 if self service; $.50 if done by Clerk; $1.00 for mail requesters first copy, $.50 each add'l. Certification fee: $4.50. Fee payee: Clerk of Judicial Records. Business checks accepted. Prepayment is required.

Court of Common Pleas - Criminal

Lackawanna County Courthouse, Scranton, PA 18503; 570-963-6759; Fax: 570-963-6459. Hours: 9AM-4PM (EST). *Felony, Misdemeanor.*

Criminal Records: Access: Mail, fax, in person. Both court and visitors may perform in person searches. Search fee: $10.00 per name. Required to search: name, years to search, DOB, SSN. Criminal records computerized since 10/95, on dockets from 1983, archived from 1941, indexed by defendant only.

General Information: Public Access terminal is available. No juvenile records released. SASE required. Turnaround time 1-2 days. Fax notes: Will not fax results. Copy fee: $.50 per page. Certification fee: $8.00. Fee payee: Clerk of Judicial Records. Business checks accepted. Prepayment is required.

Register of Wills Registrar of Wills, County Courthouse, 200 N Washington Ave, Scranton, PA 18503; 570-963-6708; Fax: 570-963-6377. Hours: 9AM-4PM (EST). *Probate.*

Lancaster County

Court of Common Pleas - Civil

50 N Duke St, PO Box 83480, Lancaster, PA 17608-3480; 717-299-8282; Fax: 717-293-7210. Hours: 8:30AM-5PM (EST). *Civil, Eviction.*

www.co.lancaster.pa.us/directory.htm#judicial

Civil Records: Access: Phone, fax, mail, online, in person. Both court and visitors may perform in person searches. Search fee: $5.00 per name. Required to search: name, years to search; also helpful: address. Civil cases indexed by defendant, plaintiff. Civil records on computer from 7/87, in files from 1987, judgments on dockets from 1800s, others archived from 1800s. Access to remote online records requires a monthly fee of $25 plus $.18 per minute. Search by name or case number. Call Nancy Malloy at 717-299-8252 for more information.

General Information: Public Access terminal is available. No naturalization records released. SASE required. Turnaround time 2-3 days. Fax notes: $2.00 for first page, $1.00 each add'l. Fee higher for out of state faxing. Copy fee: $1.00 per page. Certification fee: $3.00. Fee payee: Prothonotary. Business checks accepted. Prepayment is required.

Court of Common Pleas - Criminal

Clerk of Courts, 50 North Duke St, Lancaster, PA 17602; 717-299-8275. 8:30AM-5PM *Felony, Misdemeanor.*

Criminal Records: Access: Mail, in person. Both court and visitors may perform in person searches. Search fee: $15.00 per name. Required to search: name, years to search. Criminal records on computer from 1988, archived from 1901.

General Information: Public Access terminal is available. No juvenile records released. SASE required. Turnaround time 2 days. Copy fee: $.50 per copy or $1.00 for docket page including disposition; however, there is no copy fee if court does the search. Certification fee: $8.00. Fee payee: Clerk of Courts. Only cashiers checks and money orders accepted. Prepayment is required.

Register of Wills 50 N. Duke St., Lancaster, PA 17602; 717-299-8243; Fax: 717-295-3522. Hours: 8:30AM-5PM (EST). *Probate.*

www.co.lancaster.pa.us/wills.htm

Lawrence County

Court of Common Pleas - Criminal/Civil

430 Court St, New Castle, PA 16101-3593; 724-656-2143; Fax: 724-656-1988. Hours: 8AM-4PM (EST). *Felony, Misdemeanor, Civil, Eviction.*

Civil Records: Access: Fax, mail, online, in person. Both court and visitors may perform in person searches. Search fee: $10.00 per name. Required to search: name, years to search. Civil cases indexed by defendant, plaintiff. Civil records on computer from 1987, on Russell Index from 1937. Online access is available through a private company. For information, call Infocon at 814-472-6066.

Criminal Records: Access: Fax, mail, online, in person. Both court and visitors may perform in person searches. Search fee: $10.00 per name. Required to search: name, years to search, signed release; also helpful: DOB, SSN. Criminal records on computer from 1987, on Russell Index from 1937. Online access is available through a private company. For information, call Infocon at 814-472-6066.

General Information: No adoption, juvenile, impounded, or juvenile sex crime victim records released. SASE requested. Turnaround time ASAP. Fax notes: No fee to fax results. Fax Fee: Local $1.00 plus $.50 per pg; Long distance $3.00 plus $.50 per pg. Copy fee: $.50 per page. Certification fee: $1.50. Fee payee: Prothonotary. Business checks accepted. Prepayment is required.

Register of Wills 430 Court St, New Castle, PA 16101-3593; 724-656-2128/2159; Fax: 724-656-1966. Hours: 8AM-4PM (EST). *Probate.*

General Information: Public Access terminal is available. Fee payee: Register of Wills, Lawrence County. Prepayment is required.

Lebanon County

Court of Common Pleas - Civil Municipal Bldg, Rm 104, 400 S 8th St, Lebanon, PA 17042; 717-274-2801 X2120. Hours: 8:30AM-4:30PM (EST). *Civil, Eviction.*

Civil Records: Access: Main, in person. Visitors must perform in person searches for themselves. No search fee. Required to search: name, years to search; also helpful: address. Civil cases indexed by defendant, plaintiff. Civil records on computer from 1985, on files from 1883. Docket number required for phone access.

General Information: Public Access terminal is available. No mental health records released. Copy fee: $.50 per page. Certification fee: $8.00. Fee payee: Prothonotary. Personal checks accepted. Prepayment is required.

Court of Common Pleas - Criminal Municipal Bldg Rm 104, 400 S 8th St, Lebanon, PA 17042; 717-274-2801 X2247. Hours: 8:30AM-4:30PM (EST). *Felony, Misdemeanor.*

Criminal Records: Access: Phone, mail, in person. Both court and visitors may perform in person searches. Search fee: $16.00 per name. Required to search: name, years to search. Criminal records on computer from 1986, indexed from 1800s. Action number required for phone access.

General Information: Public Access terminal is available. No juvenile records released. SASE required. Turnaround time varies. Copy fee: $.50 per page. Certification fee: $8.00. Fee payee: Clerk of Court. Personal checks accepted. Prepayment is required.

Register of Wills Municipal Bldg, Rm 105, 400 S 8th St, Lebanon, PA 17042; 717-274-2801 X2215; Fax: 717-274-8094. 8:30AM-4:30PM (EST). *Probate.*

Lehigh County

Court of Common Pleas - Civil 455 W Hamilton St, Allentown, PA 18101-1614; 610-782-3148; Fax: 610-770-3840. Hours: 8:30AM-4:30PM (EST). *Civil, Eviction.*

www.lccpa.org

Civil Records: Access: Mail, online, in person. Visitors must perform in person searches for themselves. No search fee. Required to search: name, years to search, DOB or SSN. Civil cases indexed by defendant, plaintiff. Civil records on computer since 1985, on microfilm from 1812, some in books. Access to the county online system requires a monthly usage fee. Search by name or case number. Call Lehigh Cty Computer Svcs Dept at 610-782-3286 for more information.

General Information: Public Access terminal is available. No sealed, confidential, or impounded records released. Copy fee: $.50 per page; docket printout $3.00. Certification fee: $4.50. Fee payee: Clerk of Courts-Civil. Personal checks accepted.

Court of Common Pleas - Criminal 455 W Hamilton St, Allentown, PA 18101-1614; 610-782-3077; Fax: 610-770-6797. Hours: 8:30AM-4:30PM (EST). *Felony, Misdemeanor.*

www.lccpa.org

Criminal Records: Access: Fax, mail, online, in person. Both court and visitors may perform in person searches. Search fee: $10.00 per name. Fee includes copy of certified docket. Required to search: name, years to search, DOB. Criminal records on computer from 1990, on alpha index from 1962 to 1990, on microfilm from 1812. Access to the countywide criminal online system requires a monthly usage fee. Search by name or case number. Call Lehigh Cty Computer Svcs Dept at 610-782-3286 for more information.

General Information: Public Access terminal is available. No juvenile or impounded records released. SASE required. Turnaround time 1 week. Fax notes: No fee to fax results. Copy fee: $.50. Docket printout mailed $2.00. Certification fee: $5.00. Fee payee: Clerk of Courts-Criminal. Personal checks accepted. Prepayment is required.

Register of Wills 455 W Hamilton, Allentown, PA 18101-1614; 610-820-3170; Fax: 610-820-3439. Hours: 8AM-4PM (EST). *Probate.*

Luzerne County

Court of Common Pleas - Civil 200 N River St, Wilkes Barre, PA 18711-1001; 570-825-1745; Fax: 570-825-1757. Hours: 9AM-4:30PM (EST). *Civil, Eviction.*

Civil Records: Access: Phone, mail, in person. Both court and visitors may perform in person searches. Search fee: $15.75 per name for 5 years, $1.50 each add'l year, and $1.50 each reference cited. Required to search: name, years to search, address. Civil cases indexed by defendant, plaintiff. Civil records partially on microfiche and archives, on dockets from 1935.

General Information: No mental, sealed records released. SASE required. Turnaround time 3 days. Fax notes: Fee to fax results is $1.50 per page. Copy fee: $1.00 per page. Certification fee: $4.75. Fee payee: Prothonotary. Personal checks accepted. Credit cards accepted: Visa, MasterCard, AmEx. Prepayment is required.

Court of Common Pleas - Criminal 200 N River St, Wilkes Barre, PA 18711; 570-825-1585; Fax: 570-825-1843. Hours: 8AM-4:30PM (EST). *Felony, Misdemeanor.*

Criminal Records: Access: Phone, fax, mail, in person. Both court and visitors may perform in person searches. Search fee: $10.00 per name. Required to search: name, years to search, DOB or SSN. Criminal records on computer, microfiche and archived from 1989, on files from 1972. Records from 1933 to 1959 destroyed in flood.

General Information: No "M" number (confidential custody case) records released. SASE not required. Turnaround time 1-2 days. Fax notes: No fee to fax results. Copy fee: $.35 per page. Certification fee: $7.00. Fee payee: Clerk of Courts. Personal checks accepted. Credit cards accepted: Visa, MasterCard, Discover. Prepayment is required.

Register of Wills 200 N River St, Wilkes Barre, PA 18711; 570-825-1672. Hours: 9AM-4:30PM (EST). *Probate.*

Lycoming County

Court of Common Pleas - Criminal/Civil 48 W 3rd St, Williamsport, PA 17701; 570-327-2251. Hours: 8:30AM-5PM (EST). *Felony, Misdemeanor, Civil, Eviction.*

Civil Records: Access: In person only. Visitors must perform in person searches for themselves. No search fee. Required to search: name, years to search; also helpful: address. Civil cases indexed by defendant, plaintiff. Civil records on computer from 1983, on dockets from 1795.

Criminal Records: Access: Mail, in person. Both court and visitors may perform in person searches. Search fee: $10.00 per name. Required to search: name, years to search, DOB; also helpful: address. Criminal records on computer from 1910.

General Information: Public Access terminal is available. No juvenile, cases involving minors, mental records released. SASE required. Turnaround time same day. Copy fee: $.50 per page. Certification fee: $5.00. Fee payee: Prothonotary. Personal checks accepted. Prepayment is required.

Register of Wills Lycoming Co Courthouse, 48 W 3rd St, Williamsport, PA 17701; 570-327-2258. Hours: 8:30AM-5PM (EST). *Probate.*

McKean County

Court of Common Pleas - Criminal & Civil PO Box 273, Smethport, PA 16749; 814-887-3270; Fax: 814-887-3219. Hours: 8:30AM-4:30PM (EST). *Felony, Misdemeanor, Civil, Eviction.*

Civil Records: Access: Phone, fax, mail, in person. Both court and visitors may perform in person searches. Search fee: $12.00 per name. Required to search: name, years to search. Civil cases indexed by defendant, plaintiff. Civil records on computer since 1994, on microfiche from 1952 to 1962, on dockets from 1872.

Criminal Records: Access: Mail, in person. Both court and visitors may perform in person searches. Search fee: $10.00 per name. Required to search: name, years to search, DOB. Criminal records on computer since 1994, on dockets from 1872.

General Information: Public Access terminal is available. No sex related, juvenile, mental health records released. SASE required. Turnaround time same day. Fax notes: $2.00 per page. Copy fee: $.50 per page. Computer search copy fee: $1.00 per page. Certification fee: $3.50. Fee payee: Prothonotary or Clerk of Courts. Personal checks accepted. Prepayment is required.

Register of Wills PO Box 202, Smethport, PA 16749-0202; 814-887-3260; Fax: 814-887-2712. Hours: 8:30AM-4:30PM (EST). *Probate.*

Mercer County

Court of Common Pleas - Civil 105 Mercer County Courthouse, Mercer, PA 16137; 724-662-3800. Hours: 8:30AM-4:30PM (EST). *Civil, Eviction.*

Civil Records: Access: Mail, online, in person. Both court and visitors may perform in person searches. Search fee: $5.00 per name. Required to search: name, years to search. Civil cases indexed by defendant, plaintiff. Civil records on computer since 1994; prior records on dockets from 1930s, archived from 1700s. Include SSN and DOB in your search. Online access is available through a private company. For information, call Infocon at 814-472-6066.

General Information: Public Access terminal is available. No mental, sealed records released. SASE required. Turnaround time 1-2 days. Copy fee: $.25 per page. Certification fee: $3.00. Fee payee: Prothonotary or Clerk of Courts. Business checks accepted. Prepayment is required.

Court of Common Pleas - Criminal 112 Mercer County Courthouse, Mercer, PA 16137; 724-662-3800 X2248. Hours: 8:30AM-4:30PM (EST). *Felony, Misdemeanor.*

www.mcc.co.mercer.pa.us/LOCRULES.htm

Criminal Records: Access: Mail, in person, online. Both court and visitors may perform in person searches. Search fee: $10.00 per name. Required to search: name, years to search; also helpful: DOB, SSN. Criminal records on computer since 1993, indexed since 1920, on files from 1980. Online access is available through a private company. For information, call Infocon at 814-472-6066.

General Information: Public Access terminal is available. No juvenile records released. SASE required. Turnaround time 1 day. Fax notes: Fee to fax results is $1.00 per page. Copy fee: $1.00 for first page, $.50 each add'l. Certification fee: $5.00. Fee payee: Clerk of Courts. Personal checks accepted. Prepayment required.

Register of Wills 112 Mercer County Courthouse, Mercer, PA 16137; 724-662-3800 X2253; Fax: 724-662-1530. Hours: 8:30AM-4:30PM (EST). *Probate.*

Mifflin County

Court of Common Pleas - Criminal & Civil 20 N Wayne St, Lewistown, PA 17044; 717-248-8146; Fax: 717-248-5275. Hours: 8AM-4:30PM (EST). *Felony, Misdemeanor, Civil, Eviction.*

Civil Records: Access: In person only. Visitors must perform in person searches for themselves. No search fee. Required to search: name, years to search. Civil cases indexed by defendant, plaintiff. Civil records on computer from 1993, on microfiche from 1971-1989, prior on books. Online access is available through a private company. For information, call Infocon at 814-472-6066.

Criminal Records: Access: In person only. Visitors must perform in person searches for themselves. No search fee. Required to search: name, years to search. Criminal records on computer from 1993, on microfiche from 1971-1989, prior on books. Online access is available through a private company. For information, call Infocon at 814-472-6066.

General Information: Public Access terminal is available. No juvenile, mental health records released. Fax notes: Will fax back if fees are prepaid. Copy fee: $.50 per page. Certification fee: $4.50. Fee payee: Clerk of Courts. Personal checks accepted. Prepayment is required.

Register of Wills 20 N. Wayne St., Lewistown, PA 17044; 717-242-1449. Hours: 8AM-4:30PM M-F (EST). *Probate.*

Monroe County

Court of Common Pleas - Civil Monroe County Courthouse, Stroudsburg, PA 18360; 570-420-3570. Hours: 8:30AM-4:30PM (EST). *Civil, Eviction.*

Civil Records: Access: Mail, in person. Both court and visitors may perform in person searches. No search fee. Required to search: name, years to search. Civil cases indexed by defendant, plaintiff. Civil records indexed on computer 1995 to present, prior in dockets.

General Information: Public Access terminal is available. No juvenile records released. SASE not required. Turnaround time 1 day. Copy fee: $.50 per page. Certification fee: $3.00. Fee payee: Monroe County Prothonotary. Only cashiers checks and money orders accepted. Prepayment is required.

Court of Common Pleas - Criminal Monroe County Courthouse Rm 312, Stroudsburg, PA 18360-2190; 570-517-3385. Hours: 8:30AM-4:30PM (EST). *Felony, Misdemeanor.*

Criminal Records: Access: Mail, in person. Both court and visitors may perform in person searches. Search fee: $5.00 per name. Required to search: name, years to search; also helpful: address, DOB, SSN. Criminal records on computer since 1995; prior on dockets.

General Information: Public Access terminal is available. No sex related, juvenile, adoption records released. SASE not required. Turnaround time 1 day. Copy fee: $1.00 per page. Certification fee: $10.00. Fee payee: Clerk of Court. Only cashiers checks and money orders accepted. Prepayment is required.

Register of Wills Monroe County Courthouse, Stroudsburg, PA 18360; 570-517-3359; Fax: 570-420-3537. Hours: 8:30AM-4:30PM (EST). *Probate.*

Montgomery County

Court of Common Pleas - Civil PO Box 311, Airy & Swede St, Norristown, PA 19404-0311; 610-278-3360. Hours: 8:30AM-4:15PM (EST). *Civil, Eviction.*

www.montcopa.org

Civil Records: Access: Online, in person. Visitors must perform in person searches for themselves. No search fee. Required to search: name, years to search. Civil cases indexed by defendant, plaintiff. Civil records on computer from 4/82, on microfilm from 1800s. Court and other records are available free online at www1.montcopa.org/. The system is experimental and may or may not be adapted full time. A pay service, offering remote dial-up, is also available. For info, call the helpdesk at 610-292-4931. There is a $10 registration fee plus $.15 per minute of usage.

General Information: Public Access terminal is available. No mental health, divorce, sealed records released. SASE required. Copy fee: $.25 per page. Certification fee: $4.50. Fee payee: Prothonotary. Personal checks accepted. Prepayment is required.

Court of Common Pleas - Criminal PO Box 311, Airy & Swede St, Norristown, PA 19404-0311; 610-278-3346. Hours: 8:30AM-4:15PM (EST). *Felony, Misdemeanor.*

www.montcopa.org

Criminal Records: Access: Mail, online, in person. Both court and visitors may perform in person searches. Search fee: $15.00 per name. Required to search: name, years to search, DOB, signed release. Criminal records on computer from 10/84, prior archived and on microfiche. Court and other records are available free online at www1.montcopa.org/. The system is experimental and may or may not be adapted full time. A pay service, offering remote dial-up, is also available. For info, call the helpdesk at 610-292-4931. There is a $10 registration fee plus $.15 per minute of usage.

General Information: Public Access terminal is available. No impounded, sealed records released. SASE required. Turnaround time 5 days. Copy fee: $7.00 per page. Certification fee: $10.00. Fee payee: Clerk of Courts. Business checks accepted. Credit cards accepted: Visa, MasterCard, Discover. Accepted in person only. Prepayment is required.

Register of Wills Airy & Swede St, PO Box 311, Norristown, PA 19404; 610-278-3400; Fax: 610-278-3240. Hours: 8:30AM-4:15PM (EST). *Probate.*

www.montcopa.org

Montour County

Court of Common Pleas - Criminal & Civil Montour County Courthouse, 29 Mill St, Danville, PA 17821; 570-271-3010; Fax: 570-271-3089. Hours: 9AM-4PM (EST). *Felony, Misdemeanor, Civil, Eviction.*

Civil Records: Access: Phone, fax, mail, in person. Both court and visitors may perform in person searches. Search fee: $10.00 per name. Required to search: name, years to search. Civil cases indexed by defendant, plaintiff. Civil records on books since 1991, on microfiche since 1939, on computer back to 1996. Actual files kept for 20 years.

Criminal Records: Access: Phone, fax, mail, in person. Both court and visitors may perform in person searches. Search fee: $10.00 per name. Required to search: name, years to search, DOB, SSN. Criminal records on books since 1991, on microfiche since 1939, on computer back to 1996. Actual files kept for 20 years.

General Information: Public Access terminal is available. No sex related, juvenile or adoption records released. SASE required. Turnaround time 1-2 days. Copy fee: $.50 per page. Certification fee: $3.00. Fee payee: Prothonotary. Personal checks accepted. Prepayment is required.

Register of Wills 29 Mill St, Danville, PA 17821; 570-271-3012; Fax: 570-271-3071. Hours: 9AM-4PM (EST). *Probate.*

Northampton County

Court of Common Pleas - Civil Gov't Center, 669 Washington St Rm 207, Easton, PA 18042-7498; 610-559-3060. Hours: 8:30AM-4:30PM (EST). *Civil, Eviction.*

Civil Records: Access: In person only. Visitors must perform in person searches for themselves. No search fee. Required to search: name, years to search; also helpful: address. Civil cases indexed by defendant, plaintiff. Civil records on computer since 1/85 (Civil) and 2/90 (Judgments).

General Information: Public Access terminal is available. No impounded or PSA abuse records released. Copy fee: $1.00 per page. Certification fee: $4.75. Fee payee: Clerk of Court-Civil or Prothonotary's Office. Business checks accepted. Local personal check, certified check accepted. Prepayment is required.

Court of Common Pleas - Criminal 669 Washington St, Easton, PA 18042-7494; 610-559-3000 X2114; Fax: 610-262-4391. Hours: 8:30AM-4:30PM (EST). *Felony, Misdemeanor.*

Criminal Records: Access: Fax, mail, in person. Both court and visitors may perform in person searches. Search fee: $10.00 per name. Required to search: name, years to search, DOB; also helpful: SSN. Criminal records on computer from 1984, on files from 1800s.

General Information: Public Access terminal is available. No juvenile, expunged records released. SASE not required. Turnaround time same day. Fax notes: No fee to fax results. Copy fee: $.50 per page. Certification fee: $8.00. Fee payee: Criminal Division. Business checks accepted. Credit cards accepted: Visa, MasterCard. Prepayment is required.

Register of Wills Government Center, 669 Washington St, Easton, PA 18042; 610-559-3094; Fax: 610-559-3735. Hours: 8:30AM-4:30PM (EST). *Probate.*

Northumberland County

Court of Common Pleas - Civil County Courthouse, 201 Market St, Rm #7, Sunbury, PA 17801-3468; 570-988-4151. Hours: 9AM-5PM M; 9AM-4:30PM T-F (EST). *Civil, Eviction.*

Civil Records: Access: Mail, in person. Both court and visitors may perform in person searches. Search fee: $7.00 per name. Required to search: name, years to search. Civil cases indexed by defendant, plaintiff. Civil records on file from 1772.

General Information: Public Access terminal is available. No adult abuse, involuntary treatment records released. SASE required. Turnaround time 1-2 days. Copy fee: $1.00 2st page; $.25. Each add'l. Certification fee: $4.00 plus $1.00 each add'l page. Fee payee: Northumberland Prothonotary. Business checks accepted. Prepayment is required.

Court of Common Pleas - Criminal County Courthouse, 201 Market St, Rm 7, Sunbury, PA 17801-3468; 570-988-4148. Hours: 9AM-5PM M; 9AM-4:30PM T-F (EST). *Felony, Misdemeanor.*

Criminal Records: Access: Mail, in person. Both court and visitors may perform in person searches. Search fee: $10.00 per name. Required to search: name, years to search, DOB; also helpful: SSN. Criminal records indexed in office from 1945, on dockets from 1772, archived from 1700s to 1945.

General Information: Public Access terminal is available. No juvenile records released. SASE required. Turnaround time 1-2 days. Copy fee: $1.00 for first page, $.25 each add'l. First copy for in person requests is $.25. Certification fee: $4.00 plus $1.00 each additional page. Fee payee: Clerk of Courts Office. Personal checks accepted. Prepayment is required.

Register of Wills County Courthouse, 201 Market St, Sunbury, PA 17801; 570-988-4143. Hours: 9AM-4:30PM (EST). *Probate.*

Perry County

Court of Common Pleas - Criminal & Civil PO Box 325, New Bloomfield, PA 17068; 717-582-2131 X240. Hours: 8AM-4PM (EST). *Felony, Misdemeanor, Civil, Eviction.*

Civil Records: Access: In person only. Visitors must perform in person searches for themselves. No search fee. Required to search: name, years to search. Civil cases indexed by defendant, plaintiff. Civil records on dockets from 1800s.

Criminal Records: Access: Phone, fax, mail, in person. Both court and visitors may perform in person searches. Search fee: $10.00 per name. Required to search: name, years to search; also helpful: DOB, SSN. Criminal records on dockets from 1950.

General Information: No juvenile records released. SASE required. Turnaround time 1 week, phone turnaround immediate. Fax notes: No fee to fax results. Copy fee: $.40 per page. Certification fee: $5.00. Fee payee: Prothonotary or Clerk of Courts. Personal checks accepted. Will bill to attorneys & abstract companies upon approval.

Register of Wills PO Box 223, New Bloomfield, PA 17068; 717-582-2131; Fax: 717-582-8570. Hours: 8AM-4PM (EST). *Probate.*

Philadelphia County

Court of Common Pleas - Civil First Judicial District of PA, Room 284, City Hall, Philadelphia, PA 19107; 215-686-6656; Fax: 215-567-7380. Hours: 9AM-5PM (EST). *Civil.*

Civil Records: Access: Mail, online, in person. Both court and visitors may perform in person searches. Search fee: $35.00 per name. Required to search: name, years to search. Civil cases indexed by defendant,

plaintiff. Civil records on computer from 1/82 to present, archived on files from 1700s to 1982. Access to 1st Judicial District Civil Trial records are available free online at http://dns2.phila.gov:8080. Search by name, judgment and docket information.

General Information: Public Access terminal is available. No mental health, divorce, abuse, adoption records released. SASE required. Turnaround time 1-5 days. Copy fee: $.50 per page. Certification fee: $30.00. Fee payee: Prothonotary. Business checks accepted. Prepayment is required.

Clerk of Quarter Session 1301 Filbert St #310, Philadelphia, PA 19107; 215-683-7700 X01 & X02. Hours: 8AM-5PM (EST). *Felony, Misdemeanor.*

Criminal Records: Access: Mail, in person. Both court and visitors may perform in person searches. Search fee: $10.00 per name. Required to search: name, years to search, DOB, signed release; also helpful: address, SSN, race, sex. Criminal records on computer and microfiche from 1969, archived from 1800s.

General Information: No sealed, grand jury, mental records released. SASE required. Turnaround time 1-2. Copy fee: $.25 per page. Certification fee: $12.50. Fee payee: Clerk of Quarter Sessions. Business checks accepted. Prepayment is required.

Municipal Court 34 S 11th St, 5th floor, Philadelphia, PA 19107; 215-686-7997; Fax: 215-569-9254. Hours: 9AM-5PM (EST). *Felony, Misdemeanor, Civil Actions Under $10,000, Eviction.*

Note: Court has jurisdiction over certain criminal offenses with jail terms up to five years.

Civil Records: Access: Mail, in person. Only the court performs in person searches; visitors may not. No search fee. Required to search: name, years to search, address. Civil cases indexed by defendant, plaintiff. Civil records on computer from 1969. Include SSN and DOB if possible.

Criminal Records: Access: Mail, in person. Only the court performs in person searches; visitors may not. No search fee. Required to search: name, years to search, address, DOB, signed release. Criminal records on computer from 1969.

General Information: SASE required. Turnaround time 1-5 days. Copy fee: $.50 per page. Certification fee: $3.00. Fee payee: Prothonotary. Only cashiers checks and money orders accepted. Prepayment is required.

Register of Wills City Hall Rm 180, Philadelphia, PA 19107; 215-686-6250/6282; Fax: 215-686-6293. Hours: 8:30AM-4:30PM (EST). *Probate.*

Pike County

Court of Common Pleas - Criminal & Civil 412 Broad St, Milford, PA 18337; 570-296-7231. Hours: 8:30AM-4:30PM (EST). *Felony, Misdemeanor, Civil, Eviction.*

Civil Records: Access: Phone, mail, online, in person. Both court and visitors may perform in person searches. No search fee. Required to search: name, years to search. Civil cases indexed by defendant, plaintiff. Civil records on files for 100 yrs, computerized since 1995. Online access is available through a private company. See note at beginning of section. The court will only do searches from 01/95 forward.

Criminal Records: Access: Phone, mail, online, in person. Both court and visitors may perform in person searches. Search fee: $10.00 per name. Required to search: name, years to search. Criminal records on files for 100 yrs, computerized since 1995. Online access to criminal records is available through a private company. For information, call Infocon at 814-472-6066. The court will only do searches from 01/95 forward.

General Information: Public Access terminal is available. No juvenile, adoption, sealed records

released. SASE required. Turnaround time varies. Copy fee: $.25 per page. Certification fee: $2.50 per page. Fee payee: Prothonotary. Personal checks accepted. Personal checks not exceeding $25.00 accepted. Prepayment is required.

Register of Wills 506 Broad St, Milford, PA 18337; 570-296-3508. Hours: 8:30AM-4:30PM (EST). *Probate.*

Potter County

Court of Common Pleas - Criminal & Civil 1 E 2nd St Rm 23, Coudersport, PA 16915; 814-274-9740; Fax: 814-274-3361. Hours: 8:30AM-4:30PM (EST). *Felony, Misdemeanor, Civil, Eviction.*

Civil Records: Access: Phone, fax, mail, in person. Both court and visitors may perform in person searches. No search fee. Required to search: name, years to search. Civil cases indexed by defendant, plaintiff. Civil records on dockets from early 1900s to 11/97; on computer since.

Criminal Records: Access: Phone, fax, mail, in person. Both court and visitors may perform in person searches. No search fee. Required to search: name, years to search, DOB. Criminal records on card index from 1983 to 6/27/97; on computer since.

General Information: Public Access terminal is available. No juvenile records released. SASE required. Turnaround time 2 weeks, phone turnaround immediate (unless lengthy search). Fax notes: No fee to fax results if limited. Copy fee: $.25 per page. Certification fee: $5.00. Fee payee: Prothonotary or Clerk of Courts. Personal checks accepted. Prepayment is required.

Register of Wills 1 E 2nd St, Coudersport, PA 16915; 814-274-8370. Hours: 8:30AM-4:30PM (EST). *Probate.*

Schuylkill County

Court of Common Pleas - Civil 401 N 2nd St, Pottsville, PA 17901-2528; 570-628-1270; Fax: 570-628-1261. Hours: 8:30AM-4:30PM (EST). *Civil, Eviction.*

Civil Records: Access: Mail, in person. Both court and visitors may perform in person searches. Search fee: $5.00 per name. Required to search: name, years to search. Civil cases indexed by defendant, plaintiff. Civil records (suits) on computer from 1989, judgments on dockets from 1800s.

General Information: Public Access terminal is available. No master reports or sealed records released. SASE requested. Turnaround time 1 day. Copy fee: $.25 per page. Certification fee: $4.00 per page. Fee payee: Prothonotary. Personal checks accepted. Will bill copy fees.

Court of Common Pleas - Criminal 410 N 2nd St, Pottsville, PA 17901; 570-622-5570 X1133; Fax: 570-628-1143. Hours: 9AM-4PM (EST). *Felony, Misdemeanor.*

Criminal Records: Access: Fax, mail, in person. Both court and visitors may perform in person searches. Search fee: $10.00 plus $5.00 automation fee per name. Required to search: name, years to search, DOB; also helpful: SSN. Criminal records on computer from 4/88, on dockets from 1800s.

General Information: No juvenile records released. SASE not required. Turnaround time same day. Fax notes: No fee to fax results. Copy fee: $.25 per page. Certification fee: $8.00. Fee payee: Clerk of Courts. Business checks accepted. Prepayment is required.

Register of Wills Courthouse 401 N 2nd St, Pottsville, PA 17901-2520; 570-628-1377; Fax: 570-628-1384. Hours: 9AM-4PM (EST). *Probate.*

Snyder County

Court of Common Pleas - Criminal & Civil Snyder County Courthouse, PO Box 217, Middleburg, PA 17842; 570-837-4202. Hours: 8:30AM-4PM (EST). *Felony, Misdemeanor, Civil, Eviction.*

Civil Records: Access: Mail, in person. Both court and visitors may perform in person searches. Search fee: $10.00 per name. Required to search: name, years to search. Civil cases indexed by defendant, plaintiff. Civil records on dockets from 1800s, some on microfilm.

Criminal Records: Access: Mail, in person. Both court and visitors may perform in person searches. Search fee: $15.00 per name. Required to search: name, years to search. Criminal records on dockets from 1800s, some on microfilm.

General Information: No juvenile records released. SASE required. Turnaround time 2 days. Copy fee: $.35 per page. Certification fee: $4.00. Fee payee: Prothonotary or Clerk of Courts. No personal checks. Prepayment is required.

Register of Wills County Courthouse, PO Box 217, Middleburg, PA 17842; 570-837-4224. Hours: 8:30AM-4PM (EST). *Probate.*

Somerset County

Court of Common Pleas - Civil 111 E Union St Suite 190, Somerset, PA 15501; 814-445-1428; Fax: 814-444-9270. Hours: 8:30AM-4PM (EST). *Civil, Eviction.*

Civil Records: Access: Phone, fax, mail, in person. Both court and visitors may perform in person searches. Search fee: $12.00 per name. Required to search: name, years to search. Civil cases indexed by defendant, plaintiff. Civil records on computer from 1/92, on microfiche from 1920 to 1972, on dockets (Russell System for all other years prior to 1992). Hard copy must follow fax request.

General Information: Public Access terminal is available. No commitment records released. SASE required. Turnaround time 2-3 days. Fax notes: $.50 per page. Copy fee: $.50 per page. Certification fee: $2.00. Fee payee: Prothonotary of Somerset Co. Business checks accepted. Prepayment is required.

Court of Common Pleas - Criminal 111 E Union St Suite 180, Somerset, PA 15501; 814-445-1435. 8:30AM-4PM (EST). *Felony, Misdemeanor.*

Criminal Records: Access: Phone, mail, in person. Both court and visitors may perform in person searches. Search fee: $5.00 per name. Required to search: name, years to search, DOB; also helpful: SSN. Criminal records on microfilm from 1920, archive dates uncertain.

General Information: No impounded records released. SASE not required. Turnaround time same day, phone turnaround immediate. Copy fee: $.50 per copy. Certification fee: $1.00. Fee payee: Clerk of Courts. Personal checks accepted. Will bill copy fees.

Register of Wills 111 E Union St Suite 170, Somerset, PA 15501-0586; 814-445-1548; Fax: 814-445-7991. Hours: 8:30AM-4PM (EST). *Probate.*

Sullivan County

Court of Common Pleas - Criminal & Civil Main Street, Laporte, PA 18626; 570-946-7351; Probate phone: 570-946-7351; Fax: 570-946-4213. Hours: 8:30AM-4PM (EST). *Felony, Misdemeanor, Civil, Eviction, Probate.*

Note: Includes the Register of Wills.

Civil Records: Access: Mail, in person. Visitors must perform in person searches for themselves. No search fee. Required to search: name, years to search. Civil

cases indexed by defendant, plaintiff. Civil records on dockets from 1847 to present and on computer from August 2000.

Criminal Records: Access: Mail, in person. Visitors must perform in person searches for themselves. No search fee. Required to search: name, years to search; also helpful: SSN. Criminal records on dockets from 1847 to present and on computer from August 2000.

General Information: No juvenile records released. SASE required. Turnaround time same day. Copy fee: $2.00 per page. Certification fee: $3.00 per page. Fee payee: Prothonotary or Clerk of Courts. Personal checks accepted. Prepayment is required.

Susquehanna County

Court of Common Pleas - Civil Susquehanna Courthouse, PO Box 218, Montrose, PA 18801; 570-278-4600 X120. Hours: 8:30AM-4:30PM (EST). *Civil, Eviction.*

Civil Records: Access: Mail, fax, in person. Both court and visitors may perform in person searches. No search fee. Required to search: name, years to search. Civil cases indexed by defendant, plaintiff. Civil records on dockets from 1800s.

General Information: Public Access terminal is available. No juvenile records released. SASE required. Turnaround time same day. Copy fee: $1.00 per page. Certification fee: $3.00. Fee payee: Prothonotary. Personal checks accepted. Prepayment is required.

Court of Common Pleas - Criminal Susquehanna Courthouse, PO Box 218, Montrose, PA 18801; 570-278-4600 X321. Hours: 8:30AM-4:30PM (EST). *Felony, Misdemeanor.*

Criminal Records: Access: Mail, in person. Both court and visitors may perform in person searches. Search fee: $5.00 per name. Required to search: name, years to search; also helpful: DOB, SSN. Criminal records on dockets from 1800s, archived from 1971, computerized since 08/96.

General Information: Public Access terminal is available. No juvenile records released. SASE required. Turnaround time same day. Copy fee: $1.00 per page. Certification fee: $3.00. Fee payee: Clerk of Courts. Personal checks accepted. Prepayment is required.

Register of Wills Susquehanna County Courthouse, PO Box 218, Montrose, PA 18801; 570-278-4600 X112; Fax: 570-278-9268. Hours: 8:30AM-4:30PM (EST). *Probate.*

Tioga County

Court of Common Pleas - Criminal & Civil 116 Main St, Wellsboro, PA 16901; 570-724-9281. Hours: 9AM-4:30PM (EST). *Felony, Misdemeanor, Civil, Eviction.*

Civil Records: Access: In person only. Visitors must perform in person searches for themselves. No search fee. Required to search: name. Civil cases indexed by defendant. Civil records on dockets from 1827.

Criminal Records: Access: Mail, in person. Both court and visitors may perform in person searches. Search fee: $5.00 per name per year. Required to search: name, years to search. Criminal records on dockets from 1827.

General Information: No mental health, juvenile, abuse (14 or younger) records released. SASE required. Turnaround time same day when possible. Copy fee: $.25 per page. Certification fee: $4.50. Fee payee: Tioga County Prothonotary. Personal checks accepted. Prepayment is required.

Register of Wills 116 Main St, Wellsboro, PA 16901; 570-724-9260. Hours: 9AM-4:30PM (EST). *Probate.*

Union County

Court of Common Pleas - Criminal & Civil 103 S 2nd St, Lewisburg, PA 17837; 570-524-8751. Hours: 8:30AM-4:30PM (EST). *Felony, Misdemeanor, Civil, Eviction.*

Civil Records: Access: Phone, mail, in person. Both court and visitors may perform in person searches. No search fee. Required to search: name, years to search. Civil cases indexed by defendant, plaintiff. Civil records on computer from 1988, on microfiche (orphans court 1813 to 1988, marriage 1885 to 1998), on dockets from 1800s to 1988.

Criminal Records: Access: Phone, mail, in person. Both court and visitors may perform in person searches. No search fee. Required to search: name, years to search. Criminal records on computer from 1988, on microfiche (orphans court 1813 to 1988, marriage 1885 to 1998), on dockets from 1800s to 1988.

General Information: Public Access terminal is available. No juvenile records released. SASE required. Turnaround time same day. Copy fee: $.25 per page. Certification fee: $4.00. Fee payee: Prothonotary or Clerk of Courts. Personal checks accepted. Prepayment is required.

Register of Wills 103 S 2nd St, Lewisburg, PA 17837-1996; 570-524-8761. Hours: 8:30AM-4:30PM (EST). *Probate.*

Venango County

Court of Common Pleas - Criminal & Civil Venango County Courthouse, 1168 Liberty St, Franklin, PA 16323; 814-432-9577; Fax: 814-432-9573. Hours: 8:30AM-4:30PM (EST). *Felony, Misdemeanor, Civil, Eviction.*

www.co.venango.pa.us

Civil Records: Access: Mail, in person. Both court and visitors may perform in person searches. Search fee: $5.00 per name. Required to search: name, years to search. Civil cases indexed by defendant, plaintiff. Civil records on computer from 1993, on dockets from 1800s.

Criminal Records: Access: Mail, in person. Both court and visitors may perform in person searches. Search fee: $5.00 per name. Required to search: name, years to search, DOB; also helpful: SSN. Criminal records on computer from 1993, on dockets from 1800s.

General Information: Public Access terminal is available. No juvenile records released. SASE required. Turnaround time same day. Fax notes: Fee to fax results is $1.00 per page. Copy fee: $.50 per page. Certification fee: $7.00. Fee payee: Peggy L Miller, Clerk of Courts. Personal checks accepted. Prepayment is required.

Register of Wills/Recorder of Deeds 1168 Liberty St, Franklin, PA 16323; 814-432-9534; Fax: 814-432-9569. 8:30AM-4:30PM (EST). *Probate.*

Warren County

Court of Common Pleas - Criminal & Civil 4th & Market St, Warren, PA 16365; 814-728-3530; Fax: 814-728-3452. Hours: 8:30AM-4:30PM (EST). *Felony, Misdemeanor, Civil, Eviction.*

http://users.penn.com/~wrncourt

Civil Records: Access: Fax, mail, in person. Both court and visitors may perform in person searches. Search fee: $20.00 per name. Required to search: name, years to search. Civil cases indexed by defendant, plaintiff. Civil records on computer from 1987, on dockets from 1800s.

Criminal Records: Access: Fax, mail, in person. Both court and visitors may perform in person searches. Search fee: $20.00 per name. Required to search: name, years to search; also helpful: DOB. Criminal records on computer from 1987, on dockets from 1800s.

General Information: No juvenile records released. SASE required. Turnaround time 2 days. Fax notes: No fee to fax results. Copy fee: $1.00 per page. Certification fee: $4.00. Fee payee: Prothonotary or Clerk of Courts. Business checks accepted. Prepayment is required.

Register of Wills Courthouse, 204 4th Ave, Warren, PA 16365; 814-728-3430. Hours: 8:30AM-4:30PM (EST). *Probate.*

Washington County

Court of Common Pleas - Civil 1 S Main St Suite 1001, Washington, PA 15301; 724-228-6770. Hours: 9AM-4:30PM (EST). *Civil, Eviction.*

www.co.washington.pa.us

Civil Records: Access: Online, in person. Visitors must perform in person searches for themselves. No search fee. Required to search: name, years to search. Civil cases indexed by defendant, plaintiff. Civil records on computer from 1987, prior on dockets to 1800s. Civil records online access to be available in Summer, 2001. See the web site.

General Information: Public Access terminal is available. Copy fee: $1.50 per page. Certification fee: $4.50. Fee payee: Prothonotary. Only cashiers checks and money orders accepted. Checks from attorneys accepted. Prepayment is required.

Court of Common Pleas - Criminal Courthouse Ste 1005, 1 S Main St, Washington, PA 15301; 724-228-6787; Fax: 724-228-6890. Hours: 9AM-4:30PM (EST). *Felony, Misdemeanor.*

www.co.washington.pa.us

Criminal Records: Access: Mail, in person. Both court and visitors may perform in person searches. Search fee: $10.00 per name. Required to search: name, years to search, DOB; also helpful: address, SSN. Criminal records on computer since 10/87, prior on dockets, archived from 1800s.

General Information: No juvenile records released. SASE required. Turnaround time over 1 week. Copy fee: $.50 per page. Certification fee: $8.00. Fee payee: Clerk of Courts. Personal checks accepted. Prepayment is required.

Register of Wills Courthouse, 1 S Main St Suite 1002, Washington, PA 15301; 724-228-6775. Hours: 9AM-4:30PM (EST). *Probate.*

Wayne County

Court of Common Pleas - Criminal & Civil 925 Court St, Honesdale, PA 18431; 570-253-5970 X200; Fax: 570-253-0687. Hours: 8:30AM-4:30PM (EST). *Felony, Misdemeanor, Civil, Eviction.*

Civil Records: Access: In person only. Visitors must perform in person searches for themselves. No search fee. Required to search: name, years to search. Civil cases indexed by defendant, plaintiff. Civil records on daily docket entries, computerized since 1996.

Criminal Records: Access: In person only. Visitors must perform in person searches for themselves. No search fee. Required to search: name, years to search. Criminal records on daily docket entries, computerized since 1996.

General Information: Public Access terminal is available. Juvenile records not released. Copy fee: $.50 per page. Certification fee: No certification fee. Personal checks accepted. Prepayment is required.

Register of Wills 925 Court St, Honesdale, PA 18431; 570-253-5970 X212. Hours: 8:30AM-4:30PM (EST). *Probate.*

Westmoreland County

Court of Common Pleas - Civil Courthouse Sq, Rm 501, PO Box 1630, Greensburg, PA 15601-1168; 724-830-3502; Fax: 724-830-3517. Hours: 8:30AM-4PM (EST). *Civil, Eviction.*

Civil Records: Access: Online, in person. Visitors must perform in person searches for themselves. No search fee. Required to search: name, years to search. Civil cases indexed by defendant, plaintiff. Civil records on computer from 9/85, on dockets from 1700s. Access to the remote online system requires $100 setup (no set-up if accessed via Internet) plus $20 monthly minimum fee. The system includes civil, criminal, prothonotary indexes, and recorder information. For information, call 724-830-3874.

General Information: Public Access terminal is available. No final divorce, mental health records released. Copy fee: $.50 per page. Computer print out: $1.00 per page. Certification fee: $4.75. Fee payee: Prothonotary. Business checks accepted. Prepayment is required.

Court of Common Pleas - Criminal Criminal Division, 203 Courthouse Square, Greensburg, PA 15601-1168; 724-830-3734; Fax: 724-830-3472/850-3979. Hours: 8:30AM-4PM (EST). *Felony, Misdemeanor.*

Criminal Records: Access: Fax, mail, online, in person. Both court and visitors may perform in person searches. Search fee: $10.00 per name. Required to search: name, years to search, signed release; also helpful: DOB, SSN. Criminal records on computer from 1941, on microfiche from 1793 to 1950, archived from 1773. Access to the criminal online system requires $100 setup plus $20 monthly minimum fee. The system includes civil, criminal, prothonotary indexes. For information, call 724-830-3874.

General Information: Public Access terminal is available. No juvenile records released. SASE not required. Turnaround time 1 day. Fax notes: $10.00 per document. Copy fee: $.50 per page. Computer copy $.50 per page. Certification fee: $5.00. Fee payee: Clerk of Courts. Personal checks accepted. Attorney's check accepted. Prepayment is required.

Register of Wills 2 N Main St, #301, Greensburg, PA 15601; 724-830-3177; Fax: 724-850-3976. Hours: 8:30AM-4PM (EST). *Probate.*

Wyoming County

Court of Common Pleas - Criminal & Civil Wyoming County Courthouse, Tunkhannock, PA 18657; 570-836-3200 X232-234. Hours: 8:30AM-4PM (EST). *Felony, Misdemeanor, Civil, Eviction.*

Civil Records: Access: In person only. Visitors must perform in person searches for themselves. No search fee. Required to search: name, years to search. Civil cases indexed by defendant, plaintiff. Civil records on dockets from 1800s.

Criminal Records: Access: In person only. Visitors must perform in person searches for themselves. No search fee. Required to search: name, years to search; also helpful: DOB. Criminal records on dockets from 1800s.

General Information: Public Access terminal is available. No juvenile records released. Copy fee: $.25 per page. Certification fee: $7.00. Fee payee: Prothonotary or Clerk of Courts. Personal checks accepted. Prepayment is required.

Register of Wills County Courthouse, 1 Courthouse Sq, Tunkhannock, PA 18657; 570-836-3200 X235. Hours: 8:30AM-4PM (EST). *Probate.*

York County

Court of Common Pleas - Civil York County Courthouse, 28E Market St, York, PA 17401; 717-771-9611. Hours: 8:30AM-4:30PM (EST). *Civil.*

Civil Records: Access: Online, in person, mail. Visitors must perform in person searches for themselves. No search fee. Required to search: name, years to search. Civil cases indexed by defendant, plaintiff. Civil records on computer from mid-1988, on dockets from 1800s, archived from mid-1700s. Access to the remote online system requires $.75 per minute plus a $200.00 setup fee. For more information, call 717-771-9235.

General Information: Public Access terminal is available. No mental health records released. SASE required. Turnaround time 1 day. Copy fee: $1.00 per page. Certification fee: $4.50. Fee payee: Prothonotary. Only cashiers checks and money orders accepted. Prepayment is required.

Court of Common Pleas - Criminal York County Courthouse 28 E Market St, York, PA 17401; 717-771-9612; Fax: 717-771-9096. Hours: 8:30AM-4:30PM (EST). *Felony, Misdemeanor.*

Criminal Records: Access: Fax, mail, online, in person. Both court and visitors may perform in person searches. Search fee: $5.00 per name. Required to search: name, years to search. Criminal records on computer from 1987, on dockets from 1942, archived from 1700s. Access to the remote online system is available for criminal records from mid-1988 forward. Usage fee is $.75 per minute plus a $200.00 setup fee. For more information, call 717-771-9321.

General Information: Public Access terminal is available. No sex crime, juvenile records released. SASE required. Turnaround time 1-2 weeks. Fax notes: No fee to fax results. Copy fee: $.50 per page. Certification fee: $10.00. Fee payee: Clerk of Courts. Personal checks accepted. Prepayment is required.

Register of Wills York County Courthouse 28 E Market St, York, PA 17401; 570-771-9263; Fax: 570-771-4678. Hours: 8:30AM-4:15PM (EST). *Probate.*

Pennsylvania Recording Offices

ORGANIZATION

67 counties, 67 recording offices and 134 UCC filing offices. Each county has two different recording offices: the Prothonotary - their term for "Clerk" - accepted UCC and tax lien filings until 07/01/2001, and the Recorder of Deeds maintains real estate records. The entire state is in the Eastern Time Zone (EST).

REAL ESTATE RECORDS

County Recorders of Deeds will not perform real estate searches. Copy fees and certification fees vary.

UCC RECORDS

This was a dual filing state. Until 07/1/2001, financing statements were filed both at the state level and with the Prothonotary, except for real estate related collateral, which were filed with the Recorder of Deeds. Now, only relaest related collateral is filed locally. Some county offices will not perform UCC searches. Use search request form UCC-11. Search fees are usually $59.00 per debtor name. Copies usually cost $.50-$2.00 per page. Counties also charge $5.00 per financing statement found on a search.

TAX LIEN RECORDS

All federal and state tax liens on personal property and on real property are filed with the Prothonotary. Usually, tax liens on personal property are filed in the judgment index of the Prothonotary. Some Prothonotaries will perform tax lien searches. Search fees are usually $5.00 per name.

OTHER LIENS

Judgment, municipal, mechanics.

STATEWIDE ONLINE INFO:

The Infocon County Access System provides direct dial-up access to real estate record information for 15 Penn. counties - Armstrong, Bedford, Blair, Butler, Clarion, Clinton, Erie, Franklin, Huntingdon, Juaniata, Lawrence, Mercer, Mifflin, Pike, and Potter. Set up entails a $25.00 base set-up fee plus $25.00 per county. The monthly usage fee minimum is $25.00, plus time charges. For Information, call Infocon at 814-472-6066.

Adams County Prothonotary

County Prothonotary, 111-117 Baltimore Street, Gettysburg, PA 17325. 717-334-6781; Fax 717-334-0532.
Will search UCC records. See Recorder for real estate records. **Other Phone Numbers:** Assessor 717-337-9837.

Adams County Recorder

County Recorder of Deeds, 111-117 Baltimore Street, County Courthouse Room 102, Gettysburg, PA 17325. 717-337-9826; Fax 717-334-1758.
Will not search UCC records, but only real estate related UCC filed here. No tax liens filed here. Will not search real estate records. **Other Phone Numbers:** Assessor 717-334-6781 x216; Treasurer 717-334-6781 x221.

Allegheny County Prothonotary

County Prothonotary, 414 Grant Street, City County Building, Pittsburgh, PA 15219. 412-350-4203 R/E Recording: 412-355-4226; http://www2.county.allegheny.pa.us/realestate/
Will search UCC records. UCC search includes tax liens if requested. See Recorder for real estate records. **Online Access:** Assessor. Online access to the certified values database is available free at the web site. **Other Phone Numbers:** Assessor 412-350-4625.

Allegheny County Recorder

County Recorder of Deeds, 101 County Office Building, 542 Forbes Avenue, Pittsburgh, PA 15219-2947. 412-350-4226; Fax 412-350-6877.
Will search UCC records, but only real estate related UCC filed here. No tax liens filed here. Will not search real estate records. **Other Phone Numbers:** Assessor 412-355-4625; Treasurer 412-355-4100.

Armstrong County Prothonotary

County Prothonotary, County Courthouse, 500 East Market Street, Kittanning, PA 16201. 724-543-2500 R/E Recording: 724-548-3280 UCC Recording: 724-548-3251; Fax 724-548-3351.
Will search UCC records. This agency will not do a tax lien search. See Recorder for real estate records. **Online** **Access:** Tax Liens. Online access: see Recorder of Deeds. **Other Phone Numbers:** Assessor 724-548-3487; Treasurer 724-548-3271; Elections 724-548-3222.

Armstrong County Recorder

County Recorder of Deeds, County Courthouse, 500 Market St., Kittanning, PA 16201-1495. 724-548-3256; Fax 724-548-3236.
Will search UCC records. No tax liens filed here. Will not search real estate records. **Online Access:** Real Estate, Marriage, Probate Records. Access is available through a private company. For information, call Infocon at 814-472-6066. **Other Phone Numbers:** Assessor 724-548-3489.

Beaver County Prothonotary

County Prothonotary, Third Street, County Courthouse, Beaver, PA 15009. 724-728-5700 x283.
Will search UCC records. This agency will not do a tax lien search. See Recorder for real estate records.

Beaver County Recorder

County Recorder of Deeds, 3rd Street, County Courthouse, Beaver, PA 15009. County Recorder of Deeds, R/E and UCC Recording 724-728-5700; Fax 724-728-3630. http://www.co.beaver.pa.us
Will not search UCC records, but only real estate related UCCs filed here. No tax liens filed here. Will not search real estate records. **Online Access:** Real Estate. Online access to the Recorder's digitized images database is to be available free at www.co.beaver.pa.us/Recorder/index.htm. Historical documents will be added. **Other Phone Numbers:** Assessor 724-728-5700; Treasurer 724-728-5700; Elections 724-728-5700.

Bedford County Prothonotary

County Prothonotary, County Courthouse, Corner of Penn & Julliana, Bedford, PA 15522. 814-623-4833; Fax 814-623-4831.
Will search UCC records. UCC search includes tax liens if requested. See Recorder for real estate records. **Online Access:** Tax Liens. Online access: see Recorder of Deeds.

Bedford County Recorder

County Recorder, 200 South Juliana Street, County Courthouse, Bedford, PA 15522. County Recorder, R/E and UCC Recording 814-623-4836; Fax 814-624-0488. http://www.bedford.net/regrec/home.html
Will search UCC records. No tax liens filed here. Will not search real estate records. **Online Access:** Real Estate, Assessor, Probate, Marriage Records. Access is available through a private company. For information, call Infocon at 814-472-6066. **Other Phone Numbers:** Assessor 814-623-4842; Treasurer 814-623-4846; Elections 814-623-4807; Vital Records 814-623-4833.

Berks County Prothonotary

County Prothonotary, 633 Court St., Reading, PA 19601. 610-478-6980; Fax 610-478-6969.
Will search UCC records. See Recorder for real estate records.

Berks County Recorder

Recorder of Deeds, 633 Court St., 3rd Floor, Reading, PA 19601. Recorder of Deeds, R/E and UCC Recording 610-478-3380; Fax 610-478-3359. http://www.berksrecofdeeds.com
Will not search UCC records. No tax liens filed here. Will not search real estate records. **Online Access:** Vital Records, Probate. Online access to the Registry of Wills' databases are available free at http://www.berksregofwills.com including county marriage, estate, birth and death records. Estate and marriage records are current. **Other Phone Numbers:** Assessor 610-478-6262; Treasurer 610-478-6640; Elections 610-478-6490.

Blair County Prothonotary

County Prothonotary, P.O. Box 719, Hollidaysburg, PA 16648. 814-693-3080.
Will search UCC records. This agency will not do a tax lien search. See Recorder for real estate records. **Online Access:** Tax Liens. Online access: see Recorder of Deeds.

Blair County Recorder

County Recorder of Deeds, 423 Allegheny St., Suite 145, Hollidaysburg, PA 16648. County Recorder of Deeds, R/E and UCC Recording 814-693-3095.
Will search UCC records, but only real estate related UCC filed here. No tax liens filed here. Will not search real estate records. **Online Access:** Real Estate, Marriage, Probate Records. Access is available through a private company. For information, call Infocon at 814-472-6066. **Other Phone Numbers:** Assessor 814-695-5541 x223.

Bradford County Prothonotary

County Prothonotary, Courthouse, 301 Main St., Towanda, PA 18848. 570-265-1705.
Will search UCC records. This agency will not do a tax lien search. See Recorder for real estate records.

Bradford County Recorder

County Recorder of Deeds, 301 Main Street, Courthouse, Towanda, PA 18848. County Recorder of Deeds, R/E and UCC Recording 570-265-1702; Fax 570-265-1721.
Will search UCC records. No tax liens filed here. Will not search real estate records. **Other Phone Numbers:** Assessor 570-265-1714; Treasurer 570-265-1700.

Bucks County Prothonotary

County Prothonotary, 55 East Court St., Courthouse, Doylestown, PA 18901. 215-348-6198 UCC Recording: 215-348-6183; Fax 215-348-6184. www.buckscounty.org/courts.htm
Will search UCC records. This agency will not do a tax lien search. See Recorder for real estate records.

Bucks County Recorder

County Recorder of Deeds, Courthouse, 55 E. Court St., Doylestown, PA 18901-4367. 215-348-6209.
Will search UCC records, but only real estate related UCC filed here. No tax liens filed here. All RE transactions and assessment records on-line **Online Access:** Assessor, Real Estate, Tax Lien, Probate Records. Access to County records requires a Sprint ID number and payment of $24 annual Sprint fee, plus $.60 per minute of use. Records date back to 1980. Lending agency and Register of Wills data is available. For information, contact Jack Morris at 215-348-6579. **Other Phone Numbers:** Assessor 215-348-6219; Treasurer 215-348-6244.

Butler County Prothonotary

County Prothonotary, P.O. Box 1208, Butler, PA 16003-1208. 724-284-5214.
Will search UCC records. This agency will not do a tax lien search. See Recorder for real estate records. **Online Access:** Tax Liens. Online access: see Recorder of Deeds.

Butler County Recorder

County Recorder of Deeds, P.O. Box 1208, Butler, PA 16003-1208. 724-284-5340 R/E Recording: 724-285-4731; Fax 724-285-9099.
Will search UCC records. No tax liens filed here. **Online Access:** Marriage, Probate Records. Access is available through a private company. For information, call Infocon at 814-472-6066. **Other Phone Numbers:** Assessor 724-284-5316; Treasurer 724-284-5149.

Cambria County Prothonotary

County Prothonotary, 200 S. Center St., Ebensburg, PA 15931. 814-472-1637 R/E Recording: 814-472-1473; Fax 814-472-5632.
Will search UCC records. This agency will not do a tax lien search. See Recorder for real estate records. **Other**

Phone Numbers: Assessor 814-472-1451; Treasurer 814-472-1643; Elections 814-472-1460.

Cambria County Recorder

Recorder of Deeds, Cambria County Courthouse, 200 S. Center St., Ebensburg, PA 15931. 814-472-1470 R/E Recording: 814-472-1473 UCC Recording: 814-472-1473; Fax 814-472-1412.
Will search UCC records. No tax liens filed here. **Other Phone Numbers:** Assessor 814-472-5440 x450; Treasurer 814-472-5440 x345; Elections 814-472-1464; Register of Wills 814-472-1440.

Cameron County Prothonotary

County Prothonotary, 20 E. 5th Street, Emporium, PA 15834. 814-486-3349; Fax 814-486-0464.
Will search UCC records. See Recorder for real estate records.

Cameron County Recorder

County Recorder of Deeds, 20 E. 5th Street, Emporium, PA 15834. 814-486-3349; Fax 814-486-0464.
Will search UCC records. No tax liens filed here. **Other Phone Numbers:** Assessor 814-486-0723; Treasurer 814-486-3348.

Carbon County Prothonotary

County Prothonotary, P.O. Box 130, Jim Thorpe, PA 18229-0127. 570-325-2481 R/E Recording: 570-325-2651 (Recorder of Deeds) UCC Recording: 570-325-2481 (Prothonotary); Fax 570-325-8047. www.aopc.org/counties/carbon
Will not search UCC records. This agency will not do a tax lien search. See Recorder for real estate records. **Other Phone Numbers:** Assessor 570-325-5254; Treasurer 570-325-2251; Elections 570-325-4801.

Carbon County Recorder

County Recorder of Deeds, P.O. Box 87, Jim Thorpe, PA 18229. 570-325-2651.
Will search UCC records, but only real estate related UCC filed here. No tax liens filed here. Will not search real estate records. **Other Phone Numbers:** Assessor 570-325-3697; Treasurer 570-325-2251.

Centre County Prothonotary

County Prothonotary, Allegheny & High, County Courthouse, Bellefonte, PA 16823. 814-355-6796 R/E Recording: 814-355-6801.
Will search UCC records. This agency will not do a tax lien search. See Recorder for real estate records. **Other Phone Numbers:** Assessor 814-355-6721; Treasurer 814-355-6810; Elections 814-355-6703.

Centre County Recorder

County Recorder of Deeds, 414 Holmes Ave. #1, Bellefonte, PA 16823. 814-355-6801 R/E Recording: 814-355-6701; Fax 814-355-8680.
Will search UCC records. No tax liens filed here. Will not search real estate records. **Other Phone Numbers:** Assessor 814-355-6721; Treasurer 814-355-6810.

Chester County Prothonotary

County Prothonotary, 2 North High Street, Suite 130, County Courthouse, West Chester, PA 19380. 610-344-6111; Fax 610-344-5903. http://www.chesco.org/gengovt.html
Will search UCC records. See Recorder for real estate records.

Chester County Recorder

County Sourcebook of Deeds, Suite 100, 235 West Market St., West Chester, PA 19382-2616. 610-344-6330; Fax 610-344-6408. http://www.chesco.org/gengovt.html

Will search UCC records. No tax liens filed here. Will not search real estate records. **Online Access:** Assessor, Tax Lien, Real Estate, Vital Statistics, Probate Records. Internet access to countywide records including court records requires a sign-up and credit card payment. Application fee is $50. There is a $10.00 per month minimum (no charge for no activity); and $.10 each transaction beyond 100. Sign-up and/or logon at http://epin.chesco.org/. County data is also available as reports, labels, magnetic tape, and diskette. Also, genealogical and older vital statistics are available free at http://www.chesco.org/archives. **Other Phone Numbers:** Assessor 610-344-6105; Treasurer 610-344-6370.

Clarion County Prothonotary

County Prothonotary, Main Street, Courthouse, Clarion, PA 16214-1092. 814-226-4000; Fax 814-226-8069.
Will search UCC records. See Recorder for real estate records. **Online Access:** Tax Liens. Online access: see Recorder of Deeds.

Clarion County Recorder

County Recorder of Deeds, Courthouse, Corner of 5th Ave. & Main St., Clarion, PA 16214. 814-226-4000 x2500 R/E Recording: 814-226-4000 x2501 UCC Recording: 814-226-4000 x2501; Fax 814-226-1117.
Will search UCC records. No tax liens filed here. Will not search real estate records. **Online Access:** Assessor, Real Estate, Voter Registration Records. Access is available through a private company. For information, call Infocon at 814-472-6066. **Other Phone Numbers:** Assessor 814-226-4000 x2301; Treasurer 814-226-4000 x2861.

Clearfield County Prothonotary

County Prothonotary, P.O. Box 549, Clearfield, PA 16830. 814-765-2641 UCC Recording: 814-765-2641 x1330; Fax 814-765-6089.
Will search UCC records. See Recorder for real estate records. **Other Phone Numbers:** Assessor 814-765-2641 x1128; Treasurer 814-765-2641 x1381; Appraiser/Auditor 814-765-2641 x1129; Elections 814-765-2641 x1140.

Clearfield County Recorder

County Recorder of Deeds, P.O. Box 361, Clearfield, PA 16830. County Recorder of Deeds, R/E and UCC Recording 814-765-2641 x1350; Fax 814-765-6089.
Will search UCC records. No tax liens filed here. Will not search real estate records. **Other Phone Numbers:** Assessor 814-765-2641 x5997; Treasurer 814-765-2641 x5985; Elections 814-765-2641 x5996.

Clinton County Prothonotary

County Prothonotary, 230 E. Water St., Courthouse, Lock Haven, PA 17745. 570-893-4007.
Will search UCC records. This agency will not do a tax lien search. See Recorder for real estate records. **Online Access:** Tax Liens. Online access: see Recorder of Deeds.

Clinton County Recorder

County Recorder of Deeds, P.O. Box 943, Lock Haven, PA 17745. 570-893-4010 R/E Recording: 570-893-4020 UCC Recording: 570-893-4020; Fax 570-893-4273.
Will search UCC records, but only real estate related UCC filed here. No tax liens filed here. Will not search real estate records. **Online Access:** Real Estate, Probate Records. Access is available through a private company. For information, call Infocon at 814-472-6066. **Other Phone Numbers:** Assessor 570-893-4034; Treasurer 570-893-4004.

Columbia County Prothonotary

County Prothonotary, P.O. Box 380, Bloomsburg, PA 17815. 570-389-5614 R/E Recording: 570-389-5635 UCC Recording: 570-389-5617.
Will search UCC records. This agency will not do a tax lien search. See Recorder for real estate records. **Other Phone Numbers:** Assessor 570-389-5646; Treasurer 570-389-5626; Elections 570-389-5640.

Columbia County Recorder

County Recorder of Deeds, P.O. Box 380, Bloomsburg, PA 17815. County Recorder of Deeds, R/E and UCC Recording 570-389-5632; Fax 570-389-5636. http://www.columbiapa.org/county/offices.html
Will not search UCC records. Only real estate related UCC filed here. No tax liens filed here. Will not search real estate records. **Other Phone Numbers:** Assessor 570-389-5645; Treasurer 570-389-5626; Appraiser/ Auditor 570-389-5645; Elections 570-389-5640.

Crawford County Prothonotary

County Prothonotary, 903 Diamond Park, County Courthouse, Meadville, PA 16335. 814-333-7324; Fax 814-337-5416.
Will search UCC records. See Recorder for real estate records.

Crawford County Recorder

County Recorder of Deeds, Courthouse, 903 Diamond Park, Meadville, PA 16335. 814-333-7339 R/E Recording: 814-336-1151; Fax 814-337-5296.
Will search UCC records, but only real estate related UCC filed here. No tax liens filed here. Will not search real estate records. **Other Phone Numbers:** Assessor 814-336-1151 x302; Treasurer 814-333-1151 x332.

Cumberland County Prothonotary

County Prothonotary, 1 Courthouse Square, County Courthouse, Carlisle, PA 17013-3387. 717-240-7832.
Will search UCC records. This agency will not do a tax lien search. See Recorder for real estate records.

Cumberland County Recorder

County Recorder of Deeds, County Courthouse, 1 Courthouse Square, Carlisle, PA 17013. County Recorder of Deeds, R/E and UCC Recording 717-240-6370 UCC Recording: 717-240-5370; Fax 717-240-6490.
Will not search UCC records No tax liens filed here. Will not search real estate records. **Other Phone Numbers:** Assessor 717-240-6350; Treasurer 717-240-6380; Elections 717-240-6385.

Dauphin County Prothonotary

County Prothonotary, P.O. Box 945, Harrisburg, PA 17108. 717-255-2697.
Will search UCC records. Tax liens not included in UCC search. See Recorder for real estate records.

Dauphin County Recorder

County Recorder of Deeds, P.O. Box 12000, Harrisburg, PA 17108. 717-255-2802; Fax 717-257-1521.
Will not search UCC records. No tax liens filed here. Will not search real estate records. **Other Phone Numbers:** Assessor 717-255-2735; Treasurer 717-255-2676.

Delaware County Prothonotary

County Prothonotary, Delaware County Government Center Bldg., 201 West Front St., Room 127, Media, PA 19063. 610-891-5009.
Will search UCC records. This agency will not do a tax lien search. See Recorder for real estate records.

Delaware County Recorder

County Recorder of Deeds, 201 W. Front Street, Room 107, Government Center Building, Media, PA 19063. 610-891-4148 R/E Recording: 610-891-4144; http://www2.co.delaware.pa.us/pa/default.htm
Will not search UCC records, but only real estate related UCC filed here. No tax liens filed here. Will not search real estate records. **Online Access:** Assessor, Deeds, Real Estate Records. Online access to the public access system is available free - temporarily - at the web site. Records go back to 1982. Also, property tax records are available free on the Internet at http://taxrecords.com. **Other Phone Numbers:** Assessor 610-891-4880; Treasurer 610-891-4272; Elections 610-891-4938.

Elk County Prothonotary

County Prothonotary, P.O. Box 237, Ridgway, PA 15853-0237. 814-776-5344; Fax 814-776-5303.
Will search UCC records. See Recorder for real estate records. **Other Phone Numbers:** Assessor 814-776-5340; Treasurer 814-776-5322; Elections 814-776-5337.

Elk County Recorder

County Recorder of Deeds, P.O. Box 314, Ridgway, PA 15853-0314. County Recorder of Deeds, R/E and UCC Recording 814-776-5349; Fax 814-776-5382.
Will search UCC records, but only real estate related UCC filed here. No tax liens filed here. Will not search real estate records. **Other Phone Numbers:** Assessor 814-776-5340; Treasurer 814-776-5322; Elections 814-776-5337.

Erie County Prothonotary

County Prothonotary, 140 West 6th Street, Room 120, Erie, PA 16501-1080. 814-451-6078.
Will search UCC records. This agency will not do a tax lien search. Cannot search UCCs filed after June 30, 2001. See Recorder for real estate records. **Online Access:** Tax Liens. Online access: see Recorder of Deeds.

Erie County Recorder

County Recorder of Deeds, P.O. Box 1849, Erie, PA 16507-0849. 814-451-6246; Fax 814-451-6213.
Will search UCC records. No tax liens filed here. Will not search real estate records. **Online Access:** Real Estate, Marriage, Probate. Access is available through a private company. For information, call Infocon at 814-472-6066. **Other Phone Numbers:** Assessor 814-451-6225; Treasurer 814-451-6080.

Fayette County Prothonotary

County Prothonotary, 61 East Main Street, Courthouse, Uniontown, PA 15401. 724-430-1272 R/E Recording: 724-430-1238.
Will search UCC records. This agency will not do a tax lien search. See Recorder for real estate records.

Fayette County Recorder

County Recorder of Deeds, 61 East Main Street, Courthouse, Uniontown, PA 15401-3389. County Recorder of Deeds, R/E and UCC Recording 724-430-1238 UCC Recording: 724-430-1272; Fax 724-430-1238.
Will search UCC records. No tax liens filed here. Will not search real estate records. **Other Phone Numbers:** Assessor 724-430-1350; Treasurer 724-430-1256; Elections 724-430-1289; Vital Records 724-430-1206.

Forest County Prothonotary

County Prothonotary, P.O. Box 423, Tionesta, PA 16353. 814-755-3526; Fax 814-755-8837.

Will search UCC records. See Recorder for real estate records.

Forest County Recorder

County Recorder of Deeds, P.O. Box 423, Tionesta, PA 16353. 814-755-3526 R/E Recording: 814-755-3537; Fax 814-755-8837.
Will search UCC records. No tax liens filed here. Will not search real estate records. **Other Phone Numbers:** Assessor 814-755-3532; Treasurer 814-755-3536.

Franklin County Prothonotary

County Prothonotary, 157 Lincoln Way East, County Court House, Chambersburg, PA 17201. 717-261-3860 R/E Recording: 717-261-3872; Fax 717-264-6772.
Will search UCC records. See Recorder for real estate records. **Online Access:** Tax Liens. Online access: see Recorder of Deeds. **Other Phone Numbers:** Assessor 717-261-3801; Treasurer 717-261-3119; Elections 717-261-3886; UCC/Personal Property 717-261-3858.

Franklin County Recorder

County Recorder of Deeds, 157 Lincoln Way East, Chambersburg, PA 17201. 717-264-4125; Fax 717-267-3438.
Will search UCC records. No tax liens filed here. Will not search real estate records. **Online Access:** Real Estate, Probate Records. Access is available through a private company. For information, call Infocon at 814-472-6066. **Other Phone Numbers:** Assessor 717-261-3801; Treasurer 717-261-3120.

Fulton County Prothonotary

County Prothonotary, 201 North Second Street, Fulton County Courthouse, McConnellsburg, PA 17233-1198. 717-485-4212.
Will not search UCC records. UCC search includes tax liens if requested. See Recorder for real estate records.

Fulton County Recorder

County Recorder of Deeds, 201 North Second Street, Fulton County Courthouse, McConnellsburg, PA 17233-1198. County Recorder of Deeds, R/E and UCC Recording 717-485-4212.
Will not search UCC records, No tax liens filed here. Will not search real estate records. **Other Phone Numbers:** Assessor 717-485-3208; Treasurer 717-485-4454.

Greene County Prothonotary

County Prothonotary, 10 East High St., Room 105, Waynesburg, PA 15370. 724-852-5289.
Will not search UCC records. UCC search includes tax liens if requested. See Recorder for real estate records.

Greene County Recorder

County Recorder of Deeds, 10 E High St, Courthouse, Waynesburg, PA 15370. County Recorder of Deeds, R/E and UCC Recording 724-852-5283 UCC Recording: 724-852-5289; http://county.greenepa.net
Will search UCC records, but only real estate related UCC filed here. No tax liens filed here. Will not search real estate records. **Other Phone Numbers:** Assessor 724-852-5211; Treasurer 724-852-5225; Elections 724-852-5230.

Huntingdon County Prothonotary

County Prothonotary, P.O. Box 39, Huntingdon, PA 16652-1486. 814-643-1610 R/E Recording: 814-643-2740; Fax 814-643-4271.
Will search UCC records. See Recorder for real estate records. **Online Access:** Tax Liens. Online access: see Recorder of Deeds. **Other Phone Numbers:** Assessor 814-643-1000; Treasurer 814-643-3523; Elections 814-643-3091.

Huntingdon County Recorder

County Recorder of Deeds, 223 Penn Street, Courthouse, Huntingdon, PA 16652. County Recorder of Deeds, R/E and UCC Recording 814-643-2740; Fax 814-643-8152.

Will not search UCC records. No tax liens filed here. Will not search real estate records. **Online Access:** Real Estate, Marriage, Probate. Access is available through a private company. For information, call Infocon at 814-472-6066. **Other Phone Numbers:** Assessor 814-643-1000; Treasurer 814-643-3523; Elections 814-643-3091.

Indiana County Prothonotary

Prothonotary & Clerk of Courts, 825 Philadelphia Street, Courthouse, 1st Floor, Indiana, PA 15701-3934. 724-465-3855 R/E Recording: 724-465-3860; Fax 724-465-3868.

Will search UCC records. See Recorder for real estate records. **Other Phone Numbers:** Assessor 724-465-3812; Treasurer 724-465-3845; Elections 724-465-3852; Vital Records 724-656-3100.

Indiana County Recorder

County Recorder of Deeds, 825 Philadelphia Street, Courthouse, Indiana, PA 15701. County Recorder of Deeds, R/E and UCC Recording 724-465-3860; Fax 724-465-3863.

Will search UCC records. No tax liens filed here. Will not search real estate records. **Other Phone Numbers:** Assessor 724-465-3812; Treasurer 724-465-3845.

Jefferson County Prothonotary

County Prothonotary, 200 Main Street, Court House, Room 102, Brookville, PA 15825. 814-849-1606 R/E Recording: 814-849-1610 UCC Recording: 814-849-1625; Fax 814-849-1607.

Will search UCC records. This agency will not do a tax lien search. See Recorder for real estate records.

Jefferson County Recorder

County Recorder of Deeds, 200 Main Street, Courthouse, Brookville, PA 15825. County Recorder of Deeds, R/E and UCC Recording 814-849-1610; Fax 814-849-1677.

Will search UCC records. No tax liens filed here. Will not search real estate records. **Other Phone Numbers:** Assessor 814-849-1637; Treasurer 814-849-1609; Elections 814-849-1603.

Juniata County Prothonotary

County Prothonotary, Courthouse, Mifflintown, PA 17059. 717-436-7715 R/E Recording: 717-436-7709; Fax 717-436-7734.

Will search UCC records. This agency will not do a tax lien search. See Recorder for real estate records. **Other Phone Numbers:** Assessor 717-436-7740; Treasurer 717-436-7742; Elections 717-436-7706.

Juniata County Recorder

County Recorder of Deeds, P.O. Box 68, Mifflintown, PA 17059. County Recorder of Deeds, R/E and UCC Recording 717-436-7709; Fax 717-436-7756.

Will not search UCC records. No tax liens filed here. Will not search real estate records. **Online Access:** Real Estate, Marriage, Probate. Access is available through a private company. For information, call Infocon at 814-472-6066. **Other Phone Numbers:** Assessor 717-436-7740; Treasurer 717-436-7742; Prothonotary 717-436-7715.

Lackawanna County Prothonotary

County Clerk of Judicial Records, P.O. Box 133, Scranton, PA 18503. 570-963-6723.

Will search UCC records. This agency will not do a tax lien search. See Recorder for real estate records.

Lackawanna County Recorder

County Recorder of Deeds, 200 North Washington, Courthouse, Scranton, PA 18503. County Recorder of Deeds, R/E and UCC Recording 570-963-6775.

Will search UCC records, but only real estate related UCC filed here. No tax liens filed here. Will not search real estate records. **Other Phone Numbers:** Assessor 570-963-6728; Treasurer 570-963-6731.

Lancaster County Prothonotary

County Prothonotary, P.O. Box 83480, Lancaster, PA 17608-3480. 717-299-8282 R/E Recording: 717-299-8238; Fax 717-293-7210.

Will search UCC records. See Recorder for real estate records. **Online Access:** Real Estate. Online access to county property information is available free from the GIS Dept. at www.co.lancaster.pa.us/GIS/disclaimer.html. **Other Phone Numbers:** Assessor 717-299-8381; Treasurer 717-299-8222; Elections 717-299-8293.

Lancaster County Recorder

County Recorder of Deeds, 50 North Duke Street, Lancaster, PA 17602. 717-299-8238; http://www.co.lancaster.pa.us

Will search UCC records, but only real estate related UCC filed here. No tax liens filed here. Will not search real estate records. **Online Access:** Assessor, Real Estate, Tax Lien Records. Two online resources are available. Access to County online records requires $25 monthly plus $.18 per minute of use. This system holds 5 years data. It uses Windows. Lending agency and Register of Wills information is available. For information, contact Nancy Malloy at 717-299-8252. Assessor records on the County GIS database are available free on the Internet at www.co.lancaster.pa.us/GIS/disclaimer.html. Click on "Lancaster. Search" then choose municipality; then "Go." Search by parcel number, owner name, address, or map. **Other Phone Numbers:** Assessor 717-299-8381; Treasurer 717-299-8222.

Lawrence County Prothonotary

County Prothonotary, 430 Court Street, Government Center, New Castle, PA 16101-3593. 724-656-1943 R/E Recording: 724-656-2128 UCC Recording: 724-656-2143; Fax 724-656-1988.

Will search UCC records. This agency will not do a tax lien search. See Recorder for real estate records. **Online Access:** Tax Liens. Online access: see Recorder of Deeds. **Other Phone Numbers:** Assessor 724-656-2191; Treasurer 724-656-1978; Elections 724-656-2161; Vital Records 724-656-3100.

Lawrence County Recorder

County Recorder of Deeds, 430 Court Street, Government Center, New Castle, PA 16101. 724-656-2127; Fax 724-656-1966.

Will search UCC records. No tax liens filed here. Will not search real estate records. **Online Access:** Real Estate, Assessor, Marriage, Probate. Access is available through a private company. For information, call Infocon at 814-472-6066. **Other Phone Numbers:** Assessor 724-656-2191; Treasurer 724-656-2183.

Lebanon County Prothonotary

County Prothonotary, 400 South 8th Street, Lebanon, PA 17042. County Prothonotary, R/E and UCC Recording 717-274-2801.

Will search UCC records. This agency will not do a tax lien search. See Recorder for real estate records. **Other Phone Numbers:** Assessor 717-274-2801; Treasurer 717-274-2801; Appraiser/Auditor 717-274-2801; Elections 717-274-2801; Vital Records 717-274-2801.

Lebanon County Recorder

County Recorder of Deeds, 400 South 8th Street, Room 107, Lebanon, PA 17042. 717-274-2801 R/E Recording: 717-274-2801 x2224 UCC Recording: 717-274-2801 x2225.

Will not search UCC. No tax liens filed here. Will not search real estate records. **Other Phone Numbers:** Assessor 717-274-2801 x2250; Treasurer 717-274-2801 x2229.

Lehigh County Prothonotary

County Prothonotary, 455 W. Hamilton St., Allentown, PA 18101-1614. 610-782-3148; Fax 610-770-3840. http://www.lccpa.org/depts/clerkofcourtsgeninfo.html

The City of Bethlehem is in both Northampton and Lehigh counties. Will search UCC records. This agency will not do a tax lien search. See Recorder for real estate records.

Lehigh County Recorder

County Recorder of Deeds, 455 W. Hamilton Street, Allentown, PA 18101. 610-782-3162 R/E Recording: 610-820-3162; Fax 610-820-2039.

Will search UCC records. No tax liens filed here. Will not search real estate records. **Online Access:** Assessor, Real Estate, Tax Lien, Marriage Records. The system is open 24 hours daily; there are set-up and usage fees. Records go back to 1984. Lending agency information is available. Court records are also available. Call Lehigh City Computer Svcs Dept at 610-782-3286 for more information. **Other Phone Numbers:** Assessor 610-820-3038; Treasurer 610-820-3113.

Luzerne County Prothonotary

County Prothonotary, 200 North River Street, County Court House, Wilkes-Barre, PA 18711-1001. 570-825-6189 UCC Recording: 570-825-1749; Fax 570-825-1757.

Will search UCC records. See Recorder for real estate records.

Luzerne County Recorder

County Recorder of Deeds, 200 North River Street, Courthouse, Wilkes-Barre, PA 18711. County Recorder of Deeds, R/E and UCC Recording 570-825-1641; Fax 570-970-4580.

Will search UCC records, but only real estate related UCC filed here. No tax liens filed here. Will not search real estate records. **Other Phone Numbers:** Assessor 570-825-1539; Treasurer 570-825-1786.

Lycoming County Prothonotary

County Prothonotary, 48 West Third Street, Williamsport, PA 17701. 570-327-2251.

Will search UCC records. This agency will not do a tax lien search. See Recorder for real estate records.

Lycoming County Recorder

County Recorder of Deeds, 48 West Third Street, Williamsport, PA 17701. County Recorder of Deeds, R/E and UCC Recording 570-327-2263; Fax 570-327-2511.

Will search UCC records, but only real estate related UCC filed here. No tax liens filed here. Will not search real estate records. **Other Phone Numbers:** Assessor 570-327-2302; Treasurer 570-327-2249.

McKean County Prothonotary

County Prothonotary, P.O. Box 273, Smethport, PA 16749. 814-887-3271 R/E Recording: 814-887-3253; Fax 814-887-3219.

Will search UCC records. See Recorder for real estate records. **Other Phone Numbers:** Assessor 814-887-3214; Treasurer 814-887-3220; Elections 814-887-3203.

McKean County Recorder

Recorder of Deeds, P.O. Box 3426, Smethport, PA 16749. 814-887-3253 R/E Recording: 814-887-3250 UCC Recording: 814-887-3250; Fax 814-887-3255. Will search UCC records. No tax liens filed here. Will not search real estate records. **Other Phone Numbers:** Assessor 814-887-3215; Treasurer 814-887-3220; Elections 814-887-3203; Vital Records 814-887-3260.

Mercer County Prothonotary

County Prothonotary, 105 Mercer County Courthouse, Mercer, PA 16137-0066. 724-662-3800. Will search UCC records. This agency will not do a tax lien search. See Recorder for real estate records. **Online Access:** Tax Liens. Online access: see Recorder of Deeds.

Mercer County Recorder

County Recorder of Deeds, Box 109 Courthouse, Mercer, PA 16137. 724-662-3800 x2274 R/E Recording: 724-662-3800; Fax 724-662-2096. Will search UCC records. No tax liens filed here. Will not search real estate records. **Online Access:** Real Estate, Assessor. Access is available through a private company. For information, call Infocon at 814-472-6066. **Other Phone Numbers:** Assessor 724-662-3800 x505; Treasurer 724-662-3800 x257.

Mifflin County Prothonotary

County Prothonotary, 20 North Wayne Street, Lewistown, PA 17044. 717-248-8146; Fax 717-248-5275. Will search UCC records. See Recorder for real estate records. **Online Access:** Tax Liens. Online access: see Recorder of Deeds.

Mifflin County Recorder

County Recorder of Deeds, 20 North Wayne Street, Lewistown, PA 17044. 717-242-1449 R/E Recording: 717-248-6733; Fax 717-248-3695. Will search UCC records, but only real estate related UCC filed here. No tax liens filed here. Will not search real estate records. **Online Access:** Real Estate, Assessor, Probate Records. Access is available through a private company. For information, call Infocon at 814-472-6066. **Other Phone Numbers:** Assessor 717-248-5783; Treasurer 717-248-8439.

Monroe County Prothonotary

County Prothonotary, N. 7th & Monroe Street, Courthouse, Room 303, Stroudsburg, PA 18360-2190. 570-420-3570. Will search UCC records. Tax liens included in UCC search if requested. Additional $1.00 per item found. See Recorder for real estate records.

Monroe County Recorder

County Recorder of Deeds, 7th & Monroe Street, Courthouse, Stroudsburg, PA 18360-2185. 570-420-3530 R/E Recording: 570-420-3400; Fax 570-420-3537. Will search UCC records. No tax liens filed here. Will not search real estate records. **Other Phone Numbers:** Assessor 570-420-3412; Treasurer 570-420-3510.

Montgomery County Prothonotary

County Prothonotary, P.O. Box 311, Norristown, PA 19404. 610-278-3360; Fax 610-278-5994.

Will search UCC records. This agency will not do a tax lien search. See Recorder for real estate records.

Montgomery County Recorder

County Recorder of Deeds, P.O. Box 311, Norristown, PA 19404-0311. 610-278-3289 R/E Recording: 610-278-3868; Fax 610-278-3869. http://www.montcopa.org
Will search UCC records, but only real estate related UCC filed here. No tax liens filed here. Will not search real estate records. **Online Access:** Assessor, Real Estate, Tax Lien. Two onlines sources are available. Access to County online records requires a $10 sign up fee plus $.15 per minute of use. Records date back to 1990. Lending agency and prothonotary information are available on the system. For information or to sign up, contact Berkheimer Assoc. at 800-360-8989. Also, records on the County PIR database are available free on the Internet at www.montcopa.org/reassessment/boahome0.htm. Click on "Instructions" to learn how to use the search features, then search by parcel number, name, address, or municipality. **Other Phone Numbers:** Assessor 610-278-3761; Treasurer 610-278-3066; Elections 610-278-3075.

Montour County Prothonotary

County Prothonotary, 29 Mill Street, Courthouse, Danville, PA 17821. 570-271-3010 R/E Recording: 570-271-3012; Fax 570-271-3089. Will search UCC records. Tax liens not included in UCC search. See Recorder for real estate records. **Other Phone Numbers:** Assessor 570-271-3006; Treasurer 570-271-3016; Elections 570-271-3000; Vital Records 570-271-3010.

Montour County Recorder

Register & Recorder, 29 Mill Street, Courthouse, Danville, PA 17821. 570-271-3012; Fax 570-271-3071. Will search UCC records. No tax liens filed here. **Other Phone Numbers:** Assessor 570-271-3006; Treasurer 570-271-3016; Appraiser/Auditor 570-271-3006; Elections 570-271-3000.

Northampton County Prothonotary

County Prothonotary, 669 Washington St., 2nd Floor, Room 207, Easton, PA 18042-7498. 610-559-3060. The City of Bethlehem is in both Northampton and Lehigh counties. Will search UCC records. This agency will not do a tax lien search. See Recorder for real estate records.

Northampton County Recorder

County Recorder of Deeds, 669 Washington Streets, Government Center, Easton, PA 18042. 610-559-3077; Fax 610-559-3103. The City of Bethlehem is in both Northampton and Lehigh counties. Will search UCC records, but only real estate related UCC filed here. No tax liens filed here. Will not search real estate records. **Other Phone Numbers:** Assessor 610-559-3160.

Northumberland County Prothonotary

County Prothonotary, 201 Market Streets, Courthouse, Room 7, Sunbury, PA 17801-3468. 570-988-4151 R/E Recording: 570-988-4143. Will search UCC records. This agency will not do a tax lien search. See Recorder for real estate records. **Other Phone Numbers:** Assessor 570-988-4112; Treasurer 570-988-4161; Elections 570-988-4211.

Northumberland County Recorder

County Recorder of Deeds, 2nd & Market Streets, Court House, Sunbury, PA 17801. 570-988-4140.

Will search UCC records, but only real estate related UCC filed here. No tax liens filed here. Will not search real estate records. **Other Phone Numbers:** Assessor 570-988-4312; Treasurer 570-988-4160.

Perry County Prothonotary

County Prothonotary, P.O. Box 325, New Bloomfield, PA 17068-0325. 717-582-2131. Will search UCC records. This agency will not do a tax lien search. See Recorder for real estate records.

Perry County Recorder

County Recorder of Deeds, P.O. Box 223, New Bloomfield, PA 17068. 717-582-2131. Will search UCC records, but only real estate related UCC filed here. No tax liens filed here. Will not search real estate records. **Other Phone Numbers:** Assessor 717-582-8984 x3; Treasurer 717-582-8984 x4.

Philadelphia County Prothonotary

County Prothonotary, Broad & Market Streets, City Hall Room 262, Philadelphia, PA 19107. 215-686-6664. Will search UCC records. Tax liens not included in UCC search. See Recorder for real estate records.

Philadelphia County Recorder

County Recorder of Deeds, Broad & Market Streets, City Hall Room 153, Philadelphia, PA 19107. 215-686-2260 R/E Recording: 215-686-2291. Will search UCC records, but only real estate related UCC filed here. No tax liens filed here. Will not search real estate records. **Other Phone Numbers:** Assessor 215-686-4334; Treasurer 215-686-2312.

Pike County Prothonotary

County Prothonotary, 412 Broad Street, Milford, PA 18337. 570-296-7231. Will search UCC records. This agency will not do a tax lien search. See Recorder for real estate records. **Online Access:** Tax Liens. Online access: see Recorder of Deeds.

Pike County Recorder

County Recorder of Deeds, 506 Broad Street, Milford, PA 18337. 570-296-3508 R/E Recording: 570-296-7231. Will search UCC records, but only real estate related UCC filed here. No tax liens filed here. Will not search real estate records. **Online Access:** Probate. Access is available through a private company. For information, call Infocon at 814-472-6066. **Other Phone Numbers:** Assessor 570-296-3417; Treasurer 570-296-3441.

Potter County Prothonotary

County Prothonotary, Courthouse, Room 23, 1 E. 2nd St., Coudersport, PA 16915. 814-274-9740 R/E Recording: 814-274-8370; Fax 814-274-8284. Will search UCC records. See Recorder for real estate records. **Online Access:** Tax Liens. Online access: see Recorder of Deeds. **Other Phone Numbers:** Assessor 814-274-0488; Treasurer 814-274-9775; Elections 814-274-8467; Vital Records 814-274-9740.

Potter County Recorder

County Recorder of Deeds, Courthouse, Room 20, Coudersport, PA 16915. 814-274-8370. Will search UCC records, but only real estate related UCC filed here. No tax liens filed here. Will not search real estate records. **Online Access:** Real Estate, Assessor, Probate Records. Access is available through a private company. For information, call Infocon at 814-472-6066. **Other Phone Numbers:** Assessor 814-247-0488; Treasurer 814-274-9775.

Schuylkill County Prothonotary

County Prothonotary, 401 N. Second St., Pottsville, PA 17901-2520. 570-628-1270 R/E Recording: 570-628-1480; Fax 570-628-1261.
Will search UCC records. UCC search includes tax liens if requested. $5.00 per 5 year judgment search See Recorder for real estate records. **Other Phone Numbers:** Assessor 570-628-1025; Treasurer 570-628-1433; Elections 570-628-3040.

Schuylkill County Recorder

County Recorder of Deeds, 401 N. Second St., Pottsville, PA 17901. 570-628-1480.
Will search UCC records, but only real estate related UCC filed here. No tax liens filed here. Will not search real estate records. **Other Phone Numbers:** Assessor 570-628-1024; Treasurer 570-628-1433.

Snyder County Prothonotary

County Prothonotary, P.O. Box 217, Middleburg, PA 17842-0217. 570-837-4202; Fax 570-837-4275.
Will search UCC records. See Recorder for real estate records.

Snyder County Recorder

County Recorder of Deeds, P.O. Box 217, Middleburg, PA 17842-0217. County Recorder of Deeds, R/E and UCC Recording 570-837-4225; Fax 570-837-4299.
Will not search real estate records. **Other Phone Numbers:** Assessor 570-837-4218; Treasurer 570-837-4221.

Somerset County Prothonotary

County Prothonotary, 111 East Union St., Suite 190, Somerset, PA 15501. 814-445-1428 R/E Recording: 814-445-1547; Fax 814-444-9270.
Will search UCC records. Will not search tax liens. See Recorder for real estate records. **Other Phone Numbers:** Assessor 814-445-1536; Treasurer 814-445-1482; Elections 814-445-1549.

Somerset County Recorder

County Recorder of Deeds, 300 N Center Ave, #400, Suite 140, Somerset, PA 15501. 814-445-1547.
Will search UCC records, but only real estate related UCC filed here. No tax liens filed here. Will not search real estate records. **Other Phone Numbers:** Assessor 814-445-8931; Treasurer 814-445-2071.

Sullivan County Prothonotary

County Prothonotary, Main Street, Courthouse, Laporte, PA 18626. County Prothonotary, R/E and UCC Recording 570-946-7351.
Will not search UCC records. This agency will not do a tax lien search. See Recorder for real estate records. **Other Phone Numbers:** Assessor 570-946-5061; Treasurer 570-946-7331; Elections 570-946-5201.

Sullivan County Recorder

County Recorder of Deeds, Main Street, Courthouse, Laporte, PA 18626. County Recorder of Deeds, R/E and UCC Recording 570-946-7351.
Will not search UCC records, but only real estate related UCC filed here. No tax liens filed here. Will not search real estate records. **Other Phone Numbers:** Assessor 570-946-5061; Treasurer 570-946-7331; Elections 570-946-5201.

Susquehanna County Prothonotary

County Prothonotary, P.O. Box 218, Montrose, PA 18801-0218. 570-278-4600 x121; Fax 570-278-9268.
Will search UCC records. See Recorder for real estate records.

Susquehanna County Recorder

Recorder of Deeds, P.O. Box 218, Montrose, PA 18801. 570-278-4600 x112/3 R/E Recording: 570-278-4600 x112 UCC Recording: 570-278-4600 x112; Fax 570-278-9268.
Will search UCC records. No tax liens filed here. Will not search real estate records. **Other Phone Numbers:** Assessor 570-278-4600 x150; Treasurer 570-278-4600 x130; Vital Records 570-278-4600 x112.

Tioga County Prothonotary

County Prothonotary, 116 Main Street, Courthouse, Wellsboro, PA 16901. 570-724-9281.
Will not search UCC records. This agency will not do a tax lien search. See Recorder for real estate records.

Tioga County Recorder

County Recorder of Deeds, 116 Main Street, Courthouse, Wellsboro, PA 16901. 570-724-9260 R/E Recording: 570-724-1906.
Will search UCC records, but only real estate related UCC filed here. No tax liens filed here. Will not search real estate records. **Other Phone Numbers:** Assessor 570-724-9117; Treasurer 570-723-9213.

Union County Prothonotary

County Prothonotary, 103 South 2nd Street, Courthouse, Lewisburg, PA 17837. 570-524-8751 R/E Recording: 570-524-8761 UCC Recording: 570-524-8761.
Will not search UCC records. UCC search does not include tax liens. See Recorder for real estate records. **Other Phone Numbers:** Assessor 570-524-8611; Treasurer 570-524-8781.

Union County Recorder

County Recorder of Deeds, 103 South 2nd Street, Courthouse, Lewisburg, PA 17837-1996. 570-524-8761; http://www.unionco.org
Will not search UCC records, but only real estate related UCC filed here. Mail requests must include a stamped self-addressed envelope. No tax liens filed here. Will not search real estate records. **Other Phone Numbers:** Assessor 570-524-8611; Treasurer 570-524-8781.

Venango County Prothonotary

County Prothonotary, Courthouse, Franklin, PA 16323. 814-432-9577; Fax 814-432-9569.
Will search UCC records. UCC search includes tax liens if requested. See Recorder for real estate records.

Venango County Recorder

County Recorder of Deeds, P.O. Box 831, Franklin, PA 16323. 814-432-9539 R/E Recording: 814-437-6871; Fax 814-432-9569. http://www.co.venango.pa.us/Directory/Default.htm
Will not search UCC records. No tax liens filed here. Will not search real estate records. **Other Phone Numbers:** Assessor 814-432-9516; Treasurer 814-432-9525; Elections 814-432-9514; Vital Records 814-432-9535.

Warren County Prothonotary

County Prothonotary, 4th & Market Streets, Courthouse, Warren, PA 16365. 814-723-7550; Fax 814-723-8115.
Will search UCC records. See Recorder for real estate records.

Warren County Recorder

County Recorder of Deeds, 4th & Market Streets, Courthouse, Warren, PA 16365. 814-723-7550.
Will search UCC records, but only real estate related UCC filed here. No tax liens filed here. Will not search real estate records. **Other Phone Numbers:** Assessor 814-723-7550; Treasurer 814-723-7550.

Washington County Prothonotary

County Prothonotary, 1 S. Main St., Suite 1001, Courthouse, Washington, PA 15301. 724-228-6770.
Will search UCC records. This agency will not do a tax lien search. See Recorder for real estate records.

Washington County Recorder

County Prothonotary, Washington County Courthouse, 1 South Main St., Room 1006, Washington, PA 15301. County Prothonotary, R/E and UCC Recording 724-228-6806 UCC Recording: 724-228-6770; Fax 724-228-6737. http://www.co.washington.pa.us/
Will search UCC records. No tax liens filed here. **Online Access:** Assessor, Real Estate Records. Records are available on the county online system. Records date back to 1952. Register of Wills information and lending agency information is also available. For information, call 724-228-6766. **Other Phone Numbers:** Assessor 724-228-6850; Treasurer 724-228-6780; Elections 724-228-6750.

Wayne County Prothonotary

County Prothonotary, 925 Court Street, Courthouse, Honesdale, PA 18431-1996. 570-253-5970 x200/5 R/E Recording: 570-253-5970 x212 UCC Recording: 570-253-5970 x205; Fax 570-253-0687.
Will search UCC records. This agency will not do a tax lien search. See Recorder for real estate records. **Other Phone Numbers:** Assessor 570-253-5970 x216; Treasurer 570-253-5970 x125; Elections 570-253-5970 x165; Vital Records 570-253-5970 x200.

Wayne County Recorder

County Recorder of Deeds, 925 Court Street, Honesdale, PA 18431-1996. County Recorder of Deeds, R/E and UCC Recording 570-253-5970 x212; http://www.co-wayne-pa-us.org
Will search UCC records, but only real estate related UCC filed here. Mail requests must include a SASE. No tax liens filed here. Will not search real estate records. **Other Phone Numbers:** Assessor 570-253-5970 x216; Treasurer 570-253-5970 x125; Elections 570-253-5970 x165.

Westmoreland County Prothonotary

County Prothonotary, PO Box 1630, Courthouse Square Room 501, Greensburg, PA 15601. 724-830-3516.
Will search UCC records. UCC search includes tax liens if requested. See Recorder for real estate records.

Westmoreland County Recorder

Recorder of Deeds, Greensburg, PA 15601. 724-830-3526 R/E Recording: 724-830-3000; Fax 724-832-8757.
Will search UCC records. No tax liens filed here. Will not search real estate records. **Online Access:** Real Estate, Tax Lien Records. The online system costs $100 setup plus $20 per month minimum fee, and a per minute charge of $.50 after 40 minutes. The system also includes civil, criminal, prothonotary indexes. Recorder information dates back to 1957. No tax lien information is available, only UCC liens. For information, call 724-830-3874. **Other Phone Numbers:** Assessor 724-830-3490; Treasurer 724-830-3173.

Wyoming County Prothonotary

County Prothonotary, 1 Courthouse Square, Wyoming County Courthouse, Tunkhannock, PA 18657-1219. 717-836-3200.

Will search UCC records. This agency will not do a tax lien search. See Recorder for real estate records.

Wyoming County Recorder

County Recorder of Deeds, 1 Courthouse Square, Tunkhannock, PA 18657. 717-836-3200 x235/6 R/E Recording: 717-836-3200.

Will search UCC records, but only real estate related UCC filed here. No tax liens filed here. Will not search real estate records. **Other Phone Numbers:** Assessor 717-836-3200 x261; Treasurer 717-836-3200 x287.

York County Prothonotary

County Prothonotary, 28 East Market Street, York, PA 17401. 717-771-9611; Fax 717-771-4629.

Will search UCC records. See Recorder for real estate records.

York County Recorder

County Recorder of Deeds, 28 East Market Street, York, PA 17401. 717-771-9608 R/E Recording: 717-771-9295; Fax 717-771-9582. http://www.york-county.org

Will search UCC records. No tax liens filed here. Will not search real estate records. **Online Access:** Property Information. Parcel numbers are available to the public on the website under "Assessment Office.". **Other Phone Numbers:** Assessor 717-771-9220; Treasurer 717-771-9603.

Pennsylvania County Locator

You will usually be able to find the city name in the City/County Cross Reference below. In that case, it is a simple matter to determine the county from the cross reference. However, only the official US Postal Service city names are included in this index. There are an additional 40,000 place names that people use in their addresses. Therefore, we have also included a ZIP/City Cross Reference immediately following the City/County Cross Reference.

If you know the ZIP Code but the city name does not appear in the City/County Cross Reference index, look up the ZIP Code in the ZIP/City Cross Reference, find the city name, then look up the city name in the City/County Cross Reference. For example, you want to know the county for an address of Menands, NY 12204. There is no "Menands" in the City/County Cross Reference. The ZIP/City Cross Reference shows that ZIP Codes 12201-12288 are for the city of Albany. Looking back in the City/County Cross Reference, Albany is in Albany County.

City/County Cross Reference

AARONSBURG Centre
ABBOTTSTOWN (17301) Adams(71), York(29)
ABINGTON Montgomery
ACKERMANVILLE Northampton
ACME Westmoreland
ACOSTA Somerset
ADAH Fayette
ADAMSBURG Westmoreland
ADAMSTOWN Lancaster
ADAMSVILLE (16110) Crawford(91), Mercer(9)
ADDISON Somerset
ADRIAN Armstrong
AIRVILLE York
AKRON Lancaster
ALBA Bradford
ALBION (16401) Erie(91), Crawford(9)
ALBION Erie
ALBRIGHTSVILLE (18210) Carbon(87), Monroe(13)
ALBURTIS (18011) Berks(62), Lehigh(38)
ALDENVILLE Wayne
ALEPPO Greene
ALEXANDRIA Huntingdon
ALIQUIPPA Beaver
ALLENPORT Washington
ALLENSVILLE (17002) Mifflin(88), Huntingdon(12)
ALLENTOWN Lehigh
ALLENWOOD (17810) Union(51), Lycoming(49)
ALLISON Fayette
ALLISON PARK Allegheny
ALLPORT Clearfield
ALTOONA Blair
ALUM BANK Bedford
ALVERDA Indiana
ALVERTON Westmoreland
AMBERSON Franklin
AMBLER Montgomery
AMBRIDGE (15003) Beaver(95), Allegheny(5)
AMITY Washington
ANALOMINK Monroe
ANDREAS (18211) Schuylkill(87), Carbon(13)
ANITA Jefferson
ANNVILLE Lebanon
ANTES FORT Lycoming
APOLLO (15613) Armstrong(52), Westmoreland(48)
AQUASHICOLA Carbon
ARCADIA Indiana
ARCHBALD Lackawanna
ARCOLA Montgomery
ARDARA Westmoreland
ARDMORE (19003) Montgomery(64), Delaware(36)
ARENDTSVILLE Adams
ARISTES Columbia
ARMAGH Indiana
ARMBRUST Westmoreland

ARNOT Tioga
ARONA Westmoreland
ARTEMAS (17211) Bedford(94), Fulton(6)
ASHFIELD Carbon
ASHLAND Schuylkill
ASHVILLE (16613) Cambria(99), Blair(1)
ASPERS Adams
ASTON Delaware
ATGLEN (19310) Chester(98), Lancaster(2)
ATHENS Bradford
ATLANTIC Crawford
ATLASBURG Washington
AUBURN Schuylkill
AUDUBON Montgomery
AULTMAN Indiana
AUSTIN (16720) Potter(84), Cameron(12), McKean(4)
AVELLA Washington
AVIS Clinton
AVONDALE Chester
AVONMORE Westmoreland
BADEN (15005) Beaver(88), Allegheny(12)
BAINBRIDGE Lancaster
BAIRDFORD Allegheny
BAKERS SUMMIT Bedford
BAKERSTOWN Allegheny
BALA CYNWYD Montgomery
BALLY Berks
BANGOR Northampton
BARNESBORO (15714) Cambria(96), Indiana(5)
BARNESVILLE Schuylkill
BART Lancaster
BARTO (19504) Montgomery(58), Berks(42)
BARTONSVILLE Monroe
BATH Northampton
BAUSMAN Lancaster
BEACH HAVEN Luzerne
BEACH LAKE (18405) Wayne(92), Pike(8)
BEALLSVILLE Washington
BEAR CREEK Luzerne
BEAR LAKE Warren
BEAVER Beaver
BEAVER FALLS Beaver
BEAVER MEADOWS (18216) Carbon(52), Luzerne(48)
BEAVER SPRINGS Snyder
BEAVERDALE Cambria
BEAVERTOWN Snyder
BECCARIA Clearfield
BECHTELSVILLE (19505) Montgomery(79), Berks(21)
BEDFORD Bedford
BEDMINSTER Bucks
BEECH CREEK (16822) Clinton(81), Centre(19)
BELLE VERNON (15012) Fayette(55), Westmoreland(43), Washington(1)
BELLEFONTE Centre
BELLEVILLE Mifflin
BELLWOOD Blair

BELSANO Cambria
BENDERSVILLE Adams
BENEZETT Elk
BENSALEM Bucks
BENTLEYVILLE Washington
BENTON (17814) Columbia(77), Luzerne(17), Sullivan(4), Lycoming(3)
BERLIN Somerset
BERNVILLE Berks
BERRYSBURG Dauphin
BERWICK (18603) Columbia(85), Luzerne(15)
BERWYN (99999) Chester(99), Delaware(1)
BESSEMER Lawrence
BETHEL Berks
BETHEL PARK Allegheny
BETHLEHEM (18015) Northampton(74), Lehigh(26)
BETHLEHEM (18017) Northampton(93), Lehigh(7)
BETHLEHEM (18018) Lehigh(57), Northampton(43)
BETHLEHEM Lehigh
BETHLEHEM Northampton
BEYER Indiana
BIG COVE TANNERY Fulton
BIG RUN Jefferson
BIGLER Clearfield
BIGLERVILLE (17307) Adams(99), Cumberland(1)
BIRCHRUNVILLE Chester
BIRD IN HAND Lancaster
BIRDSBORO Berks
BLACK LICK Indiana
BLAIN Perry
BLAIRS MILLS Huntingdon
BLAIRSVILLE (15717) Indiana(91), Westmoreland(9)
BLAKESLEE Monroe
BLANCHARD Centre
BLANDBURG Cambria
BLANDON Berks
BLOOMING GLEN Bucks
BLOOMSBURG Columbia
BLOSSBURG Tioga
BLUE BALL Lancaster
BLUE BELL Montgomery
BLUE RIDGE SUMMIT Franklin
BOALSBURG Centre
BOBTOWN Greene
BODINES Lycoming
BOILING SPRINGS Cumberland
BOLIVAR Westmoreland
BOSWELL Somerset
BOVARD Westmoreland
BOWERS Berks
BOWMANSDALE Cumberland
BOWMANSTOWN Carbon
BOWMANSVILLE Lancaster
BOYERS Butler
BOYERTOWN (19512) Berks(95), Montgomery(6)

BOYNTON Somerset
BRACKENRIDGE Allegheny
BRACKNEY Susquehanna
BRADDOCK Allegheny
BRADENVILLE Westmoreland
BRADFORD McKean
BRADFORDWOODS Allegheny
BRANCHDALE Schuylkill
BRANCHTON Butler
BRANDAMORE Chester
BRANDY CAMP Elk
BRAVE Greene
BREEZEWOOD (15533) Bedford(99), Fulton(1)
BREINIGSVILLE Lehigh
BRIDGEPORT Montgomery
BRIDGEVILLE (15017) Allegheny(94), Washington(6)
BRIER HILL Fayette
BRISBIN Clearfield
BRISTOL Bucks
BROAD TOP Huntingdon
BROCKPORT (15823) Elk(69), Jefferson(31)
BROCKTON Schuylkill
BROCKWAY (15824) Jefferson(99), Clearfield(2)
BRODHEADSVILLE Monroe
BROGUE York
BROOKHAVEN Delaware
BROOKLYN Susquehanna
BROOKVILLE Jefferson
BROOMALL Delaware
BROWNFIELD Fayette
BROWNSTOWN Lancaster
BROWNSVILLE (15417) Fayette(63), Washington(37)
BRUIN Butler
BRUSH VALLEY Indiana
BRYN ATHYN Montgomery
BRYN MAWR (19010) Delaware(53), Montgomery(47)
BUCK HILL FALLS Monroe
BUCKINGHAM Bucks
BUENA VISTA Allegheny
BUFFALO MILLS (15534) Somerset(90), Bedford(11)
BULGER Washington
BUNOLA Allegheny
BURGETTSTOWN Washington
BURLINGTON Bradford
BURNHAM Mifflin
BURNSIDE Clearfield
BURNT CABINS (17215) Fulton(75), Huntingdon(25)
BUSHKILL Pike
BUTLER Butler
BYRNEDALE Elk
CABOT (16023) Butler(99), Armstrong(1)
CADOGAN Armstrong
CAIRNBROOK Somerset
CALIFORNIA Washington
CALLENSBURG Clarion

CALLERY Butler
CALUMET Westmoreland
CALVIN Huntingdon
CAMBRA Luzerne
CAMBRIDGE SPRINGS (16403) Crawford(94), Erie(6)
CAMP HILL (17011) Cumberland(98), York(2)
CAMP HILL Cumberland
CAMPBELLTOWN Lebanon
CAMPTOWN Bradford
CANADENSIS (18325) Monroe(71), Pike(29)
CANONSBURG Washington
CANTON (17724) Bradford(87), Tioga(8), Lycoming(4)
CARBONDALE (18407) Lackawanna(99), Susquehanna(1)
CARDALE Fayette
CARLISLE Cumberland
CARLTON (16311) Mercer(96), Venango(4)
CARMICHAELS Greene
CARNEGIE Allegheny
CARROLLTOWN Cambria
CARVERSVILLE Bucks
CASHTOWN Adams
CASSANDRA Cambria
CASSVILLE Huntingdon
CASTANEA Clinton
CATASAUQUA (18032) Lehigh(69), Northampton(31)
CATAWISSA (17820) Columbia(97), Montour(3)
CECIL Washington
CEDAR RUN Lycoming
CEDARS Montgomery
CENTER VALLEY Lehigh
CENTERPORT Berks
CENTERVILLE Crawford
CENTRAL CITY Somerset
CENTRALIA Columbia
CENTRE HALL Centre
CHADDS FORD (19317) Delaware(65), Chester(35)
CHALFONT Bucks
CHALKHILL Fayette
CHAMBERSBURG Franklin
CHAMBERSVILLE Indiana
CHAMPION (15622) Westmoreland(37), Fayette(36), Somerset(27)
CHANDLERS VALLEY Warren
CHARLEROI Washington
CHATHAM Chester
CHELTENHAM Montgomery
CHERRY TREE (15724) Indiana(63), Cambria(24), Clearfield(13)
CHERRYVILLE Northampton
CHEST SPRINGS Cambria
CHESTER Delaware
CHESTER HEIGHTS Delaware
CHESTER SPRINGS Chester
CHESTNUT RIDGE Fayette
CHESWICK Allegheny
CHEYNEY (19319) Delaware(97), Chester(3)
CHICORA (16025) Butler(97), Armstrong(4)
CHINCHILLA Lackawanna
CHRISTIANA Lancaster
CLAIRTON Allegheny
CLARENCE Centre
CLARENDON Warren
CLARIDGE Westmoreland
CLARINGTON (15828) Forest(50), Jefferson(50)
CLARION Clarion
CLARK Mercer
CLARKS MILLS Mercer
CLARKS SUMMIT Lackawanna
CLARKSBURG Indiana
CLARKSVILLE (15322) Greene(62), Washington(38)

CLAYSBURG (16625) Bedford(77), Blair(23)
CLAYSVILLE Washington
CLEARFIELD Clearfield
CLEARVILLE Bedford
CLIFFORD Susquehanna
CLIFTON HEIGHTS Delaware
CLIMAX Armstrong
CLINTON (15026) Beaver(79), Allegheny(15), Washington(6)
CLINTONVILLE Venango
CLUNE Indiana
CLYMER Indiana
COAL CENTER Washington
COAL TOWNSHIP Northumberland
COALDALE Schuylkill
COALPORT (16627) Clearfield(71), Cambria(29)
COATESVILLE Chester
COBURN Centre
COCHRANTON (16314) Crawford(70), Mercer(29)
COCHRANVILLE Chester
COCOLAMUS Juniata
CODORUS York
COGAN STATION Lycoming
COKEBURG Washington
COLEBROOK Lebanon
COLLEGEVILLE Montgomery
COLMAR Montgomery
COLUMBIA Lancaster
COLUMBIA CROSS ROADS (16914) Bradford(93), Tioga(8)
COLUMBUS Warren
COLVER Cambria
COMMODORE Indiana
CONCORD Franklin
CONCORDVILLE Delaware
CONESTOGA Lancaster
CONFLUENCE (15424) Somerset(81), Fayette(19)
CONNEAUT LAKE Crawford
CONNEAUTVILLE Crawford
CONNELLSVILLE Fayette
CONNOQUENESSING Butler
CONSHOHOCKEN Montgomery
CONWAY Beaver
CONYNGHAM Luzerne
COOKSBURG (16217) Forest(63), Clarion(37)
COOLSPRING Jefferson
COOPERSBURG (18036) Lehigh(88), Bucks(12)
COOPERSTOWN (16317) Venango(68), Crawford(32)
COPLAY Lehigh
CORAL Indiana
CORAOPOLIS Allegheny
CORNWALL Lebanon
CORRY (16407) Erie(87), Warren(7), Crawford(6)
CORSICA (15829) Jefferson(80), Clarion(20)
COUDERSPORT Potter
COULTERS Allegheny
COUPON Cambria
COURTNEY Washington
COVINGTON Tioga
COWANESQUE Tioga
COWANSVILLE Armstrong
CRABTREE Westmoreland
CRALEY York
CRANBERRY Venango
CRANBERRY TWP Butler
CRANESVILLE Erie
CREAMERY Montgomery
CREEKSIDE (15732) Indiana(90), Armstrong(10)
CREIGHTON Allegheny
CRESCO (99999) Monroe(98), Pike(1)
CRESSON Cambria
CRESSONA Schuylkill

CROSBY McKean
CROSS FORK (17729) Potter(73), Clinton(27)
CROWN Clarion
CROYDON Bucks
CRUCIBLE Greene
CRUM LYNNE Delaware
CRYSTAL SPRING Fulton
CUDDY Allegheny
CUMBOLA Schuylkill
CURLLSVILLE Clarion
CURRYVILLE Blair
CURTISVILLE Allegheny
CURWENSVILLE Clearfield
CUSTER CITY McKean
CYCLONE McKean
DAGUS MINES Elk
DAISYTOWN Washington
DALLAS (18612) Luzerne(97), Wyoming(3)
DALLAS Luzerne
DALLASTOWN York
DALMATIA (17017) Northumberland(62), Dauphin(38)
DALTON (18414) Lackawanna(78), Wyoming(22)
DAMASCUS Wayne
DANBORO Bucks
DANIELSVILLE Northampton
DANVILLE (17821) Montour(81), Northumberland(16), Columbia(3)
DANVILLE Montour
DARBY Delaware
DARLINGTON Beaver
DARRAGH Westmoreland
DAUBERVILLE Berks
DAUPHIN Dauphin
DAVIDSVILLE Somerset
DAWSON Fayette
DAYTON (16222) Armstrong(53), Indiana(44), Jefferson(3)
DE LANCEY Jefferson
DE YOUNG Elk
DEFIANCE Bedford
DELANO Schuylkill
DELAWARE WATER GAP Monroe
DELMONT Westmoreland
DELTA York
DENBO Washington
DENVER Lancaster
DERRICK CITY McKean
DERRY Westmoreland
DEVAULT Chester
DEVON Chester
DEWART Northumberland
DICKERSON RUN Fayette
DICKINSON Cumberland
DICKSON CITY Lackawanna
DILLINER Greene
DILLSBURG (99999) York(98), Cumberland(1)
DILLTOWN Indiana
DIMOCK Susquehanna
DINGMANS FERRY Pike
DISTANT Armstrong
DIXONVILLE Indiana
DONEGAL Westmoreland
DONORA Washington
DORNSIFE Northumberland
DOUGLASSVILLE Berks
DOVER York
DOWNINGTOWN Chester
DOYLESBURG Franklin
DOYLESTOWN Bucks
DRAVOSBURG Allegheny
DRESHER Montgomery
DREXEL HILL Delaware
DRIFTING Clearfield
DRIFTON Luzerne
DRIFTWOOD (15832) Cameron(95), Elk(5)
DRUMORE Lancaster
DRUMS Luzerne
DRY RUN Franklin

DU BOIS Clearfield
DUBLIN Bucks
DUDLEY Huntingdon
DUKE CENTER McKean
DUNBAR Fayette
DUNCANNON Perry
DUNCANSVILLE Blair
DUNLEVY Washington
DUNLO Cambria
DUQUESNE Allegheny
DURHAM Bucks
DURYEA Luzerne
DUSHORE (18614) Sullivan(98), Wyoming(2)
DYSART (16636) Cambria(97), Blair(3)
EAGLES MERE Sullivan
EAGLEVILLE Montgomery
EARLINGTON Montgomery
EARLVILLE Berks
EAST BERLIN (17316) Adams(67), York(33)
EAST BRADY (16028) Clarion(53), Armstrong(48)
EAST BUTLER Butler
EAST EARL Lancaster
EAST FREEDOM Blair
EAST GREENVILLE (18041) Montgomery(73), Lehigh(21), Bucks(4), Berks(2)
EAST HICKORY Forest
EAST MC KEESPORT Allegheny
EAST MILLSBORO Fayette
EAST PETERSBURG Lancaster
EAST PITTSBURGH Allegheny
EAST PROSPECT York
EAST SMETHPORT McKean
EAST SMITHFIELD Bradford
EAST SPRINGFIELD Erie
EAST STROUDSBURG Monroe
EAST TEXAS Lehigh
EAST VANDERGRIFT Westmoreland
EAST WATERFORD (17021) Juniata(89), Huntingdon(5), Franklin(4), Perry(3)
EASTON Northampton
EAU CLAIRE Butler
EBENSBURG Cambria
EBERVALE Luzerne
EDGEMONT Delaware
EDINBORO (16412) Erie(74), Crawford(26)
EDINBORO Erie
EDINBURG Lawrence
EDMON Armstrong
EFFORT Monroe
EIGHTY FOUR Washington
ELCO Washington
ELDERSVILLE Washington
ELDERTON Armstrong
ELDRED McKean
ELGIN Erie
ELIZABETH Allegheny
ELIZABETHTOWN (17022) Lancaster(88), Dauphin(12)
ELIZABETHVILLE Dauphin
ELKINS PARK Montgomery
ELKLAND Tioga
ELLIOTTSBURG Perry
ELLSWORTH Washington
ELLWOOD CITY (16117) Lawrence(53), Beaver(47)
ELM Lancaster
ELMHURST Lackawanna
ELMORA Cambria
ELRAMA Washington
ELTON Cambria
ELVERSON (19520) Chester(77), Berks(23)
ELYSBURG (17824) Northumberland(85), Columbia(15)
EMEIGH Cambria
EMIGSVILLE York
EMLENTON (16373) Venango(52), Butler(25), Clarion(23)

EMMAUS Lehigh
EMPORIUM (15834) Cameron(99), Elk(1)
ENDEAVOR Forest
ENOLA Cumberland
ENON VALLEY (16120) Lawrence(80),
  Beaver(20)
ENTRIKEN Huntingdon
EPHRATA Lancaster
EQUINUNK Wayne
ERIE Erie
ERNEST Indiana
ERWINNA Bucks
ESSINGTON Delaware
ETTERS York
EVANS CITY Butler
EVERETT Bedford
EVERSON Fayette
EXCELSIOR Northumberland
EXPORT Westmoreland
EXTON Chester
FACTORYVILLE (18419) Wyoming(76),
  Lackawanna(23), Susquehanna(1)
FAIRBANK Fayette
FAIRCHANCE Fayette
FAIRFIELD Adams
FAIRHOPE Somerset
FAIRLESS HILLS Bucks
FAIRMOUNT CITY (16224) Clarion(96),
  Armstrong(4)
FAIRVIEW Erie
FAIRVIEW VILLAGE Montgomery
FALLENTIMBER (16639) Cambria(95),
  Clearfield(5)
FALLS (18615) Wyoming(89), Luzerne(9),
  Lackawanna(3)
FALLS CREEK (15840) Jefferson(93),
  Clearfield(7)
FANNETTSBURG Franklin
FARMINGTON Fayette
FARRANDSVILLE Clinton
FARRELL Mercer
FAWN GROVE York
FAYETTE CITY Fayette
FAYETTEVILLE (17222) Franklin(95),
  Adams(5)
FEASTERVILLE TREVOSE Bucks
FELTON York
FENELTON Butler
FERNDALE Bucks
FINLEYVILLE (15332) Washington(86),
  Allegheny(14)
FIRST NAT BANK Erie
FISHER Clarion
FISHERTOWN Bedford
FLEETVILLE Lackawanna
FLEETWOOD Berks
FLEMING Centre
FLICKSVILLE Northampton
FLINTON Cambria
FLOURTOWN Montgomery
FOGELSVILLE Lehigh
FOLCROFT Delaware
FOLSOM Delaware
FOMBELL (16123) Beaver(98),
  Lawrence(2)
FORBES ROAD Westmoreland
FORCE Elk
FORD CITY Armstrong
FORD CLIFF Armstrong
FOREST CITY (18421) Susquehanna(60),
  Wayne(22), Lackawanna(18)
FOREST GROVE Bucks
FORESTVILLE Butler
FORKSVILLE Sullivan
FORT HILL Somerset
FORT LITTLETON Fulton
FORT LOUDON (17224) Franklin(99),
  Fulton(1)
FORT WASHINGTON Montgomery
FOUNTAINVILLE Bucks
FOXBURG Clarion
FRACKVILLE Schuylkill

FRANCONIA Montgomery
FRANKLIN Venango
FRANKLINTOWN York
FREDERICK Montgomery
FREDERICKSBURG (17026) Lebanon(90),
  Berks(10)
FREDERICKTOWN Washington
FREDONIA Mercer
FREEBURG Snyder
FREEDOM Beaver
FREELAND Luzerne
FREEPORT (16229) Armstrong(76),
  Butler(16), Westmoreland(7),
  Allegheny(2)
FRENCHVILLE Clearfield
FRIEDENS Somerset
FRIEDENSBURG Schuylkill
FRIENDSVILLE Susquehanna
FROSTBURG Jefferson
FRYBURG Clarion
FURLONG Bucks
GAINES (16921) Tioga(95), Potter(5)
GALETON Potter
GALLITZIN (16641) Cambria(97), Blair(3)
GANS Fayette
GAP (17527) Lancaster(92), Chester(8)
GARARDS FORT Greene
GARDENVILLE Bucks
GARDNERS (17324) Adams(63),
  Cumberland(37)
GARLAND Warren
GARRETT Somerset
GASTONVILLE Washington
GEIGERTOWN Berks
GENESEE Potter
GEORGETOWN Beaver
GERMANSVILLE Lehigh
GETTYSBURG Adams
GIBBON GLADE Fayette
GIBSON Susquehanna
GIBSONIA (15044) Allegheny(97), Butler(4)
GIFFORD McKean
GILBERT Monroe
GILBERTON Schuylkill
GILBERTSVILLE Montgomery
GILLETT Bradford
GIPSY Indiana
GIRARD Erie
GIRARDVILLE Schuylkill
GLADWYNE Montgomery
GLASGOW Cambria
GLASSPORT Allegheny
GLEN CAMPBELL (15742) Indiana(90),
  Clearfield(10)
GLEN HOPE Clearfield
GLEN LYON Luzerne
GLEN MILLS (19342) Delaware(98),
  Chester(2)
GLEN RICHEY Clearfield
GLEN RIDDLE LIMA Delaware
GLEN ROCK York
GLENMOORE Chester
GLENOLDEN Delaware
GLENSHAW Allegheny
GLENSIDE Montgomery
GLENVILLE York
GLENWILLARD Allegheny
GOODVILLE Lancaster
GORDON Schuylkill
GORDONVILLE Lancaster
GOULDSBORO (18424) Wayne(52),
  Lackawanna(31), Luzerne(15),
  Monroe(3)
GOWEN CITY Northumberland
GRADYVILLE Delaware
GRAMPIAN Clearfield
GRAND VALLEY Warren
GRANTHAM Cumberland
GRANTVILLE (17028) Dauphin(90),
  Lebanon(10)
GRANVILLE Mifflin
GRANVILLE SUMMIT Bradford

GRAPEVILLE Westmoreland
GRASSFLAT Clearfield
GRATZ Dauphin
GRAY Somerset
GRAYSVILLE Greene
GREAT BEND Susquehanna
GREELEY Pike
GREEN LANE (18054) Montgomery(83),
  Bucks(17)
GREEN PARK Perry
GREENCASTLE Franklin
GREENOCK Allegheny
GREENSBORO Greene
GREENSBURG Westmoreland
GREENTOWN Pike
GREENVILLE (16125) Mercer(95),
  Crawford(5)
GRINDSTONE Fayette
GROVE CITY (16127) Mercer(92),
  Butler(5), Venango(3)
GROVER Bradford
GUYS MILLS (16327) Crawford(99),
  Venango(2)
GWYNEDD Montgomery
GWYNEDD VALLEY Montgomery
HADLEY Mercer
HALIFAX Dauphin
HALLSTEAD Susquehanna
HAMBURG Berks
HAMILTON Jefferson
HAMLIN Wayne
HANNASTOWN Westmoreland
HANOVER (17331) York(83), Adams(17)
HANOVER York
HARBORCREEK Erie
HARFORD Susquehanna
HARLEIGH Luzerne
HARLEYSVILLE Montgomery
HARMONSBURG Crawford
HARMONY (16037) Butler(91),
  Lawrence(5), Beaver(4)
HARRISBURG Dauphin
HARRISON CITY Westmoreland
HARRISON VALLEY Potter
HARRISONVILLE Fulton
HARRISVILLE (16038) Butler(80),
  Venango(20)
HARTLETON Union
HARTSTOWN Crawford
HARVEYS LAKE (18618) Luzerne(83),
  Wyoming(17)
HARWICK Allegheny
HASTINGS (16646) Cambria(99),
  Clearfield(1)
HATBORO (19040) Montgomery(96),
  Bucks(4)
HATFIELD (19440) Montgomery(91),
  Bucks(9)
HAVERFORD (19041) Montgomery(75),
  Delaware(25)
HAVERTOWN Delaware
HAWK RUN Clearfield
HAWLEY (18428) Wayne(71), Pike(29)
HAWTHORN Clarion
HAZEL HURST McKean
HAZLETON Luzerne
HEGINS Schuylkill
HEILWOOD Indiana
HELFENSTEIN Schuylkill
HELLERTOWN (18055) Northampton(97),
  Bucks(3)
HENDERSONVILLE Washington
HENRYVILLE Monroe
HEREFORD Berks
HERMAN Butler
HERMINIE Westmoreland
HERMITAGE Mercer
HERNDON (17830) Northumberland(98),
  Dauphin(2)
HERRICK CENTER Susquehanna
HERSHEY (17033) Dauphin(97),
  Lebanon(3)

HESSTON Huntingdon
HIBBS Fayette
HICKORY Washington
HIDDEN VALLEY Somerset
HIGHSPIRE Dauphin
HILLER Fayette
HILLIARDS Butler
HILLSDALE Indiana
HILLSGROVE (18619) Sullivan(95),
  Lycoming(5)
HILLSVILLE Lawrence
HILLTOWN Bucks
HOLBROOK Greene
HOLICONG Bucks
HOLLIDAYSBURG Blair
HOLLSOPPLE Somerset
HOLMES Delaware
HOLTWOOD Lancaster
HOME Indiana
HOMER CITY Indiana
HOMESTEAD Allegheny
HONESDALE Wayne
HONEY BROOK (19344) Chester(90),
  Lancaster(10)
HONEY GROVE (17035) Juniata(98),
  Perry(2)
HOOKSTOWN Beaver
HOOVERSVILLE Somerset
HOP BOTTOM Susquehanna
HOPELAND Lancaster
HOPEWELL Bedford
HOPWOOD Fayette
HORSHAM Montgomery
HOSTETTER Westmoreland
HOUSTON Washington
HOUTZDALE Clearfield
HOWARD Centre
HUGHESVILLE Lycoming
HUMMELS WHARF Snyder
HUMMELSTOWN Dauphin
HUNKER Westmoreland
HUNLOCK CREEK Luzerne
HUNTINGDON Huntingdon
HUNTINGDON VALLEY (19006)
  Montgomery(94), Bucks(6)
HUNTINGTON MILLS Luzerne
HUSTONTOWN (17229) Fulton(90),
  Huntingdon(11)
HUTCHINSON Westmoreland
HYDE Clearfield
HYDE PARK Westmoreland
HYDETOWN Crawford
HYNDMAN (15545) Bedford(75),
  Somerset(25)
HYNER Clinton
ICKESBURG Perry
IDAVILLE Adams
IMLER Bedford
IMMACULATA Chester
IMPERIAL Allegheny
INDIAN HEAD Fayette
INDIANA Indiana
INDIANOLA Allegheny
INDUSTRY Beaver
INGOMAR Allegheny
INTERCOURSE Lancaster
IRVINE Warren
IRVONA Clearfield
IRWIN Westmoreland
ISABELLA Fayette
JACKSON Susquehanna
JACKSON CENTER Mercer
JACOBS CREEK Westmoreland
JAMES CITY Elk
JAMES CREEK (16657) Huntingdon(97),
  Bedford(4)
JAMESTOWN (16134) Crawford(91),
  Mercer(9)
JAMISON Bucks
JEANNETTE Westmoreland
JEFFERSON Greene
JENKINTOWN Montgomery

JENNERS Somerset
JENNERSTOWN Somerset
JERMYN Lackawanna
JEROME Somerset
JERSEY MILLS Lycoming
JERSEY SHORE (17740) Lycoming(89),
    Clinton(11)
JERSEY SHORE Lycoming
JESSUP Lackawanna
JIM THORPE Carbon
JOFFRE Washington
JOHNSONBURG Elk
JOHNSTOWN (15905) Cambria(86),
    Somerset(14)
JOHNSTOWN Cambria
JONES MILLS Westmoreland
JONESTOWN Lebanon
JOSEPHINE Indiana
JULIAN Centre
JUNEAU Indiana
JUNEDALE Carbon
KANE (16735) McKean(97), Elk(3)
KANTNER Somerset
KARNS CITY (16041) Butler(89),
    Armstrong(12)
KARTHAUS (16845) Clearfield(60),
    Centre(41)
KEISTERVILLE Fayette
KELAYRES Schuylkill
KELTON Chester
KEMBLESVILLE Chester
KEMPTON (19529) Berks(62), Lehigh(38)
KENNERDELL Venango
KENNETT SQUARE Chester
KENT Indiana
KERSEY Elk
KIMBERTON Chester
KING OF PRUSSIA Chester
KING OF PRUSSIA Montgomery
KINGSLEY Susquehanna
KINGSTON Luzerne
KINTNERSVILLE Bucks
KINZERS Lancaster
KIRKWOOD Lancaster
KITTANNING Armstrong
KLEINFELTERSVILLE Lebanon
KLINGERSTOWN (17941) Schuylkill(79),
    Northumberland(21)
KNOX Clarion
KNOX DALE Jefferson
KNOXVILLE Tioga
KOPPEL Beaver
KOSSUTH Clarion
KREAMER Snyder
KRESGEVILLE Monroe
KULPMONT Northumberland
KULPSVILLE Montgomery
KUNKLETOWN (18058) Monroe(95),
    Carbon(5)
KUTZTOWN (19530) Berks(87), Lehigh(13)
KYLERTOWN Clearfield
LA BELLE Fayette
LA JOSE Clearfield
LA PLUME Lackawanna
LACEYVILLE (18623) Wyoming(45),
    Bradford(36), Susquehanna(20)
LACKAWAXEN Pike
LAFAYETTE HILL Montgomery
LAHASKA Bucks
LAIRDSVILLE Lycoming
LAKE ARIEL (18436) Wayne(85),
    Lackawanna(15)
LAKE CITY Erie
LAKE COMO Wayne
LAKE HARMONY Carbon
LAKE LYNN Fayette
LAKE WINOLA Wyoming
LAKEVILLE Wayne
LAKEWOOD Wayne
LAMAR Clinton
LAMARTINE Clarion
LAMPETER Lancaster

LANCASTER Lancaster
LANDENBERG Chester
LANDINGVILLE Schuylkill
LANDISBURG Perry
LANDISVILLE Lancaster
LANESBORO Susquehanna
LANGELOTH Washington
LANGHORNE Bucks
LANSDALE Montgomery
LANSDOWNE Delaware
LANSE Clearfield
LANSFORD Carbon
LAPORTE Sullivan
LARIMER Westmoreland
LATROBE Westmoreland
LATTIMER MINES Luzerne
LAUGHLINTOWN Westmoreland
LAURELTON Union
LAURYS STATION Lehigh
LAVELLE Schuylkill
LAWN Lebanon
LAWRENCE Washington
LAWRENCEVILLE Tioga
LAWTON Susquehanna
LE RAYSVILLE (18829) Bradford(93),
    Susquehanna(7)
LEBANON Lebanon
LECK KILL (17836) Northumberland(88),
    Schuylkill(12)
LECKRONE Fayette
LECONTES MILLS Clearfield
LEDERACH Montgomery
LEECHBURG (15656) Armstrong(55),
    Westmoreland(45)
LEEPER Clarion
LEESPORT Berks
LEETSDALE Allegheny
LEHIGH VALLEY Lehigh
LEHIGH VALLEY Northampton
LEHIGHTON Carbon
LEHMAN Luzerne
LEISENRING Fayette
LEMASTERS Franklin
LEMONT Centre
LEMONT FURNACE Fayette
LEMOYNE Cumberland
LENHARTSVILLE Berks
LENNI Delaware
LENOXVILLE Susquehanna
LEOLA Lancaster
LEROY Bradford
LEVITTOWN Bucks
LEWIS RUN McKean
LEWISBERRY York
LEWISBURG Union
LEWISTOWN Mifflin
LEWISVILLE Chester
LIBERTY (16930) Tioga(75), Lycoming(25)
LIBRARY Allegheny
LICKINGVILLE Clarion
LIGHT STREET Columbia
LIGONIER Westmoreland
LILLY Cambria
LIMEKILN Berks
LIMEPORT Lehigh
LIMESTONE Clarion
LINCOLN UNIVERSITY Chester
LINDEN Lycoming
LINE LEXINGTON (18932) Bucks(93),
    Montgomery(8)
LINESVILLE Crawford
LIONVILLE Chester
LISTIE Somerset
LITITZ Lancaster
LITTLE MEADOWS (18830)
    Susquehanna(94), Bradford(6)
LITTLESTOWN Adams
LIVERPOOL (17045) Perry(65),
    Juniata(28), Snyder(7)
LLEWELLYN Schuylkill
LOCK HAVEN (99999) Clinton(99),
    Lycoming(1)

LOCUST GAP Northumberland
LOCUSTDALE Schuylkill
LOGANTON Clinton
LOGANVILLE York
LONG POND Monroe
LOPEZ Sullivan
LORETTO Cambria
LOST CREEK Schuylkill
LOWBER Westmoreland
LOYALHANNA Westmoreland
LOYSBURG Bedford
LOYSVILLE Perry
LUCERNEMINES Indiana
LUCINDA Clarion
LUDLOW McKean
LUMBERVILLE Bucks
LURGAN Franklin
LUTHERSBURG Clearfield
LUXOR Westmoreland
LUZERNE Luzerne
LYKENS Dauphin
LYNDELL Chester
LYNDORA Butler
LYON STATION Berks
MACKEYVILLE Clinton
MACUNGIE (18062) Lehigh(87), Berks(13)
MADERA Clearfield
MADISON Westmoreland
MADISONBURG Centre
MAHAFFEY (15757) Clearfield(99),
    Indiana(1)
MAHANOY CITY Schuylkill
MAHANOY PLANE Schuylkill
MAINESBURG Tioga
MAINLAND Montgomery
MALVERN Chester
MAMMOTH Westmoreland
MANCHESTER York
MANHEIM (17545) Lancaster(98),
    Lebanon(2)
MANNS CHOICE Bedford
MANOR Westmoreland
MANORVILLE Armstrong
MANSFIELD Tioga
MAPLETON DEPOT Huntingdon
MAR LIN Schuylkill
MARBLE Clarion
MARCHAND Indiana
MARCUS HOOK Delaware
MARIANNA Washington
MARIENVILLE (16239) Forest(98),
    Clarion(2)
MARIETTA Lancaster
MARION Franklin
MARION CENTER Indiana
MARION HEIGHTS Northumberland
MARKLETON Somerset
MARKLEYSBURG Fayette
MARS (16046) Butler(84), Allegheny(17)
MARSHALLS CREEK Monroe
MARSTELLER Cambria
MARTIN Fayette
MARTINDALE Lancaster
MARTINS CREEK Northampton
MARTINSBURG (16662) Blair(98),
    Bedford(2)
MARY D Schuylkill
MARYSVILLE (17053) Perry(97),
    Cumberland(3)
MASONTOWN Fayette
MATAMORAS Pike
MATHER Greene
MATTAWANA Mifflin
MAXATAWNY Berks
MAYPORT (16240) Jefferson(44),
    Clarion(29), Armstrong(27)
MAYTOWN Lancaster
MC ALISTERVILLE Juniata
MC CLELLANDTOWN Fayette
MC CLURE (17841) Mifflin(83), Snyder(17)
MC CONNELLSBURG Fulton
MC CONNELLSTOWN Huntingdon

MC DONALD (15057) Washington(84),
    Allegheny(16)
MC ELHATTAN Clinton
MC EWENSVILLE Northumberland
MC GRANN Armstrong
MC INTYRE Indiana
MC KEAN Erie
MC KEES ROCKS Allegheny
MC KEESPORT (15131) Allegheny(92),
    Westmoreland(8)
MC KEESPORT Allegheny
MC KNIGHTSTOWN Adams
MC SHERRYSTOWN Adams
MC VEYTOWN Mifflin
MCADOO (18237) Schuylkill(98),
    Carbon(2)
MEADOW LANDS Washington
MEADVILLE Crawford
MECHANICSBURG (17055)
    Cumberland(99), York(1)
MECHANICSVILLE Bucks
MEDIA Delaware
MEHOOPANY Wyoming
MELCROFT Fayette
MENDENHALL Chester
MENGES MILLS York
MENTCLE Indiana
MERCER Mercer
MERCERSBURG (17236) Franklin(99),
    Fulton(2)
MERION STATION Montgomery
MERRITTSTOWN Fayette
MERTZTOWN (19539) Berks(90),
    Lehigh(10)
MESHOPPEN (18630) Susquehanna(54),
    Wyoming(46)
MEXICO Juniata
MEYERSDALE Somerset
MIDDLEBURG Snyder
MIDDLEBURY CENTER Tioga
MIDDLEPORT Schuylkill
MIDDLETOWN Dauphin
MIDLAND Beaver
MIDWAY Washington
MIFFLIN Juniata
MIFFLINBURG Union
MIFFLINTOWN Juniata
MIFFLINVILLE Columbia
MILAN Bradford
MILANVILLE Wayne
MILDRED Sullivan
MILESBURG Centre
MILFORD Pike
MILFORD SQUARE Bucks
MILL CREEK (17060) Huntingdon(98),
    Mifflin(2)
MILL HALL Clinton
MILL RUN Fayette
MILL VILLAGE Erie
MILLERSBURG Dauphin
MILLERSTOWN (17062) Perry(77),
    Juniata(23)
MILLERSVILLE Lancaster
MILLERTON (16936) Tioga(87),
    Bradford(13)
MILLHEIM Centre
MILLMONT Union
MILLRIFT Pike
MILLS Potter
MILLSBORO Washington
MILLVILLE (17846) Columbia(98),
    Lycoming(3)
MILNESVILLE Luzerne
MILROY Mifflin
MILTON (17847) Northumberland(98),
    Montour(3)
MINERAL POINT Cambria
MINERAL SPRINGS Clearfield
MINERSVILLE Schuylkill
MINGOVILLE Centre
MINISINK HILLS Monroe
MIQUON Montgomery

MODENA Chester
MOHNTON (19540) Berks(93),
   Lancaster(7)
MOHRSVILLE Berks
MONACA Beaver
MONESSEN Westmoreland
MONOCACY STATION Berks
MONONGAHELA (15063) Washington(94),
   Allegheny(6)
MONROETON Bradford
MONROEVILLE Allegheny
MONT ALTO Franklin
MONT CLARE Montgomery
MONTANDON Northumberland
MONTGOMERY Lycoming
MONTGOMERYVILLE Montgomery
MONTOURSVILLE Lycoming
MONTROSE Susquehanna
MOOSIC (18507) Lackawanna(99),
   Luzerne(1)
MORANN Clearfield
MORGAN Allegheny
MORGANTOWN (19543) Berks(71),
   Lancaster(27), Chester(2)
MORRIS (16938) Tioga(70), Lycoming(30)
MORRIS RUN Tioga
MORRISDALE Clearfield
MORRISVILLE Bucks
MORTON Delaware
MOSCOW (18444) Lackawanna(91),
   Wayne(9)
MOSHANNON Centre
MOUNT AETNA Berks
MOUNT BETHEL Northampton
MOUNT BRADDOCK Fayette
MOUNT CARMEL Northumberland
MOUNT GRETNA Lebanon
MOUNT HOLLY SPRINGS Cumberland
MOUNT JEWETT McKean
MOUNT JOY Lancaster
MOUNT MORRIS Greene
MOUNT PLEASANT (15666)
   Westmoreland(94), Fayette(7)
MOUNT PLEASANT MILLS (17853)
   Snyder(87), Juniata(13)
MOUNT POCONO Monroe
MOUNT UNION (17066) Huntingdon(70),
   Mifflin(30)
MOUNT WOLF York
MOUNTAIN TOP Luzerne
MOUNTAINHOME Monroe
MOUNTVILLE Lancaster
MUIR Schuylkill
MUNCY (17756) Lycoming(90),
   Northumberland(8), Montour(2)
MUNCY VALLEY (17758) Sullivan(81),
   Lycoming(19)
MUNSON (16860) Clearfield(69),
   Centre(31)
MURRYSVILLE Westmoreland
MUSE Washington
MYERSTOWN (17067) Lebanon(89),
   Berks(11)
NANTICOKE Luzerne
NANTY GLO Cambria
NARBERTH Montgomery
NARVON (17555) Lancaster(96),
   Chester(2), Berks(2)
NATRONA HEIGHTS Allegheny
NAZARETH Northampton
NEEDMORE Fulton
NEELYTON Huntingdon
NEFFS Lehigh
NELSON Tioga
NEMACOLIN Greene
NESCOPECK (18635) Luzerne(83),
   Columbia(17)
NESQUEHONING (18240) Carbon(84),
   Schuylkill(16)
NEW ALBANY (18833) Bradford(89),
   Sullivan(11)
NEW ALEXANDRIA Westmoreland

NEW BALTIMORE Somerset
NEW BEDFORD Lawrence
NEW BERLIN Union
NEW BERLINVILLE Berks
NEW BETHLEHEM (16242) Clarion(71),
   Armstrong(29)
NEW BLOOMFIELD Perry
NEW BRIGHTON Beaver
NEW BUFFALO Perry
NEW CASTLE Lawrence
NEW COLUMBIA Union
NEW CUMBERLAND (17070)
   Cumberland(60), York(40)
NEW DERRY Westmoreland
NEW EAGLE Washington
NEW ENTERPRISE Bedford
NEW FLORENCE (15944) Indiana(83),
   Westmoreland(17)
NEW FREEDOM York
NEW FREEPORT Greene
NEW GALILEE (16141) Beaver(67),
   Lawrence(33)
NEW GENEVA Fayette
NEW GERMANTOWN Perry
NEW HOLLAND Lancaster
NEW HOPE Bucks
NEW KENSINGTON (15068)
   Westmoreland(92), Allegheny(8)
NEW KENSINGTON Westmoreland
NEW KINGSTOWN Cumberland
NEW LONDON Chester
NEW MILFORD Susquehanna
NEW MILLPORT Clearfield
NEW OXFORD Adams
NEW PARIS Bedford
NEW PARK York
NEW PHILADELPHIA Schuylkill
NEW PROVIDENCE Lancaster
NEW RINGGOLD Schuylkill
NEW SALEM Fayette
NEW STANTON Westmoreland
NEW TRIPOLI Lehigh
NEW WILMINGTON (16142) Mercer(67),
   Lawrence(33)
NEW WILMINGTON Lawrence
NEWBURG (17240) Cumberland(72),
   Franklin(28)
NEWELL Fayette
NEWFOUNDLAND (18445) Wayne(85),
   Pike(14)
NEWMANSTOWN (17073) Lebanon(99),
   Lancaster(1)
NEWPORT Perry
NEWRY Blair
NEWTON HAMILTON Mifflin
NEWTOWN Bucks
NEWTOWN SQUARE Delaware
NEWVILLE Cumberland
NICHOLSON (18446) Wyoming(49),
   Susquehanna(48), Lackawanna(4)
NICKTOWN Cambria
NINEVEH Greene
NISBET Lycoming
NORMALVILLE Fayette
NORRISTOWN Chester
NORRISTOWN Montgomery
NORTH APOLLO Armstrong
NORTH BEND Clinton
NORTH EAST Erie
NORTH SPRINGFIELD Erie
NORTH VERSAILLES Allegheny
NORTH WALES (19454) Montgomery(80),
   Bucks(20)
NORTH WALES Montgomery
NORTH WASHINGTON Butler
NORTHAMPTON Northampton
NORTHPOINT (15763) Indiana(78),
   Jefferson(22)
NORTHUMBERLAND Northumberland
NORVELT Westmoreland
NORWOOD Delaware

NOTTINGHAM (19362) Chester(99),
   Lancaster(1)
NOXEN (18636) Wyoming(85),
   Luzerne(15)
NU MINE Armstrong
NUANGOLA Luzerne
NUMIDIA Columbia
NUREMBERG (18241) Schuylkill(90),
   Luzerne(10)
OAK RIDGE Armstrong
OAKDALE Allegheny
OAKLAND MILLS Juniata
OAKMONT Allegheny
OAKS Montgomery
OHIOPYLE Fayette
OIL CITY Venango
OLANTA Clearfield
OLD FORGE Lackawanna
OLD ZIONSVILLE Lehigh
OLEY Berks
OLIVEBURG Jefferson
OLIVER Fayette
OLYPHANT Lackawanna
ONEIDA Schuylkill
ONO Lebanon
ORANGEVILLE Columbia
ORBISONIA (17243) Huntingdon(95),
   Fulton(3), Juniata(2)
OREFIELD Lehigh
ORELAND Montgomery
ORRSTOWN Franklin
ORRTANNA Adams
ORSON Wayne
ORVISTON Centre
ORWIGSBURG Schuylkill
OSCEOLA Tioga
OSCEOLA MILLS (16666) Clearfield(97),
   Blair(3)
OSTERBURG Bedford
OTTSVILLE Bucks
OXFORD (19363) Chester(96),
   Lancaster(5)
PALM (18070) Montgomery(59), Berks(41)
PALMERTON Carbon
PALMYRA (17078) Lebanon(92),
   Dauphin(9)
PAOLI Chester
PARADISE Lancaster
PARDEESVILLE Luzerne
PARKER (16049) Butler(63), Clarion(22),
   Armstrong(15)
PARKER FORD Chester
PARKESBURG Chester
PARKHILL Cambria
PARRYVILLE Carbon
PATTON Cambria
PAUPACK Pike
PAXINOS Northumberland
PAXTONVILLE Snyder
PEACH BOTTOM Lancaster
PEACH GLEN Adams
PECKVILLE Lackawanna
PEN ARGYL Northampton
PENFIELD Clearfield
PENN Westmoreland
PENN RUN Indiana
PENNS CREEK Snyder
PENNS PARK Bucks
PENNSBURG (18073) Montgomery(91),
   Bucks(9)
PENNSYLVANIA FURNACE (16865)
   Centre(97), Huntingdon(3)
PENRYN Lancaster
PEQUEA Lancaster
PERKASIE Bucks
PERKIOMENVILLE Montgomery
PERRYOPOLIS Fayette
PETERSBURG Huntingdon
PETROLIA Butler
PHILADELPHIA Delaware
PHILADELPHIA Montgomery
PHILADELPHIA Philadelphia

PHILIPSBURG (16866) Centre(70),
   Clearfield(30)
PHOENIXVILLE (19460) Chester(98),
   Montgomery(2)
PICTURE ROCKS Lycoming
PILLOW Dauphin
PINE BANK Greene
PINE FORGE Berks
PINE GROVE Schuylkill
PINE GROVE MILLS Centre
PINEVILLE Bucks
PIPERSVILLE Bucks
PITCAIRN Allegheny
PITMAN (17964) Schuylkill(94),
   Northumberland(6)
PITTSBURGH (15241) Allegheny(99),
   Washington(1)
PITTSBURGH Allegheny
PITTSFIELD Warren
PITTSTON (18641) Luzerne(92),
   Lackawanna(8)
PITTSTON Luzerne
PLAINFIELD Cumberland
PLEASANT HALL Franklin
PLEASANT MOUNT Wayne
PLEASANT UNITY Westmoreland
PLEASANTVILLE (16341) Venango(82),
   Forest(18)
PLUMSTEADVILLE Bucks
PLUMVILLE Indiana
PLYMOUTH Luzerne
PLYMOUTH MEETING Montgomery
POCONO LAKE Monroe
POCONO LAKE PRESERVE Monroe
POCONO MANOR Monroe
POCONO PINES Monroe
POCONO SUMMIT Monroe
POCOPSON Chester
POINT MARION Fayette
POINT PLEASANT Bucks
POLK (16342) Venango(85), Mercer(15)
POMEROY Chester
PORT ALLEGANY (16743) McKean(97),
   Potter(3)
PORT CARBON Schuylkill
PORT CLINTON Schuylkill
PORT MATILDA Centre
PORT ROYAL Juniata
PORT TREVORTON Snyder
PORTAGE (15946) Cambria(94), Blair(3),
   Bedford(3)
PORTERS SIDELING York
PORTERSVILLE (16051) Butler(81),
   Lawrence(20)
PORTLAND Northampton
POTTERSDALE (16871) Clearfield(59),
   Clinton(41)
POTTS GROVE Northumberland
POTTSTOWN Chester
POTTSTOWN Montgomery
POTTSVILLE Schuylkill
POYNTELLE Wayne
PRESTO Allegheny
PRESTON PARK Wayne
PRICEDALE Westmoreland
PROMPTON Wayne
PROSPECT Butler
PROSPECT PARK Delaware
PROSPERITY (15329) Washington(86),
   Greene(14)
PULASKI (16143) Lawrence(54),
   Mercer(46)
PUNXSUTAWNEY (15767) Jefferson(95),
   Indiana(5), Clearfield(1)
QUAKAKE Schuylkill
QUAKERTOWN Bucks
QUARRYVILLE Lancaster
QUECREEK Somerset
QUEEN Bedford
QUENTIN Lebanon
QUINCY Franklin
RAILROAD York

RALSTON Lycoming
RAMEY Clearfield
RANSOM Lackawanna
RAVINE Schuylkill
REA Washington
READING Berks
REAMSTOWN Lancaster
REBERSBURG Centre
REBUCK Northumberland
RECTOR Westmoreland
RED HILL Montgomery
RED LION York
REEDERS Monroe
REEDSVILLE Mifflin
REFTON Lancaster
REHRERSBURG Berks
REINHOLDS (17569) Lancaster(75),
    Berks(25)
RENFREW Butler
RENO Venango
RENOVO Clinton
REPUBLIC Fayette
REVERE Bucks
REVLOC Cambria
REW McKean
REXMONT Lebanon
REYNOLDSVILLE Jefferson
RHEEMS Lancaster
RICES LANDING Greene
RICEVILLE Crawford
RICHBORO Bucks
RICHEYVILLE Washington
RICHFIELD (17086) Juniata(53),
    Snyder(47)
RICHLAND (17087) Lebanon(51),
    Berks(49)
RICHLANDTOWN Bucks
RIDDLESBURG Bedford
RIDGWAY Elk
RIDLEY PARK Delaware
RIEGELSVILLE (18077) Bucks(89),
    Northampton(11)
RILLTON Westmoreland
RIMERSBURG Clarion
RINGGOLD Jefferson
RINGTOWN Schuylkill
RIVERSIDE Northumberland
RIXFORD McKean
ROARING BRANCH (17765) Tioga(80),
    Lycoming(19), Bradford(1)
ROARING SPRING (16673) Blair(68),
    Bedford(32)
ROBERTSDALE (16674) Huntingdon(91),
    Fulton(9)
ROBESONIA (19551) Berks(92),
    Lebanon(6), Lancaster(3)
ROBINSON Indiana
ROCHESTER Beaver
ROCHESTER MILLS Indiana
ROCK GLEN Luzerne
ROCKHILL FURNACE Huntingdon
ROCKTON Clearfield
ROCKWOOD Somerset
ROGERSVILLE Greene
ROME Bradford
RONCO Fayette
RONKS Lancaster
ROSCOE Washington
ROSSITER (15772) Indiana(98),
    Jefferson(2)
ROSSVILLE York
ROULETTE Potter
ROUSEVILLE Venango
ROUZERVILLE Franklin
ROWLAND Pike
ROXBURY Franklin
ROYERSFORD Montgomery
RUFFS DALE Westmoreland
RURAL RIDGE Allegheny
RURAL VALLEY Armstrong
RUSHLAND Bucks
RUSHVILLE Susquehanna

RUSSELL Warren
RUSSELLTON Allegheny
SABINSVILLE (16943) Tioga(64),
    Potter(36)
SACRAMENTO Schuylkill
SADSBURYVILLE Chester
SAEGERTOWN Crawford
SAGAMORE (16250) Armstrong(94),
    Crawford(6)
SAINT BENEDICT Cambria
SAINT BONIFACE Cambria
SAINT CLAIR Schuylkill
SAINT JOHNS Luzerne
SAINT MARYS Elk
SAINT MICHAEL Cambria
SAINT PETERS Chester
SAINT PETERSBURG Clarion
SAINT THOMAS Franklin
SALFORD Montgomery
SALFORDVILLE Montgomery
SALINA Westmoreland
SALISBURY Somerset
SALIX Cambria
SALONA Clinton
SALTILLO Huntingdon
SALTSBURG Indiana
SANDY LAKE Mercer
SANDY RIDGE Centre
SARVER (16055) Butler(95), Armstrong(4)
SASSAMANSVILLE Montgomery
SAXONBURG Butler
SAXTON (16678) Bedford(96),
    Huntingdon(4)
SAYLORSBURG Monroe
SAYRE Bradford
SCENERY HILL Washington
SCHAEFFERSTOWN Lebanon
SCHELLSBURG Bedford
SCHENLEY Armstrong
SCHNECKSVILLE Lehigh
SCHUYLKILL HAVEN Schuylkill
SCHWENKSVILLE Montgomery
SCIOTA Monroe
SCOTLAND Franklin
SCOTRUN Monroe
SCOTTDALE (15683) Westmoreland(85),
    Fayette(15)
SCRANTON Lackawanna
SEANOR Somerset
SELINSGROVE Snyder
SELLERSVILLE Bucks
SELTZER (17974) Schuylkill(91), York(9)
SEMINOLE Armstrong
SENECA Venango
SEVEN VALLEYS York
SEWARD (15954) Indiana(91),
    Westmoreland(9)
SEWICKLEY (15143) Allegheny(94),
    Beaver(6)
SEWICKLEY Allegheny
SHADE GAP Huntingdon
SHADY GROVE Franklin
SHAMOKIN Northumberland
SHAMOKIN DAM Snyder
SHANKSVILLE Somerset
SHARON Mercer
SHARON HILL Delaware
SHARPSVILLE Mercer
SHARTLESVILLE Berks
SHAVERTOWN Luzerne
SHAWANESE Luzerne
SHAWNEE ON DELAWARE Monroe
SHAWVILLE Clearfield
SHEAKLEYVILLE Mercer
SHEFFIELD Warren
SHELOCTA (15774) Indiana(51),
    Armstrong(49)
SHENANDOAH Schuylkill
SHEPPTON Schuylkill
SHERMANS DALE (17090) Perry(95),
    Cumberland(5)

SHICKSHINNY (18655) Luzerne(93),
    Columbia(7)
SHINGLEHOUSE (16748) Potter(73),
    McKean(27)
SHIPPENSBURG (17257)
    Cumberland(63), Franklin(37)
SHIPPENVILLE Clarion
SHIPPINGPORT Beaver
SHIRLEYSBURG Huntingdon
SHOEMAKERSVILLE Berks
SHOHOLA Pike
SHREWSBURY York
SHUNK Sullivan
SIDMAN Cambria
SIGEL (15860) Jefferson(70), Elk(24),
    Clarion(7)
SILVER SPRING Lancaster
SILVERDALE Bucks
SINNAMAHONING Cameron
SIPESVILLE Somerset
SIX MILE RUN Bedford
SKIPPACK Montgomery
SKYTOP Monroe
SLATE RUN Lycoming
SLATEDALE Lehigh
SLATINGTON Lehigh
SLICKVILLE Westmoreland
SLIGO Clarion
SLIPPERY ROCK (16057) Butler(93),
    Lawrence(4), Mercer(3)
SLOVAN Washington
SMETHPORT McKean
SMICKSBURG Indiana
SMITHFIELD Fayette
SMITHMILL Clearfield
SMITHTON Westmoreland
SMOCK Fayette
SMOKERUN Clearfield
SMOKETOWN Lancaster
SNOW SHOE Centre
SNYDERSBURG Clarion
SNYDERTOWN (17877) Columbia(50),
    Northumberland(50)
SOLEBURY Bucks
SOMERSET Somerset
SONESTOWN Sullivan
SOUDERSBURG Lancaster
SOUDERTON (18964) Montgomery(95),
    Bucks(5)
SOUTH CANAAN Wayne
SOUTH FORK Cambria
SOUTH GIBSON Susquehanna
SOUTH HEIGHTS Beaver
SOUTH MONTROSE Susquehanna
SOUTH MOUNTAIN Franklin
SOUTH STERLING Wayne
SOUTHAMPTON Bucks
SOUTHEASTERN Chester
SOUTHVIEW Washington
SOUTHWEST Westmoreland
SPANGLER Cambria
SPARTANSBURG (16434) Crawford(97),
    Warren(3)
SPINNERSTOWN Bucks
SPRAGGS Greene
SPRANKLE MILLS Jefferson
SPRING CHURCH Armstrong
SPRING CITY Chester
SPRING CREEK Warren
SPRING GLEN (17978) Schuylkill(94),
    Dauphin(6)
SPRING GROVE York
SPRING HOUSE Montgomery
SPRING MILLS Centre
SPRING MOUNT Montgomery
SPRING RUN Franklin
SPRINGBORO (16435) Crawford(98),
    Erie(2)
SPRINGDALE Allegheny
SPRINGFIELD Delaware
SPRINGS Somerset
SPRINGTOWN Bucks

SPRINGVILLE (18844) Susquehanna(98),
    Wyoming(2)
SPROUL Blair
SPRUCE CREEK Huntingdon
STAHLSTOWN Westmoreland
STAR JUNCTION Fayette
STARFORD Indiana
STARLIGHT Wayne
STARRUCCA (18462) Wayne(97),
    Susquehanna(3)
STATE COLLEGE Centre
STATE LINE Franklin
STEELVILLE Chester
STERLING (18463) Wayne(71), Pike(29)
STEVENS Lancaster
STEVENSVILLE Bradford
STEWARTSTOWN York
STILLWATER (17878) Columbia(71),
    Luzerne(29)
STOCKDALE Washington
STOCKERTOWN Northampton
STONEBORO (16153) Mercer(98),
    Venango(2)
STONY RUN Berks
STOYSTOWN Somerset
STRABANE Washington
STRASBURG Lancaster
STRATTANVILLE Clarion
STRAUSSTOWN Berks
STRONGSTOWN (15957) Indiana(60),
    Cambria(40)
STROUDSBURG Monroe
STUMP CREEK Jefferson
STURGEON Allegheny
SUGAR GROVE Warren
SUGAR RUN Bradford
SUGARLOAF Luzerne
SUMMERDALE Cumberland
SUMMERHILL Cambria
SUMMERVILLE (15864) Jefferson(66),
    Clarion(34)
SUMMIT HILL (99999) Carbon(99),
    Schuylkill(1)
SUMMIT STATION Schuylkill
SUMNEYTOWN Montgomery
SUNBURY Northumberland
SUPLEE Chester
SUSQUEHANNA (18847)
    Susquehanna(97), Wayne(3)
SUTERSVILLE Westmoreland
SWARTHMORE Delaware
SWEET VALLEY Luzerne
SWENGEL Union
SWIFTWATER Monroe
SYBERTSVILLE Luzerne
SYCAMORE Greene
SYKESVILLE Jefferson
SYLVANIA Bradford
TAFTON Pike
TALMAGE Lancaster
TAMAQUA Schuylkill
TAMIMENT Pike
TANNERSVILLE Monroe
TARENTUM Allegheny
TARRS Westmoreland
TATAMY Northampton
TAYLOR Lackawanna
TAYLORSTOWN Washington
TELFORD (18969) Montgomery(60),
    Bucks(41)
TEMPLE Berks
TEMPLETON Armstrong
TERRE HILL Lancaster
THOMASVILLE York
THOMPSON (18465) Susquehanna(88),
    Wayne(12)
THOMPSONTOWN Juniata
THORNDALE Chester
THORNTON Delaware
THREE SPRINGS (17264) Huntingdon(95),
    Fulton(5)
TIDIOUTE (16351) Warren(97), Forest(3)

TIMBLIN Jefferson
TIOGA Tioga
TIONA Warren
TIONESTA (16353) Forest(71), Clarion(29)
TIPTON Blair
TIRE HILL Somerset
TITUSVILLE (16354) Crawford(90),
  Venango(9)
TOBYHANNA Monroe
TODD Huntingdon
TOPTON Berks
TORRANCE Westmoreland
TOUGHKENAMON Chester
TOWANDA Bradford
TOWER CITY (17980) Schuylkill(94),
  Dauphin(6)
TOWNVILLE Crawford
TRAFFORD (15085) Westmoreland(98),
  Allegheny(2)
TRANSFER Mercer
TREICHLERS Northampton
TREMONT Schuylkill
TRESCKOW Carbon
TREVORTON Northumberland
TREXLERTOWN Lehigh
TROUT RUN Lycoming
TROUTVILLE Clearfield
TROXELVILLE Snyder
TROY (16947) Bradford(95), Tioga(5)
TRUMBAUERSVILLE Bucks
TUNKHANNOCK Wyoming
TURBOTVILLE (17772) Montour(51),
  Northumberland(47), Columbia(2)
TURKEY CITY Clarion
TURTLE CREEK Allegheny
TURTLEPOINT McKean
TUSCARORA Schuylkill
TWIN ROCKS Cambria
TYLER HILL Wayne
TYLERSBURG Clarion
TYLERSPORT Montgomery
TYLERSVILLE Clinton
TYRONE (16686) Blair(96), Huntingdon(3)
ULEDI Fayette
ULSTER Bradford
ULYSSES Potter
UNION CITY (16438) Crawford(60),
  Erie(40)
UNION DALE (18470) Susquehanna(94),
  Wayne(6)
UNIONTOWN Fayette
UNIONVILLE Chester
UNITED Westmoreland
UNITY HOUSE Pike
UNITYVILLE (17774) Lycoming(96),
  Columbia(4)
UNIVERSITY PARK Centre
UPPER BLACK EDDY Bucks
UPPER DARBY Delaware
UPPERSTRASBURG Franklin
URSINA Somerset

UTICA (16362) Venango(55), Mercer(40),
  Crawford(5)
UWCHLAND Chester
VALENCIA (16059) Butler(93),
  Allegheny(7)
VALIER Jefferson
VALLEY FORGE Chester
VALLEY FORGE Montgomery
VALLEY VIEW Schuylkill
VAN VOORHIS Washington
VANDERBILT Fayette
VANDERGRIFT (15690)
  Westmoreland(82), Armstrong(18)
VENANGO Crawford
VENETIA Washington
VENUS Venango
VERONA Allegheny
VESTABURG Washington
VICKSBURG Union
VILLA MARIA Lawrence
VILLANOVA (19085) Delaware(53),
  Montgomery(47)
VINTONDALE (15961) Indiana(93),
  Cambria(7)
VIRGINVILLE Berks
VOLANT (16156) Lawrence(51),
  Mercer(49)
VOWINCKEL (16260) Clarion(73),
  Forest(27)
WAGONTOWN Chester
WALLACETON Clearfield
WALLINGFORD Delaware
WALNUT BOTTOM Cumberland
WALNUTPORT Northampton
WALSTON Jefferson
WALTERSBURG Fayette
WAMPUM (16157) Lawrence(62),
  Beaver(38)
WAPWALLOPEN Luzerne
WARFORDSBURG Fulton
WARMINSTER Bucks
WARREN Warren
WARREN CENTER Bradford
WARRENDALE Allegheny
WARRINGTON Bucks
WARRIORS MARK (16877) Centre(67),
  Huntingdon(33)
WASHINGTON Washington
WASHINGTON BORO Lancaster
WASHINGTON CROSSING Bucks
WASHINGTONVILLE Montour
WATERFALL Fulton
WATERFORD (16441) Erie(92),
  Crawford(8)
WATERVILLE Lycoming
WATSONTOWN (17777)
  Northumberland(98), Montour(2)
WATTSBURG Erie
WAVERLY Lackawanna
WAYMART Wayne

WAYNE (19087) Delaware(49),
  Chester(39), Montgomery(12)
WAYNE Delaware
WAYNESBORO Franklin
WAYNESBURG Greene
WEATHERLY (18255) Carbon(99),
  Luzerne(1)
WEBSTER Westmoreland
WEEDVILLE Elk
WEIKERT Union
WELLERSBURG Somerset
WELLS TANNERY Fulton
WELLSBORO Tioga
WELLSVILLE York
WENDEL Westmoreland
WERNERSVILLE Berks
WEST ALEXANDER Washington
WEST CHESTER Chester
WEST DECATUR Clearfield
WEST ELIZABETH Allegheny
WEST FINLEY (15377) Washington(91),
  Greene(10)
WEST GROVE Chester
WEST HICKORY Forest
WEST LEBANON Indiana
WEST LEISENRING Fayette
WEST MIDDLESEX (16159) Mercer(98),
  Lawrence(2)
WEST MIDDLETOWN Washington
WEST MIFFLIN Allegheny
WEST MILTON Union
WEST NEWTON (15089)
  Westmoreland(98), Allegheny(2)
WEST PITTSBURG Lawrence
WEST POINT Montgomery
WEST SALISBURY Somerset
WEST SPRINGFIELD Erie
WEST SUNBURY Butler
WEST WILLOW Lancaster
WESTFIELD (16950) Tioga(92), Potter(8)
WESTLAND Washington
WESTLINE McKean
WESTMORELAND CITY Westmoreland
WESTON Luzerne
WESTOVER Clearfield
WESTPORT Clinton
WESTTOWN Chester
WEXFORD Allegheny
WHEATLAND Mercer
WHITE Fayette
WHITE DEER Union
WHITE HAVEN (18661) Luzerne(86),
  Carbon(14)
WHITE MILLS Wayne
WHITEHALL Lehigh
WHITNEY Westmoreland
WICKHAVEN Fayette
WICONISCO Dauphin
WIDNOON Armstrong
WILBURTON Columbia
WILCOX (15870) Elk(98), McKean(2)

WILDWOOD Allegheny
WILKES BARRE Luzerne
WILLIAMSBURG (16693) Blair(99),
  Huntingdon(1)
WILLIAMSON Franklin
WILLIAMSPORT Lycoming
WILLIAMSTOWN Dauphin
WILLOW GROVE Montgomery
WILLOW HILL Franklin
WILLOW STREET Lancaster
WILMERDING Allegheny
WILMORE Cambria
WINBURNE Clearfield
WIND GAP Northampton
WIND RIDGE Greene
WINDBER (15963) Somerset(86),
  Cambria(14)
WINDSOR York
WINFIELD (17889) Union(61), Snyder(39)
WITMER Lancaster
WOMELSDORF Berks
WOOD Bedford
WOODBURY Bedford
WOODLAND Clearfield
WOODLYN Delaware
WOODWARD Centre
WOOLRICH Clinton
WORCESTER Montgomery
WORTHINGTON (16262) Armstrong(98),
  Butler(2)
WORTHVILLE Jefferson
WOXALL Montgomery
WRIGHTSVILLE York
WYALUSING Bradford
WYANO Westmoreland
WYCOMBE Bucks
WYNCOTE Montgomery
WYNNEWOOD (19096) Montgomery(96),
  Delaware(4)
WYOMING Luzerne
WYSOX Bradford
YATESBORO Armstrong
YEAGERTOWN Mifflin
YORK York
YORK HAVEN York
YORK NEW SALEM York
YORK SPRINGS (17372) Adams(97),
  York(3)
YOUNGSTOWN Westmoreland
YOUNGSVILLE Warren
YOUNGWOOD Westmoreland
YUKON Westmoreland
ZELIENOPLE (16063) Butler(83),
  Beaver(17)
ZIEGLERVILLE Montgomery
ZION GROVE (17985) Schuylkill(92),
  Columbia(8)
ZIONHILL Bucks
ZIONSVILLE (18092) Lehigh(96), Berks(4)
ZULLINGER Franklin

ZIP/City Cross Reference

ZIP	City	ZIP	City	ZIP	City	ZIP	City
15001-15001	ALIQUIPPA	15024-15024	CHESWICK	15045-15045	GLASSPORT	15064-15064	MORGAN
15003-15003	AMBRIDGE	15025-15025	CLAIRTON	15046-15046	GLENWILLARD	15065-15065	NATRONA HEIGHTS
15004-15004	ATLASBURG	15026-15026	CLINTON	15047-15047	GREENOCK	15066-15066	NEW BRIGHTON
15005-15005	BADEN	15027-15027	CONWAY	15049-15049	HARWICK	15067-15067	NEW EAGLE
15006-15006	BAIRDFORD	15028-15028	COULTERS	15050-15050	HOOKSTOWN	15068-15069	NEW KENSINGTON
15007-15007	BAKERSTOWN	15030-15030	CREIGHTON	15051-15051	INDIANOLA	15071-15071	OAKDALE
15009-15009	BEAVER	15031-15031	CUDDY	15052-15052	INDUSTRY	15072-15072	PRICEDALE
15010-15010	BEAVER FALLS	15032-15032	CURTISVILLE	15053-15053	JOFFRE	15074-15074	ROCHESTER
15012-15012	BELLE VERNON	15033-15033	DONORA	15054-15054	LANGELOTH	15075-15075	RURAL RIDGE
15014-15014	BRACKENRIDGE	15034-15034	DRAVOSBURG	15055-15055	LAWRENCE	15076-15076	RUSSELLTON
15015-15015	BRADFORDWOODS	15035-15035	EAST MC KEESPORT	15056-15056	LEETSDALE	15077-15077	SHIPPINGPORT
15017-15017	BRIDGEVILLE	15036-15036	ELDERSVILLE	15057-15057	MC DONALD	15078-15078	SLOVAN
15018-15018	BUENA VISTA	15037-15037	ELIZABETH	15059-15059	MIDLAND	15081-15081	SOUTH HEIGHTS
15019-15019	BULGER	15038-15038	ELRAMA	15060-15060	MIDWAY	15082-15082	STURGEON
15020-15020	BUNOLA	15042-15042	FREEDOM	15061-15061	MONACA	15083-15083	SUTERSVILLE
15021-15021	BURGETTSTOWN	15043-15043	GEORGETOWN	15062-15062	MONESSEN	15084-15084	TARENTUM
15022-15022	CHARLEROI	15044-15044	GIBSONIA	15063-15063	MONONGAHELA	15085-15085	TRAFFORD

15086-15086 WARRENDALE	15365-15365 TAYLORSTOWN	15492-15492 WICKHAVEN	15661-15661 LOYALHANNA
15087-15087 WEBSTER	15366-15366 VAN VOORHIS	15501-15501 SOMERSET	15662-15662 LUXOR
15088-15088 WEST ELIZABETH	15367-15367 VENETIA	15502-15502 HIDDEN VALLEY	15663-15663 MADISON
15089-15089 WEST NEWTON	15368-15368 VESTABURG	15510-15510 SOMERSET	15664-15664 MAMMOTH
15090-15090 WEXFORD	15370-15370 WAYNESBURG	15520-15520 ACOSTA	15665-15665 MANOR
15091-15091 WILDWOOD	15376-15376 WEST ALEXANDER	15521-15521 ALUM BANK	15666-15666 MOUNT PLEASANT
15095-15096 WARRENDALE	15377-15377 WEST FINLEY	15522-15522 BEDFORD	15668-15668 MURRYSVILLE
15101-15101 ALLISON PARK	15378-15378 WESTLAND	15530-15530 BERLIN	15670-15670 NEW ALEXANDRIA
15102-15102 BETHEL PARK	15379-15379 WEST MIDDLETOWN	15531-15531 BOSWELL	15671-15671 NEW DERRY
15104-15104 BRADDOCK	15380-15380 WIND RIDGE	15532-15532 BOYNTON	15672-15672 NEW STANTON
15106-15106 CARNEGIE	15401-15401 UNIONTOWN	15533-15533 BREEZEWOOD	15673-15673 NORTH APOLLO
15108-15108 CORAOPOLIS	15410-15410 ADAH	15534-15534 BUFFALO MILLS	15674-15674 NORVELT
15110-15110 DUQUESNE	15411-15411 ADDISON	15535-15535 CLEARVILLE	15675-15675 PENN
15112-15112 EAST PITTSBURGH	15412-15412 ALLENPORT	15536-15536 CRYSTAL SPRING	15676-15676 PLEASANT UNITY
15116-15116 GLENSHAW	15413-15413 ALLISON	15537-15537 EVERETT	15677-15677 RECTOR
15120-15120 HOMESTEAD	15415-15415 BRIER HILL	15538-15538 FAIRHOPE	15678-15678 RILLTON
15122-15123 WEST MIFFLIN	15416-15416 BROWNFIELD	15539-15539 FISHERTOWN	15679-15679 RUFFS DALE
15126-15126 IMPERIAL	15417-15417 BROWNSVILLE	15540-15540 FORT HILL	15680-15680 SALINA
15127-15127 INGOMAR	15419-15419 CALIFORNIA	15541-15541 FRIEDENS	15681-15681 SALTSBURG
15129-15129 LIBRARY	15420-15420 CARDALE	15542-15542 GARRETT	15682-15682 SCHENLEY
15130-15135 MC KEESPORT	15421-15421 CHALKHILL	15544-15544 GRAY	15683-15683 SCOTTDALE
15136-15136 MC KEES ROCKS	15422-15422 CHESTNUT RIDGE	15545-15545 HYNDMAN	15684-15684 SLICKVILLE
15137-15137 NORTH VERSAILLES	15423-15423 COAL CENTER	15546-15546 JENNERS	15685-15685 SOUTHWEST
15139-15139 OAKMONT	15424-15424 CONFLUENCE	15547-15547 JENNERSTOWN	15686-15686 SPRING CHURCH
15140-15140 PITCAIRN	15425-15425 CONNELLSVILLE	15548-15548 KANTNER	15687-15687 STAHLSTOWN
15142-15142 PRESTO	15427-15427 DAISYTOWN	15549-15549 LISTIE	15688-15688 TARRS
15143-15143 SEWICKLEY	15428-15428 DAWSON	15550-15550 MANNS CHOICE	15689-15689 UNITED
15144-15144 SPRINGDALE	15429-15429 DENBO	15551-15551 MARKLETON	15690-15690 VANDERGRIFT
15145-15145 TURTLE CREEK	15430-15430 DICKERSON RUN	15552-15552 MEYERSDALE	15691-15691 WENDEL
15146-15146 MONROEVILLE	15431-15431 DUNBAR	15553-15553 NEW BALTIMORE	15692-15692 WESTMORELAND CITY
15147-15147 VERONA	15432-15432 DUNLEVY	15554-15554 NEW PARIS	15693-15693 WHITNEY
15148-15148 WILMERDING	15433-15433 EAST MILLSBORO	15555-15555 QUECREEK	15695-15695 WYANO
15189-15189 SEWICKLEY	15434-15434 ELCO	15557-15557 ROCKWOOD	15696-15696 YOUNGSTOWN
15201-15290 PITTSBURGH	15435-15435 FAIRBANK	15558-15558 SALISBURY	15697-15697 YOUNGWOOD
15301-15301 WASHINGTON	15436-15436 FAIRCHANCE	15559-15559 SCHELLSBURG	15698-15698 YUKON
15310-15310 ALEPPO	15437-15437 FARMINGTON	15560-15560 SHANKSVILLE	15701-15705 INDIANA
15311-15311 AMITY	15438-15438 FAYETTE CITY	15561-15561 SIPESVILLE	15710-15710 ALVERDA
15312-15312 AVELLA	15439-15439 GANS	15562-15562 SPRINGS	15711-15711 ANITA
15313-15313 BEALLSVILLE	15440-15440 GIBBON GLADE	15563-15563 STOYSTOWN	15712-15712 ARCADIA
15314-15314 BENTLEYVILLE	15442-15442 GRINDSTONE	15564-15564 WELLERSBURG	15713-15713 AULTMAN
15315-15315 BOBTOWN	15443-15443 HIBBS	15565-15565 WEST SALISBURY	15714-15714 BARNESBORO
15316-15316 BRAVE	15444-15444 HILLER	15601-15606 GREENSBURG	15715-15715 BIG RUN
15317-15317 CANONSBURG	15445-15445 HOPWOOD	15610-15610 ACME	15716-15716 BLACK LICK
15320-15320 CARMICHAELS	15446-15446 INDIAN HEAD	15611-15611 ADAMSBURG	15717-15717 BLAIRSVILLE
15321-15321 CECIL	15447-15447 ISABELLA	15612-15612 ALVERTON	15720-15720 BRUSH VALLEY
15322-15322 CLARKSVILLE	15448-15448 JACOBS CREEK	15613-15613 APOLLO	15721-15721 BURNSIDE
15323-15323 CLAYSVILLE	15449-15449 KEISTERVILLE	15615-15615 ARDARA	15722-15722 CARROLLTOWN
15324-15324 COKEBURG	15450-15450 LA BELLE	15616-15616 ARMBRUST	15723-15723 CHAMBERSVILLE
15325-15325 CRUCIBLE	15451-15451 LAKE LYNN	15617-15617 ARONA	15724-15724 CHERRY TREE
15327-15327 DILLINER	15454-15454 LECKRONE	15618-15618 AVONMORE	15725-15725 CLARKSBURG
15329-15329 PROSPERITY	15455-15455 LEISENRING	15619-15619 BOVARD	15727-15727 CLUNE
15330-15330 EIGHTY FOUR	15456-15456 LEMONT FURNACE	15620-15620 BRADENVILLE	15728-15728 CLYMER
15331-15331 ELLSWORTH	15458-15458 MC CLELLANDTOWN	15621-15621 CALUMET	15729-15729 COMMODORE
15332-15332 FINLEYVILLE	15459-15459 MARKLEYSBURG	15622-15622 CHAMPION	15730-15730 COOLSPRING
15333-15333 FREDERICKTOWN	15460-15460 MARTIN	15623-15623 CLARIDGE	15731-15731 CORAL
15334-15334 GARARDS FORT	15461-15461 MASONTOWN	15624-15624 CRABTREE	15732-15732 CREEKSIDE
15336-15336 GASTONVILLE	15462-15462 MELCROFT	15625-15625 DARRAGH	15733-15733 DE LANCEY
15337-15337 GRAYSVILLE	15463-15463 MERRITTSTOWN	15626-15626 DELMONT	15734-15734 DIXONVILLE
15338-15338 GREENSBORO	15464-15464 MILL RUN	15627-15627 DERRY	15736-15736 ELDERTON
15339-15339 HENDERSONVILLE	15465-15465 MOUNT BRADDOCK	15628-15628 DONEGAL	15737-15737 ELMORA
15340-15340 HICKORY	15466-15466 NEWELL	15629-15629 EAST VANDERGRIFT	15738-15738 EMEIGH
15341-15341 HOLBROOK	15467-15467 NEW GENEVA	15630-15630 EDMON	15739-15739 ERNEST
15342-15342 HOUSTON	15468-15468 NEW SALEM	15631-15631 EVERSON	15740-15740 FROSTBURG
15344-15344 JEFFERSON	15469-15469 NORMALVILLE	15632-15632 EXPORT	15741-15741 GIPSY
15345-15345 MARIANNA	15470-15470 OHIOPYLE	15633-15633 FORBES ROAD	15742-15742 GLEN CAMPBELL
15346-15346 MATHER	15472-15472 OLIVER	15634-15634 GRAPEVILLE	15744-15744 HAMILTON
15347-15347 MEADOW LANDS	15473-15473 PERRYOPOLIS	15635-15635 HANNASTOWN	15745-15745 HEILWOOD
15348-15348 MILLSBORO	15474-15474 POINT MARION	15636-15636 HARRISON CITY	15746-15746 HILLSDALE
15349-15349 MOUNT MORRIS	15475-15475 REPUBLIC	15637-15637 HERMINIE	15747-15747 HOME
15350-15350 MUSE	15476-15476 RONCO	15638-15638 HOSTETTER	15748-15748 HOMER CITY
15351-15351 NEMACOLIN	15477-15477 ROSCOE	15639-15639 HUNKER	15750-15750 JOSEPHINE
15352-15352 NEW FREEPORT	15478-15478 SMITHFIELD	15640-15640 HUTCHINSON	15751-15751 JUNEAU
15353-15353 NINEVEH	15479-15479 SMITHTON	15641-15641 HYDE PARK	15752-15752 KENT
15354-15354 PINE BANK	15480-15480 SMOCK	15642-15642 IRWIN	15753-15753 LA JOSE
15357-15357 RICES LANDING	15482-15482 STAR JUNCTION	15644-15644 JEANNETTE	15754-15754 LUCERNEMINES
15358-15358 RICHEYVILLE	15483-15483 STOCKDALE	15646-15646 JONES MILLS	15756-15756 MC INTYRE
15359-15359 ROGERSVILLE	15484-15484 ULEDI	15647-15647 LARIMER	15757-15757 MAHAFFEY
15360-15360 SCENERY HILL	15485-15485 URSINA	15650-15650 LATROBE	15758-15758 MARCHAND
15361-15361 SOUTHVIEW	15486-15486 VANDERBILT	15655-15655 LAUGHLINTOWN	15759-15759 MARION CENTER
15362-15362 SPRAGGS	15488-15488 WALTERSBURG	15656-15656 LEECHBURG	15760-15760 MARSTELLER
15363-15363 STRABANE	15489-15489 WEST LEISENRING	15658-15658 LIGONIER	15761-15761 MENTCLE
15364-15364 SYCAMORE	15490-15490 WHITE	15660-15660 LOWBER	15762-15762 NICKTOWN

Zip	City	Zip	City	Zip	City	Zip	City
15763-15763	NORTHPOINT	15958-15958	SUMMERHILL	16172-16172	NEW WILMINGTON	16362-16362	UTICA
15764-15764	OLIVEBURG	15959-15959	TIRE HILL	16201-16201	KITTANNING	16364-16364	VENUS
15765-15765	PENN RUN	15960-15960	TWIN ROCKS	16210-16210	ADRIAN	16365-16367	WARREN
15767-15767	PUNXSUTAWNEY	15961-15961	VINTONDALE	16211-16211	BEYER	16368-16369	IRVINE
15770-15770	RINGGOLD	15962-15962	WILMORE	16212-16212	CADOGAN	16370-16370	WEST HICKORY
15771-15771	ROCHESTER MILLS	15963-15963	WINDBER	16213-16213	CALLENSBURG	16371-16371	YOUNGSVILLE
15772-15772	ROSSITER	16001-16003	BUTLER	16214-16214	CLARION	16372-16372	CLINTONVILLE
15773-15773	SAINT BENEDICT	16016-16020	BOYERS	16215-16215	KITTANNING	16373-16373	EMLENTON
15774-15774	SHELOCTA	16021-16021	BRANCHTON	16216-16216	CLIMAX	16374-16374	KENNERDELL
15775-15775	SPANGLER	16022-16022	BRUIN	16217-16217	COOKSBURG	16375-16375	LAMARTINE
15776-15776	SPRANKLE MILLS	16023-16023	CABOT	16218-16218	COWANSVILLE	16388-16388	MEADVILLE
15777-15777	STARFORD	16024-16024	CALLERY	16220-16220	CROWN	16401-16401	ALBION
15778-15778	TIMBLIN	16025-16025	CHICORA	16221-16221	CURLLSVILLE	16402-16402	BEAR LAKE
15779-15779	TORRANCE	16027-16027	CONNOQUENESSING	16222-16222	DAYTON	16403-16403	CAMBRIDGE SPRINGS
15780-15780	VALIER	16028-16028	EAST BRADY	16223-16223	DISTANT	16404-16404	CENTERVILLE
15781-15781	WALSTON	16029-16029	EAST BUTLER	16224-16224	FAIRMOUNT CITY	16405-16405	COLUMBUS
15783-15783	WEST LEBANON	16030-16030	EAU CLAIRE	16225-16225	FISHER	16406-16406	CONNEAUTVILLE
15784-15784	WORTHVILLE	16033-16033	EVANS CITY	16226-16226	FORD CITY	16407-16407	CORRY
15801-15801	DU BOIS	16034-16034	FENELTON	16228-16228	FORD CLIFF	16410-16410	CRANESVILLE
15821-15821	BENEZETT	16035-16035	FORESTVILLE	16229-16229	FREEPORT	16411-16411	EAST SPRINGFIELD
15822-15822	BRANDY CAMP	16036-16036	FOXBURG	16230-16230	HAWTHORN	16412-16412	EDINBORO
15823-15823	BROCKPORT	16037-16037	HARMONY	16232-16232	KNOX	16413-16413	ELGIN
15824-15824	BROCKWAY	16038-16038	HARRISVILLE	16233-16233	LEEPER	16415-16415	FAIRVIEW
15825-15825	BROOKVILLE	16039-16039	HERMAN	16234-16234	LIMESTONE	16416-16416	GARLAND
15827-15827	BYRNEDALE	16040-16040	HILLIARDS	16235-16235	LUCINDA	16417-16417	GIRARD
15828-15828	CLARINGTON	16041-16041	KARNS CITY	16236-16236	MC GRANN	16420-16420	GRAND VALLEY
15829-15829	CORSICA	16045-16045	LYNDORA	16238-16238	MANORVILLE	16421-16421	HARBORCREEK
15831-15831	DAGUS MINES	16046-16046	MARS	16239-16239	MARIENVILLE	16422-16422	HARMONSBURG
15832-15832	DRIFTWOOD	16048-16048	NORTH WASHINGTON	16240-16240	MAYPORT	16423-16423	LAKE CITY
15834-15834	EMPORIUM	16049-16049	PARKER	16242-16242	NEW BETHLEHEM	16424-16424	LINESVILLE
15840-15840	FALLS CREEK	16050-16050	PETROLIA	16244-16244	NU MINE	16426-16426	MC KEAN
15841-15841	FORCE	16051-16051	PORTERSVILLE	16245-16245	OAK RIDGE	16427-16427	MILL VILLAGE
15845-15845	JOHNSONBURG	16052-16052	PROSPECT	16246-16246	PLUMVILLE	16428-16428	NORTH EAST
15846-15846	KERSEY	16053-16053	RENFREW	16248-16248	RIMERSBURG	16430-16430	NORTH SPRINGFIELD
15847-15847	KNOX DALE	16054-16054	SAINT PETERSBURG	16249-16249	RURAL VALLEY	16432-16432	RICEVILLE
15848-15848	LUTHERSBURG	16055-16055	SARVER	16250-16250	SAGAMORE	16433-16433	SAEGERTOWN
15849-15849	PENFIELD	16056-16056	SAXONBURG	16253-16253	SEMINOLE	16434-16434	SPARTANSBURG
15851-15851	REYNOLDSVILLE	16057-16057	SLIPPERY ROCK	16254-16254	SHIPPENVILLE	16435-16435	SPRINGBORO
15853-15853	RIDGWAY	16058-16058	TURKEY CITY	16255-16255	SLIGO	16436-16436	SPRING CREEK
15856-15856	ROCKTON	16059-16059	VALENCIA	16256-16256	SMICKSBURG	16438-16438	UNION CITY
15857-15857	SAINT MARYS	16061-16061	WEST SUNBURY	16257-16257	SNYDERSBURG	16440-16440	VENANGO
15860-15860	SIGEL	16063-16063	ZELIENOPLE	16258-16258	STRATTANVILLE	16441-16441	WATERFORD
15861-15861	SINNAMAHONING	16066-16066	CRANBERRY TWP	16259-16259	TEMPLETON	16442-16442	WATTSBURG
15863-15863	STUMP CREEK	16101-16108	NEW CASTLE	16260-16260	VOWINCKEL	16443-16443	WEST SPRINGFIELD
15864-15864	SUMMERVILLE	16110-16110	ADAMSVILLE	16261-16261	WIDNOON	16444-16444	EDINBORO
15865-15865	SYKESVILLE	16111-16111	ATLANTIC	16262-16262	WORTHINGTON	16475-16475	ALBION
15866-15866	TROUTVILLE	16112-16112	BESSEMER	16263-16263	YATESBORO	16501-16565	ERIE
15868-15868	WEEDVILLE	16113-16113	CLARK	16301-16301	OIL CITY	16601-16603	ALTOONA
15870-15870	WILCOX	16114-16114	CLARKS MILLS	16311-16311	CARLTON	16611-16611	ALEXANDRIA
15901-15915	JOHNSTOWN	16115-16115	DARLINGTON	16312-16312	CHANDLERS VALLEY	16613-16613	ASHVILLE
15920-15920	ARMAGH	16116-16116	EDINBURG	16313-16313	CLARENDON	16614-16614	BAKERS SUMMIT
15921-15921	BEAVERDALE	16117-16117	ELLWOOD CITY	16314-16314	COCHRANTON	16616-16616	BECCARIA
15922-15922	BELSANO	16120-16120	ENON VALLEY	16316-16316	CONNEAUT LAKE	16617-16617	BELLWOOD
15923-15923	BOLIVAR	16121-16121	FARRELL	16317-16317	COOPERSTOWN	16619-16619	BLANDBURG
15924-15924	CAIRNBROOK	16123-16123	FOMBELL	16319-16319	CRANBERRY	16620-16620	BRISBIN
15925-15925	CASSANDRA	16124-16124	FREDONIA	16321-16321	EAST HICKORY	16621-16621	BROAD TOP
15926-15926	CENTRAL CITY	16125-16125	GREENVILLE	16322-16322	ENDEAVOR	16622-16622	CALVIN
15927-15927	COLVER	16127-16127	GROVE CITY	16323-16323	FRANKLIN	16623-16623	CASSVILLE
15928-15928	DAVIDSVILLE	16130-16130	HADLEY	16326-16326	FRYBURG	16624-16624	CHEST SPRINGS
15929-15929	DILLTOWN	16131-16131	HARTSTOWN	16327-16327	GUYS MILLS	16625-16625	CLAYSBURG
15930-15930	DUNLO	16132-16132	HILLSVILLE	16328-16328	HYDETOWN	16627-16627	COALPORT
15931-15931	EBENSBURG	16133-16133	JACKSON CENTER	16329-16329	IRVINE	16629-16629	COUPON
15934-15934	ELTON	16134-16134	JAMESTOWN	16331-16331	KOSSUTH	16630-16630	CRESSON
15935-15935	HOLLSOPPLE	16136-16136	KOPPEL	16332-16332	LICKINGVILLE	16631-16631	CURRYVILLE
15936-15936	HOOVERSVILLE	16137-16137	MERCER	16333-16333	LUDLOW	16633-16633	DEFIANCE
15937-15937	JEROME	16140-16140	NEW BEDFORD	16334-16334	MARBLE	16634-16634	DUDLEY
15938-15938	LILLY	16141-16141	NEW GALILEE	16335-16335	MEADVILLE	16635-16635	DUNCANSVILLE
15940-15940	LORETTO	16142-16142	NEW WILMINGTON	16340-16340	PITTSFIELD	16636-16636	DYSART
15942-15942	MINERAL POINT	16143-16143	PULASKI	16341-16341	PLEASANTVILLE	16637-16637	EAST FREEDOM
15943-15943	NANTY GLO	16145-16145	SANDY LAKE	16342-16342	POLK	16638-16638	ENTRIKEN
15944-15944	NEW FLORENCE	16146-16146	SHARON	16343-16343	RENO	16639-16639	FALLENTIMBER
15945-15945	PARKHILL	16148-16148	HERMITAGE	16344-16344	ROUSEVILLE	16640-16640	FLINTON
15946-15946	PORTAGE	16150-16150	SHARPSVILLE	16345-16345	RUSSELL	16641-16641	GALLITZIN
15948-15948	REVLOC	16151-16151	SHEAKLEYVILLE	16346-16346	SENECA	16644-16644	GLASGOW
15949-15949	ROBINSON	16153-16153	STONEBORO	16347-16347	SHEFFIELD	16645-16645	GLEN HOPE
15951-15951	SAINT MICHAEL	16154-16154	TRANSFER	16350-16350	SUGAR GROVE	16646-16646	HASTINGS
15952-15952	SALIX	16155-16155	VILLA MARIA	16351-16351	TIDIOUTE	16647-16647	HESSTON
15953-15953	SEANOR	16156-16156	VOLANT	16352-16352	TIONA	16648-16648	HOLLIDAYSBURG
15954-15954	SEWARD	16157-16157	WAMPUM	16353-16353	TIONESTA	16650-16650	HOPEWELL
15955-15955	SIDMAN	16159-16159	WEST MIDDLESEX	16354-16354	TITUSVILLE	16651-16651	HOUTZDALE
15956-15956	SOUTH FORK	16160-16160	WEST PITTSBURG	16360-16360	TOWNVILLE	16652-16654	HUNTINGDON
15957-15957	STRONGSTOWN	16161-16161	WHEATLAND	16361-16361	TYLERSBURG	16655-16655	IMLER

16656-16656 IRVONA	16840-16840 HAWK RUN	17011-17012 CAMP HILL	17101-17177 HARRISBURG
16657-16657 JAMES CREEK	16841-16841 HOWARD	17013-17013 CARLISLE	17201-17201 CHAMBERSBURG
16659-16659 LOYSBURG	16843-16843 HYDE	17014-17014 COCOLAMUS	17210-17210 AMBERSON
16660-16660 MC CONNELLSTOWN	16844-16844 JULIAN	17015-17015 COLEBROOK	17211-17211 ARTEMAS
16661-16661 MADERA	16845-16845 KARTHAUS	17016-17016 CORNWALL	17212-17212 BIG COVE TANNERY
16662-16662 MARTINSBURG	16847-16847 KYLERTOWN	17017-17017 DALMATIA	17213-17213 BLAIRS MILLS
16663-16663 MORANN	16848-16848 LAMAR	17018-17018 DAUPHIN	17214-17214 BLUE RIDGE SUMMIT
16664-16664 NEW ENTERPRISE	16849-16849 LANSE	17019-17019 DILLSBURG	17215-17215 BURNT CABINS
16665-16665 NEWRY	16850-16850 LECONTES MILLS	17020-17020 DUNCANNON	17217-17217 CONCORD
16666-16666 OSCEOLA MILLS	16851-16851 LEMONT	17021-17021 EAST WATERFORD	17219-17219 DOYLESBURG
16667-16667 OSTERBURG	16852-16852 MADISONBURG	17022-17022 ELIZABETHTOWN	17220-17220 DRY RUN
16668-16668 PATTON	16853-16853 MILESBURG	17023-17023 ELIZABETHVILLE	17221-17221 FANNETTSBURG
16669-16669 PETERSBURG	16854-16854 MILLHEIM	17024-17024 ELLIOTTSBURG	17222-17222 FAYETTEVILLE
16670-16670 QUEEN	16855-16855 MINERAL SPRINGS	17025-17025 ENOLA	17223-17223 FORT LITTLETON
16671-16671 RAMEY	16856-16856 MINGOVILLE	17026-17026 FREDERICKSBURG	17224-17224 FORT LOUDON
16672-16672 RIDDLESBURG	16858-16858 MORRISDALE	17027-17027 GRANTHAM	17225-17225 GREENCASTLE
16673-16673 ROARING SPRING	16859-16859 MOSHANNON	17028-17028 GRANTVILLE	17228-17228 HARRISONVILLE
16674-16674 ROBERTSDALE	16860-16860 MUNSON	17029-17029 GRANVILLE	17229-17229 HUSTONTOWN
16675-16675 SAINT BONIFACE	16861-16861 NEW MILLPORT	17030-17030 GRATZ	17231-17231 LEMASTERS
16677-16677 SANDY RIDGE	16863-16863 OLANTA	17031-17031 GREEN PARK	17232-17232 LURGAN
16678-16678 SAXTON	16864-16864 ORVISTON	17032-17032 HALIFAX	17233-17233 MC CONNELLSBURG
16679-16679 SIX MILE RUN	16865-16865 PENNSYLVANIA	17033-17033 HERSHEY	17235-17235 MARION
16680-16680 SMITHMILL	FURNACE	17034-17034 HIGHSPIRE	17236-17236 MERCERSBURG
16681-16681 SMOKERUN	16866-16866 PHILIPSBURG	17035-17035 HONEY GROVE	17237-17237 MONT ALTO
16682-16682 SPROUL	16868-16868 PINE GROVE MILLS	17036-17036 HUMMELSTOWN	17238-17238 NEEDMORE
16683-16683 SPRUCE CREEK	16870-16870 PORT MATILDA	17037-17037 ICKESBURG	17239-17239 NEELYTON
16684-16684 TIPTON	16871-16871 POTTERSDALE	17038-17038 JONESTOWN	17240-17240 NEWBURG
16685-16685 TODD	16872-16872 REBERSBURG	17039-17039 KLEINFELTERSVILLE	17241-17241 NEWVILLE
16686-16686 TYRONE	16873-16873 SHAWVILLE	17040-17040 LANDISBURG	17243-17243 ORBISONIA
16689-16689 WATERFALL	16874-16874 SNOW SHOE	17041-17041 LAWN	17244-17244 ORRSTOWN
16691-16691 WELLS TANNERY	16875-16875 SPRING MILLS	17042-17042 LEBANON	17246-17246 PLEASANT HALL
16692-16692 WESTOVER	16876-16876 WALLACETON	17043-17043 LEMOYNE	17247-17247 QUINCY
16693-16693 WILLIAMSBURG	16877-16877 WARRIORS MARK	17044-17044 LEWISTOWN	17249-17249 ROCKHILL FURNACE
16694-16694 WOOD	16878-16878 WEST DECATUR	17045-17045 LIVERPOOL	17250-17250 ROUZERVILLE
16695-16695 WOODBURY	16879-16879 WINBURNE	17046-17046 LEBANON	17251-17251 ROXBURY
16698-16698 HOUTZDALE	16881-16881 WOODLAND	17047-17047 LOYSVILLE	17252-17252 SAINT THOMAS
16699-16699 CRESSON	16882-16882 WOODWARD	17048-17048 LYKENS	17253-17253 SALTILLO
16701-16701 BRADFORD	16901-16901 WELLSBORO	17049-17049 MC ALISTERVILLE	17254-17254 SCOTLAND
16720-16720 AUSTIN	16910-16910 ALBA	17051-17051 MC VEYTOWN	17255-17255 SHADE GAP
16724-16724 CROSBY	16911-16911 ARNOT	17052-17052 MAPLETON DEPOT	17256-17256 SHADY GROVE
16725-16725 CUSTER CITY	16912-16912 BLOSSBURG	17053-17053 MARYSVILLE	17257-17257 SHIPPENSBURG
16726-16726 CYCLONE	16914-16914 COLUMBIA CROSS	17054-17054 MATTAWANA	17260-17260 SHIRLEYSBURG
16727-16727 DERRICK CITY	ROADS	17055-17055 MECHANICSBURG	17261-17261 SOUTH MOUNTAIN
16728-16728 DE YOUNG	16915-16915 COUDERSPORT	17056-17056 MEXICO	17262-17262 SPRING RUN
16729-16729 DUKE CENTER	16917-16917 COVINGTON	17057-17057 MIDDLETOWN	17263-17263 STATE LINE
16730-16730 EAST SMETHPORT	16918-16918 COWANESQUE	17058-17058 MIFFLIN	17264-17264 THREE SPRINGS
16731-16731 ELDRED	16920-16920 ELKLAND	17059-17059 MIFFLINTOWN	17265-17265 UPPERSTRASBURG
16732-16732 GIFFORD	16921-16921 GAINES	17060-17060 MILL CREEK	17266-17266 WALNUT BOTTOM
16733-16733 HAZEL HURST	16922-16922 GALETON	17061-17061 MILLERSBURG	17267-17267 WARFORDSBURG
16734-16734 JAMES CITY	16923-16923 GENESEE	17062-17062 MILLERSTOWN	17268-17268 WAYNESBORO
16735-16735 KANE	16925-16925 GILLETT	17063-17063 MILROY	17270-17270 WILLIAMSON
16738-16738 LEWIS RUN	16926-16926 GRANVILLE SUMMIT	17064-17064 MOUNT GRETNA	17271-17271 WILLOW HILL
16740-16740 MOUNT JEWETT	16927-16927 HARRISON VALLEY	17065-17065 MOUNT HOLLY SPRINGS	17272-17272 ZULLINGER
16743-16743 PORT ALLEGANY	16928-16928 KNOXVILLE	17066-17066 MOUNT UNION	17294-17294 BLUE RIDGE SUMMIT
16744-16744 REW	16929-16929 LAWRENCEVILLE	17067-17067 MYERSTOWN	17301-17301 ABBOTTSTOWN
16745-16745 RIXFORD	16930-16930 LIBERTY	17068-17068 NEW BLOOMFIELD	17302-17302 AIRVILLE
16746-16746 ROULETTE	16932-16932 MAINESBURG	17069-17069 NEW BUFFALO	17303-17303 ARENDTSVILLE
16748-16748 SHINGLEHOUSE	16933-16933 MANSFIELD	17070-17070 NEW CUMBERLAND	17304-17304 ASPERS
16749-16749 SMETHPORT	16935-16935 MIDDLEBURY CENTER	17071-17071 NEW GERMANTOWN	17306-17306 BENDERSVILLE
16750-16750 TURTLEPOINT	16936-16936 MILLERTON	17072-17072 NEW KINGSTOWN	17307-17307 BIGLERVILLE
16751-16751 WESTLINE	16937-16937 MILLS	17073-17073 NEWMANSTOWN	17309-17309 BROGUE
16801-16801 STATE COLLEGE	16938-16938 MORRIS	17074-17074 NEWPORT	17310-17310 CASHTOWN
16802-16802 UNIVERSITY PARK	16939-16939 MORRIS RUN	17075-17075 NEWTON HAMILTON	17311-17311 CODORUS
16803-16805 STATE COLLEGE	16940-16940 NELSON	17076-17076 OAKLAND MILLS	17312-17312 CRALEY
16820-16820 AARONSBURG	16941-16941 GENESEE	17077-17077 ONO	17313-17313 DALLASTOWN
16821-16821 ALLPORT	16942-16942 OSCEOLA	17078-17078 PALMYRA	17314-17314 DELTA
16822-16822 BEECH CREEK	16943-16943 SABINSVILLE	17080-17080 PILLOW	17315-17315 DOVER
16823-16823 BELLEFONTE	16945-16945 SYLVANIA	17081-17081 PLAINFIELD	17316-17316 EAST BERLIN
16825-16825 BIGLER	16946-16946 TIOGA	17082-17082 PORT ROYAL	17317-17317 EAST PROSPECT
16826-16826 BLANCHARD	16947-16947 TROY	17083-17083 QUENTIN	17318-17318 EMIGSVILLE
16827-16827 BOALSBURG	16948-16948 ULYSSES	17084-17084 REEDSVILLE	17319-17319 ETTERS
16828-16828 CENTRE HALL	16950-16950 WESTFIELD	17085-17085 REXMONT	17320-17320 FAIRFIELD
16829-16829 CLARENCE	17001-17001 CAMP HILL	17086-17086 RICHFIELD	17321-17321 FAWN GROVE
16830-16830 CLEARFIELD	17002-17002 ALLENSVILLE	17087-17087 RICHLAND	17322-17322 FELTON
16832-16832 COBURN	17003-17003 ANNVILLE	17088-17088 SCHAEFFERSTOWN	17323-17323 FRANKLINTOWN
16833-16833 CURWENSVILLE	17004-17004 BELLEVILLE	17089-17089 CAMP HILL	17324-17324 GARDNERS
16834-16834 DRIFTING	17005-17005 BERRYSBURG	17090-17090 SHERMANS DALE	17325-17325 GETTYSBURG
16835-16835 FLEMING	17006-17006 BLAIN	17093-17093 SUMMERDALE	17327-17327 GLEN ROCK
16836-16836 FRENCHVILLE	17007-17007 BOILING SPRINGS	17094-17094 THOMPSONTOWN	17329-17329 GLENVILLE
16837-16837 GLEN RICHEY	17008-17008 BOWMANSDALE	17097-17097 WICONISCO	17331-17333 HANOVER
16838-16838 GRAMPIAN	17009-17009 BURNHAM	17098-17098 WILLIAMSTOWN	17337-17337 IDAVILLE
16839-16839 GRASSFLAT	17010-17010 CAMPBELLTOWN	17099-17099 YEAGERTOWN	17339-17339 LEWISBERRY

ZIP	Place	ZIP	Place	ZIP	Place	ZIP	Place
17340-17340	LITTLESTOWN	17580-17580	TALMAGE	17843-17843	BEAVER SPRINGS	17981-17981	TREMONT
17342-17342	LOGANVILLE	17581-17581	TERRE HILL	17844-17844	MIFFLINBURG	17982-17982	TUSCARORA
17343-17343	MC KNIGHTSTOWN	17582-17582	WASHINGTON BORO	17845-17845	MILLMONT	17983-17983	VALLEY VIEW
17344-17344	MC SHERRYSTOWN	17583-17583	WEST WILLOW	17846-17846	MILLVILLE	17985-17985	ZION GROVE
17345-17345	MANCHESTER	17584-17584	WILLOW STREET	17847-17847	MILTON	18001-18003	LEHIGH VALLEY
17346-17346	MENGES MILLS	17585-17585	WITMER	17850-17850	MONTANDON	18010-18010	ACKERMANVILLE
17347-17347	MOUNT WOLF	17601-17699	LANCASTER	17851-17851	MOUNT CARMEL	18011-18011	ALBURTIS
17349-17349	NEW FREEDOM	17701-17705	WILLIAMSPORT	17853-17853	MOUNT PLEASANT	18012-18012	AQUASHICOLA
17350-17350	NEW OXFORD	17720-17720	ANTES FORT		MILLS	18013-18013	BANGOR
17352-17352	NEW PARK	17721-17721	AVIS	17855-17855	NEW BERLIN	18014-18014	BATH
17353-17353	ORRTANNA	17722-17722	BODINES	17856-17856	NEW COLUMBIA	18015-18025	BETHLEHEM
17354-17354	PORTERS SIDELING	17723-17723	JERSEY SHORE	17857-17857	NORTHUMBERLAND	18030-18030	BOWMANSTOWN
17355-17355	RAILROAD	17724-17724	CANTON	17858-17858	NUMIDIA	18031-18031	BREINIGSVILLE
17356-17356	RED LION	17726-17726	CASTANEA	17859-17859	ORANGEVILLE	18032-18032	CATASAUQUA
17358-17358	ROSSVILLE	17727-17727	CEDAR RUN	17860-17860	PAXINOS	18034-18034	CENTER VALLEY
17360-17360	SEVEN VALLEYS	17728-17728	COGAN STATION	17861-17861	PAXTONVILLE	18035-18035	CHERRYVILLE
17361-17361	SHREWSBURY	17729-17729	CROSS FORK	17862-17862	PENNS CREEK	18036-18036	COOPERSBURG
17362-17362	SPRING GROVE	17730-17730	DEWART	17864-17864	PORT TREVORTON	18037-18037	COPLAY
17363-17363	STEWARTSTOWN	17731-17731	EAGLES MERE	17865-17865	POTTS GROVE	18038-18038	DANIELSVILLE
17364-17364	THOMASVILLE	17734-17734	FARRANDSVILLE	17866-17866	COAL TOWNSHIP	18039-18039	DURHAM
17365-17365	WELLSVILLE	17735-17735	GROVER	17867-17867	REBUCK	18040-18040	EASTON
17366-17366	WINDSOR	17737-17737	HUGHESVILLE	17868-17868	RIVERSIDE	18041-18041	EAST GREENVILLE
17368-17368	WRIGHTSVILLE	17738-17738	HYNER	17870-17870	SELINSGROVE	18042-18045	EASTON
17370-17370	YORK HAVEN	17739-17739	JERSEY MILLS	17872-17872	SHAMOKIN	18046-18046	EAST TEXAS
17371-17371	YORK NEW SALEM	17740-17740	JERSEY SHORE	17876-17876	SHAMOKIN DAM	18049-18049	EMMAUS
17372-17372	YORK SPRINGS	17742-17742	LAIRDSVILLE	17877-17877	SNYDERTOWN	18050-18050	FLICKSVILLE
17375-17375	PEACH GLEN	17743-17743	LEROY	17878-17878	STILLWATER	18051-18051	FOGELSVILLE
17401-17415	YORK	17744-17744	LINDEN	17880-17880	SWENGEL	18052-18052	WHITEHALL
17501-17501	AKRON	17745-17745	LOCK HAVEN	17881-17881	TREVORTON	18053-18053	GERMANSVILLE
17502-17502	BAINBRIDGE	17747-17747	LOGANTON	17882-17882	TROXELVILLE	18054-18054	GREEN LANE
17503-17503	BART	17748-17748	MC ELHATTAN	17883-17883	VICKSBURG	18055-18055	HELLERTOWN
17504-17504	BAUSMAN	17749-17749	MC EWENSVILLE	17884-17884	WASHINGTONVILLE	18056-18056	HEREFORD
17505-17505	BIRD IN HAND	17750-17750	MACKEYVILLE	17885-17885	WEIKERT	18058-18058	KUNKLETOWN
17506-17506	BLUE BALL	17751-17751	MILL HALL	17886-17886	WEST MILTON	18059-18059	LAURYS STATION
17507-17507	BOWMANSVILLE	17752-17752	MONTGOMERY	17887-17887	WHITE DEER	18060-18060	LIMEPORT
17508-17508	BROWNSTOWN	17754-17754	MONTOURSVILLE	17888-17888	WILBURTON	18062-18062	MACUNGIE
17509-17509	CHRISTIANA	17756-17756	MUNCY	17889-17889	WINFIELD	18063-18063	MARTINS CREEK
17512-17512	COLUMBIA	17758-17758	MUNCY VALLEY	17901-17901	POTTSVILLE	18064-18064	NAZARETH
17516-17516	CONESTOGA	17759-17759	NISBET	17920-17920	ARISTES	18065-18065	NEFFS
17517-17517	DENVER	17760-17760	NORTH BEND	17921-17921	ASHLAND	18066-18066	NEW TRIPOLI
17518-17518	DRUMORE	17762-17762	PICTURE ROCKS	17922-17922	AUBURN	18067-18067	NORTHAMPTON
17519-17519	EAST EARL	17763-17763	RALSTON	17923-17923	BRANCHDALE	18068-18068	OLD ZIONSVILLE
17520-17520	EAST PETERSBURG	17764-17764	RENOVO	17925-17925	BROCKTON	18069-18069	OREFIELD
17521-17521	ELM	17765-17765	ROARING BRANCH	17927-17927	CENTRALIA	18070-18070	PALM
17522-17522	EPHRATA	17767-17767	SALONA	17929-17929	CRESSONA	18071-18071	PALMERTON
17527-17527	GAP	17768-17768	SHUNK	17930-17930	CUMBOLA	18072-18072	PEN ARGYL
17528-17528	GOODVILLE	17769-17769	SLATE RUN	17931-17932	FRACKVILLE	18073-18073	PENNSBURG
17529-17529	GORDONVILLE	17770-17770	SONESTOWN	17933-17933	FRIEDENSBURG	18074-18074	PERKIOMENVILLE
17532-17532	HOLTWOOD	17771-17771	TROUT RUN	17934-17934	GILBERTON	18076-18076	RED HILL
17533-17533	HOPELAND	17772-17772	TURBOTVILLE	17935-17935	GIRARDVILLE	18077-18077	RIEGELSVILLE
17534-17534	INTERCOURSE	17773-17773	TYLERSVILLE	17936-17936	GORDON	18078-18078	SCHNECKSVILLE
17535-17535	KINZERS	17774-17774	UNITYVILLE	17938-17938	HEGINS	18079-18079	SLATEDALE
17536-17536	KIRKWOOD	17776-17776	WATERVILLE	17939-17939	HELFENSTEIN	18080-18080	SLATINGTON
17537-17537	LAMPETER	17777-17777	WATSONTOWN	17941-17941	KLINGERSTOWN	18081-18081	SPRINGTOWN
17538-17538	LANDISVILLE	17778-17778	WESTPORT	17942-17942	LANDINGVILLE	18083-18083	STOCKERTOWN
17540-17540	LEOLA	17779-17779	WOOLRICH	17943-17943	LAVELLE	18084-18084	SUMNEYTOWN
17543-17543	LITITZ	17801-17801	SUNBURY	17944-17944	LLEWELLYN	18085-18085	TATAMY
17545-17545	MANHEIM	17810-17810	ALLENWOOD	17945-17945	LOCUSTDALE	18086-18086	TREICHLERS
17547-17547	MARIETTA	17812-17812	BEAVER SPRINGS	17946-17946	LOST CREEK	18087-18087	TREXLERTOWN
17549-17549	MARTINDALE	17813-17813	BEAVERTOWN	17948-17948	MAHANOY CITY	18088-18088	WALNUTPORT
17550-17550	MAYTOWN	17814-17814	BENTON	17949-17949	MAHANOY PLANE	18091-18091	WIND GAP
17551-17551	MILLERSVILLE	17815-17815	BLOOMSBURG	17951-17951	MAR LIN	18092-18092	ZIONSVILLE
17552-17552	MOUNT JOY	17820-17820	CATAWISSA	17952-17952	MARY D	18098-18099	EMMAUS
17554-17554	MOUNTVILLE	17821-17822	DANVILLE	17953-17953	MIDDLEPORT	18101-18195	ALLENTOWN
17555-17555	NARVON	17823-17823	DORNSIFE	17954-17954	MINERSVILLE	18201-18201	HAZLETON
17557-17557	NEW HOLLAND	17824-17824	ELYSBURG	17957-17957	MUIR	18210-18210	ALBRIGHTSVILLE
17560-17560	NEW PROVIDENCE	17825-17825	EXCELSIOR	17959-17959	NEW PHILADELPHIA	18211-18211	ANDREAS
17562-17562	PARADISE	17827-17827	FREEBURG	17960-17960	NEW RINGGOLD	18212-18212	ASHFIELD
17563-17563	PEACH BOTTOM	17828-17828	GOWEN CITY	17961-17961	ORWIGSBURG	18214-18214	BARNESVILLE
17564-17564	PENRYN	17829-17829	HARTLETON	17963-17963	PINE GROVE	18216-18216	BEAVER MEADOWS
17565-17565	PEQUEA	17830-17830	HERNDON	17964-17964	PITMAN	18218-18218	COALDALE
17566-17566	QUARRYVILLE	17831-17831	HUMMELS WHARF	17965-17965	PORT CARBON	18219-18219	CONYNGHAM
17567-17567	REAMSTOWN	17832-17832	MARION HEIGHTS	17966-17966	RAVINE	18220-18220	DELANO
17568-17568	REFTON	17833-17833	KREAMER	17967-17967	RINGTOWN	18221-18221	DRIFTON
17569-17569	REINHOLDS	17834-17834	KULPMONT	17968-17968	SACRAMENTO	18222-18222	DRUMS
17570-17570	RHEEMS	17835-17835	LAURELTON	17970-17970	SAINT CLAIR	18223-18223	EBERVALE
17572-17573	RONKS	17836-17836	LECK KILL	17972-17972	SCHUYLKILL HAVEN	18224-18224	FREELAND
17575-17575	SILVER SPRING	17837-17837	LEWISBURG	17974-17974	SELTZER	18225-18225	HARLEIGH
17576-17576	SMOKETOWN	17839-17839	LIGHT STREET	17976-17976	SHENANDOAH	18229-18229	JIM THORPE
17577-17577	SOUDERSBURG	17840-17840	LOCUST GAP	17978-17978	SPRING GLEN	18230-18230	JUNEDALE
17578-17578	STEVENS	17841-17841	MC CLURE	17979-17979	SUMMIT STATION	18231-18231	KELAYRES
17579-17579	STRASBURG	17842-17842	MIDDLEBURG	17980-17980	TOWER CITY	18232-18232	LANSFORD

18234-18234	LATTIMER MINES	18431-18431	HONESDALE	18660-18660	WAPWALLOPEN	18949-18949	PLUMSTEADVILLE
18235-18235	LEHIGHTON	18433-18433	JERMYN	18661-18661	WHITE HAVEN	18950-18950	POINT PLEASANT
18237-18237	MCADOO	18434-18434	JESSUP	18690-18690	DALLAS	18951-18951	QUAKERTOWN
18239-18239	MILNESVILLE	18435-18435	LACKAWAXEN	18701-18703	WILKES BARRE	18953-18953	REVERE
18240-18240	NESQUEHONING	18436-18436	LAKE ARIEL	18704-18704	KINGSTON	18954-18954	RICHBORO
18241-18241	NUREMBERG	18437-18437	LAKE COMO	18705-18706	WILKES BARRE	18955-18955	RICHLANDTOWN
18242-18242	ONEIDA	18438-18438	LAKEVILLE	18707-18707	MOUNTAIN TOP	18956-18956	RUSHLAND
18243-18243	PARDEESVILLE	18439-18439	LAKEWOOD	18708-18708	SHAVERTOWN	18957-18957	SALFORD
18244-18244	PARRYVILLE	18440-18440	LA PLUME	18709-18709	LUZERNE	18958-18958	SALFORDVILLE
18245-18245	QUAKAKE	18441-18441	LENOXVILLE	18710-18774	WILKES BARRE	18960-18960	SELLERSVILLE
18246-18246	ROCK GLEN	18443-18443	MILANVILLE	18801-18801	MONTROSE	18962-18962	SILVERDALE
18247-18247	SAINT JOHNS	18444-18444	MOSCOW	18810-18810	ATHENS	18963-18963	SOLEBURY
18248-18248	SHEPPTON	18445-18445	NEWFOUNDLAND	18812-18812	BRACKNEY	18964-18964	SOUDERTON
18249-18249	SUGARLOAF	18446-18446	NICHOLSON	18813-18813	BROOKLYN	18966-18966	SOUTHAMPTON
18250-18250	SUMMIT HILL	18447-18448	OLYPHANT	18814-18814	BURLINGTON	18968-18968	SPINNERSTOWN
18251-18251	SYBERTSVILLE	18449-18449	ORSON	18815-18815	CAMPTOWN	18969-18969	TELFORD
18252-18252	TAMAQUA	18451-18451	PAUPACK	18816-18816	DIMOCK	18970-18970	TRUMBAUERSVILLE
18254-18254	TRESCKOW	18452-18452	PECKVILLE	18817-18817	EAST SMITHFIELD	18971-18971	TYLERSPORT
18255-18255	WEATHERLY	18453-18453	PLEASANT MOUNT	18818-18818	FRIENDSVILLE	18972-18972	UPPER BLACK EDDY
18256-18256	WESTON	18454-18454	POYNTELLE	18820-18820	GIBSON	18974-18974	WARMINSTER
18301-18301	EAST STROUDSBURG	18455-18455	PRESTON PARK	18821-18821	GREAT BEND	18976-18976	WARRINGTON
18320-18320	ANALOMINK	18456-18456	PROMPTON	18822-18822	HALLSTEAD	18977-18977	WASHINGTON
18321-18321	BARTONSVILLE	18457-18457	ROWLAND	18823-18823	HARFORD		CROSSING
18322-18322	BRODHEADSVILLE	18458-18458	SHOHOLA	18824-18824	HOP BOTTOM	18979-18979	WOXALL
18323-18323	BUCK HILL FALLS	18459-18459	SOUTH CANAAN	18825-18825	JACKSON	18980-18980	WYCOMBE
18324-18324	BUSHKILL	18460-18460	SOUTH STERLING	18826-18826	KINGSLEY	18981-18981	ZIONHILL
18325-18325	CANADENSIS	18461-18461	STARLIGHT	18827-18827	LANESBORO	18991-18991	WARMINSTER
18326-18326	CRESCO	18462-18462	STARRUCCA	18828-18828	LAWTON	19001-19001	ABINGTON
18327-18327	DELAWARE WATER GAP	18463-18463	STERLING	18829-18829	LE RAYSVILLE	19002-19002	AMBLER
18328-18328	DINGMANS FERRY	18464-18464	TAFTON	18830-18830	LITTLE MEADOWS	19003-19003	ARDMORE
18330-18330	EFFORT	18465-18465	THOMPSON	18831-18831	MILAN	19004-19004	BALA CYNWYD
18331-18331	GILBERT	18466-18466	TOBYHANNA	18832-18832	MONROETON	19006-19006	HUNTINGDON VALLEY
18332-18332	HENRYVILLE	18469-18469	TYLER HILL	18833-18833	NEW ALBANY	19007-19007	BRISTOL
18333-18333	KRESGEVILLE	18470-18470	UNION DALE	18834-18834	NEW MILFORD	19008-19008	BROOMALL
18334-18334	LONG POND	18471-18471	WAVERLY	18837-18837	ROME	19009-19009	BRYN ATHYN
18335-18335	MARSHALLS CREEK	18472-18472	WAYMART	18839-18839	RUSHVILLE	19010-19010	BRYN MAWR
18336-18336	MATAMORAS	18473-18473	WHITE MILLS	18840-18840	SAYRE	19012-19012	CHELTENHAM
18337-18337	MILFORD	18501-18505	SCRANTON	18842-18842	SOUTH GIBSON	19013-19013	CHESTER
18340-18340	MILLRIFT	18507-18507	MOOSIC	18843-18843	SOUTH MONTROSE	19014-19014	ASTON
18341-18341	MINISINK HILLS	18508-18515	SCRANTON	18844-18844	SPRINGVILLE	19015-19015	BROOKHAVEN
18342-18342	MOUNTAINHOME	18517-18517	TAYLOR	18845-18845	STEVENSVILLE	19016-19016	CHESTER
18343-18343	MOUNT BETHEL	18518-18518	OLD FORGE	18846-18846	SUGAR RUN	19017-19017	CHESTER HEIGHTS
18344-18344	MOUNT POCONO	18519-18519	DICKSON CITY	18847-18847	SUSQUEHANNA	19018-19018	CLIFTON HEIGHTS
18346-18346	POCONO SUMMIT	18522-18577	SCRANTON	18848-18848	TOWANDA	19019-19019	PHILADELPHIA
18347-18347	POCONO LAKE	18601-18601	BEACH HAVEN	18850-18850	ULSTER	19020-19020	BENSALEM
18348-18348	POCONO LAKE	18602-18602	BEAR CREEK	18851-18851	WARREN CENTER	19021-19021	CROYDON
	PRESERVE	18603-18603	BERWICK	18853-18853	WYALUSING	19022-19022	CRUM LYNNE
18349-18349	POCONO MANOR	18610-18610	BLAKESLEE	18854-18854	WYSOX	19023-19023	DARBY
18350-18350	POCONO PINES	18611-18611	CAMBRA	18901-18901	DOYLESTOWN	19025-19025	DRESHER
18351-18351	PORTLAND	18612-18612	DALLAS	18910-18910	BEDMINSTER	19026-19026	DREXEL HILL
18352-18352	REEDERS	18614-18614	DUSHORE	18911-18911	BLOOMING GLEN	19027-19027	ELKINS PARK
18353-18353	SAYLORSBURG	18615-18615	FALLS	18912-18912	BUCKINGHAM	19028-19028	EDGEMONT
18354-18354	SCIOTA	18616-18616	FORKSVILLE	18913-18913	CARVERSVILLE	19029-19029	ESSINGTON
18355-18355	SCOTRUN	18617-18617	GLEN LYON	18914-18914	CHALFONT	19030-19030	FAIRLESS HILLS
18356-18356	SHAWNEE ON	18618-18618	HARVEYS LAKE	18915-18915	COLMAR	19031-19031	FLOURTOWN
	DELAWARE	18619-18619	HILLSGROVE	18916-18916	DANBORO	19032-19032	FOLCROFT
18357-18357	SKYTOP	18621-18621	HUNLOCK CREEK	18917-18917	DUBLIN	19033-19033	FOLSOM
18360-18360	STROUDSBURG	18622-18622	HUNTINGTON MILLS	18918-18918	EARLINGTON	19034-19034	FORT WASHINGTON
18370-18370	SWIFTWATER	18623-18623	LACEYVILLE	18920-18920	ERWINNA	19035-19035	GLADWYNE
18371-18371	TAMIMENT	18624-18624	LAKE HARMONY	18921-18921	FERNDALE	19036-19036	GLENOLDEN
18372-18372	TANNERSVILLE	18625-18625	LAKE WINOLA	18922-18922	FOREST GROVE	19037-19037	GLEN RIDDLE LIMA
18373-18373	UNITY HOUSE	18626-18626	LAPORTE	18923-18923	FOUNTAINVILLE	19038-19038	GLENSIDE
18401-18401	ALDENVILLE	18627-18627	LEHMAN	18924-18924	FRANCONIA	19039-19039	GRADYVILLE
18403-18403	ARCHBALD	18628-18628	LOPEZ	18925-18925	FURLONG	19040-19040	HATBORO
18405-18405	BEACH LAKE	18629-18629	MEHOOPANY	18926-18926	GARDENVILLE	19041-19041	HAVERFORD
18407-18407	CARBONDALE	18630-18630	MESHOPPEN	18927-18927	HILLTOWN	19043-19043	HOLMES
18410-18410	CHINCHILLA	18631-18631	MIFFLINVILLE	18928-18928	HOLICONG	19044-19044	HORSHAM
18411-18411	CLARKS SUMMIT	18632-18632	MILDRED	18929-18929	JAMISON	19046-19046	JENKINTOWN
18413-18413	CLIFFORD	18634-18634	NANTICOKE	18930-18930	KINTNERSVILLE	19047-19049	LANGHORNE
18414-18414	DALTON	18635-18635	NESCOPECK	18931-18931	LAHASKA	19050-19050	LANSDOWNE
18415-18415	DAMASCUS	18636-18636	NOXEN	18932-18932	LINE LEXINGTON	19052-19052	LENNI
18416-18416	ELMHURST	18637-18637	NUANGOLA	18933-18933	LUMBERVILLE	19053-19053	FEASTERVILLE
18417-18417	EQUINUNK	18640-18641	PITTSTON	18934-18934	MECHANICSVILLE		TREVOSE
18419-18419	FACTORYVILLE	18642-18642	DURYEA	18935-18935	MILFORD SQUARE	19054-19059	LEVITTOWN
18420-18420	FLEETVILLE	18643-18643	PITTSTON	18936-18936	MONTGOMERYVILLE	19061-19061	MARCUS HOOK
18421-18421	FOREST CITY	18644-18644	WYOMING	18938-18938	NEW HOPE	19063-19063	MEDIA
18424-18424	GOULDSBORO	18651-18651	PLYMOUTH	18940-18940	NEWTOWN	19064-19064	SPRINGFIELD
18425-18425	GREELEY	18653-18653	RANSOM	18942-18942	OTTSVILLE	19065-19065	MEDIA
18426-18426	GREENTOWN	18654-18654	SHAWANESE	18943-18943	PENNS PARK	19066-19066	MERION STATION
18427-18427	HAMLIN	18655-18655	SHICKSHINNY	18944-18944	PERKASIE	19067-19067	MORRISVILLE
18428-18428	HAWLEY	18656-18656	SWEET VALLEY	18946-18946	PINEVILLE	19070-19070	MORTON
18430-18430	HERRICK CENTER	18657-18657	TUNKHANNOCK	18947-18947	PIPERSVILLE	19072-19072	NARBERTH

19073-19073 NEWTOWN SQUARE	19350-19350 LANDENBERG	19436-19436 GWYNEDD	19511-19511 BOWERS
19074-19074 NORWOOD	19351-19351 LEWISVILLE	19437-19437 GWYNEDD VALLEY	19512-19512 BOYERTOWN
19075-19075 ORELAND	19352-19352 LINCOLN UNIVERSITY	19438-19438 HARLEYSVILLE	19516-19516 CENTERPORT
19076-19076 PROSPECT PARK	19353-19353 LIONVILLE	19440-19440 HATFIELD	19517-19517 DAUBERVILLE
19078-19078 RIDLEY PARK	19354-19354 LYNDELL	19441-19441 HARLEYSVILLE	19518-19518 DOUGLASSVILLE
19079-19079 SHARON HILL	19355-19355 MALVERN	19442-19442 KIMBERTON	19519-19519 EARLVILLE
19080-19080 WAYNE	19357-19357 MENDENHALL	19443-19443 KULPSVILLE	19520-19520 ELVERSON
19081-19081 SWARTHMORE	19358-19358 MODENA	19444-19444 LAFAYETTE HILL	19522-19522 FLEETWOOD
19082-19082 UPPER DARBY	19360-19360 NEW LONDON	19446-19446 LANSDALE	19523-19523 GEIGERTOWN
19083-19083 HAVERTOWN	19362-19362 NOTTINGHAM	19450-19450 LEDERACH	19525-19525 GILBERTSVILLE
19085-19085 VILLANOVA	19363-19363 OXFORD	19451-19451 MAINLAND	19526-19526 HAMBURG
19086-19086 WALLINGFORD	19365-19365 PARKESBURG	19452-19452 MIQUON	19529-19529 KEMPTON
19087-19089 WAYNE	19366-19366 POCOPSON	19453-19453 MONT CLARE	19530-19530 KUTZTOWN
19090-19090 WILLOW GROVE	19367-19367 POMEROY	19454-19455 NORTH WALES	19533-19533 LEESPORT
19091-19091 MEDIA	19369-19369 SADSBURYVILLE	19456-19456 OAKS	19534-19534 LENHARTSVILLE
19092-19093 PHILADELPHIA	19370-19370 STEELVILLE	19457-19457 PARKER FORD	19535-19535 LIMEKILN
19094-19094 WOODLYN	19371-19371 SUPLEE	19460-19460 PHOENIXVILLE	19536-19536 LYON STATION
19095-19095 WYNCOTE	19372-19372 THORNDALE	19462-19462 PLYMOUTH MEETING	19538-19538 MAXATAWNY
19096-19096 WYNNEWOOD	19373-19373 THORNTON	19464-19465 POTTSTOWN	19539-19539 MERTZTOWN
19098-19098 HOLMES	19374-19374 TOUGHKENAMON	19468-19468 ROYERSFORD	19540-19540 MOHNTON
19099-19255 PHILADELPHIA	19375-19375 UNIONVILLE	19470-19470 SAINT PETERS	19541-19541 MOHRSVILLE
19301-19301 PAOLI	19376-19376 WAGONTOWN	19472-19472 SASSAMANSVILLE	19542-19542 MONOCACY STATION
19310-19310 ATGLEN	19380-19383 WEST CHESTER	19473-19473 SCHWENKSVILLE	19543-19543 MORGANTOWN
19311-19311 AVONDALE	19390-19390 WEST GROVE	19474-19474 SKIPPACK	19544-19544 MOUNT AETNA
19312-19312 BERWYN	19395-19395 WESTTOWN	19475-19475 SPRING CITY	19545-19545 NEW BERLINVILLE
19316-19316 BRANDAMORE	19397-19399 SOUTHEASTERN	19477-19477 SPRING HOUSE	19547-19547 OLEY
19317-19317 CHADDS FORD	19401-19404 NORRISTOWN	19478-19478 SPRING MOUNT	19548-19548 PINE FORGE
19318-19318 CHATHAM	19405-19405 BRIDGEPORT	19480-19480 UWCHLAND	19549-19549 PORT CLINTON
19319-19319 CHEYNEY	19406-19406 KING OF PRUSSIA	19481-19485 VALLEY FORGE	19550-19550 REHRERSBURG
19320-19320 COATESVILLE	19407-19407 AUDUBON	19486-19486 WEST POINT	19551-19551 ROBESONIA
19330-19330 COCHRANVILLE	19408-19408 EAGLEVILLE	19487-19487 KING OF PRUSSIA	19554-19554 SHARTLESVILLE
19331-19331 CONCORDVILLE	19409-19409 FAIRVIEW VILLAGE	19488-19489 NORRISTOWN	19555-19555 SHOEMAKERSVILLE
19333-19333 DEVON	19420-19420 ARCOLA	19490-19490 WORCESTER	19557-19557 STONY RUN
19335-19335 DOWNINGTOWN	19421-19421 BIRCHRUNVILLE	19492-19492 ZIEGLERVILLE	19559-19559 STRAUSSTOWN
19339-19340 CONCORDVILLE	19422-19422 BLUE BELL	19493-19496 VALLEY FORGE	19560-19560 TEMPLE
19341-19341 EXTON	19423-19423 CEDARS	19501-19501 ADAMSTOWN	19562-19562 TOPTON
19342-19342 GLEN MILLS	19424-19424 BLUE BELL	19503-19503 BALLY	19564-19564 VIRGINVILLE
19343-19343 GLENMOORE	19425-19425 CHESTER SPRINGS	19504-19504 BARTO	19565-19565 WERNERSVILLE
19344-19344 HONEY BROOK	19426-19426 COLLEGEVILLE	19505-19505 BECHTELSVILLE	19567-19567 WOMELSDORF
19345-19345 IMMACULATA	19428-19429 CONSHOHOCKEN	19506-19506 BERNVILLE	19601-19640 READING
19346-19346 KELTON	19430-19430 CREAMERY	19507-19507 BETHEL	
19347-19347 KEMBLESVILLE	19432-19432 DEVAULT	19508-19508 BIRDSBORO	
19348-19348 KENNETT SQUARE	19435-19435 FREDERICK	19510-19510 BLANDON	

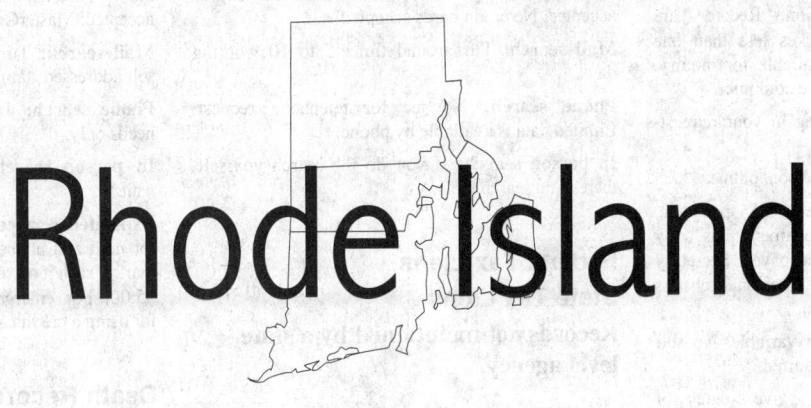

Rhode Island

General Help Numbers:

Governor's Office
222 State House
Providence, RI 02903-1196
http://www.governor.state.ri.us

401-222-2080
Fax 401-861-5894
8:30AM-4:30PM

Attorney General's Office
150 S Main St
Providence, RI 02903
http://www.riag.state.ri.us

401-274-4400
Fax 401-222-1302
8:30AM-4:30PM

State Court Administrator
Supreme Court
250 Benefit St
Providence, RI 02903
http://www.courts.state.ri.us/supreme/index.htm

401-222-3272
Fax 401-222-3599
8:30AM-4:30PM

State Archives
State Archives & Public Records Admin.
337 Westminster St
Providence, RI 02903
http://www.state.ri.us/archives

401-222-2353
Fax 401-222-3199
8:30AM-4:30PM M-SA

State Specifics:

Capital: Providence
                          Providence County

Time Zone: EST

Number of Counties: 5

Population: 1,048,319

Web Site: www.state.ri.us

State Agencies

Criminal Records

Department of Attorney General, Bureau of Criminal Identification, 150 S Main Street, Providence, RI 02903; 401-274-4400, 8:30AM-4:30PM.

http://www.riag.org

Searching: Criminal records are only released to law enforcement agencies or with a signed notarized authorization from the subject. All arrests and convictions are reported. You may also obtain records at the county level. They require a picture ID of the requester and SSN and will call the Notary on the authorization for verification.

Access by: mail, in person.

Fee & Payment: The fee is $5.00 per name. Fee payee: Department of Attorney General. Prepayment required. Personal checks accepted. No credit cards accepted.

Mail search: Turnaround time: up to 2 weeks. A self addressed stamped envelope is requested.

In person search: Turnaround time is while you wait.

Corporation Records
Fictitious Name
Limited Partnerships
Limited Liability Company Records
Limited Liability Partnerships
Not For Profit Entities

Secretary of State, Corporations Division, 100 N Main St, Providence, RI 02903-1335; 401-222-3040, 401-222-1356 (Fax), 8:30AM-4:30PM.

http://155.212.254.78/corporations.htm

Indexing & Storage: Records are available from the beginning of the Division. Records are computerized since 1984. It takes less than one day before new records are available for inquiry. Records are indexed on an inhouse computer.

Searching: Include the following in your request- full name of business.

Access by: mail, phone, fax, in person, online.

Fee & Payment: The copy fee is $.15 per page. Certification costs $5.00 per document plus copy fees. There is no search fee. Fee payee: Secretary of State. Prepayment required. Personal checks accepted. No credit cards accepted.

Mail search: Turnaround time: variable. No self addressed stamped envelope is required.

Phone search: They will give date of incorporation, registered agent, one officer, status, and whether domestic or foreign.

Fax search: Same criteria as searching by mail.

In person search: Searching is available in person.

Online search: At the web, search filings for active and inactive Rhode Island and foreign business corporations, non-profit corporations, limited partnerships, limited liability companies, and limited liability partnerships. Weekly lisiting of new corporations are also available. There is no fee.

Other access: The corporation database may be purchased on CD.

Trademarks/Servicemarks

Secretary of State, Trademark Section, 100 N Main St, Providence, RI 02903-1335; 401-222-1487, 401-222-3879 (Fax), 8:30AM-4:30PM.

http://www.sec.state.ri.us

Indexing & Storage: Records are available from the beginning of the Division. It takes less than one day before new records are available for inquiry.

Searching: All records are open to the public. Include the following in your request- trademark/servicemark name, registration number and applicant name, if known.

Access by: mail, phone, fax.

Fee & Payment: There is no search fee. The copy fee is $.15 per page.

Mail search: Turnaround time: 3 to 5 days. No self addressed stamped envelope is required.

Phone search: No fee for telephone request. Limited verification information available.

Fax search: Fax searching available.

Uniform Commercial Code

UCC Division, Secretary of State, 100 North Main St, Providence, RI 02903; 401-222-2249, 8:30AM-4:30PM.

http://155.212.254.78/corporations.htm

Indexing & Storage: Records are indexed on hard copy.

Searching: Use search request form UCC-11. All tax liens are filed at the city/town level. Include the following in your request-debtor name.

Access by: mail, phone, in person.

Fee & Payment: The search fee is $5.00 per name, copies are $.15 each. Fee payee: Secretary

of State. Prepayment required. Personal checks accepted. No credit cards accepted.

Mail search: Turnaround time: 5 to 10 working days.

Phone search: No fee for telephone request. Limited data is available by phone.

In person search: If you do the search yourself, there is no search fee.

Federal Tax Liens
State Tax Liens
Records not maintained by a state level agency.

Note: All records are located at the county level.

Sales Tax Registrations

Taxation Division, Sales & Use Tax Office, One Capitol Hill, Providence, RI 02908-5800; 401-222-2937, 401-222-6006 (Fax), 8:30AM-4PM.

http://www.tax.state.ri.us

Indexing & Storage: Records are available from the 1960's. All current permits are on the computer, all inactive records are kept on microfiche. New records are available for inquiry immediately.

Searching: This agency will only confirm that a business is registered. They will provide no other information. Include the following in your request-business name. They will also search by tax permit number.

Access by: mail, phone, fax, in person.

Fee & Payment: There is no search fee nor a copy fee, unless extensive documents are requested.

Mail search: Turnaround time: 7 to 10 days. A self addressed stamped envelope is requested.

Phone search: It will take 24 hours for a response.

Fax search: Same criteria as mail searching.

In person search: It will take 24 hours for a response.

Birth Certificates

State Department of Health, Division of Vital Records, 3 Capitol Hill, Room 101, Providence, RI 02908-5097; 401-222-2812, 401-222-2811, 8:30AM-4:30PM.

http://www.healthri.org/vital/vital.htm

Note: If the record is less than 100 years old, it can also be obtained from the city or town where birth occurred.

Indexing & Storage: Records are available from 1900 to present. New records are available for inquiry immediately. Records are indexed on microfiche, inhouse computer.

Searching: Investigative searches must have a signed release form from person of record or immediate family member. Include the following in your request-full name, names of parents, mother's maiden name, date of birth, place of birth.

Access by: mail, phone, in person.

Fee & Payment: The fee is $15.00 for 2 years searched and $.50 for each additional year. Fee payee: General Treasurer, State of Rhode Island. Prepayment required. Credit cards for emergencies

only. Personal checks accepted. Credit cards accepted: MasterCard, Visa, AmEx, Discover.

Mail search: Turnaround time: 4 to 6 weeks. A self addressed stamped envelope is requested.

Phone search: This is for emergency, expedited needs only.

In person search: Turnaround time while you wait.

Expedited service: Expedited service is available for mail and phone searches. For a 1 week service, mark "rush" on envelope and send in an extra $5.00. For emergencies, add an additional $5.00 for using a credit card and $15.50 for shipping.

Death Records

State Department of Health, Division of Vital Records, 3 Capitol Hill, Room 101, Providence, RI 02908-5097; 401-222-2812, 401-222-2811, 8:30AM-4:30PM.

http://www.healthri.org/vital/vital.htm

Note: Records less than 50 years old can be obtained at the town or city where death took place.

Indexing & Storage: Records are available from 1951 to present. For records from 1853 to 1950, contact RI Archives at 401-222-2353. New records are available for inquiry immediately. Records are indexed on microfiche, inhouse computer.

Searching: Investigative searches must have a signed release from immediate family member. Include the following in your request-full name, date of death, place of death, names of parents, mother's maiden name. Any other identifying information is helpful.

Access by: mail, phone, in person.

Fee & Payment: The fee is $15.00 for 2 years searched and $.50 for each additional year. Fee payee: General Treasurer, State of Rhode Island. Prepayment required. Credit cards are for emergency use only. Personal checks accepted. Credit cards accepted: MasterCard, Visa, AmEx, Discover.

Mail search: Turnaround time: 4 to 6 weeks. A self addressed stamped envelope is requested.

Phone search: See expedited services.

In person search: Searching is available in person.

Expedited service: Expedited service is available for mail and phone searches. You must mark "RUSH" on the outside of the envelope and enclose an extra $5.00, if you want 1 week turnaround time. For true emergencies, you can phone in. Add $5.00 fee for use of credit card and provide return express pre-paid package.

Marriage Certificates

State Department of Health, Division of Vital Records, 3 Capitol Hill, Room 101, Providence, RI 02908-5097; 401-222-2812, 401-222-2811, 8:30AM-4:30PM M-F.

http://www.healthri.org/vital/vital.htm

Note: The record may be obtained from the town or city where the marriage took place, if the record is less than 100 years old.

Indexing & Storage: Records are available from 1900 to present. New records are available for inquiry immediately. Records are indexed on microfiche, inhouse computer.

Searching: Investigative searches must have a signed release form from persons of record or immediate family member. Include the following in your request-names of husband and wife, date of marriage, place or county of marriage, wife's maiden name.

Access by: mail, phone, in person.

Fee & Payment: The search fee is $15.00 for 2 years searched and $.50 for each additional year. Fee payee: General Treasurer, State of Rhode Island. Prepayment required. Credit card use is for emergencies only. Personal checks accepted. Credit cards accepted: MasterCard, Visa, AmEx, Discover.

Mail search: Turnaround time: 4 to 6 weeks. A self addressed stamped envelope is requested.

Phone search: See expedited services.

In person search: Searching is available in person.

Expedited service: Expedited service is available for mail and phone searches. For 1 week turnaround, send an extra $5.00 and mark "RUSH" on the outside of the envelope. For true emergencies, you can order by phone. Add $5.00 fee for use of credit card and provide return express pre-paid package.

Divorce Records

Records not maintained by a state level agency.

Note: Divorce records are found at one of the 4 county Family Courts.

Workers' Compensation Records

Department of Labor & Training, Division of Workers' Compensation, PO Box 20190, Cranston, RI 02920 (Courier: 1511 Pontiac Ave, Cranston, RI 02920); 401-462-8100, 8:30AM-4PM.

http://www.dlt.state.ri.us

Indexing & Storage: Records are available from 1950s. New records are available for inquiry immediately. Records are indexed on inhouse computer.

Searching: Records are not available for employment screening. A first report of injury is not public, by law. Records are released to claimant, attorneys, employer and insurer only if connected to case. Include the following in your request-claimant name, Social Security Number, file number (if known), reason for information request, specific records that you need copies of. Records of insurance carrier coverage only are available for no charge by phone or mail. The following data is not released: medical records.

Access by: mail, in person.

Fee & Payment: The search fee is $15 per hour. Copies are $.15 per page. There is a $.40 per page fee for return by fax. Fee payee: Department of Labor. Prepayment is required for first time requesters. Personal checks accepted. No credit cards accepted.

Mail search: Turnaround time: 1 to 2 weeks. A self addressed stamped envelope is requested.

In person search: Proof of identity is required.

Driver Records

Division of Motor Vehicles, Driving Record Clerk, Operator Control, 286 Main Street, Pawtucket, RI 02860; 401-588-3010, 8:30AM-4:30PM.

http://www.dmv.state.ri.us

Note: Copies of tickets may be obtained without fee by writing to the Traffic Tribunal at the address listed above.

Indexing & Storage: Records are available for 3 years for accidents and moving violations, 5 years for alcohol-related violations or suspensions, 3 years after reinstatement for suspensions. Surrendered licenses are purged 3 years after expiration. It takes 20 days after received from courts before new records are available for inquiry.

Searching: Information is not made available for the purpose of commercial solicitation or trade. A description of proposed use must be submitted in advance for departmental approval of high volume requesters. Include the following in your request-driver's license number, full name, date of birth. The following data is not released: Social Security Numbers.

Access by: mail, in person.

Fee & Payment: The fee is $16 per record request. This is the highest fee in the nation for a driving record. Fee payee: Division of Motor Vehicles. Prepayment required. Personal checks accepted. No credit cards accepted.

Mail search: Turnaround time: 1 week. A self addressed stamped envelope is requested.

In person search: Although you may request a record in person, results must be picked up the next day or mailed back.

Other access: Rhode Island offers a tape retrieval system for high volume users.

Vehicle Ownership
Vehicle Identification

Registry of Motor Vehicles, c/o Registration Files, 286 Main Street, Pawtucket, RI 02860; 401-588-3020 x2552, 8:30AM-3:30PM.

http://www.dmv.state.ri.us

Indexing & Storage: Records are available for 3 years for title information, for 10 years for registration information. It takes 20 days from issue before new records are available for inquiry.

Searching: Request must be in writing and the purpose stated. Records will not be released for commercial or solicitation purposes. Casual requesters cannot obtain records.

Access by: mail, in person.

Fee & Payment: The fee is $10.00 per record request. The state will release lien information. There is a full charge for a no record found request. Fee payee: Registry of Motor Vehicles. Prepayment required. Personal checks accepted. No credit cards accepted.

Mail search: Turnaround time: 1 week. A self addressed stamped envelope is requested.

In person search: Records are not released in person, but are mailed.

Other access: Bulk retrieval of vehicle and ownership information is limited to statistical purposes.

Accident Reports

Rhode Island State Police, Accident Record Division, 311 Danielson Pike, North Scituate, RI 02857; 401-444-1143, 401-444-1133 (Fax), 10AM-4PM M,T,TH,F.

http://risp.state.ri.us

Indexing & Storage: Records are available for the past 2 years plus the current year. Accidents before that are stored in archives. Hard copy files are indexed. It takes 7-14 days before new records are available for inquiry.

Searching: Include the following in your request-reason for information request, full name, date of accident, location of accident.

Access by: mail, phone, in person.

Fee & Payment: The fee is $5.00 per record. Fee payee: Treasurer - State of Rhode Island. Prepayment required. Personal checks accepted. No credit cards accepted.

Mail search: Turnaround time: 1 week. A self addressed stamped envelope is requested.

Phone search: No fee for telephone request. The office will let a requester know if a report is available, but information will not be given over the phone.

In person search: Same day processing is available, provided report has been received.

Vessel Ownership
Vessel Registration

Dept of Environmental Management, Office of Boat Registration, 235 Promenade, Rm 360, Providence, RI 02908; 401-222-6647, 401-222-1181 (Fax), 8:30AM-3:30PM M-F.

http://www.state.ri.us/dem

Indexing & Storage: Records are available from the late 1970s to the present. Records are computer indexed for the last 3 years. This is a title state, lien information shows on the title record. All boats over 14 ft must be titled and registered.

Searching: All requests must be in writing on the agency's request form. Call or write for the form. Records cannot be purchased for solicitation or commercial purposes. The name or registration number or RI number is needed for a request.

Access by: mail, in person.

Fee & Payment: There is no fee.

Mail search: Turnaround time: 1 to 2 weeks. No self addressed stamped envelope is required.

In person search: No fee for request. Turnaround time varies.

Legislation Records

Secretary of State, State House, Room 38, Public Information Center, Providence, RI 02903; 401-222-3983 (Bill Status Only), 401-222-2473 (State Library), 401-222-1356 (Fax), 8:30AM-4:30PM.

http://www.sec.state.ri.us

Note: All bills are available at the State Law Library. Current session bills are available from the office of Public Information.

Indexing & Storage: Records are available for current session only.

Searching: One may search by bill number, subject, word, sponsor, etc.

Access by: mail, phone, fax, in person, online.

Fee & Payment: Copies are made by the Office of Public Information, $.15 per page. There is no search fee.

Mail search: No self addressed stamped envelope is required.

Phone search: Records are available by phone.

Fax search: Fax searching available.

In person search: There are public access terminals available.

Online search: The site search http://dirac.rilin.state.ri.us/BillStatus/webclass1.asp provides two excellent means to search enactments and measures by keywords or bill numbers.

Voter Registration
Records not maintained by a state level agency.

Note: The Local Board of Canvassers keeps records at the town and city level. Although records are open, they may not be purchased for commercial purposes.

GED Certificates

Department of Education, GED Testing, 255 Westminster, Providence, RI 02908; 401-222-4600 x2181, 7:30AM-4PM.

Searching: Include the following in your request- Social Security Number, date of birth. A signed release is also required for a verification or transcript copy.

Access by: mail, phone, in person.

Fee & Payment: The fee for a transcript is $3.00 or duplicate diploma. There is no fee for a verification. Fee payee: General Treasurer, State of Rhode Island. Prepayment required. Personal checks accepted. No credit cards accepted.

Mail search: Turnaround time: 1 week. No self addressed stamped envelope is required.

Phone search: Limited data is available.

In person search: Searching is available in person.

Hunting License Information
Fishing License Information

RI DEM, Boat Registration & Licensing, 235 Promenade, Providence, RI 02908; 401-222-3576 (License Issue Only), 401-222-1181 (Fax), 8:30AM-3:30PM.

http://www.state.ri.us/dem

Indexing & Storage: Records are available for the current year only. Agents have hard copies.

Searching: Although all records are considered open, commercial use of the records is not permitted. Include the following in your request- date of application, date of birth, address. Also, include where purchased. Requests must be in writing.

Access by: mail, phone, fax, in person.

Fee & Payment: There is no fee for a short search or confirmation. Otherwise, for extensive searches the rate $15.00 per hour. Fee payee: RI DEM. Prepayment required. Personal checks accepted. No credit cards accepted.

Mail search: Turnaround time: 1 week to 10 days.

Phone search: They will confirm only.

Fax search: Same criteria as mail searches.

In person search: They will return by mail.

Rhode Island State Licensing Agencies

Licenses Searchable Online

Acupuncturist #13................................www.health.state.ri.us/l2k/license.htm
Asbestos Abatement Worker #13................www.health.state.ri.us/l2k/license.htm
Athletic Trainer #13..............................www.health.state.ri.us/l2k/license.htm
Audiologist #13...................................www.health.state.ri.us/l2k/license.htm
Barber #13...www.health.state.ri.us/l2k/license.htm
Cable Installer #04...............................www.crb.state.ri.us/search.asp
Charter School #16................................www.ridoe.net/charterschools/list.htm
Chimney Sweep #04..............................www.crb.state.ri.us/search.asp
Chiropractor #13..................................www.health.state.ri.us/l2k/license.htm
Clinical Lab Scientist/Technician #07...........http://63.72.31.182
Clinical Lab Scientist-Cytogenetic #07.........http://63.72.31.182
Dentist #13..www.health.state.ri.us/l2k/license.htm
Dietitian/Nutritionist #13.........................www.health.state.ri.us/l2k/license.htm
Electrologist #13..................................www.health.state.ri.us/l2k/license.htm
Electron Microscopy, Clinical Lab Scientist #07http://63.72.31.182
Embalmer #13.....................................www.health.state.ri.us/l2k/license.htm
Emergency Medical Technician #13..............www.health.state.ri.us/l2k/license.htm
Funeral Director #13..............................www.health.state.ri.us/l2k/license.htm
Hazardous Waste Transporter #09...............www.state.ri.us/dem/programs/benviron/waste/transpor/index.htm
Hearing Aid Dispenser #13.......................www.health.state.ri.us/l2k/license.htm
Histologic Technician, Clinical #07...............http://63.72.31.182
Lobbyist #25......................................www.lobbyist.net/RhodeIsl/RHOLOB.htm
Marriage Therapist #13...........................www.health.state.ri.us/l2k/license.htm
Medical Doctor #24...............................www.docboard.org/ri/df/search.htm
Medical Waste Transporter #09..................www.state.ri.us/dem/programs/benviron/waste/transpor/index.htm
Midwife #13.......................................www.health.state.ri.us/l2k/license.htm
Notary Public #15.................................www.corps.state.ri.us/notaries/notaries.htm
Nurse #13...www.health.state.ri.us/l2k/license.htm
Nursing Assistant #13.............................www.health.state.ri.us/l2k/license.htm
Nursing Home Administrator #13.................www.health.state.ri.us/l2k/license.htm
Occupational Therapist #13.......................www.health.state.ri.us/l2k/license.htm
Optometrist #13...................................www.odfinder.org/LicSearch.asp
Osteopathic Physician #13........................www.docboard.org/ri/df/search.htm
Pharmacy #03.....................................www.health.state.ri.us/l2k/license.htm
Physical Therapist #13............................www.health.state.ri.us/l2k/license.htm
Podiatrist #13.....................................www.health.state.ri.us/l2k/license.htm
Prosthetist #13....................................www.health.state.ri.us/l2k/license.htm
Psychologist #13..................................www.health.state.ri.us/l2k/license.htm
Residential Building Contractor #04..............www.crb.state.ri.us/search.asp
Respiratory Care Practitioner #13................www.health.state.ri.us/l2k/license.htm
Sanitarian #13....................................www.health.state.ri.us/l2k/license.htm
Security Alarm Installer #04......................www.crb.state.ri.us/search.asp
Septic Transporter #09...........................www.state.ri.us/dem/programs/benviron/waste/transpor/index.htm
Social Worker #13.................................www.health.state.ri.us/l2k/license.htm
Speech Pathologist #13...........................www.health.state.ri.us/l2k/license.htm
Tattoo Artist #13..................................www.health.state.ri.us/l2k/license.htm
Underground Sprinkler Installer #04..............www.crb.state.ri.us/search.asp
Veterinarian #13..................................www.health.state.ri.us/l2k/license.htm

Licensing Quick Finder

Acupuncturist #13 401-222-2827
Alarm Agent/Company #11 401-222-3857
Arborist #10 401-647-3367
Architect #05.......................................401-222-2565
Asbestos Abatement Worker #13..........401-222-3601
Athletic Trainer #13 401-222-5888
Attorney #21.......................................401-222-3272
Auctioneer #11....................................401-222-3857
Audiologist #13....................................401-222-2827
Automobile Body Shop #11 401-222-3857
Automobile Glass Installer #11 401-222-3857
Automobile Wrecker #11 401-222-3857
Bank #05 401-222-2405

Barber/Barber Shop #13......................401-222-2827
Barber Instructor #13...........................401-222-2827
Beekeeper #09.....................401-222-2781 x4510
Blaster #19 401-294-0861
Bondsman #18.....................................401-222-3212
Boxer #05 401-222-6541
Cable Installer #04 401-222-1268
Cattle Dealer #09 ....401-222-2781 x4510
Charter School #16 401-222-4600
Chemical Dependency Professional/Supervisor #06
....401-233-2215
Chimney Sweep #04 401-222-1268
Chiropractor #13 401-222-2827

Clinical Lab Scientist/Technician #07 401-222-2877
Clinical Lab Scientist-Cytogenetic #07 ..401-222-2827
Clinical Supervisor, Recognized #06.....401-233-2215
Controlled Substance Wholesaler #03 ..401-222-2837
Court Reporter #26 401-222-3215
Cytotechnologist #13............................401-222-2827
Dental Hygienist #13 401-222-2151
Dentist #13 401-222-2151
Dietitian/Nutritionist #13.......................401-222-5888
Electrician #08 401-462-8527
Electrologist #13 401-222-2827
Electron Microscopy, Clinical Lab Scientist #07.........
....401-222-2827

Elevator Inspector #08...........................401-462-8527
Elevator Mechanic #08 401-462-8527
Embalmer #13 401-222-2827
Emergency Medical Technician #13......401-222-2401
Engineer #02 401-222-2038
Esthetician #13 401-222-2827
Facility Designer #09 401-222-6820
Family Day Care Home Provider #22....401-222-4741
Family Group Day Care Home Provider #22 ....
....401-222-4741
Fire Alarm Installer #19 401-294-0861
Fire Extinguisher Installer/Service #19..401-294-0861
Fireworks Shooter #19 401-294-0861
Fisher, Commercial #09 401-222-6647
Funeral Director #13.............................401-222-2827
Fur Buyer #09 401-222-6647
Hairdresser/Hairdresser Instructor #13..401-222-2827
Hazardous Waste Transport #9 ..401-222-4700 x7517
Hearing Aid Dispenser #13....................401-222-2827
Histologic Technician, Clinical #07........401-222-2827
Hoisting Engineer #08 401-462-8527
Hypodermic Needles & Syringes Dispenser #03.........
....401-222-2837
Insurance Adjuster #05.........................401-222-2223
Insurance Appraiser #05 401-222-2223
Insurance Broker #05 401-222-2223
Insurance Producer #05 401-222-2223
Insurance Solicitor #05.........................401-222-2223
Investment Advisor #05.........................401-222-3048
Landscape Architect #02 401-222-2038
Landscaper #05 401-222-2565
Lifeguard #12 401-222-2632
Liquor Control #05................................401-222-2562
Lobbyist #25 401-222-6616
Manicurist/ Manicurist Shop #13 401-222-2827
Marriage Therapist #13 401-222-2827
Medical Doctor #24 401-222-3855
Medical Waste Transporter #9....401-222-4700 x7517
Mental Health Counselor #13 401-222-2827

Midwife #13 401-222-5700
Mobile Home Park #11 401-222-3857
Mobile/Manufactured Home Mfg./Dealer #11 ....
....401-222-3857
Money Broker #05.................................401-222-2405
Mortgage Broker #05.............................401-222-2405
Notary Public #15..................................401-222-1487
Nuclear Medicine Technologist #13 401-222-5700
Nurse #13 401-222-2827
Nurse-LPN #13 401-222-5888
Nurseryman #09 ....401-222-2781 x4510
Nursing Assistant #13 401-222-5888
Nursing Home Administrator #13...........401-222-5888
Occupational Therapist #13...................401-222-2827
Optician #13..401-222-2827
Optometrist #13 401-222-2827
Osteopathic Physician #13....................401-222-3855
Park Ranger #12....................................401-222-2632
Pesticide Applicator #09 ....401-222-2781 x4510
Pharmacist/Pharmacy Technician #03 ..401-222-2837
Pharmacy #03..401-222-2837
Pharmacy, Non-residence #03...............401-222-2837
Physical Therapist #13..........................401-222-2827
Physical Therapist Assistant #13 401-222-2827
Physician Assistant #13.........................401-222-2827
Physicians Controlled Substance #03 ...401-222-2837
Pipefitter #08..401-462-8527
Plumber/Plumber Journeyman #13........401-222-2827
Plumber, Master #13 401-222-2827
Podiatrist #13 401-222-2827
Prevention Specialist/Supervisor (Social Work) #06 ...
....401-233-2215
Prosthetist #13......................................401-222-2827
Psychologist #13...................................401-222-2827
Public Accountant-CPA #01...................401-222-3185
Pyrotechnic Operator #19......................401-294-0861
Radiographer #13..................................401-222-2827
Reading Specialist #16..........................401-222-2675
Real Estate Appraiser #05....................401-222-2255

Real Estate Broker/Salesperson #05 401-222-2255
Refrigeration Technician #08 401-462-8527
Residential Building Contractor #04 401-222-1268
Respiratory Care Practitioner #13.........401-222-2827
Salvage Yard #11..................................401-222-3857
Sanitarian #13 401-222-2827
School Coach #16..................................401-222-2675
School Guidance Counselor #16 401-222-2675
School Principal/Superintendent/Supervisor #16 ....
....401-222-2675
School Psychologist/Social Worker #16 401-222-2675
Securities Broker/Dealer #05 401-222-3048
Securities Broker/Dealer Sales Representative #05....
....401-222-3048
Securities Sales Representative #05.....401-222-3048
Security Alarm Installer #04 401-222-1268
Septic Transporter #09 ....401-222-4700 x7517
Sewage Disposal System Installer #9 ...401-222-6820
Sheet Metal Technician #08 401-462-8527
Sheet Metal Worker #08........................401-462-8527
Ship Pilot #20.......................................401-783-5551
Social Worker #13.................................401-222-2827
Speech Pathologist #13.........................401-222-2827
Surveyor #05...401-222-2565
Surveyor Firm #02.................................401-222-2038
Tattoo Artist #13...................................401-222-2827
Teacher #16...401-222-2675
Telecommunications Technician #08 401-462-8527
Trapper #09 401-222-6647
Travel Agent #05...................................401-222-3857
Underground Sprinkler Installer #04.......401-222-1268
Vendor Employee #05 401-222-2405
Veterinarian #13....................................401-222-2827
Waste Water Treatment Plant Operator #09.............
....401-222-6820
Wildlife Propagator #09 401-222-6647
Wildlife Rehabilitator #23 401-789-0281
Woods Operator #10..............................401-647-3367
Wrestler #05 401-222-6541

Licensing Agency Information

#01 Board of Accountancy, 233 Richmond St, #236, Providence, RI 02903-4236; 401-222-3185, Fax: 401-222-6654.

#03 Board of Pharmacy, 3 Capitol Hill, Rm 205, Providence, RI 02908; 401-222-2837, Fax: 401-222-2158. www.health.state.ri.us

#04 Contractors' Registration Board, 1 Capitol Hill, 2nd Fl, Providence, RI 02908; 401-222-1270, Fax: 401-222-2599. www.crb.state.ri.us
Direct web site URL to search for licensees: www.crb.state.ri.us/search.asp. You can search online using name or registration #

#05 Business Regulation Department, 233 Richmond St, Providence, RI 02903-4232; 401-222-2246. www.dbr.state.ri.us

#06 Certification of Chemical Dependency Professionals, 345 Waterman Ave, Smithfield, RI 02917; 401-233-2215, Fax: 401-233-0690.

#07 Clinical Laboratory Advisory Board, 3 Capitol Hill, Rm 104, Providence, RI 02908; 401-222-2827, Fax: 401-222-1272. www.health.state.ri.us

#08 Department of Labor & Training, PO Box 20247 (1511 Pontiac Av), Providence, RI 02920-0943; 401-462-8527, Fax: 401-462-8528.

#09 Department of Environmental Management, 235 Promenade St, #260, Providence, RI 02908-5767; 401-222-4700, Fax: 401-222-6802. www.state.ri.us/dem/programs/index.htm

#10 Division of Forest Environment, 1037 Hartford Pike, North Scituate, RI 02857; 401-647-3367, Fax: 401-647-3590.

#11 Division of Licensing & Consumer Protection, 233 Richmond St, Providence, RI 02903; 401-222-3857, Fax: 401-222-6654. www.dbr.state.ri.us

#12 Division of Parks & Recreation, 2321 Hartford Ave, Johnston, RI 02919; 401-222-2632, Fax: 401-934-0610.
www.riparks.com/employment.htm

#13 Health Department, 3 Capitol Hill, Providence, RI 02908-5097; 401-222-2827, Fax: 401-222-1272.
www.health.state.ri.us/l2k/license.htm

#15 Office of Secretary of State, 100 N Main St, Providence, RI 02903; 401-222-2249, Fax: 401-222-3879. www.state.ri.us/
Direct web site URL to search for licensees: www.state.ri.us/ To Search, there are separate buttons for the Notary Public Section or Lobbyist.

#16 Office of Teacher Certification, 255 Westminster St, Providence, RI 02903; 401-222-4600, Fax: 401-222-2048.
www.ridoe.net

#18 Superior Court, 250 Benefit St, Rm 533, Providence, RI 02903; 401-222-3212, Fax: 401-272-4645. Direct written requests to Judge Jos. F. Rodgers, Jr.

#19 State Fire Marshall's Office, 24 Conway Ave, Quansit-Davisville Industrial Pk, North Kingston, RI 02852; 401-294-0861, Fax: 401-295-9092.

#20 Pilotage Commission, 301 Great Island Rd, Galilee, RI 02882; 401-783-5551, Fax: 401-783-7285.

#21 Supreme Court, 250 Benefit St, Providence, RI 02903; 401-222-3272, Fax: 401-222-3599. www.courts.state.ri.us/supreme/barex.html

#22 Department of Children, Youth & Famillies, 610 Mt. Pleasant Ave, Providence, RI 02908; 401-222-4741.

#23 Department of Environmental Management, Box 218, West Kingston, RI 02892; 401-789-0281, Fax: 401-783-7490.
www.state.ri.us/dem

#24 Department of Health, 3 Capitol Hill Rm 205, Providence, RI 02908; 401-222-3855, Fax: 401-222-2158.

#25 Office of Secretary of State, 100 N Main St, Providence, RI 02903; 401-222-2249, Fax: 401-222-3879. www.state.ri.us/
Direct web site URL to search for licensees: www.state.ri.us/ To Search, there are separate buttons for the Notary Public Section or Lobbyist.

#26 Court Administrator Office, 250 Benefit St, #506, Providence, RI 02903; 401-222-3215.

Rhode Island Federal Courts

The following list indicates the district and division name for each county in the state.

County/Court Cross Reference

Bristol .... Providence

Kent.. Providence

Newport.. Providence

Providence.. Providence

Washington... Providence

US District Court

District of Rhode Island

Providence Division Clerk's Office, Two Exchange Terrace, Federal Bldg, Providence, RI 02903 (Courier Address: Use mail address for courier delivery), 401-752-7200, Fax: 401-752-7247.

Counties: All counties in Rhode Island.

Indexing/Storage: Cases are indexed by defendant and plaintiff as well as by case number. New cases are available in the index 1-2 days after filing date. Both computer and card indexes are maintained. Computer indexing is since 1991. Anything prior to that is maintained on card index. Open records are located at this court. District wide searches are available from this court.

Fee & Payment: The fee is $20.00 per item (one party name or case number). Payment may be made by money order, cashier check, personal check. Prepayment is required. Payee: Clerk, US District Court. Certification fee: $7.00 per document. Copy fee: $.50 per page. You are allowed to make your own copies. These copies cost $.25 per page. Naturalization records are at the Federal Records Center in Waltham, MA.

Phone Search: Only the case number or name will be released over the phone.

Mail Search: Always enclose a stamped self addressed envelope.

In Person: In person searching is available.

PACER: Sign-up number is 800-676-6856. Access fee is $.60 per minute. Toll-free access: 888-421-6861. Local access: 401-752-7262. Case records are available back to December 1988. Records are never purged. New records are available online after 2 days. PACER is available online at http://pacer.rid.uscourts.gov.

US Bankruptcy Court

District of Rhode Island

Providence Division 6th Floor, 380 Westminster St, Providence, RI 02903 (Courier Address: Use mail address for courier delivery), 401-528-4477, Fax: 401-528-4470.

http://www.rib.uscourts.gov

Counties: All counties in Rhode Island.

Indexing/Storage: Cases are indexed by debtor and creditors as well as by case number. New cases are available in the index 1 day after filing date. A computer index is maintained. Open records are located at this court.

Fee & Payment: The fee is $20.00 per item (one party name or case number). Payment may be made by money order, cashier check, personal check, Visa or Mastercard. Prepayment is required. Checks from debtors not accepted. Payee: Clerk, US Bankruptcy Court. Certification fee: $7.00 per document. Copy fee: $.50 per page. You are allowed to make your own copies. These copies cost $.20 per page.

Phone Search: Only docket information is available by phone. An automated voice case information service (VCIS) is available. Call VCIS at 800-843-2841 or 401-528-4476.

Fax Search: The fees for a fax request are the same as for a mail request. The fee is $15.00 per item.

Mail Search: Always enclose a stamped self addressed envelope.

In Person: In person searching is available.

PACER: Sign-up number is 800-676-6856. Access fee is $.60 per minute. Toll-free access: 800-610-9310. Local access: 401-528-4062. Case records are available back to 1990. Records are purged every three years. New civil records are available online after 1 day. PACER is available online at http://pacer.rib.uscourts.gov.

Rhode Island County Courts

Court	Jurisdiction	No. of Courts	How Organized
Superior Courts*	General	4	4 Divisions
District Courts*	Limited	4	6 Divisions
Municipal Courts	Municipal	16	
Probate Courts*	Probate	39	39 Cities/ Towns
Family Courts	Special	4	4 Divisions
Workers' Compen- sation Court	Special	1	

* Profiled in this Sourcebook.

Court	CIVIL								
	Tort	Contract	Real Estate	Min. Claim	Max. Claim	Small Claims	Estate	Eviction	Domestic Relations
Superior Courts*	X	X	X	$5000	No Max				
District Courts*	X	X	X	$1500	$10,000	$1500		X	
Municipal Courts									
Probate Courts*							X		
Family Courts									X
Workers' Compensa- tion Court									

Court	CRIMINAL				
	Felony	Misdemeanor	DWI/DUI	Preliminary Hearing	Juvenile
Superior Courts*	X				
District Courts*		X	X	X	
Municipal Courts					
Probate Courts*					
Family Courts					X
Workers' Compensa- tion Court					

ADMINISTRATION   Court Administrator, Supreme Court, 250 Benefit St, Providence, RI, 02903; 401-222-3272, Fax: 401-222-3599. www.courts.state.ri.us

COURT STRUCTURE   Rhode Island has five counties, but only four Superior/District Court Locations (2nd-Newport, 3rd-Kent, 4th-Washignton, and 6th-Providence/Bristol Districts). Bristol and Providence counties are completely merged at the Providence location. Civil claims between $5000 and $10,000 may be filed in either Superior or District Court at the discretion of the filer.

ONLINE ACCESS   The Superior (civil, criminal, family) and Appellate courts are online internally for court personnel only.

There are plans to place criminal record data on the Internet. For more information, call Tracy Williams at 401-222-3000.

PROBATE COURTS   Probate is handled by the Town Clerk at the 39 cities and towns across Rhode Island.

📖 📖 📖 📖 📖 📖 📖

Bristol County

Superior & District Courts, RI.
Note: All civil and criminal cases are handled by the Providence County courts.

Barrington Town Hall 283 County Road, Barrington, RI 02806; 401-247-1900; Fax: 401-245-5003. Hours: 8:30AM-4:30PM (EST). *Probate.*

Bristol Town Hall 10 Court Street, Bristol, RI 02809; 401-253-7000 x21; Fax: 401-253-3080. Hours: 8:30AM-4PM (EST). *Probate.*

Warren Town Hall 514 Main Street, Warren, RI 02885; 401-245-7340; Fax: 401-245-7421. Hours: 9AM-4PM (EST). *Probate.*

Kent County

Superior Court 222 Quaker Lane, Warwick, RI 02886; 401-822-1311. Hours: 8:30AM-4:30PM (EST). *Felony, Civil Actions Over $10,000.*

www.courts.state.ri.us

Civil Records: Access: In person only. Visitors must perform in person searches for themselves. No search fee. Required to search: name, years to search. Civil cases indexed by defendant, plaintiff. Civil records on computer from 1987.
Criminal Records: Access: In person only. Visitors must perform in person searches for themselves. No search fee. Required to search: name, years to search, signed release; also helpful: DOB. Criminal records on computer from 1987.
General Information: Public Access terminal is available. (Records available from 1997.) No adoption, confidential or sealed records released. Copy fee: $.15 per page. Certification fee: $3.00. Exemplified copies $9.00 and $3.00 per page. Fee payee: Clerk of Superior Court. Personal checks accepted. Prepayment is required.

3rd Division District Court 222 Quaker Lane, Warwick, RI 02886-0107; 401-822-1771. Hours: 8:30AM-4:30PM (EST). *Misdemeanor, Civil Actions Under $10,000, Eviction, Small Claims.*

Civil Records: Access: In person only. Visitors must perform in person searches for themselves. No search fee. Required to search: name, years to search. Civil cases indexed by defendant, plaintiff. Civil records for 1995-1997 on index cards. Archives stored at Rhode Island Judicial Records Center, 1 Hill St, Pawtucket, RI 02860, 401-277-3249. Records destroyed after 10 years, but remain in docket books.
Criminal Records: Access: In person only. Visitors must perform in person searches for themselves. No search fee. Required to search: name, years to search, DOB, signed release. Criminal records for 1995-1997 on index cards. Archives stored at Rhode Island Judicial Records Center. Records destroyed after 10 years, but remain in docket books.
General Information: No mental or sealed records released. Copy fee: $.50 per page. Certification fee: $3.00. Fee payee: 3rd District Court. Personal checks accepted. Credit cards accepted: Visa, AmEx. Prepayment is required.

Coventry Town Hall 1670 Flat River Road, Coventry, RI 02816; 401-822-9174; Fax: 401-822-9132. Hours: 8:30AM-4:30PM (EST). *Probate.*

East Greenwich Town Hall 125 Main St (PO Box 11), East Greenwich, RI 02818; 401-886-8603; Fax: 401-886-8625. Hours: 8:30AM-4:30PM (EST). *Probate.*

Warwick City Hall 3275 Post Road, Warwick, RI 02886; 401-738-2000; Fax: 401-738-6639. Hours: 8:30AM-4:30PM (EST). *Probate.*

West Greenwich Town Hall 280 Victory Highway, West Greenwich, RI 02817; 401-397-5016; Fax: 401-392-3805. Hours: 9AM-4PM M,T,Th,F; 9AM-4PM, 7-9PM W (EST). *Probate.*

West Warwick Town Hall 1170 Main Street, West Warwick, RI 02893-4829; 401-822-9201; Fax: 401-822-9266. Hours: 8:30AM-4:30PM; 8:30AM-4PM June 1st-Labor Day (EST). *Probate.*

Newport County

Superior Court Florence K Murray Judicial Complex, 45 Washington Sq, Newport, RI 02840; 401-841-8330. Hours: 8:30AM-4:30PM (July and August till 4PM) (EST). *Felony, Civil Actions Over $10,000.*

Civil Records: Access: Mail, in person. Both court and visitors may perform in person searches. No search fee. Required to search: name, years to search. Civil cases indexed by defendant, plaintiff. Civil records on computer from 1989. Prior records archived at Rhode Island Records Center.
Criminal Records: Access: Mail, in person. Both court and visitors may perform in person searches. No search fee. Required to search: name, years to search, DOB. Criminal records on computer from 1983, index from 1968. Prior records archived at Records Center.
General Information: Public Access terminal is available. No child molestation or sexual assault records released. SASE required. Turnaround time 1 day. Copy fee: $.50 per page. Certification fee: $1.00. Fee payee: Clerk Superior Court. Personal checks accepted. Prepayment is required.

2nd District Court 45 Washington Square, Newport, RI 02840; 401-841-8350. Hours: 8:30AM-4:30PM (4PM-summer months) (EST). *Misdemeanor, Civil Actions Under $10,000, Eviction, Small Claims.*

Civil Records: Access: In person only. Visitors must perform in person searches for themselves. No search fee. Required to search: name, years to search. Civil cases indexed by defendant, plaintiff. Civil records on index cards for past 3 years, prior archived at Pawtucket Judicial Records Center.
Criminal Records: Access: In person only. Visitors must perform in person searches for themselves. No search fee. Required to search: name.
General Information: No juvenile, family court, sealed, expunged or ordered by judge or adoption records released. Copy fee: $.25 per page. Certification fee: $1.00. Fee payee: 2nd District Court. Personal checks accepted. Prepayment is required.

Jamestown Town Hall 93 Narragansett Avenue, Jamestown, RI 02835; 401-423-7200; Fax: 401-423-7230. Hours: 8AM-4:30PM (EST). *Probate.*

Little Compton Town Hall 40 Commons, PO Box 226, Little Compton, RI 02837; 401-635-4400; Fax: 401-635-2470. Hours: 8AM-4PM (EST). *Probate.*

Middletown Town Hall 350 East Main Road, Middletown, RI 02842; 401-847-0009; Fax: 401-845-0406. Hours: 8AM-5PM (EST). *Probate.*

Newport City Hall 43 Broadway, Newport, RI 02840; 401-846-9600; Fax: 401-849-8757. Hours: 8:30AM-5PM (EST). *Probate.*

Portsmouth Town Hall 2200 East Main Road, PO Box 115, Portsmouth, RI 02871; 401-683-2101. Hours: 9AM-4PM (EST). *Probate.*

Providence County

Providence/Bristol Superior Court 250 Benefit St, Providence, RI 02903; 401-222-3250. Hours: 8:30AM-4:30PM (EST). *Felony, Civil Actions Over $10,000.*

www.courts.state.ri.us

Note: All civil and criminal cases are handled by the Providence County courts.

Civil Records: Access: Phone, mail, in person. Visitors must perform in person searches for themselves. No search fee. Required to search: name, years to search. Civil cases indexed by defendant, plaintiff. Civil records on computer since 1983.
Criminal Records: Access: In person only. Visitors must perform in person searches for themselves. No search fee. Required to search: name, years to search, DOB. Criminal records on computer since 1983.
General Information: Public Access terminal is available. No adoption, confidential or sealed records released. Copy fee: $.15 per page. Certification fee: $3.00. Fee payee: Providence Superior Court. Personal checks accepted. Prepayment is required.

6th Division District Court 1 Dorrance Plaza 2nd Floor, Providence, RI 02903; 401-222-6710. Hours: 8:30AM-4:30PM (EST). *Misdemeanor, Civil Actions Under $10,000, Eviction, Small Claims.*

Note: All civil and criminal cases are handled by the Providence County courts.

Civil Records: Access: Mail, phone, in person. Both court and visitors may perform in person searches. No search fee. Required to search: name, years to search. Civil cases indexed by defendant, plaintiff. Civil records on card files to present. Phone access limited to one name.
Criminal Records: Access: Mail, phone, in person. Both court and visitors may perform in person searches. No search fee. Required to search: name, years to search. Criminal records for misdemeanor on computer from 1989. Phone requests limited to one name.
General Information: No adoption, confidential or sealed records released. SASE required. Turnaround time varies. Copy fee: $.50 per page. Certification fee: $1.00. Fee payee: 6th Division District Court. Personal checks accepted. Prepayment is required.

Burrillville Town Hall 105 Harrisville Main Street, Harrisville, RI 02830; 401-568-4300; Fax: 401-568-0490. Hours: 8:30AM-4:30PM (EST). *Probate.*

Central Falls City Hall 580 Broad Street, Central Falls, RI 02863; 401-727-7400; Fax: 401-727-7476. Hours: 8:30AM-4:30PM (EST). *Probate.*

Cranston City Hall 869 Park Avenue, Cranston, RI 02910; 401-461-1000; Fax: 401-461-9650. Hours: 8:30AM-4:30PM (EST). *Probate.*

Cumberland Town Hall 45 Broad Street, PO Box 7, Cumberland, RI 02864; 401-728-2400 x37; Fax: 401-724-1103. Hours: 8:30AM-4:30PM (EST). *Probate.*

East Providence City Hall 145 Taunton Avenue, East Providence, RI 02914; 401-435-7500; Fax: 401-438-7501. Hours: 8AM-4PM (EST). *Probate.*

Foster Town Hall 181 Howard Hill Road, Foster, RI 02825; 401-392-9200; Fax: 401-392-9201. Hours: 9AM-4PM (EST). *Probate.*

Glocester Town Hall 1145 Putnam Pike, Glocester/ Chepachet, RI 02814; 401-568-6206; Fax: 401-568-5850. Hours: 8AM-4:30PM (EST). *Probate.*

Johnston Town Hall 1385 Hartford Avenue, Johnston, RI 02919; 401-351-6618/401-553-8830 (Direct Phone); Fax: 401-553-8835. Hours: 8:30AM-4:30PM (EST). *Probate.*

www.johnson.ri.com

Online access to probate court records is available at http://johnston-ri.com/probate.asp. Search by last name.

Lincoln Town Hall 100 Old River Road, Lincoln, RI 02865; 401-333-1100; Fax: 401-333-3648. Hours: 9AM-4:30PM (EST). *Probate.*

Note: Court meets fourth Monday at 9 AM.

North Providence Town Hall 2000 Smith Street, North Providence, RI 02911; 401-232-0900; Fax: 401-233-1409. Hours: 8:30AM-4:30PM (EST). *Probate.*

North Smithfield Town Hall 1 Main Street, Slatersville, RI 02876; 401-767-2200 x305; Fax: 401-766-0016. Hours: 8AM-4PM (EST). *Probate.*

Pawtucket City Hall 137 Roosevelt Avenue, Pawtucket, RI 02860; 401-728-0500; Fax: 401-728-8932. Hours: 8:30AM-4:30PM (EST). *Probate.*

Providence City Hall 25 Dorrance Street, Providence, RI 02903; 401-421-7740; Fax: 401-861-6208. Hours: 8:45AM-4:15PM (EST). *Probate.*

Note: All civil and criminal cases are handled by the Providence County courts.

Scituate Town Hall 195 Danielson Pike, PO Box 328, North Scituate, RI 02857; 401-647-2822; Fax: Call first. Hours: 8:30AM-4PM (EST). *Probate.*

Smithfield Town Hall 64 Farnum Pike, Smithfield, RI 02917; 401-233-1000; Fax: 401-232-7244. Hours: 9AM-4PM (EST). *Probate.*

Woonsocket City Hall 169 Main Street, Woonsocket, RI 02895; 401-762-6400; Fax: 401-765-0022. Hours: 8:30AM-4PM (EST). *Probate.*

Washington County

Superior Court 4800 Towerhill Rd, Wakefield, RI 02879; 401-782-4121. Hours: 8:30AM-4:30PM (Sept-June) 8:30AM-4PM (July & Aug) (EST). *Felony, Civil Actions Over $10,000.*

Civil Records: Access: Phone, mail, in person. Both court and visitors may perform in person searches. No search fee. Required to search: name, years to search. Civil cases indexed by defendant, plaintiff. Civil records on computer from 1984, on index prior to 1984. Archived at Record Center, 401-277-3249. Phone requests taken only after 3PM.

Criminal Records: Access: Mail, in person. Both court and visitors may perform in person searches. No search fee. Required to search: name, years to search; also helpful: DOB. Criminal records on computer from 1984, on index prior to 1984. Archived at Record Center, 401-277-3249.

General Information: No confidential or sealed records released. SASE required. Turnaround time 1 week. Copy fee: $.15 per page. Certification fee: $3.00. Fee payee: Washington Superior Court. Personal checks accepted.

4th District Court 4800 Towerhill Rd, Wakefield, RI 02879; 401-782-4131. Hours: 8:30AM-4:30PM (EST). *Misdemeanor, Civil Actions Under $10,000, Eviction, Small Claims.*

Civil Records: Access: In person only. Visitors must perform in person searches for themselves. No search fee. Required to search: name, years to search. Civil cases indexed by defendant, plaintiff. Civil records on index cards.

Criminal Records: Access: In person only. Visitors must perform in person searches for themselves. No search fee. Required to search: name, years to search; also helpful: DOB. Criminal records available on computer beginning in 1996.

General Information: Public Access terminal is available. No family court records released. Copy fee: $.50 per page. Certification fee: $1.00. Fee payee: Court Clerk. Personal checks accepted. Prepayment is required.

Charlestown Town Hall 4540 South County Trail, Charlestown, RI 02813; 401-364-1200; Fax: 401-364-1238. Hours: 8:30AM-4:30PM (EST). *Probate.*

Exeter Town Hall 675 Ten Rod Road, Exeter, RI 02822; 401-294-3891; Fax: 401-295-1248. Hours: 9AM-4PM (EST). *Probate.*

Note: Probate Court held fourth Monday monthly at 2:00 PM.

Hopkinton Town Hall 1 Town House Road, Hopkinton, RI 02833; 401-377-7777; Fax: 401-377-7788. Hours: 8:30AM-4:30PM or by appointment (EST). *Probate.*

Narragansett Town Hall 25 Fifth Avenue, Narragansett, RI 02882; 401-789-1044 X621; Fax: 401-783-9637. Hours: 8:30AM-4:30PM (EST). *Probate.*

New Shoreham Town Hall Old Town Road, PO Drawer 220, Block Island, RI 02807; 401-466-3200; Fax: 401-466-3219. Hours: 9AM-3PM (EST). *Probate.*

North Kingstown Town Hall 80 Boston Neck Road, North Kingstown, RI 02852-5762; 401-294-3331; Fax: 401-885-7373. Hours: 8:30AM-4:30PM (EST). *Probate.*

www.northkingstown.org

Richmond Town Hall 5 Richmond Townhouse Rd., Wyoming, RI 02898; 401-539-2497; Fax: 401-539-1089. Hours: 9AM-4PM; 8:30 AM on second Tuesday (EST). *Probate.*

South Kingstown Town Hall 180 High Street, Wakefield, RI 02879; 401-789-9331; Fax: 401-789-5280. Hours: 8:30AM-4:30PM (EST). *Probate.*

Westerly Town Hall 45 Broad Street, Westerly, RI 02891; 401-348-2500; Fax: 401-348-2571. Hours: 8:30AM-4:30PM (EST). *Probate.*

Rhode Island Recording Offices

ORGANIZATION

5 counties and 39 towns, 39 recording offices. The recording officer is Town/City Clerk (Recorder of Deeds). The Town/City Clerk usually also serves as the Recorder of Deeds. There is no county administration in Rhode Island that handles recording. The entire state is in the Eastern Time Zone (EST). Be aware that the recordings in the counties of Bristol, Newport, and Providence can relate to property located in other cities/ towns even though each of these three cities bears the same name as the county.

Towns will not perform real estate searches. Copy fees are usually $1.50 per page. Certification usually costs $3.00 per document.

REAL ESTATE RECORDS

Towns will not perform real estate searches. Copy fees are usually $1.50 per page. Certification usually costs $3.00 per document.

UCC RECORDS

Financing statements are filed at the state level, except for farm related and real estate related collateral, which are filed with the Town/City Clerk. Most recording offices will not perform UCC searches. Use search request form UCC-11. Copy fees are usually $1.50 per page. Certification usually costs $3.00 per document.

TAX LIEN RECORDS

All federal and state tax liens on personal property and on real property are filed with the Recorder of Deeds. Towns will not perform tax lien searches.

OTHER LIENS

Mechanics, municipal, lis pendens.

Barrington Town

Town Clerk, 283 County Road, Town Hall, Barrington, RI 02806. 401-247-1900.
Will search UCC records. This agency will not do a tax lien search. Will not search real estate records. **Other Phone Numbers:** Assessor 401-247-1900.

Bristol Town

Town Clerk, 10 Court Street, Town Hall, Bristol, RI 02809. 401-253-7000.
Will search UCC records. This agency will not do a tax lien search. Will not search real estate records.

Burrillville Town

Town Clerk, 105 Harrisville Main Street, Town Hall, Harrisville, RI 02830-1499. 401-568-4300 R/E Recording: 401-568-4300 x13 UCC Recording: 401-568-4300 x13; Fax 401-568-0490.
Will not search UCC records. Will not search real estate records. **Other Phone Numbers:** Assessor 401-568-9452; Treasurer 401-568-9451; Appraiser/Auditor 401-568-9452; Elections 401-568-9454; Vital Records 401-568-4300 x11.

Central Falls City

City Clerk, 580 Broad Street, City Hall, Central Falls, RI 02863. City Clerk, R/E and UCC Recording 401-727-7400; Fax 401-727-7406.
Will not search UCC records. This agency will not do a tax lien search. Will not search real estate records. **Other Phone Numbers:** Assessor 401-727-7430; Treasurer 401-727-7470; Elections 401-727-7450; Vital Records 401-727-7400.

Charlestown Town

Town Clerk, 4540 South County Trail, Charlestown, RI 02813. 401-364-1200; Fax 401-364-1238. http://www.riconnect.com/chasplan/
Will not search UCC records. Will not search real estate records. **Other Phone Numbers:** Assessor 401-364-1233.

Coventry Town

Town Clerk, 1670 Flat River Road, Town Hall, Coventry, RI 02816-8911. 401-822-9174; Fax 401-822-9132.
Will search UCC records. Will not search real estate records. **Other Phone Numbers:** Assessor 401-822-9163.

Cranston City

City Clerk, 869 Park Avenue, City Hall, Cranston, RI 02910. 401-461-1000 x3130.
Will search UCC records. This agency will not do a tax lien search. Will not search real estate records.

Cumberland Town

Town Clerk, P.O. Box 7, Cumberland, RI 02864-0808. 401-728-2400 R/E Recording: 401-728-2400 x35 UCC Recording: 401-728-2400 x35; Fax 401-724-1103.
Will search UCC records. This agency will not do a tax lien search. Will not search real estate records. **Other Phone Numbers:** Assessor 401-728-2400 x13; Treasurer 401-728-2400 x28; Appraiser/Auditor 401-728-2400 x15; Elections 401-728-2400 x40; Vital Records 401-728-2400 x33.

East Greenwich Town

Town Clerk, P.O. Box 111, East Greenwich, RI 02818. 401-886-8603 R/E Recording: 401-886-8602 UCC Recording: 401-886-8602; Fax 401-886-8625. http://www.eastgreenwichri.com
Will search UCC records. Will not search real estate records. **Other Phone Numbers:** Assessor 401-886-8614; Treasurer 401-886-8608; Elections 401-886-8603; Vital Records 401-886-8602.

East Providence City

Town Clerk, 145 Taunton Avenue, City Hall, East Providence, RI 02914. 401-435-7500 R/E Recording: 401-435-7594 UCC Recording: 401-435-7594; Fax 401-435-7501. www.eastprovidence.com
Will search UCC records. Will not search real estate records. **Other Phone Numbers:** Assessor 401-435-7574; Treasurer 401-435-7560; Elections 401-435-7503; Vital Records 401-435-7596.

Exeter Town

Town Clerk, 675 Ten Rod Road, Town Hall, Exeter, RI 02822. Town Clerk, R/E and UCC Recording 401-294-3891; Fax 401-295-1248. www.town.exeter.ri.us
Will search UCC records. Will not search real estate records. **Online Access:** Assessor. Records on the Town of Exeter assessor database are available free online at http://140.239.211.227/Exeter_RI. **Other Phone Numbers:** Assessor 401-294-5734; Treasurer 401-267-1024; Appraiser/Auditor 401-294-2287; Elections 401-294-3891; Vital Records 401-884-4740.

Foster Town

Town Clerk, 181 Howard Hill Road, Town Hall, Foster, RI 02825-1227. Town Clerk, R/E and UCC Recording 401-392-9200; Fax 401-392-9201. townoffoster@worldnet.com
Will search UCC records. This agency will not do a tax lien search. Will not search real estate records. **Other Phone Numbers:** Assessor 401-392-9202; Treasurer 401-392-9207; Elections 401-392-9200; Vital Records 401-392-9200.

Glocester Town

Town Clerk, P.O. Drawer B, Glocester/ Chepachet, RI 02814-0702. Town Clerk, R/E and UCC Recording 401-568-6206; Fax 401-568-5850. http://www.glocesterri.org/townclerk.htm
Will not search UCC records. Will not search real estate records. **Other Phone Numbers:** Assessor 401-568-3329; Treasurer 401-568-3342; Elections 401-568-6206; Vital Records 401-568-6206; Tax Collector 401-568-5110.

Hopkinton Town

Town Clerk, 1 Town House Road, Town Hall, Hopkinton, RI 02833. Town Clerk, R/E and UCC Recording 401-377-7777; Fax 401-377-7788.
Will not search UCC records. Will not search real estate records. **Other Phone Numbers:** Assessor 401-377-7780; Treasurer 401-377-7766; Elections 401-377-7777; Vital Records 401-377-7777.

Jamestown Town

Town Clerk, 93 Narragansett Avenue, Town Hall, Jamestown, RI 02835. Town Clerk, R/E and UCC Recording 401-423-7200; Fax 401-423-7230.
Will search UCC records. Will not search real estate records. **Other Phone Numbers:** Assessor 401-423-7200; Treasurer 401-423-7200; Appraiser/Auditor 401-423-7200; Elections 401-423-7200; Vital Records 401-423-7200.

Johnston Town

Town Clerk, 1385 Hartford Avenue, Town Hall, Johnston, RI 02919. 401-351-6618; Fax 401-331-4271. http://johnston-ri.com/probate.asp
Will search UCC records. Will not search real estate records. **Online Access:** Probate. Probate records on the Town of Johnson lookup database are available free online at the web site.

Lincoln Town

Town Clerk, P.O. Box 100, Lincoln, RI 02865. Town Clerk, R/E and UCC Recording 401-333-1100; Fax 401-333-3648. www.lincolnri.com
Will not search real estate records. **Other Phone Numbers:** Assessor 401-333-1100; Treasurer 401-333-1100; Appraiser/Auditor 401-333-1100; Elections 401-333-1100; Vital Records 401-333-1100.

Little Compton Town

Town Clerk, P.O. Box 226, Little Compton, RI 02837-0226. 401-635-4400; Fax 401-635-2470.
Will search UCC records. Will not search real estate records.

Middletown Town

Town Clerk, 350 East Main Road, Town Hall, Middletown, RI 02842. 401-847-0009; Fax 401-848-0500.
Will search UCC records. Will not search real estate records. **Online Access:** Assessor. Records on the Town of Middletown assessor database are available free online at http://140.239.211.227/MiddletownRI. **Other Phone Numbers:** Assessor 401-847-7300.

Narragansett Town

Town Clerk, 25 Fifth Avenue, Town Hall, Narragansett, RI 02882. 401-789-1044; Fax 401-783-9637.
Will search UCC records. This agency will not do a tax lien search. Will not search real estate records. **Other Phone Numbers:** Assessor 401-789-1044 x236.

New Shoreham Town

Town Clerk, P.O. Drawer 220, Block Island, RI 02807. 401-466-3200; Fax 401-466-3219.
Will not search UCC records. Will not search real estate records. **Other Phone Numbers:** Assessor 401-466-3217.

Newport City

City Clerk, 43 Broadway, Town Hall, Newport, RI 02840-2798. 401-846-9600.
Will search UCC records. This agency will not do a tax lien search. Will not search real estate records.

North Kingstown Town

Town Clerk, 80 Boston Neck Road, Town Hall, North Kingstown, RI 02852. 401-294-3331 R/E Recording: 401-294-3331 x125 UCC Recording: 401-294-3331 x125; Fax 401-885-7373. www.northkingstown.org
Will search UCC records. Will not search real estate records. **Other Phone Numbers:** Assessor 401-294-3331 x110; Treasurer 401-294-3331 x148; Elections 401-294-3331 x129; Vital Records 401-294-3331 x122.

North Providence Town

Town Clerk, 2000 Smith Street, Town Hall, North Providence, RI 02911. 401-232-0900; Fax 401-233-1409.
Will search UCC records. This agency will not do a tax lien search. Will not search real estate records. **Other Phone Numbers:** Assessor 401-232-0900 x245; Treasurer 401-232-0900 x218.

North Smithfield Town

Town Clerk, 1 Main Street, Town Hall, Slatersville, RI 02876. Town Clerk, R/E and UCC Recording 401-767-2200; Fax 401-766-0016.
Will not search UCC records. Will not search real estate records. **Other Phone Numbers:** Assessor 401-767-2202; Elections 401-767-2200 x316.

Pawtucket City

Town Clerk, 137 Roosevelt Avenue, City Hall, Pawtucket, RI 02860. 401-728-0500 R/E Recording: 401-728-0500 x262 UCC Recording: 401-728-0500 x262; Fax 401-728-8932.
Will search UCC records. Will not search real estate records. **Other Phone Numbers:** Assessor 401-728-0500 x338; Treasurer 401-728-0500 x244; Elections 401-728-0500 x207; Vital Records 401-728-0500 x224.

Portsmouth Town

Town Clerk, P.O. Box 155, Portsmouth, RI 02871. 401-683-2101.
Will search UCC records. This agency will not do a tax lien search. Will not search real estate records. **Online Access:** Assessor. Records on the Town of Portsmouth assessor database are available free online at http://140.239.211.227/PortsmouthRI.

Providence City

City Clerk, 25 Dorrance Street, City Hall, Providence, RI 02903. 401-421-7740 x312.
Will search UCC records. This agency will not do a tax lien search. Will not search real estate records.

Richmond Town

Town Clerk, 5 Richmond Townhouse Rd., Town Hall, Wyoming, RI 02898. Town Clerk, R/E and UCC Recording 401-539-2497; Fax 401-539-1089.
Will search UCC records. Will not search real estate records. **Other Phone Numbers:** Assessor 401-539-2130; Treasurer 401-539-2498; Elections 401-539-2497; Vital Records 401-539-2497.

Scituate Town

Town Clerk, PO Box 328, North Scituate, RI 02857-0328. Town Clerk, R/E and UCC Recording 401-647-2822; Fax 401-647-7220. http://www.scituateri.org/townhall.htm
Will not search UCC records. This agency will not do a tax lien search. Will not search real estate records. **Other Phone Numbers:** Assessor 401-647-2919; Treasurer 401-647-2547.

Smithfield Town

Town Clerk, 64 Farnum Pike, Town Hall, Esmond, RI 02917. Town Clerk, R/E and UCC Recording 401-233-1000; Fax 401-232-7244.
Will search UCC records. Will not search real estate records. **Other Phone Numbers:** Assessor 401-233-1014; Treasurer 401-233-1005; Elections 401-233-1000; Vital Records 401-233-1000.

South Kingstown Town

Town Clerk, P.O. Box 31, Wakefield, RI 02880. 401-789-9331 R/E Recording: 401-789-9331 x234; Fax 401-788-9792. http://www.southkingstownri.com
Will search UCC records. This agency will not do a tax lien search. Will not search real estate records. **Online**

Access: Real Estate, Assessor. Online access to the property values database is available free at http://www.southkingstownri.com/code/propvalues_search.cfm. **Other Phone Numbers:** Assessor 401-789-9331 x220; Treasurer 401-789-9331 x209; Elections 401-789-9331 x231; Vital Records 401-789-9331 x230.

Tiverton Town

Town Clerk, 343 Highland Road, Town Hall, Tiverton, RI 02878. 401-625-6700; Fax 401-624-8640.
Will search UCC records. This agency will not do a tax lien search. Will not search real estate records. **Other Phone Numbers:** Assessor 401-625-5609.

Warren Town

Town Clerk, 514 Main Street, Town Hall, Warren, RI 02885. Town Clerk, R/E and UCC Recording 401-245-7340; Fax 401-245-7421.
Will search UCC records. Will not search real estate records. **Other Phone Numbers:** Assessor 401-245-7342; Treasurer 401-245-7341; Appraiser/Auditor 401-245-7342; Elections 401-245-7340; Vital Records 401-245-7340; Town Manager 401-245-7554.

Warwick City

City Clerk, 3275 Post Road, Warwick, RI 02886. 401-738-2000 R/E Recording: 401-738-2000 x6218 UCC Recording: 401-738-2000 x6218; Fax 401-738-6639. www.warwickri.com
Will search UCC records. Will not search real estate records. **Other Phone Numbers:** Assessor 401-738-2000 x6016; Treasurer 401-738-2000 x6228; Elections 401-738-2000 x6223; Vital Records 401-738-2000 x6215.

West Greenwich Town

Town Clerk, 280 Victory Highway, Town Hall, West Greenwich, RI 02817. 401-397-5016; Fax 401-392-3805.
Will search UCC records. Will not search real estate records.

West Warwick Town

Town Clerk, 1170 Main Street, Town Hall, West Warwick, RI 02893-4829. Town Clerk, R/E and UCC Recording 401-822-9201; Fax 401-822-9266.
Will search UCC records. Will not search real estate records. **Other Phone Numbers:** Assessor 401-822-9208; Treasurer 401-822-9216; Elections 401-822-9201; Vital Records 401-822-9201.

Westerly Town

Town Clerk, 45 Broad Street, Town Hall, Westerly, RI 02891. 401-348-2500; Fax 401-348-2571.
Will search UCC records. Will not search real estate records.

Woonsocket City

Town Clerk, 169 Main Street, City Hall, Woonsocket, RI 02895. 401-762-6400 R/E Recording: 401-767-9248 UCC Recording: 401-767-9248; Fax 401-765-4569.
Will search UCC records. Will not search real estate records. **Other Phone Numbers:** Assessor 401-762-6400 x109; Treasurer 401-767-9280; Elections 401-767-9224; Vital Records 401-767-8875

Rhode Island County Locator

You will usually be able to find the city name in the City/County Cross Reference below. In that case, it is a simple matter to determine the county from the cross reference. However, only the official US Postal Service city names are included in this index. There are an additional 40,000 place names that people use in their addresses. Therefore, we have also included a ZIP/City Cross Reference immediately following the City/County Cross Reference.

If you know the ZIP Code but the city name does not appear in the City/County Cross Reference index, look up the ZIP Code in the ZIP/City Cross Reference, find the city name, then look up the city name in the City/County Cross Reference. For example, you want to know the county for an address of Menands, NY 12204. There is no "Menands" in the City/County Cross Reference. The ZIP/City Cross Reference shows that ZIP Codes 12201-12288 are for the city of Albany. Looking back in the City/County Cross Reference, Albany is in Albany County.

City/County Cross Reference

ADAMSVILLE Newport	EXETER Washington	MANVILLE Providence	RUMFORD Providence
ALBION Providence	FISKEVILLE Providence	MAPLEVILLE Providence	SAUNDERSTOWN Washington
ASHAWAY Washington	FORESTDALE Providence	MIDDLETOWN Newport	SHANNOCK Washington
BARRINGTON Bristol	FOSTER Providence	NARRAGANSETT Washington	SLATERSVILLE Providence
BLOCK ISLAND Washington	GLENDALE Providence	NEWPORT Newport	SLOCUM Washington
BRADFORD Washington	GREENE Kent	NORTH KINGSTOWN Washington	SMITHFIELD Providence
BRISTOL Bristol	GREENVILLE Providence	NORTH PROVIDENCE Providence	TIVERTON Newport
CAROLINA Washington	HARMONY Providence	NORTH SCITUATE Providence	WAKEFIELD Washington
CENTRAL FALLS Providence	HARRISVILLE Providence	NORTH SMITHFIELD Providence	WARREN Bristol
CHARLESTOWN Washington	HOPE Providence	OAKLAND Providence	WARWICK Kent
CHEPACHET Providence	HOPE VALLEY Washington	PASCOAG Providence	WEST GREENWICH Kent
CLAYVILLE Providence	HOPKINTON Washington	PAWTUCKET Providence	WEST KINGSTON Washington
COVENTRY Kent	JAMESTOWN Newport	PEACE DALE Washington	WEST WARWICK Kent
CRANSTON Providence	JOHNSTON Providence	PORTSMOUTH Newport	WESTERLY Washington
CUMBERLAND Providence	KENYON Washington	PROVIDENCE Providence	WOOD RIVER JUNCTION Washington
EAST GREENWICH Kent	KINGSTON Washington	PRUDENCE ISLAND Bristol	WOONSOCKET Providence
EAST PROVIDENCE Providence	LINCOLN Providence	RIVERSIDE Providence	WYOMING Washington
ESCOHEAG Washington	LITTLE COMPTON Newport	ROCKVILLE Washington	

ZIP/City Cross Reference

02801-02801	ADAMSVILLE	02827-02827	GREENE	02863-02863	CENTRAL FALLS	02893-02893	WEST WARWICK
02802-02802	ALBION	02828-02828	GREENVILLE	02864-02864	CUMBERLAND	02894-02894	WOOD RIVER JUNCTION
02804-02804	ASHAWAY	02829-02829	HARMONY	02865-02865	LINCOLN	02895-02895	WOONSOCKET
02806-02806	BARRINGTON	02830-02830	HARRISVILLE	02871-02871	PORTSMOUTH	02896-02896	NORTH SMITHFIELD
02807-02807	BLOCK ISLAND	02831-02831	HOPE	02872-02872	PRUDENCE ISLAND	02898-02898	WYOMING
02808-02808	BRADFORD	02832-02832	HOPE VALLEY	02873-02873	ROCKVILLE	02901-02909	PROVIDENCE
02809-02809	BRISTOL	02833-02833	HOPKINTON	02874-02874	SAUNDERSTOWN	02910-02910	CRANSTON
02812-02812	CAROLINA	02835-02835	JAMESTOWN	02875-02875	SHANNOCK	02911-02911	NORTH PROVIDENCE
02813-02813	CHARLESTOWN	02836-02836	KENYON	02876-02876	SLATERSVILLE	02912-02912	PROVIDENCE
02814-02814	CHEPACHET	02837-02837	LITTLE COMPTON	02877-02877	SLOCUM	02914-02914	EAST PROVIDENCE
02815-02815	CLAYVILLE	02838-02838	MANVILLE	02878-02878	TIVERTON	02915-02915	RIVERSIDE
02816-02816	COVENTRY	02839-02839	MAPLEVILLE	02879-02880	WAKEFIELD	02916-02916	RUMFORD
02817-02817	WEST GREENWICH	02840-02841	NEWPORT	02881-02881	KINGSTON	02917-02917	SMITHFIELD
02818-02818	EAST GREENWICH	02842-02842	MIDDLETOWN	02882-02882	NARRAGANSETT	02918-02918	PROVIDENCE
02822-02822	EXETER	02852-02854	NORTH KINGSTOWN	02883-02883	PEACE DALE	02919-02919	JOHNSTON
02823-02823	FISKEVILLE	02857-02857	NORTH SCITUATE	02885-02885	WARREN	02920-02921	CRANSTON
02824-02824	FORESTDALE	02858-02858	OAKLAND	02886-02889	WARWICK	02940-02940	PROVIDENCE
02825-02825	FOSTER	02859-02859	PASCOAG	02891-02891	WESTERLY		
02826-02826	GLENDALE	02860-02862	PAWTUCKET	02892-02892	WEST KINGSTON		

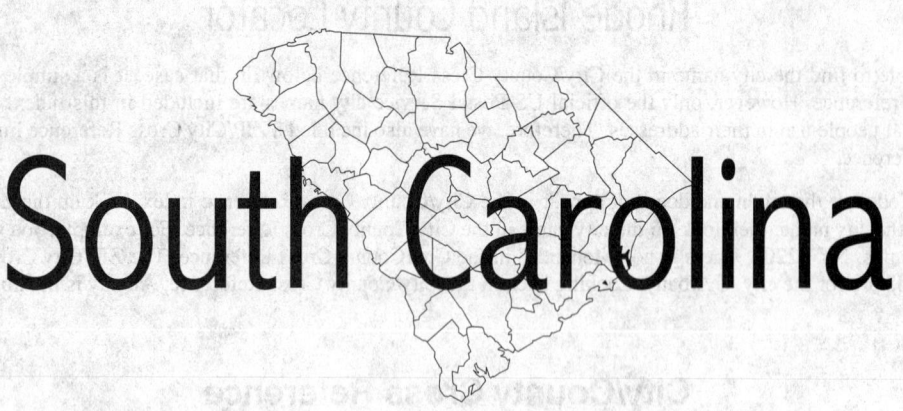

South Carolina

General Help Numbers:

Governor's Office
PO Box 11829
Columbia, SC 29211
http://www.state.sc.us/governor

803-734-9400
Fax 803-734-9413
8AM-6PM

Attorney General's Office
PO Box 11549
Columbia, SC 29211
http://www.scattorneygeneral.org

803-734-3970
Fax 803-734-4323
8:30AM-5:30PM

State Court Administrator
1015 Sumter St, 2nd Floor
Columbia, SC 29201
http://www.judicial.state.sc.us/
courtadmin/index.cfm

803-734-1800
Fax 803-734-1821
8:30AM-5PM M-F

State Archives
8301 Parklane Rd
Columbia, SC 29223
http://www.state.sc.us/scdah

803-896-6100
Fax 803-896-6198
9AM-9PM TU-FR
9-6 SA, 1-6 SU

State Specifics:

Capital:	Columbia Richland County
Time Zone:	EST
Number of Counties:	46
Population:	4,012,012
Web Site:	www.myscgov.com/SCSGPortal/ static/home_tem1.html

State Agencies

Criminal Records

South Carolina Law Enforcement Division (SLED), Criminal Records Section, PO Box 21398, Columbia, SC 29221 (Courier: 4400 Broad River Rd, Columbia, SC 29210); 803-896-7043, 803-896-7022 (Fax), 8:30AM-5PM.

http://www.sled.state.sc.us

Note: Sex offender data is available online at www.scattorneygeneral.com/public/registry.html.

Indexing & Storage: Records are available from the 1960s. New records are available for inquiry immediately. Records are indexed on inhouse computer.

Searching: Criminal records are open without restrictions. Include the following in your request-full name, any aliases, date of birth, sex, race. The SSN is optional.

Access by: mail, in person, online.

Fee & Payment: The search fee is $25.00 per individual. The fee is $8.00 for non-profit organizations, pre-approval is required. Fee payee: SLED. Prepayment required. Business and company checks are accepted. No credit cards accepted.

Mail search: Turnaround time: 5 to 7 days. The will return by overnight delivery service if prepaid and materials provided. A self addressed stamped envelope is requested.

In person search: Turnaround time is within minutes.

Online search: SLED offers commercial access to criminal record history from 1960 forward on the web site. Fees are $25.00 per screening or $8.00 if for a charitable organization. Credit card ordering accepted. Visit the web site or call 803-896-7219 for details.

Fictitious Name
Assumed Name
Trade Names
Records not maintained by a state level agency.

Note: Records are found at the county level.

Corporation Records
Trademarks/Servicemarks
Limited Partnerships, Limited
Liability Company Records

Corporation Division, Capitol Complex, PO Box 11350, Columbia, SC 29211 (Courier: Edgar A. Brown Bldg, 1205 Pendelton St. Room 525, Columbia, SC 29201); 803-734-2158, 803-734-2164 (Fax), 8:30PM-5PM.

http://www.scsos.com

Note: Trademarks and service marks are not on the computer but are in this department.

Indexing & Storage: Records are available from 1800's on. In house computer records are from 1985 on. Older records are stored at the State Archives. New records are available for inquiry immediately. Records are indexed on microfilm, inhouse computer.

Searching: Include the following in your request-full name of business. In addition to the articles of incorporation, corporation records include the following information: Prior (merged) names, Inactive and Reserved names. Annual Reports, Officer and Directors are kept in the State Department of Revenue.

Access by: mail, phone, in person, online.

Fee & Payment: Fees: $1.00 per page for the first document and $.50 per page for each additional document. If record is to be certified, then fee is $3.00 for first page. Fee payee: Secretary of State. Prepayment required. Personal checks accepted. No credit cards accepted.

Mail search: Turnaround time: 1 to 2 days. A self addressed stamped envelope is requested.

Phone search: No fee for telephone request. They will provide basic information only.

In person search: Information requests are available.

Online search: This free web-based program is called the Online Business Filings search page. The database at www.scsos.com/corp_search.htm provides access to basic filing information about any entity filed with the office. Registered agents' names and addresses, dates of business filings and types of filings are all available. The database is updated every 48 hours.

Annual Reports
Directors and Officers

Department of Revenue, Office Services/Records, 301 Gervias St, Columbia, SC 29201; 803-898-5751, 803-898-5888 (Fax), 8:30AM-5PM.

Indexing & Storage: Records are available from 1990 on. Records are indexed on inhouse computer, hard copy.

Searching: Information on partnerships and on taxes is not public. Include the following in your request-full name of business.

Access by: mail, phone, fax, in person.

Fee & Payment: Fees: $2.63 per year for annual reports. Fee payee: South Carolina Department of Revenue. Prepayment required. Personal checks accepted. No credit cards accepted.

Mail search: Turnaround time: 1 week. A self addressed stamped envelope is requested.

Phone search: No fee for up to 2 corporations. They will give officers and registered agent information.

Fax search: Turnaround is usually in 1 day.

In person search: You may request information in person, but will not receive copies the same day.

Uniform Commercial Code

UCC Division, Secretary of State, PO Box 11350, Columbia, SC 29211 (Courier: Edgar Brown Bldg, 1205 Pendelton St #525, Columbia, SC 29201); 803-734-1961, 803-734-2164 (Fax), 8:30AM-5PM.

http://www.scsos.com/ucc.htm

Indexing & Storage: Records are available from 1968. Records are computerized since 1985.

Searching: Use search request Form UCC-4 for in-state and UCC-11 for out-of-state. All tax liens are filed at the county level. Include the following in your request-debtor name.

Access by: mail, phone, fax, in person, online.

Fee & Payment: Fees are $5.00 for the first debtor name and $2.00 for each additional name on a request. However, there is no $5.00 search fee if file number given. Copies are $2.00 per financing statement, plus $1.00 for each page of attachments. Fee payee: Secretary of State. Prepayment required. Personal checks accepted. No credit cards accepted.

Mail search: Turnaround time: 5 to 10 days. A self addressed stamped envelope is requested.

Phone search: No fee for telephone request. The staff will look-up file numbers at no charge.

Fax search: There is an additional $5.00 fee for faxing in and $10.00 fee for faxing back.

In person search: You may request information in person.

Online search: "Direct Access" is open 24 hours daily, there are no fees. Inquiry is by debtor name. The system provides for copies to be faxed automatically. Call 803-734-2345 for registration information.

Federal Tax Liens
State Tax Liens
Records not maintained by a state level agency.

Note: Tax lien data is found at the county level.

Sales Tax Registrations

Revenue Department, Sales Tax Registration Section, PO Box 125, Columbia, SC 29214 (Courier: 301 Gervais St, Columbia, SC 29214); 803-898-5872, 803-898-5888 (Fax), 8:30AM-4:45PM.

http://www.dor.state.sc.us

Indexing & Storage: Records are available for 4 to 5 years, then are archived on hard copy. Records are indexed on inhouse computer.

Searching: This agency will only confirm that a business is registered. They will provide no other information. Include the following in your request-business name. They can also search by tax permit number, owner name, or federal ID.

Access by: mail, phone, fax, in person.

Mail search: Turnaround time: 7 days. A self addressed stamped envelope is requested. No fee for mail request.

Phone search: No fee for telephone request.

Fax search: Fax searching available.

In person search: No fee for request.

Birth Certificates

South Carolina DHEC, Vital Records, 2600 Bull St, Columbia, SC 29201-1797; 803-898-3630, 803-898-3631 (Order Line), 877-284-1008 (Expedite), 803-799-0301 (Fax), 8:30AM-4:30PM.

http://www.scdhec.net/vr/index.htm

Note: A "short form" wallet size birth certificate can be obtained from any SC county. This form will not show parent names.

Indexing & Storage: Records are available from January 1, 1915 to present. It takes 2 months before new records are available for inquiry. Records are indexed on microfiche, inhouse computer.

Searching: Records will only be released to the registrant (if 18 or older), parents, guardian or legal representative. Include the following in your request-full name, names of parents, mother's maiden name, date of birth, place of birth. Two types of certificates are issued: wallet-size; photocopy certification (actual birth certificate).

Access by: mail, phone, fax, in person.

Fee & Payment: The fee is $12.00 per name. Add $3.00 per copy for additional copies of same certificate. Add $5.00 for use of credit card. Fee payee: DHEC. Prepayment required. Credit cards accepted for phone and fax requests only. Personal checks accepted. Credit cards accepted: MasterCard, Visa, Discover.

Mail search: Turnaround time: 3 to 4 weeks. No self addressed stamped envelope is required.

Phone search: Phone requests are accepted, using a credit card. See expedited service.

Fax search: Same criteria as phone searches. Is considered expedited.

In person search: Turnaround time is within 1 hour.

Expedited service: Expedited service is available for mail, phone and fax searches. To have search "expedited" to a 3-4 day turnaround, fee is an extra $5.00 and must use a credit card for add'l $5.00. Overnight shipping is available for an extra fee.

Death Records

South Carolina DHEC, Vital Records, 2600 Bull St, Columbia, SC 29201-1797; 803-898-3630, 803-898-3631 (Order Line), 803-799-0301 (Fax), 8:30AM-4:30PM.

http://www.scdhec.net/vr/index.htm

Indexing & Storage: Records are available from January 1, 1915 to date. New records are available for inquiry immediately. Records are indexed on microfiche, inhouse computer.

Searching: Copies are available to those who show a direct, tangible interest in a determination of a personal or property right. If less than 5 years, records are at county also. Include the following in your request-full name, date of death, place of death.

Access by: mail, phone, fax, in person.

Fee & Payment: The search fee is $12.00 per name. Add $3.00 per copy for additional copies. Add $5.00 for use of credit card. Fee payee: DHEC. Prepayment required. Credit cards accepted for phone and fax requests only. Personal checks accepted. Credit cards accepted: MasterCard, Visa, AmEx, Discover.

Mail search: Turnaround time: 3 to 4 weeks. No self addressed stamped envelope is required.

Phone search: Phone requests are accepted, using a credit card. See expedited service.

Fax search: See expedited service.

In person search: Turnaround time within 1 hour.

Expedited service: Expedited service is available for mail, phone and fax searches. To have the request expedited (3-4 days turnaround), fee is $5.00. To use a credit card there is an additional $5.00 fee. Overnight shipping is $11.00.

Marriage Certificates

South Carolina DHEC, Vital Records, 2600 Bull St, Columbia, SC 29201-1797; 803-898-3630, 803-898-3631 (Order Line), 803-799-0301 (Fax), 8:30AM-4:30PM.

http://www.scdhec.net/vr/index.htm

Note: Copies may also be obtained from the Probate Judge in the county where license was issued.

Indexing & Storage: Records are available from July 1, 1950 to present. New records are available for inquiry immediately. Records are indexed on microfiche, inhouse computer.

Searching: Records are released only to the subjects, their adult children, former or present spouses and legal representatives. Others may obtain a statement of marriage date and place. Include the following in your request-names of husband and wife, date of marriage, place or county of marriage.

Access by: mail, phone, fax, in person.

Fee & Payment: The search fee is $12.00 per name, add $3.00 for each additional copy. Use of credit card is additional $5.00. Fee payee: DHEC. Prepayment required. Credit cards accepted for phone and fax searches only. Personal checks accepted. Credit cards accepted: MasterCard, Visa, AmEx, Discover.

Mail search: Turnaround time: 3 weeks. No self addressed stamped envelope is required.

Phone search: Phone requests are accepted, using a credit card. See expedited service.

Fax search: See expedited service.

In person search: Turnaround time within 1 hour.

Expedited service: Expedited service is available for mail, phone and fax searches. To have request expedited is an additional $5.00 plus $5.00 credit card fee. Overnight delivery is $11.00.

Divorce Records

South Carolina DHEC, Vital Records, 2600 Bull St, Columbia, SC 29201-1797; 803-898-3630, 803-898-3631 (Order Line), 803-799-0301 (Fax), 8:30AM-4:30PM.

http://www.scdhec.net/vr/index.htm

Indexing & Storage: Records are available from July 1, 1962 to present. New records are available for inquiry immediately. Records are indexed on microfiche, inhouse computer.

Searching: Records are available only to the parties, their adult children, a present or former spouse, and their legal representatives. Others may obtain a statement of the date and county of the event. Include the following in your request-names of husband and wife, date of divorce, place of divorce.

Access by: mail, phone, fax, in person.

Fee & Payment: The fee is $12.00 per name. Add $3.00 per copy for additional copies. Use of credit card is $5.00. Fee payee: DHEC. Prepayment required. Credit cards accepted for phone and fax requests only. Personal checks accepted. Credit cards accepted: MasterCard, Visa, AmEx, Discover.

Mail search: Turnaround time: 3 weeks. No self addressed stamped envelope is required.

Phone search: Phone requests are accepted, using a credit card. See expedited service.

Fax search: See expedited service.

In person search: Turnaround time within 1 hour.

Expedited service: Expedited service is available for mail, phone and fax searches. The fee for expedited service of 3-4 days turnaround time is $5.00. Use of a credit card is an additional $5.00. Overnight shipping is $11.00.

Workers' Compensation Records

Workers Compensation Commission, PO Box 1715, Columbia, SC 29202 (Courier: 1612 Marion St, Columbia, SC 29201); 803-737-5700, 803-737-5768 (Fax), 8:30AM-5PM.

http://www.state.sc.us/wcc

Indexing & Storage: Records are available from 1983 on the computer. Some of the older records are at this office and the rest are at the State Archives. Call office first for location of records. New records are available for inquiry immediately. Records are indexed on inhouse computer, books (volumes). Records are normally destroyed after 5 years after closing.

Searching: Must have a signed release form from claimant and you must specify what records you want. Include the following in your request-claimant name, Social Security Number, date of accident.

Access by: mail, fax, in person.

Fee & Payment: The search fee is $6.00 per record and includes a computer printout. File copies cost $20.00 for the first up to 20 pages and $.50 for each additional page. Fee payee: SC Workers Compensation Commission. Prepayment required. Personal checks accepted. No credit cards accepted.

Mail search: Turnaround time: 1 week. A self addressed stamped envelope is requested.

Fax search: You can request by fax, but reply is sent by mail, same turnaround time.

In person search: Records are still returned by mail.

Driver License Information
Driver Records

Division of Motor Vehicles, Driver Records Section, PO Box 1498, Columbia, SC 29216-0028 (Courier: 955 Park St, Columbia, SC 29201); 803-737-4000, 803-737-1077 (Fax), 8:30AM-5PM.

http://www.state.sc.us/dps/dmv

Note: Copies of tickets are available from this department for a fee of $2.00 per record.

Indexing & Storage: Records are available for up to 10 years for moving violations, DWIs and suspensions. Records provided to the public are limited to 3 or 10 years. The state will show moving violations regardless of whether the fine was not paid and license suspended. It takes 1 to 4 weeks before new records are available for inquiry.

Searching: Driving records and Identification card information is confidential by statute. Requests must fall within the guidelines of DPPA. Casual requesters must submit consent of subject if personal information is to be released. The driver's license number or full name and DOB are required to order a record. The following data is not released: Social Security Numbers or personal information (height, weight, sex, eye color, etc.).

Access by: mail, in person, online.

Fee & Payment: The fee is $6.00 per record request. Fee payee: Department of Public Safety. Prepayment required. Personal checks accepted. No credit cards accepted.

Mail search: Turnaround time: 3 days. Fee and return address must be submitted with each request.No self addressed stamped envelope is required.

In person search: Most DMV Branch offices in the state will process up to 10 while you wait.

Online search: The online system offers basic driver data, for a 3 year or a 10 year record. This is a single inquiry process. Network charges will be incurred as well as initial set-up and a security deposit. The system is up between 8 AM and 7 PM. Fee is $2.00 per record. Access is through the AAMVAnet (IBMIN), which requesters much "join." Call Libby Thomasson at 803-737-1546 for further information.

Other access: Magnetic tape and cassette batch processing is available. The agency, also, will sell all or portions of its driver license file in bulk format.

Vehicle Ownership
Vehicle Identification

Division of Motor Vehicles, Title and Registration Records Section, PO Box 1498, Columbia, SC 29216 (Courier: 955 Park St, Columbia, SC 29201); 803-737-4000, 8:30AM-5PM.

http://www.state.sc.us/dps/dmv

Note: For Registration, use PO Box address with ZIP 29216-0022; use ZIP 29216-0024 for Titles.

Indexing & Storage: Records are available for 10 years for titles, 3 years for registration. The index to the records is computerized since 1984. It takes one day before new records are available for inquiry.

Searching: Information regarding the name, address and telephone number will not be released to the public, unless the requester completes form provided by department. Information is not provided to casual requesters. Requesters must be in compliance with DPPA.

Access by: mail, phone, fax, in person.

Fee & Payment: The fee is $10.00 per record request for all records, including lien information. Fee payee: Department of Public Safety. Prepayment required. A deposit account is available for ongoing requesters by mail or phone. Personal checks accepted. No credit cards accepted.

Mail search: Turnaround time: 3 days. No self addressed stamped envelope is required.

Phone search: Telephone searching is available for pre-approved, ongoing requesters. A deposit is required.

Fax search: This is only available to pre-approved, ongoing requesters. A deposit is required.

In person search: You may search in person.

Other access: South Carolina offers a variety of bulk retrieval programs where permitted by law. The maximum amount of records that can be retrieved is 100,000. For more information, call Titles or Registration at 803-737-4000.

Expedited service: Expedited service is available for fax searches. Turnaround time: 1 to 2 days. Must have a deposit account. The fax number is 803-737-2299.

Accident Reports

Accident Reports, PO Box 1498, Columbia, SC 29216-0040 (Courier: 955 Park St, Columbia, SC 29201); 803-737-4000, 803-737-4483 (Fax), 8:30AM-5PM.

Indexing & Storage: Records are available for 10 years to present. The records are indexed on computer. It takes one week after receipt from enforcement agency before new records are available for inquiry. Records are indexed on inhouse computer.

Searching: Must have full name of all the drivers involved in the accident. Include the following in your request-full name, date of accident, driver's license number, county.

Access by: mail, phone, in person.

Fee & Payment: The fees are $10.00 for accident research and $10.00 for insurance research. You may call to find out if record is on file. Fee payee: Department of Public Safety. Ongoing requesters may open an account with a $100.00 deposit and then will be billed monthly. Personal checks accepted. No credit cards accepted now, but may the near future.

Mail search: Turnaround time: 7 to 10 days. Information requests are available.A self addressed stamped envelope is requested.

Phone search: Five records per day may be requested with a pre-approved account.

In person search: Records will be processed while you wait.

Vessel Ownership
Vessel Registration

Dept of Natural Resources, Registration & Titles, PO Box 167, Columbia, SC 29202; 803-734-3857, 803-734-4138 (Fax), 8:30AM-5PM.

http://www.dnr.state.sc.us

Indexing & Storage: Records are available from 1958 to present. Active records remain on computer as long as they are active. Inactive records are put on microfiche seven years after becoming inactive.

Searching: All motorized boats must be titled and registered. Sailboats lest than 14' must be titled, and if used with propulsion then registered. To search, one of the following is required: name and address, hull ID #, title #, or SC (serial) #. The following data is not released: Social Security Numbers.

Access by: mail, fax, in person.

Fee & Payment: The search fee for all types of searches is $3.00 per record if no motor, and $6.00 per record if motor. Fee payee: SC Dept of Natural Resources. Prepayment required. Personal checks accepted. No credit cards accepted.

Mail search: Turnaround time: 7 to 20 days. No self addressed stamped envelope is required.

Fax search: Fax requests must be prepaid.

In person search: Turnaround time is usually same day.

Other access: Bulk data is available. The fee is $200 for up to 20,000 records, then $10 for each 1,000 additional records.

Legislation Records

South Carolina Legislature, 937 Assembly Street, Rm 220, Columbia, SC 29201; 803-734-2060, 803-734-2145 (Older Bills), 9AM-5PM.

http://www.leginfo.state.sc.us

Note: Older passed bills are found at the Legislative Council on the 2nd floor, 803-734-2145.

Indexing & Storage: Records are available for current session only. The session is a 2 year session. Records are indexed on microfiche.

Searching: Include the following in your request-bill number.

Access by: mail, phone, fax, in person, online.

Fee & Payment: There is no fee unless the bill is long. They will compute the charge. Fee payee: South Carolina Legislative Printing. They will invoice. Personal checks accepted. No credit cards accepted.

Mail search: Turnaround time: variable. Information requests are available.No self addressed stamped envelope is required.

Phone search: You may call for copies of bills.

Fax search: Fax searching available.

In person search: Searching is available in person.

Online search: Bill text and status data can be found at the web site.

Voter Registration

State Election Commission, Records, PO Box 5987, Columbia, SC 29205; 803-734-9060, 803-734-9366 (Fax), 8:30AM-5PM.

http://www.state.sc.us/scsec

Indexing & Storage: Records are available for all active records.

Searching: Records are open to the public. To search, provide the name with the county or DOB. The following data is not released: Social Security Numbers.

Access by: mail, phone, fax, in person.

Fee & Payment: There is no search fee unless extensive time involved. Copies are $.20 each. Fee payee: State Election Commission. Prepayment required. No credit cards accepted.

Mail search: Turnaround time: 1 to 2 days.

Phone search: Records are available by phone.

Fax search: Same criteria as mail searching.

In person search: Searching is available in person.

Other access: Lists, labels, diskettes, and magnetic tapes are available with a variety of sort features. The minimum charge varies from $75 to $160 depending on the media.

GED Certificates

GED Testing Office, 402 Rutledge Bldg, 1429 Senate St, Columbia, SC 29201; 803-734-8347, 803-734-8336 (Fax), 8:30AM-5PM M-F.

http://www.state.sc.us/sde

Indexing & Storage: It takes 6 weeks before new records are available for inquiry.

Searching: To search, all of the following is required: a signed release, name, Social Security Number, and approximate date of. Specify if for civilian or military use.

Access by: mail, fax.

Fee & Payment: There is no fee for a verification. There is a $5.00 fee for a copy of a transcript by mail, $3.00 if by fax. Fee payee: SC Dept of Education. Prepayment required. Cash and money orders are accepted. No credit cards accepted.

Mail search: Turnaround time is 3-5 days.No self addressed stamped envelope is required.

Fax search: Must call for verification within a day of faxed release.

Hunting License Information
Fishing License Information
Records not maintained by a state level agency.

Note: They do not have a central database. Licenses are kept on file within the License Division by the county and agent where the license was sold.

South Carolina State Licensing Agencies

Licenses Searchable Online

Accounting Practitioner-AP #02 .... http://167.7.126.243/Lookup/Cpa.asp
Acupuncturist #39 .... http://167.7.126.243/Lookup/Medical.asp
Alcoholic Beverage Sunday Sales #34 .... www.sctax.org/tax/sundaysales.html
Animal Health Technician #43 .... http://167.7.126.243/lookup/vet.asp
Architect #03 .... http://167.7.126.243/Lookup/Architects.asp
Architectural Partnership/Corporation #03 .... http://167.7.126.243/Lookup/Architects.asp
Attorney #48 .... www.scbar.org/lawyer_directory.asp
Auction Company #50 .... http://167.7.126.243/Lookup/Auctioneers.asp
Auctioneer/Auctioneer Apprentice #50 .... http://167.7.126.243/Lookup/Auctioneers.asp
Audiologist #22 .... http://167.7.126.243/Lookup/Speech.asp
Barber Instructor/School #47 .... http://167.7.126.243/lookup/barbers.asp
Barber Shop #47 .... http://167.7.126.243/lookup/barbers.asp
Barber/Barber Apprentice #47 .... http://167.7.126.243/lookup/barbers.asp
Bodywork Therapist #47 .... http://167.7.126.243/Lookup/Massage.asp
Building/Housing Inspector #21 .... http://167.7.126.243/Lookup/BuildingCodes.asp
Burglar Alarm Contractor #24 .... http://167.7.126.243/Lookup/Contractors.asp
Chiropractor #04 .... http://167.7.126.243/lookup/Chiropractic.asp
Contractor, General & Mechanical #24 .... http://167.7.126.243/Lookup/Contractors.asp
Cosmetologist #05 .... http://167.7.126.243/lookup/cosmetology.asp
Counselor, Professional #08 .... http://167.7.126.243/lookup/Counselors.asp
Dentist #06 .... http://167.7.126.243/Lookup/Dentistry.asp
Embalmer #11 .... http://167.7.126.243/Lookup/Funeral.asp
Emergency Medical Service (Ambulance Co) #27 www.scems.com/emsassn/members.html
Engineer #07 .... http://167.7.126.243/Lookup/Engineers.asp
Forester #38 .... http://167.7.126.243/Lookup/Foresters.asp
Funeral Director/Funeral Home #11 .... http://167.7.126.243/Lookup/Funeral.asp
Geologist #20 .... http://167.7.126.243/Lookup/Geologists.asp
Home Builder, Residential #45 .... http://167.7.126.243/Lookup/ResidentialBuilders.asp
Inspector, Mech./Elec./Plumbing/Provisional #21 . http://167.7.126.243/Lookup/BuildingCodes.asp
Landscape Architect #40 .... www.dnr.state.sc.us/water/envaff/prolicense/prolicense.html
Lobbyist #37 .... www.lpitr.state.sc.us/reports/ethrpt.htm
Manicurist #05 .... http://167.7.126.243/lookup/barbers.asp
Manufactured House Manufacturer/Dealer #41 ..... http://167.7.126.243/Lookup/Mh.asp
Manufactured House Seller/Installer/Repair #41 ... http://167.7.126.243/Lookup/Mh.asp
Marriage & Family Therapist #08 .... http://167.7.126.243/lookup/Counselors.asp
Massage Therapist #47 .... http://167.7.126.243/Lookup/Massage.asp
Medical Doctor #39 .... http://167.7.126.243/Lookup/Medical.asp
Nurse #12 .... http://167.7.126.243/lookup/nurses.asp
Nurse-LPN #12 .... http://167.7.126.243/lookup/nurses.asp
Nursing Home Administrator #32 .... http://167.7.126.243/Lookup/LTC.asp
Occupational Therapist/Assistant #13 .... http://167.7.126.243/Lookup/OT.asp
Optician #14 .... http://167.7.126.243/Lookup/Opticians.asp
Optometrist #09 .... http://167.7.126.243/Lookup/Optometry.asp
Osteopathic Physician #39 .... http://167.7.126.243/Lookup/Medical.asp
Pharmacist/Pharmacy Technicians #15 .... http://167.7.126.243/lookup/pharmacy.asp
Pharmacy/Drug Outlets #15 .... http://167.7.126.243/lookup/pharmacy.asp
Physical Therapist/Therapist Assistant #16 .... http://167.7.126.243/Lookup/PT.asp
Physician Assistant #39 .... http://167.7.126.243/Lookup/Medical.asp
Podiatrist #17 .... http://167.7.126.243/Lookup/Podiatry.asp
Psycho-Educational Specialist #08 .... http://167.7.126.243/lookup/Counselors.asp
Psychologist #18 .... http://167.7.126.243/Lookup/Psychology.asp
Public Accountant-CPA #02 .... http://167.7.126.243/Lookup/Cpa.asp
Residential Care, Community #32 .... http://167.7.126.243/Lookup/LTC.asp

Respiratory Care Practitioner #39 .... http://167.7.126.243/Lookup/Medical.asp
Social Worker #18 .... http://167.7.126.243/Lookup/SW.asp
Soil Classifier #40... www.dnr.state.sc.us/water/envaff/prolicense/prolicense.html
Solid Waste Landfill #30 .... www.scdhec.net/lwm/html/min.html
Specialty Contractor (Residential Construct.) #45 http://167.7.126.243/Lookup/ResidentialBuilders.asp
Speech-Language Pathologist #22....................... http://167.7.126.243/Lookup/Speech.asp
Sprinkler Systems Contractor #24....................... http://167.7.126.243/Lookup/Contractors.asp
Surveyor #07 .... http://167.7.126.243/Lookup/Engineers.asp
Veterinarian #43 .... http://167.7.126.243/lookup/vet.asp

Licensing Quick Finder

Accounting Practitioner-AP #02 803-896-4492
Acupuncturist #39 803-896-4500
Agricultural Dealer/Handler #25 803-737-9696
Alcoholic Beverage Sunday Sales #34..803-898-5864
Alcoholic Beverage Vendors/Mfg.s/Wholesalers #34
....803-898-5864
Amusement Ride #46...........................803-734-9711
Animal Health Technician #43 803-896-4598
Architect #03.......................................803-896-4408
Architectural Partnership/Corp. #03 803-896-4408
Athletic Contest #49 803-896-4498
Athletic Trainer #49 803-896-4498
Attorney #48 803-799-6653
Auction Company #50 803-896-4853
Auctioneer/Auctioneer Apprentice #50 ..803-896-4853
Audiologist #22 803-896-4650
Bank #10 803-734-2001
Barber Instructor/School #47 803-896-4588
Barber Shop #47 803-896-4588
Barber/Barber Apprentice #47 803-896-4588
Bodywork Therapist #47.......................803-896-4588
Boxer/Boxing Professional #49 803-896-4498
Building/Housing Inspector #21 803-896-4688
Burglar Alarm Contractor #24 803-896-4686
Butterfat Tester #25 803-737-9700
Chiropractor #04 803-896-4587
Constable #51.....................................803-896-7014
Contact Lens License #14 803-896-4681
Contractor, General & Mechanical #24..803-896-4686
Cosmetologist #05 803-896-4494
Cosmetology Instructor/School #05.......803-896-4494
Counselor, Professional #08..................803-896-4658
Dental Hygienist #06 803-896-4599
Dental Specialist #06...........................803-896-4599
Dental Technician #06..........................803-896-4599
Dentist #06 803-896-4599
Electrician #42 803-933-1209
Elevator Service #46 803-734-9711
Embalmer #11 803-896-4497
Emergency Medical Service (Ambulance Co) #27 ......
....803-737-7204
Emergency Medical Technician #27.......803-737-7204
Engineer #07 803-896-4422
Esthetician #05 803-896-4494
Feed Mfg./Product #25.........................803-737-9700

Financial Institution #10.......................803-734-2001
Forester #38 803-896-4498
Funeral Director #11.............................803-896-4497
Funeral Home #11 803-896-4497
Geologist #20......................................803-896-4498
Hair Care Master Specialist #47 803-896-4588
Hearing Aid Dispenser/Fitter #29 803-737-7370
Heating & Air/Gas Fitting #42 803-933-1209
Home Builder, Residential #45..............803-896-4696
Inspector, Mech./Elec./Plumbing/Provisional #21 ......
....803-896-4688
Insurance Agent #31 803-737-5757
Investment Advisor #01........................803-734-9916
Landscape Architect #40 803-734-9100
Liquor Permit - Special Event #34.........803-898-5864
Lobbyist #37 803-253-4192
Manicurist #05 803-896-4494
Manufactured House Mfg./Dealer #41...803-896-4682
Manufactured House Salesperson/Installer/Repair #41
....803-896-4682
Marriage & Family Therapist #08 803-896-4658
Massage Therapist #47 803-896-4588
Medical Doctor #39 803-896-4500
Midwife #29 803-737-7370
Mine Site #30......................................803-896-4000
Nail Technician #05..............................803-896-4494
Nurse #12 803-896-4550
Nurse-LPN #12 803-896-4550
Nursing Home Administrator #32 803-896-4544
Occupational Therapist/Assistant #13 ..803-896-4683
Optician #14..803-896-4681
Optician Apprentice #14 803-896-4681
Optometrist #09 803-869-4679
Osteopathic Physician #39 803-896-4500
Percolation Test Technician #36...........803-896-4430
Pesticide Applicator #33 803-646-2155
Pesticide Dealer #33 803-646-2155
Pharmacist/Pharmacy Technician #15 ..803-896-4700
Pharmacy/Drug Outlets #15..................803-896-4700
Physical Therapist/Therapist Assistant #16 ....
....803-896-4655
Physician Assistant #39.......................803-896-4500
Pilot #35 803-896-6280
Pipefitter #42 803-933-1209
Plumbing #42......................................803-933-1209

Podiatrist #17......................................803-896-4685
Polygraph Examiner #51 803-896-7292
Private Detective #51 803-896-7014
Property Manager #44..........................803-896-4400
Psycho-Educational Specialist #08 803-896-4658
Psychologist #18.................................803-896-4661
Public Accountant-CPA #02..................803-896-4492
Pyrotechnic Technician #19..................803-896-4420
Pyrotechnic Wholesaler/Facility/Jobber #19 ....
....803-896-4420
Real Estate Appraiser #44 803-896-4400
Real Estate Broker #44........................803-896-4400
Residential Care, Community #32..........803-896-4544
Respiratory Care Practitioner #39 803-896-4500
Sanitarian #28.....................................803-896-0646
School Guidance Counselor #26 803-898-3224
School Media Communications Specialist #26 ....
....803-896-3224
School Principal/Supervisor/Superintendent #26 ....
....803-896-3224
Securities Agent #01 803-734-9916
Securities Broker/Dealer #01 803-734-9916
Security Guard/Security Company #51 .803-896-7014
Seed Salesperson #25 803-737-9690
Shampoo Assistant #47........................803-896-4588
Sheet Metal #42..................................803-933-1209
Social Worker #18 803-896-4665
Soil Classifier #40 803-734-9100
Solid Waste Landfill #30 803-896-4149
Solid Waste Landfill Operator #30.........803-896-4149
Specialty Contractor (Residential Construction) #45
....803-896-4696
Speech-Language Pathologist #22 803-896-4650
Sprinkler Systems Contractor #24.........803-896-4686
Surveyor #07 803-896-4422
Swimming Pool/Spa Operator #36 803-896-4430
Teacher #26..803-896-3224
Timeshare/Land Salesperson #44 803-896-4400
Veterinarian #43..................................803-896-4598
Waste Water Treatment Plant Operator #36..............
....803-896-4430
Water Treatment #36 803-896-4430
Weighmaster #025...............................803-737-9696
Well Driller #36....................................803-896-4430
Wrestler/Wrestling Professional #49 803-896-4498

Licensing Agency Information

#01 Attorney Generals Office, PO Box 11549 (1000 Assembly St, Rembert C. Dennis Building), Columbia, SC 29211-1549; 803-734-9916, Fax: 803-734-0032.
www.scsecurities.org/brokerdealer.html

#02 Department of Labor, Licensing & Regulation, PO Box 11329 (3600 Forest Dr, #101), Columbia, SC 29211; 803-896-4492, Fax: 803-896-4554.
www.llr.state.sc.us/bac.htm
Direct web site URL to search for licensees: http://167.7.126.243/Lookup/Cpa.asp. You can search online using last name, license #

#03 Department of Labor, Licensing & Regulation, PO Box 11419 (110 Centerview Dr, #201), Columbia, SC 29211; 803-896-4408, Fax: 803-734-4410.
www.llr.state.sc.us/boards.htm
Direct web site URL to search for licensees: www.llr.state.sc.us/dss/dss_menu.htm. You can search online using last name, license #, city

#04 Department of Labor, Licensing & Regulation, PO Box 11329 (110 Centerview Dr, #306), Columbia, SC 29211-1329; 803-896-4587, Fax: 803-896-4719.
www.llr.state.sc.us/POL/Chiropractors
Direct web site URL to search for licensees: http://167.7.126.243/lookup/Chiropractic.asp. You can search online using last name, license #

#05 Department of Labor, Licensing & Regulation, PO Box 11329 (110 Centerview Dr), Columbia, SC 29211-1329; 803-896-4494, Fax: 803-896-4484.
www.llr.state.sc.us/POL/Cosmetology
Direct web site URL to search for licensees: http://167.7.126.243/lookup/cosmetology.asp. You can search online using name or license # See also Board of Barber examiners for Shampoo Assistants and Master Hair Care Specialist

#06 Department of Labor, Licensing & Regulation, PO Box 11329 (110 Centerview Dr), Columbia, SC 29211-1329; 803-896-4599, Fax: 803-896-4596.
www.llr.state.sc.us/POL/Dentistry
Direct web site URL to search for licensees: http://167.7.126.243/Lookup/Dentistry.asp. You can search online using name, license #

#07 Department of Labor, Licensing & Regulation, PO Box 11597 (110 Centerview Dr, #201), Columbia, SC 29211-1597; 803-896-4422, Fax: 803-896-4427.
www.llr.state.sc.us/POL/Engineers
Direct web site URL to search for licensees: http://167.7.126.243/Lookup/Engineers.asp

#08 Department of Labor, Licensing & Regulation, PO Box 11329 (110 Centerview, #306), Columbia, SC 29211; 803-896-4658, Fax: 803-896-4719.
www.llr.state.sc.us/POL/Counselors
Direct web site URL to search for licensees: http://167.7.126.243/lookup/Counselors.asp. You can search online using name, license #

#09 Department of Labor, Licensing & Regulation, PO Box 11329 (110 Centerview Dr.), Columbia, SC 29211-1329; 803-896-4679, Fax: 803-896-4719.
www.llr.state.sc.us/POL/Optometry

Direct web site URL to search for licensees: http://167.7.126.243/Lookup/Optometry.asp. You can search online using name or license #

#10 Board of Financial Institutions, PO Box 12549 (1015 Sumter St, Rm 309), Columbia, SC 29201; 803-734-2001, Fax: 803-734-2013.

#11 Department of Labor, Licensing & Regulation, PO Box 11329 (110 Centerview Dr, #104), Columbia, SC 29211-1329; 803-896-4497, Fax: 803-896-4554.
www.llr.state.sc.us/POL/Funeral
Direct web site URL to search for licensees: http://167.7.126.243/Lookup/Funeral.asp

#12 Department of Labor, Licensing & Regulation, PO Box 12367 (110 Centerview Dr, #202), Columbia, SC 29211-2367; 803-896-4550, Fax: 803-896-4525.
www.llr.state.sc.us/POL/Nursing
Direct web site URL to search for licensees: http://167.7.126.243/lookup/nurses.asp. You can search online using last name. License #

#13 Department of Labor, Licensing & Regulation, PO Box 11329 (110 Centerview Dr, #306), Columbia, SC 29211; 803-896-4683, Fax: 803-896-4719.
www.llr.state.sc.us/POL/OccupationalTherapy
Direct web site URL to search for licensees: http://167.7.126.243/Lookup/OT.asp. You can search online using name, city, license #

#14 Department of Labor, Licensing & Regulation, PO Box 11329 (110 Centerview Dr.), Columbia, SC 29211-1329; 803-896-4681, Fax: 803-896-4719.
www.llr.state.sc.us/POL/Opticians
Direct web site URL to search for licensees: http://167.7.126.243/Lookup/Opticians.asp. You can search online using agency select, then search by name

#15 Department of Labor, Licensing & Regulation, 110 Centerview Dr, Kingstree Bldg, #306, Columbia, SC 29211-1927; 803-896-4700, Fax: 803-896-4596.
www.llr.state.sc.us/POL/Pharmacy/
Direct web site URL to search for licensees: http://167.7.126.243/lookup/pharmacy.asp. You can search online using name or license #

#16 Department of Labor, Licensing & Regulation, PO Box 11329 (110 Centerview Dr,), Columbia, SC 29211; 803-896-4655, Fax: 803-896-4719.
www.llr.state.sc.us/POL/PhysicalTherapy/Default.htm
Direct web site URL to search for licensees: http://167.7.126.243/Lookup/PT.asp. You can search online using last name, city, license #

#17 Department of Labor, Licensing & Regulation, PO Box 11289 (110 Centerview Dr, #202), Columbia, SC 29211-1289; 803-896-4685, Fax: 803-896-4515.
www.llr.state.sc.us/POL/Podiatry/Default.htm
Direct web site URL to search for licensees: http://167.7.126.243/Lookup/Podiatry.asp. You can search online using name or license #

#18 Department of Labor, Licensing & Regulation, PO Box 11329 (100 Centerview Dr), Columbia, SC 29211-1329; 803-896-4664, Fax: 803-896-4687.
www.llr.state.sc.us/pol.asp

Direct web site URL to search for licensees: http://167.7.126.243/index.asp. You can search online using name, city, license number.

#19 Department of Labor, Licensing & Regulation, PO Box 11847 (110 Centerview Dr, #201), Columbia, SC 29211-1329; 803-896-4400, Fax: 803-896-4404.
www.llr.state.sc.us/POL/Pyrotechnic

#20 Department of Labor, Licensing & Regulation, PO Box 11329 (110 Centerview Dr, #104), Columbia, SC 29211-1329; 803-896-4498, Fax: 803-896-4484.
www.llr.state.sc.us/POL/Geologists
Direct web site URL to search for licensees: http://167.7.126.243/Lookup/Geologists.asp. You can search online using name or license #

#21 Department of Labor, Licensing & Regulation, PO Box 11329 (110 Centerview Dr, #102), Columbia, SC 29211-1329; 803-896-4688, Fax: 803-896-4814.
www.llr.state.sc.us/POL/BuildingCodes
Direct web site URL to search for licensees: http://167.7.126.243/Lookup/BuildingCodes.asp

#22 Department of Labor, Licensing & Regulation, PO Box 11329 (110 Centerview Dr, #306), Columbia, SC 29211-1329; 803-896-4650, Fax: 803-896-4719.
www.llr.state.sc.us/POL/Speech
Direct web site URL to search for licensees: http://167.7.126.243/Lookup/Speech.asp. You can search online using name or license #

#24 Department of Labor, Licensing & Regulation, PO Box 11329 (110 Centerview Dr, #201), Columbia, SC 29211-1329; 803-896-4686, Fax: 803-896-4364.
www.llr.state.sc.us/POL/Contractors/
Direct web site URL to search for licensees: http://167.7.126.243/Lookup/Contractors.asp. You can search online using company or individual name.

#25 Department of Agriculture, PO Box 11280, Columbia, SC 29211; 803-734-2210, Fax: 803-734-2192.

#26 Department of Education, 1429 Senate St, Columbia, SC 29201; 803-734-8466, Fax: 803-734-2873.
www.scteachers.org

#27 Department of Health & Environmental Control, 2600 Bull St, Columbia, SC 29201; 803-737-7204, Fax: 803-545-4212.
www.scems.com

#28 Department of Health & Environmental Control, 2600 Bull St, Columbia, SC 29201; 803-896-0646, Fax: 803-896-0645.
www.scdhec.net

#29 Department of Health & Environmental Control, 2600 Bull St, Columbia, SC 29201; 803-737-7370, Fax: 803-545-4212.
www.scdhec.net/hs

#30 Department of Health & Environmental Control, 2600 Bull St, Columbia, SC 29201; 803-896-4000, Fax: 803-896-4001.
www.scdhec.net
Direct web site URL to search for licensees: www.scdhec.net/lwm/html/min.html To search for Landfill Operators, you must search by county.

#31 Department of Insurance, PO Box 100105, Columbia, SC 29202-3105; 803-737-6095, Fax: 803-737-6232.
www.state.sc.us/doi

#32 Department of Labor, Licensing & Regulation, PO Box 11329, Columbia, SC 29211; 803-896-4544, Fax: 803-896-4555.
www.llr.state.sc.us/POL/LongTermHealthCare
Direct web site URL to search for licensees:
http://167.7.126.243/Lookup/LTC.asp

#33 Department of Pesticide Regulation, 511 Winghouse Rd, Pendelton, SC 29670; 864-646-2155, Fax: 864-646-2179.

#34 Department of Revenue & Taxation, PO Box 125, Columbia, SC 29214; 803-898-5864, Fax: 803-898-5899.
www.sctax.org/tax/abl.html

#35 Division of Aeronautics, PO Box 280068, Columbia, SC 29228-0068; 803-896-6270, Fax: 803-896-6277.

#36 Department of Labor, Licensing & Regulation, PO Box 11329, Columbia, SC 29211; 803-896-4430, Fax: 803-896-4424.
www.llr.state.sc.us/boards.htm
Direct web site URL to search for licensees:
www.llr.state.sc.us/ecb.htm

#37 Ethics Commission, 5000 Thurmond Mall #250, Columbia, SC 29201; 803-253-4193, Fax: 803-253-7539.
www.state.sc.us/ethics.htm
Direct web site URL to search for licensees:
www.lpitr.state.sc.us/reports/ethrpt.htm

#38 Department of Labor, Licensing & Regulation, PO Box 11329, Columbia, SC 29211-1329; 803-896-4498, Fax: 803-896-4595.
www.llr.state.sc.us/brf.htm
Direct web site URL to search for licensees:
www.llr.state.sc.us/dss/dss_menu.htm. You can

search online using agency select, then search by name.

#39 Department of Labor, Licensing & Regulation, PO Box 11289 (110 Centerview Dr, #202), Columbia, SC 29211-1289; 803-896-4500, Fax: 803-896-4515.
www.llr.state.sc.us/POL/Medical
Direct web site URL to search for licensees:
http://167.7.126.243/Lookup/Medical.asp. You can search online using medical board, name.

#40 Department of Natural Resources, 2221 Devine St, #222, Columbia, SC 29205-2474; 803-734-9100, Fax: 803-734-9200.
www.dnr.state.sc.us
Direct web site URL to search for licensees:
www.dnr.state.sc.us/water/envaff/prolicense/prolicense.html

#41 Department of Labor, Licensing & Regulation, PO Box 11329 (110 Centerview Dr, #102), Columbia, SC 29211-1329; 803-896-4682, Fax: 803-896-4814.
www.llr.state.sc.us/POL/ManufacturedHousing
Direct web site URL to search for licensees:
http://167.7.126.243/Lookup/Mh.asp

#42 Municipal Association of South Carolina, 1411 Gervais St, Columbia, SC 29211-2109; 803-933-1209, Fax: 803-933-1299.
http://masc.state.sc.us

#43 Department of Labor, Licensing & Regulation, PO Box 11329, Columbia, SC 29211-1329; 803-896-4598, Fax: 803-896-4719.
www.llr.state.sc.us/POL/Veterinary
Direct web site URL to search for licensees:
http://167.7.126.243/lookup/vet.asp. You can search online using name or license number.

#44 Real Estate Commission, PO Box 11847, Columbia, SC 29211-1847; 803-896-4400, Fax: 803-896-4404.
www.llr.state.sc.us/rec.htm

#45 Department of Labor, Licensing & Regulation, PO Box 11329 (110 Centerview Dr, #201), Columbia, SC 29211-1329; 803-896-4696, Fax: 803-896-4656.
www.llr.state.sc.us/POL/ResidentialBuilders
Direct web site URL to search for licensees:
http://167.7.126.243/Lookup/ResidentialBuilders.asp

#46 Department of Labor, Licensing & Regulation, PO Box 11329, Columbia, SC 29211-1329; 803-734-9711, Fax: 803-737-9119.
www.llr.state.sc.us/

#47 Department of Labor, Licensing & Regulation, PO Box 11329 (110 Centerview Dr, #104), Columbia, SC 29211-1329; 803-896-4588, Fax: 803-896-4484.
www.llr.state.sc.us/pol.asp
Direct web site URL to search for licensees:
http://167.7.126.243/index.asp. You can search online using name or license #

#48 Supreme Court, PO Box 608 (950 Taylor St), Columbia, SC 29202; 803-799-6653, Fax: 803-799-4118.

#49 Department of Labor, Licensing & Regulation, PO Box 11329 (110 Centerview Dr), Columbia, SC 29211; 803-896-4498, Fax: 803-896-4595.
www.llr.state.sc.us/POL/Athletic

#50 Department of Labor, Licensing & Regulation, PO Box 11329 (110 Centerview Dr, #104), Columbia, SC 29211-1329; 803-896-4853, Fax: 803-896-4484.
www.llr.state.sc.us/POL/Auctioneers
Direct web site URL to search for licensees:
http://167.7.126.243/Lookup/Auctioneers.asp. You can search online using Auctioneers, name

#51 Law Enforcement Division, 4400 Broad River Rd, Columbia, SC 29210; 803-737-9000, Fax: 803-896-7037.

South Carolina Federal Courts

The following list indicates the district and division name for each county in the state. If the bankruptcy court location is different from the district court, then the location of the bankruptcy court appears in parentheses.

County/Court Cross Reference

Abbeville	Greenwood (Columbia)	Greenwood	Greenwood (Columbia)
Aiken	Greenwood (Columbia)	Hampton	Beaufort (Columbia)
Allendale	Greenwood (Columbia)	Horry	Florence (Columbia)
Anderson	Anderson (Columbia)	Jasper	Beaufort (Columbia)
Bamberg	Greenwood (Columbia)	Kershaw	Columbia
Barnwell	Greenwood (Columbia)	Lancaster	Greenwood (Columbia)
Beaufort	Beaufort (Columbia)	Laurens	Greenville (Columbia)
Berkeley	Charleston (Columbia)	Lee	Columbia
Calhoun	Greenwood (Columbia)	Lexington	Columbia
Charleston	Charleston (Columbia)	Marion	Florence (Columbia)
Cherokee	Spartanburg (Columbia)	Marlboro	Florence (Columbia)
Chester	Spartanburg (Columbia)	McCormick	Greenwood (Columbia)
Chesterfield	Florence (Columbia)	Newberry	Greenwood (Columbia)
Clarendon	Charleston (Columbia)	Oconee	Anderson (Columbia)
Colleton	Charleston (Columbia)	Orangeburg	Greenwood (Columbia)
Darlington	Florence (Columbia)	Pickens	Anderson (Columbia)
Dillon	Florence (Columbia)	Richland	Columbia
Dorchester	Charleston (Columbia)	Saluda	Greenwood (Columbia)
Edgefield	Greenwood (Columbia)	Spartanburg	Spartanburg (Columbia)
Fairfield	Greenwood (Columbia)	Sumter	Columbia
Florence	Florence (Columbia)	Union	Spartanburg (Columbia)
Georgetown	Charleston (Columbia)	Williamsburg	Florence (Columbia)
Greenville	Greenville (Columbia)	York	Spartanburg (Columbia)

US District Court

District of South Carolina

Anderson Division c/o Greenville Division, PO Box 10768, Greenville, SC 29603 (Courier Address: 300 E Washington St, Greenville, SC 29601), 864-241-2700.

http://www.scd.uscourts.gov

Counties: Anderson, Oconee, Pickens.

Indexing/Storage: Cases are indexed by as well as by case number. New cases are available in the index after filing date. Open records are located at the Division.

Fee & Payment: The fee is no charge per item (one party name or case number). Payment may be made by money order, cashier check. Business checks are not accepted. Personal checks are not accepted.

Phone Search: Searching not available by phone.

Mail Search: A stamped self addressed envelope is not required.

In Person: In person searching is available.

PACER: Sign-up number is 800-676-6856. Access fee is $.60 per minute. Toll-free access: 800-831-6162. Local access: 803-765-5871. Case records are available back to January 1990. Records are never purged. New records are available online after 1 day. PACER is available online at http://pacer.scd.uscourts.gov.

Opinions Online: Court opinions are available online at http://www.law.sc.edu/dsc/dsc.htm

Beaufort Division c/o Charleston Division, PO Box 835, Charleston, SC 29402 (Courier Address: 85 Broad St, Hollings Judicial Center, Charleston, SC 29401), 843-579-1401, Fax: 803-579-1402.

http://www.scd.uscourts.gov

Counties: Beaufort, Hampton, Jasper.

Indexing/Storage: Cases are indexed by as well as by case number. New cases are available in the index after filing date. Open records are located at the Division. Civil records are sent to Federal Records Center 1 year after case close. Criminal records are sent 5 years after case close.

Fee & Payment: The fee is no charge per item (one party name or case number). Payment may be made by money order, cashier check. Business checks are not accepted. Personal checks are not accepted.

Phone Search: Searching not available by phone.

Mail Search: Always enclose a stamped self addressed envelope.

In Person: In person searching is available.

PACER: Sign-up number is 800-676-6856. Access fee is $.60 per minute. Toll-free access: 800-831-6162. Local access: 803-765-5871. Case records are available back to January 1990. Records are never purged. New records are available online after 1 day. PACER is available online at http://pacer.scd.uscourts.gov.

Opinions Online: Court opinions are available online at http://www.law.sc.edu/dsc/dsc.htm

Charleston Division PO Box 835, Charleston, SC 29402 (Courier Address: 85 Broad St, Hollings Judicial Center, Charleston, SC 29401), 843-579-1401, Fax: 803-579-1402.

http://www.scd.uscourts.gov

Counties: Berkeley, Charleston, Clarendon, Colleton, Dorchester, Georgetown.

Indexing/Storage: Cases are indexed by defendant and plaintiff as well as by case number. New cases are available in the index 1-2 days after filing date. A computer index is maintained. Older records are indexed on cards and microfiche. Open records are located at this court. District wide searches are available for information from 1980 from this court.

Fee & Payment: The fee is $20.00 per item (one party name or case number). Payment may be made by money order, cashier check, personal check. Prepayment is required. Payee: US District Court. Certification fee: $7.00 per document. Copy fee: $.50 per page.

Phone Search: Only docket information is available by phone.

Mail Search: Always enclose a stamped self addressed envelope.

In Person: In person searching is available.

PACER: Sign-up number is 800-676-6856. Access fee is $.60 per minute. Toll-free access: 800-831-6162. Local access: 803-765-5871. Case records are available back to January 1990. Records are never purged. New records are available online after 1 day. PACER is available online at http://pacer.scd.uscourts.gov.

Opinions Online: Court opinions are available online at http://www.law.sc.edu/dsc/dsc.htm

Columbia Division

1845 Assembly St, Columbia, SC 29201 (Courier Address: Use mail address for courier delivery), 803-765-5816.

http://www.scd.uscourts.gov

Counties: Kershaw, Lee, Lexington, Richland, Sumter.

Indexing/Storage: Cases are indexed by defendant and plaintiff as well as by case number. New cases are available in the index 1 month after filing date. A computer index is maintained. Older records are also indexed on microfiche. Open records are located at this court. District wide searches are available from this court.

Fee & Payment: The fee is $20.00 per item (one party name or case number). Payment may be made by money order, cashier check, personal check. Prepayment is required. Payee: Clerk, US District Court. Certification fee: $7.00 per document. Copy fee: $.50 per page.

Phone Search: Searching is not available by phone. If a case number, caption and judge are provided, docket info is given. The court will not search case numbers or captions on the phone.

Fax Search: Will accept fax search request. Response will be sent through the mail when payment is received.

Mail Search: A stamped self addressed envelope is not required.

In Person: In person searching is available.

PACER: Sign-up number is 800-676-6856. Access fee is $.60 per minute. Toll-free access: 800-831-6162. Local access: 803-765-5871. Case records are available back to January 1990. Records are never purged. New records are available online after 1 day. PACER is available online at http://pacer.scd.uscourts.gov.

Opinions Online: Court opinions are available online at http://www.law.sc.edu/dsc/dsc.htm

Florence Division

PO Box 2317, Florence, SC 29503 (Courier Address: 401 W Evans St, McMillan Federal Bldg., Room 361, Florence, SC 29501), 843-676-3820, Fax: 843-676-3831.

http://www.scd.uscourts.gov

Counties: Chesterfield, Darlington, Dillon, Florence, Horry, Marion, Marlboro, Williamsburg.

Indexing/Storage: Cases are indexed by defendant and plaintiff as well as by case number. New cases are available in the index 24-48 hours after filing date. A card index is maintained. Open records are located at this court. District wide searches are available from this court.

Fee & Payment: The fee is $20.00 per item (one party name or case number). Payment may be made by money order, cashier check, personal check. Prepayment is required. Payee: Clerk, US District Court. Certification fee: $7.00 per document. Copy fee: $.50 per page.

Phone Search: Searching not available by phone.

Fax Search: Will accept fax for price quote.

Mail Search: Always enclose a stamped self addressed envelope.

In Person: In person searching is available.

PACER: Sign-up number is 800-676-6856. Access fee is $.60 per minute. Toll-free access: 800-831-6162. Local access: 803-765-5871. Case records are available back to January 1990. Records are never purged. New records are

available online after 1 day. PACER is available online at http://pacer.scd.uscourts.gov.

Opinions Online: Court opinions are available online at http://www.law.sc.edu/dsc/dsc.htm

Greenville Division

PO Box 10768, Greenville, SC 29603 (Courier Address: 300 E Washington St, Greenville, SC 29601), 864-241-2700, Fax: 864-241-2711.

http://www.scd.uscourts.gov

Counties: Greenville, Laurens.

Indexing/Storage: Cases are indexed by defendant and plaintiff as well as by case number. New cases are available in the index 24 hours after filing date. A computer index is maintained. The computer index is from 1991 on. Older records are indexed on microfiche. Open records are located at this court.

Fee & Payment: The fee is $20.00 per item (one party name or case number). Payment may be made by money order, cashier check, personal check. Prepayment is required. Payee: Clerk, US District Court. Certification fee: $7.00 per document. Copy fee: $.50 per page.

Phone Search: Only the case number, parties and attorneys' names will be released over the phone.

Mail Search: A stamped self addressed envelope is not required.

In Person: In person searching is available.

PACER: Sign-up number is 800-676-6856. Access fee is $.60 per minute. Toll-free access: 800-831-6162. Local access: 803-765-5871. Case records are available back to January 1990. Records are never purged. New records are available online after 1 day. PACER is available online at http://pacer.scd.uscourts.gov.

Opinions Online: Court opinions are available online at http://www.law.sc.edu/dsc/dsc.htm

Greenwood Division

c/o Greenville Division, PO Box 10768, Greenville, SC 29603 (Courier Address: 300 E Washington St, Greenville, SC 29601), 864-241-2700, Fax: 864-241-2711.

http://www.scd.uscourts.gov

Counties: Abbeville, Aiken, Allendale, Bamberg, Barnwell, Calhoun, Edgefield, Fairfield, Greenwood, Lancaster, McCormick, Newberry, Orangeburg, Saluda.

Indexing/Storage: Cases are indexed by as well as by case number. New cases are available in the index after filing date. Open records are located at the Division.

Fee & Payment: The fee is no charge per item (one party name or case number). Payment may be made by money order, cashier check. Business checks are not accepted. Personal checks are not accepted.

Phone Search: Searching not available by phone.

Mail Search: A stamped self addressed envelope is not required.

In Person: In person searching is available.

PACER: Sign-up number is 800-676-6856. Access fee is $.60 per minute. Toll-free access: 800-831-6162. Local access: 803-765-5871. Case records are available back to January 1990. Records are never purged. New records are available online after 1 day. PACER is available online at http://pacer.scd.uscourts.gov.

Opinions Online: Court opinions are available online at http://www.law.sc.edu/dsc/dsc.htm

Spartanburg Division

c/o Greenville Division, PO Box 10768, Greenville, SC 29603 (Courier Address: 300 E Washington St, Greenville, SC 29601), 864-241-2700, Fax: 864-241-2711.

http://www.scd.uscourts.gov

Counties: Cherokee, Chester, Spartanburg, Union, York.

Indexing/Storage: Cases are indexed by as well as by case number. New cases are available in the index after filing date. Open records are located at the Division.

Fee & Payment: The fee is no charge per item (one party name or case number). Payment may be made by money order, cashier check. Business checks are not accepted. Personal checks are not accepted.

Phone Search: Searching not available by phone.

Mail Search: A stamped self addressed envelope is not required.

In Person: In person searching is available.

PACER: Sign-up number is 800-676-6856. Access fee is $.60 per minute. Toll-free access: 800-831-6162. Local access: 803-765-5871. Case records are available back to January 1990. Records are never purged. New records are available online after 1 day. PACER is available online at http://pacer.scd.uscourts.gov.

Opinions Online: Court opinions are available online at http://www.law.sc.edu/dsc/dsc.htm

US Bankruptcy Court

District of South Carolina

Columbia Division

PO Box 1448, Columbia, SC 29202 (Courier Address: 1100 Laurel St, Columbia, SC 29201), 803-765-3004.

http://www.scb.uscourts.gov

Counties: All counties in South Carolina.

Indexing/Storage: Cases are indexed by debtor as well as by case number. New cases are available in the index 1-2 days after filing date. Creditor lists are available through PACER. Both computer and card indexes are maintained. Open records are located at this court. The bankruptcy information maintained at the US Bankruptcy Court, Columbia Division encompasses all bankruptcy information available for the District of South Carolina.

Fee & Payment: The fee is $20.00 per item (one party name or case number). Payment may be made by money order, cashier check, personal check. Prepayment is required. Debtor's checks are not accepted. Payee: Clerk, US Bankruptcy Court. Certification fee: $7.00 per document. Copy fee: $.50 per page.

Phone Search: An automated voice case information service (VCIS) is available. Call VCIS at 800-669-8767 or 803-765-5211.

Mail Search: Always enclose a stamped self addressed envelope.

In Person: In person searching is available.

PACER: Sign-up number is 800-676-6856. Access fee is $.60 per minute. Toll-free access: 800-410-2988. Local access: 803-765-5965. Case records are available back to November 1988. Records are never purged. New civil records are available online after 1 day. PACER is available online at http://pacer.scb.uscourts.gov.

South Carolina County Courts

Court	Jurisdiction	No. of Courts	How Organized
Circuit Courts*	General	46	16 Circuits
Magistrate Courts*	Limited	182	
Municipal Courts	Municipal	160	
Probate Courts*	Probate	46	
Family Courts	Special	46	16 Circuits

* Profiled in this Sourcebook.

Court	CIVIL								
	Tort	Contract	Real Estate	Min. Claim	Max. Claim	Small Claims	Estate	Eviction	Domestic Relations
Circuit Courts*	X	X	X	$5000	No Max	$7500			
Magistrate Courts	X		X	$0	$7500	$7500		X	
Municipal Courts									
Probate Courts*							X		
Family Courts									X

Court	CRIMINAL				
	Felony	Misdemeanor	DWI/DUI	Preliminary Hearing	Juvenile
Circuit Courts*	X	X	X		
Magistrate Courts*		X	X	X	
Municipal Courts		X	X	X	
Probate Courts*					
Family Courts					X

ADMINISTRATION
Court Administration, 1015 Sumter St, 2nd Floor, Columbia, SC, 29201; 803-734-1800, Fax: 803-734-1355. www.judicial.state.sc.us

COURT STRUCTURE
The 46 SC counties are divided among sixteen judicial circuits. The circuit courts are in operation at the county level and consist of a court of general sessions (criminal) and a court of common pleas (civil). A family court is also in operation at the county level. The Magistrate and Municipal Courts only handle misdemeanor cases involving a $500.00 fine and/or 30 days or less jail time.

The maximum civil claim monetary amount for the Magistrate Courts increased from $2500 to $5000 as of January 1, 1996. In 2001, this civil limit was raised to $7,500.

ONLINE ACCESS
The judicial Department is developing a statewide court case management system. Only Charleston County offers Internet access to court records at present.

ADDITIONAL INFORMATION
If requesting a record in writing, it is recommended that the words "request that General Session, Common Pleas, and Family Court records be searched" be included in the request.

Most South Carolina courts will not conduct searches. However, if a name and case number are provided, many will pull and copy the record. Search fees vary widely as they are set by each county individually.

Abbeville County

Circuit Court PO Box 99, Abbeville, SC 29620; 864-459-5074; Fax: 864-459-9188. Hours: 9AM-5PM *Felony, Misdemeanor, Civil Actions Over $7,500.*

Civil Records: Access: In person only. Visitors must perform in person searches for themselves. No search fee. Required to search: name, years to search. Civil cases indexed by defendant, plaintiff. Civil records on card index from 1870.

Criminal Records: Access: In person only. Visitors must perform in person searches for themselves. No search fee. Required to search: name, years to search; also helpful: SSN. Criminal records on card index from 1870.

General Information: No adoption, juvenile, sealed or expunged records released. Copy fee: $.25 per page. Certification fee: No certification fee. Fee payee: Clerk of Court. Personal checks accepted. Prepayment is required.

Abbeville Magistrate Court 101 Church St, PO Drawer 1156, Abbeville, SC 29620; 864-459-2080/2053; Fax: 864-459-8245. Hours: 9AM-5PM (EST). *Misdemeanor, Civil Actions Under $7,500, Eviction, Small Claims.*

Probate Court PO Box 70, Abbeville, SC 29620; 864-459-4626; Fax: 864-459-4982. Hours: 9AM-5PM (EST). *Probate.*

Aiken County

Circuit Court PO Box 583, Aiken, SC 29802; 803-642-1715. Hours: 8:30AM-5PM (EST). *Felony, Misdemeanor, Civil Actions Over $7,500.*

Civil Records: Access: In person only. Both court and visitors may perform in person searches. No search fee. Required to search: name, years to search. Civil cases indexed by defendant, plaintiff. Civil records on computer from 1988; on microfiche, archives and card index from 1800s.

Criminal Records: Access: In person only. Both court and visitors may perform in person searches. Search fee: $10.00 per hour. Required to search: name, years to search, DOB; also helpful: SSN. Criminal records on computer from 1988; on microfiche, archives and card index from 1800s.

General Information: Public Access terminal is available. No adoption, juvenile, sealed or expunged records released. Copy fee: $.25 per page. Certification fee: $1.00. Fee payee: Clerk of Court. Only cashiers checks and money orders accepted. Prepayment is required.

Aiken Magistrate Court 1680 Richland Ave W, Ste 70, Aiken, SC 29801; 803-642-1744/1747. *Civil Actions Under $7,500, Eviction, Small Claims.*

Graniteville Magistrate Court 14 Masonic Shopping Ctr, Graniteville, SC 29829; 803-663-6634/6635; Fax: 803-663-6635. Hours: 9AM-5PM (EST). *Civil Actions Under $7,500, Misdemeanor, Eviction, Small Claims.*

Note: Misdemeanor records accessed same as civil

Langley Magistrate Court PO Box 769, Langley, SC 29834; 803-593-5171/5172; Fax: 803-593-8402. *Civil Actions Under $7,500, Eviction, Small Claims.*

Monetta Magistrate Court 5697 Columbia Hwy N, PO Box 190, Monetta, SC 29105; 803-685-7125; Fax: 803-685-7988. *Civil Actions Under $7,500, Eviction, Small Claims.*

New Ellenton Magistrate Court PO Box 40, New Ellenton, SC 29809; 803-652-3609; Fax: 803-652-2653. Hours: 9AM-1PM, 2-4:30PM (EST). *Civil Actions Under $7,500, Eviction, Small Claims.*

North Augusta Magistrate Court PO Box 6493, North Augusta, SC 29861; 803-202-3580/3581; Fax: 803-202-3583. *Civil Actions Under $7,500, Eviction, Small Claims.*

Probate Court PO Box 1576 (109 Park Ave), Aiken, SC 29802; 803-642-2000; Fax: 803-642-2007. Hours: 8:30AM-5PM (EST). *Probate.*

Allendale County

Circuit Court PO Box 126, Allendale, SC 29810; 803-584-2737; Fax: 803-584-7058. Hours: 9AM-5PM *Felony, Misdemeanor, Civil Actions Over $7,500.*

Civil Records: Access: Phone, mail, in person. Both court and visitors may perform in person searches. Search fee: $5.00 per name. Required to search: name, years to search. Civil cases indexed by defendant, plaintiff. Civil records on computer 1988, card index from 1919.

Criminal Records: Access: Phone, mail, in person. Both court and visitors may perform in person searches. Search fee: $5.00 per name. Required to search: name, years to search, DOB, signed release; also helpful: SSN. Criminal records kept on computer for 3 years.

General Information: Public Access terminal is available. No adoption, juvenile, sealed or expunged records released. SASE required. Turnaround time 2 days. Copy fee: $.25 per page. Certification fee: $2.00. Fee payee: Clerk of Court. Personal checks accepted. Prepayment is required.

Allendale Magistrate Court 531 N Main St, Allendale, SC 29810; 803-584-3755; Fax: 803-584-7980. Hours: 9AM-5PM (EST). *Civil Actions Under $7,500, Eviction, Small Claims.*

Fairfax Magistrate Court 115 N Hampton Ave, PO Box 421, Fairfax, SC 29827; 803-632-3871/3468; Fax: 803-632-2113. *Civil Actions Under $7,500, Eviction, Small Claims.*

Probate Court PO Box 603, Courthouse Complex, Allendale, SC 29810; 803-584-3157; Fax: 803-584-7042. Hours: 9AM-5PM (EST). *Probate.*

Anderson County

Circuit Court PO Box 8002, Anderson, SC 29622; 864-260-4053; Fax: 864-260-4715. Hours: 8:30AM-5PM (EST). *Felony, Misdemeanor, Civil Actions Over $7,500.*

Civil Records: Access: In person only. Visitors must perform in person searches for themselves. No search fee. Required to search: name, years to search. Civil cases indexed by defendant, plaintiff. Civil records on computer from 1994, prior on cards. Mail searches available to state agencies only.

Criminal Records: Access: In person only. Visitors must perform in person searches for themselves. No search fee. Required to search: name, years to search, DOB, SSN, signed release. Criminal records on computer from 1994, prior on cards. Same as civil.

General Information: Public Access terminal is available. No adoption, juvenile, sealed or expunged records released. Copy fee: $.50 per page. Certification fee: No certification fee. Fee payee: Clerk of Court. Personal checks accepted. Prepayment is required.

Anderson Magistrate Court PO Box 8002, Anderson, SC 29622; 864-260-4156/4055; Fax: 864-260-4144. *Civil Actions Under $7,500, Eviction, Small Claims.*

Honea Path Magistrate Court PO Box 505, Honea Path, SC 29654; 864-369-0015; Fax: 864-369-0015. *Civil Actions Under $7,500, Eviction, Small Claims.*

Iva Magistrate Court 719 E Front St, PO Box 1163, Iva, SC 29655; 864-348-3456; Fax: 864-348-3456. *Civil Actions Under $7,500, Eviction, Small Claims.*

Note: The court holds warrants and criminal actions with sentences of 30 days and/or $500 fine

Pelzer Magistrate Court PO Box 824, Pelzer, SC 29669; 864-947-5225; Fax: 864-947-5225. *Civil Actions Under $7,500, Eviction, Small Claims, Misdemeanor.*

Note: The Civil action limit raises to $7,500 on January 1, 2001.

Pendleton Magistrate Court 2301 Six and Twenty Rd, Pendleton, SC 29670; Fax: 864-656-0714. *Civil Actions Under $7,500, Eviction, Small Claims.*

Piedmont Magistrate Court 104 Gin Rd, PO Box 51312, Piedmont, SC 29673; 864-845-7620; Fax: 864-295-5962. Hours: 9AM-5PM (EST). *Civil Actions Under $7,500, Eviction, Small Claims.*

Starr Magistrate Court 7626 Hwy 815, PO Box 247, Starr, SC 29684; 864-352-3157; Fax: 864-352-3157. *Civil Actions Under $7,500, Eviction, Small Claims.*

Williamston Magistrate Court 12 W Main St, PO Box 125, Williamston, SC 29697; 864-847-8580; Fax: 864-847-8580. *Civil Actions Under $7,500, Eviction, Small Claims.*

Probate Court PO Box 8002, Anderson, SC 29622; 864-260-4049; Fax: 864-260-4811. Hours: 8AM-5PM (EST). *Probate.*

Bamberg County

Circuit Court PO Box 150, Bamberg, SC 29003; 803-245-3025; Fax: 803-245-3088. Hours: 9AM-5PM (EST). *Felony, Misdemeanor, Civil Actions Over $7,500.*

Civil Records: Access: Mail, in person. Both court and visitors may perform in person searches. Search fee: $5.00 per name. Required to search: name, years to search. Civil cases indexed by defendant, plaintiff. Civil records on index books, files back to 1890.

Criminal Records: Access: Mail, in person. Both court and visitors may perform in person searches. Search fee: $5.00 per name. Required to search: name, years to search, DOB; also helpful: SSN. Criminal records on index books, files back to 1890.

General Information: No adoption, juvenile, sealed or expunged records released. SASE required. Turnaround time 1-2 days. Copy fee: $.50 per page. Certification fee: No certification fee. Fee payee: Clerk of Court. Personal checks accepted. Prepayment is required.

Bamberg Magistrate Court PO Box 187, Bamberg, SC 29003; 803-245-3016; Fax: 803-245-3085. *Civil Actions Under $7,500, Eviction, Small Claims.*

Probate Court PO Box 180, Bamberg, SC 29003; 803-245-3008; Fax: 803-245-3008. Hours: 9AM-5PM (EST). *Probate.*

Barnwell County

Circuit Court PO Box 723, Barnwell, SC 29812; 803-541-1020; Fax: 803-541-1025. Hours: 9AM-5PM (EST). *Felony, Misdemeanor, Civil Actions Over $7,500.*

Civil Records: Access: In person only. Visitors must perform in person searches for themselves. No search fee. Required to search: name, years to search. Civil cases indexed by defendant. Civil records on computer from 1988.

Criminal Records: Access: In person only. Visitors must perform in person searches for themselves. No search fee. Required to search: name, years to search, DOB, SSN. Criminal records on computer from 1988.

General Information: No adoption, juvenile, sealed or expunged records released. Copy fee: $.50 per page. Certification fee: $1.00. Fee payee: Clerk of Court. Personal checks accepted. Prepayment is required.

Barnwell Magistrate Court PO Box 1205, Barnwell, SC 29812; 803-541-1035; Fax: 83-541-1055. Hours: 9AM-Noon, 1-5PM (EST). *Civil Actions Under $7,500, Eviction, Small Claims.*

Blackville Magistrate Court 5997 Lartique St, Blackville, SC 29817; 803-284-2765; Fax: 803-284-9107. *Civil Actions Under $7,500, Eviction, Small Claims.*

Williston Magistrate Court PO Box 485, Williston, SC 29853; 803-266-3700; Fax: 803-266-5496. Hours: 9AM-5PM (EST). *Civil Actions Under $7,500, Eviction, Small Claims.*

Probate Court Room 108, County Courthouse, Barnwell, SC 29812; 803-541-1032; Fax: 803-541-1012. Hours: 9AM-5PM (EST). *Probate.*

Beaufort County

Circuit Court PO Drawer 1128, Beaufort, SC 29901; 843-470-5218; Fax: 843-470-5248. Hours: 8AM-5PM (EST). *Felony, Misdemeanor, Civil Actions Over $7,500.*

Civil Records: Access: Mail, in person. Visitors must perform in person searches for themselves. No search fee. Required to search: name, years to search. Civil cases indexed by defendant, plaintiff. Civil records on computer back to 1985; prior in index books.

Criminal Records: Access: In person only. Visitors must perform in person searches for themselves. No search fee. Required to search: name, years to search, DOB; also helpful: SSN. Criminal records on computer back to 1985; prior in index books.

General Information: No adoption, juvenile, sealed or expunged records released. Copy fee: $.25 per page. Certification fee: $1.00. Fee payee: Clerk of Court. Personal checks accepted. Prepayment is required.

Beaufort Magistrate Court PO Box 4865, Beaufort, SC 29903-4865; 843-470-5201; Fax: 843-470-5206. Hours: 8AM-4PM (EST). *Misdemeanors, Civil Actions Under $7,500, Eviction, Small Claims, Traffic.*

Bluffton Magistrate Court PO Box 840, Bluffton, SC 29910; 843-757-1500; Fax: 843-757-1527. *Civil Actions Under $7,500, Eviction, Small Claims.*

Hilton Head Magistrate Court PO Box 22895, Hilton Head, SC 29925; 843-842-4260; Fax: 843-842-4261. *Civil Actions Under $7,500, Eviction, Small Claims.*

Lobeco Magistrate Court PO Box 845, Lobeco, SC 29931-0845; 843-846-3902; Fax: 843-846-0823. Hours: 5:30PM-7:30PM M, W (EST). *Civil Actions Under $7,500, Eviction, Small Claims.*

St Helena Island Magistrate Court PO Box 126, St Helena Island, SC 29920; 843-838-3212; Fax: 843-838-8545. *Civil Actions Under $7,500, Eviction, Small Claims.*

Probate Court PO Box 1083, Beaufort, SC 29901-1083; 843-470-5319; Fax: 843-470-5324. Hours: 8AM-5PM (EST). *Probate.*

Berkeley County

Circuit Court PO Box 219, Moncks Corner, SC 29461; 843-719-4400. Hours: 9AM-5PM (EST). *Felony, Misdemeanor, Civil Actions Over $7,500.*

Civil Records: Access: In person only. Visitors must perform in person searches for themselves. No search fee. Required to search: name, years to search. Civil cases indexed by defendant, plaintiff. Civil records on computer from early 1980s, prior on books.

Criminal Records: Access: In person only. Visitors must perform in person searches for themselves. No search fee. Required to search: name, years to search, DOB, SSN. Criminal records on computer from early 1980s, prior on books.

General Information: Public Access terminal is available. No adoption, juvenile, sealed or expunged records released. Certification fee: No certification fee. Personal checks accepted.

Goose Creek Magistrate Court 538 Redbank Rd, Goose Creek, SC 29445; 843-553-7080; Fax: 843-553-7074. Hours: 9AM-5PM (EST). *Civil Actions Under $7,500, Eviction, Small Claims.*

Moncks Corner Magistrate Court 103 Gulledge St, PO Box 875, Moncks Corner, SC 29461; 843-719-4220 or 723-3800 X4220; Fax: 843-719-4534. Hours: 9AM-5PM (EST). *Civil Actions Under $7,500, Eviction, Small Claims.*

St Stephen Magistrate Court PO Box 1433, St Stephen, SC 29479; 843-567-7400; Fax: 843-567-6028. *Civil Actions Under $7,500, Eviction, Small Claims.*

Summerville Magistrate Court 1306 Alexander Ct, Summerville, SC 29483; 843-719-4384. *Civil Actions Under $7,500, Eviction, Small Claims.*

Probate Court 300 B California Ave, Moncks Corner, SC 29461; 843-719-4519; Fax: 843-719-4527. Hours: 9AM-5PM (EST). *Probate.*

Calhoun County

Circuit Court 302 S Huff Dr, St Matthews, SC 29135; 803-874-3524; Fax: 803-874-1942. Hours: 9AM-5PM (EST). *Felony, Misdemeanor, Civil Actions Over $7,500.*

Civil Records: Access: Mail, in person. Both court and visitors may perform in person searches. Search fee: $5.00 per name. Required to search: name, years to search. Civil cases indexed by defendant, plaintiff. Civil records on computer from 1982, prior on index books from 1912.

Criminal Records: Access: Mail, in person. Both court and visitors may perform in person searches. Search fee: $5.00 per name. Required to search: name, years to search, DOB. Criminal records on computer from 1982, prior on index books from 1912.

General Information: No adoption, juvenile, sealed or expunged records released. SASE required. Turnaround time 1 day. Copy fee: $.25 per page. Certification fee: No certification fee. Fee payee: Clerk of Court. Personal checks accepted. Prepayment is required.

Cameron Magistrate Court Cameron Town Hall, PO Box 663, Cameron, SC 29030; 803-823-2266; Fax: 803-823-2328. Hours: 3-6PM M & Th (EST). *Civil Actions Under $7,500, Eviction, Small Claims.*

Cameron/Lone Starr Magistrate Court Rt 1 Box 541, Cameron, SC 29030; 803-826-6000. *Civil Actions Under $7,500, Eviction, Small Claims.*

St Matthews Magistrate Court 112 W Bridge St, PO Box 191, St Matthews, SC 29135; 803-874-1112; Fax: 803-874-1111. *Civil Actions Under $7,500, Eviction, Small Claims.*

Probate Court 302 South F.R. Huff Dr, St Matthews, SC 29135; 803-874-3514; Fax: 803-874-1942. *Probate.*

Charleston County

Circuit Court PO Box 70219, Charleston, SC 29415; 843-740-5700; Fax: 843-740-5887. Hours: 8:30AM-5PM (EST). *Felony, Misdemeanor, Civil Actions Over $7,500.*

www3.charlestoncounty.org

Civil Records: Access: Mail, online, in person. Both court and visitors may perform in person searches. Search fee: $10.00 per name. Required to search: name, years to search. Civil cases indexed by defendant, plaintiff. Civil records on computer from 1988, microfiche and archives from mid 1800s. Access to civil records (from 1988 forward), judgments and lis pendens are available free online at www3.charleston county.org/connect.

Criminal Records: Access: Mail, online, in person. Both court and visitors may perform in person searches. Search fee: $10.00 per name. Required to search: name, years to search, DOB; also helpful: SSN. Criminal records on computer from 4/90, prior on books and microfilm from 1900s. The Internet offers access to records from 04/92 forward. Search by name or case number. There is no fee.

General Information: Public Access terminal is available. No adoption, juvenile, sealed or expunged records released. SASE required. Turnaround time 3 days. Fax notes: No fee to fax results. Copy fee: $.25 per page. Certification fee: $1.00. Fee payee: Clerk of Court. Business checks accepted. Prepayment required.

Charleston Magistrate Court 4050 Bridgeview Dr, #200, PO Box 60037, Charleston, SC 29419; 843-745-2217/2219; Fax: 843-745-2317. Hours: 8:30AM-4:30PM (EST). *Civil Actions Under $7,500, Eviction, Small Claims.*

Note: County magistrate courts records from 1998 forward can be searched free at www3.charleston county.org/connect.

Charleston Magistrate Court 1720 Sam Rittenberg Blvd Unit 11, PO Box 31861, Charleston, SC 29417; 843-766-6531; Fax: 843-571-4751. *Civil Actions Under $7,500, Eviction, Small Claims.*

Note: County magistrate courts records from 1998 forward can be searched free at www3.charleston county.org/connect.

Charleston Magistrate Court 995 Morrison Dr, PO Box 941, Charleston, SC 29402; 843-724-6719; Fax: 843-745-6785. Hours: 9AM-5PM (EST). *Civil Actions Under $7,500, Eviction.*

Note: County magistrate courts records from 1998 forward can be searched free at www3.charleston county.org/connect.

East Cooper Magistrate Court 1189 Iron Bridge Rd, Ste 300, PO Box 584, Mt Pleasant, SC 29465; 843-856-1205; Fax: 843-856-1188. Hours: 8AM-12, 1-4:30PM (EST). *Misdemeanor, Civil Actions Under $7,500, Eviction.*

www3.charlestoncounty.org/docs/CoC/index.html

Note: court records from 1998 forward can be searched free at www3.charlestoncounty.org/connect.

Edisto Island Magistrate Court 8070 Indigo Hill Rd, PO Box 216, Edisto Island, SC 29438; 843-869-2909; Fax: 843-869-4460. *Civil Actions Under $7,500, Eviction, Traffic.*

Note: court records from 1998 forward can be searched free at www3.charlestoncounty.org/connect.

James Island Magistrate Court PO Box 12226, James Island, SC 29422; 843-795-1140; Fax: 843-406-2753. Hours: 8:30AM-5PM (EST). *Misdemeanor, Civil Actions Under $7,500, Eviction, Small Claims.*

Note: court records from 1998 forward can be searched free at www3.charlestoncounty.org/connect.

Johns Island Magistrate Court 1521 Main Rd, Johns Island, SC 29455; 843-559-1218; Fax: 843-559-2378. *Civil Actions Under $7,500, Eviction, Small Claims.*

Note: court records from 1998 forward can be searched free at www3.charlestoncounty.org/connect.

McClellanville Magistrate Court 9888 Randall Rd, PO Box 7, McClellanville, SC 29458; 843-887-3334; Fax: 843-887-3901. Hours: 9AM-Noon, 1Pm-4PM M,W (EST). *Civil Actions Under $7,500, Eviction, Small Claims.*

Note: court records from 1998 forward can be searched free at www3.charlestoncounty.org/connect.

North Charleston Magistrate Court 2144 Melbourne St, Rm 103, North Charleston, SC 29405; 843-740-5860. *Civil Actions Under $7,500, Small Claims.*

Note: court records from 1998 forward can be searched free at www3.charlestoncounty.org/connect.

North Charleston Magistrate Court 7272 Cross County Rd, PO Box 61870, North Charleston, SC 29419; 843-767-2743/767-3141; Fax: 843-760-6887. *Civil Actions Under $7,500, Eviction, Small Claims.*

Note: court records from 1998 forward can be searched free at www3.charlestoncounty.org/connect.

North Charleston Magistrate Court 2036 Cherokee St, PO Box 71316, North Charleston, SC 29416; 843-745-2215; Fax: 843-745-2334. *Civil Actions Under $7,500, Eviction, Small Claims.*

Note: County magistrate courts records from 1998 forward can be searched free at www3.charleston county.org/connect.

Ravenel Magistrate Court 5962 Hwy 165, #200, Ravenel, SC 29470; 843-889-8332; Fax: 843-889-9202. *Civil Actions Under $7,500, Eviction, Small Claims.*

Note: court records from 1998 forward can be searched free at www3.charlestoncounty.org/connect.

Probate Court 2144 Melbourne Ave, North Charleston, SC 29405; 843-740-5890; Fax: 843-740-5897. Hours: 8:30AM-5PM (EST). *Probate.*

Cherokee County

Circuit Court PO Drawer 2289, Gaffney, SC 29342; 864-487-2571; Fax: 864-487-2754. Hours: 8:30AM-5PM (EST). *Felony, Misdemeanor, Civil Actions Over $7,500.*

Civil Records: Access: In person only. Visitors must perform in person searches for themselves. No search fee. Required to search: name, years to search. Civil cases indexed by defendant, plaintiff. Civil records on computer from 1994, prior on books.

Criminal Records: Access: In person only. Visitors must perform in person searches for themselves. No

search fee. Required to search: name, years to search. Criminal records on computer from 1994, prior on books.

General Information: Public Access terminal is available. No adoption, juvenile, sealed or expunged records released. Copy fee: $1.00 per page. Certification fee: $1.00. Fee payee: Clerk of Court. Business checks accepted. Prepayment is required.

Blacksburg Magistrate Court 101 S Shelby St, PO Box 427, Blacksburg, SC 29702; 864-839-2492; Fax: 864-839-3415. *Civil Actions Under $7,500, Eviction, Small Claims.*

Cherokee County Magistrate Court 312 E Frederick St, PO Box 336, Gaffney, SC 29342-0336; 864-487-2533/2501; Fax: 864-902-8425. Hours: 8:30AM-5PM (EST). *Civil Actions Under $7,500, Eviction, Small Claims.*

Note: Civil Action minimum raises to $7,500 on January 1, 2001.

Probate Court 1434 N Limestone St, Peachtree Ctr, Gaffney, SC 29340; 864-487-2583; Fax: 864-902-8426. Hours: 9AM-5PM (EST). *Probate.*

Chester County

Circuit Court PO Drawer 580, Chester, SC 29706; 803-385-2605; Fax: 803-581-7975. Hours: 8:30AM-5PM (EST). *Felony, Misdemeanor, Civil Actions Over $7,500.*

Civil Records: Access: Mail, in person. Both court and visitors may perform in person searches. Search fee: $2.00 per name. Required to search: name, years to search, address. Civil cases indexed by defendant, plaintiff. Civil records on computer from 1989, microfiche from 1927.

Criminal Records: Access: Mail, in person. Both court and visitors may perform in person searches. Search fee: $2.00 per name. Required to search: name, years to search, DOB, signed release; also helpful: SSN. Criminal records on computer from 1994, docket books prior.

General Information: Public Access terminal is available. No adoption, juvenile, sealed or expunged records released. SASE not required. Turnaround time 3 days. Copy fee: $.50 per page. Certification fee: $1.00. Fee payee: Clerk of Court. Personal checks accepted. Prepayment is required.

Chester Magistrate Court 2740 Dawson Dr, PO Box 727, Chester, SC 29706; 803-581-5136; Fax: 803-581-5552. *Civil Actions Under $7,500, Eviction, Small Claims.*

Richburg Magistrate Court 203-B N Main St, PO Box 148, Richburg, SC 29729; 803-789-5010. *Civil Actions Under $7,500, Eviction, Small Claims.*

Probate Court PO Drawer 580, Chester, SC 29706; 803-385-2604; Fax: 803-581-5180. Hours: 8:30AM-5PM (EST). *Probate.*

Chesterfield County

Circuit Court PO Box 529, Chesterfield, SC 29709; 843-623-2574; Fax: 843-623-6944. 8:30AM-5PM *Felony, Misdemeanor, Civil Actions Over $7,500.*

Civil Records: Access: Mail, in person. Both court and visitors may perform in person searches. Search fee: $5.00 per name. Required to search: name, years to search. Civil cases indexed by defendant, plaintiff. Civil records on docket books.

Criminal Records: Access: Mail, in person. Both court and visitors may perform in person searches. Search fee: $5.00 per name. Required to search: name, years to search; also helpful: DOB, SSN. Criminal records on docket books.

General Information: No adoption, juvenile, sealed or expunged records released. SASE required. Turnaround time 3 days. Copy fee: $.25 per page. Certification fee: No certification fee. Fee payee: Clerk of Court. Personal checks accepted. Prepayment is required.

Cheraw Magistrate Court Route 2, Box 727, Cheraw, SC 29520; 843-537-7139; Fax: 843-537-8404. *Civil Actions Under $7,500, Eviction, Small Claims.*

Cheraw Magistrate Court 105 State Rd, PO Box 364, Cheraw, SC 29520; 843-537-3323; Fax: 843-537-1670. *Civil Actions Under $7,500, Eviction, Small Claims.*

Cheraw Magistrate Court Hinson Hill Rd, Rt 1 Box 366-A, Cheraw, SC 29520; 843-623-2955. *Civil Actions Under $7,500, Eviction, Small Claims.*

Chesterfield Magistrate Court Rte 1 Box 40, Chesterfield, SC 29709; 843-623-7929; Fax: 843-623-7929. *Civil Actions Under $7,500, Eviction, Small Claims.*

McBee Magistrate Court Rt 2 Box 650, McBee, SC 29101; 843-335-8467. *Civil Actions Under $7,500, Eviction, Small Claims.*

Pageland Magistrate Court 310 W McGregor St, PO Box 133, Pageland, SC 29728; 843-672-5685. Hours: 10AM-3PM (EST). *Civil Actions Under $7,500, Eviction, Small Claims.*

Patrick Magistrate Court Rt 1 Box 385, Patrick, SC 29584; 843-498-6398. *Civil Actions Under $7,500, Eviction, Small Claims.*

Ruby Magistrate Court 300 Deaton St, PO Box 131, Ruby, SC 29741; 843-634-6597. *Civil Actions Under $7,500, Eviction, Small Claims.*

Probate Court County Courthouse, 200 W Main St, Chesterfield, SC 29709; 843-623-2376; Fax: 843-623-3945. Hours: 8:30AM-5PM (EST). *Probate.*

Clarendon County

Circuit Court PO Drawer E, Manning, SC 29102; 803-435-4444. Hours: 8:30AM-5PM (EST). *Felony, Misdemeanor, Civil Actions Over $7,500.*

Civil Records: Access: Mail, in person. Both court and visitors may perform in person searches. Search fee: $27.00. Includes all copy fees. Required to search: name, years to search. Civil cases indexed by defendant, plaintiff. Civil records on computer from 1988, index books from 1865.

Criminal Records: Access: Mail, in person. Both court and visitors may perform in person searches. Search fee: $27.00. Includes copy fees. Required to search: name, years to search. Criminal records on computer from 1983, index books from 1865.

General Information: Public Access terminal is available. No adoption, juvenile, sealed or expunged records released. SASE required. Turnaround time 5 days. Copy fee: $.25 per page. Certification fee: $1.00. Fee payee: Clerk of Court. Personal checks accepted. Prepayment is required.

Manning Magistrate Court 10 Keitt St, PO Box 371, Manning, SC 29102; 803-435-2670/8925; Fax: 803-435-8905. Hours: 8:30AM-5PM (EST). *Civil Actions Under $7,500, Eviction, Small Claims.*

Summerton Magistrate Court 216 Main St, PO Box 386, Summerton, SC 29148; 803-485-8228. *Civil Actions Under $7,500, Eviction, Small Claims.*

Probate Court PO Box 307, Manning, SC 29102; 803-435-8774; Fax: 803-435-8258. Hours: 8:30AM-5PM (EST). *Probate.*

Colleton County

Circuit Court PO Box 620, Walterboro, SC 29488; 843-549-5791; Fax: 843-549-2875. Hours: 8:30AM-5PM (EST). *Felony, Misdemeanor, Civil Actions Over $7,500.*

Civil Records: Access: Phone, fax, mail, in person. Both court and visitors may perform in person searches. Search fee: $5.00 per name. Required to search: name, years to search. Civil cases indexed by defendant, plaintiff. Civil records on computer from 1986, on index books from 1865.

Criminal Records: Access: Phone, fax, mail, in person. Both court and visitors may perform in person searches. Search fee: $5.00 per name. Required to search: name, years to search; also helpful: SSN, DOB. Criminal records on computer from 1986, on index books from 1865.

General Information: No adoption, juvenile, PTI, sealed or expunged records released. SASE required. Turnaround time 2 days. Fax notes: Extra fee to fax back results. Copy fee: $.25 per page. Certification fee: $1.00. Fee payee: Clerk of Court. Business checks accepted. Prepayment is required.

Green Pond Magistrate Court 8464 Ace Basin Prky, Green Pond, SC 29446; 843-844-8486; Fax: 843-844-8835. Hours: 9AM-5PM (EST). *Civil Actions Under $7,500, Eviction, Small Claims.*

Walterboro Magistrate Court 217 Brown St, Walterboro, SC 29488; 843-549-2417; Fax: 843-549-2211. *Civil Actions Under $7,500, Eviction, Small Claims.*

Walterboro Magistrate Court 492 Benton Farm Rd, Walterboro, SC 29488; 843-538-3637/3903; Fax: 843-538-5173. Hours: 8:30AM-5PM (EST). *Civil Actions Under $7,500, Eviction, Small Claims.*

Walterboro Magistrate Court 40-B Klein St, PO Box 1732, Walterboro, SC 29488; 843-549-1122; Fax: 843-549-9010. Hours: 8AM-5PM (EST). *Civil Actions Under $7,500, Eviction, Small Claims.*

Probate Court PO Box 1036, Walterboro, SC 29488-0031; 843-549-7216; Fax: 843-549-5571. Hours: 8:30AM-5PM (EST). *Probate.*

Darlington County

Circuit Court PO Box 1177, Darlington, SC 29540; 843-398-4339. Hours: 8:30AM-5PM (EST). *Felony, Misdemeanor, Civil Actions Over $7,500.*

Civil Records: Access: In person only. Visitors must perform in person searches for themselves. No search fee. Required to search: name, years to search. Civil cases indexed by defendant, plaintiff. Civil records on computer from 1989, on index books from 1805.

Criminal Records: Access: In person only. Visitors must perform in person searches for themselves. No search fee. Required to search: name, years to search; also helpful: DOB, SSN. Criminal records on computer from 1989, on index books from 1805. Will give disposition & sentence over phone if case number given.

General Information: No adoption, juvenile, sealed or expunged records released. Copy fee: $1.00 per page. Certification fee: No certification fee. Fee payee: Clerk of Court. Business checks accepted. Prepayment required.

Darlington Magistrate Court 200 Camp Rd, Darlington, SC 29532; 843-398-4220; Fax: 843-332-7212. Hours: 8:30AM-5PM (EST). *Civil Actions Under $7,500, Eviction, Small Claims.*

Hartsville Magistrate Court 404 S 4th St, PO Box 1765, Hartsville, SC 29550; 843-332-9661; Fax: 843-332-1603. Hours: 7:30AM-5PM (EST). *Civil Actions Under $7,500, Eviction, Small Claims.*

Lamar Magistrate Court 117 Main St, PO Box 505, Lamar, SC 29069; 843-326-5441; Fax: 843-326-5280. *Civil Actions Under $7,500, Eviction, Small Claims.*

Society Hill Magistrate Court PO Box 447, Society Hill, SC 29593; 843-378-4601. *Civil Actions Under $7,500, Eviction, Small Claims.*

Probate Court #1 Public Sq - Courthouse Rm 208, Darlington, SC 29532; 843-398-4310; Fax: 843-398-4172. Hours: 8:30AM-5PM (EST). *Probate.*

Dillon County

Circuit Court PO Drawer 1220, Dillon, SC 29536; 843-774-1425. Hours: 8:30AM-5PM (EST). *Felony, Misdemeanor, Civil Actions Over $7,500.*

Civil Records: Access: Mail, in person. Both court and visitors may perform in person searches. Search fee: $5.00 per name. Required to search: name, years to search. Civil cases indexed by defendant, plaintiff. Civil records on computer from 1990, on docket books prior.

Criminal Records: Access: Mail, in person. Both court and visitors may perform in person searches. Search fee: $5.00 per name. Required to search: name, years to search; also helpful: DOB, SSN. Criminal records on computer from 1990, on docket books prior.

General Information: No adoption, juvenile, sealed or expunged records released. SASE required. Turnaround time 1 day. Copy fee: $.25 per page. Certification fee: No certification fee. Fee payee: Clerk of Court. Personal checks accepted. Prepayment is required.

Dillon Magistrate Court 200 S 5th Ave, PO Box 1016, Dillon, SC 29536; 843-774-1407; Fax: 843-774-1453. Hours: 7PM-9PM (EST). *Civil Actions Under $7,500, Eviction, Small Claims.*

Dillon Magistrate Court 200 S 5th Ave, PO Box 1281, Dillon, SC 29536; 843-774-1454. *Civil Actions Under $7,500, Eviction, Small Claims.*

Hamer Magistrate Court 143 Elkins Road, PO Box 1, Hamer, SC 29547; 843-774-2041; Fax: 843-774-1453. *Civil Actions Under $7,500, Eviction, Small Claims.*

Lake View Magistrate Court PO Box 272, Lake View, SC 29563; 843-759-2181. *Civil Actions Under $7,500, Eviction, Small Claims.*

Probate Court PO Box 189, Dillon, SC 29536; 843-774-1423; Fax: 843-841-3732. Hours: 8:30AM-5PM (EST). *Probate.*

Dorchester County

Circuit Court 101 Ridge St, St George, SC 29477; 843-563-0160. Hours: 8:30AM-5PM (EST). *Felony, Misdemeanor, Civil Actions Over $7,500.*

Civil Records: Access: In person only. Visitors must perform in person searches for themselves. No search fee. Required to search: name, years to search. Civil cases indexed by defendant, plaintiff. Civil records on index books back to 1950s, on computer since.

Criminal Records: Access: In person only. Visitors must perform in person searches for themselves. No search fee. Required to search: name, years to search, DOB, signed release; also helpful: SSN. Criminal records on index books back to 1950s, on computer since.

General Information: No adoption, juvenile, sealed or expunged records released. Copy fee: $.25 per page.

Certification fee: $1.00. Fee payee: Clerk of Court. Personal checks accepted. Prepayment is required.

Dorchester County Court 102 Sears St, St George, SC 29477; 843-563-0130; Fax: 843-563-0123. Hours: 8AM-5PM (EST). *Civil Actions Under $7,500, Eviction, Small Claims.*

Civil Records: Access: Mail. No search fee.

General Information: Turnaround time 5-7 days. Fee payee: County Treasurer. Prepayment is required.

St George Magistrate Court 102 Sears St, St. George, SC 29477; 843-832-0130; Fax: 843-563-0123. Hours: 8:30AM-5PM (EST). *Civil Actions Under $7,500, Eviction, Small Claims.*

Summerville Magistrate Court 212 Deming Way Box 10, Summerville, SC 29483; 843-832-0370; Fax: 843-832-0371. *Civil Actions Under $7,500, Eviction, Small Claims.*

Probate Court 101 Ridge St, County Courthouse, St George, SC 29477; 843-563-0105; Fax: 843-563-0245. Hours: 8:30AM-5PM (EST). *Probate.*

Edgefield County

Circuit Court PO Box 34, Edgefield, SC 29824; 803-637-4082; Fax: 803-637-4117. Hours: 8:30AM-5PM (EST). *Felony, Misdemeanor, Civil Actions Over $7,500.*

Civil Records: Access: Mail, in person. Both court and visitors may perform in person searches. Search fee: $5.00 per name. Required to search: name, years to search. Civil cases indexed by defendant, plaintiff. Civil records archived from 1839; on computer back to 1989.

Criminal Records: Access: Mail, in person. Both court and visitors may perform in person searches. Search fee: $5.00 per name. Required to search: name, years to search, DOB; also helpful: SSN. Criminal records archived from 1839; on computer back to 1989.

General Information: No adoption, juvenile, sealed or expunged records released. SASE required. Turnaround time 1 day. Fax notes: Will not fax results. Copy fee: $.50 per page. Certification fee: $1.00. Fee payee: Clerk of Court. Business checks accepted. Prepayment is required.

Edgefield Magistrate Court 129 Courthouse Sq, PO Box 664, Edgefield, SC 29824; 803-637-4090; Fax: 803-637-4101. Hours: 8:30AM-4:30PM (EST). *Civil Actions Under $7,500, Eviction, Small Claims.*

Probate Court 124 Courthouse Square, Edgefield, SC 29824; 803-637-4076; Fax: 803-637-7157. Hours: 8:30AM-5PM (EST). *Probate.*

Fairfield County

Circuit Court PO Drawer 299, Winnsboro, SC 29180; 803-712-6526. Hours: 9AM-5PM (EST). *Felony, Misdemeanor, Civil Actions Over $7,500.*

Civil Records: Access: In person only. Visitors must perform in person searches for themselves. No search fee. Required to search: name, years to search. Civil cases indexed by defendant, plaintiff. Civil records on docket books. The court provides an index, but will not do record searching.

Criminal Records: Access; In person only. Visitors must perform in person searches for themselves. No search fee. Required to search: name, years to search, DOB; also helpful: SSN. Criminal records on docket books.

General Information: No adoption, juvenile, sealed or expunged records released. Fax notes: Will not fax results. Copy fee: $.25 per page. Certification fee: $1.00. Fee payee: Clerk of Court. Personal checks accepted. Prepayment is required.

Winnsboro Magistrate Court 115-B South Congress St, PO Box 423, Winnsboro, SC 29180; 803-635-4525; Fax: 803-635-5717. 9AM-5PM (EST). *Civil Actions Under $7,500, Eviction, Small Claims.*

Probate Court PO Box 385, Winnsboro, SC 29180; 803-635-1411 X25; Fax: 803-635-2767. Hours: 9AM-5PM (EST). *Probate.*

Florence County

Circuit Court Drawer E, City Complex (180 N Irby St), Florence, SC 29501; 843-665-3031. Hours: 8:30AM-5PM (EST). *Felony, Misdemeanor, Civil Actions Over $7,500.*

www.florenceco.org/clerk.html

Civil Records: Access: Mail, in person. Both court and visitors may perform in person searches. Search fee: $5.00 per name. Required to search: name, years to search. Civil cases indexed by defendant, plaintiff. Civil records on computer from 1984, on microfiche and docket books from 1900s.
Criminal Records: Access: Mail, in person. Both court and visitors may perform in person searches. Search fee: $5.00 per name. Required to search: name, years to search, DOB; also helpful: SSN. Criminal records on computer from 1984, on microfiche and docket books from 1900s.
General Information: No adoption, juvenile, sealed or expunged records released. SASE required. Turnaround time 10-14 days. Copy fee: $.50. Certification fee: $1.00. Fee payee: Clerk of Court. Personal checks accepted. Prepayment is required.

Florence Magistrate Court 180 N Irby St (MSC-W), Florence, SC 29501; 843-665-0031; Fax: 843-661-7800. *Civil Actions Under $7,500, Eviction, Small Claims.*

Johnsonville Magistrate Court 461 S Railroad Ave, Johnsonville, SC 29555; 843-386-3965; Fax: 843-386-3623. Hours: 8:30AM-5PM M,T,W (EST). *Civil Actions Under $7,500, Eviction, Small Claims.*

Lake City Magistrate Court PO Box 39, Lake City, SC 29560; 843-394-5461; Fax: 843-394-3865. Hours: 8:30AM-5PM (EST). *Civil Actions Under $7,500, Eviction, Small Claims.*

Olanta Magistrate Court PO Box 362, Olanta, SC 29114; 843-396-9656. Hours: 8:30AM-5PM (EST). *Civil Actions Under $7,500, Eviction, Small Claims.*

Pamplico Magistrate Court 124 Third Ave East, PO Box 367, Pamplico, SC 29583; 843-493-0072; Fax: 843-493-5391. Hours: 8:30AM-5PM T-F (EST). *Civil Actions Under $7,500, Misdemeanor, Eviction, Small Claims, Traffic.*

Timmonsville Magistrate Court 8265 S Warren St, PO Box 190, Timmonsville, SC 29161; 843-346-7472; Fax: 843-346-0660. Hours: 8:30-5PM *Civil Actions Under $7,500, Eviction, Small Claims.*

Probate Court 180 N Irby, MSC-L, Florence, SC 29501; 843-665-3085; Fax: 843-665-3068. Hours: 8:30AM-5PM (EST). *Probate.*

Georgetown County

Circuit Court PO Box 421270, Georgetown, SC 29442; 843-546-5011; Civil phone: 843-527-6388; Criminal phone: 843-527-6314; Fax: 843-546-2144. Hours: 8:30AM-5PM (EST). *Felony, Misdemeanor, Civil Actions Over $7,500.*
Civil Records: Access: In person only. Visitors must perform in person searches for themselves. No search fee. Required to search: name, years to search. Civil

cases indexed by defendant, plaintiff. Civil records on index from 1926.
Criminal Records: Access: In person only. Visitors must perform in person searches for themselves. No search fee. Required to search: name, years to search, DOB; also helpful: SSN. Criminal records on index from 1926.
General Information: No adoption, juvenile, sealed or expunged records released. Copy fee: $.50 per page. Certification fee: $1.00 per page. Fee payee: Clerk of Court. Business checks accepted. Prepayment required.

Andrews Magistrate Court 110 N Morgan Ave, Andrews, SC 29510; 843-264-8811; Fax: 843-264-5177. Hours: 8:30AM-5PM (EST). *Civil Actions Under $7,500, Eviction, Small Claims.*

Georgetown Magistrate Court 1277 N Frasier St, PO Box 1838, Georgetown, SC 29442; 843-545-8140; Fax: 843-545-8142. *Civil Actions Under $7,500, Eviction, Small Claims.*

Georgetown Magistrate Court 333 Cleland St, PO Box 807, Georgetown, SC 29442; 843-546-4650; Fax: 843-527-1703. Hours: 8AM-5PM (EST). *Civil Actions Under $7,500, Eviction, Small Claims.*

Hemingway Magistrate Court 9174 Pleasant Hill Dr, Hemingway, SC 29554; 843-558-9711; Fax: 843-558-9711. *Civil Actions Under $7,500, Eviction, Small Claims.*

Murrells Inlet Magistrate Court 4450 Murrells Inlet Rd, PO Box 859, Murrells Inlet, SC 29576; 843-651-6292; Fax: 843-651-6685. Hours: 8AM-5PM *Civil Actions Under $7,500, Eviction, Small Claims.*

Pawleys Island Magistrate Court 291 Parkersville Rd, PO Box 1830, Pawleys Island, SC 29585; 843-237-8995; Fax: 843-237-3244. Hours: 8AM-5PM (EST). *Civil Actions Under $7,500, Eviction, Small Claims.*

Probate Court PO Box 421270, Georgetown, SC 29442; 843-527-6325; Fax: 843-546-4730. Hours: 8:30AM-5PM (EST). *Probate.*

Greenville County

Circuit Court 305 E. North St, Greenville, SC 29601; 864-467-8551; Fax: 864-467-8540. Hours: 8:30AM-5PM (EST). *Felony, Misdemeanor, Civil Actions Over $7,500.*

www.greenvillecounty.org

Civil Records: Access: In person only. Visitors must perform in person searches for themselves. No search fee. Required to search: name, years to search. Civil cases indexed by defendant, plaintiff. Civil records on computer from 1985, on docket books from 1900s.
Criminal Records: Access: In person only. Visitors must perform in person searches for themselves. No search fee. Required to search: name, years to search, DOB, SSN, signed release. Criminal records on computer from 1985, on docket books from 1900s.
General Information: Public Access terminal is available. No adoption, juvenile, sealed or expunged records released. Copy fee: $.25 per page. Certification fee: $1.00 per page. Fee payee: Clerk of Court. Prepayment is required.

Greenville Magistrate Court 4 McGhee St, Greenville, SC 29601; 864-467-5312; Fax: 864-467-5105. *Civil Actions Under $7,500, Eviction, Small Claims.*

Greenville Magistrate Court 720 S Washington Ave, Greenville, SC 29611; 864-269-0991. Hours: 8:30AM-5PM (EST). *Civil Actions Under $7,500, Eviction, Small Claims.*

Greenville Magistrate Court 6247 White Horse Rd, Greenville, SC 29611; 864-294-4810; Fax: 864-294-4801. Hours: 8:30AM-5PM (EST). *Civil Actions Under $7,500, Eviction, Small Claims.*

Piedmont Magistrate Court 8150 August Rd, Piedmont, SC 29673; 864-277-9555; Fax: 864-277-8345. *Civil Actions Under $7,500, Eviction, Small Claims.*

Simpsonville Magistrate Court 3600 Grandview Dr, Simpsonville, SC 296180; 864-963-3457; Fax: 864-963-0029. *Civil Actions Under $7,500, Eviction, Small Claims.*

Taylors Magistrate Court 2801 Wade Hampton Blvd, Taylors, SC 29687; 864-244-2922; Fax: 864-268-1333. Hours: 8:30AM-5PM (EST). *Civil Actions Under $7,500, Eviction, Small Claims.*

Travelers Rest Magistrate Court 114 N Poinsett Hwy, Travelers Rest, SC 29690; 864-834-6910; Fax: 864-834-6911. Hours: 9AM-4PM (EST). *Civil Actions Under $7,500, Eviction, Small Claims.*

Probate Court 301 University Ridge, Ste 1200, Greenville, SC 29601; 864-467-7170; Fax: 864-467-7198. Hours: 8:30AM-5PM (EST). *Probate.*

www.greenvillecounty.org

Greenwood County

Circuit Court Courthouse, Rm 114, 528 Monument St, Greenwood, SC 29646; 864-942-8547; Fax: 864-943-8693. Hours: 8:30AM-5PM (EST). *Felony, Misdemeanor, Civil Actions Over $7,500.*

Civil Records: Access: Mail, in person. Both court and visitors may perform in person searches. Search fee: $2.00 per name. Required to search: name, years to search. Civil cases indexed by defendant, plaintiff. Civil records on docket books from 1897; on computer since.
Criminal Records: Access: Mail, in person. Both court and visitors may perform in person searches. Search fee: $2.00 per name. Required to search: name, years to search, DOB; also helpful: SSN. Criminal records on alpha index from 1897; on computer since. The court will not perform party name searches for in-person requesters.
General Information: No adoption, juvenile, sealed or expunged records released. SASE required. Turnaround time 1-2 days. Copy fee: $.25 per page. Certification fee: $2.00. Fee payee: Clerk of Court. Business checks accepted. Prepayment is required.

Greenwood Magistrate Court Greenood County Courthouse, Rm 106, Greenwood, SC 29646; 864-942-8655; Fax: 864-942-8663. *Civil Actions Under $7,500, Eviction, Small Claims.*

Probate Court PO Box 1210, Greenwood, SC 29648; 864-942-8625; Fax: 864-942-8620. Hours: 8:30AM-5PM (EST). *Probate.*

Hampton County

Circuit Court PO Box 7, Hampton, SC 29924; 803-943-7510. Hours: 8AM-5PM (EST). *Felony, Civil Actions Over $7,500.*
Civil Records: Access: In person only. Visitors must perform in person searches for themselves. No search fee. Required to search: name, years to search. Civil cases indexed by defendant, plaintiff. Civil records on docket books, archived from 1878.
Criminal Records: Access: In person only. Visitors must perform in person searches for themselves. No search fee. Required to search: name, years to search, DOB; also helpful: SSN. Criminal records on docket books, archived from 1878.

General Information: No adoption, juvenile, sealed or expunged records released. Copy fee: $.50 per page. Certification fee: $1.00. Fee payee: Clerk of Court. Personal checks accepted. Prepayment is required.

Estill Magistrate Court 140 E Railroad Ave, PO Box 969, Estill, SC 29918; 803-625-3232; Fax: 803-625-2148. *Civil Actions Under $7,500, Eviction, Small Claims.*

Varnville Magistrate Court Law Enforcement Ctr, 900 Cemetery Rd, PO Box 1299, Varnville, SC 29944; 803-943-7511; Fax: 843-943-7557. Hours: 8:30AM-4:30PM (EST). *Misdemeanor, Civil Actions Under $7,500, Eviction, Small Claims.*

Probate Court PO Box 601, Hampton, SC 29924; 803-943-7512; Fax: 843-943-7596. Hours: 8AM-5PM (EST). *Probate.*

Horry County

Circuit Court PO Box 677, Conway, SC 29526; 843-248-1270; Fax: 843-248-1341. Hours: 8AM-5PM (EST). *Felony, Misdemeanor, Civil Actions Over $7,500.*

Civil Records: Access: Phone, mail, in person. Both court and visitors may perform in person searches. Search fee: $3.00 per name. Required to search: name, years to search. Civil cases indexed by defendant, plaintiff. Civil records on computer from 1987, on alpha index from 1920s.

Criminal Records: Access: Phone, mail, in person. Both court and visitors may perform in person searches. Search fee: $3.00 per name. Required to search: name, years to search, DOB, SSN, signed release. Criminal records on computer from 1987, on alpha index from 1920s.

General Information: Public Access terminal is available. No adoptions, juvenile, sealed or expunged records released. SASE required. Turnaround time 2 days. Copy fee: $.50 per page. Certification fee: $1.00. Fee payee: Clerk of Court. Business checks accepted.

Aynor Magistrate Court PO Box 115, Aynor, SC 29511; 843-358-5508; Fax: 843-358-0704. Hours: 8AM-5PM (EST). *Civil Actions Under $7,500, Eviction, Small Claims.*

Conway Magistrate Court 1316 First Ave, PO Box 1236, Conway, SC 29528; 843-248-1373; Fax: 843-248-1536. Hours: 8AM-5PM (EST). *Civil Actions Under $7,500, Eviction, Small Claims.*

Conway Magistrate Court 4152 J Reuben Long Ave, Conway, SC 29526; 843-365-9222; Fax: 843-365-0348. *Civil Actions Under $7,500, Eviction, Small Claims.*

Green Sea Magistrate Court 5527 Hwy #9, PO Box 153, Green Sea, SC 29545; 843-392-1219; Fax: 843-392-1834. *Civil Actions Under $7,500, Eviction, Small Claims.*

Little River Summary Court 107 Highway 57 N, Little River, SC 29566; 843-399-5443; Fax: 843-399-6792. Hours: 8AM-5PM (EST). *Civil Actions Under $7,500, Eviction, Small Claims.*

Civil Records: Access: Mail. No search fee.
General Information: Turnaround time 5-7 days. Fee payee: Magistrate District 7.

Loris Magistrate Court 3817 Walnut St, Loris, SC 29569; 843-756-7918/6674; Fax: 843-756-1355. *Civil Actions Under $7,500, Eviction, Small Claims.*

Myrtle Beach Magistrate Court 1201 21st North Ave, Myrtle Beach, SC 29577; 843-444-6127; Fax: 843-444-6131. *Civil Actions Under $7,500, Eviction, Small Claims.*

Surfside Beach Magistrate Court 1106 Glenns Bay Rd, Surfside Beach, SC 29575; 843-238-3277/3677; Fax: 843-238-3591. Hours: 8AM-5PM (EST). *Misdemeanor, Civil Actions Under $7,500, Eviction, Small Claims.*

Probate Court PO Box 288, Conway, SC 29528; 843-248-1294; Fax: 843-248-1298. Hours: 8AM-5PM (EST). *Probate.*

Jasper County

Circuit Court PO Box 248, Ridgeland, SC 29936; 843-726-7710. Hours: 8:30AM-5PM (EST). *Felony, Misdemeanor, Civil Actions Over $7,500.*

Civil Records: Access: Mail, in person. Both court and visitors may perform in person searches. No search fee. Required to search: name, years to search. Civil cases indexed by defendant, plaintiff. Civil records on computer back to 1999; prior on books.

Criminal Records: Access: Mail, in person. Both court and visitors may perform in person searches. Search fee: $5.00 per name. Required to search: name, years to search, DOB; also helpful: SSN, signed release. Criminal records on computer back to 1999; prior on books.

General Information: Public Access terminal is available. No adoption, juvenile, sealed or expunged records released. SASE required. Turnaround time 2 days. Fax notes: Fee to fax results is $2.00 per document. Copy fee: $1.00 per page. Certification fee: $1.00. Fee payee: Clerk of Court. Personal checks accepted. Prepayment is required.

Hardeeville Magistrate Court 21 Martin St, PO Box 1169, Hardeeville, SC 29927; 843-784-2131; Fax: 843-784-3422. *Civil Actions Under $7,500, Eviction, Small Claims.*

Ridgeland Magistrate Court 111 W Adams St, PO Box 665, Ridgeland, SC 29936; 843-726-7737; Fax: 843-726-7745. *Civil Actions Under $7,500, Eviction, Small Claims.*

Ridgeland Magistrate Court PO Box 75, Ridgeland, SC 29936; 843-726-8590; Fax: 843-726-7745. *Civil Actions Under $7,500, Eviction, Small Claims.*

Probate Court PO Box 1028, Ridgeland, SC 29936; 843-726-7719; Fax: 843-726-7782. Hours: 9AM-5PM (EST). *Probate.*

Kershaw County

Circuit Court County Courthouse, Rm 313, PO Box 1557, Camden, SC 29020; 803-425-1500 x623; Fax: 803-425-1505. Hours: 8:30AM-5PM (EST). *Felony, Misdemeanor, Civil Actions Over $7,500.*

Civil Records: Access: In person only. Visitors must perform in person searches for themselves. No search fee. Required to search: name, years to search. Civil cases indexed by defendant, plaintiff. Civil records archived from 1800.

Criminal Records: Access: In person only. Visitors must perform in person searches for themselves. No search fee. Required to search: name, years to search, DOB; also helpful: SSN. Criminal records archived from 1800.

General Information: Public Access terminal is available. No adoption, juvenile, sealed or expunged records released. Copy fee: $.50 per page. Certification fee: $1.00. Fee payee: Clerk of Court. Personal checks accepted. Prepayment is required.

Bethune Magistrate Court 202 N Main St, PO Box 215, Bethune, SC 29009; 843-334-8460; Fax: 843-334-8450. *Civil Actions Under $7,500, Eviction, Small Claims.*

Camden Magistrate Court County Courthouse #118, 1121 Broad St, PO Box 1528, Camden, SC 29020; 803-425-1500 X386; Fax: 803-425-6044. Hours: 9AM-5PM (EST). *Civil Actions Under $7,500, Eviction, Small Claims.*

Probate Court 1121 Broad St, Rm 302, Camden, SC 29020; 803-425-1500; Fax: 803-425-1526. Hours: 9AM-5PM (EST). *Probate.*

Lancaster County

Circuit Court PO Box 1809, Lancaster, SC 29721; 803-285-1581; Fax: 803-285-6497. Hours: 8:30AM-5PM (EST). *Felony, Misdemeanor, Civil Actions Over $7,500.*

Civil Records: Access: Mail, in person. Both court and visitors may perform in person searches. Search fee: $5.00 per name. Required to search: name, years to search. Civil cases indexed by defendant, plaintiff. Civil records on computer from 1987, microfiche from 1937, alpha index from 1764.

Criminal Records: Access: Mail, in person. Both court and visitors may perform in person searches. Search fee: $5.00 per name. Required to search: name, years to search, DOB; also helpful: SSN. Criminal records on computer from 1987, microfiche from 1937, alpha index from 1764.

General Information: No adoption, juvenile, sealed or expunged records released. SASE required. Turnaround time 5 days. Copy fee: $.25 per page. Certification fee: $2.50. Fee payee: Clerk of Court. Personal checks accepted. Prepayment is required.

Lancaster Magistrate Court 101 South Wylie St, PO Box 1809, Lancaster, SC 29720; 803-283-3983; Fax: 803-285-3361. *Civil Actions Under $7,500, Eviction, Small Claims.*

Probate Court PO Box 1809, Lancaster, SC 29721; 803-283-3379; Fax: 803-283-3370. Hours: 8:30AM-5PM (EST). *Probate.*

Laurens County

Circuit Court PO Box 287, Laurens, SC 29360; 864-984-3538. Hours: 9AM-5PM (EST). *Felony, Misdemeanor, Civil Actions Over $7,500.*

Civil Records: Access: Mail, in person. Both court and visitors may perform in person searches. Search fee: $5.00 per name. Required to search: name, years to search. Civil cases indexed by defendant, plaintiff. Civil records on index books back to 1800s; on computer back to 1980.

Criminal Records: Access: Mail, in person. Both court and visitors may perform in person searches. Search fee: $5.00 per name. Required to search: name, years to search, DOB; also helpful: SSN. Criminal records on index books back to 1950s; on computer back to 1980.

General Information: No adoption, juvenile, sealed or expunged records released. SASE required. Turnaround time 2-3 days. Copy fee: $.50 per page. Certification fee: $1.00 per page. Fee payee: Clerk of Court. Personal checks accepted. Prepayment is required.

Clinton Magistrate Court 203 W Pitts St, Clinton, SC 29325; 864-833-5879; Fax: 864-833-7502. *Civil Actions Under $7,500, Eviction, Small Claims.*

Gray Court Magistrate Court 329 Main St, Town Hall, PO Box 438, Gray Court, SC 29645; 864-876-4390. *Civil Actions Under $7,500, Eviction, Small Claims.*

Laurens Magistrate Court PO Box 925, Laurens, SC 29360; 864-683-4485. *Civil Actions Under $7,500, Eviction, Small Claims.*

Probate Court PO Box 194, Laurens, SC 29360; 864-984-7315; Fax: 864-984-3779. Hours: 9AM-5PM (EST). *Probate.*

Lee County

Circuit Court PO Box 387, Bishopville, SC 29010; 803-484-5341; Fax: 803-484-1632. Hours: 9AM-5PM *Felony, Misdemeanor, Civil Actions Over $7,500.*

Civil Records: Access: Mail, in person. Both court and visitors may perform in person searches. Search fee: $5.00 per name. Required to search: name, years to search. Civil cases indexed by defendant, plaintiff. Civil records on computer from 1991, on archives from 1900s.
Criminal Records: Access: Mail, in person. Both court and visitors may perform in person searches. Search fee: $2.00 per name. Required to search: name, years to search, DOB; also helpful: SSN. Criminal records on computer from 1991, on archives from 1900s.
General Information: No adoption, juvenile, sealed or expunged records released. SASE required. Turnaround time 2 days. Copy fee: $.25 per page. $1.00 minimum. Certification fee: $1.00. Fee payee: Clerk of Court. Business checks accepted. Prepayment is required.

Bishopville Magistrate Court 115 Greg St, PO Box 2, Bishopville, SC 29010; 843-484-6463; Fax: 864-486-5163. *Civil Actions Under $7,500, Eviction, Small Claims.*

Dalzell Magistrate Court 2071 Rembert Church Rd, Dalzell, SC 29040; 803-484-6463; Fax: 803-484-5043. *Civil Actions Under $7,500, Eviction, Small Claims.*

Mayesville Magistrate Court 475 Lower Lee School Rd, Mayesville, SC 29104; 803-428-6762; Fax: 803-484-6463. *Civil Actions Under $7,500, Eviction, Small Claims.*

Probate Court PO Box 24, Bishopville, SC 29010; 803-484-5341 X338; Fax: 803-484-6881. Hours: 9AM-5PM (EST). *Probate.*

Lexington County

Circuit Court Lexington County Courthouse, Rm 107, 139 East Main St, Lexington, SC 29072; 803-359-8212; Fax: 803-359-8314. Hours: 8AM-5PM (EST). *Felony, Misdemeanor, Civil Actions Over $7,500.*

Civil Records: Access: Mail, in person. Both court and visitors may perform in person searches. Search fee: $3.00 per name. Required to search: name, years to search. Civil cases indexed by defendant, plaintiff. Civil records on index from 1936.
Criminal Records: Access: Fax, mail, in person. Both court and visitors may perform in person searches. Search fee: $3.00 per name. Required to search: name, years to search, DOB, SSN. Criminal records on computer since 1983.
General Information: No adoption, juvenile, sealed or expunged records released. SASE required. Turnaround time 3 days. Copy fee: $.25 per page. Certification fee: $1.00. Fee payee: County of Lexington. Personal checks accepted. Prepayment is required.

Batesburg Leesville Magistrate Court 231 W Church St, Batesburg, SC 29006; 803-359-8330/532-9204/9205; Fax: 803-532-0357. Hours: 8:30AM-5PM (EST). *Civil Actions Under $7,500, Eviction, Small Claims.*

Cayce Magistrate Court 650 Knox Abbott Dr, Cayce, SC 29033; 803-796-7100; Fax: 803-796-7635. *Civil Actions Under $7,500, Eviction, Small Claims.*

Columbia Magistrate Court 108 Harbison Blvd, Columbia, SC 29212; 803-781-7584/7585; Fax: 803-749-4050. *Misdemeanor, Civil Actions Under $7,500, Eviction, Small Claims.*

Lexington Magistrate Court 304 S Lakeshore Dr, Lexington, SC 29072; 803-359-8221; Fax: 803-359-8155. *Civil Actions Under $7,500, Eviction, Small Claims.*

Swansea Magistrate Court 500 Charlie Rast Rd, PO Box 457, Swansea, SC 29160; 803-568-3616; Fax: 803-568-4078. *Civil Actions Under $7,500, Eviction, Small Claims.*

Probate Court County Courthouse, Rm 110, 139 E Main St, Lexington, SC 29072-3488; 803-359-8324; Fax: 803-359-8199. Hours: 8AM-5PM (EST). *Probate.*

Marion County

Circuit Court PO Box 295, Marion, SC 29571; 843-423-8240. Hours: 8:30AM-5PM (EST). *Felony, Misdemeanor, Civil Actions Over $7,500.*

Civil Records: Access: In person only. Visitors must perform in person searches for themselves. No search fee. Required to search: name, years to search. Civil cases indexed by defendant, plaintiff. Civil records on computer since 1988; prior records on index cards from 1800s.
Criminal Records: Access: In person only. Visitors must perform in person searches for themselves. No search fee. Required to search: name, years to search, DOB; also helpful: SSN. Criminal records on computer since 1988; prior records on index cards from 1800s.
General Information: No adoption, juvenile, sealed or expunged records released. Copy fee: $.25 per page. Certification fee: $1.00.

Gresham Magistrate Court PO Box 35, Gresham, SC 29546; 843-362-0180. Hours: 8:30AM-5PM (EST). *Civil Actions Under $7,500, Eviction, Small Claims.*

Marion Magistrate Court 2715 W Highway 76, #B, Mullins, SC 29574-6015; 843-423-8208; Fax: 843-423-8394. Hours: 8:30AM-4PM (EST). *Civil Actions Under $7,500, Eviction, Small Claims.*

Mullins Magistrate Court 2715 US Highway 76, #B, Mullins, SC 29574; 843-423-8208 X231; Fax: 843-423-8394. Hours: 8:30AM-12:30PM, 1:30PM-5PM (EST). *Civil Actions Under $7,500, Eviction, Small Claims.*

Probate Court PO Box 583, Marion, SC 29571; 843-423-8244; Fax: 843-423-5026. Hours: 8:30AM-5PM (EST). *Probate.*

Marlboro County

Circuit Court PO Drawer 996, Bennettsville, SC 29512; 843-479-5613; Fax: 843-479-5640. Hours: 8:30AM-5PM (EST). *Felony, Misdemeanor, Civil Actions Over $7,500.*

Civil Records: Access: Mail, in person. Both court and visitors may perform in person searches. Search fee: $5.00 per name. Required to search: name, years to search. Civil cases indexed by defendant, plaintiff. Civil records on computer from 1985, on index from 1786.
Criminal Records: Access: Mail, in person. Both court and visitors may perform in person searches. Search fee: $5.00 per name. Required to search: name, years to search, DOB; also helpful: SSN. Criminal records on computer from 1985, on index from 1786.
General Information: Public Access terminal is available. No adoption, juvenile, sealed or expunged records released. SASE required. Turnaround time 1 day. Copy fee: $.25 per page. Certification fee: $2.00. Fee payee: Clerk of Court. Personal checks accepted. Prepayment is required.

Bennettsville Magistrate Court 211 N Marlboro St, PO Box 418, Bennettsville, SC 29512; 843-479-5620; Fax: 843-479-5646. Hours: 10AM-5PM M-Th; Civil 4-5PM (EST). *Civil Actions Under $7,500, Eviction, Small Claims.*

Note: Court is again active.

Marlboro County Summary Court PO Box 418, Bennettsville, SC 29512; 843-479-5620/5621; Fax: 843-479-5646. Hours: 8:30AM-4:30PM (EST). *Civil Actions Under $7,500, Eviction, Small Claims.*

Civil Records: Access: Mail. No search fee.
General Information: Turnaround time 5-7 days. Fee payee: County Treasurer. Prepayment is required.

Probate Court PO Box 455, Bennettsville, SC 29512; 843-479-5610; Fax: 843-479-5668. Hours: 8:30AM-5PM (EST). *Probate.*

McCormick County

Circuit Court 133 S Mine St, McCormick, SC 29835; 864-465-2195; Fax: 864-465-0071. Hours: 9AM-5PM (EST). *Felony, Misdemeanor, Civil Actions Over $7,500.*

Civil Records: Access: Mail, in person. Visitors must perform in person searches for themselves. No search fee. Required to search: name, years to search. Civil cases indexed by defendant, plaintiff. Civil records on index books from 1916.
Criminal Records: Access: Mail, in person. Both court and visitors may perform in person searches. Search fee: $5.00 per name. Required to search: name, years to search, DOB; also helpful: SSN. Criminal records on index books from 1916.
General Information: No adoption, juvenile, sealed or expunged records released. SASE required. Turnaround time 30 days. Copy fee: $.35 per page. Certification fee: $1.00. Fee payee: Clerk of Court. Prepayment is required.

McCormick Magistrate Court 109 Augusta St, PO Box 1116, McCormick, SC 29835; 864-465-2316; Fax: 864-465-2582. Hours: 9AM-5PM (EST). *Civil Actions Under $7,000, Eviction, Small Claims.*

Probate Court 133 S Mine St #101, McCormick, SC 29835; 864-465-2630; Fax: 864-465-0071. Hours: 9AM-5PM (EST). *Probate.*

Newberry County

Circuit Court PO Box 278, Newberry, SC 29108; 803-321-2110; Fax: 803-321-2102. Hours: 8:30AM-5PM (EST). *Felony, Misdemeanor, Civil Actions Over $7,500.*

Civil Records: Access: Mail, in person. Both court and visitors may perform in person searches. No search fee. Required to search: name, years to search. Civil cases indexed by defendant, plaintiff. Civil records on computer from 1983, docket books from 1776.
Criminal Records: Access: In person only. Visitors must perform in person searches for themselves. No search fee. Required to search: name, years to search, DOB; also helpful: SSN. Criminal records on computer from 1983, docket books from 1776.
General Information: Public Access terminal is available. No adoption, juvenile, sealed, PTI or expunged records released. Turnaround time 1 week. Copy fee: $.20 per page. Certification fee: $1.00. Fee payee: Clerk of Court. Only cashiers checks and money orders accepted. Prepayment is required.

Little Mountain Magistrate Court 824 Main St, PO Box 95, Little Mountain, SC 29075; 803-345-1040; Fax: 803-945-7222. *Civil Actions Under $7,500, Eviction, Small Claims.*

Newberry Magistrate Court 3239 Louis Rich Rd, Newberry, SC 29108; 803-321-2144/2145; Fax: 803-321-2172. Hours: 8:30-5PM (EST). *Civil Actions Under $7,500, Eviction, Small Claims.*

Whitmire Magistrate Court 116 Duncan St, Whitmire, SC 29178. Hours: 1-5PM T,TH (EST). *Civil Actions Under $7,500, Eviction, Small Claims.*

Probate Court PO Box 442, Newberry, SC 29108; 803-321-2118; Fax: 803-321-2119. Hours: 8:30AM-5PM (EST). *Probate.*

Oconee County

Circuit Court PO Box 678, Walhalla, SC 29691; 864-638-4280. Hours: 8:30AM-5PM (EST). *Felony, Misdemeanor, Civil Actions Over $7,500.*

Civil Records: Access: In person only. Visitors must perform in person searches for themselves. No search fee. Required to search: name, years to search. Civil cases indexed by defendant, plaintiff. Civil records on index cards from 1868; on computer back to 1994.
Criminal Records: Access: In person only. Visitors must perform in person searches for themselves. No search fee. Required to search: name, years to search; also helpful: DOB, SSN, signed release. Criminal records on index cards from 1868; on computer back to 1994.
General Information: Public Access terminal is available. No adoption, juvenile, sealed or expunged records released. Copy fee: $1.00 for first page, $.50 each add'l. Certification fee: No certification fee. Fee payee: Clerk of Court. Personal checks accepted. Prepayment is required.

County Summary Court 208 Booker Dr, Walhalla, SC 29691; 864-638-4125; Fax: 864-638-4229. *Civil Actions Under $7,500, Eviction, Small Claims.*

Civil Records: Access: Mail. No search fee.
General Information: Turnaround time 5-7 days. Fee payee: County Treasurer. Prepayment is required.

Walhalla Magistrate Court 208 Booker Dr, County Mail Rm, 415 S Pine St, Walhalla, SC 29691; 864-638-4125/4229; Fax: 864-638-4229. Hours: 8:30AM-5PM (EST). *Civil Actions Under $7,500, Eviction, Small Claims.*

Probate Court PO Box 471, Walhalla, SC 29691; 864-638-4275; Fax: 864-638-4278. Hours: 8:30AM-5PM (EST). *Probate.*

Orangeburg County

Circuit Court PO Box 9000, Orangeburg, SC 29116; 803-533-6260; Fax: 803-534-3848. Hours: 8:30AM-5PM (EST). *Felony, Misdemeanor, Civil Actions Over $7,500.*

Civil Records: Access: In person only. Visitors must perform in person searches for themselves. No search fee. Required to search: name, years to search. Civil cases indexed by defendant, plaintiff. Civil records on index cards from 1924.
Criminal Records: Access: In person only. Visitors must perform in person searches for themselves. No search fee. Required to search: name, years to search, DOB; also helpful: SSN. Criminal records on index cards from 1924.
General Information: No adoption, juvenile, sealed or expunged records released. Copy fee: $.50 per page. Certification fee: $1.00. Fee payee: Clerk of Court. Personal checks accepted.

Bowman Magistrate Court 6803 Charleston Highway, PO Box 365, Bowman, SC 29018; 803-829-2831. *Civil Actions Under $7,500, Eviction, Small Claims.*

Branchville Magistrate Court 7644 Freedom Rd, PO Box 85, Branchville, SC 29432; 803-274-8820; Fax: 803-274-8820. *Civil Actions Under $7,500, Eviction, Small Claims.*

Elloree Magistrate Court 2614 Cleveland St, PO Box 436, Elloree, SC 29047; 803-897-4626; Fax: 803-897-2165. *Civil Actions Under $7,500, Eviction, Small Claims.*

Eutawville Magistrate Court 300 Porcher Ave, PO Box 188, Eutawville, SC 29048; 803-492-3697/533-5879; Fax: 803-496-5850. *Civil Actions Under $7,500, Eviction, Small Claims.*

Holly Hill Magistrate Court 1006 Peake St, PO Box 154, Holly Hill, SC 29059; 803-496-9533; Fax: 803-496-9533. *Civil Actions Under $7,500, Eviction, Small Claims.*

North Magistrate Court 9305 North Rd, PO Box 321, North, SC 29112; 803-247-2101. *Civil Actions Under $7,500, Eviction, Small Claims.*

Norway Magistrate Court 8413 Savannah Hwy, PO Box 67, Norway, SC 29113; 803-263-4100; Fax: 803-263-4292. *Civil Actions Under $7,500, Eviction, Small Claims.*

Orangeburg County Magistrate Court 1520 Ellis Ave NE, PO Box 9000, Orangeburg, SC 29116; 803-533-5880/5879; Fax: 803-533-5806. Hours: 8:30AM-5PM (EST). *Civil Actions Under $7,500, Eviction, Small Claims.*

Orangeburg Magistrate Court 2345 Norway Rd, Orangeburg, SC 29115; 803-535-4129/534-8933. *Civil Actions Under $7,500, Eviction, Small Claims.*

Springfield Magistrate Court 7558 Festival Trail Rd, PO Box 125, Springfield, SC 29146; 803-258-3315; Fax: 803-258-3951. Hours: 9AM-5PM (EST). *Civil Actions Under $7,500, Eviction, Small Claims.*

Probate Court PO Drawer 9000, Orangeburg, SC 29116-9000; 803-533-6280; Fax: 803-533-6279. Hours: 8:30AM-5PM (EST). *Probate.*

Pickens County

Circuit Court PO Box 215, Pickens, SC 29671; 864-898-5866; Fax: 864-898-5863. Hours: 8:30AM-5PM (EST). *Felony, Misdemeanor, Civil Actions Over $7,500.*

Civil Records: Access: Mail, in person. Both court and visitors may perform in person searches. Search fee: $2.00 per name. Required to search: name, years to search. Civil cases indexed by defendant, plaintiff. Civil records on computer from 1990, on index from 1970.
Criminal Records: Access: Mail, in person. Both court and visitors may perform in person searches. Search fee: $2.00 per name. Required to search: name, years to search, DOB; also helpful: SSN. Criminal records on computer from 1990, on index from 1970.
General Information: No adoption, juvenile, sealed or expunged records released. SASE required. Turnaround time 1 day. Copy fee: $.25 per page. Certification fee: $1.00. Fee payee: Clerk of Court. Personal checks accepted. Prepayment is required.

Clemson Magistrate Court 115-B Commons Way, Central, SC 29630; 864-639-8084; Fax: 864-639-8084. Hours: 8:30AM-5PM (EST). *Civil Actions Under $7,500, Eviction, Small Claims.*

Easley Magistrate Court 135 Folger Ave, West End Hall, Easley, SC 29640; 864-850-7076; Fax: 864-850-7075. *Civil Actions Under $7,500, Eviction, Small Claims.*

Liberty Magistrate Court 431 E Main St, Liberty, SC 29657; 864-850-3500; Fax: 864-850-3501. Hours: 8:30AM-5PM (EST). *Misdemeanor, Civil Actions Under $7,500, Eviction, Small Claims.*

Pickens Magistrate Court 216-A, Law Enforcement Ctr Rd, Pickens, SC 29671; 864-898-5551/5552; Fax: 864-898-5546. Hours: 8:30AM-5PM (EST). *Civil Actions Under $7,500, Eviction, Small Claims.*

Probate Court 222 McDaniel Ave B-16, Pickens, SC 29671; 864-898-5903; Fax: 864-898-5924. Hours: 8:30AM-5PM (EST). *Probate.*

Richland County

Circuit Court PO Box 2766, Columbia, SC 29202; 803-748-4684; Fax: 803-748-5039. Hours: 8:30AM-5PM (EST). *Felony, Misdemeanor, Civil Actions Over $7,500.*

Civil Records: Access: Mail, in person. Both court and visitors may perform in person searches. Search fee: $2.00 per name. Required to search: name, years to search. Civil cases indexed by defendant, plaintiff. Civil records on computer from 1975. Many prior records indexed.
Criminal Records: Access: In person only. Visitors may perform in person searches for themselves. No search fee. Required to search: name, years to search; also helpful: DOB, SSN. Criminal records on index.
General Information: Public Access terminal is available. No adoption, juvenile, sealed or expunged records released. SASE required. Turnaround time 1 day. Copy fee: $.50 for first page, $.15 each add'l. Certification fee: No certification fee. Fee payee: Richland County Clerk. Personal checks accepted. Prepayment is required.

Columbia Magistrate Court 4919 Rhett St, Columbia, SC 29203; 803-754-2250; Fax: 803-754-8783. *Civil Actions Under $7,500, Eviction, Small Claims.*

Columbia Magistrate Court 1400 Huger St, PO Box 192, Columbia, SC 29202; 803-779-0280; Fax: 803-748-4952. *Civil Actions Under $7,500, Eviction, Small Claims.*

Columbia Magistrate Court 1601 B Shop Rd, PO Box 9305, Columbia, SC 29201; 803-799-1779; Fax: 803-748-5009. Hours: 8:30AM-5PM (EST). *Civil Actions Under $7,500, Eviction, Small Claims.*

Columbia Magistrate Court 6941 A North Trenholm Rd, Columbia, SC 29206; 803-782-2807; Fax: 803-782-2923. *Civil Actions Under $7,500, Eviction, Small Claims.*

Columbia Magistrate Court Richland Central Court, 1400 Huger St, PO Box 192, Columbia, SC 29202; 803-748-4741; Fax: 803-748-5046/929-6291. *Civil Actions Under $7,500, Eviction, Small Claims.*

Dutch Fork Magistrate Court 1223 St Andrews Rd, Columbia, SC 29210; 803-772-6464/6465; Fax: 803-798-6144. Hours: 9AM-5PM (EST). *Misdemeanor, Civil Actions Under $7,500, Eviction, Small Claims.*

Elgin Magistrate Court 10509 Two Notch Rd, Elgin, SC 29045; 803-788-8232; Fax: 803-865-0889. *Civil Actions Under $7,500, Eviction, Small Claims.*

Hopkins Magistrate Court 6108 Cabin Creek Rd, PO Box 70, Hopkins, SC 29061; 803-783-2424; Fax: 803-783-2425. Hours: 8:45AM-5PM (EST). *Civil Actions Under $7,500, Eviction, Small Claims.*

Lykesland Magistrate Court 1403 Caroline Rd, PO Box 9523, Columbia, SC 29290; 803-776-0454; Fax: 803-783-2667. Hours: 9AM-5PM (EST). *Civil Actions Under $7,500, Eviction, Small Claims.*

Waverly Magistrate Court 5205 Trenholm Rd #207, Forest Acres City Hall, Columbia, SC 29206; 803-738-9017/9019; Fax: 803-738-7020. *Civil Actions Under $7,500, Eviction, Small Claims.*

Probate Court PO Box 192 (1701 Main St #207), Columbia, SC 29202; 803-748-4700; Fax: 803-748-5079. Hours: 8:30AM-5PM (EST). *Probate.*

Saluda County

Circuit Court County Courthouse, Saluda, SC 29138; 864-445-3303/2168; Fax: 864-445-3772. Hours: 8:30AM-5PM (EST). *Felony, Misdemeanor, Civil Actions Over $7,500.*

Civil Records: Access: Fax, mail, in person. Both court and visitors may perform in person searches. No search fee. Required to search: name, years to search, address. Civil cases indexed by defendant, plaintiff. Civil records on computer from 1995, on index from 1897.

Criminal Records: Access: Fax, mail, in person. Both court and visitors may perform in person searches. No search fee. Required to search: name, years to search, address, DOB, signed release; also helpful: SSN. Criminal records on computer from 1995, on index from 1897. Request must be in writing.

General Information: No adoption, juvenile, sealed or expunged records released. SASE not required. Turnaround time 1 day. Copy fee: $.25 per page. Certification fee: $1.00. Fee payee: Clerk of Court. Personal checks accepted. Prepayment is required.

Saluda Magistrate Court 120 S Main St, Courthhouse Annex, Saluda, SC 29138; 864-445-2846; Fax: 864-445-3684. *Civil Actions Under $7,500, Eviction, Small Claims.*

Probate Court 100 E Church St, Saluda, SC 29138; 864-445-7110; Fax: 864-445-9726. Hours: 8:30AM-5PM (EST). *Probate.*

Spartanburg County

Circuit Court County Courthouse, 180 Magnolia St, Spartanburg, SC 29306; 864-596-2591; Fax: 864-596-2239. Hours: 8:30AM-5PM (EST). *Felony, Misdemeanor, Civil Actions Over $7,500.*

Civil Records: Access: In person only. Visitors must perform in person searches for themselves. No search fee. Required to search: name, years to search. Civil cases indexed by defendant, plaintiff. Civil records on computer from 1975, on microfiche from 1960, on alpha index from 1800s.

Criminal Records: Access: In person only. Visitors must perform in person searches for themselves. No search fee. Required to search: name, years to search, DOB, SSN, signed release. Criminal records on computer from 1975, on microfiche from 1960, on alpha index from 1800s.

General Information: Public Access terminal is available. No adoption, juvenile, sealed or expunged records released. Copy fee: $.25 per page. Certification fee: $1.00. Fee payee: Clerk of Court. Personal checks accepted. Prepayment is required.

Chesnee Magistrate Court 201 Cherokee St, Chesnee, SC 29323; 864-461-3402; Fax: 864-596-3622. *Civil Actions Under $7,500, Eviction, Small Claims.*

Inman Magistrate Court 7 Mill St, Inman, SC 29349; 864-472-4447/6247; Fax: 864-596-3622. *Civil Actions Under $7,500, Eviction, Small Claims.*

Landrum Magistrate Court 510-B North Howard Ave, Landrum, SC 29356-1117; 864-457-7245; Fax: 864-596-3622. *Civil Actions Under $7,500, Eviction, Small Claims.*

Pacolet Magistrate Court 980 Sunny Acres Rd, PO Box 416, Pacolet Mills, SC 29373; 864-474-0344/3391; Fax: 864-503-2417. Hours: 6PM-10PM M & W, 6PM-9PM Th (EST). *Civil Actions Under $7,500, Eviction, Small Claims.*

Reidville Magistrate Court 7450 Reidville Rd, PO Box 124, Reidville, SC 29375; 864-433-9223. *Civil Actions Under $7,500, Eviction, Small Claims.*

Spartanburg Magistrate Court County Courthouse, Rm 105, PO Box 5221, Spartanburg, SC 29306; 864-596-2564; Fax: 864-596-3622. *Civil Actions Under $7,500, Eviction, Small Claims.*

Probate Court 180 Magnolia St, Spartanburg, SC 29306-2392; 864-596-2556; Fax: 864-596-2011. Hours: 8:30AM-5PM (EST). *Probate.*

Sumter County

Circuit Court 141 N Main, Sumter, SC 29150; 803-436-2227; Fax: 803-436-2223. Hours: 8:30AM-5PM (EST). *Felony, Misdemeanor, Civil Actions Over $7,500.*

Civil Records: Access: Mail, in person. Both court and visitors may perform in person searches. Search fee: $5.00 per name. Required to search: name, years to search; also helpful: address. Civil cases indexed by defendant, plaintiff. Civil records on computer from 1987, microfiche and books from 1900s.

Criminal Records: Access: Mail, in person. Both court and visitors may perform in person searches. Search fee: $5.00 per name. Required to search: name, years to search, DOB, SSN, signed release; also helpful: address. Criminal records in books.

General Information: No adoption, juvenile, sealed or expunged records released. SASE required. Turnaround time 2 days. Copy fee: $.25 per page. Certification fee: $5.00. Fee payee: Sumter County Treasurer. Business checks accepted. Prepayment is required.

Mayesville Magistrate Court PO Box 236, Town Hall, Mayesville, SC 29104; 803-453-5280; Fax: 803-453-5285. *Civil Actions Under $7,500, Eviction, Small Claims.*

Pinewood Magistrate Court PO Box 41, Pinewood, SC 29125; Fax: 803-773-3113. *Civil Actions Under $7,500, Eviction, Small Claims.*

Sumter Magistrate Court 115 N Harvin St, PO Box 1394, Sumter, SC 29151; 803-436-2280; Fax: 803-436-2362. *Civil Actions Under $7,500, Eviction, Small Claims.*

Probate Court 141 N Main, Rm 111, Sumter, SC 29150; 803-436-2166; Fax: 803-436-2407. Hours: 8:30AM-5PM (EST). *Probate.*

Union County

Circuit Court PO Box 200, Union, SC 29379; 864-429-1630; Fax: 864-429-4454. Hours: 9AM-5PM (EST). *Felony, Misdemeanor, Civil Actions Over $7,500.*

Civil Records: Access: In person only. Visitors must perform in person searches for themselves. No search fee. Required to search: name, years to search. Civil cases indexed by defendant, plaintiff. All records on computer.

Criminal Records: Access: In person only. Visitors must perform in person searches for themselves. No search fee. Required to search: name, years to search; also helpful: SSN, DOB. Criminal records on computer.

General Information: Public Access terminal is available. No adoption, juvenile, sealed or expunged records released. Copy fee: $.50 per page. Certification fee: $2.00. Fee payee: Clerk of Court. Personal checks accepted. Prepayment is required.

Carlisle Magistrate Court PO Box 35, Carlisle, SC 29031; 864-427-6987. *Civil Actions Under $7,500, Eviction, Small Claims.*

Jonesville Magistrate Court 440 Pacolet St, PO Box 33, Jonesville, SC 29353; 864-674-5426; Fax: 864-674-6634. *Civil Actions Under $7,500, Eviction, Small Claims.*

Lockhart Magistrate Court 210 Main St, Union, SC 29379; 864-545-2338. *Civil Actions Under $7,500, Eviction, Small Claims.*

Union Magistrate Court 210 Main St, Courthouse, PO Box 200, Union, SC 29379; 864-429-1648; Fax: 864-429-1629. *Civil Actions Under $7,500, Eviction, Small Claims.*

Probate Court PO Box 447, Union, SC 29379; 864-429-1625; Fax: 864-429-1627. Hours: 9AM-5PM (EST). *Probate.*

Williamsburg County

Circuit Court 125 W Main St, Kingstree, SC 29556; 843-354-9321 x552; Fax: 843-354-7821. Hours: 8:30AM-5PM (EST). *Felony, Misdemeanor, Civil Actions Over $7,500.*

Civil Records: Access: Mail, in person. Both court and visitors may perform in person searches. Search fee: $5.00 per name. Required to search: name, years to search. Civil cases indexed by defendant, plaintiff. Civil records on books, archived from 1980-1989, indexed from 1806.

Criminal Records: Access: Mail, in person. Both court and visitors may perform in person searches. Search fee: $5.00 per name. Required to search: name, years to search, DOB; also helpful: SSN. Criminal records on books, archived from 1980-1989, indexed from 1806.

General Information: No adoption, juvenile, sealed or expunged records released. SASE required. Turnaround time 3 days. Copy fee: $.25 per page. Certification fee: $3.00. Fee payee: Clerk of Court. Personal checks accepted. Prepayment is required.

Hemingway Magistrate Court 206 E Broad St, PO Box 416, Hemingway, SC 29554; 843-558-2116; Fax: 843-5578-5314. *Civil Actions Under $7,500, Eviction, Small Claims.*

Kingstree Magistrate Court 10 Courthouse Sq, PO Box 673, Kingstree, SC 29556; 843-354-9602/9603; Fax: 843-354-2106. *Civil Actions Under $7,500, Eviction, Small Claims.*

Kingstree Magistrate Court Rt 4 Box 200, Kingstree, SC 29556; 843-382-9723. *Civil Actions Under $7,500, Eviction, Small Claims.*

Lane Magistrate Court Rt 2 Box 94-A, Lane, SC 29564; 843-387-5726. *Civil Actions Under $7,500, Eviction, Small Claims.*

Nesmith Magistrate Court Rt 1 Box 283, Nesmith, SC 29580; 843-382-8620. *Civil Actions Under $7,500, Eviction, Small Claims.*

Probate Court PO Box 1005, Kingstree, SC 29556; 843-354-9321 x558; Fax: 843-354-2106. Hours: 8:30AM-5PM (EST). *Probate.*

York County

Circuit Court PO Box 649, York, SC 29745; 803-688-8506. Hours: 8AM-5PM (EST). *Felony, Misdemeanor, Civil Actions Over $7,500.*

Civil Records: Access: Mail, in person. Both court and visitors may perform in person searches. Search fee: $5.00 per name. Required to search: name, years to search. Civil cases indexed by defendant, plaintiff. Civil records on computer from 1982, in books from 1932.

Criminal Records: Access: Fax, mail, in person. Both court and visitors may perform in person searches. Search fee: $5.00 per name. Required to search: name, years to search, DOB; also helpful: SSN. Criminal records on computer from 1982, in books from 1932.

General Information: No adoption, juvenile, sealed or expunged records released. SASE required. Turnaround time 1 day. Fax notes: $5.00 per document. Copy fee: $.40 per page. Certification fee: $1.00. Fee payee: Clerk of Court. Personal checks accepted. Prepayment is required.

Clover Magistrate Court 201 S Main St, PO Box 165, Clover, SC 29710; 803-222-9404. *Civil Actions Under $7,500, Eviction, Small Claims.*

Fort Mill Magistrate Court 114 Springs St, Fort Mill, SC 29715; 803-547-5572/5573; Fax: 803-547-6344. *Civil Actions Under $7,500, Eviction, Small Claims.*

Hickory Grove Magistrate Court PO Box 37, Hickory Grove, SC 29717; 803-925-2815. *Civil Actions Under $7,500, Eviction, Small Claims.*

Rock Hill Magistrate Court 529 S Cherry Rd, PO Box 11166, Rock Hill, SC 29731; 803-909-7600; Fax: 803-324-3838. *Civil Actions Under $7,500, Eviction, Small Claims.*

Rock Hill Magistrate Court 1966 Castlegate Court, Rock Hill, SC 29730; 803-628-3095; Fax: 803-328-8353. Hours: 8AM-5PM (EST). *Civil Actions Under $7,500, Eviction, Small Claims.*

York Magistrate Court 1675-1D York Hwy, York, SC 29745; 803-628-3095. *Civil Actions Under $7,500, Eviction, Small Claims.*

Probate Court PO Box 219, York, SC 29745; 803-684-8513 X8630; Fax: 803-684-8536. Hours: 8AM-5PM (EST). *Probate.*

South Carolina Recording Offices

ORGANIZATION

46 counties, 46 recording offices. The recording officer is the Register of Mesne Conveyances or Clerk of Court (varies by county). The entire state is in the Eastern Time Zone (EST).

REAL ESTATE RECORDS

Most counties will not perform real estate searches. Copy and certification fees vary. The Assessor keeps tax records.

UCC RECORDS

Financing statements are filed at the state level, except for real estate related collateral, which are filed with the Register. However, prior to 07/2001, consumer goods and farm collateral were also filed at the Register and these older records can be searched there. As a general rule, all recording offices will perform UCC searches. Searches fees are usually $5.00 per debtor name. Copy fees are usually $1.00 per page.

TAX LIEN RECORDS

All federal and state tax liens on personal property and on real property are filed with the Register of Mesne Conveyances (Clerk of Court). Some counties will perform tax lien searches. Search fees and copy fees vary.

Abbeville County

Clerk of Court, P.O. Box 99, Abbeville, SC 29620. 864-459-5074 R/E Recording: 864-459-4944 UCC Recording: 864-459-4944; Fax 864-459-9188.
Will search UCC records. This agency will not do a tax lien search. Will not search real estate records. **Other Phone Numbers:** Assessor 864-459-4921; Treasurer 864-459-2539; Appraiser/Auditor 864-459-4921; Elections 864-459-5083.

Aiken County

County Register of Mesne Conveyances, P.O. Box 537, Aiken, SC 29802-0537. County Register of Mesne Conveyances, R/E and UCC Recording 803-642-2072 UCC Recording: 803-642-2075.
Will search UCC records. Tax liens not included in UCC search. RE record owner and mortgage searches available. **Other Phone Numbers:** Assessor 803-642-1576; Treasurer 803-642-2055; Appraiser/Auditor 803-642-1576; Elections 803-642-2028.

Allendale County

Clerk of Court, P.O. Box 126, Allendale, SC 29810. 803-584-2737; Fax 803-584-7058.
Will search UCC records. This agency will not do a tax lien search. Will not search real estate records. **Other Phone Numbers:** Assessor 803-584-2572; Treasurer 803-584-3876.

Anderson County

Clerk of Court, P.O. Box 8002, Anderson, SC 29622. 864-260-4054; Fax 864-260-4443.
Will search UCC records. Will not search real estate records. **Other Phone Numbers:** Assessor 864-260-4028; Treasurer 864-260-4033.

Bamberg County

Clerk of Court, P.O. Box 150, Bamberg, SC 29003. 803-245-3025; Fax 803-245-3088.
Will search UCC records. Will not search real estate records. **Other Phone Numbers:** Assessor 803-245-3010; Treasurer 803-245-3003.

Barnwell County

Clerk of Court, P.O. Box 723, Barnwell, SC 29812-0723. 803-541-1020; Fax 803-541-1025.
Will search UCC records. Will not search real estate records. **Other Phone Numbers:** Assessor 803-541-1011; Treasurer 803-541-1050.

Beaufort County

Clerk of Court, P.O. Drawer 1197, Beaufort, SC 29901-1197. Clerk of Court, R/E and UCC Recording 843-470-2700 UCC Recording: 843-470-2715; Fax 843-470-2709. http://www.co.beaufort.sc.us
Will search UCC records. **Online Access:** Property Records, Assessor. Online access to the public records search database is available free online at http://rodweb.co.beaufort.sc.us; also, search county property information at the GIS mapping database at http://maps.co.beaufort.sc.us. A fuller records subscription service requiring registration, fees, and logon is under development. **Other Phone Numbers:** Assessor 843-470-2513; Treasurer 843-470-2766; Elections 843-470-3753.

Berkeley County

Clerk of Court, 223 North Live Oak Drive, Moncks Corner, SC 29461. 843-719-4084; Fax 843-719-4139.
Will search UCC records. Will not search real estate records. **Other Phone Numbers:** Assessor 843-761-6900 x4061; Treasurer 843-761-3800.

Calhoun County

Clerk of Court, 302 S. F.R. Huff Drive, St. Matthews, SC 29135. 803-874-3524; Fax 803-874-1942.
Will search UCC records. Will not search real estate records. **Other Phone Numbers:** Assessor 803-874-3613; Treasurer 803-874-3519.

Charleston County

Clerk of Court, P.O. Box 726, Charleston, SC 29402. Clerk of Court, R/E and UCC Recording 843-958-4800; Fax 843-958-4803. http://www.charlestoncounty.org
Will search UCC records. Will not search real estate records. **Other Phone Numbers:** Assessor 843-958-4100; Treasurer 843-958-4360; Elections 843-745-2226; Vital Records 843-740-0801.

Cherokee County

Clerk of Court, P.O. Drawer 2289, Gaffney, SC 29342. Clerk of Court, R/E and UCC Recording 864-487-2571; Fax 864-487-2754.
Will search UCC records. This agency will not do a tax lien search. Will not search real estate records. **Other Phone Numbers:** Assessor 864-487-2552; Treasurer 864-487-2551; Elections 864-487-2563; Vital Records 864-487-2571.

Chester County

Clerk of Court, P.O. Drawer 580, Chester, SC 29706. 803-385-2605; Fax 803-581-7975.
Will search UCC records. Will not search real estate records. **Other Phone Numbers:** Assessor 803-377-4177; Treasurer 803-385-2608.

Chesterfield County

Clerk of Court, P.O. Box 529, Chesterfield, SC 29709. 843-623-2574; Fax 843-623-3945.
Will search UCC records. Will not search real estate records. **Other Phone Numbers:** Assessor 843-623-7362.

Clarendon County

Clerk of Court, P.O. Drawer E, Manning, SC 29102. 803-435-4443; Fax 803-435-8258.
Will search UCC records. Will not search real estate records. **Other Phone Numbers:** Assessor 803-435-4423.

Colleton County

Clerk of Court, P.O. Box 620, Walterboro, SC 29488-0028. Clerk of Court, R/E and UCC Recording 843-549-5791; Fax 843-549-2875.
Will search UCC records. Will not search real estate records. **Other Phone Numbers:** Assessor 843-549-1213; Treasurer 843-549-2233; Elections 843-549-2842; Vital Records 843-549-1516.

Darlington County

Clerk of Court, P.O. Box 1177, Darlington, SC 29540. 843-398-4330; Fax 843-398-4172.
Will search UCC records. Will not search real estate records. **Other Phone Numbers:** Assessor 843-398-4180.

Dillon County

Clerk of Court, P.O. Drawer 1220, Dillon, SC 29536. Clerk of Court, R/E and UCC Recording 843-774-1425; Fax 843-774-1443.
Will search UCC records. UCC search includes tax liens if requested. Will not search real estate records. **Other Phone Numbers:** Assessor 843-774-1412; Treasurer 843-774-1416; Appraiser/Auditor 843-774-1412; Elections 843-774-1403; Vital Records 843-774-5611; Auditor 843-774-1418; Probate 8437741423;

Dorchester County

Clerk of Court, P.O. Box 38, St. George, SC 29477. 843-563-0106 R/E Recording: 843-832-0153 UCC Recording: 843-832-0153; Fax 843-563-0277.
Will search UCC records. Will not search real estate records. **Other Phone Numbers:** Assessor 843-563-0156; Treasurer 843-563-0165; Appraiser/Auditor 843-563-0156; Elections 843-563-0132; Vital Records 843-563-0107.

Edgefield County

Clerk of Court, P.O. Box 34, Edgefield, SC 29824. 803-637-4080 R/E Recording: 803-637-4049 UCC Recording: 803-637-4049; Fax 803-637-4117.
Will search UCC records. Will not search real estate records. **Other Phone Numbers:** Assessor 803-637-4066; Treasurer 803-637-4069; Appraiser/Auditor 803-637-4057; Elections 803-637-4072.

Fairfield County

Clerk of Court, P.O. Drawer 299, Winnsboro, SC 29180. 803-635-1411.

Will search UCC records. This agency will not do a tax lien search. Will not search real estate records. **Other Phone Numbers:** Assessor 803-635-1411; Treasurer 803-635-1411.

Florence County

Clerk of Court, MSC-E City/County Complex, Florence, SC 29501. Clerk of Court, R/E and UCC Recording 843-665-3031; Fax 843-665-3097.
Will search UCC records. Will not search real estate records. **Other Phone Numbers:** Assessor 843-665-3056; Treasurer 843-665-3041.

Georgetown County

Clerk of Court, P.O. Drawer 1270, Georgetown, SC 29442. 843-527-6315.
Will search UCC records. This agency will not do a tax lien search. Will not search real estate records. **Other Phone Numbers:** Assessor 843-546-1241; Treasurer 843-527-5179.

Greenville County

Register of Deeds, 301 University Ridge, #1300, County Square Suite 1300, Greenville, SC 29601-3655. Register of Deeds, R/E and UCC Recording 864-467-7240 UCC Recording: 864-467-7180; Fax 864-467-7107. http://www.greenvillecounty.org
Will not search UCC records. Effective July 2, 2001- Will not search Tax Liens. Will not search real estate records. **Online Access:** Real Property. Register of Deeds search database are available free online at www.greenvillecounty.org. **Other Phone Numbers:** Assessor 864-467-7300; Treasurer 864-467-7210.

Greenwood County

Clerk of Court, Courthouse, 528 Monument St., Greenwood, SC 29646. Clerk of Court, R/E and UCC Recording 864-942-8551 UCC Recording: 864-942-8613; Fax 864-942-8693. http://www.akanda.com/grnwood
Will not search UCC records. This agency will not do a tax lien search. Will not search real estate records. **Online Access:** Property Records. Records on the County Parcel Search database are available free online at www.akanda.com/grnwood/Search/search.htm. An interactive map is included. **Other Phone Numbers:** Assessor 864-942-8532; Treasurer 864-942-8528; Appraiser/Auditor 864-942-8532; Elections 864-942-8521.

Hampton County

Clerk of Court, Courthouse Square, Elm Street, Hampton, SC 29924. 803-943-7510; Fax 803-943-7596.
Will search UCC records. Will not search real estate records.

Horry County

Clerk of Court, P.O. Box 470, Conway, SC 29528. 843-248-1252; Fax 843-248-1566.
Will search UCC records. Will not search real estate records. **Other Phone Numbers:** Assessor 843-248-1361.

Jasper County

Clerk of Court, P.O. Box 248, Ridgeland, SC 29936. 843-726-7710; Fax 843-726-7782.
Will search UCC records. Will not search real estate records. **Other Phone Numbers:** Assessor 843-726-7725.

Kershaw County

Clerk of Court, P.O. Box 1557, Camden, SC 29020-1557. 803-425-1500; Fax 803-425-1505.

Will search UCC records. Tax liens not included in UCC search. Will not search real estate records. **Other Phone Numbers:** Assessor 803-425-1504.

Lancaster County

Clerk of Court, P.O. Box 1809, Lancaster, SC 29721. 803-285-1581; Fax 803-416-9388.
Will search UCC records. **Other Phone Numbers:** Assessor 803-285-6964; Treasurer 803-285-7939.

Laurens County

Clerk of Court, P.O. Box 287, Laurens, SC 29360. 864-984-3538.
Will search UCC records. This agency will not do a tax lien search. Will not search real estate records.

Lee County

Register of Deeds, P.O. Box 387, Bishopville, SC 29010. 803-484-5341 R/E Recording: 803-484-5341 x333 UCC Recording: 803-484-5341 x378; Fax 803-484-1632.
Will search UCC records. Will not search real estate records. **Other Phone Numbers:** Assessor 803-484-5341 x362; Treasurer 803-484-5341 x327.

Lexington County

Register of Deeds, 212 South Lake Drive, Lexington, SC 29072. 803-359-8404 R/E Recording: 803-359-8168 UCC Recording: 803-359-8168; Fax 803-359-8189. http://www.lex-co.com/my_lex.html
Will search UCC records. Will not search real estate records. **Online Access:** Tax Assessor. Online access to county Reassessment Information is available free at http://www.lex-co.com/my_lex.html. Click on "Assessment Information." **Other Phone Numbers:** Assessor 803-359-8190; Treasurer 803-359-8217.

Marion County

Clerk of Court, P.O. Box 295, Marion, SC 29571. 843-423-8240; Fax 843-423-8306.
Will search UCC records. This agency will not do a tax lien search. Will not search real estate records. **Other Phone Numbers:** Assessor 843-423-8225.

Marlboro County

Clerk of Court, P.O. Drawer 996, Bennettsville, SC 29512. 843-479-5613; Fax 843-479-5640.
Will search UCC records. UCC search includes tax liens if requested. Will not search real estate records.

McCormick County

Clerk of Court, 133 South Mine Street, Courthouse, Room 102, McCormick, SC 29835. 864-465-2195; Fax 864-465-0071.
Will search UCC records. Will not search real estate records. **Other Phone Numbers:** Assessor 864-465-2931; Treasurer 864-465-2332.

Newberry County

Court Clerk, P.O. Box 278, Newberry, SC 29108. Court Clerk, R/E and UCC Recording 803-321-2110; Fax 803-321-2111.
Will search UCC records. Will not search real estate records. **Other Phone Numbers:** Assessor 803-321-2125; Treasurer 803-321-2130.

Oconee County

Register of Deeds, 415 S Pine St, Walhalla, SC 29691. Register of Deeds, R/E and UCC Recording 864-638-4285.
Effective 7/2001, will not search UCC records. This agency will not do a tax lien search. Will not search real estate records. **Other Phone Numbers:** Assessor 864-638-4150; Treasurer 864-638-4162.

Orangeburg County

Clerk of Court, Box 9000, Orangeburg, SC 29116-9000. 803-533-6236; Fax 803-534-3848.
Will search UCC records. Will not search real estate records. **Other Phone Numbers:** Assessor 803-533-6220; Treasurer 803-533-6130.

Pickens County

Register of Deeds, 222 McDaniel Ave. B-5, Pickens, SC 29671. Register of Deeds, R/E and UCC Recording 864-898-5868; Fax 864-898-5924.
Will search UCC records prior to 7/2001. Search UCC records filed after 7/2001 at the Sec. of State's office only. Will not search real estate records. **Other Phone Numbers:** Assessor 864-898-5871; Treasurer 864-898-5883; Appraiser/Auditor 864-898-5878; Elections 864-898-5848; Vital Records 864-898-5965.

Richland County

Clerk of Court, P.O. Box 192, Columbia, SC 29202. 803-748-4800; Fax 803-748-4807.
Will search UCC records. Will not search real estate records. **Other Phone Numbers:** Assessor 803-748-5038.

Saluda County

Clerk of Court, Courthouse, Saluda, SC 29138. 864-445-3303; Fax 864-445-3772.
Will search UCC records. Will not search real estate records. **Other Phone Numbers:** Assessor 864-445-8121; Treasurer 864-445-2875.

Spartanburg County

County Register of Mesne Conveyances, 366 North Church Street, County Administrative Offices, Spartanburg, SC 29303. 864-596-2514.
Will search UCC records. This agency will not do a tax lien search. Will not search real estate records. **Other Phone Numbers:** Assessor 864-596-2544; Treasurer 864-596-2603.

Sumter County

Register of Deeds, Courthouse, Room 202, 141 N. Main St., Sumter, SC 29150. Register of Deeds, R/E and UCC Recording 803-436-2177 UCC Recording: 803-436-2179.
Will search UCC records. This agency will not do a tax lien search. Will not search real estate records. **Other Phone Numbers:** Assessor 803-436-2112; Treasurer 803-436-2213; Appraiser/Auditor 803-436-2112; Elections 803-436-2310.

Union County

Clerk of Court, P.O. Box 200, Union, SC 29379. 864-429-1630; Fax 864-429-1715.
Will search UCC records. This agency will not do a tax lien search. Will not search real estate records. **Other Phone Numbers:** Assessor 864-429-1650.

Williamsburg County

Clerk of Court, 125 West Main Street, Kingstree, SC 29556. 843-354-6855; Fax 843-354-5813.
Will search UCC records. Will not search real estate records. **Other Phone Numbers:** Assessor 843-354-7059.

York County

Clerk of Court, P.O. Box 649, York, SC 29745. 803-684-8510.
Will search UCC records. This agency will not do a tax lien search. Will not search real estate records. **Other Phone Numbers:** Assessor 803-684-8526; Treasurer 803-684-8528..

South Carolina County Locator

You will usually be able to find the city name in the City/County Cross Reference below. In that case, it is a simple matter to determine the county from the cross reference. However, only the official US Postal Service city names are included in this index. There are an additional 40,000 place names that people use in their addresses. Therefore, we have also included a ZIP/City Cross Reference immediately following the City/County Cross Reference.

If you know the ZIP Code but the city name does not appear in the City/County Cross Reference index, look up the ZIP Code in the ZIP/City Cross Reference, find the city name, then look up the city name in the City/County Cross Reference. For example, you want to know the county for an address of Menands, NY 12204. There is no "Menands" in the City/County Cross Reference. The ZIP/City Cross Reference shows that ZIP Codes 12201-12288 are for the city of Albany. Looking back in the City/County Cross Reference, Albany is in Albany County.

City/County Cross Reference

ABBEVILLE Abbeville
ADAMS RUN (29426) Charleston(76), Dorchester(24)
AIKEN Aiken
ALCOLU (29001) Clarendon(55), Sumter(45)
ALLENDALE Allendale
ANDERSON Anderson
ANDREWS (29510) Georgetown(75), Williamsburg(24)
ARCADIA Spartanburg
AWENDAW Charleston
AYNOR Horry
BALLENTINE Richland
BAMBERG Bamberg
BARNWELL Barnwell
BATESBURG (29006) Lexington(60), Aiken(20), Saluda(20)
BATH Aiken
BEAUFORT Beaufort
BEECH ISLAND Aiken
BELTON (29627) Anderson(94), Greenville(6)
BENNETTSVILLE Marlboro
BETHERA Berkeley
BETHUNE (29009) Kershaw(93), Chesterfield(4), Lee(4)
BISHOPVILLE (29010) Lee(99), Kershaw(2)
BLACKSBURG Cherokee
BLACKSTOCK (29014) Chester(70), Fairfield(30)
BLACKVILLE (29817) Barnwell(99), Bamberg(1)
BLAIR Fairfield
BLENHEIM Marlboro
BLUFFTON Beaufort
BLYTHEWOOD (29016) Richland(99), Fairfield(1)
BONNEAU Berkeley
BORDEN Sumter
BOWLING GREEN (29703) York(88), Cherokee(13)
BOWMAN (29018) Orangeburg(92), Dorchester(8)
BRADLEY (29819) Greenwood(98), McCormick(2)
BRANCHVILLE (29432) Orangeburg(86), Bamberg(7), Dorchester(7)
BRUNSON Hampton
BUFFALO Union
CADES (29518) Williamsburg(98), Clarendon(2)
CALHOUN FALLS (29628) Abbeville(98), McCormick(2)
CAMDEN (29020) Kershaw(98), Lee(2)
CAMERON (29030) Orangeburg(62), Calhoun(38)
CAMPOBELLO (29322) Spartanburg(98), Greenville(2)
CANADYS Colleton
CARLISLE (29031) Union(61), Chester(36), Fairfield(3)

CASSATT (29032) Kershaw(92), Lee(8)
CATAWBA York
CAYCE Lexington
CENTENARY Marion
CENTRAL (29630) Pickens(92), Anderson(8)
CHAPIN (29036) Lexington(74), Richland(21), Newberry(5)
CHAPPELLS (29037) Newberry(86), Saluda(12), Laurens(2)
CHARLESTON (29406) Charleston(75), Berkeley(25)
CHARLESTON (29414) Charleston(99), Dorchester(1)
CHARLESTON (29418) Charleston(78), Dorchester(22)
CHARLESTON (29420) Dorchester(53), Charleston(47)
CHARLESTON Berkeley
CHARLESTON Charleston
CHARLESTON AFB Charleston
CHERAW Chesterfield
CHEROKEE FALLS Cherokee
CHESNEE (29323) Spartanburg(88), Cherokee(12)
CHESTER Chester
CHESTERFIELD Chesterfield
CLARKS HILL (29821) McCormick(90), Edgefield(10)
CLEARWATER Aiken
CLEMSON Pickens
CLEVELAND (29635) Greenville(72), Pickens(28)
CLIFTON Spartanburg
CLINTON Laurens
CLIO (29525) Marlboro(98), Dillon(2)
CLOVER York
COLUMBIA (29210) Richland(70), Lexington(30)
COLUMBIA (29212) Lexington(89), Richland(11)
COLUMBIA Lexington
COLUMBIA Richland
CONESTEE Greenville
CONVERSE Spartanburg
CONWAY Horry
COOSAWATCHIE Jasper
COPE Orangeburg
CORDESVILLE Berkeley
CORDOVA Orangeburg
COTTAGEVILLE Colleton
COWARD Florence
COWPENS (29330) Spartanburg(65), Cherokee(35)
CROCKETVILLE Hampton
CROSS (29436) Berkeley(96), Orangeburg(4)
CROSS ANCHOR Spartanburg
CROSS HILL Laurens
DALE Beaufort
DALZELL (29040) Sumter(91), Lee(9)
DARLINGTON Darlington
DAUFUSKIE ISLAND Beaufort

DAVIS STATION Clarendon
DENMARK Bamberg
DILLON Dillon
DONALDS (29638) Abbeville(88), Greenwood(12)
DORCHESTER Dorchester
DRAYTON Spartanburg
DUE WEST Abbeville
DUNCAN Spartanburg
EARLY BRANCH (29916) Hampton(57), Jasper(43)
EASLEY (29642) Pickens(69), Anderson(31)
EASLEY Pickens
EASTOVER Richland
EDGEFIELD Edgefield
EDGEMOOR Chester
EDISTO ISLAND (29438) Colleton(60), Charleston(40)
EFFINGHAM Florence
EHRHARDT (29081) Bamberg(79), Colleton(21)
ELGIN (29045) Kershaw(60), Richland(39), Fairfield(1)
ELKO Barnwell
ELLIOTT Lee
ELLOREE (29047) Orangeburg(77), Calhoun(23)
ENOREE (29335) Spartanburg(86), Union(8), Laurens(7)
ESTILL Hampton
EUTAWVILLE Orangeburg
FAIR PLAY (29643) Oconee(80), Anderson(20)
FAIRFAX (29827) Allendale(96), Hampton(4)
FAIRFOREST Spartanburg
FINGERVILLE Spartanburg
FLORENCE (29501) Florence(91), Darlington(9)
FLORENCE Florence
FLOYD DALE Dillon
FOLLY BEACH Charleston
FORK Dillon
FORT LAWN Chester
FORT MILL (29715) York(98), Lancaster(2)
FORT MILL York
FOUNTAIN INN (29644) Greenville(61), Laurens(39)
FURMAN Hampton
GABLE (29051) Sumter(81), Clarendon(19)
GADSDEN Richland
GAFFNEY Cherokee
GALIVANTS FERRY Horry
GARNETT (29922) Hampton(57), Jasper(43)
GASTON (29053) Lexington(92), Calhoun(8)
GEORGETOWN Georgetown
GIFFORD Hampton
GILBERT Lexington
GLENDALE Spartanburg
GLOVERVILLE Aiken

GOOSE CREEK Berkeley
GRAMLING Spartanburg
GRANITEVILLE Aiken
GRAY COURT Laurens
GREAT FALLS (29055) Chester(91), Fairfield(9)
GREELEYVILLE (29056) Williamsburg(90), Clarendon(10)
GREEN POND Colleton
GREEN SEA Horry
GREENVILLE (29611) Greenville(95), Anderson(3), Pickens(2)
GREENVILLE Greenville
GREENWOOD (29649) Greenwood(99), Abbeville(1)
GREENWOOD Greenwood
GREER (29650) Greenville(99), Spartanburg(1)
GREER (29651) Greenville(52), Spartanburg(48)
GREER Greenville
GRESHAM Marion
GROVER Dorchester
HAMER Dillon
HAMPTON Hampton
HARDEEVILLE (29927) Jasper(99), Beaufort(1)
HARLEYVILLE Dorchester
HARTSVILLE (29550) Darlington(95), Chesterfield(4), Lee(1)
HARTSVILLE Darlington
HEATH SPRINGS (29058) Lancaster(94), Kershaw(6)
HEMINGWAY (29554) Georgetown(78), Williamsburg(20), Florence(2)
HICKORY GROVE York
HILDA Barnwell
HILTON HEAD ISLAND Beaufort
HODGES (29653) Greenwood(91), Abbeville(9)
HODGES Greenwood
HOLLY HILL (29059) Orangeburg(97), Berkeley(4)
HOLLYWOOD Charleston
HONEA PATH (29654) Anderson(59), Abbeville(32), Greenville(8), Laurens(2)
HOPKINS Richland
HORATIO Sumter
HUGER Berkeley
INMAN Spartanburg
IRMO (29063) Richland(92), Lexington(8)
ISLANDTON Colleton
ISLE OF PALMS Charleston
IVA (29655) Anderson(56), Abbeville(44)
JACKSON Aiken
JACKSONBORO Colleton
JAMESTOWN Berkeley
JEFFERSON Chesterfield
JENKINSVILLE Fairfield
JOANNA Laurens
JOHNS ISLAND Charleston
JOHNSONVILLE (29555) Florence(99), Williamsburg(1)

JOHNSTON (29832) Edgefield(93), Saluda(7)
JONESVILLE Union
KERSHAW (29067) Lancaster(74), Kershaw(26)
KINARDS (29355) Newberry(79), Laurens(22)
KINGS CREEK Cherokee
KINGSTREE Williamsburg
KLINE Barnwell
LA FRANCE Anderson
LADSON (29456) Berkeley(45), Dorchester(35), Charleston(20)
LAKE CITY (29560) Florence(91), Williamsburg(6), Clarendon(3)
LAKE VIEW Dillon
LAMAR (29069) Darlington(96), Lee(5)
LANCASTER Lancaster
LANDO Chester
LANDRUM (29356) Spartanburg(60), Greenville(40)
LANE Williamsburg
LANGLEY Aiken
LATTA (29565) Dillon(87), Marion(11), Marlboro(2)
LAURENS Laurens
LEESVILLE (29070) Lexington(84), Saluda(16)
LEXINGTON Lexington
LIBERTY (29657) Pickens(88), Anderson(13)
LIBERTY HILL Kershaw
LITTLE MOUNTAIN (29075) Newberry(80), Richland(13), Lexington(7)
LITTLE RIVER Horry
LITTLE ROCK Dillon
LIVINGSTON Orangeburg
LOBECO Beaufort
LOCKHART Union
LODGE (29082) Colleton(92), Bamberg(8)
LONE STAR Calhoun
LONG CREEK Oconee
LONGS Horry
LORIS Horry
LOWNDESVILLE Abbeville
LUGOFF (29078) Kershaw(96), Richland(4)
LURAY (29932) Hampton(52), Allendale(48)
LYDIA Darlington
LYMAN Spartanburg
LYNCHBURG (29080) Sumter(76), Lee(24)
MANNING (99999) Clarendon(99), Sumter(1)
MARIETTA (29661) Greenville(76), Pickens(24)
MARION Marion
MARTIN (29836) Allendale(89), Barnwell(11)
MAULDIN Greenville
MAYESVILLE (29104) Sumter(77), Lee(23)
MAYO Spartanburg
MC BEE (29101) Darlington(54), Chesterfield(28), Chester(19)
MC CLELLANVILLE Charleston
MC COLL Marlboro
MC CONNELLS York
MC CORMICK McCormick
MILEY Hampton
MINTURN Dillon
MODOC (29838) McCormick(82), Edgefield(18)

MONCKS CORNER Berkeley
MONETTA (29105) Aiken(77), Saluda(23)
MONTICELLO Fairfield
MONTMORENCI Aiken
MOORE Spartanburg
MOUNT CARMEL McCormick
MOUNT CROGHAN Chesterfield
MOUNT PLEASANT Charleston
MOUNTAIN REST Oconee
MOUNTVILLE Laurens
MULLINS Marion
MURRELLS INLET (29576) Horry(53), Georgetown(47)
MYRTLE BEACH Horry
NEESES Orangeburg
NESMITH Williamsburg
NEW ELLENTON Aiken
NEW ZION (29111) Clarendon(93), Williamsburg(7)
NEWBERRY Newberry
NEWRY Oconee
NICHOLS (29581) Horry(87), Dillon(11), Marion(3)
NINETY SIX (29666) Greenwood(98), Saluda(2)
NORRIS Pickens
NORTH (29112) Orangeburg(95), Lexington(3), Calhoun(2)
NORTH AUGUSTA (29860) Edgefield(67), Aiken(33)
NORTH AUGUSTA Aiken
NORTH MYRTLE BEACH (29598) Horry(94), Florence(6)
NORTH MYRTLE BEACH Horry
NORWAY Orangeburg
OLANTA (29114) Florence(56), Sumter(43), Clarendon(1)
OLAR (29843) Bamberg(51), Barnwell(49)
ORANGEBURG (29118) Orangeburg(99), Calhoun(1)
ORANGEBURG Orangeburg
PACOLET (29372) Spartanburg(70), Union(16), Cherokee(14)
PACOLET MILLS Spartanburg
PAGELAND Chesterfield
PAMPLICO Florence
PARKSVILLE McCormick
PATRICK Chesterfield
PAULINE (29374) Spartanburg(94), Union(6)
PAWLEYS ISLAND Georgetown
PEAK Newberry
PELION Lexington
PELZER (29669) Anderson(67), Greenville(33)
PENDLETON (29670) Anderson(99), Pickens(1)
PERRY Aiken
PICKENS Pickens
PIEDMONT (29673) Greenville(50), Anderson(50)
PINELAND (29934) Jasper(79), Hampton(21)
PINEVILLE Berkeley
PINEWOOD (29125) Sumter(65), Clarendon(35)
PINOPOLIS Berkeley
PLUM BRANCH (29845) McCormick(97), Edgefield(3)
POMARIA Newberry
PORT ROYAL Beaufort

POSTON Florence
PROSPERITY (29127) Newberry(98), Saluda(2)
RAINS Marion
RAVENEL (29470) Charleston(87), Dorchester(13)
REEVESVILLE Dorchester
REIDVILLE Spartanburg
REMBERT (29128) Sumter(86), Kershaw(8), Lee(6)
RICHBURG Chester
RICHLAND Oconee
RIDGE SPRING (29129) Aiken(51), Saluda(36), Edgefield(13)
RIDGELAND (29936) Jasper(88), Beaufort(12)
RIDGEVILLE (29472) Dorchester(62), Colleton(22), Berkeley(16)
RIDGEWAY (29130) Fairfield(51), Kershaw(44), Richland(5)
RIMINI (29131) Sumter(65), Clarendon(35)
RION Fairfield
ROCK HILL York
ROEBUCK Spartanburg
ROUND O Colleton
ROWESVILLE Orangeburg
RUBY Chesterfield
RUFFIN Colleton
RUSSELLVILLE Berkeley
SAINT GEORGE Dorchester
SAINT HELENA ISLAND Beaufort
SAINT MATTHEWS (29135) Calhoun(95), Orangeburg(5)
SAINT STEPHEN Berkeley
SALEM Oconee
SALLEY (29137) Aiken(84), Orangeburg(16)
SALTERS Williamsburg
SALUDA (29138) Saluda(94), Greenwood(4), Aiken(2)
SANDY SPRINGS Anderson
SANTEE Orangeburg
SARDINIA Clarendon
SCOTIA Hampton
SCRANTON Florence
SEABROOK Beaufort
SELLERS (29592) Dillon(81), Marion(19)
SENECA Oconee
SHARON York
SHAW A F B Sumter
SHELDON Beaufort
SILVERSTREET Newberry
SIMPSONVILLE Greenville
SIX MILE Pickens
SLATER Greenville
SMOAKS (29481) Colleton(94), Bamberg(6)
SMYRNA York
SOCIETY HILL (29593) Darlington(89), Chesterfield(11)
SPARTANBURG (29307) Spartanburg(97), Cherokee(3)
SPARTANBURG Spartanburg
SPRINGFIELD (29146) Orangeburg(73), Aiken(27)
STARR Anderson
STARTEX Spartanburg
STATE PARK Richland
SULLIVANS ISLAND Charleston
SUMMERTON Clarendon

SUMMERVILLE (29483) Dorchester(70), Berkeley(30)
SUMMERVILLE (29485) Dorchester(90), Charleston(10)
SUMMERVILLE Dorchester
SUMTER (29153) Sumter(96), Lee(4)
SUMTER Sumter
SUNSET Pickens
SWANSEA (29160) Lexington(67), Calhoun(32), Orangeburg(1)
SYCAMORE Allendale
TAMASSEE Oconee
TATUM Marlboro
TAYLORS Greenville
TIGERVILLE Greenville
TILLMAN Jasper
TIMMONSVILLE (29161) Florence(81), Darlington(19)
TOWNVILLE (29689) Anderson(89), Oconee(11)
TRAVELERS REST Greenville
TRENTON (29847) Edgefield(54), Aiken(46)
TRIO Williamsburg
TROY (29848) Greenwood(88), McCormick(10), Saluda(2)
TURBEVILLE (29162) Clarendon(99), Sumter(2)
ULMER (29849) Allendale(83), Barnwell(17)
UNA Spartanburg
UNION Union
VAN WYCK Lancaster
VANCE Orangeburg
VARNVILLE (29944) Hampton(93), Jasper(7)
VAUCLUSE Aiken
WADMALAW ISLAND Charleston
WAGENER Aiken
WALHALLA Oconee
WALLACE Marlboro
WALTERBORO Colleton
WARD Saluda
WARE SHOALS (29692) Greenwood(42), Laurens(41), Abbeville(17)
WARRENVILLE Aiken
WATERLOO Laurens
WEDGEFIELD Sumter
WELLFORD Spartanburg
WEST COLUMBIA Lexington
WEST UNION Oconee
WESTMINSTER Oconee
WESTVILLE Kershaw
WHITE OAK Fairfield
WHITE ROCK Richland
WHITE STONE Spartanburg
WHITMIRE (29178) Newberry(82), Union(17), Laurens(1)
WILLIAMS Colleton
WILLIAMSTON Anderson
WILLISTON (29853) Barnwell(53), Aiken(47)
WINDSOR Aiken
WINNSBORO (29180) Fairfield(94), Richland(6)
WISACKY Lee
WOODRUFF (29388) Spartanburg(98), Laurens(2)
YEMASSEE (29945) Colleton(61), Beaufort(24), Hampton(9), Jasper(6)
YORK York

ZIP/City Cross Reference

29001-29001	ALCOLU	29015-29015	BLAIR	29033-29033	CAYCE	29042-29042	DENMARK
29002-29002	BALLENTINE	29016-29016	BLYTHEWOOD	29036-29036	CHAPIN	29044-29044	EASTOVER
29003-29003	BAMBERG	29018-29018	BOWMAN	29037-29037	CHAPPELLS	29045-29045	ELGIN
29006-29006	BATESBURG	29020-29020	CAMDEN	29038-29038	COPE	29046-29046	ELLIOTT
29009-29009	BETHUNE	29030-29030	CAMERON	29039-29039	CORDOVA	29047-29047	ELLOREE
29010-29010	BISHOPVILLE	29031-29031	CARLISLE	29040-29040	DALZELL	29048-29048	EUTAWVILLE
29014-29014	BLACKSTOCK	29032-29032	CASSATT	29041-29041	DAVIS STATION	29051-29051	GABLE

ZIP	City	ZIP	City	ZIP	City	ZIP	City
29052-29052	GADSDEN	29333-29333	DRAYTON	29511-29511	AYNOR	29666-29666	NINETY SIX
29053-29053	GASTON	29334-29334	DUNCAN	29512-29512	BENNETTSVILLE	29667-29667	NORRIS
29054-29054	GILBERT	29335-29335	ENOREE	29516-29516	BLENHEIM	29669-29669	PELZER
29055-29055	GREAT FALLS	29336-29336	FAIRFOREST	29518-29518	CADES	29670-29670	PENDLETON
29056-29056	GREELEYVILLE	29338-29338	FINGERVILLE	29519-29519	CENTENARY	29671-29671	PICKENS
29058-29058	HEATH SPRINGS	29340-29342	GAFFNEY	29520-29520	CHERAW	29672-29672	SENECA
29059-29059	HOLLY HILL	29346-29346	GLENDALE	29525-29525	CLIO	29673-29673	PIEDMONT
29061-29061	HOPKINS	29348-29348	GRAMLING	29526-29528	CONWAY	29675-29675	RICHLAND
29062-29062	HORATIO	29349-29349	INMAN	29530-29530	COWARD	29676-29676	SALEM
29063-29063	IRMO	29351-29351	JOANNA	29532-29532	DARLINGTON	29677-29677	SANDY SPRINGS
29065-29065	JENKINSVILLE	29353-29353	JONESVILLE	29536-29536	DILLON	29678-29679	SENECA
29067-29067	KERSHAW	29355-29355	KINARDS	29540-29540	DARLINGTON	29680-29681	SIMPSONVILLE
29069-29069	LAMAR	29356-29356	LANDRUM	29541-29541	EFFINGHAM	29682-29682	SIX MILE
29070-29070	LEESVILLE	29360-29360	LAURENS	29542-29542	FLOYD DALE	29683-29683	SLATER
29071-29073	LEXINGTON	29364-29364	LOCKHART	29543-29543	FORK	29684-29684	STARR
29074-29074	LIBERTY HILL	29365-29365	LYMAN	29544-29544	GALIVANTS FERRY	29685-29685	SUNSET
29075-29075	LITTLE MOUNTAIN	29368-29368	MAYO	29545-29545	GREEN SEA	29686-29686	TAMASSEE
29078-29078	LUGOFF	29369-29369	MOORE	29546-29546	GRESHAM	29687-29687	TAYLORS
29079-29079	LYDIA	29370-29370	MOUNTVILLE	29547-29547	HAMER	29688-29688	TIGERVILLE
29080-29080	LYNCHBURG	29372-29372	PACOLET	29550-29551	HARTSVILLE	29689-29689	TOWNVILLE
29081-29081	EHRHARDT	29373-29373	PACOLET MILLS	29554-29554	HEMINGWAY	29690-29690	TRAVELERS REST
29082-29082	LODGE	29374-29374	PAULINE	29555-29555	JOHNSONVILLE	29691-29691	WALHALLA
29101-29101	MC BEE	29375-29375	REIDVILLE	29556-29556	KINGSTREE	29692-29692	WARE SHOALS
29102-29102	MANNING	29376-29376	ROEBUCK	29560-29560	LAKE CITY	29693-29693	WESTMINSTER
29104-29104	MAYESVILLE	29377-29377	STARTEX	29563-29563	LAKE VIEW	29695-29695	HODGES
29105-29105	MONETTA	29378-29378	UNA	29564-29564	LANE	29696-29696	WEST UNION
29106-29106	MONTICELLO	29379-29379	UNION	29565-29565	LATTA	29697-29697	WILLIAMSTON
29107-29107	NEESES	29384-29384	WATERLOO	29566-29566	LITTLE RIVER	29698-29698	GREENVILLE
29108-29108	NEWBERRY	29385-29385	WELLFORD	29567-29567	LITTLE ROCK	29702-29702	BLACKSBURG
29111-29111	NEW ZION	29386-29386	WHITE STONE	29568-29568	LONGS	29703-29703	BOWLING GREEN
29112-29112	NORTH	29388-29388	WOODRUFF	29569-29569	LORIS	29704-29704	CATAWBA
29113-29113	NORWAY	29390-29391	DUNCAN	29570-29570	MC COLL	29706-29706	CHESTER
29114-29114	OLANTA	29401-29403	CHARLESTON	29571-29571	MARION	29709-29709	CHESTERFIELD
29115-29118	ORANGEBURG	29404-29404	CHARLESTON AFB	29572-29572	MYRTLE BEACH	29710-29710	CLOVER
29122-29122	PEAK	29405-29425	CHARLESTON	29573-29573	MINTURN	29712-29712	EDGEMOOR
29123-29123	PELION	29426-29426	ADAMS RUN	29574-29574	MULLINS	29714-29714	FORT LAWN
29124-29124	PERRY	29429-29429	AWENDAW	29575-29575	MYRTLE BEACH	29715-29716	FORT MILL
29125-29125	PINEWOOD	29430-29430	BETHERA	29576-29576	MURRELLS INLET	29717-29717	HICKORY GROVE
29126-29126	POMARIA	29431-29431	BONNEAU	29577-29579	MYRTLE BEACH	29718-29718	JEFFERSON
29127-29127	PROSPERITY	29432-29432	BRANCHVILLE	29580-29580	NESMITH	29719-29719	KINGS CREEK
29128-29128	REMBERT	29433-29433	CANADYS	29581-29581	NICHOLS	29720-29722	LANCASTER
29129-29129	RIDGE SPRING	29434-29434	CORDESVILLE	29582-29582	NORTH MYRTLE BEACH	29724-29724	LANDO
29130-29130	RIDGEWAY	29435-29435	COTTAGEVILLE	29583-29583	PAMPLICO	29726-29726	MC CONNELLS
29132-29132	RION	29436-29436	CROSS	29584-29584	PATRICK	29727-29727	MOUNT CROGHAN
29133-29133	ROWESVILLE	29437-29437	DORCHESTER	29585-29585	PAWLEYS ISLAND	29728-29728	PAGELAND
29135-29135	SAINT MATTHEWS	29438-29438	EDISTO ISLAND	29587-29587	MYRTLE BEACH	29729-29729	RICHBURG
29137-29137	SALLEY	29439-29439	FOLLY BEACH	29589-29589	RAINS	29730-29734	ROCK HILL
29138-29138	SALUDA	29440-29442	GEORGETOWN	29590-29590	SALTERS	29741-29741	RUBY
29142-29142	SANTEE	29445-29445	GOOSE CREEK	29591-29591	SCRANTON	29742-29742	SHARON
29143-29143	SARDINIA	29446-29446	GREEN POND	29592-29592	SELLERS	29743-29743	SMYRNA
29145-29145	SILVERSTREET	29447-29447	GROVER	29593-29593	SOCIETY HILL	29744-29744	VAN WYCK
29146-29146	SPRINGFIELD	29448-29448	HARLEYVILLE	29594-29594	TATUM	29745-29745	YORK
29147-29147	STATE PARK	29449-29449	HOLLYWOOD	29596-29596	WALLACE	29801-29808	AIKEN
29148-29148	SUMMERTON	29450-29450	HUGER	29597-29598	NORTH MYRTLE BEACH	29809-29809	NEW ELLENTON
29150-29151	SUMTER	29451-29451	ISLE OF PALMS	29601-29617	GREENVILLE	29810-29810	ALLENDALE
29152-29152	SHAW A F B	29452-29452	JACKSONBORO	29620-29620	ABBEVILLE	29812-29812	BARNWELL
29153-29154	SUMTER	29453-29453	JAMESTOWN	29621-29626	ANDERSON	29813-29813	HILDA
29160-29160	SWANSEA	29455-29455	JOHNS ISLAND	29627-29627	BELTON	29814-29814	KLINE
29161-29161	TIMMONSVILLE	29456-29456	LADSON	29628-29628	CALHOUN FALLS	29816-29816	BATH
29162-29162	TURBEVILLE	29457-29457	JOHNS ISLAND	29630-29630	CENTRAL	29817-29817	BLACKVILLE
29163-29163	VANCE	29458-29458	MC CLELLANVILLE	29631-29634	CLEMSON	29819-29819	BRADLEY
29164-29164	WAGENER	29461-29461	MONCKS CORNER	29635-29635	CLEVELAND	29821-29821	CLARKS HILL
29166-29166	WARD	29464-29465	MOUNT PLEASANT	29636-29636	CONESTEE	29822-29822	CLEARWATER
29168-29168	WEDGEFIELD	29468-29468	PINEVILLE	29638-29638	DONALDS	29824-29824	EDGEFIELD
29169-29172	WEST COLUMBIA	29469-29469	PINOPOLIS	29639-29639	DUE WEST	29826-29826	ELKO
29175-29175	WESTVILLE	29470-29470	RAVENEL	29640-29642	EASLEY	29827-29827	FAIRFAX
29176-29176	WHITE OAK	29471-29471	REEVESVILLE	29643-29643	FAIR PLAY	29828-29828	GLOVERVILLE
29177-29177	WHITE ROCK	29472-29472	RIDGEVILLE	29644-29644	FOUNTAIN INN	29829-29829	GRANITEVILLE
29178-29178	WHITMIRE	29474-29474	ROUND O	29645-29645	GRAY COURT	29831-29831	JACKSON
29180-29180	WINNSBORO	29475-29475	RUFFIN	29646-29649	GREENWOOD	29832-29832	JOHNSTON
29201-29292	COLUMBIA	29476-29476	RUSSELLVILLE	29650-29652	GREER	29834-29834	LANGLEY
29301-29319	SPARTANBURG	29477-29477	SAINT GEORGE	29653-29653	HODGES	29835-29835	MC CORMICK
29320-29320	ARCADIA	29479-29479	SAINT STEPHEN	29654-29654	HONEA PATH	29836-29836	MARTIN
29321-29321	BUFFALO	29481-29481	SMOAKS	29655-29655	IVA	29838-29838	MODOC
29322-29322	CAMPOBELLO	29482-29482	SULLIVANS ISLAND	29656-29656	LA FRANCE	29839-29839	MONTMORENCI
29323-29323	CHESNEE	29483-29485	SUMMERVILLE	29657-29657	LIBERTY	29840-29840	MOUNT CARMEL
29324-29324	CLIFTON	29487-29487	WADMALAW ISLAND	29658-29658	LONG CREEK	29841-29841	NORTH AUGUSTA
29325-29325	CLINTON	29488-29488	WALTERBORO	29659-29659	LOWNDESVILLE	29842-29842	BEECH ISLAND
29329-29329	CONVERSE	29492-29492	CHARLESTON	29661-29661	MARIETTA	29843-29843	OLAR
29330-29330	COWPENS	29493-29493	WILLIAMS	29662-29662	MAULDIN	29844-29844	PARKSVILLE
29331-29331	CROSS ANCHOR	29501-29506	FLORENCE	29664-29664	MOUNTAIN REST	29845-29845	PLUM BRANCH
29332-29332	CROSS HILL	29510-29510	ANDREWS	29665-29665	NEWRY	29846-29846	SYCAMORE

29847-29847	TRENTON	29910-29910	BLUFFTON	29922-29922	GARNETT	29934-29934	PINELAND
29848-29848	TROY	29911-29911	BRUNSON	29923-29923	GIFFORD	29935-29935	PORT ROYAL
29849-29849	ULMER	29912-29912	COOSAWATCHIE	29924-29924	HAMPTON	29936-29936	RIDGELAND
29850-29850	VAUCLUSE	29913-29913	CROCKETVILLE	29925-29926	HILTON HEAD ISLAND	29938-29938	HILTON HEAD ISLAND
29851-29851	WARRENVILLE	29914-29914	DALE	29927-29927	HARDEEVILLE	29939-29939	SCOTIA
29853-29853	WILLISTON	29915-29915	DAUFUSKIE ISLAND	29928-29928	HILTON HEAD ISLAND	29940-29940	SEABROOK
29856-29856	WINDSOR	29916-29916	EARLY BRANCH	29929-29929	ISLANDTON	29941-29941	SHELDON
29860-29861	NORTH AUGUSTA	29918-29918	ESTILL	29931-29931	LOBECO	29943-29943	TILLMAN
29899-29899	MC CORMICK	29920-29920	SAINT HELENA ISLAND	29932-29932	LURAY	29944-29944	VARNVILLE
29901-29906	BEAUFORT	29921-29921	FURMAN	29933-29933	MILEY	29945-29945	YEMASSEE

South Dakota

General Help Numbers:

Governor's Office
State Capitol, 500 E Capitol Ave   605-773-3212
Pierre, SD 57501-5070   Fax 605-773-4711
http://www.state.sd.us/governor/index.htm   8AM-5PM

Attorney General's Office
State Capitol, 500 E Capitol Ave   605-773-3215
Pierre, SD 57501-5070   Fax 605-773-4106
http://www.state.sd.us/attorney/index.html   8AM-5PM

State Court Administrator
State Capitol Bldg   605-773-3474
500 E Capitol Ave   Fax 605-773-5627
Pierre, SD 57501-5059   8AM-5PM
http://www.state.sd.us/state/judicial

State Archives
Cultural Heritage Center/State Archives   605-773-3804
900 Governors Dr   Fax 605-773-6041
Pierre, SD 57501-2217   9AM-4:30PM
http://www.state.sd.us/deca/cultural/archives.htm

State Specifics:

Capital: Pierre
         Hughes County

Time Zone: CST*
* South Dakota's eighteen western-most counties are MST: They are: Bennett, Butte, Corson, Custer, Dewey, Fall River, Haakon, Harding, Jackson, Lawrence, Meade, Mellette, Pennington, Perkins, Shannon, Stanley, Todd, Ziebach,

Number of Counties: 66

Population: 754,844

Web Site: www.state.sd.us

State Agencies

Criminal Records

Division of Criminal Investigation, Identification Section, 500 E Capitol, Pierre, SD 57501-5070; 605-773-3331, 605-773-4629 (Fax), 8AM-5PM.

http://www.state.sd.us/attorney/attorney.html

Note: The state Court Administrator's Office has a statewide database of criminal record information from the state's circuit courts. For more information about setting up a commercial account, contact Jill Smith at 605-773-3474.

Indexing & Storage: Records are available for 10 years for misdemeanors and lifetime for felonies. Records are indexed on inhouse computer.

Searching: Include the following in your request- date of birth, full name, set of fingerprints, signed release form. The form requires identifying information: color of hair and eyes, height, weight, date of birth, Social Security Number. The following data is not released: juvenile records, minor traffic violations or out-of-state or federal charges.

Access by: mail.

Fee & Payment: The fee is $15.00 per name. Fee payee: Division of Criminal Investigation. Prepayment required. Personal checks accepted. No credit cards accepted.

Mail search: Turnaround time: 5 to 10 working days. Upon receipt of those requirements, they will conduct a search of their files and supply a copy of any criminal history that is found or a statement that there is no criminal history. A self addressed stamped envelope is requested.

Corporation Records
Limited Partnerships
Limited Liability Company Records
Trademarks/Servicemarks

Corporation Division, Secretary of State, 500 E Capitol Ave, Suite B-05, Pierre, SD 57501-5070; 605-773-4845, 605-773-5666 (Trademarks), 605-773-4550 (Fax), 8AM-5PM.

http://www.state.sd.us/sos/sos.htm

Indexing & Storage: Records are available from the founding of the state. New records are available for inquiry immediately. Records are indexed on microfiche, inhouse computer.

Searching: Trademarks may be search via e-mail at kea.warne@state.sd.us. Include the following in your request-full name of business. In addition to the articles of incorporation, corporation records include the following information: Annual Reports, Officers, Directors, Prior (merged) names, Inactive and Reserved names.

Access by: mail, phone, in person.

Fee & Payment: There is no fee for a general search. A Certificate of Good Standing is available for a fee of $10.00. Copies are $1.00 per page, add $5.00 for certification. Fee payee: Secretary of State. Prepayment required. Personal checks accepted. Credit cards accepted: MasterCard, Visa.

Mail search: Turnaround time: 1 to 3 days. A self addressed stamped envelope is requested.

Phone search: They will provide basic information only.

In person search: Turnaround time is immediate.

Expedited service: Expedited service is available for mail and phone searches. Add $10.00 per request.

Fictitious Name
Assumed Name
Records not maintained by a state level agency.

Note: Records are located at the county level.

Uniform Commercial Code
Federal Tax Liens

UCC Division, Secretary of State, 500 East Capitol, Pierre, SD 57501-5077; 605-773-4422, 605-773-4550 (Fax), 8AM-5PM.

http://www.state.sd.us/sos/sos.htm

Indexing & Storage: Records are available for all active records. Records are indexed on computer.

Searching: Use search request form UCC-11. The search includes federal tax liens on businesses. Federal tax liens on businesses and all state tax liens on individuals are filed at the county level. Include the following in your request-debtor name.

Access by: mail, phone, fax, in person, online.

Fee & Payment: The fee is $10.00 per debtor name, copies are $1.00 per page. Fee payee: Secretary of State. Prepayment required. Credit cards accepted: MasterCard, Visa.

Mail search: Turnaround time: 1 to 2 days. A self addressed stamped envelope is requested.

Phone search: Limited information is given over the phone. Reports can be ordered.

Fax search: Use of a credit card is required.

In person search: Searching is available in person.

Online search: Dakota Fast File is the filing and searching service available from the web site. This is a commercial service that requires registration and a $360 fee per year. A certified search is also available.

Expedited service: Expedited service is available for mail, phone and fax searches. Turnaround time: 1 day. Add $10.00 per debtor name.

State Tax Liens
Records not maintained by a state level agency.

Note: Records are filed at the county level.

Sales Tax Registrations

Revenue Department, Business Tax Division, 445 E Capitol, Pierre, SD 57501-3100; 605-773-3311, 605-773-5129 (Fax), 8AM-5PM.

http://www.state.sd.us/revenue

Indexing & Storage: Records are available from 1990 on computer. Records have been placed on microfilm from 1970 to 1996.

Searching: This agency will only confirm if a business is registered and licensed. They will provide no other information. Include the following in your request-business name. Also search by tax permit number or owner name.

Access by: mail, phone, fax, in person.

Mail search: Turnaround time: 2 to 3 weeks. A self addressed stamped envelope is requested. No fee for mail request.

Phone search: No fee for telephone request.

Fax search: There is no fee, turnaround time is 2-3 weeks.

In person search: No fee for request. Usually requests can be processed while you wait.

Birth Certificates

South Dakota Department of Health, Vital Records, 600 E Capitol, Pierre, SD 57501-2536; 605-773-4961, 605-773-5683 (Fax), 8AM-5PM.

http://www.state.sd.us/doh/VitalRec/index.htm

Indexing & Storage: Records are available from 1905 to present. New records are available for inquiry immediately.

Searching: Include the following in your request-full name, names of parents, mother's maiden name, date of birth, place of birth. Any county Register of Deeds can provide a computer generated birth certificate for the same fee. The following data is not released: sealed records.

Access by: mail, phone, in person, online.

Fee & Payment: The fee is $10.00. Use of a credit card is an additional $10.00 expedited fee. Fee payee: South Dakota Department of Health. Prepayment required. Personal checks accepted. Credit cards accepted: MasterCard, Visa, AmEx, Discover.

Mail search: Turnaround time: 2 to 3 days. No self addressed stamped envelope is required.

Phone search: You must use a credit card, considered expedited service.

In person search: Turnaround time 30 minutes.

Online search: You can search free at the web site for birth records over 100 years old. You can order recent (less than 100 years) birth records at the web site, for a fee.

Expedited service: Expedited service is available for web and phone searches. Turnaround time: overnight delivery. Add $19.50 for delivery and use of credit card.

Death Records

South Dakota Department of Health, Vital Records, 600 E Capitol, Pierre, SD 57501-2536; 605-773-4961, 605-773-5683 (Fax), 8AM-5PM.

http://www.state.sd.us/doh/VitalRec/index.htm

Indexing & Storage: Records are available from 1905 to present. New records are available for inquiry immediately.

Searching: Include the following in your request-full name, date of death, place of death. The following data is not released: sealed records.

Access by: mail, phone, in person, online.

Fee & Payment: The fee is $10.00 per record. There is an additional $10.00 fee if a credit card is used. Fee payee: South Dakota Department of Health. Prepayment required. Personal checks accepted. Credit cards accepted: MasterCard, Visa, AmEx, Discover.

Mail search: Turnaround time: 2 to 3 days. No self addressed stamped envelope is required.

Phone search: You must use a credit card.

In person search: Turnaround time is 30 minutes.

Online search: Records may be ordered online at the web site.

Expedited service: Expedited service is available for Internet and phone searches. Turnaround time: overnight delivery. Add $19.50 for delivery and fee for credit card use.

Marriage Certificates

South Dakota Department of Health, Vital Records, 600 E Capitol, Pierre, SD 57501-2536; 605-773-4961, 605-773-5683 (Fax), 8AM-5PM.

http://www.state.sd.us/doh/VitalRec/index.htm

Indexing & Storage: Records are available from 1905 to present. New records are available for inquiry immediately.

Searching: Include the following in your request-names of husband and wife, date of marriage, place or county of marriage. Also include wife's maiden name.

Access by: mail, phone, in person, online.

Fee & Payment: The fee is $7.00 per record. There is an additional $10.00 expedited fee if a credit card is used. Fee payee: South Dakota Department of Health. Prepayment required. Personal checks accepted. Credit cards accepted: MasterCard, Visa, AmEx, Discover.

Mail search: Turnaround time: 2 to 3 days. No self addressed stamped envelope is required.

Phone search: You must use a credit card.

In person search: Turnaround time is 30 minutes.

Online search: Records may be ordered online at the web site.

Expedited service: Expedited service is available for Internet and phone searches. Turnaround time: overnight delivery. Add $19.50 for express delivery and use of credit card.

Divorce Records

South Dakota Department of Health, Vital Records, 600 E Capitol, Pierre, SD 57501-2536; 605-773-4961, 605-773-5683 (Fax), 8AM-5PM.

http://www.state.sd.us/doh/VitalRec/index.htm

Indexing & Storage: Records are available from 1905 to present. New records are available for inquiry immediately.

Searching: Include the following in your request- names of husband and wife, date of divorce, place of divorce. The following data is not released: sealed records.

Access by: mail, phone, in person, online.

Fee & Payment: The fee is $7.00 per record. There is an additional $10.00 expedited fee if a credit card is used. Fee payee: South Dakota Department of Health. Prepayment required. Personal checks accepted. Credit cards accepted: MasterCard, Visa, AmEx, Discover.

Mail search: Turnaround time: 2 to 3 days. No self addressed stamped envelope is required.

Phone search: You must use a credit card.

In person search: Turnaround time 30 minutes.

Online search: Records may be ordered at the web site.

Expedited service: Expedited service is available for Internet and phone searches. Turnaround time: overnight delivery. Add $19.50 for express delivery and use of credit card.

Workers' Compensation Records

Labor Department, Workers Compensation Division, 700 Governors Dr, Pierre, SD 57501; 605-773-3681, 605-773-4211 (Fax), 8AM-5PM.

http://www.state.sd.us/dol/dol.htm

Indexing & Storage: Records are available from 1982. New records are available for inquiry immediately. Records are indexed on inhouse computer.

Searching: Must have a signed release form from the claimant. Must also specify which records you are requesting. A computer search will only go back to July 1989. Fraud reports and sealed files are not released. Include the following in your request-claimant name, Social Security Number, date of accident.

Access by: mail, in person.

Fee & Payment: Search fee is $20.00, copies are included. Fee payee: Division of Labor Management. Prepayment required. Personal checks accepted. No credit cards accepted.

Mail search: Turnaround time: 1 week. A self addressed stamped envelope is requested.

In person search: By going in person you will only eliminate the mail time.

Driver Records

Dept of Commerce & Regulation, Office of Driver Licensing, 118 W Capitol, Pierre, SD 57501; 605-773-6883, 605-773-3018 (Fax), 8AM-5PM.

http://www.state.sd.us/dcr/dl/sddriver.htm

Note: Ticket information is maintained at the local courts, not at the state.

Indexing & Storage: Records are available for 3 years for moving violations and DWIs. Speeding violations less than 10 mph over and out-of-state speeding violations (except for commercial drivers), suspensions and revocations are not listed on the record. It takes 1 to 3 weeks before new records are available for inquiry.

Searching: Casual requesters can only obtain records with the written permission of the subjects. All other requesters must certify for what reason they are obtaining the information and comply with DPPA policies. Include the following in your request-full name, date of birth. A secondary search will be done with the license number if no record is found on the name search. The following data is not released: Social Security Numbers.

Access by: mail, phone, in person, online.

Fee & Payment: The fee is $4.00 per record. The agency charges sales tax, if record request comes from a South Dakota address. Fee payee: Dept of Commerce and Regulation. Prepayment required. Personal checks accepted. No credit cards accepted.

Mail search: Turnaround time: 48 hours. A self addressed stamped envelope is requested.

Phone search: Pre-approved accounts may order via the telephone. This is a very limited access.

In person search: Turnaround time while you wait.

Online search: The system is open for batch requests 24 hours a day. There is a minimum of 250 requests daily. It generally takes 10 minutes to process a batch. The current fee is $4.00 per record and there are some start-up costs. For more information, call 605-773-6883.

Other access: Lists are available to the insurance industry.

Vehicle Ownership
Vehicle Identification
Vessel Ownership
Vessel Registration

Division of Motor Vehicles, Information Section, 445 E Capitol Ave, Pierre, SD 57501-3100; 605-773-3541, 605-773-5129 (Fax), 8AM-5PM.

http://www.state.sd.us/revenue/motorvcl.htm

Indexing & Storage: Records are available for 20 years to present. The DMV took over the registration and title process for boats in 1992. All boats (except canoes, inflatables, kayaks) over 12 ft in length must be titled and registered. Motorized boats 12 foot and under need to be registered. It takes 2 weeks before new records are available for inquiry.

Searching: The state requires all requests for vehicle related records be on the Division DPPA Form. Casual requesters (individuals) can only obtain information with written permission of the subject. All requests must be in writing.

Access by: mail, in person.

Fee & Payment: The fee for VIN, plate, owner, title, or lien searches is $2.00 per record. A title history is $5.00 Fee payee: Division of Motor Vehicles. Prepayment required. Personal checks accepted. No credit cards accepted.

Mail search: Turnaround time: 1 day to 1 week. Must provide details regarding the reasons for

requesting the information. A self addressed stamped envelope is requested.

In person search: You may request records in person, but the request must be in writing on the Division DPPA Form.

Accident Reports

Department of Transportation, Accident Records, 700 E. Broadway, Pierre, SD 57501-2586; 605-773-3868, 605-773-4870 (Fax), 8AM-5PM.

Indexing & Storage: Records are available for 10 years to present. It takes 2 weeks from receipt from law enforcement agency before new records are available for inquiry.

Searching: Include the following in your request-full name, date of accident, location of accident.

Access by: mail, in person.

Fee & Payment: The fee is $4.00 per record. Fee payee: Accident Records. Prepayment required. Personal checks accepted. No credit cards accepted.

Mail search: Turnaround time: 5 days. A self addressed stamped envelope is requested.

In person search: Normal turnaround time is immediate if the record is on file.

Legislation Records

South Dakota Legislature, Capitol Bldg - Legislative Research Council, 500 E Capitol Ave, Pierre, SD 57501; 605-773-3251, 605-773-4576 (Fax), 8AM-5PM.

http://legis.state.sd.us

Note: Signed bills are found at the Secretary of State's office, 605-773-3537. Pending legislation may be obtained here during the session.

Indexing & Storage: Records are available from 1951 on. It takes less than 24 hours before new records are available for inquiry.

Searching: Search by bill number, subject, sponsor or by keyword.

Access by: mail, phone, in person, online.

Fee & Payment: Fees are not charged for documents, unless one purchases a subscription to all the bills or journals.

Mail search: Turnaround time: same day. Single copies of legislation can be requested by mail. No self addressed stamped envelope is required.

Phone search: You may order bills by phone.

In person search: Searching is available in person.

Online search: Information is available at their web site at no charge. The site is very thorough and has enrolled version of bills.

Voter Registration
Records not maintained by a state level agency.

Note: The county auditors hold records. There are no restrictions on usage.

GED Certificates

Department of Labor, AEL/GED/Literacy, 700 Governors Drive, Pierre, SD 57501-2291; 605-773-4463, 605-773-4236 (Fax), 8AM-5PM.

http://www.state.sd.us/dol/GED/index.html

Note: You may e-mail requests to marcia.hess@state.sd.us.

Searching: The SSN, approximate date of test and DOB are needed to verify a record. In addition, a signed release is required for a copy of a transcript.

Access by: mail, fax, in person.

Fee & Payment: There is no fee for first two requests, then there is a $5.00 fee per transcript.

Mail search: Turnaround time: 1 day. No self addressed stamped envelope is required. No fee for mail request.

Fax search: Results will available in 1 hour.

In person search: No fee for request. You can wait for results.

Hunting License Information
Fishing License Information

Game, Fish & Parks Department, License Division, 412 W Missouri, Pierre, SD 57501; 605-773-3926, 605-773-5842 (Fax), 8AM-5PM.

http://www.state.sd.us/gfp

Indexing & Storage: Records are available for current and previous years only.

Searching: Requests must be in writing. They will release address data. The DOB and address are helpful.

Access by: mail, in person.

Fee & Payment: The fee depends on the extent of the names and the search. The state refuses to quote a price at this time. Fee payee: Dept of game & Fish. Prepayment required. Personal checks accepted. No credit cards accepted.

Mail search: Turnaround time: 1 to 2 days.

In person search: Searching is available in person.

Other access: Mailing lists are available. There is a $75.00 set up fee $75.00 per 1000 names, with a minimum of $90.00. They have records for big game licensees.

South Dakota State Licensing Agencies

Licenses Searchable Online

Ambulance Service #20 .... www.state.sd.us/doh/ems/direct.pdf
Animal Remedy (medicine/drug for animals) #19 www.state.sd.us/doa/das/hp-af-ar.htm
Architect #23 .... www.state.sd.us/dcr/engineer/Roster/index.cfm
Assessor #23 .... www.state.sd.us/dcr/engineer/Roster/index.cfm
Auctioneer #28 .... www.state.sd.us/dcr/realestate/roster/index.cfm
Barber Shop #04 .... www.state.sd.us/dcr/barber/roster.htm
Chiropractor #05 .... prill@mitchell.com
Counselor #06 .... www.state.sd.us/dcr/counselor/roster.htm
Engineer #23 .... www.state.sd.us/dcr/engineer/Roster/index.cfm
Engineer, Petroleum Environmental #23 .... www.state.sd.us/dcr/engineer/Roster/index.cfm
Fertilizer #19 .... www.state.sd.us/doa/das/hp-fert.htm
Home Inspector #28 .... www.state.sd.us/dcr/realestate/roster/index.cfm
Landscape Architect #23 .... www.state.sd.us/dcr/engineer/Roster/index.cfm
Lobbyist #27 .... www.lobbyist.net/SouthDak/SOULOB.htm
Marriage & Family Therapist #06 .... www.state.sd.us/dcr/counselor/roster.htm
Optometrist #09 .... www.odfinder.org/LicSearch.asp
Pesticide Applicator/Dealer #19 .... www.state.sd.us/doa/das/
Petroleum Release Remediator #23 .... www.state.sd.us/dcr/engineer/Roster/index.cfm
Plumber #34 .... www.state.sd.us/dcr/plumbing/
Property Manager, Real Estate #28 .... www.state.sd.us/dcr/realestate/roster/index.cfm
Public Accountant-CPA #03 .... www.state.sd.us/dcr/accountancy/annreg.pdf
Real Estate Broker #28 .... www.state.sd.us/dcr/realestate/roster/index.cfm
Real Estate Salesperson #28 .... www.state.sd.us/dcr/realestate/roster/index.cfm
Remediator #23 .... www.state.sd.us/dcr/engineer/Roster/index.cfm
Surveyor #23 .... www.state.sd.us/dcr/engineer/Roster/index.cfm
Timeshare Real Estate #28 .... www.state.sd.us/dcr/realestate/roster/index.cfm
Waste Water Collection System Operator #12 .. www.state.sd.us/denr/databases/operator/index.cfm
Waste Water Treatment Plant Operator #12 ..... www.state.sd.us/denr/databases/operator/index.cfm
Water Distributor #12 .... www.state.sd.us/denr/databases/operator/index.cfm
Water Treatment Plant Operator #12 .... www.state.sd.us/denr/databases/operator/index.cfm

Licensing Quick Finder

Abstractor #01 605-869-2269
Acupuncturist #05 605-343-7440
Alcoholic Beverage Distributor #21 605-773-3311
Ambulance Service #20 605-773-4031
Animal Feed Seller/Producer #19 605-773-4432
Animal Remedy (medicine/drug for animals) #19 605-773-4432
Appliance Contractor/Journeyman/Apprentice #34 605-773-3429
Architect #23 605-394-2510
Asbestos Abatement Worker #36 605-773-5559
Assessor #23 605-394-2510
Athletic Trainer #10 605-334-8343
Attorney #32 605-224-7554
Auctioneer #28 605-773-3600
Audiologist #30 605-642-1600
Bail Bond Agent #37 605-773-3513
Bank #02 605-773-3421
Barber #04 605-642-1600
Barber Shop #04 605-642-1600
Beauty Shop/Salon #18 605-773-6193
Brokerage Firm #31 605-733-4013
Bus Driver #17 605-773-6883
Business Opportunities Broker #31 605-733-4823
Chiropractor #05 605-343-7440
Cigarette Wholesaler #21 605-773-3311
Clinical Nurse Specialist #11 605-362-2760
Cosmetologist/ Cosmetology Salon #18 605-773-6193
Cosmetology Instructor #18 605-773-6193
Counselor #06 605-331-2927
Court/Shorthand Reporter #38 605-773-3474
Dental Assistant #07 605-224-1282
Dental Hygienist #07 605-224-1282
Dentist #07 605-224-1282

Dietitian/Nutritionist #10 605-334-8343
Drug Wholesaler #13 605-362-2737
Electrical Inspector #33 605-773-3573
Electrician #33 605-773-3573
Emergency Medical Technician #20 605-773-4031
Engineer #23 605-394-2510
Engineer, Petroleum Envmtl. #23 605-394-2510
Esthetician #18 605-773-6193
Fertilizer #19 605-773-4432
Franchise Sales #31 605-733-4823
Funeral Director/Embalmer #29 605-642-1600
Funeral Establishment #29 605-642-1600
Funeral Service #15 605-642-1600
Gaming #24 605-773-6050
Hearing Aid Dispenser #30 605-642-1600
Home Inspector #28 605-773-3600
Insurance Agent #17 605-773-3513
Investment Advisor #31 605-733-4013
Land Surveyor #17 605-394-2510
Landscape Architect #23 605-394-2510
Law Enforcement Officer #25 605-773-3584
Livestock Dealer #16 605-773-3321
Loan Production #02 605-773-3421
Lobbyist #27 605-773-5666
Manicurist/Nail Technician #18 605-773-6193
Marriage & Family Therapist #06 605-331-2927
Medical Assistant #10 605-334-8343
Medical Doctor #10 605-334-8343
Midwife Nurse #11 605-362-2760
Milk Grader/Hauler #19 605-773-4294
Milk Tester/Sampler #19 605-773-4294
Mobile Home Contractor #34 605-773-3429
Money Lending License #02 605-773-3421
Money Order Business #02 605-773-3421

Mortgage Broker/Lender #02 605-773-3421
Nail Salon #18 605-773-6193
Notary Public #27 605-773-5666
Nurse #11 605-362-2760
Nurse Anesthetist #11 605-362-2760
Nurse-RN #11 605-362-2760
Nurses' Aide #08 605-339-2071
Nurses' Aide (testing only) #35 605-331-5040
Nursing Home Administrator #08 605-331-5040
Occupational Therapist/Assistant #10 ... 605-334-8343
Optometrist #09 605-347-2136
Osteopathic Physician #10 605-334-8343
Paramedic #20 605-773-4031
Pesticide Applicator/Dealer #19 605-773-4432
Petroleum Release Remedictor #23 605-394-2510
Pharmacist/Pharmacy #13 605-362-2737
Physical Therapist/Assistant #10 605-334-8343
Physician/Medical Assistant #10 605-334-8343
Plumber #34 605-773-3429
Podiatrist #14 605-642-1600
Polygraph Examiner #25 605-773-3584
Property Manager, Real Estate #28 605-773-3600
Psychologist #26 605-642-1600
Public Accountant-CPA #03 605-367-5770
Racing #24 605-773-6050
Radiologist #05 605-343-7440
Radiology (Dental) #07 605-224-1282
Real Estate Broker/Salesperson #28 605-773-3600
Remediator #23 605-394-2510
Respiratory Care Practitioner #10 605-334-8343
School Bus Driver #17 605-773-6883
School Counselor #22 605-773-3553
School Principal/Superintendent #22 605-773-3553
Securities Agent/Broker/Dealer #31 605-733-4013

Sewage & Water Installation Contractor/Installer #34
....605-773-3429
Social Worker #15.................................605-642-1600
Surveyor #23 605-394-2510
Teacher #22..605-773-3553
Timeshare Real Estate #28 605-773-3600
Truck Driver #17 605-773-6883

Veterinarian/Veterinary Technician #16.605-773-3321
Veterinary Corporation #16...................605-773-3321
Waste Water Collection System Operator #12...........
....605-773-4208
Waste Water Treatment Plant Operator #12...............
....605-773-4208
Water Conditioning Plumbing Installer #34 ....

....605-773-3429
Water Distributor #12 605-773-4208
Water Treatment Operator #39 605-773-4208
Water Treatment Plant Operator #12 605-773-4205
Well Driller #36......................................605-773-5559

Licensing Agency Information

#01 Abstractors Board of Examiners, PO Box 187, Kennebec, SD 57544-0187; 605-869-2269, Fax: 605-869-2269.
www.state.sd.us/dcr/abstractors/abst-hom.htm

#02 Department of Commerce & Regulation, 217 1/2 W Missouri, Pierre, SD 57501-4590; 605-773-3421, Fax: 605-773-5367.
www.state.sd.us/dcr/bank

#03 Board of Accountancy, 301 E 14th St, #200, Sioux Falls, SD 57104-5022; 605-367-5770, Fax: 605-367-5773.
www.state.sd.us/dcr/accountancy
Direct web site URL to search for licensees: www.state.sd.us/dcr/accountancy/annreg.pdf   To search on this pdf search page, scroll down through the alphabetical listings.

#04 Board of Barber Examiners, 135 E Illinois, Spearfish, SD 57783; 605-642-1600, Fax: 605-642-1756.
www.state.sd.us/dcr/barber/barber-h.htm
Direct web site URL to search for licensees: www.state.sd.us/dcr/barber/roster.htm

#05 Board of Chiropractic Examiners, 1406 Mt Rushmore Road, Rapid City, SD 57701; 605-343-7440, Fax: 605-342-7868.
www.state.sd.us/dcr/chiropractic/
Direct web site URL to search for licensees: prill@mitchell.com. You can search online using downloadble form at main internet site

#06 Board of Counselor Examiners, PO Box 1822, Sioux Falls, SD 57101-1822; 605-331-2927, Fax: 605-331-2043.
www.state.sd.us/dcr/counselor/couns-ho.htm
Direct web site URL to search for licensees: www.state.sd.us/dcr/counselor/roster.htm

#07 Board of Dentistry, 106 W Capitol, #7, Pierre, SD 57501; 605-224-1282, Fax: 605-224-7426.
www.state.sd.us/dcr/dentistry/dent-hom.htm

#08 Board of Examiners for Nursing Home Administrators, PO Box 632, Sioux Falls, SD 57101-0632; 605-331-5040, Fax: 605-331-2043.
www.state.sd.us/dcr/nursinghome/nurhom-h.hml

#09 Board of Examiners in Optometry, PO Box 370, Sturgis, SD 57785-0370; 605-347-2136, Fax: 605-347-5823.
www.state.sd.us/dcr/optometry/optom-ho.htm
Direct web site URL to search for licensees: www.odfinder.org/LicSearch.asp.   Search online using national database by name, city or state.

#10 Board of Medical & Osteopathic Examiners, 1323 S Minnesota Ave, Sioux Falls, SD 57105-0685; 605-334-8343, Fax: 605-336-0270.

#11 Board of Nursing, 4300 S Louise Ave, Sioux Falls, SD 57106-3124; 605-362-2760, Fax: 605-362-2768.
www.state.sd.us/dcr/nursing/nurs-hom.htm

#12 Board of Operator Certification, 523 E Capitol Ave, Foss Bldg, Pierre, SD 57501; 605-773-3754, Fax: 605-773-5286.

www.state.sd.us/denr/enviro/wastewtr.htm
Direct web site URL to search for licensees: www.state.sd.us/denr/databases/operator/index.cfm. You can search online using name, type of certificate, employer name, and region of state.

#13 Board of Pharmacy, 4305 S Louise Ave, #104, Sioux Falls, SD 57106-3115; 605-362-2737, Fax: 605-362-2738.
www.state.sd.us/dcr/pharmacy/pharm-ho.htm

#14 Board of Podiatry Examiners, 135 E Illinois, #214, Spearfish, SD 57783; 605-642-1600, Fax: 605-642-1756.
www.state.sd.us/dcr/podiatry/pod-home.htm

#15 Board of Social Work Examiners, 135 E Illinois, #214, Spearfish, SD 57783; 605-642-1600, Fax: 605-642-1756.
www.state.sd.us/dcr/socialwork/soc-hom.htm

#16 Board of Veterinary Medical Examiners, 411 S Fort St, Pierre, SD 57501-4503; 605-773-3321, Fax: 605-773-5459.
www.dca.ca.gov/slpab/

#17 Department of Commerce & Regulation, 118 W Capitol Ave, Pierre, SD 57501-2000; 605-773-3178, Fax: 605-773-3018.
www.state.sd.us/dcr/dcr.html

#18 Cosmetology Commission, 500 E Capitol, Pierre, SD 57501-5070; 605-773-6193, Fax: 605-773-7175.   www.state.sd.us/dcr/cosmo/

#19 Department of Agriculture, 523 E Capitol, Foss Bldg, Pierre, SD 57501-3182; 605-773-3375, Fax: 605-773-3481. www.state.sd.us/doa/das/

#20 Department of Health, 600 E Capitol Ave, Pierre, SD 57501-3185; 605-773-4031, Fax: 605-773-5904. www.state.sd.us/doh/ems

#21 Department of Revenue, 445 E Capitol Ave, Pierre, SD 57501-3185; 605-773-3311, Fax: 605-773-5129. www.state.sd.us/revenue

#22 Education & Cultural Affairs Department, 700 Governors Dr, Pierre, SD 57501-2291; 605-773-3553, Fax: 605-773-6139. www.state.sd.us/deca/

#23 Engineering, 2040 W Main St, #304, Rapid City, SD 57702-2447; 605-394-2510, Fax: 605-395-2509.
www.state.sd.us/dcr/engineer
Direct web site URL to search for licensees: www.state.sd.us/dcr/engineer/Roster/index.cfm.
You can search online using last name, profession, license number, or business.

#24 Gaming Commission, 118 W Capitol, Pierre, SD 57501-5070; 605-773-6050, Fax: 605-773-6053.
www.state.sd.us/dcr/gaming/gam-hom.htm

#25 Law Enforcement Standards & Training Commission, Division of Criminal Justice Training Center, Pierre, SD 57501; 605-773-3584, Fax: 605-773-4629.

#27 Office of Secretary of State, 500 E Capitol Ave, State Capitol Bldg, #204, Pierre, SD 57501-5070; 605-773-3537, Fax: 605-773-6580.
www.state.sd.us/state/executive/sos/SOS.HTM;
www.state.sd.us/state/executive/sos/lobbyist.htm;
www.state.sd.us/state/executive/sos/Notaries/notarycover.htm

#28 Real Estate Commission, 118 W Capitol, Pierre, SD 57501; 605-773-3600, Fax: 605-773-4356.
www.state.sd.us/dcr/realestate/Real-hom.htm
Direct web site URL to search for licensees: www.state.sd.us/dcr/realestate/roster/index.cfm.
You can search online using name, city, state, firm name, and license type.

#29 Board of Funeral Services, 135 E Illinois, #214, Spearfish, SD 57783; 605-642-1600, Fax: 605-642-1756.
www.state.sd.us/dcr/funeral/fun-hom.htm

#30 Board of Licensing, 135 E Illinois Way, Spearfish, SD 57783-0654; 605-642-1600, Fax: 605-642-1756.
www.state.sd.us/dcr/hearing/hear-hom.htm

#31 Division of Securities, 118 W Capitol Ave, Pierre, SD 57501-2017; 605-773-4823, Fax: 605-773-5953.
www.state.sd.us/dcr/securities/security.htm

#32 State Bar, 222 E Capitol Ave, Pierre, SD 57501-2596; 605-224-7554, Fax: 605-224-0282.
www.sdbar.org

#33 Electrical Commission, 118 W Capitol, Pierre, SD 57501-5070; 605-773-3573, Fax: 605-773-6213.
www.state.sd.us/dcr/electrical/ELEC_HOM.htm

#34 Plumbing Commission, 118 W Capitol Ave, Pierre, SD 57501; 605-773-3429, Fax: 605-773-5405. www.state.sd.us/der/plumbing
Direct web site URL to search for licensees: www.state.sd.us/dcr/plumbing/

#35 Healthcare Administration, Nurses Aide Testing, 804 N Western Av, Souix Falls, SD 57104-2098; 605-339-2071, Fax: 605-339-1354.

#36 Department of Environment & Natural Resources, 523 E Capitol Ave, Pierre, SD 57501-3182; 605-773-5559.

#37 Division of Insurance, 910 E Sioux Ave, Pierre, SD 57501; 605-773-3513.

#38 Supreme Court, Capitol Bldg, 500 E Capitol, Pierre, SD 57501; 605-773-3474, Fax: 605-773-5627. www.ujs.state.sd.us

#39 Department of Environment & Natural Resources, 523 E Capitol Ave, Pierre, SD 57501; 605-773-4208.

South Dakota Federal Courts

The following list indicates the district and division name for each county in the state. If the bankruptcy court location is different from the district court, then the location of the bankruptcy court appears in parentheses.

County/Court Cross Reference

County	Court	County	Court
Aurora	Sioux Falls	Hyde	Pierre
Beadle	Sioux Falls	Jackson	Pierre
Bennett	Rapid City (Pierre)	Jerauld	Pierre
Bon Homme	Sioux Falls	Jones	Pierre
Brookings	Sioux Falls	Kingsbury	Sioux Falls
Brown	Aberdeen (Pierre)	Lake	Sioux Falls
Brule	Sioux Falls	Lawrence	Rapid City (Pierre)
Buffalo	Pierre	Lincoln	Sioux Falls
Butte	Aberdeen (Pierre)	Lyman	Pierre
Campbell	Aberdeen (Pierre)	Marshall	Aberdeen (Pierre)
Charles Mix	Sioux Falls	McCook	Sioux Falls
Clark	Aberdeen (Pierre)	McPherson	Aberdeen (Pierre)
Clay	Sioux Falls	Meade	Rapid City (Pierre)
Codington	Aberdeen (Pierre)	Mellette	Pierre
Corson	Aberdeen (Pierre)	Miner	Sioux Falls
Custer	Rapid City (Pierre)	Minnehaha	Sioux Falls
Davison	Sioux Falls	Moody	Sioux Falls
Day	Aberdeen (Pierre)	Pennington	Rapid City (Pierre)
Deuel	Aberdeen (Pierre)	Perkins	Rapid City (Pierre)
Dewey	Pierre	Potter	Pierre
Douglas	Sioux Falls	Roberts	Aberdeen (Pierre)
Edmunds	Aberdeen (Pierre)	Sanborn	Sioux Falls
Fall River	Rapid City (Pierre)	Shannon	Rapid City (Pierre)
Faulk	Pierre	Spink	Aberdeen (Pierre)
Grant	Aberdeen (Pierre)	Stanley	Pierre
Gregory	Pierre	Sully	Pierre
Haakon	Pierre	Todd	Pierre
Hamlin	Aberdeen (Pierre)	Tripp	Pierre
Hand	Pierre	Turner	Sioux Falls
Hanson	Sioux Falls	Union	Sioux Falls
Harding	Rapid City (Pierre)	Walworth	Aberdeen (Pierre)
Hughes	Pierre	Yankton	Sioux Falls
Hutchinson	Sioux Falls	Ziebach	Pierre

US District Court

District of South Dakota

Aberdeen Division c/o Pierre Division, Federal Bldg & Courthouse, 225 S Pierre St, Room 405, Pierre, SD 57501 (Courier Address: Use mail address for courier delivery), 605-224-5849, Fax: 605-224-0806.

http://www.sdd.uscourts.gov

Counties: Brown, Butte, Campbell, Clark, Codington, Corson, Day, Deuel, Edmunds, Grant, Hamlin, McPherson, Marshall, Roberts, Spink, Walworth. Judge Battey's closed case records are located at the Rapid City Division.

Indexing/Storage: Cases are indexed by as well as by case number. New cases are available in the index after filing date. Open records are located at the Division.

Fee & Payment: The fee is no charge per item (one party name or case number). Payment may be made by money order, cashier check. Business checks are not accepted. Personal checks are not accepted.

Phone Search: Searching not available by phone.

Mail Search: Always enclose a stamped self addressed envelope.

In Person: In person searching is available.

PACER: Sign-up number is 800-676-6856. Access fee is $.60 per minute. Toll-free access: 888-318-3413. Local access: 605-330-4393. Court does not allow electronic access to criminal cases. Case records are available back to 1991. Records are purged every six months. New records are available online after 1 day. PACER is available online at http://pacer.sdd.uscourts.gov.

Pierre Division Federal Bldg & Courthouse, Room 405, 225 S Pierre St, Pierre, SD 57501 (Courier Address: Use mail address for courier delivery), 605-224-5849, Fax: 605-224-0806.

http://www.sdd.uscourts.gov

Counties: Buffalo, Dewey, Faulk, Gregory, Haakon, Hand, Hughes, Hyde, Jackson, Jerauld, Jones, Lyman, Mellette, Potter, Stanley, Sully, Todd, Tripp, Ziebach.

Indexing/Storage: Cases are indexed by defendant and plaintiff as well as by case number. New cases are available in the index 1 day after filing date. Both computer and card indexes are maintained. Open records are located at this court.

Fee & Payment: The fee is $20.00 per item (one party name or case number). Payment may be made by money order, cashier check, personal check. Prepayment is required. Payee: Clerk, US District Court. Certification fee: $7.00 per document. Copy fee: $.50 per page.

Phone Search: Only docket information is available by phone.

Fax Search: Will accept fax for a price quote only.

Mail Search: Always enclose a stamped self addressed envelope.

In Person: In person searching is available.

PACER: Sign-up number is 800-676-6856. Access fee is $.60 per minute. Toll-free access: 888-318-3413. Local access: 605-330-4393. Court does not allow electronic access to criminal cases. Case records are available back to 1991. Records are purged every six months. New records are available online after 1 day. PACER is available online at http://pacer.sdd.uscourts.gov.

Rapid City Division
Clerk's Office, Room 302, 515 9th St, Rapid City, SD 57701 (Courier Address: Use mail address for courier delivery), 605-342-3066, Fax: 605-343-4367.

http://www.sdd.uscourts.gov

Counties: Bennett, Custer, Fall River, Harding, Lawrence, Meade, Pennington, Perkins, Shannon. Judge Battey's closed cases are located here.

Indexing/Storage: Cases are indexed by defendant and plaintiff as well as by case number. New cases are available in the index 24 hours after filing date. Both computer and card indexes are maintained. Open records are located at this court.

Fee & Payment: The fee is $20.00 per item (one party name or case number). Payment may be made by money order, cashier check, business check. Personal checks are not accepted. Prepayment is required. Payee: Clerk, US District Court. Certification fee: $7.00 per document. Copy fee: $.50 per page.

Phone Search: Only docket information available by telephone.

Mail Search: A stamped self addressed envelope is not required.

In Person: In person searching is available.

PACER: Sign-up number is 800-676-6856. Access fee is $.60 per minute. Toll-free access: 888-318-3413. Local access: 605-330-4393. Court does not allow electronic access to criminal cases. Case records are available back to 1991. Records are purged every six months. New records are available online after 1 day. PACER is available online at http://pacer.sdd.uscourts.gov.

Sioux Falls Division
P.O. Box 5060, Sioux Falls, SD 57117-5060 (Courier Address: Room 128, US Courthouse, 400 S Phillips Ave, Sioux Falls, SD 57104-6851), 605-330-4447, Fax: 605-330-4312.

http://www.sdd.uscourts.gov

Counties: Aurora, Beadle, Bon Homme, Brookings, Brule, Charles Mix, Clay, Davison, Douglas, Hanson, Hutchinson, Kingsbury, Lake, Lincoln, McCook, Miner, Minnehaha, Moody, Sanborn, Turner, Union, Yankton.

Indexing/Storage: Cases are indexed by defendant and plaintiff as well as by case number. New cases are available in the index 1 day after filing date. Both computer and card indexes are maintained. Open records are located at this court.

Fee & Payment: The fee is $20.00 per item (one party name or case number). Payment may be made by money order, cashier check, personal check. Prepayment is required. Payee: Clerk, US District Court. Certification fee: $7.00 per document. Copy fee: $.50 per page.

Phone Search: Only docket information for civil cases will be released over the phone.

Fax Search: To send a fax request, you must set up an account with the court. The fee for a fax request is $15.00 per name and $1.50 per page sent. The fee is $1.50 per page sent.

Mail Search: Always enclose a stamped self addressed envelope.

In Person: In person searching is available.

PACER: Sign-up number is 800-676-6856. Access fee is $.60 per minute. Toll-free access: 888-318-3413. Local access: 605-330-4393. Court does not allow electronic access to criminal cases. Case records are available back to 1991. Records are purged every six months. New records are available online after 1 day. PACER is available online at http://pacer.sdd.uscourts.gov.

US Bankruptcy Court
District of South Dakota

Pierre Division Clerk, Room 203, Federal Bldg, 225 S Pierre St, Pierre, SD 57501 (Courier Address: Use mail address for courier delivery), 605-224-6013, Fax: 605-224-9808.

http://www.sdb.uscourts.gov

Counties: Bennett, Brown, Buffalo, Butte, Campbell, Clark, Codington, Corson, Custer, Day, Deuel, Dewey, Edmunds, Fall River, Faulk, Grant, Gregory, Haakon, Hamlin, Hand, Harding, Hughes, Hyde, Jackson, Jerauld, Jones, Lawrence, Lyman, Marshall, McPherson, Meade,Mellette, Pennington, Perkins, Potter, Roberts, Shannon, Spink, Stanley, Sully, Todd, Tripp, Walworth, Ziebach.

Indexing/Storage: Cases are indexed by debtor and creditors as well as by case number. New cases are available in the index immediately after filing date. A computer index is maintained. Open records are located at this court. District wide searches are available for information from 10/1/91 from this court.

Fee & Payment: The fee is $20.00 per item (one party name or case number). Payment may be made by money order, cashier check, in-state business check. Personal checks are not accepted. Prepayment is required. Payee: Clerk, US Bankruptcy Court. Certification fee: $7.00 per document. Copy fee: $.50 per page.

Phone Search: Only docket information is available by phone. An automated voice case information service (VCIS) is available. Call VCIS at 800-768-6218 or 605-330-4559.

Fax Search: Will accept fax searches. Will fax docket listings at no extra charge.

Mail Search: Always enclose a stamped self addressed envelope.

In Person: In person searching is available.

PACER: Sign-up number is 800-676-6856. Access fee is $.60 per minute. Toll-free access: 800-261-3167. Local access: 605-330-4342. Case records are available back to October 1, 1991. Records are never purged. New civil records are available online after 1 day. PACER is available online at http://pacer.sdb.uscourts.gov.

Sioux Falls Division
PO Box 5060, Sioux Falls, SD 57117-5060 (Courier Address: Room 104, 400 S Phillips Ave, Sioux Falls, SD 57102), 605-330-4541, Fax: 605-330-4548.

http://www.sdb.uscourts.gov

Counties: Aurora, Beadle, Bon Homme, Brookings, Brule, Charles Mix, Clay, Davison, Douglas, Hanson, Hutchinson, Kingsbury, Lake, Lincoln, McCook, Miner, Minnehaha, Moody, Sanborn, Turner, Union, Yankton.

Indexing/Storage: Cases are indexed by debtor and creditors as well as by case number. New cases are available in the index 1 day after filing date. A computer index is maintained. Open records are located at this court. District wide searches are available for information from 10/1/91 from this court.

Fee & Payment: The fee is $20.00 per item (one party name or case number). Payment may be made by money order, cashier check, in-state business check. Personal checks are not accepted. Prepayment is required. Payee: Clerk, US Bankruptcy Court. Certification fee: $7.00 per document. Copy fee: $.50 per page.

Phone Search: Only docket information is available by phone. An automated voice case information service (VCIS) is available. Call VCIS at 800-768-6218 or 605-330-4559.

Fax Search: Will accept fax search at $15.00 fee. Will fax docket listing at no extra charge.

Mail Search: Always enclose a stamped self addressed envelope.

In Person: In person searching is available.

PACER: Sign-up number is 800-676-6856. Access fee is $.60 per minute. Toll-free access: 800-261-3167. Local access: 605-330-4342. Case records are available back to October 1, 1991. Records are never purged. New civil records are available online after 1 day. PACER is available online at http://pacer.sdb.uscourts.gov.

South Dakota County Courts

Court	Jurisdiction	No. of Courts	How Organized
Circuit Courts*	General	66	7 Circuits
Magistrate Courts		66	

* Profiled in this Sourcebook.

CIVIL									
Court	Tort	Contract	Real Estate	Min. Claim	Max. Claim	Small Claims	Estate	Eviction	Domestic Relations
Circuit Courts*	X	X	X	$0	No Max	$8000	X	X	X
Magistrate Courts				$0	$10,000	$8000	X	X	X

CRIMINAL					
Court	Felony	Misdemeanor	DWI/DUI	Preliminary Hearing	Juvenile
Circuit Courts*	X	X	X	X	X
Magistrate Courts		X	X	X	

ADMINISTRATION
State Court Administrator, State Capitol Building, 500 E Capitol Av, Pierre, SD, 57501; 605-773-3474, Fax: 605-773-5627. www.state.sd.us/state/judicial

COURT STRUCTURE
The state re-aligned their circuits from 8 to 7 effective June, 2000.

South Dakota has a statewide criminal record search database, administrated by the State Court Administrator's Office in Pierre. All criminal record information from July 1, 1989 forward, statewide, is contained in the database. To facilitate quicker access for the public, the state has designated 10 county record centers to process all mail or ongoing commercial accounts' criminal record requests. All mail requests are forwarded to, and commercial account requests are assigned to one of 10 specific county court clerks for processing a statewide search. Note that walk-in requesters seeking a single or minimum of requests may still obtain a record from their local county court. Five counties (Buffalo, Campbell, Dewey, McPherson, and Ziebach) do not have computer terminals in-house. The criminal records from these counties are entered into the database by court personnel from another location.

The search fee is $15.00 per record. State authorized commercial accounts may order and receive records by fax, there is an additional $5.00 fee unless a non-toll free line is used.

Requesters who wish to set up a commercial account are directed to contact Jill Gusso at the Court Administrator's Office in Pierre at the address mentioned above, or at jill.gusso@ujs.state.sd.us.

ONLINE ACCESS
There is no statewide online access computer system currently available. Larger courts are being placed on computer systems at a rate of 4 to 5 courts per year. Access is intended for internal use only. Smaller courts place their information on computer cards that are later sent to Pierre for input by the state office.

ADDITIONAL INFORMATION
Most South Dakota courts do not allow the public to perform searches, but rather require the court clerk to do them for a fee of $15.00 per name (increased from $5.00 as of July 1, 1997). A special Record Search Request Form must be used. Searches will be returned with a disclaimer stating that the clerk is not responsible for the completeness of the search. Clerks are not required to respond to telephone or Fax requests. Many courts are not open all day so they prefer written requests.

Aurora County

Circuit Court PO Box 366, Plankinton, SD 57368; 605-942-7165; Fax: 605-942-7170. Hours: 8AM-Noon, 1-5PM (CST). *Felony, Misdemeanor, Civil, Eviction, Small Claims, Probate.*

Civil Records: Access: Fax, mail, in person. Both court and visitors may perform in person searches. Search fee: $15.00 per name. Required to search: name, years to search; also helpful: address. Civil cases indexed by defendant, plaintiff. Civil records on manual index since 1879, some computerized since 1988.

Criminal Records: Access: Fax, mail, in person. Only the court performs in person searches; visitors may not. Search fee: $15.00 per name. Required to search: name, years to search, signed release; also helpful: address, DOB, SSN. Criminal records are computerized since 07/89 on a statewide system. Mail requests are forwarded to Douglas County for processing.

General Information: No juvenile, sealed, dismissed, adoption or mental health records released. SASE required. Turnaround time 1 day. Fax notes: $1.00 per page to fax back, $5.00 minimum. Copy fee: $.20 per page. Certification fee: $2.00. Fee payee: Aurora County Clerk of Court. Business checks accepted. Prepayment is required.

Beadle County

Circuit Court PO Box 1358, Huron, SD 57350; 605-353-7165. Hours: 8AM-5PM (CST). *Felony, Misdemeanor, Civil, Eviction, Small Claims, Probate.*

Civil Records: Access: Mail, in person. Only the court performs in person searches; visitors may not. Search fee: $15.00 per name. Required to search: name, years to search. Civil cases indexed by defendant, plaintiff. Civil records on computer from 1990 (limited), cards from 1900. Not for public use.

Criminal Records: Access: Mail, in person. Only the court performs in person searches; visitors may not. Search fee: $15.00 per name. Required to search: name, years to search, DOB; also helpful: SSN. Criminal records are computerized since 07/89 on a statewide system. Mail requests are forwarded to Hand County for processing.

General Information: No juvenile, sealed, dismissed, adoption, or mental health records released. Turnaround time up to 2 weeks. Copy fee: $.20 per page. Certification fee: $2.00. Fee payee: Beadle County Clerk of Court. Personal checks accepted. Out of state checks not accepted. Prepayment is required.

Bennett County

Circuit Court PO Box 281, Martin, SD 57551; 605-685-6969. Hours: 8AM-4:30PM (MST). *Felony, Misdemeanor, Civil, Eviction, Small Claims, Probate.*

Civil Records: Access: Mail, in person. Only the court performs in person searches; visitors may not. Search fee: $15.00 per name. Required to search: name, years to search; also helpful: address. Civil cases indexed by defendant, plaintiff. Civil records on index from 1912.

Criminal Records: Access: Mail, in person. Only the court performs in person searches; visitors may not. Search fee: $15.00 per name. Required to search: name, years to search, DOB; also helpful: address. Criminal records are computerized since 07/89 on a statewide system. All mail requests are forwarded to Potter County for processing.

General Information: No juvenile, sealed, dismissed, or mental health records released. SASE required. Turnaround time 48 hours. Application form available. Copy fee: $.20 per page. Certification fee: $3.00. Fee payee: Bennett County Clerk of Courts. Business checks accepted. Prepayment is required.

Bon Homme County

Circuit Court PO Box 6, Tyndall, SD 57066; 605-589-4215; Fax: 605-589-4245. Hours: 8AM-4:30PM (CST). *Felony, Misdemeanor, Civil, Eviction, Small Claims, Probate.*

Civil Records: Access: Fax, mail, in person. Both court and visitors may perform in person searches. Search fee: $15.00 per name. Required to search: name, years to search; also helpful: address. Civil cases indexed by defendant, plaintiff. Civil records on alpha index books from 1877. Requests should be in writing.

Criminal Records: Access: Mail, in person. Only the court performs in person searches; visitors may not. Search fee: $15.00 per name. Required to search: name, years to search, DOB, signed release; also helpful: address, SSN. Criminal records are computerized since 07/89 on a statewide system. All mail requests are forwarded to Douglas County for processing.

General Information: No juvenile, sealed, dismissed, or mental health records released. SASE required. Turnaround time 3 days to 1 week. Fax notes: $1.00 per page. $5.00 minimum, unless call is local or toll free. Copy fee: $.25 per page. Certification fee: $2.00. Fee payee: Bon Homme County Clerk of Court. Personal checks accepted. Prepayment is required.

Brookings County

Circuit Court 314 6th Ave, Brookings, SD 57006; 605-688-4200; Fax: 605-688-4952. Hours: 8AM-5PM (CST). *Felony, Misdemeanor, Civil, Eviction, Small Claims, Probate.*

Civil Records: Access: Mail, in person. Only the court performs in person searches; visitors may not. Search fee: $15.00 per name. Required to search: name, years to search; also helpful: address. Civil cases indexed by defendant, plaintiff. Civil records on alpha index books from 1900s.

Criminal Records: Access: Mail, in person. Only the court performs in person searches; visitors may not.

Search fee: $15.00 per name. Required to search: name, years to search, DOB; also helpful: address, SSN. Criminal records on computer since July 1989 on a statewide system. All mail requests are forwarded to Hand County for processing.

General Information: No juvenile, sealed, dismissed, or mental health records released. SASE required. Turnaround time 3 days. Fax notes: Fee to fax results is $1.00 per page; $5.00 minimum. Copy fee: $.20 per page. Certification fee: $2.00. Fee payee: Brookings County Clerk of Court. Only cashiers checks and money orders accepted. Prepayment is required.

Brown County

Circuit Court 101 1st Ave SE, Aberdeen, SD 57401; 605-626-2451; Fax: 605-626-2491. Hours: 8AM-5PM (CST). *Felony, Misdemeanor, Civil, Eviction, Small Claims, Probate.*

Civil Records: Access: Mail, in person. Both court and visitors may perform in person searches. Search fee: $15.00 per name. Required to search: name, years to search; also helpful: address. Civil cases indexed by defendant, plaintiff. Civil records on registers from 1975 (misdemeanor), registers from 1900s (civil).

Criminal Records: Access: Mail, in person. Only the court performs in person searches; visitors may not. Search fee: $15.00 per name. Required to search: name, years to search, DOB; also helpful: address, signed release, SSN. Criminal records on computer since 07/89 on a statewide system. All mail requests are forwarded to Edmunds County for processing.

General Information: No juvenile, sealed, dismissed, or mental health records released. SASE required. Turnaround time 1-3 days. Copy fee: $.20 per page. Certification fee: $2.00. Fee payee: Brown County Clerk of Court. Personal checks accepted. Prepayment is required.

Brule County

Circuit Court 300 S Courtland #111, Chamberlain, SD 57325-1599; 605-734-5443; Fax: 605-734-5443. Hours: 8AM-Noon, 1-5PM (CST). *Felony, Misdemeanor, Civil, Eviction, Small Claims, Probate.*

Civil Records: Access: Fax, mail, in person. Both court and visitors may perform in person searches. Search fee: $15.00 per name. Required to search: name, years to search; also helpful: address. Civil cases indexed by defendant, plaintiff. Civil records on index books or docket books from 1875.

Criminal Records: Access: Fax, mail, in person. Only the court performs in person searches; visitors may not. Search fee: $15.00 per name. Required to search: name, years to search, DOB; also helpful: address, SSN. Criminal records on computer since July 1989 on a statewide system. All mail requests are forwarded to Miner County for processing. Fax requests accepted for commercial accounts only and are forwarded as well.

General Information: No juvenile, sealed, dismissed, or mental health records released. SASE required. Turnaround time 3-5 days. Fax notes: $1.00 per page. $5.00 minimum. Copy fee: $.25 per page. Certification fee: $2.00. Fee payee: Brule County Clerk of Court. Personal checks accepted. Prepayment is required.

Buffalo County

Circuit Court PO Box 148, Gann Valley, SD 57341; 605-293-3234; Fax: 605-293-3240. Hours: 9AM-Noon (CST). *Felony, Misdemeanor, Civil, Eviction, Small Claims, Probate.*

Civil Records: Access: Mail, in person. Only the court performs in person searches; visitors may not. Search fee: $15.00 per name. Required to search: name, years to search; also helpful: address. Civil cases indexed by defendant, plaintiff. All data on alpha index from 1915.

Criminal Records: Access: Mail, in person. Only the court performs in person searches; visitors may not.

Search fee: $15.00 per name. Required to search: name, years to search, DOB; also helpful: address, SSN. Criminal records are on books, but computerized on the statewide computer system since 07/89. This office does not have a computer hook-up. All mail requests are forwarded to Miner County for processing.

General Information: No juvenile, sealed, dismissed, or mental health records released. SASE required. Turnaround time 1 week. Copy fee: $.20 per page. Certification fee: $2.00. Fee payee: Buffalo County Clerk of Court. Personal checks accepted. Prepayment is required.

Butte County

Circuit Court PO Box 237, Belle Fourche, SD 57717; 605-892-2516; Fax: 605-892-2836. Hours: 8AM-Noon, 1-5PM (MST). *Felony, Misdemeanor, Civil, Eviction, Small Claims, Probate.*

Civil Records: Access: Mail, in person. Only the court performs in person searches; visitors may not. Search fee: $15.00 per name. Required to search: name, years to search; also helpful: address. Civil cases indexed by defendant, plaintiff. All data on alpha index from 1900s.

Criminal Records: Access: Mail, in person. Only the court performs in person searches; visitors may not. Search fee: $15.00 per name. Required to search: name, years to search; also helpful: address. Criminal records on computer since 07/89 on a statewide system. All mail requests are forwarded to Lawrence County for processing.

General Information: No juvenile, sealed, dismissed, or mental health records released. SASE required. Turnaround time varies. Copy fee: $.20 per page. Certification fee: $2.00. Fee payee: Butte County Clerk of Court. Personal checks accepted. Prepayment is required.

Campbell County

Circuit Court PO Box 146, Mound City, SD 57646; 605-955-3536; Fax: 605-955-3308. Hours: 8AM-Noon T-W-F (CST). *Felony, Misdemeanor, Civil, Small Claims, Probate.*

Civil Records: Access: Mail, in person. Both court and visitors may perform in person searches. Search fee: $15.00 per name. Required to search: name, years to search; also helpful: address. Civil cases indexed by defendant, plaintiff. All data on alpha index from 1800s.

Criminal Records: Access: Mail, in person. Only the court performs in person searches; visitors may not. Search fee: $15.00 per name. Required to search: name, years to search, DOB; also helpful: address, SSN. Although records are computerized at the state level, this office has records and indices on paper. All mail requests are forwarded to Edmunds County for processing.

General Information: No juvenile, sealed, dismissed, or mental health records released. SASE required. Turnaround time varies. Copy fee: $.10 per page. Certification fee: $2.00. Fee payee: Campbell County Clerk of Court. Only cashiers checks and money orders accepted. Prepayment is required.

Charles Mix County

Circuit Court PO Box 640, Lake Andes, SD 57356; 605-487-7511; Fax: 605-487-7547. Hours: 8AM-4:30PM (CST). *Felony, Misdemeanor, Civil, Eviction, Small Claims, Probate.*

Civil Records: Access: Fax, mail, in person. Both court and visitors may perform in person searches. Search fee: $15.00 per name. Required to search: name, years to search; also helpful: address. Civil cases indexed by defendant, plaintiff. Civil records on alpha index books from 1917.

Criminal Records: Access: Fax, mail, in person. Only the court performs in person searches; visitors may not. Search fee: $15.00 per name. Required to search: name, years to search, DOB; also helpful: address, SSN. Criminal records on computer since 07/89 on a statewide system located in Douglas County. All mail and fax requests are forwarded to Douglas County for processing.

General Information: No juvenile, sealed, dismissed, or mental health records released. SASE required. Turnaround time 2-5 days. Fax notes: $1.00 per page. $5.00 minimum. Copy fee: $.20 per page. Certification fee: $2.00. Fee payee: Charles Mix County Clerk of Court. Personal check accepted with SSN or DL#. Prepayment is required.

Clark County

Circuit Court PO Box 294, Clark, SD 57225; 605-532-5851. Hours: 8AM-Noon, 1-5PM (CST). *Felony, Misdemeanor, Civil, Eviction, Small Claims, Probate.*

Civil Records: Access: Mail, in person. Only the court performs in person searches; visitors may not. Search fee: $15.00 per name. Required to search: name, years to search; also helpful: address. Civil cases indexed by defendant, plaintiff. Civil records on alpha index cards from 1969.

Criminal Records: Access: Mail, in person. Only the court performs in person searches; visitors may not. Search fee: $15.00 per name. Required to search: name, years to search, DOB; also helpful: address, SSN. Criminal records on computer since 1986 on a statewide system. All mail requests are forwarded to Hand County for processing.

General Information: No juvenile, sealed, dismissed, or mental health records released. SASE required. Turnaround time 1-4 days. Copy fee: $.20 per page. Certification fee: $2.50. Fee payee: Clark County Clerk of Court. Personal checks accepted. Prepayment is required.

Clay County

Circuit Court PO Box 377, Vermillion, SD 57069; 605-677-6755; Fax: 605-677-8885. Hours: 8AM-5PM (CST). *Felony, Misdemeanor, Civil, Eviction, Small Claims, Probate.*

Civil Records: Access: Mail, in person. Both court and visitors may perform in person searches. Search fee: $15.00 per name. Required to search: name, years to search; also helpful: address. Civil cases indexed by defendant, plaintiff. Civil records on computer from 1989 and alpha index books from 1800s.

Criminal Records: Access: Mail, in person. Only the court performs in person searches; visitors may not. Search fee: $15.00 per name. Required to search: name, years to search, DOB; also helpful: address, SSN. Criminal records on computer since 07/89 on a statewide system. All mail requests are forwarded to Douglas County for processing.

General Information: No juvenile, sealed, dismissed, or mental health records released. SASE required. Turnaround time 2-4 days. Copy fee: $.10 per page. Certification fee: $2.00. Fee payee: Clay County Clerk of Court. Personal checks accepted. Prepayment is required.

Codington County

Circuit Court PO Box 1054, Watertown, SD 57201; 605-882-5095; Fax: 605-882-5106. Hours: 8AM-5PM (CST). *Felony, Misdemeanor, Civil, Eviction, Small Claims, Probate.*

Civil Records: Access: Mail, in person. Only the court performs in person searches; visitors may not. Search fee: $15.00 per name. Required to search: name, years to search. Civil cases indexed by defendant, plaintiff. Civil records on computer from 1991 and alpha index cards back to 1890.

Criminal Records: Access: Mail, in person. Only the court performs in person searches; visitors may not. Search fee: $15.00 per name. Required to search: name,

years to search, DOB. Criminal records on computer since 07/89 on a statewide system. Mail requests for dates 1989 to present are forwarded to Hand County for processing. Prior to 1989 processed in Codington County.

General Information: No juvenile, sealed, dismissed, or mental health records released. SASE required. Turnaround time 2 days. Copy fee: $.20 per page. Certification fee: $2.00. Fee payee: Codington County Clerk of Court. Business checks accepted. Prepayment is required.

Corson County

Circuit Court PO Box 175, McIntosh, SD 57641; 605-273-4201; Fax: 605-273-4233. Hours: 9:30AM-2:30PM (MST). *Felony, Misdemeanor, Civil, Eviction, Small Claims, Probate.*

Civil Records: Access: Mail, in person. Both court and visitors may perform in person searches. Search fee: $15.00 per name. Required to search: name, years to search; also helpful: address. Civil cases indexed by defendant, plaintiff. All data on alpha index from 1940s.

Criminal Records: Access: Mail, in person. Only the court performs in person searches; visitors may not. Search fee: $15.00 per name. Required to search: name, years to search, DOB; also helpful: address, SSN. Criminal records are computerized. All phone requests are forwarded to Lawrence County for processing.

General Information: No juvenile, sealed, dismissed, adoption or mental health records released. SASE not required. Turnaround time 1 day. Copy fee: $.20 per page. Certification fee: $2.00. Fee payee: Corson County Clerk of Court. Personal checks accepted. Prepayment is required.

Custer County

Circuit Court 420 Mt Rushmore Rd, Custer, SD 57730; 605-673-4816; Fax: 605-673-3416. Hours: 8AM-5PM (MST). *Felony, Misdemeanor, Civil, Eviction, Small Claims, Probate.*

Civil Records: Access: Mail, in person. Only the court performs in person searches; visitors may not. Search fee: $15.00 per name. Required to search: name, years to search; also helpful: address. Civil cases indexed by defendant, plaintiff. Probate on microfiche from 1915, all other data on docket books and index cards from 1960s.

Criminal Records: Access: Mail, in person. Only the court performs in person searches; visitors may not. Search fee: $15.00 per name. Required to search: name, years to search, DOB, signed release; also helpful: address, SSN. Criminal records on computer since 07/89 on a statewide system. Criminal searches are performed through the Search Center at Harding County Clerk, POB 534, Buffalo, SD 57720.

General Information: No juvenile, sealed, dismissed, or mental health records released. SASE required. Turnaround time 2 days. Copy fee: $.25 per page. Certification fee: $2.00. Fee payee: Custer County Clerk of Court. Personal checks accepted. Prepayment is required.

Davison County

Circuit Court PO Box 927, Mitchell, SD 57301; 605-995-4705; Fax: 605-995-3134. Hours: 8AM-5PM (CST). *Felony, Misdemeanor, Civil, Eviction, Small Claims, Probate.*

Civil Records: Access: Mail, in person. Both court and visitors may perform in person searches. Search fee: $15.00 per name. Required to search: name, years to search; also helpful: address. Civil cases indexed by defendant. All data on alpha index from 1900s.

Criminal Records: Access: Mail, in person. Only the court performs in person searches; visitors may not. Search fee: $15.00 per name. Required to search: name, years to search, DOB; also helpful: address, SSN.

Criminal records are computerized since 07/89 on a statewide system. All mail request are forwarded to Miner County for processing.

General Information: No juvenile, sealed, dismissed, or mental health records released. SASE required. Turnaround time 1 week. Copy fee: $.25 per page. Certification fee: $2.00. Fee payee: Davison County Clerk of Court. Personal checks accepted. Out of state checks not accepted. Prepayment is required.

Day County

Circuit Court 710 W 1st St, Webster, SD 57274; 605-345-3771; Fax: 605-345-3818. Hours: 8AM-5PM (CST). *Felony, Misdemeanor, Civil, Small Claims, Probate.*

Civil Records: Access: Mail, in person. Only the court performs in person searches; visitors may not. Search fee: $15.00 per name. Required to search: name, years to search; also helpful: address. Civil cases indexed by defendant. Civil records on docket books from 1800s.

Criminal Records: Access: Mail, in person. Only the court performs in person searches; visitors may not. Search fee: $15.00 per name. Required to search: name, years to search, DOB; also helpful: address, SSN. Criminal records on computer since 1982 on a statewide system. All mail requests are forwarded to Edmunds County for processing.

General Information: No juvenile, sealed, dismissed, or mental health records released. SASE required. Turnaround time 1 week. Copy fee: $.20 per page. Certification fee: $2.00. Fee payee: Day County Clerk of Court. Prepayment is required.

Deuel County

Circuit Court PO Box 308, Clear Lake, SD 57226; 605-874-2120. Hours: 8AM-5PM (CST). *Felony, Misdemeanor, Civil, Eviction, Small Claims, Probate.*

Civil Records: Access: Mail, in person. Only the court performs in person searches; visitors may not. Search fee: $15.00 per name. Required to search: name, years to search; also helpful: address. Civil cases indexed by defendant, plaintiff. Civil records on docket books from late 1800s.

Criminal Records: Access: Mail, in person. Only the court performs in person searches; visitors may not. Search fee: $15.00 per name. Required to search: name, years to search, DOB, signed release; also helpful: address, SSN. Criminal records on computer since 07/89 on a statewide system. All mail requests are forwarded to Hand County for processing.

General Information: No juvenile, sealed, dismissed, or mental health records released. SASE required. Turnaround time 1-2 days. Copy fee: $.20 per page. Certification fee: $2.00. Fee payee: Deuel County Clerk of Court. Personal checks accepted. Prepayment is required.

Dewey County

Circuit Court PO Box 96, Timber Lake, SD 57656; 605-865-3566. Hours: 9:30AM-Noon, 1-2:30PM (MST). *Felony, Misdemeanor, Civil, Eviction, Small Claims, Probate.*

Civil Records: Access: Mail, in person. Both court and visitors may perform in person searches. Search fee: $15.00 per name. Required to search: name, years to search; also helpful: address. Civil cases indexed by defendant, plaintiff. All data on alpha index and docket books from 1900s; computerized back to 1999.

Criminal Records: Access: Mail, in person. Only the court performs in person searches; visitors may not. Search fee: $15.00 per name. Required to search: name, years to search, DOB; also helpful: address, SSN, signed release. Criminal records data on alpha index and docket books from 1900s; computerized back to 1999. All mail requests are forwarded to Lawrence County for processing.

General Information: No juvenile, adoption, sealed, dismissed, or mental health records released. SASE required. Turnaround time 2 days to 1 week. Fax notes: Fee to fax results is $1.00 per page; $5.00 per document. Copy fee: $.25 per page. Certification fee: $2.00. Fee payee: Dewey County Clerk of Court. Personal checks accepted. Prepayment is required.

Douglas County

Circuit Court PO Box 36, Armour, SD 57313; 605-724-2585. Hours: 8AM-Noon, 1-5PM (CST). *Felony, Misdemeanor, Civil, Eviction, Small Claims, Probate.*

Civil Records: Access: Mail, in person. Both court and visitors may perform in person searches. Search fee: $15.00 per name. Required to search: name, years to search; also helpful: address. Civil cases indexed by defendant. Civil records on docket books from 1800s.

Criminal Records: Access: Fax, mail, in person. Only the court performs in person searches; visitors may not. Search fee: $15.00 per name. Required to search: name, years to search, DOB, signed release; also helpful: address, SSN. Criminal records are computerized since 07/89 on a statewide system. Fax requests are for commercial accounts only.

General Information: No juvenile, sealed, dismissed, or mental health records released. SASE required. Turnaround time 1-2 weeks. Will release limited civil data over phone. Copy fee: $.50 per page. Certification fee: $2.00. Fee payee: Douglas County Clerk of Court. Personal checks accepted. Prepayment is required.

Edmunds County

Circuit Court PO Box 384, Ipswich, SD 57451; 605-426-6671; Fax: 605-426-6323. Hours: 8AM-Noon, 1-5PM (CST). *Felony, Misdemeanor, Civil, Eviction, Small Claims, Probate.*

Civil Records: Access: Fax, mail, in person. Both court and visitors may perform in person searches. Search fee: $15.00 per name. Required to search: name, years to search; also helpful: address. Civil cases indexed by defendant, plaintiff. Civil records on docket books from late 1800s.

Criminal Records: Access: Fax, mail, in person. Only the court performs in person searches; visitors may not. Search fee: $15.00 per name. Required to search: name, years to search, DOB; also helpful: SSN, signed release. Criminal records on computer since 07/89; prior records on docket books. Fax requests are for commercial accounts only. Results are statewide.

General Information: No juvenile, sealed or mental health records released. SASE required. Turnaround time 1 day to 1 week. Fax notes: Fee is $1.00 per page, $5.00 minimum. Copy fee: $.25 per page. Certification fee: $2.00. Fee payee: Edmunds County Clerk of Court. Personal checks accepted. Prepayment is required.

Fall River County

Circuit Court 906 N River St, Hot Springs, SD 57747; 605-745-5131. 8AM-5PM (MST). *Felony, Misdemeanor, Civil, Eviction, Small Claims, Probate.*

Note: Also handles cases for Shannon County. Specify which county in any search request.

Civil Records: Access: Mail, in person. Only the court performs in person searches; visitors may not. Search fee: $15.00 per name. Required to search: name, years to search; also helpful: address. Civil cases indexed by defendant, plaintiff. Civil records on computer from 1992, files from 1800s archived off site.

Criminal Records: Access: Mail, in person. Only the court performs in person searches; visitors may not. Search fee: $15.00 per name. Required to search: name, years to search, DOB; also helpful: address, SSN. Criminal records on computer since 07/89 on a statewide system.

General Information: No juvenile, sealed, adoption, or mental health records released. SASE required.

Turnaround time 1 week. Copy fee: $.25 per page. Certification fee: $2.00. Fee payee: Fall River County Clerk of Court. Personal checks accepted. Prepayment is required.

Faulk County

Circuit Court PO Box 357, Faulkton, SD 57438; 605-598-6223; Fax: 605-598-6680. Hours: 1:00PM-5:00PM (CST). *Felony, Misdemeanor, Civil, Eviction, Small Claims, Probate.*

Civil Records: Access: Mail, in person. Both court and visitors may perform in person searches. Search fee: $15.00 per name. Required to search: name, years to search; also helpful: address. Civil cases indexed by defendant. Civil records on docket books from 1900s.

Criminal Records: Access: Mail, in person. Only the court performs in person searches; visitors may not. Search fee: $15.00 per name. Required to search: name, years to search, DOB; also helpful: address, SSN. Criminal records are computerized since 07/89 on a statewide system. All mail requests are forwarded to Edmunds County for processing.

General Information: No juvenile, sealed, dismissed, adoption, or mental health records released. SASE required. Turnaround time 2-3 days. Copy fee: $.20 per page. Certification fee: $2.00. Fee payee: Faulk County Clerk of Court. Personal checks accepted. Prepayment is required.

Grant County

Circuit Court PO Box 509, Milbank, SD 57252; 605-432-5482. Hours: 8AM-Noon, 1-5PM (CST). *Felony, Misdemeanor, Civil, Eviction, Small Claims, Probate.*

Civil Records: Access: Mail, in person. Only the court performs in person searches; visitors may not. Search fee: $15.00 per name. Required to search: name, years to search; also helpful: address. Civil cases indexed by defendant, plaintiff. Civil records on computer from 1995, docket books from 1800s.

Criminal Records: Access: Mail, in person. Only the court performs in person searches; visitors may not. Search fee: $15.00 per name. Required to search: name, years to search, DOB; also helpful: address, SSN. Criminal records on computer since 07/89 on a statewide system. All mail requests are forwarded to and processed by Hand County.

General Information: No juvenile, sealed, dismissed, adoption or mental health records released. SASE required. Turnaround time 1 week by mail, immediate by phone if on computer. Copy fee: $.25 per page. Certification fee: $2.00. Fee payee: Grant County Clerk of Court. Prepayment is required.

Gregory County

Circuit Court PO Box 430, Burke, SD 57523; 605-775-2665. Hours: 8AM-Noon, 1-5PM (CST). *Felony, Misdemeanor, Civil, Eviction, Small Claims, Probate.*

Civil Records: Access: Mail, in person. Only the court performs in person searches; visitors may not. Search fee: $15.00 per name. Required to search: name, years to search; also helpful: address. Civil cases indexed by defendant, plaintiff. Civil records on docket books from late 1800s.

Criminal Records: Access: Mail, in person. Only the court performs in person searches; visitors may not. Search fee: $15.00 per name. Required to search: name, years to search, DOB, signed release; also helpful: address, SSN. Criminal records on computer back to 07/89 on a statewide system. All mail requests are forwarded to Potter County for processing.

General Information: No juvenile, sealed, dismissed, or mental health records released. SASE required. Turnaround time 1 week. Fax notes: Will fax results for a fee. Copy fee: $.20 per page. Certification fee: $2.00. Fee payee: Gregory County Clerk of Court. Only

cashiers checks and money orders accepted. Prepayment is required.

Haakon County

Circuit Court PO Box 70, Philip, SD 57567; 605-859-2627. Hours: 8AM-Noon (MST). *Felony, Misdemeanor, Civil, Eviction, Small Claims, Probate.*

Civil Records: Access: Mail, in person. Only the court performs in person searches; visitors may not. Search fee: $15.00 per name. Required to search: name, years to search; also helpful: address. Civil records on register from 1915.

Criminal Records: Access: Mail, in person. Only the court performs in person searches; visitors may not. Search fee: $15.00 per name. Required to search: name, years to search, DOB; also helpful: address, SSN. Criminal records are computerized since 07/89 on a statewide system. All mail requests are forwarded to Potter County for processing.

General Information: No juvenile, sealed, dismissed, or mental health records released. SASE required. Turnaround time 1 day. Fax notes: Fee to fax results is $1.00 per page; $5.00 minimum. Copy fee: $.20 per page. Certification fee: $2.00. Fee payee: Haakon County Clerk of Court. Personal checks accepted. Local checks accepted. Prepayment is required.

Hamlin County

Circuit Court PO Box 256, Hayti, SD 57241; 605-783-3751; Fax: 605-783-3201. Hours: 9AM-Noon, 1-4PM (CST). *Felony, Misdemeanor, Civil, Eviction, Small Claims, Probate.*

Civil Records: Access: Mail, in person. Only the court performs in person searches; visitors may not. Search fee: $15.00 per name. Required to search: name, years to search; also helpful: address. Civil cases indexed by defendant, plaintiff. Civil records on docket books from 1800s.

Criminal Records: Access: Mail, in person. Only the court performs in person searches; visitors may not. Search fee: $15.00 per name. Required to search: name, years to search, DOB; also helpful: address, SSN. Criminal records on computer since 07/89 on a statewide system.

General Information: No juvenile, sealed, dismissed, or mental health records released. SASE required. Turnaround time 1 day. Copy fee: $.20 per page. Certification fee: $2.00. Fee payee: Hamlin County Clerk of Court. Personal checks accepted. Prepayment is required.

Hand County

Circuit Court PO Box 122, Miller, SD 57362; 605-853-3337; Fax: 605-853-3779. Hours: 8AM-5PM (CST). *Felony, Misdemeanor, Civil, Eviction, Small Claims, Probate.*

Civil Records: Access: Mail, in person. Only the court performs in person searches; visitors may not. Search fee: $15.00 per name. Required to search: name, years to search; also helpful: address. Civil cases indexed by defendant. All data on alpha index and docket books from late 1800s.

Criminal Records: Access: Fax, mail, in person. Only the court performs in person searches; visitors may not. Search fee: $15.00 per name. Required to search: name, years to search, DOB; also helpful: address, SSN. Criminal records on computer since 07/89 on a statewide system. Fax requesting for commercial accounts only.

General Information: No juvenile, sealed, dismissed, or mental health records released. SASE required. Turnaround time 1 day. Copy fee: $.20 per page. Certification fee: $2.00. Fee payee: Hand County Clerk of Court. Business checks accepted. Prepayment is required.

Hanson County

Circuit Court PO Box 127, Alexandria, SD 57311; 605-239-4446; Fax: 605-239-9446. Hours: 8AM-5PM *Felony, Misdemeanor, Civil, Small Claims, Probate.*

Civil Records: Access: Fax, mail, in person. Both court and visitors may perform in person searches. Search fee: $15.00 per name. Required to search: name, years to search; also helpful: address. Civil cases indexed by defendant, plaintiff. Civil records on docket books from 1902.

Criminal Records: Access: Mail, in person. Only the court performs in person searches; visitors may not. Search fee: $15.00 per name. Required to search: name, years to search, DOB; also helpful: address, SSN. Criminal records computerized since 07/89 on a statewide system. All mail requests forwarded to Miner County for processing.

General Information: No juvenile, sealed, dismissed, adoption or mental health records released. SASE required. Turnaround time varies. Fax notes: $5.00 per document. $1.00 per page after 5 pages. Copy fee: $.15 per page. Certification fee: $2.00. Fee payee: Hanson County Clerk of Court. Personal checks accepted. Prepayment is required.

Harding County

Circuit Court PO Box 534, Buffalo, SD 57720; 605-375-3351. Hours: 9:30AM-Noon, 1-2:30PM (MST). *Felony, Misdemeanor, Civil, Eviction, Small Claims, Probate.*

Note: This court is the designated search center of Harding and Pennington County criminal records.

Civil Records: Access: Mail, in person. Both court and visitors may perform in person searches. Search fee: $15.00 per name. Required to search: name, years to search; also helpful: address. Civil cases indexed by defendant. Civil records in archives from 1909 to 1920, index books from 1920.

Criminal Records: Access: Fax, mail, in person. Only the court performs in person searches; visitors may not. Search fee: $15.00 per name. Required to search: name, years to search, DOB; also helpful: address, SSN. Criminal records are computerized since 07/89 on a statewide system. Fax requests for commercial accounts only.

General Information: No juvenile, sealed, dismissed, or mental health records released. SASE required. Turnaround time 1 week. Fax notes: $1.00 per page. $5.00 minimum, unless call is local or toll free. Copy fee: $.20 per page. Certification fee: $2.00. Fee payee: Harding County Clerk of Court. Personal checks accepted. Prepayment is required.

Hughes County

Circuit Court 104 E Capital, Pierre, SD 57501; 605-773-3713. Hours: 8AM-5PM (CST). *Felony, Misdemeanor, Civil, Eviction, Small Claims, Probate.*

Civil Records: Access: Mail, in person. Only the court performs in person searches; visitors may not. Search fee: $15.00 per name. Required to search: name, years to search; also helpful: address. Civil cases indexed by defendant, plaintiff. Civil records on microfiche from 1948 to 1973. From 1974 forward have hard copy file, starting 1991 index and docketing on computer.

Criminal Records: Access: Mail, in person. Only the court performs in person searches; visitors may not. Search fee: $15.00 per name. Required to search: name, years to search, DOB; also helpful: address. Criminal records on computer since 1988 on a statewide system. All mail requests are forwarded to Potter County for processing.

General Information: No juvenile, adoption, any record sealed by the Court or mental health records released. SASE required. Turnaround time approx 2 days. Copy fee: $.20 per page. Certification fee: $2.00.

Fee payee: Hughes County Clerk of Court. Personal checks accepted. Prepayment is required.

Hutchinson County

Circuit Court 140 Euclid Rm 36, Olivet, SD 57052-2103; 605-387-4215; Fax: 605-387-4209. Hours: 8AM-Noon, 1-5PM (CST). *Felony, Misdemeanor, Civil, Eviction, Small Claims, Probate.*

Civil Records: Access: Fax, mail, in person. Only the court performs in person searches; visitors may not. Search fee: $15.00 per name. Required to search: name, years to search; also helpful: address. Civil cases indexed by defendant, plaintiff. Civil records on docket books and index cards from 1800s, on computer since 1994.

Criminal Records: Access: Fax, mail, in person. Only the court performs in person searches; visitors may not. Search fee: $15.00 per name. Required to search: name, years to search, DOB; also helpful: address, SSN. Older records on docket books and index cards, records since 07/89 are computerized on a statewide system. All fax and mail requests are forwarded to Douglas County for processing.

General Information: No juvenile, sealed, dismissed, adoption or mental health records released. SASE required. Turnaround time 1 day. Fax notes: $5.00 per document. No fee if call is toll free, for commercial accounts only. Copy fee: $.10 per page. Certification fee: $2.00. Fee payee: Hutchinson County Clerk of Court. Business checks accepted. Prepayment required.

Hyde County

Circuit Court PO Box 306, Highmore, SD 57345; 605-852-2512; Fax: 605-852-3178. Hours: 8AM-12PM (CST). *Felony, Misdemeanor, Civil, Eviction, Small Claims, Probate.*

Civil Records: Access: Fax, mail, in person. Only the court performs in person searches; visitors may not. Search fee: $15.00 per name. Required to search: name, years to search; also helpful: address. Civil cases indexed by defendant, plaintiff. Civil records on docket books from 1920s.

Criminal Records: Access: Fax, mail, in person. Only the court performs in person searches; visitors may not. Search fee: $15.00 per name. Required to search: name, years to search, DOB; also helpful: address, SSN. Criminal records are computerized since 07/89 on a statewide system. All fax and mail requests are forwarded to Potter County for processing.

General Information: No juvenile, sealed, dismissed, or mental health records released. SASE required. Turnaround time 1-3 days. Fax notes: $5.00 per document. There is no fee if call is local or toll free. Copy fee: $.25 per page. Certification fee: $2.00. Fee payee: Hyde County Clerk of Courts. Personal checks accepted. Prepayment is required.

Jackson County

Circuit Court PO Box 128, Kadoka, SD 57543; 605-837-2121. Hours: 8AM-Noon, 1-5PM (MST). *Felony, Misdemeanor, Civil, Eviction, Small Claims, Probate.*

Civil Records: Access: Mail, in person. Only the court performs in person searches; visitors may not. Search fee: $15.00 per name. Required to search: name, years to search; also helpful: address. Civil cases indexed by defendant. Civil records on "Register of Action" from 1915.

Criminal Records: Access: Mail, in person. Only the court performs in person searches; visitors may not. Search fee: $15.00 per name. Required to search: name, years to search, DOB; also helpful: address, SSN. Criminal records on computer since 07/89 on a statewide system. All mail requests are forwarded to Potter County for processing.

General Information: No juvenile, sealed, dismissed, or mental health records released. SASE required. Turnaround time 1-2 days. Copy fee: $.20 per page. Certification fee: $2.00. Fee payee: Jackson County Clerk of Court. Personal checks accepted. Prepayment is required.

Jerauld County

Circuit Court PO Box 435, Wessington Springs, SD 57382; 605-539-1202; Fax: 605-539-1203. Hours: 8AM-5PM (CST). *Felony, Misdemeanor, Civil, Eviction, Small Claims, Probate.*

Civil Records: Access: Mail, in person. Only the court performs in person searches; visitors may not. Search fee: $15.00 per name. Required to search: name, years to search; also helpful: address. Civil cases indexed by defendant. Civil records on docket books from 1900s.

Criminal Records: Access: Fax, mail, in person. Only the court performs in person searches; visitors may not. Search fee: $15.00 per name. Required to search: name, years to search, DOB; also helpful: address, SSN. Criminal records are computerized since 1989 on a statewide system. Fax requesting for commercial accounts only.

General Information: No juvenile, sealed, dismissed, or mental health records released. SASE required. Turnaround time 2 days. Fax notes: $5.00 per page. No fee is call is local or toll free. Copy fee: $.25 per page. Certification fee: $2.00. Fee payee: Jerauld County Clerk of Court. Personal checks accepted. Prepayment is required.

Jones County

Circuit Court PO Box 448, Murdo, SD 57559; 605-669-2361. Hours: 8AM-Noon, 1-5PM (CST). *Felony, Misdemeanor, Civil, Eviction, Small Claims, Probate.*

Note: Criminal cases and records at Potter County.

Civil Records: Access: Mail, in person. Only the court performs in person searches; visitors may not. Search fee: $15.00 per name. Required to search: name, years to search; also helpful: address. Civil cases indexed by defendant, plaintiff. Civil records on docket books from 1900s.

Criminal Records: Access: Mail, in person. Only the court performs in person searches; visitors may not. Search fee: $15.00 per name. Required to search: name, years to search, DOB, SSN; also helpful: address. Criminal records are computerized since 07/89 on a statewide system. Records on books go back to 1917. All requests are forwarded to Potter County for processing.

General Information: No juvenile, sealed, dismissed, or mental health records released. SASE required. Turnaround time 3 days to 1 week. Fax notes: Fee to fax results is $1.00 per page; minimum $5.00. Copy fee: $.20 per page. Certification fee: $2.00. Fee payee: Jones County Clerk of Court (civil cases); Potter County Clerk of Court (criminal cases). Business checks accepted. Prepayment is required.

Kingsbury County

Circuit Court PO Box 176, De Smet, SD 57231-0176; 605-854-3811; Fax: 605-854-3811. Hours: 8AM-Noon, 1-5PM (CST). *Felony, Misdemeanor, Civil, Eviction, Small Claims, Probate.*

Civil Records: Access: Mail, in person. Both court and visitors may perform in person searches. Search fee: $15.00 per name. Required to search: name, years to search; also helpful: address. Civil cases indexed by defendant, plaintiff. Civil records on computer printed index from 1978 and bound books from 1890.

Criminal Records: Access: Mail, in person. Only the court performs in person searches; visitors may not. Search fee: $15.00 per name. Required to search: name, years to search, DOB; also helpful: address, SSN. Criminal records on computer since 07/89 on a statewide system. All mail requests are forwarded to Hand County for processing.

General Information: No juvenile, sealed, dismissed, adoption or mental health records released. SASE required. Turnaround time same day. Copy fee: $.20 per page. Certification fee: $2.00. Fee payee: Kingsbury County Clerk of Court. Personal checks accepted. Prepayment is required.

Lake County

Circuit Court 200 E Center St, Madison, SD 57042; 605-256-5644. 8AM-Noon, 1-5PM (CST). *Felony, Misdemeanor, Civil, Eviction, Small Claims, Probate.*

Civil Records: Access: Mail, in person. Only the court performs in person searches; visitors may not. Search fee: $15.00 per name. Required to search: name, years to search; also helpful: address. Civil cases indexed by defendant. Civil records on computer from 1985, docket books from 1800s.

Criminal Records: Access: Mail, in person. Only the court performs in person searches; visitors may not. Search fee: $15.00 per name. Required to search: name, years to search, DOB, signed release; also helpful: address, SSN. Criminal records on computer since 1989 on a statewide system; prior records on docket books since 1800s. All mail requests are forwarded to Miner County for processing.

General Information: No juvenile, sealed, dismissed, or mental health records released. SASE required. Turnaround time 1 day. Copy fee: $.20 per page. Certification fee: $2.00. Fee payee: Lake County Clerk of Court. Personal checks accepted. Prepayment is required.

Lawrence County

Circuit Court PO Box 626, Deadwood, SD 57732; 605-578-2040. Hours: 8AM-5PM (MST). *Felony, Misdemeanor, Civil, Eviction, Small Claims, Probate.*

Civil Records: Access: Mail, in person. Only the court performs in person searches; visitors may not. Search fee: $15.00 per name. Required to search: name, years to search; also helpful: address. Civil cases indexed by defendant, plaintiff. Civil records on computer from 1989 and index books from 1800s.

Criminal Records: Access: Fax, mail, in person. Only the court performs in person searches; visitors may not. Search fee: $15.00 per name. Required to search: name, years to search, DOB; also helpful: address, SSN. Criminal records on computer since 07/89 on a statewide system. Fax requesting only available for commercial accounts.

General Information: No juvenile, sealed, dismissed, or mental health records released. SASE required. Turnaround time 2 weeks. Fax notes: $5.00 per document. No fee for local or toll free calls. Copy fee: $.20 per page. Certification fee: $2.00. Fee payee: Lawrence County Clerk of Court. Personal checks accepted. Prepayment is required.

Lincoln County

Circuit Court Clerk of Courts, 100 E 5th St, Canton, SD 57013; 605-987-5891. 8AM-5PM (CST). *Felony, Misdemeanor, Civil, Eviction, Small Claims, Probate.*

Civil Records: Access: Mail, in person. Only the court performs in person searches; visitors may not. Search fee: $15.00 per name. Required to search: name, years to search; also helpful: address. Civil cases indexed by defendant, plaintiff. Civil records on docket books from 1900s. Visitor may search written index pre-1993; only the court searches computer records 1994 forward.

Criminal Records: Access: Mail, in person. Only the court performs in person searches; visitors may not. Search fee: $15.00 per name. Required to search: name, years to search, DOB; also helpful: address, SSN. Criminal records on computer since 07/89 on a

statewide system. All mail requests are forwarded to Douglas County.

General Information: No juvenile, sealed, dismissed, adoption or mental health records released. SASE required. Turnaround time 2 days, longer for probate. Copy fee: $.20 per page. Certification fee: $2.00. Fee payee: Lincoln County Clerk of Court. Personal checks accepted. Prepayment is required.

Lyman County

Circuit Court PO Box 235, Kennebec, SD 57544; 605-869-2277. Hours: 8AM-5PM (CST). *Felony, Misdemeanor, Civil, Eviction, Small Claims, Probate.*

Civil Records: Access: Mail, in person. Both court and visitors may perform in person searches. Search fee: $15.00 per name. Required to search: name, years to search; also helpful: address. Civil cases indexed by defendant, plaintiff. Civil records on docket books from 1900s; on computer back one year.

Criminal Records: Access: Mail, in person. Only the court performs in person searches; visitors may not. Search fee: $15.00 per name. Required to search: name, years to search, DOB; also helpful: address, SSN. Criminal records on computer since 07/89 on a statewide system. All mail requests forwarded to Potter county for processing.

General Information: No juvenile, sealed, dismissed, or mental health records released. SASE required. Turnaround time 1 week. Fax notes: Fee to fax results is $1.00 per page. Copy fee: $.20 per page. Certification fee: $2.00. Fee payee: Lyman County Clerk of Court. Personal checks accepted. Prepayment is required.

Marshall County

Circuit Court PO Box 130, Britton, SD 57430; 605-448-5213. Hours: 8AM-Noon, 1-5PM (CST). *Felony, Misdemeanor, Civil, Eviction, Small Claims, Probate.*

Civil Records: Access: Phone, mail, in person. Only the court performs in person searches; visitors may not. Search fee: $15.00 per name. Required to search: name, years to search; also helpful: address. Civil cases indexed by defendant, plaintiff. Civil records on docket books from 1800s.

Criminal Records: Access: Phone, mail, in person. Only the court performs in person searches; visitors may not. Search fee: $15.00 per name. Required to search: name, years to search, DOB; also helpful: address, SSN. Criminal records are computerized since 07/89 on a statewide system. All mail requests forwarded to Edmunds County for processing.

General Information: Public Access terminal is available. No juvenile, sealed, dismissed, or mental health records released. SASE required. Turnaround time 1 week. Copy fee: $.20 per page. Certification fee: $2.00. Fee payee: Marshall County Clerk of Court. Personal checks accepted. Prepayment is required.

McCook County

Circuit Court PO Box 504, Salem, SD 57058; 605-425-2781; Fax: 605-425-3144. Hours: 8AM-5PM (CST). *Felony, Misdemeanor, Civil, Eviction, Small Claims, Probate.*

Civil Records: Access: Mail, in person. Both court and visitors may perform in person searches. Search fee: $15.00 per name. Required to search: name, years to search; also helpful: address. Civil cases indexed by defendant, plaintiff. Civil records in index and docket books from late 1800s.

Criminal Records: Access: Mail, in person. Only the court performs in person searches; visitors may not. Search fee: $15.00 per name. Required to search: name, years to search, DOB, signed release; also helpful: address, SSN. Criminal records are computerized since 07/89 on a statewide system. All mail requests are forwarded to Miner County for processing. In person requests must be written.

General Information: No juvenile, sealed, dismissed, or mental health records released. SASE required. Turnaround time 1 day. Copy fee: $.20 per page. Certification fee: $2.00. Fee payee: McCook County Clerk of Court. Personal checks accepted. Prepayment is required.

McPherson County

Circuit Court PO Box 248, Leola, SD 57456; 605-439-3361; Fax: 605-439-3394. Hours: 8AM-Noon (CST). *Felony, Misdemeanor, Civil, Eviction, Small Claims, Probate.*

Civil Records: Access: Mail, in person. Both court and visitors may perform in person searches. Search fee: $15.00 per name. Required to search: name, years to search; also helpful: address. Civil cases indexed by defendant, plaintiff. Civil records on register of action from 1910, records are not computerized. There is no fee if case number is known for in person searchers.

Criminal Records: Access: Mail, in person. Only the court performs in person searches; visitors may not. Search fee: $15.00 per name. Required to search: name, years to search, DOB, signed release; also helpful: address, SSN. Criminal records on register of action from 1910, records are not computerized. All mail requests are forwarded to Edmunds County for processing.

General Information: No juvenile, sealed, dismissed, adoption or mental health records released. SASE required. Turnaround time 1 day to 1 week. Copy fee: $.25 per page. Certification fee: $2.00. Fee payee: McPherson County Clerk of Court. Personal checks accepted. Prepayment is required.

Meade County

Circuit Court PO Box 939, Sturgis, SD 57785; 605-347-4411; Fax: 605-347-3526. Hours: 8AM-Noon, 1-5PM (MST). *Felony, Misdemeanor, Civil, Eviction, Small Claims, Probate.*

Civil Records: Access: Mail, in person. Both court and visitors may perform in person searches. Search fee: $15.00 per name. Required to search: name, years to search; also helpful: address. Civil cases indexed by defendant, plaintiff. Civil records on index cards and docket books from 1800s.

Criminal Records: Access: Mail, in person. Only the court performs in person searches; visitors may not. Search fee: $15.00 per name. Required to search: name, years to search, DOB, signed release; also helpful: address, SSN. Criminal records on computer since 07/89 on a statewide system. All mail requests are forwarded to Lawrence County for processing.

General Information: No juvenile, sealed, dismissed, or mental health records released. SASE required. Turnaround time 1 day to 2 weeks. Copy fee: $.20 per page. Certification fee: $2.00. Fee payee: Meade County Clerk of Courts. Personal checks accepted. Prepayment is required.

Mellette County

Circuit Court PO Box 257, White River, SD 57579; 605-259-3230; Fax: 605-259-3194. Hours: 8AM-Noon (CST). *Felony, Misdemeanor, Civil, Eviction, Small Claims, Probate.*

Civil Records: Access: Phone, mail, in person. Both court and visitors may perform in person searches. Search fee: $15.00 per name. Required to search: name, years to search; also helpful: address. Civil cases indexed by defendant. Civil records on index cards and docket books from 1900s.

Criminal Records: Access: Phone, mail, in person. Only the court performs in person searches; visitors may not. Search fee: $15.00 per name. Required to search: name, years to search, DOB, signed release; also helpful: address, SSN. Criminal records are computerized since 07/89 on a statewide system. All mail requests are forwarded to Potter County for processing.

General Information: No juvenile, sealed, dismissed, or mental health records released. SASE not required. Turnaround time 3 days, Probate up to 1 month. Copy fee: $.20 per page. Certification fee: $2.00. Fee payee: Mellette County Clerk of Court. Personal checks accepted. Prepayment is required.

Miner County

Circuit Court PO Box 265, Howard, SD 57349; 605-772-4612; Fax: 605-772-4412. Hours: 8AM-noon; 1-5PM (CST). *Felony, Misdemeanor, Civil, Eviction, Small Claims, Probate.*

Civil Records: Access: Mail, in person. Both court and visitors may perform in person searches. Search fee: $15.00 per name. Required to search: name, years to search. Civil cases indexed by defendant, plaintiff. Civil records on docket books from 1800s.

Criminal Records: Access: Fax, mail, in person. Only the court performs in person searches; visitors may not. Search fee: $15.00 per name. Required to search: name, years to search, DOB; also helpful: SSN. Criminal records are computerized since 07/89. This is a statewide search.

General Information: No juvenile, sealed, dismissed or mental health records released. SASE required. Turnaround time 2 days. Fax notes: $5.00 per document. There is no fee is call is local or toll free. Copy fee: $.25 per page. Certification fee: $2.00 per page. Fee payee: Miner County Clerk of Court. Personal checks accepted. Prepayment is required.

Minnehaha County

Circuit Court 425 N Dakota Ave, Sioux Falls, SD 57104; 605-367-5900; Fax: 605-367-5916. Hours: 8AM-5PM (CST). *Felony, Misdemeanor, Civil, Eviction, Small Claims, Probate.*

Civil Records: Access: Mail, in person. Only the court performs in person searches; visitors may not. Search fee: $15.00 per name. Required to search: name, years to search; also helpful: address. Civil cases indexed by defendant, plaintiff. Civil records on computer from 1989, docket books from 1800s.

Criminal Records: Access: Mail, in person. Only the court performs in person searches; visitors may not. Search fee: $15.00 per name. Required to search: name, years to search, DOB, signed release; also helpful: address, SSN. Criminal records on computer since 07/89. All mail requests are forwarded to either Jerauld or Sanborn counties for processing. This is a statewide system.

General Information: No juvenile, sealed, dismissed or mental health records released. SASE required. Turnaround time 2 weeks. Copy fee: $.20 per page. Certification fee: $2.00. Fee payee: Minnehaha County Clerk of Court. Personal checks accepted. Prepayment is required.

Moody County

Circuit Court 101 E Pipestone, Flandreau, SD 57028; 605-997-3181; Fax: 605-997-3861. Hours: 8AM-5PM (CST). *Felony, Misdemeanor, Civil, Eviction, Small Claims, Probate.*

Civil Records: Access: Mail, in person. Only the court performs in person searches; visitors may not. Search fee: $15.00 per name. Required to search: name, years to search; also helpful: address. Civil cases indexed by defendant, plaintiff. Civil records on computer from 1992 and docket books from 1800s.

Criminal Records: Access: Mail, in person. Only the court performs in person searches; visitors may not. Search fee: $15.00 per name. Required to search: name, years to search, DOB; also helpful: address, SSN. Criminal records on computer since 07/89 on a

statewide index. All mail requests are forwarded to Miner County of processing.

General Information: No juvenile, sealed, dismissed, adoption or mental health records released. SASE required. Turnaround time 2-3 days. Copy fee: $.20 per page. Certification fee: $2.00. Fee payee: Moody County Clerk of Court. Personal checks accepted. Prepayment is required.

Pennington County

Circuit Court PO Box 230, Rapid City, SD 57709; 605-394-2575. Hours: 8AM-5PM (MST). *Felony, Misdemeanor, Civil, Eviction, Small Claims, Probate.*

Note: If prior to 1989, mail requests should be sent to Pennington County Clerk - arrest date and charge is required to conduct search. If 1989 to present, mail to Harding County Clerk, POB 534, Buffalo, SD 57720, 605-375-3351.

Civil Records: Access: Mail, in person. Only the court performs in person searches; visitors may not. Search fee: $15.00 per name. Required to search: name, years to search; also helpful: address. Civil records on computer from 1991, cards and docket books from 1800s.

Criminal Records: Access: Mail, in person. Only the court performs in person searches; visitors may not. Search fee: $15.00 per name. Required to search: name, years to search, DOB; also helpful: address, SSN. Criminal records are computerized since 1989 on a statewide system.

General Information: No juvenile, sealed, dismissed, or mental health records released. SASE required. Turnaround time 1 week. Copy fee: $.25 per page. Certification fee: $2.00. Fee payee: Clerk of Courts. Personal checks accepted. Prepayment is required.

Perkins County

Circuit Court PO Box 426, Bison, SD 57620-0426; 605-244-5626; Fax: 605-244-7110. Hours: 8AM-Noon, 1-5PM (MST). *Felony, Misdemeanor, Civil, Eviction, Small Claims, Probate.*

Civil Records: Access: Fax, mail, in person. Both court and visitors may perform in person searches. Search fee: $15.00 per name. Required to search: name, years to search. Civil cases indexed by defendant, plaintiff. Civil records on docket books from 1908.

Criminal Records: Access: Fax, mail, in person. Only the court performs in person searches; visitors may not. Search fee: $15.00 per name. Required to search: name, years to search, DOB, signed release. Criminal records are computerized from 07/89 on a statewide system. All fax and mail requests are forwarded to Lawrence County for processing.

General Information: No juvenile, sealed or mental health records released. SASE requested. Turnaround time varies. Fax notes: $1.00 per page. $5.00 minimum, no fee for toll free calls. Copy fee: $.25 per page. Certification fee: $2.00. Fee payee: Perkins County Clerk of Courts. Only cashiers checks and money orders accepted. Prepayment is required.

Potter County

Circuit Court 201 S Exene, Gettysburg, SD 57442; 605-765-9472. Hours: 8AM-Noon, 1-5PM (CST). *Felony, Misdemeanor, Civil, Eviction, Small Claims, Probate.*

Civil Records: Access: Mail, in person. Only the court performs in person searches; visitors may not. Search fee: $15.00 per name. Required to search: name, years to search; also helpful: address. Civil cases indexed by defendant, plaintiff. Civil records on index cards and docket books from 1889.

Criminal Records: Access: Fax, mail, in person. Only the court performs in person searches; visitors may not. Search fee: $15.00 per name. Required to search: name, years to search, DOB, signed release; also helpful:

address, SSN. Criminal records are indexed on computer since 07/89 on a statewide system.

General Information: No juvenile, sealed, dismissed, adoption or mental health records released. SASE required. Turnaround time 1-2 days. Fax notes: $5.00 per document. Faxing is for commercial accounts only, no fee if call is toll free. Copy fee: $.15 per page. Certification fee: $2.00. Fee payee: Potter County Clerk of Court. Personal checks accepted. Prepayment is required.

Roberts County

Circuit Court 411 2nd Ave E, Sisseton, SD 57262; 605-698-3395; Fax: 605-698-7894. Hours: 8AM-5PM (CST). *Felony, Misdemeanor, Civil, Eviction, Small Claims, Probate.*

Civil Records: Access: Mail, in person. Only the court performs in person searches; visitors may not. Search fee: $15.00 per name. Required to search: name, years to search; also helpful: address. Civil cases indexed by defendant, plaintiff. Civil records on computer from 1992, microfilm from 1920 to 1975 and original files from 1986.

Criminal Records: Access: Mail, in person. Only the court performs in person searches; visitors may not. Search fee: $15.00 per name. Required to search: name, years to search, DOB; also helpful: address, SSN. Criminal records on computer since 1988 on a state wide system. Criminal search requests should be sent to Edmunds County (PO Box 384, Ipswich SD 57451; 605-426-6323 fax) for processing.

General Information: No juvenile, sealed, dismissed, adoption or mental health records released. SASE required. Turnaround time 2-3 days. Copy fee: $.20 per page. Certification fee: $2.00. Fee payee: Roberts County Clerk of Court or, Edmunds City Clerk, if a criminal search. Personal checks accepted. Prepayment is required.

Sanborn County

Circuit Court PO Box 56, Woonsocket, SD 57385; 605-796-4515; Fax: 605-796-4509. Hours: 8AM-5PM (CST). *Felony, Misdemeanor, Civil, Eviction, Small Claims, Probate.*

Civil Records: Access: Mail, in person. Only the court performs in person searches; visitors may not. Search fee: $15.00 per name. Required to search: name, years to search; also helpful: address. Civil cases indexed by defendant, plaintiff. Civil records on docket books from 1890s.

Criminal Records: Access: Fax, mail, in person. Only the court performs in person searches; visitors may not. Search fee: $15.00 per name. Required to search: name, years to search, DOB; also helpful: address, SSN. Criminal records are computerized since 1989 on a statewide system.

General Information: No juvenile, sealed, dismissed, or mental health records released. SASE required. Turnaround time 1 week. Fax notes: $1.00 per page. $5.00 minimum, no fee if toll free. Copy fee: $.25 per page. Certification fee: $2.00. Fee payee: Sanborn County Clerk of Courts. Personal checks accepted. No two party checks. Prepayment is required.

Shannon County

Circuit Court 906 N River St, Hot Springs, SD 57747; 605-745-5131. 8AM-5PM (MST). *Felony, Misdemeanor, Civil, Eviction, Small Claims, Probate.*

Note: Also handles cases for Fall River County. Specify which county in your search request.

Civil Records: Access: Mail, in person. Only the court performs in person searches; visitors may not. Search fee: $15.00 per name. Required to search: name, years to search; also helpful: address. Civil cases indexed by defendant, plaintiff. Civil records on computer from 1991, index books from 1889.

Criminal Records: Access: Mail, in person. Only the court performs in person searches; visitors may not. Search fee: $15.00 per name. Required to search: name, years to search, DOB; also helpful: address, SSN. Criminal records on computer since 07/89 on a statewide system. All mail requests are forwarded to Fall River County for processing.

General Information: No juvenile, sealed, adoption, or mental health records released. SASE required. Turnaround time 1 week. Copy fee: $.25 per page. Certification fee: $2.00. Fee payee: Shannon County Clerk of Court. Personal checks accepted. Prepayment is required.

Spink County

Circuit Court 210 E 7th Ave, Redfield, SD 57469; 605-472-4535; Fax: 605-472-4352. Hours: 8AM-5PM (CST). *Felony, Misdemeanor, Civil, Eviction, Small Claims, Probate.*

Civil Records: Access: Phone, fax, mail, in person. Only the court performs in person searches; visitors may not. Search fee: $15.00 per name. Required to search: name, years to search; also helpful: address. Civil cases indexed by defendant, plaintiff. Civil records on docket books from 1882.

Criminal Records: Access: Phone, fax, mail, in person. Only the court performs in person searches; visitors may not. Search fee: $15.00 per name. Required to search: name, years to search, DOB; also helpful: address, SSN. Criminal records on computer since 1988 on a statewide system. All fax and mail requests are forwarded to Edmunds County for processing.

General Information: No juvenile, sealed, dismissed, or mental health records released. SASE required. Turnaround time 1 day. Fax notes: $5.00 per document. No fee if call is toll free, must be a commercial account. Copy fee: $.20 per page. Certification fee: $2.00. Fee payee: Spink County Clerk of Court. Personal checks accepted. Prepayment is required.

Stanley County

Circuit Court PO Box 758, Fort Pierre, SD 57532; 605-773-3992; Fax: 605-773-6330. Hours: 8AM-5PM (CST). *Felony, Misdemeanor, Civil, Eviction, Small Claims, Probate.*

Civil Records: Access: Mail, in person. Both court and visitors may perform in person searches. Search fee: $15.00 per name. Required to search: name, years to search; also helpful: address. Civil cases indexed by defendant, plaintiff. Civil records on docket books from 1973.

Criminal Records: Access: Mail, in person. Only the court performs in person searches; visitors may not. Search fee: $15.00 per name. Required to search: name, years to search, DOB; also helpful: address, SSN. Criminal records on computer since 1989 on a statewide system. All mail requests are forwarded to Potter County for processing.

General Information: No juvenile, sealed, dismissed, or mental health records released. SASE required. Turnaround time 1-2 days. Copy fee: $.20 per page. Certification fee: $2.00. Fee payee: Stanley County Clerk of Court. Personal checks accepted. Prepayment is required.

Sully County

Circuit Court PO Box 188, Onida, SD 57564; 605-258-2535; Fax: 605-258-2382. Hours: 8AM-Noon (CST). *Felony, Misdemeanor, Civil, Eviction, Small Claims, Probate.*

Civil Records: Access: Mail, in person. Only the court performs in person searches; visitors may not. Search fee: $15.00 per name. Required to search: name, years to search; also helpful: address. Civil cases indexed by defendant, plaintiff. Civil records on docket books from 1900s.

Criminal Records: Access: Mail, in person. Only the court performs in person searches; visitors may not. Search fee: $15.00 per name. Required to search: name, years to search; also helpful: address. Criminal records on computer since 07/89 on statewide system. All mail requests are forwarded to Potter County for processing.

General Information: No juvenile, sealed, dismissed, or mental health records released. SASE required. Turnaround time 1-2 days. Copy fee: $.25 per page. Certification fee: $2.00. Fee payee: Sully County Clerk of Court. No personal checks. Prepayment is required.

Todd County

Circuit Court 200 E 3rd St, PO Box 311, Winner, SD 57580; 605-842-2266; Fax: 605-842-2267. Hours: 8AM-5PM (MST). *Felony, Misdemeanor, Civil, Eviction, Small Claims, Probate.*

Civil Records: Access: Mail, in person. Only the court performs in person searches; visitors may not. Search fee: $15.00 per name. Required to search: name, years to search; also helpful: address. Civil cases indexed by defendant, plaintiff. Civil records on docket books from 1920s.

Criminal Records: Access: Mail, in person. Only the court performs in person searches; visitors may not. Search fee: $15.00 per name. Required to search: name, years to search, DOB, signed release; also helpful: address, SSN. Criminal records on computer since 07/89 on statewide system. All mail requests are forwarded to Potter County for processing.

General Information: No juvenile, sealed, dismissed, or mental health records released. SASE required. Turnaround time 2 days. Copy fee: $.20 per page. Certification fee: $2.00. Fee payee: Todd County Clerk of Court. Personal checks accepted. Prepayment required.

Tripp County

Circuit Court 200 E 3rd St, PO Box 377, Winner, SD 57580; 605-842-2266; Fax: 605-842-2267. Hours: 8AM-5PM (CST). *Felony, Misdemeanor, Civil, Eviction, Small Claims, Probate.*

Civil Records: Access: Mail, in person. Only the court performs in person searches; visitors may not. Search fee: $15.00 per name. Required to search: name, years to search; also helpful: address. Civil cases indexed by defendant, plaintiff. Civil records on docket books from 1920s.

Criminal Records: Access: Mail, in person. Only the court performs in person searches; visitors may not. Search fee: $15.00 per name. Required to search: name, years to search, DOB, signed release; also helpful: address, SSN. Criminal records on computer since 1989 on statewide system. All mail requests are forwarded to Potter County for processing.

General Information: No juvenile, sealed, dismissed, or mental health records released. SASE required. Turnaround time 2 days. Copy fee: $.20 per page. Certification fee: $2.00. Fee payee: Tripp County Clerk of Court. Personal checks accepted. Prepayment is required.

Turner County

Circuit Court PO Box 446, Parker, SD 57053; 605-297-3115; Fax: 605-297-2115. Hours: 8AM-5PM (CST). *Felony, Misdemeanor, Civil, Eviction, Small Claims, Probate.*

Civil Records: Access: Mail, in person. Only the court performs in person searches; visitors may not. Search fee: $15.00 per name. Required to search: name, years to search; also helpful: address. Civil cases indexed by defendant, plaintiff. Civil records on index cards and docket books from 1900s.

Criminal Records: Access: Mail, in person. Only the court performs in person searches; visitors may not. Search fee: $15.00 per name. Required to search: name,

years to search, DOB, signed release; also helpful: address, SSN. Criminal records on computer since 07/89 on a statewide system. All mail requests are forwarded to Douglas County for processing.

General Information: No juvenile, sealed, dismissed, or mental health records released. SASE required. Turnaround time 2 days. Fax notes: Fee to fax results is $1.00 per page; $5.00 minimum. Copy fee: $.25 per page. Certification fee: $2.00. Fee payee: Turner County Clerk of Courts. Prepayment is required.

Union County

Circuit Court PO Box 757, Elk Point, SD 57025; 605-356-2132; Fax: 605-356-3687. Hours: 8:30AM-5PM (CST). *Felony, Misdemeanor, Civil, Eviction, Small Claims, Probate.*

Civil Records: Access: Fax, mail, in person. Only the court performs in person searches; visitors may not. Search fee: $15.00 per name. Required to search: name, years to search; also helpful: address. Civil cases indexed by defendant, plaintiff. Civil records on computer from 1990, docket books from 1900s.

Criminal Records: Access: Fax, mail, in person. Only the court performs in person searches; visitors may not. Search fee: $15.00 per name. Required to search: name, years to search, DOB; also helpful: address, SSN. Criminal records on computer since 1988 on a statewide system, on docket books from 1900s. All mail requests for years 1988 to present are forwarded to Douglas County for processing.

General Information: No juvenile, sealed, dismissed, or mental health records released. SASE required. Turnaround time 1-2 days. Fax notes: Fee to fax results is $5.00 or $1.00 per page, whichever is greater. Copy fee: $.20 per page. Certification fee: $2.00. Fee payee: Union County Clerk of Court. Personal checks accepted. Prepayment is required.

Walworth County

Circuit Court PO Box 328, Selby, SD 57472; 605-649-7311; Fax: 605-649-7624. Hours: 8AM-5PM (CST). *Felony, Misdemeanor, Civil, Eviction, Small Claims, Probate.*

Civil Records: Access: Mail, in person. Only the court performs in person searches; visitors may not. Search fee: $15.00 per name. Required to search: name, years to search; also helpful: address. Civil cases indexed by defendant, plaintiff. Civil records on index cards and docket books from 1900s.

Criminal Records: Access: Mail, in person. Only the court performs in person searches; visitors may not. Search fee: $15.00 per name. Required to search: name, years to search, DOB, signed release; also helpful: address, SSN. Criminal records on computer since 07/89 in a statewide system. All mail requests are forwarded to Edmunds County for processing.

General Information: No juvenile, sealed, dismissed, or mental health records released. SASE required. Turnaround time 1-2 days. Copy fee: $.20 per page. Certification fee: $2.00. Fee payee: Walworth County Clerk of Court. Personal checks accepted. Prepayment is required.

Yankton County

Circuit Court PO Box 155, Yankton, SD 57078; 605-668-3080. Hours: 8AM-5PM (CST). *Felony, Misdemeanor, Civil, Eviction, Small Claims, Probate.*

Civil Records: Access: Mail, in person. Both court and visitors may perform in person searches. Search fee: $15.00 per name. Required to search: name, years to search; also helpful: address. Civil cases indexed by defendant, plaintiff. Civil records on computer from 1991, docket books from 1900s. Visitors only have access to the book index.

Criminal Records: Access: Mail, in person. Both court and visitors may perform in person searches. Search

fee: $15.00 per name. Must be a state authorized account. Required to search: name, years to search, DOB; also helpful: address, SSN. Criminal records on computer since 07/89 on a statewide system, Class II offenses not accessible on computer to public. Visitors only have access to the book index. All mail requests are forwarded to Douglas County for processing.

General Information: No juvenile, sealed, dismissed, or mental health records released. SASE required. Turnaround time 1 week. Copy fee: $.20 per page. Certification fee: $2.00. Fee payee: Yankton County Clerk of Court. Personal checks accepted. Prepayment is required.

Ziebach County

Circuit Court PO Box 306, Dupree, SD 57623; 605-365-5159. Hours: 9:30AM-Noon, 1-2:30PM (MST). *Felony, Misdemeanor, Civil, Eviction, Small Claims, Probate.*

Civil Records: Access: Mail, in person. Only the court performs in person searches; visitors may not. Search fee: $15.00 per name. Required to search: name, years to search; also helpful: address. Civil cases indexed by defendant. Civil records on index books from 1900s.

Criminal Records: Access: Mail, in person. Only the court performs in person searches; visitors may not.

Search fee: $15.00 per name. Required to search: name, years to search, DOB; also helpful: address, SSN. Criminal records on index books from 1900s. All mail requests are forwarded to Lawrence County for processing.

General Information: No juvenile, sealed, dismissed, adoption or mental health records released. SASE required. Turnaround time 2-3 days. Copy fee: $.10 per page. Certification fee: $2.00. Fee payee: Ziebach County Clerk of Court. Personal checks accepted. Prepayment is required.

South Dakota Recording Offices

ORGANIZATION

66 counties, 66 recording offices. The recording officer is. Register of Deeds. 48 counties are in the Central Time Zone (CST) and 18 are in the Mountain Time Zone (MST).

REAL ESTATE RECORDS

Many counties will perform real estate searches. Search fees and copy fees vary. Certification usually costs $1.00 per document.

UCC RECORDS

Financing statements are filed at the state level, except for real estate related collateral, which are filed with the Register of Deeds. All recording offices will perform UCC searches. All counties have access to a statewide database of UCC filings. Use search request form UCC-11. Searches fees are usually $10.00 per debtor name. Copy fees are usually $1.00 per page.

TAX LIEN RECORDS

Federal and state tax liens on personal property of businesses are filed with the Secretary of State. Other federal and state tax liens are filed with the county Register of Deeds. Most counties will perform tax lien searches. Search fees and copy fees vary.

OTHER LIENS

Mechanics, motor vehicle, materials.

Aurora County

Register of Deeds, P.O. Box 397, Plankinton, SD 57368. 605-942-7161; Fax 605-942-7751.
Will search UCC records. Will not search real estate records. **Other Phone Numbers:** Assessor 605-942-7164; Treasurer 605-942-7162.

Beadle County

Register of Deeds, P.O. Box 55, Huron, SD 57350-0055. 605-353-8412 R/E Recording: 605-352-3168; Fax 605-353-8402.
Will search UCC records. Will not search real estate records. **Other Phone Numbers:** Assessor 605-353-8408; Treasurer 605-353-8405; Elections 605-353-8400; Vital Records 605-353-8412.

Bennett County

Register of Deeds, P.O. Box 433, Martin, SD 57551-0433. 605-685-6054; Fax 605-685-6311.
Will search UCC records. Will not search real estate records. **Other Phone Numbers:** Assessor 605-685-6991; Treasurer 605-685-6092.

Bon Homme County

Register of Deeds, P.O. Box 3, Tyndall, SD 57066. 605-589-4217 R/E Recording: 605-589-3302.
Will search UCC records. UCC search includes tax liens if requested. Will not search real estate records. **Other Phone Numbers:** Assessor 605-589-3462.

Brookings County

Register of Deeds, 314 6th Avenue, Courthouse, Brookings, SD 57006-2084. 605-696-8240 R/E Recording: 605-692-2724; Fax 605-696-8245.
Will search UCC records. UCC search includes tax liens if requested. RE record owner and mortgage searches available. **Other Phone Numbers:** Assessor 605-696-8220; Treasurer 605-696-8250; Appraiser/Auditor 605-696-8301; Elections 605-696-8220; Vital Records 605-696-8240.

Brown County

Register of Deeds, P.O. Box 1307, Aberdeen, SD 57402-1307. 605-626-7140 R/E Recording: 605-622-7140; Fax 605-626-4010.
Will search UCC records. Will not search real estate records. **Other Phone Numbers:** Assessor 605-622-7133.

Brule County

Register of Deeds, 300 South Courtland, Suite 110, Chamberlain, SD 57325. 605-734-5310.
Will search UCC records. Will not search real estate records. **Other Phone Numbers:** Assessor 605-734-5335.

Buffalo County

Register of Deeds, P.O. Box 174, Gannvalley, SD 57341. 605-293-3239; Fax 605-293-3240.
Will search UCC records. Will not search real estate records. **Other Phone Numbers:** Assessor 605-293-3236; Treasurer 605-293-3236.

Butte County

Register of Deeds, 839 Fifth Avenue, Belle Fourche, SD 57717. 605-892-2912.
Will search UCC records. Will not search real estate records. **Other Phone Numbers:** Assessor 605-892-3950; Treasurer 605-892-4456.

Campbell County

Register of Deeds, P.O. Box 148, Mound City, SD 57646-0148. Register of Deeds, R/E and UCC Recording 605-955-3505; Fax 605-955-3308.
Will search UCC records. Will not search real estate records. **Other Phone Numbers:** Assessor 605-955-3577; Treasurer 605-955-3388; Appraiser/Auditor 605-955-3577; Elections 605-955-3366; Vital Records 605-955-3505.

Charles Mix County

Register of Deeds, P.O. Box 206, Lake Andes, SD 57356-0206. Register of Deeds, R/E and UCC Recording 605-487-7141; Fax 605-487-7221.
Will search UCC records. **Other Phone Numbers:** Assessor 605-487-7382; Treasurer 605-487-7142; Elections 605-487-7131; Vital Records 605-487-7141.

Clark County

Register of Deeds, P.O. Box 294, Clark, SD 57225-0294. 605-532-5363 R/E Recording: 605-632-5363 UCC Recording: 605-632-5363; Fax 605-532-5931.
Will search UCC records. Real Estate search fee-$10.00. **Other Phone Numbers:** Assessor 605-532-3751; Treasurer 605-532-5911; Elections 605-532-5921; Vital Records 605-632-5363.

Clay County

Register of Deeds, 211 West Main Street, Suite 202, Vermillion, SD 57069. 605-677-7130 R/E Recording: 605-624-2871.
Will search UCC records. UCC search includes tax liens if requested. Will not search real estate records. **Other Phone Numbers:** Assessor 605-677-7140; Treasurer 605-677-7123; Elections 605-677-7120; Vital Records 605-677-7130.

Codington County

Register of Deeds, 14 1st Avenue S.E., Watertown, SD 57201-3695. 605-882-6278 R/E Recording: 605-886-4719; Fax 602-882-5230.
Will search UCC records. Will not search real estate records. **Other Phone Numbers:** Assessor 605-886-6274; Treasurer 605-886-6285; Elections 605-882-6297; Vital Records 605-882-6278.

Corson County

Register of Deeds, P.O. Box 256, McIntosh, SD 57641-0256. 605-273-4395; Fax 605-273-4304.
Will search UCC records. Will not search real estate records. **Other Phone Numbers:** Assessor 605-273-4354; Treasurer 605-273-4552.

Custer County

Register of Deeds, 420 Mount Rushmore Road, Custer, SD 57730-1934. 605-673-2784; Fax 605-673-3439.
Will search UCC records. Will not search real estate records. **Other Phone Numbers:** Assessor 605-673-4817; Treasurer 605-673-2282.

Davison County

Register of Deeds, 200 East 4th, Courthouse, Mitchell, SD 57301-2692. 605-995-8616 R/E Recording: 605-996-2209; Fax 605-995-8648.
http://www.davisoncounty.org/registerofdeeds.html
Will search UCC records. Tax Lien Search per debtor name- $5.00. Will not search real estate records. **Other Phone Numbers:** Assessor 605-995-8613; Treasurer 605-995-8617; Appraiser/Auditor 605-995-8613; Elections 605-995-8608; Vital Records 605-995-8616; Court Clerk 605-995-8105.

Day County

Register of Deeds, 711 West First Street, Webster, SD 57274-1396. Register of Deeds, R/E and UCC Recording 605-345-4162; Fax 605-345-4162.
Will search UCC records. UCC search includes tax liens if requested. Will not search real estate records.

Other Phone Numbers: Assessor 605-345-3151; Treasurer 605-345-3081; Elections 605-345-3103; Vital Records 605-345-4162.

Deuel County

Register of Deeds, P.O. Box 307, Clear Lake, SD 57226. Register of Deeds, R/E and UCC Recording 605-874-2268; Fax 605-874-1306.
Will search UCC records. **Other Phone Numbers:** Assessor 605-874-2229; Treasurer 605-874-2483; Elections 605-874-2312; Vital Records 605-874-2268.

Dewey County

Register of Deeds, P.O. Box 117, Timber Lake, SD 57656-0117. Register of Deeds, R/E and UCC Recording 605-865-3661; Fax 605-865-3691.
Will search UCC records. Will search R/E records. **Other Phone Numbers:** Assessor 605-865-3573; Treasurer 605-865-3501; Appraiser/Auditor 605-865-3730; Elections 605-865-3672; Vital Records 605-865-3661.

Douglas County

Register of Deeds, P.O. Box 267, Armour, SD 57313-0267. 605-724-2204; Fax 605-724-2204.
Will search UCC records. **Other Phone Numbers:** Assessor 605-724-2688.

Edmunds County

Register of Deeds, P.O. Box 386, Ipswich, SD 57451-0386. Register of Deeds, R/E and UCC Recording 605-426-6431; Fax 605-426-6257.
Will search UCC records. This agency will not do a tax lien search. Will not search real estate records. **Other Phone Numbers:** Assessor 605-426-6841; Treasurer 605-426-6801; Appraiser/Auditor 605-426-6841; Elections 605-426-6762; Vital Records 605-426-6431.

Fall River County

Register of Deeds, 906 North River Street, Hot Springs, SD 57747. 605-745-5139; Fax 605-745-6835.
Will search UCC records. **Other Phone Numbers:** Assessor 605-745-5136; Treasurer 605-745-5145.

Faulk County

Register of Deeds, P.O. Box 309, Faulkton, SD 57438. 605-598-6228; Fax 605-598-6680.
Will search UCC records. This agency will not do a tax lien search. RE owner, mortgage, and property transfer searches available. **Other Phone Numbers:** Assessor 605-598-6225; Treasurer 605-598-6232; Vital Records 605-598-6228.

Grant County

Register of Deeds, P.O. Box 587, Milbank, SD 57252. Register of Deeds, R/E and UCC Recording 605-432-4752.
Will search UCC records. UCC search includes tax liens if requested. Will not search real estate records. **Other Phone Numbers:** Assessor 605-432-6532; Treasurer 605-432-5651; Appraiser/Auditor 605-432-6532; Elections 605-432-6711; Vital Records 605-432-4752.

Gregory County

Register of Deeds, P.O. Box 437, Burke, SD 57523. 605-775-2624; Fax 605-775-2596.
Will search UCC records. Will not search real estate records. **Other Phone Numbers:** Assessor 605-775-2673; Treasurer 605-775-2605.

Haakon County

Register of Deeds, P.O. Box 100, Philip, SD 57567-0100. 605-859-2785 R/E Recording: 605-859-2627.

Will search UCC records. UCC search includes tax liens if requested. Will not search real estate records. **Other Phone Numbers:** Assessor 605-859-2824; Treasurer 605-859-2612.

Hamlin County

Register of Deeds, P.O. Box 56, Hayti, SD 57241. 605-783-3206.
Will not search UCC records. This agency will not do a tax lien search. Will not search real estate records. **Other Phone Numbers:** Assessor 605-783-3331; Treasurer 605-783-3441.

Hand County

Register of Deeds, 415 West 1st Avenue, Miller, SD 57362-1346. Register of Deeds, R/E and UCC Recording 605-853-3512; Fax 605-853-2769.
Will search UCC records. Will not search real estate records. **Other Phone Numbers:** Assessor 605-853-2115; Treasurer 605-853-2136; Appraiser/Auditor 605-853-2182; Vital Records 605-853-3512.

Hanson County

Register of Deeds, P.O. Box 500, Alexandria, SD 57311-0500. Register of Deeds, R/E and UCC Recording 605-239-4512; Fax 605-239-4296.
Will search UCC records. **Other Phone Numbers:** Assessor 605-239-4445; Treasurer 605-239-4723; Appraiser/Auditor 605-239-4445; Elections 605-239-4714; Vital Records 605-239-4512.

Harding County

Register of Deeds, P.O. Box 101, Buffalo, SD 57720. 605-375-3321; Fax 605-375-3318.
Will search UCC records. Tax liens not included in UCC search. RE record owner and mortgage searches available. **Other Phone Numbers:** Assessor 605-375-3234; Treasurer 605-375-3542.

Hughes County

Register of Deeds, 104 East Capital, Pierre, SD 57501. 605-773-7495 R/E Recording: 605-224-7891; Fax 605-773-7479.
Will search UCC records. Will search real estate records. No fee for search. **Other Phone Numbers:** Assessor 605-224-5883; Treasurer 605-224-9231; Elections 605-773-7451; Vital Records 605-773-7495.

Hutchinson County

Register of Deeds, 140 Euclid Street, Room 37, Olivet, SD 57052-2103. 605-387-4217 R/E Recording: 605-387-2838; Fax 605-387-4209.
Will search UCC records. Will not search real estate records. **Other Phone Numbers:** Assessor 605-387-4210; Treasurer 605-387-4213; Appraiser/Auditor 605-387-4210; Elections 605-387-4217.

Hyde County

Register of Deeds, P.O. Box 342, Highmore, SD 57345. 605-852-2517.
Will search UCC records. UCC search includes tax liens if requested. Will not search real estate records. **Other Phone Numbers:** Assessor 605-852-2570; Treasurer 605-852-2510.

Jackson County

Register of Deeds, P.O. Box 248, Kadoka, SD 57453. 605-837-2420.
Will search UCC records. UCC search includes tax liens if requested. Will not search real estate records. **Other Phone Numbers:** Assessor 605-837-2424; Treasurer 605-837-2423.

Jerauld County

Register of Deeds, P.O. Box 452, Wessington Springs, SD 57382-0452. 605-539-1221.
Will search UCC records. UCC search includes tax liens if requested. RE owner, mortgage, and property transfer searches available. **Other Phone Numbers:** Assessor 605-539-9701; Treasurer 605-539-1241.

Jones County

Register of Deeds, P.O. Box 446, Murdo, SD 57559. 605-669-2132.
Will search UCC records. UCC search includes tax liens if requested. Will not search real estate records. **Other Phone Numbers:** Assessor 605-669-2122; Treasurer 605-669-2122.

Kingsbury County

Register of Deeds, P.O. Box 146, De Smet, SD 57231-0146. 605-854-3591; Fax 605-854-3833.
Will search UCC records. Will not search real estate records. **Other Phone Numbers:** Assessor 605-854-3593; Treasurer 605-854-3411.

Lake County

Register of Deeds, P.O. Box 266, Madison, SD 57042. 605-256-7614 R/E Recording: 605-256-2068; Fax 605-256-7622.
Will search UCC records. **Other Phone Numbers:** Assessor 605-256-7605; Treasurer 605-256-7618.

Lawrence County

Register of Deeds, P.O. Box 565, Deadwood, SD 57732. 605-578-3930.
Will search UCC records. Tax liens not included in UCC search. RE record owner searches available. **Other Phone Numbers:** Assessor 605-578-3680.

Lincoln County

Register of Deeds, 100 East 5th, Canton, SD 57013-1789. 605-987-5661 R/E Recording: 605-987-2581; Fax 605-987-5932.
Will search UCC records. UCC search includes tax liens if requested. RE owner, mortgage, and property transfer searches available. **Other Phone Numbers:** Assessor 605-987-2571.

Lyman County

Register of Deeds, P.O. Box 98, Kennebec, SD 57544-0098. Register of Deeds, R/E and UCC Recording 605-869-2297; Fax 605-869-2203.
Will search UCC records. **Other Phone Numbers:** Assessor 605-869-2206; Treasurer 605-869-2295; Appraiser/Auditor 605-869-2206; Elections 605-869-2247; Vital Records 605-869-2297.

Marshall County

Register of Deeds, P.O. Box 130, Britton, SD 57430. Register of Deeds, R/E and UCC Recording 605-448-2352; Fax 605-448-2116.
Will search UCC records. Will not search real estate records unless provided with legal description. **Other Phone Numbers:** Assessor 605-448-5291; Treasurer 605-448-2451; Elections 605-448-2401; Vital Records 605-448-2352.

McCook County

Register of Deeds, P.O. Box 338, Salem, SD 57058-0338. 605-425-2701; Fax 605-425-2534.
Will search UCC records. Tax liens not included in UCC search. RE record owner searches available. **Other Phone Numbers:** Assessor 605-425-2681; Treasurer 605-425-2721.

McPherson County

Register of Deeds, P.O. Box 129, Leola, SD 57456. 605-439-3151; Fax 605-439-3394.
Will search UCC records. Will not search real estate records. **Other Phone Numbers:** Assessor 605-439-3663; Treasurer 605-439-3544.

Meade County

Register of Deeds, 1425 Sherman Street, Sturgis, SD 57785. 605-347-2356; Fax 605-347-5925.
Will search UCC records. Will not search real estate records. **Other Phone Numbers:** Assessor 605-347-3818; Treasurer 605-347-5871.

Mellette County

Register of Deeds, P.O. Box 183, White River, SD 57579-0183. 605-259-3371.
Will search UCC records. UCC search includes tax liens if requested. RE record owner and mortgage searches available. **Other Phone Numbers:** Assessor 605-259-3150; Treasurer 605-259-3151.

Miner County

Register of Deeds, P.O. Box 546, Howard, SD 57349. 605-772-5621; Fax 605-772-4148. www.howardsd.com
Will search UCC records. **Other Phone Numbers:** Assessor 605-772-4241; Treasurer 605-772-4652.

Minnehaha County

Register of Deeds, 415 North Dakota Avenue, Sioux Falls, SD 57104-2465. 605-367-4223 R/E Recording: 605-335-4220; Fax 605-367-8314.
Will search UCC records. UCC search includes federal tax liens only Will not search real estate records. **Other Phone Numbers:** Assessor 605-335-4228; Treasurer 605-335-4212.

Moody County

Register of Deeds, P.O. Box 247, Flandreau, SD 57028-0247. Register of Deeds, R/E and UCC Recording 605-997-3151.
Will search UCC records. This agency will not do a tax lien search. Will not search real estate records. **Other Phone Numbers:** Assessor 605-997-3101; Treasurer 605-997-3171.

Pennington County

Register of Deeds, 315 St. Joe Street, Rapid City, SD 57701. Register of Deeds, R/E and UCC Recording 605-394-2177.
Will search UCC records. Tax liens not included in UCC search. RE record owner searches available. **Other Phone Numbers:** Assessor 605-394-2175; Treasurer 605-394-2161; Elections 605-394-2153; Vital Records 605-394-2177.

Perkins County

Register of Deeds, P.O. Box 127, Bison, SD 57620. Register of Deeds, R/E and UCC Recording 605-244-5620; Fax 605-244-7289.

Will search UCC records. **Other Phone Numbers:** Assessor 605-244-5623; Treasurer 605-244-5613.

Potter County

Register of Deeds, 201 South Exene, Gettysburg, SD 57442. 605-765-9467; Fax 605-765-2836.
Will search UCC records. Will not search real estate records. **Other Phone Numbers:** Assessor 605-765-2481; Treasurer 605-765-9403; Elections 605-765-9408; Vital Records 605-765-9467.

Roberts County

Register of Deeds, 411 East 2nd Avenue, Sisseton, SD 57262. 605-698-7152.
Will search UCC records. UCC search includes tax liens if requested. Mortgage searches available. **Other Phone Numbers:** Assessor 605-698-3205; Treasurer 605-698-7245.

Sanborn County

Register of Deeds, P.O. Box 295, Woonsocket, SD 57385. 605-796-4516; Fax 605-796-4509.
Will search UCC records. Will not search real estate records. **Other Phone Numbers:** Assessor 605-796-4514; Treasurer 605-796-4512.

Shannon County

Register of Deeds, 906 North River Street, Hot Springs, SD 57747. 605-745-5139.
Will search UCC records. UCC search includes tax liens if requested. No separate searches RE owner, mortgage, and property transfer searches available. **Other Phone Numbers:** Assessor 605-745-5141; Treasurer 605-745-5145.

Spink County

Register of Deeds, P.O. Box 266, Redfield, SD 57469-0266. Register of Deeds, R/E and UCC Recording 605-472-0150; Fax 605-472-2410.
Will search UCC records. **Other Phone Numbers:** Assessor 605-472-2891; Treasurer 605-472-0880; Elections 605-472-1825; Vital Records 605-472-0150.

Stanley County

Register of Deeds, P.O. Box 596, Fort Pierre, SD 57532. Register of Deeds, R/E and UCC Recording 605-223-2610; Fax 605-223-9948.
Will search UCC records. UCC search includes tax liens if requested. RE owner, mortgage, and property transfer searches available. **Other Phone Numbers:** Assessor 605-223-2746; Treasurer 605-223-2648; Elections 605-223-2673; Vital Records 605-223-2610.

Sully County

Register of Deeds, P.O. Box 265, Onida, SD 57564. Register of Deeds, R/E and UCC Recording 605-258-2331; Fax 605-258-2884. www.sdcounties.org/sully
Will search UCC records. Will not search real estate records. **Other Phone Numbers:** Assessor 605-258-2522; Treasurer 605-258-2444; Appraiser/Auditor 605-258-2522; Elections 605-258-2541; Vital Records 605-258-2331.

Todd County

Register of Deeds, 200 E 3rd St, 200 E. 3rd St., Winner, SD 57580-1806. 605-842-2208; Fax 605-842-3621.
Will search UCC records. **Other Phone Numbers:** Assessor 605-856-4633; Treasurer 605-842-1700.

Tripp County

Register of Deeds, 200 E 3rd St, Courthouse, 200 E. 3rd St., Winner, SD 57580-1806. 605-842-2208; Fax 605-842-3621.
Will search UCC records. Property transfer searches available. **Other Phone Numbers:** Assessor 605-842-2300; Treasurer 605-842-1700.

Turner County

Register of Deeds, P.O. Box 485, Parker, SD 57053-0485. 605-297-3443; Fax 605-297-5556.
Will search UCC records. Will not search real estate records. **Other Phone Numbers:** Assessor 605-297-4420; Treasurer 605-297-4425.

Union County

Register of Deeds, P.O. Box 490, Elk Point, SD 57025-0490. 605-356-2191 R/E Recording: 605-356-2041; Fax 605-356-3047.
Will search UCC records. Will not search real estate records. **Other Phone Numbers:** Assessor 605-356-2252; Treasurer 605-356-2391; Elections 605-356-2101; Vital Records 605-356-2191.

Walworth County

Register of Deeds, P.O. Box 159, Selby, SD 57472-0159. 605-649-7057 R/E Recording: 605-649-7311; Fax 605-649-7867.
Will search UCC records. This agency will not do a tax lien search. RE record owner and mortgage searches available. **Other Phone Numbers:** Assessor 605-649-7737; Treasurer 605-649-7737.

Yankton County

Register of Deeds, P.O. Box 694, Yankton, SD 57078. 605-665-2422 R/E Recording: 605-65-2422; Fax 605-668-9682.
Will search UCC records. Tax liens not included in UCC search. Will not search real estate records. Last deed of record only. **Other Phone Numbers:** Assessor 605-665-5962; Treasurer 605-665-2143.

Ziebach County

Register of Deeds, P.O. Box 68, Dupree, SD 57623. 605-365-5165.
Will search UCC records. This agency will not do a tax lien search. Will not search real estate records. **Other Phone Numbers:** Assessor 605-365-5129; Treasurer 605-365-5173.

South Dakota County Locator

You will usually be able to find the city name in the City/County Cross Reference below. In that case, it is a simple matter to determine the county from the cross reference. However, only the official US Postal Service city names are included in this index. There are an additional 40,000 place names that people use in their addresses. Therefore, we have also included a ZIP/City Cross Reference immediately following the City/County Cross Reference.

If you know the ZIP Code but the city name does not appear in the City/County Cross Reference index, look up the ZIP Code in the ZIP/City Cross Reference, find the city name, then look up the city name in the City/County Cross Reference. For example, you want to know the county for an address of Menands, NY 12204. There is no "Menands" in the City/County Cross Reference. The ZIP/City Cross Reference shows that ZIP Codes 12201-12288 are for the city of Albany. Looking back in the City/County Cross Reference, Albany is in Albany County.

City/County Cross Reference

ABERDEEN Brown
AGAR Sully
AKASKA Walworth
ALCESTER (57001) Union(82), Lincoln(18)
ALEXANDRIA (57311) Hanson(98), Hutchinson(2)
ALLEN Bennett
ALPENA (57312) Jerauld(54), Beadle(44), Sanborn(2)
AMHERST (57421) Marshall(96), Brown(4)
ANDOVER (57422) Day(87), Brown(13)
ARDMORE Fall River
ARLINGTON (57212) Kingsbury(61), Brookings(35), Hamlin(4)
ARMOUR (57313) Douglas(75), Charles Mix(25)
ARTESIAN Sanborn
ASHTON (57424) Spink(92), Faulk(8)
ASTORIA (57213) Deuel(68), Brookings(32)
AURORA (57002) Brookings(98), Moody(2)
AVON (57315) Bon Homme(99), Charles Mix(2)
BADGER Kingsbury
BALTIC Minnehaha
BANCROFT Kingsbury
BARNARD Brown
BATESLAND (57716) Shannon(90), Bennett(10)
BATH Brown
BEAVER CREEK Tripp
BELLE FOURCHE Butte
BELVIDERE (57521) Jackson(80), Mellette(21)
BERESFORD (57004) Union(49), Lincoln(37), Clay(14)
BETHLEHEM Meade
BIG STONE CITY (57216) Grant(89), Roberts(11)
BISON (57620) Perkins(99), Harding(1)
BLACK HAWK (57718) Meade(99), Pennington(2)
BLUNT (57522) Hughes(90), Sully(10)
BONESTEEL Gregory
BOWDLE (57428) Edmunds(75), Walworth(25), McPherson(1)
BOX ELDER (57719) Pennington(86), Meade(15)
BRADLEY Clark
BRANDON Minnehaha
BRANDT Deuel
BRENTFORD Spink
BRIDGEWATER (57319) McCook(70), Hutchinson(16), Turner(13)
BRISTOL Day
BRITTON Marshall
BROOKINGS (57006) Brookings(99), Moody(1)
BROOKINGS Brookings
BRUCE Brookings
BRYANT (57221) Hamlin(73), Clark(18), Kingsbury(10)
BUFFALO Harding
BUFFALO GAP (57722) Custer(75), Fall River(19), Shannon(6)
BUFFALO RIDGE Minnehaha
BULLHEAD Corson

BURBANK (57010) Clay(81), Union(20)
BURKE Gregory
CAMP CROOK Harding
CANISTOTA McCook
CANOVA (57321) Miner(66), Hanson(22), McCook(12)
CANTON Lincoln
CAPUTA Pennington
CARPENTER (57322) Beadle(52), Spink(25), Clark(23)
CARTER (57526) Tripp(76), Todd(18), Mellette(6)
CARTHAGE (57323) Miner(76), Kingsbury(20), Sanborn(4)
CASTLEWOOD (57223) Hamlin(99), Deuel(1)
CAVOUR Beadle
CEDARBUTTE Mellette
CENTERVILLE (57014) Turner(57), Clay(23), Lincoln(20)
CHAMBERLAIN (57325) Brule(99), Buffalo(1)
CHAMBERLAIN Brule
CHANCELLOR (57015) Turner(97), Minnehaha(3)
CHERRY CREEK Ziebach
CHESTER (57016) Lake(97), Minnehaha(3)
CLAIRE CITY Roberts
CLAREMONT (57432) Brown(77), Marshall(23)
CLARK Clark
CLEAR LAKE (57226) Deuel(97), Hamlin(3)
COLMAN (57017) Moody(96), Lake(4)
COLOME Tripp
COLTON (57018) Minnehaha(98), Lake(2)
COLUMBIA Brown
CONDE (57434) Spink(70), Brown(19), Clark(6), Day(4)
CORONA (57227) Roberts(90), Grant(10)
CORSICA (57328) Douglas(98), Aurora(1)
CORSON Minnehaha
CREIGHTON Pennington
CRESBARD (57435) Faulk(89), Edmunds(11)
CROCKER Clark
CROOKS Minnehaha
CUSTER (57730) Custer(97), Pennington(3)
DALLAS (57529) Tripp(53), Gregory(48)
DANTE Charles Mix
DAVIS (57021) Turner(98), Lincoln(3)
DE SMET Kingsbury
DEADWOOD Lawrence
DELL RAPIDS (57022) Minnehaha(88), Moody(12)
DELMONT (57330) Douglas(65), Charles Mix(24), Hutchinson(11)
DIMOCK (57331) Hutchinson(65), Douglas(21), Davison(15)
DOLAND Spink
DRAPER (57531) Jones(99), Lyman(1)
DUPREE (57623) Ziebach(90), Dewey(10)
EAGLE BUTTE Dewey
EDEN Marshall

EDGEMONT (57735) Custer(57), Fall River(43)
EGAN Moody
ELK POINT Union
ELKTON (57026) Brookings(91), Moody(9)
ELLSWORTH AFB Meade
ELM SPRINGS Meade
EMERY (57332) Hanson(51), Hutchinson(34), McCook(15)
ENNING Meade
ERWIN (57233) Kingsbury(95), Hamlin(5)
ESTELLINE (57234) Hamlin(61), Deuel(30), Brookings(9)
ETHAN (57334) Davison(60), Hanson(28), Hutchinson(12)
EUREKA (57437) McPherson(76), Campbell(24)
FAIRBURN Custer
FAIRFAX Gregory
FAIRVIEW Lincoln
FAITH (57626) Perkins(57), Meade(37), Ziebach(6)
FAULKTON Faulk
FEDORA (57337) Miner(90), Sanborn(10)
FERNEY Brown
FIRESTEEL (57628) Dewey(53), Corson(47)
FLANDREAU Moody
FLORENCE (57235) Codington(98), Day(3)
FORT MEADE Meade
FORT PIERRE (57532) Stanley(97), Lyman(3)
FORT THOMPSON Buffalo
FRANKFORT Spink
FREDERICK Brown
FREEMAN (57029) Hutchinson(74), Turner(26)
FRUITDALE Butte
FULTON (57340) Hanson(93), Miner(7)
GANN VALLEY (57341) Buffalo(97), Brule(4)
GARDEN CITY Clark
GARRETSON Minnehaha
GARY Deuel
GAYVILLE (57031) Yankton(78), Clay(22)
GEDDES (57342) Charles Mix(98), Douglas(2)
GETTYSBURG (57442) Potter(97), Sully(2), Dewey(2)
GLAD VALLEY Ziebach
GLENCROSS (57630) Dewey(92), Corson(8)
GLENHAM (57631) Walworth(77), Campbell(23)
GOODWIN (57238) Deuel(55), Codington(41), Hamlin(4)
GREGORY Gregory
GRENVILLE Day
GROTON Brown
HAMILL (57534) Tripp(89), Lyman(11)
HARRISBURG Lincoln
HARRISON Douglas
HARROLD (57536) Hughes(82), Sully(15), Hyde(3)
HARTFORD Minnehaha
HAYES (57537) Stanley(93), Haakon(8)
HAYTI (57241) Hamlin(98), Codington(2)

HAZEL (57242) Hamlin(68), Codington(33)
HECLA Brown
HENRY (57243) Codington(95), Clark(5)
HERMOSA (57744) Pennington(58), Custer(41), Shannon(1)
HERREID Campbell
HERRICK Gregory
HETLAND Kingsbury
HIGHMORE (57345) Hyde(96), Faulk(3)
HILL CITY Pennington
HITCHCOCK (57348) Beadle(65), Spink(35)
HOLABIRD Hyde
HOSMER (57448) Edmunds(66), McPherson(34)
HOT SPRINGS (57747) Fall River(98), Custer(2)
HOUGHTON Brown
HOVEN (57450) Walworth(53), Potter(47)
HOWARD Miner
HOWES Meade
HUDSON (57034) Lincoln(97), Union(3)
HUMBOLDT (57035) Minnehaha(97), McCook(3)
HURLEY Turner
HURON Beadle
IDEAL Tripp
INTERIOR (57750) Jackson(86), Pennington(14)
IONA (57542) Lyman(97), Gregory(3)
IPSWICH Edmunds
IRENE (57037) Yankton(85), Clay(9), Turner(7)
IROQUOIS (57353) Kingsbury(64), Beadle(35)
ISABEL (57633) Dewey(73), Corson(20), Ziebach(7)
JAVA (57452) Walworth(68), Campbell(32)
JEFFERSON Union
KADOKA Jackson
KAYLOR Hutchinson
KELDRON Corson
KENNEBEC Lyman
KEYSTONE Pennington
KIMBALL (57355) Brule(91), Jerauld(6), Buffalo(3)
KRANZBURG Codington
KYLE (57752) Shannon(87), Jackson(13)
LABOLT Grant
LAKE ANDES Charles Mix
LAKE CITY Marshall
LAKE NORDEN (57248) Hamlin(76), Kingsbury(25)
LAKE PRESTON Kingsbury
LANE Jerauld
LANGFORD (57454) Marshall(87), Day(13)
LANTRY Dewey
LEAD Lawrence
LEBANON Potter
LEMMON (57638) Perkins(98), Corson(2)
LENNOX (57039) Lincoln(92), Turner(8)
LEOLA (57456) McPherson(98), Edmunds(2)
LESTERVILLE (57040) Yankton(95), Bon Homme(5)
LETCHER (57359) Sanborn(75), Aurora(14), Davison(11)

LINN (57483) Hand(48), Faulk(35), Spink(17)
LITTLE EAGLE Corson
LODGEPOLE Perkins
LONG VALLEY Jackson
LONGLAKE McPherson
LOWER BRULE Lyman
LUDLOW Harding
LYONS Minnehaha
MADISON Lake
MAHTO Corson
MANDERSON Shannon
MANSFIELD (57460) Brown(61), Spink(20), Faulk(12), Edmunds(8)
MARCUS Meade
MARION (57043) Turner(91), McCook(7), Hutchinson(2)
MARTIN Bennett
MARTY Charles Mix
MARVIN (57251) Grant(98), Roberts(2)
MC INTOSH Corson
MC LAUGHLIN Corson
MEADOW (57644) Perkins(86), Corson(8), Ziebach(7)
MECKLING Clay
MELLETTE (57461) Spink(98), Brown(2)
MENNO (57045) Hutchinson(80), Yankton(17), Turner(2)
MIDLAND (57552) Haakon(47), Stanley(35), Jackson(11), Mellette(5), Jones(2)
MILBANK Grant
MILESVILLE Haakon
MILLER (57362) Hand(99), Buffalo(1)
MINA (57462) Edmunds(83), Brown(17)
MISSION Todd
MISSION HILL Yankton
MISSION RIDGE Stanley
MITCHELL (57301) Davison(97), Hanson(3)
MOBRIDGE Walworth
MONROE (57047) McCook(79), Turner(21)
MONTROSE (57048) McCook(75), Minnehaha(23), Lake(1)
MORRISTOWN Corson
MOUND CITY Campbell
MOUNT VERNON (57363) Davison(91), Aurora(6), Sanborn(4)
MUD BUTTE (57758) Meade(53), Perkins(38), Butte(9)
MURDO (57559) Jones(94), Mellette(6)
NEMO Lawrence
NEW EFFINGTON Roberts
NEW HOLLAND Douglas
NEW UNDERWOOD (57761) Pennington(69), Meade(31)
NEWELL (57760) Butte(95), Harding(4), Meade(1)
NISLAND Butte
NORRIS (57560) Mellette(64), Bennett(27), Jackson(9)
NORTH SIOUX CITY Union

NORTHVILLE (57465) Spink(60), Faulk(40)
NUNDA Lake
OACOMA Lyman
OELRICHS Fall River
OGLALA Shannon
OKATON Jones
OKREEK Todd
OLDHAM (57051) Kingsbury(95), Miner(4), Lake(1)
OLIVET Hutchinson
ONAKA (57466) Faulk(82), Edmunds(18)
ONIDA (57564) Sully(97), Hyde(3)
OPAL Meade
ORAL Fall River
ORIENT (57467) Hand(77), Faulk(24)
ORTLEY (57256) Grant(70), Roberts(17), Codington(6), Day(6)
OWANKA (57767) Pennington(78), Meade(22)
PARADE Dewey
PARKER (57053) Turner(94), McCook(4), Minnehaha(2)
PARKSTON (57366) Hutchinson(91), Douglas(9)
PARMELEE (57566) Todd(75), Mellette(25)
PEEVER Roberts
PHILIP (57567) Haakon(76), Jackson(24)
PICKSTOWN Charles Mix
PIEDMONT Meade
PIERPONT Day
PIERRE (57501) Hughes(98), Sully(2)
PINE RIDGE Shannon
PLANKINTON Aurora
PLATTE (57369) Charles Mix(86), Brule(10), Douglas(3), Aurora(1)
POLLOCK Campbell
PORCUPINE Shannon
PRAIRIE CITY (57649) Perkins(95), Harding(5)
PRESHO Lyman
PRINGLE Custer
PROVO Fall River
PUKWANA (57370) Brule(85), Buffalo(15)
QUINN (57775) Pennington(72), Haakon(19), Jackson(9)
RALPH Harding
RAMONA (57054) Lake(96), Kingsbury(4)
RAPID CITY Pennington
RAVINIA Charles Mix
RAYMOND (57258) Clark(89), Spink(11)
RED OWL Meade
REDFIELD (57469) Spink(93), Hand(6), Faulk(2)
REDIG Harding
REE HEIGHTS (57371) Hand(98), Hyde(2)
RELIANCE (57569) Lyman(98), Tripp(2)
RENNER Minnehaha
REVA (57651) Harding(50), Perkins(50)
REVILLO (57259) Grant(80), Deuel(20)
RIDGEVIEW Dewey
ROCHFORD Pennington
ROCKHAM (57470) Faulk(51), Hand(49)

ROSCOE Edmunds
ROSEBUD Todd
ROSHOLT Roberts
ROSLYN (57261) Day(98), Marshall(2)
ROWENA Minnehaha
RUTLAND Lake
SAINT CHARLES Gregory
SAINT FRANCIS Todd
SAINT LAWRENCE Hand
SAINT ONGE (57779) Lawrence(86), Butte(14)
SALEM McCook
SCENIC (57780) Pennington(96), Shannon(4)
SCOTLAND (57059) Bon Homme(85), Hutchinson(14)
SELBY Walworth
SENECA (57473) Faulk(78), Potter(22)
SHADEHILL Perkins
SHERMAN Minnehaha
SINAI Brookings
SIOUX FALLS (57106) Minnehaha(93), Lincoln(7)
SIOUX FALLS (57108) Lincoln(93), Minnehaha(7)
SIOUX FALLS Minnehaha
SISSETON (57262) Roberts(95), Marshall(5)
SMITHWICK Fall River
SOUTH SHORE (57263) Codington(77), Grant(23)
SPEARFISH Lawrence
SPENCER (57374) Hanson(51), McCook(49)
SPRINGFIELD Bon Homme
STEPHAN Hyde
STICKNEY (57375) Aurora(98), Davison(2)
STOCKHOLM (57264) Grant(97), Codington(3)
STRANDBURG (57265) Grant(78), Deuel(17), Codington(5)
STRATFORD (57474) Brown(92), Spink(8)
STURGIS (57785) Meade(98), Lawrence(2)
SUMMIT (57266) Grant(71), Roberts(29)
TABOR (57063) Bon Homme(84), Yankton(16)
TEA (57064) Lincoln(94), Turner(6)
TIMBER LAKE Dewey
TOLSTOY (57475) Potter(52), Edmunds(47), Walworth(1)
TORONTO (57268) Deuel(65), Brookings(35)
TRAIL CITY (57657) Corson(87), Dewey(14)
TRENT Moody
TRIPP (57376) Hutchinson(82), Bon Homme(17), Charles Mix(1)
TULARE (57476) Spink(82), Hand(18)
TURTON Spink
TUTHILL Bennett
TWIN BROOKS Grant
TYNDALL Bon Homme

UNION CENTER Meade
UTICA Yankton
VALE (57788) Butte(51), Meade(49)
VALLEY SPRINGS Minnehaha
VEBLEN (57270) Marshall(91), Roberts(9)
VERMILLION Clay
VIBORG (57070) Turner(87), Yankton(13)
VIENNA (57271) Clark(94), Hamlin(6)
VIRGIL Beadle
VIVIAN (57576) Lyman(91), Jones(9)
VOLGA (57071) Brookings(96), Lake(4)
VOLIN (57072) Yankton(73), Clay(27)
WAGNER Charles Mix
WAKONDA (57073) Clay(95), Turner(5)
WAKPALA Corson
WALKER Corson
WALL Pennington
WALLACE (57272) Codington(84), Clark(15), Day(1)
WANBLEE (57577) Jackson(97), Bennett(3)
WARD Moody
WARNER Brown
WASTA (57791) Pennington(83), Meade(17)
WATAUGA Corson
WATERTOWN Codington
WAUBAY (57273) Day(85), Roberts(15), Grant(1)
WAVERLY Codington
WEBSTER (57274) Day(98), Clark(2)
WENTWORTH Lake
WESSINGTON (57381) Beadle(55), Hand(45)
WESSINGTON SPRINGS (57382) Jerauld(91), Aurora(6), Beadle(3)
WESTPORT (57481) Brown(63), McPherson(28), Edmunds(10)
WEWELA Tripp
WHITE Brookings
WHITE LAKE (57383) Aurora(98), Brule(2)
WHITE OWL Meade
WHITE RIVER Mellette
WHITEHORSE Dewey
WHITEWOOD (57793) Lawrence(62), Meade(38)
WILLOW LAKE Clark
WILMOT (57279) Roberts(99), Grant(1)
WINFRED (57076) Miner(50), Lake(50)
WINNER Tripp
WITTEN Tripp
WOLSEY Beadle
WOOD Mellette
WOONSOCKET (57385) Sanborn(81), Jerauld(17), Aurora(2)
WORTHING Lincoln
WOUNDED KNEE Shannon
YALE Beadle
YANKTON Yankton
ZEONA (57795) Perkins(67), Butte(33)

ZIP/City Cross Reference

57001-57001	ALCESTER	57025-57025	ELK POINT	57043-57043	MARION	57062-57062	SPRINGFIELD
57002-57002	AURORA	57026-57026	ELKTON	57044-57044	MECKLING	57063-57063	TABOR
57003-57003	BALTIC	57027-57027	FAIRVIEW	57045-57045	MENNO	57064-57064	TEA
57004-57004	BERESFORD	57028-57028	FLANDREAU	57046-57046	MISSION HILL	57065-57065	TRENT
57005-57005	BRANDON	57029-57029	FREEMAN	57047-57047	MONROE	57066-57066	TYNDALL
57006-57007	BROOKINGS	57030-57030	GARRETSON	57048-57048	MONTROSE	57067-57067	UTICA
57010-57010	BURBANK	57031-57031	GAYVILLE	57049-57049	NORTH SIOUX CITY	57068-57068	VALLEY SPRINGS
57012-57012	CANISTOTA	57032-57032	HARRISBURG	57050-57050	NUNDA	57069-57069	VERMILLION
57013-57013	CANTON	57033-57033	HARTFORD	57051-57051	OLDHAM	57070-57070	VIBORG
57014-57014	CENTERVILLE	57034-57034	HUDSON	57052-57052	OLIVET	57071-57071	VOLGA
57015-57015	CHANCELLOR	57035-57035	HUMBOLDT	57053-57053	PARKER	57072-57072	VOLIN
57016-57016	CHESTER	57036-57036	HURLEY	57054-57054	RAMONA	57073-57073	WAKONDA
57017-57017	COLMAN	57037-57037	IRENE	57055-57055	RENNER	57074-57074	WARD
57018-57018	COLTON	57038-57038	JEFFERSON	57056-57056	ROWENA	57075-57075	WENTWORTH
57020-57020	CROOKS	57039-57039	LENNOX	57057-57057	RUTLAND	57076-57076	WINFRED
57021-57021	DAVIS	57040-57040	LESTERVILLE	57058-57058	SALEM	57077-57077	WORTHING
57022-57022	DELL RAPIDS	57041-57041	LYONS	57059-57059	SCOTLAND	57078-57079	YANKTON
57024-57024	EGAN	57042-57042	MADISON	57061-57061	SINAI	57101-57110	SIOUX FALLS

Zip	Town	Zip	Town	Zip	Town	Zip	Town
57115-57115	BUFFALO RIDGE	57339-57339	FORT THOMPSON	57471-57471	ROSCOE	57649-57649	PRAIRIE CITY
57117-57198	SIOUX FALLS	57340-57340	FULTON	57472-57472	SELBY	57650-57650	RALPH
57201-57201	WATERTOWN	57341-57341	GANN VALLEY	57473-57473	SENECA	57651-57651	REVA
57202-57202	WAVERLY	57342-57342	GEDDES	57474-57474	STRATFORD	57652-57652	RIDGEVIEW
57212-57212	ARLINGTON	57344-57344	HARRISON	57475-57475	TOLSTOY	57653-57653	SHADEHILL
57213-57213	ASTORIA	57345-57345	HIGHMORE	57476-57476	TULARE	57656-57656	TIMBER LAKE
57214-57214	BADGER	57346-57346	STEPHAN	57477-57477	TURTON	57657-57657	TRAIL CITY
57216-57216	BIG STONE CITY	57348-57348	HITCHCOCK	57479-57479	WARNER	57658-57658	WAKPALA
57217-57217	BRADLEY	57349-57349	HOWARD	57481-57481	WESTPORT	57659-57659	WALKER
57218-57218	BRANDT	57350-57350	HURON	57501-57501	PIERRE	57660-57660	WATAUGA
57219-57219	BRISTOL	57353-57353	IROQUOIS	57520-57520	AGAR	57661-57661	WHITEHORSE
57220-57220	BRUCE	57354-57354	KAYLOR	57521-57521	BELVIDERE	57701-57702	RAPID CITY
57221-57221	BRYANT	57355-57355	KIMBALL	57522-57522	BLUNT	57706-57706	ELLSWORTH AFB
57223-57223	CASTLEWOOD	57356-57356	LAKE ANDES	57523-57523	BURKE	57708-57708	BETHLEHEM
57224-57224	CLAIRE CITY	57357-57357	RAVINIA	57526-57526	CARTER	57709-57709	RAPID CITY
57225-57225	CLARK	57358-57358	LANE	57528-57528	COLOME	57714-57714	ALLEN
57226-57226	CLEAR LAKE	57359-57359	LETCHER	57529-57529	DALLAS	57716-57716	BATESLAND
57227-57227	CORONA	57361-57361	MARTY	57531-57531	DRAPER	57717-57717	BELLE FOURCHE
57229-57229	CROCKER	57362-57362	MILLER	57532-57532	FORT PIERRE	57718-57718	BLACK HAWK
57231-57231	DE SMET	57363-57363	MOUNT VERNON	57533-57533	GREGORY	57719-57719	BOX ELDER
57232-57232	EDEN	57364-57364	NEW HOLLAND	57534-57534	HAMILL	57720-57720	BUFFALO
57233-57233	ERWIN	57365-57365	OACOMA	57536-57536	HARROLD	57722-57722	BUFFALO GAP
57234-57234	ESTELLINE	57366-57366	PARKSTON	57537-57537	HAYES	57724-57724	CAMP CROOK
57235-57235	FLORENCE	57367-57367	PICKSTOWN	57538-57538	HERRICK	57725-57725	CAPUTA
57236-57236	GARDEN CITY	57368-57368	PLANKINTON	57540-57540	HOLABIRD	57729-57729	CREIGHTON
57237-57237	GARY	57369-57369	PLATTE	57541-57541	IDEAL	57730-57730	CUSTER
57238-57238	GOODWIN	57370-57370	PUKWANA	57542-57542	IONA	57732-57732	DEADWOOD
57239-57239	GRENVILLE	57371-57371	REE HEIGHTS	57543-57543	KADOKA	57735-57735	EDGEMONT
57241-57241	HAYTI	57373-57373	SAINT LAWRENCE	57544-57544	KENNEBEC	57736-57736	ELM SPRINGS
57242-57242	HAZEL	57374-57374	SPENCER	57547-57547	LONG VALLEY	57737-57737	ENNING
57243-57243	HENRY	57375-57375	STICKNEY	57548-57548	LOWER BRULE	57738-57738	FAIRBURN
57244-57244	HETLAND	57376-57376	TRIPP	57551-57551	MARTIN	57741-57741	FORT MEADE
57245-57245	KRANZBURG	57379-57379	VIRGIL	57552-57552	MIDLAND	57742-57742	FRUITDALE
57246-57246	LABOLT	57380-57380	WAGNER	57553-57553	MILESVILLE	57744-57744	HERMOSA
57247-57247	LAKE CITY	57381-57381	WESSINGTON	57555-57555	MISSION	57745-57745	HILL CITY
57248-57248	LAKE NORDEN	57382-57382	WESSINGTON SPRINGS	57557-57557	MISSION RIDGE	57747-57747	HOT SPRINGS
57249-57249	LAKE PRESTON	57383-57383	WHITE LAKE	57559-57559	MURDO	57748-57748	HOWES
57251-57251	MARVIN	57384-57384	WOLSEY	57560-57560	NORRIS	57750-57750	INTERIOR
57252-57253	MILBANK	57385-57385	WOONSOCKET	57562-57562	OKATON	57751-57751	KEYSTONE
57255-57255	NEW EFFINGTON	57386-57386	YALE	57563-57563	OKREEK	57752-57752	KYLE
57256-57256	ORTLEY	57399-57399	HURON	57564-57564	ONIDA	57754-57754	LEAD
57257-57257	PEEVER	57401-57402	ABERDEEN	57566-57566	PARMELEE	57755-57755	LUDLOW
57258-57258	RAYMOND	57420-57420	AKASKA	57567-57567	PHILIP	57756-57756	MANDERSON
57259-57259	REVILLO	57421-57421	AMHERST	57568-57568	PRESHO	57757-57757	MARCUS
57260-57260	ROSHOLT	57422-57422	ANDOVER	57569-57569	RELIANCE	57758-57758	MUD BUTTE
57261-57261	ROSLYN	57424-57424	ASHTON	57570-57570	ROSEBUD	57759-57759	NEMO
57262-57262	SISSETON	57426-57426	BARNARD	57571-57571	SAINT CHARLES	57760-57760	NEWELL
57263-57263	SOUTH SHORE	57427-57427	BATH	57572-57572	SAINT FRANCIS	57761-57761	NEW UNDERWOOD
57264-57264	STOCKHOLM	57428-57428	BOWDLE	57574-57574	TUTHILL	57762-57762	NISLAND
57265-57265	STRANDBURG	57429-57429	BRENTFORD	57576-57576	VIVIAN	57763-57763	OELRICHS
57266-57266	SUMMIT	57430-57430	BRITTON	57577-57577	WANBLEE	57764-57764	OGLALA
57268-57268	TORONTO	57432-57432	CLAREMONT	57578-57578	WEWELA	57765-57765	OPAL
57269-57269	TWIN BROOKS	57433-57433	COLUMBIA	57579-57579	WHITE RIVER	57766-57766	ORAL
57270-57270	VEBLEN	57434-57434	CONDE	57580-57580	WINNER	57767-57767	OWANKA
57271-57271	VIENNA	57435-57435	CRESBARD	57584-57584	WITTEN	57769-57769	PIEDMONT
57272-57272	WALLACE	57436-57436	DOLAND	57585-57585	WOOD	57770-57770	PINE RIDGE
57273-57273	WAUBAY	57437-57437	EUREKA	57601-57601	MOBRIDGE	57772-57772	PORCUPINE
57274-57274	WEBSTER	57438-57438	FAULKTON	57620-57620	BISON	57773-57773	PRINGLE
57276-57276	WHITE	57439-57439	FERNEY	57621-57621	BULLHEAD	57774-57774	PROVO
57278-57278	WILLOW LAKE	57440-57440	FRANKFORT	57622-57622	CHERRY CREEK	57775-57775	QUINN
57279-57279	WILMOT	57441-57441	FREDERICK	57623-57623	DUPREE	57776-57776	REDIG
57301-57301	MITCHELL	57442-57442	GETTYSBURG	57625-57625	EAGLE BUTTE	57777-57777	RED OWL
57311-57311	ALEXANDRIA	57445-57445	GROTON	57626-57626	FAITH	57778-57778	ROCHFORD
57312-57312	ALPENA	57446-57446	HECLA	57628-57628	FIRESTEEL	57779-57779	SAINT ONGE
57313-57313	ARMOUR	57448-57448	HOSMER	57629-57629	GLAD VALLEY	57780-57780	SCENIC
57314-57314	ARTESIAN	57449-57449	HOUGHTON	57630-57630	GLENCROSS	57782-57782	SMITHWICK
57315-57315	AVON	57450-57450	HOVEN	57631-57631	GLENHAM	57783-57783	SPEARFISH
57317-57317	BONESTEEL	57451-57451	IPSWICH	57632-57632	HERREID	57785-57785	STURGIS
57319-57319	BRIDGEWATER	57452-57452	JAVA	57633-57633	ISABEL	57787-57787	UNION CENTER
57321-57321	CANOVA	57454-57454	LANGFORD	57634-57634	KELDRON	57788-57788	VALE
57322-57322	CARPENTER	57455-57455	LEBANON	57636-57636	LANTRY	57790-57790	WALL
57323-57323	CARTHAGE	57456-57456	LEOLA	57638-57638	LEMMON	57791-57791	WASTA
57324-57324	CAVOUR	57457-57457	LONGLAKE	57639-57639	LITTLE EAGLE	57792-57792	WHITE OWL
57325-57326	CHAMBERLAIN	57460-57460	MANSFIELD	57640-57640	LODGEPOLE	57793-57793	WHITEWOOD
57328-57328	CORSICA	57461-57461	MELLETTE	57641-57641	MC INTOSH	57794-57794	WOUNDED KNEE
57329-57329	DANTE	57462-57462	MINA	57642-57642	MC LAUGHLIN	57795-57795	ZEONA
57330-57330	DELMONT	57465-57465	NORTHVILLE	57643-57643	MAHTO	57799-57799	SPEARFISH
57331-57331	DIMOCK	57466-57466	ONAKA	57644-57644	MEADOW		
57332-57332	EMERY	57467-57467	ORIENT	57645-57645	MORRISTOWN		
57334-57334	ETHAN	57468-57468	PIERPONT	57646-57646	MOUND CITY		
57335-57335	FAIRFAX	57469-57469	REDFIELD	57647-57647	PARADE		
57337-57337	FEDORA	57470-57470	ROCKHAM	57648-57648	POLLOCK		

Tennessee

General Help Numbers:

Governor's Office

State Capitol, 1st Floor   615-741-2001
Nashville, TN 37243-0001   Fax 615-532-9711
http://www.state.tn.us/governor   8AM-5PM

Attorney General's Office

425 5th Ave North   615-741-3491
Nashville, TN 37243-0497   Fax 615-741-2009
http://www.attorneygeneral.state.tn.us   8AM-4:30PM

State Court Administrator

Nashville City Center   615-741-2687
511 Union St, Suite 600   Fax 615-741-6285
Nashville, TN 37219   8AM-4:30PM
http://www.tsc.state.tn.us

State Archives

State Library & Archives Division   615-741-7996
403 7th Ave N   Fax 615-741-6471
Nashville, TN 37243-0312   8AM-6PM M-SA
http://www.state.tn.us/sos/statelib/tslahome.htm

State Specifics:

Capital: Nashville
Davidson County

Time Zone: CST*
     * Tennessee's twenty-nine eastern-most counties are EST:
They are: Anderson, Blount, Bradley, Campbell, Carter, Claiborne,
Cocke, Grainger, Greene, Hamilton, Hancock, Hawkins, Jefferson,
Johnson, Knox, Loudon, McMinn, Meigs, Monroe, Morgan, Polk,
Rhea, Roane, Scott, Sevier, Sullivan, Unicoi, Union, Washington.

Number of Counties: 95

Population: 5,689,283

Web Site: www.state.tn.us

State Agencies

Criminal Records

Access to Records is Restricted

Tennessee Bureau of Investigation, Records and Identification Unit, 1148 Foster Ave, Menzler-Nix Bldg, Nashville, TN 37210; 615-741-0430, 24 hours daily.

http://www.tbi.state.tn.us

Note: The record database is not open to the general public or employers. It can only be accessed by those who have specific authorization per state law. However, the state maintains a web site (http://www.ticic.state.tn.us) that permits searching of sexual offenders, missing children, and people placed on parole from another state but reside in TN.

Corporation Records
Limited Partnership Records
Fictitious Name
Assumed Name
Limited Liability Company Records

Division of Business Svcs; Corporations, Department of State, 312 Eighth Ave. N, 6th Fl, Nashville, TN 37243; 615-741-2286, 615-741-7310 (Fax), 8AM-4:30PM.

http://www.state.tn.us/sos

Indexing & Storage: Records are available from 1875 to present. Records are computerized and are on microfilm from 1979. Records are indexed on inhouse computer.

Searching: All information is considered public record. Include the following in your request-full name of business. In addition to the articles of incorporation, corporation records include the following information: Annual Reports, Officers, Directors, DBAs (assumed names only), Prior (merged) names, Inactive and Reserved names.

Access by: mail, phone, in person, online.

Fee & Payment: Certification costs $20.00. Corp., LLC, LP, and LLP records cost $20.00 per copy, which includes certification. Fee payee: Secretary of State. Prepayment required. Personal checks accepted. No credit cards accepted.

Mail search: Turnaround time: 1 to 3 days. Certificates are usually processed in 1 day.No self addressed stamped envelope is required.

Phone search: Limited information is given over the phone. Requests for certificates must be in writing.

In person search: Turnaround time is immediate unless certified documents are ordered which are ready the next day.

Online search: There is a free online search at http://www.tennesseeanytime.org/sosname. While this is intended for business name availability, details are given on existing entities.

Other access: Some data can be purchased in bulk or list format. Call 615-532-9007 for more details.

Trademarks/Servicemarks
Trade Names

Secretary of State, Trademarks/Tradenames Division, 312 8th Ave North, 6th Fl, Nashville, TN 37243-0306; 615-741-0531, 615-741-7310 (Fax), 8AM-4:30PM.

http://www.state.tn.us/sos/service.htm

Indexing & Storage: Records are available from the 1950s to present. It takes 2 to 3 days before new records are available for inquiry. Records are indexed on microfilm.

Searching: Include the following in your request-trademark/servicemark name, name of owner, date of application.

Access by: mail, phone, in person, online.

Fee & Payment: There is no search fee, but copies are $1.00 per page. Fee payee: Secretary of State. Personal checks accepted. No credit cards accepted.

Mail search: Turnaround time: 1 to 3 days. A self addressed stamped envelope is requested.

Phone search: No fee for telephone request.

In person search: Turnaround time is while you wait.

Online search: The Internet provides a record search of TN Trademarks, newest records are 3 days old.

Other access: The agency will provide a file update every three months for $1.00 per page. Requests must be in writing.

Uniform Commercial Code
State Tax Liens
Federal Tax Liens

Division Of Business Services, Secretary of State, 312 Eighth Ave N, 6th Fl, Nashville, TN 37243; 615-741-3276, 615-741-7310 (Fax), 8AM-4:30PM.

http://www.state.tn.us/sos

Indexing & Storage: Records are available from 1964. Records are computerized from 03/01/96.

Searching: Use search request form UCC-11. Federal tax liens are filed at the county level. Include the following in your request-debtor name.

Access by: mail, in person, online.

Fee & Payment: The fee is $15.00 per document, copies are $1.00 per page. Fee payee: Secretary of State. Prepayment required. Personal checks accepted. No credit cards accepted.

Mail search: Turnaround time: 1 to 2 days. A self addressed stamped envelope is requested.

In person search: The results are mailed in 3-5 days.

Online search: Free access at http://ndweb.state.tn.us/cgi-bin/nd_CGI_50/ietm/PgUCCSearch.

Sales Tax Registrations
Access to Records is Restricted

Revenue Department, Tax Enforcement Division, Andrew Jackson Bldg, 500 Deaderick St, Nashville, TN 37242-0100; 615-741-7071, 615-532-6339 (Fax), 8AM-4:30PM.

Note: This agency refuses to make any information about registrants available.

Birth Certificates

Tennessee Department of Health, Office of Vital Records, 421 5th Ave North, 1st floor, Nashville, TN 37247; 615-741-1763, 615-741-0778 (Credit card order), 615-726-2559 (Fax), 8AM-4PM.

http://www.state.tn.us/health/vr

Indexing & Storage: Records are available from 1914 to present. For birth records prior to 1914, contact the State Library and Archives at 615-741-2764. Short forms are only available since 1949. New records are available for inquiry immediately. Records are indexed on index cards, inhouse computer.

Searching: Must have a signed release form from person of record or immediate family member for certified copy. Medical and health information is not released. Include the following in your request-full name, names of parents, mother's maiden name, date of birth, place of birth, relationship to person of record. Daytime phone helpful.

Access by: mail, phone, fax, in person, online.

Fee & Payment: $10.00 for the long (copy of actual certificate) form; $5.00 for the short computerized form. Add $2.00 per name per copy for additional copies. Fee payee: Tennessee Vital Records. Prepayment required. Personal checks accepted. Credit cards accepted: MasterCard, Visa, AmEx, Discover.

Mail search: Turnaround time: 2 to 3 weeks. No self addressed stamped envelope is required.

Phone search: You must use credit cards with fax or phone requests. There is an additional $10.00 fee. Phone service is available from 8AM to 4PM.

Fax search: Fax requests are handled like phone requests.

In person search: Wait time is 15 minutes.

Online search: Records may be ordered from the web site, but are returned by mail.

Expedited service: Expedited service is available for fax or online searches. Turnaround time: 1 day. Phone and fax records ordered by credit card, for $10.00 extra, can be returned overnight for an additional fee.

Death Records

Tennessee Department of Health, Office of Vital Records, 421 5th Ave North, 1st floor, Nashville,

TN 37247; 615-741-1763, 615-741-0778 (Credit card order), 615-726-2559 (Fax), 8AM-4PM.

http://www.state.tn.us/health/vr

Indexing & Storage: Records are available for 50 years. Previous records are at the State Archives at 615-726-2559. It takes 3 months or less before new records are available for inquiry. Records are indexed on index cards, inhouse computer.

Searching: Must have a signed release form from immediate family member. Cause of death is restricted to immediate family members or their representatives and must be specifically requested. Include the following in your request-full name, names of parents, mother's maiden name, date of death, place of death, reason for information request, relationship to person of record. Daytime phone helpful.

Access by: mail, phone, fax, in person, online.

Fee & Payment: The fee is $5.00 per name. Fee payee: Tennessee Vital Records. Prepayment required. Personal checks accepted. Credit cards accepted: MasterCard, Visa, AmEx, Discover.

Mail search: Turnaround time: 2 to 3 weeks. No self addressed stamped envelope is required.

Phone search: You must use a credit card for an additional fee of $10.00. Turnaround time is one day.

Fax search: Same criteria as phone requests.

In person search: Wait is 15 minutes.

Online search: Records may be ordered online at the web site, but are returned by mail. The Cleveland (Tennessee) Public Library staff and volunteers have published the 1914-1925 death records of thirty-three counties at http://www.state.tn.us/sos/statelib/pubsvs/death.htm#index. It should be noted that the records of children under two years of age have been omitted from this project.

Expedited service: Expedited service is available for fax or online searches. Turnaround time: 24 hours. Add $10.00 per request. For credit card orders only. Add fees for overnight shipping.

Marriage Certificates

Tennessee Department of Health, Office of Vital Records, 421 5th Ave North, 1st floor, Nashville, TN 37247; 615-741-1763, 615-741-0778 (Credit card order), 615-726-2559 (Fax), 8AM-4PM.

http://www.state.tn.us/health/vr

Indexing & Storage: Records are available for 50 years. It takes 1 month before new records are available for inquiry. Records are indexed on index cards, inhouse computer.

Searching: Must have a signed release form from persons of record or immediate family member for certified copy. Information on race or previous marriages is only released for statistical purposes. Include the following in your request-names of husband and wife, date of marriage, place or county of marriage.

Access by: mail, phone, fax, in person, online.

Fee & Payment: The search fee is $10.00. Add $2.00 for each additional copy. Fee payee: Tennessee Vital Records. Prepayment required. Personal checks accepted. Credit cards accepted: MasterCard, Visa, AmEx, Discover.

Mail search: Turnaround time: 2 to 3 weeks. No self addressed stamped envelope is required.

Phone search: You must use a credit card for an additional $10.00 fee. Records are processed in 24 hours.

Fax search: Same criteria as phone searching.

In person search: Wait time is about 15 minutes.

Online search: Records may be ordered from the web site, but are returned by mail.

Expedited service: Expedited service is available for fax or online searches. Turnaround time: 24 hours if received. Add $10.00 per name. You must use a credit card. Add fees if overnight shipping desired ($11.75).

Divorce Records

Tennessee Department of Health, Office of Vital Records, 421 5th Ave North, 1st floor, Nashville, TN 37247-0460; 615-741-1763, 615-741-0778 (Credit card order), 615-726-2559 (Fax), 8AM-4PM.

http://www.state.tn.us/health/vr

Indexing & Storage: Records are available for 50 years. It takes 2 weeks to 2 months before new records are available for inquiry. Records are indexed on index cards, inhouse computer.

Searching: Must have a signed release form from person of record or immediate family member. Information on previous marriages and education is released for statistical use only. Include the following in your request-names of husband and wife, date of divorce, place of divorce.

Access by: mail, phone, fax, in person, online.

Fee & Payment: The search fee is $10.00. There is an additional $2 charge for an extra copy. Fee payee: Tennessee Vital Records. Prepayment required. Personal checks accepted. Credit cards accepted: MasterCard, Visa, AmEx, Discover.

Mail search: Turnaround time: 2 to 3 weeks. No self addressed stamped envelope is required.

Phone search: You must use a credit card and there is an additional fee of $10.00. Records are processed in one day.

Fax search: Same criteria as phone searching.

In person search: Orders in by 10:30AM are available that same day at 3PM, otherwise next day at 3PM.

Online search: Records may be ordered online, but are returned by mail.

Expedited service: Expedited service is available for fax or online searches. Turnaround time: 24 hours. Add $10.00 per request. This requires use of credit card. Add fees if overnight delivery is desired ($11.75).

Workers' Compensation Records

Tennessee Department of Labor, Workers Compensation Division, 710 James Robertson Pwy, 2nd Floor, Nashville, TN 37243-0661; 615-741-2395, 615-532-1468 (Fax), 8AM-4:30PM.

http://www.state.tn.us/labor-wfd

Indexing & Storage: Records are available from 09/91 on computer, from 1987 to present on microfiche. Prior records are maintained on index cards.

Searching: Unless you have a signed authorization from the injured party or are an attorney representing the injured party, a court order is required to obtain records. This information is not considered public record;

however, they'll tell if a claim is on file. The SSN, company name, date of injury, and claim # is required for searching records after 1987, prior record searching requires the name of the company involved.

Access by: mail, fax, in person.

Fee & Payment: The search fee is $5.00, copy fee is $.25 per page. Fee payee: State of Tennessee Treasurer. Personal checks accepted. No credit cards accepted.

Mail search: Turnaround time: within 2 weeks. They will invoice you for copies and postage.No self addressed stamped envelope is required.

Fax search: This will not effect turnaround time.

In person search: Records are still returned in 2 weeks, but you can pick them up.

Driver Records

Dept. of Safety, Financial Responsibility Section, Attn: Driving Records, 1150 Foster Ave, Nashville, TN 37210; 615-741-3954, 8AM-4:30PM.

http://www.state.tn.us/safety

Note: Tickets are available from this office for a $5.00 fee per record.

Indexing & Storage: Records are available for past 3 years for convictions, if valid; 7 years if the license is suspended, restricted, or revoked. It takes 30 days or more before new records are available for inquiry.

Searching: Tennessee passed legislation similar to DPPA. Casual requesters must have written notarized authorization to receive record information with address data if subject opted out. The driver's license number and last name or DOB are needed when ordering.

Access by: mail, in person, online.

Fee & Payment: The fee is $5.00 per record. Fee payee: Tennessee Department of Safety. Prepayment required. Certified checks or money orders are preferred. MasterCard & Visa accepted in person only.

Mail search: Turnaround time: 2 weeks. No self addressed stamped envelope is required.

In person search: Up to 10 requests will be processed while you wait at this location or at offices in Nashville, Memphis, Knoxville, Chattanooga, and various Driver License Testing Centers.

Online search: Driving records are available to subscribers, signup at www.tennesseeanytime.org. There is a $75 registration fee. Records are available 24 hours daily on an interactive basis. Records are $5.00 each. Suggested only for ongoing users. Call 1-866-886-3468 for more information.

Other access: Magnetic tape retrieval is available for high volume users. Purchase of the DL file is available for approved requesters.

Vehicle Ownership
Vehicle Identification

Titling and Registration Division, Information Unit, 44 Vantage Way #160, Nashville, TN 37243-8050; 615-741-3101 (Titles), 8AM-4:30PM.

http://www.state.tn.us/safety

Indexing & Storage: Records are available for 5 years to present. It takes 12 weeks before new records are available for inquiry.

Searching: The state follows the DPPA guidelines for permissible requesters. Records are not released to casual requesters without consent. The state recommends use of their form. Include the following in your request-make or yr or VIN, purpose of request, copy of requester's photo ID.

Access by: mail, in person.

Fee & Payment: The fee is $1.00 for name or plate searches, $5.00 for current title data, and $15.00 for a complete title history. Fee payee: Titling and Registration. Prepayment required. Personal checks accepted. No credit cards accepted.

Mail search: Turnaround time: 2 to 4 weeks. A self addressed stamped envelope is requested.

In person search: Turnaround time is while you wait, unless photocopy of actual document is required. The office closes at 4PM for walk-in customers. Photo ID required.

Accident Reports

Financial Responsibility Section, Records Unit, 1150 Foster Avenue, Nashville, TN 37210; 615-741-3954, 8AM-4:30PM.

http://www.state.tn.us/safety

Note: Also, you can obtain accident reports from the investigating agency.

Indexing & Storage: Records are available from 1991 to present. It takes 30 days before new records are available for inquiry.

Searching: Include the following in your request-full name, date of accident, location of accident. Also, include the county of the accident and DL of driver(s).

Access by: mail, in person.

Fee & Payment: The fee is $4.00 per record copy. Fee payee: Tennessee Department of Safety. Prepayment required. Agency prefers money orders and certified checks. Personal checks not accepted. MasterCard & Visa accepted for in person only.

Mail search: Turnaround time: 2 weeks. No self addressed stamped envelope is required.

In person search: Turnaround time is generally while you wait.

Vessel Ownership
Vessel Registration

Wildlife Resources Agency, Boating Division, PO Box 40747, Nashville, TN 37204; 615-781-6585, 615-741-4606 (Fax), 8AM-4:30PM.

http://www.state.tn.us/twra

Note: All liens are filed with the Secretary of State.

Indexing & Storage: Records are available for the past 3 years. Records are indexed on computer. The state does not issue titles. All motorized boats and all sailboats must be registered. It takes 30 days before new records are available for inquiry.

Searching: To search, one of the following is required: Tennessee ID #, hull id #, name, or SSN.

Access by: mail, phone, fax, in person.

Fee & Payment: There is no fee to do 1 or 2 searches; however, large lists may incur a charge.

Mail search: Turnaround time: 2 days. No self addressed stamped envelope is required.

Phone search: Whether a phone search will be performed depends on how busy the personnel is at the time of the call. Phone searches are only verbal verifications and require a Tennessee ID # to search.

Fax search: Turnaround time is 2 days. Results will be sent by mail.

In person search: Turnaround time is usually immediate, when staff available.

Other access: Records can be purchased in bulk. There is a minimum $272.50 fee if on labels and $240.00 minimum fee if on tape. Call Charlie Freeman at 615-781-6500 for more details.

Legislation Records

Tennessee General Assembly, Office of Legislative Information Services, Rachel Jackson Bldg, 1st Floor, Nashville, TN 37243; 615-741-3511 (Status), 615-741-0927 (Bill Room), 8AM-4:30PM.

http://www.legislature.state.tn.us

Indexing & Storage: Records are available for the current and past session only. Earlier records are maintained in the State Library & Archives.

Searching: Include the following in your request-bill number, topic of bill.

Access by: mail, phone, in person, online.

Fee & Payment: No fee to search, copy fee is $.25 per page. Fee payee: State of Tennessee. Personal checks accepted. No credit cards accepted.

Mail search: Turnaround time: same day. No self addressed stamped envelope is required.

Phone search: You may call for information.

In person search: You may request information in person.

Online search: Bill information can be viewed at the Internet site. The Tennessee Code is also available from the web page.

Voter Registration

Records not maintained by a state level agency.

Note: Records are held by the Administrator of Elections at the county level. Records can only be purchased for political related purposes.

GED Certificates

Department of Labor & Workforce Development, GED Records - Davy Crockett Tower, 500 James Robertson Parkway, 2nd Fl, Nashville, TN 37245; 615-741-7054, 615-532-4899 (Fax), 8AM-4:30PM.

http://www.state.tn.us/labor-wfd/AE/aeged.htm

Searching: Include the following in your request-date of birth, Social Security Number, signed release. Include your daytime telephone number. Year diploma issued also helpful.

Access by: mail, fax, in person.

Fee & Payment: There is no fee for a verification.

Mail search: Turnaround time: 7 to 10 working days. No self addressed stamped envelope is required.

Fax search: Turnaround time is generally in 3 days.

In person search: Searching is available in person.

Hunting License Information

Fishing License Information

Access to Records is Restricted

Wildlife Resources Agency, Sportsman License Division, PO Box 40747, Nashville, TN 37204; 615-781-6585, 615-741-4606 (Fax), 8AM-4:30PM.

http://state.tn.us/twra

Note: There is not a central database of hunting or fishing licenses. You must contact the vendor where the license was sold. The Sportman License Division (615-781-6585) does hold information on 45,000 sportsman licenses (boating, etc).

Tennessee State Licensing Agencies

Licenses Searchable Online

Accounting Firm #03.. www.state.tn.us/cgi-bin/commerce/roster2.pl
Alarm Contractor #03 .... www.state.tn.us/cgi-bin/commerce/roster2.pl
Alcohol & Drug Abuse Counselor #07 .... http://170.142.76.180/cgi-bin/licensure.pl
Animal Euthanasia Technician #07 .... http://170.142.76.180/cgi-bin/licensure.pl
Architect #03 .... www.state.tn.us/cgi-bin/commerce/roster2.pl
Athletic Trainer #07.. http://170.142.76.180/cgi-bin/licensure.pl
Auction Company #03 .... www.state.tn.us/cgi-bin/commerce/roster2.pl
Auctioneer #03 .... www.state.tn.us/cgi-bin/commerce/roster2.pl
Audiologist #07.. http://170.142.76.180/cgi-bin/licensure.pl
Barber/Barber Technician #03................................. www.state.tn.us/cgi-bin/commerce/roster2.pl
Barber School/Barber Shop #03.............................. www.state.tn.us/cgi-bin/commerce/roster2.pl
Boxing/Racing Personnel #03 .... www.state.tn.us/cgi-bin/commerce/roster2.pl
Chiropractor/Chiropractic Therapy Assistant #07........ http://170.142.76.180/cgi-bin/licensure.pl
Collection Agent #03.. www.state.tn.us/cgi-bin/commerce/roster2.pl
Collection Manager #03 .... www.state.tn.us/cgi-bin/commerce/roster2.pl
Contractor #03... www.state.tn.us/cgi-bin/commerce/roster2.pl
Cosmetologist #03.. www.state.tn.us/cgi-bin/commerce/roster2.pl
Cosmetology School/Shop #03 .... www.state.tn.us/cgi-bin/commerce/roster2.pl
Counselor, Associate/Professional #07 .... http://170.142.76.180/cgi-bin/licensure.pl
Dental Hygienist #07.. http://170.142.76.180/cgi-bin/licensure.pl
Dentist/Dental Assistant #07 .... http://170.142.76.180/cgi-bin/licensure.pl
Electrologist #07.. http://170.142.76.180/cgi-bin/licensure.pl
Electrology Instructor/School #07............................ http://170.142.76.180/cgi-bin/licensure.pl
Embalmer #03.. www.state.tn.us/cgi-bin/commerce/roster2.pl
Emergency Medical Personnel/Dispatcher #07........... http://170.142.76.180/cgi-bin/licensure.pl
Emergency Medical Service #07 .... http://170.142.76.180/cgi-bin/licensure.pl
Engineer #03 .... www.state.tn.us/cgi-bin/commerce/roster2.pl
First Responder EMS #07.. http://170.142.76.180/cgi-bin/licensure.pl
Funeral & Burial Cemetery/Establishment #03 .... www.state.tn.us/cgi-bin/commerce/roster2.pl
Funeral & Burial Director/Apprentice #03.................. www.state.tn.us/cgi-bin/commerce/roster2.pl
Geologist #03 .... www.state.tn.us/cgi-bin/commerce/roster2.pl
Hearing Aid Dispenser #07 .... http://170.142.76.180/cgi-bin/licensure.pl
Home Improvement #03 .... www.state.tn.us/cgi-bin/commerce/roster2.pl
Insurance Agent #03... www.state.tn.us/cgi-bin/commerce/roster2.pl
Insurance Firm #03... www.state.tn.us/cgi-bin/commerce/roster2.pl
Interior Designer #03 .... www.state.tn.us/cgi-bin/commerce/roster2.pl
Landscape Architect #03... www.state.tn.us/cgi-bin/commerce/roster2.pl
Landscape Architect Firm #03.................................. www.state.tn.us/cgi-bin/commerce/roster2.pl
Lobbyist #10.. www.state.tn.us/tref/lobby/lobby.htm
Marriage & Family Therapist #07 .... http://170.142.76.180/cgi-bin/licensure.pl
Massage Therapist/Establishment #07...................... http://170.142.76.180/cgi-bin/licensure.pl
Medical Doctor #06... http://170.142.76.180/cgi-bin/licensure.pl
Medical Laboratory Personnel #06 .... http://170.142.76.180/cgi-bin/licensure.pl
Midwife #07 .... http://170.142.76.180/cgi-bin/licensure.pl
Motor Vehicle Auction #03 .... www.state.tn.us/cgi-bin/commerce/roster2.pl
Motor Vehicle Dealer #03.. www.state.tn.us/cgi-bin/commerce/roster2.pl
Motor Vehicle Salesperson #03................................ www.state.tn.us/cgi-bin/commerce/roster2.pl
Nurse-RN-LPN #06... http://170.142.76.180/cgi-bin/licensure.pl
Nursery #11... www.state.tn.us/agriculture/regulate/regulat1.html
Nursery Plant Dealer #11 .... www.state.tn.us/agriculture/regulate/regulat1.html
Nurses' Aide #06.. http://170.142.76.180/cgi-bin/licensure.pl
Nursing Home Administrator #07 .... http://170.142.76.180/cgi-bin/licensure.pl
Occupational Therapist/Assistant #07 .... http://170.142.76.180/cgi-bin/licensure.pl
Optician, Dispensing #07.. http://170.142.76.180/cgi-bin/licensure.pl
Optometrist #07... www.odfinder.org/LicSearch.asp
Orthopedic Physician Assistant #06 .... http://170.142.76.180/cgi-bin/licensure.pl
Osteopathic Physician #06...................................... http://170.142.76.180/cgi-bin/licensure.pl
Pastoral Therapist, Clinical #07 .... http://170.142.76.180/cgi-bin/licensure.pl
Personnel Leasing #03 .... www.state.tn.us/cgi-bin/commerce/roster2.pl
Pharmacy/Pharmacist #03....................................... www.state.tn.us/cgi-bin/commerce/roster2.pl
Pharmacy Researcher #03....................................... www.state.tn.us/cgi-bin/commerce/roster2.pl
Physical Therapist/Assistant #06 .... http://170.142.76.180/cgi-bin/licensure.pl
Physician Assistant #06.. http://170.142.76.180/cgi-bin/licensure.pl
Podiatrist #07 .... http://170.142.76.180/cgi-bin/licensure.pl

Polygraph Examiner #03...www.state.tn.us/cgi-bin/commerce/roster2.pl
Private Investigative Company #03 ....www.state.tn.us/cgi-bin/commerce/roster2.pl
Private Investigator #03 ....www.state.tn.us/cgi-bin/commerce/roster2.pl
Psychological Examiner #07 ....http://170.142.76.180/cgi-bin/licensure.pl
Psychologist #07 ....http://170.142.76.180/cgi-bin/licensure.pl
Public Accountant-CPA #03 ....www.state.tn.us/cgi-bin/commerce/roster2.pl
Racetrack #03 ....www.state.tn.us/cgi-bin/commerce/roster2.pl
Real Estate Appraiser #03 ....www.state.tn.us/cgi-bin/commerce/roster2.pl
Real Estate Broker #03 ....www.state.tn.us/cgi-bin/commerce/roster2.pl
Real Estate Firm #03 ....www.state.tn.us/cgi-bin/commerce/roster2.pl
Real Estate Sales Agent #03.....................................www.state.tn.us/cgi-bin/commerce/roster2.pl
Respiratory Care Therapist/Technician/Assistant #06. http://170.142.76.180/cgi-bin/licensure.pl
Security Company #03..www.state.tn.us/cgi-bin/commerce/roster2.pl
Security Guard #03...www.state.tn.us/cgi-bin/commerce/roster2.pl
Security Trainer #03...www.state.tn.us/cgi-bin/commerce/roster2.pl
Social Worker, Master/Clinical #07 ....http://170.142.76.180/cgi-bin/licensure.pl
Speech Pathologist #07 ....http://170.142.76.180/cgi-bin/licensure.pl
Timeshare Agent #03...www.state.tn.us/cgi-bin/commerce/roster2.pl
Veterinarian #07 ....http://170.142.76.180/cgi-bin/licensure.pl
X-ray Operator #06 ....http://170.142.76.180/cgi-bin/licensure.pl
X-ray Technologist, Podiatry #06 ....http://170.142.76.180/cgi-bin/licensure.pl

Licensing Quick Finder

Accounting Firm #03 615-741-9771
Aesthetician #03 615-741-2515
Alarm Contractor #03 615-741-9771
Alcohol & Drug Abuse Counselor #07 ...615-532-5097
Alcohol Package Store #01 615-741-1602
Animal Euthanasia Technician #07 615-532-3202
Animal/Livestock Dealer #11 615-837-5183
Architect #03 615-741-3221
Athletic Trainer #07 615-532-3202
Attorney #12 615-741-3234
Auction Company #03 615-741-9771
Auctioneer #03.......................................615-741-3226
Audiologist #07 615-532-3202
Barber #03 615-741-9771
Barber School/Barber Technician #3.....615-741-9771
Barber Shop #03 615-741-9771
Bed & Breakfast #14 615-741-7206
Boiler Operator #08...............................901-385-5077
Boxing/Racing Personnel #03................615-741-9771
Camp #14..615-741-7206
Chiropractor/Chiropractic Therapy Assistant #07.......
....615-532-3202
Clinical Lab Technician/Personnel #6 ...615-532-3202
Collection Agent #03 615-741-1741
Collection Manager #03.........................615-741-9771
Contractor #03 615-741-8307
Cosmetologist #03 615-741-2515
Cosmetology School #03........................615-741-9771
Cosmetology Shop #03 615-741-9771
Counselor, Associate/Professional #7...615-532-3202
Court Reporter/Stenographer #02.........423-756-0221
Dental Hygienist #07 615-532-3202
Dentist/Dental Assistant #07.................615-532-3202
Dietitian/Nutritionist #07.......................615-532-3202
Electrologist #07 615-532-3202
Electrology Instructor/School #07..........615-532-3202
Elevator Inspector #15...........................615-741-2123
Embalmer #03 615-741-9771
Emergency Medical Personnel/Dispatcher #07 ....
....615-532-3202
Emergency Medical Service #07...........615-532-3202
Engineer #03 615-741-3221
Environmentalist #07..............................615-532-3202
Fire Protection Sprinkler System Contractor #03 ....
....615-741-7190
First Responder EMS #07 615-532-3202

Food Service Establishment #14...........615-741-7206
Funeral & Burial Cemetery/Establishment #03 ....
....615-741-9771
Funeral & Burial Dir./Apprentice #03 615-741-9771
Geologist #03..615-741-9771
Health Care Facility #06 615-532-3202
Hearing Aid Dispenser #07 615-532-3202
Home Improvement #03 615-741-9771
Hotel #14 615-741-7206
Insurance Agent #03 615-741-9771
Insurance Firm #03 615-741-9771
Interior Designer #03..............................615-741-9771
Investment Advisor #03 615-741-2947
Landscape Architect #03 615-741-3221
Landscape Architect Firm #03 615-741-9771
Liquor Sale/Permit #01 615-741-1602
Lobbyist #10 615-741-7959
Manicurist #03 615-741-2515
Marriage & Family Therapist #07 615-532-3202
Massage Therapist/Establishment #07..615-532-5083
Medical Doctor #06 615-532-3202
Medical Laboratory Personnel #06........615-532-3202
Medical Professional - Disciplinary Tracking #06........
....615-532-3202
Midwife #07 615-532-3202
Milk Tester/Sampler #11 615-837-5177
Motor Vehicle Auction #03.....................615-741-9771
Motor Vehicle Dealer #03 615-741-9771
Motor Vehicle Salesperson #03 615-741-9771
Notary Public #09...................................615-741-3699
Nurse-RN/LPN #06 615-532-3202
Nursery #11 615-837-5338
Nursery Plant Dealer #11 615-837-5338
Nurses' Aide #06....................................615-532-3202
Nursing Home Administrator #07 615-532-3202
Occupational Therapist/Assistant #07 ...615-532-3202
Optician, Dispensing #07.......................615-532-3202
Optometrist #07 615-532-3202
Orthopedic Physician Assistant #06 615-532-3202
Osteopathic Physician #06 615-532-3202
Pastoral Therapist, Clinical #07 615-532-3202
Personnel Leasing #03..........................615-741-9771
Pest Control Operator #11 615-837-5135
Pharmacist/Pharmacy #03.....................615-741-9771
Pharmacy Researcher #03.....................615-741-9771
Physical Therapist/Assistant #06 615-532-3202

Physician Assistant #06.........................615-532-3202
Plumber/Plumbing Company #08...........901-385-5077
Podiatrist #07 615-532-3202
Polygraph Examiner #03 615-741-9771
Private Investigative Company #03.........615-741-9771
Private Investigator #03..........................615-741-9771
Private Security Guard #03.....................615-741-4827
Psychological Examiner #07 615-532-3202
Psychologist #07 615-532-3202
Public Accountant-CPA #03....................615-741-2550
Racetrack #03...615-741-9771
Radiation Therapy Technician #06.........615-532-3202
Radiologic Technologist #06...................615-532-3202
Real Estate Appraiser #03 615-741-9771
Real Estate Broker #03 615-741-9771
Real Estate Firm #03..............................615-741-9771
Real Estate Sales Agent #03 615-741-1831
Refrigeration Installer/Contractor #08....901-385-5077
Respiratory Care Therapist/Technician/Assistant #06
....615-532-3202
School Administrative Supervisor #05 ...615-532-4885
School Counselor #05.............................615-532-4885
School Librarian #05 615-532-4885
Securities Broker/Dealer/Agent #03 615-741-2947
Security Company #03 615-741-9771
Security Guard #03 615-741-9771
Security Trainer #03...............................615-741-9771
Service Technician (Weigh Scales) #11 615-837-5109
Shampoo Technician #03 615-741-2515
Shorthand Reporter #02 423-756-0221
Social Worker, Master/Clinical #07 615-532-3202
Speech Pathologist #07..........................615-532-3202
Surveyor #03 615-741-3611
Swimming Pool #14 615-741-7206
Tattoo Artist/Apprentice #14 615-741-7206
Teacher #05..615-532-4885
Timeshare Agent #03 615-741-2273
Veterinarian #07......................................615-532-3202
Water Treatment Plant Operator #13 615-898-8090
Weigher, Public (Bulk Products, Aggregates) #11 ......
....615-837-5109
Weighmaster #11 615-837-5109
Wine Production/Sale/Transport #01.....615-741-1602
X-ray Operator #06 615-532-3202
X-ray Technologist, Podiatry #06 615-532-6280

Licensing Agency Information

#01 Alcoholic Beverage Commission, 226 Capitol Blvd Bldg, #300, Nashville, TN 37243-0755; 615-741-1602, Fax: 615-741-0847.

#03 Department of Commerce & Insurance, 500 James Robertson Pky, 2nd Fl, Nashville, TN 37243; 615-741-9771, Fax: 615-532-2965.
www.state.tn.us/commerce
Direct web site URL to search for licensees: www.state.tn.us/cgi-bin/commerce/roster2.pl

#05 Department of Education, 710 James Robertson Pky, Andrew Johnson Tower, 5th Fl, Nashville, TN 37243-0377; 615-532-4885, Fax: 615-532-1448.
www.state.tn.us/education/lic_home.htm

#06 Department of Health, 425 5th Ave N, Cordell Hull Bldg, 1st Fl, Nashville, TN 37247-1010; 615-532-3202.
http://170.142.76.180/bmf-bin/BMFproflist.pl
Direct web site URL to search for licensees: http://170.142.76.180/cgi-bin/licensure.pl

#07 Department of Health, 425 5th Ave N, Cordell Hull Bldg, 1st Fl, Nashville, TN 37247-1010; 615-532-3202.
http://170.142.76.180/bmf-bin/BMFproflist.pl
Direct web site URL to search for licensees: http://170.142.76.180/cgi-bin/licensure.pl You can check for disciplinary actions against of any of the licensed professionals of this agency by visiting http://170.142.76.180/cgi-bin/licensure.pl.

#08 Mechanical Licensing Board, 6465 Mullins Station Rd, Memphis, TN 38134; 901-385-5054, Fax: 901-385-5198.

#09 Office of Secretary of State, 312 8th Av N, 6th Fl, W R Snodgrass Tower, Nashville, TN 37243-0306; 615-741-3699, Fax: 615-741-7310.
www.state.tn.us/sos/sos.htm

#10 Registry of Election Finance, 404 James Robertson Pky, #1614, Nashville, TN 37243; 615-741-7959, Fax: 615-532-8902.
www.state.tn.us/tref

#11 Department of Agriculture, Melrose Station, Nashville, TN 37204; 615-837-5120, Fax: 615-837-5335.
www.state.tn.us/agriculture

#12 Board of Law Examiners, 706 Church St, #100, Nashville, TN 37243-0740; 615-741-3234, Fax: 615-741-5867.
www.state.tn.us/lawexaminers

#13 Water & Wastewater Certification Program, 2022 Blanton Dr, Fleming Training Ctr, Murfreesboro, TN 37129; 615-898-8090.

#14 Department of Health, 415 5th Ave N, Cordell Hull Bldg 6th Fl, Nashville, TN 37247-3901; 615-741-7206, Fax: 615-741-8510.
www.state.tn.us/health

#15 Department of Labor, 710 James Robertson Pky, Andrew Johnson Tower 4th Fl, Nashville, TN 37243; 615-741-2123.

Tennessee Federal Courts

The following list indicates the district and division name for each county in the state. If the bankruptcy court location is different from the district court, then the location of the bankruptcy court appears in parentheses.

County/Court Cross Reference

County	District	Division
Anderson	Eastern	Knoxville
Bedford	Eastern	Winchester (Chattanooga)
Benton	Western	Jackson
Bledsoe	Eastern	Chattanooga
Blount	Eastern	Knoxville
Bradley	Eastern	Chattanooga
Campbell	Eastern	Knoxville
Cannon	Middle	Nashville
Carroll	Western	Jackson
Carter	Eastern	Greeneville (Knoxville)
Cheatham	Middle	Nashville
Chester	Western	Jackson
Claiborne	Eastern	Knoxville
Clay	Middle	Cookeville (Nashville)
Cocke	Eastern	Greeneville (Knoxville)
Coffee	Eastern	Winchester (Chattanooga)
Crockett	Western	Jackson
Cumberland	Middle	Cookeville (Nashville)
Davidson	Middle	Nashville
De Kalb	Middle	Cookeville (Nashville)
Decatur	Western	Jackson
Dickson	Middle	Nashville
Dyer	Western	Memphis
Fayette	Western	Memphis
Fentress	Middle	Cookeville (Nashville)
Franklin	Eastern	Winchester (Chattanooga)
Gibson	Western	Jackson
Giles	Middle	Columbia (Nashville)
Grainger	Eastern	Knoxville
Greene	Eastern	Greeneville (Knoxville)
Grundy	Eastern	Winchester (Chattanooga)
Hamblen	Eastern	Greeneville (Knoxville)
Hamilton	Eastern	Chattanooga
Hancock	Eastern	Greeneville (Knoxville)
Hardeman	Western	Jackson
Hardin	Western	Jackson
Hawkins	Eastern	Greeneville (Knoxville)
Haywood	Western	Jackson
Henderson	Western	Jackson
Henry	Western	Jackson
Hickman	Middle	Columbia (Nashville)
Houston	Middle	Nashville
Humphreys	Middle	Nashville
Jackson	Middle	Cookeville (Nashville)
Jefferson	Eastern	Knoxville
Johnson	Eastern	Greeneville (Knoxville)
Knox	Eastern	Knoxville
Lake	Western	Jackson
Lauderdale	Western	Memphis
Lawrence	Middle	Columbia (Nashville)
Lewis	Middle	Columbia (Nashville)
Lincoln	Eastern	Winchester (Chattanooga)
Loudon	Eastern	Knoxville
Macon	Middle	Cookeville (Nashville)
Madison	Western	Jackson
Marion	Eastern	Chattanooga
Marshall	Middle	Columbia (Nashville)
Maury	Middle	Columbia (Nashville)
McMinn	Eastern	Chattanooga
McNairy	Western	Jackson
Meigs	Eastern	Chattanooga
Monroe	Eastern	Knoxville
Montgomery	Middle	Nashville
Moore	Eastern	Winchester (Chattanooga)
Morgan	Eastern	Knoxville
Obion	Western	Jackson
Overton	Middle	Cookeville (Nashville)
Perry	Western	Jackson
Pickett	Middle	Cookeville (Nashville)
Polk	Eastern	Chattanooga
Putnam	Middle	Cookeville (Nashville)
Rhea	Eastern	Chattanooga
Roane	Eastern	Knoxville
Robertson	Middle	Nashville
Rutherford	Middle	Nashville
Scott	Eastern	Knoxville
Sequatchie	Eastern	Chattanooga
Sevier	Eastern	Knoxville
Shelby	Western	Memphis
Smith	Middle	Cookeville (Nashville)
Stewart	Middle	Nashville
Sullivan	Eastern	Greeneville (Knoxville)
Sumner	Middle	Nashville
Tipton	Western	Memphis
Trousdale	Middle	Nashville
Unicoi	Eastern	Greeneville (Knoxville)
Union	Eastern	Knoxville
Van Buren	Eastern	Winchester (Chattanooga)
Warren	Eastern	Winchester (Chattanooga)
Washington	Eastern	Greeneville (Knoxville)
Wayne	Middle	Columbia (Nashville)
Weakley	Western	Jackson
White	Middle	Cookeville (Nashville)
Williamson	Middle	Nashville
Wilson	Middle	Nashville

US District Court

Eastern District of Tennessee

Chattanooga Division Clerk's Office, PO Box 591, Chattanooga, TN 37401 (Courier Address: Room 309, 900 Georgia Ave, Chattanooga, TN 37402), 423-752-5200.

http://www.tned.uscourts.gov

Counties: Bledsoe, Bradley, Hamilton, McMinn, Marion, Meigs, Polk, Rhea, Sequatchie.

Indexing/Storage: Cases are indexed by defendant and plaintiff as well as by case number. New cases are available in the index 1-2 days after filing date. Both computer and card indexes are maintained. Open records are located at this court.

Fee & Payment: The fee is $20.00 per item (one party name or case number). Payment may be made by money order, cashier check, personal check. Prepayment is required. Payee: Clerk, US District Court. Certification fee: $7.00 per document. Copy fee: $.50 per page.

Phone Search: Only docket information available by telephone.

Mail Search: Always enclose a stamped self addressed envelope.

In Person: In person searching is available.

PACER: Sign-up number is 800-676-6856. Access fee is. Toll-free access: 800-869-1265. Local access: 423-545-4647. Case records are available back to 1994. Records are never purged. New records are available online after 1 day. PACER is available online at http://pacer.tned.uscourts.gov.

Greeneville Division 101 Summer St W, Greenville, TN 37743 (Courier Address: Use mail address for courier delivery), 423-639-3105.

http://www.tned.uscourts.gov

Counties: Carter, Cocke, Greene, Hamblen, Hancock, Hawkins, Johnson, Sullivan, Unicoi, Washington.

Indexing/Storage: Cases are indexed by defendant and plaintiff as well as by case number. New cases are available in the index immediately after filing date. Both computer and card indexes are maintained. Open records are located at this court.

Fee & Payment: The fee is $20.00 per item (one party name or case number). Payment may be made by money order, cashier check, personal check. Prepayment is required. Payee: Clerk, US District Court. Certification fee: $7.00 per document. Copy fee: $.50 per page.

Phone Search: Only docket information is available by phone.

Mail Search: A stamped self addressed envelope is not required.

In Person: In person searching is available.

PACER: Sign-up number is 800-676-6856. Access fee is. Toll-free access: 800-869-1265. Local access: 423-545-4647. Case records are available back to 1994. Records are never purged. New records are available online after 1 day. PACER is available online at http://pacer.tned.uscourts.gov.

Knoxville Division Clerk's Office, 800 Market St, Knoxville, TN 37902 (Courier Address: Use mail address for courier delivery), 865-545-4279.

http://www.tned.uscourts.gov

Counties: Anderson, Blount, Campbell, Claiborne, Grainger, Jefferson, Knox, Loudon, Monroe, Morgan, Roane, Scott, Sevier, Union.

Indexing/Storage: Cases are indexed by defendant and plaintiff as well as by case number. New cases are available in the index 1-2 days after filing date. Both computer and card indexes are maintained. Computerized index as of June 1, 1992. Index cards prior to June 1, 1992. Open records are located at this court.

Fee & Payment: The fee is $20.00 per item (one party name or case number). Payment may be made by money order, cashier check, personal check. Prepayment is required. Payee: Clerk, US District Court. Certification fee: $7.00 per document. Copy fee: $.50 per page.

Phone Search: Only docket information is available by phone.

Mail Search: A stamped self addressed envelope is not required.

In Person: In person searching is available.

PACER: Sign-up number is 800-676-6856. Access fee is. Toll-free access: 800-869-1265. Local access: 423-545-4647. Case records are available back to 1994. Records are never purged. New records are available online after 1 day. PACER is available online at http://pacer.ohsd.uscourts.gov.

Winchester Division PO Box 459, Winchester, TN 37398 (Courier Address: 200 S Jefferson St, Room 201, Winchester, TN 37397), 931-967-1444.

http://www.tned.uscourts.gov

Counties: Bedford, Coffee, Franklin, Grundy, Lincoln, Moore, Van Buren, Warren.

Indexing/Storage: Cases are indexed by defendant and plaintiff as well as by case number. New cases are available in the index 1-2 days after filing date. A computer index is maintained. Open records are located at this court. Office has just begun maintaining records in 1997.

Fee & Payment: The fee is $20.00 per item (one party name or case number). Payment may be made by money order, cashier check, personal check. Prepayment is required. Payee: Clerk, US District Court. Certification fee: $7.00 per document. Copy fee: $.50 per page.

Phone Search: Only docket information available by telephone.

Mail Search: Always enclose a stamped self addressed envelope.

In Person: In person searching is available.

PACER: Sign-up number is 800-676-6856. Access fee is. Toll-free access: 800-869-1265. Local access: 423-545-4647. Case records are available back to 1994. Records are never purged. New records are available online after 1 day. PACER is available online at http://pacer.tned.uscourts.gov.

US Bankruptcy Court

Eastern District of Tennessee

Chattanooga Division Historic US Courthouse, 31 E 11th St, Chattanooga, TN 37402 (Courier Address: Use mail address for courier delivery), 423-752-5163.

http://www.tneb.uscourts.gov

Counties: Bedford, Bledsoe, Bradley, Coffee, Franklin, Grundy, Hamilton, Lincoln, Marion, McMinn, Meigs, Moore, Polk, Rhea, Sequatchie, Van Buren, Warren.

Indexing/Storage: Cases are indexed by debtor and creditors as well as by case number. New cases are available in the index 2 days after filing date. The court needs the name of the debtor and to obtain positive identification, a social security number or address is needed. A computer index is maintained. Open records are located at this court.

Fee & Payment: The fee is $20.00 per item (one party name or case number). Payment may be made by money order, cashier check, business check. Personal checks are not accepted. Will invoice for copy fees only. Payee: US Bankruptcy Court. Certification fee: $7.00 per document. Copy fee: $.50 per page.

Phone Search: The court will only confirm bankruptcy filings over the phone and will only honor up to three requests per phone call per day. An automated voice case information service (VCIS) is available. Call VCIS at 800-767-1512 or 423-752-5272.

Mail Search: A stamped self addressed envelope is not required.

In Person: In person searching is available.

PACER: Sign-up number is 800-676-6856. Access fee is $.60 per minute. Toll-free access: 888-833-9512. Local access: 423-752-5136. Case records are available back to January 1986. Records are purged as deemed necessary. New civil records are available online after 1 day. PACER is available online at http://pacer.tneb.uscourts.gov.

Jackson Division Room 107, 111 S Highland Ave, Jackson, TN 38301 (Courier Address: Use mail address for courier delivery), 731-421-9300.

http://www.tnwb.uscourts.gov

Counties: Benton, Carroll, Chester, Crockett, Decatur, Gibson, Hardeman, Hardin, Haywood, Henderson, Henry, Lake, Madison, McNairy, Obion, Perry, Weakley.

Indexing/Storage: Cases are indexed by debtor as well as by case number. New cases are available in the index 1-2 days after filing date. A computer index is maintained. Open records are located at this court.

Fee & Payment: The fee is $20.00 per item (one party name or case number). Payment may be made by money order, cashier check, business check. Personal checks are not accepted. Prepayment is required. A search fee is charged only when certification of the search is issued. Payee: US Bankruptcy Court. Copy fee: $.50 per page.

Phone Search: Only docket information is available by phone. An automated voice case information service (VCIS) is available. Call VCIS at 888-381-4961 or 901-328-3622.

Mail Search: A stamped self addressed envelope is not required.

In Person: In person searching is available.

PACER: Sign-up number is 800-676-6856. Access fee is $.60 per minute. Toll-free access: 800-406-0190. Local access: 423-752-5136. Case records are available back to 1989. Records are never purged. New civil records are available online after 2 days.

Knoxville Division 800 Market St #330, Howard H Baker Jr US Courthouse, Knoxville, TN 37902 (Courier Address: Use mail address for courier delivery), 865-545-4279.

http://www.tneb.uscourts.gov

Counties: Anderson, Blount, Campbell, Carter, Claiborne, Cocke, Grainger, Greene, Hamblen, Hancock, Hawkins, Jefferson, Johnson, Knox, Loudon, Monroe, Morgan, Roane, Scott, Sevier, Sullivan, Unicoi, Union, Washington.

Indexing/Storage: Cases are indexed by debtor as well as by case number. New cases are available in the index 2-3 days after filing date. Both computer and card indexes are maintained. Open records are located at this court. District wide searches are possible for limited information from 1/86 from this court.

Fee & Payment: The fee is $20.00 per item (one party name or case number). Payment may be made by money order, cashier check, personal check. Prepayment is required. Payee: Clerk, US Bankruptcy Court. Certification fee: $7.00 per document. Copy fee: $.50 per page.

Phone Search: The court will only confirm debtor names, SSN, address, attorney, trustee, chapter filed, date of filing, date of discharge/dismissal, date case closed, in addition to limited information regarding motions, hearings, etc. An automated voice case information service (VCIS) is available. Call VCIS at 800-767-1512 or 423-752-5272.

Mail Search: Always enclose a stamped self addressed envelope.

In Person: In person searching is available.

PACER: Sign-up number is 800-676-6856. Access fee is $.60 per minute. Toll-free access: 888-833-9512. Local access: 423-752-5136. Case records are available back to January 1986. Records are purged as deemed necessary. New civil records are available online after 1 day. PACER is available online at http://pacer.tneb.uscourts.gov.

US District Court

Middle District of Tennessee

Columbia Division c/o Nashville Division, 800 US Courthouse, 801 Broadway, Nashville, TN 37203 (Courier Address: Use mail address for courier delivery), 615-736-5498.

http://www.tnmd.uscourts.gov

Counties: Giles, Hickman, Lawrence, Lewis, Marshall, Maury, Wayne.

Indexing/Storage: Cases are indexed by as well as by case number. New cases are available in the index after filing date. Open records are located at the Division.

Fee & Payment: The fee is no charge per item (one party name or case number). Payment may be made by money order, cashier check. Business checks are not accepted. Personal checks are not accepted.

Phone Search: Searching is not available by phone.

Mail Search: A stamped self addressed envelope is not required.

In Person: In person searching is available.

PACER: Sign-up number is 800-676-6856. Access fee is $.60 per minute. Toll-free access: 800-458-2994. Local access: 615-736-7164. Case records are available back three years. Records are purged every year. New records are available online after 1 day. PACER is available online at http://pacer.tnmd.uscourts.gov.

Cookeville Division c/o Nashville Division, 800 US Courthouse, 801 Broadway, Nashville, TN 37203 (Courier Address: Use mail address for courier delivery), 615-736-5498, Fax: 615-736-7488.

Counties: Clay, Cumberland, De Kalb, Fentress, Jackson, Macon, Overton, Pickett, Putnam, Smith, White.

Indexing/Storage: Cases are indexed by defendant and plaintiff as well as by case number. New cases are available in the index 1 month after filing date. A computer index is maintained. Records are also indexed on microfiche. Open records are located at the Division.

Fee & Payment: The fee is $20.00 per item (one party name or case number). Payment may be made by money order, cashier check, business check. Personal checks are not accepted. Prepayment is required. Payee: Clerk, US District Court. Certification fee: $7.00 per document. Copy fee: $.50 per page.

Phone Search: Only docket information is available by phone.

Mail Search: Always enclose a stamped self addressed envelope.

In Person: In person searching is available.

PACER: Sign-up number is 800-676-6856. Access fee is $.60 per minute. Toll-free access: 800-458-2994. Local access: 615-736-7164. Case records are available back three years. Records are purged every year. New records are available online after 1 day. PACER is available online at http://pacer.tnmd.uscourts.gov.

Nashville Division 800 US Courthouse, 801 Broadway, Nashville, TN 37203 (Courier Address: Use mail address for courier delivery), 615-736-5498, Fax: 615-736-7488.

Counties: Cannon, Cheatham, Davidson, Dickson, Houston, Humphreys, Montgomery, Robertson, Rutherford, Stewart, Sumner, Trousdale, Williamson, Wilson.

Indexing/Storage: Cases are indexed by defendant and plaintiff as well as by case number. New cases are available in the index immediately after filing date. A computer index is maintained. Records are also indexed on microfiche. Open records are located at this court.

Fee & Payment: The fee is $20.00 per item (one party name or case number). Payment may be made by money order, cashier check, personal check. Prepayment is required. Payee: Clerk, US District Court. Certification fee: $7.00 per document. Copy fee: $.50 per page.

Phone Search: Only docket information is available by phone.

Fax Search: Will accept fax search at $15.00 per name.

Mail Search: A stamped self addressed envelope is not required.

In Person: In person searching is available.

PACER: Sign-up number is 800-676-6856. Access fee is $.60 per minute. Toll-free access: 800-458-2994. Local access: 615-736-7164. Case records are available back three years. Records are purged every year. New records are available online after 1 day. PACER is available online at http://pacer.tnmd.uscourts.gov.

US Bankruptcy Court

Middle District of Tennessee

Nashville Division PO Box 24890, Nashville, TN 37202-4890 (Courier Address: Customs House, Room 200, 701 Broadway, Nashville, TN 37203), 615-736-5584.

http://www.tnmb.uscourts.gov

Counties: Cannon, Cheatham, Clay, Cumberland, Davidson, De Kalb, Dickson, Fentress, Giles, Hickman, Houston, Humphreys, Jackson, Lawrence, Lewis, Macon, Marshall, Maury, Montgomery, Overton, Pickett, Putnam, Robertson, Rutherford, Smith, Stewart, Sumner, Trousdale, Wayne, White, Williamson, Wilson.

Indexing/Storage: Cases are indexed by debtor as well as by case number. New cases are available in the index 24 hours after filing date. Both computer and card indexes are maintained. Open records are located at this court.

Fee & Payment: The fee is $20.00 per item (one party name or case number). Payment may be made by money order, cashier check, business check. Personal checks are not accepted. Prepayment is required. Payee: Clerk, US Bankruptcy Court. Certification fee: $7.00 per document. Copy fee: $.50 per page.

Phone Search: Only docket information is available by phone. An automated voice case information service (VCIS) is available. Call VCIS at 800-767-1512 or 423-752-5272.

Mail Search: Always enclose a stamped self addressed envelope.

In Person: In person searching is available.

PACER: Sign-up number is 615-736-5577. Access fee is. Case records are available back to September 1989. Records are never purged. New civil records are available online after 1 day. PACER is available online at http://pacer.tnmb.uscourts.gov.

Other Online Access: Search all cases online clicking on "Database Access" and then choosing "NIBS case information" from the pop-up menu on the main page.

US District Court

Western District of Tennessee

Jackson Division Rm 26, US Courthouse 262, 111 S Highland, Jackson, TN 38301 (Courier Address: Use mail address for courier delivery), 731-421-9200, Fax: 731-421-9210.

http://www.tnwd.uscourts.gov

Counties: Benton, Carroll, Chester, Crockett, Decatur, Gibson, Hardeman, Hardin, Haywood, Henderson, Henry, Lake, McNairy, Madison, Obion, Perry, Weakley.

Indexing/Storage: Cases are indexed by defendant and plaintiff as well as by case number. New cases are available in the index 1-2 days after filing date. A computer index is maintained. Open records are located at this court.

Fee & Payment: The fee is $20.00 per item (one party name or case number). Payment may be made by money order, cashier check, personal check, Visa, Mastercard. Prepayment is required. Payee: Clerk, US District Court. Certification fee: $7.00 per document. Copy fee: $.50 per page.

Phone Search: Only docket information is available by phone.

Mail Search: Always enclose a stamped self addressed envelope.

In Person: In person searching is available.

PACER: Sign-up number is 800-676-6856. Access fee is $.60 per minute. Toll-free access: 800-407-4456. Local access: 901-495-1259. Case records are available back to 1993. Records are purged as deemed necessary. New records are available online after 2 days.

Memphis Division Federal Bldg, Room 242, 167 N Main, Memphis, TN 38103 (Courier Address: Use mail address for courier delivery), 901-495-1200, Fax: 901-495-1250.

http://www.tnwd.uscourts.gov

Counties: Dyer, Fayette, Lauderdale, Shelby, Tipton.

Indexing/Storage: Cases are indexed by defendant and plaintiff as well as by case number. New cases are available in the index 1-2 days after filing date. A computer index is maintained. Open records are located at this court.

Fee & Payment: The fee is $20.00 per item (one party name or case number). Payment may be made by money order, cashier check, personal check, Visa, Mastercard. Prepayment is required. Payee: Clerk, US District Court. Certification fee: $7.00 per document. Copy fee: $.50 per page.

Phone Search: Only docket information is available by phone.

Fax Search: Will accept fax searches with credit card number. Will fax docket listings at $.50 per page.

Mail Search: Always enclose a stamped self addressed envelope.

In Person: In person searching is available.

PACER: Sign-up number is 800-676-6856. Access fee is $.60 per minute. Toll-free access: 800-407-4456. Local access: 901-495-1259. Case records are available back to 1993. Records are purged as deemed necessary. New records are available online after 2 days.

US Bankruptcy Court

Western District of Tennessee

Memphis Division Suite 413, 200 Jefferson Ave, Memphis, TN 38103 (Courier Address: Use mail address for courier delivery), 901-328-3500, Fax: 901-328-3500.

http://www.tnwb.uscourts.gov

Counties: Dyer, Fayette, Lauderdale, Shelby, Tipton.

Indexing/Storage: Cases are indexed by debtor as well as by case number. New cases are available in the index 2 days after filing date. A computer index is maintained. Open records are located at this court.

Fee & Payment: The fee is $20.00 per item (one party name or case number). Payment may be made by money order, cashier check, business check. Personal checks are not accepted. Prepayment is required. In general, if the cost of copies exceeds the amount of the check, the court will bill for the excess by mail. Payee: Clerk, US Bankruptcy Court. Certification fee: $7.00 per document. Copy fee: $.50 per page.

Phone Search: Only docket information is available by phone. An automated voice case information service (VCIS) is available. Call VCIS at 888-381-4961 or 901-328-3622.

Mail Search: A stamped self addressed envelope is not required.

In Person: In person searching is available.

PACER: Sign-up number is 800-676-6856. Access fee is $.60 per minute. Toll-free access: 800-406-0190. Local access: 901-328-3617. Case records are available back to 1989. Records are never purged. New civil records are available online after 2 days. PACER is available online at http://pacer.tnwb.uscourts.gov.

Tennessee County Courts

Court	Jurisdiction	No. of Courts	How Organized
Circuit Courts*	General	15	31 Districts
Chancery Courts*	General	87	31 Districts
General Sessions Courts*	Limited	16	By County
Combined Circuit/ General Sessions*		87	By County
Municipal Courts	Municipal	300	
Probate Courts*	Probate	2	By County
Juvenile Courts	Special	17	By County

* Profiled in this Sourcebook.

Court	CIVIL								
	Tort	Contract	Real Estate	Min. Claim	Max. Claim	Small Claims	Estate	Eviction	Domestic Relations
Circuit Courts*	X	X	X	$0	No Max				X
Chancery Court*	X	X	X	$0	No Max		X		X
General Sessions Courts*	X	X	X	$0	$15,000	X	X		X
Municipal Courts									
Probate Courts*							X		
Juvenile Courts									X

Court	CRIMINAL				
	Felony	Misdemeanor	DWI/DUI	Preliminary Hearing	Juvenile
Circuit Courts*	X	X	X		
Criminal Courts*	X				
Chancery Court*					
General Sessions Courts*		X	X	X	X
Municipal Courts		X	X		
Probate Courts*					
Juvenile Courts					X

ADMINISTRATION   Administrative Office of the Courts, 511 Union St (Nashville City Center) #600, Nashville, TN, 37243-0607; 615-741-2687, Fax: 615-741-6285. www.tsc.state.tn.us

COURT STRUCTURE   Criminal cases are handled by the Circuit Courts and General Sessions Courts. All General Sessions Courts have raised the maximum civil case limit to $15,000 from $10,000. The Chancery Courts, in addition to handling probate, also hear certain types of equitable civil cases. Combined courts vary by county, and the counties of Davidson, Hamilton, Knox, and Shelby have separate Criminal Courts.

ONLINE ACCESS   There is currently no statewide, online computer system available, internal or external. The Tennessee Administrative Office of Courts (AOC) has provided computers and CD-ROM readers to state judges, and a computerization project (named TnCIS) to implement statewide court automation started in January 1997.

PROBATE COURTS   Probate is handled in the Chancery or County Courts, except in Shelby and Davidson Counties where it is handled by the Probate Court.

Anderson County

7th District Circuit Court & General Sessions 100 Main St, Clinton, TN 37716; 865-457-5400. Hours: 8AM-4:30PM (EST). *Felony, Misdemeanor, Civil, Eviction, Small Claims.*

Civil Records: Access: In person only. Visitors must perform in person searches for themselves. No search fee. Required to search: name, years to search. Civil cases indexed by defendant, plaintiff. Civil records on computer from 1988, archived from 1947.

Criminal Records: Access: In person only. Visitors must perform in person searches for themselves. No search fee. Required to search: name, years to search, DOB, SSN. Criminal records on computer from 1988, archived from 1947.

General Information: Public Access terminal is available. No juvenile records released. Copy fee: $1.00 per page. Certification fee: $4.00. Fee payee: Circuit Court Clerk or General Sessions Clerk. Personal checks accepted. Prepayment is required.

Chancery Court Anderson County Courthouse, PO Box 501, Clinton, TN 37717; 865-457-5400; Fax: 865-457-6267. Hours: 8:30AM-4:30PM (EST). *Civil, Probate.*

Civil Records: Access: Phone, mail, in person. Both court and visitors may perform in person searches. No search fee. Required to search: name, years to search. Civil cases indexed by defendant, plaintiff. Civil records on computer 1992 to present, prior records on another system.

General Information: No adoption or mental health records released. Copy fee: $2.00 for first page, $1.00 each add'l. Certification fee: $4.00. Fee payee: Clerk and Master. Personal checks accepted. Prepayment is required.

Bedford County

17th District Circuit Court & General Sessions 1 Public Sq, Suite 200, Shelbyville, TN 37160; 931-684-3223. Hours: 8AM-4PM M-Th, 8AM-5PM Fri (CST). *Felony, Misdemeanor, Civil, Eviction, Small Claims.*

Civil Records: Access: In person only. Visitors must perform in person searches for themselves. No search fee. Required to search: name, years to search. Civil cases indexed by defendant, plaintiff. Civil records on archives and books from 1934.

Criminal Records: Access: In person only. Visitors must perform in person searches for themselves. No search fee. Required to search: name, years to search, DOB; also helpful: SSN. Criminal records on archives and books from 1934.

General Information: No juvenile, adoptions, mental health, expunged or sealed records released. Certification fee: $1.50. Fee payee: Thomas Smith, Clerk. Personal checks accepted. Prepayment is required.

Chancery Court Chancery Court, 1 Public Sq, Suite 302, Shelbyville, TN 37160; 931-684-1672. Hours: 8AM-4PM M-Th, 8AM-5PM Fri (CST). *Civil, Probate.*

Civil Records: Access: In person only. Visitors must perform in person searches for themselves. No search fee. Required to search: name, years to search. Civil cases indexed by defendant, plaintiff. Civil records on books from 9/82 (probate), prior records back to 1800s filed in county clerk's office.

General Information: No adoption records released. Turnaround time same day. Copy fee: $.50 per page. Certification fee: $5.00. Fee payee: Clerk and Master. Personal checks accepted. Prepayment is required.

Benton County

24th District Circuit Court - General Sessions & Juvenile 1 East Court Sq Rm 207, Camden, TN 38320; 731-584-6711; Fax: 731-584-0475. Hours: 8AM-4PM M-Th; 8AM-5PM F (CST). *Felony, Misdemeanor, Civil, Eviction, Small Claims.*

Civil Records: Access: In person only. Both court and visitors may perform in person searches. No search fee. Required to search: name, years to search. Civil cases indexed by defendant, plaintiff. Civil records computerized since 1995. Public can only use docket books to search, older records archived to 1800s.

Criminal Records: Access: In person only. Both court and visitors may perform in person searches. No search fee. Required to search: name, years to search. Criminal records computerized since 1995. Public can only use docket books to search, older records archived to 1800s.

General Information: No juvenile records released without judge approval. Copy fee: $1.00 per page. Certification fee: $3.00. Fee payee: Circuit Court Clerk or General Session. Business checks accepted. Prepayment is required.

Chancery Court 1 E Court Sq, Courthouse Rm 206, Camden, TN 38320; 731-584-4435; Fax: 731-584-1407. Hours: 8AM-4PM M-Th; 8AM-5PM F (CST). *Civil, Probate.*

Civil Records: Access: In person only. Visitors must perform in person searches for themselves. No search fee. Required to search: name, years to search. Civil cases indexed by defendant, plaintiff. Civil records in books since 1880.

General Information: Public Access terminal is available. No adoption or sealed records released. Certification fee: $6.00. Fee payee: Clerk & Master. No personal checks accepted. Prepayment is required.

Bledsoe County

12th District Circuit Court & General Sessions PO Box 455, Pikeville, TN 37367; 423-447-6488; Fax: 423-447-6856. Hours: 8AM-4PM (CST). *Felony, Misdemeanor, Civil, Eviction, Small Claims.*

Civil Records: Access: In person only. Visitors must perform in person searches for themselves. No search fee. Required to search: name, years to search. Civil cases indexed by plaintiff. Civil records archived from 1920 in books.

Criminal Records: Access: In person only. Visitors must perform in person searches for themselves. No search fee. Required to search: name, years to search. Criminal records archived from 1920 in books.

General Information: Public Access terminal is available. No juvenile records released. Certification fee: No certification fee. Prepayment is required.

Chancery Court PO Box 413, Pikeville, TN 37367; 423-447-2484; Fax: 423-447-6856. Hours: 8AM-4PM (CST). *Civil, Probate.*

Civil Records: Access: Phone, fax, mail, in person. Both court and visitors may perform in person searches. No search fee. Required to search: name, years to search. Civil cases indexed by defendant, plaintiff. Civil records on books since 1856.

General Information: No juvenile or adoption records released. Turnaround time 3 days. Fax notes: $1.00 per page. Copy fee: $1.00 per page. Certification fee: $2.00 per page. Fee payee: Bledsoe County Clerk and Master. Personal checks accepted.

Blount County

5th District Circuit Court & General Sessions 926 E Lamar Alexander Pkwy, Maryville, TN 37804-6201; 865-273-5400; Fax: 865-273-5411. Hours: 8AM-4:30PM (EST). *Felony, Misdemeanor, Civil, Eviction, Small Claims.*

Civil Records: Access: Mail, in person. Both court and visitors may perform in person searches. Search fee: $15.00 per name. Required to search: name, years to search. Civil cases indexed by defendant, plaintiff. Civil records archived in books back to 1991; on computer back to 1996.

Criminal Records: Access: Mail, in person. Both court and visitors may perform in person searches. Search fee: $15.00 per name. Required to search: name, years to search. Criminal records archived in books back to 1991; on computer back to 1996.

General Information: No juvenile records released. Turnaround time 3-6 days. Copy fee: $1.00 per page. Certification fee: $5.00. Fee payee: Circuit Court Clerk or General Session. Business checks accepted. Prepayment is required.

Circuit Court 926 E Lamar Alexander Parkway, Maryville, TN 37804; 865-273-5400; Probate phone: 865-273-5800; Fax: 865-273-5411. Hours: 8AM-4:30PM (EST). *Misdemeanor, Civil, Probate.*

Note: Probate is at the County Court located at 345 Court Street.

Civil Records: Access: Mail, in person. Both court and visitors may perform in person searches. Search fee: $15.00 per name. Required to search: name, years to search. Civil cases indexed by defendant. Civil records on books.

Criminal Records: Access: Mail, in person. Both court and visitors may perform in person searches. Search fee: $15.00 per name. Required to search: name, years to search. Criminal records on books.

General Information: Public Access terminal is available. No juvenile records released. Copy fee: $1.00 per page. Certification fee: $2.00. Fee payee: Circuit Court Clerk. Only cashiers checks and money orders accepted. Prepayment is required.

Bradley County

10th District Criminal, Circuit & General Sessions Court Courthouse, Rm 205, 155 N Ocoee St, Cleveland, TN 37311-5068; 423-476-0692; Fax: 423-476-0488. Hours: 8:30AM-4:30PM M-Th, 8:30AM-5PM Fri (EST). *Felony, Misdemeanor, Civil, Eviction, Small Claims.*

Civil Records: Access: Mail, in person. Both court and visitors may perform in person searches. Search fee: $25.00 per name. Required to search: name, years to search. Civil cases indexed by defendant, plaintiff. Civil records archived from 1955, on computer from 1990.

Criminal Records: Access: Mail, in person. Both court and visitors may perform in person searches. Search fee: $25.00 per name plus $2.00 data charge. Required to search: name, years to search, DOB; also helpful: SSN. Criminal records archived from 1955, on computer from 1990.

General Information: No juvenile records released. Turnaround time 10 days. Fax notes: Fee to fax results is $1.00 per page. Copy fee: $.30 per page. Certification fee: $10.00. Fee payee: Circuit Court Clerk or General Session. Personal checks accepted. Prepayment is required.

Chancery Court Chancery Court, 155 N. Ocoee St, Cleveland, TN 37311; 423-476-0526. Hours: 8:30AM-4:30PM M-Th, 8:30AM-5PM Fri (EST). *Civil, Probate.*

Civil Records: Access: Mail, in person. Both court and visitors may perform in person searches. No search fee.

Required to search: name, years to search. Civil cases indexed by defendant, plaintiff. Civil records filed in books.

General Information: No adoption records released. Turnaround time same day. Copy fee: $.25 per page. Certification fee: $5.00. Fee payee: Clerk and Master. Personal checks accepted.

Campbell County

8th District Criminal, Circuit & General Sessions Court PO Box 26, Jacksboro, TN 37757; 423-562-2624. Hours: 8AM-4:30PM (EST). *Felony, Misdemeanor, Civil, Eviction, Small Claims.*

Civil Records: Access: Mail, in person. Both court and visitors may perform in person searches. No search fee. Required to search: name, years to search. Civil cases indexed by defendant, plaintiff. Civil records on computer since 1991. On microfiche from 1987 and archived since court started located at La Follette Library, La Follette, TN 37766.

Criminal Records: Access: Mail, in person. Both court and visitors may perform in person searches. No search fee. Required to search: name, years to search, DOB, SSN. Criminal records on computer since 1991. On microfiche from 1987 and archived since court started located at La Follette Library, La Follette, TN 37766.

General Information: No juvenile, adoption and judicial hospitalization records released. Turnaround time depends on type of search. Copy fee: $1.00 per page. Certification fee: $3.00. Fee payee: Circuit Court Clerk or General Session. Business checks accepted. Prepayment is required.

Chancery Court PO Box 182 (570 Main St, #110), Jacksboro, TN 37757; 423-562-3496. Hours: 8AM-4:30PM (EST). *Civil, Probate.*

Civil Records: Access: In person only. Visitors must perform in person searches for themselves. No search fee. Required to search: name, years to search. Civil cases indexed by defendant, plaintiff. Civil records filed in books, microfiche available at LaFollette Library.

General Information: No adoption records released. SASE preferred. Turnaround time 1-2 days. Fax notes: Fee to fax results is $1.00 per page and $.50 per document. Copy fee: $1.00 per page. Certification fee: $4.00. Payee: Clerk & Master. Business checks accepted.

Cannon County

16th District Circuit Court & General Sessions County Courthouse Public Sq, Woodbury, TN 37190; 615-563-4461; Fax: 615-563-6391. Hours: 8AM-4PM M,T,Th,F; 8AM-Noon Wed (CST). *Felony, Misdemeanor, Civil, Eviction, Small Claims.*

Civil Records: Access: In person only. Visitors must perform in person searches for themselves. No search fee. Required to search: name, years to search. Civil cases indexed by defendant, plaintiff. Civil records archived on books from 1980s.

Criminal Records: Access: In person only. Visitors must perform in person searches for themselves. No search fee. Required to search: name, years to search, DOB. Criminal records archived on books from 1980s.

General Information: No juvenile records released. Copy fee: $1.00 per page. Certification fee: $3.00. Fee payee: Circuit Court Clerk or General Session. Personal checks accepted. Prepayment is required.

County Court County Courthouse Public Square, Woodbury, TN 37190; 615-563-4278/5936; Fax: 615-563-5696. Hours: 8AM-4PM M,T,Th,F; 8AM-Noon Sat (CST). *Probate.*

Carroll County

24th District Circuit Court & General Sessions 99 Court Sq #103, Huntingdon, TN 38344; 731-986-1929. Hours: 8AM-4PM (CST). *Felony, Misdemeanor, Civil, Eviction, Small Claims.*

Civil Records: Access: In person only. Visitors must perform in person searches for themselves. No search fee. Required to search: name, years to search. Civil cases indexed by defendant, plaintiff. Civil records archived from 1925; on computer from 1988.

Criminal Records: Access: In person only. Visitors must perform in person searches for themselves. No search fee. Required to search: name, years to search, DOB. Criminal records archived from 1925; on computer from 1988.

General Information: Public Access terminal is available. Copy fee: $.50 per page. No copies by mail. Certification fee: $6.00. Fee payee: Circuit Court Clerk or General Session. Only cashiers checks and money orders accepted. Prepayment is required.

Chancery Court 99 Court Sq, #103, Huntingdon, TN 38344; 731-986-1920. Hours: 8AM-4PM (CST). *Civil, Probate.*

Civil Records: Access: Mail, in person. Both court and visitors may perform in person searches. No search fee. Required to search: name, years to search. Civil cases indexed by defendant, plaintiff. Civil records on computer since 6/88, prior records on books.

General Information: No adoption or sealed documents released. SASE required ($.52 postage). Turnaround time 5-10 days. Copy fee: $1.00 per page and $3.00 per document. Certification fee: $6.00. Fee payee: Clerk and Master. No out-of-state checks, money orders and cashiers checks accepted. Prepayment is required.

Carter County

1st District Criminal, Circuit & General Sessions Court Carter County Justice Center, 900 E Elk Ave, Elizabethton, TN 37643; 423-542-1835; Fax: 423-542-3742. Hours: 8AM-5PM (EST). *Felony, Misdemeanor, Civil, Eviction, Small Claims.*

Civil Records: Access: In person only. Visitors must perform in person searches for themselves. No search fee. Required to search: name, years to search. Civil cases indexed by defendant, plaintiff. Civil records archived from 1800s (partial lost in fire), on computer from 4-92.

Criminal Records: Access: In person only. Visitors must perform in person searches for themselves. No search fee. Required to search: name, years to search. Criminal records archived from 1800s (partial lost in fire), on computer from 4-92.

General Information: Public Access terminal is available. No juvenile, psychiatric or expunged records released. Certification fee: $4.00 plus $1.00 each add'l page. Fee payee: Circuit Court Clerk or General Session. Personal checks accepted. Prepayment is required.

County Court 801 E Elk, Elizabethton, TN 37643; 423-542-1814; Fax: 423-547-1502. Hours: 8AM-5PM (EST). *Probate.*

Cheatham County

23rd District Circuit Court & General Sessions 100 Public Sq, Ashland City, TN 37015; 615-792-3272; Civil phone: 615-792-4866; Fax: 615-792-3203. Hours: 8AM-4PM (CST). *Felony, Misdemeanor, Civil, Eviction, Small Claims.*

Note: Circuit Court is room 225, General sessions is in room 223.

Civil Records: Access: Mail, in person. Both court and visitors may perform in person searches. Search fee:

$5.00 per name. Required to search: name, years to search. Civil cases indexed by defendant, plaintiff. Civil records archived on books from 1946 in office, since court started in storage and on computer from 1990.

Criminal Records: Access: Mail, in person. Both court and visitors may perform in person searches. Search fee: $5.00 per name. Required to search: name, years to search. Criminal records archived on books from 1946 in office, since court started in storage and on computer from 1990.

General Information: No juvenile records released. SASE required. Turnaround time 2-3 days. Copy fee: $2.50 per document. Certification fee: $5.00. Fee payee: Circuit Court, or General Sessions Clerk. Prepayment is required.

Chancery Court Clerk & Master, Suite 106, Ashland City, TN 37015; 615-792-4620. Hours: 8AM-4PM (CST). *Civil, Probate.*

Civil Records: Access: In person only. Visitors must perform in person searches for themselves. No search fee. Required to search: name, years to search. Civil cases indexed by defendant, plaintiff. Civil records on computer.

General Information: No adoption records released. SASE required. Turnaround time same day. Copy fee: $1.00 per page. Certification fee: $2.00. Fee payee: Chancery Court. Personal checks accepted. Prepayment is required.

Chester County

26th District Circuit Court & General Sessions PO Box 133, Henderson, TN 38340; 731-989-2454. Hours: 8AM-4PM (CST). *Felony, Misdemeanor, Civil, Eviction, Small Claims.*

Civil Records: Access: Phone, fax, mail, in person. Both court and visitors may perform in person searches. No search fee. Required to search: name, years to search. Civil cases indexed by defendant, plaintiff. Civil records in books and archived from 1892.

Criminal Records: Access: Phone, mail, in person. Both court and visitors may perform in person searches. No search fee. Required to search: name, years to search, DOB. Criminal records in books and archived from 1892.

General Information: No juvenile records released. Turnaround time 2 days. Copy fee: $1.00 per page. Certification fee: No certification fee. Fee payee: Circuit Court, or General Sessions Clerk. Prepayment is required.

Chancery Court Clerk & Master, PO Box 262, Henderson, TN 38340; 731-989-7171; Fax: 731-989-7176. Hours: 8AM-4PM (CST). *Civil, Probate.*

Civil Records: Access: In person only. Visitors must perform in person searches for themselves. No search fee. Required to search: name, years to search. Civil cases indexed by defendant, plaintiff. Civil records on books.

General Information: No adoption or sealed records released. Certification fee: $5.00. Fee payee: Clerk and Master. Personal checks accepted.

Claiborne County

8th District Criminal, Circuit & General Sessions Court PO Drawer 570, Tazewell, TN 37879; 423-626-8181; Fax: 423-626-5631. Hours: 8:30AM-4PM M-F, 8:30AM-Noon Sat (EST). *Felony, Misdemeanor, Civil, Eviction, Small Claims.*

Civil Records: Access: Mail, fax, in person. Both court and visitors may perform in person searches. Search fee: $10.00 per name. Required to search: name, years to search. Civil cases indexed by defendant, plaintiff. Civil records archived since 1932; on computer back to 1986.

Criminal Records: Access: Mail, fax, in person. Both court and visitors may perform in person searches. Search fee: $10.00 per name. Required to search: name, years to search. Criminal records archived since 1932; on computer back to 1986.

General Information: Public Access terminal is available. No adoption records released. SASE required. Turnaround time 2-3 days. Fax notes: Fee to fax results is $.25 per page. Copy fee: $.25 per page. Certification fee: $5.00. Fee payee: Circuit Court Clerk or General Sessions. Business checks accepted. In-state personal checks accepted. Prepayment is required.

Chancery Court PO Box 180, Tazewell, TN 37879; 423-626-3284; Fax: 423-626-3604. Hours: 8:30AM-Noon, 1-4PM (EST). *Civil, Probate.*

Civil Records: Access: Mail, in person. Both court and visitors may perform in person searches. No search fee. Required to search: name, years to search. Civil cases indexed by defendant, plaintiff. Civil records kept on books back to 1932; recent on computer.

General Information: No adoption records released. Turnaround time 1-2 days. Copy fee: $.25 per page. Certification fee: $5.00. Fee payee: Clerk and Master. Personal checks accepted. Prepayment is required.

Clay County

13th District Criminal, Circuit & General Sessions Court PO Box 749, Celina, TN 38551; 931-243-2557. Hours: 8AM-4PM (CST). *Felony, Misdemeanor, Civil, Eviction, Small Claims.*

Civil Records: Access: In person only. Visitors must perform in person searches for themselves. No search fee. Required to search: name, years to search. Civil cases indexed by defendant, plaintiff. Civil records archived from early 1900s, on microfiche from 1986.

Criminal Records: Access: In person only. Visitors must perform in person searches for themselves. No search fee. Required to search: name, years to search; also helpful: SSN. Criminal records archived from early 1900s, on microfiche from 1986.

General Information: No juvenile records released. Copy fee: $.25 per page. Certification fee: No certification fee. Fee payee: Circuit Court, or General Sessions Clerk. Personal checks accepted. Prepayment is required.

Chancery Court PO Box 332, Celina, TN 38551; 931-243-3145. Hours: 8AM-4PM M,T,Th,F; 8AM-Noon W (CST). *Civil, Probate.*

Civil Records: Access: Mail, in person. Both court and visitors may perform in person searches. No search fee. Required to search: name, years to search. Civil cases indexed by defendant, plaintiff. Civil records on books.

General Information: No juvenile records released. Turnaround time 1 week. Copy fee: $1.00 per page. Certification fee: No certification fee. Fee payee: Clerk & Master. Personal checks accepted. Prepayment is required.

Cocke County

4th District Circuit Court 111 Court Ave Rm 201, Newport, TN 37821; 423-623-6124; Fax: 423-625-3889. Hours: 8:30AM-5PM (EST). *Felony, Misdemeanor, Civil Actions Over $15,000.*

Civil Records: Access: Phone, fax, mail, in person. Both court and visitors may perform in person searches. Search fee: $3.00 per name. Required to search: name, years to search. Civil cases indexed by defendant, plaintiff. Civil records archived from late 1800s.

Criminal Records: Access: Phone, fax, mail, in person. Both court and visitors may perform in person searches. Search fee: $3.00 per name. Required to search: name, years to search, DOB. Criminal records archived from late 1800s.

General Information: No divorce or sealed records released. SASE not required. Turnaround time ASAP. Copy fee: $.25 per page. Certification fee: $5.00. Fee payee: Circuit Court. Personal checks accepted.

General Sessions 111 Court Ave, Newport, TN 37821; 423-623-8619; Fax: 423-623-9808. Hours: 8AM-4PM (EST). *Misdemeanor, Civil Actions Under $15,000, Eviction, Small Claims.*

Civil Records: Access: Phone, mail, in person. Both court and visitors may perform in person searches. Search fee: $3.00 per name. Required to search: name, years to search. Civil cases indexed by defendant, plaintiff. Civil records on books.

Criminal Records: Access: Phone, mail, in person. Both court and visitors may perform in person searches. Search fee: $3.00 per name. Required to search: name, years to search. Criminal records on books.

General Information: SASE required. Turnaround time varies. Copy fee: $3.00 per document. Certification fee: $3.00. Fee payee: General Sessions Court. Business checks accepted. Prepayment is required.

Chancery Court Courthouse Annex, 360 E Main St, Suite 103, Newport, TN 37821; 423-623-3321; Fax: 423-625-3642. 8AM-4:30PM (EST). *Civil, Probate.*

Civil Records: Access: Phone, mail, in person. Only the court performs in person searches; visitors may not. No search fee. Required to search: name, years to search. Civil cases indexed by defendant, plaintiff. Civil records on computer since 1980, on books from 1930.

General Information: No sealed records released. Turnaround time 1 week. Copy fee: $1.00 per document. Certification fee: $3.00. Fee payee: Chancery Court, Clerk and Master. Personal checks accepted. Prepayment is required.

Coffee County

14th District Circuit Court & General Sessions PO Box 629, Manchester, TN 37349; 931-723-5110. Hours: 8AM-4:30PM (CST). *Felony, Misdemeanor, Civil, Eviction, Small Claims.*

Civil Records: Access: Mail, in person. Both court and visitors may perform in person searches. Search fee: $5.00 if July 1, 1996 to present; 10 year check is $10.00; beyond 10 years add $5.00 per year. Required to search: name, years to search. Civil cases indexed by defendant, plaintiff. Civil records archived from late 1800s, indexed chronologically by court date.

Criminal Records: Access: Mail, in person. Both court and visitors may perform in person searches. Search fee: Same fees as civil. Required to search: name, years to search, DOB; also helpful: SSN. Criminal records archived from late 1800s, indexed chronologically by court date.

General Information: Public Access terminal is available. No juvenile record released. Turnaround time 1 week. Copy fee: $1.00 per page. Certification fee: $3.50. Fee payee: General Sessions Clerk. Personal checks accepted. Prepayment is required.

Chancery Court 300 Hillsboro Blvd, Rm 102, Manchester, TN 37355; 931-723-5132. Hours: 8AM-4:30PM (CST). *Civil, Probate.*

Civil Records: Access: Mail, in person. Both court and visitors may perform in person searches. No search fee. Required to search: name, years to search. Civil cases indexed by defendant, plaintiff. Civil records on books after 1980, before 1980 filed in County Clerk's Office.

General Information: No juvenile or adoption records released. Copy fee: $.50 per page. Certification fee: $2.00. Fee payee: Chancery Court. Personal checks accepted. Prepayment is required.

Crockett County

Circuit Court & General Sessions 1 South Bell St, Ste 6 Courthouse, Alamo, TN 38001; 731-696-5462; Fax: 731-696-2605. Hours: 8AM-4PM (CST). *Felony, Misdemeanor, Civil, Eviction, Small Claims.*

Civil Records: Access: Mail, fax, in person. Both court and visitors may perform in person searches. Search fee: $10.00 per name. Required to search: name, years to search. Civil cases indexed by defendant, plaintiff. Civil records archived since court started, records prior to 1986 on docket books. All requests must be in writing.

Criminal Records: Access: Mail, fax, in person. Both court and visitors may perform in person searches. Search fee: $10.00 per name. Required to search: name, years to search, DOB; also helpful: SSN, sex. Criminal records on docket books, on computer from 1993. All requests must be in writing.

General Information: Public Access terminal is available. No adoption or mental records released. SASE requested. Turnaround time 1-2 days. Copy fee: $1.00 per page. Certification fee: $6.00. Fee payee: Circuit Court, or General Sessions Clerk. Business checks accepted. Prepayment is required.

Chancery Court 1 South Bells St, Suite 5, Alamo, TN 38001; 731-696-5458; Fax: 731-696-3028. Hours: 8AM-4PM (CST). *Civil, Probate.*

Civil Records: Access: Mail, in person. Both court and visitors may perform in person searches. No search fee. Required to search: name, years to search. Civil cases indexed by defendant, plaintiff. Civil records on books.

General Information: No adoption records released. SASE required. Turnaround time 1-3 days. Copy fee: $1.00 per page. Certification fee: $3.00. Plus $1.00 per page. Fee payee: Chancery Court Clerk. Personal checks accepted. Prepayment is required.

Cumberland County

13th District Criminal, Circuit & General Sessions Court 2 N Main St, Suite 302, Crossville, TN 38555; 931-484-6647; Fax: 931-456-5013. Hours: 8AM-4PM (CST). *Felony, Misdemeanor, Civil, Eviction, Small Claims.*

Civil Records: Access: In person only. Visitors must perform in person searches for themselves. No search fee. Required to search: name, years to search. Civil cases indexed by defendant, plaintiff. Civil records archived on books from 1940s approx.; on computer back to 1996.

Criminal Records: Access: In person only. Visitors must perform in person searches for themselves. No search fee. Required to search: name, years to search, DOB; also helpful: SSN. Criminal records archived on books from 1940s approx.; on computer back to 1996.

General Information: Public Access terminal is available. No sealed records released. Certification fee: No certification fee. Only cashiers checks and money orders accepted. Prepayment is required.

Chancery Court 2 N Main St, Suite 101, Crossville, TN 38555-4583; 931-484-4731. Hours: 8AM-4PM (CST). *Civil, Probate.*

Civil Records: Access: Mail, in person. Only the court performs in person searches; visitors may not. No search fee. Required to search: name, years to search. Civil cases indexed by defendant, plaintiff. Civil records on computer since 1991, on books since 1900s.

General Information: No juvenile, adoption records released. SASE requested. Turnaround time 2 days. Copy fee: $.50 per page. Certification fee: $1.00 per page. Fee payee: Clerk and Master. Personal checks accepted. Prepayment is required.

Davidson County

20th District Criminal Court
Metro Courthouse, Rm 305, Nashville, TN 37201; 615-862-5600; Fax: 615-862-5676. Hours: 8AM-4PM (CST). *Felony, Misdemeanor.*

www.nashville.org.ccrt

Criminal Records: Access: Mail, online, in person. Both court and visitors may perform in person searches. Search fee: $15.00 per name. Required to search: name, years to search, DOB, signed release; also helpful: SSN, race. Records from the Metropolitan Nashville and Davidson County Criminal Court database are available free online at www.nashville.org/ccrt. Search the criminal court dockets by date. Also, the City of Nashville sponsors an Internet site at www.police.nashville.org/justice/default.asp.
General Information: No records unauthorized by statutes released. SASE required. Turnaround time 2-3 days. Copy fee: $.25 per page. Certification fee: $6.00. Fee payee: Circuit Court Clerk. Personal checks accepted. Credit cards accepted: Visa, MasterCard, Discover. Visa, MC, Discover. Prepayment is required.

Circuit Court
506 Metro Courthouse, Nashville, TN 37201; 615-862-5181. Hours: 8AM-4:30PM (CST). *Civil.*

www.nashville.org/cir

Civil Records: Access: Mail, in person. Both court and visitors may perform in person searches. No search fee. Required to search: name, years to search. Civil cases indexed by defendant, plaintiff. Civil records archived on books from 1800s, on computer from 1974.
General Information: Public Access terminal is available. No juvenile or adoption records released. Turnaround time 2-3 days. Copy fee: $.50 per page. Certification fee: $2.00 per page. Fee payee: Circuit Court Clerk. Prepayment is required.

General Sessions Court
211 Union St, #202, Nashville, TN 37201; 615-862-5195; Fax: 615-862-5924. Hours: 8AM-4:30PM (CST). *Civil Actions Under $15,000, Eviction, Small Claims.*

www.nashville.org/cir

Civil Records: Access: In person only. Visitors must perform in person searches for themselves. No search fee. Required to search: name, years to search.
General Information: Public Access terminal is available. No juvenile records released. Copy fee: $1.00 per page. Certification fee: $3.00 per page. Fee payee: General Sessions Court Clerk. Prepayment is required.

Probate Court
408 Metro Courthouse #105, Nashville, TN 37201; 615-862-5980; Fax: 615-862-5994. Hours: 8AM-4:30 (CST). *Probate.*

De Kalb County

13th District Criminal, Circuit & General Sessions Court
1 Public Sq, Rm 303, Smithville, TN 37166; 615-597-5711. Hours: 8AM-4:30PM M,T,W,Th; 8AM-5PM Fri (CST). *Felony, Misdemeanor, Civil, Eviction, Small Claims.*

Civil Records: Access: In person only. Both court and visitors may perform in person searches. No search fee. Required to search: name, years to search. Civil cases indexed by defendant, plaintiff. Civil records archived in office last 10 years. Prior to 1982, records are not very accurate because of fire.
Criminal Records: Access: In person only. Visitors must perform in person searches for themselves. No search fee. Required to search: name, years to search, DOB; also helpful: SSN. Criminal records archived in office last 10 years. Prior to 1982, records are not very accurate because of fire.
General Information: No juvenile records released. Copy fee: $1.00 per page. Certification fee: $6.00. Fee

payee: Circuit Court, or General Sessions Clerk. Personal checks accepted. Prepayment is required.

Chancery Court
1 Public Square, Rm 302, Smithville, TN 37166; 615-597-4360. Hours: 8AM-4PM (CST). *Civil, Probate.*

Civil Records: Access: In person only. Visitors must perform in person searches for themselves. No search fee. Required to search: name, years to search. Civil cases indexed by defendant, plaintiff. Civil records on books.
General Information: Public Access terminal is available. No adoption, juvenile records released. Fax notes: Do not fax. Copy fee: $1.00 per page. Certification fee: $6.00. Fee payee: Clerk and Master. Personal checks accepted. Prepayment is required.

Decatur County

24th District Circuit Court & General Sessions
PO Box 488, Decaturville, TN 38329; 731-852-3125; Fax: 731-852-2130. Hours: 8AM-4PM M,T,Th,F; 8AM-Noon W & Sat (CST). *Felony, Misdemeanor, Civil, Eviction, Small Claims.*

Civil Records: Access: In person only. Visitors must perform in person searches for themselves. No search fee. Required to search: name, years to search. Civil cases indexed by defendant, plaintiff. Civil records archived on books from 1927.
Criminal Records: Access: In person only. Visitors must perform in person searches for themselves. No search fee. Required to search: name, years to search, DOB, SSN, signed release. Criminal records archived on books from 1927.
General Information: No adoption records released. No copy fee. Certification fee: No certification fee. Fee payee: Circuit Court. Business checks accepted. Prepayment is required.

Chancery Court
Clerk & Master, Decaturville, TN 38329; 731-852-3422; Fax: 731-852-2130. Hours: 9M-4PM M,T,Th,F; 9AM-Noon Sat (CST). *Civil, Probate.*

Civil Records: Access: In person only. Visitors must perform in person searches for themselves. No search fee. Required to search: name, years to search. Civil cases indexed by plaintiff. Probate records in books since 1869 for probate, civil records in books since 1958.
General Information: No adoption records released. SASE required. Turnaround time 2 days. Copy fee: $.25 per page. Certification fee: $2.00. Fee payee: Elizabeth Carpenter, Clerk and Master. Personal checks accepted.

Dickson County

23rd District Circuit Court
Court Square, PO Box 220, Charlotte, TN 37036; 615-789-7010; Probate phone: 615-789-4171; Fax: 615-789-7018. Hours: 8AM-4PM (CST). *Felony, Misdemeanor, Civil Actions Over $15,000.*

Civil Records: Access: Phone, fax, mail, in person. Both court and visitors may perform in person searches. Search fee: $6.00 per name. Required to search: name, years to search. Civil cases indexed by defendant, plaintiff. Civil records archived from 1800s, on computer from 1986, some records back to 1974.
Criminal Records: Access: Phone, fax, mail, in person. Both court and visitors may perform in person searches. Search fee: $6.00 per name. Required to search: name, years to search; also helpful: DOB. Criminal records archived from 1800s, on computer from 1986, some records back to 1974.
General Information: No adoption records released. SASE required. Turnaround time 1 day. Fax notes: $6.00 per document. Copy fee: $.25 per page. Certification fee: $2.00. Fee payee: Circuit Court Clerk. Personal checks accepted. Prepayment is required.

General Sessions
PO Box 217, Charlotte, TN 37036; 615-789-5414; Fax: 615-789-3456. Hours: 8AM-4PM (CST). *Civil Actions Under $15,000, Eviction, Small Claims.*

Civil Records: Access: Phone, mail, in person. Both court and visitors may perform in person searches. Search fee: $6.00. Required to search: name, years to search. Civil cases indexed by defendant. Civil records archived since court began, on computer from Aug 1991.
General Information: No sealed or expunged records released. SASE required. Turnaround time 2-3 days. Copy fee: $.50 per page. Certification fee: $3.00. Fee payee: General Sessions. Personal checks accepted. Prepayment is required.

County Court
Court Square, PO Box 220, Charlotte, TN 37036; 615-789-4171. Hours: 8AM-4PM (CST). *Probate.*

Dyer County

29th District Circuit Court & General Sessions
PO Box 1360, Dyersburg, TN 38025; 731-286-7809; Fax: 731-288-7728. Hours: 8:30AM-4:30PM (CST). *Felony, Misdemeanor, Civil, Eviction, Small Claims.*

Civil Records: Access: Mail, in person. Both court and visitors may perform in person searches. Search fee: $25.00 per name. Required to search: name, years to search. Civil cases indexed by defendant, plaintiff. Civil records archived since 1990.
Criminal Records: Access: Mail, in person. Both court and visitors may perform in person searches. Search fee: $25.00 per name. Required to search: name, years to search, DOB, SSN. Criminal records archived since 1990.
General Information: Public Access terminal is available. No juvenile records released. SASE not required. Turnaround time 1 week. No copy fee. Certification fee: No certification fee. Fee payee: Circuit Court, or General Sessions Clerk. Personal checks accepted. Prepayment is required.

Chancery Court
PO Box 1360, Dyersburg, TN 38024; 731-286-7818; Fax: 731-286-7812. Hours: 8:30AM-4:30PM M-Th, 8:30AM-5PM Fri (CST). *Civil, Probate.*

Civil Records: Access: Mail, in person. Both court and visitors may perform in person searches. No search fee. Required to search: name, years to search. Civil cases indexed by defendant, plaintiff. Civil records on books.
General Information: No adoption, juvenile records released. SASE requested. Turnaround time 1 week. Copy fee: $.50 per page. Certification fee: $1.00. Fee payee: Chancery Court Clerk. Personal checks accepted. Prepayment is required.

Fayette County

25th District Circuit Court & General Sessions
PO Box 670, Somerville, TN 38068; 901-465-5205; Fax: 901-465-5215. Hours: 9AM-5PM (CST). *Felony, Misdemeanor, Civil, Eviction, Small Claims.*

Civil Records: Access: Mail, in person. Both court and visitors may perform in person searches. Search fee: $10.00. Required to search: name, years to search. Civil cases indexed by defendant, plaintiff. Civil records on computer since 1991, prior records archived since court began, some older records destroyed by fire.
Criminal Records: Access: Mail, in person. Both court and visitors may perform in person searches. Search fee: $10.00. Required to search: name, years to search, DOB, SSN. Criminal records on computer since 1991, prior records archived since court began, some older records destroyed by fire.

General Information: Public Access terminal is available. No adoption or sealed records released. SASE required. Turnaround time 2-5 days to search books, immediate for computer records. Copy fee: $.25 per page. Certification fee: $6.00. Fee payee: Circuit Court, or General Sessions Clerk. Personal checks accepted. Prepayment is required.

Chancery Court PO Drawer 220, Somerville, TN 38068; 901-465-5220; Fax: 901-465-5215. Hours: 9AM-5PM (CST). *Civil, Probate.*

Civil Records: Access: In person only. Visitors must perform in person searches for themselves. No search fee. Required to search: name, years to search. Civil cases indexed by defendant, plaintiff. Civil records on computer since 10/92; on books.

General Information: No adoption records released. Copy fee: $1.00 per page. Certification fee: $4.00 plus $2.00 per page. Fee payee: Clerk and Master. Personal checks accepted.

Fentress County

8th District Criminal, Circuit & General Sessions Court PO Box 699, Jamestown, TN 38556; 931-879-7919. Hours: 8AM-4PM M-F; 8AM-Noon Sat (CST). *Felony, Misdemeanor, Civil, Eviction, Small Claims.*

Civil Records: Access: Mail, in person. Both court and visitors may perform in person searches. Search fee: $25.00 per name. Required to search: name, years to search. Civil cases indexed by defendant, plaintiff. Civil records archived from 1800s.

Criminal Records: Access: Mail, in person. Both court and visitors may perform in person searches. Search fee: $25.00 per name. Required to search: name, years to search, DOB, SSN. Criminal records archived from 1800s.

General Information: No juvenile records released. SASE required. Turnaround time 5 days. Copy fee: $.25 per page. Certification fee: $2.00. Fee payee: Circuit Court Clerk or General Session. Personal checks accepted.

Chancery Court PO Box 66, Jamestown, TN 38556; 931-879-8615; Fax: 931-879-4236. Hours: 9AM-5PM M,T,Th,F; 9AM-Noon Wed (CST). *Civil, Probate.*

Civil Records: Access: Mail, in person. Both court and visitors may perform in person searches. No search fee. Required to search: name, years to search. Civil cases indexed by defendant, plaintiff. Civil records in books.

General Information: No sealed or adoption records released. Turnaround time 1-5 days. Copy fee: $.25 per page. Certification fee: $4.00. Fee payee: Clerk and Master. Personal checks accepted. Prepayment is required.

Franklin County

12th District Circuit Court & General Sessions 1 South Jefferson St, Winchester, TN 37398; 931-967-2923; Fax: 931-962-1479. Hours: 8AM-4:30PM (CST). *Felony, Misdemeanor, Civil, Eviction, Small Claims.*

Civil Records: Access: Mail, in person. Both court and visitors may perform in person searches. Search fee: $10.00 per name. Required to search: name, years to search. Civil cases indexed by defendant, plaintiff. Civil records archived on docket books from 1940s, on computer since mid 1991.

Criminal Records: Access: Mail, in person. Both court and visitors may perform in person searches. Search fee: $10.00 per name. Required to search: name, years to search, DOB; also helpful: SSN. Criminal records archived on docket books from 1940s, on computer since mid 1991.

General Information: Public Access terminal is available. No juvenile records released. Turnaround time 1 week. Copy fee: $.25 per page. Certification fee: $4.00. Fee payee: Circuit Court Clerk or General Session. Business checks accepted.

County Court 1 South Jefferson St, Winchester, TN 37398; 931-962-1485; Fax: 931-962-3394. Hours: 8AM-4:30PM; *AM-Noon Sat (CST). *Probate.*

Gibson County

28th District Circuit Court & General Sessions 295 N College, PO Box 147, Trenton, TN 38382; 731-855-7615; Fax: 731-855-7676. Hours: 8AM-4:30PM (CST). *Felony, Misdemeanor, Civil, Eviction, Small Claims.*

Civil Records: Access: Fax, mail, in person. Both court and visitors may perform in person searches. Search fee: $5.00 per name. Required to search: name, years to search; also helpful: address. Civil cases indexed by defendant, plaintiff. Civil records archived in vault mid 1800s, in office since 1982. On computer since 1990.

Criminal Records: Access: Fax, mail, in person. Both court and visitors may perform in person searches. Search fee: $5.00 per name. Required to search: name, years to search; also helpful: address, DOB, SSN. Criminal records archived in vault mid 1800s, in office since 1982. On computer since 1990.

General Information: Public Access terminal is available. No adoption or expunged records released. SASE requested. Turnaround time 1-3 days. Fax notes: No fee to fax results. Copy fee: $.25 per page. $3.00 maximum fee. Certification fee: $5.00. Fee payee: Circuit Court Clerk. Business checks accepted. In-state checks accepted.

Chancery Court Clerk & Master, PO Box 290, Trenton, TN 38382; 731-855-7639; Fax: 731-855-7655. Hours: 8AM-4:30PM (CST). *Civil, Probate.*

Civil Records: Access: In person only. Visitors must perform in person searches for themselves. No search fee. Required to search: name, years to search. Civil cases indexed by defendant, plaintiff. Probate records in this office since 9/82, prior records filed in County Clerk's office, computerized records go back to 1967.

General Information: No adoption, commitment records released. SASE requested. Turnaround time 1 week. Fax notes: $10.00 per document. Copy fee: $1.00 per page. Certification fee: $4.00. Fee payee: Clerk & Master. Personal checks accepted. Prepayment is required.

Giles County

22nd District Circuit Court & General Sessions PO Box 678, Pulaski, TN 38478; 931-363-5311; Fax: 931-424-4790. Hours: 8AM-4PM *Felony, Misdemeanor, Civil, Eviction, Small Claims.*

Civil Records: Access: Phone, mail, fax, in-person. Both court and visitors may perform in person searches. Search fee: $20.00 per name. Fee applies only to pre-1990 searches. Required to search: name, years to search. Civil cases indexed by defendant, plaintiff. Civil records on computer from 1/90, remaining records filed in docket books.

Criminal Records: Access: Phone, mail, fax, in person. Both court and visitors may perform in person searches. Search fee: $20.00 per name. Fee applies only to pre-1990 searches. Required to search: name, years to search, DOB; also helpful: SSN. Criminal records on computer from 1/90, remaining records filed in docket books.

General Information: Public Access terminal is available. No juvenile records released without signed release. SASE required. Turnaround time 1 week. Copy fee: $.25 per page. Certification fee: $6.00. Fee payee: Circuit Court Clerk. Prepayment is required.

County Court PO Box 678, Pulaski, TN 38478; 931-363-1509; Fax: 931-424-6101. Hours: 8AM-4PM M-F (CST). *Probate.*

Grainger County

4th District Circuit Court & General Sessions PO Box 157, Rutledge, TN 37861; 865-828-3605; Fax: 423-828-3339. Hours: 8:30AM-4:30PM (EST). *Felony, Misdemeanor, Civil, Eviction, Small Claims.*

Civil Records: Access: In person only. Visitors must perform in person searches for themselves. No search fee. Required to search: name, years to search. Civil cases indexed by defendant, plaintiff. Civil records archived from 1977 in office.

Criminal Records: Access: In person only. Visitors must perform in person searches for themselves. No search fee. Required to search: name, years to search, DOB, SSN. Criminal records archived from 1977 in office.

General Information: No sealed records released. Copy fee: $.25 per page. Certification fee: $4.00. Fee payee: Circuit Court Clerk. Business checks accepted. Prepayment is required.

Chancery Court Clerk & Master, PO Box 160, Rutledge, TN 37861; 865-828-4436; Fax: 865-828-8714. Hours: 8:30AM-4:30PM M,T,Th,F, 8:30AM-Noon Wed (EST). *Civil, Probate.*

Civil Records: Access: Phone, fax, mail, in person. Both court and visitors may perform in person searches. No search fee. Required to search: name, years to search. Civil cases indexed by defendant, plaintiff. Civil records on books.

General Information: No adoption records released. SASE requested. Turnaround time varies. Copy fee: $1.00 per page. Certification fee: $4.00. Fee payee: Clerk & Master. Personal checks accepted. Prepayment is required.

Greene County

3rd District Criminal, Circuit & General Sessions Court 101 S Main, Geene County Courthouse, Suite 302, Greeneville, TN 37743; 423-798-1760; Fax: 423-798-1763. Hours: 8AM-4:30PM *Felony, Misdemeanor, Civil, Eviction, Small Claims.*

Civil Records: Access: In person only. Visitors must perform in person searches for themselves. No search fee. Required to search: name, years to search. Civil cases indexed by defendant, plaintiff. Civil records archived since court started, on computer from end of 1990.

Criminal Records: Access: In person only. Visitors must perform in person searches for themselves. No search fee. Required to search: name, years to search. Criminal records archived since court started, on computer from end of 1990.

General Information: No adoption records released. Copy fee: $1.00 per page. Certification fee: $3.00. Fee payee: Circuit Court Clerk. Personal checks accepted. Prepayment is required.

County Court 204 N Cutler St, #200, County Court Annex, Greeneville, TN 37745; 423-798-1708; Fax: 423-798-1822. Hours: 8AM-4:30PM (EST). *Probate.*

Grundy County

12th District Circuit Court & General Sessions PO Box 161, Altamont, TN 37301; 931-692-3368; Fax: 931-692-2414. Hours: 8AM-4PM M-Th; 8AM-5PM F (CST). *Felony, Misdemeanor, Civil, Eviction, Small Claims.*

Civil Records: Access: Mail, fax, in person. Both court and visitors may perform in person searches. Search fee: $10.00 per name. Fee is per court. Required to search: name, years to search. Civil cases indexed by defendant, plaintiff. Civil records on computer since 1993, prior records in books to 1990. Before 1990 on microfiche since 1868.

Criminal Records: Access: Mail, fax, in person. Both court and visitors may perform in person searches. Search fee: $10.00 per name. Fee is per court. Required to search: name, years to search, DOB; also helpful: SSN. Criminal records on computer since 1993, prior records in books to 1990. Before 1990 on microfiche since 1868.

General Information: No juvenile records released. Turnaround time 5 days. Fax notes: Fee to fax results is $4.00 per document. Copy fee: $1.00 per page. Certification fee: $5.00. Fee payee: Circuit Court Clerk. Prepayment is required.

Chancery Court PO Box 174, Altamont, TN 37301; 931-692-3455; Fax: 931-692-4125. Hours: 8AM-4PM M-Th; 8AM-5pm F (CST). *Civil, Probate.*

Civil Records: Access: Phone, mail, in person. Both court and visitors may perform in person searches. Search fee: $5.00 per name. Required to search: name, years to search. Civil cases indexed by defendant, plaintiff. Civil records on computer since 1993, on books back to 1990.

General Information: No adoption records released. SASE requested. Turnaround time 5 days. Copy fee: $.25 per page. Certification fee: $2.00. Fee payee: Clerk & Master. Personal checks accepted. Prepayment is required.

Hamblen County

3rd District, Criminal, Circuit & General Sessions Court 510 Allison St, Morristown, TN 37814; 423-586-5640; Fax: 423-585-2764. Hours: 8AM-4PM M-Th, 8AM-5PM Fri, 9-11:30AM Sat (CST). *Felony, Misdemeanor, Civil, Eviction, Small Claims.*

Civil Records: Access: Mail, in person. Both court and visitors may perform in person searches. Search fee: $5.00 per name. Required to search: name, years to search. Civil cases indexed by defendant, plaintiff. Civil records archived to early 1900s, on computer to 1989.

Criminal Records: Access: Mail, in person. Both court and visitors may perform in person searches. Search fee: $5.00 per name. Required to search: name, years to search, DOB; also helpful: SSN. Criminal records archived from early 1900s, on computer from 1989.

General Information: No adoption records released. SASE required. Turnaround time 1 day. Copy fee: $.25 per page. Certification fee: $4.00. Fee payee: Circuit Court Clerk or General Sessions. Personal checks accepted. Prepayment is required.

Chancery Court 511 West 2nd North St, Morristown, TN 37814; 423-586-9112; Fax: 423-587-9798. 8AM-4PM M-Th; 8AM-4:30PM F (CST). *Civil.*

Civil Records: Access: Phone, fax, mail, in person. Both court and visitors may perform in person searches. No search fee. Required to search: name, years to search. Civil cases indexed by defendant, plaintiff. Civil records on computer from 1979; prior on books.

General Information: No adoption records released. Turnaround time 3-5 days. Fax notes: $1.00 per page. Copy fee: $.50 per page. Certification fee: $2.00. Fee payee: Clerk & Master. Only cashiers checks and money orders accepted. Prepayment is required.

Hamilton County

11th District General Sessions Civil Division, 600 Market St, Room 111, Chattanooga, TN 37402; 423-209-7630; Fax: 423-209-7631. Hours: 7AM-4PM (EST). *Civil Actions Under $15,000, Eviction, Small Claims.*

www.hamiltontn.gov/courts/sessions/default.htm

Civil Records: Access: Phone, mail, in person, online. Both court and visitors may perform in person searches. No search fee. Required to search: name, years to search. Civil cases indexed by defendant, plaintiff. Civil records archived on docket books, on computer from 6/1985. Online access to current court dockets is available free at www.hamiltontn.gov/courts/CircuitClerk/dockets/default.htm.

General Information: Public Access terminal is available. No mental health records released. Turnaround time 3-4 days. Copy fee: $1.00 per page. Certification fee: $4.00. Fee payee: Sessions Court Clerk. Personal checks accepted. Prepayment is required.

11th Judicial District Civil Court Room 500 Courthouse, 625 Georgia Ave, Chattanooga, TN 37402; 423-209-6700. Hours: 8AM-4PM (EST). *Civil Actions Over $15,000.*

www.hamiltontn.gov/courts/circuit

Civil Records: Access: Mail, in person, online. Both court and visitors may perform in person searches. No search fee. Required to search: name, years to search. Civil cases indexed by defendant, plaintiff. Civil records archived from 1900s, on computer back to 7/89. Court minutes are on microfiche. Online access to current court dockets are available free at www.hamiltontn.gov/courts/CircuitClerk/dockets/default.htm.

General Information: Public Access terminal is available. No adoptions or judicial hospitalization records released. Turnaround time 1 week. Fax notes: Will fax results to local numbers only. Copy fee: $2.00 per page. Certification fee: $4.00. Fee payee: Circuit Court Clerk. Personal checks accepted. Prepayment is required.

11th District Criminal Court 600 Market St, Room 102, Chattanooga, TN 37402; 423-209-7500; Fax: 423-209-7501. Hours: 8AM-4PM (EST). *Felony, Misdemeanor.*

Criminal Records: Access: Mail, in person, online. Both court and visitors may perform in person searches. Search fee: $10.00 per name. Required to search: name, years to search, DOB, signed release; also helpful: SSN. Criminal records on computer since 1985, prior records in books. Online access to current court dockets are available free at www.hamiltontn.gov/courts/CircuitClerk/dockets/default.htm.

General Information: Public Access terminal is available. No juvenile records released. Turnaround time 1 week. Copy fee: $1.00 per page. Certification fee: $2.00. Fee payee: Circuit Court Clerk. Personal checks accepted. Prepayment is required.

Chancery Court Chancery Court, Clerk & Master, 201 E 7th St, Rm 300, Chattanooga, TN 37402; 423-209-6600; Fax: 423-209-6601. Hours: 8AM-4PM (EST). *Civil, Probate.*

www.hamilton.gov/courts/clerkmaster

Civil Records: Access: Phone, mail, in person. Both court and visitors may perform in person searches. No search fee. Required to search: name, years to search. Civil cases indexed by defendant, plaintiff. Civil records on index cards from 1919, on dockets from 6/56, microfilm: wills since 1862, inventories since 1911, settlements since 1869, bonds and letters since 1878.

General Information: Public Access terminal is available. No mental health, adoption records released. SASE required. Turnaround time 2-3 days. Fax notes: $1.00 per page. Copy fee: $1.00 per page 1-5 pages; $2.00 each 5-10 pages; $.25 over 10. Certification fee: $4.00 ($10 if Act of Congress) plus $2.00 per page. Fee payee: Hamilton County Clerk and Master. Personal checks accepted. Prepayment is required.

Hancock County

3rd District, Criminal, Circuit & General Sessions Court PO Box 347, Sneedville, TN 37869; 423-733-2954; Fax: 423-733-2119. Hours: 8AM-4PM (EST). *Felony, Misdemeanor, Civil, Eviction, Small Claims.*

Civil Records: Access: Mail, in person. Both court and visitors may perform in person searches. Search fee: $4.00 per name. Required to search: name, years to search. Civil cases indexed by plaintiff. Civil records archived on books from 1934.

Criminal Records: Access: Mail, in person. Both court and visitors may perform in person searches. Search fee: $4.00 per name. Required to search: name, years to search, DOB; also helpful: SSN. Criminal records archived on books from 1934.

General Information: Public Access terminal is available. No juvenile records released. Turnaround time 3-4 days. Copy fee: $.25 per page. Certification fee: $3.00. Fee payee: Circuit Court Clerk. Personal checks accepted. Prepayment is required.

Chancery Court PO Box 277, Sneedville, TN 37869; 423-733-4524; Fax: 423-733-2762. Hours: 9AM-4PM (EST). *Civil, Probate.*

Civil Records: Access: Mail, in person. Both court and visitors may perform in person searches. No search fee. Required to search: name, years to search. Civil cases indexed by defendant, plaintiff. Civil records on books.

General Information: No adoption records released. SASE requested. Turnaround time 2 days. Copy fee: $.50 per page. Certification fee: $1.00. Fee payee: Clerk & Master. Personal checks accepted. Prepayment is required.

Hardeman County

25th District Circuit Court & General Sessions Courthouse, 100 N Main, Bolivar, TN 38008; 731-658-6524; Fax: 731-658-4584. Hours: 8:30AM-4:30PM M-Th, 8AM-5PM Fri (CST). *Felony, Misdemeanor, Civil, Eviction, Small Claims.*

Civil Records: Access: In person only. Visitors must perform in person searches for themselves. No search fee. Required to search: name, years to search. Civil cases indexed by defendant, plaintiff. Civil records on computer since 12/92, archived General Sessions from 1960 and Circuit from 1800s.

Criminal Records: Access: In person only. Visitors must perform in person searches for themselves. No search fee. Required to search: name, years to search, DOB, SSN, signed release. Criminal records on computer since 12/92, archived General Sessions from 1960 and Circuit from 1800s.

General Information: No juvenile records released. Copy fee: $1.00 per page. Certification fee: $4.00 per document. Fee payee: Circuit Court Clerk. Only cashiers checks and money orders accepted. Hardeman county personal checks accepted. Prepayment is required.

Chancery Court PO Box 45, Bolivar, TN 38008; 731-658-3142; Fax: 731-658-4580. Hours: 8:30AM-4:30PM M-Th, 8:30AM-5PM Fri (CST). *Civil, Probate.*

Civil Records: Access: Phone, mail, fax, in person. Both court and visitors may perform in person searches. No search fee. Required to search: name, years to search. Civil cases indexed by defendant, plaintiff. Civil records on books back to 1825; computerized back to 1975.

General Information: No mental health, adoption records released. SASE requested. Turnaround time 1 day. Fax notes: Fee to fax results is $.25 per page. Copy fee: $.25 per page. Additional fee for postage. Certification fee: $4.00. Fee payee: Chancery Court Clerk. Business checks accepted. Prepayment required.

Hardin County

24th District Circuit Court & General Sessions 601 Main St, Savannah, TN 38372; 731-925-3583; Fax: 731-926-2955. Hours: 8AM-4:30PM M,T,Th,F, 8AM-Noon Wed (CST). *Felony, Misdemeanor, Civil, Eviction, Small Claims.*

Civil Records: Access: In person only. Visitors must perform in person searches for themselves. No search fee. Required to search: name, years to search. Civil cases indexed by defendant, plaintiff. Civil records archived on books and on microfiche from 1800s, on computer from 1996.

Criminal Records: Access: In person only. Visitors must perform in person searches for themselves. No search fee. Required to search: name, years to search. Criminal records archived on books and on microfiche from 1800s, on computer from 1996.

General Information: No juvenile records released. Certification fee: $5.00. Fee payee: Circuit Court Clerk. Hardin county personal checks accepted. Prepayment is required.

County Court 601 Main St, Savannah, TN 38372; 731-925-3921. Hours: 8AM-4:30PM M,T,TH,F, 8AM-12PM Wed & Sat (CST). *Probate.*

Hawkins County

3rd District Criminal, Circuit & General Sessions Court PO Box 9, Rogersville, TN 37857; 423-272-3397; Fax: 423-272-9646. Hours: 8AM-4PM (EST). *Felony, Misdemeanor, Civil, Eviction, Small Claims.*

Civil Records: Access: In person only. Visitors must perform in person searches for themselves. No search fee. Required to search: name, years to search. Civil cases indexed by defendant, plaintiff. Civil records archived on books from 1800s.

Criminal Records: Access: In person only. Visitors must perform in person searches for themselves. No search fee. Required to search: name, years to search. Criminal records archived on books from 1800s.

General Information: No juvenile records released. Copy fee: $1.00 per page. Certification fee: $4.00 ($6 if Acts of Congress) plus $2.00 per page. Fee payee: Circuit Court Clerk. No personal checks accepted.

Chancery Court PO Box 908, Rogersville, TN 37857; 423-272-8150. Hours: 8AM-4PM (EST). *Civil, Probate.*

Civil Records: Access: In person only. Visitors must perform in person searches for themselves. No search fee. Required to search: name, years to search. Civil cases indexed by defendant, plaintiff. Civil records on index books from 1927 to present.

General Information: No adoption records released. Copy fee: $1.00 per page. Certification fee: $2.00. Fee payee: Hawkins County Clerk and Master. Personal checks accepted. Prepayment is required.

Haywood County

28th District Circuit Court & General Sessions 1 N Washington Ave, Brownsville, TN 38012; 731-772-1112; Fax: 731-772-3864. Hours: 8:30AM-5PM (CST). *Felony, Misdemeanor, Civil, Eviction, Small Claims.*

Civil Records: Access: Phone, mail, in person. Both court and visitors may perform in person searches. No search fee. Required to search: name, years to search. Civil cases indexed by defendant, plaintiff. Civil records on computer since 1993, prior archived since the 1800s.

Criminal Records: Access: Phone, mail, in person. Both court and visitors may perform in person searches. No search fee. Required to search: name, years to search, DOB; also helpful: SSN. Criminal records on computer since 1993, prior archived since the 1800s.

General Information: No juvenile records released. Turnaround time dependent upon search. Copy fee: $1.00 per page. Certification fee: $3.50. Fee payee: Circuit Court Clerk. Personal checks accepted. Prepayment is required.

Chancery Court 1 N Washington, PO Box 356, Brownsville, TN 38012; 731-772-0122; Fax: 731-772-3864. Hours: 8:30AM-5PM (CST). *Civil, Probate.*

Civil Records: Access: In person only. Visitors must perform in person searches for themselves. No search fee. Required to search: name, years to search. Civil cases indexed by defendant, plaintiff. Probate records on books since 9/82; other records go back to 1800s.

General Information: No adoption or sealed records released. Turnaround time 2 days. Copy fee: $1.00 per page. Certification fee: $5.00. Fee payee: Chancery Court. Personal checks accepted. Prepayment required.

Henderson County

26th District Circuit Court & General Sessions Henderson County Courthouse, Lexington, TN 38351; 731-968-2031; Fax: 731-967-9441 (criminal). Hours: 8AM-4:30PM M,T,Th,F (CST). *Felony, Misdemeanor, Civil, Eviction, Small Claims.*

Civil Records: Access: Mail, in person. Both court and visitors may perform in person searches. Search fee: $6.00 per name. Required to search: name, years to search. Civil cases indexed by defendant, plaintiff. Civil records on cards or books, archived from 1800s; on computer back 5 years.

Criminal Records: Access: Mail, in person. Both court and visitors may perform in person searches. Search fee: $6.00 per name. Required to search: name, years to search, DOB; also helpful- SSN. Criminal records on cards or books, archived from 1800s; on computer back 5 years.

General Information: Public Access terminal is available. No sealed indictment records released. SASE required. Turnaround time 1-2 weeks. Fax notes: Fee to fax results is $10.00 per document. Copy fee: $1.00 per page. Certification fee: $6.00. Fee payee: Circuit Court Clerk. Personal checks accepted. Prepayment required.

Chancery Court 17 Monroe Rm 2, 2nd Fl, Lexington, TN 38351; 731-968-2801; Fax: 731-967-5380. Hours: 8AM-4:30PM (till noon on Wed) (CST). *Civil, Probate.*

Civil Records: Access: In person only. Visitors must perform in person searches for themselves. No search fee. Required to search: name, years to search. Civil cases indexed by defendant, plaintiff. Civil records on computer back to 6/2000; prior in books.

General Information: No confidential adoption records released. SASE required. Turnaround time dependent on search length. Fax notes: Fee to fax results is $2.00 per page. Copy fee: $2.00 per page. Certification fee: $2.00. Fee payee: Chancery Court. Only cashiers checks and money orders accepted. Prepayment is required.

Henry County

24th District Circuit Court & General Sessions PO Box 429, Paris, TN 38242; 731-642-0461. Hours: 8AM-4:30PM (CST). *Felony, Misdemeanor, Civil, Eviction, Small Claims.*

Civil Records: Access: Phone, mail, in person. Both court and visitors may perform in person searches. No search fee. Required to search: name, years to search. Civil cases indexed by defendant, plaintiff. Civil records archived from 1820s (you search) or 1900s (they search); General Sessions on computer from 1991.

Criminal Records: Access: Phone, mail, in person. Both court and visitors may perform in person searches. No search fee. Required to search: name, years to search, DOB; also helpful: SSN. Criminal records archived from 1820s (you search) or 1900s (they search); General Sessions on computer from 1991.

General Information: No juvenile records released. Turnaround time 1-2 weeks. Copy fee: $.25 per page. Certification fee: $2.00. Fee payee: Circuit Court Clerk or General Sessions. Personal checks accepted.

County Court PO Box 24, Paris, TN 38242; 731-642-2412; Fax: 731-644-0947. Hours: 8AM-4:30PM (CST). *Probate.*

Hickman County

21st District Circuit Court & General Sessions 104 College Ave #204, Centerville, TN 37033; 931-729-2211; Fax: 931-729-6141. Hours: 8AM-4PM (CST). *Felony, Misdemeanor, Civil, Eviction, Small Claims.*

Civil Records: Access: In person only. Visitors must perform in person searches for themselves. No search fee. Required to search: name, years to search. Civil cases indexed by defendant, plaintiff. Civil records on computer since 1991, prior records on books.

Criminal Records: Access: In person only. Visitors must perform in person searches for themselves. No search fee. Required to search: name, years to search. Criminal records on computer since 1991, prior records on books.

General Information: No juvenile records released. Copy fee: $1.00 per page. Certification fee: $5.00. Fee payee: Circuit Court Clerk. No personal checks accepted. Prepayment is required.

Chancery Court 104 College Ave #202, Centerville, TN 37033; 931-729-2522; Fax: 931-729-6141. Hours: 8AM-4PM (CST). *Civil, Probate.*

Civil Records: Access: Mail, in person. Both court and visitors may perform in person searches. No search fee. Required to search: name, years to search. Civil cases indexed by defendant, plaintiff. Civil records on books since 1965.

General Information: No confidential or adoption records released. SASE requested. Turnaround time 1 week. Copy fee: $.25 per page. Certification fee: $3.00. Fee payee: Clerk & Master. Personal checks accepted.

Houston County

23rd District Circuit Court & General Sessions PO Box 403, Erin, TN 37061; 931-289-4673; Fax: 931-289-5182. Hours: 8AM-4:30PM *Felony, Misdemeanor, Civil, Eviction, Small Claims.*

Civil Records: Access: Phone, fax, mail, in person. Only the court performs in person searches; visitors may not. Search fee: $5.00 per name. Required to search: name, years to search. Civil cases indexed by defendant, plaintiff. Civil records archived from 1930s in books.

Criminal Records: Access: Phone, fax, mail, in person. Only the court performs in person searches; visitors may not. Search fee: $5.00 per name. Required to search: name, years to search, DOB; also helpful: SSN. Criminal records archived from 1930s in books.

General Information: No juvenile records released. SASE required. Turnaround time 1-2 days. Copy fee: $.25 per page. Certification fee: $3.50. Fee payee: Circuit Court Clerk. Personal checks accepted. Prepayment is required.

Chancery Court PO Box 332, Erin, TN 37061; 931-289-3870; Fax: 931-289-5679. Hours: 8AM-4PM (CST). *Civil, Probate.*

Civil Records: Access: Mail, in person. Both court and visitors may perform in person searches. No search fee. Required to search: name, years to search. Civil cases indexed by defendant, plaintiff. Civil records on books.

General Information: No adoption records released. Turnaround time 2 days. Copy fee: $.25 per page.

Certification fee: $3.50. Fee payee: Clerk & Master. Personal checks accepted. Prepayment is required.

Humphreys County

23rd District Circuit Court & General Sessions Room 106, Waverly, TN 37185; 931-296-2461; Fax: 931-296-1651. Hours: 8AM-4:30PM *Felony, Misdemeanor, Civil, Eviction, Small Claims.*

Civil Records: Access: Phone, fax, mail, in person. Both court and visitors may perform in person searches. Search fee: $1.00 per name per year. If more than 15 years, the fee is a flat $25.00. Required to search: name, years to search. Civil cases indexed by defendant, plaintiff. Civil records archived from early 1900s, on computer back to 1989.

Criminal Records: Access: Phone, fax, mail, in person. Both court and visitors may perform in person searches. Search fee: $1.00 per name per year. If more than 15 years, the fee is a flat $25.00. Required to search: name, years to search, DOB, SSN, signed release. Criminal records archived from early 1900s, on computer back to 1989.

General Information: No expunged records released. SASE required. Turnaround time same day. Copy fee: $.25 per page. Certification fee: $2.00 for the document seal plus $2.00 per page. Fee payee: Donna McLeod, Rm 106 Courthouse, Waverly TN. Business checks accepted. Prepayment is required.

County Court Clerk, Room 2 Courthouse Annex, Waverly, TN 37185; 931-296-7671; Fax: 931-296-5011. Hours: 8AM-4:30PM (CST). *Probate.*

Jackson County

15th District Criminal, Circuit & General Sessions Court PO Box 205, Gainesboro, TN 38562; 931-268-9314; Fax: 931-268-4555. Hours: 8AM-4PM M,T,Th,F; 8AM-3PM W; 8AM-Noon Sat (CST). *Felony, Misdemeanor, Civil, Eviction, Small Claims.*

Civil Records: Access: Fax, mail, in person. Both court and visitors may perform in person searches. Search fee: $5.00 per name. Required to search: name, years to search. Civil cases indexed by defendant, plaintiff. Civil records archived from 1900s in books.

Criminal Records: Access: Fax, mail, in person. Both court and visitors may perform in person searches. Search fee: $5.00 per name. Required to search: name, years to search, DOB; also helpful: SSN. Criminal records archived from 1900s in books.

General Information: No juvenile records released. SASE required. Turnaround time 1 week. Copy fee: $.50 per page (first 24 are free). Certification fee: $5.00. Fee payee: Circuit Court Clerk. Business checks accepted. Prepayment is required.

Chancery Court PO Box 733, Gainesboro, TN 38562-0733; 931-268-9216; Fax: 931-268-9060. 8AM-4PM M,T,Th,F; 8AM-3PM W (CST). *Probate.*
www.jacksonco.com

Jefferson County

4th District Circuit Court & General Sessions PO Box 671, Dandridge, TN 37725; 865-397-2786; Fax: 865-397-4894. Hours: 8AM-4PM M-F; 8-11AM Sat (EST). *Felony, Misdemeanor, Civil, Eviction, Small Claims.*

Civil Records: Access: Mail, in person. Both court and visitors may perform in person searches. No search fee. Required to search: name, years to search. Civil cases indexed by defendant, plaintiff. Civil records archived from early 1900s on books.

Criminal Records: Access: Mail, in person. Both court and visitors may perform in person searches. No search fee. Required to search: name, years to search, DOB,

SSN, signed release. Criminal records archived from early 1900s on books.

General Information: No adoption or juvenile records released. Turnaround time 1 week. Copy fee: $.25 per page. Certification fee: $3.00. Copy fee included in cert fee. Fee payee: Circuit Court Clerk. Personal checks accepted.

County Court PO Box 710, Dandridge, TN 37725; 865-397-2935; Fax: 865-397-3839. Hours: 8AM-4PM M-F, 8AM-11PM Sat (EST). *Probate.*

Johnson County

1st District Criminal, Circuit & General Sessions Court PO Box 73, Mountain City, TN 37683; 423-727-9012; Fax: 423-727-7047. Hours: 8:30AM-5PM (EST). *Felony, Misdemeanor, Civil, Eviction, Small Claims.*

Civil Records: Access: Phone, mail, in person. Both court and visitors may perform in person searches. Search fee: $5.00 per name. Required to search: name, years to search. Civil cases indexed by defendant, plaintiff. Civil records in docket books, sessions 1976, criminal & circuit 1800s.

Criminal Records: Access: Phone, mail, in person. Both court and visitors may perform in person searches. Search fee: $5.00 per name. Required to search: name, years to search, DOB. Criminal records in docket books, sessions 1976, criminal & circuit 1800s.

General Information: No adoption, expunged or juvenile records released. SASE required. Turnaround time 2-3 days. Copy fee: $2.00 per page. Certification fee: $2.00. Fee payee: Circuit Court Clerk. Only cashiers checks and money orders accepted. Prepayment is required.

Chancery Court PO Box 196, Mountain City, TN 37683; 423-727-7853; Fax: 423-727-7047. Hours: 8:30AM-5PM (EST). *Civil, Probate.*

Civil Records: Access: Mail, in person. Both court and visitors may perform in person searches. No search fee. Required to search: name, years to search. Civil cases indexed by defendant, plaintiff. Civil records on books and files.

General Information: No adoption records released. SASE required. Turnaround time same day. Copy fee: $1.00 per page. Certification fee: $2.00 plus $2.00 per page. Fee payee: Clerk & Master. Only cashiers checks and money orders accepted. Prepayment is required.

Knox County

6th District Criminal Court 400 Main Ave, Room 149, Knoxville, TN 37902; 865-215-2492; Fax: 865-215-4291. Hours: 8AM-5PM M-Th; 8AM-4:30PM F (EST). *Felony, Misdemeanor.*

Criminal Records: Access: Fax, mail, in person. Only the court performs in person searches; visitors may not. Search fee: $5.00 per name. Required to search: name, years to search, DOB; also helpful: address, SSN, signed release. Criminal records on computer back to 1980; on books from 1962.

General Information: No sealed records released. SASE not required. Turnaround time 48 hours. Fax notes: $2.00 for first page, $1.00 each add'l. Copy fee: $2.00 per page. Certification fee: $2.00. Fee payee: Criminal Court Clerk. Personal checks accepted. Prepayment is required.

Circuit Court 400 Main Ave, Room M-30, PO Box 379, Knoxville, TN 37901; 865-215-2400; Fax: 865-215-4251. Hours: 8AM-5PM; 4:30 PM Fri. (EST). *Civil Actions Over $15,000.*

Civil Records: Access: Phone, fax, mail, in person. Both court and visitors may perform in person searches. Search fee: $5.00. Required to search: name, years to search. Civil cases indexed by defendant, plaintiff. Civil

records on computer from 1986, prior records archived and on microfilm.

General Information: Public Access terminal is available. No adoption or sealed records released. Turnaround time 2-3 days. Copy fee: $1.00 per page. Certification fee: $2.00. Fee payee: Circuit Court Clerk. Personal checks accepted. Credit cards accepted: Visa, MC. Prepayment is required.

General Sessions 300 Main Ave, RM 318, PO Box 379, Knoxville, TN 37901; 865-215-2518. Hours: 8AM-4:30PM (EST). *Civil Actions Under $15,000, Eviction, Small Claims.*

Civil Records: Access: Mail, in person. Both court and visitors may perform in person searches. Search fee: $5.00. Required to search: name, years to search. Civil cases indexed by defendant, plaintiff. Civil records on books and computer.

General Information: No juvenile or adoption records released. Turnaround time 1 week. Copy fee: $1.50 per page. Certification fee: $3.50. Fee payee: General Sessions Court. Personal checks accepted. Credit cards accepted: Visa, MasterCard. Prepayment is required.

Chancery Court 400 Main Ave, Knoxville, TN 37902; 865-215-2555 (Chancery); Probate phone: 865-215-2389; Fax: 865-215-2920. Hours: 8AM-4:30PM (EST). *Civil, Probate.*

Civil Records: Access: Phone, fax, mail, in person. Visitors must perform in person searches for themselves. No search fee. Required to search: name, years to search. Civil cases indexed by defendant, plaintiff. Civil records on computer since 1978, prior records on books.

General Information: No commitment or adoption records released. Turnaround time 1-2 days. Fax notes: $1.00 per page. Copy fee: $1.00 per page. Certification fee: $2.00. Fee payee: Chancery or Probate Court. Personal checks accepted. Prepayment is required.

Lake County

29th District Circuit Court & General Sessions 227 Church St, PO Box 11, Tiptonville, TN 38079; 731-253-7137; Fax: 731-253-8930. Hours: 8AM-4PM M-W & F; 8AM-Noon Th (CST). *Felony, Misdemeanor, Civil, Eviction, Small Claims.*

Civil Records: Access: In person only. Visitors must perform in person searches for themselves. No search fee. Required to search: name, years to search. Civil cases indexed by defendant, plaintiff. Civil records archived on books in office up to 30 yrs, vault records before 1960.

Criminal Records: Access: In person only. Visitors must perform in person searches for themselves. No search fee. Required to search: name, years to search, DOB; also helpful: SSN. Criminal records archived on books in office up to 30 yrs, vault records before 1960.

General Information: No sealed records released. Copy fee: $1.00 per page. Certification fee: $3.00. Fee payee: Circuit Court Clerk. Personal checks accepted.

Chancery Court PO Box 12, Tiptonville, TN 38079; 731-253-8926. Hours: 9AM-4PM M-W & F; 8AM-Noon Th (CST). *Civil, Probate.*

Civil Records: Access: Mail, in person. Both court and visitors may perform in person searches. No search fee. Required to search: name, years to search. Civil cases indexed by defendant. Civil records on books and files from 1984, prior records filed in county clerks office.

General Information: Turnaround time 3-5 days. Copy fee: $.50 per page. Certification fee: $4.00. Fee payee: Clerk and Master. Personal checks accepted. Prepayment is required.

Lauderdale County

25th District Circuit Court Lauderdale County Justice Center, 675 Hwy 51 S, PO Box 509, Ripley, TN 38063; 731-635-0101; Fax: 731-221-8663. Hours: 8AM-4:30PM (CST). *Felony, Misdemeanor, Civil Actions Over $15,000.*

Civil Records: Access: Mail, in person. Both court and visitors may perform in person searches. Search fee: $10.00 per name. Required to search: name, years to search. Civil cases indexed by defendant, plaintiff. Civil records archived on books from 1800s to 1992, on computer since 1992.

Criminal Records: Access: Mail, in person. Both court and visitors may perform in person searches. Search fee: $10.00 per name. Required to search: name, years to search; also helpful: DOB, SSN. Criminal records archived on books from 1800s to 1992, on computer since 1992.

General Information: Public Access terminal is available. No sealed or adoption records released. SASE required. Turnaround time 2-3 days. Copy fee: $1.00 per page. Certification fee: $10.00. Fee payee: Circuit Court Clerk. Business checks accepted. Prepayment is required.

General Sessions Court PO Box 509, Ripley, TN 38063; 731-635-2572; Fax: 731-635-9682. Hours: 8AM-4:30PM (CST). *Civil Actions Under $15,000, Eviction, Small Claims.*

Civil Records: Access: Mail, in person. Both court and visitors may perform in person searches. Search fee: $10.00 per name. Required to search: name, years to search. Civil cases indexed by defendant, plaintiff. Civil records on computer since 1992, records prior to 1984 on docket books.

General Information: Public Access terminal is available. No confidential records released. SASE required. Turnaround time 2-3 days. Copy fee: $1.00 per page. Certification fee: $5.00. Fee payee: General Sessions. Business checks accepted. Prepayment is required.

County Court Courthouse, 100 Court Sq, Ripley, TN 38063; 731-635-2561. Hours: 8AM-4:30PM M,T,Th,F; 8AM-Noon W & Sat (CST). *Probate.*

Lawrence County

22nd District Circuit Court & General Sessions NBU #12 240 W Gaines, Lawrenceburg, TN 38464; 931-762-4398; Fax: 931-766-4471. Hours: 8AM-4:30PM (CST). *Felony, Misdemeanor, Civil, Eviction, Small Claims.*

Civil Records: Access: In person only. Visitors must perform in person searches for themselves. No search fee. Required to search: name, years to search. Civil cases indexed by defendant, plaintiff. Civil records archived on books since court started in 1940s.

Criminal Records: Access: In person only. Visitors must perform in person searches for themselves. No search fee. Required to search: name, years to search, DOB, SSN. Criminal records archived on books since court started in 1940s.

General Information: Public Access terminal is available. No expunged records released. Certification fee: $5.00. Fee payee: Circuit Court Clerk. Business checks accepted. Prepayment is required.

County Court 240 Gaines St, NBU #12, Lawrenceburg, TN 38464; 931-762-7700. Hours: 8AM-4:30PM (CST). *Civil, Probate.*

Civil Records: Access: In person only. Visitors must perform in person searches for themselves. No search fee. Required to search: name, years to search. Civil cases indexed by defendant, plaintiff. Civil records on books.

General Information: No juvenile or adoption records released. Certification fee: $2.00. Fee payee: Circuit Court Clerk. Personal checks accepted. Prepayment is required.

Lewis County

21st Judicial District Circuit Court & General Sessions Courthouse 110 Park Avenue N, Rm 201, Hohenwald, TN 38462; 931-796-3724; Fax: 931-796-6010. Hours: 8AM-4:30PM (CST). *Felony, Misdemeanor, Civil, Eviction, Small Claims.*

Civil Records: Access: In person only. Visitors must perform in person searches for themselves. No search fee. Required to search: name, years to search. Civil cases indexed by defendant, plaintiff. Civil records archived 15 years in office, 1800s in vault.

Criminal Records: Access: In person only. Visitors must perform in person searches for themselves. No search fee. Required to search: name, years to search; also helpful: SSN. Criminal records archived 15 years in office, 1800s in vault.

General Information: No juvenile, adoption records released. Copy fee: $1.00 per page. Certification fee: $2.00 per document plus $2.00 per page. Fee payee: Circuit Court Clerk. Personal checks accepted.

Chancery Court Lewis County Courthouse, 110 Park Ave N, Rm 208, Hohenwald, TN 38462; 931-796-3734; Fax: 931-796-6010. Hours: 8AM-4:30PM (CST). *Civil, Probate.*

Civil Records: Access: Phone, mail, in person. Both court and visitors may perform in person searches. No search fee. Required to search: name, years to search. Civil cases indexed by defendant, plaintiff. Civil records on computer since 10/94, prior records on books.

General Information: No juvenile or adoption records released. Copy fee: $1.00 per page. Certification fee: $2.00. Fee payee: Clerk & Master. Personal checks accepted. Prepayment is required.

Lincoln County

17th Judicial District Circuit Court & General Sessions 112 Main Ave S, Rm 203, Fayetteville, TN 37334; 931-433-2334; Fax: 931-438-1577. Hours: 8AM-4PM (CST). *Felony, Misdemeanor, Civil, Eviction, Small Claims.*

Civil Records: Access: Phone, fax, mail, in person. Both court and visitors may perform in person searches. Search fee: $10.00 per name. Fee is for 5 years. Add $1.00 for each add'l year. Required to search: name, years to search. Civil cases indexed by defendant, plaintiff. Civil records archived on books since court started.

Criminal Records: Access: Phone, fax, mail, in person. Both court and visitors may perform in person searches. Search fee: $10.00 per name. Fee is for 5 years. Add $1.00 for each add'l year. Required to search: name, years to search, DOB. Criminal records archived on books since court started.

General Information: No probation records released. SASE required. Turnaround time 1-2 days. Fax notes: $2.00 per page. Copy fee: $1.00 per page. Certification fee: $4.00. Fee payee: Circuit Court Clerk. Business checks accepted.

Chancery Court 112 Main Ave, Rm B109, Fayetteville, TN 37334; 931-433-1482; Fax: 931-433-9979. Hours: 8AM-4PM (CST). *Civil, Probate.*

Civil Records: Access: In person only. Visitors must perform in person searches for themselves. No search fee. Required to search: name, years to search. Civil cases indexed by defendant, plaintiff. Civil records archived on books.

General Information: No adoption, divorce records released. Fax notes: Fee to fax results is $1.00 per page.

Certification fee: $4.00. Fee payee: Clerk & Master. Personal checks accepted.

Loudon County

9th District Criminal & Circuit Court PO Box 280, Loudon, TN 37774; 865-458-2042; Fax: 865-458-2043. Hours: 8AM-4:30PM (EST). *Felony, Misdemeanor, Civil, Eviction, Small Claims.*

Note: General Sessions & Juvenile Court located at 12680 Hwy 11 W Suite 3, Lenoir City, TN 37771, 423-986-3505.

Civil Records: Access: Mail, in person. Both court and visitors may perform in person searches. Search fee: $5.00 per name. Required to search: name, years to search. Civil cases indexed by defendant, plaintiff. Civil records archived from 1830 on books, on computer from Aug 1990.

Criminal Records: Access: Mail, in person. Both court and visitors may perform in person searches. Search fee: $5.00 per name. Required to search: name, years to search. Criminal records archived from 1800s on books, on computer from Aug 1990.

General Information: No juvenile, adoption records released. SASE requested. Turnaround time 2-4 days. Copy fee: $1.00 per page. Certification fee: $2.00. Fee payee: Circuit Court or general Sessions Court. Prepayment is required.

County Court 101 Mulberry St #200, Loudon, TN 37774; 865-458-2726; Fax: 865-458-9891. Hours: 8AM-5:30PM Mon, 8AM-4:30PM T-F (EST). *Probate.*

Macon County

15th District Criminal, Circuit & General Sessions Court County Court Clerk, Rm 202, Lafayette, TN 37083; 615-666-2354; Fax: 615-666-3001. Hours: 8AM-4:30PM M-Th; 8AM-5PM F (CST). *Felony, Misdemeanor, Civil, Eviction, Small Claims.*

Civil Records: Access: In person only. Visitors must perform in person searches for themselves. No search fee. Required to search: name, years to search. Civil cases indexed by defendant, plaintiff. Civil records archived in office from 1975, rest in records room from 1960; on computer since.

Criminal Records: Access: In person only. Visitors must perform in person searches for themselves. No search fee. Required to search: name, years to search, DOB; also helpful: SSN. Criminal records archived in office from 1975, rest in records room from 1960, on computer since.

General Information: Public Access terminal is available. No juvenile or adoption records released. Copy fee: $1.00 per page. Certification fee: $5.00. Fee payee: Circuit Court Clerk. Personal checks accepted. Prepayment is required.

County Court County Court Clerk, Rm 104, Lafayette, TN 37083; 615-666-2333; Fax: 615-666-5323. Hours: 8AM-4:30PM M-W, Closed Thu, 8AM-5PM Fri, 8AM-1:30PM Sat (CST). *Probate.*

Madison County

26th District Circuit Court 515 S Liberty St, Jackson, TN 38301; 731-423-6035. Hours: 8AM-4PM *Felony, Misdemeanor, Civil Actions Over $15,000.*

Civil Records: Access: In person only. Visitors must perform in person searches for themselves. No search fee. Required to search: name, years to search. Civil cases indexed by defendant, plaintiff. Civil records archived on books in office from 1963; on computer back to 1995.

Criminal Records: Access: In person only. Visitors must perform in person searches for themselves. No search fee. Required to search: name, years to search;

also helpful: DOB, SSN. Criminal records computerized since 1995, on books from 1965.

General Information: Public Access terminal is available. No sealed records released. Copy fee: $.50 per page. Searcher can bring own paper then no charges for copies. Certification fee: $5.00. Fee payee: Circuit Court Clerk. Only cashiers checks and money orders accepted. Prepayment is required.

General Sessions 515 S Liberty St, Jackson, TN 38301; 731-423-6018. Hours: 8AM-4PM (CST). *Civil Actions Under $15,000, Eviction, Small Claims.*

Civil Records: Access: Mail, in person. Both court and visitors may perform in person searches. No search fee. Required to search: name, years to search. Civil cases indexed by defendant, plaintiff. Civil records computerized since 04/98, archived on books in office from 1982, rest stored elsewhere from 1950s.

General Information: Turnaround time 1 week. Copy fee: $1.50 per page. Certification fee: $4.00. Fee payee: General Sessions Court. Only cashiers checks and money orders accepted.

Probate Division - General Sessions Division II 110 Irby St, PO Box 1504, Jackson, TN 38302-1504; 731-988-3025; Fax: 731-422-6044. Hours: 8:30-12, 1-4PM (CST). *Probate.*

Marion County

12th District Circuit Court & General Sessions PO Box 789, Courthouse Sq, Jasper, TN 37347; 423-942-2134; Fax: 423-942-4160. Hours: 8AM-4PM (CST). *Felony, Misdemeanor, Civil, Eviction, Small Claims.*

Civil Records: Access: Phone, mail, in person. Both court and visitors may perform in person searches. No search fee. Required to search: name, years to search. Civil cases indexed by defendant, plaintiff. Civil records on computer from 1988, prior records archived on books and microfiche since 1922.

Criminal Records: Access: Phone, mail, in person. Both court and visitors may perform in person searches. No search fee. Required to search: name, years to search, DOB; also helpful: SSN. Criminal records on computer from 1988, prior records archived on books and microfiche since 1922.

General Information: Public Access terminal is available. No adoption records released. Turnaround time 1 week. Copy fee: $3.00 per page. Certification fee: $3.00. Fee payee: Circuit Court Clerk. Personal checks accepted.

Chancery Court PO Box 789, Jasper, TN 37347; 423-942-2601; Fax: 423-942-0291. Hours: 8AM-4PM (CST). *Civil, Probate.*

Civil Records: Access: Mail, in person. Both court and visitors may perform in person searches. No search fee. Required to search: name, years to search. Civil cases indexed by defendant, plaintiff. Civil records on computer since 07/94, prior records on books.

General Information: No adoption records released. SASE requested. Turnaround time 1 day. Copy fee: $.50 per page. Certification fee: $3.00. Fee payee: Clerk and Master. Personal checks accepted. Prepayment is required.

Marshall County

17th District Circuit Court & General Sessions Courthouse, Lewisburg, TN 37091; 931-359-0536; Fax: 931-359-0543. Hours: 8AM-4PM *Felony, Misdemeanor, Civil, Eviction, Small Claims.*

Civil Records: Access: In person only. Visitors must perform in person searches for themselves. No search fee. Required to search: name, years to search. Civil cases indexed by plaintiff. Civil records archived on books, but no date specified.

Criminal Records: Access: In person only. Visitors must perform in person searches for themselves. No search fee. Required to search: name, years to search; also helpful: DOB, SSN. Criminal records in docket books.

General Information: No adoption records released. Copy fee: $1.00 per page. Certification fee: $4.50. Fee payee: Circuit Court Clerk. Personal checks accepted. Prepayment is required.

County Court 1107 Courthouse Annex, Lewisburg, TN 37091; 931-359-2181; Fax: 931-359-0543. Hours: 8AM-4PM (CST). *Probate.*

Maury County

Circuit Court & General Sessions Maury County Courthouse, 41 Public Square, Columbia, TN 38401; 931-381-3690; Fax: 931-381-3985. Hours: 8AM-4PM (CST). *Felony, Misdemeanor, Civil, Eviction, Small Claims, Probate.*

Civil Records: Access: Phone, fax, mail, in person. Both court and visitors may perform in person searches. No search fee. Required to search: name, years to search. Civil cases indexed by defendant, plaintiff. Civil records on books since 1984; on computer back to 1989.

Criminal Records: Access: In person only. Visitors must perform in person searches for themselves. No search fee. Required to search: name, years to search, DOB; also helpful: SSN. Criminal records on computer back to 1989.

General Information: Public Access terminal is available. No juvenile records released. Turnaround time 1 week. Fax notes: $1.00 per page. Copy fee: $1.00 per page. Certification fee: $6.00. Fee payee: Circuit Court Clerk. Personal checks accepted.

McMinn County

10th District Criminal, Circuit & General Sessions Court PO Box 506, Athens, TN 37303; 423-745-1923; Fax: 423-745-1642. Hours: 8:30AM-4PM (EST). *Felony, Misdemeanor, Civil, Eviction, Small Claims, Probate.*

Civil Records: Access: Phone, fax, mail, in person. Both court and visitors may perform in person searches. Search fee: $3.00 per name. Required to search: name, years to search; also helpful: address. Civil cases indexed by defendant, plaintiff. Civil records archived approximately 20 years; computerized back to 1996. Phone access is limited to three names.

Criminal Records: Access: Phone, fax, mail, in person. Both court and visitors may perform in person searches. Search fee: $3.00. Required to search: name, years to search, DOB, SSN; also helpful: address. Criminal records archived approximately 20 years; computerized back to 1996. Phone access is limited to three names.

General Information: No juvenile, adoption records released. Turnaround time 5-10 days. Fax notes: Fee to fax results is $2.00 per page. Copy fee: $2.00 per page. Certification fee: $4.00. Fee payee: Circuit Court Clerk. Business checks accepted.

McNairy County

25th District Circuit Court & General Sessions 300 Industrial Drive, Selmer, TN 38375; 731-645-1015; Fax: 731-645-1003. Hours: 8AM-4:30PM M-F; 8AM-Noon Sat (CST). *Felony, Misdemeanor, Civil, Eviction, Small Claims.*

Civil Records: Access: Mail, in person. Both court and visitors may perform in person searches. Search fee: $5.00 per name. Required to search: name, years to search. Civil cases indexed by defendant, plaintiff. Civil records archived on docket books since 1966.

Criminal Records: Access: Mail, in person. Both court and visitors may perform in person searches. Search

fee: $5.00 per name. Required to search: name, years to search, DOB, SSN. Criminal records archived on docket books since 1966.

General Information: Public Access terminal is available. No juvenile records released. Turnaround time 1-2 days. Copy fee: $.25 per page. Certification fee: $3.00. Fee payee: Circuit Court Clerk. Personal checks accepted. Prepayment is required.

Chancery Court Chancery Court, Clerk & Master, Courthouse, Rm 205, Selmer, TN 38375; 731-645-5446; Fax: 731-645-3656. Hours: 8AM-4PM M,T,Th,F; Closed W (CST). *Civil, Probate.*

Civil Records: Access: In person only. Visitors must perform in person searches for themselves. No search fee. Required to search: name, years to search. Civil cases indexed by defendant, plaintiff. Civil records on books.

General Information: No adoption records released. Copy fee: $.50. Certification fee: No certification fee. Fee payee: Clerk & Master. Personal checks accepted.

Meigs County

9th District Criminal, Circuit & General Sessions Court PO Box 205, Decatur, TN 37322; 423-334-5821; Fax: 423-334-4819. Hours: 8AM-5PM M,T,Th,F; 8AM-12PM Sat (EST). *Felony, Misdemeanor, Civil, Eviction, Small Claims.*

Civil Records: Access: Mail, in person. Both court and visitors may perform in person searches. No search fee. Required to search: name, years to search. Civil cases indexed by defendant, plaintiff. Civil records archived in office from 1930s, records in storage go further. They refer all name searches to an outside agency.

Criminal Records: Access: Mail, in person. Both court and visitors may perform in person searches. No search fee. Required to search: name, years to search. Criminal records archived in office from 1930s, records in storage go further. They refer all name searches to an outside agency.

General Information: No juvenile records released. SASE requested. Turnaround time 24 hours. Copy fee: $.25 per page. Certification fee: $5.00. Fee payee: Circuit Court Clerk. Personal checks accepted. Prepayment is required.

Chancery Court PO Box 5, Decatur, TN 37322; 423-334-5243. Hours: 8AM-5PM M,T,Th,F; 8:30AM-Noon Wed (EST). *Civil, Probate.*

Civil Records: Access: In person only. Visitors must perform in person searches for themselves. No search fee. Required to search: name, years to search. Civil cases indexed by defendant, plaintiff. Civil records on dockets since 1940.

General Information: No adoption records released. Copy fee: $.25 per page. Certification fee: $5.50. Fee payee: Meigs County Chancery Court. Personal checks accepted. Prepayment is required.

Monroe County

10th District, Circuit & General Sessions Court 105 College St, Madisonville, TN 37354; 423-442-2396; Fax: 423-442-9538. Hours: 8AM-4:30PM (EST). *Felony, Misdemeanor, Civil, Eviction, Small Claims.*

Civil Records: Access: Mail, in person. Both court and visitors may perform in person searches. Search fee: $10.00 per name. Required to search: name, years to search. Civil cases indexed by defendant, plaintiff. Civil records on computer since 1991, records on books in office for 10 years, unspecified prior to then.

Criminal Records: Access: Mail, in person. Both court and visitors may perform in person searches. Search fee: $10.00 per name. Required to search: name, years to search. Criminal records on computer since 1991, records on books in office for 10 years, unspecified prior to then.

General Information: Public Access terminal is available. No juvenile records released. Turnaround time 2 days. Copy fee: $1.00 per page. Certification fee: $4.00. Fee payee: Circuit Court Clerk. Personal checks accepted. Prepayment is required.

Chancery Court PO Box 56, Madisonville, TN 37354; 423-442-2644; Probate phone: 423-442-4573; Fax: 423-420-0048. Hours: 8:30AM-4:30PM (EST). *Civil, Probate.*

Civil Records: Access: Mail, in person. Both court and visitors may perform in person searches. No search fee. Required to search: name, years to search. Civil cases indexed by defendant. Civil records on computer since 1993, prior records on books.

General Information: No adoption, sealed records released. SASE requested. Turnaround time 2-3 days. Copy fee: $2.00 per page. Certification fee: $4.00. Fee payee: Chancery Court. Personal checks accepted. Prepayment is required.

Montgomery County

19th District Circuit Court PO Box 384, Clarksville, TN 37041-0384; 931-648-5700; Fax: 931-648-5731. Hours: 8:30AM-4:30PM (CST). *Felony, Civil Actions Over $10,000.*

Civil Records: Access: In person only. Visitors must perform in person searches for themselves. No search fee. Required to search: name, years to search. Civil cases indexed by defendant, plaintiff. Civil records archived on books in office from 1970s, on microfiche from 1950s.

Criminal Records: Access: In person only. Visitors must perform in person searches for themselves. No search fee. Required to search: name, years to search, DOB, signed release; also helpful: SSN. Criminal records on computer since 1997; prior records archived on books from 1970s & on microfiche from 1950s.

General Information: No juvenile records released. Copy fee: $.50 per page. Certification fee: $6.00. Fee payee: Circuit Court Clerk. Business checks accepted. Prepayment is required.

General Sessions 120 Commerce St, Clarksville, TN 37040; Civil phone: 931-648-5769; Criminal phone: 931-648-5771. Hours: 8:30AM-4:30PM (CST). *Misdemeanor, Civil Actions Under $15,000, Eviction, Small Claims.*

Civil Records: Access: Fax, mail, in person. Both court and visitors may perform in person searches. No search fee. Required to search: name, years to search. Civil cases indexed by defendant, plaintiff. Civil records on books, archived but data not given.

Criminal Records: Access: Fax, mail, in person. Both court and visitors may perform in person searches. No search fee. Required to search: name, years to search, DOB; also helpful: SSN. Criminal records on books, archived but data not given.

General Information: Public Access terminal is available. Turnaround time 1-2 weeks. Fax notes: $2.00 per page. Copy fee: $.50 per page. Certification fee: $6.00. Fee payee: General Sessions Court. Business checks accepted. Prepayment is required.

Chancery Court Chancery Court, Clerk & Master, Montgomery County Courthouse, Clarksville, TN 37040; 931-648-5703. Hours: 8AM-4:30PM (CST). *Civil, Probate.*

Civil Records: Access: In person only. Visitors must perform in person searches for themselves. No search fee. Required to search: name, years to search. Civil cases indexed by defendant, plaintiff. Civil records on books and microfilm.

General Information: Public Access terminal is available. No adoption or sealed records released. Copy

fee: $1.00 per page. Certification fee: $2.00. Fee payee: Clerk & Master. Business checks accepted. Prepayment is required.

Moore County

17th District Circuit Court & General Sessions Courthouse, PO Box 206, Lynchburg, TN 37352; 931-759-7208; Fax: 931-759-5673. Hours: 8AM-4:30PM MTWF; 8AM-Noon Sat (CST). *Felony, Misdemeanor, Civil, Eviction, Small Claims.*

Civil Records: Access: Mail, in person. Both court and visitors may perform in person searches. Search fee: $5.00 per name. Required to search: name, years to search. Civil cases indexed by defendant, plaintiff. Civil records archived to 1862, on docket books and microfiche from 1862 to 1980s.

Criminal Records: Access: Mail, in person. Both court and visitors may perform in person searches. Search fee: $5.00 per name. Required to search: name, years to search. Criminal records archived to 1862, on docket books and microfiche from 1862 to 1980s.

General Information: No juvenile records released. SASE required. Turnaround time 7-10 days. Copy fee: $2.00 per page. Certification fee: $2.00. Fee payee: Circuit Court Clerk. Only cashiers checks and money orders accepted. Prepayment is required.

Chancery Court PO Box 206, Lynchburg, TN 37352; 931-759-7028; Fax: 931-759-5610. Hours: 8AM-4:30PM M-W,F; 8AM-Noon Sat (CST). *Civil, Probate.*

Civil Records: Access: In person only. Visitors must perform in person searches for themselves. No search fee. Required to search: name, years to search. Civil cases indexed by plaintiff. Civil records on books.

General Information: No adoption or sealed records released. Copy fee: $.50 per page. Certification fee: $5.00. Fee payee: Clerk and Master. Only cashiers checks and money orders accepted. Prepayment is required.

Morgan County

9th District Criminal, Circuit & General Sessions Court PO Box 163, Wartburg, TN 37887; 423-346-3503. Hours: 8AM-4PM (EST). *Felony, Misdemeanor, Civil, Eviction, Small Claims.*

Civil Records: Access: In person only. Visitors must perform in person searches for themselves. No search fee. Required to search: name, years to search. Civil cases indexed by defendant, plaintiff. Civil records archived on books from 1855.

Criminal Records: Access: In person only. Visitors must perform in person searches for themselves. No search fee. Required to search: name, years to search; also helpful: DOB, SSN. Criminal records archived on books from 1855.

General Information: No sealed records released. Copy fee: $1.00 per page. Certification fee: $6.00. Fee payee: Circuit Court Clerk. Only cashiers checks and money orders accepted. Prepayment is required.

Chancery Court PO Box 789, Wartburg, TN 37887; 423-346-3881. Hours: 8AM-4PM (EST). *Civil, Probate.*

Civil Records: Access: Phone, mail, in person. Both court and visitors may perform in person searches. No search fee. Required to search: name, years to search. Civil cases indexed by defendant, plaintiff. Civil records in books since 1883, on microfiche since 1939.

General Information: No adoption or conservatorship records released. SASE required. Turnaround time 1-8 days. Copy fee: $.50 per page. Certification fee: $10.00. Fee payee: Clerk & Master. Personal checks accepted. Prepayment is required.

Obion County

27th District Circuit Court 7 Court House Square, Union City, TN 38261; 731-885-1372; Fax: 731-885-7515. Hours: 8:30AM-4:30PM (CST). *Felony, Misdemeanor, Civil Actions Over $10,000.*

Civil Records: Access: Mail, in person. Both court and visitors may perform in person searches. Search fee: $5.00 per name. Required to search: name, years to search. Civil cases indexed by defendant, plaintiff. Civil records for criminal archived on books from 1969, civil on books from 1974, rest are located elsewhere.

Criminal Records: Access: Mail, in person. Both court and visitors may perform in person searches. Search fee: $5.00. Misdemeanor records are $5.00 per year. Required to search: name, years to search, DOB, SSN. Criminal records for criminal archived on books from 1969, civil on books from 1974, rest are located elsewhere.

General Information: No adoption records released. SASE required. Turnaround time 2 days. Copy fee: $1.00 per page. Certification fee: $3.00. Fee payee: Circuit Court. Business checks accepted. Prepayment is required.

General Sessions 9 Bill Burnett Circle, Union City, TN 38281-0236; 731-885-1811; Fax: 731-885-7515. Hours: 8:30AM-4:30PM (CST). *Civil Actions Under $15,000, Eviction, Small Claims.*

Civil Records: Access: Mail, in person. Both court and visitors may perform in person searches. Search fee: $5.00 5 years & under; $10.00 over 5 years. Required to search: name. Civil cases indexed by defendant, plaintiff. Civil records kept in office for last 10 years.

General Information: No juvenile or adoption records released. SASE required. Turnaround time 2 days. Copy fee: $1.00 per page. Certification fee: $3.00. Fee payee: Circuit Court Clerk. Personal checks accepted. Prepayment is required.

Chancery Court PO Box 187, Union City, TN 38281; 731-885-2562; Fax: 731-885-7515. Hours: 8:30AM-4:30PM (CST). *Civil, Probate.*

Civil Records: Access: Phone, mail, in person. Both court and visitors may perform in person searches. No search fee. Required to search: name, years to search. Civil cases indexed by defendant, plaintiff. Civil records (probate) from 9/82 on books in Chancery office, prior records on books in County Clerk's office.

General Information: No adoption or sealed records released. Copy fee: $1.00 per page. Certification fee: $2.00 per page plus $4.00. Fee payee: Clerk and Master. Personal checks accepted. Prepayment is required.

Overton County

13th District Criminal, Circuit & General Sessions Court Overton County Courthouse, 100 E Court Sq, Livingston, TN 38570; 931-823-2312; Fax: 931-823-9728. Hours: 8AM-4:30PM M,T,Th,F, 8AM-Noon Wed & Sat (CST). *Felony, Misdemeanor, Civil, Eviction, Small Claims.*

Civil Records: Access: Mail, in person. Both court and visitors may perform in person searches. No search fee. Required to search: name, years to search. Civil cases indexed by defendant, plaintiff. Civil records archived on books from late 1800s.

Criminal Records: Access: Mail, in person. Both court and visitors may perform in person searches. No search fee. Required to search: name, years to search, DOB, SSN, signed release. Criminal records archived on books from late 1800s.

General Information: No juvenile records released. Turnaround time 3-5 days. Copy fee: $.25 per page. Certification fee: $5.00. Fee payee: Circuit Court Clerk. Business checks accepted. Prepayment is required.

County Court Courthouse Annex, University St, Livingston, TN 38570; 931-823-2631; Fax: 931-823-7036. Hours: 8AM-4:30PM M,T,Th,F; 8AM-Noon W & Sat (CST). *Probate.*

Perry County

21st District Circuit Court & General Sessions
PO Box 91, Linden, TN 37096; 931-589-2218. Hours: 8AM-4PM (CST). *Felony, Misdemeanor, Civil, Eviction, Small Claims.*

Civil Records: Access: Mail, in person. Both court and visitors may perform in person searches. No search fee. Required to search: name, years to search. Civil cases indexed by defendant, plaintiff. Civil records archived on books from 1941, on microfiche (limited) at library.
Criminal Records: Access: Mail, in person. Both court and visitors may perform in person searches. No search fee. Required to search: name, years to search, DOB, SSN. Criminal records archived on books from 1941, on microfiche (limited) at library.
General Information: No adoption records released. SASE required. Turnaround time 2-3 days. Copy fee: $.25 per page. Certification fee: $4.00. Fee payee: Circuit Court Clerk. Personal checks accepted.

Chancery Court PO Box 251, Linden, TN 37096; 931-589-2217; Fax: 931-589-2350. Hours: 8AM-4PM (CST). *Civil, Probate.*

Civil Records: Access: In person only. Visitors must perform in person searches for themselves. No search fee. Required to search: name, years to search. Civil cases indexed by defendant, plaintiff. Civil records (probate) on books from 1982, prior records in County Clerks office.
General Information: No adoption records released. SASE required. Copy fee: $1.50 per page. Certification fee: $5.00. Fee payee: Clerk and Master. Local checks accepted. Prepayment is required.

Pickett County

13th District, Criminal, Circuit & General Sessions Court
PO Box 5, Byrdstown, TN 38549; 931-864-3958; Fax: 931-864-6885. Hours: 8AM-4PM (CST). *Felony, Misdemeanor, Civil, Eviction, Small Claims.*

Civil Records: Access: Mail, in person. Both court and visitors may perform in person searches. No search fee. Required to search: name, years to search. Civil cases indexed by defendant. Civil records archived on books but not specific.
Criminal Records: Access: Mail, in person. Both court and visitors may perform in person searches. No search fee. Required to search: name, years to search; also helpful: SSN. Criminal records not computerized, all on books.
General Information: No adoption or juvenile records released. Turnaround time 3-4 days. Copy fee: $.25 per page. Certification fee: $4.00. Fee payee: Circuit Court Clerk. Personal checks accepted.

County Court PO Box 5 Courthoue Square, Byrdstown, TN 38549; 931-864-3879. Hours: 8AM-4PM M,T,Th,F, 8AM-Noon W & Sat (CST). *Probate.*

Polk County

10th District Criminal, Circuit & General Sessions Court
PO Box 256, Benton, TN 37307; 423-338-4524; Fax: 423-338-8611. Hours: 8:30AM-4:30PM M-F (EST). *Felony, Misdemeanor, Civil, Eviction, Small Claims.*

Civil Records: Access: Mail, in person. Both court and visitors may perform in person searches. Search fee: $5.00 per name. Required to search: name, years to search. Civil cases indexed by defendant, plaintiff. Civil records archived from 1936.

Criminal Records: Access: Mail, in person. Both court and visitors may perform in person searches. Search fee: $5.00 per name. Required to search: name, years to search, DOB, SSN. Criminal records archived from 1936.
General Information: No juvenile records released. SASE required. Turnaround time 3 days. Copy fee: $5.00 per document. Certification fee: Certification fee varies according to document size. Fee payee: Circuit Court Clerk. Personal checks accepted. Prepayment is required.

Chancery Court PO Drawer L, Benton, TN 37307; 423-338-4522; Fax: 423-338-4553. Hours: 8:30AM-4:30PM (EST). *Civil, Probate.*

Civil Records: Access: Mail, in person. Both court and visitors may perform in person searches. Search fee: $5.00 per name. Fee varies by document. Required to search: name, years to search. Civil cases indexed by defendant, plaintiff. Civil records on books.
General Information: No adoption records released. Copy fee: $1.00 per page. Certification fee: $5.50. Fee payee: Chancery Court. Personal checks accepted.

Putnam County

13th District Criminal, Circuit & General Sessions Court
421 E Spring St, 1C-49A, Cookeville, TN 38501; 931-528-1508. Hours: 8AM-4PM (CST). *Felony, Misdemeanor, Civil, Eviction, Small Claims.*

Civil Records: Access: Mail, in person. Both court and visitors may perform in person searches. No search fee. Required to search: name, years to search. Civil cases indexed by defendant, plaintiff. Civil records archived in office from 1980s, unknown before then.
Criminal Records: Access: Mail, in person. Both court and visitors may perform in person searches. No search fee. Required to search: name, years to search; also helpful: SSN. Criminal records not computerized.
General Information: No juvenile or adoption records released. Turnaround time 3-5 days. Copy fee: $.25 per page. Certification fee: $4.00. Fee payee: Circuit Court Clerk. Business checks accepted. Prepayment is required.

County Court PO Box 220, Cookeville, TN 38503-0220; 931-526-7106; Fax: 931-372-8201. Hours: 8AM-4:30PM (CST). *Probate.*

Rhea County

12th District Circuit & General Sessions Court
1475 Market St Rm 200, Dayton, TN 37321; 423-775-7805; Probate phone: 423-775-7806; Fax: 423-775-7895. Hours: 8AM-4:30PM (EST). *Felony, Misdemeanor, Civil, Eviction, Small Claims, Probate.*

Note: Probate located at the Rhea County Clerk and Master's Office.

Civil Records: Access: In person only. Visitors must perform in person searches for themselves. No search fee. Required to search: name, years to search. Civil cases indexed by defendant, plaintiff. Civil records in docket books.
Criminal Records: Access: In person only. Visitors must perform in person searches for themselves. No search fee. Required to search: name, years to search, DOB; also helpful: SSN. Criminal records in docket books.
General Information: No adoption records released. Certification fee: $4.50. Fee payee: Circuit Court Clerk. Personal checks accepted. Prepayment is required.

Roane County

9th District Criminal, Circuit & General Sessions Court
PO Box 73, Kingston, TN 37763; 865-376-2390; Fax: 865-717-4141. Hours: 8:30AM-6PM Mon; 8:30AM-4:30PM T-F (EST). *Felony, Misdemeanor, Civil, Eviction, Small Claims.*

Note: General Sessions phone is 865-376-5584, their records are separate.

Civil Records: Access: Mail, fax, in person. Both court and visitors may perform in person searches. Search fee: $5.00 per name. Required to search: name, years to search. Civil cases indexed by defendant, plaintiff. Civil records archived since court started, General Sessions and Circuit are on computer since 1991.
Criminal Records: Access: Mail, fax, in person. Both court and visitors may perform in person searches. Search fee: $5.00 per name. Required to search: name, years to search, DOB; also helpful, SSN, signed release. Criminal records archived since court started, General Sessions and Circuit are on computer since 1991.
General Information: No adoption, expunged records released. SASE required. Turnaround time 2-3 days. Copy fee: $.50 per page. Certification fee: $5.00. Fee payee: Circuit Court Clerk. Business checks accepted. Prepayment is required.

Chancery Court PO Box 402, Kingston, TN 37763; 865-376-2487; Fax: 865-376-1228. Hours: 8:30AM-6PM Mon, 8:30AM-4:30PM T-F (EST). *Civil, Probate.*

Civil Records: Access: Phone, mail, in person. Both court and visitors may perform in person searches. No search fee. Required to search: name, years to search. Civil cases indexed by defendant, plaintiff. Civil records on books; on computer since 7/95. Tax records on computer since 1982.
General Information: No adoption records released. SASE not required. Turnaround time same day. Fax notes: Fee to fax results is $1.00 per page. Copy fee: $.50 per page. Certification fee: $2.00. Fee payee: Clerk and Master. Personal checks accepted.

Robertson County

19th District Circuit Court & General Sessions
Room 200, Springfield, TN 37172; 615-382-2324; Fax: 615-384-8246. Hours: 8AM-4:30PM *Felony, Misdemeanor, Civil, Eviction, Small Claims.*

Civil Records: Access: Phone, fax, mail, in person. Both court and visitors may perform in person searches. Search fee: $5.00 per name. Required to search: name, years to search. Civil cases indexed by defendant, plaintiff. Civil records archived in office from 1980s, archived from 1800s located elsewhere.
Criminal Records: Access: Phone, fax, mail, in person. Both court and visitors may perform in person searches. Search fee: $5.00 per name. Required to search: name, years to search; also helpful: DOB, SSN. Criminal records archived in office from 1980s, archived from 1800s located elsewhere. No long distance outgoing faxing.
General Information: Public Access terminal is available. No sealed records released. SASE required. Turnaround time 15 days. Copy fee: $.25 per page. Certification fee: $5.00. Fee payee: Circuit Court Clerk. Personal checks accepted. Prepayment is required.

Chancery Court 101 Robertson, County Courthouse, Springfield, TN 37172; 615-384-5650. Hours: 8:30AM-4:30PM (CST). *Civil, Probate.*

Civil Records: Access: Mail, in person. Both court and visitors may perform in person searches. No search fee. Required to search: name, years to search. Civil cases indexed by defendant, plaintiff. Civil records in books since 1982, all chancery records on books.

General Information: No adoption records released. SASE required. Turnaround time 1-2 days. Copy fee: $1.00 per page. Certification fee: $2.00. Fee payee: Clerk & Master. Personal checks accepted. Prepayment is required.

Rutherford County

16th District Circuit Court Room 201, Murfreesboro, TN 37130; Civil phone: 615-898-7820; Criminal phone: 615-898-7812; Fax: 615-849-9553. Hours: 8AM-4:15PM (CST). *Felony, Misdemeanor, Civil Actions Over $15,000.*

Civil Records: Access: In person only. Visitors must perform in person searches for themselves. No search fee. Required to search: name, years to search. Civil cases indexed by defendant, plaintiff. Civil records archived since court started, criminal on computer since 1990.

Criminal Records: Access: In person only. Visitors must perform in person searches for themselves. No search fee. Required to search: name, years to search, DOB, signed release; also helpful: SSN. Criminal records archived since court started, criminal on computer since 1990.

General Information: Public Access terminal is available. No expunged, sealed criminal records released. Copy fee: $1.00 per page. Certification fee: $2.00 per page. Fee payee: Circuit Court Clerk. Personal checks accepted.

General Sessions Court Judicial Bldg, Room 101, Murfreesboro, TN 37130; 615-898-7831; Fax: 615-898-7835. Hours: 8AM-4:15PM (CST). *Civil Actions Under $10,000, Eviction, Small Claims.*

Civil Records: Access: In person only. Visitors must perform in person searches for themselves. No search fee. Required to search: name, years to search. Civil cases indexed by defendant, plaintiff. Civil records archived but not specified, on computer from 07/90.

General Information: Public Access terminal is available. No juvenile records released. Copy fee: $1.00 per page. Certification fee: $4.00. Fee payee: General Sessions Court. Personal checks accepted. Prepayment is required.

County Court 319 N Maple St, Murfreesboro, TN 37130; 615-898-7798; Fax: 615-898-7830. Hours: 8AM-4PM M-Th; 8AM-5PM F (CST). *Probate.*

Scott County

8th District Criminal, Circuit & General Sessions Court PO Box 330, Huntsville, TN 37756; 423-663-2440. Hours: 8AM-4:30PM (EST). *Felony, Misdemeanor, Civil, Eviction, Small Claims, Probate.*

Civil Records: Access: Phone, mail, in person. Both court and visitors may perform in person searches. Search fee: $7.00 per name per year. Required to search: name, years to search. Civil cases indexed by defendant, plaintiff. Civil records archived in docket books but not specified, on computer from 1991.

Criminal Records: Access: Phone, mail, in person. Both court and visitors may perform in person searches. Search fee: $7.00 per name per year. Fee varies according to info requested. Required to search: name, years to search, DOB; also helpful: SSN. Criminal records archived in docket books but not specified, on computer from 1991.

General Information: No juvenile records released. SASE required. Turnaround time same week. Fax notes: No fee to fax results. Copy fee: $.25 per page. Certification fee: $1.00. Fee payee: Circuit Court Clerk. Personal checks accepted.

Sequatchie County

12th District Circuit Court & General Sessions PO Box 551, Dunlap, TN 37327; 423-949-2618; Fax: 423-949-2902. Hours: 8AM-4PM (CST). *Felony, Misdemeanor, Civil, Eviction, Small Claims.*

Civil Records: Access: Phone, fax, mail, in person. Both court and visitors may perform in person searches. No search fee. Required to search: name, years to search. Civil cases indexed by defendant, plaintiff. Civil records archived on books but not specified.

Criminal Records: Access: Phone, fax, mail, in person. Both court and visitors may perform in person searches. No search fee. Required to search: name, years to search, DOB; also helpful: SSN. Criminal records not computerized.

General Information: No adoption records released. Turnaround time 1 week. Fax notes: No fee to fax results. Copy fee: $.25 per page. Certification fee: No certification fee. Fee payee: Circuit Court Clerk. Personal checks accepted.

Chancery Court PO Box 1651, Dunlap, TN 37327; 423-949-3670; Fax: 423-949-2579. Hours: 8AM-4PM (CST). *Civil, Probate.*

Civil Records: Access: Fax, mail, in person. Both court and visitors may perform in person searches. No search fee. Required to search: name, years to search. Civil cases indexed by defendant, plaintiff. Civil records on books.

General Information: No sealed or adoption records released. Turnaround time 1 week. Fax notes: $1.00 per page. Copy fee: $1.00 per page. Certification fee: $2.00. Fee payee: Clerk and Master. Personal checks accepted. Prepayment is required.

Sevier County

Circuit Court & General Sessions 125 Court Ave 204 E, Sevierville, TN 37862; 865-453-5536; Fax: 865-774-9792. Hours: 8AM-4:30PM M-Th, 8AM-6PM Fri (EST). *Felony, Misdemeanor, Civil, Eviction, Small Claims.*

Note: The courts are separate; Circuit is on the 2nd floor and Sessions on the 1st floor. They share the fax. Call Sessions direct at 865-453-6116.

Civil Records: Access: Fax, mail, in person. Both court and visitors may perform in person searches. Search fee: $1.00 per name. Required to search: name, years to search. Civil cases indexed by defendant, plaintiff. Civil records computerized since 1994. Records before 1980s difficult to locate.

Criminal Records: Access: Fax, mail, in person. Both court and visitors may perform in person searches. Search fee: $1.00 per name. Required to search: name, years to search; also helpful: SSN. Criminal records computerized since 1990.

General Information: No expunged records released. SASE not required. Turnaround time 1 week. Fax notes: $1.00 per page. Copy fee: $1.00 per page. Certification fee: $3.00. Fee payee: Circuit Court or General Sessions Clerk. Personal checks accepted.

County Court 125 Court Ave, #202, Sevierville, TN 37862; 865-453-5502; Fax: 865-453-6830. Hours: 8AM-4:30PM (EST). *Probate.*

Shelby County

Circuit Court 140 Adams Ave, Rm 224, Memphis, TN 38103; 901-545-4006; Fax: 901-545-4723. Hours: 8AM-4:30PM (CST). *Civil Actions Over $15,000.*

Civil Records: Access: Fax, mail, in person. Both court and visitors may perform in person searches. Search fee: $5.00 per name. Required to search: name; also helpful: years to search. Civil cases indexed by defendant, plaintiff. Civil records archived from early

1900s, on computer from 1991, on microfiche from 1980.

General Information: No juvenile or adoption records released. Turnaround time 5-8 days. Fax notes: $1.00 per page. Copy fee: $1.00 per page. Certification fee: $5.00. Fee payee: Circuit Court Clerk. Personal checks accepted. Prepayment is required.

30th District Criminal Court 201 Poplar, Room 401, 4th Flr, Memphis, TN 38103; 901-545-5001; Fax: 901-545-3679. Hours: 8AM-4:30PM (CST). *Felony.*

www.co.shelby.tn.us

Criminal Records: Access: Fax, mail, in person. Both court and visitors may perform in person searches. Search fee: $5.00 per name. Required to search: name, years to search, DOB, SSN. Criminal records on computer for approximately 15 years, prior records archived since court started.

General Information: Public Access terminal is available. No expunged or sealed records released. Turnaround time 2 days. Fax notes: Fee to fax results is $5.00 per document. Copy fee: $2.00 per page. Certification fee: $5.00. Fee payee: Criminal Court Clerk. Business checks accepted. Credit cards accepted: Visa, MasterCard. Prepayment is required.

General Sessions - Civil 140 Adams, Room 106, Memphis, TN 38103; 901-576-4031. Hours: 8AM-4:30PM (CST). *Civil Actions Under $25,000, Eviction, Small Claims.*

http://geberalsessionscourt.co.shelby.tn.us

Civil Records: Access: In person only. Visitors must perform in person searches for themselves. No search fee. Required to search: name, years to search. Civil cases indexed by defendant, plaintiff. Civil records archived 10 years in office, (prior records unsure), some microfiche and on computer from 1982.

General Information: Public Access terminal is available. No mental commitment records released. SASE requested. Turnaround time 1 week. Copy fee: $1.50 per page. Certification fee: $6.00. Fee payee: General Sessions Court Clerk. Personal checks accepted. Prepayment is required.

General Sessions - Criminal 201 Poplar, Room 81, Memphis, TN 38103; 901-545-5100; Fax: 901-545-3655. 8AM-4:30PM (CST). *Misdemeanor.*

www.generalsessionscourt.co.shelby.tn.us

Criminal Records: Access: Mail, in person. Both court and visitors may perform in person searches. Search fee: $10.00 per name. Use of terminal is $10.00 each 20 minutes. Required to search: name, years to search, DOB; also helpful: SSN. Criminal records on computer since 1982, prior records archived since court started.

General Information: Public Access terminal is available. No mental records released. SASE not required. Turnaround time 2-5 days. Copy fee: $1.50 per page. Certification fee: $14.00. Fee payee: General Sessions Court. Personal checks accepted. Prepayment is required.

Probate Court 140 Adams, Room 124, Memphis, TN 38103; 901-576-4040; Fax: 901-576-4746. Hours: 8AM-4:30PM (CST). *Probate.*

Smith County

15th District Criminal, Circuit & General Sessions Court 211 Main St, Carthage, TN 37030; 615-735-0500; Fax: 615-735-8261. Hours: 8AM-4PM M-F; 8AM-Noon Sat (CST). *Felony, Misdemeanor, Civil, Eviction, Small Claims.*

Civil Records: Access: Mail, in person. Both court and visitors may perform in person searches. No search fee. Required to search: name, years to search. Civil cases indexed by defendant, plaintiff. Civil records on computer from 3/92, prior records archived on books, questionable to dates.

Criminal Records: Access: Phone, mail, in person. Both court and visitors may perform in person searches. No search fee. Required to search: name, years to search. Criminal records on computer from 3/92, prior records archived on books, questionable to dates.

General Information: Public Access terminal is available. No juvenile records released. Turnaround time 1-2 days. Copy fee: $.25 per page. Certification fee: $6.00. Fee payee: Circuit Court Clerk. Only cashiers checks and money orders accepted. Prepayment is required.

Chancery Court 211 N Main St, Carthage, TN 37030; 615-735-2092; Fax: 615-735-8261. Hours: 8AM-4PM (CST). *Civil, Probate.*

Civil Records: Access: Fax, mail, in person. Only the court performs in person searches; visitors may not. No search fee. Required to search: name, years to search. Civil cases indexed by defendant, plaintiff. Civil records on books back to 1811.

General Information: No adoption records released. SASE requested. Turnaround time 1 day. Fax notes: Fee to fax results is $1.00 per page. Copy fee: $.50 per page. Certification fee: $4.00. Fee payee: Clerk and Master. Personal checks accepted. Prepayment is required.

Stewart County

23rd District Circuit Court & General Sessions PO Box 193, Dover, TN 37058; 931-232-7042; Fax: 931-232-3111. Hours: 8AM-4:30PM (CST). *Felony, Misdemeanor, Civil, Eviction, Small Claims.*

Civil Records: Access: Mail, in person. Both court and visitors may perform in person searches. No search fee. Required to search: name, years to search. Civil cases indexed by plaintiff. Civil records archived on books from 1800s, on computer through 8/94.

Criminal Records: Access: Mail, in person. Both court and visitors may perform in person searches. No search fee. Required to search: name, years to search. Criminal records archived on books from 1800s, on computer through 8/94.

General Information: No expunged records released. Turnaround time 1-10 days. Certification fee: No certification fee.

Chancery Court PO Box 102, Dover, TN 37058; 931-232-5665; Fax: 931-232-3111. Hours: 8AM-4:30PM (CST). *Civil, Probate.*

Civil Records: Access: Mail, in person. Only the court performs in person searches; visitors may not. No search fee. Required to search: name, years to search. Civil cases indexed by defendant, plaintiff. Civil records on books.

General Information: No adoption records released. SASE required. Turnaround time 1 week. Copy fee: $.25 per page. Certification fee: $4.00. Fee payee: Clerk and Master. Personal checks accepted. Prepayment is required.

Sullivan County

Bristol Circuit Court - Civil Division Courthouse, Rm 211, 801 Anderson St, Bristol, TN 37620; 423-989-4354. Hours: 8AM-5PM (EST). *Civil.*

Civil Records: Access: Mail, in person. Both court and visitors may perform in person searches. No search fee. Required to search: name, years to search. Civil cases indexed by defendant, plaintiff. Civil records archived from 1930s (minute books, unsure of docket books), on computer from 1986.

General Information: Public Access terminal is available. No adoption or sealed records released. Turnaround time 1-2 weeks. Copy fee: $1.00 per page. Certification fee: $5.00 for the seal and $2.00 each

additional page after 1st. Fee payee: Circuit Court Clerk. Personal checks accepted.

Kingsport Circuit Court - Civil Division 225 W Center St, Kingsport, TN 37660; 423-224-1724. Hours: 8AM-5PM (EST). *Civil Actions Over $15,000.*

Civil Records: Access: Phone, mail, in person. Both court and visitors may perform in person searches. No search fee. Required to search: name, years to search. Civil cases indexed by defendant, plaintiff. Civil records archived from 1920s, on computer from 1985.

General Information: No juvenile, adoption records released. SASE requested. Turnaround time 2-3 days. Copy fee: $1.00 per page. Certification fee: $5.00. Fee payee: Circuit Court Clerk. Personal checks accepted. Prepayment is required.

2nd District Circuit Court 140 Blockville ByPass, PO Box 585, Blountville, TN 37617; 423-323-5158. 8AM-5PM (EST). *Felony, Misdemeanor.*

Criminal Records: Access: Mail, in person. Both court and visitors may perform in person searches. No search fee. Required to search: name, years to search, DOB; also helpful: SSN. Criminal records on computer since 12/83; prior records archived since the 1800s.

General Information: Public Access terminal is available. No juvenile records released. Turnaround time 1 week. Copy fee: $1.00 per page. Certification fee: $7.00 for first page then $2.00 each additional. Fee payee: Circuit Court Clerk. Personal checks accepted.

Bristol General Sessions Courthouse, 801 Broad St, Rm 211, Bristol, TN 37620; 423-989-4352. Hours: 8AM-4:30PM (EST). *Misdemeanor, Civil Actions Under $10,000, Eviction, Small Claims.*

Civil Records: Access: Phone, mail, in person. Both court and visitors may perform in person searches. No search fee. Required to search: name, years to search. Civil cases indexed by defendant, plaintiff. Civil records archived since court started (stored in Blountville), on computer from 1986.

Criminal Records: Access: Phone, mail, in person. Both court and visitors may perform in person searches. No search fee. Required to search: name, years to search, DOB, SSN, signed release. Criminal records archived since court started (stored in Blountville), on computer from 1986.

General Information: Public Access terminal is available. No juvenile records released. SASE required. Turnaround time depends on search. Copy fee: $1.00 per page. Certification fee: $4.00. Fee payee: Circuit Court Clerk. Personal checks accepted.

Chancery Court PO Box 327, Blountville, TN 37617; 423-323-6483; Fax: 423-279-3280. Hours: 8AM-5PM (EST). *Civil, Probate.*

Civil Records: Access: Mail, in person. Both court and visitors may perform in person searches. No search fee. Required to search: name, years to search. Civil cases indexed by defendant, plaintiff. Civil records on books back to 1867; computerized records go back to 1996.

General Information: No adoption records released. Copy fee: Varies by length of document. Certification fee: $2.50. Fee payee: Chancery Court. Personal checks accepted.

Kingsport General Sessions 200 Shelby St, Kingsport, TN 37660; 423-274-1711. Hours: 8AM-5PM (EST). *Misdemeanor, Civil Actions Under $15,000, Eviction, Small Claims.*

Civil Records: Access: Phone, mail, in person. Both court and visitors may perform in person searches. No search fee. Required to search: name, years to search. Civil cases indexed by defendant, plaintiff. Civil records archived in office from 1973, on computer from 1988.

Criminal Records: Access: Phone, mail, in person. Both court and visitors may perform in person searches. No search fee. Required to search: name, years to

search; also helpful: SSN. Criminal records archived in office from 1973, on computer from 1988.

General Information: Public Access terminal is available. No juvenile records released. Turnaround time 2-3 days. Fax notes: Fee to fax results is $1.00 per page. Copy fee: $1.00 per page. Certification fee: $2.00 per page. Fee payee: General Sessions Clerk. Personal checks accepted. Prepayment is required.

Sumner County

18th District Criminal, Circuit & General Sessions Court Public Sq, PO Box 549, Gallatin, TN 37066; 615-452-4367; Fax: 615-451-6027. Hours: 8AM-4:30PM (CST). *Felony, Misdemeanor, Civil, Eviction, Small Claims.*

Civil Records: Access: In person only. Visitors must perform in person searches for themselves. No search fee. Required to search: name, years to search. Civil cases indexed by defendant, plaintiff. Civil records archived on books in office from 1950.

Criminal Records: Access: In person only. Visitors must perform in person searches for themselves. No search fee. Required to search: name, years to search. Criminal records archived on books in office from 1950; computerized back to 1997.

General Information: Public Access terminal is available. No juvenile, adoption records released. Copy fee: $1.00 per page. Certification fee: $4.00. Fee payee: Circuit Court Clerk. Only cashiers checks and money orders accepted. Prepayment is required.

Chancery Court Room 300, Sumner County Courthouse, Gallatin, TN 37066; 615-452-4282; Fax: 615-451-6031. 8AM-4:30PM (CST). *Civil, Probate.*

Civil Records: Access: Phone, fax, mail, in person. Both court and visitors may perform in person searches. No search fee. Required to search: name, years to search. Civil cases indexed by defendant, plaintiff. Civil records on books.

General Information: No juvenile or adoption records released. Turnaround time 1-2 days. Copy fee: $1.00 per page. Certification fee: $4.00 plus $2.00 per page. Fee payee: Clerk and Master. Personal checks accepted. Prepayment is required.

Tipton County

25th District Circuit Court & General Sessions 1801 S College, Rm 102, Covington, TN 38019; 901-475-3310. Hours: 8AM-5PM (CST). *Felony, Misdemeanor, Civil, Eviction, Small Claims.*

Civil Records: Access: Mail, in person. Both court and visitors may perform in person searches. Search fee: $10.00 per name per court. $25.00 for computer info before 07/91. Required to search: name, years to search. Civil cases indexed by defendant, plaintiff. Civil records on computer from July 1991, prior records on docket books.

Criminal Records: Access: Mail, in person. Both court and visitors may perform in person searches. Search fee: $10.00 per name per court. Required to search: name, years to search, DOB; also helpful: SSN. Criminal records on computer from July 1991, prior records on docket books.

General Information: Public Access terminal is available. No juvenile or adoption records released. SASE requested. Turnaround time 1 week. Copy fee: $.50 per page. Certification fee: $5.00. Fee payee: Circuit Court Clerk or General Sessions. Personal checks accepted. Prepayment is required.

Chancery Court Tipton County Justice Ctr., 1801 S College #110, Covington, TN 38019; 901-476-0209; Fax: 901-476-0246. 8AM-5PM (CST). *Civil, Probate.*

Civil Records: Access: Phone, mail, in person. Both court and visitors may perform in person searches. No search fee. Required to search: name, years to search.

Civil cases indexed by defendant, plaintiff. Civil records on books since 1982, on computer since 1991.

General Information: No adoption records released. SASE required. Turnaround time ASAP. Copy fee: $.50 per page. Certification fee: $4.00 plus $2.00 per page. Fee payee: Tipton County Chancery Court. Personal checks accepted. Prepayment is required.

Trousdale County

15th District Criminal, Circuit & General Sessions Court
200 East Main St, Rm 5, Hartsville, TN 37074; 615-374-3411; Fax: 615-374-1100. Hours: 8AM-4:30PM (CST). *Felony, Misdemeanor, Civil, Eviction, Small Claims.*

Civil Records: Access: In person only. Visitors must perform in person searches for themselves. No search fee. Required to search: name, years to search. Civil cases indexed by defendant, plaintiff. Civil records archived on books since 1927.

Criminal Records: Access: In person only. Visitors must perform in person searches for themselves. No search fee. Required to search: name, years to search. Criminal records archived on books since 1927.

General Information: No juvenile or adoption records released. Copy fee: $1.00 per page. Certification fee: $3.00. Fee payee: Circuit Court Clerk. Only cashiers checks & money orders accepted. Prepayment required.

Chancery Court
Courthouse Room 1, 200 E Main St, Hartsville, TN 37074; 615-374-2996; Fax: 615-374-1100. Hours: 8AM-4:30PM (CST). *Civil, Probate.*

Civil Records: Access: In person only. Visitors must perform in person searches for themselves. No search fee. Required to search: name, years to search. Civil cases indexed by defendant, plaintiff. Civil records on book since 9/80, prior records in County Clerks office.

General Information: No adoption or sealed records released. Copy fee: $.50 per page. Certification fee: $3.00. Plus $.50 per page. Fee payee: Clerk and Master. Personal checks accepted. Prepayment is required.

Unicoi County

1st District Criminal, Circuit & General Sessions Court
PO Box 2000, Erwin, TN 37650; 423-743-3541. Hours: 8AM-5PM (EST). *Felony, Misdemeanor, Civil, Eviction, Small Claims.*

Civil Records: Access: Mail, in person. Both court and visitors may perform in person searches. Search fee: $10.00 per name. Required to search: name, years to search. Civil cases indexed by defendant, plaintiff. Civil records archived on books from 1932 (felonies) and 1961 (misdemeanors).

Criminal Records: Access: Mail, in person. Both court and visitors may perform in person searches. Search fee: $10.00 per name. Required to search: name, years to search, DOB. Criminal records archived on books from 1932 (felonies) and 1961 (misdemeanors).

General Information: Public Access terminal is available. No adoption records released. Turnaround time 2 days. Copy fee: $.25 per page. Certification fee: $4.50. Fee payee: Circuit Court Clerk. Personal checks accepted. Prepayment is required.

Probate Court
PO Box 340, Erwin, TN 37650; 423-743-3381; Fax: 423-743-3219. Hours: 9AM-5PM M-F, 9AM-Noon Sat (EST). *Probate.*

Union County

8th District Criminal, Circuit & General Sessions Court
901 E Main Street, #220, Maynardville, TN 37807; 865-992-5493. Hours: 8AM-4PM Mon-Thur; 8AM-6PM Fri (EST). *Felony, Misdemeanor, Civil, Eviction, Small Claims.*

Civil Records: Access: Mail, in person. Both court and visitors may perform in person searches. Search fee: $10.00 per name. Required to search: name, years to

search. Civil cases indexed by defendant, plaintiff. Civil records archived on books from 1969.

Criminal Records: Access: Mail, in person. Both court and visitors may perform in person searches. Search fee: $10.00 per name. Required to search: name, years to search, DOB, SSN. Criminal records archived on books from 1969.

General Information: No sealed records released. Turnaround time 1 week. Copy fee: $.25 per page. Certification fee: $4.00. Fee payee: Circuit Court Clerk. Personal checks accepted.

Chancery Court
901 Main St #215, Maynardville, TN 37807-3510; 865-992-5942. Hours: 8AM-4PM (6PM F) (EST). *Civil, Probate.*

Civil Records: Access: Phone, mail, in person. Both court and visitors may perform in person searches. No search fee. Required to search: name, years to search. Civil cases indexed by plaintiff. Civil records on books back to 1969.

General Information: No adoption records released. Turnaround time 1 week. Fax notes: Fee to fax results is $.50 per page. Copy fee: $.50 per page. Certification fee: $4.00. Fee payee: Union County Clerk and Master. Personal checks accepted.

Van Buren County

31st District Circuit Court & General Sessions
PO Box 126, Spencer, TN 38585; 931-946-2153; Fax: 931-946-7572. Hours: 8AM-5PM (CST). *Felony, Misdemeanor, Civil, Eviction, Small Claims.*

Civil Records: Access: Mail, in person. Both court and visitors may perform in person searches. Search fee: $10.00 per name. Required to search: name, years to search. Civil cases indexed by defendant. Civil records archived on books, date unspecified.

Criminal Records: Access: Mail, in person. Both court and visitors may perform in person searches. Search fee: $10.00 per name. Required to search: name, years to search, DOB; also helpful: SSN. Criminal records archived on books, date unspecified.

General Information: No juvenile records released. Turnaround time 2 weeks. Copy fee: $.25 per page. Certification fee: $3.00. Fee payee: Circuit Court Clerk. Only cashiers checks and money orders accepted.

County Court
PO Box 126, Spencer, TN 38585; 931-946-2121; Fax: 931-946-2388. Hours: 8AM-4PM M,T,Th,F, 8AM-Noon Wed & Sat (CST). *Probate.*

Warren County

31st District Circuit Court & General Sessions
111 Court Sq, PO Box 639, McMinnville, TN 37111; 931-473-2373; Fax: 931-473-3726. Hours: 8AM-4:30PM M-Th; 8AM-5PM F (CST). *Felony, Misdemeanor, Civil, Eviction, Small Claims.*

Civil Records: Access: Mail, in person. Both court and visitors may perform in person searches. Search fee: $5.00 per name. Required to search: name, years to search. Civil cases indexed by defendant, plaintiff. Civil records on computer since 1988 (general sessions), archived in office from 1939 (Circuit).

Criminal Records: Access: Mail, in person. Both court and visitors may perform in person searches. Search fee: $5.00 per name. Required to search: name, years to search, DOB, SSN, offense, date of offense. Criminal records on computer since 1988 (general sessions), archived in office from 1939 (Circuit).

General Information: No adoption or juvenile records released. Turnaround time 1-2 days. Copy fee: $1.00 per page. Certification fee: $2.00. Fee payee: Circuit Court Clerk. Personal checks accepted. Prepayment is required.

Chancery Court
PO Box 639, McMinnville, TN 37111; 931-473-2364; Fax: 931-473-3232. 8AM-4:30PM M-Th, 8AM-5PM F (CST). *Civil, Probate.*

Civil Records: Access: Mail, in person. Both court and visitors may perform in person searches. No search fee. Required to search: name, years to search. Civil cases indexed by defendant, plaintiff. Civil records on books.

General Information: No adoption records released. SASE required. Turnaround time 1 week. Copy fee: $2.00 per page. Certification fee: Certification is $4.00 for first page, $2.00 each add'l. Fee payee: Clerk and Master. Personal checks accepted.

Washington County

1st District Circuit Court & General Sessions
PO Box 356, Jonesborough, TN 37659; 423-753-1611; Fax: 423-753-1809. Hours: 8AM-5PM (EST). *Felony, Misdemeanor, Civil, Eviction, Small Claims.*

Civil Records: Access: Mail, in person. Both court and visitors may perform in person searches. Search fee: $5.00 per name. Required to search: name, years to search. Civil cases indexed by defendant, plaintiff. Civil records archived from 1800s, on computer from 1989.

Criminal Records: Access: Mail, in person. Both court and visitors may perform in person searches. Search fee: $5.00 per name. Required to search: name, years to search, DOB, SSN. Criminal records archived from 1800s, on computer from 1989.

General Information: Public Access terminal is available. No sealed, juvenile, adoption records released. SASE requested. Turnaround time 1 week. Copy fee: $2.00 per page. Certification fee: $4.00. Fee payee: Circuit Court Clerk. Personal checks accepted. Prepayment is required.

General Sessions
101 E Market St, Johnson City, TN 37604; 423-461-1412; Fax: 423-926-4862. Hours: 8AM-5PM (EST). *Civil Actions Under $15,000, Eviction, Small Claims.*

Civil Records: Access: Mail, in person. Both court and visitors may perform in person searches. Search fee: $5.00 per name. Required to search: name, years to search. Civil cases indexed by defendant, plaintiff. Civil records archived since court started, computerized since 1990.

General Information: Public Access terminal is available. No sealed records released. SASE requested. Turnaround time 1-2 weeks. Copy fee: $2.00 per page. Certification fee: $8.00. Fee payee: Circuit Court Clerk. In-state checks accepted. Prepayment is required.

Johnson City Law Court - Civil
101 E Market St, Johnson City, TN 37604; 423-461-1475; Fax: 423-926-4862. Hours: 8AM-5PM (EST). *Civil Actions Over $15,000.*

Civil Records: Access: Mail, in person. Both court and visitors may perform in person searches. Search fee: $5.00 per name. Required to search: name, years to search. Civil cases indexed by defendant, plaintiff. Civil records on computer from 1988.

General Information: No sealed records released. SASE requested. Turnaround time 1 week. Copy fee: $2.00 per page. Certification fee: $4.00. Fee payee: Circuit Court Clerk. Personal checks accepted. Out of state checks not accepted. Prepayment is required.

Probate Court
PO Box 218, Jonesborough, TN 37659; 423-753-1623; Fax: 423-753-4716. Hours: 8AM-5PM (EST). *Probate.*

Wayne County

22nd District Circuit Court & General Sessions
PO Box 869, Waynesboro, TN 38485; 931-722-5519; Fax: 931-722-5994. Hours: 8AM-4PM M,T,Th,F, 8AM-Noon W & Sat (CST). *Felony, Misdemeanor, Civil, Eviction, Small Claims.*

Civil Records: Access: Phone, mail, in person. Both court and visitors may perform in person searches. Search fee: $5.00 per name. Required to search: name, years to search. Civil cases indexed by defendant, plaintiff. Civil records archived on books from 1800s.

Criminal Records: Access: Phone, mail, in person. Both court and visitors may perform in person searches. Search fee: $5.00 per name. Required to search: name, years to search, DOB, SSN. Criminal records archived on books from 1800s.

General Information: No juvenile or adoption records released. Turnaround time 7-10 days. Certification fee: Same as copy fee. Fee payee: Circuit Court Clerk. Personal checks accepted. Prepayment is required.

Chancery Court
PO Box 101, Waynesboro, TN 38485; 931-722-5517; Fax: 931-722-5994. Hours: 8AM-4PM (CST). *Civil, Probate.*

Civil Records: Access: Mail, in person. Both court and visitors may perform in person searches. No search fee. Required to search: name, years to search. Civil cases indexed by defendant, plaintiff. Civil records on books.

General Information: No adoption records released. SASE requested. Turnaround time 2 days. No copy fee. Certification fee: $3.00. Fee payee: Clerk and Master. Personal checks accepted. Prepayment is required.

Weakley County

27th District Circuit Court & General Sessions
PO Box 28, Dresden, TN 38225; 731-364-3455; Fax: 731-364-6765. Hours: 8AM-4:30PM *Felony, Misdemeanor, Civil, Eviction, Small Claims.*

Civil Records: Access: In person only. Visitors must perform in person searches for themselves. No search fee. Required to search: name, years to search. Civil cases indexed by defendant, plaintiff. Civil records archived on since court started, on books.

Criminal Records: Access: In person only. Visitors must perform in person searches for themselves. No search fee. Required to search: name, years to search, DOB; also helpful: SSN. Criminal records archived on since court started, on books.

General Information: No adoption or sealed records released. Copy fee: $2.00 per page. Certification fee: $6.00. Fee payee: Circuit Court Clerk. Personal checks accepted. Prepayment is required.

Chancery Court
PO Box 197, Dresden, TN 38225; 731-364-3454; Fax: 731-364-5247. Hours: 8AM-4:30PM (CST). *Civil, Probate.*

Civil Records: Access: Mail, in person. Both court and visitors may perform in person searches. No search fee. Required to search: name, years to search. Civil cases indexed by defendant, plaintiff. Civil records on computer since 1982, prior records in books to 1930; Probate to 1800s.

General Information: No adoption or sealed records released. Turnaround time 1 week. Copy fee: $1.00 per page. Certification fee: $5.00. Fee payee: Clerk and Master. Personal checks accepted. Prepayment is required.

White County

13th District Criminal, Circuit & General Sessions Court
Courthouse, Room 304, Sparta, TN 38583; 931-836-3205; Fax: 931-836-3526. Hours: 8AM-5PM (CST). *Felony, Misdemeanor, Civil, Eviction, Small Claims.*

Civil Records: Access: In person only. Visitors must perform in person searches for themselves. No search fee. Required to search: name, years to search. Civil cases indexed by defendant, plaintiff. Civil records archived since court started.

Criminal Records: Access: In person only. Visitors must perform in person searches for themselves. No search fee. Required to search: name, years to search, DOB; also helpful: SSN. Criminal records archived since court started.

General Information: No juvenile, adoption records released. Certification fee: $3.50. Fee payee: Circuit Court Clerk. Personal checks accepted. Prepayment is required.

Chancery Court
White County Courthouse, Room 303, Sparta, TN 38583; 931-836-3787. Hours: 8AM-4PMn (CST). *Civil, Probate.*

Civil Records: Access: Phone, in person. Visitors must perform in person searches for themselves. No search fee. Required to search: name, years to search. Civil cases indexed by defendant, plaintiff. Civil records kept in books and files.

General Information: No adoption records released. Certification fee: $2.00. Fee payee: Clerk and Master. Personal checks accepted. Prepayment is required.

Williamson County

21st District Circuit Court & General Sessions
Room 107, Franklin, TN 37064; 615-790-5454; Fax: 615-790-5432. Hours: 8AM-4:30PM *Felony, Misdemeanor, Civil, Eviction, Small Claims.*

Civil Records: Access: Mail, in person. Both court and visitors may perform in person searches. Search fee: $15.00 per name. Required to search: name, years to search. Civil cases indexed by defendant, plaintiff. Civil records archived on books from 1810, on computer from 1992.

Criminal Records: Access: Mail, in person. Both court and visitors may perform in person searches. Search fee: $12.00 per name. Misdemeanor search is $30.00. Required to search: name, years to search, DOB; also helpful: SSN. Criminal records archived on books from 1810, on computer from 1992.

General Information: SASE not required. Turnaround time 3 days. Certification fee: $4.00. Fee payee: Circuit Court Clerk. Personal checks accepted. Prepayment is required.

Chancery Court
Clerk & Master, Franklin, TN 37064; 615-790-5428; Fax: 615-790-5626. Hours: 8AM-4:30PM (CST). *Civil, Probate.*

Civil Records: Access: Phone, mail, in person. Both court and visitors may perform in person searches. No search fee. Required to search: name, years to search. Civil cases indexed by defendant, plaintiff. Civil records on computer since 1991, prior records on books since 1800s (no probate on computer).

General Information: No adoption, sealed records released. SASE requested. Copy fee: $1.00 per page. Fee payee: Clerk and Master. Local checks accepted.

Wilson County

15th District Criminal, Circuit & General Sessions Court
PO Box 518, Lebanon, TN 37088-0518; 615-444-2042; Fax: 615-449-3420. Hours: 8AM-4PM M-Th, 8AM-5PM F (CST). *Felony, Misdemeanor, Civil, Eviction, Small Claims.*

Civil Records: Access: In person only. Visitors must perform in person searches for themselves. No search fee. Required to search: name, years to search. Civil cases indexed by defendant, plaintiff. Civil records archived in office from 1982, from 1800s located elsewhere, on computer from 10/91, on microfiche from 1940s.

Criminal Records: Access: In person only. Visitors must perform in person searches for themselves. No search fee. Required to search: name, years to search, DOB, SSN. Criminal records archived in office from 1982, from 1800s located elsewhere, on computer from 10/91, on microfiche from 1940s.

General Information: No adoption, juvenile records released. Copy fee: $.25 per page. Certification fee: $6.00. Plus $2.00 each additional page. Fee payee: Circuit Court Clerk. Business checks accepted. Prepayment is required.

County Court
PO Box 918, Lebanon, TN 37088-0918; 615-443-2627; Fax: 615-443-2628. Hours: 8AM-4:30PM M-Th, 8AM-5PM Fri (CST). *Probate.*

Tennessee Recording Offices

ORGANIZATION   95 counties, 96 recording offices. The recording officer is the Register of Deeds. Sullivan County has two offices. 66 counties are in the Central Time Zone (CST) and 29 are in the Eastern Time Zone (EST).

REAL ESTATE RECORDS   Counties will not perform real estate searches. Certified copies usually cost $1.00 per page. Tax records are kept at the Assessor's Office.

UCC RECORDS   Financing statements are filed at the state level, except for real estate related collateral, which are filed with the Register of Deeds. However, prior to 07/2001, consumer goods and farm collateral were also filed at the Register of Deeds and these older records can be searched there. Many recording offices will not perform UCC searches. Use search request form UCC-11. Search fees and copy fees vary.

TAX LIEN RECORDS   All federal tax liens are filed with the county Register of Deeds. State tax liens are filed with the Secretary of State or the Register of Deeds. Counties will not perform tax lien searches.

OTHER LIENS   Judgment, materialman, mechanics, trustee.

Anderson County

Register of Deeds, 100 North Main Street, Courthouse, Room 205, Clinton, TN 37716-3688. 865-457-5400; Fax 865-457-1638.
Will search UCC records prior to 7/2001 and current fixture (land) files. Will not search real estate records. **Other Phone Numbers:** Assessor 865-457-5400 x225.

Bedford County

Register of Deeds, 108 Northside Square, Shelbyville, TN 37160. 931-684-5719; Fax 931-685-2086.
Will search UCC records prior to 7/2001 and current fixture (land) files. Will not search real estate records. **Other Phone Numbers:** Assessor 931-684-6390; Treasurer 931-684-4363.

Benton County

Register of Deeds, 1 E. Court Sq., Suite 105, Camden, TN 38320-2070. 731-584-6661.
Will search UCC records prior to 7/2001 and current fixture (land) files. This agency will not do a tax lien search. Will not search real estate records. **Other Phone Numbers:** Assessor 731-584-7615.

Bledsoe County

Register of Deeds, P.O. Box 385, Pikeville, TN 37367. Register of Deeds, R/E and UCC Recording 423-447-2020; Fax 423-447-6856.
Will search UCC records prior to 7/2001 and current fixture (land) files. Will not search real estate records. **Other Phone Numbers:** Assessor 423-447-6548; Treasurer 423-447-2369; Appraiser/Auditor 423-447-6548; Elections 423-447-2776.

Blount County

Register of Deeds, 349 Court Street, Maryville, TN 37804-5906. 865-273-5880; Fax 865-273-5890. http://www.blount.state.tn.us/register.htm
Will search UCC records prior to 7/2001 and current fixture (land) files. Will not search real estate records. **Other Phone Numbers:** Assessor 865-982-5130.

Bradley County

Register of Deeds, P.O. Box 579, Cleveland, TN 37364-0579. 423-476-0513; Fax 423-478-8888.
Will not search UCC records. Will not search real estate records. **Other Phone Numbers:** Assessor 423-476-0505.

Campbell County

Register of Deeds, P.O. Box 85, Jacksboro, TN 37757. 423-562-3864; Fax 423-562-9833.
Will search UCC records prior to 7/2001 and current fixture (land) files. Tax liens not included in UCC search. Will not search real estate records. **Other Phone Numbers:** Assessor 423-562-3201.

Cannon County

Register of Deeds, Courthouse, Woodbury, TN 37190. 615-563-2041; Fax 615-563-5696.
Will search UCC records prior to 7/2001 and current fixture (land) files. **Other Phone Numbers:** Assessor 615-563-5437.

Carroll County

Register of Deeds, Carroll County Office Complex, 625 High St., Suite 104, Huntingdon, TN 38344. 731-986-1952; Fax 731-986-1955.
Will search UCC records prior to 7/2001 and current fixture (land) files. Will not search real estate records. **Other Phone Numbers:** Assessor 731-986-1975.

Carter County

Register of Deeds, 801 East Elk Avenue, Elizabethton, TN 37643. 423-542-1830.
Will search UCC records prior to 7/2001 and current fixture (land) files. This agency will not do a tax lien search. Will not search real estate records. **Other Phone Numbers:** Assessor 423-542-1806.

Cheatham County

Register of Deeds, P.O. Box 453, Ashland City, TN 37015. 615-792-4317; Fax 615-792-2039.
Will search UCC records prior to 7/2001 and current fixture (land) files. Will not search real estate records. **Other Phone Numbers:** Assessor 615-792-5371; Treasurer 615-792-4298.

Chester County

Register of Deeds, P.O. Box 292, Henderson, TN 38340. 731-989-4991.
Will search UCC records prior to 7/2001 and current fixture (land) files. This agency will not do a tax lien search. Will not search real estate records. **Other Phone Numbers:** Assessor 731-989-4882; Treasurer 731-989-3993.

Claiborne County

Register of Deeds, P.O. Box 117, Tazewell, TN 37879. 423-626-3325.
Will search UCC records prior to 7/2001 and current fixture (land) files. This agency will not do a tax lien search. RE record owner and property searches available. **Other Phone Numbers:** Assessor 423-626-3276; Treasurer 423-626-3275.

Clay County

Register of Deeds, P.O. Box 430, Celina, TN 38551. 931-243-3298.
Will search UCC records prior to 7/2001 and current fixture (land) files. UCC search includes tax liens. Will not search real estate records. **Other Phone Numbers:** Assessor 931-243-2599; Treasurer 931-243-2310.

Cocke County

Register of Deeds, 111 Court Ave., Room 102, Courthouse, Newport, TN 37821-3102. 423-623-7540.
Will search UCC records prior to 7/2001 and current fixture (land) files. This agency will not do a tax lien search. Will not search real estate records. **Other Phone Numbers:** Assessor 423-623-7024; Trustee 423-623-3037.

Coffee County

Register of Deeds, P.O. Box 178, Manchester, TN 37349. 931-723-5130; Fax 931-723-8232.
Will search UCC records prior to 7/2001 and current fixture (land) files. Will not search real estate records. **Other Phone Numbers:** Assessor 931-723-5126.

Crockett County

Register of Deeds, County Courthouse, 1 S Bells St #2, 1 S. Bells St., Suite 2, Alamo, TN 38001. 731-696-5455.
Will search UCC records prior to 7/2001 and current fixture (land) files. UCC search includes tax liens if requested. Will not search real estate records. **Other Phone Numbers:** Assessor 731-696-5456; Treasurer 731-696-5454.

Cumberland County

Register of Deeds, 2 North Main St., Suite 204, Crossville, TN 38555-4583. 931-484-5559.
Will not search UCC records. This agency will not do a tax lien search. Will not search real estate records. **Other Phone Numbers:** Assessor 931-484-5745; Elections 931-484-4919; Trustee 931-484-5730.

Davidson County

Register of Deeds, 103 Metro Courthouse, Nashville, TN 37201-5028. 615-862-6790; Fax 615-880-2039. http://www.nashville.org
Will not search UCC records. Will not search real estate records. **Online Access:** Property Records. Property records on the Metropolitan Planning Commission City of Nashville database are available free online at www.nashville.org/mpc/maps/index.html. Click on "Go straight to maps.". **Other Phone Numbers:** Assessor 615-862-6080.

De Kalb County

Register of Deeds, One Public Square, Rm 201, Smithville, TN 37166. 615-597-4153; Fax 615-597-7420.
Will search UCC records prior to 7/2001 and current fixture (land) files. This agency will not do a tax lien search. Will not search real estate records. **Other Phone Numbers:** Assessor 615-597-5925; Trustee 615-597-5176.

Decatur County

Register of Deeds, P.O. Box 488, Decaturville, TN 38329. 731-852-3712.
Will search UCC records prior to 7/2001 and current fixture (land) files. This agency will not do a tax lien search. Will not search real estate records. **Other Phone Numbers:** Assessor 731-852-3117; Treasurer 731-852-3723.

Dickson County

Register of Deeds, P.O. Box 220, Charlotte, TN 37036. 615-789-4171; Fax 615-789-3893.
Will search UCC records prior to 7/2001 and current fixture (land) files. Will not search real estate records. **Other Phone Numbers:** Assessor 615-789-4171.

Dyer County

Register of Deeds, P.O. Box 1360, Dyersburg, TN 38025-1360. 731-286-7806; Fax 731-288-7724.
Will search UCC records prior to 7/2001 and current fixture (land) files. Will not search real estate records. **Other Phone Numbers:** Assessor 731-286-7805; Treasurer 731-286-7802.

Fayette County

Register of Deeds, P.O. Box 99, Somerville, TN 38068-0099. 901-465-5251.
Will search UCC records prior to 7/2001 and current fixture (land) files. This agency will not do a tax lien search. Will not search real estate records. **Other Phone Numbers:** Assessor 901-465-5226.

Fentress County

Register of Deeds, P.O. Box 341, Jamestown, TN 38556. Register of Deeds, R/E and UCC Recording 931-879-7818; Fax 931-879-1579.
Will not search UCC records. Will not search real estate records. **Other Phone Numbers:** Assessor 931-879-9194; Treasurer 931-879-7717; Appraiser/Auditor 931-879-8294; Elections 931-879-7162; Vital Records 931-879-8014.

Franklin County

Register of Deeds, P.O. Box 101, Winchester, TN 37398-0101. 931-967-2840.
Will search UCC records prior to 7/2001 and current fixture (land) files. This agency will not do a tax lien search. Will not search real estate records. **Other Phone Numbers:** Assessor 931-967-3869; Treasurer 931-967-2962.

Gibson County

Register of Deeds, Courthouse, 1 Court Square, Trenton, TN 38382. 731-855-7628; Fax 731-855-7650.
Will search UCC records prior to 7/2001 and current fixture (land) files. Will not search real estate records.

Giles County

Register of Deeds, P.O. Box 678, Pulaski, TN 38478. 931-363-5137; Fax 931-424-6101. http://www.usit.net/giles/Government/register.htm
Will search UCC records prior to 7/2001 and current fixture (land) files. This agency will not do a tax lien search. Will not search real estate records. **Other Phone**

Numbers: Assessor 931-363-2166; Trustee 931-363-1676.

Grainger County

Register of Deeds, P.O. Box 174, Rutledge, TN 37861. 865-828-3523; Fax 865-828-4284.
Will search UCC records prior to 7/2001 and current fixture (land) files. **Other Phone Numbers:** Assessor 865-828-5858; Trustee 865-828-3514.

Greene County

Register of Deeds, Courthouse, 101 S. Main St. Suite 201, Greeneville, TN 37743. 423-639-0196 R/E Recording: 423-639-1726 UCC Recording: 423-639-1726.
Will not search UCC records. This agency will not do a tax lien search. Will not search real estate records. **Other Phone Numbers:** Assessor 423-638-1738; Treasurer 423-639-1705.

Grundy County

Register of Deeds, P.O. Box 35, Altamont, TN 37301-0035. 931-692-3621; Fax 931-692-3627.
Will search UCC records prior to 7/2001 and current fixture (land) files. Will not search real estate records. **Other Phone Numbers:** Assessor 931-692-3596.

Hamblen County

Register of Deeds, 511 West 2nd North Street, Morristown, TN 37814. 423-586-6551; Fax 423-587-9798.
Will search UCC records prior to 7/2001 and current fixture (land) files. Will not search real estate records.

Hamilton County

Register of Deeds, 625 Georgia Ave., Court House, Room 400, Chattanooga, TN 37402. 423-209-6560; Fax 423-209-6561. http://www.hamiltontn.gov/register
Will search UCC records prior to 7/2001 and current fixture (land) files. This agency will not do a tax lien search. Will not search real estate records. **Online Access:** Real Estate. Two sources for records exist. The County Register of Deeds subscription service is available online for $50 per month and $1.00 per fax page. Search by name, address, or book & page. For further information, call 423-209-6560. Also, unofficial property records are available free online from a private company at http://216.205.78.218/Samples/Hamilton Search.html. Site is under construction. **Other Phone Numbers:** Assessor 423-209-7300; Treasurer 423-209-7270.

Hancock County

Register of Deeds, P.O. Box 72, Sneedville, TN 37869. 423-733-4545.
Will search UCC records prior to 7/2001 and current fixture (land) files. This agency will not do a tax lien search. Will not search real estate records. **Other Phone Numbers:** Assessor 423-733-2332.

Hardeman County

Register of Deeds, Courthouse, 100 N Main St., Bolivar, TN 38008. 731-658-3476; Fax 731-658-3075.
Will not search UCC records. This agency will not do a tax lien search. Will not search real estate records. **Other Phone Numbers:** Assessor 731-658-6522.

Hardin County

Register of Deeds, Courthouse, Savannah, TN 38372. 731-925-4936.
Will search UCC records prior to 7/2001 and current fixture (land) files. This agency will not do a tax lien search. Will not search real estate records. **Other Phone Numbers:** Assessor 731-925-9031; Treasurer 731-925-8180.

Hawkins County

Register of Deeds, P.O. Box 235, Rogersville, TN 37857. 423-272-8304; Fax 423-921-3170.
Will search UCC records prior to 7/2001 and current fixture (land) files. Will not search real estate records. **Other Phone Numbers:** Assessor 423-272-8505.

Haywood County

Register of Deeds, 1 North Washington, Courthouse, Brownsville, TN 38012. 731-772-0332.
Will search UCC records prior to 7/2001 and current fixture (land) files. This agency will not do a tax lien search. Will not search real estate records. **Other Phone Numbers:** Assessor 731-772-0432; Treasurer 731-772-1722.

Henderson County

Register of Deeds, Courthouse, Lexington, TN 38351. 731-968-2941.
Will search UCC records prior to 7/2001 and current fixture (land) files. This agency will not do a tax lien search. Will not search real estate records.

Henry County

Register of Deeds, P.O. Box 44, Paris, TN 38242. Register of Deeds, R/E and UCC Recording 731-642-4081; Fax 731-642-2123. www.ustitlesearch.com
Will not search UCC records. Will not search real estate records. **Other Phone Numbers:** Assessor 731-642-0162; Elections 731-642-0411; Trustee 731-642-6633.

Hickman County

Register of Deeds, #1 Courthouse, Centerville, TN 37033-1639. Register of Deeds, R/E and UCC Recording 931-729-4882.
Will search UCC records prior to 7/2001 and current fixture (land) files. This agency will not do a tax lien search. Will not search real estate records. **Other Phone Numbers:** Assessor 931-729-2169.

Houston County

Register of Deeds, P.O. Box 412, Erin, TN 37061. 931-289-3510; Fax 931-289-4240.
Will search UCC records prior to 7/2001 and current fixture (land) files. Will not search real estate records. **Other Phone Numbers:** Assessor 931-289-3929.

Humphreys County

Register of Deeds, 102 Thompson Street, Courthouse Annex, Room 3, Waverly, TN 37185. Register of Deeds, R/E and UCC Recording 931-296-7681.
Will not search UCC records. This agency will not do a tax lien search. Will not search real estate records. **Other Phone Numbers:** Assessor 931-615-2919; Treasurer 931-296-2414.

Jackson County

Register of Deeds, P.O. Box 301, Gainesboro, TN 38562. Register of Deeds, R/E and UCC Recording 931-268-9012.
Will not search UCC records. This agency will not do a tax lien search. Will not search real estate records. **Other Phone Numbers:** Assessor 931-268-0246; Treasurer 931-268-9417; Elections 931-268-9284.

Jefferson County

Register of Deeds, P.O. Box 58, Dandridge, TN 37725. 865-397-2918.
Will not search UCC records, but will do an index name search back 3 years only. This agency will not do a tax lien search. Will not search real estate records. **Other Phone Numbers:** Assessor 865-397-3326; Treasurer 865-397-2101.

Johnson County

Register of Deeds, 222 Main Street, Mountain City, TN 37683. 423-727-7841; Fax 423-727-7047.
Will search UCC records prior to 7/2001 and current fixture (land) files. Will not search real estate records. **Other Phone Numbers:** Assessor 423-727-7692.

Knox County

Register of Deeds, 400 W. Main Avenue, Room 224, Knoxville, TN 37902. 865-215-2330.
Will search UCC records prior to 7/2001 and current fixture (land) files. This agency will not do a tax lien search. Will not search real estate records. **Online Access:** Real Property. Real property records are available free online through a private company at http://216.205.78.218/samples/KnoxSearch.html. Site is under construction. **Other Phone Numbers:** Assessor 865-521-2360; Treasurer 865-521-2305.

Lake County

Register of Deeds, 229 Church St., Box 5, Courthouse, Tiptonville, TN 38079. Register of Deeds, R/E and UCC Recording 731-253-7462; Fax 731-253-6815.
Will search UCC records. Will not search real estate records. **Other Phone Numbers:** Assessor 731-253-7200.

Lauderdale County

Register of Deeds, Courthouse, Ripley, TN 38063. 731-635-2171; Fax 731-635-9682.
Will search UCC records prior to 7/2001 and current fixture (land) files. Will not search real estate records. **Other Phone Numbers:** Assessor 731-635-9561; Treasurer 731-635-0712.

Lawrence County

Register of Deeds, 240 West Gaines Street, N.B.U. #18, Lawrenceburg, TN 38464. 931-766-4100; Fax 931-766-5602.
Will search UCC records prior to 7/2001 and current fixture (land) files. Will not search real estate records.

Lewis County

Register of Deeds, Courthouse, Room 104, 110 N. Park Ave., Hohenwald, TN 38462. 931-796-2255.
Will search UCC records. This agency will not do a tax lien search. Will not search real estate records. **Other Phone Numbers:** Assessor 931-796-5848; Elections 931-796-362.

Lincoln County

Register of Deeds, 112 Main Ave S, Rm 104, 112 Main St., Fayetteville, TN 37334. Register of Deeds, R/E and UCC Recording 931-433-5366; Fax 931-433-9312.
Will not search UCC records. This agency will not do a tax lien search. Will not search real estate records. **Other Phone Numbers:** Assessor 931-433-5409; Treasurer 931-433-1371; Elections 931-433-6220.

Loudon County

Register of Deeds, P.O. Box 395, Loudon, TN 37774. 865-458-2605; Fax 865-458-9028.
Will search UCC records prior to 7/2001 and current fixture (land) files. Will not search real estate records.

Macon County

Register of Deeds, Courthouse, Room 102, Lafayette, TN 37083. 615-666-2353; Fax 615-666-5323.
Will search UCC records prior to 7/2001 and current fixture (land) files. Will not search real estate records. **Other Phone Numbers:** Assessor 615-666-3688; Trustee 615-666-3624.

Madison County

Register of Deeds, Courthouse, Room 109, 100 Main St., Jackson, TN 38301. 731-423-6028; Fax 731-422-1171.
Will search UCC records prior to 7/2001 and current fixture (land) files. Will not search real estate records. **Other Phone Numbers:** Assessor 731-423-6100; Treasurer 731-423-6027.

Marion County

Register of Deeds, P.O. Box 789, Jasper, TN 37347. 423-942-2573.
Will search UCC records prior to 7/2001 and current fixture (land) files. This agency will not do a tax lien search. Will not search real estate records.

Marshall County

Register of Deeds, 1103 Courthouse Annex, Lewisburg, TN 37091. 931-359-4933.
Will not search UCC records. This agency will not do a tax lien search. Will not search real estate records. **Other Phone Numbers:** Assessor 931-359-3238.

Maury County

Register of Deeds, P.O. Box 769, Columbia, TN 38402-0769. 931-381-3690 x358 R/E Recording: 931-381-3690 x355 UCC Recording: 931-381-3690 x355; www.titlesearcher.com
Will not search real estate records. **Other Phone Numbers:** Assessor 931-381-3690 x253.

McMinn County

Register of Deeds, 6 East Madison, Athens, TN 37303. 423-745-1232; Fax 423-745-0095.
Will search UCC records prior to 7/2001 and current fixture (land) files. Will not search real estate records. **Other Phone Numbers:** Assessor 423-745-2743; Trustee 423-745-1291.

McNairy County

Register of Deeds, P.O. Box 158, Selmer, TN 38375. 731-645-3656; Fax 731-645-3656.
Will search UCC records prior to 7/2001 and current fixture (land) files. Tax liens not included in UCC search. RE record owner and mortgage searches available. **Other Phone Numbers:** Assessor 731-645-5146.

Meigs County

Register of Deeds, P.O. Box 245, Decatur, TN 37322. 423-334-5228.
Will search UCC records prior to 7/2001 and current fixture (land) files. This agency will not do a tax lien search. Will not search real estate records. **Other Phone Numbers:** Assessor 423-334-5231; Trustee 423-334-5119.

Monroe County

Register of Deeds, 103 College Street - Suite 4, Madisonville, TN 37354. 423-442-2440.
Will search UCC records prior to 7/2001 and current fixture (land) files. This agency will not do a tax lien search. Will not search real estate records. **Other Phone Numbers:** Assessor 423-442-2440; Treasurer 423-442-2920.

Montgomery County

Register of Deeds, 350 Pageant Ln, Suite 404, Clarksville, TN 37040. 931-648-5713; Fax 931-553-5157.
Will Search UCC records prior to 7/2001 and current fixture (land) files. Will not search real estate records. **Other Phone Numbers:** Assessor 931-648-5709; Trustee 931-648-5710.

Moore County

Register of Deeds, P.O. Box 206, Lynchburg, TN 37352. 931-759-7913; Fax 931-759-6394.
Will search UCC records prior to 7/2001 and current fixture (land) files. This agency will not do a tax lien search. Will not search real estate records. **Other Phone Numbers:** Assessor 931-759-7044.

Morgan County

Register of Deeds, P.O. Box 311, Wartburg, TN 37887. 423-346-3105.
Will search UCC records prior to 7/2001 and current fixture (land) files. This agency will not do a tax lien search. Will not search real estate records. **Other Phone Numbers:** Assessor 423-346-3130.

Obion County

Register of Deeds, P.O. Box 514, Union City, TN 38261. Register of Deeds, R/E and UCC Recording 731-885-9351; Fax 731-885-7515.
Will not search UCC records. Will not search real estate records. **Other Phone Numbers:** Assessor 731-885-2931; Elections 731-885-1901.

Overton County

Register of Deeds, 317 East University St., Room 150, Livingston, TN 38570. 931-823-4011.
Will not search UCC records. This agency will not do a tax lien search. Will not search real estate records.

Perry County

Register of Deeds, PO Box 62, Linden, TN 37096-0062. Register of Deeds, R/E and UCC Recording 931-589-2210; Fax 931-589-2215.
Will search UCC records prior to 7/2001 and current fixture (land) files. UCC search includes tax liens if requested. Will not search real estate records. **Other Phone Numbers:** Assessor 931-589-2277; Treasurer 931-589-2313.

Pickett County

Register of Deeds, P.O. Box 5, Byrdstown, TN 38549. 931-864-3316; Fax 931-864-6615.
Will search UCC records prior to 7/2001 and current fixture (land) files. Will not search real estate records. **Other Phone Numbers:** Assessor 931-864-3114.

Polk County

Register of Deeds, P.O. Box 293, Benton, TN 37307. 423-338-4537.
Will search UCC records prior to 7/2001 and current fixture (land) files. This agency will not do a tax lien search. Will not search real estate records. **Other Phone Numbers:** Assessor 423-338-4505; Trustee 423-338-4545.

Putnam County

Register of Deeds, P.O. Box 487, Cookeville, TN 38503-0487. 931-526-7101.
Will search UCC records prior to 7/2001 and current fixture (land) files. This agency will not do a tax lien search. Will not search real estate records. **Other Phone Numbers:** Assessor 931-528-8428; Treasurer 931-528-8845.

Rhea County

Register of Deeds, 1475 Market Street, Dayton, TN 37321. Register of Deeds, R/E and UCC Recording 423-775-7841; Fax 423-775-7895.
Will search UCC records prior to 7/2001 and current fixture (land) files. This agency will not do a tax lien search. Will not search real estate records. **Other Phone Numbers:** Assessor 423-775-7840; Treasurer 423-775-7810.

Roane County

Register of Deeds, P.O. Box 181, Kingston, TN 37763. 865-376-4673.
Will not search UCC records. This agency will not do a tax lien search. Will not search real estate records. **Other Phone Numbers:** Assessor 865-376-4362; Trustee 865-376-4938.

Robertson County

Register of Deeds, 525 S. Brown St., Springfield, TN 37172. 615-384-3772.
Will search UCC records prior to 7/2001 and current fixture (land) files. This agency will not do a tax lien search. Will not search real estate records.

Rutherford County

Register of Deeds, P.O. Box 5050, Murfreesboro, TN 37133-5050. 615-898-7870; Fax 615-898-7987.
Will search UCC records prior to 7/2001 and current fixture (land) files. Will not search real estate records. **Other Phone Numbers:** Assessor 615-898-7750.

Scott County

Register of Deeds, P.O. Box 61, Huntsville, TN 37756. 423-663-2417.
Will search UCC records prior to 7/2001 and current fixture (land) files. This agency will not do a tax lien search. Will not search real estate records. **Other Phone Numbers:** Assessor 423-663-2420; Treasurer 423-663-2598.

Sequatchie County

Register of Deeds, P.O. Box 174, Dunlap, TN 37327. Register of Deeds, R/E and UCC Recording 423-949-2512; Fax 423-949-6554.
Will not search UCC records. Will not search real estate records. **Other Phone Numbers:** Assessor 423-949-3534.

Sevier County

Register of Deeds, 125 Court Avenue, Courthouse Suite 209W, Sevierville, TN 37862. Register of Deeds, R/E and UCC Recording 865-453-2758; www.titlesearcher.com
Will not search UCC records. This agency will not do a tax lien search. Will not search real estate records. **Other Phone Numbers:** Assessor 865-453-3242; Appraiser/Auditor 865-453-3242; Elections 865-453-6985; Trustee 865-453-2767.

Shelby County

Register of Deeds, P.O. Box 3823, Memphis, TN 38173-0823. 901-545-4366; Fax 901-545-3837. http://www.assessor.shelby.tn.us/page1.cfm
Will search UCC records prior to 7/2001 and current fixture (land) files. Will not search real estate records. **Online Access:** Property Records. Property records on the assessor database are available free online at www.assessor.shelby.tn.us/page1.cfm. **Other Phone Numbers:** Assessor 901-576-4200.

Smith County

Register of Deeds, 122 Turner High Circle, Suite 113, Carthage, TN 37030. 615-735-1760; Fax 615-735-8263.
Will search UCC records prior to 7/2001 and current fixture (land) files. Will not search real estate records. **Other Phone Numbers:** Assessor 615-735-1750.

Stewart County

Register of Deeds, P.O. Box 57, Dover, TN 37058. 931-232-5990.

Will search UCC records prior to 7/2001 and current fixture (land) files. This agency will not do a tax lien search. Will not search real estate records. **Other Phone Numbers:** Assessor 931-232-5252; Trustee 931-232-7026.

Sullivan County (Blountville Office)

Register of Deeds, 3411 Hwy 126, #101, Blountville, TN 37617. Register of Deeds, R/E and UCC Recording 423-323-6420; Fax 423-279-2771.
Will not search UCC records. Will not search real estate records. **Other Phone Numbers:** Assessor 423-323-6455; Appraiser/Auditor 423-323-6455; Elections 423-323-6444; Vital Records 423-279-2777; Trustee 423-323-6464.

Sullivan County (Bristol Office)

Register of Deeds, 801 Anderson St., Bristol, TN 37620. 423-989-4370.
Will search UCC records prior to 7/2001 and current fixture (land) files. This agency will not do a tax lien search. Will not search real estate records. **Other Phone Numbers:** Assessor 423-323-6455; Treasurer 423-323-6464.

Sumner County

Register of Deeds, P.O. Box 299, Gallatin, TN 37066-0299. Register of Deeds, R/E and UCC Recording 615-452-3892; http://www.deeds.sumnertn.org
Will search UCC records prior to 7/2001 and current fixture (land) files. This agency will not do a tax lien search. Will not search real estate records. **Online Access:** Property, Recording. Online access to the Register of Deeds website requires a $25.00 set-up fee and $50.00 monthly user fee. For information, call the Registrar at 615-452-3892 or download the User Agreement from the website. **Other Phone Numbers:** Assessor 615-452-2412; Trustee 615-452-1260.

Tipton County

Register of Deeds, P.O. Box 644, Covington, TN 38019-0644. Register of Deeds, R/E and UCC Recording 901-476-0204; Fax 901-476-0227.
Will not search UCC records. This agency will not do a tax lien search. Will not search real estate records. **Other Phone Numbers:** Assessor 901-476-0213; Treasurer 901-476-0211; Elections 901-476-0223.

Trousdale County

Register of Deeds, 200 E. Main St. #8, Hartsville, TN 37074-1706. 615-374-2921; Fax 615-374-1100.
Will search UCC records prior to 7/2001 and current fixture (land) files. This agency will not do a tax lien search. Will not search real estate records. **Other Phone Numbers:** Assessor 615-374-2553.

Unicoi County

Register of Deeds, P.O. Box 305, Erwin, TN 37650-0305. 423-743-6104.
Will not search UCC records. This agency will not do a tax lien search. Will not search real estate records. **Other Phone Numbers:** Assessor 423-743-3801.

Union County

Register of Deeds, 901 Main St #108, Maynardville, TN 37807. 865-992-8024.
Will search UCC records prior to 7/2001 and current fixture (land) files. This agency will not do a tax lien search. Will not search real estate records. **Other Phone Numbers:** Assessor 865-992-3211; Trustee 865-992-5943.

Van Buren County

Register of Deeds, P.O. Box 9, Spencer, TN 38585. 931-946-7363; Fax 931-946-7363.
Will not search UCC records. Will not search real estate records. **Other Phone Numbers:** Assessor 931-946-2451.

Warren County

Register of Deeds, P.O. Box 128, McMinnville, TN 37111. Register of Deeds, R/E and UCC Recording 931-473-2926 UCC Recording: 931-473-8663; Fax 931-474-2114.
Will search UCC records prior to 7/2001 and current fixture (land) files. This agency will not do a tax lien search. Will not search real estate records. **Other Phone Numbers:** Assessor 931-473-3450.

Washington County

Register of Deeds, P.O. Box 5, Jonesboro, TN 37659. 423-753-1644; Fax 423-753-1743.
Will search UCC records prior to 7/2001 and current fixture (land) files. Will not search real estate records. **Other Phone Numbers:** Assessor 423-753-1670.

Wayne County

Register of Deeds, P.O. Box 465, Waynesboro, TN 38485. 931-722-5518; Fax 931-722-5518.
Will search UCC records prior to 7/2001 and current fixture (land) files. Will not search real estate records. **Other Phone Numbers:** Assessor 931-722-5282; Treasurer 931-722-3269; Appraiser/Auditor 931-722-5282; Elections 931-722-3517.

Weakley County

Register of Deeds, P.O. Box 45, Dresden, TN 38225-0045. 731-364-3646; Fax 731-364-5389.
Will search UCC records prior to 7/2001 and current fixture (land) files. Will not search real estate records. **Other Phone Numbers:** Assessor 731-364-3677; Trustee 731-364-3643.

White County

Register of Deeds, P.O. Box 86, Sparta, TN 38583-0086. 931-836-2817; Fax 931-836-8418.
Will search UCC records prior to 7/2001 and current fixture (land) files. Will not search real estate records. **Other Phone Numbers:** Assessor 931-836-3840.

Williamson County

Register of Deeds, P.O. Box 808, Franklin, TN 37065-0808. Register of Deeds, R/E and UCC Recording 615-790-5706; http://www.rod.williamson-tn.org
Will search UCC records. This agency will not do a tax lien search. Will not search real estate records. **Other Phone Numbers:** Assessor 615-790-5708; Treasurer 615-790-5709; Appraiser/Auditor 615-790-5708; Elections 615-790-5712.

Wilson County

Register of Deeds, P.O. Box 176, Lebanon, TN 37087-0176. Register of Deeds, R/E and UCC Recording 615-443-2611; Fax 615-443-3288. http://www.register.co.wilson.tn.us
Will not search UCC records. Will not search real estate records. **Online Access:** Real Estate, Liens, Recording. Online access to the Register of Deeds database requires a $10 registration fee then $25.00 per month usage fee. Includes indexes and images back to 11/1999, expanding to include 1994. **Other Phone Numbers:** Assessor 615-444-8661; Treasurer 615-444-0894.

Tennessee County Locator

You will usually be able to find the city name in the City/County Cross Reference below. In that case, it is a simple matter to determine the county from the cross reference. However, only the official US Postal Service city names are included in this index. There are an additional 40,000 place names that people use in their addresses. Therefore, we have also included a ZIP/City Cross Reference immediately following the City/County Cross Reference.

If you know the ZIP Code but the city name does not appear in the City/County Cross Reference index, look up the ZIP Code in the ZIP/City Cross Reference, find the city name, then look up the city name in the City/County Cross Reference. For example, you want to know the county for an address of Menands, NY 12204. There is no "Menands" in the City/County Cross Reference. The ZIP/City Cross Reference shows that ZIP Codes 12201-12288 are for the city of Albany. Looking back in the City/County Cross Reference, Albany is in Albany County.

City/County Cross Reference

ADAMS (37010) Robertson(61), Montgomery(39)
ADAMSVILLE (38310) McNairy(62), Hardin(38)
AFTON Greene
ALAMO Crockett
ALCOA Blount
ALEXANDRIA (37012) De Kalb(79), Wilson(11), Smith(10)
ALLARDT Fentress
ALLONS (38541) Overton(67), Clay(33)
ALLRED Overton
ALPINE (38543) Overton(82), Pickett(18)
ALTAMONT Grundy
ANDERSONVILLE (37705) Anderson(69), Union(31)
ANTIOCH Davidson
APISON Hamilton
ARDMORE (38449) Giles(79), Lincoln(21)
ARLINGTON (38002) Shelby(82), Fayette(18)
ARNOLD AFB Coffee
ARRINGTON (37014) Williamson(60), Rutherford(40)
ARTHUR Claiborne
ASHLAND CITY (37015) Cheatham(94), Davidson(4), Montgomery(2)
ATHENS McMinn
ATOKA (38004) Tipton(94), Shelby(6)
ATWOOD (38220) Carroll(95), Gibson(5)
AUBURNTOWN (37016) Cannon(70), Wilson(31)
BAKEWELL Hamilton
BATH SPRINGS Decatur
BAXTER (38544) Putnam(92), De Kalb(8)
BEAN STATION Grainger
BEECH BLUFF (38313) Madison(53), Chester(25), Henderson(22)
BEECHGROVE (37018) Coffee(95), Bedford(5)
BEERSHEBA SPRINGS Grundy
BELFAST Marshall
BELL BUCKLE (37020) Bedford(78), Rutherford(22)
BELLS (38006) Crockett(83), Haywood(12), Madison(5)
BELVIDERE Franklin
BENTON Polk
BETHEL SPRINGS (38315) McNairy(67), Chester(33)
BETHPAGE (37022) Sumner(74), Trousdale(24), Macon(2)
BIG ROCK Stewart
BIG SANDY Benton
BIRCHWOOD (37308) Hamilton(83), Meigs(17)
BLAINE (37709) Union(57), Grainger(40), Knox(3)
BLOOMINGTON SPRINGS (38545) Jackson(62), Putnam(39)
BLOUNTVILLE Sullivan
BLUFF CITY Sullivan
BOGOTA Dyer

BOLIVAR Hardeman
BON AQUA (37025) Hickman(78), Dickson(19), Williamson(3)
BRADEN Fayette
BRADFORD Gibson
BRADYVILLE (37026) Cannon(90), Coffee(10)
BRENTWOOD (37027) Williamson(79), Davidson(21)
BRENTWOOD Williamson
BRICEVILLE Anderson
BRIGHTON (38011) Tipton(98), Shelby(3)
BRISTOL Sullivan
BROWNSVILLE Haywood
BRUCETON (38317) Carroll(95), Benton(5)
BRUNSWICK Shelby
BRUSH CREEK Smith
BUCHANAN Henry
BUENA VISTA (38318) Carroll(97), Benton(3)
BUFFALO VALLEY (38548) Putnam(77), Smith(23)
BULLS GAP (37711) Greene(61), Hawkins(35), Hamblen(4)
BUMPUS MILLS Stewart
BURLISON Tipton
BURNS Dickson
BUTLER (37640) Johnson(66), Carter(34)
BYBEE Cocke
BYRDSTOWN (38549) Pickett(99), Fentress(1)
CALHOUN (37309) McMinn(95), Polk(5)
CAMDEN Benton
CAMPAIGN Warren
CARTHAGE Smith
CARYVILLE Campbell
CASTALIAN SPRINGS (37031) Sumner(59), Trousdale(42)
CEDAR GROVE Carroll
CEDAR HILL (37032) Robertson(94), Cheatham(5), Montgomery(1)
CELINA (38551) Clay(99), Jackson(1)
CENTERVILLE Hickman
CHAPEL HILL (37034) Marshall(85), Bedford(15)
CHAPMANSBORO (37035) Cheatham(98), Montgomery(1)
CHARLESTON (37310) Bradley(98), Polk(2)
CHARLOTTE (37036) Dickson(93), Cheatham(7)
CHATTANOOGA (37405) Hamilton(89), Marion(11)
CHATTANOOGA (37419) Hamilton(86), Marion(14)
CHATTANOOGA Hamilton
CHESTNUT MOUND Smith
CHEWALLA McNairy
CHRISTIANA Rutherford
CHUCKEY (37641) Greene(89), Washington(11)
CHURCH HILL Hawkins

CLAIRFIELD (37715) Claiborne(84), Campbell(16)
CLARKRANGE Fentress
CLARKSBURG Carroll
CLARKSVILLE Montgomery
CLEVELAND Bradley
CLIFTON (38425) Wayne(68), Hardin(27), Perry(5)
CLINTON Anderson
COALFIELD Morgan
COALMONT Grundy
COKERCREEK Monroe
COLLEGE GROVE (37046) Williamson(85), Rutherford(14)
COLLEGEDALE Hamilton
COLLIERVILLE (38017) Shelby(79), Fayette(22)
COLLIERVILLE Shelby
COLLINWOOD Wayne
COLUMBIA Maury
COMO Henry
CONASAUGA Polk
COOKEVILLE (38501) Putnam(93), Jackson(7)
COOKEVILLE (38506) Putnam(75), Overton(19), White(6)
COOKEVILLE Putnam
COPPERHILL Polk
CORDOVA Shelby
CORNERSVILLE (37047) Marshall(79), Giles(19), Lincoln(1)
CORRYTON (37721) Knox(76), Union(24)
COSBY (37722) Cocke(84), Sevier(17)
COTTAGE GROVE (38224) Henry(96), Weakley(5)
COTTONTOWN (37048) Sumner(90), Robertson(10)
COUNCE Hardin
COVINGTON Tipton
COWAN Franklin
CRAB ORCHARD Cumberland
CRAWFORD Overton
CROCKETT MILLS Crockett
CROSS PLAINS Robertson
CROSSVILLE Cumberland
CRUMP Hardin
CULLEOKA (38451) Maury(88), Marshall(12)
CUMBERLAND CITY (37050) Stewart(75), Montgomery(16), Houston(10)
CUMBERLAND FURNACE (37051) Dickson(63), Montgomery(37)
CUMBERLAND GAP Claiborne
CUNNINGHAM (37052) Montgomery(98), Dickson(2)
CYPRESS INN Wayne
DANDRIDGE (37725) Jefferson(98), Sevier(2)
DARDEN Henderson
DAYTON Rhea
DECATUR (37322) Meigs(94), McMinn(6)
DECATURVILLE (38329) Decatur(97), Henderson(3)

DECHERD (37324) Franklin(97), Grundy(3)
DEER LODGE (37726) Morgan(85), Fentress(16)
DEL RIO Cocke
DELANO (37325) Polk(71), McMinn(26), Hamilton(3)
DELLROSE Lincoln
DENMARK Madison
DENVER Humphreys
DICKSON (37055) Dickson(99), Hickman(1)
DICKSON Dickson
DIXON SPRINGS (37057) Trousdale(49), Macon(28), Smith(23)
DOVER Stewart
DOWELLTOWN De Kalb
DOYLE (38559) White(91), Van Buren(9)
DRESDEN Weakley
DRUMMONDS Tipton
DUCK RIVER Hickman
DUCKTOWN Polk
DUFF Campbell
DUKEDOM Weakley
DUNLAP (37327) Sequatchie(93), Bledsoe(7)
DYER Gibson
DYERSBURG Dyer
EADS (38028) Fayette(60), Shelby(40)
EAGAN Claiborne
EAGLEVILLE (37060) Rutherford(87), Bedford(8), Williamson(5)
EATON Gibson
EIDSON (37731) Hawkins(92), Hancock(8)
ELBRIDGE Obion
ELGIN Scott
ELIZABETHTON Carter
ELKTON Giles
ELLENDALE Shelby
ELMWOOD Smith
ELORA (37328) Lincoln(86), Franklin(13)
ENGLEWOOD (37329) McMinn(92), Monroe(8)
ENVILLE (38332) Chester(90), McNairy(10)
ERIN (37061) Houston(87), Humphreys(12), Montgomery(1)
ERWIN (37650) Unicoi(94), Washington(6)
ESTILL SPRINGS (37330) Franklin(94), Coffee(6)
ETHRIDGE (38456) Lawrence(81), Giles(19)
ETOWAH McMinn
EVA Benton
EVENSVILLE Rhea
FAIRVIEW (37062) Williamson(98), Dickson(2)
FALL BRANCH (37656) Greene(50), Washington(43), Sullivan(8)
FARNER (37333) Polk(97), Lincoln(3)
FAYETTEVILLE Lincoln
FINGER (38334) McNairy(83), Chester(17)
FINLEY Dyer
FIVE POINTS Lawrence
FLAG POND Unicoi

FLINTVILLE (37335) Lincoln(98), Franklin(2)
FOSTERVILLE Rutherford
FOWLKES Dyer
FRANKEWING (38459) Giles(59), Lincoln(41)
FRANKLIN (37064) Williamson(99), Davidson(1)
FRANKLIN Williamson
FRIENDSHIP (38034) Crockett(80), Dyer(20)
FRIENDSVILLE (37737) Blount(93), Loudon(7)
FRUITVALE Crockett
GADSDEN Crockett
GAINESBORO Jackson
GALLATIN Sumner
GALLAWAY Fayette
GATES (38037) Lauderdale(72), Haywood(28)
GATLINBURG Sevier
GEORGETOWN (37336) Bradley(61), Hamilton(31), Meigs(8)
GERMANTOWN Shelby
GIBSON Gibson
GLADEVILLE Wilson
GLEASON (99999) Weakley(99), Henry(1)
GOODLETTSVILLE (37072) Davidson(61), Sumner(29), Robertson(10)
GOODLETTSVILLE Davidson
GOODSPRING Giles
GORDONSVILLE Smith
GRAND JUNCTION (38039) Hardeman(73), Fayette(27)
GRANDVIEW (37337) Rhea(53), Cumberland(40), Pickett(8)
GRANVILLE (38564) Jackson(89), Putnam(11)
GRAYSVILLE (37338) Rhea(64), Sequatchie(18), Bledsoe(12), Hamilton(6)
GREENBACK (37742) Loudon(73), Blount(27)
GREENBRIER Robertson
GREENEVILLE Greene
GREENFIELD Weakley
GRIMSLEY Fentress
GRUETLI LAAGER Grundy
GUILD Marion
GUYS McNairy
HALLS (38040) Lauderdale(83), Crockett(12), Dyer(5)
HAMPSHIRE (38461) Maury(60), Lewis(38), Hickman(2)
HAMPTON Carter
HARRIMAN (37748) Roane(89), Morgan(11)
HARRISON Hamilton
HARROGATE Claiborne
HARTFORD Cocke
HARTSVILLE (37074) Trousdale(86), Macon(14)
HEISKELL (37754) Anderson(64), Knox(30), Union(6)
HELENWOOD Scott
HENDERSON (38340) Chester(91), Hardeman(9)
HENDERSONVILLE Sumner
HENNING Lauderdale
HENRY Henry
HERMITAGE (37076) Davidson(96), Wilson(4)
HICKMAN (38567) Smith(96), De Kalb(4)
HICKORY VALLEY (38042) Hardeman(98), Fayette(2)
HICKORY WITHE Fayette
HILHAM (38568) Overton(67), Jackson(18), Clay(15)
HILLSBORO Coffee
HIXSON Hamilton
HOHENWALD Lewis

HOLLADAY (38341) Benton(93), Decatur(4), Henderson(3)
HOLLOW ROCK Carroll
HORNBEAK Obion
HORNSBY (38044) Hardeman(89), McNairy(8), Chester(4)
HUMBOLDT (38343) Gibson(79), Crockett(15), Madison(7)
HUNTINGDON Carroll
HUNTLAND Franklin
HUNTSVILLE Scott
HURON (99999) Henderson(99), Chester(1)
HURRICANE MILLS Humphreys
IDLEWILD Gibson
INDIAN MOUND (37079) Stewart(81), Montgomery(20)
IRON CITY (38463) Lawrence(62), Wayne(38)
ISABELLA Polk
JACKS CREEK Chester
JACKSBORO Campbell
JACKSON (38305) Madison(97), Carroll(3)
JACKSON Madison
JAMESTOWN Fentress
JASPER Marion
JEFFERSON CITY Jefferson
JELLICO Campbell
JOELTON (37080) Davidson(59), Cheatham(41)
JOHNSON CITY (37601) Washington(73), Carter(27)
JOHNSON CITY Washington
JONESBOROUGH Washington
KELSO Lincoln
KENTON (38233) Gibson(72), Obion(28)
KINGSPORT (37660) Sullivan(96), Hawkins(4)
KINGSPORT (37663) Sullivan(98), Washington(2)
KINGSPORT Sullivan
KINGSTON Roane
KINGSTON SPRINGS Cheatham
KNOXVILLE (37931) Knox(97), Anderson(3)
KNOXVILLE Knox
KODAK (37764) Sevier(84), Knox(12), Jefferson(4)
KYLES FORD Hancock
LA FOLLETTE Campbell
LA GRANGE Fayette
LA VERGNE (37086) Rutherford(97), Davidson(3)
LA VERGNE Rutherford
LACONIA Fayette
LAFAYETTE Macon
LAKE CITY (37769) Anderson(79), Campbell(21)
LANCASTER (38569) Smith(77), De Kalb(24)
LANCING Morgan
LASCASSAS (37085) Rutherford(76), Wilson(24)
LAUREL BLOOMERY Johnson
LAVINIA Carroll
LAWRENCEBURG (38464) Lawrence(94), Giles(3), Wayne(3)
LEBANON (37087) Wilson(97), Trousdale(3)
LEBANON (37090) Wilson(98), Smith(2)
LEBANON Wilson
LENOIR CITY (37771) Loudon(91), Roane(9)
LENOIR CITY Loudon
LENOX Dyer
LEOMA (38468) Lawrence(90), Giles(11)
LEWISBURG (37091) Marshall(96), Bedford(4)
LEXINGTON Henderson
LIBERTY (37095) De Kalb(78), Cannon(18), Wilson(4)

LIMESTONE (37681) Greene(56), Washington(44)
LINDEN (37096) Perry(98), Wayne(1)
LIVINGSTON Overton
LOBELVILLE (37097) Perry(95), Humphreys(5)
LONE MOUNTAIN Claiborne
LOOKOUT MOUNTAIN Hamilton
LORETTO Lawrence
LOUDON (37774) Loudon(94), Roane(5)
LOUISVILLE Blount
LOWLAND Hamblen
LUPTON CITY Hamilton
LURAY Chester
LUTTRELL (37779) Union(92), Knox(6), Grainger(2)
LUTTS Wayne
LYLES Hickman
LYNCHBURG (37352) Moore(97), Franklin(3)
LYNNVILLE (38472) Giles(93), Marshall(6), Maury(1)
MACON Fayette
MADISON Davidson
MADISONVILLE (37354) Monroe(99), McMinn(1)
MANCHESTER Coffee
MANSFIELD Henry
MARTIN Weakley
MARYVILLE (37801) Blount(89), Monroe(11)
MARYVILLE (37803) Blount(99), Monroe(2)
MARYVILLE Blount
MASCOT (37806) Knox(97), Grainger(3)
MASON (38049) Fayette(78), Tipton(22)
MAURY CITY Crockett
MAYNARDVILLE (99999) Union(99), Knox(1)
MC DONALD (37353) Bradley(89), Hamilton(11)
MC EWEN (37101) Humphreys(97), Hickman(3)
MC KENZIE (38201) Carroll(78), Weakley(12), Henry(10)
MC LEMORESVILLE Carroll
MC MINNVILLE (37110) Warren(99), Cannon(1)
MC MINNVILLE Warren
MEDINA (38355) Madison(51), Gibson(49)
MEDON (38356) Madison(58), Hardeman(30), Chester(12)
MEMPHIS Shelby
MERCER (38392) Madison(69), Hardeman(31)
MICHIE McNairy
MIDDLETON Hardeman
MIDWAY Greene
MILAN Gibson
MILLEDGEVILLE (38359) Chester(75), McNairy(25)
MILLIGAN COLLEGE Carter
MILLINGTON (38053) Shelby(83), Tipton(17)
MILLINGTON Shelby
MILTON (37118) Rutherford(67), Wilson(26), Cannon(8)
MINOR HILL Giles
MISTON Dyer
MITCHELLVILLE Sumner
MOHAWK Greene
MONROE (38573) Overton(67), Pickett(33)
MONTEAGLE (37356) Marion(85), Grundy(15)
MONTEREY (38574) Putnam(67), Overton(18), Cumberland(14), Fentress(2)
MOORESBURG (37811) Hawkins(99), Grainger(2)
MORLEY Campbell
MORRIS CHAPEL (38361) Hardin(91), McNairy(9)

MORRISON (37357) Warren(57), Coffee(30), Cannon(11), Grundy(2)
MORRISTOWN Hamblen
MOSCOW Fayette
MOSHEIM Greene
MOSS Clay
MOUNT CARMEL Hawkins
MOUNT JULIET (37122) Wilson(96), Rutherford(3)
MOUNT JULIET Wilson
MOUNT PLEASANT (38474) Maury(94), Lewis(3), Giles(2)
MOUNT VERNON Monroe
MOUNTAIN CITY Johnson
MOUNTAIN HOME Washington
MULBERRY Lincoln
MUNFORD Tipton
MURFREESBORO Rutherford
NASHVILLE (37221) Davidson(97), Williamson(3)
NASHVILLE Davidson
NEW JOHNSONVILLE Humphreys
NEW MARKET Jefferson
NEW TAZEWELL (37825) Claiborne(88), Union(12)
NEW TAZEWELL Claiborne
NEWBERN Dyer
NEWCOMB Campbell
NEWPORT Cocke
NIOTA (37826) McMinn(99), Meigs(1)
NOLENSVILLE (37135) Williamson(90), Rutherford(6), Davidson(5)
NORENE Wilson
NORMANDY (37360) Coffee(53), Bedford(41), Moore(5)
NORRIS Anderson
NUNNELLY Hickman
OAK RIDGE (37830) Anderson(93), Roane(6), Knox(2)
OAK RIDGE Anderson
OAKDALE Morgan
OAKFIELD Madison
OAKLAND Fayette
OBION (38240) Obion(94), Dyer(6)
OCOEE Polk
OLD HICKORY (37138) Davidson(69), Wilson(31)
OLDFORT (37362) Bradley(70), Polk(30)
OLIVEHILL (38475) Hardin(85), Wayne(15)
OLIVER SPRINGS (37840) Morgan(47), Roane(34), Anderson(19)
ONEIDA Scott
ONLY Hickman
OOLTEWAH Hamilton
ORLINDA Robertson
OZONE Cumberland
PALL MALL (38577) Pickett(55), Fentress(45)
PALMER (37365) Grundy(92), Sequatchie(7), Marion(1)
PALMERSVILLE Weakley
PALMYRA Montgomery
PARIS (38242) Henry(99), Weakley(1)
PARROTTSVILLE Cocke
PARSONS Decatur
PEGRAM (37143) Cheatham(86), Davidson(14)
PELHAM Grundy
PETERSBURG (37144) Lincoln(53), Marshall(36), Bedford(9), Moore(2), Giles(1)
PETROS Morgan
PHILADELPHIA (37846) Loudon(58), Roane(25), Monroe(15), McMinn(2)
PICKWICK DAM Hardin
PIGEON FORGE Sevier
PIKEVILLE (37367) Bledsoe(90), Cumberland(10)
PINEY FLATS Sullivan
PINSON (38366) Madison(51), Chester(50)
PIONEER (37847) Scott(66), Campbell(35)
PLEASANT HILL Cumberland

PLEASANT SHADE (37145) Smith(73), Macon(16), Jackson(12)
PLEASANT VIEW (37146) Cheatham(69), Robertson(31)
PLEASANTVILLE Hickman
POCAHONTAS (38061) Hardeman(63), McNairy(37)
PORTLAND (37148) Sumner(93), Robertson(7)
POWDER SPRINGS (37848) Grainger(61), Union(39)
POWELL (37849) Knox(82), Anderson(18)
PRIMM SPRINGS (38476) Hickman(38), Williamson(37), Maury(25)
PROSPECT Giles
PRUDEN Claiborne
PULASKI Giles
PURYEAR Henry
QUEBECK White
RAMER McNairy
READYVILLE (37149) Rutherford(66), Cannon(34)
REAGAN (38368) Henderson(79), Chester(21)
RED BOILING SPRINGS (37150) Macon(76), Clay(23)
RELIANCE (37369) Monroe(54), Polk(45), McMinn(1)
RICEVILLE McMinn
RICKMAN Overton
RIDDLETON Smith
RIDGELY (38080) Lake(78), Dyer(17), Obion(5)
RIDGETOP Robertson
RIPLEY (38063) Lauderdale(94), Haywood(6)
RIVES Obion
ROAN MOUNTAIN Carter
ROBBINS (37852) Scott(92), Morgan(8)
ROCK ISLAND (38581) Warren(90), Van Buren(9)
ROCKFORD (37853) Blount(95), Knox(5)
ROCKVALE (37153) Rutherford(91), Bedford(9)
ROCKWOOD (37854) Roane(70), Cumberland(19), Morgan(11)
ROGERSVILLE Hawkins
ROSSVILLE Fayette
RUGBY (37733) Morgan(67), Knox(33)
RUSSELLVILLE Hamblen
RUTHERFORD Gibson
RUTLEDGE Grainger
SAINT ANDREWS Franklin
SAINT BETHLEHEM Montgomery
SAINT JOSEPH Lawrence

SALE CREEK Hamilton
SALTILLO Hardin
SAMBURG Obion
SANTA FE Maury
SARDIS (38371) Hardin(66), Henderson(35)
SAULSBURY Hardeman
SAVANNAH Hardin
SCOTTS HILL (38374) Decatur(98), Henderson(2)
SELMER McNairy
SEQUATCHIE Marion
SEVIERVILLE (37876) Sevier(98), Jefferson(2)
SEVIERVILLE Sevier
SEWANEE Franklin
SEYMOUR (37865) Sevier(80), Blount(20)
SHADY VALLEY Johnson
SHARON Weakley
SHARPS CHAPEL Union
SHAWANEE Claiborne
SHELBYVILLE Bedford
SHERWOOD Franklin
SHILOH (38376) Hardin(83), McNairy(17)
SIGNAL MOUNTAIN (37377) Hamilton(94), Sequatchie(6)
SILERTON (38377) Hardeman(67), Chester(33)
SILVER POINT (38582) Putnam(77), De Kalb(23)
SLAYDEN Dickson
SMARTT Warren
SMITHVILLE (37166) De Kalb(89), Warren(10), Cannon(1)
SMYRNA Rutherford
SNEEDVILLE (37869) Hancock(75), Hawkins(20), Claiborne(5)
SODDY DAISY (37379) Hamilton(97), Sequatchie(3)
SODDY DAISY Hamilton
SOMERVILLE Fayette
SOUTH FULTON (38257) Obion(94), Weakley(6)
SOUTH PITTSBURG Marion
SOUTHSIDE Montgomery
SPARTA (38583) White(88), De Kalb(6), Putnam(3), Cumberland(2)
SPEEDWELL (37870) Claiborne(76), Campbell(12), Union(12)
SPENCER Van Buren
SPRING CITY Rhea
SPRING CREEK Madison
SPRING HILL (37174) Maury(80), Williamson(19)

SPRINGFIELD (37172) Robertson(99), Sumner(1)
SPRINGVILLE Henry
STANTON (38069) Haywood(92), Fayette(9)
STANTONVILLE McNairy
STEWART (37175) Stewart(51), Houston(49)
STRAWBERRY PLAINS (37871) Knox(48), Jefferson(38), Sevier(14)
SUGAR TREE (38380) Decatur(58), Benton(42)
SUMMERTOWN (38483) Lawrence(71), Lewis(23), Giles(4), Maury(2)
SUMMITVILLE Coffee
SUNBRIGHT (37872) Morgan(95), Scott(5)
SURGOINSVILLE Hawkins
SWEETWATER (37874) Monroe(88), Loudon(6), McMinn(6)
TAFT Lincoln
TALBOTT (37877) Hamblen(60), Jefferson(40)
TALLASSEE Blount
TAZEWELL (37879) Claiborne(99), Hancock(1)
TELFORD Washington
TELLICO PLAINS Monroe
TEN MILE (37880) Roane(67), Meigs(33)
TENNESSEE RIDGE (37178) Houston(53), Stewart(48)
THOMPSONS STATION Williamson
THORN HILL (37881) Grainger(88), Hancock(11)
TIGRETT Dyer
TIPTON Tipton
TIPTONVILLE Lake
TOONE Hardeman
TOWNSEND Blount
TRACY CITY Grundy
TRADE Johnson
TREADWAY Hancock
TRENTON Gibson
TREZEVANT Carroll
TRIMBLE (38259) Dyer(88), Obion(8), Gibson(4)
TROY Obion
TULLAHOMA (37388) Coffee(77), Franklin(19), Moore(3), Bedford(1)
TURTLETOWN Polk
UNICOI Unicoi
UNION CITY Obion
UNIONVILLE (37180) Bedford(94), Rutherford(5)
VANLEER (37181) Dickson(90), Houston(10)

VIOLA Warren
VONORE (37885) Monroe(97), Loudon(3)
WALLAND Blount
WALLING White
WARTBURG Morgan
WARTRACE (37183) Bedford(77), Coffee(18), Moore(5)
WASHBURN (37888) Grainger(72), Union(28)
WATAUGA (37694) Carter(76), Sullivan(19), Washington(5)
WATERTOWN (37184) Wilson(97), Smith(3)
WATTS BAR DAM Rhea
WAVERLY Humphreys
WAYNESBORO (38485) Wayne(98), Lewis(3)
WESTMORELAND (37186) Sumner(59), Macon(41)
WESTPOINT (38486) Lawrence(83), Wayne(17)
WESTPORT (38387) Carroll(91), Benton(9)
WHITE BLUFF (37187) Dickson(93), Cheatham(7)
WHITE HOUSE (37188) Robertson(57), Sumner(43)
WHITE PINE (37890) Jefferson(92), Hamblen(8)
WHITES CREEK Davidson
WHITESBURG (37891) Hamblen(68), Hawkins(32)
WHITESIDE Marion
WHITEVILLE (38075) Hardeman(73), Haywood(14), Fayette(13)
WHITLEYVILLE (38588) Jackson(77), Clay(16), Macon(7)
WHITWELL (37397) Marion(96), Sequatchie(4)
WILDER Fentress
WILDERSVILLE Henderson
WILLIAMSPORT (38487) Maury(68), Hickman(32)
WILLISTON Fayette
WINCHESTER Franklin
WINFIELD Scott
WINONA Scott
WOODBURY (37190) Cannon(98), Warren(2)
WOODLAND MILLS Obion
WOODLAWN Montgomery
WYNNBURG Lake
YORKVILLE Gibson
YUMA (38390) Carroll(83), Henderson(17)

ZIP/City Cross Reference

ZIP	City		ZIP	City		ZIP	City		ZIP	City
37010-37010	ADAMS		37035-37035	CHAPMANSBORO		37070-37070	GOODLETTSVILLE		37101-37101	MC EWEN
37011-37011	ANTIOCH		37036-37036	CHARLOTTE		37071-37071	GLADEVILLE		37110-37111	MC MINNVILLE
37012-37012	ALEXANDRIA		37037-37037	CHRISTIANA		37072-37072	GOODLETTSVILLE		37115-37116	MADISON
37013-37013	ANTIOCH		37040-37044	CLARKSVILLE		37073-37073	GREENBRIER		37118-37118	MILTON
37014-37014	ARRINGTON		37046-37046	COLLEGE GROVE		37074-37074	HARTSVILLE		37119-37119	MITCHELLVILLE
37015-37015	ASHLAND CITY		37047-37047	CORNERSVILLE		37075-37075	HENDERSONVILLE		37121-37122	MOUNT JULIET
37016-37016	AUBURNTOWN		37048-37048	COTTONTOWN		37076-37076	HERMITAGE		37127-37133	MURFREESBORO
37018-37018	BEECHGROVE		37049-37049	CROSS PLAINS		37077-37077	HENDERSONVILLE		37134-37134	NEW JOHNSONVILLE
37019-37019	BELFAST		37050-37050	CUMBERLAND CITY		37078-37078	HURRICANE MILLS		37135-37135	NOLENSVILLE
37020-37020	BELL BUCKLE		37051-37051	CUMBERLAND FURNACE		37079-37079	INDIAN MOUND		37136-37136	NORENE
37022-37022	BETHPAGE		37052-37052	CUNNINGHAM		37080-37080	JOELTON		37137-37137	NUNNELLY
37023-37023	BIG ROCK		37054-37054	DENVER		37082-37082	KINGSTON SPRINGS		37138-37138	OLD HICKORY
37024-37024	BRENTWOOD		37055-37056	DICKSON		37083-37083	LAFAYETTE		37140-37140	ONLY
37025-37025	BON AQUA		37057-37057	DIXON SPRINGS		37085-37085	LASCASSAS		37141-37141	ORLINDA
37026-37026	BRADYVILLE		37058-37058	DOVER		37086-37086	LA VERGNE		37142-37142	PALMYRA
37027-37027	BRENTWOOD		37059-37059	DOWELLTOWN		37087-37088	LEBANON		37143-37143	PEGRAM
37028-37028	BUMPUS MILLS		37060-37060	EAGLEVILLE		37089-37089	LA VERGNE		37144-37144	PETERSBURG
37029-37029	BURNS		37061-37061	ERIN		37090-37090	LEBANON		37145-37145	PLEASANT SHADE
37030-37030	CARTHAGE		37062-37062	FAIRVIEW		37091-37091	LEWISBURG		37146-37146	PLEASANT VIEW
37031-37031	CASTALIAN SPRINGS		37063-37063	FOSTERVILLE		37095-37095	LIBERTY		37147-37147	PLEASANTVILLE
37032-37032	CEDAR HILL		37064-37065	FRANKLIN		37096-37096	LINDEN		37148-37148	PORTLAND
37033-37033	CENTERVILLE		37066-37066	GALLATIN		37097-37097	LOBELVILLE		37149-37149	READYVILLE
37034-37034	CHAPEL HILL		37067-37069	FRANKLIN		37098-37098	LYLES		37150-37150	RED BOILING SPRINGS

ZIP	Place	ZIP	Place	ZIP	Place	ZIP	Place
37151-37151	RIDDLETON	37360-37360	NORMANDY	37726-37726	DEER LODGE	37881-37881	THORN HILL
37152-37152	RIDGETOP	37361-37361	OCOEE	37727-37727	DEL RIO	37882-37882	TOWNSEND
37153-37153	ROCKVALE	37362-37362	OLDFORT	37729-37729	DUFF	37885-37885	VONORE
37155-37155	SAINT BETHLEHEM	37363-37363	OOLTEWAH	37730-37730	EAGAN	37886-37886	WALLAND
37160-37162	SHELBYVILLE	37364-37364	CLEVELAND	37731-37731	EIDSON	37887-37887	WARTBURG
37165-37165	SLAYDEN	37365-37365	PALMER	37732-37732	ELGIN	37888-37888	WASHBURN
37166-37166	SMITHVILLE	37366-37366	PELHAM	37733-37733	RUGBY	37890-37890	WHITE PINE
37167-37167	SMYRNA	37367-37367	PIKEVILLE	37737-37737	FRIENDSVILLE	37891-37891	WHITESBURG
37171-37171	SOUTHSIDE	37369-37369	RELIANCE	37738-37738	GATLINBURG	37892-37892	WINFIELD
37172-37172	SPRINGFIELD	37370-37370	RICEVILLE	37742-37742	GREENBACK	37893-37893	WINONA
37174-37174	SPRING HILL	37371-37371	ATHENS	37743-37745	GREENEVILLE	37901-37999	KNOXVILLE
37175-37175	STEWART	37372-37372	SAINT ANDREWS	37748-37748	HARRIMAN	38001-38001	ALAMO
37178-37178	TENNESSEE RIDGE	37373-37373	SALE CREEK	37752-37752	HARROGATE	38002-38002	ARLINGTON
37179-37179	THOMPSONS STATION	37374-37374	SEQUATCHIE	37753-37753	HARTFORD	38004-38004	ATOKA
37180-37180	UNIONVILLE	37375-37375	SEWANEE	37754-37754	HEISKELL	38006-38006	BELLS
37181-37181	VANLEER	37376-37376	SHERWOOD	37755-37755	HELENWOOD	38007-38007	BOGOTA
37183-37183	WARTRACE	37377-37377	SIGNAL MOUNTAIN	37756-37756	HUNTSVILLE	38008-38008	BOLIVAR
37184-37184	WATERTOWN	37378-37378	SMARTT	37757-37757	JACKSBORO	38010-38010	BRADEN
37185-37185	WAVERLY	37379-37379	SODDY DAISY	37760-37760	JEFFERSON CITY	38011-38011	BRIGHTON
37186-37186	WESTMORELAND	37380-37380	SOUTH PITTSBURG	37762-37762	JELLICO	38012-38012	BROWNSVILLE
37187-37187	WHITE BLUFF	37381-37381	SPRING CITY	37763-37763	KINGSTON	38014-38014	BRUNSWICK
37188-37188	WHITE HOUSE	37382-37382	SUMMITVILLE	37764-37764	KODAK	38015-38015	BURLISON
37189-37189	WHITES CREEK	37383-37383	SEWANEE	37765-37765	KYLES FORD	38017-38017	COLLIERVILLE
37190-37190	WOODBURY	37384-37384	SODDY DAISY	37766-37766	LA FOLLETTE	38018-38018	CORDOVA
37191-37191	WOODLAWN	37385-37385	TELLICO PLAINS	37769-37769	LAKE CITY	38019-38019	COVINGTON
37201-37250	NASHVILLE	37387-37387	TRACY CITY	37770-37770	LANCING	38021-38021	CROCKETT MILLS
37301-37301	ALTAMONT	37388-37388	TULLAHOMA	37771-37772	LENOIR CITY	38023-38023	DRUMMONDS
37302-37302	APISON	37389-37389	ARNOLD AFB	37773-37773	LONE MOUNTAIN	38024-38025	DYERSBURG
37303-37303	ATHENS	37391-37391	TURTLETOWN	37774-37774	LOUDON	38027-38027	COLLIERVILLE
37304-37304	BAKEWELL	37394-37394	VIOLA	37777-37777	LOUISVILLE	38028-38028	EADS
37305-37305	BEERSHEBA SPRINGS	37395-37395	WATTS BAR DAM	37778-37778	LOWLAND	38029-38029	ELLENDALE
37306-37306	BELVIDERE	37396-37396	WHITESIDE	37779-37779	LUTTRELL	38030-38030	FINLEY
37307-37307	BENTON	37397-37397	WHITWELL	37801-37804	MARYVILLE	38033-38033	FOWLKES
37308-37308	BIRCHWOOD	37398-37398	WINCHESTER	37806-37806	MASCOT	38034-38034	FRIENDSHIP
37309-37309	CALHOUN	37401-37499	CHATTANOOGA	37807-37807	MAYNARDVILLE	38036-38036	GALLAWAY
37310-37310	CHARLESTON	37501-37501	MEMPHIS	37809-37809	MIDWAY	38037-38037	GATES
37311-37312	CLEVELAND	37601-37615	JOHNSON CITY	37810-37810	MOHAWK	38039-38039	GRAND JUNCTION
37313-37313	COALMONT	37616-37616	AFTON	37811-37811	MOORESBURG	38040-38040	HALLS
37314-37314	COKERCREEK	37617-37617	BLOUNTVILLE	37813-37816	MORRISTOWN	38041-38041	HENNING
37315-37315	COLLEGEDALE	37618-37618	BLUFF CITY	37818-37818	MOSHEIM	38042-38042	HICKORY VALLEY
37316-37316	CONASAUGA	37620-37625	BRISTOL	37819-37819	NEWCOMB	38043-38043	HICKORY WITHE
37317-37317	COPPERHILL	37640-37640	BUTLER	37820-37820	NEW MARKET	38044-38044	HORNSBY
37318-37318	COWAN	37641-37641	CHUCKEY	37821-37822	NEWPORT	38045-38045	LACONIA
37320-37320	CLEVELAND	37642-37642	CHURCH HILL	37824-37825	NEW TAZEWELL	38046-38046	LA GRANGE
37321-37321	DAYTON	37643-37644	ELIZABETHTON	37826-37826	NIOTA	38047-38047	LENOX
37322-37322	DECATUR	37645-37645	MOUNT CARMEL	37828-37828	NORRIS	38048-38048	MACON
37323-37323	CLEVELAND	37650-37650	ERWIN	37829-37829	OAKDALE	38049-38049	MASON
37324-37324	DECHERD	37656-37656	FALL BRANCH	37830-37831	OAK RIDGE	38050-38050	MAURY CITY
37325-37325	DELANO	37657-37657	FLAG POND	37840-37840	OLIVER SPRINGS	38052-38052	MIDDLETON
37326-37326	DUCKTOWN	37658-37658	HAMPTON	37841-37841	ONEIDA	38053-38054	MILLINGTON
37327-37327	DUNLAP	37659-37659	JONESBOROUGH	37842-37842	OZONE	38056-38056	MISTON
37328-37328	ELORA	37660-37669	KINGSPORT	37843-37843	PARROTTSVILLE	38057-38057	MOSCOW
37329-37329	ENGLEWOOD	37680-37680	LAUREL BLOOMERY	37845-37845	PETROS	38058-38058	MUNFORD
37330-37330	ESTILL SPRINGS	37681-37681	LIMESTONE	37846-37846	PHILADELPHIA	38059-38059	NEWBERN
37331-37331	ETOWAH	37682-37682	MILLIGAN COLLEGE	37847-37847	PIONEER	38060-38060	OAKLAND
37332-37332	EVENSVILLE	37683-37683	MOUNTAIN CITY	37848-37848	POWDER SPRINGS	38061-38061	POCAHONTAS
37333-37333	FARNER	37684-37684	MOUNTAIN HOME	37849-37849	POWELL	38063-38063	RIPLEY
37334-37334	FAYETTEVILLE	37686-37686	PINEY FLATS	37851-37851	PRUDEN	38066-38066	ROSSVILLE
37335-37335	FLINTVILLE	37687-37687	ROAN MOUNTAIN	37852-37852	ROBBINS	38067-38067	SAULSBURY
37336-37336	GEORGETOWN	37688-37688	SHADY VALLEY	37853-37853	ROCKFORD	38068-38068	SOMERVILLE
37337-37337	GRANDVIEW	37690-37690	TELFORD	37854-37854	ROCKWOOD	38069-38069	STANTON
37338-37338	GRAYSVILLE	37691-37691	TRADE	37857-37857	ROGERSVILLE	38070-38070	TIGRETT
37339-37339	GRUETLI LAAGER	37692-37692	UNICOI	37860-37860	RUSSELLVILLE	38071-38071	TIPTON
37340-37340	GUILD	37694-37694	WATAUGA	37861-37861	RUTLEDGE	38074-38074	BOLIVAR
37341-37341	HARRISON	37699-37699	PINEY FLATS	37862-37862	SEVIERVILLE	38075-38075	WHITEVILLE
37342-37342	HILLSBORO	37701-37701	ALCOA	37863-37863	PIGEON FORGE	38076-38076	WILLISTON
37343-37343	HIXSON	37705-37705	ANDERSONVILLE	37864-37864	SEVIERVILLE	38077-38077	WYNNBURG
37345-37345	HUNTLAND	37707-37707	ARTHUR	37865-37865	SEYMOUR	38079-38079	TIPTONVILLE
37346-37346	ISABELLA	37708-37708	BEAN STATION	37866-37866	SHARPS CHAPEL	38080-38080	RIDGELY
37347-37347	JASPER	37709-37709	BLAINE	37867-37867	SHAWANEE	38083-38083	MILLINGTON
37348-37348	KELSO	37710-37710	BRICEVILLE	37868-37868	PIGEON FORGE	38088-38088	CORDOVA
37349-37349	MANCHESTER	37711-37711	BULLS GAP	37869-37869	SNEEDVILLE	38101-38137	MEMPHIS
37350-37350	LOOKOUT MOUNTAIN	37713-37713	BYBEE	37870-37870	SPEEDWELL	38138-38139	GERMANTOWN
37351-37351	LUPTON CITY	37714-37714	CARYVILLE	37871-37871	STRAWBERRY PLAINS	38140-38182	MEMPHIS
37352-37352	LYNCHBURG	37715-37715	CLAIRFIELD	37872-37872	SUNBRIGHT	38183-38183	GERMANTOWN
37353-37353	MC DONALD	37716-37717	CLINTON	37873-37873	SURGOINSVILLE	38184-38197	MEMPHIS
37354-37354	MADISONVILLE	37719-37719	COALFIELD	37874-37874	SWEETWATER	38201-38201	MC KENZIE
37355-37355	MANCHESTER	37721-37721	CORRYTON	37876-37876	SEVIERVILLE	38220-38220	ATWOOD
37356-37356	MONTEAGLE	37722-37722	COSBY	37877-37877	TALBOTT	38221-38221	BIG SANDY
37357-37357	MORRISON	37723-37723	CRAB ORCHARD	37878-37878	TALLASSEE	38222-38222	BUCHANAN
37358-37358	MOUNT VERNON	37724-37724	CUMBERLAND GAP	37879-37879	TAZEWELL	38223-38223	COMO
37359-37359	MULBERRY	37725-37725	DANDRIDGE	37880-37880	TEN MILE	38224-38224	COTTAGE GROVE

Zip Range	City	Zip Range	City	Zip Range	City	Zip Range	City
38225-38225	DRESDEN	38332-38332	ENVILLE	38387-38387	WESTPORT	38505-38506	COOKEVILLE
38226-38226	DUKEDOM	38333-38333	EVA	38388-38388	WILDERSVILLE	38541-38541	ALLONS
38229-38229	GLEASON	38334-38334	FINGER	38389-38389	YORKVILLE	38542-38542	ALLRED
38230-38230	GREENFIELD	38336-38336	FRUITVALE	38390-38390	YUMA	38543-38543	ALPINE
38231-38231	HENRY	38337-38337	GADSDEN	38391-38391	DENMARK	38544-38544	BAXTER
38232-38232	HORNBEAK	38338-38338	GIBSON	38392-38392	MERCER	38545-38545	BLOOMINGTON
38233-38233	KENTON	38339-38339	GUYS	38393-38393	CHEWALLA		SPRINGS
38235-38235	MC LEMORESVILLE	38340-38340	HENDERSON	38401-38402	COLUMBIA	38547-38547	BRUSH CREEK
38236-38236	MANSFIELD	38341-38341	HOLLADAY	38425-38425	CLIFTON	38548-38548	BUFFALO VALLEY
38237-38238	MARTIN	38342-38342	HOLLOW ROCK	38449-38449	ARDMORE	38549-38549	BYRDSTOWN
38240-38240	OBION	38343-38343	HUMBOLDT	38450-38450	COLLINWOOD	38550-38550	CAMPAIGN
38241-38241	PALMERSVILLE	38344-38344	HUNTINGDON	38451-38451	CULLEOKA	38551-38551	CELINA
38242-38242	PARIS	38345-38345	HURON	38452-38452	CYPRESS INN	38552-38552	CHESTNUT MOUND
38251-38251	PURYEAR	38346-38346	IDLEWILD	38453-38453	DELLROSE	38553-38553	CLARKRANGE
38253-38253	RIVES	38347-38347	JACKS CREEK	38454-38454	DUCK RIVER	38554-38554	CRAWFORD
38254-38254	SAMBURG	38348-38348	LAVINIA	38455-38455	ELKTON	38555-38555	CROSSVILLE
38255-38255	SHARON	38351-38351	LEXINGTON	38456-38456	ETHRIDGE	38556-38556	JAMESTOWN
38256-38256	SPRINGVILLE	38352-38352	LURAY	38457-38457	FIVE POINTS	38557-38558	CROSSVILLE
38257-38257	SOUTH FULTON	38355-38355	MEDINA	38459-38459	FRANKEWING	38559-38559	DOYLE
38258-38258	TREZEVANT	38356-38356	MEDON	38460-38460	GOODSPRING	38560-38560	ELMWOOD
38259-38259	TRIMBLE	38357-38357	MICHIE	38461-38461	HAMPSHIRE	38562-38562	GAINESBORO
38260-38260	TROY	38358-38358	MILAN	38462-38462	HOHENWALD	38563-38563	GORDONSVILLE
38261-38261	UNION CITY	38359-38359	MILLEDGEVILLE	38463-38463	IRON CITY	38564-38564	GRANVILLE
38271-38271	WOODLAND MILLS	38361-38361	MORRIS CHAPEL	38464-38464	LAWRENCEBURG	38565-38565	GRIMSLEY
38281-38281	UNION CITY	38362-38362	OAKFIELD	38468-38468	LEOMA	38567-38567	HICKMAN
38301-38308	JACKSON	38363-38363	PARSONS	38469-38469	LORETTO	38568-38568	HILHAM
38310-38310	ADAMSVILLE	38365-38365	PICKWICK DAM	38471-38471	LUTTS	38569-38569	LANCASTER
38311-38311	BATH SPRINGS	38366-38366	PINSON	38472-38472	LYNNVILLE	38570-38570	LIVINGSTON
38313-38313	BEECH BLUFF	38367-38367	RAMER	38473-38473	MINOR HILL	38573-38573	MONROE
38314-38314	JACKSON	38368-38368	REAGAN	38474-38474	MOUNT PLEASANT	38574-38574	MONTEREY
38315-38315	BETHEL SPRINGS	38369-38369	RUTHERFORD	38475-38475	OLIVEHILL	38575-38575	MOSS
38316-38316	BRADFORD	38370-38370	SALTILLO	38476-38476	PRIMM SPRINGS	38577-38577	PALL MALL
38317-38317	BRUCETON	38371-38371	SARDIS	38477-38477	PROSPECT	38578-38578	PLEASANT HILL
38318-38318	BUENA VISTA	38372-38372	SAVANNAH	38478-38478	PULASKI	38579-38579	QUEBECK
38320-38320	CAMDEN	38374-38374	SCOTTS HILL	38481-38481	SAINT JOSEPH	38580-38580	RICKMAN
38321-38321	CEDAR GROVE	38375-38375	SELMER	38482-38482	SANTA FE	38581-38581	ROCK ISLAND
38324-38324	CLARKSBURG	38376-38376	SHILOH	38483-38483	SUMMERTOWN	38582-38582	SILVER POINT
38326-38326	COUNCE	38377-38377	SILERTON	38485-38485	WAYNESBORO	38583-38583	SPARTA
38327-38327	CRUMP	38378-38378	SPRING CREEK	38486-38486	WESTPOINT	38585-38585	SPENCER
38328-38328	DARDEN	38379-38379	STANTONVILLE	38487-38487	WILLIAMSPORT	38587-38587	WALLING
38329-38329	DECATURVILLE	38380-38380	SUGAR TREE	38488-38488	TAFT	38588-38588	WHITLEYVILLE
38330-38330	DYER	38381-38381	TOONE	38501-38503	COOKEVILLE	38589-38589	WILDER
38331-38331	EATON	38382-38382	TRENTON	38504-38504	ALLARDT		

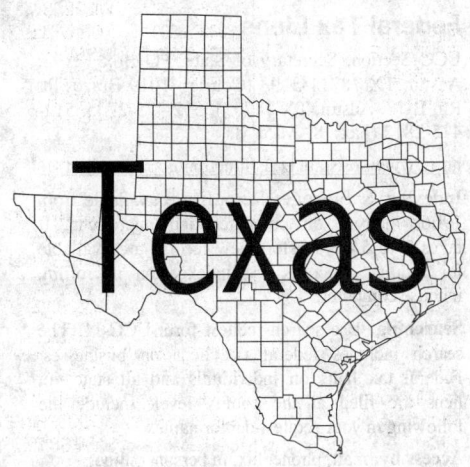

General Help Numbers:

Governor's Office
PO Box 12428
Austin, TX 78711-2428
http://www.governor.state.tx.us

512-463-2000
Fax 512-463-1849
7:30AM-5:30PM

Attorney General's Office
PO Box 12548
Austin, TX 78711-2548
http://www.oag.state.tx.us

512-463-2100
Fax 512-463-2063
7:30AM-5:30PM

State Court Administrator
PO Box 12066
Austin, TX 78711-2066
http://www.oca.courts.state.tx.us

512-463-1625
Fax 512-463-1648
8AM-5PM

State Archives
PO Box 12927
Austin, TX 78711-2927
http://www.tsl.state.tx.us

512-463-5455
Fax 512-463-5436
8AM-5PM
Genealogy 8-5 TU-SA

State Specifics:

Capital: Austin
                            Travis County

Time Zone: CST*
* Texas' two western-most counties are MST:
They are: El Paso and Hudspeth,

Number of Counties: 254

Population: 20,851,820

Web Site: www.state.tx.us

State Agencies

Criminal Records

Crime Records Service, Correspondence Section, PO Box 15999, Austin, TX 78761-5999 (Courier: 5805 N Lamar, Austin, TX 78752); 512-424-5079, 8AM-5PM.

http://records.txdps.state.tx.us/dps/default.cfm

Note: Since 1/1/93, per Chapter 60, Code of Criminal Procedure, disposition after reported said date includes complete information regarding charge, date of conviction, and county. Data prior to this date may not be complete.

Indexing & Storage: Records are available for many years. New records are available for inquiry immediately.

Searching: To obtain ALL arrest information (conviction and non-conviction), must have a signed release from the person of record and full set of their fingerprints. Sex offender data is available online at http://records.txdps.state.tx.us/so_caveats.cfm. To obtain conviction data only, submit full name, sex, race, and DOB. The SSN is helpful, but not required. No letter of authorization is needed for the conviction only report. Turnaround time is 24-48 hours.

Access by: mail, in person, online.

Fee & Payment: The fee is $15.00 for the full search using fingerprints and $10.00 for the conviction only search. Fee payee: Texas Department of Safety. Prepayment required. Credit cards are accepted for Internet searches only. Personal checks accepted. Credit cards accepted: MasterCard, Visa.

Mail search: The turnaround time for requests with fingerprints is 4 weeks; the $10.00 non-fingerprint request turnaround time is 1-2 weeks.No self addressed stamped envelope is required.

In person search: Turnaround time is 24 hours for the non-fingerprint search and 24-48 hours for the fingerprint search.

Online search: Records can be pulled from the web site. Requesters must establish an account and have a pre-paid bank to work from. The fee established by the Department (Sec. 411.135(b)) is $3.15 per request plus a $.57 handling fee when credit purchased.

Corporation Records
Fictitious Name
Limited Partnership Records
Limited Liability Company Records
Assumed Name
Trademarks/Servicemarks

Secretary of State, Corporation Section, PO Box 13697, Austin, TX 78711-3697 (Courier: J Earl Rudder Bldg, 1019 Brazos, B-13, Austin, TX 78701); 512-463-5555 (Information), 512-463-5578 (Copies), 512-463-5709 (Fax), 8AM-5PM.

http://www.sos.state.tx.us

Indexing & Storage: Records are available from the 1800s. Records are indexed on inhouse computer, online.

Searching: New records are available immediately on the computer, but it takes 12 days before new records are available to be copied. Include the following in your request-full name of business, corporation file number. In addition to the articles of incorporation, corporation records include the following information: Public Information Reports (extracted information from the database only), Officers, Directors, DBAs, Prior (merged) names, Inactive and Reserved names.

Access by: mail, phone, fax, in person, online.

Fee & Payment: Certification is $10.00 plus $1.00 per document page. Copies are $.10 per page. Fee payee: Secretary of State. Prepayment required. Credit card transaction charge is 2.1% of the total amount charged. Frequent requesters may set up a pre-paid billing account. Personal checks accepted. Credit cards accepted: MasterCard, Visa, Discover.

Mail search: Turnaround time: 3 to 5 days. No self addressed stamped envelope is required.

Phone search: No fee for telephone request.

Fax search: Fax requests cost an additional $2.00 per page plus expedited fees.

In person search: Public access terminals are available for walk-in requesters.

Online search: There are 2 online methods available. Dial-up access is available M-TH from 7 AM to 8 PM (6PM on Fridays). There is a $3.00 fee for each record searched (secured party searches are $10.00). Filing procedures and forms are available from the web site or from 900-263-0060 ($1.00 per minute). General corporation information is available at no fee at http://open.cpa.state.tx.us from the State Comptroller's office.

Other access: The agency makes portions of its database available for purchase. Call 512-475-2755 for more information.

Expedited service: Expedited service is available for mail, phone and in person searches. Add $25.00 per document. Add $5.00 per certificate for copies. Will process by close of business day following receipt.

Uniform Commercial Code
Federal Tax Liens

UCC Section, Secretary of State, PO Box 13193, Austin, TX 78711-3193 (Courier: 1019 Brazos St, Rm B-13, Austin, TX 78701); 512-475-2705, 512-475-2812 (Fax), 8AM-5PM.

http://www.sos.state.tx.us/function/ucc/cover.htm

Indexing & Storage: Records are available from 1966, indexed on computer and microfiche. It takes 3 to 5 days before new records are available for inquiry. Records are indexed on microfilm, inhouse computer.

Searching: Use search request form UCC-11. The search includes federal tax liens on businesses. Federal tax liens on individuals and all state tax liens are filed at the county level. Include the following in your request-debtor name.

Access by: mail, phone, fax, in person, online.

Fee & Payment: Using the approved form - $10.00 per debtor name; other forms - $25.00 per debtor name; copies - $1.50 per page with a minimum of $5.00. Effective 01/01/00, a version of the UCC-11 was designated as the standard form. Fee payee: Secretary of State. Personal checks accepted. Credit cards accepted: MasterCard, Visa, Discover.

Mail search: Turnaround time: 1 to 2 weeks. No self addressed stamped envelope is required.

Phone search: Debtor names, up to 10 filings per debtor searched, will be released. No collateral is listed.

Fax search: There is an additional fee of $15.00.

In person search: You may request information in person.

Online search: Direct dial-up is open from 7 AM to 6 PM. The fee is $3.00 per search, $10.00 for a secured party search. General information and forms can be found at the web site.

Other access: The state offers the database for sale, contact the Information Services Dept at (512) 463-5609 for further details.

Expedited service: Expedited service is available for mail, in-person and phone searches. Turnaround time: 24 hours. Add $15.00 per from. Expedited mail service is offered. Also, you can include your Fed Ex number for fastest return.

State Tax Liens
Records not maintained by a state level agency.

Note: Records are located at the county level.

Sales Tax Registrations

Controller of Public Accounts, PO Box 13528, Austin, TX 78711-3528 (Courier: LBJ Office Bldg, 111 E 17th St, Austin, TX 78774); 800-252-5555, 800-252-1386 (Searches), 512-475-1610 (Fax), 8AM-5PM.

http://www.window.state.tx.us

Searching: This agency will provide the following business information: business name, address, phone number, tax permit number, a list of officers & directors, and the registered agent for a corporation. Audit results are not released. Include the following in your request-business name. They will also search by tax permit number.

Access by: mail, phone, in person, online.

Fee & Payment: There is no search fee. Fee payee: Comptroller of Public Accounts. Personal checks accepted. No credit cards accepted.

Mail search: Turnaround time: 10 working days. If more than 3 businesses are requested, the agency prefers that you request by mail.No self addressed stamped envelope is required. No fee for mail request.

Phone search: No fee for telephone request. The agency will provide responses to 3 business names or less over the phone.

In person search: No fee for request. They will verify information or will mail a letter.

Online search: Go to http://aixtcp.cpa.state.tx.us/star to search 16,000+ documents by index or collection. This office makes general corporation information available at http://open.cpa.state.tx.us. There is no fee.

Birth Certificates

Texas Department of Health, Bureau of Vital Statistics, PO Box 12040, Austin, TX 78711-2040 (Courier: 1100 W 49th St, Austin, TX 78756-3191); 512-458-7111, 512-458-7506 (Fax), 8AM-5PM.

http://www.tdh.state.tx.us/bvs

Indexing & Storage: Records are available from 1903 to present. It takes receipt from local registration officials before new records are available for inquiry. Records are indexed on microfiche, index cards, inhouse computer.

Searching: Must have a signed, notarized release form from person of record or immediate family member and name and address of requester for records less than 50 years old. Include the following in your request-full name, names of parents, mother's maiden name, date of birth, place of birth, relationship to person of record, reason for information request. Must send a copy of requester's photo ID or show a photo ID for in-person searches. The following data is not released: Social Security Numbers.

Access by: mail, fax, in person, online.

Fee & Payment: The search fee is $11.00 per name. Fee payee: Bureau of Vital Statistics. Prepayment required. Credit cards accepted for fax requests only. Personal checks accepted. Credit cards accepted: MasterCard, Visa.

Mail search: Turnaround time: 6 to 8 weeks. No self addressed stamped envelope is required.

Fax search: See expedited service.

In person search: Turnaround time 1-2 hours.

Online search: The birth database 1950-present of the Department of Health is available at http://userdb.rootsweb.com/tx/birth/summary/search.cgi. As of March 2000, Birth Indexes from 1926-1995 are available at http://userdb.rootsweb.com/tx/birth/general/search.cgi Search by surname, given name, county, year and gender.

Other access: Birth Indexes from 1926-1995 are available on CD-Rom and microfiche.

Expedited service: Expedited service is available for fax searches. Turnaround time: 48 to 96 hours. The total fee for expedited service is $21.00; ($11.00 for search, $5.00 for expedited service, and $5.00 for overnight service fee), add $6.75 if delivery to PO box or rural route.

Death Records

Texas Department of Health, Bureau of Vital Statistics, PO Box 12040, Austin, TX 78711-2040 (Courier: 1100 W 49th St, Austin, TX 78756-3191); 512-458-7111, 512-458-7506 (Fax), 8AM-5PM.

http://www.tdh.state.tx.us/bvs

Indexing & Storage: Records are available from 1903 to present. Records are indexed on microfiche, index cards, inhouse computer.

Searching: Must have a signed release form from immediate family member and requester's name and current address for records less than 25 years old. Include the following in your request-full name, date of death, place of death, Social Security Number, relationship to person of record, reason for information request. You must include a copy of requesters' photo ID or show a photo ID for in person requests. The following data is not released: Social Security Numbers.

Access by: mail, fax, in person, online.

Fee & Payment: The search fee is $9.00 per name. Add $3.00 per name per copy for each additional copy. Fee payee: Bureau of Vital Statistics. Prepayment required. Credit cards accepted for fax requests only. Personal checks accepted. Credit cards accepted: MasterCard, Visa.

Mail search: Turnaround time: 6 to 8 weeks. No self addressed stamped envelope is required.

Fax search: See expedited service.

In person search: Turnaround time 1-2 hours.

Online search: The database of the Texas Department of Health is available at http://userdb.rootsweb.com/tx/death/search.cgi?. As of March 2000, Death Indexes from 1964-1998 are available. You may search by surname, given name, county, year or gender.

Other access: Death Indexes from 1964-1998 are available on CD-Rom and microfiche.

Expedited service: Expedited service is available for fax searches. Turnaround time: 48 to 96 hours. The total expedited service fee is $19.00; ($9.00 search fee, $5.00 expedited service fee, and $5.00 overnight service fee), add $6.75 if delivery to PO box or rural route.

Marriage Certificates

Texas Department of Health, Bureau of Vital Statistics, 1100 W 49th St, Austin, TX 78756 (Courier: 1100 W 49th St, Austin, TX 78756-3191); 512-458-7111, 512-458-7506 (Fax), 8AM-5PM.

http://www.tdh.state.tx.us/bvs

Indexing & Storage: Records are available from 1966 to present. It takes delivery from the county clerk before new records are available for inquiry. Records are indexed on microfiche, index cards, inhouse computer.

Searching: They only have a copy of the application form and an index to the county record. The actual certificate must be obtained from the county recorder of record. Include the following in your request-names of husband and wife, date of marriage, place or county of marriage. The following data is not released: Social Security Numbers.

Access by: mail, fax, in person, online.

Fee & Payment: The search fee is $9.00 per record. Fee payee: Bureau of Vital Statistics. Prepayment required. Credit cards accepted for fax

requests only. Personal checks accepted. Credit cards accepted: MasterCard, Visa.

Mail search: Turnaround time: 6 to 12 weeks. No self addressed stamped envelope is required.

Fax search: See expedited service.

In person search: Turnaround time while you wait.

Online search: The marriage records database 1966-1997 of the Department of Health is available at http://userdb.rootsweb.com/tx/marriage/search.cgi. Search by husband or wife name, county, or year.

Expedited service: Expedited service is available for fax searches. Turnaround time: 48 to 96 hours. Total expedited service fee is $19.00; ($9.00 search fee, $5.00 expedited service fee, and $5.00 overnight service fee), add $6.75 if delivery to PO box or rural route.

Divorce Records

Texas Department of Health, Bureau of Vital Statistics, PO Box 12040, Austin, TX 78711-2040 (Courier: 1100 W 49th St, Austin, TX 78756-3191); 512-458-7111, 512-458-7506 (Fax), 8AM-5PM.

http://www.tdh.state.tx.us/bvs

Indexing & Storage: Records are available from 1968 to present. It takes delivery from the county clerk before new records are available for inquiry. Records are indexed on microfiche, index cards, inhouse computer.

Searching: They only have the a report of divorce form and an index that directs you to the county court of record. A copy of the actual record must be obtained at the county level. Include the following in your request-names of husband and wife, date of divorce, year divorce case began, case number (if known).

Access by: mail, fax, in person, online.

Fee & Payment: The search fee is $9.00 per name. Fee payee: Bureau of Vital Statistics. Prepayment required. Credit cards accepted for fax requests only. Personal checks accepted. Credit cards accepted: MasterCard, Visa.

Mail search: Turnaround time: 6 to 12 weeks. No self addressed stamped envelope is required.

Fax search: See expedited service.

In person search: Turnaround time 1-2 hours.

Online search: The divorce records database 1968-1997 of the Department of Health is available at http://userdb.rootsweb.com/tx/divorce/search.cgi. Search by husband or wife name, county, or year.

Expedited service: Expedited service is available for fax searches. Turnaround time: 48 to 96 hours. The total expedited service fee is $19.00; ($9.00 search fee, $5.00 expedited service fee, and $5.00 overnight service fee), add $6.75 if delivery to PO box or rural route.

Workers' Compensation Records

Texas Workers' Compensation Commission, Southfield Building, 4000 South, IH-35, MS-92B, Austin, TX 78704-7491; 512-804-4000, 512-804-4990 (Reprographics Department), 512-804-4993 (Fax), 8AM-5PM.

Indexing & Storage: Records are available from 1962. Records are indexed on inhouse computer.

Searching: A signed, notarized release is required to obtain file copies. Use Form TWCC-153. Include the following in your request-claimant name, Social Security Number, date of accident. The file number is required to receive copies. If you don't know the file number or date of accident, you must submit Form TWCC-155.

Access by: mail, fax.

Fee & Payment: The fees for TWCC-153 are $1.00 for certification, $1.00 for the first page and $.30 each additional page. The fees for TWCC-155 are $15.00 search fee and $1.00 for certification. Fee payee: Texas Workers' Compensation Commission. Prepayment required. An invoice will be sent, copies are held until payment received. Personal checks accepted. No credit cards accepted.

Mail search: Turnaround time: 4 to 6 weeks. No self addressed stamped envelope is required.

Fax search: Same as by mail, but only TWCC-153 available by fax

Expedited service: Expedited service is available for mail and phone searches. They will call and advise exact fees needed to pre-pay. There will be a minimum of $25.00.

Driver Records

Department of Public Safety, Driver Records Section, PO Box 15999, Austin, TX 78761-5999 (Courier: 5805 N Lamar Blvd, Austin, TX 78752); 512-424-2032, 8AM-5PM.

http://www.txdps.state.tx.us

Note: Tickets are only available from the court system.

Indexing & Storage: Records are available for 5 years for moving violations and suspensions, indefinite for DWIs, 11 years for SR judgments. Non-moving violations do not appear on the record. It takes 30 days before new records are available for inquiry.

Searching: Class type listings from the driver's record are not provided. Casual requesters must use Form DR-1A. This form contains the written consent if personal information is requested by a casual user. The name and driver's license number or date of birth, are needed when ordering. The following data is not released: Social Security Numbers or medical records.

Access by: mail, in person.

Fee & Payment: Driving record fees are $6.00 for a 3 year driving record, $10.00 if certified or $5.00 if by tape. A license statue including latest address is $4.00 per report. There is a full charge for a "no record found." Fee payee: Texas Department of Public Safety. Prepayment required. Personal checks accepted. No credit cards accepted.

Mail search: Turnaround time: 7 to 10 days. No self addressed stamped envelope is required.

In person search: Normal turnaround time is same day.

Other access: Magnetic tape retrieval is available for high volume users.

Vehicle Ownership
Vehicle Identification

Department of Transportation, Vehicle Titles and Registration, 40th St and Jackson, Austin, TX 78779-0001; 512-465-7611, 512-465-7736 (Fax), 8AM-5PM.

http://www.dot.state.tx.us

Note: A "Request for Texas Motor Vehicle Information", form VTR-275, which includes a signed statement certifying that the information will be used in compliance with state and federal laws and that the information is needed for a "lawful and legitimate purpose" is required.

Indexing & Storage: Records are available as long as there is activity. If no activity for 3 years, record is purged. Title history information is available on microfiche for 16 years to present. It takes 48 hours after entry into the system before new records are available for inquiry.

Searching: For plate checks, include a signed statement showing the information is needed for "lawful and legitimate purposes." The state does not permit name searches. Personal information is not released without consent to casual requesters. Use Form VTR-275 for vehicle history. The following data is not released: Social Security Numbers.

Access by: mail, online.

Fee & Payment: The current fee for VIN and plate checks is $2.30 per record. If you want to do a title search on an RV or mobile home (either attached or unattached), the fee is $5.75 or $6.75 certified. Fee payee: Department of Transportation. Prepayment required. Personal checks accepted. No credit cards accepted.

Mail search: Turnaround time: 7 to 10 days. A self addressed stamped envelope is requested.

Online search: Online access is available for pre-approved accounts. A $200 deposit is required, there is a $23 charge per month and $.12 fee per inquiry. Searching by name is not permitted. For more information, contact Production Data Control.

Other access: The state offers tape cartridge retrieval for customized searches or based on the entire database. Weekly updates are available. There are approximately 32,000,000 records in the database.

Accident Reports

Texas Department of Public Safety, Accident Records Bureau, PO Box 15999, Austin, TX 78761-5999 (Courier: 5805 N Lamar Blvd, Austin, TX 78752); 512-424-2600, 8AM-5PM.

http://www.txdps.state.tx.us

Indexing & Storage: Records are available for 10 years to present. It takes 30 days before new records are available for inquiry.

Searching: Accident reports investigated by DPS are open to the public; however, the driver reports are confidential. Those copies may only be provided to the driver who submitted and signed the report. Items required to search include two or more of following: full name of any person involved, specific city/county location, and date of incident.

Access by: mail, in person.

Fee & Payment: Fees: $4.00 per uncertified report and $6.00 per certified report. There is a $4.00 charge for a no record found search. Fee payee: Texas Department of Public Safety. Prepayment required. Personal checks accepted. No credit cards accepted.

Mail search: Turnaround time: 4 to 6 weeks. No self addressed stamped envelope is required.

In person search: Up to 5 requests will be processed immediately.

Vessel Ownership
Vessel Registration

Parks & Wildlife Dept, 4200 Smith School Rd, Austin, TX 78744; 512-389-4828, 800-262-8755, 8AM-5PM.

http://www.tpwd.state.tx.us/boat/boat.htm

Indexing & Storage: Records are available from 1976 to 1988 for titled boats, then from 1989 to present for all boats. Records are indexed on computer. All motorized boats must be registered and titled. All sailboats 14 ft and over must be registered and titled. Lien data shows on all reports.

Searching: The written request must include: name & address of requestor, TX #, motor # and/or serial numbers, and the statement "The use of the information obtained will be for lawful purposes."

Access by: mail, in person.

Fee & Payment: There is a $1.50 fee for a record check and a $6.00 fee for a complete history from microfilm. Fee payee: TX Parks & Wildlife Dept. Prepayment required. Personal checks accepted. No credit cards accepted.

Mail search: Turnaround time: 2 to 3 weeks. Turnaround time is often longer in the summer. No self addressed stamped envelope is required.

In person search: Histories are returned by mail.

Other access: Records are released in bulk format; however, requesters are screened for lawful purpose. The agency requires a copy of any item mailed or distributed as a result of purchase. media includes tape, labels, and printed lists.

Legislation Records

Legislative Reference Library, PO Box 12488, Austin, TX 78711-2488 (Courier: State Capitol Building, 2N.3, 1100 Congress, Austin, TX 78701); 512-463-1252 (Bill Status), 512-463-0252 (Senate Bill Copies), 512-463-1144 (House Bill Copies), 512-475-4626 (Fax), 8AM-5PM.

http://www.lrl.state.tx.us

Note: They ask that you call first to obtain location of bills. The sessions meet in odd number years from January through May.

Indexing & Storage: Records are available from the beginning of the Legislature in the Library. Records are computerized since 1989 and are on microfiche from 1973 to 1980.

Searching: Include the following in your request-bill number, year.

Access by: mail, fax, in person, online.

Fee & Payment: There is no search fee. There is no copy fee if under 10 pages; if over it is $.20 per page plus any shipping costs. Will express ship with requester's proper account number of the shipping company. Fee payee: Legislative Reference Library. Prepayment required. Business checks or money orders are preferred. No credit cards accepted.

Mail search: Turnaround time: variable. No self addressed stamped envelope is required.

Fax search: Result will be returned by fax if under 10 pages.

In person search: Searching is available in person.

Online search: The web is a thorough searching site of bills and status.

Voter Registration
Access to Records is Restricted

Secretary of State, Elections Division, PO Box 12060, Austin, TX 78711-2060; 800-252-8683, 512-475-2811 (Fax), 8AM-5PM.

http://www.sos.state.tx.us

Note: To do individual look-ups, one must go to the Tax Assessor-Collector at the county level Records are open. The state will sell the entire database, for non-commercial purposes, in a variety of media and sort formats.

GED Certificates

Texas Education Agency, GED Records, 1701 N Congress Ave, Austin, TX 78701-1494; 512-463-9292, 512-305-9493 (Fax), 7AM-6PM.

http://www.tea.state.tx.us/ged

Indexing & Storage: Records are available from 1944 to present. It takes 2 weeks before new records are available for inquiry. Records are indexed on mainframe computer.

Searching: To search, the name and Social Security Number are required.

Access by: mail, phone, fax, in person.

Fee & Payment: There is no fee for verification or transcripts. However, if the subject did not pay the GED fees and the record is prior to 1994, a fee may be charged to the requester.

Mail search: Turnaround time: 1 to 2 days. No self addressed stamped envelope is required.

Phone search: Verifications are available by phone.

Fax search: Fax requests require a signed release. Turnaround time: Same day.

In person search: Searching is available in person.

Hunting License Information
Fishing License Information

TX Parks & Wildlife Department, License Section, 4200 Smith School Rd, Austin, TX 78744; 512-389-4820, 512-389-4330 (Fax), 8AM-5PM.

http://www.tpwd.state.tx.us

Indexing & Storage: Records are available from 09/01/96 forward and are computerized.

Searching: All requests must be in writing on their official Form, unless request is for self. They will release address, status, and date of issue. Include the driver's license number and/or SSN and or DOB. Requests must be in writing and signed by requester. Include requester's address and phone.

Access by: mail, fax.

Fee & Payment: There is no fee.

Mail search: Turnaround time: 1 to 3 days. Up to 5 names can be requested by mail.

Fax search: Up to 5 names can be requested by fax. Results are mailed unless you have a toll free fax number.

Other access: The license database is for sale. For fees and procedures call 512-389-8069.

Texas State Licensing Agencies

Licenses Searchable Online

Air Conditioning/Refrigeration Contractor #14 .... www.license.state.tx.us/LicenseSearch/
Appraiser #47 .... www.talcb.state.tx.us
Architectural Barrier #14 .... www.license.state.tx.us/LicenseSearch/
Attorney #40 .... www.texasbar.com
Auctioneer #14 .... www.license.state.tx.us/LicenseSearch/
Audiologist #22 .... www.tdh.state.tx.us/hcqs/plc/speech.htm
Bank Agency, Foreign #01 .... www.banking.state.tx.us/asp/fba/lookup.asp
Bank, State Chartered #01 .... www.banking.state.tx.us/asp/bank/lookup.asp
Barber School #02 .... www.tsbbe.state.tx.us/schoolr.htm
Boiler Inspector/Installer #14 .... www.license.state.tx.us/LicenseSearch/
Boxing/Combative Sports Event #14 .... www.license.state.tx.us/LicenseSearch/
Career Counselor #14 .... www.license.state.tx.us/LicenseSearch/
Check Seller #01 .... www.banking.state.tx.us/asp/soc/lookup.asp
Chiropractor #25 .... www.tbce.state.tx.us
Counselor, Professional #41 .... www.tdh.state.tx.us/hcqs/plc/lpcrost.txt
Currency Exchange #01 .... www.banking.state.tx.us/asp/cex/lookup.asp
Dental Hygienist #23 .... www.tsbde.state.tx.us/dbsearch/
Dental Laboratory #23 .... www.tsbde.state.tx.us/dbsearch/
Dentist #23 .... www.tsbde.state.tx.us/dbsearch/
Dietitian #22 .... www.tdh.state.tx.us/hcqs/plc/dtrost.txt
ECA #27 .... http://160.42.108.3/ems_web/blh_html_page1.htm
Elevator/Escalator #14 .... www.license.state.tx.us/LicenseSearch/
Emergency Medical Technician #27 .... http://160.42.108.3/ems_web/blh_html_page1.htm
Funeral Establishment/Preneed Funeral Home #15 . www.banking.state.tx.us/asp/pfc/lookup.asp
Funeral Prepaid Permit Holder #01 .... www.banking.state.tx.us/asp/pfc/lookup.asp
Health Facility, Occupational/Physical Therapy #17 www.ecptote.state.tx.us/license/ftverif.php
Hearing Instrument Dispenser/Fitter #22 .... www.tdh.state.tx.us/hcqs/plc/fdhi.htm
Industrialized Housing #14 .... www.license.state.tx.us/LicenseSearch/
Insurance Adjuster #48 .... www.tdi.state.tx.us/general/forms/colists.html
Insurance Agency/Agent #48 .... www.tdi.state.tx.us/general/forms/colists.html
Insurance Company #48 .... www.tdi.state.tx.us/general/forms/colists.html
Lobbyist #50 .... www.lobbyist.net/Texas/TEXLOB.htm
Marriage & Family Therapist #31 .... www.tdh.state.tx.us/hcqs/plc/mft.htm#rosters
Massage Therapist #28 .... www.tdh.state.tx.us/hcqs/plc/mtrost.txt
Massage Therapist, Temporary #28 .... www.tdh.state.tx.us/hcqs/plc/mtrostt.txt
Massage Therapy Establishment #28 .... www.tdh.state.tx.us/hcqs/plc/mtroste.txt
Massage Therapy School/Instructor #28 .... www.tdh.state.tx.us/hcqs/plc/mtrosts.txt
Medical Doctor #30 .... www.docboard.org/tx/df/txsearch.htm
Occupational Therapist/Assistant #17 .... www.ecptote.state.tx.us/license/otverif.php
Optometrist #51 .... www.odfinder.org/LicSearch.asp
Orthotics & Prosthetics Facility #26 .... www.tdh.state.tx.us/hcqs/plc/op_fac.htm
Orthotist/Prosthetist #26 .... www.tdh.state.tx.us/hcqs/plc/oprost.txt
Paramedic #27 .... http://160.42.108.3/ems_web/blh_html_page1.htm
Perpetual Care Cemetery #01 .... www.banking.state.tx.us/asp/pcc/lookup.asp
Personal Employment Service #14 .... www.license.state.tx.us/LicenseSearch/
Pharmacist #24 .... www.tsbp.state.tx.us/dbsearch/pht_search.asp
Pharmacy #24 .... www.tsbp.state.tx.us/dbsearch/phy_search.asp
Physical Therapist/Assistant #17 .... www.ecptote.state.tx.us/license/ptverif.php
Physicist, Medical #26 .... www.tdh.state.tx.us/hcqs/plc/mprost.txt
Polygraph Examiner #34 .... http://polygraph.org/states/tape/members_roster.htm
Polygraph Examiner of Sex Offenders #26 .... www.tdh.state.tx.us/hcqs/plc/csp.htm
Property Tax Consultant #14 .... www.license.state.tx.us/LicenseSearch/
Radiologic Technologist #25 .... www.tdh.state.tx.us/hcqs/plc/mrtrost.txt

Radiology Technician #26...............................www.tdh.state.tx.us/hcqs/plc/mrtrost.txt
Real Estate Broker/Salesperson #52......................www.trec.state.tx.us/publicinfo/
Real Estate Inspector #52....................................www.trec.state.tx.us/publicinfo/
Representative Offices (Banking) #01 ....www.banking.state.tx.us/asp/rep/lookup.asp
Respiratory Care Practitioner #29 ....www.tdh.state.tx.us/hcqs/plc/rcrost.txt
Service Contract Provider #14...............................www.license.state.tx.us/LicenseSearch/
Sex Offender Treatment Provider #26 ....www.tdh.state.tx.us/hcqs/plc/csotrost.txt
Social Worker #26...www.tdh.state.tx.us/hcqs/plc/lsw/lsw_default.htm#roster
Speech-Language Pathologist #22..........................www.tdh.state.tx.us/hcqs/plc/speech.htm
Staff Leasing #14...www.license.state.tx.us/LicenseSearch/
Talent Agency #14...www.license.state.tx.us/LicenseSearch/
Temporary Common Worker #14.............................www.license.state.tx.us/LicenseSearch/
Transportation Service Provider #54 ....www.license.state.tx.us/LicenseSearch/
Trust Company #01 ....www.banking.state.tx.us/asp/trustco/lookup.asp
Vehicle Protection Provider #14 ....www.license.state.tx.us/LicenseSearch/
Water Well & Pump Installer #14............................www.license.state.tx.us/LicenseSearch/
Weather Modification Service #14...........................www.license.state.tx.us/LicenseSearch/

Licensing Quick Finder

Acupuncturist #30 512-305-7030
Agricultural Specialities, Perishable #11 512-463-7604
Air Conditioning/Refrigeration Contractor #14.............
....512-463-6599
Alcoholic Beverage Dist./Mfg./Retailer #46.............
....512-206-3360
Appraiser #47 512-465-3950
Architect #61..512-305-9000
Architectural Barrier #14.......................512-463-6599
Asbestos Abatement Contractor #12.....512-834-6600
Asbestos Air Monitoring Technician #12 512-834-6600
Asbestos Consultant/Inspector #12.......512-834-6600
Asbestos Management Planner #12 512-834-6600
Asbestos Worker #12 512-834-6600
Athletic Agent #38 512-475-1769
Athletic Trainer #21..............................512-834-6615
Attorney #40 512-463-1463
Auctioneer #14.....................................512-463-6599
Audiologist #22 512-834-6627
Audiology Assistant #25 512-834-6627
Bank Agency, Foreign #01 512-475-1300
Bank, State Chartered #01 512-475-1300
Barber #02..512-305-8475
Barber School #02................................512-305-8475
Barber Shop #02...................................512-305-8475
Beauty Shop/Salon #08.........................512-467-8206
Boiler Inspector/Installer #14 800-722-7843
Boxing/Combative Sports Event #14 512-463-5101
Career Counselor #14...........................512-463-6599
Check Seller #01..................................512-475-1290
Child Care Facility/Administrator #49 512-438-3269
Chiropractor #25...................................512-305-6700
Contact Lens Dispenser #26.................512-834-4515
Cosmetologist #08................................512-467-8206
Counselor, Professional #41.................512-834-6658
County Librarian #44 512-463-5466
Court Reporter #09...............................512-463-1630
Currency Exchange #01........................512-475-1290
Day Care Center #49 512-438-3269
Day Care, Residential #49....................512-438-3269
Dental Assistant #23 512-463-6400
Dental Hygienist #23.............................512-434-6400
Dental Laboratory #23...........................512-463-6400
Dentist #23 512-463-6400
Dietitian #22...512-834-6601
Dog Racing/Dog Racing Personnel #36 ....
....512-833-6697
ECA #27...512-834-6700
Elevator/Escalator #14 512-463-6599

Emergency Medical Technician #27.......512-834-6700
Engineer #05 512-440-7723
Engineering Firm #05 512-440-7723
Family Home Day Care #49...................512-438-3269
Farm/Agricultural Service Co. #11 512-462-1441
Fire Alarm System Contractor #53.........512-305-7931
Fire Extinguisher Contractor #53...........512-305-7931
Fire Inspector #56 512-918-7100
Fire Investigator #56.............................512-918-7100
Fire Protection Sprinkler System Contractor #53 ....
....512-305-7931
Fire Suppression Specialist #56............512-918-7100
Firefighter #56......................................512-918-7100
Fireworks Display #53 512-305-7931
Fish Farmer #11 512-463-7602
Fishing Guide #45................................512-389-4818
Funeral Director #15.............................512-936-2474
Funeral Establishment/Preneed Funeral Home #15....
....512-936-2474
Funeral Prepaid Permit Holder #01 512-475-1290
Health Facility, Occupational/Physical Therapy #17....
....512-305-6900
Health Related Registry #26.................512-834-6602
Hearing Instru. Dispenser/Fitter #22......512-834-6784
Home Equity & Secondary Mortgage Lenders #07 .....
....512-936-7600
Home Health Agency #26......................512-834-6646
Horse Racing/Horse Racing Personnel #36 ....
....512-833-6697
Industrialized Housing #14 512-463-7353
Insurance Adjuster #48.........................512-322-3503
Insurance Agency #48..........................512-322-3503
Insurance Agent #48.............................512-322-3503
Insurance Company #48........................512-322-3507
Interior Designer #61............................512-305-9000
Interpreter for the Deaf #06 512-407-3250
Investment Advisor #39........................512-305-8332
Irrigator #57...512-239-6719
Laboratory Certification #25..................512-463-6400
Landscape Architect #61 512-305-9000
Law Enforcement Officer #58 512-936-7700
Lead Abatement Project Designer #55..512-834-6612
Lead Abatement Worker #55 512-834-6612
Lead Firm #55......................................512-834-6612
Lead Inspector #55...............................512-834-6612
Lead Risk Assessor #55.......................512-834-6612
Lead Supervisor #55.............................512-834-6612
Lead Training Program Providers #55...512-834-6612
Loan Company #07...............................512-936-7600

Lobbyist #50 512-463-5800
LPG-Liquefied Petroleum Gas Technician #11 ....
....512-462-1441
Manicurist/Manicurist Shop #02............512-305-8475
Marriage & Family Therapist #31 512-834-6657
Massage Therapist #28 512-834-6616
Massage Therapist, Temporary #28......512-834-6616
Massage Therapy Establishment #28 ...512-834-6616
Massage Therapy School #28 512-834-6616
Massage Therapy School Instructor #28 512-834-6616
Medical Doctor #30 512-305-7030
Medical Laboratory Practitioner #22......512-834-6602
Medication Aide #13..............................512-231-5827
Midwife, Direct Entry #25......................512-458-7700
Notary Public #33.................................512-463-5705
Nurse, Advance Regist. Practice #25....512-305-7400
Nurse-RN #25.......................................512-231-5829
Nurses' Aide #13...................................512-231-5829
Nursing Facility Administrator #13..........512-231-5825
Nursing Home Administrator #32 512-231-5825
Occupational Therapist/Assistant #17 ...512-305-6900
Optician #26..512-834-6661
Optometrist #51 512-305-8500
Orthotics & Prosthetics Facility #26.......512-834-4520
Orthotist/Prosthetist #26 512-834-4520
Paramedic #27......................................512-834-6700
Pawn Shop #07.....................................512-936-7600
Perfusionist #26 512-834-6751
Perpetual Care Cemetery #01 512-475-1290
Personal Employment Service #14 512-463-6599
Pesticide Applicator/Dealer #10 512-463-7476
Pharmacist #24.....................................512-305-8000
Pharmacy #24.......................................512-305-8000
Physical Therapist/Assistant #17 512-305-6900
Physician Assistant #30........................512-305-7030
Physicist, Medical #26..........................512-834-6655
Plumber Journeyman #03............ 512-458-2145 x227
Plumber, Master #03.............. 512-458-2145 x227
Plumbing Inspector #03 ...... 512-458-2145 x227
Podiatrist #20..512-305-7000
Polygraph Examiner #34 512-424-2058
Polygraph Examiner of Sex Offenders #26................
....512-834-6655
Private Investigator #35........................512-463-5545
Property Tax Consultant #14.................512-463-6599
Psychological Associate #19 512-305-7700
Psychologist #19..................................512-305-7700
Psychologist Associate #25..................512-305-7700
Public Accountant-CPA #43..................512-305-7853

Radiologic Technologist #25	512-834-6617	Securities Agent/Salesperson #39	512-305-8332	Tax Appraisal Professional #59	512-305-7300
Radiology Technician #26	512-834-6617	Securities Broker #39	512-305-8332	Teacher #42	512-469-3000
Real Estate Broker #52	512-459-6544	Securities Dealer #39	512-305-8332	Temporary Common Worker #14	512-463-6599
Real Estate Inspector #52	512-459-6544	Security Agency, Private #35	512-463-5545	Transportation Service Provider #54	512-465-3500
Real Estate Salesperson #52	512-459-6544	Seed Dealer #11	979-542-3691	Trust Company #01	512-475-1300
Representative Offices (Banking) #01	512-475-1300	Service Contract Provider #14	512-463-6599	Underground Storage Tank Installer #60	512-239-2191
Respiratory Care Practitioner #29	512-834-6632	Sex Offender Treatment Provider #26	512-834-4530	Vehicle Protection Provider #14	512-463-6599
Sanitarian #22	512-834-6635	Shorthand Reporter #09	512-463-1630	Veterinarian #18	512-305-7555
Sanitation Code Enforcement Ofc. #22	512-834-6635	Social Worker #26	512-719-3521	Water Well & Pump Installer #14	512-463-7880
Savings & Loan Association #37	512-475-1350	Speech-Language Pathologist #22	512-834-6627	Weather Modification Service #14	512-463-6599
Savings Bank #37	512-475-1350	Staff Leasing #14	512-475-2896	Weigher, Public #11	512-463-7607
School Psychology Specialist #19	512-305-7700	Surveyor #04	512-452-9427	Wig Specialist #02	512-305-8475
School Psychology Specialist #25	512-305-7700	Talent Agency #14	512-463-6599		

Licensing Agency Information

#01 Banking Department, 2601 N Lamar Blvd, Austin, TX 78705-4294; 512-475-1300, Fax: 512-475-1313.
www.banking.state.tx.us
Direct web site URL to search for licensees: www.banking.state.tx.us/itds.htm. You can search online using alphabetical lists

#02 Board of Barber Examiners, 333 Guadalupe, #2-110, Austin, TX 78701; 512-305-8475, Fax: 512-305-6800.
www.tsbbe.state.tx.us Cost of bulk record request is estimated based on amount of information requested.

#03 Board of Plumbing Examiners, PO Box 4200, Austin, TX 78765-4200; 512-458-2145, Fax: 512-450-0637.
www.tsbpe.state.tx.us

#04 Board of Professional Land Surveying, 7701 N Lamar, #400, Austin, TX 78752; 512-452-9427, Fax: 512-452-7711.
www.txls.state.tx.us

#05 Board of Registration for Professional Engineers; 1917 IH35 S (78760), Austin, TX 78741; 512-440-7723, Fax: 512-442-1414.
www.tbpe.state.tx.us Licensing data may be availabe online at the web site as early as October, 2000.

#06 Commission for the Deaf & Hard of Hearing, 4800 N Lamar Blvd, #310, Austin, TX 78711; 512-407-3250 Voice; 512-407-3251 TTY, Fax: 512-451-9316.
http://link.tsl.texas.gov/tx/TCDHH

#07 Office of Consumer Credit Commissioner, 2601 N Lamar Blvd, Austin, TX 78705-4207; 512-936-2600, Fax: 512-936-7610.
www.occc.state.tx.us

#08 Cosmetology Commission, 5717 Balcones Dr, Austin, TX 78755; 512-467-8206, Fax: 512-419-9914.

#09 Court Reporter Certification Board, PO Box 131131, Austin, TX 78711-3131; 512-463-1630, Fax: 512-463-1117.
www.crcb.state.tx.us

#10 Department of Agriculture, 1700 Congress Ave, Austin, TX 78711; 512-463-7476, Fax: 512-475-1618.
www.agr.state.tx.us/pesticide/index.html

#11 Department of Agriculture, PO Box 12847 (1700 N Congress, Stephen F Austin Bldg), Austin, TX 78711; 512-463-7476, Fax: 512-463-7582.
www.agr.state.tx.us

#12 Department of Health, 1100 W 49th St, Austin, TX 78756; 512-834-6600, Fax: 512-834-6644.
www.tdh.state.tx.us/beh/asbmain.htm

#13 Department of Human Services, Mail Code Y979, Austin, TX 78714-9030; 512-231-5800, Fax: 512-834-6764.
www.dhs.state.tx.us

#14 Department of Licensing & Regulation, PO Box 12157 (920 Colorado), Austin, TX 78711-2157; 512-463-6599, Fax: 512-475-2854.
www.license.state.tx.us
Direct web site URL to search for licensees: www.license.state.tx.us/LicenseSearch

#15 Funeral Service Commission, 510 S Congress Ave, #206, Austin, TX 78704-1718; 512-936-2474, Fax: 512-479-5064.
www.tfsc.state.tx.us

#17 Executive Council on Physical Therapy & Occupational Therapy Examiners, 333 Guadalupe St, Tower 2, #510, Austin, TX 78701; 512-305-6900, Fax: 512-305-6951.
www.ecptote.state.tx.us
Direct web site URL to search for licensees: www.ecptote.state.tx.us/serv/verification/default.html

#18 Health Department, 333 Guadalupe, Tower 2, #330, Austin, TX 78701-3998; 512-305-7555, Fax: 512-305-7556.
www.texasonline.state.tx.us/tbvme

#19 Board of Examiners of Psychologists, 333 Guadalupe, #2-450, Austin, TX 78701; 512-305-7700, Fax: 512-305-7701.
www.tsbep.state.tx.us

#20 Board of Podiactric Medical Examiners, 333 Guadalupe, #2-320, Austin, TX 78701; 512-305-7000, Fax: 512-305-7003.

#21 Health Department, 1100 W 49th St, Austin, TX 78756; 512-834-6615, Fax: 512-834-6677.
www.tdh.state.tx.us/hcqs/plc/at.htm

#22 Health Department, 1100 W 49th St, Austin, TX 78756-3183; 512-834-6635, Fax: 512-834-6707.
www.tdh.state.tx.us/license.htm
Direct web site URL to search for licensees: www.tdh.state.tx.us/license.htm

#23 Health Department, 333 Guadalupe, Tower 3, #800, Austin, TX 78701; 512-463-6400, Fax: 512-463-7452.
www.tsbde.state.tx.us

#24 Health Department, 333 Guadalupe, Tower 3, #600, Box 21, Austin, TX 78701-3942; 512-305-8000, Fax: 512-305-8082.
www.tsbp.state.tx.us
Direct web site URL to search for licensees: www.tsbp.state.tx.us/dbsearch/index.htm. You can search online using status, license number, name, city, county, and ZIP Code.

#25 Health Department, 323 Guadalupe, Tower 3, #825, Austin, TX 78701; 512-458-7111, Fax: 512-305-6705.
www.tdh.state.tx.us

#26 Health Department, 1100 W 49th St, Austin, TX 78756; 512-834-6658, Fax: 512-834-6789.
www.tdh.state.tx.us/hfl/hfl-web.htm
Direct web site URL to search for licensees: www.tdh.state.tx.us/license.htm

#27 Health Department, 1100 W 49th St, Austin, TX 78756; 512-458-6700, Fax: 512-834-6736.
www.tdh.state.tx.us/hcqs/ems/emshome.htm
Direct web site URL to search for licensees: http://160.42.108.3/ems_web/blh_html_page1.htm You can search online using name and/or city

#28 Health Department, 1100 W 49th St, Austin, TX 78756; 512-834-6616, Fax: 512-834-6677.
www.tdh.state.tx.us/hcqs/plc/massage.htm

#29 Health Department, 1100 W 49th St, Austin, TX 78756; 512-834-6632, Fax: 512-834-4518.
www.tdh.state.tx.us/hcqs/plc/resp.htm

#30 Board of Medical Examiners, PO Box 2018, Austin, TX 78768-2018; 512-305-7030, Fax: 512-463-9416.
www.tsbme.state.tx.us
Direct web site URL to search for licensees: www.docboard.org/tx/df/txsearch.htm. You can search online using name, license #.

#31 Health Department, 1100 W 49th St, Austin, TX 78756; 512-834-6628, Fax: 512-834-6677.
www.tdh.state.tx.us/hcqs/plc/mft.htm
Direct web site URL to search for licensees: www.tdh.state.tx.us/license.htm. You can search online using alphabetical lists

#32 Department of Human Services, PO Box 149030 - Mail Code yana, Austin, TX 78714-9030; 512-231-5825, Fax: 512-834-6764.
www.dhs.state.tx.us/programs/credentialing/

#33 Office of Secretary of State, 1019 Brazos, Rm 214, Austin, TX 78711-2887; 512-463-5705. www.sos.state.tx.us

#34 Polygraph Examiner Board, PO Box 4087, Austin, TX 78773-4087; 512-424-2058, Fax: 512-424-5739.
http://polygraph.org/states/tape
Direct web site URL to search for licensees: http://polygraph.org/states/tape/members_roster.htm

#35 Private Investigators/Security Agencies Board, 4930 S Congress, Capitol Station, Austin, TX 78711; 512-463-5545, Fax: 512-707-2041. www.tcps.state.tx.us

#36 Racing Commission, 8505 Cross Park Dr, #110, Austin, TX 78754; 512-833-6699, Fax: 512-833-6907.
www.txrc.state.tx.us

#37 Savings & Loan Department, 2601 N Lamar Blvd, #201, Austin, TX 78705-4241; 112-475-1350, Fax: 512-475-1360.
www.tsld.state.tx.us

#38 Secretary of State, PO Box 12887 (10119 Bravos), Austin, TX 78711-2887; 512-475-1769, Fax: 512-475-2815.
www.sos.state.tx.us

#39 Securities Board, 200 E 10th St, 5th Fl, Austin, TX 78701; 512-305-8300, Fax: 512-305-8310.
www.ssb.state.tx.us

#40 State Bar of Texas, 1414 Colorado, #300, Austin, TX 78701-1627; 512-463-1463 x1383, Fax: 512-462-1475.
www.texasbar.com
Direct web site URL to search for licensees: www.texasbar.com

#41 Board of Examiners for Professional Counselors, 1100 W 49th St, Austin, TX 78756; 512-834-6658, Fax: 512-834-6789.
www.tdh.state.tx.us/hcqs/plc/lpc.htm

#42 Board for Educator Certification, 1001 Trinity, Austin, TX 78701-2603; 512-469-3000, Fax: 512-469-3018.
www.sbec.state.tx.us

#43 Board of Public Accountancy, 333 Guadalupe St, Tower III, #900, Austin, TX 78701; 512-305-7800, Fax: 512-505-7875.
www.tsbpa.state.tx.us

#44 Library & Archives Commission, 1201 Brazos, Austin, TX 78711-2927; 512-463-5466, Fax: 512-463-8800.
www.tsl.state.tx.us

#45 State Parks & Wildlife Department, 4200 Smith School Rd, Austin, TX 78744; 512-389-4818, Fax: 512-389-4349.
www.tpwd.state.tx.us

#46 Alcoholic Beverage Commission, PO Box 13127 (5806 Mesa Dr), Austin, TX 78711; 512-206-3333, Fax: 512-451-0240.
www.tabc.state.tx

#47 Appraisers Licensing & Certification Board, 1101 Camino La Costa, Austin, TX 78752; 512-465-3950, Fax: 512-465-3953.
www.talcb.state.tx.us
Direct web site URL to search for licensees: www.talcb.state.tx.us

#48 Department of Insurance, 333 Guadalupe, Austin, TX 78701; 512-463-6169, Fax: 512-475-2025.
www.tdi.state.tx.us
Direct web site URL to search for licensees: www.tdi.state.tx.us/general/forms/colists.html.
You can search online using downloadable lists

#49 Department of Protective & Regulatory Services, 701 W 51st St, #E-550, Austin, TX 78714-9030; 512-438-4800, Fax: 512-438-3848.
www.tdprs.state.tx.us

#50 Ethics Commission, PO Box 12070, Austin, TX 78711-2070; 512-463-5800, Fax: 512-463-5777.
www.ethics.state.tx.us
Direct web site URL to search for licensees: www.ethics.state.tx.us/filinginfo/loblists.htm

#51 Optometry Board, 333 Guadalupe St, #2-420, Austin, TX 78701-3942; 512-305-8500, Fax: 512-305-8501.
www.tded.state.tx.us/guide/REGULATORYBODIES.html

Direct web site URL to search for licensees: www.odfinder.org/LicSearch.asp. Search online using national database by name, city or state.

#52 Real Estate Commission, PO Box 12188, Austin, TX 78711-2188; 512-459-6544, Fax: 512-465-3698.
www.trec.state.tx.us
Direct web site URL to search for licensees: www.trec.state.tx.us/publicinfo. You can search online using name and license number.

#53 State Fire Marshal, 333 Guadalupe, Austin, TX 78701; 512-305-7900, Fax: 512-305-7922.
www.tdi.state.tx.us/fire/fmli.html

#54 Department of Transportation, 4203 Bull Creek, Austin, TX 78731; 512-465-3500, Fax: 512-465-3535.
www.dot.state.tx.us

#55 Department of Health, Toxic Substances Control Division, 1100 W 49th St, Austin, TX 78756-3199; 512-834-6612, Fax: 512-834-6644.
www.tdh.state.tx.us/beh/web.htm

#56 Commission on Fire Protection, 12675 Research Blvd, PO Box 2286, Austin, TX 78768-2286; 512-918-7100, Fax: 512-239-4917.
www.tcfp.state.tx.us

#57 Natural Resource Conservation Comm MC178, PO Box 13087, Austin, TX 78711-3087; 512-239-6719, Fax: 512-239-0533.
www.tnrcc.state.tx.us

#58 Commission on Law Enforcement Officer, 1033 La Posada #240, Austin, TX 78752; 512-936-7700.

#59 Board of Tax Professional Examiners, 333 Guadalupe St, Tower II #520, Austin, TX 78701; 512-305-7300.

#60 Natural Resource Conservation Commission, PO Box 13087, Austin, TX 78711-3087; 512-239-2191.

#61 Board of Architectural Examiners, 333 Guadalupe #2-350, Austin, TX 78701-3942; 512-305-9000.

Texas Federal Courts

The following list indicates the district and division name for each county in the state. If the bankruptcy court location is different from the district court, then the location of the bankruptcy court appears in parentheses.

County/Court Cross Reference

County	District	Division
Anderson	Eastern	Tyler
Andrews	Western	Midland (Midland/Odessa)
Angelina	Eastern	Texarkana (Beaumont)
Aransas	Southern	Corpus Christi
Archer	Northern	Wichita Falls
Armstrong	Northern	Amarillo
Atascosa	Western	San Antonio
Austin	Southern	Houston
Bailey	Northern	Lubbock
Bandera	Western	San Antonio
Bastrop	Western	Austin
Baylor	Northern	Wichita Falls
Bee	Southern	Corpus Christi
Bell	Western	Waco
Bexar	Western	San Antonio
Blanco	Western	Austin
Borden	Northern	Lubbock
Bosque	Western	Waco
Bowie	Eastern	Texarkana
Brazoria	Southern	Galveston (Houston)
Brazos	Southern	Houston
Brewster	Western	Pecos (Midland/Odessa)
Briscoe	Northern	Amarillo
Brooks	Southern	Corpus Christi
Brown	Northern	San Angelo (Lubbock)
Burleson	Western	Austin
Burnet	Western	Austin
Caldwell	Western	Austin
Calhoun	Southern	Victoria (Corpus Christi)
Callahan	Northern	Abilene (Lubbock)
Cameron	Southern	Brownsville (Corpus Christi)
Camp	Eastern	Marshall
Carson	Northern	Amarillo
Cass	Eastern	Marshall
Castro	Northern	Amarillo
Chambers	Southern	Galveston (Houston)
Cherokee	Eastern	Tyler
Childress	Northern	Amarillo
Clay	Northern	Wichita Falls
Cochran	Northern	Lubbock
Coke	Northern	San Angelo (Lubbock)
Coleman	Northern	San Angelo (Lubbock)
Collin	Eastern	Sherman (Plano)
Collingsworth	Northern	Amarillo
Colorado	Southern	Houston
Comal	Western	San Antonio
Comanche	Northern	Fort Worth
Concho	Northern	San Angelo (Lubbock)
Cooke	Eastern	Sherman (Plano)
Coryell	Western	Waco
Cottle	Northern	Wichita Falls
Crane	Western	Midland (Midland/Odessa)
Crockett	Northern	San Angelo (Lubbock)
Crosby	Northern	Lubbock
Culberson	Western	Pecos (Midland/Odessa)
Dallam	Northern	Amarillo
Dallas	Northern	Dallas
Dawson	Northern	Lubbock
De Witt	Southern	Victoria (Houston)
Deaf Smith	Northern	Amarillo
Delta	Eastern	Sherman (Plano)
Denton	Eastern	Sherman (Plano)
Dickens	Northern	Lubbock
Dimmit	Western	San Antonio
Donley	Northern	Amarillo
Duval	Southern	Corpus Christi
Eastland	Northern	Abilene (Lubbock)
Ector	Western	Midland (Midland/Odessa)
Edwards	Western	Del Rio (San Antonio)
El Paso	Western	El Paso
Ellis	Northern	Dallas
Erath	Northern	Fort Worth
Falls	Western	Waco
Fannin	Eastern	Sherman (Plano)
Fayette	Southern	Houston
Fisher	Northern	Abilene (Lubbock)
Floyd	Northern	Lubbock
Foard	Northern	Wichita Falls
Fort Bend	Southern	Houston
Franklin	Eastern	Texarkana
Freestone	Western	Waco
Frio	Western	San Antonio
Gaines	Northern	Lubbock
Galveston	Southern	Galveston (Houston)
Garza	Northern	Lubbock
Gillespie	Western	Austin
Glasscock	Northern	San Angelo (Lubbock)
Goliad	Southern	Victoria (Corpus Christi)
Gonzales	Western	San Antonio
Gray	Northern	Amarillo
Grayson	Eastern	Sherman (Plano)
Gregg	Eastern	Tyler
Grimes	Southern	Houston
Guadalupe	Western	San Antonio
Hale	Northern	Lubbock
Hall	Northern	Amarillo
Hamilton	Western	Waco
Hansford	Northern	Amarillo
Hardeman	Northern	Wichita Falls
Hardin	Eastern	Beaumont
Harris	Southern	Houston
Harrison	Eastern	Marshall
Hartley	Northern	Amarillo
Haskell	Northern	Abilene (Lubbock)
Hays	Western	Austin
Hemphill	Northern	Amarillo
Henderson	Eastern	Tyler
Hidalgo	Southern	McAllen (Corpus Christi)
Hill	Western	Waco
Hockley	Northern	Lubbock
Hood	Northern	Fort Worth
Hopkins	Eastern	Sherman (Plano)
Houston	Eastern	Texarkana (Beaumont)
Howard	Northern	Abilene (Lubbock)
Hudspeth	Western	Pecos (Midland/Odessa)
Hunt	Northern	Dallas

County	District	Location
Hutchinson	Northern	Amarillo
Irion	Northern	San Angelo (Lubbock)
Jack	Northern	Fort Worth
Jackson	Southern	Victoria (Corpus Christi)
Jasper	Eastern	Beaumont
Jeff Davis	Western	Pecos (Midland/Odessa)
Jefferson	Eastern	Beaumont
Jim Hogg	Southern	Laredo (Houston)
Jim Wells	Southern	Corpus Christi
Johnson	Northern	Dallas
Jones	Northern	Abilene (Lubbock)
Karnes	Western	San Antonio
Kaufman	Northern	Dallas
Kendall	Western	San Antonio
Kenedy	Southern	Corpus Christi
Kent	Northern	Lubbock
Kerr	Western	San Antonio
Kimble	Western	Austin
King	Northern	Wichita Falls
Kinney	Western	Del Rio (San Antonio)
Kleberg	Southern	Corpus Christi
Knox	Northern	Wichita Falls
La Salle	Southern	Laredo (Corpus Christi)
Lamar	Eastern	Sherman (Plano)
Lamb	Northern	Lubbock
Lampasas	Western	Austin
Lavaca	Southern	Victoria (Houston)
Lee	Western	Austin
Leon	Western	Waco
Liberty	Eastern	Beaumont
Limestone	Western	Waco
Lipscomb	Northern	Amarillo
Live Oak	Southern	Corpus Christi
Llano	Western	Austin
Loving	Western	Pecos (Midland/Odessa)
Lubbock	Northern	Lubbock
Lynn	Northern	Lubbock
Madison	Southern	Houston
Marion	Eastern	Marshall
Martin	Western	Midland (Midland/Odessa)
Mason	Western	Austin
Matagorda	Southern	Galveston (Houston)
Maverick	Western	Del Rio (San Antonio)
McCulloch	Western	Austin
McLennan	Western	Waco
McMullen	Southern	Laredo (Houston)
Medina	Western	San Antonio
Menard	Northern	San Angelo (Lubbock)
Midland	Western	Midland (Midland/Odessa)
Milam	Western	Waco
Mills	Northern	San Angelo (Lubbock)
Mitchell	Northern	Abilene (Lubbock)
Montague	Northern	Wichita Falls
Montgomery	Southern	Houston
Moore	Northern	Amarillo
Morris	Eastern	Marshall
Motley	Northern	Lubbock
Nacogdoches	Eastern	Texarkana (Beaumont)
Navarro	Northern	Dallas
Newton	Eastern	Beaumont
Nolan	Northern	Abilene (Lubbock)
Nueces	Southern	Corpus Christi
Ochiltree	Northern	Amarillo
Oldham	Northern	Amarillo
Orange	Eastern	Beaumont
Palo Pinto	Northern	Fort Worth
Panola	Eastern	Tyler
Parker	Northern	Fort Worth
Parmer	Northern	Amarillo
Pecos	Western	Pecos (Midland/Odessa)
Polk	Eastern	Texarkana (Beaumont)
Potter	Northern	Amarillo
Presidio	Western	Pecos (Midland/Odessa)
Rains	Eastern	Tyler
Randall	Northern	Amarillo
Reagan	Northern	San Angelo (Lubbock)
Real	Western	San Antonio
Red River	Eastern	Sherman (Plano)
Reeves	Western	Pecos (Midland/Odessa)
Refugio	Southern	Victoria (Corpus Christi)
Roberts	Northern	Amarillo
Robertson	Western	Waco
Rockwall	Northern	Dallas
Runnels	Northern	San Angelo (Lubbock)
Rusk	Eastern	Tyler
Sabine	Eastern	Texarkana (Beaumont)
San Augustine	Eastern	Texarkana (Beaumont)
San Jacinto	Southern	Houston
San Patricio	Southern	Corpus Christi
San Saba	Western	Austin
Schleicher	Northern	San Angelo (Lubbock)
Scurry	Northern	Lubbock
Shackelford	Northern	Abilene (Lubbock)
Shelby	Eastern	Texarkana (Beaumont)
Sherman	Northern	Amarillo
Smith	Eastern	Tyler
Somervell	Western	Waco
Starr	Southern	McAllen (Corpus Christi)
Stephens	Northern	Abilene (Lubbock)
Sterling	Northern	San Angelo (Lubbock)
Stonewall	Northern	Abilene (Lubbock)
Sutton	Northern	San Angelo (Lubbock)
Swisher	Northern	Amarillo
Tarrant	Northern	Fort Worth
Taylor	Northern	Abilene (Lubbock)
Terrell	Western	Del Rio (San Antonio)
Terry	Northern	Lubbock
Throckmorton	Northern	Abilene (Lubbock)
Titus	Eastern	Texarkana
Tom Green	Northern	San Angelo (Lubbock)
Travis	Western	Austin
Trinity	Eastern	Texarkana (Beaumont)
Tyler	Eastern	Texarkana (Beaumont)
Upshur	Eastern	Marshall
Upton	Western	Midland (Midland/Odessa)
Uvalde	Western	Del Rio (San Antonio)
Val Verde	Western	Del Rio (San Antonio)
Van Zandt	Eastern	Tyler
Victoria	Southern	Victoria (Corpus Christi)
Walker	Southern	Houston
Waller	Southern	Houston
Ward	Western	Pecos (Midland/Odessa)
Washington	Western	Austin
Webb	Southern	Laredo (Houston)
Wharton	Southern	Houston
Wheeler	Northern	Amarillo
Wichita	Northern	Wichita Falls
Wilbarger	Northern	Wichita Falls
Willacy	Southern	Brownsville (Corpus Christi)
Williamson	Western	Austin
Wilson	Western	San Antonio
Winkler	Western	Pecos (Midland/Odessa)
Wise	Northern	Fort Worth
Wood	Eastern	Tyler
Yoakum	Northern	Lubbock
Young	Northern	Wichita Falls
Zapata	Southern	Laredo (Houston)
Zavala	Western	Del Rio (San Antonio)

US District Court

Eastern District of Texas

Beaumont Division PO Box 3507, Beaumont, TX 77704 (Courier Address: Room 104, 300 Willow, Beaumont, TX 77701), 409-654-7000.

http://www.txed.uscourts.gov

Counties: Delta*, Fannin*, Hardin, Hopkins*, Jasper, Jefferson, Lamar*, Liberty, Newton, Orange, Red River. Counties marked with an asterisk are called the Paris Division, whose case records are maintained here.

Indexing/Storage: Cases are indexed by defendant and plaintiff as well as by case number. New cases are available in the index immediately after filing date. A computer index is maintained. Records are also indexed on microfiche. Open records are located at this court. District wide searches are available for records from 3/86 from this division. This division maintains records for the Paris Division also.

Fee & Payment: The fee is $20.00 per item (one party name or case number). Payment may be made by money order, cashier check, personal check. Prepayment is required. Payee: Clerk, US District Court. Certification fee: $7.00 per document. Copy fee: $.50 per page. You are allowed to make your own copies. These copies cost $.25 per page. Copies are made from a public copy machine. Certified search requests are $25.00.

Phone Search: Only docket information is available by phone.

Mail Search: A stamped self addressed envelope is not required.

In Person: In person searching is available.

PACER: Sign-up number is 800-676-6856. Access fee is $.60 per minute. Toll-free access: 888-837-7816. Local access: 903-590-1104. Case records are available back to 1992. Records are purged once per year. New records are available online after 1 day. PACER is available online at http://pacer.txed.uscourts.gov.

Lufkin Division 104 N. Third St., Lufkin, TX 75901 (Courier Address: Use mail address for courier delivery), 936-632-2739.

http://www.txed.uscourts.gov

Counties: Angelina, Houston, Nacogdoches, Polk, Sabine, San Augustine, Shelby, Trinity, Tyler.

Indexing/Storage: Cases are indexed by defendant and plaintiff as well as by case number. New cases are available in the index 1 day after filing date. Both computer and card indexes are maintained. Records are also indexed on microfiche. Open records are located at this court.

Fee & Payment: The fee is $20.00 per item (one party name or case number). Payment may be made by money order, cashier check, personal check. Prepayment is required. Payee: US District Court. Certification fee: $7.00 per document. Copy fee: $.50 per page. You are allowed to make your own copies. These copies cost $.50 per page.

Phone Search: Only docket information is available by phone.

Mail Search: Always enclose a stamped self addressed envelope.

In Person: In person searching is available.

PACER: Sign-up number is 800-676-6856. Access fee is. New records are available online after 1 day. PACER is available online at http://pacer.txed.uscourts.gov.

Marshall Division PO Box 1499, Marshall, TX 75671-1499 (Courier Address: 100 E Houston, Marshall, TX 75670), 903-935-2912, Fax: 903-938-2651.

http://www.txed.uscourts.gov

Counties: Camp, Cass, Harrison, Marion, Morris, Upshur.

Indexing/Storage: Cases are indexed by defendant and plaintiff as well as by case number. New cases are available in the index 1 day after filing date. Both computer and card indexes are maintained. Records are also indexed on microfiche. Open records are located at this court.

Fee & Payment: The fee is $20.00 per item (one party name or case number). Payment may be made by money order, cashier check, personal check. Prepayment is required. Payee: US District Court. Certification fee: $7.00 per document. Copy fee: $.50 per page. You are allowed to make your own copies. These copies cost $.50 per page.

Phone Search: Only docket information is available by phone.

Mail Search: Always enclose a stamped self addressed envelope.

In Person: In person searching is available.

PACER: Sign-up number is 800-676-6856. Access fee is $.60 per minute. Toll-free access: 888-837-7816. Local access: 903-590-1104. Case records are available back to 1992. Records are purged once per year. New records are available online after 1 day. PACER is available online at http://pacer.txed.uscourts.gov.

Sherman Division 101 E Pecan St, Sherman, TX 75090 (Courier Address: Use mail address for courier delivery), 903-892-2921.

http://www.txed.uscourts.gov

Counties: Collin, Cooke, Denton, Grayson.

Indexing/Storage: Cases are indexed by defendant and plaintiff as well as by case number. New cases are available in the index 1 day after filing date. Both computer and card indexes are maintained. Records are also indexed on microfiche. Open records are located at this court. District wide searches are available from this division.

Fee & Payment: The fee is $20.00 per item (one party name or case number). Payment may be made by money order, cashier check, personal check. Prepayment is required. Payee: Clerk, US District Court. Certification fee: $7.00 per document. Copy fee: $.50 per page.

Phone Search: Docket information available by phone.

Mail Search: Always enclose a stamped self addressed envelope.

In Person: In person searching is available.

PACER: Sign-up number is 800-676-6856. Access fee is $.60 per minute. Toll-free access: 888-837-7816. Local access: 903-590-1104. Case records are available back to 1992. Records are purged once per year. New records are available online after 1 day. PACER is available online at http://pacer.txed.uscourts.gov.

Texarkana Division Clerk's Office, 500 State Line Ave, Room 301, Texarkana, TX 75501 (Courier Address: Use mail address for courier delivery), 903-794-8561, Fax: 903-794-0600.

http://www.txed.uscourts.gov

Counties: Bowie, Franklin, Titus.

Indexing/Storage: Cases are indexed by defendant and plaintiff as well as by case number. New cases are available in the index 1-2 days after filing date. Both computer and card indexes are maintained. Records are also indexed on microfiche. Open records are located at this court. There is no set time when cases are sent to the Fort Worth Federal Records Center.

Fee & Payment: The fee is $20.00 per item (one party name or case number). Payment may be made by money order, cashier check, personal check. Prepayment is required. Payee: Clerk, US District Court. Certification fee: $7.00 per document. Copy fee: $.50 per page.

Phone Search: Searching is not available by phone.

Mail Search: Always enclose a stamped self addressed envelope.

In Person: In person searching is available.

PACER: Sign-up number is 800-676-6856. Access fee is $.60 per minute. Toll-free access: 888-837-7816. Local access: 903-590-1104. Case records are available back to 1992. Records are purged once per year. New records are available online after 1 day. PACER is available online at http://pacer.txed.uscourts.gov.

Tyler Division Clerk, Room 106, 211 W Ferguson, Tyler, TX 75702 (Courier Address: Use mail address for courier delivery), 903-590-1000.

http://www.txed.uscourts.gov

Counties: Anderson, Cherokee, Gregg, Henderson, Panola, Rains, Rusk, Smith, Van Zandt, Wood.

Indexing/Storage: Cases are indexed by defendant and plaintiff as well as by case number. New cases are available in the index 1-2 days after filing date. Both computer and card indexes are maintained. Records are also indexed on microfiche. Open records are located at this court. There is no set time when cases are sent to the Fort Worth Federal Records Center.

Fee & Payment: The fee is $20.00 per item (one party name or case number). Payment may be made by money order, cashier check, personal check. Prepayment is required. Payee: Clerk, US District Court. Certification fee: $7.00 per document. Copy fee: $.50 per page. You are allowed to make your own copies. These copies cost $.25 per page.

Phone Search: Only docket information is available by phone.

Mail Search: A stamped self addressed envelope is not required.

In Person: In person searching is available.

PACER: Sign-up number is 800-676-6856. Access fee is $.60 per minute. Toll-free access: 888-837-7816. Local access: 903-590-1104. Case records are available back to 1992. Records are purged once per year. New records are available online after 1 day. PACER is available online at http://pacer.txed.uscourts.gov.

US Bankruptcy Court

Eastern District of Texas

Beaumont Division Suite 100, 300 Willow, Beaumont, TX 77701 (Courier Address: Use mail address for courier delivery), 409-839-2617.

http://www.txeb.uscourts.gov

Counties: Angelina, Hardin, Houston, Jasper, Jefferson, Liberty, Nacogdoches, Newton, Orange, Polk, Sabine, San Augustine, Shelby, Trinity, Tyler.

Indexing/Storage: Cases are indexed by debtor as well as by case number. New cases are available in the index 1 day after filing date. A computer index is maintained. Open records are located at this court.

Fee & Payment: The fee is $20.00 per item (one party name or case number). Payment may be made by money order, cashier check, personal check. Prepayment is required. Debtor's checks are not accepted. Payee: Clerk, US Bankruptcy Court. Certification fee: $7.00 per document. Copy fee: $.50 per page. You are allowed to make your own copies. These copies cost $.25 per page. The searcher must fill out a card with their phone number, the date and the case number.

Phone Search: Only docket information is available by phone. An automated voice case information service (VCIS) is available. Call VCIS at 800-466-1694 or 903-590-1217.

Mail Search: Always enclose a stamped self addressed envelope.

In Person: In person searching is available.

PACER: Sign-up number is 800-676-6856. Access fee is $.60 per minute. Toll-free access: 800-466-1681. Local access: 903-590-1220. Case records are available back to 1989. Records are purged every six months. New civil records are available online after 1 day. PACER is available online at http://pacer.txeb.uscourts.gov.

Marshall Division c/o Tyler Division, 200 E Ferguson, Tyler, TX 75702 (Courier Address: Use mail address for courier delivery), 903-590-1212, Fax: 903-590-1226.

http://www.txeb.uscourts.gov

Counties: Camp, Cass, Harrison, Marion, Morris, Upshur.

Indexing/Storage: Cases are indexed by as well as by case number. New cases are available in the index after filing date. Open records are located at the Division.

Fee & Payment: The fee is no charge per item (one party name or case number). Payment may be made by money order, cashier check. Business checks are not accepted. Personal checks are not accepted.

Phone Search: An automated voice case information service (VCIS) is available. Call VCIS at 800-466-1694 or 903-590-1217.

Mail Search: A stamped self addressed envelope is not required.

In Person: In person searching is available.

PACER: Sign-up number is 800-676-6856. Access fee is $.60 per minute. Toll-free access: 800-466-1681. Local access: 903-590-1220. Case records are available back to 1989. Records are purged every six months. New civil records are available online after 1 day. PACER is available online at http://pacer.txeb.uscourts.gov.

Plano Division Suite 300B, 660 N Central Expressway, Plano, TX 75074 (Courier Address: Use mail address for courier delivery), 972-509-1240, Fax: 972-509-1245.

http://www.txeb.uscourts.gov

Counties: Collin, Cooke, Delta, Denton, Fannin, Grayson, Hopkins, Lamar, Red River.

Indexing/Storage: Cases are indexed by debtor and creditors as well as by case number. New cases are available in the index 24 hours after filing date. A computer index is maintained. Open records are located at this court.

Fee & Payment: The fee is $20.00 per item (one party name or case number). Payment may be made by money order, cashier check, personal check. Prepayment is required. Payee: Clerk, US Bankruptcy Court. Certification fee: $7.00 per document. Copy fee: $.50 per page. You are allowed to make your own copies. These copies cost $.25 per page.

Phone Search: Only docket information is available by phone. An automated voice case information service (VCIS) is available. Call VCIS at 800-466-1694 or 903-590-1217.

Mail Search: Always enclose a stamped self addressed envelope.

In Person: In person searching is available.

PACER: Sign-up number is 800-676-6856. Access fee is $.60 per minute. Toll-free access: 800-466-1681. Local access: 903-590-1220. Case records are available back to 1989. Records are purged every six months. New civil records are available online after 1 day.

Texarkana Division c/o Plano Division, Suite 300B, 660 N Central Expressway, Plano, TX 75074 (Courier Address: Use mail address for courier delivery), 972-509-1240, Fax: 972-509-1245.

http://www.txeb.uscourts.gov

Counties: Bowie, Franklin, Titus.

Indexing/Storage: Cases are indexed by as well as by case number. New cases are available in the index after filing date. Open records are located at the Division.

Fee & Payment: The fee is no charge per item (one party name or case number). Payment may be made by money order, cashier check. Business checks are not accepted. Personal checks are not accepted.

Phone Search: An automated voice case information service (VCIS) is available. Call VCIS at 800-466-1694 or 903-590-1217.

Mail Search: Always enclose a stamped self addressed envelope.

In Person: In person searching is available.

PACER: Sign-up number is 800-676-6856. Access fee is $.60 per minute. Toll-free access: 800-466-1681. Local access: 903-590-1220. Case records are available back to 1989. Records are purged every six months. New civil records are available online after 1 day.

Tyler Division 200 E Ferguson, 2nd Floor, Tyler, TX 75702 (Courier Address: Use mail address for courier delivery), 903-590-1212, Fax: 903-590-1226.

http://www.txeb.uscourts.gov

Counties: Anderson, Cherokee, Gregg, Henderson, Panola, Rains, Rusk, Smith, Van Zandt, Wood.

Indexing/Storage: Cases are indexed by debtor as well as by case number. New cases are available in the index 1 day after filing date. Both computer and card indexes are maintained. Records are also indexed on microfiche. Card index is only for cases prior to October 1987. Open records are located at this court. District wide searches are available for information from 10/87 from this court. This court maintains automated case records and all finance records for the other divisions in this district.

Fee & Payment: The fee is $20.00 per item (one party name or case number). Payment may be made by money order, cashier check, personal check. Prepayment is required. Payee: Clerk, US Bankruptcy Court. Certification fee: $7.00 per document. Copy fee: $.50 per page. You are allowed to make your own copies. These copies cost $.25 per page.

Phone Search: This court will answer questions pertaining to information not available from VCIS. An automated voice case information service (VCIS) is available. Call VCIS at 800-466-1694 or 903-590-1217.

Mail Search: A stamped self addressed envelope is not required.

In Person: In person searching is available.

PACER: Sign-up number is 800-676-6856. Access fee is $.60 per minute. Toll-free access: 800-466-1681. Local access: 903-590-1220. Case records are available back to 1989. Records are purged every six months. New civil records are available online after 1 day. PACER is available online at http://pacer.txeb.uscourts.gov.

US District Court

Northern District of Texas

Abilene Division PO Box 1218, Abilene, TX 79604 (Courier Address: Room 2008, 341 Pine St, Abilene, TX 79601), 915-677-6311.

http://www.txnd.uscourts.gov

Counties: Callahan, Eastland, Fisher, Haskell, Howard, Jones, Mitchell, Nolan, Shackelford, Stephens, Stonewall, Taylor, Throckmorton.

Indexing/Storage: Cases are indexed by defendant and plaintiff as well as by case number. New cases are available in the index 2 days after filing date. Both computer and card indexes are maintained. A computer index is planned for early 1996. Open records are located at this court. District wide searches can be conducted from this court for information from 1983.

Fee & Payment: The fee is $20.00 per item (one party name or case number). Payment may be made by money order, cashier check, personal check. Prepayment is required. Payee: Clerk, US District Court. Certification fee: $7.00 per document. Copy fee: $.50 per page.

Phone Search: Only a name or case number will be released over the phone.

Mail Search: A stamped self addressed envelope is not required.

In Person: In person searching is available.

PACER: Sign-up number is 800-676-6856. Access fee is $.60 per minute. Toll-free access: 800-684-2393. Local access: 214-753-2449. Case records are available back to June 1991. Records are purged once per year. New records are available online after 1 day. PACER is available online at http://pacer.txnd.uscourts.gov.

Amarillo Division 205 E 5th St, Amarillo, TX 79101 (Courier Address: Use mail address for courier delivery), 806-324-2352.

http://www.txnd.uscourts.gov

Counties: Armstrong, Briscoe, Carson, Castro, Childress, Collingsworth, Dallam, Deaf Smith, Donley, Gray, Hall, Hansford, Hartley, Hemphill, Hutchinson, Lipscomb, Moore, Ochiltree, Oldham, Parmer, Potter, Randall, Roberts, Sherman, Swisher, Wheeler.

Indexing/Storage: Cases are indexed by defendant and plaintiff as well as by case number. New cases are available in the index immediately after filing date. Both computer and card indexes are maintained. Records are also indexed on microfiche. Open records are located at this court.

Fee & Payment: The fee is $20.00 per item (one party name or case number). Payment may be made by money order, cashier check, personal check. Prepayment is required. Payee: Clerk, US District Court. Certification fee: $7.00 per document. Copy fee: $.50 per page.

Phone Search: No party information is released over the phone. Only pleadings are released over the phone.

Mail Search: A stamped self addressed envelope is not required.

In Person: In person searching is available.

PACER: Sign-up number is 800-676-6856. Access fee is $.60 per minute. Toll-free access: 800-684-2393. Local access: 214-753-2449. Case records are available back to June 1991. Records are purged once per year. New records are available online after 1 day. PACER is available online at http://pacer.txnd.uscourts.gov.

Dallas Division Room 14A20, 1100 Commerce St, Dallas, TX 75242 (Courier Address: Use mail address for courier delivery), 214-753-2200.

http://www.txnd.uscourts.gov

Counties: Dallas, Ellis, Hunt, Johnson, Kaufman, Navarro, Rockwall.

Indexing/Storage: Cases are indexed by defendant and plaintiff as well as by case number. New cases are available in the index 2 days after filing date. A computer index is maintained. Computer index goes back to 1990 for the entire district. Records are also indexed on microfiche since 1957. Open records are located at this court. District wide searches are available for information from 1957 forward from this division.

Fee & Payment: The fee is $20.00 per item (one party name or case number). Payment may be made by money order, cashier check, personal check, Visa, Mastercard. Prepayment is required. Payee: Clerk, US District Court. Certification fee: $7.00 per document. Copy fee: $.50 per page. You are allowed to make your own copies. These copies cost $.25 per page.

Phone Search: Only computerized docket information will be released over the phone.

Mail Search: Always enclose a stamped self addressed envelope.

In Person: In person searching is available.

PACER: Sign-up number is 800-676-6856. Access fee is $.60 per minute. Toll-free access: 800-684-2393. Local access: 214-753-2449. Case records are available back to June 1991. Records are purged once per year. New records are available online after 1 day. PACER is available online at http://pacer.txnd.uscourts.gov.

Fort Worth Division Clerk's Office, 501 W Tenth St, Room 310, Fort Worth, TX 76102 (Courier Address: Use mail address for courier delivery), 817-978-3132.

http://www.txnd.uscourts.gov

Counties: Comanche, Erath, Hood, Jack, Palo Pinto, Parker, Tarrant, Wise.

Indexing/Storage: Cases are indexed by defendant and plaintiff as well as by case number. New cases are available in the index 1 day after filing date. A computer index is maintained. Computer records go back to 1990 for civil cases and 1993 for criminal cases. Records are also indexed on microfiche. Open records are located at this court. District wide searches for information from 1957 are available from this court.

Fee & Payment: The fee is $20.00 per item (one party name or case number). Payment may be made by money order, cashier check, personal check. Prepayment is required. Payee: Clerk, US District Court. Certification fee: $7.00 per document. Copy fee: $.50 per page. You are allowed to make your own copies. These copies cost $.25 per page.

Phone Search: The court will only release minimal information about a case when the caller already has a case number. They will not search for case numbers over the phone.

Mail Search: A stamped self addressed envelope is not required.

In Person: In person searching is available.

PACER: Sign-up number is 800-676-6856. Access fee is $.60 per minute. Toll-free access: 800-684-2393. Local access: 214-753-2449. Case records are available back to June 1991. Records are purged once per year. New records are available online after 1 day. PACER is available online at http://pacer.txnd.uscourts.gov.

Lubbock Division Clerk, Room 209, 1205 Texas Ave, Lubbock, TX 79401 (Courier Address: Use mail address for courier delivery), 806-472-7624.

http://www.txnd.uscourts.gov

Counties: Bailey, Borden, Cochran, Crosby, Dawson, Dickens, Floyd, Gaines, Garza, Hale, Hockley, Kent, Lamb, Lubbock, Lynn, Motley, Scurry, Terry, Yoakum.

Indexing/Storage: Cases are indexed by defendant and plaintiff as well as by case number. New cases are available in the index 1 day after filing date. Both computer and card indexes are maintained. Records are also indexed on microfiche. Open records are located at this court. No records have been sent to the Federal Records Center.

Fee & Payment: The fee is $20.00 per item (one party name or case number). Payment may be made by money order, cashier check, personal check. Prepayment is required. Payee: Clerk, US District Court. Certification fee: $7.00 per document. Copy fee: $.50 per page.

Phone Search: Searching not available by phone.

Mail Search: Always enclose a stamped self addressed envelope.

In Person: In person searching is available.

PACER: Sign-up number is 800-676-6856. Access fee is $.60 per minute. Toll-free access: 800-684-2393. Local access: 214-753-2449. Case records are available back to June 1991. Records are purged once per year. New records are

available online after 1 day. PACER is available online at http://pacer.txnd.uscourts.gov.

San Angelo Division Clerk's Office, Room 202, 33 E Twohig, San Angelo, TX 76903 (Courier Address: Use mail address for courier delivery), 915-655-4506, Fax: 915-658-6826.

http://www.txnd.uscourts.gov

Counties: Brown, Coke, Coleman, Concho, Crockett, Glasscock, Irion, Menard, Mills, Reagan, Runnels, Schleicher, Sterling, Sutton, Tom Green.

Indexing/Storage: Cases are indexed by defendant and plaintiff as well as by case number. New cases are available in the index immediately after filing date. A card index is maintained. Records are also indexed on microfiche. Open records are located at this court. Civil records are retained for 3 years. Criminal records are retained for 7 to 8 years.

Fee & Payment: The fee is $20.00 per item (one party name or case number). Payment may be made by money order, cashier check, personal check. Prepayment is required. Payee: Clerk, US District Court. Certification fee: $7.00 per document. Copy fee: $.50 per page.

Phone Search: Only docket information available.

Fax Search: Fax requests cost the same as mail requests and require prepayment.

Mail Search: Always enclose a stamped self addressed envelope.

In Person: In person searching is available.

PACER: Sign-up number is 800-676-6856. Access fee is $.60 per minute. Toll-free access: 800-684-2393. Local access: 214-753-2449. Case records are available back to June 1991. Records are purged once per year. New records are available online after 1 day. PACER is available online at http://pacer.txnd.uscourts.gov.

Wichita Falls Division PO Box 1234, Wichita Falls, TX 76307 (Courier Address: Room 203, 1000 Lamar, Wichita Falls, TX 76301), 940-767-1902, Fax: 940-767-2526.

http://www.txnd.uscourts.gov

Counties: Archer, Baylor, Clay, Cottle, Foard, Hardeman, King, Knox, Montague, Wichita, Wilbarger, Young.

Indexing/Storage: Cases are indexed by defendant and plaintiff as well as by case number. New cases are available in the index immediately after filing date. A card index is maintained. Records are also indexed on microfiche. Open records are located at this court.

Fee & Payment: The fee is $20.00 per item (one party name or case number). Payment may be made by money order, cashier check, personal check. Prepayment is required. Payee: Clerk, US District Court. Certification fee: $7.00 per document. Copy fee: $.50 per page.

Phone Search: Only docket information available.

Fax Search: Will accept fax for price quote only.

Mail Search: Always enclose a stamped self addressed envelope.

In Person: In person searching is available.

PACER: Sign-up number is 800-676-6856. Access fee is $.60 per minute. Toll-free access: 800-684-2393. Local access: 214-753-2449. Case records are available back to June 1991. Records are purged once per year. New records are available online after 1 day. PACER is available online at http://pacer.txnd.uscourts.gov.

US Bankruptcy Court

Northern District of Texas

Amarillo Division PO Box 15960, Amarillo, TX 79105 (Courier Address: 624 Polk St, Suite 100, Amarillo, TX 79101), 806-324-2302.

http://www.txnb.uscourts.gov

Counties: Armstrong, Briscoe, Carson, Castro, Childress, Collingsworth, Dallam, Deaf Smith, Donley, Gray, Hall, Hansford, Hartley, Hemphill, Hutchinson, Lipscomb, Moore, Ochiltree, Oldham, Parmer, Potter, Randall, Roberts, Sherman, Swisher, Wheeler.

Indexing/Storage: Cases are indexed by debtor as well as by case number. New cases are available in the index immediately after filing date. Both computer and card indexes are maintained. Card index available prio to June 1988. Open records are located at this court.

Fee & Payment: The fee is $20.00 per item (one party name or case number). Payment may be made by money order, cashier check, business check. Personal checks are not accepted. Prepayment is required. Law firm checks are accepted. Payee: Clerk, US Bankruptcy Court. Certification fee: $7.00 per document. Copy fee: $.50 per page. You are allowed to make your own copies. These copies cost $.50 per page. The search fee is required should the court have to pull the file and count pages and the fee is $15.00 per case file. The court does not charge to do a name search.

Phone Search: Only docket information is available by phone. An automated voice case information service (VCIS) is available. Call VCIS at 800-886-9008 or 214-753-2128.

Mail Search: Always enclose a stamped self addressed envelope.

In Person: In person searching is available.

PACER: Sign-up number is 800-676-6856. Access fee is $.60 per minute. Toll-free access: 888-225-1738. Local access: 214-753-2134. Case records are available back to 1994. Records are purged every six months. New civil records are available online after 1 day. PACER is available online at https://pacer.txnb.uscourts.gov.

Dallas Division 1100 Commerce St, Suite 12A24, Dallas, TX 75242-1496 (Courier Address: Use mail address for courier delivery), 214-753-2000.

http://www.txnb.uscourts.gov

Counties: Dallas, Ellis, Hunt, Johnson, Kaufman, Navarro, Rockwall.

Indexing/Storage: Cases are indexed by debtor and creditors as well as by case number. New cases are available in the index 1-2 days after filing date. Both computer and card indexes are maintained. Open records are located at this court. District wide searches are available for records from 8/92 to the present from this division. This court maintains records for the Wichita Falls Division.

Fee & Payment: The fee is $20.00 per item (one party name or case number). Payment may be made by money order. Business checks are not accepted. Personal checks are not accepted. There is no search fee for searching docket sheets or claim registers. Prepayment is required. Payee: Clerk, US Bankruptcy Court. Certification fee: $7.00 per document. Copy fee: $.50 per page.

Phone Search: Only docket information is available by phone. An automated voice case information service (VCIS) is available. Call VCIS at 800-886-9008 or 214-753-2128.

Mail Search: Always enclose a stamped self addressed envelope.

In Person: In person searching is available.

PACER: Sign-up number is 800-676-6856. Access fee is $.60 per minute. Toll-free access: 888-225-1738. Local access: 214-753-2134. Case records are available back to 1994. Records are purged every six months. New civil records are available online after 1 day. PACER is available online at https://pacer.txnb.uscourts.gov.

Fort Worth Division 501 W 10th, Suite 147, Fort Worth, TX 76102 (Courier Address: Use mail address for courier delivery), 817-333-6000, Fax: 817-333-6001.

http://www.txnb.uscourts.gov

Counties: Comanche, Erath, Hood, Jack, Palo Pinto, Parker, Tarrant, Wise.

Indexing/Storage: Cases are indexed by debtor as well as by case number. New cases are available in the index 1-2 days after filing date. Both computer and card indexes are maintained. Records up to 1986 are on index cards. Complete August 1, 1992 through the present are indexed on computer. From 1987 to August 1, 1992, records are indexed manually. Open records are located at this court. Closed cases are held in house as long as there is space to store them. They are sent opnce at year end to the Fort Worth Federal Records Center.

Fee & Payment: The fee is $20.00 per item (one party name or case number). Payment may be made by money order, cashier check, personal check. Prepayment is required. Debtor's checks are not accepted. Payee: Clerk, US Bankruptcy Court. Certification fee: $7.00 per document. Copy fee: $.50 per page. You are allowed to make your own copies. These copies cost $.25 per page.

Phone Search: Only docket information is available by phone. A record can be searched over the phone by debtor's name for records from 1987 to the present. An automated voice case information service (VCIS) is available. Call VCIS at 800-886-9008 or 214-753-2128.

Mail Search: Always enclose a stamped self addressed envelope.

In Person: In person searching is available.

PACER: Sign-up number is 800-676-6856. Access fee is $.60 per minute. Toll-free access: 888-225-1738. Local access: 214-753-2134. Case records are available back to 1994. Records are purged every six months. New civil records are available online after 1 day. PACER is available online at https://pacer.txnb.uscourts.gov.

Lubbock Division 306 Federal Bldg, 1205 Texas Ave, Lubbock, TX 79401-4002 (Courier Address: Use mail address for courier delivery), 806-472-5000.

http://www.txnb.uscourts.gov

Counties: Bailey, Borden, Brown, Callahan, Cochran, Cooke, Coleman, Concho, Crockett, Crosby, Dawson, Dickens, Eastland, Fisher, Floyd, Gaines, Garza, Glasscock, Hale, Haskell, Hockley, Howard, Irion, Jones, Kent, Lamb, Lubbock, Lynn, Menard, Mills, Mitchell,Motley, Nolan, Reagan, Runnels, Schleicher, Scurry, Shackelford, Stephens, Sterling, Stonewall, Sutton, Taylor, Terry, Throckmorton, Tom Green, Yoakum.

Indexing/Storage: Cases are indexed by debtor as well as by case number. New cases are available in the index 1-2 days after filing date. A computer index is maintained. Open records are located at this court.

Fee & Payment: The fee is $20.00 per item (one party name or case number). Payment may be made by money order, cashier check, business check. Personal checks are not accepted. Prepayment is required. Debtor's checks are not accepted. Payee: Clerk, US Bankruptcy Court. Certification fee: $7.00 per document. Copy fee: $.50 per page.

Phone Search: Only docket information is available by phone. A record can be searched over the phone by debtor's name for records from 1987 to the present. An automated voice case information service (VCIS) is available. Call VCIS at 800-886-9008 or 214-753-2128.

Mail Search: Always enclose a stamped self addressed envelope.

In Person: In person searching is available.

PACER: Sign-up number is 800-676-6856. Access fee is $.60 per minute. Toll-free access: 888-225-1738. Local access: 214-753-2134. Case records are available back to 1994. Records are purged every six months. New civil records are available online after 1 day. PACER is available online at https://pacer.txnb.uscourts.gov.

Wichita Falls Division c/o Dallas Division, Suite 12A24, 1100 Commerce St, Dallas, TX 75242-1496 (Courier Address: Use mail address for courier delivery), 214-753-2000.

http://www.txnb.uscourts.gov

Counties: Archer, Baylor, Clay, Cottle, Foard, Hardeman, King, Knox, Montague, Wichita, Wilbarger, Young.

Indexing/Storage: Cases are indexed by as well as by case number. New cases are available in the index after filing date. Open records are located at the Division.

Fee & Payment: The fee is no charge per item (one party name or case number). Payment may be made by money order, cashier check. Business checks are not accepted. Personal checks are not accepted.

Phone Search: An automated voice case information service (VCIS) is available. Call VCIS at 800-886-9008 or 214-753-2128.

Mail Search: Always enclose a stamped self addressed envelope.

In Person: In person searching is available.

PACER: Sign-up number is 800-676-6856. Access fee is $.60 per minute. Toll-free access: 888-225-1738. Local access: 214-753-2134. Case records are available back to 1994. Records are purged every six months. New civil records are available online after 1 day. PACER is available online at https://pacer.txnb.uscourts.gov.

US District Court

Southern District of Texas

Brownsville Division 600 E Harrison St Rm 101, Brownsville, TX 78520-7114 (Courier Address: Use mail address for courier delivery., 600 E Harrison St #101,), 956-548-2500, Fax: 956-548-2598.

http://www.txsd.uscourts.gov

Counties: Cameron, Willacy.

Indexing/Storage: Cases are indexed by defendant and plaintiff as well as by case number. New cases are available in the index 2 days after filing date. Both computer and card indexes are maintained. Records are also indexed on microfiche. Open records are located at this court.

Fee & Payment: The fee is $20.00 per item (one party name or case number). Payment may be made by money order, cashier check, personal check. Prepayment is required. Payee: Clerk, US District Court. Certification fee: $7.00 per document. Copy fee: $.50 per page.

Phone Search: Only docket information is available by phone.

Mail Search: Always enclose a stamped self addressed envelope.

In Person: In person searching is available.

PACER: Sign-up number is 800-676-6856. Access fee is $.60 per minute. Toll-free access: 800-998-9037. Local access: 713-250-5046, 713-250-5000. Case records are available back to June 1990. Records are purged every six months. New records are available online after 1 day. PACER is available online at http://pacer.txs.uscourts.gov.

Corpus Christi Division Clerk's Office, 1133 N. Shoreline Blvd., #208, Corpus Christi, TX 78401 (Courier Address: Use mail address for courier delivery), 361-888-3142.

http://www.txsd.uscourts.gov

Counties: Aransas, Bee, Brooks, Duval, Jim Wells, Kenedy, Kleberg, Live Oak, Nueces, San Patricio.

Indexing/Storage: Cases are indexed by defendant and plaintiff as well as by case number. New cases are available in the index 3 to 5 days after filing date. A computer index is maintained. Records are also indexed on microfiche. Open records are located at this court.

Fee & Payment: The fee is $20.00 per item (one party name or case number). Payment may be made by money order, cashier check, personal check. Prepayment is required. Payee: Clerk, US District Court. Certification fee: $7.00 per document. Copy fee: $.50 per page.

Phone Search: Searching is not available by phone.

Mail Search: Always enclose a stamped self addressed envelope.

In Person: In person searching is available.

PACER: Sign-up number is 800-676-6856. Access fee is $.60 per minute. Toll-free access: 800-998-9037. Local access: 713-250-5046, 713-250-5000. Case records are available back to June 1990. Records are purged every six months. New records are available online after 1 day. PACER is available online at http://pacer.txs.uscourts.gov.

Galveston Division Clerk's Office, PO Drawer 2300, Galveston, TX 77553 (Courier Address: 601 Rosenberg, Room 411, Galveston, TX 77550), 409-766-3530.

http://www.txsd.uscourts.gov

Counties: Brazoria, Chambers, Galveston, Matagorda.

Indexing/Storage: Cases are indexed by defendant and plaintiff as well as by case number. New cases are available in the index 1 day after filing date. Both computer and card indexes are maintained. Records are also indexed on microfiche. Open records are located at this court.

Fee & Payment: The fee is $20.00 per item (one party name or case number). Payment may be made by money order, cashier check, business check. Personal checks are not accepted. Prepayment is required. Payee: Clerk, US District Court. Certification fee: $7.00 per document. Copy fee: $.50 per page. You are allowed to make your own copies. These copies cost $.50 per page.

Phone Search: Only the status of the case and the trial settings will be released over the phone.

Mail Search: Always enclose a stamped self addressed envelope.

In Person: In person searching is available.

PACER: Sign-up number is 800-676-6856. Access fee is $.60 per minute. Toll-free access: 800-998-9037. Local access: 713-250-5046, 713-250-5000. Case records are available back to June 1990. Records are purged every six months. New records are available online after 1 day. PACER is available online at http://pacer.txs.uscourts.gov.

Houston Division PO Box 61010, Houston, TX 77208 (Courier Address: Room 1217, 515 Rusk, Houston, TX 77002), 713-250-5500.

http://www.txsd.uscourts.gov

Counties: Austin, Brazos, Colorado, Fayette, Fort Bend, Grimes, Harris, Madison, Montgomery, San Jacinto, Walker, Waller, Wharton.

Indexing/Storage: Cases are indexed by defendant and plaintiff as well as by case number. New cases are available in the index 2 days after filing date. Mail searches must be coordinated through the court's copy service (IKON). Call 713-236-0903. They charge $8.12 per search plus $.29 per page for copies. Both computer and card indexes are maintained. Records are also indexed on microfiche. Open records are located at this court. District wide searches are available for information from 1979 forward from this court. Criminal docketing for the district is performed in Houston.

Fee & Payment: The fee is $20.00 per item (one party name or case number). Payment may be made by money order, cashier check, personal check. Prepayment is required. Payee: Clerk, US District Court. Certification fee: $7.00 per document. Copy fee: $.50 per page.

Phone Search: Searching is not available by phone.

Mail Search: A stamped self addressed envelope is not required.

In Person: In person searching is available.

PACER: Sign-up number is 800-676-6856. Access fee is $.60 per minute. Toll-free access: 800-998-9037. Local access: 713-250-5046, 713-250-5000. Case records are available back to June 1990. Records are purged every six months. New records are available online after 1 day. PACER is available online at http://pacer.txs.uscourts.gov.

Laredo Division PO Box 597, Laredo, TX 78042-0597 (Courier Address: Room 319, 1300 Matamoros, Laredo, TX 78040), 956-723-3542, Fax: 956-726-2289.

http://www.txsd.uscourts.gov

Counties: Jim Hogg, La Salle, McMullen, Webb, Zapata.

Indexing/Storage: Cases are indexed by defendant and plaintiff as well as by case number. New cases are available in the index immediately after filing date. The style of the case is needed to search. A computer index is maintained. Open records are located at this court.

Fee & Payment: The fee is $20.00 per item (one party name or case number). Payment may be made by cashier check. Business checks are not accepted. Personal checks are not accepted. Payee: Clerk, US District Court. Certification fee: $7.00 per document. Copy fee: $.50 per page.

Phone Search: Searching is not available by phone.

Mail Search: A stamped self addressed envelope is not required.

In Person: In person searching is available.

PACER: Sign-up number is 800-676-6856. Access fee is $.60 per minute. Toll-free access: 800-998-9037. Local access: 713-250-5046, 713-250-5000. Case records are available back to June 1990. Records are purged every six months. New records are available online after 1 day. PACER is available online at http://pacer.txs.uscourts.gov.

McAllen Division Suite 1011, 1701 W Business Hwy 83, McAllen, TX 78501 (Courier Address: Use mail address for courier delivery), 956-618-8065.

http://www.txsd.uscourts.gov

Counties: Hidalgo, Starr.

Indexing/Storage: Cases are indexed by defendant and plaintiff as well as by case number. New cases are available in the index 1 day after filing date. Both computer and card indexes are maintained. Open records are located at this court. This court has only been in operation for about 4 years. They have sent no records to the Fort Worth Federal Records Center.

Fee & Payment: The fee is $20.00 per item (one party name or case number). Payment may be made by money order, cashier check, business check. Personal checks are not accepted. Prepayment is required. Payee: Clerk, US District Court. Certification fee: $7.00 per document. Copy fee: $.50 per page.

Phone Search: Only docket information available by phone.

Mail Search: Always enclose a stamped self addressed envelope.

In Person: In person searching is available.

PACER: Sign-up number is 800-676-6856. Access fee is $.60 per minute. Toll-free access: 800-998-9037. Local access: 713-250-5046, 713-250-5000. Case records are available back to June 1990. Records are purged every six months. New records are available online after 1 day. PACER is available online at http://pacer.txs.uscourts.gov.

Victoria Division Clerk US District Court, PO Box 1638, Victoria, TX 77902 (Courier Address: Room 406, 312 S Main, Victoria, TX 77901), 361-788-5000.

http://www.txsd.uscourts.gov

Counties: Calhoun, De Witt, Goliad, Jackson, Lavaca, Refugio, Victoria.

Indexing/Storage: Cases are indexed by defendant and plaintiff as well as by case number. New cases are available in the index 2 days after filing date. Both computer and card indexes are maintained. Open records are located at this court.

Fee & Payment: The fee is $20.00 per item (one party name or case number). Payment may be made by money order, cashier check, personal check. Prepayment is required. Payee: Clerk, US District Court. Certification fee: $7.00 per document. Copy fee: $.50 per page. You are allowed to make your own copies. These copies cost $.50 per page.

Phone Search: Only docket information is available by phone.

Mail Search: Always enclose a stamped self addressed envelope.

In Person: In person searching is available.

PACER: Sign-up number is 800-676-6856. Access fee is $.60 per minute. Toll-free access: 800-998-9037. Local access: 713-250-5046, 713-250-5000. Case records are available back to June 1990. Records are purged every six months. New records are available online after 1 day. PACER is available online at http://pacer.txs.uscourts.gov.

US Bankruptcy Court

Southern District of Texas

Corpus Christi Division 1133 N. Shoreline Blvd. - 3rd Fl., Corpus Christi, TX 78401 (Courier Address: Use mail address for courier delivery), 361-888-3484.

http://www.txsd.uscourts.gov

Counties: Aransas, Bee, Brooks, Calhoun, Cameron, Duval, Goliad, Hidalgo, Jackson, Jim Wells, Kenedy, Kleberg, Lavaca, Live Oak, Nueces, Refugio, San Patricio, Starr, Victoria, Willacy.Files from Brownsville, Corpus Christi, and McAllen are maintained here.

Indexing/Storage: Cases are indexed by debtor as well as by case number. New cases are available in the index 1-2 days after filing date. A computer index is maintained. Records are also indexed on microfiche. Open records are located at this court. Until further notice as of 9/1/97, this office will continue to hold case records for the Victoria Division.

Fee & Payment: The fee is $20.00 per item (one party name or case number). Payment may be made by money order, cashier check, personal check. Prepayment is required. Payee: Clerk, US Bankruptcy Court. Certification fee: $7.00 per document. Copy fee: $.50 per page. You are allowed to make your own copies. These copies cost $.25 per page. There are dollar and coin-operated copiers available for public use.

Phone Search: An automated voice case information service (VCIS) is available. Call VCIS at 800-745-4459 or 713-250-5049.

Mail Search: Always enclose a stamped self addressed envelope.

In Person: In person searching is available.

PACER: Sign-up number is 800-676-6856. Access fee is $.60 per minute. Toll-free access: 800-998-9037. Local access: 713-250-5046, 713-250-5000. Case records are available back to June 1, 1991. Records are purged every six months.

New civil records are available online after 1-3 days. PACER is available online at http://pacer.txs.uscourts.gov.

Houston Division Room 1217, 515 Rusk Ave, Houston, TX 77002 (Courier Address: Use mail address for courier delivery), 713-250-5500.

http://www.txsd.uscourts.gov

Counties: Austin, Brazoria, Brazos, Chambers, Colorado, De Witt, Fayette, Fort Bend, Galveston, Grimes, Harris, Jim Hogg*, La Salle*, Madison, Matagorda, McMullen*, Montgomery, San Jacinto, Walker,Waller, Wharton, Webb* Zapata*. Open case records for the counties marked with an asterisk are being moved to the Laredo Division.

Indexing/Storage: Cases are indexed by debtor as well as by case number. New cases are available in the index 1-2 days after filing date. Both computer and card indexes are maintained. Records are also indexed on microfiche. Open records are located at this court. Some case files are maintained here from as early as 1978. Case files for the new Laredo Division are being moved to 1300 Matamors, Laredo, TX 78040, 956-726-2236 as of 9/1/97.

Fee & Payment: The fee is $20.00 per item (one party name or case number). Payment may be made by money order, cashier check, personal check. Prepayment is required. Payee: Clerk, US Bankruptcy Court. Certification fee: $7.00 per document. Copy fee: $.50 per page.

Phone Search: Only docket information is available by phone. An automated voice case information service (VCIS) is available. Call VCIS at 800-745-4459 or 713-250-5049.

Mail Search: Always enclose a stamped self addressed envelope.

In Person: In person searching is available.

PACER: Sign-up number is 800-676-6856. Access fee is $.60 per minute. Toll-free access: 800-998-9037. Local access: 713-250-5046, 713-250-5000. Case records are available back to June 1, 1991. Records are purged every six months. New civil records are available online after 1-3 days. PACER is available online at http://pacer.txs.uscourts.gov.

US District Court

Western District of Texas

Austin Division Room 130, 200 W 8th St, Austin, TX 78701 (Courier Address: Use mail address for courier delivery), 512-916-5896.

http://www.txwd.uscourts.gov

Counties: Bastrop, Blanco, Burleson, Burnet, Caldwell, Gillespie, Hays, Kimble, Lampasas, Lee, Llano, McCulloch, Mason, San Saba, Travis, Washington, Williamson.

Indexing/Storage: Cases are indexed by defendant and plaintiff as well as by case number. New cases are available in the index 1 day after filing date. A computer index is maintained. Records are also indexed on microfiche. Open records are located at this court.

Fee & Payment: The fee is $20.00 per item (one party name or case number). Payment may be made by money order, cashier check, personal check. Prepayment is required. Payee: Clerk, US District Court. Certification fee: $7.00 per document. Copy fee: $.50 per page. You are

allowed to make your own copies. These copies cost $.35 per page.

Phone Search: Only docket information is available by phone. The caller must have the case number.

Mail Search: Always enclose a stamped self addressed envelope.

In Person: In person searching is available.

PACER: Sign-up number is 800-676-6856. Access fee is $.60 per minute. Toll-free access: 888-869-6365. Local access: 210-472-5256. Case records are available back to 1994. Records are purged every six months. New records are available online after 1 day. PACER is available online at http://pacer.txwd.uscourts.gov.

Del Rio Division Room L100, 111 E Broadway, Del Rio, TX 78840 (Courier Address: Use mail address for courier delivery), 830-703-2054.

http://www.txwd.uscourts.gov

Counties: Edwards, Kinney, Maverick, Terrell, Uvalde, Val Verde, Zavala.

Indexing/Storage: Cases are indexed by defendant and plaintiff as well as by case number. New cases are available in the index 1 month after filing date. A computer index is maintained. Open records are located at this court.

Fee & Payment: The fee is $20.00 per item (one party name or case number). Payment may be made by money order, cashier check, personal check. Prepayment is required. Payee: Clerk, US District Court. Certification fee: $7.00 per document. Copy fee: $.50 per page.

Phone Search: Only docket information is available by phone.

Mail Search: Always enclose a stamped self addressed envelope.

In Person: In person searching is available.

PACER: Sign-up number is 800-676-6856. Access fee is $.60 per minute. Toll-free access: 888-869-6365. Local access: 210-472-5256. Case records are available back to 1994. Records are purged every six months. New records are available online after 1 day. PACER is available online at http://pacer.txwd.uscourts.gov.

El Paso Division US District Clerk's Office, Room 350, 511 E San Antonio, El Paso, TX 79901 (Courier Address: Use mail address for courier delivery), 915-534-6725.

http://www.txwd.uscourts.gov

Counties: El Paso.

Indexing/Storage: Cases are indexed by defendant and plaintiff as well as by case number. New cases are available in the index 1-2 days after filing date. Both computer and card indexes are maintained. Microfiche also available. Open records are located at this court.

Fee & Payment: The fee is $20.00 per item (one party name or case number). Payment may be made by money order, cashier check, personal check. Prepayment is required. Payee: Clerk, US District Court. Certification fee: $7.00 per document. Copy fee: $.50 per page. You are allowed to make your own copies. These copies cost $.25 per page.

Phone Search: Only docket information is available by phone.

Mail Search: Always enclose a stamped self addressed envelope.

In Person: In person searching is available.

PACER: Sign-up number is 800-676-6856. Access fee is $.60 per minute. Toll-free access: 888-869-6365. Local access: 210-472-5256. Case records are available back to 1994. Records are purged every six months. New records are available online after 1 day. PACER is available online at http://pacer.txwd.uscourts.gov.

Midland Division
Clerk, US District Court, 200 E Wall St, Rm 107, Midland, TX 79701 (Courier Address: Use mail address for courier delivery), 915-686-4001.

http://www.txwd.uscourts.gov

Counties: Andrews, Crane, Ector, Martin, Midland, Upton.

Indexing/Storage: Cases are indexed by defendant and plaintiff as well as by case number. New cases are available in the index immediately after filing date. Both computer and card indexes are maintained. Records are also indexed on microfiche. Open records are located at this court.

Fee & Payment: The fee is $20.00 per item (one party name or case number). Payment may be made by money order, cashier check, personal check. Prepayment is required. Payee: Clerk, US District Court. Certification fee: $7.00 per document. Copy fee: $.50 per page. You are allowed to make your own copies. These copies cost $.25 per page. To do your own copies, you must bring your own change. They will not provide change.

Phone Search: Most information will be released over the phone.

Mail Search: Always enclose a stamped self addressed envelope.

In Person: In person searching is available.

PACER: Sign-up number is 800-676-6856. Access fee is $.60 per minute. Toll-free access: 888-869-6365. Local access: 210-472-5256. Case records are available back to 1994. Records are purged every six months. New records are available online after 1 day. PACER is available online at http://pacer.txwd.uscourts.gov.

Pecos Division
US Courthouse, 410 S Cedar St, Pecos, TX 79772 (Courier Address: Use mail address for courier delivery), 915-445-4228.

http://www.txwd.uscourts.gov

Counties: Brewster, Culberson, Hudspeth, Jeff Davis, Loving, Pecos, Presidio, Reeves, Ward, Winkler.

Indexing/Storage: Cases are indexed by defendant and plaintiff as well as by case number. New cases are available in the index immediately after filing date. A card index is maintained. Open records are located at this court.

Fee & Payment: The fee is $20.00 per item (one party name or case number). Payment may be made by money order, cashier check, personal check. Prepayment is required. Debtor's checks are not accepted. Payee: Clerk, US District Court. Certification fee: $7.00 per document. Copy fee: $.50 per page. You are allowed to make your own copies. These copies cost $.25 per page.

Phone Search: Searching is not available by phone.

Mail Search: Always enclose a stamped self addressed envelope.

In Person: In person searching is available.

PACER: Sign-up number is 800-676-6856. Access fee is $.60 per minute. Toll-free access:

888-869-6365. Local access: 210-472-5256. Case records are available back to 1994. Records are purged every six months. New records are available online after 1 day. PACER is available online at http://pacer.txwd.uscourts.gov.

San Antonio Division
US Clerk's Office, 655 E Durango Blvd, Suite G-65, San Antonio, TX 78206 (Courier Address: Use mail address for courier delivery), 210-472-6550.

http://www.txwd.uscourts.gov

Counties: Atascosa, Bandera, Bexar, Comal, Dimmit, Frio, Gonzales, Guadalupe, Karnes, Kendall, Kerr, Medina, Real, Wilson.

Indexing/Storage: Cases are indexed by defendant and plaintiff as well as by case number. New cases are available in the index 1-2 days after filing date. A computer index is maintained. Records are also indexed on microfiche. Open records are located at this court.

Fee & Payment: The fee is $20.00 per item (one party name or case number). Payment may be made by money order, cashier check, personal check. Prepayment is required. Payee: Clerk, US District Court. Certification fee: $7.00 per document. Copy fee: $.50 per page. You are allowed to make your own copies. These copies cost $.35 per page.

Phone Search: Only docket information is available by phone.

Mail Search: Always enclose a stamped self addressed envelope.

In Person: In person searching is available.

PACER: Sign-up number is 800-676-6856. Access fee is $.60 per minute. Toll-free access: 888-869-6365. Local access: 210-472-5256. Case records are available back to 1994. Records are purged every six months. New records are available online after 1 day. PACER is available online at http://pacer.txwd.uscourts.gov.

Waco Division
Clerk, Room 303, 800 Franklin, Waco, TX 76701 (Courier Address: Use mail address for courier delivery), 254-750-1501.

http://www.txwd.uscourts.gov

Counties: Bell, Bosque, Coryell, Falls, Freestone, Hamilton, Hill, Leon, Limestone, McLennan, Milam, Robertson, Somervell.

Indexing/Storage: Cases are indexed by defendant and plaintiff as well as by case number. New cases are available in the index 1-2 days after filing date. A card index is maintained. Open records are located at this court.

Fee & Payment: The fee is $20.00 per item (one party name or case number). Payment may be made by money order, cashier check, personal check. Prepayment is required. Payee: Clerk, US District Court. Certification fee: $7.00 per document. Copy fee: $.50 per page. You are allowed to make your own copies. These copies cost $.25 per page.

Phone Search: Only docket information is available by phone.

Mail Search: Always enclose a stamped self addressed envelope.

In Person: In person searching is available.

PACER: Sign-up number is 800-676-6856. Access fee is $.60 per minute. Toll-free access: 888-869-6365. Local access: 210-472-5256. Case records are available back to 1994. Records are purged every six months. New records are

available online after 1 day. PACER is available online at http://pacer.txwd.uscourts.gov.

US Bankruptcy Court
Western District of Texas

Austin Division Homer Thornberry Judicial Bldg, 903 San Antonio, Room 322, Austin, TX 78701 (Courier Address: Use mail address for courier delivery), 512-916-5237.

http://www.txwb.uscourts.gov

Counties: Bastrop, Blanco, Burleson, Burnet, Caldwell, Gillespie, Hays, Kimble, Lampasas, Lee, Llano, Mason, McCulloch, San Saba, Travis, Washington, Williamson.

Indexing/Storage: Cases are indexed by debtor and creditors as well as by case number. New cases are available in the index 24 hours after filing date. A computer index is maintained. Records are also indexed on microfiche. Open records are located at this court.

Fee & Payment: The fee is $20.00 per item (one party name or case number). Payment may be made by money order, cashier check, personal check, Visa or Mastercard. Prepayment is required. Debtor's checks are not accepted. Payee: US Bankruptcy Court. Certification fee: $7.00 per document. Copy fee: $.50 per page. You are allowed to make your own copies. These copies cost $.25 per page. Xerox copy service available in lobby. Fee is $.25 per page plus tax.

Phone Search: Only docket information is available by phone. An automated voice case information service (VCIS) is available. Call VCIS at 888-436-7477 or 210-472-4023.

Mail Search: Always enclose a stamped self addressed envelope.

In Person: In person searching is available.

PACER: Sign-up number is 800-676-6856. Access fee is $.60 per minute. Toll-free access: 888-372-5708. Local access: 210-472-6262. Case records are available back to May 1, 1987. Records are purged every 6-8 months. New civil records are available online after 1 day. PACER is available online at http://pacer.txwb.uscourts.gov.

Electronic Filing: Electronic filing information is available online at http://ecf.txwb.uscourts.gov

El Paso Division PO Box 971040, El Paso, TX 79925 (Courier Address: 8515 Lockheed, El Paso, TX 79997-1040), 915-779-7362, Fax: 915-779-5693.

http://www.txwb.uscourts.gov

Counties: El Paso.

Indexing/Storage: Cases are indexed by debtor as well as by case number. New cases are available in the index 24 hours after filing date. A computer index is maintained. The computer index goes back to 1987. Prior to that there is a card index to 1987 and microfiche up to 1980. Open records are located at this court.

Fee & Payment: The fee is $20.00 per item (one party name or case number). Payment may be made by money order, cashier check, personal check. Prepayment is required. Payee: Clerk, US Bankruptcy Court. Certification fee: $7.00 per document. Copy fee: $.50 per page. You are allowed to make your own copies. These copies cost $.25 per page.

Phone Search: Only docket information is available by phone. An automated voice case information service (VCIS) is available. Call VCIS at 888-436-7477 or 210-472-4023.

Mail Search: Always enclose a stamped self addressed envelope.

In Person: In person searching is available.

PACER: Sign-up number is 800-676-6856. Access fee is $.60 per minute. Toll-free access: 888-372-5708. Local access: 210-472-6262. Case records are available back to May 1, 1987. Records are purged every 6-8 months. New civil records are available online after 1 day. PACER is available online at http://pacer.txwb.uscourts.gov.

Electronic Filing: Electronic filing information is available online at http://ecf.txwb.uscourts.gov

Midland/Odessa Division
US Post Office Annex, Room P-163, 100 E Wall St, Midland, TX 79701 (Courier Address: Use mail address for courier delivery), 915-683-1650.

http://www.txwb.uscourts.gov

Counties: Andrews, Brewster, Crane, Culberson, Ector, Hudspeth, Jeff Davis, Loving, Martin, Midland, Pecos, Presidio, Reeves, Upton, Ward, Winkler.

Indexing/Storage: Cases are indexed by debtor as well as by case number. New cases are available in the index immediately after filing date. Both computer and card indexes are maintained. Records are also indexed on microfiche. Open records are located at this court. Records from the Pecos Division, which has been closed, have been transferred here.

Fee & Payment: The fee is $20.00 per item (one party name or case number). Payment may be made by money order, cashier check, personal check. Prepayment is required. Payee: Clerk, US Bankruptcy Court. Certification fee: $7.00 per document. Copy fee: $.50 per page. You are allowed to make your own copies. These copies cost $.25 per page. To do your own copies, you must bring your own change. They will not provide change.

Phone Search: Only docket information is available by phone. An automated voice case information service (VCIS) is available. Call VCIS at 888-436-7477 or 210-472-4023.

Mail Search: Always enclose a stamped self addressed envelope.

In Person: In person searching is available.

PACER: Sign-up number is 800-676-6856. Access fee is $.60 per minute. Toll-free access: 888-372-5708. Local access: 210-472-6262. Case records are available back to May 1, 1987. Records are purged every 6-8 months. New civil records are available online after 1 day. PACER is available online at http://pacer.txwb.uscourts.gov.

Electronic Filing: Electronic filing information is available online at http://ecf.txwb.uscourts.gov

San Antonio Division
PO Box 1439, San Antonio, TX 78295 (Courier Address: 615 E Houston St, San Antonio, TX 78205), 210-472-6720, Fax: 210-472-5916.

http://www.txsd.uscourts.gov/

Counties: Atascosa, Bandera, Bexar, Comal, Dimmit, Edwards, Frio, Gonzales, Guadalupe, Karnes, Kendall, Kerr, Kinney, Maverick, Medina, Real, Terrell, Uvalde, Val Verde, Wilson, Zavala.

Indexing/Storage: Cases are indexed by debtor as well as by case number. New cases are available in the index 24 hours after filing date. A computer index is maintained. Open records are located at this court. District wide searches are available for records within a 10 year span from this division.

Fee & Payment: The fee is $20.00 per item (one party name or case number). Payment may be made by cashier check. Business checks are not accepted, American Express, Visa, or Mastercard. Personal checks are not accepted. You are allowed to make your own copies. These copies cost $.35 per page. There is a copy service on site.

Phone Search: Call VCIS at 888-436-7477 or 210-472-4023.

Mail Search: Always enclose a stamped self addressed envelope.

In Person: In person searching is available.

PACER: Sign-up number is 800-676-6856. Access fee is $.60 per minute. Toll-free access: 888-372-5708. Local access: 210-472-6262. Case records are available back to May 1, 1987. Records are purged every 6-8 months. New civil records are available online after 1 day. Records are purged every 6-8 months. New civil records are available online after 1 day.

Waco Division
St. Charles Place, Ste. 20, 600 Austin Ave, Waco, TX 76701 (Courier Address: Use mail address for courier delivery), 254-754-1481, Fax: 254-754-8385.

http://www.txwb.uscourts.gov

Counties: Bell, Bosque, Coryell, Falls, Freestone, Hamilton, Hill, Leon, Limestone, McLennan, Milam, Robertson, Somervell.

Indexing/Storage: Cases are indexed by debtor as well as by case number. New cases are available in the index 1 day after filing date. A computer index is maintained. Records are also indexed on microfiche. Open records are located at this court.

Fee & Payment: The fee is $20.00 per item (one party name or case number). Payment may be made by money order, cashier check, personal check. Prepayment is required. Payee: Clerk, US Bankruptcy Court. Certification fee: $7.00 per document. Copy fee: $.50 per page. You are allowed to make your own copies. These copies cost $.25 per page.

Phone Search: Only docket information is available by phone. An automated voice case information service (VCIS) is available. Call VCIS at 888-436-7477 or 210-472-4023.

Mail Search: Always enclose a stamped self addressed envelope.

In Person: In person searching is available.

PACER: Sign-up number is 800-676-6856. Access fee is $.60 per minute. Toll-free access: 888-372-5708. Local access: 210-472-6262. Case records are available back to May 1, 1987. Records are purged every 6-8 months. New civil records are available online after 1 day. PACER is available online at http://pacer.txwb.uscourts.gov.

Electronic Filing: Electronic filing information is available online at http://ecf.txwb.uscourts.gov

Texas County Courts

Court	Jurisdiction	No. of Courts	How Organized
District Courts*	General	186	406 Districts
County Courts*	Limited	182	
Combined Courts*		72	
Justice of the Peace Courts	Municipal	838	
Municipal Courts	Municipal	854	
Probate Courts*	Probate	8	

* Profiled in this Sourcebook.

Court	CIVIL								
	Tort	Contract	Real Estate	Min. Claim	Max. Claim	Small Claims	Estate	Eviction	Domestic Relations
District Courts*	X	X	X	$200	No Max				X
County Courts*	X	X	X	$200	Varies		X		X
Justice of the Peace Courts	X	X	X	$0	$5000	$5000		X	
Municipal Courts									
Probate Courts*							X		

Court	CRIMINAL				
	Felony	Misdemeanor	DWI/DUI	Preliminary Hearing	Juvenile
District Courts*	X				X
County Courts*		X	X		X
Justice of the Peace Courts		X		X	
Municipal Courts		X			
Probate Courts*					

ADMINISTRATION Office of Court Administration, PO Box 12066, Austin, TX, 78711; 512-463-1625, Fax: 512-463-1648. www.courts.state.tx.us

COURT STRUCTURE The legal court structure for Texas takes up 30 pages in the "Texas Judicial Annual Report." Generally, Texas District Courts have general civil jurisdiction and exclusive felony jurisdiction, along with typical variations such as contested probate and divorce.

The County Court structure includes two forms of courts - "Constitutional" and "at Law" - which come in various configurations depending upon the county. County Courts' upper claim limits vary from $5,000 to $100,000. For civil matters up to $5000, we recommend searchers start at the Constitutional County Court as they, generally, offer a shorter waiting time for cases in urban areas. In addition, keep in mind that the Municipal Courts have, per the Texas manual, "limited civil penalties in cases involving dangerous dogs." In some counties the District Court or County Court handles evictions.

District Courts handle felonies. County Courts handle misdemeanors and general civil cases.

ONLINE ACCESS Statewide appellate court case information is searchable for free on the Internet at www.info.courts.state.tx.us/appindex/appindex.exe. A number of individual county courts also offer online access to their records.

PROBATE COURTS Probate is handled in Probate Court in the 18 largest counties and in District Courts or County Courts at Law elsewhere. However, the County Clerk is responsible for the records in every county.

Anderson County

District Court PO Box 1159, Palestine, TX 75802-1159; 903-723-7412. Hours: 8AM-Noon, 1-5PM (CST). *Felony, Civil.*

Civil Records: Access: Mail, in person. Both court and visitors may perform in person searches. Search fee: $5.00 per name. Required to search: name, years to search. Civil cases indexed by defendant, plaintiff. Civil records on computer from 1984; prior on card index.

Criminal Records: Access: Mail, in person. Both court and visitors may perform in person searches. Search fee: $5.00 per name. Required to search: name, years to search, DOB; also helpful: SSN. Criminal records on computer from 1984; prior on card index.

General Information: Public Access terminal is available. No juvenile or adoption records released. SASE required. Turnaround time 2 days. Fax notes: Do not fax. Copy fee: $1.00 per page. Certification fee: $1.00 per page. Fee payee: Anderson County District Clerk. Personal checks accepted. Prepayment is required.

County Court 500 N Church, Palestine, TX 75801; 903-723-7432. Hours: 8AM-5PM (CST). *Misdemeanor, Civil, Probate.*

Civil Records: Access: Mail, in person. Both court and visitors may perform in person searches. Search fee: $5.00 per name. Required to search: name, years to search. Civil cases indexed by defendant, plaintiff. Civil records on computer from 1982, land cases from 1983.

Criminal Records: Access: Mail, in person. Both court and visitors may perform in person searches. Search fee: $5.00 per name. Required to search: name, years to search, DOB. Criminal records on computer from 1969.

General Information: Public Access terminal is available. SASE required. Turnaround time 1 week. Copy fee: $1.00 per page. Certification fee: $5.00. Fee payee: County Clerk. Personal checks accepted. Prepayment is required.

Andrews County

District Court PO Box 328, Andrews, TX 79714; 915-524-1417. Hours: 8AM-5PM (CST). *Felony, Civil.*

Civil Records: Access: Mail, in person. Only the court performs in person searches; visitors may not. Search fee: $5.00 per name. Required to search: name, years to search. Civil cases indexed by defendant, plaintiff. Civil records computerized since 1975.

Criminal Records: Access: Mail, in person. Only the court performs in person searches; visitors may not. Search fee: $5.00 per name. Required to search: name, years to search, DOB; also helpful: SSN. Criminal records computerized since 1975; prior to 1910.

General Information: No juvenile, mental, sealed, terminations or adoption records released. SASE required. Turnaround time 1 day. Fax notes: Do not fax. Copy fee: $1.00 for first page, $.25 each add'l. Certification fee: $2.00. Fee payee: District Clerk. Personal checks accepted. Prepayment is required.

County Court PO Box 727, Andrews, TX 79714; 915-524-1426. Hours: 8AM-5PM (CST). *Misdemeanor, Civil, Probate.*

Civil Records: Access: Phone, mail, in person. Both court and visitors may perform in person searches. Search fee: $5.00 per name. Required to search: name, years to search. Civil cases indexed by defendant, plaintiff. Civil records on computer since 1980; prior records in manual index.

Criminal Records: Access: Phone, mail, in person. Both court and visitors may perform in person searches. Search fee: $5.00 per name. Required to search: name, years to search, DOB or SSN; also helpful: sex. Criminal records on computer since 1985; prior records in manual index.

General Information: No juvenile, mental, sealed, or adoption records released. SASE not required. Turnaround time 1 day. Copy fee: $1.00 per page. Certification fee: $5.00. Fee payee: F. Wm. Hoermann County Clerk. Personal checks accepted if instate. Prepayment is required.

Angelina County

District Court PO Box 908, Lufkin, TX 75902; 936-634-4312; Fax: 936-634-5915. Hours: 8AM-5PM (CST). *Felony, Civil.*

Civil Records: Access: Mail, in person. Both court and visitors may perform in person searches. Search fee: $5.00 per name. Required to search: name, years to search. Civil cases indexed by defendant, plaintiff. Civil records on computer for 5 years, on index books from 1800s. Must state whether search is on plaintiff or defendant.

Criminal Records: Access: Mail, in person. Both court and visitors may perform in person searches. Search fee: $5.00 per name. Required to search: name, years to search, DOB; also helpful: SSN. Criminal records on computer from 1984, on index books from 1800s.

General Information: Public Access terminal is available. No juvenile, mental, sealed, or adoption records released. SASE required. Turnaround time 2-3 days. Copy fee: $1.00 per page. Certification fee: $2.00. Fee payee: District Clerk. Personal checks accepted. Prepayment is required.

County Court PO Box 908, Lufkin, TX 75902; 936-634-8339; Fax: 936-634-8460. Hours: 8AM-5PM (CST). *Misdemeanor, Civil, Probate.*

Civil Records: Access: Mail, in person. Both court and visitors may perform in person searches. Search fee: $10.00 per name. Will search back to 1984. Required to search: name, years to search. Civil cases indexed by defendant, plaintiff. Civil records on index books.

Criminal Records: Access: Mail, in person. Both court and visitors may perform in person searches. Search fee: $10.00 per name. Will search back to 1984. Required to search: name, years to search; also helpful: DOB. Criminal records on computer from 1984.

General Information: No juvenile, mental, sealed, or adoption records released. SASE required. Turnaround time 1-2 days. Copy fee: $1.00 per page. Certification fee: $5.00. Fee payee: County Clerk. Business checks accepted. Prepayment is required.

Aransas County

District Court 301 North Live Oak, Rockport, TX 78382; 361-790-0128; Fax: 361-790-5211. Hours: 8AM-5PM (CST). *Felony, Civil.*

Civil Records: Access: Mail, in person. Both court and visitors may perform in person searches. Search fee: $5.00 per name. Required to search: name, years to search. Civil cases indexed by defendant, plaintiff. Civil records in index books from 1800s.

Criminal Records: Access: Mail, in person. Both court and visitors may perform in person searches. Search fee: $5.00 per name. Required to search: name, years to search. Criminal records in index books from 1800s.

General Information: No juvenile, mental, sealed, or adoption records released. SASE required. Turnaround time 1-2 days. Copy fee: $1.00 per page. Certification fee: $1.00. Fee payee: District Clerk. Personal checks accepted. Prepayment is required.

County Court 301 N Live Oak, Rockport, TX 78382; 361-790-0122. Hours: 8AM-4:30PM (CST). *Misdemeanor, Civil, Probate.*

Civil Records: Access: Mail, fax, in person. Both court and visitors may perform in person searches. Search fee: $5.00 per name. Required to search: name, years to search. Civil cases indexed by defendant, plaintiff. Civil records in index books from 1947, computerized records go back to 1998.

Criminal Records: Access: Mail, fax, in person. Both court and visitors may perform in person searches. Search fee: $5.00 per name. Required to search: name, years to search, DOB. Criminal records in index books from 1947; computerized records go back to 1995.

General Information: Public Access terminal is available. No juvenile, mental, sealed, or adoption records released. SASE not required. Turnaround time 2 days. Copy fee: $1.00 per page. Certification fee: $5.00. Fee payee: County Clerk. Personal checks accepted. Prepayment is required.

Archer County

District & County Court PO Box 815, Archer City, TX 76351; 940-574-4615. Hours: 8:30AM-5PM (CST). *Felony, Misdemeanor, Civil, Eviction, Probate.*

Civil Records: Access: Phone, mail, in person. Both court and visitors may perform in person searches. Search fee: $5.00 per name. Fee is per index searched. Required to search: name, years to search. Civil cases indexed by defendant, plaintiff. Civil records on computer from 1986, in index books from 1900s.

Criminal Records: Access: Phone, mail, in person. Both court and visitors may perform in person searches. Search fee: $5.00 per name. Fee is per index searched. Required to search: name, years to search. Criminal records on computer from 1986, in index books from 1900s.

General Information: No juvenile, mental, sealed, or adoption records released. SASE required. Turnaround time 1 day. Copy fee: $1.00 per page. Certification fee: $1.00. County Court certification fee is $5.00. Fee payee: County Clerk or District Clerk. Personal checks accepted. Prepayment is required.

Armstrong County

District & County Court PO Box 309, Claude, TX 79019; 806-226-2081; Fax: 806-226-5301. Hours: 8AM-Noon, 1-5PM (CST). *Felony, Misdemeanor, Civil, Eviction, Probate.*

Civil Records: Access: Mail, in person. Both court and visitors may perform in person searches. Search fee: $5.00 per name. Required to search: name, years to search. Civil cases indexed by defendant, plaintiff. Civil records in index books from 1800s.

Criminal Records: Access: Mail, in person. Both court and visitors may perform in person searches. Search fee: $5.00 per name. Required to search: name, years to search. Criminal records in index books from 1800s; computerized back to 1992.

General Information: No juvenile, mental, sealed, or adoption records released. SASE required. Turnaround time 1-2 days. Copy fee: $1.00 per page. Certification fee: $5.00. Fee payee: County Clerk. Personal checks accepted. Prepayment is required.

Atascosa County

District Court #52 Courthouse Circle, Jourdanton, TX 78026; 830-769-3011. Hours: 8AM-Noon, 1-5PM (CST). *Felony, Civil.*

Civil Records: Access: Mail, in person. Both court and visitors may perform in person searches. Search fee: $5.00 per name. Required to search: name, years to search; also helpful: address. Civil cases indexed by defendant, plaintiff. Civil records in index books.

Criminal Records: Access: Mail, in person. Both court and visitors may perform in person searches. Search fee: $5.00 per name. Required to search: name, years to search; also helpful: DOB, SSN. Criminal records in index books.

General Information: No juvenile, mental, sealed, or adoption records released. SASE required. Turnaround time 6 days. Fax notes: Fee to fax results is $2.00 per page. Copy fee: $1.00 per page. Certification fee: $1.00. Fee payee: District Clerk. Personal checks accepted.

County Court Circle Dr Rm 6-1, Jourdanton, TX 78026; 830-767-2511. Hours: 8AM-5PM (CST). *Misdemeanor, Civil, Probate.*

Civil Records: Access: Mail, in person. Both court and visitors may perform in person searches. No search fee. Required to search: name, years to search. Civil cases indexed by defendant, plaintiff. Civil records in index books from 1900s; on computer back to 2000.

Criminal Records: Access: In person only. Visitors must perform in person searches for themselves. No search fee. Required to search: name, years to search. Criminal records in index books from 1900s; on computer back to 2000.

General Information: No juvenile, mental, sealed, or adoption records released. SASE required. Turnaround time same day. Copy fee: $1.00 per page. Certification fee: $5.00. Fee payee: County Clerk. Personal checks accepted. Prepayment is required.

Austin County

District Court 1 East Main, Bellville, TX 77418-1598; 979-865-5911 X121. Hours: 8AM-Noon, 1-5PM (CST). *Felony, Civil.*

www.austincountyonline.com/dclerk.html

Civil Records: Access: Mail, in person. Both court and visitors may perform in person searches. Search fee: $5.00 per name. Required to search: name, years to search. Civil cases indexed by defendant, plaintiff. Civil records in index books from 1843; on computer back to 1995.

Criminal Records: Access: Mail, in person. Both court and visitors may perform in person searches. Search fee: $5.00 per name. Required to search: name, years to search; also helpful: DOB, SSN. Criminal records in index books from 1843; on computer back to 1996.

General Information: Public Access terminal is available. No juvenile, mental, sealed, or adoption records released. SASE required. Turnaround time same day. Fax notes: Fee to fax results is $2.00 per document. Copy fee: $1.00 per page. Certification fee: $1.00 per page. This fee includes copy fee. Fee payee: District Clerk. Personal checks accepted. Prepayment is required.

County Court at Law 1 E Main, Bellville, TX 77418; 979-865-5911; Fax: 979-865-0336. Hours: 8AM-5PM (CST). *Misdemeanor, Civil, Probate.*

Civil Records: Access: Mail, in person. Both court and visitors may perform in person searches. Search fee: $5.00 per name. Required to search: name, years to search. Civil cases indexed by defendant, plaintiff. Civil records on computer from 06/95, index books from 1843.

Criminal Records: Access: Mail, in person. Both court and visitors may perform in person searches. Search fee: $5.00 per name. Required to search: name, years to search, DOB; also helpful: SSN. Criminal records on computer from 05/95, index books from 1876.

General Information: No juvenile, mental, sealed, or adoption records released. SASE required. Turnaround time 2 days. Copy fee: $1.00 per page. Certification fee: $5.00. Fee payee: Carrie Gregor, County Clerk. Personal checks accepted. Prepayment is required.

Bailey County

District Court 300 S 1st St, Muleshoe, TX 79347; 806-272-3165; Fax: 806-272-3879. Hours: 8AM-5PM (CST). *Felony, Civil.*

Civil Records: Access: Phone, mail, in person. Both court and visitors may perform in person searches. Search fee: $5.00 per name. Required to search: name, years to search. Civil cases indexed by defendant, plaintiff. Civil records in index books, archived from 1925.

Criminal Records: Access: Phone, mail, in person. Both court and visitors may perform in person searches.

Search fee: $5.00 per name. Required to search: name, years to search. Criminal records in index books, archived from 1925.

General Information: No juvenile, mental, sealed, or adoption records released. SASE required. Turnaround time 1 day. Copy fee: $1.00 per page. Certification fee: $1.00. Fee payee: District Clerk. Personal checks accepted. Prepayment is required.

County Court 300 S 1st St, Muleshoe, TX 79347; 806-272-3044; Fax: 806-272-3538. Hours: 8AM-5PM (CST). *Misdemeanor, Civil, Probate.*

Civil Records: Access: Mail, in person. Both court and visitors may perform in person searches. Search fee: $10.00 per name. Required to search: name, years to search. Civil cases indexed by defendant, plaintiff. Civil records in index books, archived from 1925.

Criminal Records: Access: Mail, in person. Both court and visitors may perform in person searches. Search fee: $10.00 per name. Required to search: name, years to search. Criminal records in index books, archived from 1925.

General Information: No juvenile, mental, sealed, or adoption records released. SASE required. Turnaround time 10 days. Copy fee: $1.00 per page. Certification fee: $5.00. Fee payee: County Clerk. Personal checks accepted. Prepayment is required.

Bandera County

District & County Court PO Box 823, Bandera, TX 78003; 830-796-3332; Fax: 830-796-8323. Hours: 8AM-5PM (CST). *Felony, Misdemeanor, Civil, Eviction, Probate.*

Note: The District Clerk can be reached at PO Box 2688 and 830-796-4606. PO box and phone above is for County Clerk.

Civil Records: Access: Fax, mail, in person. Both court and visitors may perform in person searches. Search fee: $5.00 per name. Required to search: name, years to search; also helpful: address. Civil cases indexed by defendant, plaintiff. Civil records on computer from 1988, index books from 1857.

Criminal Records: Access: Fax, mail, in person. Both court and visitors may perform in person searches. Search fee: $5.00 per name. Required to search: name, years to search, signed release; also helpful: address, DOB, SSN. Criminal records on computer from 1988, index books from 1857.

General Information: No juvenile, mental or sealed records released. SASE required. Turnaround time 2 days. Fax notes: Fee to fax results is $2.00 for first page, $1.00 each add'l. Copy fee: $1.00 per page. Certification fee: $5.00. Fee payee: Bandera County Clerk. Personal checks accepted. Prepayment is required.

Bastrop County

District Court PO Box 770, Bastrop, TX 78602; 512-332-7244. Hours: 8AM-5PM (CST). *Felony, Civil.*

Civil Records: Access: Mail, in person. Both court and visitors may perform in person searches. Search fee: $5.00 per name. Required to search: name, years to search. Civil cases indexed by defendant, plaintiff. Civil records on microfilm from 1986, archived from early 1800s.

Criminal Records: Access: Mail, in person. Both court and visitors may perform in person searches. Search fee: $5.00 per name. Required to search: name, years to search, signed release. Criminal records on computer since 1989; prior on microfilm from 1986, archived from early 1800s.

General Information: No juvenile, mental, sealed, or adoption records released. SASE required. Turnaround time 1 day. Copy fee: $.25 per page. Certification fee: $1.00. Fee payee: District Clerk. Personal checks accepted.

County Court PO Box 577, Bastrop, TX 78602; 512-332-7234. Hours: 8AM-Noon, 1-5PM (CST). *Misdemeanor, Probate.*

Criminal Records: Access: Phone, mail, in person. Both court and visitors may perform in person searches. Search fee: $5.00 per name. Required to search: name, years to search, DOB, SSN. Criminal records on computer since 1986, prior on index books.

General Information: No juvenile, mental, sealed, or adoption records released. SASE required. Turnaround time 1-2 days. Fax notes: Fee to fax results is $1.00 per page. Copy fee: $1.00 per page. Certification fee: $5.00. Fee payee: Bastrop County Clerk. Personal checks accepted. Prepayment is required.

Baylor County

District & County Court PO Box 689, Seymour, TX 76380; 940-888-3322. Hours: 8:30AM-5PM (CST). *Felony, Misdemeanor, Civil, Eviction, Probate.*

Civil Records: Access: Phone, mail, in person. Both court and visitors may perform in person searches. Search fee: $10.00 per name. Required to search: name, years to search. Civil cases indexed by defendant, plaintiff. Civil records on index cards and books.

Criminal Records: Access: Phone, mail, in person. Both court and visitors may perform in person searches. Search fee: $10.00 per name. Required to search: name, years to search. Criminal records on index cards and books from 1900s.

General Information: No juvenile, mental, sealed, or adoption records released. SASE required. Turnaround time 1-2 days. Copy fee: $1.00 per page. Certification fee: $2.00. $5.00 for County Court certification. Fee payee: Baylor County Clerk. Personal checks accepted. Prepayment is required.

Bee County

District Court PO Box 666, Beeville, TX 78104-0666; 361-362-3242; Fax: 361-362-3282. Hours: 8AM-5PM (CST). *Felony, Civil.*

Civil Records: Access: Mail, in person. Both court and visitors may perform in person searches. Search fee: $5.00 per name. Required to search: name, years to search. Civil cases indexed by defendant, plaintiff. Civil records on index books from 1911.

Criminal Records: Access: Mail, in person. Both court and visitors may perform in person searches. Search fee: $5.00 per name. Required to search: name, years to search, signed release. Criminal records on index books from 1911.

General Information: No juvenile, mental, sealed, or adoption records released. SASE required. Turnaround time 1-3 days. Copy fee: $1.00 per page. Certification fee: $2.00. Fee payee: District Clerk. Personal checks accepted.

County Court 105 W Corpus Christi St, Rm 103, Beeville, TX 78102; 361-362-3245; Fax: 361-362-3247. Hours: 8AM-Noon, 1-5PM (CST). *Misdemeanor, Civil, Probate.*

Civil Records: Access: Phone, fax, mail, in person. Both court and visitors may perform in person searches. Search fee: $5.00 per name. Required to search: name, years to search. Civil cases indexed by defendant, plaintiff. Civil records on index books from 1859.

Criminal Records: Access: Phone, fax, mail, in person. Both court and visitors may perform in person searches. Search fee: $5.00 per name. Add $1.00 for certificate. Required to search: name, years to search, DOB; also helpful: SSN. Criminal records on index books from 1859.

General Information: No juvenile, mental, sealed, or adoption records released. SASE required. Turnaround time 1 day. Fax notes: Fee to fax results is $2.00 per page. Copy fee: $1.00 per page. Certification fee: $5.00.

Fee payee: County Clerk. Personal checks accepted. Prepayment is required.

Bell County

District Court 104 S Main St, PO Box 909, Belton, TX 76513; 254-933-5197; Fax: 254-933-5199. Hours: 8AM-5PM (CST). *Felony, Civil.*

Civil Records: Access: Mail, in person. Both court and visitors may perform in person searches. Search fee: $10.00 per name. Required to search: name, years to search. Civil cases indexed by defendant, plaintiff. Civil records on computer from 1987, alpha index from 1982, chrono from 1800.

Criminal Records: Access: Mail, in person. Both court and visitors may perform in person searches. Search fee: $10.00 per name. Required to search: name, years to search, DOB; also helpful, SSN, signed release, cause number. Criminal records on computer from 1987, alpha index from 1982, chrono from 1800.

General Information: Public Access terminal is available. No juvenile, mental, sealed, or adoption records released. SASE required. Turnaround time 1-2 days. Copy fee: $.50 per page. Certification fee: $1.00 per page. Fee payee: District Clerk, Bell County. Only cashiers checks and money orders accepted. Prepayment is required.

County Court PO Box 480, Belton, TX 76513; 254-933-5165; Civil phone: 254-933-5174; Criminal phone: 254-933-5170; Fax: 254-933-5176. Hours: 8AM-5PM (CST). *Misdemeanor, Civil, Probate.*

Civil Records: Access: Mail, in person. Both court and visitors may perform in person searches. Search fee: $5.00 per name. Required to search: name, years to search. Civil cases indexed by defendant, plaintiff. Civil records on computer since September, 1989.

Criminal Records: Access: Mail, in person. Both court and visitors may perform in person searches. Search fee: $5.00 per name. Required to search: name, years to search, DOB, SSN. Records on computer since 1986.

General Information: Public Access terminal is available. No juvenile, mental, sealed, or adoption records released. SASE not required. Turnaround time 3-5 days. Copy fee: $1.00 per page. Certification fee: $1.00. Fee payee: County Clerk. Local checks only. Prepayment is required.

Bexar County

District Court 100 Dolorosa, County Courthouse, Chief Court Clerk, San Antonio, TX 78205; 210-220-2083; Fax: 210-335-2942. Hours: 8AM-5PM (CST). *Felony, Civil.*

www.co.bexar.tx.us/dclerk

Civil Records: Access: Mail, fax, online, in person. Both court and visitors may perform in person searches. Search fee: $5.00 per name. Required to search: name, years to search. Civil cases indexed by defendant, plaintiff. Civil records on computer from 1982-present, chrono index from 1909. Access to the remote online system requires a $100 setup fee, plus a $25 monthly fee, plus inquiry fees. Call Jennifer Mann at 210-335-0212 for more information.

Criminal Records: Access: Mail, fax, online, in person. Both court and visitors may perform in person searches. Search fee: $5.00 per name. Required to search: name, years to search, signed release, DOB. Criminal records on computer from 1982-present, chrono index from 1909. Online access to criminal records is the same as civil.

General Information: Public Access terminal is available. No juvenile, mental, sealed, or adoption records released. SASE required. Turnaround time up to 10 days. Fax notes: Fee to fax results is $.50 per page. Copy fee: $.50 per page. Certification fee: $1.00 per page. Fee payee: District Clerk. Only cashiers checks and money orders accepted. Prepayment is required.

County Court - Civil Central Filing Department 100 Dolorosa, San Antonio, TX 78205-3083; 210-335-2231. 8AM-5PM (CST). *Civil.*

Note: There are twelve hearing locations in this county where open cases are held. All closed cases are forwarded here.

Civil Records: Access: Phone, fax, mail, in person. Both court and visitors may perform in person searches. Search fee: $5.00 per name. Fee is for 10 year search. Required to search: name, years to search. Civil cases indexed by defendant, plaintiff. Civil records on computer back 10 years, index books prior.

General Information: Public Access terminal is available. No mental, sealed records released. SASE required. Turnaround time 1-2 days. Copy fee: $1.00 per page. Certification fee: $5.00. Fee payee: County Clerk. Personal checks accepted. Prepayment required.

County Court - Criminal 300 Dolorosa, Suite 4101, San Antonio, TX 78205; 210-335-2238. Hours: 8AM-5PM (CST). *Misdemeanor.*

www.co.bexar.tx.us/dclerk

Criminal Records: Access: Mail, online, in person. Both court and visitors may perform in person searches. Search fee: $5.00 per name. Fee is per ten year period. Required to search: name, years to search, DOB, signed release; also helpful: SSN. Criminal records on computer since 1974, alpha index since 1983, on card index form 1909. Access to the criminal online system requires a $100 setup fee, plus a $25 monthly fee, plus inquiry fees. Call Jennifer Mann at 210-335-0212 for more information.

General Information: Public Access terminal is available. No sealed records released. SASE requested. Turnaround time 2-3 days. Copy fee: $1.00 per page. Certification fee: $5.00 plus $1.00 per page. Fee payee: County Clerk. Personal checks accepted. Checks must be in state. Prepayment is required.

Probate Court #2 100 Dolorosa St, Rm 117, San Antonio, TX 78205; 210-335-2546. Hours: 8AM-5PM (CST). *Probate.*

www.co.bexar.tx.us/pcourt/probatecourts.htm

Blanco County

District & County Court PO Box 65, Johnson City, TX 78636; 830-868-7357. Hours: 8AM-5PM (CST). *Felony, Misdemeanor, Civil, Eviction, Probate.*

Civil Records: Access: Mail, in person. Both court and visitors may perform in person searches. Search fee: $5.00 per name. Required to search: name, years to search. Civil cases indexed by defendant, plaintiff. Civil records on computer from 1994, index books before.

Criminal Records: Access: Mail, in person. Both court and visitors may perform in person searches. Search fee: $5.00 per name. Required to search: name, years to search, DOB; also helpful: SSN. Criminal records on computer from 1994, index books before.

General Information: Public Access terminal is available. No juvenile, mental, sealed, or adoption records released. SASE required. Turnaround time 1 day. Copy fee: $1.00 per page. Certification fee: $5.00. Fee payee: County Clerk. Personal checks accepted. Prepayment is required.

Borden County

District & County Court PO Box 124, Gail, TX 79738; 806-756-4312. Hours: 8AM-5PM (CST). *Felony, Misdemeanor, Civil, Eviction, Probate.*

Civil Records: Access: Mail, in person. Both court and visitors may perform in person searches. Search fee: $5.00 per name. Required to search: name, years to search. Civil cases indexed by defendant, plaintiff. Civil records in index books, archived from 1900.

Criminal Records: Access: Mail, in person. Only the court performs in person searches; visitors may not. Search fee: $5.00 per name. Required to search: name, years to search. Criminal records in index books, archived from 1900.

General Information: No juvenile, mental, sealed, or adoption records released. SASE required. Turnaround time 1 week. Fax notes: Fee to fax results is $1.00 per page. Copy fee: $1.00 per page. Certification fee: $1.00. Fee payee: District Clerk. Personal checks accepted. Prepayment is required.

Bosque County

District Court Main & Morgan St, Po Box 674, Meridian, TX 76665; 254-435-2334. Hours: 8AM-5PM (CST). *Felony, Civil.*

Civil Records: Access: Mail, in person. Both court and visitors may perform in person searches. Search fee: $5.00 per name. Required to search: name, years to search. Civil cases indexed by defendant, plaintiff. Civil records on computer from 1990, files/books from 1870s.

Criminal Records: Access: Mail, in person. Both court and visitors may perform in person searches. Search fee: $5.00 per name. Required to search: name, years to search, DOB or SSN. Criminal records on books/files from 1856.

General Information: No juvenile, mental, sealed, or adoption records released. SASE required. Turnaround time 1 day. Copy fee: $1.00 per page. Certification fee: $1.00. Payee: District Clerk. Personal checks accepted.

County Court PO Box 617, Meridian, TX 76665; 254-435-2201; Fax: 254-435-2152. Hours: 8AM-5PM (CST). *Misdemeanor, Civil, Probate.*

Civil Records: Access: Mail, in person. Both court and visitors may perform in person searches. Search fee: $5.00 per name. Required to search: name, years to search. Civil cases indexed by defendant, plaintiff. Civil records in index books from 1854.

Criminal Records: Access: Mail, in person. Both court and visitors may perform in person searches. Search fee: $5.00 per name. Required to search: name, years to search, DOB, signed release. Criminal records in index books from 1854.

General Information: Public Access terminal is available. No juvenile, mental, sealed, or adoption records released. SASE required. Turnaround time 1-2 days. Copy fee: $1.00 per page. Certification fee: $5.00. Fee payee: County Clerk. Personal checks accepted. In state checks only. Prepayment is required.

Bowie County

District & County Court 710 James Bowie Dr, PO Box 248, New Boston, TX 75570; 903-628-6750; Probate phone: 903-628-6740. Hours: 8AM-5PM (CST). *Felony, Misdemeanor, Civil, Probate.*

Note: Probate records are at this address in the County Clerk's office.

Civil Records: Access: Mail, in person. Both court and visitors may perform in person searches. Search fee: $5.00 per name. Required to search: name, years to search. Civil cases indexed by defendant, plaintiff. Civil records on computer from 1978, on microfiche from 1900s, chrono index from 1800s.

Criminal Records: Access: Mail, in person. Both court and visitors may perform in person searches. Search fee: $5.00 per name. Required to search: name, years to search, DOB. Criminal records on computer from 1978, on microfiche from 1900s, chrono index from 1800s.

General Information: No juvenile, mental, sealed, or adoption records released. SASE required. Turnaround time 1 day. Copy fee: $1.00 per page. Certification fee: $2.00. Fee payee: District Clerk. Personal checks accepted.

Brazoria County

District Court 111 E Locus #500, Angleton, TX 77515-4678; 979-864-1316. Hours: 8AM-5PM (CST). *Felony, Civil.*

Civil Records: Access: Phone, mail, in person. Both court and visitors may perform in person searches. Search fee: $5.00 per name. Fee is per 10 year period. Required to search: name, years to search. Civil cases indexed by defendant, plaintiff. Civil records on computer from 1986, index chrono to 1900, prior alpha.

Criminal Records: Access: Phone, mail, in person. Both court and visitors may perform in person searches. Search fee: $5.00 per name. Fee is per 10 year period. Required to search: name, years to search, DOB, signed release; also helpful: SSN. Criminal records on computer from 1986, index chrono to 1900, prior alpha.

General Information: Public Access terminal is available. No juvenile, mental, sealed, or adoption records released. SASE required. Turnaround time up to 1 week. Copy fee: $1.00 per page. Certification fee: $1.00. Fee payee: District Clerk. Only cashiers checks and money orders accepted. Prepayment is required.

County Court 111 E Locust #200, Angleton, TX 77515; Civil phone: 979-864-1385; Criminal phone: 979-864-1380; Fax: 979-848-1031 (civil); -1020 (Crim.). 8AM-5PM (CST). *Misdemeanor, Civil.*

Civil Records: Access: Fax, mail, in person. Both court and visitors may perform in person searches. Search fee: $5.00 per name. Required to search: name, years to search. Civil cases indexed by defendant, plaintiff. Civil records on computer from 1984; prior on books or microfiche back to 1800s. Fee must be prepaid before faxing search request.

Criminal Records: Access: Fax, mail, in person. Both court and visitors may perform in person searches. Search fee: $5.00 per name. Required to search: name, years to search, DOB. Criminal records on computer from 1984; prior on books or microfiche back to 1800s.

General Information: Public Access terminal is available. No juvenile, mental, sealed records released. SASE required. Turnaround time 2 days. Copy fee: $1.00 per page. Certification fee: $5.00 per document. Fee payee: Joyce Hudman, County Clerk. Personal checks accepted. Prepayment is required.

Probate Court 111 E Locust #200, Angleton, TX 77515; 979-864-1367; Fax: 979-864-1830. Hours: 8AM-5PM (CST). *Probate.*

Brazos County

District Court 300 E 26th St #216 (PO Box 2208), Bryan, TX 77806; 979-361-4233; Fax: 979-361-0197. Hours: 8AM-5PM (CST). *Felony, Civil.*

www.co.brazos.tx.us/disclerk

Civil Records: Access: Mail, in person. Both court and visitors may perform in person searches. Search fee: $5.00 per name. Required to search: name, years to search. Civil cases indexed by defendant, plaintiff. Civil records on computer, index chrono from 1800s.

Criminal Records: Access: Mail, in person. Both court and visitors may perform in person searches. Search fee: $5.00 per name. Required to search: name, years to search; also helpful: DOB, SSN. Criminal records on computer, index chrono from 1800s.

General Information: No juvenile, mental, sealed, or adoption records released. SASE required. Turnaround time 1-2 days. Copy fee: $.50 per page. Certification fee: $1.00 per page. Fee payee: District Clerk. Personal checks accepted. Prepayment is required.

County Court 300 E 26th St #120, Bryan, TX 77803; 979-361-4128. Hours: 8AM-5PM (CST). *Misdemeanor, Civil, Probate.*

Note: Court holds misdemeanor records prior to 1986 only. Newer cases are at the District Court.

Civil Records: Access: Mail, in person. Both court and visitors may perform in person searches. Search fee: $5.00 per name. Required to search: name, years to search. Civil cases indexed by defendant, plaintiff. Civil records on computer from 1986, index chrono to 1958.

Criminal Records: Access: Mail, in person. Both court and visitors may perform in person searches. Search fee: $5.00 per name. Required to search: name, years to search, DOB. Criminal records on computer from 1986, index chrono from 1958.

General Information: Public Access terminal is available. No juvenile, mental, sealed, or adoption records released. SASE required. Turnaround time 2-3 days. Copy fee: $1.00 per page. Certification fee: $5.00. Fee payee: County Clerk. Only cashiers checks and money orders accepted. Prepayment is required.

Brewster County

District Court PO Box 1024, Alpine, TX 79831; 915-837-6216; Fax: 915-837-6217. Hours: 9AM-12, 1-5PM (CST). *Felony, Civil.*

Civil Records: Access: Phone, fax, mail, in person. Both court and visitors may perform in person searches. No search fee. Required to search: name; also helpful: years to search. Civil cases indexed by defendant, plaintiff. Civil records are computerized since 1994, indexed from 1899.

Criminal Records: Access: Phone, fax, mail, in person. Both court and visitors may perform in person searches. No search fee. Required to search: name, DOB; also helpful: years to search. Criminal records are computerized since 1994, indexed from 1899.

General Information: Turnaround time 1-2 days. Fax notes: No fee for local calls. Copy fee: $1.00 per page. Certification fee: $1.00. Fee payee: District Clerk. Personal checks accepted. Prepayment is required.

County Court PO Box 119 (201 W Avenue E), Alpine, TX 79831; 915-837-3366; Fax: 915-837-6217. 9AM-5PM (CST). *Misdemeanor, Civil Probate.*

Civil Records: Access: Mail, fax, in person. Both court and visitors may perform in person searches. Search fee: $10.00 per name. Required to search: name, years to search. Civil cases indexed by defendant, plaintiff. Civil records in index books from 1800s.

Criminal Records: Access: Mail, fax, in person. Both court and visitors may perform in person searches. Search fee: $10.00 per name. Required to search: name, years to search, DOB, signed release; also helpful: SSN. Criminal records in index books from 1800s.

General Information: No juvenile, mental, sealed, or adoption records released. SASE required. Turnaround time 1 week. Fax notes: Fee to fax results is $2.00 per page. Copy fee: $1.00 per page. Certification fee: $5.00. Fee payee: County Clerk. Personal checks accepted. Prepayment is required.

Briscoe County

District & County Court PO Box 555, Silverton, TX 79257; 806-823-2134; Fax: 806-823-2359. Hours: 8AM-5PM (CST). *Felony, Misdemeanor, Civil, Eviction, Probate.*

Civil Records: Access: Fax, mail, in person. Both court and visitors may perform in person searches. Search fee: $5.00 per name. Required to search: name, years to search. Civil cases indexed by defendant, plaintiff. Civil records in index books from 1892.

Criminal Records: Access: Fax, mail, in person. Both court and visitors may perform in person searches. Search fee: $5.00 per name. Required to search: name, years to search, DOB. Criminal records in index books from 1892.

General Information: No juvenile, mental, sealed, or adoption records released. SASE required. Turnaround time 1 day. Copy fee: $1.00 per page. Certification fee:

$5.00. Fee payee: District or County Clerk. Personal checks accepted. Prepayment is required.

Brooks County

District Court PO Box 534, Falfurrias, TX 78355; 361-325-5604; Fax: 361-325-5679. Hours: 8AM-5PM (CST). *Felony, Civil.*

Civil Records: Access: Phone, fax, mail, online, in person. Both court and visitors may perform in person searches. Search fee: $5.00 per name. Required to search: name, years to search; also helpful: address. Civil cases indexed by defendant, plaintiff. Civil records on computer since 1992, index books since 1920. Civil information available free online at www.idocket.com.

Criminal Records: Access: Phone, fax, mail, online, in person. Both court and visitors may perform in person searches. Search fee: $5.00 per name. Required to search: name, years to search; also helpful: address, DOB, SSN. Criminal records on computer since 1992, index books since 1920, microfiche since 1939. Online access to criminal records is the same as civil.

General Information: No juvenile, mental, sealed, or adoption records released. SASE required. Turnaround time 1 week. Fax notes: Fee to fax results is $1.00 per page. Copy fee: $1.00 per page. Certification fee: $2.00. Fee payee: District Clerk. Business checks accepted. Prepayment is required.

County Court PO Box 427, Falfurrias, TX 78355; 361-325-5604 X245,246,248. Hours: 8AM-5PM (CST). *Misdemeanor, Civil, Probate.*

Civil Records: Access: Phone, fax, mail, in person. Both court and visitors may perform in person searches. Search fee: $10.00 per name. Required to search: name, years to search. Civil cases indexed by plaintiff. Civil records in index books since 1911.

Criminal Records: Access: Phone, fax, mail, in person. Both court and visitors may perform in person searches. Search fee: $10.00 per name. Required to search: name, years to search, DOB. Criminal records in index books since 1911.

General Information: No juvenile, mental, sealed, or adoption records released. SASE required. Turnaround time 1-2 days. Fax notes: $5.00 for first page, $2.00 each add'l. Copy fee: $1.00 per page. Certification fee: $5.00. Payee: County Clerk. Personal checks accepted.

Brown County

District Court 200 S Broadway, Brownwood, TX 76801; 915-646-5514. 8:30AM-5PM *Felony, Civil.*

Civil Records: Access: Mail, in person. Both court and visitors may perform in person searches. Search fee: $5.00 per name. Required to search: name, years to search. Civil cases indexed by defendant, plaintiff. Civil records on computer since 1995; prior records on books to 1930s.

Criminal Records: Access: Mail, in person. Both court and visitors may perform in person searches. Search fee: $5.00 per name. Required to search: name, years to search. Criminal records on computer since 1995; prior records on books to 1930s.

General Information: Public Access terminal is available. No juvenile, mental, sealed, or adoption records released. SASE required. Turnaround time 2-3 days. Fax notes: Do not fax. Copy fee: $1.00 per page. Certification fee: $1.00 per page. Fee payee: District Clerk. Business checks accepted. Prepayment required.

County Court 200 S Broadway, Brownwood, TX 76801; 915-643-2594. Hours: 8:30AM-5PM (CST). *Misdemeanor, Civil, Probate.*

Civil Records: Access: Mail, in person. Both court and visitors may perform in person searches. Search fee: $5.00 per name. Required to search: name, years to search. Civil cases indexed by defendant, plaintiff. Civil records on computer from 1987, on microfiche from 1900s.

Criminal Records: Access: Mail, in person. Both court and visitors may perform in person searches. Search fee: $5.00 per name. Required to search: name, years to search; also helpful: DOB, SSN. Criminal records on computer from 1987, on microfiche from 1900s.

General Information: Public Access terminal is available. No juvenile, mental, sealed records released. SASE required. Turnaround time 1-2 days. Copy fee: $1.00 per page. Certification fee: $5.00. Fee payee: Brown County Clerk. Personal checks accepted. Prepayment is required.

Burleson County

District Court 100 West Buck #303, Caldwell, TX 77836; 979-567-2336. Hours: 8AM-12, 1-5PM (CST). *Felony, Civil.*

Civil Records: Access: Mail, in person. Both court and visitors may perform in person searches. Search fee: $5.00 per name. Required to search: name, years to search. Civil cases indexed by defendant, plaintiff. Civil records on microfilm from 1980, index books prior.

Criminal Records: Access: Mail, in person. Both court and visitors may perform in person searches. Search fee: $5.00 per name. Required to search: name, years to search. Criminal records on microfilm from 1980, index books prior.

General Information: No juvenile, mental, sealed, or adoption records released. SASE or toll-free phone number required. Turnaround time 1-2 days. Fax notes: Will fax to toll-free number. Copy fee: $1.00 per page. Certification fee: $1.00 per page. Fee payee: District Clerk. Personal checks accepted. Prepayment required.

County Court 100 West Buck #203, Caldwell, TX 77836; 979-567-2329; Fax: 979-567-2376. Hours: 8AM-5PM (CST). *Misdemeanor, Civil, Probate.*

Civil Records: Access: Mail, fax, in person. Visitors must perform in person searches for themselves. No search fee. Required to search: name, years to search. Civil cases indexed by defendant, plaintiff. Civil records on computer back to 9/1981; prior on books.

Criminal Records: Access: Mail, fax, in person. Visitors must perform in person searches for themselves. No search fee. Required to search: name, years to search, DOB, SSN. Civil records on computer back to 9/1981; prior on books.

General Information: No juvenile, mental, or sealed records released. SASE required. Turnaround time 2-4 days. Fax notes: Fee to fax results is $1.00 per page. Copy fee: $1.00 per page. Certification fee: $5.00. Fee payee: County Clerk. Personal checks accepted. Prepayment is required.

Burnet County

District Court 220 S Pierce, Burnet, TX 78611; 512-756-5450. Hours: 8AM-5PM (CST). *Felony, Civil.*

Civil Records: Access: Mail, in person. Both court and visitors may perform in person searches. Search fee: $5.00 per name. Required to search: name, years to search. Civil cases indexed by defendant, plaintiff. Civil records on computer from 1991, index books to 1856.

Criminal Records: Access: Mail, in person. Both court and visitors may perform in person searches. Search fee: $5.00 per name. Required to search: name, years to search; also helpful: DOB, SSN. Criminal records on computer from 1988, index book from 1856.

General Information: No juvenile, mental, sealed, or adoption records released. SASE required. Turnaround time 2 days. Copy fee: $1.00 per page. Certification fee: $2.00. Fee payee: District Clerk. Personal checks accepted. Prepayment is required.

County Court 220 S Pierce, Burnet, TX 78611; 512-756-5403; Fax: 512-756-5410. Hours: 8AM-5PM (CST). *Misdemeanor, Civil, Probate.*

Civil Records: Access: Fax, mail, in person. Both court and visitors may perform in person searches. Search fee: $10.00 per name. Required to search: name, years to search. Civil cases indexed by defendant, plaintiff. Civil records on computer from 1989, on microfiche from 1852.

Criminal Records: Access: Fax, mail, in person. Both court and visitors may perform in person searches. Search fee: $10.00 per name. Required to search: name, years to search, offense, date of offense. Criminal records on computer from 1989, on microfiche to 1852.

General Information: Public Access terminal is available. No juvenile, mental, sealed, or adoption records released. SASE required. Turnaround time 2 days. Fax notes: $1.00 per page. Copy fee: $1.00 per page. Certification fee: $5.00. Fee payee: County Clerk. Personal checks accepted. Prepayment is required.

Caldwell County

District Court 201 E San Antonio St, Lockhart, TX 78644; 512-398-1806. Hours: 8:30AM-Noon, 1-5PM (CST). *Felony, Civil.*

Civil Records: Access: Phone, fax, mail, in person. Both court and visitors may perform in person searches. Search fee: $5.00 per name. Required to search: name, years to search. Civil cases indexed by defendant, plaintiff. Civil records on computer since 1988, index books from 1900s.

Criminal Records: Access: Phone, fax, mail, in person. Both court and visitors may perform in person searches. Search fee: $5.00 per name. Required to search: name, years to search; also helpful: DOB, SSN. Criminal records on computer since 1988, index books from 1900s.

General Information: No juvenile, mental, sealed, or adoption records released. SASE required. Turnaround time 1-3 days. Copy fee: $1.00 per page. Certification fee: $1.00. Fee payee: District Clerk. Personal checks accepted. Prepayment is required.

County Court PO Box 906, Lockhart, TX 78644; 512-398-1804. Hours: 8:30AM-Noon, 1-5PM (CST). *Misdemeanor, Civil, Probate.*

Civil Records: Access: Mail, in person. Both court and visitors may perform in person searches. Search fee: $5.00 per name. Required to search: name, years to search. Civil cases indexed by defendant, plaintiff. Civil records in index books since 1967.

Criminal Records: Access: Mail, in person. Both court and visitors may perform in person searches. Search fee: $5.00 per name. Required to search: name, years to search, DOB, offense, date of offense. Criminal records in index books since 1967.

General Information: Public Access terminal is available. No juvenile, mental, sealed, or adoption records released. SASE not required. Turnaround time 2-4 days. Copy fee: $1.00 per page. Certification fee: $5.00. Fee payee: Caldwell County Clerk. Personal checks accepted. Prepayment is required.

Calhoun County

District Court 211 S Ann, Port Lavaca, TX 77979; 361-553-4630. Hours: 8AM-5PM (CST). *Felony, Civil.*

Civil Records: Access: Mail, in person. Both court and visitors may perform in person searches. Search fee: $5.00 per name. Required to search: name, years to search. Civil cases indexed by defendant, plaintiff. Civil records in index books from 1852.

Criminal Records: Access: Mail, in person. Both court and visitors may perform in person searches. Search fee: $5.00 per name. Required to search: name, years to search, signed release; also helpful: DOB. Criminal records in index books from 1852.

General Information: No juvenile, mental, sealed, or adoption records released. SASE required. Turnaround time 1 day. Copy fee: $1.00 per page. Certification fee: $1.00. Fee payee: District Clerk. Personal checks accepted. Prepayment is required.

County Court 211 S Ann, Port Lavaca, TX 77979; 361-553-4411; Fax: 361-553-4420. Hours: 8AM-5PM (CST). *Misdemeanor, Civil, Probate.*

Civil Records: Access: Phone, mail, in person. Both court and visitors may perform in person searches. Search fee: $5.00 per name. Required to search: name, years to search. Civil cases indexed by defendant, plaintiff. Civil records in index books from 1852.

Criminal Records: Access: Phone, mail, in person. Both court and visitors may perform in person searches. Search fee: $5.00 per name. Required to search: name, years to search. Criminal records in index books from 1852.

General Information: No juvenile, mental, sealed, or adoption records released. SASE required. Turnaround time 1-2 days. Copy fee: $1.00 per page. Certification fee: $5.00. Fee payee: County Clerk. Personal checks accepted. Prepayment is required.

Callahan County

District Court 100 W 4th St Suite 300, Baird, TX 79504-5396; 915-854-1800. Hours: 8AM-5PM (CST). *Felony, Civil.*

Civil Records: Access: Mail, in person. Both court and visitors may perform in person searches. Search fee: $5.00 per name. Required to search: name, years to search. Civil cases indexed by defendant, plaintiff. Civil records in index books since 1879.

Criminal Records: Access: Mail, in person. Both court and visitors may perform in person searches. Search fee: $5.00 per name. Required to search: name, years to search. Criminal records in index books since 1879.

General Information: No juvenile, mental, sealed, or adoption records released. SASE required. Turnaround time 1-2 days. Copy fee: $1.00 per page. Certification fee: No certification fee. Fee payee: District Clerk. Personal checks accepted. Prepayment is required.

County Court 100 W 4th St, Suite 104, Baird, TX 79504-5300; 915-854-1217; Fax: 915-854-1227. 8AM-5PM (CST). *Misdemeanor, Civil, Probate.*

Civil Records: Access: Phone, fax, mail, in person. Both court and visitors may perform in person searches. Search fee: $6.00 per name. Required to search: name, years to search. Civil cases indexed by defendant, plaintiff. Civil records on computer from 1992, index books from 1800s.

Criminal Records: Access: Phone, fax, mail, in person. Both court and visitors may perform in person searches. Search fee: $6.00 per name. Required to search: name, years to search. Criminal records on computer from 1992, index books from 1800s.

General Information: Public Access terminal is available. (Public access for land records only.) No juvenile, mental, sealed, or adoption records released. SASE required. Turnaround time 1 day. Fax notes: Fee to fax results is $1.50 per page. Copy fee: $1.00 per page. Certification fee: $5.00. Fee payee: Jeanie Bohannon, County Clerk. Personal checks accepted. Prepayment is required.

Cameron County

District Court 974 E Harrison St, Brownsville, TX 78520; 956-544-0839. Hours: 8AM-Noon, 1-5PM (CST). *Felony, Civil.*

Civil Records: Access: Mail, online, in person. Both court and visitors may perform in person searches. Search fee: $5.00 per name. Required to search: name, years to search. Civil cases indexed by defendant, plaintiff. Civil records on computer from 1989. Online access is available 24 hours daily. The $125 setup fee includes software, there is a $30 monthly access fee also. For more information, call Eric at 956-544-0838 X475.

Criminal Records: Access: Mail, in person. Only the court performs in person searches; visitors may not.

Search fee: $5.00 per name. Required to search: name, years to search, DOB, SSN, signed release, offense. Criminal records on computer since 1987.

General Information: Public Access terminal is available. (Civil only.) No juvenile, mental, sealed, or adoption records released. SASE required. Turnaround time 1 week. On cases prior to 1990 turnaround time could be more than 1 week. Copy fee: $1.00 per page. Certification fee: No certification fee. Fee payee: Cameron County District Clerk. Personal checks accepted. Prepayment is required.

County Court No. 1, 2 & 3 PO Box 2178, Brownsville, TX 78522-2178; 956-544-0848; Fax: 956-544-0894. Hours: 8AM-5PM (CST). *Misdemeanor, Civil, Probate.*

Civil Records: Access: Fax, mail, in person. Both court and visitors may perform in person searches. Search fee: $5.00 per name. Required to search: name, years to search. Civil cases indexed by defendant, plaintiff. Civil records on optical imaging since 1994, on computer from 1987, index books from 1912.

Criminal Records: Access: Fax, mail, in person. Both court and visitors may perform in person searches. Search fee: $5.00 per name. Required to search: name, years to search, DOB. Criminal records on optical imaging since 1994, on computer from 1987, index books from 1912.

General Information: Public Access terminal is available. No juvenile, mental, sealed, or adoption records released. SASE required. Turnaround time 1-2 days. Fax notes: $4.25 for first page, $2.25 each add'l. Must receive payment prior to faxing. Copy fee: $1.00 per page. Certification fee: $5.00. Fee payee: Joe G Rivera, County Clerk. Personal checks accepted. Prepayment is required.

Camp County

District Court 126 Church St Rm 203, Pittsburg, TX 75686; 903-856-3221; Fax: 903-856-0560. Hours: 8AM-5PM (CST). *Felony, Civil.*

Civil Records: Access: Mail, fax, in person. Both court and visitors may perform in person searches. Search fee: $5.00 per name. Required to search: name, years to search. Civil cases indexed by defendant, plaintiff. Civil records in index books from 1874.

Criminal Records: Access: Mail, in person. Both court and visitors may perform in person searches. Search fee: $5.00 per name. Required to search: name, years to search, signed release. Criminal records in index books from 1874.

General Information: No juvenile, mental, sealed, or adoption records released. SASE not required. Turnaround time 1 week. Fax notes: Fee to fax results is $.25 per page. Copy fee: $.25 per page. Certification fee: $2.00 for 1st page, $.25 each add'l. Fee payee: District Clerk. Personal checks accepted. Prepayment is required.

County Court 126 Church St Rm 102, Pittsburg, TX 75686; 903-856-2731; Fax: 903-856-2309. Hours: 8AM-Noon, 1-5PM *Misdemeanor, Civil, Probate.*

Civil Records: Access: Fax, mail, in person. Both court and visitors may perform in person searches. Search fee: $10.00 per name. Required to search: name, years to search. Civil cases indexed by defendant, plaintiff. Civil records in index books from 1960. Fax access is only allowed with prepayment of fees.

Criminal Records: Access: Fax, mail, in person. Both court and visitors may perform in person searches. Search fee: $10.00 per name. Required to search: name, years to search, signed release, offense. Criminal records in index books from 1960.

General Information: No juvenile, mental, sealed, or adoption records released. SASE required. Turnaround time 1 day. Copy fee: $.50 per page. Certification fee:

$5.00 plus $1.00 per page. Fee payee: Camp County Clerk. Personal checks accepted. Prepayment required.

Carson County

District & County Court PO Box 487, Panhandle, TX 79068; 806-537-3623; Fax: 806-537-3724. Hours: 8AM-Noon, 1-5PM (CST). *Felony, Misdemeanor, Civil, Eviction, Probate.*

Civil Records: Access: Mail, fax, in person. Both court and visitors may perform in person searches. Search fee: $5.00 per name. Required to search: name, years to search. Civil cases indexed by defendant, plaintiff. Civil records on computer from 1981, index books from 1800s.

Criminal Records: Access: Mail, fax, in person. Both court and visitors may perform in person searches. Search fee: $5.00 per name. Required to search: name, years to search. Criminal records on computer from 1981, index books from 1800s.

General Information: No juvenile, mental, sealed, or adoption records released. SASE required. Turnaround time 1 day. Copy fee: $1.00 per page. Certification fee: $5.00 per page. Fee payee: Carson County Clerk. Personal checks accepted. Prepayment is required.

Cass County

District Court PO Box 510, Linden, TX 75563; 903-756-7514. Hours: 8AM-5PM (CST). *Felony, Civil.*

Civil Records: Access: Mail, in person. Both court and visitors may perform in person searches. Search fee: $5.00 per name. Required to search: name, years to search. Civil cases indexed by defendant, plaintiff. Civil records on computer from 1985, index books from 1900s.

Criminal Records: Access: Mail, in person. Both court and visitors may perform in person searches. Search fee: $5.00 per name. Required to search: name, years to search. Criminal records on computer from 1985, index books from 1900s.

General Information: Public Access terminal is available. No juvenile, mental, sealed, or adoption records released. SASE required. Turnaround time 1 day. Fax notes: Fee to fax results is $.25 per minute; minimum $3.00. Copy fee: $1.00 per page. Fee payee: District Clerk. Personal checks accepted. Prepayment is required.

County Court PO Box 449, Linden, TX 75563; 903-756-5071. Hours: 8AM-5PM (CST). *Misdemeanor, Probate.*

Criminal Records: Access: Mail, in person. Both court and visitors may perform in person searches. Search fee: $10.00 per name. Required to search: name, years to search. Criminal records in index books from 1983.

General Information: No juvenile, mental, sealed, or adoption records released. SASE required. Turnaround time 1 day. Copy fee: $1.00 per page. Certification fee: $5.00 plus $1.00 per page. Fee payee: County Clerk. Personal checks accepted. Prepayment is required.

Castro County

District & County Court 100 E Bedford, Rm 101, Dimmitt, TX 79027; 806-647-3338. Hours: 8AM-5PM (CST). *Felony, Misdemeanor, Civil, Probate.*

Civil Records: Access: Mail, in person. Both court and visitors may perform in person searches. Search fee: $5.00 per name. If record is older than 10 years, then search fee is $10.00. Required to search: name, years to search. Civil cases indexed by defendant, plaintiff. Civil records in index books.

Criminal Records: Access: Mail, in person. Both court and visitors may perform in person searches. Search fee: $5.00 per name. Required to search: name, years to search; also helpful: DOB, SSN. Criminal records in index books.

General Information: No juvenile, mental, sealed, or adoption records released. SASE required. Turnaround time 1 day. Copy fee: $1.00 per page. Certification fee: $5.00. Fee payee: County or District Court Clerk. Personal checks accepted. Prepayment is required.

Chambers County

District Clerk Drawer NN, Anahuac, TX 77514; 409-267-8276. Hours: 8AM-Noon, 1-5PM (CST). *Felony, Civil.*

Civil Records: Access: Mail, in person. Both court and visitors may perform in person searches. Search fee: $5.00 per name. Required to search: name, years to search. Civil cases indexed by defendant, plaintiff. Civil records on computer back to 1800s.

Criminal Records: Access: Mail, in person. Both court and visitors may perform in person searches. Search fee: $5.00 per name. Required to search: name, years to search. Criminal records on computer back to 1800s.

General Information: No juvenile, mental, sealed, or adoption records released. SASE required. Turnaround time 1 day. Copy fee: $1.00 per page. Certification fee: $5.00. Fee payee: R B Scherer Jr, District Clerk. Personal checks accepted. Prepayment is required.

County Court PO Box 728, Anahuac, TX 77514; 409-267-8309; Fax: 409-267-4453. Hours: 8AM-5PM (CST). *Misdemeanor, Civil, Probate.*

Civil Records: Access: Mail, in person. Both court and visitors may perform in person searches. Search fee: $5.00 per name. Required to search: name, years to search; also helpful: address. Civil cases indexed by defendant, plaintiff. Civil records on computer from 1987, index books from 1875.

Criminal Records: Access: Mail, in person. Both court and visitors may perform in person searches. Search fee: $5.00 per name. Required to search: name, years to search, DOB, offense; also helpful: address. Criminal records on computer from 1987, index books from 1875.

General Information: No juvenile or mental records released. SASE required. Turnaround time 2-3 days. Copy fee: $1.00 per page. Certification fee: $5.00. Fee payee: Chambers County Clerk. Personal checks accepted. Prepayment is required.

Cherokee County

District Court Drawer C, Rusk, TX 75785; 903-683-4533. 8AM-Noon, 1-5PM (CST). *Felony, Civil.*

Civil Records: Access: Mail, fax, in person. Both court and visitors may perform in person searches. Search fee: $5.00 per name. Required to search: name, years to search. Civil cases indexed by defendant, plaintiff. Civil records on computer from 1991, index books from 1848.

Criminal Records: Access: Mail, fax, in person. Both court and visitors may perform in person searches. Search fee: $5.00 per name. Required to search: name, years to search. Criminal records on computer from 1991, index books from 1848.

General Information: No juvenile, mental, sealed, or adoption records released. SASE required. Turnaround time 1-2 days. Copy fee: $.50 per page. Certification fee: $1.00 per page. Fee payee: District Clerk. Personal checks accepted. Prepayment is required.

County Court Cherokee County Clerk, PO Box 420, Rusk, TX 75785; 903-683-2350; Fax: 903-683-5931. Hours: 8AM-5PM (CST). *Misdemeanor, Civil, Probate.*

Civil Records: Access: Mail, in person. Both court and visitors may perform in person searches. Search fee: $5.00 per name. Required to search: name, years to search. Civil cases indexed by defendant, plaintiff. Civil records on computer from 1987, index books from 1846.

Criminal Records: Access: Mail, in person. Both court and visitors may perform in person searches. Search fee: $10.00 per name. Required to search: name, years to search. Criminal records on computer from 1987, index books from 1846.

General Information: No juvenile, mental, sealed, or adoption records released. SASE required. Turnaround time 2-4 days. Copy fee: $1.00 per page. Certification fee: $5.00. Fee payee: County Clerk. Personal checks accepted. Prepayment is required.

Childress County

District & County Court Courthouse Box 4, Childress, TX 79201; 940-937-6143; Fax: 940-937-3479. Hours: 8:30AM-Noon, 1-5PM (CST). *Felony, Misdemeanor, Civil, Eviction, Probate.*

Civil Records: Access: Mail, in person. Both court and visitors may perform in person searches. Search fee: $5.00 per name. Required to search: name, years to search. Civil cases indexed by defendant, plaintiff. Civil records on computer from 1992, index books from 1920.

Criminal Records: Access: Mail, in person. Both court and visitors may perform in person searches. Search fee: $5.00 per name. Required to search: name, years to search, DOB. Criminal records on computer from 1992, index books from 1920.

General Information: No juvenile, mental, sealed, or adoption records released. SASE not required. Turnaround time 1 day. Copy fee: $1.00 per page. Certification fee: $1.00. County Court certification fee is $5.00. Fee payee: District or County Clerk. Personal checks accepted. Prepayment is required.

Clay County

District Clerk PO Box 568, Henrietta, TX 76365; 940-538-4561; Fax: 940-538-4431. Hours: 8AM-Noon, 1-5PM (CST). *Felony, Civil.*

Civil Records: Access: Mail, in person. Both court and visitors may perform in person searches. Search fee: $5.00 per name. Required to search: name, years to search. Civil cases indexed by defendant, plaintiff. Civil records in index books from 1873.

Criminal Records: Access: Mail, in person. Both court and visitors may perform in person searches. Search fee: $5.00 per name. Required to search: name, years to search. Criminal records in index books from 1873.

General Information: No juvenile, mental, sealed, or adoption records released. SASE required. Turnaround time 1-2 days. Fax notes: Will not fax results. Copy fee: $.50 per page. Certification fee: $1.00 per page. Fee payee: District Clerk. Personal checks accepted. Prepayment is required.

County Court PO Box 548, Henrietta, TX 76365; 940-538-4631. Hours: 8AM-5PM (CST). *Misdemeanor, Civil, Probate.*

Civil Records: Access: Mail, in person. Both court and visitors may perform in person searches. Search fee: $5.00 per name. Required to search: name, years to search. Civil cases indexed by defendant, plaintiff. Civil records in index books from 1873.

Criminal Records: Access: Mail, in person. Both court and visitors may perform in person searches. Search fee: $5.00 per name. Required to search: name, years to search. Criminal records in index books from 1873.

General Information: No juvenile, mental, sealed, or adoption records released. SASE required. Turnaround time 2-4 days. Copy fee: $1.00 per page. Certification fee: $5.00. Fee payee: County Clerk. Personal checks accepted. Prepayment is required.

Cochran County

District & County Court County Courthouse Rm 102, Morton, TX 79346; 806-266-5450; Fax: 806-266-9027. Hours: 8AM-5PM (CST). *Felony, Misdemeanor, Civil, Eviction, Probate.*

Note: E-mail address for search requests is cclerk@door.net.

Civil Records: Access: Phone, fax, mail, in person, e-mail. Both court and visitors may perform in person searches. Search fee: $5.00 per name. Required to search: name, years to search. Civil cases indexed by defendant, plaintiff. Civil records in index books from 1920.

Criminal Records: Access: Fax, mail, in person, e-mail. Both court and visitors may perform in person searches. Search fee: $5.00 per name. Required to search: name, years to search, DOB; also helpful: sex. Criminal records in index books from 1920.

General Information: No juvenile, mental, sealed, or adoption records released. SASE required. Turnaround time 1 day. Fax notes: Fee to fax is $5.00 plus $1.00 per page. Copy fee: $1.00 per page. Certification fee: $5.00. Fee payee: District or County Clerk. Personal checks accepted. Prepayment is required.

Coke County

District & County Court PO Box 150, Robert Lee, TX 76945; 915-453-2631; Fax: 915-453-2650. Hours: 8AM-5PM (CST). *Felony, Misdemeanor, Civil, Eviction, Probate.*

Civil Records: Access: Mail, in person. Both court and visitors may perform in person searches. Search fee: $5.00 per name. Required to search: name, years to search. Civil cases indexed by defendant, plaintiff. Civil records in index books since 1889.

Criminal Records: Access: Mail, in person. Both court and visitors may perform in person searches. Search fee: $5.00 per name. Required to search: name, years to search. Criminal records in index books since 1889.

General Information: No juvenile, mental, sealed, or adoption records released. SASE not required. Turnaround time 2 days. Fax notes: $2.00 per page. Copy fee: $1.00 per page. Certification fee: $5.00. Fee payee: Coke County Clerk. Personal checks accepted. Prepayment is required.

Coleman County

District Court PO Box 512, Coleman, TX 76834; 915-625-2568. 8AM-4:30PM (CST). *Felony, Civil.*

Civil Records: Access: Mail, in person. Both court and visitors may perform in person searches. Search fee: $5.00 per name. Required to search: name, years to search. Civil cases indexed by defendant, plaintiff. Civil records in index books since 1934.

Criminal Records: Access: Mail, in person. Both court and visitors may perform in person searches. Search fee: $5.00 per name. Required to search: name, years to search, DOB, SSN. Criminal records in index books since 1931.

General Information: No juvenile, mental, sealed, or adoption records released. SASE required. Turnaround time up to 5 days. Fax notes: Do not fax. Copy fee: $1.00 per page. Certification fee: $1.00. Fee payee: District Clerk. Personal checks accepted. Prepayment is required.

County Court PO Box 591, Coleman, TX 76834; 915-625-2889. Hours: 8AM-5PM (CST). *Misdemeanor, Civil, Probate.*

Civil Records: Access: Mail, in person. Both court and visitors may perform in person searches. Search fee: $5.00 per name. Required to search: name, years to search. Civil cases indexed by defendant, plaintiff. Civil records in index books from 1971.

Criminal Records: Access: Mail, in person. Both court and visitors may perform in person searches. Search fee: $5.00 per name. Required to search: name, years to search. Criminal records in index books from 1900s.

General Information: No juvenile, mental, sealed, or adoption records released. SASE required. Turnaround time 1-2 days. Copy fee: $1.00 per page. Certification fee: $5.00. Fee payee: County Clerk. Personal checks accepted. Prepayment is required.

Collin County

District Clerk PO Box 578, McKinney, TX 75070; Civil phone: 972-548-4320; Criminal phone: 972-548-4430. Hours: 8AM-4:30PM (CST). *Felony, Civil.*

Civil Records: Access: Mail, online, in person. Both court and visitors may perform in person searches. Search fee: $5.00 per name. Required to search: name, years to search. Civil cases indexed by defendant, plaintiff. Civil records on computer and microfiche from 1986 (some records are on computer through the 1970s), index books from 1846. Online is available 7am to 7pm M-Sat, 6 to 6 on Sun. The access fee is $.12 a minute, there is a monthly minimum of $31.13. Procomm Plus is suggested. Subscribers also receive fax call-back service. Call Patty Ostrom at 972-548-4503 for subscription information.

Criminal Records: Access: Mail, online, in person. Both court and visitors may perform in person searches. Search fee: $5.00 per name. Required to search: name, years to search, DOB. Criminal records on computer and microfiche from 1986 (some records are on computer through the 1970s), index books from 1846. Online access to criminal records is the same as civil.

General Information: Public Access terminal is available. No juvenile, mental, sealed, or adoption records released. SASE required. Turnaround time 2-3 days. Copy fee: $1.00 per page. Certification fee: No certification fee. Fee payee: District Clerk. Personal checks accepted. Prepayment is required.

County Court 1800 N Grovers #110, McKinney, TX 75069; 972-548-6420; Fax: 972-548-6433. Hours: 8AM-5PM (CST). *Misdemeanor, Civil, Probate.*

Civil Records: Access: Phone, mail, online, in person. Both court and visitors may perform in person searches. Search fee: $5.00 per name. Required to search: name, years to search. Civil cases indexed by defendant, plaintiff. Civil records on computer and microfiche from 1975, index books prior. Online is available 7am to 7pm M-Sat, 6 to 6 on Sun. The access fee is $.12 a minute, there is a monthly minimum of $31.13. Procomm Plus is suggested. Call Patty Ostrom at 972-548-4503 for subscription information.

Criminal Records: Access: Phone, mail, online, in person. Both court and visitors may perform in person searches. Search fee: $5.00 per name. Required to search: name, DOB. Criminal records computerized since early 1970s. Online access to criminal records is the same as civil.

General Information: Public Access terminal is available. No juvenile, mental, sealed, or adoption records released. SASE required. Turnaround time 2-4 days. Copy fee: $1.00 per page. Certification fee: $5.00. Fee payee: County Clerk. Personal checks accepted. Prepayment is required.

Collingsworth County

District & County Court County Courthouse, Rm 3, 800 West Ave, Box 10, Wellington, TX 79095; 806-447-2408; Fax: 806-447-5418. Hours: 9AM-5PM (CST). *Felony, Misdemeanor, Civil, Eviction, Probate.*

Civil Records: Access: Mail, in person. Both court and visitors may perform in person searches. Search fee: $10.00 per name. Required to search: name, years to search. Civil cases indexed by defendant, plaintiff. Civil records on microfilm from 1984, on index books from 1800s.

Criminal Records: Access: Mail, in person. Both court and visitors may perform in person searches. Search fee: $10.00 per name. Required to search: name, years to search, DOB. Criminal records on microfilm from 1984, on index books from 1800s.

General Information: No juvenile, mental health, sealed, or adoption records released. SASE required. Turnaround time 2 days. Copy fee: $1.00 per page. Certification fee: $5.00. Fee payee: Collingsworth County Clerk. Personal checks accepted. Prepayment is required.

Colorado County

District Court County Courthouse, 400 Spring St, Columbus, TX 78934; 979-732-2536. Hours: 8AM-Noon, 1-5PM (CST). *Felony, Civil.*

Civil Records: Access: Mail, in person. Both court and visitors may perform in person searches. Search fee: $5.00 per name. Required to search: name, years to search. Civil cases indexed by defendant, plaintiff. Civil records in index books from 1837.

Criminal Records: Access: Mail, in person. Both court and visitors may perform in person searches. Search fee: $5.00 per name. Required to search: name, years to search. Criminal records in index books from 1837.

General Information: No juvenile, mental, sealed, or adoption records released. SASE required. Turnaround time 1 day. Copy fee: $.50 per page. Certification fee: $2.00. Fee payee: District Clerk. Personal checks accepted. Prepayment is required.

County Court PO Box 68, County Courthouse, Columbus, TX 78934; 979-732-2155; Fax: 979-732-8852. Hours: 8AM-5PM (CST). *Misdemeanor, Civil, Probate.*

Civil Records: Access: Mail, in person. Both court and visitors may perform in person searches. Search fee: $10.00 per name. Required to search: name, years to search. Civil cases indexed by defendant, plaintiff. Civil records in index books from 1850.

Criminal Records: Access: Mail, in person. Both court and visitors may perform in person searches. Search fee: $10.00 per name. Required to search: name, years to search. Criminal records in index books from 1850.

General Information: No juvenile, mental, sealed, or adoption records released. SASE required. Turnaround time 1-2 days. Copy fee: $1.00 per page. Certification fee: $5.00. Fee payee: County Clerk. Personal checks accepted. Prepayment is required.

Comal County

District Court 150 N Seguin Ste 304, New Braunfels, TX 78130-5161; 830-620-5574; Fax: 830-608-2006. Hours: 8AM-4:30PM (CST). *Felony, Civil.*

www.co.comal.tx.us

Civil Records: Access: Fax, mail, in person, online. Both court and visitors may perform in person searches. Search fee: $5.00 per name. Required to search: name, years to search. Civil cases indexed by defendant, plaintiff. Civil records on computer from 1984, index books from 1846. Online access to county judicial records is available free at www.co.comal.tx.us/Search/judsrch.htm. Search by either party name.

Criminal Records: Access: Fax, mail, in person, online. Both court and visitors may perform in person searches. Search fee: $5.00 per name. Required to search: name, years to search, DOB; also helpful: SSN, sex. Criminal records on computer from 1984, index books from 1846. Online access to county criminal judicial records is available free at www.co.comal.tx.us/Search/judsrch.htm. Search by defendant name.

General Information: Public Access terminal is available. No juvenile, sealed, or adoption records released. SASE required. Turnaround time 3 days. Fax notes: $5.00 per page. Fee is for incoming & outgoing faxes. Copy fee: $1.00 for first page, $.25 each add'l. Certification fee: $1.00 per page. Fee payee: District Clerk. Personal checks accepted. Prepayment required.

County Court at Law 100 Main Plaza, Ste 303, New Braunfels, TX 78130; 830-620-5582; Fax: 830-608-2021. Hours: 8AM-4:30PM (CST). *Misdemeanor, Civil, Probate.*

www.co.comal.tx.us

Civil Records: Access: Phone, fax, mail, in person, online. Both court and visitors may perform in person searches. Search fee: $5.00 per name. Required to search: name, years to search. Civil cases indexed by defendant, plaintiff. Civil records on computer since 1977. Online access to county judicial records is available free at www.co.comal.tx.us/Search/judsrch.htm. Search by either party name.

Criminal Records: Access: Phone, fax, mail, in person. Both court and visitors may perform in person searches. Search fee: $5.00 per name. Required to search: name, years to search; also helpful: address, DOB. Criminal records on computer since 1977. Online access to county criminal judicial records is available free at www.co.comal.tx.us/Search/judsrch.htm. Search by defendant name.

General Information: Public Access terminal is available. No juvenile, mental, sealed or adoption records released. Turnaround time 1 week. Fax notes: $1.00 per page. Copy fee: $1.00 per page. Certification fee: $5.00. Fee payee: County Court at Law. Only cashiers checks and money orders accepted. Prepayment is required.

Comanche County

District Court County Courthouse, Box 206, Comanche, TX 76442; 915-356-2342; Fax: 915-356-2150. 8:30AM-Noon, 1-5PM (CST). *Felony, Civil.*

Civil Records: Access: Mail, in person. Only the court performs in person searches; visitors may not. Search fee: $5.00 per name. Required to search: name, years to search. Civil cases indexed by defendant, plaintiff. Civil records on computer to 1990, index books to 1876.

Criminal Records: Access: Mail, in person. Only the court performs in person searches; visitors may not. Search fee: $5.00 per name. Required to search: name, years to search. Criminal records on computer from 1990, index books from 1876.

General Information: No juvenile, mental, sealed, or adoption records released. SASE required. Turnaround time 1 day. Copy fee: $1.00 per page. Certification fee: $2.00. Fee payee: District Clerk. Personal checks accepted. Prepayment is required.

County Court County Courthouse, Comanche, TX 76442; 915-356-2655. Hours: 8:30AM-5PM (CST). *Misdemeanor, Civil, Probate.*

Civil Records: Access: Mail, in person. Both court and visitors may perform in person searches. Search fee: $5.00 per name. Required to search: name, years to search. Civil cases indexed by defendant, plaintiff. Civil records in index books from 1856.

Criminal Records: Access: Mail, in person. Both court and visitors may perform in person searches. Search fee: $5.00 per name. Required to search: name, years to search. Criminal records in index books from 1856.

General Information: No juvenile, mental, sealed, or adoption records released. SASE required. Turnaround time 1 day. Copy fee: $1.00 per page. Certification fee: $5.00. Fee payee: County Clerk. Personal checks accepted. Prepayment is required.

Concho County

District & County Court PO Box 98, Paint Rock, TX 76866; 915-732-4322; Fax: 915-732-2040. Hours: 8:30AM-5PM (CST). *Felony, Misdemeanor, Civil, Eviction, Probate.*

Civil Records: Access: Phone, mail, in person. Both court and visitors may perform in person searches. Search fee: $10.00 per name. Required to search: name, years to search. Civil cases indexed by defendant, plaintiff. Civil records in index books from 1879; computerized back to 1994.

Criminal Records: Access: Phone, mail, in person. Both court and visitors may perform in person searches. Search fee: $10.00 per name. Required to search: name, years to search, DOB; also helpful: SSN. Criminal records in index books from 1879; computerized back to 1994.

General Information: No juvenile, mental, sealed, or adoption records released. SASE required. Turnaround time 1 week. Fax notes: Fee to fax results is $1.00 per page. Copy fee: $1.00 per page. Certification fee: $5.00. Fee payee: District or County Clerk. Personal checks accepted. Prepayment is required.

Cooke County

District Court County Courthouse, 100 S Dixon, Gainesville, TX 76240; 940-668-5450. Hours: 8AM-5PM (CST). *Felony, Civil.*

Civil Records: Access: Mail, in person. Both court and visitors may perform in person searches. Search fee: $5.00 per name. Required to search: name, years to search. Civil cases indexed by defendant, plaintiff. Civil records on microfiche from late 1900s, index books from 1800s. Must request specifically if you wish to go back more than 10 years.

Criminal Records: Access: Mail, in person. Both court and visitors may perform in person searches. Search fee: $5.00 per name. Required to search: name, years to search. Criminal records on microfiche from late 1900,s, index books from 1800s.

General Information: No juvenile, mental, sealed, or adoption records released. SASE required. Turnaround time 2 days. Copy fee: $.50 per page. Certification fee: $1.00. Fee payee: District Clerk. Personal checks accepted. Prepayment is required.

County Court County Courthouse, Gainesville, TX 76240; 940-668-5422. Hours: 8AM-5PM (CST). *Misdemeanor, Civil, Probate.*

Civil Records: Access: Mail, in person. Both court and visitors may perform in person searches. Search fee: $5.00 per name. Required to search: name, years to search. Civil cases indexed by defendant, plaintiff. Civil records in index books and original papers to late 1850s.

Criminal Records: Access: Mail, in person. Both court and visitors may perform in person searches. Search fee: $5.00 per name. Required to search: name, years to search, DOB. Criminal records in index books and original papers from late 1850s.

General Information: No juvenile, mental, sealed, or adoption records released. SASE not required. Turnaround time 1 day. Copy fee: $1.00 per page. Certification fee: $5.00. Fee payee: Cooke County Clerk. Personal checks accepted. Prepayment required.

Coryell County

District Court PO Box 4, Gatesville, TX 76528; 254-865-5911; Fax: 254-865-5064. Hours: 8AM-5PM (CST). *Felony, Civil.*

Civil Records: Access: Fax, mail, in person. Both court and visitors may perform in person searches. Search fee: $5.00 per name. Required to search: name, years to search. Civil cases indexed by defendant, plaintiff. Civil records in index books from 1854; computerized back to 2000.

Criminal Records: Access: Fax, mail, in person. Both court and visitors may perform in person searches. Search fee: $5.00 per name. Required to search: name, years to search, DOB, SSN. Criminal records in index books from 1854; computerized back to 2000.

General Information: Public Access terminal is available. No juvenile, sealed, or adoption records released. SASE required. Turnaround time 1 day. Fax notes: Fee to fax results is $1.00 per page. Copy fee: $1.00 per page. Certification fee: No certification fee. Fee payee: District Clerk. Personal checks accepted. Prepayment is required.

County Court PO Box 237, Gatesville, TX 76528; 254-865-5016; Fax: 254-865-8631. Hours: 8AM-Noon, 1-5PM (CST). *Misdemeanor, Civil, Probate.*

Civil Records: Access: Fax, mail, in person. Both court and visitors may perform in person searches. Search fee: $10.00 per name. Required to search: name, years to search. Civil cases indexed by defendant, plaintiff. Civil records on computer from 1991, index books from 1846.

Criminal Records: Access: Fax, mail, in person. Both court and visitors may perform in person searches. Search fee: $10.00 per name. Required to search: name, years to search. Criminal records on computer from 1991, index books from 1846.

General Information: Public Access terminal is available. No juvenile, mental, sealed, or adoption records released. SASE required. Turnaround time 1-5 days. Fax notes: $1.00 per page. Fax fee for out of county request is $5.00 plus $1.00 per page. Copy fee: $1.00 per page. Certification fee: $5.00 plus $1.00 per page. Fee payee: County Clerk. Business checks accepted. Personal checks must be in county. Prepayment is required.

Cottle County

District & County Court PO Box 717, Paducah, TX 79248; 806-492-3823. Hours: 9AM-Noon, 1-5PM (CST). *Felony, Misdemeanor, Civil, Eviction, Probate.*

Civil Records: Access: Mail, in person. Both court and visitors may perform in person searches. Search fee: $5.00 per name. Required to search: name, years to search. Civil cases indexed by defendant, plaintiff. Civil records in index books from 1892.

Criminal Records: Access: Mail, in person. Both court and visitors may perform in person searches. Search fee: $5.00 per name. Required to search: name, years to search. Criminal records in index books from 1892.

General Information: No juvenile, mental, sealed, or adoption records released. SASE required. Turnaround time 2-3 days. Copy fee: $1.00 per page. Certification fee: $1.00. Fee payee: Cottle County Clerk. Personal checks accepted. Prepayment is required.

Crane County

District & County Court PO Box 578, Crane, TX 79731; 915-558-3581. Hours: 9AM-12 1-5PM (CST). *Felony, Misdemeanor, Civil, Eviction, Probate.*

Civil Records: Access: In person only. Visitors must perform in person searches for themselves. No search fee. Required to search: name, years to search. Civil cases indexed by defendant, plaintiff. Limited civil records on computer from 1990; index books to 1927.

Criminal Records: Access: Mail, fax, in person. Both court and visitors may perform in person searches. Search fee: $5.00 per name. Ten year search only. Required to search: name, years to search, offense. Limited criminal records on computer from 1990; index books from 1927.

General Information: Public Access terminal is available. No juvenile, mental, sealed or adoption records released. SASE required. Turnaround time 2-5 days. Copy fee: $1.00 per page. Certification fee: County = $5.00. District Court = $1.00. Fee payee:

District or County Clerk. Only cashiers checks and money orders accepted. Prepayment is required.

Crockett County

District & County Court PO Drawer C, Ozona, TX 76943; 915-392-2022. Hours: 8AM-5PM (CST). *Felony, Misdemeanor, Civil, Eviction, Probate.*

Civil Records: Access: Mail, in person. Both court and visitors may perform in person searches. Search fee: $10.00 per name. Required to search: name, years to search. Civil cases indexed by defendant, plaintiff. Civil records on computer from 1982, index books from 1800s.

Criminal Records: Access: Mail, in person. Both court and visitors may perform in person searches. Search fee: $10.00 per name. Required to search: name, years to search, DOB, SSN, signed release. Criminal records on computer from 1982, index books from 1800s.

General Information: No juvenile, mental, sealed, or adoption records released. SASE required. Turnaround time 1 week. Fax notes: Fee to fax results is $1.00 per page. Copy fee: $1.00 per page. Certification fee: $5.00. Fee payee: District or County Clerk. Personal checks accepted. Prepayment is required.

Crosby County

District Court 201 W Aspen St #207, Crosbyton, TX 79322-2500; 806-675-2071; Fax: 806-675-2433. Hours: 8AM-Noon, 1-5PM (CST). *Felony, Civil.*

Civil Records: Access: Phone, fax, mail, in person. Both court and visitors may perform in person searches. Search fee: $5.00 per name. Required to search: name, years to search. Civil cases indexed by defendant, plaintiff. Civil records in index books from 1896.

Criminal Records: Access: Phone, fax, mail, in person. Both court and visitors may perform in person searches. Search fee: $5.00 per name. Required to search: name, years to search. Criminal records in index books from 1896.

General Information: No juvenile, mental, sealed, or adoption records released. SASE required. Turnaround time 1 day. Fax notes: No fee to fax results. Only for local or toll free calls. Copy fee: $.70 for first page, $.25 each add'l. Certification fee: $1.00. Fee payee: District Clerk. Personal checks accepted. Prepayment is required.

County Court 201 W Aspen St #102, Crosbyton, TX 79322-2500; 806-675-2334. Hours: 8AM-noon, 1:00PM-5PM (CST). *Misdemeanor, Civil, Probate.*

Civil Records: Access: Mail, in person. Both court and visitors may perform in person searches. No search fee. Required to search: name, years to search. Civil cases indexed by defendant, plaintiff. Civil records on microfiche from 1990, index books from 1886.

Criminal Records: Access: Mail, in person. Both court and visitors may perform in person searches. Search fee: $5.00 per name. Required to search: name, years to search. Criminal records on microfiche from 1990, index books from 1886.

General Information: No juvenile, mental, sealed, or adoption records released. SASE not required. Turnaround time 1 day. Copy fee: $1.00 per page. Certification fee: $5.00. Fee payee: County Clerk. Personal checks accepted. Prepayment is required.

Culberson County

District & County Court PO Box 158, Van Horn, TX 79855; 915-283-2058. Hours: 8AM-5PM (CST). *Felony, Misdemeanor, Civil, Eviction, Probate.*

Civil Records: Access: Phone, mail, fax, in person. Both court and visitors may perform in person searches. Search fee: $5.00 per name. Required to search: name, years to search. Civil cases indexed by defendant, plaintiff. Civil records in index books since 1911.

Criminal Records: Access: Phone, mail, fax, in person. Both court and visitors may perform in person searches. Search fee: $5.00 per name. Required to search: name, years to search, signed release. Criminal records in index books since 1911.

General Information: No juvenile, mental, sealed, or adoption records released. SASE required. Turnaround time 2 days. Fax notes: Fee to fax results is $1.00 per page. Copy fee: $1.00 per page. Certification fee: $5.00. Fee payee: District or County Clerk. Personal checks accepted. Prepayment is required.

Dallam County

District & County Court PO Box 1352, Dalhart, TX 79022; 806-249-4751; Fax: 806-249-2252. Hours: 9AM-5PM (CST). *Felony, Misdemeanor, Civil, Probate.*

Civil Records: Access: Fax, mail, in person. Both court and visitors may perform in person searches. Search fee: $5.00 per name. Required to search: name, years to search. Civil cases indexed by defendant, plaintiff. Civil records in index books from 1800s.

Criminal Records: Access: Fax, mail, in person. Both court and visitors may perform in person searches. Search fee: $5.00 per name. Required to search: name, years to search. Criminal records in index books from 1800s.

General Information: No juvenile, mental, sealed, or adoption records released. SASE required. Turnaround time 1 day. Fax notes: $5.00 for first page, $1.00 each add'l. Copy fee: $1.00 per page. Certification fee: $5.00. Fee payee: Dallam County Clerk. Personal checks accepted. Prepayment is required.

Dallas County

District Court - Civil 600 Commerce St, Dallas, TX 75202-4606; 214-653-7421. Hours: 8AM-6:00PM (CST). *Civil.*

www.dallascounty.org

Civil Records: Access: Mail, online, in person. Both court and visitors may perform in person searches. Search fee: $5.00 per name. Required to search: name, years to search. Civil cases indexed by defendant, plaintiff. Civil records on computer since 1967; on dockets back to 1940; records prior to 1940 are maintained by Texas Historical Div. of the Dallas Public Library. Public Access System allows remote access at $1.00 per minute to these and other court and public records. Will invoice to your telephone bill. Access number is 900-263-INFO. ProComm Plus is recommended. Searching is by name or case number. Call the Public Access Administrator at 214-653-7717 for more information.

General Information: Public Access terminal is available. No sealed records released. Copy fee: $1.00 per page. Fee payee: District Clerk. Only cashiers checks and money orders accepted. Prepayment is required.

District Court - Criminal 133 N Industrial Blvd, Dallas, TX 75207-4313; 214-653-5950; Fax: 214-653-5986. Hours: 8AM-4:30PM (CST). *Felony.*

www.dallascounty.org

Criminal Records: Access: Mail, online, in person. Both court and visitors may perform in person searches. Search fee: $5.00 per name. Required to search: name, years to search, DOB. Criminal records on computer from 1972, on microfiche from 1979. Public Access System allows remote access at $1.00 per minute to these and other court and public records. Will invoice to your telephone bill. Access number is 900-263-INFO. ProComm Plus is recommended. The system is open 8am to 4:30pm. Searching is by name or case number. Call the Public Access Administrator at 214-653-6807 for more information.

General Information: Public Access terminal is available. No juvenile, mental, sealed, or adoption records released. SASE required. Turnaround time 1-2 days. Copy fee: $1.00 per page. Certification fee: $1.00 per page. Fee payee: District Clerk. Only cashiers checks and money orders accepted. Prepayment is required.

County Court - Misdemeanor 133 N Industrial Blvd, Dallas, TX 75207-4313; 214-653-5740. Hours: 8AM-4:30PM (CST). *Misdemeanor.*

www.dallascounty.org

Criminal Records: Access: Mail, online, in person. Both court and visitors may perform in person searches. Search fee: $5.00 per name. Required to search: name, years to search, DOB. Criminal records on computer from 1972; prior on microfiche. For older searches call 214-653-5763. Public Access System allows remote access at $1.00 per minute to these and other court and public records. Will invoice to your telephone bill. Access number is 900-263-INFO. ProComm Plus is recommended. Searching is by name or case number. Call the Public Access Administrator at 214-653-6807 for more information.

General Information: Public Access terminal is available. No juvenile, mental, sealed, or adoption records released. SASE required. Turnaround time 2-3 weeks. Copy fee: $.60 per page. Certification fee: $1.00 per page. Fee payee: County Clerk. Only cashiers checks and money orders accepted. Prepayment is required.

County Court - Civil 509 W Main 3rd Floor, Dallas, TX 75202; 214-653-7131. Hours: 8AM-4:30PM (CST). *Civil.*

www.dallascounty.org

Note: No civil claims limit as of 05/23/97 in Dallas County

Civil Records: Access: Phone, mail, online, in person. Both court and visitors may perform in person searches. Search fee: $5.00 per name per 10 years. Required to search: name, years to search. Civil cases indexed by defendant, plaintiff. Civil records on computer from 1964, index books from 1800s. Public Access System allows remote access at $1.00 per minute to these and other court and public records. Will invoice to your telephone bill. Access number is 900-263-INFO. ProComm Plus is recommended. Searching is by name or case number. Call the Public Access Administrator at 214-653-6807 for more information.

General Information: Public Access terminal is available. No juvenile, mental, sealed, or adoption records released. SASE required. Turnaround time 1 day. Copy fee: $1.00 per page. Certification fee: $5.00. Fee payee: Earl Bullock, County Clerk. Personal checks accepted. Prepayment is required.

Probate Court #3 Records Bldg, 2nd Floor, Dallas, TX 75202; 214-653-6166. 8AM-4:30PM *Probate.*

Note: Remote access system for civil and criminal records in this county includes probate records.

Dawson County

District Court Drawer 1268, Lamesa, TX 79331; 806-872-7373; Fax: 806-872-9513. Hours: 8:30AM-5PM (CST). *Felony, Civil.*

Civil Records: Access: Fax, mail, in person. Both court and visitors may perform in person searches. Search fee: $5.00 per name. Required to search: name, years to search. Civil cases indexed by defendant, plaintiff. Civil records in index books/files from 1900s.
Criminal Records: Access: Fax, mail, in person. Both court and visitors may perform in person searches. Search fee: $5.00 per name. Required to search: name, years to search, signed release. Criminal records in index books/files from 1900s.

General Information: No juvenile, mental, sealed, or adoption records released. SASE not required. Turnaround time 1 day. Fax notes: $1.00 per page. Copy fee: $1.00 per page. Certification fee: No certification fee. Fee payee: Dawson County District Clerk. Personal checks accepted. Prepayment is required.

County Court Drawer 1268, Lamesa, TX 79331; 806-872-3778; Fax: 806-872-2473. Hours: 8:30AM-5PM (CST). *Misdemeanor, Civil, Probate.*

Civil Records: Access: Fax, mail, in person. Both court and visitors may perform in person searches. Search fee: $5.00 per name. Required to search: name, years to search. Civil cases indexed by defendant, plaintiff. Civil records in index files since 1905; on computer back to 1998. Fees must be prepaid before fax access is allowed.
Criminal Records: Access: Mail, in person. Both court and visitors may perform in person searches. Search fee: $5.00 per name. Required to search: name, years to search, DOB; also helpful-signed release, offense, date of offense. Criminal records in index files since 1905; on computer back to 1998. Fees must be prepaid before fax access is allowed.

General Information: No juvenile, mental or sealed records released. SASE not required. Turnaround time 1 day. Fax notes: Fee to fax results is $5.00 per document and $1.00 per page. Copy fee: $1.00 per page. Certification fee: $5.00. Fee payee: County Clerk. Personal checks accepted. Prepayment is required.

De Witt County

County Court 307 N Gonzales, Cuero, TX 77954; 361-275-3724; Fax: 361-275-8994. Hours: 8AM-5PM (CST). *Misdemeanor, Probate.*

Civil Records: Access: Phone, fax, mail, in person. Search fee: $5.00 per name. Required to search: name, years to search. Civil cases indexed by defendant, plaintiff. Civil records go back to 1960s; on computer back to 1998.
Criminal Records: Access: Mail, in person. Both court and visitors may perform in person searches. Search fee: $5.00 per name. Required to search: name, years to search; also helpful: DOB, SSN. Criminal records go back to 1960s; on computer back to 1998.

General Information: No juvenile, mental, sealed, or adoption records released. SASE required. Fax notes: Fee to fax results is $1.00 per page. Copy fee: $1.00 per page. Certification fee: $1.00. Fee payee: DeWitt County Clerk. Personal checks accepted. Prepayment is required.

District Court PO Box 845, Cuero, TX 77954; 361-275-2221. Hours: 8AM-5PM (CST). *Felony, Civil.*

Civil Records: Access: Phone, mail, in person. Both court and visitors may perform in person searches. Search fee: $5.00 per name. Required to search: name, years to search. Civil cases indexed by defendant, plaintiff.
Criminal Records: Access: Mail, in person. Both court and visitors may perform in person searches. Search fee: $5.00 per name. Required to search: name, years to search, DOB, SSN, signed release. Criminal records maintained on books.
General Information: No juvenile, mental, sealed, or adoption records released. SASE required. Turnaround time 1 week. Copy fee: $1.00 per page. Certification fee: $1.00. Fee payee: District Clerk. Personal checks accepted. Prepayment is required.

Deaf Smith County

District Court 235 E Third St Rm 304, Hereford, TX 79045; 806-364-3901; Fax: 806-363-7007. Hours: 8AM-5PM (CST). *Felony, Civil.*

Civil Records: Access: Fax, mail, in person. Both court and visitors may perform in person searches. Search

fee: $5.00 per name. Required to search: name, years to search. Civil cases indexed by defendant, plaintiff. Civil records on computer from 2/1993; prior on microfiche from 5/15/1981.
Criminal Records: Access: Fax, mail, in person. Both court and visitors may perform in person searches. Search fee: $5.00 per name. Required to search: name, years to search; also helpful: DOB, SSN, case number. Criminal records on computer from 2/1993; prior on microfiche from 5/15/1981.

General Information: Public Access terminal is available. No juvenile, mental, sealed, or adoption records released. SASE not required. Turnaround time 1 day. Fax notes: Fee to fax results is $2.00 per page. Copy fee: $1.00 per page. Certification fee: $1.00. Fee payee: District Clerk. Personal checks accepted. Prepayment is required.

County Court Deaf Smith Courthouse, 235 E Third, Room 203, Hereford, TX 79045; 806-363-7077. Hours: 8AM-5PM (CST). *Misdemeanor, Civil, Probate.*

Civil Records: Access: Mail, in person. Both court and visitors may perform in person searches. Search fee: $5.00 per name. Required to search: name, years to search. Civil cases indexed by defendant, plaintiff. Civil records on computer from 1989, microfiche from 1981, index books from early 1900s.
Criminal Records: Access: Mail, in person. Both court and visitors may perform in person searches. Search fee: $5.00 per name. Required to search: name, years to search. Criminal records on computer from 1989, microfiche from 1981, index books from early 1900s.
General Information: Public Access terminal is available. No juvenile, mental, sealed, or adoption records released. SASE not required. Turnaround time 1 day. Copy fee: $1.00 per page. Certification fee: $5.00. Fee payee: County Clerk. Personal checks accepted. Prepayment is required.

Delta County

District & County Court PO Box 455, Cooper, TX 75432; 903-395-4110; Fax: 903-395-2178. Hours: 8AM-5PM (CST). *Felony, Misdemeanor, Civil, Eviction, Probate.*

Civil Records: Access: Phone, mail, in person. Both court and visitors may perform in person searches. Search fee: $5.00 per name. Required to search: name, years to search. Civil cases indexed by defendant, plaintiff. Civil records in index books from late 1800s. Phone searches must be pre-paid.
Criminal Records: Access: Phone, mail, in person. Both court and visitors may perform in person searches. Search fee: $5.00 per name. Required to search: name, years to search, DOB. Criminal records in index books from late 1800s. Phone searches must be prepaid.
General Information: No juvenile, mental, sealed, or adoption records released. SASE required. Turnaround time 1 day. Fax notes: Fee to fax is $2.50 per page plus $1.00 per document. Copy fee: $1.00 per page. Certification fee: $5.00. Fee payee: County or District Clerk. Personal checks accepted. Prepayment is required.

Denton County

District Court PO Box 2146, Denton, TX 76202; 940-565-8530; Fax: 940-565-5519. Hours: 8AM-4:30PM (CST). *Felony, Civil.*

www.co.denton.tx.us/dept/District_Clerk/dcl.htm

Civil Records: Access: Phone, mail, fax, online, in person. Both court and visitors may perform in person searches. Search fee: $5.00 per name. Required to search: name, years to search. Civil cases indexed by defendant, plaintiff. Civil records on computer from 1990, archived from 1936. Civil searches available on the web site at no charge. Search by name or cause number.

Criminal Records: Access: Mail, fax, online, in person. Both court and visitors may perform in person searches. Search fee: $5.00 per name. Required to search: name, years to search, DOB. Criminal records on computer from 1990, archived from 1936. Criminal searches are available on the web site at no charge. Records are available from 1994 forward. Access also includes sheriff bond and jail records.

General Information: Public Access terminal is available. No juvenile, mental, sealed, expunctions or adoption records released. SASE required. Turnaround time 1-2 weeks. Fax notes: Fee to fax results is $1.00 per page. Copy fee: $1.00 per page. Certification fee: $1.00. Fee payee: District Clerk. Personal checks accepted. Credit cards accepted: Visa, MasterCard.

County Court PO Box 2187, Denton, TX 76202; Civil phone: 940-565-8518; Criminal phone: 940-565-8520. 8AM-5PM (CST). *Misdemeanor, Civil, Probate.*

http://justice.co.denton.texas.us

Civil Records: Access: Mail, in person. Both court and visitors may perform in person searches. Search fee: $5.00 per name. Add $1.00 per year over first 5. Required to search: name, years to search. Civil cases indexed by defendant, plaintiff. Civil records on computer from 1989, microfiche from 1968.

Criminal Records: Access: Mail, in person. Both court and visitors may perform in person searches. Search fee: $5.00 per name. Add $1.00 per year over first 5. Required to search: name, years to search, DOB. Criminal records on computer from 1989, microfiche from 1968.

General Information: Public Access terminal is available. No juvenile, mental, sealed, or adoption records released. SASE required. Turnaround time 1-2 weeks. Copy fee: $1.00 per page. Certification fee: $5.00. Fee payee: Denton County Clerk. Only cashiers checks and money orders accepted. Prepayment is required.

Dickens County

District & County Court PO Box 120, Dickens, TX 79229; 806-623-5531; Fax: 806-623-5319. Hours: 8AM-5PM (CST). *Felony, Misdemeanor, Civil, Eviction, Probate.*

Civil Records: Access: Mail, fax, in person. Both court and visitors may perform in person searches. Search fee: $5.00 per name. Required to search: name, years to search. Civil cases indexed by defendant, plaintiff. Civil records in index books since late 1891.

Criminal Records: Access: Mail, fax, in person. Both court and visitors may perform in person searches. Search fee: $5.00 per name. Required to search: name, years to search; also helpful: DOB, SSN. Criminal records in index books since late 1891.

General Information: No juvenile, mental, sealed or adoption records released. SASE required. Turnaround time 1-2 days. Fax notes: Will not fax results. Copy fee: $1.00 per page. Certification fee: $5.00. Fee payee: District Court. Personal checks accepted. Prepayment is required.

Dimmit County

District Court 103 N 5th, Carrizo Springs, TX 78834; 830-876-2321; Fax: 830-876-5036. Hours: 8AM-5PM (CST). *Felony, Civil.*

Civil Records: Access: Mail, in person. Both court and visitors may perform in person searches. Search fee: $5.00 per name. Required to search: name, years to search; also helpful: address. Civil cases indexed by defendant, plaintiff. Civil records in index books, archived from 1936.

Criminal Records: Access: Mail, in person. Both court and visitors may perform in person searches. Search

fee: $5.00 per name. Required to search: name, years to search; also helpful: DOB, SSN. Criminal records in index books, archived from 1936.

General Information: No juvenile, mental, sealed, or adoption records released. SASE required. Turnaround time 2-3 days. Copy fee: $1.00 per page. Certification fee: $5.00. Fee payee: District Clerk. Personal checks accepted. Prepayment is required.

County Court 103 N 5th, Carrizo Springs, TX 78834; 830-876-2323 x232; Fax: 830-876-4205. Hours: 8AM-5PM (CST). *Misdemeanor, Civil, Probate.*

Civil Records: Access: Phone, fax, mail, in person. Both court and visitors may perform in person searches. Search fee: $5.00 per name. Required to search: name, years to search. Civil cases indexed by defendant, plaintiff. Civil records on microfiche from 1992, index books prior.

Criminal Records: Access: Phone, fax, mail, in person. Both court and visitors may perform in person searches. Search fee: $5.00 per name. Required to search: name, years to search, signed release, DOB; also helpful: sex, SSN. Criminal records on microfiche from 1992, index books prior.

General Information: No juvenile, mental, sealed, or adoption records released. SASE required. Turnaround time 1 day. Fax notes: Fee to fax results is $2.00 1st page; $1.00 each add'l. Copy fee: $1.00 per page. Certification fee: $5.00. Fee payee: County Clerk. Personal checks accepted. Prepayment is required.

Donley County

District & County Court PO Drawer U, Clarendon, TX 79226; 806-874-3436; Fax: 806-874-5146. Hours: 8AM-Noon, 1-5PM (CST). *Felony, Misdemeanor, Civil, Eviction, Probate.*

Civil Records: Access: Mail, in person. Both court and visitors may perform in person searches. Search fee: $5.00 per name. Required to search: name, years to search. Civil cases indexed by defendant, plaintiff. Civil records on computer from 1991, index books to 1900s.

Criminal Records: Access: Mail, in person. Both court and visitors may perform in person searches. Search fee: $5.00 per name. Required to search: name, years to search, DOB, signed release, aliases; also helpful: SSN. Criminal records on computer from 1991, index books from 1900s.

General Information: No juvenile, mental, sealed, or adoption records released. SASE required. Turnaround time 1 day. Copy fee: $1.00 per page. Certification fee: $1.00. Fee payee: County Clerk. Personal checks accepted. Prepayment is required.

Duval County

District Court PO Drawer 428, San Diego, TX 78384; 361-279-3322 X239. Hours: 8AM-5PM (CST). *Felony, Civil.*

Civil Records: Access: Mail, in person. Both court and visitors may perform in person searches. Search fee: $15.00 per name. Fee is for large cases. Required to search: name, years to search. Civil cases indexed by defendant, plaintiff. Civil records on index books from 1900s.

Criminal Records: Access: Phone, mail, in person. Both court and visitors may perform in person searches. Search fee: $15.00 per name. Fee is for large cases. Required to search: name, years to search. Criminal records not computerized, indexed in books.

General Information: No sealed, or adoption records released. SASE required. Turnaround time 1-2 days. Copy fee: $1.00 per page. Certification fee: $1.00. Fee payee: District Clerk. Personal checks accepted. Prepayment is required.

County Court PO Box 248, San Diego, TX 78384; 361-279-3322. Hours: 8AM-Noon, 1-5PM (CST). *Misdemeanor, Civil, Probate.*

Civil Records: Access: Mail, in person. Both court and visitors may perform in person searches. Search fee: $10.00 per name. Required to search: name, years to search. Civil cases indexed by defendant, plaintiff. Civil records in index books from 1800s.

Criminal Records: Access: Mail, in person. Both court and visitors may perform in person searches. Search fee: $10.00 per name. Required to search: name, years to search, offense, date of offense. Criminal records in index books from 1800s.

General Information: No juvenile, mental, sealed, or adoption records released. SASE required. Turnaround time 2 days. Copy fee: $1.00 per page. Certification fee: $5.00. Fee payee: County Clerk. Personal checks accepted. Prepayment is required.

Eastland County

District Court PO Box 670, Eastland, TX 76448; 254-629-2664; Fax: 254-629-1558. Hours: 8AM-5PM (CST). *Felony, Civil.*

Civil Records: Access: Phone, fax, mail, online, in person. Both court and visitors may perform in person searches. No search fee. Required to search: name, years to search. Civil cases indexed by defendant, plaintiff. Civil records on computer from 1930. Civil case information is available free online at www.idocket.com.

Criminal Records: Access: Phone, fax, mail, online, in person. Both court and visitors may perform in person searches. No search fee. Required to search: name, years to search. Criminal records on computer from 1976, archived from 1875. Online access to criminal records is the same as civil.

General Information: No juvenile, mental, sealed, or adoption records released. SASE required. Turnaround time 1 day. Copy fee: $1.00 per page. Certification fee: No certification fee. Fee payee: District Clerk. Personal checks accepted. Prepayment is required.

County Court PO Box 110, Eastland, TX 76448; 254-629-1583. Hours: 8AM-5PM (CST). *Misdemeanor, Probate.*

Note: No civil records after 1977; criminal and probate records only thereafter.

Criminal Records: Access: Mail, in person. Both court and visitors may perform in person searches. Search fee: $5.00 per name. Required to search: name, years to search, DOB; also helpful: SSN. Signed release required if subject is a minor. Criminal records in index books from 1873. Name searches only.

General Information: No juvenile, mental, sealed, or adoption records released. SASE not required. Turnaround time 1-2 days. Copy fee: $1.00 per page. Certification fee: $5.00. Fee payee: Eastland County Clerk. Personal checks accepted. Checks accepted (must have phone number & DL # on check). Prepayment is required.

Ector County

District Court County Courthouse, 300 N Grant, Rm 301, Odessa, TX 79761; 915-498-4290; Fax: 915-498-4292. Hours: 8AM-5PM (CST). *Felony, Civil.*

Civil Records: Access: Phone, fax, mail, in person. Both court and visitors may perform in person searches. Search fee: $5.00 per name. Required to search: name, years to search. Civil cases indexed by defendant, plaintiff. Civil records on computer from 1989, index books from 1880.

Criminal Records: Access: Phone, mail, in person. Only the court performs in person searches; visitors may not. Search fee: $5.00 per name. Required to search: name, years to search. Criminal records on computer from 1989, index books from 1880.

General Information: Public Access terminal is available. No juvenile, mental, sealed, or adoption records released. SASE required. Turnaround time 2 weeks. Fax notes: $2.00 per page. Copy fee: $.25 per page. Certification fee: $1.00 per page. Fee payee: Ector County District Clerk. Business checks accepted. Prepayment is required.

County Court PO Box 707, Odessa, TX 79760; 915-498-4130. Hours: 8AM-4:30PM (CST). *Misdemeanor, Civil, Probate.*

Civil Records: Access: Mail, in person. Both court and visitors may perform in person searches. Search fee: $5.00 per name. Required to search: name, years to search. Civil cases indexed by defendant, plaintiff. Civil records on computer from 1992, index books from 1900s.

Criminal Records: Access: Mail, in person. Both court and visitors may perform in person searches. Search fee: $5.00 per name. Required to search: name, years to search; also helpful: DOB, SSN. Criminal records on computer from 1989, index books from 1900s.

General Information: Public Access terminal is available. No juvenile, mental, sealed, or adoption records released. SASE required. Turnaround time 2 days. Copy fee: $1.00 per page. Certification fee: $5.00. Fee payee: County Clerk. Personal checks accepted. Prepayment is required.

Edwards County

District & County Court PO Box 184, Rocksprings, TX 78880; 830-683-2235; Fax: 830-683-5376. Hours: 8AM-Noon, 1-5PM (CST). *Felony, Misdemeanor, Civil, Eviction, Probate.*

Civil Records: Access: Phone, fax, mail, in person. Both court and visitors may perform in person searches. Search fee: $5.00 per name. Required to search: name, years to search. Civil cases indexed by defendant, plaintiff. Civil records on computer from 1991, Real Property on computer from 1960, index books from 1885.

Criminal Records: Access: Phone, fax, mail, in person. Both court and visitors may perform in person searches. Search fee: $10.00 per name. Required to search: name, years to search. Criminal records on computer from 1991, index books from 1960.

General Information: No juvenile, mental, sealed, or adoption records released. SASE required. Turnaround time 1 day. Fax notes: Fee to fax results is $2.50 for first page, $.50 per page thereafter. Copy fee: $1.00 per page. Certification fee: $5.00. Fee payee: Edwards County Clerk. Personal checks accepted. Prepayment is required.

El Paso County

District Court 500 East San Antonio Rm 103, El Paso, TX 79901; 915-546-2021. Hours: 8AM-4:45PM (MST). *Felony, Civil.*

Civil Records: Access: Mail, in person. Both court and visitors may perform in person searches. Search fee: $5.00 per name. Fee is per 10 year period. Required to search: name, years to search. Civil cases indexed by defendant, plaintiff. Civil records on computer from civil 1976, microfiche from 1971, index books from 1800s.

Criminal Records: Access: Mail, in person. Both court and visitors may perform in person searches. Search fee: $5.00 per name. Fee is per 10 year period. Required to search: name, years to search, DOB, signed release; also helpful: sex. Criminal records on computer from 1986, microfiche from 1971, index books from 1800s.

General Information: Public Access terminal is available. No juvenile, mental, sealed, or adoption records released. SASE required. Turnaround time 1-3 days. Copy fee: $.25 per page. Certification fee: $1.00.
Fee payee: District Clerk. Business checks accepted.

Credit cards accepted: Visa, MasterCard. Prepayment is required.

County Court 500 E San Antonio St Rm 105, El Paso, TX 79901; 915-546-2072. Hours: 8AM-4:45PM (MST). *Misdemeanor, Civil.*

Civil Records: Access: Mail, fax, in person. Both court and visitors may perform in person searches. Search fee: $5.00 per name. Required to search: name, years to search. Civil cases indexed by defendant, plaintiff. Civil records on computer from 1989, on microfiche and archived from 1952.

Criminal Records: Access: Phone, mail, fax, in person. Both court and visitors may perform in person searches. Search fee: $5.00 per name. Required to search: name, years to search, DOB, SSN. Criminal records computerized since 1989.

General Information: Public Access terminal is available. No juvenile, mental, sealed, or adoption records released. SASE required. Turnaround time up to 1 week. Copy fee: $1.00 per page. Certification fee: $5.00. Fee payee: County Clerk. Personal checks accepted. Prepayment is required.

Probate Court 500 E San Antonio, Rm 1201 A, El Paso, TX 79901; 915-546-2161; Fax: 915-533-4448. Hours: 8AM-5PM (MST). *Probate.*

Ellis County

District Court 1201 N Hiway 77 #B, Waxahachie, TX 75165; 972-923-5000. Hours: 8AM-5PM (CST). *Felony, Civil.*

Civil Records: Access: Mail, in person. Both court and visitors may perform in person searches. Search fee: $5.00 per name. Required to search: name, years to search. Civil cases indexed by defendant, plaintiff. Civil records on computer from 1992, index books from 1800s.

Criminal Records: Access: Mail, in person. Both court and visitors may perform in person searches. Search fee: $5.00 per name. Required to search: name, years to search, DOB, offense. Criminal records on computer from 1992, index books from 1800s.

General Information: Public Access terminal is available. No juvenile, mental, sealed, or adoption records released. SASE required. Turnaround time 1 week. Copy fee: $.50 per page. Certification fee: $1.00 per page. Fee payee: District Clerk's Office. Only cashiers checks and money orders accepted. Prepayment is required.

County Court PO Box 250, Waxahachie, TX 75168; 972-923-5070. Hours: 8AM-4:45PM (CST). *Misdemeanor, Civil, Probate.*

Civil Records: Access: Mail, in person. Both court and visitors may perform in person searches. Search fee: $10.00 per name. Fee is per 5 year period. Required to search: name, years to search. Civil cases indexed by defendant, plaintiff. Civil records on computer in 1995.

Criminal Records: Access: Mail, in person. Both court and visitors may perform in person searches. Search fee: $10.00 per name. Fee is per 5 year period. Required to search: name, years to search. Criminal records on computer since 1992, index books from 1965.

General Information: Public Access terminal is available. No juvenile, mental, sealed, or adoption records released. SASE required. Turnaround time 1-5 days. Copy fee: $1.00 per page. Certification fee: $5.00. Fee payee: Ellis County Clerk. Personal checks accepted. Prepayment is required.

Erath County

District Court 112 W College, Courthouse Annex, Stephenville, TX 76401; 254-965-1486; Fax: 254-965-7156. Hours: 8AM-Noon, 1-5PM (CST). *Felony, Civil.*

Civil Records: Access: Mail, fax, in person. Both court and visitors may perform in person searches. Search

fee: $5.00 per name. Fee is per name per search. Required to search: name, years to search. Civil cases indexed by defendant, plaintiff. Civil records on computer last 10 years, index books and archived from 1900.

Criminal Records: Access: Mail, fax, in person. Both court and visitors may perform in person searches. Search fee: $5.00 per name. Required to search: name, years to search, DOB; also helpful: SSN. Criminal records on computer last 10 years, index books and archived from 1900.

General Information: Public Access terminal is available. No juvenile, mental, sealed, or adoption records released. SASE required. Turnaround time 1-2 days. Fax notes: Fee to fax results is $1.00 per page. Copy fee: $1.00 per page. Certification fee: $5.00. Fee payee: District Clerk. Personal checks accepted. Prepayment is required.

County Court Erath County Courthouse, Stephenville, TX 76401; 254-965-1482. Hours: 8AM-Noon, 1-5PM (CST). *Misdemeanor, Civil, Probate.*

Civil Records: Access: Mail, in person. Both court and visitors may perform in person searches. Search fee: $10.00 per name. Required to search: name, years to search. Civil cases indexed by defendant, plaintiff. Civil records on computer back to 1993, index books since 1970.

Criminal Records: Access: Mail, in person. Both court and visitors may perform in person searches. Search fee: $10.00 per name. Required to search: name, years to search, DOB. Criminal records on computer back to 1993, index books from 1960.

General Information: Public Access terminal is available. No juvenile, mental, sealed, or adoption records released. SASE required. Turnaround time 1 week. Copy fee: $1.00 per page. Certification fee: $5.00 plus $1.00 per page. Fee payee: County Clerk. Personal checks accepted. Prepayment is required.

Falls County

District Court 3rd Floor, PO Box 229, Marlin, TX 76661; 254-883-1419. Hours: 8AM-Noon, 1-5PM (CST). *Felony, Civil.*

Civil Records: Access: Mail, in person. Both court and visitors may perform in person searches. Search fee: $5.00 per name. Required to search: name, years to search. Civil cases indexed by defendant, plaintiff. Civil records in index books.

Criminal Records: Access: Mail, in person. Both court and visitors may perform in person searches. Search fee: $5.00 per name. Required to search: name, years to search; also helpful: DOB. Criminal records in index books.

General Information: No juvenile, mental, sealed, child support or adoption records released. SASE required. Turnaround time 1-5 days. Copy fee: $1.00 per page. Certification fee: No certification fee. Fee payee: District Clerk. Personal checks accepted. Prepayment is required.

County Court PO Box 458, Marlin, TX 76661; 254-883-1408. Hours: 8AM-5PM (CST). *Misdemeanor, Civil, Probate.*

Civil Records: Access: Phone, mail, in person. Both court and visitors may perform in person searches. Search fee: $5.00 per name. Required to search: name, years to search. Civil cases indexed by defendant, plaintiff. Civil records in index books from 1985. Phone search only available if fee prepaid.

Criminal Records: Access: Phone, mail, in person. Both court and visitors may perform in person searches. Search fee: $5.00 per name. Required to search: name, years to search, DOB, SSN. Criminal records in index books from 1985. Phone search only available if fee prepaid.

General Information: No juvenile, mental, sealed, or adoption records released. SASE required. Turnaround time 1 day. Copy fee: $1.00 per page. Certification fee: $5.00. Fee payee: County Clerk. Business checks accepted. Local personal and business checks accepted. Prepayment is required.

Fannin County

District Court Fannin County Courthouse Ste 201, Bonham, TX 75418; 903-583-7459 X33; Fax: 903-640-1826. 8AM-Noon, 1-5PM (CST). *Felony, Civil.*

Civil Records: Access: Fax, mail, in person. Both court and visitors may perform in person searches. Search fee: $5.00 per name. Required to search: name, years to search. Civil cases indexed by defendant, plaintiff. Civil records in index books, archived from 1865.

Criminal Records: Access: Fax, mail, in person. Both court and visitors may perform in person searches. Search fee: $5.00 per name. Fee is for felonies only. Required to search: name, years to search, address, DOB, SSN. Criminal records on computer from 1985, books from 1975, archived from 1865.

General Information: No juvenile, mental, sealed, or adoption records released. SASE required. Turnaround time 2 days. Fax notes: No fee to fax results. Fax available to 800 numbers only. Copy fee: $1.00 per page. Certification fee: No certification fee. Fee payee: District Clerk, Fannin County. Personal checks accepted. Prepayment is required.

County Court County Courthouse, 101 E Sam Rayburn Ste 102, Bonham, TX 75418; 903-583-7486; Fax: 903-583-7811. Hours: 8AM-5PM (CST). *Misdemeanor, Civil, Probate.*

Civil Records: Access: Phone, mail, in person. Both court and visitors may perform in person searches. Search fee: $5.00 per name. Required to search: name, years to search. Civil cases indexed by defendant, plaintiff. Civil records in index books.

Criminal Records: Access: Phone, mail, in person. Both court and visitors may perform in person searches. Search fee: $5.00 per name. Required to search: name, years to search, DOB; also helpful-SSN. Criminal records on computer back to 1979; prior on index books. Phone search limited to 1 year.

General Information: No juvenile, mental, sealed, or adoption records released. SASE required. Turnaround time 1 day. Copy fee: $1.00 per page. Certification fee: $5.00. Fee payee: County Clerk. Personal checks accepted. Prepayment is required.

Fayette County

District Court Fayette County Courthouse, 151 N Washington, La Grange, TX 78945; 979-968-3548; Fax: 979-968-8621. Hours: 8AM-5PM (CST). *Felony, Civil.*

Civil Records: Access: Mail, in person. Both court and visitors may perform in person searches. Search fee: $5.00 per name. Required to search: name, years to search. Civil cases indexed by defendant, plaintiff. Civil records in index books, on computer since 1992.

Criminal Records: Access: Mail, in person. Both court and visitors may perform in person searches. Search fee: $5.00 per name. Required to search: name, years to search. Criminal records in index books, on computer since 1992.

General Information: No juvenile, mental, sealed, or adoption records released. SASE required. Turnaround time 2-3 days. Copy fee: $1.00 per page. Certification fee: $2.00. Fee payee: Fayette County District Clerk. Personal checks accepted. Prepayment is required.

County Court PO Box 59, La Grange, TX 78945; 979-968-3251. Hours: 8AM-5PM (CST). *Misdemeanor, Civil, Probate.*

Civil Records: Access: Phone, mail, in person. Both court and visitors may perform in person searches.

Search fee: $5.00 per name. Required to search: name, years to search. Civil cases indexed by defendant, plaintiff. Civil records in index books, archived from 1970.

Criminal Records: Access: Phone, mail, in person. Both court and visitors may perform in person searches. Search fee: $5.00 per name. Required to search: name, years to search. Criminal records on computer from 1980, index books prior.

General Information: No juvenile, mental, sealed, or adoption records released. SASE required. Turnaround time 1 day. Copy fee: $1.00 per page. Certification fee: $5.00 plus $1.00 per page. Fee payee: County Clerk. Personal checks accepted. Prepayment is required.

Fisher County

32nd District Court PO Box 88, Roby, TX 79543; 915-776-2279; Fax: 915-776-2815. Hours: 8AM-5PM (CST). *Felony, Civil.*

Civil Records: Access: Mail, fax, in person. Both court and visitors may perform in person searches. Search fee: $10.00 per name. Required to search: name, years to search; also helpful: address. Civil cases indexed by defendant, plaintiff. Civil records in index books from 1886.

Criminal Records: Access: Mail, fax, in person. Both court and visitors may perform in person searches. Search fee: $10.00 per name. Required to search: name, years to search, signed release; also helpful: address, DOB. Criminal records in index books from 1886.

General Information: No juvenile, mental, sealed, or adoption records released. SASE required. Turnaround time 1-2 days. Fax notes: Fee to fax results is $1.00 per page. Copy fee: $1.00 per page. Certification fee: $1.00. Fee payee: District Clerk. Business checks accepted. Prepayment is required.

County Court Box 368, Roby, TX 79543-0368; 915-776-2401. Hours: 8AM-Noon, 1-5PM (CST). *Misdemeanor, Civil, Probate.*

Civil Records: Access: Mail, in person. Both court and visitors may perform in person searches. Search fee: $5.00 per name. Required to search: name, years to search. Civil cases indexed by defendant, plaintiff. Civil records on computer from 1991, index books from 1880.

Criminal Records: Access: Mail, in person. Both court and visitors may perform in person searches. Search fee: $5.00 per name. Required to search: name, years to search, signed release, offense. Criminal records on computer from 1989, index books from 1880.

General Information: No juvenile, mental, sealed, or adoption records released. SASE required. Turnaround time 1 day. Copy fee: $1.00 per page. Certification fee: $5.00. Fee payee: Fisher County Clerk. Personal checks accepted. Prepayment is required.

Floyd County

District Court PO Box 67, Floydada, TX 79235; 806-983-4923. Hours: 8:30AM-Noon, 1-4:45PM (CST). *Felony, Civil.*

Civil Records: Access: Phone, mail, in person. Both court and visitors may perform in person searches. Search fee: $5.00 per name. Required to search: name, years to search. Civil cases indexed by defendant, plaintiff. Civil records in index books from early 1900s.

Criminal Records: Access: Mail, in person. Both court and visitors may perform in person searches. Search fee: $5.00 per name. Required to search: name, years to search. Criminal records in index books to early 1900s.

General Information: No juvenile, mental, sealed, or adoption records released. SASE required. Turnaround time 1 day. Copy fee: $.25 per page. Certification fee: $1.00. Fee payee: District Clerk. Personal checks accepted. Prepayment is required.

County Court Courthouse, Rm 101, Main Street, Floydada, TX 79235; 806-983-4900. Hours: 8:30AM-Noon, 1-5PM (CST). *Misdemeanor, Civil, Probate.*

Civil Records: Access: Phone, mail, in person. Both court and visitors may perform in person searches. Search fee: $10.00 per name. Required to search: name, years to search. Civil cases indexed by defendant, plaintiff. Civil records in index books from 1897.

Criminal Records: Access: Phone, mail, in person. Both court and visitors may perform in person searches. Search fee: $10.00 per name. Required to search: name, years to search, DOB. Criminal records in index books from 1897.

General Information: No juvenile, mental, sealed, or adoption records released. SASE not required. Turnaround time 1-5 days. Copy fee: $1.00 per page. Certification fee: $5.00. Fee payee: County Clerk. Personal checks accepted. Prepayment is required.

Foard County

District & County Court PO Box 539, Crowell, TX 79227; 940-684-1365. Hours: 9AM-4:30PM (CST). *Felony, Misdemeanor, Civil, Eviction, Probate.*

Civil Records: Access: Mail, in person. Both court and visitors may perform in person searches. Search fee: $10.00 per name. Required to search: name, years to search. Civil cases indexed by defendant, plaintiff. Civil records in index books from 1910; on computer from 1989.

Criminal Records: Access: Mail, in person. Both court and visitors may perform in person searches. Search fee: $10.00 per name. Required to search: name, years to search, DOB. Criminal records in index books from 1910; on computer from 1989.

General Information: No juvenile, mental, sealed, or adoption records released. SASE required. Turnaround time varies. Fax notes: Fee to fax results is $.25 per page. Copy fee: $1.00 per page. Certification fee: $5.00. Fee payee: District or County Clerk. Personal checks accepted. Prepayment is required.

Fort Bend County

District Court 301 Jackson, Richmond, TX 77469; 281-341-4515; Civil phone: 281-341-4562; Criminal phone: 281-341-4542; Fax: 281-341-4519. Hours: 8AM-5PM (CST). *Felony, Civil.*

www.co.fort-bend.tx.us/distclerk/index.html

Note: Physical court location is 401 Jackson.

Civil Records: Access: Phone, mail, online, in person. Both court and visitors may perform in person searches. Search fee: $5.00 per name. Required to search: name, years to search. Civil cases indexed by defendant, plaintiff. Civil records on computer from 1991, index books from early 1900s. Online searching available through a 900 number service. The access fee is $.55 per minute plus a deposit. Call 281-341-4522 for information.

Criminal Records: Access: Phone, mail, online, in person. Both court and visitors may perform in person searches. Search fee: $5.00 per name. Required to search: name, years to search, DOB, SSN. Criminal records on computer from 1981, index books from early 1900s. Criminal records from 1987 are available on the same online system described in civil records.

General Information: Public Access terminal is available. (Located at 401 Jackson, Rm 100, Richmond, TX 77469.) No juvenile, mental, sealed, termination or adoption records released. SASE required. Turnaround time 2-3 weeks. Copy fee: $.50 per page. Include $1.00 for postage. Fee for microfilm copies $.50 per page. Certification fee: No certification fee. Fee payee: District Clerk. Personal checks accepted. For legal ease account info call 281-341-4508. Prepayment is required.

County Court 301 Jackson St, #101, Richmond, TX 77469; 281-341-8685; Fax: 281-341-4520. Hours: 8AM-4PM (CST). *Misdemeanor, Civil, Probate.*

www.co.fort-bend.tx.us

Civil Records: Access: Mail, online, in person. Both court and visitors may perform in person searches. Search fee: $10.00 per name. Search fee is for each type record to be searched. Required to search: name, years to search. Civil cases indexed by defendant, plaintiff. Civil records on computer from 1986, microfiche from 1983-1994, 1994-present optical imaged. Online access to the civil records index is available free at www.co.fort-bend.tx.us/Admin_of_Justice/County_Clerk/index_info_research.htm. Includes Probate records index online.

Criminal Records: Access: Mail, online, in person. Both court and visitors may perform in person searches. Search fee: $10.00 per name. A search fee for each type record to be searched required. Required to search: name, years to search, DOB. Criminal records on computer from 1983, microfiche from 1983-1994, 1994-present optical imaged. Online access to the criminal index is the same as civil.

General Information: Public Access terminal is available. No juvenile, mental, sealed, or adoption records released. SASE not required. Turnaround time 1-2 days. Fax notes: Fee to fax results is $1.00 per page. Copy fee: $1.00 per page. Certification fee: $5.00. Fee payee: Ft Bend County Clerk. Personal checks accepted. Credit cards accepted: Visa, MC, AmEx, Discover. Prepayment is required.

Franklin County

District Court PO Box 68, Mount Vernon, TX 75457; 903-537-4786. Hours: 8AM-5PM (CST). *Felony, Civil.*

Civil Records: Access: Mail, in person. Both court and visitors may perform in person searches. Search fee: $5.00 per name. Required to search: name, years to search. Civil cases indexed by defendant, plaintiff. Civil records on computer from 1987, on microfiche from 1986, index books from 1800s.

Criminal Records: Access: Mail, in person. Both court and visitors may perform in person searches. Search fee: $5.00 per name. Required to search: name, years to search; also helpful: DOB, SSN. Criminal records on computer from 1987, on microfiche from 1986, index books from 1800s.

General Information: No juvenile, mental, sealed, or adoption records released. SASE required. Turnaround time 1 day. Copy fee: $1.00 per page. Certification fee: $5.00. Fee payee: District Clerk. Personal checks accepted. Prepayment is required.

County Court PO Box 68, Mount Vernon, TX 75457; 903-537-4252; Fax: 903-537-2418. Hours: 8AM-5PM (CST). *Misdemeanor, Civil, Probate.*

Civil Records: Access: Mail, in person. Both court and visitors may perform in person searches. Search fee: $5.00 per name. Required to search: name, years to search. Civil cases indexed by defendant, plaintiff. Civil records on computer from 1987, index books from 1847.

Criminal Records: Access: Mail, in person. Both court and visitors may perform in person searches. Search fee: $5.00 per name. Required to search: name, years to search, DOB and SSN. Criminal records on computer from 1987, index books from 1847.

General Information: No juvenile, mental, sealed, or adoption records released. SASE required. Turnaround time 1 day. Fax notes: Fee to fax results is $1.00 per page. Copy fee: $1.00 per page. Certification fee: $5.00. Fee payee: County Clerk. Personal checks accepted. Prepayment is required.

Freestone County

District Court PO Box 722, Fairfield, TX 75840; 903-389-2534. Hours: 8AM-5PM (CST). *Felony, Civil.*

Civil Records: Access: Mail, in person. Both court and visitors may perform in person searches. Search fee: $5.00 per name. Required to search: name, years to search. Civil cases indexed by defendant, plaintiff. Civil records in index books from 1800s.

Criminal Records: Access: Mail, in person. Both court and visitors may perform in person searches. Search fee: $5.00 per name. Required to search: name, years to search. Criminal records in index books from 1800s.

General Information: No juvenile, mental, sealed, or adoption records released. SASE required. Turnaround time 1 day. Copy fee: $1.00 per page. Certification fee: $1.00. Fee payee: District Clerk. Personal checks accepted.

County Court PO Box 1011, Fairfield, TX 75840; 903-389-2635. Hours: 8AM-5PM (CST). *Misdemeanor, Civil, Probate.*

Civil Records: Access: Mail, in person. Both court and visitors may perform in person searches. Search fee: $5.00 per name. Required to search: name, years to search. Civil cases indexed by defendant, plaintiff. Civil records in index books from 1967.

Criminal Records: Access: Mail, in person. Both court and visitors may perform in person searches. Search fee: $5.00 per name. Required to search: name, years to search. Criminal records in index books from 1967.

General Information: No juvenile, mental, sealed, or adoption records released. SASE required. Turnaround time 2 days. Copy fee: $1.00 per page. Certification fee: $5.00. Fee payee: Freestone County Clerk. Personal checks accepted. Prepayment is required.

Frio County

District Court 500 E San Antonio Box 8, Pearsall, TX 78061; 830-334-8073; Fax: 830-334-0047. Hours: 8AM-5PM (CST). *Felony, Civil.*

Civil Records: Access: Mail, in person. Both court and visitors may perform in person searches. Search fee: $5.00 per name. Required to search: name, years to search; also helpful: address. Civil cases indexed by defendant, plaintiff. Civil records in index books from 1890s.

Criminal Records: Access: Mail, in person. Both court and visitors may perform in person searches. Search fee: $5.00 per name. Required to search: name, years to search, DOB; also helpful: address. Criminal records in index books from 1890s.

General Information: No juvenile, mental, sealed, or adoption records released. SASE required. Turnaround time 2-3 days. Fax notes: Fee to fax results is $2.00 per page. Copy fee: $1.00 per page. Certification fee: $1.00. Fee payee: District Clerk. Business checks accepted. Prepayment is required.

County Court 500 E San Antonio St #6, Pearsall, TX 78061; 830-334-2214; Fax: 830-334-0021. Hours: 8AM-5PM (CST). *Misdemeanor, Civil, Probate.*

Civil Records: Access: Fax, mail, in person. Both court and visitors may perform in person searches. Search fee: $5.00 per name. Required to search: name, years to search. Civil cases indexed by defendant, plaintiff. Civil records in index books from 1876.

Criminal Records: Access: Fax, mail, in person. Both court and visitors may perform in person searches. Search fee: $5.00 per name. Required to search: name, years to search. Criminal records in index books from 1876.

General Information: No juvenile, mental, sealed, or adoption records released. SASE required. Turnaround time 2-4 days. Fax notes: $2.00 per page. Copy fee: $1.00 per page. Certification fee: $5.00. Fee payee:

County Clerk. Personal checks accepted. Prepayment is required.

Gaines County

District Court 101 S Main Rm 213, Seminole, TX 79360; 915-758-4013; Fax: 915-758-4036. Hours: 8AM-Noon, 1-5PM (CST). *Felony, Civil.*

Civil Records: Access: Phone, mail, in person. Only the court performs in person searches; visitors may not. Search fee: $5.00 per name. Required to search: name, years to search. Civil cases indexed by defendant, plaintiff. Civil records on computer from 1980, index books from 1900s.

Criminal Records: Access: Phone, mail, in person. Only the court performs in person searches; visitors may not. Search fee: $5.00 per name. Required to search: name, years to search. Criminal records on computer from 1980, index books from 1900s.

General Information: No juvenile, mental, sealed, or adoption records released. SASE required. Turnaround time 1 day. Copy fee: $1.00 per page. Certification fee: No certification fee. Fee payee: District Clerk. Personal checks accepted. Prepayment is required.

County Court 101 S Main Rm 107, Seminole, TX 79360; 915-758-4003. Hours: 8AM-5PM (CST). *Misdemeanor, Civil, Probate.*

Civil Records: Access: Mail, in person. Both court and visitors may perform in person searches. No search fee. Required to search: name, years to search. Civil cases indexed by defendant, plaintiff.

Criminal Records: Access: Mail, in person. Both court and visitors may perform in person searches. No search fee. Required to search: name, years to search.

General Information: No juvenile, mental, sealed, or adoption records released. SASE required. Turnaround time 1 day. Copy fee: $1.00 per page. Certification fee: $1.00. Fee payee: County Clerk. Personal checks accepted. Prepayment is required.

Galveston County

District Court 722 Moody St Rm 404, Galveston, TX 77550; 409-766-2424; Fax: 409-766-2292. Hours: 8AM-5PM (CST). *Felony, Civil.*

Civil Records: Access: Fax, mail, in person. Search fee: $5.00 per name. Required to search: name, years to search. Civil cases indexed by defendant, plaintiff. Civil records on computer from 1982, on microfiche from 1982, archived from 1849. Fax access is only allowed with prepaid accounts.

Criminal Records: Access: Fax, mail, in person. Both court and visitors may perform in person searches. Search fee: $5.00 per name. Required to search: name, years to search, DOB. Criminal records on computer from 1982, on microfiche from 1982, archived from 1849.

General Information: Public Access terminal is available. No juvenile, mental, sealed, or adoption records released. SASE required. Turnaround time 2-5 days. Copy fee: $1.00 per page. Certification fee: $1.00. Fee payee: District Clerk. Personal checks accepted. Prepayment is required.

County Court PO Box 2450, Galveston, TX 77553-2450; Civil phone: 409-766-2203; Criminal phone: 409-770-5112; Probate phone: 409-766-2022. Hours: 8AM-5PM (CST). *Misdemeanor, Civil, Probate.*

Civil Records: Access: Mail, online, in person. Both court and visitors may perform in person searches. Search fee: $5.00 per name. Required to search: name, years to search. Civil cases indexed by defendant, plaintiff. Civil records on computer from 1984, index books from 1947. Access to the GCNET remote online service requires a $200 escrow account plus a $.25 per minute fee. Fax back service is available. For more information, call Robert Dickinson at 409-770-5115.

Criminal Records: Access: Mail, online, in person. Both court and visitors may perform in person searches. Search fee: $5.00 per name. Required to search: name, years to search, DOB; also helpful: SSN. Criminal records on computer from 1984, index books from 1947. Online access is through the GCNET systems as described in civil records.

General Information: Public Access terminal is available. No juvenile, mental, sealed, or adoption records released. SASE required. Turnaround time 1-2 days. Copy fee: $1.00 per page. Certification fee: $5.00 plus $1.00 per page. Fee payee: County Clerk. Personal checks accepted. Checks are accepted with mail requests only. Prepayment is required.

Garza County

District & County Court PO Box 366, Post, TX 79356; 806-495-4430; Fax: 806-495-4431. Hours: 8AM-Noon,1-5PM (CST). *Felony, Misdemeanor, Civil, Eviction, Probate.*

Civil Records: Access: Mail, in person. Both court and visitors may perform in person searches. Search fee: $5.00 per name. Required to search: name, years to search. Civil cases indexed by defendant, plaintiff. Civil records on index books.

Criminal Records: Access: Mail, in person. Both court and visitors may perform in person searches. Search fee: $5.00 per name. Required to search: name, years to search, DOB or SSN. Criminal records on index books.

General Information: No criminal records released. Turnaround time 2-3 days. Fax notes: Fee to fax results is $4.00 per document. Copy fee: $1.00 per page. Certification fee: $5.00. Fee payee: District or County Clerk. Personal checks accepted. Prepayment required.

Gillespie County

District Court 101 W Main Rm 204, Fredericksburg, TX 78624; 830-997-6517. Hours: Public hours 8AM-5PM (CST). *Felony, Civil.*

Civil Records: Access: Mail, in person. Both court and visitors may perform in person searches. Search fee: $5.00 per name. Required to search: name, years to search. Civil cases indexed by defendant, plaintiff. Civil records in index books from 1800s. Index #1 from 1800s-1927, Index #2 from 1927-1988, Index #3 from 1989-present.

Criminal Records: Access: Mail, in person. Both court and visitors may perform in person searches. Search fee: $5.00 per name. Required to search: name, years to search; also helpful: DOB, SSN. Criminal records in index books from 1800s. Index #1 from 1800s-1927, Index #2 from 1927-1988, Index #3 from 1989-present.

General Information: No juvenile, mental, sealed, or adoption records released. SASE required. Turnaround time 1-2 days. Copy fee: $1.00 for first page, $.25 each add'l. Certification fee: $1.00 per page. Fee payee: Gillespie County District Clerk. Personal checks accepted. Prepayment is required.

County Court 101 W Main Unit #13, Fredericksburg, TX 78624; 830-997-6515; Fax: 830-997-9958. Hours: 8AM-4PM (CST). *Misdemeanor, Civil, Probate.*

Civil Records: Access: Mail, in person. Both court and visitors may perform in person searches. Search fee: $5.00 per name. Required to search: name, years to search; also helpful: address. Civil cases indexed by defendant, plaintiff. Civil records on computer from 1988, on microfiche from 1990, index books from 1900s.

Criminal Records: Access: Mail, in person. Both court and visitors may perform in person searches. Search fee: $5.00 per name. Required to search: name, years to search, aliases; also helpful: DOB, SSN. Criminal records on computer from 1988, on microfiche from 1990, index books from 1900s.

General Information: No juvenile, mental, sealed, or adoption record released. SASE required. Turnaround time 1-2 days. Copy fee: $1.00 per page. Certification fee: $10.00. Fee payee: Debbie Wahl County Clerk. No out-of-town checks accepted. Prepayment is required.

Glasscock County

District & County Court PO Box 190, 117 E Currie, Garden City, TX 79739; 915-354-2371. Hours: 8AM-4PM (CST). *Felony, Misdemeanor, Civil, Probate.*

Civil Records: Access: Mail, in person. Both court and visitors may perform in person searches. Search fee: $10.00 per name. Required to search: name, years to search. Civil cases indexed by defendant, plaintiff. Civil records in index books from 1893.

Criminal Records: Access: Mail, in person. Both court and visitors may perform in person searches. Search fee: $10.00 per name. Required to search: name, years to search, signed release. Criminal records in index books from 1893.

General Information: No juvenile, mental, or adoption records released. SASE required. Turnaround time 2 days. Copy fee: $1.00 per page. Certification fee: $5.00. Fee payee: District or County Clerk. Personal checks accepted. Prepayment is required.

Goliad County

District & County Court PO Box 50 (127 N Courthouse Sq.), Goliad, TX 77963; 361-645-2443/3294; Fax: 361-645-3858. Hours: 8AM-5PM (CST). *Felony, Misdemeanor, Civil, Probate.*

Civil Records: Access: Mail, fax, in person. Both court and visitors may perform in person searches. Search fee: $5.00 per name. Fee is per court. Required to search: name, years to search; also helpful: address. Civil cases indexed by defendant, plaintiff. Civil records on computer since 1983 (real property only), on microfiche and index books from 1870.

Criminal Records: Access: Mail, fax, in person. Both court and visitors may perform in person searches. Search fee: $5.00 per name. Fee is per court. Required to search: name, years to search; also helpful: address, DOB, SSN, offense. Criminal records on microfiche and index books from 1870.

General Information: No juvenile, mental, sealed, or adoption records released. SASE not required. Turnaround time 1-2 days. Fax notes: Fee to fax results is $1.00 per page. Copy fee: $1.00 per page. Certification fee: Certification: Fee is $5.00 for County Court; $1.00 for District Court plus $1.00 per page. Fee payee: Goliad County/District Clerk. Personal checks accepted. Prepayment is required.

Gonzales County

District Court PO Box 34, Gonzales, TX 78629-0034; 830-672-2326; Fax: 830-672-9313. Hours: 8AM-Noon 1-5PM (CST). *Felony, Civil.*

Civil Records: Access: Phone, fax, mail, in person. Both court and visitors may perform in person searches. Search fee: $5.00 per name. Required to search: name, years to search; also helpful: address. Civil cases indexed by defendant, plaintiff. Civil records on computer from 1991, index books from 1800s.

Criminal Records: Access: Phone, fax, mail, in person. Both court and visitors may perform in person searches. Search fee: $5.00 per name. Required to search: name, years to search; also helpful: address, DOB, SSN. Criminal records on computer from 1991, index books from 1800s.

General Information: No juvenile, mental, sealed, or adoption records released. SASE required. Turnaround time 1-2 days. Fax notes: Fee to fax results is $1.00 per page. Copy fee: $1.00 per page. Certification fee: No certification fee. Fee payee: District Clerk. Personal checks accepted.

County Court PO Box 77, Gonzales, TX 78629; 830-672-2801; Fax: 830-672-2636. Hours: 8AM-5PM (CST). *Misdemeanor, Civil, Probate.*

Civil Records: Access: Fax, mail, in person. Both court and visitors may perform in person searches. Search fee: $5.00 per name. Required to search: name, years to search. Civil cases indexed by defendant, plaintiff. Civil records on computer since 1993, original jackets since 1975, index books from 1900s.

Criminal Records: Access: Mail, in person. Both court and visitors may perform in person searches. Search fee: $5.00 per name. Required to search: name, years to search, offense, date of offense. Criminal records on computer since 1993, original jackets, index books from 1900s.

General Information: No mental or drug dependant commitment records released. SASE required. Turnaround time 1-2 days. Fax notes: $5.00. Copy fee: $1.00 per page. Certification fee: $5.00. Fee payee: County Clerk. Personal checks accepted. Prepayment is required.

Gray County

District Court PO Box 1139, Pampa, TX 79066-1139; 806-669-8010; Fax: 806-669-8053. Hours: 8:30AM-5PM (CST). *Felony, Civil.*

Civil Records: Access: Fax, mail, in person. Both court and visitors may perform in person searches. Search fee: $5.00 per name. Required to search: name, years to search. Civil cases indexed by defendant, plaintiff. Civil records on computer from 1965, index books from 1910. All requests must be in writing.

Criminal Records: Access: Fax, mail, in person. Both court and visitors may perform in person searches. Search fee: $5.00 per name. Required to search: name, years to search; also helpful: DOB. Criminal records on computer from 1930. All requests must be in writing.

General Information: No juvenile, mental, sealed, or adoption records released. SASE required. Turnaround time 1-2 days. Fax notes: $1.00 per page. Copy fee: $.25 per page. Certification fee: $1.00 per page. Fee payee: District Clerk. Personal checks accepted. Prepayment is required.

County & Probate Court PO Box 1902, Pampa, TX 79066-1902; 806-669-8004; Fax: 806-669-8054. Hours: 8:30AM-5PM (CST). *Misdemeanor, Civil, Probate.*

Civil Records: Access: Phone, fax, mail, in person. Both court and visitors may perform in person searches. Search fee: $5.00 per name. Fee is per index. Required to search: name, years to search. Civil cases indexed by defendant, plaintiff. Civil records on type written indices from 1900s.

Criminal Records: Access: Phone, fax, mail, in person. Both court and visitors may perform in person searches. Search fee: $5.00 per name. Fee is per index. Required to search: name, years to search, DOB. Criminal records on type written indices from 1900s.

General Information: No juvenile, mental, sealed, or adoption records released. They will not release any records with the SSN on it. SASE required. Turnaround time 1-2 days. Fax notes: $2.50 for first page, $1.00 each add'l. Copy fee: $1.00 per page. Certification fee: $5.00. Fee payee: Susan Winborne, County Clerk. Personal checks accepted. Prepayment is required.

Grayson County

District Court 200 S Crockett Rm 120-A, Sherman, TX 75090; 903-813-4352. Hours: 8AM-5PM (CST). *Felony, Civil.*

Civil Records: Access: Mail, in person. Both court and visitors may perform in person searches. Search fee: $5.00 per name. Required to search: name, years to search. Civil cases indexed by defendant, plaintiff. Civil records on computer from 1988, microfilm since 1939, index books since 1900s.

Criminal Records: Access: Mail, in person. Both court and visitors may perform in person searches. Search fee: $5.00 per name. Required to search: name, years to search, DOB; also helpful: SSN. Criminal records on computer since 1988, microfilm since 1939, index books since 1900s.

General Information: Public Access terminal is available. No juvenile, mental, sealed, expunction or adoption records released. SASE required. Turnaround time 1-2 days. Copy fee: $1.00 per page. Certification fee: $2.00. Fee payee: District Clerk. Personal checks accepted. Prepayment is required.

County Court 200 S Crockett, Sherman, TX 75090; 903-813-4336; Fax: 903-892-8300. Hours: 8AM-5PM (CST). *Misdemeanor, Civil, Probate.*

www.co.grayson.tx.us

Civil Records: Access: Mail, in person, online. Both court and visitors may perform in person searches. Search fee: $5.00 per name. Required to search: name, years to search. Civil cases indexed by defendant, plaintiff. Civil records on computer since 1992, index books since 1952. Online access to civil records is available free online at http://209.151.115.130:3004/udsrch.asp. Also includes sheriffs' bail, and sheriff's jail searching.

Criminal Records: Access: Mail, in person, online. Both court and visitors may perform in person searches. Search fee: $5.00 per name. Required to search: name, years to search, also helpful: DOB, SSN. Criminal records on computer from 1982. Online access to criminal records is the same as civil.

General Information: Public Access terminal is available. No juvenile, mental, sealed, or adoption records released. SASE required. Turnaround time 1-2 days. Fax notes: Will fax results if prepaid. Copy fee: $1.00 per page. Certification fee: $5.00. Fee payee: County Clerk. Personal checks accepted. Prepayment is required.

Gregg County

District Court PO Box 711, Longview, TX 75606; 903-237-2663. Hours: 8AM-5PM (CST). *Felony, Civil.*

www.co.gregg.tx.us/Gregg_DC.html

Civil Records: Access: Phone, fax, mail, in person, online. Both court and visitors may perform in person searches. Search fee: $5.00 per name. Required to search: name, years to search. Civil cases indexed by defendant, plaintiff. Civil records on computer back to 1981, index books from 1873. Online access to county judicial records is available free at www.co.gregg.tx.us/judsrch.htm. Search by name, cause #, status.

Criminal Records: Access: Phone, fax, mail, in person, online. Both court and visitors may perform in person searches. Search fee: $5.00 per name. Required to search: name, years to search. Criminal records on computer back to 1977, index books from 1873. Online access to criminal records is the same as civil. Also includes jail and bond search.

General Information: No juvenile, mental, sealed, or adoption records released. SASE required. Turnaround time 1-2 days. Fax notes: $1.00 per page. Copy fee: $1.00 for 1st page, $.25 each add'l. Certification fee: $1.00 per page. Fee payee: District Clerk. Only cashiers checks and money orders accepted. Prepayment is required.

County Court PO Box 3049, Longview, TX 75606; 903-236-8430. Hours: 8AM-5PM (CST). *Misdemeanor, Civil, Probate.*

www.co.gregg.tx.us/Gregg_County_Judge.html

Civil Records: Access: Mail, in person, online. Both court and visitors may perform in person searches.

Search fee: $5.00 per name. Required to search: name, years to search. Civil cases indexed by defendant, plaintiff. Civil records on computer from 1983, index books after 1983. Online access to county judicial records is available free at www.co.gregg.tx.us/judsrch.htm. Search by name, cause #, status.

Criminal Records: Access: Mail, in person, online. Both court and visitors may perform in person searches. Search fee: $5.00 per name. Required to search: name, years to search, DOB or SSN. Criminal records on computer from 1983, index books after 1983. Online access to criminal records is the same as civil. Jail and bond search also available.

General Information: Public Access terminal is available. No juvenile, mental, sealed, or adoption records released. SASE required. Turnaround time 1 week. Fax notes: Fee to fax results is $1.00 per page. Copy fee: $1.00 per page. Certification fee: $5.00. Fee payee: Gregg County Clerk. Only in-state personal checks accepted. Prepayment is required.

Grimes County

District Court PO Box 234, Anderson, TX 77830; 936-873-2111; Fax: 936-873-2415. Hours: 8AM-4:45PM (CST). *Felony, Civil.*

Civil Records: Access: Phone, fax, mail, in person. Both court and visitors may perform in person searches. Search fee: $5.00 per name. Required to search: name, years to search. Civil cases indexed by defendant, plaintiff. Civil records on computer from 1990, index books from 1800s.

Criminal Records: Access: Phone, fax, mail, in person. Both court and visitors may perform in person searches. Search fee: $5.00 per name. Required to search: name, years to search, DOB, SSN. Criminal records on computer from 1990, index books from 1800s.

General Information: No juvenile, mental, sealed, or adoption records released. SASE not required. Turnaround time 1-2 days. Copy fee: $1.00 per page. Certification fee: $1.00. Fee payee: District Clerk. Personal checks accepted. Prepayment is required.

County Court PO Box 209, Anderson, TX 77830; 936-873-2606 X251. Hours: 8AM-4:45PM (CST). *Misdemeanor, Civil, Probate.*

Civil Records: Access: Mail, in person. Only the court performs in person searches; visitors may not. Search fee: $5.00 per name. Required to search: name, years to search. Civil cases indexed by defendant, plaintiff. Civil records in index books from 1850.

Criminal Records: Access: Mail, in person. Only the court performs in person searches; visitors may not. Search fee: $5.00 per name. Required to search: name, years to search, offense, date of offense. Criminal records in index books from 1850.

General Information: No juvenile, mental, sealed, or adoption records released. SASE required. Turnaround time 1-2 days. Copy fee: $1.00 per page. Certification fee: $5.00. Fee payee: County Clerk. Personal checks accepted.

Guadalupe County

District Court 101 E Court St, Seguin, TX 78155; 830-303-4188; Fax: 830-379-1943. Hours: 8AM-5PM (CST). *Felony, Civil.*

www.co.guadalupe.tx.us/districtclerk.htm

Civil Records: Access: In person, online. Visitors must perform in person searches for themselves. No search fee. Required to search: name, years to search. Civil cases indexed by defendant, plaintiff. Civil records on computer from 1990, index books from 1846. Online access to court case information from 1990 forward is available at www.idocket.com; subscription required.

Criminal Records: Access: In person, online. Visitors must perform in person searches for themselves. No

search fee. Required to search: name, years to search, DOB; also helpful: SSN. Criminal records on computer from 1990, index books from 1846. Online access to criminal records is the same as civil.

General Information: Public Access terminal is available. No juvenile, mental, sealed, or adoption records released. Copy fee: $.20 per page. Certification fee: $1.00 per page. Fee payee: District Clerk. Personal checks accepted. Credit cards accepted: Visa, MasterCard, AmEx. Prepayment is required.

County Court 101 E Court St, Seguin, TX 78155; 830-303-4188 X266,234,232; Fax: 830-372-1206. 8AM-4:30PM (CST). *Misdemeanor, Civil, Probate.*

Civil Records: Access: Mail, in person. Both court and visitors may perform in person searches. Search fee: $5.00 per name. Required to search: name, years to search. Civil cases indexed by defendant, plaintiff. Civil records on computer from 1990, index books to 1968.

Criminal Records: Access: Mail, in person. Both court and visitors may perform in person searches. Search fee: $5.00 per name. Required to search: name, years to search, DOB; also helpful: SSN. Criminal records on computer from 1990, index books from 1968.

General Information: No juvenile, mental, sealed, or adoption records released. SASE required. Turnaround time 5 days. Copy fee: $1.00 per page. Certification fee: $5.00. Payee: County Clerk. Personal checks accepted. Checks accepted for civil fees. Prepayment is required.

Hale County

District Court 500 Broadway #200, Plainview, TX 79072-8050; 806-291-5226; Fax: 806-291-5206. Hours: 8AM-Noon; 1-5PM (CST). *Felony, Civil.*

Civil Records: Access: Phone, fax, mail, in person. Both court and visitors may perform in person searches. Search fee: $5.00 per name. Required to search: name, years to search. Civil cases indexed by defendant, plaintiff. Civil records on computer back to 1988, index cards from 1975.

Criminal Records: Access: Phone, fax, mail, in person. Both court and visitors may perform in person searches. Search fee: $5.00 per name. Required to search: name, years to search, DOB; also helpful: SSN. Criminal records on computer back to 1988, index cards from 1975.

General Information: Public Access terminal is available. No juvenile, mental, sealed, or adoption records released. SASE required. Turnaround time 1-2 days. Fax notes: Fee to fax results is $2.00 per document. Copy fee: $1.00 1st 4 pages, $.25 each additional page. Certification fee: $1.00 each. Fee payee: District Clerk. Personal checks accepted. Prepayment is required.

County Court 500 Broadway #140, Plainview, TX 79072-8030; 806-291-5261; Fax: 806-291-9810. Hours: 8AM-Noon, 1-5PM (CST). *Misdemeanor, Civil, Probate.*

Civil Records: Access: Mail, fax, in person. Both court and visitors may perform in person searches. Search fee: $5.00 per name. Required to search: name, years to search, address. Civil cases indexed by defendant, plaintiff. Civil records in index books from 1928; on computer to 1990.

Criminal Records: Access: Mail, fax, in person. Both court and visitors may perform in person searches. Search fee: $5.00 per name. Required to search: name, years to search, DOB. Criminal records in index books from 1928; on computer to 1990.

General Information: Public Access terminal is available. No juvenile, mental, sealed, or adoption records released. SASE required. Turnaround time 1-2 days. Copy fee: $1.00 per page. Certification fee: $5.00. Fee payee: County Clerk. Personal checks accepted. Checks accepted except for vital records. Prepayment is required.

Hall County

District & County Court County Courthouse, Memphis, TX 79245; 806-259-2627; Fax: 806-259-5078. Hours: 8:30AM-Noon; 1-5PM (CST). *Felony, Misdemeanor, Civil, Eviction, Probate.*

Civil Records: Access: Phone, mail, in person. Both court and visitors may perform in person searches. Search fee: $10.00 per name. Required to search: name, years to search. Civil cases indexed by defendant, plaintiff. Civil records on computer from 1992, index books from 1890.
Criminal Records: Access: Phone, mail, in person. Both court and visitors may perform in person searches. Search fee: $10.00 per name. Required to search: name, years to search, offense. Criminal records on computer from 1992, index books from 1890.
General Information: No juvenile, mental, sealed, or adoption records released. SASE required. Turnaround time 1-2 days. Copy fee: $1.00 per page. Certification fee: $5.00. Fee payee: Hall County Clerk. Personal checks accepted. Prepayment is required.

Hamilton County

District Court County Courthouse, Hamilton, TX 76531; 254-386-3417; Fax: 254-386-8610. Hours: 8AM-5PM M-Th; 8AM-4:30PM F *Felony, Civil.*

Civil Records: Access: Fax, mail, in person. Both court and visitors may perform in person searches. Search fee: $5.00 per name. Required to search: name, years to search. Civil cases indexed by defendant, plaintiff. Civil records in index books.
Criminal Records: Access: Fax, mail, in person. Both court and visitors may perform in person searches. Search fee: $5.00 per name. Required to search: name, years to search. Criminal records in index books.
General Information: No juvenile, mental, sealed, or adoption records released. SASE required. Turnaround time 2-4 days. Fax notes: No fee to fax results. Copy fee: $1.00 per page. Certification fee: $2.00. Fee payee: District Clerk. Personal checks accepted.

County Court County Courthouse, Hamilton, TX 76531; 254-386-3518; Fax: 254-386-8727. Hours: 8AM-5PM (CST). *Misdemeanor, Civil, Probate.*

Civil Records: Access: Mail, fax, in person. Both court and visitors may perform in person searches. Search fee: $5.00 per name. Required to search: name, years to search. Civil cases indexed by defendant, plaintiff. Civil records in index books; on computer since.
Criminal Records: Access: Mail, fax, in person. Both court and visitors may perform in person searches. Search fee: $5.00 per name. Required to search: name, years to search, DOB or SSN. Criminal records in index books; on computer since.
General Information: No juvenile, mental, sealed, or adoption records released. SASE required. Turnaround time 1-2 days. Fax notes: Will fax results for fee. Copy fee: $1.00 per page. Certification fee: $1.00. Fee payee: County Clerk. Personal checks accepted. Prepayment is required.

Hansford County

District & County Court PO Box 397, Spearman, TX 79081; 806-659-4110; Fax: 806-659-4168. Hours: 8:00AM-5PM (CST). *Felony, Misdemeanor, Civil, Eviction, Probate.*

Civil Records: Access: Phone, fax, mail, in person. Both court and visitors may perform in person searches. Search fee: $5.00 per name. Required to search: name, years to search. Civil cases indexed by defendant, plaintiff. Civil records on computer from 01/82, index books from 1900s.
Criminal Records: Access: Phone, fax, mail, in person. Both court and visitors may perform in person searches. Search fee: $5.00 per name. Required to

---

search: name, years to search; also helpful: DOB, SSN. Criminal records on computer since 06/92.
General Information: Public Access terminal is available. No juvenile, mental, sealed, or adoption records released. SASE required. Turnaround time 1-2 days. Fax notes: $4.00 for first page, $1.00 each add'l. Copy fee: $1.00 per page. Certification fee: $2.00 for District Court records; $5.00 for County Court records. Payee: District/County Clerk. Personal checks accepted.

Hardeman County

District & County Court PO Box 30, Quanah, TX 79252; 940-663-2901. Hours: 8:30AM-5PM (CST). *Felony, Misdemeanor, Civil, Eviction, Probate.*

Civil Records: Access: Mail, in person. Both court and visitors may perform in person searches. Search fee: $10.00 per name. Required to search: name, years to search. Civil cases indexed by defendant, plaintiff. Civil records in index books from 1900s.
Criminal Records: Access: Mail, in person. Both court and visitors may perform in person searches. Search fee: $10.00 per name. Required to search: name, years to search. Criminal records in index books from 1900s.
General Information: No juvenile, mental, sealed, or adoption records released. SASE required. Turnaround time 1-2 days. Copy fee: $1.00 per page. Certification fee: $5.00. Fee payee: District Clerk. Personal checks accepted. Prepayment is required.

Hardin County

District Court PO Box 2997, Kountze, TX 77625; 409-246-5150. Hours: 8AM-4PM (CST). *Felony, Civil.*

Civil Records: Access: Phone, mail, in person. Both court and visitors may perform in person searches. Search fee: $5.00 per name. Required to search: name, years to search. Civil cases indexed by defendant, plaintiff. Civil records in index books since 1920.
Criminal Records: Access: Phone, mail, in person. Both court and visitors may perform in person searches. Search fee: $5.00 per name. Required to search: name, years to search, DOB; also helpful: SSN, sex. Criminal records in index books since 1920.
General Information: No juvenile, mental, sealed, or adoption records released. SASE required. Turnaround time 1-2 days. Fax notes: Fee to fax results is $1.00 per page. Copy fee: $1.00 per page. Certification fee: $2.00. Fee payee: District Clerk. Business checks accepted. Prepayment is required.

County Court PO Box 38, Kountze, TX 77625; 409-246-5185. Hours: 8AM-5PM (CST). *Misdemeanor, Civil, Probate.*

Civil Records: Access: Mail, in person. Both court and visitors may perform in person searches. Search fee: $5.00 per name. Required to search: name, years to search. Civil cases indexed by defendant, plaintiff. Civil records in index books since 1850.
Criminal Records: Access: Mail, in person. Both court and visitors may perform in person searches. Search fee: $5.00 per name. Required to search: name, years to search. Criminal records on computer since 1992, index books from 1850.
General Information: No juvenile, mental, sealed, or adoption records released. SASE not required. Turnaround time 1-2 days. Copy fee: $1.00 per page. Certification fee: $5.00. Fee payee: Hardin County Clerk. Personal checks accepted. Prepayment required.

Harris County

District Court PO Box 4651, Houston, TX 77210; Civil phone: 713-755-5711; Civil phone: 713-755-5734; Fax: 713-755-5480 (civil). Hours: 8AM-6PM (CST). *Felony, Civil Over $100,000.*

www.hcdistrictclerk.com

Civil Records: Access: Phone, mail, online, in person, email. Both court and visitors may perform in person

---

searches. Search fee: $5.00 per name. Required to search: name, years to search. Civil cases indexed by defendant, plaintiff. Civil records on computer from 1969. The online subscriber fee site requires a $150 deposit, possible training fees, and $10 monthly fee plus per minute usage charges. The system includes probate, misdemeanor and traffic. Also, civil court general information is available on the Internet at www.ccl.co.harris.tx.us/civil/default.htm.
Criminal Records: Access: Phone, mail, online, in person, email. Both court and visitors may perform in person searches. Search fee: $5.00 per name. Required to search: name, years to search, DOB; also helpful: SSN. Criminal records on computer since 1976. Online access to criminal records is the same as civil. Also, Internet access to criminal records is available to qualified JIMs subscribers at www.co.harris.tx.us/subscriber/cb/submenu.htm. Records include felonies and A & B class misdemeanors.
General Information: Public Access terminal is available. No juvenile, sealed, or adoption records released. SASE required. Fax notes: Fax service requires credit card pre-payment. Copy fee: $1.00 per page. Fax requesters must be pre-approved Certification fee: $1.00. Fee payee: District Clerk, Harris County. Business check accepted from attorney with TX Bar Card number, corporate or company check with Harris Co address. Prepayment is required.

County Court, PO Box 1525, Houston, TX 77251-1525; 713-755-6421. Hours: 8AM-4:30PM (CST). *Civil Under $100,000.*

www.co.harris.tx.us/cclerk

Civil Records: Access: Phone, mail, online, in person. Both court and visitors may perform in person searches. No search fee. Required to search: name, years to search. Civil cases indexed by defendant, plaintiff. Civil records on computer and microfiche from 1963. Online access is free starting in 2001 at the web site. The system includes civil data search and county civil settings inquiry and other county clerk functions. For further information, visit the web site, send an email request to dcsa@dco.co.harris.tx.us, or call 713-755-6421. Also, civil court general information is available at www.ccl.co.harris.tx.us/civil/default.htm.
General Information: Public Access terminal is available. SASE required. Turnaround time 24-48 hours. Copy fee: $1.00 per page. Certification fee: $5.00. Fee payee: Harris County Clerk. Business checks accepted. Credit cards accepted: Visa, MasterCard, Discover, AmEx. Prepayment is required.

Probate Court 1115 Congress, 6th Floor, Houston, TX 77002; 713-755-6084; Fax: 713-755-4349. Hours: 6AM-5PM (CST). *Probate.*

Note: Probate dockets are available through the Harris County online system. Call (713) 755-7815 for information. Probate dockets are available free at http://63.101.65.71/CoolICE/ProbateCourt/pc_inquiry.

Harrison County

71st District Court PO Box 1119, Marshall, TX 75671-1119; 903-935-4845. Hours: 8AM-5PM (CST). *Felony, Civil.*

www.co.harrison.tx.us

Civil Records: Access: Mail, in person. Both court and visitors may perform in person searches. Search fee: $5.00 per name. Required to search: name, years to search; also helpful: address. Civil cases indexed by defendant, plaintiff. Civil records on computer from 1988, index books from 1845.
Criminal Records: Access: Mail, in person. Both court and visitors may perform in person searches. Search fee: $5.00 per name. Required to search: name, years to search, DOB; also helpful: address, SSN. Criminal records on computer from 1988, index books to 1845.

General Information: Public Access terminal is available. No juvenile, mental, sealed, or adoption records released. SASE required. Turnaround time 1-2 days. Copy fee: $1.00 per page. Certification fee: No certification fee. Fee payee: Harrison County District Clerk. Personal checks accepted. Prepayment is required.

County Court PO Box 1365, Marshall, TX 75671; 903-935-4858. Hours: 8AM-5PM (CST). *Misdemeanor, Civil, Probate.*

Civil Records: Access: Mail, in person. Both court and visitors may perform in person searches. Search fee: $5.00 per name. Required to search: name, years to search. Civil cases indexed by defendant, plaintiff. Civil records in docket books from 1800; on computer back to 1981.
Criminal Records: Access: Mail, in person. Both court and visitors may perform in person searches. Search fee: $5.00 per name. Required to search: name, years to search, DOB. Criminal records in docket books from 1800; on computer back to 1995.
General Information: No juvenile, mental, sealed, birth, death or adoption records released. SASE not required. Turnaround time 10 days. Fax notes: Fee to fax results is $1.00 per page. Copy fee: $1.00 per page. Certification fee: $5.00 plus $1.00 per page. Fee payee: County Clerk. Personal checks accepted. In state checks only. Prepayment is required.

Hartley County

District & County Court PO Box Q, Channing, TX 79018; 806-235-3582; Fax: 806-235-2316. Hours: 8:30AM-Noon, 1-5PM (CST). *Felony, Misdemeanor, Civil, Eviction, Probate.*

Civil Records: Access: Mail, in person. Both court and visitors may perform in person searches. Search fee: $5.00 per name. Charge is for each book searched. Required to search: name, years to search. Civil cases indexed by defendant, plaintiff. Civil records on computer from 1992, index books from 1900s. Results can be faxed if pre-paid and local call.
Criminal Records: Access: Mail, in person. Both court and visitors may perform in person searches. Search fee: $5.00 per name, per book searched (misdemeanor or felony). Required to search: name, years to search, DOB. Criminal records on computer from 1992, index books from 1900s. Results can be faxed if pre-paid and local call.
General Information: No juvenile, mental, sealed, or adoption records released. SASE required. Turnaround time 1-2 days. Copy fee: $1.00 per page. Certification fee: $5.00. Fee payee: Hartley County Clerk. Personal checks accepted. Prepayment is required.

Haskell County

District Court PO Box 27, Haskell, TX 79521; 940-864-2030. Hours: 8AM-Noon, 1-5PM M-Th; 8AM-4:30PM F (CST). *Felony, Civil.*

Civil Records: Access: Mail, in person. Both court and visitors may perform in person searches. Search fee: $5.00 per name. Required to search: name, years to search. Civil cases indexed by defendant, plaintiff. Civil records on computer from 1992, index books from 1896.
Criminal Records: Access: Mail, in person. Both court and visitors may perform in person searches. Search fee: $5.00 per name. Required to search: name, years to search, signed release. Criminal records on computer from 1992, index books from 1896.
General Information: No juvenile, mental, sealed, or adoption records released. SASE required. Turnaround time 1-2 days. Copy fee: $1.00 per page. Certification fee: $1.00. Fee payee: District Clerk. Business checks accepted. In-state checks accepted. Prepayment is required.

County Court PO Box 725, Haskell, TX 79521; 940-864-2451. Hours: 8AM-Noon, 1-5PM (CST). *Misdemeanor, Civil, Probate.*

Civil Records: Access: Phone, fax, mail, in person. Both court and visitors may perform in person searches. Search fee: $5.00 per name. Required to search: name, years to search. Civil cases indexed by defendant, plaintiff. Civil records in index books from 1903.
Criminal Records: Access: Fax, mail, in person. Both court and visitors may perform in person searches. Search fee: $5.00 per name. Required to search: name, years to search. Criminal records in index books from 1903.
General Information: No juvenile, mental, sealed, or adoption records released. SASE required. Turnaround time 1-2 days. Fax notes: $2.00 per page. Copy fee: $1.00 per page. Certification fee: $5.00. Fee payee: County Clerk. Personal checks accepted. Prepayment is required.

Hays County

District Court 110 E Martin Luther King, Suite 123, San Marcos, TX 78666; 512-393-7660; Fax: 512-393-7674. Hours: 8AM-5PM (CST). *Felony, Civil.*
www.co.hays.tx.us
Civil Records: Access: Phone, mail, in person. Both court and visitors may perform in person searches. Search fee: $5.00 per name. Required to search: name, years to search. Civil cases indexed by defendant, plaintiff. Civil records on computer from 1987, index books from 1890s.
Criminal Records: Access: Phone, mail, in person. Both court and visitors may perform in person searches. Search fee: $5.00 per name. Required to search: name, years to search; also helpful: DOB, SSN. Criminal records on computer from 1987, index books from 1890s.
General Information: Public Access terminal is available. No sealed or adoption records released. SASE required. Turnaround time 1-5 days. Copy fee: $.50 per page. Certification fee: $1.00 plus $1.00 per page. Fee payee: District Clerk. Personal checks accepted. Prepayment is required.

County Court Justice Center, 110 E Martin L King Dr, San Marcos, TX 78666; 512-393-7738; Fax: 512-393-7735. Hours: 8AM-5PM (CST). *Misdemeanor, Civil, Probate.*
www.co.hays.tx.us
Civil Records: Access: Mail, in person. Both court and visitors may perform in person searches. Search fee: $5.00 per name. Required to search: name, years to search. Civil cases indexed by defendant, plaintiff. Civil records on computer from 1988, index books from 1848.
Criminal Records: Access: Mail, in person. Both court and visitors may perform in person searches. Search fee: $5.00 per name. Required to search: name, years to search, DOB. Criminal records on computer from 1987, index books from 1848.
General Information: Public Access terminal is available. No juvenile, mental, sealed, or adoption records released. SASE not required. Turnaround time 1-2 weeks. Copy fee: $1.00 per page. Certification fee: $5.00. Fee payee: Hays County Clerk. Personal checks accepted. Prepayment is required.

Hemphill County

District & County Court PO Box 867, Canadian, TX 79014; 806-323-6212. Hours: 8AM-5PM (CST). *Felony, Misdemeanor, Civil, Eviction, Probate.*

Civil Records: Access: Phone, mail, in person. Both court and visitors may perform in person searches. Search fee: $10.00 per name. Required to search: name, years to search. Civil cases indexed by defendant, plaintiff. Civil records in index books from 1890s.

Criminal Records: Access: Phone, mail, in person. Both court and visitors may perform in person searches. Search fee: $10.00 per name. Required to search: name, years to search, DOB. Criminal records in index books from 1890s.
General Information: Public Access terminal is available. No juvenile, mental, sealed, or adoption records released. SASE required. Turnaround time 1-2 days. Fax notes: Fee to fax results is $1.00 per page. Copy fee: $1.00 per page. Certification fee: $5.00 per page. Fee payee: Hemphill County Clerk. Personal checks accepted. Prepayment is required.

Henderson County

District Court Henderson County Courthouse, Athens, TX 75751; 903-675-6115. Hours: 8AM-5PM (CST). *Felony, Civil.*

Civil Records: Access: Mail, in person. Both court and visitors may perform in person searches. Search fee: $5.00 per name. Required to search: name, years to search. Civil cases indexed by defendant, plaintiff. Civil records on computer from 1987, index books from 1849.
Criminal Records: Access: Mail, in person. Both court and visitors may perform in person searches. Search fee: $5.00 per name. Required to search: name, years to search, DOB; also helpful: SSN. Criminal records on computer from 1987, index books from 1849.
General Information: No juvenile, mental, sealed, or adoption records released. SASE required. Turnaround time 1-2 days. Copy fee: $1.00 per page. Certification fee: $2.00. Fee payee: District Clerk. Personal checks accepted. Prepayment is required.

County Court PO Box 632, Athens, TX 75751; 903-675-6140. Hours: 8AM-5PM (CST). *Misdemeanor, Civil, Probate.*

Civil Records: Access: Mail, in person. Both court and visitors may perform in person searches. Search fee: $5.00 per name. Required to search: name, years to search. Civil cases indexed by defendant, plaintiff. Civil records on computer from 1990, index books from 1900s.
Criminal Records: Access: Mail, fax, in person. Both court and visitors may perform in person searches. Search fee: $5.00 per name. Required to search: name, years to search, DOB, SSN. Criminal records on computer from 1984, index books from 1900s.
General Information: No juvenile, mental, sealed, or adoption records released. SASE required. Turnaround time 1-2 weeks. Fax notes: Fee to fax results is $2.00 per page. Copy fee: $1.00 per page. Certification fee: No certification fee. Fee payee: County Clerk. Personal checks accepted. Prepayment is required.

Hidalgo County

District Court 100 N Closner, Box 87, Edinburg, TX 78540; 956-318-2200. Hours: 8AM-5PM (CST). *Felony, Civil.*

Civil Records: Access: Mail, in person. Only the court performs in person searches; visitors may not. Search fee: $5.00 per name. Required to search: name, years to search. Civil cases indexed by defendant, plaintiff. Civil records on computer from 1987.
Criminal Records: Access: Mail, in person. Only the court performs in person searches; visitors may not. Search fee: $5.00 per name. Required to search: name, years to search, DOB. Criminal records on computer from 1987.
General Information: No juvenile, mental, sealed, or adoption records released. SASE required. Turnaround time 1-2 days. Copy fee: $1.00 per page. Certification fee: $1.00. Fee payee: District Clerk. Business checks accepted. Prepayment is required.

County Court PO Box 58, Edinburg, TX 78540; 956-318-2100. Hours: 7:30AM-5:30PM (CST). *Misdemeanor, Civil, Probate.*

Civil Records: Access: Mail, in person. Both court and visitors may perform in person searches. Search fee: $5.00 per name. Required to search: name, years to search. Civil cases indexed by defendant, plaintiff. Civil records on computer to 1985, index books before 1985.

Criminal Records: Access: Mail, in person. Both court and visitors may perform in person searches. Search fee: $5.00 per name. Required to search: name, years to search. Criminal records on computer from 1985, index books after 1985.

General Information: Public Access terminal is available. (Criminal only.) No juvenile, mental, sealed, or adoption records released. SASE required. Turnaround time 1-2 days. Copy fee: $1.00 per page. Certification fee: $5.00. Fee payee: County Clerk. Business checks accepted. Prepayment is required.

Hill County

District Court PO Box 634, Hillsboro, TX 76645; 254-582-4042. Hours: 8AM-5PM (CST). *Felony, Civil.*

Civil Records: Access: Mail, in person. Both court and visitors may perform in person searches. Search fee: $5.00 per name. Required to search: name, years to search. Civil cases indexed by defendant, plaintiff. Civil records on optical imaging from September, 1993, on computer from 1991, microfilm from 1930s to 1950s, index books from 1900s.

Criminal Records: Access: Mail, in person. Both court and visitors may perform in person searches. Search fee: $5.00 per name. Required to search: name, years to search; also helpful: DOB, SSN. Criminal records on optical imaging from September, 1993, on computer from 1989, microfilm from 1930s to 1950s, index books from 1900s.

General Information: No juvenile, mental, sealed, or adoption records released. SASE required. Turnaround time 1-2 days. Copy fee: $1.00 per page. Certification fee: $1.00. Fee payee: District Clerk. Personal checks accepted. Prepayment is required.

County Court PO Box 398, Hillsboro, TX 76645; 254-582-4030. 8AM-5PM . *Misdemeanor, Probate.*

General Information: Turnaround time 1-2 days. Fee payee: County Clerk. Prepayment is required.

Hockley County

District Court 802 Houston St, Ste 316, Levelland, TX 79336; 806-894-8527; Fax: 806-894-3891. Hours: 9AM-5PM (CST). *Felony, Civil.*

Civil Records: Access: Phone, mail, in person. Both court and visitors may perform in person searches. Search fee: $5.00 per name. Required to search: name, years to search. Civil cases indexed by defendant, plaintiff. Civil records on computer from 1992, archived from 1929.

Criminal Records: Access: Phone, mail, in person. Both court and visitors may perform in person searches. Search fee: $5.00 per name. Required to search: name, years to search. Criminal records on computer from 1992, archived from 1929.

General Information: No juvenile, mental, sealed, or adoption records released. SASE required. Turnaround time 1-2 days. Copy fee: $1.00 per page. Certification fee: $2.00. Fee payee: District Clerk. Personal checks accepted. Prepayment is required.

County Court County Courthouse, 802 Houston St Ste 213, Levelland, TX 79336; 806-894-3185. Hours: 9AM-5PM (CST). *Misdemeanor, Civil, Probate.*

Civil Records: Access: Mail, in person. Both court and visitors may perform in person searches. No search fee. Required to search: name, years to search. Civil cases

indexed by defendant, plaintiff. Civil records on computer from 1990, index books from 1960.

Criminal Records: Access: Mail, in person. Both court and visitors may perform in person searches. Search fee: $5.00 per name. Required to search: name, years to search; also helpful: DOB. Criminal records on computer from 1990, index books from 1960.

General Information: Public Access terminal is available. No juvenile, mental, sealed, or adoption records released. SASE required. Turnaround time 1-2 days. Copy fee: $1.00 per page. Certification fee: $5.00. Fee payee: Hockley County Clerk. Personal checks accepted.

Hood County

District Court County Courthouse, Granbury, TX 76048; 817-579-3236; Fax: 817-579-3239. Hours: 8AM-5PM (CST). *Felony, Civil.*

Civil Records: Access: Mail, in person. Both court and visitors may perform in person searches. Search fee: $5.00 per name. Required to search: name, years to search. Civil cases indexed by defendant, plaintiff. Civil records on computer and microfiche from 1983, index books before 1983.

Criminal Records: Access: Mail, in person. Both court and visitors may perform in person searches. Search fee: $5.00 per name. Required to search: name, years to search, DOB, SSN, signed release. Criminal records on computer and microfiche from 1983, index books before 1983.

General Information: No juvenile, mental, sealed, or adoption records released. SASE required. Turnaround time 1-2 days. Copy fee: $1.00 per page. Certification fee: $1.00. Fee payee: District Clerk. Personal checks accepted. Prepayment is required.

County Court PO Box 339, Granbury, TX 76048; 817-579-3222; Fax: 817-579-3227. Hours: 8AM-5PM (CST). *Misdemeanor, Civil, Probate.*

Civil Records: Access: Mail, in person. Both court and visitors may perform in person searches. Search fee: $5.00 per name. Required to search: name, years to search. Civil cases indexed by defendant, plaintiff. Civil records in index books.

Criminal Records: Access: Mail, in person. Both court and visitors may perform in person searches. Search fee: $5.00 per name. Required to search: name, years to search; also helpful: DOB. Criminal records on computer and microfiche from 1982, index books before 1982.

General Information: Public Access terminal is available. No juvenile, mental, sealed, or adoption records released. SASE required. Turnaround time 1 day. Copy fee: $1.00 per page. Certification fee: $5.00. Fee payee: Hood County Clerk. Personal checks accepted. Prepayment is required.

Hopkins County

District Court PO Box 391 (411 College St), Sulphur Springs, TX 75482; 903-438-4081. Hours: 8AM-5PM (CST). *Felony, Civil.*

Civil Records: Access: Mail, in person. Both court and visitors may perform in person searches. Search fee: $5.00 per name. Required to search: name, years to search. Civil cases indexed by defendant, plaintiff. Civil records on computer from 1987, index books from 1840, archived from 1890.

Criminal Records: Access: Mail, in person. Both court and visitors may perform in person searches. Search fee: $5.00 per name. Required to search: name, years to search. Criminal records on computer from 1987, index books from 1840, archived from 1890.

General Information: Public Access terminal is available. No juvenile, mental, sealed, or adoption records released. SASE required. Turnaround time 2 days. Copy fee: $1.00 per page. Certification fee: $2.00.

Fee payee: District Clerk. Personal checks accepted. Prepayment is required.

County Court PO Box 288, Sulphur Springs, TX 75483; 903-438-4074; Fax: 903-438-4007. Hours: 8AM-5PM (CST). *Misdemeanor, Civil, Probate.*

www.hopkinscountytx.org/departments.htm

Civil Records: Access: Mail, in person. Both court and visitors may perform in person searches. Search fee: $5.00 per name. Required to search: name, years to search. Civil cases indexed by defendant, plaintiff. Civil records on computer since 1992, index books to 1846.

Criminal Records: Access: Mail, in person. Both court and visitors may perform in person searches. Search fee: $5.00 per name. Required to search: name, years to search; also helpful-DOB, SSN, signed release. Criminal records on computer from 1985, index books from 1846.

General Information: Public Access terminal is available. No juvenile, mental, sealed, or adoption records released. SASE required. Turnaround time 1-2 days. Fax notes: Will not fax results. Copy fee: $1.00 per page. Certification fee: $5.00. Fee payee: County Clerk. Personal checks accepted. Prepayment required.

Houston County

District Court County Courthouse, 410 E Houston, PO Box 1186, Crockett, TX 75835; 936-544-3255 x229; Fax: 936-544-9523. Hours: 8AM-5PM (CST). *Felony, Civil.*

Civil Records: Access: Fax, mail, in person. Both court and visitors may perform in person searches. Search fee: $5.00 per name. Required to search: name, years to search. Civil cases indexed by plaintiff. Civil records on computer from 10/99, index books since 1800s.

Criminal Records: Access: Fax, mail, in person. Both court and visitors may perform in person searches. Search fee: $5.00 per name. Required to search: name, years to search, signed release; also helpful: DOB, SSN. Criminal records on computer since 10/99, index books since 1800s.

General Information: No juvenile, mental, sealed, or adoption records released. SASE required. Turnaround time 1-2 days. Fax notes: $3.50 for first page, $.50 each add'l. Copy fee: $1.00 per page. Certification fee: No certification fee. Fee payee: District Clerk. Personal checks accepted. Prepayment is required.

County Court PO Box 370, Crockett, TX 75835; 936-544-3255; Fax: 936-544-8053. Hours: 8AM-4:30 (CST). *Misdemeanor, Civil, Probate.*

Civil Records: Access: Mail, in person. Both court and visitors may perform in person searches. Search fee: $5.00 per name. Required to search: name, years to search. Civil cases indexed by defendant, plaintiff. Civil records on computer since 2000, microfiche since 1983, index books since 1881 (probate).

Criminal Records: Access: Mail, in person. Both court and visitors may perform in person searches. Search fee: $5.00 per name. Required to search: name, years to search. Criminal records on computer since 2000, index books since 1881.

General Information: Public Access terminal is available. No juvenile, mental, sealed, or adoption records released. SASE not required. Turnaround time 1-2 days. Fax notes: Will not fax results. Copy fee: $1.00 per page. Certification fee: $5.00. Fee payee: County Clerk. Personal checks accepted. Prepayment is required.

Howard County

District Court PO Box 2138, Big Spring, TX 79721; 915-264-2223; Fax: 915-264-2256. Hours: 8AM-5PM (CST). *Felony, Civil.*

Civil Records: Access: Mail, in person. Both court and visitors may perform in person searches. Search fee:

$5.00 per name. Required to search: name, years to search. Civil cases indexed by defendant, plaintiff. Civil records on computer from 1990, index books to 1881.
Criminal Records: Access: Mail, in person. Both court and visitors may perform in person searches. Search fee: $5.00 per name. Required to search: name, years to search. Criminal records on computer from 1990, index books from 1881.
General Information: No juvenile, mental, sealed or adoption records released. SASE required. Turnaround time 1-2 days. Fax notes: Fee to fax results is $1.00 per page. Copy fee: $1.00 per page. Certification fee: $1.00 per page. Fee payee: District Clerk. Personal checks accepted. Prepayment is required.

County Court PO Box 1468, Big Spring, TX 79721; 915-264-2213; Fax: 915-264-2215. Hours: 8AM-5PM (CST). *Misdemeanor, Civil, Probate.*

Civil Records: Access: Phone, mail, in person. Both court and visitors may perform in person searches. Search fee: $5.00 per name. Required to search: name, years to search. Civil cases indexed by defendant, plaintiff. Civil records in index books since 1881.
Criminal Records: Access: Phone, mail, in person. Both court and visitors may perform in person searches. Search fee: $5.00 per name. Required to search: name, years to search. Criminal records in index books since 1881.
General Information: No juvenile, mental, sealed, or adoption records released. SASE not required. Turnaround time 1-2 days. Fax notes: $5.00 per document. Copy fee: $1.00 per page. Certification fee: $5.00. Fee payee: County Clerk. Business checks accepted. Prepayment is required.

Hudspeth County

District & County Court PO Drawer 58, Sierra Blanca, TX 79851; 915-369-2301; Fax: 915-369-3005. Hours: 8AM-5PM (MST). *Felony, Misdemeanor, Civil, Eviction, Probate.*

Civil Records: Access: Phone, fax, mail, in person. Both court and visitors may perform in person searches. Search fee: $5.00 per name. Required to search: name, years to search. Civil cases indexed by defendant, plaintiff. Civil records in index books from 1900s; on computer since.
Criminal Records: Access: Phone, fax, mail, in person. Both court and visitors may perform in person searches. Search fee: $5.00 per name. Required to search: name, years to search, DOB. Criminal records in index books from 1900s; on computer since.
General Information: Public Access terminal is available. No juvenile, mental, sealed, or adoption records released. SASE required. Turnaround time 1-2 days. Fax notes: $1.00 per page. Copy fee: $1.00 per page. Certification fee: $5.00. Fee payee: District/County Clerk. Personal checks accepted. Prepayment is required.

Hunt County

District Court PO Box 1437, Greenville, TX 75403; 903-408-4172. Hours: 8AM-5PM (CST). *Felony, Civil.*

Civil Records: Access: Mail, in person. Both court and visitors may perform in person searches. Search fee: $5.00 per name. Required to search: name, years to search. Civil cases indexed by defendant, plaintiff. Civil records on computer from 1992, microfiche from 1973, index books from 1900s.
Criminal Records: Access: Mail, in person. Both court and visitors may perform in person searches. Search fee: $5.00 per name. Required to search: name, years to search, DOB. Criminal records on computer from 1992, microfiche from 1973, index books from 1900s.
General Information: Public Access terminal is available. No juvenile, sealed, or adoption records

released. SASE required. Turnaround time 1-2 days. Copy fee: $1.00 per page. Certification fee: $1.00. Fee payee: District Clerk. Personal checks accepted. Prepayment is required.

County Court PO Box 1316, Greenville, TX 75403-1316; 903-408-4130. Hours: 8AM-5PM (CST). *Misdemeanor, Civil, Probate.*

Civil Records: Access: Mail, in person. Both court and visitors may perform in person searches. Search fee: $5.00 per name. Required to search: name, years to search. Civil cases indexed by defendant, plaintiff. Civil records on computer since 1986, index books from 1940; on microfilm prior to 1986.
Criminal Records: Access: Mail, in person. Both court and visitors may perform in person searches. Search fee: $5.00 per name. Required to search: name, years to search, DOB. Criminal records on computer since 1986, index books from 1940; on microfilm prior to 1986.
General Information: Public Access terminal is available. No juvenile, mental, sealed, or adoption records released. SASE required. Turnaround time 1-2 days. Fax notes: No fee to fax results. Copy fee: $1.00 per page. Certification fee: $5.00. Fee payee: County Clerk. Personal checks accepted. Prepayment required.

Hutchinson County

District Court PO Box 580, Stinnett, TX 79083; 806-878-4017; Fax: 806-878-4042. Hours: 9AM-5PM (CST). *Felony, Civil.*

Civil Records: Access: Mail, in person. Both court and visitors may perform in person searches. Search fee: $5.00 per name. Required to search: name, years to search. Civil cases indexed by defendant, plaintiff. Civil records on computer from 1988, docket books to 1920.
Criminal Records: Access: Mail, in person. Both court and visitors may perform in person searches. Search fee: $5.00 per name. Required to search: name, years to search, signed release; also helpful: DOB, SSN. Criminal records on computer from 1988, docket books from 1920.
General Information: Public Access terminal is available. No juvenile, mental, sealed, or adoption records released. SASE required. Turnaround time 2 days. Fax notes: Fee to fax results is $1.00 per page. Copy fee: $.25 per page. $1.00 minimum. Certification fee: $1.00 per page. Fee payee: District Clerk. Personal checks accepted. Prepayment is required.

County Court PO Box 1186, Stinnett, TX 79083; 806-878-4002. Hours: 9AM-5PM (CST). *Misdemeanor, Civil, Probate.*

Civil Records: Access: Mail, in person. Both court and visitors may perform in person searches. Search fee: $5.00 per name. Required to search: name, years to search. Civil cases indexed by defendant, plaintiff. Civil records in index books from 1900s.
Criminal Records: Access: Mail, in person. Both court and visitors may perform in person searches. Search fee: $5.00 per name. Required to search: name, years to search, signed release, DOB or SSN. Criminal records on computer since 1990, index books from 1900s.
General Information: Public Access terminal is available. No juvenile, mental, sealed, or adoption records released. SASE not required. Turnaround time 2 days. Copy fee: $1.00 per page. Certification fee: $5.00. Fee payee: Carol Ann Herbst, Hutchinson County Clerk. Business checks accepted. Prepayment required.

Irion County

District & County Court PO Box 736, Mertzon, TX 76941-0736; 915-835-2421; Fax: 915-835-2008. Hours: 8AM-5PM (CST). *Felony, Misdemeanor, Civil, Eviction, Probate.*

Civil Records: Access: Mail, in person. Both court and visitors may perform in person searches. Search fee: $5.00 per name. Fee is per court. Required to search:

name, years to search. Civil cases indexed by defendant, plaintiff. Civil records in index books from 1886.
Criminal Records: Access: Mail, in person. Both court and visitors may perform in person searches. Search fee: $5.00 per name. Fee is per court. Required to search: name, years to search; also helpful: DOB, SSN. Criminal records on index books from 1886.
General Information: No juvenile, mental, or sealed records released. SASE required. Turnaround time 5-20 days. Fax notes: $1.00 per page. Copy fee: $1.00 per page. Certification fee: $1.00. County Court certification fee $5.00. Fee payee: District/County Clerk. Personal checks accepted. Prepayment required.

Jack County

District Court 100 Main, County Courthouse, Jacksboro, TX 76458; 940-567-2141; Fax: 940-567-2696. Hours: 8AM-5PM (CST). *Felony, Civil.*

Civil Records: Access: Mail, in person. Only the court performs in person searches; visitors may not. Search fee: $10.00 per name. Required to search: name, years to search. Civil cases indexed by defendant, plaintiff. Civil records in index books from 1857.
Criminal Records: Access: Mail, in person. Only the court performs in person searches; visitors may not. Search fee: $10.00 per name. Required to search: name, years to search. Criminal records in index books from 1857.
General Information: No juvenile, mental, sealed, or adoption records released. SASE required. Turnaround time 2 days. Copy fee: $.50 per page. Certification fee: $1.00. Fee payee: Jack County District Clerk. Personal checks accepted. Prepayment is required.

County Court 100 Main, Jacksboro, TX 76458; 940-567-2111. Hours: 8AM-5PM (CST). *Misdemeanor, Civil, Probate.*

Civil Records: Access: Phone, mail, in person. Both court and visitors may perform in person searches. Search fee: $5.00 per name. Required to search: name, years to search. Civil cases indexed by defendant, plaintiff. Civil records in index books from 1856.
Criminal Records: Access: Phone, mail, in person. Both court and visitors may perform in person searches. Search fee: $5.00 per name. Required to search: name, years to search. Criminal records in index books from 1856.
General Information: No juvenile, mental, sealed, or adoption records released. SASE required. Turnaround time 1-2 days. Copy fee: $1.00 per page. Certification fee: $5.00. Fee payee: Jack County Clerk. Personal checks accepted. Prepayment is required.

Jackson County

District Court 115 W Main Rm 203, Edna, TX 77957; 361-782-3812. 8AM-5PM *Felony, Civil.*

Civil Records: Access: Phone, mail, in person. Both court and visitors may perform in person searches. Search fee: $5.00 per name. Required to search: name, years to search. Civil cases indexed by defendant, plaintiff. Civil records in index books from 1850.
Criminal Records: Access: Phone, mail, in person. Both court and visitors may perform in person searches. Search fee: $5.00 per name. Required to search: name, years to search. Criminal records on microfiche from 1981, index books from 1850.
General Information: No juvenile, mental, sealed, or adoption records released. SASE required. Turnaround time 1-2 days. Copy fee: $1.00 per page. Certification fee: $1.00. Fee payee: District Clerk. Personal checks accepted. Prepayment is required.

County Court 115 W Main Rm101, Edna, TX 77957; 361-782-3563. Hours: 8AM-5PM (CST). *Misdemeanor, Civil, Probate.*

Civil Records: Access: Mail, in person. Both court and visitors may perform in person searches. Search fee:

$5.00 per name. Required to search: name, years to search. Civil cases indexed by defendant, plaintiff. Civil records in index books from 1900s; computerized back to 1993.

Criminal Records: Access: In person only. Both court and visitors may perform in person searches. Search fee: $5.00 per name. Required to search: name, years to search, DOB, offense, date of offense. Criminal records in index books from 1900s; computerized back to 1993.

General Information: Public Access terminal is available. No juvenile, mental, sealed, or adoption records released. SASE not required. Turnaround time 1-2 days. Fax notes: Fee to fax results is $4.25 for the 1st page and $2.25 per page thereafter. Copy fee: $1.00 per page. Certification fee: $5.00. Fee payee: County Clerk. Personal checks accepted. Prepayment is required.

Jasper County

District Court County Courthouse #202, PO Box 2088, Jasper, TX 75951; 409-384-2721. Hours: 8AM-4:30PM (CST). *Felony, Civil.*

Civil Records: Access: Mail, in person. Only the court performs in person searches; visitors may not. Search fee: $5.00 per name. Required to search: name, years to search. Civil cases indexed by defendant, plaintiff. Civil records on computer since 1991, index books and microfilm since 1850s.

Criminal Records: Access: Mail, in person. Only the court performs in person searches; visitors may not. Search fee: $5.00 per name. Required to search: name, years to search. Criminal records on computer since 12/96; index books and microfilm since 1850s.

General Information: No juvenile, mental, sealed, or adoption records released. SASE required. Turnaround time 1-2 days. Copy fee: $1.00 per page. Certification fee: No certification fee. Fee payee: District Clerk/Court. Personal checks accepted. Prepayment is required.

County Court Rm 103, Courthouse, Main at Lamar, PO Box 2070, Jasper, TX 75951; 409-384-9481; Fax: 409-384-7198. Hours: 8AM-5PM (CST). *Misdemeanor, Civil, Probate.*

Civil Records: Access: Phone, mail, fax, in person. Both court and visitors may perform in person searches. Search fee: $10.00 per name. There is no fee if you do the search yourself. Required to search: name, years to search. Civil cases indexed by defendant, plaintiff. Civil records in index books; on computer back to 1987.

Criminal Records: Access: Phone, mail, fax, in person. Both court and visitors may perform in person searches. Search fee: $10.00 per name. There is no fee if you do the search yourself. Required to search: name, years to search, DOB; also helpful: SSN. Criminal records in index books; on computer back to 1987.

General Information: Public Access terminal is available. No juvenile, mental, sealed, or adoption records released. SASE not required. Turnaround time 1 day. Fax notes: Fee to fax results is $3.00 1st page; $1.00 each add'l. Copy fee: $1.00 per page. Certification fee: $5.00. Fee payee: Debbie Newman County Clerk. Personal checks accepted. Personal checks require drivers license. Prepayment is required.

Jeff Davis County

District & County Court PO Box 398, Fort Davis, TX 79734; 915-426-3251; Fax: 915-426-3760. Hours: 9AM-Noon, 1-5PM (CST). *Felony, Misdemeanor, Civil, Eviction, Probate.*

Civil Records: Access: Mail, in person. Both court and visitors may perform in person searches. Search fee: $5.00 per name. Required to search: name, years to search. Civil cases indexed by defendant, plaintiff. Civil records in index books.

Criminal Records: Access: Mail, in person. Both court and visitors may perform in person searches. Search fee: $5.00 per name. Required to search: name, years to search. Criminal records in index books.

General Information: No juvenile, mental, sealed, or adoption records released. SASE required. Turnaround time 2 days. Copy fee: $1.00 per page. Certification fee: $5.00. Fee payee: County Clerk. Personal checks accepted. Prepayment is required.

Jefferson County

District Court PO Box 3707 (Pearl St Courthouse), Beaumont, TX 77704; 409-835-8580; Fax: 409-835-8527. Hours: 8AM-5PM (CST). *Felony, Civil.*

www.co.jefferson.tx.us

Civil Records: Access: Mail, online, in person. Both court and visitors may perform in person searches. Search fee: $5.00 per name. Required to search: name, years to search. Civil cases indexed by defendant, plaintiff. Civil records on computer and index books since 1940s. Online access to the civil records index is available at www.co.jefferson.tx.us/dclerk/civil_index/main.htm. Search by defendant or plaintiff by year 1985 to present. Search results are not certified unless done by the court itself.

Criminal Records: Access: Mail, online, in person. Both court and visitors may perform in person searches. Search fee: $5.00 per name. Required to search: name, years to search; also helpful: DOB, SSN. Criminal records on computer and index books since 1940s. Online access to the criminal records index is available at www.co.jefferson.tx.us/dclerk/criminal_index/main.htm. Search by name by year 1981 to present.

General Information: Public Access terminal is available. (Civil, Family & E-file on selected cases.) No juvenile, mental, sealed, or adoption records released. SASE required. Turnaround time 2-4 days. Copy fee: $1.00 per page. Certification fee: $1.00. Fee payee: District Clerk. Personal checks accepted. Prepayment is required.

County Court PO Box 1151, Beaumont, TX 77704; 409-835-8479; Fax: 409-839-2394. Hours: 8AM-5PM (CST). *Misdemeanor, Civil, Probate.*

Civil Records: Access: Fax, mail, in person. Both court and visitors may perform in person searches. Search fee: $5.00 per name. Required to search: name, years to search. Civil cases indexed by defendant, plaintiff. Civil records on computer since 11/95, index books to 1836.

Criminal Records: Access: Fax, mail, in person. Both court and visitors may perform in person searches. Search fee: $5.00 per name. Required to search: name, years to search, DOB. Criminal records on computer since 02/25/91, index books to 1836.

General Information: Public Access terminal is available. No juvenile, mental, sealed, or adoption records released. SASE required. Turnaround time 1 day. Fax notes: $3.00 for first page, $.50 each add'l. Copy fee: $1.00 per page. Certification fee: $5.00. Fee payee: County Clerk. Personal checks accepted. Prepayment is required.

Jim Hogg County

District & County Court PO Box 878, Hebbronville, TX 78361; 361-527-4031; Fax: 361-527-5843. Hours: 9AM-5PM (CST). *Felony, Misdemeanor, Civil, Eviction, Probate.*

Civil Records: Access: Mail, fax, in person. Both court and visitors may perform in person searches. Search fee: $15.00 per name. Required to search: name, years to search. Civil cases indexed by defendant, plaintiff. Civil records in index books.

Criminal Records: Access: In person only. Visitors must perform in person searches for themselves. No search fee. Required to search: name, years to search. Criminal records in index books.

General Information: No juvenile, mental, sealed, or adoption records released. SASE required. Turnaround time 2-4 days. Fax notes: Fee to fax results is $3.00 per page. Copy fee: $1.00 per page. Certification fee: $5.00. Fee payee: District Clerk. Personal checks accepted. Prepayment is required.

Jim Wells County

79th District Court PO Drawer 2219, Alice, TX 78333; 361-668-5717. Hours: 8AM-Noon, 1-5PM (CST). *Felony, Civil.*

Civil Records: Access: Mail, in person. Both court and visitors may perform in person searches. Search fee: $5.00 per name. Required to search: name, years to search. Civil cases indexed by defendant, plaintiff. Civil records on computer since 1992, index books since 1912.

Criminal Records: Access: Mail, in person. Both court and visitors may perform in person searches. Search fee: $5.00 per name. Required to search: name, years to search; also helpful: SSN. Criminal records on computer since 1992, index books since 1912.

General Information: No juvenile, mental, sealed, or adoption records released. SASE required. Turnaround time 2 days. Copy fee: $1.00 per page. Certification fee: $2.00. Fee payee: District Clerk. Personal checks accepted. Prepayment is required.

County Court PO Box 1459, 200 N Almond, Alice, TX 78333; 361-668-5702. Hours: 8:30AM-Noon, 1-5PM (CST). *Misdemeanor, Civil, Probate.*

Civil Records: Access: Phone, mail, in person. Both court and visitors may perform in person searches. Search fee: $10.00 per name. Required to search: name, years to search. Civil cases indexed by defendant, plaintiff. Civil records in index books.

Criminal Records: Access: Phone, mail, in person. Both court and visitors may perform in person searches. Search fee: $10.00 per name. Required to search: name, years to search, address, DOB. Criminal records on computer since 1986, index books also.

General Information: No juvenile, mental, sealed, or adoption records released. SASE not required. Turnaround time 1 day. Copy fee: $1.00 per page. Certification fee: $5.00. Fee payee: County Clerk. Personal checks accepted. Prepayment is required.

Johnson County

District Court PO Box 495, Cleburne, TX 76033-0495; 817-556-6843; Fax: 817-556-6120. Hours: 8AM-5PM (CST). *Felony, Civil.*

Civil Records: Access: Fax, mail, in person. Both court and visitors may perform in person searches. Search fee: $5.00 per name. Required to search: name; also helpful: years to search. Civil cases indexed by defendant, plaintiff. Civil records on computer from 1989, index books back to 1800s.

Criminal Records: Access: Fax, mail, in person. Both court and visitors may perform in person searches. Search fee: $5.00 per name. Required to search: name; also helpful: years to search, aliases. Criminal records on computer from 1989, index books back to 1800s.

General Information: Public Access terminal is available. No juvenile, mental, sealed, or adoption records released. SASE required. Turnaround time 2-4 days. Fax notes: Fee to fax results is $1.00 per page. Copy fee: $.50 per page. Certification fee: $1.00. Fee payee: District Clerk. Business checks accepted. Prepayment is required.

County Court Room 104, PO Box 662, Cleburne, TX 76033-0662; 817-556-6300. Hours: 8AM-Noon, 1-4:30PM (CST). *Misdemeanor, Civil, Probate.*

Civil Records: Access: Mail, in person. Both court and visitors may perform in person searches. Search fee: $5.00 per name. Required to search: name, years to

search. Civil cases indexed by defendant, plaintiff. Civil records on computer to 1988, index books before 1988.

Criminal Records: Access: Mail, in person. Both court and visitors may perform in person searches. Search fee: $5.00 per name. Required to search: name, years to search, and DOB or SSN. Criminal records on computer since 1988, index books before 1988.

General Information: Public Access terminal is available. No juvenile, mental, sealed, or adoption records released. SASE required. Turnaround time 1-2 days. Copy fee: $1.00 per page. Certification fee: $5.00. Fee payee: County Clerk. Business checks accepted. Prepayment is required.

Jones County

District Court PO Box 308, Anson, TX 79501; 915-823-3731; Fax: 915-823-3513 (Attn: Nona Carter). Hours: 8AM-5PM *Felony, Misdemeanor, Civil.*

Civil Records: Access: Mail, in person. Both court and visitors may perform in person searches. Search fee: $5.00 per name. Required to search: name, years to search. Civil cases indexed by defendant, plaintiff. Civil records on computer since 1990, index books since 1881.

Criminal Records: Access: Mail, in person. Both court and visitors may perform in person searches. Search fee: $5.00 per name. Required to search: name, years to search, DOB. Criminal records on computer since 1986, index books since 1881.

General Information: No juvenile, mental, sealed, or adoption records released. SASE required. Turnaround time same day. Copy fee: $1.00 per page. Certification fee: $2.00. Fee payee: Nona Carter, District Clerk. Personal checks accepted. Can set up deposit account. Prepayment is required.

Karnes County

District Court County Courthouse, 101 N Panna Maria Ave, Karnes City, TX 78118-2930; 830-780-2562; Fax: 830-780-3227. Hours: 8AM-Noon, 1-5PM (CST). *Felony, Civil.*

Civil Records: Access: Mail, in person. Both court and visitors may perform in person searches. Search fee: $5.00 per name. Required to search: name, years to search. Civil cases indexed by defendant, plaintiff. Civil records in index books.

Criminal Records: Access: Mail, in person. Both court and visitors may perform in person searches. Search fee: $5.00 per name. Required to search: name, years to search. Criminal records in index books.

General Information: No juvenile, mental, sealed, or adoption records released. SASE required. Turnaround time 1-2 days. Copy fee: $1.00 per page. Certification fee: $2.00. Fee payee: District Clerk. Personal checks accepted. Prepayment is required.

County Court 101 N Panna Maria Ave #9 Courthouse, Karnes City, TX 78118-2929; 830-780-3938; Fax: 830-780-4576. Hours: 8AM-5PM (CST). *Misdemeanor, Civil, Probate.*

Civil Records: Access: Mail, in person. Both court and visitors may perform in person searches. Search fee: $10.00 per name. Required to search: name, years to search. Civil cases indexed by defendant, plaintiff. Civil records in index books, no computerization.

Criminal Records: Access: Mail, in person. Both court and visitors may perform in person searches. Search fee: $10.00 per name. Required to search: name, years to search. Criminal records in index books, no computerization.

General Information: No juvenile, mental, sealed, or adoption records released. SASE required. Turnaround time 2 days. Fax notes: Fee to fax results is $2.00 per page. Copy fee: $1.00 per page. Certification fee: $5.00. Fee payee: Elizabeth Swize, County Clerk. Personal checks accepted. Prepayment is required.

Kaufman County

District Court County Courthouse, 100 W Mulberry St, Kaufman, TX 75142; 972-932-4331. Hours: 8AM-5PM (CST). *Felony, Civil.*

Civil Records: Access: Phone, mail, in person. Both court and visitors may perform in person searches. Search fee: $5.00 per name. Required to search: name, years to search. Civil cases indexed by defendant, plaintiff. Civil records on computer or books from 1849.

Criminal Records: Access: Phone, mail, in person. Both court and visitors may perform in person searches. Search fee: $5.00 per name. Required to search: name, years to search. Criminal records on computer or books from 1849.

General Information: No sealed, or adoption records released. SASE required. Turnaround time up to 1 week. Copy fee: $1.00 per page. Certification fee: $1.00. Fee payee: Kaufman Distric Clerk. Personal checks accepted. Prepayment is required.

County Court County Courthouse, Kaufman, TX 75142; 972-932-4331. Hours: 8AM-4:30PM (CST). *Misdemeanor, Civil, Probate.*

Civil Records: Access: Mail, in person. Only the court performs in person searches; visitors may not. Search fee: $5.00 per name. Required to search: name, years to search. Civil cases indexed by defendant, plaintiff. Civil records on computer to 1985, index books before 1985.

Criminal Records: Access: Mail, in person. Only the court performs in person searches; visitors may not. Search fee: $5.00 per name. Required to search: name, years to search. Criminal records on computer from 1985, index books before 1985.

General Information: Public Access terminal is available. No juvenile, mental, sealed, or adoption records released. SASE required. Turnaround time 10 days. Copy fee: $1.00 per page. Certification fee: $5.00. Fee payee: County Clerk. Personal checks accepted. Prepayment is required.

Kendall County

District Court 201 E. San Antonia, #201, Boerne, TX 78006; 830-249-9343. Hours: 8AM-Noon, 1-5PM (CST). *Felony, Civil.*

Civil Records: Access: Mail, in person. Both court and visitors may perform in person searches. Search fee: $5.00 per name. Required to search: name, years to search. Civil cases indexed by defendant, plaintiff. Civil records in index books.

Criminal Records: Access: Mail, in person. Both court and visitors may perform in person searches. Search fee: $5.00 per name. Required to search: name, years to search; also helpful: DOB, SSN. Criminal records in index books.

General Information: No juvenile, mental, sealed, or adoption records released. SASE required. Turnaround time 2-4 days. Copy fee: $.50 per page. Certification fee: $1.00 per page. Fee payee: District Clerk. Personal checks accepted. Prepayment is required.

County Court 201 E San Antonio #127, Boerne, TX 78006; 830-249-9343; Fax: 830-249-3472. Hours: 8AM-5PM (CST). *Misdemeanor, Probate.*

Civil Records: Access: Mail, in person. Both court and visitors may perform in person searches. Search fee: $10.00 per name. Required to search: name, years to search. Civil cases indexed by defendant, plaintiff. Civil records in index books from 1860s.

Criminal Records: Access: Mail, in person. Both court and visitors may perform in person searches. Search fee: $10.00 per name. Required to search: name, years to search. Criminal records in index books from 1860s.

General Information: No juvenile, mental, sealed, or adoption records released. SASE required. Turnaround time 2-4 days. Fax notes: No fee to fax results. Copy fee: $1.00 per page. Certification fee: $5.00. Fee payee:

County Clerk. Personal checks accepted. Prepayment is required.

Kenedy County

District & County Court PO Box 227, Sarita, TX 78385; 361-294-5220; Fax: 361-294-5218. Hours: 8:30AM-Noon, 1PM-4:30PM (CST). *Felony, Misdemeanor, Civil, Eviction, Probate.*

Civil Records: Access: Phone, mail, in person. Both court and visitors may perform in person searches. Search fee: $5.00 per name. Required to search: name, years to search. Civil cases indexed by defendant, plaintiff. Civil records on microfilm since 1991, minute books since 1921.

Criminal Records: Access: Phone, mail, in person. Both court and visitors may perform in person searches. Search fee: $5.00 per name. Required to search: name, years to search. Criminal records on microfilm since 1991, minute books since 1921.

General Information: No juvenile, mental, sealed, or adoption records released. SASE not required. Turnaround time 5 days. Copy fee: $1.00 per page. Certification fee: $5.00. Fee payee: District/County Clerk. Personal checks accepted. Prepayment required.

Kent County

District & County Court PO Box 9, Jayton, TX 79528; 806-237-3881; Fax: 806-237-2632. Hours: 8:30AM-Noon, 1-5PM (CST). *Felony, Misdemeanor, Civil, Eviction, Probate.*

Civil Records: Access: Mail, in person. Both court and visitors may perform in person searches. Search fee: $5.00 per name. Required to search: name, years to search. Civil cases indexed by defendant, plaintiff. Civil records in index books.

Criminal Records: Access: Mail, in person. Both court and visitors may perform in person searches. Search fee: $5.00 per name. Required to search: name, years to search. Criminal records in index books.

General Information: No juvenile, mental, sealed, or adoption records released. SASE required. Turnaround time as soon as possible. Copy fee: $1.00 per page. Certification fee: $5.00 plus $1.00 per page. Fee payee: County Clerk. Only cashiers checks and money orders accepted. Prepayment is required.

Kerr County

District Court 700 Main, County Courthouse, Kerrville, TX 78028; 830-792-2281. Hours: 8AM-5PM (CST). *Felony, Civil.*

Civil Records: Access: Mail, in person. Both court and visitors may perform in person searches. Search fee: $5.00 per name. Required to search: name, years to search. Civil cases indexed by defendant, plaintiff. Civil records on computer from late 1991, index books after 1991.

Criminal Records: Access: Mail, in person. Both court and visitors may perform in person searches. Search fee: $5.00 per name. Required to search: name, years to search, DOB, SSN. Criminal records on computer from late 1990, index books prior.

General Information: No juvenile, mental, sealed, or adoption records released. SASE required. Turnaround time 2-4 days. Fax notes: Fee to fax results is $1.00 per page. Copy fee: $1.00 1st page; $.25 each add'l. Certification fee: $1.00 per page. Fee payee: District Clerk. Personal checks accepted. 1989. Prepayment is required.

County Court & County Court at Law 700 Main St, #122, Kerrville, TX 78028-5389; 830-792-2255; Probate phone: 830-792-2298; Fax: 830-792-2274. Hours: 8AM-5PM (CST). *Misdemeanor, Civil, Probate.*

Civil Records: Access: Phone, mail, fax, in person. Both court and visitors may perform in person searches.

Search fee: $5.00 per name. Required to search: name, years to search. Civil cases indexed by defendant, plaintiff. Civil records on computer since 1988, microfiche since 1985, index books prior to 1985.

Criminal Records: Access: Phone, mail, fax, in person. Both court and visitors may perform in person searches. Search fee: $5.00 per name. Required to search: name, years to search, DOB; also helpful: SSN. Criminal records on computer since 1988, microfiche since 1985, index books prior to 1985.

General Information: Public Access terminal is available. No juvenile, mental, sealed, or adoption records released. SASE not required. Turnaround time 3 days. Fax notes: Fee to fax results is $1.00 per page. Copy fee: $1.00 per page. Certification fee: $5.00. Fee payee: Kerr County Clerk. Only cashiers checks and money orders accepted. Prepayment is required.

Kimble County

District & County Court 501 Main St, Junction, TX 76849; 915-446-3353; Fax: 915-446-2986. Hours: 8AM-Noon, 1-5PM (CST). *Felony, Misdemeanor, Civil, Probate.*

Civil Records: Access: Mail, in person. Both court and visitors may perform in person searches. Search fee: $5.00 per name. Required to search: name, years to search. Civil cases indexed by defendant, plaintiff. Civil records in index books (records are micro-filmed for security only).

Criminal Records: Access: Mail, in person. Both court and visitors may perform in person searches. Search fee: $5.00 per name. Required to search: name, years to search, DOB. Criminal records in index books (records are micro-filmed for security only).

General Information: No juvenile, mental, sealed, or adoption records released. SASE not required. Turnaround time 3-4 days. Copy fee: $1.00 per page. Certification fee: $5.00. Fee payee: Kimble County/District Clerk. Personal checks accepted. Prepayment is required.

King County

District & County Court PO Box 135, Guthrie, TX 79236; 806-596-4412; Fax: 806-596-4664. Hours: 9AM-Noon, 1-5PM (CST). *Felony, Misdemeanor, Civil, Eviction, Probate.*

Civil Records: Access: Mail, in person. Both court and visitors may perform in person searches. Search fee: $5.00 per name. Required to search: name, years to search. Civil cases indexed by defendant, plaintiff. Civil records in index books.

Criminal Records: Access: Mail, in person. Both court and visitors may perform in person searches. Search fee: $5.00 per name. Required to search: name, years to search, DOB. Criminal records in index books.

General Information: No juvenile, mental, sealed, or adoption records released. SASE required. Turnaround time 2-4 days. Fax notes: Fee to fax results is $5.00 per document or $1.00 per page. Copy fee: $1.00 per page. Certification fee: $5.00. Fee payee: District Clerk. Personal checks accepted. Prepayment is required.

Kinney County

District & County Court PO Drawer 9, Brackettville, TX 78832; 830-563-2521; Fax: 830-563-2644. Hours: 8AM-5PM (CST). *Felony, Misdemeanor, Civil, Probate.*

Civil Records: Access: Phone, fax, mail, in person. Both court and visitors may perform in person searches. Search fee: $10.00 per name. Required to search: name, years to search. Civil cases indexed by defendant, plaintiff. Civil records in index books from 1800s; computerized back to 1990s.

Criminal Records: Access: Phone, fax, mail, in person. Both court and visitors may perform in person searches. Search fee: $10.00 per name. Required to

search: name, years to search, DOB. Criminal records in index books from 1800s; computerized records back to 1990s.

General Information: No juvenile, mental, sealed, or adoption records released. SASE required. Turnaround time 1 week. Fax notes: $3.00 for 1st page; $2.00 each add'l. Copy fee: $1.00 per page. Certification fee: Certification fee: $5.00 County; $1.00 District. Fee payee: County & District Clerk. Personal checks accepted. Prepayment is required.

Kleberg County

District & County Court at Law PO Box 312, Kingsville, TX 78364-0312; 361-595-8561; Fax: 361-595-8525. Hours: 8AM-Noon, 1-5 PM (CST). *Felony, Civil.*

Civil Records: Access: Phone, fax, mail, in person. Both court and visitors may perform in person searches. Search fee: $5.00 per name. Required to search: name, years to search. Civil cases indexed by defendant, plaintiff. Civil records in index books since 1916.

Criminal Records: Access: Phone, fax, mail, in person. Both court and visitors may perform in person searches. Search fee: $5.00 per name. Required to search: name, years to search; also helpful: DOB, SSN. Criminal records in index books since 1916.

General Information: No sealed or adoption records released. SASE required. Turnaround time 2-3 days. Fax notes: $5.00 per document. Incoming fax fee $1.00. Copy fee: $1.00 per page. Certification fee: $1.00. Fee payee: District Clerk. Personal checks accepted. (local personal checks only). Prepayment is required.

County Court - Criminal PO Box 1327, Kingsville, TX 78364; 361-595-8548. Hours: 8AM-noon; 1-5PM (CST). *Misdemeanor, Probate.*

Note: Court also handles civil cases dealing with occupational licenses and bond forfeitures.

Criminal Records: Access: Phone, mail, in person. Both court and visitors may perform in person searches. Search fee: $5.00 per name. Required to search: name, years to search, DOB. Criminal records on computer since 1989, index books since 1913.

General Information: No juvenile or mental records released. SASE required. Turnaround time same day. Copy fee: $1.00 per page. Certification fee: $5.00. Fee payee: Kleberg County Clerk. Business checks accepted. Prepayment is required.

Knox County

District & County Court PO Box 196, Benjamin, TX 79505; 940-454-2441. Hours: 8AM-Noon, 1-5PM (CST). *Felony, Misdemeanor, Civil, Eviction, Probate.*

Civil Records: Access: Mail, in person. Both court and visitors may perform in person searches. Search fee: $10.00 per name. Required to search: name, years to search. Civil cases indexed by defendant, plaintiff. Civil records in index books.

Criminal Records: Access: Mail, in person. Both court and visitors may perform in person searches. Search fee: $5.00 for a misdemeanor search; $5.00 for a felony search. Required to search: name, years to search. Criminal records in index books.

General Information: No juvenile, mental, sealed, or adoption records released. SASE required. Turnaround time 1 day. Copy fee: $1.00 per page. Certification fee: $5.00. Fee payee: District/County Clerk. Personal checks accepted. Prepayment is required.

La Salle County

District Court PO Box 340, Cotulla, TX 78014; 830-879-4434. Hours: 8AM-5PM (CST). *Felony, Civil.*

Civil Records: Access: Mail, in person. Both court and visitors may perform in person searches. Search fee: $5.00 per name. Required to search: name, years to

search. Civil cases indexed by defendant, plaintiff. Civil records in index books.

Criminal Records: Access: Mail, in person. Both court and visitors may perform in person searches. Search fee: $5.00 per name. Required to search: name, years to search. Criminal records in index books.

General Information: No juvenile, mental, sealed, or adoption records released. SASE required. Turnaround time 1-2 days. Copy fee: $1.00 per page. Certification fee: $5.00. Fee payee: District Clerk. Personal checks accepted. Prepayment is required.

District & County Courts PO Box 340, Cotulla, TX 78014; 830-879-4432; Fax: 830-879-2933. Hours: 8AM-5PM (CST). *Misdemeanor, Civil, Eviction, Probate.*

Civil Records: Access: Mail, in person. Both court and visitors may perform in person searches. Search fee: $5.00 per name. Required to search: name, years to search. Civil cases indexed by defendant, plaintiff. Civil records on computer since 1994, prior on index books.

Criminal Records: Access: Mail, in person. Both court and visitors may perform in person searches. Search fee: $5.00 per name. Required to search: name, years to search. Criminal records on computer since 1994, prior on index books.

General Information: No juvenile, mental, sealed, or adoption records released. SASE required. Turnaround time 1-2 days. Copy fee: $1.00 per page. Certification fee: $5.00. Fee payee: County Clerk. Personal checks accepted. Prepayment is required.

Lamar County

District Court 119 N Main Rm 306, Paris, TX 75460; 903-737-2427. Hours: 8AM-5PM (CST). *Felony, Civil.*

Civil Records: Access: Mail, in person. Both court and visitors may perform in person searches. Search fee: $5.00 per name. Required to search: name, years to search. Civil cases indexed by defendant, plaintiff. Civil records on computer since January, 1994, index books prior to 1994.

Criminal Records: Access: Mail, in person. Both court and visitors may perform in person searches. Search fee: $5.00 per name. Required to search: name, years to search. Criminal records on computer since January, 1994, index books prior to 1994.

General Information: Public Access terminal is available. No juvenile, mental, sealed, or adoption records released. SASE required. Turnaround time 1-2 days. Copy fee: $1.00 per page. Certification fee: No certification fee. Fee payee: District Clerk. Personal checks accepted. Prepayment is required.

County Court 119 N Main, Paris, TX 75460; 903-737-2420. Hours: 8AM-5PM (CST). *Misdemeanor, Civil, Probate.*

Civil Records: Access: Phone, fax, mail, in person. Both court and visitors may perform in person searches. Search fee: $10.00 per name. Required to search: name, years to search. Civil cases indexed by defendant, plaintiff. Civil records in index books since 1913; on computer back to 1988.

Criminal Records: Access: Phone, fax, mail, in person. Both court and visitors may perform in person searches. Search fee: $5.00 per name. Required to search: name, years to search; also helpful- drivers license number. Criminal records on computer back to 1988, index books since 1913.

General Information: No juvenile, mental, sealed, or adoption records released. SASE not required. Turnaround time 2-3 days. Copy fee: $1.00 per page. Certification fee: $5.00. Fee payee: County Clerk. Business checks accepted. Personal checks must be local. Prepayment is required.

Lamb County

District Court 100 6th Rm 212, Courthouse, Littlefield, TX 79339; 806-385-4222. Hours: 8AM-Noon, 1-5PM (CST). *Felony, Civil.*

Civil Records: Access: Mail, in person. Both court and visitors may perform in person searches. Search fee: $5.00 per name. Required to search: name, years to search. Civil cases indexed by defendant, plaintiff. Civil records on computer since 1987; on index books back to 1940.
Criminal Records: Access: Mail, in person. Both court and visitors may perform in person searches. Search fee: $10.00 per name. Required to search: name, years to search; also helpful: DOB, SSN. Criminal records in index books to 1940s; on computer since 1987.
General Information: No juvenile, mental, sealed, or adoption records released. SASE required. Turnaround time 2-3 days. Copy fee: $1.00 per page. Certification fee: $1.00 per page. Fee payee: District Court. Personal checks accepted. Prepayment is required.

County Court County Courthouse, Rm 103, Box 3, Littlefield, TX 79339-3366; 806-385-4222 X214; Fax: 806-385-6485. Hours: 8AM-5PM (CST). *Misdemeanor, Civil, Probate.*

Civil Records: Access: Mail, in person. Both court and visitors may perform in person searches. Search fee: $5.00 per name. Required to search: name, years to search. Civil cases indexed by defendant, plaintiff. Civil records in index books.
Criminal Records: Access: Mail, in person. Both court and visitors may perform in person searches. Search fee: $5.00 per name. Required to search: name, years to search; also helpful: DOB, SSN. Criminal records in index books.
General Information: No juvenile, mental, sealed, or adoption records released. SASE required. Turnaround time 1-2 days. Copy fee: $1.00 per page. Certification fee: $5.00. Fee payee: Lamb County Clerk. Personal checks accepted. Prepayment is required.

Lampasas County

District Court PO Box 327, Lampasas, TX 76550; 512-556-8271 X22; Fax: 512-556-9463. Hours: 8AM-5PM (CST). *Felony, Civil.*

Civil Records: Access: Mail, in person. Both court and visitors may perform in person searches. Search fee: $5.00 per name. Required to search: name, years to search. Civil cases indexed by defendant, plaintiff. Civil records in index books.
Criminal Records: Access: Mail, in person. Both court and visitors may perform in person searches. Search fee: $5.00 per name. Required to search: name, years to search. Criminal records in index books; on computer since.
General Information: No juvenile, mental, sealed, or adoption records released. SASE required. Turnaround time 2-4 days. Fax notes: Fee to fax results is $1.00 per page. Copy fee: $1.00 per page. Certification fee: $2.00. Fee payee: District Clerk. Business checks accepted. Prepayment is required.

County Court PO Box 347, Lampasas, TX 76550; 512-556-8271 X37. Hours: 8AM-5PM (CST). *Misdemeanor, Civil, Probate.*

Civil Records: Access: Mail, in person. Both court and visitors may perform in person searches. Search fee: $5.00 per name. Required to search: name, years to search. Civil cases indexed by defendant, plaintiff. Civil records in index books.
Criminal Records: Access: Mail, in person. Both court and visitors may perform in person searches. Search fee: $5.00 per name. Required to search: name, years to search; also helpful: DOB, SSN. Criminal records in index books.

General Information: Public Access terminal is available. No juvenile, mental, sealed, or adoption records released. SASE required. Turnaround time 1-2 days. Copy fee: $1.00 per page. Certification fee: $5.00. Fee payee: County Clerk. Personal checks accepted. Checks must be in state. Prepayment is required.

Lavaca County

District Court PO Box 306, Hallettsville, TX 77964; 361-798-2351. Hours: 8AM-Noon, 1-5PM (CST). *Felony, Civil.*

Civil Records: Access: Phone, mail, in person. Both court and visitors may perform in person searches. Search fee: $5.00 per name. Required to search: name, years to search. Civil cases indexed by defendant, plaintiff. Civil records in index books from 1847. Information released to attorneys only.
Criminal Records: Access: Mail, in person. Both court and visitors may perform in person searches. Search fee: $5.00 per name. Required to search: name, years to search. Criminal records in index books from 1847. Information released to law enforcement only.
General Information: No juvenile, Department of Human Services, adoptions and expunction records released. SASE required. Turnaround time same day. Copy fee: $1.00 per page. Certification fee: $2.00. Fee payee: Lavaca County District Clerk. Personal checks accepted. Prepayment is required.

County Court PO Box 326, Hallettsville, TX 77964; 361-798-3612. Hours: 8AM-5PM (CST). *Misdemeanor, Civil, Probate.*

Civil Records: Access: Mail, in person. Both court and visitors may perform in person searches. Search fee: $5.00 per name per 5 years. Required to search: name, years to search, DOB; also helpful: address, SSN, DL#. Civil cases indexed by defendant, plaintiff. Civil records in index books.
Criminal Records: Access: Mail, in person. Both court and visitors may perform in person searches. Search fee: $5.00 per name per 5 years. Required to search: name, years to search; also helpful: address, DOB. Criminal records in index books.
General Information: No juvenile, mental, sealed or adoption released. SASE not required. Turnaround time same day as received. Copy fee: $1.00 per page. Certification fee: $5.00 plus 1.00 per page. Fee payee: County Clerk. Personal checks accepted. Prepayment is required.

Lee County

District Court PO Box 176, Giddings, TX 78942; 979-542-2947; Fax: 979-542-2444. Hours: 8AM-Noon, 1-5PM (CST). *Felony, Civil.*

Civil Records: Access: Mail, in person. Both court and visitors may perform in person searches. Search fee: $5.00 per name. Required to search: name, years to search. Civil cases indexed by defendant, plaintiff. Civil records on index books from 1800s.
Criminal Records: Access: Mail, in person. Both court and visitors may perform in person searches. Search fee: $5.00 per name. Required to search: name, years to search; also helpful: DOB, SSN. Criminal records on computer since 1989.
General Information: No juvenile or adoption records released. Turnaround time 1-2 days. Copy fee: $1.00 per page. Certification fee: $2.00. Fee payee: District Clerk, Lee County. Personal checks accepted. Prepayment is required.

County Court PO Box 419, Giddings, TX 78942; 979-542-3684; Fax: 979-542-2623. Hours: 8AM-5PM (CST). *Misdemeanor, Civil, Probate.*

Civil Records: Access: Mail, in person. Both court and visitors may perform in person searches. Search fee: $5.00 per name. Required to search: name, years to search. Civil cases indexed by defendant, plaintiff. Civil

records in index books since 1874 (beginning 1995 on computer).
Criminal Records: Access: Mail, in person. Both court and visitors may perform in person searches. Search fee: $5.00 per name. Required to search: name, years to search. Criminal records on computer since 1992, index books since 1874.
General Information: No juvenile, mental, sealed or adoption records released. SASE required. Turnaround time 1-3 days. Copy fee: $1.00 per page. Certification fee: $5.00. Fee payee: County Clerk. Personal checks accepted. Prepayment is required.

Leon County

District Court PO Box 39, Centerville, TX 75833; 903-536-2227. Hours: 8AM-5PM (CST). *Felony, Civil.*

Civil Records: Access: Mail, in person. Both court and visitors may perform in person searches. Search fee: $5.00 per name. Required to search: name, years to search. Civil cases indexed by defendant, plaintiff. Civil records in index books.
Criminal Records: Access: Mail, in person. Only the court performs in person searches; visitors may not. Search fee: $5.00 per name. Required to search: name, years to search. Criminal records in index books.
General Information: No juvenile, mental, sealed, or adoption records released. SASE required. Turnaround time 2-4 days. Copy fee: $1.00 per page. Certification fee: $2.00. Fee payee: District Clerk. Personal checks accepted. Prepayment is required.

County Court PO Box 98, Centerville, TX 75833; 903-536-2352. Hours: 8AM-5PM (CST). *Misdemeanor, Civil, Probate.*

Civil Records: Access: Mail, in person. Both court and visitors may perform in person searches. Search fee: $5.00 per name. Required to search: name, years to search. Civil cases indexed by defendant, plaintiff. Civil records in index books.
Criminal Records: Access: Mail, in person. Both court and visitors may perform in person searches. Search fee: $5.00 per name. Required to search: name, years to search, signed release. Criminal records in index books.
General Information: No juvenile, mental, sealed, or adoption records released. SASE not required. Turnaround time 1-3 days. Copy fee: $1.00 per page. Certification fee: $5.00. Fee payee: Leon County Clerk. Business checks accepted. Personal checks accepted in person only. Prepayment is required.

Liberty County

District Court 1923 Sam Houston Rm 303, Liberty, TX 77575; 936-336-4600. Hours: 8AM-Noon, 1-5PM (CST). *Felony, Civil.*

Civil Records: Access: Mail, in person. Both court and visitors may perform in person searches. Search fee: $5.00 per name. Required to search: name, years to search. Civil cases indexed by defendant, plaintiff. Civil records on computer since 1994, index books prior.
Criminal Records: Access: Mail, in person. Both court and visitors may perform in person searches. Search fee: $5.00 per name. Required to search: name, years to search. Criminal records on computer since 1994, index books prior.
General Information: No juvenile, mental, sealed, or adoption records released. SASE required. Turnaround time 2-4 days. Copy fee: $1.00 per page. Fee payee: District Clerk. Personal checks accepted. Prepayment is required.

County Court PO Box 369, Liberty, TX 77575; 936-336-4670. Hours: 8AM-5PM (CST). *Misdemeanor, Civil, Probate.*

Civil Records: Access: Mail, in person. Both court and visitors may perform in person searches. Search fee: $5.00 per name. Required to search: name, years to

search. Civil cases indexed by defendant, plaintiff. Civil records in index books; later on computer.

Criminal Records: Access: Mail, in person. Both court and visitors may perform in person searches. Search fee: $5.00 per name. Required to search: name, years to search, DOB, SSN, signed release. Criminal records in index books; later on computer.

General Information: No juvenile, mental, sealed, or adoption records released. SASE required. Turnaround time 2-4 days. Copy fee: $1.00 per page. Certification fee: $5.00. Fee payee: County Clerk. Business checks accepted. Personal checks accepted in person only. Prepayment is required.

Limestone County

District Court PO Box 230, Groesbeck, TX 76642; 254-729-3206; Fax: 254-729-2960. Hours: 8AM-5PM (CST). *Felony, Civil.*

Civil Records: Access: Phone, fax, mail, in person. Both court and visitors may perform in person searches. Search fee: $5.00 per name. Required to search: name, years to search. Civil cases indexed by defendant, plaintiff. Civil records on computer since September 1990, index books since 1883.

Criminal Records: Access: Phone, fax, mail, in person. Both court and visitors may perform in person searches. Search fee: $5.00 per name. Required to search: name, years to search, DOB; also helpful: SSN. Criminal records on computer since September 1990, index books since 1911.

General Information: No juvenile, mental, sealed, or adoption records released. SASE not required. Turnaround time 1 week. Fax notes: $1.00 for first page, $.25 each add'l. Copy fee: $1.00 per document or $.50 for single page. Certification fee: $2.00. Fee payee: District Clerk. Personal checks accepted.

County Court PO Box 350, Groesbeck, TX 76642; 254-729-5504; Fax: 254-729-2951. Hours: 8AM-5PM (CST). *Misdemeanor, Civil, Probate.*

Civil Records: Access: Mail, in person. Both court and visitors may perform in person searches. Search fee: $5.00 per name. Required to search: name, years to search. Civil cases indexed by defendant, plaintiff. Civil records in index books.

Criminal Records: Access: Mail, in person. Both court and visitors may perform in person searches. Search fee: $5.00 per name. Required to search: name, years to search; also helpful: DOB, SSN, signed release. Criminal records in index books.

General Information: Public Access terminal is available. No juvenile, mental, sealed, or adoption records released. SASE not required. Turnaround time 2 days. Fax notes: Fee to fax results is $2.00 per page. Copy fee: $1.00 per page. Certification fee: $5.00. Fee payee: Limestone County Clerk. Personal checks accepted. Prepayment is required.

Lipscomb County

District & County Court PO Box 70, Lipscomb, TX 79056; 806-862-3091; Fax: 806-862-3004. Hours: 8:30AM-Noon, 1-5PM (CST). *Felony, Misdemeanor, Civil, Eviction, Probate.*

Civil Records: Access: Fax, mail, in person. Both court and visitors may perform in person searches. Search fee: $5.00 per name. Required to search: name. Civil cases indexed by defendant, plaintiff. Civil records in index books since 1887; on computer back to 1999.

Criminal Records: Access: Fax, mail, in person. Both court and visitors may perform in person searches. Search fee: $5.00 per name. Required to search: name; also helpful: DOB. Criminal records in index books since 1887; on computer back to 1999.

General Information: No juvenile, mental, sealed, or adoption records released. SASE not required. Turnaround time 2 days. Fax notes: $1.00 for first page,

$.50 each add'l. Copy fee: $1.00 per page. Certification fee: $5.00 and $1.00 per district. Fee payee: County Clerk. Personal checks accepted. Prepayment is required.

Live Oak County

District Court PO Drawer 440, George West, TX 78022; 361-449-2733 X105. Hours: 8AM-5PM (CST). *Felony, Civil.*

Civil Records: Access: Phone, fax, mail, in person. Both court and visitors may perform in person searches. Search fee: $10.00 per name. Required to search: name, years to search. Civil cases indexed by defendant, plaintiff. Civil records in index books and microfiche since 1850s.

Criminal Records: Access: Phone, fax, mail, in person. Both court and visitors may perform in person searches. Search fee: $10.00 per name. Required to search: name, years to search, DOB; also helpful: SSN. Criminal records in index books and microfiche since 1850s.

General Information: No juvenile, mental, sealed, or adoption records released. SASE required. Turnaround time 1-2 days. Copy fee: $1.00 per page. Certification fee: $1.00. Fee payee: District Clerk. Personal checks accepted. Prepayment is required.

County Court PO Box 280, George West, TX 78022; 361-449-2733 X3. Hours: 8AM-5PM (CST). *Misdemeanor, Civil, Probate.*

Civil Records: Access: Mail, in person. Both court and visitors may perform in person searches. Search fee: $10.00 per name. Required to search: name, years to search. Civil cases indexed by defendant, plaintiff. Civil records in index books.

Criminal Records: Access: Mail, in person. Both court and visitors may perform in person searches. Search fee: $10.00 per name. Required to search: name, years to search. Criminal records in index books.

General Information: No juvenile, mental, sealed, or adoption records released. SASE required. Turnaround time 1-2 days. Copy fee: $1.00 per page. Certification fee: $5.00. Fee payee: County Clerk. Personal checks accepted. Prepayment is required.

Llano County

District Clerk PO Box 877, Llano, TX 78643-0877; 915-247-5036; Fax: 915-248-0492. Hours: 8AM-4:30PM (CST). *Felony, Civil.*

Civil Records: Access: Mail, in person. Both court and visitors may perform in person searches. Search fee: $5.00 per name. Fee is per 5 year period. Required to search: name, years to search. Civil cases indexed by defendant, plaintiff. Civil records in index books.

Criminal Records: Access: Mail, in person. Both court and visitors may perform in person searches. Search fee: $5.00 per name. Fee is per 5 year period. Required to search: name, years to search. Criminal records in index books.

General Information: No juvenile, mental, sealed, or adoption records released. SASE required. Turnaround time 1-3 days. Copy fee: $1.00 per page. Certification fee: $1.00 per page. Fee payee: Llano County District Clerk. Personal checks accepted. Credit cards accepted: Visa, MasterCard. 5% handling fee charged. Prepayment is required.

County Court PO Box 40, Llano, TX 78643-0040; 915-247-4455. Hours: 8AM-4:30PM (CST). *Misdemeanor, Civil, Probate.*

Civil Records: Access: Phone, mail, in person. Both court and visitors may perform in person searches. Search fee: $5.00 per name. Required to search: name, years to search. Civil cases indexed by defendant, plaintiff. Civil records on computer since 1985, index books prior.

Criminal Records: Access: Phone, mail, in person. Both court and visitors may perform in person searches. Search fee: $5.00 per name. Required to search: name, years to search; also helpful: DOB. Criminal records on computer since 1985, index books prior.

General Information: Public Access terminal is available. No juvenile, mental, sealed, or adoption records released. SASE not required. Turnaround time 2-4 days. Copy fee: $1.00 per page. Certification fee: $5.00. Payee: County Clerk. Personal checks accepted.

Loving County

District & County Court PO Box 194, Mentone, TX 79754; 915-377-2441; Fax: 915-377-2701. Hours: 9AM-Noon, 1-5PM (CST). *Felony, Misdemeanor, Civil, Eviction, Probate.*

Civil Records: Access: Phone, fax, mail, in person. Both court and visitors may perform in person searches. Search fee: $5.00 per name. Required to search: name, years to search. Civil cases indexed by defendant, plaintiff. Civil records in index books from 1935; computerized back to 1987.

Criminal Records: Access: Phone, fax, mail, in person. Both court and visitors may perform in person searches. Search fee: $5.00 per name. Required to search: name, years to search. Criminal records in index books from 1935; computerized back to 1987.

General Information: No juvenile, mental, sealed, or adoption records released. SASE required. Turnaround time 2 days. Fax notes: Fee to fax results is $1.50 per page. Copy fee: $1.00 per page. Certification fee: $5.00. Fee payee: Loving County Clerk. Personal checks accepted. Prepayment is required.

Lubbock County

District Court PO Box 10536, Lubbock, TX 79408-3536; 806-775-1623; Fax: 806-775-1382. Hours: 8AM-5PM (CST). *Felony, Civil.*

www.districtclerk.com

Civil Records: Access: Fax, mail, in person. Both court and visitors may perform in person searches. Search fee: $5.00 per name. Required to search: name, years to search. Civil cases indexed by defendant, plaintiff. Civil records on computer to 1991, in index books to 1985.

Criminal Records: Access: Fax, mail, in person. Both court and visitors may perform in person searches. Search fee: $5.00 per name. Required to search: name, years to search, DOB; also helpful: SSN. Criminal records on computer to 1991, in index books to 1985.

General Information: Public Access terminal is available. No juvenile, mental, sealed, or adoption records released. SASE required. Fax notes: $5.00 per document. Certification fee: $1.00. Fee payee: District Clerk. Personal checks accepted. Prepayment is required.

County Courts Courthouse, Room 207, PO Box 10536, Lubbock, TX 79408; 806-775-1051. Hours: 8:30AM-5PM (CST). *Misdemeanor, Civil, Probate.*

www.co.lubbock.tx.us/CClerk/county_clerk.htm

Civil Records: Access: Mail, in person. Both court and visitors may perform in person searches. Search fee: $10.00 per name. Fee is for each 5 year period. Required to search: name, years to search. Civil cases indexed by defendant, plaintiff. Civil records on computer since 1986, index books prior.

Criminal Records: Access: Mail, in person. Both court and visitors may perform in person searches. Search fee: $5.00 per name. Fee is for each 5 year period; $7.00 for more than 5 years. Required to search: name, years to search, DOB. Criminal records on computer since 1986, index books prior.

General Information: Public Access terminal is available. No juvenile, mental, sealed, or adoption records released. SASE required. Turnaround time 3-5 days. Copy fee: $1.00 per page. Certification fee: $5.00.

Fee payee: County Clerk. Personal checks accepted. Prepayment is required.

Lynn County

District Court PO Box 939, Tahoka, TX 79373; 806-998-4274; Fax: 806-998-4151. Hours: 8:30AM-5PM (CST). *Felony, Civil.*

Civil Records: Access: Fax, mail, in person. Both court and visitors may perform in person searches. Search fee: $5.00 per name. Required to search: name, years to search. Civil cases indexed by defendant, plaintiff. Civil records on computer to 1997, index books from 1916.
Criminal Records: Access: Fax, mail, in person. Both court and visitors may perform in person searches. Search fee: $5.00 per name. Required to search: name, years to search. Criminal records on computer from 1997, index books from 1916.
General Information: No juvenile, mental, sealed, or adoption records released. SASE not required. Turnaround time 2 days. Fax notes: $2.00 per page. Copy fee: $1.00 per page. Certification fee: $1.00 per page. Fee payee: District Clerk. Personal checks accepted. Prepayment is required.

County Court PO Box 937, Tahoka, TX 79373; 806-998-4750; Fax: 806-998-4988. Hours: 8:30AM-5PM (CST). *Misdemeanor, Civil, Probate.*

Civil Records: Access: Mail, in person. Both court and visitors may perform in person searches. Search fee: $5.00. Required to search: name, years to search. Civil cases indexed by defendant, plaintiff. Civil records in index books from 1903; on computer back to 1997.
Criminal Records: Access: Mail, in person. Both court and visitors may perform in person searches. Search fee: $5.00. Required to search: name, years to search. Criminal records in index books from 1903; on computer back to 1997.
General Information: No juvenile, mental, sealed, or adoption records released. SASE required. Turnaround time 2-4 days. Fax notes: Fee to fax results is $2.00 per page. Copy fee: $1.00 per page. Certification fee: $5.00. Fee payee: Lynn County Clerk. Personal checks accepted. Prepayment is required.

Madison County

District Court 101 W Main Rm 226, Madisonville, TX 77864; 936-348-9203. Hours: 8AM-Noon, 1-5PM (CST). *Felony, Civil.*

Civil Records: Access: Mail, in person. Both court and visitors may perform in person searches. Search fee: $5.00 per name. Required to search: name, years to search. Civil cases indexed by defendant, plaintiff. Civil records in index books to 1967.
Criminal Records: Access: Mail, in person. Both court and visitors may perform in person searches. Search fee: $5.00 per name. Required to search: name, years to search. Criminal records in index books to 1835.
General Information: No juvenile, mental, sealed, or adoption records released. SASE required. Turnaround time 1 day. Copy fee: $1.00 per page. Certification fee: No certification fee. Fee payee: District Clerk. Personal checks accepted. Prepayment is required.

County Court 101 W Main Rm 102, Madisonville, TX 77864; 936-348-2638; Fax: 936-348-5858. Hours: 8AM-4:30PM (CST). *Misdemeanor, Civil, Probate.*

Civil Records: Access: Mail, in person. Both court and visitors may perform in person searches. Search fee: $10.00 per name. Required to search: name, years to search. Civil cases indexed by defendant. Civil records on computer from 1982, index books back to 1965.
Criminal Records: Access: Mail, in person. Both court and visitors may perform in person searches. Search fee: $10.00 per name. Required to search: name, years to search, DOB. Criminal records on computer from 1982, index books back to 1965.

General Information: No juvenile, mental, sealed, or adoption records released. SASE required. Turnaround time as soon as fees are paid. Fax notes: Fee to fax results is $1.00 per page. Copy fee: $1.00 per page. Certification fee: $5.00. Fee payee: Madison County Clerk. Personal checks accepted. Prepayment required.

Marion County

District Court PO Box 628, Jefferson, TX 75657; 903-665-2441/2013. Hours: 8AM-5PM (CST). *Felony, Civil.*

Civil Records: Access: Mail, in person. Both court and visitors may perform in person searches. Search fee: $5.00 per name. Required to search: name, years to search. Civil cases indexed by defendant, plaintiff. Civil records on computer to 1991, index books up to 1986.
Criminal Records: Access: Mail, in person. Both court and visitors may perform in person searches. Search fee: $5.00 per name. Required to search: name, years to search. Criminal records on computer from 1991, index books up to 1986.
General Information: No juvenile, mental, sealed, or adoption records released. SASE required. Turnaround time 1 week. Copy fee: $1.00 per page. Certification fee: $1.00. Fee payee: District Clerk. Personal checks accepted. Prepayment is required.

County Court PO Box 763, Jefferson, TX 75657; 903-665-3971. Hours: 8AM-Noon, 1-5PM (CST). *Misdemeanor, Probate.*

Criminal Records: Access: Phone, mail, in person. Both court and visitors may perform in person searches. No search fee. Required to search: name, years to search. Criminal records in index books from 1966; computerized back to 1973.
General Information: No juvenile, mental, sealed, or adoption records released. SASE required. Turnaround time 2-4 days. Copy fee: $1.00 per page. Certification fee: $5.00. Fee payee: County Clerk. Personal checks accepted. Prepayment is required.

Martin County

District & County Court PO Box 906, Stanton, TX 79782; 915-756-3412. Hours: 8AM-Noon, 1-5PM (CST). *Felony, Misdemeanor, Civil, Eviction, Probate.*

Civil Records: Access: Mail, in person. Both court and visitors may perform in person searches. Search fee: $5.00 per name. Required to search: name, years to search. Civil cases indexed by defendant, plaintiff. Civil records in index books to 1900.
Criminal Records: Access: Mail, in person. Both court and visitors may perform in person searches. Search fee: $5.00 per name. Required to search: name, years to search. Criminal records in index books to 1900.
General Information: No juvenile, mental, sealed, or adoption records released. SASE required. Turnaround time 2-4 days. Fax notes: Fee to fax results is $1.00 per page. Copy fee: $1.00 per page. Certification fee: $5.00. Fee payee: County/District Clerk. Personal checks accepted. Prepayment is required.

Mason County

District & County Court PO Box 702, Mason, TX 76856; 915-347-5253; Fax: 915-347-6868. Hours: 8AM-Noon, 1-4PM (CST). *Felony, Misdemeanor, Civil, Probate.*

Civil Records: Access: Mail, in person. Both court and visitors may perform in person searches. Search fee: $10.00 per name. Required to search: name, years to search. Civil cases indexed by defendant, plaintiff. Civil records in index books to 1858; on computer back to 1993.
Criminal Records: Access: Mail, in person. Both court and visitors may perform in person searches. Search fee: $10.00 per name. Required to search: name, years

to search; also helpful: DOB, SSN. Criminal records in index books to 1858; on computer back to 1993.
General Information: No juvenile, mental, sealed, or adoption records released. SASE required. Turnaround time 2 days. Fax notes: Will not fax results. Copy fee: $1.00 per page. Certification fee: $5.00. Fee payee: County/District Clerk. Personal checks accepted. Prepayment is required.

Matagorda County

District Court 1700 7th St Rm 307, Bay City, TX 77414-5092; 979-244-7621. Hours: 8AM-Noon, 1-5PM (CST). *Felony, Civil.*

Civil Records: Access: Mail, in person. Both court and visitors may perform in person searches. Search fee: $5.00 per name. Required to search: name, years to search. Civil cases indexed by defendant, plaintiff. Civil records in index books and card files back to 1910; computerized back to 1994.
Criminal Records: Access: Mail, in person. Both court and visitors may perform in person searches. Search fee: $5.00 per name. Required to search: name, years to search, DOB. Criminal records in index books and card files back to 1910; computerized back to 1994.
General Information: No juvenile, sealed, or adoption records released. SASE required. Turnaround time 1-2 days. Fax notes: Do not fax. Copy fee: $1.00 per page. Certification fee: $2.00. Fee payee: District Clerk. Personal checks accepted. Prepayment is required.

County Court 1700 7th St Rm 202, Bay City, TX 77414-5094; 979-244-7680; Fax: 979-244-7688. 8AM-5PM (CST). *Misdemeanor, Civil, Probate.*

Civil Records: Access: Mail, in person. Both court and visitors may perform in person searches. Search fee: $5.00 per name. Required to search: name, years to search. Civil cases indexed by defendant, plaintiff. Civil records on computer from 1994, index books prior.
Criminal Records: Access: Mail, in person. Both court and visitors may perform in person searches. Search fee: $5.00 per name. Required to search: name, years to search, DOB, SSN. Criminal records on computer from 1994, index books prior.
General Information: Public Access terminal is available. No juvenile, mental, sealed, or adoption records released. SASE required. Turnaround time 1-2 days. Fax notes: Fee to fax results is $2.00 per document. Copy fee: $1.00 per page. Certification fee: $5.00. Fee payee: County Clerk. Personal checks accepted. Credit cards accepted: Visa, MasterCard. Prepayment is required.

Maverick County

District Court PO Box 3659, Eagle Pass, TX 78853; 830-773-2629. 8AM-5PM. *Felony, Civil.*

Civil Records: Access: Mail, in person. Both court and visitors may perform in person searches. Search fee: $5.00 per name. Required to search: name, years to search. Civil cases indexed by defendant, plaintiff. Civil records in index books; recent records computerized.
Criminal Records: Access: Mail, in person. Both court and visitors may perform in person searches. Search fee: $5.00 per name. Required to search: name, years to search. Criminal records in index books; recent records computerized.
General Information: No juvenile, mental, sealed, or adoption records released. SASE required. Turnaround time 2-4 days. Fax notes: Fee to fax results is $1.00 per page. Copy fee: $1.00 per page. Certification fee: $5.00. Fee payee: District Clerk. Personal checks accepted. Prepayment is required.

County Court PO Box 4050, Eagle Pass, TX 78853; 830-773-2829. Hours: 8AM-5PM (CST). *Misdemeanor, Civil, Probate.*

Civil Records: Access: Mail, in person. Both court and visitors may perform in person searches. Search fee:

$10.00 per name. Required to search: name, years to search. Civil cases indexed by defendant, plaintiff. Civil records on index books.

Criminal Records: Access: Mail, in person. Both court and visitors may perform in person searches. Search fee: $10.00 per name. Required to search: name, years to search, DOB, SSN. Criminal records on index books.

General Information: No juvenile, mental, sealed, or adoption records released. SASE not required. Turnaround time 1-2 days. Fax notes: Fee to fax results is 1.00 per page. Copy fee: $1.00 per page. Certification fee: $5.00. Fee payee: County Clerk. Personal checks accepted. Prepayment is required.

McCulloch County

District Court County Courthouse Rm 205, Brady, TX 76825; 915-597-0733; Fax: 915-597-0606. Hours: 8:30AM-5PM (CST). *Felony, Civil.*

Civil Records: Access: Mail, fax, in person, online. Both court and visitors may perform in person searches. Search fee: $5.00 per name. Required to search: name, years to search. Civil cases indexed by defendant, plaintiff. Civil records in index books. Civil case information available free online at www.idocket.com.

Criminal Records: Access: Mail, fax, in person, online. Both court and visitors may perform in person searches. Search fee: $5.00 per name. Required to search: name, years to search; also helpful: DOB, SSN. Criminal records in index books back to 1990; on computer back to 1995. Online access to criminal records is the same as civil.

General Information: Public Access terminal is available. No juvenile, mental, sealed, or adoption records released. SASE required. Turnaround time 2-4 days. Fax notes: Will not fax results. Copy fee: $1.00 per page. Certification fee: $2.00. Fee payee: District Clerk. Personal checks accepted. Prepayment required.

County Court County Courthouse, Brady, TX 76825; 915-597-0733. Hours: 8AM-5PM (CST). *Misdemeanor, Civil, Probate.*

Civil Records: Access: Mail, in person. Both court and visitors may perform in person searches. Search fee: $5.00 per name. Required to search: name, years to search. Civil cases indexed by defendant, plaintiff. Civil records in index books.

Criminal Records: Access: Mail, in person. Both court and visitors may perform in person searches. Search fee: $5.00 per name. Required to search: name, years to search. Criminal records in index books.

General Information: No juvenile, mental, sealed, or adoption records released. SASE required. Turnaround time 1-2 days. Copy fee: $1.00 per page. Certification fee: $1.00. Fee payee: County Clerk. Personal checks accepted. Prepayment is required.

McLennan County

District Court PO Box 2451, Waco, TX 76703; Civil phone: 254-757-5057; Criminal phone: 254-757-5054; Fax: 254-757-5060. Hours: 8AM-Noon, 1-5PM (CST). *Felony, Civil.*

Civil Records: Access: Fax, mail, in person. Both court and visitors may perform in person searches. Search fee: $5.00 per name. Required to search: name, years to search. Civil cases indexed by defendant, plaintiff. Civil records on computer since 1986, index books from 1850.

Criminal Records: Access: Fax, mail, in person. Both court and visitors may perform in person searches. Search fee: $5.00 per name. Required to search: name, years to search. Criminal records on computer since 1959, index books from 1850.

General Information: No juvenile, mental, sealed, or adoption records released. SASE required. Turnaround time 2 days. Copy fee: $1.00 per page. Certification fee: No certification fee. Fee payee: Joe Johnson, District

Clerk. Personal checks accepted. Credit cards accepted: Visa, MasterCard. Prepayment is required.

County Court PO Box 1727, Waco, TX 76703; 254-757-5185; Fax: 254-757-5146. Hours: 8AM-5PM (CST). *Misdemeanor, Civil, Probate.*

Civil Records: Access: Mail, in person. Both court and visitors may perform in person searches. Search fee: $5.00 per name. Required to search: name, years to search. Civil cases indexed by defendant, plaintiff. Civil records in index books back to 1876; Probate to 1850.

Criminal Records: Access: Mail, in person. Both court and visitors may perform in person searches. Search fee: $5.00 per name. Required to search: name, years to search; also helpful: DOB, SSN. Criminal records on computer since 1993; in index books to 1935.

General Information: No juvenile, mental, sealed, or adoption records released. SASE required. Turnaround time 2-4 days. Copy fee: $1.00 per page. Certification fee: $5.00. Fee payee: County Clerk. Business checks accepted. Prepayment is required. Will fax results to toll-free numbers only.

McMullen County

District & County Court PO Box 235, Tilden, TX 78072; 361-274-3215; Fax: 361-274-3618. Hours: 8AM-4PM (CST). *Felony, Misdemeanor, Civil, Eviction, Probate.*

Civil Records: Access: Mail, in person. Both court and visitors may perform in person searches. Search fee: $5.00 per name. Required to search: name, years to search. Civil cases indexed by defendant, plaintiff. Civil records in index books.

Criminal Records: Access: Mail, in person. Both court and visitors may perform in person searches. Search fee: $5.00 per name. Required to search: name, years to search. Criminal records in index books.

General Information: No juvenile, mental, sealed, or adoption records released. SASE required. Turnaround time 2-4 days. Fax notes: Will fax results for a fee. Copy fee: $1.00 per page. Certification fee: $5.00. Fee payee: County Clerk. Personal checks accepted. Prepayment is required.

Medina County

District Court County Courthouse Rm 209, Hondo, TX 78861; 830-741-6071. Hours: 8AM-Noon, 1-5PM (CST). *Felony, Civil.*

Civil Records: Access: Mail, in person. Both court and visitors may perform in person searches. Search fee: $5.00 per name. Required to search: name, years to search. Civil cases indexed by defendant, plaintiff. Civil records on computer since 1990, index books since 1849.

Criminal Records: Access: Mail, in person. Both court and visitors may perform in person searches. Search fee: $5.00 per name. Required to search: name, years to search, DOB. Criminal records on computer since 1990, index books since 1849.

General Information: Public Access terminal is available. No juvenile, mental, sealed, or adoption records released. SASE required. Turnaround time 1 week. Fax notes: Will not fax results. Copy fee: $1.00 1st page; $.50 each add'l. Certification fee: $1.00 per page. Fee payee: District Clerk. Only cashiers checks and money orders accepted. Out-of-state checks not accepted. Prepayment is required.

County Court at Law 1100 16th St, Rm 203, Hondo, TX 78861; 830-741-6061. Hours: 8AM-Noon, 1-5PM (CST). *Misdemeanor, Civil, Probate.*

Civil Records: Access: Phone, mail, in person. Both court and visitors may perform in person searches. Search fee: $5.00 per name. Required to search: name, years to search. Civil cases indexed by defendant, plaintiff. Civil records on computer since late 1993, index books prior.

Criminal Records: Access: Phone, mail, in person. Both court and visitors may perform in person searches. Search fee: $5.00 per name. Required to search: name, years to search; also helpful: address, DOB, SSN. Criminal records on computer since late 1993, index books prior.

General Information: No juvenile, mental, or sealed records released. SASE required. Turnaround time 1-2 days. Copy fee: $1.00 per page. Certification fee: $5.00. Fee payee: County Clerk. Personal checks accepted. Prepayment is required.

Menard County

District & County Court PO Box 1028, Menard, TX 76859; 915-396-4682; Fax: 915-396-2047. Hours: 8AM-Noon, 1-5PM (CST). *Felony, Misdemeanor, Civil, Eviction, Probate.*

Civil Records: Access: Fax, mail, in person. Both court and visitors may perform in person searches. Search fee: $9.00 per name. Required to search: name, years to search. Civil cases indexed by defendant, plaintiff. Civil records in index books.

Criminal Records: Access: Mail, in person. Both court and visitors may perform in person searches. Search fee: $9.00 per name. Required to search: name, years to search. Criminal records in index books.

General Information: No juvenile, mental, sealed, or adoption records released. SASE required. Turnaround time 2-4 days. Fax notes: $1.00 per page. Copy fee: $1.00 per page. Certification fee: $5.00. Fee payee: District/County Clerk. Personal checks accepted. Prepayment is required.

Midland County

District Court 200 W Wall #301, Midland, TX 79701; 915-688-1107. Hours: 8AM-5PM (CST). *Felony, Civil.*

www.co.midland.tx.us/DC/default.asp

Civil Records: Access: Mail, in person, online. Both court and visitors may perform in person searches. Search fee: $5.00 per name. Required to search: name, years to search. Civil cases indexed by defendant, plaintiff. Civil records on computer back to 1980, index books prior. Online access to the district Clerk database is available free at www.co.midland.tx.us/DC/Database/search.asp.

Criminal Records: Access: Mail, in person, online. Both court and visitors may perform in person searches. Search fee: $5.00 per name. Required to search: name, years to search. Criminal records on computer back to 1980, index books prior. Online access to criminal records is the same as civil.

General Information: Public Access terminal is available. No juvenile, mental, sealed, or adoption records released. SASE required. Turnaround time 2 days. Fax notes: Fee to fax results is $1.00 per page. Copy fee: $1.00 per page. Certification fee: No certification fee. Fee payee: District Clerk. Business checks accepted. Prepayment is required.

County Court PO Box 211, Midland, TX 79702; 915-688-1070; Fax: 915-688-8973. Hours: 8AM-5PM (CST). *Misdemeanor, Civil, Probate.*

www.co.midland.tx.us/CC/default.asp

Civil Records: Access: Mail, in person, online. Both court and visitors may perform in person searches. Search fee: $5.00 per name. Required to search: name; also helpful: years to search, address. Civil cases indexed by defendant, plaintiff. Civil records on computer since 1987, index books since 1885. Probate records on computer since 1887. Online access to the County Clerk database is available free at www.co.midland.tx.us/CC/Database/search.asp.

Criminal Records: Access: Mail, in person, online. Both court and visitors may perform in person searches. Search fee: $5.00 per name. Required to search: name;

also helpful: years to search, address, DOB, SSN. Criminal records on computer since 1978, index books since 1885. Online access to criminal records is the same as civil.

General Information: Public Access terminal is available. No juvenile, mental, sealed, or adoption records released. SASE not required. Turnaround time 1-2 days. Copy fee: $1.00 per page. Certification fee: $5.00. Fee payee: County Clerk. Only cashiers checks and money orders accepted. Prepayment is required.

Milam County

District Court PO Box 999, Cameron, TX 76520; 254-697-7052. Hours: 8AM-5PM (CST). *Felony, Civil.*

Civil Records: Access: Mail, in person. Both court and visitors may perform in person searches. Search fee: $5.00 per name. Required to search: name, years to search. Civil cases indexed by defendant, plaintiff. Civil records on microfilm and index books.

Criminal Records: Access: Mail, in person. Both court and visitors may perform in person searches. Search fee: $5.00 per name. Required to search: name, years to search. Criminal records on microfilm and index books.

General Information: No juvenile, mental, sealed, or adoption records released. SASE required. Turnaround time same day. Copy fee: $1.00 per page. Certification fee: $1.00. Fee payee: District Clerk. Only cashiers checks and money orders accepted. Prepayment is required.

County Court PO Box 191, Cameron, TX 76520; 254-697-7049; Fax: 254-697-7055. Hours: 8AM-5PM (CST). *Misdemeanor, Civil, Probate.*

Civil Records: Access: Mail, in person. Both court and visitors may perform in person searches. Search fee: $5.00 per name. Required to search: name, years to search. Civil cases indexed by defendant, plaintiff. Civil records on computer back to 1983; prior in books back to 1874.

Criminal Records: Access: Mail, in person. Both court and visitors may perform in person searches. Search fee: $5.00 per name. Required to search: name, years to search, signed release, DOB or SSN. Criminal records on computer back to 1983; prior in books back to 1874.

General Information: No juvenile, mental, sealed, or adoption records released. SASE not required. Turnaround time 1-2 days. Fax notes: Fee to fax results is $2.00 plus $1.00 per page. Copy fee: $1.00 per page. Certification fee: $5.00. Fee payee: Milam County Clerk. Personal checks accepted. Prepayment required.

Mills County

District & County Court PO Box 646, Goldthwaite, TX 76844; 915-648-2711; Fax: 915-648-2806. Hours: 8AM-Noon, 1-5PM (CST). *Felony, Misdemeanor, Civil, Probate.*

Civil Records: Access: Fax, mail, in person. Both court and visitors may perform in person searches. Search fee: $5.00 per name. Required to search: name, years to search; also helpful: cause number. Civil cases indexed by defendant, plaintiff. Civil records in index books since 1887.

Criminal Records: Access: Mail, fax, in person. Both court and visitors may perform in person searches. Search fee: $5.00 per name. Required to search: name, years to search, DOB, signed release; also helpful: cause number. Criminal records in index books since 1887.

General Information: No juvenile, mental, sealed, or adoption records released. SASE required. Turnaround time 1-2 days. Copy fee: $1.00 per page. Certification fee: $5.00. Fee payee: County-District Clerk. Personal checks accepted. Prepayment is required.

Mitchell County

District Court County Courthouse, Colorado City, TX 79512; 915-728-5918. Hours: 8AM-5PM (CST). *Felony, Civil.*

Civil Records: Access: Mail, in person. Both court and visitors may perform in person searches. Search fee: $5.00 per name. Required to search: name, years to search. Civil cases indexed by defendant, plaintiff. Civil records in index books.

Criminal Records: Access: Mail, in person. Only the court performs in person searches; visitors may not. Search fee: $5.00 per name. Required to search: name, years to search. Criminal records in index books.

General Information: No juvenile, mental, sealed, or adoption records released. SASE required. Turnaround time 1 day. Copy fee: $.35 per page. Certification fee: $1.00 per page. Fee payee: District Clerk. Personal checks accepted. Prepayment is required.

County Court 349 Oak St Rm 103, Colorado City, TX 79512; 915-728-3481; Fax: 915-728-5322. Hours: 8AM-Noon, 1-5PM (CST). *Misdemeanor, Civil, Probate.*

Civil Records: Access: Fax, mail, in person. Both court and visitors may perform in person searches. Search fee: $5.00 per name. Required to search: name, years to search. Civil cases indexed by defendant, plaintiff. Civil records in index books, on computer from 9-1-1998 to present.

Criminal Records: Access: Mail, in person. Both court and visitors may perform in person searches. Search fee: $5.00 per name. Required to search: name, years to search; also helpful: DOB. Criminal records in index books, on computer from 9-1-1998 to present.

General Information: Public Access terminal is available. (Land records on computer back to 5/1985.) No juvenile, mental, sealed, or adoption, commitment records released. Turnaround time 2-4 days. Fax notes: Fee to fax results is $3.00 for the 1st page and $1.00 per page thereafter. Copy fee: $1.00 per page. Certification fee: $5.00. Fee payee: Mitchell County Clerk. Personal checks accepted. No out of state personal checks. Money order accepted. Prepayment is required.

Montague County

District Court PO Box 155, Montague, TX 76251; 940-894-2571. Hours: 8AM-5PM (CST). *Felony, Civil.*

Civil Records: Access: Mail, in person. Both court and visitors may perform in person searches. Search fee: $5.00 per name. Required to search: name, years to search. Civil cases indexed by defendant, plaintiff. Civil records on computer and index books.

Criminal Records: Access: Mail, in person. Both court and visitors may perform in person searches. Search fee: $5.00 per name. Required to search: name, years to search. Criminal records on computer and index books.

General Information: No juvenile, mental, sealed, or adoption records released. SASE required. Turnaround time 2-4 days. Copy fee: $1.00 per page. Certification fee: $5.00. Fee payee: District Clerk. Personal checks accepted. Prepayment is required.

County Court PO Box 77, Montague, TX 76251; 940-894-2461. Hours: 8AM-5PM (CST). *Misdemeanor, Civil, Probate.*

Civil Records: Access: Mail, in person. Both court and visitors may perform in person searches. Search fee: $5.00 per name. Required to search: name, years to search. Civil cases indexed by defendant, plaintiff. Civil records on computer since 1993, index books prior.

Criminal Records: Access: Mail, in person. Both court and visitors may perform in person searches. Search fee: $5.00 per name. Required to search: name, years to search. Criminal records on computer since 1993, index books prior.

General Information: No juvenile, mental, sealed, or adoption records released. SASE required. Turnaround time 1-2 days. Fax notes: Fee to fax results is $2.50 1st page, $.75 each add'l page. Copy fee: $1.00 per page. Certification fee: $5.00. Fee payee: County Clerk. Personal checks accepted. Prepayment is required.

Montgomery County

District Court PO Box 2985, Conroe, TX 77305; 936-539-7855. Hours: 8AM-5PM M-T,Th-F; 8AM-4:30PM W (CST). *Felony, Civil.*

Civil Records: Access: Mail, in person. Both court and visitors may perform in person searches. Search fee: $5.00 per name. Required to search: name, years to search. Civil cases indexed by defendant, plaintiff. Civil records in index books, on computer since 1990.

Criminal Records: Access: Mail, in person. Both court and visitors may perform in person searches. Search fee: $5.00 per name. Required to search: name, years to search. Criminal records in index books, on computer since 1990.

General Information: Public Access terminal is available. No juvenile, mental, sealed, or adoption records released. SASE not required. Turnaround time 3-6 days. Copy fee: $1.00 per page. Certification fee: No certification fee. Fee payee: Barbara Adamick, District Clerk. Personal checks not accepted. Prepayment is required.

County Court PO Box 959, Conroe, TX 77305; 936-539-7885; Fax: 936-760-6990. Hours: 8AM-5PM (CST). *Misdemeanor, Civil, Probate.*

www.co.montgomery.tx.us

Civil Records: Access: Mail, in person. Both court and visitors may perform in person searches. Search fee: $5.00 per name. Required to search: name, years to search. Civil cases indexed by defendant, plaintiff. Civil records on computer and index books.

Criminal Records: Access: Mail, in person. Both court and visitors may perform in person searches. Search fee: $5.00 per name. Required to search: name, years to search. Criminal records on computer and index books.

General Information: Public Access terminal is available. No mental or sealed records released. SASE required. Turnaround time 2 days. Fax notes: Fee to fax results is $2.00 per page. Copy fee: $1.00 per page. Certification fee: $5.00. Fee payee: County Clerk. Personal checks accepted. Prepayment is required.

Moore County

District Court 715 Dumas Ave #109, Dumas, TX 79029; 806-935-4218; Fax: 806-935-6325. Hours: 8:30AM-5PM (CST). *Felony, Civil.*

Civil Records: Access: Mail, in person. Both court and visitors may perform in person searches. Search fee: $5.00 per name. Required to search: name, years to search. Civil cases indexed by defendant, plaintiff. Civil records on computer back to 1990; docket books and original files prior.

Criminal Records: Access: Mail, in person. Both court and visitors may perform in person searches. Search fee: $5.00 per name. Required to search: name, years to search, DOB; also helpful: SSN. Criminal records on computer to 1990; docket books and original files prior.

General Information: No juvenile, mental, sealed, or adoption records released. SASE required. Turnaround time 1 day. Copy fee: $1.00 per page. Certification fee: $1.00. Fee payee: District Clerk. Personal checks accepted. Prepayment is required.

County Court 715 Dumas Ave Rm 105, Dumas, TX 79029; 806-935-6164/2009; Fax: 806-935-9004. Hours: 8:30AM-5PM (CST). *Misdemeanor, Civil, Probate.*

Civil Records: Access: Mail, fax, in person. Both court and visitors may perform in person searches. Search fee: $5.00 per name. Required to search: name, years to search. Civil cases indexed by defendant, plaintiff. Civil records on computer back to 71987, index books prior.

Criminal Records: Access: Mail, fax, in person. Both court and visitors may perform in person searches. Search fee: $5.00 per name. Required to search: name, years to search, signed release, DOB or SSN. Criminal records on computer back to 71987, in index books prior.

General Information: Public Access terminal is available. No juvenile, mental, sealed, or adoption records released. SASE required. Turnaround time 24 hours. Fax notes: Fee to fax results is $5.00 plus $1.00 per page. Copy fee: $1.00 per page. Certification fee: $5.00. Fee payee: Moore County Clerk. Business checks accepted. Prepayment is required.

Morris County

District Court 500 Broadnax, Daingerfield, TX 75638; 903-645-2321. Hours: 8AM-5PM (CST). *Felony, Civil.*

Civil Records: Access: Mail, in person. Both court and visitors may perform in person searches. Search fee: $5.00 per name. Required to search: name, years to search. Civil cases indexed by defendant, plaintiff. Civil records in index books and file folders from 1930s. Plaintiff index only for active cases.

Criminal Records: Access: Mail, in person. Both court and visitors may perform in person searches. Search fee: $5.00 per name. Required to search: name, years to search, DOB. Criminal records in index books and file folders from 1930s. Plaintiff index only for active cases.

General Information: No juvenile, mental, sealed, or adoption records released. SASE required. Turnaround time 1 day. Copy fee: $1.00 per page. Certification fee: No certification fee. Fee payee: Morris County District Clerk. Personal checks accepted. Prepayment is required.

County Court 500 Broadnax, Daingerfield, TX 75638; 903-645-3911. Hours: 8AM-5PM (CST). *Misdemeanor, Probate.*

Criminal Records: Access: Mail, in person. Both court and visitors may perform in person searches. Search fee: $5.00 per name. Required to search: name, years to search. Criminal record on index books.

General Information: No juvenile, mental, sealed, or adoption records released. SASE not required. Turnaround time 1 day. Copy fee: $1.00 per page. Certification fee: $5.00. Fee payee: County Clerk. Personal checks accepted. Prepayment is required.

Motley County

District & County Court PO Box 660, Matador, TX 79244; 806-347-2621; Fax: 806-347-2220. Hours: 9AM-Noon, 1-5PM (CST). *Felony, Misdemeanor, Civil, Eviction, Probate.*

Civil Records: Access: Mail, fax, in person. Both court and visitors may perform in person searches. Search fee: $10.00 per name. Required to search: name, years to search, address. Civil cases indexed by defendant, plaintiff. Civil records in docket books, archived from 1891.

Criminal Records: Access: Mail, fax, in person. Only the court performs in person searches; visitors may not. Search fee: $10.00 per name. Required to search: name, years to search, DOB. Criminal records in docket books, archived from 1891.

General Information: No juvenile, mental, sealed or adoption records released. SASE required. Turnaround time 1-2 days. Copy fee: $1.00 per page. Certification fee: $2.00. Fee payee: Motley County Clerk. Personal checks accepted. Prepayment is required.

Nacogdoches County

District Court 101 W Main #215, Nacogdoches, TX 75961; 936-560-7730; Fax: 936-560-7839. Hours: 8AM-5PM (CST). *Felony, Civil.*

Civil Records: Access: Mail, in person. Both court and visitors may perform in person searches. Search fee: $5.00 per name. Required to search: name, years to search. Civil cases indexed by defendant, plaintiff. Civil records on computer from 1987, index books prior.

Criminal Records: Access: Mail, in person. Both court and visitors may perform in person searches. Search fee: $5.00 per name. Required to search: name, years to search, signed release. Criminal records on computer from 1987, index books prior.

General Information: No juvenile, mental, sealed, or adoption records released. SASE required. Turnaround time 5-6 days. Copy fee: $1.00 per page. Certification fee: No certification fee. Fee payee: Nacogdoches County. Business checks accepted. Prepayment is required.

County Court 101 W Main, Rm 205, Nacogdoches, TX 75961; 936-560-7733. Hours: 8AM-5PM (CST). *Misdemeanor, Civil, Probate.*

Civil Records: Access: Mail, in person. Both court and visitors may perform in person searches. Search fee: $5.00 per name. Required to search: name, years to search. Civil cases indexed by defendant, plaintiff. Civil records on computer since 1986, index books prior.

Criminal Records: Access: Mail, in person. Both court and visitors may perform in person searches. Search fee: $5.00 per name. Required to search: name, years to search. Criminal records on computer since 1987, index books prior.

General Information: Public Access terminal is available. No juvenile, mental, sealed, or adoption records released. SASE required. Turnaround time 2-4 days. Copy fee: $1.00 per page. Certification fee: $5.00. Fee payee: County Clerk. Personal checks accepted. Prepayment is required.

Navarro County

District Court PO Box 1439, Corsicana, TX 75151; 903-654-3040; Fax: 903-654-3088. Hours: 8AM-5PM (CST). *Felony, Civil.*

Civil Records: Access: Phone, fax, mail, online, in person. Both court and visitors may perform in person searches. Search fee: $5.00 per name. Required to search: name, years to search. Civil cases indexed by defendant, plaintiff. Civil records on computer since 1990, index books and microfiche since 1900s. Civil case information is available free online at www.idocket.com.

Criminal Records: Access: Phone, fax, mail, in person. Both court and visitors may perform in person searches. Search fee: $5.00 per name. Required to search: name, years to search. Criminal records on computer since 1990, index books and microfiche since 1900s. Online access to criminal records is the same as civil.

General Information: No juvenile, sealed, or adoption records released. SASE required. Turnaround time 1-2 days. Fax notes: $5.00 for first page, $1.00 each add'l. Copy fee: $1.00 for first page, $.25 each add'l. Certification fee: $1.00 per page. Fee payee: District Clerk. Personal checks accepted. Prepayment required.

County Court PO Box 423, Corsicana, TX 75151; 903-654-3035. Hours: 8AM-5PM (CST). *Misdemeanor, Civil, Probate.*

Civil Records: Access: Mail, in person. Both court and visitors may perform in person searches. Search fee: $5.00 per name. Fee is for 10 year period. Required to search: name, years to search. Civil cases indexed by defendant, plaintiff. Civil records in index books; on computer back to 1999.

Criminal Records: Access: Mail, in person. Both court and visitors may perform in person searches. Search fee: $5.00 per name. Fee is for 10 year period. Required to search: name, years to search, DOB or SSN. Criminal records in index books; on computer back to 1999.

General Information: Public Access terminal is available. No juvenile, mental, sealed, or adoption records released. SASE required. Turnaround time 2-4 days. Copy fee: $1.00 per page. Certification fee: $5.00. Fee payee: County Clerk. Personal checks accepted. Prepayment is required.

Newton County

District Court PO Box 535, Newton, TX 75966; 409-379-3951. Hours: 8AM-4:30PM (CST). *Felony, Civil.*

Civil Records: Access: Mail, in person. Both court and visitors may perform in person searches. Search fee: $5.00 per name. Required to search: name, years to search. Civil cases indexed by defendant, plaintiff. Civil records in index books.

Criminal Records: Access: Mail, in person. Both court and visitors may perform in person searches. Search fee: $5.00 per name. Required to search: name, years to search. Criminal records in index books.

General Information: No juvenile, mental, sealed, or adoption records released. SASE required. Turnaround time same day. Fax notes: Fee to fax results is $2.00 per page. Copy fee: $1.00 per page. Certification fee: $2.00. Fee payee: District Clerk. Personal checks accepted. Prepayment is required.

County Court PO Box 484, Newton, TX 75966; 409-379-5341; Fax: 409-379-9049. Hours: 8AM-4:30PM (CST). *Misdemeanor, Civil, Probate.*

Civil Records: Access: Mail, in person. Both court and visitors may perform in person searches. Search fee: $5.00 per name. Required to search: name, years to search. Civil cases indexed by defendant, plaintiff. Civil records on index books from 1953.

Criminal Records: Access: Mail, in person. Both court and visitors may perform in person searches. Search fee: $5.00 per name. Required to search: name, years to search. Criminal records on index books from 1953.

General Information: No juvenile, mental, sealed, or adoption records released. SASE not required. Turnaround time 1-2 days. Fax notes: Fee to fax results is $.50 per page. Copy fee: $1.00 per page. Certification fee: $5.00. Fee payee: County Clerk. Personal checks accepted. Prepayment is required.

Nolan County

District Court 100 E 3rd 200A, Sweetwater, TX 79556; 915-235-2111. Hours: 8:30AM-Noon, 1-5PM (CST). *Felony, Civil.*

Civil Records: Access: Mail, in person. Both court and visitors may perform in person searches. Search fee: $5.00 per name. Required to search: name, years to search. Civil cases indexed by defendant, plaintiff. Civil records in index books, records are not computerized.

Criminal Records: Access: Mail, in person. Only the court performs in person searches; visitors may not. Search fee: $5.00 per name. Required to search: name, years to search. Criminal records in index books, records are not computerized. Include which years to search.

General Information: No juvenile, mental, sealed, or adoption records released. SASE required. Turnaround time same day. Copy fee: $1.00 for first page, $.50 each add'l. Certification fee: $1.00 per page. Fee payee: District Clerk. Personal checks accepted. Prepayment is required.

County Court 100 East 3rd St #108, Sweetwater, TX 79556-4546; 915-235-2462. Hours: 8:30AM-Noon, 1-5PM (CST). *Misdemeanor, Civil, Probate.*

Civil Records: Access: Mail, in person. Both court and visitors may perform in person searches. Search fee: $5.00 per name. Required to search: name, years to search. Civil cases indexed by defendant, plaintiff. Civil records in index books.

Criminal Records: Access: Mail, in person. Both court and visitors may perform in person searches. Search fee: $5.00 per name. Required to search: name, years to search. Criminal records in index books.

General Information: No juvenile, mental, sealed, or adoption records released. SASE required. Turnaround time 2-4 days. Copy fee: $1.00 per page. Certification fee: $5.00. Fee payee: County Clerk. Personal checks accepted. Prepayment is required.

Nueces County

District Court PO Box 2987, Corpus Christi, TX 78403-2987; 361-888-0450; Fax: 361-888-0571. Hours: 8AM-5PM (CST). *Felony, Civil.*

www.co.nueces.tx.us/districtclerk

Civil Records: Access: Mail, in person, online. Both court and visitors may perform in person searches. Search fee: $5.00 per name. Required to search: name, years to search. Civil cases indexed by defendant, plaintiff. Civil records on computer since 1980, index books prior. Online access to civil District Court records are available free online at the web site. Search by name, company, or cause number.

Criminal Records: Access: Mail, in person, online. Both court and visitors may perform in person searches. Search fee: $5.00 per name. Required to search: name, years to search. Criminal records on computer since 1980, index books prior. Online access to criminal District Court records are available free online at the web site. Search by name, SID #, or cause number.

General Information: Public Access terminal is available. (Civil only.) No juvenile, mental, sealed, or adoption records released. SASE required. Turnaround time 2-4 days. Copy fee: $1.00 per page for civil, $.25 per page for criminal. Certification fee: $1.00. Fee payee: District Clerk. Personal checks accepted. Prepayment is required.

County Court PO Box 2987, Corpus Christi, TX 78403-2987; Civil phone: 361-888-0450; Criminal phone: 361-888-0495; Probate phone: 361-888-0365; Fax: 361-888-0571. Hours: 8AM-5PM (CST). *Misdemeanor, Civil, Probate.*

www.co.nueces.tx.us/districtclerk

Civil Records: Access: Mail, in person, online. Both court and visitors may perform in person searches. Search fee: $5.00 per name. Required to search: name, years to search. Civil cases indexed by defendant, plaintiff. Civil records on computer since 1993, index books prior. Online access to civil County Court records are available free online at the web site. Search by name, company, or cause number.

Criminal Records: Access: Mail, in person, online. Both court and visitors may perform in person searches. Search fee: $5.00 per name. Required to search: name, years to search, DOB. Criminal records on computer since 1987, index books prior. Online access to criminal County Court records are available free online at the web site. Search by name, SID #, or cause number.

General Information: Public Access terminal is available. (Civil & Criminal only.) No juvenile, mental, sealed, or adoption records released. SASE required. Turnaround time 2-4 days. Copy fee: $1.00 per page. Certification fee: $1.00. Fee payee: County Clerk. Personal checks accepted. Prepayment is required.

Ochiltree County

District Court 511 S Main, Perryton, TX 79070; 806-435-8054; Fax: 806-435-8058. Hours: 8:30AM-5PM (CST). *Felony, Civil.*

Civil Records: Access: Fax, mail, in person. Both court and visitors may perform in person searches. Search fee: $5.00 per name. Required to search: name, years to search. Civil cases indexed by defendant, plaintiff. Civil records in index books; on computer back to 1995.

Criminal Records: Access: Fax, mail, in person. Only the court performs in person searches; visitors may not. Search fee: $5.00 per name. Required to search: name, years to search. Criminal records in index books; on computer back to 1995.

General Information: No juvenile, mental, sealed, or adoption records released. SASE required. Turnaround time 2-4 days. Fax notes: No fee to fax results. Copy fee: $1.00 per page. Certification fee: $1.00. Fee payee: District Clerk. Personal checks accepted. Prepayment is required.

County Court 511 S Main St, Perryton, TX 79070; 806-435-8039; Fax: 806-435-2081. Hours: 8:30AM-Noon, 1-5PM (CST). *Misdemeanor, Civil, Probate.*

Civil Records: Access: Fax, mail, in person. Both court and visitors may perform in person searches. Search fee: $5.00 per name. Required to search: name, years to search. Civil cases indexed by defendant, plaintiff. Civil records in index books.

Criminal Records: Access: Fax, mail, in person. Both court and visitors may perform in person searches. Search fee: $5.00 per name. Required to search: name, years to search. Criminal records in index books.

General Information: No juvenile, mental, sealed, or adoption records released. SASE not required. Turnaround time usually mailed out same day of receipt. Fax notes: $3.00 for first page, $2.00 each add'l. Copy fee: $1.00 per page. Certification fee: $5.00. Fee payee: Ochiltree County Clerk. Personal checks accepted. Fax fees may be billed.

Oldham County

District & County Court PO Box 360, Vega, TX 79092; 806-267-2667. Hours: 8:30AM-Noon, 1-5PM (CST). *Felony, Misdemeanor, Civil, Eviction, Probate.*

Civil Records: Access: Mail, in person. Both court and visitors may perform in person searches. Search fee: $5.00 per name. Required to search: name, years to search. Civil cases indexed by defendant, plaintiff. Civil records in index books.

Criminal Records: Access: Mail, in person. Both court and visitors may perform in person searches. Search fee: $5.00 per name. Required to search: name, years to search. Criminal records in index books.

General Information: No juvenile, mental, sealed, or adoption records released. SASE required. Turnaround time 2-4 days. Copy fee: $1.00 per page. Certification fee: $5.00. Fee payee: Oldham County/District Clerk. Personal checks accepted. Prepayment is required.

Orange County

District Court PO Box 427, Orange, TX 77630; 409-883-7740. Hours: 8AM-5PM (CST). *Felony, Civil.*

Civil Records: Access: Mail, in person. Both court and visitors may perform in person searches. Search fee: $5.00 per name. Required to search: name, years to search. Civil cases indexed by defendant, plaintiff. Civil records on computer since 1985, index books prior.

Criminal Records: Access: Mail, in person. Both court and visitors may perform in person searches. Search fee: $5.00 per name. Required to search: name, years to search. Criminal records computerized since 1989.

General Information: Public Access terminal is available. No juvenile, mental, sealed, or adoption records released. SASE required. Turnaround time 2-4

days. Copy fee: $1.00 per page. Certification fee: $1.00. Fee payee: District Clerk. Only cashiers checks and money orders accepted. Prepayment is required.

County Court PO Box 1536, Orange, TX 77631-1536; 409-882-7055; Fax: 409-882-0379. Hours: 8:30AM-5PM (CST). *Misdemeanor, Civil, Probate.*

Civil Records: Access: Phone, fax, mail, in person. Both court and visitors may perform in person searches. No search fee. Required to search: name, years to search. Civil cases indexed by defendant, plaintiff. Civil records back to 1852; on computer back to 1985.

Criminal Records: Access: Phone, fax, mail, in person. Both court and visitors may perform in person searches. No search fee. Required to search: name, years to search. Criminal records back to 1852; on computer back to 1985.

General Information: Public Access terminal is available. No juvenile, mental, sealed, or adoption records released. SASE required. Turnaround time 7-10 days. Fax notes: Fee to fax results is $1.00 per page. Copy fee: $1.00 per page. Certification fee: $5.00. Fee payee: Karen Jo Vance, County Clerk. Personal checks accepted. Prepayment is required.

Palo Pinto County

District Court PO Box 189, Palo Pinto, TX 76484-0189; 940-659-1279. Hours: 8AM-4:30PM (CST). *Felony, Civil.*

Civil Records: Access: Mail, in person. Both court and visitors may perform in person searches. Search fee: $5.00 per name. Required to search: name, years to search. Civil cases indexed by defendant, plaintiff. Civil records on computer since 1993, index books prior.

Criminal Records: Access: Mail, in person. Both court and visitors may perform in person searches. Search fee: $5.00 per name. Required to search: name, years to search. Criminal records on computer since 1993, index books prior.

General Information: No juvenile, mental, sealed, or adoption records released. SASE required. Turnaround time 1-2 days. Copy fee: $1.00 per page. Certification fee: $1.00. Fee payee: District Clerk. Personal checks accepted. Prepayment is required.

County Court PO Box 219, Palo Pinto, TX 76484; 940-659-1277; Fax: 940-659-2590. Hours: 8:30AM-4:30PM (CST). *Misdemeanor, Civil, Probate.*

Civil Records: Access: Mail, in person. Both court and visitors may perform in person searches. Search fee: $5.00 per name. Required to search: name, years to search. Civil cases indexed by defendant, plaintiff. Civil records on computer back to 1986; index books from 1857.

Criminal Records: Access: Mail, in person. Both court and visitors may perform in person searches. Search fee: $5.00 per name. Required to search: name, years to search, DOB; also helpful: SSN. Criminal records on computer back to 1986; index books from 1857.

General Information: No juvenile, mental, sealed, or adoption records released. SASE not required. Turnaround time next day. Copy fee: $1.00 per page. Certification fee: $5.00. Fee payee: County Clerk. Personal checks accepted. Prepayment is required.

Panola County

District Court County Courthouse Rm 227, Carthage, TX 75633; 903-693-0306; Fax: 903-693-6914. Hours: 8AM-5PM (CST). *Felony, Civil.*

Civil Records: Access: Mail, in person. Both court and visitors may perform in person searches. Search fee: $5.00 per name. Required to search: name, years to search. Civil cases indexed by defendant, plaintiff. Civil records in index books from 1865; computerized back to 1994.

Criminal Records: Access: Mail, in person. Both court and visitors may perform in person searches. Search

fee: $5.00 per name. Required to search: name, years to search, DOB. Criminal records in index books from 1865; computerized back to 1994.

General Information: No juvenile, mental, sealed, or adoption records released. SASE required. Turnaround time 3 days. Fax notes: Fee to fax results is $1.00 per page. Copy fee: $1.00 per page. Certification fee: $1.00 fee per page. Fee payee: District Clerk. Personal checks accepted. Prepayment is required.

County Court County Courthouse Rm 201, Carthage, TX 75633; 903-693-0302. Hours: 8AM-5PM (CST). *Misdemeanor, Civil, Probate.*

Civil Records: Access: Mail, in person. Both court and visitors may perform in person searches. Search fee: $5.00 per name. Required to search: name, years to search. Civil cases indexed by defendant, plaintiff. Civil records in index books.

Criminal Records: Access: Mail, in person. Both court and visitors may perform in person searches. Search fee: $5.00 per name. Required to search: name, years to search, DOB. Criminal records in index books.

General Information: No juvenile, mental, sealed, or adoption records released. SASE not required. Turnaround time 2-4 days. Copy fee: $1.00 per page. Certification fee: $5.00. Fee payee: County Clerk. Personal checks accepted. Personal checks require ID. Prepayment is required.

Parker County

District Court 117 Ft. Worth Ave (PO Box 340), Weatherford, TX 76086; 817-599-6591; Civil phone: X6211; Criminal phone: X6214. Hours: 8AM-5PM (CST). *Felony, Civil.*

Civil Records: Access: Mail, in person. Both court and visitors may perform in person searches. Search fee: $5.00 per name. Required to search: name, years to search, and/or cause number. Civil cases indexed by defendant, plaintiff. Civil records in index books.

Criminal Records: Access: Mail, in person. Both court and visitors may perform in person searches. Search fee: $5.00 per name. Required to search: name, years to search, and/or cause number; also helpful: DOB, SSN. Criminal records in index books.

General Information: No juvenile, mental, sealed, or adoption records released. SASE required. Turnaround time same day. Copy fee: $1.00 for first page, $.25 each add'l. Certification fee: $1.00 per page. Fee payee: District Clerk. Personal checks accepted. Prepayment is required.

County Court County Clerk - Court Division, PO Box 819, Weatherford, TX 76086-0819; 817-594-1632. Hours: 8AM-Noon, 1-5PM *Misdemeanor, Civil.*

Civil Records: Access: Phone, mail, fax, in person. Both court and visitors may perform in person searches. Search fee: $5.00 per name. Required to search: name, years to search. Civil cases indexed by defendant, plaintiff. Civil records in index books; on computer since 8/1985.

Criminal Records: Access: Phone, mail, fax, in person. Both court and visitors may perform in person searches. Search fee: $5.00 per name. Required to search: name, years to search, DOB; also helpful - SSN, signed release. Criminal records on computer since 8/1985, index books and archived since 1900s.

General Information: Public Access terminal is available. No juvenile, mental, sealed, or adoption records released. SASE required. Turnaround time 1-2 days. Copy fee: $1.00 per page. Certification fee: $1.00. Fee payee: County Clerk. Personal checks accepted. Prepayment is required.

Probate Court 1112 Santa Fe Dr, PO Box 819, Weatherford, TX 76086; 817-594-7461. Hours: 8AM-5PM (CST). *Probate.*

Parmer County

District Court PO Box 195, Farwell, TX 79325-0195; 806-481-3419; Fax: 806-481-9416. Hours: 8:30AM-Noon, 1-5PM (CST). *Felony, Civil.*

Civil Records: Access: Fax, mail, in person. Both court and visitors may perform in person searches. Search fee: $5.00 per name. Required to search: name, years to search. Civil cases indexed by defendant, plaintiff. Civil records in index books since 1917.

Criminal Records: Access: Fax, mail, in person. Both court and visitors may perform in person searches. Search fee: $5.00 per name. Required to search: name, years to search. Criminal records in index books since 1917.

General Information: No juvenile, mental, sealed, or adoption records released. SASE required. Turnaround time 1 day. Fax notes: $1.00 per page. Copy fee: $1.00 per page. Certification fee: No certification fee. Fee payee: District Clerk. Personal checks accepted. Prepayment is required.

County Court PO Box 356, Farwell, TX 79325; 806-481-3691. Hours: 8:30AM-5PM (CST). *Misdemeanor, Civil, Probate.*

Civil Records: Access: Mail, in person. Both court and visitors may perform in person searches. Search fee: $5.00 per name. Required to search: name, years to search. Civil cases indexed by defendant, plaintiff. Civil records in index books.

Criminal Records: Access: Mail, in person. Both court and visitors may perform in person searches. Search fee: $5.00 per name. Required to search: name, years to search. Criminal records in index books.

General Information: No juvenile, mental, sealed, or adoption records released. SASE required. Turnaround time 2-4 days. Copy fee: $1.00 per page. Certification fee: $5.00. Fee payee: County Clerk. Personal checks accepted. Prepayment is required.

Pecos County

District Court 400 S Nelson, Fort Stockton, TX 79735; 915-336-3503; Fax: 915-336-6437. Hours: 8AM-5PM (CST). *Felony, Civil.*

Civil Records: Access: Fax, mail, in person. Both court and visitors may perform in person searches. Search fee: $5.00 per name. Required to search: name, years to search. Civil cases indexed by defendant, plaintiff. Civil records on computer since 1987, index books prior.

Criminal Records: Access: Fax, mail, in person. Both court and visitors may perform in person searches. Search fee: $5.00 per name. Required to search: name, years to search, DOB, signed release; also helpful-address, SSN. Criminal records on computer since 1987, index books prior.

General Information: No juvenile, mental, sealed, or adoption records released. SASE required. Turnaround time 2-4 days. Fax notes: Fee to fax results is $1.00 per page. Copy fee: $1.00 per page. Certification fee: No certification fee. Fee payee: District Clerk. Personal checks accepted. Prepayment is required.

County Court 103 W Callaghan, Fort Stockton, TX 79735; 915-336-7555; Fax: 915-336-7575. Hours: 8AM-5PM (CST). *Misdemeanor, Civil, Probate.*

Civil Records: Access: Mail, in person. Both court and visitors may perform in person searches. Search fee: $8.00 per name. Required to search: name, years to search. Civil cases indexed by defendant, plaintiff. Civil records on computer and index books to 1955.

Criminal Records: Access: Mail, in person. Both court and visitors may perform in person searches. Search fee: $8.00 per name. Required to search: name, years to search. Criminal records on computer and index books to 1955.

General Information: No juvenile, mental, sealed, or adoption records released. SASE required. Turnaround

time same day. Fax notes: Fee to fax results is $1.00 per page. Copy fee: $1.00 per page. Certification fee: $5.00. Fee payee: County Clerk. Personal checks accepted. Prepayment is required.

Polk County

District Court 101 W Church, Livingston, TX 77351; 936-327-6814. 8AM-5PM *Felony, Civil.*

Civil Records: Access: Mail, in person. Both court and visitors may perform in person searches. Search fee: $5.00 per name. Fee is per 10 year period. Required to search: name, years to search. Civil cases indexed by defendant, plaintiff. Civil records in index books.

Criminal Records: Access: Mail, in person. Both court and visitors may perform in person searches. Search fee: $5.00 per name. Fee is per 10 year period. Required to search: name, years to search; also helpful: DOB. Criminal records in index books.

General Information: No juvenile, mental, sealed, or adoption records released. SASE required. Turnaround time 2-4 days. Copy fee: $1.00 per page. Certification fee: $2.00. Fee payee: District Clerk. Personal checks accepted. Prepayment is required.

County Court PO Drawer 2119, Livingston, TX 77351; 936-327-6804; Fax: 936-327-6874. Hours: 8AM-5PM (CST). *Misdemeanor, Civil, Probate.*

Civil Records: Access: Mail, in person. Both court and visitors may perform in person searches. Search fee: $5.00 per name. Required to search: name, years to search. Civil cases indexed by defendant, plaintiff. Civil records in index books.

Criminal Records: Access: Mail, in person. Both court and visitors may perform in person searches. Search fee: $5.00 per name. Required to search: name, years to search; also helpful: DOB, SSN. Criminal records in index books; on computer back to 1982.

General Information: No juvenile, mental, sealed, or adoption records released. SASE required. Turnaround time 2-4 days. Fax notes: Fee to fax results is $2.00 per document and $1.00 per page. Copy fee: $1.00 per page. Certification fee: $5.00. Fee payee: County Clerk. Personal checks accepted. Prepayment is required.

Potter County

District Court PO Box 9570, Amarillo, TX 79105-9570; 806-379-2300. Hours: 7:30AM-5:30PM (CST). *Felony, Civil.*

www.co.potter.tx.us/districtclerk

Civil Records: Access: Phone, fax, mail, online, in person. Both court and visitors may perform in person searches. Search fee: $5.00 per name. Required to search: name, years to search. Civil cases indexed by defendant, plaintiff. Civil records on computer since 9/87, index books prior. Civil case information from 1988 forward available free online www.idocket.com.

Criminal Records: Access: Phone, fax, mail, online, in person. Both court and visitors may perform in person searches. Search fee: $5.00 per name. Required to search: name, years to search. Criminal records on computer since 9/87, index books prior. Online access to criminal records is the same as civil.

General Information: Public Access terminal is available. No juvenile, mental, sealed, or adoption records released. SASE required. Turnaround time 2-4 days. Fax notes: $1.00 per page plus 5% of transaction total for credit card fee. Copy fee: $.25 per page. Certification fee: $1.00 per page. Fee payee: District Clerk. Business checks accepted. Credit cards accepted: Visa, MasterCard. Prepayment is required.

County Court & County Courts at Law 1 & 2 PO Box 9638, Amarillo, TX 79105; 806-379-2285; Fax: 806-379-2296. Hours: 8AM-5PM (CST). *Misdemeanor, Civil, Probate.*

www.co.potter.tx.us/countyclerk/index.html

Note: Limited civil records filed here, most are with the District Clerk.

Civil Records: Access: Mail, in person. Both court and visitors may perform in person searches. Search fee: $10.00 per name. Required to search: exact name, years to search. Civil cases indexed by defendant, plaintiff. Civil records on computer since 1990, index books and microfiche since 1889. Civil case information is available from idocket: http://idocket.com/counties.htm.

Criminal Records: Access: Mail, in person. Both court and visitors may perform in person searches. Search fee: $10.00 per name. Required to search: exact name, years to search, also helpful: DOB. Criminal records on computer since 1990, index books and microfiche since 1889. Criminal case information is available from idocket at http://idocket.com/counties.htm.

General Information: Public Access terminal is available. No juvenile, mental or sealed records released. SASE required. Turnaround time 1-2 days. Copy fee: $1.00 per page. Certification fee: $5.00. Fee payee: Potter County Clerk. Personal checks accepted. Credit cards accepted: Visa, MasterCard. Prepayment is required.

Presidio County

District & County Court PO Box 789, Marfa, TX 79843; 915-729-4812; Fax: 915-729-4313. Hours: 8AM-Noon, 1-4PM (CST). *Felony, Misdemeanor, Civil, Eviction, Probate.*

Civil Records: Access: Mail, in person. Both court and visitors may perform in person searches. Search fee: $5.00 per name. Required to search: name, years to search. Civil cases indexed by defendant, plaintiff. Civil records in index books.

Criminal Records: Access: Mail, in person. Both court and visitors may perform in person searches. Search fee: $5.00 per name. Required to search: name, years to search. Criminal records in index books.

General Information: No juvenile, mental, sealed, or adoption records released. SASE required. Turnaround time 2-4 days. Copy fee: $1.00 per page. Certification fee: $5.00. Fee payee: District Clerk. Personal checks accepted. Prepayment is required.

Rains County

District & County Court PO Box 187, Emory, TX 75440; 903-473-2461. Hours: 7:30AM-4:30PM (CST). *Felony, Misdemeanor, Civil, Eviction, Probate.*

Civil Records: Access: Mail, in person. Both court and visitors may perform in person searches. Search fee: $5.00 per name. Required to search: name. Civil cases indexed by defendant, plaintiff. Civil records on computer since 1989, index books prior.

Criminal Records: Access: Mail, in person. Both court and visitors may perform in person searches. Search fee: $5.00 per name. Required to search: name; also helpful: DOB. Criminal records on computer since 1989, index books prior.

General Information: No juvenile, mental, sealed, or adoption records released. SASE required. Turnaround time same day. Copy fee: $1.00 per page. Certification fee: $5.00. Fee payee: Mary Sheppard, District/County Clerk. Personal checks accepted. Prepayment required.

Randall County

District Courts PO Box 1096, Canyon, TX 79015; 806-655-6200; Fax: 806-655-6205. Hours: 8AM-5PM (CST). *Felony, Civil.*

www.randallcounty.org

Civil Records: Access: Fax, mail, online, in person. Both court and visitors may perform in person searches. Search fee: $5.00 per name. Required to search: name, years to search. Civil cases indexed by defendant, plaintiff. Civil records in index books. Records on

computer since 1982. Civil case information is available free online at www.idocket.com.

Criminal Records: Access: Fax, mail, online, in person. Both court and visitors may perform in person searches. Search fee: $5.00 per name. Required to search: name, years to search. Criminal records on computer since 1985; prior in docket books. Online access to criminal records is the same as civil.

General Information: Public Access terminal is available. (Criminal only.) No juvenile, mental, sealed, or adoption records released. SASE not required. Turnaround time 1-2 days. Fax notes: Fee to fax results is $5.00 1st pg; $1.00 each add'l. Copy fee: $.25 per page. Certification fee: $1.00 per page. Fee payee: District Clerk. Personal checks accepted. Credit cards accepted: Visa, MasterCard. Prepayment is required.

County Court PO Box 660, Canyon, TX 79015; 806-655-6330. Hours: 8AM-5PM (CST). *Misdemeanor, Civil, Probate.*

www.randallcounty.org/cclerk/default.htm

Civil Records: Access: Phone, mail, fax, in person, email. Both court and visitors may perform in person searches. Search fee: $10.00 per name. Required to search: name, years to search. Civil cases indexed by defendant, plaintiff. Civil records in index books. Civil case information is available online from idocket at http://idocket.com/counties.htm.

Criminal Records: Access: Phone, mail, fax, in person, online, email. Both court and visitors may perform in person searches. Search fee: $10.00 per name. Required to search: name, years to search; also helpful: DOB. Criminal records on computer since 1984; prior records in index books. Criminal case information is available online from idocket at http://idocket.com/counties.htm.

General Information: Public Access terminal is available. No juvenile, mental, sealed, or adoption records released. SASE required. Turnaround time 2-4 days. Fax notes: Fee to fax results is $1.00 per page. Copy fee: $1.00 per page. Certification fee: $5.00. Fee payee: Randall County Clerk. Personal checks accepted.

Reagan County

District & County Court PO Box 100, Big Lake, TX 76932; 915-884-2442; Fax: 915-884-1503. Hours: 8:30AM-5PM (CST). *Felony, Misdemeanor, Civil, Eviction, Probate.*

Civil Records: Access: Mail, in person. Both court and visitors may perform in person searches. Search fee: $5.00 per name. Required to search: name, years to search. Civil cases indexed by defendant, plaintiff. Civil records in index books.

Criminal Records: Access: Mail, in person. Both court and visitors may perform in person searches. Search fee: $5.00 per name. Required to search: name, years to search. Criminal records in index books.

General Information: No juvenile, mental, sealed, or adoption records released. SASE required. Turnaround time same day. Fax notes: $5.00 per document; no fee to fax to toll-free number. Copy fee: $1.00 per page. Certification fee: $5.00. Fee payee: County/District Clerk. Personal checks accepted. Prepayment required.

Real County

District & County Court PO Box 750, Leakey, TX 78873; 830-232-5202; Fax: 830-232-6888. Hours: 8AM-5PM (CST). *Felony, Misdemeanor, Civil, Eviction, Probate.*

Civil Records: Access: In person only. Visitors must perform in person searches for themselves. No search fee. Squireed to search: name, years to search. Civil cases indexed by defendant, plaintiff. Civil records in index books.

Criminal Records: Access: In person only. Visitors must perform in person searches for themselves. No search fee. Required to search: name, years to search, DOB. Criminal records in index books.

General Information: No juvenile, mental, sealed, or adoption records released. Fax notes: Fee to fax results is $1.00 per page. Copy fee: $1.00 per page. Certification fee: $5.00. Fee payee: District/County Court. Personal checks accepted. Prepayment required.

Red River County

District Court 400 N Walnut, Clarksville, TX 75426; 903-427-3761; Fax: 903-427-1201. Hours: 8:30AM-Noon, 1-5PM (CST). *Felony, Civil.*

Civil Records: Access: Mail, fax, in person. Both court and visitors may perform in person searches. Search fee: $5.00 per name. Required to search: name, years to search. Civil cases indexed by defendant, plaintiff. Civil records in index books and on microfilm to 1800s.

Criminal Records: Access: Mail, fax, in person. Both court and visitors may perform in person searches. Search fee: $5.00 per name. Required to search: name, years to search. Criminal records in index books and on microfilm to 1800s.

General Information: No juvenile, mental, sealed, or adoption records released. SASE required. Turnaround time same day. Copy fee: $1.00 per page. Certification fee: $2.00. Fee is for in person certification only. Fee payee: District Clerk. Personal checks accepted. Prepayment is required.

County Court 200 N Walnut, Clarksville, TX 75426; 903-427-2401. Hours: 8:30AM-5PM (CST). *Misdemeanor, Probate.*

Criminal Records: Access: Mail, in person. Both court and visitors may perform in person searches. Search fee: $5.00 per name. Required to search: name, years to search. Criminal records on computer (name only) since 1980, in index books since 1960s.

General Information: No mental, sealed, or adoption records released. SASE required. Turnaround time 1-2 days. Copy fee: $1.00 per page. Certification fee: $5.00. Fee payee: County Clerk. Personal checks accepted. Prepayment is required.

Reeves County

District Court PO Box 848, Pecos, TX 79772; 915-445-2714; Fax: 915-445-7455. Hours: 8AM-Noon, 1-5PM (CST). *Felony, Civil.*

Civil Records: Access: Phone, mail, in person. Both court and visitors may perform in person searches. Search fee: $5.00 per name. Required to search: name, years to search. Civil cases indexed by defendant, plaintiff. Civil records on computer since 1988, index books prior.

Criminal Records: Access: Mail, in person. Both court and visitors may perform in person searches. Search fee: $5.00 per name. Required to search: name, years to search. Criminal records on computer since 1988, index books prior.

General Information: No juvenile, mental, sealed, or adoption records released. SASE required. Turnaround time 2-4 days. Copy fee: $.25 per page. Certification fee: $1.00 per page. Fee payee: District Clerk Reeves County. Personal checks accepted. Prepayment is required.

County Court PO Box 867, Pecos, TX 79772; 915-445-5467. Hours: 8AM-5PM (CST). *Misdemeanor, Civil, Probate.*

Civil Records: Access: Mail, in person. Both court and visitors may perform in person searches. Search fee: $10.00 per name. Required to search: name, years to search; also helpful: address. Civil cases indexed by defendant, plaintiff. Civil records on computer since 1990, index books prior.

Criminal Records: Access: Mail, in person. Both court and visitors may perform in person searches. Search fee: $10.00 per name. Required to search: name, years to search, DOB; also helpful: address. Criminal records on computer since 1990, index books prior.

General Information: No juvenile, mental, sealed, or adoption records released. SASE required. Turnaround time 5 days. Fax notes: $.50 per page. Copy fee: $1.00 per page. Certification fee: $5.00. Fee payee: Reeves County Clerk. Personal checks accepted.

Refugio County

District Court PO Box 736, Refugio, TX 78377; 361-526-2721. 8AM-Noon, 1-5PM *Felony, Civil.*

Civil Records: Access: Mail, in person. Both court and visitors may perform in person searches. Search fee: $5.00 per name. Required to search: name, years to search. Civil cases indexed by defendant, plaintiff. Civil records on computer since 1992, index books prior.

Criminal Records: Access: Mail, in person. Both court and visitors may perform in person searches. Search fee: $5.00 per name. Required to search: name, years to search. Criminal records on computer since 1992, index books prior.

General Information: No juvenile, mental, sealed, or adoption records released. SASE required. Turnaround time 2-4 days. Copy fee: $1.00 per page. Certification fee: $1.00. Fee payee: District Clerk. Personal checks accepted. Prepayment is required.

County Court PO Box 704, Refugio, TX 78377; 361-526-2233. Hours: 8AM-5PM (CST). *Misdemeanor, Civil, Probate.*

Civil Records: Access: Mail, in person. Both court and visitors may perform in person searches. Search fee: $10.00 per name. Required to search: name, years to search. Civil cases indexed by defendant, plaintiff. Civil records on computer since 1992, index books prior.

Criminal Records: Access: Mail, in person. Both court and visitors may perform in person searches. Search fee: $10.00 per name. Required to search: name, years to search. Criminal records on computer since 1992, index books prior.

General Information: No juvenile, mental, sealed, or adoption records released. SASE not required. Turnaround time 1-2 days. Copy fee: $1.00 per page. Certification fee: $5.00. Fee payee: Janelle Morgan, County Clerk. Personal checks accepted. Prepayment is required.

Roberts County

District & County Court PO Box 477, Miami, TX 79059; 806-868-2341. Hours: 8AM-Noon, 1-5PM (CST). *Felony, Misdemeanor, Civil, Eviction, Probate.*

Civil Records: Access: Mail, in person. Both court and visitors may perform in person searches. Search fee: $5.00 per name. Required to search: name, years to search. Civil cases indexed by defendant, plaintiff. Civil records in index books.

Criminal Records: Access: Mail, in person. Both court and visitors may perform in person searches. Search fee: $5.00 per name. Required to search: name, years to search, DOB, SSN. Criminal records in index books.

General Information: No juvenile, mental, sealed, or adoption records released. SASE required. Turnaround time 2-4 days. Fax notes: $3.00 first pg; $1.00 each add'l. Copy fee: $1.00 per page. Include postage with copy fee. Certification fee: County Court certification fee is $5.00, District is $1.00. Payee: Roberts County. Personal checks accepted. Prepayment is required.

Robertson County

District Court PO Box 250, Franklin, TX 77856; 979-828-3636. Hours: 8AM-5PM (CST). *Felony, Civil.*

Civil Records: Access: Mail, in person. Both court and visitors may perform in person searches. Search fee:

$5.00 per name. Required to search: name, years to search. Civil cases indexed by defendant, plaintiff. Civil records on computer and index books.

Criminal Records: Access: Mail, in person. Both court and visitors may perform in person searches. Search fee: $5.00 per name. Required to search: name, years to search, DOB; also helpful: SSN. Criminal records on computer and index books.

General Information: No juvenile, sealed, or adoption records released. SASE required. Turnaround time 1-2 days. Copy fee: $1.00 per page. Certification fee: $1.00 per page. Fee payee: Robertson County District Clerk. Personal checks accepted. Prepayment is required.

County Court PO Box 1029, Franklin, TX 77856; 979-828-4130. Hours: 8AM-5PM (CST). *Misdemeanor, Civil, Probate.*

Civil Records: Access: Mail, fax, in person. Both court and visitors may perform in person searches. Search fee: $5.00 per name. Required to search: name, years to search. Civil cases indexed by defendant, plaintiff. Civil records on computer back to 1989, index books to 1918.

Criminal Records: Access: Mail, fax, in person. Both court and visitors may perform in person searches. Search fee: $5.00 per name. Required to search: name, years to search, DOB. Criminal records on computer back to 1989, index books from 1918.

General Information: Public Access terminal is available. No juvenile, mental, sealed, or adoption records released. SASE not required. Turnaround time same day. Fax notes: Will not fax results. Copy fee: $1.00 per page. Certification fee: $5.00. Fee payee: Robertson County Clerk. Personal checks accepted. Prepayment is required.

Rockwall County

District Court 1101 Ridge Rd #209, Rockwall, TX 75087; 972-882-0260; Fax: 972-882-0268. Hours: 8AM-5PM (CST). *Felony, Civil.*

Civil Records: Access: Mail, in person. Both court and visitors may perform in person searches. Search fee: $5.00 per name. Fee is per 5 year period. Required to search: name, years to search. Civil cases indexed by defendant, plaintiff. Civil records on computer back to 1992, index books prior.

Criminal Records: Access: Mail, in person. Both court and visitors may perform in person searches. Search fee: $5.00 per name. Required to search: name, years to search, DOB. Criminal records on computer back to 1980, index books prior.

General Information: Public Access terminal is available. No juvenile, mental, sealed, or adoption records released. SASE required. Turnaround time 2-4 days. Copy fee: $1.00 per page. Certification fee: $1.00. Fee payee: District Clerk. Personal checks accepted. Prepayment is required.

County Court 1101 Ridge Rd #101, Rockwall, TX 75087; 972-882-0220; Fax: 972-882-0229. Hours: 8AM-5PM (CST). *Misdemeanor, Civil, Probate.*

Civil Records: Access: Phone, mail, in person. Both court and visitors may perform in person searches. Search fee: $5.00 per name. Required to search: name, years to search. Civil cases indexed by defendant, plaintiff. Civil records on computer back to 1983 and in index books from 1800s.

Criminal Records: Access: Phone, mail, in person. Both court and visitors may perform in person searches. Search fee: $5.00 per name. Required to search: name, years to search. Criminal records on computer back to 1983 and in index books from 1800s.

General Information: Public Access terminal is available. No juvenile, mental, sealed, or adoption records released. SASE required. Turnaround time 2-4 days. Fax notes: Fee to fax results is $5.00 per document. Copy fee: $1.00 per page. Certification fee:

$5.00. Fee payee: County Clerk. Personal checks accepted. Prepayment is required.

Runnels County

District Court PO Box 166, Ballinger, TX 76821; 915-365-2638; Fax: 915-365-3408. Hours: 8:30AM-5PM (CST). *Felony, Civil.*

Civil Records: Access: Phone, fax, mail, in person. Both court and visitors may perform in person searches. Search fee: $5.00 per name. Required to search: name; also helpful: years to search. Civil cases indexed by defendant, plaintiff. Civil records in index books since beginning of Courthouse.

Criminal Records: Access: Phone, fax, mail, in person. Both court and visitors may perform in person searches. Search fee: $5.00 per name. Required to search: name; also helpful: years to search, DOB, SSN. Criminal records in index books since beginning of Courthouse.

General Information: No juvenile, mental, sealed or adoption records released. SASE required. Turnaround time 1-2 days. Fax notes: $1.00 per page. Copy fee: $1.00 per page. Certification fee: $1.00. Fee payee: District Clerk. Personal checks accepted. Prepayment is required.

County Court PO Box 189, Ballinger, TX 76821; 915-365-2720. Hours: 8:30AM-Noon, 1-5PM (CST). *Misdemeanor, Civil, Probate.*

Civil Records: Access: Phone, mail, in person. Both court and visitors may perform in person searches. No search fee. Required to search: name, years to search. Civil cases indexed by defendant, plaintiff. Civil records in docket books with alphabetical index and file jacket by number.

Criminal Records: Access: Phone, mail, in person. Both court and visitors may perform in person searches. No search fee. Required to search: name, years to search; also helpful: DOB. Criminal records in docket books with alphabetical index and file jacket by number.

General Information: No juvenile or mental records released. SASE not required. Turnaround time 1-2 days. Copy fee: $1.00 per page. Certification fee: $5.00. Fee payee: County Clerk, Runnels County. Personal checks accepted. Prepayment is required.

Rusk County

District Court PO Box 1687, Henderson, TX 75653; 903-657-0353. 8AM-5PM *Felony, Civil.*

Civil Records: Access: Mail, in person. Both court and visitors may perform in person searches. Search fee: $5.00 per name. Required to search: name, years to search. Civil cases indexed by defendant, plaintiff. Civil records in index books; on computer back to 1973.

Criminal Records: Access: Mail, in person. Both court and visitors may perform in person searches. Search fee: $5.00 per name. Required to search: name, years to search, DOB, SSN, signed release. Criminal records in index books; on computer back to 1973.

General Information: No juvenile, mental, sealed, or adoption records released. SASE required. Turnaround time 2-4 days. Copy fee: $1.00 per page. Certification fee: $1.00. Fee payee: District Clerk. Only cashiers checks and money orders accepted. Prepayment is required.

County Court at Law PO Box 1687, Henderson, TX 75653-1687; 903-657-0353 (X0348 Fam Court Records). Hours: 8AM-5PM (CST). *Misdemeanor, Civil, Probate.*

Note: Misdemeanor & Probate records are at County Clerk, PO Box 758, phone 903-657-0330.

Civil Records: Access: Mail, in person. Both court and visitors may perform in person searches. Search fee: $5.00 per name. Required to search: name, years to

search. Civil cases indexed by defendant, plaintiff. Civil records in index books.

Criminal Records: Access: Mail, in person. Both court and visitors may perform in person searches. Search fee: $5.00 per name. Required to search: name, years to search, DOB, SSN. Criminal records are not computerized, are indexed in books.

General Information: No juvenile, mental, sealed, or adoption records released. SASE required. Turnaround time 2-4 days. Copy fee: $1.00 per page. Certification fee: No certification fee. Fee payee: District Clerk. Business checks accepted. Prepayment is required.

Sabine County

District Court PO Box 850, Hemphill, TX 75948; 409-787-2912. Hours: 8AM-4PM (CST). *Felony, Civil.*

Civil Records: Access: Mail, in person. Both court and visitors may perform in person searches. Search fee: $10.00 per name. Required to search: name, years to search. Civil cases indexed by defendant, plaintiff. Civil records on computer since 1993, index books prior.

Criminal Records: Access: Mail, in person. Both court and visitors may perform in person searches. Search fee: $10.00 per name. Required to search: name, years to search. Criminal records on computer since 1993, index books prior.

General Information: No juvenile, mental, sealed, or adoption records released. SASE required. Turnaround time 1-2 days. Copy fee: $1.00 per page. Certification fee: No certification fee. Fee payee: District Clerk. Personal checks accepted. Prepayment is required.

County Court PO Drawer 580, Hemphill, TX 75948-0580; 409-787-3786. Hours: 8AM-4PM (CST). *Misdemeanor, Probate.*

Criminal Records: Access: Mail, in person. Both court and visitors may perform in person searches. Search fee: $10.00 per name. Required to search: name, years to search. Criminal records on computer since 1992, index books prior.

General Information: No juvenile, mental, sealed, or adoption records released. SASE not required. Turnaround time 2 days. Copy fee: $1.00 per page. Certification fee: $5.00. Fee payee: Sabine County Clerk. Business checks accepted. Prepayment required.

San Augustine County

District Court County Courthouse Rm 202, San Augustine, TX 75972; 936-275-2231; Fax: 936-275-9579. Hours: 8AM-4:15PM (CST). *Felony, Civil.*

Civil Records: Access: Phone, mail, in person. Both court and visitors may perform in person searches. Search fee: $5.00 per name. Required to search: name, years to search. Civil cases indexed by plaintiff. Civil records in index books.

Criminal Records: Access: Phone, mail, in person. Only the court performs in person searches; visitors may not. Search fee: $5.00 per name. Required to search: name, years to search. Criminal records in index books.

General Information: No juvenile, mental, sealed, or adoption records released. SASE required. Turnaround time 2-4 days. Copy fee: $1.00 per page. Certification fee: $1.00. Fee payee: District Clerk. Personal checks accepted.

County Court County Courthouse Rm 106, San Augustine, TX 75972; 936-275-2452; Fax: 936-275-9579. Hours: 8AM-4:30PM (CST). *Misdemeanor, Civil, Probate.*

Civil Records: Access: Mail, in person. Both court and visitors may perform in person searches. Search fee: $5.00 per name. Required to search: name, years to search; also helpful: address. Civil cases indexed by defendant, plaintiff. Civil records in binders and file jackets.

Criminal Records: Access: Phone, mail, in person. Both court and visitors may perform in person searches. Search fee: $5.00 per name. Required to search: name, years to search; also helpful: address, DOB, SSN. Criminal records in binders and file jackets. Criminal information may be obtained over the phone, but copies must be paid for in advance. Will fax back if $5.00 paid in advance.

General Information: No juvenile, mental, sealed, or adoption records released. SASE required. Turnaround time 2-3 days. Copy fee: $1.00 per page. Certification fee: $5.00. Fee payee: County Clerk. Personal checks accepted. Prepayment is required.

San Jacinto County

District Court PO Box 369, Coldspring, TX 77331; 936-653-2909. Hours: 8AM-Noon, 1-5PM (CST). *Felony, Civil.*

Civil Records: Access: Mail, in person. Both court and visitors may perform in person searches. Search fee: $5.00 per name. Required to search: name, years to search. Civil cases indexed by defendant, plaintiff. Civil records in index books.

Criminal Records: Access: Mail, in person. Both court and visitors may perform in person searches. Search fee: $5.00 per name. Required to search: name, years to search. Criminal records on computer since 1986.

General Information: No juvenile, mental, sealed, or adoption records released. SASE required. Turnaround time 2-4 days. Copy fee: $1.00 per page. Certification fee: $2.00. Fee payee: District Clerk. Personal checks accepted. Prepayment is required.

County Court PO Box 669, Coldspring, TX 77331; 936-653-2324. Hours: 8AM-4:30PM (CST). *Misdemeanor, Civil, Probate.*

www.co.san-jacinto.tx.us

Civil Records: Access: Mail, in person. Both court and visitors may perform in person searches. Search fee: $5.00 per name. Required to search: name, years to search. Civil cases indexed by defendant, plaintiff. Civil records in index books.

Criminal Records: Access: Mail, in person. Both court and visitors may perform in person searches. Search fee: $5.00 per name. Required to search: name, years to search; also helpful: address, DOB, SSN. Criminal records in index books.

General Information: No juvenile, mental, sealed, or adoption records released. SASE required. Turnaround time 2 weeks. Copy fee: $1.00 per page. Certification fee: $5.00. Fee payee: County Clerk. Personal checks accepted. Only cashiers checks and money orders accepted for criminal searches. Prepayment is required.

San Patricio County

District Court PO Box 1084, Sinton, TX 78387; 361-364-6225. Hours: 8AM-5PM (CST). *Felony, Civil.*

Civil Records: Access: Mail, in person. Both court and visitors may perform in person searches. Search fee: $5.00 per name. Fee is per division. Required to search: name, years to search. Civil cases indexed by defendant, plaintiff. Civil records in index books from 1800s; computerized back to 1993.

Criminal Records: Access: Mail, in person. Both court and visitors may perform in person searches. Search fee: $5.00 per name. Fee is per division. Required to search: name, years to search. Criminal records in index books from 1800s; computerized back to 1993.

General Information: Public Access terminal is available. No juvenile, mental, sealed, or adoption records released. SASE required. Turnaround time 2-4 days. Copy fee: $1.00 per page. Certification fee: $1.00. Fee payee: District Clerk. Business checks accepted. Prepayment is required.

County Court PO Box 578, Sinton, TX 78387; 361-364-6290; Fax: 361-364-6112. Hours: 8AM-5PM (CST). *Misdemeanor, Civil, Probate.*

Civil Records: Access: Phone, mail, in person. Both court and visitors may perform in person searches. Search fee: $5.00 per name. Required to search: name, years to search; also helpful: address. Civil cases indexed by defendant, plaintiff. Civil records in index books.

Criminal Records: Access: Phone, mail, in person. Both court and visitors may perform in person searches. Search fee: $5.00 per name. Required to search: name, years to search; also helpful: address, DOB, SSN. Criminal records in index books.

General Information: No juvenile, mental, sealed, or adoption records released. SASE required. Turnaround time 2-3 days. Copy fee: $1.00 per page. Certification fee: $5.00. Fee payee: County Clerk. Personal checks accepted. Prepayment is required.

San Saba County

District & County Court County Courthouse, 500 E Wallace #202, San Saba, TX 76877; 915-372-3375. Hours: 8AM-Noon, 1-5PM (CST). *Felony, Misdemeanor, Civil, Eviction, Probate.*

Civil Records: Access: Phone, mail, in person. Both court and visitors may perform in person searches. Search fee: $10.00 per name. Required to search: name, years to search. Civil cases indexed by defendant, plaintiff. Civil records in index books.

Criminal Records: Access: Mail, in person. Both court and visitors may perform in person searches. Search fee: $10.00 per name. Required to search: name, years to search; also helpful: DOB. Criminal records in index books.

General Information: No juvenile, mental, sealed, or adoption records released. SASE required. Turnaround time 2-3 days. Copy fee: $1.00 per page. Certification fee: $5.00. Fee payee: District/County Clerk. Personal checks accepted. Prepayment is required.

Schleicher County

District & County Court PO Drawer 580, Eldorado, TX 76936; 915-853-2833; Fax: 915-853-2603. Hours: 9AM-Noon, 1-5PM (CST). *Felony, Misdemeanor, Civil, Eviction, Probate.*

Civil Records: Access: Mail, in person. Both court and visitors may perform in person searches. Search fee: $10.00 per name. Required to search: name, years to search. Civil cases indexed by defendant, plaintiff. Civil records in index books.

Criminal Records: Access: Mail, in person. Both court and visitors may perform in person searches. Search fee: $10.00 per name. Required to search: name, years to search. Criminal records in index books.

General Information: No juvenile, mental, sealed, or adoption records released. SASE required. Turnaround time 2-3 days. Copy fee: $1.00 per page. Certification fee: $5.00. Fee payee: District/County Clerk. Personal checks accepted. Prepayment is required.

Scurry County

132nd District Court 1806 25th St #402, Snyder, TX 79549; 915-573-5641. Hours: 8AM-5PM (CST). *Felony, Civil.*

Civil Records: Access: Mail, in person. Both court and visitors may perform in person searches. Search fee: $5.00 per name. Required to search: name, years to search. Civil cases indexed by defendant, plaintiff. Civil records in index books. All requests must be in writing.

Criminal Records: Access: Mail, in person. Both court and visitors may perform in person searches. Search fee: $5.00 per name. Required to search: name, years to search, address, DOB, SSN, sex. Criminal records in index books. All requests must be in writing.

General Information: No juvenile, mental, sealed, or adoption records released. SASE required. Turnaround time 2-3 days. Fax notes: Fee to fax results is $1.00 per page. Copy fee: $1.00 for first page, $.25 each add'l. Certification fee: $1.00 per page. Fee payee: District Clerk. Personal checks accepted. Prepayment required.

County Court County Courthouse, 1806 25th St Ste 300, Snyder, TX 79549; 915-573-5332. Hours: 8:30AM-5PM (CST). *Misdemeanor, Civil, Probate.*

Civil Records: Access: Mail, in person. Both court and visitors may perform in person searches. Search fee: $10.00 per name. Required to search: name, years to search. Civil cases indexed by defendant, plaintiff. Civil records in index books since 1900s; on computer back to 1995.

Criminal Records: Access: Mail, in person. Both court and visitors may perform in person searches. Search fee: $5.00 per name. Fee includes copies. Required to search: name, years to search; also helpful: address, DOB, SSN. Criminal records in index books since 1900s; on computer back to 1995. Written request always required.

General Information: Public Access terminal is available. No mental or sealed records released. SASE required. Turnaround time 1-2 days. Fax notes: Fee to fax results is $1.00 per page. Copy fee: $1.00 per page. Certification fee: $5.00. Fee payee: County Clerk Scurry County. Personal checks accepted. Personal checks must be in-state. Prepayment is required.

Shackelford County

District & County Court PO Box 247, Albany, TX 76430; 915-762-2232. Hours: 8:30AM-5PM (CST). *Felony, Misdemeanor, Civil, Probate.*

Civil Records: Access: Mail, in person. Both court and visitors may perform in person searches. Search fee: $5.00 per name. Fee is per court. Required to search: name, years to search. Civil cases indexed by defendant, plaintiff. Civil records on computer since 1987, index books since 1867.

Criminal Records: Access: Mail, in person. Both court and visitors may perform in person searches. Search fee: $5.00 per name. Fee is per court. Required to search: name, years to search. Criminal records on computer since 1987, index books since 1867.

General Information: No juvenile, mental, sealed, or adoption records released. SASE required. Turnaround time 3 days after receipt. Copy fee: $1.00 per page. Certification fee: $5.00. Fee payee: Clerk, Shackelford County. Personal checks accepted. Prepayment is required.

Shelby County

District Court PO Drawer 1953, Center, TX 75935; 936-598-4164. Hours: 8AM-4:30PM (CST). *Felony, Civil.*

Civil Records: Access: Mail, in person. Both court and visitors may perform in person searches. Search fee: $5.00 per name. Required to search: name, years to search. Civil cases indexed by defendant, plaintiff. Civil records in index books; on computer back to 2000.

Criminal Records: Access: Mail, in person. Both court and visitors may perform in person searches. Search fee: $5.00 per name. Required to search: name, years to search, signed release. Criminal records in index books; on computer back to 2000.

General Information: No juvenile, mental, sealed, or adoption records released. SASE required. Turnaround time 2-3 days. Copy fee: $1.00 per page. Certification fee: $1.00. Fee payee: District Clerk. Only cashiers checks and money orders accepted. Will accept attorney's check. Prepayment is required.

County Court PO Box 1987, Center, TX 75935; 936-598-6361; Fax: 936-598-3701. Hours: 8AM-4:30PM (CST). *Misdemeanor, Civil, Probate.*

Civil Records: Access: Mail, in person. Both court and visitors may perform in person searches. Search fee: $10.00 per name. Required to search: name, years to search. Civil cases indexed by defendant, plaintiff. Civil records in index books back to 1982; recent on computer.

Criminal Records: Access: Mail, in person. Both court and visitors may perform in person searches. Search fee: $10.00 per name. Required to search: name, years to search, signed release; also helpful: DOB, SSN. Criminal records in index books back to 1982; recent on computer. All requests must be in writing.

General Information: No juvenile, mental, sealed, or adoption records released. SASE required. Turnaround time 1-2 days. Copy fee: $1.00 per page. Certification fee: $5.00. Fee payee: Shelby County Clerk. Personal checks accepted. Prepayment is required.

Sherman County

District & County Court PO Box 270, Stratford, TX 79084; 806-366-2371; Fax: 806-366-5670. Hours: 8AM-Noon, 1-5PM (CST). *Felony, Misdemeanor, Civil, Eviction, Probate.*

Civil Records: Access: Mail, in person. Both court and visitors may perform in person searches. Search fee: $5.00 per name. Required to search: name, years to search. Civil cases indexed by defendant. Civil records on computer since 1994, index books prior.

Criminal Records: Access: Mail, in person. Both court and visitors may perform in person searches. Search fee: $5.00 per name. Required to search: name, years to search. Criminal records on computer since 1994, index books prior.

General Information: No juvenile, mental, sealed, or adoption records released. SASE required. Turnaround time 2-3 days. Copy fee: $1.00 per page. Certification fee: $5.00. Fee payee: Sherman County Clerk. Personal checks accepted. Prepayment is required.

Smith County

District Courts PO Box 1077, Tyler, TX 75710; 903-535-0666; Fax: 903-535-0683. Hours: 8AM-5PM (CST). *Felony, Civil.*

Civil Records: Access: Mail, in person. Both court and visitors may perform in person searches. Search fee: $5.00 per name. Required to search: name, years to search. Civil cases indexed by defendant, plaintiff. Civil records in index books.

Criminal Records: Access: Mail, in person. Both court and visitors may perform in person searches. Search fee: $5.00 per name. Required to search: name, years to search. Criminal records in index books.

General Information: No juvenile, mental, sealed, or adoption records released. SASE required. Turnaround time 2-3 days. Copy fee: $1.00 per page. Certification fee: $1.00. Fee payee: District Clerk. Cashiers checks and money orders accepted. Prepayment is required.

County Court PO Box 1018, Tyler, TX 75710; 903-535-0630; Fax: 903-535-0684. Hours: 8AM-5PM (CST). *Misdemeanor, Civil, Probate.*

Civil Records: Access: Mail, in person. Both court and visitors may perform in person searches. Search fee: $5.00 per name. Required to search: name, years to search. Civil cases indexed by defendant, plaintiff. Civil records in index books.

Criminal Records: Access: Mail, in person. Both court and visitors may perform in person searches. Search fee: $5.00 per name. Required to search: name, years to search; also helpful: DOB, SSN. Criminal records in index books.

General Information: No juvenile, mental, sealed, or adoption records released. SASE required. Turnaround time 2-4 days. Copy fee: $1.00 per page. $5.00 certified copies. Certification fee: $5.00. Fee payee: Smith County Clerk. Personal checks accepted. Prepayment is required.

Somervell County

District & County Court PO Box 1098, Glen Rose, TX 76043; 254-897-4427; Fax: 254-897-3233. Hours: 8AM-5PM (CST). *Felony, Misdemeanor, Civil, Eviction, Probate.*

Civil Records: Access: Mail, in person. Both court and visitors may perform in person searches. Search fee: $5.00 per name. Required to search: name, years to search; also helpful: address. Civil cases indexed by defendant, plaintiff. Civil records on computer since 1991, microfilm since 1980, index books since 1875.

Criminal Records: Access: Mail, in person. Both court and visitors may perform in person searches. Search fee: $5.00 per name. Required to search: name, years to search, DOB, SSN, signed release; also helpful: address. Criminal records on computer since 1991, microfilm since 1980, index books since 1875.

General Information: No juvenile, mental, sealed, or adoption records released. SASE not required. Turnaround time same day. Fax notes: Fee to fax results is $1.00 per page. Copy fee: $1.00 per page. Certification fee: $5.00. Fee payee: County/District Clerk. Personal checks accepted. Prepayment is required.

Starr County

County Court at Law Starr County Courthouse, Room 201, Rio Grande City, TX 78582; 956-487-2101; Fax: 956-487-6227. Hours: 8AM-5PM (CST). *Felony, Misdemeanor, Civil, Eviction, Probate.*

Civil Records: Access: Phone, fax, mail, in person. Both court and visitors may perform in person searches. Search fee: $10.00 per name. Required to search: name, years to search. Civil cases indexed by defendant, plaintiff. Civil records in index books since 1920s.

Criminal Records: Access: Mail, in person. Both court and visitors may perform in person searches. Search fee: $10.00 per name. Required to search: name, years to search, DOB; also helpful: SSN. Criminal records on computer since 1972, in index books since 1920s.

General Information: No juvenile, mental, sealed, or adoption records released. SASE requested. Turnaround time 2-4 days. Fax notes: $1.00 per page. Copy fee: $1.00 per page. Certification fee: $5.00. Fee payee: County Clerk. Personal checks accepted. Prepayment is required.

District & County Court Starr County Courthouse, Room 304, Rio Grande City, TX 78582; 956-487-2610 (Dist) 487-2954 (County); Fax: 956-487-4885. Hours: 8AM-5PM (CST). *Felony, Misdemeanor, Civil, Eviction, Probate.*

Civil Records: Access: Phone, fax, mail, in person. Both court and visitors may perform in person searches. Search fee: $7.00 per name. Required to search: name, years to search. Civil cases indexed by defendant, plaintiff. Civil records on index books from 1920s.

Criminal Records: Access: Phone, fax, mail, in person. Only the court performs in person searches; visitors may not. Search fee: $7.00 per name. Required to search: name, years to search, SSN; also helpful: DOB. Criminal records on computer since 1992; in docket books to 1800s.

General Information: No adoption records released. SASE required. Turnaround time 2 days. Fax notes: $5.00 for 1st copy; $1.00 each add'l. Copy fee: $1.00 per page. Certification fee: $5.00. Fee payee: District Clerk. Personal checks accepted. Prepayment is required.

Stephens County

District Court 200 W Walker, Breckenridge, TX 76424; 254-559-3151; Fax: 254-559-8127. Hours: 8:30AM-5PM (CST). *Felony, Civil.*

Civil Records: Access: Fax, mail, in person. Both court and visitors may perform in person searches. Search fee: $5.00 per name. Required to search: name, years to search. Civil cases indexed by defendant, plaintiff. Civil records in index books, archived from 1900.

Criminal Records: Access: Fax, mail, in person. Both court and visitors may perform in person searches. Search fee: $5.00 per name. Required to search: name, years to search. Criminal records in index books, archived from 1900.

General Information: No juvenile, mental, sealed, or adoption records released. SASE required. Turnaround time same day. Fax notes: $1.00 per page. Available to local and 800 numbers only. Copy fee: $1.00 per page. Certification fee: $1.00. Fee payee: District Clerk. Personal checks accepted. Prepayment is required.

Sterling County

District & County Court PO Box 55, Sterling City, TX 76951; 915-378-5191. Hours: 8:30AM-Noon, 1-5PM (CST). *Felony, Misdemeanor, Civil, Eviction, Probate.*

Civil Records: Access: Mail, in person. Both court and visitors may perform in person searches. No search fee. Required to search: name, years to search; also helpful: address. Civil cases indexed by defendant, plaintiff. Civil records in index books from 1900s.

Criminal Records: Access: Mail, in person. Both court and visitors may perform in person searches. No search fee. Required to search: name, years to search; also helpful: DOB, SSN. Criminal records in index books from 1900s.

General Information: No juvenile, mental, sealed, or adoption records released. SASE required. Turnaround time 1-2 days. Fax notes: Fee to fax results is $1.00 per page. Copy fee: $1.00 per page. Certification fee: $5.00. Fee payee: Sterling County/District Clerk. Personal checks accepted. Prepayment is required.

Stonewall County

District & County Court PO Drawer P, Aspermont, TX 79502; 940-989-2272. Hours: 8AM-Noon, 1-4:30PM (CST). *Felony, Misdemeanor, Civil, Eviction, Probate.*

Civil Records: Access: Phone, mail, in person. Both court and visitors may perform in person searches. No search fee. Required to search: name, years to search. Civil cases indexed by defendant, plaintiff. Civil records in index books.

Criminal Records: Access: Phone, mail, in person. Both court and visitors may perform in person searches. No search fee. Required to search: name, years to search. Criminal records in index books.

General Information: No juvenile, mental, sealed, or adoption records released. SASE required. Fax notes: Fax fee is $2.00 per page. Copy fee: $1.00 per page. Certification fee: $5.00. Fee payee: County Clerk. Personal checks accepted.

Sutton County

District & County Court 300 E Oak, Ste 3, Sonora, TX 76950; 915-387-3815. 8:30AM-4:30PM *Felony, Misdemeanor, Civil, Eviction, Probate.*

Civil Records: Access: Phone, mail, in person. Both court and visitors may perform in person searches. Search fee: $10.00 per name. Required to search: name, years to search. Civil cases indexed by defendant, plaintiff. Civil records on computer back to 1992, index books prior.

Criminal Records: Access: Mail, in person. Both court and visitors may perform in person searches. Search

---

fee: $10.00 per name. Required to search: name, years to search. Criminal records on computer back to 1992, index books prior.

General Information: No juvenile, mental, sealed, or adoption records released. SASE required. Turnaround time 2-4 days. Copy fee: $1.00 per page. Certification fee: $5.00. Fee payee: County Clerk. Personal checks accepted. Prepayment is required.

Swisher County

District & County Court County Courthouse, 119 S Maxwell, Tulia, TX 79088; 806-995-4396; Fax: 806-995-4121. Hours: 8AM-5PM (CST). *Felony, Misdemeanor, Civil, Probate.*

Civil Records: Access: Mail, fax, in person, email. Both court and visitors may perform in person searches. Search fee: $5.00 per name. Required to search: name, years to search. Civil cases indexed by defendant, plaintiff. Civil records on computer since 1992, index books prior.

Criminal Records: Access: Mail, fax, in person, email. Both court and visitors may perform in person searches. Search fee: $5.00 per name. Required to search: name, years to search, DOB and SSN. Criminal records on computer since 1992, index books prior.

General Information: No juvenile, mental, sealed, or adoption records released. SASE requested. Turnaround time 1-2 days. Fax notes: Fee to fax results is $1.00 per page. If the call is long distance, add $5.00. Copy fee: $1.00 per page. Certification fee: Certification Fee: $1.00 per page Court Records; $5.00 per document Land Records. Fee payee: County/District Clerk. Personal checks accepted. Prepayment is required.

Tarrant County

District Court 401 W Belknap, Fort Worth, TX 76196-0402; 817-884-1574 (884-1265 Family Division); Civil phone: 817-884-1240; Criminal phone: 817-884-1342; Fax: 817-884-1484. Hours: 8AM-5PM (CST). *Felony, Misdemeanor, Civil.*

www.tarrantcounty.com

Civil Records: Access: Mail, online, in person. Both court and visitors may perform in person searches. Search fee: $5.00 per name. Required to search: name, years to search. Civil cases indexed by defendant, plaintiff. Civil records on computer since 1989, file jackets prior to 1989. Access to the remote online system requires a $50 setup that includes software. The per minute fee is $.05 plus $25 per month. Call Mr. Hinojosa at 817-884-1419 for more information.

Criminal Records: Access: Mail, online, in person. Both court and visitors may perform in person searches. Search fee: $5.00 per name. Required to search: name, years to search, DOB. Criminal records on computer since 1975, microfilm since 1970, index books and case files since 1876. Online access to criminal records is same as civil.

General Information: Public Access terminal is available. No juvenile, mental, sealed, or adoption records released. SASE not required. Turnaround time 1-3 days. Copy fee: $.30 per page. Certification fee: $1.00 per page. Fee payee: Thomas A Wilder, District Clerk. Business checks accepted. Prepayment required.

Probate Court County Courthouse, 100 W Weatherford St, Probate Court #1 Rm 260A, Fort Worth, TX 76196; 817-884-1200; Fax: 817-884-3178. Hours: 8AM-4:30PM (CST). *Probate.*

Taylor County

District Court 300 Oak St, Abilene, TX 79602; 915-674-1316. 8AM-Noon, 1-5PM. *Felony, Civil.*

http://co.taylor.tx.us

Civil Records: Access: Mail, in person. Both court and visitors may perform in person searches. Search fee: $5.00 per name. Required to search: name, years to

---

search. Civil cases indexed by defendant, plaintiff. Civil records on computer since 09/01/94; prior records in index books.

Criminal Records: Access: Mail, in person. Both court and visitors may perform in person searches. Search fee: $5.00 per name. Required to search: name, years to search, DOB; also helpful: SSN. Criminal records on computer since 1981; prior records in index books.

General Information: Public Access terminal is available. No juvenile, mental, sealed, or adoption records released. SASE required. Turnaround time 4 days. Copy fee: $1.00 per page. Certification fee: No certification fee. Fee payee: Taylor County District Clerk. Business checks accepted. Prepayment is required.

County Court PO Box 5497, Abilene, TX 79608; 915-674-1202; Fax: 915-674-1279. Hours: 8AM-5PM (CST). *Misdemeanor, Civil, Probate.*

Civil Records: Access: Mail, in person. Both court and visitors may perform in person searches. Search fee: $5.00 per name. Fee is per 10 years. Required to search: name, years to search. Civil cases indexed by defendant, plaintiff. Civil records on computer less than ten years, index books prior.

Criminal Records: Access: Mail, in person. Both court and visitors may perform in person searches. Search fee: $5.00 per name. Fee is per 10 years. Required to search: name, years to search, DOB; also helpful: address, SSN. Criminal records on computer 10 years, index books prior.

General Information: No juvenile, mental, sealed, or adoption records released. SASE required. Turnaround time 2-4 days. Fax notes: No fee to fax uncertified records. Copy fee: $1.00 per page. Certification fee: $5.00. Fee payee: County Clerk. Personal checks accepted. Prepayment is required.

Terrell County

District & County Court PO Drawer 410, Sanderson, TX 79848; 915-345-2391; Fax: 915-345-2653. Hours: 9AM-Noon, 1-5PM (CST). *Felony, Misdemeanor, Civil, Probate.*

Civil Records: Access: Phone, fax, mail, in person. Both court and visitors may perform in person searches. No search fee. Required to search: name, years to search. Civil cases indexed by defendant, plaintiff. Civil records in index books.

Criminal Records: Access: Mail, in person. Both court and visitors may perform in person searches. Search fee: $5.00 per name. Required to search: name, years to search. Criminal records in index books.

General Information: No juvenile, mental, sealed, or adoption records released. Turnaround time 2-4 days. Fax notes: $8.00 for first page, $2.00 each add'l. Copy fee: $1.00 per page. Certification fee: $5.00. Fee payee: County Clerk. Personal checks accepted. Prepayment is required.

Terry County

District Court 500 W Main Rm 209E, Brownfield, TX 79316; 806-637-4202. 8:30AM-5PM *Felony, Civil.*

Civil Records: Access: Mail, in person. Both court and visitors may perform in person searches. Search fee: $5.00 per name. Required to search: name, years to search. Civil cases indexed by defendant, plaintiff. Civil records in index books.

Criminal Records: Access: Mail, in person. Only the court performs in person searches; visitors may not. Search fee: $5.00 per name. Required to search: name, years to search, DOB; also helpful: SSN. Criminal records in index books.

General Information: No juvenile, mental, sealed, or adoption records released. SASE required. Turnaround time same day. Copy fee: $1.00 per page. Certification fee: $1.00. Fee payee: District Clerk. Personal checks accepted. Prepayment is required.

County Court 500 W Main Rm 105, Brownfield, TX 79316-4398; 806-637-8551; Fax: 806-637-4874. 8:30AM-5PM (CST). *Misdemeanor, Civil, Probate.*

Civil Records: Access: Mail, in person. Both court and visitors may perform in person searches. Search fee: $10.00 per name. Required to search: name, years to search. Civil cases indexed by defendant, plaintiff. Civil records in index books.

Criminal Records: Access: Mail, in person. Both court and visitors may perform in person searches. Search fee: $10.00 per name. Required to search: name, years to search; also helpful: address, DOB, SSN. Criminal records in index books back to 1904.

General Information: No juvenile, mental, sealed, or adoption records released. SASE required. Turnaround time 1-2 days. Fax notes: Fee to fax results is $1.00 per page. Copy fee: $1.00 per page. Certification fee: $5.00. Fee payee: County Clerk. Personal checks accepted. Prepayment is required.

Throckmorton County

District & County Court PO Box 309, Throckmorton, TX 76483; 940-849-2501. Hours: 8AM-Noon, 1-5PM (CST). *Felony, Misdemeanor, Civil, Eviction, Probate.*

Civil Records: Access: Phone, mail, in person. Both court and visitors may perform in person searches. Search fee: $10.00 per name. Required to search: name, years to search; also helpful: address. Civil cases indexed by defendant, plaintiff. Civil records in index books.

Criminal Records: Access: Mail, in person. Both court and visitors may perform in person searches. Search fee: $10.00 per name. Required to search: name, years to search. Criminal records in index books.

General Information: No juvenile, mental, sealed, or adoption records released. SASE required. Turnaround time 2-4 days. Copy fee: $1.00 per page. Certification fee: No certification fee. Fee payee: County/District Clerk. Personal checks accepted. Prepayment is required.

Titus County

District Court 105 W 1st St, PO Box 492, Mount Pleasant, TX 75455; 903-577-6721. Hours: 8AM-5PM (CST). *Felony, Civil.*

Civil Records: Access: Phone, mail, in person. Both court and visitors may perform in person searches. Search fee: $5.00 per name. Required to search: name, years to search. Civil cases indexed by defendant, plaintiff. Civil records in index books from 1895; computerized back to 1998.

Criminal Records: Access: Phone, mail, in person. Both court and visitors may perform in person searches. Search fee: $5.00 per name. Required to search: name, years to search. Criminal records in index books from 1895; computerized back to 1998.

General Information: No juvenile, mental, sealed, or adoption records released. SASE required. Turnaround time 2-3 days. Copy fee: $1.00 per page. Certification fee: $5.00. Fee payee: District Clerk. Personal checks accepted. Prepayment is required.

County Court 100 W 1st St #204, Mount Pleasant, TX 75455; 903-577-6796; Fax: 903-577-6793. Hours: 8AM-5PM (CST). *Misdemeanor, Civil, Probate.*

Civil Records: Access: Mail, in person. Both court and visitors may perform in person searches. Search fee: $10.00 per name. Required to search: name, years to search; also helpful: address. Civil cases indexed by defendant, plaintiff. Civil records on computer since January 1994, index books since 1895.

Criminal Records: Access: Mail, in person. Both court and visitors may perform in person searches. Search

fee: $10.00 per name. Required to search: name, years to search; also helpful: address, DOB, SSN. Criminal records on computer since January 1994, index books since 1895.

General Information: No juvenile, mental, sealed, or adoption records released. SASE required. Turnaround time 1 week to 10 days. Copy fee: $1.00 per page. Certification fee: $5.00. Fee payee: County Clerk. Business checks accepted. Prepayment is required.

Tom Green County

District Court County Courthouse, 112 W Beauregard, San Angelo, TX 76903; 915-659-6579; Fax: 915-659-3241. 8AM-5PM (CST). *Felony, Civil.*

http://justice.co.tom-green.tx.us

Civil Records: Access: Mail, in person, online. Both court and visitors may perform in person searches. Search fee: $5.00 per name. Required to search: name, years to search; also helpful. Civil cases indexed by defendant, plaintiff. Civil records in index books from 1900s; on computer back to 1993. Online access to civil case records back to 1994 is available online at the web site. Search by name, case number, DOB.

Criminal Records: Access: Mail, in person, online. Both court and visitors may perform in person searches. Search fee: $5.00 per name. Required to search: name, years to search, DOB. Criminal records in index books from 1900s; on computer back to 1993. Online access to criminal records is the same as civil.

General Information: Public Access terminal is available. No juvenile, mental, sealed, or adoption records released. SASE required. Turnaround time 1 week. Fax notes: Fee to fax results is $1.00 per page. Copy fee: $1.00 per page. Certification fee: No certification fee. Fee payee: District Clerk. Personal checks accepted. Prepayment is required.

County Court 124 W Beauregard, San Angelo, TX 76903; 915-659-6555. Hours: 8AM-4:30PM (CST). *Misdemeanor, Civil, Probate.*

Civil Records: Access: Mail, in person. Both court and visitors may perform in person searches. Search fee: $5.00 per name. Required to search: name, years to search; also helpful: address. Civil cases indexed by defendant, plaintiff. Civil records on computer since 1994, index books prior.

Criminal Records: Access: Mail, in person. Both court and visitors may perform in person searches. Search fee: $5.00 per name. Required to search: name, years to search; also helpful: address, DOB, SSN. Criminal records on computer since 1994, index books prior.

General Information: No juvenile, mental, sealed, or adoption records released. SASE required. Turnaround time same day. Copy fee: $1.00 per page. Certification: $5.00. Payee: County Clerk. Prepayment is required.

Travis County

District Court PO Box 1748, Austin, TX 78767; Civil phone: 512-473-9457; Criminal phone: 512-473-9420; Fax: 512-473-9549 Civil; 512-708-4566 Crim. Hours: 8AM-5PM (CST). *Felony, Civil.*

Civil Records: Access: Phone, mail, in person. Both court and visitors may perform in person searches. Search fee: $5.00 per name. Add $2.00 per year prior to 1988. Required to search: name, years to search. Civil cases indexed by defendant, plaintiff. Civil records on computer since 1986, microfiche and index books.

Criminal Records: Access: Phone, mail, in person. Both court and visitors may perform in person searches. Search fee: $5.00 per name. Add $2.00 per year prior to 1988. Required to search: name, years to search, DOB. Criminal records on computer since 1988, index books prior to 1988.

General Information: Public Access terminal is available. No juvenile, mental, sealed, or adoption records released (all felony cases are public record).

SASE required. Turnaround 2-3 days, normally. Copy fee: $.50 per page. Certification fee: No certification fee. Fee payee: District Clerk. Personal checks accepted. Credit cards accepted: Visa, MasterCard, Discover. Prepayment is required.

County Court PO Box 1748, Austin, TX 78767-1748; Civil phone: 512-473-9090; Criminal phone: 512-473-9440; Probate phone: 512-473-9595; Fax: 512-473-4220. Hours: 8AM-5PM (CST). *Misdemeanor, Civil, Probate.*

www.co.travis.tx.us

Civil Records: Access: Phone, mail, in person. Both court and visitors may perform in person searches. Search fee: $5.00 per name. Fee applies to cases opened prior to June 1986. Required to search: name, years to search. Civil cases indexed by defendant, plaintiff. Civil records on computer since 06/86, microfilm prior.

Criminal Records: Access: Phone, mail, in person. Both court and visitors may perform in person searches. Search fee: $5.00 per name. $10.00 per name for microfilm. Required to search: name, years to search; also helpful: address, DOB, SSN. Criminal records on computer since 1981; prior records on microfilm.

General Information: Public Access terminal is available. No juvenile, mental, sealed, or adoption records released. SASE not required. Turnaround time 2-5 days. Copy fee: $1.00 per page. Certification fee: $5.00. Fee payee: Travis County Clerk. Personal checks accepted. Prepayment is required.

Trinity County

District Court PO Box 548, Groveton, TX 75845; 936-642-1118. Hours: 8AM-5PM (CST). *Felony, Civil.*

Civil Records: Access: In person only. Both court and visitors may perform in person searches. Search fee: $5.00 per name. Required to search: name, years to search. Civil cases indexed by defendant, plaintiff. Civil records on computer for 20 years, index books prior.

Criminal Records: Access: In person only. Both court and visitors may perform in person searches. Search fee: $5.00 per name. Required to search: name, years to search. Criminal records on computer for 20 years, index books prior.

General Information: No juvenile, mental, sealed, or adoption records released. Fax notes: Do not fax. Copy fee: $1.00 per page. Certification fee: $1.00 per page. Fee payee: District Clerk. Personal checks accepted. Prepayment is required.

County Court PO Box 456, Groveton, TX 75845; 936-642-1208; Fax: 936-642-3004. Hours: 8AM-5PM (CST). *Misdemeanor, Civil, Probate.*

Civil Records: Access: Mail, in person. Both court and visitors may perform in person searches. Search fee: $10.00 per name. Required to search: name, years to search; also helpful: address. Civil cases indexed by defendant, plaintiff. Civil records in index books. Date of birth required for searching.

Criminal Records: Access: Mail, in person. Both court and visitors may perform in person searches. Search fee: $10.00 per name. Required to search: name, years to search, SSN; also helpful: address, DOB, sex. Criminal records in index books. Date of birth required for searching.

General Information: No juvenile, mental, sealed, or adoption records released. SASE required. Turnaround time 1-2 days. Fax notes: Fee to fax results is $1.00 per page. Copy fee: $1.00 per page. Certification fee: $5.00. Fee payee: County Clerk. Personal checks accepted. Prepayment is required.

Tyler County

District Court 203 Courthouse, 100 W Bluff, Woodville, TX 75979; 409-283-2162. Hours: 8AM-Noon, 1-4:30PM (CST). *Felony, Civil.*

Civil Records: Access: Mail, in person. Both court and visitors may perform in person searches. Search fee: $5.00 per name. Required to search: name, years to search. Civil cases indexed by defendant, plaintiff. Civil records in index books.

Criminal Records: Access: Mail, in person. Both court and visitors may perform in person searches. Search fee: $5.00. Required to search: name, years to search. Criminal records in index books.

General Information: No juvenile, mental, sealed, or adoption records released. SASE required. Turnaround time same day. Copy fee: $1.00 per page. Certification fee: $2.00. Fee payee: District Clerk. Business checks accepted. Prepayment is required.

County Court County Courthouse, Rm 110, 100 W Bluff, Woodville, TX 75979; 409-283-2281; Fax: 409-283-7296. Hours: 8AM-4:30PM (CST). *Misdemeanor, Civil, Probate.*

Civil Records: Access: Mail, in person. Both court and visitors may perform in person searches. Search fee: $5.00 per name. Required to search: name, years to search. Civil cases indexed by defendant, plaintiff. Civil records on computer since 1989, microfilm since 1973, index books from 1800s.

Criminal Records: Access: Mail, in person. Both court and visitors may perform in person searches. Search fee: $5.00 per name. Required to search: name, years to search; also helpful: address, DOB, SSN. Criminal records on computer since 1989, microfilm since 1973, index books from 1800s.

General Information: Public Access terminal is available. No juvenile, mental, sealed or adoption records released. SASE not required. Turnaround time 1-2 days. Copy fee: $1.00 per page. Certification fee: $5.00. Fee payee: County Clerk. Personal checks accepted. Prepayment is required.

Upshur County

County Court PO Box 730, Gilmer, TX 75644; 903-843-4015. Hours: 8AM-5PM (CST). *Felony, Misdemeanor, Civil, Probate.*

Civil Records: Access: Phone, mail, in person. Both court and visitors may perform in person searches. Search fee: $10.00 per name. Fee is per 5 year period. Required to search: name, years to search. Civil cases indexed by defendant, plaintiff. Civil records in index books; on computer back to 1979.

Criminal Records: Access: Phone, mail, in person. Both court and visitors may perform in person searches. Search fee: $10.00 per name. Fee is per 5 year period. Required to search: name, years to search, DOB, offense. Criminal records in index books; on computer back to 1979.

General Information: Public Access terminal is available. No juvenile, mental, sealed or adoption records released. SASE required. Turnaround time same day. Copy fee: $1.00 per page. Certification fee: $5.00. Fee payee: County Clerk. Personal checks accepted. Prepayment is required.

Upton County

District & County Court PO Box 465, Rankin, TX 79778; 915-693-2861; Fax: 915-693-2129. Hours: 8AM-5PM (CST). *Felony, Misdemeanor, Civil, Eviction, Probate.*

Civil Records: Access: Fax, mail, in person. Both court and visitors may perform in person searches. Search fee: $5.00 per name. Required to search: name, years to search. Civil cases indexed by defendant, plaintiff. Civil records on computer back to 1987; in index books to 1910.

Criminal Records: Access: Fax, mail, in person. Both court and visitors may perform in person searches. Search fee: $5.00 per name. Required to search: name, years to search, signed release; also helpful: address, DOB. Criminal records on computer back to 1987; in index books to 1910.

General Information: No juvenile, mental, sealed, or adoption records released. SASE required. Turnaround time 1-2 days. Fax notes: Fee to fax results is $1.00 per page. Copy fee: $1.00 per page. Certification fee: $2.00. Fee payee: District/County Clerk. Personal checks accepted. Prepayment is required.

Uvalde County

District Court County Courthouse Suite #15, Uvalde, TX 78801; 830-278-3918. Hours: 8AM-5PM (CST). *Felony, Civil.*

Civil Records: Access: Phone, mail, in person. Both court and visitors may perform in person searches. Search fee: $5.00 per name. Required to search: name, years to search. Civil cases indexed by defendant, plaintiff. Civil records in index books. Phone access available to those with an account.

Criminal Records: Access: Phone, mail, in person. Both court and visitors may perform in person searches. Search fee: $5.00 per name. Required to search: name, years to search, DOB, SSN. Criminal records in index books.

General Information: No juvenile, mental, sealed, or adoption records released. SASE required. Turnaround time 2-3 days. Copy fee: $.75 per page. Certification fee: $1.00 per page. Fee payee: District Clerk. Personal checks accepted. Prepayment is required.

County Court PO Box 284, Uvalde, TX 78802; 830-278-6614. Hours: 8AM-5PM (CST). *Misdemeanor, Civil, Probate.*

Civil Records: Access: Mail, in person. Both court and visitors may perform in person searches. Search fee: $10.00 per name. The fee covers a 10 year search. Required to search: name, years to search. Civil cases indexed by defendant, plaintiff. Civil records in index books from 1800s.

Criminal Records: Access: Mail, in person. Both court and visitors may perform in person searches. Search fee: $10.00 per name. The fee covers a 10 year search. Required to search: name, years to search, DOB. Criminal records in index books from 1800s.

General Information: Public Access terminal is available. No juvenile, mental, sealed, or adoption records released. SASE not required. Turnaround time 1-2 days. Copy fee: $1.00 per page. Certification fee: $5.00. Fee payee: Lucille C Hutcherson, Uvalde County Clerk. Personal checks accepted. Prepayment is required.

Val Verde County

District Court PO Box 1544, Del Rio, TX 78841; 830-774-7538. Hours: 8AM-4:30PM (CST). *Felony, Civil.*

Civil Records: Access: Mail, in person. Both court and visitors may perform in person searches. Search fee: $5.00 per name. Required to search: name, years to search. Civil cases indexed by defendant, plaintiff. Civil records on computer since 1990, index books prior.

Criminal Records: Access: Mail, in person. Both court and visitors may perform in person searches. Search fee: $5.00 per name. Required to search: name, years to search. Criminal records on computer since 1990, index books prior.

General Information: Public Access terminal is available. No juvenile, mental, sealed, or adoption records released. SASE required. Turnaround time 2-5 days. Copy fee: $.50 per page. Certification fee: $1.00 per page. Fee payee: District Clerk. Business checks accepted. Local checks accepted. Prepayment is required.

County Court PO Box 1267, Del Rio, TX 78841-1267; 830-774-7564. Hours: 8AM-4:30PM (CST). *Misdemeanor, Probate.*

Criminal Records: Access: Mail, in person. Both court and visitors may perform in person searches. Search fee: $5.00 per name. Required to search: name, years to search; also helpful: address, DOB, SSN. Criminal records in index books.

General Information: No juvenile, mental, sealed, or adoption records released. SASE required. Turnaround time 1-2 days. Copy fee: $1.00 per page. Certification fee: $5.00. Fee payee: County Clerk. Personal checks accepted. Prepayment is required.

Van Zandt County

District Court 121 E Dallas St Rm 302, Canton, TX 75103; 903-567-6576; Fax: 903-567-4700. Hours: 8AM-5PM (CST). *Felony, Civil.*

Civil Records: Access: Phone, mail, in person. Both court and visitors may perform in person searches. Search fee: $5.00 per name. Required to search: name, years to search. Civil cases indexed by defendant, plaintiff. Civil records in index books.

Criminal Records: Access: Mail, in person. Both court and visitors may perform in person searches. Search fee: $5.00 per name. Required to search: name, years to search. Criminal records in index books.

General Information: No juvenile, mental, sealed, or adoption records released. SASE required. Turnaround time 2-4 days. Copy fee: $1.00 per page. Certification fee: No certification fee. Fee payee: District Clerk. Personal checks accepted. Prepayment is required.

County Court 121 E Dallas St #202, Canton, TX 75103; 903-567-6503; Fax: 903-567-6722. Hours: 8AM-5PM (CST). *Misdemeanor, Civil, Probate.*

Civil Records: Access: Mail, in person. Both court and visitors may perform in person searches. Search fee: $5.00 per name. Required to search: name, years to search. Civil cases indexed by defendant, plaintiff. Civil records in index books.

Criminal Records: Access: Mail, in person. Both court and visitors may perform in person searches. Search fee: $5.00 per name. Required to search: name, years to search; also helpful: address, DOB, SSN. Criminal records in index books.

General Information: No juvenile, mental, sealed, or adoption records released. SASE required. Turnaround time 2-4 days. Copy fee: $1.00 per page. Certification fee: $5.00. Fee payee: County Clerk. Personal checks accepted. Prepayment is required.

Victoria County

District Court PO Box 2238, Victoria, TX 77902; 361-575-0581; Fax: 361-572-5682. Hours: 8AM-5PM (CST). *Felony, Civil.*

Civil Records: Access: Fax, mail, in person. Both court and visitors may perform in person searches. Search fee: $5.00 per name. Required to search: name, years to search. Civil cases indexed by defendant, plaintiff. Civil records on computer since 1989, index books since 1800s.

Criminal Records: Access: Fax, mail, in person. Both court and visitors may perform in person searches. Search fee: $5.00 per name. Required to search: name, years to search, DOB. Criminal records on computer since 1989, index books since 1800s.

General Information: No juvenile, mental, sealed, or adoption records released. SASE required. Turnaround time 1-2 days. Fax notes: No fee for local fax; Long distance fax fee $5.00 plus $1.00 per pg. Copy fee: $1.00 per page. Certification fee: $1.00. Fee payee: District Clerk. Personal checks accepted. Prepayment is required.

County Court 115 N Bridge, Rm 103, Victoria, TX 77901; 361-575-1478; Fax: 361-575-6276. Hours: 8AM-5PM (CST). *Misdemeanor, Civil, Probate.*

Civil Records: Access: Phone, fax, mail, in person. Both court and visitors may perform in person searches. Search fee: $5.00 per name. Required to search: name, years to search. Civil cases indexed by defendant, plaintiff. Civil records on computer and Cox index.

Criminal Records: Access: Phone, fax, mail, in person. Both court and visitors may perform in person searches. Search fee: $5.00 per name. Required to search: name, years to search; also helpful: address, DOB, SSN. Criminal records on computer and Cox index.

General Information: No juvenile, mental, sealed, birth, death or adoption records released. SASE required. Turnaround time 1 day. Fax notes: $1.00 for first page, $1.00 each add'l. Copy fee: $1.00 per page. Certification fee: $5.00. Fee payee: Victoria County Clerk. Personal checks accepted. Prepayment required.

Walker County

District Court 1100 University Ave Rm 301, Huntsville, TX 77340; 936-436-4972. Hours: 8AM-Noon, 1-4:30PM (CST). *Felony, Civil.*

Civil Records: Access: Mail, in person. Both court and visitors may perform in person searches. Search fee: $5.00 per name. Required to search: name, years to search. Civil cases indexed by defendant, plaintiff. Civil records on computer and index books.

Criminal Records: Access: Mail, in person. Both court and visitors may perform in person searches. Search fee: $5.00 per name. Required to search: name, years to search. Criminal records on computer and index books.

General Information: No juvenile, mental, sealed, abortion or adoption records released. SASE required. Turnaround time 1-2 days. Copy fee: $1.00 per page. Certification fee: No certification fee. Fee payee: District Clerk. Business checks accepted. Prepayment required.

County Court PO Box 210, Huntsville, TX 77342-0210; 936-436-4922; Fax: 936-436-4928. Hours: 8AM-4:45PM (CST). *Misdemeanor, Civil, Probate.*

Civil Records: Access: Mail, in person. Both court and visitors may perform in person searches. Search fee: $5.00 per name. Required to search: name, years to search. Civil cases indexed by defendant, plaintiff. Civil records in index books.

Criminal Records: Access: Mail, in person. Both court and visitors may perform in person searches. Search fee: $5.00 per name. Required to search: name, years to search; also helpful: address, DOB, SSN. Criminal records in index books.

General Information: No juvenile, mental, sealed, or adoption records released. SASE required. Turnaround time 2-3 days. Copy fee: $1.00 per page. Certification fee: $5.00. Fee payee: County Clerk. Personal checks accepted. Prepayment is required.

Waller County

District Court 836 Austin St Rm 318, Hempstead, TX 77445; 979-826-7735. Hours: 8AM-Noon, 1-5PM (CST). *Felony, Civil.*

Civil Records: Access: Mail, in person. Both court and visitors may perform in person searches. Search fee: $5.00 per name. Required to search: name, years to search. Civil cases indexed by defendant, plaintiff. Civil records on index books.

Criminal Records: Access: Mail, in person. Both court and visitors may perform in person searches. Search fee: $5.00 per name. Required to search: name, years to search. Criminal records on computer since 9/99.

General Information: No juvenile, mental, sealed, or adoption records released. SASE required. Turnaround time 2 days. Copy fee: $1.00 per page. Certification fee:

$1.00. Fee payee: District Clerk. Personal checks accepted. Prepayment is required.

County Court 836 Austin St, Rm 217, Hempstead, TX 77445; 936-826-3357. Hours: 8AM-Noon, 1-5PM (CST). *Misdemeanor, Civil, Probate.*

Civil Records: Access: Mail, in person. Both court and visitors may perform in person searches. Search fee: $5.00 per name. Required to search: name, years to search. Civil cases indexed by defendant, plaintiff. Civil records in index books; on computer back to 1994.

Criminal Records: Access: Mail, in person. Both court and visitors may perform in person searches. Search fee: $5.00 per name. Required to search: name, years to search, signed release; also helpful: DOB, SSN. Criminal records in index books; on computer back to 1994.

General Information: No juvenile, mental, sealed, or adoption records released. SASE required. Turnaround time 2-3 days. Copy fee: $1.00 per page. Certification fee: $5.00. Fee payee: Waller County Clerk. No personal checks accepted for copies. Prepayment is required.

Ward County

District Court PO Box 440, Monahans, TX 79756; 915-943-2751; Fax: 915-943-3810. Hours: 8AM-5PM (CST). *Felony, Civil.*

Civil Records: Access: Mail, fax, in person. Both court and visitors may perform in person searches. Search fee: $5.00 per name. Required to search: name, years to search. Civil cases indexed by defendant, plaintiff. Civil records on computer since 1980, index books prior.

Criminal Records: Access: Mail, fax, in person. Both court and visitors may perform in person searches. Search fee: $5.00 per name. Required to search: name, years to search, signed release, also DOB or SSN. Criminal records on books.

General Information: No juvenile, mental, sealed, or adoption records released. SASE required. Turnaround time 1-2 days. Copy fee: $1.00 per page. Certification fee: $1.00. Fee payee: District Clerk. Business checks accepted. Prepayment is required.

County Court County Courthouse, Monahans, TX 79756; 915-943-3294; Fax: 915-943-6054. Hours: 8AM-5PM (CST). *Misdemeanor, Civil, Probate.*

Civil Records: Access: Mail, in person. Both court and visitors may perform in person searches. Search fee: $5.00 per name. Required to search: name, years to search. Civil cases indexed by defendant, plaintiff. Civil records in index books; computerized records go back 10 years. In person requests must be accompanied by written request.

Criminal Records: Access: Mail, in person. Both court and visitors may perform in person searches. Search fee: $5.00 per name. Required to search: name, years to search, DOB, signed release; also helpful: address, SSN. Criminal records in index books; computerized records go back 10 years. In person requests must be accompanied by a written request.

General Information: No juvenile, mental, sealed, or adoption records released. SASE required. Turnaround time 1-2 days. Fax notes: Fee to fax results is $3.00 per page. Copy fee: $1.00 per page. Certification fee: $5.00 plus $1.00 per page. Fee payee: County Clerk. Personal checks accepted. Prepayment is required.

Washington County

District Court 100 E Main #304, Brenham, TX 77833-3753; 979-277-6200. Hours: 8AM-5PM (CST). *Felony, Civil.*

Civil Records: Access: Mail, in person. Both court and visitors may perform in person searches. Search fee: $5.00 per name. Required to search: name, years to search. Civil cases indexed by defendant, plaintiff. Civil

records in index books since 1800s; on computer back to 1988.

Criminal Records: Access: Mail, in person. Both court and visitors may perform in person searches. Search fee: $5.00 per name. Required to search: name, years to search; also helpful: DOB. Criminal records in index books since 1800s; on computer back to 1988.

General Information: Public Access terminal is available. No juvenile, mental, sealed, or adoption records released. SASE not required. Turnaround time 1-2 days. Copy fee: $.50 per page. Certification fee: $1.00 per page. Fee payee: District Clerk. Personal checks accepted. Prepayment is required.

County Court 100 E Main #102, Brenham, TX 77833; 979-277-6200; Fax: 979-277-6278. Hours: 8AM-5PM (CST). *Misdemeanor, Civil, Probate.*

Civil Records: Access: Mail, in person. Both court and visitors may perform in person searches. Search fee: $5.00 per name. Required to search: name, years to search. Civil cases indexed by defendant, plaintiff. Civil records in index books from 1860s; computerized back to 1985. In person request must be accompanied by a written request.

Criminal Records: Access: Mail, in person. Both court and visitors may perform in person searches. Search fee: $5.00 per name. Required to search: name, years to search; also helpful: address, DOB, SSN. Criminal records in index books from 1860s; computerized back to 1985. In person requests must be accompanied by a written request.

General Information: Public Access terminal is available. No juvenile, mental, sealed, or adoption records released. SASE required. Turnaround time 1-2 days. Fax notes: Fee to fax results is $1.00 per page and must be pre-paid. Copy fee: $1.00 per page. Certification fee: $5.00 per instrument. Fee payee: Washington County Clerk. Personal checks accepted. Prepayment is required.

Webb County

District Court PO Box 667, Laredo, TX 78042-0667; 956-721-2460; Fax: 956-721-2458. Hours: 8AM-5PM (CST). *Felony, Civil.*

www.webbcounty.com

Civil Records: Access: Mail, in person. Both court and visitors may perform in person searches. Search fee: $5.00 per name. Required to search: name, years to search, address; also helpful: DOB, SSN. Civil cases indexed by defendant, plaintiff. Civil records on computer since November, 1988, index books prior.

Criminal Records: Access: Mail, in person. Both court and visitors may perform in person searches. Search fee: $5.00 per name. Required to search: name, years to search, DOB or SSN. Criminal records on computer since November, 1988, index books prior.

General Information: Public Access terminal is available. No juvenile, mental, sealed, or adoption records released. SASE required. Turnaround time 1 week. Copy fee: $1.00 per page. Certification fee: $1.00. Fee is per page of document. Fee payee: District Clerk. Personal checks accepted. Prepayment required.

County Court 1110 Victoria #201, Laredo, TX 78040; 956-721-2640; Civil phone: 956-721-2653; Criminal phone: 956-721-2651; Probate phone: 956-721-2656; Fax: 956-721-2288. Hours: 8AM-5PM (CST). *Misdemeanor, Civil Under $5,000, Probate.*

Civil Records: Access: Mail, in person. Both court and visitors may perform in person searches. Search fee: $5.00 per name. Required to search: name, years to search. Civil cases indexed by defendant, plaintiff. Civil records on computer since 1988, index books prior.

Criminal Records: Access: Mail, in person. Both court and visitors may perform in person searches. Search fee: $5.00 per name. Required to search: name, years to search, DOB; also helpful: address, SSN. Criminal records on computer since 1988, index books prior.

General Information: Public Access terminal is available. No juvenile, mental, sealed, or adoption records released. SASE required. Turnaround time 2-3 days. Copy fee: $1.00 per page. Certification fee: $5.00. Fee payee: County Clerk. Personal checks accepted. Prepayment is required.

Wharton County

District Court PO Drawer 391, Wharton, TX 77488; 979-532-5542; Fax: 979-532-1299. Hours: 8AM-5PM (CST). *Felony, Civil.*

Civil Records: Access: Mail, fax, in person. Both court and visitors may perform in person searches. Search fee: $5.00 per name. Required to search: name, years to search. Civil cases indexed by defendant, plaintiff. Civil records on computer since 1989, index books prior.

Criminal Records: Access: Mail, fax, in person. Both court and visitors may perform in person searches. Search fee: $5.00 per name. Required to search: name, years to search. Criminal records on computer since 1989, index books prior.

General Information: No juvenile, mental, sealed, or adoption records released. SASE required. Turnaround time same day. Copy fee: $1.00 per page. Certification fee: $2.00. Fee payee: District Clerk of Wharton. Personal checks accepted. Prepayment is required.

County Court PO Box 69, Wharton, TX 77488; 979-532-2381. Hours: 8AM-5PM (CST). *Misdemeanor, Civil, Probate.*

Civil Records: Access: Mail, in person. Both court and visitors may perform in person searches. Search fee: $5.00 per name per 10 years searched. Required to search: name, years to search. Civil cases indexed by defendant, plaintiff. Civil records on computer since 1991, index books since 1978, prior indexes in storage.

Criminal Records: Access: Mail, in person. Both court and visitors may perform in person searches. Search fee: $5.00 per name per 10 years searched. Required to search: name, years to search, DOB, signed release; also helpful: address, SSN, copy of ID. Criminal records on computer since 1991, index books since 1978, prior indexes in storage.

General Information: Public Access terminal is available. No juvenile, mental, sealed, or adoption records released. SASE required. Turnaround time 1-2 days. Fax notes: Fee to fax results is $2.00 plus $1.00 per page. Copy fee: $1.00 per page. Certification fee: $5.00. Fee payee: County Clerk. Business checks accepted. Prepayment is required.

Wheeler County

District Court PO Box 528, Wheeler, TX 79096; 806-826-5931; Fax: 806-826-3282. Hours: 8AM-5PM (CST). *Felony, Civil.*

Civil Records: Access: Phone, mail, in person. Both court and visitors may perform in person searches. Search fee: $5.00 per name. Required to search: name, years to search. Civil cases indexed by defendant, plaintiff. Civil records in index books.

Criminal Records: Access: Phone, mail, in person. Both court and visitors may perform in person searches. Search fee: $5.00 per name. Required to search: name, years to search. Criminal records in index books.

General Information: No juvenile, mental, sealed, or adoption records released. SASE not required. Turnaround time 2-3 days. Copy fee: $1.00. Fee is for first 10 pages. Add $.25 per add'l page. Certification fee: $1.00. Payee: District Clerk. Personal checks accepted.

County Court PO Box 465, Wheeler, TX 79096; 806-826-5544; Fax: 806-826-3282. Hours: 8AM-5PM (CST). *Misdemeanor, Civil, Probate.*

Civil Records: Access: Mail, in person. Both court and visitors may perform in person searches. Search fee:

$10.00 per name. Required to search: name, years to search. Civil cases indexed by defendant, plaintiff. Civil records on computer and index books.

Criminal Records: Access: Mail, in person. Both court and visitors may perform in person searches. Search fee: $10.00 per name. Required to search: name, years to search; also helpful: DOB, SSN. Criminal records on computer and index books.

General Information: No juvenile, mental, sealed, or adoption records released. SASE required. Turnaround time 1 day. Copy fee: $1.00 per page. Certification fee: $5.00. Fee payee: County Clerk. Business checks accepted. Prepayment is required.

Wichita County

District Court PO Box 718, Wichita Falls, TX 76307; 940-766-8190. 8AM-5PM *Felony, Civil.*

Civil Records: Access: Phone, mail, in person. Both court and visitors may perform in person searches. Search fee: $5.00 per name. Required to search: name, years to search. Civil cases indexed by defendant, plaintiff. Civil records on computer since 1984, index books prior. Phone searches must be prepaid.

Criminal Records: Access: Phone, mail, in person. Both court and visitors may perform in person searches. Search fee: $5.00 per name. Required to search: name, years to search. Criminal records on computer since 1984, index books before. Phone searches must be prepaid.

General Information: No juvenile, mental, sealed, or adoption records released. SASE required. Turnaround time 2-3 days. Copy fee: $1.00 per page. Certification fee: $1.00. Fee payee: District Clerk. Personal checks accepted. Prepayment is required.

County Court PO Box 1679, Wichita Falls, TX 76307; 940-766-8173; Probate phone: 940-766-8172. Hours: 8AM-5PM (CST). *Misdemeanor, Probate.*

Criminal Records: Access: Phone, mail, in person. Both court and visitors may perform in person searches. Search fee: $10.00 per name searched. Required to search: name, years to search; also helpful: DOB, SSN. Criminal records on computer or printed index from 1980 to present.

General Information: No juvenile, mental, sealed, or adoption records released. Mental can be released with an order from the judge. SASE required. Turnaround time within 1 week or less. Copy fee: $1.00 per page. Certification fee: $5.00 per document. Fee payee: Wichita County Clerk. No checks accepted. Prepayment is required.

Wilbarger County

District Court 1700 Wilbarger Rm 33, Vernon, TX 76384; 940-553-3411; Fax: 940-553-2316. Hours: 8AM-5PM (CST). *Felony, Civil.*

Civil Records: Access: Mail, in person. Both court and visitors may perform in person searches. Search fee: $5.00 per name. Required to search: name, years to search. Civil cases indexed by defendant, plaintiff. Civil records in index books.

Criminal Records: Access: Mail, in person. Both court and visitors may perform in person searches. Search fee: $5.00 per name. Required to search: name, years to search, DOB. Criminal records in index books.

General Information: No juvenile, mental, sealed, or adoption records released. Will return results by fax or phone if an 800 number is provided. SASE required. Turnaround time 2-3 days. Fax notes: Will fax results to toll-free number. Copy fee: $1.00 per page. Certification fee: $5.00. Fee payee: District Clerk. Business checks accepted. Prepayment is required.

County Court 1700 Wilbarger Rm 15, Vernon, TX 76384; 940-552-5486. Hours: 8AM-5PM (CST). *Misdemeanor, Civil, Probate.*

Civil Records: Access: Mail, in person. Both court and visitors may perform in person searches. Search fee: $10.00 per name. Required to search: name, years to search. Civil cases indexed by defendant. Civil records in index books.

Criminal Records: Access: Mail, in person. Both court and visitors may perform in person searches. Search fee: $10.00 per name. Required to search: name, years to search; also helpful: address, DOB, SSN. Criminal records in index books.

General Information: No juvenile, mental, sealed, or adoption records released. SASE required. Turnaround time same day. Fax notes: Fee to fax results is $1.00 per page. Copy fee: $1.00 per page. Certification fee: $5.00 plus $1.00 per page. Fee payee: County Clerk. Personal checks accepted. Prepayment is required.

Willacy County

District Court County Courthouse, Raymondville, TX 78580; 956-689-2532; Fax: 956-689-5713. Hours: 8AM-5PM (CST). *Felony, Civil.*

Civil Records: Access: Mail, in person. Both court and visitors may perform in person searches. Search fee: $8.00 per name. Required to search: name, years to search. Civil cases indexed by defendant, plaintiff. Civil records in index books.

Criminal Records: Access: Mail, in person. Both court and visitors may perform in person searches. Search fee: $8.00 per name. Required to search: name, years to search. Criminal records in index books.

General Information: No juvenile, mental, sealed, or adoption records released. SASE required. Turnaround time 2-3 days. Copy fee: $1.00 per page. Certification fee: $2.00 per page. Fee payee: District Clerk. Personal checks accepted. Prepayment is required.

County Court 540 W Hidalgo, Raymondville, TX 78580; 956-689-2710. Hours: 8AM-Noon, 1-5PM (CST). *Misdemeanor, Civil, Probate.*

Civil Records: Access: Mail, in person. Both court and visitors may perform in person searches. Search fee: $5.00 per name. Required to search: name, years to search; also helpful: address. Civil cases indexed by defendant, plaintiff. Civil records in index books.

Criminal Records: Access: Mail, in person. Both court and visitors may perform in person searches. Search fee: $5.00 per name. Required to search: name, years to search; also helpful: address, DOB, SSN. Criminal records in index books.

General Information: No juvenile, mental, sealed, or adoption records released. SASE required. Turnaround time 2-3 days. Fax notes: Fee to fax results is $2.00 per page. Copy fee: $1.00 per page. Certification fee: $5.00. Fee payee: County Clerk. Personal checks accepted. Prepayment is required.

Williamson County

District Court PO Box 24, Georgetown, TX 78627; 512-943-1212; Fax: 512-943-1222. Hours: 8AM-5PM (CST). *Felony, Civil.*

Civil Records: Access: Mail, in person. Both court and visitors may perform in person searches. Search fee: $5.00 per name. Required to search: name, years to search. Civil cases indexed by defendant, plaintiff. Civil records on computer since 1989, index books prior.

Criminal Records: Access: Mail, in person. Both court and visitors may perform in person searches. Search fee: $5.00 per name. Required to search: name, years to search, DOB, signed release; also helpful: SSN. Criminal records on computer since 1989, index books prior.

General Information: No juvenile, mental, sealed, or adoption records released. SASE required. Turnaround time 2-3 days. Copy fee: $1.00 1st pg; $.25 each add'l. Certification fee: $1.00. Fee payee: District Clerk. Personal checks accepted. Prepayment is required.

County Court 405 MLK St, Box 14, Georgetown, TX 78626; Civil phone: 512-943-1140; Criminal phone: 512-943-1150; Probate phone: 512-943-1140; Fax: 512-943-1154. Hours: 8AM-5PM (CST). *Misdemeanor, Civil, Probate.*

Civil Records: Access: Mail, in person. Both court and visitors may perform in person searches. Search fee: $10.00 per name. Required to search: name, years to search. Civil cases indexed by defendant, plaintiff. Civil records on computer since 1985, index books to 1848.
Criminal Records: Access: Mail, in person. Both court and visitors may perform in person searches. Search fee: $10.00 per name. Required to search: name, years to search; also helpful: DOB, SSN. Criminal records on computer since 1983; prior on books.
General Information: Public Access terminal is available. No juvenile, mental, sealed, or adoption records released. SASE required. Turnaround time 2 days. Fax notes: Fee to fax results is $1.00 per page. Copy fee: $1.00 per page. Certification fee: $5.00. Fee payee: County Clerk. Personal checks accepted. Prepayment is required.

Wilson County

District Court PO Box 812, Floresville, TX 78114; 830-393-7322; Fax: 830-393-7319. Hours: 8AM-Noon, 1-5PM (CST). *Felony, Civil.*

Civil Records: Access: Fax, mail, in person. Both court and visitors may perform in person searches. Search fee: $5.00 per name. Required to search: name, years to search. Civil cases indexed by defendant, plaintiff. Civil records in index books from 1960.
Criminal Records: Access: Fax, mail, in person. Both court and visitors may perform in person searches. Search fee: $5.00 per name. Required to search: name, years to search; also helpful: DOB. Criminal records in index books from 1960.
General Information: No juvenile, mental, sealed, or adoption records released. SASE required. Turnaround time 2 days. Fax notes: Fee to fax results is $3.00 for first page, $1.00 per page thereafter. Copy fee: $1.00 per page. Certification fee: $1.00. Fee payee: District Clerk. Personal checks accepted. Prepayment is required.

County Court PO Box 27, Floresville, TX 78114; 830-393-7308. Hours: 8AM-5PM (CST). *Misdemeanor, Civil, Probate.*

Civil Records: Access: Phone, mail, fax, in person. Both court and visitors may perform in person searches. No search fee. Required to search: name, years to search. Civil cases indexed by defendant, plaintiff. Civil records on computer back to 1992; on index books back to 1860.
Criminal Records: Access: Phone, mail, fax, in person. Both court and visitors may perform in person searches. No search fee. Required to search: name, years to search, DOB. Criminal records on computer back to 1992; on index books back to 1860.
General Information: No juvenile, mental, sealed, or adoption records released. SASE required. Turnaround time same day. Fax notes: Do not fax. Copy fee: $1.00 per page. Certification fee: $5.00. Fee payee: Eva S Martinez, County Clerk. Personal checks accepted. Prepayment is required.

Winkler County

District Court PO Box 1065, Kermit, TX 79745; 915-586-3359. Hours: 8AM-5PM (CST). *Felony, Civil.*

Civil Records: Access: Phone, mail, in person. Both court and visitors may perform in person searches. Search fee: $5.00 per name. Required to search: name, years to search. Civil cases indexed by defendant,

plaintiff. Civil records on computer since 1991 (child-support only), index books prior.
Criminal Records: Access: Mail, in person. Both court and visitors may perform in person searches. Search fee: $5.00 per name. Required to search: name, years to search, DOB, SSN. Criminal records on computer since 1991, index books prior.
General Information: No juvenile, mental, sealed, or adoption records released. SASE required. Turnaround time 1-2 days. Copy fee: $1.00 per page. Fee payee: District Clerk. Personal checks accepted. Prepayment is required.

County Court PO Box 1007, Kermit, TX 79745; 915-586-3401. Hours: 8AM-5PM (CST). *Misdemeanor, Civil, Probate.*

Civil Records: Access: Mail, in person. Both court and visitors may perform in person searches. Search fee: $5.00 per name. Required to search: name, years to search. Civil cases indexed by defendant, plaintiff. Civil records on computer back to 1991; prior in index books.
Criminal Records: Access: Mail, in person. Both court and visitors may perform in person searches. Search fee: $5.00 per name. Required to search: name, years to search; also helpful: address, DOB, SSN. Criminal records on computer back to 1991; prior in index books.
General Information: No juvenile, mental, sealed, or adoption records released. SASE required. Turnaround time 2-3 days. Copy fee: $1.00 per page. Certification fee: $5.00. Fee payee: County Clerk. Business checks accepted. Prepayment is required.

Wise County

District Court PO Box 308, Decatur, TX 76234; 940-627-5535; Fax: 940-627-0705. Hours: 8AM-5PM (CST). *Felony, Civil.*

Civil Records: Access: Mail, in person. Both court and visitors may perform in person searches. Search fee: $5.00 per name. Required to search: name, years to search. Civil cases indexed by defendant, plaintiff. Civil records in index books since 1896.
Criminal Records: Access: Mail, in person. Both court and visitors may perform in person searches. Search fee: $5.00 per name. Required to search: name, years to search, DOB, SSN, signed release. Criminal records in docket books.
General Information: No juvenile, mental, sealed, or adoption records released. SASE required. Turnaround time same day. Copy fee: $1.00 per page. Certification fee: $2.00. Fee payee: Wise County District Clerk. Personal checks accepted. Prepayment is required.

County Court at Law PO Box 359, Decatur, TX 76234; 940-627-3351; Fax: 940-627-2138. Hours: 8AM-5PM (CST). *Misdemeanor, Civil, Probate.*

Civil Records: Access: Mail, in person. Both court and visitors may perform in person searches. Search fee: $10.00 per name. Required to search: name, years to search. Civil cases indexed by defendant, plaintiff. Civil records in index books since sovereignty; on computer back to 1998.
Criminal Records: Access: Mail, in person. Both court and visitors may perform in person searches. Search fee: $10.00 per name. Required to search: name, years to search; also helpful: DOB, SSN. Criminal records in index books since sovereignty; on computer to 1997.
General Information: Public Access terminal is available. No mental health or sealed records released. SASE required. Turnaround time 1 day. Copy fee: $1.00 per page. Certification fee: $5.00. Fee payee: Wise County Clerk. Personal checks accepted. Prepayment is required.

Wood County

District Court PO Box 1707, Quitman, TX 75783; 903-763-2361; Fax: 903-763-1511. Hours: 8AM-Noon, 1-5PM (CST). *Felony, Civil.*

Civil Records: Access: Mail, fax, in person. Both court and visitors may perform in person searches. Search fee: $5.00 per name. Required to search: name, years to search. Civil cases indexed by defendant, plaintiff. Civil records on computer since 1990, microfilm since 1981, index books since 1890.
Criminal Records: Access: Mail, fax, in person. Both court and visitors may perform in person searches. Search fee: $5.00 per name. Required to search: name, years to search; also helpful: DOB, SSN. Criminal records on computer since 1990, microfilm since 1981, index books since 1890.
General Information: Public Access terminal is available. No juvenile, mental, sealed, or adoption records released. SASE required. Turnaround time 2-3 days. Copy fee: $1.00 per page. Certification fee: $1.00. Fee payee: District Clerk. Personal checks accepted. Prepayment is required.

County Court PO Box 1796, Quitman, TX 75783; 903-763-2711; Fax: 903-763-2902. Hours: 8AM-5PM (CST). *Misdemeanor, Civil, Probate.*

Civil Records: Access: Mail, in person. Both court and visitors may perform in person searches. Search fee: $5.00 per name. Required to search: name, years to search. Civil cases indexed by defendant, plaintiff. Civil records on computer since 1980; index books since early 1900s.
Criminal Records: Access: Mail, in person. Both court and visitors may perform in person searches. Search fee: $5.00 per name. Required to search: name, years to search; also helpful DOB, SSN, signed release, DL#. Criminal records on computer back to 1980; index books from 1965.
General Information: No mental or sealed records released. SASE required. Turnaround time same day. Copy fee: $1.00 per page. Certification fee: $5.00. Fee payee: Wood County Clerk. Personal checks accepted. Prepayment is required.

Yoakum County

District Court PO Box 899, Plains, TX 79355; 806-456-7453; Fax: 806-456-8767. Hours: 8AM-5PM (CST). *Felony, Civil.*

Civil Records: Access: Phone, fax, mail, in person. Both court and visitors may perform in person searches. Search fee: $5.00 per name. Required to search: name, years to search. Civil cases indexed by defendant, plaintiff. Civil records on computer since 1980, index books since 1907.
Criminal Records: Access: Phone, fax, mail, in person. Both court and visitors may perform in person searches. Search fee: $5.00 per name. Required to search: name, years to search, DOB; also helpful: SSN. Criminal records on computer since 1980, index books since 1930.
General Information: No juvenile, mental, sealed, or adoption records released. SASE not required. Turnaround time same day. Fax notes: $2.00 for first page, $1.00 each add'l. Copy fee: $1.00 per page. Certification fee: $1.00. Fee payee: District Clerk. Personal checks accepted. Prepayment is required.

County Court PO Box 309, Plains, TX 79355; 806-456-2721; Fax: 806-456-6175 (County Judge Office). Hours: 8AM-5PM (CST). *Misdemeanor, Civil, Probate.*

Civil Records: Access: Phone, fax, mail, in person. Both court and visitors may perform in person searches. Search fee: $5.00 per name. Required to search: name, years to search; also helpful: address. Civil cases indexed by defendant, plaintiff. Civil records in minutes books and microfilm since September, 1986, case binders (all), computer (Court Mgmnt-current).

Criminal Records: Access: Mail, in person. Both court and visitors may perform in person searches. Search fee: $5.00 per name. Required to search: name, years to search; also helpful: address, DOB, SSN. Criminal minutes books and microfilm since September, 1986, case binders (all), computer (Court Mgmnt-current).

General Information: Public Access terminal is available. No juvenile or mental records released. SASE not required. Turnaround time same day. Copy fee: $1.00 per page. Certification fee: $5.00. Fee payee: County Clerk, Yoakum County. Personal checks accepted. Prepayment is required.

Young County

District Court 516 4th St Rm 201, Courthouse, Graham, TX 76450; 940-549-0029; Fax: 940-549-4874. Hours: 8:30AM-Noon, 1-5PM (CST). *Felony, Civil.*

Civil Records: Access: Phone, fax, mail, in person. Both court and visitors may perform in person searches. Search fee: $5.00 per name. Required to search: name, years to search. Civil cases indexed by defendant, plaintiff. Civil records on computer since 1988, index books prior. Search fee must be prepaid before fax access is allowed.

Criminal Records: Access: Phone, fax, mail, in person. Both court and visitors may perform in person searches. Search fee: $5.00 per name. Required to search: name, years to search; also helpful: DOB, SSN. Criminal records on computer since 1988, index books prior.

General Information: No juvenile, mental, sealed, or adoption records released. SASE required. Turnaround time 1-2 days. Fax notes: No fee to fax results. Copy fee: $1.00 for first page, $.25 each add'l. Certification fee: $1.00 per page. Fee payee: District Clerk. Personal checks accepted. Prepayment is required.

County Court 516 4th St Rm 104, Graham, TX 76450; 940-549-8432; Fax: 940-521-0305. Hours: 8:30AM-Noon, 1-5PM (CST). *Misdemeanor, Civil, Probate.*

Civil Records: Access: Mail, in person. Both court and visitors may perform in person searches. Search fee: $10.00 per name. Required to search: name, years to

search. Civil cases indexed by defendant, plaintiff. Civil records on computer since 1991, index books prior.

Criminal Records: Access: Mail, in person. Both court and visitors may perform in person searches. Search fee: $5.00 per name. Required to search: name, years to search. Criminal records on computer since 1991, index books prior.

General Information: Public Access terminal is available. No juvenile, mental, sealed, or adoption records released. SASE not required. Turnaround time upon receipt. Fax notes: Fee to fax results is $1.00 per page. Copy fee: $1.00 per page. Certification fee: $5.00. Fee payee: Shirley Choate, County Clerk. Personal checks accepted. Prepayment is required.

Zapata County

District Court PO Box 788, Clerk's Office, Zapata, TX 78076; 956-765-9930; Fax: 956-765-9931. Hours: 8AM-Noon, 1-5PM (CST). *Felony, Civil.*

Civil Records: Access: Fax, mail, in person. Both court and visitors may perform in person searches. Search fee: $5.00 per name. Required to search: name, years to search. Civil cases indexed by plaintiff. Civil records in index books.

Criminal Records: Access: Fax, mail, in person. Both court and visitors may perform in person searches. Search fee: $5.00 per name. Required to search: name, years to search. Criminal records in index books.

General Information: No juvenile, mental, sealed, or adoption records released. SASE required. Turnaround time 1-3 days. Fax notes: $4.00 for first page, $1.00 each add'l. Copy fee: $1.00 per page. Certification fee: $5.00. Fee payee: District Clerk/County Clerk. Personal checks accepted. Prepayment is required.

County Court PO Box 789, Zapata, TX 78076; 956-765-9915; Fax: 956-765-9933. Hours: 8AM-Noon, 1-5PM (CST). *Misdemeanor, Civil, Probate.*

Civil Records: Access: Fax, mail, in person. Both court and visitors may perform in person searches. Search fee: $5.00 per name. Required to search: name, years to search. Civil cases indexed by defendant, plaintiff. Civil records in index books since 1916.

Criminal Records: Access: Fax, mail, in person. Both court and visitors may perform in person searches. Search fee: $5.00 per name. Required to search: name, years to search; also helpful: DOB, SSN. Criminal records in index books since 1916.

General Information: No juvenile, mental, sealed, or adoption records released. SASE not required. Turnaround time 1-2 days. Fax notes: $4.00 for first page, $1.00 each add'l. Copy fee: $1.00 per page. Certification fee: $5.00. Fee payee: Consuelo R Villarreal, County Clerk. Personal checks accepted. Prepayment is required.

Zavala County

District Court PO Box 704, Crystal City, TX 78839; 830-374-3456. Hours: 8AM-Noon, 1-5PM (CST). *Felony, Civil.*

Civil Records: Access: Phone, mail, in person. Both court and visitors may perform in person searches. Search fee: $5.00 per name. Required to search: name, years to search. Civil cases indexed by defendant, plaintiff. Civil records in index books from 1900s.

Criminal Records: Access: Phone, mail, in person. Both court and visitors may perform in person searches. Search fee: $5.00 per name. Required to search: name, years to search. Criminal records in index books from 1900s.

General Information: No juvenile, mental, sealed, or adoption records released. SASE required. Turnaround time 1-2 days. Copy fee: $1.00 per page. Certification fee: No certification fee. Fee payee: Zavala County District Clerk. Personal checks accepted.

County Court Zavala County Courthouse, 200 E Uvalde, Crystal City, TX 78839; 830-374-2331; Fax: 830-374-5955. Hours: 8AM-5PM (CST). *Misdemeanor, Civil, Probate.*

Civil Records: Access: Mail, in person. Both court and visitors may perform in person searches. Search fee: $10.00 per name. Required to search: name, years to search. Civil cases indexed by defendant, plaintiff. Civil records in index books from 1880s.

Criminal Records: Access: Mail, in person. Both court and visitors may perform in person searches. Search fee: $10.00 per name. Required to search: name, years to search, DOB. Criminal records in index books from 1880s.

General Information: No juvenile, mental, sealed, or adoption records released. SASE required. Turnaround time 1-2 days. Copy fee: $1.00 per page. Certification fee: $1.00. Fee payee: Zavala County Clerk. Personal checks accepted. Prepayment is required.

Texas Recording Offices

ORGANIZATION

254 counties, 254 recording offices. The recording officer is County Clerk. 252 counties are in the Central Time Zone (CST) and 2 are in the Mountain Time Zone (MST).

Certain Assessor and property information from nearly 50 counties is available for through two web sites: www.taxnetusa.com and www.txcountydata.com.

REAL ESTATE RECORDS

Some counties will perform real estate searches. Copy fees are usually $1.00 per page. Certification usually costs $5.00 per document. Each county has an "Appraisal District" which is responsible for collecting taxes.

UCC RECORDS

Financing statements are filed at the state level, except for real estate related collateral, which are filed with the County Clerk. Most all recording offices will perform UCC searches. Searches fees are usually $10.00 per debtor name using the approved UCC-11 request form, plus $15.00 for using a non-Texas form. Copy fees are usually $1.00-1.50 per page with a minimum copy fee of $5.00.

TAX LIEN RECORDS

Federal tax liens on personal property of businesses are filed with the Secretary of State. Other federal and all state tax liens are filed with the County Clerk. All counties will perform tax lien searches. Search fees and copy fees vary.

OTHER LIENS

Mechanics, judgment, hospital, labor, lis pendens.

NOTES

Over 60 Texas counties offer Assessor and Real Estate via two private company web sites. The profiles to follow indicate which counties are involved. Some counties can be accessed from either site.

www.taxnetusa.com . TaxNetUSA can be reached at 817-795-8378, or faxed at 817-795-8359.

This site offers free appraisal district and property information records for 55 Texas counties as well as a few counties in other states. The site also offers advanced and subscriptions services for 6 other counties.

At the TaxNetUSA site, user chooses "advanced search subscribers login" (fee service) or "Appraisal Districts Online Basic Search" (no fee). For a basic search, use the pull down menu in the county field to select the county to search. Select county and click go. At the county Assessor/Tax site, follow the directions for that county. Generally, but in varying degrees from county to county, the basic search allows you to access general property information: name, address, valuation, etc., and you may search by parcel number, owner name, or address. Depending on the county, more "detailed" information may be available.

TaxNetUSA's Advanced Search Information (fee) allows most counties to be searched by any combination of the following criteria: owner name, property location, city, school district, subdivision, maps co page, land area, class, tax board code, tax value, deed date and more. Fees vary and can range frorm a simple $25 search, to multiple county subscriptions that are over $1,500.00.

www.txcountydata.com

Assessor and property information records for 49 Texas counties on the TXCOUNTYDATA site are available on the Internet for no fee.

At the TXCOUNTYDATA site, click on "County Search" then use the pull down menu in the county field to select the county to search. Select county and click go. The County Info page for each county lists the Appraiser, mailing address, phone, fax, web site, e-mail. Generally, you can search any county account, owner name, address, or property ID number. Search allows you to access owner address, property address, legal description, taxing entities, exemptions, deed, account number, abstract/subdivision, neighborhood, valuation info, and/or building attributes.

Anderson County

County Clerk, 500 North Church Street, Palestine, TX 75801. 903-723-7402.
Will search UCC records prior to 7/2001 and current fixture (land) files. This agency will not do a tax lien search. Will not search real estate records. **Online Access:** Assessor, Property Tax. See note at beginning of section. **Other Phone Numbers:** Assessor 903-723-7433; Treasurer 903-723-7408; Appraiser/Auditor 903-723-2949.

Andrews County

County Clerk, P.O. Box 727, Andrews, TX 79714. County Clerk, R/E and UCC Recording 915-524-1426; Fax 915-524-1473.
Will search UCC records prior to 7/2001 and current fixture (land) files. Will not search real estate records.

Other Phone Numbers: Assessor 915-524-1409; Appraiser/Auditor 915-523-9111; Elections 915-524-1426; Vital Records 915-524-1426.

Angelina County

County Clerk, P.O. Box 908, Lufkin, TX 75902-0908. 936-634-8339; Fax 936-634-8460.
Will search UCC records prior to 7/2001 and current fixture (land) files. Tax liens not included in UCC search. Will not search real estate records. **Online Access:** Assessor, Property Tax. See note at beginning of section. **Other Phone Numbers:** Assessor 936-634-8456; Appraiser/Auditor 936-634-8456.

Aransas County

County Clerk, 301 North Live Oak, Rockport, TX 78382. County Clerk, R/E and UCC Recording 361-790-0122.
Will search UCC records prior to 7/2001 and current fixture (land) files. Tax liens not included in UCC search. Will not search real estate records. **Online Access:** Assessor, Property Tax. See note at beginning of section. **Other Phone Numbers:** Assessor 361-790-9733; Treasurer 361-790-0132; Appraiser/Auditor 361-729-9733; Elections 361-729-7431; Vital Records 361-790-0122.

Archer County

County Clerk, P.O. Box 815, Archer City, TX 76351. 940-574-4615; Fax 940-574-4625.

Will search UCC records prior to 7/2001 and current fixture (land) files. Tax liens not included in UCC search. Will not search real estate records. **Online Access:** Property Tax. See note at beginning of section. **Other Phone Numbers:** Assessor 940-574-4224; Treasurer 940-574-4822; Appraiser/Auditor 940-574-2172.

Armstrong County

County Clerk, P.O. Box 309, Claude, TX 79019-0309. County Clerk, R/E and UCC Recording 806-226-2081; Fax 806-226-5301.
Will search UCC records prior to 7/2001 and current fixture (land) files. Tax liens not included in UCC search. Will not search real estate records. **Other Phone Numbers:** Assessor 806-226-4481; Treasurer 806-226-3651; Appraiser/Auditor 806-226-4481; Elections 806-226-2081; Vital Records 806-226-2081.

Atascosa County

County Clerk, Circle Drive, Room 6-1, Jourdanton, TX 78026. 830-769-2511 R/E Recording: 830-767-2511.
Will search UCC records prior to 7/2001 and current fixture (land) files. UCC search includes tax liens if requested. Will not search real estate records. **Online Access:** Assessor, Property Tax. See note at beginning of section. **Other Phone Numbers:** Assessor 830-769-3620; Treasurer 830-769-3024; Appraiser/Auditor 830-742-3591.

Austin County

County Clerk, 1 East Main, Bellville, TX 77418-1551. County Clerk, R/E and UCC Recording 979-865-5911; Fax 979-865-0336.
Will search UCC records prior to 7/2001 and current fixture (land) files. This agency will not do a tax lien search. Will not search real estate records. **Online Access:** Assessor, Property Tax. See note at beginning of section. **Other Phone Numbers:** Assessor 979-865-9124; Treasurer 979-865-5911; Appraiser/Auditor 409-865-9124; Elections 979-865-5911; Vital Records 979-865-5911.

Bailey County

County Clerk, 300 South First, Suite 200, Muleshoe, TX 79347. County Clerk, R/E and UCC Recording 806-272-3044; Fax 806-272-3538.
Will search UCC records prior to 7/2001 and current fixture (land) files. **Other Phone Numbers:** Assessor 806-272-3022; Treasurer 806-272-3239; Appraiser/Auditor 806-272-5501.

Bandera County

County Clerk, P.O. Box 823, Bandera, TX 78003. 830-796-3332; Fax 830-796-8323.
Will search UCC records prior to 7/2001 and current fixture (land) files. UCC search includes tax liens if requested. RE owner, mortgage, and property transfer searches available. **Online Access:** Property Tax. See note at beginning of section. **Other Phone Numbers:** Assessor 830-796-3039; Appraiser/Auditor 830-796-3030.

Bastrop County

County Clerk, P.O. Box 577, Bastrop, TX 78602. 512-321-4443 R/E Recording: 512-332-7234.
Will search UCC records prior to 7/2001 and current fixture (land) files. UCC search includes tax liens if requested. RE owner, mortgage, and property transfer searches available. **Online Access:** Assessor, Property Tax. See notes at beginning of section. **Other Phone Numbers:** Assessor 512-303-2905; Treasurer 512-321-2460; Appraiser/Auditor 512-303-3536.

Baylor County

County Clerk, P.O. Box 689, Seymour, TX 76380-0689. 940-888-3322.
Will search UCC records prior to 7/2001 and current fixture (land) files. UCC search includes tax liens if requested. RE owner, mortgage, and property transfer searches available. **Other Phone Numbers:** Assessor 940-888-3169; Treasurer 940-888-3553; Appraiser/Auditor 940-888-3169.

Bee County

County Clerk, 105 West Corpus Christi Street, Room 103, Beeville, TX 78102. 361-362-3245; Fax 361-362-3247.
Will search UCC records prior to 7/2001 and current fixture (land) files. UCC search includes tax liens if requested. Will not search real estate records. **Online Access:** Property Tax. See note at beginning of section. **Other Phone Numbers:** Assessor 361-362-3250; Appraiser/Auditor 361-358-0193.

Bell County

County Clerk, P.O. Box 480, Belton, TX 76513-0480. 254-933-5171; Fax 254-933-5176.
Will search UCC records prior to 7/2001 and current fixture (land) files. Tax liens not included in UCC search. Will not search real estate records. **Online Access:** Assessor, Property Tax. TexasTax provides two methods of access to County records. Access to "Advanced Search" records requires a login and subscription fee. Subs are allowed in monthly increments. Advanced Search includes full data, maps, and Excel spreadsheet. For information, see www.texastax.com/bell/subscriptioninfo.asp. Records on "Quick Search - FREE" at www.texastax.com/bell/index/asp allows access to these County records: tax ID number, owner, parcel address, land value data. Search FREE by tax ID number, address, name, city or value. View details. **Other Phone Numbers:** Assessor 817-771-1108; Treasurer 817-933-5255; Appraiser/Auditor 254-939-5841.

Bexar County

County Clerk, Bexar County Courthouse, 100 Dolorosa, Room 108, San Antonio, TX 78205-3083. 210-335-2581; Fax 210-335-2813. http://www.bcad.org/home.htm
Will search UCC records prior to 7/2001 and current fixture (land) files. Tax liens not included in UCC search. RE owner, mortgage, and property transfer searches available. **Online Access:** Property Tax, Assessor. Online access to the county Central Appraisal District database is available free at www.bcad.org/property.htm. **Other Phone Numbers:** Appraiser/Auditor 210-335-2251.

Blanco County

County Clerk, P.O. Box 65, Johnson City, TX 78636. 830-868-7357.
Will search UCC records prior to 7/2001 and current fixture (land) files. UCC search includes tax liens if requested. Will not search real estate records. **Online Access:** Assessor, Property Tax. See note at beginning of section. **Other Phone Numbers:** Assessor 830-868-7178; Treasurer 830-868-4566; Appraiser/Auditor 830-868-4624.

Borden County

County Clerk, P.O. Box 124, Gail, TX 79738-0124. County Clerk, R/E and UCC Recording 806-756-4312; Fax 806-756-4405.
Will search UCC records prior to 7/2001 and current fixture (land) files. Tax liens not included in UCC search. Will not search real estate records. **Other Phone**

Numbers: Assessor 806-756-4415; Treasurer 806-756-4386; Appraiser/Auditor 806-756-4484; Elections 806-756-4312; Vital Records 806-756-4312.

Bosque County

County Clerk, P.O. Box 617, Meridian, TX 76665. 254-435-2201.
Will search UCC records prior to 7/2001 and current fixture (land) files. UCC search includes tax liens if requested. RE owner, mortgage, and property transfer searches available. **Other Phone Numbers:** Assessor 254-435-2201 x15; Treasurer 254-435-2201 x20; Appraiser/Auditor 254-435-2301.

Bowie County

County Clerk, P.O.Box 248, New Boston, TX 75570. 903-628-6740; Fax 903-628-6729.
Will search UCC records prior to 7/2001 and current fixture (land) files. Will not search real estate records. **Other Phone Numbers:** Assessor 903-628-2571 x229; Treasurer 903-628-2571 x230; Appraiser/Auditor 903-628-5493; Elections 903-628-6809; Vital Records 903-628-6744.

Brazoria County

County Clerk, 111 East Locust, Suite 200, Angleton, TX 77515-4654. 979-849-5711; Fax 979-864-1358. http://www.brazoriacad.org
Will search UCC records prior to 7/2001 and current fixture (land) files. **Online Access:** Assessor, Property Tax. Online access to the county Central Appraisal District database is available free at www.brazoriacad.org/search.htm. Also, see notes at beginning of section. **Other Phone Numbers:** Assessor 979-849-7792; Treasurer 979-849-5711; Appraiser/Auditor 979-849-7792.

Brazos County

County Clerk, 300 East 26th Street, Suite 120, Bryan, TX 77803. 979-361-4132 R/E Recording: 409-361-4132; Fax 979-361-4125.
Will search UCC records prior to 7/2001 and current fixture (land) files. UCC search includes tax liens if requested. Mortgage and property transfer searches available. **Online Access:** Assessor, Property Tax. See notes at beginning of section. **Other Phone Numbers:** Assessor 979-361-4480; Treasurer 979-361-4340; Appraiser/Auditor 409-774-4100.

Brewster County

County Clerk, P.O. Box 119, Alpine, TX 79831. County Clerk, R/E and UCC Recording 915-837-3366; Fax 915-837-6217.
Will search UCC records prior to 7/2001 and current fixture (land) files. Will search real estate records. Search fee is $10.00 per name. **Other Phone Numbers:** Assessor 915-837-2214; Treasurer 915-837-6200; Appraiser/Auditor 915-837-2558; Vital Records 915-837-3366.

Briscoe County

County Clerk, P.O. Box 555, Silverton, TX 79257. County Clerk, R/E and UCC Recording 806-823-2134; Fax 806-823-2359.
Will search UCC records prior to 7/2001 and current fixture (land) files. **Other Phone Numbers:** Assessor 806-823-2136; Treasurer 806-823-2131; Appraiser/Auditor 806-823-2161; Elections 806-823-2134; Vital Records 806-823-2134.

Brooks County

County Clerk, P.O. Box 427, Falfurrias, TX 78355. 361-325-5604 R/E Recording: 361-325-5604 x1; Fax 361-325-4944.

Will search UCC records. **Other Phone Numbers:** Assessor 361-325-5604 x226; Treasurer 361-325-5604 x229; Appraiser/Auditor 361-325-5681.

Brown County

County Clerk, 200 South Broadway, Courthouse, Brownwood, TX 76801. County Clerk, R/E and UCC Recording 915-643-2594.

Will search UCC records. Tax liens not included in UCC search. Will not search real estate records. **Online Access:** Assessor, Property Tax. See note at beginning of section. **Other Phone Numbers:** Assessor 915-643-1646 (Tax); Treasurer 915-646-6033; Appraiser/Auditor 915-643-5676; Elections 915-643-2594; Vital Records 915-643-2594.

Burleson County

County Clerk, 100 W Buck St #203, Caldwell, TX 77836. 979-567-2329 R/E Recording: 409-567-2329; Fax 979-567-2376.

Will search UCC records prior to 7/2001 and current fixture (land) files. Tax liens not included in UCC search. Will not search real estate records. **Online Access:** Assessor, Property Tax. See note at beginning of section. **Other Phone Numbers:** Assessor 979-567-4671; Appraiser/Auditor 409-567-2318.

Burnet County

County Clerk, 220 South Pierce Street, Burnet, TX 78611. 512-756-5406; Fax 512-756-5410.

Will search UCC records prior to 7/2001 and current fixture (land) files. Tax liens not included in UCC search. Will not search real estate records. **Online Access:** Assessor, Property Tax. See note at beginning of section. **Other Phone Numbers:** Assessor 512-756-8291; Appraiser/Auditor 512-756-8291.

Caldwell County

County Clerk, P.O. Box 906, Lockhart, TX 78644-0906. 512-398-1804; http://www.caldwellcad.org

Will search UCC records prior to 7/2001 and current fixture (land) files. Tax liens not included in UCC search. RE owner, mortgage, and property transfer searches available. **Online Access:** Assessor, Property Tax. Online access to the county Appraisal District database is available free at www.caldwell cad.org/search.htm. Search real estate or personal property. Also, see notes at beginning of section. **Other Phone Numbers:** Assessor 512-398-2391; Treasurer 512-398-1800; Appraiser/Auditor 512-398-0550.

Calhoun County

County Clerk, 211 South Ann, Port Lavaca, TX 77979. County Clerk, R/E and UCC Recording 361-553-4411; Fax 361-553-4420.

Will search UCC records. Will not search real estate records. **Other Phone Numbers:** Assessor 361-552-8808; Treasurer 361-553-4620; Appraiser/Auditor 361-552-8808; Elections 361-553-4440; Vital Records 361-553-4411.

Callahan County

County Clerk, 100 W. 4th, Ste. 104, Courthouse, Baird, TX 79504. 915-854-1217; Fax 915-854-1227.

Will search UCC records. Tax liens not included in UCC search. Will not search real estate records. **Other Phone Numbers:** Treasurer 915-854-1399; Appraiser/Auditor 915-854-1165.

Cameron County

County Clerk, P.O. Box 2178, Brownsville, TX 78520. County Clerk, R/E and UCC Recording 956-544-0815 UCC Recording: 956-550-1329; Fax 956-554-0813.

Will search UCC records prior to 7/2001 and current fixture (land) files. **Online Access:** Assessor, Property

Tax. See note at beginning of section. **Other Phone Numbers:** Assessor 956-544-0800; Treasurer 956-544-0819; Appraiser/Auditor 956-399-9322; Elections 956-544-0809; Vital Records 956-544-0817.

Camp County

County Clerk, 126 Church Street, Room 102, Pittsburg, TX 75686. County Clerk, R/E and UCC Recording 903-856-2731; Fax 903-856-2309.

Will search UCC records prior to 7/2001 and current fixture (land) files. Will not search real estate records. **Other Phone Numbers:** Assessor 903-856-3391; Treasurer 903-856-7862; Appraiser/Auditor 903-856-6538; Elections 903-856-2731; Vital Records 903-856-2731.

Carson County

County Clerk, P.O. Box 487, Panhandle, TX 79068. County Clerk, R/E and UCC Recording 806-537-3873; Fax 806-537-3623.

Will search UCC records prior to 7/2001 and current fixture (land) files. UCC search includes tax liens if requested. Will not search real estate records. **Other Phone Numbers:** Assessor 806-537-3412; Treasurer 806-537-3753; Appraiser/Auditor 806-537-3569; Elections 806-537-3873; Vital Records 806-537-3873.

Cass County

County Clerk, P.O. Box 449, Linden, TX 75563. County Clerk, R/E and UCC Recording 903-756-5071; Fax 903-756-5732.

Will search UCC records prior to 7/2001 and current fixture (land) files. **Other Phone Numbers:** Assessor 903-756-5311; Treasurer 903-756-7626; Appraiser/Auditor 903-756-7545; Elections 903-756-5071; Vital Records 903-756-5071.

Castro County

County Clerk, 100 East Bedford, Room 101, Dimmitt, TX 79027-2643. County Clerk, R/E and UCC Recording 806-647-3338.

Will search UCC records prior to 7/2001 and current fixture (land) files. UCC search includes tax liens if requested. Will not search real estate records. **Other Phone Numbers:** Assessor 806-647-5336; Treasurer 806-647-5534; Appraiser/Auditor 806-647-5131; Elections 806-647-3338; Vital Records 806-647-3338.

Chambers County

County Clerk, P.O. Box 728, Anahuac, TX 77514. 409-267-8309; Fax 409-267-4453.

Will search UCC records prior to 7/2001 and current fixture (land) files. UCC search includes tax liens if requested. Will not search real estate records. **Online Access:** Property Tax. See note at beginning of section. **Other Phone Numbers:** Assessor 409-267-8304; Treasurer 409-267-8286; Appraiser/Auditor 409-267-3795.

Cherokee County

County Clerk, P.O. Box 420, Rusk, TX 75785. County Clerk, R/E and UCC Recording 903-683-2350; Fax 903-683-5931.

Will search UCC records prior to 7/2001 and current fixture (land) files. **Other Phone Numbers:** Assessor 903-683-5478; Treasurer 903-683-4935; Appraiser/Auditor 903-683-2296; Elections 903-683-2350; Vital Records 903-683-2350.

Childress County

County Clerk, Courthouse Box 4, Childress, TX 79201. County Clerk, R/E and UCC Recording 940-937-6143; Fax 940-937-3479.

Will search UCC records. **Other Phone Numbers:** Assessor 940-937-6062; Treasurer 940-937-6271;

Appraiser/Auditor 940-937-6062; Elections 940-937-6143; Vital Records 940-937-6143.

Clay County

County Clerk, P.O. Box 548, Henrietta, TX 76365. 940-538-4631.

Will search UCC records prior to 7/2001 and current fixture (land) files. This agency will not do a tax lien search. RE owner, mortgage, and property transfer searches available. **Online Access:** Property Tax. See note at beginning of section. **Other Phone Numbers:** Assessor 940-538-4311; Appraiser/Auditor 940-538-4311.

Cochran County

County Clerk, 100 North Main, Courthouse, Morton, TX 79346-2598. 806-266-5450; Fax 806-266-9027.

Will search UCC records prior to 7/2001 and current fixture (land) files. Tax liens not included in UCC search. RE owner, mortgage, and property transfer searches available. **Other Phone Numbers:** Assessor 806-266-5171; Treasurer 806-266-5161; Appraiser/Auditor 806-266-5584.

Coke County

County Clerk, P.O. Box 150, Robert Lee, TX 76945. 915-453-2631; Fax 915-453-2650.

Will search UCC records prior to 7/2001 and current fixture (land) files. UCC search includes tax liens if requested. Will not search real estate records. **Other Phone Numbers:** Assessor 915-453-2614; Treasurer 915-453-2713; Appraiser/Auditor 915-453-4528.

Coleman County

County Clerk, P.O. Box 591, Coleman, TX 76834. 915-625-2889.

Will search UCC records. This agency will not do a tax lien search. Will not search real estate records. **Other Phone Numbers:** Assessor 915-625-4155; Treasurer 915-625-4221; Appraiser/Auditor 915-625-4155.

Collin County

County Clerk, 200 South McDonald, Annex "A", Suite 120, McKinney, TX 75069. County Clerk, R/E and UCC Recording 972-548-4134 UCC Recording: 972-548-4151; http://www.co.collin.tx.us

Will search UCC records prior to 7/2001 and current fixture (land) files. UCC search includes tax liens if requested. Will not search real estate records. **Online Access:** Property Tax. See note at beginning of section. **Other Phone Numbers:** Assessor 972-547-5020; Treasurer 972-548-4202; Appraiser/Auditor 972-578-5200; Elections 972-548-3214; Vital Records 972-548-4134.

Collingsworth County

County Clerk, Courthouse, Room 3, 800 West Ave., Wellington, TX 79095. 806-447-2408; Fax 806-447-5418.

Will search UCC records prior to 7/2001 and current fixture (land) files. Tax liens not included in UCC search. RE record owner searches available. **Other Phone Numbers:** Appraiser/Auditor 806-447-5172.

Colorado County

County Clerk, P.O. Box 68, Columbus, TX 78934. 979-732-2155 R/E Recording: 979-732-6561 or 2155; Fax 979-732-8852.

Will not search UCC records. Will search real estate records. **Other Phone Numbers:** Assessor 979-732-8222; Treasurer 979-732-2865; Appraiser/Auditor 979-732-8222.

Comal County

County Clerk, 150 N Seguin, Suite 101, Suite 104, New Braunfels, TX 78130. 830-620-5513; Fax 830-620-3410. http://www.co.comal.tx.us
Will search UCC records prior to 7/2001 and current fixture (land) files. **Other Phone Numbers:** Assessor 830-620-5521; Treasurer 830-620-5506; Appraiser/Auditor 830-625-8597; Elections 830-620-5538; Vital Records 830-620-5515.

Comanche County

County Clerk, Courthouse, Comanche, TX 76442. 915-356-2655; Fax 915-356-3710.
Will search UCC records prior to 7/2001 and current fixture (land) files. UCC search includes tax liens if requested. Will not search real estate records. **Online Access:** Assessor, Property Tax. See note at beginning of section. **Other Phone Numbers:** Assessor 915-356-3101; Treasurer 915-356-2838; Appraiser/Auditor 915-356-5253.

Concho County

County Clerk, P.O. Box 98, Paint Rock, TX 76866-0098. County Clerk, R/E and UCC Recording 915-732-4322; Fax 915-732-2040.
Will search UCC records prior to 7/2001 and current fixture (land) files. UCC search includes tax liens if requested. RE record owner and mortgage searches available. **Other Phone Numbers:** Assessor 915-732-4460; Treasurer 915-732-4279; Appraiser/Auditor 915-732-4389; Elections 915-732-4322; Vital Records 915-732-4322.

Cooke County

County Clerk, Courthouse, Gainesville, TX 76240. 940-668-5420; Fax 940-668-5440.
Will search UCC records prior to 7/2001 and current fixture (land) files. Will not search real estate records. **Other Phone Numbers:** Assessor 940-665-7651; Treasurer 940-668-5423; Appraiser/Auditor 940-665-7651.

Coryell County

County Clerk, P.O. Box 237, Gatesville, TX 76528. 254-865-5016 R/E Recording: 254-865-5016 x3; Fax 254-865-8631.
Will search UCC records prior to 7/2001 and current fixture (land) files. Will not search real estate records. **Other Phone Numbers:** Assessor 254-865-6593; Appraiser/Auditor 254-865-6593.

Cottle County

County Clerk, P.O. Box 717, Paducah, TX 79248. 806-492-3823.
Will search UCC records. UCC search includes tax liens if requested. RE owner, mortgage, and property transfer searches available. **Other Phone Numbers:** Assessor 806-492-3345; Treasurer 806-492-3738; Appraiser/Auditor 806-492-3345.

Crane County

County Clerk, P.O. Box 578, Crane, TX 79731. 915-558-3581.
Will search UCC records prior to 7/2001 and current fixture (land) files. This agency will not do a tax lien search. Will not search real estate records. **Other Phone Numbers:** Assessor 915-558-2622; Treasurer 915-558-3372; Appraiser/Auditor 915-558-1021.

Crockett County

County Clerk, P.O. Drawer C, Ozona, TX 76943. County Clerk, R/E and UCC Recording 915-392-2022; Fax 915-392-3742.
Will search UCC records prior to 7/2001 and current fixture (land) files. Will not search real estate records.

Other Phone Numbers: Assessor 915-392-2674; Treasurer 915-392-3376; Appraiser/Auditor 915-392-2674; Elections 915-392-2022; Vital Records 915-392-2022.

Crosby County

County Clerk, 201 W Aspen St, Room 102, Crosbyton, TX 79322. 806-675-2334.
Will search UCC records prior to 7/2001 and current fixture (land) files. Tax liens not included in UCC search. Will not search real estate records. **Other Phone Numbers:** Assessor 806-675-2356; Appraiser/Auditor 806-675-2356.

Culberson County

County Clerk, P.O. Box 158, Van Horn, TX 79855. 915-283-2059 x32 R/E Recording: 915-283-2059; Fax 915-283-9234.
Will search UCC records prior to 7/2001 and current fixture (land) files. **Other Phone Numbers:** Assessor 915-283-2977; Treasurer 915-283-2115; Appraiser/Auditor 915-283-2977.

Dallam County

County Clerk, P.O. Box 1352, Dalhart, TX 79022. 806-249-4751 R/E Recording: 806-244-4751 UCC Recording: 806-244-4751; Fax 806-249-2252.
Will search UCC records. Will not search real estate records. **Other Phone Numbers:** Assessor 806-244-2801; Appraiser/Auditor 806-249-6767; Elections 806-244-4751; Vital Records 806-244-4751.

Dallas County

County Clerk, Records Bldg, 2nd Floor, 509 Main St., Dallas, TX 75202-3502. 214-653-7131.
Will search UCC records prior to 7/2001 and current fixture (land) files. Tax liens not included in UCC search. Will not search real estate records. **Online Access:** Property Tax, Voter Registration. Access to the County Voter Registration Records is available free online at www.openrecords.org/records/voting/dallas_voting. Search by name or partial name. Also, online access to the Central Appraisal District database is available free at http://www.dallascad.org. Business personal property searches are to be available. Also, see note at beginning of section. **Other Phone Numbers:** Assessor 214-653-0520; Appraiser/Auditor 214-631-0520.

Dawson County

County Clerk, P.O. Drawer 1268, Lamesa, TX 79331. 806-872-3778; Fax 806-872-2473.
Will search UCC records prior to 7/2001 and current fixture (land) files. UCC search includes tax liens if requested. Will not search real estate records. **Other Phone Numbers:** Assessor 806-872-7060; Treasurer 806-872-7474; Appraiser/Auditor 806-872-7060; Elections 806-872-2124.

De Witt County

County Clerk, 307 North Gonzales, Courthouse, Cuero, TX 77954. 361-275-3724; Fax 361-275-8994.
Will search UCC records prior to 7/2001 and current fixture (land) files. Not included in UCC search, must search each location. Will not search real estate records. **Other Phone Numbers:** Appraiser/Auditor 361-275-5753.

Deaf Smith County

County Clerk, 235 East 3rd, Room 203, Hereford, TX 79045-5542. 806-363-7077; Fax 806-363-7007.
Will Search UCC records prior to 7/2001 and current fixture (land) files. Tax liens not included in UCC search. Will not search real estate records. **Online Access:** Assessor, Property Tax. See note at beginning

of section. **Other Phone Numbers:** Treasurer 806-364-0399; Appraiser/Auditor 806-364-0625.

Delta County

County Clerk, P.O. Box 455, Cooper, TX 75432. County Clerk, R/E and UCC Recording 903-395-4110; Fax 903-395-2178.
Will search UCC records. UCC search includes tax liens if requested. RE owner, mortgage, and property transfer searches available. **Other Phone Numbers:** Assessor 903-395-2718; Treasurer 903-395-4315; Appraiser/Auditor 903-395-4118; Elections 903-395-4110; Vital Records 903-395-4110.

Denton County

County Clerk, P.O. Box 2187, Denton, TX 76202-2187. 940-565-8510.
Will search UCC records prior to 7/2001 and current fixture (land) files. Tax liens not included in UCC search. RE record owner searches available. **Online Access:** Property Tax. See note at beginning of section. **Other Phone Numbers:** Assessor 940-565-8655; Appraiser/Auditor 940-56-0904.

Dickens County

County Clerk, P.O. Box 120, Dickens, TX 79229. 806-623-5531; Fax 806-623-5319.
Will search UCC records prior to 7/2001 and current fixture (land) files. UCC search includes tax liens if requested. Will not search real estate records. **Other Phone Numbers:** Appraiser/Auditor 806-623-5216.

Dimmit County

County Clerk, 103 North 5th Street, Carrizo Springs, TX 78834. 830-876-2323 x233 R/E Recording: 830-876-3569; Fax 830-876-4205.
Will search UCC records prior to 7/2001 and current fixture (land) files. Will not search real estate records. **Other Phone Numbers:** Assessor 830-876-2323 x228; Treasurer 830-876-2323 x226; Appraiser/Auditor 830-876-3420; Vital Records 830-876-2323 x233.

Donley County

County Clerk, P.O. Drawer U, Clarendon, TX 79226. County Clerk, R/E and UCC Recording 806-874-3436; Fax 806-874-5146.
Will search UCC records prior to 7/2001 and current fixture (land) files. **Other Phone Numbers:** Assessor 806-874-2193; Treasurer 806-874-2328; Appraiser/Auditor 806-874-2744; Elections 806-874-3436; Vital Records 806-874-3436.

Duval County

County Clerk, P.O. Box 248, San Diego, TX 78384. 361-279-3322 x271/2 R/E Recording: 361-279-3322 x272 UCC Recording: 361-279-3322 x272; Fax 361-279-3159.
Will search UCC records prior to 7/2001 and current fixture (land) files. UCC search includes tax liens if requested. Will not search real estate records. **Other Phone Numbers:** Assessor 361-279-3322; Treasurer 361-279-6128; Appraiser/Auditor 361-279-3305; Elections 361-279-3322 x272; Vital Records 361-279-3322 x272.

Eastland County

County Clerk, P.O. Box 110, Eastland, TX 76448-0110. 254-629-1583; Fax 254-629-8125.
Will search UCC records. Will not search real estate records. **Other Phone Numbers:** Assessor 254-629-1564; Treasurer 254-629-2672; Appraiser/Auditor 254-629-8597.

Ector County

County Clerk, P.O. Box 707, Odessa, TX 79760. 915-498-4130; Fax 915-498-4177.
Will search UCC records prior to 7/2001 and current fixture (land) files. Will not search real estate records. **Other Phone Numbers:** Assessor 915-332-6834; Treasurer 915-335-3105; Appraiser/Auditor 915-332-6834.

Edwards County

County Clerk, P.O. Box 184, Rocksprings, TX 78880-0184. 830-683-2235; Fax 830-683-5376.
Will search UCC records. UCC search includes tax liens if requested. Will not search real estate records. **Other Phone Numbers:** Assessor 830-683-2337; Treasurer 830-683-5116; Appraiser/Auditor 830-683-4189.

El Paso County

County Clerk, 500 E. San Antonio, Room 105, El Paso, TX 79901-2496. 915-546-2074.
Will search UCC records prior to 7/2001 and current fixture (land) files. UCC search includes tax liens if requested. RE owner, mortgage, and property transfer searches available. **Online Access:** Property Tax. See note at beginning of section. **Other Phone Numbers:** Assessor 915-541-4054; Appraiser/Auditor 915-780-2000.

Ellis County

County Clerk, P.O. Box 250, Waxahachie, TX 75168. 972-923-5070.
Will search UCC records prior to 7/2001 and current fixture (land) files. UCC search includes tax liens if requested. RE owner, mortgage, and property transfer searches available. **Online Access:** Property Tax. See note at beginning of section. **Other Phone Numbers:** Treasurer 972-923-5125; Appraiser/Auditor 972-937-3552.

Erath County

County Clerk, Courthouse, 100 W. Washington St., Stephenville, TX 76401. County Clerk, R/E and UCC Recording 254-965-1482; Fax 254-965-5732.
Will search UCC records prior to 7/2001 and current fixture (land) files. UCC search includes tax liens if requested. Will not search real estate records. **Online Access:** Property Tax. See note at beginning of section. **Other Phone Numbers:** Assessor 254-965-7301; Treasurer 254-965-1483; Appraiser/Auditor 254-965-7301; Elections 254-965-1482; Vital Records 254-965-1410.

Falls County

County Clerk, P.O. Box 458, Marlin, TX 76661. County Clerk, R/E and UCC Recording 254-883-1408; Fax 254-883-1406.
Will search UCC records prior to 7/2001 and current fixture (land) files. Tax liens not included in UCC search. Will not search real estate records. **Other Phone Numbers:** Assessor 254-883-1436; Treasurer 254-883-1433; Appraiser/Auditor 254-883-2543; Elections 254-883-1408; Vital Records 254-883-1408.

Fannin County

County Clerk, Courthouse, Suite 102, 101 E. Sam Rayburn Dr., Bonham, TX 75418-4346. 903-583-7486; Fax 903-583-7811.
Will search UCC records prior to 7/2001 and current fixture (land) files. UCC search includes tax liens if requested. Will not search real estate records. **Online Access:** Assessor, Property Tax. See notes at beginning of section. **Other Phone Numbers:** Assessor 903-583-9546; Appraiser/Auditor 903-583-8701.

Fayette County

County Clerk, P.O. Box 59, La Grange, TX 78945. 979-968-3251 R/E Recording: 409-968-3251.
Will search UCC records. Tax liens not included in UCC search. Will not search real estate records. **Online Access:** Assessor, Property Tax. See note at beginning of section. **Other Phone Numbers:** Assessor 979-968-3164; Treasurer 979-968-3055; Appraiser/Auditor 979-968-8383; Elections 979-968-3251; Vital Records 979-968-3251.

Fisher County

County Clerk, P.O. Box 368, Roby, TX 79543-0368. 915-776-2401; Fax 915-776-2815.
Will search UCC records. **Other Phone Numbers:** Assessor 915-776-2181; Treasurer 915-776-2351; Appraiser/Auditor 915-776-2733; Elections 915-776-2401; Vital Records 915-776-2401.

Floyd County

County Clerk, Courthouse, Room 101, 100 Main St., Floydada, TX 79235. 806-983-4900.
Will search UCC records prior to 7/2001 and current fixture (land) files. UCC search includes tax liens if requested. Will not search real estate records. **Other Phone Numbers:** Assessor 806-983-5256; Treasurer 806-983-2376; Appraiser/Auditor 806-983-5256.

Foard County

County Clerk, P.O. Box 539, Crowell, TX 79227. County Clerk, R/E and UCC Recording 940-684-1365; Fax 940-684-1947.
Will search UCC records prior to 7/2001 and current fixture (land) files. Will search R/E records. Search fee is $10.00 per name. **Other Phone Numbers:** Assessor 940-684-1225; Treasurer 940-684-1818; Appraiser/Auditor 940-684-1225; Elections 940-684-1365; Vital Records 940-684-1365.

Fort Bend County

County Clerk, 301 Jackson, Suite 101, Richmond, TX 77469. County Clerk, R/E and UCC Recording 281-341-8685; Fax 281-341-8669. http://www.co.fort-bend.tx.us
Will search UCC records prior to 7/2001 and current fixture (land) files. Tax liens not included in UCC search. Will not search real estate records. **Online Access:** Real Estate, Liens, Assessor, UCC, Marriage, Death, Birth Records. Online access to the county clerk database is available free at www.co.fort-bend.tx.us/admin_of_justice/County_Clerk/index_info_research.htm. Search the property index by name, or the plat index. And, search county UCCs, probate and court records. Also, for full records, their fee remote system is available, including images. Access fee is $.25 per minute plus set-up. For information, contact Diane Shepard at 281-341-8664. Also, see note at beginning of section for add'l fee service for tax records. **Other Phone Numbers:** Assessor 281-341-3735; Treasurer 281-341-3750; Appraiser/Auditor 281-341-8623; Elections 281-341-8670; Vital Records 281-341-8685.

Franklin County

County Clerk, P.O. Box 68, Mount Vernon, TX 75457-0068. 903-537-4252 R/E Recording: 903-537-4252 x6 UCC Recording: 903-537-4252 ext 6; Fax 903-537-2982.
Will search UCC records prior to 7/2001 and current fixture (land) files. Tax liens not included in UCC search. RE owner, mortgage, and property transfer searches available. **Online Access:** Property Tax. See note at beginning of section. **Other Phone Numbers:** Assessor 903-537-4252 x3; Treasurer 903-537-2206 x8; Appraiser/Auditor 903-537-2286; Elections 903-537-4252 x3; Vital Records 903-537-4252 ext 6.

Freestone County

County Clerk, P.O. Box 1017, Fairfield, TX 75840. 903-389-2635.
Will search UCC records. Tax liens not included in UCC search. Will not search real estate records. **Other Phone Numbers:** Assessor 903-389-2336; Treasurer 903-389-2180; Appraiser/Auditor 903-389-5510; Elections 903-389-2635; Vital Records 903-389-2635.

Frio County

County Clerk, 500 E San Antonio Street, # 6, Pearsall, TX 78061. County Clerk, R/E and UCC Recording 830-334-2214; Fax 830-334-0021.
Will search UCC records prior to 7/2001 and current fixture (land) files. Will not search real estate records. **Other Phone Numbers:** Assessor 830-334-2152; Treasurer 830-334-0040; Appraiser/Auditor 830-334-4163; Elections 830-334-2214; Vital Records 830-334-2214.

Gaines County

County Clerk, 101 S. Main, Room 107, Seminole, TX 79360. County Clerk, R/E and UCC Recording 915-758-4003 UCC Recording: 915-758-4033.
Will search UCC records. UCC search includes tax liens if requested. Will not search real estate records. **Other Phone Numbers:** Assessor 915-758-4008; Treasurer 915-758-4009; Appraiser/Auditor 915-758-3263; Vital Records 915-758-4033.

Galveston County

County Clerk, P.O. Box 2450, Galveston, TX 77553-2450. 409-766-2208 R/E Recording: 409-76-2208; http://www.galvestoncad.org/
Will search UCC records prior to 7/2001 and current fixture (land) files. UCC search includes tax liens if requested. Will not search real estate records. **Online Access:** Real Estate, Liens, Assessor Records. Several sources exist. 1. Access to County online records requires $200 escrow deposit, $25 monthly fee, plus $.25 per minute. Index records date back to 1965; image documents to 1/95. Lending agency information and fax back services are available. For information, contact Robert Dickinson at 409-770-5115. 2. Online access to the Central Appraisal District database is available free at www.galvestoncad.org/search.htm. 3. Also, see note at beginning of section. **Other Phone Numbers:** Assessor 409-762-8621 x481; Treasurer 409-762-8621 x345; Appraiser/Auditor 409-935-1980.

Garza County

County Clerk, P.O. Box 366, Post, TX 79356-0366. 806-495-4430; Fax 806-495-4431.
Will search UCC records prior to 7/2001 and current fixture (land) files. Tax liens not included in UCC search. Will not search real estate records. **Other Phone Numbers:** Appraiser/Auditor 806-495-3518.

Gillespie County

County Clerk, 101 West Main, Room 109, Unit #13, Fredericksburg, TX 78624. 830-997-6515; Fax 830-997-9958.
Will search UCC records prior to 7/2001 and current fixture (land) files. UCC search includes tax liens if requested. Will not search real estate records. **Online Access:** Assessor, Property Tax. See note at beginning of section. **Other Phone Numbers:** Assessor 830-997-9807; Treasurer 830-997-6521; Appraiser/Auditor 830-997-9807.

Glasscock County

County Clerk, P.O. Box 190, Garden City, TX 79739. County Clerk, R/E and UCC Recording 915-354-2371.
Will search UCC records prior to 7/2001 and current fixture (land) files. UCC search includes tax liens if

requested. RE owner, mortgage, and property transfer searches available. **Other Phone Numbers:** Assessor 915-354-2580; Treasurer 915-354-2415; Appraiser/Auditor 915-354-2580; Elections 915-354-2371; Vital Records 915-354-2371.

Goliad County

County Clerk, P.O. Box 50, Goliad, TX 77963. County Clerk, R/E and UCC Recording 361-645-3294; Fax 361-645-3858.

Will search UCC records prior to 7/2001 and current fixture (land) files. **Other Phone Numbers:** Assessor 361-645-2492; Treasurer 361-645-3551; Appraiser/Auditor 361-645-2492; Elections 361-645-3294; Vital Records 361-645-3294.

Gonzales County

County Clerk, P.O. Box 77, Gonzales, TX 78629. County Clerk, R/E and UCC Recording 830-672-2801; Fax 830-672-2636.

Will search UCC records. Will not search real estate records. **Other Phone Numbers:** Assessor 830-627-2841; Treasurer 830-627-2621; Appraiser/Auditor 830-672-2879; Vital Records 830-672-2801.

Gray County

County Clerk, P.O. Box 1902, Pampa, TX 79066-1902. County Clerk, R/E and UCC Recording 806-669-8004; Fax 806-669-8054.

Will search UCC records. UCC search includes tax liens if requested with extra fee Will not search real estate records. **Other Phone Numbers:** Assessor 806-665-0791; Treasurer 806-669-8009; Appraiser/Auditor 806-665-0791; Elections 806-669-8004; Vital Records 806-669-8004.

Grayson County

County Clerk, 100 West Houston #17, Sherman, TX 75090. County Clerk, R/E and UCC Recording 903-813-4239; Fax 903-870-0829. http://www.co.grayson.tx.us

Will search UCC records prior to 7/2001 and current fixture (land) files. UCC search includes tax liens. Will not search real estate records. **Online Access:** Property Tax. See note at beginning of section. **Other Phone Numbers:** Assessor 903-893-9673; Treasurer 903-813-4251; Appraiser/Auditor 903-893-9673; Vital Records 903-813-4239.

Gregg County

County Clerk, P.O. Box 3049, Longview, TX 75606. 903-236-8430 R/E Recording: 903-236-8430 x746 UCC Recording: 903-236-8430 X746; Fax 903-237-2574. http://www.co.gregg.tx.us

Will search UCC records prior to 7/2001 and current fixture (land) files. UCC search does not include tax liens Will not search real estate records. **Online Access:** Property Tax. See note at beginning of section. **Other Phone Numbers:** Assessor 903-759-0015; Treasurer 903-236-8430 X853; Appraiser/Auditor 903-238-8823; Elections 903-237-2654; Vital Records 903-236-8430 X637.

Grimes County

County Clerk, P.O. Box 209, Anderson, TX 77830. 936-873-2111 R/E Recording: 409-873-2111.

Will search UCC records prior to 7/2001 and current fixture (land) files. This agency will not do a tax lien search. Will not search real estate records. **Other Phone Numbers:** Assessor 936-873-2163; Treasurer 936-873-2111; Appraiser/Auditor 409-873-2163.

Guadalupe County

County Clerk, P.O. Box 990, Seguin, TX 78156-0990. County Clerk, R/E and UCC Recording 830-303-4188

x236; Fax 830-401-0300. http://www.guadalupecad.org/

Will search UCC records prior to 7/2001 and current fixture (land) files. Tax liens not included in UCC search. Will not search real estate records. **Online Access:** Property Tax, Assessor. Online access to the county Appraisal District database is available free at at www.guadalupecad.org/gadname.html. Name search here, but other methods are allowed at the web site above. Also, see note at beginning of section. **Other Phone Numbers:** Assessor 830-303-3421 x354; Treasurer 830-303-4188 x374; Appraiser/Auditor 830-372-2871; Elections 830-303-4188 x280; Vital Records 830-303-4188 x233.

Hale County

County Clerk, 500 Broadway #140, Plainview, TX 79072-8030. County Clerk, R/E and UCC Recording 806-291-5261 UCC Recording: 806-291-5248; Fax 806-296-9810.

Will search UCC records prior to 7/2001 and current fixture (land) files. Tax liens not included in UCC search. Will search real estate records. Written requests only. $5.00 search fee plus $10.00 per name. **Other Phone Numbers:** Assessor 806-291-5278; Treasurer 806-291-5213; Appraiser/Auditor 806-293-4226; Elections 806-291-5261; Vital Records 806-291-5219.

Hall County

County Clerk, Courthouse, Box 8, Memphis, TX 79245. 806-259-2627; Fax 806-259-5078.

Will search UCC records prior to 7/2001 and current fixture (land) files. Tax liens not included in UCC search. RE owner, mortgage, and property transfer searches available. **Other Phone Numbers:** Assessor 806-259-2125; Treasurer 806-259-2421; Appraiser/Auditor 806-259-2393.

Hamilton County

County Clerk, Main Street, Courthouse, Hamilton, TX 76531. County Clerk, R/E and UCC Recording 254-386-3518; Fax 254-386-8727.

Will search UCC records prior to 7/2001 and current fixture (land) files. Will not search real estate records. **Other Phone Numbers:** Assessor 254-386-5114; Treasurer 254-386-5315; Appraiser/Auditor 254-386-8945; Elections 254-386-3518; Vital Records 254-386-3518.

Hansford County

County Clerk, P.O. Box 397, Spearman, TX 79081. County Clerk, R/E and UCC Recording 806-659-4110; Fax 806-659-4168.

Will search UCC records prior to 7/2001 and current fixture (land) files. Will not search real estate records. **Other Phone Numbers:** Assessor 806-659-4120; Treasurer 806-659-4125; Appraiser/Auditor 806-659-5575; Elections 806-659-4110.

Hardeman County

County Clerk, P.O. Box 30, Quanah, TX 79252-0030. County Clerk, R/E and UCC Recording 940-663-2901; Fax 940-663-5161.

Will search UCC records prior to 7/2001 and current fixture (land) files. UCC search includes tax liens if requested. Will not search real estate records. **Other Phone Numbers:** Assessor 940-663-5221; Treasurer 940-663-5401; Appraiser/Auditor 940-663-2532.

Hardin County

County Clerk, P.O. Box 38, Kountze, TX 77625. County Clerk, R/E and UCC Recording 409-246-5185. Will search UCC records. This agency will not do a tax lien search. Will not search real estate records. **Other Phone Numbers:** Assessor 409-246-5180; Treasurer 409-246-5121; Appraiser/Auditor 409-246-2507.

Harris County

County Clerk, P.O. Box 1525, Houston, TX 77251-1525. 713-755-6405 R/E Recording: 713-755-6411 UCC Recording: 713-755-6439; Fax 713-755-4977. http://www.co.harris.tx.us/cclerk

Personal checks are not accepted for mail requests. Will search UCC records prior to 7/2001 and current fixture (land) files. Tax liens not included in UCC search. Will not search real estate records. **Online Access:** Real Estate, Liens, Assessor, Voter, UCC, Assumed Name, Grantor/Grantee, Vital Statistics. Two sources for County Clerk information exist. Access to the County online subscription service requires a $300 deposit and $40 per hour of use. For info, call Ken Peabody at 713-755-7151. Also, free access to records is available from the web site. Assumed Name records are found at http://63.101.65.71/CoolICE/AssumeNames/an_inquiry. UCC filings are at http://63.101.65.71/CoolICE/UniformCode/uc_inquiry. Real Property at http://63.101.65.71/CoolICE/RealProperty/rp_inquiry and www.hcad.org/Records. Vital statistics are available at http://63.101.65.71/CoolICE/VitalStats/vs_inquiry; marriage at http://63.101.65.71/CoolICE/MarriageLic/ma_inquiry. Also, search the Assessor-Collector database free at www.tax.co.harris.tx.us/dbsearch.htm. **Other Phone Numbers:** Assessor 713-683-9200; Appraiser/Auditor 713-957-5291; Elections 713-755-5792; Vital Records 713-755-6438.

Harrison County

County Clerk, P.O. Box 1365, Marshall, TX 75671. 903-935-4858.

Will search UCC records prior to 7/2001 and current fixture (land) files. UCC search includes tax liens if requested. Will not search real estate records. **Online Access:** Property Tax. See note at beginning of section. **Other Phone Numbers:** Assessor 903-935-1991; Treasurer 903-935-4820; Appraiser/Auditor 903-935-1991.

Hartley County

County Clerk, P.O. Box Q, Channing, TX 79018. County Clerk, R/E and UCC Recording 806-235-2603 UCC Recording: 806-235-3582; Fax 806-235-2316.

Will search UCC records prior to 7/2001 and current fixture (land) files. Will not search real estate records. **Other Phone Numbers:** Assessor 806-235-4515; Treasurer 806-235-3572; Appraiser/Auditor 806-235-4515; Elections 806-235-3582; Vital Records 806-235-3582; Judge 806-235-3142.

Haskell County

County Clerk, P.O. Box 725, Haskell, TX 79521-0725. 940-864-2451; Fax 940-864-6164.

Will search UCC records prior to 7/2001 and current fixture (land) files. **Other Phone Numbers:** Assessor 940-864-3805; Treasurer 940-864-3448; Appraiser/Auditor 940-864-3805.

Hays County

County Clerk, 137 N. Guadalupe, Hays County Records Building, San Marcos, TX 78666. 512-393-7330; Fax 512-393-7337. http://www.co.hays.tx.us/departments/departments.asp

Will search UCC records prior to 7/2001 and current fixture (land) files. **Online Access:** Assessor, Property Tax. See notes at beginning of section. **Other Phone Numbers:** Assessor 512-392-8167; Treasurer 512-392-3669; Appraiser/Auditor 512-268-2522; Elections 512-393-7310.

Hemphill County

County Clerk, P.O. Box 867, Canadian, TX 79014. County Clerk, R/E and UCC Recording 806-323-6212.

Will search UCC records. UCC search includes tax liens if requested. RE owner, mortgage, and property transfer searches available. **Other Phone Numbers:** Assessor 806-323-5161; Treasurer 806-323-6671; Appraiser/Auditor 806-323-8022; Elections 806-323-6212; Vital Records 806-323-6212.

Henderson County

County Clerk, P.O. Box 632, Athens, TX 75751-0632. 903-675-6140.
Will search UCC records prior to 7/2001 and current fixture (land) files. Tax liens not included in UCC search. Will not search real estate records. **Online Access:** Property Tax. See note at beginning of section. **Other Phone Numbers:** Assessor 903-675-9296; Treasurer 903-675-6119; Appraiser/Auditor 903-675-9296.

Hidalgo County

County Clerk, P.O. Box 58, Edinburg, TX 78540. 956-318-2100; Fax 956-318-2105. www.co.hidalgo.tx.us
Will search UCC records prior to 7/2001 and current fixture (land) files. This agency will not do a tax lien search. Will not search real estate records. **Online Access:** Assessor, Property Tax. See note at beginning of section. **Other Phone Numbers:** Assessor 956-318-2180; Appraiser/Auditor 956-782-2255.

Hill County

County Clerk, P.O. Box 398, Hillsboro, TX 76645. 254-582-2161.
Will search UCC records prior to 7/2001 and current fixture (land) files. Tax liens not included in UCC search. RE owner, mortgage, and property transfer searches available. **Online Access:** Property Tax. See note at beginning of section. **Other Phone Numbers:** Assessor 254-582-3862; Treasurer 254-582-2632; Appraiser/Auditor 254-582-2508.

Hockley County

County Clerk, 800 Houston St., Ste 213, Levelland, TX 79336. County Clerk, R/E and UCC Recording 806-894-3185.
Will search UCC records prior to 7/2001 and current fixture (land) files. UCC search includes tax liens if requested. Will not search real estate records. **Other Phone Numbers:** Assessor 806-894-4938; Treasurer 806-894-3718; Appraiser/Auditor 806-894-9654; Elections 806-894-3185; Vital Records 806-894-3185.

Hood County

County Clerk, P.O. Box 339, Granbury, TX 76048-0339. 817-579-3222; Fax 817-579-3227.
Will search UCC records prior to 7/2001 and current fixture (land) files. Tax liens not included in UCC search. RE owner, mortgage, and property transfer searches available. **Online Access:** Property Tax. See note at beginning of section. **Other Phone Numbers:** Assessor 817-579-3295; Treasurer 817-579-3208; Appraiser/Auditor 817-573-2471.

Hopkins County

County Clerk, P.O. Box 288, Sulphur Springs, TX 75483. 903-438-4074 R/E Recording: 903-885-3929; Fax 903-438-9007. www.hopkinscountytx.org
Will search UCC records prior to 7/2001 and current fixture (land) files. UCC search includes tax liens if requested. Will not search real estate records. **Other Phone Numbers:** Assessor 903-438-4063; Treasurer 903-438-4003; Appraiser/Auditor 903-885-2173; Elections 903-438-4074; Vital Records 903-438-4074; Tax/Assessor/Voter Registrar 903-438-4063.

Houston County

County Clerk, P.O. Box 370, Crockett, TX 75835-0370. 936-544-3255 R/E Recording: 936-544-3255 x241 UCC Recording: 936-544-3255 x241; Fax 936-544-8053.
Will search UCC records prior to 7/2001 and current fixture (land) files. UCC search includes tax liens if requested. RE owner, mortgage, and property transfer searches available. **Other Phone Numbers:** Assessor 936-544-3255 x258; Treasurer 936-544-3255 x236; Appraiser/Auditor 936-544-9655; Elections 936-544-3255 x241; Vital Records 936-544-3255 x241.

Howard County

County Clerk, P.O. Box 1468, Big Spring, TX 79721-1468. County Clerk, R/E and UCC Recording 915-264-2213 UCC Recording: 915-264-2214; Fax 915-264-2215. www.howard-county.net
As of July 1, 2001 all UCC records that are to be recorded in UCC records will be filed with the Sec of State. Tax liens not included in UCC search. Will not search real estate records. **Other Phone Numbers:** Assessor 915-264-2232; Treasurer 915-264-2218; Appraiser/Auditor 915-263-8301; Elections 915-264-2214; Vital Records 915-264-2214.

Hudspeth County

County Clerk, P.O. Drawer A, Sierra Blanca, TX 79851. County Clerk, R/E and UCC Recording 915-369-2301; Fax 915-369-2361.
Will search UCC records prior to 7/2001 and current fixture (land) files. **Other Phone Numbers:** Assessor 915-369-2331; Treasurer 915-369-3511; Appraiser/Auditor 915-369-4118; Elections 915-369-2301; Vital Records 915-369-2301.

Hunt County

County Clerk, P.O. Box 1316, Greenville, TX 75403-1316. County Clerk, R/E and UCC Recording 903-408-4130.
Will search UCC records prior to 7/2001 and current fixture (land) files. Tax liens not included in UCC search. Will not search real estate records. **Online Access:** Assessor, Property Tax. See notes at beginning of section. **Other Phone Numbers:** Assessor 903-408-4150; Treasurer 903-408-4171; Appraiser/Auditor 903-408-3510; Elections 903-408-4130; Vital Records 903-408-4130.

Hutchinson County

County Clerk, P.O. Box 1186, Stinnett, TX 79083. County Clerk, R/E and UCC Recording 806-878-4002.
Will search UCC records. UCC search includes tax liens if requested. Will not search real estate records. **Other Phone Numbers:** Assessor 806-878-4005; Treasurer 806-878-4010; Appraiser/Auditor 806-274-2294; Elections 806-878-4002; Vital Records 806-878-4002.

Irion County

County Clerk, P.O. Box 736, Mertzon, TX 76941-0736. 915-835-2421; Fax 915-835-2008.
Will search UCC records prior to 7/2001 and current fixture (land) files. **Other Phone Numbers:** Assessor 915-835-7771; Treasurer 915-835-4111; Appraiser/Auditor 915-835-3551.

Jack County

County Clerk, 100 Main Street, Jacksboro, TX 76458. County Clerk, R/E and UCC Recording 940-567-2111.
Will search UCC records. UCC search includes tax liens if requested. Will not search real estate records. **Other Phone Numbers:** Assessor 940-567-6301; Treasurer 940-567-2251; Appraiser/Auditor 940-567-

6301; Elections 940-567-2111; Vital Records 940-567-2111.

Jackson County

County Clerk, 115 West Main, Room 101, Edna, TX 77957. 361-782-3563; Fax 361-782-3645.
Will search UCC records prior to 7/2001 and current fixture (land) files. UCC search includes tax liens if requested. Will not search real estate records. **Other Phone Numbers:** Assessor 361-782-7115; Treasurer 361-782-3402; Appraiser/Auditor 361-782-7115.

Jasper County

Deputy Clerk, P.O. Box 2070, Jasper, TX 75951. Deputy Clerk, R/E and UCC Recording 409-384-2632; Fax 409-384-7198.
Will search UCC records prior to 7/2001 and current fixture (land) files. Will not search real estate records. **Other Phone Numbers:** Assessor 409-384-6896; Treasurer 409-384-2461; Appraiser/Auditor 409-384-2544; Elections 409-384-3399; Vital Records 409-384-2632.

Jeff Davis County

County Clerk, P.O. Box 398, Fort Davis, TX 79734. 915-426-3251; Fax 915-426-3760.
Will search UCC records prior to 7/2001 and current fixture (land) files. Will not search real estate records. **Other Phone Numbers:** Assessor 915-426-3213; Treasurer 915-426-3242; Appraiser/Auditor 915-857-3333.

Jefferson County

County Clerk, P.O. Box 1151, Beaumont, TX 77704-1151. County Clerk, R/E and UCC Recording 409-835-8475; Fax 409-839-2394. http://www.co.jefferson.tx.us/
Will search UCC records prior to 7/2001 and current fixture (land) files. State tax liens not included in UCC search. Will search only federal tax liens. Will not search real estate records. **Online Access:** Property Tax. See note at beginning of section. **Other Phone Numbers:** Assessor 409-835-8516; Treasurer 409-835-8509; Appraiser/Auditor 409-835-4611; Elections 409-835-8760; Vital Records 409-835-8475.

Jim Hogg County

County Clerk, P.O. Box 878, Hebbronville, TX 78361. County Clerk, R/E and UCC Recording 361-527-4031; Fax 361-527-5843.
Will search UCC records prior to 7/2001 and current fixture (land) files. **Other Phone Numbers:** Assessor 361-527-3237; Treasurer 361-527-3164; Appraiser/Auditor 361-527-4033; Elections 361-527-4031; Vital Records 361-527-4031.

Jim Wells County

County Clerk, P.O. Box 1459, Alice, TX 78333. 361-668-5702.
Will search UCC records prior to 7/2001 and current fixture (land) files. UCC search includes tax liens if requested. Will not search real estate records **Other Phone Numbers:** Assessor 361-668-9656; Treasurer 361-668-5713; Appraiser/Auditor 361-668-9656.

Johnson County

County Clerk, P.O. Box 662, Cleburne, TX 76033-0662. County Clerk, R/E and UCC Recording 817-556-6314 UCC Recording: 817-556-6310; Fax 817-556-6326. http://www.johnsoncad.com/search.htm
Will search UCC records prior to 7/2001 and current fixture (land) files. **Online Access:** Assessor, Property Tax. Records from the County Appraiser are available fee online at the web site. Also, see note at beginning of section. **Other Phone Numbers:** Assessor 817-556-6100; Treasurer 817-566-6341; Appraiser/Auditor 817-

558-8100; Elections 817-556-6311; Vital Records 817-556-6314.

Jones County

County Clerk, P.O. Box 552, Anson, TX 79501-0552. County Clerk, R/E and UCC Recording 915-823-3762; Fax 915-823-4223.
Will search UCC records prior to 7/2001 and current fixture (land) files. Will not search real estate records. **Online Access:** Assessor, Property Tax. See note at beginning of section. **Other Phone Numbers:** Assessor 915-823-2422; Treasurer 915-823-3742; Appraiser/Auditor 915-823-2422; Elections 915-823-3762; Vital Records 915-823-3762.

Karnes County

County Clerk, 101 North Panna Maria Ave., Courthouse - Suite 9, Karnes City, TX 78118-2929. County Clerk, R/E and UCC Recording 830-780-3938; Fax 830-780-4576.
Will search UCC records prior to 7/2001 and current fixture (land) files. **Other Phone Numbers:** Assessor 830-780-2431; Treasurer 830-780-2312; Appraiser/Auditor 830-780-2433; Elections 830-780-3938; Vital Records 830-780-3938.

Kaufman County

County Clerk, Courthouse, Kaufman, TX 75142. County Clerk, R/E and UCC Recording 972-932-4331; Fax 972-932-7628.
Will search UCC records prior to 7/2001 and current fixture (land) files. UCC search includes tax liens if requested. RE owner, mortgage, and property transfer searches available. **Online Access:** Assessor, Property Tax. See note at beginning of section. **Other Phone Numbers:** Assessor 972-932-6081; Treasurer 972-932-4331; Appraiser/Auditor 972-932-6081; Elections 972-932-4331; Vital Records 972-932-4331.

Kendall County

County Clerk, 201 East San Antonio, Suite 127, Boerne, TX 78006. County Clerk, R/E and UCC Recording 830-249-9343; Fax 830-249-3472. http://www.kendallcad.org
Will search UCC records. Tax liens not included in UCC search. RE owner, mortgage, and property transfer searches available. **Online Access:** Assessor, Property Tax. Online access to the county Appraisal District is available at the web site. **Other Phone Numbers:** Assessor 830-249-9343; Treasurer 830-249-9343; Appraiser/Auditor 830-249-8012; Elections 830-249-9343; Vital Records 830-249-9343.

Kenedy County

County Clerk, P.O. Box 227, Sarita, TX 78385-0227. County Clerk, R/E and UCC Recording 361-294-5220; Fax 361-294-5218.
Will search UCC records prior to 7/2001 and current fixture (land) files. UCC search includes tax liens if requested. RE owner, mortgage, and property transfer searches available. **Other Phone Numbers:** Assessor 361-294-5202; Treasurer 361-294-5304; Appraiser/Auditor 512-321-1695; Elections 361-294-5220; Vital Records 361-294-5220.

Kent County

County Clerk, P.O. Box 9, Jayton, TX 79528-0009. 806-237-3881; Fax 806-237-2632.
Will search UCC records prior to 7/2001 and current fixture (land) files. UCC search includes tax liens if requested. Mortgage searches available. **Other Phone Numbers:** Assessor 806-237-3066; Treasurer 806-237-3075; Appraiser/Auditor 806-237-3036.

Kerr County

County Clerk, Courthouse, Room 122, 700 Main, Kerrville, TX 78028-5389. County Clerk, R/E and UCC Recording 830-792-2255; Fax 830-792-2274. www.ktc.com
Will search UCC records prior to 7/2001 and current fixture (land) files. **Online Access:** Assessor, Property Tax. See note at beginning of section. **Other Phone Numbers:** Assessor 830-895-5223; Treasurer 830-257-7972; Appraiser/Auditor 830-895-5223; Elections 830-792-2255; Vital Records 830-792-2255.

Kimble County

County Clerk, 501 Main Street, Junction, TX 76849. County Clerk, R/E and UCC Recording 915-446-3353; Fax 915-446-2986.
Will search UCC records. UCC search includes tax liens if requested. Will not search real estate records. **Other Phone Numbers:** Assessor 915-446-3717; Treasurer 915-446-2847; Appraiser/Auditor 915-446-3717; Elections 915-446-3353; Vital Records 915-446-3353.

King County

County Clerk, P.O. Box 135, Guthrie, TX 79236. County Clerk, R/E and UCC Recording 806-596-4412; Fax 806-596-4664.
Will search UCC records prior to 7/2001 and current fixture (land) files. Tax liens not included in UCC search. Will not search real estate records. **Other Phone Numbers:** Assessor 806-596-4318; Treasurer 806-596-4319; Appraiser/Auditor 806-596-4318; Elections 806-596-4412; Vital Records 806-596-4412.

Kinney County

County Clerk, P.O. Drawer 9, Brackettville, TX 78832. County Clerk, R/E and UCC Recording 830-563-2521; Fax 830-563-2644.
Will search UCC records. Will not search real estate records. **Other Phone Numbers:** Assessor 830-563-2323; Treasurer 830-563-2777; Appraiser/Auditor 830-563-2323; Elections 830-563-2521; Vital Records 830-563-2521.

Kleberg County

County Clerk, P.O. Box 1327, Kingsville, TX 78364-1327. County Clerk, R/E and UCC Recording 361-595-8548.
Will search UCC records prior to 7/2001 and current fixture (land) files. UCC search includes tax liens if requested. Will not search real estate records. **Online Access:** Property Tax. See note at beginning of section. **Other Phone Numbers:** Assessor 361-595-8541; Treasurer 361-595-8535; Appraiser/Auditor 361-595-5775; Elections 361-595-8548; Vital Records 361-595-8548.

Knox County

County Clerk, P.O. Box 196, Benjamin, TX 79505. 940-454-2441; Fax 940-454-2022.
Will search UCC records prior to 7/2001 and current fixture (land) files. UCC search includes tax liens if requested. Will not search real estate records. **Other Phone Numbers:** Treasurer 817-454-2251; Appraiser/Auditor 940-454-3891.

La Salle County

County Clerk, P.O. Box 340, Cotulla, TX 78014. 830-879-2117; Fax 830-879-2933.
Will search UCC records prior to 7/2001 and current fixture (land) files. Will not search real estate records. **Other Phone Numbers:** Appraiser/Auditor 830-879-2547.

Lamar County

County Clerk, Courthouse, 119 N. Main #109, Paris, TX 75460. County Clerk, R/E and UCC Recording 903-737-2420; Fax 903-782-1100.
Will search UCC records prior to 7/2001 and current fixture (land) files. Tax liens not included in UCC search. Will not search real estate records. **Online Access:** Death Records. Cemetery records in Lamar County are available free online at http://userdb.rootsweb.com/cemeteries/TX/Lamar. **Other Phone Numbers:** Assessor 903-785-7822; Treasurer 903-737-2418; Appraiser/Auditor 903-785-7822; Elections 903-737-2420; Vital Records 903-737-2420.

Lamb County

County Clerk, 100 6th Street, Room 103 Box 3, Littlefield, TX 79339-3366. 806-385-4222 x210 R/E Recording: 806-385-4222; Fax 806-385-6485.
Will search UCC records prior to 7/2001 and current fixture (land) files. Tax liens not included in UCC search. Will not search real estate records. **Online Access:** Assessor, Property Tax. See note at beginning of section. **Other Phone Numbers:** Assessor 806-385-6474; Treasurer 806-385-3770; Appraiser/Auditor 806-385-6474.

Lampasas County

County Clerk, P.O. Box 347, Lampasas, TX 76550. 512-556-8271.
Will search UCC records prior to 7/2001 and current fixture (land) files. Tax liens not included in UCC search. Property transfer searches available. **Other Phone Numbers:** Assessor 512-556-8058; Treasurer 512-556-8058; Appraiser/Auditor 512-556-8058.

Lavaca County

County Clerk, P.O. Box 326, Hallettsville, TX 77964-0326. County Clerk, R/E and UCC Recording 361-798-3612.
Will search UCC records. This agency will not do a tax lien search. Will not search real estate records. **Other Phone Numbers:** Assessor 361-798-3600; Treasurer 361-798-2181; Appraiser/Auditor 361-798-4396; Elections 361-798-3612; Vital Records 361-798-3612.

Lee County

County Clerk, P.O. Box 419, Giddings, TX 78942. County Clerk, R/E and UCC Recording 979-542-3684; Fax 979-542-2623.
Will search UCC records prior to 7/2001 and current fixture (land) files. This agency will not do a tax lien search. RE owner, mortgage, and property transfer searches available. **Other Phone Numbers:** Assessor 979-542-2640; Treasurer 979-542-2161; Appraiser/Auditor 979-542-9618; Elections 979-542-3684.

Leon County

County Clerk, P.O. Box 98, Centerville, TX 75833. 903-536-2352 R/E Recording: 903-536-2252; Fax 903-536-2431.
Will search UCC records prior to 7/2001 and current fixture (land) files. Will not search real estate records. **Other Phone Numbers:** Assessor 903-536-2252; Treasurer 903-536-2915; Appraiser/Auditor 903-536-2352.

Liberty County

County Clerk, P.O. Box 369, Liberty, TX 77575. 936-336-4673 R/E Recording: 409-336-4673.
Will search UCC records prior to 7/2001 and current fixture (land) files. UCC search includes tax liens if requested. Will not search real estate records. **Online Access:** Assessor, Property Tax. See note at beginning

of section. **Other Phone Numbers:** Assessor 936-336-4673; Appraiser/Auditor 409-336-5722.

Limestone County

County Clerk, P.O. Box 350, Groesbeck, TX 76642. 254-729-5504 R/E Recording: 254-729-3009; Fax 254-729-2951.
Will search UCC records prior to 7/2001 and current fixture (land) files. Tax liens not included in UCC search. RE record owner searches available. **Online Access:** Assessor, Property Tax. See notes at beginning of section. **Other Phone Numbers:** Assessor 254-729-3009; Treasurer 254-729-3314; Appraiser/Auditor 254-729-5504.

Lipscomb County

County Clerk, P.O. Box 70, Lipscomb, TX 79056. 806-862-3091; Fax 806-862-3004.
Will search UCC records. **Other Phone Numbers:** Assessor 806-624-2881; Treasurer 806-862-3821; Appraiser/Auditor 806-624-2881.

Live Oak County

County Clerk, P.O. Box 280, George West, TX 78022. 361-449-2733 x3 R/E Recording: 361-449-2733.
Will search UCC records prior to 7/2001 and current fixture (land) files. Tax liens not included in UCC search. Will not search real estate records. **Other Phone Numbers:** Assessor 361-449-2641; Treasurer 361-449-2641 x109; Appraiser/Auditor 361-449-2641.

Llano County

County Clerk, 107 W. Sandstone, Llano, TX 78643-2318. 915-247-4455; Fax 915-247-2406.
Will search UCC records prior to 7/2001 and current fixture (land) files. UCC search includes tax liens if requested. Will not search real estate records. **Online Access:** Assessor, Property Tax. See note at beginning of section. **Other Phone Numbers:** Assessor 915-247-3065; Treasurer 915-247-5056; Appraiser/Auditor 915-247-3065.

Loving County

County Clerk, P.O. Box 194, Mentone, TX 79754. County Clerk, R/E and UCC Recording 915-377-2441; Fax 915-377-2701.
Will search UCC records. Will not search real estate records. **Other Phone Numbers:** Assessor 915-377-2411; Treasurer 915-377-2311; Appraiser/Auditor 915-377-2201; Elections 915-377-2441; Vital Records 915-377-2441.

Lubbock County

County Clerk, P.O. Box 10536, Lubbock, TX 79408-0536. 806-775-1060; Fax 806-775-1660. http://tax.co.lubbock.tx.us
Will search UCC records prior to 7/2001 and current fixture (land) files. Will not search real estate records. **Online Access:** Assessor, Property Tax, Voter Registration. For assessor and property tax information, see notes at beginning of section. Voter registration records from the County Assessor/Collector database are available free online at www.lubbock tax.com/registration. **Other Phone Numbers:** Assessor 806-762-5000; Appraiser/Auditor 806-762-5000.

Lynn County

County Clerk, P.O. Box 937, Tahoka, TX 79373. County Clerk, R/E and UCC Recording 806-998-4750; Fax 806-998-4988.
Will search UCC records prior to 7/2001 and current fixture (land) files. UCC search includes tax liens if requested. Will not search real estate records. **Other Phone Numbers:** Assessor 806-998-4112; Treasurer 806-998-4055; Appraiser/Auditor 806-998-5477; Elections 806-998-4750; Vital Records 806-998-4750.

Madison County

County Clerk, 101 West Main, Room 102, Madisonville, TX 77864. County Clerk, R/E and UCC Recording 936-348-2638; Fax 936-348-5858.
Will search UCC records. UCC search includes tax liens if requested. Will not search real estate records. **Other Phone Numbers:** Assessor 936-348-2783; Treasurer 936-348-5141; Appraiser/Auditor 936-348-2783; Elections 936-348-2638; Vital Records 936-348-2638.

Marion County

County Clerk, P.O. Box 763, Jefferson, TX 75657. County Clerk, R/E and UCC Recording 903-665-3971; Fax 903-665-8732.
Will search UCC records prior to 7/2001 and current fixture (land) files. Tax liens not included in UCC search. RE owner, mortgage, and property transfer searches available. **Other Phone Numbers:** Assessor 903-665-3281; Treasurer 903-665-2472; Appraiser/Auditor 903-665-2519; Elections 903-665-3971; Vital Records 903-665-3971.

Martin County

County Clerk, P.O. Box 906, Stanton, TX 79782. 915-756-3412; Fax 915-756-2992.
Will search UCC records prior to 7/2001 and current fixture (land) files. UCC search includes tax liens if requested. Will not search real estate records. **Other Phone Numbers:** Appraiser/Auditor 915-756-2823.

Mason County

County Clerk, P.O. Box 702, Mason, TX 76856-0702. County Clerk, R/E and UCC Recording 915-347-5253; Fax 915-347-6868.
Will search UCC records prior to 7/2001 and current fixture (land) files. UCC search includes tax liens if requested. Will not search real estate records. **Other Phone Numbers:** Assessor 915-347-5989; Treasurer 915-347-5251; Appraiser/Auditor 915-347-5989; Elections 915-347-5253; Vital Records 915-347-5253.

Matagorda County

County Clerk, 1700 7th Street, Room 202, Bay City, TX 77414. County Clerk, R/E and UCC Recording 979-244-7680; Fax 979-244-7688.
Will search UCC records prior to 7/2001 and current fixture (land) files. Will not search real estate records. **Other Phone Numbers:** Assessor 979-244-7670; Treasurer 979-244-7609; Appraiser/Auditor 979-244-2031; Elections 979-244-7680; Vital Records 979-244-7680.

Maverick County

County Clerk, P.O. Box 4050, Eagle Pass, TX 78853-4050. County Clerk, R/E and UCC Recording 830-773-2829; Fax 830-773-0129.
Will search UCC records prior to 7/2001 and current fixture (land) files. UCC search includes tax liens if requested. Will not search real estate records. **Online Access:** Assessor, Property Tax. See note at beginning of section. **Other Phone Numbers:** Assessor 830-773-9273; Treasurer 830-773-2413; Appraiser/Auditor 830-773-0255; Elections 830-773-2829; Vital Records 830-773-2829.

McCulloch County

County Clerk, Courthouse, Brady, TX 76825. 915-597-0733; Fax 915-597-1731.
Will search UCC records prior to 7/2001 and current fixture (land) files. **Other Phone Numbers:** Appraiser/Auditor 915-597-1627.

McLennan County

County Clerk, P.O. Box 1727, Waco, TX 76703-1727. 254-757-5078; Fax 254-757-5146.
Will search UCC records prior to 7/2001 and current fixture (land) files. Tax liens not included in UCC search. Will not search real estate records. **Online Access:** Property Tax. See note at beginning of section. **Other Phone Numbers:** Appraiser/Auditor 254-752-9864.

McMullen County

County Clerk, P.O. Box 235, Tilden, TX 78072-0235. 361-274-3215; Fax 361-274-3618.
Will search UCC records prior to 7/2001 and current fixture (land) files. Tax liens not included in UCC search. Property transfer searches available. **Other Phone Numbers:** Assessor 361-274-3214; Treasurer 361-274-3685; Appraiser/Auditor 361-274-3233.

Medina County

County Clerk, Courthouse, Room 109, 16th St., Hondo, TX 78861. County Clerk, R/E and UCC Recording 830-741-6041; Fax 830-741-6015.
Will search UCC records prior to 7/2001 and current fixture (land) files. **Other Phone Numbers:** Assessor 830-741-6100; Treasurer 830-741-6110; Appraiser/Auditor 830-741-3035; Elections 830-741-6040; Vital Records 830-741-6041.

Menard County

County Clerk, P.O. Box 1028, Menard, TX 76859. 915-396-4682 R/E Recording: 915-396-4784; Fax 915-396-2047.
Will search UCC records prior to 7/2001 and current fixture (land) files. Will not search real estate records. **Other Phone Numbers:** Appraiser/Auditor 915-396-4682.

Midland County

County Clerk, P.O. Box 211, Midland, TX 79702. County Clerk, R/E and UCC Recording 915-688-1059; Fax 915-688-8914.
Will search UCC records prior to 7/2001 and current fixture (land) files. Tax liens not included in UCC search. Will not search real estate records. **Other Phone Numbers:** Assessor 915-699-4991; Treasurer 915-688-1235; Appraiser/Auditor 915-699-4991; Elections 915-688-1222; Vital Records 915-688-1059.

Milam County

County Clerk, P.O. Box 191, Cameron, TX 76520. 254-697-7049 R/E Recording: 254-697-6596; Fax 254-697-7055.
Will search UCC records prior to 7/2001 and current fixture (land) files. UCC search includes tax liens if requested. Will not search real estate records. **Online Access:** Assessor, Property Tax. See note at beginning of section. **Other Phone Numbers:** Assessor 254-697-7017; Treasurer 254-697-7032; Appraiser/Auditor 254-697-6638; Elections 254-697-7049; Vital Records 254-697-7049.

Mills County

County Clerk, P.O. Box 646, Goldthwaite, TX 76844-0646. 915-648-2711 R/E Recording: 915-648-2253; Fax 915-648-2806.
Will search UCC records prior to 7/2001 and current fixture (land) files. Tax liens not included in UCC search. RE owner, mortgage, and property transfer searches available. **Other Phone Numbers:** Assessor 915-648-2253; Treasurer 915-648-2636; Appraiser/Auditor 915-648-2711.

Mitchell County

County Clerk, 349 Oak St. #103, Colorado City, TX 79512-6213. County Clerk, R/E and UCC Recording 915-728-3481; Fax 915-728-5322.

Will search UCC records prior to 7/2001 and current fixture (land) files. Tax liens not included in UCC search. RE owner, mortgage, and property transfer searches available. **Other Phone Numbers:** Assessor 915-728-2606; Treasurer 915-728-8356; Appraiser/Auditor 915-728-5028; Elections 915-728-2606; Vital Records 915-728-3481.

Montague County

County Clerk, P.O. Box 77, Montague, TX 76251-0077. 940-894-2461; Fax 940-894-3110.

Will search UCC records prior to 7/2001 and current fixture (land) files. Will not search real estate records. **Other Phone Numbers:** Assessor 940-894-6011; Appraiser/Auditor 940-894-2081.

Montgomery County

County Clerk, P.O. Box 959, Conroe, TX 77305. 936-539-7893 R/E Recording: 936-539-7885 UCC Recording: 936-539-7885; Fax 936-760-6990. www.co.montgomery.tx.us

Will search UCC records prior to 7/2001 and current fixture (land) files. Tax liens not included in UCC search. Will not search real estate records. **Online Access:** Assessor, Property Tax. See notes at beginning of section. **Other Phone Numbers:** Assessor 936-756-3354; Treasurer 936-759-7844; Appraiser/Auditor 936-756-3354; Elections 936-539-7843; Vital Records 936-538-8114.

Moore County

County Clerk, 715 Dumas Ave., Rm. 105, Dumas, TX 79029. 806-935-2009; Fax 806-935-9004.

Will search UCC records prior to 7/2001 and current fixture (land) files. UCC search includes tax liens if requested. Will not search real estate records. **Other Phone Numbers:** Assessor 806-935-4193; Treasurer 806-935-2019; Appraiser/Auditor 806-935-4193.

Morris County

County Clerk, 500 Broadnax Street, Daingerfield, TX 75638. 903-645-3911 R/E Recording: 903-645-5601.

Will search UCC records prior to 7/2001 and current fixture (land) files. UCC search includes tax liens if requested. Will not search real estate records. **Other Phone Numbers:** Assessor 903-645-5601; Treasurer 903-645-2916; Appraiser/Auditor 903-645-3911.

Motley County

County Clerk, P.O. Box 66, Matador, TX 79244. County Clerk, R/E and UCC Recording 806-347-2621; Fax 806-347-2220.

Will search UCC records. **Other Phone Numbers:** Assessor 806-347-2252; Treasurer 806-347-2800; Appraiser/Auditor 806-347-2273; Elections 806-347-2621; Vital Records 806-347-2621.

Nacogdoches County

County Clerk, 101 West Main, Room 205, Nacogdoches, TX 75961. County Clerk, R/E and UCC Recording 936-560-7733; Fax 936-559-5926.

Will search UCC records prior to 7/2001 and current fixture (land) files. Tax liens not included in UCC search. Will not search real estate records. **Online Access:** Property Tax. Online access to the county Central Appraisal District Appriasal Roll from TaxNetUSA is available free at www.taxnetusa.com/nacogdoches. **Other Phone Numbers:** Assessor 936-560-3447; Treasurer 936-560-7703; Appraiser/Auditor 409-560-3447; Elections 936-560-7825; Vital Records 936-560-7733.

Navarro County

County Clerk, P.O. Box 423, Corsicana, TX 75151. 903-654-3035.

Will search UCC records prior to 7/2001 and current fixture (land) files. UCC search includes tax liens if requested. Will not search real estate records. **Online Access:** Assessor, Property Tax. See note at beginning of section for "Advanced" fee service. **Other Phone Numbers:** Assessor 903-872-6161; Treasurer 903-654-3090; Appraiser/Auditor 903-872-2476.

Newton County

County Clerk, P.O. Box 484, Newton, TX 75966-0484. County Clerk, R/E and UCC Recording 409-379-5341; Fax 409-379-9049.

Will search UCC records prior to 7/2001 and current fixture (land) files. UCC search includes tax liens if requested. Will not search real estate records. **Online Access:** Assessor, Property Tax, Death. Assessor, Property Tax: see note at beginning of section. Death records in this county may be accessed over the Internet at http://www.jas.net/jas.htm (site may be temporarily down). **Other Phone Numbers:** Assessor 409-379-3710; Treasurer 409-379-8127; Appraiser/Auditor 409-379-3710; Vital Records 409-379-5341.

Nolan County

County Clerk, 100 E 3rd St #108, Sweetwater, TX 79556-0098. 915-235-2462.

Will search UCC records prior to 7/2001 and current fixture (land) files. Tax liens not included in UCC search. Will not search real estate records. **Other Phone Numbers:** Assessor 915-235-8421; Treasurer 915-236-6932; Appraiser/Auditor 915-235-8421.

Nueces County

County Clerk, P.O. Box 2627, Corpus Christi, TX 78403. County Clerk, R/E and UCC Recording 361-888-0611 UCC Recording: 361-888-0580; Fax 361-888-0329. http://www.co.nueces.tx.us

Will search UCC records prior to 7/2001 and current fixture (land) files. Tax liens not included in UCC search. Will not search real estate records. **Online Access:** Assessor, Property Tax. Records from the County Appraiser are available fee online at www.nuecescad.org/nueces3.html. Also, see notes at beginning of section. **Other Phone Numbers:** Assessor 361-888-0230; Treasurer 361-888-0515; Appraiser/Auditor 361-881-8022; Elections 361-888-0483; Vital Records 361-888-0580.

Ochiltree County

County Clerk, 511 South Main, Perryton, TX 79070. County Clerk, R/E and UCC Recording 806-435-8039; Fax 806-435-2081.

Will search UCC records prior to 7/2001 and current fixture (land) files. UCC search includes tax liens if requested. Will not search real estate records. **Other Phone Numbers:** Assessor 806-435-8025; Treasurer 806-435-8046; Appraiser/Auditor 806-435-9623; Elections 806-435-8039; Vital Records 806-435-8039.

Oldham County

County Clerk, P.O. Box 360, Vega, TX 79092. 806-267-2667.

Will search UCC records prior to 7/2001 and current fixture (land) files. UCC search includes tax liens if requested. Will not search real estate records. **Other Phone Numbers:** Appraiser/Auditor 806-267-2442.

Orange County

County Clerk, P.O. Box 1536, Orange, TX 77631-1536. County Clerk, R/E and UCC Recording 409-882-7055; Fax 409-882-0379.

Will search UCC records. Will not search real estate records. **Other Phone Numbers:** Assessor 409-882-7971; Treasurer 409-882-7991; Appraiser/Auditor 409-745-4777; Elections 409-882-7055; Vital Records 409-882-7055.

Palo Pinto County

County Clerk, P.O. Box 219, Palo Pinto, TX 76484. County Clerk, R/E and UCC Recording 940-659-1277.

Will search UCC records. Tax liens not included in UCC search. Will not search real estate records. **Other Phone Numbers:** Assessor 940-659-1281; Treasurer 940-659-1260; Appraiser/Auditor 940-659-1281; Elections 940-659-1277; Vital Records 940-659-1277.

Panola County

County Clerk, Sabine & Sycamore, Courthouse Bldg., Room 201, Carthage, TX 75633. 903-693-0302; Fax 903-693-2726.

Will search UCC records prior to 7/2001 and current fixture (land) files. UCC search includes tax liens if requested. Will not search real estate records. **Other Phone Numbers:** Assessor 903-693-0340; Treasurer 903-693-0325; Appraiser/Auditor 903-693-2891.

Parker County

County Clerk, P.O. Box 819, Weatherford, TX 76086. 817-599-6591.

Will search UCC records prior to 7/2001 and current fixture (land) files. UCC search includes tax liens if requested. Will not search real estate records. **Online Access:** Assessor, Property Tax. See note at beginning of section for "Advanced" fee service. **Other Phone Numbers:** Assessor 817-599-7671; Treasurer 817-596-0078; Appraiser/Auditor 817-596-0077.

Parmer County

County Clerk, P.O. Box 356, Farwell, TX 79325. County Clerk, R/E and UCC Recording 806-481-3691; Fax 806-481-9154.

Will search UCC records prior to 7/2001 and current fixture (land) files. UCC search includes tax liens if requested. Will not search real estate records. **Other Phone Numbers:** Assessor 806-481-3845; Treasurer 806-481-9152; Appraiser/Auditor 806-481-1405; Elections 806-481-3691; Vital Records 806-481-3691.

Pecos County

County Clerk, 103 West Callaghan Street, Fort Stockton, TX 79735. 915-336-7555; Fax 915-336-7557.

Will search UCC records prior to 7/2001 and current fixture (land) files. Will not search real estate records. **Other Phone Numbers:** Assessor 915-336-7587; Treasurer 915-336-3461; Appraiser/Auditor 915-336-7587.

Polk County

County Clerk, P.O. Drawer 2119, Livingston, TX 77351. County Clerk, R/E and UCC Recording 936-327-6804; Fax 936-327-6874.

Will search UCC records prior to 7/2001 and current fixture (land) files. Tax liens not included in UCC search. Will not search real estate records. **Other Phone Numbers:** Assessor 936-327-6801; Treasurer 936-327-6816; Appraiser/Auditor 936-327-2174; Elections 936-327-6852; Vital Records 936-327-6804; Court Clerk 936-327-6805.

Potter County

County Clerk, P.O. Box 9638, Amarillo, TX 79105. 806-379-2275; Fax 806-379-2296. http://www.prad.org

Will search UCC records prior to 7/2001 and current fixture (land) files. Tax liens not included in UCC search. Will not search real estate records. **Online**

Access: Assessor, Property Tax. Two sources exist. Records on the Potter-Randall Appraisal District database are available free online at www.prad.org/search.html. Records periodically updated; for current tax information call Potter (806-342-2600) or Randall (806-665-6287). See note at beginning of section for "Advanced" fee service. **Other Phone Numbers:** Assessor 806-358-1601; Treasurer 806-379-2236; Appraiser/Auditor 806-358-1601.

Presidio County

County Clerk, P.O. Box 789, Marfa, TX 79843. County Clerk, R/E and UCC Recording 915-729-4812; Fax 915-729-4313.
Will search UCC records prior to 7/2001 and current fixture (land) files. **Other Phone Numbers:** Assessor 915-729-4081; Treasurer 915-729-4076; Appraiser/Auditor 915-729-3431; Elections 915-729-4812; Vital Records 915-729-4812.

Rains County

County Clerk, P.O. Box 187, Emory, TX 75440. County Clerk, R/E and UCC Recording 903-473-2461. Will search UCC records prior to 7/2001 and current fixture (land) files. UCC search does not include tax liens. Will not search real estate records. **Other Phone Numbers:** Assessor 903-473-2391; Treasurer 903-473-2310; Appraiser/Auditor 903-473-2391; Elections 903-473-2461; Vital Records 903-473-2461.

Randall County

County Clerk, P.O. Box 660, Canyon, TX 79015. County Clerk, R/E and UCC Recording 806-655-6330; Fax 806-656-6430. http://www.prad.org
Will search UCC records prior to 7/2001 and current fixture (land) files. Tax liens not included in UCC search. Will not search real estate records. **Online Access:** Assessor, Property Tax. Two sources exist. Randall County records are combined online with Potter County; see Potter County for access information. Also, see notes at beginning of section. **Other Phone Numbers:** Assessor 806-358-1414; Treasurer 806-655-6256; Appraiser/Auditor 806-358-1601; Elections 806-655-6363; Vital Records 806-655-6332.

Reagan County

County Clerk, P.O. Box 100, Big Lake, TX 76932. County Clerk, R/E and UCC Recording 915-884-2442; Fax 915-884-1503.
Will search UCC records prior to 7/2001 and current fixture (land) files. UCC search includes tax liens if requested. Will not search real estate records. **Other Phone Numbers:** Assessor 915-884-2131; Treasurer 915-884-2090; Appraiser/Auditor 915-884-3275; Elections 915-884-2442; Vital Records 915-884-2442.

Real County

County Clerk, P.O. Box 750, Leakey, TX 78873-0750. 830-232-5202; Fax 830-232-6888. http://www.realcountytexas.com
Will search UCC records prior to 7/2001 and current fixture (land) files. **Other Phone Numbers:** Assessor 830-232-6210; Treasurer 830-232-6627; Appraiser/Auditor 830-232-6248.

Red River County

County Clerk, 200 North Walnut, Courthouse Annex, Clarksville, TX 75426-3075. County Clerk, R/E and UCC Recording 903-427-2401; Fax 903-427-5510.
Will search UCC records prior to 7/2001 and current fixture (land) files. Tax liens not included in UCC search. RE record owner searches available. **Other Phone Numbers:** Assessor 903-427-3009; Treasurer 903-427-3748; Appraiser/Auditor 903-427-4181; Elections 903-427-2401; Vital Records 903-427-2401.

Reeves County

County Clerk, P.O. Box 867, Pecos, TX 79772. County Clerk, R/E and UCC Recording 915-445-5467; Fax 915-445-5096.
Will search UCC records prior to 7/2001 and current fixture (land) files. Will not search real estate records. **Other Phone Numbers:** Assessor 915-445-5122; Treasurer 915-445-2631; Appraiser/Auditor 915-445-5122; Elections 915-445-5467; Vital Records 915-445-5467.

Refugio County

County Clerk, P.O. Box 704, Refugio, TX 78377. 361-526-2233.
Will search UCC records prior to 7/2001 and current fixture (land) files. UCC search includes tax liens if requested. RE record owner and property searches available. **Other Phone Numbers:** Assessor 361-526-5994; Treasurer 361-526-4223; Appraiser/Auditor 361-526-5994.

Roberts County

County Clerk, P.O. Box 477, Miami, TX 79059-0477. 806-868-2341; Fax 806-868-3381.
Will not search UCC records. Will not search real estate records. **Other Phone Numbers:** Assessor 806-868-3611; Treasurer 806-868-3201; Appraiser/Auditor 806-868-5281; Vital Records 806-868-2341.

Robertson County

County Clerk, P.O. Box 1029, Franklin, TX 77856. County Clerk, R/E and UCC Recording 979-828-4130; Fax 979-828-1260.
Will search UCC records prior to 7/2001 and current fixture (land) files. UCC search includes tax liens if requested. Will not search real estate records. **Other Phone Numbers:** Assessor 979-828-3337; Treasurer 979-828-3201; Appraiser/Auditor 979-828-5800; Elections 979-828-4130; Vital Records 979-828-4130.

Rockwall County

County Clerk, 1101 Ridge Rd., S-101, Rockwall, TX 75087. County Clerk, R/E and UCC Recording 972-882-0220 UCC Recording: 972-882-0225; Fax 972-882-0229.
Will search UCC records prior to 7/2001 and current fixture (land) files. UCC search includes tax liens if requested. Will not search real estate records. **Online Access:** Assessor, Property Tax. See notes at beginning of section. **Other Phone Numbers:** Assessor 972-882-0250; Treasurer 972-882-0290; Appraiser/Auditor 972-771-2034; Elections 972-882-0220; Vital Records 972-882-0220.

Runnels County

County Clerk, P.O. Box 189, Ballinger, TX 76821-0189. 915-365-2720; Fax 915-365-3408.
Will search UCC records prior to 7/2001 and current fixture (land) files. Tax liens not included in UCC search. Will not search real estate records. **Other Phone Numbers:** Assessor 915-365-3583; Treasurer 915-365-2428; Appraiser/Auditor 915-365-3583.

Rusk County

County Clerk, P.O. Box 758, Henderson, TX 75653-0758. 903-657-0330.
Will search UCC records prior to 7/2001 and current fixture (land) files. UCC search includes tax liens if requested. Will not search real estate records. **Online Access:** Property Tax. See note at beginning of section. **Other Phone Numbers:** Appraiser/Auditor 903-657-3578.

Sabine County

County Clerk, P.O. Drawer 580, Hemphill, TX 75948-0580. County Clerk, R/E and UCC Recording 409-787-3786; Fax 409-787-2044.
Will search UCC records. **Other Phone Numbers:** Assessor 409-787-2777; Treasurer 409-787-2210; Appraiser/Auditor 409-787-2777; Elections 409-787-3786; Vital Records 409-787-3786.

San Augustine County

County Clerk, 106 Courthouse, 100 W. Columbia, San Augustine, TX 75972-1335. 936-275-2452 R/E Recording: 409-275-2452; Fax 936-275-9579.
Will search UCC records prior to 7/2001 and current fixture (land) files. Will not search real estate records. **Other Phone Numbers:** Assessor 936-275-2300; Treasurer 936-275-9472; Appraiser/Auditor 936-275-3496.

San Jacinto County

County Clerk, P.O. Box 669, Coldspring, TX 77331. County Clerk, R/E and UCC Recording 936-653-2324. Will search UCC records prior to 7/2001 and current fixture (land) files. This agency will not do a tax lien search. RE owner, mortgage, and property transfer searches available. **Online Access:** Assessor, Property Tax. See note at beginning of section. **Other Phone Numbers:** Assessor 936-653-3292; Treasurer 936-653-2353; Appraiser/Auditor 936-653-4481; Elections 936-653-2324; Vital Records 936-653-2324.

San Patricio County

County Clerk, P.O. Box 578, Sinton, TX 78387. 361-364-6290 R/E Recording: 361-364-6290 x241 UCC Recording: 361-364-6290 x241; Fax 361-364-3825.
Will search UCC records prior to 7/2001 and current fixture (land) files. Tax liens not included in UCC search. Will not search real estate records. **Online Access:** Property Tax. See note at beginning of section. **Other Phone Numbers:** Assessor 361-364-6150; Treasurer 361-364-6228; Appraiser/Auditor 361-364-5402; Elections 361-364-6290 x238; Vital Records 361-364-6290 x238.

San Saba County

County Clerk, 500 East Wallace, San Saba, TX 76877. 915-372-3614; Fax 915-372-5746.
Will search UCC records prior to 7/2001 and current fixture (land) files. Will not search real estate records. **Other Phone Numbers:** Appraiser/Auditor 915-372-5031.

Schleicher County

County Clerk, P.O. Drawer 580, Eldorado, TX 76936. 915-853-2833; Fax 915-853-2603.
Will search UCC records prior to 7/2001 and current fixture (land) files. Will not search real estate records. **Other Phone Numbers:** Assessor 915-853-3066; Appraiser/Auditor 915-853-2671.

Scurry County

County Clerk, 1806 25th Street, Suite 300, Snyder, TX 79549-2530. 915-573-5332; Fax 915-573-7396.
Will search UCC records prior to 7/2001 and current fixture (land) files. Will not search real estate records. **Other Phone Numbers:** Assessor 915-573-9316; Treasurer 915-573-5382; Appraiser/Auditor 915-573-8549.

Shackelford County

County Clerk, P.O. Box 247, Albany, TX 76430. County Clerk, R/E and UCC Recording 915-762-2232. Will search UCC records. Tax liens not included in UCC search. **Other Phone Numbers:** Assessor 915-762-2207; Treasurer 915-762-2232; Appraiser/Auditor

915-762-2207; Elections 915-762-2232; Vital Records 915-762-2232.

Shelby County

County Clerk, P.O. Box 1987, Center, TX 75935. 936-598-6361 R/E Recording: 409-598-6361.
Will search UCC records prior to 7/2001 and current fixture (land) files. UCC search includes tax liens if requested. Will not search real estate records. **Other Phone Numbers:** Assessor 936-598-4441; Treasurer 936-598-3581; Appraiser/Auditor 409-598-6171.

Sherman County

County Clerk, P.O. Box 270, Stratford, TX 79084. 806-366-2371; Fax 806-366-5670.
Will search UCC records prior to 7/2001 and current fixture (land) files. **Other Phone Numbers:** Assessor 806-396-2150; Treasurer 806-396-5842; Appraiser/Auditor 806-396-5566.

Smith County

County Clerk, P.O. Box 1018, Tyler, TX 75710. 903-535-0650; Fax 903-535-0684.
Will search UCC records prior to 7/1/2001. **Online Access:** Property Tax. See note at beginning of section. **Other Phone Numbers:** Assessor 903-535-0835; Treasurer 903-535-0555; Appraiser/Auditor 903-510-8600; Elections 903-535-0657; Vital Records 903-535-0650.

Somervell County

County/District Clerk, P.O. Box 1098, Glen Rose, TX 76043. County/District Clerk, R/E and UCC Recording 254-897-4427; Fax 254-897-3233.
Will search UCC records prior to 7/2001 and current fixture (land) files. This agency will not do a tax lien search. Will not search real estate records. **Online Access:** Assessor, Property Tax. See note at beginning of section. **Other Phone Numbers:** Assessor 254-897-2419; Treasurer 254-897-4814; Appraiser/Auditor 254-897-4094; Elections 254-897-4427; Vital Records 254-897-4427.

Starr County

County Clerk, Courthouse, Rio Grande City, TX 78582. 956-487-2954; Fax 956-487-6227.
Will search UCC records. UCC search includes tax liens if requested. RE owner, mortgage, and property transfer searches available. **Other Phone Numbers:** Appraiser/Auditor 956-487-5613; Vital Records 956-487-2101.

Stephens County

County Clerk, Courthouse, Breckenridge, TX 76424. 254-559-3700.
Will search UCC records prior to 7/2001 and current fixture (land) files. UCC search includes tax liens if requested. Will not search real estate records. **Other Phone Numbers:** Assessor 254-559-2732; Treasurer 254-559-3181; Appraiser/Auditor 254-559-8233.

Sterling County

County Clerk, P.O. Box 55, Sterling City, TX 76951-0055. 915-378-5191.
Will search UCC records prior to 7/2001 and current fixture (land) files. UCC search includes tax liens if requested. Will not search real estate records. **Other Phone Numbers:** Assessor 915-378-7711; Treasurer 915-378-8511; Appraiser/Auditor 915-378-7711.

Stonewall County

County Clerk, P.O. Drawer P, Aspermont, TX 79502. 940-989-2272.
Will search UCC records prior to 7/2001 and current fixture (land) files. UCC search includes tax liens if

requested. RE owner, mortgage, and property transfer searches available. **Other Phone Numbers:** Assessor 940-989-2633; Treasurer 940-989-3520; Appraiser/Auditor 940-989-3363.

Sutton County

County Clerk, Sutton County Annex, 300 E. Oak, Suite 3, Sonora, TX 76950. 915-387-3815.
Will search UCC records prior to 7/2001 and current fixture (land) files. UCC search includes tax liens if requested. RE owner, mortgage, and property transfer searches available. **Other Phone Numbers:** Assessor 915-387-2809; Treasurer 915-387-2886; Appraiser/Auditor 915-387-2809.

Swisher County

County Clerk, Courthouse, 119 S. Maxwell, Tulia, TX 79088. 806-995-3294; Fax 806-995-4121.
Will search UCC records. UCC search includes tax liens if requested. Will not search real estate records. **Online Access:** Assessor, Property Tax. See notes at beginning of section. **Other Phone Numbers:** Appraiser/Auditor 806-995-4118.

Tarrant County

County Clerk, 100 West Weatherford, Courthouse, Room 180, Ft. Worth, TX 76196. 817-884-1550; http://www.tad.org/
Will search UCC records prior to 7/2001 and current fixture (land) files. This agency will not do a tax lien search. Will not search real estate records. **Online Access:** Property Tax, Assessor. Online access to the county Appraisal District Property data is available free at www.tad.org/Datasearch/datasearch.htm. Also, see note at beginning of section. **Other Phone Numbers:** Assessor 817-284-0024; Appraiser/Auditor 817-284-0024.

Taylor County

County Clerk, P.O. Box 5497, Abilene, TX 79608. 915-674-1202; Fax 915-674-1279. http://www.taylorcad.org/
Will search UCC records prior to 7/2001 and current fixture (land) files. Tax liens not included in UCC search. Will not search real estate records. **Online Access:** Assessor, Property Tax. Online access to the county Central Appraisal District database is available free at www.taylorcad.org/tayname.html. Search is by name, but other methods are available via the web site listed above. Also, see note at beginning of section. **Other Phone Numbers:** Assessor 915-672-4870; Treasurer 915-674-1231; Appraiser/Auditor 915-676-9381; Elections 915-674-1216; Vital Records 915-674-1202.

Terrell County

County Clerk, P.O. Drawer 410, Sanderson, TX 79848. 915-345-2391; Fax 915-345-2653.
Will search UCC records prior to 7/2001 and current fixture (land) files. **Other Phone Numbers:** Appraiser/Auditor 915-345-2251.

Terry County

County Clerk, 500 West Main, Room 105, Brownfield, TX 79316-4398. County Clerk, R/E and UCC Recording 806-637-8551; Fax 806-637-4874.
Will search UCC records prior to 7/2001 and current fixture (land) files. Will not search real estate records. **Other Phone Numbers:** Assessor 806-637-6966; Treasurer 806-637-3616; Appraiser/Auditor 806-637-6966; Elections 806-637-8551; Vital Records 806-637-8551.

Throckmorton County

County Clerk, P.O. Box 309, Throckmorton, TX 76483. County Clerk, R/E and UCC Recording 940-849-2501; Fax 940-849-3220.
Will search UCC records prior to 7/2001 and current fixture (land) files. **Other Phone Numbers:** Assessor 940-849-9421; Treasurer 940-849-2921; Appraiser/Auditor 940-849-5691; Elections 940-849-2501; Vital Records 940-849-2501.

Titus County

County Clerk, 100 W. 1 St., 2nd Floor, Suite 204, Mount Pleasant, TX 75455. 903-577-6796; Fax 903-572-5078.
Will search UCC records prior to 7/2001 and current fixture (land) files. UCC search includes tax liens if requested. Will not search real estate records. **Other Phone Numbers:** Assessor 903-572-6712; Treasurer 903-572-8723; Appraiser/Auditor 903-577-7939.

Tom Green County

County Clerk, 124 West Beauregard, San Angelo, TX 76903-5835. 915-659-6552 R/E Recording: 915-659-3262.
Will search UCC records prior to 7/2001 and current fixture (land) files. Tax liens not included in UCC search. Will not search real estate/UCC records. **Other Phone Numbers:** Appraiser/Auditor 915-658-5575; Vital Records 915-659-6556.

Travis County

County Clerk, P.O. Box 1748, Austin, TX 78701. 512-473-9188; Fax 512-473-9075. http://www.traviscad.org/
Will search UCC records prior to 7/2001 and current fixture (land) files. Tax liens not included in UCC search. RE owner, mortgage, and property transfer searches available. **Online Access:** Assessor, Property Tax. Online access to the Central Appraisal District database is available free at www.traviscad.org/search.htm. Also search business personal property. Also, See note at beginning of section. **Other Phone Numbers:** Assessor 512-473-9473; Treasurer 512-473-9000; Appraiser/Auditor 512-834-9317.

Trinity County

County Clerk, P.O. Box 456, Groveton, TX 75845. County Clerk, R/E and UCC Recording 936-642-1208; Fax 936-642-3004.
Will search UCC records. Tax liens not included in UCC search. Will not search real estate records. **Other Phone Numbers:** Assessor 936-642-1637; Treasurer 936-642-1443; Appraiser/Auditor 936-642-1502; Elections 936-642-1208; Vital Records 936-642-1208.

Tyler County

County Clerk, 110 W. Bluff, Room 110, Woodville, TX 75979. 409-283-2281 R/E Recording: 409-283-2281 x10 UCC Recording: 409-283-2281 x13.
Will search UCC records prior to 7/2001 and current fixture (land) files. Tax liens not included in UCC search. RE owner, mortgage, and property transfer searches available. **Other Phone Numbers:** Assessor 409-283-2734; Treasurer 409-283-3054; Appraiser/Auditor 409-283-3736; Elections 409-283-2281 x10; Vital Records 409-283-2281 x15.

Upshur County

County Clerk, P.O. Box 730, Gilmer, TX 75644. 903-843-4014 R/E Recording: 903-843-4015 UCC Recording: 903-843-4015; Fax 903-843-5492.
Will search UCC records prior to 7/2001 and current fixture (land) files. Tax liens not included in UCC search. RE owner, mortgage, and property transfer searches available. **Online Access:** Assessor, Property

Tax. See note at beginning of section. **Other Phone Numbers:** Assessor 903-843-3083; Treasurer 903-843-4027; Appraiser/Auditor 903-843-3041; Elections 903-843-1614; Vital Records 903-843-4015.

Upton County

County Clerk, P.O. Box 465, Rankin, TX 79778. County Clerk, R/E and UCC Recording 915-693-2861; Fax 915-693-2129.

Will search UCC records. **Other Phone Numbers:** Assessor 915-652-3222; Treasurer 915-693-2401; Appraiser/Auditor 915-652-3221; Elections 915-693-2861; Vital Records 915-693-2861.

Uvalde County

County Clerk, P.O. Box 284, Uvalde, TX 78802-0284. 830-278-6614 R/E Recording: 830-278-614.

Will search UCC records prior to 7/2001 and current fixture (land) files. UCC search includes tax liens if requested. RE owner, mortgage, and property transfer searches available. **Other Phone Numbers:** Assessor 830-278-3225; Treasurer 830-278-5821; Appraiser/Auditor 830-278-1106.

Val Verde County

County Clerk, P.O. Box 1267, Del Rio, TX 78841-1267. 830-774-7564.

Will search UCC records prior to 7/2001 and current fixture (land) files. Tax liens not included in UCC search. Will not search real estate records. **Other Phone Numbers:** Treasurer 210-774-4602; Appraiser/Auditor 830-774-4602.

Van Zandt County

County Clerk, 121 East Dallas St, Courthouse - Room 202, Canton, TX 75103. 903-567-6503; Fax 903-567-6722.

Will search UCC records prior to 7/2001 and current fixture (land) files. UCC search includes tax liens if requested. Will not search real estate records. **Online Access:** Property Tax. See note at beginning of section. **Other Phone Numbers:** Appraiser/Auditor 903-567-6171.

Victoria County

County Clerk, P.O. Box 2410, Victoria, TX 77902. County Clerk, R/E and UCC Recording 361-575-1478; Fax 361-575-6276.

Will search UCC records prior to 7/2001 and current fixture (land) files. Tax liens not included in UCC search. Will not search real estate records. **Online Access:** Assessor, Property Tax. See notes at beginning of section. **Other Phone Numbers:** Assessor 361-576-3671; Treasurer 361-576-8588; Appraiser/Auditor 361-576-3621; Elections 361-576-0124; Vital Records 361-575-1478.

Walker County

County Clerk, P.O. Box 210, Huntsville, TX 77342-0210. 936-436-4922; Fax 936-436-4928.

Will search UCC records prior to 7/2001 and current fixture (land) files. UCC search includes tax liens if requested. RE owner, mortgage, and property transfer searches available. **Other Phone Numbers:** Appraiser/Auditor 936-295-0402.

Waller County

County Clerk, 836 Austin Street, Room 217, Hempstead, TX 77445. County Clerk, R/E and UCC Recording 979-826-7711.

Will search UCC records prior to 7/2001 and current fixture (land) files. This agency will not do a tax lien search. Will not search real estate records. **Online Access:** Assessor, Property Tax. See note at beginning of section. **Other Phone Numbers:** Assessor 979-826-

7620; Treasurer 979-826-7707; Appraiser/Auditor 409-396-6100; Elections 979-826-7643; Vital Records 979-826-7711.

Ward County

County Clerk, Corner of 4 & Allen, Monahans, TX 79756. County Clerk, R/E and UCC Recording 915-943-3294; Fax 915-942-6054.

Will search UCC records. Will not search real estate records. **Other Phone Numbers:** Assessor 915-943-3224; Treasurer 915-943-2841; Appraiser/Auditor 915-943-3224; Elections 915-943-3294; Vital Records 915-943-3294.

Washington County

County Clerk, 100 East Main, Suite 102, Brenham, TX 77833. 979-277-6200; Fax 979-277-6278.

Will search UCC records prior to 7/2001 and current fixture (land) files. Will not search real estate records. **Online Access:** Assessor, Property Tax. See note at beginning of section. **Other Phone Numbers:** Assessor 979-836-5674; Treasurer 979-277-6200; Appraiser/Auditor 979-277-6528.

Webb County

County Clerk, P.O. Box 29, Laredo, TX 78042. 956-721-2640; Fax 956-721-2288. http://www.webbcad.org

Will search UCC records prior to 7/2001 and current fixture (land) files. UCC search includes tax liens if requested. RE owner, mortgage, and property transfer searches available. **Online Access:** Appraiser, Property Tax. Online access to the county Central Appraisal District database is available at www.webbcad.org/search1.htm. Also, See note at beginning of section. **Other Phone Numbers:** Assessor 956-721-2323; Treasurer 956-721-2215; Appraiser/Auditor 956-718-4091.

Wharton County

County Clerk, P.O. Box 69, Wharton, TX 77488. County Clerk, R/E and UCC Recording 979-532-2381; Fax 979-532-8426.

Will search UCC records prior to 7/2001 and current fixture (land) files. UCC search includes tax liens if requested. Will not search real estate records. **Online Access:** Assessor, Property Tax. See note at beginning of section. **Other Phone Numbers:** Appraiser/Auditor 409-532-8931; Vital Records 979-532-2381.

Wheeler County

County Clerk, P.O. Box 465, Wheeler, TX 79096. 806-826-5544; Fax 806-826-3282.

Will search UCC records prior to 7/2001 and current fixture (land) files. UCC search includes tax liens if requested. RE owner, mortgage, and property transfer searches available. **Other Phone Numbers:** Assessor 806-826-5900; Treasurer 806-826-3122; Appraiser/Auditor 806-826-5900.

Wichita County

County Clerk, P.O. Box 1679, Wichita Falls, TX 76307-1679. County Clerk, R/E and UCC Recording 940-766-8160; Fax 940-716-8554.

Will search UCC records prior to 7/2001 and current fixture (land) files. Tax liens not included in UCC search. Will not search real estate records. **Online Access:** Property Tax. See note at beginning of section. **Other Phone Numbers:** Assessor 940-322-2435; Treasurer 940-766-8245; Appraiser/Auditor 940-322-2435; Elections 940-766-8174; Vital Records 940-766-81644.

Wilbarger County

County Clerk, Courthouse, 1700 Main St. #15, Vernon, TX 76384. County Clerk, R/E and UCC Recording 940-552-5486.

Will search UCC records prior to 7/2001 and current fixture (land) files. UCC search includes tax liens if requested. RE owner, mortgage, and property transfer searches available. **Online Access:** Property Tax. See note at beginning of section. **Other Phone Numbers:** Assessor 940-552-9341; Treasurer 940-553-2302; Appraiser/Auditor 940-553-1857; Elections 940-552-5486; Vital Records 940-552-5486.

Willacy County

County Clerk, 540 West Hidalgo Avenue, Courthouse Building, First Floor, Raymondville, TX 78580. County Clerk, R/E and UCC Recording 956-689-2710; Fax 956-689-0937.

Will search UCC records prior to 7/2001 and current fixture (land) files. Tax liens not included in UCC search. Will not search real estate records. **Other Phone Numbers:** Assessor 956-689-3621; Treasurer 956-689-2772; Appraiser/Auditor 956-689-5979; Elections 956-689-2710; Vital Records 956-689-2710.

Williamson County

County Clerk, P.O. Box 18, Georgetown, TX 78627-0018. 512-943-1515; Fax 512-943-1616.

Will search UCC records prior to 7/2001 and current fixture (land) files. Tax liens not included in UCC search. Will not search real estate records. **Online Access:** Assessor, Property Tax. TexasTax provides free access to County tax assessor information online at www.texastax.com/search/default.asp?County=william son. Also, see note at beginning of section. **Other Phone Numbers:** Assessor 512-863-7569; Treasurer 512-930-4424; Appraiser/Auditor 512-930-3787.

Wilson County

County Clerk, P.O. Box 27, Floresville, TX 78114. County Clerk, R/E and UCC Recording 830-393-7308; Fax 830-393-7334.

Will search UCC records prior to 7/2001 and current fixture (land) files. UCC search includes tax liens if requested. RE record owner searches available. **Online Access:** Assessor, Property Tax. See note at beginning of section. **Other Phone Numbers:** Assessor 830-393-7313; Treasurer 830-393-7310; Appraiser/Auditor 830-393-3065; Elections 830-393-7368; Vital Records 830-393-7308.

Winkler County

County Clerk, P.O. Box 1007, Kermit, TX 79745. 915-586-3401.

Will search UCC records prior to 7/2001 and current fixture (land) files. Tax liens not included in UCC search. Will not search real estate records. **Other Phone Numbers:** Assessor 915-586-3465; Treasurer 915-586-6604; Appraiser/Auditor 915-586-2832.

Wise County

County Clerk, P.O. Box 359, Decatur, TX 76234. 940-627-3351; Fax 940-627-2138.

Will search UCC records prior to 7/2001 and current fixture (land) files. Will not search real estate records. **Online Access:** Property Tax. See note at beginning of section. **Other Phone Numbers:** Assessor 940-627-3523; Treasurer 940-627-3540; Appraiser/Auditor 940-627-3081.

Wood County

County Clerk, P.O. Box 1756, Quitman, TX 75783. 903-763-2711; Fax 903-763-5641.

Will search UCC records prior to 7/2001 and current fixture (land) files. UCC search includes tax liens if

requested. Will not search real estate records. **Online Access:** Assessor, PropertyTax. See note at beginning of section. **Other Phone Numbers:** Assessor 903-763-4946; Treasurer 903-763-4186; Appraiser/Auditor 903-763-4891.

Yoakum County

County Clerk, P.O. Box 309, Plains, TX 79335. 806-456-2721; Fax 806-456-2258.

Will search UCC records prior to 7/2001 and current fixture (land) files. UCC search includes tax liens if requested. RE record owner and property transfer searches $5.00. **Other Phone Numbers:** Assessor 806-456-7102; Treasurer 806-456-8794; Appraiser/Auditor 806-456-7101.

Young County

County Clerk, 516 Fourth St #104, 516 Fourth St., Room 104, Graham, TX 76450-3063. 940-549-8432

R/E Recording: 940-539-8432 UCC Recording: 940-539-8432; Fax 940-521-0305.

Will search UCC records prior to 7/2001 and current fixture (land) files. Tax liens not included in UCC search. Will not search real estate records. **Other Phone Numbers:** Assessor 940-549-1393; Treasurer 940-549-2633; Appraiser/Auditor 940-549-2392; Elections 940-549-5132; Vital Records 940-539-8432; 940-539-8433.

Zapata County

County Clerk, P.O. Box 789, Zapata, TX 78076. 956-765-9915; Fax 956-765-9933.

Will search UCC records prior to 7/2001 and current fixture (land) files. UCC search includes tax liens if requested. RE owner, mortgage, and property transfer searches available. **Online Access:** Property Tax. See note at beginning of section. **Other Phone Numbers:** Assessor 956-765-9971; Treasurer 956-765-9925; Appraiser/Auditor 956-765-9971.

Zavala County

County Clerk, Zavala Courthouse, Crystal City, TX 78839. 830-374-2331; Fax 830-374-5955.

Will search UCC records prior to 7/2001 and current fixture (land) files. UCC search includes tax liens if requested. RE owner, mortgage, and property transfer searches available. **Other Phone Numbers:** Assessor 830-347-3475; Treasurer 830-374-2442; Appraiser/Auditor 830-374-3476.

Texas County Locator

You will usually be able to find the city name in the City/County Cross Reference below. In that case, it is a simple matter to determine the county from the cross reference. However, only the official US Postal Service city names are included in this index. There are an additional 40,000 place names that people use in their addresses. Therefore, we have also included a ZIP/City Cross Reference immediately following the City/County Cross Reference.

If you know the ZIP Code but the city name does not appear in the City/County Cross Reference index, look up the ZIP Code in the ZIP/City Cross Reference, find the city name, then look up the city name in the City/County Cross Reference. For example, you want to know the county for an address of Menands, NY 12204. There is no "Menands" in the City/County Cross Reference. The ZIP/City Cross Reference shows that ZIP Codes 12201-12288 are for the city of Albany. Looking back in the City/County Cross Reference, Albany is in Albany County.

City/County Cross Reference

ABBOTT (76621) Hill(91), McLennan(9)
ABERNATHY (79311) Hale(73), Lubbock(27)
ABILENE (79601) Taylor(79), Jones(15), Callahan(3), Shackelford(3)
ABILENE (79602) Taylor(94), Callahan(6)
ABILENE Taylor
ACE Polk
ACKERLY Dawson
ADDISON (75001) Dallas(98), Collin(2)
ADKINS (78101) Bexar(75), Wilson(25)
ADRIAN (79001) Deaf Smith(50), Oldham(50)
AFTON Dickens
AGUA DULCE Nueces
AIKEN Floyd
ALAMO Hidalgo
ALANREED Gray
ALBA (75410) Wood(88), Rains(12)
ALBANY Shackelford
ALEDO (76008) Parker(79), Tarrant(21)
ALICE Jim Wells
ALIEF Harris
ALLEN Collin
ALLEYTON Colorado
ALLISON Wheeler
ALPINE Brewster
ALTAIR Colorado
ALTO Cherokee
ALVARADO Johnson
ALVIN (77511) Brazoria(94), Galveston(6)
ALVIN Brazoria
ALVORD Wise
AMARILLO (79103) Potter(77), Randall(23)
AMARILLO (79106) Potter(91), Randall(9)
AMARILLO (79109) Randall(75), Potter(25)
AMARILLO (79118) Randall(95), Potter(6)
AMARILLO (79121) Randall(97), Potter(3)
AMARILLO Potter
AMARILLO Randall
AMHERST Lamb
ANAHUAC Chambers
ANDERSON Grimes
ANDREWS Andrews
ANGLETON Brazoria
ANNA Collin
ANNONA Red River
ANSON Jones
ANTHONY El Paso
ANTON (79313) Hockley(74), Lamb(20), Lubbock(5), Hale(2)
APPLE SPRINGS Trinity
AQUILLA Hill
ARANSAS PASS (78336) San Patricio(77), Aransas(22)
ARANSAS PASS San Patricio
ARCHER CITY Archer
ARGYLE Denton
ARLINGTON Tarrant
ARMSTRONG Kenedy
ARP Smith
ART Mason
ARTESIA WELLS La Salle
ARTHUR CITY Lamar
ASHERTON Dimmit

ASPERMONT Stonewall
ATASCOSA Bexar
ATHENS Henderson
ATLANTA Cass
AUBREY Denton
AUSTIN (78728) Travis(97), Williamson(4)
AUSTIN (78729) Williamson(92), Travis(8)
AUSTIN (78736) Travis(91), Hays(9)
AUSTIN (78737) Hays(53), Travis(47)
AUSTIN (78750) Travis(59), Williamson(41)
AUSTIN Travis
AUSTIN Williamson
AUSTWELL Refugio
AVALON Ellis
AVERY (75554) Red River(88), Bowie(12)
AVINGER (75630) Marion(56), Cass(44)
AXTELL (76624) McLennan(97), Limestone(3)
AZLE (76020) Parker(51), Tarrant(48)
AZLE Parker
BACLIFF Galveston
BAGWELL Red River
BAILEY Fannin
BAIRD Callahan
BALLINGER Runnels
BALMORHEA Reeves
BANDERA Bandera
BANGS (76823) Brown(64), Coleman(36)
BANQUETE Nueces
BARDWELL Ellis
BARKER Harris
BARKSDALE (78828) Edwards(72), Real(28)
BARNHART (76930) Irion(55), Crockett(46)
BARRY (75102) Navarro(97), Ellis(3)
BARSTOW Ward
BARTLETT (76511) Bell(60), Williamson(36), Milam(4)
BASTROP Bastrop
BATESVILLE Zavala
BATSON Hardin
BAY CITY Matagorda
BAYSIDE Refugio
BAYTOWN (77520) Harris(82), Chambers(18)
BAYTOWN (77521) Harris(96), Chambers(4)
BAYTOWN Harris
BEASLEY Fort Bend
BEAUMONT Jefferson
BEBE Gonzales
BECKVILLE Panola
BEDFORD Tarrant
BEDIAS Grimes
BEEVILLE Bee
BELLAIRE Harris
BELLEVUE (76228) Clay(83), Montague(17)
BELLS Grayson
BELLVILLE Austin
BELMONT Gonzales
BELTON Bell
BEN ARNOLD Milam
BEN BOLT Jim Wells
BEN FRANKLIN Delta

BEN WHEELER Van Zandt
BENAVIDES Duval
BEND San Saba
BENJAMIN Knox
BERCLAIR Goliad
BERGHEIM Kendall
BERTRAM Burnet
BIG BEND NATIONAL PARK Brewster
BIG LAKE Reagan
BIG SANDY (75755) Upshur(92), Wood(9)
BIG SPRING (79720) Howard(99), Glasscock(1)
BIG SPRING Howard
BIG WELLS Dimmit
BIGFOOT (78005) Frio(84), Atascosa(16)
BIROME Hill
BISHOP Nueces
BIVINS Cass
BLACKWELL (79506) Nolan(83), Coke(17)
BLANCO (78606) Blanco(84), Comal(16)
BLANKET (76432) Brown(98), Comanche(2)
BLEDSOE Cochran
BLEIBLERVILLE Austin
BLESSING Matagorda
BLOOMBURG Cass
BLOOMING GROVE (76626) Navarro(98), Ellis(2)
BLOOMINGTON Victoria
BLOSSOM Lamar
BLUE RIDGE (75424) Collin(98), Fannin(2)
BLUEGROVE Clay
BLUFF DALE (76433) Hood(83), Somervell(10), Erath(8)
BLUFFTON Llano
BLUM Hill
BOERNE (78006) Kendall(83), Bexar(14), Comal(3)
BOERNE (78015) Bexar(64), Kendall(31), Comal(5)
BOGATA Red River
BOLING Wharton
BON WIER Newton
BONHAM Fannin
BOOKER (79005) Lipscomb(73), Ochiltree(27)
BORGER Hutchinson
BOVINA Parmer
BOWIE (76230) Montague(98), Jack(2)
BOYD (76023) Wise(91), Parker(9)
BOYS RANCH (79010) Potter(75), Oldham(25)
BRACKETTVILLE Kinney
BRADY McCulloch
BRANDON Hill
BRASHEAR Hopkins
BRAZORIA Brazoria
BRECKENRIDGE Stephens
BREMOND (76629) Robertson(87), Falls(13)
BRENHAM Washington
BRIDGE CITY Orange
BRIDGEPORT Wise
BRIGGS Burnet

BRISCOE (79011) Hemphill(66), Wheeler(34)
BROADDUS San Augustine
BRONSON (75930) Sabine(63), San Augustine(37)
BRONTE (76933) Runnels(68), Coke(33)
BROOKELAND (75931) Jasper(52), Sabine(48)
BROOKESMITH (76827) Brown(99), Coleman(2)
BROOKSHIRE (77423) Waller(87), Fort Bend(13)
BROOKSTON Lamar
BROWNFIELD Terry
BROWNSBORO (75756) Henderson(99), Van Zandt(1)
BROWNSVILLE Cameron
BROWNWOOD Brown
BRUCEVILLE (76630) McLennan(96), Falls(5)
BRUNI (78344) Webb(94), Duval(6)
BRYAN (77807) Brazos(89), Robertson(11)
BRYAN (77808) Brazos(92), Robertson(8)
BRYAN Brazos
BRYSON Jack
BUCHANAN DAM Llano
BUCKHOLTS Milam
BUDA (78610) Hays(88), Travis(12)
BUFFALO (75831) Leon(83), Freestone(17)
BUFFALO GAP Taylor
BULA (79320) Bailey(82), Lamb(18)
BULLARD (75757) Smith(83), Cherokee(17)
BULVERDE Comal
BUNA Jasper
BURKBURNETT Wichita
BURKETT Coleman
BURKEVILLE Newton
BURLESON (76028) Johnson(78), Tarrant(22)
BURLESON Johnson
BURLINGTON (76519) Milam(67), Bell(28), Falls(6)
BURNET Burnet
BURTON Washington
BUSHLAND Potter
BYERS Clay
BYNUM Hill
CACTUS Moore
CADDO Stephens
CADDO MILLS Hunt
CALDWELL Burleson
CALL (75933) Newton(68), Jasper(32)
CALLIHAM McMullen
CALVERT Robertson
CAMDEN Polk
CAMERON Milam
CAMP WOOD Real
CAMPBELL Hunt
CAMPBELLTON (78008) Atascosa(91), Live Oak(9)
CANADIAN (79014) Hemphill(99), Lipscomb(1)
CANTON Van Zandt

CANUTILLO El Paso
CANYON Randall
CANYON LAKE Comal
CARBON Eastland
CAREY Childress
CARLSBAD Tom Green
CARLTON Hamilton
CARMINE Fayette
CARRIZO SPRINGS Dimmit
CARROLLTON (75007) Denton(90),
  Dallas(10)
CARROLLTON Dallas
CARROLLTON Denton
CARTHAGE Panola
CASON Morris
CASTELL (76831) Mason(60), Llano(40)
CASTROVILLE Medina
CAT SPRING (78933) Colorado(97),
  Austin(3)
CATARINA Dimmit
CAYUGA Anderson
CEDAR CREEK (78612) Bastrop(95),
  Travis(5)
CEDAR HILL Dallas
CEDAR LANE Matagorda
CEDAR PARK (78613) Williamson(98),
  Travis(2)
CEDAR PARK Williamson
CEE VEE Cottle
CELESTE (75423) Hunt(97), Fannin(3)
CELINA Collin
CENTER Shelby
CENTER POINT Kerr
CENTERVILLE Leon
CENTRALIA Trinity
CHALK Cottle
CHANDLER Henderson
CHANNELVIEW Harris
CHANNING (79018) Hartley(82),
  Moore(18)
CHAPMAN RANCH Nueces
CHAPPELL HILL (77426) Washington(87),
  Austin(13)
CHARLOTTE Atascosa
CHATFIELD Navarro
CHEROKEE (76832) San Saba(99),
  Llano(1)
CHESTER (75936) Tyler(90), Polk(10)
CHICO Wise
CHICOTA Lamar
CHILDRESS (79201) Childress(98), Hall(1)
CHILLICOTHE (79225) Hardeman(85),
  Wilbarger(15)
CHILTON Falls
CHINA Jefferson
CHINA SPRING (76633) McLennan(99),
  Bosque(1)
CHIRENO Nacogdoches
CHRIESMAN Burleson
CHRISTINE Atascosa
CHRISTOVAL (76935) Tom Green(74),
  Schleicher(26)
CIBOLO (78108) Guadalupe(71),
  Bexar(28), Comal(1)
CISCO (76437) Eastland(96), Callahan(3),
  Stephens(1)
CLARENDON (79226) Donley(83),
  Armstrong(12), Hall(4), Briscoe(2)
CLARKSVILLE Red River
CLAUDE Armstrong
CLAY Burleson
CLAYTON Panola
CLEBURNE Johnson
CLEVELAND (77327) Liberty(43), San
  Jacinto(29), Montgomery(28)
CLEVELAND Liberty
CLIFTON Bosque
CLINT El Paso
CLUTE Brazoria
CLYDE Callahan
COAHOMA (79511) Howard(95), Borden(5)
COLDSPRING San Jacinto

COLEMAN Coleman
COLLEGE STATION Brazos
COLLEGEPORT Matagorda
COLLEYVILLE Tarrant
COLLINSVILLE (76233) Grayson(72),
  Cooke(28)
COLMESNEIL Tyler
COLORADO CITY Mitchell
COLUMBUS Colorado
COMANCHE Comanche
COMBES Cameron
COMFORT (78013) Kendall(88), Kerr(12)
COMMERCE Hunt
COMO Hopkins
COMSTOCK Val Verde
CONCAN Uvalde
CONCEPCION Duval
CONCORD (77850) Leon(88), Brazos(13)
CONE Crosby
CONROE Montgomery
CONVERSE Bexar
COOKVILLE Titus
COOLIDGE (76635) Limestone(94),
  McLennan(6)
COOPER Delta
COPEVILLE Collin
COPPELL Dallas
COPPERAS COVE (76522) Coryell(99),
  Lampasas(1)
CORPUS CHRISTI Nueces
CORRIGAN Polk
CORSICANA Navarro
COST Gonzales
COTTON CENTER Hale
COTULLA La Salle
COUPLAND (78615) Williamson(89),
  Travis(11)
COVINGTON Hill
COYANOSA Pecos
CRANDALL Kaufman
CRANE Crane
CRANFILLS GAP (76637) Bosque(92),
  Hamilton(8)
CRAWFORD McLennan
CRESSON (76035) Hood(59), Parker(35),
  Johnson(6)
CROCKETT Houston
CROSBY Harris
CROSBYTON Crosby
CROSS PLAINS (76443) Callahan(96),
  Brown(3)
CROWELL Foard
CROWLEY (76036) Tarrant(72),
  Johnson(28)
CRYSTAL CITY Zavala
CUERO De Witt
CUMBY Hopkins
CUNEY Cherokee
CUNNINGHAM Lamar
CUSHING (75760) Nacogdoches(94),
  Rusk(6)
CYPRESS Harris
D HANIS Medina
DAINGERFIELD Morris
DAISETTA Liberty
DALE (78616) Caldwell(94), Bastrop(7)
DALHART (79022) Dallam(73), Hartley(27)
DALLARDSVILLE Polk
DALLAS (75252) Collin(96), Dallas(4)
DALLAS (75287) Collin(52), Denton(47),
  Dallas(1)
DALLAS Dallas
DAMON (77430) Fort Bend(61),
  Brazoria(39)
DANBURY Brazoria
DANCIGER Brazoria
DANEVANG Wharton
DARROUZETT Lipscomb
DAVILLA Milam
DAWN Deaf Smith
DAWSON (76639) Navarro(88),
  McLennan(12)

DAYTON (77535) Liberty(94), Chambers(6)
DE BERRY Panola
DE KALB Bowie
DE LEON Comanche
DE SOTO Dallas
DEANVILLE Burleson
DECATUR Wise
DEER PARK Harris
DEL RIO Edwards
DEL RIO Val Verde
DEL VALLE (78617) Travis(88),
  Bastrop(12)
DELL CITY Hudspeth
DELMITA (78536) Starr(88), Hidalgo(13)
DENISON Grayson
DENNIS Parker
DENTON Denton
DENVER CITY (79323) Yoakum(97),
  Gaines(3)
DEPORT Lamar
DESDEMONA (76445) Eastland(90),
  Comanche(9)
DETROIT (75436) Red River(93), Lamar(7)
DEVERS Liberty
DEVINE Medina
DEWEYVILLE Newton
DIANA (75640) Upshur(71), Harrison(27),
  Marion(2)
DIBOLL Angelina
DICKENS Dickens
DICKINSON Galveston
DIKE Hopkins
DILLEY Frio
DIME BOX Lee
DIMMITT Castro
DINERO Live Oak
DOBBIN Montgomery
DODD CITY Fannin
DODGE Walker
DODSON (79230) Collingsworth(67),
  Childress(33)
DONIE (75838) Freestone(60),
  Limestone(39), Leon(1)
DONNA Hidalgo
DOOLE McCulloch
DOSS Gillespie
DOUCETTE Tyler
DOUGHERTY Floyd
DOUGLASS Nacogdoches
DOUGLASSVILLE Cass
DRIFTWOOD Hays
DRIPPING SPRINGS (78620) Hays(90),
  Travis(10)
DRISCOLL Nueces
DRYDEN Terrell
DUBLIN (76446) Erath(84), Comanche(16)
DUMAS Moore
DUMONT (79232) Dickens(69), King(31)
DUNCANVILLE Dallas
DUNN Scurry
DYESS AFB Taylor
EAGLE LAKE (77434) Colorado(98),
  Wharton(2)
EAGLE PASS Maverick
EARLY Brown
EARTH (79031) Lamb(75), Castro(17),
  Bailey(9)
EAST BERNARD (77435) Wharton(90),
  Fort Bend(10)
EASTLAND Eastland
EASTON Gregg
ECLETO Karnes
ECTOR Fannin
EDCOUCH Hidalgo
EDDY (76524) McLennan(98), Falls(2)
EDEN Concho
EDGEWOOD Van Zandt
EDINBURG Hidalgo
EDMONSON Hale
EDNA Jackson
EDROY San Patricio
EGYPT Wharton

EL CAMPO Wharton
EL INDIO Maverick
EL PASO (79938) El Paso(98),
  Hudspeth(2)
EL PASO El Paso
ELBERT Throckmorton
ELDORADO Schleicher
ELECTRA (76360) Wichita(88),
  Wilbarger(12)
ELGIN (78621) Bastrop(76), Travis(14),
  Williamson(7), Lee(3)
ELIASVILLE Young
ELKHART (75839) Anderson(99),
  Houston(1)
ELLINGER Fayette
ELM MOTT McLennan
ELMATON Matagorda
ELMENDORF (78112) Bexar(97),
  Wilson(3)
ELMO Kaufman
ELSA Hidalgo
ELYSIAN FIELDS Harrison
EMORY (75440) Rains(99), Wood(1)
ENCINAL La Salle
ENCINO Brooks
ENERGY Comanche
ENLOE Delta
ENNIS Ellis
ENOCHS Bailey
EOLA (76937) Tom Green(87), Concho(13)
ERA Cooke
ESTELLINE Hall
ETOILE Nacogdoches
EULESS Tarrant
EUSTACE (75124) Henderson(96), Van
  Zandt(4)
EVADALE Jasper
EVANT Coryell
FABENS El Paso
FAIRFIELD Freestone
FALCON HEIGHTS Starr
FALFURRIAS (78355) Brooks(96), Jim
  Wells(4)
FALLS CITY (78113) Wilson(57),
  Karnes(43)
FANNIN Goliad
FARMERSVILLE (75442) Collin(99),
  Hunt(1)
FARNSWORTH Ochiltree
FARWELL (79325) Parmer(91), Bailey(9)
FATE Rockwall
FAYETTEVILLE (78940) Fayette(85),
  Colorado(9), Austin(6)
FENTRESS Caldwell
FERRIS (75125) Ellis(83), Dallas(17)
FIELDTON Lamb
FISCHER (78623) Hays(52), Comal(48)
FLAT Coryell
FLATONIA Fayette
FLINT Smith
FLOMOT (79234) Motley(84), Floyd(16)
FLORENCE (76527) Williamson(97),
  Bell(2)
FLORESVILLE Wilson
FLOWER MOUND Denton
FLOYDADA (79235) Floyd(97), Crosby(2)
FLUVANNA (79517) Scurry(71),
  Borden(30)
FLYNN Leon
FOLLETT Lipscomb
FORESTBURG (76239) Montague(85),
  Cooke(15)
FORNEY (75126) Kaufman(97),
  Rockwall(3)
FORRESTON Ellis
FORSAN Howard
FORT DAVIS Jeff Davis
FORT HANCOCK Hudspeth
FORT MC KAVETT Menard
FORT STOCKTON Pecos
FORT WORTH (76108) Tarrant(93),
  Parker(7)

FORT WORTH (76126) Tarrant(88), Parker(12)
FORT WORTH (76177) Tarrant(93), Denton(7)
FORT WORTH (76178) Tarrant(99), Denton(2)
FORT WORTH Tarrant
FOWLERTON (78021) La Salle(63), McMullen(25), Atascosa(13)
FRANCITAS Jackson
FRANKLIN Robertson
FRANKSTON (75763) Henderson(78), Anderson(22)
FRED Tyler
FREDERICKSBURG (78624) Gillespie(75), Kendall(24)
FREDONIA (76842) Mason(96), San Saba(5)
FREEPORT Brazoria
FREER Duval
FRESNO Fort Bend
FRIENDSWOOD (77546) Galveston(67), Harris(32)
FRIENDSWOOD Galveston
FRIONA (79035) Parmer(98), Deaf Smith(2)
FRISCO (75034) Collin(85), Denton(15)
FRISCO (75035) Collin(98), Denton(2)
FRITCH (79036) Hutchinson(95), Carson(5)
FROST (76641) Navarro(98), Ellis(2)
FRUITVALE Van Zandt
FULSHEAR Fort Bend
FULTON Aransas
GAIL Borden
GAINESVILLE Cooke
GALENA PARK Harris
GALLATIN Cherokee
GALVESTON Galveston
GANADO Jackson
GARCIASVILLE Starr
GARDEN CITY (79739) Glasscock(88), Reagan(12)
GARDENDALE Ector
GARLAND (75048) Dallas(90), Collin(10)
GARLAND Dallas
GARRISON (75946) Nacogdoches(54), Rusk(46)
GARWOOD Colorado
GARY (75643) Panola(92), Shelby(8)
GATESVILLE (76528) Coryell(98), Bell(2)
GATESVILLE Coryell
GAUSE Milam
GENEVA Sabine
GEORGE WEST Live Oak
GEORGETOWN Williamson
GERONIMO Guadalupe
GIDDINGS Lee
GILCHRIST Galveston
GILLETT Karnes
GILMER Upshur
GIRARD Kent
GIRVIN Pecos
GLADEWATER (75647) Gregg(59), Upshur(31), Smith(10)
GLEN FLORA Wharton
GLEN ROSE Somervell
GLIDDEN Colorado
GOBER Fannin
GODLEY Johnson
GOLDEN Wood
GOLDSBORO (79519) Taylor(46), Runnels(42), Coleman(12)
GOLDSMITH Ector
GOLDTHWAITE Mills
GOLIAD Goliad
GONZALES Gonzales
GOODFELLOW AFB Tom Green
GOODRICH Polk
GORDON (76453) Palo Pinto(96), Erath(4)
GORDONVILLE Grayson

GOREE (76363) Knox(98), Haskell(1), Throckmorton(1)
GORMAN (76454) Eastland(76), Comanche(25)
GOULDBUSK Coleman
GRAFORD Palo Pinto
GRAHAM Young
GRANBURY (76048) Hood(98), Somervell(2)
GRANBURY (76049) Hood(97), Parker(3)
GRAND PRAIRIE (75050) Dallas(74), Tarrant(26)
GRAND PRAIRIE (75051) Dallas(87), Tarrant(13)
GRAND PRAIRIE (75052) Dallas(68), Tarrant(32)
GRAND PRAIRIE Dallas
GRAND SALINE Van Zandt
GRANDFALLS Ward
GRANDVIEW (76050) Johnson(96), Hill(2), Ellis(2)
GRANGER Williamson
GRAPELAND (75844) Houston(87), Anderson(13)
GRAPEVINE Tarrant
GREENVILLE Hunt
GREENWOOD Wise
GREGORY San Patricio
GROESBECK Limestone
GROOM (79039) Carson(58), Gray(39), Armstrong(2), Donley(2)
GROVES Jefferson
GROVETON Trinity
GRULLA Starr
GRUVER (79040) Hansford(65), Sherman(35)
GUERRA (78360) Jim Hogg(80), Starr(20)
GUNTER Grayson
GUSTINE Comanche
GUTHRIE King
GUY (77444) Fort Bend(72), Brazoria(28)
HALE CENTER (79041) Hale(98), Lamb(3)
HALLETTSVILLE Lavaca
HALLSVILLE Harrison
HALTOM CITY Tarrant
HAMILTON Hamilton
HAMLIN (79520) Jones(95), Fisher(5)
HAMSHIRE (77622) Jefferson(83), Chambers(17)
HANKAMER Chambers
HAPPY (79042) Randall(59), Swisher(28), Castro(8), Armstrong(5)
HARDIN Liberty
HARGILL Hidalgo
HARKER HEIGHTS Bell
HARLETON (75651) Harrison(94), Marion(6)
HARLINGEN Cameron
HARPER (78631) Gillespie(97), Kerr(3)
HARROLD Wilbarger
HART (79043) Castro(92), Lamb(9)
HARTLEY Hartley
HARWOOD (78632) Gonzales(81), Caldwell(19)
HASKELL Haskell
HASLET (76052) Tarrant(90), Denton(6), Wise(4)
HASSE Comanche
HAWKINS Wood
HAWLEY Jones
HEARNE Robertson
HEBBRONVILLE Jim Hogg
HEDLEY Donley
HEIDENHEIMER Bell
HELOTES (78023) Bexar(87), Medina(8), Bandera(5)
HEMPHILL Sabine
HEMPSTEAD Waller
HENDERSON Rusk
HENRIETTA Clay
HEREFORD (79045) Deaf Smith(97), Castro(3)

HERMLEIGH (79526) Scurry(95), Fisher(5)
HEWITT McLennan
HEXT Menard
HICO (76457) Hamilton(87), Erath(13)
HIDALGO Hidalgo
HIGGINS (79046) Lipscomb(72), Hemphill(28)
HIGH ISLAND Galveston
HIGHLANDS Harris
HILLISTER Tyler
HILLSBORO Hill
HITCHCOCK Galveston
HOBSON Karnes
HOCHHEIM De Witt
HOCKLEY (77447) Harris(62), Waller(21), Montgomery(17)
HOLLAND Bell
HOLLIDAY Archer
HONDO Medina
HONEY GROVE Fannin
HOOKS Bowie
HOUSTON (77031) Harris(99), Fort Bend(1)
HOUSTON (77053) Fort Bend(59), Harris(41)
HOUSTON (77083) Harris(59), Fort Bend(41)
HOUSTON (77085) Harris(93), Fort Bend(7)
HOUSTON (77099) Harris(97), Fort Bend(3)
HOUSTON Harris
HOWE Grayson
HUBBARD (76648) Hill(96), Navarro(3), Limestone(1)
HUFFMAN Harris
HUFSMITH Harris
HUGHES SPRINGS (75656) Cass(92), Morris(9)
HULL (77564) Liberty(92), Hardin(8)
HUMBLE (77339) Harris(84), Montgomery(16)
HUMBLE Harris
HUNGERFORD Wharton
HUNT (78024) Kerr(98), Real(2)
HUNTINGTON Angelina
HUNTSVILLE Walker
HURST Tarrant
HUTCHINS Dallas
HUTTO Williamson
HYE Blanco
IDALOU Lubbock
IMPERIAL Pecos
INDUSTRY Austin
INEZ Victoria
INGLESIDE San Patricio
INGRAM Kerr
IOLA Grimes
IOWA PARK Wichita
IRA (79527) Scurry(80), Borden(20)
IRAAN Pecos
IREDELL (76649) Bosque(89), Erath(11)
IRENE Hill
IRVING Dallas
ITALY Ellis
ITASCA Hill
IVANHOE Fannin
JACKSBORO Jack
JACKSONVILLE Cherokee
JARRELL Williamson
JASPER Jasper
JAYTON Kent
JEFFERSON (75657) Marion(93), Cass(6), Harrison(1)
JERMYN Jack
JEWETT (75846) León(61), Limestone(39)
JOAQUIN (75954) Shelby(94), Panola(6)
JOHNSON CITY Blanco
JOINERVILLE Rusk
JONESBORO (76538) Coryell(90), Hamilton(10)

JONESVILLE (75659) Harrison(86), Rusk(14)
JOSEPHINE Collin
JOSHUA Johnson
JOURDANTON Atascosa
JUDSON Gregg
JUNCTION Kimble
JUSTICEBURG Garza
JUSTIN Denton
KAMAY Wichita
KARNACK Harrison
KARNES CITY Karnes
KATY (77450) Harris(81), Fort Bend(19)
KATY (77493) Harris(84), Waller(14), Fort Bend(2)
KATY (77494) Fort Bend(78), Harris(19), Waller(3)
KATY Harris
KAUFMAN Kaufman
KEENE Johnson
KELLER Tarrant
KEMAH Galveston
KEMP (75143) Kaufman(71), Henderson(29)
KEMPNER (76539) Coryell(48), Lampasas(43), Bell(6), Burnet(3)
KENDALIA Kendall
KENDLETON Fort Bend
KENEDY Karnes
KENNARD (75847) Houston(91), Trinity(9)
KENNEDALE Tarrant
KENNEY Austin
KERENS Navarro
KERMIT Winkler
KERRICK Dallam
KERRVILLE Kerr
KILDARE Cass
KILGORE (75662) Gregg(94), Rusk(6)
KILGORE Gregg
KILLEEN (76544) Bell(52), Coryell(49)
KILLEEN Bell
KINGSBURY Guadalupe
KINGSLAND Llano
KINGSVILLE Kleberg
KIRBYVILLE Jasper
KIRKLAND Childress
KIRVIN Freestone
KLONDIKE Delta
KNICKERBOCKER Tom Green
KNIPPA Uvalde
KNOTT Howard
KNOX CITY (79529) Knox(98), Haskell(2)
KOPPERL Bosque
KOSSE (76653) Limestone(86), Falls(6), Robertson(5), McLennan(4)
KOUNTZE Hardin
KRESS (79052) Swisher(91), Hale(8)
KRUM Denton
KURTEN Brazos
KYLE (78640) Hays(97), Caldwell(3)
LA BLANCA Hidalgo
LA COSTE (78039) Medina(87), Bexar(13)
LA FERIA Cameron
LA GRANGE Fayette
LA JOYA Hidalgo
LA MARQUE Galveston
LA PORTE Harris
LA PRYOR Zavala
LA SALLE Jackson
LA VERNIA (78121) Wilson(55), Guadalupe(45)
LA VILLA Hidalgo
LA WARD Jackson
LADONIA Fannin
LAIRD HILL Rusk
LAKE CREEK Delta
LAKE DALLAS Denton
LAKE JACKSON Brazoria
LAKEVIEW Hall
LAMESA Dawson
LAMPASAS (76550) Lampasas(98), Burnet(2)

LANCASTER (75146) Dallas(99), Ellis(1)
LANCASTER Dallas
LANE CITY Wharton
LANEVILLE Rusk
LANGTRY Val Verde
LAREDO Webb
LARUE Henderson
LASARA Willacy
LATEXO Houston
LAUGHLIN A F B Val Verde
LAVON Collin
LAWN (79530) Taylor(95), Runnels(5)
LAZBUDDIE Parmer
LEAGUE CITY Galveston
LEAKEY Real
LEANDER (78641) Travis(67), Williamson(33)
LEANDER Travis
LEANDER Williamson
LEDBETTER (78946) Fayette(73), Lee(13), Washington(13)
LEESBURG (75451) Camp(92), Upshur(5), Wood(3)
LEESVILLE Gonzales
LEFORS Gray
LEGGETT Polk
LELIA LAKE Donley
LEMING Atascosa
LENORAH Martin
LEON JUNCTION Coryell
LEONA (75850) Leon(99), Madison(1)
LEONARD (75452) Fannin(49), Collin(35), Hunt(16)
LEROY McLennan
LEVELLAND Hockley
LEWISVILLE Denton
LEXINGTON (78947) Lee(98), Milam(2)
LIBERTY Liberty
LIBERTY HILL (78642) Williamson(98), Burnet(2)
LILLIAN Johnson
LINCOLN Lee
LINDALE Smith
LINDEN Cass
LINDSAY Cooke
LINGLEVILLE Erath
LINN (78563) Hidalgo(78), Starr(22)
LIPAN (76462) Hood(56), Palo Pinto(24), Parker(20)
LIPSCOMB Lipscomb
LISSIE Wharton
LITTLE ELM Denton
LITTLE RIVER Bell
LITTLEFIELD (79339) Lamb(97), Hockley(3)
LIVERPOOL Brazoria
LIVINGSTON Polk
LLANO Llano
LOCKHART Caldwell
LOCKNEY (79241) Floyd(97), Swisher(2)
LODI Marion
LOHN McCulloch
LOLITA Jackson
LOMETA (76853) Lampasas(92), Mills(6), San Saba(2)
LONDON (76854) Kimble(76), Menard(20), Mason(4)
LONE OAK (75453) Hunt(79), Rains(20), Hopkins(2)
LONE STAR (75668) Morris(64), Marion(35), Cass(1)
LONG BRANCH (75669) Panola(95), Rusk(5)
LONG MOTT Calhoun
LONGVIEW (75601) Gregg(93), Harrison(7)
LONGVIEW (75602) Gregg(86), Harrison(14)
LONGVIEW (75603) Gregg(86), Rusk(14)
LONGVIEW (75605) Gregg(99), Harrison(1)
LONGVIEW Gregg

LOOP Gaines
LOPENO Zapata
LORAINE (79532) Mitchell(94), Scurry(4), Nolan(3)
LORENA (76655) McLennan(99), Falls(1)
LORENZO (79343) Crosby(68), Lubbock(32)
LOS EBANOS Hidalgo
LOS FRESNOS Cameron
LOS INDIOS Cameron
LOTT (76656) Falls(99), Bell(1)
LOUISE (77455) Wharton(84), Jackson(15), Colorado(1)
LOVELADY (75851) Houston(96), Trinity(4)
LOVING Young
LOWAKE Concho
LOZANO Cameron
LUBBOCK (79407) Lubbock(94), Hockley(6)
LUBBOCK Lubbock
LUEDERS (79533) Jones(57), Shackelford(39), Haskell(5)
LUFKIN Angelina
LULING (78648) Caldwell(93), Guadalupe(7)
LUMBERTON Hardin
LYFORD (78569) Willacy(93), Hidalgo(7)
LYONS Burleson
LYTLE (78052) Atascosa(68), Medina(23), Bexar(9)
MABANK (75147) Henderson(70), Kaufman(28), Van Zandt(3)
MACDONA Bexar
MADISONVILLE Madison
MAGNOLIA (77355) Montgomery(98), Waller(2)
MAGNOLIA Montgomery
MAGNOLIA SPRINGS Bowie
MAGNOLIA SPRINGS Jasper
MALAKOFF Henderson
MALONE Hill
MANCHACA (78652) Travis(71), Hays(30)
MANOR Travis
MANSFIELD (76063) Tarrant(91), Johnson(9)
MANVEL Brazoria
MAPLE Bailey
MARATHON Brewster
MARBLE FALLS (78654) Burnet(56), Blanco(38), Llano(5), Travis(1)
MARBLE FALLS Burnet
MARFA Presidio
MARIETTA Cass
MARION (78124) Guadalupe(99), Bexar(1)
MARKHAM Matagorda
MARLIN Falls
MARQUEZ Leon
MARSHALL Harrison
MART (76664) McLennan(92), Limestone(7), Falls(1)
MARTINDALE (78655) Caldwell(64), Guadalupe(37)
MARTINSVILLE Nacogdoches
MARYNEAL Nolan
MASON Mason
MASTERSON Moore
MATADOR Motley
MATAGORDA Matagorda
MATHIS (78368) San Patricio(97), Live Oak(3)
MAUD Bowie
MAURICEVILLE Orange
MAXWELL (78656) Caldwell(94), Hays(6)
MAY Brown
MAYDELLE Cherokee
MAYPEARL Ellis
MAYSFIELD Milam
MC CAMEY Upton
MC CAULLEY Fisher
MC COY Atascosa
MC DADE Bastrop

MC GREGOR (76657) McLennan(98), Coryell(2)
MC KINNEY Collin
MC LEOD Cass
MC NEIL Travis
MC QUEENEY Guadalupe
MCADOO (79243) Dickens(54), Crosby(46)
MCALLEN Hidalgo
MCFADDIN Victoria
MCLEAN (79057) Gray(73), Wheeler(21), Donley(6)
MEADOW (79345) Terry(93), Lynn(6), Taylor(1)
MEDINA (78055) Bandera(98), Kerr(2)
MEGARGEL Archer
MELISSA Collin
MELVIN (76858) McCulloch(83), Concho(17)
MEMPHIS (79245) Hall(99), Collingsworth(1)
MENARD (76859) Menard(87), Kimble(14)
MENTONE Loving
MERCEDES Hidalgo
MERETA Tom Green
MERIDIAN Bosque
MERIT Hunt
MERKEL (79536) Taylor(76), Jones(24)
MERTENS (76666) Hill(89), Navarro(11)
MERTZON Irion
MESQUITE Dallas
MEXIA (76667) Limestone(97), Freestone(3)
MEYERSVILLE (77974) De Witt(70), Victoria(30)
MIAMI (79059) Roberts(84), Gray(16)
MICO Medina
MIDFIELD Matagorda
MIDKIFF Upton
MIDLAND Midland
MIDLOTHIAN Ellis
MIDWAY (75852) Madison(82), Walker(12), Leon(6)
MILAM Sabine
MILANO (76556) Milam(98), Burleson(2)
MILES (76861) Tom Green(51), Runnels(47), Concho(2)
MILFORD (76670) Ellis(71), Navarro(25), Hill(4)
MILLERSVIEW Concho
MILLICAN Brazos
MILLSAP (76066) Parker(94), Palo Pinto(6)
MINDEN Rusk
MINEOLA (75773) Wood(86), Smith(14)
MINERAL Bee
MINERAL WELLS (76067) Palo Pinto(97), Parker(3)
MINERAL WELLS Palo Pinto
MINGUS (76463) Erath(60), Palo Pinto(39), Eastland(2)
MIRANDO CITY Webb
MISSION Hidalgo
MISSOURI CITY (77489) Fort Bend(96), Harris(4)
MISSOURI CITY Fort Bend
MOBEETIE (79061) Wheeler(87), Gray(9), Hemphill(4)
MONAHANS Ward
MONT BELVIEU Chambers
MONTAGUE Montague
MONTALBA (75853) Anderson(95), Henderson(5)
MONTGOMERY Montgomery
MOODY (76557) McLennan(68), Bell(31), Coryell(2)
MOORE (78057) Frio(87), Medina(13)
MORAN (76464) Shackelford(82), Stephens(11), Callahan(7)
MORGAN Bosque
MORGAN MILL Erath
MORSE (79062) Hutchinson(71), Hansford(21), Bee(7)
MORTON (79346) Cochran(98), Bailey(2)

MOSCOW Polk
MOULTON Lavaca
MOUND Coryell
MOUNT CALM (76673) Hill(65), Limestone(25), McLennan(10)
MOUNT ENTERPRISE Rusk
MOUNT PLEASANT Titus
MOUNT VERNON Franklin
MOUNTAIN HOME Kerr
MUENSTER Cooke
MULDOON Fayette
MULESHOE (79347) Bailey(92), Parmer(5), Lamb(2)
MULLIN Mills
MUMFORD Robertson
MUNDAY (76371) Knox(98), Haskell(2)
MURCHISON (75778) Henderson(85), Van Zandt(15)
MYRA Cooke
NACOGDOCHES Nacogdoches
NADA Colorado
NAPLES (75568) Morris(63), Cass(37)
NASH Bowie
NATALIA Medina
NAVAL AIR STATION/ JRB Tarrant
NAVASOTA (77868) Grimes(96), Brazos(3)
NAVASOTA Brazos
NAZARETH Castro
NECHES Anderson
NEDERLAND Jefferson
NEEDVILLE Fort Bend
NEMO (76070) Somervell(84), Johnson(16)
NEVADA Collin
NEW BADEN Robertson
NEW BOSTON Bowie
NEW BRAUNFELS (78130) Comal(82), Guadalupe(18)
NEW BRAUNFELS Comal
NEW CANEY Montgomery
NEW DEAL Lubbock
NEW HOME Lynn
NEW LONDON Rusk
NEW SUMMERFIELD Cherokee
NEW ULM (78950) Colorado(98), Austin(3)
NEW WAVERLY (77358) Walker(49), San Jacinto(37), Montgomery(14)
NEWARK Wise
NEWCASTLE (76372) Young(76), Throckmorton(24)
NEWGULF Wharton
NEWPORT Clay
NEWTON (75966) Newton(89), Jasper(11)
NIXON (78140) Gonzales(92), Wilson(5), Guadalupe(3)
NOCONA Montague
NOLAN Nolan
NOLANVILLE Bell
NOME Jefferson
NORDHEIM De Witt
NORMANGEE (77871) Madison(91), Leon(10)
NORMANNA Bee
NORTH HOUSTON Harris
NORTH RICHLAND HILLS Tarrant
NORTH ZULCH (77872) Madison(98), Grimes(2)
NORTON Runnels
NOTREES Ector
NOVICE (79538) Runnels(73), Coleman(27)
NURSERY Victoria
O BRIEN Haskell
OAKHURST San Jacinto
OAKLAND Colorado
OAKVILLE Live Oak
OAKWOOD (75855) Leon(57), Freestone(43)
ODELL Wilbarger
ODEM San Patricio
ODESSA (79765) Ector(54), Midland(46)
ODESSA (79766) Ector(91), Midland(9)
ODESSA Ector

ODONNELL (79351) Dawson(40), Lynn(37), Borden(21), Terry(1)
OGLESBY (76561) Coryell(84), McLennan(16)
OILTON Webb
OKLAUNION Wilbarger
OLD GLORY (79540) Stonewall(96), Haskell(4)
OLD OCEAN Brazoria
OLDEN Eastland
OLMITO Cameron
OLNEY (76374) Young(97), Archer(2)
OLTON (79064) Lamb(82), Hale(18)
OMAHA (75571) Morris(99), Titus(1)
ONALASKA Polk
ORANGE (77632) Orange(98), Newton(2)
ORANGE Orange
ORANGE GROVE Jim Wells
ORANGEFIELD Orange
ORCHARD Fort Bend
ORE CITY (75683) Upshur(59), Marion(40), Harrison(1)
ORLA Reeves
OTTINE Gonzales
OTTO Falls
OVALO (79541) Taylor(90), Callahan(10)
OVERTON (75684) Rusk(79), Smith(21)
OZONA (76943) Crockett(79), Val Verde(21)
PADUCAH (79248) Cottle(85), King(12), Foard(4)
PAIGE (78659) Lee(64), Bastrop(36)
PAINT ROCK Concho
PALACIOS Matagorda
PALESTINE Anderson
PALMER Ellis
PALO PINTO Palo Pinto
PALUXY Hood
PAMPA Gray
PANDORA Wilson
PANHANDLE Carson
PANNA MARIA Karnes
PANOLA Panola
PARADISE Wise
PARIS Lamar
PASADENA Harris
PATTISON Waller
PATTONVILLE Lamar
PAWNEE Bee
PEACOCK Stonewall
PEAR VALLEY McCulloch
PEARLAND (77581) Brazoria(96), Harris(4)
PEARLAND Brazoria
PEARSALL Frio
PEASTER Parker
PECAN GAP Delta
PECOS Reeves
PEGGY Atascosa
PENDLETON Bell
PENELOPE Hill
PENITAS Hidalgo
PENNINGTON (75856) Trinity(65), Houston(35)
PENWELL Ector
PEP (79353) Hockley(86), Cochran(14)
PERRIN (76486) Parker(38), Palo Pinto(38), Jack(24)
PERRY Falls
PERRYTON Ochiltree
PETERSBURG (79250) Hale(48), Lubbock(23), Floyd(18), Crosby(11)
PETROLIA Clay
PETTUS Bee
PETTY Lamar
PFLUGERVILLE Travis
PHARR Hidalgo
PICKTON Hopkins
PIERCE Wharton
PILOT POINT (76258) Denton(96), Grayson(4)
PINEHURST Montgomery
PINELAND Sabine

PIPE CREEK Bandera
PITTSBURG (75686) Camp(88), Titus(6), Upshur(5), Morris(1)
PLACEDO Victoria
PLAINS Yoakum
PLAINVIEW Hale
PLANO (75093) Collin(98), Denton(2)
PLANO Collin
PLANTERSVILLE (77363) Grimes(97), Waller(3)
PLEASANTON Atascosa
PLEDGER Matagorda
PLUM Fayette
POINT Rains
POINT COMFORT Calhoun
POINTBLANK San Jacinto
POLLOK Angelina
PONDER (76259) Denton(99), Wise(1)
PONTOTOC (76869) Mason(50), Llano(25), San Saba(25)
POOLVILLE (76487) Parker(75), Wise(23), Jack(3)
PORT ARANSAS Nueces
PORT ARTHUR Jefferson
PORT BOLIVAR Galveston
PORT ISABEL Cameron
PORT LAVACA Calhoun
PORT MANSFIELD Willacy
PORT NECHES Jefferson
PORT O CONNOR Calhoun
PORTER Montgomery
PORTLAND San Patricio
POST (79356) Garza(96), Lynn(3), Crosby(1)
POTEET Atascosa
POTH Wilson
POTTSBORO Grayson
POTTSVILLE Hamilton
POWDERLY Lamar
POWELL Navarro
POYNOR Henderson
PRAIRIE HILL Limestone
PRAIRIE LEA Caldwell
PRAIRIE VIEW Waller
PREMONT (78375) Jim Wells(98), Duval(2)
PRESIDIO Presidio
PRICE Rusk
PRIDDY Mills
PRINCETON Collin
PROCTOR Comanche
PROGRESO Hidalgo
PROSPER (75078) Collin(97), Denton(3)
PURDON Navarro
PURMELA (76566) Coryell(92), Hamilton(8)
PUTNAM Callahan
PYOTE Ward
QUAIL Collingsworth
QUANAH Hardeman
QUEEN CITY Cass
QUEMADO (78877) Maverick(98), Kinney(2)
QUINLAN (75474) Hunt(97), Kaufman(3)
QUITAQUE (79255) Briscoe(52), Motley(29), Floyd(17), Hall(2)
QUITMAN Wood
RAINBOW Somervell
RALLS Crosby
RANDOLPH Fannin
RANGER (76470) Eastland(86), Stephens(14)
RANKIN Upton
RANSOM CANYON Lubbock
RATCLIFF Houston
RAVENNA Fannin
RAYMONDVILLE Willacy
RAYWOOD Liberty
REAGAN Falls
REALITOS Duval
RED OAK (75154) Ellis(82), Dallas(18)
RED ROCK Bastrop
REDFORD Presidio

REDWATER Bowie
REESE AIR FORCE BASE Lubbock
REFUGIO Refugio
REKLAW (75784) Rusk(52), Cherokee(48)
RHOME Wise
RICE (75155) Navarro(92), Ellis(9)
RICHARDS (77873) Montgomery(94), Grimes(6)
RICHARDSON (75080) Dallas(86), Collin(14)
RICHARDSON (75082) Collin(78), Dallas(22)
RICHARDSON Dallas
RICHLAND Navarro
RICHLAND SPRINGS (76871) San Saba(94), McCulloch(6)
RICHMOND Fort Bend
RIESEL (76682) McLennan(94), Falls(6)
RINGGOLD (76261) Montague(85), Clay(15)
RIO FRIO Real
RIO GRANDE CITY Starr
RIO HONDO Cameron
RIO MEDINA Medina
RIO VISTA (76093) Johnson(96), Hill(4)
RISING STAR (76471) Eastland(87), Brown(10), Comanche(3)
RIVERSIDE Walker
RIVIERA Kleberg
ROANOKE (76262) Denton(58), Tarrant(42)
ROANOKE Denton
ROANS PRAIRIE Grimes
ROARING SPRINGS (79256) Motley(55), Dickens(45)
ROBERT LEE (76945) Coke(84), Tom Green(16)
ROBSTOWN Nueces
ROBY Fisher
ROCHELLE McCulloch
ROCHESTER Haskell
ROCK ISLAND Colorado
ROCKDALE Milam
ROCKLAND Tyler
ROCKPORT Aransas
ROCKSPRINGS Edwards
ROCKWALL (75087) Rockwall(98), Collin(2)
ROCKWOOD Coleman
ROGERS (76569) Bell(94), Milam(6)
ROMA Starr
ROMAYOR Liberty
ROOSEVELT Kimble
ROPESVILLE (79358) Hockley(82), Lubbock(18)
ROSANKY (78953) Bastrop(80), Caldwell(20)
ROSCOE (79545) Nolan(93), Scurry(4), Fisher(3)
ROSEBUD (76570) Falls(87), Milam(11), Bell(2)
ROSENBERG Fort Bend
ROSHARON (77583) Brazoria(77), Fort Bend(23)
ROSS McLennan
ROSSER Kaufman
ROSSTON Cooke
ROTAN (79546) Fisher(98), Stonewall(2)
ROUND MOUNTAIN Blanco
ROUND ROCK (78664) Williamson(98), Travis(2)
ROUND ROCK Williamson
ROUND TOP (78954) Fayette(96), Austin(4)
ROUND TOP Fayette
ROWENA (76875) Runnels(97), Concho(3)
ROWLETT (75088) Dallas(90), Rockwall(10)
ROWLETT Dallas
ROXTON Lamar
ROYALTY Ward
ROYSE CITY (75189) Hunt(56), Collin(45)

RULE (79547) Haskell(96), Stonewall(4)
RULE Haskell
RUNGE (78151) Karnes(93), De Witt(5), Goliad(2)
RUSK Cherokee
RYE Liberty
SABINAL Uvalde
SABINE PASS Jefferson
SACUL Nacogdoches
SADLER Grayson
SAINT HEDWIG Bexar
SAINT JO (76265) Montague(97), Cooke(3)
SALADO Bell
SALINENO Starr
SALT FLAT Hudspeth
SALTILLO Hopkins
SAMNORWOOD Collingsworth
SAN ANGELO (76904) Tom Green(99), Irion(1)
SAN ANGELO Tom Green
SAN ANTONIO (78223) Bexar(95), Wilson(5)
SAN ANTONIO (78253) Bexar(90), Medina(10)
SAN ANTONIO (78264) Bexar(94), Atascosa(6)
SAN ANTONIO (78266) Comal(95), Bexar(5)
SAN ANTONIO Bexar
SAN AUGUSTINE San Augustine
SAN BENITO Cameron
SAN DIEGO (78384) Duval(81), Jim Wells(19)
SAN ELIZARIO El Paso
SAN FELIPE Austin
SAN ISIDRO Starr
SAN JUAN Hidalgo
SAN MARCOS (78666) Hays(93), Guadalupe(6)
SAN MARCOS Hays
SAN PERLITA Willacy
SAN SABA San Saba
SAN YGNACIO Zapata
SANDERSON Terrell
SANDIA (78383) Jim Wells(49), Nueces(40), Live Oak(11)
SANDY Blanco
SANFORD Hutchinson
SANGER Denton
SANTA ANNA Coleman
SANTA ELENA Starr
SANTA FE Galveston
SANTA MARIA Cameron
SANTA ROSA Cameron
SANTO Palo Pinto
SARAGOSA Reeves
SARATOGA Hardin
SARITA Kenedy
SATIN Falls
SAVOY Fannin
SCHERTZ (78154) Guadalupe(90), Bexar(8), Comal(2)
SCHULENBURG (78956) Fayette(95), Lavaca(5)
SCHWERTNER Williamson
SCOTLAND Archer
SCOTTSVILLE Harrison
SCROGGINS (75480) Franklin(98), Wood(2)
SCURRY Kaufman
SEABROOK Harris
SEADRIFT Calhoun
SEAGOVILLE (75159) Dallas(86), Kaufman(14)
SEAGRAVES (79359) Gaines(77), Yoakum(12), Terry(11)
SEALY Austin
SEBASTIAN Willacy
SEGUIN Guadalupe
SELMAN CITY Rusk
SEMINOLE Gaines
SEYMOUR (76380) Baylor(98), Knox(2)

SHAFTER Presidio
SHALLOWATER (79363) Lubbock(94), Hockley(5), Hale(1)
SHAMROCK (79079) Wheeler(95), Collingsworth(6)
SHAMROCK Wheeler
SHEFFIELD Pecos
SHELBYVILLE Shelby
SHEPHERD San Jacinto
SHEPPARD AFB Wichita
SHERIDAN Colorado
SHERMAN Grayson
SHINER (77984) Lavaca(91), Gonzales(9)
SHIRO (77876) Grimes(80), Walker(20)
SIDNEY Comanche
SIERRA BLANCA Hudspeth
SILSBEE (99999) Hardin(99), Tyler(1)
SILVER Coke
SILVERTON (79257) Briscoe(97), Swisher(2), Floyd(1)
SIMMS Bowie
SIMONTON Fort Bend
SINTON (78387) San Patricio(94), Bee(6)
SKELLYTOWN (79080) Hutchinson(68), Carson(33)
SKIDMORE Bee
SLATON (79364) Lubbock(96), Lynn(4)
SLIDELL Wise
SMILEY Gonzales
SMITHVILLE (78957) Bastrop(56), Fayette(44)
SMYER Hockley
SNOOK Burleson
SNYDER Scurry
SOMERSET (78069) Atascosa(74), Bexar(26)
SOMERVILLE Burleson
SONORA Sutton
SOUR LAKE Hardin
SOUTH BEND Young
SOUTH HOUSTON Harris
SOUTH PADRE ISLAND Cameron
SOUTH PLAINS Floyd
SOUTHLAKE Tarrant
SOUTHLAND Garza
SOUTHMAYD Grayson
SPADE Lamb
SPEAKS Lavaca
SPEARMAN (79081) Hansford(97), Hutchinson(2), Ochiltree(1)
SPICEWOOD (78669) Travis(95), Burnet(5)
SPLENDORA (77372) Montgomery(90), Liberty(10)
SPRING Harris
SPRING Montgomery
SPRING BRANCH Comal
SPRINGLAKE (79082) Lamb(88), Castro(12)
SPRINGTOWN (76082) Parker(93), Wise(7)
SPUR (79370) Dickens(94), Crosby(5), Kent(1)
SPURGER (77660) Tyler(96), Hardin(4)
STAFFORD (77477) Fort Bend(89), Harris(11)
STAFFORD Fort Bend
STAMFORD (79503) Jones(92), Haskell(8)
STAMFORD (79553) Jones(94), Haskell(6)
STANTON (79782) Martin(91), Glasscock(9)
STAPLES Guadalupe
STAR Mills
STEPHENVILLE Erath
STERLING CITY (76951) Sterling(97), Glasscock(3)
STINNETT (79083) Hutchinson(77), Moore(23)
STOCKDALE Wilson
STONEWALL (78671) Gillespie(99), Blanco(1)
STOWELL Chambers

STRATFORD (79084) Sherman(96), Dallam(4)
STRAWN (76475) Palo Pinto(79), Eastland(18), Stephens(4)
STREETMAN (75859) Freestone(63), Navarro(37)
SUBLIME Lavaca
SUDAN (79371) Lamb(71), Bailey(29)
SUGAR LAND Fort Bend
SULLIVAN CITY Hidalgo
SULPHUR BLUFF Hopkins
SULPHUR SPRINGS Hopkins
SUMMERFIELD (79085) Castro(79), Parmer(14), Oldham(7)
SUMNER Lamar
SUNDOWN Hockley
SUNNYVALE Dallas
SUNRAY (79086) Moore(69), Sherman(31)
SUNSET (76270) Wise(73), Montague(27)
SUTHERLAND SPRINGS Wilson
SWEENY (77480) Matagorda(91), Brazoria(9)
SWEET HOME Lavaca
SWEETWATER (79556) Nolan(95), Fisher(5)
SYLVESTER (79560) Fisher(93), Jones(7)
TAFT San Patricio
TAHOKA Lynn
TALCO (75487) Franklin(79), Titus(21)
TALPA Coleman
TARPLEY Bandera
TARZAN Martin
TATUM Rusk
TAYLOR Williamson
TEAGUE Freestone
TEHUACANA Limestone
TELEGRAPH (76883) Edwards(67), Kimble(33)
TELEPHONE Fannin
TELFERNER Lavaca
TELL (79259) Childress(63), Hall(37)
TEMPLE Bell
TENAHA (75974) Shelby(65), Panola(35)
TENNESSEE COLONY Anderson
TENNYSON Coke
TERLINGUA Brewster
TERRELL (75160) Kaufman(91), Hunt(9)
TERRELL Kaufman
TEXARKANA Bowie
TEXARKANA Miller
TEXAS CITY Galveston
TEXLINE Dallam
THE COLONY Denton
THICKET Hardin
THOMASTON De Witt
THOMPSONS Fort Bend
THORNDALE (76577) Milam(90), Williamson(10)
THORNTON (76687) Limestone(81), Robertson(19)
THRALL (76578) Williamson(99), Milam(1)
THREE RIVERS Live Oak
THROCKMORTON Throckmorton
TILDEN McMullen
TIMPSON (75975) Shelby(91), Panola(5), Rusk(4)
TIOGA (76271) Grayson(82), Cooke(19)
TIVOLI (77990) Refugio(86), Calhoun(15)
TOKIO (79376) Yoakum(71), Terry(29)
TOLAR Hood
TOM BEAN Grayson
TOMBALL Harris
TORNILLO El Paso
TOW Llano
TOYAH Reeves
TOYAHVALE Reeves
TRENT (79561) Taylor(43), Nolan(36), Fisher(11), Jones(10)
TRENTON Fannin
TRINIDAD Henderson
TRINITY (75862) Trinity(92), Walker(6), Houston(2)

TROUP (75789) Smith(87), Cherokee(13)
TROY (76579) Bell(99), Falls(1)
TRUSCOTT Knox
TULETA Bee
TULIA Swisher
TURKEY (79261) Hall(91), Briscoe(9)
TUSCOLA Taylor
TYE Taylor
TYLER Smith
TYNAN Bee
UMBARGER Randall
UNIVERSAL CITY Bexar
UTOPIA Uvalde
UVALDE Uvalde
VALENTINE (79854) Presidio(53), Jeff Davis(47)
VALERA Coleman
VALLEY MILLS (76689) McLennan(49), Bosque(36), Coryell(16)
VALLEY SPRING Llano
VALLEY VIEW (76272) Cooke(99), Denton(1)
VAN (75790) Van Zandt(87), Smith(13)
VAN ALSTYNE (75495) Grayson(60), Collin(40)
VAN HORN Culberson
VAN VLECK Matagorda
VANCOURT (76955) Tom Green(88), Concho(12)
VANDERBILT Jackson
VANDERPOOL Bandera
VEGA (79092) Deaf Smith(53), Oldham(47)
VENUS (76084) Johnson(67), Ellis(33)
VERA (76383) Knox(91), Baylor(9)
VERIBEST Tom Green
VERNON Wilbarger
VICTORIA (77905) Victoria(96), Goliad(4)
VICTORIA Victoria
VIDOR Orange
VILLAGE MILLS Hardin
VOCA McCulloch
VON ORMY (78073) Bexar(72), Atascosa(28)
VOSS Coleman
VOTAW Hardin
VOTH Jefferson
WACO McLennan
WADSWORTH Matagorda
WAELDER (78959) Gonzales(48), Fayette(43), Bastrop(6), Caldwell(3)
WAKA Ochiltree
WALBURG Williamson
WALL Tom Green
WALLER (77484) Waller(64), Harris(35), Grimes(2)
WALLIS (77485) Austin(52), Fort Bend(48)
WALLISVILLE Chambers
WALNUT SPRINGS (76690) Bosque(88), Somervell(10), Erath(2)
WARDA Fayette
WARING Kendall
WARREN Tyler
WASHINGTON Washington
WASKOM Harrison
WATER VALLEY Tom Green
WAXAHACHIE Ellis
WAYSIDE Armstrong
WEATHERFORD (76087) Parker(96), Hood(4)
WEATHERFORD Parker
WEBSTER Harris
WEESATCHE Goliad
WEIMAR Colorado
WEINERT Haskell
WEIR Williamson
WELCH (79377) Dawson(54), Terry(46)
WELLBORN Brazos
WELLINGTON Collingsworth
WELLMAN Terry
WELLS Cherokee
WESLACO Hidalgo
WEST (76691) McLennan(99), Hill(1)

WEST COLUMBIA Brazoria
WEST POINT Fayette
WESTBROOK Mitchell
WESTHOFF De Witt
WESTMINSTER Collin
WESTON Collin
WHARTON Wharton
WHEELER Wheeler
WHEELOCK (77882) Robertson(80), Brazos(20)
WHITE DEER (79097) Carson(90), Gray(10)
WHITE OAK Gregg
WHITEFACE Cochran
WHITEHOUSE Smith
WHITESBORO (76273) Grayson(79), Cooke(21)
WHITEWRIGHT (75491) Grayson(96), Fannin(4)
WHITHARRAL Hockley
WHITNEY Hill
WHITSETT Live Oak
WHITT (76490) Parker(55), Palo Pinto(46)
WHON Coleman
WICHITA FALLS (76301) Wichita(94), Clay(5), Archer(1)
WICHITA FALLS (76302) Wichita(84), Clay(9), Archer(7)
WICHITA FALLS (76308) Wichita(92), Archer(8)
WICHITA FALLS Wichita
WICKETT Ward
WIERGATE Newton
WILDORADO (79098) Deaf Smith(55), Oldham(26), Randall(13), Potter(5)
WILLIS Montgomery
WILLOW CITY Gillespie
WILLS POINT (75169) Van Zandt(70), Hunt(20), Kaufman(10)
WILMER Dallas
WILSON Lynn
WIMBERLEY Hays
WINCHESTER Fayette
WINDOM Fannin
WINDTHORST (76389) Archer(62), Clay(29), Jack(9)
WINFIELD Titus
WINGATE (79566) Taylor(58), Runnels(38), Nolan(4)
WINK Winkler
WINNIE (77665) Chambers(87), Jefferson(13)
WINNSBORO (75494) Wood(82), Franklin(14), Hopkins(3)
WINONA Smith
WINTERS (79567) Runnels(97), Taylor(3)
WODEN Nacogdoches
WOLFE CITY Hunt
WOLFFORTH (79382) Lubbock(98), Hockley(2)
WOODLAKE Trinity
WOODLAWN Harrison
WOODSBORO Refugio
WOODSON (76491) Throckmorton(96), Stephens(5)
WOODVILLE Tyler
WOODWAY McLennan
WORTHAM (76693) Freestone(77), Navarro(15), Limestone(8)
WRIGHTSBORO Gonzales
WYLIE (75098) Collin(87), Dallas(11), Rockwall(2)
YANCEY Medina
YANTIS Wood
YOAKUM (77995) Lavaca(55), De Witt(43), Victoria(2)
YORKTOWN De Witt
ZAPATA Zapata
ZAVALLA (75980) Angelina(99), Jasper(1)
ZEPHYR (76890) Brown(97), Mills(2)

ZIP/City Cross Reference

ZIP Range	City	ZIP Range	City	ZIP Range	City	ZIP Range	City
73301-73344	AUSTIN	75158-75158	SCURRY	75482-75483	SULPHUR SPRINGS	75692-75692	WASKOM
75001-75001	ADDISON	75159-75159	SEAGOVILLE	75485-75485	WESTMINSTER	75693-75693	WHITE OAK
75002-75002	ALLEN	75160-75161	TERRELL	75486-75486	SUMNER	75694-75694	WOODLAWN
75006-75008	CARROLLTON	75163-75163	TRINIDAD	75487-75487	TALCO	75701-75713	TYLER
75009-75009	CELINA	75164-75164	JOSEPHINE	75488-75488	TELEPHONE	75750-75750	ARP
75010-75011	CARROLLTON	75165-75165	WAXAHACHIE	75489-75489	TOM BEAN	75751-75751	ATHENS
75013-75013	ALLEN	75166-75166	LAVON	75490-75490	TRENTON	75754-75754	BEN WHEELER
75014-75017	IRVING	75167-75168	WAXAHACHIE	75491-75491	WHITEWRIGHT	75755-75755	BIG SANDY
75019-75019	COPPELL	75169-75169	WILLS POINT	75492-75492	WINDOM	75756-75756	BROWNSBORO
75020-75021	DENISON	75172-75172	WILMER	75493-75493	WINFIELD	75757-75757	BULLARD
75023-75026	PLANO	75173-75173	NEVADA	75494-75494	WINNSBORO	75758-75758	CHANDLER
75027-75028	FLOWER MOUND	75180-75181	MESQUITE	75495-75495	VAN ALSTYNE	75759-75759	CUNEY
75029-75029	LEWISVILLE	75182-75182	SUNNYVALE	75496-75496	WOLFE CITY	75760-75760	CUSHING
75030-75030	ROWLETT	75185-75187	MESQUITE	75497-75497	YANTIS	75762-75762	FLINT
75034-75035	FRISCO	75189-75189	ROYSE CITY	75501-75507	TEXARKANA	75763-75763	FRANKSTON
75037-75039	IRVING	75201-75398	DALLAS	75550-75550	ANNONA	75764-75764	GALLATIN
75040-75049	GARLAND	75401-75404	GREENVILLE	75551-75551	ATLANTA	75765-75765	HAWKINS
75050-75054	GRAND PRAIRIE	75407-75407	PRINCETON	75554-75554	AVERY	75766-75766	JACKSONVILLE
75056-75056	THE COLONY	75409-75409	ANNA	75555-75555	BIVINS	75770-75770	LARUE
75057-75057	LEWISVILLE	75410-75410	ALBA	75556-75556	BLOOMBURG	75771-75771	LINDALE
75058-75058	GUNTER	75411-75411	ARTHUR CITY	75558-75558	COOKVILLE	75772-75772	MAYDELLE
75060-75063	IRVING	75412-75412	BAGWELL	75559-75559	DE KALB	75773-75773	MINEOLA
75065-75065	LAKE DALLAS	75413-75413	BAILEY	75560-75560	DOUGLASSVILLE	75778-75778	MURCHISON
75067-75067	LEWISVILLE	75414-75414	BELLS	75561-75561	HOOKS	75779-75779	NECHES
75068-75068	LITTLE ELM	75415-75415	BEN FRANKLIN	75562-75562	KILDARE	75780-75780	NEW SUMMERFIELD
75069-75070	MC KINNEY	75416-75416	BLOSSOM	75563-75563	LINDEN	75782-75782	POYNOR
75074-75075	PLANO	75417-75417	BOGATA	75564-75564	LODI	75783-75783	QUITMAN
75076-75076	POTTSBORO	75418-75418	BONHAM	75565-75565	MC LEOD	75784-75784	REKLAW
75078-75078	PROSPER	75420-75420	BRASHEAR	75566-75566	MARIETTA	75785-75785	RUSK
75080-75083	RICHARDSON	75421-75421	BROOKSTON	75567-75567	MAUD	75788-75788	SACUL
75084-75084	IRVING	75422-75422	CAMPBELL	75568-75568	NAPLES	75789-75789	TROUP
75085-75085	RICHARDSON	75423-75423	CELESTE	75569-75569	NASH	75790-75790	VAN
75086-75086	PLANO	75424-75424	BLUE RIDGE	75570-75570	NEW BOSTON	75791-75791	WHITEHOUSE
75087-75087	ROCKWALL	75425-75425	CHICOTA	75571-75571	OMAHA	75792-75792	WINONA
75088-75088	ROWLETT	75426-75426	CLARKSVILLE	75572-75572	QUEEN CITY	75798-75799	TYLER
75090-75092	SHERMAN	75428-75429	COMMERCE	75573-75573	REDWATER	75801-75802	PALESTINE
75093-75094	PLANO	75431-75431	COMO	75574-75574	SIMMS	75831-75831	BUFFALO
75097-75097	WESTON	75432-75432	COOPER	75599-75599	TEXARKANA	75832-75832	CAYUGA
75098-75098	WYLIE	75433-75433	CUMBY	75601-75615	LONGVIEW	75833-75833	CENTERVILLE
75099-75099	COPPELL	75434-75434	CUNNINGHAM	75630-75630	AVINGER	75834-75834	CENTRALIA
75101-75101	BARDWELL	75435-75435	DEPORT	75631-75631	BECKVILLE	75835-75835	CROCKETT
75102-75102	BARRY	75436-75436	DETROIT	75633-75633	CARTHAGE	75838-75838	DONIE
75103-75103	CANTON	75437-75437	DIKE	75636-75636	CASON	75839-75839	ELKHART
75104-75104	CEDAR HILL	75438-75438	DODD CITY	75637-75637	CLAYTON	75840-75840	FAIRFIELD
75105-75105	CHATFIELD	75439-75439	ECTOR	75638-75638	DAINGERFIELD	75844-75844	GRAPELAND
75106-75106	CEDAR HILL	75440-75440	EMORY	75639-75639	DE BERRY	75845-75845	GROVETON
75110-75110	CORSICANA	75441-75441	ENLOE	75640-75640	DIANA	75846-75846	JEWETT
75114-75114	CRANDALL	75442-75442	FARMERSVILLE	75641-75641	EASTON	75847-75847	KENNARD
75115-75115	DE SOTO	75443-75443	GOBER	75642-75642	ELYSIAN FIELDS	75848-75848	KIRVIN
75116-75116	DUNCANVILLE	75444-75444	GOLDEN	75643-75643	GARY	75849-75849	LATEXO
75117-75117	EDGEWOOD	75446-75446	HONEY GROVE	75644-75644	GILMER	75850-75850	LEONA
75118-75118	ELMO	75447-75447	IVANHOE	75647-75647	GLADEWATER	75851-75851	LOVELADY
75119-75120	ENNIS	75448-75448	KLONDIKE	75650-75650	HALLSVILLE	75852-75852	MIDWAY
75121-75121	COPEVILLE	75449-75449	LADONIA	75651-75651	HARLETON	75853-75853	MONTALBA
75123-75123	DE SOTO	75450-75450	LAKE CREEK	75652-75654	HENDERSON	75855-75855	OAKWOOD
75124-75124	EUSTACE	75451-75451	LEESBURG	75656-75656	HUGHES SPRINGS	75856-75856	PENNINGTON
75125-75125	FERRIS	75452-75452	LEONARD	75657-75657	JEFFERSON	75858-75858	RATCLIFF
75126-75126	FORNEY	75453-75453	LONE OAK	75658-75658	JOINERVILLE	75859-75859	STREETMAN
75127-75127	FRUITVALE	75454-75454	MELISSA	75659-75659	JONESVILLE	75860-75860	TEAGUE
75132-75132	FATE	75455-75456	MOUNT PLEASANT	75660-75660	JUDSON	75861-75861	TENNESSEE COLONY
75134-75134	LANCASTER	75457-75457	MOUNT VERNON	75661-75661	KARNACK	75862-75862	TRINITY
75135-75135	CADDO MILLS	75458-75458	MERIT	75662-75663	KILGORE	75865-75865	WOODLAKE
75137-75138	DUNCANVILLE	75459-75459	HOWE	75666-75666	LAIRD HILL	75880-75880	TENNESSEE COLONY
75140-75140	GRAND SALINE	75460-75462	PARIS	75667-75667	LANEVILLE	75882-75882	PALESTINE
75141-75141	HUTCHINS	75468-75468	PATTONVILLE	75668-75668	LONE STAR	75884-75886	TENNESSEE COLONY
75142-75142	KAUFMAN	75469-75469	PECAN GAP	75669-75669	LONG BRANCH	75901-75915	LUFKIN
75143-75143	KEMP	75470-75470	PETTY	75670-75672	MARSHALL	75925-75925	ALTO
75144-75144	KERENS	75471-75471	PICKTON	75680-75680	MINDEN	75926-75926	APPLE SPRINGS
75146-75146	LANCASTER	75472-75472	POINT	75681-75681	MOUNT ENTERPRISE	75928-75928	BON WIER
75147-75147	MABANK	75473-75473	POWDERLY	75682-75682	NEW LONDON	75929-75929	BROADDUS
75148-75148	MALAKOFF	75474-75474	QUINLAN	75683-75683	ORE CITY	75930-75930	BRONSON
75149-75150	MESQUITE	75475-75475	RANDOLPH	75684-75684	OVERTON	75931-75931	BROOKELAND
75151-75151	CORSICANA	75476-75476	RAVENNA	75685-75685	PANOLA	75932-75932	BURKEVILLE
75152-75152	PALMER	75477-75477	ROXTON	75686-75686	PITTSBURG	75933-75933	CALL
75153-75153	POWELL	75478-75478	SALTILLO	75687-75687	PRICE	75934-75934	CAMDEN
75154-75154	RED OAK	75479-75479	SAVOY	75688-75688	SCOTTSVILLE	75935-75935	CENTER
75155-75155	RICE	75480-75480	SCROGGINS	75689-75689	SELMAN CITY	75936-75936	CHESTER
75157-75157	ROSSER	75481-75481	SULPHUR BLUFF	75691-75691	TATUM	75937-75937	CHIRENO

75938-75938	COLMESNEIL	76129-76179	FORT WORTH	76445-76445	DESDEMONA	76623-76623	AVALON
75939-75939	CORRIGAN	76180-76180	NORTH RICHLAND HILLS	76446-76446	DUBLIN	76624-76624	AXTELL
75941-75941	DIBOLL	76181-76181	FORT WORTH	76448-76448	EASTLAND	76626-76626	BLOOMING GROVE
75942-75942	DOUCETTE	76182-76182	NORTH RICHLAND HILLS	76449-76449	GRAFORD	76627-76627	BLUM
75943-75943	DOUGLASS	76185-76199	FORT WORTH	76450-76450	GRAHAM	76628-76628	BRANDON
75944-75944	ETOILE	76201-76208	DENTON	76452-76452	ENERGY	76629-76629	BREMOND
75946-75946	GARRISON	76225-76225	ALVORD	76453-76453	GORDON	76630-76630	BRUCEVILLE
75947-75947	GENEVA	76226-76226	ARGYLE	76454-76454	GORMAN	76631-76631	BYNUM
75948-75948	HEMPHILL	76227-76227	AUBREY	76455-76455	GUSTINE	76632-76632	CHILTON
75949-75949	HUNTINGTON	76228-76228	BELLEVUE	76457-76457	HICO	76633-76633	CHINA SPRING
75951-75951	JASPER	76230-76230	BOWIE	76458-76458	JACKSBORO	76634-76634	CLIFTON
75954-75954	JOAQUIN	76233-76233	COLLINSVILLE	76459-76459	JERMYN	76635-76635	COOLIDGE
75956-75956	KIRBYVILLE	76234-76234	DECATUR	76460-76460	LOVING	76636-76636	COVINGTON
75958-75958	MARTINSVILLE	76238-76238	ERA	76461-76461	LINGLEVILLE	76637-76637	CRANFILLS GAP
75959-75959	MILAM	76239-76239	FORESTBURG	76462-76462	LIPAN	76638-76638	CRAWFORD
75960-75960	MOSCOW	76240-76241	GAINESVILLE	76463-76463	MINGUS	76639-76639	DAWSON
75961-75964	NACOGDOCHES	76244-76244	KELLER	76464-76464	MORAN	76640-76640	ELM MOTT
75966-75966	NEWTON	76245-76245	GORDONVILLE	76465-76465	MORGAN MILL	76641-76641	FROST
75968-75968	PINELAND	76246-76246	GREENWOOD	76466-76466	OLDEN	76642-76642	GROESBECK
75969-75969	POLLOK	76247-76247	JUSTIN	76467-76467	PALUXY	76643-76643	HEWITT
75972-75972	SAN AUGUSTINE	76248-76248	KELLER	76468-76468	PROCTOR	76645-76645	HILLSBORO
75973-75973	SHELBYVILLE	76249-76249	KRUM	76469-76469	PUTNAM	76648-76648	HUBBARD
75974-75974	TENAHA	76250-76250	LINDSAY	76470-76470	RANGER	76649-76649	IREDELL
75975-75975	TIMPSON	76251-76251	MONTAGUE	76471-76471	RISING STAR	76650-76650	IRENE
75976-75976	WELLS	76252-76252	MUENSTER	76472-76472	SANTO	76651-76651	ITALY
75977-75977	WIERGATE	76253-76253	MYRA	76474-76474	SIDNEY	76652-76652	KOPPERL
75978-75978	WODEN	76255-76255	NOCONA	76475-76475	STRAWN	76653-76653	KOSSE
75979-75979	WOODVILLE	76258-76258	PILOT POINT	76476-76476	TOLAR	76654-76654	LEROY
75980-75980	ZAVALLA	76259-76259	PONDER	76481-76481	SOUTH BEND	76655-76655	LORENA
75990-75990	WOODVILLE	76261-76261	RINGGOLD	76483-76483	THROCKMORTON	76656-76656	LOTT
76001-76007	ARLINGTON	76262-76262	ROANOKE	76484-76484	PALO PINTO	76657-76657	MC GREGOR
76008-76008	ALEDO	76263-76263	ROSSTON	76485-76485	PEASTER	76660-76660	MALONE
76009-76009	ALVARADO	76264-76264	SADLER	76486-76486	PERRIN	76661-76661	MARLIN
76010-76019	ARLINGTON	76265-76265	SAINT JO	76487-76487	POOLVILLE	76664-76664	MART
76020-76020	AZLE	76266-76266	SANGER	76490-76490	WHITT	76665-76665	MERIDIAN
76021-76022	BEDFORD	76267-76267	SLIDELL	76491-76491	WOODSON	76666-76666	MERTENS
76023-76023	BOYD	76268-76268	SOUTHMAYD	76501-76508	TEMPLE	76667-76667	MEXIA
76028-76028	BURLESON	76270-76270	SUNSET	76511-76511	BARTLETT	76670-76670	MILFORD
76031-76033	CLEBURNE	76271-76271	TIOGA	76513-76513	BELTON	76671-76671	MORGAN
76034-76034	COLLEYVILLE	76272-76272	VALLEY VIEW	76518-76518	BUCKHOLTS	76673-76673	MOUNT CALM
76035-76035	CRESSON	76273-76273	WHITESBORO	76519-76519	BURLINGTON	76675-76675	OTTO
76036-76036	CROWLEY	76299-76299	ROANOKE	76520-76520	CAMERON	76676-76676	PENELOPE
76039-76040	EULESS	76301-76310	WICHITA FALLS	76522-76522	COPPERAS COVE	76677-76677	PERRY
76041-76041	FORRESTON	76311-76311	SHEPPARD AFB	76523-76523	DAVILLA	76678-76678	PRAIRIE HILL
76043-76043	GLEN ROSE	76351-76351	ARCHER CITY	76524-76524	EDDY	76679-76679	PURDON
76044-76044	GODLEY	76352-76352	BLUEGROVE	76525-76525	EVANT	76680-76680	REAGAN
76048-76049	GRANBURY	76354-76354	BURKBURNETT	76526-76526	FLAT	76681-76681	RICHLAND
76050-76050	GRANDVIEW	76357-76357	BYERS	76527-76527	FLORENCE	76682-76682	RIESEL
76051-76051	GRAPEVINE	76360-76360	ELECTRA	76528-76528	GATESVILLE	76684-76684	ROSS
76052-76052	HASLET	76363-76363	GOREE	76530-76530	GRANGER	76685-76685	SATIN
76053-76054	HURST	76364-76364	HARROLD	76531-76531	HAMILTON	76686-76686	TEHUACANA
76055-76055	ITASCA	76365-76365	HENRIETTA	76533-76533	HEIDENHEIMER	76687-76687	THORNTON
76058-76058	JOSHUA	76366-76366	HOLLIDAY	76534-76534	HOLLAND	76689-76689	VALLEY MILLS
76059-76059	KEENE	76367-76367	IOWA PARK	76537-76537	JARRELL	76690-76690	WALNUT SPRINGS
76060-76060	KENNEDALE	76369-76369	KAMAY	76538-76538	JONESBORO	76691-76691	WEST
76061-76061	LILLIAN	76370-76370	MEGARGEL	76539-76539	KEMPNER	76692-76692	WHITNEY
76063-76063	MANSFIELD	76371-76371	MUNDAY	76540-76547	KILLEEN	76693-76693	WORTHAM
76064-76064	MAYPEARL	76372-76372	NEWCASTLE	76548-76548	HARKER HEIGHTS	76701-76711	WACO
76065-76065	MIDLOTHIAN	76373-76373	OKLAUNION	76550-76550	LAMPASAS	76712-76712	WOODWAY
76066-76066	MILLSAP	76374-76374	OLNEY	76552-76552	LEON JUNCTION	76714-76799	WACO
76067-76068	MINERAL WELLS	76377-76377	PETROLIA	76554-76554	LITTLE RIVER	76801-76801	BROWNWOOD
76070-76070	NEMO	76379-76379	SCOTLAND	76555-76555	MAYSFIELD	76802-76802	EARLY
76071-76071	NEWARK	76380-76380	SEYMOUR	76556-76556	MILANO	76803-76804	BROWNWOOD
76073-76073	PARADISE	76384-76385	VERNON	76557-76557	MOODY	76820-76820	ART
76077-76077	RAINBOW	76388-76388	WEINERT	76558-76558	MOUND	76821-76821	BALLINGER
76078-76078	RHOME	76389-76389	WINDTHORST	76559-76559	NOLANVILLE	76823-76823	BANGS
76082-76082	SPRINGTOWN	76401-76402	STEPHENVILLE	76561-76561	OGLESBY	76824-76824	BEND
76084-76084	VENUS	76424-76424	BRECKENRIDGE	76564-76564	PENDLETON	76825-76825	BRADY
76086-76088	WEATHERFORD	76426-76426	BRIDGEPORT	76565-76565	POTTSVILLE	76827-76827	BROOKESMITH
76092-76092	SOUTHLAKE	76427-76427	BRYSON	76566-76566	PURMELA	76828-76828	BURKETT
76093-76093	RIO VISTA	76429-76429	CADDO	76567-76567	ROCKDALE	76831-76831	CASTELL
76094-76094	ARLINGTON	76430-76430	ALBANY	76569-76569	ROGERS	76832-76832	CHEROKEE
76095-76095	BEDFORD	76431-76431	CHICO	76570-76570	ROSEBUD	76834-76834	COLEMAN
76096-76096	ARLINGTON	76432-76432	BLANKET	76571-76571	SALADO	76836-76836	DOOLE
76097-76097	BURLESON	76433-76433	BLUFF DALE	76573-76573	SCHWERTNER	76837-76837	EDEN
76098-76098	AZLE	76435-76435	CARBON	76574-76574	TAYLOR	76841-76841	FORT MC KAVETT
76099-76099	GRAPEVINE	76436-76436	CARLTON	76577-76577	THORNDALE	76842-76842	FREDONIA
76101-76116	FORT WORTH	76437-76437	CISCO	76578-76578	THRALL	76844-76844	GOLDTHWAITE
76117-76117	HALTOM CITY	76439-76439	DENNIS	76579-76579	TROY	76845-76845	GOULDBUSK
76118-76126	FORT WORTH	76442-76442	COMANCHE	76596-76599	GATESVILLE	76848-76848	HEXT
76127-76127	NAVAL AIR STATION/ JRB	76443-76443	CROSS PLAINS	76621-76621	ABBOTT	76849-76849	JUNCTION
		76444-76444	DE LEON	76622-76622	AQUILLA	76852-76852	LOHN

ZIP Range	City	ZIP Range	City	ZIP Range	City	ZIP Range	City
76853-76853	LOMETA	77367-77367	RIVERSIDE	77484-77484	WALLER	77660-77660	SPURGER
76854-76854	LONDON	77368-77368	ROMAYOR	77485-77485	WALLIS	77661-77661	STOWELL
76855-76855	LOWAKE	77369-77369	RYE	77486-77486	WEST COLUMBIA	77662-77662	VIDOR
76856-76856	MASON	77371-77371	SHEPHERD	77487-77487	SUGAR LAND	77663-77663	VILLAGE MILLS
76857-76857	MAY	77372-77372	SPLENDORA	77488-77488	WHARTON	77664-77664	WARREN
76858-76858	MELVIN	77373-77373	SPRING	77489-77489	MISSOURI CITY	77665-77665	WINNIE
76859-76859	MENARD	77374-77374	THICKET	77491-77494	KATY	77670-77670	VIDOR
76861-76861	MILES	77375-77375	TOMBALL	77496-77496	SUGAR LAND	77701-77708	BEAUMONT
76862-76862	MILLERSVIEW	77376-77376	VOTAW	77497-77497	STAFFORD	77709-77709	VOTH
76864-76864	MULLIN	77377-77377	TOMBALL	77501-77508	PASADENA	77710-77710	BEAUMONT
76865-76865	NORTON	77378-77378	WILLIS	77510-77510	SANTA FE	77711-77711	LUMBERTON
76866-76866	PAINT ROCK	77379-77383	SPRING	77511-77512	ALVIN	77713-77726	BEAUMONT
76867-76867	PEAR VALLEY	77384-77385	CONROE	77514-77514	ANAHUAC	77801-77808	BRYAN
76869-76869	PONTOTOC	77386-77393	SPRING	77515-77516	ANGLETON	77830-77830	ANDERSON
76870-76870	PRIDDY	77396-77396	HUMBLE	77517-77517	SANTA FE	77831-77831	BEDIAS
76871-76871	RICHLAND SPRINGS	77401-77402	BELLAIRE	77518-77518	BACLIFF	77833-77834	BRENHAM
76872-76872	ROCHELLE	77404-77404	BAY CITY	77519-77519	BATSON	77835-77835	BURTON
76873-76873	ROCKWOOD	77406-77406	RICHMOND	77520-77522	BAYTOWN	77836-77836	CALDWELL
76874-76874	ROOSEVELT	77410-77410	CYPRESS	77530-77530	CHANNELVIEW	77837-77837	CALVERT
76875-76875	ROWENA	77411-77411	ALIEF	77531-77531	CLUTE	77838-77838	CHRIESMAN
76877-76877	SAN SABA	77412-77412	ALTAIR	77532-77532	CROSBY	77839-77839	CLAY
76878-76878	SANTA ANNA	77413-77413	BARKER	77533-77533	DAISETTA	77840-77845	COLLEGE STATION
76880-76880	STAR	77414-77414	BAY CITY	77534-77534	DANBURY	77850-77850	CONCORD
76882-76882	TALPA	77415-77415	CEDAR LANE	77535-77535	DAYTON	77852-77852	DEANVILLE
76883-76883	TELEGRAPH	77417-77417	BEASLEY	77536-77536	DEER PARK	77853-77853	DIME BOX
76884-76884	VALERA	77418-77418	BELLVILLE	77538-77538	DEVERS	77855-77855	FLYNN
76885-76885	VALLEY SPRING	77419-77419	BLESSING	77539-77539	DICKINSON	77856-77856	FRANKLIN
76886-76886	VERIBEST	77420-77420	BOLING	77541-77542	FREEPORT	77857-77857	GAUSE
76887-76887	VOCA	77422-77422	BRAZORIA	77545-77545	FRESNO	77859-77859	HEARNE
76888-76888	VOSS	77423-77423	BROOKSHIRE	77546-77546	FRIENDSWOOD	77861-77861	IOLA
76890-76890	ZEPHYR	77426-77426	CHAPPELL HILL	77547-77547	GALENA PARK	77862-77862	KURTEN
76901-76906	SAN ANGELO	77428-77428	COLLEGEPORT	77549-77549	FRIENDSWOOD	77863-77863	LYONS
76908-76908	GOODFELLOW AFB	77429-77429	CYPRESS	77550-77555	GALVESTON	77864-77864	MADISONVILLE
76909-76909	SAN ANGELO	77430-77430	DAMON	77560-77560	HANKAMER	77865-77865	MARQUEZ
76930-76930	BARNHART	77431-77431	DANCIGER	77561-77561	HARDIN	77866-77866	MILLICAN
76932-76932	BIG LAKE	77432-77432	DANEVANG	77562-77562	HIGHLANDS	77867-77867	MUMFORD
76933-76933	BRONTE	77433-77433	CYPRESS	77563-77563	HITCHCOCK	77868-77869	NAVASOTA
76934-76934	CARLSBAD	77434-77434	EAGLE LAKE	77564-77564	HULL	77870-77870	NEW BADEN
76935-76935	CHRISTOVAL	77435-77435	EAST BERNARD	77565-77565	KEMAH	77871-77871	NORMANGEE
76936-76936	ELDORADO	77436-77436	EGYPT	77566-77566	LAKE JACKSON	77872-77872	NORTH ZULCH
76937-76937	EOLA	77437-77437	EL CAMPO	77568-77568	LA MARQUE	77873-77873	RICHARDS
76939-76939	KNICKERBOCKER	77440-77440	ELMATON	77571-77572	LA PORTE	77875-77875	ROANS PRAIRIE
76940-76940	MERETA	77441-77441	FULSHEAR	77573-77574	LEAGUE CITY	77876-77876	SHIRO
76941-76941	MERTZON	77442-77442	GARWOOD	77575-77575	LIBERTY	77878-77878	SNOOK
76943-76943	OZONA	77443-77443	GLEN FLORA	77577-77577	LIVERPOOL	77879-77879	SOMERVILLE
76945-76945	ROBERT LEE	77444-77444	GUY	77578-77578	MANVEL	77880-77880	WASHINGTON
76949-76949	SILVER	77445-77445	HEMPSTEAD	77580-77580	MONT BELVIEU	77881-77881	WELLBORN
76950-76950	SONORA	77446-77446	PRAIRIE VIEW	77581-77581	PEARLAND	77882-77882	WHEELOCK
76951-76951	STERLING CITY	77447-77447	HOCKLEY	77582-77582	RAYWOOD	77901-77905	VICTORIA
76953-76953	TENNYSON	77448-77448	HUNGERFORD	77583-77583	ROSHARON	77950-77950	AUSTWELL
76955-76955	VANCOURT	77449-77450	KATY	77584-77584	PEARLAND	77951-77951	BLOOMINGTON
76957-76957	WALL	77451-77451	KENDLETON	77585-77585	SARATOGA	77954-77954	CUERO
76958-76958	WATER VALLEY	77452-77452	KENNEY	77586-77586	SEABROOK	77957-77957	EDNA
77001-77299	HOUSTON	77453-77453	LANE CITY	77587-77587	SOUTH HOUSTON	77960-77960	FANNIN
77301-77306	CONROE	77454-77454	LISSIE	77588-77588	PEARLAND	77961-77961	FRANCITAS
77315-77315	NORTH HOUSTON	77455-77455	LOUISE	77590-77592	TEXAS CITY	77962-77962	GANADO
77325-77325	HUMBLE	77456-77456	MARKHAM	77597-77597	WALLISVILLE	77963-77963	GOLIAD
77326-77326	ACE	77457-77457	MATAGORDA	77598-77598	WEBSTER	77964-77964	HALLETTSVILLE
77327-77328	CLEVELAND	77458-77458	MIDFIELD	77611-77611	BRIDGE CITY	77967-77967	HOCHHEIM
77331-77331	COLDSPRING	77459-77459	MISSOURI CITY	77612-77612	BUNA	77968-77968	INEZ
77332-77332	DALLARDSVILLE	77460-77460	NADA	77613-77613	CHINA	77969-77969	LA SALLE
77333-77333	DOBBIN	77461-77461	NEEDVILLE	77614-77614	DEWEYVILLE	77970-77970	LA WARD
77334-77334	DODGE	77462-77462	NEWGULF	77615-77615	EVADALE	77971-77971	LOLITA
77335-77335	GOODRICH	77463-77463	OLD OCEAN	77616-77616	FRED	77972-77972	LONG MOTT
77336-77336	HUFFMAN	77464-77464	ORCHARD	77617-77617	GILCHRIST	77973-77973	MCFADDIN
77337-77337	HUFSMITH	77465-77465	PALACIOS	77619-77619	GROVES	77974-77974	MEYERSVILLE
77338-77339	HUMBLE	77466-77466	PATTISON	77622-77622	HAMSHIRE	77975-77975	MOULTON
77340-77344	HUNTSVILLE	77467-77467	PIERCE	77623-77623	HIGH ISLAND	77976-77976	NURSERY
77345-77347	HUMBLE	77468-77468	PLEDGER	77624-77624	HILLISTER	77977-77977	PLACEDO
77348-77349	HUNTSVILLE	77469-77469	RICHMOND	77625-77625	KOUNTZE	77978-77978	POINT COMFORT
77350-77350	LEGGETT	77470-77470	ROCK ISLAND	77626-77626	MAURICEVILLE	77979-77979	PORT LAVACA
77351-77351	LIVINGSTON	77471-77471	ROSENBERG	77627-77627	NEDERLAND	77982-77982	PORT O CONNOR
77353-77355	MAGNOLIA	77473-77473	SAN FELIPE	77629-77629	NOME	77983-77983	SEADRIFT
77356-77356	MONTGOMERY	77474-77474	SEALY	77630-77632	ORANGE	77984-77984	SHINER
77357-77357	NEW CANEY	77475-77475	SHERIDAN	77639-77639	ORANGEFIELD	77985-77985	SPEAKS
77358-77358	NEW WAVERLY	77476-77476	SIMONTON	77640-77643	PORT ARTHUR	77986-77986	SUBLIME
77359-77359	OAKHURST	77477-77477	STAFFORD	77650-77650	PORT BOLIVAR	77987-77987	SWEET HOME
77360-77360	ONALASKA	77478-77479	SUGAR LAND	77651-77651	PORT NECHES	77988-77988	TELFERNER
77362-77362	PINEHURST	77480-77480	SWEENY	77655-77655	SABINE PASS	77989-77989	THOMASTON
77363-77363	PLANTERSVILLE	77481-77481	THOMPSONS	77656-77656	SILSBEE	77990-77990	TIVOLI
77364-77364	POINTBLANK	77482-77482	VAN VLECK	77657-77657	LUMBERTON	77991-77991	VANDERBILT
77365-77365	PORTER	77483-77483	WADSWORTH	77659-77659	SOUR LAKE	77993-77993	WEESATCHE

77994-77994	WESTHOFF	78145-78145	PAWNEE	78564-78564	LOPENO	78661-78661	PRAIRIE LEA
77995-77995	YOAKUM	78146-78146	PETTUS	78565-78565	LOS EBANOS	78662-78662	RED ROCK
78001-78001	ARTESIA WELLS	78147-78147	POTH	78566-78566	LOS FRESNOS	78663-78663	ROUND MOUNTAIN
78002-78002	ATASCOSA	78148-78150	UNIVERSAL CITY	78567-78567	LOS INDIOS	78664-78664	ROUND ROCK
78003-78003	BANDERA	78151-78151	RUNGE	78568-78568	LOZANO	78665-78665	SANDY
78004-78004	BERGHEIM	78152-78152	SAINT HEDWIG	78569-78569	LYFORD	78666-78667	SAN MARCOS
78005-78005	BIGFOOT	78154-78154	SCHERTZ	78570-78570	MERCEDES	78669-78669	SPICEWOOD
78006-78006	BOERNE	78155-78156	SEGUIN	78572-78573	MISSION	78670-78670	STAPLES
78007-78007	CALLIHAM	78159-78159	SMILEY	78575-78575	OLMITO	78671-78671	STONEWALL
78008-78008	CAMPBELLTON	78160-78160	STOCKDALE	78576-78576	PENITAS	78672-78672	TOW
78009-78009	CASTROVILLE	78161-78161	SUTHERLAND SPRINGS	78577-78577	PHARR	78673-78673	WALBURG
78010-78010	CENTER POINT	78162-78162	TULETA	78578-78578	PORT ISABEL	78674-78674	WEIR
78011-78011	CHARLOTTE	78163-78163	BULVERDE	78579-78579	PROGRESO	78675-78675	WILLOW CITY
78012-78012	CHRISTINE	78164-78164	YORKTOWN	78580-78580	RAYMONDVILLE	78676-78676	WIMBERLEY
78013-78013	COMFORT	78201-78299	SAN ANTONIO	78582-78582	RIO GRANDE CITY	78677-78677	WRIGHTSBORO
78014-78014	COTULLA	78330-78330	AGUA DULCE	78583-78583	RIO HONDO	78680-78683	ROUND ROCK
78015-78015	BOERNE	78332-78333	ALICE	78584-78584	ROMA	78691-78691	PFLUGERVILLE
78016-78016	DEVINE	78335-78336	ARANSAS PASS	78585-78585	SALINENO	78701-78789	AUSTIN
78017-78017	DILLEY	78338-78338	ARMSTRONG	78586-78586	SAN BENITO	78801-78802	UVALDE
78019-78019	ENCINAL	78339-78339	BANQUETE	78588-78588	SAN ISIDRO	78827-78827	ASHERTON
78021-78021	FOWLERTON	78340-78340	BAYSIDE	78589-78589	SAN JUAN	78828-78828	BARKSDALE
78022-78022	GEORGE WEST	78341-78341	BENAVIDES	78590-78590	SAN PERLITA	78829-78829	BATESVILLE
78023-78023	HELOTES	78342-78342	BEN BOLT	78591-78591	SANTA ELENA	78830-78830	BIG WELLS
78024-78024	HUNT	78343-78343	BISHOP	78592-78592	SANTA MARIA	78832-78832	BRACKETTVILLE
78025-78025	INGRAM	78344-78344	BRUNI	78593-78593	SANTA ROSA	78833-78833	CAMP WOOD
78026-78026	JOURDANTON	78347-78347	CHAPMAN RANCH	78594-78594	SEBASTIAN	78834-78834	CARRIZO SPRINGS
78027-78027	KENDALIA	78349-78349	CONCEPCION	78595-78595	SULLIVAN CITY	78836-78836	CATARINA
78028-78029	KERRVILLE	78350-78350	DINERO	78596-78596	WESLACO	78837-78837	COMSTOCK
78039-78039	LA COSTE	78351-78351	DRISCOLL	78597-78597	SOUTH PADRE ISLAND	78838-78838	CONCAN
78040-78049	LAREDO	78352-78352	EDROY	78598-78598	PORT MANSFIELD	78839-78839	CRYSTAL CITY
78050-78050	LEMING	78353-78353	ENCINO	78599-78599	WESLACO	78840-78842	DEL RIO
78052-78052	LYTLE	78355-78355	FALFURRIAS	78602-78602	BASTROP	78843-78843	LAUGHLIN A F B
78053-78053	MC COY	78357-78357	FREER	78603-78603	BEBE	78847-78847	DEL RIO
78054-78054	MACDONA	78358-78358	FULTON	78604-78604	BELMONT	78850-78850	D HANIS
78055-78055	MEDINA	78359-78359	GREGORY	78605-78605	BERTRAM	78851-78851	DRYDEN
78056-78056	MICO	78360-78360	GUERRA	78606-78606	BLANCO	78852-78853	EAGLE PASS
78057-78057	MOORE	78361-78361	HEBBRONVILLE	78607-78607	BLUFFTON	78860-78860	EL INDIO
78058-78058	MOUNTAIN HOME	78362-78362	INGLESIDE	78608-78608	BRIGGS	78861-78861	HONDO
78059-78059	NATALIA	78363-78364	KINGSVILLE	78609-78609	BUCHANAN DAM	78870-78870	KNIPPA
78060-78060	OAKVILLE	78368-78368	MATHIS	78610-78610	BUDA	78871-78871	LANGTRY
78061-78061	PEARSALL	78369-78369	MIRANDO CITY	78611-78611	BURNET	78872-78872	LA PRYOR
78062-78062	PEGGY	78370-78370	ODEM	78612-78612	CEDAR CREEK	78873-78873	LEAKEY
78063-78063	PIPE CREEK	78371-78371	OILTON	78613-78613	CEDAR PARK	78877-78877	QUEMADO
78064-78064	PLEASANTON	78372-78372	ORANGE GROVE	78614-78614	COST	78879-78879	RIO FRIO
78065-78065	POTEET	78373-78373	PORT ARANSAS	78615-78615	COUPLAND	78880-78880	ROCKSPRINGS
78066-78066	RIO MEDINA	78374-78374	PORTLAND	78616-78616	DALE	78881-78881	SABINAL
78067-78067	SAN YGNACIO	78375-78375	PREMONT	78617-78617	DEL VALLE	78883-78883	TARPLEY
78069-78069	SOMERSET	78376-78376	REALITOS	78618-78618	DOSS	78884-78884	UTOPIA
78070-78070	SPRING BRANCH	78377-78377	REFUGIO	78619-78619	DRIFTWOOD	78885-78885	VANDERPOOL
78071-78071	THREE RIVERS	78379-78379	RIVIERA	78620-78620	DRIPPING SPRINGS	78886-78886	YANCEY
78072-78072	TILDEN	78380-78380	ROBSTOWN	78621-78621	ELGIN	78931-78931	BLEIBLERVILLE
78073-78073	VON ORMY	78381-78382	ROCKPORT	78622-78622	FENTRESS	78932-78932	CARMINE
78074-78074	WARING	78383-78383	SANDIA	78623-78623	FISCHER	78933-78933	CAT SPRING
78075-78075	WHITSETT	78384-78384	SAN DIEGO	78624-78624	FREDERICKSBURG	78934-78934	COLUMBUS
78076-78076	ZAPATA	78385-78385	SARITA	78626-78628	GEORGETOWN	78935-78935	ALLEYTON
78101-78101	ADKINS	78387-78387	SINTON	78629-78629	GONZALES	78938-78938	ELLINGER
78102-78104	BEEVILLE	78389-78389	SKIDMORE	78630-78630	CEDAR PARK	78940-78940	FAYETTEVILLE
78107-78107	BERCLAIR	78390-78390	TAFT	78631-78631	HARPER	78941-78941	FLATONIA
78108-78108	CIBOLO	78391-78391	TYNAN	78632-78632	HARWOOD	78942-78942	GIDDINGS
78109-78109	CONVERSE	78393-78393	WOODSBORO	78634-78634	HUTTO	78943-78943	GLIDDEN
78111-78111	ECLETO	78401-78480	CORPUS CHRISTI	78635-78635	HYE	78944-78944	INDUSTRY
78112-78112	ELMENDORF	78501-78505	MCALLEN	78636-78636	JOHNSON CITY	78945-78945	LA GRANGE
78113-78113	FALLS CITY	78516-78516	ALAMO	78638-78638	KINGSBURY	78946-78946	LEDBETTER
78114-78114	FLORESVILLE	78520-78526	BROWNSVILLE	78639-78639	KINGSLAND	78947-78947	LEXINGTON
78115-78115	GERONIMO	78535-78535	COMBES	78640-78640	KYLE	78948-78948	LINCOLN
78116-78116	GILLETT	78536-78536	DELMITA	78641-78641	LEANDER	78949-78949	MULDOON
78117-78117	HOBSON	78537-78537	DONNA	78642-78642	LIBERTY HILL	78950-78950	NEW ULM
78118-78118	KARNES CITY	78538-78538	EDCOUCH	78643-78643	LLANO	78951-78951	OAKLAND
78119-78119	KENEDY	78539-78540	EDINBURG	78644-78644	LOCKHART	78952-78952	PLUM
78121-78121	LA VERNIA	78543-78543	ELSA	78645-78646	LEANDER	78953-78953	ROSANKY
78122-78122	LEESVILLE	78545-78545	FALCON HEIGHTS	78648-78648	LULING	78954-78954	ROUND TOP
78123-78123	MC QUEENEY	78547-78547	GARCIASVILLE	78650-78650	MC DADE	78956-78956	SCHULENBURG
78124-78124	MARION	78548-78548	GRULLA	78651-78651	MC NEIL	78957-78957	SMITHVILLE
78125-78125	MINERAL	78549-78549	HARGILL	78652-78652	MANCHACA	78959-78959	WAELDER
78130-78132	NEW BRAUNFELS	78550-78553	HARLINGEN	78653-78653	MANOR	78960-78960	WARDA
78133-78133	CANYON LAKE	78557-78557	HIDALGO	78654-78654	MARBLE FALLS	78961-78961	ROUND TOP
78135-78135	NEW BRAUNFELS	78558-78558	LA BLANCA	78655-78655	MARTINDALE	78962-78962	WEIMAR
78140-78140	NIXON	78559-78559	LA FERIA	78656-78656	MAXWELL	78963-78963	WEST POINT
78141-78141	NORDHEIM	78560-78560	LA JOYA	78657-78657	MARBLE FALLS	79001-79001	ADRIAN
78142-78142	NORMANNA	78561-78561	LASARA	78658-78658	OTTINE	79002-79002	ALANREED
78143-78143	PANDORA	78562-78562	LA VILLA	78659-78659	PAIGE	79003-79003	ALLISON
78144-78144	PANNA MARIA	78563-78563	LINN	78660-78660	PFLUGERVILLE	79005-79005	BOOKER

79007-79008	BORGER	79220-79220	AFTON	79366-79366	RANSOM CANYON	79701-79712	MIDLAND
79009-79009	BOVINA	79221-79221	AIKEN	79367-79367	SMYER	79713-79713	ACKERLY
79010-79010	BOYS RANCH	79222-79222	CAREY	79369-79369	SPADE	79714-79714	ANDREWS
79011-79011	BRISCOE	79223-79223	CEE VEE	79370-79370	SPUR	79718-79718	BALMORHEA
79012-79012	BUSHLAND	79224-79224	CHALK	79371-79371	SUDAN	79719-79719	BARSTOW
79013-79013	CACTUS	79225-79225	CHILLICOTHE	79372-79372	SUNDOWN	79720-79721	BIG SPRING
79014-79014	CANADIAN	79226-79226	CLARENDON	79373-79373	TAHOKA	79730-79730	COYANOSA
79015-79016	CANYON	79227-79227	CROWELL	79376-79376	TOKIO	79731-79731	CRANE
79018-79018	CHANNING	79229-79229	DICKENS	79377-79377	WELCH	79733-79733	FORSAN
79019-79019	CLAUDE	79230-79230	DODSON	79378-79378	WELLMAN	79734-79734	FORT DAVIS
79021-79021	COTTON CENTER	79231-79231	DOUGHERTY	79379-79379	WHITEFACE	79735-79735	FORT STOCKTON
79022-79022	DALHART	79232-79232	DUMONT	79380-79380	WHITHARRAL	79738-79738	GAIL
79024-79024	DARROUZETT	79233-79233	ESTELLINE	79381-79381	WILSON	79739-79739	GARDEN CITY
79025-79025	DAWN	79234-79234	FLOMOT	79382-79382	WOLFFORTH	79740-79740	GIRVIN
79027-79027	DIMMITT	79235-79235	FLOYDADA	79383-79383	NEW HOME	79741-79741	GOLDSMITH
79029-79029	DUMAS	79236-79236	GUTHRIE	79401-79464	LUBBOCK	79742-79742	GRANDFALLS
79031-79031	EARTH	79237-79237	HEDLEY	79489-79489	REESE AIR FORCE BASE	79743-79743	IMPERIAL
79032-79032	EDMONSON	79238-79238	KIRKLAND	79490-79499	LUBBOCK	79744-79744	IRAAN
79033-79033	FARNSWORTH	79239-79239	LAKEVIEW	79501-79501	ANSON	79745-79745	KERMIT
79034-79034	FOLLETT	79240-79240	LELIA LAKE	79502-79502	ASPERMONT	79748-79748	KNOTT
79035-79035	FRIONA	79241-79241	LOCKNEY	79503-79503	STAMFORD	79749-79749	LENORAH
79036-79036	FRITCH	79243-79243	MCADOO	79504-79504	BAIRD	79752-79752	MC CAMEY
79039-79039	GROOM	79244-79244	MATADOR	79505-79505	BENJAMIN	79754-79754	MENTONE
79040-79040	GRUVER	79245-79245	MEMPHIS	79506-79506	BLACKWELL	79755-79755	MIDKIFF
79041-79041	HALE CENTER	79247-79247	ODELL	79508-79508	BUFFALO GAP	79756-79756	MONAHANS
79042-79042	HAPPY	79248-79248	PADUCAH	79510-79510	CLYDE	79758-79758	GARDENDALE
79043-79043	HART	79250-79250	PETERSBURG	79511-79511	COAHOMA	79759-79759	NOTREES
79044-79044	HARTLEY	79251-79251	QUAIL	79512-79512	COLORADO CITY	79760-79769	ODESSA
79045-79045	HEREFORD	79252-79252	QUANAH	79516-79516	DUNN	79770-79770	ORLA
79046-79046	HIGGINS	79255-79255	QUITAQUE	79517-79517	FLUVANNA	79772-79772	PECOS
79051-79051	KERRICK	79256-79256	ROARING SPRINGS	79518-79518	GIRARD	79776-79776	PENWELL
79052-79052	KRESS	79257-79257	SILVERTON	79519-79519	GOLDSBORO	79777-79777	PYOTE
79053-79053	LAZBUDDIE	79258-79258	SOUTH PLAINS	79520-79520	HAMLIN	79778-79778	RANKIN
79054-79054	LEFORS	79259-79259	TELL	79521-79521	HASKELL	79779-79779	ROYALTY
79056-79056	LIPSCOMB	79261-79261	TURKEY	79525-79525	HAWLEY	79780-79780	SARAGOSA
79057-79057	MCLEAN	79311-79311	ABERNATHY	79526-79526	HERMLEIGH	79781-79781	SHEFFIELD
79058-79058	MASTERSON	79312-79312	AMHERST	79527-79527	IRA	79782-79782	STANTON
79059-79059	MIAMI	79313-79313	ANTON	79528-79528	JAYTON	79783-79783	TARZAN
79061-79061	MOBEETIE	79314-79314	BLEDSOE	79529-79529	KNOX CITY	79785-79785	TOYAH
79062-79062	MORSE	79316-79316	BROWNFIELD	79530-79530	LAWN	79786-79786	TOYAHVALE
79063-79063	NAZARETH	79320-79320	BULA	79532-79532	LORAINE	79788-79788	WICKETT
79064-79064	OLTON	79322-79322	CROSBYTON	79533-79533	LUEDERS	79789-79789	WINK
79065-79066	PAMPA	79323-79323	DENVER CITY	79534-79534	MC CAULLEY	79821-79821	ANTHONY
79068-79068	PANHANDLE	79324-79324	ENOCHS	79535-79535	MARYNEAL	79830-79832	ALPINE
79070-79070	PERRYTON	79325-79325	FARWELL	79536-79536	MERKEL	79834-79834	BIG BEND NATIONAL
79072-79073	PLAINVIEW	79326-79326	FIELDTON	79537-79537	NOLAN		PARK
79077-79077	SAMNORWOOD	79329-79329	IDALOU	79538-79538	NOVICE	79835-79835	CANUTILLO
79078-79078	SANFORD	79330-79330	JUSTICEBURG	79539-79539	O BRIEN	79836-79836	CLINT
79079-79079	SHAMROCK	79331-79331	LAMESA	79540-79540	OLD GLORY	79837-79837	DELL CITY
79080-79080	SKELLYTOWN	79336-79338	LEVELLAND	79541-79541	OVALO	79838-79838	FABENS
79081-79081	SPEARMAN	79339-79339	LITTLEFIELD	79543-79543	ROBY	79839-79839	FORT HANCOCK
79082-79082	SPRINGLAKE	79342-79342	LOOP	79544-79544	ROCHESTER	79842-79842	MARATHON
79083-79083	STINNETT	79343-79343	LORENZO	79545-79545	ROSCOE	79843-79843	MARFA
79084-79084	STRATFORD	79344-79344	MAPLE	79546-79546	ROTAN	79845-79845	PRESIDIO
79085-79085	SUMMERFIELD	79345-79345	MEADOW	79547-79548	RULE	79846-79846	REDFORD
79086-79086	SUNRAY	79346-79346	MORTON	79549-79550	SNYDER	79847-79847	SALT FLAT
79087-79087	TEXLINE	79347-79347	MULESHOE	79553-79553	STAMFORD	79848-79848	SANDERSON
79088-79088	TULIA	79350-79350	NEW DEAL	79556-79556	SWEETWATER	79849-79849	SAN ELIZARIO
79091-79091	UMBARGER	79351-79351	ODONNELL	79560-79560	SYLVESTER	79850-79850	SHAFTER
79092-79092	VEGA	79353-79353	PEP	79561-79561	TRENT	79851-79851	SIERRA BLANCA
79093-79093	WAKA	79355-79355	PLAINS	79562-79562	TUSCOLA	79852-79852	TERLINGUA
79094-79094	WAYSIDE	79356-79356	POST	79563-79563	TYE	79853-79853	TORNILLO
79095-79095	WELLINGTON	79357-79357	RALLS	79565-79565	WESTBROOK	79854-79854	VALENTINE
79096-79096	WHEELER	79358-79358	ROPESVILLE	79566-79566	WINGATE	79855-79855	VAN HORN
79097-79097	WHITE DEER	79359-79359	SEAGRAVES	79567-79567	WINTERS	79901-88595	EL PASO
79098-79098	WILDORADO	79360-79360	SEMINOLE	79601-79606	ABILENE		
79101-79189	AMARILLO	79363-79363	SHALLOWATER	79607-79607	DYESS AFB		
79201-79201	CHILDRESS	79364-79364	SLATON	79608-79699	ABILENE		

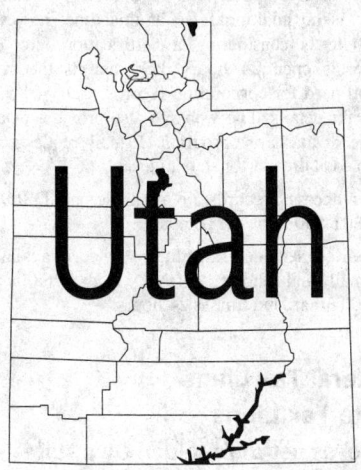

General Help Numbers:

Governor's Office
210 State Capitol   801-538-1000
Salt Lake City, UT 84114   Fax 801-538-1528
http://www.governor.state.ut.us   8AM-5PM

Attorney General's Office
236 State Capitol   801-538-9600
Salt Lake City, UT 84114   Fax 801-538-1121
http://attorneygeneral.utah.gov   8AM-5:30PM

State Court Administrator
450 S State   801-578-3800
Salt Lake City, UT 84114   Fax 801-578-3843
http://courtlink.utcourts.gov   8AM-5PM

State Archives
PO Box 141021   801-538-3012
Salt Lake City, UT 84114-1021   Fax 801-538-3354
http://www.archives.state.ut.us   8AM-5PM M-F

State Specifics:

Capital:	Salt Lake City
	Salt Lake County
Time Zone:	MST
Number of Counties:	29
Population:	2,233,169
Web Site:	www.state.ut.us

State Agencies

Criminal Records

Bureau of Criminal Identification, Box 148280, Salt Lake City, UT 84114-8280 (Courier: 3888 West 5400 South, Salt Lake City, UT 84119); 801-965-4445, 801-965-4749 (Fax), 8AM-5PM.

http://www.bci.state.ut.us

Note: Records are not open to the public or employers, unless the form has been filled out by the subject, fingerprints are submitted, and the sunject's signature is notarized. Those agencies authorized by law do not need to submit fingerprints, but still must have subject's notarized signature.

Searching: Sex offender data is available online at www.udc.state.ut.us/offenders/sexoffenders/sexoffenderssearch.html. Include the following in your request-name, DOB, SSN, driver's license #, notarized signature of subject, fingerprints.

Access by: mail.

Fee & Payment: The fee is $10.00. Fee payee: Utah Bureau of Criminal Investigation Personal checks accepted.

Mail search: Turnaround time is 7-10 days. Records are available by mail with submission of proper form.

Corporation Records
Limited Liability Company Records
Fictitious Name
Limited Partnership Records
Assumed Name
Trademarks/Servicemarks

Commerce Department, Corporate Division, PO Box 146705, Salt Lake City, UT 84114-6705 (Courier: 160 E 300 S, 2nd fl, Salt Lake City, UT 84111); 801-530-4849 (Call Center), 801-530-6205 (Certified Records), 801-530-6034 (Non-Certified), 801-530-6363 (Cert. Of Existence), 801-530-6111 (Fax), 8AM-5PM.

http://www.commerce.state.ut.us

Indexing & Storage: Records are available for active entities only. Records are indexed on inhouse computer and via the Internet.

Searching: Include the following in your request-full name of business. In addition to the articles of incorporation, corporation records include the following information: Annual Reports, Officers, Directors, DBAs, Prior (merged) names and Reserved names.

Access by: mail, phone, fax, in person, online.

Fee & Payment: Certified records are $10.00 per record. Copies are $.30 per page. Fax transmittals are $5.00 for the first page and $1.00 each page after. There are higher fees for other specific reports. Fee payee: State of Utah. Prepayment required. Personal checks accepted. Credit cards accepted: MasterCard, Visa.

Mail search: Turnaround time: 5-10 days. A self addressed stamped envelope is requested. Copies cost $.30 per page.

Phone search: Copies cost $.30 per page. They will answer questions on name availability, status, agent and officer information.

Fax search: Turnaround time is 5-10 days.

In person search: Copies cost $.30 per page.

Online search: A business entity/principle search service is available on the eUtah web site at www.state.ut.us/egov_services/services.html. Basic information (name, address, agent) is free, detailed data is a available for minimal fees, but registration is required. The eUtah web site also offers an Unclaimed Property search page.

Other access: State allows e-mail access for orders of Certification of Existence at orders@br.state.ut.us.

Expedited service: Expedited service is available. Turnaround time: 24 hours. Add $75.00 per business name.

Uniform Commercial Code

Department of Commerce, UCC Division, Box 146705, Salt Lake City, UT 84114-6705 (Courier: 160 E 300 South, Heber M Wells Bldg, 2nd Floor, Salt Lake City, UT 84111); 801-530-4849, 801-530-6438 (Fax), 8AM-5PM.

http://www.commerce.state.ut.us

Indexing & Storage: Records are available from 1965. Records are computerized since 1995.

Searching: Use search request form UCC-11. All tax liens are filed at the county level. Include the following in your request-debtor name. File number(s) and/or debtor name(s), name and address of requesting party, and daytime phone number are required.

Access by: mail, fax, in person, online.

Fee & Payment: For a certified search, the fee is $10.00 per file number certified, copies are $.30 per page. For uncertified searches, the fee is only $.30 per page. Fee payee: State of Utah. They will bill for copy charges. Personal checks accepted. Credit cards accepted: MasterCard, Visa.

Mail search: Turnaround time: ten working days. A self addressed stamped envelope is requested.

Fax search: Same fees and turnaround time as mail search apply. They will invoice.

In person search: Searching is available in person.

Online search: User fee is $10.00 per month. There is no additional fee at this time; however, the state is considering a certification fee. The system is open 24 hours daily and is the same system used for corporation records. Call 801-530-6643 for details. The web site also provides details of the "Datashare" program. E-mail requests are accepted at orders@br.state.ut.us.

Other access: Records are available on CD-ROM. Call 801-530-2267 for details.

Expedited service: Expedited service is available for mail and phone searches. Add $75.00 per name. Turnaround time is 24 hours.

Federal Tax Liens
State Tax Liens
Records not maintained by a state level agency.

Note: Records are found at the local level.

Sales Tax Registrations

Tax Commission, Taxpayer Services, 210 N 1950 W, Salt Lake City, UT 84134; 801-297-2200, 801-297-7697 (Fax), 8AM-5PM.

http://www.tax.ex.state.ut.us

Note: General forms and tax law information can be downloaded from the web site.

Indexing & Storage: Records are available for 15 years for business records, for 10 years for individual records.

Searching: Requester must have written consent. This agency will only confirm that a business is registered and active if a tax permit number is provided. They will provide no other information. Records are not accessible by the public; access is limited to the owner(s) of the account(s). You can show power of attorney to access, also. Requests must be in writing.

Access by: mail, in person.

Fee & Payment: Copies are $6.50 per record. Fee payee: Utah Tax Commission. Prepayment required. Personal checks accepted. No credit cards accepted.

Mail search: Turnaround time: 1 to 2 weeks. No self addressed stamped envelope is required.

In person search: Turnaround time is 24 hours.

Birth Certificates

Department of Health, Office of Vital Records & Statistics, Box 141012, Salt Lake City, UT 84114-1012 (Courier: 288 N 1460 W, Salt Lake City, UT 84114); 801-538-6105, 801-538-6380 (Voice, credit card orders), 801-538-9467 (Fax), 9AM-5PM (walk-in counter closes at 4:30 PM).

http://hlunix.state.ut.us/bvr/home.html

Note: Must have a signed release from person of record or immediate family member.

Indexing & Storage: Records are available from 1905 on. Index computer files go back to 1978. Indexes are not available to the public. New records are available for inquiry immediately.

Searching: At the web site you can download an application at the Forms link on the navigation bar. Follow the instructions on the application and mail it or bring it to the Service Window in-person. Or, you may write a letter. Include the following in

your request-full name, names of parents, mother's maiden name, date of birth, place of birth, relationship to person of record, reason for information request. Be sure to sign the request and include a daytime phone number. You may phone, fax or email to request an application form. The following data is not released: medical records.

Access by: mail, phone, fax, in person.

Fee & Payment: Search fee is $9.00 or specify a 5-year period to search for $12.00 (add'l 5-year periods are add'l charge of $12.00). Fee is $50.00 if the entire index must be searched. Add $5.00 per name for second copies. Fee payee: Vital Records. Prepayment required. Personal checks accepted. Credit cards accepted: MasterCard, Visa, AmEx, Discover.

Mail search: Turnaround time: 2 to 3 weeks. No self addressed stamped envelope is required.

Phone search: See expedited service.

Fax search: See expedited service.

In person search: Turnaround time 15 to 30 minutes.

Expedited service: Expedited service is available for mail, phone and fax searches. Turnaround time: overnight delivery. Add $10.00. Also, you must use a credit card which is an additional $5.00. Overnight return is $14.50 for FedEx or $10.50 express mail.

Death Records

Department of Health, Office of Vital Records & Statistics, Box 141012, Salt Lake City, UT 84114-1012 (Courier: 288 N 1460 W, Salt Lake City, UT 84114); 801-538-6105, 801-538-6380 (Voice, credit card orders), 801-538-9467 (Fax), 9AM-5PM (walk-in counter closes at 4:30 PM).

http://hlunix.state.ut.us/bvr/html/certificates.html

Note: Certificates can be obtained by an immediate family member or with written permission from the immediate family.

Indexing & Storage: Records are available from 1905 on. Index computer files go back since 1978. Indexes are not available to the public. New records are available for inquiry immediately.

Searching: At the web site you can download an application at the Forms link on the navigation bar. Follow the instructions on the application and mail it or bring it to the Service Window in-person. Or, you may write a letter. Include the following in your request-full name, date of death, place of death, relationship to person of record, reason for information request. If you do not know the date of death, include last known date alive. You may phone, fax or email to request an application form.

Access by: mail, phone, fax, in person.

Fee & Payment: Search fee is $9.00, add $5.00 per name for second copies. Fee payee: Vital Records. Prepayment required. Personal checks accepted. Credit cards accepted: MasterCard, Visa, AmEx, Discover.

Mail search: Turnaround time: 2 weeks. No self addressed stamped envelope is required.

Phone search: See expedited service.

Fax search: See expedited service.

In person search: Turnaround time 15 to 30 minutes.

Expedited service: Expedited service is available for mail, phone and fax searches. Turnaround time: overnight delivery. Expedite fee is $10.00

plus you must use a credit card which is an additional $5.00. Add $14.50 for FedEx or $10.50 express mail for overnight service.

Marriage Certificates

Department of Health, Office of Vital Records & Statictics, Box 141012, Salt Lake City, UT 84114-1012 (Courier: 288 N 1460 W, Salt Lake City, UT 84114); 801-535-6105, 801-538-6380 (Voice, credit card orders), 801-538-9467 (Fax), 9AM-5PM (walk-in counter closes at 4:30 PM).

http://hlunix.state.ut.us/bvr/html/certificates.html

Note: Records are certification summaries and not copies of the original records. Marriage records not held by the state can be found at the County Recorder in county where marriage took place. Actual copies can only be obtained by an immediate family member or with written permission from the immediate family.

Indexing & Storage: Records are available 1978 to 1998.

Searching: At the web site you can download an application at the Forms link on the navigation bar. Follow the instructions on the application and mail it or bring it to the Service Window in-person. Or, you may write a letter. Include the following in your request-date & place of occurrence, groom's name, bride's maiden name. You may phone, fax or email to request an application form.

Access by: mail, phone, fax, in person.

Fee & Payment: $9.00 for an abstract only. If a five year search is required, the fee is $12.00 and add $12.00 for each additional five years searched. It costs $50.00 to search the entire database. Fee payee: Vital Records. Prepayment required Personal checks accepted Credit cards accepted: MasterCard, Visa, AmEx, Discover.

Mail search: Turnaround time: 2-3 weeks.

Phone search: See expedited service.

Fax search: See expedited service.

In person search: Turnaround time 15 to 30 minutes.

Expedited service: Expedited service is available for mail, phone and fax searches. Turnaround time: same day service. You must use a credit card which is an additional $15.00. For express mail or FedEx, add current fee.

Divorce Records

Department of Health, Office of Vital Records & Statistics, Box 141012, Salt Lake City, UT 84114-1012 (Courier: 288 N 1460 W, Salt Lake City, UT 84114); 801-535-6105, 801-538-6380 (Voice, credit card orders), 801-538-9467 (Fax), 9AM-5PM (walk-in counter closes at 4:30 PM).

http://hlunix.state.ut.us/bvr/html/certificates.html

Note: Records provided are certification summaries and not copies of actual records. Divorce records not held by the state can be found at the Clerk of the Court in the county issuing the decree. Actual copies can only be obtained from the state by an immediate family member or with written permission from the immediate family.

Indexing & Storage: Records are available from 1978 to August, 1997.

Searching: At the web site you can download an application at the Forms link on the navigation bar. Follow the instructions on the application and mail it or bring it to the Service Window in person.

Include the following in your request-date and place of occurrence, date and place of marriage, husband's name, wife's name. You may phone or fax to request an application form.

Access by: mail, phone, fax.

Fee & Payment: $9.00 for an abstract only. If search involved, fee is $12.00 for each five years searched or $50.00 to search entire database. Fee payee: Vital Records. Prepayment required Credit card orders, add $15.00 Personal checks accepted Credit cards accepted: Visa, MasterCard, Discover, AmEx.

Mail search: Turnaround time: 2-3 weeks.

Phone search: See expedited service.

Fax search: See expedited service.

Expedited service: For mail and credit card phone orders only. Turnaround time: same day service. For express mail or FedEx, add current fee.

Workers' Compensation Records

Labor Commission, Division of Industrial Accidents, PO Box 146610, Salt Lake City, UT 84114-6610 (Courier: 160 E 300 S, 3rd Floor, Salt Lake City, UT 84114); 801-530-6800, 801-530-6804 (Fax), 8AM-5PM.

http://www.labor.state.ut.us

Indexing & Storage: Records are available from 1970 to 1988 on microfiche, from 1989 to present on computer.

Searching: Must have a notarized release from claimant (not over 90 days old). If a conditional job has been offered, then include a statement of such with employer's signature. Include the following in your request-Social Security Number, date of birth. Phone or fax to request form.

Access by: mail, fax, in person.

Fee & Payment: The search fee is $15.00 per name, copies are $.50 per page. Fee payee: Division of Industrial Accidents. Prepayment required. Personal checks accepted. No credit cards accepted.

Mail search: Turnaround time: 2 to 3 days. Include your telephone number so they can call with the total charge, which must be paid before records are released.No self addressed stamped envelope is required.

Fax search: Prepayment is required.

In person search: Same criteria as mail requests.

Driver Records

Department of Public Safety, Driver License Division, Customer Service Section, PO Box 30560, Salt Lake City, UT 84130-0560 (Courier: 4501 South 2700 West, 3rd Floor South, Salt Lake City, UT 84119); 801-965-4437, 801-965-4496 (Fax), 8AM-5PM.

http://www.dl.state.ut.us

Note: Copies of tickets can be purchased for $5.00 per record. However, if the ticket information came to the state via magnetic tape, the state will refer the requester to the court.

Indexing & Storage: Records are available for 3 years for moving violations, 6 years for DWIs and 3 years for suspensions (alcohol related suspensions are 6 years). Records on commercial drivers are kept for 10 years. It takes 2 weeks to 6 months before new records are available for inquiry.

Searching: Interstate speeding convictions less than 10 mph over are not shown unless there is written consent. Accidents are reported only if driver had citation. Addresses removed from report to comply with DPPA. Requests must comply with DPPA permissible uses. The driver's full name and DOB and/or license number are needed when ordering. Also helpful: SSN. The following data is not released: medical records or addresses.

Access by: mail, in person.

Fee & Payment: The fee is $4.25 per record. Fee payee: Department of Public Safety. Prepayment required. Personal checks accepted. No credit cards accepted.

Mail search: Turnaround time: approx. 1 week. Will FedEx if requester has account or submits pre-paid envelope.A self addressed stamped envelope is requested.

In person search: Up to 10 requests can be processed immediately; any additional requests are available the next day. Driving records can be obtained at any one of 17 branch offices throughout the state.

Other access: Magnetic tape inquiry is available for high volume users. The state will not sell its DL file to commercial vendors.

Accident Reports

Driver's License Division, Accident Reports Section, PO Box 30560, Salt Lake City, UT 84130-0560 (Courier: 4501 South 2700 West, 3rd Floor South, Salt Lake City, UT 84119); 801-965-4428, 8AM-5PM.

Indexing & Storage: Records are available for 10 years to present and are indexed on microfilm. It takes 2 weeks to 6 months before new records are available for inquiry.

Searching: Include the following in your request-full name, date of accident, location of accident. The following data is not released: medical records, Social Security Numbers or addresses.

Access by: mail, fax, in person.

Fee & Payment: The fee is $5.00 per record. Fee payee: Department of Public Safety. Prepayment required. The state will allow ongoing requesters to pre-pay with an account. Personal checks accepted. No credit cards accepted.

Mail search: Turnaround time: 2 weeks. A self addressed stamped envelope is requested.

Fax search: Money must be received up front before records can be returned by fax.

In person search: Records will be mailed, or can be picked up if pre-paid.

Vehicle Ownership
Vehicle Identification
Vessel Ownership
Vessel Registration

State Tax Commission, Motor Vehicle Records Section, 210 North 1950 West, Salt Lake City, UT 84134; 801-297-3507, 801-297-3578 (Fax), 8AM-5PM.

http://www.dmv-utah.com

Indexing & Storage: Records are available from 1979. All boats 1985 or newer must be titled. All motors over 25 HP must be titled. All boats, except canoes, must be registered. It takes 2 weeks before new records are available for inquiry.

Searching: Access is not open to casual requesters without consent of subject. The name or the vehicle ID or registration number or hull ID is needed to search. The following data is not released: medical records or Social Security Numbers.

Access by: mail, phone, in person, online.

Fee & Payment: The current fee is $2.00 per record and $6.50 for each microfilm record requested. State has established accounts for dealerships and financial institutions requesting lien-holder information. Fee payee: State Tax Commission. Prepayment required. Personal checks accepted. No credit cards accepted.

Mail search: Turnaround time: 2 days. Boat records can take as long as 1 week to process. A self addressed stamped envelope is requested.

Phone search: Searching is available for pre-approved, established accounts.

In person search: Turnaround time while you wait for small amounts.

Online search: Motor Vehicle Dept. Driver records are available online, also titles, liens, and registration searches are available at www.state.ut.us/egov_services/services.html; registration is required.

Other access: Utah offers a bulk or batch format for obtaining registration information on magnetic tape or paper. A written request stating the purpose of the usage is required. Call 801-297-2700 for further information.

Legislation Records

Utah Legislature, Research and General Counsel, 436 State Capitol, Salt Lake City, UT 84114, 801-538-1588 (Bill Room), 801-538-1032 (Older Passed Bills), 801-538-1712 (Fax), 8AM-5PM.

http://www.le.state.ut.us

Note: Sessions start 3rd Monday in January.

Indexing & Storage: Records are available from 1980 to 1989 on microfiche and from 1990 forward on computer.

Searching: Bill room only has current bills. Include the following in your request-bill number, topic of bill.

Access by: mail, phone, fax, in person, online.

Fee & Payment: There is no search fee, copy fee is $.10 per page if over 10 pages. Fee payee: State of Utah. Personal checks accepted. No credit cards accepted.

Mail search: Turnaround time: variable. No self addressed stamped envelope is required.

Phone search: Records are available by phone.

Fax search: The fee is $1.00 per page.

In person search: It is necessary to call first and make an appointment.

Online search: Web site contains bill information and also the Utah Code.

Voter Registration
Access to Records is Restricted

Office of Lt Governor, Elections Office, 115 State Capitol, Salt Lake City, UT 84114; 801-538-1041, 801-538-1133 (Fax), 8AM-5PM.

http://www.governor.state.ut.us/elections

Note: Individual record requests are referred to the county clerk offices. Records that have not been secured by the registrant are open to the public; however, the counties will not release the SSN or DL. The entire state voter registration database can be purchased from this office for approximately $1,000.

GED Certificates

State Office of Education, GED Testing, Attn Records, 250 East 500 South, Salt Lake City, UT 84111; 801-538-7870, 801-538-7868 (Fax), 8AM-5PM.

http://www.usoe.k12.ut.us/adulted/ged/index.html

Indexing & Storage: Records are available from 1965 to present. It takes 1 to 3 months before new records are available for inquiry.

Searching: Include the following in your request-Social Security Number, signed release, name at time of testing, current name if different. The following information is not required to search, but is very helpful: date/year of test, date of birth, and city of test.

Access by: mail, phone, fax, in person.

Fee & Payment: There is no fee for verification.

Mail search: Turnaround time: 1 to 2 days. No self addressed stamped envelope is required.

Phone search: Phone searches require that a signed release is faxed prior to the phone call.

Fax search: Same criteria as phone searching.

In person search: Searchers should call first.

Hunting License Information
Fishing License Information

Utah Division of Wildlife Resources, PO Box 146301, Salt Lake City, UT 84114-6301 (Courier: 1594 West North Temple, #2110, Salt Lake City, UT 84116); 801-538-4700, 801-538-4709 (Fax), 8AM-5PM.

http://www.nr.state.ut.us?dwr/dwr.htm

Indexing & Storage: Records are available from 1988 on. the last 3 previous years are kept on computer. Records are indexed on inhouse computer.

Searching: Must use the official request form supplied by this agency. You must show a reasonable purpose in order to obtain information. Include the following in your request-name. DOB and SSN are helpful. The following data is not released: telephone numbers.

Access by: mail.

Fee & Payment: Fees are based upon actual cost of computer time, personnel time plus copy fee of $.25 per page. Fee payee: Utah Division of Wildlife Resources. Prepayment required. Personal checks accepted. No credit cards accepted.

Mail search: Turnaround time: variable. No self addressed stamped envelope is required.

Other access: Draw lists are provided for a small fee at the time of big game drawing.

Utah State Licensing Agencies

Licenses Searchable Online

Accounting Firm #05 .... https://secure.e-utah.org/llv
Acupuncturist #05 .... https://secure.e-utah.org/llv
Alarm Company #05 .... https://secure.e-utah.org/llv
Alarm Company Agent/Response Runner #05 .... https://secure.e-utah.org/llv
Animal Euthanasia Agency #05 .... https://secure.e-utah.org/llv
Arbitrator, Alternate Dispute Resolution #05 .... https://secure.e-utah.org/llv
Architect #05 .... https://secure.e-utah.org/llv
Athletic Judge #05 .... https://secure.e-utah.org/llv
Bank #10 .... www.dfi.state.ut.us/Banks.htm
Barber #05 .... https://secure.e-utah.org/llv
Barber School/Instructor #05 .... https://secure.e-utah.org/llv
Boxer #05 .... https://secure.e-utah.org/llv
Building Inspector/Trainee #05 .... https://secure.e-utah.org/llv
Building Trades, General #05 .... https://secure.e-utah.org/llv
Chiropractor #05 .... https://secure.e-utah.org/llv
Consumer Lender #10 .... www.dfi.state.ut.us/consumer.htm
Contractor #05 .... https://secure.e-utah.org/llv
Controlled Substance Precursor Distributor #05 .... https://secure.e-utah.org/llv
Cosmetologist #05 .... https://secure.e-utah.org/llv
Cosmetology School/Instructor #05 .... https://secure.e-utah.org/llv
Counselor Trainee, Professional #05 .... https://secure.e-utah.org/llv
Counselor, Professional #05 .... https://secure.e-utah.org/llv
Credit Union #10 .... www.dfi.state.ut.us/CreditUn.htm
Deception Detection Examiner/Intern #05 .... https://secure.e-utah.org/llv
Dental Hygienist #05 .... https://secure.e-utah.org/llv
Dental Hygienist with Local Anesthesia #05 .... https://secure.e-utah.org/llv
Dentist #05 .... https://secure.e-utah.org/llv
Dietitian #05 .... https://secure.e-utah.org/llv
Electrician, Apprentice/Journeyman/Master #05 .... https://secure.e-utah.org/llv
Electrologist #05 .... https://secure.e-utah.org/llv
Employee Leasing Company #05 .... https://secure.e-utah.org/llv
Engineer #05 .... https://secure.e-utah.org/llv
Engineer, Structural Professional #05 .... https://secure.e-utah.org/llv
Environmental Health Specialist/Specialist-In-Training #05 https://secure.e-utah.org/llv
Escrow Agent #10 .... www.dfi.state.ut.us/OtherInt.htm
Funeral Service Establishment #05 .... https://secure.e-utah.org/llv
Health Care Assistant #05 .... https://secure.e-utah.org/llv
Health Facility Administrator #05 .... https://secure.e-utah.org/llv
Hearing Aid Specialist #05 .... https://secure.e-utah.org/llv
Hearing Instrument Intern #05 .... https://secure.e-utah.org/llv
Industrial Loan #10 .... www.dfi.state.ut.us/IndustLn.htm
Laboratory, Analytical #05 .... https://secure.e-utah.org/llv
Landscape Architect #05 .... https://secure.e-utah.org/llv
Manufactured Housing Dealer/Salesperson #05 .... https://secure.e-utah.org/llv
Marriage & Family Therapist/Therapist Trainee #05 .... https://secure.e-utah.org/llv
Massage Technician/Apprentice #05 .... https://secure.e-utah.org/llv
Mediator, Alternate Dispute Resolution #05 .... https://secure.e-utah.org/llv
Medical Doctor/Surgeon #05 .... https://secure.e-utah.org/llv
Midwife Nurse #05 .... https://secure.e-utah.org/llv

Mortgage Broker, Residential #02	www.commerce.state.ut.us/re/lists/agntbrkr.txt
Mortgage Lender #10	www.dfi.state.ut.us/mortgage.htm
Naturopath #05	https://secure.e-utah.org/llv
Naturopathic Physician #05	https://secure.e-utah.org/llv
Negotiator, Alternate Dispute Resolution #05	https://secure.e-utah.org/llv
Nuclear Pharmacy #05	https://secure.e-utah.org/llv
Nurse #05	https://secure.e-utah.org/llv
Nurse-LPN #05	https://secure.e-utah.org/llv
Occupational Therapist/Assistant #05	https://secure.e-utah.org/llv
Optometrist #05	https://secure.e-utah.org/llv
Osteopathic Physician #05	https://secure.e-utah.org/llv
Pharmaceutical Administration Facility #05	https://secure.e-utah.org/llv
Pharmaceutical Dog Trainer #05	https://secure.e-utah.org/llv
Pharmaceutical Researcher #05	https://secure.e-utah.org/llv
Pharmaceutical Teaching Organization #05	https://secure.e-utah.org/llv
Pharmaceutical Whlse./Dist./Mfg. #05	https://secure.e-utah.org/llv
Pharmacist/Pharmacist Intern #05	https://secure.e-utah.org/llv
Pharmacy Out-of-State Mail Service #05	https://secure.e-utah.org/llv
Pharmacy Retail/Branch #05	https://secure.e-utah.org/llv
Pharmacy Technician #05	https://secure.e-utah.org/llv
Pharmacy, Institutional/Hospital #05	https://secure.e-utah.org/llv
Physical Therapist #05	https://secure.e-utah.org/llv
Physician Assistant #05	https://secure.e-utah.org/llv
Plumber, Apprentice/Journeyman #05	https://secure.e-utah.org/llv
Podiatrist #05	https://secure.e-utah.org/llv
Pre-Need Provider/Sales Agent #05	https://secure.e-utah.org/llv
Probation Provider, Private #05	https://secure.e-utah.org/llv
Psychologist #05	https://secure.e-utah.org/llv
Public Accountant-CPA #05	https://secure.e-utah.org/llv
Radiology Practical Technician #05	https://secure.e-utah.org/llv
Radiology Technologist #05	https://secure.e-utah.org/llv
Real Estate Agent #02	www.commerce.state.ut.us/re/lists/agntbrkr.txt
Real Estate Appraiser #02	www.commerce.state.ut.us/re/lists/apprais.txt
Real Estate Broker #02	www.commerce.state.ut.us/re/lists/agntbrkr.txt
Real Estate Establishment #05	https://secure.e-utah.org/llv
Recreational Therapist #05	https://secure.e-utah.org/llv
Recreational Vehicle Dealer #05	https://secure.e-utah.org/llv
Residential Electrician Trainee/Journeyman/Master #05	https://secure.e-utah.org/llv
Residential Plumber/Jouneyman/Apprentice #05	https://secure.e-utah.org/llv
Respiratory Care Practitioner #05	https://secure.e-utah.org/llv
Sanitarian #05	https://secure.e-utah.org/llv
Security Company #05	https://secure.e-utah.org/llv
Security Officer, Armed/Unarmed Private #05	https://secure.e-utah.org/llv
Shorthand Reporter #05	https://secure.e-utah.org/llv
Social Service Aide/Worker/Trainee #05	https://secure.e-utah.org/llv
Social Worker #05	https://secure.e-utah.org/llv
Social Worker, Clinical #05	https://secure.e-utah.org/llv
Speech Pathologist/Audiologist #05	https://secure.e-utah.org/llv
Substance Abuse Counselor #05	https://secure.e-utah.org/llv
Surveyor #05	https://secure.e-utah.org/llv
Veterinarian/Veterinary Intern #05	https://secure.e-utah.org/llv
Veterinary Pharmaceutical Outlet #05	https://secure.e-utah.org/llv

Licensing Quick Finder

Accounting Firm #05	801-530-6628
Acupuncturist #05	801-530-6628
Alarm Company #05	801-530-6628
Alarm Company Agent/Response Runner #05	801-530-6628
Animal Euthanasia Agency #05	801-530-6628
Arbitrator, Alternate Dispute Resolution #05	801-530-6628
Architect #05	801-530-6628
Athletic Event Promoter #05	801-530-6628
Athletic Judge #05	801-530-6628
Athletic Manager #05	801-530-6628
Attorney #09	801-531-9077
Bank #10	801-538-8835
Barber #05	801-530-6628
Barber School/Instructor #05	801-530-6628
Beekeeper #03	801-538-7184
Boxer #05	801-530-6628
Brand Inspector #03	801-538-7161
Building Inspector/Trainee #05	801-530-6628
Building Trades, General #05	801-530-6628
Burglar Alarm Agent #11	801-965-4484
Bus Driver #11	801-965-4406
Chiropractor #05	801-530-6628
Consumer Lender #10	801-538-8830
Contractor #05	801-530-6628
Controlled Substance Precursor Dist. #05	801-530-6628
Cosmetologist #05	801-530-6628
Cosmetology School/Instructor #05	801-530-6628
Counselor Trainee, Professional #05	801-530-6628
Counselor, Professional #05	801-530-6628
Credit Union #10	801-538-8840
Deception Detection Examiner/Intern #05	801-530-6628
Dental Hygienist #05	801-530-6628
Dentist #05	801-530-6628
Dietitian #05	801-530-6628
Egg & Poultry Inspector #03	801-538-7124
Electrician, Apprentice/Journeyman/Master #05	801-530-6628
Electrologist #05	801-530-6628
Employee Leasing Company #05	801-530-6628
Endowment Care-Cemetery #05	801-530-6628
Engineer #05	801-530-6628
Engineer, Structural Professional #05	801-530-6628
Environmental Health Specialist/Specialist-In-Training #05	801-530-6628
Escrow Agent #10	801-538-8842
Feed #03	801-538-7183
Food & Dairy Inspector #03	801-538-7124
Funeral Service Director/Apprentice #5	801-530-6628
Funeral Service Establishment #5	801-530-6628
Geologist #07	801-537-3300
Grain & Seed #03	801-538-7183
Health Care Assistant #05	801-530-6628
Health Facility Administrator #05	801-530-6628
Hearing Aid Specialist #05	801-530-6628
Hearing Instrument Intern #05	801-530-6628
Industrial Loan #10	801-538-8841
Insurance Agent #08	801-538-3855
Insurance Establishment #08	801-538-3855
Interpreter for the Deaf #12	801-263-4860
Laboratory, Analytical #05	801-530-6628
Landscape Architect #05	801-530-6628
Liquor License #01	801-977-6800
Liquor Store (Retail Liquor License) #1	801-977-6800
Manufactured Housing Dealer/Salesperson #05	801-530-6628
Marriage & Family Therapist/Therapist Trainee #05	801-530-6628
Massage Technician/Apprentice #05	801-530-6628
Meat Inspector #03	801-538-7161
Mediator, Alternate Dispute Resolution #05	801-530-6628
Medical Doctor/Surgeon #05	801-530-6628
Midwife Nurse #05	801-530-6628
Mortgage Broker, Residential #02	801-530-6747
Mortgage Lender #10	801-538-8830
Naturopath #05	801-530-6628
Naturopathic Physician #05	801-530-6628
Notary Public #04	801-530-6078
Nuclear Pharmacy #05	801-530-6628
Nurse #05	801-530-6628
Nurse-LPN #05	801-530-6628
Occupational Therapist/Assistant #05	801-530-6628
Optometrist #05	801-530-6628
Osteopathic Physician #05	801-530-6628
Pesticide Dealer/Applicator #03	801-538-7188
Pharmaceutical Admin. Facility #05	801-530-6628
Pharmaceutical Dog Trainer #05	801-530-6628
Pharmaceutical Researcher #05	801-530-6628
Pharmaceutical Teaching Organization #05	801-530-6628
Pharmaceutical Whlse./Dist./Mfg. #05	801-530-6628
Pharmacist/Pharmacist Intern #05	801-530-6628
Pharmacy Out-of-State Mail Svc #05	801-530-6628
Pharmacy Retail/Branch #05	801-530-6628
Pharmacy Technician #05	801-530-6628
Pharmacy, Institutional/Hospital #05	801-530-6628
Physical Therapist #05	801-530-6628
Physician Assistant #05	801-530-6628
Plumber, Apprentice/Journeyman #05	801-530-6628
Podiatrist #05	801-530-6628
Polygraph Examiner #11	801-965-4484
Pre-Need Provider/Sales Agent #05	801-530-6628
Probation Provider, Private #05	801-530-6628
Psychological Assistant #05	801-530-6628
Psychologist #05	801-530-6628
Public Accountant-CPA #05	801-530-6628
Radiology Practical Technician #05	801-530-6628
Radiology Technologist #05	801-530-6628
Real Estate Broker/Agent #02	801-530-6747
Real Estate Appraiser #02	801-530-6747
Real Estate Establishment #05	801-530-6628
Recreational Therapist #05	801-530-6628
Recreational Vehicle Dealer #05	801-530-6628
Referee #05	801-530-6628
Residential Electrician Trainee/Journeyman/Master #05	801-530-6628
Residential Plumber/Jouneyman/Apprentice #05	801-530-6628
Respiratory Care Practitioner #05	801-530-6628
Sanitarian #05	801-530-6628
Savings & Loan #10	801-538-8842
School Administrator #06	801-538-7751
School Librarian #06	801-538-7751
Securities Broker/Dealer #05	801-530-6628
Security Company #05	801-530-6628
Security Guard #11	801-965-4484
Security Officer, Armed/Unarmed #05	801-530-6628
Shorthand Reporter #05	801-530-6628
Social Service Aide/Worker/Trainee #5	801-530-6628
Social Worker #05	801-530-6628
Social Worker, Clinical #05	801-530-6628
Speech Pathologist/Audiologist #05	801-530-6628
Substance Abuse Counselor #05	801-530-6628
Surveyor #05	801-530-6628
Taxi Driver/Chauffeur #11	801-965-4406
Teacher #06	801-538-7751
Third Party Payment Issuer #10	801-538-8842
Truck Driver #11	801-965-4406
Veterinarian/Veterinary Intern #05	801-530-6628
Veterinary Pharmaceutical Outlet #05	801-530-6628
Weights & Measures #03	801-538-7158

Licensing Agency Information

#01 Alcoholic Beverage Control Department, PO Box 30408, Salt Lake City, UT 84130-0408; 801-977-6800, Fax: 801-977-6888.
www.alcbev.state.ut.us

#02 Commerce Department, 160 E 300 S, 2nd Fl, Salt Lake City, UT 84145-0806; 801-530-6747, Fax: 801-530-6749.
www.commerce.state.ut.us/re/udre1.htm
Direct web site URL to search for licensees: www.commerce.state.ut.us/re/lists/data.htm. You can search online using alphabetical lists

#03 Department of Agriculture, PO Box 146500, Salt Lake City, UT 84114-6500; 801-538-7100, Fax: 801-538-7126.

#04 Department of Commerce, 160 E 300 S, Salt Lake City, UT 84114-6705; 801-530-4849.
www.commerce.state.ut.us/corporat/notarypublic.htm

#05 Department of Commerce, PO Box 146741 (160 E 300 S, Heber M Wells Bldg), Salt Lake City, UT 84114-6741; 801-530-6628, Fax: 801-530-6511.
www.commerce.state.ut.us/dopl
Direct web site URL to search for licensees: https://secure.e-utah.org/llv. You can search online using alphabetical lists.

#06 Educator Licensing, 250 E 500 S, Salt Lake City, UT 84111; 801-538-7751, Fax: 801-538-7973.
www.usoe.k12.ut.us

#07 Geological Survey Department, PO Box 146100, Salt Lake City, UT 84114-6100; 801-537-3300, Fax: 801-537-3400.

#08 Insurance Department, 3110 State Office Bldg, Salt Lake City, UT 84114-6901; 801-538-3855, Fax: 801-538-3829.
www.insurance.state.ut.us

Direct web site URL to search for licensees: www.commerce.state.ut.us/web/commerce/DOPL/current.htm Or, from www.insurance.state.ut.us, click on "Industry Services."

#09 State Bar Association, 645 S 200 E, Salt Lake City, UT 84111; 801-531-9077, Fax: 801-531-0660.
www.utahbar.com

#10 Department of Financial Institutions, 324 S State #201, PO Box 89, Salt Lake City, UT 84110-0089; 801-538-8830, Fax: 801-538-8894.
www.dfi.state.ut.us

#11 Department of Public Safety, 4501 S 2700 W, Salt Lake City, UT 84130-0560; 801-965-4406.

#12 Division of Services for the Deaf & Hard of Hearing, 5709 S 1500 W, Salt Lake City, UT 84123; 801-263-4870, Fax: 801-263-4865.
www.usor.state.ut.us/dsdhh

Utah Federal Courts

County/Court Cross Reference

All counties report to Salt Lake City.

US District Court

District of Utah

Clerk's Office, Room 150, 350 S Main St, Salt Lake City, UT 84101-2180 (Courier Address: Use mail address for courier delivery), 801-524-6100, Fax: 801-526-1175.

http://www.utd.uscourts.gov

Counties: All counties in Utah. Although all cases are heard here, the district is divided into Northern and Central Divisions. The Northern Division includes the counties of Box Elder, Cache, Rich, Davis, Morgan and Weber, and the Central Division includes allother counties.

Indexing/Storage: Cases are indexed by defendant and plaintiff as well as by case number. New cases are available in the index 1 day after filing date. A computer index is maintained. Older records are on microfiche. Open records are located at this court.

Fee & Payment: The fee is $20.00 per item (one party name or case number). Payment may be made by money order, cashier check, personal check, Visa, Mastercard. Prepayment is required. Payee: Clerk, US District Court. Certification fee: $7.00 per document. Copy fee: $.50 per page. You are allowed to make your own copies. These copies cost $.15 per page. Public terminals are available.

Phone Search: Only limited information will be released over the telephone.

Mail Search: A stamped self addressed envelope is not required.

In Person: In person searching is available.

PACER: Sign-up number is 800-676-6856. Access fee is $.60 per minute. Toll-free access: 800-314-3423. Local access: 801-524-4221. PACER is available online at http://pacer.utd.uscourts.gov. Case records are available back to July 1, 1989. Records are never purged. New records are available online after 1 day. PACER is available online at http://pacer.utd.uscourts.gov.

US Bankruptcy Court

District of Utah

Clerk of Court, Frank E Moss Courthouse, 350 S Main St, Room 301, Salt Lake City, UT 84101 (Courier Address: Use mail address for courier delivery), 801-524-6687, Fax: 801-524-4409.

http://www.utb.uscourts.gov

Counties: All counties in Utah. Although all cases are handled here, the court divides itself into two divisions. The Northern Division includes the counties of Box Elder, Cache, Rich, Davis, Morgan and Weber, and the Central Division includes the remainingcounties. Court is held once per week in Ogden for Northern cases.

Indexing/Storage: Cases are indexed by debtor and creditors as well as by case number. New cases are available in the index as soon as the work load permits after filing date. A computer index is maintained. Open records are located at this court.

Fee & Payment: The fee is $20.00 per item (one party name or case number). Payment may be made by money order, cashier check, personal check. Prepayment is required. Debtor's checks are not accepted. Payee: Clerk, US Bankruptcy Court. Certification fee: $7.00 per document. Copy fee: $.50 per page.

Phone Search: Only docket information is available by phone. An automated voice case information service (VCIS) is available. Call VCIS at 800-733-6740 or 801-524-3107.

Fax Search: The court has a contract with a copy service that will accept fax requests. Call for more information. The court has a contract with a copy service that will fax docket listings for a fee. Call for more information.

Mail Search: Always enclose a stamped self addressed envelope.

In Person: In person searching is available.

PACER: Sign-up number is 800-676-6856. Access fee is $.60 per minute. Toll-free access: 800-718-1188. Local access: 801-524-5760. Case records are available back to January 1985. Records are purged after 12 months. New civil records are available online after 2 days or more. PACER is available online at http://pacer.utb.uscourts.gov.

Opinions Online: Court opinions are available online at http://www.utb.uscourts.gov/OPINIONS/opin.htm.

Utah County Courts

Court	Jurisdiction	No. of Courts	How Organized
District Courts*	General	41	8 Districts
Justice Courts	Limited	128	128 Cities/ Counties
Juvenile Courts	Special		8 Juvenile Districts

* Profiled in this Sourcebook.

	CIVIL								
Court	Tort	Contract	Real Estate	Min. Claim	Max. Claim	Small Claims	Estate	Eviction	Domestic Relations
District Courts*	X	X	X	$20,000	No Max	$2000	X	X	X
Justice Courts	X	X		$0	$1000	$2000			
Juvenile Courts									

	CRIMINAL				
Court	Felony	Misdemeanor	DWI/DUI	Preliminary Hearing	Juvenile
District Courts*	X	X	X	X	
Justice Courts		X	X		
Juvenile Courts					X

ADMINISTRATION

Court Administrator, 450 S State Street, Salt Lake City, UT, 84114; 801-578-3800, Fax: 801-578-3843. http://courtlink.utcourts.gov

COURT STRUCTURE

41 District Courts are arranged in eight judicial districts. Effective July 1, 1996, each Circuit Court (the lower court) was combined with District Court (the higher court) in each county. It is reported that branch courts in larger counties such as Salt Lake which were formerly Circuit Courts have been elevated to District Courts, with full jurisdiction over felony as well as misdemeanor cases. Many misdemeanors are handled at Justice Courts, which are limited jurisdiction.

ONLINE ACCESS

Case information from all Utah District Court locations is available through XChange. Fees include $25.00 registration and $30.00 per month plus $.10 per minute for usage, over 120 minutes. Information about XChange and the subscription agreement can be found at http://courtlink.utcourts.gov/howto/access or call 801-238-7877. Records go back seven to ten years.

ADDITIONAL INFORMATION

The Administrative Office of Courts provides a search service to the public. One can search on a particular case or the case history of individuals. Information on this service can be found at http://courtlink.utcourts.gov/howto/access. Include the county or geographic region. UT Code Rule 4-202.08 sets fees for record searches at $21.00 per hour, billed on 15 minute increments, with the first 15 minutes free and the copy fee at $.25 per page.

📖📖📖📖📖📖

Beaver County

5th Judicial District Court PO Box 1683, Beaver, UT 84713; 435-438-5309; Fax: 435-438-5395. Hours: 8AM-5PM (MST). *Felony, Misdemeanor, Civil, Eviction, Probate.*

Civil Records: Access: Fax, mail, in person, online. Both court and visitors may perform in person searches. Search fee: $13.00 per hour. Required to search: name, years to search. Civil cases indexed by defendant, plaintiff. Civil records archived from 1800s, are on computer back to 1997. Online access available through XChange. See state introduction.

Criminal Records: Access: Fax, mail, in person, online. Both court and visitors may perform in person searches. Search fee: $13.00 per hour. Required to search: name, years to search, DOB. Criminal records archived from 1800s, are on computer back to 1997. Online access available through XChange. See state introduction.

General Information: Public Access terminal is available. No adoption, juvenile, sealed records released. SASE required. Turnaround time 2-7 days. Fax notes: Fee to fax results is $.25 per page. Copy fee: $.25 per page. Certification fee: $2.00 plus $.50 per page. Fee payee: Beaver County Court. Personal checks accepted. Prepayment is required.

Box Elder County

1st District Court 43 N Main, PO Box 873, Brigham City, UT 84302; 435-734-4600; Fax: 435-734-4610. Hours: 8AM-5PM (MST). *Felony, Misdemeanor, Civil, Eviction, Small Claims, Probate.*

Civil Records: Access: Phone, fax, mail, online, in person. Both court and visitors may perform in person searches. Search fee: $13.00 per name. Required to search: name, years to search. Civil cases indexed by defendant, plaintiff. Civil records on computer from 3/87, books, microfiche, archived from 1856. Online access available through XChange. See state introduction.

Criminal Records: Access: Fax, mail, online, in person. Both court and visitors may perform in person searches. Search fee: $13.00 per name. Required to search: name, years to search; also helpful: DOB, SSN. Criminal records on computer from 3/87, books, microfiche, archived from 1856. Online access available through XChange. See state introduction.

General Information: Public Access terminal is available. No adoptions, sealed records released. SASE required. Turnaround time 1 week. Fax notes: Fee to fax results is $.50 per page. Copy fee: $.25 per page. Certification fee: $2.00. Fee payee: 1st District Court. Personal checks accepted. Credit cards accepted: Visa, MasterCard. Prepayment is required.

Cache County

1st District Court 140 N. 100 W., Logan, UT 84321; 435-750-1300; Fax: 435-750-1355. Hours: 8AM-5PM (MST). *Felony, Misdemeanor, Civil, Eviction, Small Claims, Probate.*

http://courtlink.utcourts.gov/howto/access/index.htm

Civil Records: Access: Phone, mail, online, in person. Both court and visitors may perform in person searches. Search fee: $10.00 per hour. Required to search: name, years to search. Civil cases indexed by defendant, plaintiff. Civil records on computer from 11-87, archived from 1983, microfiche in Salt Lake City. Online access available through XChange. See state introduction.

Criminal Records: Access: Phone, mail, online, in person. Both court and visitors may perform in person searches. Search fee: $10.00 per hour. Required to search: name, years to search; also helpful: DOB, SSN. Criminal records on computer from 11-87, archived from 1983, microfiche in Salt Lake City. Online access available through XChange. See state introduction.

General Information: Public Access terminal is available. No sealed records released. SASE required. Turnaround time 2 weeks. Fax notes: Fee to fax results is $2.00 per page. Copy fee: $.25 per page. Certification fee: $2.00 plus $.50 per page. Fee payee: 1st Judicial District. Personal checks accepted. Credit cards accepted: Visa, MasterCard. Credit cards accepted in person only. Prepayment is required.

Carbon County

7th District Court 149 E. 100 South, Price, UT 84501; 435-636-3400; Fax: 435-637-7349. Hours: 8AM-5PM (MST). *Felony, Misdemeanor, Civil, Eviction, Small Claims, Probate.*

Civil Records: Access: Phone, mail, online, in person. Both court and visitors may perform in person searches. Search fee: $10.00 per hour. First 20 minutes no charge. Required to search: name, years to search. Civil cases indexed by defendant, plaintiff. Civil records on computer from 1988, on microfiche from 1985, archived prior to 1988. Online access available through XChange. See state introduction.

Criminal Records: Access: Phone, mail, online, in person. Both court and visitors may perform in person searches. Search fee: $10.00 per hour. First 20 minutes no charge. Required to search: name, years to search, DOB; also helpful: SSN. Criminal records on computer from 1988, on microfiche from 1985, archived prior to 1988. Online access available through XChange. See state introduction.

General Information: Public Access terminal is available. No sealed records released. SASE required. Turnaround time 48 hrs after receipt. Fax notes: Fee to fax results is $2.00 1st page, $1.00 each add'l. Copy fee: $.25 per page. Certification fee: $2.00 plus $.50 per page. Fee payee: 7th District Court. Personal checks accepted. Credit cards accepted: Visa. Will bill fax fees.

Daggett County

8th District Court PO Box 219, Manila, UT 84046; 435-784-3154; Fax: 435-784-3335. Hours: 9AM-Noon, 1-5PM (MST). *Felony, Misdemeanor, Civil, Eviction, Probate.*

Civil Records: Access: Phone, fax, mail, in person. Both court and visitors may perform in person searches. No search fee. Required to search: name, years to search. Civil cases indexed by defendant, plaintiff. Civil records archived from 1918. Fax access requires prior approval.

Criminal Records: Access: Fax, mail, in person. Both court and visitors may perform in person searches. No search fee. Required to search: name, years to search, DOB, signed release. Criminal records archived from 1918. Same as civil.

General Information: No sealed records released. SASE required. Turnaround time 10 days. Signature and record request form required. Fax notes: Fee to fax results is $.50 per page. Copy fee: $.25 per page. Certification fee: $2.00 plus $.50 per page. Fee payee: Daggett County. Personal checks accepted. Prepayment is required.

Davis County

2nd District Court PO Box 769, Farmington, UT 84025; 385-447-3800; Fax: 385-447-3881. Hours: 8AM-5PM (MST). *Felony, Class A Misdemeanor, Civil, Probate.*

Civil Records: Access: Phone, mail, online, in person. Both court and visitors may perform in person searches. Search fee: $10.00 per hour. First 30 minutes no charge. Required to search: name, years to search. Civil cases indexed by defendant, plaintiff. Civil records on computer back to 1989, prior on microfiche and archived. Online access available through XChange. See state introduction.

Criminal Records: Access: Phone, mail, online, in person. Both court and visitors may perform in person searches. Search fee: $10.00 per hour. First 30 minutes no charge. Required to search: name, years to search, DOB; also helpful: SSN. Criminal records on computer back to 1989, prior on microfiche and archived. Online access available via XChange. See state introduction.

General Information: Public Access terminal is available. No adoption, criminal pre-sentence investigation records released. SASE required. Turnaround time 2-3 days. Fax notes: Will fax results, not fee indicated. Copy fee: $.25 per page. Certified copies $.50 per page. Certification fee: $2.00. Fee payee: 2nd District Court. Personal checks accepted. Prepayment is required.

2nd District Court - Bountiful Department
805 South Main, Bountiful, UT 84010; 385-397-7008; Fax: 385-397-7010. Hours: 8AM-5PM (MST). *Felony, Misdemeanor, Civil, Eviction, Small Claims, Probate.*

Civil Records: Access: Phone, mail, online, in person. Both court and visitors may perform in person searches. No search fee. Required to search: name, years to search; also helpful: address. Civil cases indexed by defendant, plaintiff. Civil records on computer since 10/86. For in person searching, call ahead. Online access available via XChange. See state introduction.

Criminal Records: Access: Phone, mail, online, in person. Both court and visitors may perform in person searches. No search fee. Required to search: name, years to search, DOB, signed release. Criminal records on computer since 10/86. Online access available through XChange. See state introduction. For in person searching, call ahead.

General Information: Public Access terminal is available. SASE required. Turnaround time 5 days. Copy fee: $.25 per page. Certification fee: $2.50. Fee payee: District Court. Personal checks accepted. Prepayment is required.

2nd District Court - Layton Department
425 Wasatch Dr, Layton, UT 84041; 385-546-2484; Fax: 385-546-8224. Hours: 8AM-5PM (MST). *Felony, Misdemeanor, Civil, Eviction, Small Claims, Probate.*

Civil Records: Access: Online, in person. Visitors must perform in person searches for themselves. No search fee. Required to search: name, years to search. Civil cases indexed by defendant, plaintiff. Civil records on computer from 1988, archived from start of court. Computer index alpha and case number, archives by alpha from 1982, prior to 1982 not indexed. Online access available through XChange. See state introduction.

Criminal Records: Access: Mail, online, in person. Both court and visitors may perform in person searches. Search fee: $10.00 for 30 minutes after first 10. Required to search: name, years to search; also helpful: DOB, SSN. Criminal records on computer from 1988, archived from start of court. Computer index alpha and case number, archives by alpha from 1982, prior to 1982 not indexed. Online access available through XChange. See state introduction.

General Information: Public Access terminal is available. No confidential records, probation reports, sealed records released. SASE requested. Turnaround time 1 day. Copy fee: $.25 per page. Certification fee: $2.00. Fee payee: Layton Circuit Court. Personal checks accepted.

Duchesne County

8th District Court PO Box 990, Duchesne, UT 84021; 435-738-2753; Fax: 435-738-2754. Hours: 8AM-5PM (MST). *Felony, Misdemeanor, Civil, Eviction, Small Claims, Probate.*

Civil Records: Access: Phone, mail, fax, online, in person. Both court and visitors may perform in person searches. Search fee: $10.00 per hour. First 20 minutes no charge. Required to search: name, years to search. Civil cases indexed by defendant, plaintiff. Civil records on computer from 1988, civil on microfiche from 1915 to 1980. Online access available through XChange. See state introduction.

Criminal Records: Access: Phone, mail, fax, online, in person. Both court and visitors may perform in person searches. Search fee: $10.00 per hour. First 20 minutes no charge. Required to search: name, years to search, DOB, SSN. Criminal records on computer since 1988; index books back 13 years prior; earlier archived. Online access available through XChange. See state introduction.

General Information: Public Access terminal is available. No confidential records released. SASE required. Turnaround time 1-5 days. Fax notes: Fee to fax results is $1.00 per page. Copy fee: $.25 per page; $.50 if certified. Certification fee: $2.00. Fee payee: 8th District Court. Personal checks accepted. Prepayment is required.

8th District Court - Roosevelt Department
PO Box 1286, Roosevelt, UT 84066; 435-722-0235; Fax: 435-722-0236. Hours: 8AM-5PM (MST). *Felony, Misdemeanor, Civil, Eviction, Probate.*

Civil Records: Access: Mail, online, in person. Both court and visitors may perform in person searches. Search fee: $10.00 per hour. First 20 minutes no charge. Required to search: name, years to search. Civil cases indexed by defendant, plaintiff. Civil records on computer since 1988. Online access available through XChange. See state introduction.

Criminal Records: Access: Mail, online, in person. Both court and visitors may perform in person searches. Search fee: $10.00 per hour. First 20 minutes no charge. Required to search: name, years to search; also helpful: DOB. Criminal records on computer since 1988. Online access available through XChange. See state introduction.

General Information: Public Access terminal is available. No confidential, sealed, expunged or juvenile records released. Turnaround time 2-5 days. Copy fee: $.25 per page. Certification fee: $2.00 plus $.50 per page. Personal checks accepted. Prepayment is required.

Emery County

7th District Court PO Box 635, Castle Dale, UT 84513; 435-381-2619; Fax: 435-381-5625. Hours: 8AM-5PM (MST). *Felony, Misdemeanor, Civil, Eviction, Probate.*

Note: Phone for hearing impaired is 800-992-0172.

Civil Records: Access: Phone, fax, mail, in person, online. Both court and visitors may perform in person searches. Search fee: $10.00 per hour. First 20 minutes no charge. Required to search: name, years to search. Civil cases indexed by defendant, plaintiff. Civil records on computer from 1997, microfiche and archived from start of district court. Online access available through XChange. See state introduction.

Criminal Records: Access: Phone, fax, mail, in person, online. Both court and visitors may perform in person searches. Search fee: $10.00 per hour. First 20 minutes no charge. Required to search: name, years to search, DOB. Criminal records on computer from 1997, microfiche and archived from start of district court. Online access available through XChange. See state introduction.

General Information: Public Access terminal is available. No adoption, sealed records released. SASE required. Turnaround time 1 week unless large request. Fax notes: $2.00 for first page, $1.00 each add'l. Copy fee: $.25 per page. Certification fee: $2.00 plus $.50 per page. Fee payee: 7th District Court. Personal checks accepted. Prepayment is required.

Garfield County

6th District Court PO Box 77, Panguitch, UT 84759; 435-676-8826 X104; Fax: 435-676-8239. Hours: 9AM-5PM (MST). *Felony, Misdemeanor, Civil, Eviction, Small Claims, Probate.*

Civil Records: Access: Phone, fax, mail, in person. Both court and visitors may perform in person searches. Search fee: $13.00 per hour. Required to search: name, years to search. Civil cases indexed by defendant, plaintiff. Civil records archived for 100 years; on computer back to 2000.

Criminal Records: Access: Fax, mail, in person. Both court and visitors may perform in person searches. Search fee: $13.00 per hour. Required to search: name, years to search. Criminal records archived for 100 years; on computer back to 2000.

General Information: No adoption records released. SASE not required. Turnaround time 1 day. Fax notes: Fee to fax results is $1.00 for 1st page, $.50 each add'l. Copy fee: $.25 per page. Certification fee: $2.00 plus $.50 per page. Fee payee: 6th District Court. Personal checks accepted. Prepayment is required.

Grand County

7th District Court 125 E. Center, Moab, UT 84532; 435-259-1349; Fax: 435-259-4081. Hours: 8AM-5PM (MST). *Felony, Misdemeanor, Civil, Eviction, Probate.*

Civil Records: Access: Phone, mail, online, in person. Both court and visitors may perform in person searches. No search fee. Required to search: name, years to search. Civil cases indexed by defendant. District records on computer from Spring 1990, Circuit from spring 1989, archived since court started. Online access available through XChange. See state introduction.

Criminal Records: Access: Phone, mail, online, in person. Both court and visitors may perform in person searches. Search fee: None for 1st 20 minutes; $10.00 per hour thereafter. Required to search: name, years to search; also helpful: DOB, SSN. District records on computer from spring 1990, Circuit from spring 1989, archived since court started. Online access available through XChange. See state introduction.

General Information: Public Access terminal is available. No adoption, expunged records released. SASE required. Turnaround time same day. Fax notes: $2.00 for 1st page; $1.00 each add'l. Copy fee: $.25 per page. Certification fee: $2.00 plus $.50 per page. Fee payee: 7th District Court. Personal checks accepted. Credit cards accepted: Visa, MasterCard. Prepayment is required.

Iron County

5th District Court 40 North 100 East, Cedar City, UT 84720; 435-586-7440; Fax: 435-586-4801. Hours: 8AM-5PM (MST). *Felony, Misdemeanor, Civil, Eviction, Small Claims, Probate.*

Note: Hearing location also in Parawon, but records held here.

Civil Records: Access: Mail, online, in person. Both court and visitors may perform in person searches. Search fee: Per hour charges vary. Required to search: name. Civil cases indexed by defendant, plaintiff. District records on computer from 4/89, former Circuit Court records on computer from 1987, archived from 1900. Online access available through XChange. See state introduction.

Criminal Records: Access: Mail, online, in person. Both court and visitors may perform in person searches. Search fee: Per hour charge varies. Required to search: name, years to search, DOB, SSN. District records on computer from 4/89, former Circuit Court records on computer from 1987, archived from 1900. Online access available via XChange. See state introduction.

General Information: Public Access terminal is available. No sealed records released. SASE required. Turnaround time 2-3 days. Copy fee: $.50 per page. Certification fee: $2.00. Fee payee: 5th District Court. Personal checks accepted. Prepayment is required.

Juab County

4th District Court 160 N. Main, PO Box 249, Nephi, UT 84648; 435-623-0901; Fax: 435-623-0922. Hours: 8AM-5PM (MST). *Felony, Misdemeanor, Civil, Eviction, Probate.*

Civil Records: Access: Phone, mail, online, in person. Both court and visitors may perform in person searches. Search fee: $13.00 per hour. First 15 minutes are no charge. Required to search: name, years to search. Civil cases indexed by defendant, plaintiff. Civil records on computer from 11/94, archived since court started. Online access available through XChange. See state introduction.

Criminal Records: Access: Phone, mail, online, in person. Both court and visitors may perform in person searches. Search fee: $13.00 per hour. First 15 minutes are no charge. Required to search: name, years to search. Criminal records on computer from 11/94, archived since court started. Online access available through XChange. See state introduction.

General Information: Public Access terminal is available. All records must be viewed in this office. SASE required. Turnaround time 1 week. Copy fee: $.25 per page. Certification fee: $2.00 plus $.50 per page. Fee payee: 4th Circuit or District Court. Personal checks accepted. Prepayment is required.

Kane County

6th District Court 76 North Main, Kanab, UT 84741; 435-644-2458; Fax: 435-644-2052. Hours: 8AM-5PM (MST). *Felony, Misdemeanor, Civil, Eviction, Small Claims, Probate.*

Civil Records: Access: Phone, fax, mail, in person. Only the court performs in person searches; visitors may not. Search fee: First 15 minutes of search if free, thereafter $25.00 per hour. Required to search: name,

years to search. Civil cases indexed by defendant, plaintiff. Civil records on computer from 1985, archived since court started.

Criminal Records: Access: Phone, fax, mail, in person. Only the court performs in person searches; visitors may not. Search fee: First 15 minutes of search if free, thereafter $25.00 per hour. Required to search: name, years to search. Criminal records on computer from 1985, archived since court started.

General Information: No sealed, expunged records released. SASE requested. Turnaround time 2-3 days. Fax notes: Fee to fax results is $.50 per page. Copy fee: $.25 per page. Certification fee: $2.00. Fee payee: Kane County. Personal checks accepted. Prepayment is required.

Millard County

4th District Court 765 S Highway 99, #6, Fillmore, UT 84631; 435-743-6223; Fax: 435-743-6923. Hours: 8AM-5PM (MST). *Felony, Misdemeanor, Civil, Eviction, Small Claims, Probate.*

Civil Records: Access: Phone, mail, online, in person. Both court and visitors may perform in person searches. Search fee: $10.00 per hour. Required to search: name, years to search. Civil cases indexed by defendant, plaintiff. Civil records on computer from 1988, archived from 1896. Online access available through XChange. See state introduction.

Criminal Records: Access: Phone, mail, online, in person. Both court and visitors may perform in person searches. Search fee: $10.00 per hour. Required to search: name, years to search. Criminal records on computer from 1988, archived from 1896. Online access available via XChange. See state introduction.

General Information: Public Access terminal is available. No pre-sentence, expunged or sealed records released. SASE required. Turnaround time 1 day. Copy fee: $.25 per page. Certification fee: $2.00. Fee payee: 4th District Court. Business checks accepted. Prepayment is required.

Morgan County

2nd District Court PO Box 886, Morgan, UT 84050; 385-845-4020; Fax: 385-829-6176. Hours: 8AM-5PM (MST). *Felony, Misdemeanor, Civil, Eviction, Small Claims, Probate.*

Civil Records: Access: Phone, fax, mail, online, in person. Both court and visitors may perform in person searches. Search fee: $13.00 per hour. If less than 10 minutes, no charge. Required to search: name, years to search. Civil cases indexed by defendant, plaintiff. Civil records on computer since 1992; on microfiche, books, archived from 1862. Online access available through XChange. See state introduction.

Criminal Records: Access: Phone, fax, mail, online, in person. Both court and visitors may perform in person searches. Search fee: $13.00 per hour. If less than 10 minutes, no charge. Required to search: name, years to search, DOB; also helpful: SSN. Criminal records on computer since 1992, prior in books. Online access available through XChange. See state introduction.

General Information: Public Access terminal is available. No sealed records released. Turnaround time same day. Fax notes: No fee to fax results. Copy fee: $.25 per page. Certification fee: $2.00. Fee payee: Morgan District or Circuit Court. Personal checks accepted. Prepayment is required.

Piute County

6th District Court PO Box 99, Junction, UT 84740; 435-577-2840; Fax: 435-577-2433. Hours: 9AM-Noon, 1-5PM (MST). *Felony, Misdemeanor, Civil, Eviction, Small Claims, Probate.*

Civil Records: Access: Mail, in person. Both court and visitors may perform in person searches. Search fee: $10.00 per hour. Required to search: name, years to search. Civil cases indexed by defendant, plaintiff. Civil records archived from 1889.

Criminal Records: Access: Mail, in person. Both court and visitors may perform in person searches. Search fee: $10.00 per hour. Required to search: name, years to search. Criminal records archived from 1889.

General Information: No sealed records released. SASE required. Turnaround time 2-3 days. Copy fee: $.50 per page. Certification fee: $2.00. Fee payee: Piute County District Court. Personal checks accepted. Search fees may be billed if prior arrangements have been made.

Rich County

1st District Court PO Box 218, Randolph, UT 84064; 435-793-2415; Fax: 435-793-2410. Hours: 9AM-5PM (MST). *Felony, Misdemeanor, Civil, Eviction, Small Claims, Probate.*

Civil Records: Access: Phone, fax, mail, in person. Both court and visitors may perform in person searches. Search fee: $10.00 per hour. Required to search: name, years to search; also helpful: address. Civil cases indexed by defendant, plaintiff. Civil records archived since court started.

Criminal Records: Access: Phone, fax, mail, in person. Both court and visitors may perform in person searches. Search fee: $10.00 per hour. Required to search: name, years to search; also helpful: address, DOB, SSN. Criminal records archived since court started.

General Information: No sealed records released. SASE required. Turnaround time 2-3 days. Copy fee: $.25 per page. Certification: $2.00. Payee: Rich County. Personal checks accepted. Prepayment is required.

Salt Lake County

3rd District Court 450 South State Street, Salt Lake City, UT 84111; 801-238-7300; Fax: 801-238-7404. Hours: 8AM-5PM (MST). *Felony, Misdemeanor, Civil, Eviction, Small Claims, Probate.*

Note: An automated court information line allows phone access to court dates, fine balances, and judgment/divorce decrees (case or citation number required) at 801-238-7830.

Civil Records: Access: Phone, mail, online, in person. Both court and visitors may perform in person searches. Search fee: $10.00 per hour. First 20 minutes no charge. Required to search: name, years to search. Civil cases indexed by defendant, plaintiff. Civil records on computer from 1988, microfiche from 1940, archived from 1800s. Online access available through XChange. See state introduction.

Criminal Records: Access: Phone, mail, online, in person. Both court and visitors may perform in person searches. Search fee: $10.00 per hour. First 20 minutes no charge. Required to search: name, years to search, DOB, SSN. Criminal records on computer from 1988, microfiche from 1940, archived from 1800s. Online access available via XChange. See state introduction.

General Information: Public Access terminal is available. No juvenile or adoption records released. Turnaround time 2-3 days. Copy fee: $1.00 per page. Certification fee: $5.00. Fee payee: 3rd District Court. Personal checks accepted. Prepayment is required.

3rd District Court - Murray Department

5022 S. State St, Murray, UT 84107; 801-281-7700; Fax: 801-281-7736. Hours: 8AM-5PM (MST). *Felony, Misdemeanor, Civil, Eviction, Small Claims.*

Civil Records: Access: Fax, mail, online, in person. Both court and visitors may perform in person searches. Search fee: $10.00 per name. Required to search: name, years to search. Civil cases indexed by defendant, plaintiff. Civil records on computer from 1985, archived from 1979. Online access available through XChange.

See state introduction. Fax access requires pre-arrangement.

Criminal Records: Access: Fax, mail, online, in person. Both court and visitors may perform in person searches. Search fee: $10.00 per name. Required to search: name, years to search, DOB. Criminal records on computer from 1985, archived from 1979. Online access to criminal records is the same as civil.

General Information: Public Access terminal is available. No sealed records released. SASE required. Turnaround time 1 week. Fax notes: No fee to fax results. Copy fee: $.25 per page. Certification fee: $2.00 plus $.50 per page. Fee payee: Murray District Court. Personal checks accepted. Prepayment is required.

3rd District Court - Salt Lake City

450 South State St, Salt Lake City, UT 84111; 801-238-7480; Fax: 801-238-7396. Hours: 8AM-5PM (MST). *Felony, Misdemeanor, Civil, Eviction, Small Claims, Probate.*

Note: An automated court information line allows phone access to court dates, fine balances, and judgment/divorce decrees (case or citation number required) at 801-238-7830.

Civil Records: Access: Mail, online, in person. Both court and visitors may perform in person searches. No search fee. Required to search: name, years to search. Civil cases indexed by defendant, plaintiff. Civil records on computer from 1986, archived after satisfaction or dismissal, destroyed prior to 1985. Online access available through XChange. See state introduction.

Criminal Records: Access: Mail, online, in person. Both court and visitors may perform in person searches. Search fee: First 20 minutes no charge. Required to search: name, years to search, DOB; also helpful: SSN. Criminal records on computer from 1986, archived after satisfaction or dismissal, destroyed prior to 1985. Online access available via XChange. See state introduction.

General Information: Public Access terminal is available. No confidential records released. Turnaround time 2-3 days. Copy fee: $.50 per page. Certification fee: $2.00. Fee payee: 3rd Circuit Court. Business checks accepted. Credit cards: Visa, MasterCard.

3rd District Court - Sandy Department

210 West 10,000 South, Sandy, UT 84070-3282; 801-565-5714; Fax: 801-565-5703. Hours: 8AM-5PM (MST). *Felony, Misdemeanor, Civil, Eviction, Small Claims.*

Civil Records: Access: Phone, mail, online, in person. Both court and visitors may perform in person searches. Search fee: $13.00 per hour. Required to search: name, years to search. Civil cases indexed by defendant, plaintiff. Civil records on computer from 1986, civil archived from 1985. Online access available through XChange. See state introduction.

Criminal Records: Access: Phone, mail, online, in person. Both court and visitors may perform in person searches. Search fee: $13.00 per hour. Required to search: name, years to search. Criminal records on computer from 1986, civil archived from 1985. Online access available via XChange. See state introduction.

General Information: Public Access terminal is available. (Available by appointment.) No police reports, pre-sentence records released. SASE required. Turnaround time 1-2 weeks. Copy fee: $.50 per page. Certification fee: $2.00. Fee payee: 3rd District Court-Sandy Dept. Personal checks accepted. No two-party checks. Credit cards accepted: Visa, MasterCard. Prepayment is required.

3rd District Court - West Valley Department

3636 S. Constitution Blvd, West Valley, UT 84119; 801-982-2400; Fax: 801-967-9857. Hours: 8AM-5PM (MST). *Felony, Misdemeanor, Civil, Eviction, Small Claims, Probate.*

Civil Records: Access: Mail, online, in person. Both court and visitors may perform in person searches. Search fee: $10.00 per hour. Required to search: name,

years to search. Civil cases indexed by defendant, plaintiff. Civil records on computer since 1986, archived from 1983. Online access available through XChange. See state introduction.

Criminal Records: Access: Mail, online, in person. Both court and visitors may perform in person searches. Search fee: $10.00 per hour. Required to search: name, years to search. Criminal records on computer since 1986, archived from 1983. Online access available through XChange. See state introduction.

General Information: Public Access terminal is available. No sealed records released. SASE required. Turnaround time 1 week. Copy fee: $.25 per page. Certification fee: $2.00. Fee payee: 3rd District Court. Personal checks accepted. Prepayment is required.

San Juan County

7th District Court PO Box 68, Monticello, UT 84535; 435-587-2122; Fax: 435-587-2372. Hours: 8AM-5PM (MST). *Felony, Misdemeanor, Civil, Eviction, Probate.*

Civil Records: Access: Phone, mail, fax, online, in person. Both court and visitors may perform in person searches. Search fee: $10.00 per hour. Required to search: name, years to search. Civil cases indexed by defendant, plaintiff. Civil records on computer since 1991; on index books from 1919 to 1991. Online access available through XChange. See state introduction.

Criminal Records: Access: Mail, fax, online, in person. Both court and visitors may perform in person searches. Search fee: $10.00 per hour. Required to search: name, years to search. Criminal records on computer since 1991; on index books from 1919 to 1991. Online access available through XChange. See state introduction.

General Information: Public Access terminal is available. No juvenile records released. SASE required. Turnaround time 1 week. Fax notes: Fee to fax results is $1.00 per page. Copy fee: $.25 per page. Certification fee: $2.00 plus $.50 per page. Fee payee: 7th District Court. Personal checks accepted. Credit cards accepted: Visa, MasterCard. Visa, MC accepted in person only. Prepayment is required.

Sanpete County

6th District Court 160 N. Main, Manti, UT 84642; 435-835-2131; Fax: 435-835-2135. Hours: 8:30AM-5PM (MST). *Felony, Misdemeanor, Civil, Eviction, Small Claims, Probate.*

Civil Records: Access: Phone, fax, mail, in person, online. Both court and visitors may perform in person searches. Search fee: $13.00 per hour after first 15 minutes free. Required to search: name, years to search. Civil cases indexed by defendant, plaintiff. Civil records on computer from 1986. Online access available through XChange. See state introduction.

Criminal Records: Access: Phone, fax, mail, in person, online. Both court and visitors may perform in person searches. Search fee: $13.00 per hour. Required to search: name, years to search; also helpful: DOB. Criminal records on computer from 1986. Online access available through XChange. See state introduction.

General Information: Public Access terminal is available. No criminal, expunged, or sealed records released. SASE requested. Turnaround time 10 days. Fax notes: $3.50 for first page, $2.50 each add'l. Copy fee: $.25 per page. Certification fee: $2.00 plus $.50 per page. Fee payee: 6th District Court. Personal checks accepted. Prepayment is required.

Sevier County

6th District Court 895 E 300 N, Richfield, UT 84701-2345; 435-896-2700; Fax: 435-896-8047. Hours: 8AM-5PM (MST). *Felony, Misdemeanor, Civil, Eviction, Probate.*

Civil Records: Access: Phone, fax, mail, online, in person. Both court and visitors may perform in person searches. Search fee: $10.00 per hour. For search requiring 20 minutes or less, no charge. Required to search: name, years to search. Civil cases indexed by defendant, plaintiff. Circuit records on computer from 1989, District on computer from 1991. Online access available through XChange. See state introduction.
Criminal Records: Access: Phone, fax, mail, online, in person. Both court and visitors may perform in person searches. Search fee: $10.00 per hour. Required to search: name, years to search, DOB, SSN. Circuit records on computer from 1989, District on computer from 1991. Online access available through XChange. See state introduction.
General Information: Public Access terminal is available. No sealed records released. Turnaround time 2-3 days. Fax notes: $2.00 for first page, $1.00 each add'l. Copy fee: $.50 per page. Certification fee: $2.00. Fee payee: 6th District Court. Personal checks accepted. Prepayment is required.

Summit County

3rd District Court PO Box 128, Coalville, UT 84017; 435-336-4451 X3274 & 3202; Fax: 435-336-3030. Hours: 8AM-5PM (MST). *Felony, Misdemeanor, Civil, Eviction, Probate.*

Civil Records: Access: Mail, online, in person. Both court and visitors may perform in person searches. Search fee: $10.00 per hour. Required to search: name, years to search. Civil cases indexed by defendant, plaintiff. All indexes on computer, records archived. Online access available through XChange. See state introduction.
Criminal Records: Access: Mail, online, in person. Both court and visitors may perform in person searches. Search fee: $10.00 per hour. Required to search: name, years to search. Criminal records indexes on computer, records archived. Online access available through XChange. See state introduction.
General Information: Public Access terminal is available. No sealed probate records released. SASE required. Turnaround time 2-3 days. Copy fee: $.25 per page. Certification fee: $2.00 plus $.50 each additional page. Fee payee: 3rd District Court. Personal checks accepted. Prepayment is required.

3rd District Court - Park City Department,
6300 N Silver Creek, Park City, UT 84098; 435-615-4300. *Felony, Misdemeanor, Civil, Eviction, Small Claims.*

Note: 6/1/2001 merged with Coalville Dept. address above, Park City, Utah, 435-615-4300.

Tooele County

3rd District Court 47 S. Main, Tooele, UT 84074; 435-843-3210; Fax: 435-882-8524. Hours: 8AM-5PM (MST). *Felony, Misdemeanor, Civil, Eviction, Small Claims, Probate.*

Civil Records: Access: Fax, mail, online, in person. Both court and visitors may perform in person searches. Search fee: $10.00 per hour. First 20 minutes no charge. Required to search: name, years to search. Civil cases indexed by defendant, plaintiff. Civil records on computer from 1982, archived since court started. Online access available through XChange. See state introduction.
Criminal Records: Access: Fax, mail, online, in person. Both court and visitors may perform in person searches. Search fee: $10.00 per hour. First 20 minutes

no charge. Required to search: name, years to search; also helpful: SSN. Criminal records on computer back to 1989, archived since court started. Online access available through XChange. See state introduction.
General Information: Public Access terminal is available. No adoption records released. SASE required. Turnaround time 2-3 days. Fax notes: Fee to fax results is $.25 per page. Copy fee: $.25 per page. Certification fee: $2.00. Fee payee: 3rd District Court. Personal checks accepted. Prepayment is required.

Uintah County

8th District Court PO Box 1015, Vernal, UT 84078; 435-789-7534; Fax: 435-789-0564. Hours: 8AM-5PM (MST). *Felony, Misdemeanor, Civil, Eviction, Probate.*

Civil Records: Access: Mail, online, in person. Both court and visitors may perform in person searches. Search fee: $10.00 per hour. First 20 minutes no charge. Required to search: name, years to search. Civil cases indexed by defendant, plaintiff. Circuit records on computer from 1987, everything else from 1989, archived since court started. Online access available through XChange. See state introduction.
Criminal Records: Access: Mail, online, in person. Both court and visitors may perform in person searches. Search fee: $10.00 per hour. First 20 minutes no charge. Required to search: name, years to search. Circuit records on computer from 1987, everything else from 1989, archived since court started. Online access available through XChange. See state introduction.
General Information: Public Access terminal is available. No sealed records released. SASE required. Turnaround time 2-3 days. Copy fee: $.25 per page. Certification fee: $2.00 plus $.50 per page. Fee payee: 8th District Court. Personal checks accepted. Prepayment is required.

Utah County

4th District Court 125 North, 100 West, Provo, UT 84601; 385-429-1000; Fax: 385-429-1033. Hours: 8AM-5PM (MST). *Felony, Misdemeanor, Civil, Eviction, Small Claims, Probate.*

http://courtlink.utcourts.gov

Civil Records: Access: Phone, mail, fax, in person. Both court and visitors may perform in person searches. Search fee: $13.00 per hour. Required to search: name, years to search. Civil cases indexed by defendant, plaintiff. Civil and probate on computer from 1986, judgments, tax liens, and divorce decrees on microfiche from 1900 to 1975, archived from 1900s. Online access available through XChange. See state introduction.
Criminal Records: Access: Phone, mail, fax, in person. Both court and visitors may perform in person searches. Search fee: $13.00 per hour. Required to search: name, years to search, DOB. Felony on computer from 1989; archived from 1900s. Online access available through XChange. See state introduction.
General Information: Public Access terminal is available. No sealed records released. SASE required. Turnaround time 7-10 days. Fax notes: Do not fax. Copy fee: $.25 per page. Certification fee: $2.00 for 1st page and $.25 per page thereafter. Fee payee: 4th District Court. Personal checks accepted. Credit cards accepted: Visa, MasterCard. Accepted in person only. Prepayment is required.

4th District Court - Orem Department 97 E
Center, Orem, UT 84057; 385-764-5870/5864; Fax: 385-226-5244. Hours: 8AM-5PM (MST). *Misdemeanor, Civil, Eviction, Small Claims.*

Civil Records: Access: Mail, online, in person. Only the court performs in person searches; visitors may not. Search fee: $10.00 per hour. First 20 minutes no charge. Required to search: name, years to search. Civil cases

indexed by defendant, plaintiff. Civil records on computer since 1988. Access available remotely through XChange. See state introduction.
Criminal Records: Access: Mail, online, in person. Only the court performs in person searches; visitors may not. Search fee: $10.00 per hour. First 20 minutes no charge. Required to search: name, years to search; also helpful: DOB. Criminal records on computer since 1988. Access to criminal available remotely through XChange. See state introduction.
General Information: Public Access terminal is available. No sealed, expunged or confidential records released. Turnaround time 5-7 days. Copy fee: $.25 per page. Certification fee: $2.00 plus $.50 per page. Fee payee: 4th District Court. Personal checks accepted. Credit cards accepted: Visa, MasterCard. Prepayment is required.

4th District Court - Spanish Forks Department 40 S Main St, Spanish Forks, UT 84660; 385-798-8674; Fax: 385-798-1377. Hours: 8AM-5PM (MST). *Felony, Misdemeanor, Civil, Eviction, Small Claims.*

Civil Records: Access: Phone, fax, mail, online, in person. Both court and visitors may perform in person searches. Search fee: $10.00 per hour. First 20 minutes no charge. Required to search: name, years to search. Civil cases indexed by defendant, plaintiff. Civil records on computer since 1988. Access available remotely through XChange. See state introduction.
Criminal Records: Access: Phone, fax, mail, online, in person. Both court and visitors may perform in person searches. Search fee: $10.00 per hour. First 20 minutes no charge. Required to search: name, years to search; also helpful: DOB. Criminal records on computer since 1988. Access to criminal available remotely through XChange. See state introduction.
General Information: No sealed, expunged or confidential records released. Turnaround time 5-7 days. Fax notes: No fee to fax results. Fax requires prior arrangement. Copy fee: $.25 per page. Certification fee: $2.00 plus $.50 per page. Fee payee: 4th District Court. Personal checks accepted. Credit cards accepted: Visa, MasterCard. Prepayment is required.

4th District Court - American Fork Department 98 N Center St, American Fork, UT 84003-1626; 385-756-9654; Fax: 385-763-0153. Hours: 8AM-5PM (MST). *Misdemeanor, Civil, Eviction, Small Claims.*

Civil Records: Access: Mail, online, in person. Both court and visitors may perform in person searches. Search fee: $10.00 per hour. First 20 minutes no charge. Required to search: name, years to search. Civil cases indexed by defendant, plaintiff. Civil records on computer since 1988. Access available remotely through XChange. See state introduction.
Criminal Records: Access: Mail, online, in person. Both court and visitors may perform in person searches. Search fee: $10.00 per hour. First 20 minutes no charge. Required to search: name, years to search; also helpful: DOB. Access to criminal available remotely through XChange. See state introduction.
General Information: No sealed, expunged or confidential records released. SASE required. Turnaround time 5-7 days. Copy fee: $.25 per page. Certification fee: $2.00 plus $.50 per page. Fee payee: 4th District Court. Personal checks accepted. Credit cards accepted: Visa, MasterCard. Prepayment is required.

Wasatch County

4th District Court PO Box 730, Heber City, UT 84032; 435-654-4676; Fax: 435-654-5281. Hours: 8AM-5PM (MST). *Felony, Misdemeanor, Civil, Eviction, Small Claims, Probate.*

Civil Records: Access: Phone, fax, mail, online, in person. Both court and visitors may perform in person searches. No search fee. Required to search: name, years to search. Civil cases indexed by defendant, plaintiff. Civil records on computer since 01/95; records archived since court started. Online access available through XChange. See state introduction.
Criminal Records: Access: Phone, fax, mail, online, in person. Both court and visitors may perform in person searches. No search fee. Required to search: name, years to search; also helpful: DOB, signed release. Criminal records on computer since 01/95; records archived since court started. Online access available through XChange. See state introduction.
General Information: Public Access terminal is available. No adoption records released. SASE required. Turnaround time 1-2 days. Fax notes: Fee to fax results is $1.00 plus $.25 per page. Copy fee: $.25 per page. Certification fee: $2.00 plus $.50 per page. Fee payee: 4th District Court. Personal checks accepted. Prepayment is required.

Washington County

5th District Court 220 North 200 East, St. George, UT 84770; Civil phone: 435-986-5701; Criminal phone: 435-986-5700; Fax: 435-986-5723. Hours: 8AM-5PM (MST). *Felony, Misdemeanor, Civil, Eviction, Small Claims, Probate.*

Civil Records: Access: Mail, online, in person. Both court and visitors may perform in person searches. No search fee. Required to search: name. Civil cases indexed by defendant, plaintiff. District Court records on computer from April, 1990; Circuit Court on computer from 1987. Online access available through XChange. See state introduction.
Criminal Records: Access: Mail, online, in person. Both court and visitors may perform in person searches. No search fee. Required to search: name, years to search. District Court records on computer from April,

1990; Circuit Court on computer from 1987. Online access available through XChange. See state introduction.
General Information: Public Access terminal is available. No mental health, adoption records released. SASE required. Turnaround time 2-3 days. Copy fee: $.25 per page. Certification fee: $2.00 plus $.50 per page. Fee payee: 5th District Court. Personal checks accepted. Credit cards accepted: Visa, MasterCard. Prepayment is required.

Wayne County

6th District Court PO Box 189, Loa, UT 84747; 435-836-2731; Fax: 435-836-2479. Hours: 9AM-5PM (MST). *Felony, Misdemeanor, Civil, Eviction, Small Claims, Probate.*

Civil Records: Access: Phone, mail, fax, in person. Both court and visitors may perform in person searches. Search fee: $10.00 per hour. Required to search: name, years to search. Civil cases indexed by defendant, plaintiff. Civil records archived since court started; computerized from Jan. 2001.
Criminal Records: Access: Phone, mail, fax, in person. Both court and visitors may perform in person searches. Search fee: $10.00 per hour. Required to search: name, years to search; also helpful: SSN. Criminal records archived since court started; computerized from Jan. 2001.
General Information: No sealed records released. SASE required. Turnaround time 2-3 days. Fax notes: Fee to fax results is $1.00 per page. Copy fee: $.25 per page. Certification fee: $2.00. Fee payee: 6th District Court. Personal checks accepted. Prepayment required.

Weber County

2nd District Court 2525 Grant Ave, Ogden, UT 84401; Civil phone: 385-395-1091; Criminal phone: 385-395-1102; Probate phone: 385-395-1173. Hours: 8AM-5PM (MST). *Felony, Misdemeanor, Civil, Eviction, Small Claims, Probate.*

Note: An automated court information line allows phone access to court dates, fine balances, and judgment/divorce decrees (case or citation number required) at 801-395-1111.

Civil Records: Access: Phone, mail, online, in person. Both court and visitors may perform in person searches. Search fee: $13.00 per hour. First 20 minutes no charge. Required to search: name, years to search. Civil cases indexed by defendant, plaintiff. Civil records on computer from 1980, books prior to that. Online access available through XChange. See state introduction.
Criminal Records: Access: Phone, mail, online, in person. Both court and visitors may perform in person searches. Search fee: $13.00 per hour. First 20 minutes no charge. Required to search: name, years to search, DOB, SSN. Criminal records on computer from 1980, books prior to that. Online access available through XChange. See state introduction.
General Information: Public Access terminal is available. No adoption, voluntary commitments, expunged criminal records released. SASE required. Turnaround time 2-9 days. Copy fee: $.25 per page. Certification fee: $2.00 plus $.50 per page. Fee payee: Ogden District Court. Personal checks accepted. Credit cards accepted: Visa, MasterCard. Prepayment is required.

2nd District Court - Roy Department 5051
South 1900 West, Roy, UT 84067; 385-774-1051; Fax: 385-774-1060. Hours: 8AM-5PM (MST). *Felony, Misdemeanor.*

Note: Civil and small claims records here only prior to 01/01/90. Newer records maintained in Ogden

Criminal Records: Access: Mail, online, in person. Both court and visitors may perform in person searches. Search fee: $10.00 per hour. First 20 minutes no charge. Required to search: name, years to search, signed release; also helpful: address, DOB. Criminal records on computer since January 1987. Online access available through XChange. See state introduction.

General Information: No sealed, expunged or juvenile records released. Turnaround time 5 days. Copy fee: $.25 per page. Certification fee: $2.00 plus $.50 per page. Fee payee: Roy District Court. Personal checks accepted. Credit cards accepted: Visa, MasterCard. Prepayment is required.

Utah Recording Offices

ORGANIZATION

29 counties 29 recording offices. The recording officers are County Recorder and Clerk of District Court (state tax liens). The entire state is in the Mountain Time Zone (MST).

REAL ESTATE RECORDS

County Recorders will not perform real estate searches. Copy fees vary, and certification fees are usually $2.00 per document.

UCC RECORDS

Financing statements are filed at the state level, except for real estate related collateral, which are filed with the Register of Deeds (and at the state level in certain cases). Many filing offices will not perform UCC searches. Copy fees vary. Certification usually costs $2.00 per document.

TAX LIEN RECORDS

All federal tax liens are filed with the County Recorder. They do not perform searches. All state tax liens are filed with Clerk of District Court, many of which have on-line access. Refer to the County Court section for information about Utah District Courts.

Beaver County

County Recorder, P.O. Box 431, Beaver, UT 84713. 435-438-6480; Fax 435-438-6481.
Will search UCC records. UCC search does not include federal tax liens. Will not search real estate records. **Other Phone Numbers:** Assessor 435-438-6400; Treasurer 435-438-6410; Appraiser/Auditor 435-438-6460.

Box Elder County

County Recorder, 1 South Main, Courthouse, Brigham City, UT 84302-2599. 435-734-2031; Fax 435-734-2038.
Will search UCC records. Will not search real estate records. **Other Phone Numbers:** Assessor 435-734-3333; Treasurer 435-734-3333; Appraiser/Auditor 435-734-3317.

Cache County

County Recorder, 179 North Main Street, Logan, UT 84321. 435-752-5561; Fax 435-753-7120.
Will search UCC records. Will not search real estate records. **Other Phone Numbers:** Assessor 435-716-7100; Treasurer 435-716-8394; Appraiser/Auditor 435-716-7123.

Carbon County

County Recorder, Courthouse Building, 120 East Main, Price, UT 84501. 435-636-3244; Fax 435-637-6757.
Will search UCC records. Will not search real estate records. **Other Phone Numbers:** Assessor 435-636-3249; Treasurer 435-636-3258; Appraiser/Auditor 435-636-3227.

Daggett County

County Recorder, P.O. Box 219, Manila, UT 84046-0219. 435-784-3210; Fax 435-784-3335.
Will not search UCC records. Will not search real estate records. **Other Phone Numbers:** Assessor 435-784-3222; Treasurer 435-784-3154; Appraiser/Auditor 435-784-3210; Elections 435-784-5154.

Davis County

County Recorder, P.O. Box 618, Farmington, UT 84025. 801-451-3225 R/E Recording: 385-451-3225; http://www.co.davis.ut.us
Will not search UCC or tax lien records. Will not search real estate records. **Online Access:** Real Estate, Liens. Access to the county land records database requires written registration and $15.00 per month fee plus $.10 per transaction. Records go back to 1981. For information and sign-up, contact Janet at 801-451-3347. **Other Phone Numbers:** Assessor 385-451-3252; Treasurer 385-451-3243; Appraiser/Auditor 385-451-

3214; Elections 385-451-3213; Vital Records 801-451-3337.

Duchesne County Recorder

County Recorder, P.O. Box 916, Duchesne, UT 84021. County Recorder, R/E and UCC Recording 435-738-1160; Fax 435-738-5522.
Will not search UCC records. Will not search real estate records. **Other Phone Numbers:** Assessor 435-738-1115; Treasurer 435-738-1193; Appraiser/Auditor 435-738-1123; Elections 435-738-1101.

Emery County

County Recorder, P.O. Box 698, Castle Dale, UT 84513-0698. 435-381-2414; Fax 435-381-5529.
Will search UCC records. Will not search real estate records. **Other Phone Numbers:** Assessor 435-381-2474; Treasurer 435-381-2510; Appraiser/Auditor 435-381-5106.

Garfield County

County Recorder, P.O. Box 77, Panguitch, UT 84759. 435-676-1112 x112; Fax 435-676-8239.
Will search UCC records. Will not search real estate records. **Other Phone Numbers:** Assessor 435-676-1107; Treasurer 435-676-1109; Appraiser/Auditor 435-676-8826 x100.

Grand County

County Recorder & Deputies, 125 East Center St., Moab, UT 84532. County Recorder & Deputies, R/E and UCC Recording 435-259-1331; Fax 435-259-1320.
Will not search UCC records. Will not search real estate records. **Other Phone Numbers:** Assessor 435-295-1329; Treasurer 435-295-1337,8,9; Appraiser/Auditor 435-259-1322.

Iron County

County Recorder, P.O. Box 506, Parowan, UT 84761. 435-477-8350.
Will not search UCC records. This agency will not do a tax lien search. Will not search real estate records. **Other Phone Numbers:** Assessor 435-477-8311; Treasurer 435-477-8360; Appraiser/Auditor 435-477-8331.

Juab County

County Recorder, 160 North Main, Nephi, UT 84648. 435-623-3430.
Will search UCC records. This agency will not do a federal tax lien search. Will not search real estate records. **Other Phone Numbers:** Assessor 435-623-3425; Treasurer 435-623-0096; Appraiser/Auditor 435-623-3410.

Kane County

County Recorder, 76 North Main #14, Kanab, UT 84741. 435-644-2360.
Will not search UCC records. This agency will not do a federal tax lien search. Will not search real estate records. **Other Phone Numbers:** Assessor 435-644-2649; Treasurer 435-644-5659; Appraiser/Auditor 435-644-2458.

Millard County

County Recorder, 50 South Main, Fillmore, UT 84631. County Recorder, R/E and UCC Recording 435-743-6210; Fax 435-743-4221.
Will not search UCC records. Will not search real estate records. **Other Phone Numbers:** Assessor 435-743-5719; Treasurer 435-743-5322; Appraiser/Auditor 435-743-5227.

Morgan County

County Recorder, P.O. Box 886, Morgan, UT 84050. 385-829-3277; Fax 385-829-6176.
Will search UCC records. Will not search real estate records. **Other Phone Numbers:** Assessor 385-845-4000; Treasurer 385-845-4030; Appraiser/Auditor 385-845-4011.

Piute County

County Recorder, P.O. Box 116, Junction, UT 84740. 435-577-2505; Fax 435-577-2433.
Will search UCC records. This agency will not do a federal tax lien search. Will not search real estate records. **Other Phone Numbers:** Assessor 435-577-2988; Treasurer 435-577-2505; Appraiser/Auditor 435-577-2840.

Rich County

County Recorder, P.O. Box 322, Randolph, UT 84064. 435-793-2005.
Will search UCC records. This agency will not do a federal tax lien search. Will not search real estate records. **Other Phone Numbers:** Assessor 435-793-5215; Treasurer 435-793-5155; Appraiser/Auditor 435-793-2415.

Salt Lake County

County Recorder, 2001 South State Street, Room N-1600, Salt Lake City, UT 84190-1150. 801-468-3391; http://www.co.slc.ut.us
Will search UCC records. This agency will not do a federal tax lien search. Will not search real estate records. **Online Access:** Assessor. Two sources are available. Records on the county Truth-In-Tax Information web site are available free online at www.co.slc.ut.us/valnotice. Also, Assessor, real estate, appraisal, abstracts, and GIS mapping are available for

$150.00 fee on the online system at http://rec.co.slc.ut.us/polaris/default.cfm. Search by GIS, name, or property information. Register online or call 801-468-3013. **Other Phone Numbers:** Assessor 801-468-2165; Treasurer 801-468-3140; Appraiser/ Auditor 801-468-3389.

San Juan County

County Recorder, P.O. Box 789, Monticello, UT 84535. 435-587-3228; Fax 435-587-2425.
Will not search UCC records. This agency will not do a tax lien search. Will not search real estate records. **Other Phone Numbers:** Assessor 435-587-3221; Treasurer 435-547-3237; Appraiser/Auditor 435-587-3223.

Sanpete County

County Recorder, 160 North Main, Manti, UT 84642. 435-835-2181; Fax 435-835-2143.
Will search UCC records. This agency will not do a federal tax lien search. Will not search real estate records. **Other Phone Numbers:** Assessor 435-835-2111; Treasurer 435-835-2101; Appraiser/Auditor 435-835-2142.

Sevier County

County Recorder, 250 North Main, Richfield, UT 84701. 435-896-9262 x210; Fax 435-896-8888.
Will not search UCC records. Will not search real estate records. **Other Phone Numbers:** Assessor 435-896-9262 x230; Treasurer 435-896-9262 x240; Appraiser/ Auditor 435-896-9262 x203.

Summit County

County Recorder, P.O. Box 128, Coalville, UT 84017. 435-336-3238; Fax 435-336-3055.
Will not search UCC records. Will not search real estate records. **Other Phone Numbers:** Assessor 435-336-3248; Treasurer 435-336-3266; Appraiser/Auditor 435-336-3254.

Tooele County

County Recorder, 47 South Main Street, Courthouse, Tooele, UT 84074-2194. County Recorder, R/E and UCC Recording 435-843-3180; Fax 435-882-7317. http://www.co.tooele.ut.us
Will search UCC records. Will not search real estate records. **Online Access:** Property Tax. Online access to the property information database may be operational at www.co.tooele.ut.us/taxinfo.html. **Other Phone Numbers:** Assessor 435-843-3101; Treasurer 435-843-3191; Appraiser/Auditor 435-843-3130; Elections 435-843-3140; Vital Records 435-843-2300.

Uintah County

County Recorder, 147 East Main St., County Building, Vernal, UT 84078. 435-781-5461 R/E Recording: 435-781-5398; Fax 435-781-5319. http://www.co.uintah.ut.us/recorder/rec.htm
Will not search UCC records. This agency will not do a tax lien search. Will not search real estate records. **Online Access:** Property. Online access to the counrty recorder's land records is available free at www.co.uintah.ut.us/recorder/landinfo.html. **Other Phone Numbers:** Assessor 435-781-5349; Treasurer 435-781-5362; Appraiser/Auditor 435-781-5360.

Utah County

County Recorder, P.O. Box 122, Provo, UT 84603. County Recorder, R/E and UCC Recording 801-370-8179; Fax 801-370-8181. http://www.co.utah.ut.us
Will search UCC records. This agency will not do a federal tax lien search. Will not search real estate records. **Online Access:** Real Estate, Liens, Assessor. Online access to the land records database and also map searching is available free at www.co.utah.ut.us/omninet/land. Indexes go back to 1978; parcel indexes back to 1981. Document images go back to 1994. Building and GIS information is also available online. **Other Phone Numbers:** Assessor 801-370-8275; Treasurer 801-370-8255; Appraiser/Auditor 801-370-8108; Elections 801-370-8226; Vital Records 801-370-4526.

Wasatch County

County Recorder, 25 North Main, Heber, UT 84032. 435-654-3211; http://www.co.wasatch.ut.us/d/
Will not search UCC records. This agency will not do a tax lien search. Will not search real estate records. **Online Access:** Real Property. The county GIS Dept. plans to have "metadata" (property information) available free online from its GIS mapping site at www.co.wasatch.ut.us/d/dpgis.html. **Other Phone Numbers:** Assessor 435-654-3211 x302; Treasurer 435-654-3211 x306; Appraiser/Auditor 435-654-3211 x309.

Washington County

County Recorder, 197 East Tabernacle, St. George, UT 84770. County Recorder, R/E and UCC Recording 435-634-5709; Fax 435-634-5718.
Will not search UCC records. Will not search real estate records. **Other Phone Numbers:** Assessor 435-634-5703; Treasurer 435-652-5856; Appraiser/Auditor 435-634-5712.

Wayne County

County Recorder, P.O. Box 187, Loa, UT 84747-0187. 435-836-2765; Fax 435-836-2479.
Will search UCC records. **Other Phone Numbers:** Assessor 435-836-2709; Treasurer 435-836-2765; Appraiser/Auditor 435-836-2731.

Weber County

County Recorder, 2380 Washington Blvd, Suite 370, Ogden, UT 84401. 801-399-8441; http://www.co.weber.ut.us
Will search UCC records. UCC search includes federal tax liens if requested. RE record owner searches available. **Online Access:** Real Estate. Property records on the County Parcel Search site are available free online at www.co.weber.ut.us/netapps/Parcel/main.htm. **Other Phone Numbers:** Assessor 385-399-8122; Treasurer 385-399-8480; Appraiser/Auditor 385-399-8573.

Utah County Locator

You will usually be able to find the city name in the City/County Cross Reference below. In that case, it is a simple matter to determine the county from the cross reference. However, only the official US Postal Service city names are included in this index. There are an additional 40,000 place names that people use in their addresses. Therefore, we have also included a ZIP/City Cross Reference immediately following the City/County Cross Reference.

If you know the ZIP Code but the city name does not appear in the City/County Cross Reference index, look up the ZIP Code in the ZIP/City Cross Reference, find the city name, then look up the city name in the City/County Cross Reference. For example, you want to know the county for an address of Menands, NY 12204. There is no "Menands" in the City/County Cross Reference. The ZIP/City Cross Reference shows that ZIP Codes 12201-12288 are for the city of Albany. Looking back in the City/County Cross Reference, Albany is in Albany County.

City/County Cross Reference

ALPINE Utah
ALTAMONT Duchesne
ALTON Kane
ALTONAH Duchesne
AMERICAN FORK Utah
ANETH San Juan
ANNABELLA Sevier
ANTIMONY Garfield
AURORA Sevier
AXTELL Sanpete
BEAR RIVER CITY Box Elder
BEAVER Beaver
BERYL Iron
BICKNELL Wayne
BINGHAM CANYON Salt Lake
BLANDING San Juan
BLUEBELL Duchesne
BLUFF San Juan
BONANZA Uintah
BOULDER Garfield
BOUNTIFUL Davis
BRIAN HEAD Iron
BRIDGELAND Duchesne
BRIGHAM CITY Box Elder
BRYCE Garfield
BRYCE CANYON Garfield
CACHE JUNCTION Cache
CANNONVILLE Garfield
CASTLE DALE Emery
CEDAR CITY Iron
CEDAR VALLEY Utah
CENTERFIELD Sanpete
CENTERVILLE Davis
CENTRAL Washington
CHESTER Sanpete
CIRCLEVILLE Piute
CISCO Grand
CLARKSTON Cache
CLAWSON Emery
CLEARFIELD Davis
CLEVELAND Emery
COALVILLE Summit
COLLINSTON Box Elder
CORINNE Box Elder
CORNISH Cache
CROYDON Morgan
DAMMERON VALLEY Washington
DELTA Millard
DEWEYVILLE Box Elder
DRAPER Salt Lake
DUCHESNE Duchesne
DUCK CREEK VILLAGE Kane
DUGWAY Tooele
DUTCH JOHN Daggett
EAST CARBON Carbon
ECHO Summit
EDEN Weber
ELBERTA Utah
ELMO Emery
ELSINORE Sevier
EMERY Emery
ENTERPRISE Washington
EPHRAIM Sanpete
ESCALANTE Garfield
EUREKA Juab

FAIRVIEW (84629) Sanpete(66), Utah(33), San Juan(2)
FARMINGTON Davis
FAYETTE Sanpete
FERRON Emery
FIELDING Box Elder
FILLMORE Millard
FORT DUCHESNE Uintah
FOUNTAIN GREEN Sanpete
FRUITLAND Duchesne
GARDEN CITY Rich
GARLAND Box Elder
GARRISON Millard
GLENDALE Kane
GLENWOOD Sevier
GOSHEN Utah
GRANTSVILLE Tooele
GREEN RIVER Emery
GREENVILLE Beaver
GREENWICH (84732) Sevier(71), Piute(29)
GROUSE CREEK Box Elder
GUNLOCK Washington
GUNNISON Sanpete
GUSHER Uintah
HANKSVILLE Wayne
HANNA Duchesne
HATCH Garfield
HEBER CITY Wasatch
HELPER Carbon
HENEFER Summit
HENRIEVILLE Garfield
HIAWATHA Carbon
HILDALE Washington
HILL AFB Davis
HINCKLEY Millard
HOLDEN Millard
HONEYVILLE Box Elder
HOOPER (84315) Weber(93), Davis(7)
HOWELL Box Elder
HUNTINGTON Emery
HUNTSVILLE Weber
HURRICANE Washington
HYDE PARK Cache
HYRUM Cache
IBAPAH Tooele
IVINS Washington
JENSEN Uintah
JOSEPH Sevier
JUNCTION Piute
KAMAS Summit
KANAB Kane
KANARRAVILLE Iron
KANOSH Millard
KAYSVILLE Davis
KENILWORTH Carbon
KINGSTON Piute
KOOSHAREM Sevier
LA SAL San Juan
LA VERKIN Washington
LAKE POWELL San Juan
LAKETOWN Rich
LAPOINT Uintah
LAYTON Davis
LEAMINGTON Millard

LEEDS Washington
LEHI Utah
LEVAN Juab
LEWISTON Cache
LINDON Utah
LOA Wayne
LOGAN Cache
LYMAN Wayne
LYNNDYL Millard
MAGNA Salt Lake
MANILA Daggett
MANTI Sanpete
MANTUA Box Elder
MAPLETON Utah
MARYSVALE Piute
MAYFIELD Sanpete
MEADOW Millard
MENDON Cache
MEXICAN HAT San Juan
MIDVALE Salt Lake
MIDWAY Wasatch
MILFORD Beaver
MILLVILLE Cache
MINERSVILLE Beaver
MOAB Grand
MODENA Iron
MONA Juab
MONROE Sevier
MONTEZUMA CREEK San Juan
MONTICELLO San Juan
MONUMENT VALLEY San Juan
MORGAN Morgan
MORONI Sanpete
MOUNT CARMEL Kane
MOUNT PLEASANT Sanpete
MOUNTAIN HOME Duchesne
MYTON (84052) Duchesne(74), Uintah(26)
NEOLA Duchesne
NEPHI Juab
NEW HARMONY Washington
NEWCASTLE Iron
NEWTON Cache
NORTH SALT LAKE Davis
OAK CITY Millard
OAKLEY Summit
OASIS Millard
OGDEN (84405) Weber(91), Davis(9)
OGDEN Weber
ORANGEVILLE Emery
ORDERVILLE Kane
OREM Utah
PANGUITCH Garfield
PARADISE Cache
PARAGONAH Iron
PARK CITY Summit
PARK VALLEY Box Elder
PAROWAN Iron
PAYSON Utah
PEOA Summit
PINE VALLEY Washington
PLEASANT GROVE Utah
PLYMOUTH Box Elder
PORTAGE Box Elder
PRICE Carbon
PROVIDENCE Cache

PROVO Utah
RANDLETT Uintah
RANDOLPH Rich
REDMOND Sevier
RICHFIELD Sevier
RICHMOND Cache
RIVERSIDE Box Elder
RIVERTON Salt Lake
ROCKVILLE Washington
ROOSEVELT (84066) Duchesne(96), Uintah(4)
ROY Weber
RUSH VALLEY Tooele
SAINT GEORGE Washington
SALEM Utah
SALINA Sevier
SALT LAKE CITY Salt Lake
SANDY Salt Lake
SANTA CLARA Washington
SANTAQUIN Utah
SCIPIO Millard
SEVIER Sevier
SIGURD Sevier
SMITHFIELD Cache
SNOWVILLE Box Elder
SOUTH JORDAN Salt Lake
SPANISH FORK Utah
SPRING CITY Sanpete
SPRINGDALE (84767) Washington(73), Garfield(27)
SPRINGVILLE Utah
STERLING Sanpete
STOCKTON Tooele
SUMMIT Iron
SUNNYSIDE Carbon
SYRACUSE Davis
TABIONA Duchesne
TALMAGE Duchesne
TEASDALE Wayne
THOMPSON Grand
TOOELE Tooele
TOQUERVILLE Washington
TORREY Wayne
TREMONTON Box Elder
TRENTON Cache
TRIDELL Uintah
TROPIC Garfield
VERNAL Uintah
VERNON Tooele
VEYO Washington
VIRGIN Washington
WALES Sanpete
WALLSBURG Wasatch
WASHINGTON Washington
WELLINGTON Carbon
WELLSVILLE Cache
WENDOVER Tooele
WEST JORDAN Salt Lake
WHITEROCKS Uintah
WILLARD Box Elder
WOODRUFF Rich
WOODS CROSS Davis

ZIP/City Cross Reference

ZIP	City	ZIP	City	ZIP	City	ZIP	City
84001-84001	ALTAMONT	84078-84079	VERNAL	84523-84523	FERRON	84714-84714	BERYL
84002-84002	ALTONAH	84080-84080	VERNON	84525-84525	GREEN RIVER	84715-84715	BICKNELL
84003-84003	AMERICAN FORK	84082-84082	WALLSBURG	84526-84526	HELPER	84716-84716	BOULDER
84004-84004	ALPINE	84083-84083	WENDOVER	84527-84527	HIAWATHA	84717-84717	BRYCE CANYON
84006-84006	BINGHAM CANYON	84084-84084	WEST JORDAN	84528-84528	HUNTINGTON	84718-84718	CANNONVILLE
84007-84007	BLUEBELL	84085-84085	WHITEROCKS	84529-84529	KENILWORTH	84719-84719	BRIAN HEAD
84008-84008	BONANZA	84086-84086	WOODRUFF	84530-84530	LA SAL	84720-84721	CEDAR CITY
84010-84011	BOUNTIFUL	84087-84087	WOODS CROSS	84531-84531	MEXICAN HAT	84722-84722	CENTRAL
84013-84013	CEDAR VALLEY	84088-84088	WEST JORDAN	84532-84532	MOAB	84723-84723	CIRCLEVILLE
84014-84014	CENTERVILLE	84090-84094	SANDY	84533-84533	LAKE POWELL	84724-84724	ELSINORE
84015-84016	CLEARFIELD	84095-84095	SOUTH JORDAN	84534-84534	MONTEZUMA CREEK	84725-84725	ENTERPRISE
84017-84017	COALVILLE	84097-84097	OREM	84535-84535	MONTICELLO	84726-84726	ESCALANTE
84018-84018	CROYDON	84098-84098	PARK CITY	84536-84536	MONUMENT VALLEY	84728-84728	GARRISON
84020-84020	DRAPER	84101-84199	SALT LAKE CITY	84537-84537	ORANGEVILLE	84729-84729	GLENDALE
84021-84021	DUCHESNE	84201-84244	OGDEN	84539-84539	SUNNYSIDE	84730-84730	GLENWOOD
84022-84022	DUGWAY	84301-84301	BEAR RIVER CITY	84540-84540	THOMPSON	84731-84731	GREENVILLE
84023-84023	DUTCH JOHN	84302-84302	BRIGHAM CITY	84542-84542	WELLINGTON	84732-84732	GREENWICH
84024-84024	ECHO	84304-84304	CACHE JUNCTION	84601-84606	PROVO	84733-84733	GUNLOCK
84025-84025	FARMINGTON	84305-84305	CLARKSTON	84620-84620	AURORA	84734-84734	HANKSVILLE
84026-84026	FORT DUCHESNE	84306-84306	COLLINSTON	84621-84621	AXTELL	84735-84735	HATCH
84027-84027	FRUITLAND	84307-84307	CORINNE	84622-84622	CENTERFIELD	84736-84736	HENRIEVILLE
84028-84028	GARDEN CITY	84308-84308	CORNISH	84623-84623	CHESTER	84737-84737	HURRICANE
84029-84029	GRANTSVILLE	84309-84309	DEWEYVILLE	84624-84624	DELTA	84738-84738	IVINS
84030-84030	GUSHER	84310-84310	EDEN	84626-84626	ELBERTA	84739-84739	JOSEPH
84031-84031	HANNA	84311-84311	FIELDING	84627-84627	EPHRAIM	84740-84740	JUNCTION
84032-84032	HEBER CITY	84312-84312	GARLAND	84628-84628	EUREKA	84741-84741	KANAB
84033-84033	HENEFER	84313-84313	GROUSE CREEK	84629-84629	FAIRVIEW	84742-84742	KANARRAVILLE
84034-84034	IBAPAH	84314-84314	HONEYVILLE	84630-84630	FAYETTE	84743-84743	KINGSTON
84035-84035	JENSEN	84315-84315	HOOPER	84631-84631	FILLMORE	84744-84744	KOOSHAREM
84036-84036	KAMAS	84316-84316	HOWELL	84632-84632	FOUNTAIN GREEN	84745-84745	LA VERKIN
84037-84037	KAYSVILLE	84317-84317	HUNTSVILLE	84633-84633	GOSHEN	84746-84746	LEEDS
84038-84038	LAKETOWN	84318-84318	HYDE PARK	84634-84634	GUNNISON	84747-84747	LOA
84039-84039	LAPOINT	84319-84319	HYRUM	84635-84635	HINCKLEY	84749-84749	LYMAN
84040-84041	LAYTON	84320-84320	LEWISTON	84636-84636	HOLDEN	84750-84750	MARYSVALE
84042-84042	LINDON	84321-84323	LOGAN	84637-84637	KANOSH	84751-84751	MILFORD
84043-84043	LEHI	84324-84324	MANTUA	84638-84638	LEAMINGTON	84752-84752	MINERSVILLE
84044-84044	MAGNA	84325-84325	MENDON	84639-84639	LEVAN	84753-84753	MODENA
84046-84046	MANILA	84326-84326	MILLVILLE	84640-84640	LYNNDYL	84754-84754	MONROE
84047-84047	MIDVALE	84327-84327	NEWTON	84642-84642	MANTI	84755-84755	MOUNT CARMEL
84049-84049	MIDWAY	84328-84328	PARADISE	84643-84643	MAYFIELD	84756-84756	NEWCASTLE
84050-84050	MORGAN	84329-84329	PARK VALLEY	84644-84644	MEADOW	84757-84757	NEW HARMONY
84051-84051	MOUNTAIN HOME	84330-84330	PLYMOUTH	84645-84645	MONA	84758-84758	ORDERVILLE
84052-84052	MYTON	84331-84331	PORTAGE	84646-84646	MORONI	84759-84759	PANGUITCH
84053-84053	NEOLA	84332-84332	PROVIDENCE	84647-84647	MOUNT PLEASANT	84760-84760	PARAGONAH
84054-84054	NORTH SALT LAKE	84333-84333	RICHMOND	84648-84648	NEPHI	84761-84761	PAROWAN
84055-84055	OAKLEY	84334-84334	RIVERSIDE	84649-84649	OAK CITY	84762-84762	DUCK CREEK VILLAGE
84056-84056	HILL AFB	84335-84335	SMITHFIELD	84650-84650	OASIS	84763-84763	ROCKVILLE
84057-84059	OREM	84336-84336	SNOWVILLE	84651-84651	PAYSON	84764-84764	BRYCE
84060-84060	PARK CITY	84337-84337	TREMONTON	84652-84652	REDMOND	84765-84765	SANTA CLARA
84061-84061	PEOA	84338-84338	TRENTON	84653-84653	SALEM	84766-84766	SEVIER
84062-84062	PLEASANT GROVE	84339-84339	WELLSVILLE	84654-84654	SALINA	84767-84767	SPRINGDALE
84063-84063	RANDLETT	84340-84340	WILLARD	84655-84655	SANTAQUIN	84770-84771	SAINT GEORGE
84064-84064	RANDOLPH	84341-84341	LOGAN	84656-84656	SCIPIO	84772-84772	SUMMIT
84065-84065	RIVERTON	84401-84414	OGDEN	84657-84657	SIGURD	84773-84773	TEASDALE
84066-84066	ROOSEVELT	84501-84501	PRICE	84660-84660	SPANISH FORK	84774-84774	TOQUERVILLE
84067-84067	ROY	84510-84510	ANETH	84662-84662	SPRING CITY	84775-84775	TORREY
84068-84068	PARK CITY	84511-84511	BLANDING	84663-84663	SPRINGVILLE	84776-84776	TROPIC
84069-84069	RUSH VALLEY	84512-84512	BLUFF	84664-84664	MAPLETON	84779-84779	VIRGIN
84070-84070	SANDY	84513-84513	CASTLE DALE	84665-84665	STERLING	84780-84780	WASHINGTON
84071-84071	STOCKTON	84515-84515	CISCO	84667-84667	WALES	84781-84781	PINE VALLEY
84072-84072	TABIONA	84516-84516	CLAWSON	84701-84701	RICHFIELD	84782-84782	VEYO
84073-84073	TALMAGE	84518-84518	CLEVELAND	84710-84710	ALTON	84783-84783	DAMMERON VALLEY
84074-84074	TOOELE	84520-84520	EAST CARBON	84711-84711	ANNABELLA	84784-84784	HILDALE
84075-84075	SYRACUSE	84521-84521	ELMO	84712-84712	ANTIMONY	84790-84790	SAINT GEORGE
84076-84076	TRIDELL	84522-84522	EMERY	84713-84713	BEAVER		

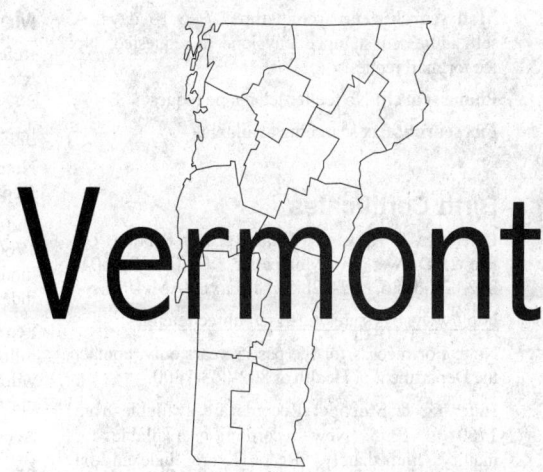

Vermont

General Help Numbers:

Governor's Office

Pavillion Office Bldg   802-828-3333
109 State St   Fax 802-828-3339
Montpelier, VT 05609   7:45AM-4:30PM
http://www.gov.state.vt.us

Attorney General's Office

109 State St   802-828-3171
Montpelier, VT 05609-1001   Fax 802-828-2154
http://www.state.vt.us/atg   7:45AM-4:30PM

State Court Administrator

Administrative Office of Courts   802-828-3278
111 State St   Fax 802-828-3457
Montpelier, VT 05609-0701   7:45AM-4:30PM
http://www.state.vt.us/courts/admin.htm

State Archives

State Archives Division   802-828-2308
26 Terrace-Redstone Bldg   Fax 802-828-2496
Montpelier, VT 05609-1103   7:45AM-4:30PM
http://vermont-archives.org

State Specifics:

Capital: Montpelier
      Washington County

Time Zone: EST

Number of Counties: 14

Population: 608,827

Web Site: www.state.vt.us

State Agencies

Criminal Records

Access to Records is Restricted

State Repository, Vermont Criminal Information Center, 103 S. Main St., Waterbury, VT 05671-2101; 802-244-8727, 802-241-5552 (Fax), 8AM-4:30PM.

http://www.dps.state.vt.us

Note: Records are not available to the public and can only be access by those authorized by law. This includes employers with employees working with children, the elderly, or the disabled. Otherwise, suggest searching at the county level.

Corporation Records
Limited Liability Company Records
Limited Liability Partnerships
Limited Partnerships
Trademarks/Servicemarks

Secretary of State, Corporation Division, 81 River St, Drawer 9, Montpelier, VT 05609-1101; 802-828-2386, 802-828-2853 (Fax), 7:45AM-4:30PM.

http://www.sec.state.vt.us/soshome.htm

Indexing & Storage: Records are available from beginning of record keeping. Records are on computer if active. Inactive records are indexed by a card file.

Searching: Include the following in your request-full name of business.

Access by: mail, phone, fax, in person, online.

Fee & Payment: There is no search fee. Copies are \$.10 per page or \$.25 per page if on microfiche. The fee for certification is \$5.00, or \$1.00 per page when copies pulled. Fee payee: Secretary of State. Personal checks accepted. No credit cards accepted.

Mail search: Turnaround time: 3 to 5 days.

Phone search: They will only confirm if business is active.

Fax search: Same criteria as mail searching. They will return a page or two by fax, if local number, otherwise results are mailed.

In person search: Searching is available in person.

Online search: Corporate and trademark records can be accessed from the Internet for no fee. All records are available. Also, the web site offers a "Trade Name Finder."

Other access: There is an option on the Internet to download the entire corporation (and tradename) database.

Uniform Commercial Code

UCC Division, Secretary of State, 81 River St, Drawer 4, Montpelier, VT 05609-1101; 802-828-2386, 802-828-2853 (Fax), 7:45AM-4:30PM.

http://www.sec.state.vt.us/corps/corpindex.htm

Indexing & Storage: Records are available from 1967. All active records are computerized. It takes 3 to 5 days before new records are available for inquiry.

Searching: Use search request form UCC-11. All tax liens are filed at the town/city level. Include the following in your request-debtor name, business name.

Access by: mail, fax, in person, online.

Fee & Payment: Searches are $10.00 per name. The copy fee is $2.00 per page. If there are attachments, they are an additional $5.00 per page. If results are to be returned by fax, add $2.00 per page. Fee payee: Secretary of State. Personal checks accepted. No credit cards accepted.

Mail search: Turnaround time: 4 days. A self addressed stamped envelope is requested.

Fax search: Same criteria as mail searching.

In person search: Turnaround time depends on workload, may not be immediate.

Online search: Searches are available from the Internet site. You can search by debtor or business name, there is no fee.

Federal Tax Liens
State Tax Liens
Records not maintained by a state level agency.

Note: Records are found at the local town level.

Sales Tax Registrations

Administrative Agency/Tax Department, Business Tax Division, 109 State St, Montpelier, VT 05609-1401; 802-828-2551, 802-828-5787 (Fax), 7:45AM-4:30PM.

Indexing & Storage: Records are available for 4 years on computer database, then records are archived.

Searching: This agency will only confirm that a business is registered. Records are considered confidential. They will provide no other information. Include the following in your request-business name. They will also search by tax permit number, owner name or federal tax ID.

Access by: mail, phone, fax.

Mail search: Turnaround time: 7 to 10 days. A self addressed stamped envelope is requested. No fee for mail request.

Phone search: No fee for telephone request.

Fax search: Fax searching available.

Birth Certificates

Reference & Research, Vital Records Section, US Rte 2, Drawer 33, Montpelier, VT 05633-7601; 802-828-3286, 802-828-3710 (Fax), 8AM-4PM.

http://www.bgs.state.vt.us/gsc/pubrec/referen

Note: For records for the past 5 years only, contact the Department of Health at 802-863-7300.

Indexing & Storage: Records are available from 1760 to 1995. New records are available for inquiry immediately. Records are indexed on index cards, inhouse computer.

Searching: The records are open to the public. Include the following in your request-full name, names of parents, mother's maiden name, date of birth, place of birth.

Access by: mail, phone, fax, in person.

Fee & Payment: The search fee is $7.00 per name. Fee payee: VT Vital Records. Prepayment required. Use of credit card is only for expedited service. Personal checks accepted. Credit cards accepted: MasterCard, Visa, AmEx, Discover.

Mail search: Turnaround time: 2 to 3 days. A self addressed stamped envelope is requested.

Phone search: See expedited service.

Fax search: See expedited service.

In person search: You may view the records for no charge.

Expedited service: Expedited service is available for fax searches. Turnaround time: 1 to 2 days. Add $5.00 for use of credit card and $15.50 for overnight shipping.

Death Records

Reference & Research, Vital Records, US Rte 2, Drawer 33, Montpelier, VT 05633-7601; 802-828-3286, 8AM-4PM.

http://www.bgs.state.vt.us/gsc/pubrec/referen

Note: For records up to 5 years old, contact the Department of Health at 802-863-7300.

Indexing & Storage: Records are available from 1760 to 1995. New records are available for inquiry immediately. Records are indexed on index cards, inhouse computer.

Searching: Records are open to the public. Include the following in your request-full name, date of death, place of death, names of parents.

Access by: mail, phone, in person.

Fee & Payment: The search fee is $7.00 per name. Fee payee: VT Vital Records. Prepayment required. Credit card for expedited service only. Personal checks accepted. No credit cards accepted.

Mail search: Turnaround time: 2 to 3 days. A self addressed stamped envelope is requested.

Phone search: See expedited service.

In person search: You may view records at no charge.

Marriage Certificates

Reference & Research, Vital Records Section, US Rte 2, Drawer 33, Montpelier, VT 05633-7601; 802-828-3286, 8AM-4PM.

http://www.bgs.state.vt.us/gsc/pubrec/referen

Note: For records up to 5 years old, contact the VT Department of Health at 802-863-7300.

Indexing & Storage: Records are available from 1760 to 1995. New records are available for inquiry immediately. Records are indexed on index cards, inhouse computer.

Searching: Records are open. Include the following in your request-names of husband and wife, date of marriage, place or county of marriage, names of parents.

Access by: mail, in person.

Fee & Payment: The search fee is $7.00 per name. Fee payee: VT Vital Records. Prepayment required. Personal checks accepted. No credit cards accepted.

Mail search: Turnaround time: 2 to 3 days. A self addressed stamped envelope is requested.

In person search: Records may be viewed in person at no charge.

Divorce Records

Research & Reference, Vital Records Section, US Rte 2, Drawer 33, Montpelier, VT 05633-7601; 802-828-3286, 8AM-4PM.

http://www.bgs.state.vt.us/gsc/pubrec/referen

Note: For records less than 5 years old, contact the VT Department of health at 802-863-7300.

Indexing & Storage: Records are available from 1760 to 1995. New records are available for inquiry immediately. Records are indexed on index cards, inhouse computer.

Searching: Records are open. Include the following in your request-names of husband and wife, date of divorce, place of divorce.

Access by: mail, in person.

Fee & Payment: The search fee is $7.00 per name. Fee payee: VT Vital Records. Prepayment required. Personal checks accepted. No credit cards accepted.

Mail search: Turnaround time: 2 to 3 days. A self addressed stamped envelope is requested.

In person search: There is no fee to view records.

Workers' Compensation Records

Labor and Industry, Workers Compensation Division, Drawer 20, Montpelier, VT 05620-3401 (Courier: National Life Bldg, Montpelier, VT 05620); 802-828-2286, 802-828-2195 (Fax), 7:45AM-4:30PM.

http://www.state.vt.us/labind/wcindex.htm

Indexing & Storage: Records are available from 1997 on. Records prior to 1997 are in the State Archives. New records are available for inquiry immediately. Records are indexed on inhouse computer.

Searching: Must have a signed release from the claimant. You also will get only the employer's first report of injury. Include the following in your request-claimant name, Social Security Number, place of employment at time of accident. The following data is not released: medical records.

Access by: mail, phone, fax, in person.

Fee & Payment: No search fee, copy fee is $.04 per page. Fee payee: State of Vermont. Personal checks accepted. No credit cards accepted.

Mail search: Turnaround time: 2 weeks. A self addressed stamped envelope is requested.

Phone search: No fee for telephone request. They will indicate if there was a first report filed. They will release no additional information.

Fax search: Turnaround time is 2 weeks.

In person search: Turnaround time is while you wait if staff is available.

Driver Records
Driver License Information

Department of Motor Vehicles, DI - Records Unit, 120 State St, Montpelier, VT 05603-0001; 802-828-2050, 802-828-2098 (Fax), 7:45AM-4:30PM.

http://www.aot.state.vt.us/dmv/dmvhp.htm

Note: This office is closed on Wed. mornings. Ticket information is available from the Vermont Judicial Bureau, PO Box 607, White River Junction, VT 05001, 802-295-8869. There is no charge, but no information is given over the phone.

Indexing & Storage: Records are available for convictions and accidents. Records are sold as 3 year records or as complete (8+ years) records. It takes 5-7 days normally before new records are available for inquiry.

Searching: Written authorization from the subject releases personal information to a requester. Include the following in your request-name, DOB, signed release. Mail or walk-in requesters need the driver's full name and DOB; the license number is optional. Online requesters need only the license number, but the last name and DOB are helpful. The following data is not released: addresses, Social Security Numbers, medical information or personal information (height, weight, sex, eye color, etc.).

Access by: mail, in person, online.

Fee & Payment: Fees: $4.00 for 3 year record; $8.00 for the "complete" record. There is a full charge for a "no record found." Fee payee: Vermont Department of Motor Vehicles. Prepayment required. Personal checks accepted. No credit cards accepted.

Mail search: Turnaround time: 5 to 7 days. A self addressed stamped envelope is requested.

In person search: Normal turnaround time is while you wait.

Online search: Online access costs $4.00 per 3 year record. The system is called "GovNet." Two methods are offered-single inquiry and batch mode. The system is open 24 hours a day, 7 days a week (except for file maintenance periods). Only the license number is needed when ordering, but it is suggested to submit the name and DOB also.

Other access: The state will sell its license file to approved requesters, but customization is not available.

Accident Reports

Department of Motor Vehicles, Accident Report Section, 120 State St, Montpelier, VT 05603; 802-828-2050, 7:45AM-4PM.

Note: The office is closed Wednesday mornings.

Indexing & Storage: Records are available for 5 years to present. Only records involving damage in excess of $1,000 or if injuries involved are reportable. It takes 45 days after the incident before new records are available for inquiry.

Searching: Include the following in your request-full name, date of accident, location of accident. If accident involves a criminal action it may take up to 3 months after accident date to get the report. The following data is not released: Social Security Numbers.

Access by: mail, in person.

Fee & Payment: The fee is $12.00 for the police report and $6.00 for a copy of the individual's report. For insurance information of the accident the fee is $4.00. Fee payee: Vermont Department of Motor Vehicles. Prepayment required. Personal checks accepted. No credit cards accepted.

Mail search: Turnaround time: 3 weeks. A self addressed stamped envelope is requested.

In person search: Searching is available in person.

Vehicle Ownership
Vehicle Identification
Vessel Ownership
Vessel Registration

Department of Motor Vehicles, Registration & License Information/Records, 120 State St, Montpelier, VT 05603; 802-828-2000, 7:45AM-4:30PM (on Wed only 1PM-4:30PM).

http://www.dmv.state.vt.us

Indexing & Storage: Records are available from 1971 to present. Vessel records go back to the late 1970s and are removed after 14 years of inactivity. All motorized boats must be registered. It takes 1 to 3 weeks before new records are available for inquiry.

Searching: You must have name and DOB or plate # or VIN. To receive personal information, you must include signed release by individual. The following data is not released: Social Security Numbers, residence addresses, bulk information or lists for commercial purposes or medical information.

Access by: mail, in person.

Fee & Payment: $4.00 for each group (1-4) of registration records and $15.00 for an ownership (lien) search. Vessel fees are diffeent: registration check is $4.00, title search with lien is $7.50. Statsitical research is $25.00 per hour. Fee payee: Vermont Department of Motor Vehicles. Prepayment required. Personal checks accepted. No credit cards accepted.

Mail search: Turnaround time: 7 to 10 days. A self addressed stamped envelope is requested.

In person search: The turnaround time is generally 30 minutes for vehicle records. Vessel records are returned by mail.

Other access: High volume requesters can obtain records via magnetic tape. Bulk release of the database is not available except for statistical purposes. Apply to the Commissioner's Office.

Legislation Records

Vermont General Assembly, State House-Legislative Council, 115 State Street, Drawer 33, Montpelier, VT 05633; 802-828-2231, 802-828-2424 (Fax), 8AM-4:30PM.

http://www.leg.state.vt.us

Indexing & Storage: Records are available from 1940 at Legislative Council. Records are indexed on inhouse computer.

Searching: Include the following in your request-bill number, topic of bill.

Access by: mail, phone, fax, in person, online.

Fee & Payment: There is no fee.

Mail search: Turnaround time: same day. No self addressed stamped envelope is required.

Phone search: Records are available by phone.

Fax search: Fax searching available.

In person search: No fee for request. A public access terminal is available in the public lobby of the legislature.

Online search: The web site offers access to bill information.

Other access: A subscription service is available for bill text.

Voter Registration
Records not maintained by a state level agency.

Note: There is no statewide database. All records are kept at the municipal level.

GED Certificates

Department of Education, GED Testing, 120 State Street, Montpelier, VT 05620; 802-828-5161, 802-828-3146 (Fax), 8AM-4:30PM.

Searching: Include the following in your request-date of birth, Social Security Number, signed release.

Access by: mail, fax, in person.

Fee & Payment: The fee is $3.00 for a transcript copy. Fee payee: Treasurer, State of Vermont. Prepayment required. No credit cards accepted.

Mail search: Turnaround time: 1 week.

Fax search: Same criteria as mail searching.

In person search: Searching is available in person.

Hunting License Information
Fishing License Information
Records not maintained by a state level agency.

Note: They do maintain a central database on computer. Vendors forward records on a yearly basis (July).

Vermont State Licensing Agencies

Licenses Searchable Online

Accounting Firm #15 .... www.sec.state.vt.us/seek/lrspseek.htm
Acupuncturist #15 .... www.sec.state.vt.us/seek/lrspseek.htm
Appraiser #12 .... www.sec.state.vt.us/seek/lrspseek.htm
Architect #15 .... www.sec.state.vt.us/seek/lrspseek.htm
Auctioneer #15 .... www.sec.state.vt.us/seek/lrspseek.htm
Barber #15... www.sec.state.vt.us/seek/lrspseek.htm
Boxing Manager/Promoter #15.................. www.sec.state.vt.us/seek/lrspseek.htm
Chiropractor #15...................................... www.sec.state.vt.us/seek/lrspseek.htm
Cosmetologist #15 .... www.sec.state.vt.us/seek/lrspseek.htm
Dental Assistant #15................................ www.sec.state.vt.us/seek/lrspseek.htm
Dental Hygienist #15................................ www.sec.state.vt.us/seek/lrspseek.htm
Dentist #15 .... www.sec.state.vt.us/seek/lrspseek.htm
Dietitian #15 .... www.sec.state.vt.us/seek/lrspseek.htm
Embalmer #12.. www.sec.state.vt.us/seek/lrspseek.htm
Engineer #15 .... www.sec.state.vt.us/seek/lrspseek.htm
Esthetician #15.. www.sec.state.vt.us/seek/lrspseek.htm
Funeral Director #12 .... www.sec.state.vt.us/seek/lrspseek.htm
Hearing Aid Dispenser #15 .... www.sec.state.vt.us/seek/lrspseek.htm
Lobbyist #15.. www.sec.state.vt.us/seek/lbylseek.htm
Manicurist #15 .... www.sec.state.vt.us/seek/lrspseek.htm
Marriage & Family Therapist #15 .... www.sec.state.vt.us/seek/lrspseek.htm
Medical Doctor/Surgeon #15 .... www.docboard.org/vt/df/vtsearch.htm
Mental Health Counselor, Clinical #15...... www.sec.state.vt.us/seek/lrspseek.htm
Naturopathic Physician #15 .... www.sec.state.vt.us/seek/lrspseek.htm
Notary Public #15 .... www.sec.state.vt.us/seek/not_seek.htm
Nurse/Nurse Practitioner/LNA #15 .... www.sec.state.vt.us/seek/lrspseek.htm
Nursing Home Administrator #15 .... www.sec.state.vt.us/seek/lrspseek.htm
Occupational Therapist #15 .... www.sec.state.vt.us/seek/lrspseek.htm
Optician #15 .... www.sec.state.vt.us/seek/lrspseek.htm
Optometrist #15....................................... www.sec.state.vt.us/seek/lrspseek.htm
Osteopathic Physician #15....................... www.sec.state.vt.us/seek/lrspseek.htm
Pharmacy/ Pharmacist #15....................... www.sec.state.vt.us/seek/lrspseek.htm
Physical Therapist/Assistant #15 .... www.sec.state.vt.us/seek/lrspseek.htm
Physician Assistant #15........................... www.docboard.org/vt/df/vtsearch.htm
Podiatrist #15 .... www.docboard.org/vt/df/vtsearch.htm
Private Investigator #15 .... www.sec.state.vt.us/seek/lrspseek.htm
Psychoanalyst #15................................... www.sec.state.vt.us/seek/lrspseek.htm
Psychologist #15 .... www.sec.state.vt.us/seek/lrspseek.htm
Psychotherapist #15 .... www.sec.state.vt.us/seek/lrspseek.htm
Public Accountant-CPA #15...................... www.sec.state.vt.us/seek/lrspseek.htm
Racing Promoter #15................................ www.sec.state.vt.us/seek/lrspseek.htm
Radiologic Technologist #15 .... www.sec.state.vt.us/seek/lrspseek.htm
Real Estate Appraiser #12 .... www.sec.state.vt.us/seek/lrspseek.htm
Real Estate Broker/Agent #12 .... www.sec.state.vt.us/seek/lrspseek.htm
Real Estate Salesperson #12.................... www.sec.state.vt.us/seek/lrspseek.htm
Security Guard #15................................... www.sec.state.vt.us/seek/lrspseek.htm
Social Worker, Clinical #15...................... www.sec.state.vt.us/seek/lrspseek.htm
Surveyor #15 .... www.sec.state.vt.us/seek/lrspseek.htm
Tattoo Artist #15 .... www.sec.state.vt.us/seek/lrspseek.htm
Veterinarian #15 .... www.sec.state.vt.us/seek/lrspseek.htm

Licensing Quick Finder

Accounting Firm #15 802-828-2363
Acupuncturist #15 802-828-2373
Alcohol & Drug Abuse Counselor #18 ...802-878-7776
Appraiser #12 802-828-3183
Architect #15..802-828-2373
Armed Courier #15................................802-828-2837
Asbestos Abatement Contractor/Worker #19.............
....802-863-7231
Attorney #02 802-828-3281
Auctioneer #15......................................802-828-3183
Barber #15...802-828-2837
Boiler & Pressure Vessel Inspector #9 ..802-828-2107
Boxing Manager/Promoter #15 802-828-2363
Chiropractor #15 802-828-2363
Cosmetologist #15 802-828-2363
Dealer/Repairer Weighing & Measuring Devices #04
....802-244-2436
Dental Assistant #15 802-828-2363
Dental Hygienist #15 802-828-2363
Dentist #15 802-828-2363
Dietitian #15..802-828-2363
Driver Training School/instructor #11 802-828-2114
Electrician #08 802-828-2107
Embalmer #12 802-828-3183
Emergency Care Attendant #07 802-863-7310
Emergency Medical Technician #07......802-863-7310
Engineer #15 802-828-2363
Esthetician #15 802-828-2363
Fire Alarm System Installer/Dealer #8 ...802-828-2107
Funeral Director #12..............................802-828-3183
Guard Dog Handler #15 802-828-2363
Hearing Aid Dispenser #15 802-828-2363
Horse Racing Trainers/Owners/Professional #17 ....
....802-786-5050

Insurance Adjuster #05.........................802-828-3303
Insurance Agent/Consultant #05............802-828-3303
Insurance Appraiser #05 802-828-3303
Insurance Broker #05 802-828-3303
Investment Advisor #05 802-828-3420
Issuer Agent #05...................................802-828-3420
Lead Abatement Contr./Worker #19......802-863-7231
Lightning Rod Installer/Dealer #08 802-828-2107
Liquor, Retail #10 802-828-2339
Liquor, Wholesale #10...........................802-828-2339
Livestock Dealer #04 802-828-2421
Lobbyist #15 802-828-2464
Lottery Retailer #16...............................802-479-5686
Manicurist #15 802-828-2363
Marriage & Family Therapist #15 802-828-2363
Meat Inspection Laboratory #04.............802-244-4510
Medical Doctor/Surgeon #15 802-828-2673
Mental Health Counselor, Clinical #15...802-828-2363
Milk & Cream Tester #04 802-244-4510
Naturopathic Physician #15 802-828-2363
Notary Public #15..................................802-828-2464
Nurse/Nurse Practitioner/LNA #15 802-828-2396
Nursing Home Administrator #15 802-828-2363
Occupational Therapist #15 802-828-2363
Optician #15..802-828-2363
Optometrist #15 802-828-2373
Osteopathic Physician #15 802-828-2373
Pari-Mutuel Seller #17 802-786-5050
Peddler #15 802-828-2363
Pediatrist #15 802-828-2673
Pesticide Applicator #04 802-244-2431
Pharmacy/Pharmacist #15.....................802-828-2363
Photographer, Itinerant #15 802-828-2363
Physical Therapist/Assistant #15 802-828-2363

Physician Assistant #15........................802-828-2673
Plumber #08 802-828-2107
Podiatrist #15..802-828-2363
Polygraph Examiner #03 802-244-8781
Private Investigator #15.........................802-828-2363
Psychoanalyst #15 802-828-2373
Psychologist #15...................................802-828-2373
Psychotherapist #15..............................802-828-2363
Public Accountant-CPA #15...................802-828-2363
Public Adjuster #05 802-828-3303
Race Driver/Track Personnel #15 802-828-2363
Racing Promoter #15 802-828-2363
Radiologic Technologist #15..................802-828-2363
Real Estate Appraiser #12.....................802-828-3183
Real Estate Broker/Agent #12 802-828-3228
Real Estate Salesperson #12 802-828-3228
School Guidance Counselor #06 802-828-2445
School Librarian/Media Specialist #06...802-828-2445
School Principal/Superintendant #06 802-828-2445
Securities Broker/Dealer #05 802-828-3420
Securities Sales Representative #05......802-828-3420
Security Guard #15................................802-828-2363
Social Worker, Clinical #15....................802-828-2363
Surveyor #15 802-828-3183
Tattoo Artist #15....................................802-828-2363
Teacher #06...802-828-2445
Vehicle Dealer #11 802-828-2038
Vendor, Itinerant #15.............................802-828-2363
Veterinarian #15....................................802-828-2363
Vocational Education Teacher #06 802-828-2445
Waste Water Treatment Plant Operator #01................
....802-241-3822
Well Driller #01......................................802-241-3400

Licensing Agency Information

#01 Agency of Natural Resources, 103 S Main St, The Sewing Bldg, Waterbury, VT 05671-0405; 802-241-3822, Fax: 802-241-2596.

#02 Board of Bar Examiners, 109 State St, Montpelier, VT 05609-0702; 802-828-3281, Fax: 802-828-3457.
www.state.vt.us/courts/

#03 Commission of Public Safety, 103 S Main St, Waterbury State Complex, Waterbury, VT 05671-2101; 802-244-8781, Fax: 802-244-1106.

#04 Department of Agriculture, 103 S Main St, Waterbury, VT 05671; 802-244-4510, Fax: 802-241-3008.
www.clt.agr.state.us

#05 Department of Banking, 89 Main St City Ctr, Drawer 20, Montpelier, VT 05620-3101; 802-828-3420, Fax: 802-828-2896.
www.state.vt.us/bis/

#06 Department of Education, 120 State St, Montpelier, VT 05620-2501; 802-828-2445, Fax: 802-828-5107.
www.state.vt.us/educ/license

#07 Department of Health, 108 Cherry St, Burlington, VT 05402; 802-863-7310, Fax: 802-863-7577.
www.state.vt.us/health/ems

#08 Department of Labor & Industry, Drawer 20, National Life Bldg, Montpelier, VT 05620-3401; 802-828-2107, Fax: 802-828-2195.
www.state.vt.us/labind

#09 Department of Labor & Industry, 372 Hurricane Ln #102, Williston, VT 05495-2080; 802-658-2199, Fax: 802-863-7410.

#10 Department of Liquor Control, PO Drawer 20, Montpelier, VT 05620-4501; 802-828-2339, Fax: 802-828-2803.
www.sec.state.vt.us

#11 Department of Motor Vehicles, 120 State St, Montpelier, VT 05603; 802-828-2114, Fax: 802-828-2092.
www.dmv.state.vt.us

#12 Real Estate Commission, 81 Riverside St. Heritage Bldg, Montpelier, VT 05609-1106; 802-828-3228, Fax: 802-828-2368.
www.sec.state.vt.us

Direct web site URL to search for licensees: www.sec.state.vt.us/seek/lrspseek.htm. You can search online using last name; first name optional. Also, search profession lists.

#15 Secretary of State, 109 State St, Montpelier, VT 05609; 802-828-2673, Fax: 802-828-5450.
www.vtprofessionals.org
Direct web site URL to search for licensees: www.sec.state.vt.us/seek/lrspseek.htm. You can search online using name.

#16 Lottery Commission, PO Box 420 (379 S Barre Rd), South Barre, VT 05670-0429; 802-479-5686, Fax: 802-479-4294.
www.vtlottery.com

#17 Racing Commission, 128 Merchants Row, Rutland, VT 05701; 802-786-5050, Fax: 802-786-5051.

#18 Alcohol & Drug Abuse Certification Board, PO Box 135, St. Albans, VT 05478-0135; 802-878-7776, Fax: 802-879-6211.
www.vtboard.org/vtboard/

#19 Department of Health, PO Box 70, Burlington, VT 05402; 802-863-7231, Fax: 802-863-7483.
www.state.vt.us/health

Vermont Federal Courts

The following list indicates the district and division name for each county in the state. If the bankruptcy court location is different from the district court, then the location of the bankruptcy court appears in parentheses.

County/Court Cross Reference

Addison	Rutland	Lamoille	Burlington (Rutland)
Bennington	Rutland	Orange	Rutland
Caledonia	Burlington (Rutland)	Orleans	Burlington (Rutland)
Chittenden	Burlington (Rutland)	Rutland	Rutland
Essex	Burlington (Rutland)	Washington	Burlington (Rutland)
Franklin	Burlington (Rutland)	Windham	Rutland
Grand Isle	Burlington (Rutland)	Windsor	Rutland

US District Court

District of Vermont

Burlington Division Clerk's Office, PO Box 945, Burlington, VT 05402-0945 (Courier Address: Room 506, 11 Elmwood Ave, Burlington, VT 05401), 802-951-6301.

http://www.vtd.uscourts.gov

Counties: Caledonia, Chittenden, Essex, Franklin, Grand Isle, Lamoille, Orleans, Washington. However, cases from all counties in the state are assigned randomly to either Burlington or Brattleboro. Brattleboro is a hearing location only, not listed here.

Indexing/Storage: Cases are indexed by defendant and plaintiff as well as by case number. New cases are available in the index 1 working day after filing date. Both computer and card indexes are maintained. New cases filed January 1, 1991 to present are on the automated in house system. Pre-1991 cases are indexed on microfiche or microfilm. Open records are located at this court.

Fee & Payment: The fee is $20.00 per item (one party name or case number). Payment may be made by money order, cashier check, personal check. Prepayment is required. Payee: Clerk, US District Court. Certification fee: $7.00 per document. Copy fee: $.50 per page. You are allowed to make your own copies. These copies cost $.50 per page.

Phone Search: Only general information which can be accessed by computer will be released over the phone.

Mail Search: Always enclose a stamped self addressed envelope.

In Person: In person searching is available.

PACER: Sign-up number is 800-676-6856. Access fee is $.60 per minute. Toll-free access: 800-263-9396. Local access: 802-951-6623. Case records are available back to January 1991. Records are never purged. New records are available online after 1 day.

Other Online Access: Search records on the Internet using RACER at https://racer.vtd. uscourts.gov/perl/bkplog.html. Access fee is 7 cents per page.

Rutland Division PO Box 607, Rutland, VT 05702-0607 (Courier Address: 151 West St, Rutland, VT 05701), 802-773-0245.

http://www.vtd.uscourts.gov

Counties: Addison, Bennington, Orange, Rutland, Windsor, Windham. However, cases from all counties in the state are randomly assigned to either Burlington or Brattleboro. Rutland is a hearing location only, not listed here.

Indexing/Storage: Cases are indexed by defendant and plaintiff as well as by case number. New cases are available in the index 1 day after filing date. A computer index is maintained. New cases filed January 1, 1991 to present are on the automated in house system. Pre-1991 cases are indexed on microfiche or microfilm. Open records are located at this court. There is no judge sitting in Rutland itself, but one is in Brattleboro.

Fee & Payment: The fee is $20.00 per item (one party name or case number). Payment may be made by money order, cashier check, personal check. Prepayment is required. Payee: Clerk, US District Court. Certification fee: $7.00 per document. Copy fee: $.50 per page. You are allowed to make your own copies. These copies cost $.50 per page.

Phone Search: Only docket information is available by phone.

Mail Search: Always enclose a stamped self addressed envelope.

In Person: In person searching is available.

PACER: Sign-up number is 800-676-6856. Access fee is $.60 per minute. Toll-free access: 800-263-9396. Local access: 802-951-6623. Case records are available back to January 1991. Records are never purged. New records are available online after 1 day.

Other Online Access: Search records on the Internet using RACER at https://racer.vtd.uscourts. gov/perl/bkplog.html. Access fee is 7 cents per page.

US Bankruptcy Court

District of Vermont

Rutland Division PO Box 6648, Rutland, VT 05702-6648 (Courier Address: 67 Merchants Row, Rutland, VT 05701), 802-776-2000, Fax: 802-776-2020.

http://www.vtb.uscourts.gov

Counties: All counties in Vermont.

Indexing/Storage: Cases are indexed by debtor and creditors as well as by case number. New cases are available in the index immediately after filing date. A computer index is maintained. Open records are located at this court.

Fee & Payment: The fee is $20.00 per item (one party name or case number). Payment may be made by money order, cashier check, personal check, Visa or Mastercard. Prepayment is required. Payee: US Bankruptcy Court. Certification fee: $7.00 per document. Copy fee: $.50 per page.

Phone Search: Docket information is available by phone. An automated voice case information service (VCIS) is available. Call VCIS at 800-260-9956 or 802-776-2007.

Fax Search: Will accept fax searches with credit card. Copy fees apply to faxed dockets.

Mail Search: A stamped self addressed envelope is not required.

In Person: In person searching is available.

PACER: Sign-up number is 800-676-6856. Access fee is $.60 per minute. Toll-free access: 800-260-9968. Local access: 802-776-2006. Case records are available back to 1992 (limited information prior). Records are never purged. New civil records are available online after 1 day. PACER is available online at http://pacer.vtb.uscourts.gov.

Electronic Filing: Electronic filing information is available online at https://ecf.vtb.uscourts.gov

Vermont County Courts

Court	Jurisdiction	No. of Courts	How Organized
Superior Courts*	General	11	14 Counties
District Courts*	Limited	11	3 Circuits
Combined Courts*		3	
Probate Courts*	Probate	18	
Family Courts	Special	14	14 Counties
Environmental Court	Special	1	

* Profiled in this Sourcebook.

Court	CIVIL								
	Tort	Contract	Real Estate	Min. Claim	Max. Claim	Small Claims	Estate	Eviction	Domestic Relations
Superior Courts*	X	X	X	$0	No Max	$3500		X	
District Courts*									
Probate Courts*							X		
Family Courts									X

Court	CRIMINAL				
	Felony	Misdemeanor	DWI/DUI	Preliminary Hearing	Juvenile
Superior Courts*					
District Courts*	X	X	X	X	
Probate Courts*					
Family Courts					X

ADMINISTRATION
Administrative Office of Courts, Court Administrator, 109 State St, Montpelier, VT, 05609-0701; 802-828-3278, Fax: 802-828-3457. www.vermontjudiciary.org

COURT STRUCTURE
As of September, 1996, all small claims came under the jurisdiction of Superior Court, the court of general jurisdiction. All counties have a diversion program in which first offenders go through a process that includes a letter of apology, community service, etc. and, after 2 years, the record is expunged. These records are never released.

The Vermont Judicial Bureau has jurisdiction over Traffic, Municipal Ordinance, and Fish and Game, Minors in Possession, and hazing.

ONLINE ACCESS
There is no online computer access to the public; however, some courts offer calendar data over the Internet.

ADDITIONAL INFORMATION
There are statewide certification and copy fees, as follows: Certification Fee - $5.00 per document plus copy fee; Copy Fee - $.25 per page with a $1.00 minimum.

Addison County

Superior Court 7 Mahady Ct, Middlebury, VT 05753; 802-388-7741. Hours: 8:30AM-4:30PM (EST). *Civil, Eviction, Small Claims.*

Civil Records: Access: Mail, in person. Only the court performs in person searches; visitors may not. No search fee. Required to search: name, years to search. Civil cases indexed by defendant, plaintiff. Civil records on index cards and recording books.

General Information: No sealed or unserved records released. Turnaround time 2-3 days. Copy fee: $.25 per page. Certification fee: $5.00. Fee payee: Addison County Clerk. Personal checks accepted. Credit cards accepted. Prepayment is required.

District Court 7 Mahady Ct, Middlebury, VT 05753; 802-388-4237. Hours: 8AM-4:30PM (EST). *Felony, Misdemeanor.*

Criminal Records: Access: Phone, mail, in person. Only the court performs in person searches; visitors may not. Search fee: $1.00 per name. Required to search: name, years to search, DOB. Criminal records on computer since mid 1991; prior on dockets and index cards.

General Information: No adoptions, juvenile, sealed, or expunged records released. Turnaround time up to 1 week. Copy fee: $.25 per page. Certification fee: $5.00. Fee payee: Addison District Court. Personal checks accepted. Prepayment is required.

Probate Court 7 Mahady Court, Middlebury, VT 05753; 802-388-2612. 8AM-4:30PM (EST). *Probate.*

Bennington County

Superior Court 207 South St, PO Box 4157, Bennington, VT 05201; 802-447-2700; Fax: 802-447-2703. 8AM-4:30PM *Civil, Eviction, Small Claims.*

Civil Records: Access: Phone, mail, in person. Both court and visitors may perform in person searches. No search fee. Required to search: name, years to search. Civil cases indexed by defendant, plaintiff. Civil records on computer from 1989, index from 1968.

General Information: No deposition, adoption, juvenile, sealed or expunged records released.

Turnaround time 2-3 days. Copy fee: $.25 per page. Certification fee: $5.00. Fee payee: Bennington County. Personal checks accepted. Prepayment is required.

District Court 200 Veterans Memorial Dr #13, Bennington, VT 05201; 802-447-2727; Fax: 802-447-2750. 7:45AM-4:30PM (EST). *Felony, Misdemeanor.*

Criminal Records: Access: Phone, mail, in person. Both court and visitors may perform in person searches. No search fee. Required to search: name, years to search, DOB. Criminal records on index cards and docket books.

General Information: No sealed, diversion case records released. SASE requested. Turnaround time varies. Copy fee: $.25 per page. $1.00 minimum. Certification fee: $5.00. Fee payee: District Court or Vermont District Court. Personal checks accepted. Prepayment is required.

Probate Court - Bennington District 207 South St, PO Box 65, Bennington, VT 05201; 802-447-2705; Fax: 802-447-2703 (Attn: Probate Court). Hours: 9AM-Noon, 1:30-4PM (EST). *Probate.*

Probate Court - Manchester District PO Box 446, Manchester, VT 05254; 802-362-1410. Hours: 8AM-Noon, 1-4:20PM (EST). *Probate.*

Caledonia County

Superior Court 1126 Main St #1, St Johnsbury, VT 05819; 802-748-6600; Fax: 802-748-6603. Hours: 8AM-4:30PM (EST). *Civil, Eviction, Small Claims.*

Civil Records: Access: Phone, fax, mail, in person. Only the court performs in person searches; visitors may not. No search fee. Required to search: name, years to search. Civil cases indexed by defendant, plaintiff. Civil records on computer from 1992, in archives before 1985, index from 1985, all other records on index cards.

General Information: No adoption, juvenile, sealed or expunged records released. SASE requested. Turnaround time 1 week. Fax notes: $2.00 per page. Copy fee: Superior Court $1.00 minimum; Family Court $.25 per page, $1.00 minimum. Certification fee: $5.00 plus $.25 per page. Payee: Caledonia Superior Court. Personal checks accepted. Prepayment required.

District Court 1126 Main St #1, St Johnsbury, VT 05819; 802-748-6610; Fax: 802-748-6603. Hours: 8AM-4:30PM (EST). *Felony, Misdemeanor.*

Criminal Records: Access: Fax, mail, in person. Both court and visitors may perform in person searches. No search fee. Required to search: name, years to search; also helpful: DOB. Criminal records on computer since 1991, prior on index cards.

General Information: Public Access terminal is available. No adoptions, juvenile, sealed or expunged records released. SASE not required. Turnaround time less than a week. Fax notes: $2.00 per page. Copy fee: $.25 per page. $1.00 minimum. Certification fee: $5.00. Fee payee: Caledonia District Court. Personal checks accepted.

Probate Court 27 Main St, PO Box 406, St Johnsbury, VT 05819; 802-748-6605; Fax: 802-748-6603. Hours: 8AM-4:30PM (EST). *Probate.*

Chittenden County

Superior Court 175 Main St.(PO Box 187), Burlington, VT 05402; 802-863-3467. Hours: 8AM-4:30PM (EST). *Civil, Eviction, Small Claims.*

http://court.co.chittenden.vt.us/superior

Civil Records: Access: Phone, mail, in person. Only the court performs in person searches; visitors may not. No search fee. Required to search: name, years to search. Civil cases indexed by defendant, plaintiff. Civil records on computer back to 1983, small claims since 1996, prior records on books from 1800s.

General Information: No adoption, juvenile, sealed or expunged records released. Turnaround time 1 week. Fax notes: Will not fax results. Copy fee: $.25 per page. $1.00 minimum. Certification fee: $5.00. Fee payee: Chittenden County Superior Court. Personal checks accepted. Prepayment is required.

District Court 32 Cherry St #300, Burlington, VT 05401; 802-651-1800. Hours: 8AM-4:30PM (EST). *Felony, Misdemeanor.*

Criminal Records: Access: Mail, in person. Both court and visitors may perform in person searches. No search fee. Required to search: name, years to search; also helpful: DOB. Criminal records on new computer from 6/90, on old computer from 6/85 to 06/90, books by alpha name from 12/69 to 1980; index cards from 1970.

General Information: Public Access terminal is available. No adoption, juvenile, sealed or expunged records released. Turnaround time 1-2 days. Copy fee: $.25 per page. Certification fee: $5.00. Fee payee: Vermont District Court. Personal checks accepted. Prepayment is required.

Probate Court PO Box 511, Burlington, VT 05402; 802-651-1518. 8AM-4:30PM (EST). *Probate.*

Essex County

District & Superior Court Box 75, Guildhall, VT 05905; 802-676-3910; Fax: 802-676-3463. Hours: 8AM-4:30PM (EST). *Felony, Misdemeanor, Civil, Eviction, Small Claims.*

www.state.vt.us/courts

Civil Records: Access: Phone, fax, mail, in person. Only the court performs in person searches; visitors may not. No search fee. Required to search: name, years to search. Civil cases indexed by defendant, plaintiff. Civil records indexed from 1974; on computer from 5/94. Calendar information on web site. Will not accept phone requests for more than 2 names.

Criminal Records: Access: Phone, fax, mail, in person. Only the court performs in person searches; visitors may not. No search fee. Required to search: name, years to search, DOB. Criminal records indexed from 1974; on computer from 5/94. Calendar information on web site. Will not accept phone requests for more than 2 names.

General Information: No adoptions, juvenile, sealed or expunged records released. Turnaround time 1 week. Fax notes: $1.00 per page. Copy fee: $.25 per page. $1.00 minimum. Certification fee: $5.00 plus $.25 per page. Fee payee: Depends on court (superior or district). Only cashiers checks and money orders accepted. Prepayment is required.

Probate Court PO Box 426, Island Pond, VT 05846; 802-723-4770; Fax: 802-723-4770. Hours: 8:30AM-Noon, 1-3:30PM (EST). *Probate.*

Franklin County

Superior Court Box 808 Church St, St Albans, VT 05478; 802-524-3863; Fax: 802-524-7996. Hours: 8AM-4:30PM (EST). *Civil, Eviction, Small Claims.*

Civil Records: Access: Phone, fax, mail, in person. Only the court performs in person searches; visitors may not. No search fee. Required to search: name, years to search. Civil cases indexed by defendant, plaintiff. Civil records on computer since 1996; prior on index cards from 1840.

General Information: No adoption, juvenile, sealed or expunged records released. SASE required. Turnaround time 1 week. Fax notes: $2.00 per page. Copy fee: $.25 per page. $1.00 minimum. Certification fee: $5.00. Fee payee: Franklin Superior Court. Personal checks accepted. Prepayment is required.

District Court 36 Lake St, St Albans, VT 05478; 802-524-7997; Fax: 802-524-7946. Hours: 8AM-4:30PM (EST). *Felony, Misdemeanor.*

Criminal Records: Access: Phone, mail, in person. Only the court performs in person searches; visitors may not. No search fee. Required to search: name, years to search; also helpful: DOB, SSN. Criminal records on computer since 1987.

General Information: Public Access terminal is available. No adoption, juvenile, sealed or expunged records released. Turnaround time 7-10 days. Fax notes: Fee to fax results is $1.00 per document and $.25 per page. Copy fee: $.25 per page. Certification fee: $5.00. Fee payee: Vermont District Court. Personal checks accepted. Prepayment is required.

Franklin Probate Court 17 Church St, St Albans, VT 05478; 802-524-4112. Hours: 8AM-Noon, 1-4:30PM (EST). *Probate.*

Grand Isle County

District & Superior Court PO Box 7, North Hero, VT 05474; 802-372-8350; Fax: 802-372-3221. Hours: 8AM-4:30PM (EST). *Felony, Misdemeanor, Civil, Eviction, Small Claims.*

Civil Records: Access: Phone, fax, mail, in person. Both court and visitors may perform in person searches. No search fee. Required to search: name, years to search. Civil cases indexed by defendant, plaintiff. Civil records on computer from 1990, on index 1940.

Criminal Records: Access: Phone, fax, mail, in person. Both court and visitors may perform in person searches. No search fee. Required to search: name, years to search; also helpful: DOB, SSN. Criminal records on computer from 1990, on index from 1940.

General Information: No adoption, juvenile, sealed or expunged records released. Turnaround time 1-2 days. Fax notes: Do not fax. Copy fee: $.25 per page. $1.00 minimum. Certification fee: $5.00. Fee payee: Grand Isle Superior or District Court. Personal checks accepted. Prepayment is required.

Probate Court PO Box 7, North Hero, VT 05474; 802-372-8350; Fax: 802-372-3221. Hours: 8AM-4:30PM (EST). *Probate.*

Lamoille County

Superior Court Box 490, Hyde Park, VT 05655; 802-888-2207. 8AM-4:30PM (EST). *Civil, Eviction, Small Claims.*

Civil Records: Access: Mail, in person. Only the court performs in person searches; visitors may not. No search fee. Required to search: name, years to search. Civil cases indexed by defendant, plaintiff. Civil records on computer from 1989, index from 1970s.

General Information: No adoption, juvenile, sealed or expunged records released. SASE required. Turnaround time 1 week. Copy fee: $.25 per page. Certification fee: $5.00. Fee payee: Lamoille Superior Court. Personal checks accepted.

District Court PO Box 489, Hyde Park, VT 05655-0489; 802-888-3887; Fax: 802-888-2591. Hours: 8AM-4:30PM (EST). *Felony, Misdemeanor.*

Criminal Records: Access: Fax, mail, in person. Only the court performs in person searches; visitors may not. No search fee. Required to search: name, DOB; also helpful: years to search. Criminal records on computer since 06/88; prior on index cards.

General Information: No adoption, juvenile, sealed or expunged records released. SASE required. Turnaround time 3 days if record on-site, 1 week if off-site. Fax notes: No fee to fax results. They will only fax returns to toll free calls. Copy fee: $.25 per page. $1.00 minimum. Certification fee: $5.00. Fee payee: Vermont District Court. Personal checks accepted. Prepayment required.

Probate Court PO Box 102, Hyde Park, VT 05655-0102; 802-888-3306; Fax: 802-888-1347. Hours: 8AM-noon, 1:30-4:30PM (EST). *Probate.*

Orange County

District & Superior Court 5 Court St, Chelsea, VT 05038-9746; 802-685-4870; Fax: 802-685-3246. Hours: 8AM-4:30PM (EST). *Felony, Misdemeanor, Civil, Eviction, Small Claims.*

Civil Records: Access: Fax, mail, in person. Only the court performs in person searches; visitors may not. No search fee. Required to search: name, years to search; also helpful: address. Civil cases indexed by defendant, plaintiff. Civil records on computer from 7/94, on index from 1967.
Criminal Records: Access: Phone, fax, mail, in person. Only the court performs in person searches; visitors may not. No search fee. Required to search: name, years to search, DOB; also helpful: address. Criminal records on computer from 1990, on index from 1967.
General Information: No adoption, juvenile, sealed or expunged records released. Turnaround time 1 week. Fax notes: Fee to fax results is $1.00 per page. Copy fee: $.25 per page. $1.00 minimum. Certification fee: $5.00. Fee payee: Clerk of Court. Personal checks accepted. Prepayment is required.

Probate Court 5 Court Street, Chelsea, VT 05038-9746; 802-685-4610; Fax: 802-685-3246. Hours: 8AM-Noon, 1-4:30PM (EST). *Probate.*

Note: The Bradford and Randolph Districts were consolidated into this one probate court as of June 1994.

Orleans County

Superior Court 247 Main St #1, Newport, VT 05855-1203; 802-334-3344; Fax: 802-334-3385. 8AM-4:30PM (EST). *Civil, Eviction, Small Claims.*

Civil Records: Access: Phone, fax, mail, in person. Only the court performs in person searches; visitors may not. No search fee. Required to search: name; also helpful: years to search. Civil cases indexed by defendant, plaintiff. Civil records on computer since 1994; prior records on index from 1800s.
General Information: No juvenile records released. SASE required. Turnaround time 1 week. Fax notes: $2.00 per page. Copy fee: $.25 per page. $1.00 minimum. Certification fee: $5.00. Fee payee: Orleans Superior Court. Personal checks accepted. Prepayment is required.

District Court 217 Main St, #4, Newport VT 05855 802-334-3325. 8AM-4:30PM. *Felony, Misdemeanor.*

Criminal Records: Access: Phone, mail, in person. Both court and visitors may perform in person searches. No search fee. Required to search: name, years to search, DOB. Criminal records on computer since 01/91; prior on index cards back to 1971. History checks of three or more names must be in writing.
General Information: No adoption, juvenile, sealed or expunged records released. SASE required. Turnaround time 1 week. Fax notes: Will not fax results. Copy fee: $.25 per page. $1.00 minimum; Add $4.00 if copies retrieved from public records. Certification fee: $5.00. Fee payee: District Court of Vermont. Personal checks accepted. Prepayment is required.

Probate Court 247 Main St, Newport, VT 05855; 802-334-3366. 8AM-Noon, 1-4:30PM (EST). *Probate.*

Rutland County

Superior Court 83 Center St, Rutland, VT 05701; 802-775-4394. Hours: 8AM-4:30PM (EST). *Civil, Eviction, Small Claims.*

Civil Records: Access: Mail, in person. Only the court performs in person searches; visitors may not. No

search fee. Required to search: name, years to search. Civil cases indexed by defendant, plaintiff. Civil records on computer from 1987, on index from late 1700s.
General Information: No adoption, juvenile, sealed or expunged records released. SASE required. Turnaround time 1 week. Copy fee: $.25 per page. $1.00 minimum. Certification fee: $5.00. Fee payee: Rutland Superior Court. Personal checks accepted. Prepayment required.

District Court 92 State St, Rutland, VT 05701-2886; 802-786-5880. Hours: 8AM-4:30PM (EST). *Felony, Misdemeanor.*

Criminal Records: Access: Phone, mail, in person. Both court and visitors may perform in person searches. No search fee. Required to search: name, years to search, DOB; also helpful: SSN. Criminal records on computer since 1985.
General Information: Public Access terminal is available. No sealed, expunged records released. SASE required. Turnaround time 1 week. Copy fee: $.25 per page. $1.00 minimum. Certification fee: $5.00. Fee payee: District Court of Vermont. Personal checks accepted.

Probate Court - Fair Haven District 3 North Park Place, Fair Haven, VT 05743; 802-265-3380. Hours: 8AM-4PM (EST). *Probate.*

Probate Court - Rutland District 83 Center St, Rutland, VT 05701; 802-775-0114. Hours: 8AM-4:30PM (EST). *Probate.*

Washington County

Superior Court 65 State St, Montpelier, VT 05602-3594; 802-828-2091. Hours: 8AM-4:30PM (EST). *Civil, Eviction, Small Claims.*

Civil Records: Access: Phone, mail, in person. Only the court performs in person searches; visitors may not. No search fee. Required to search: name, years to search; also helpful: address. Civil cases indexed by defendant, plaintiff. Civil records on computer from 1987, archives from 1900s.
General Information: No adoption, juvenile or expunged records released. SASE requested. Turnaround time 1-2 days. Copy fee: $.25 per page. $1.00 minimum. Certification fee: $5.00. Fee payee: Washington County Superior Court. Personal checks accepted.

District Court 255 N Main, Barre, VT 05641; 802-479-4252. Hours: 8AM-4:30PM (EST). *Felony, Misdemeanor.*

Criminal Records: Access: Phone, mail, in person. Both court and visitors may perform in person searches. No search fee. Required to search: name, years to search; also helpful: DOB. Criminal records on computer since 1989; prior records in index form 1970s.
General Information: No adoption, juvenile, sealed or expunged records released. SASE requested. Turnaround time 3-5 days. Copy fee: $.25 per page. $1.00 minimum. Certification fee: $5.00. Fee payee: Washington District Court. Personal checks accepted.

Probate Court 10 Elm Street #2, Montpelier, VT 05601; 802-828-3405. Hours: 8AM-Noon, 1-4:30PM M-Th; 8AM-Noon, 1-4PM F (EST). *Probate.*

Windham County

Superior Court Box 207, Newfane, VT 05345; 802-365-7979; Fax: 802-365-4360. Hours: 9AM-4PM (EST). *Civil, Eviction, Small Claims.*

Civil Records: Access: Phone, fax, mail, in person. Both court and visitors may perform in person searches. No search fee. Required to search: name, years to search. Civil cases indexed by defendant, plaintiff. Civil records on computer from 1994, on index from 1919. Fax available only in emergency.

General Information: No adoption, juvenile, sealed or expunged records released. SASE required. Turnaround time 1-2 days. Fax notes: No fee to fax results. Copy fee: $.25 per page. $1.00 minimum. Certification fee: $5.00. Fee payee: Windham Superior Court. Personal checks accepted. Prepayment is required.

District Court 30 Putney Rd, Brattleboro, VT 05301; 802-257-2800; Fax: 802-257-2853. Hours: 8AM-4:30PM (EST). *Felony, Misdemeanor.*

Criminal Records: Access: Phone, fax, mail, in person. Both court and visitors may perform in person searches. No search fee. Required to search: name, years to search; also helpful: address, DOB, SSN. Criminal records on computer since 1990; prior on index cards and docket books.
General Information: No adoption, juvenile, sealed or expunged records released. SASE requested. Turnaround time 5-7 days. Fax notes: $.25 per page. Copy fee: $.25 per page. Certification fee: $5.00. Fee payee: Vermont District Court. Personal checks accepted. Prepayment is required.

Probate Court - Marlboro District PO Box 523, Brattleboro, VT 05302; 802-257-2898. Hours: 8AM-Noon, 1-4:30PM (EST). *Probate.*

Probate Court - Westminster District PO Box 47, Bellows Falls, VT 05101-0047; 802-463-3019. Hours: 8AM-Noon,1-4:30PM (EST). *Probate.*

Windsor County

Superior Court Box 458, Woodstock, VT 05091; 802-457-2121; Fax: 802-457-3446. Hours: 8AM-4:30PM (EST). *Civil, Eviction, Small Claims.*

Civil Records: Access: Phone, mail, in person. Only the court performs in person searches; visitors may not. No search fee. Required to search: name, years to search. Civil cases indexed by defendant, plaintiff. Civil records on computer since 1990.
General Information: No adoption, juvenile, sealed or expunged records released. SASE required. Turnaround time 1-2 weeks. Copy fee: $.25 per page. $1.00 minimum. Certification fee: $5.00. Fee payee: Windsor County Clerk or Windsor Superior Court. Personal checks accepted. Prepayment is required.

District Court Windsor Circuit Unit 1, 82 Railroad Row, White River Junction, VT 05001-1962; 802-295-8865. Hours: 8AM-4:30PM (EST). *Felony, Misdemeanor.*

Criminal Records: Access: Phone, mail, in person. Only the court performs in person searches; visitors may not. No search fee. Required to search: name, years to search; also helpful: DOB, SSN. Criminal records on computer from 1989, index from 1968.
General Information: No adoption, juvenile, sealed or expunged records released. SASE requested. Turnaround time 7 days. Copy fee: $.25 per page. $1.00 minimum. Certification fee: $5.00. Fee payee: Vermont District Court. Personal checks accepted. Prepayment is required.

Probate Court - Hartford District PO Box 275, Woodstock, VT 05091; 802-457-1503; Fax: 802-457-3446. Hours: 8AM-Noon, 1-4:30PM (EST). *Probate.*

Probate Court - Windsor District PO Box 402, Rt. 106, Cota Fuel Bldg, North Springfield, VT 05150; 802-886-2284; Fax: 802-886-2285. Hours: 8AM-Noon, 1-4:30PM (EST). *Probate..*

Vermont Recording Offices

ORGANIZATION

14 counties and 246 towns/cities, 246 recording offices. The recording officer is Town/City Clerk. There is no county administration in Vermont. Many towns are so small that their mailing addresses are in different towns. Four towns/cities have the same name as counties - Barre, Newport, Rutland, and St. Albans. The entire state is in the Eastern Time Zone (EST).

REAL ESTATE RECORDS

Most towns/cities will not perform real estate searches. Copy fees and certification fees vary. Certified copies are generally very expensive at $6.00 per page total. Deed copies usually cost $2.00 flat.

UCC RECORDS

This was a dual filing state until 12/31/94. From 01/01/95, only consumer goods and real estate related collateral were filed with Town/City Clerks. Starting 07/01/2001, only real estate collateral is filed at the local level. Most recording offices will perform UCC searches. Use search request form UCC-11. Search fees are usually $10.00 per name, and copy fees vary.

TAX LIEN RECORDS

All federal and state tax liens on personal property and on real property are filed with the Town/City Clerk in the lien/attachment book and indexed in real estate records. Most towns/cities will not perform tax lien searches.

OTHER LIENS

Mechanics, local tax, judgment, foreclosure.

Addison Town

Town Clerk, 7099 VT Rte 22A, Addison, VT 05491. 802-759-2020; Fax 802-759-2233.
Will search UCC records. Will not search real estate records. **Other Phone Numbers:** Assessor 802-388-4041.

Albany Town

Town Clerk, P.O. Box 284, Albany, VT 05820-0284. 802-755-6100.
Will search UCC records. Will not search real estate records.

Alburg Town

Town Clerk, P.O. Box 346, Alburg, VT 05440-0346. 802-796-3468; Fax 802-796-3939.
Will search UCC records. Will not search real estate records.

Andover Town

Town Clerk, 953 Weston-Andover Rd., Andover, VT 05143. 802-875-2765; Fax 802-875-6647.
Will search UCC records. Will not search real estate records.

Arlington Town

Town Clerk, P.O. Box 304, Arlington, VT 05250. 802-375-2332; Fax 802-375-6474.
Will search UCC records. Will not search real estate records. **Other Phone Numbers:** Assessor 802-375-9022; Treasurer 802-375-1260.

Athens Town

Town Clerk, 56 Brookline Rd., Athens, VT 05143. 802-869-3370; Fax 802-869-3370.
Will search UCC records. Tax liens not included in UCC search. Will not search real estate records. **Other Phone Numbers:** Assessor 802-869-2246.

Bakersfield Town

Town Clerk, Box 203, Bakersfield, VT 05441. 802-827-4495; Fax 802-527-3106.
Will search UCC records.

Baltimore Town

Town Clerk, 1902 Baltimore Rd., Baltimore, VT 05143. 802-263-5419; Fax 802-263-9423.
Will search UCC records. Will not search real estate records.

Barnard Town

Town Clerk, P.O. Box 274, Barnard, VT 05031-0274. 802-234-9211.
Will search UCC records. This agency will not do a tax lien search. Will not search real estate records.

Barnet Town

Town Clerk, Box 15, Barnet, VT 05821-0015. 802-633-2256; Fax 802-633-4315.
Will search UCC records.

Barre City

Town Clerk, Box 418, Barre, VT 05641. Town Clerk, R/E and UCC Recording 802-476-0242; Fax 802-476-0264.
Will search UCC records. Will not search real estate records. **Other Phone Numbers:** Assessor 802-476-0244; Treasurer 802-476-0242; Appraiser/Auditor 802-476-0244; Elections 802-476-0242; Vital Records 802-476-0242.

Barre Town

Town Clerk, P.O. Box 124, Websterville, VT 05678-0124. Town Clerk, R/E and UCC Recording 802-479-9391; Fax 802-479-9332.
Will search UCC records. Will not search real estate records. **Other Phone Numbers:** Assessor 802-479-2595; Treasurer 802-479-9391; Appraiser/Auditor 802-479-2595; Elections 802-479-9391; Vital Records 802-479-9391; Town Manager 802-479-9331 802-479-9391.

Barton Town

Town Clerk, P.O. Box 657, Barton, VT 05822-1386. 802-525-6222; Fax 802-525-8856.
Will search UCC records. **Other Phone Numbers:** Assessor 802-525-6222.

Belvidere Town

Town Clerk, 3996 Vermont Rt 109, Belvidere Center, VT 05492. 802-644-2498.
Will not search UCC records. This agency will not do a tax lien search. Will not search real estate records.

Bennington Town

Town Clerk, 205 South Street, Bennington, VT 05201. 802-442-1043; Fax 802-442-1068.
Will search UCC records. Will not search real estate records. **Other Phone Numbers:** Assessor 802-442-1043.

Benson Town

Town Clerk, P.O. Box 163, Benson, VT 05731-0163. 802-537-2611; Fax 802-537-2611.
Will search UCC records. Will not search real estate records.

Berkshire Town

Town Clerk, RFD 1, Box 2560, Enosburg Falls, VT 05450. 802-933-2335; Fax 802-933-5913.
Will search UCC records. This agency will not do a tax lien search. Will not search real estate records.

Berlin Town

Town Clerk, 108 Shed Rd., Berlin, VT 05602. Town Clerk, R/E and UCC Recording 802-229-9298.
Will search UCC records. This agency will not do a tax lien search. Will not search real estate records. **Other Phone Numbers:** Assessor 802-229-4880; Treasurer 802-229-9298; Elections 802-229-9298; Vital Records 802-229-9298.

Bethel Town

Town Clerk, RD 2, Box 85, Bethel, VT 05032. 802-234-9722; Fax 802-234-6840.
Will search UCC records. Will not search real estate records.

Bloomfield Town

Town Clerk, P.O. Box 336, No. Stratford, NH, 03590. 802-962-5191; Fax 802-962-5191.
Will search UCC records. Will not search real estate records.

Bolton Town

Town Clerk, RD 1, Box 445, Waterbury, VT 05676. 802-434-3064; Fax 802-434-6404.
Will search UCC records. Will not search real estate records. **Other Phone Numbers:** Treasurer 802-434-5075.

Bradford Town

Town Clerk, P.O. Box 339, Bradford, VT 05033-0339. 802-222-4727; Fax 802-222-3520.
Will search UCC records. Will not search real estate records.

Braintree Town

Town Clerk, RD 1, Box 361A, Randolph, VT 05060. 802-728-9787; Fax 802-728-9787.

Will search UCC records. This agency will not do a tax lien search. Will not search real estate records. **Other Phone Numbers:** Assessor 802-728-9787.

Brandon Town

Town Clerk, 49 Center Street, Brandon, VT 05733. Town Clerk, R/E and UCC Recording 802-247-5721; Fax 802-247-5481. http://www.town.brandon.vt.us
Will search UCC records. Will not search real estate records. **Other Phone Numbers:** Assessor 802-247-0226; Treasurer 802-247-5721; Appraiser/Auditor 802-247-0226; Elections 802-247-5721; Vital Records 802-247-5721.

Brattleboro Town

Town Clerk, 230 Main Street, Brattleboro, VT 05301-2885. 802-254-4541; Fax 802-257-2312. http://www.brattleboro.org/
Will search UCC records. Will not search real estate records. **Other Phone Numbers:** Assessor 802-254-4541 x119.

Bridgewater Town

Town Clerk, P.O. Box 14, Bridgewater, VT 05034. Town Clerk, R/E and UCC Recording 802-672-3334; Fax 802-672-5395.
Will search UCC records. **Other Phone Numbers:** Assessor 802-672-3334; Treasurer 802-672-3334.

Bridport Town

Town Clerk, Box 27, Bridport, VT 05734-0027. Town Clerk, R/E and UCC Recording 802-758-2483.
Town clerk will perform searches as a private contractor. Will search UCC records. This agency will not do a tax lien search. Will not search real estate records. **Other Phone Numbers:** Assessor 802-758-2483; Treasurer 802-758-2483.

Brighton Town

Town Clerk, P.O. Box 377, Island Pond, VT 05846. 802-723-4405; Fax 802-723-4405.
Will search UCC records.

Bristol Town

Town Clerk, Box 249, Bristol, VT 05443. 802-843-3180; Fax 802-843-3127.
Will search UCC records. Will not search real estate records.

Brookfield Town

Town Clerk, P.O. Box 463, Brookfield, VT 05036-0463. 802-276-3352; Fax 802-276-3926.
Will search UCC records. This agency will not do a tax lien search. Will not search real estate records. **Other Phone Numbers:** Treasurer 802-728-2118.

Brookline Town

Town Clerk, PO Box 403, Brookline, VT 05345. 802-365-4648.
Will search UCC records. This agency will not do a tax lien search. Will not search real estate records. **Other Phone Numbers:** Assessor 802-365-4232.

Brownington Town

Town Clerk, 509 Dutton Brook Ln, Orleans, VT 05860. 802-754-8401; Fax 802-754-8401.
Will search UCC records. UCC search includes tax liens if requested. RE owner, mortgage, and property transfer searches available. **Other Phone Numbers:** Treasurer 802-754-6559.

Brunswick Town

Town Clerk, 4495 Vermont Rte. 102, RFD 1, Box 470, Brunswick, VT 05905. Town Clerk, R/E and UCC Recording 802-962-5283.

Will search UCC records. UCC search includes tax liens. RE owner, mortgage, and property transfer searches available. **Other Phone Numbers:** Assessor 802-962-3450; Treasurer 802-962-5283; Elections 802-962-5283; Vital Records 802-962-5283.

Burlington City

Town Clerk, City Hall, Room 20, 149 Church St., Burlington, VT 05401. 802-865-7135; Fax 802-865-7014.
Will search UCC records. Will not search real estate records.

Cabot Town

Town Clerk, P.O. Box 36, Cabot, VT 05647-0036. Town Clerk, R/E and UCC Recording 802-563-2279; Fax 802-563-2423.
Will search UCC records. Will not search real estate records. **Other Phone Numbers:** Assessor 802-563-2279; Treasurer 802-563-2279; Appraiser/Auditor 802-563-2279; Elections 802-563-2279; Vital Records 802-563-2279.

Calais Town

Town Clerk, 668 West County Rd., Calais, VT 05648. Town Clerk, R/E and UCC Recording 802-223-5952 UCC Recording: 802-223-5952

802-223-5952.
Will search UCC records. This agency will not do a tax lien search. Will not search real estate records. **Other Phone Numbers:** Assessor 802-223-5952; Treasurer 802-223-5952; Appraiser/Auditor 802-223-5952; Elections 802-223-5952; Vital Records 802-223-5952.

Cambridge Town

Town Clerk, P.O. Box 127, Jeffersonville, VT 05464. Town Clerk, R/E and UCC Recording 802-644-2251; Fax 802-644-8348.
Will search UCC records. **Other Phone Numbers:** Appraiser/Auditor 802-644-2200; Vital Records 802-644-2251.

Canaan Town

Town Clerk, P.O. Box 159, Canaan, VT 05903-0159. Town Clerk, R/E and UCC Recording 802-266-3370; Fax 802-266-7085.
Will search UCC records. UCC search includes tax liens if requested. RE owner, mortgage, and property transfer searches available. **Other Phone Numbers:** Assessor 802-266-3370; Treasurer 802-266-3370; Appraiser/Auditor 802-266-3370; Elections 802-266-3370.

Castleton Town

Town Clerk, P.O. Box 727, Castleton, VT 05735. Town Clerk, R/E and UCC Recording 802-468-2212; Fax 802-468-5482.
Will search UCC records. **Other Phone Numbers:** Treasurer 802-468-5319; Appraiser/Auditor 802-468-2751; Elections 802-468-2212; Vital Records 802-468-2212.

Cavendish Town

Town Clerk, P.O. Box 126, Cavendish, VT 05142-0126. Town Clerk, R/E and UCC Recording 802-226-7292; Fax 802-226-7790.
Will search UCC records. Will not search real estate records. **Other Phone Numbers:** Assessor 802-226-7292; Treasurer 802-226-7292; Appraiser/Auditor 802-226-7292; Elections 802-226-7292; Vital Records 802-226-7292.

Charleston Town

Town Clerk, 5063 Vermont Rt 105, West Charleston, VT 05872-7902. 802-895-2814; Fax 802-895-2814.

Will not search UCC records. Will not search real estate records.

Charlotte Town

Town Clerk, P.O. Box 119, Charlotte, VT 05445-0119. Town Clerk, R/E and UCC Recording 802-425-3071; Fax 802-425-4241.
Will search UCC records. **Other Phone Numbers:** Assessor 802-425-3855; Treasurer 802-425-3071; Appraiser/Auditor 802-425-3855; Elections 802-425-3071; Vital Records 802-425-3071; Planning & Zoning 802-425-3533.

Chelsea Town

Town Clerk, P.O. Box 266, Chelsea, VT 05038. 802-685-4460.
Will search UCC records. UCC search includes tax liens if requested. RE owner, mortgage, and property transfer searches available.

Chester Town

Town Clerk, P.O. Box 370, Chester, VT 05143. 802-875-2173; Fax 802-875-2237.
Will search UCC records.

Chittenden Town

Town Clerk, Holden Road, Town Hall, Chittenden, VT 05737. 802-483-6647.
Chittenden is in Rutland County, not Chittenden County. Uninformed secured parties continue to attempt filings at the county level even though there is no county filing in Vermont. Will search UCC records. This agency will not do a tax lien search. Will not search real estate records. **Other Phone Numbers:** Treasurer 802-483-647.

Clarendon Town

Town Clerk, P.O. Box 30, North Clarendon, VT 05759-0030. Town Clerk, R/E and UCC Recording 802-775-4274; Fax 802-775-4274.
Will search UCC records. Will not search real estate records. **Other Phone Numbers:** Assessor 802-775-1536; Treasurer 802-775-1536; Appraiser/Auditor 802-775-1536; Elections 802-775-4274; Vital Records 802-775-4274.

Colchester Town

Town Clerk, P.O. Box 55, Colchester, VT 05446. 802-655-0812 UCC Recording: 802-654-0700; Fax 802-654-0757. http://www.colchestervt.org
Will search UCC records. Will not search real estate records. **Other Phone Numbers:** Assessor 802-655-0863; Treasurer 802-655-0812; Elections 203-654-0700; Vital Records 203-654-0700.

Concord Town

Town Clerk, P.O. Box 317, Concord, VT 05824-0317. Town Clerk, R/E and UCC Recording 802-695-2220; Fax 802-695-2220.
Will search UCC records. Will not search real estate records. **Other Phone Numbers:** Assessor 802-695-2220; Treasurer 802-695-2220; Appraiser/Auditor 802-695-2220; Elections 802-695-2220; Vital Records 802-695-2220.

Corinth Town

Town Clerk, P.O. Box 461, Corinth, VT 05039. Town Clerk, R/E and UCC Recording 802-439-5850; Fax 802-439-5850.
Will not search UCC records. Will not search real estate records. **Other Phone Numbers:** Assessor 802-439-5098; Treasurer 802-439-5850; Elections 802-439-5850; Vital Records 802-439-5850.

Cornwall Town

Town Clerk, 2629 Route 30, Cornwall, VT 05753-9299. 802-462-2775; Fax 802-462-2606.
Will search UCC records. **Other Phone Numbers:** Assessor 802-462-2855.

Coventry Town

Town Clerk, P.O. Box 104, Coventry, VT 05825. 802-754-2288; Fax 802-754-2288.
Will search UCC records. Will not search real estate records.

Craftsbury Town

Town Clerk, Box 55, Craftsbury, VT 05826. 802-586-2823; Fax 802-586-2823.
Will search UCC records. **Other Phone Numbers:** Assessor 802-586-2835.

Danby Town

Town Clerk, Box 231, Danby, VT 05739-0231. Town Clerk, R/E and UCC Recording 802-293-5136; Fax 802-293-5311.
Will search UCC records. **Other Phone Numbers:** Assessor 802-293-5136; Treasurer 802-293-5136; Appraiser/Auditor 802-293-5136; Elections 802-293-5136; Vital Records 802-293-5136.

Danville Town

Town Clerk, P.O. Box 183, Danville, VT 05828. 802-684-3352; Fax 802-684-9606.
Will search UCC records. Will not search real estate records.

Derby Town

Town Clerk, P.O. Box 25, Derby, VT 05829. 802-766-4906; Fax 802-766-2027.
Will search UCC records. Will search real estate records. **Other Phone Numbers:** Assessor 802-766-4906; Treasurer 802-766-4906; Appraiser/Auditor 802-766-2012; Elections 802-766-4906; Vital Records 802-766-4906.

Dorset Town

Town Clerk, Mad Tom Road, Town Hall, East Dorset, VT 05253. 802-362-1178; Fax 802-362-5156.
Will search UCC records. Will not search real estate records. **Other Phone Numbers:** Assessor 802-362-0162.

Dover Town

Town Clerk, P.O. Box 527, Dover, VT 05356-0527. Town Clerk, R/E and UCC Recording 802-464-5100; Fax 802-464-8721. www.dovervt.com
Will search UCC records. Will not search real estate records. **Other Phone Numbers:** Assessor 802-464-8720; Treasurer 802-464-5100; Appraiser/Auditor 802-464-8720; Elections 802-464-5100; Vital Records 802-464-5100.

Dummerston Town

Town Clerk, 1523 Middle Rd., Dummerston, VT 05346. 802-257-1496; Fax 802-257-4671.
Will search UCC records. Will not search real estate records.

Duxbury Town

Town Clerk, RD 2, Box 1260, Waterbury, VT 05676. 802-244-6660.
Will search UCC records. This agency will not do a tax lien search. Will not search real estate records.

East Haven Town

Town Clerk, P.O. Box 10, East Haven, VT 05837-0010. Town Clerk, R/E and UCC Recording 802-467-3772.
Will search UCC records. This agency will not do a tax lien search. Will not search real estate records. **Other Phone Numbers:** Assessor 802-467-3772; Treasurer 802-467-3772; Appraiser/Auditor 802-467-3772; Elections 802-467-3772; Vital Records 802-467-3772.

East Montpelier Town

Town Clerk, P.O. Box 157, East Montpelier, VT 05651-0157. Town Clerk, R/E and UCC Recording 802-223-3313; Fax 802-223-3314.
Will search UCC records. This agency will not do a tax lien search. Will not search real estate records. **Other Phone Numbers:** Assessor 802-223-3313; Treasurer 802-223-3313; Appraiser/Auditor 802-223-3313; Elections 802-223-3313.

Eden Town

Town Clerk, 71 Old Schoolhouse Rd., Eden Mills, VT 05653. 802-635-2528; Fax 802-635-1724.
Will search UCC records. Will not search real estate records. **Other Phone Numbers:** Assessor 802-635-2528; Vital Records 802-635-2528.

Elmore Town

Town Clerk, P.O. Box 123, Lake Elmore, VT 05657. 802-888-2637.
Will search UCC records. This agency will not do a tax lien search. Will not search real estate records.

Enosburg Town

Town Clerk, P.O. Box 465, Enosburg Falls, VT 05450. Town Clerk, R/E and UCC Recording 802-933-4421; Fax 802-933-4832.
Will search UCC records. Will not search real estate records. **Other Phone Numbers:** Assessor 802-933-4421; Treasurer 802-933-4421; Appraiser/Auditor 802-933-4421; Elections 802-933-4421; Vital Records 802-933-4421.

Essex Town

Town Clerk, 81 Main Street, Essex Junction, VT 05452. Town Clerk, R/E and UCC Recording 802-879-0413; Fax 802-878-1353. www.essex.org
Will search UCC records. Will not search real estate records. **Other Phone Numbers:** Assessor 802-878-1345; Treasurer 802-879-0413; Appraiser/Auditor 802-878-1345; Elections 802-879-0413; Vital Records 802-879-0413.

Fair Haven Town

Town Clerk, 3 North Park Place, Fair Haven, VT 05743. 802-265-3610; Fax 802-265-2158.
Will search UCC records. Will not search real estate records. **Other Phone Numbers:** Treasurer 802-265-3010.

Fairfax Town

Town Clerk, P.O. Box 27, Fairfax, VT 05454. Town Clerk, R/E and UCC Recording 802-849-6111.
Will search UCC records. This agency will not do a tax lien search. Will not search real estate records. **Other Phone Numbers:** Assessor 802-849-6111; Treasurer 802-849-6111; Vital Records 802-849-6111.

Fairfield Town

Town Clerk, P.O. Box 5, Fairfield, VT 05455. 802-827-3261.
Will search UCC records. This agency will not do a tax lien search. Will not search real estate records.

Fairlee Town

Town Clerk, P.O. Box 95, Fairlee, VT 05045-0095. Town Clerk, R/E and UCC Recording 802-333-4363; Fax 802-333-9214.
Will search UCC records. Will not search real estate records. **Other Phone Numbers:** Assessor 802-333-4363; Treasurer 802-333-4363.

Fayston Town

Town Clerk, 866 N. Fayston Rd., No. Fayston, VT 05660. 802-496-2454.
Will search UCC records. This agency will not do a tax lien search. Will not search real estate records. **Other Phone Numbers:** Assessor 802-496-9849.

Ferrisburgh Town

Town Clerk, P.O. Box 6, Ferrisburgh, VT 05456-0006. 802-877-3429; Fax 802-877-6757.
Will search UCC records. Will not search real estate records.

Fletcher Town

Town Clerk, 2141 Cambridge Rd, Cambridge, VT 05444. 802-849-6616; Fax 802-849-2500.
Will search UCC records. Will not search real estate records.

Franklin Town

Town Clerk, P.O. Box 82, Franklin, VT 05457-0082. Town Clerk, R/E and UCC Recording 802-285-2101.
Will search UCC records. This agency will not do a tax lien search. Will not search real estate records. **Other Phone Numbers:** Assessor 802-285-2101; Treasurer 802-285-2101; Appraiser/Auditor 802-285-2101; Elections 802-285-2101; Vital Records 802-285-2101.

Georgia Town

Town Clerk, 47 Town Common Road North, St. Albans, VT 05478. Town Clerk, R/E and UCC Recording 802-524-3524; Fax 802-524-3543.
Will search UCC records. **Other Phone Numbers:** Assessor 802-524-3543; Treasurer 802-524-3524; Appraiser/Auditor 802-524-3543; Elections 802-524-3524; Vital Records 802-524-3524; Town Administrator 802-524-9794.

Glover Town

Town Clerk, 51 Bean Hill, Glover, VT 05839. 802-525-6227 R/E Recording: 802-525-6226 UCC Recording: 802-525-6226; Fax 802-525-6227.
Will search UCC records. Will not search real estate records. **Other Phone Numbers:** Assessor 802-525-6226; Treasurer 802-525-6226; Appraiser/Auditor 802-525-6226; Elections 802-525-6226; Vital Records 802-525-6226.

Goshen Town

Town Clerk, 50 Carlisle Hill Rd., Goshen, VT 05733. 802-247-6455.
Will search UCC records. This agency will not do a tax lien search. Will not search real estate records.

Grafton Town

Town Clerk, P.O. Box 180, Grafton, VT 05146. 802-843-2419.
Will search UCC records. This agency will not do a tax lien search. Will not search real estate records.

Granby Town

Town Clerk, P.O. Box 56, Granby, VT 05840. 802-328-3611; Fax 802-328-3611.
Will search UCC records. **Other Phone Numbers:** Assessor 802-328-2683.

Grand Isle Town Clerk

Town Clerk, PO Box 49, Grand Isle, VT 05458. 802-372-8830; Fax 802-372-8815.
Will search UCC records. Will not search real estate records.

Granville Town

Town Clerk, P.O. Box 66, Granville, VT 05747-0066. 802-767-4403; Fax 802-767-3968.
Will search UCC records. This agency will not do a tax lien search. Will not search real estate records. **Other Phone Numbers:** Assessor 802-767-4403.

Greensboro Town

Town Clerk, Box 119, Greensboro, VT 05841. 802-533-2911.
Will search UCC records. This agency will not do a tax lien search. Will not search real estate records.

Groton Town

Town Clerk, 314 Scott Highway, Groton, VT 05046. Town Clerk, R/E and UCC Recording 802-584-3276; Fax 802-584-3276.
Will search UCC records. Will not search real estate records. **Other Phone Numbers:** Assessor 802-584-3276; Treasurer 802-584-3276; Appraiser/Auditor 802-584-3131; Elections 802-584-3276; Vital Records 802-584-3276.

Guildhall Town

Town Clerk, P.O. Box 10, Guildhall, VT 05905. 802-676-3797; Fax 802-676-3518.
Will search UCC records. Will not search real estate records.

Guilford Town

Town Clerk, 236 School Rd., Guilford, VT 05301-8319. 802-254-6857; Fax 802-257-5764.
Will search UCC records. Will not search real estate records.

Halifax Town

Town Clerk, P.O. Box 45, West Halifax, VT 05358. 802-368-7390; Fax 802-368-7390.
Will search UCC records. This agency will not do a tax lien search. Will not search real estate records. **Other Phone Numbers:** Treasurer 802-368-7698.

Hancock Town

Town Clerk, P.O. Box 100, Hancock, VT 05748. 802-767-3660; Fax 802-767-3660.
Will search UCC records. This agency will not do a tax lien search. Will not search real estate records. **Other Phone Numbers:** Assessor 802-767-3301; Treasurer 802-767-3660; Appraiser/Auditor 802-767-3660; Elections 802-767-3660; Vital Records 802-767-3660.

Hardwick Town

Town Clerk, Box 523, Hardwick, VT 05843. Town Clerk, R/E and UCC Recording 802-472-5971; Fax 802-472-6865.
Will search UCC records. Will not search real estate records. **Other Phone Numbers:** Assessor 802-472-5971; Treasurer 802-472-5971; Appraiser/Auditor 802-472-5971; Elections 802-472-5971.

Hartford Town

Town Clerk, 171 Bridge Street, White River Junction, VT 05001-1920. Town Clerk, R/E and UCC Recording 802-295-2785; http://www.hartford-vt.org
Will search UCC records. This agency will not do a tax lien search. Will not search real estate records. **Other Phone Numbers:** Assessor 802-295-9353; Treasurer 802-295-9353; Appraiser/Auditor 802-295-3077; Elections 802-295-2785; Vital Records 802-295-2785.

Hartland Town

Town Clerk, P.O. Box 349, Hartland, VT 05048-0349. Town Clerk, R/E and UCC Recording 802-436-2444; Fax 802-436-2444.
Will search UCC records. **Other Phone Numbers:** Assessor 802-436-2464; Treasurer 802-436-2464; Elections 802-436-2444; Vital Records 802-436-2444.

Highgate Town

Town Clerk, P.O. Box 67, Highgate Center, VT 05459. 802-868-4697.
Will search UCC records. This agency will not do a tax lien search. Will not search real estate records.

Hinesburg Town

Town Clerk, P.O. Box 133, Hinesburg, VT 05461. 802-482-2281; Fax 802-482-5404.
Will search UCC records. Will not search real estate records. **Other Phone Numbers:** Assessor 802-482-3619.

Holland Town

Town Clerk, 120 School Rd., Holland/Derby Line, VT 05830. 802-895-4440; Fax 802-895-4440.
Will search UCC records. Will not search real estate records.

Hubbardton Town

Town Clerk, RR 1, Box 2828, Fair Haven, VT 05743-9502. 802-273-2951.
Will search UCC records. UCC search includes tax liens if requested. RE owner, mortgage, and property transfer searches available.

Huntington Town

Town Clerk, 4930 Main Rd., Huntington, VT 05462. Town Clerk, R/E and UCC Recording 802-434-2032; Fax 802-434-4779.
Will search UCC records. This agency will not do a tax lien search. Will not search real estate records. **Other Phone Numbers:** Assessor 802-434-5783; Treasurer 802-434-2032; Appraiser/Auditor 802-434-5783; Elections 802-434-2032; Vital Records 802-434-2032; Administrator 802-434-4779.

Hyde Park Town

Town Clerk, P.O. Box 98, Hyde Park, VT 05655-0098. Town Clerk, R/E and UCC Recording 802-888-2300; Fax 802-888-6878.
Will search UCC records. **Other Phone Numbers:** Assessor 802-888-2300; Treasurer 802-888-2300; Appraiser/Auditor 802-888-2300; Elections 802-888-2300; Vital Records 802-888-2300.

Ira Town

Town Clerk, 808 Route 133, West Rutland, VT 05777. 802-235-2745 R/E Recording: 802-235-2247 UCC Recording: 802-235-2247.
Will search UCC records. This agency will not do a tax lien search. Will not search real estate records. **Other Phone Numbers:** Assessor 802-235-2247; Treasurer 802-235-2747; Appraiser/Auditor 802-235-2747; Elections 802-235-2747; Vital Records 802-235-2747.

Irasburg Town

Town Clerk, Box 51, Irasburg, VT 05845. 802-754-2242.
Will search UCC records. This agency will not do a tax lien search. Will not search real estate records.

Isle La Motte Town

Town Clerk, P.O. Box 250, Isle La Motte, VT 05463. 802-928-3434; Fax 802-928-3002.
Will search UCC records. Will not search real estate records.

Jamaica Town

Town Clerk, P.O. Box 173, Jamaica, VT 05343. 802-874-4681.
Will search UCC records. This agency will not do a tax lien search. Will not search real estate records. **Other Phone Numbers:** Assessor 802-874-4908.

Jay Town

Town Clerk, 1036 Vermont Rte. 242, Jay, VT 05859-9820. 802-988-2996.
Will search UCC records. This agency will not do a tax lien search. Will not search real estate records.

Jericho Town

Town Clerk, P.O. Box 67, Jericho, VT 05465. 802-899-4936; Fax 802-899-5549.
Will search UCC records. Will not search real estate records. **Other Phone Numbers:** Assessor 802-899-2640.

Johnson Town

Town Clerk, P.O. Box 383, Johnson, VT 05656. 802-635-2611; Fax 802-635-9523.
Will search UCC records. Will not search real estate records.

Killington Town

Town Clerk, P.O. Box 429, Killington, VT 05751-0429. 802-422-3243; Fax 802-422-3030. http://www.killingtontown.com/staff.htm
Formerly known as the Town of Sherburne. Will search UCC records. Will not search real estate records. **Other Phone Numbers:** Treasurer 802-422-3241.

Kirby Town

Town Clerk, Town of Kirby, 346 Town Hall Rd., Lyndonville, VT 05851-9802. Town Clerk, R/E and UCC Recording 802-626-9386; Fax 802-626-9386.
Will search UCC records. **Other Phone Numbers:** Assessor 802-626-9386; Treasurer 802-626-9386; Appraiser/Auditor 802-626-9386; Elections 802-626-9386; Vital Records 802-626-9386.

Landgrove Town

Town Clerk, Box 508, Londonderry, VT 05148. 802-824-3716; Fax 802-824-3716.
Will search UCC records. Will not search real estate records. **Other Phone Numbers:** Assessor 802-824-3716.

Leicester Town

Town Clerk, 44 Schoolhouse Rd., Leicester, VT 05733. 802-247-5961.
Will search UCC records. This agency will not do a tax lien search. Will not search real estate records.

Lemington Town

Town Clerk, 2549 RIver Rd., VT 102, Lemington, VT 05903. 802-277-4814.
Will search UCC records. UCC search includes tax liens if requested. RE owner, mortgage, and property transfer searches available.

Lincoln Town

Town Clerk, 62 Quaker St., Lincoln, VT 05443. 802-453-2980; Fax 802-453-2975.
Will search UCC records.

Londonderry Town

Town Clerk, P.O. Box 118, South Londonderry, VT 05155-0118. 802-824-3356.
Will search UCC records. UCC search includes tax liens if requested. RE owner, mortgage, and property transfer searches available.

Lowell Town

Town Clerk, 2170 VT Rt. 100, Lowell, VT 05847-0007. 802-744-6559; Fax 802-744-2357.
Will not search UCC records. Will not search real estate records.

Ludlow Town

Town Clerk, P.O. Box 307, Ludlow, VT 05149. 802-228-3232; Fax 802-228-2813.
Will search UCC records. Will not search real estate records. **Other Phone Numbers:** Assessor 802-228-7206.

Lunenburg Town

Town Clerk, P.O. Box 54, Lunenburg, VT 05906. 802-892-5959.
Will search UCC records. This agency will not do a tax lien search. Will not search real estate records.

Lyndon Town

Town Clerk, P.O. Box 167, Lyndonville, VT 05851. 802-626-5785; Fax 802-626-1265.
Will search UCC records. Will not search real estate records. **Other Phone Numbers:** Assessor 802-626-5785.

Maidstone Town

Town Clerk, P.O. Box 118, Maidstone, VT 05905-0118. Town Clerk, R/E and UCC Recording 802-676-3210; Fax 802-676-3210.
Will search UCC records. **Other Phone Numbers:** Elections 802-676-3210; Vital Records 802-676-3210.

Manchester Town

Town Clerk, P.O. Box 830, Manchester Center, VT 05255. 802-362-1315; Fax 802-362-1315.
Will search UCC records. Will not search real estate records. **Other Phone Numbers:** Assessor 802-362-1373; Treasurer 802-362-1197; Town Manager 802-362-1313; Planning/Zoning 802-362-4824;

Marlboro Town

Town Clerk, P.O. Box E, Marlboro, VT 05344-0305. 802-254-2181; Fax 802-257-2447.
Will search UCC records. This agency will not do a tax lien search. Will do minor checking on specifically-named records, but at the discretion of the Town Clerk.

Marshfield Town

Town Clerk, 122 School St., Room 1, Marshfield, VT 05658. 802-426-3305; Fax 802-426-3045.
Will search UCC records. **Other Phone Numbers:** Assessor 802-426-3798.

Mendon Town

Town Clerk, 34 US Route 4, Mendon, VT 05701. Town Clerk, R/E and UCC Recording 802-775-1662; Fax 802-773-9682.
Will search UCC records. Will not search real estate records. **Other Phone Numbers:** Assessor 802-496-9689; Treasurer 802-775-1662; Elections 802-775-1662; Vital Records 802-775-1662.

Middlebury Town

Town Clerk, Municipal Building, 94 Main St., Middlebury, VT 05753-1334. 802-388-4041.

Will search UCC records. This agency will not do a tax lien search. Will not search real estate records.

Middlesex Town

Town Clerk, 5 Church St., Middlesex, VT 05602. Town Clerk, R/E and UCC Recording 802-223-5915 UCC Recording: 802-223-5915

802-223-5915; Fax 802-223-0569.
Will search UCC records. Will not search real estate records. **Other Phone Numbers:** Assessor 802-223-5915

802-223-5915; Treasurer 802-223-5915; Appraiser/Auditor 802-223-5915; Elections 802-223-5915; Vital Records 802-223-5915
802-223-5915.

Middletown Springs Town

Town Clerk, P.O. Box 1232, Middletown Springs, VT 05757-1197. 802-235-2220; Fax 802-235-2066.
Will search UCC records. This agency will not do a tax lien search. Will not search real estate records.

Milton Town

Town Clerk, P.O. Box 18, Milton, VT 05468. 802-893-4111; Fax 802-893-1005.
Will search UCC records. Will not search real estate records. **Other Phone Numbers:** Assessor 802-893-4325.

Monkton Town

Town Clerk, RR 1, Box 2015, North Ferrisburg, VT 05473-9509. 802-453-3800.
Will search UCC records. This agency will not do a tax lien search. Will not search real estate records.

Montgomery Town

Town Clerk, P.O. Box 356, Montgomery Center, VT 05471-0356. Town Clerk, R/E and UCC Recording 802-326-4719; Fax 802-326-4939.
Will search UCC records. **Other Phone Numbers:** Assessor 802-326-4719; Treasurer 802-326-4719; Appraiser/Auditor 802-326-4719; Elections 802-326-4719; Vital Records 802-326-4719.

Montpelier City

Town Clerk, 39 Main Street, City Hall, Montpelier, VT 05602. 802-223-9500; Fax 802-223-9518.
Will search UCC records. **Other Phone Numbers:** Assessor 802-223-9504.

Moretown Town

Town Clerk, P.O. Box 666, Moretown, VT 05660. 802-496-3645.
Will search UCC records. This agency will not do a tax lien search. Will not search real estate records.

Morgan Town

Town Clerk, P.O. Box 45, Morgan, VT 05853-0045. 802-895-2927; Fax 802-895-4204.
Will search UCC records. This agency will not do a tax lien search. Will do simple REsearches.

Morristown Town

Town Clerk, P.O. Box 748, Morrisville, VT 05661-0748. 802-888-6370; Fax 802-888-6375.
Will search UCC records. Will not search real estate records.

Mount Holly Town

Town Clerk, P.O. Box 248, Mount Holly, VT 05758. Town Clerk, R/E and UCC Recording 802-259-2391; Fax 802-259-2391.
Will search UCC records. Will not search real estate records. **Other Phone Numbers:** Assessor 802-259-

---

2391; Treasurer 802-259-2391; Appraiser/Auditor 802-259-2391; Elections 802-259-2391; Vital Records 802-259-2391.

New Haven Town

Town Clerk, 78 North St., New Haven, VT 05472. 802-453-3516.
Will search UCC records. Tax liens not included in UCC search. RE record owner searches available.

Newark Town

Town Clerk, RFD 1, Box 50C, West Burke, VT 05871. 802-467-3336.
Will search UCC records. This agency will not do a tax lien search. Will not search real estate records.

Newbury Town

Town Clerk, P.O. Box 126, Newbury, VT 05051. 802-866-5521.
Will search UCC records. UCC search includes tax liens if requested. RE owner, mortgage, and property transfer searches available.

Newfane Town

Town Clerk, P.O. Box 36, Newfane, VT 05345-0036. 802-365-7772; Fax 802-365-7692.
Will search UCC records. Will not search real estate records.

Newport City

Town Clerk, 222 Main Street, Newport, VT 05855. Town Clerk, R/E and UCC Recording 802-334-2112; Fax 802-334-2964.
Will search UCC records. Will not search real estate records. **Other Phone Numbers:** Assessor 802-334-6992; Treasurer 802-334-2112; Appraiser/Auditor 802-334-6992; Elections 802-334-2112; Vital Records 802-334-2112.

Newport Town

Town Clerk, P.O. Box 85, Newport Center, VT 05857. 802-334-6442; Fax 802-334-6442.
Will search UCC records. Will not search real estate records.

North Hero Town

Town Clerk, P.O. Box 38, North Hero, VT 05474-0038. Town Clerk, R/E and UCC Recording 802-372-6926; Fax 802-372-3806.
Will search UCC records. **Other Phone Numbers:** Assessor 802-372-6926; Treasurer 802-372-6926; Appraiser/Auditor 802-372-6926; Elections 802-372-6926; Vital Records 802-372-6926.

Northfield Town

Town Clerk, 51 South Main Street, Northfield, VT 05663. 802-485-5421; Fax 802-485-8426.
Will search UCC records. **Other Phone Numbers:** Assessor 802-485-6004; Treasurer 802-485-5421; Elections 802-485-5421; Vital Records 802-485-5421.

Norton Town

Town Clerk, P.O. Box 148, Norton, VT 05907. Town Clerk, R/E and UCC Recording 802-822-9935.
Will search UCC records. This agency will not do a tax lien search. Will not search real estate records. **Other Phone Numbers:** Treasurer 802-822-9935; Elections 802-822-9935; Vital Records 802-822-9935.

Norwich Town

Town Clerk, P.O. Box 376, Norwich, VT 05055. 802-649-1419; Fax 802-649-0123.
Will search UCC records. Will not search real estate records. **Other Phone Numbers:** Assessor 802-649-1116.

Orange Town

Town Clerk, P.O. Box 233, East Barre, VT 05649. 802-479-2673; Fax 802-479-2673.
Will search UCC records. Will not search real estate records.

Orwell Town

Town Clerk, P.O. Box 32, Orwell, VT 05760-0032. 802-948-2032.
Will search UCC records. UCC search includes tax liens if requested. Will not search real estate records. **Other Phone Numbers:** Assessor 802-948-2032.

Panton Town

Town Clerk, P.O. Box 174, Vergennes, VT 05491-0174. 802-475-2333; Fax 802-475-2785.
Will search UCC records. This agency will not do a tax lien search. Will not search real estate records. **Other Phone Numbers:** Assessor 802-496-9689.

Pawlet Town

Town Clerk, P.O. Box 128, Pawlet, VT 05761-0128. 802-325-3309; Fax 802-325-6109.
Will search UCC records. Will not search real estate records. **Other Phone Numbers:** Assessor 802-325-3309.

Peacham Town

Town Clerk, Box 244, Peacham, VT 05862. 802-592-3218.
Will search UCC records. This agency will not do a tax lien search. Will not search real estate records.

Peru Town

Town Clerk, Box 127, Peru, VT 05152. 802-824-3065; Fax 802-824-3065.
Will search UCC records. Will not search real estate records.

Pittsfield Town

Town Clerk, P.O. Box 556, Pittsfield, VT 05762-0556. 802-746-8170.
Will search UCC records. UCC search includes tax liens if requested. RE owner, mortgage, and property transfer searches available. **Other Phone Numbers:** Assessor 802-746-8113; Treasurer 802-746-8050.

Pittsford Town

Town Clerk, P.O. Box 10, Pittsford, VT 5763. 802-483-2931 R/E Recording: 802-483-2931 x12 UCC Recording: 802-483-2931 x12; Fax 802-483-6612.
Will search UCC records. **Other Phone Numbers:** Assessor 802-483-2275; Treasurer 802-483-2931 x12; Appraiser/Auditor 802-483-2931 x12; Elections 802-483-2931 x12; Vital Records 802-483-2931 x12.

Plainfield Town

Town Clerk, P.O. Box 217, Plainfield, VT 5667. 802-454-8461; Fax 802-454-8461.
Will not search UCC records. Records are available for searching M/W/F 7:30AM-4PM. Will not search real estate records.

Plymouth Town

Town Clerk, 68 Town Office Rd., Plymouth, VT 05056. 802-672-3655; Fax 802-672-5466.
Will search UCC records. Will not search real estate records.

Pomfret Town

Town Clerk, P.O. Box 286, North Pomfret, VT 05053. 802-457-3861.
Will search UCC records. This agency will not do a tax lien search. Will not search real estate records.

Poultney Town

Town Clerk, 9 Main St., Suite 2, Poultney, VT 05764. 802-287-5761.
Husband and wife considered as one debtor for searching fee computation. Partnership name plus two partner names considered one name on filing for fee computation. See Filing Facts for further clarification. Will search UCC records. This agency will not do a tax lien search. Will not search real estate records. **Other Phone Numbers:** Assessor 802-287-5761.

Pownal Town

Town Clerk, P.O. Box 411, Pownal, VT 05261. Town Clerk, R/E and UCC Recording 802-823-7757; Fax 802-823-0116.
Will search UCC records. **Other Phone Numbers:** Assessor 802-823-5644.

Proctor Town

Town Clerk, 45 Main Street, Proctor, VT 05765. 802-459-3333; Fax 802-459-2356.
Will search UCC records. Will not search real estate records.

Putney Town

Town Clerk, P.O. Box 233, Putney, VT 05346. 802-387-5862.
Will search UCC records. This agency will not do a tax lien search. Will not search real estate records.

Randolph Town

Town Clerk, Drawer B, Randolph, VT 05060. 802-728-5682; Fax 802-728-5818.
Will search UCC records. Will not search real estate records.

Reading Town

Town Clerk, P.O. Box 72, Reading, VT 05062. Town Clerk, R/E and UCC Recording 802-484-7250; Fax 802-454-7250.
Will search UCC records. Will not search real estate records. **Other Phone Numbers:** Assessor 802-484-7250; Treasurer 802-484-7250; Appraiser/Auditor 802-484-7250; Elections 802-484-7250; Vital Records 802-484-7250.

Readsboro Town

Town Clerk, P.O. Box 246, Readsboro, VT 05350. 802-423-5405; Fax 802-423-5423.
Will search UCC records. Will not search real estate records.

Richford Town

Town Clerk, P.O. Box 236, Richford, VT 05476-0236. Town Clerk, R/E and UCC Recording 802-848-7751; Fax 802-848-7752. www.richfordvt.com
Will search UCC records. Will not search real estate records. **Other Phone Numbers:** Assessor 802-848-7751; Treasurer 802-848-7751; Appraiser/Auditor 802-848-7751; Elections 802-848-7751; Vital Records 802-848-7751.

Richmond Town

Town Clerk, P.O. Box 285, Richmond, VT 05477. 802-434-2221; Fax 802-434-5570.
Will search UCC records. Will not search real estate records.

Ripton Town

Town Clerk, Box 10, Ripton, VT 05766-0010. 802-388-2266.
Will search UCC records. This agency will not do a tax lien search. Will not search real estate records.

Rochester Town

Town Clerk, P.O. Box 238, Rochester, VT 05767-0238. 802-767-3631; Fax 802-767-6028.
Will search UCC records. Will not search real estate records. **Other Phone Numbers:** Assessor 802-767-9872; Treasurer 802-767-3631; Elections 802-767-3631; Vital Records 802-767-3631.

Rockingham Town

Town Clerk, P.O. Box 339, Bellows Falls, VT 05101-0339. Town Clerk, R/E and UCC Recording 802-463-4336; Fax 802-463-1228.
Will search UCC records. This agency will not do a tax lien search. Will not search real estate records. **Other Phone Numbers:** Assessor 802-463-1229; Treasurer 802-463-3964; Elections 802-463-4336; Vital Records 802-463-4336; Health & Zoning 802-463-3964.

Roxbury Town

Town Clerk, Box 53, Roxbury, VT 05669. Town Clerk, R/E and UCC Recording 802-485-7840; Fax 802-485-7860.
Will search UCC records. **Other Phone Numbers:** Assessor 802-485-7840; Treasurer 802-485-7860; Appraiser/Auditor 802-485-7840; Elections 802-485-7840; Vital Records 802-485-7860.

Royalton Town

Town Clerk, P.O. Box 680, South Royalton, VT 05068-0680. 802-763-7207; Fax 802-763-7967.
Will search UCC records. Will not search real estate records. **Other Phone Numbers:** Assessor 802-763-2202; Second phone 802-763-7967.

Rupert Town

Town Clerk, Box 140, West Rupert, VT 05776. Town Clerk, R/E and UCC Recording 802-394-7728; Fax 802-394-7728.
Will search UCC records. This agency will not do a tax lien search. Will not search real estate records. **Other Phone Numbers:** Assessor 802-394-7728; Treasurer 802-394-7728; Elections 802-394-7728; Vital Records 802-394-7728.

Rutland City

Town Clerk, P.O. Box 969, Rutland, VT 05702. 802-773-1801 R/E Recording: 802-773-1800 UCC Recording: 802-773-1800.
Will search UCC records. This agency will not do a tax lien search. Will not search real estate records. **Other Phone Numbers:** Assessor 802-773-1800; Treasurer 802-773-1800; Elections 802-773-1800.

Rutland Town

Town Clerk, P.O. Box 225, Center Rutland, VT 05736. Town Clerk, R/E and UCC Recording 802-773-2528; Fax 802-773-7295.
Will search UCC records. Will not search real estate records. **Other Phone Numbers:** Assessor 802-773-2528; Treasurer 802-773-2528.

Ryegate Town

Town Clerk, P.O. Box 332, Ryegate, VT 05042. Town Clerk, R/E and UCC Recording 802-584-3880; Fax 802-584-3880.
Will search UCC records. Will not search real estate records. **Other Phone Numbers:** Assessor 802-584-3880; Treasurer 802-584-3880; Appraiser/Auditor 802-584-3880; Elections 802-584-3880; Vital Records 802-584-3880.

Salisbury Town

Town Clerk, P.O. Box 66, Salisbury, VT 05769-0066. 802-352-4228; Fax 802-352-9832.
Will search UCC records.

Sandgate Town

Town Clerk, 3266 Sandgate Rd., Sandgate, VT 05250. 802-375-9075; Fax 802-375-8350.
Will search UCC records. This agency will not do a tax lien search. Will not search real estate records. **Other Phone Numbers:** Assessor 802-375-9075; Treasurer 802-375-9075; Appraiser/Auditor 802-375-9075; Elections 802-375-9075; Vital Records 802-375-9075.

Searsburg Town

Town Clerk, P.O. Box 157, Wilmington, VT 05363. Town Clerk, R/E and UCC Recording 802-464-8081.
Will search UCC records. Tax liens not included in UCC search. RE owner, mortgage, and property transfer searches available. **Other Phone Numbers:** Assessor 802-464-8081; Treasurer 802-464-8081; Elections 802-464-8081; Vital Records 802-464-8081.

Shaftsbury Town

Town Clerk, P.O. Box 409, Shaftsbury, VT 05262. 802-442-4038; Fax 802-442-0955.
Will search UCC records. Will not search real estate records. **Other Phone Numbers:** Assessor 802-442-5740; Treasurer 802-442-6242.

Sharon Town

Town Clerk, P.O. Box 250, Sharon, VT 05065. 802-763-8268.
Will search UCC records. This agency will not do a tax lien search. Will not search real estate records.

Sheffield Town

Town Clerk, Box 165, Sheffield, VT 05866-0165. 802-626-8862.
Will search UCC records. This agency will not do a tax lien search. Will not search real estate records. **Other Phone Numbers:** Assessor 802-626-9273.

Shelburne Town

Town Clerk, P.O. Box 88, Shelburne, VT 05482. Town Clerk, R/E and UCC Recording 802-985-5116; Fax 802-985-9550.
Will search UCC records. Will not search real estate records. **Other Phone Numbers:** Assessor 802-985-5115; Treasurer 802-985-5116; Elections 802-985-5116; Vital Records 802-985-5116; 802-985-5117.

Sheldon Town

Town Clerk, P.O. Box 66, Sheldon, VT 05483. 802-933-2524; Fax 802-933-4951.
Will search UCC records. This agency will not do a tax lien search. RE record owner searches available.

Shoreham Town

Town Clerk, 297 Main St., Shoreham, VT 05770-9759. 802-897-5841; Fax 802-897-2545.
Will search UCC records. **Other Phone Numbers:** Assessor 802-897-5542.

Shrewsbury Town

Town Clerk, 9823 Cold River Rd., Shrewsbury, VT 05738. 802-492-3511; Fax 802-492-3511.
Will search UCC records. Will not search real estate records. **Other Phone Numbers:** Treasurer 802-492-3558.

South Burlington City

Town Clerk, 575 Dorset Street, South Burlington, VT 05403. 802-658-7952; Fax 802-658-4748.
Will search UCC records. Will not search real estate records.

South Hero Town

Town Clerk, P.O. Box 175, South Hero, VT 05486. Town Clerk, R/E and UCC Recording 802-372-5552.
Will search UCC records. This agency will not do a tax lien search. Will not search real estate records. **Other Phone Numbers:** Assessor 802-372-5552; Treasurer 802-372-5552; Elections 802-372-5552; Vital Records 802-372-5552.

Springfield Town

Town Clerk, 96 Main Street, Springfield, VT 05156. Town Clerk, R/E and UCC Recording 802-885-2104; Fax 802-885-1617.
Will search UCC records. **Other Phone Numbers:** Assessor 802-885-2104; Treasurer 802-885-2104.

St. Albans City

Town Clerk, P.O. Box 867, St. Albans, VT 05478-0867. Town Clerk, R/E and UCC Recording 802-524-1501.
Will search UCC records. This agency will not do a tax lien search. Will not search real estate records. **Other Phone Numbers:** Assessor 802-524-1502; Treasurer 802-524-1501; Appraiser/Auditor 802-524-1502; Elections 802-524-1501; Water/Sewer 802-524-1504; Accounting 802-524-1506;

St. Albans Town

Town Clerk, P.O. Box 37, St. Albans Bay, VT 05481. 802-524-2415; Fax 802-524-9609.
Will search UCC records. Will not search real estate records. **Other Phone Numbers:** Assessor 802-524-7589.

St. George Town

Town Clerk, 1 Barber Rd., St. George, VT 05495. 802-482-5272; Fax 802-482-5548.
Will search UCC records. **Other Phone Numbers:** Assessor 802-496-9689.

St. Johnsbury Town

Town Clerk, 1187 Main St., Suite 2, St. Johnsbury, VT 05819-2288. 802-748-4331; Fax 802-748-1268.
Will search UCC records. Will not search real estate records. **Other Phone Numbers:** Assessor 802-748-4272.

Stamford Town

Town Clerk, 986 Main Rd., Stamford, VT 05352-9601. Town Clerk, R/E and UCC Recording 802-694-1361.
Will search UCC records. This agency will not do a tax lien search. Will not search real estate records. **Other Phone Numbers:** Assessor 802-694-1361; Treasurer 802-694-1361; Appraiser/Auditor 802-694-1361; Elections 802-694-1361; Vital Records 802-694-1361.

Stannard Town

Town Clerk, P.O. Box 94, Greensboro Bend, VT 05842-0094. 802-533-2577.
Will search UCC records. This agency will not do a tax lien search. Will not search real estate records.

Starksboro Town

Town Clerk, P.O. Box 91, Starksboro, VT 05487-0091. Town Clerk, R/E and UCC Recording 802-453-2639; Fax 802-453-7293.
Will search UCC records. Will not search real estate records. **Other Phone Numbers:** Assessor 802-453-6364; Treasurer 802-453-2639; Elections 802-453-2639; Vital Records 802-453-2639.

Stockbridge Town

Town Clerk, P.O. Box 39, Stockbridge, VT 05772-0039. 802-234-9371; Fax 802-234-9371.

Will search UCC records. Will not search real estate records. **Other Phone Numbers:** Assessor 802-234-9371.

Stowe Town

Town Clerk, P.O. Box 248, Stowe, VT 05672. Town Clerk, R/E and UCC Recording 802-253-6133; Fax 802-253-6143.
Will search UCC records. Will not search real estate records. **Other Phone Numbers:** Assessor 802-253-6144; Treasurer 802-253-6133; Appraiser/Auditor 802-253-6144; Elections 802-253-6133; Vital Records 802-253-6133.

Strafford Town

Town Clerk, P.O. Box 27, Strafford, VT 05072. 802-765-4411; Fax 802-765-9621.
Will search UCC records. UCC search includes tax liens if requested. Will not search real estate records.

Stratton Town

Town Clerk, P.O. Box 166, West Wardsboro, VT 05360. 802-896-6184; Fax 802-896-6630.
Will search UCC records.

Sudbury Town

Town Clerk, 4694 Route 30, Sudbury, VT 05733. Town Clerk, R/E and UCC Recording 802-623-7296.
Will search UCC records. This agency will not do a tax lien search. Will not search real estate records. **Other Phone Numbers:** Assessor 802-623-7296; Treasurer 802-623-7296; Appraiser/Auditor 802-623-7296; Elections 802-623-7296; Vital Records 802-623-7296.

Sunderland Town

Town Clerk, P.O. Box 295, East Arlington, VT 05252. 802-375-6106.
Will search UCC records. This agency will not do a tax lien search. Will not search real estate records. **Other Phone Numbers:** Assessor 802-362-2284.

Sutton Town

Town Clerk, Box 106, Sutton, VT 05867. 802-467-3377; Fax 802-467-1052.
Will search UCC records.

Swanton Town

Town Clerk, P.O. Box 711, Swanton, VT 05488. Town Clerk, R/E and UCC Recording 802-868-4421; Fax 802-868-4957.
Will search UCC records. Will not search real estate records. **Other Phone Numbers:** Assessor 802-868-4421; Treasurer 802-868-4421; Appraiser/Auditor 802-868-4421; Elections 802-868-4421; Vital Records 802-868-4421.

Thetford Town

Town Clerk, P.O. Box 126, Thetford Center, VT 05075-0126. 802-785-2922; Fax 802-785-2031.
Will search UCC records. Will not search real estate records.

Tinmouth Town

Town Clerk, 515 North End Rd., Tinmouth, VT 05773. Town Clerk, R/E and UCC Recording 802-446-2498; Fax 802-446-2498.
Will search UCC records. Will not search real estate records. **Other Phone Numbers:** Assessor 802-446-2498; Treasurer 802-446-2498; Appraiser/Auditor 802-446-2498; Elections 802-446-2498; Vital Records 802-446-2498.

Topsham Town

Town Clerk, P.O. Box 69, Topsham, VT 05076. Town Clerk, R/E and UCC Recording 802-439-5505; Fax 802-439-5505.
Will not search UCC records. This agency will not do a tax lien search. Will not search real estate records. **Other Phone Numbers:** Assessor 802-439-5505; Treasurer 802-439-5505; Elections 802-439-5505; Vital Records 802-439-5505.

Town of Burke

Town Clerk, 212 School St, West Burke, VT 05871. Town Clerk, R/E and UCC Recording 802-467-3717; Fax 802-467-8623.
Will search UCC records. Will not search real estate records. **Other Phone Numbers:** Assessor 802-467-3717; Treasurer 802-467-3717.

Town of Mount Tabor

Town Clerk, P.O. Box 245, Mt. Tabor, VT 05739. 802-293-5282; Fax 802-293-5287.
Will search UCC records. **Other Phone Numbers:** Treasurer 802-293-5741.

Townshend Town

Town Clerk, P.O. Box 223, Townshend, VT 05353-0223. 802-365-7300.
Will search UCC records. This agency will not do a tax lien search. Will not search real estate records.

Troy Town

Town Clerk, P.O. Box 80, North Troy, VT 05859. 802-988-2663.
Will search UCC records. UCC search includes tax liens if requested. Will not search real estate records.

Tunbridge Town

Town Clerk, P.O. Box 6, Tunbridge, VT 05077. Town Clerk, R/E and UCC Recording 802-889-5521; Fax 802-889-3744.
Will search UCC records. Will not search real estate records. **Other Phone Numbers:** Assessor 802-889-5521; Treasurer 802-889-5521; Appraiser/Auditor 802-889-3571; Elections 802-889-5521; Vital Records 802-889-5521.

Underhill Town

Town Clerk, P.O. Box 32, Underhill, VT 05490. Town Clerk, R/E and UCC Recording 802-899-4434; Fax 802-899-2137.
Will search UCC records. Will not search real estate records. **Other Phone Numbers:** Assessor 802-899-4434; Treasurer 802-899-4434; Appraiser/Auditor 802-899-4434; Elections 802-899-4434; Vital Records 802-899-4434.

Vergennes City

Town Clerk, P.O. Box 35, Vergennes, VT 05491-0035. 802-877-2841; Fax 802-877-1157.
Will search UCC records.

Vernon Town

Town Clerk, 567 Governor Hunt Rd., Vernon, VT 05354. Town Clerk, R/E and UCC Recording 802-257-0292; Fax 802-254-3561.
Will search UCC records. Will not search real estate records. **Other Phone Numbers:** Assessor 802-257-0292; Treasurer 802-257-0292; Appraiser/Auditor 802-257-0292; Elections 802-257-0292; Vital Records 802-257-0292.

Vershire Town

Town Clerk, 6894 Vermont Rte. 113, Vershire, VT 05079. Town Clerk, R/E and UCC Recording 802-685-2227.
Will search UCC records. UCC search includes tax liens if requested. Will not search real estate records. **Other Phone Numbers:** Assessor 802-685-2227; Treasurer 802-685-2227.

Victory Town

Town Clerk, HCR 60 Box 511, North Concord, VT 05858. 802-328-3907.
Will search UCC records. This agency will not do a tax lien search. Will not search real estate records.

Waitsfield Town

Town Clerk, 9 Bridge St, Bridge Street, Waitsfield, VT 05673-0390. 802-496-2218; Fax 802-496-9284.
Will search UCC records. This agency will not do a tax lien search. Will not search real estate records. **Other Phone Numbers:** Assessor 802-496-9689.

Walden Town

Town Clerk, 12 Vt. Rte. 215, West Danville, VT 05873. 802-563-2220; Fax 802-563-3008.
Will search UCC records. This agency will not do a tax lien search. Will not search real estate records.

Wallingford Town

Town Clerk, P.O. Box 327, Wallingford, VT 05773. 802-446-2336; Fax 802-446-3174. http://www.wallingfordvt.com
Will search UCC records. This agency will not do a tax lien search. Will not search real estate records. **Other Phone Numbers:** Assessor 802-446-2336.

Waltham Town

Town Clerk, P.O. Box 175, Vergennes, VT 05491. 802-877-3641; Fax 802-877-3641.
Will search UCC records. UCC search includes tax liens if requested. Will not search real estate records.

Wardsboro Town

Town Clerk, P.O. Box 48, Wardsboro, VT 05355-0048. 802-896-6055; Fax 802-896-1000.
Will search UCC records.

Warren Town

Town Clerk, P.O. Box 337, Warren, VT 05674. 802-496-2709.
Will search UCC records. This agency will not do a tax lien search. Will not search real estate records.

Washington Town

Town Clerk, Clerk's Office, Rte. 100, Washington, VT 05675. 802-883-2218.
Will search UCC records. UCC search includes tax liens if requested. RE record owner searches available.

Waterbury Town

Town Clerk, 51 South Main Street, Waterbury, VT 05676. 802-244-8447; Fax 802-244-1014.
Will search UCC records. Will not search real estate records.

Waterford Town

Town Clerk, P.O. Box 56, Lower Waterford, VT 05848. 802-748-2122; Fax 802-748-8196.
Will search UCC records. Will not search real estate records.

Waterville Town

Town Clerk, PO Box 31, Waterville, VT 05492. Town Clerk, R/E and UCC Recording 802-644-8865; Fax 802-644-8865.
Will search UCC records. Will not search real estate records. **Other Phone Numbers:** Assessor 802-644-8865; Treasurer 802-644-8865; Appraiser/Auditor 802-644-8865; Elections 802-644-8865; Vital Records 802-644-8865.

Weathersfield Town

Town Clerk, P.O. Box E, Weathersfield, VT 05030-0304. 802-674-2626.
Will search UCC records. This agency will not do a tax lien search. Will not search real estate records. **Other Phone Numbers:** Assessor 802-674-2626.

Wells Town

Town Clerk, P.O. Box 585, Wells, VT 05774. 802-645-0486.
Will search UCC records. UCC search includes tax liens if requested. Will not search real estate records.

West Fairlee Town

Town Clerk, Box 615, West Fairlee, VT 05083. 802-333-9696; Fax 802-333-9696.
Will search UCC records. Will not search real estate records.

West Haven Town

Town Clerk, 2919 Main Rd., Fair Haven, VT 05743-9610. 802-265-4880; Fax 802-265-4880.
Will search UCC records. **Other Phone Numbers:** Assessor 802-265-7996; Treasurer 802-265-3675; Vital Records 802-265-4880.

West Rutland Town

Town Clerk, 35 Marble St., West Rutland, VT 05777. 802-438-2204; Fax 802-438-5133.
Will search UCC records. **Other Phone Numbers:** Assessor 802-438-2263.

West Windsor Town

Town Clerk, Box 6, Brownsville, VT 05037. Town Clerk, R/E and UCC Recording 802-484-7212; Fax 802-484-3518.
Will search UCC records. Will not search real estate records. **Other Phone Numbers:** Assessor 802-484-7212; Treasurer 802-484-7212; Appraiser/Auditor 802-484-7212.

Westfield Town

Town Clerk, 1257 Vermont Rte. 100, Westfield, VT 05874. 802-744-2484; Fax 802-744-2484.
Will search UCC records. UCC search includes tax liens if requested. Will not search real estate records. **Other Phone Numbers:** Assessor 802-744-2484; Treasurer 802-744-2484.

Westford Town

Town Clerk, 1713 Vermont Route 128, Westford, VT 05494. 802-878-4587; Fax 802-879-6503.
Will not search UCC records and tax lien records. Will not search real estate records.

Westminster Town

Town Clerk, P.O. Box 147, Westminster, VT 05158-0147. 802-722-4091; Fax 802-722-4255.
Will search UCC records. Will not search real estate records.

Westmore Town

Town Clerk, 54 Hinton Hill Rd., Orleans, VT 05860. 802-525-3007; Fax 802-525-3007.

Will search UCC records. Will not search real estate records.

Weston Town

Town Clerk, P.O. Box 98, Weston, VT 05161. 802-824-6645; Fax 802-824-4121.
Will search UCC records. Will not search real estate records.

Weybridge Town

Town Clerk, 1727 Quaker Village Rd., Weybridge, VT 05753. Town Clerk, R/E and UCC Recording 802-545-2450; Fax 802-545-2450.
Will search UCC records. Will not search real estate records. **Other Phone Numbers:** Assessor 802-545-2450; Treasurer 802-545-2450; Appraiser/Auditor 802-545-2450; Elections 802-545-2450; Vital Records 802-545-2450.

Wheelock Town

Town Clerk, P.O. Box 1328, Lyndonville, VT 05851-0428. Town Clerk, R/E and UCC Recording 802-626-9094; Fax 802-626-9094.
Will search UCC records. UCC search includes tax liens if requested. RE record owner searches available. **Other Phone Numbers:** Assessor 802-626-8311; Treasurer 802-626-9094; Elections 802-626-9094; Vital Records 802-626-9094.

Whiting Town

Town Clerk, 29 S. Main St., Whiting, VT 05778. Town Clerk, R/E and UCC Recording 802-623-7813.
Will search UCC records. UCC search includes tax liens if requested. RE owner, mortgage, and property transfer searches available. **Other Phone Numbers:** Assessor 802-623-7813; Treasurer 802-623-7813.

Whitingham Town

Town Clerk, P.O. Box 529, Jacksonville, VT 05342. 802-368-7887; Fax 802-368-7519.
Will search UCC records. UCC search includes tax liens if requested. RE owner, mortgage, and property transfer searches available. **Other Phone Numbers:** Assessor 802-368-2400; Treasurer 802-368-2801.

Williamstown Town

Town Clerk, P.O. Box 646, Williamstown, VT 05679. 802-433-5455.
Will search UCC records. UCC search includes tax liens if requested. RE record owner searches available.

Williston Town

Town Clerk, 7900 Williston Rd., Williston, VT 05495. 802-878-5121.
St. George is a separate town with a Williston mailing address. Will search UCC records. This agency will not do a tax lien search. Will not search real estate records. **Other Phone Numbers:** Assessor 802-878-1091; Appraiser/Auditor 802-878-1091.

Wilmington Town

Town Clerk, P.O. Box 217, Wilmington, VT 05363-0217. Town Clerk, R/E and UCC Recording 802-464-5836; Fax 802-464-1238.
Will search UCC records. Will not search real estate records. **Other Phone Numbers:** Assessor 802-464-8591; Treasurer 802-464-8591; Appraiser/Auditor 802-464-8591; Elections 802-464-5836; Vital Records 802-464-5836.

Windham Town

Town Clerk, RR 1, Box 109, West Townshend, VT 05359. 802-874-4211.
Will search UCC records. This agency will not do a tax lien search. Will not search real estate records.

Windsor Town

Town Clerk, P.O. Box 47, Windsor, VT 05089. Town Clerk, R/E and UCC Recording 802-674-5610; Fax 802-674-1017.
Will search UCC records. Will not search real estate records. **Other Phone Numbers:** Assessor 802-674-5414; Treasurer 802-674-6788; Appraiser/Auditor 802-674-5414; Elections 802-674-5610; Vital Records 802-674-5610.

Winhall Town

Town Clerk, Box 389, Bondville, VT 05340. 802-297-2122.

Will search UCC records. This agency will not do a tax lien search. Will not search real estate records. **Other Phone Numbers:** Assessor 802-297-2119.

Winooski City

Town Clerk, 27 West Allen Street, Winooski, VT 05404. 802-655-6419; Fax 802-655-6414.
Will search UCC records. Will not search real estate records. **Other Phone Numbers:** Assessor 802-655-6410.

Wolcott Town

Town Clerk, P.O. Box 100, Wolcott, VT 05680-0100. 802-888-2746; Fax 802-888-2746.
Will search UCC records. **Other Phone Numbers:** Assessor 802-888-2746; Treasurer 802-888-2746; Appraiser/Auditor 802-888-6858.

Woodbury Town

Town Clerk, P.O. Box 123, Woodbury, VT 05681. 802-456-7051.
Will search UCC records. This agency will not do a tax lien search. Will not search real estate records. **Other Phone Numbers:** Assessor 802-456-8836.

Woodford Town

Town Clerk, HRC 65 Box 600, Bennington, VT 05201. 802-442-4895; Fax 802-442-4895.
Will search UCC records. Will not search real estate records.

Woodstock Town

Town Clerk, 31 The Green, Woodstock, VT 05091. 802-457-3611; Fax 802-457-2329.
Will search UCC records. Will not search real estate records. **Other Phone Numbers:** Assessor 802-457-2607.

Worcester Town

Town Clerk, Drawer 161, Worcester, VT 05682-0161. 802-223-6942; Fax 802-229-5216. www.vermont town.com
Will search UCC records. Will not search real estate records.

Vermont County Locator

You will usually be able to find the city name in the City/County Cross Reference below. In that case, it is a simple matter to determine the county from the cross reference. However, only the official US Postal Service city names are included in this index. There are an additional 40,000 place names that people use in their addresses. Therefore, we have also included a ZIP/City Cross Reference immediately following the City/County Cross Reference.

If you know the ZIP Code but the city name does not appear in the City/County Cross Reference index, look up the ZIP Code in the ZIP/City Cross Reference, find the city name, then look up the city name in the City/County Cross Reference. For example, you want to know the county for an address of Menands, NY 12204. There is no "Menands" in the City/County Cross Reference. The ZIP/City Cross Reference shows that ZIP Codes 12201-12288 are for the city of Albany. Looking back in the City/County Cross Reference, Albany is in Albany County.

City/County Cross Reference

ADAMANT Washington
ALBANY Orleans
ALBURG Grand Isle
ARLINGTON Bennington
ASCUTNEY Windsor
AVERILL Essex
BAKERSFIELD Franklin
BARNARD Windsor
BARNET Caledonia
BARRE (05641) Washington(98),
   Orange(2)
BARTON Orleans
BEEBE PLAIN Orleans
BEECHER FALLS Essex
BELLOWS FALLS Windham
BELMONT Rutland
BELVIDERE CENTER Lamoille
BENNINGTON Bennington
BENSON Rutland
BETHEL Windsor
BOMOSEEN Rutland
BONDVILLE (05340) Bennington(97),
   Windham(3)
BRADFORD Orange
BRANDON (05733) Rutland(82),
   Addison(18)
BRATTLEBORO Windham
BRIDGEWATER Windsor
BRIDGEWATER CORNERS Windsor
BRIDPORT Addison
BRISTOL Addison
BROOKFIELD Orange
BROWNSVILLE Windsor
BURLINGTON Chittenden
CABOT (05647) Washington(99),
   Caledonia(1)
CALAIS Washington
CAMBRIDGE (05444) Chittenden(79),
   Lamoille(14), Franklin(7)
CAMBRIDGEPORT Windham
CANAAN Essex
CASTLETON Rutland
CAVENDISH Windsor
CENTER RUTLAND Rutland
CHARLOTTE Chittenden
CHELSEA Orange
CHESTER Windsor
CHESTER DEPOT Windsor
CHITTENDEN Rutland
COLCHESTER Chittenden
CONCORD Essex
CORINTH Orange
COVENTRY Orleans
CRAFTSBURY (05826) Orleans(98),
   Caledonia(2)
CRAFTSBURY COMMON (05827)
   Orleans(98), Caledonia(2)
CUTTINGSVILLE Rutland
DANBY Rutland
DANVILLE Caledonia
DERBY Orleans
DERBY LINE Orleans
DORSET Bennington

EAST ARLINGTON Bennington
EAST BARRE (05649) Washington(93),
   Orange(8)
EAST BERKSHIRE Franklin
EAST BURKE Caledonia
EAST CALAIS Washington
EAST CHARLESTON Orleans
EAST CORINTH Orange
EAST DORSET (05253) Bennington(85),
   Rutland(15)
EAST DOVER Windham
EAST FAIRFIELD Franklin
EAST HARDWICK Caledonia
EAST HAVEN Essex
EAST MIDDLEBURY Addison
EAST MONTPELIER Washington
EAST POULTNEY Rutland
EAST RANDOLPH Orange
EAST RYEGATE Caledonia
EAST SAINT JOHNSBURY Caledonia
EAST THETFORD Orange
EAST WALLINGFORD Rutland
EDEN Lamoille
EDEN MILLS Lamoille
ELY Orange
ENOSBURG FALLS Franklin
ESSEX Chittenden
ESSEX JUNCTION Chittenden
FAIR HAVEN Rutland
FAIRFAX (05454) Chittenden(89),
   Franklin(11)
FAIRFIELD Franklin
FAIRLEE Orange
FERRISBURG Addison
FLORENCE Rutland
FOREST DALE Rutland
FRANKLIN Franklin
GAYSVILLE Windsor
GILMAN Essex
GLOVER Orleans
GRAFTON Windham
GRANBY Essex
GRAND ISLE Grand Isle
GRANITEVILLE (05654) Washington(64),
   Orange(36)
GRANVILLE Addison
GREENSBORO (05841) Orleans(95),
   Caledonia(5)
GREENSBORO BEND Orleans
GROTON Caledonia
GUILDHALL (05905) Essex(97),
   Chittenden(3)
HANCOCK Addison
HARDWICK Caledonia
HARTFORD Windsor
HARTLAND Windsor
HARTLAND FOUR CORNERS Windsor
HIGHGATE CENTER Franklin
HIGHGATE SPRINGS Franklin
HINESBURG (05461) Chittenden(97),
   Addison(3)
HUNTINGTON Chittenden
HYDE PARK Lamoille

HYDEVILLE Rutland
IRASBURG Orleans
ISLAND POND Essex
ISLE LA MOTTE Grand Isle
JACKSONVILLE Windham
JAMAICA Windham
JEFFERSONVILLE (99999) Lamoille(99),
   Franklin(1)
JERICHO Chittenden
JOHNSON Lamoille
JONESVILLE Chittenden
KILLINGTON Rutland
LAKE ELMORE Lamoille
LONDONDERRY Windham
LOWELL Orleans
LOWER WATERFORD Caledonia
LUDLOW Windsor
LUNENBURG Essex
LYNDON Caledonia
LYNDON CENTER Caledonia
LYNDONVILLE Caledonia
MANCHESTER Bennington
MANCHESTER CENTER Bennington
MARLBORO Windham
MARSHFIELD (05658) Washington(97),
   Caledonia(3)
MC INDOE FALLS (05050) Caledonia(67),
   Orange(33)
MIDDLEBURY Addison
MIDDLETOWN SPRINGS Rutland
MILTON (05468) Chittenden(96),
   Franklin(4)
MONKTON Addison
MONTGOMERY Franklin
MONTGOMERY CENTER (05471)
   Franklin(86), Orleans(14)
MONTPELIER Washington
MORETOWN Washington
MORGAN Orleans
MORRISVILLE Lamoille
MOSCOW Lamoille
MOUNT HOLLY (05758) Rutland(98),
   Windsor(2)
NEW HAVEN Addison
NEWBURY Orange
NEWFANE Windham
NEWPORT Orleans
NEWPORT CENTER Orleans
NORTH BENNINGTON Bennington
NORTH CLARENDON Rutland
NORTH CONCORD Essex
NORTH FERRISBURG (05473)
   Addison(97), Chittenden(4)
NORTH HARTLAND Windsor
NORTH HERO Grand Isle
NORTH HYDE PARK Lamoille
NORTH MONTPELIER Washington
NORTH POMFRET Windsor
NORTH POWNAL Bennington
NORTH SPRINGFIELD Windsor
NORTH THETFORD Orange
NORTH TROY Orleans
NORTHFIELD Washington

NORTHFIELD FALLS Washington
NORTON Essex
NORWICH Windsor
ORLEANS Orleans
ORWELL (05760) Addison(96), Rutland(4)
PASSUMPSIC Caledonia
PAWLET (05761) Rutland(86),
   Bennington(14)
PEACHAM Caledonia
PERKINSVILLE Windsor
PERU Bennington
PITTSFIELD (05762) Rutland(95),
   Windsor(5)
PITTSFORD Rutland
PLAINFIELD Washington
PLYMOUTH Windsor
POST MILLS Orange
POULTNEY Rutland
POWNAL Bennington
PROCTOR Rutland
PROCTORSVILLE Windsor
PUTNEY Windham
QUECHEE Windsor
RANDOLPH Orange
RANDOLPH CENTER Orange
READING (05062) Windsor(98), Orange(2)
READSBORO Bennington
RICHFORD Franklin
RICHMOND Chittenden
ROCHESTER (05767) Windsor(96),
   Addison(2), Rutland(2)
ROXBURY (05669) Washington(61),
   Addison(29), Orange(10)
RUPERT Bennington
RUTLAND Rutland
SAINT ALBANS Franklin
SAINT ALBANS BAY Franklin
SAINT JOHNSBURY Caledonia
SAINT JOHNSBURY CENTER Caledonia
SALISBURY Addison
SAXTONS RIVER Windham
SHAFTSBURY Bennington
SHARON Windsor
SHEFFIELD Caledonia
SHELBURNE Chittenden
SHELDON Franklin
SHELDON SPRINGS Franklin
SHOREHAM Addison
SOUTH BARRE Washington
SOUTH BURLINGTON Chittenden
SOUTH HERO Grand Isle
SOUTH LONDONDERRY Windham
SOUTH NEWFANE Windham
SOUTH POMFRET Windsor
SOUTH ROYALTON Windsor
SOUTH RYEGATE (05069) Caledonia(99),
   Orange(1)
SOUTH STRAFFORD Orange
SOUTH WOODSTOCK Windsor
SPRINGFIELD Windsor
STARKSBORO Addison
STOCKBRIDGE Windsor
STOWE Lamoille

STRAFFORD Orange
SUTTON Caledonia
SWANTON Franklin
TAFTSVILLE Windsor
THETFORD Orange
THETFORD CENTER Orange
TOWNSHEND Windham
TROY Orleans
TUNBRIDGE Orange
UNDERHILL Chittenden
UNDERHILL CENTER Chittenden
VERGENNES Addison
VERNON Windham
VERSHIRE Orange
WAITSFIELD Washington
WALLINGFORD Rutland

WARDSBORO Windham
WARREN Washington
WASHINGTON Orange
WATERBURY (05676) Washington(95), Chittenden(6)
WATERBURY Washington
WATERBURY CENTER (05677) Washington(98), Lamoille(2)
WATERVILLE Lamoille
WEBSTERVILLE Washington
WELLS Rutland
WELLS RIVER Orange
WEST BURKE Caledonia
WEST CHARLESTON Orleans
WEST DANVILLE Caledonia
WEST DOVER Windham

WEST DUMMERSTON Windham
WEST FAIRLEE Orange
WEST GLOVER Orleans
WEST HALIFAX Windham
WEST HARTFORD Windsor
WEST NEWBURY Orange
WEST PAWLET (05775) Rutland(82), Bennington(18)
WEST RUPERT Bennington
WEST RUTLAND Rutland
WEST TOPSHAM Orange
WEST TOWNSHEND Windham
WEST WARDSBORO Windham
WESTFIELD Orleans
WESTFORD Chittenden
WESTMINSTER Windham

WESTMINSTER STATION Windham
WESTON Windsor
WHITE RIVER JUNCTION Windsor
WHITING (05778) Addison(94), Rutland(6)
WHITINGHAM Windham
WILDER Windsor
WILLIAMSTOWN Orange
WILLIAMSVILLE Windham
WILLISTON Chittenden
WILMINGTON Windham
WINDSOR Windsor
WINOOSKI Chittenden
WOLCOTT Lamoille
WOODBURY Washington
WOODSTOCK Windsor
WORCESTER Washington

ZIP/City Cross Reference

ZIP Range	City	ZIP Range	City	ZIP Range	City	ZIP Range	City
05001-05009	WHITE RIVER JUNCTION	05149-05149	LUDLOW	05452-05453	ESSEX JUNCTION	05671-05671	WATERBURY
05030-05030	ASCUTNEY	05150-05150	NORTH SPRINGFIELD	05454-05454	FAIRFAX	05672-05672	STOWE
05031-05031	BARNARD	05151-05151	PERKINSVILLE	05455-05455	FAIRFIELD	05673-05673	WAITSFIELD
05032-05032	BETHEL	05152-05152	PERU	05456-05456	FERRISBURG	05674-05674	WARREN
05033-05033	BRADFORD	05153-05153	PROCTORSVILLE	05457-05457	FRANKLIN	05675-05675	WASHINGTON
05034-05034	BRIDGEWATER	05154-05154	SAXTONS RIVER	05458-05458	GRAND ISLE	05676-05676	WATERBURY
05035-05035	BRIDGEWATER CORNERS	05155-05155	SOUTH LONDONDERRY	05459-05459	HIGHGATE CENTER	05677-05677	WATERBURY CENTER
05036-05036	BROOKFIELD	05156-05156	SPRINGFIELD	05460-05460	HIGHGATE SPRINGS	05678-05678	WEBSTERVILLE
05037-05037	BROWNSVILLE	05158-05158	WESTMINSTER	05461-05461	HINESBURG	05679-05679	WILLIAMSTOWN
05038-05038	CHELSEA	05159-05159	WESTMINSTER STATION	05462-05462	HUNTINGTON	05680-05680	WOLCOTT
05039-05039	CORINTH	05161-05161	WESTON	05463-05463	ISLE LA MOTTE	05681-05681	WOODBURY
05040-05040	EAST CORINTH	05201-05201	BENNINGTON	05464-05464	JEFFERSONVILLE	05682-05682	WORCESTER
05041-05041	EAST RANDOLPH	05250-05250	ARLINGTON	05465-05465	JERICHO	05701-05702	RUTLAND
05042-05042	EAST RYEGATE	05251-05251	DORSET	05466-05466	JONESVILLE	05730-05730	BELMONT
05043-05043	EAST THETFORD	05252-05252	EAST ARLINGTON	05468-05468	MILTON	05731-05731	BENSON
05045-05045	FAIRLEE	05253-05253	EAST DORSET	05469-05469	MONKTON	05732-05732	BOMOSEEN
05046-05046	GROTON	05254-05254	MANCHESTER	05470-05470	MONTGOMERY	05733-05733	BRANDON
05047-05047	HARTFORD	05255-05255	MANCHESTER CENTER	05471-05471	MONTGOMERY CENTER	05734-05734	BRIDPORT
05048-05048	HARTLAND	05257-05257	NORTH BENNINGTON	05472-05472	NEW HAVEN	05735-05735	CASTLETON
05049-05049	HARTLAND FOUR CORNERS	05260-05260	NORTH POWNAL	05473-05473	NORTH FERRISBURG	05736-05736	CENTER RUTLAND
05050-05050	MC INDOE FALLS	05261-05261	POWNAL	05474-05474	NORTH HERO	05737-05737	CHITTENDEN
05051-05051	NEWBURY	05262-05262	SHAFTSBURY	05476-05476	RICHFORD	05738-05738	CUTTINGSVILLE
05052-05052	NORTH HARTLAND	05301-05304	BRATTLEBORO	05477-05477	RICHMOND	05739-05739	DANBY
05053-05053	NORTH POMFRET	05340-05340	BONDVILLE	05478-05479	SAINT ALBANS	05740-05740	EAST MIDDLEBURY
05054-05054	NORTH THETFORD	05341-05341	EAST DOVER	05481-05481	SAINT ALBANS BAY	05741-05741	EAST POULTNEY
05055-05055	NORWICH	05342-05342	JACKSONVILLE	05482-05482	SHELBURNE	05742-05742	EAST WALLINGFORD
05056-05056	PLYMOUTH	05343-05343	JAMAICA	05483-05483	SHELDON	05743-05743	FAIR HAVEN
05058-05058	POST MILLS	05344-05344	MARLBORO	05485-05485	SHELDON SPRINGS	05744-05744	FLORENCE
05059-05059	QUECHEE	05345-05345	NEWFANE	05486-05486	SOUTH HERO	05745-05745	FOREST DALE
05060-05060	RANDOLPH	05346-05346	PUTNEY	05487-05487	STARKSBORO	05746-05746	GAYSVILLE
05061-05061	RANDOLPH CENTER	05350-05350	READSBORO	05488-05488	SWANTON	05747-05747	GRANVILLE
05062-05062	READING	05351-05351	SOUTH NEWFANE	05489-05489	UNDERHILL	05748-05748	HANCOCK
05065-05065	SHARON	05352-05352	READSBORO	05490-05490	UNDERHILL CENTER	05750-05750	HYDEVILLE
05067-05067	SOUTH POMFRET	05353-05353	TOWNSHEND	05491-05491	VERGENNES	05751-05751	KILLINGTON
05068-05068	SOUTH ROYALTON	05354-05354	VERNON	05492-05492	WATERVILLE	05753-05753	MIDDLEBURY
05069-05069	SOUTH RYEGATE	05355-05355	WARDSBORO	05494-05494	WESTFORD	05757-05757	MIDDLETOWN SPRINGS
05070-05070	SOUTH STRAFFORD	05356-05356	WEST DOVER	05495-05495	WILLISTON	05758-05758	MOUNT HOLLY
05071-05071	SOUTH WOODSTOCK	05357-05357	WEST DUMMERSTON	05601-05633	MONTPELIER	05759-05759	NORTH CLARENDON
05072-05072	STRAFFORD	05358-05358	WEST HALIFAX	05640-05640	ADAMANT	05760-05760	ORWELL
05073-05073	TAFTSVILLE	05359-05359	WEST TOWNSHEND	05641-05641	BARRE	05761-05761	PAWLET
05074-05074	THETFORD	05360-05360	WEST WARDSBORO	05647-05647	CABOT	05762-05762	PITTSFIELD
05075-05075	THETFORD CENTER	05361-05361	WHITINGHAM	05648-05648	CALAIS	05763-05763	PITTSFORD
05076-05076	EAST CORINTH	05362-05362	WILLIAMSVILLE	05649-05649	EAST BARRE	05764-05764	POULTNEY
05077-05077	TUNBRIDGE	05363-05363	WILMINGTON	05650-05650	EAST CALAIS	05765-05765	PROCTOR
05079-05079	VERSHIRE	05401-05402	BURLINGTON	05651-05651	EAST MONTPELIER	05766-05766	MIDDLEBURY
05081-05081	WELLS RIVER	05403-05403	SOUTH BURLINGTON	05652-05652	EDEN	05767-05767	ROCHESTER
05083-05083	WEST FAIRLEE	05404-05404	WINOOSKI	05653-05653	EDEN MILLS	05768-05768	RUPERT
05084-05084	WEST HARTFORD	05405-05406	BURLINGTON	05654-05654	GRANITEVILLE	05769-05769	SALISBURY
05085-05085	WEST NEWBURY	05407-05407	SOUTH BURLINGTON	05655-05655	HYDE PARK	05770-05770	SHOREHAM
05086-05086	WEST TOPSHAM	05439-05439	COLCHESTER	05656-05656	JOHNSON	05772-05772	STOCKBRIDGE
05088-05088	WILDER	05440-05440	ALBURG	05657-05657	LAKE ELMORE	05773-05773	WALLINGFORD
05089-05089	WINDSOR	05441-05441	BAKERSFIELD	05658-05658	MARSHFIELD	05774-05774	WELLS
05091-05091	WOODSTOCK	05442-05442	BELVIDERE CENTER	05660-05660	MORETOWN	05775-05775	WEST PAWLET
05101-05101	BELLOWS FALLS	05443-05443	BRISTOL	05661-05661	MORRISVILLE	05776-05776	WEST RUPERT
05141-05141	CAMBRIDGEPORT	05444-05444	CAMBRIDGE	05662-05662	MOSCOW	05777-05777	WEST RUTLAND
05142-05142	CAVENDISH	05445-05445	CHARLOTTE	05663-05663	NORTHFIELD	05778-05778	WHITING
05143-05143	CHESTER	05446-05446	COLCHESTER	05664-05664	NORTHFIELD FALLS	05819-05819	SAINT JOHNSBURY
05144-05144	CHESTER DEPOT	05447-05447	EAST BERKSHIRE	05665-05665	NORTH HYDE PARK	05820-05820	ALBANY
05146-05146	GRAFTON	05448-05448	EAST FAIRFIELD	05666-05666	NORTH MONTPELIER	05821-05821	BARNET
05148-05148	LONDONDERRY	05449-05449	COLCHESTER	05667-05667	PLAINFIELD	05822-05822	BARTON
		05450-05450	ENOSBURG FALLS	05669-05669	ROXBURY	05823-05823	BEEBE PLAIN
		05451-05451	ESSEX	05670-05670	SOUTH BARRE	05824-05824	CONCORD

05825-05825	COVENTRY	05841-05841	GREENSBORO	05859-05859	NORTH TROY	05901-05901	AVERILL
05826-05826	CRAFTSBURY	05842-05842	GREENSBORO BEND	05860-05860	ORLEANS	05902-05902	BEECHER FALLS
05827-05827	CRAFTSBURY COMMON	05843-05843	HARDWICK	05861-05861	PASSUMPSIC	05903-05903	CANAAN
05828-05828	DANVILLE	05845-05845	IRASBURG	05862-05862	PEACHAM	05904-05904	GILMAN
05829-05829	DERBY	05846-05846	ISLAND POND	05863-05863	SAINT JOHNSBURY	05905-05905	GUILDHALL
05830-05830	DERBY LINE	05847-05847	LOWELL		CENTER	05906-05906	LUNENBURG
05832-05832	EAST BURKE	05848-05848	LOWER WATERFORD	05866-05866	SHEFFIELD	05907-05907	NORTON
05833-05833	EAST CHARLESTON	05849-05849	LYNDON	05867-05867	SUTTON		
05836-05836	EAST HARDWICK	05850-05850	LYNDON CENTER	05868-05868	TROY		
05837-05837	EAST HAVEN	05851-05851	LYNDONVILLE	05871-05871	WEST BURKE		
05838-05838	EAST SAINT	05853-05853	MORGAN	05872-05872	WEST CHARLESTON		
	JOHNSBURY	05855-05855	NEWPORT	05873-05873	WEST DANVILLE		
05839-05839	GLOVER	05857-05857	NEWPORT CENTER	05874-05874	WESTFIELD		
05840-05840	GRANBY	05858-05858	NORTH CONCORD	05875-05875	WEST GLOVER		

Virginia

General Help Numbers:

Governor's Office
Capitol Bldg, 3rd Floor   804-786-2211
Richmond, VA 23219   Fax 804-371-6351
http://www.thedigitaldominion.com/index.cfm   8:30AM-
5:30PM

Attorney General's Office
900 E Main St   804-786-2071
Richmond, VA 23219   Fax 804-786-1991
http://www.oag.state.va.us   8:30AM-5PM

State Court Administrator
Administrative Office of Courts   804-786-6455
100 N 9th St, 3rd Floor   Fax 804-786-4542
Richmond, VA 23219   8AM-5PM
http://www.courts.state.va.us

State Archives
800 E. Broad St   804-692-3500
Richmond, VA 23219-8000   Fax 804-692-3556
http://www.lva.lib.va.us   9AM-5PM M-SA

State Specifics:

Capital: Richmond
                                Richmond City County

Time Zone: EST

Number of Counties: 95

Population: 7,078,515

Web Site: www.state.va.us

State Agencies

Criminal Records
Virginia State Police, CCRE, PO Box 85076, Richmond, VA 23261-5076 (Courier: 7700 Midlothian Turnpike, Richmond, VA 23235); 804-674-2084, 804-674-2277 (Fax), 8AM-5PM.

http://www.vsp.state.va.us

Note: Dissemination of information is governed by Section 19.2-389 Code of Virginia.

Indexing & Storage: Records are available from 1966. New records are available for inquiry immediately. Records are indexed on inhouse computer.

Searching: Must have a signed release form from person of record, including notarized signatures for both subject and requester. Must use their form "SP-167." Arrest records one year old without a disposition are not released. Include the following in your request-full name, date of birth, Social Security Number, sex, race.

Access by: mail, online.

Fee & Payment: The fee is $15.00 per name. Fee payee: Virginia State Police. Prepayment required. Pay by certified check or money order. MasterCard and Visa are accepted.

Mail search: Turnaround time: 4 to 6 weeks. A self addressed stamped envelope is requested.

Online search: Certain entities, including screening companies, are entitled to online access. The system is ONLY available to IN-STATE accounts. Fees are same as manual submission with exception of required software package purchase. The system is windows oriented, but will not handle networks. The PC user must be a stand alone system. There is a minimum usage requirement of 25 requests per month. Turnaround time is 24-72 hours. Fee is $15.00 per record.

Corporation Records
Limited Liability Company Records
Fictitious Name
Limited Partnership Records

State Corporation Commission, Clerks Office, PO Box 1197, Richmond, VA 23218-1197 (Courier: Tyler Bldg, 1st Floor, 1300 E Main St, Richmond, VA 23219); 804-371-9733, 804-371-9133 (Fax), 8:15AM-5PM.

http://www.state.va.us/scc/division/clk/index.htm

Indexing & Storage: Records are available for all active entities on computer. Older inactive records must be researched from the State Library.

Searching: Records are public and are open for inspection. Include the following in your request-full name of business. In addition to the articles of incorporation, corporation records, the following information is available: Annual Reports, Officers, Directors, DBAs, Prior (merged) names, Inactive (back to 1976 on computer) and Reserved names, and Registered Agents.

Access by: mail, phone, fax, in person, online.

Fee & Payment: Plain copies cost $1.00 per page for the first two pages and $.50 for each additional page thereafter. Certification is $3.00. Fee payee: Treasurer of Virginia. Prepayment required. Requesters with billing accounts are encouraged to fax orders. Personal checks accepted. No credit cards accepted.

Mail search: Turnaround time: 3 to 5 days. Be sure to include your phone number and contact person with all written requests.No self addressed stamped envelope is required.

Phone search: No fee for telephone request. Agency will provide only limited information (screen data only) and name availability over the phone.

Fax search: Turnaround time is 3-5 days.

In person search: Information is available via public access terminals. Certificates for Fact and Good Standing are generally available in 1-3 days.

Online search: There is a dial-up system, called Direct Access, for registered accounts. There are no fees. A wealth of information is available on this system. For more details, call 804-371-9819 or visit www.state.va.us/scc/division/clk/diracc.htm. Download the application from the web site.

Other access: Magnetic tape purchase is offered to those who wish the entire database.

Trademarks/Servicemarks

State Corporation Commission, Virginia Securities Division, PO Box 1197 (1300 Main St, 9th Fl), Richmond, VA 23218; 804-371-9051, 804-371-9911 (Fax), 8:15AM-5PM.

http://www.state.va.us/sec

Indexing & Storage: Records are available from as early as the 1920s. Records are computerized since the 1970s. Records are normally destroyed after they have been inactive for 1 year.

Access by: mail, phone, fax, in person.

Fee & Payment: There is no search fee. The copy fee is $2.00 for the first 2 pages and $.50 each additional page. Fee payee: Treasurer of Virginia. Prepayment required. Personal checks accepted. No credit cards accepted.

Mail search: Turnaround time: 1 to 2 days.

Phone search: Limited to 1 or 2 searches per call.

Fax search: Fax searching available.

In person search: You may make copies at $.50 per page.

Uniform Commercial Code
Federal Tax Liens

UCC Division, State Corporation Commission, PO Box 1197, Richmond, VA 23218-1197 (Courier: 1300 E Main St, 1st Floor, Richmond, VA 23219); 804-371-9733, 804-371-9744 (Fax), 8:15AM-5PM.

http://www.state.va.us/scc/division/clk/index.htm

Indexing & Storage: Records are available from the 1960s on microfiche and from mid 1992 on computer.

Searching: Use search request form UCC-11. The search includes federal tax liens on businesses if specifically requested. Federal tax liens on individuals and all state tax liens are filed at the local level, which may be a county or independent city. Include the following in your request-debtor name. Turnaround time for copies of UCC searches is 10 days, 5 days for most other orders (financing statements, list of filings, etc).

Access by: mail, phone, fax, in person, online.

Fee & Payment: Search request - $7.00; copies - $1.00 for each of the first 2 pages and $.50 for each additional page; certification - $1.00. Fee payee: State Corporation Commission. Prepayment required. Personal checks accepted. No credit cards accepted.

Mail search: A self addressed stamped envelope is requested.

Phone search: No fee for telephone request. They will do limited verification on a yes or no basis.

Fax search: Only available to those with billing accounts. Limit of 10 pages on return.

In person search: Cut-off time for same day service for Good Standings and Certificates is 3 PM if research not required.

Online search: This is a free, non-Internet service. Accounts must be registered. This is the same system used for corporation records. Call 804-371-9819 and ask for a registration packet.

State Tax Liens
Records not maintained by a state level agency.

Note: All information is found at the local city or county level.

Sales Tax Registrations

Taxation Department, Sales - Taxpayer Assistance, PO Box 1115, Richmond, VA 23218-1115 (Courier: 2220 W Broad St, Richmond, VA 23220); 804-367-8037, 804-786-2670 (Fax), 8:30AM-4:30PM.

http://www.state.va.us/tax/tax.html

Note: Registration information of businesses is available from the Corporation Commission.

Indexing & Storage: Records are available for three years on computer, then put on microfilm for ten years, then purged.

Searching: This agency will provide no information without a written, signed, notarized authorization from the business itself; they will then provide the business name, address, phone, and tax permit number. Include the following in your request-business name, tax permit number.

Access by: mail.

Mail search: Turnaround time: 1 week to 10 days. No self addressed stamped envelope is required. No fee for mail request.

Birth Certificates

State Health Department, Office of Vital Records, PO Box 1000, Richmond, VA 23218-1000 (Courier: 1601 Willow Lawn Drive, #275, Richmond, VA 23220); 804-662-6200, 804-644-2550 (Fax), 8AM-4:45PM, Closed on major holidays.

http://www.vdh.state.va.us/vitalrec/f_08.htm

Note: An application for certification may be downloaded form web site.

Indexing & Storage: Records are available from 1912 on. Records from 1853 to 1896 are located at the State Archives. New records are available for inquiry immediately. Records are indexed on microfiche, inhouse computer.

Searching: Vital records are available to immediate family members only. Birth records are public information 100 years after the date of the event. Include the following in your request-name at birth, date of birth, place of birth, mother's maiden name, father's name, relationship to the person on the certificate. Include your area code and daytime phone number, your return address, and be sure to sign your request.

Access by: mail, phone, fax, in person.

Fee & Payment: The fee is $8.00 per certificate, $10.00 per authentication. The payee for authentication is the Secretary of the Commonweatlh. Fee payee: The State Health Department. Prepayment required. Personal checks accepted. Credit cards accepted: MasterCard, Visa, AmEx, Discover.

Mail search: Turnaround time: 4 to 6 weeks. No self addressed stamped envelope is required.

Phone search: You must use a credit card. See Expedited Service.

Fax search: You must use a credit card. See Expedited Service.

In person search: Turnaround time 15 minutes.

Expedited service: Expedited service is available from VitalChek Express Service. Phone (877) 572-6333, select option #2. Webside: www.vitalchek.com; e-mail: vitals.reply@vitalchek.com. Turnaround time: 2 - 5 days. Provider: Federal Express $22.50 plus $8.00/1st copy and $8.00 each copy thereafter. Add $10.00 for authentication.

Death Records

State Health Department, Office of Vital Records, PO Box 1000, Richmond, VA 23218-1000 (Courier: 1601 Willow Lawn Drive, #275, Richmond, VA 23220); 804-662-6200, 804-644-2550 (Fax), 8AM-4:45PM, Closed on major holidays.

http://www.vdh.state.va.us/vitalrec/f_08.htm

Note: An application for certification may be downloaded form web site.

Indexing & Storage: Records are available from 1912 on. Records from 1853 to 1896 are located at the State Archives. New records are available for inquiry immediately. Records are indexed on microfiche, inhouse computer.

Searching: Vital records are available to immediate family members only. Death records are public information 50 years after the date of the event. Include the following in your request-name of deceased, date of death, place of death, relationship to the deceased, reason for the certificate. Include your area code and daytime phone number, your return address, and be sure to sign your request.

Access by: mail, phone, fax, in person.

Fee & Payment: The fee is $8.00 per certificate, $10.00 per authentication. The payee for authentication is the Secretary of the Commonweatlh. Fee payee: The State Health Department. Prepayment required. Personal checks accepted. Credit cards accepted: MasterCard, Visa, AmEx, Discover.

Mail search: Turnaround time: 4 to 6 weeks. No self addressed stamped envelope is required.

Phone search: You must use a credit card. See Expedited Service.

Fax search: You must use a credit card. See Expedited Service.

In person search: Turnaround time 15 minutes.

Expedited service: Expedited service is available from VitalChek Express Service. Phone (877) 572-6333, select option #2. Webside: www.vitalchek.com; e-mail: vitals.reply@vitalchek.com. Turnaround time: 2 - 5 days. Provider: Federal Express $22.50 plus $8.00/1st copy and $8.00 each copy thereafter. Add $10.00 for authentication.

Marriage Certificates

State Health Department, Office of Vital Records, PO Box 1000, Richmond, VA 23218-1000 (Courier: 1601 Willow Lawn Drive, #275, Richmond, VA 23220); 804-662-6200, 804-644-2550 (Fax), 8AM-4:45PM, Closed on major holidays.

http://www.vdh.state.va.us/vitalrec/f_08.htm

Note: An application for certification may be downloaded form web site.

Indexing & Storage: Records are available from 1853 to present. New records are available for inquiry immediately. Records are indexed on microfiche, inhouse computer.

Searching: Vital records are available to immediate family members only. Marriage records are public information 50 years after the date of the event. Include the following in your request-name, date of marriage, place of marriage, relationship to the person on the certificate, reason for the certificate. Include your area code and daytime phone number, your return address, and be sure to sign your request.

Access by: mail, phone, fax, in person.

Fee & Payment: The fee is $8.00 per certificate, $10.00 per authentication. The payee for authentication is the Secretary of the Commonweatlh. Fee payee: The State Health Department. Prepayment required. Personal checks accepted. Credit cards accepted: MasterCard, Visa, AmEx, Discover.

Mail search: Turnaround time: 4 to 6 weeks. No self addressed stamped envelope is required.

Phone search: You must use a credit card. See Expedited Service.

Fax search: You must use a credit card. See Expedited Service.

In person search: Turnaround time 15 minutes.

Expedited service: Expedited service is available from VitalChek Express Service. Phone (877) 572-6333, select option #2. Webside: www.vitalchek.com; e-mail: vitals.reply@vitalchek.com. Turnaround time: 2 - 5 days. Provider: Federal Express $22.50 plus $8.00/1st copy and $8.00 each copy thereafter. Add $10.00 for authentication.

Divorce Records

State Health Department, Office of Vital Records, PO Box 1000, Richmond, VA 23218-1000 (Courier: 1601 Willow Lawn Drive, #275, Richmond, VA 23220); 804-662-6200, 804-644-2550 (Fax), 8AM-4:45PM, Closed on major holidays.

http://www.vdh.state.va.us/vitalrec/f_08.htm

Note: An application for certification may be downloaded form web site.

Indexing & Storage: Records are available 1918 to present. New records are available for inquiry immediately. Records are indexed on microfiche, inhouse computer.

Searching: Vital records are available to immediate family members only. Divorce records are public information 50 years after the date of the event. Include the following in your request-name, date of divorce, place of divorce, relationship to the person on the certificate, reason for the certificate. Include your area code and daytime phone number, your return address, and be sure to sign your request.

Access by: mail, phone, fax, in person.

Fee & Payment: The fee is $8.00 per certificate, $10.00 per authentication. The payee for authentication is the Secretary of the Commonweatlh. Fee payee: The State Health Department. Prepayment required. Personal checks accepted. Credit cards accepted: MasterCard, Visa, AmEx, Discover.

Mail search: Turnaround time: 4 to 6 weeks. No self addressed stamped envelope is required.

Phone search: You must use a credit card. See Expedited Service.

Fax search: You must use a credit card. See Expedited Service.

In person search: Turnaround time 15 minutes.

Expedited service: Expedited service is available from VitalChek Express Service. Phone (877) 572-6333, select option #2. Webside: www.vitalchek.com; e-mail: vitals.reply@vitalchek.com. Turnaround time: 2 - 5 days. Provider: Federal Express $22.50 plus $8.00/1st copy and $8.00 each copy thereafter. Add $10.00 for authentication.

Workers' Compensation Records

Workers' Compensation Commission, 1000 DMV Dr, Richmond, VA 23220; 804-367-8633, 804-367-9740 (Fax), 8:15AM-5PM.

Indexing & Storage: Records are available from 1977 on. New records are available for inquiry immediately. Records are indexed on microfilm, inhouse computer.

Searching: To receive file copies, you must have a notarized release from the claimant. They will release a "yes or no" answer when presented with a list. Awards issued are public information. Include the following in your request-claimant name, Social Security Number, claim number. All requests must be in writing. The following data is not released: sealed records.

Access by: mail, in person.

Fee & Payment: The search fee is $10.00. No copy fee for first 10 pages, then $.50 per page. Fee payee: Treasurer - State of Virginia. Prepayment required. Personal checks accepted. No credit cards accepted.

Mail search: Turnaround time: 1 to 4 days.

In person search: Request must be in writing.

Driver Records

Motorist Records Services, Attn: Records Request Work Center, PO Box 27412, Richmond, VA 23269; 804-367-0538, 8:30AM-5:30PM M-F; 8:30AM-12:30PM S.

http://www.dmv.state.va.us

Note: Copies of tickets from non-computerized courts are available at this address for $6.00 per record only to driver or driver's authorized representative. Ticket information from computerized courts must be obtained from each court.

Indexing & Storage: Records are available for 3 years for moving violations & misc convictions, 5 years for speeding & unauthorized use of a motor vehicle, 11 years for 3 reckless driving offenses and DWI, and 24 months from the complied date for suspensions. It takes 12 days from receipt before new records are available for inquiry. Records are indexed on inhouse computer.

Searching: Access is for DPPA permissible users only. Casual requesters cannot obtain records without consent. Include the following in your request-full name, date of birth, sex. Insurance records display 5 years, employment records the last 7 years. Surrendered licenses are purged after 5 years.

Access by: mail, in person, online.

Fee & Payment: The current fee is $6.00 for mail or walk-in requests and $5.00 for online or tape requests. Add $5.00 for certification. Fee payee: Department of Motor Vehicles. Prepayment required. Personal checks accepted. No credit cards accepted.

Mail search: Turnaround time: 5 days. The driver's name, DOB, and sex must "match" to get a record. Request must be on a DMV form or on letterhead.A self addressed stamped envelope is requested.

In person search: Normal turnaround time is while you wait. There are 72 field offices where records can be requested.

Online search: Online service is provided by the Virginia Information Providers Network (VIPNet). Online reports are provided via the Internet on an interactive basis 24 hours daily. There is a $50 annual administrative fee and records are $5.00 each. Go to www.vipnet.org for more information or call 804-786-4718.

Other access: Magnetic tape ordering for batch requests is available from VIPnet. No records are sold for marketing purposes.

Accident Reports

Department of Motor Vehicles, Customer Record Requests, Rm 517, PO Box 27412, Richmond, VA 23269; 804-367-0538, 804-367-0390 (Fax), 8:30AM-5:30PM M-F; 8:30AM-12:30PM S.

http://www.dmv.state.va.us

Indexing & Storage: Records are available for 40 months to present. Records are indexed on computer.

Searching: All requests must be in writing. Only information released to general public are the names, date, location, witnesses, and one investigating officer (Per 46.2-379). Full information is available to involved parties. Include the following in your request-full name, date of accident, location of accident.

Access by: mail, fax, in person.

Fee & Payment: The fee is $6.00 per report. Fee payee: Department of Motor Vehicles. Prepayment required. Personal checks accepted. Credit cards accepted: MasterCard, Visa.

Mail search: Turnaround time: 5 days.

Fax search: Must pay with a credit card.

In person search: Turnaround time is while you wait, if personnel available.

Vehicle Ownership
Vehicle Identification

Motorist Records Services, Customer Records Request Section, PO Box 27412, Richmond, VA 23269; 804-367-0538, 8:30AM-5:30PM M-F; 8:30AM-12:30PM S.

http://www.dmv.state.va.us

Note: Lien information is only released to lending institutions and collection agencies.

Indexing & Storage: It takes 12 days from receipt before new records are available for inquiry.

Searching: Casual requesters cannot obtain records without consent. High volume requesters must sign an agreement or contract and will be assigned a user number. Records cannot be purchased and resold for marketing purposes. Private investigators who are registered as compliance agents by the Department of Justice Services may obtain address information by submitting a license plate number.

Access by: mail, phone, in person, online.

Fee & Payment: The fee is $6.00 for vehicle ownership and registration information or $6.00 per vehicle on a name search. There is a full charge for a "no record found." Fee payee: Department of Motor Vehicles. Prepayment required. Personal checks accepted. No credit cards accepted.

Mail search: Turnaround time: 5 days. A self addressed stamped envelope is requested.

Phone search: Phone requesting is available for pre-approved accounts. There is a limit to 5 requests a day.

In person search: Turnaround time: while you wait, usually limited to five at one time.

Online search: The online system, managed by the Virginia Information Providers Network (VIPNet), is an interactive system open 24 hours daily. There is an annual $50 administration fee and records are $5.00 each. All accounts must be approved by both the DMV and VIPNet. Contact Rodney Willett at 804-786-4718 to request an information use agreement application. The URL is www.vipnet.org.

Other access: Bulk release of vehicle or ownership information is not available except for statistical and vehicle recall purposes.

Vessel Ownership
Vessel Registration

Game & Inland Fisheries Dept, 4010 W Broad St, Richmond, VA 23230-1528; 804-367-6135, 804-367-1064 (Fax), 8:15AM-5PM.

http://www.dgif.state.va.us

Indexing & Storage: Records are available from 1960 to the present. Records are indexed on computer from 1984 to the present. All motorized boats must be registered. All motorboats, or sailboats if over 18 ft are titled. Lien information will show on record.

Searching: All requests must be in writing. One of the following is required for a search: name, SSN, title #, hull #.

Access by: mail, in person, online.

Fee & Payment: If history or extensive research is required, there is a fee of $15.00 per boat. For simple record searches there is no fee, unless over 5 records are requested then the fee is $5.00 per record. Fee payee: Game & Inland Fisheries Dept. Prepayment required. No credit cards accepted.

Mail search: Turnaround time: 3 to 4 working days. No self addressed stamped envelope is required.

In person search: Turnaround time is usually immediate.

Online search: The VA boat registration database may be searched on the web at www.vipnet.org. There is both a free service and a more advanced pay service, but both require a subscription which is $50.00 a year. Other motor vehicle records are available.

Legislation Records

House of Delegates, Information & Public Relations, PO Box 406, Richmond, VA 23218 (Courier: 1st Floor, State Capitol Bldg, 9th and Grace Streets, Richmond, VA 23219); 804-698-1500, 877-391-3228 (Toll Free), 804-786-3215 (Fax), 8AM-5PM.

http://legis.state.va.us/vaonline/v.htm

Indexing & Storage: Records are available from 1994 on computer. Final disposition reports and patron reports are on microfiche from 1975 to 1996.

Searching: A request in writing to the Clerk of the House of Delegates is necessary to obtain a member's voting record and statements of economic interests. Include the following in your request-bill number, topic of bill, year. The name of the bill sponsor (patron) and topic of bill are helpful.

Access by: mail, phone, in person, online.

Fee & Payment: There is no search fee. The copy fee is $.50 per page over 10 and additional charges for other records. Fee payee: Treasurer of Virginia. Personal checks accepted. No credit cards accepted.

Mail search: Turnaround time: 1 to 2 days. No self addressed stamped envelope is required.

Phone search: Records are available by phone.

In person search: Searching is available in person.

Online search: Information can be found on the web site. There is no fee.

Other access: Lists of General Assembly members, information on General Assembly, documents summarizing bills introduced and enacted are all available through this office.

Voter Registration
Access to Records is Restricted

State Board of Elections, 200 N 9th Street, #101, Richmond, VA 23219; 804-786-6551, 804-371-0194 (Fax), 8:30AM-5PM.

http://www.sbe.state.va.us

Note: Individual searches must be done at the county or city level with the General Registrars. The state will sell all or portions of its statewide database (95 counties, 40 cities) to organizations promoting voter registration and participation.

GED Certificates

Virginia Dept of Education, GED Services, PO Box 2120, Richmond, VA 23218-2120; 804-225-2020, 804-786-7243 (Fax), 8:15AM-5PM.

http://www.pen.k12.va.us

Searching: To search, all of the following is required: a signed release, name, DOB, SSN, year of test and location of test.

Access by: mail, fax, in person.

Fee & Payment: There is no fee for a verification or for a transcript, but duplicate certificates are $10.00. Fee payee: VA Department of Education - GED Srvs. Prepayment required. Only money orders and cashier's checks are accepted. No credit cards accepted.

Mail search: Turnaround time: 1 to 2 days. No self addressed stamped envelope is required.

Fax search: Same criteria as mail searching.

In person search: Turnaround time is typically immediate.

Hunting License Information
Fishing License Information
Records not maintained by a state level agency.

Note: They do not have a central database.

Virginia State Licensing Agencies

Licenses Searchable Online

Accountant/Accounting Firm/Sponsor #10............ www.dpor.state.va.us/regulantlookup/
Acupuncturist #06... www.vipnet.org/dhp/cgi-bin/search_publicdb.cgi
Air Conditioning Contractor #10 .... www.dpor.state.va.us/regulantlookup/
Architect #10 .... www.dpor.state.va.us/regulantlookup/
Asbestos Related Occupation #10 .... www.dpor.state.va.us/regulantlookup/
Auctioneer #10 .... www.dpor.state.va.us/regulantlookup/
Barber #10.. www.dpor.state.va.us/regulantlookup/
Boxer #10 .... www.dpor.state.va.us/regulantlookup/
Carpenter #10... www.dpor.state.va.us/regulantlookup/
Cemetery Company #10 .... www.dpor.state.va.us/regulantlookup/
Chiropractor #06... www.vipnet.org/dhp/cgi-bin/search_publicdb.cgi
Clinical Nurse Specialist #06................................ www.vipnet.org/dhp/cgi-bin/search_publicdb.cgi
Contractor #10.. www.dpor.state.va.us/regulantlookup/
Cosmetologist/Cosmetology School/Business #10www.dpor.state.va.us/regulantlookup/
Dental Hygienist #06.. www.vipnet.org/dhp/cgi-bin/search_publicdb.cgi
Dentist #06 .... www.vipnet.org/dhp/cgi-bin/search_publicdb.cgi
Electrical Contractor #10...................................... www.dpor.state.va.us/regulantlookup/
Embalmer #06... www.vipnet.org/dhp/cgi-bin/search_publicdb.cgi
Engineer #10 .... www.dpor.state.va.us/regulantlookup/
Funeral Director #06 .... www.vipnet.org/dhp/cgi-bin/search_publicdb.cgi
Gas Fitter #10... www.dpor.state.va.us/regulantlookup/
Geologist #10 .... www.dpor.state.va.us/regulantlookup/
Hearing Aid Specialist #10 .... www.dpor.state.va.us/regulantlookup/
Heating & Air Conditioning Mechanic #10............ www.dpor.state.va.us/regulantlookup/
Heating Contractor #10... www.dpor.state.va.us/regulantlookup/
Interior Designer #10 .... www.dpor.state.va.us/regulantlookup/
Landscape Architect #10...................................... www.dpor.state.va.us/regulantlookup/
Lead-Related Occupation #10............................... www.dpor.state.va.us/regulantlookup/
Lobbyist #11... www.soc.state.va.us/databa.htm
Marriage & Family Therapist #06 .... www.vipnet.org/dhp/cgi-bin/search_publicdb.cgi
Medical Doctor #06... www.vipnet.org/dhp/cgi-bin/search_publicdb.cgi
Medical Equipment Supplier #06........................... www.vipnet.org/dhp/cgi-bin/search_publicdb.cgi
Nail Technician #10 .... www.dpor.state.va.us/regulantlookup/
Nurse/Nurse's Aide #06 .... www.vipnet.org/dhp/cgi-bin/search_publicdb.cgi
Nurse-LPN #06... www.vipnet.org/dhp/cgi-bin/search_publicdb.cgi
Nurse-RN #06... www.vipnet.org/dhp/cgi-bin/search_publicdb.cgi
Nursing Home Administrator/Preceptor #06 .... www.vipnet.org/dhp/cgi-bin/search_publicdb.cgi
Occupational Therapist #06 .... www.vipnet.org/dhp/cgi-bin/search_publicdb.cgi
Optician #10.. www.dpor.state.va.us/regulantlookup/
Optometrist #06.. www.odfinder.org/LicSearch.asp
Osteopathic Physician #06.................................... www.vipnet.org/dhp/cgi-bin/search_publicdb.cgi
Pharmacist/Pharmacy #06.................................... www.vipnet.org/dhp/cgi-bin/search_publicdb.cgi
Physical Therapist #06.. www.vipnet.org/dhp/cgi-bin/search_publicdb.cgi
Physician #06 .... www.vipnet.org/dhp/cgi-bin/search_publicdb.cgi
Pilot, Branch #10 .... www.dpor.state.va.us/regulantlookup/
Plumber #10.. www.dpor.state.va.us/regulantlookup/
Podiatrist #06 .... www.vipnet.org/dhp/cgi-bin/search_publicdb.cgi
Polygraph Examiner #10....................................... www.dpor.state.va.us/regulantlookup/
Property Association #10 .... www.dpor.state.va.us/regulantlookup/
Psychologist, Clinical/Applied #06........................ www.vipnet.org/dhp/cgi-bin/search_publicdb.cgi
Psychology School #06... www.vipnet.org/dhp/cgi-bin/search_publicdb.cgi
Public Accountant-CPA #10.................................. www.dpor.state.va.us/regulantlookup/
Real Estate Agent/Business/School #10............... www.dpor.state.va.us/regulantlookup/
Real Estate Appraiser/Appraiser Business #10..... www.dpor.state.va.us/regulantlookup/
Respiratory Care Practitioner #06 .... www.vipnet.org/dhp/cgi-bin/search_publicdb.cgi
Social Worker, Clinical #06.................................. www.vipnet.org/dhp/cgi-bin/search_publicdb.cgi
Soil Scientist #10 .... www.dpor.state.va.us/regulantlookup/
Speech Pathologist/Audiologist #06 .... www.vipnet.org/dhp/cgi-bin/search_publicdb.cgi
Substance Abuse Treatment Practitioner #06....... www.vipnet.org/dhp/cgi-bin/search_publicdb.cgi
Surveyor #10 .... www.dpor.state.va.us/regulantlookup/
Veterinarian/Veterinary Technician #06 .... www.vipnet.org/dhp/cgi-bin/search_publicdb.cgi
Waste Management Facility Operator #10 .... www.dpor.state.va.us/regulantlookup/
Waste Water Treatment Plant Operator #10 .... www.dpor.state.va.us/regulantlookup/
Wrestler #10.. www.dpor.state.va.us/regulantlookup/

Licensing Quick Finder

Accountant/Accounting Firm #10 804-367-8500
Acupuncturist #06 804-662-9908
Air Conditioning Contractor #10 804-367-8511
Alcoholic Beverage Distributor #01 804-213-4400
Architect #10.......................................804-367-8506
Asbestos Related Occupation #10 804-367-8595
Attorney/Attorney Associate #14...........804-775-0500
Auctioneer #10....................................804-367-8506
Barber #10...804-367-8509
Boxer #10...804-367-0186
Cardiac Technical Professional #15......804-371-3500
Carpenter #10......................................804-367-8511
Cemetery Company #10........................804-367-2039
Chiropractor #06..................................804-662-9908
Clinical Nurse Specialist #06 804-662-9909
Contractor #10.....................................804-367-8511
Cosmetologist/Cosmetology School/Business #10 .....
....804-367-8509
Counselor, Professional #06.................804-662-9912
Dental Hygienist #06 804-662-9906
Dentist #06 804-662-9906
Electrical Contractor #10 804-367-8511
Embalmer #06 804-662-9907
Emergency Medical Technician #15......804-371-3500
Engineer #10 804-367-8506
Funeral Director #06.............................804-662-9907
Gas Fitter #10 804-367-8511
Geologist #10.......................................804-367-2406
Hearing Aid Specialist #10...................804-367-8509
Heating & Air Conditioning Mechanic #10 ....
....804-367-8511
Heating Contractor #10 804-367-8511
Horse Racing #13 804-966-7400
Insurance Agent/Agency #02................804-371-9631

Interior Designer #10............................804-367-8506
Investment Advisor/Advisor Agency #12804-371-9686
Landscape Architect #10 804-367-8506
Lead-Related Occupation #10 804-367-8595
Lobbyist #11...804-786-2441
Marriage & Family Therapist #06 804-662-9912
Medical Doctor #06 804-662-9908
Medical Equipment Supplier #06...........804-662-9921
Nail Technician #10...............................804-367-8505
Notary Public #09.................................804-786-2441
Nurse/Nurse's Aide #06........................804-662-9909
Nurse-LPN #06 804-662-9909
Nurse-RN #06.......................................804-662-9900
Nursing Home Administrator/Preceptor #06 ....
....804-662-9111
Occupational Therapist #06 804-662-9908
Optician #10..804-367-8509
Optometrist #06 804-662-9910
Osteopathic Physician #06 804-662-9908
Paramedic #15......................................804-371-3500
Personal Protection Specialist #05........804-786-0460
Pesticide Applicator (Commercial) #4 ...804-786-3798
Pesticide Applicator (Private) #04 804-786-3798
Pesticide Business #04 804-786-3798
Pharmacist/Pharmacy #06....................804-662-9921
Physical Therapist #06 804-662-9908
Physician #06 804-662-9968
Pilot, Branch #10..................................804-367-8514
Plumber #10..804-367-8511
Podiatrist #06 804-662-9908
Polygraph Examiner #10 804-367-8506
Private Investigator #05........................804-786-0460
Property Association #10 804-367-8500
Psychologist, Clinical/Applied #06.........804-662-9913

Psychology School #06 804-662-9913
Public Accountant-CPA #10...................804-367-8505
Real Estate Agent/Firm/School #10 804-367-8526
Real Estate Appraiser/Appraiser Business #10 ....
....804-367-2039
Rehabilitation Provider #06....................804-662-9912
Respiratory Care Practitioner #06 804-662-9908
School Guidance Counselor #08 804-225-2022
School Library Media Specialist #08 804-225-2022
School Principal/Superintendent #08 804-225-2022
Securities Broker/Dealer/Dealer Agent #12 ....
....804-371-9686
Securities Brokerage #12 804-371-9187
Security Officer, Unarmed/Armed #05....804-786-0460
Security Technician (Electronic Security) #05.............
....804-786-0460
Shock/Trauma Professional #15 804-371-3500
Shorthand Reporter #03 703-768-8122
Social Worker, Clinical #06 804-662-9914
Soil Scientist #10 804-367-2785
Speech Pathologist/Audiologist #06.......804-662-9111
Substance Abuse Counselor #06...........804-662-9912
Substance Abuse Treatment Practitioner #06..............
....804-662-9912
Surveyor #10 804-367-8506
Teacher #08..804-225-2022
Veterinarian/Veterinary Technician #6....804-662-9915
Veterinary Facility #06...........................804-662-9915
Waste Management Facility Operator #10 ....
....804-367-8595
Waste Water Treatment Plant Operator #10.............
....804-367-8505
Wrestler #10 804-367-0186

Licensing Agency Information

#01 Alcoholic Beverage Control Board, 2901 Hermitage Rd, Richmond, VA 23220; 804-213-4400, Fax: 804-213-4586.
www.abc.state.va.us

#02 Bureau of Insurance, PO Box 1157, Richmond, VA 23209; 804-371-9801, Fax: 804-371-9511.
www.state.va.us/sec

#03 CSR Contact Person, 2404 Belle Haven Meadows, Alexandria, VA 22306; 703-768-8122, Fax: 703-768-8921.

#04 Department of Agriculture & Consumer Services, PO Box 1163, Richmond, VA 23218; 804-786-3798, Fax: 804-371-8598 Admin ofc.; 786-9149 lic. app..
www.vdacs.state.va.us/perticides

#05 Department of Criminal Justice, 805 E Broad St, 9th Fl, Richmond, VA 23219; 804-786-4000, Fax: 804-786-6344.
www.dcjs.state.va.us

#06 Department of Health Professions, 6606 W Broad St, 4th Fl, Richmond, VA 23230-1717; 804-662-9900, Fax: 804-662-9943.

www.dhp.state.va.us
Direct web site URL to search for licensees: www.vipnet.org/dhp/cgi-bin/search_publicdb.cgi

#08 Office of Professional Licensure, PO Box 2120 (101 N 14th St, James Monroe Bldg.), Richmond, VA 23218-2120; 804-225-2022, Fax: 804-225-2031.
www.pen.k12.va.us

#09 Office of Secretary of Commonwealth, PO Box 1795, Richmond, VA 23218; 804-786-2441, Fax: 804-371-0017.
www.soc.state.va.us

#10 Department of Professional & Occupation Regulation, 3600 W Broad St, Richmond, VA 23230-4917; 804-367-8500, Fax: 804-367-2475.
www.state.va.us/dpor
Direct web site URL to search for licensees: www.dpor.state.va.us/regulantlookup/

#11 Secretary of the Commonwealth, PO Box 2454, Richmond, VA 23219-2454; 804-781-2441, Fax: 804-371-0017.
www.soc.state.va.us
Direct web site URL to search for licensees: www.soc.state.va.us/databa.htm. You can search

online using registration year, principal name, and lobbyist name.

#12 Corporation Commission, PO Box 1197 (1300 E Main, 9th Fl), Richmond, VA 23218; 804-371-9187, Fax: 804-371-9911.
www.state.va.us/sec/division/SRF/webpages/homepageJavaB.htm

#13 Virginia Racing Commission, 10700 Horsemans Road , PO Box 208, New Kent, VA 23124; 804-966-7400, Fax: 804-966-7418.
www.vrc.state.va.us

#14 State Bar Association, 707 E Main St, #1500, Richmond, VA 23219-2800; 804-775-0500, Fax: 804-775-0501.
www.vsb.org

#15 Department of Health, 1538 E Parham Rd, Richmond, VA 23228; 804-371-3500, Fax: 804-371-3543.
www.voh.state.va.us/oems

Virginia Federal Courts

The following list indicates the district and division name for each county in the state. If the bankruptcy court location is different from the district court, then the location of the bankruptcy court appears in parentheses.

County/Court Cross Reference

County	District	Division
Accomack	Eastern	Norfolk
Albemarle	Western	Charlottesville (Lynchburg)
Alexandria City	Eastern	Alexandria
Alleghany	Western	Roanoke (Harrisonburg)
Amelia	Eastern	Richmond
Amherst	Western	Lynchburg
Appomattox	Western	Lynchburg
Arlington	Eastern	Alexandria
Augusta	Western	Harrisonburg
Bath	Western	Harrisonburg
Bedford	Western	Lynchburg
Bedford City	Western	Lynchburg
Bland	Western	Roanoke
Botetourt	Western	Roanoke
Bristol City	Western	Abingdon (Roanoke)
Brunswick	Eastern	Richmond
Buchanan	Western	Abingdon (Roanoke)
Buckingham	Western	Lynchburg
Buena Vista City	Western	Lynchburg (Harrisonburg)
Campbell	Western	Lynchburg
Caroline	Eastern	Richmond
Carroll	Western	Roanoke
Charles City	Eastern	Richmond
Charlotte	Western	Danville (Lynchburg)
Charlottesville City	Western	Charlottesville (Lynchburg)
Chesapeake City	Eastern	Norfolk
Chesterfield	Eastern	Richmond
Clarke	Western	Harrisonburg
Clifton Forge City	Western	Roanoke (Harrisonburg)
Colonial Heights City	Eastern	Richmond
Covington City	Western	Roanoke (Harrisonburg)
Craig	Western	Roanoke
Culpeper	Western	Charlottesville (Lynchburg)
Cumberland	Western	Lynchburg
Danville City	Western	Danville (Lynchburg)
Dickenson	Western	Big Stone Gap (Roanoke)
Dinwiddie	Eastern	Richmond
Emporia City	Eastern	Richmond
Essex	Eastern	Richmond
Fairfax	Eastern	Alexandria
Fairfax City	Eastern	Alexandria
Falls Church City	Eastern	Alexandria
Fauquier	Eastern	Alexandria
Floyd	Western	Roanoke
Fluvanna	Western	Charlottesville (Lynchburg)
Franklin	Western	Roanoke
Franklin City	Eastern	Norfolk
Frederick	Western	Harrisonburg
Fredericksburg City	Eastern	Richmond
Galax City	Western	Roanoke
Giles	Western	Roanoke
Gloucester	Eastern	Newport News
Goochland	Eastern	Richmond
Grayson	Western	Roanoke
Greene	Western	Charlottesville (Lynchburg)
Greensville	Eastern	Richmond
Halifax	Western	Danville (Lynchburg)
Hampton City	Eastern	Newport News
Hanover	Eastern	Richmond
Harrisonburg City	Western	Harrisonburg
Henrico	Eastern	Richmond
Henry	Western	Danville (Lynchburg)
Highland	Western	Harrisonburg
Hopewell City	Eastern	Richmond
Isle of Wight	Eastern	Norfolk
James City	Eastern	Newport News
King George	Eastern	Richmond
King William	Eastern	Richmond
King and Queen	Eastern	Richmond
Lancaster	Eastern	Richmond
Lee	Western	Big Stone Gap (Roanoke)
Lexington City	Western	Lynchburg (Harrisonburg)
Loudoun	Eastern	Alexandria
Louisa	Western	Charlottesville (Lynchburg)
Lunenburg	Eastern	Richmond
Lynchburg City	Western	Lynchburg
Madison	Western	Charlottesville (Lynchburg)
Manassas City	Eastern	Alexandria
Manassas Park City	Eastern	Alexandria
Martinsville City	Western	Lynchburg
Mathews	Eastern	Newport News
Mecklenburg	Eastern	Richmond
Middlesex	Eastern	Richmond
Montgomery	Western	Roanoke
Nelson	Western	Charlottesville (Lynchburg)
New Kent	Eastern	Richmond
Newport News City	Eastern	Newport News
Norfolk City	Eastern	Norfolk
Northampton	Eastern	Norfolk
Northumberland	Eastern	Richmond
Norton City	Western	Big Stone Gap (Roanoke)
Nottoway	Eastern	Richmond
Orange	Western	Charlottesville (Lynchburg)
Page	Western	Harrisonburg
Patrick	Western	Danville (Lynchburg)
Petersburg City	Eastern	Richmond
Pittsylvania	Western	Danville (Lynchburg)
Poquoson City	Eastern	Newport News
Portsmouth City	Eastern	Norfolk
Powhatan	Eastern	Richmond

Prince Edward	Eastern	Richmond		Southampton	Eastern	Norfolk
Prince George	Eastern	Richmond		Spotsylvania	Eastern	Richmond
Prince William	Eastern	Alexandria		Stafford	Eastern	Alexandria
Pulaski	Western	Roanoke		Staunton City	Western	Harrisonburg
Radford City	Western	Roanoke		Suffolk City	Eastern	Norfolk
Rappahannock	Western	Charlottesville (Harrisonburg)		Surry	Eastern	Richmond
Richmond	Eastern	Richmond		Sussex	Eastern	Richmond
Richmond City	Eastern	Richmond		Tazewell	Western	Abingdon (Roanoke)
Roanoke	Western	Roanoke		Virginia Beach City	Eastern	Norfolk
Roanoke City	Western	Roanoke		Warren	Western	Harrisonburg
Rockbridge	Western	Lynchburg (Harrisonburg)		Washington	Western	Abingdon (Roanoke)
Rockingham	Western	Harrisonburg		Waynesboro City	Western	Harrisonburg
Russell	Western	Abingdon (Roanoke)		Westmoreland	Eastern	Richmond
Salem City	Western	Roanoke		Williamsburg City	Eastern	Newport News
Scott	Western	Big Stone Gap (Roanoke)		Winchester City	Western	Harrisonburg
Shenandoah	Western	Harrisonburg		Wise	Western	Big Stone Gap (Roanoke)
Smyth	Western	Abingdon (Roanoke)		Wythe	Western	Roanoke
South Boston City	Western	Danville (Lynchburg)		York	Eastern	Newport News

US District Court

Eastern District of Virginia

Alexandria Division 401 Courthouse Square, Alexandria, VA 22314 (Courier Address: Use mail address for courier delivery), 703-299-2100.

http://www.vaed.uscourts.gov

Counties: Arlington, Fairfax, Fauquier, Loudoun, Prince William, Stafford, City of Alexandria, City of Fairfax, City of Falls Church, City of Manassas, City of Manassas Park.

Indexing/Storage: Cases are indexed by defendant and plaintiff as well as by case number. New cases are available in the index 1 day after filing date. A computer index is maintained. Records are indexed and stored in numerical order. Open records are located at this court.

Fee & Payment: The fee is $20.00 per item (one party name or case number). Payment may be made by money order, cashier check, personal check. Prepayment is required. Payee: Clerk, US District Court. Certification fee: $7.00 per document. Copy fee: $.50 per page.

Phone Search: Only docket information is available by phone.

Mail Search: Always enclose a stamped self addressed envelope.

In Person: In person searching is available.

PACER: Sign-up number is 800-676-6856. Access fee is $.60 per minute. Toll-free access: 800-852-5186. Local access: 703-299-2158. Case records are available back to June 1990. New records are available online after 1 day. PACER is available online at http://pacer.vaed.uscourts.gov.

Newport News Division Clerk's Office, PO Box 494, Newport News, VA 23607 (Courier Address: USPO Bldg, Room 201, 101 25th St, Newport News, VA 23607), 757-223-4600.

http://www.vaed.uscourts.gov

Counties: Gloucester, James City, Mathews, York, City of Hampton, City of Newport News, City of Poquoson, City of Williamsburg.

Indexing/Storage: Cases are indexed by defendant and plaintiff as well as by case number.

New cases are available in the index 1 day after filing date. A computer index is maintained. Open records are located at this court.

Fee & Payment: The fee is $20.00 per item (one party name or case number). Payment may be made by money order, cashier check, personal check. Prepayment is required. Payee: Clerk, US District Court. Certification fee: $7.00 per document. Copy fee: $.50 per page.

Phone Search: Only docket information is available by phone. The court will not honor requests for lists of names over the phone.

Mail Search: Always enclose a stamped self addressed envelope.

In Person: In person searching is available.

PACER: Sign-up number is 800-676-6856. Access fee is $.60 per minute. Toll-free access: 800-852-5186. Local access: 703-299-2158. Case records are available back to June 1990. New records are available online after 1 day. PACER is available online at http://pacer.vaed.uscourts.gov.

Norfolk Division US Courthouse, Room 193, 600 Granby St, Norfolk, VA 23510 (Courier Address: Use mail address for courier delivery), 757-222-7204.

http://www.vaed.uscourts.gov

Counties: Accomack, City of Chesapeake, City of Franklin, Isle of Wight, City of Norfolk, Northampton, City of Portsmouth, City of Suffolk, Southampton, City of Virginia Beach.

Indexing/Storage: Cases are indexed by defendant and plaintiff as well as by case number. New cases are available in the index 1 day after filing date. Both computer and card indexes are maintained. Records are also indexed by microfiche from January 1981 to June 1991. Records prior to 1981 are in the card index. Open records are located at this court.

Fee & Payment: The fee is $20.00 per item (one party name or case number). Payment may be made by money order, cashier check, business check. Personal checks are not accepted. Prepayment is required. Payee: Clerk, US District Court. Certification fee: $7.00 per document. Copy fee: $.50 per page.

Phone Search: Searching is not available by phone. Only limited docket information is available by phone.

Mail Search: Always enclose a stamped self addressed envelope.

In Person: In person searching is available.

PACER: Sign-up number is 800-676-6856. Access fee is $.60 per minute. Toll-free access: 800-852-5186. Local access: 703-299-2158. Case records are available back to June 1990. New records are available online after 1 day. PACER is available online at http://pacer.vaed.uscourts.gov.

Richmond Division Lewis F Powell, Jr Courthouse Bldg, 1000 E Main St, Room 305, Richmond, VA 23219-3525 (Courier Address: Use mail address for courier delivery), 804-916-2200.

Counties: Amelia, Brunswick, Caroline, Charles City, Chesterfield, Dinwiddie, Essex, Goochland, Greensville, Hanover, Henrico, King and Queen, King George, King William, Lancaster, Lunenburg, Mecklenburg, Middlesex, New Kent, Northumberland, Nottoway, City ofPetersburg, Powhatan, Prince Edward, Prince George, Richmond, City of Richmond, Spotsylvania, Surry, Sussex, Westmoreland, City of Colonial Heights, City of Emporia, City of Fredericksburg, City of Hopewell.

Indexing/Storage: Cases are indexed by defendant and plaintiff as well as by case number. New cases are available in the index 1 day after filing date. A computer index is maintained. Records are indexed by case number and stored at the court. Open records are located at this court.

Fee & Payment: The fee is $20.00 per item (one party name or case number). Payment may be made by money order, cashier check, personal check. Prepayment is required. Payee: Clerk's Office, US District Court. Certification fee: $7.00 per document. Copy fee: $.50 per page.

Phone Search: Only docket information is available by phone. The court will not honor requests for lists of names over the phone.

Mail Search: A stamped self addressed envelope is not required.

In Person: In person searching is available.

PACER: Sign-up number is 800-676-6856. Access fee is $.60 per minute. Toll-free access:

800-852-5186. Local access: 703-299-2158. Case records are available back to June 1990. New records are available online after 1 day. PACER is available online at http://pacer.vaed.uscourts.gov.

US Bankruptcy Court

Eastern District of Virginia

Alexandria Division PO Box 19247, Alexandria, VA 22320-0247 (Courier Address: Suite 100, 200 S Washington St, Alexandria, VA 22314), 703-258-1200.

http://www.vaeb.uscourts.gov

Counties: City of Alexandria, Arlington, Fairfax, City of Fairfax, City of Falls Church, Fauquier, Loudoun, City of Manassas, City of Manassas Park, Prince William, Stafford.

Indexing/Storage: Cases are indexed by debtor as well as by case number. New cases are available in the index 2 days after filing date. A creditor register is also kept for each case. Both computer and card indexes are maintained. Index card are for cases prior to December 1989. Open records are located at this court.

Fee & Payment: The fee is $20.00 per item (one party name or case number). Payment may be made by money order, cashier check, personal check. Prepayment is required. Debtor's checks are not accepted. Payee: Clerk, US Bankruptcy Court. Certification fee: $7.00 per document. Copy fee: $.50 per page.

Phone Search: Docket information is available by phone. An automated voice case information service (VCIS) is available. Call VCIS at 800-326-5879 or 804-771-2736.

Mail Search: Always enclose a stamped self addressed envelope.

In Person: In person searching is available.

PACER: Sign-up number is 800-676-6856. Access fee is $.60 per minute. Toll-free access: 800-890-2858. Local access: 703-258-1234. Use of PC Anywhere v4.0 suggested. Case records are available back to mid 1989. Records are never purged. New civil records are available online after 1 day.

Electronic Filing: Electronic filing information is available online at http://ecf.vaeb.uscourts.gov

Other Online Access: Search records using the Internet. Searching is currently free. To search by name - www.vaeb.uscourts.gov/home/SearchNM. html. To search by case number - www.vaeb.uscourts.gov/home/SearchCSNUM.htm l. More options available from main site.

Newport News Division c/o Norfolk Bankruptcy Court, PO Box 1938, Norfolk, VA 23501-1938 (Courier Address: Walter E Hoffman US Courthouse, Room 400, 600 Granby St, Norfolk, VA 23510), 757-222-7500.

http://www.vaeb.uscourts.gov

Counties: Newport News City. Records are at the Norfolk Bankruptcy Court.

Phone Search: Call for name, case number, chapter, filing date, judge, attorney for debtor, trustee, Social Security number and date discharged. An automated voice case information service (VCIS) is available. Call VCIS at 800-326-5879 or 804-771-2736.

Mail Search: Always enclose a stamped self addressed envelope.

PACER: Sign-up number is 800-676-6856. Access fee is $.60 per minute. Toll-free access: 800-890-2785. Local access: 757-595-1365. New civil records are available online after 7 days.

Electronic Filing: Electronic filing information is available online at http://ecf.vaeb.uscourts.gov

Other Online Access: Search records using the Internet. Searching is currently free. To search by name - www.vaeb.uscourts.gov/home/SearchNM. html. To search by case number - www.vaeb.uscourts.gov/home/SearchCSNUM.htm l. More options available from main site.

Norfolk Division PO Box 1938, Norfolk, VA 23501-1938 (Courier Address: Walter E Hoffman US Courthouse, Room 400, 600 Granby St, Norfolk, VA 23510), 757-222-7500.

http://www.vaeb.uscourts.gov

Counties: Accomack, City of Cape Charles, City of Chesapeake, City of Franklin, Gloucester, City of Hampton, Isle of Wight, James City, Matthews, City of Norfolk, Northampton, City of PoquosonCity of Portsmouth, Southampton, City of Suffolk,City of Virginia Beach, City of Williamsburg, York.

Indexing/Storage: Cases are indexed by debtor as well as by case number. New cases are available in the index 2 days after filing date. A computer index is maintained. Open records are located at this court.

Fee & Payment: The fee is $20.00 per item (one party name or case number). Payment may be made by money order, cashier check, personal check. Prepayment is required. The search fee checks should be made to the clerk. The searcher must use Ikon Management Services for copies. The copy fee checks should be made to Ikon Management Services. Debtor checks are not accepted. Payee: Clerk, US Bankruptcy Court. Certification fee: $7.00 per document. Copy fee: $.50 per page. The fee for copies made by court personnel is $.31 per page.

Phone Search: Call for name, case number, chapter, filing date, judge, attorney for debtor, trustee, Social Security number and date discharged. An automated voice case information service (VCIS) is available. Call VCIS at 800-326-5879 or 804-771-2736.

Mail Search: Always enclose a stamped self addressed envelope.

In Person: In person searching is available.

PACER: Sign-up number is 800-676-6856. Access fee is $.60 per minute. Toll-free access: 800-890-2954. Local access: 757-222-7441. New civil records are available online after 7 days.

Electronic Filing: Electronic filing information is available online at http://ecf.vaeb.uscourts.gov

Other Online Access: Search records using the Internet. Searching is currently free; search by name - www.vaeb.uscourts.gov/home/SearchNM. html. To search by case number - www.vaeb.uscourts.gov/home/SearchCSNUM.htm l. More options available from main site.

Richmond Division Office of the clerk, 1100 E Main St, Room 310, Richmond, VA 23219-3515 (Courier Address: 1100 E Main St, Room 301, Richmond, VA 23219), 804-916-2400.

http://www.vaeb.uscourts.gov

Counties: Amelia, Brunswick, Caroline, Charles City, Chesterfield, City of Colonial Heights, Dinwiddie, City of Emporia, Essex, City of Fredericksburg, Goochland, Greensville, Hanover, Henrico, City of Hopewell, King and Queen, King George, King William,Lancaster, Lunenburg, Mecklenburg, Middlesex, New Kent, Northumberland, Nottoway, City of Petersburg, Powhatan, Prince Edward, Prince George, Richmond, City of Richmond, Spotsylvania, Surry, Sussex, Westmoreland.

Indexing/Storage: Cases are indexed by debtor as well as by case number. New cases are available in the index 1 day after filing date. A computer index is maintained. Open records are located at this court.

Fee & Payment: The fee is $20.00 per item (one party name or case number). Payment may be made by money order, cashier check, personal check. Prepayment is required. The court will not send statements. Debtor checks are not accepted. Dave Jones & Assoc Copy Svc handles search requests. You must fax your request to them at 804-780-0652. They will call you back with the fees. Payee: Clerk, US Bankruptcy Court. Certification fee: $7.00 per document. Copy fee: $.50 per page.

Phone Search: Only docket information is available by phone. An automated voice case information service (VCIS) is available. Call VCIS at 800-326-5879 or.

Mail Search: Always enclose a stamped self addressed envelope.

In Person: In person searching is available.

PACER: Sign-up number is. Access fee is. Toll-free access: 800-890-2829. Local access: 804-916-2484. New records are available online after.

Electronic Filing: Electronic filing information is available online at http://ecf.vaeb.uscourts.gov

Other Online Access: Search records using the Internet. Searching is currently free. To search by name - www.vaeb.uscourts.gov/home/SearchNM. html. To search by case number - www.vaeb.uscourts.gov/home/SearchCSNUM.htm l. More options available from main site.

US District Court

Western District of Virginia

Abingdon Division Clerk's Office, PO Box 398, Abingdon, VA 24212 (Courier Address: 180 W Main St, Abingdon, VA 24210), 540-628-5116, Fax: 540-628-1028.

http://www.vawd.uscourts.gov

Counties: Buchanan, City of Bristol, Russell, Smyth, Tazewell, Washington.

Indexing/Storage: Cases are indexed by defendant and plaintiff as well as by case number. New cases are available in the index immediately after filing date. Both computer and card indexes are maintained. Open records are located at this court.

Fee & Payment: The fee is $20.00 per item (one party name or case number). Payment may be made by money order, cashier check, personal check. Court will bill for searches and copies. Payee: Clerk, US District Court. Certification fee: $7.00 per document. Copy fee: $.50 per page. You are allowed to make your own copies. These copies cost $.10 per page.

Phone Search: Docket information available by phone.

Fax Search: Will accept fax for searches from 1992 to present only.

Mail Search: A stamped self addressed envelope is not required.

In Person: In person searching is available.

PACER: Sign-up number is 800-676-6856. Access fee is. Toll-free access: 888-279-7848. Local access: 540-857-5140. Case records are available back to Mid 1990. Records are never purged. New records are available online after 1 day. PACER is available online at http://pacer.vawd.uscourts.gov.

Big Stone Gap Division PO Box 490, Big Stone Gap, VA 24219 (Courier Address: 322 Wood Ave E, Room 203, Big Stone Gap, VA 24219), 540-523-3557, Fax: 540-523-6214.

http://www.vawd.uscourts.gov

Counties: Dickenson, Lee, Scott, Wise, City of Norton.

Indexing/Storage: Cases are indexed by defendant and plaintiff as well as by case number. New cases are available in the index immediately after filing date. The style of the case is needed to conduct a search. A civil action number is very helpful. A computer index is maintained. A microfilm index is also maintained for older cases. Open records are located at this court.

Fee & Payment: The fee is $20.00 per item (one party name or case number). Payment may be made by money order, cashier check, personal check. Payee: Clerk, US District Court. Certification fee: $7.00 per document. Copy fee: $.50 per page. You are allowed to make your own copies. These copies cost $.50 per page.

Phone Search: Only docket information available.

Mail Search: Always enclose a stamped self addressed envelope.

In Person: In person searching is available.

PACER: Sign-up number is 800-676-6856. Access fee is. Toll-free access: 888-279-7848. Local access: 540-857-5140. Case records are available back to Mid 1990. Records are never purged. New records are available online after 1 day.

Charlottesville Division Clerk, Room 304, 255 W Main St, Charlottesville, VA 22902 (Courier Address: Use mail address for courier delivery), 804-296-9284.

http://www.vawd.uscourts.gov

Counties: Albemarle, Culpeper, Fluvanna, Greene, Louisa, Madison, Nelson, Orange, Rappahannock, City of Charlottesville.

Indexing/Storage: Cases are indexed by defendant and plaintiff as well as by case number. New cases are available in the index immediately after filing date. Both computer and card indexes are maintained. Records are indexed on microfiche from 1981 to 1991, and on card prior to that. Open records are located at this court. District wide searches are available from this court for any information within the district.

Fee & Payment: The fee is $20.00 per item (one party name or case number). Payment may be made by money order, cashier check, personal check. Prepayment is required. Payee: Clerk, US District Court. Certification fee: $7.00 per document. Copy fee: $.50 per page. You are allowed to make your own copies. These copies cost $.50 per page. Court only searches computer index. You may search microfiche index.

Phone Search: Searching not available by phone.

Mail Search: Always enclose a stamped self addressed envelope.

In Person: In person searching is available.

PACER: Sign-up number is 800-676-6856. Access fee is. Toll-free access: 888-279-7848. Local access: 540-857-5140. Case records are available back to Mid 1990. Records are never purged. New records are available online after 1 day. PACER is available online at http://pacer.vawd.uscourts.gov.

Danville Division PO Box 52, Danville, VA 24543-0053 (Courier Address: Dan Daniel Post Office Bldg, Room 202, 700 Main St, Danville, VA 24541), 804-793-7147, Fax: 804-793-0284.

http://www.vawd.uscourts.gov

Counties: Charlotte, Halifax, Henry, Patrick, Pittsylvania, City of Danville, City of Martinsville, City of South Boston.

Indexing/Storage: Cases are indexed by defendant and plaintiff as well as by case number. New cases are available in the index immediately after filing date. Both computer and card indexes are maintained. Open records are located at this court.

Fee & Payment: The fee is $20.00 per item (one party name or case number). Payment may be made by money order, cashier check, personal check. Prepayment is required. Payee: Clerk, US District Court. Certification fee: $7.00 per document. Copy fee: $.50 per page.

Phone Search: If there is an expedited request and the $15.00 search fee is prepaid, the court will call to give the information, and follow with a written response.

Mail Search: A stamped self addressed envelope is not required.

In Person: In person searching is available.

PACER: Sign-up number is 800-676-6856. Access fee is. Toll-free access: 888-279-7848. Local access: 540-857-5140. Case records are available back to Mid 1990. Records are never purged. New records are available online after 1 day. PACER is available online at http://pacer.vawd.uscourts.gov.

Harrisonburg Division Clerk, PO Box 1207, Harrisonburg, VA 22801 (Courier Address: Post Office Bldg, 116 N Main St, Room 314, Harrisonburg, VA 22801), 540-434-3181.

http://www.vawd.uscourts.gov

Counties: Augusta, Bath, Clarke, Frederick, Highland, Page, Rockingham, Shenandoah, Warren, City of Harrisonburg, City of Staunton, City of Waynesboro, City of Winchester.

Indexing/Storage: Cases are indexed by defendant and plaintiff as well as by case number. New cases are available in the index 1-2 days after filing date. Both computer and card indexes are maintained. Records are indexed on computer for civil cases from 1991 and criminal cases from 1993. Open records are located at this court. District wide searches are available from this court 1-2 days after it is filed, but the court prefers that searches be conducted where the case is filed.

Fee & Payment: The fee is $20.00 per item (one party name or case number). Payment may be made by money order, cashier check, personal check. Prepayment is required. Payee: Clerk, US District Court. Certification fee: $7.00 per document. Copy fee: $.50 per page.

Phone Search: Limited information available by phone.

Mail Search: A stamped self addressed envelope is not required.

In Person: In person searching is available.

PACER: Sign-up number is 800-676-6856. Access fee is. Toll-free access: 888-279-7848. Local access: 540-857-5140. Case records are available back to Mid 1990. Records are never purged. New records are available online after 1 day. PACER is available online at http://pacer.vawd.uscourts.gov.

Lynchburg Division Clerk, PO Box 744, Lynchburg, VA 24505 (Courier Address: Room 212, 1100 Main St, Lynchburg, VA 24504), 804-847-5722.

http://www.vawd.uscourts.gov

Counties: Amherst, Appomattox, Bedford, Buckingham, Campbell, Cumberland, Rockbridge, City of Bedford, City of Buena Vista, City of Lexington, City of Lynchburg.

Indexing/Storage: Cases are indexed by defendant and plaintiff as well as by case number. New cases are available in the index immediately after filing date. Both computer and card indexes are maintained. The computer index goes back to 1989. Open records are located at this court.

Fee & Payment: The fee is $20.00 per item (one party name or case number). Payment may be made by money order, cashier check, personal check. Prepayment is required. Payee: Clerk, US District Court. Certification fee: $7.00 per document. Copy fee: $.50 per page.

Phone Search: Only docket information available.

Mail Search: A stamped self addressed envelope is not required.

In Person: In person searching is available.

PACER: Sign-up number is 800-676-6856. Access fee is. Toll-free access: 888-279-7848. Local access: 540-857-5140. Case records are available back to Mid 1990. Records are never purged. New records are available online after 1 day. PACER is available online at http://pacer.vawd.uscourts.gov.

Roanoke Division Clerk, PO Box 1234, Roanoke, VA 24006 (Courier Address: 210 Franklin Rd SW, Roanoke, VA 24011), 540-857-5100, Fax: 540-857-5110.

http://www.vawd.uscourts.gov

Counties: Alleghany, Bland, Botetourt, Carroll, Craig, Floyd, Franklin, Giles, Grayson, Montgomery, Pulaski, Roanoke, Wythe, City of Covington, City of Clifton Forge, City of Galax, City of Radford, City of Roanoke, City of Salem.

Indexing/Storage: Cases are indexed by defendant and plaintiff as well as by case number. New cases are available in the index immediately after filing date. Both computer and card indexes are maintained. Records are also indexed on microfiche. The automated in house system is available for records from 1992. Open records are located at this court. District wide searches are available for all records from this court.

Fee & Payment: The fee is $20.00 per item (one party name or case number). Payment may be made by money order, cashier check, personal check. Prepayment is required. Payee: Clerk, US District Court. Certification fee: $7.00 per document. Copy fee: $.50 per page.

Phone Search: If there is an expedited request and the $15.00 search fee is prepaid, the court will call to give the information. However, a written response will follow.

Mail Search: A stamped self addressed envelope is not required.

In Person: In person searching is available.

PACER: Sign-up number is 800-676-6856. Access fee is. Toll-free access: 888-279-7848. Local access: 540-857-5140. Case records are available back to Mid 1990. Records are never purged. New records are available online after 1 day. PACER is available online at http://pacer.vawd.uscourts.gov.

US Bankruptcy Court

Western District of Virginia

Harrisonburg Division PO Box 1407, Harrisonburg, VA 22803 (Courier Address: 116 N Main St, Harrisonburg, VA 22801), 540-434-8327, Fax: 540-434-9715.

http://www.vawb.uscourts.gov

Counties: Alleghany, Augusta, Bath, City of Buena Vista, Clarke, City of Clifton Forge, City of Covington, Frederick, City of Harrisonburg, Highland, City of Lexington, Page, Rappahannock, Rockbridge, Rockingham, Shenandoah, City of Staunton, Warren, City ofWaynesboro, City of Winchester.

Indexing/Storage: Cases are indexed by debtor as well as by case number. New cases are available in the index immediately after filing date. Both computer and card indexes are maintained. The computer index goes back to 1986. Older cases are on a card index. Open records are located at this court.

Fee & Payment: The fee is $20.00 per item (one party name or case number). Payment may be made by money order, cashier check, business check. Personal checks are not accepted. Prepayment is required. Payee: Clerk, US Bankruptcy Court. Certification fee: $7.00 per document. Copy fee: $.50 per page.

Phone Search: Only docket information is available by phone, and only if it is available from the computer.

Mail Search: Always enclose a stamped self addressed envelope.

In Person: In person searching is available.

PACER: Sign-up number is 800-676-6856. Access fee is $.60 per minute. Toll-free access: 800-248-0329. Local access: 540-434-8373. Case records are available back to March 1986. Records are never purged. New civil records are available online after 1 day.

Other Online Access: Search records on the Internet using RACER at https://pacer.vawb.uscourts.gov/Perl/bkplog.html. Access fee is 7 cents per page.

Lynchburg Division PO Box 6400, Lynchburg, VA 24505 (Courier Address: 1100 Main St, Room 226, Lynchburg, VA 24504), 804-845-0317.

http://www.vawb.uscourts.gov

Counties: Albemarle, Amherst, Appomattox, Bedford, City of Bedford, Buckingham, Campbell, Charlotte, City of Charlottesville, Culpeper, Cumberland, City of Danville, Fluvanna, Greene, Halifax, Henry, Louisa, City of Lynchburg, Madison, City of Martinsville,Nelson, Orange, Patrick, Pittsylvania, City of South Boston.

Indexing/Storage: Cases are indexed by debtor as well as by case number. New cases are available in the index 24 hours after filing date. A computer index is maintained. The computer index goes back to 1986. Open records are located at this court.

Fee & Payment: The fee is $20.00 per item (one party name or case number). Payment may be made by money order, cashier check, business check. Personal checks are not accepted. Prepayment is required. Payee: Clerk, US Bankruptcy Court. Certification fee: $7.00 per document. Copy fee: $.50 per page.

Phone Search: Only the name, date filed and chapter will be released over the phone.

Mail Search: Always enclose a stamped self addressed envelope.

In Person: In person searching is available.

PACER: Sign-up number is 800-676-6856. Access fee is $.60 per minute. Toll-free access: 800-248-2469. Local access: 804-528-9003. Case records are available back to 1986. New civil records are available online after 1 day.

Other Online Access: Search records on the Internet using RACER at https://pacer.vawb.uscourts.gov/Perl/bkplog.html. Access fee is 7 cents per page.

Roanoke Division PO Box 2390, Roanoke, VA 24010 (Courier Address: Commonwealth Bldg, 210 Church Ave, Roanoke, VA 24011), 540-857-2391, Fax: 540-857-2873.

http://www.vawb.uscourts.gov

Counties: Bland, Botetourt, City of Bristol, Buchanan, Carroll, Craig, Dickenson, Floyd, Franklin, City of Galax, Giles, Grayson, Lee, Montgomery, City of Norton, Pulaski, City of Radford, Roanoke, City of Roanoke, Russell, City of Salem, Scott, Smyth, Tazewell,Washington, Wise, Wythe.

Indexing/Storage: Cases are indexed by debtor and creditors as well as by case number. New cases are available in the index same day if possible after filing date. A computer index is maintained. Records are indexed numerically (for example: 7-92-00123 = office number, year and 5 digit case number). Open records are located at this court.

Fee & Payment: The fee is $20.00 per item (one party name or case number). Payment may be made by money order, cashier check. Business checks are not accepted. Personal checks are not accepted. Prepayment is required. Only firm checks will be accepted. Payee: Clerk, US Bankruptcy Court. Certification fee: $7.00 per document. Copy fee: $.50 per page.

Phone Search: Searching is not available by phone. Only the number of pages of the requested items will be given over the phone.

Mail Search: Always enclose a stamped self addressed envelope.

In Person: In person searching is available.

PACER: Sign-up number is 800-676-6856. Access fee is $.60 per minute. Toll-free access: 800-249-9839. Local access: 540-857-2319. Case records are available back to 1988. Records are never purged. New civil records are available online after 1 day.

Other Online Access: Search records on the Internet using RACER at https://pacer.vawb.uscourts.gov/Perl/bkplog.html. Access fee is 7 cents per page.

Virginia County Courts

Court	Jurisdiction	No. of Courts	How Organized
Circuit Courts*	General	117	31 Circuits
District Courts*	Limited	123	
Combined Courts*		5	

* Profiled in this Sourcebook.

Court	CIVIL								
	Tort	Contract	Real Estate	Min. Claim	Max. Claim	Small Claims	Estate	Eviction	Domestic Relations
Circuit Courts*	X	X	X	$15,000	No Max		X		X
District Courts*	X	X	X	$0	$15,000			X	X

Court	CRIMINAL				
	Felony	Misdemeanor	DWI/DUI	Preliminary Hearing	Juvenile
Circuit Courts*	X				
District Courts*		X	X	X	X

ADMINISTRATION

Executive Secretary, Administrative Office of Courts, 100 N 9th St 3rd Fl, Supreme Court Bldg, Richmond, VA, 23219; 804-786-6455, Fax: 804-786-4542.

www.courts.state.va.us

COURT STRUCTURE

117 Circuit Courts in 31 districts are the courts of general jurisdiction. There are 123 District Courts of limited jurisdiction. Please note that a district can comprise a county or a city. Records of civil action from $3000 to $15,000 can be at either the Circuit or District Court as either can have jurisdiction. It is necessary to check both record locations as there is no concurrent database nor index.

The upper limit for civil actions in District Court was raised from $10,000 to $15,000 as of July 1, 1997.

ONLINE ACCESS

Two online, statewide public access computer system are available. The first is the Law Office Public Access System (LOPAS). The system allows remote access to the court case indexes and abstracts from most of the state's courts. In order to determine which courts are on LOPAS, you must obtain an ID and password (instructions below), and search on the system. A summary list of included courts is not available. Searching is by specific court; there is no combined index.

The system contains opinions from the Supreme Court and the Court of Appeals as well as criminal and civil case information from Circuit and District Courts. The number of years of information provided varies widely from court to court, depending on when the particular court joined the Courts Automated Information System (CAIS). There are no sign-up or other fees to use LOPAS. Access is granted on a request-by-request basis. Anyone wishing to establish an account or receive information on LOPAS must contact Ken Mittendorf, Director of MIS, Supreme Court of Virginia, 100 N 9th St, Richmond VA 23219 or by phone at 804-786-6455 or Fax at 804-786-4542.

Virginia also has the "Circuit Court Case Information Pilot Project" which includes free access to records from these Circuit Courts: Arlington, Augusta, Bedford, Botetourt, Carroll, Chesapeake City, Danville City, Dickenson, Fauquier, Floyd, Franklin City, Fredericksburg City, Gloucester, Hampton City, Henry, Hopewell City, Isle of Wight, King George, Louisa, Martinsville City, Nelson, Newport News City, Norfolk City, Nottoway, Orange, Petersburg City, Pulaski, Radford City, Richmond City, Roanoke City, Rockingham, Russell, Tazewell, Warren, Waynesboro City, Williamsburg/James City, Winchester, Wise, York.

ADDITIONAL INFORMATION

In most jurisdictions, the certification fee is $2.00 per document plus copy fee. The copy fee is $.50 per page.

Accomack County

2nd Circuit Court PO Box 126, Accomac, VA 23301; 757-787-5776; Fax: 757-787-1849. Hours: 9AM-5PM (EST). *Felony, Civil Actions Over $15,000, Probate.*

Civil Records: Access: Fax, mail, online, in person. Both court and visitors may perform in person searches. No search fee. Required to search: name, years to search. Civil cases indexed by defendant, plaintiff. Civil records on microfiche and archived from 1663; on computer back to 1984. For information about the statewide online system, LOPAS, see the state introduction.

Criminal Records: Access: Fax, mail, online, in person. Both court and visitors may perform in person searches. No search fee. Required to search: name, years to search, DOB; also helpful: SSN. Criminal records on microfiche and archived from 1663; on computer back to 1984. Online access to criminal records is the same as civil.

General Information: Public Access terminal is available. No juvenile, sealed, probate, tax return or adoption records released. SASE not required. Turnaround time 1-2 days. Fax notes: Fee to fax results is $2.00 1st page, $.50 each add'l. Copy fee: $.50 per page. Certification fee: $2.00. Fee payee: Samuel H Cooper Jr, Clerk of Court. Personal checks accepted.

2A General District Court PO Box 276, Accomac, VA 23301; 757-787-0920. Hours: 9AM-5PM (EST). *Misdemeanor, Civil Actions Under $15,000, Eviction, Small Claims.*

Civil Records: Access: Phone, mail, online, in person. Both court and visitors may perform in person searches. No search fee. Required to search: name, years to search. Civil cases indexed by defendant. Civil records on computer from 11/88, index cards from 1985. For information about the statewide online system, LOPAS, see the state introduction.

Criminal Records: Access: Phone, mail, online, in person. Both court and visitors may perform in person searches. No search fee. Required to search: name, years to search, DOB; also helpful: SSN. Criminal records on computer from 11/88, index cards from 1985. Online access to criminal records is the same as civil.

General Information: Public Access terminal is available. No juvenile, sealed, adoption records released. SASE required. Turnaround time 1-3 days. Copy fee: $1.00 for first 2 pages. Add $.50 per page thereafter. Certification fee: No certification fee. Fee payee: Accomack District Court. Personal checks accepted. Credit cards accepted: Visa, MasterCard. Prepayment is required.

Albemarle County

16th Circuit & District Court 501 E Jefferson St, Charlottesville, VA 22902; 804-972-4085; Fax: 804-972-4071. Hours: 8:30AM-4:30PM (EST). *Felony, Misdemeanor, Civil, Eviction, Probate.*

Civil Records: Access: Mail, online, in person. Both court and visitors may perform in person searches. No search fee. Required to search: name, years to search. Civil records on microfiche from 1980 to present and archived from 1700s to 1990. For information about the statewide online system, LOPAS, see the state introduction.

Criminal Records: Access: Mail, online, in person. Both court and visitors may perform in person searches. No search fee. Required to search: name, years to search. Criminal records on microfiche from 1980 to present and archived from 1700s to 1990. Online access to criminal records is the same as civil.

General Information: No juvenile, sealed records released. Turnaround time 7-10 days. Copy fee: $.50

per page. Certification fee: $2.00. Fee payee: Albemarle Clerk of Court. Personal checks accepted. Prepayment is required.

Alexandria City

18th Circuit Court 520 King St. #307, Alexandria, VA 22314; 703-838-4044. Hours: 9AM-5PM (EST). *Felony, Civil Actions Over $15,000, Probate.*

http://ci.alexandria.va.us/city/courts/circuitcourt.html

Civil Records: Access: In person only. Visitors must perform in person searches for themselves. No search fee. Required to search: name, years to search. Civil cases indexed by defendant, plaintiff. Civil records on computer from 1983 to present, microfiche from 1970s to present.

Criminal Records: Access: In person only. Visitors must perform in person searches for themselves. No search fee. Required to search: name, years to search; also helpful: DOB. Criminal records on computer since 7/87.

General Information: Public Access terminal is available. No juvenile, sealed, adoption or expunged records released. Copy fee: $.50 per page. Certification fee: $2.00. Fee payee: Clerk of Court. Only cashiers checks and money orders accepted. Prepayment is required.

18th Judicial District Court 520 King St #201, PO Box 20206, Alexandria, VA 22314; 703-838-4041 (traffic); Civil phone: 703-838-4021; Criminal phone: 703-838-4030. Hours: 8AM-4PM (EST). *Misdemeanor, Civil Actions Under $15,000, Eviction, Small Claims.*

Civil Records: Access: Online, in person. Visitors must perform in person searches for themselves. No search fee. Required to search: name, years to search. Civil cases indexed by defendant. Civil records on computer from 1991 to present, index cards prior to 1986. For information about the statewide online system, LOPAS, see the state introduction.

Criminal Records: Access: Online, in person. Visitors must perform in person searches for themselves. No search fee. Required to search: name. Criminal records on computer from 1991 to present, index cards prior to 1986. Online access to criminal records is the same as civil.

General Information: Public Access terminal is available. No copy fee. Certification fee: No certification fee.

Alleghany County

25th Circuit Court PO Box 670, Covington, VA 24426; 540-965-1730; Fax: 540-965-1732. Hours: 8:30AM-5PM M-F; 9AM-Noon Sat (EST). *Felony, Civil Actions Over $15,000, Probate.*

www.alleghanycountyclerk.com

Civil Records: Access: Online, in person. Visitors must perform in person searches for themselves. No search fee. Required to search: name. Civil cases indexed by plaintiff. Civil records available from 1822, some on microfilm. For information about the statewide online system, LOPAS, see the state introduction.

Criminal Records: Access: Online, in person. Visitors must perform in person searches for themselves. No search fee. Required to search: name. Criminal records available from 1822, some on microfilm. Online access to criminal records is the same as civil.

General Information: No juvenile, adoption or sealed records released. Copy fee: $.50 per page. Certification fee: $2.00. Fee payee: Michael D Wolfe, Clerk of Court. Personal checks accepted. Prepayment is required.

25th General District Court PO Box 139, Covington, VA 24426; 540-965-1720; Fax: 540-965-1722. Hours: 9AM-5PM (EST). *Misdemeanor, Civil Actions Under $15,000, Eviction, Small Claims.*

Civil Records: Access: Fax, mail, online, in person. Both court and visitors may perform in person searches. No search fee. Required to search: name, years to search. Civil cases indexed by defendant, plaintiff. Civil records on computer from 1/90, prior on index cards. For information about the statewide online system, LOPAS, see the state introduction.

Criminal Records: Access: Fax, mail, online, in person. Both court and visitors may perform in person searches. No search fee. Required to search: name, years to search; also helpful: DOB, SSN. Criminal records on computer from 1/90, prior on index cards. Online access to criminal records is the same as civil.

General Information: Public Access terminal is available. No juvenile, sealed records released. SASE requested. Turnaround time 1-2 days. Fax notes: No fee to fax results. Copy fee: $1.00 each for first 2 pages; $.50 each add'l. Certification fee: No certification fee. Personal checks accepted. Credit cards accepted: Visa, MasterCard. Acpted for fines and cost only.

Amelia County

11th Circuit Court PO Box 6309 (1 E Main St, B-5), PO Box 237, Amelia, VA 23068; 804-561-2128. Hours: 8:30AM-4:30PM (EST). *Felony, Civil Actions Over $15,000, Probate.*

Note: Will search on telephone request if not busy.

Civil Records: Access: Mail, online, in person. Both court and visitors may perform in person searches. No search fee. Required to search: name, years to search. Civil cases indexed by defendant, plaintiff. Civil records on microfiche 1735 to present, indexed on books. For information about the statewide online system, LOPAS, see the state introduction.

Criminal Records: Access: Mail, online, in person. Both court and visitors may perform in person searches. No search fee. Required to search: name, years to search, DOB; also helpful: SSN. Criminal records on microfiche 1735 to present, indexed on books. Online access to criminal records is the same as civil.

General Information: No juvenile, sealed records released. SASE required. Turnaround time 3-5 days. Copy fee: $.50 per page. Certification fee: $3.00. Fee payee: Amelia County Circuit Court. Personal checks accepted. Prepayment is required.

11th General District Court PO Box 24, Amelia, VA 23002; 804-561-2456; Fax: 804-561-6956. Hours: 8:30AM-4:30PM (EST). *Misdemeanor, Civil Actions Under $15,000, Eviction, Small Claims.*

Civil Records: Access: Mail, online, in person. Both court and visitors may perform in person searches. No search fee. Required to search: name, years to search. Civil cases indexed by defendant, plaintiff. Civil records on computer since 12/20/92, prior records on index cards. For information about the statewide online system, LOPAS, see the state introduction.

Criminal Records: Access: Mail, online, in person. Both court and visitors may perform in person searches. No search fee. Required to search: name, years to search, DOB; also helpful: SSN. Criminal records on computer since 12/20/92, prior records on index cards. Online access to criminal records is the same as civil.

General Information: Public Access terminal is available. No juvenile, sealed records released. SASE required. Turnaround time 1-14 days. Copy fee: $1.00 for 1st two pages, $.50 each add'l page. Certification fee: No certification fee. Fee payee: Amelia District Court. Personal checks accepted. Prepayment is required.

Amherst County

24th Circuit Court PO Box 462, Amherst, VA 24521; 804-946-9321; Fax: 804-946-9323. Hours: 8AM-5PM (EST). *Felony, Civil Actions Over $15,000, Probate.*

Civil Records: Access: Online, in person. Visitors must perform in person searches for themselves. No search fee. Required to search: name, years to search. Civil cases indexed by defendant, plaintiff. Civil records on index books from 1761. For information about the statewide online system, LOPAS, see the state introduction.

Criminal Records: Access: Online, in person. Visitors must perform in person searches for themselves. No search fee. Required to search: name, years to search, date of offense. Criminal records on index books from 1761. Online access to criminal records is the same as civil.

General Information: No juvenile, sealed or adoption records released. Copy fee: $.50 per page. Certification fee: $2.00. Fee payee: Clerk of Circuit Court. Personal checks accepted. Prepayment is required.

24th General District Court PO Box 513, Amherst, VA 24521; 804-946-9351; Fax: 804-946-9359. Hours: 8AM-4:30PM (EST). *Misdemeanor, Civil Actions Under $15,000, Eviction, Small Claims.*

Note: Has handled misdemeanor cases since 1985.

Civil Records: Access: Online, in person. Visitors must perform in person searches for themselves. No search fee. Required to search: name, years to search. Civil cases indexed by defendant, plaintiff. Civil records on computer from 1989, cards 10 years prior. For information about the statewide online system, LOPAS, see the state introduction.

Criminal Records: Access: Online, in person. Visitors must perform in person searches for themselves. No search fee. Required to search: name, years to search, DOB, SSN. Criminal records on computer from 1989, cards 10 years prior. Online access to criminal records is the same as civil.

General Information: Public Access terminal is available. No sealed records released. Copy fee: $1.00 per page. Certification fee: $2.00. Fee payee: Clerk of Court. Personal checks accepted. Credit cards accepted: Visa, MasterCard. Prepayment is required.

Appomattox County

10th Circuit Court PO Box 672, Appomattox, VA 24522; 804-352-5275; Fax: 804-352-2781. 8:30AM-4:30PM *Felony, Civil Actions Over $15,000, Probate.*

Civil Records: Access: Online, in person. Visitors must perform in person searches for themselves. No search fee. Required to search: name, years to search. Civil cases indexed by defendant, plaintiff. Civil records on books from 1892 to present; on computer since. For information about the statewide online system, LOPAS, see the state introduction.

Criminal Records: Access: Online, in person. Visitors must perform in person searches for themselves. No search fee. Required to search: name, years to search. Criminal records on books from 1892 to present; on computer since. Online access to criminal records is the same as civil.

General Information: Public Access terminal is available. No juvenile, sealed records released. Copy fee: $.50 per page. Certification fee: No certification fee. Fee payee: Clerk of Circuit Court. Personal checks accepted. Prepayment is required.

10th General District Court PO Box 187, Appomattox, VA 24522; 804-352-5540; Fax: 804-352-0717. Hours: 8:30AM-4:30PM (EST). *Misdemeanor, Civil Actions Under $15,000, Eviction, Small Claims.*

Civil Records: Access: Fax, mail, online, in person. Both court and visitors may perform in person searches.

No search fee. Required to search: name, years to search. Civil cases indexed by defendant, plaintiff. Civil records on card file from 1985 to present, prior to 1985 in Circuit Court. For information about the statewide online system, LOPAS, see the state introduction.

Criminal Records: Access: Fax, mail, online, in person. Both court and visitors may perform in person searches. No search fee. Required to search: name, years to search; also helpful: SSN. Criminal records on card file from 1985 to present, prior to 1985 in Circuit Court. Online access to criminal records is the same as civil.

General Information: Public Access terminal is available. No juvenile, sealed records released. Turnaround time 1-5 days. Fax notes: No fee to fax results. Copy fee: $1.00 1st page; $.50 each add'l. Certification fee: No certification fee. Fee payee: General District Court. Personal checks accepted. Credit cards accepted: Visa, MasterCard.

Arlington County

17th Circuit Court 1425 N Courthouse Rd, Arlington, VA 22201; 703-358-7010. Hours: 8AM-5PM *Felony, Civil Actions Over $15,000, Probate.*

http://158.59.15.115/arlington

Civil Records: Access: Online, in person. Visitors must perform in person searches for themselves. No search fee. Required to search: name, years to search. Civil cases indexed by defendant, plaintiff. Civil records on computer from 1987; prior on books from mid-1930 to present. Online access is available free at http://208.210.219.132/courtinfo/vacircuit/select.jsp?court=. For information about the statewide online system, LOPAS, see the state introduction.

Criminal Records: Access: Online, in person. Visitors must perform in person searches for themselves. No search fee. Required to search: name, years to search. Criminal records on computer from 1987; prior on books from mid-1930 to present. Online access to criminal records is the same as civil.

General Information: Public Access terminal is available. (Criminal only.) No juvenile, adoption or sealed records released. Mail requests not accepted. Copy fee: $.50 per page. Certification fee: $2.00. Fee payee: Clerk of Court. Personal checks accepted. Prepayment is required.

17th General District Court 1425 N Courthouse Rd, Rm 2500, Arlington, VA 22201; 703-228-4485; Fax: 703-228-4593. Hours: 8AM-4PM (EST). *Misdemeanor, Civil Actions Under $15,000, Eviction, Small Claims.*

Note: Phone access limited to 4 requests.

Civil Records: Access: Phone, mail, online, in person. Both court and visitors may perform in person searches. No search fee. Required to search: name, years to search. Civil cases indexed by defendant. Civil records on computer back to 1990, books from early 1970s. For information about the statewide online system, LOPAS, see the state introduction.

Criminal Records: Access: Phone, mail, online, in person. Both court and visitors may perform in person searches. No search fee. Required to search: name, years to search, DOB; also helpful-SSN, case number. Criminal records on computer back to 1990, books from early 1970s. Online access to criminal records is the same as civil.

General Information: Public Access terminal is available. No juvenile, sealed records released. Turnaround time 1-2 days. Fax notes: Will not fax results. Copy fee: $.50 per page. Certification fee: $2.00. Fee payee: Clerk of Court. Personal checks accepted. Prepayment is required.

Augusta County

25th Circuit Court PO Box 689, Staunton, VA 24402-0689; 540-245-5321; Fax: 540-245-5318. Hours: 8AM-5PM (EST). *Felony, Civil Actions Over $15,000, Probate.*

Note: Court prefers that searches be done in person. Mail access is limited; they will only search back to 1987. Phone available for very short search only.

Civil Records: Access: Fax, mail, online, in person. Both court and visitors may perform in person searches. No search fee. Required to search: name, years to search. Civil cases indexed by defendant, plaintiff. Civil records on computer from 1987 to present, books from 1745 to 1986. Online access is available free at http://208.210.219.132/courtinfo/vacircuit/select.jsp?court=. For information about the statewide online system, LOPAS, see the state introduction.

Criminal Records: Access: Fax, mail, online, in person. Both court and visitors may perform in person searches. No search fee. Required to search: name, years to search; also helpful: DOB, SSN. Criminal records go back to 1987 felonies only. Online access to criminal records is the same as civil.

General Information: Public Access terminal is available. No juvenile, adoption or sealed records released. SASE required. Turnaround time 1-2 days. Copy fee: $.50 per page. Certification fee: $2.00. Fee payee: Clerk, Augusta County Circuit Court. Personal checks accepted.

25th General District Court 6 E Johnson St, 2nd Floor, Staunton, VA 24401; 540-245-5300; Fax: 540-245-5302. Hours: 8:30AM-4:30PM (EST). *Misdemeanor, Civil Actions Under $15,000, Eviction, Small Claims.*

Civil Records: Access: Mail, online, in person. Both court and visitors may perform in person searches. No search fee. Required to search: name, years to search. Civil cases indexed by defendant, plaintiff. Civil records kept for 10 years on computer, then archived or destroyed. For information about the statewide online system, LOPAS, see the state introduction.

Criminal Records: Access: Mail, online, in person. Both court and visitors may perform in person searches. No search fee. Required to search: name, years to search. Criminal records kept for 10 years on computer, then archived or destroyed. Online access to criminal records is the same as civil.

General Information: Public Access terminal is available. No juvenile, sealed records released. SASE requested. Turnaround time 2-3 days. Copy fee: $.50 per page. Certification fee: No certification fee. Fee payee: Augusta General District Court. Personal checks accepted. Credit cards accepted: Visa, MasterCard. Prepayment is required.

Bath County

25th Circuit Court PO Box 180, Warm Springs, VA 24484; 540-839-7226; Fax: 540-839-7222. Hours: 8:30AM-4:30PM (EST). *Felony, Civil Actions Over $15,000, Probate.*

Civil Records: Access: Mail, online, in person. Both court and visitors may perform in person searches. No search fee. Required to search: name, years to search. Civil cases indexed by defendant, plaintiff. Civil records on books from 1791 to present. For information about the statewide online system, LOPAS, see the state introduction.

Criminal Records: Access: Online, in person. Visitors must perform in person searches for themselves. No search fee. Required to search: name, years to search; also helpful: DOB, SSN. Criminal records on books from 1791 to present. Online access to criminal records is the same as civil.

General Information: No juvenile, sealed or adoption records released. Turnaround time 1-2 days. Copy fee: $.50 per page. Certification fee: $3.00. Fee payee: Bath County Circuit Court. Personal checks accepted. Prepayment is required.

25th General District Court PO Box 96, Warm Springs, VA 24484; 540-839-7241; Fax: 540-839-7248. Hours: 8:30AM-4:30PM (EST). *Misdemeanor, Civil Actions Under $15,000, Eviction, Small Claims.*

Civil Records: Access: Phone, fax, mail, online, in person. Both court and visitors may perform in person searches. No search fee. Required to search: name, years to search. Civil cases indexed by defendant, plaintiff. Civil records on files from 1985 to present, Prior records in Circuit Court. For information about the statewide online system, LOPAS, see the state introduction.

Criminal Records: Access: Phone, fax, mail, online, in person. Both court and visitors may perform in person searches. No search fee. Required to search: name, years to search, DOB; also helpful: SSN. Criminal records on files back 10 years, Prior records in Circuit Court. Online access to criminal records is the same as civil.

General Information: Public Access terminal is available. No juvenile, sealed records released. SASE requested. Turnaround time 2 days, will give immediate response on phone if not an extensive search. Copy fee: $.50 per page. Certification fee: No certification fee. Fee payee: Bath County Combined Court. Personal checks accepted. Credit cards accepted: Visa, MasterCard.

Bedford County

County Circuit Court 1635 Venture Blvd, Bedford, VA 24523; 540-586-7632; Fax: 540-586-6197. Hours: 8:30AM-5PM (EST). *Felony, Civil Actions Over $15,000, Probate.*

Civil Records: Access: Online, in person. Visitors must perform in person searches for themselves. No search fee. Required to search: name, years to search. Civil cases indexed by defendant, plaintiff. Civil records on computer from 1988, index books. Online access is available free at http://208.210.219.132/courtinfo/vacircuit/select.jsp?court=. For information about the statewide online system, LOPAS, see the state introduction.

Criminal Records: Access: Online, in person. Visitors must perform in person searches for themselves. No search fee. Required to search: name, years to search, DOB; also helpful: SSN, race, sex. Criminal records on computer from 1988, index books. Online access to criminal records is the same as civil.

General Information: Public Access terminal is available. No juvenile, sealed records released. Copy fee: $.50 per page. Certification fee: $2.00 per page. Fee payee: Bedford Clerk of Court. Personal checks accepted. Prepayment is required.

24th General District Court 1635 Venture Blvd #500, Bedford, VA 24523; 540-586-7637; Fax: 540-586-7684. 8AM-4PM (EST). *Misdemeanor, Civil Actions Under $15,000, Eviction, Small Claims.*

Civil Records: Access: Mail, online, in person. Visitors must perform in person searches for themselves. Search fee: $5.00 per name. Required to search: name, years to search. Civil cases indexed by defendant. Civil records on computer for ten years. Date of birth or SSN also helpful in searching. For information about the statewide online system, LOPAS, see the state introduction.

Criminal Records: Access: Mail, online, in person. Both court and visitors may perform in person searches. Search fee: $5.00 per name. Required to search: name, years to search; also helpful: DOB, SSN. Criminal records on computer for ten years. Date of birth or SSN

also helpful in searching. Online access to criminal records is the same as civil.

General Information: Public Access terminal is available. No sealed records released. SASE required. Turnaround time 1-5 days. Copy fee: $1.00 1st 2 pages, $.50 each additional page. Certification fee: No certification fee. Fee payee: Bedford General District Court. Personal checks accepted. Credit cards accepted: Visa, MasterCard. Prepayment is required.

Bedford City

Circuit & District Courts, VA.

Note: See Bedford County

Bland County

27th Circuit Court PO Box 295, Bland, VA 24315; 540-688-4562; Fax: 540-688-4562. Hours: 8AM-6PM (EST). *Felony, Civil Actions Over $15,000, Probate.*

Civil Records: Access: Phone, fax, mail, online, in person. Both court and visitors may perform in person searches. Search fee: $10.00 per name. Required to search: name, years to search. Civil cases indexed by defendant, plaintiff. Civil records on books from 1861 to present. For information about the statewide online system, LOPAS, see the state introduction.

Criminal Records: Access: Phone, fax, mail, online, in person. Both court and visitors may perform in person searches. Search fee: $10.00 per name. Required to search: name, years to search, signed release; also helpful: SSN. Criminal records on books from 1861 to present. Online access to criminal records is the same as civil.

General Information: No juvenile, sealed or adoption records released. Turnaround time 2 days. Fax notes: $1.00 per page. Copy fee: $.50 per page. Certification fee: $2.00. Fee payee: Clerk of Court. Personal checks accepted. Prepayment is required.

27th General District Court PO Box 157, Bland, VA 24315; 540-688-4433; Fax: 540-688-4789. Hours: 8AM-5PM (EST). *Misdemeanor, Civil Actions Under $15,000, Eviction, Small Claims.*

Civil Records: Access: Phone, fax, mail, online, in person. Both court and visitors may perform in person searches. No search fee. Required to search: name, years to search. Civil cases indexed by defendant. Civil records on computer from 4/23/92, card index back to 1985. For information about the statewide online system, LOPAS, see the state introduction. Phone access limited to specific cases only.

Criminal Records: Access: Phone, fax, mail, online, in person. Both court and visitors may perform in person searches. No search fee. Required to search: name, years to search; also helpful: DOB, SSN. Criminal records on computer from 4/23/92, card index back to 1985. Online access to criminal records is the same as civil. Phone access limited to specific cases only.

General Information: Public Access terminal is available. No juvenile, sealed or adoption records released. SASE requested. Turnaround time 1-2 days. Copy fee: $1.00 1st 2 pages, $.50 each additional page. Certification fee: No certification fee. Fee payee: General District Court. Personal checks accepted. Credit cards accepted: Visa, MasterCard.

Botetourt County

25th Circuit Court PO Box 219, Fincastle, VA 24090; 540-473-8274; Fax: 540-473-8209. Hours: 8:30AM-4:30PM (EST). *Felony, Civil Actions Over $15,000, Probate.*

Civil Records: Access: Mail, online, in person. Both court Sand visitors may perform in person searches. No search fee. Required to search: name, years to search. Civil cases indexed by defendant, plaintiff. Civil records on computer 7/1/91 to present, books back to 1770.

Online access is available free at http://208.210.219.132/courtinfo/vacircuit/select.jsp?court=. For information about the statewide online system, LOPAS, see the state introduction.

Criminal Records: Access: Mail, online, in person. Both court and visitors may perform in person searches. No search fee. Required to search: name, years to search, DOB, SSN. Criminal records on computer 7/1/91 to present, books back to 1770. Online access to criminal records is the same as civil.

General Information: Public Access terminal is available. No juvenile, sealed or adoption records released. SASE required. Turnaround time same day. Copy fee: $.50 per page. Certification fee: $2.00. Fee payee: Clerk of Court. Personal checks accepted. Prepayment is required.

25th General District Court PO Box 205, Fincastle, VA 24090-0205; 540-473-8244; Fax: 540-473-8344. Hours: 8AM-4PM (EST). *Misdemeanor, Civil Actions Under $15,000, Eviction, Small Claims.*

Civil Records: Access: Mail, online, in person. Both court and visitors may perform in person searches. No search fee. Required to search: name, years to search. Civil cases indexed by defendant, plaintiff. Civil records on computer from 1988 to present. Civil records on files back to 1964, others back to 1974. For information about the statewide online system, LOPAS, see the state introduction.

Criminal Records: Access: Mail, online, in person. Both court and visitors may perform in person searches. No search fee. Required to search: name, years to search. Criminal records on computer from 1991 to present. Civil records on files back to 1964, others back to 1974. Online access to criminal records is the same as civil.

General Information: Public Access terminal is available. No juvenile, sealed records released. SASE requested. Turnaround time 1-2 days. No copy fee. Certification fee: No certification fee. Personal checks accepted. Checks that require verification calls not accepted. Credit cards accepted: Visa, MasterCard.

Bristol City

28th Circuit Court 497 Cumberland St, Bristol, VA 24201; 540-645-7321; Fax: 540-645-7345. Hours: 9AM-5PM (EST). *Felony, Civil Actions Over $15,000, Probate.*

Civil Records: Access: Mail, online, in person. Both court and visitors may perform in person searches. No search fee. Required to search: name, years to search. Civil cases indexed by defendant, plaintiff. Civil records indexed from 1890 to present. For information about the statewide online system, LOPAS, see the state introduction.

Criminal Records: Access: Online, in person. Visitors must perform in person searches for themselves. No search fee. Required to search: name, years to search. Criminal records indexed from 1890 to present. Online access to criminal records is the same as civil.

General Information: No juvenile, sealed or adoption records released. SASE required. Turnaround time up to 1 week. Copy fee: $.50 per page. Certification fee: $2.00. Fee payee: Clerk of Circuit Court. Personal checks accepted. Prepayment is required.

28th General District Court 497 Cumberland St, Bristol, VA 24201; 540-645-7341; Fax: 540-645-7342. Hours: 8AM-5PM (EST). *Misdemeanor, Civil Actions Under $15,000, Eviction, Small Claims.*

Civil Records: Access: Mail, fax, online, in person. Both court and visitors may perform in person searches. No search fee. Required to search: name, years to search. Civil cases indexed by defendant, plaintiff. Civil records on computer from 1989, card file 1983 to 1988. For information about the statewide online system, LOPAS, see the state introduction.

Criminal Records: Access: Mail, fax, online, in person. Visitors must perform in person searches for themselves. No search fee. Required to search: name, years to search, DOB, SSN. Criminal records on computer from 1989, card file 1983 to 1988. Online access to criminal records is the same as civil.
General Information: Public Access terminal is available. No juvenile, sealed records released. SASE requested. Turnaround time 1-2 days. Copy fee: $.50 per page. Certification fee: $2.00. Fee payee: General District Court. Personal checks accepted. Credit cards accepted: Visa, MasterCard.

Brunswick County

6th Circuit Court 216 N Main St, Lawrenceville, VA 23868; 804-848-2215; Fax: 804-848-4307. Hours: 8:30AM-5PM (EST). *Felony, Civil, Probate.*

Civil Records: Access: Online, in person. Visitors must perform in person searches for themselves. No search fee. Required to search: name, years to search. Civil cases indexed by defendant, plaintiff. Civil records in books; on computer since 1992. For information about the statewide online system, LOPAS, see the state introduction.
Criminal Records: Access: Online, in person. Visitors must perform in person searches for themselves. No search fee. Required to search: name, years to search. Criminal records in books; on computer since 1992. Online access to criminal records is the same as civil.
General Information: Public Access terminal is available. (Available for land records and wills. No case information.) No juvenile, sealed or adoption records released. Fax notes: Will fax results to 800 number and to accounts. Copy fee: $.50 per page. Certification fee: $2.00. Fee payee: Clerk of Court. Personal checks accepted.

6th General District Court, 202 Main St, Lawrenceville, VA 23868-0066; 804-848-2315; Fax: 804-848-2550. Hours: 8:30AM-4:30PM (EST). *Misdemeanor, Civil Actions Under $15,000, Eviction, Small Claims.*

Civil Records: Access: Mail, in person. Only the court performs in person searches; visitors may not. No search fee. Required to search: name, years to search. Civil cases indexed by defendant, plaintiff. Civil records computerized since 1988. For information about the statewide online system, LOPAS, see state introduction.
Criminal Records: Access: Mail, in person. Only the court performs in person searches; visitors may not. No search fee. Required to search: name, years to search, DOB; also helpful: SSN, signed release. Criminal records computerized since 1990 (expunged).
General Information: Public Access terminal is available. No juvenile, sealed records released. SASE required. Turnaround time 1-2 days. No copy fee. Certification fee: No certification fee.

Buchanan County

29th Circuit PO Box 929, Grundy, VA 24614; 540-935-6575. Hours: 8:30AM-5PM (EST). *Felony, Misdemeanor, Civil Actions Over $15,000, Probate.*

Civil Records: Access: Phone, mail, online, in person. Both court and visitors may perform in person searches. No search fee. Required to search: name, years to search; also helpful: address. Civil cases indexed by defendant, plaintiff. Civil records on books prior to 1991. For information about the statewide online system, LOPAS, see the state introduction.
Criminal Records: Access: Phone, mail, online, in person. Both court and visitors may perform in person searches. No search fee. Required to search: name, years to search, DOB; also helpful: address, SSN. Criminal records on books prior to 1991; on computer back to 1977. Online access to criminal records is the same as civil.

General Information: Public Access terminal is available. No juvenile, sealed records released. Turnaround time 1-2 days. Fax notes: Fee to fax results is $3.00 per document. Copy fee: $.50 per page. Certification fee: $.50. Fee payee: Clerk of Circuit Court. Personal checks accepted.

29th Judicial District Court PO Box 654, Grundy, VA 24614; 540-935-6526; Fax: 540-935-5479. Hours: 8AM-4PM (EST). *Civil Actions Under $15,000, Eviction, Small Claims.*

Civil Records: Access: Fax, mail, in person. Both court and visitors may perform in person searches. No search fee. Required to search: name; also helpful: years to search. Civil cases indexed by defendant, plaintiff. Civil Records are indexed for 10 years, on computer to 1993.
General Information: Turnaround time is 1 week. Fax notes: will fax back to toll-free or local numbers only. Copy fee: No search fee. Certification fee: No certification fee. Fee payee: General District Court. Personal checks accepted. Credit cards: Visa, MasterCard.

Buckingham County

10th Circuit Court Route 60, PO Box 107, Buckingham, VA 23921; 804-969-4734; Fax: 804-969-2043. Hours: 8:30AM-4:30PM (EST). *Felony, Civil Actions Over $15,000, Probate.*

Civil Records: Access: Mail, online, in person. Both court and visitors may perform in person searches. No search fee. Required to search: name, years to search. Civil cases indexed by defendant, plaintiff. Civil records on books from 1869 to present. For information about the statewide online system, LOPAS, see the state introduction. Simple requests only by mail.
Criminal Records: Access: Mail, online, in person. Both court and visitors may perform in person searches. No search fee. Required to search: name, years to search; also helpful: DOB. Criminal records on books from 1869 to present. Online access to criminal records is the same as civil.
General Information: No juvenile, sealed or adoption records released. Copy fee: $.50 per page. Certification fee: $2.00. Fee payee: Clerk of Court. Personal checks accepted.

Buckingham General District Court PO Box 127, Buckingham, VA 23921; 804-969-4755; Fax: 804-969-1762. Hours: 8:30AM-4:30PM (EST). *Misdemeanor, Civil Actions Under $15,000, Eviction, Small Claims.*

Civil Records: Access: Mail, online, in person. Only the court performs in person searches; visitors may not. No search fee. Required to search: name, years to search. Civil cases indexed by defendant. Civil records on computer or hard copy from 1993, prior records on index cards. For information about the statewide online system, LOPAS, see the state introduction.
Criminal Records: Access: Mail, online, in person. Only the court performs in person searches; visitors may not. No search fee. Required to search: name, years to search, DOB, SSN, signed release. Criminal records on computer or hard copy from 1993, prior records on index cards. Online access to criminal records is the same as civil.
General Information: No juvenile, sealed records released. Turnaround time 2 weeks. Copy fee: $.50 per page. Certification fee: $2.00. Fee payee: Buckingham. Personal checks accepted. Credit cards accepted: Visa, MasterCard.

Buena Vista City

25th Circuit & District Court 2039 Sycamore Ave, Buena Vista, VA 24416; 540-261-8627 X626/627; Fax: 540-261-8625. Hours: 8:30AM-5PM (EST). *Felony, Misdemeanor, Civil, Eviction, Probate.*

Civil Records: Access: Mail, online, in person. Both court and visitors may perform in person searches. No search fee. Required to search: name, years to search. Civil cases indexed by defendant, plaintiff. Civil records on manual records 1892 to present. For information about the statewide online system, LOPAS, see the state introduction.
Criminal Records: Access: Mail, online, in person. Both court and visitors may perform in person searches. No search fee. Required to search: name, years to search. Criminal records on manual records 1892 to present. Online access to criminal records is the same as civil.
General Information: Public Access terminal is available. No juvenile, sealed records released. SASE required. Turnaround time 1 day. Fax notes: $.50 per page. Copy fee: $.50 per page. Certification fee: $3.00. Fee payee: Buena Vista Circuit Court. Personal checks accepted. Prepayment is required.

Campbell County

24th Circuit Court State RD 501 Village Hwy, PO Box 7, Rustburg, VA 24588; 804-592-9517. Hours: 8:30AM-4:30PM (EST). *Felony, Civil Actions Over $15,000, Probate.*

Civil Records: Access: Mail, online, in person. Both court and visitors may perform in person searches. No search fee. Required to search: name, years to search. Civil cases indexed by defendant, plaintiff. Civil records on index books. For information about the statewide online system, LOPAS, see the state introduction.
Criminal Records: Access: Mail, online, in person. Both court and visitors may perform in person searches. No search fee. Required to search: name, years to search; also helpful: DOB. Criminal records on index books. Online access to criminal records is the same as civil.
General Information: No juvenile, sealed or adoption records released. SASE required. Turnaround 2-10 days. Copy fee: $.50 per page. Certification fee: $2.00. Fee payee: Clerk of Court. Personal checks accepted.

24th General District Court 1st Floor, New Courthouse Bldg, PO Box 97, Rustburg, VA 24588; 804-332-9546; Fax: 804-332-9694. Hours: 8AM-4PM (EST). *Misdemeanor, Civil Actions Under $15,000, Eviction, Small Claims.*

Civil Records: Access: Online, in person. Visitors must perform in person searches for themselves. No search fee. Required to search: name, years to search. Civil cases indexed by defendant, plaintiff. Civil records on computer for 10 years. For information about the statewide online system, LOPAS, see the state introduction.
Criminal Records: Access: Online, in person. Visitors must perform in person searches for themselves. No search fee. Required to search: name, years to search. Criminal records on computer for 10 years. Online access to criminal records is the same as civil.
General Information: Public Access terminal is available. (Not available for criminal or civil information.) Copy fee: $1.00 for 1st 2 copies then $.50 per copy thereafter. Certification fee: No certification fee. Fee payee: Clerk of Court. Prepayment is required.

Caroline County

15th Circuit Court Main St & Courthouse Ln, PO Box 309, Bowling Green, VA 22427-0309; 804-633-5800. Hours: 9AM-5PM (EST). *Felony, Civil Actions Over $15,000, Probate.*

Civil Records: Access: Online, in person. Visitors must perform in person searches for themselves. No search fee. Required to search: name, years to search. Civil cases indexed by defendant, plaintiff. Civil records on books from early 1800s to present. For information about the statewide online system, LOPAS, see the state introduction.

Criminal Records: Access: Online, in person. Visitors must perform in person searches for themselves. No search fee. Required to search: name, years to search; also helpful: DOB. Criminal records on books from early 1800s to present. Online access to criminal records is the same as civil.

General Information: No juvenile, sealed, adoption records released. Copy fee: $.50 per page. Certification fee: $2.00. Fee payee: Clerk of Court. Personal checks accepted. Accepted for payment of fines & costs only. Not accepted over the phone. Prepayment is required.

15th General District Court PO Box 511, Bowling Green, VA 22427; 804-633-5720; Fax: 804-633-3033. Hours: 8AM-4PM (EST). *Misdemeanor, Civil Actions Under $15,000, Eviction, Small Claims.*

Civil Records: Access: Mail, online, in person. Both court and visitors may perform in person searches. No search fee. Required to search: name, years to search. Civil cases indexed by defendant, plaintiff. Civil records on computer from 1/92, index cards from 1991. For information about the statewide online system, LOPAS, see the state introduction.

Criminal Records: Access: Mail, online, in person. Both court and visitors may perform in person searches. No search fee. Required to search: name, years to search. Criminal records on computer from 1/92, index cards from 1991. Online access to criminal records is the same as civil.

General Information: Public Access terminal is available. Fax notes: Will not fax results. Certification fee: No certification fee.

Carroll County

27th Circuit Court PO Box 218, Hillsville, VA 24343; 540-728-3117. Hours: 8AM-5PM (EST). *Felony, Civil Actions Over $15,000, Probate.*

Civil Records: Access: Mail, online, in person. Both court and visitors may perform in person searches. Search fee: $5.00 per name. Required to search: name, years to search, also helpful: SSN. Civil cases indexed by defendant, plaintiff. Civil records on books from 1842 to present. Online access is available free at http://208.210.219.132/courtinfo/vacircuit/select.jsp?court=. For information about the statewide online system, LOPAS, see the state introduction.

Criminal Records: Access: Mail, online, in person. Both court and visitors may perform in person searches. Search fee: $5.00 per name. Required to search: name, years to search; also helpful: SSN. Criminal records on books from 1842 to present. Online access to criminal records is the same as civil.

General Information: No juvenile, sealed, adoption records released. SASE requested. Turnaround time 3-5 days. Copy fee: $.50 per page. Certification fee: $2.00. Fee payee: Clerk of Court. Personal checks accepted. Prepayment is required.

Carroll Combined District Court PO Box 698, Hillsville, VA 24343; 540-728-7751; Fax: 540-728-2582. Hours: 8AM-4:30PM (EST). *Misdemeanor, Civil Actions Under $15,000, Eviction, Small Claims.*

Civil Records: Access: In person only. Visitors must perform in person searches for themselves. No search fee. Required to search: name, years to search. Civil cases indexed by defendant, plaintiff. Civil records on books from 1800s, on computer from 1988; no plaintiff index prior to computerization. For information about the statewide online system, LOPAS, see the state introduction.

Criminal Records: Access: In person only. Visitors must perform in person searches for themselves. No search fee. Criminal records on books from 1800s, on computer from 1988; no prior plaintiff index.

General Information: Public Access terminal is available. No juvenile, sealed records released. No copy fee. Certification fee: No certification fee. Fee payee: General District Court. Personal checks accepted. Credit cards accepted: Visa, MasterCard. Prepayment is required.

Charles City

9th Circuit Court 10700 Courthouse Rd, PO Box 86, Charles City, VA 23030-0086; 804-829-9212; Fax: 804-829-5647. Hours: 8:30AM-4:30PM (EST). *Felony, Civil Actions Over $15,000, Probate.*

Civil Records: Access: Mail, online, in person. Both court and visitors may perform in person searches. No search fee. Required to search: name, years to search. Civil cases indexed by defendant, plaintiff. Civil records on computer from 1990, on books from 1789. For information about the statewide online system, LOPAS, see the state introduction.

Criminal Records: Access: Mail, online, in person. Both court and visitors may perform in person searches. No search fee. Required to search: name, years to search, DOB, SSN, signed release. Criminal records on computer from 1990, on books from 1789. Online access to criminal records is the same as civil.

General Information: No juvenile, sealed records released. Turnaround time 2-5 days. Fax notes: Fee to fax results is $.50 per page. Copy fee: $.50 per page. Certification fee: $2.00. Fee payee: Clerk of Circuit Court. Personal checks accepted. Prepayment required.

9th General District Court Charles City Courthouse, 10700 Courthouse Rd, Charles City, VA 23030; 804-829-9224; Fax: 504-829-5109. Hours: 8:30AM-4PM (EST). *Misdemeanor, Civil Actions Under $15,000, Eviction, Small Claims.*

Civil Records: Access: Mail, online, in person. Both court and visitors may perform in person searches. No search fee. Required to search: name, years to search. Civil cases indexed by defendant, plaintiff. Civil records on computer back to 1989; on books from 1700s. For information about the statewide online system, LOPAS, see the state introduction.

Criminal Records: Access: Mail, online, in person. Both court and visitors may perform in person searches. No search fee. Required to search: name, years to search, DOB, SSN. Criminal records on computer back to 1989; on books from 1700s. Online access to criminal records is the same as civil.

General Information: Public Access terminal is available. No juvenile, sealed records released. Turnaround time 3 days. Fax notes: Will not fax results. No copy fee. Certification fee: $2.00. Fee payee: Circuit Court. Personal checks accepted. Prepayment required.

Charlotte County

10th Circuit Court 115 LeGrande Ave PO Box 38, Charlotte Courthouse, VA 23923; 804-542-5147. Hours: 8:30AM-4:30PM (EST). *Felony, Civil Actions Over $15,000, Probate.*

Civil Records: Access: In person only. Visitors must perform in person searches for themselves. No search fee. Sourcired to search: name, years to search. Civil cases indexed by defendant, plaintiff. Civil records on books from 1765, in folders by case number.

Criminal Records: Access: In person only. Visitors must perform in person searches for themselves. No search fee. Required to search: name, years to search, DOB. Criminal records on books from 1765, in folders by case number.

General Information: No juvenile, sealed records released. Copy fee: $.50 per page. Certification fee: $3.00. Fee payee: Clerk of Circuit Court. Personal checks accepted. Prepayment is required.

Charlotte General District Court PO Box 127, Charlotte Courthouse, VA 23923; 804-542-5600; Fax: 804-542-5902. Hours: 8:30AM-4:30PM (EST). *Misdemeanor, Civil Actions Under $15,000, Eviction, Small Claims.*

Civil Records: Access: Online, in person. Visitors must perform in person searches for themselves. No search fee. Required to search: name, years to search. Civil cases indexed by defendant, plaintiff. Civil records on computer back to 5/95, on books from 1988. For information about the statewide online system, LOPAS, see the state introduction.

Criminal Records: Access: Online, in person. Visitors must perform in person searches for themselves. No search fee. Required to search: name, years to search, DOB; also helpful-SSN, signed release. Criminal records on computer back to 5/95, on books from 1988. Online access to criminal records is the same as civil.

General Information: Public Access terminal is available. No juvenile, sealed records released. Fax notes: Fee to fax results is $.50 per page. Copy fee: $.50 per page. Certification fee: No certification fee. Fee payee: Clerk of General District Court. Personal checks accepted. Credit cards accepted: Visa, MasterCard.

Charlottesville City

16th Judicial Circuit Court 315 E High St, Charlottesville, VA 22902; 804-295-3182. Hours: 8:30AM-4:30PM (EST). *Felony, Civil Actions Over $15,000, Probate.*

Civil Records: Access: Online, in person. Visitors must perform in person searches for themselves. No search fee. Required to search: name, years to search. Civil cases indexed by defendant, plaintiff. Civil records on books from 1888 to present. For information about the statewide online system, LOPAS, see the state introduction.

Criminal Records: Access: Online, in person. Visitors must perform in person searches for themselves. No search fee. Required to search: name, years to search; also helpful: DOB. Criminal records on books from 1888 to present. Online access to criminal records is the same as civil.

General Information: No juvenile, sealed or adoption records released. Copy fee: $.50 per page. Certification fee: $2.00. Fee payee: Charlottesville Circuit Court Clerk's Office. Personal checks accepted. No out of state checks accepted. Prepayment is required.

Charlottesville General District Court 606 E Market St, PO Box 2677, Charlottesville, VA 22902; 804-970-3385; Fax: 804-970-3387. Hours: 8:30AM-4:30PM (EST). *Misdemeanor, Civil Actions Under $15,000, Eviction, Small Claims.*

Civil Records: Access: Mail, online, in person. Both court and visitors may perform in person searches. No search fee. Required to search: name, years to search. Civil cases indexed by defendant, plaintiff. Civil records on computer from 1986 to present, on books 1982-1986, records kept for 10 years. For information about the statewide online system, LOPAS, see the state introduction.

Criminal Records: Access: Mail, online, in person. Both court and visitors may perform in person searches. No search fee. Required to search: name, years to search; also helpful: DOB, SSN. Criminal records on computer from 1986 to present, on books 1982-1986, records kept for 10 years. Online access to criminal records is the same as civil.

General Information: Public Access terminal is available. No juvenile, sealed, confidential records released. SASE required. Turnaround time 3 days. Copy fee: $1.00 for first page, $.50 each add'l. Certification fee: No certification fee. Fee payee: General District Court. Personal checks accepted. Prepayment is required.

Chesapeake City

1st Circuit Court 307 Albemarle Dr, #300A, Chesapeake, VA 23322-5579; 757-382-3000; Fax: 757-382-3035. Hours: 8:30AM-5PM (EST). *Felony, Civil Actions Over $15,000, Probate.*

Civil Records: Access: Mail, fax, online, in person. Visitors must perform in person searches for themselves. No search fee. Required to search: name, years to search. Civil cases indexed by defendant, plaintiff. Civil records on books from 1637, on computer from 1989. Online access is available free at http://208.210.219.132/courtinfo/vacircuit/select.jsp?court=. For information about the statewide online system, LOPAS, see the state introduction.

Criminal Records: Access: Mail, fax, online, in person. Visitors must perform in person searches for themselves. No search fee. Required to search: name, years to search, DOB; also helpful: SSN, sex, signed release. Criminal records on books from 1637, on computer from 1989. Online access to criminal records is the same as civil.

General Information: Public Access terminal is available. No juvenile, sealed records released. SASE required. Turnaround time 1 week. Fax notes: Fee to fax results is $.50 per page. Copy fee: $.50 per page. Certification fee: $2.50. Fee payee: Clerk of Circuit Court. Personal checks accepted. Prepayment is required.

1st General District Court 307 Albemarle Dr #100, Chesapeake, VA 23322; Civil phone: 757-382-3143; Criminal phone: 757-382-3134; Fax: 757-382-3171. Hours: 8AM-4PM (EST). *Misdemeanor, Civil Actions Under $15,000, Eviction, Small Claims.*

Note: Indicate division (civil, criminal or traffic) in address.

Civil Records: Access: Mail, online, in person. Both court and visitors may perform in person searches. Search fee: $15.00 per name. Required to search: name, years to search. Civil cases indexed by defendant, plaintiff. Civil records on books from 1700. For information about the statewide online system, LOPAS, see the state introduction. Mail access by specific case only.

Criminal Records: Access: Mail, online, in person. Both court and visitors may perform in person searches. No search fee. Required to search: name, years to search, DOB; also helpful: SSN. Criminal records on books from 1700. Online access to criminal records is the same as civil.

General Information: Public Access terminal is available. No juvenile, sealed records released. Turnaround time 2-14 days. Copy fee: $1.00 per page. Certification fee: $2.00. Fee payee: General District Court. Personal checks accepted. Credit cards accepted: Visa, MasterCard. Prepayment is required.

Chesterfield County

12th Circuit Court 9500 Courthouse Rd, PO Box 125, Chesterfield, VA 23832; 804-748-1241; Fax: 804-796-5625. Hours: 8:30AM-5PM (EST). *Felony, Civil Actions Over $15,000, Probate.*

www.co.chesterfield.va.us/cc-main.htm

Civil Records: Access: Mail, online, in person. Both court and visitors may perform in person searches. Search fee: $3.00 per name. Required to search: name,

years to search. Civil cases indexed by defendant, plaintiff. Civil records on computer from 1988 to present, prior on index books. For information about the statewide online system, LOPAS, see the state introduction.

Criminal Records: Access: Mail, online, in person. Only the court performs in person searches; visitors may not. Search fee: $3.00 per name. Required to search: name, years to search; also helpful: DOB, SSN. Criminal records on computer from 1988 to present, prior on index books. Online access to criminal records is the same as civil.

General Information: Public Access terminal is available. (Civil only.) No juvenile, adoption, sealed records released. SASE required. Turnaround time 1-2 days. Copy fee: $.50 per page. Certification fee: $2.00. Fee payee: Chesterfield Circuit Court. Personal checks accepted. Prepayment is required.

12th General District Court PO Box 144, Chesterfield, VA 23832; 804-748-1231. Hours: 8AM-4PM (EST). *Misdemeanor, Civil Actions Under $15,000, Eviction, Small Claims.*

Civil Records: Access: Mail, online, in person. Both court and visitors may perform in person searches. No search fee. Required to search: name, years to search. Civil cases indexed by defendant, plaintiff. Civil records on computer from 1986 to present, index books from 1975 to 1986. For information about the statewide online system, LOPAS, see the state introduction.

Criminal Records: Access: Mail, online, in person. Both court and visitors may perform in person searches. No search fee. Required to search: name, years to search, DOB, SSN. Criminal records on computer from 1986 to present, index books from 1975 to 1986. Online access to criminal records is the same as civil.

General Information: Public Access terminal is available. No sealed records released. Turnaround time 2 days. Copy fee: $.50 per page. Certification fee: $2.00. Personal checks accepted. Credit cards accepted: Visa, MasterCard.

Clarke County

26th Circuit Court PO Box 189, Berryville, VA 22611; 540-955-5116; Fax: 540-955-0284. Hours: 9AM-5PM (EST). *Felony, Civil Actions Over $15,000, Probate.*

Civil Records: Access: Phone, mail, fax, online, in person. Both court and visitors may perform in person searches. No search fee. Required to search: name, years to search. Civil cases indexed by defendant, plaintiff. Civil records on books from 1920s. For information about the statewide online system, LOPAS, see the state introduction.

Criminal Records: Access: Online, in person. Visitors must perform in person searches for themselves. No search fee. Required to search: name, years to search, signed release. Criminal records on books from 1920s. Online access to criminal records is the same as civil.

General Information: No juvenile, sealed or adoption records released. No criminal records by mail. SASE requested. Turnaround time 1-2 days. Fax notes: Fee to fax results is $.50 per page. Copy fee: $.50 per page. Certification fee: No certification fee. Fee payee: Clerk of Court. Personal checks accepted. Prepayment required.

General District Court 104 N Church St (PO Box 612), Berryville, VA 22611; 540-955-5128; Fax: 540-955-1195. Hours: 8:30AM-4:30PM (EST). *Misdemeanor, Civil Actions Under $15,000, Eviction, Small Claims.*

www.co.clarke.va.us

Civil Records: Access: Online, in person. Visitors must perform in person searches for themselves. No search fee. Required to search: name, years to search. Civil cases indexed by defendant, plaintiff. Civil records on

computer from 1992, on index cards for 1991. For information about the statewide online system, LOPAS, see the state introduction.

Criminal Records: Access: Online, in person. Visitors must perform in person searches for themselves. No search fee. Required to search: name, years to search, DOB, SSN, date of conviction, charge; also helpful: docket number, defendant's name. Criminal records on computer from 1992, on index cards for 1991. Online access to criminal records is the same as civil.

General Information: Public Access terminal is available. Copy fee: $.50 per page. Fee payee: Clarke County General District Court. Personal checks accepted. Personal checks require name and address. Prepayment is required.

Clifton Forge City

25th Circuit Court PO Box 670, Covington, VA 24426; 540-965-1730. Hours: 9AM-5PM (EST). *Felony, Civil Actions Over $15,000, Probate.*

Note: This court closed 7/1/01 and was combined with the Alleghany County Circuit Court.

25th General District Court PO Box 139, Covington, VA 24426; 540-965-1720; Fax: 540-965-1720. Hours: 9AM-5PM (EST). *Misdemeanor, Civil Actions Under $15,000, Eviction, Small Claims.*

Note: As of 7/1/2001, the Clifton Forge Court is combined with the Alleghany County District Court to form the 25th Combined District Court.

Colonial Heights City

12th Circuit Court 401 Temple Ave, PO Box 3401, Colonial Heights, VA 23834; 804-520-9364. Hours: 8:30AM-5PM (EST). *Felony, Civil Actions Over $15,000, Probate.*

Civil Records: Access: Mail, online, in person. Both court and visitors may perform in person searches. Search fee: $5.00 per name. Required to search: name, years to search. Civil cases indexed by defendant, plaintiff. Civil records on books from 1961, on computer from 1991. For information about the statewide online system, LOPAS, see the state introduction.

Criminal Records: Access: Mail, online, in person. Both court and visitors may perform in person searches. Search fee: $5.00 per name. Required to search: name, years to search; also helpful: DOB, SSN. Criminal records on books from 1961, on computer from 1991. Online access to criminal records is the same as civil.

General Information: No juvenile, sealed or adoption records released. SASE required. Turnaround time 2 days. Copy fee: $.50 per page. Certification fee: $2.00. Fee payee: Clerk of Circuit Court. Personal checks accepted. Prepayment is required.

12th General District Court 401 Temple Ave, PO Box 279, Colonial Heights, VA 23834; 804-520-9346 (Dial 0); Fax: 804-520-9370. Hours: 8AM-4PM (EST). *Misdemeanor, Civil Actions Under $15,000, Eviction, Small Claims.*

Civil Records: Access: Mail, fax, online, in person. Both court and visitors may perform in person searches. No search fee. Required to search: name, years to search. Civil cases indexed by defendant, plaintiff. Civil records on computer from 1989 to present, index cards from 1985. For information about the statewide online system, LOPAS, see the state introduction.

Criminal Records: Access: Mail, fax, online, in person. Both court and visitors may perform in person searches. No search fee. Required to search: name, years to search, DOB, SSN. Criminal records on computer from 1989 to present, index cards from 1985. Online access to criminal records is the same as civil.

General Information: Public Access terminal is available. No juvenile, sealed records released.

Turnaround time 1 week. Copy fee: $.50 per page. Certification fee: $2.00. Fee payee: Colonial Heights Combined Court. Personal checks accepted. Credit cards accepted: Visa, MasterCard. Prepayment is required.

Covington City

Circuit & District Courts, VA.

Note: See Alleghany County

Craig County

25th Circuit Court PO Box 185, New Castle, VA 24127-0185; 540-864-6141. Hours: 9AM-5PM (EST). *Felony, Civil Actions Over $15,000, Probate.*

Civil Records: Access: Online, in person. Visitors must perform in person searches for themselves. No search fee. Required to search: name, years to search. Civil cases indexed by defendant. Civil records on books from mid 1800s. For information about the statewide online system, LOPAS, see the state introduction.

Criminal Records: Access: Online, in person. Visitors must perform in person searches for themselves. No search fee. Required to search: name, years to search; also helpful: SSN. Criminal records on books from mid 1800s. Online access to criminal records is the same as civil.

General Information: No juvenile, sealed or adoption records released. Copy fee: $.50 per page. Certification fee: $2.00. Fee payee: Clerk of Court. Personal checks accepted. Prepayment is required.

25th General District Court Craig County General District Court, PO Box 232, New Castle, VA 24127; 540-864-5989. Hours: 8:15AM-4:45PM (EST). *Misdemeanor, Civil Actions Under $15,000, Eviction, Small Claims.*

Civil Records: Access: Online, in person. Visitors must perform in person searches for themselves. No search fee. Required to search: name, years to search. Civil cases indexed by defendant, plaintiff. Civil records in files 10 years back. For information about the statewide online system, LOPAS, see the state introduction. Lengthy searches must be performed in person.

Criminal Records: Access: Online, in person. Visitors must perform in person searches for themselves. No search fee. Required to search: name, years to search; also helpful: SSN. Criminal records in files 10 years back. Online access to criminal records is the same as civil. Lengthy searches must be performed in person.

General Information: Public Access terminal is available. No juvenile, sealed records released. Copy fee: $.50 for first page, $1.00 each add'l. Certification fee: No certification fee. Fee payee: Craig County District Court. Personal checks accepted. Credit cards accepted: Visa, MasterCard.

Culpeper County

16th Circuit Court 135 W Cameron St, Culpeper, VA 22701-3097; 540-727-3438. Hours: 8:30AM-4:30PM (EST). *Felony, Civil Actions Over $15,000, Probate.*

Civil Records: Access: Online, in person. Visitors must perform in person searches for themselves. No search fee. Required to search: name, years to search. Civil cases indexed by defendant, plaintiff. Civil records on computer from 1991, docket books from 1800s. For information about the statewide online system, LOPAS, see the state introduction.

Criminal Records: Access: Online, in person. Visitors must perform in person searches for themselves. No search fee. Required to search: name, years to search, signed release. Criminal records on computer from 1991, docket books from 1800s. Online access to criminal records is the same as civil.

General Information: Public Access terminal is available. No juvenile, sealed records released. Copy

fee: $.50 per page. Certification fee: $2.00. Fee payee: Clerk of Court. Personal checks accepted. Prepayment is required.

16th General District Court 135 W Cameron St, Culpeper, VA 22701; 540-727-3417; Fax: 540-727-3474. Hours: 8:30AM-4:30PM (EST). *Misdemeanor, Civil Actions Under $15,000, Eviction, Small Claims.*

Civil Records: Access: Mail, online, in person. Both court and visitors may perform in person searches. No search fee. Required to search: name, years to search. Civil cases indexed by defendant, plaintiff. Civil records on computer from 1987 to present, prior on index cards. For information about the statewide online system, LOPAS, see the state introduction.

Criminal Records: Access: Mail, online, in person. Both court and visitors may perform in person searches. No search fee. Required to search: name, years to search. Criminal records on computer from 1987 to present, prior on index cards. Online access to criminal records is the same as civil.

General Information: Public Access terminal is available. No juvenile, sealed records released. SASE required. Turnaround time 1-5 days. Copy fee: $.50 per page. Certification fee: No certification fee. Fee payee: General District Court. Personal checks accepted. Prepayment is required.

Cumberland County

10th Circuit Court PO Box 8, Cumberland, VA 23040; 804-492-4442. Hours: 8:30AM-4:30PM (EST). *Felony, Civil Actions Over $15,000, Probate.*

Civil Records: Access: Online, in person. Visitors must perform in person searches for themselves. No search fee. Required to search: name, years to search. Civil cases indexed by defendant, plaintiff. Civil records in files. For information about the statewide online system, LOPAS, see the state introduction. Phone access only available for simple requests.

Criminal Records: Access: Online, in person. Visitors must perform in person searches for themselves. No search fee. Required to search: name, years to search. Criminal records in files. Online access to criminal records is the same as civil.

General Information: No juvenile, sealed records released. Copy fee: $.50 per page. Certification fee: No certification fee. Fee payee: Clerk of Circuit Court. Personal checks accepted. Prepayment is required.

10th General District Court PO Box 24, Cumberland, VA 23040; 804-492-4848; Fax: 804-492-9455. Hours: 8:30AM-4:30PM (EST). *Misdemeanor, Civil Actions Under $15,000, Eviction, Small Claims.*

Civil Records: Access: Phone, fax, mail, online, in person. Only the court performs in person searches; visitors may not. No search fee. Required to search: name, years to search. Civil cases indexed by defendant, plaintiff. Civil records on books from 1990, on computer from 1993. For information about the statewide online system, LOPAS, see the state introduction.

Criminal Records: Access: Phone, fax, mail, online, in person. Only the court performs in person searches; visitors may not. No search fee. Required to search: name, years to search; also helpful: DOB, SSN, sex. Criminal records on books from 1990, on computer from 1993. Online access to criminal records is the same as civil.

General Information: No juvenile, sealed records released. SASE required. Turnaround time 2 days. Copy fee: $1.00 per page. Certification fee: No certification fee. Fee payee: Clerk of District Court. Personal checks accepted. Credit cards accepted: Visa, MasterCard.

Danville City

22nd Circuit Court PO Box 3300, Danville, VA 24543; 804-799-5168; Fax: 804-799-6502. Hours: 8:30AM-5PM (EST). *Felony, Civil Actions Over $15,000, Probate.*

Civil Records: Access: Online, in person. Visitors must perform in person searches for themselves. No search fee. Required to search: name, years to search. Civil cases indexed by defendant, plaintiff. Civil records in index books from 1841, judgments on computer since 1990. Online access is available free at http://208.210.219.132/courtinfo/vacircuit/select.jsp?court=. For information about the statewide online system, LOPAS, see the state introduction.

Criminal Records: Access: Online, in person. Visitors must perform in person searches for themselves. No search fee. Required to search: name, years to search. Criminal records in index books from 1841. Criminal records on computer from 1988. Online access to criminal records is the same as civil.

General Information: No juvenile, sealed or adoption records released. Copy fee: $.50 per page. Certification fee: $2.00. Fee payee: Gerald A Gibson, Clerk. Personal checks accepted. Prepayment is required.

22nd General District Court PO Box 3300, Danville, VA 24543; 804-799-5179; Fax: 804-797-8814. Hours: 8:30AM-4:30PM (EST). *Misdemeanor, Civil Actions Under $15,000, Eviction, Small Claims.*

Civil Records: Access: Phone, fax, mail, online, in person. Both court and visitors may perform in person searches. No search fee. Required to search: name, years to search. Civil cases indexed by defendant, plaintiff. Civil records on computer from 1987 to present. For information about the statewide online system, LOPAS, see the state introduction.

Criminal Records: Access: Phone, fax, mail, online, in person. Both court and visitors may perform in person searches. No search fee. Required to search: name, years to search. Criminal records on computer from 1987 to present. Online access to criminal records is the same as civil.

General Information: Public Access terminal is available. No juvenile, sealed records released. SASE requested. Turnaround time 2 days. Copy fee: $1.00 1st 2 pages, $.50 each additional page. Certification fee: No certification fee. Fee payee: General District Court. Personal checks accepted. Credit cards accepted: Visa, MasterCard.

Dickenson County

29th Circuit Court PO Box 190, Clintwood, VA 24228; 540-926-1616; Fax: 540-926-6465. Hours: 8:30AM-4:30PM (EST). *Felony, Civil Actions Over $15,000, Probate.*

Civil Records: Access: Phone, mail, online, in person. Both court and visitors may perform in person searches. No search fee. Required to search: name, years to search. Civil cases indexed by defendant, plaintiff. Civil records on computer from 1989, index book from 1880. Online access is available free at http://208.210.219.132/courtinfo/vacircuit/select.jsp?court=. For information about the statewide online system, LOPAS, see the state introduction.

Criminal Records: Access: Phone, mail, online, in person. Both court and visitors may perform in person searches. No search fee. Required to search: name, years to search, DOB; also helpful: SSN. Criminal records on computer from 1989, index book from 1880. Online access to criminal records is the same as civil.

General Information: Public Access terminal is available. No juvenile, sealed, adoption, confidential records released. SASE requested. Turnaround time 1 week. Copy fee: $.50 per page. Certification fee: $2.00. Fee payee: Joe Tate, Clerk of Circuit Court. Personal checks accepted. Prepayment is required.

29th General District Court PO Box 128, Clintwood, VA 24228; 540-926-1630; Fax: 540-926-4815. Hours: 8:30AM-4:30PM (EST). *Misdemeanor, Civil Actions Under $15,000, Eviction, Small Claims.*

Civil Records: Access: Phone, mail, in person. Both court and visitors may perform in person searches. No search fee. Required to search: name, years to search. Civil cases indexed by defendant. Civil records on index cards 10 yrs back, on computer from 5/93. For information about the statewide online system, LOPAS, see the state introduction.

Criminal Records: Access: Phone, mail, in person. Both court and visitors may perform in person searches. No search fee. Required to search: name, years to search. Criminal records on index cards 10 yrs back, on computer from 5/93. Online access to criminal records is the same as civil.

General Information: Public Access terminal is available. No juvenile, sealed records released. SASE requested. Turnaround time 1 week. Copy fee: $.10 per page. Certification fee: No certification fee. Fee payee: Dickenson Combined Court or General District Court. Personal checks accepted. Credit cards accepted: Visa, MasterCard.

Dinwiddie County

11th Circuit Court PO Box 63, Dinwiddie, VA 23841; 804-469-4540. Hours: 8:30AM-4:30PM (EST). *Felony, Civil Actions Over $15,000, Probate.*

Civil Records: Access: Mail, online, in person. Both court and visitors may perform in person searches. No search fee. Required to search: name, years to search; also helpful: address. Civil cases indexed by defendant, plaintiff. Civil records on index cards from 1833; deeds on computer since 1989. For information about the statewide online system, LOPAS, see state introduction.

Criminal Records: Access: Mail, online, in person. Both court and visitors may perform in person searches. No search fee. Required to search: name, years to search; also helpful: DOB, SSN. Criminal records on index cards from 1833; deeds on computer since 1989. Online access to criminal records is the same as civil.

General Information: No juvenile, sealed or expunged records released. SASE requested. Turnaround time 3 days. Copy fee: $.50 per page. Certification fee: $2.00 plus $.50 per page. Fee payee: Clerk of Court. Personal checks accepted.

11th General District Court PO Box 280, Dinwiddie, VA 23841; 804-469-4533; Fax: 804-469-4412. Hours: 8:30AM-4:30PM (EST). *Misdemeanor, Civil Actions Under $15,000, Eviction, Small Claims.*

Civil Records: Access: Mail, online, in person. Only the court performs in person searches; visitors may not. No search fee. Required to search: name, years to search. Civil cases indexed by defendant, plaintiff. Civil records on index cards from 1800s, on computer from 1989. For information about the statewide online system, LOPAS, see the state introduction.

Criminal Records: Access: Mail, online, in person. Only the court performs in person searches; visitors may not. No search fee. Required to search: name, years to search. Criminal records on index cards from 1800s, on computer from 1989. Online access to criminal records is the same as civil.

General Information: No juvenile, sealed records released. SASE required. Turnaround time 3 days. Copy fee: $1.00 per page. Certification fee: $2.00. Fee payee: District Court. Personal checks accepted. Credit cards accepted: Visa, MasterCard. Prepayment is required.

Emporia City

Circuit Court, VA.

Note: See Greensville County

6th General District Court 315 S Main, Emporia, VA 23847; 804-634-5400. Hours: 8:30AM-4:30PM (EST). *Misdemeanor, Civil Actions Under $15,000, Eviction, Small Claims.*

Civil Records: Access: Online, in person. Visitors must perform in person searches for themselves. No search fee. Required to search: name, years to search. Civil cases indexed by defendant, plaintiff. Civil records on computer back to 1991. For information about the statewide online system, LOPAS, see the state introduction.

Criminal Records: Access: Mail, online, in person. Only the court performs in person searches; visitors may not. No search fee. Required to search: name, years to search. Criminal records on computer back to 1991. Online access to criminal records is the same as civil.

General Information: Public Access terminal is available. No juvenile records released. Turnaround time 1-2 days. No copy fee. Certification fee: No certification fee. Personal checks accepted.

Essex County

15th Circuit Court PO Box 445, 305 prince St, Tappahannock, VA 22560; 804-443-3541. Hours: 8:30AM-5PM (EST). *Felony, Civil Actions Over $15,000, Probate.*

Civil Records: Access: In person only. Visitors must perform in person searches for themselves. No search fee. Required to search: name, years to search. Civil cases indexed by defendant, plaintiff. Civil records on books from 1656; deed index on computer back to 1977.

Criminal Records: Access: In person only. Visitors must perform in person searches for themselves. No search fee. Required to search: name, years to search. Criminal records on books from 1656.

General Information: No juvenile, sealed records released. Copy fee: $.50 per page. Certification fee: $2.00. Fee payee: Clerk of Court. Personal checks accepted. Prepayment is required.

15th General District Court PO Box 66, Tappahannock, VA 22560; 804-443-3744; Fax: 804-443-4122. Hours: 8AM-12:30PM, 1-4:30PM (EST). *Misdemeanor, Civil Actions Under $15,000, Eviction, Small Claims.*

Civil Records: Access: Mail, online, in person. Both court and visitors may perform in person searches. No search fee. Required to search: name, years to search. Civil cases indexed by defendant, plaintiff. Civil records on computer from 5/92, prior on index cards. For information about the statewide online system, LOPAS, see the state introduction.

Criminal Records: Access: Online, in person. Visitors must perform in person searches for themselves. No search fee. Required to search: name, years to search, DOB, SSN. Criminal records on computer from 5/92, prior on index cards. Online access to criminal records is the same as civil.

General Information: Public Access terminal is available. No juvenile, sealed records released. Turnaround time 1-2 days. No copy fee. Certification fee: No certification fee. Fee payee: General District Court. Personal checks accepted. Credit cards accepted: Visa, MasterCard. Prepayment is required.

Fairfax County

19th Circuit Court 4110 Chain Bridge Rd, Fairfax, VA 22030; Civil phone: 703-591-8507; Criminal phone: 703-246-2228. Hours: 8AM-4PM (EST). *Felony, Civil Actions Over $15,000, Probate.*

www.co.fairfax.va.us/courts

Civil Records: Access: Mail, in person. Visitors must perform in person searches for themselves. No search fee. Required to search: name, years to search. Civil

cases indexed by defendant, plaintiff. Civil records on computer from 1979, index cards from 1940s.

Criminal Records: Access: Mail, in person. Visitors must perform in person searches for themselves. No search fee. Required to search: name, years to search, DOB; also helpful: SSN. Criminal records on computer from 1979, index cards from 1940s.

General Information: Public Access terminal is available. No juvenile, sealed records released. Copy fee: $.50 per page. Certification fee: $2.00. Fee payee: Fairfax Circuit Court. Personal checks accepted. In-state personal checks accepted. Credit cards accepted: Visa, MasterCard. Prepayment is required.

19th General District Court 4110 Chain Bridge Rd, Fairfax, VA 22030; 703-246-2153; Civil phone: 703-246-3012; Criminal phone: 703-691-7320; Fax: 703-591-2349. Hours: 8AM-4PM (EST). *Misdemeanor, Civil Actions Under $15,000, Eviction, Small Claims.*

www.co.fairfax.va.us/courts

Note: Traffic division at 703-691-7320.

Civil Records: Access: Phone, in person. Visitors must perform in person searches for themselves. No search fee. Required to search: name, years to search. Civil cases indexed by defendant, plaintiff. Civil records on microfiche for 10 years.

Criminal Records: Access: Phone, in person. Only the court performs in person searches; visitors may not. No search fee. Required to search: name, years to search; also helpful: DOB, SSN. Criminal records on microfiche for 10 years.

General Information: No juvenile, sealed records released. Copy fee: $.50 per page. Certification fee: No certification fee. Fee payee: Fairfax General District Court. Personal checks accepted. Prepayment required.

Fairfax City

Circuit Court, VA.

Note: See Fairfax County

19th General District Court 10455 Armstrong St #304, Fairfax, VA 22030; 703-385-7866; Fax: 703-352-3195. Hours: 8:30AM-4:30PM (EST). *Misdemeanor.*

Note: Find Circuit Court cases and General District civil cases for this city in the Fairfax County listing

Criminal Records: Access: Mail, in person. Only the court performs in person searches; visitors may not. No search fee. Required to search: name, years to search; also helpful: SSN. Criminal records on computer and index from 1985.

General Information: No juvenile or sealed records released. SASE requested. Turnaround time same day. Copy fee: $1.00 for first 2 pages; each add'l page $.50. Certification fee: No certification fee. Fee payee: General District Court. Personal checks accepted. Credit cards accepted: Visa, MasterCard.

Falls Church City

Circuit Court, VA.

Note: See Arlington County

17th District Courts Combined Falls Church District, 300 Park Ave, Falls Church, VA 22046-3305; 703-248-5096 (GDC); Civil phone: 703-248-5098; Fax: 703-241-1407. Hours: 8AM-4PM (EST). *Misdemeanor, Civil Actions Under $15,000, Eviction, Small Claims.*

www.ci.falls-church.va.us

Note: Small claims phone is 703-248-5157; juvenile and domestic relations is 703-248-5099.

Civil Records: Access: Fax, online. Only the court performs in person searches; visitors may not. No search fee. Required to search: name, years to search. Civil cases indexed by defendant, plaintiff. Civil records on computer from 1989, microfiche back to 1980. For information about the statewide online system, LOPAS, see the state introduction.

Criminal Records: Access: Fax, online, in person. Only the court performs in person searches; visitors may not. No search fee. Required to search: name, years to search; also helpful: DOB, SSN. Criminal records on computer and microfiche back to 1989. Online access to criminal records is the same as civil.

General Information: No juvenile, sealed records released. Fax notes: No fee to fax results. Copy fee: $.50 per page. Certification fee: No certification fee. Fee payee: Falls Church District Court. Personal checks accepted. Credit cards accepted: Visa, MasterCard. Prepayment is required.

Fauquier County

20th Circuit Court 40 Culpeper St, Warrenton, VA 20186-3298; 540-347-8610. Hours: 8AM-4:30PM (EST). *Felony, Civil Actions Over $15,000, Probate.*

http://co.fauquier.va.us/services/ccc/index.html

Civil Records: Access: Online, in person. Visitors must perform in person searches for themselves. No search fee. Required to search: name, years to search. Civil cases indexed by defendant, plaintiff. Civil records on computer back to 1988. Online access is available free at http://208.210.219.132/courtinfo/vacircuit/select.jsp ?court=. For information about the statewide online system, LOPAS, see the state introduction.

Criminal Records: Access: Online, in person. Visitors must perform in person searches for themselves. No search fee. Required to search: name, years to search. Criminal records on computer back to 1988. Online access to criminal records is the same as civil.

General Information: No juvenile, sealed, adoption records released. Copy fee: $.50 per page. Certification fee: $2.00. Fee payee: Clerk of Fauquier Circuit Court. Personal checks accepted. Prepayment is required.

20th General District Court 6 Court St, Warrenton, VA 20186; Civil phone: 540-347-8676; Criminal phone: 540-347-8624; Fax: 540-347-5756. Hours: 8:30AM-4:30PM (EST). *Misdemeanor, Civil Actions Under $15,000, Eviction, Small Claims.*

Civil Records: Access: Online, in person. Visitors must perform in person searches for themselves. No search fee. Required to search: name, years to search. Civil cases indexed by defendant, plaintiff. Civil records on computer from 12/86, prior on file cards. For information about the statewide online system, LOPAS, see the state introduction.

Criminal Records: Access: Online, in person. Visitors must perform in person searches for themselves. No search fee. Required to search: name, years to search. Criminal records on computer from 12/86; criminal records only go back 10 years. Online access to criminal records is the same as civil.

General Information: Public Access terminal is available. No juvenile, sealed records released. Copy fee: $1.00 1st 2 pages, $.50 each additional page. Certification fee: No certification fee. Fee payee: General District Court. Personal checks accepted.

Floyd County

27th Circuit Court 100 East Main St, #200, Floyd, VA 24091; 540-745-9330. Hours: 8:30AM-4:30PM M-F, 8:30AM-Noon Sat (EST). *Felony, Civil Actions Over $15,000, Probate.*

Civil Records: Access: Online, in person. Visitors must perform in person searches for themselves. No search fee. Required to search: name, years to search. Civil cases indexed by defendant, plaintiff. Civil records on files from 1831. Online access is available free at http://208.210.219.132/courtinfo/vacircuit/select.jsp?co urt=. For information about the statewide online system, LOPAS, see the state introduction.

Criminal Records: Access: Online, in person. Visitors must perform in person searches for themselves. No search fee. Required to search: name, years to search; also helpful: DOB, SSN. Criminal records on files from 1831. Online access to criminal records is the same as civil.

General Information: No juvenile, sealed records released. Copy fee: $.50 per page. Certification fee: $2.00. Fee payee: Clerk of Circuit Court. Personal checks accepted. Prepayment is required.

27th General District Court 100 East Main St, Floyd, VA 24091-2101; 540-745-9327; Fax: 540-745-9329. Hours: 8AM-4:30PM (EST). *Misdemeanor, Civil Actions Under $15,000, Eviction, Small Claims.*

Civil Records: Access: Phone, fax, mail, online, in person. Both court and visitors may perform in person searches. No search fee. Required to search: name, years to search. Civil cases indexed by defendant, plaintiff. Phone search results may be of limited content. For information about the statewide online system, LOPAS, see the state introduction.

Criminal Records: Access: Phone, fax mail, online, in person. Both court and visitors may perform in person searches. No search fee. Required to search: name, years to search, DOB. Phone search results may be of limited content. For information about the statewide online system, LOPAS, see the state introduction.

General Information: Public Access terminal is available. No juvenile, sealed records released. SASE required. Turnaround time 1 week. Copy fee: $.50 per page. Certification fee: No certification fee. Fee payee: Clerk of District Court. Prepayment is required.

Fluvanna County

16th Circuit Court PO Box 299, Palmyra, VA 22963; 804-589-8011; Fax: 804-589-6004. Hours: 8:30AM-4:30PM (EST). *Felony, Civil Actions Over $15,000, Probate.*

Civil Records: Access: Mail, in person. Both court and visitors may perform in person searches. Search fee: $5.00 per name. Required to search: name, years to search. Civil cases indexed by defendant, plaintiff. Civil records on index books from 1777; computerized back to 1985. For information about the statewide online system, LOPAS, see the state introduction.

Criminal Records: Access: Mail, in person. Both court and visitors may perform in person searches. Search fee: $5.00 per name. Required to search: name, years to search, DOB; also helpful: SSN. Criminal records on index books from 1777; computerized back to 1985.

General Information: Public Access terminal is available. No juvenile or sealed records released. SASE required. Turnaround time same 1-2 days. Fax notes: Fee to fax results is $2.00 per document. Copy fee: $.50 per page. Certification fee: $2.00. Fee payee: Clerk of Circuit Court. Personal checks accepted. Prepayment is required.

16th General District Court Fluvanna County Courthouse, PO Box 417, Palmyra, VA 22963; 804-589-8022; Fax: 804-589-6934. Hours: 8:30AM-4:30PM (EST). *Misdemeanor, Civil Actions Under $15,000, Eviction, Small Claims.*

Civil Records: Access: Online, in person. Visitors must perform in person searches for themselves. No search fee. Required to search: name, years to search. Civil cases indexed by defendant, plaintiff. Civil records on computer since 12/91, on books since 1984. For information about the statewide online system, LOPAS, see the state introduction.

Criminal Records: Access: Online, in person. Visitors must perform in person searches for themselves. No search fee. Required to search: name, years to search; also helpful: DOB, SSN. Criminal records on computer since 12/91, on books since 1984. Online access to criminal records is the same as civil.

General Information: Public Access terminal is available. No juvenile records released. Copy fee: $.50 per page. Certification fee: No certification fee. Fee payee: Fluvanna District Court. Personal checks accepted. Prepayment is required.

Franklin City

5th Circuit Court PO Box 190, Courtland, VA 23837; 757-653-2200. Hours: 8:30AM-5PM (EST). *Felony, Civil Actions Over $15,000, Probate.*

Note: Southampton County serves as the Circuit Court for the city of Franklin.

Civil Records: Access: Mail, online, in person. Both court and visitors may perform in person searches. Search fee: $5.00 per name. Required to search: name, years to search. Civil cases indexed by defendant, plaintiff. Civil records on computer since 1989, prior on docket books since 1700s. Online access is available free at http://208.210.219.132/courtinfo/vacircuit/ select.jsp?court=. For information about the statewide online system, LOPAS, see the state introduction.

Criminal Records: Access: Mail, online, in person. Both court and visitors may perform in person searches. Search fee: $5.00 per name. Required to search: name, years to search; also helpful: SSN. Criminal records on computer since 1989, prior on docket books since 1700s. Online access to criminal records is the same as civil.

General Information: Public Access terminal is available. No juvenile records released. Turnaround time 2-5 days. Copy fee: $.50. Fee for first 2 pages. Add $.50 per page thereafter. Certification fee: No certification fee. Fee payee: Clerk of the Circuit Court. Personal checks accepted. Credit cards accepted: Visa, MasterCard.

Circuit Court, VA.

Note: See Franklin County

22nd General District Court PO Box 569, Rocky Mount, VA 24151; 540-483-3060; Fax: 540-483-3036. 8:30AM-4:30PM *Misdemeanor, Civil Actions Under $15,000, Eviction, Small Claims.*

Civil Records: Access: Online, in person. Visitors must perform in person searches for themselves. No search fee. Required to search: name, years to search. Civil cases indexed by defendant, plaintiff. Civil records file on computer from 1991. For information about the statewide online system, LOPAS, see the state introduction.

Criminal Records: Access: Online, in person. Visitors must perform in person searches for themselves. No search fee. Required to search: name, years to search. Criminal records file on computer from 1991. Online access to criminal records is the same as civil.

General Information: Public Access terminal is available. Copy fee: $.25 per page. Certification fee: No certification fee. Personal checks accepted. Credit cards accepted: Visa, MasterCard.

Frederick County

Circuit Court 5 North Kent St, Winchester, VA 22601; 540-667-5770. Hours: 9AM-5PM (EST). *Felony, Misdemeanor, Civil, Probate.*

www.winfredclerk.com

Civil Records: Access: Mail, in person. Both court and visitors may perform in person searches. No search fee. Required to search: name, years to search. Civil cases indexed by defendant, plaintiff. Civil records on books from 1970s. For information about the statewide online system, LOPAS, see the state introduction. Mail access limited to simple requests.

Criminal Records: Access: In person only. Visitors must perform in person searches for themselves. No search fee. Required to search: name, years to search.

Criminal records on books from 1970s. Online access to criminal records is the same as civil.

General Information: Public Access terminal is available. No juvenile, sealed or adoption records released. Turnaround time 1-2 days. Copy fee: $.50 per page. Certification fee: $3.00. Fee payee: Clerk of Circuit Court. Personal checks accepted. Prepayment is required.

26th District Court 5 North Kent St, Winchester, VA 22601; 540-722-7208; Fax: 540-722-1063. Hours: 8AM-5PM (EST). *Misdemeanor, Civil Actions up to $15,000.*

Civil Records: Access: Phone, fax, mail, in person. Both court and visitors may perform in person searches. No search fee. Required to search: name, years to search.

Criminal Records: Access: In person only. Visitors must perform in person searches for themselves. No search fee. Required to search: name, years to search.

General Information: Public Access terminal is available. Turnaround time 2-4 days. Copy fee: $.50 per page. Certification fee: $.50. Fee payee: Frederick District Court. Personal checks accepted. Prepayment is required.

Fredericksburg City

15th Circuit Court 815 Princess Anne St, PO Box 359, Fredericksburg, VA 22404-0359; 540-372-1066. Hours: 8AM-4PM (EST). *Felony, Civil Actions Over $15,000, Probate.*

Civil Records: Access: Online, in person. Visitors must perform in person searches for themselves. No search fee. Required to search: name, years to search. Civil cases indexed by defendant, plaintiff. Civil records on index books from 1765. Online access is available free at http://208.210.219.132/courtinfo/vacircuit/select.jsp ?court=. For information about the statewide online system, LOPAS, see the state introduction.

Criminal Records: Access: Online, in person. Visitors must perform in person searches for themselves. No search fee. Required to search: name, years to search, DOB; also helpful: SSN. Criminal records on index books from 1765. Online access to criminal records is the same as civil.

General Information: Public Access terminal is available. No juvenile, probate tax returns, sealed or adoption records released. Copy fee: $.50 per page. Certification fee: $2.00. Fee payee: Clerk of Circuit Court. Personal checks accepted.

15th General District Court PO Box 180, Fredericksburg, VA 22404; 540-372-1044. Hours: 8AM-4PM (EST). *Misdemeanor, Civil Actions Under $15,000, Eviction, Small Claims.*

Civil Records: Access: Mail, online, in person. Both court and visitors may perform in person searches. No search fee. Required to search: name, years to search. Civil cases indexed by defendant, plaintiff. Civil records on computer from 1987, prior on index books. For information about the statewide online system, LOPAS, see the state introduction.

Criminal Records: Access: Mail, online, in person. Both court and visitors may perform in person searches. No search fee. Required to search: name, years to search, DOB, SSN. Criminal records on computer from 1987, prior on index books. Online access to criminal records is the same as civil.

General Information: Public Access terminal is available. No sealed records released. Turnaround time 1-10 days. Copy fee: $.50 per page. Certification fee: $2.00. Fee payee: Fredricksburg District Court. Personal checks accepted. Prepayment is required.

Galax City

Circuit Court, VA.

Note: See Carroll County for Hillsville area and Grayson County for Independence area

27th General District Court 353 N Main St, PO Box 214, Galax, VA 24333-0214; 540-236-8731; Fax: 540-236-2754. Hours: 8:30AM-4:30PM (EST). *Misdemeanor, Civil Actions Under $15,000, Eviction, Small Claims.*

Note: Circuit Court jurisdiction for this city can be in Carroll County or Grayson County depending on side of the side the offense occurred.

Civil Records: Access: Mail, online, in person. Both court and visitors may perform in person searches. No search fee. Required to search: name, years to search. Civil cases indexed by defendant, plaintiff. Civil records on computer since 1990, prior on index books. For information about the statewide online system, LOPAS, see the state introduction.

Criminal Records: Access: Mail, online, in person. Both court and visitors may perform in person searches. No search fee. Required to search: name, years to search. Criminal records on computer since 1990, prior on index books. Online access to criminal records is the same as civil.

General Information: Public Access terminal is available. No juvenile, sealed records released. Turnaround time 1-5 days. Copy fee: $.25 per page. Certification fee: No certification fee. Fee payee: Clerk of District Court Galax District. Personal checks accepted. Credit cards accepted: Visa, MasterCard. Prepayment is required.

Giles County

27th Circuit Court 501 Wenonah Ave, PO Box 502, Pearisburg, VA 24134; 540-921-1722; Fax: 540-921-3825. Hours: 9AM-5PM (EST). *Felony, Civil Actions Over $15,000, Probate.*

Civil Records: Access: Mail, online, in person. Both court and visitors may perform in person searches. No search fee. Required to search: name, years to search. Civil cases indexed by defendant, plaintiff. Civil records (financial) on computer since 1990, on index cards from 1985. For information about the statewide online system, LOPAS, see the state introduction.

Criminal Records: Access: Mail, online, in person. Both court and visitors may perform in person searches. No search fee. Required to search: name, years to search, DOB; also helpful: SSN. Criminal records (financial) on computer since 1990, on index cards from 1985. Online access to criminal records is the same as civil.

General Information: No juvenile, sealed records released. Turnaround time 1-2 days. Copy fee: $.50 per page. Certification fee: $3.00. Fee payee: Clerk of Circuit Court. Personal checks accepted. Prepayment is required.

27th General District Court 120 N Main St, #1, Pearisburg, VA 24134; 540-921-3533; Fax: 540-921-2752. Hours: 8:30AM-4:30PM (EST). *Misdemeanor, Civil Actions Under $15,000, Eviction, Small Claims.*

Civil Records: Access: Fax, mail, online, in person. Both court and visitors may perform in person searches. No search fee. Required to search: name, years to search. Civil cases indexed by defendant, plaintiff. Civil records on computer since 1990, prior on index cards back 10 years. For information about the statewide online system, LOPAS, see the state introduction.

Criminal Records: Access: Fax, mail, online, in person. Both court and visitors may perform in person searches. No search fee. Required to search: name, years to search; also helpful: SSN. Criminal records on computer since 1990, prior on index cards back 10

years. Online access to criminal records is the same as civil.

General Information: Public Access terminal is available. No juvenile, sealed records released. Turnaround time 3-7 days. Fax notes: Fee to fax results is $1.00 per page. Copy fee: $1.00 for first page, $.50 each add'l. Certification fee: No certification fee. Fee payee: General District Court. Personal checks accepted. Credit cards accepted: Visa, MasterCard.

Gloucester County

9th Circuit Court Box N, Gloucester, VA 23061-0570; 804-693-2502; Fax: 804-693-2186. Hours: 8AM-4:30PM *Felony, Civil Actions Over $15,000, Probate.* www.co.gloucester.va.us

Civil Records: Access: Phone, fax, mail, online, in person. Both court and visitors may perform in person searches. No search fee. Required to search: name, years to search. Civil cases indexed by defendant, plaintiff. Civil records on index books from 1862; on computer since 1990. Online access is available free at http://208.210.219.132/courtinfo/vacircuit/select.jsp?court=. For information about the statewide online system, LOPAS, see the state introduction.

Criminal Records: Access: Phone, Fax, mail, online, in person. Both court and visitors may perform in person searches. No search fee. Required to search: name, years to search, DOB. Criminal records on index books from 1862; on computer since 1990. Online access to criminal records is the same as civil.

General Information: Public Access terminal is available. No juvenile, sealed or adoption records released. SASE requested. Turnaround time 1 day. Fax notes: $1.00 per page. Copy fee: $.50 per page. Certification fee: $2.00. Fee payee: Clerk of Circuit Court. Personal checks accepted.

9th General District Court PO Box 873, Gloucester, VA 23061; 804-693-4860; Fax: 804-693-6669. Hours: 8:30AM-4:30PM (EST). *Misdemeanor, Civil Actions Under $15,000, Eviction, Small Claims.*

Civil Records: Access: Fax, mail, online, in person. Both court and visitors may perform in person searches. No search fee. Required to search: name, years to search. Civil cases indexed by defendant, plaintiff. Civil records on index books from 1865; computerized back to 1992. For information about the statewide online system, LOPAS, see the state introduction.

Criminal Records: Access: Fax, mail, online, in person. Both court and visitors may perform in person searches. No search fee. Required to search: name, years to search; also helpful: DOB, SSN. Criminal records on index books from 1865; computerized back to 1992. Online access to criminal records is the same as civil.

General Information: Public Access terminal is available. No juvenile, sealed records released. SASE requested. Turnaround time 1 week. Fax notes: No fee to fax results. Copy fee: $.50 per page. Certification fee: No certification fee. Fee payee: Clerk of General District Court/Gloucester District Court. Personal checks accepted. Credit cards accepted: Visa, MasterCard. Prepayment is required.

Goochland County

16th Circuit Court PO Box 196, Goochland, VA 23063; 804-556-5353. Hours: 8:30AM-5PM (EST). *Felony, Civil Actions Over $15,000, Probate.*

Civil Records: Access: Online, in person. Visitors must perform in person searches for themselves. No search fee. Required to search: name, years to search. Civil cases indexed by defendant, plaintiff. Civil records on index books from 1850. For information about the statewide online system, LOPAS, see the state introduction.

Criminal Records: Access: Online, in person. Visitors must perform in person searches for themselves. No search fee. Required to search: name, years to search. Criminal records on index books from 1850. Online access to criminal records is the same as civil.

General Information: No juvenile, sealed or adoption records released. Copy fee: $.50 per page. Certification fee: $1.00. Fee payee: Clerk of Circuit Court. Personal checks accepted. Prepayment is required.

General District Court PO Box 47, Goochland, VA 23063; 804-556-5309. Hours: 8:30AM-4:30PM (EST). *Misdemeanor, Civil Actions Under $15,000, Eviction, Small Claims.*

Civil Records: Access: Online, in person. Visitors must perform in person searches for themselves. No search fee. Required to search: name, years to search. Civil cases indexed by defendant, plaintiff. Civil records on index books and computer back to 1989. For information about the statewide online system, LOPAS, see the state introduction.

Criminal Records: Access: Online, in person. Visitors must perform in person searches for themselves. No search fee. Required to search: name, years to search, DOB. Criminal records on index books and computer back to 1989. Online access to criminal records is the same as civil.

General Information: Public Access terminal is available. No juvenile records released. No copy fee. Certification fee: No certification fee. Fee payee: Clerk of General District Court, Goochland District Court. Credit cards accepted: Visa, MasterCard. Prepayment is required.

Grayson County

27th Circuit Court PO Box 130, Independence, VA 24348; 540-773-2231; Fax: 540-773-3338. Hours: 8AM-5PM (EST). *Felony, Civil Actions Over $15,000, Probate.*

Civil Records: Access: Mail, online, in person. Both court and visitors may perform in person searches. No search fee. Required to search: name, years to search. Civil cases indexed by defendant, plaintiff. Civil records on index books since 1793. For information about the statewide online system, LOPAS, see the state introduction.

Criminal Records: Access: Mail, online, in person. Both court and visitors may perform in person searches. No search fee. Required to search: name, years to search, DOB. Criminal records on index books since 1793. Online access to criminal records is the same as civil.

General Information: Public Access terminal is available. No juvenile, sealed or adoption records released. SASE requested. Turnaround time 2-3 days. Copy fee: $.50 per page. Certification fee: $2.00. Fee payee: Clerk of Circuit Court. Personal checks accepted. Prepayment is required.

27th General District Court PO Box 280, Independence, VA 24348; 540-773-2011. Hours: 8AM-4:30PM (EST). *Misdemeanor, Civil Actions Under $15,000, Eviction, Small Claims.*

Civil Records: Access: Mail, online, in person. Both court and visitors may perform in person searches. No search fee. Required to search: name, years to search. Civil cases indexed by defendant. Civil records on index books from 1800s, on computer from 1989. For information about the statewide online system, LOPAS, see the state introduction.

Criminal Records: Access: Mail, online, in person. Both court and visitors may perform in person searches. No search fee. Required to search: name, years to search; also helpful: DOB, SSN. Criminal records on index books from 1800s, on computer from 1989. Online access to criminal records is the same as civil.

General Information: Public Access terminal is available. No juvenile, sealed records released. Turnaround time 1 week. No copy fee. Certification fee: No certification fee.

Greene County

16th Circuit Court PO Box 386, Stanardsville, VA 22973; 804-985-5208; Fax: 804-985-6723. Hours: 8:15AM-4:30PM; Recording until 4:15 PM (EST). *Felony, Civil Actions Over $15,000, Probate.*

Civil Records: Access: Mail, online, in person. Both court and visitors may perform in person searches. No search fee. Required to search: name, years to search. Civil cases indexed by defendant, plaintiff. Civil records on index books from 1838. For information about the statewide online system, LOPAS, see the state introduction.

Criminal Records: Access: Mail, online, in person. Both court and visitors may perform in person searches. Search fee: $10.00 per name. Required to search: name, years to search. Criminal records on index books from 1838. Online access to criminal records is the same as civil.

General Information: No juvenile, sealed or adoption records released. SASE required. Turnaround time 7-10 days. Copy fee: $.50 per page. Certification fee: No certification fee. Fee payee: Clerk of Circuit Court or Green County Circuit. Personal checks accepted. Prepayment is required.

16th General District Court Greene County Courthouse (PO Box 245), Stanardsville, VA 22973; 434-985-5224; Fax: 434-985-1448. Hours: 8:30AM-4PM (EST). *Misdemeanor, Civil Actions Under $15,000, Eviction, Small Claims.*

Civil Records: Access: Fax, mail, online, in person. Both court and visitors may perform in person searches. No search fee. Required to search: name, years to search. Civil cases indexed by defendant, plaintiff. Civil records on index books from 1838, on computer back to 10/93. For information about the statewide online system, LOPAS, see the state introduction.

Criminal Records: Access: In person only. Visitors must perform in person searches for themselves. No search fee. Required to search: name, years to search, DOB; also helpful: SSN. Criminal records on computer back to 1/92, prior on cards, books. Online access to criminal records is the same as civil.

General Information: Public Access terminal is available. No juvenile, sealed records released. Turnaround time 1 week. Fax notes: No fee to fax results. Copy fee: $.50 per page. Certification fee: No certification fee. Fee payee: Clerk of General District Court or Greene County Combined Court. Personal checks accepted. Credit cards accepted: Visa, MasterCard. Prepayment is required.

Greensville County

6th Circuit Court PO Box 631, Emporia, VA 23847; 804-348-4215. Hours: 9AM-5PM (EST). *Felony, Civil Actions Over $15,000, Probate.*

Civil Records: Access: Online, in person. Visitors must perform in person searches for themselves. No search fee. Required to search: name, years to search. Civil cases indexed by defendant, plaintiff. Civil records on index books from 1781; on computer since 1989. For information about the statewide online system, LOPAS, see the state introduction.

Criminal Records: Access: Online, in person. Visitors must perform in person searches for themselves. No search fee. Required to search: name, years to search. Criminal records on index books from 1781; on computer since 1989. Online access to criminal records is the same as civil.

General Information: No juvenile, sealed records released. Copy fee: $.50 per page. Certification fee:

$2.00. Fee payee: Clerk of Circuit Court. Business checks accepted. Prepayment is required.

Greenville/Emporia Combined Court 315 S Main, Emporia, VA 23847; 804-348-4266. Hours: 8:30AM-4:30PM (EST). *Misdemeanor, Civil Actions Under $15,000, Eviction, Small Claims.*

Civil Records: Access: Online, in person. Visitors must perform in person searches for themselves. No search fee. Required to search: name, years to search. Civil cases indexed by defendant, plaintiff. Civil records on index books from 1800s; on computer back 10 years. For information about the statewide online system, LOPAS, see the state introduction.

Criminal Records: Access: Online, in person. Visitors must perform in person searches for themselves. No search fee. Required to search: name, years to search, DOB; also helpful: SSN. Criminal records on index books from 1800s; on computer back 10 years. Online access to criminal records is the same as civil.

General Information: Public Access terminal is available. No juvenile, sealed records released. Copy fee: $.50 per page. Certification fee: No certification fee. Fee payee: Clerk of General District Court. Personal checks accepted.

Halifax County

10th Circuit Court PO Box 729, Halifax, VA 24558; 804-476-6211. Hours: 8:30AM-5PM (EST). *Felony, Civil Actions Over $15,000, Probate.*

Civil Records: Access: Online, in person. Visitors must perform in person searches for themselves. No search fee. Required to search: name, years to search. Civil cases indexed by defendant, plaintiff. Civil records on computer from 1988, on index books from 1752. For information about the statewide online system, LOPAS, see the state introduction.

Criminal Records: Access: Mail, online, in person. Only the court performs in person searches; visitors may not. Search fee: $5.00 per name. Required to search: name, years to search. Criminal records on computer from 1988, on index books from 1752. Online access to criminal records is the same as civil.

General Information: No juvenile, sealed records released. Turnaround time 1-5 days. Copy fee: $.50 per page. Certification fee: $.50 per page. Fee payee: Circuit Court. Personal checks accepted. Prepayment required.

10th General District Court Halifax County Courthouse, PO Box 458, Halifax, VA 24558; 804-476-3385; Fax: 804-476-3387. Hours: 8:30AM-4:30PM (EST). *Misdemeanor, Civil Actions Under $15,000, Eviction, Small Claims.*

Civil Records: Access: Fax, mail, online, in person. Both court and visitors may perform in person searches. No search fee. Required to search: name, years to search, address. Civil cases indexed by defendant, plaintiff. Civil records on computer from 1989, on index books from 1700s. For information about the statewide online system, LOPAS, see the state introduction.

Criminal Records: Access: Fax, mail, online, in person. Both court and visitors may perform in person searches. No search fee. Required to search: name, years to search, address, DOB; also helpful: SSN. Criminal records on computer from 1989, on index books from 1700s. Online access to criminal records is the same as civil.

General Information: Public Access terminal is available. (Available Tues, Thurs & Fri all day, also Wed afternoons.) No juvenile, sealed records released. Turnaround time within 7 days. Fax notes: Fax fee only charged for excessive number of pages. Copy fee: $.50 per page. Certification fee: No certification fee. Fee payee: General District Court. Personal checks accepted. Prepayment is required.

Hampton City

8th Circuit Court 101 King's Way, PO Box 40, Hampton, VA 23669-0040; 757-727-6105. Hours: 8:30AM-5PM (EST). *Felony, Civil Actions Over $15,000, Probate.*

Civil Records: Access: Mail, online, in person. Both court and visitors may perform in person searches. Search fee: $10.00 per name. Required to search: name, years to search. Civil cases indexed by defendant, plaintiff. Civil records on index books since 1865. Online access is available free at http://208.210.219.132/courtinfo/vacircuit/select.jsp?court=. For information about the statewide online system, LOPAS, see the state introduction.

Criminal Records: Access: Mail, online, in person. Both court and visitors may perform in person searches. Search fee: $10.00 per name. Required to search: name, years to search. Criminal records on index books since 1865. Online access to criminal records is the same as civil.

General Information: No pre-sentence, criminal correspondence, chancery, judges notes or medical records released. SASE preferred. Turnaround time 3 days. Copy fee: $.50 per page. Certification fee: $2.00. Fee payee: Clerk of Court. Personal checks accepted. No out of state checks accepted. Prepayment required.

8th General District Court Courthouse, PO Box 70, Hampton, VA 23669-0070; Civil phone: 757-727-6480; Criminal phone: 757-727-6260/6262. Hours: 8AM-4PM (EST). *Misdemeanor, Civil Actions Under $15,000, Eviction, Small Claims.*

Civil Records: Access: Online, in person. Visitors must perform in person searches for themselves. No search fee. Required to search: name, years to search. Civil cases indexed by defendant, plaintiff. Civil records on index books from early 1900s, on computer from 1985. For information about the statewide online system, LOPAS, see the state introduction. Mail access limited to specific case & 2 names.

Criminal Records: Access: Online, in person. Visitors must perform in person searches for themselves. No search fee. Required to search: name, years to search. Criminal records on index books from early 1900s, on computer from 1985. Online access to criminal records is the same as civil.

General Information: Public Access terminal is available. No sealed records released. Copy fee: $.50 each. Certification fee: No certification fee. Fee payee: Hampton District Court. Personal checks accepted. Credit cards accepted. Accepted for fines only. Prepayment is required.

Hanover County

15th Circuit Court 7507 Library Dr, PO Box 39, Hanover, VA 23069; 804-365-6151; Fax: 804-365-6278. Hours: 8:30AM-4:30PM (EST). *Felony, Civil Actions Over $15,000, Probate.*

Civil Records: Access: Online, in person. Visitors must perform in person searches for themselves. No search fee. Required to search: name, years to search. Civil cases indexed by defendant, plaintiff. Civil records index in books, older records date from 1850. For information about the statewide online system, LOPAS, see the state introduction.

Criminal Records: Access: Online, in person. Visitors must perform in person searches for themselves. No search fee. Required to search: name, years to search. Criminal records index in books, older records date from 1850. Online access to criminal records is the same as civil.

General Information: Public Access terminal is available. No juvenile, sealed records released. Copy fee: $.50 per page. Certification fee: $2.00. Fee payee: Clerk of Circuit Court. Personal checks accepted. Prepayment is required.

15th General District Court Hanover County Courthouse, PO Box 176, Hanover, VA 23069; 804-365-6191; Fax: 804-365-6290. Hours: 8AM-4PM (EST). *Misdemeanor, Civil Actions Under $15,000, Eviction, Small Claims.*

Civil Records: Access: Mail, online, in person. Both court and visitors may perform in person searches. No search fee. Required to search: name, years to search. Civil cases indexed by defendant, plaintiff. Civil records on index books back to 1991; on computer back to 1992. For information about the statewide online system, LOPAS, see the state introduction.

Criminal Records: Access: Online, in person. Visitors must perform in person searches for themselves. No search fee. Required to search: name, years to search, DOB; also helpful: SSN. Criminal records on index books back to 1991; on computer back to 1992. Online access to criminal records is the same as civil.

General Information: Public Access terminal is available. Copy fee: $1.00 for first page, $.50 each add'l. Certification fee: No certification fee. Fee payee: Hanover General District Court. Personal checks accepted. Credit cards accepted: Visa, MasterCard.

Harrisonburg City

Circuit & District Courts, VA.

Note: See Rockingham County

Henrico County

14th Circuit Court PO Box 27032, Richmond, VA 23273-7032; Civil phone: 804-501-5422; Criminal phone: 804-501-4758. Hours: 8AM-4:30PM (EST). *Felony, Civil Actions Over $15,000, Probate.*

Civil Records: Access: Mail, online, in person. Visitors must perform in person searches for themselves. No search fee. Required to search: name, years to search. Civil cases indexed by defendant, plaintiff. Civil records on computer from 11/88, on index cards from 1850. For information about the statewide online system, LOPAS, see the state introduction.

Criminal Records: Access: Mail, online, in person. Visitors must perform in person searches for themselves. No search fee. Required to search: name, years to search, DOB. Criminal records on computer from 11/88, on index cards from 1850. Online access to criminal records is the same as civil.

General Information: Public Access terminal is available. No juvenile, judges notes, adoption sealed records released. SASE required. Turnaround time 3-5 days. Copy fee: $.50 per page. Certification fee: $2.00 per document. Fee payee: Clerk of Circuit Court. Personal checks accepted. Prepayment is required.

14th General District Court PO Box 27032, Richmond, VA 23273; Civil phone: 804-501-4727; Criminal phone: 804-501-4723; Fax: 804-501-4141. Hours: 8AM-4PM (EST). *Misdemeanor, Civil Actions Under $15,000, Eviction, Small Claims.*

Civil Records: Access: Online, in person. Visitors must perform in person searches for themselves. No search fee. Required to search: name, years to search. Civil cases indexed by defendant. Civil records on computer from 07/85. For information about the statewide online system, LOPAS, see the state introduction.

Criminal Records: Access: Online, in person. Visitors must perform in person searches for themselves. No search fee. Required to search: name, years to search, DOB. Criminal records on computer from 1990. Online access to criminal records is the same as civil.

General Information: Public Access terminal is available. No juvenile, sealed records released. Copy fee: $1.00 per page. Certification fee: No certification fee. Fee payee: Clerk of General District Court. Personal checks accepted. Credit cards accepted. Not accepted over the phone. Prepayment is required.

Henry County

21st Circuit Court 3160 Kings Mountain Rd Suite B, Martinsville, VA 24112; 540-634-4880. 9AM-5PM (EST). *Felony, Civil Actions Over $15,000, Probate.*

Civil Records: Access: Online, in person. Visitors must perform in person searches for themselves. No search fee. Required to search: name, years to search. Civil cases indexed by defendant, plaintiff. Civil records on computer since 04/92; prior on index books. Online access is available free at http://208.210.219.132/courtinfo/vacircuit/select.jsp?court=. For information about the statewide online system, LOPAS, see the state introduction.

Criminal Records: Access: Online, in person. Visitors must perform in person searches for themselves. No search fee. Required to search: name, years to search, DOB; also helpful: SSN. Criminal records computerized since 07/92. Online access to criminal records is the same as civil.

General Information: Public Access terminal is available. No juvenile, expungments, sealed or adoption records released. Fax notes: Fee to fax results is $.50 per page. Copy fee: $.50 per page. Certification fee: $2.00. Fee payee: Clerk of Circuit Court. Personal checks accepted. Prepayment is required.

21st General District Court 3160 King's Mountain Rd Ste A, Martinsville, VA 24112; 540-634-4815; Fax: 540-634-4825. 9AM-5PM *Misdemeanor, Civil Actions Under $15,000, Eviction, Small Claims.*

Civil Records: Access: Online, in person. Visitors must perform in person searches for themselves. No search fee. Required to search: name, years to search; also helpful: address. Civil cases indexed by defendant, plaintiff. Civil records on computer from 1991. For information about the statewide online system, LOPAS, see the state introduction.

Criminal Records: Access: Online, in person. Visitors must perform in person searches for themselves. No search fee. Required to search: name, years to search, DOB; also helpful: address, SSN. Criminal records on computer from 1991. Online access to criminal records is the same as civil.

General Information: Public Access terminal is available. No sealed records released. Only attorneys are allowed copies, public cannot. Certification fee: No certification fee.

Highland County

25th Circuit Court PO Box 190, Monterey, VA 24465; 540-468-2447; Fax: 540-468-3447. Hours: 8:45AM-4:30PM (EST). *Felony, Civil Actions Over $15,000, Probate.*

Civil Records: Access: Mail, online, in person. Both court and visitors may perform in person searches. No search fee. Required to search: name, years to search. Civil cases indexed by defendant, plaintiff. Civil records on index books from 1868. For information about the statewide online system, LOPAS, see state introduction.

Criminal Records: Access: Mail, online, in person. Both court and visitors may perform in person searches. No search fee. Required to search: name, years to search. Criminal records on index books from 1868. Online access to criminal records is the same as civil.

General Information: No juvenile, sealed records released. Turnaround time up to 1 week. Copy fee: $.50 per page. Certification fee: $2.00. Fee payee: Clerk of Circuit Court. Personal checks accepted. Prepayment is required.

25th General District Court Highland County Courthouse, PO Box 88, Monterey, VA 24465; 540-468-2445; Fax: 540-468-3447. Hours: 8:30AM-5:00PM (EST). *Misdemeanor, Civil Actions Under $15,000, Eviction, Small Claims.*

Civil Records: Access: Fax, mail, online, in person. Both court and visitors may perform in person searches. No search fee. Required to search: name, years to search. Civil cases indexed by defendant, plaintiff. Civil records on index books from 1885; computerized back to 1993. For information about the statewide online system, LOPAS, see the state introduction.

Criminal Records: Access: Fax, mail, online, in person. Both court and visitors may perform in person searches. No search fee. Required to search: name, years to search; also helpful: DOB, SSN, signed release. Criminal records on index books from 1885; computerized back to 1993. Online access to criminal records is the same as civil.

General Information: Public Access terminal is available. No juvenile, sealed records released. SASE requested. Turnaround time 2-3 days. Copy fee: $1.00 copy fee for first 2 pages. Add $.50 per page thereafter. Certification fee: No certification fee. Fee payee: General District Court. Personal checks accepted. Prepayment is required.

Hopewell City

6th Circuit Court 100 E Broadway, PO Box 354, 2nd Fl, Room 251, Hopewell, VA 23860; 804-541-2239; Fax: 804-541-2438. Hours: 8:30AM-4:30PM (EST). *Felony, Civil Actions Over $15,000, Probate.*

Civil Records: Access: Mail, online, in person. Both court and visitors may perform in person searches. No search fee. Required to search: name, years to search. Civil cases indexed by defendant, plaintiff. Civil records on index books since 1916. Online access is available free at http://208.210.219.132/courtinfo/vacircuit/select.jsp?court=. For information about the statewide online system, LOPAS, see the state introduction.

Criminal Records: Access: Online, in person. Visitors must perform in person searches for themselves. No search fee. Required to search: name, years to search, DOB. Criminal records on index books since 1916. Online access to criminal records is the same as civil.

General Information: Public Access terminal is available. No juvenile, sealed records released. SASE required. Turnaround time 1 week. Copy fee: $.50 per page. Certification fee: $2.00. Payee: Clerk of Circuit Court. Personal checks accepted. Prepayment required.

Hopewell District Court 100 E Broadway, Hopewell, VA 23860; 804-541-2257; Fax: 804-541-2364. Hours: 8:30AM-4:30PM (EST). *Misdemeanor, Civil Actions Under $15,000, Eviction, Small Claims.*

Civil Records: Access: Mail, online, in person. Both court and visitors may perform in person searches. No search fee. Required to search: name, years to search. Civil cases indexed by defendant, plaintiff. Civil records on index books from early 1900s, on computer from 1988. For information about the statewide online system, LOPAS, see the state introduction.

Criminal Records: Access: Mail, online, in person. Both court and visitors may perform in person searches. No search fee. Required to search: name, years to search, DOB; also helpful: SSN. Criminal records on index books from early 1900s, on computer from 1988. Online access to criminal records is the same as civil.

General Information: Public Access terminal is available. No juvenile, sealed or domestic relations records released. SASE requested. Turnaround time 3-5 days. Copy fee: $.50 per page. Certification fee: $2.00. Fee payee: Clerk of General District Court. Personal checks accepted. Credit cards: Visa, MasterCard.

Isle of Wight County

5th Circuit Court 17122 Monument Circle, PO Box 110, Isle of Wight, VA 23397; 757-357-3191. Hours: 9AM-5PM (EST). *Felony, Civil Actions Over $15,000, Probate.*

Note: The Clerk can be reached at 757-365-6233.

Civil Records: Access: Online, in person. Visitors must perform in person searches for themselves. No search fee. Required to search: name, years to search. Civil cases indexed by defendant, plaintiff. Civil records on index books from 1800s; on computer since 1983. Online access is available free at http://208.210.219.132/courtinfo/vacircuit/select.jsp?court=. For information about the statewide online system, LOPAS, see the state introduction.

Criminal Records: Access: Online, in person. Visitors must perform in person searches for themselves. No search fee. Required to search: name, years to search, DOB. Criminal records on index books from 1800s; on computer since 6/1948. Online access to criminal records is the same as civil.

General Information: Public Access terminal is available. No juvenile, sealed records released. Copy fee: $.50 per page. Certification fee: $2.00. Fee payee: Clerk of Circuit Court. Personal checks accepted. Prepayment is required.

5th General District Court Isle of Wight Courthouse, PO Box 122, Isle of Wight, VA 23397; 757-365-6243; Fax: 757-365-6246. Hours: 8AM-4PM (EST). *Misdemeanor, Civil Actions Under $15,000, Eviction, Small Claims.*

Note: The Clerk can be reached at 757-365-6244.

Civil Records: Access: Online, in person. Visitors must perform in person searches for themselves. No search fee. Required to search: name, years to search. Civil cases indexed by defendant, plaintiff. Civil records on index books back to 1800s; on computer since 1994. For information about the statewide online system, LOPAS, see the state introduction.

Criminal Records: Access: Online, in person. Visitors must perform in person searches for themselves. No search fee. Required to search: name, years to search. Criminal records on index books back to 1800s; on computer since 1994. Online access to criminal records is the same as civil.

General Information: Juvenile, sealed, adoption records not released. Copy fee: $.50 per page. Certification fee: $2.00. Fee payee: Clerk of GDC. Personal checks accepted. Credit cards accepted: Visa, MasterCard. Prepayment is required.

James City

Williamsburg-James City Circuit Court

5201 Monticello Ave #6, Williamsburg, VA 23188-8218; 757-564-2242; Fax: 757-564-2329. Hours: 8:30AM-4:00PM (EST). *Felony, Civil Actions Over $15,000, Probate.*

Civil Records: Access: Mail, online, in person. Both court and visitors may perform in person searches. Search fee: $2.00 per name. Required to search: name, years to search. Civil cases indexed by defendant, plaintiff. Civil records on computer since 1987, archived from 1970, prior on index books. Online access is available free at http://208.210.219.132/courtinfo/vacircuit/select.jsp?court=. For information about the statewide online system, LOPAS, see the state introduction.

Criminal Records: Access: Mail, online, in person. Both court and visitors may perform in person searches. Search fee: $2.00 per name. Required to search: name, years to search, DOB; also helpful: SSN. Criminal records on computer since 1987, archived from 1970, prior on index books. Online access to criminal records is the same as civil.

General Information: Public Access terminal is available. No juvenile, sealed, adoption records released. SASE required. Turnaround time 1-2 days. Fax notes: Fee to fax results is $1.00 per page. Copy fee: $.50 per page. Certification fee: $2.00. Fee payee: Clerk of Circuit Court. Personal checks accepted. Prepayment is required.

9th General District Court James City Courthouse, 5201 Monticello Ave #2, Williamsburg, VA 23188-8218; 757-564-2400; Fax: 757-564-2410. Hours: 7:30AM-4PM (EST). *Misdemeanor, Civil Actions Under $15,000, Eviction, Small Claims.*

Civil Records: Access: Fax, mail, in person. Both court and visitors may perform in person searches. No search fee. Required to search: name, years to search. Civil cases indexed by defendant, plaintiff. Civil records on index books from 1991, on computer from 1991. For information about the statewide online system, LOPAS, see the state introduction.

Criminal Records: Access: Fax, mail, in person. Both court and visitors may perform in person searches. No search fee. Required to search: name, years to search, DOB; also helpful: SSN. Criminal records on index books from 1991, on computer from 1991. Online access to criminal records is the same as civil.

General Information: Public Access terminal is available. No juvenile, sealed records released. SASE requested. Turnaround time 10 days. Copy fee: Charges will be incurred if extensive searching or copies are needed. Certification fee: No certification fee. Fee payee: General District Court. Personal checks accepted. Credit cards accepted: Visa, MasterCard.

King and Queen County

9th Circuit Court PO Box 67, King & Queen Court House, VA 23085; 804-785-5984; Fax: 804-785-5698. Hours: 9AM-5PM (EST). *Felony, Civil Actions Over $15,000, Probate.*

Civil Records: Access: Online, in person. Visitors must perform in person searches for themselves. No search fee. Required to search: name, years to search. Civil cases indexed by plaintiff. Civil records archived from 1864. For information about the statewide online system, LOPAS, see the state introduction.

Criminal Records: Access: Online, in person. Visitors must perform in person searches for themselves. No search fee. Required to search: name, years to search. Criminal records archived from 1864. Online access to criminal records is the same as civil.

General Information: Public Access terminal is available. No juvenile, sealed or adoption records released. Copy fee: $.50 per page. Certification fee: $1.00. Fee payee: Clerk of Circuit Court. Personal checks accepted. Prepayment is required.

King & Queen General District Court PO Box 86, King & Queen Courthouse, VA 23085-0086; 804-785-5982; Fax: 804-785-5694. Hours: 8:30AM-4:30PM (EST). *Misdemeanor, Civil Actions Under $15,000, Eviction.*

Civil Records: Access: Fax, mail, online, in person. Both court and visitors may perform in person searches. No search fee. Required to search: name, years to search. Civil cases indexed by defendant, plaintiff. Civil records on computer back to 1991. For information about the statewide online system, LOPAS, see the state introduction.

Criminal Records: Access: Fax, mail, online, in person. Both court and visitors may perform in person searches. No search fee. Required to search: name, years to search, DOB; also helpful: SSN, signed release. Criminal records on computer back to 1991. Online access to criminal records is the same as civil.

General Information: Public Access terminal is available. Turnaround time 1-5 days. Fax notes: No fee to fax results. Copy fee: $1.00 for first page, $.50 each add'l. Certification fee: No certification fee. Fee payee: General District Court. Personal checks accepted. Prepayment is required.

King George County

15th Circuit Court 9483 Kings Highway #3, King George, VA 22485; 540-775-3322. Hours: 8:30AM-4:30PM *Felony, Civil Actions Over $15,000, Probate.*

Civil Records: Access: Mail, online, in person. Both court and visitors may perform in person searches. Search fee: $10.00 per name. Required to search: name, years to search. Civil cases indexed by defendant, plaintiff. Civil records on index books from 1800s. Online access is available free at http:// 208.210.219.132/courtinfo/vacircuit/select.jsp?court=. For information about the statewide online system, LOPAS, see the state introduction.

Criminal Records: Access: Mail, online, in person. Both court and visitors may perform in person searches. Search fee: $10.00 per name. Required to search: name, years to search. Criminal records on index books from 1800s. Online access to criminal records is the same as civil.

General Information: No sealed records released. SASE required. Turnaround time 1-2 days. Copy fee: $.50 per page. Certification fee: $2.00. Fee payee: Clerk of Circuit court. Personal checks accepted. Prepayment is required.

15th Judicial District King George Combined Court County Courthouse PO Box 279, King George, VA 22485; 540-775-3573. Hours: 8AM-4:30PM (EST). *Misdemeanor, Civil Actions Under $15,000, Eviction, Small Claims.*

Civil Records: Access: Mail, online, in person. Both court and visitors may perform in person searches. No search fee. Required to search: name, years to search. Civil cases indexed by defendant, plaintiff. Civil records on index books from early 1900s. For information about the statewide online system, LOPAS, see the state introduction. Records prior to 1988 written request only.

Criminal Records: Access: Mail, online, in person. Both court and visitors may perform in person searches. No search fee. Required to search: name, years to search, DOB; also helpful: SSN. Criminal records on index books from early 1900s. Online access to criminal records is the same as civil.

General Information: Public Access terminal is available. No juvenile, sealed records released. Turnaround time 1-5 days. Copy fee: $1.00 per page. Certification fee: $2.00. Fee payee: Clerk of General District Court. Personal checks accepted. Credit cards accepted: Visa, MasterCard. Prepayment is required.

King William County

9th Circuit Court 227 Courthouse Lane, PO Box 216, King William, VA 23086; 804-769-4938. Hours: 8:30AM-4:30PM (EST). *Felony, Civil Actions Over $15,000, Probate.*

Civil Records: Access: Mail, in person. Both court and visitors may perform in person searches. No search fee. Required to search: name, years to search. Civil cases indexed by defendant, plaintiff. Civil records on index books from 1800s.

Criminal Records: Access: Mail, in person. Both court and visitors may perform in person searches. No search fee. Required to search: name, years to search, DOB; also helpful: SSN. Criminal records on index books from 1800s.

General Information: Public Access terminal is available. No juvenile, sealed records released. SASE required. Turnaround time 1 week. Copy fee: $.50 per page. Certification fee: $1.00. Fee payee: Clerk of Circuit Court. Personal checks accepted. Prepayment is required.

King William General District Court PO Box 5, King William, VA 23086; 804-769-4948; Fax: 804-769-4971. Hours: 8:30AM-4:30PM (EST). *Misdemeanor, Civil Actions Under $15,000, Eviction, Small Claims.*

Civil Records: Access: Fax, mail, online, in person. Both court and visitors may perform in person searches. No search fee. Required to search: name, years to search. Civil cases indexed by defendant, plaintiff. Civil records on computer since 1992. For information about the statewide online system, LOPAS, see the state introduction.

Criminal Records: Access: Fax, mail, online, in person. Both court and visitors may perform in person searches. No search fee. Required to search: name, years to search, DOB; also helpful: signed release, SSN. Criminal records on computer back to 1992. Online access to criminal records is the same as civil.

General Information: Public Access terminal is available. No juvenile, sealed records released. SASE requested. Turnaround time 1-5 days. Fax notes: No fee to fax results. Copy fee: $1.00 for first page, $.50 each add'l. Certification fee: No certification fee. Fee payee: General District Court. Personal checks accepted.

Lancaster County

15th Circuit Court Courthouse Building, PO Box 99, Lancaster, VA 22503; 804-462-5611. Hours: 8:30AM-4:30PM (EST). *Felony, Civil Actions Over $15,000, Probate.*

Civil Records: Access: Mail, online, in person. Both court and visitors may perform in person searches. No search fee. Required to search: name, years to search. Civil cases indexed by defendant, plaintiff. Civil records on index books from 1845. For information about the statewide online system, LOPAS, see state introduction.

Criminal Records: Access: Mail, online, in person. Both court and visitors may perform in person searches. No search fee. Required to search: name, years to search. Criminal records on index books from 1845. Online access to criminal records is the same as civil.

General Information: Public Access terminal is available. No juvenile, sealed records released. Turnaround time same day. Copy fee: $.50 per page. Certification fee: $2.00. Fee payee: Clerk of Circuit Court. Personal checks accepted. Out of state checks not accepted. Prepayment is required.

15th General District Court PO 129, Lancaster, VA 22503; 804-462-0012. Hours: 8:30AM-4:30PM (EST). *Misdemeanor, Civil Actions Under $15,000, Eviction, Small Claims.*

Civil Records: Access: Mail, online, in person. Both court and visitors may perform in person searches. No search fee. Required to search: name, years to search. Civil cases indexed by defendant. Civil records on computer from 11/93. For information about the statewide online system, LOPAS, see the state introduction.

Criminal Records: Access: Mail, online, in person. Both court and visitors may perform in person searches. No search fee. Required to search: name, years to search, DOB; also helpful: SSN. Criminal records on computer from 11/93. Online access to criminal records is the same as civil.

General Information: Public Access terminal is available. No sealed records released. Copy fee: $1.00 per page. Fee is for excessive number of pages. Certification fee: No certification fee. Fee payee: Clerk of General District Court. Personal checks accepted. Prepayment is required.

Lee County

30th Circuit Court PO Box 326, Jonesville, VA 24263; 540-346-7763; Fax: 540-346-3440. Hours: 8:30AM-5PM M-F, 9AM-Noon Sat (EST). *Felony, Civil Actions Over $15,000, Probate.*

Civil Records: Access: Phone, fax, mail, online, in person. Both court and visitors may perform in person searches. No search fee. Required to search: name, years to search. Civil cases indexed by defendant, plaintiff. Civil records on index books from 1800s. For information about the statewide online system, LOPAS, see the state introduction. Phone & fax access limited to short searches.

Criminal Records: Access: Phone, fax, mail, online, in person. Both court and visitors may perform in person searches. No search fee. Required to search: name, years to search, DOB; also helpful: SSN. Criminal records on index books from 1800s. Online access to criminal records is the same as civil.

General Information: Public Access terminal is available. No juvenile, sealed records released. Turnaround time 1-3 days. Copy fee: $.50 per page. Certification fee: $2.00. Fee payee: Clerk of Circuit Court. Personal checks accepted. Prepayment required.

30th General District Court Lee County Courthouse, PO Box 306, Jonesville, VA 24263; 540-346-7729; Fax: 540-346-7701. Hours: 8AM-4:30PM (EST). *Misdemeanor, Civil Actions Under $15,000, Eviction, Small Claims.*

Civil Records: Access: Mail, online, in person. Both court and visitors may perform in person searches. No search fee. Required to search: name, years to search. Civil cases indexed by defendant, plaintiff. Civil records on index books from 1800s, on computer from 11/7/90. For information about the statewide online system, LOPAS, see the state introduction.

Criminal Records: Access: Mail, online, in person. Both court and visitors may perform in person searches. No search fee. Required to search: name, years to search. Criminal records on index books from 1800s, on computer from 11/7/90. Online access to criminal records is the same as civil.

General Information: Public Access terminal is available. No juvenile, sealed records released. Turnaround time 1-2 days. Copy fee: $1.00 for first page, $.50 each add'l. Certification fee: No certification fee. Fee payee: Clerk of General District Court. Personal checks accepted. Prepayment is required.

Lexington City

Circuit & District Courts, VA.

Note: See Rockbridge County

Loudoun County

20th Circuit Court 18 E Market Street, Leesburg, VA 20178; 703-777-0386; Fax: 703-777-0676. 9AM-5PM *Felony, Civil Actions Over $15,000, Probate.*

Civil Records: Access: Phone, mail, online, in person. Both court and visitors may perform in person searches. No search fee. Required to search: name, years to search. Civil cases indexed by defendant, plaintiff. Civil records on computer since 1986; prior on index books from 1700s. For information about the statewide online system, LOPAS, see the state introduction. Phone access limited to simple requests. Mail access for deeds & wills only.

Criminal Records: Access: Online, in person. Both court and visitors may perform in person searches. No search fee. Required to search: name, years to search, DOB; also helpful: SSN. Criminal records on computer since 1986; prior on index books from 1700s. Online access to criminal records is the same as civil.

General Information: No juvenile, sealed or adoption records released. Turnaround time 1 week. Copy fee:

$.50 per page. Certification fee: $2.50. Fee payee: Clerk of Circuit Court. Business checks accepted. Personal checks accepted if in-state. Prepayment is required.

20th General District Court 18 E Market St, 2nd Flr, Leesburg, VA 20176; 703-777-0312; Fax: 703-777-0311. Hours: 8AM-4PM (EST). *Misdemeanor, Civil Actions Under $15,000, Eviction.*

Civil Records: Access: Phone, mail, fax, online, in person. Both court and visitors may perform in person searches. No search fee. Required to search: name, years to search. Civil cases indexed by defendant, plaintiff. Civil records on computer back 10 years. For information about the statewide online system, LOPAS, see the state introduction.
Criminal Records: Access: Mail, fax, online, in person. Both court and visitors may perform in person searches. No search fee. Required to search: name, years to search. Criminal records on computer back 10 years. Online access to criminal records is the same as civil.
General Information: Public Access terminal is available. SASE required. Turnaround time 7-10 days. Copy fee: $.50 per page. Certification fee: No certification fee. Personal checks accepted. Credit cards accepted: Visa, MasterCard. Prepayment is required.

Louisa County

16th Circuit Court Box 37, Louisa, VA 23093; 540-967-5312; Fax: 540-967-2705. Hours: 8:30AM-5PM (EST). *Felony, Civil Actions Over $15,000, Probate.*

Civil Records: Access: Online, in person. Visitors must perform in person searches for themselves. No search fee. Required to search: name, years to search. Civil cases indexed by defendant, plaintiff. Civil records archived from 1742; on computer back to 1989. Online access is available free at http://208.210.219.132/courtinfo/vacircuit/select.jsp?court=. For information about the statewide online system, LOPAS, see the state introduction.
Criminal Records: Access: Online, in person. Both court and visitors may perform in person searches. No search fee. Required to search: name, years to search, DOB or SSN. Criminal records archived from 1742; on computer back to 1989. Online access to criminal records is the same as civil.
General Information: No juvenile, sealed records released. Copy fee: $.50 per page. Certification fee: $2.00. Fee payee: Clerk of Circuit Court. Personal checks accepted. Prepayment is required.

16th General District Court PO Box 452, Louisa, VA 23093; 540-967-5330; Fax: 540-967-2369. Hours: 8:30AM-4:30PM (EST). *Misdemeanor, Civil Actions Under $15,000, Eviction, Small Claims.*

Civil Records: Access: Online, in person. Visitors must perform in person searches for themselves. No search fee. Required to search: name, years to search. Civil cases indexed by defendant, plaintiff. Civil records archived from 1762, on computer from 1990. For information about the statewide online system, LOPAS, see the state introduction.
Criminal Records: Access: Online, in person. Visitors must perform in person searches for themselves. No search fee. Required to search: name, years to search. Criminal records archived from 1762, on computer from 1990. Online access to criminal records is the same as civil.
General Information: Public Access terminal is available. No juvenile, sealed records released. Copy fee: $1.00 for first page, $.50 each add'l. Fee payee: Louisa District Court. Personal checks accepted. Prepayment is required.

Lunenburg County

10th Circuit Court 11435 Courthouse Rd, Lunenburg, VA 23952; 804-696-2230; Fax: 804-696-3931. Hours: 8:30AM-4:30PM (EST). *Felony, Civil Actions Over $15,000, Probate.*

Civil Records: Access: Fax, mail, online, in person. Both court and visitors may perform in person searches. No search fee. Required to search: name, years to search. Civil cases indexed by defendant, plaintiff. Civil records on index books from 1700s. For information about the statewide online system, LOPAS, see the state introduction.
Criminal Records: Access: Fax, mail, online, in person. Both court and visitors may perform in person searches. No search fee. Required to search: name, years to search. Criminal records on index books from 1700s. Online access to criminal records is the same as civil.
General Information: No juvenile, sealed records released. Turnaround time 1-2 days. Fax notes: No fee to fax results. Copy fee: $.50 per page. Certification fee: $2.00. Fee payee: Clerk of Circuit Court. Personal checks accepted. Prepayment is required.

10th General District Court 11413 Courthouse Road, Lunenburg, VA 23952; 804-696-5508; Fax: 804-696-3665. Hours: 8:30AM-4:30PM (EST). *Misdemeanor, Civil Actions Under $15,000, Eviction, Small Claims.*

Civil Records: Access: Mail, online, in person. Both court and visitors may perform in person searches. No search fee. Required to search: name, years to search. Civil cases indexed by defendant, plaintiff. Civil records computerized since 1995, on index books and cards from 1991, prior to 1985 at Circuit Court:. For information about the statewide online system, LOPAS, see the state introduction.
Criminal Records: Access: Mail, online, in person. Both court and visitors may perform in person searches. No search fee. Required to search: name, years to search, DBO, SSN. Criminal records computerized since 1995, on index books and cards from 1991, prior to 1985 at Circuit Court:. Online access to criminal records is the same as civil.
General Information: Public Access terminal is available. No juvenile records released. SASE required. Turnaround time 3 days. Certification fee: No certification fee. Personal checks accepted. Credit cards accepted: Visa, MasterCard.

Lynchburg City

24th Circuit Court 900 Court St, PO Box 4, Lynchburg, VA 24505-0004; 804-847-1590; Fax: 804-847-1864. Hours: 8:30AM-4:45PM (EST). *Felony, Civil Actions Over $15,000, Probate.*

Civil Records: Access: Mail, online, in person. Both court and visitors may perform in person searches. No search fee. Required to search: name, years to search. Civil cases indexed by defendant, plaintiff. Civil records on index books from 1800s, on computer since 1988. For information about the statewide online system, LOPAS, see the state introduction.
Criminal Records: Access: Mail, online, in person. Both court and visitors may perform in person searches. No search fee. Required to search: name, years to search; also helpful: DOB, SSN. Criminal records on index books from 1800s, on computer since 1988. Online access to criminal records is the same as civil.
General Information: Public Access terminal is available. No juvenile, sealed records released. SASE required. Turnaround time 3 days. Copy fee: $.50 per page. Certification fee: $2.00. Fee payee: Clerk of Circuit Court. Personal checks accepted. Prepayment is required.

24th General District Court - Civil Division 905 Court St, PO Box 60, Lynchburg, VA 24505; 804-847-1639; Fax: 804-847-1779. Hours: 8AM-4PM (EST). *Civil Actions Under $15,000, Eviction, Small Claims.*

Civil Records: Access: Mail, online, in person. Both court and visitors may perform in person searches. No search fee. Required to search: name, years to search; also helpful: address. Civil cases indexed by defendant, plaintiff. Civil records on index books from 1800s, on computer since 1987. For information about the statewide online system, LOPAS, see the state introduction.
General Information: Public Access terminal is available. No juvenile, sealed records released. Turnaround time 1-2 weeks. Copy fee: $1.00 for first 2 pages, $.50 each add'l. Certification fee: No certification fee. Fee payee: Lynchburg General District Court. Personal checks accepted.

24th General District Court - Criminal Division 905 Court St, Lynchburg, VA 24504; 804-847-1560; Fax: 804-847-1779. Hours: 8AM-4PM (EST). *Misdemeanor.*

Criminal Records: Access: Online, in person. Visitors must perform in person searches for themselves. No search fee. Required to search: name, years to search. Criminal records on index books from 1800s, on computer since 1987. For information about the statewide online system, LOPAS, see the state introduction. Mail access limited to specific cases only, not name searches.
General Information: Public Access terminal is available. No juvenile, sealed records released. Copy fee: $1.00 for first 2 pages, $.50 each add'l. Certification fee: No certification fee. Fee payee: Lynchburg General District Court. Personal checks accepted.

Madison County

16th Circuit Court 100 Court Square, Main St (PO Box 220), Madison, VA 22727; 540-948-6888; Fax: 540-948-3759. Hours: 8:30AM-4:30PM (EST). *Felony, Civil Actions Over $15,000, Probate.*

Civil Records: Access: Mail, online, in person. Visitors must perform in person searches for themselves. No search fee. Required to search: name, years to search. Civil cases indexed by defendant, plaintiff. Civil records on index books from 1792, on computer since 1989. For information about the statewide online system, LOPAS, see the state introduction.
Criminal Records: Access: Mail, online, in person. Visitors must perform in person searches for themselves. No search fee. Required to search: name, years to search, DOB; also helpful: SSN. Criminal records on index books from 1792, on computer since 1989. Online access to criminal records is the same as civil.
General Information: Public Access terminal is available. No juvenile, sealed records released. Turnaround time 1 week. Copy fee: $.50 per page. Certification fee: $2.00. Fee payee: Clerk of Circuit Court. Personal checks accepted. Prepayment is required.

16th General District Court Madison County Courthouse, PO Box 470, Madison, VA 22727; 540-948-4657; Fax: 540-948-5649. Hours: 8:30AM-4:30PM (EST). *Misdemeanor, Civil Actions Under $15,000, Eviction, Small Claims.*

Civil Records: Access: Phone, fax, mail, online, in person. Only the court performs in person searches; visitors may not. No search fee. Required to search: name, years to search. Civil cases indexed by defendant, plaintiff. Civil records on index books from 1800s, from 1992 on computer. For information about the statewide online system, LOPAS, see the state introduction.

Criminal Records: Access: Phone, fax, mail, online, in person. Only the court performs in person searches; visitors may not. No search fee. Required to search: name, years to search; also helpful: address, DOB, SSN. Criminal records on index books from 1800s, from 1992 on computer. Online access to criminal records is the same as civil.

General Information: No juvenile, sealed or pre-trial records released. Turnaround time 3-4 days. Fax notes: No fee to fax results. No copy fee. Certification fee: No certification fee.

Manassas City

Circuit & District Courts, VA.

Note: See Prince William County

Manassas Park City

Circuit & District Courts, VA.

Note: See Prince William County

Martinsville City

21st Circuit Court PO Box 1206, Martinsville, VA 24114-1206; 540-656-5106; Fax: 540-656-5232. Hours: 9AM-5PM (EST). *Felony, Civil Actions Over $15,000, Probate.*

Civil Records: Access: Online, in person. Visitors must perform in person searches for themselves. No search fee. Required to search: name, years to search. Civil cases indexed by defendant, plaintiff. Civil records on computer since 1988, on index books from 1942. Online access is available free at http://208.210.219.132/courtinfo/vacircuit/select.jsp?court=. For information about the statewide online system, LOPAS, see the state introduction.

Criminal Records: Access: Online, in person. Visitors must perform in person searches for themselves. No search fee. Required to search: name, years to search; also helpful: DOB, SSN. Criminal records on computer since 1988, on index books from 1942. Online access to criminal records is the same as civil.

General Information: Public Access terminal is available. No juvenile, sealed records released. Copy fee: $.50 per page. Certification fee: $2.00. Fee payee: Clerk of Circuit Court. Personal checks accepted.

21st General District Court PO Box 1402, Martinsville, VA 24112; 540-656-5125; Fax: 540-638-8584. Hours: 9AM-5PM (EST). *Misdemeanor, Civil Actions Under $15,000, Eviction, Small Claims.*

Civil Records: Access: Online, in person. Visitors must perform in person searches for themselves. No search fee. Required to search: name, years to search. Civil cases indexed by defendant, plaintiff. Civil records on computer since 1991. For information about the statewide online system, LOPAS, see the state introduction.

Criminal Records: Access: Online, in person. Visitors must perform in person searches for themselves. No search fee. Required to search: name, years to search. Criminal records on computer since 1991. Online access to criminal records is the same as civil.

General Information: No sealed or expunged records released. Copy fee: Copies not available. Certification fee: No certification fee.

Mathews County

9th Circuit Court PO Box 463, Mathews, VA 23109; 804-725-2550. Hours: 8AM-4PM (EST). *Felony, Civil Actions Over $15,000, Probate.*

Civil Records: Access: Online, in person. Visitors must perform in person searches for themselves. No search fee. Required to search: name, years to search. Civil cases indexed by defendant. Civil records on index books from 1800s. For information about the statewide online system, LOPAS, see the state introduction.

Criminal Records: Access: Mail, online, in person. Both court and visitors may perform in person searches. No search fee. Required to search: name, years to search; also helpful: DOB, SSN. Criminal records on index books from 1800s. Online access to criminal records is the same as civil.

General Information: No juvenile, sealed records released. SASE required. Turnaround time 1-3 days. Copy fee: $.50 per page. Certification fee: $2.00. Fee payee: Clerk of Circuit Court. Personal checks accepted. Prepayment is required.

9th General District Court PO Box 169, Saluda, VA 23149; 804-758-4312. Hours: 8:30AM-4:30PM (EST). *Misdemeanor, Civil Actions Under $15,000, Eviction, Small Claims.*

Civil Records: Access: Mail, online, in person. Both court and visitors may perform in person searches. No search fee. Required to search: name, years to search. Civil cases indexed by defendant. Civil records on index books from 1800s; on computer 10 years back. For information about the statewide online system, LOPAS, see the state introduction.

Criminal Records: Access: Mail, online, in person. Both court and visitors may perform in person searches. No search fee. Required to search: name, years to search, DOB, date of offense; also helpful: SSN. Criminal records on index books from 1800s; on computer 10 years back. Online access to criminal records is the same as civil.

General Information: Public Access terminal is available. No juvenile, sealed records released. SASE required. Turnaround time 7-10 days. Copy fee: $.50 per page. Certification fee: No certification fee. Fee payee: Clerk of General District Court. Personal checks accepted. Prepayment is required.

Mecklenburg County

10th Circuit Court PO Box 530, Boydton, VA 23917; 804-738-6191; Fax: 804-738-6861. Hours: 8:30AM-4:30PM (EST). *Felony, Civil Actions Over $15,000, Probate.*

Civil Records: Access: Online, in person. Visitors must perform in person searches for themselves. No search fee. Required to search: name, years to search. Civil cases indexed by defendant, plaintiff. Civil records on index books from 1800s, on computer from 1/93. For information about the statewide online system, LOPAS, see the state introduction.

Criminal Records: Access: Online, in person. Visitors must perform in person searches for themselves. No search fee. Required to search: name, years to search. Criminal records on index books from 1800s, on computer from 1/93. Online access to criminal records is the same as civil.

General Information: Public Access terminal is available. No juvenile, sealed or direct indictments (drug offenses) records released. Copy fee: $.50 per page. Certification fee: $2.00. Fee payee: Clerk of Circuit Court. Personal checks accepted. Prepayment is required.

10th General District Court 1294 Jefferson Street (PO Box 306), Boydton, VA 23917; 804-738-6191 X223; Fax: 804-738-0761. Hours: 8:30AM-4:30PM (EST). *Misdemeanor, Civil Actions Under $15,000, Eviction, Small Claims.*

Civil Records: Access: Fax, mail, online, in person. Both court and visitors may perform in person searches. Search fee: $5.00. Required to search: name, years to search. Civil cases indexed by defendant, plaintiff. Civil records on computer since 1991. For information about the statewide online system, LOPAS, see the state introduction.

Criminal Records: Access: Fax, mail, online, in person. Both court and visitors may perform in person searches. Search fee: $5.00. Required to search: name,

years to search; also helpful: DOB, SSN. Criminal records on computer since 1991. Online access to criminal records is the same as civil.

General Information: Public Access terminal is available. Sealed, and adoption records not released. Copy fee: $.50 per page. Certification fee: No certification fee. Fee payee: Clerk of General District Court. Personal checks accepted. Credit cards accepted: Visa, MasterCard.

Middlesex County

9th Circuit Court PO Box 158, Saluda, VA 23149; 804-758-5317; Fax: 804-758-0792. Hours: 8:30AM-4:30PM (EST). *Felony, Civil Actions Over $15,000, Probate.*

Civil Records: Access: Online, in person. Visitors must perform in person searches for themselves. No search fee. Required to search: name, years to search. Civil cases indexed by defendant, plaintiff. Civil records on index books from 1800s. For information about the statewide online system, LOPAS, see the state introduction.

Criminal Records: Access: Online, in person. Visitors must perform in person searches for themselves. No search fee. Required to search: name, years to search. Criminal records on index books from 1800s. Online access to criminal records is the same as civil.

General Information: No juvenile, sealed records released. Copy fee: $.50 per page. Certification fee: $2.00. Fee payee: Clerk of Circuit Court. Personal checks accepted. Prepayment is required.

9th General District Court PO Box 169, Saluda, VA 23149; 804-758-4312. Hours: 8:30AM-4:30PM (EST). *Misdemeanor, Civil Actions Under $15,000, Eviction, Small Claims.*

Civil Records: Access: Mail, online, in person. Both court and visitors may perform in person searches. No search fee. Required to search: name, years to search. Civil cases indexed by defendant. Civil records on index books from 1800s; on computer back 10 years. For information about the statewide online system, LOPAS, see the state introduction.

Criminal Records: Access: Mail, online, in person. Both court and visitors may perform in person searches. No search fee. Required to search: name, years to search. Criminal records on index books from 1800s; on computer back 10 years. Online access to criminal records is the same as civil.

General Information: Public Access terminal is available. No juvenile, sealed records released. SASE required. Turnaround time 2-3 days. Copy fee: $.50 per page. Certification fee: No certification fee. Fee payee: Clerk of General District Court. Personal checks accepted. Prepayment is required.

Montgomery County

27th Circuit Court PO Box 6309, Christiansburg, VA 24068; 540-382-5760; Fax: 540-382-6937. Hours: 8:30AM-4:30PM (EST). *Felony, Civil Actions Over $15,000, Probate.*

Civil Records: Access: Phone, mail, online, in person. Both court and visitors may perform in person searches. No search fee. Required to search: name, years to search. Civil cases indexed by defendant, plaintiff. Civil records on index books from 1800s, on computer from 1/94. For information about the statewide online system, LOPAS, see the state introduction. Phone & mail access limited to cases filed 7/93 to present.

Criminal Records: Access: Online, in person. Visitors must perform in person searches for themselves. No search fee. Required to search: name, years to search; also helpful: DOB, SSN. Criminal records on computer since 9/93, prior in books. Online access to criminal records is the same as civil.

General Information: Public Access terminal is available. No juvenile, sealed records released. SASE requested. Copy fee: $.50 per page. Certification fee: $2.00. Fee payee: Clerk of Circuit Court. Personal checks accepted. Prepayment is required.

27th General District Court
Montgomery County Courthouse, 1 E Main St, Suite 201, Christiansburg, VA 24073; 540-382-5735; Fax: 540-382-6988. 8:30AM-4:30PM (EST). *Misdemeanor, Civil Actions Under $15,000, Eviction, Small Claims.*

Civil Records: Access: Fax, mail, online, in person. Both court and visitors may perform in person searches. No search fee. Required to search: name, years to search. Civil cases indexed by defendant, plaintiff. Civil records on computerized records go back ten years. For information about the statewide online system, LOPAS, see the state introduction.

Criminal Records: Access: Fax, mail, online, in person. Both court and visitors may perform in person searches. No search fee. Required to search: name, years to search. Computerized records go back ten years. Online access to criminal records is the same as civil.

General Information: Public Access terminal is available. No juvenile records released. Turnaround time 5 days. Copy fee: $.50 per page. Certification fee: No certification fee. Fee payee: Clerk General District Court. Personal checks accepted.

Nelson County

24th Circuit Court
PO Box 10, Lovingston, VA 22949; 804-263-4069; Fax: 804-263-8313. Hours: 8AM-5PM (EST). *Felony, Civil Actions Over $15,000, Probate.*

Civil Records: Access: Online, in person. Visitors must perform in person searches for themselves. No search fee. Required to search: name, years to search. Civil cases indexed by defendant, plaintiff. Civil records on index books from 1800s, deeds on computer from 7/93. Online access is available free at http://208.210.219.132/courtinfo/vacircuit/select.jsp?court=. For information about the statewide online system, LOPAS, see the state introduction.

Criminal Records: Access: Online, in person. Visitors must perform in person searches for themselves. No search fee. Required to search: name, years to search; also helpful- DOB, SSN. Criminal records on index books from 1800s, deeds on computer from 7/93. Online access to criminal records is the same as civil.

General Information: Public Access terminal is available. (Deeds and marriage licenses from 6/30/93 and financing statements from 06/30/94 are on terminal.) No juvenile, sealed records released. Copy fee: $.50 per page. Certification fee: $2.00. Fee payee: Clerk of Circuit Court. Personal checks accepted. Prepayment is required.

24th General District Court
Nelson County Courthouse, 84 Courthouse St, PO Box 55, Lovingston, VA 22949; 804-263-4245; Fax: 804-263-4264. Hours: 8AM-4:30PM (EST). *Misdemeanor, Civil Actions Under $15,000, Eviction, Small Claims.*

Civil Records: Access: Fax, mail, online, in person. Both court and visitors may perform in person searches. No search fee. Required to search: name, years to search. Civil cases indexed by defendant, plaintiff. Civil records on computer from 1993, indexed from 1990. For information about the statewide online system, LOPAS, see the state introduction.

Criminal Records: Access: Fax, mail, online, in person. Both court and visitors may perform in person searches. No search fee. Required to search: name, years to search. Criminal records on computer from 1993, indexed from 1990. Online access to criminal records is the same as civil.

General Information: Public Access terminal is available. No sealed records released. SASE required. Turnaround time 3-4 days. Fax notes: No fee to fax results. Copy fee: $.50 per page. Certification fee: No certification fee. Fee payee: Clerk of General District Court. Personal checks accepted. Prepayment is required.

New Kent County

9th Circuit Court
PO Box 98, 2001 Court House Circle, New Kent, VA 23124; 804-966-9520; Fax: 804-966-9528. Hours: 8:30AM-4:30PM (EST). *Felony, Civil Actions Over $15,000, Probate.*

Civil Records: Access: Online, in person. Visitors must perform in person searches for themselves. No search fee. Required to search: name, years to search. Civil cases indexed by defendant, plaintiff. Civil records on index books from 1865, some on cards; computerized back to 1992. For information about the statewide online system, LOPAS, see the state introduction.

Criminal Records: Access: Online, in person. Visitors must perform in person searches for themselves. No search fee. Required to search: name, years to search, DOB, SSN. Criminal records on index books from 1865, some on cards; computerized back to 1992. Online access to criminal records is the same as civil.

General Information: Public Access terminal is available. No juvenile, sealed, adoption records released. Copy fee: $.50 per page. Certification fee: $.50. Fee payee: Circuit Court. Personal checks accepted. Prepayment is required.

9th General District Court
PO Box 127, New Kent, VA 23124; 804-966-9530; Fax: 804-966-9535. Hours: 8:30AM-4:30PM (EST). *Misdemeanor, Civil Actions Under $15,000, Eviction, Small Claims.*

Civil Records: Access: Mail, online, in person. Both court and visitors may perform in person searches. No search fee. Required to search: name, years to search. Civil cases indexed by defendant, plaintiff. Civil records on computer since 1989. For information about the statewide online system, LOPAS, see the state introduction.

Criminal Records: Access: Mail, online, in person. Both court and visitors may perform in person searches. No search fee. Required to search: name, years to search; also helpful: DOB, SSN. Criminal records on computer since 1989. Online access to criminal records is the same as civil.

General Information: Public Access terminal is available. No juvenile, sealed records released. SASE required. Turnaround time 5 days. Copy fee: $1.00 per page. Certification fee: No certification fee. Fee payee: General District Court. Personal checks accepted. Credit cards accepted: Visa, MasterCard. Prepayment is required.

Newport News City

7th Circuit Court
2500 Washington Ave, Newport News, VA 23607; 757-926-8561; Fax: 757-926-8531. Hours: 8AM-4:45PM (EST). *Felony, Civil Actions Over $15,000, Probate.*

Civil Records: Access: Mail, online, in person. Both court and visitors may perform in person searches. No search fee. Required to search: name, years to search. Civil cases indexed by defendant, plaintiff. Civil records on computer from 1987, prior on index books. Online access is available free at http://208.210.219.132/courtinfo/vacircuit/select.jsp?court=. For information about the statewide online system, LOPAS, see the state introduction. Mail access only available for old records.

Criminal Records: Access: Online, in person. Visitors must perform in person searches for themselves. No search fee. Required to search: name, years to search. Criminal records on computer from 1987, on index

books from 1985 to 1987, prior on judgment books. Online access to criminal records is the same as civil.

General Information: Public Access terminal is available. No adoption, juvenile, sealed records released. SASE requested. Turnaround time 1 day. Copy fee: $.50 per page. Certification fee: $2.00. Fee payee: Clerk of Circuit Court. Personal checks accepted. In state checks only. Prepayment is required.

7th General District Court
2500 Washington Ave, Newport News, VA 23607; Civil phone: 757-926-3520; Criminal phone: 757-926-8811; Fax: 757-926-8496. Hours: 7:30AM-4PM (EST). *Misdemeanor, Civil Actions Under $15,000, Eviction, Small Claims.*

Civil Records: Access: Phone, fax, mail, online, in person. Visitors must perform in person searches for themselves. No search fee. Required to search: name, years to search. For information about the statewide online system, LOPAS, see the state introduction.

Criminal Records: Access: Phone, fax, mail, online, in person. Both court and visitors may perform in person searches. No search fee. Required to search: name, years to search. Criminal records on computer on index cards since 1985, prior records at Circuit Court. Online access to criminal records is the same as civil.

General Information: Public Access terminal is available. No juvenile, sealed records released. Turnaround time 1-2 days. Copy fee: $1.00 for first page, $.50 each add'l. Certification fee: No certification fee. Fee payee: General District Court. Personal checks accepted. Credit cards accepted: Visa, MasterCard. Prepayment is required.

Norfolk City

4th Circuit Court
100 St Paul's Blvd, Norfolk, VA 23510; 757-664-4380; Fax: 757-664-4581. Hours: 9AM-5PM (EST). *Felony, Civil Actions Over $15,000, Probate.*

Civil Records: Access: Mail, online, in person. Both court and visitors may perform in person searches. No search fee. Required to search: name, years to search. Civil cases indexed by defendant, plaintiff. Civil records on computer from 1987, docket books back to 1800s. Online access is available free at http://208.210.219.132/courtinfo/vacircuit/select.jsp?court=. For information about the statewide online system, LOPAS, see the state introduction.

Criminal Records: Access: Online, in person. Visitors must perform in person searches for themselves. No search fee. Required to search: name, years to search; also helpful: DOB, SSN. Criminal records on computer from 1987, docket books back to 1800s. Online access to criminal records is the same as civil.

General Information: Public Access terminal is available. No juvenile, sealed records released. Turnaround time 2-3 days. Copy fee: $.50 per page. Certification fee: $2.00. Fee payee: Clerk of Circuit Court. Personal checks accepted. Prepayment is required.

4th General District Court
811 E City Hall Ave, Norfolk, VA 23510; 757-664-4910; Civil phone: 757-664-4913/4; Criminal phone: 757-664-4915/6. Hours: 8AM-4PM (EST). *Misdemeanor, Civil Actions Under $15,000, Eviction, Small Claims.*

Civil Records: Access: Mail, online, in person. Both court and visitors may perform in person searches. Search fee: $10.00 per name. Required to search: name, years to search. Civil cases indexed by defendant, plaintiff. Civil records in files, on computer from 1986. For information about the statewide online system, LOPAS, see the state introduction.

Criminal Records: Access: Mail, online, in person. Both court and visitors may perform in person searches. Search fee: $10.00 per name. Required to search: name, years to search. Criminal records in files, on computer from 1986. Online access to criminal records is the same as civil.

General Information: Public Access terminal is available. No juvenile, sealed, or adoption records released. Turnaround time within 1-2 weeks. Copy fee: $1.00 per document. Certification fee: No certification fee. Fee payee: Norfolk General District Court. Personal checks accepted. Prepayment is required.

Northampton County

2nd Circuit Court PO Box 36, Eastville, VA 23347; 757-678-0465; Fax: 757-678-5410. 9AM-5PM (EST). *Felony, Civil Actions Over $15,000, Probate.*

Civil Records: Access: Phone, fax, mail, online, in person. Both court and visitors may perform in person searches. No search fee. Required to search: name, years to search. Civil cases indexed by defendant, plaintiff. Civil records on index books from 1800s. For information about the statewide online system, LOPAS, see the state introduction.

Criminal Records: Access: Phone, fax, mail, online, in person. Both court and visitors may perform in person searches. No search fee. Required to search: name, years to search, DOB. Criminal records on index books from 1800s. Online access to criminal records is the same as civil.

General Information: No juvenile, sealed records released. SASE required. Turnaround time 1 week. Fax notes: $.50 per page. Copy fee: $.50 per page. Certification fee: $1.00. Fee payee: Clerk of Circuit Court. Personal checks accepted. Credit cards accepted: Visa. Prepayment is required.

Northampton General District Court PO Box 125, Eastville, VA 23347; 757-678-0466. Hours: 8AM-5PM (EST). *Misdemeanor, Civil Actions Under $15,000, Eviction, Small Claims.*

Civil Records: Access: Mail, online, in person. Only the court performs in person searches; visitors may not. No search fee. Required to search: name, years to search. Civil cases indexed by defendant, plaintiff. Civil records on computer since 1990. For information about the statewide online system, LOPAS, see the state introduction.

Criminal Records: Access: Mail, online, in person. Only the court performs in person searches; visitors may not. No search fee. Required to search: name, years to search, DOB or SSN. Criminal records on computer since 1990. Online access to criminal records is the same as civil.

General Information: No juvenile, sealed records released. SASE required. Turnaround time 1-2 days. Copy fee: $.50 per page. Certification fee: No certification fee. Fee payee: General District Court. Personal checks accepted.

Northumberland County

15th Circuit Court PO Box 217, Heathsville, VA 22473; 804-580-3700; Fax: 804-580-2261. Hours: 8:30AM-4:45PM (EST). *Felony, Civil Actions Over $15,000, Probate.*

Civil Records: Access: Mail, online, in person. Both court and visitors may perform in person searches. No search fee. Required to search: name, years to search. Civil cases indexed by defendant, plaintiff. Civil records on index books from 1650. For information about the statewide online system, LOPAS, see the state introduction.

Criminal Records: Access: Mail, online, in person. Both court and visitors may perform in person searches. No search fee. Required to search: name, years to search, DOB. Criminal records on index books from 1650. Online access to criminal records is the same as civil.

General Information: No juvenile, sealed records released. Turnaround time 1-2 days. Copy fee: $.50 per

page. Certification fee: No certification fee. Fee payee: Clerk of Circuit Court. Personal checks accepted.

15th General District Court Northumberland Courthouse, PO Box 114, Heathsville, VA 22473; 804-580-4323; Fax: 804-580-6702. Hours: 8AM-4:30PM (EST). *Misdemeanor, Civil Actions Under $15,000, Eviction, Small Claims.*

Civil Records: Access: Online, in person. Visitors must perform in person searches for themselves. No search fee. Required to search: name, years to search. Civil cases indexed by defendant, plaintiff. Civil records on index books; on computer since 1994. For information about the statewide online system, LOPAS, see the state introduction.

Criminal Records: Access: Online, in person. Visitors must perform in person searches for themselves. No search fee. Required to search: name, years to search, DOB; also helpful: SSN. Criminal records on index books back to 1990; on computer since 1994. Online access to criminal records is the same as civil.

General Information: Public Access terminal is available. No juvenile, sealed records released. Copy fee: $1.00 for first page, $.10 each add'l. Certification fee: No certification fee. Fee payee: Clerk of District Court. Personal checks accepted. Credit cards accepted: Visa, MasterCard. Prepayment is required.

Norton City

Circuit & District Courts, VA.

Note: See Wise County

Nottoway County

11th Circuit Court Courthouse, PO Box 25, Nottoway, VA 23955; 804-645-9043; Fax: 804-645-2201. Hours: 8:30AM-4:30PM (EST). *Felony, Civil Actions Over $15,000, Probate.*

Civil Records: Access: Mail, online, in person. Both court and visitors may perform in person searches. No search fee. Required to search: name, years to search. Civil cases indexed by defendant, plaintiff. Civil records on index books from late 1700s. Online access is available free at http://208.210.219.132/courtinfo/vacircuit/select.jsp?court=. For information about the statewide online system, LOPAS, see the state introduction.

Criminal Records: Access: Online, in person. Visitors must perform in person searches for themselves. No search fee. Required to search: name, years to search; also helpful: DOB, SSN. Criminal records on index books from late 1700s. Online access to criminal records is the same as civil.

General Information: Public Access terminal is available. No juvenile, sealed records released. SASE required. Turnaround time 1-2 days. Copy fee: $.50 per page. Certification fee: $2.00. Fee payee: Clerk's Office. Personal checks accepted. Prepayment is required.

11th General District Court Courthouse, Nottoway, VA 23955; 804-645-9312. Hours: 8AM-4:15PM (EST). *Misdemeanor, Civil Actions Under $15,000, Eviction, Small Claims.*

Civil Records: Access: Mail, online, in person. Both court and visitors may perform in person searches. No search fee. Required to search: name, years to search. Civil cases indexed by defendant, plaintiff. Civil records on index cards from 1986, on computer from 1989. Only court can search prior to 1989. For information about the statewide online system, LOPAS, see the state introduction.

Criminal Records: Access: Mail, online, in person. Both court and visitors may perform in person searches. No search fee. Required to search: name, years to search; also helpful: DOB, SSN. Criminal records on index cards from 1986, on computer from 1989. Only court can search prior to 1989. Online access to criminal records is the same as civil.

General Information: Public Access terminal is available. No juvenile records released. SASE required. Turnaround time 2-3 days. Copy fee: $1.00 for first page, $.50 each add'l. Certification fee: No certification fee. Fee payee: Nottoway District Court. Personal checks accepted. Prepayment is required.

Orange County

16th Circuit Court PO Box 230, Orange, VA 22960; 540-672-4030; Fax: 540-672-2939. Hours: 8:30AM-4:30PM (EST). *Felony, Civil Actions Over $15,000, Probate.*

Civil Records: Access: Online, in person. Both court and visitors may perform in person searches. No search fee. Required to search: name, years to search. Civil cases indexed by defendant, plaintiff. Civil records on computer since 1989, in index books from 1734 for deeds, from 1853 for births, from 1912 for marriages. Online access is available free at http://208.210.219.132/courtinfo/vacircuit/select.jsp?court=. For information about the statewide online system, LOPAS, see the state introduction.

Criminal Records: Access: Phone, fax, mail, online, in person. Both court and visitors may perform in person searches. No search fee. Required to search: name, years to search, DOB; also helpful: SSN. Criminal records on computer since 1989, in index books from 1734. Online access to criminal records is the same as civil.

General Information: Public Access terminal is available. No juvenile, sealed records released. Turnaround time 1 week-10 days. Fax notes: No fee to fax results. Copy fee: $.50 per page. Certification fee: No certification fee. Fee payee: Clerk of Circuit Court. Personal checks accepted. Prepayment is required.

16th General District Court Orange County Courthouse, PO Box 821, Orange, VA 22960; 540-672-3150; Fax: 540-672-9438. Hours: 8:30AM-4:30PM (EST). *Misdemeanor, Civil Actions Under $15,000, Eviction, Small Claims.*

Civil Records: Access: Mail, online, in person. Only the court performs in person searches; visitors may not. No search fee. Required to search: name, years to search. Civil cases indexed by defendant, plaintiff. Civil records on index books from 1800s, on computer from 1990. For information about the statewide online system, LOPAS, see the state introduction.

Criminal Records: Access: Mail, online, in person. Only the court performs in person searches; visitors may not. No search fee. Required to search: name, years to search, DOB; also helpful: SSN. Criminal records on index books from 1800s, on computer from 1990. Online access to criminal records is the same as civil.

General Information: No juvenile, sealed records released. Turnaround time 1-2 days. Copy fee: $1.00 for first page, $.50 each add'l. Certification fee: No certification fee. Fee payee: Clerk of District Court. In-state checks accepted. Credit cards accepted: Visa, MasterCard. Prepayment is required.

Page County

26th Circuit Court 116 S Court St, Suite A, Luray, VA 22835; 540-743-4064; Fax: 540-743-2338. Hours: 9AM-5PM (EST). *Felony, Civil Actions Over $15,000, Probate.*

Civil Records: Access: Online, in person. Visitors must perform in person searches for themselves. No search fee. Required to search: name, years to search. Civil cases indexed by defendant, plaintiff. Civil records on index books from 1831. For information about the statewide online system, LOPAS, see the state introduction.

Criminal Records: Access: Online, in person. Visitors must perform in person searches for themselves. No search fee. Required to search: name, years to search,

DOB; also helpful: SSN. Criminal records on index books from 1831. Online access to criminal records is the same as civil.

General Information: No juvenile, sealed records released. Copy fee: $.50 per page. Certification fee: $2.00. Fee payee: Ron Wilson, Clerk. Personal checks accepted. No second party checks accepted. Prepayment is required.

26th General District Court 116 S Court St, Luray, VA 22835; 540-743-5705. Hours: 8AM-4:30PM (EST). *Misdemeanor, Civil Actions Under $15,000, Eviction, Small Claims.*

Civil Records: Access: Mail, online, in person. Both court and visitors may perform in person searches. No search fee. Required to search: name, years to search. Civil cases indexed by defendant, plaintiff. Civil records on computer back to 1/90. For information about the statewide online system, LOPAS, see the state introduction.

Criminal Records: Access: Mail, online, in person. Both court and visitors may perform in person searches. No search fee. Required to search: name, years to search; also helpful: DOB, SSN. Criminal records on computer back to 1/90. Online access to criminal records is the same as civil.

General Information: Public Access terminal is available. No sealed records released. SASE requested. Turnaround time 7-10 days. Certification fee: $1.00. Fee payee: District Court. Personal checks accepted.

Patrick County

21st Circuit Court PO Box 148, Stuart, VA 24171; 540-694-7213. Hours: 9AM-5PM (EST). *Felony, Civil Actions Over $15,000, Probate.*

Civil Records: Access: In person only. Visitors must perform in person searches for themselves. No search fee. Required to search: name, years to search. Civil cases indexed by plaintiff. Civil records on index books from 1791. For information about the statewide online system, LOPAS, see the state introduction.

Criminal Records: Access: Online, in person. Visitors must perform in person searches for themselves. No search fee. Required to search: name, years to search; also helpful: DOB, SSN. Criminal records on index books from 1791. Online access to criminal records is the same as civil.

General Information: No juvenile, sealed records released. Copy fee: $.50 per page. Certification fee: $2.00. Fee payee: Clerk of Circuit Court. Personal checks accepted. Prepayment is required.

21st General District Court PO Box 149, Stuart, VA 24171; 540-694-7258; Fax: 540-694-5614. Hours: 8:30AM-5PM (EST). *Misdemeanor, Civil Actions Under $15,000, Eviction, Small Claims.*

Civil Records: Access: Mail, online, in person. Both court and visitors may perform in person searches. No search fee. Required to search: name, years to search. Civil cases indexed by defendant, plaintiff. Civil records archived from 1916, on computer from 10/94. For information about the statewide online system, LOPAS, see the state introduction.

Criminal Records: Access: Mail, online, in person. Both court and visitors may perform in person searches. No search fee. Required to search: name, years to search, DOB; also helpful: SSN. Criminal records archived from 1916, on computer from 10/94. Online access to criminal records is the same as civil.

General Information: Public Access terminal is available. No juvenile, sealed records released. SASE requested. Turnaround time 1 week. No copy fee. Certification fee: No certification fee. Personal checks accepted.

Petersburg City

11th Circuit Court 7 Courthouse Ave, Petersburg, VA 23803; 804-733-2367; Fax: 804-732-5548. Hours: 8AM-4:30PM (EST). *Felony, Civil Actions Over $15,000, Probate.*

Civil Records: Access: Online, in person. Visitors must perform in person searches for themselves. No search fee. Required to search: name, years to search. Civil cases indexed by defendant, plaintiff. Civil records on index books back to 1784. Online access is available free at http://208.210.219.132/courtinfo/vacircuit/select.jsp?court=. For information about the statewide online system, LOPAS, see the state introduction.

Criminal Records: Access: Online, in person. Visitors must perform in person searches for themselves. No search fee. Required to search: name, years to search; also helpful: DOB, SSN. Criminal records on index books back to 1784. Online access to criminal records is the same as civil.

General Information: No juvenile, sealed or adoption records released. Copy fee: $.50 per page. Certification fee: $2.00. Fee payee: Petersburg Circuit Court Clerk. Personal checks accepted. Out of state checks not accepted. Prepayment is required.

11th Judicial District Court 35 E Tabb St, Petersburg, VA 23803; 804-733-2374; Civil phone: X4153; Criminal phone: X4152; Fax: 804-733-2375 (Attn: Civil or Crimnal). Hours: 8AM-4PM (EST). *Misdemeanor, Civil Actions Under $15,000, Eviction, Small Claims.*

Civil Records: Access: Fax, mail, online, in person. Both court and visitors may perform in person searches. No search fee. Required to search: name, years to search. Civil cases indexed by defendant, plaintiff. Civil records on index books back to 1980. For information about the statewide online system, LOPAS, see the state introduction.

Criminal Records: Access: Fax, mail, online, in person. Both court and visitors may perform in person searches. No search fee. Required to search: name, years to search, DOB; also helpful: SSN. Criminal records indexed on books for 10 years; on computer back to 1988. Online access to criminal records is the same as civil.

General Information: Public Access terminal is available. No sealed records released. Turnaround time 1 week. Copy fee: $1.00 for first 2 pages. Add $.50 per page thereafter. Certification fee: $1.00 plus $.50 per page after second. Fee payee: General District Court. Personal checks accepted. In state checks accepted. Prepayment is required.

Pittsylvania County

22nd Circuit Court PO Drawer 31, Chatham, VA 24531; 804-432-7887. Hours: 8:30AM-5PM (EST). *Felony, Civil Actions Over $15,000, Probate.*

Civil Records: Access: Online, in person. Visitors must perform in person searches for themselves. No search fee. Required to search: name, years to search. Civil cases indexed by defendant, plaintiff. Civil records on index books back to 1767. For information about the statewide online system, LOPAS, see the state introduction.

Criminal Records: Access: Online, in person. Visitors must perform in person searches for themselves. No search fee. Required to search: name, years to search, DOB, SSN. Criminal records on index books back to 1767. Online access to criminal records is the same as civil.

General Information: No juvenile, sealed records released. Copy fee: $.50 per page. Certification fee: $2.00. Fee payee: Clerk of Circuit Court. Personal checks accepted. Prepayment is required.

22nd General District Court Pittsylvania Courthouse Annex 2nd Flr, PO Box 695, Chatham, VA 24531; 804-432-7879; Fax: 804-432-7915. Hours: 8:30AM-4:30PM (EST). *Misdemeanor, Civil Actions Under $15,000, Eviction, Small Claims.*

www.courts.state.va.us/courts/gd/Pittsylvania/home.html

Civil Records: Access: Online, in person. Visitors must perform in person searches for themselves. No search fee. Required to search: name, years to search. Civil cases indexed by defendant, plaintiff. Civil records on computer since 1991. For information about the statewide online system, LOPAS, see the state introduction.

Criminal Records: Access: Online, in person. Visitors must perform in person searches for themselves. No search fee. Required to search: name, years to search. Criminal records on computer since 1991. Online access to criminal records is the same as civil.

General Information: Public Access terminal is available. No juvenile, sealed records released. Fax notes: Fee to fax results is $.25 per page. Copy fee: $.25 per page. Certification fee: No certification fee. Fee payee: General District Court. Personal checks accepted.

Poquoson City

Circuit & District Courts, VA.

Note: See York County

Portsmouth City

Circuit Court PO Drawer 1217, Portsmouth, VA 23705; 757-393-8671; Fax: 757-399-4826. Hours: 8:30AM-5PM (EST). *Felony, Civil Actions Over $15,000, Probate.*

Civil Records: Access: Online, in person. Visitors must perform in person searches for themselves. No search fee. Required to search: name, years to search. Civil cases indexed by defendant, plaintiff. Civil records on computer from 1988, prior on index books. For information about the statewide online system, LOPAS, see the state introduction. Phone access limited to simple requests.

Criminal Records: Access: Mail, online, in person. Both court and visitors may perform in person searches. Search fee: $5.00 per name. Required to search: name, years to search; also helpful: DOB. Criminal records on computer since 1987, prior indexed on books. Online access to criminal records is the same as civil.

General Information: Public Access terminal is available. No juvenile, sealed records released. Copy fee: $.50 per page. Certification fee: $2.50. Fee payee: Walter M Edmonds, Clerk. Business checks accepted. Credit cards accepted: Visa, MasterCard. Prepayment is required.

General District Court PO Box 129, Portsmouth, VA 23705; Civil phone: 757-393-8624; Criminal phone: 757-393-8681; Fax: 757-393-8634. Hours: 8:30AM-4:30PM (EST). *Misdemeanor, Civil Actions Under $15,000, Eviction, Small Claims.*

Note: Traffic Division: 757-393-8506.

Civil Records: Access: Online, in person. Visitors must perform in person searches for themselves. No search fee. Required to search: name, years to search. Civil cases indexed by defendant, plaintiff. Civil records on computer from 4/87, from 1981 to 4/87 paper files only. For information about the statewide online system, LOPAS, see the state introduction.

Criminal Records: Access: Mail, fax, online, in person. Both court and visitors may perform in person searches. Search fee: $7.00 per name. Required to search: name, years to search; also helpful: DOB, SSN. Criminal records on computer from 7/91, case (paper files) maintained for 10 years. Online access to criminal records is the same as civil.

General Information: Public Access terminal is available. Juvenile, sealed records not released. SASE required. Turnaround time within 14 days. No copy fee. Certification fee: No certification fee. Fee payee: Clerk of General District Court. Personal checks accepted. Credit cards accepted: Visa, MasterCard.

Powhatan County

11th Circuit Court PO Box 37, Powhatan, VA 23139-0037; 804-598-5660; Fax: 804-598-5608. Hours: 8:30AM-5PM (EST). *Felony, Civil Actions Over $15,000, Probate.*

Civil Records: Access: Mail, in person. Visitors must perform in person searches for themselves. No search fee. Required to search: name, years to search. Civil cases indexed by defendant, plaintiff. Civil records on index books from 1777, on computer from 1993. Phone access limited to simple requests only.

Criminal Records: Access: In person only. Visitors must perform in person searches for themselves. No search fee. Required to search: name, years to search, signed release; also helpful: SSN. Criminal records on index books from 1777, on computer from 1993.

General Information: Public Access terminal is available. No juvenile, sealed records released. SASE required. Turnaround time 1-2 weeks. Copy fee: $.50 per page. Certification fee: $2.00. Fee payee: Clerk of Court. Personal checks accepted. Will bill copy fees.

11th Judicial District Court Courthouse, 3880 D Old Buckingham Rd, Powhatan, VA 23139; 804-598-5665; Fax: 804-598-5648. Hours: 8:30AM-5PM (EST). *Misdemeanor, Civil Actions Under $15,000, Eviction, Small Claims.*

Civil Records: Access: Phone, fax, mail, online, in person. Only the court performs in person searches; visitors may not. No search fee. Required to search: name, years to search. Civil cases indexed by defendant. Civil records on index cards for 10 yrs, on computer from 1992. For information about the statewide online system, LOPAS, see the state introduction.

Criminal Records: Access: Phone, fax, mail, online, in person. Only the court performs in person searches; visitors may not. No search fee. Required to search: name, years to search, DOB; also helpful: SSN. Criminal records on index cards for 10 yrs, on computer from 1993. Online access to criminal records is the same as civil.

General Information: No juvenile, sealed records released. Turnaround time 1 week. Fax notes: No fee to fax results. Local faxing only. Copy fee: $.50 each for 1st two; $25. Each add'l. Certification fee: No certification fee. Fee payee: Powhatan District Court. Personal checks accepted.

Prince Edward County

Circuit Court 111 South Street, Court House, Farmville, VA 23901; 434-392-5145. Hours: 8:30AM-4:30PM *Felony, Civil Actions Over $15,000, Probate.*

Civil Records: Access: Online, in person. Visitors must perform in person searches for themselves. No search fee. Required to search: name, years to search. Civil cases indexed by defendant, plaintiff. Civil records on computer from 1990, books from 1930s. For information about the statewide online system, LOPAS, see the state introduction. The court will only provide copies of specified documents at the cost of the time to locate and cost of copies.

Criminal Records: Access: Online, in person. Visitors must perform in person searches for themselves. No search fee. Required to search: name, years to search, DOB; also helpful: SSN. Criminal records on computer from 1990, books from 1930s. Online access to criminal records is the same as civil.

General Information: Public Access terminal is available. No juvenile, sealed records released. Copy fee: $.50 per page. Certification fee: $2.00. Fee payee: Clerk of Circuit Court. Personal checks accepted. Prepayment is required.

General District Court PO Box 41, Farmville, VA 23901-0041; 434-392-4024; Fax: 434-392-3800. Hours: 8:30AM-4:30PM (EST). *Misdemeanor, Civil Actions Under $15,000, Eviction, Small Claims.*

Civil Records: Access: Mail, online, in person. Both court and visitors may perform in person searches. No search fee. Required to search: name, years to search; also helpful: address. Civil cases indexed by defendant, plaintiff. Civil records on computer from 1991. For information about the statewide online system, LOPAS, see the state introduction.

Criminal Records: Access: Mail, online, in person. Both court and visitors may perform in person searches. No search fee. Required to search: name, years to search; also helpful: DOB, SSN. Criminal records on computer from 1991. Online access to criminal records is the same as civil.

General Information: Public Access terminal is available. No juvenile, sealed records released. SASE required. Turnaround time 1 week. Copy fee: $1.00 per page. Certification fee: No certification fee. Fee payee: Clerk of District Court. Personal checks accepted. Prepayment is required.

Prince George County

6th Circuit Court PO Box 98, Prince George, VA 23875; 804-733-2640; Fax: 804-761-5721. Hours: 8:30AM-5PM (EST). *Felony, Civil Actions Over $15,000, Probate.*

Civil Records: Access: Mail, online, in person. Both court and visitors may perform in person searches. Search fee: $5.00 per name. Required to search: name, years to search. Civil cases indexed by defendant, plaintiff. Civil records on index books since 1930s, computerized since 04/96. For information about the statewide online system, LOPAS, see state introduction.

Criminal Records: Access: Mail, online, in person. Both court and visitors may perform in person searches. Search fee: $5.00 per name. Required to search: name, years to search, DOB; also helpful: SSN. Criminal records on index books since 1930s, computerized since 04/96. Online access to criminal records is the same as civil.

General Information: Public Access terminal is available. No juvenile or sealed records released. SASE required. Turnaround time 1-2 days. Copy fee: $.50 per page. Certification fee: No certification fee. Fee payee: Clerk of the Circuit Court. Personal checks accepted. Prepayment is required.

6th General District Court P.C. Courthouse, PO Box 187, Prince George, VA 23875; 804-733-2783. Hours: 8:30AM-4:30PM (EST). *Misdemeanor, Civil Actions Under $15,000, Eviction, Small Claims.*

Civil Records: Access: Mail, online, in person. Both court and visitors may perform in person searches. No search fee. Required to search: name, years to search. Civil cases indexed by defendant, plaintiff. Civil records on computer since 1991, prior on books since 1985. For information about the statewide online system, LOPAS, see the state introduction.

Criminal Records: Access: Mail, online, in person. Both court and visitors may perform in person searches. No search fee. Required to search: name, years to search; also helpful: SSN. Criminal records on computer since 1991, prior on books since 1985. Online access to criminal records is the same as civil.

General Information: Public Access terminal is available. No juvenile records released. Turnaround time 1-2 weeks. No copy fee. Certification fee: No certification fee. Fee payee: Prince George Combined Court. Personal checks accepted.

Prince William County

31st Circuit Court 9311 Lee Ave, Manassas, VA 20110; 703-792-6015; Fax: 703-792-4721. Hours: 8:30AM-5PM (EST). *Felony, Civil Actions Over $15,000, Probate.*

www.pwcgov.org/ccourt

Civil Records: Access: In person only. Visitors must perform in person searches for themselves. No search fee. Required to search: name, years to search. Civil cases indexed by defendant, plaintiff. Civil records on computer since 1989; prior on microfiche or books.

Criminal Records: Access: Mail, in person. Both court and visitors may perform in person searches. Search fee: $10.00 per name. Required to search: name, years to search, DOB; also helpful: SSN. Criminal records on computer since 1989; prior on microfiche or books.

General Information: Public Access terminal is available. No juvenile records released. Turnaround time 1 week. Copy fee: $.50 per page. Certification fee: $2.00. Fee payee: Clerk of Circuit Court. Personal checks accepted.

31st General District Court 9311 Lee Ave, Manassas, VA 20110; Civil phone: 703-792-6149; Criminal phone: 703-792-6141; Fax: 703-792-6121. Hours: 8AM-4PM (EST). *Misdemeanor, Civil Actions Under $15,000, Eviction, Small Claims.*

www.courts.state.va.us/courts/gd/Prince_William/home.html

Civil Records: Access: Phone, mail, online, in person. Both court and visitors may perform in person searches. No search fee. Required to search: name, years to search. Civil cases indexed by defendant, plaintiff. Civil records on computer since 1986, on index cards since 1985. For information about the statewide online system, LOPAS, see the state introduction.

Criminal Records: Access: Phone, mail, online, in person. Both court and visitors may perform in person searches. No search fee. Required to search: name, years to search. Criminal records on computer go back 10 years. Online access to criminal records is the same as civil.

General Information: Public Access terminal is available. No juvenile or sealed records released. SASE required. Turnaround time 10 days. Copy fee: $1.00 copy fee for first 2 pages. Add $.50 per page thereafter. Certification fee: No certification fee. Fee payee: Clerk G.D.C. Personal checks accepted. Prepayment required.

Pulaski County

27th Circuit Court 45 3rd St NW Suite 101, Pulaski, VA 24301; 540-980-7825; Fax: 540-980-7835. Hours: 8:30AM-4:30PM (EST). *Felony, Civil Actions Over $15,000, Probate.*

www.pulaskicircuitcourt.com

Civil Records: Access: Online, in person. Visitors must perform in person searches for themselves. No search fee. Required to search: name, years to search. Civil cases indexed by defendant, plaintiff. Civil records on index books from 1800s; online since 1998. Online access to court records is available free at http://records.pulaskicircuitcourt.com/splash.jsp. Registration required; search by name, document type or number. Also, online access is available free at http://208.210.219.132/courtinfo/vacircuit/select.jsp?court=.

Criminal Records: Access: Online, in person. Visitors must perform in person searches for themselves. No search fee. Required to search: name, years to search, DOBV; also helpful: SSN. Criminal records on index books from 1800s, online since 1998. Online access to criminal records is the same as civil. This agency will perform no record checks and refer all requests to the State Police.

General Information: No juvenile, sealed records released. Copy fee: $.50 per page. Certification fee: $1.00. Fee payee: Clerk of Court. Personal checks accepted. Prepayment is required.

27th General District Court
45 3rd St NW Ste 102, Pulaski, VA 24301; 540-980-7470; Fax: 540-980-7792. Hours: 8:30AM-4:30PM (EST). *Misdemeanor, Civil Actions Under $15,000, Eviction, Small Claims.*

Civil Records: Access: Online, in person. Visitors must perform in person searches for themselves. No search fee. Required to search: name, years to search. Civil cases indexed by defendant, plaintiff. Civil records on computer since 1987; no records prior due to courthouse fire. For information about the statewide online system, LOPAS, see the state introduction.
Criminal Records: Access: Online, in person. Visitors must perform in person searches for themselves. No search fee. Required to search: name, years to search, DOB; also helpful: SSN. Criminal records on computer since 1987; no records prior due to courthouse fire. Online access to criminal records is the same as civil.
General Information: Public Access terminal is available. No juvenile, sealed records released. Copy fee: $.50 per page. Certification fee: No certification fee. Fee payee: Clerk of General District Court. Personal checks accepted. Credit cards accepted: Visa, MasterCard. Credit cards accepted for fines & costs only. Prepayment is required.

Radford City

27th Circuit Court
619 2nd St, Radford, VA 24141; 540-731-3610; Fax: 540-731-3612. Hours: 8AM-5PM (no machine receipts after 4:30PM) (EST). *Felony, Civil Actions Over $15,000, Probate.*

Civil Records: Access: Fax, mail, online, in person. Both court and visitors may perform in person searches. No search fee. Required to search: name, years to search. Civil cases indexed by defendant, plaintiff. Civil records on computer back to 6/2000. Online access is available free at http://208.210.219.132/courtinfo/vacircuit/ select.jsp?court=. For information about the statewide online system, LOPAS, see state introduction.
Criminal Records: Access: Fax, mail, online, in person. Both court and visitors may perform in person searches. No search fee. Required to search: name, years to search, DOB, signed release; also helpful: SSN. Criminal records on computer back to 6/2000. Online access to criminal records is the same as civil.
General Information: Public Access terminal is available. No juvenile, sealed or adoption records released. SASE required. Turnaround time same day. Fax notes: $.50 per page. Copy fee: $.50 per page. Certification fee: $2.00. Fee payee: Radford Circuit Court. Personal checks accepted. Prepayment required.

27th General District Court
619 2nd St, Radford, VA 24141; 540-731-3609; Fax: 540-731-3692. Hours: 8:30AM-4:30PM (EST). *Misdemeanor, Civil Actions Under $15,000, Eviction, Small Claims.*

Civil Records: Access: Mail, online, in person. Both court and visitors may perform in person searches. Search fee: A search fee may be required. Required to search: name, years to search. Civil cases indexed by defendant, plaintiff. For information about the statewide online system, LOPAS, see the state introduction.
Criminal Records: Access: Fax, mail, online, in person. Both court and visitors may perform in person searches. Search fee: None, unless it is a lengthy search. Required to search: name, years to search, DOB, SSN, signed release. Criminal records on computer since 1989. Online access to criminal records is the same as civil.
General Information: Public Access terminal is available. No juvenile, sealed records released. Turnaround time 7 days. Fax notes: $.50 per page. Copy fee: $.50 per page. Certification fee: No

certification fee. Fee payee: District Court. Personal checks accepted. Prepayment is required.

Rappahannock County

20th Circuit Court
238 Gay Street (PO Box 517), Washington, VA 22747; 540-675-3621. Hours: 8:30AM-4:30PM (EST). *Felony, Civil Actions Over $15,000, Probate.*

Civil Records: Access: Mail, online, in person. Both court and visitors may perform in person searches. No search fee. Required to search: name, years to search. Civil cases indexed by defendant, plaintiff. Civil records computerized since 1995, on index cards from 1833, early records archived. For information about the statewide online system, LOPAS, see the state introduction. Mail access limited to specific cases only. Court will only do searches as time permits.
Criminal Records: Access: Mail, online, in person. Both court and visitors may perform in person searches. Search fee: Searches performed only as time permits. Required to search: name, years to search; also helpful: DOB, SSN. Criminal records computerized since 1995, on index cards from 1833, early records archived. Online access to criminal records is the same as civil. Mail access limited to specific cases only.
General Information: Public Access terminal is available. No juvenile, sealed records released. SASE required. Turnaround time 1-2 days. Copy fee: $.50 per page. Fee payee: Clerk of the Circuit Court. Personal checks accepted. Prepayment is required.

20th Combined District Court
PO Box 206, Washington, VA 22747; 540-675-3518. Hours: 8:30AM-4:30PM (EST). *Misdemeanor, Civil Actions Under $15,000, Eviction, Small Claims.*

Civil Records: Access: Mail, online, in person. Both court and visitors may perform in person searches. No search fee. Required to search: name, years to search. Civil cases indexed by defendant, plaintiff. Civil records on index cards back to 1985, prior in Circuit Court. For information about the statewide online system, LOPAS, see the state introduction.
Criminal Records: Access: Mail, online, in person. Both court and visitors may perform in person searches. No search fee. Required to search: name, years to search, DOB; also helpful: SSN. Criminal records on index cards back to 1985, prior in Circuit Court. Online access to criminal records is the same as civil.
General Information: Public Access terminal is available. No juvenile, sealed records released. SASE requested. Turnaround time up to 2 weeks. Copy fee: $.25 per page. Certification fee: No certification fee. Fee payee: Clerk of General District Court. Personal checks accepted. Credit cards accepted: Visa, MasterCard.

Richmond County

15th Circuit Court
101 Court Circle, PO Box 1000, Warsaw, VA 22572; 804-333-3781; Fax: 804-333-5396. Hours: 9AM-5PM (EST). *Felony, Civil Actions Over $15,000, Probate.*

Civil Records: Access: Phone, mail, in person. Both court and visitors may perform in person searches. No search fee. Required to search: name, years to search; also helpful: address, SS#. Civil cases indexed by defendant, plaintiff. Civil records archived from 1692. For information about the statewide online system, LOPAS, see the state introduction.
Criminal Records: Access: Mail, in person. Both court and visitors may perform in person searches. No search fee. Required to search: name, years to search, DOB; also helpful: address. Criminal records archived from 1692.
General Information: No juvenile, sealed records released. SASE requested. Turnaround time same day. Copy fee: $.50 per page; $1.00 per page if genealogy records. Certification fee: $2.00. Fee payee: Clerk of

Circuit Court. Personal checks accepted. Prepayment is required.

15th Judicial District Court
Richmond County Courthouse, PO Box 1000, Warsaw, VA 22572; 804-333-4616; Fax: 804-333-3741. Hours: 8AM-4:30PM (EST). *Misdemeanor, Civil Actions Under $15,000, Eviction, Small Claims.*

Civil Records: Access: Mail, online, in person. Both court and visitors may perform in person searches. No search fee. Required to search: name, years to search. Civil cases indexed by defendant, plaintiff. Civil records archived 10 years back; on computer from 1994. For information about the statewide online system, LOPAS, see the state introduction.
Criminal Records: Access: Mail, online, in person. Both court and visitors may perform in person searches. No search fee. Required to search: name, years to search; also helpful: DOB, SSN. Criminal records archived 10 years back; on computer from 1994. Online access to criminal records is the same as civil.
General Information: Public Access terminal is available. No juvenile, sealed records released. SASE requested. Turnaround time 2 days. Certification fee: No certification fee. Personal checks accepted.

Richmond City

13th Circuit Court - Division I
John Marshall Courts Building, 400 N 9th St, Richmond, VA 23219; 804-646-6505; Civil phone: 804-646-6536; Criminal phone: 804-646-6553. Hours: 8:45AM-4:45PM (EST). *Felony, Civil Actions Over $15,000, Probate.*

www.vipnet.org/vipnet/clerks/richmondjohnmarshall.html

Note: Also search for felony records at the Manchester Courthouse location.

Civil Records: Access: Mail, online, in person. Visitors must perform in person searches for themselves. No search fee. Required to search: name, years to search. Civil cases indexed by defendant, plaintiff. Civil records on computer from 1987. On microfilm from 1980, on card index from 1970s, on index books from 1600s. Online access is available free at http://208.210.219.132/courtinfo/vacircuit/select.jsp?court=. For information about the statewide online system, LOPAS, see the state introduction.
Criminal Records: Access: Mail, online, in person. Visitors must perform in person searches for themselves. No search fee. Required to search: name, years to search; also helpful: DOB, SSN. Criminal records on computer from 1987. On microfilm from 1980, on card index from 1970s, on index books from 1600s. Online access to criminal records is the same as civil.
General Information: Public Access terminal is available. No juvenile, sealed records released. Copy fee: $.50 per page. Certification fee: $2.00. Fee payee: Bevill M Dean, Clerk. Personal checks accepted. Prepayment is required.

13th General District Court - Civil Division
400 N 9th St Rm 203, Richmond, VA 23219; 804-646-6461. Hours: 8AM-4PM (EST). *Civil Actions Under $15,000, Eviction, Small Claims.*

Civil Records: Access: Phone, mail, online, in person. Both court and visitors may perform in person searches. No search fee. Required to search: name, years to search. Civil cases indexed by defendant, plaintiff. Civil records computerized since 1993, in index books from 1973. Records destroyed after 20 years & 10 years after 1985. Prior to 02/94, date of judgment needed. For information about the statewide online system, LOPAS, see the state introduction.
General Information: Public Access terminal is available. No juvenile, sealed records released. Turnaround time 1-2 days. Copy fee: $.50 per page.

Certification fee: $3.00. Fee payee: Clerk of General District Court, Civil Division. Business checks accepted. Prepayment is required.

13th General District Court - Division II

905 Decatur St, Richmond, VA 23224; 804-646-5387; Fax: 804-232-7862. Hours: 8AM-4PM (EST). *Misdemeanor, Traffic.*

Criminal Records: Access: Mail, online, in person. Both court and visitors may perform in person searches. No search fee. Required to search: name, years to search, DOB; also helpful: SSN. Criminal records on computer from 1986, on index cards from 1980 to 1985, records prior to 1980 destroyed. For information about the statewide online system, LOPAS, see the state introduction.
General Information: Public Access terminal is available. No juvenile, sealed records released. Turnaround time 1-5 days. Copy fee: $1.00 per page. Certification fee: $2.00. Fee payee: Clerk of General District Court. Personal checks accepted. Prepayment is required.

Richmond City - Manchester County

13th Circuit Court

Manchester Courthouse, 10th and Hull St, Richmond, VA 23224-4070; 804-646-8470; Fax: 804-646-8122. Hours: 8:45AM-4:45PM (EST). *Felony.*

www.vipnet.org/vipnet/clerks/richmondmanchester.html
Note: Also search for felony records at the Division I location.

Civil Records: Access: Mail, online, in person. Only the court performs in person searches; visitors may not. No search fee. Required to search: name, years to search. Civil cases indexed by defendant, plaintiff. Civil records on computer from 1989, on index cards from 1961 to 1988, prior archived in Richmond. Online access is available free at http://208.210.219.132/courtinfo/vacircuit/select.jsp?court=. For information about the statewide online system, LOPAS, see the state introduction.
Criminal Records: Access: Mail, online, in person. Only the court performs in person searches; visitors may not. No search fee. Required to search: name, years to search. Criminal records on computer from 1989, on index cards from 1961 to 1988, prior archived in Richmond. Online access to criminal records is the same as civil.
General Information: No juvenile, sealed, adoption records released. SASE required. Turnaround time 1-2 days. Copy fee: $.50 per page. Certification fee: $2.00. Fee payee: Clerk of Circuit Court. Business checks accepted. Credit cards accepted: Visa, MasterCard. Prepayment is required.

Roanoke County

23rd Judicial Circuit Court

PO Box 1126, Salem, VA 24153-1126; 540-387-6261. Hours: 8:30AM-4:30PM (EST). *Felony, Civil Actions Over $15,000, Probate.*

www.co.roanoke.va.us
Civil Records: Access: Online, in person. Visitors must perform in person searches for themselves. No search fee. Required to search: name, years to search. Civil cases indexed by defendant, plaintiff. Civil records on computer from 1986, on index books from 1838 to 1986, prior records to Botetourt County. For information about the statewide online system, LOPAS, see the state introduction.
Criminal Records: Access: Online, in person. Visitors must perform in person searches for themselves. No search fee. Required to search: name, years to search, DOB; also helpful: SSN. Criminal records on computer from 1986, on index books from 1838 to 1986, prior records to Botetourt County. Online access to criminal records is the same as civil.

General Information: No juvenile, sealed records released. Copy fee: $.50 per page. Certification fee: $2.00. Fee payee: Clerk of Circuit Court. Personal checks accepted. Prepayment is required.

23rd General District Court

PO Box 997, Salem, VA 24153; 540-387-6168; Fax: 540-387-6066. Hours: 8:15AM-4:30PM (EST). *Misdemeanor, Civil Actions Under $15,000, Eviction, Small Claims.*

www.co.roanoke.va.us
Civil Records: Access: Mail, online, in person. Both court and visitors may perform in person searches. No search fee. Required to search: name, years to search. Civil cases indexed by defendant, plaintiff. Some records on computer from 1968, on index cards from 1985, on docket sheets from 1950s to 1985, prior at Circuit Court or Archives. For information about the statewide online system, LOPAS, see state introduction.
Criminal Records: Access: Mail, online, in person. Both court and visitors may perform in person searches. No search fee. Required to search: name, years to search, DOB; also helpful: SSN. Some records on computer from 1968, on index cards from 1985, on docket sheets from 1950s to 1985, prior at Circuit Court or Archives. Online access to criminal records is the same as civil.
General Information: Public Access terminal is available. No sealed records released. SASE required. Turnaround time 5 days. Copy fee: $.50 per page. Certification fee: No certification fee. Fee payee: General. Personal checks accepted. Credit cards accepted: Visa, MasterCard. Not accepted for copy fees.

Roanoke City

23rd Circuit Court

PO Box 2610, Roanoke, VA 24010-2610; Civil phone: 540-853-6702; Criminal phone: 540-853-6723. Hours: 8:30AM-4:30PM (EST). *Felony, Civil Actions Over $15,000, Probate.*

www.co.roanoke.va.us
Civil Records: Access: Mail, online, in person. Visitors must perform in person searches for themselves. No search fee. Required to search: name, years to search. Civil cases indexed by defendant, plaintiff. Civil records on computer from 1986, civil on microfiche from 1884, criminal on index books from 1800s, prior archived. Online access is available free at http://208.210.219.132/courtinfo/vacircuit/select.jsp?court=. For information about the statewide online system, LOPAS, see the state introduction.
Criminal Records: Access: Mail, online, in person. Visitors must perform in person searches for themselves. No search fee. Required to search: name, years to search, DOB; also helpful: SSN. Criminal records on computer from 1986, civil on microfiche from 1884, criminal on index books from 1800s, prior archived. Online access to criminal records is the same as civil.
General Information: Public Access terminal is available. No juvenile, sealed records released. Copy fee: $.50 per page. Certification fee: $2.00. Fee payee: Clerk of Circuit Court. Personal checks accepted. Prepayment is required.

General District Court

315 W Church Ave, 2nd Flr, Roanoke, VA 24016-5007; Civil phone: 540-853-2364; Criminal phone: 540-853-2361. Hours: 8AM-4PM (EST). *Misdemeanor, Civil Actions Under $15,000, Eviction, Small Claims.*

Civil Records: Access: Mail, online, in person. Both court and visitors may perform in person searches. No search fee. Required to search: name, years to search. Civil cases indexed by defendant, plaintiff. Civil records on computer from 1986, prior on index cards. For information about the statewide online system, LOPAS, see the state introduction.
Criminal Records: Access: Online, in person. Visitors must perform in person searches for themselves. No

search fee. Required to search: name, years to search, DOB; also helpful: SSN. Criminal records on computer from 1986, prior on index cards. Online access to criminal records is the same as civil.
General Information: Public Access terminal is available. (Records available from past 10 years.) No juvenile, sealed, adoptions records released. Turnaround time 5 days. Copy fee: $1.00 1st 2 pages, $.50 each additional page. Certification fee: No certification fee. Fee payee: General District Court. Business checks accepted. Credit cards accepted: Visa, MasterCard. Prepayment is required.

Rockbridge County

25th Circuit Court

Courthouse Square, 2 S Main St, Lexington, VA 24450; 540-463-2232; Fax: 540-463-3850. Hours: 8:30AM-4:30PM (EST). *Felony, Civil Actions Over $15,000, Probate.*

Civil Records: Access: Phone, mail, online, in person. Both court and visitors may perform in person searches. No search fee. Required to search: name, years to search. Civil cases indexed by defendant, plaintiff. Civil records on computer from 1985, on index books from 1778. Criminal records are easily obtained from the late 1960s. Prior records are not easily accessible. For information about the statewide online system, LOPAS, see the state introduction.
Criminal Records: Access: Online, in person. Visitors must perform in person searches for themselves. No search fee. Required to search: name, years to search, DOB; also helpful: SSN. Criminal records on computer from 1985, on index books from 1778. Criminal records are easily obtained from the late 1960s. Prior records are not easily accessible. Online access to criminal records is the same as civil.
General Information: Public Access terminal is available. No juvenile, sealed records released. Turnaround time 2-3 days. Copy fee: $.50 per page. Certification fee: $2.50. Fee payee: Clerk of Circuit Court. Personal checks accepted. Prepayment required.

District Court

150 S Main St, Lexington, VA 24450; 540-463-3631. Hours: 8:30AM-4:30PM (EST). *Misdemeanor, Civil Actions Under $15,000, Eviction, Small Claims.*

Lexington-Rockbridge is a combined district court.

Civil Records: Access: Mail, online, in person. Both court and visitors may perform in person searches. No search fee. Required to search: name, years to search. Civil cases indexed by defendant, plaintiff. Civil records on computer from 1989, on index cards from 1985 to 1989, prior to 1985 at Circuit Court. Records destroyed after 10 years. For information about the statewide online system, LOPAS, see the state introduction.
Criminal Records: Access: Mail, online, in person. Both court and visitors may perform in person searches. No search fee. Required to search: name, years to search, DOB; also helpful: SSN. Criminal records on computer from late 1989, on index cards from 1985 to 1989, prior to 1985 at Circuit Court. Online access to criminal records is the same as civil.
General Information: Public Access terminal is available. No juvenile, sealed records released. SASE required. Turnaround time 5-7 days. Copy fee: $1.00 each for 1st two; $.50 each add'l. Certification fee: No certification fee.

Rockingham County

26th Circuit Court

Courthouse, Harrisonburg, VA 22801; Civil phone: 540-564-3114; Criminal phone: 540-564-3118; Fax: 540-564-3127. Hours: 9AM-5PM (EST). *Felony, Civil Actions Over $15,000, Probate.*

Civil Records: Access: Online, in person. Visitors must perform in person searches for themselves. No search fee. Required to search: name, years to search. Civil cases indexed by defendant, plaintiff. Civil records on index cards from the beginning of the county. Online access is available free at http://208.210.219.132/courtinfo/vacircuit/select.jsp?court=. For information about the statewide online system, LOPAS, see the state introduction.

Criminal Records: Access: Online, in person. Visitors must perform in person searches for themselves. No search fee. Required to search: name, years to search. Criminal records on index cards from the beginning of the county. Online access to criminal records is the same as civil.

General Information: Public Access terminal is available. (Deeds only.) No juvenile, sealed records released. Copy fee: $.50 per page. Certification fee: $2.00. Fee payee: Clerk of Circuit Court. Personal checks accepted. Prepayment is required.

26th General District Court
53 Court Square, Harrisonburg, VA 22801; Civil phone: 540-564-3135; Criminal phone: 540-564-3130; Fax: 540-564-3096. Hours: 8AM-4PM (EST). *Misdemeanor, Civil Actions Under $15,000, Eviction, Small Claims.*

Civil Records: Access: Phone, mail, online, in person. Both court and visitors may perform in person searches. No search fee. Required to search: name, years to search. Civil cases indexed by defendant, plaintiff. Civil records on computer from 1988, on index cards from 1978, prior at Circuit Court. For information about the statewide online system, LOPAS, see the state introduction.

Criminal Records: Access: Phone, mail, online, in person. Both court and visitors may perform in person searches. No search fee. Required to search: name, years to search, DOB; also helpful: SSN. Criminal records on computer from 1987, on index cards from 1985, prior at Circuit Court. Online access to criminal records is the same as civil.

General Information: Public Access terminal is available. No juvenile, sealed, adoption records released. SASE required. Turnaround time up to 1 week. Copy fee: $.50 per page. Certification fee: Cert fee included in copy fee. Fee payee: General District Court. Personal checks accepted. Credit cards accepted: Visa, MasterCard. Prepayment is required.

Russell County

29th Circuit Court
PO Box 435, Lebanon, VA 24266; 540-889-8023; Fax: 540-889-8003. Hours: 8:30AM-5PM (6PM M,W,F) (EST). *Felony, Civil Actions Over $15,000, Probate.*

Civil Records: Access: Fax, mail, online, in person. Both court and visitors may perform in person searches. No search fee. Required to search: name, years to search. Civil cases indexed by defendant, plaintiff. Civil records on computer from 1990, archived from 1809. Online access is available free at http://208.210.219.132/courtinfo/vacircuit/select.jsp?court=. For information about the statewide online system, LOPAS, see the state introduction. Fax access limited to short searches.

Criminal Records: Access: Fax, mail, online, in person. Both court and visitors may perform in person searches. No search fee. Required to search: name, years to search, signed release. Criminal records on computer from 1990, archived from 1809. Online access to criminal records is the same as civil.

General Information: No juvenile, sealed records released. Turnaround time 1-5 days. Copy fee: $.50 per page. Certification fee: No certification fee. Fee payee: Clerk of Circuit Court. Personal checks accepted. Prepayment is required.

29th General District Court
Russell County Courthouse, PO Box 65, Lebanon, VA 24266; 540-889-8051; Fax: 540-889-8091. Hours: 8:30AM-4:30PM (EST). *Misdemeanor, Civil Actions Under $15,000, Eviction, Small Claims.*

Civil Records: Access: Phone, fax, mail, online, in person. Both court and visitors may perform in person searches. No search fee. Required to search: name. Civil cases indexed by defendant, plaintiff. Civil records on computer back to 1993. For information about the statewide online system, LOPAS, see the state introduction.

Criminal Records: Access: Phone, fax, mail, online, in person. Both court and visitors may perform in person searches. No search fee. Required to search: name, DOB; also helpful: SSN. Criminal records on computer back to 1993; other records back to 1990. Online access to criminal records is the same as civil.

General Information: Public Access terminal is available. No juvenile, sealed records released. Turnaround time 2-5 days. Fax notes: No fee to fax results. No copy fee. Certification fee: No certification fee. Personal checks accepted. Credit cards accepted: Visa, MasterCard.

Salem City

23rd Circuit Court
2 E Calhoun St, PO Box 891, Salem, VA 24153; 540-375-3067; Fax: 540-375-4039. Hours: 8:30AM-5PM (EST). *Felony, Civil Actions Over $15,000, Probate.*

Civil Records: Access: Mail, online, in person. Both court and visitors may perform in person searches. No search fee. Required to search: name, years to search. Civil cases indexed by defendant, plaintiff. Civil records on computer from 1985, on index books from 1968, prior at Roanoke Circuit Court. For information about the statewide online system, LOPAS, see the state introduction.

Criminal Records: Access: Online, in person. Visitors must perform in person searches for themselves. No search fee. Required to search: name, years to search, DOB; also helpful: SSN. Criminal records on computer from 1985, on index books from 1968, prior at Roanoke Circuit Court. Online access to criminal records is the same as civil.

General Information: Public Access terminal is available. No juvenile, sealed or adoption records released. SASE required. Turnaround time 2 weeks. Copy fee: $.50 per page. Certification fee: $2.00. Fee payee: Clerk of Circuit Court. Personal checks accepted. Prepayment is required.

23rd General District Court
2 E Calhoun St, Salem, VA 24153; 540-375-3044; Fax: 540-375-4024. Hours: 8AM-4PM (EST). *Misdemeanor, Civil Actions Under $15,000, Eviction, Small Claims.*

Civil Records: Access: Online, in person. Visitors must perform in person searches for themselves. No search fee. Required to search: name, years to search. Civil cases indexed by defendant, plaintiff. Civil records on computer from 1987, on index cards from 1986, prior records at City of Salem Circuit Court. For information about the statewide online system, LOPAS, see the state introduction.

Criminal Records: Access: Online, in person. Visitors must perform in person searches for themselves. No search fee. Required to search: name, years to search, DOB, SSN. Criminal records on computer from 1987, on index cards from 1986, prior records at City of Salem Circuit Court. Online access to criminal records is the same as civil.

General Information: Public Access terminal is available. No juvenile, sealed records released. Copy fee: $.50 per page. Certification fee: $2.00. Fee payee: General District Court. Personal checks accepted. Prepayment is required.

Scott County

30th Circuit Court
104 E Jackson St, Suite 2, Gate City, VA 24251; 540-386-3801. Hours: 8:30AM-5PM (EST). *Felony, Civil Actions Over $15,000, Probate.*

Civil Records: Access: Phone, mail, online in person. Both court and visitors may perform in person searches. Search fee: $10.00 per name. Required to search: name, years to search. Civil cases indexed by defendant, plaintiff. Civil records on index books back to 1815; on computer back to 1999. For information about the statewide online system, LOPAS, see the state introduction.

Criminal Records: Access: Mail, online, in person. Both court and visitors may perform in person searches. Search fee: $10.00 per name. Required to search: name, years to search, DOB; also helpful: SSN. Criminal records on index books back to 1815; on computer back to 1999. Online access to criminal records is the same as civil.

General Information: Public Access terminal is available. No juvenile, sealed records released. SASE required. Turnaround time 3-4 days. Fax notes: Fee to fax results is $2.00 per page. Copy fee: $.50 per page. Certification fee: $1.50. Fee payee: Mark A. "Bo" Taylor, Clerk. Personal checks accepted. Will bill phone requests.

30th General District Court
104 E Jackson St, Suite 9, Gate City, VA 24251; 540-386-7341. Hours: 8AM-4PM (EST). *Misdemeanor, Civil Actions Under $15,000, Eviction, Small Claims.*

Civil Records: Access: Mail, online, in person. Only the court performs in person searches; visitors may not. No search fee. Required to search: name, years to search. Civil cases indexed by plaintiff. Civil records on index books, on computer from 1990. For information about the statewide online system, LOPAS, see the state introduction.

Criminal Records: Access: Mail, online, in person. Only the court performs in person searches; visitors may not. No search fee. Required to search: name, years to search, DOB; also helpful: SSN. Criminal records on index books, on computer from 1990. Online access to criminal records is the same as civil.

General Information: No juvenile, sealed records released. SASE required. Turnaround time up to 1-2 days. Copy fee: $1.00 per page. Certification fee: No certification fee. Fee payee: General District Court. Personal checks accepted. Prepayment is required.

Shenandoah County

26th Circuit Court
112 S Main St, PO Box 406, Woodstock, VA 22664; 540-459-6150; Fax: 540-459-6155. Hours: 9AM-5PM (EST). *Felony, Civil Actions Over $15,000, Probate.*

Civil Records: Access: Mail, online, in person. Both court and visitors may perform in person searches. No search fee. Required to search: name, years to search. Civil cases indexed by defendant, plaintiff. Civil records on computer from 1986, on index cards from 1772. For information about the statewide online system, LOPAS, see the state introduction. Mail access limited to specific cases only.

Criminal Records: Access: Online, in person. Visitors must perform in person searches for themselves. No search fee. Required to search: name, years to search, DOB; also helpful: SSN. Criminal records on computer from 1986, on index cards from 1772. Online access to criminal records is the same as civil.

General Information: No juvenile, sealed records released. SASE required. Turnaround time 1-2 days. Copy fee: $.50 per page. Certification fee: $2.00. Fee payee: Clerk of Circuit Court. Personal checks accepted. Prepayment is required.

26th General District Court 103 N Main St, PO Box 189, Woodstock, VA 22664; 540-459-6130; Fax: 540-459-6139. Hours: 8:30AM-4:30PM (EST). *Misdemeanor, Civil Actions Under $15,000, Eviction, Small Claims.*

Civil Records: Access: Mail, online, in person. Visitors must perform in person searches for themselves. No search fee. Required to search: name, years to search. Civil cases indexed by defendant, plaintiff. Civil records on computer from 1992, on index cards from 1985, prior at Circuit Court. For information about the statewide online system, LOPAS, see the state introduction.

Criminal Records: Access: Online, in person. Visitors must perform in person searches for themselves. No search fee. Required to search: name, years to search, DOB; also helpful: SSN. Criminal records on computer from 1992, on index cards from 1985, prior at Circuit Court. For information about the statewide online system, LOPAS, see the state introduction. This agency will not do criminal record checks and refer all requesters to the State Police or the online system.

General Information: Public Access terminal is available. No sealed or adoption records relapsed. Copy fee: $1.00 for first page; $.50 each add'l. Certification fee: No certification fee. Fee payee: General District Court. Personal checks accepted. Visa/MC credit cards accepted. Accepted for criminal fines only. Prepayment is required.

Smyth County

28th Circuit Court PO Box 1025, Marion, VA 24354; 540-782-4044; Fax: 540-782-4045. Hours: 9AM-5PM (EST). *Felony, Civil Actions Over $15,000, Probate.*

Civil Records: Access: Mail, fax, online, in person. Both court and visitors may perform in person searches. Search fee: $10.00 per name. Required to search: name, years to search. Civil cases indexed by defendant, plaintiff. Civil records on index cards from 1832, most are computerized since 01/90. For information about the statewide online system, LOPAS, see the state introduction.

Criminal Records: Access: Mail, fax, online, in person. Both court and visitors may perform in person searches. Search fee: $10.00 per name. Required to search: name, years to search; also helpful: DOB, SSN. Criminal records on index cards from 1832, most are computerized since 01/90. Online access to criminal records is the same as civil.

General Information: Public Access terminal is available. (Not available for criminal or civil information.) No juvenile, sealed or adoption records released. SASE requested. Turnaround time 1 week. Fax notes: Fee to fax results is $1.oo per page. Copy fee: $.50 per page. Certification fee: $2.00. Fee payee: Clerk of Circuit Court. Personal checks accepted. Prepayment is required.

28th General District Court Smythe County Courthouse, Rm 231, 109 W Main St, Marion, VA 24354; 540-782-4047; Fax: 540-782-4048. Hours: 8:30AM-4:30PM (EST). *Misdemeanor, Civil Actions Under $15,000, Eviction, Small Claims.*

Civil Records: Access: Phone, mail, online, in person. Both court and visitors may perform in person searches. No search fee. Required to search: name, years to search; also helpful: address. Civil cases indexed by defendant, plaintiff. Civil records on computer back to 7/90. For information about the statewide online system, LOPAS, see the state introduction.

Criminal Records: Access: Phone, mail, online, in person. Both court and visitors may perform in person searches. No search fee. Required to search: name, years to search, DOB; also helpful: SSN. Criminal

records on computer back to 7/90. Online access to criminal records is the same as civil.

General Information: Public Access terminal is available. No juvenile, sealed records released. Turnaround time 1-2 days. Copy fee: $.50 per page. Certification fee: No certification fee. Fee payee: General District Court. Personal checks accepted. Credit cards accepted: Visa, MasterCard. Prepayment is required.

South Boston City

Circuit & District Courts, VA.

Note: See Halifax County

Southampton County

5th Circuit Court PO Box 190, Courtland, VA 23837; 757-653-2200. Hours: 8:30AM-5PM (EST). *Felony, Civil Actions Over $15,000, Probate.*

Civil Records: Access: Mail, online, in person. Both court and visitors may perform in person searches. Search fee: $5.00 per name. Required to search: name, years to search. Civil cases indexed by defendant, plaintiff. Civil records on index books from 1749. For information about the statewide online system, LOPAS, see the state introduction.

Criminal Records: Access: Mail, online, in person. Both court and visitors may perform in person searches. No search fee. Required to search: name, years to search. Criminal records on index books from 1749. Online access to criminal records is the same as civil.

General Information: Public Access terminal is available. No juvenile, sealed, adoption records released. Turnaround time 1-5 days. Copy fee: $.50 per page. Certification fee: $2.00. Fee payee: Clerk of Circuit Court. Personal checks accepted. Prepayment is required.

5th General District Court PO Box 347, Courtland, VA 23837; 757-653-2673. Hours: 8:30AM-4:30PM (EST). *Misdemeanor, Civil Actions Under $15,000, Eviction, Small Claims.*

Civil Records: Access: Mail, online, in person. Both court and visitors may perform in person searches. No search fee. Required to search: name, years to search. Civil cases indexed by defendant. Civil records on index cards, docket books and computer from 1985, prior records at Circuit Court. For information about the statewide online system, LOPAS, see the state introduction.

Criminal Records: Access: Mail, online, in person. Both court and visitors may perform in person searches. No search fee. Required to search: name, years to search, DOB; also helpful: SSN. Criminal records on index cards, docket books and computer from 1985, prior records at Circuit Court. Online access to criminal records is the same as civil.

General Information: Public Access terminal is available. No juvenile, sealed, adoption records released. Turnaround time 1-5 days. Fax notes: Fee to fax results is $2.00 per document. Copy fee: $1.00 1st 2 pages; $.50 each add'l page. Certification fee: No certification fee. Fee payee: Clerk of General District Court. Personal checks accepted. Credit cards accepted. Prepayment is required.

Spotsylvania County

15th Circuit Court 9113 Courthouse Rd, PO Box 96, Spotsylvania, VA 22553; 540-582-7090; Fax: 540-582-2169. Hours: 8AM-4:30PM (EST). *Felony, Civil Actions Over $15,000, Probate.*

Civil Records: Access: Online, in person. Visitors must perform in person searches for themselves. No search fee. Requried to search: name, years to search. Civil cases indexed by defendant, plaintiff. Civil records on computer from 1996, on index books from late 1700s. For information about the statewide online system,

LOPAS, see the state introduction. Mail access limited to specific case only.

Criminal Records: Access: Online, in person. Visitors must perform in person searches for themselves. No search fee. Required to search: name, years to search, DOB, SSN. Criminal records on computer from 1996, on index books from late 1700s. Online access to criminal records is the same as civil.

General Information: Public Access terminal is available. No juvenile, sealed, adoption records released. Copy fee: $.50 per page. Certification fee: $2.00. Fee payee: Clerk of Circuit Court. Personal checks accepted. Prepayment is required.

15th General District Court Judicial Center, PO Box 339, Spotsylvania, VA 22553; 540-582-7110. Hours: 8AM-4PM (EST). *Misdemeanor, Civil Actions Under $15,000, Eviction, Small Claims.*

Civil Records: Access: Mail, online, in person. Both court and visitors may perform in person searches. No search fee. Required to search: name, years to search. Civil cases indexed by defendant, plaintiff. Civil records on computer back 10 years, prior at Circuit Court. For information about the statewide online system, LOPAS, see the state introduction.

Criminal Records: Access: Mail, online, in person. Both court and visitors may perform in person searches. No search fee. Required to search: name, years to search. Criminal records on computer back 10 years. Online access to criminal records is the same as civil.

General Information: Public Access terminal is available. No juvenile, sealed records released. Turnaround time 5 days. Copy fee: $.50 per page. Certification fee: $2.00. Fee payee: Clerk of General District Court. Personal checks accepted. Prepayment is required.

Stafford County

15th Circuit Court PO Box 69, Stafford, VA 22554; 540-658-8750. Hours: 8:30AM-4PM (EST). *Felony, Civil Actions Over $15,000, Probate.*

Civil Records: Access: Mail, online, in person. Both court and visitors may perform in person searches. No search fee. Required to search: name, years to search. Civil cases indexed by defendant, plaintiff. Civil records in index books from 1699. For information about the statewide online system, LOPAS, see the state introduction.

Criminal Records: Access: Mail, online, in person. Both court and visitors may perform in person searches. No search fee. Required to search: name, years to search, DOB; also helpful: SSN. Criminal records in index books from 1699. Online access to criminal records is the same as civil.

General Information: Public Access terminal is available. No juvenile, sealed records released. Turnaround time up to 10 days. Copy fee: $.50 per page. Certification fee: $2.00. Fee payee: Clerk of Circuit Court. Personal checks accepted.

15th General District Court 1300 Courthouse Rd, PO Box 940, Stafford, VA 22555; 540-658-8763; Fax: 540-720-4834. Hours: 8AM-4PM (EST). *Misdemeanor, Civil Actions Under $15,000, Eviction, Small Claims.*

Civil Records: Access: Fax, mail, online, in person. Both court and visitors may perform in person searches. No search fee. Required to search: name, years to search. Civil cases indexed by defendant, plaintiff. Civil records on computer since 1986, prior at Circuit Court. For information about the statewide online system, LOPAS, see the state introduction.

Criminal Records: Access: Fax, mail, online, in person. Both court and visitors may perform in person searches. No search fee. Required to search: name, years to search. Criminal records on computer since

1986, prior at Circuit Court. Online access to criminal records is the same as civil.

General Information: Public Access terminal is available. No sealed records released. SASE requested. Turnaround time 2-7 days. Fax notes: No fee to fax results. Copy fee: $.50 per page. Certification fee: No certification fee. Fee payee: Clerk of General District Court. Personal checks accepted. Credit cards accepted: Visa, MasterCard. Prepayment is required.

Staunton City

25th Circuit Court PO Box 1286, Staunton, VA 24402-1286; 540-332-3874; Fax: 540-332-3970. Hours: 8:30AM-5PM (EST). *Felony, Civil Actions Over $15,000, Probate.*

Civil Records: Access: Mail, online, in person. Visitors must perform in person searches for themselves. No search fee. Required to search: name, years to search. Civil cases indexed by defendant, plaintiff. Civil records on index books since 1802; on computer back to 1988. For information about the statewide online system, LOPAS, see the state introduction.

Criminal Records: Access: Online, in person. Visitors must perform in person searches for themselves. No search fee. Required to search: name, years to search. Criminal records on index books since 1802; on computer back to 1988. Online access to criminal records is the same as civil.

General Information: Public Access terminal is available. No juvenile, sealed or adoption records released. Fax notes: Fee to fax results is $.50 per page. Copy fee: $.50 per page. Certification fee: $2.00. Fee payee: Clerk of Circuit Court. Personal checks accepted. Prepayment is required.

25th General District Court 113 E Beverly St, Staunton, VA 24401-4390; 540-332-3878; Fax: 540-332-3985. 8:30AM-4:30P. *Misdemeanor, Civil Actions Under $15,000, Eviction, Small Claims.*

Civil Records: Access: Mail, online, in person. Both court and visitors may perform in person searches. No search fee. Required to search: name, years to search; also helpful: address. Civil cases indexed by defendant, plaintiff. Civil records on computer from 11/94, on index cards from 1990, prior at Circuit Court. For information about the statewide online system, LOPAS, see the state introduction.

Criminal Records: Access: Mail, online, in person. Both court and visitors may perform in person searches. No search fee. Required to search: name, years to search, DOB; also helpful: SSN. Criminal records indexed on computer since 1991. Online access to criminal records is the same as civil.

General Information: Public Access terminal is available. Turnaround time 1-5 days. Copy fee: $.50 per page. Certification fee: No certification fee. Fee payee: Staunton General District Court. Personal checks accepted. Credit cards accepted: Visa, MasterCard. Credit cards accepted for criminal & traffic cases only. Prepayment is required.

Suffolk City

Suffolk Circuit Court PO Box 1604, Suffolk, VA 23439-1604; 757-923-2251; Fax: 757-934-3490. Hours: 8:30AM-5PM (EST). *Felony, Civil Actions Over $15,000, Probate.*

Civil Records: Access: Online, in person. Visitors must perform in person searches for themselves. No search fee. Required to search: name, years to search. Civil cases indexed by defendant, plaintiff. Civil records on computer from 1989, on index books from 1866. For information about the statewide online system, LOPAS, see the state introduction.

Criminal Records: Access: Online, in person. Visitors must perform in person searches for themselves. No search fee. Required to search: name, years to search.

Criminal records on computer from 1989, on index books from 1866. Online access to criminal records is the same as civil.

General Information: No juvenile, sealed, adoption records released. Copy fee: $.50 per page. Certification fee: $1.50. Fee payee: Clerk of Circuit Court. Personal checks accepted. Credit cards accepted: Visa, MasterCard. Prepayment is required.

5th General District Court 150 N Main St, PO Box 1648, Suffolk, VA 23434; 757-923-2281; Fax: 757-925-1790. 8AM-4PM (EST). *Misdemeanor, Civil Actions up to $15,000, Eviction, Small Claims.*

Civil Records: Access: Mail, online, in person. Both court and visitors may perform in person searches. No search fee. Required to search: name, years to search. Civil cases indexed by defendant, plaintiff. Civil records on computer from 1987, prior on index cards. Records destroyed after 10 years. For information about the statewide online system, LOPAS, see the state introduction.

Criminal Records: Access: Online, in person. Visitors must perform in person searches for themselves. No search fee. Required to search: name, years to search, DOB; also helpful: SSN. Criminal records on computer from 1987, prior on index cards. Online access to criminal records is the same as civil.

General Information: Public Access terminal is available. No juvenile, sealed, adoptions records released. SASE required. Turnaround time 1 week. Copy fee: $.50 per page. Certification fee: No certification fee. Fee payee: Suffolk General District Court. Personal checks accepted. Credit cards accepted: Visa, MasterCard. Prepayment is required.

Surry County

6th Circuit Court 28 Colonial Trail East, PO Box 203, Surry, VA 23883; 757-294-3161; Fax: 757-294-0471. Hours: 9AM-5PM (EST). *Felony, Civil Actions Over $15,000, Probate.*

Civil Records: Access: In person only. Visitors must perform in person searches for themselves. No search fee. Required to search: name, years to search. Civil cases indexed by defendant, plaintiff. Civil records on cards.

Criminal Records: Access: In person only. Visitors must perform in person searches for themselves. No search fee. Required to search: name, years to search, DOB; also helpful: SSN. Criminal records on cards.

General Information: Juvenile, sealed records not released. Copy fee: $.50 per page. Certification fee: No certification fee. Fee payee: Circuit Clerk. Business checks accepted.

6th General District Court Hwy 10 and School St, PO Box 332, Surry, VA 23883; 757-294-5201; Fax: 757-294-0312. Hours: 8:30AM-4:30PM (EST). *Misdemeanor, Civil Actions Under $15,000, Eviction, Small Claims.*

Civil Records: Access: Online, in person. Visitors must perform in person searches for themselves. No search fee. Required to search: name, years to search. Civil cases indexed by defendant, plaintiff. Civil records on computer since 11/93, on books from 1985, prior at Circuit Court. For information about the statewide online system, LOPAS, see the state introduction.

Criminal Records: Access: Online, in person. Visitors must perform in person searches for themselves. No search fee. Required to search: name, years to search, DOB; also helpful: SSN. Criminal records on computer since 11/93, on books from 1985, prior at Circuit Court. Online access to criminal records is the same as civil.

General Information: Public Access terminal is available. No juvenile, sealed, adoption records released. No copy fee. Certification fee: No certification fee.

Sussex County

6th Circuit Court PO Box 1337, Sussex, VA 23884; 804-246-5511 X3276; Fax: 804-246-2203. Hours: 9AM-5PM (EST). *Felony, Civil Actions Over $15,000, Probate.*

Civil Records: Access: Mail, online, in person. Only the court performs in person searches; visitors may not. No search fee. Required to search: name, years to search. Civil cases indexed by defendant, plaintiff. Civil records on index books from 1754; on computer back to 1991. For information about the statewide online system, LOPAS, see the state introduction.

Criminal Records: Access: Mail, online, in person. Visitors must perform in person searches for themselves. No search fee. Required to search: name, years to search, DOB, SSN, signed release. Criminal records on index books from 1754; on computer back to 1991. Online access to criminal records is the same as civil.

General Information: No juvenile, sealed, adoption, confidential, or probate records released. Turnaround time 1-2 days. Fax notes: Fee to fax results is $1.00 per page. Copy fee: $.50 per page. Certification fee: $2.00. Fee payee: Clerk of Circuit Court. Personal checks accepted. Prepayment is required.

6th Judicial District Sussex Court Sussex Cnty Courthouse 15098 Courthouse Rd Rt 735, PO Box 1315, Sussex, VA 23884; 804-246-5511 X3241; Fax: 804-246-6604. Hours: 8:30AM-4:30PM (EST). *Misdemeanor, Civil Actions Under $15,000, Eviction, Small Claims.*

Civil Records: Access: Online, in person. Both court and visitors may perform in person searches. No search fee. Required to search: name, years to search. Civil cases indexed by defendant, plaintiff. Civil records on computer from 9/88, on index cards from 1985, prior in Circuit Court. For information about the statewide online system, LOPAS, see the state introduction.

Criminal Records: Access: Online, in person. Visitors must perform in person searches for themselves. No search fee. Required to search: name, years to search, DOB; also helpful: SSN. Criminal records on computer from 9/88, on index cards from 1985, prior in Circuit Court. Online access to criminal records is the same as civil.

General Information: Public Access terminal is available. No juvenile, sealed, adoption records released. Copy fee: $1.00 minimum for first 2 pages, thereafter $.50 per page. Certification fee: No certification fee. Fee payee: Sussex District Court. Personal checks accepted. Credit cards accepted: Visa, MasterCard. Prepayment is required.

Tazewell County

29th Circuit Court PO Box 968, Tazewell, VA 24651-0968; 540-988-7541 X311-312; Fax: 540-988-7501. Hours: 8AM-4:30PM (EST). *Felony, Civil Actions Over $15,000, Probate.*

Civil Records: Access: Mail, online, in person. Both court and visitors may perform in person searches. No search fee. Required to search: name, years to search. Civil cases indexed by defendant, plaintiff. Civil records on index cards from 1800s. Online access is available free at http://208.210.219.132/courtinfo/vacircuit/select.jsp?court=. For information about the statewide online system, LOPAS, see the state introduction.

Criminal Records: Access: Mail, online, in person. Both court and visitors may perform in person searches. No search fee. Required to search: name, years to search, signed release. Criminal records on computer from 1992. Online access to criminal records is the same as civil.

General Information: Public Access terminal is available. (Only for deeds, wills, and other recordings.) No juvenile, sealed records released. Turnaround time

1-3 days. Copy fee: $.50 per page. Certification fee: $2.00. Fee payee: Clerk of Circuit Court. Personal checks accepted. Prepayment is required.

29th General District Court
PO Box 566, Tazewell, VA 24651; 540-988-9057; Fax: 540-988-6202. Hours: 8AM-4:30PM (EST). *Misdemeanor, Civil Actions Under $15,000, Eviction, Small Claims.*

Civil Records: Access: Mail, fax, online, in person. Both court and visitors may perform in person searches. No search fee. Required to search: name, years to search. Civil cases indexed by defendant, plaintiff. Civil records on computer back to 1991, prior records to 1985 at Circuit Court. For information about the statewide online system, LOPAS, see the state introduction. Mail access is limited to two searches.
Criminal Records: Access: Mail, fax, online, in person. Both court and visitors may perform in person searches. No search fee. Required to search: name, years to search, DOB; also helpful: SSN, signed release. Criminal records on computer back to 1991, prior records to 1985 at Circuit Court. Online access to criminal records is the same as civil.
General Information: Public Access terminal is available. No juvenile, sealed, adoption records released. SASE requested. Turnaround time 1-3 days. Fax notes: Fee to fax results is $1.00 per document and $1.00 per page. Copy fee: $.50 per page. Certification fee: No certification fee. Fee payee: Clerk of General District Court. Personal checks accepted. Credit cards accepted: Visa, MasterCard.

Virginia Beach City

2nd Circuit Court
2425 Nimmo Parkway, Virginia Beach, VA 23456-9017; 757-427-4181; Fax: 757-426-5686. Hours: 8:30AM-5PM (EST). *Felony, Civil Actions Over $15,000, Probate.*

www.virginia-beach.va.us/courts

Civil Records: Access: Online, in person. Visitors must perform in person searches for themselves. No search fee. Required to search: name, years to search. Civil cases indexed by defendant, plaintiff. Civil records on computer from 1986, on files from 1960s. For information about the statewide online system, LOPAS, see the state introduction.
Criminal Records: Access: Online, in person. Visitors must perform in person searches for themselves. No search fee. Required to search: name, years to search, DOB; also helpful: SSN. Criminal records on computer from 1986, on files from 1960s. Online access to criminal records is the same as civil.
General Information: Public Access terminal is available. No juvenile, sealed, presentencing probation report, judges notes or adoption records released. Copy fee: $.50 per page. Certification fee: $2.00. Fee payee: Clerk of Circuit Court. Personal checks accepted. Prepayment is required.

2nd General District Court
2425 Nimmo Parkway, Judicial Center, Virginia Beach, VA 23456-9057; 757-427-8531 Court Info Line; Civil phone: 757-427-4277; Criminal phone: 757-427-4707; Fax: 757-426-5672. Hours: 8:30AM-4PM (EST). *Misdemeanor, Civil Actions Under $15,000, Eviction, Small Claims.*

www.vbgov.com

Note: Records may be available online in 2002; check web site.
Civil Records: Access: Phone, fax, mail, online, in person. Both court and visitors may perform in person searches. Search fee: $10.00 per name. Required to search: name, years to search. Civil cases indexed by defendant, plaintiff. Civil records on computer from 1987, on docket books and cards from 1978. For information about the statewide online system, LOPAS, see the state introduction.

Criminal Records: Access: Phone, fax, mail, online, in person. Both court and visitors may perform in person searches. Search fee: $10.00 per name. Required to search: name, years to search, DOB; also helpful: SSN. Criminal records on computer back ten years, then destroyed. Online access to criminal records is the same as civil.
General Information: Public Access terminal is available. No juvenile, sealed, adoption or mental records released. Turnaround time 3-4 weeks. Fax notes: No fee to fax results. Copy fee: $.50 per page. Certification fee: No certification fee. Fee payee: Clerk of General District Court. Personal checks accepted. Prepayment is required.

Warren County

Circuit Court
1 East Main St, Front Royal, VA 22630; 540-635-2435; Fax: 540-636-3274. Hours: 9AM-5PM (EST). *Felony, Civil Actions Over $15,000, Probate.*

www.courts.state.va.us/courts/circuit/warren/home.html

Civil Records: Access: Phone, fax, mail, online, in person. Both court and visitors may perform in person searches. No search fee. Required to search: name, years to search. Civil cases indexed by defendant, plaintiff. Civil records on archives from 1836; on computer since. Online access is available free at http://208.210.219.132/courtinfo/vacircuit/select.jsp?court=. For information about the statewide online system, LOPAS, see the state introduction. Phone access limited to specific case only.
Criminal Records: Access: Phone, fax, mail, online, in person. Both court and visitors may perform in person searches. No search fee. Required to search: name, years to search, DOB; also helpful: SSN. Criminal records on archives from 1836; on computer since. Online access to criminal records is the same as civil.
General Information: Public Access terminal is available. No juvenile, sealed, adoption records released. SASE required. Turnaround time 1-2 days. Copy fee: $.50 per page. Certification fee: $2.00. Fee payee: William A Hall, Clerk. Personal checks accepted.

26th General District Court
1 East Main St, Front Royal, VA 22630; 540-635-2335; Fax: 540-636-8233. Hours: 8:15AM-4:15PM (EST). *Misdemeanor, Civil Actions Under $15,000, Eviction, Small Claims.*

Civil Records: Access: Mail, fax, online, in person. Both court and visitors may perform in person searches. No search fee. Required to search: name, years to search. Civil cases indexed by defendant. Civil records in archives back to 1836, on computer from 1989. For information about the statewide online system, LOPAS, see the state introduction.
Criminal Records: Access: Mail, fax, online, in person. Both court and visitors may perform in person searches. No search fee. Required to search: name, years to search; also helpful: SSN. Criminal records in archives back to 1836, on computer from 1989. Online access to criminal records is the same as civil.
General Information: Public Access terminal is available. No juvenile, sealed records released. SASE required. Turnaround time 2-3 days. Copy fee: $.50 per page. Certification fee: No certification fee. Fee payee: General District Court. Personal checks accepted. Credit cards accepted: Visa, MasterCard.

Washington County

Circuit Court
PO Box 289, Abingdon, VA 24212-0289; 540-676-6224/6226; Fax: 540-676-6218. Hours: 7:30AM-5PM; Recording Hours: 8:30AM-4PM (EST). *Felony, Civil Actions Over $15,000, Probate.*

Civil Records: Access: Mail, online, in person. Both court and visitors may perform in person searches. No search fee. Required to search: name, years to search. Civil cases indexed by defendant, plaintiff. Civil records on archives from 1777, on computer from 1991. For information about the statewide online system, LOPAS, see the state introduction.
Criminal Records: Access: Online, in person. Visitors must perform in person searches for themselves. No search fee. Required to search: name, years to search. Criminal records on archives from 1777, on computer from 1991. Online access to criminal records is the same as civil.
General Information: Public Access terminal is available. No juvenile, sealed or adoption records released. SASE required. Turnaround time 1 week. Copy fee: $.50 per page. Certification fee: $2.00. Fee payee: Clerk, Circuit Court. Personal checks accepted. Will bill copy fees.

28th General District Court
191 E Main St, Abingdon, VA 24210; 540-676-6279; Fax: 540-676-6293. Hours: 8:30AM-5PM (EST). *Misdemeanor, Civil Actions Under $15,000, Eviction, Small Claims.*

Civil Records: Access: Mail, online, in person. Both court and visitors may perform in person searches. No search fee. Required to search: name, years to search. Civil cases indexed by defendant, plaintiff. Civil records on archives from 1777, on computer from 1987. For information about the statewide online system, LOPAS, see the state introduction.
Criminal Records: Access: Fax, mail, online, in person. Both court and visitors may perform in person searches. No search fee. Required to search: name, years to search. Criminal records on archives from 1777, on computer from 1987. Online access to criminal records is the same as civil.
General Information: Public Access terminal is available. No sealed records released. SASE required. Turnaround time 1-2 days. Copy fee: $1.00 for first page, $.50 each add'l. Certification fee: $2.00. Fee payee: General District Court. Personal checks accepted. Credit cards accepted: Visa, MasterCard. Prepayment is required.

Waynesboro City

25th Circuit Court
250 S Wayne Ave, PO Box 910, Waynesboro, VA 22980; 540-942-6616; Fax: 540-942-6774. Hours: 8:30AM-5PM (EST). *Felony, Civil Actions Over $15,000, Probate.*

Civil Records: Access: Online, in person. Visitors must perform in person searches for themselves. No search fee. Required to search: name, years to search. Civil cases indexed by defendant, plaintiff. Civil records on computer from 11/88 (some), all on index books from 5/48. Online access is available free at http://208.210.219.132/courtinfo/vacircuit/select.jsp?court=. For information about the statewide online system, LOPAS, see the state introduction.
Criminal Records: Access: Online, in person. Visitors must perform in person searches for themselves. No search fee. Required to search: name, years to search, DOB; also helpful: SSN. Criminal records on computer from 11/88 (some), all on index books from 5/48. Online access to criminal records is the same as civil.
General Information: No juvenile, sealed, adoptions released. Copy fee: $.50 per page. Certification fee: $2.00. Fee payee: Clerk of Circuit Court. Personal checks accepted. Prepayment is required.

25th General District Court - Waynesboro
250 S Wayne, PO Box 1028, Waynesboro, VA 22980; 540-942-6636; Fax: 540-942-6666. Hours: 8:30AM-4:30PM (EST). *Misdemeanor, Civil Actions Under $15,000, Eviction, Small Claims.*

Civil Records: Access: Mail, fax, online, in person. Both court and visitors may perform in person searches. No search fee. Required to search: name, years to search. Civil cases indexed by defendant, plaintiff. Civil records on computer 10 years. For information about the statewide online system, LOPAS, see the state introduction.

Criminal Records: Access: Mail, fax, online, in person. Both court and visitors may perform in person searches. No search fee. Required to search: name, years to search. Criminal records on computer for 10 years. Online access to criminal records is the same as civil.

General Information: Public Access terminal is available. Turnaround time up to 1 week. No copy fee. Certification fee: No certification fee. Fee payee: General District. Personal checks accepted. Credit cards accepted: Visa, MasterCard.

Westmoreland County

15th Circuit Court PO Box 307, Montross, VA 22520; 804-493-0108; Fax: 804-493-0393. 9AM-5PM (EST). *Felony, Civil Actions Over $15,000, Probate.*

Civil Records: Access: Online, in person. Visitors must perform in person searches for themselves. No search fee. Required to search: name, years to search. Civil cases indexed by defendant, plaintiff. Civil records on index books from 1653; on computer back to 8/2000. For information about the statewide online system, LOPAS, see the state introduction.

Criminal Records: Access: Online, in person. Visitors must perform in person searches for themselves. No search fee. Required to search: name, years to search, DOB; also helpful: SSN. Criminal records on index books from 1653; on computer back to 8/2000. Online access to criminal records is the same as civil.

General Information: Public Access terminal is available. No juvenile, sealed, adoption records released. Copy fee: $.50 per page. Certification fee: $3.00. Fee payee: Clerk of Circuit Court. Personal checks accepted. Will bill copy fees.

15th General District Court PO Box 688, Montross, VA 22520; 804-493-0105; Hours: 8AM-4:30PM (EST). *Misdemeanor, Civil Actions Under $15,000, Small Claims.*

Civil Records: Access: Mail, online, in person. Both court and visitors may perform in person searches. No search fee. Required to search: name, years to search. Civil cases indexed by defendant, plaintiff. Civil records on index books/cards for 10 years. For information about the statewide online system, LOPAS, see the state introduction.

Criminal Records: Access: Mail, online, in person. Both court and visitors may perform in person searches. No search fee. Required to search: name, years to search; also helpful: DOB, SSN. Criminal records on index books/cards for 10 years. Online access to criminal records is the same as civil.

General Information: Public Access terminal is available. All records public. SASE required. Turnaround time 1 week. Copy fee: $1.00 for first page, $.50 each add'l. Certification fee: No certification fee. Fee payee: General District Court. Personal checks accepted. Attorney checks accepted. Credit cards accepted: Visa, MasterCard. Prepayment is required.

Williamsburg City

Circuit & District Courts, VA.

Note: See James City

Winchester City

26th Circuit Court 5 N Kent St, Winchester, VA 22601; 540-667-5770; Fax: 540-667-6638. Hours: 9AM-5PM (EST). *Felony, Civil Actions Over $15,000, Probate.*

www.winfredclerk.com

Note: The Winchester Court and the Frederick County Court Clerks are housed in the same judicial center. The offices share microfilming and deed indexing systems.

Civil Records: Access: Online, in person. Visitors must perform in person searches for themselves. No search fee. Required to search: name, years to search. Civil cases indexed by defendant, plaintiff. Civil records on computer from 1985 to present, on index books from 1790. Online access is available free at http:// 208.210.219.132/courtinfo/vacircuit/select.jsp?court=. For information about the statewide online system, LOPAS, see the state introduction.

Criminal Records: Access: Mail, online, in person. Both court and visitors may perform in person searches. No search fee. Required to search: name, years to search; also helpful: DOB, SSN. Criminal records on computer from 1985 to present, on index books from 1790. Online access to criminal records is the same as civil.

General Information: No juvenile, sealed, adoption records released. SASE required. Turnaround time same day. Copy fee: $.50 per page. Certification fee: $2.00. Fee payee: Clerk of Circuit Court. Personal checks accepted. Prepayment is required.

26th General District Court 5 N Kent St, PO Box 526, Winchester, VA 22604; 540-722-7208; Fax: 540-722-1063. 8AM-4PM (EST). *Misdemeanor, Civil Actions Under $15,000, Eviction, Small Claims.*

Civil Records: Access: Phone, mail, online, in person. Both court and visitors may perform in person searches. No search fee. Required to search: name, years to search. Civil cases indexed by defendant, plaintiff. Civil records on computer from 1987, on index cards from 1985 to 1987, prior at Circuit Court. For information about the statewide online system, LOPAS, see the state introduction.

Criminal Records: Access: Mail, online, in person. Both court and visitors may perform in person searches. No search fee. Required to search: name, years to search, DOB, SSN, signed release. Criminal records on computer from 1987, on index cards from 1985 to 1987, prior at Circuit Court. Online access to criminal records is the same as civil. Forms for criminal searches available from State Police.

General Information: Public Access terminal is available. No sealed records released. Turnaround time 1-2 days. Copy fee: $.50 per page. Certification fee: $2.00. Fee payee: Clerk of General District Court. Personal checks accepted. Prepayment is required.

Wise County

30th Circuit Court PO Box 1248, Wise, VA 24293-1248; 540-328-6111; Fax: 540-328-6111. Hours: 8:30AM-5PM (EST). *Felony, Civil Actions Over $15,000, Probate.*

Civil Records: Access: Phone, fax, mail, online, in person. Both court and visitors may perform in person searches. Search fee: $10.00 per name. Required to search: name, years to search; also helpful: address. Civil cases indexed by defendant, plaintiff. Civil records on archives from 1856. Online access is available free at http://208.210.219.132/courtinfo/vacircuit/select.jsp?court=. For information about the statewide online system, LOPAS, see the state introduction. Also, court indexes are available at www.courtbar.org. Registration and a fee is required. Records go back to June, 2000.

Criminal Records: Access: Phone, fax, mail, online, in person. Both court and visitors may perform in person searches. Search fee: $10.00 per name. Required to search: name, years to search, DOB; also helpful: SSN. Criminal records on archives from 1856. For information about the statewide online system, LOPAS, see the state introduction. For other online access, see the civil records section, above.

General Information: Public Access terminal is available. No juvenile, sealed or adoption records released. Turnaround time 2-3 days. Copy fee: $.50 per page. Certification fee: $2.00 plus copy fee. Fee payee:

Clerk of Circuit Court. Personal checks accepted. Prepayment is required.

30th General District Court Wise County Courthouse, PO Box 829, Wise, VA 24293; 540-328-3426; Fax: 540-328-4576. Hours: 8AM-4PM (EST). *Misdemeanor, Civil Actions Under $15,000, Eviction, Small Claims.*

Civil Records: Access: Phone, mail, online, in person. Both court and visitors may perform in person searches. No search fee. Required to search: name, years to search. Civil cases indexed by defendant, plaintiff. Civil records on computer back 10 years. For information about the statewide online system, LOPAS, see the state introduction. Also, court indexes are available at www.courtbar.org. Registration and a fee is required. Records go back to June, 2000.

Criminal Records: Access: Phone, mail, online, in person. Both court and visitors may perform in person searches. No search fee. Required to search: name, years to search; also helpful: DOB, SSN. Criminal records on computer back 10 years. For information about the statewide online system, LOPAS, see the state introduction. For other online access, see the civil records section, above.

General Information: Public Access terminal is available. No juvenile, sealed records released. Turnaround time 5 days. Copy fee: $.50 per page. Certification fee: No certification fee. Fee payee: General District Court. Personal checks accepted. Credit cards accepted. Prepayment is required.

Wythe County

27th Circuit Court 225 S Fourth St, Rm 105, Wytheville, VA 24382; 540-223-6050; Fax: 540-223-6057. Hours: 8:30AM-5PM (EST). *Felony, Civil Actions Over $15,000, Probate.*

Civil Records: Access: Mail, online, in person. Both court and visitors may perform in person searches. No search fee. Required to search: name, years to search. Civil cases indexed by defendant, plaintiff. Civil records on computer from 1989, on index cards/books from 1950s (some back to 1790s). For information about the statewide online system, LOPAS, see the state introduction.

Criminal Records: Access: Mail, online, in person. Both court and visitors may perform in person searches. No search fee. Required to search: name, years to search; also helpful: DOB, SSN. Criminal records on computer from 1989, on index cards/books from 1950s (some back to 1790s). For information about the statewide online system, LOPAS, see the state introduction.

General Information: No juvenile, sealed, adoption records released. SASE required. Turnaround time 1-2 days. Copy fee: $.50 per page. Certification fee: No certification fee. Fee payee: Clerk of Circuit Court. Personal checks accepted. Credit cards accepted: Visa, MasterCard. Prepayment is required.

Wythe General District Court 245 S. Fourth St., # 205, Wytheville, VA 24382-2595; 540-223-6075; Fax: 540-223-6087. 8AM-4:30PM *Misdemeanor, Civil Actions Under $15,000, Eviction, Small Claims.*

Civil Records: Access: Online, in person. Visitors must perform in person searches for themselves. No search fee. Required to search: name, years to search. Civil cases indexed by defendant, plaintiff. Civil records on computer from 1/91, prior at Circuit Court. For information about the statewide online system, LOPAS, see the state introduction.

Criminal Records: Access: Online, in person. Visitors must perform in person searches for themselves. No search fee. Required to search: name, years to search; also helpful: DOB, SSN. Criminal records on computer from 1/91. For information about the statewide online system, LOPAS, see the state introduction.

General Information: Public Access terminal is available. Copy fee: $.50 per page. Fee is only applied to requests for excessive amounts of information. Certification fee: No certification fee. Fee payee: General District Court. Personal checks accepted. Credit cards accepted: Visa, MasterCard.

York County

9th Circuit Court PO Box 371, Yorktown, VA 23690; 757-890-3350; Fax: 757-890-3364. Hours: 8:15AM-5PM (EST). *Felony, Civil Actions Over $15,000, Probate.*

Note: Also includes city of Poquoson.

Civil Records: Access: Online, in person. Visitors must perform in person searches for themselves. No search fee. Required to search: name, years to search. Civil cases indexed by defendant, plaintiff. Civil records on index books from 1633, computerized since 1986. Online access is available free at http://208.210.219.132/courtinfo/vacircuit/select.jsp?court=.

For information about the statewide online system, LOPAS, see the state introduction.

Criminal Records: Access: Mail, online, in person. Both court and visitors may perform in person searches. Search fee: $5.00 per name. Required to search: name, years to search, DOB; also helpful: SSN. Criminal records on index books from 1633, computerized since 1986. For information about the statewide online system, LOPAS, see the state introduction.

General Information: Public Access terminal is available. No juvenile, sealed, adoption records released. SASE required. Turnaround time 1 week. Copy fee: $.50 per page. Certification fee: $2.00. Fee payee: Clerk of Circuit Court. Personal checks accepted. Prepayment is required.

9th Judicial District Court York County GDC, PO Box 316, Yorktown, VA 23690-0316; 757-890-3450; Fax: 757-890-3459. Hours: 8:30AM-4:30PM (EST). *Misdemeanor, Civil Actions Under $15,000, Eviction, Small Claims.*

www.yorkcounty.gov

Civil Records: Access: Fax, mail, online, in person. Both court and visitors may perform in person searches. No search fee. Required to search: name, years to search. Civil cases indexed by defendant, plaintiff. Civil records on computer back to 1990; prior at Circuit Court. For information about the statewide online system, LOPAS, see the state introduction.

Criminal Records: Access: Fax, mail, online, in person. Both court and visitors may perform in person searches. No search fee. Required to search: name, years to search. Criminal records on computer back to 1991; prior to 1985 at Circuit Court. For information about the statewide online system, LOPAS, see the state introduction.

General Information: Public Access terminal is available. No juvenile, sealed, adoption records released. Turnaround time 5 days. Fax notes: $1.00 for first page, $.50 each add'l. Copy fee: $1.00 for first page, $.50 each add'l. Certification fee: No certification fee.

Virginia Recording Offices

ORGANIZATION
95 counties and 41 independent cities, 123 recording offices. The recording officer is Clerk of Circuit Court. Fifteen independent cities share the Clerk of Circuit Court with the county - Bedford, Covington (Alleghany County), Emporia (Greenville County), Fairfax, Falls Church (Arlington or Fairfax County), Franklin (Southhampton County), Galax (Carroll County), Harrisonburg (Rockingham County), Lexington (Rockbridge County), Manassas and Manassas Park (Prince William County), Norton (Wise County), Poquoson (York County), South Boston (Halifax County), and Williamsburg (James City County. Charles City and James City are counties, not cities. The City of Franklin is not in Franklin County, the City of Richmond is not in Richmond County, and the City of Roanoke is not in Roanoke County. The entire state is in the Eastern Time Zone (EST).

REAL ESTATE RECORDS
Only a few Clerks of Circuit Court will perform real estate searches. Copy fees and certification fees vary. The independent cities may have separate Assessor Offices.

UCC RECORDS
This was a dual filing state. Until 07/2001, financing statements were filed at the state level and with the Clerk of Circuit Court, except for consumer goods, farm and real estate related collateral, which were filed only with the Clerk of Circuit Court. Now, only real estate related collateral is filed at the county level. Some recording offices will perform UCC searches. Use search request form UCC-11. Searches fees and copy fees vary.

TAX LIEN RECORDS
Federal tax liens on personal property of businesses are filed with the State Corporation Commission. Other federal and all state tax liens are filed with the county Clerk of Circuit Court. They are usually filed in a "Judgment Lien Book." Most counties will not perform tax lien searches.

OTHER LIENS
Judgment, mechanics, hospital, lis pendens.

STATEWIDE ONLINE INFO:
A growing number of Virginia counties and cities provide free access to real estate related information via the Internet.

Accomack County

Clerk of Circuit Court, P.O. Box 126, Accomac, VA 23301-0126. 757-787-5776; Fax 757-787-1849.
Will search UCC records. This agency will not do a tax lien search. Will not search real estate records. **Other Phone Numbers:** Assessor 757-787-5729.

Albemarle County

Clerk of Circuit Court, 501 E. Jefferson St., Room 225, Charlottesville, VA 22902-5176. 804-972-4083; Fax 804-293-0298.
Will search UCC records. Will not search real estate records. **Other Phone Numbers:** Assessor 804-296-5856.

Alexandria City

Clerk of Circuit Court, 520 King Street, Room 307, Alexandria, VA 22314. 703-838-4070.
Will search UCC records. This agency will not do a tax lien search. Will not search real estate records. **Other Phone Numbers:** Assessor 703-838-4646; Treasurer 703-838-6420.

Alleghany County

Clerk of Circuit Court, P.O. Box 670, Covington, VA 24426-0670. Clerk of Circuit Court, R/E and UCC Recording 540-965-1730; Fax 540-965-1732. http://www.alleghanycountyclerk.com
Will not search UCC records. Will not search real estate records. **Other Phone Numbers:** Assessor 540-965-1640; Treasurer 540-965-1630.

Amelia County

Clerk of Circuit Court, P.O. Box 237, Amelia Court House, VA 23002-0237. 804-561-2128.
Will not search UCC records. This agency will not do a tax lien search. Will not search real estate records. **Other Phone Numbers:** Assessor 804-561-2158; Treasurer 804-561-2145; Elections 804-561-3460.

Amherst County

Clerk of Circuit Court, P.O. Box 462, Amherst, VA 24521. 804-946-9321.
Will search UCC records. This agency will not do a tax lien search. Will not search real estate records. **Other Phone Numbers:** Assessor 804-946-9310; Treasurer 804-946-9318.

Appomattox County

Clerk of Circuit Court, P.O. Box 672, Appomattox, VA 24522. 804-352-5275; Fax 804-352-2781.
Will search UCC records. Will not search real estate records. **Other Phone Numbers:** Assessor 804-352-7450; Treasurer 804-352-5200.

Arlington County

Clerk of Circuit Court, 1425 N. Courthouse Rd 6th Floor, Arlington, VA 22201. 703-228-7242.
Will search UCC records. This agency will not do a tax lien search. Will not search real estate records. **Online Access:** Real Estate, Assessor. Property records on the County assessor database are available free at www.co.arlington.va.us/REAssessments/Scripts/DreaDefault.asp. **Other Phone Numbers:** Assessor 703-228-3920.

Augusta County

Clerk of Circuit Court, P.O. Box 689, Staunton, VA 24402-0689. 540-245-5321; Fax 540-245-5318.
Will search UCC records. This agency will not do a tax lien search. Will not search real estate records. **Other Phone Numbers:** Assessor 540-245-5647; Treasurer 540-245-5660.

Bath County

Clerk of Circuit Court, P.O. Box 180, Warm Springs, VA 24484. 540-839-7226.
Will search UCC records. This agency will not do a tax lien search. Will not search real estate records. **Other Phone Numbers:** Assessor 540-839-7231; Treasurer 540-839-7256.

Bedford County

Clerk of Circuit Court, P.O. Box 235, Bedford, VA 24523. 540-586-7632.
Will search UCC records. This agency will not do a tax lien search. Will not search real estate records. **Online Access:** Property Tax. County real estate records on the Bedford County Commissioner of the Revenue site are available free online at http://208.206.84.33/realestate2/. Records on the City of Bedford (www.ci.bedford.va.us) Property Tax database are available free online at http://www.ci.bedford.va.us/taxf.shtml. Search by name, address or tax map reference number. **Other Phone Numbers:** Assessor 540-586-7626; Treasurer 540-586-7670.

Bland County

Clerk of Circuit Court, P.O. Box 295, Bland, VA 24315-0295. 540-688-4562; Fax 540-688-4562.
Will search UCC records. This agency will not do a tax lien search. Will not search real estate records. **Other Phone Numbers:** Assessor 540-688-4291; Treasurer 540-688-3741.

Botetourt County

Clerk of Circuit Court, P.O. Box 219, Fincastle, VA 24090. 540-473-8274.
Will search UCC records. This agency will not do a tax lien search. Will not search real estate records. **Other Phone Numbers:** Assessor 540-473-8254; Treasurer 540-473-8254.

Bristol City

Clerk of Circuit Court, 497 Cumberland Street, Room 210, Bristol, VA 24201. 540-645-7321; Fax 540-645-7345.
Will search UCC records. Will not search real estate records. **Other Phone Numbers:** Assessor 540-645-7316; Treasurer 540-645-7311.

Brunswick County

Clerk of Circuit Court, 216 N. Main St., Lawrenceville, VA 23868. 804-848-2215; Fax 804-848-4307.
Will not search UCC records. Will not search real estate records. **Other Phone Numbers:** Assessor 804-848-2313; Treasurer 804-848-2512.

Buchanan County

Clerk of Circuit Court, P.O. Box 929, Grundy, VA 24614. Clerk of Circuit Court, R/E and UCC Recording 540-935-6567; Fax 540-935-6574.
Will search UCC records. Will search real estate records. **Other Phone Numbers:** Assessor 540-935-6542; Treasurer 540-935-6551; Elections 540-935-6534; Vital Records 540-935-6575.

Buckingham County

Clerk of Circuit Court, P.O. Box 107, Buckingham, VA 23921. 804-969-4734; Fax 804-959-2043.
Will search UCC records. Will not search real estate records. **Other Phone Numbers:** Assessor 804-969-4181.

Buena Vista City

Clerk of Circuit Court, 2039 Sycamore Ave., Buena Vista, VA 24416. 540-261-8627 R/E Recording: 540-261-8623 UCC Recording: 540-261-8626; Fax 540-261-8623.
Will search UCC records. This agency will not do a tax lien search. Will not search real estate records. **Other Phone Numbers:** Assessor 540-261-8611; Treasurer 540-261-8621; Elections 540-261-8605.

Campbell County

Clerk of Circuit Court, P.O. Box 7, Rustburg, VA 24588. 804-592-9517.
Will search UCC records. Tax liens not included in UCC search. Will not search real estate records. **Other Phone Numbers:** Treasurer 804-332-9590.

Caroline County

Clerk of Circuit Court, P.O. Box 309, Bowling Green, VA 22427-0309. 804-633-5800.
Will search UCC records. This agency will not do a tax lien search. Will not search real estate records.

Carroll County

Clerk of Circuit Court, P.O. Box 218, Hillsville, VA 24343-0218. 540-728-3117; Fax 540-728-0255.
Will search UCC records. Will not search real estate records. **Online Access:** Real Estate. Online access to Carroll county property information is available free on the GIS mapping site at http://arcims.webgis.net/webgis/carroll_grayson. No name searching at this time. Access to Town of Hillsville property information is available on the gis mapping site at http://arcims.webgis.net/webgis/hillsville. **Other Phone Numbers:** Assessor 540-728-3281.

Charles City County

Clerk of Circuit Court, P.O. Box 86, Charles City, VA 23030-0086. 804-829-9212; Fax 804-829-5647.
Will search UCC records. Will not search real estate records.

Charlotte County

Clerk of Circuit Court, P.O. Box 38, Charlotte Court House, VA 23923. 804-542-5147; Fax 804-542-4336.
Will search UCC records. Will not search real estate records. **Other Phone Numbers:** Assessor 804-542-5546; Treasurer 804-542-5725.

Charlottesville City

Clerk of Circuit Court, 315 East High Street, Charlottesville, VA 22902. 804-295-3182.
Will search UCC records. This agency will not do a tax lien search. Will not search real estate records. **Other Phone Numbers:** Assessor 804-970-3136; Treasurer 804-296-5851.

Chesapeake City

Clerk of Circuit Court, 307 Albemarle Dr, #300, Chesapeake, VA 23322. Clerk of Circuit Court, R/E and UCC Recording 757-382-3026 UCC Recording: 757-382-3031; Fax 757-436-3034.
Will search UCC records. Will not search real estate records. **Other Phone Numbers:** Assessor 757-382-6235; Treasurer 757-382-6281.

Chesterfield County Circuit Court

Clerk of Circuit Court, P.O. Box 40, Chesterfield, VA 23832-0125. Clerk of Circuit Court, R/E and UCC Recording 804-748-1241; Fax 804-796-5625.
Will not search UCC records. Will not search real estate records. **Other Phone Numbers:** Assessor 804-748-1321; Treasurer 804-748-1201; Elections 804-748-1471.

Clarke County

Clerk of Circuit Court, P.O. Box 189, Berryville, VA 22611. 540-955-5116; Fax 540-955-0284.
Will search UCC records. Will not search real estate records. **Other Phone Numbers:** Assessor 540-955-5108; Treasurer 540-955-5160.

Clifton Forge City

Clerk of Circuit Court, P.O. Box 27, Clifton Forge, VA 24422. 540-863-2508.
As of July 1, 2001, all governmental functions were transferred to Alleghany County. Will search UCC records. This agency will not do a tax lien search. Will not search real estate records. **Other Phone Numbers:** Assessor 540-863-2506.

Colonial Heights City

Clerk of Circuit Court, P.O. Box 3401, Colonial Heights, VA 23834. 804-520-9364.
Will not search UCC records. This agency will not do a tax lien search. Will not search real estate records. **Other Phone Numbers:** Assessor 804-520-9272.

Craig County

Clerk of Circuit Court, P.O. Box 185, New Castle, VA 24127-0185. 540-864-6141.
Will search UCC records. This agency will not do a tax lien search. Will not search real estate records. **Other Phone Numbers:** Assessor 540-864-6241; Treasurer 540-864-5641.

Culpeper County

Clerk of Circuit Court, 135 West Cameron St., Room 103, Culpeper, VA 22701. Clerk of Circuit Court, R/E and UCC Recording 540-727-3438.
Will search UCC records. This agency will not do a tax lien search. Will not search real estate records. **Other Phone Numbers:** Assessor 540-727-3443; Treasurer 540-727-3442.

Cumberland County

Clerk of Circuit Court, P.O. Box 8, Cumberland, VA 23040. 804-492-4442; Fax 804-492-4876.
Will search UCC records. **Other Phone Numbers:** Assessor 804-492-4280; Treasurer 804-492-4297.

Danville City

Clerk of Circuit Court, P.O. Box 3300, Danville, VA 24543. 804-799-5168; Fax 804-799-6502.
Will search UCC records. This agency will not do a tax lien search. Will not search real estate records. **Online Access:** Real Estate, Liens. Access to Danville City online records is free; signup is required. Records date back to 1993. Lending agency information is available. For information, contact Leigh Ann Thomas at 804-799-5168. **Other Phone Numbers:** Assessor 804-799-5120; Treasurer 804-799- 5140.

Dickenson County

Clerk of Circuit Court, P.O. Box 190, Clintwood, VA 24228. 540-926-1616; Fax 540-926-6465.
Will search UCC records. **Other Phone Numbers:** Assessor 540-926-1646; Treasurer 540-926-1610.

Dinwiddie County

Clerk of Circuit Court, P.O. Box 63, Dinwiddie, VA 23841. 804-469-4540.
Will search UCC records. This agency will not do a tax lien search. Will not search real estate records. **Other Phone Numbers:** Assessor 804-469-4507; Treasurer 804-469-4510.

Essex County

Clerk of Circuit Court, P.O. Box 445, Tappahannock, VA 22560. Clerk of Circuit Court, R/E and UCC Recording 804-443-3541; Fax 804-445-1216.
Will not search UCC records. This agency will not do a tax lien search. Will not search real estate records. **Other Phone Numbers:** Assessor 804-443-2661; Treasurer 804-443-4371; Elections 804-443-4611.

Fairfax County

Clerk of Circuit Court, 4110 Chain Bridge Road, 3rd Floor, Fairfax, VA 22030. 703-246-4100; http://www.co.fairfax.va.us
As of 1/1/88, Falls Church filings for zip codes 22041, 22042, 22043 and 22044 are filed in Fairfax County. Will search UCC records. This agency will not do a tax lien search. Will not search real estate records. **Online Access:** Real Estate, Property Tax. Records on the Dept. of Tax Administration Real Estate Assessment database are available free online at www.co.fairfax.va.us/dta/re/notice.asp Also, the Automated Information System operates Monday-Saturday 7AM-7PM at 703-222-6740. Hear about property descriptions, assessed values and sales prices. Fax-back service is available. **Other Phone Numbers:** Assessor 703-222-8234.

Fauquier County

Clerk of Circuit Court, First Floor, 40 CulpeperSt., Warrenton, VA 20186. 540-347-8608 R/E Recording: 540-347-8697; http://www.co.fauquier.va.us/services/ccc/index.html
Will not search UCC records. This agency will not do a tax lien search. Will not search real estate records. **Other Phone Numbers:** Assessor 540-347-8614; Treasurer 540-347-8691.

Floyd County

Clerk of Circuit Court, 100 East Main Street, Room 200, Floyd, VA 24091. 540-745-9330.
Will not search UCC records. This agency will not do a tax lien search. Will not search real estate records. **Online Access:** Real Estate. Online access to county property information is available free at the gis mapping site at http://arcims.webgis.net/webgis/floyd/default.asp. No name searching at this time. **Other Phone Numbers:** Assessor 540-745-9345; Treasurer 540-745-9357.

Fluvanna County

Clerk of Circuit Court, P.O. Box 299, Palmyra, VA 22963-0299. Clerk of Circuit Court, R/E and UCC Recording 804-589-8011; Fax 804-589-6004.
Will not search UCC records. This agency will not do a tax lien search. Will not search real estate records. **Other Phone Numbers:** Assessor 804-589-8322; Treasurer 804-589-8012; Appraiser/Auditor 804-589-8322; Elections 804-589-3593; Vital Records 804-589-8021.

Franklin County

Clerk of Circuit Court, P.O. Box 567, Rocky Mount, VA 24151. 540-483-3065; Fax 540-483-3042.
Will search UCC records. Will not search real estate records. **Other Phone Numbers:** Assessor 757-562-8547.

Frederick County

Clerk of Circuit Court, 5 North Kent Street, Winchester, VA 22601. 540-667-5770; Fax 540-545-8711. http://www.winfredclerk.com/standard.htm
Do not confuse this county with Fredericksburg, VA or Frederick, MD. Also, the City of Winchester has a separate filing office. Will search UCC records. Tax liens not included in UCC search. Will not search real estate records. **Other Phone Numbers:** Assessor 540-662-5303; Treasurer 540-662-6611.

Fredericksburg City

Clerk of Circuit Court, P.O. Box 359, Fredericksburg, VA 22404. 540-372-1066.
Many Fredericksburg addresses are outside the city limits, in Stafford County or Spotsylvania County. Many residents are not themselves aware of this. Check debtor location carefully. Will search UCC records. This agency will not do a tax lien search. Will not search real estate records. **Other Phone Numbers:** Assessor 540-372-1004.

Giles County

Clerk of Circuit Court, 501 Wenonah Avenue, Pearisburg, VA 24134-0501. 540-921-1722; Fax 540-921-3825.
Will search UCC records. Will not search real estate records. **Other Phone Numbers:** Assessor 540-921-3321; Treasurer 540-921-1240.

Gloucester County

Clerk of Circuit Court, P.O. Box N, Gloucester, VA 23061-0570. 804-693-2502; Fax 804-693-2186.
Will search UCC records. **Other Phone Numbers:** Assessor 804-693-3451; Treasurer 804-693-2141.

Goochland County

Clerk of Circuit Court, P.O. Box 196, Goochland, VA 23063. 804-556-5353.
Will search UCC records. This agency will not do a tax lien search. Will not search real estate records. **Other Phone Numbers:** Assessor 804-556-5307.

Grayson County

Clerk of Circuit Court, P.O. Box 130, Independence, VA 24348-0130. 540-773-2231; Fax 540-773-3338.
Will search UCC records. This agency will not do a tax lien search. Will not search real estate records. **Online Access:** Real Estate. Online access to Grayson county property information is available free on the gis mapping site at http://arcims.webgis.net/webgis/carroll_grayson. No name searching at this time. **Other Phone Numbers:** Assessor 540-773-2022; Treasurer 540-773-2571.

Greene County

Clerk of Circuit Court, P.O. Box 386, Stanardsville, VA 22973-0386. 804-985-5208; Fax 804-985-6723.
Will search UCC records. Will not search real estate records. **Other Phone Numbers:** Assessor 804-985-5211; Treasurer 804-985-5214.

Greensville County

Clerk of Circuit Court, P.O. Box 631, Emporia, VA 23847. 804-348-4215; Fax 804-348-4020.
Will search UCC records. Will not search real estate records. **Other Phone Numbers:** Assessor 804-348-4229; Treasurer 804-348-4208.

Halifax County

Clerk of Circuit Court, P.O. Box 729, Halifax, VA 24558. 804-476-6211; Fax 804-476-2890.
Will search UCC records. Will not search real estate records. **Other Phone Numbers:** Assessor 804-476-2773; Treasurer 804-476-2025.

Hampton City

Clerk of Circuit Court, P.O. Box 40, Hampton, VA 23669-0040. 757-727-6896.
Will search UCC records. This agency will not do a tax lien search. Will not search real estate records. **Other Phone Numbers:** Assessor 757-727-6363; Treasurer 757-727-6374.

Hanover County

Clerk of Circuit Court, P.O. Box 39, Hanover, VA 23069-0039. 804-537-6150.
Will search UCC records. This agency will not do a tax lien search. Will not search real estate records. **Other Phone Numbers:** Assessor 804-537-6029.

Henrico County

Clerk of Circuit Court, P.O. Box 27032, Richmond, VA 23273. 804-501-4202.
Will search UCC records. This agency will not do a tax lien search. Will check book & page for name and date for RE. **Other Phone Numbers:** Assessor 804-501-5580.

Henry County

Clerk of Circuit Court, 3160 Kings Mountain Rd. #B, Martinsville, VA 24112. Clerk of Circuit Court, R/E and UCC Recording 540-634-4880; http://henry county.neocom.net
Will not search UCC records. This agency will not do a tax lien search. Will not search real estate records. **Online Access:** Real Estate, Assessor. Online access to county porperty information is available free at the gis mapping site at www.webgis.net/henry. **Other Phone Numbers:** Assessor 540-634-4610; Treasurer 540-624-4675; Appraiser/Auditor 540-634-4610; Elections 540-634-4697; Vital Records 540-634-4880.

Highland County

Clerk of Circuit Court, P.O. Box 190, Monterey, VA 24465-0190. 540-468-2447; Fax 540-468-3447.
Will search UCC records. Will not search real estate records. **Other Phone Numbers:** Assessor 540-468-2142; Treasurer 540-465-2265.

Hopewell City

Clerk of Circuit Court, P.O. Box 354, Hopewell, VA 23860. 804-541-2239.
Will search UCC records. This agency will not do a tax lien search. Will not search real estate records. **Other Phone Numbers:** Assessor 804-541-2234; Treasurer 804-541-2240.

Isle of Wight County

Clerk of Circuit Court, P.O. Box 110, Isle of Wight, VA 23397. 757-357-3191 x233.
Will search UCC records. This agency will not do a tax lien search. Will not search real estate records. **Other Phone Numbers:** Assessor 757-365-6219; Treasurer 757-357-3191.

James City County

Clerk of Circuit Court, 5201 Monticello Ave #6, Williamsburg, VA 23188. 757-564-2242 R/E Recording: 757-564-2349; http://www.regis.state.va.us/jcc/public/index.htm
This office also handles filings for the City of WIlliamsburg. Will search UCC records. This agency will not do a tax lien search. Will not search real estate records. **Online Access:** Real Estate. Records on the James City County Property Information database are available free online at the web site. **Other Phone Numbers:** Assessor 757-253-6650; Treasurer 757-229-6705.

King and Queen County

Clerk of Circuit Court, P.O. Box 67, King and Queen Court House, VA 23085. Clerk of Circuit Court, R/E and UCC Recording 804-785-5984; Fax 804-785-5698.
Will not search UCC records. Will not search real estate records. **Other Phone Numbers:** Assessor 804-785-5976; Treasurer 804-785-5978; Elections 804-785-5980.

King George County

Clerk of Circuit Court, 9483 Kings Highway, #3, King George, VA 22485. Clerk of Circuit Court, R/E and UCC Recording 540-775-3322.
Will search UCC records. UCC search includes tax liens if requested. RE owner, mortgage, and property transfer searches available. **Other Phone Numbers:** Assessor 540-775-4664; Treasurer 540-775-2571.

King William County

Clerk of Circuit Court, P.O. Box 216, King William, VA 23086. 804-769-4936; Fax 804-769-4991.
Will search UCC records. This agency will not do a tax lien search. RE owner, mortgage, and property transfer searches available. **Other Phone Numbers:** Assessor 804-769-4942; Treasurer 804-769-4931.

Lancaster County

Clerk of Circuit Court, P.O. Box 99, Lancaster, VA 22503. 804-462-5611; Fax 804-462-9978.
Will search UCC records. This agency will not do a tax lien search. Will not search real estate records. **Other Phone Numbers:** Assessor 804-462-7920; Treasurer 804-462-5630; Elections 804-462-5277.

Lee County

Clerk of Circuit Court, P.O. Box 326, Jonesville, VA 24263. 540-346-7763; Fax 540-346-3440.
Will search UCC records. Will not search real estate records. **Other Phone Numbers:** Assessor 540-346-7722; Treasurer 540-346-7716.

Loudoun County

Clerk of Circuit Court, P.O. Box 550, Leesburg, VA 20178. Clerk of Circuit Court, R/E and UCC Recording 703-777-0270; http://www.co.loudoun.va.us/1-gov.htm
Will search UCC records. This agency will not do a tax lien search. Will not search real estate records. **Other Phone Numbers:** Assessor 703-777-0260; Treasurer 703-777-0280.

Louisa County

Clerk of Circuit Court, P.O. Box 37, Louisa, VA 23093. 540-967-5312.
Will search UCC records. This agency will not do a tax lien search. Will not search real estate records. **Other Phone Numbers:** Assessor 540-967-3450.

Lunenburg County

Clerk of Circuit Court, Courthouse, Lunenburg, VA 23952. 804-696-2230.
Will search UCC records. This agency will not do a tax lien search. Will not search real estate records. **Other Phone Numbers:** Assessor 804-696-2516.

Lynchburg City

Clerk of Circuit Court, P.O. Box 4, Lynchburg, VA 24505. 804-847-1590; Fax 804-847-1864.
Will search UCC records. This agency will not do a tax lien search. Will not search real estate records. **Other**

Phone Numbers: Assessor 804-847-1510; Treasurer 804-847-1520.

Madison County

Clerk of Circuit Court, P.O. Box 220, Madison, VA 22727-0220. 540-948-6888; Fax 540-948-3759. Will search UCC records. Will not search real estate records. **Other Phone Numbers:** Assessor 540-948-4421; Treasurer 540-948-4409.

Martinsville City

Clerk of Circuit Court, P.O. Box 1206, Martinsville, VA 24114-1206. 540-656-5106; Fax 540-656-5232. Will search UCC records. This agency will not do a tax lien search. Will not search real estate records.

Mathews County

Clerk of Circuit Court, P.O. Box 463, Mathews, VA 23109-0463. 804-725-2550. Will search UCC records. UCC search includes tax liens if requested. Will not search real estate records.

Mecklenburg County

Clerk of Circuit Court, P.O. Box 530, Boydton, VA 23917-0530. 804-738-6191. Will search UCC records. This agency will not do a tax lien search. Will not search real estate records.

Middlesex County

Clerk of Circuit Court, P.O. Box 158, Saluda, VA 23149. Clerk of Circuit Court, R/E and UCC Recording 804-758-5317. Will search UCC records. This agency will not do a tax lien search. Will not search real estate records. **Other Phone Numbers:** Assessor 804-758-5331; Treasurer 804-758-5302; Appraiser/Auditor 804-758-5331; Elections 804-758-4420.

Montgomery County

Clerk of Circuit Court, PO Box 6309, 1 East Main #B5, Christiansburg, VA 24068. 540-382-5760; Fax 540-382-6937. http://www.montva.com Will not search UCC records. Will not search real estate records. **Online Access:** Real Estate, Property Tax. Access to the county Tax Parcel Information System database is available free online at www.webgis.net/montgomery/index.htm. Select what to search and click next. Records on the Town of Blacksburg GIS site are available free online at www.webgis.net/blacksburg. Use map or enter an owner name. Find owner name, address, land or building value. **Other Phone Numbers:** Assessor 540-382-5717; Treasurer 540-382-5723; Appraiser/Auditor 540-382-5715; Elections 540-382-5741; Vital Records 540-382-5760; Office of Public Information 540-381-6887.

Nelson County

Clerk of Circuit Court, P.O. Box 10, Lovingston, VA 22949. 804-263-4069; Fax 804-263-8313. Will search UCC records. This agency will not do a tax lien search. Will not search real estate records. **Other Phone Numbers:** Assessor 804-263-4009; Treasurer 804-263-4079.

New Kent County

Clerk of Circuit Court, P.O. Box 98, New Kent, VA 23124-0098. Clerk of Circuit Court, R/E and UCC Recording 804-966-9520; Fax 804-966-9528. Will not search UCC records. Will not search real estate records. **Other Phone Numbers:** Assessor 804-966-9610; Treasurer 804-966-9615.

Newport News City

Clerk of Circuit Court, 2500 Washington Avenue, Courthouse, Newport News, VA 23607. 757-926-8561 R/E Recording: 757-926-8355 UCC Recording: 757-926-8349; Fax 757-926-8531. http://www.newport-news.va.us Will search UCC records. Will not search real estate records. **Online Access:** Assessor, Real Estate. Online access to the City's "Real Estate on the Web" database is available free at http://216.54.20.244/reisweb1. Search by address or parcel number; new "advanced search" may include name searching. **Other Phone Numbers:** Assessor 757-247-8671; Treasurer 757-247-8731.

Norfolk City

Clerk of Circuit Court, 100 St. Paul's Blvd., Norfolk, VA 23510-2773. 757-664-4380; http://206.246.226.47/RealEstate Will search UCC records. UCC search includes tax liens if requested. RE owner, mortgage, and property transfer searches available. **Online Access:** Real Estate, Assessor. Records on the City of Norfolk Real Estate Property Assessment database are available free online at http://206.246.226.47/RealEstate/search.html. **Other Phone Numbers:** Assessor 757-64-4732; Treasurer 757-441-2931.

Northampton County

Clerk of Circuit Court, P.O. Box 36, Eastville, VA 23347-0036. 757-678-0465; Fax 757-678-5410. Will search UCC records. Will not search real estate records. **Other Phone Numbers:** Assessor 757-678-0446; Treasurer 757-678-0450.

Northumberland County

Clerk of Circuit Court, P.O. Box 217, Heathsville, VA 22473. 804-580-3700. Will search UCC records. This agency will not do a tax lien search. RE record owner searches available. **Other Phone Numbers:** Assessor 804-580-4600; Treasurer 804-580-5201.

Nottoway County

Clerk of Circuit Court, P.O. Box 25, Nottoway, VA 23955. 804-645-9043; Fax 804-645-2201. Will search UCC records. Will not search real estate records. **Other Phone Numbers:** Assessor 804-645-9317.

Orange County

Clerk of Circuit Court, P.O. Box 230, Orange, VA 22960. Clerk of Circuit Court, R/E and UCC Recording 540-672-4030; Fax 540-672-2939. Will search UCC records. Will not search real estate records. **Other Phone Numbers:** Assessor 540-672-4441; Treasurer 540-672-2656.

Page County Circuit Court

Clerk of Circuit Court, 116 South Court Street, Suite A, Luray, VA 22835. Clerk of Circuit Court, R/E and UCC Recording 540-743-4064; Fax 540-743-2338. Will not search UCC records. Will not search real estate records. **Other Phone Numbers:** Assessor 540-743-3840; Treasurer 540-743-3975; Elections 540-743-3986.

Patrick County

Clerk of Circuit Court, P.O. Box 148, Stuart, VA 24171-0148. Clerk of Circuit Court, R/E and UCC Recording 540-694-7213; Fax 540-694-6943. Will not search UCC records. Will not search real estate records. **Other Phone Numbers:** Assessor 540-684-7131; Treasurer 540-694-7257; Elections 540-694-7206.

Petersburg City

Clerk of Circuit Court, 7 Courthouse Ave., Petersburg, VA 23803. 804-733-2367; Fax 804-732-5548. Will search UCC records. Will not search real estate records. **Other Phone Numbers:** Assessor 804-733-2315; Treasurer 804-733-2321.

Pittsylvania County

Clerk of Circuit Court, P.O. Drawer 31, Chatham, VA 24531. 804-432-7887. Will search UCC records. This agency will not do a tax lien search. Will not search real estate records. **Online Access:** Real Estate. See Danville City for Real Estate and Lien records online for Danville City. **Other Phone Numbers:** Assessor 804-656-6211.

Portsmouth City

Clerk of Circuit Court, P.O. Drawer 1217, Portsmouth, VA 23705. 757-393-8671 R/E Recording: 757-393-8530; Fax 757-399-4826. Will search UCC records. This agency will not do a tax lien search. Will not search real estate records. **Other Phone Numbers:** Assessor 757-393-8631; Treasurer 757-393-8651; Appraiser/Auditor 757-393-8771; Elections 757-393-8644.

Powhatan County

Clerk of Circuit Court, P.O. Box 37, Powhatan, VA 23139-0037. 804-598-5660. Will search UCC records. This agency will not do a tax lien search. Will not search real estate records. **Other Phone Numbers:** Assessor 804-598-5617; Treasurer 804-598-5626.

Prince Edward County

Clerk of Circuit Court, P.O. Box 304, Farmville, VA 23901. 804-392-5145. Will search UCC records. This agency will not do a tax lien search. Will not search real estate records. **Other Phone Numbers:** Assessor 804-392-3231; Treasurer 804-392-3404.

Prince George County

Clerk of Circuit Court, P.O. Box 98, Prince George, VA 23875-0098. 804-733-2640. Will search UCC records. This agency will not do a tax lien search. Will not search real estate records. **Other Phone Numbers:** Assessor 804-733-2616; Treasurer 804-733-2620.

Prince William County

Clerk of Circuit Court, 9311 Lee Avenue, Room 300, Manassas, VA 20110-5598. 703-792-6035; Fax 703-792-6083. www.pwcgov.org/ccourt Will search UCC records. Will not search real estate records. **Online Access:** Property Records. Records on the county Property Information database are available free online at www.pwcgov.org/realestate/LandRover.asp. **Other Phone Numbers:** Assessor 703-792-6780; Vital Records 703-792-6045 (marriage only).

Pulaski County

Clerk of Circuit Court, Suite 101, 45 3rd St. NW, Pulaski, VA 24301. 540-980-7825; Fax 540-980-7835. Will search UCC records. This agency will not do a tax lien search. Will not search real estate records. **Other Phone Numbers:** Assessor 540-980-7753; Treasurer 540-980-7785.

Radford City

Clerk of Circuit Court, 619 Second Street, Courthouse, Radford, VA 24141. 540-731-3610; Fax 540-731-3612. Will search UCC records. This agency will not do a tax lien search. Will not search real estate records. **Other**

Phone Numbers: Treasurer 540-731-3661; Elections 540-731-3639.

Rappahannock County

Clerk of Circuit Court, P.O. Box 517, Washington, VA 22747-1517. 540-675-3621.
Will search UCC records. This agency will not do a tax lien search. Will not search real estate records. **Other Phone Numbers:** Assessor 540-675-3513; Treasurer 540-675-3334.

Richmond City

Clerk of Circuit Court, 400 N. 9th St., Richmond, VA 23219. 804-780-6520.
The City of Richmond is not in Richmond County. It is bordered by Henrico and Chesterfield Counties. Will search UCC records. This agency will not do a tax lien search. Will not search real estate records. **Other Phone Numbers:** Assessor 804-780-5600.

Richmond County

Clerk of Circuit Court, P.O. Box 1000, Warsaw, VA 22572-1000. 804-333-3781; Fax 804-333-5396. http://www.co.richmond.va.us/
The City of Richmond is a separate filing office and is not located in this county. The following ZIP Codes are the only ones for this county: 22572, 22460, 22472, 22548, and part of 22435. Will search UCC records. Tax liens included with UCC search if requested. RE record owner searches available. **Other Phone Numbers:** Assessor 804-333-5062; Treasurer 804-333-3555; Appraiser/Auditor 804-333-5062; Elections 804-333-4772; Vital Records 804-333-3781.

Roanoke City

Clerk of Circuit Court, Box 2610, Roanoke, VA 24010-2610. 540-853-6702.
Will search UCC records. This agency will not do a tax lien search. **Online Access:** Property Records. Online access to Roanoke City property records are available free at www.webgis.net/RoanokeCity. **Other Phone Numbers:** Assessor 540-981-2523; Treasurer 540-333-3555.

Roanoke County

Clerk of Circuit Court, P.O. Box 1126, Salem, VA 24153-1126. 540-387-6205; Fax 540-387-6145.
Will search UCC records. Will not search real estate records. **Other Phone Numbers:** Assessor 703-772-2035.

Rockbridge County

Clerk of Circuit Court, 2 South Main Street, Court House, Lexington, VA 24450-2599. Clerk of Circuit Court, R/E and UCC Recording 540-463-2232; Fax 540-463-3850.
Will search UCC records. Will not search real estate records. **Other Phone Numbers:** Assessor 540-463-2613; Treasurer 540-772-2056; Appraiser/Auditor 540-463-3431; Elections 540-463-7203.

Rockingham County

Clerk of Circuit Court, Courthouse, Harrisonburg, VA 22801. 540-564-3110; Fax 540-564-3127.
Will search UCC records. Will not search real estate records.

Russell County

Clerk of Circuit Court, P.O. Box 435, Lebanon, VA 24266. 540-889-8023; Fax 540-889-8003.
Will search UCC records. Will not search real estate records. **Other Phone Numbers:** Assessor 540-889-8014; Treasurer 540-889-8028.

Salem City

Clerk of Circuit Court, P.O. Box 891, Salem, VA 24153. 540-375-3067; Fax 540-375-4039.
Will search UCC records. Will not search real estate records.

Scott County

Clerk of Circuit Court, 104 East Jackson Street, Courthouse, Suite 2, Gate City, VA 24251-3417. 540-386-3801.
Will search UCC records. UCC search includes tax liens if requested. Will not search real estate records. **Other Phone Numbers:** Assessor 540-386-3801; Treasurer 540-386-7742; Registrar 540-386-6691.

Shenandoah County

Clerk of Circuit Court, P.O. Box 406, Woodstock, VA 22664-0406. 540-459-6150; Fax 540-459-6155.
Will search UCC records. Will not search real estate records. **Other Phone Numbers:** Assessor 540-459-6170; Treasurer 540-459-6180.

Smyth County

Clerk of Circuit Court, P.O. Box 1025, Marion, VA 24354. Clerk of Circuit Court, R/E and UCC Recording 540-782-4044; Fax 540-783-4045.
Will not search UCC records. Will not search real estate records. **Other Phone Numbers:** Assessor 540-782-4040; Treasurer 540-782-4059.

Southampton County

Clerk of Circuit Court, P.O. Box 190, Courtland, VA 23837. 757-653-9245.
Will not search UCC records. This agency will not do a tax lien search. Will not search real estate records. **Other Phone Numbers:** Assessor 757-653-3030; Treasurer 757-653-3025.

Spotsylvania County

Clerk of Circuit Court, P.O. Box 96, Spotsylvania, VA 22553-0096. 540-582-7090; Fax 540-582-2169.
Will search UCC records. Will not search real estate records.

Stafford County

Clerk of Circuit Court, P.O. Box 69, Stafford, VA 22555. 540-659-8752.
Will search UCC records. This agency will not do a tax lien search. Will not search real estate records. **Other Phone Numbers:** Assessor 540-658-4132; Treasurer 540-659-8700.

Staunton City

Clerk of Circuit Court, P.O. Box 1286, Staunton, VA 24402-1286. Clerk of Circuit Court, R/E and UCC Recording 540-332-3874; Fax 540-332-3970. http://www.staunton.va.us/cityhall/spinhall.htm
Will not search UCC records. Will not search real estate records. **Other Phone Numbers:** Assessor 540-332-3827; Treasurer 540-332-3833; Appraiser/Auditor 540-332-3827; Elections 540-332-3840.

Suffolk City

Clerk of Circuit Court, P.O. Box 1604, Suffolk, VA 23439-1604. 757-923-2251 R/E Recording: 757-923-2264 UCC Recording: 757-923-2347.
Will search UCC records. This agency will not do a tax lien search. Will not search real estate records. **Other Phone Numbers:** Assessor 757-923-2400.

Surry County

Clerk of Circuit Court, P.O. Box 203, Surry, VA 23883-0203. 757-294-3161.

Will search UCC records. This agency will not do a tax lien search. Will not search real estate records. **Other Phone Numbers:** Assessor 757-294-3000; Treasurer 757-294-5206.

Sussex County

Clerk of Circuit Court, P.O. Box 1337, Sussex, VA 23884. 804-246-5511 x3274.
Will search UCC records. This agency will not do a tax lien search. Will not search real estate records. **Other Phone Numbers:** Assessor 804-246-5511 x3222; Treasurer 804-246-5511 x3223.

Tazewell County

Clerk of Circuit Court, P.O. Box 968, Tazewell, VA 24651-0968. 540-988-7541; Fax 540-988-7501.
Will search UCC records. **Other Phone Numbers:** Assessor 540-988-7541 x305; Treasurer 540-988-7541 x315.

Virginia Beach City

Clerk of Circuit Court, Judicial Center, 2305 Judicial Blvd., Virginia Beach, VA 23456-9017. 757-427-8818; Fax 757-426-5686.
Will search UCC records. Will not search real estate records. **Other Phone Numbers:** Assessor 757-427-4601.

Warren County

Clerk of Circuit Court, 1 East Main Street, Front Royal, VA 22630-3382. Clerk of Circuit Court, R/E and UCC Recording 540-635-2435; Fax 540-636-3274. http://www.courts.state.va.us
Will search UCC records. Will not search real estate records. **Other Phone Numbers:** Assessor 540-635-2651; Treasurer 540-635-2215; Elections 540-635-4327.

Washington County

Clerk of Circuit Court, P.O. Box 289, Abingdon, VA 24212. 540-676-6226; Fax 540-676-6218.
Will search UCC records. Will not search real estate records. **Online Access:** Real Estate, Assessor. Online access to Town of Abington property information is available free on the GIS mapping site at www.webgis.net/abingdon. **Other Phone Numbers:** Assessor 540-676-6270; Treasurer 540-676-6272.

Waynesboro City

Clerk of Circuit Court, P.O. Box 910, Waynesboro, VA 22980. 540-942-6616.
Will search UCC records. This agency will not do a tax lien search. Will not search real estate records. **Other Phone Numbers:** Assessor 540-942-6621 or 5513; Treasurer 540-942-6606.

Westmoreland County

Clerk of Circuit Court, P.O. Box 307, Montross, VA 22520. 804-493-0108.
Will not search UCC records. This agency will not do a tax lien search. Will not search real estate records. **Other Phone Numbers:** Assessor 804-493-0113; Treasurer 804-493-0124.

Winchester City

Clerk of Circuit Court, 5 N. Kent Street, Winchester, VA 22601. Clerk of Circuit Court, R/E and UCC Recording 540-667-5770; Fax 540-667-6638. http://www.winfredclerk.com
Will not search UCC records. This agency will not do a tax lien search. Will not search real estate records. **Other Phone Numbers:** Assessor 540-667-1815.

Wise County

Clerk of Circuit Court, P.O. Box 1248, Wise, VA 24293. 540-328-6111; Fax 540-328-0039. http://www.courtbar.org

Will not search UCC records. Will not search real estate records. **Online Access:** Assessor, Real Estate, Liens, Probate, Marriage Records. Includes City of Norton. Premium User fee is $395 annually or $39 per month. Genealogists have two plans: the 150-year marriage and probate database is $99 annually or $10 per month. Database index and images include the Court's orders, land documents from 1970 including links to real estate tax assessments, fifty-year real estate transfer histories, tax maps, plat maps, delinquent taxes, and permit images. Probate and marriage records, with recent document images from probate. Access the judgment lien index for the past 20 years; UCC-1 indices for the past five years. Also, property information is available free at http://arcims.webgis.net/webgis/wise. **Other Phone Numbers:** Assessor 540-328-3556; Treasurer 540-328-3666.

Wythe County

Clerk of Circuit Court, 225 South Fourth Street, Room 105, Wytheville, VA 24382. Clerk of Circuit Court, R/E and UCC Recording 540-223-6050; Fax 540-223-6057.

Will search UCC records. Will not search real estate records. **Online Access:** Real Estate. Online access to property information is available at the gis mapping site at http://arcims.webgis.net/webgis/wythe. No name searching at this time. **Other Phone Numbers:** Assessor 540-223-6015; Treasurer 540-223-6070; Appraiser/Auditor 540-223-6015; Elections 540-223-6038.

York County

Clerk of Circuit Court, P.O. Box 371, Yorktown, VA 23690. 757-890-3350; Fax 757-890-3364. http://www.yorkcounty.gov/circuitcourt

Will search UCC records. Will not search real estate records. **Online Access:** Property Records. Property records from the County GIS site are available free online at http://206.246.204.37. **Other Phone Numbers:** Assessor 757-890-3270; Treasurer 757-890-3420.

Virginia County Locator

You will usually be able to find the city name in the City/County Cross Reference below. In that case, it is a simple matter to determine the county from the cross reference. However, only the official US Postal Service city names are included in this index. There are an additional 40,000 place names that people use in their addresses. Therefore, we have also included a ZIP/City Cross Reference immediately following the City/County Cross Reference.

If you know the ZIP Code but the city name does not appear in the City/County Cross Reference index, look up the ZIP Code in the ZIP/City Cross Reference, find the city name, then look up the city name in the City/County Cross Reference. For example, you want to know the county for an address of Menands, NY 12204. There is no "Menands" in the City/County Cross Reference. The ZIP/City Cross Reference shows that ZIP Codes 12201-12288 are for the city of Albany. Looking back in the City/County Cross Reference, Albany is in Albany County.

City/County Cross Reference

ABINGDON Washington
ACCOMAC Accomack
ACHILLES Gloucester
AFTON (22920) Nelson(67), Albemarle(33)
ALBERTA Brunswick
ALDIE Loudoun
ALEXANDRIA (22302) Alexandria City(95), Fairfax(5)
ALEXANDRIA (22311) Alexandria City(92), Fairfax(8)
ALEXANDRIA (22312) Fairfax(76), Alexandria City(24)
ALEXANDRIA Alexandria City
ALEXANDRIA Fairfax
ALFONSO Lancaster
ALTAVISTA Campbell
ALTON Halifax
AMELIA COURT HOUSE Amelia
AMHERST (24521) Amherst(99), Nelson(1)
AMISSVILLE (20106) Culpeper(61), Rappahannock(35), Fauquier(4)
AMISSVILLE Rappahannock
AMMON Dinwiddie
AMONATE Tazewell
ANDERSONVILLE Buckingham
ANDOVER Wise
ANNANDALE Fairfax
APPALACHIA Wise
APPOMATTOX (24522) Appomattox(97), Buckingham(2), Charlotte(1)
ARARAT Patrick
ARCOLA Loudoun
ARK Gloucester
ARLINGTON Arlington
ARODA Madison
ARRINGTON (22922) Nelson(95), Amherst(5)
ARVONIA Buckingham
ASHBURN Loudoun
ASHLAND Hanover
ASSAWOMAN Accomack
ATKINS Smyth
ATLANTIC Accomack
AUGUSTA SPRINGS Augusta
AUSTINVILLE (24312) Carroll(61), Wythe(39)
AXTON (24054) Pittsylvania(52), Henry(48)
AYLETT King William
BACOVA Bath
BANCO Madison
BANDY Tazewell
BANK AMERICARD Roanoke City
BARBOURSVILLE (22923) Orange(53), Albemarle(24), Greene(24)
BARHAMSVILLE New Kent
BARREN SPRINGS (24313) Wythe(90), Pulaski(10)
BASKERVILLE Mecklenburg
BASSETT (24055) Henry(96), Franklin(4)
BASTIAN (24314) Bland(91), Tazewell(9)
BASYE Shenandoah
BATESVILLE Albemarle
BATTERY PARK Isle of Wight

BAVON Mathews
BEALETON Fauquier
BEAUMONT Goochland
BEAVERDAM (23015) Hanover(81), Caroline(10), Spotsylvania(8)
BEAVERLETT Mathews
BEDFORD (24523) Bedford(76), Bedford City(24)
BEE Dickenson
BELLAMY Gloucester
BELLE HAVEN Accomack
BELSPRING Pulaski
BEN HUR Lee
BENA Gloucester
BENT MOUNTAIN Roanoke
BENTONVILLE (22610) Warren(98), Page(2)
BERGTON Rockingham
BERRYVILLE Clarke
BIG ISLAND Bedford
BIG ROCK Buchanan
BIG STONE GAP (24219) Wise(98), Lee(2)
BIRCHLEAF Dickenson
BIRDSNEST Northampton
BISHOP Tazewell
BLACKSBURG Montgomery
BLACKSTONE (23824) Nottoway(93), Brunswick(6)
BLACKWATER (24221) Lee(64), Scott(36)
BLAIRS Pittsylvania
BLAKES Mathews
BLAND Bland
BLOXOM Accomack
BLUE GRASS Highland
BLUE RIDGE (24064) Botetourt(52), Bedford(48)
BLUEFIELD Tazewell
BLUEMONT (20135) Loudoun(94), Clarke(6)
BLUEMONT Loudoun
BOHANNON Mathews
BOISSEVAIN Tazewell
BOONES MILL (24065) Franklin(81), Roanoke(19)
BOSTON (22713) Culpeper(87), Rappahannock(13)
BOWLING GREEN Caroline
BOYCE Clarke
BOYDTON Mecklenburg
BOYKINS Southampton
BRACEY (23919) Mecklenburg(93), Brunswick(7)
BRANCHVILLE Southampton
BRANDY STATION Culpeper
BREAKS Dickenson
BREMO BLUFF Fluvanna
BRIDGEWATER (22812) Rockingham(79), Augusta(21)
BRIGHTWOOD Madison
BRISTOL (24202) Washington(92), Bristol City(5), Scott(3)
BRISTOL Bristol City
BRISTOW Prince William

BROAD RUN (20137) Fauquier(82), Prince William(18)
BROAD RUN Fauquier
BROADFORD (24316) Smyth(50), Tazewell(50)
BROADWAY (22815) Rockingham(96), Shenandoah(4)
BRODNAX (23920) Brunswick(81), Mecklenburg(19)
BROOKE Stafford
BROOKNEAL (24528) Campbell(94), Charlotte(6)
BROWNSBURG Rockbridge
BRUCETOWN Frederick
BRUINGTON King and Queen
BUCHANAN Botetourt
BUCKINGHAM Buckingham
BUENA VISTA (24416) Buena Vista City(79), Rockbridge(21)
BUFFALO JUNCTION (99999) Mecklenburg(99), Halifax(1)
BUMPASS (23024) Louisa(81), Spotsylvania(17), Hanover(3)
BURGESS Northumberland
BURKE Fairfax
BURKES GARDEN Tazewell
BURKEVILLE (23922) Nottoway(94), Prince Edward(7)
BURR HILL Orange
CALLANDS (24530) Pittsylvania(99), Henry(1)
CALLAO Northumberland
CALLAWAY Franklin
CALVERTON Fauquier
CANA Carroll
CAPE CHARLES Northampton
CAPEVILLE Northampton
CAPRON Southampton
CARDINAL Mathews
CARET (22436) Essex(97), Caroline(3)
CARROLLTON Isle of Wight
CARRSVILLE Isle of Wight
CARSON (23830) Prince George(57), Dinwiddie(29), Sussex(14)
CARTERSVILLE Cumberland
CASANOVA Fauquier
CASCADE Pittsylvania
CASTLETON (22716) Rappahannock(96), Culpeper(4)
CASTLEWOOD Russell
CATAWBA (24070) Roanoke(72), Montgomery(27), Craig(1)
CATHARPIN Prince William
CATLETT Fauquier
CAUTHORNVILLE King and Queen
CEDAR BLUFF (24609) Russell(94), Tazewell(6)
CENTER CROSS Essex
CENTREVILLE Fairfax
CERES (24318) Smyth(72), Bland(28)
CHAMPLAIN (22438) Essex(84), Caroline(16)
CHANCE Essex

CHANTILLY Fairfax
CHANTILLY Loudoun
CHARLES CITY Charles City
CHARLOTTE COURT HOUSE (23923) Charlotte(93), Prince Edward(7)
CHARLOTTESVILLE (22901) Albemarle(82), Charlottesville City(18)
CHARLOTTESVILLE (22902) Charlottesville City(64), Albemarle(36)
CHARLOTTESVILLE (22903) Charlottesville City(67), Albemarle(33)
CHARLOTTESVILLE (22906) Charlottesville City(99), Albemarle(1)
CHARLOTTESVILLE Albemarle
CHARLOTTESVILLE Charlottesville City
CHASE CITY (23924) Mecklenburg(98), Charlotte(1)
CHATHAM Pittsylvania
CHECK Floyd
CHERITON Northampton
CHESAPEAKE Chesapeake City
CHESTER Chesterfield
CHESTER GAP Rappahannock
CHESTERFIELD Chesterfield
CHILHOWIE (24319) Smyth(77), Washington(23)
CHINCOTEAGUE Accomack
CHRISTCHURCH Middlesex
CHRISTIANSBURG Montgomery
CHURCH ROAD (23833) Dinwiddie(91), Amelia(9)
CHURCH VIEW Middlesex
CHURCHVILLE Augusta
CITY OFFICES Roanoke City
CLAREMONT Surry
CLARKSVILLE Mecklenburg
CLAUDVILLE Patrick
CLEAR BROOK Frederick
CLEVELAND (24225) Russell(96), Dickenson(4)
CLIFFORD Amherst
CLIFTON Fairfax
CLIFTON FORGE (24422) Clifton Forge City(64), Alleghany(36)
CLINCHBURG Washington
CLINCHCO Dickenson
CLINTWOOD Dickenson
CLOVER Halifax
CLOVERDALE Botetourt
CLUSTER SPRINGS Halifax
COBBS CREEK Mathews
COBHAM Albemarle
COEBURN (24230) Wise(92), Dickenson(7), Scott(1)
COLEMAN FALLS Bedford
COLES POINT Westmoreland
COLLINSVILLE Henry
COLOGNE King and Queen
COLONIAL BEACH Westmoreland
COLONIAL HEIGHTS (23834) Colonial Heights City(66), Chesterfield(34)
COLUMBIA (23038) Goochland(63), Cumberland(29), Fluvanna(7)

CONCORD (24538) Campbell(83), Appomattox(17)
COPPER HILL (24079) Floyd(92), Franklin(4), Roanoke(3)
CORBIN Caroline
COURTLAND (23837) Southampton(97), Sussex(3)
COVESVILLE Albemarle
COVINGTON (24426) Alleghany(59), Covington City(41)
CRADDOCKVILLE Accomack
CRAIGSVILLE Augusta
CREWE Nottoway
CRIDERS Rockingham
CRIMORA Augusta
CRIPPLE CREEK Wythe
CRITZ Patrick
CROCKETT Wythe
CROSS JUNCTION Frederick
CROZET Albemarle
CROZIER Goochland
CRYSTAL HILL Halifax
CULLEN (23934) Prince Edward(53), Charlotte(47)
CULPEPER Culpeper
CUMBERLAND (23040) Cumberland(93), Buckingham(7)
DABNEYS Louisa
DAHLGREN King George
DALEVILLE Botetourt
DAMASCUS Washington
DANTE (24237) Dickenson(68), Russell(32)
DANVILLE (24540) Danville City(59), Pittsylvania(42)
DANVILLE (24541) Danville City(72), Pittsylvania(28)
DANVILLE Danville City
DARLINGTN HTS Prince Edward
DAVENPORT Buchanan
DAVIS WHARF Accomack
DAYTON Rockingham
DEERFIELD Augusta
DELAPLANE Fauquier
DELTAVILLE Middlesex
DENDRON Surry
DEWITT Dinwiddie
DIGGS Mathews
DILLWYN (23936) Buckingham(97), Cumberland(3)
DINWIDDIE Dinwiddie
DISPUTANTA (23842) Prince George(96), Sussex(4)
DOE HILL Highland
DOGUE King George
DOLPHIN Brunswick
DORAN Tazewell
DOSWELL (23047) Hanover(78), Caroline(22)
DRAKES BRANCH (23937) Charlotte(90), Lunenburg(10)
DRAPER (24324) Pulaski(95), Wythe(5)
DREWRYVILLE Southampton
DRY FORK Pittsylvania
DRYDEN Lee
DUBLIN Pulaski
DUFFIELD (24244) Scott(84), Lee(16)
DUGSPUR Carroll
DULLES Loudoun
DUMFRIES Prince William
DUNDAS (23938) Brunswick(87), Lunenburg(13)
DUNGANNON Scott
DUNN LORING Fairfax
DUNNSVILLE Essex
DUTTON (23050) Gloucester(53), Mathews(47)
DYKE (22935) Greene(65), Albemarle(35)
EAGLE ROCK (24085) Botetourt(95), Alleghany(5)
EARLYSVILLE Albemarle
EAST STONE GAP Wise

EASTVILLE Northampton
EBONY Brunswick
EDINBURG Shenandoah
EDWARDSVILLE Northumberland
EGGLESTON Giles
ELBERON Surry
ELK CREEK Grayson
ELKTON (22827) Rockingham(86), Page(14)
ELKWOOD Culpeper
ELLISTON (24087) Montgomery(93), Roanoke(7)
EMORY Washington
EMPORIA (23847) Greensville(70), Emporia City(26), Southampton(3), Sussex(2)
ESMONT Albemarle
ETLAN Madison
EVERGREEN Appomattox
EVINGTON (24550) Campbell(90), Bedford(10)
EWING Lee
EXETER Wise
EXMORE Northampton
FABER (22938) Nelson(96), Albemarle(4)
FAIRFAX (22030) Fairfax City(50), Fairfax(50)
FAIRFAX (22031) Fairfax(96), Fairfax City(4)
FAIRFAX (22032) Fairfax(96), Fairfax City(4)
FAIRFAX Fairfax
FAIRFAX Fairfax City
FAIRFAX STATION Fairfax
FAIRFIELD Rockbridge
FALLS CHURCH (22042) Fairfax(98), Falls Church City(2)
FALLS CHURCH (22044) Fairfax(96), Falls Church City(4)
FALLS CHURCH (22046) Falls Church City(70), Fairfax(31)
FALLS CHURCH Fairfax
FALLS CHURCH Falls Church City
FALLS MILLS Tazewell
FANCY GAP Carroll
FARMVILLE (23901) Prince Edward(73), Cumberland(24), Buckingham(2)
FARMVILLE Prince Edward
FARNHAM Richmond
FERRUM (24088) Franklin(97), Patrick(3)
FIELDALE Henry
FIFE Goochland
FINCASTLE Botetourt
FISHERS HILL Shenandoah
FISHERSVILLE Augusta
FLINT HILL Rappahannock
FLOYD Floyd
FONESWOOD Richmond
FORD (23850) Dinwiddie(86), Amelia(14)
FOREST (24551) Bedford(87), Campbell(13)
FORK UNION Fluvanna
FORT BELVOIR Fairfax
FORT BLACKMORE Scott
FORT DEFIANCE Augusta
FORT EUSTIS Newport News City
FORT LEE (23801) Prince George(97), Petersburg City(3)
FORT MITCHELL Lunenburg
FORT MONROE Hampton City
FORT VALLEY Shenandoah
FOSTER Mathews
FRANKLIN (23851) Franklin City(46), Southampton(46), Isle of Wight(8)
FRANKTOWN Northampton
FREDERICKSBURG (22401) Fredericksburg City(97), Spotsylvania(3)
FREDERICKSBURG (22407) Spotsylvania(97), Fredericksburg City(2)
FREDERICKSBURG (22408) Spotsylvania(94), Caroline(3), Fredericksburg City(2)

FREDERICKSBURG Fredericksburg City
FREDERICKSBURG Stafford
FREE UNION (22940) Albemarle(80), Greene(20)
FREEMAN (23856) Brunswick(96), Greensville(4)
FRIES (24330) Grayson(93), Carroll(7)
FRONT ROYAL Warren
FT MYER Arlington
FULKS RUN Rockingham
GAINESVILLE (20155) Prince William(96), Fauquier(4)
GAINESVILLE Prince William
GALAX (24333) Grayson(51), Galax City(38), Carroll(11)
GARRISONVILLE Stafford
GASBURG Brunswick
GATE CITY Scott
GLADE SPRING Washington
GLADEHILL Franklin
GLADSTONE (24553) Nelson(71), Appomattox(12), Buckingham(10), Amherst(7)
GLADYS Campbell
GLASGOW Rockbridge
GLEN ALLEN Hanover
GLEN ALLEN Henrico
GLEN LYN Giles
GLEN WILTON Botetourt
GLOUCESTER Gloucester
GLOUCESTER POINT Gloucester
GOLDBOND Giles
GOLDVEIN Fauquier
GOOCHLAND Goochland
GOODE Bedford
GOODVIEW Bedford
GORDONSVILLE (22942) Orange(67), Louisa(30), Albemarle(3)
GORE Frederick
GOSHEN (24439) Rockbridge(91), Augusta(9)
GRAVES MILL Madison
GREAT AMERICAN MAGAZINE Hampton City
GREAT FALLS (22066) Fairfax(97), Loudoun(3)
GREEN BAY (23942) Prince Edward(73), Lunenburg(27)
GREENBACKVILLE Accomack
GREENBUSH Accomack
GREENVILLE Augusta
GREENWAY Fairfax
GREENWOOD Albemarle
GRETNA Pittsylvania
GRIMSTEAD Mathews
GROTTOES (24441) Rockingham(74), Augusta(26)
GRUNDY Buchanan
GUM SPRING (23065) Goochland(75), Louisa(25)
GWYNN Mathews
HACKSNECK Accomack
HADENSVILLE Goochland
HAGUE Westmoreland
HALIFAX Halifax
HALLIEFORD Mathews
HALLWOOD Accomack
HAMILTON Loudoun
HAMPDEN SYDNEY Prince Edward
HAMPTON (23665) York(51), Hampton City(49)
HAMPTON Hampton City
HANDSOM Southampton
HANOVER (23069) Hanover(43), Caroline(38), King William(19)
HARBORTON Accomack
HARDY (24101) Franklin(91), Bedford(8), Roanoke(1)
HARDYVILLE Middlesex
HARMAN Buchanan
HARRISONBURG (22801) Harrisonburg City(83), Rockingham(17)

HARRISONBURG Harrisonburg City
HARRISONBURG Rockingham
HARTFIELD Middlesex
HARTWOOD Stafford
HAYES Gloucester
HAYMARKET Prince William
HAYNESVILLE Richmond
HAYSI (24256) Dickenson(88), Buchanan(12)
HAYWOOD Madison
HEAD WATERS Highland
HEATHSVILLE Northumberland
HENRY (24102) Franklin(91), Henry(9)
HERNDON Fairfax
HIGHLAND SPRINGS Henrico
HIGHTOWN Highland
HILLSVILLE (99999) Carroll(99), Wythe(1)
HILTONS (24258) Scott(97), Washington(3)
HINTON Rockingham
HIWASSEE (24347) Pulaski(88), Montgomery(11), Carroll(1)
HONAKER (24260) Russell(88), Buchanan(12)
HOOD Madison
HOPEWELL (23860) Hopewell City(75), Prince George(25)
HORNTOWN Accomack
HORSEPEN Tazewell
HOT SPRINGS (24445) Bath(59), Alleghany(42)
HOWARDSVILLE (24562) Albemarle(62), Buckingham(38)
HUDDLESTON Bedford
HUDGINS Mathews
HUME Fauquier
HUNTLY Rappahannock
HURLEY Buchanan
HURT Pittsylvania
HUSTLE Essex
HYACINTH Northumberland
INDEPENDENCE Grayson
INDIAN VALLEY (24105) Floyd(97), Carroll(3)
IRON GATE Alleghany
IRVINGTON Lancaster
ISLE OF WIGHT Isle of Wight
IVANHOE (24350) Wythe(71), Carroll(24), Grayson(5)
IVOR (23866) Southampton(54), Isle of Wight(46)
IVY Albemarle
JAMAICA Middlesex
JAMES STORE Gloucester
JAMESTOWN James City
JAMESVILLE Northampton
JARRATT (23867) Greensville(93), Sussex(8)
JARRATT Greensville
JAVA (24565) Pittsylvania(87), Halifax(13)
JEFFERSONTON Culpeper
JENKINS BRIDGE Accomack
JERSEY King George
JETERSVILLE (23083) Amelia(99), Nottoway(1)
JEWELL RIDGE (24622) Tazewell(64), Buchanan(36)
JONESVILLE Lee
JORDAN MINES Alleghany
KEELING Pittsylvania
KEEN MOUNTAIN Buchanan
KEENE Albemarle
KEEZLETOWN Rockingham
KELLER Accomack
KENBRIDGE Lunenburg
KENTS STORE (23084) Goochland(46), Louisa(30), Fluvanna(24)
KEOKEE Lee
KESWICK (22947) Albemarle(97), Louisa(2)
KEYSVILLE (23947) Charlotte(52), Lunenburg(39), Prince Edward(10)

KILMARNOCK (22482)
  Northumberland(54), Lancaster(46)
KING AND QUEEN COURT HOUS King
  and Queen
KING GEORGE King George
KING WILLIAM King William
KINSALE Westmoreland
LA CROSSE (23950) Mecklenburg(89),
  Brunswick(11)
LACEY SPRING Rockingham
LACKEY York
LADYSMITH Caroline
LAHORE Orange
LAMBSBURG Carroll
LANCASTER Lancaster
LANEVIEW (22504) Essex(88),
  Middlesex(12)
LANEXA (23089) New Kent(75), James
  City(25)
LAUREL FORK (24352) Carroll(95),
  Floyd(5)
LAWRENCEVILLE Brunswick
LEBANON Russell
LEE MONT Accomack
LEESBURG Loudoun
LEON Madison
LEWISETTA Northumberland
LEXINGTON (24450) Rockbridge(61),
  Lexington City(39)
LIGHTFOOT York
LIGNUM Culpeper
LINCOLN Loudoun
LINDEN (22642) Warren(85), Fauquier(15)
LINVILLE Rockingham
LITTLE PLYMOUTH King and Queen
LIVELY Lancaster
LOCUST DALE Madison
LOCUST GROVE (22508) Orange(87),
  Spotsylvania(13)
LOCUST HILL Middlesex
LOCUSTVILLE Accomack
LONG ISLAND (24569) Pittsylvania(90),
  Halifax(8), Campbell(3)
LORETTO Essex
LORTON Fairfax
LOTTSBURG Northumberland
LOUISA (23093) Louisa(93), Goochland(6)
LOVETTSVILLE Loudoun
LOVINGSTON Nelson
LOW MOOR Alleghany
LOWRY Bedford
LUNENBURG Lunenburg
LURAY Page
LYNCH STATION (24571) Campbell(93),
  Bedford(7)
LYNCHBURG (24501) Lynchburg City(92),
  Campbell(8)
LYNCHBURG (24502) Lynchburg City(62),
  Campbell(37), Bedford(1)
LYNCHBURG (24503) Lynchburg City(69),
  Bedford(31)
LYNCHBURG (24504) Lynchburg City(87),
  Campbell(12)
LYNCHBURG Lynchburg City
LYNDHURST (22952) Augusta(98),
  Nelson(2)
MACHIPONGO Northampton
MACON Powhatan
MADISON Madison
MADISON HEIGHTS Amherst
MADISON MILLS Madison
MAIDENS (23102) Goochland(79),
  Louisa(14), Hanover(7)
MANAKIN SABOT Goochland
MANASSAS (20109) Prince William(90),
  Manassas City(10)
MANASSAS (20110) Manassas City(83),
  Prince William(17)
MANASSAS (20111) Prince William(70),
  Manassas Park City(30)
MANASSAS Manassas City
MANASSAS Manassas Park City

MANASSAS Prince William
MANGOHICK King William
MANNBORO Amelia
MANQUIN King William
MAPPSVILLE Accomack
MARION Smyth
MARIONVILLE Northampton
MARKHAM Fauquier
MARSHALL Fauquier
MARTINSVILLE (24112) Henry(56),
  Martinsville City(43), Franklin(1)
MARTINSVILLE Martinsville City
MARYUS Gloucester
MASCOT King and Queen
MASSIES MILL Nelson
MATHEWS Mathews
MATTAPONI King and Queen
MAURERTOWN Shenandoah
MAVISDALE Buchanan
MAX MEADOWS Wythe
MAXIE Buchanan
MC CLURE Dickenson
MC COY Montgomery
MC DOWELL Highland
MC GAHEYSVILLE Rockingham
MC KENNEY Dinwiddie
MC LEAN Fairfax
MEADOWS OF DAN (24120) Patrick(60),
  Floyd(31), Carroll(9)
MEADOWVIEW Washington
MEARS Accomack
MECHANICSVILLE Hanover
MEHERRIN (23954) Prince Edward(65),
  Lunenburg(35)
MELFA Accomack
MENDOTA Washington
MEREDITHVILLE Brunswick
MERRIFIELD Fairfax
MERRY POINT Lancaster
MIDDLEBROOK (24459) Augusta(77),
  Rockbridge(23)
MIDDLEBURG (20117) Loudoun(98),
  Fauquier(2)
MIDDLEBURG Loudoun
MIDDLETOWN (22645) Frederick(59),
  Warren(40)
MIDDLETOWN Warren
MIDLAND Fauquier
MIDLOTHIAN (23113) Chesterfield(97),
  Powhatan(3)
MIDLOTHIAN Chesterfield
MILES Mathews
MILFORD Caroline
MILLBORO Bath
MILLERS TAVERN Essex
MILLWOOD Clarke
MINE RUN Orange
MINERAL (23117) Louisa(85),
  Spotsylvania(9), Goochland(6)
MINT SPRING Augusta
MITCHELLS Culpeper
MOBJACK Mathews
MODEST TOWN Accomack
MOLLUSK Lancaster
MONETA (24121) Bedford(63),
  Franklin(37)
MONROE Amherst
MONTEBELLO Nelson
MONTEREY Highland
MONTPELIER (23192) Hanover(95),
  Louisa(5)
MONTPELIER STATION Orange
MONTROSS Westmoreland
MONTVALE Bedford
MOON Mathews
MORATTICO Lancaster
MOSELEY (23120) Chesterfield(95),
  Powhatan(5)
MOUNT CRAWFORD (22841)
  Rockingham(91), Augusta(10)
MOUNT HOLLY Westmoreland
MOUNT JACKSON Shenandoah

MOUNT SIDNEY Augusta
MOUNT SOLON Augusta
MOUNT VERNON Fairfax
MOUTH OF WILSON Grayson
MUSTOE Highland
NARROWS (24124) Giles(96), Bland(4)
NARUNA Campbell
NASSAWADOX Northampton
NATHALIE Halifax
NATURAL BRIDGE Rockbridge
NATURAL BRIDGE STATION Rockbridge
NAXERA Gloucester
NELLYSFORD Nelson
NELSON Mecklenburg
NELSONIA Accomack
NEW CANTON (23123) Buckingham(94),
  Cumberland(6)
NEW CASTLE Craig
NEW CHURCH Accomack
NEW HOPE Augusta
NEW KENT (23124) New Kent(95),
  Hanover(5)
NEW MARKET (22844) Shenandoah(97),
  Rockingham(3)
NEW POINT Mathews
NEW RIVER Pulaski
NEWBERN Pulaski
NEWINGTON Fairfax
NEWPORT (24128) Giles(79), Craig(15),
  Montgomery(7)
NEWPORT NEWS (23605) Newport News
  City(82), Hampton City(19)
NEWPORT NEWS Newport News City
NEWSOMS Southampton
NEWTOWN King and Queen
NICKELSVILLE (24271) Scott(98),
  Russell(2)
NINDE King George
NOKESVILLE (20181) Prince William(98),
  Fauquier(2)
NOKESVILLE Prince William
NORA Dickenson
NORFOLK (23505) Norfolk City(94),
  Northampton(6)
NORFOLK Norfolk City
NORGE James City
NORTH (23128) Gloucester(68),
  Mathews(32)
NORTH GARDEN Albemarle
NORTH TAZEWELL Tazewell
NORTON (24273) Norton City(91), Wise(9)
NORWOOD Nelson
NOTTOWAY Nottoway
NUTTSVILLE Lancaster
OAK HALL Accomack
OAKPARK Madison
OAKTON Fairfax
OAKWOOD Buchanan
OCCOQUAN Prince William
OILVILLE (23129) Goochland(97),
  Hanover(3)
OLDHAMS Westmoreland
ONANCOCK Accomack
ONEMO Mathews
ONLEY Accomack
OPHELIA Northumberland
ORANGE (22960) Orange(98), Madison(2)
ORDINARY Gloucester
ORISKANY Botetourt
ORKNEY SPRINGS Shenandoah
ORLEAN Fauquier
OYSTER Northampton
PAEONIAN SPRINGS Loudoun
PAINT BANK Craig
PAINTER Accomack
PALMYRA Fluvanna
PAMPLIN (23958) Appomattox(62), Prince
  Edward(28), Charlotte(10)
PARIS (20130) Fauquier(84), Loudoun(16)
PARIS Fauquier
PARKSLEY Accomack
PARROTT Pulaski

PARTLOW Spotsylvania
PATRICK SPRINGS Patrick
PEARISBURG Giles
PEMBROKE Giles
PENHOOK (24137) Franklin(78),
  Pittsylvania(22)
PENN LAIRD Rockingham
PENNINGTON GAP Lee
PETERSBURG (23803) Petersburg
  City(54), Dinwiddie(24), Chesterfield(22)
PETERSBURG (23805) Petersburg
  City(61), Prince George(27),
  Dinwiddie(12)
PETERSBURG Petersburg City
PHENIX Charlotte
PHILOMONT Loudoun
PILGRIMS KNOB Buchanan
PILOT (24138) Floyd(57), Montgomery(43)
PINEY RIVER Nelson
PITTSVILLE Pittsylvania
PLAIN VIEW King and Queen
PLEASANT VALLEY Rockingham
POCAHONTAS Tazewell
POQUOSON Poquoson City
PORT HAYWOOD Mathews
PORT REPUBLIC Rockingham
PORT ROYAL Caroline
PORTSMOUTH Portsmouth City
POUND Wise
POUNDING MILL Tazewell
POWHATAN (23139) Powhatan(99),
  Cumberland(1)
PRATTS Madison
PRINCE GEORGE Prince George
PROSPECT (23960) Prince Edward(99),
  Appomattox(1)
PROVIDENCE FORGE (23140) New
  Kent(56), Charles City(44)
PULASKI Pulaski
PUNGOTEAGUE Accomack
PURCELLVILLE Loudoun
QUANTICO Prince William
QUANTICO Stafford
QUICKSBURG Shenandoah
QUINBY Accomack
QUINQUE Greene
QUINTON New Kent
RADFORD (24141) Radford City(67),
  Pulaski(29), Montgomery(3), Floyd(1)
RADFORD Radford City
RADIANT Madison
RANDOLPH (23962) Charlotte(86),
  Halifax(15)
RAPHINE (24472) Rockbridge(89),
  Augusta(11)
RAPIDAN (22733) Culpeper(51),
  Orange(49)
RAPPAHANNOCK ACADEMY Caroline
RAVEN (24639) Tazewell(68),
  Buchanan(29), Russell(3)
RAWLINGS Brunswick
RECTORTOWN Fauquier
RED ASH Tazewell
RED HOUSE (23963) Charlotte(73),
  Campbell(17), Appomattox(10)
RED OAK (23964) Charlotte(73),
  Mecklenburg(27)
REDART Mathews
REDWOOD Franklin
REEDVILLE Northumberland
REGINA Lancaster
REMINGTON (22734) Fauquier(85),
  Culpeper(15)
REPUBLICAN GROVE Halifax
RESCUE Isle of Wight
RESTON Fairfax
REVA (22735) Culpeper(89), Madison(11)
RHOADESVILLE Orange
RICE (23966) Prince Edward(63),
  Amelia(37)
RICH CREEK Giles
RICHARDSVILLE Culpeper

RICHLANDS Tazewell
RICHMOND (23222) Richmond City(65), Henrico(35)
RICHMOND (23223) Henrico(50), Richmond City(50)
RICHMOND (23224) Richmond City(93), Chesterfield(7)
RICHMOND (23225) Richmond City(86), Chesterfield(14)
RICHMOND (23226) Richmond City(52), Henrico(48)
RICHMOND (23227) Henrico(60), Richmond City(40)
RICHMOND (23230) Henrico(56), Richmond City(45)
RICHMOND (23231) Henrico(83), Richmond City(15), Charles City(3)
RICHMOND (23233) Henrico(94), Goochland(6)
RICHMOND (23234) Chesterfield(59), Richmond City(41)
RICHMOND (23235) Chesterfield(73), Richmond City(28)
RICHMOND Chesterfield
RICHMOND Goochland
RICHMOND Henrico
RICHMOND Richmond City
RIDGEWAY Henry
RILEYVILLE Page
RINER (24149) Montgomery(79), Floyd(21)
RINGGOLD Pittsylvania
RIPPLEMEAD Giles
RIXEYVILLE Culpeper
ROANOKE (24012) Roanoke City(80), Roanoke(17), Botetourt(3)
ROANOKE (24014) Roanoke(51), Roanoke City(50)
ROANOKE (24018) Roanoke(85), Roanoke City(15)
ROANOKE (24019) Roanoke(70), Botetourt(17), Roanoke City(13)
ROANOKE Botetourt
ROANOKE Montgomery
ROANOKE Roanoke
ROANOKE Roanoke City
ROCHELLE Madison
ROCKBRIDGE BATHS Rockbridge
ROCKVILLE (23146) Hanover(75), Goochland(25)
ROCKY GAP Bland
ROCKY MOUNT Franklin
ROLLINS FORK King George
ROSE HILL Lee
ROSEDALE Russell
ROSELAND (22967) Nelson(93), Amherst(7)
ROSELAND Amherst
ROUND HILL Loudoun
ROWE (24646) Buchanan(86), Russell(14)
RUBY Stafford
RUCKERSVILLE (22968) Greene(91), Albemarle(9)
RURAL RETREAT (24368) Wythe(64), Smyth(36)
RUSTBURG Campbell
RUTHER GLEN (22546) Caroline(99), Hanover(1)
RUTHVILLE Charles City
SAINT CHARLES Lee
SAINT PAUL (24283) Wise(96), Russell(3), Dickenson(1)
SAINT STEPHENS CHURCH (23148) King and Queen(89), Essex(11)
SALEM (24153) Salem City(63), Roanoke(37)
SALEM Salem City
SALTVILLE (24370) Smyth(65), Washington(35)

SALUDA (23149) Gloucester(69), Middlesex(27), King and Queen(4)
SANDSTON Henrico
SANDY HOOK Goochland
SANDY LEVEL Pittsylvania
SANFORD Accomack
SAXE Charlotte
SAXIS Accomack
SCHLEY Gloucester
SCHUYLER (22969) Nelson(54), Albemarle(46)
SCOTTSBURG Halifax
SCOTTSVILLE (24590) Albemarle(74), Buckingham(13), Fluvanna(13)
SEAFORD York
SEALSTON King George
SEAVIEW Northampton
SEDLEY (23878) Southampton(98), Sussex(2)
SELMA Alleghany
SEVEN MILE FORD Smyth
SEVERN Gloucester
SHACKLEFORDS King and Queen
SHADOW Mathews
SHARPS Richmond
SHAWSVILLE Montgomery
SHENANDOAH Page
SHILOH King George
SHIPMAN Nelson
SHORTT GAP Buchanan
SINGERS GLEN Rockingham
SKIPPERS (23879) Greensville(92), Sussex(8)
SKIPWITH Mecklenburg
SMITHFIELD Isle of Wight
SOMERSET (22972) Orange(98), Madison(2)
SOMERVILLE Fauquier
SOUTH BOSTON Halifax
SOUTH HILL (23970) Mecklenburg(98), Lunenburg(2)
SPARTA Caroline
SPEEDWELL (24374) Wythe(98), Smyth(2)
SPENCER (24165) Henry(89), Patrick(11)
SPERRYVILLE (22740) Culpeper(72), Rappahannock(26), Madison(3)
SPOTSYLVANIA Spotsylvania
SPOTTSWOOD (24475) Augusta(96), Rockbridge(4)
SPOUT SPRING Appomattox
SPRING GROVE (23881) Prince George(53), Surry(47)
SPRINGFIELD Fairfax
STAFFORD Stafford
STAFFORDSVILLE Giles
STANARDSVILLE Greene
STANLEY Page
STANLEYTOWN Henry
STAR TANNERY (22654) Frederick(75), Shenandoah(25)
STATE FARM Goochland
STAUNTON (24401) Staunton City(75), Augusta(25)
STAUNTON Augusta
STAUNTON Staunton City
STEELES TAVERN Augusta
STEPHENS CITY (22655) Frederick(99), Warren(1)
STEPHENSON Frederick
STERLING Loudoun
STERLING PARK Loudoun
STEVENSBURG Culpeper
STEVENSVILLE King and Queen
STONEGA Wise
STONY CREEK (23882) Sussex(60), Dinwiddie(40)
STRASBURG (22657) Shenandoah(74), Warren(26)

STRASBURG Shenandoah
STRATFORD Westmoreland
STUART Patrick
STUARTS DRAFT Augusta
STUDLEY Hanover
SUFFOLK Suffolk City
SUGAR GROVE Smyth
SUMERDUCK Fauquier
SUPPLY Essex
SURRY Surry
SUSAN Mathews
SUSSEX Sussex
SUTHERLAND Dinwiddie
SUTHERLIN (24594) Pittsylvania(93), Halifax(7)
SWEET BRIAR Amherst
SWOOPE Augusta
SWORDS CREEK Russell
SYRIA Madison
TANGIER Accomack
TANNERSVILLE Tazewell
TAPPAHANNOCK (22560) Essex(97), King and Queen(3)
TASLEY Accomack
TAZEWELL Tazewell
TEMPERANCEVILLE Accomack
THAXTON Bedford
THE PLAINS Fauquier
THORNBURG Spotsylvania
TIMBERVILLE (22853) Rockingham(88), Shenandoah(12)
TOANO James City
TOMS BROOK Shenandoah
TOPPING Middlesex
TOWNSEND Northampton
TRAMMEL Dickenson
TREVILIANS Louisa
TRIANGLE Prince William
TROUT DALE (24378) Grayson(89), Smyth(11)
TROUTVILLE (24175) Botetourt(99), Roanoke(1)
TROY (22974) Fluvanna(47), Louisa(32), Albemarle(20)
TURBEVILLE Halifax
TYRO Nelson
UNION HALL Franklin
UNIONVILLE Orange
UNIVERSITY OF RICHMOND Richmond City
UPPERVILLE (20184) Fauquier(66), Loudoun(34)
UPPERVILLE Fauquier
URBANNA Middlesex
VALENTINES Brunswick
VANSANT Buchanan
VERNON HILL (24597) Halifax(81), Pittsylvania(19)
VERONA Augusta
VESTA Patrick
VESUVIUS (24483) Rockbridge(57), Amherst(23), Nelson(20)
VICTORIA Lunenburg
VIENNA Fairfax
VIEWTOWN (22746) Culpeper(73), Rappahannock(27)
VILLAGE Richmond
VILLAMONT Bedford
VINTON (24179) Roanoke(56), Bedford(44)
VIRGILINA (24598) Halifax(84), Mecklenburg(16)
VIRGINIA BEACH Virginia Beach City
VOLNEY Grayson
WACHAPREAGUE Accomack
WAKE Middlesex
WAKEFIELD (23888) Sussex(51), Southampton(26), Surry(22)

WALKERTON (23177) King and Queen(79), King William(21)
WARDTOWN Northampton
WARE NECK Gloucester
WARFIELD Brunswick
WARM SPRINGS Bath
WARNER Middlesex
WARRENTON Fauquier
WARSAW Richmond
WASHINGTON Rappahannock
WATER VIEW Middlesex
WATERFORD Loudoun
WATTSVILLE Accomack
WAVERLY (23890) Sussex(96), Surry(4)
WAVERLY Sussex
WAYNESBORO (22980) Waynesboro City(82), Augusta(18)
WEBER CITY Scott
WEEMS Lancaster
WEIRWOOD Northampton
WEST AUGUSTA Augusta
WEST MCLEAN Fairfax
WEST POINT (23181) King William(89), New Kent(8), James City(3)
WESTMORELAND Westmoreland
WEYERS CAVE (24486) Augusta(98), Rockingham(2)
WHITE HALL Albemarle
WHITE MARSH Gloucester
WHITE PLAINS Brunswick
WHITE POST (22663) Frederick(71), Clarke(26), Warren(3)
WHITE STONE Lancaster
WHITETOP Grayson
WHITEWOOD Buchanan
WICOMICO Gloucester
WICOMICO CHURCH Northumberland
WILLIAMSBURG (23185) James City(47), York(28), Williamsburg City(23), Charles City(1)
WILLIAMSBURG (23188) James City(72), York(27), Williamsburg City(1)
WILLIAMSBURG Williamsburg City
WILLIAMSVILLE (24487) Bath(63), Highland(38)
WILLIS (24380) Floyd(93), Carroll(7)
WILLIS WHARF Northampton
WILSONS Dinwiddie
WINCHESTER (22601) Winchester City(94), Frederick(7)
WINCHESTER Frederick
WINCHESTER Winchester City
WINDSOR Isle of Wight
WINGINA (24599) Nelson(85), Buckingham(15)
WIRTZ Franklin
WISE Wise
WITHAMS Accomack
WOLFORD Buchanan
WOLFTOWN Madison
WOODBERRY FOREST Madison
WOODBRIDGE Prince William
WOODFORD (22580) Caroline(94), Spotsylvania(6)
WOODLAWN Carroll
WOODS CROSS ROADS Gloucester
WOODSTOCK Shenandoah
WOODVILLE Rappahannock
WOOLWINE Patrick
WYLLIESBURG Charlotte
WYTHEVILLE Wythe
YALE Sussex
YARDS Tazewell
YORKTOWN York
ZACATA Westmoreland
ZANONI Gloucester
ZUNI (23898) Isle of Wight(79), Southampton(21)

ZIP/City Cross Reference

20101-20104	DULLES	22212-22246	ARLINGTON	22610-22610	BENTONVILLE	22827-22827	ELKTON
20105-20105	ALDIE	22301-22336	ALEXANDRIA	22611-22611	BERRYVILLE	22830-22830	FULKS RUN
20106-20106	AMISSVILLE	22401-22412	FREDERICKSBURG	22620-22620	BOYCE	22831-22831	HINTON
20107-20107	ARCOLA	22427-22428	BOWLING GREEN	22622-22622	BRUCETOWN	22832-22832	KEEZLETOWN
20108-20113	MANASSAS	22430-22430	BROOKE	22623-22623	CHESTER GAP	22833-22833	LACEY SPRING
20115-20116	MARSHALL	22432-22432	BURGESS	22624-22624	CLEAR BROOK	22834-22834	LINVILLE
20117-20118	MIDDLEBURG	22433-22433	BURR HILL	22625-22625	CROSS JUNCTION	22835-22835	LURAY
20119-20119	CATLETT	22435-22435	CALLAO	22626-22626	FISHERS HILL	22840-22840	MC GAHEYSVILLE
20120-20122	CENTREVILLE	22436-22436	CARET	22627-22627	FLINT HILL	22841-22841	MOUNT CRAWFORD
20124-20124	CLIFTON	22437-22437	CENTER CROSS	22630-22630	FRONT ROYAL	22842-22842	MOUNT JACKSON
20128-20128	ORLEAN	22438-22438	CHAMPLAIN	22637-22637	GORE	22843-22843	MOUNT SOLON
20129-20129	PAEONIAN SPRINGS	22442-22442	COLES POINT	22638-22638	WINCHESTER	22844-22844	NEW MARKET
20130-20130	PARIS	22443-22443	COLONIAL BEACH	22639-22639	HUME	22845-22845	ORKNEY SPRINGS
20131-20131	PHILOMONT	22446-22446	CORBIN	22640-22640	HUNTLY	22846-22846	PENN LAIRD
20132-20134	PURCELLVILLE	22448-22448	DAHLGREN	22641-22641	STRASBURG	22847-22847	QUICKSBURG
20135-20135	BLUEMONT	22451-22451	DOGUE	22642-22642	LINDEN	22848-22848	PLEASANT VALLEY
20136-20136	BRISTOW	22454-22454	DUNNSVILLE	22643-22643	MARKHAM	22849-22849	SHENANDOAH
20137-20137	BROAD RUN	22456-22456	EDWARDSVILLE	22644-22644	MAURERTOWN	22850-22850	SINGERS GLEN
20138-20138	CALVERTON	22460-22460	FARNHAM	22645-22645	MIDDLETOWN	22851-22851	STANLEY
20139-20139	CASANOVA	22461-22461	FONESWOOD	22646-22646	MILLWOOD	22853-22853	TIMBERVILLE
20140-20140	RECTORTOWN	22463-22463	GARRISONVILLE	22649-22649	MIDDLETOWN	22901-22911	CHARLOTTESVILLE
20141-20142	ROUND HILL	22469-22469	HAGUE	22650-22650	RILEYVILLE	22920-22920	AFTON
20143-20143	CATHARPIN	22471-22471	HARTWOOD	22652-22652	FORT VALLEY	22922-22922	ARRINGTON
20144-20144	DELAPLANE	22472-22472	HAYNESVILLE	22654-22654	STAR TANNERY	22923-22923	BARBOURSVILLE
20146-20149	ASHBURN	22473-22473	HEATHSVILLE	22655-22655	STEPHENS CITY	22924-22924	BATESVILLE
20151-20153	CHANTILLY	22476-22476	HUSTLE	22656-22656	STEPHENSON	22929-22929	COBHAM
20155-20156	GAINESVILLE	22480-22480	IRVINGTON	22657-22657	STRASBURG	22931-22931	COVESVILLE
20158-20159	HAMILTON	22481-22481	JERSEY	22660-22660	TOMS BROOK	22932-22932	CROZET
20160-20160	LINCOLN	22482-22482	KILMARNOCK	22663-22663	WHITE POST	22935-22935	DYKE
20163-20167	STERLING	22485-22485	KING GEORGE	22664-22664	WOODSTOCK	22936-22936	EARLYSVILLE
20168-20169	HAYMARKET	22488-22488	KINSALE	22701-22701	CULPEPER	22937-22937	ESMONT
20170-20172	HERNDON	22501-22501	LADYSMITH	22709-22709	ARODA	22938-22938	FABER
20175-20178	LEESBURG	22503-22503	LANCASTER	22711-22711	BANCO	22939-22939	FISHERSVILLE
20180-20180	LOVETTSVILLE	22504-22504	LANEVIEW	22712-22712	BEALETON	22940-22940	FREE UNION
20181-20182	NOKESVILLE	22507-22507	LIVELY	22713-22713	BOSTON	22942-22942	GORDONSVILLE
20184-20185	UPPERVILLE	22508-22508	LOCUST GROVE	22714-22714	BRANDY STATION	22943-22943	GREENWOOD
20186-20188	WARRENTON	22509-22509	LORETTO	22715-22715	BRIGHTWOOD	22945-22945	IVY
20190-20191	RESTON	22511-22511	LOTTSBURG	22716-22716	CASTLETON	22946-22946	KEENE
20192-20192	HERNDON	22513-22513	MERRY POINT	22718-22718	ELKWOOD	22947-22947	KESWICK
20193-20196	RESTON	22514-22514	MILFORD	22719-22719	ETLAN	22948-22948	LOCUST DALE
20197-20197	WATERFORD	22517-22517	MOLLUSK	22720-22720	GOLDVEIN	22949-22949	LOVINGSTON
20198-20198	THE PLAINS	22520-22520	MONTROSS	22721-22721	GRAVES MILL	22952-22952	LYNDHURST
20199-20199	DULLES	22523-22523	MORATTICO	22722-22722	HAYWOOD	22953-22953	MADISON MILLS
22002-22002	AMISSVILLE	22524-22524	MOUNT HOLLY	22723-22723	HOOD	22954-22954	MASSIES MILL
22003-22003	ANNANDALE	22526-22526	NINDE	22724-22724	JEFFERSONTON	22957-22957	MONTPELIER STATION
22009-22015	BURKE	22528-22528	NUTTSVILLE	22725-22725	LEON	22958-22958	NELLYSFORD
22026-22026	DUMFRIES	22529-22529	OLDHAMS	22726-22726	LIGNUM	22959-22959	NORTH GARDEN
22027-22027	DUNN LORING	22530-22530	OPHELIA	22727-22727	MADISON	22960-22960	ORANGE
22030-22038	FAIRFAX	22534-22534	PARTLOW	22728-22728	MIDLAND	22963-22963	PALMYRA
22039-22039	FAIRFAX STATION	22535-22535	PORT ROYAL	22729-22729	MITCHELLS	22964-22964	PINEY RIVER
22040-22047	FALLS CHURCH	22538-22538	RAPPAHANNOCK	22730-22730	OAKPARK	22965-22965	QUINQUE
22060-22060	FORT BELVOIR		ACADEMY	22731-22731	PRATTS	22967-22967	ROSELAND
22066-22066	GREAT FALLS	22539-22539	REEDVILLE	22732-22732	RADIANT	22968-22968	RUCKERSVILLE
22067-22067	GREENWAY	22542-22542	RHOADESVILLE	22733-22733	RAPIDAN	22969-22969	SCHUYLER
22079-22079	LORTON	22544-22544	ROLLINS FORK	22734-22734	REMINGTON	22971-22971	SHIPMAN
22081-22082	MERRIFIELD	22545-22545	RUBY	22735-22735	REVA	22972-22972	SOMERSET
22092-22092	HERNDON	22546-22546	RUTHER GLEN	22736-22736	RICHARDSVILLE	22973-22973	STANARDSVILLE
22093-22093	ASHBURN	22547-22547	SEALSTON	22737-22737	RIXEYVILLE	22974-22974	TROY
22095-22095	HERNDON	22548-22548	SHARPS	22738-22738	ROCHELLE	22976-22976	TYRO
22096-22096	RESTON	22552-22552	SPARTA	22739-22739	SOMERVILLE	22980-22980	WAYNESBORO
22101-22102	MC LEAN	22553-22553	SPOTSYLVANIA	22740-22740	SPERRYVILLE	22987-22987	WHITE HALL
22103-22103	WEST MCLEAN	22554-22555	STAFFORD	22741-22741	STEVENSBURG	22989-22989	WOODBERRY FOREST
22106-22109	MC LEAN	22558-22558	STRATFORD	22742-22742	SUMERDUCK	23001-23001	ACHILLES
22116-22120	MERRIFIELD	22560-22560	TAPPAHANNOCK	22743-22743	SYRIA	23002-23002	AMELIA COURT HOUSE
22121-22121	MOUNT VERNON	22565-22565	THORNBURG	22746-22746	VIEWTOWN	23003-23003	ARK
22122-22122	NEWINGTON	22567-22567	UNIONVILLE	22747-22747	WASHINGTON	23004-23004	ARVONIA
22124-22124	OAKTON	22568-22568	MINE RUN	22748-22748	WOLFTOWN	23005-23005	ASHLAND
22125-22125	OCCOQUAN	22570-22570	VILLAGE	22749-22749	WOODVILLE	23009-23009	AYLETT
22134-22135	QUANTICO	22572-22572	WARSAW	22801-22807	HARRISONBURG	23011-23011	BARHAMSVILLE
22150-22161	SPRINGFIELD	22576-22576	WEEMS	22810-22810	BASYE	23014-23014	BEAUMONT
22172-22172	TRIANGLE	22577-22577	WESTMORELAND	22811-22811	BERGTON	23015-23015	BEAVERDAM
22180-22185	VIENNA	22578-22578	WHITE STONE	22812-22812	BRIDGEWATER	23017-23017	BELLAMY
22191-22194	WOODBRIDGE	22579-22579	WICOMICO CHURCH	22815-22815	BROADWAY	23018-23018	BENA
22199-22199	LORTON	22580-22580	WOODFORD	22820-22820	CRIDERS	23021-23021	BOHANNON
22201-22210	ARLINGTON	22581-22581	ZACATA	22821-22821	DAYTON	23022-23022	BREMO BLUFF
22211-22211	FT MYER	22601-22604	WINCHESTER	22824-22824	EDINBURG	23023-23023	BRUINGTON

Zip	Place	Zip	Place	Zip	Place	Zip	Place
23024-23024	BUMPASS	23156-23156	SHACKLEFORDS	23480-23480	WACHAPREAGUE	23923-23923	CHARLOTTE COURT
23025-23025	CARDINAL	23160-23160	STATE FARM	23482-23482	WARDTOWN		HOUSE
23027-23027	CARTERSVILLE	23161-23161	STEVENSVILLE	23483-23483	WATTSVILLE	23924-23924	CHASE CITY
23030-23030	CHARLES CITY	23162-23162	STUDLEY	23486-23486	WILLIS WHARF	23927-23927	CLARKSVILLE
23031-23031	CHRISTCHURCH	23163-23163	SUSAN	23487-23487	WINDSOR	23930-23930	CREWE
23032-23032	CHURCH VIEW	23168-23168	TOANO	23488-23488	WITHAMS	23934-23934	CULLEN
23035-23035	COBBS CREEK	23169-23169	TOPPING	23501-23551	NORFOLK	23936-23936	DILLWYN
23038-23038	COLUMBIA	23170-23170	TREVILIANS	23601-23603	NEWPORT NEWS	23937-23937	DRAKES BRANCH
23039-23039	CROZIER	23173-23173	UNIVERSITY OF	23604-23604	FORT EUSTIS	23938-23938	DUNDAS
23040-23040	CUMBERLAND		RICHMOND	23605-23630	NEWPORT NEWS	23939-23939	EVERGREEN
23043-23043	DELTAVILLE	23175-23175	URBANNA	23631-23631	HAMPTON	23941-23941	FORT MITCHELL
23045-23045	DIGGS	23176-23176	WAKE	23651-23651	FORT MONROE	23942-23942	GREEN BAY
23047-23047	DOSWELL	23177-23177	WALKERTON	23653-23661	HAMPTON	23943-23943	HAMPDEN SYDNEY
23050-23050	DUTTON	23178-23178	WARE NECK	23662-23662	POQUOSON	23944-23944	KENBRIDGE
23054-23054	FIFE	23180-23180	WATER VIEW	23663-23681	HAMPTON	23947-23947	KEYSVILLE
23055-23055	FORK UNION	23181-23181	WEST POINT	23690-23693	YORKTOWN	23950-23950	LA CROSSE
23056-23056	FOSTER	23183-23183	WHITE MARSH	23694-23694	LACKEY	23952-23952	LUNENBURG
23058-23060	GLEN ALLEN	23184-23184	WICOMICO	23696-23696	SEAFORD	23954-23954	MEHERRIN
23061-23061	GLOUCESTER	23185-23188	WILLIAMSBURG	23701-23709	PORTSMOUTH	23955-23955	NOTTOWAY
23062-23062	GLOUCESTER POINT	23190-23190	WOODS CROSS ROADS	23801-23801	FORT LEE	23958-23958	PAMPLIN
23063-23063	GOOCHLAND	23191-23191	ZANONI	23803-23806	PETERSBURG	23959-23959	PHENIX
23064-23064	GRIMSTEAD	23192-23192	MONTPELIER	23821-23821	ALBERTA	23960-23960	PROSPECT
23065-23065	GUM SPRING	23218-23298	RICHMOND	23822-23822	AMMON	23962-23962	RANDOLPH
23066-23066	GWYNN	23301-23301	ACCOMAC	23824-23824	BLACKSTONE	23963-23963	RED HOUSE
23067-23067	HADENSVILLE	23302-23302	ASSAWOMAN	23827-23827	BOYKINS	23964-23964	RED OAK
23068-23068	HALLIEFORD	23303-23303	ATLANTIC	23828-23828	BRANCHVILLE	23966-23966	RICE
23069-23069	HANOVER	23304-23304	BATTERY PARK	23829-23829	CAPRON	23967-23967	SAXE
23070-23070	HARDYVILLE	23306-23306	BELLE HAVEN	23830-23830	CARSON	23968-23968	SKIPWITH
23071-23071	HARTFIELD	23307-23307	BIRDSNEST	23831-23831	CHESTER	23970-23970	SOUTH HILL
23072-23072	HAYES	23308-23308	BLOXOM	23832-23832	CHESTERFIELD	23974-23974	VICTORIA
23075-23075	HIGHLAND SPRINGS	23310-23310	CAPE CHARLES	23833-23833	CHURCH ROAD	23976-23976	WYLLIESBURG
23076-23076	HUDGINS	23313-23313	CAPEVILLE	23834-23834	COLONIAL HEIGHTS	24000-24050	ROANOKE
23079-23079	JAMAICA	23314-23314	CARROLLTON	23836-23836	CHESTER	24053-24053	ARARAT
23081-23081	JAMESTOWN	23315-23315	CARRSVILLE	23837-23837	COURTLAND	24054-24054	AXTON
23083-23083	JETERSVILLE	23316-23316	CHERITON	23838-23838	CHESTERFIELD	24055-24055	BASSETT
23084-23084	KENTS STORE	23320-23328	CHESAPEAKE	23839-23839	DENDRON	24058-24058	BELSPRING
23085-23085	KING AND QUEEN	23336-23337	CHINCOTEAGUE	23840-23840	DEWITT	24059-24059	BENT MOUNTAIN
	COURT HOUS	23341-23341	CRADDOCKVILLE	23841-23841	DINWIDDIE	24060-24063	BLACKSBURG
23086-23086	KING WILLIAM	23345-23345	DAVIS WHARF	23842-23842	DISPUTANTA	24064-24064	BLUE RIDGE
23089-23089	LANEXA	23347-23347	EASTVILLE	23843-23843	DOLPHIN	24065-24065	BOONES MILL
23090-23090	LIGHTFOOT	23350-23350	EXMORE	23844-23844	DREWRYVILLE	24066-24066	BUCHANAN
23091-23091	LITTLE PLYMOUTH	23354-23354	FRANKTOWN	23845-23845	EBONY	24067-24067	CALLAWAY
23092-23092	LOCUST HILL	23356-23356	GREENBACKVILLE	23846-23846	ELBERON	24068-24068	CHRISTIANSBURG
23093-23093	LOUISA	23357-23357	GREENBUSH	23847-23847	EMPORIA	24069-24069	CASCADE
23101-23101	MACON	23358-23358	HACKSNECK	23850-23850	FORD	24070-24070	CATAWBA
23102-23102	MAIDENS	23359-23359	HALLWOOD	23851-23851	FRANKLIN	24072-24072	CHECK
23103-23103	MANAKIN SABOT	23389-23389	HARBORTON	23856-23856	FREEMAN	24073-24073	CHRISTIANSBURG
23105-23105	MANNBORO	23395-23395	HORNTOWN	23857-23857	GASBURG	24076-24076	CLAUDVILLE
23106-23106	MANQUIN	23396-23396	OAK HALL	23860-23860	HOPEWELL	24077-24077	CLOVERDALE
23107-23107	MARYUS	23397-23397	ISLE OF WIGHT	23866-23866	IVOR	24078-24078	COLLINSVILLE
23108-23108	MASCOT	23398-23398	JAMESVILLE	23867-23867	JARRATT	24079-24079	COPPER HILL
23109-23109	MATHEWS	23399-23399	JENKINS BRIDGE	23868-23868	LAWRENCEVILLE	24082-24082	CRITZ
23110-23110	MATTAPONI	23401-23401	KELLER	23870-23870	JARRATT	24083-24083	DALEVILLE
23111-23111	MECHANICSVILLE	23404-23404	LOCUSTVILLE	23872-23872	MC KENNEY	24084-24084	DUBLIN
23112-23113	MIDLOTHIAN	23405-23405	MACHIPONGO	23873-23873	MEREDITHVILLE	24085-24085	EAGLE ROCK
23115-23115	MILLERS TAVERN	23407-23407	MAPPSVILLE	23874-23874	NEWSOMS	24086-24086	EGGLESTON
23116-23116	MECHANICSVILLE	23408-23408	MARIONVILLE	23875-23875	PRINCE GEORGE	24087-24087	ELLISTON
23117-23117	MINERAL	23409-23409	MEARS	23876-23876	RAWLINGS	24088-24088	FERRUM
23119-23119	MOON	23410-23410	MELFA	23878-23878	SEDLEY	24089-24089	FIELDALE
23120-23120	MOSELEY	23412-23412	MODEST TOWN	23879-23879	SKIPPERS	24090-24090	FINCASTLE
23123-23123	NEW CANTON	23413-23413	NASSAWADOX	23881-23881	SPRING GROVE	24091-24091	FLOYD
23124-23124	NEW KENT	23414-23414	NELSONIA	23882-23882	STONY CREEK	24092-24092	GLADEHILL
23125-23125	NEW POINT	23415-23415	NEW CHURCH	23883-23883	SURRY	24093-24093	GLEN LYN
23126-23126	NEWTOWN	23416-23416	OAK HALL	23884-23884	SUSSEX	24094-24094	GOLDBOND
23127-23127	NORGE	23417-23417	ONANCOCK	23885-23885	SUTHERLAND	24095-24095	GOODVIEW
23128-23128	NORTH	23418-23418	ONLEY	23887-23887	VALENTINES	24101-24101	HARDY
23129-23129	OILVILLE	23419-23419	OYSTER	23888-23888	WAKEFIELD	24102-24102	HENRY
23130-23130	ONEMO	23420-23420	PAINTER	23889-23889	WARFIELD	24104-24104	HUDDLESTON
23131-23131	ORDINARY	23421-23421	PARKSLEY	23890-23891	WAVERLY	24105-24105	INDIAN VALLEY
23138-23138	PORT HAYWOOD	23422-23422	PUNGOTEAGUE	23893-23893	WHITE PLAINS	24111-24111	MC COY
23139-23139	POWHATAN	23423-23423	QUINBY	23894-23894	WILSONS	24112-24115	MARTINSVILLE
23140-23140	PROVIDENCE FORGE	23424-23424	RESCUE	23897-23897	YALE	24120-24120	MEADOWS OF DAN
23141-23141	QUINTON	23426-23426	SANFORD	23898-23898	ZUNI	24121-24121	MONETA
23146-23146	ROCKVILLE	23427-23427	SAXIS	23899-23899	CLAREMONT	24122-24122	MONTVALE
23147-23147	RUTHVILLE	23429-23429	SEAVIEW	23901-23909	FARMVILLE	24124-24124	NARROWS
23148-23148	SAINT STEPHENS	23430-23431	SMITHFIELD	23911-23911	ANDERSONVILLE	24126-24126	NEWBERN
	CHURCH	23432-23439	SUFFOLK	23915-23915	BASKERVILLE	24127-24127	NEW CASTLE
23149-23149	SALUDA	23440-23440	TANGIER	23917-23917	BOYDTON	24128-24128	NEWPORT
23150-23150	SANDSTON	23441-23441	TASLEY	23919-23919	BRACEY	24129-24129	NEW RIVER
23153-23153	SANDY HOOK	23442-23442	TEMPERANCEVILLE	23920-23920	BRODNAX	24130-24130	ORISKANY
23154-23154	SCHLEY	23443-23443	TOWNSEND	23921-23921	BUCKINGHAM	24131-24131	PAINT BANK
23155-23155	SEVERN	23450-23479	VIRGINIA BEACH	23922-23922	BURKEVILLE	24132-24132	PARROTT

24133-24133	PATRICK SPRINGS	24279-24279	POUND	24433-24433	DOE HILL	24563-24563	HURT
24134-24134	PEARISBURG	24280-24280	ROSEDALE	24435-24435	FAIRFIELD	24565-24565	JAVA
24136-24136	PEMBROKE	24281-24281	ROSE HILL	24437-24437	FORT DEFIANCE	24566-24566	KEELING
24137-24137	PENHOOK	24282-24282	SAINT CHARLES	24438-24438	GLEN WILTON	24569-24569	LONG ISLAND
24138-24138	PILOT	24283-24283	SAINT PAUL	24439-24439	GOSHEN	24570-24570	LOWRY
24139-24139	PITTSVILLE	24285-24285	STONEGA	24440-24440	GREENVILLE	24571-24571	LYNCH STATION
24141-24143	RADFORD	24289-24289	TRAMMEL	24441-24441	GROTTOES	24572-24572	MADISON HEIGHTS
24146-24146	REDWOOD	24290-24290	WEBER CITY	24442-24442	HEAD WATERS	24574-24574	MONROE
24147-24147	RICH CREEK	24292-24292	WHITETOP	24445-24445	HOT SPRINGS	24576-24576	NARUNA
24148-24148	RIDGEWAY	24293-24293	WISE	24448-24448	IRON GATE	24577-24577	NATHALIE
24149-24149	RINER	24301-24301	PULASKI	24450-24450	LEXINGTON	24578-24578	NATURAL BRIDGE
24150-24150	RIPPLEMEAD	24311-24311	ATKINS	24457-24457	LOW MOOR	24579-24579	NATURAL BRIDGE
24151-24151	ROCKY MOUNT	24312-24312	AUSTINVILLE	24458-24458	MC DOWELL		STATION
24153-24157	SALEM	24313-24313	BARREN SPRINGS	24459-24459	MIDDLEBROOK	24580-24580	NELSON
24161-24161	SANDY LEVEL	24314-24314	BASTIAN	24460-24460	MILLBORO	24581-24581	NORWOOD
24162-24162	SHAWSVILLE	24315-24315	BLAND	24463-24463	MINT SPRING	24585-24585	REPUBLICAN GROVE
24165-24165	SPENCER	24316-24316	BROADFORD	24464-24464	MONTEBELLO	24586-24586	RINGGOLD
24167-24167	STAFFORDSVILLE	24317-24317	CANA	24465-24465	MONTEREY	24588-24588	RUSTBURG
24168-24168	STANLEYTOWN	24318-24318	CERES	24467-24467	MOUNT SIDNEY	24589-24589	SCOTTSBURG
24171-24171	STUART	24319-24319	CHILHOWIE	24468-24468	MUSTOE	24590-24590	SCOTTSVILLE
24174-24174	THAXTON	24322-24322	CRIPPLE CREEK	24469-24469	NEW HOPE	24592-24592	SOUTH BOSTON
24175-24175	TROUTVILLE	24323-24323	CROCKETT	24471-24471	PORT REPUBLIC	24593-24593	SPOUT SPRING
24176-24176	UNION HALL	24324-24324	DRAPER	24472-24472	RAPHINE	24594-24594	SUTHERLIN
24177-24177	VESTA	24325-24325	DUGSPUR	24473-24473	ROCKBRIDGE BATHS	24595-24595	SWEET BRIAR
24178-24178	VILLAMONT	24326-24326	ELK CREEK	24474-24474	SELMA	24597-24597	VERNON HILL
24179-24179	VINTON	24327-24327	EMORY	24475-24475	SPOTTSWOOD	24598-24598	VIRGILINA
24184-24184	WIRTZ	24328-24328	FANCY GAP	24476-24476	STEELES TAVERN	24599-24599	WINGINA
24185-24185	WOOLWINE	24330-24330	FRIES	24477-24477	STUARTS DRAFT	24601-24601	AMONATE
24201-24209	BRISTOL	24333-24333	GALAX	24479-24479	SWOOPE	24602-24602	BANDY
24210-24212	ABINGDON	24340-24340	GLADE SPRING	24482-24482	VERONA	24603-24603	BIG ROCK
24215-24215	ANDOVER	24343-24343	HILLSVILLE	24483-24483	VESUVIUS	24604-24604	BISHOP
24216-24216	APPALACHIA	24347-24347	HIWASSEE	24484-24484	WARM SPRINGS	24605-24605	BLUEFIELD
24217-24217	BEE	24348-24348	INDEPENDENCE	24485-24485	WEST AUGUSTA	24606-24606	BOISSEVAIN
24218-24218	BEN HUR	24350-24350	IVANHOE	24486-24486	WEYERS CAVE	24607-24607	BREAKS
24219-24219	BIG STONE GAP	24351-24351	LAMBSBURG	24487-24487	WILLIAMSVILLE	24608-24608	BURKES GARDEN
24220-24220	BIRCHLEAF	24352-24352	LAUREL FORK	24501-24515	LYNCHBURG	24609-24609	CEDAR BLUFF
24221-24221	BLACKWATER	24354-24354	MARION	24517-24517	ALTAVISTA	24612-24612	DORAN
24224-24224	CASTLEWOOD	24360-24360	MAX MEADOWS	24520-24520	ALTON	24613-24613	FALLS MILLS
24225-24225	CLEVELAND	24361-24361	MEADOWVIEW	24521-24521	AMHERST	24614-24614	GRUNDY
24226-24226	CLINCHCO	24363-24363	MOUTH OF WILSON	24522-24522	APPOMATTOX	24618-24618	HARMAN
24228-24228	CLINTWOOD	24366-24366	ROCKY GAP	24523-24523	BEDFORD	24619-24619	HORSEPEN
24230-24230	COEBURN	24368-24368	RURAL RETREAT	24526-24526	BIG ISLAND	24620-24620	HURLEY
24236-24236	DAMASCUS	24370-24370	SALTVILLE	24527-24527	BLAIRS	24622-24622	JEWELL RIDGE
24237-24237	DANTE	24373-24373	SEVEN MILE FORD	24528-24528	BROOKNEAL	24624-24624	KEEN MOUNTAIN
24239-24239	DAVENPORT	24374-24374	SPEEDWELL	24529-24529	BUFFALO JUNCTION	24627-24627	MAVISDALE
24243-24243	DRYDEN	24375-24375	SUGAR GROVE	24530-24530	CALLANDS	24628-24628	MAXIE
24244-24244	DUFFIELD	24377-24377	TANNERSVILLE	24531-24531	CHATHAM	24630-24630	NORTH TAZEWELL
24245-24245	DUNGANNON	24378-24378	TROUT DALE	24533-24533	CLIFFORD	24631-24631	OAKWOOD
24246-24246	EAST STONE GAP	24379-24379	VOLNEY	24534-24534	CLOVER	24634-24634	PILGRIMS KNOB
24248-24248	EWING	24380-24380	WILLIS	24535-24535	CLUSTER SPRINGS	24635-24635	POCAHONTAS
24250-24250	FORT BLACKMORE	24381-24381	WOODLAWN	24536-24536	COLEMAN FALLS	24637-24637	POUNDING MILL
24251-24251	GATE CITY	24382-24382	WYTHEVILLE	24538-24538	CONCORD	24639-24639	RAVEN
24256-24256	HAYSI	24401-24407	STAUNTON	24539-24539	CRYSTAL HILL	24640-24640	RED ASH
24258-24258	HILTONS	24411-24411	AUGUSTA SPRINGS	24540-24544	DANVILLE	24641-24641	RICHLANDS
24260-24260	HONAKER	24412-24412	BACOVA	24549-24549	DRY FORK	24646-24646	ROWE
24263-24263	JONESVILLE	24413-24413	BLUE GRASS	24550-24550	EVINGTON	24647-24647	SHORTT GAP
24265-24265	KEOKEE	24415-24415	BROWNSBURG	24551-24551	FOREST	24649-24649	SWORDS CREEK
24266-24266	LEBANON	24416-24416	BUENA VISTA	24553-24553	GLADSTONE	24651-24651	TAZEWELL
24269-24269	MC CLURE	24421-24421	CHURCHVILLE	24554-24554	GLADYS	24656-24656	VANSANT
24270-24270	MENDOTA	24422-24422	CLIFTON FORGE	24555-24555	GLASGOW	24657-24657	WHITEWOOD
24271-24271	NICKELSVILLE	24426-24426	COVINGTON	24556-24556	GOODE	24658-24658	WOLFORD
24272-24272	NORA	24430-24430	CRAIGSVILLE	24557-24557	GRETNA		
24273-24273	NORTON	24431-24431	CRIMORA	24558-24558	HALIFAX		
24277-24277	PENNINGTON GAP	24432-24432	DEERFIELD	24562-24562	HOWARDSVILLE		

Washington

General Help Numbers:

Governor's Office
PO Box 40002
Olympia, WA 98504-0002
http://www.governor.wa.gov

360-902-4111
Fax 360-753-4110
8AM-5PM

Attorney General's Office
PO Box 40100
Olympia, WA 98504-0100
http://www.wa.gov/ago

360-753-6200
Fax 360-664-0988
8AM-5PM

State Court Administrator
Temple of Justice
PO Box 41174
Olympia, WA 98504-1174
http://www.courts.wa.gov

360-357-2121
Fax 360-357-2127
8AM-5PM

State Archives
State Archives
PO Box 40238
Olympia, WA 98504-0238
http://www.secstate.wa.gov/archives

360-753-5485
Fax 360-664-8814
8:30AM-4:30PM

State Specifics:

Capital: Olympia
                                            Thurston County

Time Zone: PST

Number of Counties: 39

Population: 5,894,121

Web Site: http://access.wa.gov

State Agencies

Criminal Records

Washington State Patrol, Identification Section, PO Box 42633, Olympia, WA 98504-2633 (Courier: 3000 Pacific Ave. SE #204, Olympia, WA 98501); 360-705-5100, 8AM-5PM.

http://www.wa.gov/wsp/wsphome.htm

Indexing & Storage: Records are available from 1974. Criminal history information is retained at the Identification Section until the offender is age seventy, or ten years from the last date of arrest, whichever is longer. New records are available for inquiry immediately. Records are indexed on inhouse computer.

Searching: They will release arrest records without disposition if less than 1 year old. Include the following in your request-date of birth, Social Security Number, sex, race, name and address of subject. You can also submit fingerprints, but it is not required. The following data is not released: non-conviction information.

Access by: mail, online.

Fee & Payment: Prepayment required. Fee payee: Washington State Patrol. Money orders or cashier's checks preferred. Personal checks accepted.

Mail search: Turnaround time: 7 to 10 days. The fee for a name check is $10.00 per individual. For

a fingerprint check, the fee is $25.00 per individual. No self addressed stamped envelope is required.

Online search: The State Court Administrator's office maintains a database of criminal records in their JIS-Link. Records do not include arrests unless case is filed. There is a $100.00 set-up fee and a $25.00 per hour access charge. Call 360-357-2407 for packet. WSP offers access through a system called WATCH, which can be accessed from their web site. The fee is $10.00. The exact DOB and exact spelling of the name is required. Credit cards are accepted for payment. To set up a WATCH account, call (360) 705-5100 or e-mail to criminhis@wsp.gov.

Corporation Records
Trademarks/Servicemarks
Limited Partnerships
Limited Liability Company Records

Secretary of State, Corporations Division, PO Box 40234, Olympia, WA 98504-0234 (Courier: Dolliver Bldg, 801 Capitol Way South, Olympia, WA 98501); 360-753-7115, 360-664-8781 (Fax), 8AM-4PM.

http://www.secstate.wa.gov/corps

Indexing & Storage: Records are available for initial filing documents. Annual reports for the past 5 years are on microfilm.

Searching: All of the information here is public record. Include the following in your request-full name of business, UBI number if available. The copies for a limited partnership are different than corporation documents. Any single document is $1.00 per page plus $.20 per copy.

Access by: mail, phone, in person, online.

Fee & Payment: Directors, Officers list is $4.00 per corporate name. Photocopies fee is $10.00 per document, $20.00 if the document needs to be certified. If file exceeds 100 pages, a surcharge of $13.00 per 50 pages is added. Trademark documents are $.50 per page. Fee payee: Secretary of State. Prepayment required. The state allows ongoing requesters to order from a deposit account. Personal checks accepted. No credit cards accepted.

Mail search: Turnaround time: variable.

Phone search: Information requests are available at this department for limited information. You can also order documents to be mailed to you.

In person search: Turnaround time is while you wait.

Online search: From the Dept of Licensing; subscription is $18 per month, access is $60 per hour plus line charges of $.09-37 per minute. A $200 deposit is required to start. Hours are from 5 AM to 9 PM. Call Darla at 360-664-1530 for more information. A free, non-commercial look-up service is provided at the web site. Information is updated weekly. Also, the Department of Revenue has a non-commercial use site for tax license and registration at http://dov.wa.gov/prd.

Expedited service: Expedited service is available for mail and phone searches. Turnaround time: immediate. Add $20.00 per document.

Trade Names

Master License Service, Business & Professions Div, PO Box 9034, Olympia, WA 98507-9034 (Courier: 405 Black Lake Blvd, Olympia, WA 98507); 360-664-1400, 900-463-6000 (Trade Name Search), 360-753-9668 (Fax), 8AM-5PM.

http://www.wa.gov/dol

Indexing & Storage: Records are available from 1984 (note that everyone re-registered trade names in 1984).

Searching: Searching may be done by business name, business address, owner's name, or UBI number. The following data is not released: Social Security Numbers, personal information (height, weight, sex, eye color, etc.), date of birth or addresses.

Access by: mail, phone, in person, online.

Fee & Payment: The search fee is $4.00, which includes 3 business/owner names. A name variation is considered a separate name. Certification costs an additional $2.00. Fee payee: Washington State Treasurer. Prepayment required. Personal checks accepted. No credit cards accepted.

Mail search: Response time is generally one week.No self addressed stamped envelope is required.

Phone search: The 900 number fee is $4.95 for the first minute and $.50 for each additional minute. Average search is 2 minutes.

In person search: Copies cost $.25 per page. Turnaround time is while you wait.

Online search: This is the same system for corporation and UCC records. A deposit is required (depends on usage), access is $60 per hour plus a $.09-.37 phone charge. Hours are 5 AM to 9 PM daily. Call Field Access at 360-664-1400 to set up a contractual agreement.

Other access: Records can be purchased on cartridges or 9 track tapes. Information includes date of registration, owner name, state ID numbers, and cancel date if cancelled. Call same number and ask for Jody Miller.

Expedited service: Expedited service is available for fax searches. Must have an account with a deposit.

Uniform Commercial Code
Federal Tax Liens

Department of Licensing, UCC Records, PO Box 9660, Olympia, WA 98507-9660 (Courier: 405 Black Lake Blvd, Olympia, WA 98502); 360-664-1530, 360-586-1404 (Fax), 8AM-5PM.

http://www.wa.gov/dol/bpd/uccfront.htm

Note: The state plans to make electronic filing, search and payment options available at the end of 2001.

Indexing & Storage: Records are available from 1967. Records are computerized since 1985. However, only currently active plus 1 full year are accessible.

Searching: Use search request form UCC-11R. The search includes all notices of federal tax liens. State tax liens are filed at the county level. Include the following in your request-debtor name.

Access by: mail, fax, online.

Fee & Payment: A request for information is $18.80. A request for information with copies is $26.57. Use form UCC-11. Fee payee: Department of Licensing. Prepayment required. Credit cards are accepted for fax searching only. Personal checks accepted. Credit cards accepted: MasterCard, Visa.

Mail search: Turnaround time: 7 to 10 days. No self addressed stamped envelope is required.

Fax search: Established accounts may receive fax results, $1.00 each for first 5 pages, $.50 each additional.

Online search: Subscription fee is $18.00 per month. Online access costs $60.00 per hour. There is a deposit of $200 required which is replenished at end of the month. Line charges will vary from $.09 to.37 per minute. Hours are from 5 AM to 9 PM. Call Darla at 360-664-1530 for more information.

Other access: The database may be purchased on magnetic tape or microfilm.

State Tax Liens
Records not maintained by a state level agency.

Note: State tax liens are filed at the county level.

Sales Tax Registrations

Revenue Department, Taxpayer Services, PO Box 47498, Olympia, WA 98504-7478 (Courier: 415 Gen Admin Bldg, Olympia, WA 98501); 360-786-6100, 800-647-7706, 360-664-0456 (Fax), 8AM-5PM.

http://www.dor.wa.gov

Indexing & Storage: Records are available from 1984 and are indexed on microfiche.

Searching: This agency will provide any disclosable information found on the face of the tax application such as business name, address, opening date, DBA, owner type, account status, and SIC code. Include the following in your request-business name. They will also search by tax registration number.

Access by: mail, phone, fax, online.

Mail search: Turnaround time: 5 days. A self addressed stamped envelope is requested. No fee for mail request.

Phone search: No fee for telephone request. Only "public registration" information is available.

Fax search: Turnaround time is 5 days.

Online search: The agency provides a state business records database with free access on the Internet. Lookups are by owner names, DBAs, and tax reporting numbers. Results show a myriad of data.

Birth Certificates

Department of Health, Center for Health Statistics, PO Box 9709, Olympia, WA 98507-9709 (Courier: 1112 S Quince St, 1st Fl, Olympia, WA 98501); 360-236-4300 (Main Number), 360-236-4313 (Credit Card Ordering), 360-352-2586 (Fax), 8AM - 4:30PM.

http://www.doh.wa.gov

Indexing & Storage: Records are available from July 1, 1907 to present. It takes 2-3 months before new records are available for inquiry. Records are indexed on microfiche, inhouse computer.

Searching: The data on the lower portion of form is confidential. Include the following in your request-full name, names of parents, mother's maiden name, date of birth, place of birth. Please specify if father is not listed on birth certificate.

Access by: mail, phone, fax, in person.

Fee & Payment: The search fee is $13.00 per record. Fee payee: Dept of Health. Prepayment required. Personal checks accepted.

Mail search: Turnaround time: 7 to 8 weeks. Must send your current address and daytime phone number with request.A self addressed stamped envelope is requested.

Phone search: You must use a credit card for a $11.00 additional fee. Phone ordering is from 9-12 and 1-4, M-F. next day processing and mail-out.

Fax search: Same criteria as phone searching. Certificate can be returned by fax for an additional $5.00 (non-certified).

In person search: There is no counter service, but there is a drop box. Requests are returned by mail.

Expedited service: Expedited service is available for phone searches. Turnaround time: next working day mail. You must use a credit card for an additional $11.00 fee and courier or Express Mail are additional costs.

Death Records

Department of Health, Vital Records, PO Box 9709, Olympia, WA 98507-9709 (Courier: 1112 S Quince St, 1st Fl, Olympia, WA 98501); 360-236-4300 (Main Number), 360-236-4313 (Credit Card Ordering), 360-352-2586 (Fax), 8 AM - 4:30 PM.

http://www.doh.wa.gov

Indexing & Storage: Records are available from July 1, 1907 to present. It takes 2-6 months before new records are available for inquiry. Records are indexed on microfiche, inhouse computer.

Searching: A written request is required, there is no public viewing. Include the following in your request-full name, date of death, place of death.

Access by: mail, phone, fax, in person.

Fee & Payment: The fee for a certified record in $13.00. Fee payee: Dept of Health. Prepayment required. Personal checks accepted.

Mail search: Turnaround time: 7 to 8 weeks. Must send your current address and daytime phone number with request.A self addressed stamped envelope is requested.

Phone search: You must use a credit card for an additional $11.00 fee. Records are processed the next day. Credit card orders are taken between 9-12 and 1-4.

Fax search: Same criteria as phone searching. Non-certified copies can be returned by fax for $5.00 per page.

In person search: There is no counter service, they have a drop box. Requests are returned by mail.

Expedited service: Expedited service is available for phone and in person searches. Turnaround time: overnight delivery. You must use a credit card for an additional $11.00 fee and courier or Express Mail are additional costs.

Marriage Certificates

Department of Health, Vital Records, PO Box 9709, Olympia, WA 98507-9709 (Courier: 1112 S Quince St, 1st Fl, Olympia, WA 98501); 360-236-4300 (Main Number), 360-236-4313 (Credit Card Ordering), 360-352-2586 (Fax), 8 AM - 4:30 PM.

http://www.doh.wa.gov

Indexing & Storage: Records are available from 1968 to present. It takes 2-4 months before new records are available for inquiry. Records are indexed on microfiche, inhouse computer.

Searching: Written request is required, there is no public viewing. Include the following in your request-names of husband and wife, date of marriage, place or county of marriage.

Access by: mail, phone, fax, in person.

Fee & Payment: The search fee is $13.00. Fee payee: Dept of Health. Prepayment required. Personal checks accepted.

Mail search: Turnaround time: 7 to 8 weeks. Must send your current address and daytime phone number with request.A self addressed stamped envelope is requested.

Phone search: You must use a credit card for an additional $11.00 fee. Turnaround time is next day. Credit card ordering is between 9-12 and 1-4.

Fax search: Same criteria as phone searching. Non-certified records can be returned by fax for an additional $5.00 per record.

In person search: There is no counter service, a drop box is available. Requests are returned by mail.

Expedited service: Expedited service is available for phone and in person searches. Turnaround time: overnight delivery. You must use a credit card for an additional $11.00 fee and courier or Express Mail are additional costs.

Divorce Records

Department of Health, Vital Records, PO Box 9709, Olympia, WA 98507-9709 (Courier: 1112 S Quince St, 1st Fl, Olympia, WA 98501); 360-753-4300 (Main Number), 360-753-4313 (Credit Card Ordering), 360-352-2586 (Fax), 8AM - 4:30PM.

http://www.doh.wa.gov

Indexing & Storage: Records are available from 1968 to present. It takes 2-4 months before new records are available for inquiry. Records are indexed on microfiche, inhouse computer.

Searching: Include the following in your request-names of husband and wife, date of divorce, place of divorce.

Access by: mail, phone, fax, in person.

Fee & Payment: The search fee is $13.00. Fee payee: Dept of Health. Prepayment required. Personal checks accepted.

Mail search: Turnaround time: 5 weeks. Must send your current address and daytime phone number with request.A self addressed stamped envelope is requested.

Phone search: Phone requesters are required to use a credit card for an additional $11.00 fee. The request is processed the next day. Credit card ordering between 9-12 and 1-4.

Fax search: Same criteria as phone searching. Non-certified documents can be returned for an additional $5.00 per record.

In person search: There is no counter service, a drop box is used. All requests are returned by mail.

Expedited service: Expedited service is available for phone and in person searches. Turnaround time: overnight delivery. You must use a credit card for an additional $11.00 fee and courier or Express Mail are additional costs.

Workers' Compensation Records

Labor and Industries, Public Disclosure Unit, PO Box 44285, Olympia, WA 98504-4285 (Courier: 7273 Linderson Way SW, Tumwater, WA 98501); 360-902-4937, 360-902-5529 (Fax), 8AM-5PM.

http://www.wa.gov/LNI

Indexing & Storage: Records are available for the past 3 years. Prior records are at the State Archives, but you must go through this office for those records. It takes 1 month before new records are available for inquiry. Records are indexed on microfiche.

Searching: Must have signed release from the claimant. Written request only. Claims information is not released except as provided under Title 51 of the Revised Code of Washington (RCW). No out-of-state subpoenas are honored. Include the following in your request-claimant name, Social Security Number, claim number. The DOB is helpful. The following data is not released: chemically-related illness.

Access by: mail, in person.

Fee & Payment: Fees depend on extensive of file and search. First $20.00 in duplication fees are free. Fee payee: L & I Cashier. Personal checks accepted. No credit cards accepted.

Mail search: Turnaround time: 2 to 3 days. The record information that they send back is taken from microfiche only. No hard file copies released.

In person search: Must schedule by appointment.

Driver Records

Department of Licensing, Driver Record Section, PO Box 9030, Olympia, WA 98507-9030 (Courier: 1125 Washington Street SE, Olympia, WA 98504); 360-902-3921, 360-902-3900 (General Information), 360-586-9044 (Fax), 8AM-4:30PM.

http://www.wa.gov/dol

Note: Copies of tickets may be requested by the driver or driver's authorized representative. The fee is $.75 per ticket; the first 4 are free.

Indexing & Storage: Records are available for 5 years from conviction date for violations, actions, and accidents. The state offers a 3 year record (primarily for insurance) and a full record (primarily for employment). It takes 2 to 3 weeks or more before new records are available for inquiry.

Searching: All mail or walk-in requests require a signed authorization from the driver, exceptions are for ongoing, pre-approved accounts. Casual requesters cannot obtain records without consent. Either the license number or name and DOB are needed for a request. The license number is based upon a code of the name and DOB. This code can be confusing (O or 0, *'s) so it is suggested you try name and DOB first. The following data is not released: Social Security Numbers.

Access by: mail, in person.

Fee & Payment: The fee is $4.50 per record. Fee payee: Washington State Treasurer. Prepayment required. Personal checks accepted. No credit cards accepted.

Mail search: Turnaround time: 2 weeks. There is no charge for a no record found.A self addressed stamped envelope is requested.

In person search: Turnaround time is immediate for up to 5 requests. There is no charge for a no record found.

Other access: Tape retrieval is offered for high volume requesters.

Vehicle Ownership
Vehicle Identification
Vessel Ownership
Vessel Registration

Department of Licensing, Vehicle Records, PO Box 2957, Olympia, WA 98507-2957 (Courier: 1125 S Washington MS-48001, Olympia, WA

98504); 360-902-3780, 360-902-3827 (Fax), 8AM-5PM.

http://www.wa.gov/dol

Note: It is recommended that on-going, high volume users enter into a disclosure agreement with this agency; contact: Shirley at 360-902-3760.

Indexing & Storage: Records are available for 10 years to present. All motorized boats and sailboats must be titled. All boats must be registered unless under 16 ft with less than a 10 hp motor. It takes 2 to 3 weeks before new records are available for inquiry. Records are indexed on inhouse computer.

Searching: Washington has strict access guidelines that restrict casual requesters. Permitted requesters include attorneys, PI's, insurance companies, and business entities for use in the normal course of business. A special form is required. Include the following in your request-VIN, license plate number. Records cannot be searched by owner or driver name. Requests must be in writing.

Access by: mail, phone, in person, online.

Fee & Payment: The fee for microfilm or microfiche searches is $.75. Fee for photocopy or printouts is $.15 each; no charge under $4.50. There is no charge to "view" a record.

Mail search: Turnaround time: 2 weeks. No self addressed stamped envelope is required.

Phone search: VIPS (Vehicle/Vessel Information Processing System) is a touch-tone ordering available for pre-approved, high volume accounts. The system processes by plate number, VIN, WN# & HIN, and is open 24/7. For more information, call 360-902-3760.

In person search: Searching is available in person.

Online search: This is a commercial subscription service. All accounts must be pre-approved. Access is via the Internet. Known as IVIPS, the system processes the same as the phone search. A $25.00 deposit is required and there is a $.04 fee per hit. For more information, call 360-902-3760.

Other access: Large bulk lists cannot be released for any commercial purposes. Lists are released to non-profit entities and for statistical purposes. For more information, call 360-902-3760.

Accident Reports

State Patrol, Collision Reports, PO Box 42628, Olympia, WA 98504-2628; 360-570-5220, 360-493-9417 (Fax), 8AM-5PM.

http://www.wa.gov/wsp/wsphome.htm

Indexing & Storage: Records are available for 6 years plus the present year. It takes 2 to 3 weeks before new records are available for inquiry.

Searching: Per RCW 46.52.080, the reports are only available to those involved or those who have a "proper interest." Include the following in your request-name, date of accident, location of accident. It is strongly suggested to use their request form - Form 300-345-008. The agency will fax a copy of the form, upon request.

Access by: mail, in person.

Fee & Payment: The fee is $5.00 per record. Fee payee: Washington State Patrol. Prepayment required. Personal checks accepted. No credit cards accepted.

Mail search: Turnaround time: 2 weeks. A self addressed stamped envelope is requested.

In person search: Walk-in requesters may receive the report with proper credentials, if personnel are available to do the search.

Legislation Records

Washington Legislature, State Capitol-Legislative Info Center, PO Box 40600, Olympia, WA 98504-0600; 360-753-5000 (Information), 800-562-6000 (Local Only), 360-786-7573 (Bill Room), 360-786-1293 (Fax), 9AM-5PM.

http://www.leg.wa.gov

Indexing & Storage: Records are available for past 2 years. Records are indexed on microfiche.

Searching: Include the following in your request-bill number, topic of bill, year.

Access by: mail, phone, fax, in person, online.

Fee & Payment: There is no search fee, unless extensive research is required.

Mail search: Turnaround time: 1 to 2 days. There is a limit of one copy per bill.No self addressed stamped envelope is required.

Phone search: Records are available by phone.

Fax search: Turnaround is 1 to 2 days.

In person search: Searching is available in person.

Online search: The web site offers bill text and status look-up.

Other access: There is an array of subscription services available from the legislative Bill Room. Data available includes bill sets, final digest, roll call transcripts, summaries, budget notes, and various reports. Call the Bill Room for a price list.

Voter Registration
Access to Records is Restricted

Secretary of State, Election Division, PO Box 40220, Olympia, WA 98504; 360-902-4152, 360-586-5629 (Fax), 8AM-5PM.

http://www.secstate.wa.gov/elections

Note: All voter information is kept at the local level by the County Auditor (except King County

where records are kept by the Dept of Records and Elections). Individual look-ups will not receive SSNs, DOBs, or telephone numbers.

GED Certificates

State Board for Community & Technical Colleges, GED Records, PO Box 42495, Olympia, WA 98504-2495 (Courier: 319 7th Ave, Olympia, WA 98504); 360-753-6748, 360-664-8808 (Fax), 8AM-5PM.

http://www.sbctc.ctc.edu

Searching: Include the following in your request-name, Social Security Number, date of birth, signed release. Also, the city, date of test, and any previous name the record could be under are helpful.

Access by: mail, fax, in person.

Fee & Payment: There is no fee for either verification or a transcript.

Mail search: Turnaround time: 1 week. No self addressed stamped envelope is required.

Fax search: Same criteria as mail searching.

In person search: Verification is while you wait.

Hunting License Information
Fishing License Information

Department of Fish & Wildlife, Attn: Public Disclosure Officer, 600 Capitol Way, N, Olympia, WA 98501-1091; 360-902-2253, 360-902-2171 (Fax), 8AM-5PM.

http://www.wa.gov/wdfw

Indexing & Storage: Records are available for 3 years. It takes up to 3 months before new records are available for inquiry.

Searching: Records cannot be purchased for commercial list purposes. All requests must be in writing.

Access by: fax, in person, online.

Fee & Payment: There is no fee unless a lengthy list is presented, then $.15 per page. No self addressed stamped envelope is required. No searching by mail.

Fax search: Fax searching available.

In person search: Searching is available in person.

Online search: You may send an e-mail request; check the web site for the exact address.

Other access: The database can be purchased for non-commercial purposes only.

Washington State Licensing Agencies

Licenses Searchable Online

Announcer, Athletic Event (Ring) #27	https://wws2.wa.gov/dol/profquery/
Architect #26	https://wws2.wa.gov/dol/profquery/LicenseeSearch.asp
Athletic Inspector #27	https://wws2.wa.gov/dol/profquery
Athletic Judge/Timekeeper #27	https://wws2.wa.gov/dol/profquery
Athletic Manager #27	https://wws2.wa.gov/dol/profquery
Athletic Physician #27	https://wws2.wa.gov/dol/profquery
Athletic Promoter/Matchmaker #27	https://wws2.wa.gov/dol/profquery
Attorney #23	www.wsba.org/directory/default.htm
Auction Company #27	https://wws2.wa.gov/dol/profquery
Auctioneer #27	https://wws2.wa.gov/dol/profquery
Bail Bond Agent/Agency #15	https://wws2.wa.gov/dol/profquery
Barber #18	https://wws2.wa.gov/dol/profquery
Barber Instructor #18	https://wws2.wa.gov/dol/profquery
Beauty Shop/Salon #18	https://wws2.wa.gov/dol/profquery
Boxer #27	https://wws2.wa.gov/dol/profquery
Bulk Hauler #14	https://wws2.wa.gov/dol/profquery
Cemetery & Funeral-Related Profession #06	https://wws2.wa.gov/dol/profquery
Collection Agency #27	https://wws2.wa.gov/dol/profquery
Contractor, General #12	https://wws2.wa.gov/lni/bbip/contractor.asp
Cosmetologist #18	https://wws2.wa.gov/dol/profquery
Cosmetology Instructor #18	https://wws2.wa.gov/dol/profquery
Cosmetology School #18	https://wws2.wa.gov/dol/profquery
Crematory #06	https://wws2.wa.gov/dol/profquery
Electrical Administrator #12	https://wws2.wa.gov/lni/bbip/contractor.asp
Electrical Contractor #12	https://wws2.wa.gov/lni/bbip/contractor.asp
Electrician #12	https://wws2.wa.gov/lni/bbip/contractor.asp
Embalmer #06	https://wws2.wa.gov/dol/profquery
Employment Agency #27	https://wws2.wa.gov/dol/profquery
Engineer #27	https://wws2.wa.gov/dol/profquery/LicenseeSearch.asp
Esthetician/Esthetician Instructor #18	https://wws2.wa.gov/dol/profquery
Funeral Director #06	https://wws2.wa.gov/dol/profquery
Funeral Establishment #06	https://wws2.wa.gov/dol/profquery
Geologist #14	https://wws2.wa.gov/dol/profquery
Insurance Company #25	www.insurance.wa.gov/tableofcontents/annualreptins.htm
Land Surveyors #27	https://wws2.wa.gov/dol/profquery/LicenseeSearch.asp
Landscape Architect #26	https://wws2.wa.gov/dol/profquery/LicenseeSearch.asp
Limosine Carrier #14	https://wws2.wa.gov/dol/profquery
Liquor Store #19	www.liq.wa.gov/services/storesearch.asp
Manicurist/Manicurist Instructor #18	https://wws2.wa.gov/dol/profquery
Manufactured Home Dealer #14	https://wws2.wa.gov/dol/profquery
Mobile Home/Travel Trailer Dealer #14	https://wws2.wa.gov/dol/profquery
Notary Public #17	https://wws2.wa.gov/dol/profquery/
Optometrist #11	www.odfinder.org/LicSearch.asp
Plumber #12	https://wws2.wa.gov/lni/bbip/contractor.asp
Private Investigative Agency #15	https://wws2.wa.gov/dol/profquery
Private Investigator, Armed/Unarmed #15	https://wws2.wa.gov/dol/profquery
Real Estate Appraiser #16	https://wws2.wa.gov/dol/profquery
Real Estate Broker #16	https://wws2.wa.gov/dol/profquery
Real Estate Sales Occupation #16	https://wws2.wa.gov/dol/profquery
Scrap Processor #14	https://wws2.wa.gov/dol/profquery
Security Guard #15	https://wws2.wa.gov/dol/profquery
Snowmobile Dealer #14	https://wws2.wa.gov/dol/profquery
Surveyor #00	www.wa.gov/dol/bpd/plisls.htm
Tow Truck Operator #14	https://wws2.wa.gov/dol/profquery
Travel Agency #14	https://wws2.wa.gov/dol/profquery
Travel Seller #14	https://wws2.wa.gov/dol/profquery
Vehicle Dealer Manufacturer #14	https://wws2.wa.gov/dol/profquery
Vehicle Dealer, Miscellaneous #14	https://wws2.wa.gov/dol/profquery
Vehicle Transporter #14	https://wws2.wa.gov/dol/profquery
Wrecker #14	https://wws2.wa.gov/dol/profquery
Wrestler #27	https://wws2.wa.gov/dol/profquery

Licensing Quick Finder

Acupuncturist #10	360-586-7759
Alien Bank #07	360-902-8704
Animal Technician #10	360-586-6355
Announcer, Athletic Event (Ring) #27	360-753-3713
Applicator, Commercial #05	877-301-4555
Applicator, Private Commercial #05	877-301-4555
Architect #26	360-664-1388
Athlete, Professional #27	360-753-3713
Athletic Inspector #27	360-753-3713
Athletic Judge/Timekeeper #27	360-753-3713
Athletic Manager #27	360-753-3713
Athletic Physician #27	360-753-3713
Athletic Promoter/Matchmaker #27	360-753-3713
Attorney #23	206-727-8200
Auction Company #27	360-753-4553
Auctioneer #27	360-753-4553
Audiologist #11	360-753-1817
Bail Bond Agent/Agency #15	360-586-4567
Bank #07	360-902-8704
Barber #18	360-586-6387
Barber Instructor #18	360-586-6387
Beauty Shop/Salon #18	360-586-6387
Boiler Inspector #13	360-902-5270
Boxer #27	360-753-3713
Bulk Hauler #14	360-902-3703
Business Opportunity Offering #07	360-902-8760
Cemetery & Funeral-Related Profession #06	360-664-1555
Check Casher/Seller #07	360-902-8703
Chiropractor #10	360-753-0776
Collection Agency #27	360-664-1389
Commodities #07	360-902-8760
Consumer Loan Company #07	360-902-8703
Contractor, General #12	360-902-5226
Cosmetologist #18	360-586-6387
Cosmetology Instructor #18	360-586-6387
Cosmetology School #18	360-586-6387
Counselor #10	360-664-9098
Court Reporter #27	360-753-1061
Credit Union #07	360-902-8701
Crematory #06	360-664-1555
Demonstration & Research Applicator #05	877-301-4555
Dental Hygienist #10	360-586-1867
Dentist #10	360-586-6898
Dietitian #10	360-586-6351
Egg Inspector #04	360-902-1830
Electrical Administrator #12	360-902-5269
Electrical Contractor #12	360-902-5269
Electrician #12	360-902-5269
Embalmer #06	360-664-1555
Emergency Medical Technician #10	360-705-6700
Employment Agency #27	360-664-1389
Engineer #27	360-664-1575
ESA Pathology #20	360-725-6400
Escrow Company/Officers #07	360-902-8703
Esthetician/Esthetician Instructor #18	360-586-6387
Firearms Dealer #15	360-753-2803
Fishing, Commercial #08	360-902-2464
Franchise #07	360-902-8760
Fruit/Vegetable Inspector #04	360-902-1832
Funeral Director #06	360-664-1555
Funeral Establishment #06	360-664-1555
Gaming #24	360-438-7654
Geologist #14	360-902-3703
Grain Inspector/Weigher/Sampler #28	360-753-1484
Health Care Assistant #10	360-753-1230
Hearing Instrument Fitter/Dispenser #11	360-753-1817
Home Health Care Agency #09	360-705-6611
Horse Racing #22	360-459-6462
Hospital #09	360-705-6611
Hypnotherapist #11	360-586-8584
Insurance Agent/Broker #25	360-407-0341
Insurance Broker, Resident/Non-Resident #25	360-407-0341
Insurance Company #25	360-407-0341
Insurance Corporation, Resident #25	360-407-0341
Investment Advisors #07	360-902-8760
Kick Boxer #27	360-753-3713
Land Surveyor #27	360-664-1575
Landscape Architect #26	360-664-1388
Limosine Carrier #14	360-902-3703
Liquor Store #19	360-664-1600
Livestock Brand Recording #03	360-902-1855
Manicurist/Manicurist Instructor #18	360-586-6387
Manufactured Home Dealer #14	360-902-3703
Marriage & Family Therapist #10	360-586-4566
Massage Therapist #11	360-586-6351
Medical Doctor #11	360-753-2287
Mental Health Counselor #10	360-586-8584
Midwife #11	360-664-4218
Mobile Home/Travel Trailer Dealer #14	360-902-3703
Mortgage Broker #07	360-902-8703
Naturopathic Physician #11	360-664-3230
Notary Public #17	360-664-1550
Nurse/Nursing Assistant #11	360-586-1923
Nurse-LPN #11	360-664-4226
Nursing Home #09	360-493-2500
Nursing Home Administrator #11	360-753-3729
Occupational Therapist #11	360-664-8662
Ocularist #11	360-753-3576
Optician #11	360-753-3576
Optometrist #11	360-753-4614
Osteopathic Physician #11	360-586-8438
Pest Control Consultant #05	877-301-4555
Pest Control Operator/Consultant, Public #05	877-301-4555
Pesticide Dealer Manager #05	877-301-4555
Pesticide Operator/Applicator #05	877-301-4555
Pesticide Private Application #05	877-301-4555
Pharmacist #10	360-236-4825
Pharmacy Technician #10	360-236-4825
Physical Therapist #11	360-753-0876
Physician Assistant #11	360-664-3909
Pilot, Marine, Commercial #02	206-515-3904
Plumber #12	360-902-5207
Podiatrist #11	360-586-8438
Private Investigative Agency #15	360-664-9070
Private Investigative Trainer #15	360-664-9070
Private Investigator, Arm/Unarmed #15	360-664-9070
Psychologist #11	360-753-2147
Public Accountant-CPA #01	360-753-2585
Radiologic Technologist #11	360-586-6100
Real Estate Appraiser #16	360-753-1062
Real Estate Broker #16	360-753-2262
Real Estate Sales Occupation #16	360-753-2250
Referee #27	360-753-3713
Respiratory Therapist #11	360-586-8437
Savings & Loan/Savings Bank #07	306-902-8704
School Counselor #20	360-725-6400
School Nurse #20	360-725-6400
School Occupational/Physical Therapist #20	360-725-6400
School Principal/Superintendent #20	360-725-6400
School Program Administrator #20	360-725-6400
School Psychologist/Social Worker #20	360-725-6400
Scrap Processor #14	360-902-3703
Securities Broker/Dealer #07	360-902-8760
Securities Salesperson #07	306-902-8760
Security Guard #15	360-664-9070
Sex Offender Treatment Provider #11	360-753-2147
Snowmobile Dealer #14	360-902-3703
Social Worker #10	360-586-4566
Speech-Language Pathologist #11	360-753-1817
Sport Fishing #08	360-902-2464
Teacher #21	360-753-6773
Tow Truck Operator #14	360-902-3703
Travel Agency #14	360-902-3703
Travel Seller #14	360-902-3703
Trust Company #07	360-902-8704
Vehicle Dealer Mfg. #14	360-902-3703
Vehicle Dealer, Miscellaneous #14	360-902-3703
Vehicle Transporter #14	360-902-3703
Vessel Dealer #14	360-902-3703
Veterinarian #10	360-586-4566
Veterinary Medical Clerk #10	360-586-4566
Weights & Measures #03	360-902-1857
Wrecker #14	360-902-3703
Wrestler #27	360-753-3713
X-ray Technician #11	360-586-6100

Licensing Agency Information

#01 Board of Accountancy, PO Box 9131, Olympia, WA 98507-9131; 360-753-2585, Fax: 360-664-9190. www.cpaboard.wa.gov

#02 Board of Pilotage Commissioners, 2911 2nd Ave, Seattle, WA 98121-1012; 206-515-3904, Fax: 206-515-3969.

#03 Department of Agriculture, 1111 Washington St, Olympia, WA 98504-2560; 360-902-1850, Fax: 360-902-2086.
www.wa.gov/agr

#04 Department of Agriculture, PO Box 42560 (1111 Washington St SE), Olympia, WA 98504-2560; 360-902-1800.
www.wa.gov/agr/food.htm

#05 Department of Agriculture, PO Box 42589, Olympia, WA 98504-2589; 360-902-2010, Fax: 360-902-2093.
www.wa.gov/agr/pmd/index.htm

#06 Department of Licensing, PO Box 9012, Olympia, WA 98507-9012; 360-664-1555, Fax: 360-586-4414. www.wa.gov/dol/bpd

#07 Department of Financial Institutions, PO Box 41200, Olympia, WA 98504-1200; 360-902-8700, Fax: 360-586-5068.
www.wa.gov/dfi

#08 Department of Fish & Wildlife, 600 Capitol Way N, Olympia, WA 98501-1091; 360-902-2253, Fax: 360-902-2171.
www.wa.gov/wdfw

#09 Department of Health, PO Box 47852, Olympia, WA 98504-7852; 360-705-6611, Fax: 360-705-6654. www.wa.gov/health

#10 Department of Health, PO Box 47860, Olympia, WA 98504-7860; 360-586-5846, Fax: 360-586-4359.
www.doh.wa.gov/Topics/topics.htm#Licensing

#11 Department of Health, PO Box 47860 (1112 SE Quince St), Olympia, WA 98504-7860; 360-753-3576, Fax: 360-586-0745.
www.doh.wa.gov

#12 Department of Labor & Industries, PO Box 44000, Olympia, WA 98504-4000; 360-902-5800, Fax: 360-902-5292.
www.lni.wa.gov
Direct web site URL to search for licensees: www.lni.wa.gov/contractors/contractor.asp. You can search online using name, registration number, uniform business identifier number, and city.

#13 Department of Labor & Industries, PO Box 44410, Olympia, WA 98504-4410; 360-902-5270, Fax: 360-902-5292.
www.wa.gov/lni

#14 Department of Licensing, 1125 Washington St SE, Olympia, WA 98507-9039; 360-902-3703, Fax: 360-586-6703.
www.wa.gov/dol/

#15 Licensing Dept, Public Protection Unit, PO Box 9649, Olympia, WA 98507-9649; 360-664-9070, Fax: 360-570-7888.
www.wa.gov/dol

#16 Department of Licensing, PO Box 9015, Olympia, WA 98507-9015; 360-753-2250, Fax: 360-586-0998.
www.wa.gov/dol/bpd/refront.htm

#17 Department of Licensing, PO Box 9027 (405 Black Wake Blvd SW), Olympia, WA 98507-9027; 360-664-1550, Fax: 360-664-2550.
www.wa.gov/dol
Direct web site URL to search for licensees: https://wws2.wa.gov/dol/profquery/LicenseSearch.asp

#18 Department of Licensing, PO Box 9012, 405 Black Lake Blvd, Olympia, WA 98507-9026; 360-586-6387, Fax: 360-664-2550.
www.wa.gov/dol/bpd/cosfront.htm

#19 Liquor Control Board, 3000 Paciic Ave. SE, Olympia, WA 98504-3075; 360-664-1600.
www.liq.wa.gov/default.asp
Direct web site URL to search for licensees: www.liq.wa.gov/services/storesearch.asp. You can search online using county, city, and store number.

#20 Superintendent of Public Instruction, PO Box 47200 (Old Capitol Bldg), Olympia, WA 98504-7200; 360-725-6400, Fax: 360-586-0145.
www.k12.wa.us/cert

#21 Teacher Certification, PO Box 47200, Olympia, WA 98504-7200; 360-753-6773, Fax: 360-586-0145.
www.k12.wa.us/cert

#22 Horse Racing Commission, 7912 Martin Way, #D, Olympia, WA 98516-5703; 360-459-6462, Fax: 360-459-6461.
www.whrc.wa.gov/licensing/index.htm

#23 Bar Association, 2101 4th Ave, 4th Fl, Seattle, WA 98121-2599; 206-727-8200, Fax: 206-727-8320.
www.wsba.org
Direct web site URL to search for licensees: www.wsba.org/directory/default.htm

#24 Gambling Commission, PO Box 42400, Olympia, WA 98504-2400; 360-438-7654 x358, Fax: 360-438-7503.
www.wa.gov/gambling/wsgc.htm

#25 Insurance Licensing, 4224 6th Ave SE, Rowesix Bldg 5, Olympia, WA 98504-0257; 360-407-0341, Fax: 360-438-7629.
www.insurance.wa.gov/

#26 Department of Licensing, Architects & Landscape Architects, PO Box 9045, Olympia, WA 98507-9045; 360-664-1388, Fax: 360-664-2551.
www.wa.gov/dol/bpd/arcfront.htm
Direct web site URL to search for licensees: www.wa.gov/dol/bpd/licquery.htm. You can search online using last name or license number

#27 Department of Licensing, PO Box 9649, Olympia, WA 98507-9649; 360-753-3713, Fax: 360-664-2550.
www.wa.gov/dol/

#28 Department of Agriculture, 3939 Cleveland Av SE, Olympia, WA 98501; 360-902-1921, Fax: 360-586-5257.
www.wa.gov/agr/pmd/index.htm

Washington Federal Courts

The following list indicates the district and division name for each county in the state. If the bankruptcy court location is different from the district court, then the location of the bankruptcy court appears in parentheses.

County/Court Cross Reference

County	District	Division	County	District	Division
Adams	Eastern	Spokane	Lewis	Western	Tacoma
Asotin	Eastern	Spokane	Lincoln	Eastern	Spokane
Benton	Eastern	Spokane	Mason	Western	Tacoma
Chelan	Eastern	Spokane	Okanogan	Eastern	Spokane
Clallam	Western	Tacoma (Seattle)	Pacific	Western	Tacoma
Clark	Western	Tacoma	Pend Oreille	Eastern	Spokane
Columbia	Eastern	Spokane	Pierce	Western	Tacoma
Cowlitz	Western	Tacoma	San Juan	Western	Seattle
Douglas	Eastern	Spokane	Skagit	Western	Seattle
Ferry	Eastern	Spokane	Skamania	Western	Tacoma
Franklin	Eastern	Spokane	Snohomish	Western	Seattle
Garfield	Eastern	Spokane	Spokane	Eastern	Spokane
Grant	Eastern	Spokane	Stevens	Eastern	Spokane
Grays Harbor	Western	Tacoma	Thurston	Western	Tacoma
Island	Western	Seattle	Wahkiakum	Western	Tacoma
Jefferson	Western	Tacoma (Seattle)	Walla Walla	Eastern	Spokane
King	Western	Seattle	Whatcom	Western	Seattle
Kitsap	Western	Tacoma (Seattle)	Whitman	Eastern	Spokane
Kittitas	Eastern	Yakima (Spokane)	Yakima	Eastern	Yakima (Spokane)
Klickitat	Eastern	Yakima (Spokane)			

US District Court

Eastern District of Washington

Spokane Division PO Box 1493, Spokane, WA 99210-1493 (Courier Address: Room 840, W 920 Riverside, Spokane, WA 99201), 509-353-2150.

http://www.waed.uscourts.gov

Counties: Adams, Asotin, Benton, Chelan, Columbia, Douglas, Ferry, Franklin, Garfield, Grant, Lincoln, Okanogan, Pend Oreille, Spokane, Stevens, Walla Walla, Whitman. Also, some cases from Kittitas, Klickitat and Yakima are heard here.

Indexing/Storage: Cases are indexed by defendant and plaintiff as well as by case number. New cases are available in the index 2-3 days after filing date. A computer index is maintained. Records are also indexed on microfiche. Search must be in Spokane Division for all cases before 1989. Open records are located at this court. Judge McDonald's records are maintained in Yakima (Yakima County). All other cases are kept in the Spokane Division.

Fee & Payment: The fee is $20.00 per item (one party name or case number). Payment may be made by money order, cashier check, personal check. Prepayment is required. Payee: Clerk, US District Court. Certification fee: $7.00 per document. Copy fee: $.50 per page.

Phone Search: Searching not available by phone.

Mail Search: A stamped self addressed envelope is not required.

In Person: In person searching is available.

PACER: Sign-up number is 800-676-6856. Access fee is $.60 per minute. Toll-free access: 888-372-5706. Local access: 509-353-2395. Case records are available back to July 1989. Records are purged every six months. New records are available online after 2-3 days. PACER is available online at http://pacer.waed.uscourts.gov.

Yakima Division PO Box 2706, Yakima, WA 98907 (Courier Address: Room 215, 25 S 3rd St, Yakima, WA 98901), 509-575-5838.

http://www.waed.uscourts.gov

Counties: Kittitas, Klickitat, Yakima. Cases assigned primarily to Judge McDonald are here. Some cases from Kittitas, Klickitat and Yakima are heard in Spokane.

Indexing/Storage: Cases are indexed by defendant and plaintiff as well as by case number. New cases are available in the index 1 day after filing date. A computer index is maintained. Search must be in Spokane Division for all cases before 1989. Open records are located at this court. Judge McDonald's records are maintained in Yakima. All other cases are kept in the Spokane Division.

Fee & Payment: The fee is $20.00 per item (one party name or case number). Payment may be made by money order, cashier check, business check. Personal checks are not accepted. Prepayment is required. Payee: Clerk, US District Court. Certification fee: $7.00 per document. Copy fee: $.50 per page.

Phone Search: Some docket information is available by phone.

Mail Search: Always enclose a stamped self addressed envelope.

In Person: In person searching is available.

PACER: Sign-up number is 800-676-6856. Access fee is $.60 per minute. Toll-free access: 888-372-5706. Local access: 509-353-2395. Case records are available back to July 1989. Records are purged every six months. New records are available online after 2-3 days. PACER is available online at http://pacer.waed.uscourts.gov.

US Bankruptcy Court

Eastern District of Washington

Spokane Division PO Box 2164, Spokane, WA 99210-2164 (Courier Address: W 904 Riverside, Suite 304, Spokane, WA 99201), 509-353-2404.

http://www.waeb.uscourts.gov

Counties: Adams, Asotin, Benton, Chelan, Columbia, Douglas, Ferry, Franklin, Garfield, Grant, Kittitas, Klickitat, Lincoln, Okanogan, Pend Oreille, Spokane, Stevens, Walla Walla, Whitman, Yakima.

Indexing/Storage: Cases are indexed by debtor and creditors as well as by case number. New cases are available in the index immediately after filing date. Open records are located at this court.

Fee & Payment: The fee is $20.00 per item (one party name or case number). Payment may be made by money order, cashier check, business check. Personal checks are not accepted. Prepayment is not required for copy requests. Copies will be provided with a bill through the mail. Payee: Clerk, US Bankruptcy Court.

Certification fee: $7.00 per document. Copy fee: $.50 per page.

Phone Search: Only docket information is available by phone. Press extension 6.

Mail Search: Always enclose a stamped self addressed envelope.

In Person: In person searching is available.

PACER: Sign-up number is. Access fee is. New records are available online after.

Other Online Access: Search records on the Internet using RACER at is http://204.227.177.194. Records go back to 1997. Access fee of 7 cents per page is planned.

US District Court

Western District of Washington

Seattle Division Clerk of Court, 215 US Courthouse, 1010 5th Ave, Seattle, WA 98104 (Courier Address: Use mail address for courier delivery), 206-553-5598.

http://www.wawd.uscourts.gov

Counties: Island, King, San Juan, Skagit, Snohomish, Whatcom.

Indexing/Storage: Cases are indexed by defendant and plaintiff as well as by case number. New cases are available in the index 10 days after filing date. Both computer and card indexes are maintained. Records are also indexed on microfiche. Open records are located at this court.

Fee & Payment: The fee is $20.00 per item (one party name or case number). Payment may be made by money order, cashier check, personal check. Prepayment is required. Payee: Clerk, US District Court. Certification fee: $7.00 per document. Copy fee: $.50 per page. You are allowed to make your own copies. These copies cost $.25 per page. An outside copy service will make copies for $.11 per page.

Phone Search: Docket information is available by phone for civil cases since 1988 and criminal cases since 1992.

Mail Search: A stamped self addressed envelope is not required.

In Person: In person searching is available.

PACER: Sign-up number is 800-676-6856. Access fee is $.60 per minute. Toll-free access: 800-520-8604. Local access: 206-553-2288. Case records are available back to 1988. Records are never purged. New civil records are available online after 4 days. New criminal records are available online after 2 days. PACER is available online at http://pacer.wawd.uscourts.gov.

Electronic Filing: Electronic filing information is available online at https://ecf.wawb.uscourts.gov

Tacoma Division Clerk's Office, Room 3100, 1717 Pacific Ave, Tacoma, WA 98402-3200 (Courier Address: Use mail address for courier delivery), 253-593-6313.

http://www.wawd.uscourts.gov

Counties: Clallam, Clark, Cowlitz, Grays Harbor, Jefferson, Kitsap, Lewis, Mason, Pacific, Pierce, Skamania, Thurston, Wahkiakum.

Indexing/Storage: Cases are indexed by defendant and plaintiff as well as by case number. New cases are available in the index immediately after filing date. A computer index is maintained. District wide searches are available for information from 1989. Microfiche and card indexes are available for older records. Open records are located at this court.

Fee & Payment: The fee is $20.00 per item (one party name or case number). Payment may be made by money order, cashier check, personal check. Prepayment is required. There is a $25.00 service fee if a check is returned. Payee: Clerk, US District Court. Certification fee: $7.00 per document. Copy fee: $.50 per page.

Phone Search: Only docket information is available by phone.

Mail Search: Always enclose a stamped self addressed envelope.

In Person: In person searching is available.

PACER: Sign-up number is 800-676-6856. Access fee is $.60 per minute. Toll-free access: 800-520-8604. Local access: 206-553-2288. Case records are available back to 1988. Records are never purged. New civil records are available online after 4 days. New criminal records are available online after 2 days. PACER is available online at http://pacer.wawd.uscourts.gov.

US Bankruptcy Court

Western District of Washington

Seattle Division Clerk of Court, 315 Park Place Bldg, 1200 6th Ave, Seattle, WA 98101 (Courier Address: Use mail address for courier delivery), 206-553-7545, Fax: 206-553-0131.

http://www.wawb.uscourts.gov

Counties: Clallam, Island, Jefferson, King, Kitsap, San Juan, Skagit, Snohomish, Whatcom.

Indexing/Storage: Cases are indexed by debtor and creditors as well as by case number. New cases are available in the index 1 day after filing date. Both computer and card indexes are maintained. Open cases are stored by case number. Closed cases are stored by year closed and then by case number. Open records are located at this court.

Fee & Payment: The fee is $20.00 per item (one party name or case number). Payment may be made by money order, cashier check, personal check. Prepayment is required. Payee: Clerk, US Bankruptcy Court. Certification fee: $7.00 per document. Copy fee: $.50 per page. You are

allowed to make your own copies. These copies cost $.15 per page. An outside copy service is available at $.35 per page.

Phone Search: An automated voice case information service (VCIS) is available. Call VCIS at 888-436-7477 or 206-553-8543.

Fax Search: Will accept fax search request if no copies requested.

Mail Search: Always enclose a stamped self addressed envelope.

In Person: In person searching is available.

PACER: Sign-up number is 800-676-6856. Access fee is $.60 per minute. Toll-free access: 800-704-4492. Local access: 206-553-0060. Case records are available back to June 1995. Records are never purged. New civil records are available online after 2 days. PACER is available online at http://pacer.wawb.uscourts.gov.

Electronic Filing: Electronic filing information is available online at https://ecf.wawb.uscourts.gov

Tacoma Division Suite 2100, 1717 Pacific Ave, Tacoma, WA 98402-3233 (Courier Address: Use mail address for courier delivery), 253-593-6310.

http://www.wawb.uscourts.gov

Counties: Clark, Cowlitz, Grays Harbor, Lewis, Mason, Pacific, Pierce, Skamania, Thurston, Wahkiakum.

Indexing/Storage: Cases are indexed by debtor as well as by case number. New cases are available in the index 1 day after filing date. Records can be searched by debtor's name from 1987 to the present. A computer index is maintained. Open records are located at this court.

Fee & Payment: The fee is $20.00 per item (one party name or case number). Payment may be made by money order, cashier check. Business checks are not accepted. Personal checks are not accepted. Prepayment is required. Attorney checks are accepted. Payee: Clerk, US Bankruptcy Court. Certification fee: $7.00 per document. Copy fee: $.50 per page. You are allowed to make your own copies. These copies cost $.15 per page. An outside copy service is available for $.10 per page.

Phone Search: An automated voice case information service (VCIS) is available. Call VCIS at 888-436-7477 or 206-553-8543.

Mail Search: A stamped self addressed envelope is not required.

In Person: In person searching is available.

PACER: Sign-up number is 800-676-6856. Access fee is $.60 per minute. Toll-free access: 800-704-4492. Local access: 206-553-0060. Case records are available back to June 1995. Records are never purged. New civil records are available online after 2 days. PACER is available online at http://pacer.wawb.uscourts.gov.

Electronic Filing: Electronic filing information is available online at https://ecf.wawb.uscourts.gov

Washington County Courts

Court	Jurisdiction	No. of Courts	How Organized
Superior Courts*	General	39	29 Districts
District Courts*	Limited	65	39 Counties
Municipal Courts	Municipal	131	131 Cities

* Profiled in this Sourcebook.

CIVIL									
Court	Tort	Contract	Real Estate	Min. Claim	Max. Claim	Small Claims	Estate	Eviction	Domestic Relations
Superior Courts*	X	X	X	$50,000	No Max		X	X	X
District Courts*	X	X		$0	$50,000	$2500			
Municipal Courts									

CRIMINAL					
Court	Felony	Misdemeanor	DWI/DUI	Preliminary Hearing	Juvenile
Superior Courts*	X				X
District Courts*		X	X	X	
Municipal Courts		X	X		

ADMINISTRATION   Court Administrator, Temple of Justice, PO Box 41174, Olympia, WA, 98504; 360-357-2121, Fax: 360-357-2127. www.courts.wa.gov

COURT STRUCTURE   District Courts retain civil records for 10 years from date of final disposition, then the records are destroyed. District Courts retain criminal records forever.

Washington has a mandatory arbitration requirement for civil disputes for $35,000 or less. However, either party may request a trial in Superior Court if dissatisfied with the arbitrator's decision.

The limit for civil actions in District Court has been increased from $25,000 to $35,000.

ONLINE ACCESS   Appellate, Superior, and District Court records are available online. The Superior Court Management Information System (SCOMIS), the Appellate Records System (ACORDS) and the District/Municipal Court Information System (DISCIS) are on the Judicial Information System's JIS-Link. Case records available through JIS-Link from 1977 include criminal, civil, domestic, probate, and judgments. JIS-Link is generally available 24-hours daily. Equipment requirements are a PC running Windows or MS-DOS. There is a one-time installation fee of $100.00 per site, and a connect time charge of $25.00 per hour (approximately $.42 per minute), plus a surcharge of $.85 per session. For additional information and/or a registration packet, contact: JISLink Coordinator, Office of the Administrator for the Courts, 1206 S Quince St., PO Box 41170, Olympia WA 98504-1170, 360-357-2407 or visit the web site at www.courts.wa.gov/jislink.

ADD'L INFORMATION   SASE is required in every jurisdiction that responds to written search requests.

📖 📖 📖 📖 📖 📖 📖

Adams County

Superior Court 210 W Broadway (PO Box 187), Ritzville, WA 99169-0187; 509-659-3257; Fax: 509-659-0118. Hours: 8:30AM-Noon, 1-4:30PM (PST). *Felony, Civil, Eviction, Probate.*

Civil Records: Access: Phone, fax, mail, online, in person. Only the court performs in person searches; visitors may not. Search fee: $20.00 per hour. Required to search: name, years to search; also helpful: address. Civil cases indexed by defendant, plaintiff. Civil records on computer from 1985, archived from 1900s. Index available remotely online from JIS-Link; see www.courts.wa.gov/jislink (also, see state introduction).

Criminal Records: Access: Phone, fax, mail, online, in person. Only the court performs in person searches; visitors may not. Search fee: $20.00 per hour. Required to search: name, years to search; also helpful: address, DOB, SSN. Criminal records on computer from 1985, archived from 1900s. Online access to criminal records is the same as civil. (Also see state introduction.).

General Information: No sealed, juvenile, adoption, paternity, mental health, sex offenders (victims) records released. SASE required. Turnaround time 1 week. Fax notes: $1.00 per page. Copy fee: $.50 per page. Certification fee: $2.00 plus $1.00 each additional page. Fee payee: Adams County Clerk. Business checks accepted. Prepayment is required.

Othello District Court 165 N 1st, Othello, WA 99344; 509-488-3935; Fax: 509-488-3480. Hours: 8:30AM-4:30PM (PST). *Misdemeanor, Civil Actions Under $50,000, Small Claims.*

Civil Records: Access: Phone, fax, mail, online, in person. Only the court performs in person searches; visitors may not. No search fee. Required to search: name, years to search; also helpful: address. Civil cases indexed by defendant, plaintiff. Civil records on computer from 1992, on index cards. Index available remotely online from JIS-Link; see www.courts.wa.gov/jislink (also, see state introduction).

Criminal Records: Access: Phone, fax, mail, online, in person. Only the court performs in person searches; visitors may not. No search fee. Required to search:

name, years to search; also helpful: address, DOB, SSN. Criminal records on computer from 1992, on index cards. Online access to criminal records is the same as civil. (Also see state introduction.).

General Information: No sealed, juvenile, adoption, paternity, mental health, sex offenders (victims) or (sometimes) DUI records released. SASE required. Turnaround time 1-3 days. Fax notes: No fee to fax results. Copy fee: $2.50 for first page, $1.00 each add'l. Certification fee: $2.50 plus $1.00 per page after first. Fee payee: Othello District Court. Personal checks accepted. Prepayment is required.

Ritzville District Court 210 W Broadway, Ritzville, WA 99169; 509-659-1002; Fax: 509-659-0118. Hours: 8:30AM-4:30PM (PST). *Misdemeanor, Civil Actions Under $50,000, Small Claims.*

Civil Records: Access: Fax, mail, online, in person. Only the court performs in person searches; visitors may not. No search fee. Required to search: name, years to search; also helpful: address. Civil cases indexed by defendant, plaintiff. Civil records on computer from 10/90. Index available remotely online from JIS-Link; see www.courts.wa.gov/jislink (also, see state introduction).

Criminal Records: Access: Fax, mail, online, in person. Only the court performs in person searches; visitors may not. No search fee. Required to search: name, years to search, DOB; also helpful: address, SSN. Criminal records on computer from 10/90. Online access to criminal records is the same as civil. (Also see state introduction.).

General Information: No sealed, juvenile, adoption, paternity, mental health, sex offenders (victims) or (sometimes) DUI records released. SASE required. Turnaround time 2 days. Fax notes: No fee to fax results. Copy fee: $1.00 per page. Certification fee: $5.00. Fee payee: Ritzville District Court. Personal checks accepted. Prepayment is required.

Asotin County

Superior Court PO Box 159, Asotin, WA 99402-0159; 509-243-2081; Fax: 509-243-4978. Hours: 8AM-5PM (PST). *Felony, Civil, Eviction, Probate.*

Civil Records: Access: Phone, fax, mail, online, in person. Only the court performs in person searches; visitors may not. No search fee. Required to search: name, years to search; also helpful: address. Civil cases indexed by defendant, plaintiff. Civil records on computer from mid 1985, on microfiche from 1970s, archived from 1895. Index available remotely online from JIS-Link; see www.courts.wa.gov/jislink (also, see state introduction).

Criminal Records: Access: Phone, fax, mail, online, in person. Only the court performs in person searches; visitors may not. No search fee. Required to search: name, years to search; also helpful: address, DOB, SSN. Criminal records on computer from mid 1985, on microfiche from 1970s, archived from 1895. Online access to criminal records is the same as civil. (Also see state introduction.).

General Information: No sealed, juvenile, adoption, paternity, mental health, sex offenders (victims) or (sometimes) DUI records released. SASE required. Turnaround time 1 day. Copy fee: $2.00 for first page, $1.00 each add'l. Certification fee: Cert fee included in copy fee. Fee payee: Asotin County Clerk. Personal checks accepted. Prepayment is required.

District Court PO Box 429, Asotin, WA 99402-0429; 509-243-2027; Fax: 509-243-2091. Hours: 8AM-5PM (PST). *Misdemeanor, Civil Actions Under $50,000, Small Claims.*

Civil Records: Access: Fax, mail, online, in person. Only the court performs in person searches; visitors may not. Search fee: $5.00 per name. Required to search: name, years to search; also helpful: address.

Civil cases indexed by defendant, plaintiff. Civil records on computer since 1993; prior records on log books. Index available remotely online from JIS-Link; see www.courts.wa.gov/jislink (also, see state introduction).

Criminal Records: Access: Fax, mail, online, in person. Only the court performs in person searches; visitors may not. Search fee: $5.00 per name. Required to search: name, years to search; also helpful: address, DOB, SSN. Criminal records on computer from 1989. Online access to criminal records is the same as civil. (Also see state introduction.).

General Information: No sealed, juvenile, adoption, paternity, mental health, sex offenders (victims) or (sometimes) DUI records released. SASE required. Turnaround time up to 2 weeks. Fax notes: No fee to fax results. Copy fee: $.25 per page. Certification fee: $6.00. Fee payee: Asotin County District Court. Personal checks accepted. Prepayment is required.

Benton County

Superior Court 7320 W Quinault, Kennewick, WA 99336-7690; 509-735-8388. Hours: 8AM-Noon, 1-4PM (PST). *Felony, Civil, Probate.*

Civil Records: Access: Mail, in person. Only the court performs in person searches; visitors may not. Search fee: $20.00 per hour. Required to search: name, years to search; also helpful: address. Civil cases indexed by defendant, plaintiff. Civil records on computer from 1979, pre-1979 on index books. Index available remotely online from JIS-Link; see www.courts.wa.gov/jislink (also, see state introduction).

Criminal Records: Access: Mail, in person. Only the court performs in person searches; visitors may not. Search fee: $20.00 per hour. Required to search: name, years to search; also helpful: address, DOB, SSN. Criminal records on computer from 1979, pre-1979 on index books. Online access to criminal records is the same as civil. (Also see state introduction.).

General Information: No sealed, dependency, adoption, paternity, mental health, sex offenders (victims). SASE required. Turnaround time 10 days. Fax notes: $3.00 for first page, $1.00 each add'l. Copy fee: $.25 per page. Certification fee: $2.00 plus $1.00 per page after first. Fee payee: Benton County Clerk. Personal checks accepted. Prepayment is required.

District Court 7320 W Quinault, Kennewick, WA 99336; 509-735-8476; Fax: 509-736-3069. Hours: 7:30AM-Noon, 1-4:30PM (PST). *Misdemeanor, Civil Actions Under $50,000, Small Claims.*

Civil Records: Access: Mail, fax, online, in person. Both court and visitors may perform in person searches. Search fee: $10.00 per name. Required to search: name, years to search; also helpful: address. Civil cases indexed by defendant, plaintiff. Civil records on computer from 7/91. Index available remotely online from JIS-Link; see www.courts.wa.gov/jislink (also, see state introduction).

Criminal Records: Access: Mail, fax, online, in person. Both court and visitors may perform in person searches. Search fee: $10.00 per name. Required to search: name, years to search, DOB, signed release; also helpful: address, SSN. Criminal records on computer from 7/91. Online access to criminal records is the same as civil. (Also see state introduction.).

General Information: Public Access terminal is available. No sealed, juvenile, adoption, paternity, mental health, sex offenders (victims) or (sometimes) DUI records released. SASE requested. Turnaround time 10 days. Fax notes: Will not fax results. Copy fee: First 50 copies free, then $.05 each. Certification fee: $5.00. Fee payee: Benton County District Court. Personal checks accepted. Credit cards accepted: Visa, MasterCard. Prepayment is required.

Chelan County

Superior Court 350 Orondo (PO Box 3025), Wenatchee, WA 98807-3025; 509-664-5380; Fax: 509-664-2611. Hours: 9AM-5PM (PST). *Felony, Civil, Eviction, Probate.*

www.co.chelan.wa.us

Civil Records: Access: Phone, fax, mail, online, in person. Both court and visitors may perform in person searches. Search fee: $20.00 per hour. Required to search: name, years to search. Civil cases indexed by defendant, plaintiff. Civil records on computer since 1984; prior on microfilm 1900-1984. Index available online from JIS-Link; see www.courts.wa.gov/jislink (also, see state introduction).

Criminal Records: Access: Phone, fax, mail, online, in person. Both court and visitors may perform in person searches. Search fee: $20.00 per hour. Required to search: name, years to search; also helpful: address, DOB, SSN. Criminal records on computer since 1984; prior on microfilm 1900-1984. Online access to criminal records is the same as civil. (Also see state introduction.).

General Information: Public Access terminal is available. No sealed, juvenile, adoption, paternity, mental health, sex offenders (victims) records released. SASE required. Turnaround time 1 day. Fax notes: $3.00 for first page, $1.00 each add'l. Copy fee: $2.00 for first page, $1.00 each add'l. Certification fee: The certification fee is included in the copy fee. Fee payee: Chelan County Clerk. Personal checks and credit cards accepted. Prepayment is required.

Chelan County District Court PO Box 2182, Courthouse 4th Fl, Wenatchee, WA 98807; 509-664-5393; Fax: 509-664-5456. Hours: 8:30AM-4:30PM (PST). *Misdemeanor, Civil Actions Under $50,000, Small Claims.*

Civil Records: Access: Fax, mail, online, in person. Both court and visitors may perform in person searches. Search fee: $15.00 per name. Required to search: name; also helpful: years to search, address. Civil cases indexed by defendant, plaintiff. Civil records on computer from 1984. Records destroyed 10 years after date of last action. Index available remotely online from JIS-Link; see www.courts.wa.gov/jislink (also, see state introduction).

Criminal Records: Access: Fax, mail, online, in person. Both court and visitors may perform in person searches. Search fee: $15.00 per name. Required to search: name, DOB, signed release; also helpful: years to search, address, SSN, aliases. Criminal records on computer. Criminal files may be destroyed 5 years after close of case, infractions destroyed 3 years after close. Online access to criminal records is the same as civil. (Also see state introduction.).

General Information: Public Access terminal is available. (For records since 1986.) No sealed, domestic violence victim info, alcohol/probation evaluation records released. SASE required. Turnaround time 1 week. Copy fee: $2.00 for first page, $1.00 each add'l. Certification fee: $5.00. Fee payee: Chelan County District Court. Personal checks accepted. Prepayment is required.

Clallam County

Superior Court 223 E Fourth St, (PO Box 863), Port Angeles, WA 98362-3098; 360-417-2333; Fax: 360-417-2495. Hours: 8AM-5PM (PST). *Felony, Civil, Eviction, Probate.*

www.clallam.net/scourt

Civil Records: Access: Phone, mail, in person. Both court and visitors may perform in person searches. Search fee: $20.00 per hour. Required to search: name, years to search; also helpful: address. Civil cases indexed by defendant, plaintiff. Civil records on computer from 10/83, on microfiche from 1914, some records on index cards.

Criminal Records: Access: Phone, mail, online, in person. Both court and visitors may perform in person searches. Search fee: $20.00 per hour. Required to search: name, years to search; also helpful: address, DOB. Criminal records on computer from 10/95, on microfiche from 1914, some records on index cards. Criminal Index available remotely online from JIS-Link; see www.courts.wa.gov/jislink (also, see state introduction).

General Information: Public Access terminal is available. No sealed, juvenile, adoption, paternity, mental health, sex offenders (victims) records released. SASE required. Turnaround time 1 week plus. Fax notes: Fee to fax results is $3.00 plus $1.00 per page. Copy fee: $.10 per page. Certification fee: $2.00 plus $1.00 per page after first. Fee payee: Clerk. Business checks accepted. Prepayment is required.

District One Court
223 E 4th St, Port Angeles, WA 98362; 360-417-2285; Fax: 360-417-2470. Hours: 8AM-5PM (PST). *Misdemeanor, Civil Actions Under $50,000, Small Claims.*

www.wa.gov/clallam/dcourt/index.html

Civil Records: Access: Mail, fax, online, in person. Visitors must perform in person searches for themselves. No search fee. Required to search: name, years to search; also helpful: address. Civil cases indexed by defendant, plaintiff. Civil records on computer from 1986. Index available remotely online from JIS-Link; see www.courts.wa.gov/jislink (also, see state introduction).

Criminal Records: Access: Mail, fax, online, in person. Visitors must perform in person searches for themselves. No search fee. Required to search: name, years to search, DOB, signed release; also helpful: address, SSN, nationality. Criminal records on computer from 1986. Online access to criminal records is the same as civil. (Also see state introduction.).

General Information: Public Access terminal is available. No sealed, juvenile, adoption, paternity, mental health, sex offenders (victims) or (sometimes) DUI records released. Turnaround time up to 1 week. Copy fee: $.10 per page. Certification fee: $5.00 per document. Fee payee: Clallam County Clerk, District 1 Court. Personal checks accepted. Prepayment required.

District Two Court
PO Box 1937, Forks, WA 98331; 360-374-6383; Fax: 360-374-2100. Hours: 8AM-5PM (PST). *Misdemeanor, Civil Actions Under $50,000, Small Claims.*

Civil Records: Access: Mail, online, in person. Both court and visitors may perform in person searches. No search fee. Required to search: name, years to search; also helpful: address. Civil cases indexed by defendant, plaintiff. Civil records on computer from 1986, on index cards from 1982-1986. Index available remotely online from JIS-Link; see www.courts.wa.gov/jislink (also, see state introduction).

Criminal Records: Access: Mail, online, in person. Only the court performs in person searches; visitors may not. No search fee. Required to search: name, years to search; also helpful: address, DOB, SSN. Criminal records on computer from 1986, on index cards from 1982-1986. Online access to criminal records is the same as civil. (Also see state introduction.).

General Information: Public Access terminal is available. No sealed, juvenile, adoption, paternity, mental health, sex offenders (victims) or (sometimes) DUI records released. Turnaround time 1 week. Fax notes: Fee to fax results in $1.00 per page. Copy fee: $.15 per page. Certification fee: $5.00. Fee payee: Clallam County District II Court. Personal checks accepted.

Clark County

Superior Court
1200 Franklin St, PO Box 5000, Vancouver, WA 98666; 360-397-2049; Civil phone: 360-397-2292; Criminal phone: 360-397-2295. Hours: 8:30AM-4:30PM *Felony, Civil, Eviction, Probate.*

www.co.clark.wa.us/law/supcourt.htm

Civil Records: Access: Phone, mail, online, in person, email. Both court and visitors may perform in person searches. Search fee: $20.00 per hour. Required to search: name, years to search. Civil cases indexed by defendant, plaintiff. Civil records on computer from 1979 indexed, on microfiche from 1960, and index books prior to 1979. Index available remotely online from JIS-Link; see www.courts.wa.gov/jislink (also, see state introduction).

Criminal Records: Access: Phone, mail, online, in person. Both court and visitors may perform in person searches. Search fee: $20.00 per hour. Required to search: name, years to search, DOB; also helpful: address, signed release. Criminal records on computer since 1988, prior to 1988 on microfilm. Online access to criminal records is the same as civil. (Also see state introduction.).

General Information: Public Access terminal is available. No sealed, juvenile, adoption, paternity, mental health, sex offenders (victims). Turnaround time 1-3 days. Copy fee: $2.00 for first page, $1.00 each add'l. Certification fee: $2.00. Fee payee: County Clerk. Only cashiers checks, money orders and attorney checks accepted. Prepayment is required.

District Court
PO Box 9806, Vancouver, WA 98666; Civil phone: 360-397-2411; Criminal phone: 360-397-2424; Fax: 360-737-6044. Hours: 8:30AM-4:30PM (PST). *Misdemeanor, Civil Actions Under $50,000, Small Claims.*

www.co.clark.wa.us/law/distct.htm

Civil Records: Access: Phone, fax, mail, online, in person. Only the court performs in person searches; visitors may not. No search fee. Required to search: name, years to search; also helpful: address. Civil cases indexed by defendant, plaintiff. Civil records on computer for approximately ten years. Index available remotely online from JIS-Link; see www.courts.wa.gov/jislink (also, see state introduction).

Criminal Records: Access: Fax, mail, online, in person. Only the court performs in person searches; visitors may not. No search fee. Required to search: name, DOB, signed release; also helpful: years to search, address, SSN. Criminal records on computer for approximately five years. Online access to criminal records is the same as civil. (Also see state introduction.).

General Information: No sealed, juvenile, adoption, paternity, mental health, sex offenders (victims) or (sometimes) DUI records released. Turnaround time 1 week. Fax notes: No fee to fax results. Copy fee: $.15 per page. Certification fee: $5.00. Fee payee: Clark County District Court. Personal checks accepted. Prepayment is required.

Columbia County

Superior Court
341 E Main St, Dayton, WA 99328; 509-382-4321; Fax: 509-382-4830. Hours: 8:30AM-Noon, 1-4:30PM (PST). *Felony, Civil, Eviction, Probate.*

Civil Records: Access: Phone, fax, mail, online, in person. Only the court performs in person searches; visitors may not. Search fee: $20.00 per hour. Required to search: name, years to search. Civil cases indexed by defendant, plaintiff. Civil records on computer from 1987, some records on index cards and books, archived from 1900s. Index available remotely online from JIS-Link; see www.courts.wa.gov/jislink (also, see state introduction).

Criminal Records: Access: Phone, fax, mail, online, in person. Only the court performs in person searches; visitors may not. Search fee: $20.00 per hour. Required to search: name, years to search. Criminal records on computer from 1987, some records on index cards and books, archived from 1900s. Online access to criminal records is the same as civil. (Also see state introduction).

General Information: No sealed, juvenile, adoption, paternity, mental health, sex offenders (victims). SASE required. Turnaround time 1 week. Copy fee: $1.00 per page. Certification fee: $2.00 plus $1.00 per page after first. Fee payee: Columbia County Clerk. Personal checks accepted. Prepayment is required.

District Court
341 E Main St, Dayton, WA 99328-1361; 509-382-4812; Fax: 509-382-4830. Hours: 8:30AM-4:30PM (PST). *Misdemeanor, Civil Actions Under $50,000, Small Claims.*

Civil Records: Access: Mail, online, in person. Both court and visitors may perform in person searches. No search fee. Required to search: name, years to search; also helpful: address. Civil cases indexed by plaintiff. Civil records on computer since 05/96; prior on index books. Index available remotely online from JIS-Link; see www.courts.wa.gov/jislink (also, see state introduction).

Criminal Records: Access: Mail, online, in person. Both court and visitors may perform in person searches. Search fee: Fee may be charged if more than 1 case. Required to search: name, years to search, DOB, signed release; also helpful: address, SSN. Criminal records on computer from 1993, on books prior. Online access to criminal records is the same as civil. (Also see state introduction.).

General Information: No sealed, juvenile, adoption, paternity, mental health, sex offenders (victims) or (sometimes) DUI records released. SASE required. Turnaround time 7-10 days. Copy fee: $1.00 per page. Certification fee: $5.00 per page. Fee payee: District Court. Personal checks accepted. Prepayment required.

Cowlitz County

Superior Court
312 SW First Ave, Kelso, WA 98626-1724; 360-577-3016; Fax: 360-577-2323. Hours: 8:30-5:30PM (PST). *Felony, Civil, Eviction, Probate.*

www.co.cowlitz.wa.us/Dptpages/superct.htm

Civil Records: Access: Phone, fax, mail, online, in person. Both court and visitors may perform in person searches. Search fee: $10.00 per name. Required to search: name, years to search; also helpful: address. Civil cases indexed by defendant, plaintiff. Civil records on computer from 1981, on microfilm through 1989, hard copy files from 1990 to present. Index available remotely online from JIS-Link; see www.courts.wa.gov/jislink (also, see state introduction).

Criminal Records: Access: Phone, fax, mail, online, in person. Both court and visitors may perform in person searches. Search fee: $10.00 per name. Required to search: name, years to search; also helpful: address, DOB, SSN. Criminal records on computer from 1981, on microfilm through 1989, hard copy files from 1987 to present. Online access to criminal records is the same as civil. (Also see state introduction.).

General Information: Public Access terminal is available. No sealed, juvenile, adoption, paternity, mental health records released. SASE required. Turnaround time 2 days. Fax notes: Will fax if prepayment received. Copy fee: $2.00 for first page, $1.00 each add'l. Certification fee: Included in copy fee. Fee payee: Cowlitz County Superior Court Clerk. Business checks accepted. Prepayment is required.

District Court 312 SW First Ave, Kelso, WA 98626-1724; 360-577-3073. Hours: 8:30AM-5PM (PST). *Misdemeanor, Civil Actions Under $50,000, Small Claims.*

Civil Records: Access: Mail, online, in person. Only the court performs in person searches; visitors may not. No search fee. Required to search: name, years to search; also helpful: address. Civil cases indexed by defendant, plaintiff. Civil records on index cards from 1985. Index available remotely online from JIS-Link; see www.courts.wa.gov/jislink (also, see state introduction).

Criminal Records: Access: Mail, online, in person. Only the court performs in person searches; visitors may not. No search fee. Required to search: name, years to search, DOB; also helpful: address, SSN. Criminal records on index cards from 1985. Online access to criminal records is the same as civil. (Also see state introduction.).

General Information: No sealed, adoption, paternity, mental health records released. Turnaround time 2 weeks. Copy fee: $.25 per page. Certification fee: $5.00. Fee payee: District Court. No personal checks accepted. Prepayment is required.

Douglas County

Superior Court PO Box 488, Waterville, WA 98858-0516; 509-745-9063; Fax: 509-745-8027. Hours: 8AM-5PM (PST). *Felony, Civil, Eviction, Probate.*

Note: Clerk is reached at 509-745-8529.

Civil Records: Access: Phone, fax, mail, online, in person. Only the court performs in person searches; visitors may not. Search fee: $20.00 per hour. Required to search: name, years to search; also helpful: address. Civil cases indexed by defendant, plaintiff. Civil records on computer from 1985, archived and on microfiche from 1883, some records on index books. Index available remotely online from JIS-Link; see www.courts.wa.gov/jislink (also, see state introduction.)

Criminal Records: Access: Phone, fax, mail, online, in person. Only the court performs in person searches; visitors may not. Search fee: $20.00 per hour. Required to search: name, years to search, DOB; also helpful: address, SSN. Criminal records on computer from 1985, archived and on microfiche from 1883, some records on index books. Online access to criminal records is the same as civil. (Also see state introduction.).

General Information: No sealed, juvenile, adoption, paternity, mental health, sex offenders (victims). SASE required. Turnaround time 1 week. Fax notes: $2.00 for first page, $1.00 each add'l. Copy fee: $2.00 for first page, $1.00 each add'l. Certification fee: $2.00 plus $1.00 per page after first. Fee payee: Douglas County Clerk. Business checks accepted. Prepayment is required.

District Court - Bridgeport 1206 Columbia Ave (PO Box 730), Bridgeport, WA 98813-0730; 509-686-2034; Fax: 509-686-4671. Hours: 8:30AM-4:30PM (PST). *Misdemeanor, Small Claims.*

Note: If record not found in this court, request forwarded to East Wenatchee (South) court.

Civil Records: Access: Fax, mail, online, in person. Only the court performs in person searches; visitors may not. Please use the court's "Request for Information" form. Search fee: $10.00 per name. Required to search: name, years to search; also helpful: address. Civil cases indexed by defendant. Civil records on computer back to 02/95. Index available remotely online from JIS-Link; see www.courts.wa.gov/jislink (also, see state introduction).

Criminal Records: Access: Fax, mail, online, in person. Only the court performs in person searches; visitors may not. Please use the court's "Request for

Information" form. Search fee: $10.00 per name. Required to search: name, years to search; also helpful: address, DOB, SSN. Criminal records on computer back to 02/95. Online access to criminal records is the same as civil. (Also see state introduction.).

General Information: No sealed, juvenile, adoption, paternity, mental health, sex offenders (victims) or (sometimes) DUI records released. SASE required. Turnaround time 10 days. Fax notes: Will not fax results. Copy fee: $1.00 per page. Certification fee: $5.00 per page. Fee payee: Douglas County District Court Bridgeport. Personal checks accepted. Prepayment is required.

District Court - East Wenatchee 110 3rd St NE, East Wenatchee, WA 98802; 509-884-3536; Fax: 509-884-5973. 8:30AM-4:30PM (PST). *Misdemeanor, Civil Actions Under $50,000, Small Claims.*

www.douglascountywa.net/dep_dis.html

Note: If record not found in this court, request forwarded to Bridgeport Branch (North) County District Court.

Civil Records: Access: Fax, mail, online, in person. Only the court performs in person searches; visitors may not. Search fee: $10.00 per hour. Required to search: name, years to search; also helpful: address. Civil cases indexed by defendant, plaintiff. Civil records on index cards from 1982. Index available remotely online from JIS-Link; see www.courts.wa.gov/jislink (also, see state introduction).

Criminal Records: Access: Fax, mail, online, in person. Only the court performs in person searches; visitors may not. Search fee: $10.00 per hour. Required to search: name, years to search; also helpful: address, DOB, SSN. Criminal records on computer back 5 years. Online access to criminal records is the same as civil. (Also see state introduction.).

General Information: No sealed, juvenile, adoption, paternity, mental health, sex offenders (victims) or (sometimes) DUI records released. SASE required. Turnaround time 1 week. Fax notes: $1.00 for first page, $1.00 each add'l. Local faxing only. Copy fee: $1.00 per page. Certification fee: $5.00. Fee payee: Douglas District Court. Personal checks accepted. Prepayment is required.

Ferry County

Superior Court 350 E Delaware #4, Republic, WA 99166; 509-775-5245. Hours: 8AM-4PM (PST). *Felony, Civil, Probate.*

Civil Records: Access: Phone, mail, online, in person. Both court and visitors may perform in person searches. Search fee: $20.00 per hour. Required to search: name, years to search; also helpful: address. Civil cases indexed by defendant, plaintiff. Civil records on computer since 1987. Index available remotely online from JIS-Link; see www.courts.wa.gov/jislink (also, see state introduction).

Criminal Records: Access: Phone, mail, online, in person. Both court and visitors may perform in person searches. Search fee: $20.00 per hour. Required to search: name, years to search; also helpful: address, DOB. Criminal records on computer since 1987. Online access to criminal records is the same as civil. (Also see state introduction.).

General Information: Public Access terminal is available. No sealed, juvenile, adoption, paternity, mental health or sex offenders (victims). SASE required. Turnaround time 1-4 days. Copy fee: $2.00 for first page, $1.00 each add'l. Certification fee: $2.00 plus $1.00 each additional page. Fee payee: Ferry County Clerk. Business checks accepted. Prepayment required.

District Court 350 E Delaware Ave #6, Republic, WA 99166-9747; 509-775-5244; Fax: 509-775-5221. Hours: 8AM-4PM (PST). *Misdemeanor, Civil Actions Under $50,000, Small Claims.*

Civil Records: Access: Fax, mail, online, in person. Only the court performs in person searches; visitors may not. No search fee. Required to search: name, years to search; also helpful: address. Civil cases indexed by case number. Civil records on computer back to 1995; others back to 1993. Index available remotely online from JIS-Link; see www.courts.wa.gov/jislink (also, see state introduction).

Criminal Records: Access: Mail, fax, online, in person. Only the court performs in person searches; visitors may not. No search fee. Required to search: name, years to search, DOB; also helpful: address, SSN, signed release. Criminal records on computer back to 1995; others back to 1993. Online access to criminal records is the same as civil. (Also see state introduction.).

General Information: No sealed, juvenile, adoption, paternity, mental health, sex offenders (victims) or (sometimes) DUI records released. SASE required. Turnaround time 1 week. Fax notes: No fee to fax results. Copy fee: $2.00 for first page, $1.00 each add'l. Certification fee: $5.00. Fee payee: Ferry County District Court. Personal checks accepted. Prepayment is required.

Franklin County

Superior Court 1016 N 4th St, Pasco, WA 99301; 509-545-3525. Hours: 8:30AM-5PM (PST). *Felony, Civil, Eviction, Probate.*

www.co.franklin.wa.us

Civil Records: Access: Mail, online, in person. Only the court performs in person searches; visitors may not. Search fee: $20.00 per hour. Required to search: name, years to search; also helpful: address. Civil cases indexed by defendant, plaintiff. Civil records on computer from 7/83, on index books, archived from 1900s. Index available remotely online from JIS-Link; see www.courts.wa.gov/jislink (also, see state introduction).

Criminal Records: Access: Mail, online, in person. Only the court performs in person searches; visitors may not. Search fee: $20.00 per hour. Required to search: name, years to search, DOB; also helpful: address, SSN. Criminal records on computer from 7/83, on index books, archived from 1900s. Online access to criminal records is the same as civil. (Also see state introduction.).

General Information: No sealed, juvenile, adoption, paternity, mental health, sex offenders (victims). SASE required. Turnaround time 1 week. Fax notes: Fee to fax results is $3.00 per page. Copy fee: $2.00 for first page, $1.00 each add'l. Certification fee: $2.00 plus $1.00 per page after first. Fee payee: Franklin County Superior Court Clerk. Business checks accepted. Prepayment is required.

District Court 1016 N 4th St, Pasco, WA 99301; 509-545-3593; Fax: 509-545-3588. Hours: 8:30AM-Noon, 1-5PM (PST). *Misdemeanor, Civil Actions Under $50,000, Small Claims.*

Civil Records: Access: Mail, online, in person. Only the court performs in person searches; visitors may not. Search fee: $10.00 per name. Required to search: name, years to search; also helpful: address. Civil cases indexed by defendant, plaintiff. Civil records on computer from 1993, prior on index cards. Index available remotely online from JIS-Link; see www.courts.wa.gov/jislink (also, see state introduction).

Criminal Records: Access: Mail, online, in person. Only the court performs in person searches; visitors may not. Search fee: $10.00 per name. Required to search: name, years to search, DOB; also helpful:

address, SSN. Criminal records on computer from 1987, prior on index cards. Online access to criminal records is the same as civil. (Also see state introduction.).

General Information: Public Access terminal is available. No sealed, juvenile, adoption, paternity, mental health, sex offenders (victims) or (sometimes) DUI records released. SASE required. Turnaround time 2-3 days. Copy fee: $.25 per page. Certification fee: $5.00. Fee payee: Franklin District Court. Personal checks accepted. Prepayment is required.

Garfield County

Superior Court PO Box 915, Pomeroy, WA 99347-0915; 509-843-3731; Fax: 509-843-1224. Hours: 8:30AM-Noon, 1-5PM (PST). *Felony, Civil, Eviction, Probate.*

www.co.garfield.wa.us

Civil Records: Access: Phone, fax, mail, online, in person. Both court and visitors may perform in person searches. Search fee: $8.00 per hour. Required to search: name, years to search; also helpful: address. Civil cases indexed by defendant, plaintiff. Civil records on docket books, archived from 1882. Index available remotely online from JIS-Link; see www.courts.wa.gov/jislink (also, see state introduction).

Criminal Records: Access: Phone, fax, mail, online, in person. Both court and visitors may perform in person searches. Search fee: $8.00 per hour. Required to search: name, years to search; also helpful: address, DOB, SSN. Criminal records on docket books, archived from 1882. Online access to criminal records is the same as civil. (Also see state introduction.).

General Information: No sealed, juvenile, adoption, paternity, mental health, sex offenders (victims). SASE requested. Turnaround time 1 week. Fax notes: $.50 per page. Copy fee: $1.00 per page. Certification fee: $2.00 plus $1.00 per page after first. Fee payee: Garfield County Clerk. Personal checks accepted. Prepayment is required.

District Court PO Box 817, Pomeroy, WA 99347-0817; 509-843-1002. 8:30AM-5PM *Misdemeanor, Civil Actions Under $50,000, Small Claims.*

Civil Records: Access: Mail, online, in person. Only the court performs in person searches; visitors may not. Search fee: $3.00 per name. Required to search: name, years to search; also helpful: address. Civil cases indexed by defendant. Civil records on index cards. Index available remotely online from JIS-Link; see www.courts.wa.gov/jislink (also, see state introduction).

Criminal Records: Access: Mail, online, in person. Only the court performs in person searches; visitors may not. Search fee: $3.00 per name. Required to search: name, years to search, DOB; also helpful: address, SSN. Criminal records on index cards. Online access to criminal records is the same as civil. (Also see state introduction.).

General Information: No sealed, juvenile, adoption, mental health, sex offenders (victims) or (sometimes) DUI records released. Turnaround time 1 week. Copy fee: $1.00 for first page, $.50 each add'l. Certification fee: $5.00. Fee payee: Garfield County District Court. Personal checks accepted. Prepayment is required.

Grant County

Superior Court PO Box 37, Ephrata, WA 98823-0037; 509-754-2011 X448; Fax: 509-754-5638. Hours: 8AM-5PM (PST). *Felony, Civil, Eviction, Probate.*

Civil Records: Access: Phone, mail, online, in person. Both court and visitors may perform in person searches. Search fee: $10.00 per name. Required to search: name, years to search; also helpful: address. Civil cases indexed by defendant, plaintiff. Civil records on computer from 1982, and some on index cards, archived from 1909. Index available remotely online

from JIS-Link; see www.courts.wa.gov/jislink (also, see state introduction).

Criminal Records: Access: Phone, mail, online, in person. Both court and visitors may perform in person searches. Search fee: $10.00 per name. Required to search: name, years to search; also helpful: address, DOB, SSN. Criminal records on computer from 1982, and some on index cards, archived from 1909. Online access to criminal records is the same as civil. (Also see state introduction.).

General Information: Public Access terminal is available. No sealed, juvenile, adoption, paternity, mental health, sex offenders (victims) records released. SASE required. Turnaround time 2 weeks. Copy fee: $2.00 for first page, $1.00 each add'l. Certification fee: $2.00 plus $1.00 per page after first. Fee payee: Grant County Clerk's Office. Business checks accepted. Prepayment is required.

District Court PO Box 37, Ephrata, WA 98823-0037; 509-754-2011 X318; Fax: 509-754-6099. Hours: 8AM-5PM (PST). *Misdemeanor, Civil Actions Under $50,000, Small Claims.*

Civil Records: Access: Mail, online, in person. Only the court performs in person searches; visitors may not. Search fee: $20.00 per name. Required to search: name, years to search; also helpful: address. Civil cases indexed by defendant, plaintiff. Civil records on computer from 3/91, on index cards. Index available remotely online from JIS-Link; see www.courts.wa.gov/jislink (also, see state introduction).

Criminal Records: Access: Mail, online, in person. Only the court performs in person searches; visitors may not. Search fee: $20.00 per name. Required to search: name, years to search, DOB; also helpful: address, SSN. Criminal records on computer from 3/91, on index cards. Online access to criminal records is the same as civil. (Also see state introduction.).

General Information: No sealed, probation, juvenile, adoption, paternity, mental health, sex offenders (victims) or (sometimes) DUI records released. Turnaround time up to 30 days. Copy fee: $2.00 for first page, $1.00 each add'l. Certification fee: $5.00 per page. Fee payee: Grant County District Court. Personal checks accepted. Prepayment is required.

Grays Harbor County

Superior Court 102 W Broadway, Rm 203, Montesano, WA 98563-3606; 360-249-3842; Fax: 360-249-6381. Hours: 8AM-5PM (PST). *Felony, Civil, Eviction, Probate.*

Civil Records: Access: Phone, fax, mail, online, in person. Both court and visitors may perform in person searches. Search fee: $20.00 per name. No fee for records before 1980. Required to search: name, years to search; also helpful: address. Civil cases indexed by defendant, plaintiff. Civil records on computer from 12/80, on microfiche from 1856, on index cards. Index available remotely online from JIS-Link; see www.courts.wa.gov/jislink (also, see state introduction).

Criminal Records: Access: Phone, fax, mail, online, in person. Both court and visitors may perform in person searches. Search fee: $20.00 per name. No fee for records before 1980. Required to search: name, years to search; also helpful: address, DOB, SSN. Criminal records on computer from 12/80, on microfiche from 1856, on index cards. Online access to criminal records is the same as civil. (Also see state introduction.).

General Information: No sealed, juvenile, adoption, paternity, mental health, sex offenders (victims). SASE required. Turnaround time 2 days. Fax notes: No fee to fax results. Fax available in emergency only. Copy fee: $2.00 for first page, $1.00 each add'l. Certification fee: Included in copy fee. Fee payee: Grays Harbor County Clerk. Business checks accepted. Prepayment is required.

District Court No 1 102 W Broadway, Rm 202, PO Box 647, Montesano, WA 98563-0647; 360-249-3441; Fax: 360-249-6382. Hours: 8AM-Noon, 1-5PM (PST). *Misdemeanor, Civil Actions Under $50,000, Small Claims.*

www.co.grays-harbor.wa.us/info/judicial

Civil Records: Access: Phone, fax, mail, online, in person. Only the court performs in person searches; visitors may not. No search fee. Required to search: name, years to search; also helpful: address. Civil cases indexed by defendant, plaintiff. Civil records on computer from 4/91, on index cards. Index available remotely online from JIS-Link; see www.courts.wa.gov/jislink (also, see state introduction).

Criminal Records: Access: Phone, fax, mail, online, in person. Only the court performs in person searches; visitors may not. No search fee. Required to search: name, years to search, DOB; also helpful: address, SSN. Criminal records on computer from 4/91, on index cards. Online access to criminal records is the same as civil.

General Information: Public Access terminal is available. No sealed, juvenile, adoption, paternity, mental health, sex offenders (victims) records released. SASE required. Turnaround time 1 week. Copy fee: $.25 per page. Certification fee: $5.00. Fee payee: Grays Harbor District Court #1. Personal checks accepted. Prepayment is required.

District Court No 2 PO Box 142, Aberdeen, WA 98520-0035; 360-532-7061; Fax: 360-532-7704. Hours: 8AM-Noon, 1-5PM (PST). *Misdemeanor, Civil Actions Under $50,000, Small Claims.*

www.co.grays-harbor.wa.us

Civil Records: Access: Phone, fax, mail, online, in person. Only the court performs in person searches; visitors may not. No search fee. Required to search: name, years to search; also helpful: address. Civil cases indexed by defendant, plaintiff. Civil records on computer from 4/91, on index cards. Index available remotely online from JIS-Link; see www.courts.wa.gov/jislink (also, see state introduction).

Criminal Records: Access: Phone, fax, mail, online, in person. Only the court performs in person searches; visitors may not. No search fee. Required to search: name, years to search, DOB; also helpful: address, SSN. Criminal records on computer from 4/91, on index cards. Online access to criminal records is the same as civil. (Also see state introduction.).

General Information: No sealed, juvenile, adoption, paternity, mental health, sex offenders (victims) or (sometimes) DUI records released. SASE required. Turnaround time 1 week. Fax notes: No fee to fax results. Copy fee: $.25 per page. Certification fee: $5.00. Fee payee: Grays Harbor District Court #2. Personal checks accepted. Prepayment is required.

Island County

Superior Court PO Box 5000, Coupeville, WA 98239-5000; 360-679-7359. Hours: 8AM-4:30PM (PST). *Felony, Civil, Eviction, Probate.*

Civil Records: Access: Phone, fax, mail, online, in person. Both court and visitors may perform in person searches. Search fee: $20.00 per hour. Required to search: name, years to search; also helpful: address. Civil cases indexed by defendant, plaintiff. Civil records on computer from 7/1984, microfiche from 1889. Archived in Bellingham, WA. Index available remotely online from JIS-Link; see www.courts.wa.gov/jislink (also, see state introduction).

Criminal Records: Access: Phone, mail, online, in person. Both court and visitors may perform in person searches. Search fee: $20.00 per hour. Required to search: name, years to search; also helpful: address, DOB, SSN. Criminal records on computer from 7/1984, microfiche from 1889. Archived in Bellingham,

WA. Online access to criminal records is the same as civil. (Also see state introduction.).

General Information: No sealed, dependency, truancy, adoption, paternity, mental health, sex offenders (victims). SASE required. Turnaround time 1 week. Copy fee: $.25 per page. Certification fee: $2.00 first page and $1.00 each add'l. Fee payee: Island county Clerk. Business checks accepted. Prepayment required.

District Court 800 S 8th Ave, Oak Harbor, WA 98277; 360-675-5988; Fax: 360-675-8231. Hours: 8AM-4:30PM (PST). *Misdemeanor, Civil Actions Under $50,000, Small Claims.*

Note: Records requests are done as time permits. Bottom of priority list.

Civil Records: Access: Fax, mail, online, in person. Both court and visitors may perform in person searches. No search fee. Required to search: name, years to search; also helpful: address. Civil cases indexed by defendant. Civil records on computer from 1991, on index by alpha. Index available remotely online from JIS-Link; see www.courts.wa.gov/jislink (also, see state introduction).

Criminal Records: Access: Fax, mail, online, in person. Only the court performs in person searches; visitors may not. No search fee. Required to search: name, years to search, DOB; also helpful: address, SSN. Criminal records on computer from 1991, on index by alpha. Online access to criminal records is the same as civil. (Also see state introduction.).

General Information: No sealed, juvenile, adoption, paternity, mental health, sex offenders (victims) or (sometimes) DUI records released. SASE required. Turnaround time 1-7 days. Fax notes: $1.00 per page. Copy fee: $.25 per page. Certification fee: $5.00. Fee payee: Island District Court. Personal checks accepted. Prepayment is required.

Jefferson County

Superior Court PO Box 1220, Port Townsend, WA 98368-0920; 360-385-9125. Hours: 9AM-5PM (PST). *Felony, Civil, Eviction, Probate.*

Civil Records: Access: Phone, mail, online, in person. Both court and visitors may perform in person searches. Search fee: $8.00 per hour. Required to search: name, years to search. Civil cases indexed by defendant, plaintiff. Civil records on computer from 1983, on microfiche from 1890s. Archive in Bellingham, WA. Index available remotely online from JIS-Link; see www.courts.wa.gov/jislink (also, see state introduction).

Criminal Records: Access: Phone, mail, online, in person. Both court and visitors may perform in person searches. Search fee: $8.00 per hour. Required to search: name, years to search; also helpful: DOB. Criminal records on computer from 1983, on microfiche from 1890s. Archive in Bellingham, WA. Online access to criminal records is the same as civil. (Also see state introduction.).

General Information: No sealed, juvenile, adoption, paternity, mental health records released. SASE required. Turnaround time 2 days. Copy fee: $1.00 for first page, $.50 each add'l. Certification fee: $2.00 plus $1.00 per page after first. Fee payee: County Clerk. Personal checks accepted. Out of state checks not accepted. Prepayment is required.

District Court PO Box 1220, Port Townsend, WA 98368-0920; 360-385-9135; Fax: 360-385-9367. Hours: 8AM-5PM (PST). *Misdemeanor, Civil Actions Under $50,000, Small Claims.*

www.co.jefferson.wa.us

Civil Records: Access: Phone, fax, mail, online, in person. Only the court performs in person searches; visitors may not. No search fee. Required to search: name, years to search; also helpful: address. Civil cases indexed by defendant. Civil records on DISCIS computer from 1993, on computer from '90-'93, on log

books prior to 1990. Physical files kept 10 years from disposition per retention schedule. Index available remotely online from JIS-Link; see www.courts.wa.gov/jislink (also, see state introduction).

Criminal Records: Access: Phone, fax, mail, online, in person. Only the court performs in person searches; visitors may not. No search fee. Required to search: name, DOB; also helpful: years to search, address, SSN. Criminal records on DISCIS computer from 1993, on computer from '90-'93, on log books prior to 1990. Physical files kept 10 years from disposition per retention schedule. Online access to criminal records is the same as civil. (Also see state introduction.).

General Information: No sealed, juvenile, adoption, paternity, mental health, sex offenders (victims) records released. SASE required. Turnaround time 1 week. Copy fee: $.15 per page. Certification fee: $6.00. Personal checks accepted. Prepayment is required.

King County

Superior Court 516 Third Ave, E-609 Courthouse, Seattle, WA 98104-2386; 206-296-9300, 800-325-6165 in state. Hours: 8:30AM-4:30AM (PST). *Felony, Civil, Eviction, Probate.*

www.metrokc.gov/kcscc

Civil Records: Access: Mail, online, in person. Both court and visitors may perform in person searches. Search fee: $20.00 per hour. Fee $25.00 minimum including copies. Required to search: name, years to search; also helpful: address. Civil cases indexed by defendant, plaintiff. Civil records on computer since 1979; prior records on microfiche back to 1935. Index available remotely online from JIS-Link; see www.courts.wa.gov/jislink (also, see state introduction).

Criminal Records: Access: Mail, online, in person. Both court and visitors may perform in person searches. Search fee: $20.00 per hour. Fee is $25.00 if number of pages unknown. Required to search: name, years to search; also helpful: address, DOB, SSN. Criminal records on computer since 1979; prior records on microfiche back to 1938. Online access to criminal records is the same as civil. (Also see state introduction.).

General Information: Public Access terminal is available. No sealed, juvenile, adoption, paternity, mental health, sex offenders (victims). SASE required. Turnaround time 2 weeks. Copy fee: $.15 per page. Microfiche/computer image copy fee: $.25 per page. Certification fee: $2.00 plus $1.00 per page after first. Fee payee: King County Superior Court Clerk. Personal checks accepted. In state personal checks only. Prepayment is required.

District Court (Aukeen Division) 1210 S Central, Kent, WA 98032-7426; 206-296-7740. Hours: 8:30AM-4:30PM (PST). *Misdemeanor, Civil Actions Under $50,000, Small Claims.*

www.metrookc.gov/kcdc

Civil Records: Access: Mail, online, in person. Only the court performs in person searches; visitors may not. No search fee. Required to search: name, years to search; also helpful: address. Civil cases indexed by defendant, plaintiff. Civil records on computer 5 years back. Index available remotely online from JIS-Link; see www.courts.wa.gov/jislink (also, see state introduction).

Criminal Records: Access: Mail, online, in person. Only the court performs in person searches; visitors may not. No search fee. Required to search: name, years to search, DOB; also helpful: address, SSN. Criminal records on computer 5 years back. Online access to criminal records is the same as civil. (Also see state introduction.).

General Information: No sealed, juvenile, adoption, paternity, mental health, sex offenders (victims) or (sometimes) DUI records released. SASE required.

Turnaround time 1 day. Copy fee: $.15 per page. Certification fee: $5.00. Fee payee: Aukeen District Court. Personal checks accepted. Prepayment is required.

District Court (Bellevue Div) 585 112th Ave SE, Bellevue, WA 98004; 206-296-3650; Fax: 206-296-0589. 8:30AM-4:30PM (PST). *Misdemeanor, Civil Actions Under $50,000, Small Claims.*

Civil Records: Access: Phone, mail, online, in person. Both court and visitors may perform in person searches. No search fee. Required to search: name, years to search; also helpful: address. Civil cases indexed by defendant, plaintiff. Civil records on computer for past 10 years. Index available remotely online from JIS-Link; see www.courts.wa.gov/jislink (also, see state introduction).

Criminal Records: Access: Phone, mail, online, in person. Both court and visitors may perform in person searches. No search fee. Required to search: name, years to search, DOB; also helpful: address, SSN. Criminal records on computer from 1987. Criminal records may be removed after 5 years from disposition. Online access to criminal records is the same as civil. (Also see state introduction.).

General Information: No sealed, juvenile, adoption, paternity, mental health, sex offenders (victims) or (sometimes) DUI records released. Turnaround time cannot be guaranteed for written requests. Copy fee: $.15 per page. Certification fee: $5.00. Fee payee: KCDC, Bellevue Division. Personal checks accepted. Credit cards accepted: Visa, MasterCard. Prepayment is required.

District Court (Federal Way Division) 33506 10th Pl South, Federal Way, WA 98003-6396; 206-296-7784; Fax: 206-296-0590. Hours: 8:30AM-4:30PM (PST). *Misdemeanor, Civil Actions Under $50,000, Small Claims.*

www.metrokc.gov/kcdc

Civil Records: Access: Phone, mail, online, in person. Only the court performs in person searches; visitors may not. No search fee. Required to search: name, years to search; also helpful: address. Civil cases indexed by defendant, plaintiff. Civil records on computer back 10 years. Index available remotely online from JIS-Link; see www.courts.wa.gov/jislink (also, see state introduction).

Criminal Records: Access: Phone, mail, online, in person. Only the court performs in person searches; visitors may not. No search fee. Required to search: name, years to search, DOB, signed release; also helpful: address. Criminal records on computer back 5 years. Online access to criminal records is the same as civil. (Also see state introduction.).

General Information: No sealed, adoption, paternity, mental health, sex offenders (victims) or (sometimes) DUI records released. SASE required. Turnaround time up to 7 days. Copy fee: $.15 per page. Certification fee: $5.00. Fee payee: Federal Way Division King County District Court. Personal checks accepted. Credit cards accepted: Visa, MasterCard. Prepayment is required.

District Court (Issaquah Division) 5415 220th Ave SW, Issaquah, WA 98029-6839; 206-296-7688; Fax: 206-296-0591. Hours: 8:30AM-4:30PM (PST). *Misdemeanor, Civil Actions Under $50,000, Small Claims.*

www.metrokc.gov/kcdc

Civil Records: Access: Mail, online, in person. Only the court performs in person searches; visitors may not. No search fee. Required to search: name, years to search; also helpful: address. Civil cases indexed by defendant, plaintiff. Civil records on computer back 10 years. Index available remotely online from JIS-Link; see www.courts.wa.gov/jislink (also, see state introduction).

Criminal Records: Access: Mail, online, in person. Only the court performs in person searches; visitors may not. No search fee. Required to search: name, years to search, DOB, signed release; also helpful: address. Criminal records on computer back 5 years. Online access to criminal records is the same as civil. (Also see state introduction.).

General Information: No sealed, juvenile, sex offenders (victims) or (sometimes) DUI records released. SASE required. Turnaround time 1-5 days. Copy fee: $.15 per page. Certification fee: $6.00. Fee payee: Issaquah Division. Personal checks accepted. Prepayment is required.

District Court (Renton Division) 3407 NE 2nd St, Renton, WA 98056-4193; 206-296-3532, 800-325-6165 in state; Fax: 206-296-0593. Hours: 8:30AM-4:30PM (PST). *Misdemeanor, Civil Actions Under $50,000, Small Claims.*

www.metrokc.gov

Civil Records: Access: Phone, fax, mail, online, in person. Only the court performs in person searches; visitors may not. No search fee. Required to search: name, years to search; also helpful: address. Civil cases indexed by defendant, plaintiff. Civil records on computer back 10 years. Index available remotely online from JIS-Link; see www.courts.wa.gov/jislink (also, see state introduction).

Criminal Records: Access: Phone, fax, mail, online, in person. Only the court performs in person searches; visitors may not. No search fee. Required to search: name, years to search, signed release; also helpful: address, DOB, SSN. Criminal records on computer back 5 years. Online access to criminal records is the same as civil. (Also see state introduction.).

General Information: No sealed, juvenile, adoption, paternity, mental health, sex offenders (victims) or (sometimes) DUI records released. SASE requested. Turnaround time 2-3 days. Copy fee: $.15 per page. Certification fee: $5.00. Fee payee: Renton District Court. Personal checks accepted. Credit cards accepted: Visa/MC. Prepayment is required.

District Court (Seattle Division) 516 Third Ave E-327 Courthouse, Seattle, WA 98104-3273; 206-296-3565. 8:30AM-4:30PM (PST). *Misdemeanor, Civil Actions Under $50,000, Small Claims.*

www.metrokc.gov/kcdc

Civil Records: Access: Mail, online, in person. Both court and visitors may perform in person searches. No search fee. Required to search: name, years to search; also helpful: address. Civil cases indexed by defendant, plaintiff. Civil records on computer from back 10 years. Index available remotely online from JIS-Link; see www.courts.wa.gov/jislink (also, see state introduction).

Criminal Records: Access: Mail, online, in person. Both court and visitors may perform in person searches. No search fee. Required to search: name, years to search, DOB, signed release; also helpful: address, SSN. Criminal records on computer from back 10 years. Online access to criminal records is the same as civil. (Also see state introduction.).

General Information: Public Access terminal is available. (10 minute limit. 90% of info available to public, other 10% can only be searched by court staff.) No sealed, juvenile, adoption, paternity, mental health, sex offenders (victims), treatment plans or (sometimes) DUI records released. SASE required. Turnaround time 10 days. Copy fee: $.15 per page. Certification fee: $5.00. Fee payee: King County District Court, Seattle. Personal checks accepted. Credit cards accepted: Visa, MasterCard. Prepayment is required.

District Court (Shoreline Division) 18050 Meridian Ave N, Shoreline, WA 98133-4642; 206-296-3679; Fax: 206-296-0594. Hours: 8:30AM-4:30PM (PST). *Misdemeanor, Civil Actions Under $50,000, Small Claims.*

www.metrokc.gov/kcdc

Civil Records: Access: Phone, fax, mail, online, in person. Both court and visitors may perform in person searches. No search fee. Required to search: name, years to search; also helpful: address. Civil cases indexed by defendant, plaintiff. Civil records on computer from 1985. Index available remotely online from JIS-Link; see www.courts.wa.gov/jislink (also, see state introduction).

Criminal Records: Access: Phone, fax, mail, online, in person. Both court and visitors may perform in person searches. No search fee. Required to search: name, years to search; also helpful: address, DOB, SSN. Criminal records on computer from 1987. Online access to criminal records is the same as civil. (Also see state introduction.).

General Information: Public Access terminal is available. No sealed, juvenile, adoption, paternity, mental health, sex offenders (victims) or (sometimes) DUI records released. SASE required. Turnaround time 1 week. Fax notes: No fee to fax results. Copy fee: $.25 per page. Certification fee: $5.00. Fee payee: King County District Court. Personal checks accepted. Credit cards accepted: Visa, MasterCard. Prepayment is required.

District Court (Southwest Division - Vashon) 19021 99th SW (PO Box 111), Vashon, WA 98070-0111; 206-296-3664; Fax: 206-296-0578. Hours: 8:30AM-Noon, 1:15-4:30PM 2nd & 4th F of the month (PST). *Misdemeanor, Civil Actions Under $50,000, Small Claims.*

www.metrokc.gov/kcdc

Civil Records: Access: Fax, mail, online, in person. Only the court performs in person searches; visitors may not. No search fee. Required to search: name, years to search; also helpful: address. Civil cases indexed by defendant, plaintiff. Civil records on computer back 5 years. Index available remotely online from JIS-Link; see www.courts.wa.gov/jislink (also, see state introduction).

Criminal Records: Access: Fax, mail, online, in person. Only the court performs in person searches; visitors may not. No search fee. Required to search: name, years to search; also helpful: address, DOB, SSN. Criminal records on computer from 1987. Online access to criminal records is the same as civil. (Also see state introduction.).

General Information: No sealed, juvenile, adoption, paternity, mental health, sex offenders (victims) or (sometimes) DUI records released. Turnaround time 1 day. Fax notes: No fee to fax results. Copy fee: $.15 per page. Certification fee: $5.00. Fee payee: Vashon District Court. Personal checks accepted. Prepayment is required.

District Court (Southwest Division) 601 SW 149th St, Seattle, WA 98166; 206-296-0133; Fax: 206-296-0585. Hours: 8:30AM-4:30PM (PST). *Misdemeanor, Civil Actions Under $50,000, Small Claims.*

Civil Records: Access: Mail, online, in person. Only the court performs in person searches; visitors may not. No search fee. Required to search: name, years to search; also helpful: address. Civil cases indexed by defendant, plaintiff. Civil records on computer back 10 years. Index available remotely online from JIS-Link; see www.courts.wa.gov/jislink (also, see state introduction).

Criminal Records: Access: Mail, online, in person. Only the court performs in person searches; visitors

may not. No search fee. Required to search: name, years to search, DOB, signed release; also helpful: address. Criminal records on computer back 5 years. Online access to criminal records is the same as civil. (Also see state introduction.).

General Information: No sealed, juvenile, sex offenders (victims) or (sometimes) DUI records released. SASE requested. Turnaround time 2-4 days. Copy fee: $.15 per page. Certification fee: $5.00. Fee payee: Southwest Division, King County District Court. Personal checks accepted. Credit cards accepted: Visa, MasterCard. Prepayment is required.

District Court NE Division 8601 160th Ave NE, Redmond, WA 98052-3548; 206-296-3667. Hours: 8:30AM-4:30PM (PST). *Misdemeanor, Civil Actions Under $50,000, Small Claims.*

www.metrokc.gov/kcdc

Civil Records: Access: Mail, online, in person. Both court and visitors may perform in person searches. No search fee. Required to search: name, years to search; also helpful: address. Civil cases indexed by defendant, plaintiff. Civil records on computer back 10 years. Index available remotely online from JIS-Link; see www.courts.wa.gov/jislink (also, see state introduction).

Criminal Records: Access: Mail, online, in person. Both court and visitors may perform in person searches. No search fee. Required to search: name, years to search, DOB; also helpful: address. Criminal records on computer back 5 years. Online access to criminal records is the same as civil. (Also see state introduction.).

General Information: Public Access terminal is available. No sealed, juvenile, adoption, paternity, mental health, sex offenders (victims) or (sometimes) DUI records released. Turnaround time 1-2 weeks. Copy fee: $.15 per page. Certification fee: $5.00. Fee payee: King County District Court. Personal checks accepted. Credit cards accepted: Visa, MasterCard. Prepayment is required.

Kitsap County

Superior Court 614 Division St, MS34, Port Orchard, WA 98366-4699; 360-337-7164; Fax: 360-337-4927. Hours: 8AM-4:30PM (PST). *Felony, Civil, Eviction, Probate.*

www.wa.gov/kitsap/departments/clerk/index.html

Civil Records: Access: Mail, online, in person. Both court and visitors may perform in person searches. Search fee: $20.00 per hour. Fee is for up to 5 names. Required to search: name, years to search. Civil cases indexed by defendant, plaintiff. Civil records on computer from 1978, on microfiche and archived from 1889. Index available remotely online from JIS-Link; see www.courts.wa.gov/jislink (also, see state introduction).

Criminal Records: Access: Mail, online, in person. Both court and visitors may perform in person searches. Search fee: $20.00 per hour. Fee is for up to 5 names. Required to search: name, years to search; also helpful: address, DOB, SSN. Criminal records on computer from 1978, on microfiche and archived from 1889. Online access to criminal records is the same as civil. (Also see state introduction.).

General Information: Public Access terminal is available. No dependencies, adoption or mental illness records released. SASE required. Turnaround time 2 weeks. Copy fee: $2.00 for first page, $1.00 each add'l. Certification fee: Certification fee included in copy fee. Fee payee: Kitsap County Clerk. Personal checks accepted. Out-of state personal checks not accepted. Prepayment is required.

District Court 614 Division St, MS 25, Port Orchard, WA 98366-4614; 360-337-7109; Fax: 360-337-4865. 8:30AM-4:30PM (PST). *Misdemeanor, Civil Actions Under $50,000, Small Claims.*

Civil Records: Access: Phone, fax, mail, online, in person. Only the court performs in person searches; visitors may not. No search fee. Required to search: name, years to search; also helpful: address. Civil cases indexed by defendant, plaintiff. Civil records on computer from 10/95, prior in archives. Index available remotely online from JIS-Link; see www.courts.wa.gov/jislink (also, see state introduction).

Criminal Records: Access: Phone, fax, mail, online, in person. Only the court performs in person searches; visitors may not. No search fee. Required to search: name, years to search; also helpful: address, DOB, SSN. Criminal records on computer from 6/89, prior in archives. Online access to criminal records is the same as civil. (Also see state introduction.).

General Information: No dependencies, adoption and mental illness records released. Turnaround time 1 week. Fax notes: No fee to fax results. Local faxing only. Copy fee: $.15 per page. Certification fee: $5.00. Fee payee: Kitsap County District Court. Personal checks accepted. Prepayment is required.

District Court North 614 Division St, MS-25, Port Orchard, WA 98366; 360-337-7109; Fax: 360-337-4865. Hours: 8:30AM-12:15PM; 1:15-4:30PM (PST). *Misdemeanor, Civil Actions Under $50,000, Small Claims.*

Note: The court physical address is 19050 Jensen Way NE, Poulsbo, WA.

Civil Records: Access: Mail, online, in person. Only the court performs in person searches; visitors may not. No search fee. Required to search: name, years to search. Civil cases indexed by defendant, plaintiff. Civil records on computer back 8 years, on index cards for 10 years. Index available remotely online from JIS-Link; see www.courts.wa.gov/jislink (also, see state introduction). Send all mail requests to Port Orchard District court.

Criminal Records: Access: Mail, online, in person. Only the court performs in person searches; visitors may not. No search fee. Required to search: name, signed release; also helpful: years to search, DOB. Criminal records on computer back 8 years, on index cards for 10 years. Online access to criminal records is the same as civil. (Also see state introduction.). Send all mail requests to Port Orchard District Court.

General Information: No dependencies, adoption and mental illness records released. Copy fee: $.15 per page. Certification fee: $5.00. Fee payee: District Court North, Kitsap County. Only cashiers checks and money orders accepted. Prepayment is required.

Kittitas County

Superior Court 205 W 5th Rm 210, Ellensburg, WA 98926; 509-962-7531; Fax: 509-962-7667. Hours: 9AM-Noon, 1-5PM (PST). *Felony, Misdemeanor, Civil, Eviction, Probate.*

Civil Records: Access: Phone, fax, mail, online, in person. Only the court performs in person searches; visitors may not. Search fee: $10.00 per name. Required to search: name, years to search; also helpful: address. Civil cases indexed by defendant, plaintiff. Civil records on computer from 1982, on microfiche and archived from 1890. Some records on index cards. Index available remotely online from JIS-Link; see www.courts.wa.gov/jislink (also, see state introduction).

Criminal Records: Access: Phone, fax, mail, online, in person. Only the court performs in person searches; visitors may not. Search fee: $10.00 per name. Required to search: name, years to search; also helpful: address, DOB, SSN. Criminal records on computer from 1982, on microfiche and archived from 1890. Some records

on index cards. Online access to criminal records is the same as civil. (Also see state introduction.).

General Information: No dependencies, adoption, and mental illness records released. Turnaround time 2 days. Fax notes: No fee to fax results. Fax available in emergency only. Copy fee: $1.00 per page. Certification fee: $2.00. Fee payee: Kittitas County Clerk. Personal checks accepted. Prepayment is required.

District Court Lower Kittitas 205 W 5th, Rm 180, Ellensburg, WA 98926; 509-962-7511. Hours: 9AM-5PM (PST). *Misdemeanor, Civil Actions Under $50,000, Small Claims.*

Civil Records: Access: Mail, online, in person. Only the court performs in person searches; visitors may not. No search fee. Required to search: name, years to search. Civil cases indexed by defendant, plaintiff. Civil records on computer from 8/91, archived back 10 years, some on index cards. Records retained for 20 years. Index available remotely online from JIS-Link; see www.courts.wa.gov/jislink (also, see state introduction).

Criminal Records: Access: Mail, online, in person. Only the court performs in person searches; visitors may not. No search fee. Required to search: name, years to search, DOB. Criminal records on computer from 8/91, archived back 10 years, some on index cards. Records retained for 20 years. Online access to criminal records is the same as civil. (Also see state introduction.).

General Information: No dependencies, adoption, and mental illness records released. SASE required. Turnaround time 7-10 days. Copy fee: $.25 per page. Certification fee: $5.00. Fee payee: Kittitas County District Court. Personal checks accepted. Prepayment is required.

District Court Upper Kittitas 618 E First, Cle Elum, WA 98922; 509-674-5533; Fax: 509-674-4209. Hours: 8AM-5PM (PST). *Misdemeanor, Civil Actions Under $50,000, Small Claims.*

Civil Records: Access: Fax, mail, online, in person. Only the court performs in person searches; visitors may not. No search fee. Required to search: name, years to search. Civil cases indexed by defendant, plaintiff. Civil records on computer since 8/91; prior records archived from 1890, some on index cards. Records retained for 10 years. Index available remotely online from JIS-Link; see www.courts.wa.gov/jislink (also, see state introduction).

Criminal Records: Access: Fax, mail, online, in person. Only the court performs in person searches; visitors may not. No search fee. Required to search: name, years to search, DOB; also helpful: SSN. Criminal records on computer since 08/91; prior records archived from 1890, some on index cards. Records retained for 5 years. Online access to criminal records is the same as civil. (Also see state introduction.).

General Information: Public Access terminal is available. (For records since 1997.) No dependencies, adoption, and mental illness records released. Turnaround time 1 week. Fax notes: No fee to fax results. There is no additional fee for faxing, but same fees as copies or certification fees. Copy fee: $.25 per page. Certification fee: $5.00. Fee payee: UKCDC. Personal checks accepted. Credit cards accepted: Visa, MasterCard. Prepayment is required.

Klickitat County

Superior Court Superior Court Clerk, 205 S Columbus, Rm 204, Goldendale, WA 98620; 509-773-5744. Hours: 9AM-5PM (PST). *Felony, Civil, Eviction, Probate.*

Civil Records: Access: Phone, mail, online, in person. Only the court performs in person searches; visitors may not. Search fee: $8.00 per hour. Required to search: name, years to search; also helpful: address. Civil cases indexed by defendant, plaintiff. Civil records on

computer from 9/87. Index available remotely online from JIS-Link; see www.courts.wa.gov/jislink (also, see state introduction).

Criminal Records: Access: Phone, mail, online, in person. Only the court performs in person searches; visitors may not. Search fee: $8.00 per hour. Required to search: name, years to search; also helpful: address, DOB, SSN. Criminal records on computer from 9/87; prior on books back to 1886. Online access to criminal records is the same as civil. (Also see state introduction.).

General Information: No dependencies, adoption, and mental illness records released. SASE required. Turnaround time 2 weeks. Copy fee: $2.00 for first page, $1.00 each add'l. Certification fee: $2.00 plus $1.00 per page after first. Fee payee: Klickitat County Clerk. No personal checks accepted. Prepayment is required.

East District Court 205 S Columbus, MS-CH11, Goldendale, WA 98620-9290; 509-773-4670. Hours: 8AM-12, 1-5pm (PST). *Misdemeanor, Civil Actions Under $50,000, Small Claims.*

Civil Records: Access: Phone, mail, fax, online, in person. Both court and visitors may perform in person searches. No search fee. Required to search: name, years to search. Civil cases indexed by defendant, plaintiff. Civil records on computer from 4/93, on index cards prior. Retained for 10 years. Index available remotely online from JIS-Link; see www.courts.wa.gov/jislink (also, see state introduction).

Criminal Records: Access: Phone, mail, fax, online, in person. Both court and visitors may perform in person searches. No search fee. Required to search: name, years to search, DOB. Criminal records on computer from 4/93, on index cards prior. Retained for 10 years. Online access to criminal records is the same as civil. (Also see state introduction.).

General Information: No dependencies, adoption, and mental illness records released. SASE required. Turnaround time 1 week. Copy fee: 1st 10 pages free, each additional page $.15. Certification fee: $5.00. Fee payee: East District Court. Personal checks accepted. Prepayment is required.

West District Court PO Box 435, White Salmon, WA 98672-0435; 509-493-1190; Fax: 509-493-4469. Hours: 8AM-5PM (PST). *Misdemeanor, Civil Actions Under $50,000, Small Claims.*

Civil Records: Access: Mail, in person. Only the court performs in person searches; visitors may not. No search fee. Required to search: name, years to search. Civil cases indexed by defendant, plaintiff. Civil records on computer from 5/93, on docket books. Index available remotely online from JIS-Link; see www.courts.wa.gov/jislink (also, see state introduction).

Criminal Records: Access: Mail, in person. Only the court performs in person searches; visitors may not. No search fee. Required to search: name, years to search, DOB; also helpful: address. Criminal records on computer from 5/93, on docket books. Online access to criminal records is the same as civil. (Also see state introduction.).

General Information: No dependencies, adoption, sealed and mental illness records released. SASE required. Turnaround time 3-5 days. Copy fee: $2.00 for first page, $1.00 each add'l. Certification fee: $5.00. Fee payee: West District Court. Personal checks accepted. Prepayment is required.

Lewis County

Superior Court 360 NW North St, MS:CLK 01, Chehalis, WA 98532-1900; 360-740-2704; Fax: 360-748-1639. Hours: 8AM-5PM (PST). *Felony, Misdemeanor, Civil, Eviction, Probate.*

Civil Records: Access: Phone, mail, online, in person. Only the court performs in person searches; visitors may not. Search fee: $8.00 per hour. Required to search: name, years to search; also helpful: address. Civil cases indexed by defendant, plaintiff. Civil records on computer from 1983, archived from 1900s. Index available remotely online from JIS-Link; see www.courts.wa.gov/jislink (also, see state introduction). **Criminal Records:** Access: Phone, mail, online, in person. Only the court performs in person searches; visitors may not. Search fee: $8.00 per hour. Required to search: name, years to search; also helpful: address, DOB, SSN. Criminal records on computer from 1983, archived from 1900s. Online access to criminal records is the same as civil. (Also see state introduction.). **General Information:** No dependencies, adoption, paternity, and mental illness records released. SASE required. Turnaround time up to 7 days. Fax notes: Fee to fax results is $.50 per page. Copy fee: $2.00 for first page, $1.00 each add'l. Certification fee: $3.00. Fee payee: Lewis County Clerk. Personal checks accepted. Prepayment is required.

District Court PO Box 336, Chehalis, WA 98532-0336; 360-740-1203; Fax: 360-740-2779. Hours: 8AM-5PM (PST). *Misdemeanor, Civil Actions Under $50,000, Small Claims.*

Civil Records: Access: Fax, mail, online, in person. Both court and visitors may perform in person searches. No search fee. Required to search: name, years to search. Civil cases indexed by defendant, plaintiff. Civil records on computer from 1983, on index cards. Records retained 10 years. Index available remotely online from JIS-Link; see www.courts.wa.gov/jislink (also, see state introduction). **Criminal Records:** Access: Fax, mail, online, in person. Both court and visitors may perform in person searches. No search fee. Required to search: name, years to search, DOB, sex, signed release; also helpful: address, SSN. Criminal records on computer since 1981. Records retained for 5 years. Online access to criminal records is the same as civil. (Also see state introduction.). **General Information:** No dependencies, adoption, and mental illness records released. SASE required. Turnaround time 1 week. Fax notes: No fee to fax results. Copy fee: $.25 per page. Certification fee: $5.00 per page. Fee payee: Lewis County District Court. Personal checks accepted. Prepayment is required.

Lincoln County

Superior Court Box 68, Davenport, WA 99122-0396; 509-725-1401; Fax: 509-725-1150. Hours: 8AM-5PM *Felony, Misdemeanor, Civil, Eviction, Probate.*

Civil Records: Access: Mail, online, in person. Only the court performs in person searches; visitors may not. Search fee: $20.00 per hour. Required to search: name, years to search; also helpful: address. Civil cases indexed by defendant, plaintiff. Civil records on computer and microfiche from 11/82, archived from 1903. Index available remotely online from JIS-Link; see www.courts.wa.gov/jislink (also, see state introduction). **Criminal Records:** Access: Mail, online, in person. Only the court performs in person searches; visitors may not. Search fee: $20.00 per hour. Required to search: name, years to search; also helpful: address, DOB, SSN. Criminal records on computer and microfiche from 11/82, archived from 1903. Online access to criminal records is the same as civil. (Also see state introduction.). **General Information:** No dependencies, adoption, and mental illness records released. SASE required. Turnaround time same day. Copy fee: $2.00 for first page, $1.00 each add'l. Certification fee: $2.00. Fee payee: Lincoln County Clerk. Business checks accepted. Prepayment is required.

District Court PO Box 329, Davenport, WA 99122-0329; 509-725-2281. Hours: 8AM-5PM (PST). *Misdemeanor, Civil Actions Under $50,000, Small Claims.*

Note: Small office with limited time allowable for searches.

Civil Records: Access: Mail, fax, online, in person. Both court and visitors may perform in person searches. Search fee: $25.00 per hour. Required to search: name, years to search. Civil cases indexed by defendant. Civil records on computer back to 6/93, in books from 1985. Index available remotely online from JIS-Link; see www.courts.wa.gov/jislink (also, see state introduction). **Criminal Records:** Access: Mail, fax, online, in person. Only the court performs in person searches; visitors may not. Search fee: $25.00 per hour. Required to search: name, years to search, DOB. Criminal records on computer back to 6/93, in books from 1985. Online access to criminal records is the same as civil. (Also see state introduction.). **General Information:** Public Access terminal is available. No dependencies, adoption, and mental illness records released. SASE required. Turnaround time 1 week. Copy fee: $2.00 for first page, $1.00 each add'l. Certification fee: $6.00 plus $1.00 per page after first. Fee payee: Lincoln County District Court. Business checks accepted. Prepayment is required.

Mason County

Superior Court PO Box 340, Shelton, WA 98584; 360-427-9670 X346. Hours: 8:30AM-5PM (PST). *Felony, Civil, Eviction, Probate.*

www.co.mason.wa.us/Clerk/clerk.htm

Civil Records: Access: Phone, mail, online, in person. Both court and visitors may perform in person searches. Search fee: $20.00 per hour. Required to search: name, years to search; also helpful: address. Civil cases indexed by defendant, plaintiff. Civil records on computer from 1982, on microfiche and archived from 1890, on index or docket books prior to 1982. Index available remotely online from JIS-Link; see www.courts.wa.gov/jislink (also, see state introduction). **Criminal Records:** Access: Phone, mail, online, in person. Both court and visitors may perform in person searches. Search fee: $20.00 per hour. Required to search: name, years to search; also helpful: address, DOB. Criminal records on computer from 1982, on microfiche and archived from 1890, on index or docket books prior to 1982. Online access to criminal records is the same as civil. (Also see state introduction.). **General Information:** No dependencies, adoption, and mental illness records released. SASE required. Turnaround time 1 week. Fax notes: Will not fax results. Copy fee: $2.00 for 1st page, $1.00 each add'l. Certification fee: $2.00 plus $1.00 per page after first. Fee payee: Mason County Clerk. Attorney checks accepted. Prepayment is required.

District Court PO Box "O", Shelton, WA 98584-0090; 360-427-9670 X339; Fax: 360-427-7776. Hours: 8:30AM-5PM (PST). *Misdemeanor, Civil Actions Under $50,000, Small Claims.*

Civil Records: Access: Mail, in person. Only the court performs in person searches; visitors may not. Search fee: $20.00 per name. Fee is for extensive searching. Required to search: name, years to search; also helpful: address. Civil cases indexed by defendant, plaintiff. Civil records on computer from 12/92, prior on index book. Index available remotely online from JIS-Link; see www.courts.wa.gov/jislink (also, see state introduction). **Criminal Records:** Access: Mail, in person. Only the court performs in person searches; visitors may not. Search fee: Will charge $20.00 for extensive search. Required to search: name, years to search, DOB, signed release; also helpful: address, SSN. Criminal records on

computer from 12/92, prior on index book. Online access to criminal records is the same as civil. (Also see state introduction.). **General Information:** No dependencies, adoption, and mental illness records released. SASE required. Turnaround time 1 week. Copy fee: $.15 per page. Certification fee: $5.00. Fee payee: Mason County District Court. Personal checks accepted. Prepayment is required.

Okanogan County

Superior Court PO Box 72, Okanogan, WA 98840; 509-422-7275; Fax: 509-422-7277. Hours: 8AM-5PM (PST). *Felony, Misdemeanor, Civil, Eviction, Probate.*

Civil Records: Access: Phone, fax, mail, online, in person. Both court and visitors may perform in person searches. Search fee: $20.00 per hour. Required to search: name, years to search; also helpful: address. Civil cases indexed by defendant, plaintiff. Civil records on computer from 1994, on hand-written indexes from 1895. Index available remotely online from JIS-Link; see www.courts.wa.gov/jislink (also, see state introduction). **Criminal Records:** Access: Phone, fax, mail, online, in person. Both court and visitors may perform in person searches. Search fee: $20.00 per hour. Required to search: name, years to search; also helpful: address, DOB, SSN. Criminal records on computer from 1994, on hand-written indexes from 1895. Online access to criminal records is the same as civil. (Also see state introduction.). **General Information:** No dependencies, adoption, and mental illness records released. SASE required. Turnaround time 1-7 days. Copy fee: $1.00 per page. Certification fee: $2.00 plus $1.00 per page after first. Fee payee: Okanogan County Clerk. Personal checks accepted. Prepayment is required.

District Court PO Box 980, Okanogan, WA 98840-0980; 509-422-7170; Fax: 509-422-7174. Hours: 8AM-5PM (PST). *Misdemeanor, Civil Actions Under $50,000, Small Claims.*

Civil Records: Access: Phone, fax, mail, in person, online. Both court and visitors may perform in person searches. No search fee. Required to search: name, years to search. Civil cases indexed by defendant, plaintiff. Civil records on computer from 8/91, prior on index cards. Index available remotely online from JIS-Link; see www.courts.wa.gov/jislink (also, see state introduction). **Criminal Records:** Access: Phone, fax, mail, in person, online. Both court and visitors may perform in person searches. No search fee. Required to search: name, years to search, DOB. Criminal records on computer from 8/91, prior on index cards. Online access to criminal records is the same as civil. (Also see state introduction.). **General Information:** No dependencies, adoption, alcohol related evaluations, mental illness records released. SASE requested. Turnaround time 7 days. Fax notes: $1.00 for first page, $.50 each add'l. Copy fee: $1.00 for first page, $.50 each add'l. Certification fee: $5.00. Fee payee: Okanogan County District Court. Personal checks accepted. Prepayment is required.

Pacific County

Superior Court PO Box 67, South Bend, WA 98586; 360-875-9320; Fax: 360-875-9321. Hours: 8AM-4PM M-Th; 8AM-5PM F (PST). *Felony, Civil, Eviction, Probate.*

Civil Records: Access: Phone, mail, online, in person. Both court and visitors may perform in person searches. Search fee: $20.00 per hour if searching before 1984. Required to search: name, years to search. Civil cases indexed by defendant, plaintiff. Civil records on computer from 2/84, archived from 1887, some on docket books. Index available remotely online from JIS-Link; see www.courts.wa.gov/jislink (also, see state introduction).

Criminal Records: Access: Phone, mail, online, in person. Both court and visitors may perform in person searches. Search fee: $20.00 per hour if searching before 1984. Required to search: name, years to search. Criminal records on computer from 2/84, archived from 1887, some on docket books. Online access to criminal records is the same as civil. (Also see state introduction.).

General Information: No dependencies, adoption, and mental illness records released. Turnaround time varies. Copy fee: $2.00 for first page, $1.00 each add'l; Non-certified: $.15 per page. Certification fee: $2.00. Fee payee: Pacific County Clerk. Personal checks accepted. Prepayment is required.

District Court North Box 134, South Bend, WA 98586-0134; 360-875-9354; Fax: 360-875-9351. Hours: 9AM-4PM (PST). *Misdemeanor, Civil Actions Under $50,000, Small Claims.*

Civil Records: Access: Phone, fax, mail, online, in person. Both court and visitors may perform in person searches. No search fee. Required to search: name, years to search; also helpful: address. Civil cases indexed by defendant, plaintiff. Civil records on computer back to 3/93, prior on index cards. Civil records retained 10 years. Index available remotely online from JIS-Link; see www.courts.wa.gov/jislink (also, see state introduction).

Criminal Records: Access: Phone, fax, mail, online, in person. Both court and visitors may perform in person searches. No search fee. Required to search: name, DOB; also helpful: years to search, address, SSN. Criminal Records retained forever, on computer back to 03/93. Online access to criminal records is the same as civil. (Also see state introduction.).

General Information: No dependencies, MVRs, defendant case histories, adoption, and mental illness records released. SASE required. Turnaround time 1 week. Fax notes: No fee to fax results. Copy fee: $2.00 for first page, $1.00 each add'l. Certification fee: $5.00. Fee payee: North District Court. Personal checks accepted. Prepayment is required.

District Court South PO Box 794, Ilwaco, WA 98624; 360-642-9417; Fax: 360-642-9416. Hours: 8AM-Noon, 1-5PM (PST). *Misdemeanor, Civil Actions Under $50,000, Small Claims.*

Civil Records: Access: Phone, fax, mail, online, in person. Only the court performs in person searches; visitors may not. No search fee. Required to search: name, years to search; also helpful: address. Civil cases indexed by defendant, plaintiff. Civil records on computer for current and open cases. Records retained for 10 years. Index available remotely online from JIS-Link; see www.courts.wa.gov/jislink (also, see state introduction).

Criminal Records: Access: Phone, fax, mail, online, in person. Only the court performs in person searches; visitors may not. No search fee. Required to search: name; also helpful: years to search, address, DOB, SSN. Criminal records on computer for current and open cases. Records retained for 10 years. Online access to criminal records is the same as civil. (Also see state introduction.).

General Information: No dependencies, adoption, and mental illness records released. SASE required. Turnaround time 1 week. Fax notes: No fee to fax results. Copy fee: $1.00 for first page, $.10 each add'l. Fee payee: South District Court. Personal checks accepted. Prepayment is required.

Pend Oreille County

Superior Court 229 S Garden Ave (PO Box 5020), Newport, WA 99156-5020; 509-447-2435; Fax: 509-447-2734. Hours: 8AM-4:30PM (PST). *Felony, Civil, Eviction, Probate.*

Civil Records: Access: Mail, in person. Both court and visitors may perform in person searches. Search fee: $20.00 per hour. Required to search: name, years to search; also helpful: address. Civil cases indexed by defendant, plaintiff. Civil records on computer and microfiche from 9/82, archived from 1911, on docket books prior to 9/82. Index available remotely online from JIS-Link; see www.courts.wa.gov/jislink (also, see state introduction).

Criminal Records: Access: Phone, mail, in person. Both court and visitors may perform in person searches. No search fee. Required to search: name, years to search; also helpful: address, DOB, SSN. Criminal records on computer and microfiche from 9/82, archived from 1911, on docket books prior to 9/82. Online access to criminal records is the same as civil. (Also see state introduction.).

General Information: No dependencies, adoption, and mental illness records released. SASE required. Turnaround time same day. Fax notes: Fee to fax results is $3.00 for the 1st page and $1.00 per page thereafter. Copy fee: $2.00 for first page, $1.00 each add'l. Certification fee: $2.00. Fee payee: Pend Oreille County Clerk. Personal checks accepted. Prepayment is required.

District Court PO Box 5030, 229 S Garden Ave, Newport, WA 99156-5030; 509-447-4110; Civil phone: 800-359-1506; Fax: 509-447-5724. Hours: 8AM-4:30PM (PST). *Misdemeanor, Civil Actions Under $50,000, Small Claims.*

Civil Records: Access: Phone, fax, mail, online, in person. Only the court performs in person searches; visitors may not. No search fee. Required to search: name, years to search; also helpful: address. Civil cases indexed by defendant, plaintiff. Civil records on DISCIS computer from 10/92, on computer from 1989, archived from 1972. Records retained for 10 years. Index available remotely online from JIS-Link; see www.courts.wa.gov/jislink (also, see state introduction).

Criminal Records: Access: Fax, mail, online, in person. Only the court performs in person searches; visitors may not. No search fee. Required to search: name, DOB; also helpful: years to search, address, SSN. Criminal records on DISCIS computer from 10/92, on computer from 1989, archived from 1972. Records retained for 10 years. Online access to criminal records is the same as civil. (Also see state introduction.).

General Information: Public Access terminal is available. No dependencies, adoption, and mental illness records released. SASE required. Turnaround time 10 days. Fax notes: No fee to fax results. Copy fee: $.25 per page. Certification fee: $5.00. Fee payee: Pend Oreille County District Court. Personal checks accepted. Prepayment is required.

Pierce County

Superior Court 930 Tacoma Ave South, Rm 110, Tacoma, WA 98402; 253-798-7455; Fax: 253-798-3428. Hours: 8:30AM-4:30PM (PST). *Felony, Civil, Eviction, Probate.*

www.co.pierce.wa.us/abtus/ourorg/supct/abtussup.htm

Civil Records: Access: Mail, online, in person. Both court and visitors may perform in person searches. Search fee: $10.00 per hour. Required to search: name, years to search; also helpful: address. Civil cases indexed by defendant, plaintiff. Civil records on computer from 5/81, archived from 7/23/80. Online Superior Court case information, inmates, attorneys, and scheduled proceedings is available free at www.co.pierce.wa.us/cfapps/linx/headerindex.cfm?sour

ce=search.cfm&activeTab=search. Also, a statewide index is available remotely online (see state introduction).

Criminal Records: Access: Mail, online, in person. Both court and visitors may perform in person searches. Search fee: $10.00 per hour. Required to search: name, years to search, DOB; also helpful: address, SSN. Criminal records on computer from 5/81, archived from 7/23/80. Online access to criminal records is the same as civil. Also, a statewide case index is available remotely online (see state introduction).

General Information: No sealed, juvenile, adoption, paternity, mental health, sex offenders (victims) or (sometimes) DUI records released. SASE required. Turnaround time same day. Fax notes: Will fax results; $5.00 minimum. Copy fee: $2.00 for first page, $1.00 each add'l. Certification fee: $2.00 plus $1.00 per page after first. Fee payee: Pierce County Clerk. Business checks accepted. Prepayment is required.

District Court #1 - Civil 1902 96th St S., Tacoma, WA 98444; 253-798-7474; Fax: 253-798-6310. Hours: 8:30AM-4:30PM (PST). *Civil Actions Under $50,000, Small Claims.*

www.co.pierce.wa.us/abtus/ourorg/distct/abtusd1.htm

Civil Records: Access: Mail, fax, online, in person. Both court and visitors may perform in person searches. No search fee. Required to search: name, years to search, DOB; also helpful: address. Civil cases indexed by defendant, plaintiff. Civil records on computer from 1990; Records go back 5 years. Index available remotely online from JIS-Link; see www.courts.wa.gov/jislink (also, see state introduction).

General Information: No sealed, juvenile, adoption, paternity, mental health, sex offenders (victims) or some DUI records released. SASE required. Turnaround time 1-2 weeks. Copy fee: $1.00 for first page, $.50 each add'l. Certification fee: $5.00. Fee payee: Pierce County District Court #1. Personal checks accepted. Credit cards accepted: Visa, MasterCard.

District Court #1 - Criminal 930 Tacoma Ave S, Rm 601, Tacoma, WA 98402-2175; 253-798-7474; Fax: 253-798-6166. Hours: 8:30AM-4:30PM (PST). *Misdemeanor.*

www.co.pierce.wa.us/abtus/ourorg/distct/abtusd1.htm

Criminal Records: Access: Mail, fax, online, in person. Both court and visitors may perform in person searches. No search fee. Required to search: name, years to search, DOB; also helpful: address, SSN. Criminal records on computer from 8/1990. Criminal Index available remotely online from JIS-Link; see www.courts.wa.gov/jislink (also, see state introduction).

General Information: No sealed, juvenile, adoption, paternity, mental health, sex offenders (victims) or some DUI records released. SASE required. Turnaround time 1-2 weeks. Copy fee: $1.00 for first page, $.50 each add'l. Certification fee: $5.00. Fee payee: Pierce County District Court #1. Personal checks accepted. Credit cards accepted: Visa, MasterCard.

District Court #2 6659 Kimball Dr, Suite E-503, Gig Harbor, WA 98335-1229; 253-851-5131; Fax: 253-858-2184. Hours: 8:30AM-4:30PM (PST). *Misdemeanor, Civil Actions Under $50,000, Small Claims.*

www.co.pierce.wa.us/abtus/ourorg/distct/abtusd2.htm

Civil Records: Access: Phone, fax, mail, in person. Both court and visitors may perform in person searches. Search fee: $10.00 per name. Fee if records retrieved from archives. Required to search: name, years to search; also helpful: address. Civil cases indexed by defendant, plaintiff. Civil records on computer from 8/92, log books prior. Index available remotely online from JIS-Link; see www.courts.wa.gov/jislink (also, see state introduction).

Criminal Records: Access: Phone, fax, mail, in person. Both court and visitors may perform in person searches. Search fee: $10.00 per name. Fee is charged if records retrieved from archives. Required to search: name, DOB; also helpful: years to search, address, SSN. Criminal records on computer from 8/92, log books prior. Online access to criminal records is the same as civil. (Also see state introduction.).

General Information: No sealed, judge's notes, treatment or probation report records released. SASE required. Turnaround time 1-2 weeks if archive material needed. Fax notes: No fee to fax results. Copy fee: $1.00 for first page, $.50 each add'l. Certification fee: $6.00. Fee payee: District Court No 2. Personal checks accepted. Credit cards accepted: Visa, MasterCard.

District Court #3 PO Box 105 (201 Center St), Eatonville, WA 98328-0105; 360-832-6000; Fax: 360-832-8911. 8:30AM-4:30PM (PST). *Misdemeanor, Civil Actions Under $50,000, Small Claims.*

www.co.pierce.wa.us/abtus/ourorg/distct/abtusd3.htm

Civil Records: Access: Fax, mail, online, in person. Only the court performs in person searches; visitors may not. No search fee. Required to search: name, years to search; also helpful: address. Civil cases indexed by defendant, plaintiff. Civil records on computer from Aug 1992, on index cards. Index available remotely online from JIS-Link; see www.courts.wa.gov/jislink (also, see state introduction). Fax requests must be on letterhead.

Criminal Records: Access: Mail, online, in person. Only the court performs in person searches; visitors may not. No search fee. Required to search: name, DOB; also helpful: years to search, address, SSN. Criminal records on computer from Aug 1992, on index cards. Online access to criminal records is the same as civil. (Also see state introduction.).

General Information: No sealed, juvenile, adoption, paternity, mental health, sex offenders (victims) or (sometimes) DUI records released. Turnaround time 1-2 days. Fax notes: No fee to fax results. Copy fee: $.25 per page. Certification fee: $5.00. Fee payee: Pierce County District Court #3. Personal checks accepted. Prepayment is required.

District Court #4 PO Box 110 (811 Main St), Buckley, WA 98321-0110; 360-829-0411; Fax: 360-829-3098. Hours: 8:30AM-4PM (PST). *Misdemeanor, Civil Actions Under $50,000, Small Claims.*

www.co.pierce.wa.us/abtus/ourorg/distct/abtusd4.htm

Civil Records: Access: Phone, mail, online, in person. Both court and visitors may perform in person searches. No search fee. Required to search: name, years to search; also helpful: address. Civil cases indexed by defendant, plaintiff. Civil records on index cards. Index available remotely online from JIS-Link; see www.courts.wa.gov/jislink (also, see state introduction).

Criminal Records: Access: Phone, mail, online, in person. Both court and visitors may perform in person searches. No search fee. Required to search: name, years to search; also helpful: address, DOB, SSN. Criminal records on index cards. Online access to criminal records is the same as civil. (Also see state introduction.).

General Information: No unclosed case records released. SASE required. Turnaround time 1 week. Copy fee: $.15 per page. Certification fee: $5.00. Fee payee: Pierce County District Court #4. Personal checks accepted. Prepayment is required.

San Juan County

Superior Court 350 Court St, #7, Friday Harbor, WA 98250; 360-378-2163; Fax: 360-378-3967. Hours: 8AM-4:30PM (PST). *Felony, Misdemeanor, Civil, Eviction, Probate.*

www.co.san-juan.wa.us

Civil Records: Access: Phone, fax, mail, online, in person. Both court and visitors may perform in person searches. Search fee: $20.00 per hour. Required to search: name, years to search; also helpful: address, case number. Civil cases indexed by defendant, plaintiff. Civil records on computer from 1987, on microfiche and archived from 1890s. Index available remotely online from JIS-Link; see www.courts.wa.gov/jislink (also, see state introduction).

Criminal Records: Access: Phone, fax, mail, online, in person. Both court and visitors may perform in person searches. Search fee: $20.00 per hour. Required to search: name, years to search; also helpful: address, DOB, SSN, case number. Criminal records on computer from 1987, on microfiche and archived from 1890s. Online access to criminal records is the same as civil. (Also see state introduction.).

General Information: No dependencies, adoption, and mental illness records released. SASE required. Turnaround time 3 days. Fax notes: $5.00 for first page, $1.00 each add'l. Copy fee: $2.00 for first page, $1.00 each add'l. Certification fee: $2.00. Fee payee: San Juan County Clerk. Personal checks accepted. Credit cards accepted. Prepayment is required.

District Court PO Box 127, Friday Harbor, WA 98250-0127; 360-378-4017; Fax: 360-378-4099. Hours: 8:30AM-4:30PM (PST). *Misdemeanor, Civil Actions Under $50,000, Small Claims.*

Civil Records: Access: Mail, in person. Only the court performs in person searches; visitors may not. No search fee. Required to search: name, years to search; also helpful: address. Civil cases indexed by defendant, plaintiff. Civil records on computer from 1993, on index cards prior. Records retained for 10 years. Index available remotely online from JIS-Link; see www.courts.wa.gov/jislink (also, see state introduction).

Criminal Records: Access: Mail, in person. Only the court performs in person searches; visitors may not. No search fee. Required to search: name, years to search, signed release; also helpful: address, DOB, SSN. Criminal records on computer from 1993, log book prior. Retained 5 years. Online access to criminal records is the same as civil. (Also see state introduction.).

General Information: No dependencies, adoption, confidential social files and mental illness records released. SASE required. Turnaround time 1-3 days. Copy fee: $2.00 for first page, $1.00 each add'l. Certification fee: $5.00. Fee payee: San Juan County District Court. Personal checks accepted. Credit cards are accepted through OfficialPayments.Com or 1-877-876-7619. You will need to provide them with your case # or ticket #. Prepayment is required.

Skagit County

Superior Court PO Box 837, Mount Vernon, WA 98273-0837; 360-336-9440. Hours: 8:30AM-4:30PM (PST). *Felony, Civil, Eviction, Probate.*

Civil Records: Access: Mail, online, in person. Both court and visitors may perform in person searches. Search fee: $20.00 per hour. Required to search: name, years to search. Civil cases indexed by defendant, plaintiff. Civil records on computer from 10/81, on microfilm and archived from 1878. Index available remotely online from JIS-Link; see www.courts.wa.gov/jislink (also, see state introduction).

Criminal Records: Access: Mail, online, in person. Both court and visitors may perform in person searches. Search fee: $20.00 per hour. Required to search: name,

years to search. Criminal records on computer from 10/81, on microfilm and archived from 1878. Online access to criminal records is the same as civil. (Also see state introduction.).

General Information: Public Access terminal is available. No dependencies, adoption, and mental illness, juvenile offender prior to 07/01/78 records released. SASE required. Turnaround time 5 days. Copy fee: $.15 each, do-it-yourself. Self made copies cannot be certified. Certification fee: copies are $2.00 for first page, $1.00 each add'l. Fee payee: Skagit County Clerk. Only cashiers checks and money orders accepted. Prepayment is required.

District Court PO Box 340, Mount Vernon, WA 98273-0340; 360-336-9319; Fax: 360-336-9318. Hours: 8:30AM-4:30PM (PST). *Misdemeanor, Civil Actions Under $50,000, Small Claims.*

Civil Records: Access: Phone, fax, mail, online, in person. Both court and visitors may perform in person searches. No search fee. Required to search: name, years to search; also helpful: address. Civil cases indexed by defendant, plaintiff. Civil records on computer from 1986, archived for 12 years. Open records retained for 10 years. Index available remotely online from JIS-Link; see www.courts.wa.gov/jislink (also, see state introduction). Mail search requires special form.

Criminal Records: Access: Phone, fax, mail, online, in person. Both court and visitors may perform in person searches. No search fee. Required to search: name, years to search, DOB; also helpful: SSN. Criminal records prior to 1995 only retained for 5 years. Online access to criminal records is the same as civil. (Also see state introduction.).

General Information: No dependencies, alcohol, adoption, and mental illness records released. SASE required. Turnaround time 3-4 days. Copy fee: $.50 per page. Certification fee: $5.00. Fee payee: District Court, Skagit County. Personal checks accepted. Prepayment is required.

Skamania County

Superior Court PO Box 790, Stevenson, WA 98648; 509-427-9431; Fax: 509-427-7386. Hours: 8:30AM-5PM (PST). *Felony, Civil, Eviction, Probate.*

Civil Records: Access: Phone, mail, online, in person. Only the court performs in person searches; visitors may not. Search fee: $20.00 per hour. Required to search: name, years to search; also helpful: address. Civil cases indexed by defendant, plaintiff. Civil records on computer from 1984, on microfiche and archived from 1900. Index available remotely online from JIS-Link; see www.courts.wa.gov/jislink (also, see state introduction).

Criminal Records: Access: Phone, mail, online, in person. Only the court performs in person searches; visitors may not. Search fee: $20.00 per hour. Required to search: name, years to search; also helpful: address, DOB. Criminal records on computer from 1984, on microfiche and archived from 1900. Online access to criminal records is the same as civil. (Also see state introduction.).

General Information: No dependencies, adoption, and mental illness records released. SASE required. Turnaround time same day. Copy fee: $2.00 first page, $1.00 each add'l. Certification fee: Same as copy fee. Fee payee: Skamania County Clerk. Personal checks accepted. Prepayment is required.

District Court PO Box 790, Stevenson, WA 98648; 509-427-9430; Fax: 509-427-7386. Hours: 8:30AM-5PM (PST). *Misdemeanor, Civil Actions Under $50,000, Small Claims.*

Civil Records: Access: Phone, fax, mail, online, in person. Both court and visitors may perform in person searches. Search fee: $10.00 per hour. Required to

search: name, years to search; also helpful: address. Civil cases indexed by defendant, plaintiff. Civil records on computer from 5/91. Records retained for 10 years. Index available remotely online from JIS-Link; see www.courts.wa.gov/jislink (also, see state introduction).
Criminal Records: Access: Phone, fax, mail, online, in person. Both court and visitors may perform in person searches. Search fee: $10.00 per hour. Required to search: name, years to search; also helpful: address, DOB, SSN. Criminal records on computer from 5/91. Records retained for 10 years. Online access to criminal records is the same as civil. (Also see state introduction.).
General Information: No dependencies, adoption, and mental illness records released. SASE required. Turnaround time 2-3 days. Fax notes: No fee to fax results. Copy fee: $2.00 for first page, $1.00 each add'l. Certification fee: $6.00. Fee payee: Skamania County District Court. Personal checks accepted. Prepayment is required.

Snohomish County

Superior Court 3000 Rockefeller, MS 605, Everett, WA 98201; 425-388-3466. Hours: 8:30AM-5PM (PST). *Felony, Civil Actions, Eviction, Probate.*
www.co.snohomish.wa.us
Civil Records: Access: Phone, mail, online, in person. Both court and visitors may perform in person searches. Search fee: $20.00 per hour. Required to search: name, years to search. Civil cases indexed by defendant, plaintiff. Civil records on computer from 1978, prior on database index. Index available remotely online from JIS-Link; see www.courts.wa.gov/jislink (also, see state introduction).
Criminal Records: Access: Phone, mail, online, in person. Both court and visitors may perform in person searches. Search fee: $20.00 per hour. Required to search: name, years to search. Criminal records on computer from 1978, prior on database index. Online access to criminal records is the same as civil. (Also see state introduction.).
General Information: Public Access terminal is available. No sealed, juvenile, adoption, paternity, mental health, sex offenders (victims). SASE requested. Turnaround time 1 week. Copy fee: $.10 per page. Certification fee: $2.00 plus $1.00 per page after first. Fee payee: County Clerk or Snohomish County Clerk's Office. Business checks accepted. No credit cards or personal checks. Prepayment is required.

Cascade Division District Court 415 E Burke St, Arlington, WA 98223; 360-652-9552; Fax: 360-435-0873. Hours: 8:30AM-5PM (PST). *Misdemeanor, Civil Actions Under $50,000, Small Claims.*
Civil Records: Access: Mail, online, in person. Only the court performs in person searches; visitors may not. Search fee: $5.00 per name. Required to search: name, years to search; also helpful: address. Civil cases indexed by defendant, plaintiff. Civil records on computer from 1985. Index available remotely online from JIS-Link; see www.courts.wa.gov/jislink (also, see state introduction).
Criminal Records: Access: Mail, online, in person. Only the court performs in person searches; visitors may not. Search fee: $5.00 per name. Required to search: name, years to search, DOB; also helpful: address, SSN. Criminal records on computer from 1987. Online access to criminal records is the same as civil. (Also see state introduction.).
General Information: Public Access terminal is available. No sealed, juvenile, adoption, paternity, mental health, sex offenders (victims) or some DUI records released. Turnaround time 1 week. Copy fee: $.15 per page. Certification fee: $5.00. Fee payee: Cascade Division. Personal checks accepted. Credit cards accepted: Visa, MasterCard. Prepayment is required.

Everett Division District Court 3000 Rockefeller Ave MS 508, Everett, WA 98201; 425-388-3331; Civil phone: 425-388-3595; Fax: 425-388-3565. Hours: 8:30AM-5PM (PST). *Misdemeanor, Civil Actions Under $50,000, Small Claims.*
Civil Records: Access: Fax, mail, online, in person. Both court and visitors may perform in person searches. No search fee. Required to search: complete name, years to search; also helpful: address. Civil cases indexed by defendant, plaintiff. Civil records on computer back to 1986. Index available remotely online from JIS-Link; see www.courts.wa.gov/jislink (also, see state introduction).
Criminal Records: Access: Fax, mail, online, in person. Only the court performs in person searches; visitors may not. No search fee. Required to search: complete name, years to search, DOB; also helpful: address, SSN. Criminal records on computer back to 1986. Online access to criminal records is the same as civil. (Also see state introduction.).
General Information: Public Access terminal is available. Limited DUI records released. SASE required. Turnaround time 1 week. Fax notes: No fee to fax results. Copy fee: $.15 per page. Certification fee: $5.00. Fee payee: Everett District Court. Personal checks accepted. Credit cards accepted: Visa, MC, AmEx, Discover. Prepayment is required.

Evergreen Division District Court 14414 179th Ave SE, PO Box 625, Monroe, WA 98272-0625; 360-805-6776; Fax: 360-805-6755. Hours: 8:30AM-5PM (PST). *Misdemeanor, Civil Actions Under $50,000, Small Claims.*
Civil Records: Access: Phone, mail, in person. Only the court performs in person searches; visitors may not. No search fee. Required to search: name, years to search; also helpful: address. Civil cases indexed by defendant, plaintiff. Civil records on computer back 10 years, file retained for 5 years. Index available remotely online from JIS-Link; see www.courts.wa.gov/jislink (also, see state introduction).
Criminal Records: Access: Mail, in person. Only the court performs in person searches; visitors may not. No search fee. Required to search: name, years to search; also helpful: address, DOB. Criminal records on computer archived 3 years after closure by state. Online access to criminal records is the same as civil. (Also see state introduction.).
General Information: No sealed, juvenile, adoption, paternity, mental health, sex offenders (victims) or some DUI records released. SASE requested. Turnaround time 1 week. Copy fee: $.15 per page. Certification fee: $5.00. Fee payee: Evergreen District Court. Personal checks accepted. Prepayment is required.

South Division District Court 20520 68th Ave W, Lynnwood, WA 98036-7406; 425-774-8803; Fax: 425-744-6820. Hours: 8:30AM-5PM (PST). *Misdemeanor, Civil Actions Under $50,000, Small Claims.*
Civil Records: Access: Mail, online, in person. No search fee. Required to search: name, years to search. Civil cases indexed by defendant. Civil records on computer since 1987. Index available remotely online from JIS-Link; see www.courts.wa.gov/jislink (also, see state introduction).
Criminal Records: Access: Mail, online, in person. Only the court performs in person searches; visitors may not. No search fee. Required to search: name, years to search. Criminal records on computer since 1989. Online access to criminal records is the same as civil. (Also see state introduction.).
General Information: No sealed, juvenile, adoption, paternity, mental health, sex offenders (victims) or some DUI records released. SASE requested. Turnaround time 2-4 days. Copy fee: $.15 per page. Certification

fee: $5.00. Fee payee: South District Court. Personal checks accepted. Prepayment is required.

Spokane County

Superior Court W 1116 Broadway, Spokane, WA 99260; 509-477-2211. Hours: 8:30AM-5PM (PST). *Felony, Civil, Eviction, Probate.*
Civil Records: Access: Phone, mail, online, in person. Both court and visitors may perform in person searches. Search fee: $10.00 per hour. Required to search: name, years to search. Civil cases indexed by defendant, plaintiff. Civil records on computer from 1973, archives back to 1800s, docket books prior to computer. Index available remotely online from JIS-Link; see www.courts.wa.gov/jislink (also, see state introduction).
Criminal Records: Access: Phone, mail, online, in person. Both court and visitors may perform in person searches. Search fee: $10.00 per hour. Required to search: name, years to search; also helpful: DOB. Criminal records on computer from 1973, archives back to 1800s, docket books prior to computer. Online access to criminal records is the same as civil. (Also see state introduction.).
General Information: No sealed, juvenile dependency, adoption, paternity, mental health records released. SASE required. Turnaround time 1-3 days. Copy fee: $2.00 for first page, $1.00 each add'l. Certification fee: $2.00 plus $1.00 each additional page. Fee payee: Spokane County Clerk. Personal checks accepted. Prepayment is required.

District Court 1100 Mallon W, Spokane, WA 99260; 509-477-4770. Hours: 8:30AM-5PM (PST). *Misdemeanor, Civil Actions Under $50,000, Small Claims.*
www.spokanecounty.org/districtcourt
Civil Records: Access: Mail, online, in person. Both court and visitors may perform in person searches. No search fee. Required to search: name, years to search; also helpful: address. Civil cases indexed by defendant, plaintiff. Civil records on computer for 10 years; prior on index cards or microfiche. Index available remotely online from JIS-Link; see www.courts.wa.gov/jislink (also, see state introduction).
Criminal Records: Access: Mail, online, in person. Both court and visitors may perform in person searches. No search fee. Required to search: name, years to search, signed release; also helpful: address, DOB. Criminal records are computer since 1984, but searches are only done for five years time. Online access to criminal records is the same as civil. (Also see state introduction.).
General Information: SASE required. Turnaround time 1 week. Copy fee: $1.00 per page. Certification fee: $5.00. Fee payee: Spokane County District Court. Business checks accepted. Personal checks accepted for civil records only. Prepayment is required.

Stevens County

Superior Court 215 S Oak Rm 206, Colville, WA 99114; 509-684-7575. Hours: 8AM-Noon, 1-4:30PM (PST). *Felony, Civil, Eviction, Probate.*
Civil Records: Access: Phone, mail, online, in person. Only the court performs in person searches; visitors may not. Search fee: $8.00 per hour. Required to search: name, years to search; also helpful: address. Civil cases indexed by defendant, plaintiff. Civil records on computer from 10-82, microfiche from 1889-1982, archives 1889, index cards prior to 1982. Index available remotely online from JIS-Link; see www.courts.wa.gov/jislink (also, see state introduction).
Criminal Records: Access: Mail, online, in person. Only the court performs in person searches; visitors may not. Search fee: $8.00 per hour. Required to search: name, years to search, DOB; also helpful: address, SSN. Criminal records on computer from 10-82, microfiche

from 1889-1982, archives 1889, index cards prior to 1982. Online access to criminal records is the same as civil. (Also see state introduction.).

General Information: No sealed, juvenile, adoption, paternity, mental health, sex offenders (victims). SASE required. Turnaround time same day. Copy fee: $2.00 for 1st page, $1.00 each add'l pg. Certification fee: Included in copy fee. Fee payee: Stevens County Clerk. Personal checks accepted. Prepayment is required.

District Court 215 S Oak Rm 213, Colville, WA 99114; 509-684-5249; Fax: 509-684-7571. Hours: 8AM-Noon, 1-4:30PM (PST). *Misdemeanor, Civil Actions Under $50,000, Small Claims.*

www.co.stevens.wa.us/distcourt/departments.htm

Civil Records: Access: Mail, online, in person. Only the court performs in person searches; visitors may not. Search fee: $8.00 per name. Required to search: name, years to search; also helpful: address. Civil cases indexed by defendant. Civil records on computer from 1/93, prior on docket books to 1988. Index available remotely online from JIS-Link; see www.courts.wa.gov/jislink (also, see state introduction).

Criminal Records: Access: Mail, online, in person. Only the court performs in person searches; visitors may not. Search fee: $8.00 per name. Required to search: name, years to search, DOB; also helpful: address, SSN, signed release. Criminal records on computer from 07/93, prior on docket books to 1988. Online access to criminal records is the same as civil. (Also see state introduction.).

General Information: No sealed, juvenile, adoption, paternity, mental health, sex offenders (victims) or some DUI records released. Turnaround time 1 week. Fax notes: Fee to fax results is $1.00 per page. Copy fee: $.15 per page. Certification fee: $5.00. Fee payee: Stevens County District Court. Business checks accepted. Prepayment is required.

Thurston County

Superior Court 2000 Lakeridge Dr SW, Bldg 2, Olympia, WA 98502; 360-786-5430. Hours: 8AM-5PM *Felony, Misdemeanor, Civil, Eviction, Probate.*

www.co.thurston.wa.us/clerk

Civil Records: Access: Phone, mail, in person, e-mail. Both court and visitors may perform in person searches. Search fee: $20.00 per hour. Required to search: name, years to search; also helpful: address. Civil cases indexed by defendant, plaintiff. Civil records on computer from 07/78, archives back to 1850s. Index available remotely online from JIS-Link; see www.courts.wa.gov/jislink (also, see state introduction).

Criminal Records: Access: Phone, mail, in person, E-mail. Both court and visitors may perform in person searches. Search fee: $20.00 per hour. Required to search: name, years to search, DOB, signed release; also helpful: address, SSN. Criminal records on computer from 07/78, archives back to 1850s. Online access to criminal records is the same as civil. (Also see state introduction.).

General Information: Public Access terminal is available. No sealed, juvenile, adoption, paternity, mental health, sex offenders (victims). SASE required. Turnaround time 1-7 days. Copy fee: $2.00 for first page, $1.00 each add'l. Certification fee: Certification fee is $2.00 first page and $1.00 each additional. Fee payee: Thurston County Clerk. Business checks accepted. Prepayment is required.

District Court 2000 Lakeridge Dr SW, Bldg 3, Olympia, WA 98502; 360-786-5450; Fax: 360-754-3359. Hours: 9AM-5PM (PST). *Misdemeanor, Civil Actions Under $50,000, Small Claims.*

Civil Records: Access: Phone, fax, mail, online, in person. Both court and visitors may perform in person searches. No search fee. Required to search: name, years to search; also helpful: address. Civil cases

indexed by defendant, plaintiff. Civil records on computer from 1983. Index available remotely online from JIS-Link; see www.courts.wa.gov/jislink (also, see state introduction).

Criminal Records: Access: Phone, fax, mail, online, in person. Both court and visitors may perform in person searches. No search fee. Required to search: name, years to search; also helpful: address, DOB, SSN. Criminal records on computer from 1988. Online access to criminal records is the same as civil. (Also see state introduction.).

General Information: No sealed, juvenile, adoption, paternity, mental health, sex offenders (victims) or some DUI records released. SASE required. Turnaround time 2 week. Copy fee: $.25 per page. Certification fee: $5.00. Fee payee: Thurston County District Court. Personal checks accepted. Prepayment is required.

Wahkiakum County

Superior Court PO Box 116, Cathlamet, WA 98612; 360-795-3558; Fax: 360-795-8813. Hours: 8AM-4PM (PST). *Felony, Misdemeanor, Civil, Eviction, Probate.*

Civil Records: Access: Mail, online, in person. Both court and visitors may perform in person searches. Search fee: $20.00 per hour. Required to search: name, years to search. Civil cases indexed by defendant, plaintiff. Civil records on computer from 1988, archives from 1850s. Index available remotely online from JIS-Link; see www.courts.wa.gov/jislink (also, see state introduction).

Criminal Records: Access: Mail, online, in person. Both court and visitors may perform in person searches. Search fee: $20.00 per hour. Required to search: name, years to search; also helpful: address, DOB, SSN. Criminal records on computer from 1988, archives from 1850s. Online access to criminal records is the same as civil. (Also see state introduction.).

General Information: No sealed, juvenile, adoption, paternity, mental health, sex offenders (victims). SASE required. Turnaround time 1 day. Copy fee: $1.00 per page. Certification fee: No certification fee. Fee payee: County Clerk. Personal checks accepted. Prepayment is required.

District Court PO Box 144, Cathlamet, WA 98612; 360-795-3461; Fax: 360-795-6506. Hours: 8AM-4PM (PST). *Misdemeanor, Civil Actions Under $50,000, Small Claims.*

Civil Records: Access: Phone, fax, mail, online, in person. Both court and visitors may perform in person searches. No search fee. Required to search: name, years to search; also helpful: address. Civil cases indexed by defendant, plaintiff. Civil records on computer from 1997, index cards back 10 years, archived prior. Index available remotely online from JIS-Link; see www.courts.wa.gov/jislink (also, see state introduction).

Criminal Records: Access: Phone, fax, mail, online, in person. Both court and visitors may perform in person searches. No search fee. Required to search: name, years to search; also helpful: DOB. Criminal records on computer from 1997, index cards back 10 years, archived prior. Online access to criminal records is the same as civil. (Also see state introduction.).

General Information: No sealed, juvenile, adoption, paternity, mental health, sex offenders (victims) or some DUI records released. SASE required. Turnaround time 2 days. Fax notes: No fee to fax results. Copy fee: $.25 per page. Certification fee: $5.00. Fee payee: Wahkiakum District Court. Personal checks accepted. Prepayment is required.

Walla Walla County

Superior Court PO Box 836, Walla Walla, WA 99362; 509-527-3221; Fax: 509-527-3214. Hours: 9AM-4PM (PST). *Felony, Civil, Eviction, Probate.*

Civil Records: Access: Phone, mail, online, in person. Only the court performs in person searches; visitors may not. Search fee: $20.00 per hour. Required to search: name, years to search; also helpful: address. Civil cases indexed by defendant, plaintiff. Civil records on computer from 7/81, prior in docket books. Index available remotely online from JIS-Link; see www.courts.wa.gov/jislink (also, see state introduction).

Criminal Records: Access: Phone, mail, online, in person. Only the court performs in person searches; visitors may not. Search fee: $20.00 per hour. Required to search: name, years to search, DOB; also helpful: address, SSN. Criminal records on computer from 7/81, prior in docket books. Online access to criminal records is the same as civil. (Also see state introduction.).

General Information: No sealed, juvenile, adoption, paternity, mental health, sex offenders (victims). Personal checks not accepted. Turnaround time 1 day. Fax notes: Will not fax results. Copy fee: $2.00 for first page, $1.00 each add'l. Certification fee: $2.00 plus $1.00 each add'l page. Fee payee: Walla Walla County Clerk. Only cashiers checks and money orders accepted. Prepayment is required.

District Court 317 W Rose St, Walla Walla, WA 99362; 509-527-3236. Hours: 9AM-4PM (PST). *Misdemeanor, Civil Actions Under $50,000, Small Claims.*

Civil Records: Access: Mail, online, in person. Only the court performs in person searches; visitors may not. Search fee: $5.00 per name. Required to search: name, years to search. Civil cases indexed by defendant, plaintiff. Civil records on computer from 7/87, on index books. Records retained for 10 years. Index available remotely online from JIS-Link; see www.courts.wa.gov/jislink (also, see state introduction).

Criminal Records: Access: Mail, online, in person. Only the court performs in person searches; visitors may not. Search fee: $5.00 per name. Required to search: name, years to search, signed release; also helpful: address, DOB, SSN. Criminal records on computer from 7/87, on index books. Records retained for 10 years. Online access to criminal records is the same as civil. (Also see state introduction.).

General Information: No sealed, juvenile, adoption, paternity, mental health, sex offenders (victims) or some DUI records released. SASE required. Turnaround time 1-3 days. Copy fee: $1.00 for first page, $.50 each add'l. Certification fee: $5.00. Fee payee: Walla Walla District Court. Personal checks accepted. Prepayment required.

Whatcom County

Superior Court PO Box 1144, Bellingham, WA 98227; 360-676-6777; Fax: 360-676-6693. Hours: 8:30-4:30PM (PST). *Felony, Civil, Eviction, Probate.*

Note: Extension 50014 for criminal; 50018 for civil.

Civil Records: Access: Phone, fax, mail, online, in person. Only the court performs in person searches; visitors may not. Search fee: No search fee if record is on computer. Required to search: name, years to search; also helpful: address. Civil cases indexed by defendant, plaintiff. Civil records on computer from 1980, archives back to 1800s, index cards. Index available remotely online from JIS-Link; see www.courts.wa.gov/jislink (also, see state introduction).

Criminal Records: Access: Phone, fax, mail, online, in person. Only the court performs in person searches; visitors may not. No search fee. Required to search: name, years to search; also helpful: address, DOB, SSN. Criminal records on computer from 1980, archives back to 1800s, index cards. Online access to criminal records is the same as civil. (Also see state introduction.).

General Information: No sealed, juvenile, adoption, paternity, mental health, sex offenders (victims). SASE required. Turnaround time up to 1 week. Copy fee: $2.00 for first page, $1.00 each add'l. Certification fee: Included in copy fee. Fee payee: Whatcom County Clerk. Only cashiers checks and money orders accepted. Prepayment is required.

District Court 311 Grand Ave, Bellingham, WA 98225; 360-676-6770; Fax: 360-738-2452. Hours: 8AM-4:30PM (PST). *Misdemeanor, Civil Actions Under $50,000, Small Claims.*

www.co.whatcom.wa.us

Civil Records: Access: Mail, online, in person. Only the court performs in person searches; visitors may not. No search fee. Required to search: name, years to search; also helpful: address. Civil cases indexed by defendant, plaintiff. Civil records on computer 10 years back. Index available remotely online from JIS-Link; see www.courts.wa.gov/jislink (also, see state introduction).

Criminal Records: Access: Mail, online, in person. Only the court performs in person searches; visitors may not. No search fee. Required to search: name, years to search; also helpful: address, DOB, SSN. Criminal records on computer 10 years back. Online access to criminal records is the same as civil. (Also see state introduction.).

General Information: No sealed, juvenile, adoption, paternity, mental health, sex offenders (victims) or some DUI records released. Turnaround time 2 days. Copy fee: $.25 per page. Certification fee: $5.00. Fee payee: Whatcom District Court. Personal checks accepted. Prepayment is required.

Whitman County

Superior Court Box 390, Colfax, WA 99111; 509-397-6240; Fax: 509-397-3546. Hours: 8AM-5PM (PST). *Felony, Civil, Eviction, Probate.*

www.palouse.org/whitman/services/SCourt/index.htm

Civil Records: Access: Phone, fax, mail, online, in person. Both court and visitors may perform in person searches. Search fee: $8.00 per hour. Required to search: name, years to search; also helpful: address. Civil cases indexed by defendant, plaintiff. Civil records on computer from 1985, archives back to 1887. Index available remotely online from JIS-Link; see www.courts.wa.gov/jislink (also, see state introduction).

Criminal Records: Access: Phone, fax, mail, online, in person. Both court and visitors may perform in person searches. Search fee: $8.00 per hour. Required to search: name, years to search; also helpful: address, DOB, SSN. Criminal records on computer from 1985, archives back to 1887. Online access to criminal records is the same as civil. (Also see state introduction.).

General Information: No sealed, juvenile, adoption, paternity, mental health, sex offenders (victims). SASE

required. Turnaround time 1 week. Fax notes: $4.00 for first page, $1.00 each add'l. Copy fee: $.15 per page. Certification fee: $2.00 plus $1.00 per page after first. Fee payee: Whitman County Clerk. Personal checks accepted. Prepayment is required.

District Court 400 N Main St, PO Box 230, Colfax, WA 99111; 509-397-6260; Fax: 509-397-5584. Hours: 8AM-5PM; Public Hours: 8:30AM-4:30PM (PST). *Misdemeanor, Civil Actions Under $50,000, Small Claims.*

www.palouse.org/whitman/services/dcourt

Civil Records: Access: Phone, fax, mail, online, in person. Only the court performs in person searches; visitors may not. Search fee: $8.00 per hour. Required to search: name, years to search; also helpful: address. Civil cases indexed by defendant, plaintiff. Civil records on DISCIS computer system from 7/91, prior on index log. Index available remotely online from JIS-Link; see www.courts.wa.gov/jislink (also, see state introduction).

Criminal Records: Access: Phone, fax, mail, online, in person. Only the court performs in person searches; visitors may not. Search fee: $8.00 per hour. Required to search: name, years to search, DOB; also helpful: address, SSN. Criminal records on DISCIS computer system from 7/91, prior on index log. Online access to criminal records is the same as civil. (Also see state introduction.).

General Information: No sealed, juvenile, adoption, paternity, mental health, sex offenders (victims) or some DUI records released. SASE required. Turnaround time 1 week. Fax notes: Fee to fax results is $3.00. Copy fee: $.15 per page. Certification fee: $6.00. Fee payee: Whitman County. Personal checks accepted. Prepayment is required.

District Court PO Box 249, Pullman, WA 99163; 509-332-2065; Fax: 509-332-5740. Hours: 8AM-5PM (PST). *Misdemeanor, Civil Actions Under $50,000, Small Claims.*

Civil Records: Access: Fax, mail, online, in person. Only the court performs in person searches; visitors may not. Search fee: $8.00 per hour. Required to search: name, years to search; also helpful: address. Civil cases indexed by defendant, plaintiff. Civil records on DISCIS computer system from 7/91; '89-'91 on index. Index available remotely online from JIS-Link; see www.courts.wa.gov/jislink (also, see state introduction).

Criminal Records: Access: Fax, mail, online, in person. Only the court performs in person searches; visitors may not. Search fee: $8.00 per hour. Required to search: name, years to search; also helpful: address, DOB, SSN. Criminal records on DISCIS computer system from 7/91; '89-'91 on index. Online access to criminal records is the same as civil. (Also see state introduction.).

General Information: No sealed, juvenile, adoption, paternity, mental health, sex offenders (victims) or some DUI records released. SASE required. Turnaround time 1 week. Fax notes: No fee to fax results. Copy fee: $.15

per page. Certification fee: $6.00. Fee payee: Whitman District Court. Personal checks accepted.

Yakima County

Superior Court 128 N 2nd St, Rm 323, Yakima, WA 98901; 509-574-1430. Hours: 8:30AM-4:30PM (PST). *Felony, Civil, Domestic Relations, Probate.*

Civil Records: Access: Phone, mail, in person. Only the court performs in person searches; visitors may not. Search fee: $20.00 per hour. Required to search: name, years to search. Civil cases indexed by defendant, plaintiff. Civil records on computer from 1978, archives back to 1890s. Index available remotely online from JIS-Link; see www.courts.wa.gov/jislink (also, see state introduction).

Criminal Records: Access: Phone, mail, in person. Only the court performs in person searches; visitors may not. Search fee: $20.00 per hour. Required to search: name, years to search; also helpful: DOB. Criminal records on computer from 1978, archives back to 1890s. Online access to criminal records is the same as civil. (Also see state introduction.).

General Information: No sealed, juvenile, adoption, paternity, mental health, sex offenders (victims). SASE required. Turnaround time varies. Copy fee: $.15 per page. Microfilm copies $.25 per page. $1.00 minimum. Certification fee: $2.00 plus $1.00 per page after first. Fee payee: Yakima County Clerk. Business checks accepted, no personal. Prepayment is required.

District Court 128 N 2nd St, Rm 225, Yakima, WA 98901-2631; 509-574-1800; Fax: 509-574-1831. Hours: 8:30AM-4:30PM (PST). *Misdemeanor, Civil Actions Under $50,000, Small Claims.*

www.co.yakima.wa.us/courts

Civil Records: Access: Phone, fax, mail, online, in person. Both court and visitors may perform in person searches. No search fee. Required to search: name, years to search; also helpful: address. Civil cases indexed by defendant, plaintiff. Civil records on computer from 1984, generally. Index available remotely online from JIS-Link; see www.courts.wa.gov/jislink (also, see state introduction).

Criminal Records: Access: Phone, fax, mail, online, in person. Both court and visitors may perform in person searches. No search fee. Required to search: name, years to search, DOB; also helpful: address, case number, DRL, SSN. Criminal records on computer from 1984, generally. Online access to criminal records is the same as civil. (Also see state introduction.).

General Information: No sealed or some DUI records released. SASE requested. Turnaround time 2 days. Fax notes: No fee to fax results. Copy fee: $.15 per page. Certification fee: $5.00. Fee payee: Yakima County District Court. Personal checks accepted. Credit cards accepted: Visa. Prepayment is required.

Washington Recording Offices

ORGANIZATION   39 counties, 39 recording offices. The recording officer is County Auditor. County records are usually combined in a Grantor/Grantee index. The entire state is in the Pacific Time Zone (PST).

REAL ESTATE RECORDS   Many County Auditors will perform real estate searches, including record owner. Search fees and copy fees vary. Copies usually cost $1.00 per page and $2.00 for certification per document. If the Auditor does not provide searches, contact the Assessor for record owner information. Contact the Treasurer (Finance Department in King County) for information about unpaid real estate taxes.

UCC RECORDS   Financing statements are filed at the state level, except for real estate related collateral, which are filed with the County Auditor. Most recording offices will perform UCC searches. Use search request form UCC-11R. Searches fees and copy fees vary.

TAX LIEN RECORDS   All federal tax liens on personal property are filed with the Department of Licensing. Other federal and all state tax liens are filed with the County Auditor. Most counties will perform tax lien searches. Search fees are usually $8.00 per hour.

Asotin County

County Auditor, P.O. Box 129, Asotin, WA 99402. 509-243-2084 R/E Recording: 509-246-4164; Fax 509-243-2087.
Will search UCC records. **Other Phone Numbers:** Assessor 509-243-2016; Treasurer 509-243-2014; Appraiser/Auditor 509-243-2084.

Benton County

County Auditor, P.O. Box 470, Prosser, WA 99350. 509-786-5616; Fax 509-786-5528.
The county also has a second recording office located at 5600 W. Canal, Ste B, Kenniwick, WA 99336. Will search UCC records. UCC search includes tax liens if requested. Will search tax liens separately Will search RE names(s) for a range of years at $8.00 per hour. **Other Phone Numbers:** Assessor 509-786-2046; Treasurer 509-786-2255; Appraiser/Auditor 509-736-3085.

Chelan County

County Auditor, P.O. Box 400, Wenatchee, WA 98807. County Auditor, R/E and UCC Recording 509-664-5432 UCC Recording: 509-664-5439; Fax 509-664-5246. http://www.co.chelan.wa.us
Will search UCC records. **Other Phone Numbers:** Assessor 509-664-5365; Treasurer 509-664-5405; Appraiser/Auditor 509-664-5431; Elections 509-664-5431; Vital Records 509-236-4300.

Clallam County

Chief Deputy Auditor, PO Box 3030, Port Angeles, WA 98362. Chief Deputy Auditor, R/E and UCC Recording 360-417-2220; Fax 360-417-2517. http://www.clallam.net
Will search UCC records. Will not search real estate records. **Other Phone Numbers:** Assessor 360-417-2204; Treasurer 360-417-2373; Appraiser/Auditor 360-417-2221; Elections 360-417-2217; Vital Records 360-417-2303.

Clark County

County Auditor, P.O. Box 5000, Vancouver, WA 98666-5000. County Auditor, R/E and UCC Recording 360-397-2208; Fax 360-397-6007. http://www.co.clark.wa.us/auditor
Will search UCC records. Will not search real estate records. **Online Access:** Real Estate, Liens, Vital Statistics, Recording. Online access to County Auditor's database is available at http://auditor.co.clark.wa.us/auditor_new/index.cfm. Court documents are excluded from this index. **Other Phone Numbers:** Assessor 360-397-2391; Treasurer 360-397-2252; Appraiser/

Auditor 360-397-2345; Elections 360-397-2345; Vital Records 360-397-2243; Auditor Main Line 360-397-2241.

Columbia County

County Auditor, 341 East Main St., Dayton, WA 99328-1361. County Auditor, R/E and UCC Recording 509-382-4541; Fax 509-382-4830. http://www.columbiaco.com
Will search UCC records. UCC search includes tax liens if requested. Will search separately Will not search real estate records. **Other Phone Numbers:** Assessor 509-382-2131; Treasurer 509-382-2641; Appraiser/Auditor 509-382-4541; Elections 509-382-4541.

Cowlitz County

County Auditor, 207 Fourth Avenue North, Kelso, WA 98626. County Auditor, R/E and UCC Recording 360-577-3006; Fax 360-414-5552. http://www.co.cowlitz.wa.us/departme.htm
Will search UCC records. UCC search includes tax liens if requested. Will search separately RE record owner and mortgage searches available. All searches by name only. **Other Phone Numbers:** Assessor 360-577-3010; Treasurer 360-577-3060; Appraiser/Auditor 360-577-3005; Elections 360-577-3002.

Douglas County

County Auditor, P.O. Box 456, Waterville, WA 98858. 509-884-9422 x400 R/E Recording: 509-745-8527 x400; Fax 509-884-9468.
Will search UCC records. **Other Phone Numbers:** Assessor 509-884-9442; Treasurer 509-884-9428; Appraiser/Auditor 509-884-9403.

Ferry County

County Auditor, 350 East Delaware #2, Republic, WA 99166. 509-775-5200 R/E Recording: 509-775-5202 UCC Recording: 509-775-5202; Fax 509-775-5208.
Will search UCC records. **Other Phone Numbers:** Assessor 509-775-5203; Treasurer 509-775-5238; Appraiser/Auditor 509-775-5208; Elections 509-775-5208; Vital Records 509-775-5200.

Franklin County

County Auditor, PO Box 1451, Pasco, WA 99301. County Auditor, R/E and UCC Recording 509-545-3536; Fax 509-545-2142.
Will search UCC records. This agency will not do a tax lien search. Will not search real estate records. **Other Phone Numbers:** Assessor 509-545-3506; Treasurer 509-545-3518; Appraiser/Auditor 509-545-3538;

Elections 509-545-3538; Vital Records 509-586-0207 X229.

Garfield County

County Auditor, P.O. Box 278, Pomeroy, WA 99347-0278. County Auditor, R/E and UCC Recording 509-843-1411; Fax 509-843-3941.
Will search UCC records. UCC search includes tax liens if requested. Will not search real estate records. **Other Phone Numbers:** Assessor 509-843-3632; Treasurer 509-843-1531; Appraiser/Auditor 509-843-1411; Elections 509-843-1411; Vital Records 509-843-1411.

Grant County

County Auditor, P.O. Box 37, Ephrata, WA 98823. 509-754-2011 x333.
Will search UCC records. Will not perform tax lien searches Will not search real estate records. **Other Phone Numbers:** Assessor 509-754-2011 x310; Treasurer 509-754-2011 x353; Appraiser/Auditor 509-754-2011 x377.

Grays Harbor County

County Auditor, 101 W. Broadway, Ste. 2, Montesano, WA 98563. 360-249-4232 x331 R/E Recording: 360-249-4232; Fax 360-249-3330.
Will search UCC records. Will not search real estate records. **Other Phone Numbers:** Assessor 360-249-4121; Treasurer 360-249-3751; Appraiser/Auditor 360-249-4232.

Island County

Deputy Auditor, P.O. Box 5000, Coupeville, WA 98239. Deputy Auditor, R/E and UCC Recording 360-679-7366; Fax 360-240-5553. http://www.islandcounty.net
Will not search UCC records due to incompleteness of their records. Will not search real estate records. **Other Phone Numbers:** Assessor 360-679-7303; Treasurer 360-678-5111; Appraiser/Auditor 360-679-7366; Elections 360-679-7366.

Jefferson County

County Auditor, P.O. Box 563, Port Townsend, WA 98368. 360-385-9116; Fax 360-385-9228. http://www.co.jefferson.wa.us/departments.htm
Will search UCC records. Will not search real estate records. **Online Access:** Assessor, Real Estate. Online access to the "Recorded Document Search" database is available at www.co.jefferson.wa.us/_hidden/disclaimer.htm. Records on the County Property (Tax Parcel) Database Tool are also available as well as plats

& survey images. **Other Phone Numbers:** Assessor 360-385-9105; Treasurer 360-385-9150; Appraiser/ Auditor 360-385-9119.

King County

Superintendent of Records, 500 4th Avenue, Room 311, Administration Building, Room 311, Seattle, WA 98104. Superintendent of Records, R/E and UCC Recording 206-296-1570; Fax 206-205-8396. http://www.metrokc.gov
Will search UCC records. Will search real estate records. Fee is $8.00 per name per 5-year search. **Online Access:** Real Estate, Liens, Marriage. Online access to the county recorder's database is available free at http://www.metrokc.gov/recelec/records. also, property records on Dept. of Developmental and Environmental Resources database are available free online at www.metrokc.gov/ddes/gis/parcel. After the disclaimer page, search by parcel number, address, street intersection, or map. **Other Phone Numbers:** Assessor 206-296-7300; Treasurer 206-296-3850; Appraiser/Auditor 206-296-8683; Elections 206-296-1565; Vital Records 206-296-4768; Finance Dept 206-296-3850.

Kitsap County

County Auditor, 614 Division Street, Room 106 /MS 31, Port Orchard, WA 98366. 360-337-4935 R/E Recording: 360-337-7133; Fax 360-337-4645.
Will search UCC records. UCC search includes tax liens if requested. Will not search real estate records. **Other Phone Numbers:** Assessor 360-876-7160; Treasurer 360-876-7135; Appraiser/Auditor 360-227-7129; Elections 360-337-7128.

Kittitas County

County Auditor, 205 West 5th, Room 105, Ellensburg, WA 98926-3129. 509-962-7504 R/E Recording: 509-962-7557; Fax 509-962-7687.
Will search UCC records. **Other Phone Numbers:** Assessor 509-962-7501; Treasurer 509-962-7535; Appraiser/Auditor 509-962-7503; Elections 509-962-7503; Vital Records 509-962-7504; Health Department 509-962-7504.

Klickitat County

County Auditor, 205 S. Columbus Avenue, MS-CH-2, Goldendale, WA 98620. County Auditor, R/E and UCC Recording 509-773-4001; Fax 509-773-4244. http://www.klickitatcounty.org
Will search UCC records. **Other Phone Numbers:** Assessor 509-773-3715; Treasurer 509-773-4664; Appraiser/Auditor 509-773-4001; Elections 509-773-4001; Vital Records 509-773-4001; Toll Free Auditor 800-583-8050.

Lewis County

County Auditor, P.O. Box 29, Chehalis, WA 98532-0029. County Auditor, R/E and UCC Recording 360-740-1163; Fax 360-740-1421.
Will search UCC records. Will not search real estate records. **Other Phone Numbers:** Assessor 360-740-1392; Treasurer 360-740-1115; Appraiser/Auditor 360-740-1164.

Lincoln County

County Auditor, P.O. Box 28, Davenport, WA 99122. County Auditor, R/E and UCC Recording 509-725-4971; Fax 509-725-0820.
Will search UCC records. **Other Phone Numbers:** Assessor 509-725-7011; Treasurer 509-725-5061; Appraiser/Auditor 509-725-4971; Elections 509-725-4971; Vital Records 509-725-4971.

Mason County

County Auditor, P.O. Box 400, Shelton, WA 98584. 360-427-9670 R/E Recording: 360-427-9670 x468 UCC Recording: 360-427-9670 x467; Fax 360-427-8425. http://auditor.co.mason.wa.us/
Will search UCC records. Will not search real estate records. **Other Phone Numbers:** Assessor 360-427-9670 x491; Treasurer 360-427-9670 x484; Appraiser/Auditor 360-427-9670 x470; Elections 360-427-9670 x469; Vital Records 360-427-9670 x467.

Okanogan County

County Auditor, P.O. Box 1010, Okanogan, WA 98840. 509-422-7240.
Will search UCC records. This agency will not do a tax lien search. Will not search real estate records. **Other Phone Numbers:** Assessor 509-422-7190; Treasurer 509-422-7180; Appraiser/Auditor 509-422-7240.

Pacific County

County Auditor, P.O. Box 97, South Bend, WA 98586-9903. 360-875-9318 R/E Recording: 360-875-9309 x313; Fax 360-875-9333. http://www.co.pacific.wa.us/directory.htm
Will search UCC records. Tax liens not included in UCC search. Will not perform title searches of real estate records; will search for individual documents. **Other Phone Numbers:** Assessor 360-875-9301; Treasurer 360-875-9421; Appraiser/Auditor 360-875-9317 x313; Elections 360-875-9317; Vital Records 360-875-9318.

Pend Oreille County

County Auditor, P.O. Box 5015, Newport, WA 99156. 509-447-3185; Fax 509-447-2475.
Will search UCC records. Tax liens are filed with County Treasurer Will not search real estate records. **Other Phone Numbers:** Assessor 509-447-4312; Treasurer 509-447-3612; Appraiser/Auditor 509-447-3185.

Pierce County

County Auditor, 2401 South 35th Street, Room 200, Tacoma, WA 98409. 253-798-7440 R/E Recording: 206-591-7440; Fax 253-798-2761.
Will search UCC records. **Online Access:** Assessor. Property records on County Assessor-Treasurer database are available free online at www.co.pierce.wa.us/CFApps/atr/TIMSNet/index.htm. After the disclaimer page, search by parcel number or site address. **Other Phone Numbers:** Assessor 253-798-6111; Treasurer 253-798-6111; Appraiser/Auditor 253-798-7430.

San Juan County

County Auditor, P.O. Box 638, Friday Harbor, WA 98250. 360-378-2161; Fax 360-378-6256.
Will search UCC records. UCC search includes tax liens if requested. Will not search real estate records. **Other Phone Numbers:** Assessor 360-378-4729; Treasurer 360-378-2171; Appraiser/Auditor 360-378-3357.

Skagit County

County Auditor, P.O. Box 1306, Mount Vernon, WA 98273-1306. 360-336-9420; Fax 360-336-9429.
Will search UCC records. UCC search includes tax liens if requested. Will not search real estate records. **Other Phone Numbers:** Assessor 360-336-9370; Treasurer 360-336-9350; Appraiser/Auditor 360-336-9305.

Skamania County

County Auditor, P.O. Box 790, Stevenson, WA 98648-0790. County Auditor, R/E and UCC Recording 509-

427-9420; Fax 509-427-4165. http://www.wacounties.org/waco/county/skamania.html
Will search UCC records. **Other Phone Numbers:** Assessor 509-427-9400; Treasurer 509-427-9410; Appraiser/Auditor 509-427-9420; Elections 509-427-9420; Vital Records 509-427-9420.

Snohomish County

County Auditor, Dept. R., M/S # 204, 3000 Rockefeller Avenue, Everett, WA 98201. County Auditor, R/E and UCC Recording 425-388-3483; Fax 425-259-2777.
Will search UCC records. UCC search includes tax liens if requested. Mortgage and property transfer searches available. **Online Access:** Real Estate, Assessor, Tax Liens, Marriage, Recordings. Online access to the Auditor's office database is available free at http://198.238.192.100/default1.htm. Search on the OPR, map, or marriage page. **Other Phone Numbers:** Assessor 425-388-3433; Treasurer 425-388-3366; Appraiser/ Auditor 425-388-3444; Elections 425-388-3444.

Spokane County

County Auditor, West 1116 Broadway, Spokane, WA 99260. 509-477-2270 R/E Recording: 509-456-2217; Fax 509-477-6451.
Will search UCC records. **Other Phone Numbers:** Assessor 509-456-3696; Treasurer 509-456-4713; Appraiser/Auditor 509-477-2320.

Stevens County

County Auditor, 215 South Oak St., Colville, WA 99114. County Auditor, R/E and UCC Recording 509-684-7512; Fax 509-684-8310.
Will search UCC records. Tax liens not included in UCC search. RE owner, mortgage, and property transfer searches available. **Other Phone Numbers:** Treasurer 509-684-2593; Appraiser/Auditor 509-684-7514; Elections 509-684-7514; Auditor 509-684-6161.

Thurston County

County Auditor, 2000 Lakeridge Drive SW, Olympia, WA 98502. 360-786-5405; Fax 360-786-5223.
Will search UCC records. Will not search real estate records. **Online Access:** Assessor, Real Estate. Assessor and property information on Thurston GeoData database are available free online at www.geodata.org/scripts/esrimap.dll?name=TGCMAP &Cmd=Map. **Other Phone Numbers:** Assessor 360-786-5410; Treasurer 360-786-5550; Appraiser/Auditor 360-786-5408.

Wahkiakum County

County Auditor, P.O. Box 543, Cathlamet, WA 98612. 360-795-3219; Fax 360-795-0824.
Will search UCC records. UCC search includes tax liens if requested. Will not search real estate records. **Other Phone Numbers:** Assessor 360-795-3791; Treasurer 360-795-8005; Appraiser/Auditor 360-795-3219; Elections 360-795-3219; Vital Records 360-795-6207.

Walla Walla County

County Auditor, P.O. Box 1856, Walla Walla, WA 99362-0356. 509-527-3204; Fax 509-526-4806. http://www.co.walla-walla.wa.us/auditor1.htm
Will search UCC records. UCC search includes tax liens if requested. Will not search real estate records. **Other Phone Numbers:** Assessor 509-527-3216; Treasurer 509-527-3212; Appraiser/Auditor 509-527-3204.

Whatcom County

County Auditor, 311 Grand Avenue, Bellingham, WA 98225. 360-676-6740 R/E Recording: 360-676-6741 x50061; Fax 360-738-4556. http://www.co.whatcom.wa.us

Will search UCC records. **Online Access:** Assessor, Real Estate. Online acess to the assessor parcel database information system is available free at http://www.co.whatcom.wa.us/cgibin/db2www/assessor/search/RPSearch.ndt/disclaimer. **Other Phone Numbers:** Assessor 360-676-6790; Treasurer 360-676-6774; Appraiser/Auditor 360-676-6745.

Whitman County

County Auditor, P.O. Box 350, Colfax, WA 99111-0350. 509-397-6270 R/E Recording: 509-397-6270509-397-6270 UCC Recording: 509-392-6270; Fax 509-397-6351. www.whitmancounty.org

Will search UCC records. UCC searches cost $8.00 per hour. Will not search real estate records. **Other Phone Numbers:** Assessor 509-397-6220; Treasurer 509-397-6230; Appraiser/Auditor 509-397-6270; Elections 509-397-6270; Vital Records 509-397-6270.

Yakima County

County Auditor, 128 N. 2nd St., #117, Yakima, WA 98901. County Auditor, R/E and UCC Recording 509-574-1330; Fax 509-574-1341. http://www.pan.co.yakima.wa.us

Will search UCC records. Will not search real estate records. **Online Access:** Assessor, Real Estate. Assessor and property information on County Assessor database are available free online at www.co.yakima.wa.us/assessor/propinfo/asr_info.asp.

Other Phone Numbers: Assessor 509-574-1100; Treasurer 509-575-4091; Appraiser/Auditor 509-574-1340.

Washington County Locator

You will usually be able to find the city name in the City/County Cross Reference below. In that case, it is a simple matter to determine the county from the cross reference. However, only the official US Postal Service city names are included in this index. There are an additional 40,000 place names that people use in their addresses. Therefore, we have also included a ZIP/City Cross Reference immediately following the City/County Cross Reference.

If you know the ZIP Code but the city name does not appear in the City/County Cross Reference index, look up the ZIP Code in the ZIP/City Cross Reference, find the city name, then look up the city name in the City/County Cross Reference. For example, you want to know the county for an address of Menands, NY 12204. There is no "Menands" in the City/County Cross Reference. The ZIP/City Cross Reference shows that ZIP Codes 12201-12288 are for the city of Albany. Looking back in the City/County Cross Reference, Albany is in Albany County.

City/County Cross Reference

ABERDEEN Grays Harbor
ACME Whatcom
ADDY Stevens
ADNA Lewis
AIRWAY HEIGHTS Spokane
ALBION Whitman
ALLYN Mason
ALMIRA (99103) Lincoln(87), Grant(13)
AMANDA PARK Grays Harbor
AMBOY (98601) Clark(98), Cowlitz(2)
ANACORTES Skagit
ANATONE Asotin
ANDERSON ISLAND Pierce
APPLETON Klickitat
ARDENVOIR Chelan
ARIEL Cowlitz
ARLINGTON Snohomish
ASHFORD Pierce
ASOTIN Asotin
AUBURN King
BAINBRIDGE ISLAND Kitsap
BARING King
BATTLE GROUND Clark
BAY CENTER Pacific
BEAVER Clallam
BELFAIR Mason
BELLEVUE King
BELLINGHAM Whatcom
BELMONT Whitman
BENGE Adams
BENTON CITY Benton
BEVERLY Grant
BICKLETON (99322) Klickitat(96),
   Yakima(4)
BINGEN Klickitat
BLACK DIAMOND King
BLAINE Whatcom
BLAKELY ISLAND San Juan
BOTHELL King
BOTHELL Snohomish
BOW Skagit
BOYDS Ferry
BREMERTON Kitsap
BREWSTER Okanogan
BRIDGEPORT Douglas
BRINNON Jefferson
BROWNSTOWN Yakima
BRUSH PRAIRIE Clark
BUCKLEY Pierce
BUCODA Thurston
BUENA Yakima
BURBANK Walla Walla
BURLEY Kitsap
BURLINGTON Skagit
BURTON King
CAMAS Clark
CAMP MURRAY Pierce
CARBONADO Pierce
CARLSBORG Clallam
CARLTON Okanogan
CARNATION King
CARROLLS Cowlitz
CARSON Skamania

CASHMERE Chelan
CASTLE ROCK Cowlitz
CATHLAMET Wahkiakum
CENTERVILLE Klickitat
CENTRALIA (98531) Lewis(97),
   Thurston(4)
CHATTAROY Spokane
CHEHALIS Lewis
CHELAN Chelan
CHELAN FALLS Chelan
CHENEY Spokane
CHEWELAH Stevens
CHIMACUM Jefferson
CHINOOK Pacific
CINEBAR Lewis
CLALLAM BAY Clallam
CLARKSTON Asotin
CLAYTON (99110) Stevens(75),
   Spokane(25)
CLE ELUM Kittitas
CLEARLAKE Skagit
CLINTON Island
COLBERT Spokane
COLFAX Whitman
COLLEGE PLACE Walla Walla
COLTON Whitman
COLVILLE Stevens
CONCONULLY Okanogan
CONCRETE Skagit
CONNELL (99326) Franklin(91), Adams(9)
CONWAY Skagit
COPALIS BEACH Grays Harbor
COPALIS CROSSING Grays Harbor
COSMOPOLIS (98537) Grays Harbor(97),
   Pacific(3)
COUGAR Cowlitz
COULEE CITY (99115) Grant(78),
   Douglas(22)
COULEE DAM (99116) Okanogan(83),
   Douglas(15), Grant(2)
COUPEVILLE Island
COWICHE Yakima
CRESTON Lincoln
CUNNINGHAM Adams
CURLEW Ferry
CURTIS Lewis
CUSICK Pend Oreille
CUSTER Whatcom
DALLESPORT Klickitat
DANVILLE Ferry
DARRINGTON (98241) Snohomish(75),
   Skagit(26)
DAVENPORT (99999) Lincoln(99),
   Stevens(1)
DAYTON Columbia
DEER HARBOR San Juan
DEER PARK (99006) Spokane(86),
   Stevens(12), Pend Oreille(1)
DEMING Whatcom
DIXIE Walla Walla
DOTY Lewis
DRYDEN Chelan
DUPONT Pierce

DUVALL King
EAST OLYMPIA Thurston
EAST WENATCHEE Douglas
EASTON Kittitas
EASTSOUND San Juan
EATONVILLE Pierce
EDMONDS Snohomish
EDWALL (99008) Lincoln(65), Spokane(35)
ELBE (98330) Pierce(80), Lewis(20)
ELECTRIC CITY Grant
ELK (99009) Spokane(67), Pend
   Oreille(33)
ELLENSBURG Kittitas
ELMA Grays Harbor
ELMER CITY Okanogan
ELTOPIA Franklin
ENDICOTT Whitman
ENTIAT Chelan
ENUMCLAW (98022) King(98), Pierce(2)
EPHRATA Grant
ETHEL Lewis
EVANS Stevens
EVERETT Snohomish
EVERSON Whatcom
FAIRCHILD AIR FORCE BASE Spokane
FAIRFIELD Spokane
FALL CITY King
FARMINGTON Whitman
FEDERAL WAY King
FERNDALE Whatcom
FORD (99013) Stevens(50), Spokane(46),
   Lincoln(4)
FORKS Clallam
FOUR LAKES Spokane
FOX ISLAND Pierce
FREELAND Island
FREEMAN Spokane
FRIDAY HARBOR San Juan
FRUITLAND Stevens
GALVIN Lewis
GARFIELD Whitman
GEORGE Grant
GIFFORD Stevens
GIG HARBOR Pierce
GLENOMA Lewis
GLENWOOD Klickitat
GOLD BAR (98251) Snohomish(98),
   King(2)
GOLDENDALE Klickitat
GOOSE PRAIRIE Yakima
GRAHAM Pierce
GRAND COULEE (99133) Grant(88),
   Douglas(7), Lincoln(4)
GRANDVIEW Yakima
GRANGER Yakima
GRANITE FALLS Snohomish
GRAPEVIEW Mason
GRAYLAND Grays Harbor
GRAYS RIVER Wahkiakum
GREENACRES Spokane
GREENBANK Island
HAMILTON Skagit
HANSVILLE Kitsap

HARRAH Yakima
HARRINGTON Lincoln
HARTLINE Grant
HATTON Adams
HAY Whitman
HEISSON Clark
HOBART King
HOODSPORT Mason
HOOPER Whitman
HOQUIAM Grays Harbor
HUMPTULIPS Grays Harbor
HUNTERS Stevens
HUSUM Klickitat
ILWACO Pacific
INCHELIUM Ferry
INDEX Snohomish
INDIANOLA Kitsap
IONE Pend Oreille
ISSAQUAH King
JOYCE Clallam
KAHLOTUS Franklin
KALAMA Cowlitz
KAPOWSIN Pierce
KELLER (99140) Ferry(83), Stevens(17)
KELSO Cowlitz
KENMORE King
KENNEWICK Benton
KENT King
KETTLE FALLS (99141) Stevens(91),
   Ferry(9)
KEYPORT Kitsap
KINGSTON Kitsap
KIRKLAND King
KITTITAS Kittitas
KLICKITAT Klickitat
LA CENTER Clark
LA CONNER Skagit
LA GRANDE Pierce
LA PUSH Clallam
LACEY Thurston
LACROSSE Whitman
LAKE STEVENS Snohomish
LAKEBAY Pierce
LAKEWOOD Snohomish
LAMONA Lincoln
LAMONT (99017) Whitman(99), Lincoln(1)
LANGLEY Island
LATAH Spokane
LAURIER Ferry
LEAVENWORTH Chelan
LEBAM Pacific
LIBERTY LAKE Spokane
LILLIWAUP Mason
LINCOLN Lincoln
LIND Adams
LITTLEROCK Thurston
LONG BEACH Pacific
LONGBRANCH Pierce
LONGMIRE Pierce
LONGVIEW Cowlitz
LOOMIS Okanogan
LOON LAKE Stevens
LOPEZ ISLAND San Juan

LUMMI ISLAND Whatcom
LYLE Klickitat
LYMAN Skagit
LYNDEN Whatcom
LYNNWOOD Snohomish
MABTON Yakima
MALAGA Chelan
MALDEN Whitman
MALO Ferry
MALONE Grays Harbor
MALOTT Okanogan
MANCHESTER Kitsap
MANSFIELD Douglas
MANSON Chelan
MAPLE FALLS Whatcom
MAPLE VALLEY King
MARBLEMOUNT Skagit
MARCUS Stevens
MARLIN (98832) Grant(98), Adams(2)
MARSHALL Spokane
MARYSVILLE Snohomish
MATLOCK Mason
MATTAWA Grant
MAZAMA Okanogan
MCCLEARY Grays Harbor
MCKENNA Pierce
MEAD Spokane
MEDICAL LAKE Spokane
MEDINA King
MENLO Pacific
MERCER ISLAND King
MESA Franklin
METALINE Pend Oreille
METALINE FALLS Pend Oreille
METHOW Okanogan
MICA Spokane
MILTON (98354) Pierce(92), King(8)
MINERAL Lewis
MOCLIPS Grays Harbor
MOHLER Lincoln
MONITOR Chelan
MONROE Snohomish
MONTESANO Grays Harbor
MORTON Lewis
MOSES LAKE Grant
MOSSYROCK Lewis
MOUNT VERNON Skagit
MOUNTLAKE TERRACE Snohomish
MOXEE Yakima
MUKILTEO Snohomish
NACHES Yakima
NAHCOTTA Pacific
NAPAVINE Lewis
NASELLE (98638) Pacific(92),
   Wahkiakum(9)
NEAH BAY Clallam
NEILTON Grays Harbor
NESPELEM Okanogan
NEWMAN LAKE Spokane
NEWPORT (99156) Pend Oreille(52),
   Spokane(48)
NINE MILE FALLS (99026) Spokane(55),
   Stevens(45)
NOOKSACK Whatcom
NORDLAND Jefferson
NORTH BEND King
NORTH BONNEVILLE Skamania
NORTHPORT Stevens
OAK HARBOR Island

OAKESDALE Whitman
OAKVILLE (98568) Grays Harbor(98),
   Thurston(3)
OCEAN PARK Pacific
OCEAN SHORES Grays Harbor
ODESSA (99159) Lincoln(80), Adams(20)
OKANOGAN Okanogan
OLALLA Kitsap
OLD NATIONAL BANK Spokane
OLGA San Juan
OLYMPIA Thurston
OMAK Okanogan
ONALASKA Lewis
ORCAS San Juan
ORIENT Ferry
ORONDO Douglas
OROVILLE Okanogan
ORTING Pierce
OTHELLO (99344) Adams(80), Grant(15),
   Franklin(5)
OTIS ORCHARDS Spokane
OUTLOOK Yakima
OYSTERVILLE Pacific
PACIFIC King
PACIFIC BEACH Grays Harbor
PACKWOOD Lewis
PALISADES Douglas
PALOUSE Whitman
PARADISE INN Pierce
PARKER Yakima
PASCO (99301) Franklin(95), Walla
   Walla(5)
PASCO Franklin
PATEROS Okanogan
PATERSON Benton
PE ELL Lewis
PESHASTIN Chelan
PLYMOUTH Benton
POINT ROBERTS Whatcom
POMEROY (99347) Garfield(95), Asotin(2),
   Columbia(2)
PORT ANGELES Clallam
PORT GAMBLE Kitsap
PORT HADLOCK Jefferson
PORT LUDLOW Jefferson
PORT ORCHARD Kitsap
PORT TOWNSEND Jefferson
POULSBO Kitsap
PRESCOTT (99348) Walla Walla(98),
   Columbia(2)
PRESTON King
PROSSER (99350) Benton(96), Klickitat(4)
PULLMAN Whitman
PUYALLUP Pierce
QUILCENE Jefferson
QUINAULT Grays Harbor
QUINCY Grant
RAINIER Thurston
RANDLE Lewis
RAVENSDALE King
RAYMOND Pacific
REARDAN (99029) Spokane(64),
   Lincoln(36)
REDMOND King
REDONDO King
RENTON King
REPUBLIC (99166) Ferry(99),
   Okanogan(1)
RETSIL Kitsap

RICE Stevens
RICHLAND Benton
RIDGEFIELD Clark
RITZVILLE Adams
RIVERSIDE Okanogan
ROCHESTER Thurston
ROCK ISLAND Douglas
ROCKFORD Spokane
ROCKPORT (98283) Skagit(96),
   Whatcom(4)
ROLLINGBAY Kitsap
RONALD Kittitas
ROOSEVELT Klickitat
ROSALIA (99170) Spokane(75),
   Whitman(25)
ROSBURG Wahkiakum
ROSLYN Kittitas
ROY Pierce
ROYAL CITY Grant
RYDERWOOD Cowlitz
SAINT JOHN Whitman
SALKUM Lewis
SATSOP Grays Harbor
SEABECK (98380) Kitsap(98), Mason(2)
SEAHURST King
SEATTLE King
SEAVIEW Pacific
SEDRO WOOLLEY (98284) Skagit(97),
   Whatcom(3)
SEKIU Clallam
SELAH Yakima
SEQUIM (98382) Clallam(98), Jefferson(2)
SEQUIM Jefferson
SHAW ISLAND San Juan
SHELTON Mason
SILVANA Snohomish
SILVER CREEK Lewis
SILVERDALE Kitsap
SILVERLAKE Cowlitz
SKAMOKAWA Wahkiakum
SKYKOMISH King
SNOHOMISH Snohomish
SNOQUALMIE King
SNOQUALMIE PASS King
SOAP LAKE Grant
SOUTH BEND Pacific
SOUTH CLE ELUM Kittitas
SOUTH COLBY Kitsap
SOUTH PRAIRIE Pierce
SOUTHWORTH Kitsap
SPANAWAY Pierce
SPANGLE Spokane
SPOKANE Spokane
SPRAGUE (99032) Lincoln(86), Adams(14)
SPRINGDALE Stevens
STANWOOD (98292) Snohomish(63),
   Island(37)
STARBUCK Columbia
STARTUP Snohomish
STEHEKIN Chelan
STEILACOOM Pierce
STEPTOE Whitman
STEVENSON Skamania
STRATFORD Grant
SULTAN Snohomish
SUMAS Whatcom
SUMNER Pierce
SUNNYSIDE Yakima
SUQUAMISH Kitsap

TACOMA Pierce
TAHOLAH Grays Harbor
TAHUYA Mason
TEKOA (99033) Spokane(63), Whitman(37)
TENINO Thurston
THE CRESCENT STORE Spokane
THORNTON Whitman
THORP Kittitas
TIETON Yakima
TOKELAND Pacific
TOLEDO Lewis
TONASKET Okanogan
TOPPENISH Yakima
TOUCHET Walla Walla
TOUTLE Cowlitz
TRACYTON Kitsap
TROUT LAKE Klickitat
TUMTUM Stevens
TWISP Okanogan
UNDERWOOD Skamania
UNION Mason
UNIONTOWN Whitman
UNIVERSITY PLACE Pierce
USK (99180) Pend Oreille(85),
   Spokane(15)
VADER Lewis
VALLEY Stevens
VALLEYFORD Spokane
VANCOUVER Clark
VANTAGE Kittitas
VASHON King
VAUGHN Pierce
VERADALE Spokane
WAHKIACUS Klickitat
WAITSBURG (99361) Walla Walla(87),
   Columbia(13)
WALDRON San Juan
WALLA WALLA Walla Walla
WALLULA Walla Walla
WAPATO Yakima
WARDEN Grant
WASHOUGAL (98671) Clark(77),
   Skamania(23)
WASHTUCNA Adams
WATERVILLE Douglas
WAUCONDA Okanogan
WAUNA Pierce
WAVERLY Spokane
WELLPINIT Stevens
WENATCHEE Chelan
WEST RICHLAND Benton
WESTPORT Grays Harbor
WHITE SALMON Klickitat
WHITE SWAN Yakima
WILBUR (99185) Lincoln(99), Ferry(1)
WILKESON Pierce
WILSON CREEK Grant
WINLOCK Lewis
WINTHROP Okanogan
WISHRAM Klickitat
WOODINVILLE (98072) King(87),
   Snohomish(13)
WOODLAND (98674) Cowlitz(60),
   Clark(40)
YACOLT Clark
YAKIMA Yakima
YELM Thurston
ZILLAH Yakima

City/County Cross Reference

Zip Range	City	Zip Range	City	Zip Range	City	Zip Range	City
98001-98002	AUBURN	98020-98020	EDMONDS	98029-98029	ISSAQUAH	98042-98042	KENT
98003-98003	FEDERAL WAY	98021-98021	BOTHELL	98031-98032	KENT	98043-98043	MOUNTLAKE TERRACE
98004-98009	BELLEVUE	98022-98022	ENUMCLAW	98033-98034	KIRKLAND	98045-98045	NORTH BEND
98010-98010	BLACK DIAMOND	98023-98023	FEDERAL WAY	98035-98035	KENT	98046-98046	LYNNWOOD
98011-98012	BOTHELL	98024-98024	FALL CITY	98036-98037	LYNNWOOD	98047-98047	PACIFIC
98013-98013	BURTON	98025-98025	HOBART	98038-98038	MAPLE VALLEY	98050-98050	PRESTON
98014-98014	CARNATION	98026-98026	EDMONDS	98039-98039	MEDINA	98051-98051	RAVENSDALE
98015-98015	BELLEVUE	98027-98027	ISSAQUAH	98040-98040	MERCER ISLAND	98052-98053	REDMOND
98019-98019	DUVALL	98028-98028	KENMORE	98041-98041	BOTHELL	98054-98054	REDONDO

98055-98059	RENTON	98305-98305	BEAVER	98527-98527	BAY CENTER	98626-98626	KELSO
98060-98060	SEATTLE	98310-98314	BREMERTON	98528-98528	BELFAIR	98628-98628	KLICKITAT
98061-98061	ROLLINGBAY	98315-98315	SILVERDALE	98530-98530	BUCODA	98629-98629	LA CENTER
98062-98062	SEAHURST	98320-98320	BRINNON	98531-98531	CENTRALIA	98631-98631	LONG BEACH
98063-98063	FEDERAL WAY	98321-98321	BUCKLEY	98532-98532	CHEHALIS	98632-98632	LONGVIEW
98064-98064	KENT	98322-98322	BURLEY	98533-98533	CINEBAR	98635-98635	LYLE
98065-98065	SNOQUALMIE	98323-98323	CARBONADO	98535-98535	COPALIS BEACH	98637-98637	NAHCOTTA
98068-98068	SNOQUALMIE PASS	98324-98324	CARLSBORG	98536-98536	COPALIS CROSSING	98638-98638	NASELLE
98070-98070	VASHON	98325-98325	CHIMACUM	98537-98537	COSMOPOLIS	98639-98639	NORTH BONNEVILLE
98071-98071	AUBURN	98326-98326	CLALLAM BAY	98538-98538	CURTIS	98640-98640	OCEAN PARK
98072-98072	WOODINVILLE	98327-98327	DUPONT	98539-98539	DOTY	98641-98641	OYSTERVILLE
98073-98073	REDMOND	98328-98328	EATONVILLE	98540-98540	EAST OLYMPIA	98642-98642	RIDGEFIELD
98082-98082	BOTHELL	98329-98329	GIG HARBOR	98541-98541	ELMA	98643-98643	ROSBURG
98083-98083	KIRKLAND	98330-98330	ELBE	98542-98542	ETHEL	98644-98644	SEAVIEW
98092-98092	AUBURN	98331-98331	FORKS	98544-98544	GALVIN	98645-98645	SILVERLAKE
98093-98093	FEDERAL WAY	98332-98332	GIG HARBOR	98546-98546	GRAPEVIEW	98647-98647	SKAMOKAWA
98101-98109	SEATTLE	98333-98333	FOX ISLAND	98547-98547	GRAYLAND	98648-98648	STEVENSON
98110-98110	BAINBRIDGE ISLAND	98334-98334	SEQUIM	98548-98548	HOODSPORT	98649-98649	TOUTLE
98111-98199	SEATTLE	98335-98335	GIG HARBOR	98550-98550	HOQUIAM	98650-98650	TROUT LAKE
98201-98208	EVERETT	98336-98336	GLENOMA	98552-98552	HUMPTULIPS	98651-98651	UNDERWOOD
98220-98220	ACME	98337-98337	BREMERTON	98554-98554	LEBAM	98660-98668	VANCOUVER
98221-98221	ANACORTES	98338-98338	GRAHAM	98555-98555	LILLIWAUP	98670-98670	WAHKIACUS
98222-98222	BLAKELY ISLAND	98339-98339	PORT HADLOCK	98556-98556	LITTLEROCK	98671-98671	WASHOUGAL
98223-98223	ARLINGTON	98340-98340	HANSVILLE	98557-98557	MCCLEARY	98672-98672	WHITE SALMON
98224-98224	BARING	98342-98342	INDIANOLA	98558-98558	MCKENNA	98673-98673	WISHRAM
98225-98228	BELLINGHAM	98343-98343	JOYCE	98559-98559	MALONE	98674-98674	WOODLAND
98230-98231	BLAINE	98344-98344	KAPOWSIN	98560-98560	MATLOCK	98675-98675	YACOLT
98232-98232	BOW	98345-98345	KEYPORT	98561-98561	MENLO	98682-98687	VANCOUVER
98233-98233	BURLINGTON	98346-98346	KINGSTON	98562-98562	MOCLIPS	98801-98801	WENATCHEE
98235-98235	CLEARLAKE	98348-98348	LA GRANDE	98563-98563	MONTESANO	98802-98802	EAST WENATCHEE
98236-98236	CLINTON	98349-98349	LAKEBAY	98564-98564	MOSSYROCK	98807-98807	WENATCHEE
98237-98237	CONCRETE	98350-98350	LA PUSH	98565-98565	NAPAVINE	98811-98811	ARDENVOIR
98238-98238	CONWAY	98351-98351	LONGBRANCH	98566-98566	NEILTON	98812-98812	BREWSTER
98239-98239	COUPEVILLE	98352-98352	SUMNER	98568-98568	OAKVILLE	98813-98813	BRIDGEPORT
98240-98240	CUSTER	98353-98353	MANCHESTER	98569-98569	OCEAN SHORES	98814-98814	CARLTON
98241-98241	DARRINGTON	98354-98354	MILTON	98570-98570	ONALASKA	98815-98815	CASHMERE
98243-98243	DEER HARBOR	98355-98355	MINERAL	98571-98571	PACIFIC BEACH	98816-98816	CHELAN
98244-98244	DEMING	98356-98356	MORTON	98572-98572	PE ELL	98817-98817	CHELAN FALLS
98245-98245	EASTSOUND	98357-98357	NEAH BAY	98575-98575	QUINAULT	98819-98819	CONCONULLY
98246-98246	BOW	98358-98358	NORDLAND	98576-98576	RAINIER	98821-98821	DRYDEN
98247-98247	EVERSON	98359-98359	OLALLA	98577-98577	RAYMOND	98822-98822	ENTIAT
98248-98248	FERNDALE	98360-98360	ORTING	98579-98579	ROCHESTER	98823-98823	EPHRATA
98249-98249	FREELAND	98361-98361	PACKWOOD	98580-98580	ROY	98824-98824	GEORGE
98250-98250	FRIDAY HARBOR	98362-98363	PORT ANGELES	98581-98581	RYDERWOOD	98826-98826	LEAVENWORTH
98251-98251	GOLD BAR	98364-98364	PORT GAMBLE	98582-98582	SALKUM	98827-98827	LOOMIS
98252-98252	GRANITE FALLS	98365-98365	PORT LUDLOW	98583-98583	SATSOP	98828-98828	MALAGA
98253-98253	GREENBANK	98366-98367	PORT ORCHARD	98584-98584	SHELTON	98829-98829	MALOTT
98255-98255	HAMILTON	98368-98368	PORT TOWNSEND	98585-98585	SILVER CREEK	98830-98830	MANSFIELD
98256-98256	INDEX	98370-98370	POULSBO	98586-98586	SOUTH BEND	98831-98831	MANSON
98257-98257	LA CONNER	98371-98375	PUYALLUP	98587-98587	TAHOLAH	98832-98832	MARLIN
98258-98258	LAKE STEVENS	98376-98376	QUILCENE	98588-98588	TAHUYA	98833-98833	MAZAMA
98259-98259	LAKEWOOD	98377-98377	RANDLE	98589-98589	TENINO	98834-98834	METHOW
98260-98260	LANGLEY	98378-98378	RETSIL	98590-98590	TOKELAND	98836-98836	MONITOR
98261-98261	LOPEZ ISLAND	98380-98380	SEABECK	98591-98591	TOLEDO	98837-98837	MOSES LAKE
98262-98262	LUMMI ISLAND	98381-98381	SEKIU	98592-98592	UNION	98840-98840	OKANOGAN
98263-98263	LYMAN	98382-98382	SEQUIM	98593-98593	VADER	98841-98841	OMAK
98264-98264	LYNDEN	98383-98383	SILVERDALE	98595-98595	WESTPORT	98843-98843	ORONDO
98266-98266	MAPLE FALLS	98384-98384	SOUTH COLBY	98596-98596	WINLOCK	98844-98844	OROVILLE
98267-98267	MARBLEMOUNT	98385-98385	SOUTH PRAIRIE	98597-98597	YELM	98845-98845	PALISADES
98270-98271	MARYSVILLE	98386-98386	SOUTHWORTH	98599-98599	OLYMPIA	98846-98846	PATEROS
98272-98272	MONROE	98387-98387	SPANAWAY	98601-98601	AMBOY	98847-98847	PESHASTIN
98273-98274	MOUNT VERNON	98388-98388	STEILACOOM	98602-98602	APPLETON	98848-98848	QUINCY
98275-98275	MUKILTEO	98390-98390	SUMNER	98603-98603	ARIEL	98849-98849	RIVERSIDE
98276-98276	NOOKSACK	98392-98392	SUQUAMISH	98604-98604	BATTLE GROUND	98850-98850	ROCK ISLAND
98277-98278	OAK HARBOR	98393-98393	TRACYTON	98605-98605	BINGEN	98851-98851	SOAP LAKE
98279-98279	OLGA	98394-98394	VAUGHN	98606-98606	BRUSH PRAIRIE	98852-98852	STEHEKIN
98280-98280	ORCAS	98395-98395	WAUNA	98607-98607	CAMAS	98853-98853	STRATFORD
98281-98281	POINT ROBERTS	98396-98396	WILKESON	98609-98609	CARROLLS	98855-98855	TONASKET
98283-98283	ROCKPORT	98397-98397	LONGMIRE	98610-98610	CARSON	98856-98856	TWISP
98284-98284	SEDRO WOOLLEY	98398-98398	PARADISE INN	98611-98611	CASTLE ROCK	98857-98857	WARDEN
98286-98286	SHAW ISLAND	98401-98424	TACOMA	98612-98612	CATHLAMET	98858-98858	WATERVILLE
98287-98287	SILVANA	98430-98430	CAMP MURRAY	98613-98613	CENTERVILLE	98859-98859	WAUCONDA
98288-98288	SKYKOMISH	98431-98466	TACOMA	98614-98614	CHINOOK	98860-98860	WILSON CREEK
98290-98291	SNOHOMISH	98467-98467	UNIVERSITY PLACE	98616-98616	COUGAR	98862-98862	WINTHROP
98292-98292	STANWOOD	98471-98499	TACOMA	98617-98617	DALLESPORT	98901-98909	YAKIMA
98293-98293	STARTUP	98501-98508	OLYMPIA	98619-98619	GLENWOOD	98920-98920	BROWNSTOWN
98294-98294	SULTAN	98509-98509	LACEY	98620-98620	GOLDENDALE	98921-98921	BUENA
98295-98295	SUMAS	98512-98516	OLYMPIA	98621-98621	GRAYS RIVER	98922-98922	CLE ELUM
98296-98296	SNOHOMISH	98520-98520	ABERDEEN	98622-98622	HEISSON	98923-98923	COWICHE
98297-98297	WALDRON	98522-98522	ADNA	98623-98623	HUSUM	98925-98925	EASTON
98303-98303	ANDERSON ISLAND	98524-98524	ALLYN	98624-98624	ILWACO	98926-98926	ELLENSBURG
98304-98304	ASHFORD	98526-98526	AMANDA PARK	98625-98625	KALAMA	98929-98929	GOOSE PRAIRIE

98930-98930	GRANDVIEW	99022-99022	MEDICAL LAKE	99130-99130	GARFIELD	99181-99181	VALLEY
98932-98932	GRANGER	99023-99023	MICA	99131-99131	GIFFORD	99185-99185	WILBUR
98933-98933	HARRAH	99025-99025	NEWMAN LAKE	99133-99133	GRAND COULEE	99201-99299	SPOKANE
98934-98934	KITTITAS	99026-99026	NINE MILE FALLS	99134-99134	HARRINGTON	99301-99302	PASCO
98935-98935	MABTON	99027-99027	OTIS ORCHARDS	99135-99135	HARTLINE	99320-99320	BENTON CITY
98936-98936	MOXEE	99029-99029	REARDAN	99136-99136	HAY	99321-99321	BEVERLY
98937-98937	NACHES	99030-99030	ROCKFORD	99137-99137	HUNTERS	99322-99322	BICKLETON
98938-98938	OUTLOOK	99031-99031	SPANGLE	99138-99138	INCHELIUM	99323-99323	BURBANK
98939-98939	PARKER	99032-99032	SPRAGUE	99139-99139	IONE	99324-99324	COLLEGE PLACE
98940-98940	RONALD	99033-99033	TEKOA	99140-99140	KELLER	99326-99326	CONNELL
98941-98941	ROSLYN	99034-99034	TUMTUM	99141-99141	KETTLE FALLS	99327-99327	CUNNINGHAM
98942-98942	SELAH	99036-99036	VALLEYFORD	99143-99143	LACROSSE	99328-99328	DAYTON
98943-98943	SOUTH CLE ELUM	99037-99037	VERADALE	99144-99144	LAMONA	99329-99329	DIXIE
98944-98944	SUNNYSIDE	99039-99039	WAVERLY	99146-99146	LAURIER	99330-99330	ELTOPIA
98946-98946	THORP	99040-99040	WELLPINIT	99147-99147	LINCOLN	99332-99332	HATTON
98947-98947	TIETON	99101-99101	ADDY	99148-99148	LOON LAKE	99333-99333	HOOPER
98948-98948	TOPPENISH	99102-99102	ALBION	99149-99149	MALDEN	99335-99335	KAHLOTUS
98950-98950	VANTAGE	99103-99103	ALMIRA	99150-99150	MALO	99336-99338	KENNEWICK
98951-98951	WAPATO	99104-99104	BELMONT	99151-99151	MARCUS	99341-99341	LIND
98952-98952	WHITE SWAN	99105-99105	BENGE	99152-99152	METALINE	99343-99343	MESA
98953-98953	ZILLAH	99107-99107	BOYDS	99153-99153	METALINE FALLS	99344-99344	OTHELLO
99001-99001	AIRWAY HEIGHTS	99109-99109	CHEWELAH	99154-99154	MOHLER	99345-99345	PATERSON
99003-99003	CHATTAROY	99110-99110	CLAYTON	99155-99155	NESPELEM	99346-99346	PLYMOUTH
99004-99004	CHENEY	99111-99111	COLFAX	99156-99156	NEWPORT	99347-99347	POMEROY
99005-99005	COLBERT	99113-99113	COLTON	99157-99157	NORTHPORT	99348-99348	PRESCOTT
99006-99006	DEER PARK	99114-99114	COLVILLE	99158-99158	OAKESDALE	99349-99349	MATTAWA
99008-99008	EDWALL	99115-99115	COULEE CITY	99159-99159	ODESSA	99350-99350	PROSSER
99009-99009	ELK	99116-99116	COULEE DAM	99160-99160	ORIENT	99352-99352	RICHLAND
99011-99011	FAIRCHILD AIR FORCE	99117-99117	CRESTON	99161-99161	PALOUSE	99353-99353	WEST RICHLAND
	BASE	99118-99118	CURLEW	99163-99165	PULLMAN	99356-99356	ROOSEVELT
99012-99012	FAIRFIELD	99119-99119	CUSICK	99166-99166	REPUBLIC	99357-99357	ROYAL CITY
99013-99013	FORD	99121-99121	DANVILLE	99167-99167	RICE	99359-99359	STARBUCK
99014-99014	FOUR LAKES	99122-99122	DAVENPORT	99169-99169	RITZVILLE	99360-99360	TOUCHET
99015-99015	FREEMAN	99123-99123	ELECTRIC CITY	99170-99170	ROSALIA	99361-99361	WAITSBURG
99016-99016	GREENACRES	99124-99124	ELMER CITY	99171-99171	SAINT JOHN	99362-99362	WALLA WALLA
99017-99017	LAMONT	99125-99125	ENDICOTT	99173-99173	SPRINGDALE	99363-99363	WALLULA
99018-99018	LATAH	99126-99126	EVANS	99174-99174	STEPTOE	99371-99371	WASHTUCNA
99019-99019	LIBERTY LAKE	99127-99127	SAINT JOHN	99176-99176	THORNTON	99401-99401	ANATONE
99020-99020	MARSHALL	99128-99128	FARMINGTON	99179-99179	UNIONTOWN	99402-99402	ASOTIN
99021-99021	MEAD	99129-99129	FRUITLAND	99180-99180	USK	99403-99403	CLARKSTON

West Virginia

General Help Numbers:

Governor's Office
Office of the Governor　　　　　　　304-558-2000
1900 Kanawha Blvd, East　　　　　Fax 304-342-7025
Charleston, WV 25305-0370　　　　8AM-6PM M-TH;
　　　　　　　　　　　　　　　　　　8AM-5PM F

http://www.state.wv.us/governor

Attorney General's Office
1900 Kanawha Blvd. Rm 26E　　　　304-558-2021
Charleston, WV 25305-9924　　　Fax 304-558-0140
http://www.state.wv.us/wvag　　　　8:30AM-5PM

State Court Administrator
State Supreme Court of Appeals　　　304-558-0145
1900 Kanawha Blvd, Bldg 1, Rm E 100Fax 304-558-1212
Charleston, WV 25305-0830　　　　　9AM-5PM
http://www.state.wv.us/wvsca/AO.htm

State Archives
Archives & History Section　　　　　304-558-0220
1900 Kanawha Blvd E　　　　　　Fax 304-558-2779
Charleston, WV 25305-0300　　9AM-5PM M-F, 1-5 SA
http://www.wvculture.org/history/wvsamenu.html

State Specifics:

Capital:　　　　　　　　　　　　　　Charleston
　　　　　　　　　　　　　　　　Kanawha County

Time Zone:　　　　　　　　　　　　　　　　EST

Number of Counties:　　　　　　　　　　　　55

Population:　　　　　　　　　　　　1,808,344

Web Site:　　　　　　　　　　　www.state.wv.us

State Agencies

Criminal Records

State Police, Criminal Identification Bureau, Records Section, 725 Jefferson Rd, South Charleston, WV 25309; 304-746-2277, 304-746-2402 (Fax), 8:30AM-4:30PM.

http://www.wvstatepolice.com

Note: The state will also sell an "incident report" of a specific criminal action for $15.00, call 304-746-2178. Sex offender data is available online at www.state.wv.us/~ag/dci/so/so_registration.html.

Indexing & Storage: Records are available from 1938 on computer.

Searching: You must use their "39A Card." The report will include all arrests. To search, the following information must be provided - signed release, index fingerprints, name, Social Security Number, date of birth, race, sex, and the "39A Card." All records are returned by mail. Search can be initiated in person, results mailed.

Access by: mail.

Fee & Payment: The search fee is $20.00 per record. Fee payee: West Virginia State Police. Prepayment required. Personal checks accepted. No credit cards accepted.

Mail search: Turnaround time: 5 to 10 days.

Corporation Records
Limited Liability Company Records
Limited Partnerships
Trademarks/Servicemarks
Limited Liability Partnerships

Secretary of State, Corporation Division, State Capitol Bldg, Room W139, Charleston, WV 25305-0776; 304-558-8000, 304-558-0900 (Fax), 8:30AM-4:30PM.

http://www.state.wv.us/sos/corp/default.htm

Indexing & Storage: Records are available for current active companies. It takes 24 hours before new records are available for inquiry. Records are indexed on inhouse computer.

Searching: Include the following in your request-full name of business. In addition to the initial organizing documents, business records include: Annual Reports, Officers, Directors, Prior (merged) names, Reserved names, mergers and amendments, agents of process and capital stock allocation of corporations.

Access by: mail, phone, fax, in person, online.

Fee & Payment: For plain copies, the fee is $1.00 for the first page and $.50 each additional page. For certified documents, the fee is $15.00 plus $5.00 for each amendment. Officer search is $5.00 plus $.50 a page if over 5 pages. Fee payee: Secretary of State. Prepayment required. Personal checks accepted. Credit cards accepted: MasterCard, Visa, AmEx, Discover.

Mail search: Turnaround time: 24 hours. No self addressed stamped envelope is required.

Phone search: They will confirm if a company is active, they will only do three searches per phone call.

Fax search: Fax searching available.

In person search: Searching is available in person.

Online search: Corporation and business types records on the Secretary of State Business Organization Information System are available free online at www.state.wv.us/wvcorporations/ verifylogon.asp. Search by organization name.

Uniform Commercial Code

UCC Division, Secretary of State, Bldg 1, West Wing, Rm 131, Charleston, WV 25305-0440; 304-558-6000, 304-558-0900 (Fax), 8:30AM-4:30PM.

http://www.state.wv.us/sos

Note: The agency may place limited information under the web site in the future.

Indexing & Storage: Records are available from July 1, 1964. Records are indexed on inhouse computer.

Searching: Use search request form UCC-11. All tax liens are filed at the county level. Terminated filings are not researched. Include the following in your request-debtor name.

Access by: mail, phone, fax, in person.

Fee & Payment: The fee is $5.00 per search and $.50 per copy. Fee payee: Secretary of State. Prepayment required. Pre-paid accounts are accepted, but do not send excess amount-search request may be returned. Personal checks accepted. Credit cards accepted: MasterCard, Visa, AmEx, Discover.

Mail search: Turnaround time: 1 day. A self addressed stamped envelope is requested.

Phone search: They will bill for telephone searches.

Fax search: Same fees as phone or mail searches. Turnaround time in 24 hours.

In person search: Searching is available in person.

Federal Tax Liens
State Tax Liens
Records not maintained by a state level agency.

Note: All tax liens are filed at the county level.

Sales Tax Registrations

WV State Tax Department, Office of Business Registration, PO Box 11425, Charleston, WV 25339 (Courier: 1001 E Lee St E, Charleston, WV 25330); 304-558-8500, 304-558-8733 (Fax), 8:30AM-4:30PM.

http://www.wv.state/taxdiv

Indexing & Storage: Records are available for the current year plus four years. It takes 4 to 6 weeks before new records are available for inquiry.

Searching: This agency will provide only confirmation if permit is registered or not. They will provide no other data. Include the following in your request-business name. They will also search by tax permit number.

Access by: mail, phone, fax, in person.

Mail search: Turnaround time: 2 weeks or less. A self addressed stamped envelope is requested. No fee for mail request.

Phone search: No fee for telephone request.

Fax search: Fax searching available.

In person search: No fee for request. Records are still returned by mail.

Birth Certificates

Bureau of Public Health, Vital Records, 350 Capitol St, Rm 165, Charleston, WV 25305-3701; 304-558-2931, 304-343-2169 (Fax), 8AM-4PM.

http://www.wvdhhr.org/bph/oehp/hsc

Indexing & Storage: Records are available from 1917 to present. New records are available for inquiry immediately. Records are indexed on microfiche, inhouse computer.

Searching: Records released to immediate family members only. Include the following in your request-full name, names of parents, mother's maiden name, date of birth, place of birth.

Access by: mail, phone, in person, online.

Fee & Payment: The fee is $5.00 per name, add $10.00 for using credit card. Fee payee: Vital Registration. Prepayment required. Personal checks accepted. Credit cards accepted: MasterCard, Visa, AmEx, Discover.

Mail search: Turnaround time: 3 to 4 weeks. A self addressed stamped envelope is requested.

Phone Search: See expedited service.

In person search: Turnaround time 15 minutes.

Online search: Online ordering is available at www.vitalchek.com.

Expedited service: Expedited service is available for mail and phone searches. To order by credit card and have 1 week turnaround time add $15.00. Add overnight delivery fees if desired.

Death Records

Bureau of Public Health, Vital Records, 350 Capitol St, Rm 165, Charleston, WV 25305-3701; 304-558-2931, 302-343-2169 (Fax), 8AM-4PM.

http://www.wvdhhr.org/bph/oehp/hsc

Indexing & Storage: Records are available from 1917 on. New records are available for inquiry immediately. Records are indexed on microfiche, inhouse computer.

Searching: Record released to immediate family or anyone with a verifiable, specific interest only. Include the following in your request-full name, date of death, place of death, names of parents, Social Security Number.

Access by: mail, phone, fax, in person, online.

Fee & Payment: The fee is $5.00 per name. Add $10.00 for use of credit card. Fee payee: Vital Registration. Prepayment required. Personal checks accepted. Credit cards accepted: MasterCard, Visa, AmEx, Discover.

Mail search: Turnaround time: 4 to 6 weeks. A self addressed stamped envelope is requested.

Phone search: See expedited service.

Fax search: Access is provided by VitalChek. Use of credit card is required.

In person search: Turnaround time 15 minutes.

Online search: Order online at www.vitalchek.com.

Expedited service: Expedited service is available for mail and phone searches. Add $15.00 for using a credit card and 1 week expedited service. Add overnight service fees if desired.

Marriage Certificates

Bureau of Public Health, Vital Records, 350 Capitol St, Rm 165, Charleston, WV 25305-3701; 304-558-2931, 304-343-2169 (Fax), 8AM-4PM.

http://www.wvdhhr.org/bph/oehp/hsc

Indexing & Storage: Records are available from 1921 on. Records certified from 1964 on. New records are available for inquiry immediately. Records are indexed on microfiche, inhouse computer.

Searching: You must be a family member or show cause to receive the record. Include the following in your request-names of husband and wife, date of marriage, place or county of marriage.

Access by: mail, phone, fax, in person.

Fee & Payment: The fee is $5.00 per name. Add $10.00 for use of credit card. Fee payee: Vital Registration. Prepayment required. Personal checks accepted. Credit cards accepted: MasterCard, Visa, AmEx, Discover.

Mail search: Turnaround time: 3 to 4 weeks. A self addressed stamped envelope is requested.

Phone search: See expedited service.

Fax search: Available from VitalChek. Use of credit card required.

In person search: Turnaround time 15 minutes.

Expedited service: Expedited service is available for mail and phone searches. Turnaround time: overnight delivery. $15.00 fee expedited service included using a credit card. Add overnight delivery fees, if desired.

Divorce Records

Records not maintained by a state level agency.

Note: Records are maintained by the Clerk of Court in the county of divorce.

Workers' Compensation Records

Workers Compensation Division, Records Management, 4510 Pennsylvania, Charleston, WV 25302; 304-558-5587, 304-558-1908 (Fax), 8AM-4:30PM.

http://www.state.wv.us/bep

Indexing & Storage: Records are available from 1916. New records are available for inquiry immediately. Records are indexed on microfiche.

Searching: Must have a signed release from claimant or be a representative of the employer. They suggest the use of their WC910 Form. You may call for a copy of this form, but they will release no information over the phone. Include the following in your request-claimant name, Social Security Number, date of accident, file number (if known). The following data is not released: psychiatric information.

Access by: mail, in person.

Fee & Payment: There are no fees unless extensive copies or searching is needed.

Mail search: Turnaround time: 5 to 10 days. Turnaround time is 1-2 days for microfiche copies and 5-10 days if paper copies are required.A self addressed stamped envelope is requested.

In person search: Turnaround time is usually 1 or more days.

Driver License Information

Driver Records

Division of Motor Vehicles, 1800 Kanawha Blvd, Building 3, Rm 118, State Capitol Complex, Charleston, WV 25317; 304-558-0238, 304-558-0037 (Fax), 8:30AM-4:30PM.

http://www.state.wv.us/dmv

Note: Ticket information is available from this office for the convictee only (no fee). Others must request ticket information from the court system.

Indexing & Storage: Records are available for 3 years for all violations including DWIs and suspensions. Convictions not shown on the record include speeding 10 mph or less over limit on interstate, driving on expired license, and overweight or overlength violations (truckers). It takes 1 week to 3 months (DUIs immediately) before new records are available for inquiry.

Searching: Casual requesters cannot obtain personal information on subjects who have not given consent. Accidents are not reported on records. The driver's license number and last name are required for a request.

Access by: mail, in person, online.

Fee & Payment: The fee is $5.00 per record including no record founds. Fee payee: Division of Motor Vehicles. Prepayment required. Personal checks accepted. No credit cards accepted.

Mail search: Turnaround time: 24 hours. A self addressed stamped envelope is requested.

In person search: Up to seven requests may be received immediately at the counter. Branch offices in 9 cities can issue instant records.

Online search: Online access is available in either interactive or batch mode. The system is open 24 hours a day. Batch requesters receive return transmission about 3 AM. Users must access through AAMVAnet. A contract is required and accounts must pre-pay. Fee is $5.00 per record. For more information, call Lacy Morgan at (304) 558-3915.

Other access: The state will sell its DL file to commercial vendors, but records cannot be re-sold.

Vehicle Ownership
Vehicle Identification
Vessel Ownership
Vessel Registration

Division of Motor Vehicles, Information Services, 1606 Washington St East, Charleston, WV 25311; 304-558-0282, 304-558-1012 (Fax), 8:30AM-4:30PM.

http://www.state.wv.us/dmv

Note: This agency maintains records for unattached mobile homes.

Indexing & Storage: Records are available from 1959 for vehicles, from 1975 for boat registrations, and from 1980 for boat titles. All motorized boats and all sailboats must be registered and titled. It takes 1 to 3 days before new records are available for inquiry.

Searching: High volume requesters must be approved after stating purpose of requests. Casual requesters cannot receive personal information. If doing search by name, it is suggested to also submit address. Boat records can be searched by hull number or WV number. The following data is not released: Social Security Numbers or medical information.

Access by: mail, in person.

Fee & Payment: The fee is $1.00 for registration information, $2.00 per vehicle for lien information, and $15.00 for a complete title history (which includes lien information), and $5.00 for message forwarding. Fee payee: Division of Motor Vehicles. Prepayment required. Do not overpay, they do not have the capacity to refund. Personal checks accepted. No credit cards accepted.

Mail search: Turnaround time: 3 to 5 days. Return address must appear clearly on the request.A self addressed stamped envelope is requested.

In person search: Turnaround time is while you wait if the record is on computer, or 2 days for photocopies.

Other access: The entire state's vehicle file can be purchased. Costs for customized runs depend on programming time. Further resale is prohibited. Call Lynda Osborne 304-558-0282 for more information.

Accident Reports

Department of Public Safety, Traffic Records Section, 725 Jefferson Rd, South Charleston, WV 25309-1698; 304-746-2128, 304-746-2206 (Fax), 8:30AM-4:30PM.

http://www.wv.statepolice.com

Note: It is suggested to send a letter explaining purpose of request and state if involved in some manner.

Indexing & Storage: Records are available of incidents investigated by the state police for the past 10 years. It takes 1 to 3 weeks before new records are available for inquiry.

Searching: If the State Police did not investigate the incident, the report must be obtained from the local investigating jurisdiction. Include the following in your request-name, date of accident, location of accident. The following data is not released: juvenile records.

Access by: mail, phone, fax, in person.

Fee & Payment: The fee is $10.00 per record. If certified, the cost is $15.00. Fee payee: Superintendent, Division of Public Safety. Prepayment required. Personal checks accepted. No credit cards accepted.

Mail search: Turnaround time: 2 to 3 weeks. A self addressed stamped envelope is requested.

Phone search: Records are available by phone.

Fax search: For an extra $5.00 per record, the agency will send data by fax.

In person search: Turnaround time is same day, if record is readily available.

Legislation Records

West Virginia State Legislature, State Capitol, Documents, Charleston, WV 25305; 304-347-4830, 800-642-8650 (Local), 8:30AM-4:30PM.

http://www.legis.state.wv.us

Note: Sessions start 2nd Wed. in January.

Indexing & Storage: Records are available for current session only. Records are indexed on books (volumes).

Searching: Include the following in your request-bill number, topic of bill.

Access by: mail, phone, fax, in person, online.

Fee & Payment: There is no fee.

Mail search: Turnaround time: 2 days. There is a limit of 7 bills per mailing. Indicate if the bill is pending by House or Senate, or if bill is passed.No self addressed stamped envelope is required.

Phone search: Records are available by phone.

Fax search: Same criteria as mail searching.

In person search: Searching is available in person.

Online search: The Internet site allows one to search for status and/or text of bills.

Voter Registration

Records not maintained by a state level agency.

Note: Voter information is held by the county clerks. There is no statewide system. All information is public record.

GED Certificates

Dept of Education, GED Office, 1900 Kanawha Blvd E, Bldg 6, Rm 250, Charleston, WV 25305-0330; 304-558-6315, 304-558-6317.

http://wvabe.state.k12.wv.us/ged/index.htm

Searching: To search, all of the following is a required: a signed release, name, year of test, date of birth, Social Security Number, city of test, and a copy of or presentation of a photo ID and daytime phone number.

Access by: mail.

Fee & Payment: There is no fee for verification. Copies of transcripts are $5.00 each. Fee payee: WV DOE Vocational Division. Prepayment required. No credit cards accepted.

Mail search: Turnaround time: 7 to 10 days. No self addressed stamped envelope is required.

Hunting License Information
Fishing License Information

Natural Resources Department, Licensing Division, 1900 Kanawha Blvd E, Bldg 3, Room 624, Charleston, WV 25305; 304-558-2758, 304-558-6208 (Fax), 8:30AM-4:30PM.

http://www.wvweb.com/www/hunting

Indexing & Storage: Records are available for current year only. Records are indexed on inhouse computer.

Searching: All requests must be in writing. Records are considered public records. Include the following in your request-full name, driver's license number.

Access by: mail.

Fee & Payment: The search fee is $29.00, but only if a record is found. Fee payee: Natural Resources Department. Personal checks accepted. Credit cards accepted: MasterCard, Visa.

Mail search: Turnaround time: 5 to 10 working days. No self addressed stamped envelope is required.

Other access: The agency sells mailing lists. Request must be in writing and certain restrictions apply. Call the number above for further details.

West Virginia State Licensing Agencies

Licenses Searchable Online

Attorney #14	www.wvbar.org/BARINFO/mdirectory/index.htm
Lobbyist #39	www.lobbyist.net/WestVirg/WESLOB.htm
Optometrist #41	www.odfinder.org/LicSearch.asp
Public Accountant-CPA #01	www.state.wv.us/scripts/wvboa/default.cfm
Radiologic Technologist #09	www.state.wv.us/rtboe/RTLIST.pdf

Licensing Quick Finder

Aesthetician #03 304-558-2924
Animal Technician #22 304-558-2016
Architect #02..304-528-5825
Asbestos Worker #42 304-558-2981
Athletic Trainer #26 304-558-7010
Attorney #14 304-558-7815
Barber #03 304-558-2924
Boat & Canoe Expedition Provider #29 .304-558-2783
Boating Business, Whitewater #29........304-558-2783
Charitable Organization #36 304-558-6000
Chiropractor #04 304-772-1424
Contractor, General #24 .... 304-558-7890x122
Cosmetologist #03 304-558-2924
Counselor LPC, Professional #10 304-746-2512
Counselor, Professional #10.................304-746-2512
Credit Service Organization #36 304-558-6000
Dental Hygienist #06.............................304-252-8266
Dentist #06 304-252-8266
Educational Audiologist #26..................304-558-7010
Electrician #40 304-558-2191
Embalmer #05 304-558-0302
Emergency Medical Technician-Paramedic #27 ....
....304-558-3956
Engineer #33 304-558-3554
First Responder #27...............................304-558-3956
Fishing Guide #29 304-558-2783
Forester #20 304-924-6266
Forestry Technician #20 304-924-6266

Fundraiser, For-Profit Professional #37.800-982-8297
Funeral Director; Funeral Home #05 304-558-0302
Hearing Aid Specialist #12....................304-558-7886
Insurance Agent #30 304-558-3354
Insurance Solicitor #30..........................304-558-3354
Investment Advisor/Representative #38 304-558-2257
Landscape Architect #13.......................304-293-2141
Lobbyist #39 304-558-0664
Manicurist #03 304-558-2924
Medical Doctor #15 304-558-2921
Midwife Nurse #08 304-558-3596
Mine Electrician #32 304-558-1425
Mine Surveyor/Foreman #32 304-558-1425
Miner #32 304-558-1425
Notary Public #36..................................304-558-6000
Nurse #08 304-558-3596
Nurse Anesthetist #08 304-558-3596
Nurse-LPN #08 304-558-3572
Nursing Home Administrator #31 304-759-0722
Occupational Therapist/Assistant #16 ...304-329-0480
Optometrist #41 304-627-2106
Osteopathic Physician/Physician Assistant #17..........
....304-723-4638
Pesticide Applicator #25 304-558-2209
Pharmacist #18 304-558-0558
Physical Therapist/Assistant #19 304-627-2251
Physician Assistant #15.........................304-558-2921
Podiatrist #15...304-558-2921

Polygraph Examiner #28 .... 304-558-7890 x122
Private Detective #36 304-558-6000
Psychologist #11 304-558-0604
Public Accountant-CPA #01...................304-558-3557
Radiologic Technologist #09 304-787-4398
Rafting Outfitter, Whitewater #29 304-558-2783
Real Estate Appraiser #34.....................304-558-3919
Real Estate Broker/Salesperson #35 304-558-3555
Sanitarian, Registered/In Training #23 ..304-558-2981
School Counselor #26 304-558-7010
School Nurse #26....................................304-558-7010
School Principal #26...............................304-558-7010
School Psychologist #26 304-558-7010
School Social Services/Attendance Investigator #26
....304-558-7010
School Superintendent #26 304-558-7010
Securities Agent #38 304-558-2257
Securities Broker/Dealer #38 304-558-2257
Security Guard #36 304-558-6000
Shooting Reserve #29 304-558-2783
Shot Firer #32 304-558-1425
Social Worker #21 304-558-8816
Speech/Language Pathologist #26 304-558-7010
Supervisor of Instruction #26 304-558-7010
Surveyor #07 304-465-1653
Teacher #26..304-558-7010
Telemarketer #37 800-982-8297
Veterinarian #22.....................................304-558-2016

Licensing Agency Information

#01 Board of Accountancy, 812 Quarrier St, L&S Bldg, #200, Charleston, WV 25301-2695; 304-558-3557, Fax: 304-558-1325.
www.state.wv.us/wvboa
Direct web site URL to search for licensees: www.state.wv.us/scripts/wvboa/default.cfm. You can search online using last name, city, and ZIP Code.

#02 Board of Architects, PO Box 589, Huntington, WV 25710-0589; 304-528-5825, Fax: 304-528-5826.
http://wvbrdarch.org
Direct web site URL to search for licensees: http://wvbrdarch.org/cgi-wvbrdarch/wvbrdarch_licdb/wvbrdarch/architects/query_form. You can search online using name and registration number.

#03 Board of Barbers & Cosmetologists, 1716 Pennsylvania Ave, #7, Charleston, WV 25302; 304-558-2924, Fax: 304-558-3450.

#04 Board of Chiropractic Examiners, PO Box 153, St Albans, WV 25177; 304-722-1424, Fax: 304-722-1425.
www.state.wv.us/wvboc Licenses verified in writing only; $5.00 fee each.

#05 Board of Embalmers & Funeral Directors, 179 Summers St, #305, Charleston, WV 25301-2131; 304-558-0302, Fax: 304-558-0660.

#06 Board of Examiners for Dentists/Dental Hygienists, PO Drawer 1459, Beckley, WV 25802-1459; 304-252-8266, Fax: 304-252-2779.

#07 Board of Examiners for Land Surveyors, PO Box 1248, Oakhill, WV 25901; 304-465-1653, Fax: 304-465-1653 *51.

#08 Board of Examiners for Nurses, 101 Dee Dr, Charleston, WV 25311-1620; 304-558-3596, Fax: 304-558-3666.
www.state.wv.us/nurses/rn

#09 Board of Examiners for Radiologic Technology, PO Box 638, Cool Ridge, WV 25825; 304-787-4398, Fax: 304-787-4398.
www.state.wv.us/rtboe
Direct web site URL to search for licensees: www.state.wv.us/rtboe/RTLIST.pdf. You can search online using alphabetical list

#10 Board of Examiners in Counseling, 100 Angus E Peyton Dr, South Charleston, WV 25303-1600; 304-746-2512, Fax: 305-746-1942.
www.marshall.edu/schoolcoun/boe.html

#11 Board of Examiners of Psychologists, PO Box 3955, Charleston, WV 25339-3955; 304-558-0604, Fax: 304-558-0608.

#12 Board of Hearing-Aid Dealers, 701 Jefferson Rd, South Charleston, WV 25309-1638; 304-558-7886, Fax: 304-558-7886.
www.state.wv.us/bep/lmi/license/liclist.htm

#13 Board of Landscape Architects, PO Box 4231, Star City, WV 26504; 304-293-2141 x4490, Fax: 304-293-3752.

#14 Board of Law Examiners, 1900 Kanawha Blvd, Bldg 1, #E-400, Charleston, WV 25305-0837; 304-558-7815, Fax: 304-558-0831.
www.wvbar.org
Direct web site URL to search for licensees: www.wvbar.org/BARINFO/mdirectory/index.htm. You can search online using alphabetical lists

#15 Board of Medicine, 101 Dee Dr, Charleston, WV 25311-1620; 304-558-2921, Fax: 304-558-2084.

#16 Board of Occupational Therapy, 119 S Price St, Kingwood, WV 26537; 304-329-0480, Fax: 304-329-0480.
www.wvbot.org

#17 Board of Osteopathy, 334 Penco Rd, Weirton, WV 26062-3813; 304-723-4638, Fax: 304-723-6723.

#18 Board of Pharmacy, 232 Capitol St, Charleston, WV 25301-2206; 304-558-0558, Fax: 304-558-0572.
www.wvop.com

#19 WV Board of Physical Therapy, 153 W Main St, #103, Clarksburg, WV 26301; 304-627-2251, Fax: 304-627-2253.
www.wvbopt.com

#20 Board of Registration for Foresters, 8 Kepner St, Buckhannon, WV 26201; 304-924-6266, Fax: 304-924-6142.

#21 Board of Social Work Examiners, PO Box 5459, Charleston, WV 25361; 304-558-8816, Fax: 304-558-4189.

#22 Board of Veterinary Medicine, 1900 Kanawha Blvd E, Charleston, WV 25305-0119; 304-558-2016, Fax: 304-558-0891.

#23 Bureau of Public Health, 815 Quarrier St, Charleston, WV 25301-2616; 304-558-2981, Fax: 304-558-1071.

#24 Contractor Licensing Board, 1900 Kanawha Blvd E, Bldg 3, Rm 319, Charleston, WV 25305; 304-558-7890 x122.
www.state.wv.us/labor

#25 Department of Agriculture, State Capitol Complex, Bldg1, Rm M28, Charleston, WV 25305; 304-558-2209, Fax: 304-558-3594.
www.state.wv.us/agriculture

#26 Department of Education, 1900 Washington St E, Rm B252, Charleston, WV 25305; 304-558-7010, Fax: 304-558-0882.
http://wvde.state.wv.us

#27 Office of EMS, 350 Capitol St #515, Charleston, WV 25301-3716; 304-558-3956, Fax: 304-558-1437.

#28 Department of Labor, State Capitol Complex, Bldg. 6, Rm 749B, Charleston, WV 25305; 304-558-7890 x122, Fax: 304-558-3797.
www.state.wv.us/labor

#29 Division of Natural Resources, 1900 Kanawha Blvd, East Bldg 3, Rm 837, Charleston, WV 25305; 304-558-2783, Fax: 304-558-1170.
www.dnr.state.wv.us

#30 Insurance Commissioner, 1124 Smith St, Charleston, WV 25301; 304-558-0610, Fax: 304-558-4966.
www.state.wv.us/insurance No longer licenses insurance brokers.

#31 Nursing Home Administrators Licensing Board, 5303 Kensington Dr, Cross Lanes, WV 25313; 304-759-0722, Fax: 304-759-0724.

#32 Office of Miners Health Safety & Training, 1615 Washington St E, Charleston, WV 25311; 304-558-1425, Fax: 304-558-1282.
state.wv.us/mhst

#33 Board of Registration for Professional Engineers, 608 Union Bldg, Charleston, WV 25301-2703; 304-558-3554, Fax: 304-558-6232.

#34 Real Estate Appraiser Licensing & Certification Bd, 2110 Kanawah Blvd E, #101, Charleston, WV 25311; 304-558-3919, Fax: 304-558-3983.

www.state.wv.us/appraise

#35 Real Estate Commission, 1033 Quarrier St, #400, Charleston, WV 25301-2315; 304-558-3555, Fax: 304-558-6442.
www.state.wv.us/wvrec/

#36 Secretary of State, 1900 Kanawha Blvd, Bldg 1, #157-K, Charleston, WV 25305-0770; 304-558-6000, Fax: 304-558-0900.
www.state.wv.us/sos

#37 Department of Tax & Revenue, PO Box 3784, Charleston, WV 25337; 304-558-0211.
www.state.wv.us/taxrev/

#38 State Auditor's Office, State Capitol, Rm W110, Charleston, WV 25305; 304-558-2257, Fax: 304-558-4211.
www.wvauditor.com

#39 Ethics Commission, 1207 Quarrier St, 4th Fl, Charleston, WV 25301; 304-558-0664, Fax: 304-558-2169.
www.state.wv.us/ethics Online searching at the web site is planned

#40 State Fire Marshall, 1207 Quarrier, 2nd Fl, Charleston, WV 25301; 304-558-2191, Fax: 304-558-2537.
www.wvfiremarshal.org

#41 Board of Optometry, 101 Michael St, Clarksburg, WV 26301-3937; 304-627-2106, Fax: 304-627-2282.
Direct web site URL to search for licensees: www.odfinder.org/LicSearch.asp

#42 Department of Health & Human Resources, 815 Quarrier St, Charleston, WV 25301; 304-558-2981.

West Virginia Federal Courts

The following list indicates the district and division name for each county in the state. If the bankruptcy court location is different from the district court, then the location of the bankruptcy court appears in parentheses.

County/Court Cross Reference

County	District	Division
Barbour	Northern	Elkins (Wheeling)
Berkeley	Northern	Martinsburg (Wheeling)
Boone	Southern	Charleston
Braxton	Northern	Clarksburg (Wheeling)
Brooke	Northern	Wheeling
Cabell	Southern	Huntington (Charleston)
Calhoun	Northern	Clarksburg (Wheeling)
Clay	Southern	Charleston
Doddridge	Northern	Clarksburg (Wheeling)
Fayette	Southern	Beckley (Charleston)
Gilmer	Northern	Clarksburg (Wheeling)
Grant	Northern	Elkins (Wheeling)
Greenbrier	Southern	Beckley (Charleston)
Hampshire	Northern	Martinsburg (Wheeling)
Hancock	Northern	Wheeling
Hardy	Northern	Elkins (Wheeling)
Harrison	Northern	Clarksburg (Wheeling)
Jackson	Southern	Parkersburg (Charleston)
Jefferson	Northern	Martinsburg (Wheeling)
Kanawha	Southern	Charleston
Lewis	Northern	Clarksburg (Wheeling)
Lincoln	Southern	Huntington (Charleston)
Logan	Southern	Charleston
Marion	Northern	Clarksburg (Wheeling)
Marshall	Northern	Wheeling
Mason	Southern	Huntington (Charleston)
McDowell	Southern	Bluefield (Charleston)
Mercer	Southern	Bluefield (Charleston)
Mineral	Northern	Elkins (Wheeling)
Mingo	Southern	Huntington (Charleston)
Monongalia	Northern	Clarksburg (Wheeling)
Monroe	Southern	Bluefield (Charleston)
Morgan	Northern	Martinsburg (Wheeling)
Nicholas	Southern	Beckley (Charleston)
Ohio	Northern	Wheeling
Pendleton	Northern	Elkins (Wheeling)
Pleasants	Northern	Clarksburg (Wheeling)
Pocahontas	Northern	Elkins (Wheeling)
Preston	Northern	Elkins (Wheeling)
Putnam	Southern	Charleston
Raleigh	Southern	Beckley (Charleston)
Randolph	Northern	Elkins (Wheeling)
Ritchie	Northern	Clarksburg (Wheeling)
Roane	Southern	Charleston
Summers	Southern	Bluefield (Charleston)
Taylor	Northern	Clarksburg (Wheeling)
Tucker	Northern	Elkins (Wheeling)
Tyler	Northern	Clarksburg (Wheeling)
Upshur	Northern	Elkins (Wheeling)
Wayne	Southern	Huntington (Charleston)
Webster	Northern	Elkins (Wheeling)
Wetzel	Northern	Wheeling
Wirt	Southern	Parkersburg (Charleston)
Wood	Southern	Parkersburg (Charleston)
Wyoming	Southern	Beckley (Charleston)

US District Court

Northern District of West Virginia

Clarksburg Division PO Box 2857, Clarksburg, WV 26302-2857 (Courier Address: 500 W Pike St, Rm 301, Clarksburg, WV 26301), 304-622-8513, Fax: 304-623-4551.

http://www.wvnd.uscourts.gov

Counties: Braxton, Calhoun, Doddridge, Gilmer, Harrison, Lewis, Marion, Monongalia, Pleasants, Ritchie, Taylor, Tyler.

Indexing/Storage: Cases are indexed by defendant and plaintiff as well as by case number. New cases are available in the index 1-2 days after filing date. A card index is maintained. Open records are located at this court.

Fee & Payment: The fee is $20.00 per item (one party name or case number). Payment may be made by money order, cashier check. Business checks are not accepted. Personal checks are not accepted. Prepayment is required. Money orders are preferred unless it is a known person or business. Payee: Clerk, US District Court.

Certification fee: $7.00 per document. Copy fee: $.50 per page.

Phone Search: Only docket information is available by phone.

Mail Search: A stamped self addressed envelope is not required.

In Person: In person searching is available.

PACER: Sign-up number is 800-676-6856. Access fee is $.60 per minute. Toll-free access: 888-513-7959. Local access: 304-233-7424. Case records are available back to October 1994. Records are purged every 5 years. New records are available online after 1 day. PACER is available online at http://pacer.wvnd.uscourts.gov.

Elkins Division PO Box 1518, Elkins, WV 26241 (Courier Address: 2nd Floor, 300 3rd St, Elkins, WV 26241), 304-636-1445, Fax: 304-636-5746.

http://www.wvnd.uscourts.gov

Counties: Barbour, Grant, Hardy, Mineral, Pendleton, Pocahontas, Preston, Randolph, Tucker, Upshur, Webster.

Indexing/Storage: Cases are indexed by defendant and plaintiff as well as by case number.

New cases are available in the index 1 day after filing date. Both computer and card indexes are maintained. Civil cases are indexed on computer from October 1994 forward, and criminal cases from October 1995 forward. Open records are located at this court. District-wide searches are available from this court. A case number and cause of action will be released.

Fee & Payment: The fee is $20.00 per item (one party name or case number). Payment may be made by money order, cashier check. Business checks are not accepted. Personal checks are not accepted. Prepayment is required. Money orders are preferred unless it is a known person or business. Payee: Clerk, US District Court. Certification fee: $7.00 per document. Copy fee: $.50 per page. You are allowed to make your own copies. These copies cost $.50 per page. If court personnel help, the search fee will be charged.

Phone Search: Only docket information is available by phone.

Fax Search: Will accept search requests by fax with $15.00 fee. The fee is $1.00 per page.

Mail Search: A stamped self addressed envelope is not required.

In Person: In person searching is available.

PACER: Sign-up number is 800-676-6856. Access fee is $.60 per minute. Toll-free access: 888-513-7959. Local access: 304-233-7424. Case records are available back to October 1994. Records are purged every 5 years. New records are available online after 1 day. PACER is available online at http://pacer.wvnd.uscourts.gov.

Martinsburg Division Room 207, 217 W King St, Martinsburg, WV 25401 (Courier Address: Use mail address for courier delivery), 304-267-8225, Fax: 304-264-0434.

http://www.wvnd.uscourts.gov

Counties: Berkeley, Hampshire, Jefferson, Morgan.

Indexing/Storage: Cases are indexed by defendant and plaintiff as well as by case number. New cases are available in the index 2 days after filing date. Both computer and card indexes are maintained. The computer index is from 1994 forward. Open records are located at this court.

Fee & Payment: The fee is $20.00 per item (one party name or case number). Payment may be made by money order, cashier check. Business checks are not accepted. Personal checks are not accepted. Prepayment is required. Payee: Clerk, US District Court. Certification fee: $7.00 per document. Copy fee: $.50 per page.

Phone Search: Limited docket information is available by phone.

Mail Search: Always enclose a stamped self addressed envelope.

In Person: In person searching is available.

PACER: Sign-up number is 800-676-6856. Access fee is $.60 per minute. Toll-free access: 888-513-7959. Local access: 304-233-7424. Case records are available back to October 1994. Records are purged every 5 years. New records are available online after 1 day. PACER is available online at http://pacer.wvnd.uscourts.gov.

Wheeling Division Clerk, PO Box 471, Wheeling, WV 26003 (Courier Address: 12th & Chapline Sts, Wheeling, WV 26003), 304-232-0011, Fax: 304-233-2185.

http://www.wvnd.uscourts.gov

Counties: Brooke, Hancock, Marshall, Ohio, Wetzel.

Indexing/Storage: Cases are indexed by defendant and plaintiff as well as by case number. New cases are available in the index immediately after filing date. Both computer and card indexes are maintained. Civil cases on computer since October 1994, and criminal cases since October 1995. Open records are located at this court. Records have not yet been sent to the Federal Records Center from this office.

Fee & Payment: The fee is $20.00 per item (one party name or case number). Payment may be made by money order, cashier check, personal check. Prepayment is required. Payee: Clerk, US District Court. Certification fee: $7.00 per document. Copy fee: $.50 per page. You are allowed to make your own copies. These copies cost Not Applicable per page.

Phone Search: All information that is not sealed is available for release over the phone.

Mail Search: Always enclose a stamped self addressed envelope.

In Person: In person searching is available.

PACER: Sign-up number is 800-676-6856. Access fee is $.60 per minute. Toll-free access:

888-513-7959. Local access: 304-233-7424. Case records are available back to October 1994. Records are purged every 5 years. New records are available online after 1 day. PACER is available online at http://pacer.wvnd.uscourts.gov.

US Bankruptcy Court
Northern District of West Virginia

Wheeling Division PO Box 70, Wheeling, WV 26003 (Courier Address: 12th & Chapline Sts, Wheeling, WV 26003), 304-233-1655.

http://www.wvnb.uscourts.gov

Counties: Barbour, Berkeley, Braxton, Brooke, Calhoun, Doddridge, Gilmer, Grant, Hampshire, Hancock, Hardy, Harrison, Jefferson, Lewis, Marion, Marshall, Mineral, Monongalia, Morgan, Ohio, Pendleton, Pleasants, Pocahontas, Preston, Randolph, Ritchie, Taylor,Tucker, Tyler, Upshur, Webster, Wetzel.

Indexing/Storage: Cases are indexed by debtor as well as by case number. New cases are available in the index 24 hours after filing date. A card index is maintained. Open records are located at this court.

Fee & Payment: The fee is $20.00 per item (one party name or case number). Payment may be made by money order, cashier check, personal check. Prepayment is required. Payee: Clerk, US Bankruptcy Court. Certification fee: $7.00 per document. Copy fee: $.50 per page.

Phone Search: Only docket information is available by phone. An automated voice case information service (VCIS) is available.

Mail Search: Always enclose a stamped self addressed envelope.

In Person: In person searching is available.

PACER: Sign-up number is 800-676-6856. Access fee is $.60 per minute. Toll-free access: 800-809-3016. Local access: 304-233-2871. Case records are available back to early 1990. Records are never purged. New civil records are available online after 1 day. PACER is available online at http://pacer.wvnb.uscourts.gov.

US District Court
Southern District of West Virginia

Beckley Division PO Drawer 5009, Beckley, WV 25801 (Courier Address: 110 N. Heber, Beckley, WV 25801), 304-253-7481, Fax: 304-253-3252.

http://www.wvsd.uscourts.gov

Counties: Fayette, Greenbrier, Raleigh, Sumners, Wyoming.

Indexing/Storage: Cases are indexed by defendant and plaintiff as well as by case number. New cases are available in the index immediately after filing date. A card index is maintained. Open records are located at this court.

Fee & Payment: The fee is $20.00 per item (one party name or case number). Payment may be made by money order, cashier check, personal check. Prepayment is required. Payee: Clerk, US District Court. Certification fee: $7.00 per document. Copy fee: $.50 per page. You are allowed to make your own copies. These copies cost $.50 per page.

Phone Search: Only docket information is available by phone.

Fax Search: There is no charge for information on names only.

Mail Search: Always enclose a stamped self addressed envelope.

In Person: In person searching is available.

PACER: Sign-up number is 800-676-6856. Access fee is $.60 per minute. Local access: 304-347-5681. Case records are available back to 1991. New records are available online after 1 day. PACER is available online at http://pacer.wvsd.uscourts.gov.

Bluefield Division Clerk's Office, PO Box 4128, Bluefield, WV 24701 (Courier Address: 601 Federal St, Bluefield, WV 24701), 304-327-9798.

http://www.wvsd.uscourts.gov

Counties: McDowell, Mercer, Monroe.

Indexing/Storage: Cases are indexed by defendant and plaintiff as well as by case number. New cases are available in the index immediately after filing date. A card index is maintained. Open records are located at this court.

Fee & Payment: The fee is $20.00 per item (one party name or case number). Payment may be made by money order, cashier check, personal check. Prepayment is required. Payee: Clerk, US District Court. Certification fee: $7.00 per document. Copy fee: $.50 per page. You are allowed to make your own copies. These copies cost $.50 per page.

Phone Search: One name may be searched by phone.

Fax Search: Fax requests are accepted.

Mail Search: Always enclose a stamped self addressed envelope.

In Person: In person searching is available.

PACER: Sign-up number is 800-676-6856. Access fee is $.60 per minute. Local access: 304-347-5681. Case records are available back to 1991. New records are available online after 1 day. PACER is available online at http://pacer.wvsd.uscourts.gov.

Charleston Division PO Box 3924, Charleston, WV 25339 (Courier Address: 300 Virginia St E, #24, Charleston, WV 25339), 304-347-3000.

http://www.wvsd.uscourts.gov/

Counties: Boone, Clay, Jackson, Kanawha, Lincoln, Logan, Mingo, Nicholas, Putnam, Roane.

Indexing/Storage: Cases are indexed by defendant and plaintiff as well as by case number. New cases are available in the index immediately after filing date. Both computer and card indexes are maintained. Open records are located at this court. The fee to retrieve a record that has been sent to the Records Center is $25.00.

Fee & Payment: The fee is $20.00 per item (one party name or case number). Payment may be made by money order, cashier check, personal check. Prepayment is required. Payee: Clerk, US District Court. Certification fee: $7.00 per document. Copy fee: $.50 per page. You are allowed to make your own copies. These copies cost $.50 per page.

Phone Search: Only docket information is available by phone.

Fax Search: The court plans to accept fax requests beginning in October 1998. Call for more information.

Mail Search: A stamped self addressed envelope is not required.

In Person: In person searching is available.

PACER: Sign-up number is 800-676-6856. Access fee is $.60 per minute. Local access: 304-347-5681. Case records are available back to 1991. New records are available online after 1 day. PACER is available online at http://pacer.wvsd.uscourts.gov.

Huntington Division Clerk of Court, PO Box 1570, Huntington, WV 25716 (Courier Address: Room 101, 845 5th Ave, Huntington, WV 25701), 304-529-5588, Fax: 304-529-5131.

http://www.wvsd.uscourts.gov

Counties: Cabell, Mason, Wayne.

Indexing/Storage: Cases are indexed by defendant and plaintiff as well as by case number. New cases are available in the index immediately after filing date. Both computer and card indexes are maintained. Open records are located at this court.

Fee & Payment: The fee is $20.00 per item (one party name or case number). Payment may be made by money order, cashier check, personal check. Prepayment is required. Payee: Clerk, US District Court. Certification fee: $7.00 per document. Copy fee: $.50 per page. You are allowed to make your own copies. These copies cost $.50 per page.

Phone Search: Only docket information is available by phone.

Fax Search: Fax requests will be accepted, but for a maximum of 1-2 names.

Mail Search: Always enclose a stamped self addressed envelope.

In Person: In person searching is available.

PACER: Sign-up number is 800-676-6856. Access fee is $.60 per minute. Local access: 304-347-5681. Case records are available back to 1991. New records are available online after 1 day. PACER is available online at http://pacer.wvsd.uscourts.gov.

Parkersburg Division Clerk of Court, PO Box 1526, Parkersburg, WV 26102 (Courier Address: Room 5102, 425 Julianna St, Parkersburg, WV 26101), 304-420-6490, Fax: 304-420-6363.

http://www.wvsd.uscourts.gov

Counties: Wirt, Wood.

Indexing/Storage: Cases are indexed by defendant and plaintiff as well as by case number. New cases are available in the index immediately after filing date. Both computer and card indexes are maintained. Open records are located at this court.

Fee & Payment: The fee is $20.00 per item (one party name or case number). Payment may be made by money order, cashier check, personal check. Prepayment is required. Payee: Clerk, US District Court. Certification fee: $7.00 per document. Copy fee: $.50 per page. You are allowed to make your own copies. These copies cost $.50 per page.

Phone Search: Only docket information is available by phone.

Fax Search: Fax requests are accepted, but for a maximum of 1-2 names only.

Mail Search: Always enclose a stamped self addressed envelope.

In Person: In person searching is available.

PACER: Sign-up number is 800-676-6856. Access fee is $.60 per minute. Local access: 304-347-5681. Case records are available back to 1991. New records are available online after 1 day. PACER is available online at http://pacer.wvsd.uscourts.gov.

US Bankruptcy Court

Southern District of West Virginia

Charleston Division PO Box 3924, Charleston, WV 25339 (Courier Address: 300 Virginia St E, Room 2400, Charleston, WV 25301), 304-347-3000.

http://www.wvsd.uscourts.gov

Counties: Boone, Cabell, Clay, Fayette, Greenbrier, Jackson, Kanawha, Lincoln, Logan, Mason, McDowell, Mercer, Mingo, Monroe, Nicholas, Putnam, Raleigh, Roane, Summers, Wayne, Wirt, Wood, Wyoming.

Indexing/Storage: Cases are indexed by debtor as well as by case number. New cases are available in the index 1-2 days after filing date. Both computer and card indexes are maintained. Card index is maintained to December 1, 1988 after which index is on computer. Open records are located at this court.

Fee & Payment: The fee is $20.00 per item (one party name or case number). Payment may be made by money order, cashier check, personal check, Visa or Mastercard. Prepayment is required. Credit cards accepted only from law firms. Payee: Clerk, US Bankruptcy Court. Certification fee: $7.00 per document. Copy fee: $.50 per page.

Phone Search: Only docket information is available by phone. An automated voice case information service (VCIS) is available.

Mail Search: A stamped self addressed envelope is not required.

In Person: In person searching is available.

PACER: Sign-up number is 800-676-6856. Access fee is $.60 per minute. Local access: 304-347-5678, 304-347-5679. Case records are available back to 1988. Records are purged every 6 months. New civil records are available online after 1 day. PACER is available online at http://pacer.wvsb.uscourts.gov.

West Virginia County Courts

Court	Jurisdiction	No. of Courts	How Organized
Circuit Courts*	General	55	31 Circuits
Magistrate Courts*	Limited	55	55 Counties
Municipal Courts	Municipal	122	

* Profiled in this Sourcebook.

Court	CIVIL								
	Tort	Contract	Real Estate	Min. Claim	Max. Claim	Small Claims	Estate	Eviction	Domestic Relations
Circuit Courts*	X	X	X	$300	No Max		X		X
Magistrate Courts*	X	X		$0	$5000	$3000		X	X
Municipal Courts									

Court	CRIMINAL				
	Felony	Misdemeanor	DWI/DUI	Preliminary Hearing	Juvenile
Circuit Courts*	X				X
Magistrate Courts*		X	X	X	
Municipal Courts			X		

ADMINISTRATION
Administrative Office, Supreme Court of Appeals, 1900 Kanawha Blvd, 1 E 100 State Capitol, Charleston, WV, 25305; 304-558-0145, Fax: 304-558-1212.

www.state.wv.us/wvsca

COURT STRUCTURE
The 55 Circuit Courts are the courts of general jurisdiction. Effective October 1999, a family court division was created within the circuit court of each county. Probate is handled by the Circuit Court. Records are held at the County Commissioner's Office.

ONLINE ACCESS
The Court system continues to develop toward a statewide system that will allow access to public records. Magistrate Courts will be on a common server/Winterm system by 2002. Several courts's public records are online via private providers. Contact Kit Thorton, Counsel for Law and Technology at 304-588-0145.

ADDITIONAL INFORMATION
There is a statewide requirement that search turnaround times not exceed five business days. However, most courts do far better than that limit. Release of public information is governed by WV Code Sec.29B-1-1 et seq.

📖 📖 📖 📖 📖 📖 📖

Barbour County

Circuit Court 8 N Main St, Philippi, WV 26416; 304-457-3454; Fax: 304-457-2790. Hours: 8:30AM-4:30PM *Felony, Civil Actions Over $5,000, Probate.*

Note: Probate is handled by the County Clerk at this address.

Civil Records: Access: Phone, mail, in person. Both court and visitors may perform in person searches. No search fee. Required to search: name, years to search. Civil cases indexed by defendant, plaintiff. Civil records on microfiche from 1843 to 1980s on index cards back to 1862, on dockets back to 1843.

Criminal Records: Access: Phone, mail, in person. Both court and visitors may perform in person searches. No search fee. Required to search: name, years to search. Criminal records on microfiche from 1843 to 1980s on index cards back to 1862, on dockets back to 1843.

General Information: Public Access terminal is available. No sealed, juvenile, adoptions, mental health, expunged records released. SASE requested. Turnaround time 1 day. Fax notes: No fee to fax results if one or two pages only. Copy fee: $.50 per page. Certification fee: $1.00. Fee payee: Barbour County Circuit Clerk. Personal checks accepted. Prepayment is required.

Magistrate Court PO Box 541, Philippi, WV 26416; 304-457-3676; Fax: 304-457-4999. Hours: 8:30AM-4:30PM (EST). *Misdemeanor, Civil Actions Under $5,000, Eviction, Small Claims.*

Civil Records: Access: In person, mail. Both court and visitors may perform in person searches. No search fee. Phone access limited to one name searched from 8/93 on only.

Criminal Records: Access: In person, mail. Visitors must perform in person searches for themselves. No search fee. Required to search: name, years to search.

General Information: Turnaround time varies.

Berkeley County

Circuit Court 110 W King St, Martinsburg, WV 25401-3210; 304-264-1918; Probate phone: 304-264-1940. Hours: 9AM-5PM (EST). *Felony, Civil Actions Over $5,000, Probate.*

Note: Probate is handled by Fiduciary Records Clerk, 100 W King St, Room 2, Martinsburg, WV 25401.

Civil Records: Access: Fax, mail, in person. Both court and visitors may perform in person searches. No search fee. Required to search: name, years to search. Civil cases indexed by defendant, plaintiff. Civil records on computer from January 1990, on index books from 1800s.

Criminal Records: Access: In person only. Visitors must perform in person searches for themselves. No search fee. Required to search: name, years to search; also helpful: DOB, SSN. Criminal records on computer from January 1990, on index books from 1800s.

General Information: Public Access terminal is available. No sealed, juvenile, adoptions, mental health, guardianship records released. SASE not required. Turnaround time 1 week. Fax notes: $2.00 per page. Copy fee: $.50 per page. Certification fee: No certification fee. Fee payee: Clerk of Circuit Court. Business checks accepted.

Magistrate Court 120 W John St, Martinsburg, WV 25401; 304-264-1956; Fax: 304-263-9154. Hours: 9AM-4PM (EST). *Misdemeanor, Civil Actions Under $5,000, Eviction, Small Claims.*

Civil Records: Access: Fax, mail, in person. Both court and visitors may perform in person searches. No search fee.

Criminal Records: Access: In person only. Both court and visitors may perform in person searches. No search fee. Required to search: name, years to search; also helpful: address, DOB, SSN.

General Information: Public Access terminal is available.

Boone County

Circuit Court 200 State St, Madison, WV 25130; 304-369-3925; Probate phone: 304-369-7337; Fax: 304-369-7326. Hours: 8AM-4PM (EST). *Felony, Civil Actions Over $5,000, Probate.*

Note: Probate is handled by County Clerk, 200 State St, Madison, WV 25130.

Civil Records: Access: Phone, fax, mail, in person. Both court and visitors may perform in person searches. No search fee. Required to search: name, years to search. Civil cases indexed by defendant, plaintiff. Civil records on computer from 1984 to present, on index books 1956 to present, on dockets back to 1900.

Criminal Records: Access: Phone, fax, mail, in person. Both court and visitors may perform in person searches. No search fee. Required to search: name, years to search, signed release. Criminal records on computer from 1984 to present, on index books 1956 to present, on dockets back to 1864.

General Information: No sealed, juvenile, adoptions, mental health, expunged records released. SASE requested. Turnaround time 1 day. Fax notes: Fee to fax results is $3.00 per document. Copy fee: $.50 per page. Certification fee: No certification fee. Fee payee: Circuit Clerk. Business checks accepted. Prepayment required.

Magistrate Court 200 State St., Madison, WV 25130; 304-369-7364; Fax: 304-369-1932. Hours: 8AM-4PM (EST). *Misdemeanor, Civil Actions Under $5,000, Eviction, Small Claims.*

Civil Records: Access: In person, mail. Both court and visitors may perform in person searches. No search fee.

Criminal Records: Access: In person, mail. Visitors must perform in person searches for themselves. No search fee. Required to search: name, years to search; also helpful: DOB, SSN.

General Information: Turnaround time 2-3 weeks.

Braxton County

Circuit Court 300 Main St, Sutton, WV 26601; 304-765-2837; Fax: 304-765-2947. Hours: 8AM-4PM (EST). *Felony, Civil Actions Over $5,000, Probate.*

Civil Records: Access: Phone, fax, mail, in person. Both court and visitors may perform in person searches. No search fee. Required to search: name, years to search. Civil cases indexed by defendant, plaintiff. Civil records on microfiche 1806-1910; on dockets back to 1810.

Criminal Records: Access: Phone, fax, mail, in person. Both court and visitors may perform in person searches. No search fee. Required to search: name, years to search, signed release. Criminal records on microfiche 1806 to 1910, on dockets back to 1810.

General Information: No adoption, juvenile, mental hygiene records released. SASE required. Turnaround time 2-3 days. Fax notes: $3.00 for first page, $1.00 each add'l. Copy fee: $.50 per page. Certification fee: No certification fee. Fee payee: JW Morris, Clerk. Personal checks accepted. Prepayment is required.

Magistrate Court 307 Main St, Sutton, WV 26601; 304-765-5678; Fax: 304-765-3756. Hours: 8:30AM-4:30PM (EST). *Misdemeanor, Civil Actions Under $5,000, Eviction, Small Claims.*

Civil Records: Access: Mail, fax, in person. Both court and visitors may perform in person searches. Search fee: $.50 per page found. Records go back to 1977; on computer back to 1998.

Criminal Records: Access: Mail, fax, in person. Both court and visitors may perform in person searches. Search fee: $.50 per page found. Required to search: name, years to search, DOB; also helpful: address, SSN, signed release. Records go back to 1977; on computer back to 1998.

General Information: Turnaround time 1-2 weeks. Fax notes: Fee to fax results is $2.00 per page. Copy fee: $.50 per page. Fee payee: Braxton County Magistrate Court. Prepayment is required.

Brooke County

Circuit Court Brooke County Courthouse, Wellsburg, WV 26070; 304-737-3662; Probate phone: 304-737-3661. Hours: 9AM-5PM (EST). *Felony, Civil Actions Over $5,000, Probate.*

Note: Probate is handled by County Clerk, 632 Main St, Courthouse, Wellsburg, WV 26070.

Civil Records: Access: Mail, in person. Both court and visitors may perform in person searches. No search fee. Required to search: name; also helpful: years to search. Civil cases indexed by defendant, plaintiff. Civil records on dockets and files from prior to 1960 to present, in boxes back to 1800s.

Criminal Records: Access: Mail, in person. Both court and visitors may perform in person searches. No search fee. Required to search: name; also helpful: years to search, DOB, SSN. Criminal records on dockets and files from prior to 1960 to present, in boxes back to 1800s.

General Information: No divorce, juvenile, mental hygiene, adoption records released. Turnaround time same day, unless in archives. Copy fee: $.50 per page. Certification fee: $.50 per page. Fee payee: Brooke County Circuit Clerk. Personal checks accepted. Prepayment is required.

Magistrate Court 632 Main St, Wellsburg, WV 26070; 304-737-1321; Fax: 304-737-1509. Hours: 9AM-4PM (EST). *Misdemeanor, Civil Actions Under $5,000, Eviction, Small Claims.*

Civil Records: Access: In person only. Visitors must perform in person searches for themselves. No search fee. Civil records go back to 1977; computerized back to 1996.

Criminal Records: Access: In person only. Visitors must perform in person searches for themselves. No search fee. Required to search: name; also helpful: DOB, SSN, signed release. Criminal records go back to 1977; computerized back to 1996.

Cabell County

Circuit Court PO Box 0545, Huntington, WV 25710-0545; 304-526-8622; Fax: 304-526-8699. Hours: 8:30AM-4:30PM (EST). *Felony, Civil Actions Over $5,000, Probate.*

Civil Records: Access: Mail, in person. Both court and visitors may perform in person searches. No search fee. Required to search: name, years to search. Civil cases indexed by defendant, plaintiff. Civil records on computer from 1990 to present. On index books back to 1854.

Criminal Records: Access: In person only. Visitors must perform in person searches for themselves. No search fee. Required to search: name, years to search; also helpful: address, DOB, SSN. Criminal records on computer from 1990 to present. On index books back to 1854. Requests are directed to the state Criminal Investigation Bureau.

General Information: Public Access terminal is available. No sealed, juvenile, adoptions, mental health, guardianship records released. SASE required. Turnaround time 1 day. Copy fee: $.50 per page. Certification fee: No certification fee. Fee payee: Clerk of Circuit Court. Business checks accepted. Prepayment is required.

Magistrate Court 750 5th Ave, Basement, Rm B 113 Courthouse, Huntington, WV 25701; 304-526-8642; Fax: 304-526-8646. Hours: 8:30AM-4:30PM (EST). *Misdemeanor, Civil Actions Under $5,000, Eviction, Small Claims.*

Civil Records: Access: In person only. Visitors must perform in person searches for themselves. No search fee. Records go back to 1996 (1987-95 in storage); on computer back to 1991.

Criminal Records: Access: In person only. Visitors must perform in person searches for themselves. No search fee. Required to search: name. Records go back to 1996 (1987-95 in storage); on computer to 1991.

General Information: Public Access terminal is available. Fax notes: Fee to fax results is $2.00 per page. Copy fee: $.25 per page. Certification fee: $.50 per page. Fee payee: Magistrate Court Clerk. Prepayment is required.

Calhoun County

Circuit Court PO Box 266, Grantsville, WV 26147; 304-354-6910; Fax: 304-354-6910. Hours: 8:30AM-4PM (EST). *Felony, Civil Actions Over $5,000, Probate.*

Civil Records: Access: Phone, fax, mail, in person. Both court and visitors may perform in person searches. No search fee. Required to search: name, years to search. Civil cases indexed by defendant, plaintiff. Civil records on index books from 1800s.

Criminal Records: Access: Phone, fax, mail, in person. Both court and visitors may perform in person searches. No search fee. Required to search: name, years to search; also helpful: DOB, SSN. Criminal records on dockets from 1900s.

General Information: No adoption, juvenile, divorce, domestic relations, guardianship/conservatorship records released. Turnaround time same day received. Fax notes: $3.00 for first page, $.50 each add'l. Copy fee: $.50 per page. Certification fee: $1.00. Fee payee: Circuit Clerk. Personal checks accepted.

Magistrate Court PO Box 186, Grantsville, WV 26147; 304-354-6698; Fax: 304-354-6698. Hours: 8:30AM-4PM (EST). *Misdemeanor, Civil Actions Under $5,000, Eviction, Small Claims.*

Civil Records: Access: In person, mail. Both court and visitors may perform in person searches. No search fee.

Criminal Records: Access: In person, mail. Both court and visitors may perform in person searches. No search fee. Required to search: name; also helpful: years to search, DOB, SSN.

General Information: Turnaround time 1 week.

Clay County

Circuit Court PO Box 129, Clay, WV 25043; 304-587-4256; Fax: 304-587-4346. Hours: 8AM-4PM (EST). *Felony, Civil Actions Over $5,000, Probate.*

Civil Records: Access: In person only. Visitors must perform in person searches for themselves. No search fee. Required to search: name, years to search, address.

Civil cases indexed by defendant, plaintiff. Civil records on docket books and index books back to 1962, microfilm back to 1858; computerized back to 1998.

Criminal Records: Access: Phone, fax, mail, in person. Only the court performs in person searches; visitors may not. Court will do name only searches if time allows. No search fee. Required to search: name, years to search, address, DOB, SSN. Criminal records on docket books and index books back to 1962, microfilm back to 1858; computerized back to 1998.

General Information: Public Access terminal is available. No juvenile, guardianship, conservatorship or mental health records released. SASE required. Turnaround time 3 days. Fax notes: Fee to fax results is $.50 per page. Copy fee: $.50 per page. Certification fee: No certification fee. Fee payee: Clerk of the Circuit Court. Personal checks accepted. Prepayment required.

Magistrate Court PO Box 393, Clay, WV 25043; 304-587-2131; Fax: 304-587-2727. Hours: 8:30AM-4:30PM (EST). *Misdemeanor, Civil Actions Under $5,000, Eviction, Small Claims.*

Civil Records: Access: In person, mail. Both court and visitors may perform in person searches. No search fee.

Criminal Records: Access: In person, mail. Both court and visitors may perform in person searches. No search fee. Required to search: name, offense; also helpful: years to search, DOB, SSN.

General Information: Turnaround time 5 days.

Doddridge County

Circuit Court 118 E. Court St, West Union, WV 26456; 304-873-2331. Hours: 8:30AM-4PM (EST). *Felony, Civil Actions Over $5,000, Probate.*

Civil Records: Access: Phone, mail, in person. Both court and visitors may perform in person searches. No search fee. Required to search: name, years to search. Civil cases indexed by defendant, plaintiff. Civil records on index books 1960 to present, archived from 1845 to 1960; computerized records go back to 1999.

Criminal Records: Access: Phone, mail, fax, in person. Both court and visitors may perform in person searches. No search fee. Required to search: name, years to search. Criminal records in index books and files from 1948; computerized records go back to 1999.

General Information: No juvenile, adoption, mental, domestic records released. SASE required. Turnaround time 1-5 days. Copy fee: $.50 per page. Certification fee: No certification fee. Fee payee: Clerk of Circuit Court. Personal checks accepted. Prepayment required.

Magistrate Court PO Box 207, West Union, WV 26456; 304-873-2694; Fax: 304-873-2643. Hours: 8AM-4PM (EST). *Misdemeanor, Civil Actions Under $5,000, Eviction, Small Claims.*

Civil Records: Access: In person, mail. Both court and visitors may perform in person searches. No search fee.

Criminal Records: Access: In person, mail. Both court and visitors may perform in person searches. No search fee. Required to search: name, years to search; also helpful: offense.

General Information: Turnaround time 5 days.

Fayette County

Circuit Court 100 Court St, Fayetteville, WV 25840; Civil phone: 304-574-4249; Criminal phone: 304-574-4303/4250; Probate phone: 304-574-4226. Hours: 8AM-4PM (EST). *Felony, Civil Actions Over $5,000, Probate.*

Note: Probate is handled by County Clerk, PO Box 569, Fayetteville, WV 25840.

Civil Records: Access: Phone, mail, in person. Both court and visitors may perform in person searches. No search fee. Required to search: name; also helpful: years to search. Civil cases indexed by defendant, plaintiff.

Civil records on computer since 1995; prior records on file 1850 to present.

Criminal Records: Access: Mail, in person. Both court and visitors may perform in person searches. No search fee. Required to search: name, years to search; also helpful: DOB, SSN. Criminal records on computer since 1995; prior records on file 1850 to present.

General Information: No divorce, adoption, mental, juvenile records released. SASE not required. Turnaround time 1 week. Copy fee: $.50 per page. Certification fee: $2.00. Fee payee: Circuit Clerk of Fayette County. Personal checks accepted. Prepayment is required.

Magistrate Court 100 Church St, Fayetteville, WV 25840; 304-574-4279; Fax: 304-574-2458. Hours: 8AM-9PM M-F, 8AM-Noon Sat (EST). *Misdemeanor, Civil Actions Under $5,000, Eviction, Small Claims.*

Civil Records: Access: In person only. Visitors must perform in person searches for themselves. No search fee. Civil records on computer back to 1997.

Criminal Records: Access: In person only. Visitors must perform in person searches for themselves. No search fee. Required to search: name, years to search. Criminal records on computer back to 1997.

General Information Public access terminal available.

Gilmer County

Circuit Court Gilmer County Courthouse, Glenville, WV 26351; 304-462-7241; Fax: 304-462-5134. Hours: 8AM-4PM (EST). *Felony, Civil Actions Over $5,000, Probate.*

Civil Records: Access: Phone, mail, fax, in person. Both court and visitors may perform in person searches. No search fee. Required to search: name, years to search. Civil cases indexed by defendant, plaintiff. Civil records on dockets and files from 1845 to present; computerized back to 1999.

Criminal Records: Access: Phone, mail, fax, in person. Both court and visitors may perform in person searches. No search fee. Required to search: name, years to search. Criminal records on dockets and files from 1845 to present; computerized back to 1999.

General Information: No juvenile, mental, confidential records released. SASE not required. Turnaround time 1 day. Fax notes: Fee to fax results is $1.50 per page with a $3.00 minimum. Copy fee: $.50 per page. Certification fee: No certification fee. Fee payee: Circuit Clerk. Personal checks accepted.

Magistrate Court Courthouse Annex, Glenville, WV 26351; 304-462-7812; Fax: 304-462-8582. Hours: 8:30AM-4PM (EST). *Misdemeanor, Civil Actions Under $5,000, Eviction, Small Claims.*

Civil Records: Access: In person, mail. Both court and visitors may perform in person searches. No search fee.

Criminal Records: Access: In person, mail. Both court and visitors may perform in person searches. No search fee. Required to search: name, years to search; also helpful: DOB, SSN.

General Information: Records on computer back to 2000. Public access terminal available. Mail turnaround time 1-5 days. Will fax results, $2.00 per document.

Grant County

Circuit Court 5 Highland Ave, Petersburg, WV 26847; 304-257-4545; Fax: 304-257-2593 (Attn: Circuit Court). Hours: 8:30AM-4:30PM (EST). *Felony, Civil Actions Over $5,000, Probate.*

Civil Records: Access: Fax, mail, in person. Both court and visitors may perform in person searches. No search fee. Required to search: name, years to search; also helpful: address. Civil cases indexed by defendant, plaintiff. Civil records on index cards (current cases only), on index books back to 1866.

Criminal Records: Access: Fax, mail, in person. Both court and visitors may perform in person searches. No search fee. Required to search: name, years to search, DOB, SSN; also helpful: address. Criminal records on index cards (current cases only), on index books back to 1866.

General Information: No juvenile, guardianship, adoptions, mental, domestic order records released. SASE required. Turnaround time 1-2 days. Fax notes: Fee to fax results is $1.50 for first page, $.75 each page thereafter. Copy fee: $.50 per page. Certification fee: $1.50. Fee payee: Circuit Clerk. Business checks accepted. In-state personal checks accepted. Prepayment is required.

Magistrate Court 5 Highland Ave (PO Box 216), Petersburg, WV 26847; 304-257-4637/1289; Fax: 304-257-9501. Hours: 8:30AM-4:30PM (EST). *Misdemeanor, Civil Actions Under $5,000, Eviction, Small Claims.*

Civil Records: Access: Fax, mail, in person. Only the court performs in person searches; visitors may not. Search fee: No search fee. Records on computer back to 1994.

Criminal Records: Access: Fax, mail, in person. Only the court performs in person searches; visitors may not. No search fee. Required to search: name, years to search. Records on computer back to 1994; prior back to 1977.

General Information: Turnaround time 1-2 days. Certification fee: $.50 per page. Fee payee: Grant County Magistrate Court. Prepayment is required.

Greenbrier County

Circuit Court PO Drawer 751, Lewisburg, WV 24901; 304-647-6626; Fax: 304-647-6666. Hours: 8:30AM-4:30PM (EST). *Felony, Civil Actions Over $5,000, Probate.*

Civil Records: Access: Mail, in person. Both court and visitors may perform in person searches. Search fee: $5.00 per name. Required to search: name, years to search. Civil cases indexed by defendant, plaintiff. Civil records indexed by general and docket books from 1800s; computerized back to 1994.

Criminal Records: Access: Mail, in person. Both court and visitors may perform in person searches. Search fee: $5.00 per name. Required to search: name, years to search; also helpful: DOB, SSN, signed release. Criminal records indexed by general and docket books from 1800s; computerized back to 1994. No information given over the telephone on criminal matters except to authorized personnel.

General Information: No juvenile, adoptions, mental health records released. Turnaround time 1-2 days. Fax notes: Fee to fax results is $2.50 per page. Copy fee: $.50 per page. Certification fee: $1.00. Fee payee: Clerk of Circuit Court. Personal checks accepted.

Magistrate Court 200 North Court St, Lewisburg, WV 24901; 304-647-6632; Fax: 304-647-3612. Hours: 8:30AM-4:30PM (EST). *Misdemeanor, Civil Actions Under $5,000, Eviction, Small Claims.*

Civil Records: Access: Phone, mail, in person. Both court and visitors may perform in person searches. No search fee. Civil records on computer back to 1989; other records back to 1987.

Criminal Records: Access: Mail, in person. Both court and visitors may perform in person searches. No search fee. Required to search: name, years to search; also helpful: DOB, SSN. Civil records on computer back to 1989; other records back to 1987.

General Information: Turnaround time 1-2 days. Fax notes: Fee to fax results is $2.00 per page. Certification fee: $.75 plus $.25 per page. Fee payee: Greenbrier County Magistrate Court. Prepayment is required.

Hampshire County

Circuit Court PO Box 343, Romney, WV 26757; 304-822-5022; Probate phone: 304-822-5112. Hours: 9AM-4PM M-F 5PM-8PM Friday evening (EST). *Felony, Civil Actions Over $5,000, Probate.*

Note: Probate handled by County Clerk, PO Box 806, Romney, WV 26757.

Civil Records: Access: Fax, mail, in person. Both court and visitors may perform in person searches. No search fee. Required to search: name, years to search. Civil cases indexed by defendant, plaintiff. Civil records on index files from 1957 to present, on index cards in storage 1885 to 1957.

Criminal Records: Access: Fax, mail, in person. Both court and visitors may perform in person searches. Search fee: $10.00 per name. Required to search: name, years to search. Criminal records on index files from 1957 to present, on index cards in storage 1885 to 1957.

General Information: No juvenile, divorce or adoption records released. SASE required. Turnaround time 2 days. Copy fee: $.50 per page. Certification fee: $1.50. Fee payee: Clerk of Circuit Court. Personal checks accepted. Will bill to attorneys.

Magistrate Court 239 W Birch Ln, PO Box 881, Romney, WV 26757; 304-822-4311; Fax: 304-822-3981. Hours: 8:30AM-4PM (EST). *Misdemeanor, Civil Actions Under $5,000, Eviction, Small Claims.*

Civil Records: Access: Mail, fax, in person. Both court and visitors may perform in person searches. No search fee. Civil records go back to 1977; on computer back to 1993.

Criminal Records: Access: Mail, fax, in person. Both court and visitors may perform in person searches. No search fee. Required to search: name, years to search; also helpful: DOB, SSN. Criminal records go back to 1977; on computer back to 1993.

General Information: Public Access terminal is available. Turnaround time 5 days. Fax notes: Will fax back to toll-free numbers no charge. Certification fee: $.50 per page. Fee payee: Magistrate Court Clerk. Prepayment is required.

Hancock County

Circuit Court PO Box 428, New Cumberland, WV 26047; 304-564-3311; Fax: 304-564-5014. Hours: 8:30AM-4:30PM (EST). *Felony, Civil Actions Over $5,000, Probate.*

Note: Probate can be reached at PO Box 367.

Civil Records: Access: Fax, mail, in person, online. Both court and visitors may perform in person searches. Search fee: $5.00 per name. Required to search: name, years to search; also helpful: address. Civil cases indexed by defendant, plaintiff. Civil records on computer since 1972. Limited online access to court records is available via a pay service, see www.swcg-inc.com/courts.htm or call 800-795-8543. $125 set-up fee plus a $38.00 or $120 monthly fee plan.

Criminal Records: Access: Fax, mail, in person, online. Both court and visitors may perform in person searches. Search fee: $5.00 per name. Required to search: name, years to search, signed release; also helpful: address, DOB, SSN. Criminal records on computer since 1972. Online access to criminal records is the same as civil.

General Information: Public Access terminal is available. No adoption, juvenile, mental hygiene released. SASE required. Turnaround time same day. Fax notes: Fee to fax results is $2.00 per page. Copy fee: $.50 per page. Certification fee: $1.50. Fee payee: Clerk of Circuit Court. Personal checks accepted.

Magistrate Court 106 Court St, New Cumberland, WV 26047; 304-564-3355; Fax: 304-564-3852. Hours: 8:30-4:30PM M-W, F; 8AM-9PM Th (EST). *Misdemeanor, Civil Actions Under $5,000, Eviction, Small Claims.*

Civil Records: Access: In person, mail. Both court and visitors may perform in person searches. No search fee. Phone, fax and mail access limited.

Criminal Records: Access: In person, mail. Both court and visitors may perform in person searches. No search fee. Required to search: name, years to search; also helpful: DOB, SSN. Phone, fax and mail access limited.

General Information: Turnaround time 1-2 days.

Hardy County

Circuit Court 204 Washington St, RM 237, Moorefield, WV 26836; 304-538-7869; Fax: 304-538-6197. Hours: 9AM-4PM (EST). *Felony, Civil Actions Over $5,000, Probate.*

Civil Records: Access: In person only. Both court and visitors may perform in person searches. No search fee. Required to search: name, years to search. Civil cases indexed by defendant, plaintiff. Civil records on docket books back to 1960 (chrono index in front of book).

Criminal Records: Access: Phone, in person. Both court and visitors may perform in person searches. No search fee. Required to search: name, years to search, DOB; also helpful: SSN. Criminal records on docket books back to 1960 (chrono index in front of book).

General Information: No juvenile, mental, domestic records released. Copy fee: $.50 per page. Certification fee: $1.00. Fee payee: Clerk of Circuit Court. Personal checks accepted. Prepayment is required.

Magistrate Court 204 Washington St, Moorefield, WV 26836; 304-538-6836; Fax: 304-538-2072. Hours: 9AM-4PM (EST). *Misdemeanor, Civil Actions Under $5,000, Eviction, Small Claims.*

Civil Records: Access: Fax, mail, in person. Both court and visitors may perform in person searches. No search fee. Civil records on computer back to 1990; others back to 1977.

Criminal Records: Access: Fax, mail, in person. Both court and visitors may perform in person searches. No search fee. Required to search: name, years to search; also helpful: DOB, SSN. Criminal records on computer back to 1990; others back to 1977.

General Information: Public Access terminal is available. SASE required. Turnaround time 10 days, 2 days if on computer. Fax notes: Fee to fax results is $2.00 per page. Certification fee: $.50 per page. Fee payee: Hardy County Magistrate Court. Prepayment is required.

Harrison County

Circuit Court 301 W. Main, Suite 301, Clarksburg, WV 26301-2967; 304-624-8640; Probate phone: 304-624-8673; Fax: 304-624-8710. Hours: 8:30AM-4PM (EST). *Felony, Civil Actions Over $5,000, Probate.*

Note: Probate is handled by County Clerk, 301 W Main St, Courthouse, Clarksburg, WV 26301.

Civil Records: Access: In person only. Visitors must perform in person searches for themselves. No search fee. Required to search: name, years to search. Civil cases indexed by defendant, plaintiff. Civil records on computer from 1990 to present. On index books back to mid-1800s.

Criminal Records: Access: In person only. Visitors must perform in person searches for themselves. No search fee. Required to search: name, years to search; also helpful: DOB, SSN. Criminal records on computer from 1990 to present. On index books back to mid-1800s.

General Information: Public Access terminal is available. No adoption, juvenile, guardianship, mental health records released. Copy fee: $.50 per page.

Certification fee: No certification fee. Fee payee: Harrison County Circuit Clerk. Only cashiers checks and money orders accepted. Prepayment is required.

Magistrate Court 306 Washington Ave Rm 222, Clarksburg, WV 26301; 304-624-8645; Fax: 304-624-8740. Hours: 8AM-4PM (EST). *Misdemeanor, Civil Actions Under $5,000, Eviction, Small Claims.*

Civil Records: Access: In person, mail. Both court and visitors may perform in person searches. No search fee.

Criminal Records: Access: In person, mail. Both court and visitors may perform in person searches. No search fee. Required to search: name, years to search; also helpful: DOB, SSN.

General Information: Turnaround time 5 days.

Jackson County

Circuit Court PO Box 427, Ripley, WV 25271; 304-372-2011 X329; Fax: 304-372-6205. Hours: 9AM-4PM M-F, 9AM-Noon Sat (EST). *Felony, Civil Actions Over $5,000, Probate.*

Civil Records: Access: Phone, mail, in person. Both court and visitors may perform in person searches. No search fee. Required to search: name, years to search. Civil cases indexed by defendant, plaintiff. Civil records on index books back to 1800s.

Criminal Records: Access: Phone, mail, in person. Both court and visitors may perform in person searches. No search fee. Required to search: name, years to search; also helpful: DOB, SSN. Criminal records on index books back to 1800s.

General Information: No juvenile, mental, adoption, domestic records released. SASE required. Turnaround time 1-2 days. Copy fee: $.50 per page. Certification fee: $.50 per page. Fee payee: Clerk of Circuit Court. Only cashiers checks and money orders accepted. Prepayment is required.

Magistrate Court PO Box 368, Ripley, WV 25271; 304-372-2011; Fax: 304-372-7132. Hours: 9AM-4PM (EST). *Misdemeanor, Civil Actions Under $5,000, Eviction, Small Claims.*

Civil Records: Access: In person only. Visitors must perform in person searches for themselves. No search fee.

Criminal Records: Access: In person only. Visitors must perform in person searches for themselves. No search fee. Required to search: name, years to search; also helpful: DOB, SSN.

Jefferson County

Circuit Court PO Box 584, Charles Town, WV 25414; 304-728-3231; Fax: 304-728-3398. Hours: 9AM-5PM (EST). *Felony, Civil Actions Over $5,000.*

Civil Records: Access: In person only. Visitors must perform in person searches for themselves. No search fee. Required to search: name, years to search. Civil cases indexed by defendant, plaintiff. Civil records on computer back to 01/85; on index books 1960 to 1985. On dockets back 1960 back to 1800s in storage.

Criminal Records: Access: In person only. Visitors must perform in person searches for themselves. No search fee. Required to search: name, years to search. Criminal records on computer back to 01/85; on index books 1960 to 1985. On dockets back 1960 back to 1800s in storage.

General Information: Public Access terminal is available. No juvenile, mental health records released. Fax notes: Fee to fax results is $2.00 per page. Copy fee: $.50 per page. Certification fee: $3.00. Fee payee: Circuit Clerk. Personal checks accepted. Prepayment is required.

Magistrate Court PO Box 607, Charles Town, WV 25414; 304-728-3233; Fax: 304-728-3235. Hours: 7:30AM-4:30PM (EST). *Misdemeanor, Civil Actions Under $5,000, Eviction, Small Claims.*

Civil Records: Access: Mail, fax, in person. Both court and visitors may perform in person searches. No search fee. Civil records on computer back to 1996; others go back to 1977.

Criminal Records: Access: Mail, fax, in person. Both court and visitors may perform in person searches. No search fee. Required to search: name, years to search, DOB; also helpful: SSN, signed release. Criminal records on computer back to 1996; others go back to 1977.

General Information: Turnaround time 5 days. Fax notes: No fee to fax results. Certification fee: $.50 per page. Fee payee: Magistrate Clerk. Prepayment is required.

Kanawha County

Circuit Court PO Box 2351, Charleston, WV 25328; 304-357-0440; Probate phone: 304-357-0130; Fax: 304-357-0473. Hours: 8AM-5PM (EST). *Felony, Civil Actions Over $5,000, Probate.*

Note: Probate is handled by County Clerk, 409 Virginia St East, Charleston, WV 25301.

Civil Records: Access: In person, online. Visitors must perform in person searches for themselves. No search fee. Required to search: name, years to search; also helpful: address. Civil cases indexed by defendant, plaintiff. Civil records on computer from 7/1989 to present. On microfiche back to 1800s. Limited online access to court records is available via a pay service, see www.swcg-inc.com/courts.htm or call 800-795-8543. $125 set-up fee plus a $38.00 or $120 monthly fee plan.

Criminal Records: Access: In person, online. Visitors must perform in person searches for themselves. No search fee. Required to search: name, years to search; also helpful: address, DOB, SSN. Criminal records on computer from 7/1989 to present. On microfiche back to 1800s. Online access to criminal records is the same as civil.

General Information: Public Access terminal is available. No juvenile, neglect, adoption, domestic, guardianship, mental health or conservatorship records released. Copy fee: $.50 per page. Certification fee: No certification fee. Fee payee: Kanawha Circuit Clerk. Business checks accepted. Prepayment is required.

Magistrate Court 111 Court St, Charleston, WV 25333; 304-357-0400; Fax: 304-357-0205. Hours: 8:30AM-4:30PM (EST). *Misdemeanor, Civil Actions Under $5,000, Eviction, Small Claims.*

Civil Records: Access: In person, mail. Both court and visitors may perform in person searches. No search fee.

Criminal Records: Access: In person, mail. Both court and visitors may perform in person searches. No search fee. Required to search: name, years to search; also helpful: DOB, SSN.

General Information: Turnaround time 14 days.

Lewis County

Circuit Court PO Box 69, Weston, WV 26452; 304-269-8210; Fax: 304-269-8249. Hours: 8:30AM-4:30PM (EST). *Felony, Civil Actions Over $5,000, Probate.*

Civil Records: Access: Phone, fax, mail, in person. Only the court performs in person searches; visitors may not. No search fee. Required to search: name, years to search. Civil cases indexed by defendant, plaintiff. Civil records on index books 1977 to 1992; on computer back to 1984. No index for chancery books back to 1800s.

Criminal Records: Access: Phone, fax, mail, in person. Only the court performs in person searches; visitors may not. No search fee. Required to search:

name, years to search; also helpful: SSN. Criminal records on index books 1977 to 1992; on computer back to 1984. No index for chancery books back to 1800s.

General Information: No adoption, juvenile, domestic records released. SASE not required. Turnaround time 2 days. Fax notes: Fee to fax results is $2.00 per page. Copy fee: $.50 per page. Certification fee: $.50 per page. Fee payee: Clerk of Circuit Court. Business checks accepted.

Magistrate Court 111 Court St, PO Box 260, Weston, WV 26452; 304-269-8230; Fax: 304-269-8253. Hours: 8:30AM-Noon, 1-4:30PM (EST). *Misdemeanor, Civil Actions Under $5,000, Eviction, Small Claims.*

Civil Records: Access: In person, mail. Both court and visitors may perform in person searches. No search fee.

Criminal Records: Access: In person, mail. Both court and visitors may perform in person searches. No search fee. Required to search: name, years to search; also helpful: DOB, SSN.

General Information: Turnaround time 5 days.

Lincoln County

Circuit Court PO Box 338, Hamlin, WV 25523; 304-824-7887; Fax: 304-824-7909. Hours: 9AM-4:30PM (EST). *Felony, Civil Actions Over $5,000, Probate.*

Civil Records: Access: Phone, mail, in person. Both court and visitors may perform in person searches. No search fee. Required to search: name, years to search. Civil cases indexed by defendant, plaintiff. Civil records computerized since 1991, on index books 1971 to present, on docket books back to 1909.

Criminal Records: Access: Phone, mail, in person. Both court and visitors may perform in person searches. No search fee. Required to search: name, years to search, DOB, SSN; also helpful: address. Criminal records computerized since 1991, on index books 1971 to present, on docket books back to 1909.

General Information: Public Access terminal is available. No juvenile, adoption, divorce or mental hygiene records released. SASE not required. Turnaround time immediate to next day. Copy fee: $.50 per page. Certification fee: No certification fee. Fee payee: Clerk of Circuit Court. Personal checks accepted. Prepayment is required.

Magistrate Court PO Box 573, Hamlin, WV 25523; 304-824-5001 x235; Fax: 304-824-5280. Hours: 9AM-4PM (EST). *Misdemeanor, Civil Actions Under $5,000, Eviction, Small Claims.*

Note: Searches performed by court only on second and fourth Thursday of each month.

Civil Records: Access: In person, mail. Only the court performs in person searches; visitors may not. No search fee.

Criminal Records: Access: In person, mail. Only the court performs in person searches; visitors may not. No search fee. Required to search: name, years to search; also helpful: DOB, SSN.

General Information: Turnaround time 1-14 days.

Logan County

Circuit Court Logan County Courthouse, Rm 311, Logan, WV 25601; 304-792-8550; Fax: 304-792-8555. Hours: 8:30AM-4:30PM (EST). *Felony, Civil Actions Over $5,000, Probate.*

Civil Records: Access: Mail, fax, in person. Both court and visitors may perform in person searches. No search fee. Required to search: name, years to search. Civil cases indexed by defendant, plaintiff. Civil records on index books back to 1860s, on computer from 1995.

Criminal Records: Access: Mail, fax, in person. Both court and visitors may perform in person searches. No

search fee. Required to search: name, years to search. Criminal records on index books back to 1860s, on computer from 1995.

General Information: No adoptions, juvenile, domestic records released. SASE not required. Turnaround time 1-2 days. Fax notes: Fee to fax results is $1.00 per page. Copy fee: $.50 per page. Certification fee: $1.50 plus $.50 per page after first 2. Fee payee: Clerk of Circuit Court. Only cashiers checks and money orders accepted. Will bill to attorneys.

Magistrate Court Logan County Courthouse, 300 Stratton St, Logan, WV 25601; 304-792-8651; Fax: 304-752-0790. Hours: 8:30AM-Noon; 1-4:30PM (EST). *Misdemeanor, Civil Actions Under $5,000, Eviction, Small Claims.*

Civil Records: Access: In person, mail. Both court and visitors may perform in person searches. No search fee.

Criminal Records: Access: In person, mail. Both court and visitors may perform in person searches. No search fee. Required to search: name, years to search; also helpful: address, DOB, SSN.

General Information: Turnaround time 5 days.

Marion County

Circuit Court PO Box 1269, Fairmont, WV 26554; 304-367-5360; Fax: 304-367-5374. Hours: 8:30AM-4:30PM (EST). *Felony, Civil Actions Over $3,000.*

Civil Records: Access: Phone, fax, mail, in person. Both court and visitors may perform in person searches. No search fee. Required to search: name, years to search. Civil cases indexed by defendant, plaintiff. Civil records on computer from Jan. 1988 to present. On docket books from 1849 to 1988.

Criminal Records: Access: In person only. Visitors must perform in person searches for themselves. No search fee. Required to search: name, years to search; also helpful: DOB, SSN. Criminal records on computer from Jan. 1988 to present. On docket books from 1849 to 1988. The court refers all written requests to the Dept of Public Safety.

General Information: Public Access terminal is available. No adoptions, juvenile, mental or guardianship records released. SASE not required. Turnaround time 2-3 days. Fax notes: $5.00 for first page, $2.00 each add'l. Fax fee: After 10 pages fee is $1.00 per page. Copy fee: $.50 per page. Certification fee: $.50 per page. Fee payee: Clerk of Circuit Court. Business checks accepted. Prepayment is required.

Magistrate Court 200 Jackson St, Fairmont, WV 26554; 304-367-5330; Fax: 304-367-5337. Hours: 8:30AM-4:30PM M-W, F; 8:30AM-9PM Th (EST). *Misdemeanor, Civil Actions Under $5,000, Eviction, Small Claims.*

Civil Records: Access: In person, mail. Only the court performs in person searches; visitors may not. No search fee.

Criminal Records: Access: In person, mail. Only the court performs in person searches; visitors may not. No search fee. Required to search: name, years to search; also helpful: DOB, SSN.

General Information: Turnaround time 5-15 days, ASAP for phone requests, time permitting. Copy fee: $.25 per copy. Fee payee: Marion County Magistrate Clerk. Prepayment is required.

Marshall County

Circuit Court Marshall County Courthouse, 7th St, Moundsville, WV 26041; 304-845-2130; Fax: 304-845-3948. Hours: 8:30AM-4:30PM M-Th; 8:30AM-5:30PM F (EST). *Felony, Civil Actions Over $5,000.*

Civil Records: Access: Fax, mail, in person. Both court and visitors may perform in person searches. No search fee. Required to search: name, years to search. Civil cases indexed by defendant, plaintiff. Civil records on computer since 01/98; prior records on index books and in files from 1836 to present.

Criminal Records: Access: Fax, mail, in person. Both court and visitors may perform in person searches. No search fee. Required to search: name, years to search; also helpful: DOB, SSN. Criminal records on computer since 01/98; prior records on index books and in files from 1836 to present.

General Information: No juvenile, mental, adoption, sealed, conservatorship, guardianship or divorce records released. SASE not required. Turnaround time 1-2 days. Fax notes: Fee to fax results is $.50 per page. Copy fee: $.25 per page. Certification fee: $1.00. Fee payee: Clerk of Circuit Court. Personal checks accepted. Will bill to attorneys.

Mason County

Circuit Court Mason County Courthouse, Point Pleasant, WV 25550; 304-675-4400; Fax: 304-675-7419. Hours: 8:30AM-4:30PM (EST). *Felony, Civil Actions Over $5,000, Probate.*

Civil Records: Access: Phone, mail, in person. Both court and visitors may perform in person searches. No search fee. Required to search: name, years to search. Civil cases indexed by defendant, plaintiff. Civil records on computer from 1994. No time limit on open cases. Index books with data back to 1800s.

Criminal Records: Access: In person only. Visitors must perform in person searches for themselves. No search fee. Required to search: name, years to search. Criminal records on computer from 1994. No time limit on open cases. Index books with data back to 1800s.

General Information: Public Access terminal is available. No divorce or juvenile records released. SASE not required. Turnaround time 1-2 days. Fax notes: Fee to fax results is $2.00 per page. Copy fee: $.50 per page. Certification fee: No certification fee. Fee payee: Circuit Court Clerk. Personal checks accepted. Will bill mail requests.

Magistrate Court Corner of 6th St and Viand, Point Pleasant, WV 25550; 304-675-6840; Fax: 304-675-5949. Hours: 8:30AM-4:30PM (EST). *Misdemeanor, Civil Actions Under $5,000, Eviction, Small Claims.*

Civil Records: Access: In person, mail. Both court and visitors may perform in person searches. No search fee.

Criminal Records: Access: In person, mail. Both court and visitors may perform in person searches. No search fee. Required to search: name, years to search.

General Information: Turnaround time 3-4 days.

McDowell County

Circuit Court PO Box 400, Welch, WV 24801; 304-436-8535; Probate phone: 304-436-8544. Hours: 9AM-5PM (EST). *Felony, Civil Actions Over $5,000, Probate.*

Note: Probate is handled by County Clerk, 90 Wyoming St, Ste 109, Welch, WV 24801.

Civil Records: Access: Mail, in person. Both court and visitors may perform in person searches. No search fee. Required to search: name, years to search. Civil cases indexed by defendant, plaintiff. Civil records on index books back to 1800s; on computer back to 1999.

Criminal Records: Access: Mail, in person. Both court and visitors may perform in person searches. No search fee. Required to search: name, years to search; also helpful: DOB, SSN. Criminal records on index books back to 1800s; on computer back to 1999.

General Information: No sealed, juvenile, adoption, mental health, guardianship records released. SASE required. Turnaround time 1 week. Copy fee: $.50 per page. Certification fee: No certification fee. Fee payee: Clerk of Circuit Court. Business checks accepted. Prepayment is required.

Magistrate Court PO Box 447, Welch, WV 24801; 304-436-8587; Fax: 304-436-8575. Hours: 9AM-5PM (EST). *Misdemeanor, Civil Actions Under $5,000, Eviction, Small Claims.*

Civil Records: Access: In person only. Visitors must perform in person searches for themselves. No search fee.

Criminal Records: Access: In person, mail. Both court and visitors may perform in person searches. No search fee. Required to search: name, years to search; also helpful: DOB, SSN.

General Information: Turnaround time 5 days.

Mercer County

Circuit Court 1501 W. Main St, Princeton, WV 24740; 304-487-8369; Probate phone: 304-425-8336; Fax: 304-425-1598. Hours: 8:30AM-4:30PM (EST). *Felony, Civil Actions Over $5,000, Probate.*

Note: Probate Court records are at the same address but separate office and phone.

Civil Records: Access: Phone, fax, mail, in person. Both court and visitors may perform in person searches. No search fee. Required to search: name, years to search. Civil cases indexed by defendant, plaintiff. Civil records on computer from Oct. 1989 to present. On index books from 1930 to 1989 (Cott System). On index cards back to 1890s.

Criminal Records: Access: Phone, fax, mail, in person. Both court and visitors may perform in person searches. No search fee. Required to search: name, years to search; also helpful: DOB, SSN. Criminal records on computer from Oct. 1989 to present. On index books from 1930 to 1989 (Cott System). On index cards back to 1890s.

General Information: No juvenile, adoption, mental health, guardianship or conservatorship records released. Turnaround time 1-2 days. Fax notes: $2.00 per page. Copy fee: $.50 per page. Certification fee: $.50 per page. Fee payee: Circuit Court Clerk. Business checks accepted.

Magistrate Court 120 Scott Street, Princeton, WV 24740; 304-425-7952. Hours: 8:30AM-4:30PM (EST). *Misdemeanor, Civil Actions Under $5,000, Eviction, Small Claims.*

Civil Records: Access: In person only. Visitors must perform in person searches for themselves. No search fee. Civil records from 1977; computerized back to 1984.

Criminal Records: Access: In person only. Visitors must perform in person searches for themselves. No search fee. Required to search: name, years to search; also helpful: address, DOB, SSN. Criminal records from 1977; computerized back to 1984.

General Information: Public Access terminal is available. Certification fee: $.50. Fee payee: Mercer County Magistrate Court. Prepayment is required.

Mineral County

Circuit Court 150 Armstrong St, Keyser, WV 26726; 304-788-1562; Fax: 304-788-4109. Hours: 8:30AM-5PM (EST). *Felony, Civil Actions Over $5,000, Probate.*

Civil Records: Access: Fax, mail, in person, online. Both court and visitors may perform in person searches. Search fee: $5.00 per name. Required to search: name, years to search. Civil cases indexed by defendant, plaintiff. Civil records on computer January 1991 to present, on dockets from 1920s. Limited online access to court records is available via a pay service, see www.swcg-inc.com/courts.htm or call 800-795-8543. $125 set-up fee plus a $38.00 or $120 monthly fee plan. Fax access not guaranteed.

Criminal Records: Access: Fax, mail, in person, online. Both court and visitors may perform in person searches. Search fee: $5.00 per name. Required to

search: name, years to search; also helpful: DOB, SSN. Criminal records on computer January 1991 to present, on dockets from 1920s. Online access to criminal records is the same as civil. Fax access not guaranteed.

General Information: No juvenile, adoption, divorce, mental hygiene, conservatorship or guardianship records released. SASE requested. Turnaround time 2-4 days. Fax notes: No fee to fax results. Copy fee: $.50 per page. Certification fee: No certification fee. Fee payee: Clerk of Circuit Court. Personal checks accepted.

Magistrate Court 105 West St, Keyser, WV 26726; 304-788-2625; Fax: 304-788-9835. Hours: 8:30AM-4:30PM (EST). *Misdemeanor, Civil Actions Under $5,000, Eviction, Small Claims.*

Civil Records: Access: Mail, in person. Both court and visitors may perform in person searches. Search fee: No search fee. Required to search: name, years to search. Civil records on computer back to 1991.

Criminal Records: Access: Mail, in person. Both court and visitors may perform in person searches. No search fee. Required to search: name, years to search; also helpful: DOB, SSN. Records on computer back to 1991; prior back to 1977.

General Information: Public Access terminal is available. Turnaround time: time permitting. Certification fee: $.50 per page. Fee payee: Magistrate Court. Prepayment is required.

Mingo County

Circuit Court PO Box 435, Williamson, WV 25661; 304-235-0320; Probate phone: 304-235-0330. Hours: 8:30AM-4:30PM M-W,F, 8:30AM-6:30PM Th (EST). *Felony, Civil Actions Over $5,000, Probate.*

Note: Probate is handled by County Clerk, 75 E 2nd Ave, Williamson, WV 25661.

Civil Records: Access: Mail, in person. Only the court performs in person searches; visitors may not. Search fee: $10.00 per name. Required to search: name, years to search. Civil cases indexed by defendant, plaintiff. Civil records on computer from 1/1991 to present, civil on index books back to 1960, chancery books back to 1800s (written or in person only).

Criminal Records: Access: Mail, in person. Only the court performs in person searches; visitors may not. Search fee: $10.00 per name. Required to search: name, years to search; also helpful: DOB. Criminal records on computer since 1/91, Index books back to 1955.

General Information: Public Access terminal is available. No adoption, mental hygiene, juvenile records released. Turnaround time 1-2 days. Copy fee: $.50 per page. Certification fee: $2.00. Fee payee: Mingo County Circuit Clerk. Personal checks accepted. Prepayment is required.

Magistrate Court PO Box 986, Williamson, WV 25661; 304-235-2445; Fax: 304-235-3179. Hours: 8:30AM-4:30PM (EST). *Misdemeanor, Civil Actions Under $5,000, Eviction, Small Claims.*

Civil Records: Access: Phone, mail, fax, in person. Only the court performs in person searches; visitors may not. No search fee. Required to search: name, years to search; also helpful: DOB. Civil records go back to 1977; on computer back to 1998.

Criminal Records: Access: Phone, mail, fax, in person. Only the court performs in person searches; visitors may not. No search fee. Required to search: name, years to search; also helpful: DOB, SSN. Criminal records go back to 1977; on computer back to 1998.

General Information: Turnaround time 1 week, sooner for phone requests. Fax notes: Fee to fax is $2.00 per page; will fax free to toll-free. Copy fee: $.25 per page. Certification fee: $.50 per page. Fee payee: Magistrate Court.

Monongalia County

Circuit Court County Courthouse, 243 High St Rm 110, Morgantown, WV 26505; 304-291-7240; Probate phone: 304-291-7230; Fax: 304-291-7273. Hours: 9AM-7PM M; 9AM-5PM T-F (EST). *Felony, Civil Actions Over $5,000, Probate.*

Note: A disclaimer for the Clerk must be included by mail requesters. Probate is handled by County Clerk, 243 High St, Room 123, Morgantown, WV 26505.

Civil Records: Access: Mail, in person. Both court and visitors may perform in person searches. Search fee: $5.00 per name. Required to search: name, years to search. Civil cases indexed by defendant, plaintiff. Civil records on computer from 1/90 to present, on index book separated by plaintiff and defendant back to 1865.
Criminal Records: Access: Mail, in person. Both court and visitors may perform in person searches. Search fee: $5.00 per name. Required to search: name, years to search; also helpful: DOB, SSN. Criminal records on computer from 1/90 to present, on index book separated by plaintiff and defendant back to 1865.
General Information: Public Access terminal is available. No juvenile, divorce, mental hygiene, divorce, adoption, guardianship, conservatorship or domestic records released. SASE required. Turnaround time 1 day. Fax notes: Fee to fax results is $1.00 per page. Copy fee: $.50 per page. Certification fee: No certification fee. Fee payee: Circuit Clerk. Business checks accepted. Prepayment is required.

Magistrate Court 265 Spruce St, Morgantown, WV 26505; 304-291-7296; Fax: 304-284-7313. Hours: 8AM-7PM (EST). *Misdemeanor, Civil Actions Under $5,000, Eviction, Small Claims.*

Civil Records: Access: Mail, fax, in person. Both court and visitors may perform in person searches. Search fee: No search fee. Required to search: name, years to search. Records on computer 2 years back; prior in books back to 1977.
Criminal Records: Access: Mail, fax, online, in person. Both court and visitors may perform in person searches. No search fee. Required to search: name, years to search; also helpful: DOB, SSN, signed release. Records on computer 2 years back; prior in books back to 1977.
General Information: Turnaround time 10-14 days. Fax notes: Will not fax results. Certification fee: $.50 per page. Fee payee: Magistrate Court. Prepayment is required.

Monroe County

Circuit Court PO Box 350, Union, WV 24983-0350; 304-772-3017; Fax: 304-772-4087. Hours: 8AM-4PM (EST). *Felony, Civil Actions Over $5,000.*

Civil Records: Access: Phone, mail, in person. Both court and visitors may perform in person searches. No search fee. Required to search: name, years to search. Civil cases indexed by defendant, plaintiff. Civil records on index books 1799 to present; on computer back to 2000.
Criminal Records: Access: Phone, mail, in person. Both court and visitors may perform in person searches. No search fee. Required to search: name, years to search; also helpful: DOB, SSN. Criminal records on index books 1799 to present; on computer back to 2000.
General Information: Public Access terminal is available. No juvenile, adoption, divorce records released. SASE requested. Turnaround time 1 week. Copy fee: $.50 per page. Include postage with copy fee. Certification fee: $1.00. Fee payee: Clerk of Circuit Court. Personal checks accepted. Prepayment is required.

Magistrate Court PO Box 4, Union, WV 24983; 304-772-3321/3176; Fax: 304-772-4357. Hours: 8:30AM-4:30PM (EST). *Misdemeanor, Civil Actions Under $5,000, Eviction, Small Claims.*

Civil Records: Access: In person, mail. Both court and visitors may perform in person searches. No search fee.
Criminal Records: Access: In person, mail. Both court and visitors may perform in person searches. No search fee. Required to search: name, years to search; also helpful: DOB, SSN.
General Information: Turnaround time 1-2 days. Fax notes: $2.00.

Morgan County

Circuit Court 77 Fairfax St, Ste 2A, Berkeley Springs, WV 25411-1501; 304-258-8554; Fax: 304-258-7319. Hours: 9AM-5PM MTTh, 9AM-1PM Wed, 9AM-7PM Fri (EST). *Felony, Civil Actions Over $5,000, Probate.*

Civil Records: Access: In person only. Visitors must perform in person searches for themselves. No search fee. Required to search: name, years to search. Civil cases indexed by defendant, plaintiff. Civil records on computer back to 1/93, index cards back to 1960; in person searching only on index books back to 1800s.
Criminal Records: Access: In person only. Visitors must perform in person searches for themselves. No search fee. Required to search: name, years to search; also helpful-DOB, SSN, signed release. Criminal records on computer back to 1/93, index cards back to 1960; in person searching only on index books back to 1800s.
General Information: Public Access terminal is available. No juvenile, adoption, mental health, divorce records released. Copy fee: $.50 per page. Certification fee: No certification fee. Fee payee: Betty R Moss-Miller, Circuit Clerk. Only cashiers checks and money orders accepted. Will bill to attorneys.

Magistrate Court 202 Fairfax St, Berkeley Springs, WV 25411; 304-258-8631; Fax: 304-258-8639. Hours: 9AM-4:30PM (EST). *Misdemeanor, Civil Actions Under $5,000, Eviction, Small Claims.*

Civil Records: Access: In person only. Visitors must perform in person searches for themselves. No search fee.
Criminal Records: Access: In person only. Visitors must perform in person searches for themselves. No search fee. Required to search: name, years to search; also helpful: DOB, SSN. Phone, fax and mail access limited.

Nicholas County

Circuit Court 700 Main St, Summersville, WV 26651; 304-872-7810; Probate phone: 304-872-7820. Hours: 8:30AM-4:30PM (EST). *Felony, Civil Actions Over $5,000, Probate.*

Note: Probate is handled by County Clerk, 700 Main St, Ste 2, Summersville, WV 26651.

Civil Records: Access: Mail, in person, online. Both court and visitors may perform in person searches. No search fee. Required to search: name, years to search. Civil cases indexed by defendant, plaintiff. Civil records on computer since 1994; prior records on index cards from 1976 to 1994 on dockets back to 1818. Limited online access to court records is available via a pay service, see www.swcg-inc.com/courts.htm or call 800-795-8543. $125 set-up fee plus a $38.00 or $120 monthly fee plan.
Criminal Records: Access: Mail, in person, online. Both court and visitors may perform in person searches. No search fee. Required to search: name, years to search; also helpful: DOB, SSN. Criminal records on computer since 1994; prior records on index cards from 1976 to 1994 on dockets back to 1818. Online access to criminal records is the same as civil.

General Information: Public Access terminal is available. No divorce, juvenile, adoption, mental, guardianship records released. SASE required. Turnaround time 1 week. Copy fee: $.50 per page. Certification fee: No certification fee. Fee payee: Circuit Clerk. Personal checks accepted.

Magistrate Court 511 Church St, Suite 206 2nd Flr, Summersville, WV 26651; 304-872-7829; Fax: 304-872-7888. Hours: 8:30AM-4:30PM (EST). *Misdemeanor, Civil Actions Under $5,000, Eviction, Small Claims.*

Civil Records: Access: Mail, in person. Visitors must perform in person searches for themselves. No search fee. Civil records on computer back to 1990.
Criminal Records: Access: Mail, in person. Visitors must perform in person searches for themselves. No search fee. Required to search: name, years to search; also helpful: DOB, SSN. Criminal records on computer back to 1990.
General Information: Public Access terminal is available. Certification fee: $.50 per page. Fee payee: Magistrate Court.

Ohio County

Circuit Court 1500 Chapline St, City & County Bldg Rm 403, Wheeling, WV 26003; 304-234-3613; Fax: 304-232-0550. Hours: 8:30AM-5PM (EST). *Felony, Civil Actions Over $5,000, Probate.*

Civil Records: Access: Fax, mail, in person, online. Both court and visitors may perform in person searches. Search fee: $5.00 per name. Required to search: name, years to search. Civil cases indexed by defendant, plaintiff. Civil records on computer from Oct 1986 to present, on index books back to 1800s. Limited online access to court records is available via a pay service, see www.swcg-inc.com/courts.htm or call 800-795-8543. $125 set-up fee plus a $38.00 or $120 monthly fee plan.
Criminal Records: Access: Fax, mail, in person, online. Both court and visitors may perform in person searches. Search fee: $5.00 per name. Required to search: name, years to search; also helpful: DOB, SSN. Criminal records on computer from Oct 1986 to present, on index books back to 1800s. Online access to criminal records is the same as civil.
General Information: Public Access terminal is available. No domestic, juvenile, mental, adoption records released. SASE required. Turnaround time 1 week for accounts only. Fax notes: Fee to fax is $2.00 per page. Copy fee: $.50 per page. Certification fee: $1.50. Fee payee: Ohio County Circuit Court. Business checks accepted. Prepayment is required.

Magistrate Court Courthouse Annex, 26 15th St, Wheeling, WV 26003; 304-234-3709; Fax: 304-234-3898. Hours: 8:30AM-4:30PM (EST). *Misdemeanor, Civil Actions Under $5,000, Eviction, Small Claims.*

Civil Records: Access: In person, mail. Both court and visitors may perform in person searches. No search fee. Phone, fax and mail access limited.
Criminal Records: Access: In person, mail. Both court and visitors may perform in person searches. No search fee. Required to search: name, years to search; also helpful: DOB, SSN. Phone, fax and mail access limited.
General Information: Turnaround time 1 week.

Pendleton County

Circuit Court PO Box 846, Franklin, WV 26807; 304-358-7067; Fax: 304-358-2152. Hours: 8:30AM-4PM (EST). *Felony, Civil Actions Over $5,000, Probate.*

Civil Records: Access: Phone, fax, mail, in person. Both court and visitors may perform in person searches. No search fee. Required to search: name, years to search. Civil cases indexed by defendant, plaintiff. Civil records on index books back to 1800s.

Criminal Records: Access: Phone, fax, mail, in person. Both court and visitors may perform in person searches. No search fee. Required to search: name, years to search; also helpful: DOB, SSN. Criminal records on index books back to 1800s.

General Information: No juvenile, divorce records released. SASE required. Turnaround time 2-3 days. Fax notes: $2.00 per page. Copy fee: $.50 per page. Certification fee: No certification fee. Fee payee: Pendleton County Circuit Clerk. Personal checks accepted. Local checks accepted.

Magistrate Court PO Box 637, Franklin, WV 26807; 304-358-2343; Fax: 304-358-3870. Hours: 8:30AM-4PM (EST). *Misdemeanor, Civil Actions Under $5,000, Eviction, Small Claims.*

Civil Records: Access: In person, mail. Both court and visitors may perform in person searches. No search fee.

Criminal Records: Access: In person, mail. Both court and visitors may perform in person searches. No search fee. Required to search: name, years to search.

General Information: Turnaround time 3-5 days, will tell phone requesters if request is from 1994-present.

Pleasants County

Circuit Court 301 Court Lane, Rm 201, St. Mary's, WV 26170; 304-684-3513; Probate phone: 304-684-3542; Fax: 304-684-3514. Hours: 8:30AM-4:30PM (EST). *Felony, Civil Actions Over $5,000, Probate.*

Note: Probate is handled by County Clerk, 301 Court Lane, Room 101, St Mary's, WV 26170.

Civil Records: Access: In person only. Visitors must perform in person searches for themselves. No search fee. Required to search: name, years to search. Civil cases indexed by defendant, plaintiff. Civil records on computer from Jan 1960 to present, on index cards from 1960 to present, on index books back to 1800s.

Criminal Records: Access: In person only. Visitors must perform in person searches for themselves. No search fee. Required to search: name, years to search. Criminal records on computer from Jan 1960 to present, on index cards from 1960 to present, on index books back to 1800s.

General Information: No domestic, marriage, adoption, juvenile or mental health records released. Copy fee: $.50 per page. Certification fee: $.50 per page. Fee payee: Gail E Mote, Circuit Clerk. Personal checks accepted. Will bill to attorneys.

Magistrate Court 301 Court Lane, Rm B-6, St Mary's, WV 26170; 304-684-7197; Fax: 304-684-3882. Hours: 8:30AM-4:30PM (EST). *Misdemeanor, Civil Actions Under $5,000, Eviction, Small Claims.*

Civil Records: Access: Phone, mail, fax, in person. Only the court performs in person searches; visitors may not. Search fee: None, but there is a copy fee. Required to search: name, years to search; also helpful: DOB or SSN. Records go back to 1977, on computer since mid-2000. Will do some searches over the phone while caller holds.

Criminal Records: Access: Phone, mail, fax, in person. Only the court performs in person searches; visitors may not. Search fee: None, but there is a copy fee. Required to search: name, years to search; also helpful: DOB, SSN. Records go back to 1977, on computer since mid-2000. Will do some searches over the phone while caller holds.

General Information: Public Access terminal is available. Turnaround time 1-2 days. Fax notes: Fee to fax results is $2.00 per page. Certification fee: $.50 per page. Fee payee: Pleasants County Magistrate Court. Prepayment is required.

Pocahontas County

Circuit Court 900-D 10th Ave, Marlinton, WV 24954; 304-799-4604. Hours: 9AM-4:30PM (EST). *Felony, Civil Actions Over $5,000, Probate.*

Civil Records: Access: Phone, mail, in person. Only the court performs in person searches; visitors may not. No search fee. Required to search: name, years to search; also helpful: address. Civil cases indexed by defendant, plaintiff. Civil records on index books from 1948 to present, order books back to 1800s.

Criminal Records: Access: In person only. Visitors must perform in person searches for themselves. No search fee. Required to search: name, years to search; also helpful: DOB, SSN. Criminal records on index books from 1948 to present, order books back to 1800s.

General Information: No juvenile, domestic cases involving finances, adoption, guardianship records released. SASE required. Turnaround time same day. Copy fee: $.50 per page. Certification fee: No certification fee. Fee payee: Clerk of Circuit Court. Personal checks accepted. Prepayment is required.

Magistrate Court 900 10th Ave, Marlinton, WV 24954; 304-799-6603/4200; Fax: 304-799-6331. Hours: 9AM-4:30PM (EST). *Misdemeanor, Civil Actions Under $5,000, Eviction, Small Claims.*

Civil Records: Access: In person only. Visitors must perform in person searches for themselves. No search fee.

Criminal Records: Access: In person only. Visitors must perform in person searches for themselves. No search fee. Required to search: name, years to search; also helpful: DOB, SSN.

Preston County

Circuit Court 101 W. Main St, Rm 301, Kingwood, WV 26537; 304-329-0047; Probate phone: 304-329-0070; Fax: 304-329-1417. Hours: 9AM-5PM M-Th, 9AM-7PM Fri (EST). *Felony, Civil Actions Over $5,000, Probate.*

Note: Probate is handled by County Clerk, 101 W Main St, Room 201, Kingwood, WV 26537.

Civil Records: Access: Phone, fax, mail, in person. Only the court performs in person searches; visitors may not. No search fee. Required to search: name, years to search. Civil cases indexed by defendant, plaintiff. Civil records on computer from 1/80 to present, on index books 1965 to 1980, chancery file from 1869 to 1965.

Criminal Records: Access: Phone, fax, mail, in person. Only the court performs in person searches; visitors may not. No search fee. Required to search: name, years to search; also helpful: DOB, SSN. Criminal records on docket books from 1869 to 1979, records on computer since 1979.

General Information: No juvenile, adoption, domestic, mental hygiene records released. SASE required. Turnaround time 1 week. Fax notes: Fee to fax results is $2.00 per page. Copy fee: $.50 per page. Certification fee: No certification fee. Fee payee: Betsy Castle, Circuit Clerk. Personal checks accepted. Prepayment is required.

Magistrate Court 328 Tunnelton, Kingwood, WV 26537; 304-329-2764; Fax: 304-329-0855. Hours: 8:30AM-4:30PM (EST). *Misdemeanor, Civil Actions Under $5,000, Eviction, Small Claims.*

Civil Records: Access: In person, mail. Both court and visitors may perform in person searches. No search fee.

Criminal Records: Access: In person, mail. Both court and visitors may perform in person searches. No search fee. Required to search: name, years to search; also helpful: DOB, SSN.

General Information: Public Access terminal is available. Turnaround time 1 week.

Putnam County

Circuit Court Putnam County Judicial Bldg, 3389 Winfield Rd, Winfield, WV 25213; 304-586-0203; Fax: 304-586-0221. Hours: 8AM-4PM M-W & F, 8AM-7PM Th (EST). *Felony, Civil Actions Over $5,000, Probate.*

Civil Records: Access: In person, online. Both court and visitors may perform in person searches. No search fee. Required to search: name, years to search. Civil cases indexed by defendant, plaintiff. Civil records on computer from 1989 to present, on index books back to 1800s. Limited online access to court records is available via a pay service, see www.swcg-inc.com/courts.htm or call 800-795-8543. $125 set-up fee plus a $38.00 or $120 monthly fee plan.

Criminal Records: Access: In person, online. Visitors must perform in person searches for themselves. No search fee. Required to search: name, years to search; also helpful: DOB, SSN. Criminal records on computer from 1982 to present. Online access to criminal records is the same as civil.

General Information: Public Access terminal is available. No divorce records released. Copy fee: $.50 per page. Certification fee: No certification fee. Fee payee: Circuit Clerk. Business checks accepted.

Magistrate Court 3389 Winfield Rd, Winfield, WV 25213; 304-586-0234; Fax: 304-586-0234. Hours: 8:30AM-4:30PM (EST). *Misdemeanor, Civil Actions Under $5,000, Eviction, Small Claims.*

Civil Records: Access: In person, mail. Both court and visitors may perform in person searches. No search fee.

Criminal Records: Access: In person, mail. Both court and visitors may perform in person searches. No search fee. Required to search: name, years to search; also helpful: DOB, SSN.

General Information: Turnaround time 1 week.

Raleigh County

Circuit Court 215 Main St, Beckley, WV 25801; 304-255-9135; Probate phone: 304-255-9123; Fax: 304-255-9353. Hours: 8:30AM-4:30PM (EST). *Felony, Civil Actions Over $5,000, Probate.*

Note: Probate is handled by County Clerk, 215 Main St, Courthouse, Beckley, WV 25801.

Civil Records: Access: In person only. Visitors must perform in person searches for themselves. No search fee. Required to search: name, years to search. Civil cases indexed by defendant, plaintiff. Civil records on master index books from 1977 to present. On dockets back to 1800s.

Criminal Records: Access: Phone, mail, in person. Both court and visitors may perform in person searches. No search fee. Required to search: name, years to search; also helpful: DOB, SSN. Criminal records on master index books from 1977 to present. On dockets back to 1800s.

General Information: No divorce, juvenile, adoption records released. SASE required. Fax notes: Fee to fax results is $2.00 per page. Copy fee: $.50 per page. Certification fee: No certification fee. Fee payee: Clerk of Circuit Court. Business checks accepted. Will bill to attorneys.

Magistrate Court 115 W Prince St, Suite A, Beckley, WV 25801; 304-255-9197; Fax: 304-255-9354. Hours: 8AM-4PM (EST). *Misdemeanor, Civil Actions Under $5,000, Eviction, Small Claims.*

Civil Records: Access: In person only. Visitors must perform in person searches for themselves. No search fee.

Criminal Records: Access: In person only. Visitors must perform in person searches for themselves. No search fee. Required to search: name, years to search, offense, date of offense; also helpful: DOB, SSN.

General Information: Public Access terminal is available. (For records since 1996.).

Randolph County

Circuit Court Courthouse, 2 Randolph Ave, Elkins, WV 26241; 304-636-2765; Fax: 304-637-3700. Hours: 8AM-4:30PM (EST). *Felony, Civil Actions Over $5,000, Probate.*

Civil Records: Access: In person only. Visitors must perform in person searches for themselves. No search fee. Required to search: name, years to search. Civil cases indexed by defendant, plaintiff. Civil records on computer from 1/91 to present. On index books back to late 1800s.

Criminal Records: Access: In person only. Visitors must perform in person searches for themselves. No search fee. Required to search: name, years to search. Criminal records on computer from 1/91 to present. On index books back to late 1800s.

General Information: Public Access terminal is available. No juvenile, adoption, mental health, or guardianship records released. Copy fee: $.50 per page. Certification fee: No certification fee. Fee payee: Circuit Clerk. Personal checks accepted.

Magistrate Court #11 Randolph Ave, Elkins, WV 26241; 304-636-5885; Fax: 304-636-2510. Hours: 8AM-4:30PM (EST). *Misdemeanor, Civil Actions Under $5,000, Eviction, Small Claims.*

Civil Records: Access: In person, mail. Both court and visitors may perform in person searches. No search fee.

Criminal Records: Access: In person, mail. Both court and visitors may perform in person searches. No search fee. Required to search: name, years to search; also helpful: DOB, SSN.

General Information: Turnaround time 3 days.

Ritchie County

Circuit Court 115 E. Main St, Harrisville, WV 26362; 304-643-2164 x229. Hours: 8AM-4PM (EST). *Felony, Civil Actions Over $5,000, Probate.*

Civil Records: Access: Phone, mail, in person. Both court and visitors may perform in person searches. No search fee. Required to search: name, years to search. Civil cases indexed by defendant, plaintiff. Civil records on index cards from 1960 to present. On index books back to mid-1800s.

Criminal Records: Access: Phone, mail, in person. Both court and visitors may perform in person searches. No search fee. Required to search: name, years to search; also helpful: DOB, SSN. Criminal records on index cards from 1960 to present. On index books back to mid-1800s.

General Information: No juvenile, mental health, adoption records released. SASE requested. Turnaround time 1-2 days. Copy fee: $.50 per page. Certification fee: No certification fee. Fee payee: Circuit Clerk. Personal checks accepted. Prepayment is required.

Magistrate Court 319 E. Main St, Harrisville, WV 26362; 304-643-4409; Fax: 304-643-2098. Hours: 8AM-4PM (EST). *Misdemeanor, Civil Actions Under $5,000, Eviction, Small Claims.*

Civil Records: Access: In person, mail. Both court and visitors may perform in person searches. No search fee. Civil records go back to 1977; computerized from 1990. Phone, fax and mail access limited.

Criminal Records: Access: In person, mail. Both court and visitors may perform in person searches. No search fee. Required to search: name, years to search; also helpful: DOB, SSN. Criminal records go back to 1977; computerized from 1990. Phone, fax and mail access limited.

General Information: Public Access terminal is available. Turnaround time 1-2 days, 1-2 hours for phone requests. Certification fee: $.50. Fee payee: Magistrate Court.

Roane County

Circuit Court PO Box 122, Spencer, WV 25276; 304-927-2750; Fax: 304-927-2164. Hours: 9AM-Noon, 1-4:30PM M-F; 9:30AM-Noon Sat (EST). *Felony, Civil Actions Over $5,000, Probate.*

Civil Records: Access: Phone, fax, mail, in person. Both court and visitors may perform in person searches. No search fee. Required to search: name, years to search. Civil cases indexed by defendant, plaintiff. Civil records on index books back to early 1900s; computerized records go back to 1998.

Criminal Records: Access: Phone, fax, mail, in person. Both court and visitors may perform in person searches. No search fee. Required to search: name, years to search; also helpful: DOB, SSN. Criminal records on index books back to early 1900s; computerized records go back to 1998.

General Information: Public Access terminal is available. No sealed, juvenile, adoption records released. SASE not required. Turnaround time 1-2 days, less by phone. Fax notes: $1.50 for the 1st page; $1.00 per page thereafter. Copy fee: $.50 per page. Certification fee: $.50 per page. Fee payee: Beverly Greathouse. Personal checks accepted. Local checks accepted.

Magistrate Court 201 Main St, Spencer, WV 25276; 304-927-4750; Fax: 304-927-2754. Hours: 9AM-4PM (EST). *Misdemeanor, Civil Actions Under $5,000, Eviction, Small Claims.*

Note: Record requests can be directed to 304-746-2180.

Civil Records: Access: In person only. Visitors must perform in person searches for themselves. No search fee. Required to search: name, years to search. Records on computer back to 1997; prior records go back to 1976.

Criminal Records: Access: In person only. Visitors must perform in person searches for themselves. No search fee. Required to search: name, DOB; also helpful: years to search, SSN. Records on computer back to 1997; prior records go back to 1976.

General Information: Public Access terminal is available. Certification fee: $.50 per page. Fee payee: Roane County Magistrate Court. Will bill to attorneys.

Summers County

Circuit Court PO Box 1058, Hinton, WV 25951; 304-466-7103; Fax: 304-466-7124 (Attn:Circuit Court). Hours: 8:30AM-4:30PM (EST). *Felony, Civil Actions Over $5,000, Probate.*

Civil Records: Access: Phone, fax, mail, in person. Both court and visitors may perform in person searches. No search fee. Required to search: name, years to search. Civil cases indexed by defendant, plaintiff. Civil records on index books back to 1800s.

Criminal Records: Access: Phone, fax, mail, in person. Both court and visitors may perform in person searches. No search fee. Required to search: name, years to search; also helpful: DOB, SSN. Criminal records on index books back to 1800s.

General Information: No juvenile, adoption, child abuse records released. SASE required. Turnaround time 1-2 days. Fax notes: $2.00 per page. Copy fee: $.50 per page. Certification fee: $1.00. Fee payee: Clerk of Circuit Court. Personal checks accepted. Prepayment is required.

Magistrate Court PO Box 1059, Hinton, WV 25951; 304-466-7108; Fax: 304-466-4912. Hours: 8:30AM-4:30PM (EST). *Misdemeanor, Civil Actions Under $5,000, Eviction, Small Claims.*

Civil Records: Access: Phone, fax, mail, in person. Both court and visitors may perform in person searches. No search fee. Civil records on docket books and computer back to 1977.

Criminal Records: Access: Phone, fax, mail, in person. Both court and visitors may perform in person searches. No search fee. Required to search: name, years to search; also helpful: DOB, SSN. Criminal records on docket books and computer back to 1977.

General Information: Public Access terminal is available. Turnaround time 1-2 days. Certification fee: $.50 per page. Fee payee: Magistrate Court. Prepayment is required.

Taylor County

Circuit Court 214 W. Main St, Rm 104, Grafton, WV 26354; 304-265-2480. Hours: 8:30AM-Noon, 1-4:30PM (EST). *Felony, Civil Actions Over $5,000, Probate.*

Civil Records: Access: Phone, mail, in person. Both court and visitors may perform in person searches. No search fee. Required to search: name, years to search. Civil cases indexed by defendant, plaintiff. Civil records on index books back to 1844, computerized since 1996.

Criminal Records: Access: Phone, mail, in person. Both court and visitors may perform in person searches. No search fee. Required to search: name, years to search; also helpful: DOB, SSN. Criminal records on index books back to 1844, computerized since 1996.

General Information: No juvenile, adoptions, mental health records released. SASE required; any additional fee for postage is 3X the amount. Turnaround time 2 days. Fax notes: Fee to fax results is $2.00 per page. Copy fee: $.50 per page. Certification fee: No certification fee. Fee payee: Circuit Clerk. Prepayment is required.

Magistrate Court 214 W. Main St, Grafton, WV 26354; 304-265-1322; Fax: 304-265-5708. Hours: 8:30AM-4:30PM (EST). *Misdemeanor, Civil Actions Under $5,000, Eviction, Small Claims.*

Civil Records: Access: In person, mail. Both court and visitors may perform in person searches. No search fee.

Criminal Records: Access: In person, mail. Both court and visitors may perform in person searches. No search fee. Required to search: name, years to search; also helpful: DOB, SSN.

General Information: Public Access terminal is available. Turnaround time 1-2 days.

Tucker County

Circuit Court 215 1st St #2, Parsons, WV 26287; 304-478-2606; Criminal phone: 304-746-2177; Fax: 304-478-4464. Hours: 8AM-4PM (EST). *Felony, Civil Actions Over $5,000.*

Civil Records: Access: In person only. Visitors must perform in person searches for themselves. No search fee. Required to search: name, years to search. Civil cases indexed by defendant, plaintiff. Civil records on index books to 1996; 1997 to present on computer.

Criminal Records: Access: Mail, fax, in person. Both court and visitors may perform in person searches. Written requests must include a disclaimer to release clerk of responsibility. No search fee. Required to search: name, years to search, SSN; also helpful: DOB, case number. Criminal records on index books to 1996; 1997 to present on computer.

General Information: No juvenile, domestic, adoption or mental hygiene records released. SASE required. Fax notes: Fee to fax is $1.00 per page. Copy fee: $.50 per page. Certification fee: No certification fee. Fee payee: Circuit Court Clerk. Personal checks accepted. Prepayment is required.

Magistrate Court 201 Walnut St, Parsons, WV 26287; 304-478-2665; Fax: 304-478-4836. Hours: 8:30AM-4:30PM (EST). *Misdemeanor, Civil Actions Under $5,000, Eviction, Small Claims.*

Civil Records: Access: In person, mail. Both court and visitors may perform in person searches. No search fee.

Criminal Records: Access: In person, mail. Both court and visitors may perform in person searches. No search fee. Required to search: name, years to search; also helpful: DOB, SSN.

General Information: Turnaround time 3-4 days.

Tyler County

Circuit Court PO Box 8, Middlebourne, WV 26149; 304-758-4811; Fax: 304-758-4008. Hours: 8AM-4PM (EST). *Felony, Civil Actions Over $5,000, Probate.*

Civil Records: Access: Phone, mail, fax, in person. Both court and visitors may perform in person searches. No search fee. Required to search: name, years to search. Civil cases indexed by defendant, plaintiff. Civil records on index books back to 1800s; computerized back to 1997.

Criminal Records: Access: Phone, mail, fax, in person. Both court and visitors may perform in person searches. No search fee. Required to search: name, years to search; also helpful: DOB, SSN. Criminal records on index books back to 1800s; computerized back to 1997.

General Information: No adoption, juvenile, or domestic records released. SASE required. Turnaround time 1-2 days. Fax notes: Fee to fax results is $5.00 per page. Copy fee: $.50 per page. Certification fee: No certification fee. Fee payee: Tyler County Circuit Clerk. Personal checks accepted. Prepayment is required.

Magistrate Court PO Box 127, Middlebourne, WV 26149; 304-758-2137. Hours: 9AM-4PM (EST). *Misdemeanor, Civil Actions Under $5,000, Eviction, Small Claims.*

Civil Records: Access: In person, mail. Only the court performs in person searches; visitors may not. No search fee.

Criminal Records: Access: In person, mail. Only the court performs in person searches; visitors may not. No search fee. Required to search: name, years to search; also helpful: DOB, SSN.

General Information: Turnaround time 1 week.

Upshur County

Circuit Court 38 W. Main St, Rm 304, Buckhannon, WV 26201; 304-472-2370; Probate phone: 304-472-1068; Fax: 304-472-2168. Hours: 8AM-4:30PM (EST). *Felony, Civil Actions Over $5,000, Probate.*

Note: Probate is handled by County Clerk, 40 W Main, Courthouse, Room 101, Buckhannon, WV 26201.

Civil Records: Access: Fax, mail, in person. Both court and visitors may perform in person searches. Search fee: $5.00 per name. Required to search: name, years to search. Civil cases indexed by defendant, plaintiff. Civil records on index books from 1900 to present, on computer from 1/1990.

Criminal Records: Access: Fax, mail, in person. Both court and visitors may perform in person searches. Search fee: $5.00 per name. Required to search: name, years to search; also helpful: DOB, SSN. Criminal records on computer from 1/90 to present, on index books from 1947 to 1/1990, on dockets back to 1800s.

General Information: Public Access terminal is available. No mental health, juvenile, adoption records released. SASE requested. Turnaround time 1-2 days. Fax notes: $2.00 per page. Copy fee: $.50 per page. Certification fee: $.50 per page. Fee payee: Circuit Clerk. Business checks accepted. Prepayment required.

Magistrate Court 38 W Main, Rm 204 Courthouse Annex, Buckhannon, WV 26201; 304-472-2053. Hours: 8AM-4PM (EST). *Misdemeanor, Civil Actions Under $5,000, Eviction, Small Claims.*

Civil Records: Access: Mail, in person. Both court and visitors may perform in person searches. No search fee. Civil records from 1977; computerized back to 1992.

Criminal Records: Access: Mail, in person. Both court and visitors may perform in person searches. No search fee. Required to search: name; also helpful: DOB, SSN. Criminal records from 1977; computerized back to 1992.

General Information: Public Access terminal is available. Turnaround time 1-2 days. Copy fee: $.25 + $.50 court costs. Fee payee: Magistrate Court. Prepayment is required.

Wayne County

Circuit Court PO Box 38, Wayne, WV 25570; 304-272-6359; Probate phone: 304-272-4372. Hours: 8AM-4PM M,T,W,F; 8AM-8PM Th (EST). *Felony, Civil Actions Over $5,000, Probate.*

Note: Probate is handled by County Clerk, PO Box 248, Wayne, WV 25570.

Civil Records: Access: Phone, mail, in person. Both court and visitors may perform in person searches. No search fee. Required to search: name, years to search. Civil cases indexed by defendant, plaintiff. Civil records on computer back to 1993; prior on index books from 1960 to present. Contact Circuit Clerk for books prior (to 1800s). The staff will not conduct genealogical searches.

Criminal Records: Access: In person only. Visitors must perform in person searches for themselves. No search fee. Required to search: name, years to search, SSN; also helpful: DOB. Criminal records on computer back to 1993; prior on index books from 1960 to present. Contact Circuit Clerk for books prior (to 1800s).

General Information: No juvenile, adoption, mental records released. SASE required. Turnaround time 1-2 days. Copy fee: $.50 per page. Certification fee: No certification fee. Fee payee: Clerk of Circuit Court. Business checks accepted. Prepayment is required.

Magistrate Court PO Box 667, Wayne, WV 25570; 304-272-5648/6388. Hours: 8AM-4PM (EST). *Felony, Misdemeanor, Civil Actions Under $5,000, Eviction, Small Claims.*

Civil Records: Access: phone, fax, mail, in person. Both court and visitors may perform in person searches. No search fee. Required to search: name; also helpful: years to search, DOB, SSN. Civil records go back to 1977; on computer back to 1996.

Criminal Records: Access: phone, fax, mail, in person. Both court and visitors may perform in person searches. No search fee. Required to search: name; also helpful: years to search, DOB, SSN. Criminal records go back to 1977; on computer back to 1996.

General Information: Public Access terminal is available. Turnaround time 1-2 days, usually same day for phone requests. Fax notes: $2.00 per page. Certification fee: $.50 per page. Fee payee: Wayne County Magistrate Court. Prepayment is required.

Webster County

Circuit Court 2 Court Square, Rm G-4, Webster Springs, WV 26288; 304-847-2421; Fax: 304-847-7671. Hours: 8:30AM-4PM (EST). *Felony, Civil Actions Over $5,000, Probate.*

Civil Records: Access: Phone, fax, mail, in person. Both court and visitors may perform in person searches. No search fee. Required to search: name, years to search. Civil cases indexed by defendant, plaintiff. Civil records on index cards from 1977 to present.

Criminal Records: Access: Phone, fax, mail, in person. Both court and visitors may perform in person searches. No search fee. Required to search: name, years to search; also helpful: DOB, SSN. Felony dockets back to 1800s.

General Information: No mental health, juvenile, guardianship, adoption, paternity records released. SASE requested. Turnaround time 1-2 days. Fax notes:

$1.00 per page. Copy fee: $.50 per page. Certification fee: No certification fee. Fee payee: Clerk of Circuit Court. Personal checks accepted.

Magistrate Court 2 Court Square, Rm B-1, Webster Springs, WV 26288; 304-847-2613; Fax: 304-847-7747. Hours: 8:30AM-4PM (EST). *Misdemeanor, Civil Actions Under $5,000, Eviction, Small Claims.*

Note: They recommend that criminal searches be directed to the Court Repository in Charleston, 304-746-2180.

Civil Records: Access: In person only. Visitors must perform in person searches for themselves. No search fee. Civil records go back to 1977; on computer since 2001.

Criminal Records: Access: In person only. Visitors must perform in person searches for themselves. No search fee. Required to search: name, years to search; also helpful: DOB, SSN. Criminal records go back to 1977; on computer since 2001.

General Information: Certification fee: $.50 per page. Fee payee: Magistrate Court Clerk.

Wetzel County

Circuit Court PO Box 263, New Martinsville, WV 26155; 304-455-8219; Fax: 304-455-1069. Hours: 9AM-4:30PM (EST). *Felony, Civil Actions Over $5,000.*

Civil Records: Access: Phone, mail, in person. Both court and visitors may perform in person searches. No search fee. Required to search: name, years to search. Civil cases indexed by defendant, plaintiff. Civil records on index books back to mid 1863; computerized back to 1996.

Criminal Records: Access: Phone, mail, in person. Both court and visitors may perform in person searches. No search fee. Required to search: name. Criminal records on index books back to mid 1863; computerized back to 1996.

General Information: No juvenile, domestic, adoption records released. SASE required. Turnaround time same day. Copy fee: $.50 per page. Certification fee: No certification fee. Fee payee: Circuit Clerk. Personal checks accepted.

Magistrate Court PO Box 147, New Martinsville, WV 26155; 304-455-5040\5171\2450; Fax: 304-455-2859. Hours: 8:30AM-4:30PM (EST). *Misdemeanor, Civil Actions Under $5,000, Eviction, Small Claims.*

Civil Records: Access: mail, fax, in person. Both court and visitors may perform in person searches. No search fee.

Criminal Records: Access: mail, fax, in person. Both court and visitors may perform in person searches. No search fee. Required to search: name, years to search; also helpful: DOB, SSN.

General Information: Turnaround time 1-2 days.

Wirt County

Circuit Court PO Box 465, Elizabeth, WV 26143; 304-275-6597; Fax: 304-275-3642. Hours: 8:30AM-4PM (EST). *Felony, Civil Actions Over $5,000, Probate.*

Civil Records: Access: Phone, fax, mail, in person. Both court and visitors may perform in person searches. No search fee. Required to search: name, years to search. Civil cases indexed by defendant, plaintiff. Civil records on index cards from 1848 to present; computerized back to 9/2000.

Criminal Records: Access: Phone, fax, mail, in person. Both court and visitors may perform in person searches. No search fee. Required to search: name, years to search; also helpful: DOB, SSN. Criminal records on index cards from 1848 to present; computerized back to 9/2000.

General Information: No divorce, juvenile or adoption records released. SASE required. Turnaround time same day if possible. Fax notes: No fee to fax results. Copy fee: $.50 per page. Certification fee: $.50 per document. Fee payee: Wirt County Circuit Clerk. Personal checks accepted.

Magistrate Court PO Box 249, Elizabeth, WV 26143; 304-275-3641; Fax: 304-275-3642. Hours: 8:30AM-4PM (EST). *Misdemeanor, Civil Actions Under $5,000, Eviction, Small Claims.*

Civil Records: Access: Phone, in person. Both court and visitors may perform in person searches. No search fee. Civil records go back 10 years; computerized back to 9/2000.

Criminal Records: Access: Phone, in person. Both court and visitors may perform in person searches. No search fee. Required to search: name, years to search; also helpful: address, DOB, SSN. Criminal records go back 10 years; computerized back to 9/2000.

General Information: Public Access terminal is available.

Wood County

Circuit Court Wood County Judicial, #2 Government Sq, Parkersburg, WV 26101-5353; 304-424-1700. Hours: 8:30AM-4:30PM (EST). *Felony, Civil Actions Over $5,000, Probate.*

Note: Probate is handled by County Clerk, PO Box 1474, Parkersburg, WV 26102.

Civil Records: Access: Phone, mail, in person. Both court and visitors may perform in person searches. No search fee. Required to search: name, years to search. Civil cases indexed by defendant, plaintiff. Civil records on computer from 1978 to present, on index books back to 1885.

Criminal Records: Access: Mail, in person. Both court and visitors may perform in person searches. No search fee. Required to search: name, years to search, DOB, SSN. Criminal records on computer since 1979; prior records on index back to 1885.

General Information: Public Access terminal is available. No juvenile, adoption, mental hygiene, guardianship records released. Turnaround time 1-2 days. Copy fee: $.50 per page. Certification fee: No certification fee. Fee payee: Carole Jones, Clerk. Business checks accepted. Prepayment is required.

Magistrate Court 208 Avery St, Parkersburg, WV 26101; 304-422-3444; Fax: 304-422-2451. Hours: 8:30AM-4:30PM (EST). *Misdemeanor, Civil Actions Under $5,000, Eviction, Small Claims.*

Civil Records: Access: In person, mail. Both court and visitors may perform in person searches. No search fee. Fax and mail access limited.

Criminal Records: Access: In person, mail. Both court and visitors may perform in person searches. No search fee. Required to search: name, years to search, address; also helpful: DOB, SSN. Fax and mail access limited.

General Information: Turnaround time 10 days.

Wyoming County

Circuit Court PO Box 190, Pineville, WV 24874; 304-732-8000 X238; Fax: 304-732-7262. Hours: 9AM-4PM (EST). *Felony, Civil Actions Over $5,000.*

Civil Records: Access: Phone, mail, in person. Both court and visitors may perform in person searches. No search fee. Required to search: name, years to search. Civil cases indexed by defendant, plaintiff. Civil records on index books back to 1800s.

Criminal Records: Access: Phone, mail, in person. Both court and visitors may perform in person searches. No search fee. Required to search: name, years to search; also helpful: DOB, SSN. Criminal records on index books back to 1800s.

General Information: No juvenile, mental hygiene, adoption, or sealed records released. SASE preferred. Turnaround time 1-2 days, less for phone requests. Copy fee: $.50 per page. Certification fee: $.50 per page. Fee payee: Jack Lambert, Circuit Clerk. Business checks accepted. Prepayment is required.

Magistrate Court PO Box 598, Pineville, WV 24874; 304-732-8000 X218; Fax: 304-732-7247. Hours: 9AM-4PM M-Th, 9AM-6PM Fri (EST). *Misdemeanor, Civil Actions Under $5,000, Eviction, Small Claims.*

Civil Records: Access: Mail, in person. Both court and visitors may perform in person searches. No search fee. Civil records from 1977; computerized back to 1995.

Criminal Records: Access: Mail, in person. Both court and visitors may perform in person searches. No search fee. Required to search: name, years to search; also helpful: DOB, SSN. Criminal records from 1977; computerized back to 1995.

General Information: Public Access terminal is available. Turnaround time 1-2 days. Fax notes: Fee to fax results is $2.00 per page. Copy fee: $.25 per copy. Certification fee: $.75. Fee payee: Wyoming County Magistrate Court. Prepayment is required.

West Virginia Recording Offices

ORGANIZATION — 55 counties, 55 recording offices. The recording officer is County Clerk. The entire state is in the Eastern Time Zone (EST).

REAL ESTATE RECORDS — Most County Clerks will not perform real estate searches. Copy fees are usually $1.50 up to two pages and $1.00 for each additional page. Certification usually costs $1.00 per document.

UCC RECORDS — Financing statements are filed at the state level, except for real estate related collateral, which are filed only with the Register of Deeds. Previous to 07/2001, collateral on consumer goods were are filed in both places, now they are only filed at the state level. Many recording offices will perform UCC searches. Use search request form UCC-11. Searches fees and copy fees vary.

TAX LIEN RECORDS — All federal and state tax liens are filed with the County Clerk. Most counties will not perform tax lien searches.

OTHER LIENS — Judgment, mechanics, lis pendens

Barbour County

County Clerk, 8 North Main Street, Courthouse, Philippi, WV 26416. 304-457-2232.
Will search UCC records. UCC search includes tax liens if requested. Property transfer searches available. **Other Phone Numbers:** Assessor 304-457-2336; Treasurer 304-457-2881.

Berkeley County

County Clerk, 100 West King Street, Room 1, Martinsburg, WV 25401. 304-264-1927; Fax 304-267-1794.
Will search UCC records. Will not search real estate records. **Other Phone Numbers:** Assessor 304-264-1901; Treasurer 304-264-1980; Sheriff 304-264-1980.

Boone County

County Clerk, 200 State Street, Madison, WV 25130. 304-369-7337; Fax 304-369-7329.
Will search UCC records. Will not search real estate records. **Other Phone Numbers:** Assessor 304-369-7308; Treasurer 304-369-7391.

Braxton County

County Clerk, P.O. Box 486, Sutton, WV 26601-0728. 304-765-2833; Fax 304-765-2093.
Will search UCC records. **Other Phone Numbers:** Assessor 304-765-2805; Treasurer 304-765-2830.

Brooke County

County Clerk, 632 Main Street, Courthouse, Wellsburg, WV 26070. 304-737-3661; Fax 304-737-4023.
Will search UCC records. Will not search real estate records. **Other Phone Numbers:** Assessor 304-737-3667.

Cabell County

County Clerk, Cabell County Courthouse, 750 Fifth Ave., Room 108, Huntington, WV 25701-2083. 304-526-8625; Fax 304-526-8632.
Will search UCC records. **Other Phone Numbers:** Assessor 304-526-8601; Treasurer 304-526-8672.

Calhoun County

County Clerk, P.O. Box 230, Grantsville, WV 26147-0230. 304-354-6725; Fax 304-354-6725.
Will search UCC records. Will not search real estate records. **Other Phone Numbers:** Assessor 304-354-6958; Treasurer 304-354-6333.

Clay County

County Clerk, P.O. Box 190, Clay, WV 25043. 304-587-4259; Fax 304-587-7329.
Will search UCC records. Will not search real estate records. **Other Phone Numbers:** Assessor 304-587-4258; Treasurer 304-587-4260.

Doddridge County

County Clerk, 118 East Court Street, Room 102, West Union, WV 26456-1297. 304-873-2631.
Will search UCC records. This agency will not do a tax lien search. Will not search real estate records. **Other Phone Numbers:** Assessor 304-873-1261; Treasurer 304-873-1000.

Fayette County

County Clerk, P.O. Box 569, Fayetteville, WV 25840. 304-574-4226.
Will not search UCC records. This agency will not do a tax lien search. Will not search real estate records. **Other Phone Numbers:** Assessor 304-574-4244; Treasurer 304-574-4216.

Gilmer County

County Clerk, 10 Howard Street, Courthouse, Glenville, WV 26351. 304-462-7641; Fax 304-462-5134.
Will search UCC records. Will not search real estate records. **Other Phone Numbers:** Assessor 304-462-7731; Treasurer 304-462-7441.

Grant County

County Clerk, 5 Highland Avenue, Petersburg, WV 26847. County Clerk, R/E and UCC Recording 304-257-4550; Fax 304-257-2593.
Will search UCC records. Will not search real estate records. **Other Phone Numbers:** Assessor 304-257-1050; Treasurer 304-257-1818; Appraiser/Auditor 304-257-4550; Elections 304-257-4550; Vital Records 304-257-4550; Sheriff 304-257-1818.

Greenbrier County

County Clerk, P.O. Box 506, Lewisburg, WV 24901. 304-647-6602; Fax 304-647-6666.
Will search UCC records. This agency will not do a tax lien search. Will not search real estate records. **Other Phone Numbers:** Assessor 304-647-6615; Treasurer 304-647-6609.

Hampshire County

County Clerk, P.O. Box 806, Romney, WV 26757-0806. County Clerk, R/E and UCC Recording 304-822-5112; Fax 304-822-4039.
Will search UCC records. This agency will not do a tax lien search. Will not search real estate records. **Other Phone Numbers:** Assessor 304-822-3326; Treasurer 304-822-4720; Appraiser/Auditor 304-822-3326; Elections 304-822-5112; Vital Records 304-822-5112.

Hancock County

County Clerk, P.O. Box 367, New Cumberland, WV 26047. 304-564-3311 x281 R/E Recording: 304-564-3311 x267; Fax 304-564-5941.
Will not search UCC records. Will not search real estate records. **Other Phone Numbers:** Assessor 304-564-3311 x212; Treasurer 304-564-3311 x239; Appraiser/Auditor 304-564-3311 x256; Elections 304-564-3311 x288; Vital Records 304-564-3311 x268.

Hardy County

County Clerk, 204 Washington Street, Courthouse - Room 111, Moorefield, WV 26836. 304-538-2929; Fax 304-538-6832.
Will search UCC records. Will not search real estate records. **Other Phone Numbers:** Assessor 304-538-6139; Treasurer 304-538-2593.

Harrison County

County Clerk, 301 West Main Street, Courthouse, Clarksburg, WV 26301. 304-624-8612; Fax 304-624-8673.
Will search UCC records. Will not search real estate records. **Other Phone Numbers:** Assessor 304-624-8510; Treasurer 304-624-8550.

Jackson County

County Clerk, Court & Main Streets, P.O. Box 800, Ripley, WV 25271. 304-372-2011; Fax 304-372-5259.
Will search UCC records. **Other Phone Numbers:** Assessor 304-372-2011 x356; Treasurer 304-372-2011 x305.

Jefferson County

County Clerk, P.O. Box 208, Charles Town, WV 25414. 304-728-3215; Fax 304-728-1957.
Will search UCC records. This agency will not do a tax lien search. Will not search real estate records. **Other Phone Numbers:** Assessor 304-728-3224; Treasurer 304-728-3220; Elections 304-728-3246.

Kanawha County

County Clerk, P.O. Box 3226, Charleston, WV 25332. 304-357-0130 R/E Recording: 304-357-0244 UCC Recording: 304-357-0244; Fax 304-357-0585.

Will search UCC records. Will not search real estate records. **Other Phone Numbers:** Assessor 304-357-0250; Treasurer 304-357-0210; Elections 304-357-0110; Vital Records 304-357-0710.

Lewis County

County Clerk, P.O. Box 87, Weston, WV 26452. 304-269-8215; Fax 304-269-8202.

Will search UCC records. Will not search real estate records. **Other Phone Numbers:** Assessor 304-269-8205; Treasurer 304-269-8222.

Lincoln County

County Clerk, P.O. Box 497, Hamlin, WV 25523. 304-824-3336; Fax 304-824-7972.

Will search UCC records. Will not search real estate records. **Other Phone Numbers:** Assessor 304-824-7878; Treasurer 304-824-3336.

Logan County

County Clerk, Stratton & Main Street, Courthouse, Room 101, Logan, WV 25601. 304-792-8600; Fax 304-792-8621.

Will search UCC records. This agency will not do a tax lien search. Will not search real estate records. **Other Phone Numbers:** Assessor 304-792-8525.

Marion County

County Clerk, P.O. Box 1267, Fairmont, WV 26555-1267. 304-367-5441; Fax 304-367-5448.

Will search UCC records. This agency will not do a tax lien search. Will not search real estate records. **Other Phone Numbers:** Assessor 304-367-5410; Treasurer 304-367-5303.

Marshall County

County Clerk, P.O. Box 459, Moundsville, WV 26041. 304-845-1220; Fax 304-845-5891.

Will search UCC records. Will not search real estate records. **Other Phone Numbers:** Assessor 304-845-1490; Treasurer 304-845-1400.

Mason County

County Clerk, 200 6th Street, Point Pleasant, WV 25550. County Clerk, R/E and UCC Recording 304-675-1997; Fax 304-675-2521.

Will search UCC records. **Other Phone Numbers:** Assessor 304-675-4480; Treasurer 304-675-3810; Elections 304-675-1997; Vital Records 304-675-1997.

McDowell County

County Clerk, 90 Wyoming Street, Suite 109, Welch, WV 24801-2487. 304-436-8544 R/E Recording: 304-436-8549 UCC Recording: 304-436-8542; Fax 304-436-8576.

Will search UCC records. Will not search real estate records. **Other Phone Numbers:** Assessor 304-436-8564; Treasurer 304-436-8527; Appraiser/Auditor 304-436-8528; Elections 304-436-8543; Vital Records 304-436-8542.

Mercer County

County Clerk, 1501 Main St., Princeton, WV 24740. 304-487-8312; Fax 304-487-8351.

Will search UCC records. This agency will not do a tax lien search. Will not search real estate records. **Other Phone Numbers:** Assessor 304-487-8329; Treasurer 304-425-8366.

Mineral County

County Clerk, 150 Armstrong Street, Keyser, WV 26726. 304-788-3924; Fax 304-788-4109.

Will search UCC records. This agency will not do a tax lien search. Will not search real estate records. **Other Phone Numbers:** Assessor 304-788-3753.

Mingo County

County Clerk, P.O. Box 1197, Williamson, WV 25661. 304-235-0330; Fax 304-235-0565.

Will search UCC records. Will not search real estate records. **Other Phone Numbers:** Assessor 304-235-1850.

Monongalia County

County Clerk, 243 High Street, Courthouse - Room 123, Morgantown, WV 26505-5491. 304-291-7230; Fax 304-291-7233.

Will search UCC records. **Online Access:** Assessor, Real Estate Records. Records on the County Parcel Search database are available free online at www.assessor.org/parcelweb. Search by a wide variety of criteria including owner name and address. **Other Phone Numbers:** Assessor 304-291-7222; Treasurer 304-291-7244.

Monroe County

County Clerk, P.O. Box 350, Union, WV 24983. 304-772-3096.

Will search UCC records. This agency will not do a tax lien search. Will not search real estate records. **Other Phone Numbers:** Assessor 304-772-3083; Treasurer 304-772-3018.

Morgan County

County Clerk, 77 Fairfax Street, #1A, Suite 100, Berkeley Springs, WV 25411. County Clerk, R/E and UCC Recording 304-258-8547.

Will search UCC records. This agency will not do a tax lien search. Will not search real estate records. **Other Phone Numbers:** Assessor 304-258-8570; Treasurer 304-258-8562; Elections 304-258-8547; Vital Records 304-258-8547.

Nicholas County

County Clerk, 700 Main Street, Suite 2, Summersville, WV 26651. County Clerk, R/E and UCC Recording 304-872-7820; Fax 304-872-9600.

Will search UCC records. Will not search real estate records. **Other Phone Numbers:** Assessor 304-872-3630 x42; Treasurer 304-872-3630 x42; Elections 304-872-7820; Vital Records 304-872-7820.

Ohio County

County Clerk, 205 City County Building, Wheeling, WV 26003-3589. 304-234-3656; Fax 304-234-3829.

Will search UCC records. This agency will not do a tax lien search. Will not search real estate records. **Other Phone Numbers:** Assessor 304-234-3626; Treasurer 304-234-3688.

Pendleton County

County Clerk, P.O. Box 1167, Franklin, WV 26807-0089. 304-358-2505; Fax 304-358-2473.

Will search UCC records. Will not search real estate records. **Other Phone Numbers:** Assessor 304-358-2563; Treasurer 304-358-2214.

Pleasants County

County Clerk, Courthouse, 301 Court Lane, Room 101, St. Marys, WV 26170. County Clerk, R/E and UCC Recording 304-684-3542; Fax 304-684-9315.

Will search UCC records. **Other Phone Numbers:** Assessor 304-684-3132; Treasurer 304-684-2285; Appraiser/Auditor 304-684-3542; Elections 304-684-

3542; Vital Records 304-684-3542; Sheriff 304-684-2285.

Pocahontas County

County Clerk, 900C 10th Avenue, Marlinton, WV 24954. 304-799-4549.

Will search UCC records. This agency will not do a tax lien search. Will not search real estate records. **Other Phone Numbers:** Assessor 304-799-4750; Treasurer 304-799-4710.

Preston County

County Clerk, 101 West Main Street, Room 201, Kingwood, WV 26537. 304-329-0070; Fax 304-329-0198.

Will search UCC records. This agency will not do a tax lien search. Will not search real estate records. **Other Phone Numbers:** Assessor 304-329-1220; Treasurer 304-329-0105.

Putnam County

County Clerk, 3389 Winfield Rd., Winfield, WV 25213-9705. 304-586-0202; Fax 304-586-0200.

Will search UCC records. This agency will not do a tax lien search. Will not search real estate records. **Other Phone Numbers:** Assessor 304-586-0206; Treasurer 304-586-0204.

Raleigh County

County Clerk, 215 Main Street, Courthouse, Beckley, WV 25801. 304-255-9123 R/E Recording: 304-255-9125; Fax 304-255-9352.

Will search UCC records. Will not search real estate records. **Other Phone Numbers:** Assessor 304-255-9179; Treasurer 304-255-9300; Appraiser/Auditor 304-255-9177; Elections 304-255-9127; Vital Records 304-255-9123.

Randolph County

County Clerk, P.O. Box 368, Elkins, WV 26241. 304-636-0543.

Will search UCC records. This agency will not do a tax lien search. Will not search real estate records. **Other Phone Numbers:** Assessor 304-636-2114; Treasurer 304-636-2100; Sheriff 304-636-2100.

Ritchie County

County Clerk, 115 East Main Street, Courthouse - Room 201, Harrisville, WV 26362. 304-643-2164 R/E Recording: 304-643-2164 x227 UCC Recording: 304-643-2164 x227; Fax 304-643-2906.

Will search UCC records. This agency will not do a tax lien search. Will not search real estate records. **Other Phone Numbers:** Assessor 304-643-2164 x242; Treasurer 304-643-2164 x237; Appraiser/Auditor 304-643-2164 x242; Elections 304-643-2164 x228; Vital Records 304-643-2164 x227; Sheriff 304-643-2164 x237.

Roane County

County Clerk, P.O. Box 69, Spencer, WV 25276-1411. 304-927-2860; Fax 304-927-0079.

Will search UCC records. Will not search real estate records. **Other Phone Numbers:** Assessor 304-927-3020; Treasurer 304-927-2540; Sheriff 304-927-2540.

Summers County

County Clerk, P.O. Box 97, Hinton, WV 25951-0097. 304-466-7104; Fax 304-466-7128.

Will search UCC records. This agency will not do a tax lien search. Will not search real estate records. **Other Phone Numbers:** Assessor 304-466-7126; Treasurer 304-466-7112; Sheriff 304-466-7112.

Taylor County

County Clerk, 214 West Main Street, Room 101, Courthouse, Grafton, WV 26354. 304-265-1401; Fax 304-265-3016.

Will search UCC records. This agency will not do a tax lien search. Will not search real estate records. **Other Phone Numbers:** Assessor 304-265-2420; Treasurer 304-265-5766.

Tucker County

County Clerk, 215 First St. #3, 215 First St., Parsons, WV 26287. County Clerk, R/E and UCC Recording 304-478-2414; Fax 304-478-4464.

Will search UCC records. Will not search real estate records. **Other Phone Numbers:** Assessor 304-478-3727; Treasurer 304-478-2321; Elections 304-478-2414; Vital Records 304-478-2414.

Tyler County

County Clerk, P.O. Box 66, Middlebourne, WV 26149. County Clerk, R/E and UCC Recording 304-758-2102; Fax 304-758-2126.

Will search UCC records. Will not search real estate records. **Other Phone Numbers:** Assessor 304-758-4781; Treasurer 304-758-4551; Elections 304-758-2102; Vital Records 304-758-2102.

Upshur County

County Clerk, 40 W. Main Street, Courthouse - Room 101, Buckhannon, WV 26201. County Clerk, R/E and UCC Recording 304-472-1068; Fax 304-472-1029.

Will search UCC records. Will not search real estate records. **Other Phone Numbers:** Assessor 304-472-4650; Treasurer 304-472-1180; Appraiser/Auditor 304-472-4650; Elections 304-472-1068; Vital Records 304-472-1068.

Wayne County

Clerk of County Commission, P.O. Box 248, Wayne, WV 25570. Clerk of County Commission, R/E and UCC Recording 304-272-5974; Fax 304-272-5318.

Will search UCC records. Will not search real estate records. **Other Phone Numbers:** Assessor 304-272-6357; Treasurer 304-272-6721; Vital Records 304-272-6371.

Webster County

County Clerk, Courthouse - Room G-1, 2 Court Square, Webster Springs, WV 26288-1054. 304-847-2508; Fax 304-847-5780.

Will search UCC records. This agency will not do a tax lien search. Will not search real estate records. **Other Phone Numbers:** Assessor 304-847-2110; Treasurer 304-847-2006.

Wetzel County

County Clerk, P.O. Box 156, New Martinsville, WV 26155-0156. County Clerk, R/E and UCC Recording 304-455-8224; Fax 304-455-5256.

Will search UCC records. Will not search real estate records. **Other Phone Numbers:** Assessor 304-455-8214; Treasurer 304-455-8218; Elections 304-455-8235; Vital Records 304-455-8224.

Wirt County

County Clerk, P.O. Box 53, Elizabeth, WV 26143. 304-275-4271; Fax 304-275-3418.

Will search UCC records. This agency will not do a tax lien search. Will not search real estate records. **Other Phone Numbers:** Assessor 304-275-3192; Treasurer 304-275-4222.

Wood County

County Clerk, P.O. Box 1474, Parkersburg, WV 26102-1474. 304-424-1850.

Will search UCC records. This agency will not do a tax lien search. Will not search real estate records. **Other Phone Numbers:** Assessor 304-424-1875; Treasurer 304-424-1910.

Wyoming County

County Clerk, P.O. Box 309, Pineville, WV 24874. 304-732-8000; Fax 304-732-9659.

Will search UCC records. Will not search real estate records. **Other Phone Numbers:** Assessor 304-732-8000; Treasurer 304-732-8000; Sheriff 304-732-8000.

The Sourcebook to Public Record Information
County Locator - West Virginia

West Virginia County Locator

You will usually be able to find the city name in the City/County Cross Reference below. In that case, it is a simple matter to determine the county from the cross reference. However, only the official US Postal Service city names are included in this index. There are an additional 40,000 place names that people use in their addresses. Therefore, we have also included a ZIP/City Cross Reference immediately following the City/County Cross Reference.

If you know the ZIP Code but the city name does not appear in the City/County Cross Reference index, look up the ZIP Code in the ZIP/City Cross Reference, find the city name, then look up the city name in the City/County Cross Reference. For example, you want to know the county for an address of Menands, NY 12204. There is no "Menands" in the City/County Cross Reference. The ZIP/City Cross Reference shows that ZIP Codes 12201-12288 are for the city of Albany. Looking back in the City/County Cross Reference, Albany is in Albany County.

City/County Cross Reference

ACCOVILLE Logan
ADRIAN Upshur
ADVENT Jackson
ALBRIGHT Preston
ALDERSON (24910) Greenbrier(72), Summers(18), Monroe(10)
ALKOL Lincoln
ALLEN JUNCTION Wyoming
ALLOY Fayette
ALMA Tyler
ALPOCA Wyoming
ALUM BRIDGE (26321) Lewis(96), Doddridge(4)
ALUM CREEK (25003) Kanawha(66), Lincoln(34)
ALVY Tyler
AMEAGLE Raleigh
AMHERSTDALE Logan
AMIGO Wyoming
AMMA Roane
ANAWALT McDowell
ANMOORE Harrison
ANSTED Fayette
APPLE GROVE Mason
ARBOVALE Pocahontas
ARNETT Raleigh
ARNOLDSBURG Calhoun
ARTHUR Grant
ARTHURDALE Preston
ARTIE Raleigh
ASBURY Greenbrier
ASHFORD Boone
ASHLAND McDowell
ASHTON Mason
ATHENS Mercer
AUBURN Ritchie
AUGUSTA Hampshire
AURORA Preston
AUTO Greenbrier
AVONDALE McDowell
BAISDEN Mingo
BAKER Hardy
BAKERTON Jefferson
BALD KNOB Boone
BALLARD Monroe
BALLENGEE (24919) Monroe(50), Summers(50)
BANCROFT Putnam
BARBOURSVILLE (25504) Cabell(99), Wayne(1)
BARRACKVILLE Marion
BARRETT Boone
BARTLEY McDowell
BARTOW Pocahontas
BAXTER Marion
BAYARD Grant
BEARDS FORK Fayette
BEAVER Raleigh
BECKLEY Raleigh
BECKWITH Fayette
BEECH BOTTOM Brooke
BEESON Mercer
BELINGTON Barbour
BELLE Kanawha
BELLEVILLE (26133) Wood(98), Jackson(2)
BELMONT Pleasants

BELVA (26656) Nicholas(68), Fayette(26), Clay(7)
BENS RUN Tyler
BENTREE Clay
BENWOOD Marshall
BEREA Ritchie
BERGOO Webster
BERKELEY SPRINGS Morgan
BERWIND McDowell
BETHANY (26032) Brooke(97), Ohio(3)
BEVERLY Randolph
BICKMORE Clay
BIG BEND Calhoun
BIG CREEK Logan
BIG RUN Wetzel
BIG SANDY McDowell
BIG SPRINGS Calhoun
BIM Boone
BIRCH RIVER (26610) Nicholas(87), Webster(14)
BLACKSVILLE Monongalia
BLAIR Logan
BLANDVILLE Doddridge
BLOOMERY Hampshire
BLOOMINGROSE Boone
BLOUNT Kanawha
BLUE CREEK Kanawha
BLUE JAY Raleigh
BLUEFIELD Mercer
BOB WHITE Boone
BOGGS Webster
BOLT (25817) Raleigh(94), Wyoming(7)
BOMONT Clay
BOOMER Fayette
BOOTH Monongalia
BORDERLAND Mingo
BOWDEN (26254) Tucker(73), Randolph(27)
BOZOO Monroe
BRADLEY Raleigh
BRADSHAW McDowell
BRAMWELL Mercer
BRANCHLAND (25506) Lincoln(98), Cabell(3)
BRANDONVILLE Preston
BRANDYWINE Pendleton
BREEDEN Mingo
BRENTON Wyoming
BRETZ Preston
BRIDGEPORT (26330) Harrison(94), Taylor(5), Barbour(1)
BRISTOL (26332) Harrison(97), Doddridge(3)
BROHARD (26138) Wirt(95), Calhoun(5)
BROOKS Summers
BROWNTON Barbour
BRUCETON MILLS Preston
BRUNO Logan
BUCKEYE Pocahontas
BUCKHANNON (26201) Upshur(98), Barbour(1), Lewis(1)
BUD Wyoming
BUFFALO (25033) Kanawha(76), Putnam(24)
BUNKER HILL Berkeley
BURLINGTON (26710) Mineral(91), Hampshire(9)

BURNSVILLE (26335) Braxton(57), Gilmer(43)
BURNWELL (25034) Kanawha(50), Putnam(50)
BURTON (26562) Wetzel(64), Monongalia(36)
CABIN CREEK Kanawha
CABINS Grant
CAIRO Ritchie
CALDWELL (24925) Greenbrier(88), Monroe(13)
CALVIN Nicholas
CAMDEN Lewis
CAMDEN ON GAULEY (26208) Webster(90), Nicholas(10)
CAMERON Marshall
CAMP CREEK Mercer
CANEBRAKE McDowell
CANNELTON Fayette
CANVAS Nicholas
CAPELS McDowell
CAPON BRIDGE Hampshire
CAPON SPRINGS Hampshire
CARETTA McDowell
CAROLINA Marion
CASS Pocahontas
CASSVILLE Monongalia
CEDAR GROVE Kanawha
CEDARVILLE (26611) Braxton(53), Gilmer(47)
CENTER POINT Doddridge
CENTRALIA Braxton
CENTURY Barbour
CEREDO Wayne
CHAPMANVILLE (25508) Logan(86), Boone(14)
CHARLES TOWN Jefferson
CHARLESTON Kanawha
CHARLTON HEIGHTS Fayette
CHARMCO Greenbrier
CHATTAROY Mingo
CHAUNCEY Logan
CHESTER Hancock
CHLOE (25235) Calhoun(86), Clay(14)
CIRCLEVILLE Pendleton
CLARKSBURG Harrison
CLAY (25043) Clay(95), Nicholas(5)
CLEAR CREEK Raleigh
CLEAR FORK Wyoming
CLENDENIN (25045) Kanawha(75), Roane(18), Clay(7)
CLEVELAND (26215) Upshur(75), Webster(25)
CLIFTON Mason
CLINTONVILLE Greenbrier
CLIO Roane
CLOTHIER (25047) Boone(64), Logan(36)
COAL CITY Raleigh
COAL MOUNTAIN Wyoming
COALTON Randolph
COALWOOD McDowell
COLCORD Raleigh
COLFAX Marion
COLLIERS Brooke
COMFORT Boone
COOL RIDGE (25825) Raleigh(97), Summers(3)

COPEN Braxton
CORA Logan
CORE Monongalia
CORINNE Wyoming
CORINTH Preston
COSTA Boone
COTTAGEVILLE (25239) Jackson(83), Mason(18)
COTTLE Nicholas
COVEL Wyoming
COWEN Webster
COXS MILLS (26342) Gilmer(98), Ritchie(2)
CRAB ORCHARD Raleigh
CRAIGSVILLE Nicholas
CRANBERRY Raleigh
CRAWFORD (26343) Lewis(51), Upshur(49)
CRAWLEY Greenbrier
CRESTON (26141) Wirt(72), Calhoun(28)
CRICHTON Greenbrier
CROWN HILL Kanawha
CRUM Wayne
CRUMPLER McDowell
CUCUMBER McDowell
CULLODEN (25510) Cabell(68), Putnam(20), Lincoln(12)
CUZZART Preston
CYCLONE (24827) Wyoming(96), Wayne(4)
DAILEY Randolph
DALLAS Marshall
DANESE Fayette
DANIELS Raleigh
DANVILLE Boone
DAVIN (25617) Logan(83), Wyoming(17)
DAVIS (26260) Tucker(91), Nicholas(9)
DAVISVILLE Wood
DAVY (24828) McDowell(99), Wyoming(1)
DAWES Kanawha
DAWMONT Harrison
DEEP WATER Fayette
DELBARTON Mingo
DELLSLOW Monongalia
DELRAY Hampshire
DIANA Webster
DILLE (26617) Clay(81), Nicholas(19)
DINGESS Mingo
DIXIE (25059) Nicholas(93), Fayette(7)
DOROTHY Raleigh
DOTHAN Fayette
DRENNEN Nicholas
DRY CREEK Raleigh
DRYBRANCH Kanawha
DRYFORK (26263) Tucker(58), Randolph(43)
DUCK (25063) Clay(62), Braxton(38)
DUNBAR Kanawha
DUNLOW Wayne
DUNMORE Pocahontas
DURBIN Pocahontas
EAST BANK Kanawha
EAST LYNN Wayne
ECCLES Raleigh
ECKMAN McDowell
EDGARTON Mingo
EDMOND Fayette

EGLON Preston
ELBERT McDowell
ELEANOR Putnam
ELIZABETH (26143) Wirt(86), Wood(8),
   Jackson(3), Ritchie(2)
ELK GARDEN (26717) Mineral(80),
   Grant(20)
ELKHORN McDowell
ELKINS Randolph
ELKVIEW (25071) Kanawha(99), Roane(1)
ELLAMORE Randolph
ELLENBORO (26346) Ritchie(77),
   Pleasants(23)
ELMIRA Braxton
ELTON Summers
EMMETT Logan
ENGLISH McDowell
ENTERPRISE Harrison
ERBACON Webster
ESKDALE Kanawha
ETHEL Logan
EUREKA Pleasants
EVANS (25241) Jackson(95), Mason(5)
EVERETTVILLE Monongalia
EXCHANGE Braxton
FAIRDALE Raleigh
FAIRLEA Greenbrier
FAIRMONT Marion
FAIRVIEW (26570) Monongalia(73),
   Marion(27)
FALLING ROCK Kanawha
FALLING WATERS (25419) Berkeley(75),
   Jefferson(25)
FALLS MILL Braxton
FANROCK Wyoming
FARMINGTON Marion
FAYETTEVILLE Fayette
FENWICK Nicholas
FISHER Hardy
FIVE FORKS Calhoun
FLAT TOP Mercer
FLATWOODS Braxton
FLEMINGTON (26347) Taylor(75),
   Barbour(25)
FOLA Clay
FOLLANSBEE Brooke
FOLSOM Wetzel
FOREST HILL Summers
FORT ASHBY Mineral
FORT GAY (25514) Wayne(72), Logan(28)
FORT SEYBERT Pendleton
FORT SPRING Greenbrier
FOSTER (25081) Boone(93), Kanawha(8)
FOUR STATES Marion
FRAMETOWN (26623) Braxton(97),
   Gilmer(3)
FRANKFORD Greenbrier
FRANKLIN Pendleton
FRAZIERS BOTTOM (25082) Putnam(67),
   Mason(34)
FREEMAN Mercer
FRENCH CREEK Upshur
FRENCHTON Upshur
FRIARS HILL Greenbrier
FRIENDLY (26146) Tyler(86),
   Pleasants(14)
GALLAGHER (25083) Kanawha(97),
   Fayette(3)
GALLIPOLIS FERRY Mason
GALLOWAY Barbour
GANDEEVILLE Roane
GAP MILLS Monroe
GARY McDowell
GASSAWAY Braxton
GAULEY BRIDGE (25085) Fayette(63),
   Kanawha(38)
GAY (25244) Jackson(82), Roane(19)
GENOA Wayne
GERRARDSTOWN Berkeley
GHENT Raleigh
GILBERT Mingo
GILBOA Nicholas

GILMER Gilmer
GIVEN (25245) Jackson(88), Putnam(11)
GLACE Monroe
GLADY Randolph
GLASGOW Kanawha
GLEN Clay
GLEN DALE Marshall
GLEN DANIEL Raleigh
GLEN EASTON Marshall
GLEN FERRIS Fayette
GLEN FORK Wyoming
GLEN JEAN Fayette
GLEN MORGAN Raleigh
GLEN ROGERS Wyoming
GLEN WHITE Raleigh
GLENDON Braxton
GLENGARY Berkeley
GLENHAYES Wayne
GLENVILLE Gilmer
GLENWOOD (25520) Mason(54),
   Cabell(47)
GORDON Boone
GORMANIA Grant
GRAFTON Taylor
GRANT TOWN Marion
GRANTSVILLE Calhoun
GRANVILLE Monongalia
GRASSY MEADOWS Greenbrier
GREAT CACAPON Morgan
GREEN BANK Pocahontas
GREEN SPRING Hampshire
GREEN SULPHUR SPRINGS Summers
GREENVILLE Monroe
GREENWOOD (26360) Doddridge(58),
   Ritchie(32), Tyler(10)
GRIFFITHSVILLE Lincoln
GRIMMS LANDING Mason
GYPSY Harrison
HACKER VALLEY Webster
HALLTOWN Jefferson
HAMBLETON (26269) Tucker(94),
   Monongalia(6)
HAMLIN (25523) Lincoln(94), Putnam(7)
HAMPDEN Mingo
HANDLEY Kanawha
HANOVER Wyoming
HANSFORD Kanawha
HARMAN (26270) Randolph(91),
   Pendleton(9)
HARMONY (25246) Roane(95), Jackson(5)
HARPER Raleigh
HARPERS FERRY Jefferson
HARRISON Clay
HARRISVILLE Ritchie
HARTFORD Mason
HARTS (25524) Lincoln(82), Logan(16),
   Wayne(3)
HAVACO McDowell
HAYWOOD Harrison
HAZELGREEN Ritchie
HAZELTON Preston
HEATERS Braxton
HEDGESVILLE (25427) Berkeley(91),
   Morgan(9)
HELEN Raleigh
HELVETIA (26224) Randolph(65),
   Upshur(35)
HEMPHILL McDowell
HENDERSON Mason
HENDRICKS Tucker
HENLAWSON Logan
HENSLEY McDowell
HEPZIBAH Harrison
HERNDON Wyoming
HERNSHAW Kanawha
HEWETT (25108) Boone(95), Logan(5)
HIAWATHA Mercer
HICO Fayette
HIGH VIEW Hampshire
HILLSBORO Pocahontas
HILLTOP Fayette
HINES Greenbrier

HINTON Summers
HOLDEN Logan
HOMETOWN Putnam
HORNER Lewis
HUGHESTON Kanawha
HUNDRED (26575) Wetzel(87),
   Monongalia(13)
HUNTINGTON (25701) Cabell(97),
   Wayne(4)
HUNTINGTON (25704) Wayne(57),
   Cabell(43)
HUNTINGTON Cabell
HUNTINGTON Wayne
HURRICANE Putnam
HUTTONSVILLE Randolph
IAEGER (24844) McDowell(83),
   Wyoming(17)
IDAMAY Marion
IKES FORK Wyoming
INDEPENDENCE (26374) Preston(62),
   Taylor(22), Monongalia(16)
INDORE Clay
INDUSTRIAL Harrison
INSTITUTE Kanawha
INWOOD Berkeley
IRELAND (26376) Lewis(61), Braxton(39)
ISABAN McDowell
ITMANN Wyoming
IVYDALE Clay
JACKSONBURG (26377) Wetzel(61),
   Tyler(39)
JANE LEW (26378) Lewis(64),
   Harrison(36)
JEFFREY Boone
JENKINJONES McDowell
JESSE Wyoming
JODIE Fayette
JOLO McDowell
JONBEN Raleigh
JOSEPHINE Raleigh
JULIAN Boone
JUMPING BRANCH (25969) Summers(86),
   Raleigh(15)
JUNCTION Hampshire
JUNIOR Barbour
JUSTICE Mingo
KANAWHA FALLS Fayette
KANAWHA HEAD Upshur
KEARNEYSVILLE Jefferson
KEGLEY Mercer
KELLYSVILLE Mercer
KENNA Jackson
KENOVA Wayne
KENTUCK Jackson
KERENS (26276) Randolph(67),
   Tucker(33)
KERMIT (25674) Mingo(74), Wayne(27)
KESLERS CROSS LANES Nicholas
KEYSER Mineral
KEYSTONE McDowell
KIAHSVILLE Wayne
KIEFFER Greenbrier
KILSYTH Fayette
KIMBALL McDowell
KIMBERLY Fayette
KINCAID Fayette
KINGMONT Marion
KINGSTON Fayette
KINGWOOD Preston
KIRBY (26729) Hampshire(83), Hardy(17)
KISTLER Logan
KOPPERSTON Wyoming
KYLE McDowell
LAHMANSVILLE Grant
LAKE Logan
LAKIN Mason
LANARK Raleigh
LANSING Fayette
LASHMEET Mercer
LAVALETTE Wayne
LAYLAND (25864) Raleigh(78), Fayette(22)

LE ROY (25252) Jackson(66), Roane(17),
   Wirt(17)
LECKIE McDowell
LEEWOOD Kanawha
LEFT HAND Roane
LEIVASY Nicholas
LENORE Mingo
LEON (25123) Mason(55), Putnam(46)
LERONA (25971) Mercer(95), Summers(5)
LESAGE Cabell
LESLIE Greenbrier
LESTER Raleigh
LETART Mason
LETTER GAP Gilmer
LEVELS (25431) Morgan(92),
   Hampshire(8)
LEWISBURG Greenbrier
LIBERTY (25124) Putnam(92), Jackson(5),
   Kanawha(3)
LIMA Tyler
LINDEN Roane
LINDSIDE Monroe
LINN (26384) Gilmer(90), Lewis(10)
LITTLE BIRCH Braxton
LITTLETON Wetzel
LIZEMORES Clay
LOCHGELLY Fayette
LOCKBRIDGE Summers
LOCKNEY Gilmer
LOGAN Logan
LONDON Kanawha
LONG BRANCH Fayette
LOOKOUT Fayette
LOONEYVILLE Roane
LORADO Logan
LORENTZ Upshur
LOST CITY Hardy
LOST CREEK Harrison
LOST RIVER Hardy
LUMBERPORT Harrison
LUNDALE Logan
LYBURN Logan
LYNCO Wyoming
MABEN Wyoming
MABIE Randolph
MABSCOTT Raleigh
MAC ARTHUR Raleigh
MACFARLAN Ritchie
MADISON Boone
MAHAN Fayette
MAIDSVILLE Monongalia
MALLORY Logan
MAMMOTH Kanawha
MAN Logan
MANNINGTON (26582) Marion(96),
   Wetzel(3), Harrison(1)
MAPLEWOOD Fayette
MARIANNA Wyoming
MARLINTON Pocahontas
MARTINSBURG Berkeley
MASON Mason
MASONTOWN (26542) Preston(87),
   Monongalia(13)
MATEWAN Mingo
MATHENY Wyoming
MATHIAS Hardy
MATOAKA (24736) Mercer(88),
   Wyoming(12)
MAXWELTON Greenbrier
MAYBEURY McDowell
MAYSEL Clay
MAYSVILLE Grant
MC COMAS Mercer
MC GRAWS Wyoming
MC MECHEN Marshall
MC WHORTER Harrison
MEADOR Mingo
MEADOW BLUFF Greenbrier
MEADOW BRIDGE (25976) Summers(49),
   Fayette(45), Greenbrier(5)
MEADOW CREEK Summers
MEADOWBROOK Harrison

MEDLEY Grant
METZ (26585) Marion(72), Wetzel(28)
MIAMI Kanawha
MIDDLEBOURNE Tyler
MIDKIFF Lincoln
MIDWAY Raleigh
MILAM (26838) Hardy(75), Pendleton(25)
MILL CREEK Randolph
MILLSTONE Calhoun
MILLVILLE Jefferson
MILLWOOD Jackson
MILTON Cabell
MINDEN Fayette
MINERAL WELLS Wood
MINGO Randolph
MOATSVILLE (26405) Barbour(85),
    Preston(15)
MOHAWK McDowell
MONAVILLE Logan
MONTANA MINES Marion
MONTCALM Mercer
MONTCOAL Raleigh
MONTERVILLE Randolph
MONTGOMERY (25136) Fayette(68),
    Kanawha(32)
MONTROSE (26283) Randolph(69),
    Barbour(19), Tucker(11)
MOOREFIELD Hardy
MORGANTOWN Monongalia
MOUNDSVILLE Marshall
MOUNT ALTO (25264) Mason(53),
    Jackson(47)
MOUNT CARBON Fayette
MOUNT CLARE Harrison
MOUNT GAY Logan
MOUNT HOPE (25880) Raleigh(64),
    Fayette(36)
MOUNT LOOKOUT Nicholas
MOUNT NEBO Nicholas
MOUNT OLIVE Fayette
MOUNT STORM (26739) Grant(96),
    Berkeley(4)
MOUNT ZION Calhoun
MOUNTAIN Ritchie
MOYERS Pendleton
MULLENS Wyoming
MUNDAY (26152) Calhoun(77), Wirt(24)
MURRAYSVILLE (26153) Jackson(89),
    Wood(11)
MYRA Lincoln
MYRTLE Mingo
NALLEN (26680) Fayette(81),
    Greenbrier(14), Nicholas(5)
NAOMA Raleigh
NAPIER Braxton
NAUGATUCK Mingo
NEBO (25141) Clay(75), Calhoun(25)
NELLIS Boone
NEMOURS Mercer
NEOLA Greenbrier
NETTIE Nicholas
NEW CREEK (26743) Mineral(78),
    Grant(22)
NEW CUMBERLAND Hancock
NEW HAVEN Mason
NEW MANCHESTER Hancock
NEW MARTINSVILLE Wetzel
NEW MILTON (26411) Doddridge(89),
    Gilmer(11)
NEW RICHMOND Wyoming
NEWBERNE (26409) Gilmer(56),
    Ritchie(44)
NEWBURG Preston
NEWELL Hancock
NEWHALL McDowell
NEWTON Roane
NEWTOWN Mingo
NICUT (26633) Calhoun(62), Braxton(35),
    Gilmer(3)
NIMITZ Summers
NITRO (25143) Kanawha(75), Putnam(25)
NOLAN Mingo

NORMANTOWN (25267) Gilmer(89),
    Braxton(6), Calhoun(6)
NORTH MATEWAN Mingo
NORTH SPRING Wyoming
NORTHFORK McDowell
NORTON Randolph
OAK HILL Fayette
OAKVALE Mercer
OCEANA Wyoming
ODD (25902) Raleigh(84), Mercer(16)
OHLEY Kanawha
OLD FIELDS (26845) Hardy(86),
    Hampshire(14)
OMAR Logan
ONA Cabell
ONEGO Pendleton
ORGAS Boone
ORLANDO (26412) Braxton(62), Lewis(30),
    Gilmer(9)
ORMA Calhoun
OSAGE Monongalia
OTTAWA Boone
OVAPA Clay
PADEN CITY (26159) Wetzel(64), Tyler(36)
PAGE Fayette
PAGETON McDowell
PALERMO Lincoln
PALESTINE Wirt
PANTHER McDowell
PARKERSBURG Wood
PARSONS Tucker
PAW PAW (25434) Hampshire(84),
    Morgan(16)
PAX Fayette
PAYNESVILLE McDowell
PEACH CREEK Logan
PECKS MILL Logan
PEMBERTON Raleigh
PENCE SPRINGS Summers
PENNSBORO (26415) Ritchie(98), Tyler(2)
PENTRESS Monongalia
PERKINS Gilmer
PETERSBURG Grant
PETERSTOWN Monroe
PETROLEUM (26161) Ritchie(89),
    Wood(7), Wirt(5)
PEYTONA Boone
PHILIPPI Barbour
PICKENS (26230) Randolph(89),
    Webster(11)
PIEDMONT Mineral
PINCH Kanawha
PINE GROVE Wetzel
PINEVILLE Wyoming
PINEY VIEW Raleigh
PIPESTEM (25979) Summers(74),
    Mercer(26)
PLINY Putnam
POCA Putnam
POE Nicholas
POINT PLEASANT Mason
POINTS Hampshire
POND GAP Kanawha
POOL Nicholas
PORTERS FALLS Wetzel
POWELLTON Fayette
POWHATAN McDowell
PRATT Kanawha
PREMIER McDowell
PRENTER Boone
PRICHARD Wayne
PRINCE Fayette
PRINCETON Mercer
PRINCEWICK Raleigh
PROCIOUS Clay
PROCTOR (26055) Marshall(84),
    Wetzel(16)
PROSPERITY Raleigh
PULLMAN Ritchie
PURGITSVILLE (26852) Hampshire(64),
    Hardy(24), Mineral(8), Grant(4)
PURSGLOVE Monongalia

QUINNIMONT Fayette
QUINWOOD (25981) Greenbrier(55),
    Nicholas(46)
RACHEL Marion
RACINE Boone
RAGLAND Mingo
RAINELLE (25962) Fayette(94),
    Greenbrier(6)
RALEIGH Raleigh
RAMAGE Boone
RAMSEY Fayette
RANGER (25557) Lincoln(98), Wayne(2)
RANSON Jefferson
RAVENCLIFF Wyoming
RAVENSWOOD (26164) Jackson(88),
    Wood(12)
RAWL Mingo
RAYSAL McDowell
READER Wetzel
RED CREEK Tucker
RED HOUSE (25168) Putnam(62),
    Kanawha(39)
RED JACKET Mingo
REDSTAR Fayette
REEDSVILLE Preston
REEDY (25270) Roane(98), Wirt(2)
RENICK Greenbrier
REYNOLDSVILLE Harrison
RHODELL Raleigh
RICHWOOD (26261) Nicholas(99),
    Greenbrier(1)
RIDGELEY (26753) Mineral(89),
    Marion(11)
RIDGEVIEW Boone
RIDGEWAY Berkeley
RIO Hampshire
RIPLEY Jackson
RIPPON Jefferson
RIVERTON Pendleton
RIVESVILLE (26588) Marion(81),
    Monongalia(19)
ROANOKE Lewis
ROBERTSBURG Putnam
ROBSON Fayette
ROCK Mercer
ROCK CASTLE Jackson
ROCK CAVE (26234) Upshur(94),
    Webster(6)
ROCK CREEK Raleigh
ROCK VIEW Wyoming
ROCKPORT Wood
RODERFIELD McDowell
ROMNEY Hampshire
RONCEVERTE (24970) Greenbrier(99),
    Monroe(1)
ROSEDALE (26636) Gilmer(44),
    Braxton(28), Calhoun(28)
ROSEMONT Taylor
ROSSMORE Logan
ROWLESBURG (26425) Preston(99),
    Tucker(1)
RUPERT Greenbrier
SABINE Wyoming
SAINT ALBANS Kanawha
SAINT GEORGE (26290) Tucker(95),
    Preston(5)
SAINT MARYS (26170) Pleasants(98),
    Ritchie(2)
SALEM (26426) Harrison(70),
    Doddridge(30)
SALT ROCK Cabell
SAND FORK Gilmer
SAND RIDGE Calhoun
SANDSTONE Summers
SANDYVILLE Jackson
SARAH ANN Logan
SARTON Monroe
SAULSVILLE Wyoming
SAXON (25180) Boone(91), Raleigh(9)
SCARBRO Fayette
SCOTT DEPOT Putnam

SECONDCREEK (24974) Monroe(89),
    Greenbrier(11)
SELBYVILLE (26236) Upshur(75),
    Randolph(25)
SENECA ROCKS Pendleton
SETH Boone
SHADY SPRING Raleigh
SHANKS Hampshire
SHARON Kanawha
SHARPLES Logan
SHENANDOAH JUNCTION Jefferson
SHEPHERDSTOWN Jefferson
SHERMAN Jackson
SHINNSTON (26431) Harrison(98),
    Taylor(2)
SHIRLEY Tyler
SHOALS Wayne
SHOCK (26638) Gilmer(94), Calhoun(6)
SHORT CREEK (26058) Brooke(75),
    Ohio(25)
SIAS Lincoln
SIMON Wyoming
SIMPSON Taylor
SINKS GROVE (24976) Monroe(91),
    Greenbrier(9)
SISTERSVILLE Tyler
SKELTON Raleigh
SKYGUSTY McDowell
SLAB FORK (25920) Raleigh(77),
    Wyoming(23)
SLANESVILLE Hampshire
SLATYFORK Pocahontas
SMITHBURG Doddridge
SMITHERS Fayette
SMITHFIELD (26437) Wetzel(90),
    Marion(10)
SMITHVILLE (26178) Ritchie(96), Gilmer(4)
SMOOT Greenbrier
SNOWSHOE Pocahontas
SOD Lincoln
SOPHIA Raleigh
SOUTHSIDE Mason
SPANISHBURG Mercer
SPELTER Harrison
SPENCER Roane
SPRAGUE Raleigh
SPRIGG Mingo
SPRING DALE Fayette
SPRINGFIELD Hampshire
SPURLOCKVILLE (25565) Lincoln(65),
    Boone(35)
SQUIRE McDowell
STANAFORD Raleigh
STATTS MILLS Jackson
STEPHENSON Wyoming
STIRRAT Logan
STOLLINGS Logan
STOUTS MILLS Gilmer
STRANGE CREEK (26639) Braxton(69),
    Clay(17), Nicholas(14)
STUMPTOWN (25280) Gilmer(55),
    Calhoun(45)
SUGAR GROVE Pendleton
SUMERCO Lincoln
SUMMERLEE Fayette
SUMMERSVILLE Nicholas
SUMMIT POINT Jefferson
SUNDIAL Raleigh
SUPERIOR McDowell
SURVEYOR Raleigh
SUTTON Braxton
SWEET SPRINGS Monroe
SWEETLAND Lincoln
SWISS Nicholas
SWITCHBACK McDowell
SWITZER Logan
SYLVESTER Boone
TAD Kanawha
TALCOTT Summers
TALLMANSVILLE Upshur
TANNER Gilmer
TAPLIN Logan

TARIFF Roane
TEAYS Putnam
TERRA ALTA Preston
TERRY Raleigh
THACKER Mingo
THOMAS (26292) Tucker(97), Grant(3)
THORNTON (26440) Taylor(69),
   Preston(24), Barbour(7)
THORPE McDowell
THREE CHURCHES Hampshire
THURMOND Fayette
TIOGA (26691) Nicholas(87), Webster(13)
TORNADO (25202) Kanawha(95),
   Lincoln(5)
TRIADELPHIA Ohio
TROY (26443) Gilmer(82), Doddridge(18)
TRUE Summers
TUNNELTON Preston
TURTLE CREEK Boone
TWILIGHT Boone
TWIN BRANCH McDowell
UNEEDA Boone
UNION Monroe
UPPER TRACT Pendleton
UPPERGLADE Webster
VALLEY BEND Randolph
VALLEY CHAPEL Lewis
VALLEY FORK Clay
VALLEY GROVE (26060) Ohio(99),
   Brooke(1)

VALLEY HEAD (26294) Randolph(83),
   Pocahontas(17)
VAN Boone
VARNEY Mingo
VERDUNVILLE Logan
VERNER (25650) Mingo(83), Logan(17)
VICTOR Fayette
VIENNA Wood
VIVIAN McDowell
VOLGA (26238) Barbour(66), Upshur(33),
   Harrison(2)
VULCAN Mingo
WADESTOWN (26589) Monongalia(94),
   Wetzel(6)
WAITEVILLE Monroe
WALKER (26180) Wood(93), Wirt(7)
WALKERSVILLE (26447) Lewis(86),
   Braxton(14)
WALLACE (26448) Harrison(93),
   Doddridge(5), Marion(2)
WALLBACK (25285) Clay(73), Roane(27)
WALTON Roane
WANA Monongalia
WAR McDowell
WARDENSVILLE (26851) Hardy(93),
   Hampshire(7)
WARRIORMINE McDowell
WASHINGTON Wood
WAVERLY (26184) Wood(85),
   Pleasants(14)

WAYNE Wayne
WAYSIDE (24985) Monroe(64),
   Summers(36)
WEBSTER SPRINGS Webster
WEIRTON (26062) Hancock(86),
   Brooke(14)
WELCH McDowell
WELLSBURG Brooke
WEST COLUMBIA Mason
WEST HAMLIN Lincoln
WEST LIBERTY Ohio
WEST MILFORD Harrison
WEST UNION (26456) Doddridge(92),
   Tyler(4), Ritchie(4)
WESTON Lewis
WHARNCLIFFE Mingo
WHARTON Boone
WHEELING Ohio
WHITE OAK (25989) Raleigh(98),
   Summers(2)
WHITE SULPHUR SPRINGS Greenbrier
WHITESVILLE (25209) Raleigh(90),
   Boone(10)
WHITMAN Logan
WHITMER Randolph
WICK Tyler
WIDEN Clay
WILCOE McDowell
WILEY FORD Mineral
WILEYVILLE Wetzel

WILKINSON Logan
WILLIAMSBURG Greenbrier
WILLIAMSON Mingo
WILLIAMSTOWN Wood
WILSIE Braxton
WILSONBURG Harrison
WILSONDALE (25699) Wayne(80),
   Mingo(11), Lincoln(9)
WINDSOR HEIGHTS Brooke
WINFIELD Putnam
WINIFREDE Kanawha
WINONA Fayette
WOLF PEN Wyoming
WOLF SUMMIT Harrison
WOLFCREEK Monroe
WOLFE Mercer
WOODVILLE (25572) Boone(83),
   Lincoln(17)
WORTH McDowell
WORTHINGTON (26591) Marion(96),
   Harrison(4)
WYATT Harrison
WYCO Wyoming
WYOMING Wyoming
YAWKEY Lincoln
YELLOW SPRING Hampshire
YOLYN Logan
YUKON McDowell

ZIP/City Cross Reference

ZIP	City	ZIP	City	ZIP	City	ZIP	City
24701-24701	BLUEFIELD	24846-24846	ISABAN	24919-24919	BALLENGEE	25022-25022	BLAIR
24710-24710	ALPOCA	24847-24847	ITMANN	24920-24920	BARTOW	25024-25024	BLOOMINGROSE
24712-24712	ATHENS	24848-24848	JENKINJONES	24924-24924	BUCKEYE	25025-25025	BLOUNT
24714-24714	BEESON	24849-24849	JESSE	24925-24925	CALDWELL	25026-25026	BLUE CREEK
24715-24715	BRAMWELL	24850-24850	JOLO	24927-24927	CASS	25028-25028	BOB WHITE
24716-24716	BUD	24851-24851	JUSTICE	24931-24931	CRAWLEY	25030-25030	BOMONT
24719-24719	COVEL	24852-24852	KEYSTONE	24934-24934	DUNMORE	25031-25031	BOOMER
24724-24724	FREEMAN	24853-24853	KIMBALL	24935-24935	FOREST HILL	25033-25033	BUFFALO
24726-24726	HERNDON	24854-24854	KOPPERSTON	24936-24936	FORT SPRING	25035-25035	CABIN CREEK
24729-24729	HIAWATHA	24855-24855	KYLE	24938-24938	FRANKFORD	25036-25036	CANNELTON
24731-24731	KEGLEY	24856-24856	LECKIE	24941-24941	GAP MILLS	25039-25039	CEDAR GROVE
24732-24732	KELLYSVILLE	24857-24857	LYNCO	24942-24942	GLACE	25040-25040	CHARLTON HEIGHTS
24733-24733	LASHMEET	24859-24859	MARIANNA	24943-24943	GRASSY MEADOWS	25043-25043	CLAY
24736-24736	MATOAKA	24860-24860	MATHENY	24944-24944	GREEN BANK	25044-25044	CLEAR CREEK
24737-24737	MONTCALM	24861-24861	MAYBEURY	24945-24945	GREENVILLE	25045-25045	CLENDENIN
24738-24738	NEMOURS	24862-24862	MOHAWK	24946-24946	HILLSBORO	25046-25046	CLIO
24739-24739	OAKVALE	24866-24866	NEWHALL	24950-24950	KIEFFER	25047-25047	CLOTHIER
24740-24740	PRINCETON	24867-24867	NEW RICHMOND	24951-24951	LINDSIDE	25048-25048	COLCORD
24747-24747	ROCK	24868-24868	NORTHFORK	24954-24954	MARLINTON	25049-25049	COMFORT
24751-24751	WOLFE	24869-24869	NORTH SPRING	24957-24957	MAXWELTON	25051-25051	COSTA
24801-24801	WELCH	24870-24870	OCEANA	24958-24958	MEADOW BLUFF	25053-25053	DANVILLE
24808-24808	ANAWALT	24871-24871	PAGETON	24961-24961	NEOLA	25054-25054	DAWES
24810-24810	ASHLAND	24872-24872	PANTHER	24962-24962	PENCE SPRINGS	25057-25057	DEEP WATER
24811-24811	AVONDALE	24873-24873	PAYNESVILLE	24963-24963	PETERSTOWN	25059-25059	DIXIE
24813-24813	BARTLEY	24874-24874	PINEVILLE	24966-24966	RENICK	25060-25060	DOROTHY
24815-24815	BERWIND	24877-24877	POWHATAN	24970-24970	RONCEVERTE	25061-25061	DRYBRANCH
24816-24816	BIG SANDY	24878-24878	PREMIER	24974-24974	SECONDCREEK	25062-25062	DRY CREEK
24817-24817	BRADSHAW	24879-24879	RAYSAL	24976-24976	SINKS GROVE	25063-25063	DUCK
24818-24818	BRENTON	24880-24880	ROCK VIEW	24977-24977	SMOOT	25064-25064	DUNBAR
24820-24820	CAPELS	24881-24881	RODERFIELD	24981-24981	TALCOTT	25067-25067	EAST BANK
24821-24821	CARETTA	24882-24882	SIMON	24983-24983	UNION	25070-25070	ELEANOR
24822-24822	CLEAR FORK	24883-24883	SKYGUSTY	24984-24984	WAITEVILLE	25071-25071	ELKVIEW
24823-24823	COAL MOUNTAIN	24884-24884	SQUIRE	24985-24985	WAYSIDE	25075-25075	ESKDALE
24824-24824	COALWOOD	24887-24887	SWITCHBACK	24986-24986	WHITE SULPHUR	25076-25076	ETHEL
24825-24825	CRUMPLER	24888-24888	THORPE		SPRINGS	25079-25079	FALLING ROCK
24826-24826	CUCUMBER	24889-24889	TWIN BRANCH	24991-24991	WILLIAMSBURG	25081-25081	FOSTER
24827-24827	CYCLONE	24892-24892	WAR	24993-24993	WOLFCREEK	25082-25082	FRAZIERS BOTTOM
24828-24828	DAVY	24894-24894	WARRIORMINE	25002-25002	ALLOY	25083-25083	GALLAGHER
24829-24829	ECKMAN	24895-24895	WILCOE	25003-25003	ALUM CREEK	25085-25085	GAULEY BRIDGE
24830-24830	ELBERT	24896-24896	WOLF PEN	25004-25004	AMEAGLE	25086-25086	GLASGOW
24831-24831	ELKHORN	24897-24897	WORTH	25005-25005	AMMA	25088-25088	GLEN
24832-24832	ENGLISH	24898-24898	WYOMING	25007-25007	ARNETT	25090-25090	GLEN FERRIS
24834-24834	FANROCK	24899-24899	YUKON	25008-25008	ARTIE	25093-25093	GORDON
24836-24836	GARY	24901-24901	LEWISBURG	25009-25009	ASHFORD	25095-25095	GRIMMS LANDING
24839-24839	HANOVER	24902-24902	FAIRLEA	25010-25010	BALD KNOB	25102-25102	HANDLEY
24841-24841	HAVACO	24910-24910	ALDERSON	25011-25011	BANCROFT	25103-25103	HANSFORD
24842-24842	HEMPHILL	24915-24915	ARBOVALE	25015-25015	BELLE	25105-25105	HARRISON
24843-24843	HENSLEY	24916-24916	ASBURY	25018-25018	BENTREE	25106-25106	HENDERSON
24844-24844	IAEGER	24917-24917	AUTO	25019-25019	BICKMORE	25107-25107	HERNSHAW
24845-24845	IKES FORK	24918-24918	BALLARD	25021-25021	BIM	25108-25108	HEWETT

25109-25109	HOMETOWN	25261-25261	MILLSTONE	25564-25564	SOD	25832-25832	DANIELS
25110-25110	HUGHESTON	25262-25262	MILLWOOD	25565-25565	SPURLOCKVILLE	25833-25833	DOTHAN
25111-25111	INDORE	25264-25264	MOUNT ALTO	25567-25567	SUMERCO	25836-25836	ECCLES
25112-25112	INSTITUTE	25265-25265	NEW HAVEN	25569-25569	TEAYS	25837-25837	EDMOND
25113-25113	IVYDALE	25266-25266	NEWTON	25570-25570	WAYNE	25839-25839	FAIRDALE
25114-25114	JEFFREY	25267-25267	NORMANTOWN	25571-25571	WEST HAMLIN	25840-25840	FAYETTEVILLE
25115-25115	KANAWHA FALLS	25268-25268	ORMA	25572-25572	WOODVILLE	25841-25841	FLAT TOP
25118-25118	KIMBERLY	25270-25270	REEDY	25573-25573	YAWKEY	25843-25843	GHENT
25119-25119	KINCAID	25271-25271	RIPLEY	25601-25601	LOGAN	25844-25844	GLEN DANIEL
25120-25120	KINGSTON	25272-25272	ROCK CASTLE	25606-25606	ACCOVILLE	25845-25845	GLEN FORK
25121-25121	LAKE	25274-25274	SAND RIDGE	25607-25607	AMHERSTDALE	25846-25846	GLEN JEAN
25122-25122	LEEWOOD	25275-25275	SANDYVILLE	25608-25608	BAISDEN	25847-25847	GLEN MORGAN
25123-25123	LEON	25276-25276	SPENCER	25611-25611	BRUNO	25848-25848	GLEN ROGERS
25124-25124	LIBERTY	25279-25279	STATTS MILLS	25612-25612	CHAUNCEY	25849-25849	GLEN WHITE
25125-25125	LIZEMORES	25281-25281	TARIFF	25614-25614	CORA	25851-25851	HARPER
25126-25126	LONDON	25283-25283	VALLEY FORK	25617-25617	DAVIN	25853-25853	HELEN
25130-25130	MADISON	25285-25285	WALLBACK	25620-25620	EMMETT	25854-25854	HICO
25132-25132	MAMMOTH	25286-25286	WALTON	25621-25621	GILBERT	25855-25855	HILLTOP
25133-25133	MAYSEL	25287-25287	WEST COLUMBIA	25623-25623	HAMPDEN	25856-25856	JONBEN
25134-25134	MIAMI	25301-25396	CHARLESTON	25624-25624	HENLAWSON	25857-25857	JOSEPHINE
25136-25136	MONTGOMERY	25401-25402	MARTINSBURG	25625-25625	HOLDEN	25859-25859	KILSYTH
25139-25139	MOUNT CARBON	25410-25410	BAKERTON	25628-25628	KISTLER	25860-25860	LANARK
25140-25140	NAOMA	25411-25411	BERKELEY SPRINGS	25630-25630	LORADO	25862-25862	LANSING
25141-25141	NEBO	25413-25413	BUNKER HILL	25631-25631	LUNDALE	25864-25864	LAYLAND
25142-25142	NELLIS	25414-25414	CHARLES TOWN	25632-25632	LYBURN	25865-25865	LESTER
25143-25143	NITRO	25419-25419	FALLING WATERS	25634-25634	MALLORY	25866-25866	LOCHGELLY
25147-25147	OHLEY	25420-25420	GERRARDSTOWN	25635-25635	MAN	25867-25867	LONG BRANCH
25148-25148	ORGAS	25421-25421	GLENGARY	25636-25636	MONAVILLE	25868-25868	LOOKOUT
25149-25149	OTTAWA	25422-25422	GREAT CACAPON	25637-25637	MOUNT GAY	25870-25870	MABEN
25150-25150	OVAPA	25423-25423	HALLTOWN	25638-25638	OMAR	25871-25871	MABSCOTT
25152-25152	PAGE	25425-25425	HARPERS FERRY	25639-25639	PEACH CREEK	25873-25873	MAC ARTHUR
25154-25154	PEYTONA	25427-25427	HEDGESVILLE	25643-25643	ROSSMORE	25875-25875	MC GRAWS
25156-25156	PINCH	25428-25428	INWOOD	25644-25644	SARAH ANN	25876-25876	SAULSVILLE
25158-25158	PLINY	25429-25430	KEARNEYSVILLE	25645-25645	STIRRAT	25878-25878	MIDWAY
25159-25159	POCA	25431-25431	LEVELS	25646-25646	STOLLINGS	25879-25879	MINDEN
25160-25160	POND GAP	25432-25432	MILLVILLE	25647-25647	SWITZER	25880-25880	MOUNT HOPE
25161-25161	POWELLTON	25434-25434	PAW PAW	25648-25648	TAPLIN	25882-25882	MULLENS
25162-25162	PRATT	25437-25437	POINTS	25649-25649	VERDUNVILLE	25901-25901	OAK HILL
25164-25164	PROCIOUS	25438-25438	RANSON	25650-25650	VERNER	25902-25902	ODD
25165-25165	RACINE	25440-25440	RIDGEWAY	25651-25651	WHARNCLIFFE	25904-25904	PAX
25168-25168	RED HOUSE	25441-25441	RIPPON	25652-25652	WHITMAN	25906-25906	PINEY VIEW
25169-25169	RIDGEVIEW	25442-25442	SHENANDOAH	25653-25653	WILKINSON	25907-25907	PRINCE
25173-25173	ROBSON		JUNCTION	25654-25654	YOLYN	25908-25908	PRINCEWICK
25174-25174	ROCK CREEK	25443-25443	SHEPHERDSTOWN	25661-25661	WILLIAMSON	25909-25909	PROSPERITY
25177-25177	SAINT ALBANS	25444-25444	SLANESVILLE	25665-25665	BORDERLAND	25911-25911	RALEIGH
25180-25180	SAXON	25446-25446	SUMMIT POINT	25666-25666	BREEDEN	25912-25912	RAMSEY
25181-25181	SETH	25501-25501	ALKOL	25667-25667	CHATTAROY	25913-25913	RAVENCLIFF
25182-25182	SHARON	25502-25502	APPLE GROVE	25669-25669	CRUM	25914-25914	REDSTAR
25183-25183	SHARPLES	25503-25503	ASHTON	25670-25670	DELBARTON	25915-25915	RHODELL
25185-25185	MOUNT OLIVE	25504-25504	BARBOURSVILLE	25671-25671	DINGESS	25916-25916	SABINE
25186-25186	SMITHERS	25505-25505	BIG CREEK	25672-25672	EDGARTON	25917-25917	SCARBRO
25187-25187	SOUTHSIDE	25506-25506	BRANCHLAND	25674-25674	KERMIT	25918-25918	SHADY SPRING
25193-25193	SYLVESTER	25507-25507	CEREDO	25676-25676	LENORE	25919-25919	SKELTON
25201-25201	TAD	25508-25508	CHAPMANVILLE	25678-25678	MATEWAN	25920-25920	SLAB FORK
25202-25202	TORNADO	25510-25510	CULLODEN	25682-25682	MEADOR	25921-25921	SOPHIA
25203-25203	TURTLE CREEK	25511-25511	DUNLOW	25685-25685	NAUGATUCK	25922-25922	SPANISHBURG
25204-25204	TWILIGHT	25512-25512	EAST LYNN	25686-25686	NEWTOWN	25926-25926	SPRAGUE
25205-25205	UNEEDA	25514-25514	FORT GAY	25687-25687	NOLAN	25927-25927	STANAFORD
25206-25206	VAN	25515-25515	GALLIPOLIS FERRY	25688-25688	NORTH MATEWAN	25928-25928	STEPHENSON
25208-25208	WHARTON	25517-25517	GENOA	25690-25690	RAGLAND	25931-25931	SUMMERLEE
25209-25209	WHITESVILLE	25519-25519	GLENHAYES	25691-25691	RAWL	25932-25932	SURVEYOR
25211-25211	WIDEN	25520-25520	GLENWOOD	25692-25692	RED JACKET	25934-25934	TERRY
25213-25213	WINFIELD	25521-25521	GRIFFITHSVILLE	25694-25694	THACKER	25936-25936	THURMOND
25214-25214	WINIFREDE	25523-25523	HAMLIN	25696-25696	VARNEY	25938-25938	VICTOR
25231-25231	ADVENT	25524-25524	HARTS	25697-25697	VULCAN	25942-25942	WINONA
25234-25234	ARNOLDSBURG	25526-25526	HURRICANE	25699-25699	WILSONDALE	25943-25943	WYCO
25235-25235	CHLOE	25529-25529	JULIAN	25701-25770	HUNTINGTON	25951-25951	HINTON
25239-25239	COTTAGEVILLE	25530-25530	KENOVA	25801-25802	BECKLEY	25958-25958	CHARMCO
25241-25241	EVANS	25534-25534	KIAHSVILLE	25810-25810	ALLEN JUNCTION	25961-25961	CRICHTON
25243-25243	GANDEEVILLE	25535-25535	LAVALETTE	25811-25811	AMIGO	25962-25962	RAINELLE
25244-25244	GAY	25537-25537	LESAGE	25812-25812	ANSTED	25965-25965	ELTON
25245-25245	GIVEN	25540-25540	MIDKIFF	25813-25813	BEAVER	25966-25966	GREEN SULPHUR
25247-25247	HARTFORD	25541-25541	MILTON	25814-25814	BECKWITH		SPRINGS
25248-25248	KENNA	25544-25544	MYRA	25816-25816	BLUE JAY	25967-25967	HINES
25250-25250	LAKIN	25545-25545	ONA	25817-25817	BOLT	25969-25969	JUMPING BRANCH
25251-25251	LEFT HAND	25547-25547	PECKS MILL	25818-25818	BRADLEY	25971-25971	LERONA
25252-25252	LE ROY	25550-25550	POINT PLEASANT	25820-25820	CAMP CREEK	25972-25972	LESLIE
25253-25253	LETART	25555-25555	PRICHARD	25823-25823	COAL CITY	25973-25973	LOCKBRIDGE
25256-25256	LINDEN	25557-25557	RANGER	25825-25825	COOL RIDGE	25976-25976	MEADOW BRIDGE
25258-25258	LOCKNEY	25559-25559	SALT ROCK	25826-25826	CORINNE	25977-25977	MEADOW CREEK
25259-25259	LOONEYVILLE	25560-25560	SCOTT DEPOT	25827-25827	CRAB ORCHARD	25978-25978	NIMITZ
25260-25260	MASON	25562-25562	SHOALS	25831-25831	DANESE	25979-25979	PIPESTEM

Zip	City	Zip	City	Zip	City	Zip	City
25981-25981	QUINWOOD	26230-26230	PICKENS	26415-26415	PENNSBORO	26624-26624	GASSAWAY
25984-25984	RUPERT	26234-26234	ROCK CAVE	26416-26416	PHILIPPI	26627-26627	HEATERS
25985-25985	SANDSTONE	26236-26236	SELBYVILLE	26419-26419	PINE GROVE	26629-26629	LITTLE BIRCH
25986-25986	SPRING DALE	26237-26237	TALLMANSVILLE	26421-26421	PULLMAN	26631-26631	NAPIER
25988-25988	TRUE	26238-26238	VOLGA	26422-26422	REYNOLDSVILLE	26634-26634	PERKINS
25989-25989	WHITE OAK	26241-26241	ELKINS	26423-26423	ROANOKE	26636-26636	ROSEDALE
26003-26003	WHEELING	26250-26250	BELINGTON	26424-26424	ROSEMONT	26638-26638	SHOCK
26030-26030	BEECH BOTTOM	26253-26253	BEVERLY	26425-26425	ROWLESBURG	26639-26639	STRANGE CREEK
26031-26031	BENWOOD	26254-26254	BOWDEN	26426-26426	SALEM	26641-26641	WILSIE
26032-26032	BETHANY	26257-26257	COALTON	26430-26430	SAND FORK	26651-26651	SUMMERSVILLE
26033-26033	CAMERON	26259-26259	DAILEY	26431-26431	SHINNSTON	26656-26656	BELVA
26034-26034	CHESTER	26260-26260	DAVIS	26434-26434	SHIRLEY	26660-26660	CALVIN
26035-26035	COLLIERS	26261-26261	RICHWOOD	26435-26435	SIMPSON	26662-26662	CANVAS
26036-26036	DALLAS	26263-26263	DRYFORK	26436-26436	SMITHBURG	26667-26667	DRENNEN
26037-26037	FOLLANSBEE	26264-26264	DURBIN	26437-26437	SMITHFIELD	26671-26671	GILBOA
26038-26038	GLEN DALE	26266-26266	UPPERGLADE	26438-26438	SPELTER	26674-26674	JODIE
26039-26039	GLEN EASTON	26267-26267	ELLAMORE	26440-26440	THORNTON	26675-26675	KESLERS CROSS LANES
26040-26040	MC MECHEN	26268-26268	GLADY	26443-26443	TROY	26676-26676	LEIVASY
26041-26041	MOUNDSVILLE	26269-26269	HAMBLETON	26444-26444	TUNNELTON	26678-26678	MOUNT LOOKOUT
26047-26047	NEW CUMBERLAND	26270-26270	HARMAN	26446-26446	VALLEY CHAPEL	26679-26679	MOUNT NEBO
26050-26050	NEWELL	26271-26271	HENDRICKS	26447-26447	WALKERSVILLE	26680-26680	NALLEN
26055-26055	PROCTOR	26273-26273	HUTTONSVILLE	26448-26448	WALLACE	26681-26681	NETTIE
26056-26056	NEW MANCHESTER	26275-26275	JUNIOR	26451-26451	WEST MILFORD	26684-26684	POOL
26058-26058	SHORT CREEK	26276-26276	KERENS	26452-26452	WESTON	26690-26690	SWISS
26059-26059	TRIADELPHIA	26278-26278	MABIE	26456-26456	WEST UNION	26691-26691	TIOGA
26060-26060	VALLEY GROVE	26280-26280	MILL CREEK	26461-26461	WILSONBURG	26704-26704	AUGUSTA
26062-26062	WEIRTON	26282-26282	MONTERVILLE	26462-26462	WOLF SUMMIT	26705-26705	AURORA
26070-26070	WELLSBURG	26283-26283	MONTROSE	26463-26463	WYATT	26707-26707	BAYARD
26074-26074	WEST LIBERTY	26285-26285	NORTON	26502-26507	MORGANTOWN	26710-26710	BURLINGTON
26075-26075	WINDSOR HEIGHTS	26287-26287	PARSONS	26519-26519	ALBRIGHT	26711-26711	CAPON BRIDGE
26101-26104	PARKERSBURG	26288-26288	WEBSTER SPRINGS	26520-26520	ARTHURDALE	26714-26714	DELRAY
26105-26105	VIENNA	26289-26289	RED CREEK	26521-26521	BLACKSVILLE	26716-26716	EGLON
26106-26106	PARKERSBURG	26290-26290	SAINT GEORGE	26522-26522	BOOTH	26717-26717	ELK GARDEN
26133-26133	BELLEVILLE	26291-26291	SLATYFORK	26524-26524	BRETZ	26719-26719	FORT ASHBY
26134-26134	BELMONT	26292-26292	THOMAS	26525-26525	BRUCETON MILLS	26720-26720	GORMANIA
26135-26135	BENS RUN	26293-26293	VALLEY BEND	26527-26527	CASSVILLE	26722-26722	GREEN SPRING
26136-26136	BIG BEND	26294-26294	VALLEY HEAD	26529-26529	CORE	26726-26726	KEYSER
26137-26137	BIG SPRINGS	26296-26296	WHITMER	26531-26531	DELLSLOW	26729-26729	KIRBY
26138-26138	BROHARD	26298-26298	BERGOO	26533-26533	EVERETTVILLE	26731-26731	LAHMANSVILLE
26141-26141	CRESTON	26301-26306	CLARKSBURG	26534-26534	GRANVILLE	26734-26734	MEDLEY
26142-26142	DAVISVILLE	26320-26320	ALMA	26535-26535	HAZELTON	26739-26739	MOUNT STORM
26143-26143	ELIZABETH	26321-26321	ALUM BRIDGE	26537-26537	KINGWOOD	26743-26743	NEW CREEK
26146-26146	FRIENDLY	26323-26323	ANMOORE	26541-26541	MAIDSVILLE	26750-26750	PIEDMONT
26147-26147	GRANTSVILLE	26325-26325	AUBURN	26542-26542	MASONTOWN	26753-26753	RIDGELEY
26148-26148	MACFARLAN	26327-26327	BEREA	26543-26543	OSAGE	26755-26755	RIO
26149-26149	MIDDLEBOURNE	26328-26328	BLANDVILLE	26544-26544	PENTRESS	26757-26757	ROMNEY
26150-26150	MINERAL WELLS	26330-26330	BRIDGEPORT	26546-26546	PURSGLOVE	26761-26761	SHANKS
26151-26151	MOUNT ZION	26332-26332	BRISTOL	26547-26547	REEDSVILLE	26763-26763	SPRINGFIELD
26152-26152	MUNDAY	26334-26334	BROWNTON	26554-26555	FAIRMONT	26764-26764	TERRA ALTA
26155-26155	NEW MARTINSVILLE	26335-26335	BURNSVILLE	26559-26559	BARRACKVILLE	26767-26767	WILEY FORD
26159-26159	PADEN CITY	26337-26337	CAIRO	26560-26560	BAXTER	26801-26801	BAKER
26160-26160	PALESTINE	26338-26338	CAMDEN	26561-26561	BIG RUN	26802-26802	BRANDYWINE
26161-26161	PETROLEUM	26339-26339	CENTER POINT	26562-26562	BURTON	26804-26804	CIRCLEVILLE
26162-26162	PORTERS FALLS	26342-26342	COXS MILLS	26563-26563	CAROLINA	26806-26806	FORT SEYBERT
26164-26164	RAVENSWOOD	26343-26343	CRAWFORD	26566-26566	COLFAX	26807-26807	FRANKLIN
26167-26167	READER	26346-26346	ELLENBORO	26568-26568	ENTERPRISE	26808-26808	HIGH VIEW
26169-26169	ROCKPORT	26347-26347	FLEMINGTON	26570-26570	FAIRVIEW	26810-26810	LOST CITY
26170-26170	SAINT MARYS	26348-26348	FOLSOM	26571-26571	FARMINGTON	26812-26812	MATHIAS
26173-26173	SHERMAN	26349-26349	GALLOWAY	26572-26572	FOUR STATES	26814-26814	RIVERTON
26175-26175	SISTERSVILLE	26350-26350	GILMER	26574-26574	GRANT TOWN	26815-26815	SUGAR GROVE
26178-26178	SMITHVILLE	26351-26351	GLENVILLE	26575-26575	HUNDRED	26816-26816	ARTHUR
26180-26180	WALKER	26354-26354	GRAFTON	26576-26576	IDAMAY	26817-26817	BLOOMERY
26181-26181	WASHINGTON	26361-26361	GYPSY	26578-26578	KINGMONT	26818-26818	FISHER
26184-26184	WAVERLY	26362-26362	HARRISVILLE	26581-26581	LITTLETON	26823-26823	CAPON SPRINGS
26186-26186	WILEYVILLE	26366-26366	HAYWOOD	26582-26582	MANNINGTON	26824-26824	JUNCTION
26187-26187	WILLIAMSTOWN	26369-26369	HEPZIBAH	26585-26585	METZ	26833-26833	MAYSVILLE
26201-26201	BUCKHANNON	26372-26372	HORNER	26586-26586	MONTANA MINES	26836-26836	MOOREFIELD
26202-26202	FENWICK	26374-26374	INDEPENDENCE	26587-26587	RACHEL	26838-26838	MILAM
26203-26203	ERBACON	26375-26375	INDUSTRIAL	26588-26588	RIVESVILLE	26845-26845	OLD FIELDS
26205-26205	CRAIGSVILLE	26376-26376	IRELAND	26589-26589	WADESTOWN	26847-26847	PETERSBURG
26206-26206	COWEN	26377-26377	JACKSONBURG	26590-26590	WANA	26851-26851	WARDENSVILLE
26208-26208	CAMDEN ON GAULEY	26378-26378	JANE LEW	26591-26591	WORTHINGTON	26852-26852	PURGITSVILLE
26209-26209	SNOWSHOE	26384-26384	LINN	26601-26601	SUTTON	26855-26855	CABINS
26210-26210	ADRIAN	26385-26385	LOST CREEK	26610-26610	BIRCH RIVER	26865-26865	YELLOW SPRING
26215-26215	CLEVELAND	26386-26386	LUMBERPORT	26611-26611	CEDARVILLE	26866-26866	UPPER TRACT
26217-26217	DIANA	26404-26404	MEADOWBROOK	26612-26612	CENTRALIA	26884-26884	SENECA ROCKS
26218-26218	FRENCH CREEK	26405-26405	MOATSVILLE	26615-26615	COPEN	26886-26886	ONEGO
26219-26219	FRENCHTON	26407-26407	MOUNTAIN	26617-26617	DILLE		
26222-26222	HACKER VALLEY	26408-26408	MOUNT CLARE	26618-26618	ELMIRA		
26224-26224	HELVETIA	26410-26410	NEWBURG	26619-26619	EXCHANGE		
26228-26228	KANAWHA HEAD	26411-26411	NEW MILTON	26621-26621	FLATWOODS		
26229-26229	LORENTZ	26412-26412	ORLANDO	26623-26623	FRAMETOWN		

Wisconsin

General Help Numbers:

Governor's Office
PO Box 7863   608-266-1212
Madison, WI 53707-7863   Fax 608-267-8983
http://www.wisconsin.gov/state/governor   8AM-5PM

Attorney General's Office
Justice Department   608-266-1221
PO Box 7857   Fax 608-267-2779
Madison, WI 53707-7857   8AM-5PM
http://www.doj.state.wi.us

State Court Administrator
Supreme Court   608-266-6828
PO Box 1688   Fax 608-267-0980
Madison, WI 53701-1688   8AM-5PM
http://www.courts.state.wi.us

State Archives
Archives Division   608-264-6450
816 State St   Fax 608-264-6486
Madison, WI 53706   8AM-5PM M-F, 9-4 SA
http://www.shsw.wisc.edu/archives

State Specifics:

Capital: Madison
Dane County

Time Zone: CST

Number of Counties: 72

Population: 5,363,675

Web Site: www.wisconsin.gov

State Agencies

Criminal Records

Wisconsin Department of Justice, Crime Information Bureau, Record Check Unit, PO Box 2688, Madison, WI 53701-2688 (Courier: 123 W Washington Ave, Madison, WI 53703); 608-266-5764, 608-266-7780 (Online Questions), 8AM-4:30PM.

http://www.doj.state.wi.us

Indexing & Storage: Records are available from July 1971 (when the agencies were required to save records) and are computerized. Records are indexed on inhouse computer.

Searching: Arrest records without dispositions are released. Include the following in your request-sex, race, full name, date of birth. All requests must be in writing. The following data is not released: juvenile records.

Access by: mail, fax, in person, online.

Fee & Payment: The fee is $13.00 per individual. Fee payee: Wisconsin Department of Justice. Prepayment required. Personal checks accepted. No credit cards accepted.

Mail search: Turnaround time: 7 to 10 days. A self addressed stamped envelope is requested.

Fax search: Incoming fax permitted only for customers with accounts. There must be a supply of return envelopes on hand.

In person search: Records are returned by mail.

Online search: The agency offers Internet access at http://wi-recordcheck.org. An account is required. Also, there is a free Internet service for access to the state's Circuit Courts' records. However, not all counties participate. Visit http://ccap.courts.state.wi.us.

Other access: State criminal history records can also be found at http://wi-recordcheck.org.

Registration and an account are required with the Crime Information Bureau.

Corporation Records
Limited Partnership Records
Limited Liability Company Records
Limited Liability Partnerships

Department of Financial Institutions, Division of Corporate & Consumer Services, PO Box 7846, Madison, WI 53707-7846 (Courier: 345 W Washington Ave, 3rd Floor, Madison, WI 53703); 608-261-7577, 608-267-6813 (Fax), 7:45AM-4:30PM.

http://www.wdfi.org

Indexing & Storage: Records are available from 1873. Any records that are not at this office are kept at the State Records Center or the State Archives, but you must go through this office for access. New records are available for inquiry immediately. Records are indexed on inhouse computer, microfilm.

Searching: Include the following in your request-full name of business. In addition to the articles of incorporation, corporation records include the following information: Annual Reports, Officers, Directors, Prior (merged) names, Reserved names and Name Changes.

Access by: mail, phone, in person, online.

Fee & Payment: ID reports are $5.00, simple copywork is $2.00 per document. Short form certificates of status are $5.00. Certified copies are $5.00 plus $.50 per page. In-person copies are $.10 do it yourself. Fee payee: Department of Financial Institutions. Prepayment required. Personal checks accepted. Credit cards accepted; Visa or MasterCard

Mail search: Turnaround time: 7 to 10 days. A self addressed stamped envelope is requested.

Phone search: No fee for telephone request. They will only give a verbal response from the on-screen information.

In person search: Turnaround time is while you wait.

Online search: Selected elements of the database ("CRIS" Corporate Registration System) are available online on the department's website at www.wdfi.org/corporations/crispix.

Other access: Some data is released in database format and is available for purchase in print form, cartridge or diskette.

Expedited service: Expedited service is available for mail searches. Turnaround time: 2 days. Add $25.00 per item.

Trademarks/Servicemarks
Trade Names

Secretary of State, Tradenames/Trademarks Division, PO Box 7848, Madison, WI 53707-7848 (Courier: 30 W Mifflin St, 10th Floor, Madison, WI 53702); 608-266-5653, 608-266-3159 (Fax), 7:45AM-4:30PM.

http://badger.state.wi.us/agencies/sos

Indexing & Storage: Records are available for the past 20 years. It takes 7-14 working days before new records are available for inquiry. Records are indexed on index cards.

Searching: All information is considered public record and they will release any information they have. Note that the data is not computerized. Include the following in your request-trademark/servicemark name, name of owner, date of application.

Access by: mail, phone, fax, in person.

Fee & Payment: There is no fee to see if a mark is listed. Plain copies of one records cost $2.00. For certified copies, the cost is $6.00 minimum, depending on the number of pages in the file. Fee payee: Secretary of State. Prepayment required. Personal checks accepted. No credit cards accepted.

Mail search: Turnaround time: 7 to 10 days.

Phone search: They will pull the file and give all available information over the phone.

Fax search: Same fees apply, $2.00 per copy if returned by fax. Turnaround time in 2-3 days.

In person search: You may make copies at $.10 per page.

Uniform Commercial Code
Federal Tax Liens
State Tax Liens

Department of Financial Institutions, CCS/UCC, PO Box 7847, Madison, WI 53707-7847 (Courier: 345 W Washington Ave 3rd Fl, Madison, WI 53703); 608-261-9548, 608-264-7965 (Fax), 7:45AM-4:30PM.

http://www.wdfi.org

Indexing & Storage: Records are available from 1965, if still in effect. Records 1977 to present maintained on microfiche. Records are indexed on inhouse computer.

Searching: Use search request form UCC-11. The search includes federal tax liens on businesses. Federal tax liens on individuals and state tax liens are filed at the county level, but will show up if entered on the statewide lien system. Include the following in your request-debtor name.

Access by: mail, phone, fax, in person, online.

Fee & Payment: The search fee is $10.00 per name, copies are $1.00 per page. Fee payee: Department of Financial Institutions. Prepayment required. Personal checks accepted. No credit cards accepted.

Mail search: Turnaround time: up to 5 days.

Phone search: Call for uncertified information, some data is given over the phone.

Fax search: Turnaround time is 2-7 days.

In person search: Searching is available in person.

Online search: There is free Internet access for most records. Some records may require a $1.00 fee. All requesters must be registered with a password.

Sales Tax Registrations

Revenue Department, Income, Sales, & Excise Tax Division, PO Box 8902, Madison, WI 53708-8902 (Courier: 125 S Webster, Madison, WI 53702); 608-266-2776, 608-267-1030 (Fax), 7:45AM-4:30PM.

http://www.dor.state.wi.us

Indexing & Storage: Records are available from 1963. Records are indexed on inhouse computer.

Searching: This agency will provide the data on the face of the tax permit-business name, address, tax permit number. Include the following in your request-business name, tax permit number.

Access by: mail, phone, in person.

Fee & Payment: There is no search fee, no copy fee.

Mail search: Turnaround time: 2 to 3 weeks. A self addressed stamped envelope is requested.

Phone search: Records are available by phone.

In person search: Searching is available in person.

Birth Certificates

The Center of Health Statistics, Vital Records, PO Box 309, Madison, WI 53701-0309 (Courier: One W Wilson St, Room 158, Madison, WI 53702); 608-266-1373, 608-266-1371 (Recording), 608-267-7820 (Genealogy), 608-255-2035 (Fax), 8AM-4:15PM.

http://www.dhfs.state.wi.us/VitalRecords

Indexing & Storage: Records are available from 1907 on. This office has the original records. The county of issue has a copy. New records are available for inquiry immediately. Records are indexed on microfiche.

Searching: Must have a signed release from person of record or immediate family member and include the reason for the inquiry for certified copies. Uncertified copy requests do not require a release or a reason, but cannot be expedited. Include the following in your request-full name, names of parents, mother's maiden name, date of birth, place of birth, relationship to person of record, reason for information request.

Access by: mail, fax, in person.

Fee & Payment: The fee is $12.00 per name. Add $2.00 per name per copy for additional copies. Uncertified copies are the same price. Fee payee: Vital Records. Prepayment required. Credit cards are for fax service only. Personal checks accepted. Credit cards accepted: MasterCard, Visa, AmEx, Discover.

Mail search: Turnaround time: 2 weeks. A self addressed stamped envelope is requested.

Fax search: See expedited service.

In person search: Turnaround time 2 to 4 hours.

Expedited service: Expedited service is available for fax searches. There is an additional $5.00 for use of a credit card and $15.50 for overnight shipping.

Death Records

The Center of Health Statistics, Vital Records, PO Box 309, Madison, WI 53701-0309 (Courier: One W Wilson St, Room 158, Madison, WI 53702); 608-266-1373, 608-266-1371 (Recording), 608-267-7820 (Genealogy), 608-255-2035 (Fax), 8AM-4:15PM.

http://www.dhfs.state.wi.us/VitalRecords

Indexing & Storage: Records are available from 1907 on. This office has the original records. The county of issue has a copy. New records are available for inquiry immediately. Records are indexed on microfiche.

Searching: Must have a signed release from immediate family member for certified copies. Uncertified copy requests do not require a release. Include the following in your request-full name, date of death, place of death, relationship to person of record, reason for information request.

Access by: mail, fax, in person.

Fee & Payment: The fee is $7.00 per name search. Add $2.00 per name per copy for additional copies. Uncertified copies are the same fee, but cannot be expedited. Fee payee: Vital Records. Prepayment required. Credit cards fax service only. Personal checks accepted. Credit cards accepted: MasterCard, Visa, AmEx, Discover.

Mail search: Turnaround time: 5 to 10 working days. A self addressed stamped envelope is requested.

Fax search: See expedited service.

In person search: Turnaround time 2 to 4 hours.

Expedited service: Expedited service is available for fax searches. The credit card fee is $5.00 and the overnight shipping fee is $15.50.

Marriage Certificates

The Center of Health Statistics, Vital Records, PO Box 309, Madison, WI 53701-0309 (Courier: One W Wilson St, Room 158, Madison, WI 53702); 608-266-1373, 608-266-1371 (Recording), 608-267-7820 (Genealogy), 608-255-2035 (Fax), 8AM-4:15PM.

http://www.dhfs.state.wi.us/VitalRecords

Indexing & Storage: Records are available from 1907 on. This office has the original records. The county of issue has a copy. New records are available for inquiry immediately. Records are indexed on microfiche.

Searching: Must have a signed release from the named parties for certified copies. Requests for uncertified copies do not require a release. Include the following in your request-names of husband and wife, date of marriage, place or county of marriage, reason for information request.

Access by: mail, fax, in person.

Fee & Payment: The fee is $7.00 per name search. Add $2.00 per name per copy for additional copies. The fee is the same for uncertified copies, but cannot be expedited. Fee payee: Vital Records. Prepayment required. Credit cards accepted for fax service only. Personal checks accepted. Credit cards accepted: MasterCard, Visa, AmEx, Discover.

Mail search: Turnaround time: 5 to 10 working days. A self addressed stamped envelope is requested.

Fax search: See expedited service.

In person search: Turnaround time 2 to 4 hours.

Expedited service: Available for fax requests. Using a credit card ($5.00 extra) required. Overnight shipping is $15.50.

Divorce Records

The Center of Health Statistics, Vital Records, PO Box 309, Madison, WI 53701-0309 (Courier: One W Wilson St, Room 158, Madison, WI 53702); 608-266-1373, 608-266-1371 (Recording), 608-267-7820 (Genealogy), 608-255-2035 (Fax), 8AM-4:15PM.

http://www.dhfs.state.wi.us/VitalRecords

Indexing & Storage: Records are available from 1907. Please note that this office does not house records for the years 1987, 1988 and 1989. You must search at the county level for those years.

New records are available for inquiry immediately. Records are indexed on microfiche.

Searching: Must have a signed release form from the persons of record for a certified copy. Requests for uncertified copies do not require a release. Include the following in your request-names of husband and wife, date of divorce, place of divorce, case number (if known), reason for information request.

Access by: mail, fax, in person.

Fee & Payment: The fee is $7.00 per name search. Add $2.00 per name per copy for additional copies. Uncertified copies are the same fee, but cannot be expedited. Fee payee: Vital Records. Prepayment required. Credit cards accepted for fax service only. Personal checks accepted. Credit cards accepted: MasterCard, Visa, AmEx, Discover.

Mail search: Turnaround time: 5 to 10 working days. A self addressed stamped envelope is requested.

Fax search: See expedited service.

In person search: Turnaround time 2 to 4 hours.

Expedited service: Expedited service is available for fax searches. Using a credit card (extra $5.00) is required. The overnight shipping fee is $15.50.

Workers' Compensation Records

Dept of Workforce Development, Worker's Compensation Division, PO Box 7901, Madison, WI 53707-7901 (Courier: 201 E Washington Ave, Madison, WI 53707); 608-266-1340, 7:45AM-4:30PM.

http://dwd.state.wi.us/wc

Indexing & Storage: Records are available for 12 years from last benefit payment. New records are available for inquiry immediately. Records are indexed on microfilm, inhouse computer. Records are normally destroyed after 12 years if they are inactive. May be on microfilm if there was activity in the last couple of years.

Searching: Must have release from claimant or be a party to the claim. Must also specify what records you request. Include the following in your request-claimant name, date of accident, employer. Also, submit either the claim number or the SSN. It is suggested to call first so that they can locate records.

Access by: mail, in person.

Fee & Payment: There is a $3.00 service fee plus $.20 per copy fee, $2.00 if certified. Fee payee: Workforce Department. Prepayment required. Personal checks accepted. No credit cards accepted.

Mail search: Turnaround time: 1 to 2 weeks. A self addressed stamped envelope is requested.

In person search: If you make the copies, the fee is $.10 per page, but you must BRING YOUR OWN DIMES. They will not make change. Certification is not available for walk-ins.

Driver Records

Division of Motor Vehicles, Records & Licensing Section, PO Box 7995, Madison, WI 53707-7995 (Courier: 4802 Sheboygan Ave, Room 301, Madison, WI 53707); 608-266-2353, 608-267-3636 (Fax), 7:30AM-4:30PM.

http://www.dot.state.wi.us

Note: Copies of tickets may be obtained from this address for $3.50 per citation.

Indexing & Storage: Records are available for 5 years from date of conviction for moving violations and suspensions/revocations, 10 years from date of convictions for alcohol-related violations, and 20 years withdrawal based on damage judgment. It takes no more than 15 days before new records are available for inquiry.

Searching: ID card information, juvenile record entries, arrests and medical information are confidential. Driver record information can be obtained per DPPA guidelines. The driver license number, or full name, DOB and sex are required when ordering a record. The driver's address is included as part of the search for approved requesters.

Access by: mail, phone, in person, online.

Fee & Payment: The fee is $3.00 per driving record. Fee payee: Division of Motor Vehicles. Prepayment required. Personal checks accepted. No credit cards accepted.

Mail search: Turnaround time: 3 days. No self addressed stamped envelope is required.

Phone search: Pre-approved accounts may order driving records by phone or fax. The fee is $4.00 if a human operator reads back the record or $3.00 for a digitized computer readback of record.

In person search: Turnaround time is normally within a few minutes.

Online search: Commercial online access is available for high volume users only, fee is $3.00 per record. Call 608-266-2353 for more information.

Other access: Wisconsin offers a magnetic tape retrieval system for high volume users. The state will, also, sell its license file without histories. For more information, call 608-266-1951.

Vehicle Ownership
Vehicle Identification

Department of Transportation, Vehicle Records Section, PO Box 7911, Madison, WI 53707-7911 (Courier: 4802 Sheboygan Ave, Room 205, Madison, WI 53707); 608-266-3666, 608-266-1466 (Registration Laws), 608-267-6966 (Fax), 7:30AM-4:30PM.

http://www.dot.state.wi.us

Indexing & Storage: Records are available for 7 years to present. It takes 10 to 15 days before new records are available for inquiry.

Searching: All DPPA restrictions apply. All casual or occasional requestors must submit a request form: MV2896. Depending on what record is required, records can be looked up by VIN, plate or by name & city or county.

Access by: mail, in person.

Fee & Payment: The fee is $3.00 per record, including lien searches. The photocopy fee is $.25 per page. Fee payee: Registration Fee Trust. Prepayment required. Personal checks accepted. No credit cards accepted.

Mail search: Turnaround time: 5 business days. A self addressed stamped envelope is requested.

In person search: The turnaround time is normally within a few minutes.

Other access: The state offers a variety of methods of obtaining bulk registration lists including tapes and microfiche. Tape input by a specific request list is available only to law enforcement. Call 608-266-2064 for more information. All DPPA restrictions apply.

Accident Reports

Division of Motor Vehicles, Traffic Accident Section, PO Box 7919, Madison, WI 53707-7919 (Courier: 4802 Sheboygan Ave, Room 804, Madison, WI 53707); 608-266-8753, 608-267-0606 (Fax), 7:30AM-4:30PM.

http://www.dot.state.wi.us

Indexing & Storage: Records are available for 5 years to present. It takes 30 days, on average, from receipt of report before new records are available for inquiry.

Searching: The information is public record. Records can be accessed by driver license number, by plate number, or by accident report number. If none of these items are available, the full name, DOB, and date of accident will be used. The following data is not released: juvenile records.

Access by: mail, phone, in person.

Fee & Payment: The fees are $4.05 for operator reports and $4.75 for police reports. Fee payee: Registration Fee Trust. Prepayment is required if charges are above $6.00. Personal checks accepted. No credit cards accepted.

Mail search: Turnaround time: 24 to 48 hours. No self addressed stamped envelope is required.

Phone search: 24 hour automated messaging system available to request copies.

In person search: Normal turnaround time is immediate.

Vessel Ownership
Vessel Registration

Department of Natural Resources, Boat Registration, PO Box 7236, Madison, WI 53707-7924 (Courier: 101 S Webster, Madison, WI 53703); 608-266-2107, 608-264-6130 (Fax), 7:45AM-4:30PM.

http://www.dnr.state.wi.us

Indexing & Storage: Records are available from 1978 to present. Records are indexed on computer. All motorized boats and all sailboats must be registered. All motorized boats and all sailboats, if 16 ft or over, must be titled. Lien information shows on title records.

Searching: To search one of the following is required: name, hull ID #, or boat registration #.

Access by: mail, phone, fax, in person.

Fee & Payment: There is no search fee unless the search is really involved, in which case the fee is $5.00 per name. Fee payee: DNR. Personal checks accepted. No credit cards accepted.

Mail search: Turnaround time: 1 to 2 days. No self addressed stamped envelope is required.

Phone search: Records are available by phone.

Fax search: Same criteria as mail searching.

In person search: Unless the search is a simple record check, records are returned by mail the next day.

Other access: Data is available in bulk release on disks, labels, and printed lists. For further information, call Cyndy Lawler at (608) 261-6410.

Legislation Records

Wisconsin Legislation, Legislative Reference Bureau, PO Box 2037, Madison, WI 53701-2037 (Courier: 100 N. Hamilton Street, Madison, WI 53703); 608-266-0341, 800-362-9472 (Bill Status), 608-266-5648 (Fax), 7:45AM-5PM.

http://www.legis.state.wi.us

Note: Call first if you need bill number or act number and they will find it for you. Then you must call or go to Legislative Document Room 608, 608-266-2400, for actual copies.

Indexing & Storage: Records are available from 1848 on. Records are computerized since 1995.

Searching: Drafts are not available. Include the following in your request-bill number, topic of bill.

Access by: mail, phone, in person, online.

Fee & Payment: There is no search fee. Fee payee: Wisconsin Legislature. Personal checks accepted. No credit cards accepted.

Mail search: Turnaround time: variable. No self addressed stamped envelope is required.

Phone search: There is a nominal fee for microfiche or paper copies.

In person search: Searching is available in person.

Online search: Information on current bills is available over the Internet. There is a Folio Program to search text of previous session bills.

Voter Registration
Records not maintained by a state level agency.

Note: All records are maintained at the municipal level. Although records are open to the public be advised that not all municipalities maintain voter lists. Not all voters are registered.

GED Certificates

Department of Public Instruction, GED Program, PO Box 7841, Madison, WI 53707-7841 (Courier: 125 S Webster, Madison, WI 53707); 608-267-9245, 800-441-4563, 608-264-9552 (Fax).

http://www.dpi.state.wi.us

Searching: To search, the SSN and DOB are required. For a transcript, include a signed release.

Access by: mail, phone, fax, in person.

Fee & Payment: There is no fee.

Mail search: Turnaround time: 1 week. No self addressed stamped envelope is required.

Phone search: A requester can leave a message, with all required data, and the agency will call back with verification.

Fax search: Same criteria as mail searching.

In person search: Searching is available in person.

Hunting License Information
Fishing License Information
Access to Records is Restricted

Dept of Natural Resources, Fish & Game Licensing Division, PO Box 7921, Madison, WI 53707 (Courier: 101 S Webster St, Madison, WI 53703); 608-266-2621, 608-264-6130 (Fax), 8AM-4:30PM.

http://www.dnr.state.wi.us

Note: They do not have a central database. Only vendors have the names and addresses and they supply to local county clerks. A new automated issuance system is planned that will change availability.

Wisconsin State Licensing Agencies

Licenses Searchable Online

License	URL
Accounting Firm #02	http://drlchq.state.wi.us/plsql/chq/cred_holder_query
Acupuncturist #04	http://165.189.238.43/plsql/plsql/Search_Ind_Health
Adjustment Service Company #06	www.wdfi.org/fi/lfs/licensee_lists
Aesthetics Establishment/Specialty School #02	http://drlchq.state.wi.us/plsql/chq/cred_holder_query
Aesthetics Instructor #01	http://165.189.238.43/plsql/plsql/Search_Ind_Bdp
Appraiser, General(Certified or Licensed) #01	http://165.189.238.43/plsql/plsql/Search_Ind_Bdp
Appraiser, Residential #01	http://165.189.238.43/plsql/plsql/Search_Ind_Bdp
Architect #01	http://165.189.238.43/plsql/plsql/Search_Ind_Bdp
Architectural Corporation #02	http://drlchq.state.wi.us/plsql/chq/cred_holder_query
Art Therapist #04	http://165.189.238.43/plsql/plsql/Search_Ind_Health
Auction Company #02	http://drlchq.state.wi.us/plsql/chq/cred_holder_query
Auctioneer #01	http://165.189.238.43/plsql/plsql/Search_Ind_Bdp
Audiologist #04	http://165.189.238.43/plsql/plsql/Search_Ind_Health
Bank #05	www.wdfi.org/fi/banks/licensee_lists/default.asp
Barber #01	http://165.189.238.43/plsql/plsql/Search_Ind_Bdp
Barber School #02	http://drlchq.state.wi.us/plsql/chq/cred_holder_query
Barber/Apprentice/Instructor/Manager #01	http://165.189.238.43/plsql/plsql/Search_Ind_Bdp
Boxer #01	http://165.189.238.43/plsql/plsql/Search_Ind_Bdp
Boxing Club (Amateur or Professional) #02	http://drlchq.state.wi.us/plsql/chq/cred_holder_query
Boxing Show Permit #02	http://drlchq.state.wi.us/plsql/chq/cred_holder_query
Cemetery Authority/Warehouse #02	http://drlchq.state.wi.us/plsql/chq/cred_holder_query
Cemetery Preneed Seller #01	http://165.189.238.43/plsql/plsql/Search_Ind_Bdp
Cemetery Salesperson #01	http://165.189.238.43/plsql/plsql/Search_Ind_Bdp
Charitable Organization #02	http://drlchq.state.wi.us/plsql/chq/cred_holder_query
Check Seller #06	www.wdfi.org/fi/lfs/licensee_lists
Chiropractor #04	http://165.189.238.43/plsql/plsql/Search_Ind_Health
Collection Agency #06	www.wdfi.org/fi/lfs/licensee_lists
Cosmetologist #01	http://165.189.238.43/plsql/plsql/Search_Ind_Bdp
Cosmetology School #02	http://drlchq.state.wi.us/plsql/chq/cred_holder_query
Cosmetology Instructor/Manager/Apprentice #01	http://165.189.238.43/plsql/plsql/Search_Ind_Bdp
Counselor, Professional #04	http://165.189.238.43/plsql/plsql/Search_Ind_Health
Credit Service Organization #05	www.wdfi.org/fi/cu/chartered_lists/default.asp
Credit Union #05	www.wdfi.org/fi/cu/chartered_lists/default.asp
Currency Exchange #06	www.wdfi.org/fi/lfs/licensee_lists
Dance Therapist #04	http://165.189.238.43/plsql/plsql/Search_Ind_Health
Debt Collector #06	www.wdfi.org/fi/lfs/licensee_lists
Dental Hygienist #04	http://165.189.238.43/plsql/plsql/Search_Ind_Health
Dentist #04	http://165.189.238.43/plsql/plsql/Search_Ind_Health
Designer of Engineering Systems #01	http://165.189.238.43/plsql/plsql/Search_Ind_Bdp
Dietitian #04	http://165.189.238.43/plsql/plsql/Search_Ind_Health
Drug Distributor/Manufacturer #02	http://drlchq.state.wi.us/plsql/chq/cred_holder_query
Electrologist #01	http://165.189.238.43/plsql/plsql/Search_Ind_Bdp
Electrology Establishment/Specialty School #02	http://drlchq.state.wi.us/plsql/chq/cred_holder_query
Electrology Instructor #01	http://165.189.238.43/plsql/plsql/Search_Ind_Bdp
Engineer/Engineer in Training #01	http://165.189.238.43/plsql/plsql/Search_Ind_Bdp
Engineering Corporation #02	http://drlchq.state.wi.us/plsql/chq/cred_holder_query
Firearms Permit #02	http://drlchq.state.wi.us/plsql/chq/cred_holder_query
Fund Raiser, Professional #01	http://165.189.238.43/plsql/plsql/Search_Ind_Bdp
Fund Raising Counsel #02	http://drlchq.state.wi.us/plsql/chq/cred_holder_query
Funeral Director/Director Apprentice #01	http://165.189.238.43/plsql/plsql/Search_Ind_Bdp
Funeral Establishment #02	http://drlchq.state.wi.us/plsql/chq/cred_holder_query
Funeral Preneed Seller #01	http://165.189.238.43/plsql/plsql/Search_Ind_Bdp
Geologist #01	http://165.189.238.43/plsql/plsql/Search_Ind_Bdp
Geology Firm #02	http://drlchq.state.wi.us/plsql/chq/cred_holder_query
Hearing Instrument Specialist #04	http://165.189.238.43/plsql/plsql/Search_Ind_Health
Home Inspector #01	http://165.189.238.43/plsql/plsql/Search_Ind_Bdp
Hydrologist #01	http://165.189.238.43/plsql/plsql/Search_Ind_Bdp
Hydrology Firm #02	http://drlchq.state.wi.us/plsql/chq/cred_holder_query
Insurance Company #06	http://badger.state.wi.us/agencies/oci/dir_ins.htm
Insurance Premium Finance Company #06	www.wdfi.org/fi/lfs/licensee_lists
Interior Designer #01	http://165.189.238.43/plsql/plsql/Search_Ind_Bdp
Investment Advisor/Advisor Representative #10	www.wdfi.org/fi/securities/licensing/licensee_lists/default.asp
Land Surveyor #01	http://165.189.238.43/plsql/plsql/Search_Ind_Bdp
Landscape Architect #01	http://165.189.238.43/plsql/plsql/Search_Ind_Bdp

Loan Company #06 .... www.wdfi.org/fi/lfs/licensee_lists
Loan Solicitor/Originator #05 .... www.wdfi.org/fi/mortbank/default.htm
Lobbying Organization, Principal #11 .... http://ethics.state.wi.us/Scripts/OEL2000.asp
Lobbyist #11 .... http://ethics.state.wi.us/Scripts/Lobbyists2000.asp
Manicurist Establishment/Specialty School #02 .... http://drlchq.state.wi.us/plsql/chq/cred_holder_query
Manicurist/Manicurist Instructor #01 .... http://165.189.238.43/plsql/plsql/Search_Ind_Bdp
Marriage & Family Therapist #04 .... http://165.189.238.43/plsql/plsql/Search_Ind_Health
Massage Therapist/Bodyworker #04 .... http://165.189.238.43/plsql/plsql/Search_Ind_Health
Medical Doctor/Surgeon #04 .... http://165.189.238.43/plsql/plsql/Search_Ind_Health
Midwife Nurse #04 .... http://165.189.238.43/plsql/plsql/Search_Ind_Health
Mobile Home & RV Dealer #06 .... www.wdfi.org/fi/lfs/licensee_lists
Mortgage Banker/Broker #05 .... www.wdfi.org/fi/mortbank/default.htm
Motorcycle Dealer #06 .... www.wdfi.org/fi/lfs/licensee_lists
Music Therapist #04 .... http://165.189.238.43/plsql/plsql/Search_Ind_Health
Nurse-RN-LPN #04 .... http://165.189.238.43/plsql/plsql/Search_Ind_Health
Nursing Home Administrator #01 .... http://165.189.238.43/plsql/plsql/Search_Ind_Bdp
Occupational Therapist/Therapy Assistant #04 ..... http://165.189.238.43/plsql/plsql/Search_Ind_Health
Optometrist #04 .... http://165.189.238.43/plsql/plsql/Search_Ind_Health
Payday Lender #06 .... www.wdfi.org/fi/lfs/licensee_lists
Pharmacy/Pharmacist #04 .... http://165.189.238.43/plsql/plsql/Search_Ind_Health
Physical Therapist #04 .... http://165.189.238.43/plsql/plsql/Search_Ind_Health
Physician Assistant #04 .... http://165.189.238.43/plsql/plsql/Search_Ind_Health
Podiatrist #04 .... http://165.189.238.43/plsql/plsql/Search_Ind_Health
Private Detective #01 .... http://165.189.238.43/plsql/plsql/Search_Ind_Bdp
Private Detective Agency #02 .... http://drlchq.state.wi.us/plsql/chq/cred_holder_query
Psychologist #04 .... http://165.189.238.43/plsql/plsql/Search_Ind_Health
Public Accountant #01 .... http://165.189.238.43/plsql/plsql/Search_Ind_Bdp
Real Estate Appraiser #01 .... http://165.189.238.43/plsql/plsql/Search_Ind_Bdp
Real Estate Broker/Salesperson #01 .... http://165.189.238.43/plsql/plsql/Search_Ind_Bdp
Real Estate Business Entity #02 .... http://drlchq.state.wi.us/plsql/chq/cred_holder_query
Respiratory Care Practitioner #04 .... http://165.189.238.43/plsql/plsql/Search_Ind_Health
Sales Finance Company/Loan Company #06 .... www.wdfi.org/fi/lfs/licensee_lists
Savings & Loan Sales Finance Company #06 .... www.wdfi.org/fi/lfs/licensee_lists
Savings Institution #05 .... www.wdfi.org/fi/savings_institutions/licensee_lists/default.asp
School Psychology Private Practice #04 .... http://165.189.238.43/plsql/plsql/Search_Ind_Health
Securities Broker/Dealer/Agent #10 .... www.wdfi.org/fi/securities/licensing/licensee_lists/default.asp
Security Guard #01 .... http://165.189.238.43/plsql/plsql/Search_Ind_Bdp
Social Worker #04 .... http://165.189.238.43/plsql/plsql/Search_Ind_Health
Soil Science Firm #02 .... http://drlchq.state.wi.us/plsql/chq/cred_holder_query
Soil Scientist #01 .... http://165.189.238.43/plsql/plsql/Search_Ind_Bdp
Speech Pathologist/Audiologist #04 .... http://165.189.238.43/plsql/plsql/Search_Ind_Health
Timeshare Salesperson #01 .... http://165.189.238.43/plsql/plsql/Search_Ind_Bdp
Veterinarian/Veterinary Technician #04 .... http://165.189.238.43/plsql/plsql/Search_Ind_Health

Licensing Quick Finder

Accounting Firm #02 .... 608-266-5511 X43
Acupuncturist #04 608-266-0145
Adjustment Counselor #06 608-261-9555
Adjustment Service Company #06 608-267-3776
Aesthetics Establishment/Specialty School #02 ....
.... 608-266-5511 X43
Aesthetics Instructor #01 .... 608-266-5511 X42
Appraiser, General #01 .... 608-266-5511 X43
Appraiser, Residential #01 .... 608-266-5511 X43
Architect #01 .... 608-266-5511 X43
Architectural Corporation #02 .... 608-266-5511 X43
Art Therapist #04 608-266-2811
Asbestos Worker #17 608-267-2297
Attorney #16 608-257-3838
Auction Company #02 .... 608-266-5511 X43
Auctioneer #01 .... 608-266-5511 X43
Audiologist #04 608-266-0145
Bank #05 608-261-7578
Barber #01 .... 608-266-5511 X42
Barber School #02 .... 608-266-5511 X43
Barber/Apprentice/Instructor/Manager #01 ....
.... 608-266-5511 X43
Beer Wholesaler #08 608-266-2776
Boiler Repairer #19 608-261-8500

Boxer #01 .... 608-266-5511 X442
Boxing Club (Amateur or Professional) #02 ....
.... 608-266-5511 X43
Boxing Show Permit #02 .... 608-266-5511 X43
Building Inspector #19 608-261-8500
Business Tax Registration #08 608-266-2776
Cemetery Authority/Warehouse #02 ....
.... 608-266-5511 X441
Cemetery Preneed Seller #01 ...... 608-266-5511 X441
Cemetery Salesperson #01 .... 608-266-5511 X441
Charitable Gaming #14 608-270-2555
Charitable Organization #02 .... 608-266-5511 X441
Check Seller #06 ....,............... 608-267-3776
Chiropractor #04 608-266-0145
Cigarette & Tobacco Dist./Vendor/Multiple Retailer #08
.... 608-266-2776
Cigarette & Tobacco Warehouser/Wholesaler/Jobber
#08 608-266-2776
Collection Agency #06 608-267-3776
Cosmetologist #01 .... 608-266-5511 X42
Cosmetology School #02 .... 608-266-5511 X43
Cosmetology Instructor/Manager/Apprentice #01 ....
.... 608-266-5511 X43
Counselor, Professional #04 608-266-0145

Credit Service Organization #05 608-266-9543
Credit Union #05 608-266-9543
Currency Exchange #06 608-267-3776
Dance Therapist #04 608-266-2811
Debt Collector #06 608-267-3776
Dental Hygienist #04 608-266-2811
Dentist #04 608-266-2811
Designer of Engineering Systems #01 ....
.... 608-266-5511 X42
Dietitian #04 608-266-0145
Director of Instruction #15 608-266-1027
Dog Racing #14 608-270-2555
Drug Distributor/Mfg. #02 .... 608-266-5511 X43
Electrical Inspector #19 608-261-8500
Electrician #19 608-261-8500
Electrologist #01 .... 608-266-5511 X43
Electrology Establishment/Specialty School #02 ....
.... 608-266-5511 X43
Electrology Instructor #01 .... 608-266-5511 X43
Emergency Medical Technician/Paramedic #07 ....
.... 608-266-1568
Employee Benefits Plan Admin. #12 608-267-1238
Engineer/Engineer in Training #1 ... 608-266-5511 X42
Engineering Corporation #02 .... 608-266-5511 X43

Excise Tax Permit #08	608-266-2776
Fertilizer #09	608-224-4548
Firearms Permit #02	608-266-5511 X43
Fireworks Manufacturing #19	608-261-8500
Fuel Tax Permit #08	608-266-2776
Fund Raiser, Professional #01	608-266-5511 X441
Fund Raising Counsel #02	608-266-5511 X441
Funeral Director/Director Apprentice #1	608-266-5511 X442
Funeral Establishment #02	608-266-5511 X43
Funeral Preneed Seller #01	608-266-5511 X442
Geologist #01	608-266-5511 X42
Geology Firm #02	608-266-5511 X43
Hearing Instrument Specialist #04	608-266-2811
Home Inspector #01	608-266-5511 X43
Hydrologist #01	608-266-5511 X42
Hydrology Firm #02	608-266-5511 X43
Indian Gaming Vendor #14	608-270-2555
Insurance Company #06	608-267-3776
Insurance Intermediary #12	608-266-8699
Insurance Premium Finance Company #06	608-267-3776
Interior Designer #01	608-266-5511 X43
Investment Advisor/Advisor Rep. #10	608-266-3693
Land Surveyor #01	608-266-5511 X43
Landfill Operator #18	608-267-6744
Landscape Architect #01	608-266-5511 X42
Liquor, Wholesale #08	608-266-2776
Loan Company #06	608-267-1708
Loan Solicitor/Originator #05	608-261-7578
Lobbying Organization, Principal #11	608-266-8123
Lobbyist #11	608-266-8123
Manicurist Establishment/Specialty School #02	

	608-266-5511 X43
Manicurist/Manicurist Instructor #1	608-266-5511 X43
Marriage & Family Therapist #04	608-266-0145
Massage Therapist/Bodyworker #04	608-266-2811
Medical Doctor/Surgeon #04	608-266-2811
Midwife Nurse #04	608-266-0145
Mobile Home & RV Dealer #06	608-267-3743
Mortgage Banker/Broker #05	608-261-7578
Motorcycle Dealer #06	608-267-3743
Music Therapist #04	608-266-2811
Notary Public #13	608-266-5594
Nurse-RN-LPN #04	608-266-0145
Nursing Home Administrator #01	608-266-5511 X43
Occupational Therapist/Therapy Assistant #04	608-266-2811
Optometrist #04	608-266-0145
Osteopathic Physician #04	608-266-2811
Payday Lender #06	608-267-1708
Pesticide Applicator/Application Business #09	608-224-4548
Pesticide Dealer #09	608-224-4548
Pesticide Vet Clinic #09	608-224-4548
Pharmacy/Pharmacist #04	608-266-2811
Physical Therapist #04	608-266-2811
Physician Assistant #04	608-266-2811
Plumber #19	608-261-8500
Podiatrist #04	608-266-2811
Private Detective #01	608-266-5511 X43
Private Detective Agency #02	608-266-5511 X43
Psychologist #04	608-266-0145
Public Accountant #01	608-266-5511 X42
Racing/Racing Vendor #14	608-270-2555
Real Estate Appraiser #01	608-266-5511 X42

Real Estate Broker/Salesman #1	608-266-5511 X43
Real Estate Business Entity #02	608-266-5511 X43
Respiratory Care Practitioner #04	608-266-2811
Sales Finance Company/Loan Company #06	608-267-3743
Sales Witholding Tax Registration #08	608-266-2776
Sanitarian #17	608-266-8018
Savings & Loan Sales Finance Company #06	608-267-3743
Savings Institution #05	608-261-4335
School Counselor #15	608-266-1027
School Librarian/Media Specialist #15	608-266-1027
School Nurse #15	608-266-1027
School Principal/Superintendent/Business Mgr #15	608-266-1027
School Psychologist/Social Worker #15	608-266-1027
School Psychology Private Practice #4	608-266-0145
Securities Broker/Dealer/Agent #10	608-266-3693
Security Guard #01	608-266-5511 X43
Social Worker #04	608-266-0145
Soil Science Firm #02	608-266-5511 X43
Soil Scientist #01	608-266-5511 X42
Soil Tester #19	608-261-8500
Speech Pathologist/Audiologist #04	608-266-2811
Teacher #15	608-266-1027
Timeshare Salesperson #01	608-266-5511 X43
Veterinarian/Veterinary Technician #4	608-266-2811
Viatical Settlement Broker #12	608-266-8699
Vocational Education Coordinator, Local #15	608-266-1027
Welder #19	608-261-8500
Wine Distributor, Public #08	608-266-2776

Licensing Agency Information

#01 Department of Regulation and Licensing, PO Box 8935 (1400 E Washington), Madison, WI 53708-8935; 608-266-5511, Fax: 608-267-3816. www.state.wi.us/agencies/drl/
Direct web site URL to search for licensees: http://165.189.238.43/plsql/plsql/Search_Ind_Bdp. You can search online using name or credential number

#02 Dept of Regulation & Licensing, PO Box 8935, Madison, WI 53708-8935; 608-266-5511, Fax: 608-267-3816.
http://badger.state.wi.us/agencies/drl/
Direct web site URL to search for licensees: http://drlchq.state.wi.us/plsql/chq/cred_holder_query. You can search online using name or credential number

#04 Bureau of Health Services Professions, PO Box 8935 (1400 E Washington Ave), Madison, WI 53708-8935; 608-266-0483, Fax: 608-261-7083.
www.state.wi.us/agencies/drl/
Direct web site URL to search for licensees: http://165.189.238.43/plsql/plsql/Search_Ind_Health. You can search online using name or credential number This Department recommends an internet search; if not, inquire by mail. Phone verifications may not be accepted

#05 Department of Financial Institutions, PO Box 7876, Madison, WI 53707-7876; 608-266-1622.
www.wdfi.org Division of Financial Inst. - dfi - offers both a great online list system and telephone system for verifications. This section contains banks, mortgage, and credit union sevices.

#06 Department of Financial Institutions, PO Box 7876, Madison, WI 53707-7876; 608-261-9555, Fax: 608-267-6889.

www.wdfi.org
Direct web site URL to search for licensees: www.wdfi.org/fi/lfs/licensee_lists/. You can search online using generated lists Licensed Financial Services of WS Dept. of Financial Instituitions offers an online list system for verifications.

#07 Department of Health & Family Services, 1414 E Washington, Rm 227, 53703, Madison, WI 53701-2659; 608-266-1568, Fax: 608-261-6392.
Direct web site URL to search for licensees: www.dhfs.state.wi.us/reg_licens/dohprog/ems/ems index.htm

#08 Department of Revenue, PO Box 8902, Madison, WI 53708-8902; 608-266-2776, Fax: 608-267-1030.
www.dor.state.wi.us

#09 Department of Agriculture, Trade & Consumer Protection, 2811 Agriculture Dr, Madison, WI 53708-8911; 608-224-4548, Fax: 608-224-4656.
http://datcp.state.wi.us/pesticide/pestlic.htm

#10 Department of Financial Institutions, PO Box 1768, Madison, WI 53701; 608-266-3693, Fax: 608-256-1259.
www.wdfi.org/fi/securities/
Direct web site URL to search for licensees: www.wdfi.org/fi/securities/licensing/licensee_lists /default.asp. You can search online using name, city and state.

#11 Ethics Board, 44 E Mifflin St, #601, Madison, WI 53703-2800; 608-266-8123, Fax: 608-264-9309. http://ethics.state.wi.us
Direct web site URL to search for licensees: http://ethics.state.wi.us/LobbyingRegistrationRepo rts/LobbyingOverview.htm

#12 Office of the Commissioner of Insurance, 121 E Wilson St, 53702, Madison, WI 53707-7872; 608-266-3585, Fax: 608-264-8115.
http://badger.state.wi.us/agencies/oci/oci_home.ht m

#13 Office of Secretary of State, PO Box 7848, Madison, WI 53707-7848; 608-266-5594, Fax: 608-266-3159.
http://badger.state.wi.us/agencies/sos/

#14 Department of Administration, 2005 W Beltline Hwy, #201, Madison, WI 53713; 608-270-2555, Fax: 608-270-2564.

#15 Teacher Education, PO Box 7841, Madison, WI 53707-7841; 608-266-1027, Fax: 608-264-9558.
www.dpi.state.wi.us/dpi/DLSIS/tel/index.html

#16 State Bar Association, PO Box 7158, Madison, WI 53707; 608-257-3838, Fax: 608-257-5502.
www.wisbar.org

#17 Department of Health & Family Svcs, 1 W Wilson St, Perry Manor, Madison, WI 53703; 608-267-2297.

#18 Department of Natural Resources, 101 S Webster St, PO Box 7921, Madison, WI 53707-7921; 608-267-6744.

#19 Department of Commerce, 201 W Washington Ave, PO Box 2689, Madison, WI 53707-2689; 608-261-8500.
www.commerce.state.wi.us/SB/SB-HomePage.html

Wisconsin Federal Courts

The following list indicates the district and division name for each county in the state. If the bankruptcy court location is different from the district court, then the location of the bankruptcy court appears in parentheses.

County/Court Cross Reference

County	District	Division
Adams	Western	Madison
Ashland	Western	Madison (Eau Claire)
Barron	Western	Madison (Eau Claire)
Bayfield	Western	Madison (Eau Claire)
Brown	Eastern	Milwaukee
Buffalo	Western	Madison (Eau Claire)
Burnett	Western	Madison (Eau Claire)
Calumet	Eastern	Milwaukee
Chippewa	Western	Madison (Eau Claire)
Clark	Western	Madison (Eau Claire)
Columbia	Western	Madison
Crawford	Western	Madison
Dane	Western	Madison
Dodge	Eastern	Milwaukee
Door	Eastern	Milwaukee
Douglas	Western	Madison (Eau Claire)
Dunn	Western	Madison (Eau Claire)
Eau Claire	Western	Madison (Eau Claire)
Florence	Eastern	Milwaukee
Fond du Lac	Eastern	Milwaukee
Forest	Eastern	Milwaukee
Grant	Western	Madison
Green	Western	Madison
Green Lake	Eastern	Milwaukee
Iowa	Western	Madison
Iron	Western	Madison (Eau Claire)
Jackson	Western	Madison (Eau Claire)
Jefferson	Western	Madison
Juneau	Western	Madison (Eau Claire)
Kenosha	Eastern	Milwaukee
Kewaunee	Eastern	Milwaukee
La Crosse	Western	Madison (Eau Claire)
Lafayette	Western	Madison
Langlade	Eastern	Milwaukee
Lincoln	Western	Madison (Eau Claire)
Manitowoc	Eastern	Milwaukee
Marathon	Western	Madison (Eau Claire)
Marinette	Eastern	Milwaukee
Marquette	Eastern	Milwaukee
Menominee	Eastern	Milwaukee
Milwaukee	Eastern	Milwaukee
Monroe	Western	Madison (Eau Claire)
Oconto	Eastern	Milwaukee
Oneida	Western	Madison (Eau Claire)
Outagamie	Eastern	Milwaukee
Ozaukee	Eastern	Milwaukee
Pepin	Western	Madison (Eau Claire)
Pierce	Western	Madison (Eau Claire)
Polk	Western	Madison (Eau Claire)
Portage	Western	Madison (Eau Claire)
Price	Western	Madison (Eau Claire)
Racine	Eastern	Milwaukee
Richland	Western	Madison
Rock	Western	Madison
Rusk	Western	Madison (Eau Claire)
Sauk	Western	Madison
Sawyer	Western	Madison (Eau Claire)
Shawano	Eastern	Milwaukee
Sheboygan	Eastern	Milwaukee
St. Croix	Western	Madison (Eau Claire)
Taylor	Western	Madison (Eau Claire)
Trempealeau	Western	Madison (Eau Claire)
Vernon	Western	Madison (Eau Claire)
Vilas	Western	Madison (Eau Claire)
Walworth	Eastern	Milwaukee
Washburn	Western	Madison (Eau Claire)
Washington	Eastern	Milwaukee
Waukesha	Eastern	Milwaukee
Waupaca	Eastern	Milwaukee
Waushara	Eastern	Milwaukee
Winnebago	Eastern	Milwaukee
Wood	Western	Madison (Eau Claire)

US District Court

Eastern District of Wisconsin

Milwaukee Division Clerk's Office, Room 362, 517 E Wisconsin Ave, Milwaukee, WI 53202 (Courier Address: Use mail address for courier delivery), 414-297-3372.

http://www.wied.uscourts.gov

Counties: Brown, Calumet, Dodge, Door, Florence, Fond du Lac, Forest, Green Lake, Kenosha, Kewaunee, Langlade, Manitowoc, Marinette, Marquette, Menominee, Milwaukee, Oconto, Outagamie, Ozaukee, Racine, Shawano, Sheboygan, Walworth, Washington, Waukesha, Waupaca, Waushara, Winnebago.

Indexing/Storage: Cases are indexed by defendant and plaintiff as well as by case number. New cases are available in the index immediately after filing date. The computer index for civil cases goes back to 1991 and for criminal cases back to 1993. A computer index is maintained. Open records are located at this court.

Fee & Payment: The fee is $20.00 per item (one party name or case number). Payment may be made by money order, cashier check, personal check. Prepayment is required. Payee: Clerk, US District Court. Certification fee: $7.00 per document. Copy fee: $.50 per page. You are allowed to make your own copies. These copies cost $.25 per page.

Phone Search: Docket information available by phone if you have the case number or party names.

Mail Search: Always enclose a stamped self addressed envelope.

In Person: In person searching is available.

PACER: Sign-up number is 800-676-6856. Access fee is. Toll-free access: 877-253-4862. Local access: 414-297-3361. Case records are available back to 1991. Records are never purged. New records are available online after 1 day. PACER is available online at http://pacer.wied.uscourts.gov.

US Bankruptcy Court

Eastern District of Wisconsin

Milwaukee Division Room 126, 517 E Wisconsin Ave, Milwaukee, WI 53202 (Courier Address: Use mail address for courier delivery), 414-297-3291.

http://www.wieb.uscourts.gov

Counties: Brown, Calumet, Dodge, Door, Florence, Fond du Lac, Forest, Green Lake, Kenosha, Kewaunee, Langlade, Manitowoc, Marinette, Marquette, Menominee, Milwaukee, Oconto, Outagamie, Ozaukee, Racine, Shawano, Sheboygan, Walworth, Washington, Waukesha, Waupaca, Waushara, Winnebago.

Indexing/Storage: Cases are indexed by debtor as well as by case number. New cases are available in the index 1-2 days after filing date. The computer index goes back to 1986. A computer index is maintained. Open records are located at this court.

Fee & Payment: The fee is $20.00 per item (one party name or case number). Payment may be made by money order, cashier check, personal check. Prepayment is required. Payee: Clerk, US Bankruptcy Court. Certification fee: $7.00 per document. Copy fee: $.50 per page. You are

allowed to make your own copies. These copies cost $.25 per page.

Phone Search: An automated voice case information service (VCIS) is available. Call VCIS at 877-781-7277 or 414-297-3582.

Mail Search: Always enclose a stamped self addressed envelope.

In Person: In person searching is available.

PACER: Sign-up number is 800-676-6856. Access fee is $.60 per minute. Toll-free access: 877-467-5537. Local access: 414-297-1400. Case records are available back to 1991. Records are purged aafter case is closed. New civil records are available online after 1-2 days. PACER is available online at http://pacer.wieb.uscourts.gov.

US District Court

Western District of Wisconsin

Madison Division PO Box 432, Madison, WI 53701 (Courier Address: 120 N Henry St, Madison, WI 53703), 608-264-5156.

http://www.wiw.uscourts.gov

Counties: Adams, Ashland, Barron, Bayfield, Buffalo, Burnett, Chippewa, Clark, Columbia, Crawford, Dane, Douglas, Dunn, Eau Claire, Grant, Green, Iowa, Iron, Jackson, Jefferson, Juneau, La Crosse, Lafayette, Lincoln, Marathon, Monroe, Oneida, Pepin, Pierce, Polk, Portage, Price, Richland, Rock, Rusk, Sauk, Sawyer, St. Croix, Taylor, Trempealeau, Vernon, Vilas, Washburn, Wood.

Indexing/Storage: Cases are indexed by defendant and plaintiff as well as by case number. New cases are available in the index 24 hours after filing date. A computer index is maintained. Open records are located at this court. District wide searches are available from this court.

Fee & Payment: The fee is $20.00 per item (one party name or case number). Payment may be made by money order, cashier check, personal check. Prepayment is required. Payee: Clerk, US District Court. Certification fee: $7.00 per document. Copy fee: $.50 per page.

Phone Search: Only docket information is available by phone.

Mail Search: Always enclose a stamped self addressed envelope.

In Person: In person searching is available.

PACER: Sign-up number is 800-676-6856. Access fee is $.60 per minute. Toll-free access: 800-372-8791. Local access: 608-264-5914. Case records are available back to 1990. Records are never purged. New records are available online after 1 day. PACER is available online at http://pacer.wiwd.uscourts.gov.

US Bankruptcy Court

Western District of Wisconsin

Eau Claire Division PO Box 5009, Eau Claire, WI 54702-5009 (Courier Address: 500 S Barstow Commons, Eau Claire, WI 54701), 715-839-2980, Fax: 715-839-2996.

http://www.wiw.uscourts.gov

Counties: Ashland, Barron, Bayfield, Buffalo, Burnett, Chippewa, Clark, Douglas, Dunn, Eau Claire, Iron, Jackson, Juneau, La Crosse, Lincoln,

Marathon, Monroe, Oneida, Pepin, Pierce, Polk, Portage, Price, Rusk, Sawyer, St. Croix, Taylor, Trempealeau, Vernon, Vilas, Washburn, Wood. Division has satellite offices in LaCrosse and Wausau.

Indexing/Storage: Cases are indexed by debtor as well as by case number. New cases are available in the index 1 day after filing date. A computer index is maintained. Open records are located at this court. All division records are maintained here until they are forwarded to the Chicago Federal Records Center.

Fee & Payment: The fee is $20.00 per item (one party name or case number). Payment may be made by money order, cashier check, business check. Personal checks are not accepted. Prepayment is required. Personal checks are accepted only from attorneys. Payee: Clerk, US Bankruptcy Court. Certification fee: $7.00 per document. Copy fee: $.50 per page.

Phone Search: Only limited docket information is available by phone. An automated voice case information service (VCIS) is available. Call VCIS at 800-743-8247 or 608-264-5035.

Mail Search: A stamped self addressed envelope is not required.

In Person: In person searching is available.

PACER: Sign-up number is 800-676-6856. Access fee is $.60 per minute. Toll-free access: 800-373-8708. Local access: 608-264-5630. Case records are available back to April 1991. New civil records are available online after 1 day. WebPACER is available at http://pacer.wiwb.uscourts.gov/js_index.html.

Madison Division PO Box 548, Madison, WI 53701 (Courier Address: Room 340, 120 N Henry St, Madison, WI 53703), 608-264-5178.

http://www.wiw.uscourts.gov/bankruptcy

Counties: Adams, Columbia, Crawford, Dane, Grant, Green, Iowa, Jefferson, Lafayette, Richland, Rock, Sauk.

Indexing/Storage: Cases are indexed by debtor as well as by case number. New cases are available in the index 24 hours after filing date. A computer index is maintained. Open records are located at this court.

Fee & Payment: The fee is $20.00 per item (one party name or case number). Payment may be made by money order, cashier check, business check. Personal checks are not accepted. Prepayment is required. Payee: Clerk, US Bankruptcy Court. Certification fee: $7.00 per document. Copy fee: $.50 per page.

Phone Search: Only limited docket information is available by phone. An automated voice case information service (VCIS) is available. Call VCIS at 800-743-8247 or 608-264-5035.

Fax Search: Fax requests are accepted.

Mail Search: A stamped self addressed envelope is not required.

In Person: In person searching is available.

PACER: Sign-up number is 800-676-6856. Access fee is $.60 per minute. Toll-free access: 800-373-8708. Local access: 608-264-5630. Case records are available back to April 1991. New civil records are available online after 1 day. WebPACER is available at http://pacer.wiwb.uscourts.gov/js_index.html.

Wisconsin County Courts

Court	Jurisdiction	No. of Courts	How Organized
Circuit Courts*	General	74	69 Circuits
Municipal Courts	Municipal	226	
Probate Courts*	Probate	72	

* Profiled in this Sourcebook.

Court					CIVIL				
	Tort	Contract	Real Estate	Min. Claim	Max. Claim	Small Claims	Estate	Eviction	Domestic Relations
Circuit Courts*	X	X	X	$0	No Max	$5000	X	X	X
Municipal Courts									
Probate Courts*							X		

Court	CRIMINAL				
	Felony	Misdemeanor	DWI/DUI	Preliminary Hearing	Juvenile
Circuit Courts*	X	X	X	X	X
Municipal Courts			X		X
Probate Courts*					

ADMINISTRATION
Director of State Courts, Supreme Court, PO Box 1688, Madison, WI, 53701; 608-266-6828, Fax: 608-267-0980. www.courts.state.wi.us

COURT STRUCTURE
The Circuit Court is the court of general jurisdiction. The Register in Probate maintains guardianship and mental health records, most of which are sealed but may be opened for cause with a court order. In some counties, the Register also maintains termination and adoption records, but practices vary widely across the state.

Most Registers in Probate are putting pre-1950 records on microfilm and destroying the hard copies. This is done as "time and workloads permit," so microfilm archiving is not uniform across the state.

The small claims limit was raised to $5000 in mid-1995.

ONLINE ACCESS
Wisconsin Circuit Court Access (WCCA) allows users to view circuit court case information at http://ccap.courts.state.wi.us/internetcourtaccess which is the Wisconsin court system web site. Data is available from all counties except Outagamie and Walworth. Searches can be conducted statewide or county by county. WCCA provides detailed information about circuit cases and for civil cases, the program displays judgment and judgment party information. WCCA also offers the ability to generate reports. In addition, public access terminals are available at each court. Due to statutory requirements, WCCA users will not be able to view restricted cases. There are probate records for all counties except Outagamie, Milwaukee and Walworth. Portage County offers probate records only online.

ADDITIONAL INFORMATION
The statutory fee schedule for the Circuit Courts is as follows: Search Fee - $5.00 per name; Copy Fee - $1.25 per page; Certification Fee - $5.00. In about half the Circuit Courts, no search fee is charged if the case number is provided. There is normally no search fee charged for in-person searches.

The fee schedule for probate is as follows: Search Fee - $4.00 per name; Certification Fee - $3.00 per document plus copy fee; Copy Fee - $1.00 per page.

PROBATE COURTS
Probate filing is a function of the Circuit Court; however, each county has a Register in Probate who maintains and manages the probate records. Probate records are available online at http://ccap.courts.state.wi.us/internetcourtaccess for all counties except Outagamie, Milwaukee and Walworth.

Adams County

Circuit Court PO Box 220, Friendship, WI 53934; 608-339-4208; Fax: 608-339-6414. Hours: 8AM-4:30PM (CST). *Felony, Misdemeanor, Civil, Eviction, Small Claims.*

Civil Records: Access: Phone, mail, online, in person. Both court and visitors may perform in person searches. Search fee: $5.00 per name. Required to search: name, years to search. Civil records on computer from 1993, on index cards and books from 1950. Historical societies have previous records and indexes. Organized 1848. Civil court records are available free online at http://ccap.courts.state.wi.us/internetcourtaccess/.

Criminal Records: Access: Phone, mail, online, in person. Both court and visitors may perform in person searches. Search fee: $5.00 per name. Required to search: name, years to search, DOB. Criminal records on computer from 1993, on index cards and books from 1950. Historical societies have previous records and indexes. Organized 1848. Online access to criminal records is the same as civil.

General Information: Public Access terminal is available. No juvenile, paternity, financial, PSI reports released. SASE required. Turnaround time 1-2 days. Fax notes: Fee to fax results is $1.25 per page. Copy fee: $1.25 per page. Certification fee: $5.00. Fee payee: Clerk of Court. Personal checks accepted. Prepayment is required.

Register in Probate PO Box 200, Friendship, WI 53934; 608-339-4213; Fax: 608-339-6414. Hours: 8AM-4:30PM (CST). *Probate.*

Note: Probate records are available free online; see Circuit Court.

Ashland County

Circuit Court Courthouse 210 W Main St Rm 307, Ashland, WI 54806; 715-682-7016; Fax: 715-682-7919. Hours: 8AM-Noon, 1-4PM (CST). *Felony, Misdemeanor, Civil, Eviction, Small Claims.*

Civil Records: Access: Phone, fax, mail, online, in person. Both court and visitors may perform in person searches. Search fee: $5.00 per name. Required to search: name, years to search. Civil cases indexed by defendant, plaintiff. Civil records on index cards and index books concurrently from 1960. Organized 1860. Civil court records are available free on the Internet at http://ccap.courts.state.wi.us/internetcourtaccess/.

Criminal Records: Access: Phone, fax, mail, online, in person. Both court and visitors may perform in person searches. Search fee: $5.00 per name. Required to search: name, years to search. Criminal records (some) on computer. Online access to criminal records is the same as civil.

General Information: Public Access terminal is available. No juvenile or paternity records released. SASE required. Turnaround time 1-2 days. Fax notes: $1.25 per page. Copy fee: $1.25 per page. Certification fee: $5.00. Fee payee: Clerk of Court. Personal checks accepted. Local or pre-approved checks accepted. Prepayment is required.

Register in Probate Courthouse Rm 203, 201 W Main, Ashland, WI 54806; 715-682-7009; Fax: 715-682-7919. Hours: 8AM-Noon, 1-4PM (CST). *Probate.*

Note: Probate records are available free online; see Circuit Court.

Barron County

Circuit Court Barron County Courthouse, 330 E LaSalle Ave, Barron, WI 54812; 715-537-6265; Fax: 715-537-6269. Hours: 8AM-4:30PM (CST). *Felony, Misdemeanor, Civil, Eviction, Small Claims.*

Civil Records: Access: Online, in person. Visitors must perform in person searches for themselves. No search fee. Required to search: name, years to search. Civil cases indexed by defendant, plaintiff. Civil records on computer, index cards from 1983. Organized 1859. Civil court records are available free on the Internet at http://ccap.courts.state.wi.us/internetcourtaccess/.

Criminal Records: Access: Online, in person. Visitors must perform in person searches for themselves. No search fee. Required to search: name, years to search. Criminal records on computer, index cards from 1983. Organized 1859. Online access to criminal records is the same as civil.

General Information: Public Access terminal is available. No expunged, paternity or sealed records released. Copy fee: $1.25 per page. Certification fee: $5.00. Fee payee: Clerk of Court. Personal checks accepted. Prepayment is required.

Register in Probate Courthouse Rm 218, Barron, WI 54812; 715-537-6261; Fax: 715-537-6277. Hours: 8AM-4PM (CST). *Probate.*

Note: Probate records are available free online; see Circuit Court.

Bayfield County

Circuit Court 117 E 5th, Washburn, WI 54891; 715-373-6108; Fax: 715-373-6153. Hours: 8AM-4PM (CST). *Felony, Misdemeanor, Civil, Eviction, Small Claims.*

Civil Records: Access: Mail, online, in person. Both court and visitors may perform in person searches. Search fee: $5.00 per name. Required to search: name, years to search. Civil cases indexed by defendant, plaintiff. Civil records on computer for all open cases since 1982, on index cards from 1979, index books in archives from 1845 to 1979. Civil court records are available free on the Internet at http://ccap.courts.state.wi.us/internetcourtaccess/.

Criminal Records: Access: Mail, online, in person. Both court and visitors may perform in person searches. Search fee: $5.00 per name. Required to search: name, years to search, DOB. Criminal records on computer since 1993. Online access to criminal records is the same as civil.

General Information: Public Access terminal is available. No sealed records released. SASE required. Turnaround time 1-2 days. Fax notes: Fee to fax results is $1.25 per page. Copy fee: $1.25 per page. Certification fee: $5.00. Fee payee: Clerk of Court. Personal checks accepted. Prepayment is required.

Register in Probate 117 E 5th, PO Box 86, Washburn, WI 54891; 715-373-6155; Fax: 715-373-6153. Hours: 8AM-4PM (CST). *Probate.*

Note: Probate records are available free online; see Circuit Court.

Brown County

Circuit Court PO Box 23600, Green Bay, WI 54305-3600; 920-448-4161; Fax: 920-448-4156. Hours: 8AM-4:30PM (CST). *Felony, Misdemeanor, Civil, Eviction, Small Claims.*

Civil Records: Access: Mail, online, in person. Both court and visitors may perform in person searches. Search fee: $5.00 per name. Required to search: name, years to search. Civil cases indexed by defendant, plaintiff. Civil records on computer since 1990, on microfiche from 1987-1990, archives from 1962-1990. Crossed on index cards from 1972, index books from 1982. Civil court records are available free online at http://ccap.courts.state.wi.us/internetcourtaccess/.

Criminal Records: Access: Mail, online, in person. Both court and visitors may perform in person searches. Search fee: $5.00 per name. Required to search: name, years to search, DOB. Criminal records on computer since 1990, on microfiche from 1987-1990, archives from 1962-1990. Crossed on index cards from 1972,

index books from 1982. Online access to criminal records is the same as civil.

General Information: Public Access terminal is available. No juvenile or paternity records released. SASE required. Turnaround time 10 days. Copy fee: $1.25 per page. Certification fee: $5.00. Fee payee: Brown County Clerk of Court. Personal checks accepted. Prepayment is required.

Register in Probate PO Box 23600, Green Bay, WI 54305-3600; 920-448-4275; Fax: 920-448-6208. Hours: 8AM-4:30PM (CST). *Probate.*

Note: Probate records are available free online; see Circuit Court.

Buffalo County

Circuit Court 407 S 2nd, PO Box 68, Alma, WI 54610; 608-685-6212; Fax: 608-685-6211. Hours: 8AM-4:30PM (CST). *Felony, Misdemeanor, Civil, Eviction, Small Claims.*

Civil Records: Access: Phone, fax, mail, online, in person. Both court and visitors may perform in person searches. Search fee: $5.00 per name. Required to search: name, years to search. Civil cases indexed by defendant, plaintiff. Civil records on computer from 1994, on index cards from 1979. No civil records available before 1962. Civil court records are available free on the Internet at http://ccap.courts.state.wi.us/internetcourtaccess/.

Criminal Records: Access: Phone, fax, mail, online, in person. Both court and visitors may perform in person searches. Search fee: $5.00 per name. Required to search: name, years to search. Criminal records on computer from 1994. Felonies retained 50 years; misdemeanors 20 years. No misdemeanors available before 1962. Online access to criminal records is the same as civil.

General Information: Public Access terminal is available. No closed records released. SASE required. Turnaround time 1 week. Fax notes: Fee to fax results is $1.25 per page. Copy fee: $1.25 per page. Certification fee: $5.00. Fee payee: Buffalo County Clerk of Court. Personal checks accepted. Prepayment is required.

Register in Probate 407 S 2nd, PO Box 68, Alma, WI 54610; 608-685-6202; Fax: 608-685-6211. Hours: 8AM-4:30PM (CST). *Probate.*

Note: Probate records are available free online; see Circuit Court.

Burnett County

Circuit Court 7410 County Road K #115, Siren, WI 54872; 715-349-2147. Hours: 8:30AM-4:30PM (CST). *Felony, Misdemeanor, Civil, Eviction, Small Claims.*

Civil Records: Access: Mail, online, in person. Both court and visitors may perform in person searches. Search fee: $5.00 per name. Required to search: name, years to search. Civil cases indexed by defendant, plaintiff. Civil records on computer from 10/92, on index books from 1800s. Organized 1856. Civil court records are available free on the Internet at http://ccap.courts.state.wi.us/internetcourtaccess/.

Criminal Records: Access: Mail, online, in person. Both court and visitors may perform in person searches. Search fee: $5.00 per name. Required to search: name, years to search. Criminal records on computer from 10/92, on index books from 1800s. Organized 1856. Online access to criminal records is the same as civil.

General Information: Public Access terminal is available. No paternity, juvenile, sealed or confidential records released. SASE required. Turnaround time 1-2 days. Copy fee: $1.25 per page. Certification fee: $5.00. Fee payee: Clerk of Courts. Personal checks accepted. Prepayment is required.

Register in Probate 7410 County Road K #110, Siren, WI 54872; 715-349-2177; Fax: 715-349-7659. Hours: 8:30AM-4:30PM (CST). *Probate.*

Note: Probate records are available free online; see Circuit Court.

Calumet County

Circuit Court 206 Court St, Chilton, WI 53014; 920-849-1414; Fax: 920-849-1483. Hours: 8AM-4:30PM (CST). *Felony, Misdemeanor, Civil, Eviction, Small Claims.*

Civil Records: Access: Mail, online, in person. Both court and visitors may perform in person searches. Search fee: $5.00 per name. Required to search: name, years to search. Civil cases indexed by defendant, plaintiff. Civil records on computer from 1992, index cards from 1978, index books from 1800s. Civil court records are available free on the Internet at http://ccap.courts.state.wi.us/internetcourtaccess.

Criminal Records: Access: Mail, online, in person. Both court and visitors may perform in person searches. Search fee: $5.00 per name. Required to search: name, years to search, DOB. Criminal records on computer from 1992, index cards from 1978, index books from 1800s. Online access to criminal records is the same as civil.

General Information: Public Access terminal is available. No juvenile or paternity records released. SASE required. Turnaround time 2 days. Copy fee: $1.25 per page. Certification fee: $5.00. Fee payee: Clerk of Court. Personal checks accepted. Prepayment is required.

Register in Probate 206 Court St, Chilton, WI 53014-1198; 920-849-1455; Fax: 920-849-1483. Hours: 8AM-Noon, 1-4:30PM (CST). *Probate.*

Note: Probate records are available free online; see Circuit Court.

Chippewa County

Circuit Court 711 N Bridge St, Chippewa Falls, WI 54729-1879; 715-726-7758; Fax: 715-726-7786. Hours: 8AM-4:30PM (CST). *Felony, Misdemeanor, Civil, Eviction, Small Claims.*

Civil Records: Access: Mail, fax, online, in person. Both court and visitors may perform in person searches. Search fee: $5.00 per name per case type. Required to search: name, years to search; also helpful: address. Civil cases indexed by defendant, plaintiff. Civil records on computer from 1990, index cards from 1979, index books from 1900s. Civil court records are available free on the Internet at http://ccap.courts.state.wi.us/internetcourtaccess/.

Criminal Records: Access: Mail, fax, online, in person. Both court and visitors may perform in person searches. Search fee: $5.00 per name. Required to search: name, years to search, DOB; also helpful: SSN. Criminal records on computer from 1990, index cards from 1979, index books from 1900s. Online access to criminal records is the same as civil.

General Information: Public Access terminal is available. Paternity records released only to party or attorney of record, or with written authorization. SASE required. Turnaround time 10 days or less; up to 30 days if pre-1990. Fax notes: Fee to fax results is $2.00 for 1st page and $1.00 per page thereafter. Copy fee: $1.25 per page. Certification fee: $5.00. Fee payee: Chippewa County Clerk of Courts. Personal checks accepted. Prepayment is required.

Register in Probate 711 N Bridge St, Chippewa Falls, WI 54729; 715-726-7737; Fax: 715-738-2626. Hours: 8AM-4:30PM (CST). *Probate.*

Note: Probate records are available free online; see Circuit Court.

Clark County

Circuit Court 517 Court St, Neillsville, WI 54456-1971; 715-743-5181; Fax: 715-743-5154. Hours: 8AM-5PM (CST). *Felony, Misdemeanor, Civil, Eviction, Small Claims.*

Civil Records: Access: Mail, online, in person. Both court and visitors may perform in person searches. Search fee: $5.00 per name. Required to search: name, years to search. Civil cases indexed by defendant, plaintiff. Civil records on computer from 1994, on index cards from 1981, index books from 1900s. Civil court records are available free on the Internet at http://ccap.courts.state.wi.us/internetcourtaccess/.

Criminal Records: Access: Mail, online, in person. Both court and visitors may perform in person searches. Search fee: $5.00 per name. Required to search: name, years to search. Criminal records on computer from 1994, on index cards from 1981, index books from 1900s. Online access to criminal records is the same as civil.

General Information: No sealed or paternity records released. SASE required. Turnaround time 1-2 weeks. Copy fee: $.15 per page. Certification fee: $5.00. Fee payee: Clerk of Court. Personal checks accepted. Prepayment is required.

Register in Probate 517 Court St, Rm 403, Neillsville, WI 54456; 715-743-5172; Fax: 715-743-5120. Hours: 8AM-4:30PM (CST). *Probate.*

Note: There is a $4.00 search fee. Probate records are available free online; see Circuit Court.

Columbia County

Circuit Court PO Box 587, Portage, WI 53901; 608-742-9642; Fax: 608-742-9601. Hours: 8AM-4:30PM (CST). *Felony, Misdemeanor, Civil, Eviction, Small Claims.*

Civil Records: Access: Mail, online, in person. Both court and visitors may perform in person searches. Search fee: $5.00 per name. Required to search: name, years to search. Civil cases indexed by defendant, plaintiff. Civil records on computer from 1994, on microfiche to 1960s, concurrent index cards from 1940s. Civil court records are available free online at http://ccap.courts.state.wi.us/internetcourtaccess/.

Criminal Records: Access: Mail, online, in person. Both court and visitors may perform in person searches. Search fee: $5.00 per name. Required to search: name, years to search, DOB. Criminal records on computer from 1994, on microfiche to 1960s, concurrent index cards/books from 1940s. Online access to criminal records is the same as civil.

General Information: Public Access terminal is available. No juvenile or paternity records released. SASE required. Turnaround time 1 week. Fax notes: Fee to fax results is $1.00 per page. Copy fee: $1.25 per page. Certification fee: $5.00. Fee payee: Clerk of Court. Personal checks accepted. Prepayment required.

Register in Probate 400 DeWitt, PO Box 221, Portage, WI 53901; 608-742-9636; Fax: 608-742-9601. Hours: 8AM-4:30PM (CST). *Probate.*

Note: Probate records are available free online; see Circuit Court.

Crawford County

Circuit Court 220 N Beaumont Rd, Prairie Du Chien, WI 53821; 608-326-0211. Hours: 8AM-4:30PM (CST). *Felony, Misdemeanor, Civil, Eviction, Small Claims.*

Civil Records: Access: Mail, online, in person. Both court and visitors may perform in person searches. Search fee: $5.00 per name. Required to search: name, years to search. Civil cases indexed by defendant, plaintiff. Civil records on computer from 1993, on index

cards from 1984, index books from 1900. Historical Society has archives. Civil court records are available free on the Internet at http://ccap.courts.state.wi.us/internetcourtaccess/.

Criminal Records: Access: Mail, online, in person. Both court and visitors may perform in person searches. Search fee: $5.00 per name. Required to search: name, years to search. Criminal records on computer from 1993, on index cards from 1984, index books from 1900. Historical Society has archives. Online access to criminal records is the same as civil.

General Information: Public Access terminal is available. No juvenile, paternity, mental records released. SASE required. Turnaround time 10 working days. Copy fee: $1.25 per page. Certification fee: $5.00. Fee payee: Clerk of Court. Personal checks accepted. Prepayment is required.

Register in Probate 220 N Beaumont Rd, Prairie Du Chien, WI 53821; 608-326-0206; Fax: 608-326-0288. Hours: 8AM-4:30PM (CST). *Probate.*

Note: Probate records are available free online; see Circuit Court.

Dane County

Circuit Court 210 Martin Luther King Jr Blvd, Rm GR10, Madison, WI 53703; 608-266-4311; Fax: 608-267-8859. Hours: 7:45AM-4:30PM (CST). *Felony, Misdemeanor, Civil, Eviction, Small Claims.*

www.co.dane.wi.us/clrkcort/clrkhome.htm

Civil Records: Access: Fax, mail, online, in person. Both court and visitors may perform in person searches. Search fee: $5.00 per name. Required to search: name, years to search. Civil cases indexed by defendant, plaintiff. Civil records on computer from 1981, on microfiche from 1976, defendant index books 1848. Civil court records are available free on the Internet at http://ccap.courts.state.wi.us/internetcourtaccess/.

Criminal Records: Access: Fax, mail, online, in person. Both court and visitors may perform in person searches. Search fee: $5.00 per name. Required to search: name, years to search; also helpful: DOB. Criminal records on computer from 1983. Online access to criminal records is the same as civil.

General Information: Public Access terminal is available. No "confidential records" released. SASE required. Turnaround time 2-3 days. Fax notes: $.50 per page. Copy fee: $1.25 per page. Certification fee: $5.00. Fee payee: Dane County Clerk of Courts. Personal checks accepted. Prepayment is required.

Register in Probate 210 Martin Luther King Jr Blvd, Rm 305, Madison, WI 53703-3344; 608-266-4331. Hours: 7:45AM-4:30PM (CST). *Probate.*

Note: Probate records are available free online; see Circuit Court.

Dodge County

Circuit Court 210 W Center St, Juneau, WI 53039; 920-386-3820; Fax: 920-386-3587. Hours: 8AM-4:30PM (CST). *Felony, Misdemeanor, Civil, Eviction, Small Claims.*

Civil Records: Access: Mail, online, in person. Both court and visitors may perform in person searches. Search fee: $5.00 per name. Required to search: name, years to search. Civil cases indexed by defendant, plaintiff. Civil records on computer from 1993, on index cards from 1986, microfiche from 1972, index books from 1900s. Civil court records are available free online at http://ccap.courts.state.wi.us/internetcourtaccess/.

Criminal Records: Access: Mail, online, in person. Both court and visitors may perform in person searches. Search fee: $5.00 per name. Required to search: name, years to search, DOB. Criminal records on computer from 1993, on index cards from 1986, microfiche from

1972, index books from 1900s. Online access to criminal records is the same as civil.

General Information: Public Access terminal is available. No juvenile or John Doe records released. SASE required. Turnaround time 1-2 days. Fax notes: Fee to fax results is $1.50 per page. Copy fee: $1.25 per page. Certification fee: $5.00. Fee payee: Clerk of Courts. Personal checks accepted. Prepayment is required.

Register in Probate 210 W Center St, Juneau, WI 53039-1091; 920-386-3550; Fax: 920-386-3587. Hours: 8AM-4:30PM (CST). *Probate.*

Note: $4.00 search fee; records computerized since 1992. Probate records are available free online; see Circuit Court.

Door County

Circuit Court PO Box 670, Sturgeon Bay, WI 54235; 920-746-2205; Fax: 920-746-2520. Hours: 8AM-4:30PM (CST). *Felony, Misdemeanor, Civil, Eviction, Small Claims.*

Civil Records: Access: Mail, online, in person. Both court and visitors may perform in person searches. Search fee: $5.00 per name. Required to search: name, years to search. Civil cases indexed by defendant, plaintiff. Civil records on computer from 4/93, on index cards from 1984, index books from 1900s. Civil court records are available free on the Internet at http://ccap.courts.state.wi.us/internetcourtaccess/.

Criminal Records: Access: Mail, online, in person. Both court and visitors may perform in person searches. Search fee: $5.00 per name. Required to search: name, years to search, DOB. Criminal records on computer from 4/93, on index cards from 1984, index books from 1900s. Online access to criminal records is the same as civil.

General Information: Public Access terminal is available. No financial or paternity records released. SASE required. Turnaround time 2-3 days. Fax notes: Fee to fax results is $3.00 per document. Copy fee: $1.25 per page. Certification fee: $5,00. Fee payee: Clerk of Court. Personal checks accepted.

Register in Probate PO Box 670, 421 Nebraska St, Rm C375, Sturgeon Bay, WI 54235-2470; 920-746-2482; Fax: 920-746-2470. Hours: 8AM-4:30PM (CST). *Probate.*

Note: Probate records are available free online; see Circuit Court.

Douglas County

Circuit Court 1313 Belknap, Superior, WI 54880; Civil phone: 715-395-1237; Criminal phone: 715-395-1240; Fax: 715-395-1421. Hours: 8AM-4:30PM (CST). *Felony, Misdemeanor, Civil, Eviction, Small Claims.*

Civil Records: Access: Mail, online, in person. Only the court performs in person searches; visitors may not. Search fee: $5.00 per name. Required to search: name, years to search. Civil cases indexed by defendant, plaintiff. Civil records on computer since 1994; prior records on index cards from 1976, index books from 1900s. Civil court records are available free online at http://ccap.courts.state.wi.us/internetcourtaccess/.

Criminal Records: Access: Mail, online, in person. Only the court performs in person searches; visitors may not. Search fee: $5.00 per name. Required to search: name, years to search; also helpful: DOB. Criminal records on computer since 1994; prior records on index cards from 1976, index books from 1900s. Online access to criminal records is the same as civil.

General Information: Public Access terminal is available. No juvenile or paternity records released. SASE required. Turnaround time 1-2 weeks. Copy fee: $1.25 per page. Certification fee: $5.00. Fee payee:

Clerk of Courts. Only cashiers checks and money orders accepted. Douglas County personal checks accepted. Prepayment is required.

Register in Probate 1313 Belknap, Superior, WI 54880; 715-395-1229; Fax: 715-395-1421. Hours: 8AM-4:30PM (CST). *Probate.*

Note: Probate records are available free online; see Circuit Court.

Dunn County

Circuit Court Stokke Parkway #1500, Menomonie, WI 54751; 715-232-2611. Hours: 8AM-4:30PM (CST). *Felony, Misdemeanor, Civil, Eviction, Small Claims.*

Civil Records: Access: Mail, online, in person. Both court and visitors may perform in person searches. Search fee: $5.00 per name. Required to search: name, years to search. Civil cases indexed by defendant, plaintiff. Civil records on computer from 1987, index cards from 1977, index books from 1900s, archives from 1970. Civil court records are available free online at http://ccap.courts.state.wi.us/internetcourtaccess/.

Criminal Records: Access: Mail, online, in person. Both court and visitors may perform in person searches. Search fee: $5.00 per name. Required to search: name, years to search, DOB. Criminal records on computer from 1987, index cards from 1977, index books from 1900s, archives from 1970. Online access to criminal records is the same as civil.

General Information: Public Access terminal is available. No juvenile, family financial, sealed records released. SASE not required. Turnaround time 2-3 days. Copy fee: $1.25 per page. Certification fee: $5.00. Fee payee: Clerk of Court. Personal checks accepted. Prepayment is required.

Register in Probate 615 Stokke Parkway Dr #1300, Menomonie, WI 54751; 715-232-1449; Fax: 715-232-6971. Hours: 8AM-4:30PM (CST). *Probate.*

Note: Probate records are available free online; see Circuit Court.

Eau Claire County

Circuit Court 721 Oxford Ave, Eau Claire, WI 54703; 715-839-4816; Fax: 715-839-4817. Hours: 8AM-5PM (CST). *Felony, Misdemeanor, Civil, Eviction, Small Claims.*

Civil Records: Access: Mail, online, in person. Both court and visitors may perform in person searches. Search fee: $5.00 per name and case type (civil, small claims, etc.). Required to search: name, years to search. Civil cases indexed by defendant, plaintiff. Civil records on computer from 7/92, on index cards from 1970, index books from 1968. Civil court records are available free on the Internet at http://ccap.courts.state.wi.us/internetcourtaccess/.

Criminal Records: Access: Mail, online, in person. Both court and visitors may perform in person searches. Search fee: $5.00 per name. Required to search: name, years to search, DOB. Criminal records on computer from 7/92, on index cards from 1970, index books from 1968. Online access to criminal records is the same as civil.

General Information: Public Access terminal is available. No paternity, financial disclosure, expungment or sealed records released. SASE required. Turnaround time 1-10 days. Copy fee: $1.25 per page. Certification fee: $5.00. Fee payee: Clerk of Court-Eau Claire County. Personal checks accepted. Prepayment is required.

Register in Probate 721 Oxford Ave, Eau Claire, WI 54703; 715-839-4823. 8AM-5PM (CST). *Probate.*

Note: Probate records are available free online; see Circuit Court.

Florence County

Circuit Court PO Box 410, Florence, WI 54121; 715-528-3205; Fax: 715-528-5470. Hours: 8:30AM-4PM (CST). *Felony, Misdemeanor, Civil, Eviction, Small Claims.*

Civil Records: Access: Mail, online, in person. Both court and visitors may perform in person searches. Search fee: $5.00 per name. Required to search: name, years to search. Civil cases indexed by defendant, plaintiff. Civil records on computer from 1991; prior records on index books from 1900s. Civil court records are available free on the Internet at http://ccap.courts.state.wi.us/internetcourtaccess/.

Criminal Records: Access: Mail, online, in person. Both court and visitors may perform in person searches. Search fee: $5.00 per name. Required to search: name, years to search. Criminal records on computer from 1991; prior records on index books from 1900s. Online access to criminal records is the same as civil.

General Information: Public Access terminal is available. No juvenile, mental health, adoption or guardianship records released. SASE required. Turnaround time 2 weeks. Copy fee: $1.25 per page. Certification fee: $5.00. Fee payee: Clerk of Courts. Personal checks accepted. Prepayment is required.

Register in Probate PO Box 410, Florence, WI 54121; 715-528-3205; Fax: 715-528-5470. Hours: 8:30AM-Noon, 1-4PM (CST). *Probate.*

Note: Probate records are available free online; see Circuit Court.

Fond du Lac County

Circuit Court PO Box 1355, Fond du Lac, WI 54936-1355; 920-929-3041; Fax: 920-929-3933. Hours: 8AM-4:30PM (CST). *Felony, Misdemeanor, Civil, Eviction, Small Claims.*

Civil Records: Access: Mail, online, in person. Both court and visitors may perform in person searches. Search fee: $5.00 per name. Required to search: name, years to search. Civil cases indexed by defendant, plaintiff. Civil records on computer from 1990, index cards from 1978, microfiche 1836 to 1978, archives prior to 1900s. Old files destroyed, on microfiche or in Historical Society. Civil court records are available free on the Internet at http://ccap.courts.state.wi.us/internetcourtaccess/.

Criminal Records: Access: Mail, online, in person. Both court and visitors may perform in person searches. Search fee: $5.00 per name. Required to search: name, years to search, DOB. Criminal records on computer from 1990, index cards from 1978, microfiche 1836 to 1978, archives prior to 1900s. Old files destroyed, on microfiche or in Historical Society. Online access to criminal records is the same as civil.

General Information: Public Access terminal is available. No juvenile or paternity records released. SASE required. Turnaround time 1-2 days. Fax notes: Fee to fax results is $2.00 per document. Copy fee: $1.25 per page. Certification fee: $5.00. Fee payee: Clerk of Circuit Court. Personal checks accepted. Prepayment is required.

Register in Probate PO Box 1355, Fond du Lac, WI 54936-1355; 920-929-3084; Fax: 920-929-7058. Hours: 8AM-4:30PM (CST). *Probate.*

Note: Probate records are available free online; see Circuit Court.

Forest County

Circuit Court 200 E Madison St, Crandon, WI 54520; 715-478-3323; Fax: 715-478-3211. Hours: 8:30AM-4:30PM (CST). *Felony, Misdemeanor, Civil, Eviction, Small Claims.*

Civil Records: Access: Mail, online, in person. Both court and visitors may perform in person searches. Search fee: $5.00 per name. Required to search: name, years to search. Civil cases indexed by defendant, plaintiff. Civil records on computer from 1994, on index cards from 1979, index books from 1903, Historical Society has books prior to 1903. Civil court records are available free on the Internet at http://ccap.courts.state.wi.us/internetcourtaccess/.
Criminal Records: Access: Mail, online, in person. Both court and visitors may perform in person searches. Search fee: $5.00 per name. Required to search: name, years to search, DOB. Criminal records on computer from 1994, on index cards from 1979, index books from 1903, Historical Society has books prior to 1903. Online access to criminal records is the same as civil.
General Information: Public Access terminal is available. No juvenile, paternity records released. SASE required. Turnaround time 1-2 days. Fax notes: Fee to fax results is $1.25 per page. Copy fee: $1.25 per page. Certification fee: $5.00. Fee payee: Clerk of Court. Personal checks accepted. Prepayment is required.

Register in Probate 200 E Madison St, Crandon, WI 54520; 715-478-2418; Fax: 715-478-2430. Hours: 8:30AM-4:30PM (CST). *Probate.*

Note: Probate records are available free online; see Circuit Court.

Grant County

Circuit Court PO Box 110, Lancaster, WI 53813; 608-723-2752; Fax: 608-723-7370. Hours: 8AM-4:30PM (CST). *Felony, Misdemeanor, Civil, Eviction, Small Claims.*

Civil Records: Access: Phone, mail, fax, online, in person. Both court and visitors may perform in person searches. No search fee. Required to search: name, years to search. Civil cases indexed by defendant, plaintiff. Civil records on computer from 10/93, on index books from 1900s. Civil court records are available free on the Internet at http://ccap.courts.state.wi.us/internetcourtaccess/.
Criminal Records: Access: Phone, mail, fax, online, in person. Only the court performs in person searches; visitors may not. No search fee. Required to search: name, years to search. Criminal records on computer from 10/93, on index books from 1900s. Online access to criminal records is the same as civil.
General Information: Public Access terminal is available. No juvenile, paternity records released. SASE required. Turnaround time 2 weeks. Copy fee: $1.25 per page. Certification fee: $5.00 plus $1.25 per page. Fee payee: Clerk of Court. Personal checks accepted. Prepayment is required.

Register in Probate 130 W Maple St, Lancaster, WI 53813; 608-723-2697; Fax: 608-723-7370. Hours: 8AM-4:30PM (CST). *Probate.*

Note: $4.00 search fee, records computerized since 1993. Probate records are available free online; see Circuit Court.

Green County

Circuit Court 1016 16th Ave, Monroe, WI 53566; 608-328-9433; Fax: 608-328-2835. Hours: 8AM-5PM (CST). *Felony, Misdemeanor, Civil, Eviction, Small Claims.*

Civil Records: Access: Mail, online, in person. Both court and visitors may perform in person searches. Search fee: $5.00 per name. Required to search: name,

years to search; also helpful: address. Civil cases indexed by defendant, plaintiff. Civil records on index cards from 1984, index books from 1900s; computerized back to 1994. Civil court records are available free on the Internet at http://ccap.courts.state.wi.us/internetcourtaccess/.
Criminal Records: Access: Mail, online, in person. Both court and visitors may perform in person searches. Search fee: $5.00 per name. Required to search: name, years to search; also helpful: DOB. Criminal records on index cards from 1984, index books from 1900s; computerized back to 1994. Online access to criminal records is the same as civil.
General Information: No juvenile, paternity or sealed records released. SASE required. Turnaround time 1-2 days. Copy fee: $1.25 per page. Certification fee: $5.00. Fee payee: Clerk of Court. Personal checks accepted. Prepayment is required.

Register in Probate 1016 16th Ave, Monroe, WI 53566; 608-328-9567; Fax: 608-328-2835. Hours: 8AM-12, 1PM-5PM (CST). *Probate.*

Note: Probate records are available free online; see Circuit Court.

Green Lake County

Circuit Court 492 Hill St, PO Box 3188, Green Lake, WI 54941; 920-294-4142; Fax: 920-294-4150. Hours: 8AM-4:30PM (CST). *Felony, Misdemeanor, Civil, Eviction, Small Claims.*

Civil Records: Access: Mail, online, in person. Both court and visitors may perform in person searches. Search fee: $5.00 per name. Required to search: name, years to search. Civil cases indexed by defendant, plaintiff. Civil records on computer from 4/93, on index cards since 1900s. Civil court records are available free online   at http://ccap.courts.state.wi.us/internetcourtaccess/.
Criminal Records: Access: Mail, online, in person. Both court and visitors may perform in person searches. Search fee: $5.00 per name. Required to search: name, years to search. Criminal records on computer from 4/93, on index cards since 1900s. Online access to criminal records is the same as civil.
General Information: Public Access terminal is available. No paternity or juvenile ordinance records released. SASE required. Turnaround time 1-3 days. Copy fee: $1.25 per page. Certification fee: $5.00. Fee payee: Clerk of Circuit Clerk. Personal checks accepted. Prepayment is required.

Register in Probate 492 Hill St, PO Box 3188, Green Lake, WI 54941; 920-294-4044; Fax: 920-294-4171. Hours: 8AM-4:30PM (CST). *Probate.*

www.co.green-lake.wi.us

Note: Probate records are available free online; see Circuit Court.

Iowa County

Circuit Court 222 N Iowa St, Dodgeville, WI 53533; 608-935-0395; Fax: 608-935-0386. Hours: 8:30AM-4:30PM (CST). *Felony, Misdemeanor, Civil, Eviction, Small Claims.*

Civil Records: Access: Mail, online, in person. Both court and visitors may perform in person searches. Search fee: $5.00 per name. Required to search: name, years to search. Civil cases indexed by defendant, plaintiff. Civil records on computer from 1992, index cards from 1987, archives from 1917, index books from 1829. Civil court records are available free online at http://ccap.courts.state.wi.us/internetcourtaccess/.
Criminal Records: Access: Mail, online, in person. Both court and visitors may perform in person searches. Search fee: $5.00 per name. Required to search: name, years to search, DOB. Criminal records on computer from 1992, index cards from 1987, archives from 1917,

index books from 1829. Online access to criminal records is the same as civil.
General Information: Public Access terminal is available. No adoption, paternity or mental records released. SASE required. Turnaround time same day. Fax notes: Fee to fax results is $1.25 per page. Copy fee: $1.25 per page. Certification fee: $5.00. Fee payee: Clerk of Court. Personal checks accepted. Prepayment is required.

Register in Probate 222 N Iowa St, Dodgeville, WI 53533; 608-935-0347; Fax: 608-935-0386. Hours: 8:30AM-Noon, 12;30-4:30PM (CST). *Probate.*

Note: Probate records are available free online; see Circuit Court.

Iron County

Circuit Court 300 Taconite St, Hurley, WI 54534; 715-561-4084; Fax: 715-561-4054. Hours: 8AM-4PM (CST). *Felony, Misdemeanor, Civil, Eviction, Small Claims.*

Civil Records: Access: Phone, mail, online, in person. Both court and visitors may perform in person searches. Search fee: $5.00 per name. Required to search: name, years to search. Civil cases indexed by defendant, plaintiff. Civil records on index cards from 1989, index books from 1920. Civil court records are available free on the Internet at http://ccap.courts.state.wi.us/internet courtaccess/. Phone access for title companies only.
Criminal Records: Access: Mail, online, in person. Both court and visitors may perform in person searches. Search fee: $5.00 per name. Required to search: name, years to search, DOB. Criminal records on index cards from 1989, index books from 1920. Online access to criminal records is the same as civil.
General Information: Public Access terminal is available. No juvenile or paternity records released. SASE required. Turnaround time 10 days. Copy fee: $1.25 per page. Certification fee: $5.00. Fee payee: Clerk of Court. Personal checks accepted.

Register in Probate 300 Taconite St, Hurley, WI 54534; 715-561-3434; Fax: 715-561-4054. Hours: 8AM-4PM (CST). *Probate.*

Note: Probate records are available free online; see Circuit Court.

Jackson County

Circuit Court 307 Main St, Black River Falls, WI 54615; 715-284-0208; Fax: 715-284-0270. Hours: 8AM-4:30PM (CST). *Felony, Misdemeanor, Civil, Eviction, Small Claims.*

www.co.jackson.wi.us

Civil Records: Access: Mail, online, in person. Both court and visitors may perform in person searches. Search fee: $5.00 per name. Required to search: name, years to search. Civil cases indexed by defendant, plaintiff. Civil records on computer from 6/92, on index cards from 1979, index books to 1935, files and indexes prior to 1935 destroyed. Civil court records are available free on the Internet at http://ccap.courts.state.wi.us/internetcourtaccess/.
Criminal Records: Access: Mail, online, in person. Both court and visitors may perform in person searches. Search fee: $5.00 per name. Required to search: name, years to search, DOB. Criminal records on computer from 6/92, on index cards from 1979, index books to 1935, files and indexes prior to 1935 destroyed. Online access to criminal records is the same as civil.
General Information: Public Access terminal is available. No juvenile or pre-judgment paternity records released. SASE required. Turnaround time 1-4 days. Copy fee: $1.25 per page. Certification fee: $5.00. Fee payee: Clerk of Court. Personal checks accepted. Prepayment is required.

Register in Probate 307 Main St, Black River Falls, WI 54615; 715-284-0213; Fax: 715-284-0277. Hours: 8AM-4:30PM (CST). *Probate.*

Note: Probate records are available free online; see Circuit Court.

Jefferson County

Circuit Court 320 S Main St, Jefferson, WI 53549; 920-674-7150; Fax: 920-674-7425. Hours: 8AM-4:30PM (CST). *Felony, Misdemeanor, Civil, Eviction, Small Claims.*

Civil Records: Access: Mail, online, in person. Both court and visitors may perform in person searches. Search fee: $5.00 per name. Required to search: name, years to search. Civil cases indexed by defendant, plaintiff. Civil records on computer from 1992, on index cards from 1979, index books from late 1800s. Civil court records are available free on the Internet at http://ccap.courts.state.wi.us/internetcourtaccess/.
Criminal Records: Access: Mail, online, in person. Both court and visitors may perform in person searches. Search fee: $5.00 per name. Required to search: name, years to search, DOB. Criminal records on computer from 1992, on index cards from 1979, index books from late 1800s. Online access to criminal records is the same as civil.
General Information: No juvenile or mental health records released. SASE required. Turnaround time 2-3 days. Copy fee: $1.25 per page. Certification fee: $5.00. Fee payee: Clerk of Courts. Personal checks accepted. Prepayment is required.

Register in Probate 320 S Main St, Jefferson, WI 53549; 920-674-7245; Fax: 920-675-0134. Hours: 8AM-4:30PM (CST). *Probate.*

Note: Probate records are available free online; see Circuit Court.

Juneau County

Circuit Court 220 E State St, Mauston, WI 53948; 608-847-9356; Fax: 608-847-9360. Hours: 8AM-Noon, 12:30-4:30PM (CST). *Felony, Misdemeanor, Civil, Eviction, Small Claims.*

Civil Records: Access: Mail, online, in person. Both court and visitors may perform in person searches. Search fee: $5.00 per name. Fee is per case. Required to search: name, years to search. Civil cases indexed by defendant, plaintiff. Civil records on computer from 1988, index cards from 1977, index books from 1900, microfiche from 1856-1900. Civil court records are available free on the Internet at http://ccap.courts.state.wi.us/internetcourtaccess/.
Criminal Records: Access: Mail, online, in person. Both court and visitors may perform in person searches. Search fee: $5.00 per name. Required to search: name, years to search, DOB. Criminal records on computer from 1988, index cards from 1977, index books from 1900, microfiche from 1856-1900. Online access to criminal records is the same as civil.
General Information: Public Access terminal is available. No juvenile, confidential family or paternity records released. SASE required. Turnaround time 1 week. Copy fee: $1.25 per page. Certification fee: $5.00. Fee payee: Juneau County Clerk of Court. Personal checks accepted. Prepayment is required.

Register in Probate 220 E State St Rm 205, Mauston, WI 53948; 608-847-9346; Fax: 608-847-9349. Hours: 8AM-4:30PM (CST). *Probate.*

Note: Probate records are available free online; see Circuit Court.

Kenosha County

Circuit Court 912 56th St, Kenosha, WI 53140; 262-653-2664; Fax: 262-653-2435. Hours: 8AM-5PM *Felony, Misdemeanor, Civil, Eviction, Small Claims.*

Civil Records: Access: Mail, online, in person. Both court and visitors may perform in person searches. Search fee: $5.00 per name. Required to search: name, years to search. Civil cases indexed by defendant, plaintiff. Civil records on computer from 1989, index cards from 1960, microfiche from 1850. Civil court records are available free on the Internet at http://ccap.courts.state.wi.us/internetcourtaccess/.
Criminal Records: Access: Mail, online, in person. Both court and visitors may perform in person searches. Search fee: $5.00 per name. Required to search: name, years to search; also helpful: DOB, SSN. Criminal records on computer from 1989, index cards from 1960, microfiche from 1850. Online access to criminal records is the same as civil.
General Information: Public Access terminal is available. No juvenile or paternity records released. SASE required. Turnaround time 1-2 days. Copy fee: $1.25 per page. Certification fee: $5.00. Fee payee: Clerk of Court. Personal checks accepted. Prepayment is required.

Register in Probate Courthouse Rm 304, 912 56th St, Kenosha, WI 53140; 262-653-6678; Fax: 262-653-2435. Hours: 8AM-5PM (CST). *Probate.*

Note: $4.00 per search, records indexed on computer (1992) and cards. Probate records are available free online; see Circuit Court.

Kewaunee County

Circuit Court 613 Dodge St, Kewaunee, WI 54216; 920-388-7144; Fax: 920-388-3139. Hours: 8AM-4:30PM (CST). *Felony, Misdemeanor, Civil, Eviction, Small Claims.*

Civil Records: Access: Phone, mail, online, in person. Both court and visitors may perform in person searches. Search fee: $5.00 per name. Required to search: name, years to search. Civil cases indexed by defendant, plaintiff. Civil records on index cards from 1978, index books from 1852. Civil court records are available free on the Internet at http://ccap.courts.state.wi.us/nternetcourtaccess/.
Criminal Records: Access: Phone, mail, online, in person. Both court and visitors may perform in person searches. Search fee: $5.00 per name. Required to search: name, years to search, DOB. Criminal records on index cards from 1978, index books from 1852. Online access to criminal records is the same as civil.
General Information: No paternity records released. SASE required. Turnaround time 1-2 days. Copy fee: $1.25 per page. Certification fee: $5.00. Fee payee: Clerk of Circuit Court. Personal checks accepted. Prepayment is required.

Register in Probate 613 Dodge St, Kewaunee, WI 54216; 920-388-4410; Fax: 920-388-3139. Hours: 8AM-4:30PM (CST). *Probate.*

Note: Probate records are available free online; see Circuit Court.

La Crosse County

Circuit Court 333 Vine St, La Crosse, WI 54601; 608-785-9590/9573; Fax: 608-789-7821. Hours: 8:30AM-5PM (CST). *Felony, Misdemeanor, Civil, Eviction, Small Claims.*

Civil Records: Access: Phone, mail, online, in person. Both court and visitors may perform in person searches. Search fee: $5.00 per name. Required to search: name, years to search. Civil cases indexed by defendant, plaintiff. Civil records on computer from 1993, on index cards from 1983, index books from 1917. Civil court

records are available free on the Internet at http://ccap.courts.state.wi.us/internetcourtaccess/.
Criminal Records: Access: Phone, mail, online, in person. Both court and visitors may perform in person searches. Search fee: $5.00 per name. Required to search: name, years to search; also helpful: DOB, SSN. Criminal records on computer from 1993, on index cards from 1983, index books from 1917. Online access to criminal records is the same as civil.
General Information: Public Access terminal is available. No juvenile, paternity or finances in family records released. SASE required. Turnaround time 1-2 days. Fax notes: Fee to fax results is $1.25 per page. Copy fee: $1.25 per page. Certification fee: $5.00. Fee payee: Clerk of Courts. Personal checks accepted. Prepayment is required.

Register in Probate 333 Vine St, Rm 1201, La Crosse, WI 54601; 608-785-9882. Hours: 8:30AM-5PM (CST). *Probate.*

Note: Probate records are available free online; see Circuit Court.

Lafayette County

Circuit Court 626 Main St, Darlington, WI 53530; 608-776-4832. Hours: 8AM-4:30PM (CST). *Felony, Misdemeanor, Civil, Eviction, Small Claims.*

Civil Records: Access: Mail, online, in person. Both court and visitors may perform in person searches. Search fee: $5.00 per name. Required to search: name, years to search. Civil cases indexed by defendant. Civil records on index cards from 1973, index books from 1900; computerized back to 1993. Civil court records are available free on the Internet at http://ccap.courts.state.wi.us/internetcourtaccess/.
Criminal Records: Access: Mail, online, in person. Both court and visitors may perform in person searches. Search fee: $5.00 per name. Required to search: name, years to search. Criminal records on index cards from 1973, index books from 1900; computerized back to 1993. Online access to criminal records is the same as civil.
General Information: Public Access terminal is available. No juvenile records released. SASE required. Turnaround time 2-3 days. Copy fee: $1.25 per page. Certification fee: $5.00. Fee payee: Clerk of Circuit Court. Personal checks accepted. Prepayment is required.

Register in Probate 626 Main St, Rm 302, Darlington, WI 53530; 608-776-4811. Hours: 8AM-4:30PM (CST). *Probate.*

Note: Probate records are available free online; see Circuit Court.

Langlade County

Circuit Court 800 Clermont St, Antigo, WI 54409; 715-627-6215. Hours: 8:30AM-4:30PM (CST). *Felony, Misdemeanor, Civil, Eviction, Small Claims.*

Civil Records: Access: Mail, online, in person. Both court and visitors may perform in person searches. Search fee: $5.00 per name. Required to search: name, years to search. Civil cases indexed by defendant, plaintiff. Civil records on index books from 1905. Civil court records are available free on the Internet at http://ccap.courts.state.wi.us/internetcourtaccess/.
Criminal Records: Access: Mail, online, in person. Both court and visitors may perform in person searches. Search fee: $5.00 per name. Required to search: name, years to search. Criminal records on index books from 1905. Online access to criminal records is the same as civil.
General Information: No confidential records released. SASE required. Turnaround time 2-3 days. Copy fee: $1.25 per page. Certification fee: $5.00. Fee

payee: Clerk of Court. Personal checks accepted. Prepayment is required.

Register in Probate 800 Clermont St, Antigo, WI 54409; 715-627-6213; Fax: 715-627-6329. Hours: 8:30AM-4:30PM (CST). *Probate.*

Note: There is a $4.00 search fee. Probate records are available free online; see Circuit Court.

Lincoln County

Circuit Court 1110 E Main St, Merrill, WI 54452; 715-536-0319; Fax: 715-536-0361. Hours: 8:15AM-4:30PM (CST). *Felony, Misdemeanor, Civil, Eviction, Small Claims.*

Civil Records: Access: Mail, online, in person. Both court and visitors may perform in person searches. Search fee: $5.00 per name. Required to search: name, years to search. Civil cases indexed by defendant. Civil records on computer from 1990, index cards from 1982, index books from 1900s. Civil court records are available free on the Internet at http://ccap.courts.state.wi.us/internetcourtaccess/.

Criminal Records: Access: Mail, online, in person. Both court and visitors may perform in person searches. Search fee: $5.00 per name. Required to search: name, years to search; also helpful: DOB, SSN. Criminal records on computer from 1990, index cards from 1982, index books from 1900s. Online access to criminal records is the same as civil.

General Information: No paternity or sealed records released. SASE required. Turnaround time 1-2 days. Copy fee: $1.25 per page. Certification fee: $5.00. Fee payee: Clerk of Court. Personal checks accepted. Local personal checks accepted. Prepayment is required.

Register in Probate 1110 E Main St, Merrill, WI 54452; 715-536-0342; Fax: 715-536-5230. Hours: 8:15AM-Noon, 1-4:30PM (CST). *Probate.*

Note: Probate records are available free online; see Circuit Court.

Manitowoc County

Circuit Court PO Box 2000, Manitowoc, WI 54221-2000; 920-683-4030. Hours: 8:30AM-5PM M; 8:30AM-4:30PM T-F (CST). *Felony, Misdemeanor, Civil, Eviction, Small Claims.*

Civil Records: Access: Phone, mail, online, in person. Both court and visitors may perform in person searches. Search fee: $5.00 per name. Required to search: name, years to search. Civil cases indexed by defendant, plaintiff. Civil records on computer from 1993, on index cards from 1962, index books from 1906, Historical Society has prior records. Civil court records are available free on the Internet at http://ccap.courts.state.wi.us/internetcourtaccess/. Prior written agreement with court required for phone access.

Criminal Records: Access: Phone, mail, online, in person. Both court and visitors may perform in person searches. Search fee: $5.00 per name. Required to search: name, years to search, DOB. Criminal records on computer from 1993, on index cards from 1962, index books from 1906, Historical Society has prior records. Online access to criminal records is the same as civil. Prior written agreement required for phone access.

General Information: Public Access terminal is available. No confidential records released. SASE required. Turnaround time 2-3 days. Copy fee: $1.25 per page. Certification fee: $1.25 per page. Fee payee: Clerk of Circuit Court. Personal checks accepted. Prepayment is required.

Register in Probate 1010 S 8th St Rm 116, Manitowoc, WI 54220; 920-683-4016; Fax: 920-683-5182. Hours: 8:30AM-4:30PM T-F; 8:30AM-5PM M (CST). *Probate.*

Note: Probate records are available free online; see Circuit Court.

Marathon County

Circuit Court 500 Forest St, Wausau, WI 54403; 715-261-1300; Fax: 715-261-1319 Civ; 261-1280 Crim. Hours: 8AM-5PM (Summer hours 8AM-4:30PM Memorial-Labor Day) (CST). *Felony, Misdemeanor, Civil, Eviction, Small Claims.*

Civil Records: Access: Mail, online, in person. Only the court performs in person searches; visitors may not. Search fee: $5.00 per name. Required to search: name, years to search. Civil cases indexed by defendant, plaintiff. Civil records on computer from 1992, on index cards from 1979, index books from 1900s. Civil court records are available free on the Internet at http://ccap.courts.state.wi.us/internetcourtaccess. All requests must be in writing, using their form if possible.

Criminal Records: Access: Mail, online, in person. Only the court performs in person searches; visitors may not. Search fee: $5.00 per name. Required to search: name, years to search, DOB. Criminal records on computer from 1992, on index cards from 1979, index books from 1900s. Criminal court records are available free on the Internet at http://ccap.courts.state.wi.us/internetcourtaccess. All requests must be in writing, using their form if possible.

General Information: No mental health or juvenile records released. SASE required. Turnaround time 1-3 days. Copy fee: $1.25 per page. Certification fee: $5.00. Fee payee: Clerk of Court. Personal checks accepted. Prepayment is required.

Register in Probate 500 Forest St, Wausau, WI 54403; 715-261-1260; Fax: 715-261-1269. Hours: 8AM-5PM (CST). *Probate.*

Note: Probate records are available free online; see Circuit Court.

Marinette County

Circuit Court 1926 Hall Ave, Marinette, WI 54143-1717; 715-732-7450. Hours: 8:30AM-4:30PM (CST). *Felony, Misdemeanor, Civil, Eviction, Small Claims.*

Civil Records: Access: Mail, online, in person. Both court and visitors may perform in person searches. Search fee: $5.00 per name. Required to search: name, years to search. Civil cases indexed by defendant, plaintiff. Civil records on computer from 1989, index cards from 1980, index books from 1906, prior records at Historical Society. Civil court records 1994 to present are available free on the Internet at http://ccap.courts.state.wi.us/internetcourtaccess/.

Criminal Records: Access: Mail, online, in person. Both court and visitors may perform in person searches. Search fee: $5.00 per name. Required to search: name, years to search, DOB. Criminal records on computer from 1989, index cards from 1980, index books from 1906, prior records at Historical Society. Online access to criminal records is the same as civil.

General Information: Public Access terminal is available. No paternity records released. SASE required. Turnaround time 2-3 days. Copy fee: $1.25 per page. Certification fee: $5.00. Fee payee: Clerk of Courts. Personal checks accepted. Prepayment is required.

Register in Probate 1926 Hall Ave, Marinette, WI 54143-1717; 715-732-7475; Fax: 715-732-7561. Hours: 8:30AM-4:30PM (CST). *Probate.*

Note: Probate records are available free online; see Circuit Court.

Marquette County

Circuit Court PO Box 187, Montello, WI 53949; 608-297-9102; Fax: 608-297-9188. Hours: 8AM-Noon, 12:30-4:30PM (CST). *Felony, Misdemeanor, Civil, Eviction, Small Claims.*

Civil Records: Access: Phone, mail, online, in person. Both court and visitors may perform in person searches. Search fee: $5.00 per name. Required to search: name, years to search. Civil cases indexed by defendant, plaintiff. Civil records on index books from 1900s, prior records at Historical Society; computerized back to 1996. Civil court records are available free online at http://ccap.courts.state.wi.us/internetcourtaccess/.

Criminal Records: Access: Phone, mail, online, in person. Both court and visitors may perform in person searches. Search fee: $5.00 per name. Required to search: name, years to search, DOB, full name. Criminal records on index books from 1900s, prior records at Historical Society; computerized back to 1996. Online access to criminal records is the same as civil.

General Information: Public Access terminal is available. No adoption, juvenile, paternity, guardianship, mental or termination of parental right records released. SASE not required. Turnaround time 1-2 days. Fax notes: Fee to fax results is $2.00 per page. Copy fee: $1.25 per page. Certification fee: $5.00. Fee payee: Clerk of Circuit Court. Personal checks accepted. Prepayment is required.

Register in Probate 77 W Park St, PO Box 749, Montello, WI 53949; 608-297-9105; Fax: 608-297-9188. Hours: 8AM-4:30PM (CST). *Probate.*

Note: Probate records are available free online; see Circuit Court.

Menominee County

Circuit Court PO Box 279, Keshena, WI 54135; 715-799-3313; Fax: 715-799-1322. Hours: 8AM-4:30PM (CST). *Felony, Misdemeanor, Civil, Eviction, Small Claims.*

Civil Records: Access: Mail, online, in person. Both court and visitors may perform in person searches. Search fee: $5.00 per name. Required to search: name, years to search. Civil cases indexed by defendant, plaintiff. Civil records are indexed by cards, kept in files since 1979. Older records are at the Historical Society. Civil court records are available free on the Internet at http://ccap.courts.state.wi.us/internetcourtaccess/.

Criminal Records: Access: Mail, online, in person. Both court and visitors may perform in person searches. Search fee: $5.00 per name. Required to search: name, years to search, DOB. Criminal records are indexed by cards, kept in files since 1979. Older records are at the Historical Society. Online access to criminal records is the same as civil.

General Information: Public Access terminal is available. No juvenile, mental, adoption. Turnaround time 3-4 days. Copy fee: $1.25 per page. Certification fee: $5.00. Fee payee: Clerk of Court. Personal checks accepted.

Register in Probate 311 N Main St, RM 203, Shawano, WI 54166; 715-526-8631; Fax: 715-526-8622. Hours: 8AM-4:30PM (CST). *Probate.*

Note: Tribal probate records only in Keshena (Menominee County); Non-tribal records are in Shawano County. Probate records are available free online; see Circuit Court.

Milwaukee County

Circuit Court - Civil 901 9th St Rm G-9, Milwaukee, WI 53233; 414-278-4128; Fax: 414-223-1256, 8AM-4PM (CST). *Civil, Eviction, Small Claims.*

www.co.milwaukee.wi.us/courts/court.htm

Civil Records: Access: Mail, online, in person. Both court and visitors may perform in person searches. Search fee: $5.00 per name. Required to search: name, years to search; also helpful-DOB or SSN. Civil cases indexed by defendant, plaintiff. Civil records on computer from 1985, on microfiche from 1949, prior with County Historical Society. Civil court records are available free on the Internet at http://ccap.courts.state.wi.us/internetcourtaccess/.

General Information: Public Access terminal is available. No paternity records released. SASE required. Turnaround time 1-2 weeks. Fax notes: Will not fax results. Copy fee: $1.25 per page. Certification fee: $5.00. Fee payee: Milwaukee County Clerk of Circuit Court. Personal checks accepted. Prepayment is required.

Circuit Court - Criminal Division 821 W State St, Milwaukee, WI 53233; 414-278-4538; Fax: 414-223-1262. 8AM-5PM *Felony, Misdemeanor.*

www.co.milwaukee.wi.us/courts/court.htm

Criminal Records: Access: Fax, mail, online, in person. Both court and visitors may perform in person searches. Search fee: $5.00 per name. Required to search: name, years to search, DOB. Criminal records on computer from 10/86, index books and cards prior. Criminal court records are available free on the Internet at http://ccap.courts.state.wi.us/internetcourtaccess/. Also, criminal case records on the Milwaukee Municipal Court Case Information System database are available free online at www.court.ci.mil. wi.us/home.asp. Search by Case Number, by Citation Number, or by Name.

General Information: Public Access terminal is available. No sealed records released. SASE required. Turnaround time 4 days. Fax notes: No fee to fax results. Copy fee: $1.25 per page. Certification fee: $5.00. Fee payee: Clerk of Circuit Court. Personal checks accepted. Prepayment is required.

Register in Probate 901 N 9th St Rm 207, Milwaukee, WI 53233; 414-278-4444; Fax: 414-223-1814. Hours: 8AM-4:30PM (CST). *Probate.*

Monroe County

Circuit Court 112 S Court St #203, Sparta, WI 54656-1764; 608-269-8745. 8AM-4:30PM (CST). *Felony, Misdemeanor, Civil, Eviction, Small Claims.*

Civil Records: Access: Fax, mail, online, in person. Both court and visitors may perform in person searches. Search fee: $5.00 per name. Required to search: name, years to search. Civil cases indexed by defendant, plaintiff. Civil records on computer and cards. Civil court records are available free on the Internet at http://ccap.courts.state.wi.us/internetcourtaccess/.

Criminal Records: Access: Fax, mail, online, in person. Both court and visitors may perform in person searches. Search fee: $5.00 per name. Required to search: name, years to search. Criminal records on computer and cards. Online access to criminal records is the same as civil.

General Information: Public Access terminal is available. No paternity, medical or financial records released. SASE required. Turnaround time 1 week. Fax notes: $1.25 per page. No charge to toll free lines. Copy fee: $1.25 per page. Certification fee: $5.00. Fee payee: Clerk of Court. Local checks accepted. Prepayment is required.

Register in Probate 112 S Court, Rm 301, Sparta, WI 54656-1765; 608-269-8701; Fax: 608-269-8950. Hours: 8AM-4:30PM (CST). *Probate.*

Note: Probate records are available free online; see Circuit Court.

Oconto County

Circuit Court 301 Washington St, Oconto, WI 54153; 920-834-6855; Fax: 920-834-6867. Hours: 8AM-4PM (CST). *Felony, Misdemeanor, Civil, Eviction, Small Claims.*

Civil Records: Access: Mail, online, in person. Both court and visitors may perform in person searches. Search fee: $5.00 per name. Required to search: name, years to search. Civil cases indexed by defendant, plaintiff. Civil records on computer since 1994; prior records on index books from 1930s, Historical Society has earlier records. Civil court records are available free on the Internet at http://ccap.courts.state.wi.us/internetcourtaccess/.

Criminal Records: Access: Mail, online, in person. Both court and visitors may perform in person searches. Search fee: $5.00 per name. Required to search: name, years to search, DOB. Criminal records on computer since 1994; prior records on index books from 1930s; Historical Society has earlier records. Online access to criminal records is the same as civil.

General Information: Public Access terminal is available. No juvenile or paternity records released. SASE required. Turnaround time 1-2 days. Copy fee: $1.25 per page. Certification fee: $5.00. Fee payee: Oconto County Clerk of Court. Personal checks accepted. Prepayment is required.

Register in Probate 301 Washington St, Oconto, WI 54153; 920-834-6839; Fax: 920-834-6867. Hours: 8AM-4PM (CST). *Probate.*

Note: Probate records are available free online; see Circuit Court.

Oneida County

Circuit Court PO Box 400, Rhinelander, WI 54501; 715-369-6120. Hours: 8AM-4:30PM (CST). *Felony, Misdemeanor, Civil, Eviction, Small Claims.*

Civil Records: Access: Mail, online, in person. Both court and visitors may perform in person searches. Search fee: $5.00 per name. Required to search: name, years to search. Civil cases indexed by defendant, plaintiff. Civil records on computer from 1992, index cards from 1980, index books from 1900s. Civil court records are available free on the Internet at http://ccap.courts.state.wi.us/internetcourtaccess/.

Criminal Records: Access: Mail, online, in person. Both court and visitors may perform in person searches. Search fee: $5.00 per name. Required to search: name, years to search, DOB. Criminal records on computer from 1992, index cards from 1980, index books from 1900s. Online access to criminal records is the same as civil.

General Information: Public Access terminal is available. No paternity records released. SASE not required. Turnaround time 1 week. Copy fee: $1.25 per page. Certification fee: $5.00. Fee payee: Clerk of Court. Personal checks accepted. Prepayment required.

Register in Probate PO Box 400, Rhinelander, WI 54501; 715-369-6159. Hours: 8AM-12, 1-4:30PM (CST). *Probate.*

Note: Probate records are available free online; see Circuit Court.

Outagamie County

Circuit Court 320 S Walnut St, Appleton, WI 54911; 920-832-5130; Fax: 920-832-5115. Hours: 8:30AM-5PM (CST). *Felony, Misdemeanor, Civil, Eviction, Small Claims.*

Note: Small claims and eviction records at 920-832-5135.

Civil Records: Access: In person only. Visitors must perform in person searches for themselves. No search fee. Required to search: name, years to search. Civil cases indexed by defendant, plaintiff. Civil records on computer from 10/87, index cards from 1983, index books from 1901, some records on microfiche.

Criminal Records: Access: Mail, in person. Both court and visitors may perform in person searches. Search fee: $5.00 per name. Required to search: name, years to search, DOB. Criminal records on computer from 10/87, index cards from 1983, index books from 1901, some records on microfiche.

General Information: Public Access terminal is available. No adoption or juvenile records released. SASE required. Turnaround time 2-3 days. Fax notes: Fax fee is $1.25 per page. Copy fee: $1.25 per page. Certification fee: $5.00. Fee payee: Clerk of Court. Personal checks accepted. Prepayment is required.

Register in Probate 320 S Walnut St, Appleton, WI 54911; 920-832-5601; Fax: 920-832-5115. Hours: 8:30AM-Noon, 1-5PM (CST). *Probate.*

Ozaukee County

Circuit Court 1201 S Spring St, Port Washington, WI 53074; 262-284-8409; Fax: 262-284-8491. Hours: 8:30AM-5PM (CST). *Felony, Misdemeanor, Civil, Eviction, Small Claims.*

www.co.ozaukee.wi.us/departments/clerkofcourts.htm

Civil Records: Access: Mail, online, in person. Both court and visitors may perform in person searches. Search fee: $5.00 per name. Required to search: name, years to search. Civil cases indexed by defendant, plaintiff. Civil records on computer from 1991, index cards from late 1950s. Civil court records are available free on the Internet at http://ccap.courts.state.wi.us/internetcourtaccess/.

Criminal Records: Access: Mail, online, in person. Both court and visitors may perform in person searches. Search fee: $5.00 per name. Required to search: name, years to search, DOB. Criminal records on computer from 1989.

General Information: Public Access terminal is available. No paternity records released. SASE required. Turnaround time 1 week. Copy fee: $1.25 per page. Certification fee: $5.00. Fee payee: Clerk of Court. Business checks accepted. In-state personal checks accepted. Prepayment is required.

Register in Probate PO Box 994, Port Washington, WI 53074; 262-284-8370; Fax: 262-284-8491. Hours: 8:30AM-5PM (CST). *Probate.*

Note: Probate records are available free online; see Circuit Court.

Pepin County

Circuit Court PO Box 39, Durand, WI 54736; 715-672-8861; Fax: 715-672-8521. Hours: 8:30AM-Noon, 12:30-4:30PM (CST). *Felony, Misdemeanor, Civil, Eviction, Small Claims.*

Civil Records: Access: Mail, online, in person. Both court and visitors may perform in person searches. Search fee: $5.00 per name. Required to search: name, years to search. Civil cases indexed by plaintiff. Civil records on computer from 1995, index books from 1900s. Civil court records are available free on the Internet at http://ccap.courts.state.wi.us/internetcourtaccess/.

Criminal Records: Access: Mail, online, in person. Both court and visitors may perform in person searches. Search fee: $5.00 per name. Required to search: name, years to search, DOB. Criminal records on computer from 1995, index books from 1900s. Online access to criminal records is the same as civil.

General Information: Public Access terminal is available. No minor or financial divorce records released. SASE required. Turnaround time 1 week. Copy fee: $1.25 per page. Certification fee: $5.00. Fee payee: Clerk of Court. Personal checks accepted. Prepayment is required.

Register in Probate PO Box 39, Durand, WI 54736; 715-672-8859; Fax: 715-672-8521. Hours: 8:30AM-Noon, 1-4:30PM (CST). *Probate.*

Note: Probate records are available free online; see Circuit Court.

Pierce County

Circuit Court PO Box 129, Ellsworth, WI 54011; 715-273-3531. Hours: 8AM-5PM (CST). *Felony, Misdemeanor, Civil, Eviction, Small Claims.*

Civil Records: Access: Mail, online, in person. Both court and visitors may perform in person searches. Search fee: $5.00 per name. Fee is by type of case. Required to search: name, years to search. Civil cases indexed by defendant, plaintiff. Civil records on index cards from 1979, index books from 1950s, on computer back to 1995. Archives in River Falls. Civil court records are available free on the Internet at http://ccap.courts.state.wi.us/internetcourtaccess/.

Criminal Records: Access: Mail, online, in person. Both court and visitors may perform in person searches. Search fee: $5.00 per name. Required to search: name, years to search, DOB. Criminal records on index cards from 1979, index books from 1950s; on computer back to 1995. Archives in River Falls. Online access to criminal records is the same as civil.

General Information: Public Access terminal is available. No sealed records released. SASE required. Turnaround time 2-3 days. Copy fee: $1.25 per page. Certification fee: $5.00. Fee payee: Clerk of Court. Personal checks accepted. Prepayment is required.

Register in Probate PO Box 97, Ellsworth, WI 54011; 715-273-3531 x460; Fax: 715-273-6855. Hours: 8AM-5PM (CST). *Probate.*

Note: Probate records are available free online; see Circuit Court.

Polk County

Circuit Court 100 Polk Plaza, PO Box 549, Balsam Lake, WI 54810; 715-485-9299; Fax: 715-485-9262. Hours: 8:30AM-4:30PM (CST). *Felony, Misdemeanor, Civil, Eviction, Small Claims.*

Civil Records: Access: Mail, online, in person. Both court and visitors may perform in person searches. Search fee: $5.00 per name. Required to search: name, years to search. Civil cases indexed by defendant, plaintiff. Civil records on computer. Civil court records are available free on the Internet at http://ccap.courts.state.wi.us/internetcourtaccess/.

Criminal Records: Access: Mail, online, in person. Both court and visitors may perform in person searches. Search fee: $5.00 per name. Fee is per record/file. Required to search: name, years to search, DOB. Criminal records on computer. Online access to criminal records is the same as civil.

General Information: Public Access terminal is available. No juvenile, paternity or confidential records released. SASE required. Turnaround time 2 days. Copy fee: $1.25 per page. Certification fee: $5.00. Fee payee: Clerk of Court. Personal checks accepted. Prepayment is required.

Register in Probate 100 Polk Plaza, Suite 230, Balsam Lake, WI 54810; 715-485-9238; Fax: 715-485-9275. Hours: 8:30AM-4:30PM (CST). *Probate.*

Note: Probate records are available free online; see Circuit Court.

Portage County

Circuit Court (Branches 1, 2 & 3) 1516 Church St, Stevens Point, WI 54481; 715-346-1364; Fax: 715-346-1236. Hours: 7:30AM-4:30PM (CST). *Felony, Misdemeanor, Civil, Eviction, Small Claims.*

Civil Records: Access: Mail, in person. Both court and visitors may perform in person searches. Search fee: $5.00 per name. Required to search: name, years to search. Civil cases indexed by defendant, plaintiff. Civil records on computer from 6/91, index cards from 1980, index books from 1900s.

Criminal Records: Access: Mail, in person. Both court and visitors may perform in person searches. Search fee: $5.00 per name. Required to search: name, years to search, address, DOB, SSN, signed release. Criminal records on computer from 6/91, index cards from 1980, index books from 1900s.

General Information: Public Access terminal is available. No expunged records released. SASE required. Turnaround time 10 working days. Copy fee: $1.25 per page. Certification fee: $5.00. Fee payee: Clerk of Court. Business checks accepted. Prepayment is required.

Register in Probate 1516 Church St, Stevens Point, WI 54481; 715-346-1362; Fax: 715-346-1486. Hours: 7:30AM-4:30PM (CST). *Probate.*

Note: Probate records are available free on the Internet at http://ccap.courts.state.wi.us/internetcourtaccess.

Price County

Circuit Court Courthouse, 126 Cherry St, Phillips, WI 54555; 715-339-2353; Fax: 715-339-3079. Hours: 8AM-Noon, 1-4:30PM (CST). *Felony, Misdemeanor, Civil, Eviction, Small Claims.*

Civil Records: Access: Mail, online, in person. Both court and visitors may perform in person searches. Search fee: $5.00 per name. Required to search: name, years to search. Civil cases indexed by defendant, plaintiff. Civil records on computer from 1997, prior on index books. Civil court records are available free on the Internet at http://ccap.courts.state.wi.us/internetcourtaccess/.

Criminal Records: Access: Mail, online, in person. Both court and visitors may perform in person searches. Search fee: $5.00 per name. Required to search: name, years to search, DOB; also helpful: SSN. Criminal records on computer from 1997, prior on index books. Online access to criminal records is the same as civil.

General Information: Public Access terminal is available. No confidential records per statute or order released. SASE required. Turnaround time 1-2 days. Copy fee: $1.25 per page. Certification fee: $5.00. Fee payee: Clerk of Circuit Court. Personal checks accepted. Prepayment is required.

Register in Probate Courthouse, 126 Cherry St, Phillips, WI 54555; 715-339-3078; Fax: 715-339-3079. Hours: 8AM-4:30PM (CST). *Probate.*

Note: Probate records are available free online; see Circuit Court.

Racine County

Circuit Court 730 Wisconsin Ave, Racine, WI 53403; 262-636-3333; Fax: 262-636-3341. Hours: 8AM-5PM (CST). *Felony, Misdemeanor, Civil, Eviction, Small Claims, Probate.*

Civil Records: Access: Mail, online, in person. Both court and visitors may perform in person searches. Search fee: $5.00 per name. Required to search: name, years to search. Civil cases indexed by defendant, plaintiff. Civil records on computer from 1990, index cards from 1970, archives prior to 1970. Civil court records are available free on the Internet at http://ccap.courts.state.wi.us/internetcourtaccess/.

Criminal Records: Access: Mail, online, in person. Both court and visitors may perform in person searches. Search fee: $5.00 per name. Required to search: name, years to search, DOB. Criminal records on computer from 1990, index cards from 1970, archives prior to 1970. Online access to criminal records is the same as civil.

General Information: Public Access terminal is available. No adoption, juvenile, paternity or mental commitment records released. SASE required. Turnaround time 1-2 weeks. Copy fee: $1.25 per page. Certification fee: $5.00. Fee payee: Clerk of Court. Personal checks accepted. Prepayment is required.

Register in Probate 730 Wisconsin Ave, Racine, WI 53403; 262-636-3137; Fax: 262-636-3341. Hours: 8AM-5PM (CST). *Probate.*

Note: Probate records are available free online; see Circuit Court.

Richland County

Circuit Court PO Box 655, Richland Center, WI 53581; 608-647-3956. Hours: 8:30AM-4:30PM (CST). *Felony, Misdemeanor, Civil, Eviction, Small Claims.*

Civil Records: Access: Mail, online, in person. Both court and visitors may perform in person searches. Search fee: $5.00 per name. Required to search: name, years to search. Civil cases indexed by defendant, plaintiff. Civil records on index cards from 1982, index books from 1972, archives prior to 1972, on computer back to 1993. Civil court records are available free at http://ccap.courts.state.wi.us/internetcourtaccess/.

Criminal Records: Access: Mail, online, in person. Only the court performs in person searches; visitors may not. Search fee: $5.00 per name. Required to search: name, years to search, DOB. Criminal records on index cards from 1982, index books from 1972, archives prior to 1972, on computer back t0 1993. Online access to criminal records is the same as civil.

General Information: Public Access terminal is available. No juvenile or paternity records released. SASE required. Turnaround time 1 week. Copy fee: $1.25 per page. Certification fee: $5.00. Fee payee: Clerk of Circuit Court. Personal checks accepted. Personal out-of-state checks not accepted. Prepayment is required.

Register in Probate PO Box 427, Richland Center, WI 53581; 608-647-2626; Fax: 608-647-6134. Hours: 8:30AM-Noon, 1-4:30PM (CST). *Probate.*

Note: Probate records are available free online; see Circuit Court.

Rock County

Circuit Court 51 S Main, Janesville, WI 53545; 608-743-2200; Fax: 608-743-2223. Hours: 8AM-5PM *Felony, Misdemeanor, Civil, Eviction, Small Claims.*

Civil Records: Access: Mail, online, in person. Both court and visitors may perform in person searches. Search fee: $5.00 per name. Required to search: name, years to search. Civil cases indexed by defendant, plaintiff. Civil records on computer from 6/93, on index cards from 6/91, index books from 1940, archives prior to 1940. Civil court records are available free on the Internet at http://ccap.courts.state.wi.us/internetcourtaccess/.

Criminal Records: Access: Mail, online, in person. Both court and visitors may perform in person searches. Search fee: $5.00 per name. Required to search: name, years to search, DOB. Criminal records on computer from 6/93, on index cards from 6/91, index books from 1940, archives prior to 1940. Online access to criminal records is the same as civil.

General Information: Public Access terminal is available. No juvenile, paternity or sealed records released. SASE required. Turnaround time 2-3 days. Copy fee: $1.25 per page. Certification fee: $5.00. Fee payee: Clerk of Court. Personal checks accepted. Prepayment is required.

Circuit Court - South
Janesville Courthouse, 51 S Main St, Janesville, WI 53545; 608-743-2200. Hours: 8AM-5PM (CST). *Felony, Misdemeanor, Civil, Eviction, Small Claims.*

Civil Records: Access: Mail, online, in person. Both court and visitors may perform in person searches. Search fee: $5.00 per name. Required to search: name, years to search. Civil cases indexed by defendant, plaintiff. Civil records on computer from mid-1993, on index cards from 1970s, index books from 1900s in vault. Civil court records are available free online at http://ccap.courts.state.wi.us/internetcourtaccess/.
Criminal Records: Access: Mail, online, in person. Both court and visitors may perform in person searches. Search fee: $5.00 per name. Required to search: name, years to search, DOB. Criminal records on computer from mid-1993, on index cards from 1970s, index books from 1900s in vault. Online access to criminal records is the same as civil.
General Information: Public Access terminal is available. No paternity records released. SASE required. Turnaround time 1 week. Copy fee: $1.25 per page. Certification fee: $5.00. Fee payee: Clerk of Court. Personal checks accepted. Prepayment required.

Register in Probate 51 S Main, Janesville, WI 53545; 608-757-5635. Hours: 8AM-5PM (CST). *Probate.*

Note: Probate records are available free online; see Circuit Court.

Rusk County

Circuit Court 311 Miner Ave East, #L350, Ladysmith, WI 54848; 715-532-2108. Hours: 8AM-4:30PM (CST). *Felony, Misdemeanor, Civil, Small Claims.*

Civil Records: Access: Mail, online, in person, online. Both court and visitors may perform in person searches. Search fee: $5.00 per name. Required to search: name, years to search. Civil cases indexed by defendant, plaintiff. Civil records on computer from 1992, on index cards from 1978, index books from 1900. Civil court records 1992 to present are available free on the Internet at http://ccap.courts.state.wi.us/internetcourtaccess/. Phone requests are accepted if the case number is known.
Criminal Records: Access: Mail, online, in person, online. Both court and visitors may perform in person searches. Search fee: $5.00 per name. Required to search: name, years to search, DOB. Criminal records on computer from 1992, on index cards from 1978, index books from 1900. Online access to criminal records is the same as civil. Phone requests are accepted if the case number is known.
General Information: Public Access terminal is available. No juvenile or paternity records released. SASE required. Turnaround time 5 days. Copy fee: $1.25 per page. Certification fee: $5.00. Fee payee: Clerk of Court. Personal checks accepted. Prepayment is required.

Register in Probate 311 E Miner Ave, Ladysmith, WI 54848; 715-532-2147; Fax: 715-532-2266. Hours: 8AM-4:30PM (CST). *Probate.*

Note: Probate records are available free online; see Circuit Court.

Sauk County

Circuit Court 515 Oak Street, Baraboo, WI 53913; 608-355-3287. Hours: 8AM-4:30PM (CST). *Felony, Misdemeanor, Civil, Eviction, Small Claims.*

Civil Records: Access: Mail, online, in person. Both court and visitors may perform in person searches. Search fee: $5.00 per name. Required to search: name, years to search. Civil cases indexed by defendant, plaintiff. Civil records on computer from 1990, index cards from 1980, index books from 1967. Civil court records are available free on the Internet at http://ccap.courts.state.wi.us/internetcourtaccess/.
Criminal Records: Access: Fax, mail, online, in person. Both court and visitors may perform in person searches. Search fee: $5.00 per name. Required to search: name, years to search. Criminal records on computer from 1990, index cards from 1980, index books from 1967. Online access to criminal records is the same as civil.
General Information: Public Access terminal is available. No paternity, juvenile records released. SASE required. Turnaround time 2-3 days. Fax notes: Fee to fax results is $5.00 1st page, $1.00 each add'l plus tax. Copy fee: $1.25 per page. Certification fee: $5.00. Fee payee: Clerk of Court. Personal checks accepted. Prepayment is required.

Register in Probate 515 Oak St, Baraboo, WI 53913; 608-355-3226; Fax: 608-355-3480. Hours: 8AM-4:30PM (CST). *Probate.*

Note: Probate records are available free online; see Circuit Court.

Sawyer County

Circuit Court PO Box 508, Hayward, WI 54843; 715-634-4887. Hours: 8AM-4PM (CST). *Felony, Misdemeanor, Civil, Eviction, Small Claims.*

Civil Records: Access: Mail, online, in person. Both court and visitors may perform in person searches. Search fee: $5.00 per name. Required to search: name, years to search. Civil cases indexed by defendant, plaintiff. Civil records on index cards from 7/85, prior on books. Civil court records are available free online at http://ccap.courts.state.wi.us/internetcourtaccess/.
Criminal Records: Access: Mail, online, in person. Both court and visitors may perform in person searches. Search fee: $5.00 per name. Required to search: name, years to search. Criminal records on index cards from 7/85, prior on books. Online access to criminal records is the same as civil.
General Information: Public Access terminal is available. No juvenile, probate or paternity records released. SASE required. Turnaround time 1 day. Copy fee: $1.25 per page. Certification fee: $5.00. Fee payee: Clerk of Court. Personal checks accepted. Prepayment is required.

Register in Probate PO Box 447, Hayward, WI 54843; 715-634-7519. 8AM-4PM (CST). *Probate.*

Note: Probate records are available free online; see Circuit Court.

Shawano County

Circuit Court 311 N Main Rm 206, Shawano, WI 54166; 715-526-9347; Fax: 715-526-4915. Hours: 8AM-4:30PM (CST). *Felony, Misdemeanor, Civil, Eviction, Small Claims.*

www.co.shawano.wi.us

Civil Records: Access: Fax, mail, online, in person. Both court and visitors may perform in person searches. Search fee: $5.00 per name. Required to search: name, years to search. Civil cases indexed by defendant, plaintiff. Civil records on computer from 1993, on index books from 1930s, prior in archives. Civil court records

are available free on the Internet at http://ccap.courts.state.wi.us/internetcourtaccess/.
Criminal Records: Access: Fax, mail, online, in person. Both court and visitors may perform in person searches. Search fee: $5.00 per name. Required to search: name, years to search, DOB. Criminal records on computer from 1993, on index books from 1930s, prior in archives. Online access to criminal records is the same as civil.
General Information: Public Access terminal is available. No juvenile, closed files or mental records released. SASE required. Turnaround time 10-20 days. Fax notes: $1.25 per page, add $2.50 for long distance. Copy fee: $1.25 per page. Certification fee: $5.00. Fee payee: Clerk of Court. Personal checks accepted.

Register in Probate 311 N Main, Rm 203, Shawano, WI 54166; 715-526-8631; Fax: 715-526-8622. Hours: 8AM-4:30PM (CST). *Probate.*

Note: Probate records are available free online; see Circuit Court.

Sheboygan County

Circuit Court 615 N 6th St, Sheboygan, WI 53081; 920-459-3068; Fax: 920-459-3921. Hours: 8AM-5PM (CST). *Felony, Misdemeanor, Civil, Eviction, Small Claims.*

Civil Records: Access: Mail, online, in person. Both court and visitors may perform in person searches. Search fee: $5.00 per name. Required to search: name, years to search; also helpful: address. Civil cases indexed by defendant, plaintiff. Civil records on computer since 1992; prior records on index cards from 1960, index books from 1860s, archives prior to 1971. Civil court records are available free on the Internet at http://ccap.courts.state.wi.us/internetcourtaccess/.
Criminal Records: Access: Mail, online, in person. Both court and visitors may perform in person searches. Search fee: $5.00 per name. Required to search: name, years to search, DOB; also helpful: address. Criminal records on computer since 1992; prior records on index cards from 1960, index books from 1860s, archives prior to 1971. Online access to criminal records is the same as civil.
General Information: Public Access terminal is available. No juvenile or paternity records released. SASE required. Turnaround time 2-3 days. Copy fee: $1.25 per page. Certification fee: $5.00. Fee payee: Clerk of Circuit Court. Personal checks accepted. Prepayment is required.

Register in Probate 615 N 6th St, Sheboygan, WI 53081; 920-459-3050 & 459-3202; Fax: 920-459-0541. Hours: 8AM-5PM (CST). *Probate.*

Note: There is a $4.00 search fee. Probate records are available free online; see Circuit Court.

St. Croix County

Circuit Court 1101 Carmichael Rd, Hudson, WI 54016; 715-386-4630. Hours: 8AM-5PM (CST). *Felony, Misdemeanor, Civil, Eviction, Small Claims.*

Civil Records: Access: Mail, online, in person. Both court and visitors may perform in person searches. Search fee: $5.00 per name. Required to search: name, years to search. Civil cases indexed by defendant, plaintiff. Civil records on computer from 10/92, on index cards from 1982, index books from 1900s. Civil court records are available free on the Internet at http://ccap.courts.state.wi.us/internetcourtaccess/.
Criminal Records: Access: Mail, online, in person. Both court and visitors may perform in person searches. Search fee: $5.00 per name. Required to search: name, years to search, DOB. Criminal records on computer from 10/92, on index cards from 1982, index books from 1900s. Online access to criminal records is the same as civil.

General Information: Public Access terminal is available. No juvenile forfeitures, paternity, some case specific documents or sealed records released. SASE required. Turnaround time 5-10 days. Copy fee: $1.25 per page. Certification fee: $5.00. Fee payee: Clerk of Court. Personal checks accepted. Prepayment required.

Register in Probate 1101 Carmichael Rd, Rm 2242, Hudson, WI 54016; 715-386-4618; Fax: 715-381-4401. Hours: 8AM-5PM (CST). *Probate.*

Note: Probate records are available free online; see Circuit Court.

Taylor County

Circuit Court 224 S 2nd St, Medford, WI 54451-1811; 715-748-1425; Fax: 715-748-2465. Hours: 8:30AM-4:30PM (CST). *Felony, Misdemeanor, Civil, Eviction, Small Claims.*

Civil Records: Access: Mail, online, in person. Both court and visitors may perform in person searches. Search fee: $5.00 per name. Required to search: name, years to search. Civil cases indexed by defendant, plaintiff. Civil records on computer from 1989; prior records index books from 1917. Civil court records are available free on the Internet at http://ccap.courts.state.wi.us/internetcourtaccess.

Criminal Records: Access: Mail, online, in person. Both court and visitors may perform in person searches. Search fee: $5.00 per name. Required to search: name, years to search, DOB. Criminal records on computer from 1989; prior records index books from 1917. Online access to criminal records is the same as civil.

General Information: Public Access terminal is available. No sealed records released. SASE required. Turnaround time 1-2 days. Copy fee: $1.25 per page. Certification fee: $5.00. Fee payee: Clerk of Circuit Court. Personal checks accepted. Prepayment required.

Register in Probate 224 S 2nd, Medford, WI 54451; 715-748-1435; Fax: 715-748-2465. Hours: 8:30AM-4:30PM (CST). *Probate.*

http://ccap.courts.state.wi.us/internetcourtaccess

Note: Probate records are available free online; see Circuit Court.

Trempealeau County

Circuit Court 36245 Main St, Whitehall, WI 54773; 715-538-2311. Hours: 8AM-4:30PM (CST). *Felony, Misdemeanor, Civil, Eviction, Small Claims.*

www.win.bright.net/~tremphea/circuitcourt.htm

Civil Records: Access: Fax, mail, online, in person. Both court and visitors may perform in person searches. Search fee: $5.00 per name. Required to search: name, years to search. Civil cases indexed by defendant, plaintiff. Civil records on computer from 1993, on index cards from 1987, index books from 1940, archives prior to 1940. Civil court records are available free online at http://ccap.courts.state.wi.us/internetcourtaccess/.

Criminal Records: Access: Fax, mail, online, in person. Both court and visitors may perform in person searches. Search fee: $5.00 per name. Required to search: name, years to search, DOB. Criminal records on computer from 1993, on index cards from 1987, index books from 1940, archives prior to 1940. Online access to criminal records is the same as civil.

General Information: Public Access terminal is available. No juvenile, paternity or child support records released. SASE required. Turnaround time 2-3 days. Fax notes: $2.00 per page. Copy fee: $1.25 per page. Certification fee: $5.00. Fee payee: Clerk of Circuit Court. Personal checks accepted. Prepayment is required.

Register in Probate 36245 Main St, PO Box 67, Whitehall, WI 54773; 715-538-2311 X238; Fax: 715-538-4400. Hours: 8AM-4:30PM (CST). *Probate.*

www.win.bright.net/~tremphea/circuitcourt.htm

Note: Probate records are available free online; see Circuit Court.

Vernon County

Circuit Court PO Box 426, Viroqua, WI 54665; 608-637-5340; Fax: 608-637-5554. Hours: 8:30AM-4:30PM (CST). *Felony, Misdemeanor, Civil, Eviction, Small Claims.*

Civil Records: Access: Phone, fax, mail, online, in person. Both court and visitors may perform in person searches. Search fee: $5.00 per name. Required to search: name, years to search, DOB. Civil cases indexed by defendant, plaintiff. Civil records on computer back to 1993; on index books & cards 1950 to 1992. Civil court records are available free on the Internet at http://ccap.courts.state.wi.us/internetcourtaccess/.

Criminal Records: Access: Phone, fax, mail, online, in person. Both court and visitors may perform in person searches. Search fee: $5.00 per name. Required to search: name, years to search; also helpful: DOB. Criminal records on computer back to 1993; on index books & cards 1950 to 1992. Online access to criminal records is the same as civil.

General Information: Public Access terminal is available. No paternity or juvenile records released. SASE required. Turnaround time 2-3 days. Copy fee: $.25 per page. Certification fee: $5.00. Fee payee: Clerk of Court. Personal checks accepted. Will bill to attorneys & credit agencies.

Register in Probate PO Box 448, Viroqua, WI 54665; 608-637-5347; Fax: 608-637-5554. Hours: 8:30AM-4:30PM (CST). *Probate.*

Note: Probate records are available free online; see Circuit Court.

Vilas County

Circuit Court 330 Court St, Eagle River, WI 54521; 715-479-3632; Fax: 715-479-3740. Hours: 8AM-4PM (CST). *Felony, Misdemeanor, Civil, Eviction, Small Claims.*

Civil Records: Access: Mail, online, in person. Both court and visitors may perform in person searches. Search fee: $5.00 per name. Required to search: name, years to search. Civil records on computer back to 1992, index cards from 1978, index books from 1900s. Civil court records are available free on the Internet at http://ccap.courts.state.wi.us/internetcourtaccess/.

Criminal Records: Access: Mail, online, in person. Both court and visitors may perform in person searches. Search fee: $5.00 per name. Required to search: name, years to search, DOB. Criminal records on computer back to 1992; index cards from 1978, index books from 1900s. Online access to criminal records is the same as civil.

General Information: Public Access terminal is available. No paternity records released. SASE required. Turnaround time 2 weeks. Fax notes: Fee to fax results is $1.25 per page. Copy fee: $1.25 per page. Certification fee: $5.00. Fee payee: Clerk of Circuit Court. Personal checks accepted. Prepayment required.

Register in Probate 330 Court St, Eagle River, WI 54521; 715-479-3642; Fax: 715-479-3740. Hours: 8AM-4PM (CST). *Probate.*

Note: Probate records are available free online; see Circuit Court.

Walworth County

Circuit Court PO Box 1001, Elkhorn, WI 53121-1001; 262-741-4224; Fax: 262-741-4379. Hours: 8AM-5PM (CST). *Felony, Misdemeanor, Civil, Eviction, Small Claims.*

www.co.walworth.wi.us

Civil Records: Access: Mail, in person. Both court and visitors may perform in person searches. Search fee: $5.00 per name. Required to search: name, years to search. Civil cases indexed by defendant, plaintiff. Civil records on computer from 1989, index cards/books from 1836.

Criminal Records: Access: Mail, in person. Both court and visitors may perform in person searches. Search fee: $5.00 per name. Required to search: name, years to search, DOB. Criminal records on computer from 1989, index cards/books from 1836 (organized).

General Information: Public Access terminal is available. No sealed records released. SASE required. Turnaround time 1-2 days. Copy fee: $1.25 per page. Certification fee: $5.00. Fee payee: County Clerk of Courts. Business checks accepted. Credit cards accepted: Visa, MasterCard. Credit cards accepted in person only. Prepayment is required.

Register in Probate PO Box 1001, Elkhorn, WI 53121; 262-741-4256; Fax: 262-741-4182. Hours: 8AM-5PM (CST). *Probate.*

Washburn County

Circuit Court PO Box 339, Shell Lake, WI 54871; 715-468-4677; Fax: 715-468-4678. Hours: 8AM-4:30PM (CST). *Felony, Misdemeanor, Civil, Eviction, Small Claims.*

Civil Records: Access: Mail, online, in person. Both court and visitors may perform in person searches. Search fee: $5.00 per name. Required to search: name, years to search. Civil cases indexed by defendant, plaintiff. Civil records on computer since 1993 (civil money judgments back to 1/1/90); on index books from 1883. Civil court records are available free online at http://ccap.courts.state.wi.us/internetcourtaccess/.

Criminal Records: Access: Mail, online, in person. Both court and visitors may perform in person searches. Search fee: $5.00 per name. Required to search: name, years to search; also helpful: DOB. Criminal records on computer since 1993; on index books from 1883. Online access to criminal records is the same as civil.

General Information: Public Access terminal is available. No sealed records released. SASE required. Turnaround time 2-3 days. Copy fee: $1.25 per page. Certification fee: $5.00. Fee payee: Clerk of Court. Personal checks accepted. Prepayment is required.

Register in Probate PO Box 316, Shell Lake, WI 54871; 715-468-4688; Fax: 715-468-4678. Hours: 8AM-4:30PM (CST). *Probate.*

Note: Probate records are available free online; see Circuit Court.

Washington County

Circuit Court PO Box 1986, West Bend, WI 53095-7986; 262-335-4341; Fax: 262-335-4776. Hours: 8AM-4:30PM (CST). *Felony, Misdemeanor, Civil, Eviction, Small Claims.*

www.co.washington.wi.us

Civil Records: Access: Mail, fax, online, in person. Both court and visitors may perform in person searches. Search fee: $5.00 per name. Required to search: name, years to search; also helpful: address. Civil cases indexed by defendant, plaintiff. Civil records on computer from 1986, index cards from 1976, index books from 1836. Civil court records are available free on the Internet at http://ccap.courts.state.wi.us/internetcourtaccess/.

Criminal Records: Access: Mail, fax, online, in person. Both court and visitors may perform in person searches. Search fee: $5.00 per name. Required to search: name, years to search, DOB; also helpful: address. Criminal records on computer from 1986, index cards from 1976, index books from 1836. Online access to criminal records is the same as civil.

General Information: Public Access terminal is available. No paternity records released prior to adjudication. SASE required. Turnaround time 1 week. Copy fee: $1.25 per page. Certification fee: $5.00. Fee payee: Clerk of Court. Personal checks accepted. Prepayment is required.

Register in Probate PO Box 82, West Bend, WI 53095-0082; 262-335-4334; Fax: 262-306-2224. Hours: 8AM-4:30PM (CST). *Probate.*

www.co.washington.wi.us

Note: Probate records are available free online; see Circuit Court.

Waukesha County

Circuit Court 515 W Moreland Blvd, Waukesha, WI 53188; Civil phone: 262-548-7525; Criminal phone: 262-548-7485; Fax: 262-896-8228. Hours: 8AM-4:30PM (CST). *Felony, Misdemeanor, Civil, Eviction, Small Claims.*

www.co.waukesha.wi.us/departments/courts/index.html

Civil Records: Access: Mail, online, in person. Both court and visitors may perform in person searches. Search fee: $5.00 per name. Required to search: name, years to search. Civil cases indexed by defendant, plaintiff. Civil records on computer back to 1994. Civil court records are available free on the Internet at http://ccap.courts.state.wi.us/internetcourtaccess/.

Criminal Records: Access: Mail, online, in person. Both court and visitors may perform in person searches. Search fee: $5.00 per name. Required to search: name, years to search, DOB. Criminal records on computer back to 1994. Online access to criminal records is the same as civil.

General Information: Public Access terminal is available. No paternity, mental commitment records released. SASE required. Turnaround time 2-3 days. Fax notes: Fee to fax is $3.00 per document plus $1.25 per page. Copy fee: $1.25 per page. Certification fee: $5.00. Fee payee: Clerk of Circuit Court. Personal checks accepted. Credit cards accepted. Accepted in person only. Prepayment is required.

Register in Probate 515 W Moreland, Rm 375, Waukesha, WI 53188; 262-548-7468. 8AM-4:30PM M,T,Th,F; 7:30AM-5:30PM W (CST). *Probate.*

Note: Probate records are available free online; see Circuit Court.

Waupaca County

Circuit Court 811 Harding St, Waupaca, WI 54981; 715-258-6460. Hours: 8AM-4PM (CST). *Felony, Misdemeanor, Civil, Eviction, Small Claims.*

Civil Records: Access: Mail, online, in person. Both court and visitors may perform in person searches. Search fee: $5.00 per name. Required to search: name, years to search. Civil cases indexed by defendant, plaintiff. Civil records on computer from 1992. Civil court records are available free on the Internet at http://ccap.courts.state.wi.us/internetcourtaccess/.

Criminal Records: Access: Mail, online, in person. Both court and visitors may perform in person searches. Search fee: $5.00 per name. Required to search: name, years to search. Criminal records on computer from 1992. Online access to criminal records is the same as civil.

General Information: Public Access terminal is available. No juvenile, JO, paternity excluding past judgments released. SASE required. Turnaround time 3-4 days. Copy fee: $1.25 per page. Computer document copy fee $.50 per page. Certification fee: $5.00. Fee payee: Clerk of Court. Business checks accepted. Personal in-state checks accepted. Prepayment is required.

Register in Probate 811 Harding St, Waupaca, WI 54981; 715-258-6429; Fax: 715-258-6440. Hours: 8AM-4PM (CST). *Probate.*

Note: Probate records are available free online; see Circuit Court.

Waushara County

Circuit Court PO Box 507, Wautoma, WI 54982; 920-787-0441; Fax: 920-787-0481. Hours: 8AM-4:30PM (CST). *Felony, Misdemeanor, Civil, Eviction, Small Claims.*

Civil Records: Access: Mail, fax, online, in person. Both court and visitors may perform in person searches. Search fee: $5.00 per name. fee only if court does search. Required to search: name, years to search. Civil cases indexed by defendant. Civil records on computer from 1992, index cards prior to 1978, index books from 1900s. Civil court records are available free online at http://ccap.courts.state.wi.us/internetcourtaccess/.

Criminal Records: Access: Mail, fax, online, in person. Both court and visitors may perform in person searches. Search fee: $5.00 per name. Fee applies if court does search. Required to search: name, years to search, DOB. Criminal records on computer from 1993, prior on cards and books. Online access to criminal records is the same as civil.

General Information: Public Access terminal is available. SASE required. Turnaround time 1-2 weeks. Copy fee: $1.25 per page. Certification fee: $5.00. Fee payee: Clerk of Court. Personal checks accepted. Personal in-state checks accepted, money orders for out of state requests. Prepayment is required.

Register in Probate PO Box 508, Wautoma, WI 54982; 920-787-0448. Hours: 8AM-4:30PM (CST). *Probate.*

Note: Probate records are available free online; see Circuit Court.

Winnebago County

Circuit Court PO Box 2808, Oshkosh, WI 54903-2808; 920-236-4848; Fax: 920-424-7780. Hours: 8AM-4:30PM (CST). *Felony, Misdemeanor, Civil, Eviction, Small Claims.*

Civil Records: Access: Mail, fax, online, in person. Both court and visitors may perform in person searches. Search fee: $5.00 per name. Required to search: name, years to search. Civil cases indexed by defendant, plaintiff. Civil records are on computer since 1990, prior on books and cards. organized since 1938. Civil court records are available free on the Internet at http://ccap.courts.state.wi.us/internetcourtaccess/.

Criminal Records: Access: Mail, fax, online, in person. Both court and visitors may perform in person searches. Search fee: $5.00 per name. Required to search: full name, years to search, DOB. Criminal records are on computer since 1990, prior on books and cards. organized since 1938. Online access to criminal records is the same as civil.

General Information: Public Access terminal is available. No juvenile, paternity, financial records released. SASE required. Turnaround time 1 week. Fax notes: Fee to fax results is $1.25 per page. Copy fee: $1.25 per page. Certification fee: $5.00. Fee payee: Clerk of Courts. Personal checks accepted.

Register in Probate PO Box 2808, Oshkosh, WI 54903-2808; 920-236-4833; Fax: 920-424-7536. Hours: 8AM-Noon, 1-4:30PM (CST). *Probate.*

Note: There is a $4.00 search fee. Probate records are available free online; see Circuit Court.

Wood County

Circuit Court 400 Market St, Po Box 8095, Wisconsin Rapids, WI 54494-958095; 715-421-8490. Hours: 8AM-4:30PM (CST). *Felony, Misdemeanor, Civil, Eviction, Small Claims.*

Civil Records: Access: Mail, online, in person. Both court and visitors may perform in person searches. Search fee: $5.00 per name. Required to search: name, years to search. Civil cases indexed by defendant, plaintiff. Civil records on computer from 1983, microfiche from 1856-1980s. Court records are available free on the Internet at http://ccap.courts.state.wi.us/internetcourtaccess/.

Criminal Records: Access: Mail, online, in person. Both court and visitors may perform in person searches. Search fee: $5.00 per name. Required to search: name, years to search, DOB. Criminal records on computer from 1980. Online access to criminal records is the same as civil.

General Information: Public Access terminal is available. No paternity or sealed records released. SASE required. Turnaround time 2-3 days. Copy fee: $1.25 per page. Certification fee: $5.00. Fee payee: Clerk of Court. Personal checks accepted. Prepayment is required.

Register in Probate Wood County Courthouse, PO Box 8095, Wisconsin Rapids, WI 54495-8095; 715-421-8520; Fax: 715-421-8808. Hours: 8AM-4:30PM (CST). *Probate.*

Note: Court also holds guardianships, juveniles, mental and adoption records. Probate records are available free online; see Circuit Court.

Wisconsin Recording Offices

ORGANIZATION
72 counties, 72 recording offices. The recording officers are Register of Deeds and Clerk of Court (state tax liens). The entire state is in the Central Time Zone (CST).

REAL ESTATE RECORDS
Registers will not perform real estate searches. Copy fees and certification fees vary. Assessor telephone numbers are for local municipalities or for property listing agencies. Counties do not have assessors. Copies usually cost $2.00 for the first page and $1.00 for each additional page. Certification usually costs $.25 per document. The Treasurer maintains property tax records.

UCC RECORDS
Financing statements are filed at the state level, except for real estate related collateral, which are filed with the Register of Deeds. However, prior to 07/2001, consumer goods and farm collateral were also filed at the Register of Deeds and these older records can be searched there. Nearly all recording offices will perform UCC searches, and many will accept a search by phone. Use search request form UCC-11 for mail-in searches. Searches fees are usually $10.00 per debtor name. Copy fees are usually $1.00 per page.

TAX LIEN RECORDS
Federal tax liens on personal property of businesses are filed with the Secretary of State. Other federal tax liens are filed with the county Register of Deeds. State tax liens are filed with the Clerk of Court. Refer to the County Court Records section for information about Wisconsin courts. Many Registers will perform federal tax lien searches. Search fees and copy fees vary.

OTHER LIENS
Judgment, mechanics, breeders.

Adams County

Register of Deeds, P.O. Box 219, Friendship, WI 53934-0219. 608-339-4206.
Will search UCC records. Will not search real estate records.

Ashland County

Register of Deeds, 201 West Main Street, Room 206, Ashland, WI 54806. 715-682-7008; Fax 715-682-7032.
Will search UCC records. Will not search real estate records. **Other Phone Numbers:** Treasurer 715-682-7012; Elections 715-682-7000; Vital Records 715-682-7008.

Barron County

Register of Deeds, 330 East LaSalle, Room 201, Barron, WI 54812. Register of Deeds, R/E and UCC Recording 715-537-6210; Fax 715-537-6277.
Will search UCC records. Will not search real estate records. **Other Phone Numbers:** Assessor 715-537-6313; Treasurer 715-537-6270; Vital Records 715-537-6210.

Bayfield County

Register of Deeds, P.O. Box 813, Washburn, WI 54891. 715-373-6119.
Will search UCC records. UCC search does not include federal tax liens. Will not search real estate records.

Brown County

Register of Deeds, P.O. Box 23600, Green Bay, WI 54305-3600. 920-448-4470 R/E Recording: 920-448-4439 UCC Recording: 920-448-4468; Fax 920-448-4449. http://www.co.brown.wi.us/rod
Will search UCC records. Will not search real estate records. **Online Access:** Real Estate. Online access to Register of Deeds real estate records is available by subscription at http://www.co.brown.wi.us/rod/LaredoTapestry/main.html. Registration and fees are required. A more sophisticated subscription system, named Laredo, offers full access to land records for firms operating in Wisconsin. **Other Phone Numbers:** Treasurer 920-448-4074; Elections 920-448-4016; Vital Records 920-448-4474; Automated 920-448-4470.

Buffalo County

Register of Deeds, P.O. Box 28, Alma, WI 54610-0028. 608-685-6230; Fax 608-685-6213.
Will search UCC records. Will not search real estate records. **Other Phone Numbers:** Treasurer 608-685-6215.

Burnett County

Register of Deeds, 7410 County Road K #103, Siren, WI 54872. 715-349-2183.
Will search UCC records. UCC search does not include federal tax liens. Will not search real estate records. **Other Phone Numbers:** Treasurer 715-349-2187.

Calumet County

Register of Deeds, 206 Court Street, Chilton, WI 53014. 920-849-1441; Fax 920-849-1469.
Will search UCC records. Will not search real estate records.

Chippewa County

Register of Deeds, 711 North Bridge Street, Chippewa Falls, WI 54729-1876. 715-726-7994; Fax 715-726-4582. http://www.co.chippewa.wi.us
Will search UCC records. Will not doa title search; will search for one or two records. **Other Phone Numbers:** Treasurer 715-726-7965; Elections 715-726-7980.

Clark County

Registrar, P.O. Box 384, Neillsville, WI 54456-1989. 715-743-5162 R/E Recording: 715-743-5163 UCC Recording: 715-743-5163; Fax 715-743-5154.
Will search UCC records. Will not search real estate records. **Other Phone Numbers:** Treasurer 715-743-5155; Elections 715-743-5148; Vital Records 715-743-5163.

Columbia County

Register of Deeds, P.O. Box 133, Portage, WI 53901. 608-742-9677; Fax 608-742-9602.
Will search UCC records. Will not search real estate records. **Other Phone Numbers:** Assessor 608-742-9677; Treasurer 608-742-9613.

Crawford County

Register of Deeds, 220 North Beaumont Road, Prairie du Chien, WI 53821. Register of Deeds, R/E and UCC Recording 608-326-0219; Fax 608-326-0220.
Will search UCC records. Will not search real estate records. **Other Phone Numbers:** Vital Records 608-326-0219.

Dane County

Register of Deeds, P.O. Box 1438, Madison, WI 53701. Register of Deeds, R/E and UCC Recording 608-266-4141 UCC Recording: 608-266-4143; Fax 608-267-3110. http://www.co.dane.wi.us/regdeeds/rdhome.htm
Will search UCC records. Will not search real estate records. **Online Access:** Assessor, Real Estate. Records on the geographic & land database are available free online at http://dc-web.co.dane.wi.us/dane. For fuller access, a subscription service is available. Also, parcel information is available free at http://dc-web.co.dane.wi.us/dane/html/parcelsearch.asp. Professional companies may register to use assessor/land record services at http://dc-web.co.dane.wi.us/dane/html/community.asp. Registration & login. Also, the City of Madison tax assessor database is accessible at www.ci.madison.wi.us/assessor/property.html. **Other Phone Numbers:** Vital Records 608-266-4142.

Dodge County

Register of Deeds, 127 East Oak Street, Administration Building, Juneau, WI 53039-1391. Register of Deeds, R/E and UCC Recording 920-386-3720 UCC Recording: 920-386-3723; Fax 920-386-3902.
Will search UCC records. Will not search real estate records. **Other Phone Numbers:** Assessor 920-386-3770; Treasurer 414-386-3781; Vital Records 920-386-3720.

Door County

Register of Deeds, P.O. Box 670, Sturgeon Bay, WI 54235-0670. Register of Deeds, R/E and UCC Recording 920-746-2270 UCC Recording: 608-261-9548 (Madison); Fax 920-746-2525. www.wrda.org
Will not search real estate records. **Other Phone Numbers:** Assessor 920-746-2905; Treasurer 920-746-2286; Vital Records 920-746-2270.

Douglas County

Register of Deeds, PO Box 847, Superior, WI 54880. 715-395-1463 R/E Recording: 715-395-1350; Fax 715-395-1553. http://www.douglascountywi.org
Will search UCC records. Will not search real estate records. **Other Phone Numbers:** Treasurer 715-395-1348; Elections 715-395-1397; Vital Records 715-395-1463.

Dunn County

Register of Deeds, 800 Wilson Avenue, Menomonie, WI 54751. 715-232-1228; Fax 715-232-1324.
Will search UCC records. Will not search real estate records. **Other Phone Numbers:** Assessor 715-232-1401; Treasurer 715-232-3789.

Eau Claire County

Register of Deeds, P.O. Box 718, Eau Claire, WI 54702. 715-839-4745.
Will search UCC records. UCC search does not include federal tax liens. Will not search real estate records. **Other Phone Numbers:** Treasurer 715-839-4745.

Florence County

Register of Deeds, P.O. Box 410, Florence, WI 54121-0410. 715-528-4252; Fax 715-528-5470.
Will search UCC records.

Fond du Lac County

Register of Deeds, P.O. Box 509, Fond du Lac, WI 54935-0509. 920-929-3018 R/E Recording: 920-929-3021 UCC Recording: 920-929-3022; Fax 920-929-3293. http://www.co.fond-du-lac.wi.us
Will search UCC records. This agency will not do a federal tax lien search. Will not search real estate records. **Other Phone Numbers:** Assessor 920-929-3010; Treasurer 920-929-3010; Elections 920-929-3000; Vital Records 920-929-3019.

Forest County

Register of Deeds, 200 E. Madison Street, Crandon, WI 54520. Register of Deeds, R/E and UCC Recording 715-478-3823.
Will search UCC records. UCC search does not include federal tax liens. Will not search real estate records. **Other Phone Numbers:** Treasurer 715-478-2412; Elections 715-478-2422; Vital Records 715-478-3823.

Grant County

Register of Deeds, P.O. Box 391, Lancaster, WI 53813-0391. Register of Deeds, R/E and UCC Recording 608-723-2727; Fax 608-723-4048.
Will search UCC records. Will not search real estate records. **Other Phone Numbers:** Assessor 608-723-2666; Treasurer 608-723-2604; Elections 608-723-2675; Vital Records 608-723-2727.

Green County

Register of Deeds, 1016 16th Avenue, Courthouse, Monroe, WI 53566. 608-328-9439; Fax 608-328-2835.
Will search UCC records. UCC search includes federal tax liens if requested. Will not search real estate records.

Green Lake County

Register of Deeds, P.O. Box 3188, Green Lake, WI 54941-3188. Register of Deeds, R/E and UCC Recording 920-294-4021; Fax 920-294-4165.
Will search UCC records. **Other Phone Numbers:** Treasurer 920-294-4018; Vital Records 920-294-4019.

Iowa County

Register of Deeds, 222 North Iowa Street, Dodgeville, WI 53533. 608-935-0396; Fax 608-935-3024.

Will search UCC records. Will not search real estate records.

Iron County

Register of Deeds, 300 Taconite Street, Hurley, WI 54534. Register of Deeds, R/E and UCC Recording 715-561-2945; Fax 715-561-2928.
Will search UCC records. Will not search real estate records. **Other Phone Numbers:** Assessor 715-561-2883; Treasurer 715-561-2883; Appraiser/Auditor 715-561-2883; Vital Records 715-561-2945.

Jackson County

Register of Deeds, 307 Main, Black River Falls, WI 54615. 715-284-0204; Fax 715-284-0261.
Will search UCC records. Will not search real estate records.

Jefferson County

Register of Deeds, P.O. Box 356, Jefferson, WI 53549. 920-674-7235.
Will search UCC records. Federal tax liens included in UCC search if requested. Will not search real estate records. **Other Phone Numbers:** Treasurer 414-674-7250.

Juneau County

Register of Deeds, P.O. Box 100, Mauston, WI 53948-0100. Register of Deeds, R/E and UCC Recording 608-847-9325; Fax 608-849-9369.
Will search UCC records. Will not search real estate records. **Other Phone Numbers:** Treasurer 608-847-9308; Elections 608-847-9302; Vital Records 608-847-9325.

Kenosha County

Register of Deeds, 1010 56 St., Kenosha, WI 53140. 262-653-2444 R/E Recording: 414-653-2441; Fax 262-653-2564.
Will search UCC records. Will not search real estate records. **Online Access:** Real Estate, Liens, Vital Records. The set-up fee is $500, plus $6.00 per hour usage fee. The sytem operates 24 hours daily; records date back to 5/1986. Federal tax liens are listed. Lending agency information is available. For further information, contact Joellyn Storz at 262-653-2511. **Other Phone Numbers:** Assessor 414-653-2545; Treasurer 414-653-2542; Vital Records 262-653-2444.

Kewaunee County

Register of Deeds, 613 Dodge Street, Kewaunee, WI 54216-1398. 920-388-7126; Fax 920-388-7195.
Will search UCC records. Will not search real estate records. **Other Phone Numbers:** Assessor 920-388-4410 x118.

La Crosse County

Register of Deeds, 400 North 4th Street, Room 106, Administrative Center, La Crosse, WI 54601-3200. 608-785-9644 R/E Recording: 608-785-9652 UCC Recording: 608-785-9651; Fax 608-785-9704. http://www.co.la-crosse.wi.us/departments.htm
Will search UCC records. Will not search real estate records. **Other Phone Numbers:** Assessor 608-785-7525; Treasurer 608-785-9711; Vital Records 608-785-9652.

Lafayette County

Register of Deeds, P.O. Box 170, Darlington, WI 53530. Register of Deeds, R/E and UCC Recording 608-776-4838; Fax 608-776-4991.
Will Search UCC records. **Other Phone Numbers:** Treasurer 608-776-4862; Elections 608-776-4850; Vital Records 608-776-4838.

Langlade County

Register of Deeds, 800 Clermont Street, Antigo, WI 54409. 715-627-6209; Fax 715-627-6303.
Will search UCC records. Will not search real estate records. **Other Phone Numbers:** Treasurer 715-627-6204.

Lincoln County

Register of Deeds, 1110 East Main, Courthouse, Merrill, WI 54452. Register of Deeds, R/E and UCC Recording 715-536-0318; Fax 715-536-0360. www.co.lincoln.wi.us
Will search UCC records. Will not search real estate records. **Other Phone Numbers:** Assessor 715-536-0479; Treasurer 715-536-0315; Elections 715-536-0359; Vital Records 715-536-0318.

Manitowoc County

Register of Deeds, P.O. Box 421, Manitowoc, WI 54221-0421. 920-683-4010; Fax 920-683-2702. http://www.manitowoc.org
Will search UCC records. Will not search real estate records. **Online Access:** Assessor, Real Estate. Records on the City of Manitowoc Assessor database are available free online at http://assessor.manitowoc.org/default.htm. **Other Phone Numbers:** Assessor 920-683-4425; Treasurer 920-683-4020.

Marathon County

Register of Deeds, 500 Forest Street, Courthouse, Wausau, WI 54403-5568. Register of Deeds, R/E and UCC Recording 715-261-1470; Fax 715-261-1488.
Will search UCC records. **Other Phone Numbers:** Assessor 715-843-1300; Treasurer 715-261-1150; Elections 715-261-1500; Vital Records 715-261-1470.

Marinette County

Register of Deeds, 1926 Hall Avenue, Courthouse, Marinette, WI 54143. 715-732-7550; Fax 715-732-7532.
Will search UCC records. Will not search real estate records. **Other Phone Numbers:** Treasurer 715-732-7430.

Marquette County

Register of Deeds, P.O. Box 236, Montello, WI 53949-0236. 608-297-9132; Fax 608-297-7606.
Will search UCC records. Will not search real estate records. **Other Phone Numbers:** Treasurer 608-297-9148.

Menominee County

Register of Deeds, PO Box 279, Keshena, WI 54135-0279. Register of Deeds, R/E and UCC Recording 715-799-3312; Fax 715-799-1322.
Will search UCC records. **Other Phone Numbers:** Assessor 715-799-3315; Treasurer 715-799-3001; Appraiser/Auditor 715-799-3001; Elections 715-799-3311; Vital Records 715-799-3312.

Milwaukee County

Register of Deeds, 901 North 9th Street, Milwaukee, WI 53233. Register of Deeds, R/E and UCC Recording 414-278-4005 UCC Recording: 414-278-4006; Fax 414-223-1257. http://www.co.milwaukee.wi.us
Will search UCC records. **Online Access:** Assessor, Real Estate. Ownership, Property and Assessment data as well as sales data by year on the Milwaukee City (not county) Assessor Office database are available free online at www.ci.mil.wi.us/citygov/assessor/assessments.htm. Search by address. **Other Phone Numbers:** Assessor 414-286-3651; Treasurer 414-278-4033; Elections 414-278-4060; Vital Records 414-278-4003.

Monroe County

Register of Deeds, P.O. Box 195, Sparta, WI 54656. 608-269-8716.
Will search UCC records. UCC search includes federal tax liens if requested. RE record owner searches available. **Other Phone Numbers:** Treasurer 608-269-8710.

Oconto County

Register of Deeds, 301 Washington Street, Room 2035, Oconto, WI 54153-1699. 920-834-6807; www.co.oconto.wi.us
Will search UCC records. UCC search includes federal tax liens if requested. Will not search real estate records. **Other Phone Numbers:** Treasurer 920-834-6813.

Oneida County

Register of Deeds, P.O. Box 400, Rhinelander, WI 54501. 715-369-6150; Fax 715-369-6222.
Will search UCC records. **Other Phone Numbers:** Assessor 715-369-6137; Treasurer 715-369-6137.

Outagamie County

Register of Deeds, 410 South Walnut St., CAB 205, Appleton, WI 54911-5999. Register of Deeds, R/E and UCC Recording 920-832-5095 UCC Recording: 920-832-5097; Fax 920-832-2177. http://www.co.outagamie.wi.us
Will search UCC records. Will not search real estate records. **Other Phone Numbers:** Treasurer 414-832-5065; Elections 920-832-5077; Vital Records 920-832-5095; Abstracting Phone 920-832-5114; Tax Lister 920-832-5665;

Ozaukee County

Register of Deeds, P.O. Box 994, Port Washington, WI 53074-0994. Register of Deeds, R/E and UCC Recording 262-284-8260; Fax 262-284-8100. www.co.ozaukee.wi.us
Will search UCC records. **Other Phone Numbers:** Treasurer 262-284-8280; Vital Records 262-284-8260.

Pepin County

Register of Deeds, P.O. Box 39, Durand, WI 54736. 715-672-8856; Fax 715-672-8677.
Will search UCC records. Will not search real estate records. **Other Phone Numbers:** Treasurer 715-672-8850.

Pierce County

Register of Deeds, P.O. Box 267, Ellsworth, WI 54011-0267. Register of Deeds, R/E and UCC Recording 715-273-3531 x418; Fax 715-273-6861. colson1@co.pierce.wi.us
Will search UCC records. Will not search real estate records. **Other Phone Numbers:** Assessor 715-273-3531; Treasurer 715-273-3531 x307-8; Vital Records 715-273-3531 x418.

Polk County

Register of Deeds, 100 Polk County Plaza, Suite 160, Balsam Lake, WI 54810. 715-485-9249 R/E Recording: 715-485-9240 UCC Recording: 715-485-9240; Fax 715-485-9202.
Will search UCC records. Will not search real estate records. **Other Phone Numbers:** Assessor 715-485-3161 x254; Treasurer 715-485-3161 x273; Elections 715-485-9223; Vital Records 715-485-9240.

Portage County

Register of Deeds, 1516 Church Street, County-City Building, Stevens Point, WI 54481. 715-346-1428; Fax 715-345-5361.
Will search UCC records. **Other Phone Numbers:** Assessor 715-346-1553; Treasurer 715-346-1428.

Price County

Register of Deeds, 126 Cherry, Phillips, WI 54555. 715-339-2515.
Will search UCC records. UCC search includes federal tax liens if requested. RE owner, mortgage, and property transfer searches available. **Other Phone Numbers:** Treasurer 715-339-2615.

Racine County

Register of Deeds, 730 Wisconsin Avenue, Racine, WI 53403. 262-636-3208; Fax 262-636-3851.
Will search UCC records. Will not search real estate records. **Other Phone Numbers:** Assessor 262-636-3238; Treasurer 262-636-3238.

Richland County

Register of Deeds, P.O. Box 337, Richland Center, WI 53581. Register of Deeds, R/E and UCC Recording 608-647-3011.
Will search UCC records. UCC search includes federal tax liens if requested. Will not search real estate records. **Other Phone Numbers:** Assessor 608-647-3658; Treasurer 608-647-3658.

Rock County

Register of Deeds, 51 South Main Street, Janesville, WI 53545. 608-757-5657.
Will search UCC records. UCC search does not include federal tax liens. Will not search real estate records. **Online Access:** Assessor, Real Estate. Records on the City of Janesville Assessor database are available free online at http://assessor.ci.janesville.wi.us/Assessor/query.asp. **Other Phone Numbers:** Assessor 608-757-5650.

Rusk County

Register of Deeds, 311 Miner Avenue, Ladysmith, WI 54848-0311. 715-532-2139; Fax 715-532-2194.
Will search UCC records. Will not search real estate records. **Other Phone Numbers:** Treasurer 715-532-2105.

Sauk County

Register of Deeds, 505 Broadway St., Baraboo, WI 53913. 608-355-3288; Fax 608-355-3292.
Will search UCC records. Will not search real estate records. **Other Phone Numbers:** Assessor 608-355-5581; Treasurer 608-355-3276.

Sawyer County

Register of Deeds, P.O. Box 686, Hayward, WI 54843-0686. Register of Deeds, R/E and UCC Recording 715-634-4867; Fax 715-634-6839. http://sawyercountygov.org
Will search UCC records. Will not search real estate records. **Other Phone Numbers:** Assessor 715-634-4868; Treasurer 715-634-4868; Elections 715-634-4866; Vital Records 715-634-4867.

Shawano County

Register of Deeds, 311 North Main, Shawano, WI 54166. 715-524-2129; Fax 715-524-5157.
Will search UCC records. Will not search real estate records. **Other Phone Numbers:** Assessor 715-524-9130; Treasurer 715-524-9130.

Sheboygan County

Register of Deeds, 508 New York Ave., 2nd Floor, Sheboygan, WI 53081. 920-459-3023.
Will search UCC records. UCC search includes federal tax liens if requested. Will not search real estate records. **Other Phone Numbers:** Treasurer 920-459-3015.

St. Croix County

Register of Deeds, 1101 Carmichael Rd., Hudson, WI 54016. 715-386-4652; Fax 715-386-4687.
Will search UCC records. **Other Phone Numbers:** Assessor 715-386-4677; Treasurer 715-386-4645.

Taylor County

Register of Deeds, P.O. Box 403, Medford, WI 54451-0403. 715-748-1483.
Will search UCC records. UCC search includes federal tax liens. RE owner, mortgage, and property transfer searches available. **Other Phone Numbers:** Assessor 715-748-3131; Treasurer 715-748-1466.

Trempealeau County

Register of Deeds, P.O. Box 67, Whitehall, WI 54773. 715-538-2311; http://www.tremplocounty.com
Will search UCC records. UCC search includes federal tax liens. Will not search real estate records. **Online Access:** Real Estate, Assessor. Online access to the county assessor's database is available free at http://www.tremplocounty.com/Search. **Other Phone Numbers:** Treasurer 715-538-2311 x219.

Vernon County

Register of Deeds, P.O. Box 46, Viroqua, WI 54665. Register of Deeds, R/E and UCC Recording 608-637-3571; Fax 608-637-5304.
Will search UCC records. UCC search includes federal tax liens if requested. Will not search real estate records. **Other Phone Numbers:** Assessor 608-637-3222; Treasurer 608-637-3222; Elections 608-637-3571; Vital Records 608-637-3572.

Vilas County

Register of Deeds, 330 Court St., Eagle River, WI 54521. Register of Deeds, R/E and UCC Recording 715-479-3660; Fax 715-479-3695. http://co.vilas.wi.us
Will search UCC records. Will not search real estate records. **Other Phone Numbers:** Assessor 715-479-3609; Treasurer 715-479-3610; Vital Records 715-479-3660.

Walworth County

Register of Deeds, P.O. Box 995, Elkhorn, WI 53121-0995. 262-741-4214 R/E Recording: 262-741-4233 UCC Recording: 262-741-4237; Fax 262-741-4947. www.wrda.org
Will search UCC records. Will search Real Estate records with grantor/grantee system. **Other Phone Numbers:** Assessor 262-741-4251; Treasurer 262-741-4251; Elections 262-741-4241; Vital Records 262-741-4235.

Washburn County

Register of Deeds, P.O. Box 607, Shell Lake, WI 54871. 715-468-4616 R/E Recording: 715-468-4619 UCC Recording: 715-468-4615; Fax 715-468-4658.
Will search UCC records. **Other Phone Numbers:** Assessor 715-468-7410; Treasurer 715-468-4650; Elections 715-468-4605; Vital Records 715-468-4615.

Washington County

Register of Deeds, P.O. Box 1986, West Bend, WI 53095-7986. 262-335-4318; Fax 262-335-6866. http://207.227.35.41/departments/registerofdeeds.html
Will search UCC records. Will not search real estate records. **Other Phone Numbers:** Assessor 262-335-4370; Treasurer 262-335-4325; Elections 262-335-4468.

Waukesha County

Register of Deeds, 1320 Pewaukee Rd., Room 110, Waukesha, WI 53188. 262-548-7590.

Will search UCC records. UCC search includes federal tax liens if requested. RE owner, mortgage, and property transfer searches available. **Other Phone Numbers:** Assessor 262-542-0455; Treasurer 262-548-7576.

Waupaca County

Register of Deeds, P.O. Box 307, Waupaca, WI 54981. Register of Deeds, R/E and UCC Recording 715-258-6250; Fax 715-258-6212.

Will search UCC records. Will not search real estate records. **Other Phone Numbers:** Assessor 715-258-6215; Treasurer 715-258-6220; Elections 715-258-6200; Vital Records 715-258-6250.

Waushara County

Register of Deeds, P.O. Box 338, Wautoma, WI 54982. Register of Deeds, R/E and UCC Recording 920-787-0444; Fax 920-787-0425.

Will search UCC records. Will not search real estate records. **Other Phone Numbers:** Assessor 920-787-4631; Treasurer 920-787-4631; Vital Records 920-787-0444.

Winnebago County

Register of Deeds, P.O. Box 2808, Oshkosh, WI 54903-2808. 920-236-4883 R/E Recording: 920-236-4881; Fax 920-303-3025.

Will search UCC records. Federal tax liens included in UCC search if requested for an extra $5.00. Will not search real estate records. **Online Access:** Assessor,

Real Estate. Records on the City of Menasha Tax Roll Information database are available free online at http://my.athenet.net/~mencity/search/. **Other Phone Numbers:** Assessor 920-236-4775; Treasurer 920-236-4777; Elections 920-236-4888; Vital Records 920-236-4882.

Wood County

Register of Deeds, P.O. Box 8095, Wisconsin Rapids, WI 54495. 715-421-8450.

Will search UCC records. This agency will not do a federal tax lien search. Will not search real estate records. **Other Phone Numbers:** Assessor 715-421-8484; Treasurer 715-421-8484.

Wisconsin County Locator

You will usually be able to find the city name in the City/County Cross Reference below. In that case, it is a simple matter to determine the county from the cross reference. However, only the official US Postal Service city names are included in this index. There are an additional 40,000 place names that people use in their addresses. Therefore, we have also included a ZIP/City Cross Reference immediately following the City/County Cross Reference.

If you know the ZIP Code but the city name does not appear in the City/County Cross Reference index, look up the ZIP Code in the ZIP/City Cross Reference, find the city name, then look up the city name in the City/County Cross Reference. For example, you want to know the county for an address of Menands, NY 12204. There is no "Menands" in the City/County Cross Reference. The ZIP/City Cross Reference shows that ZIP Codes 12201-12288 are for the city of Albany. Looking back in the City/County Cross Reference, Albany is in Albany County.

City/County Cross Reference

ABBOTSFORD (54405) Clark(72), Marathon(28)
ABRAMS Oconto
ADAMS Adams
ADELL Sheboygan
AFTON Rock
ALBANY (99999) Green(99), Rock(1)
ALGOMA (54201) Kewaunee(97), Door(3)
ALGOMA Kewaunee
ALLENTON (53002) Washington(99), Dodge(1)
ALMA Buffalo
ALMA CENTER Jackson
ALMENA Barron
ALMOND (54909) Portage(82), Waushara(18)
ALTOONA Eau Claire
AMBERG (99999) Marinette(99), Manitowoc(1)
AMERY Polk
AMHERST Portage
AMHERST JUNCTION Portage
ANIWA (54408) Marathon(58), Shawano(38), Langlade(4)
ANTIGO (54409) Langlade(96), Shawano(2), Marathon(2)
APPLETON (54914) Outagamie(98), Winnebago(2)
APPLETON (54915) Outagamie(67), Calumet(23), Winnebago(11)
APPLETON Outagamie
ARCADIA (54612) Trempealeau(90), Buffalo(10)
ARENA Iowa
ARGONNE Forest
ARGYLE (53504) Lafayette(71), Green(29)
ARKANSAW (54721) Pepin(88), Dunn(7), Pierce(5)
ARKDALE Adams
ARLINGTON (53911) Columbia(90), Dane(10)
ARMSTRONG CREEK (54103) Forest(84), Marinette(15), Florence(1)
ARPIN Wood
ASHIPPUN Dodge
ASHLAND (54806) Ashland(92), Bayfield(8)
ATHELSTANE (54104) Marinette(98), Oconto(1)
ATHENS (54411) Marathon(98), Taylor(2)
AUBURNDALE (54412) Wood(76), Marathon(24)
AUGUSTA Eau Claire
AVALON Rock
AVOCA Iowa
BABCOCK Wood
BAGLEY Grant
BAILEYS HARBOR Door
BALDWIN St. Croix
BALSAM LAKE Polk
BANCROFT (54921) Portage(87), Adams(10), Waushara(3)
BANGOR La Crosse

BARABOO Sauk
BARNEVELD (53507) Iowa(98), Dane(2)
BARRON Barron
BARRONETT (54813) Barron(50), Burnett(30), Washburn(20)
BASSETT Kenosha
BAY CITY Pierce
BAYFIELD Bayfield
BEAR CREEK (54922) Outagamie(53), Waupaca(47)
BEAVER DAM Dodge
BEETOWN Grant
BELDENVILLE Pierce
BELGIUM (53004) Ozaukee(98), Sheboygan(2)
BELLEVILLE (53508) Dane(78), Green(22)
BELMONT Lafayette
BELOIT Rock
BENET LAKE Kenosha
BENOIT Bayfield
BENTON Lafayette
BERLIN (54923) Green Lake(76), Waushara(21), Winnebago(3)
BIG BEND Waukesha
BIG FALLS Waupaca
BIRCHWOOD (54817) Washburn(40), Sawyer(33), Barron(24), Rusk(3)
BIRNAMWOOD (54414) Shawano(82), Marathon(18)
BLACK CREEK (54106) Outagamie(99), Shawano(2)
BLACK EARTH (53515) Dane(99), Iowa(1)
BLACK RIVER FALLS (99999) Jackson(99), Monroe(1)
BLAIR (54616) Trempealeau(96), Jackson(4)
BLANCHARDVILLE (53516) Lafayette(52), Iowa(26), Green(20), Dane(2)
BLENKER Wood
BLOOM CITY Richland
BLOOMER Chippewa
BLOOMINGTON Grant
BLUE MOUNDS (53517) Iowa(51), Dane(49)
BLUE RIVER (53518) Richland(74), Grant(24), Crawford(2)
BONDUEL (54107) Shawano(97), Outagamie(3)
BOSCOBEL (53805) Grant(78), Crawford(22)
BOULDER JUNCTION Vilas
BOWLER Shawano
BOYCEVILLE Dunn
BOYD (54726) Chippewa(66), Eau Claire(34)
BRANCH Manitowoc
BRANDON (53919) Fond du Lac(98), Green Lake(2)
BRANTWOOD Price
BRIGGSVILLE (53920) Marquette(63), Adams(37)
BRILL Barron

BRILLION (54110) Calumet(79), Manitowoc(19), Brown(2)
BRISTOL Kenosha
BRODHEAD (53520) Rock(58), Green(42)
BROKAW Marathon
BROOKFIELD Waukesha
BROOKLYN (53521) Rock(53), Green(25), Dane(22)
BROOKS Adams
BROWNSVILLE (53006) Dodge(75), Fond du Lac(25)
BROWNTOWN (53522) Green(93), Lafayette(7)
BRUCE Rusk
BRULE (54820) Douglas(84), Bayfield(16)
BRUSSELS Door
BRYANT Langlade
BURLINGTON (53105) Racine(58), Walworth(32), Kenosha(9)
BURNETT Dodge
BUTLER Waukesha
BUTTE DES MORTS Winnebago
BUTTERNUT (54514) Price(57), Ashland(38), Iron(6)
BYRON Fond du Lac
CABLE (54821) Bayfield(97), Sawyer(3)
CADOTT (54727) Chippewa(93), Eau Claire(7)
CALEDONIA Racine
CAMBRIA (53923) Columbia(78), Green Lake(22)
CAMBRIDGE (53523) Jefferson(53), Dane(47)
CAMERON Barron
CAMP DOUGLAS (54618) Monroe(51), Juneau(49)
CAMP LAKE Kenosha
CAMPBELLSPORT (53010) Fond du Lac(95), Washington(4)
CAROLINE Shawano
CASCADE (53011) Sheboygan(88), Fond du Lac(12)
CASCO (54205) Kewaunee(98), Door(2)
CASHTON (54619) Monroe(78), Vernon(21), La Crosse(1)
CASSVILLE Grant
CATARACT Monroe
CATAWBA Price
CATO Manitowoc
CAZENOVIA (53924) Richland(99), Sauk(2)
CECIL (54111) Shawano(90), Oconto(10)
CEDAR GROVE (53013) Sheboygan(81), Ozaukee(19)
CEDARBURG (53012) Ozaukee(95), Washington(5)
CENTURIA Polk
CHASEBURG Vernon
CHELSEA Taylor
CHETEK (54728) Barron(90), Rusk(9), Dunn(1)
CHILI (54420) Clark(97), Wood(4)

CHILTON (53014) Calumet(98), Manitowoc(2)
CHIPPEWA FALLS (54729) Chippewa(97), Eau Claire(3)
CHIPPEWA FALLS Chippewa
CLAM LAKE (54517) Ashland(93), Sawyer(7)
CLAYTON (54004) Polk(62), Barron(39)
CLEAR LAKE (54005) Polk(70), St. Croix(11), Barron(10), Dunn(9)
CLEVELAND (53015) Manitowoc(85), Sheboygan(15)
CLINTON (53525) Rock(97), Walworth(3)
CLINTONVILLE (54929) Waupaca(67), Shawano(32), Outagamie(1)
CLYMAN Dodge
COBB Iowa
COCHRANE Buffalo
COLBY (54421) Clark(76), Marathon(25)
COLEMAN (54112) Marinette(76), Oconto(25)
COLFAX (54730) Dunn(79), Chippewa(21)
COLGATE (53017) Washington(71), Waukesha(29)
COLLINS Manitowoc
COLOMA (54930) Waushara(85), Adams(13), Marquette(2)
COLUMBUS (53925) Columbia(83), Dodge(14), Dane(3)
COMBINED LOCKS Outagamie
COMSTOCK (54826) Barron(62), Polk(38)
CONOVER Vilas
CONRATH Rusk
COON VALLEY (54623) La Crosse(51), Vernon(50)
CORNELL Chippewa
CORNUCOPIA Bayfield
COTTAGE GROVE Dane
COUDERAY Sawyer
CRANDON Forest
CRIVITZ (54114) Marinette(91), Oconto(9)
CROSS PLAINS Dane
CUBA CITY (53807) Grant(84), Lafayette(16)
CUDAHY Milwaukee
CUMBERLAND (54829) Barron(91), Polk(9)
CURTISS (54422) Clark(95), Taylor(5)
CUSHING Polk
CUSTER (54423) Portage(98), Marathon(2)
DALE Outagamie
DALLAS Barron
DALTON (53926) Green Lake(79), Marquette(13), Columbia(8)
DANBURY (54830) Burnett(93), Douglas(7)
DANE Dane
DARIEN (53114) Walworth(77), Rock(23)
DARLINGTON Lafayette
DE FOREST (53532) Dane(99), Columbia(1)
DE PERE (54115) Brown(92), Outagamie(8)

DE SOTO (54624) Vernon(82), Crawford(18)
DEER PARK (54007) St. Croix(67), Polk(33)
DEERBROOK Langlade
DEERFIELD Dane
DELAFIELD Waukesha
DELAVAN Walworth
DELLWOOD Adams
DENMARK (54208) Brown(51), Kewaunee(41), Manitowoc(8)
DICKEYVILLE Grant
DODGE Trempealeau
DODGEVILLE Iowa
DORCHESTER (54425) Clark(84), Marathon(10), Taylor(7)
DOUSMAN (53118) Waukesha(96), Jefferson(4)
DOWNING (54734) Dunn(96), St. Croix(4)
DOWNSVILLE Dunn
DOYLESTOWN Columbia
DRESSER Polk
DRUMMOND Bayfield
DUNBAR Marinette
DURAND (54736) Pepin(84), Buffalo(15), Dunn(1)
EAGLE (53119) Waukesha(93), Walworth(5), Jefferson(3)
EAGLE RIVER (54521) Vilas(78), Oneida(20), Forest(2)
EAST ELLSWORTH Pierce
EAST TROY (53120) Walworth(98), Racine(2)
EASTMAN Crawford
EAU CLAIRE (54703) Eau Claire(90), Chippewa(11)
EAU CLAIRE Eau Claire
EAU GALLE (54737) Dunn(96), Pepin(4)
EDEN Fond du Lac
EDGAR Marathon
EDGERTON (53534) Rock(86), Dane(12), Jefferson(1)
EDGEWATER Sawyer
EDMUND Iowa
EGG HARBOR Door
ELAND (54427) Marathon(66), Shawano(34)
ELCHO (54428) Langlade(96), Oneida(4)
ELDERON Marathon
ELDORADO Fond du Lac
ELEVA (54738) Trempealeau(52), Eau Claire(47), Buffalo(2)
ELK MOUND (54739) Dunn(59), Chippewa(41)
ELKHART LAKE (53020) Sheboygan(91), Manitowoc(7), Calumet(3)
ELKHORN Walworth
ELLISON BAY Door
ELLSWORTH Pierce
ELM GROVE Waukesha
ELMWOOD (54740) Pierce(85), Dunn(15)
ELROY (53929) Juneau(73), Monroe(22), Vernon(5)
ELTON Langlade
EMBARRASS Waupaca
EMERALD St. Croix
ENDEAVOR Marquette
EPHRAIM Door
ETTRICK (54627) Trempealeau(92), Jackson(8)
EUREKA Winnebago
EVANSVILLE (53536) Rock(93), Green(7)
EXELAND (54835) Sawyer(89), Rusk(11)
FAIRCHILD (54741) Jackson(53), Eau Claire(47)
FAIRWATER Fond du Lac
FALL CREEK Eau Claire
FALL RIVER (53932) Columbia(94), Dodge(6)
FENCE (54120) Florence(61), Marinette(39)
FENNIMORE Grant

FERRYVILLE (54628) Crawford(96), Vernon(4)
FIFIELD Price
FISH CREEK Door
FLORENCE Florence
FOND DU LAC Fond du Lac
FONTANA Walworth
FOOTVILLE Rock
FOREST JUNCTION Calumet
FORESTVILLE (54213) Door(85), Kewaunee(15)
FORT ATKINSON (53538) Jefferson(97), Rock(3)
FOUNTAIN CITY Buffalo
FOX LAKE Dodge
FOXBORO Douglas
FRANCIS CREEK Manitowoc
FRANKLIN Milwaukee
FRANKSVILLE Racine
FREDERIC (54837) Polk(79), Burnett(21)
FREDONIA (53021) Ozaukee(89), Washington(11)
FREEDOM Outagamie
FREMONT (54940) Waupaca(50), Waushara(33), Winnebago(14), Outagamie(3)
FRIENDSHIP Adams
FRIESLAND Columbia
GALESVILLE Trempealeau
GALLOWAY Marathon
GAYS MILLS Crawford
GENESEE DEPOT Waukesha
GENOA Vernon
GENOA CITY (53128) Walworth(81), Kenosha(19)
GERMANTOWN Washington
GILE Iron
GILLETT (54124) Oconto(93), Menominee(4), Shawano(3)
GILLETT Oconto
GILLETT Shawano
GILMAN (54433) Taylor(80), Chippewa(20)
GILMANTON Buffalo
GLEASON (54435) Lincoln(66), Langlade(34)
GLEN FLORA Rusk
GLEN HAVEN Grant
GLENBEULAH (53023) Sheboygan(97), Fond du Lac(3)
GLENWOOD CITY (54013) St. Croix(96), Dunn(4)
GLIDDEN Ashland
GOODMAN (54125) Marinette(99), Forest(1)
GORDON Douglas
GOTHAM Richland
GRAFTON Ozaukee
GRAND MARSH Adams
GRAND VIEW Bayfield
GRANTON Clark
GRANTSBURG (54840) Burnett(98), Polk(2)
GRATIOT Lafayette
GREEN BAY Brown
GREEN LAKE Green Lake
GREEN VALLEY Shawano
GREENBUSH Sheboygan
GREENDALE Milwaukee
GREENLEAF (54126) Brown(97), Manitowoc(3)
GREENVILLE Outagamie
GREENWOOD Clark
GRESHAM Shawano
GURNEY Iron
HAGER CITY Pierce
HALES CORNERS Milwaukee
HAMMOND St. Croix
HANCOCK (54943) Waushara(82), Adams(18)
HANNIBAL Taylor
HANOVER Rock
HARSHAW Oneida

HARTFORD (53027) Washington(96), Dodge(4)
HARTLAND Waukesha
HATLEY Marathon
HAUGEN Barron
HAWKINS (54530) Rusk(70), Price(29)
HAWTHORNE Douglas
HAYWARD (54843) Sawyer(88), Washburn(12)
HAZEL GREEN (53811) Grant(92), Lafayette(7), Oneida(1)
HAZELHURST Oneida
HEAFFORD JUNCTION Lincoln
HELENVILLE Jefferson
HERBSTER Bayfield
HERTEL Burnett
HEWITT Wood
HIGH BRIDGE Ashland
HIGHLAND (53543) Iowa(93), Grant(7)
HILBERT Calumet
HILLPOINT (53937) Sauk(52), Richland(48)
HILLSBORO (54634) Vernon(71), Richland(28), Juneau(1)
HILLSDALE Barron
HINGHAM Sheboygan
HIXTON Jackson
HOLCOMBE (54745) Chippewa(90), Rusk(10)
HOLLANDALE (53544) Iowa(98), Dane(2)
HOLMEN La Crosse
HONEY CREEK Walworth
HORICON Dodge
HORTONVILLE Outagamie
HUBERTUS Washington
HUDSON St. Croix
HUMBIRD (54746) Clark(76), Jackson(24)
HURLEY Iron
HUSTISFORD Dodge
HUSTLER Juneau
INDEPENDENCE (54747) Trempealeau(86), Buffalo(14)
IOLA (54945) Waupaca(97), Portage(4)
IOLA Waupaca
IRMA Lincoln
IRON BELT Iron
IRON RIDGE Dodge
IRON RIVER Bayfield
IXONIA (53036) Jefferson(70), Dodge(25), Waukesha(5)
JACKSON Washington
JANESVILLE Rock
JEFFERSON Jefferson
JIM FALLS Chippewa
JOHNSON CREEK Jefferson
JUDA Green
JUMP RIVER Taylor
JUNCTION CITY (54443) Portage(95), Marathon(3), Wood(3)
JUNEAU Dodge
KANSASVILLE (53139) Racine(86), Kenosha(14)
KAUKAUNA (54130) Outagamie(95), Brown(3), Calumet(2)
KELLNERSVILLE Manitowoc
KEMPSTER Langlade
KENDALL (54638) Monroe(93), Juneau(4), Vernon(4)
KENNAN Price
KENOSHA Kenosha
KESHENA Menominee
KEWASKUM (53040) Washington(68), Sheboygan(18), Fond du Lac(14)
KEWAUNEE Kewaunee
KIEL (53042) Manitowoc(96), Calumet(4)
KIELER Grant
KIMBERLY Outagamie
KING Waupaca
KINGSTON Green Lake
KNAPP (54749) Dunn(90), St. Croix(10)
KOHLER Sheboygan

KRAKOW (54137) Shawano(80), Oconto(20)
LA CROSSE La Crosse
LA FARGE (54639) Vernon(93), Richland(7)
LA POINTE Ashland
LA VALLE (53941) Sauk(97), Juneau(2), Richland(1)
LAC DU FLAMBEAU (54538) Vilas(89), Oneida(6), Price(5)
LADYSMITH Rusk
LAKE DELTON Sauk
LAKE GENEVA Walworth
LAKE MILLS Jefferson
LAKE NEBAGAMON Douglas
LAKE TOMAHAWK Oneida
LAKEWOOD Oconto
LANCASTER Grant
LAND O LAKES (54540) Vilas(96), Manitowoc(4)
LANNON Waukesha
LAONA Forest
LARSEN Winnebago
LEBANON Dodge
LENA (54139) Oconto(98), Marinette(2)
LEOPOLIS Shawano
LEWIS Polk
LILY Langlade
LIME RIDGE Sauk
LINDEN Iowa
LITTLE CHUTE Outagamie
LITTLE SUAMICO Oconto
LIVINGSTON (53554) Grant(67), Iowa(33)
LODI (53555) Columbia(91), Dane(9)
LOGANVILLE Sauk
LOMIRA (53048) Dodge(98), Fond du Lac(2)
LONE ROCK (53556) Richland(89), Sauk(11)
LONG LAKE (54542) Forest(66), Florence(34)
LOWELL Dodge
LOYAL Clark
LUBLIN (54447) Taylor(98), Clark(2)
LUCK (54853) Polk(94), Burnett(6)
LUXEMBURG (54217) Kewaunee(89), Door(6), Brown(5)
LYNDON STATION (53944) Juneau(87), Sauk(13)
LYNXVILLE Crawford
LYONS Walworth
MADISON Dane
MAIDEN ROCK Pierce
MALONE (53049) Fond du Lac(94), Calumet(6)
MANAWA Waupaca
MANCHESTER Green Lake
MANITOWISH WATERS (54545) Vilas(98), Iron(2)
MANITOWOC Manitowoc
MAPLE Douglas
MAPLEWOOD Door
MARATHON Marathon
MARENGO Ashland
MARIBEL (54227) Manitowoc(99), Brown(1)
MARINETTE Marinette
MARION (54950) Shawano(56), Waupaca(44)
MARKESAN (53946) Green Lake(98), Fond du Lac(2)
MARQUETTE Green Lake
MARSHALL (53559) Dane(98), Jefferson(2)
MARSHALL FIELDS Milwaukee
MARSHFIELD (54449) Wood(93), Marathon(7)
MARSHFIELD Wood
MASON (54856) Bayfield(95), Ashland(5)
MATHER Juneau
MATTOON Shawano
MAUSTON Juneau

MAYVILLE Dodge
MAZOMANIE (53560) Dane(96), Iowa(4)
MC FARLAND Dane
MC NAUGHTON Oneida
MEDFORD Taylor
MEDINA Outagamie
MELLEN Ashland
MELROSE (54642) Jackson(95), La
   Crosse(3), Trempealeau(2)
MENASHA (54952) Winnebago(90),
   Calumet(10)
MENOMONEE FALLS Waukesha
MENOMONIE Dunn
MEQUON Ozaukee
MERCER Iron
MERRILL (54452) Lincoln(89),
   Marathon(11)
MERRILLAN (54754) Jackson(84),
   Clark(16)
MERRIMAC (53561) Sauk(87),
   Columbia(13)
MERTON Waukesha
MIDDLETON Dane
MIKANA Barron
MILAN Marathon
MILLADORE (54454) Wood(87),
   Portage(13)
MILLSTON Jackson
MILLTOWN Polk
MILTON Rock
MILWAUKEE Milwaukee
MINDORO (54644) La Crosse(98),
   Jackson(3)
MINERAL POINT (53565) Iowa(89),
   Lafayette(11)
MINOCQUA (54548) Oneida(80), Vilas(20)
MINONG (54859) Washburn(89),
   Douglas(11)
MISHICOT Manitowoc
MONDOVI (54755) Buffalo(54), Dunn(16),
   Eau Claire(15), Pepin(14)
MONROE Green
MONTELLO (53949) Marquette(99), Green
   Lake(1)
MONTFORT (53569) Iowa(50), Grant(50)
MONTICELLO Green
MONTREAL Iron
MORRISONVILLE Dane
MOSINEE (54455) Marathon(98),
   Portage(3)
MOUNT CALVARY Fond du Lac
MOUNT HOPE Grant
MOUNT HOREB Dane
MOUNT STERLING Crawford
MOUNTAIN Oconto
MUKWONAGO (53149) Waukesha(87),
   Walworth(12), Racine(1)
MUSCODA (53573) Richland(58),
   Grant(33), Iowa(9)
MUSKEGO (53150) Waukesha(98),
   Racine(2)
NASHOTAH Waukesha
NECEDAH Juneau
NEENAH Winnebago
NEILLSVILLE Clark
NEKOOSA (54457) Wood(57), Adams(40),
   Juneau(3)
NELSON Buffalo
NELSONVILLE Portage
NEOPIT Menominee
NEOSHO Dodge
NESHKORO (54960) Marquette(59),
   Waushara(35), Green Lake(6)
NEW AUBURN (54757) Chippewa(64),
   Barron(17), Dunn(13), Rusk(6)
NEW BERLIN Waukesha
NEW FRANKEN Brown
NEW GLARUS (53574) Green(98),
   Dane(2)
NEW HOLSTEIN (53061) Calumet(96),
   Fond du Lac(4)
NEW HOLSTEIN Fond du Lac

NEW LISBON Juneau
NEW LONDON (54961) Waupaca(75),
   Outagamie(25)
NEW MUNSTER Kenosha
NEW RICHMOND (54017) St. Croix(99),
   Polk(1)
NEWBURG Washington
NEWTON Manitowoc
NIAGARA (54151) Marinette(81),
   Florence(19)
NICHOLS Outagamie
NORTH FREEDOM Sauk
NORTH LAKE Waukesha
NORTH PRAIRIE Waukesha
NORWALK Monroe
OAK CREEK Milwaukee
OAKDALE Monroe
OAKFIELD (53065) Fond du Lac(91),
   Dodge(9)
OCONOMOWOC (53066) Waukesha(95),
   Jefferson(3), Dodge(2)
OCONTO Oconto
OCONTO FALLS (54154) Oconto(97),
   Shawano(3)
ODANAH Ashland
OGDENSBURG Waupaca
OGEMA Price
OJIBWA Sawyer
OKAUCHEE Waukesha
OMRO Winnebago
ONALASKA La Crosse
ONEIDA (54155) Brown(57),
   Outagamie(43)
ONTARIO (54651) Vernon(70), Monroe(31)
OOSTBURG Sheboygan
OREGON Dane
ORFORDVILLE Rock
OSCEOLA (54020) Polk(99), St. Croix(1)
OSHKOSH Winnebago
OSSEO (54758) Trempealeau(82),
   Jackson(9), Eau Claire(9)
OWEN (54460) Clark(97), Taylor(3)
OXFORD (53952) Marquette(51),
   Adams(49)
PACKWAUKEE Marquette
PALMYRA Jefferson
PARDEEVILLE (53954) Columbia(97),
   Marquette(3)
PARK FALLS (54552) Price(97), Iron(3)
PATCH GROVE Grant
PEARSON Langlade
PELICAN LAKE (54463) Oneida(97),
   Langlade(3)
PELL LAKE Walworth
PEMBINE Marinette
PEPIN Pepin
PESHTIGO (54157) Marinette(99),
   Oconto(1)
PEWAUKEE Waukesha
PHELPS Vilas
PHILLIPS Price
PHLOX Langlade
PICKEREL (54465) Langlade(62),
   Forest(38)
PICKETT (54964) Winnebago(86), Fond du
   Lac(15)
PIGEON FALLS Trempealeau
PINE RIVER Waushara
PITTSVILLE (54466) Wood(81), Clark(11),
   Jackson(8)
PLAIN Sauk
PLAINFIELD (54966) Waushara(85),
   Portage(13), Adams(2)
PLATTEVILLE (53818) Grant(96),
   Lafayette(3)
PLEASANT PRAIRIE Kenosha
PLOVER Portage
PLUM CITY (54761) Pierce(98), Dunn(1)
PLYMOUTH Sheboygan
POPLAR Douglas
PORT EDWARDS Wood
PORT WASHINGTON Ozaukee

PORT WING Bayfield
PORTAGE Columbia
PORTERFIELD Marinette
POSKIN Barron
POTOSI Grant
POTTER Calumet
POUND (54161) Marinette(54), Oconto(46)
POWERS LAKE Kenosha
POY SIPPI Waushara
POYNETTE Columbia
PRAIRIE DU CHIEN (53821) Crawford(98),
   Grant(2)
PRAIRIE DU SAC (53578) Sauk(92),
   Columbia(8)
PRAIRIE FARM (54762) Barron(90),
   Dunn(10)
PRENTICE Price
PRESCOTT Pierce
PRESQUE ISLE Vilas
PRINCETON (54968) Green Lake(94),
   Marquette(6)
PULASKI (54162) Shawano(71),
   Brown(22), Oconto(7)
RACINE (53403) Racine(98), Kenosha(2)
RACINE Racine
RADISSON Sawyer
RANDOLPH (53956) Dodge(58),
   Columbia(36), Green Lake(6)
RANDOLPH Columbia
RANDOM LAKE (53075) Sheboygan(94),
   Ozaukee(5), Washington(1)
READFIELD Waupaca
READSTOWN (54652) Vernon(94),
   Crawford(6)
REDGRANITE Waushara
REEDSBURG Sauk
REEDSVILLE (54230) Manitowoc(99),
   Brown(2)
REESEVILLE Dodge
REWEY Iowa
RHINELANDER (54501) Oneida(99),
   Lincoln(1)
RIB LAKE (54470) Taylor(97), Price(3)
RICE LAKE Barron
RICHFIELD Washington
RICHLAND CENTER Richland
RIDGELAND (54763) Dunn(94), Barron(6)
RIDGEWAY Iowa
RINGLE Marathon
RIO Columbia
RIPON (54971) Fond du Lac(82), Green
   Lake(14), Winnebago(4)
RIVER FALLS (54022) Pierce(73), St.
   Croix(28)
ROBERTS St. Croix
ROCHESTER Racine
ROCK FALLS Dunn
ROCK SPRINGS Sauk
ROCKFIELD Washington
ROCKLAND (54653) La Crosse(89),
   Monroe(11)
ROSENDALE Fond du Lac
ROSHOLT (54473) Portage(80),
   Marathon(20)
ROTHSCHILD Marathon
ROYALTON Waupaca
RUBICON Dodge
RUDOLPH (54475) Wood(85), Portage(15)
SAINT CLOUD (53079) Fond du Lac(95),
   Sheboygan(5)
SAINT CROIX FALLS Polk
SAINT FRANCIS Milwaukee
SAINT GERMAIN (54558) Vilas(90),
   Oneida(10)
SAINT JOSEPH St. Croix
SAINT NAZIANZ Manitowoc
SALEM Kenosha
SAND CREEK Dunn
SARONA (54870) Washburn(96), Barron(4)
SAUK CITY (53583) Sauk(87), Dane(13)
SAUKVILLE Ozaukee
SAXEVILLE Waushara

SAXON (54559) Iron(88), Ashland(12)
SAYNER Vilas
SCANDINAVIA (54977) Waupaca(95),
   Portage(5)
SCHOFIELD Marathon
SENECA Crawford
SEXTONVILLE Richland
SEYMOUR (54165) Outagamie(96),
   Shawano(3), Brown(1)
SHARON (53585) Walworth(82), Rock(17),
   Sauk(2)
SHAWANO Shawano
SHEBOYGAN Sheboygan
SHEBOYGAN FALLS Sheboygan
SHELDON (54766) Rusk(58), Taylor(32),
   Chippewa(10)
SHELL LAKE (54871) Washburn(69),
   Burnett(31)
SHERWOOD Calumet
SHIOCTON (54170) Outagamie(90),
   Shawano(10)
SHULLSBURG Lafayette
SILVER LAKE Kenosha
SINSINAWA Grant
SIREN (54872) Burnett(98), Polk(2)
SISTER BAY Door
SLINGER Washington
SOBIESKI Oconto
SOLDIERS GROVE (54655) Crawford(64),
   Richland(30), Vernon(6)
SOLON SPRINGS (54873) Douglas(83),
   Bayfield(17)
SOMERS Kenosha
SOMERSET St. Croix
SOUTH MILWAUKEE Milwaukee
SOUTH RANGE Douglas
SOUTH WAYNE Lafayette
SPARTA Monroe
SPENCER (54479) Marathon(58),
   Clark(42)
SPOONER (54801) Washburn(87),
   Burnett(13)
SPRING GREEN (53588) Sauk(67),
   Iowa(32), Richland(2)
SPRING VALLEY (54767) Pierce(95), St.
   Croix(4), Dunn(1)
SPRINGBROOK Washburn
SPRINGFIELD Walworth
STANLEY (54768) Chippewa(80),
   Clark(12), Eau Claire(6), Taylor(2)
STAR LAKE Vilas
STAR PRAIRIE (54026) Polk(64), St.
   Croix(36)
STETSONVILLE (54480) Taylor(95),
   Marathon(5)
STEUBEN Crawford
STEVENS POINT Portage
STITZER Grant
STOCKBRIDGE Calumet
STOCKHOLM (54769) Pierce(62),
   Pepin(39)
STODDARD (54658) Vernon(89), La
   Crosse(11)
STONE LAKE (54876) Sawyer(63),
   Washburn(38)
STOUGHTON (53589) Dane(99), Rock(1)
STRATFORD Marathon
STRUM (54770) Trempealeau(74), Eau
   Claire(26)
STURGEON BAY Door
STURTEVANT (53177) Racine(91),
   Kenosha(9)
SUAMICO Brown
SULLIVAN Jefferson
SUMMIT LAKE Langlade
SUN PRAIRIE Dane
SUPERIOR Douglas
SURING (54174) Oconto(97),
   Menominee(3)
SUSSEX Waukesha
TAYLOR (54659) Jackson(90),
   Trempealeau(10)

THERESA (53091) Dodge(95), Washington(5)
THIENSVILLE Ozaukee
THORP (54771) Clark(93), Taylor(7)
THREE LAKES (54562) Oneida(96), Forest(3)
TIGERTON (54486) Shawano(94), Waupaca(6)
TILLEDA Shawano
TISCH MILLS Manitowoc
TOMAH Monroe
TOMAHAWK (54487) Lincoln(88), Oneida(12)
TONY Rusk
TOWNSEND Oconto
TREGO Washburn
TREMPEALEAU Trempealeau
TREVOR Kenosha
TRIPOLI (54564) Oneida(43), Lincoln(42), Price(16)
TUNNEL CITY Monroe
TURTLE LAKE (54889) Barron(73), Polk(27)
TWIN LAKES Kenosha
TWO RIVERS Manitowoc
UNION CENTER Juneau
UNION GROVE (53182) Racine(92), Kenosha(8)
UNITY (54488) Clark(69), Marathon(31)

UPSON Iron
VALDERS Manitowoc
VAN DYNE (54979) Fond du Lac(88), Winnebago(12)
VERONA Dane
VESPER Wood
VIOLA (54664) Richland(84), Vernon(16)
VIROQUA (54665) Vernon(99), Crawford(1)
WABENO Forest
WALDO Sheboygan
WALES Waukesha
WALWORTH Walworth
WARRENS (54666) Monroe(84), Jackson(15)
WASCOTT Douglas
WASHBURN Bayfield
WASHINGTON ISLAND Door
WATERFORD Racine
WATERLOO (53594) Jefferson(84), Dodge(14), Dane(3)
WATERTOWN Dodge
WATERTOWN Jefferson
WAUKAU Winnebago
WAUKESHA Waukesha
WAUNAKEE Dane
WAUPACA (54981) Waupaca(92), Waushara(5), Portage(4)

WAUPUN (53963) Fond du Lac(51), Dodge(49)
WAUSAU Marathon
WAUSAUKEE Marinette
WAUTOMA (54982) Waushara(97), Marquette(3)
WAUZEKA Crawford
WEBSTER Burnett
WEST BEND Washington
WEST SALEM La Crosse
WESTBORO (54490) Taylor(96), Price(4)
WESTBY Vernon
WESTFIELD (53964) Marquette(97), Waushara(2), Adams(2)
WEYAUWEGA (54983) Waupaca(89), Waushara(11)
WEYERHAEUSER Rusk
WHEELER Dunn
WHITE LAKE (54491) Langlade(91), Oconto(9)
WHITEHALL Trempealeau
WHITELAW Manitowoc
WHITEWATER (53190) Walworth(60), Rock(29), Jefferson(11)
WILD ROSE Waushara
WILLARD Clark
WILLIAMS BAY Walworth
WILMOT Kenosha
WILSON St. Croix

WILTON Monroe
WINDSOR Dane
WINNEBAGO Winnebago
WINNECONNE (54986) Winnebago(96), Waushara(4)
WINTER Sawyer
WISCONSIN DELLS (53965) Columbia(43), Sauk(27), Adams(26), Juneau(5)
WISCONSIN RAPIDS (54494) Wood(93), Portage(7)
WISCONSIN RAPIDS Wood
WITHEE (54498) Clark(92), Taylor(8)
WITTENBERG (54499) Shawano(71), Marathon(28), Portage(1)
WONEWOC (53968) Juneau(66), Sauk(26), Vernon(6), Richland(2)
WOODFORD Lafayette
WOODLAND Dodge
WOODMAN Grant
WOODRUFF (54568) Vilas(66), Oneida(34)
WOODVILLE St. Croix
WOODWORTH Kenosha
WRIGHTSTOWN Brown
WYEVILLE Monroe
WYOCENA Columbia
ZACHOW Shawano
ZENDA Walworth

ZIP/City Cross Reference

ZIP	City	ZIP	City	ZIP	City	ZIP	City
53001-53001	ADELL	53059-53059	NEOSHO	53128-53128	GENOA CITY	53505-53505	AVALON
53002-53002	ALLENTON	53060-53060	NEWBURG	53129-53129	GREENDALE	53506-53506	AVOCA
53003-53003	ASHIPPUN	53061-53062	NEW HOLSTEIN	53130-53130	HALES CORNERS	53507-53507	BARNEVELD
53004-53004	BELGIUM	53063-53063	NEWTON	53132-53132	FRANKLIN	53508-53508	BELLEVILLE
53005-53005	BROOKFIELD	53064-53064	NORTH LAKE	53137-53137	HELENVILLE	53510-53510	BELMONT
53006-53006	BROWNSVILLE	53065-53065	OAKFIELD	53138-53138	HONEY CREEK	53511-53512	BELOIT
53007-53007	BUTLER	53066-53066	OCONOMOWOC	53139-53139	KANSASVILLE	53515-53515	BLACK EARTH
53008-53008	BROOKFIELD	53069-53069	OKAUCHEE	53140-53144	KENOSHA	53516-53516	BLANCHARDVILLE
53009-53009	BYRON	53070-53070	OOSTBURG	53146-53146	NEW BERLIN	53517-53517	BLUE MOUNDS
53010-53010	CAMPBELLSPORT	53072-53072	PEWAUKEE	53147-53147	LAKE GENEVA	53518-53518	BLUE RIVER
53011-53011	CASCADE	53073-53073	PLYMOUTH	53148-53148	LYONS	53520-53520	BRODHEAD
53012-53012	CEDARBURG	53074-53074	PORT WASHINGTON	53149-53149	MUKWONAGO	53521-53521	BROOKLYN
53013-53013	CEDAR GROVE	53075-53075	RANDOM LAKE	53150-53150	MUSKEGO	53522-53522	BROWNTOWN
53014-53014	CHILTON	53076-53076	RICHFIELD	53151-53151	NEW BERLIN	53523-53523	CAMBRIDGE
53015-53015	CLEVELAND	53078-53078	RUBICON	53152-53152	NEW MUNSTER	53525-53525	CLINTON
53016-53016	CLYMAN	53079-53079	SAINT CLOUD	53153-53153	NORTH PRAIRIE	53526-53526	COBB
53017-53017	COLGATE	53080-53080	SAUKVILLE	53154-53154	OAK CREEK	53527-53527	COTTAGE GROVE
53018-53018	DELAFIELD	53081-53083	SHEBOYGAN	53156-53156	PALMYRA	53528-53528	CROSS PLAINS
53019-53019	EDEN	53085-53085	SHEBOYGAN FALLS	53157-53157	PELL LAKE	53529-53529	DANE
53020-53020	ELKHART LAKE	53086-53086	SLINGER	53158-53158	PLEASANT PRAIRIE	53530-53530	DARLINGTON
53021-53021	FREDONIA	53088-53088	STOCKBRIDGE	53159-53159	POWERS LAKE	53531-53531	DEERFIELD
53022-53022	GERMANTOWN	53089-53089	SUSSEX	53167-53167	ROCHESTER	53532-53532	DE FOREST
53023-53023	GLENBEULAH	53090-53090	WEST BEND	53168-53168	SALEM	53533-53533	DODGEVILLE
53024-53024	GRAFTON	53091-53091	THERESA	53170-53170	SILVER LAKE	53534-53534	EDGERTON
53026-53026	GREENBUSH	53092-53092	THIENSVILLE	53171-53171	SOMERS	53535-53535	EDMUND
53027-53027	HARTFORD	53093-53093	WALDO	53172-53172	SOUTH MILWAUKEE	53536-53536	EVANSVILLE
53029-53029	HARTLAND	53094-53094	WATERTOWN	53176-53176	SPRINGFIELD	53537-53537	FOOTVILLE
53031-53031	HINGHAM	53095-53095	WEST BEND	53177-53177	STURTEVANT	53538-53538	FORT ATKINSON
53032-53032	HORICON	53097-53097	MEQUON	53178-53178	SULLIVAN	53540-53540	GOTHAM
53033-53033	HUBERTUS	53098-53098	WATERTOWN	53179-53179	TREVOR	53541-53541	GRATIOT
53034-53034	HUSTISFORD	53099-53099	WOODLAND	53181-53181	TWIN LAKES	53542-53542	HANOVER
53035-53035	IRON RIDGE	53101-53101	BASSETT	53182-53182	UNION GROVE	53543-53543	HIGHLAND
53036-53036	IXONIA	53102-53102	BENET LAKE	53183-53183	WALES	53544-53544	HOLLANDALE
53037-53037	JACKSON	53103-53103	BIG BEND	53184-53184	WALWORTH	53545-53547	JANESVILLE
53038-53038	JOHNSON CREEK	53104-53104	BRISTOL	53185-53185	WATERFORD	53549-53549	JEFFERSON
53039-53039	JUNEAU	53105-53105	BURLINGTON	53186-53188	WAUKESHA	53550-53550	JUDA
53040-53040	KEWASKUM	53108-53108	CALEDONIA	53190-53190	WHITEWATER	53551-53551	LAKE MILLS
53042-53042	KIEL	53109-53109	CAMP LAKE	53191-53191	WILLIAMS BAY	53553-53553	LINDEN
53044-53044	KOHLER	53110-53110	CUDAHY	53192-53192	WILMOT	53554-53554	LIVINGSTON
53045-53045	BROOKFIELD	53114-53114	DARIEN	53194-53194	WOODWORTH	53555-53555	LODI
53046-53046	LANNON	53115-53115	DELAVAN	53195-53195	ZENDA	53556-53556	LONE ROCK
53047-53047	LEBANON	53118-53118	DOUSMAN	53201-53234	MILWAUKEE	53557-53557	LOWELL
53048-53048	LOMIRA	53119-53119	EAGLE	53235-53235	SAINT FRANCIS	53558-53558	MC FARLAND
53049-53049	MALONE	53120-53120	EAST TROY	53237-53295	MILWAUKEE	53559-53559	MARSHALL
53050-53050	MAYVILLE	53121-53121	ELKHORN	53401-53408	RACINE	53560-53560	MAZOMANIE
53051-53052	MENOMONEE FALLS	53122-53122	ELM GROVE	53501-53501	AFTON	53561-53561	MERRIMAC
53056-53056	MERTON	53125-53125	FONTANA	53502-53502	ALBANY	53562-53562	MIDDLETON
53057-53057	MOUNT CALVARY	53126-53126	FRANKSVILLE	53503-53503	ARENA	53563-53563	MILTON
53058-53058	NASHOTAH	53127-53127	GENESEE DEPOT	53504-53504	ARGYLE	53565-53565	MINERAL POINT

53566-53566	MONROE	53946-53946	MARKESAN	54153-54153	OCONTO	54435-54435	GLEASON
53569-53569	MONTFORT	53947-53947	MARQUETTE	54154-54154	OCONTO FALLS	54436-54436	GRANTON
53570-53570	MONTICELLO	53948-53948	MAUSTON	54155-54155	ONEIDA	54437-54437	GREENWOOD
53571-53571	MORRISONVILLE	53949-53949	MONTELLO	54156-54156	PEMBINE	54439-54439	HANNIBAL
53572-53572	MOUNT HOREB	53950-53950	NEW LISBON	54157-54157	PESHTIGO	54440-54440	HATLEY
53573-53573	MUSCODA	53951-53951	NORTH FREEDOM	54159-54159	PORTERFIELD	54441-54441	HEWITT
53574-53574	NEW GLARUS	53952-53952	OXFORD	54160-54160	POTTER	54442-54442	IRMA
53575-53575	OREGON	53953-53953	PACKWAUKEE	54161-54161	POUND	54443-54443	JUNCTION CITY
53576-53576	ORFORDVILLE	53954-53954	PARDEEVILLE	54162-54162	PULASKI	54444-54444	KEMPSTER
53577-53577	PLAIN	53955-53955	POYNETTE	54165-54165	SEYMOUR	54446-54446	LOYAL
53578-53578	PRAIRIE DU SAC	53956-53957	RANDOLPH	54166-54166	SHAWANO	54447-54447	LUBLIN
53579-53579	REESEVILLE	53959-53959	REEDSBURG	54169-54169	SHERWOOD	54448-54448	MARATHON
53580-53580	REWEY	53960-53960	RIO	54170-54170	SHIOCTON	54449-54449	MARSHFIELD
53581-53581	RICHLAND CENTER	53961-53961	ROCK SPRINGS	54171-54171	SOBIESKI	54450-54450	MATTOON
53582-53582	RIDGEWAY	53962-53962	UNION CENTER	54173-54173	SUAMICO	54451-54451	MEDFORD
53583-53583	SAUK CITY	53963-53963	WAUPUN	54174-54174	SURING	54452-54452	MERRILL
53584-53584	SEXTONVILLE	53964-53964	WESTFIELD	54175-54175	TOWNSEND	54453-54453	MILAN
53585-53585	SHARON	53965-53965	WISCONSIN DELLS	54177-54177	WAUSAUKEE	54454-54454	MILLADORE
53586-53586	SHULLSBURG	53968-53968	WONEWOC	54180-54180	WRIGHTSTOWN	54455-54455	MOSINEE
53587-53587	SOUTH WAYNE	53969-53969	WYOCENA	54182-54182	ZACHOW	54456-54456	NEILLSVILLE
53588-53588	SPRING GREEN	54001-54001	AMERY	54201-54201	ALGOMA	54457-54457	NEKOOSA
53589-53589	STOUGHTON	54002-54002	BALDWIN	54202-54202	BAILEYS HARBOR	54458-54458	NELSONVILLE
53590-53591	SUN PRAIRIE	54003-54003	BELDENVILLE	54203-54203	BRANCH	54459-54459	OGEMA
53593-53593	VERONA	54004-54004	CLAYTON	54204-54204	BRUSSELS	54460-54460	OWEN
53594-53594	WATERLOO	54005-54005	CLEAR LAKE	54205-54205	CASCO	54462-54462	PEARSON
53595-53595	DODGEVILLE	54006-54006	CUSHING	54206-54206	CATO	54463-54463	PELICAN LAKE
53596-53596	SUN PRAIRIE	54007-54007	DEER PARK	54207-54207	COLLINS	54464-54464	PHLOX
53597-53597	WAUNAKEE	54009-54009	DRESSER	54208-54208	DENMARK	54465-54465	PICKEREL
53598-53598	WINDSOR	54010-54010	EAST ELLSWORTH	54209-54209	EGG HARBOR	54466-54466	PITTSVILLE
53599-53599	WOODFORD	54011-54011	ELLSWORTH	54210-54210	ELLISON BAY	54467-54467	PLOVER
53701-53794	MADISON	54012-54012	EMERALD	54211-54211	EPHRAIM	54469-54469	PORT EDWARDS
53801-53801	BAGLEY	54013-54013	GLENWOOD CITY	54212-54212	FISH CREEK	54470-54470	RIB LAKE
53802-53802	BEETOWN	54014-54014	HAGER CITY	54213-54213	FORESTVILLE	54471-54471	RINGLE
53803-53803	BENTON	54015-54015	HAMMOND	54214-54214	FRANCIS CREEK	54472-54472	MARSHFIELD
53804-53804	BLOOMINGTON	54016-54016	HUDSON	54215-54215	KELLNERSVILLE	54473-54473	ROSHOLT
53805-53805	BOSCOBEL	54017-54017	NEW RICHMOND	54216-54216	KEWAUNEE	54474-54474	ROTHSCHILD
53806-53806	CASSVILLE	54020-54020	OSCEOLA	54217-54217	LUXEMBURG	54475-54475	RUDOLPH
53807-53807	CUBA CITY	54021-54021	PRESCOTT	54220-54221	MANITOWOC	54476-54476	SCHOFIELD
53808-53808	DICKEYVILLE	54022-54022	RIVER FALLS	54226-54226	MAPLEWOOD	54479-54479	SPENCER
53809-53809	FENNIMORE	54023-54023	ROBERTS	54227-54227	MARIBEL	54480-54480	STETSONVILLE
53810-53810	GLEN HAVEN	54024-54024	SAINT CROIX FALLS	54228-54228	MISHICOT	54481-54481	STEVENS POINT
53811-53811	HAZEL GREEN	54025-54025	SOMERSET	54229-54229	NEW FRANKEN	54484-54484	STRATFORD
53812-53812	KIELER	54026-54026	STAR PRAIRIE	54230-54230	REEDSVILLE	54485-54485	SUMMIT LAKE
53813-53813	LANCASTER	54027-54027	WILSON	54232-54232	SAINT NAZIANZ	54486-54486	TIGERTON
53816-53816	MOUNT HOPE	54028-54028	WOODVILLE	54234-54234	SISTER BAY	54487-54487	TOMAHAWK
53817-53817	PATCH GROVE	54082-54082	SAINT JOSEPH	54235-54235	STURGEON BAY	54488-54488	UNITY
53818-53818	PLATTEVILLE	54101-54101	ABRAMS	54240-54240	TISCH MILLS	54489-54489	VESPER
53820-53820	POTOSI	54102-54102	AMBERG	54241-54241	TWO RIVERS	54490-54490	WESTBORO
53821-53821	PRAIRIE DU CHIEN	54103-54103	ARMSTRONG CREEK	54245-54245	VALDERS	54491-54491	WHITE LAKE
53824-53824	SINSINAWA	54104-54104	ATHELSTANE	54246-54246	WASHINGTON ISLAND	54492-54492	STEVENS POINT
53825-53825	STITZER	54106-54106	BLACK CREEK	54247-54247	WHITELAW	54493-54493	WILLARD
53826-53826	WAUZEKA	54107-54107	BONDUEL	54301-54344	GREEN BAY	54494-54495	WISCONSIN RAPIDS
53827-53827	WOODMAN	54110-54110	BRILLION	54401-54403	WAUSAU	54498-54498	WITHEE
53901-53901	PORTAGE	54111-54111	CECIL	54404-54404	MARSHFIELD	54499-54499	WITTENBERG
53910-53910	ADAMS	54112-54112	COLEMAN	54405-54405	ABBOTSFORD	54501-54501	RHINELANDER
53911-53911	ARLINGTON	54113-54113	COMBINED LOCKS	54406-54406	AMHERST	54511-54511	ARGONNE
53913-53913	BARABOO	54114-54114	CRIVITZ	54407-54407	AMHERST JUNCTION	54512-54512	BOULDER JUNCTION
53916-53917	BEAVER DAM	54115-54115	DE PERE	54408-54408	ANIWA	54513-54513	BRANTWOOD
53919-53919	BRANDON	54119-54119	DUNBAR	54409-54409	ANTIGO	54514-54514	BUTTERNUT
53920-53920	BRIGGSVILLE	54120-54120	FENCE	54410-54410	ARPIN	54515-54515	CATAWBA
53922-53922	BURNETT	54121-54121	FLORENCE	54411-54411	ATHENS	54517-54517	CLAM LAKE
53923-53923	CAMBRIA	54123-54123	FOREST JUNCTION	54412-54412	AUBURNDALE	54519-54519	CONOVER
53924-53924	CAZENOVIA	54124-54124	GILLETT	54413-54413	BABCOCK	54520-54520	CRANDON
53925-53925	COLUMBUS	54125-54125	GOODMAN	54414-54414	BIRNAMWOOD	54521-54521	EAGLE RIVER
53926-53926	DALTON	54126-54126	GREENLEAF	54415-54415	BLENKER	54524-54524	FIFIELD
53927-53927	DELLWOOD	54127-54127	GREEN VALLEY	54416-54416	BOWLER	54525-54525	GILE
53928-53928	DOYLESTOWN	54128-54128	GRESHAM	54417-54417	BROKAW	54526-54526	GLEN FLORA
53929-53929	ELROY	54129-54129	HILBERT	54418-54418	BRYANT	54527-54527	GLIDDEN
53930-53930	ENDEAVOR	54130-54130	KAUKAUNA	54420-54420	CHILI	54529-54529	HARSHAW
53931-53931	FAIRWATER	54131-54131	FREEDOM	54421-54421	COLBY	54530-54530	HAWKINS
53932-53932	FALL RIVER	54135-54135	KESHENA	54422-54422	CURTISS	54531-54531	HAZELHURST
53933-53933	FOX LAKE	54136-54136	KIMBERLY	54423-54423	CUSTER	54532-54532	HEAFFORD JUNCTION
53934-53934	FRIENDSHIP	54137-54137	KRAKOW	54424-54424	DEERBROOK	54534-54534	HURLEY
53935-53935	FRIESLAND	54138-54138	LAKEWOOD	54425-54425	DORCHESTER	54536-54536	IRON BELT
53936-53936	GRAND MARSH	54139-54139	LENA	54426-54426	EDGAR	54537-54537	KENNAN
53937-53937	HILLPOINT	54140-54140	LITTLE CHUTE	54427-54427	ELAND	54538-54538	LAC DU FLAMBEAU
53939-53939	KINGSTON	54141-54141	LITTLE SUAMICO	54428-54428	ELCHO	54539-54539	LAKE TOMAHAWK
53940-53940	LAKE DELTON	54143-54143	MARINETTE	54429-54429	ELDERON	54540-54540	LAND O LAKES
53941-53941	LA VALLE	54149-54149	MOUNTAIN	54430-54430	ELTON	54541-54541	LAONA
53942-53942	LIME RIDGE	54150-54150	NEOPIT	54432-54432	GALLOWAY	54542-54542	LONG LAKE
53943-53943	LOGANVILLE	54151-54151	NIAGARA	54433-54433	GILMAN	54543-54543	MC NAUGHTON
53944-53944	LYNDON STATION	54152-54152	NICHOLS	54434-54434	JUMP RIVER	54545-54545	MANITOWISH WATERS

54546-54546	MELLEN	54657-54657	STEUBEN	54773-54773	WHITEHALL	54890-54890	WASCOTT
54547-54547	MERCER	54658-54658	STODDARD	54774-54774	CHIPPEWA FALLS	54891-54891	WASHBURN
54548-54548	MINOCQUA	54659-54659	TAYLOR	54801-54801	SPOONER	54893-54893	WEBSTER
54550-54550	MONTREAL	54660-54660	TOMAH	54805-54805	ALMENA	54895-54895	WEYERHAEUSER
54552-54552	PARK FALLS	54661-54661	TREMPEALEAU	54806-54806	ASHLAND	54896-54896	WINTER
54554-54554	PHELPS	54662-54662	TUNNEL CITY	54810-54810	BALSAM LAKE	54901-54906	OSHKOSH
54555-54555	PHILLIPS	54664-54664	VIOLA	54812-54812	BARRON	54909-54909	ALMOND
54556-54556	PRENTICE	54665-54665	VIROQUA	54813-54813	BARRONETT	54911-54919	APPLETON
54557-54557	PRESQUE ISLE	54666-54666	WARRENS	54814-54814	BAYFIELD	54921-54921	BANCROFT
54558-54558	SAINT GERMAIN	54667-54667	WESTBY	54816-54816	BENOIT	54922-54922	BEAR CREEK
54559-54559	SAXON	54669-54669	WEST SALEM	54817-54817	BIRCHWOOD	54923-54923	BERLIN
54560-54560	SAYNER	54670-54670	WILTON	54818-54818	BRILL	54926-54926	BIG FALLS
54561-54561	STAR LAKE	54701-54703	EAU CLAIRE	54819-54819	BRUCE	54927-54927	BUTTE DES MORTS
54562-54562	THREE LAKES	54720-54720	ALTOONA	54820-54820	BRULE	54928-54928	CAROLINE
54563-54563	TONY	54721-54721	ARKANSAW	54821-54821	CABLE	54929-54929	CLINTONVILLE
54564-54564	TRIPOLI	54722-54722	AUGUSTA	54822-54822	CAMERON	54930-54930	COLOMA
54565-54565	UPSON	54723-54723	BAY CITY	54824-54824	CENTURIA	54931-54931	DALE
54566-54566	WABENO	54724-54724	BLOOMER	54826-54826	COMSTOCK	54932-54932	ELDORADO
54568-54568	WOODRUFF	54725-54725	BOYCEVILLE	54827-54827	CORNUCOPIA	54933-54933	EMBARRASS
54601-54603	LA CROSSE	54726-54726	BOYD	54828-54828	COUDERAY	54934-54934	EUREKA
54610-54610	ALMA	54727-54727	CADOTT	54829-54829	CUMBERLAND	54935-54937	FOND DU LAC
54611-54611	ALMA CENTER	54728-54728	CHETEK	54830-54830	DANBURY	54940-54940	FREMONT
54612-54612	ARCADIA	54729-54729	CHIPPEWA FALLS	54832-54832	DRUMMOND	54941-54941	GREEN LAKE
54613-54613	ARKDALE	54730-54730	COLFAX	54834-54834	EDGEWATER	54942-54942	GREENVILLE
54614-54614	BANGOR	54731-54731	CONRATH	54835-54835	EXELAND	54943-54943	HANCOCK
54615-54615	BLACK RIVER FALLS	54732-54732	CORNELL	54836-54836	FOXBORO	54944-54944	HORTONVILLE
54616-54616	BLAIR	54733-54733	DALLAS	54837-54837	FREDERIC	54945-54945	IOLA
54618-54618	CAMP DOUGLAS	54734-54734	DOWNING	54838-54838	GORDON	54946-54946	KING
54619-54619	CASHTON	54735-54735	DOWNSVILLE	54839-54839	GRAND VIEW	54947-54947	LARSEN
54620-54620	CATARACT	54736-54736	DURAND	54840-54840	GRANTSBURG	54948-54948	LEOPOLIS
54621-54621	CHASEBURG	54737-54737	EAU GALLE	54841-54841	HAUGEN	54949-54949	MANAWA
54622-54622	COCHRANE	54738-54738	ELEVA	54842-54842	HAWTHORNE	54950-54950	MARION
54623-54623	COON VALLEY	54739-54739	ELK MOUND	54843-54843	HAYWARD	54951-54951	MEDINA
54624-54624	DE SOTO	54740-54740	ELMWOOD	54844-54844	HERBSTER	54952-54952	MENASHA
54625-54625	DODGE	54741-54741	FAIRCHILD	54845-54845	HERTEL	54956-54957	NEENAH
54626-54626	EASTMAN	54742-54742	FALL CREEK	54846-54846	HIGH BRIDGE	54960-54960	NESHKORO
54627-54627	ETTRICK	54743-54743	GILMANTON	54847-54847	IRON RIVER	54961-54961	NEW LONDON
54628-54628	FERRYVILLE	54744-54744	HILLSDALE	54848-54848	LADYSMITH	54962-54962	OGDENSBURG
54629-54629	FOUNTAIN CITY	54745-54745	HOLCOMBE	54849-54849	LAKE NEBAGAMON	54963-54963	OMRO
54630-54630	GALESVILLE	54746-54746	HUMBIRD	54850-54850	LA POINTE	54964-54964	PICKETT
54631-54631	GAYS MILLS	54747-54747	INDEPENDENCE	54851-54851	LEWIS	54965-54965	PINE RIVER
54632-54632	GENOA	54748-54748	JIM FALLS	54853-54853	LUCK	54966-54966	PLAINFIELD
54634-54634	HILLSBORO	54749-54749	KNAPP	54854-54854	MAPLE	54967-54967	POY SIPPI
54635-54635	HIXTON	54750-54750	MAIDEN ROCK	54855-54855	MARENGO	54968-54968	PRINCETON
54636-54636	HOLMEN	54751-54751	MENOMONIE	54856-54856	MASON	54969-54969	READFIELD
54637-54637	HUSTLER	54754-54754	MERRILLAN	54857-54857	MIKANA	54970-54970	REDGRANITE
54638-54638	KENDALL	54755-54755	MONDOVI	54858-54858	MILLTOWN	54971-54971	RIPON
54639-54639	LA FARGE	54756-54756	NELSON	54859-54859	MINONG	54974-54974	ROSENDALE
54640-54640	LYNXVILLE	54757-54757	NEW AUBURN	54861-54861	ODANAH	54975-54975	ROYALTON
54641-54641	MATHER	54758-54758	OSSEO	54862-54862	OJIBWA	54976-54976	SAXEVILLE
54642-54642	MELROSE	54759-54759	PEPIN	54864-54864	POPLAR	54977-54977	SCANDINAVIA
54643-54643	MILLSTON	54760-54760	PIGEON FALLS	54865-54865	PORT WING	54978-54978	TILLEDA
54644-54644	MINDORO	54761-54761	PLUM CITY	54867-54867	RADISSON	54979-54979	VAN DYNE
54645-54645	MOUNT STERLING	54762-54762	PRAIRIE FARM	54868-54868	RICE LAKE	54980-54980	WAUKAU
54646-54646	NECEDAH	54763-54763	RIDGELAND	54870-54870	SARONA	54981-54981	WAUPACA
54648-54648	NORWALK	54764-54764	ROCK FALLS	54871-54871	SHELL LAKE	54982-54982	WAUTOMA
54649-54649	OAKDALE	54765-54765	SAND CREEK	54872-54872	SIREN	54983-54983	WEYAUWEGA
54650-54650	ONALASKA	54766-54766	SHELDON	54873-54873	SOLON SPRINGS	54984-54984	WILD ROSE
54651-54651	ONTARIO	54767-54767	SPRING VALLEY	54874-54874	SOUTH RANGE	54985-54985	WINNEBAGO
54652-54652	READSTOWN	54768-54768	STANLEY	54875-54875	SPRINGBROOK	54986-54986	WINNECONNE
54653-54653	ROCKLAND	54769-54769	STOCKHOLM	54876-54876	STONE LAKE	54990-54990	IOLA
54654-54654	SENECA	54770-54770	STRUM	54880-54880	SUPERIOR		
54655-54655	SOLDIERS GROVE	54771-54771	THORP	54888-54888	TREGO		
54656-54656	SPARTA	54772-54772	WHEELER	54889-54889	TURTLE LAKE		

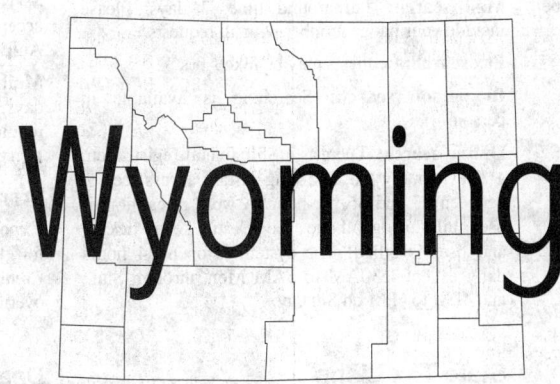

Wyoming

General Help Numbers:

Governor's Office
State Capitol Building, Rm 124   307-777-7434
Cheyenne, WY 82002-0010   Fax 307-632-3909
http://www.state.wy.us/governor/   8AM-5PM
governor_home.html

Attorney General's Office
123 State Capitol   307-777-7841
Cheyenne, WY 82002   Fax 307-777-6869
http://attorneygeneral.state.wy.us   8AM-5PM

State Court Administrator
Supreme Court Bldg   307-777-7480
2301 Capitol Ave   Fax 307-777-3447
Cheyenne, WY 82002   8AM-5PM
http://www.courts.state.wy.us

State Archives
Archives Division   307-777-7826
2301 Central Ave, Barrett Bldg   Fax 307-777-7044
Cheyenne, WY 82002   8AM-5PM M-F
    (Research Area 8AM-4:45PM)
http://commerce.state.wy.us/cr/archives

State Specifics:

Capital:	Cheyenne
	Laramie County
Time Zone:	MST
Number of Counties:	23
Population:	493,782
Web Site:	www.state.wy.us

State Agencies

Criminal Records

Division of Criminal Investigation, Criminal Record Unit, 316 W 22nd St, Cheyenne, WY 82002; 307-777-7523, 307-777-7252 (Fax), 8AM to 5PM.

http://attorneygeneral.state.wy.us/dci/index.html

Note: First, obtain a Request for Criminal Record Packet ($15.00) from address above or phone.

Indexing & Storage: Records are available from 1941 on. New records are available for inquiry immediately. Records are indexed on inhouse computer.

Searching: Must have a notarized, signed waiver from the person of record. Must also have a standard 8" x 8" orange fingerprint card (that you must get from this office) with properly rolled fingerprints of person and notarized signature of applicant. Include the following in your request- name, set of fingerprints, date of birth, Social Security Number, number of years to search. Must also fill out waiver from their office that is on the back of the fingerprint card. Major misdemeanors and felonies will indicate arrests as well as convictions. The following data is not released: juvenile records.

Access by: mail, in person.

Fee & Payment: The search fee is $15.00 plus an additional $5.00 if this office must perform the fingerprinting. The fee is only $10.00 if the applicant is part of an organization providing volunteer services. Fee payee: Office of the Attorney General. Prepayment required. Money order, cash or certified checks only. No credit cards accepted.

Mail search: Turnaround time: 2 to 4 weeks. A self addressed stamped envelope is requested.

In person search: Proper forms are required to be filled out.

Corporation Records
Limited Liability Company Records
Limited Partnership Records
Fictitious Name
Trademarks/Servicemarks

Corporations Division, Secretary of State, State Capitol, Cheyenne, WY 82002; 307-777-7311, 307-777-5339 (Fax), 8AM-5PM.

http://soswy.state.wy.us

Indexing & Storage: Records are available from 1800s on. The records on microfilm are inactive records before 1983. Newer records are on computer. New records are available for inquiry immediately. Records are indexed on microfilm, inhouse computer.

Searching: The Annual Report financial information (Appendix I Worksheet filed with Annual Report) is not released. Include the following in your request-full name of business. In addition to the articles of incorporation, corporation records include the following information: Annual Reports, Officers, Directors, DBAs, Prior (merged) names, Inactive and Reserved names.

Access by: mail, phone, fax, in person, online.

Fee & Payment: Copy fees are $.50 per page for the first 10 pages and $.15 for each additional page. Certification is $3.00. Fee payee: Secretary of State. They will invoice for copies and certificates. Prepaid accounts are available. Personal checks accepted. No credit cards accepted.

Mail search: Turnaround time: 1 to 3 days. A self addressed stamped envelope is requested.

Phone search: You may call for information.

Fax search: Turnaround time is 24-48 hours.

In person search: You may request information in person.

Online search: Information is available through the Internet site listed above. You can search by corporate name or even download the whole file. Also, they have 2 pages of excellent searching tips.

Uniform Commercial Code
Federal Tax Liens

UCC Division, Secretary of State, The Capitol, Cheyenne, WY 82002-0020 (Courier: Capitol Bldg, RM 110, Cheyenne, WY 82002); 307-777-5372, 307-777-5988 (Fax), 8AM-5PM.

http://soswy.state.wy.us

Indexing & Storage: Records are available for five years on computer, since the "beginning" on microfiche. Records are indexed on inhouse computer and microfiche.

Searching: The search includes federal tax liens on businesses. Include the following in your request-debtor name.

Access by: mail, fax, in person, online.

Fee & Payment: The search fee is $5.00. Copies cost $.50 each for the first 10 pages and $.15 for each additional page. Fee payee: Secretary of

State. Personal checks accepted. No credit cards accepted.

Mail search: Turnaround time: 7 days. Please include your phone number with all requests.

Fax search: Requests may be faxed in.

In person search: Searching is available in person.

Online search: There is a $50 annual registration, a $20 monthly fee, and long distant access fees of between $3 and $6 per hour. A word of caution, if user fails to log off the "clock" still keeps ticking and user is billed! The system is open 24 hours daily except 1:30AM to 5AM Mon. through Sun., and 4PM to 6PM on Sunday.

State Tax Liens
Records not maintained by a state level agency.

Note: There is no state income tax. All other state tax liens are filed at the county level.

Sales Tax Registrations

Department of Revenue, Excise Tax Division, Herscher Bldg, 122 W 25th St, Cheyenne, WY 82002-0110; 307-777-5200, 307-777-3652 (Fax), 8AM-5PM.

http://revenue.state.wy.us

Indexing & Storage: Records are available for at least two years: inactive files are purged every two years.

Searching: This agency will only confirm that the business is registered. They will provide no other information. Requests may be e-mailed, visit the web site for the proper e-mail address. Include the following in your request-business name. They will also search by tax permit number.

Access by: mail, phone, in person.

Fee & Payment: There may be a copy fee per page, if record is not considered confidential per statute. The fee depends on the type of record and how many copies are needed. Suggest to call first or to send a restrictive check.

Mail search: A self addressed stamped envelope is requested. No fee for mail request.

Phone search: No fee for telephone request.

In person search: No fee for request.

Birth Certificates

Wyoming Department of Health, Vital Records Services, Hathaway Bldg, Cheyenne, WY 82002; 307-777-7591, 307-635-4103 (Fax), 8AM-5PM.

http://wdhfs.state.wy.us/vital_records

Indexing & Storage: Records are available from 1909 to present. New records are available for inquiry immediately. Records are indexed on microfilm, inhouse computer.

Searching: Must have a signed release from person of record or parent or guardian. Include the following in your request-full name, names of parents, mother's maiden name, date of birth, place of birth, relationship to person of record. Must include signature on request and copy of photo ID.

Access by: mail, fax, in person.

Fee & Payment: Search fee is $12.00 per name per 5 years searched. Fee includes certification.

Use of credit card is an additional $5.00 for expedited service. Fee payee: Vital Records Services. Prepayment required. Personal checks accepted. Credit cards accepted: MasterCard, Visa, AmEx, Discover.

Mail search: Turnaround time: 3 to 4 working days. No self addressed stamped envelope is required.

Fax search: See expedited services.

In person search: Turnaround time is 15 minutes.

Expedited service: Expedited service is available for fax searches. Turnaround time: next day. Credit card is required ($5.00), records are overnighted for an additional $11.75.

Death Records

Wyoming Department of Health, Vital Records Services, Hathaway Bldg, Cheyenne, WY 82002; 307-777-7591, 307-635-4103 (Fax), 8AM-5PM.

http://wdhfs.state.wy.us/vital_records

Indexing & Storage: Records are available from 1945 to present. For prior records, contact the State Archives at 307-777-7826. New records are available for inquiry immediately. Records are indexed on microfilm, inhouse computer.

Searching: Must have a signed release form from immediate family member. The agency will verify information to family member, such as aunts and uncles, but will not release copies. Include the following in your request-full name, date of death, place of death, relationship to person of record, reason for information request. Must include signature and copy of photo ID with request.

Access by: mail, fax, in person.

Fee & Payment: Search fee is $9.00 per name if year is known; fee is $12.00 per name per 5 years if date is unknown. All copies are certified. Use of credit card for expedited service an extra $5.00. Fee payee: Vital Records Services. Prepayment required. Personal checks accepted. Credit cards accepted: MasterCard, Visa, AmEx, Discover.

Mail search: Turnaround time: 3 to 4 working days. No self addressed stamped envelope is required.

Fax search: See expedited services.

In person search: Turnaround time is 15 minutes.

Expedited service: Expedited service is available for fax searches. Turnaround time: next day. Include credit card fee and funds for overnight delivery.

Marriage Certificates

Wyoming Department of Health, Vital Records Services, Hathaway Bldg, Cheyenne, WY 82002; 307-777-7591, 307-635-4103 (Fax), 8AM-5PM.

http://wdhfs.state.wy.us/vital_records

Indexing & Storage: Records are available from 1941 to present. New records are available for inquiry immediately. Records are indexed on microfilm, inhouse computer.

Searching: Must have a signed release from persons of record. Include the following in your request-names of husband and wife, date of marriage, place or county of marriage, relationship to person of record, reason for information request, wife's maiden name. Signature and copy of photo ID must be included in request.

Access by: mail, fax, in person.

Fee & Payment: The fee is $12.00 per record and an additional $5.00 if a credit card is used fro expedited service. Fee payee: Vital Records Services. Prepayment required. Personal checks accepted. Credit cards accepted: MasterCard, Visa, AmEx, Discover.

Mail search: Turnaround time: 3 to 4 working days. No self addressed stamped envelope is required.

Fax search: See expedited services.

In person search: Turnaround time is 15 minutes.

Expedited service: Expedited service is available for fax searches. Turnaround time: next day. Include credit card fee and funds for overnight delivery.

Divorce Records

Wyoming Department of Health, Vital Records Services, Hathaway Bldg, Cheyenne, WY 82002; 307-777-7591, 307-635-4103 (Fax), 8AM-5PM.

http://wdhfs.state.wy.us/vital_records

Indexing & Storage: Records are available from 1941 to present. New records are available for inquiry immediately. Records are indexed on microfilm, inhouse computer.

Searching: Must have a signed release from person of record. Include the following in your request-names of husband and wife, date of divorce, place of divorce, relationship to person of record. Include copy of photo ID with request.

Access by: mail, phone, fax, in person.

Fee & Payment: Fee is $12.00 per record, add $5.00 if expedited service used. Fee payee: Vital Records Services. Prepayment required. Personal checks accepted. Credit cards accepted: MasterCard, Visa, AmEx, Discover.

Mail search: Turnaround time: 3 to 4 working days.

Phone search: See expedited service.

Fax search: See expedited services.

In person search: Turnaround time is 30 minutes.

Expedited service: Expedited service is available for fax searches. Turnaround time: next day. Include credit card fee ($5.00) and funds for overnight delivery.

Workers' Compensation Records

Employment Department, Workers Compensation Division, 122 W 25th St, Cheyenne, WY 82002 (Courier: Herschler Bldg, 2nd Floor E, 122 W 25th St, Cheyenne, WY 82002); 307-777-7159, 307-777-5946 (Fax), 8AM-4:30PM.

http://wydoe.state.wy.us/wscd

Indexing & Storage: Records are available from 1987 on computer. Records are on microfiche from 1919 to 1987. Searches on microfiche must include the date of injury, county of injury, employer and body part affected.

Searching: Only the injured party, employer or legal counsel for either party can obtain records from this agency. Include the following in your request-claimant name, Social Security Number. The only information released is case #, date of injury, body part, employer at time of injury, or other information specifically authorized by claimant.

Access by: mail, fax.

Fee & Payment: No search fee, copy fee is $.25 per copy.

Mail search: Turnaround time: variable. Send release form with request to Gary Lord at address above.No self addressed stamped envelope is required.

Fax search: They will fax results with appropriate request.

Driver License Information
Driver Records

Wyoming Department of Transportation, Driver Services, 5300 Bishop Blvd, Cheyenne, WY 82009-3340; 307-777-4800, 307-777-4773 (Fax), 8AM-5PM.

http://wydotweb.state.wy.us

Note: Tickets may be obtained from the address above for a fee of $5.00 per citation.

Indexing & Storage: Records are available for 3 years from offense date for moving violations, 5 years from conviction date for DWIs, and 3 to 5 years based on original charge for suspensions. Accidents are shown only if driver has no insurance. It takes 5 to 10 days before new records are available for inquiry.

Searching: Companies requesting records must identify themselves and certify the purpose for which the report is to be used and no other purpose. Casual requesters cannot obtain records with personal information without signed release from subject. The driver license number or name and DOB is needed when ordering. In addition, a SSN is required when requesting a Commercial Driver License (CDL) record. The following data is not released: medical information.

Access by: mail, in person.

Fee & Payment: The fee is $5.00 per record, $3.00 by tape. Fee payee: Department of Transportation. Prepayment required. Personal checks accepted. No credit cards accepted.

Mail search: Turnaround time: 2 days. A self addressed stamped envelope is requested.

In person search: Normal turnaround time is while you wait. Individual licensees may request a copy of their own record at any field office.

Other access: Magnetic tape retrieval is available at $3.00 per record. The entire driver license file may be purchased for $2,500.

Accident Reports

Department of Transportation, Accident Records Section, 5300 Bishop Blvd, Cheyenne, WY 82009-3340; 307-777-4450, 307-777-4250 (Fax), 8AM-5PM.

Note: The agency refers to these reports as "Crash Reports."

Indexing & Storage: Records are available from 1979 on. It takes 3 to 30 days before new records are available for inquiry.

Searching: Accident reports (done by the officer) are considered open public record reports. Reports compiled by individuals involved are closed. Include the following in your request-date of accident, location of accident, full name, date of birth.

Access by: mail, phone, in person.

Fee & Payment: The fee is $3.00 per record uncertified and $5.00 certified. If the specific year or location is not given, the fee is $25.00. Fee

payee: Department of Transportation. Prepayment required. Personal checks accepted. No credit cards accepted.

Mail search: Turnaround time: 1 week to 10 days. A self addressed stamped envelope is requested.

Phone search: Searches may be done by phone, but no copies are sent until payment is received.

In person search: In-person requests are normally processed in a few of minutes.

Vehicle Ownership
Vehicle Identification

Wyoming Dept. of Transportation, Motor Vehicle Services, 5300 Bishop Blvd, Cheyenne, WY 82009-3340 (Courier: 5300 Bishop Blvd, Cheyenne, WY 82002); 307-777-4709, 307-777-4772 (Fax), 8AM-5PM.

http://www.wydotweb.state.wy.us

Note: At the web site, click on "Vehicle Services" for detailed WY DOT vehicle information.

Indexing & Storage: Records are available for 40 years on titles and 80 years on registrations. It takes 3 to 15 days before new records are available for inquiry.

Searching: An opt in provision allows casual requesters to obtain records on subjects who opted in. Requests must be for a legitimate business purpose and requesters must sign a "Privacy Disclosure Agreement." Lien records are not available from the state and must be obtained from the one of the 23 Wyoming county clerk offices.

Access by: mail, in person.

Fee & Payment: The fee is $5.00 per record. Fee payee: Department of Transportation. Prepayment required. Personal checks accepted. No credit cards accepted.

Mail search: Turnaround time: 1 week. No self addressed stamped envelope is required.

In person search: Turnaround time is normally in a few minutes.

Other access: Bulk information is available, customized lists can be obtained. Records cannot be resold once purchased. For more information, call the Info Tech Section at 307-777-4870.

Vessel Ownership
Vessel Registration

Wyoming Game & Fish Dept, Watercraft Section, 5400 Bishop Blvd, Cheyenne, WY 82006; 307-777-4575, 307-777-4610 (Fax), 8AM-5PM M-F.

http://gf.state.wy.us

Indexing & Storage: Records are available for the last 3 years on computer. The state does not issue titles. All motorized boats with a 5 HP or larger motor must be registered.

Searching: To search you must provide one of the following: Name, Wyoming #, or Hull Id #.

Access by: mail, phone, fax, in person.

Fee & Payment: There is no search fee.

Mail search: Turnaround time: 2 to 3 days. Turnaround time is 1 week if archived info is needed.

Phone search: Records are available by phone.

Fax search: Information can be faxed back.

In person search: No fee for request. Turnaround time is immediate if the file is not archived.

Other access: Printed lists are available, call for further details.

Legislation Records

Wyoming Legislature, State Capitol, Room 213, Cheyenne, WY 82002; 307-777-7881, 8AM-5PM.

http://legisweb.state.wy.us

Note: General Session starts on the 2nd Tuesday in January. Budget session starts in February on second Monday.

Indexing & Storage: Records are available for the current session and for past bills, only as introduced. Records are indexed on books (volumes).

Searching: Include the following in your request-bill number, date of debate, topic of bill.

Access by: mail, phone, in person, online.

Fee & Payment: Copies are $.10 a page with a minimum fee of $1.00. Fee payee: Wyoming Legislature. Personal checks accepted. No credit cards accepted.

Mail search: Turnaround time: variable. No self addressed stamped envelope is required.

Phone search: Records are available by phone.

In person search: Searching is available in person.

Online search: The Internet site contains a wealth of information regarding the legislature and bills.

Voter Registration
Access to Records is Restricted

Secretary of State, Election Division, Wyoming State Capitol, Cheyenne, WY 82002-0020; 307-777-7186, 307-777-7640 (Fax), 8AM-5PM.

http://soswy.state.wy.us

Note: Individual look-ups must be done at the county level. The SSN and DOB are not released. The state will sell all or part of its database, but only for political reasons. Commercial use is not permitted.

GED Certificates

Wyoming Community College Commission, GED Program, 2020 Carey Ave, 8th Fl, Cheyenne, WY 82002; 307-777-6911, 307-777-6567 (Fax), 8AM-5PM M-F.

http://www.commission.wcc.edu

Searching: To search, all of the following is required: name, Social Security Number, and date of birth. For transcripts, a signed release is also required.

Access by: mail, fax, in person.

Fee & Payment: There is no fee for verifications or transcripts.

Mail search: Turnaround time: 2 weeks. No self addressed stamped envelope is required.

Fax search: Same criteria as mail searching.

In person search: Turnaround time is typically 10 minutes for verifications if clerical help available, otherwise mailed. All transcript copies are mailed.

Hunting License Information
Fishing License Information

Game & Fish Department, License Section, 5400 Bishop Blvd, Cheyenne, WY 82006; 307-777-4600 (Licensing Section), 307-777-4679 (Fax), 8AM-5PM.

http://gf.state.wy.us

Note: They have a central database for lottery (big game, moose, big horn sheep, elk, deer & antelope) permits only.

Indexing & Storage: Records are available from 3 years present on computer, 10 years on microfiche.

Searching: Include the following in your request-full name, date of birth, Social Security Number. The following data is not released: Social Security Numbers.

Access by: mail, phone, fax, in person.

Fee & Payment: Fees are incurred if there is extensive searching or lists are involved. Call first. Fee payee: Wyoming Game and Fish. Prepayment required. Money orders and cashier's checks are preferred. No credit cards accepted.

Wyoming State Licensing Agencies

Licenses Searchable Online

Attorney #09 .... www.wyomingbar.org/setemp.asp
Bank #23 .... http://audit.state.wy.us/banking/banks.htm
Collection Agency #24 .... http://audit.state.wy.us/banking/CAB.htm
Engineer #27 .... www.wrds.uwyo.edu/wrds/borpe/roster/roster.html
Funeral Pre-Need Agent #08 .... http://insurance.state.wy.us/search/search.asp
Geologist #18 .... http://wbpgweb.uwyo.edu/roster_search.htm
Insurance Agent #08 .... http://insurance.state.wy.us/search/search.asp
Insurance Broker, Resident #08 .... http://insurance.state.wy.us/search/search.asp
Insurance Claims Adjuster #08 .... http://insurance.state.wy.us/search/search.asp
Insurance Consultant #08 .... http://insurance.state.wy.us/search/search.asp
Insurance Service Representatives #08 ..... http://insurance.state.wy.us/search/search.asp
Insurance Solicitor #08 .... http://insurance.state.wy.us/search/search.asp
Lobbyist #36 .... www.lobbyist.net/Wyoming/WYOLOB.htm
Motor Club Agent #08 .... http://insurance.state.wy.us/search/search.asp
Optometrist #06 .... www.odfinder.org/LicSearch.asp
Public Accountant-CPA #29 .... http://cpaboard.state.wy.us/search.cfm
Public Accountant-CPA Firm #29 .... http://cpaboard.state.wy.us/search.cfm
Real Estate Agent #21 .... http://realestate.state.wy.us
Real Estate Appraiser #21 .... http://realestate.state.wy.us
Savings & Loan Association #23 .... http://audit.state.wy.us/banking/fsb.htm
Surplus Line Broker, Resident #08 .... http://insurance.state.wy.us/search/search.asp
Surveyor #27 .... www.wrds.uwyo.edu/wrds/borpe/roster/roster.html

Licensing Quick Finder

Architect #30	307-777-7788
Attorney #09	307-632-9061
Bank #23	307-777-6605
Barber/Barber Shop #02	307-754-5237
Bus Driver #41	307-777-4800
Child Care Facility #22	307-777-6595
Chiropractor #32	307-777-6529
Collection Agency #24	307-777-3497
Cosmetologist #03	307-777-3534
Cosmetologist Instructor #03	307-777-3534
Counselor, Professional #30	307-777-7788
Dental Hygienist #04	307-777-6529
Dentist #04	307-777-6529
Educational Diagnostician #35	307-777-6261
Electrician #26	307-777-7991
Embalmer #05	307-777-7788
Emergency Medical Technician #40	307-777-7955
Engineer #27	307-777-6155
Esthetician #03	307-777-3534
Funeral Director #05	307-777-7788
Funeral Pre-Need Agent #08	307-777-7344
Geologist #18	307-766-2490
Hearing Aid Specialist #07	307-777-6529
Insurance Agent #08	307-777-7344
Insurance Broker, Resident #08	307-777-7344
Insurance Claims Adjuster #08	307-777-7344
Insurance Consultant #08	307-777-7344
Insurance Service Representatives #8	307-777-7344

Insurance Solicitor #08	307-777-7344
Jockey/Jockey Apprentice #38	307-777-5887
Landscape Architect #30	307-777-7788
Law Enforcement Officer #39	307-777-7718
Lobbyist #36	307-777-7186
Manicurist/Nail Technician #03	307-777-3534
Marriage & Family Therapist #30	307-777-7788
Medical Doctor #10	307-778-7053
Mine Foreman #33	307-362-5222
Mine Inspector/Examiner #33	307-362-5222
Motor Club Agent #08	307-777-7344
Notary Public #36	307-777-5407
Nurse #37	877-626-2681
Nurse-LPN #37	877-626-2681
Nursing Assistant #37	877-626-2681
Nursing Home Administrator #12	307-432-0465
Occupational Therapist #12	307-432-0488
Occupational Therapist Assistant #12	307-432-0488
Optometrist #06	307-777-3507
Outfitter & Guide #13	307-777-5323
Pari-Mutuel Employee/Official #38	307-777-5887
Pesticide Applicator, Commercial #1	307-777-6569
Pharmacist #14	307-234-0294
Pharmacy Technician #14	307-234-0294
Physical Therapist #15	307-777-3507
Physician Assistant #10	307-778-7053
Podiatrist #19	307-777-3507
Property Tax Appraiser #25	307-777-5239

Psychiatrist #10	307-778-7053
Psychologist #16	307-777-6529
Public Accountant-CPA #29	307-777-7551
Public Accountant-CPA Firm #29	307-777-7551
Racetrack Security Employee #38	307-777-5887
Racing Event #38	307-777-5887
Racing Permittee/Employee/Official #38	307-777-5887
Radiation (Ionizing) Agent #17	307-777-3507
Radiologic Technologist/Technician #17	307-777-3507
Radiopharmaceutical Agent #17	307-778-2068
Real Estate Agent #21	307-777-7142
Real Estate Appraiser #21	307-777-7142
Savings & Loan Association #23	307-777-6605
School Counselor #35	307-777-6261
School Librarian #35	307-777-6261
School Principal/Superintendent #35	307-777-6261
Securities Agent #34	307-777-7370
Securities Broker/Dealer #34	307-777-7370
Social Worker #30	307-777-7788
Speech Pathologist/Audiologist #28	307-777-6529
Surplus Line Broker, Resident #08	307-777-7344
Surveyor #27	307-777-6155
Teacher #35	307-777-6261
Travel & Baggage Agent #08	307-777-7344
Truck Driver #41	307-777-4800
Veterinarian #20	307-777-3507
Water/Waste Water Treatment Plant Operator #42	307-777-7781

Licensing Agency Information

#01 Board of Agriculture, 2219 Carey Ave, Cheyenne, WY 82002-0100; 307-777-6569, Fax: 307-777-6593.
www.wyagric.state.wy.us

#02 Board of Barber Examiners, 441 Sunlight Dr, Powell, WY 82435; 307-754-5237.
http://soswy.state.wy.us/director/ag-bd/barber.htm

#03 Board of Cosmetology, 2515 Warren Ave, #302, Cheyenne, WY 82002; 307-777-3534, Fax: 307-777-3681.
soswy.state.wy.us/director/boards.htm

#04 Board of Dental Examiners, 2020 Carey Ave #201, Cheyenne, WY 82002; 307-777-6529, Fax: 307-777-3508.
soswy.state.wy.us/director/ag-bd/dental.htm

#05 Board of Embalming, 2020 Carey Ave, #201, Cheyenne, WY 82002; 307-777-7788, Fax: 307-777-3508.

#06 Board of Examiners in Optometry, 2020 Carey Ave, #201, Cheyenne, WY 82002; 307-777-3507, Fax: 307-777-3508.
http://soswy.state.wy.us/director/boards.htm
Direct web site URL to search for licensees: www.odfinder.org/LicSearch.asp. You can search online using national database by name, city or state.

#07 Board of Hearing Aid Specialists, 2020 Carey Ave, #201, Cheyenne, WY 82002; 307-777-6529, Fax: 307-777-3508.
soswy.state.wy/director/boards.htm

#08 Board of Insurance Agents Examiners, 122 W 25th St, Cheyenne, WY 82002-0040; 307-777-7344, Fax: 307-777-5895.
http://insurance.state.wy.us/
Direct web site URL to search for licensees: http://insurance.state.wy.us/search/search.asp

#09 Board of Law Examiners, PO Box 109 (500 Randall Ave.), Cheyenne, WY 82003; 307-632-9061, Fax: 307-630-3737.
www.wyomingbar.org
Direct web site URL to search for licensees: www.wyomingbar.org/setemp.asp. You can search online using name, city, and district.

#10 Board of Medicine, 211 W 19th St, 2nd Fl, Cheyenne, WY 82002; 307-778-7053, Fax: 307-778-2069.
http://soswy.state.wy/director/boards.htm

#12 Board of Occupational Therapy, 2020 Carey Ave, #201, Cheyenne, WY 82002; 307-432-0488, Fax: 307-432-0492.
http://soswy.state.wy.us/director/boards.htm

#13 Board of Outfitters & Professional Guides, 1750 Wland Rd, Cheyenne, WY 82002; 307-777-5323, Fax: 307-777-6715.
http://outfitte.state.wy.us/index.html

#14 Board of Pharmacy, 1720 S Poplar St, #4, Casper, WY 82601; 307-234-0294, Fax: 307-234-7226.
http://pharmacyboard.state.wy.us

#15 Board of Physical Therapy, 2020 Carey Ave, #201, Cheyenne, WY 82002; 307-777-3507, Fax: 307-777-3508.
http://soswy.state.wy.us/director/boards.htm

#16 Board of Psychology, 2020 Carey Ave, #201, Cheyenne, WY 82002; 307-777-6529, Fax: 307-777-3508.
http://soswy.state.wy.us/director/boards.htm

#17 Board of Radiologic Technologists, 2020 Carey Ave, #201, Cheyenne, WY 82002; 307-777-3507, Fax: 307-777-3508.
http://soswy.state.wy.us/director/boards.htm

#18 Board of Registration for Professional Geologists, PO Box 3008, Laramie, WY 82071-3008; 307-766-2490, Fax: 307-766-2713.
http://wbpgweb.uwyo.edu
Direct web site URL to search for licensees: http://wbpgweb.uwyo.edu/roster_search.htm

#19 Board of Registration in Podiatry, 2020 Carey Ave, #201, Cheyenne, WY 82002; 307-777-3507, Fax: 307-777-3508.
http://soswy.state.wy.us/director/boards.htm

#20 Board of Veterinary Medicine, 2020 Carey Ave, #201, Cheyenne, WY 82002; 307-777-3507, Fax: 307-777-3508.
http://soswy.state.wy.us/director/boards.htm

#21 Real Estate Appraiser Board, 2020 Carey Ave, #100, Cheyenne, WY 82002; 307-777-7142, Fax: 307-777-3796.
http://realestate.state.wy.us
Direct web site URL to search for licensees: http://realestate.state.wy.us

#22 Child Care Certification Board, 2300 Capitol Ave, Hathaway Bldg., 3rd Fl, Cheyenne, WY 82002-0490; 307-777-6595, Fax: 307-777-3659.
http://soswy.state.wy.us/director/boards.htm

#23 Department of Audit, 122 W 25th St, Herschler Bldg, 3rd Fl, Cheyenne, WY 82002; 307-777-6605, Fax: 307-777-3555.
http://audit.state.wy.us/banking/default.htm
Direct web site URL to search for licensees: http://audit.state.wy.us/banking/Links.htm

#24 Department of Audit, Herschler Bldg, 3rd Fl, Cheyenne, WY 82002; 307-777-3497, Fax: 307-777-3555.
http://audit.state.wy.us/banking/CAB.htm
Direct web site URL to search for licensees: http://audit.state.wy.us/banking/CAB.htm. You can search online using alphabetical list

#25 Department of Revenue, 122 W 25th St, Herschler Bldg, 2nd Fl W, Cheyenne, WY 82002-0110; 307-777-5239.
http://soswy.state.wy.us/director/boards.htm

#26 Electrical Board, Herschler Bldg, 1st Fl W, Cheyenne, WY 82002; 307-777-7288, Fax: 307-777-7119.
www.state.wy.us/~fire/electrical.htm

#27 Engineers & Professional Land Surveyors, 2424 Pioneer Ave, #400, Cheyenne, WY 82001; 307-777-6155, Fax: 307-777-3403.

www.wrds.uwyo.edu/wrds/borpe/borpe.html
Direct web site URL to search for licensees: www.wrds.uwyo.edu/wrds/borpe/roster/roster.html
. You can search online using name, registration number, branch, city, state, address or corporation

#28 Examiners for Speech Pathology & Audiology, 2020 Carey Ave, #201, Cheyenne, WY 82002; 307-777-6529, Fax: 307-777-3508.
http://soswy.state.wy.us/director/boards.htm

#29 Board of CPAs, 2020 Carey Ave, #100, Cheyenne, WY 82002; 307-777-7551, Fax: 307-777-3796.
http://cpaboard.state.wy.us
Direct web site URL to search for licensees: http://cpaboard.state.wy.us/search.cfm. You can search online using name, city or state

#30 Professional Licensing Boards, 2020 Carey Ave, #201, Cheyenne, WY 82002; 307-777-7788, Fax: 307-777-3508.

#32 Licensing Boards - Chiropractic Examiners, 2020 Carey Ave, #201, Cheyenne, WY 82002; 307-777-6529, Fax: 307-777-3508.
http://soswy.state.wy.us/director/boards.htm

#33 Mining Council, PO Box 1094, Rock Springs, WY 82901; 307-362-5222, Fax: 307-362-5233.

#34 Office of Secretary of State, The Capitol 200 W 24th St, Cheyenne, WY 82002-0020; 307-777-7370, Fax: 307-777-5339.
http://soswy.state.wy.us

#35 Professional Teaching Standards Board, 2300 Capitol Ave, Hathaway Bldg, Cheyenne, WY 82002; 307-777-6261, Fax: 307-777-6234.
www.k12.wy.us/ptsb

#36 Secretary of State, PO Box, Cheyenne, WY 82002-0020; 307-777-7378, Fax: 307-777-5466.
http://soswy.state.wy.us

#37 Board of Nursing, 2020 Carey Ave, #110, Cheyenne, WY 82002; 307-777-7601, Fax: 307-777-3519.
http://nursing.state.wy.us
Direct web site URL to search for licensees: http://nursing.state.wy.us/voice/voice.htm. You can search online using SSN or license number

#38 Pari-Mutuel Commission, 2515 Warren Ave, #301, Cheyenne, WY 82002; 307-777-5887, Fax: 307-777-5700.
http://paramutuel.state.wy.us

#39 P.O.S.T. Commission, 1710 Pacific Ave, Cheyenne, WY 82002; 307-777-7718.

#40 Office of Emergency Medical Svcs, 2300 Capital Ave, Hathaway Bldg, Cheyenne, WY 82002; 307-777-7955.

#41 Driver Svcs, PO Box 1708, 5300 Bishop Blvd, Cheyenne, WY 82003-1708; 307-777-4800.

#42 Department of Environmental Quality, 122 W 25th St, Herschler Bldg, Cheyenne, WY 82002; 307-777-7781.

Wyoming Federal Courts

The following list indicates the district and division name for each county in the state.

County/Court Cross Reference

Albany	Cheyenne	Natrona	Cheyenne
Big Horn	Cheyenne	Niobrara	Cheyenne
Campbell	Cheyenne	Park	Cheyenne
Carbon	Cheyenne	Platte	Cheyenne
Converse	Cheyenne	Sheridan	Cheyenne
Crook	Cheyenne	Sublette	Cheyenne
Fremont	Cheyenne	Sweetwater	Cheyenne
Goshen	Cheyenne	Teton	Cheyenne
Hot Springs	Cheyenne	Uinta	Cheyenne
Johnson	Cheyenne	Washakie	Cheyenne
Laramie	Cheyenne	Weston	Cheyenne
Lincoln	Cheyenne		

US District Court

District of Wyoming

Cheyenne Division PO Box 727, Cheyenne, WY 82003 (Courier Address: Room 2131, 2120 Capitol Ave, Cheyenne, WY 82001), 307-772-2145.

http://www.ck10.uscourts.gov/wyoming/district

Counties: All counties in Wyoming. Some criminal records are held in Casper.

Indexing/Storage: Cases are indexed by defendant and plaintiff as well as by case number. New cases are available in the index 1-2 days after filing date. A computer index is maintained. Records older than 1992 are on microfiche also. Open records are located at this court.

Fee & Payment: The fee is $20.00 per item (one party name or case number). Payment may be made by money order, cashier check, personal check. Prepayment is required. Payee: Clerk, US District Court. Certification fee: $7.00 per document. Copy fee: $.50 per page.

Phone Search: Searching is not available by phone.

Mail Search: A stamped self addressed envelope is not required.

In Person: In person searching is available.

PACER: Sign-up number is 800-676-6856. Access fee is $.60 per minute. Toll-free access: 888-417-3560. Local access: 307-772-2808. Case records are available back to 1988. Records are purged once per year. New civil records are available online after 1-2 days. New criminal records are available online after 1 day. PACER is available online at http://pacer.wyd.uscourts.gov.

US Bankruptcy Court

District of Wyoming

Cheyenne Division PO Box 1107, Cheyenne, WY 82003 (Courier Address: 6th Floor, 2120 Capitol Ave, Cheyenne, WY 82001), 307-772-2191.

http://www.wyb.uscourts.gov

Counties: All counties in Wyoming.

Indexing/Storage: Cases are indexed by debtor as well as by case number. New cases are available in the index 24 hours after filing date. Both computer and card indexes are maintained. Open records are located at this court.

Fee & Payment: The fee is $20.00 per item (one party name or case number). Payment may be made by money order, cashier check, personal check. Prepayment is required. Payee: Clerk, US Bankruptcy Court. Certification fee: $7.00 per document. Copy fee: $.50 per page.

Phone Search: An automated voice case information service (VCIS) is available. Call VCIS at 888-804-5537 or 307-772-2191.

Mail Search: Always enclose a stamped self addressed envelope.

In Person: In person searching is available.

PACER: Sign-up number is 800-676-6856. Access fee is $.60 per minute. Toll-free access: 888-804-5536. Local access: 307-772-2036. Case records are available back one year. Records are purged annually. New civil records are available online after 1 day. PACER is available online at http://pacer.wyb.uscourts.gov.

Electronic Filing: Electronic filing information is available online at https://ecf.wyb.uscourts.gov

Opinions Online: Court opinions are available online at http://www.wyb.uscourts.gov/opinion_search.htm

Wyoming County Courts

Court	Jurisdiction	No. of Courts	How Organized
District Courts*	General	23	9 Districts
Circuit Courts*	Limited	20	16 Counties
Justice of the Peace Courts*	Municipal	7	7 Counties
Municipal Courts	Municipal	80	

* Profiled in this Sourcebook.

Court	CIVIL								
	Tort	Contract	Real Estate	Min. Claim	Max. Claim	Small Claims	Estate	Eviction	Domestic Relations
District Courts*	X	X	X	$3000/ $7000	No Max		X		X
Circuit Courts*	X	X	X	$0	$7000	$3000		X	X
Justice of the Peace Courts*	X	X	X	$0	$3000	$3000			
Municipal Courts									

Court	CRIMINAL				
	Felony	Misdemeanor	DWI/DUI	Preliminary Hearing	Juvenile
District Courts*	X				X
Circuit Courts*		X	X	X	
Justice of the Peace Courts*		X	X	X	
Municipal Courts		X	X		

ADMINISTRATION   Court Administrator, 2301 Capitol Av, Supreme Court Bldg, Cheyenne, WY, 82002; 307-777-7480, Fax: 307-777-3447. www.courts.state.wy.us

COURT STRUCTURE   For their "lower" jurisdiction court, some counties have Circuit Courts and others have Justice Courts. Thus each county has a District Court ("higher" jurisdiction) and either a Circuit or Justice Court. Circuit Courts handle civil claims up to $7,000 while Justice Courts handle civil claims up to $3,000. The District Courts take cases over the applicable limit in each county.

Two counties have two Circuit Courts each: Park and Sweetwater. Fremont County has three. Cases may be filed in any of the court offices in those counties, and records requests are referred between the courts.

The Park and Sublette County Justice Courts were eliminated on January 2, 1995 and were replaced by Circuit Courts, where the Justice Court records are now located.

Probate is handled by the District Court.

ONLINE ACCESS   Wyoming's statewide case management system is for internal use only. Planning is underway for a new case management system that will ultimately allow public access.

📖 📖 📖 📖 📖 📖 📖

Albany County

2nd Judicial District Court County Courthouse, 525 Grand, Rm 305, Laramie, WY 82070; 307-721-2508. Hours: 9AM-5PM (MST). *Felony, Civil Actions Over $7,000, Probate.*

Civil Records: Access: Phone, mail, in person. Only the court performs in person searches; visitors may not. No search fee. Required to search: name; also helpful: years to search. Civil cases indexed by defendant, plaintiff. Civil records on computer from 1988, prior records on card index to 1890. Limit calls to three names.

Criminal Records: Access: Mail, in person. Only the court performs in person searches; visitors may not. Search fee: $5.00 per name. Search results can be phoned back to a toll-free number only. Required to search: name, years to search, DOB. Criminal records on computer from 1988, prior records on card index to 1890.

General Information: No sex offenses records released, signed release required for child support cases. SASE required. Turnaround time same day. Copy fee: $1.00 for first page, $.50 each add'l. Certification fee: No certification fee. Fee payee: Clerk of District Court. Personal checks accepted. Prepayment is required.

Continued...

Albany Circuit Court County Courthouse, 525 Grand, Rm 105, Laramie, WY 82070; 307-742-5747; Fax: 307-742-5610. Hours: 8AM-5PM (MST). *Misdemeanor, Civil Actions Under $7,000, Eviction, Small Claims.*

Civil Records: Access: Mail, in person. Both court and visitors may perform in person searches. Search fee: $5.00 per name. Required to search: name, years to search. Civil cases indexed by defendant, plaintiff. Civil records on computer from 1989, prior on docket books to 1984.

Criminal Records: Access: Mail, in person. Both court and visitors may perform in person searches. Search fee: $5.00 per name. Required to search: name, years to search, DOB. Criminal records on computer from 1989, prior on docket books to 1984.

General Information: No SSN or family violence records released. SASE required. Turnaround time same day. No copy fee. Certification fee: No certification fee. Fee payee: Albany Circuit Court. Personal checks accepted. In-state checks only. Prepayment is required.

Big Horn County

5th Judicial District Court PO Box 670, Basin, WY 82410; 307-568-2381; Fax: 307-568-2791. Hours: 8AM-Noon, 1-5PM (MST). *Felony, Civil Actions Over $7,000, Probate.*

Civil Records: Access: Fax, mail, in person. Both court and visitors may perform in person searches. Search fee: $5.00 per name. Required to search: name, years to search. Civil cases indexed by defendant, plaintiff. Civil records on computer 1989, on microfiche 1982, 1970 to present on cards.

Criminal Records: Access: Fax, mail, in person. Both court and visitors may perform in person searches. Search fee: $5.00 per name. Required to search: name, years to search. Criminal records on computer 1989, on microfiche 1982, 1970 to present on cards.

General Information: Some confidential records not released. SASE required. Turnaround time 24 hours. Copy fee: $1.00 for first page, $.50 each add'l. Certification fee: $.50. Fee payee: Clerk of Court. Business checks accepted. Prepayment is required.

Big Horn Circuit Court PO Box 749, Basin, WY 82410; 307-568-2367; Fax: 307-568-2554. Hours: 8AM-5PM (MST). *Misdemeanor, Civil Actions Under $7,000, Small Claims.*

Civil Records: Access: Fax, mail, in person. Both court and visitors may perform in person searches. Search fee: $5.00 per name. Required to search: name, years to search; also helpful: address. Civil cases indexed by defendant. Civil records on microfiche 1985.

Criminal Records: Access: Fax, mail, in person. Both court and visitors may perform in person searches. Search fee: $5.00 per name. Required to search: name, DOB; also helpful: SSN. Criminal records on computer since 1990, microfiche 1985.

General Information: No sex or juvenile offenses released. Turnaround time 1 day. Copy fee: $.50 per page. Certification fee: No certification fee. Fee payee: Big Horn Circuit Court. Personal checks accepted. Prepayment is required.

Campbell County

6th Judicial District Court PO Box 817, Gillette, WY 82717; 307-682-3424; Fax: 307-687-6209. Hours: 8AM-5PM (MST). *Felony, Civil Actions Over $7,000, Probate.*

Civil Records: Access: Phone, fax, mail, in person. Both court and visitors may perform in person searches. Search fee: $5.00 per name. Required to search: name, years to search. Civil cases indexed by defendant. Civil records archived from 1913; on computer back to 1983.

Criminal Records: Access: Phone, fax, mail, in person. Both court and visitors may perform in person searches. Search fee: $5.00 per name. Required to search: name, years to search. Criminal records archived from 1913; on computer back to 1983.

General Information: Public Access terminal is available. Names of victims in sex cases, confidential records not released. SASE not required. Turnaround time 1-2 days. Fax notes: $1.00 per page. Copy fee: $1.00 for first page, $.50 each add'l. Certification fee: No certification fee. Fee payee: Clerk of District Court. Personal checks accepted. Out of state checks not accepted. Prepayment is required.

Campbell Circuit Court 500 S Gillette Ave #301, Gillette, WY 82716; 307-682-2190; Fax: 307-687-6214. Hours: 8AM-5PM (MST). *Misdemeanor, Civil Actions Under $7,000, Eviction, Small Claims.*

Civil Records: Access: Mail, in person. Only the court performs in person searches; visitors may not. Search fee: $5.00 per name. Required to search: name, years to search; also helpful: address. Civil cases indexed by defendant, plaintiff. Civil records on computer since 1983, archives from 1979.

Criminal Records: Access: Mail, in person. Both court and visitors may perform in person searches. Search fee: $5.00 per name. Required to search: name, years to search, DOB; also helpful: address. Criminal records on computer since 1983, archives from 1979.

General Information: No sex related cases released. SASE requested. Turnaround time 1-2 days. Copy fee: $1.00 for first page, $.50 each add'l. Certification fee: No certification fee. Fee payee: Campbell County Court. Personal checks accepted. Prepayment is required.

Carbon County

2nd Judicial District Court PO Box 67, Rawlins, WY 82301; 307-328-2628; Fax: 307-328-2629. Hours: 8AM-5PM (MST). *Felony, Civil Actions Over $7,000, Probate.*

Civil Records: Access: Phone, fax, mail, in person. Both court and visitors may perform in person searches. No search fee. Required to search: name, years to search; also helpful: address. Civil cases indexed by defendant, plaintiff. Civil records on file from late 1800s, index cards, docket books, then computer.

Criminal Records: Access: Phone, fax, mail, in person. Both court and visitors may perform in person searches. No search fee. Required to search: name, years to search; also helpful: address, DOB, SSN. Criminal records on index cards and docket books; on computer since.

General Information: No juvenile or adoption records released. SASE required. Turnaround time 4-5 days. Fax notes: No fee to fax results. Fax available for 800 numbers only. Copy fee: $1.00 for first page, $.50 each add'l. Certification fee: No certification fee. Fee payee: Clerk 2nd Judicial District Court, Clerk of Court. Personal checks accepted. Prepayment is required.

Carbon Circuit Court Attn: Chief Clerk, Courthouse, 415 W Pine St, Rawlins, WY 82301; 307-324-6655; Fax: 307-324-9465. Hours: 8AM-5PM (MST). *Misdemeanor, Civil Actions Under $7,000, Eviction, Small Claims.*

Civil Records: Access: Phone, mail, fax, in person. Only the court performs in person searches; visitors may not. Search fee: $5.00 per name. Required to search: name, years to search; also helpful: address. Civil cases indexed by defendant, plaintiff. Civil records on computer since 3/95.

Criminal Records: Access: Mail, fax, in person. Only the court performs in person searches; visitors may not. Search fee: $5.00 per name. Required to search: name, DOB. Criminal records on computer back to 08/87.

General Information: Sex related cases not released. SASE required. Turnaround time 1 week. Copy fee: Copy fee for excessive amount of pages is $.25 per page. Certification fee: No certification fee. Fee payee: Circuit Court of Carbon County. Personal checks accepted. Prepayment is required.

Converse County

8th Judicial District Court Box 189, Douglas, WY 82633; 307-358-3165; Fax: 307-358-9783. Hours: 9AM-5PM (MST). *Felony, Civil Actions Over $7,000, Probate.*

Civil Records: Access: Phone, fax, mail, in person. Both court and visitors may perform in person searches. No search fee. Required to search: name, years to search; also helpful: address. Civil cases indexed by defendant, plaintiff. Civil records on card file from 1888.

Criminal Records: Access: Phone, fax, mail, in person. Both court and visitors may perform in person searches. Search fee: $5.00. Required to search: name, years to search; also helpful: address, DOB, SSN. Criminal records on card file from 1800.

General Information: No juvenile, adoptions or mental cases released. Turnaround time usually same day. Fax notes: $2.00 per page. Copy fee: $.25 per page. Certification fee: $1.00 plus $.50 each add'l page. Fee payee: Clerk of District Court. Only cashiers checks and money orders accepted. Prepayment is required.

Converse Circuit Court 107 N 5th Street #231, PO Box 45, Douglas, WY 82633; 307-358-2196; Fax: 307-358-2501. Hours: 8AM-5PM (MST). *Misdemeanor, Civil Actions Under $7,000, Eviction, Small Claims.*

Civil Records: Access: Mail, in person. Both court and visitors may perform in person searches. Search fee: $5.00 per name. Required to search: name, years to search. Civil cases indexed by defendant, plaintiff. Civil records on computer from 1994, card file prior.

Criminal Records: Access: Mail, in person. Both court and visitors may perform in person searches. Search fee: $5.00 per name. Required to search: name, years to search, DOB also helpful: address, SSN. Criminal records on computer from 1990, card file prior.

General Information: No sealed records released. Turnaround time 1-2 days. Copy fee: $1.00 for first page, $.50 each add'l. Certification fee: $2.00. Fee payee: Circuit Court of Converse County. Prepayment is required.

Crook County

6th Judicial District Court Box 904, Sundance, WY 82729; 307-283-2523; Fax: 307-283-2996. Hours: 8AM-5PM (MST). *Felony, High Misdemeanor, Civil Actions Over $3,000, Probate.*

Civil Records: Access: Mail, in person. Both court and visitors may perform in person searches. Search fee: $5.00 per name. Required to search: name, years to search; also helpful: address. Civil cases indexed by defendant, plaintiff. Civil records on card file from late 1800s; on computer back to 1999.

Criminal Records: Access: Mail, in person. Both court and visitors may perform in person searches. Search fee: $5.00 per name. Required to search: name, years to search; also helpful: address, DOB, SSN. Criminal records on card file from late 1800s; on computer back to 1999.

General Information: No sealed records released. SASE required. Turnaround time 2 days. Fax notes: $1.00 for 1st page, $.50 each add'l. Copy fee: $.50 per page. Certification fee: $1.00. Fee payee: Clerk of District Court. Business checks accepted. Prepayment is required.

Justice Court PO Box 117, Sundance, WY 82729; 307-283-2929; Fax: 307-283-1091. Hours: 8AM-5PM (MST). *Misdemeanor, Civil Actions Under $3,000, Small Claims.*

Civil Records: Access: Mail, fax, in person. Only the court performs in person searches; visitors may not. Search fee: $5.00 per name. Required to search: name, years to search; also helpful: address. Civil cases indexed by defendant, plaintiff. Civil records on cards, archives back to 1977; on computer back to 1992.

Criminal Records: Access: Mail, fax, in person. Only the court performs in person searches; visitors may not. Search fee: $5.00 per name. Required to search: name, years to search; also helpful: address, DOB, SSN. Criminal records on computer back to 1992.

General Information: No sex related cases released. SASE required. Turnaround time 2 days. Fax notes: Fee to fax results is $5.00 per document. Copy fee: $3.00 for first page, $1.00 each add'l. Certification fee: $1.00. Fee payee: Crook County Justice Court. Personal checks accepted. Prepayment is required.

Fremont County

9th Judicial District Court PO Box 370, Lander, WY 82520; 307-332-1134; Fax: 307-332-1143. Hours: 8AM-Noon, 1-5PM (MST). *Felony, Civil Actions Over $7,000, Probate.*

Civil Records: Access: Phone, fax, mail, in person. Both court and visitors may perform in person searches. Search fee: $5.00 per name. Required to search: name, years to search; also helpful: address. Civil cases indexed by defendant, plaintiff. Civil records on computer since 1992, in books since 1991, on microfiche since 1939 and on card file from 1898.

Criminal Records: Access: Phone, fax, mail, in person. Both court and visitors may perform in person searches. Search fee: $5.00 per name. Required to search: name, years to search; also helpful: address, DOB, SSN. Criminal records on computer since 1992, in books since 1991, on microfiche since 1939 and on card file from 1898.

General Information: Public Access terminal is available. No juvenile, involuntary hospitalization or adoption records released. SASE required. Turnaround time same day. Fax notes: No fee to fax results. Copy fee: $.50 per page. Certification fee: No certification fee. Fee payee: Clerk of District Court. Personal checks accepted.

Dubois Circuit Court Box 952, Dubois, WY 82513; 307-455-2920; Fax: 307-455-2132. Hours: 8AM-Noon (MST). *Misdemeanor, Civil Actions Under $7,000, Eviction, Small Claims.*

Note: This is a satellite of the Lander Court.

Civil Records: Access: Mail, in person. Both court and visitors may perform in person searches. Search fee: $5.00 per name. Required to search: name, years to search. Civil cases indexed by defendant, plaintiff. Civil records on index.

Criminal Records: Access: Mail, in person. Both court and visitors may perform in person searches. Search fee: $5.00 per name. Required to search: name, years to search; also helpful: DOB. Criminal records on computer since 12/96; prior records on indexes.

General Information: No juvenile, sexual data released. SASE required. Turnaround time 2 days. Copy fee: $.10 per page. Certification fee: No certification fee. Fee payee: Fremont County Court. Personal checks accepted. Prepayment is required.

Fremont Circuit Court 450 N. 2nd, Rm 230, Lander, WY 82520; 307-332-3239; Fax: 307-332-1152. Hours: 8AM-5PM (MST). *Misdemeanor, Civil Actions Over $7,000, Eviction, Small Claims.*

Civil Records: Access: Phone, fax, mail, in person. Both court and visitors may perform in person searches.

Search fee: $5.00 per name. Required to search: name, years to search; also helpful: address. Civil cases indexed by defendant, plaintiff. Civil records on computer from 1988, archive back to 1979.

Criminal Records: Access: Phone, fax, mail, in person. Both court and visitors may perform in person searches. Search fee: $5.00 per name. Required to search: name, years to search; also helpful: address, DOB, SSN. Criminal records on computer from 1988, archive back to 1979.

General Information: No juvenile or sexual data released. SASE required. Turnaround time 2 days. Fax notes: No fee to fax results. No copy fee. Certification fee: No certification fee. Fee payee: Circuit Court. Personal checks accepted. In-state checks only. Prepayment is required.

Riverton Circuit Court 818 S Federal Blvd, Riverton, WY 82501; 307-856-7259; Fax: 307-857-3635. Hours: 8AM-5PM (MST). *Misdemeanor, Civil Actions Under $7,000, Eviction, Small Claims.*

www.courts.state.wy.us/JD91.HTM

Civil Records: Access: Mail, in person. Both court and visitors may perform in person searches. Search fee: $5.00 per name. Required to search: name, years to search. Civil cases indexed by defendant, plaintiff. Civil records are computerized since 1997; prior in books to 1980.

Criminal Records: Access: Mail, in person. Only the court performs in person searches; visitors may not. Search fee: $5.00 per name. Required to search: name, years to search, DOB; also helpful: SSN. Criminal records on computer since 1989; prior in books to 1980.

General Information: No sex released cases released. SASE required. Turnaround time 2 days. Fax notes: No fee to fax results. No copy fee. Certification fee: No certification fee. Fee payee: Fremont County Court. Personal checks accepted. In state checks only. Prepayment is required.

Goshen County

8th Judicial District Court Clerk of District Court, PO Box 818, Torrington, WY 82240; 307-532-2155; Fax: 307-532-8608. Hours: 7:30AM-4PM (MST). *Felony, Civil Actions Over $7,000, Probate.*

Civil Records: Access: Mail, in person. Both court and visitors may perform in person searches. Search fee: $5.00 per name. Required to search: name, years to search; also helpful: address. Civil cases indexed by defendant, plaintiff. Civil records on index file only since 1913.

Criminal Records: Access: Mail, in person. Both court and visitors may perform in person searches. Search fee: $5.00 per name. Required to search: name, years to search; also helpful: address, DOB, SSN. Criminal records on index file only since 1913.

General Information: No juvenile records released. SASE required. Turnaround time 3-4 days. Copy fee: $1.00 for first page, $.50 each add'l. Certification fee: $.50. Fee payee: Clerk of District Court. Personal checks accepted. In-state checks only. Prepayment is required.

Goshen Circuit Court Drawer BB, Torrington, WY 82240; 307-532-2938; Civil phone: X251; Criminal phone: X249; Fax: 307-532-5101. Hours: 7AM-4PM (MST). *Misdemeanor, Civil Actions Under $7,000, Eviction, Small Claims.*

Civil Records: Access: Mail, in person. Both court and visitors may perform in person searches. Search fee: $5.00 per name. Required to search: name, years to search; also helpful: address. Civil cases indexed by defendant. Civil records on computer from 1989, prior archived.

Criminal Records: Access: Mail, in person. Both court and visitors may perform in person searches. Search fee: $5.00 per name. Required to search: name, years to

search; also helpful: address, DOB, SSN. Criminal records on computer from 1989, prior archived.

General Information: No juvenile records released. SASE required. Turnaround time 3-4 days. Copy fee: $1.00 per page. Certification fee: $5.00. Fee payee: Goshen County Court. Personal checks accepted. Prepayment is required.

Hot Springs County

5th Judicial District Court 415 Arapahoe St, Thermopolis, WY 82443; 307-864-3323; Fax: 307-864-3210. Hours: 8AM-5PM (MST). *Felony, Civil Actions Over $7,000, Probate.*

Civil Records: Access: Mail, in person. Both court and visitors may perform in person searches. Search fee: $5.00 per name. Required to search: name, years to search; also helpful: address. Civil cases indexed by defendant, plaintiff. Civil records on card index back to 1900s.

Criminal Records: Access: Mail, in person. Both court and visitors may perform in person searches. Search fee: $5.00 per name. Required to search: name, years to search, DOB, SSN; also helpful: address. Criminal records on card index back to 1900s.

General Information: No juvenile, adoption or sexual data released. SASE required. Turnaround time 1 day. Copy fee: $.25 per page. Certification fee: $.50. Fee payee: Clerk of District Court. Personal checks accepted. Prepayment is required.

Hot Springs Circuit Court 417 Arapahoe St, Thermopolis, WY 82443; 307-864-5161; Fax: 307-864-5116. Hours: 8AM-5PM (MST). *Misdemeanor, Civil Actions Under $7,000, Small Claims.*

Civil Records: Access: Mail, in person. Both court and visitors may perform in person searches. No search fee. Required to search: name, years to search. Civil cases indexed by defendant, plaintiff. Civil records on computer from 1990, prior in card file.

Criminal Records: Access: Mail, in person. Both court and visitors may perform in person searches. No search fee. Required to search: name, years to search. Criminal records on computer from 1990, prior in card file.

General Information: No closed case records released. SASE required. Turnaround time 2-3 days. No copy fee. Certification fee: No certification fee. Fee payee: Justice Court. Business checks accepted. Prepayment is required.

Johnson County

4th Judicial District Court 76 N Main, Buffalo, WY 82834; 307-684-7271; Fax: 307-684-5146. 8AM-5PM *Felony, Civil Actions Over $3,000, Probate.*

Civil Records: Access: Fax, mail, in person. Both court and visitors may perform in person searches. Search fee: $5.00 per name. Required to search: name, years to search; also helpful: address. Civil cases indexed by defendant, plaintiff. Civil records on computer from 1989, card index since 1892.

Criminal Records: Access: Fax, mail, in person. Both court and visitors may perform in person searches. Search fee: $5.00 per name. Required to search: name, years to search; also helpful: address, DOB, SSN. Criminal records on computer from 1989, card index since 1892.

General Information: No adoption or juvenile records released. SASE required. Turnaround time 1 week. Copy fee: $.50 per page. Certification fee: $.50. Fee payee: Clerk of District Court. Personal checks accepted. In-state checks only. Prepayment is required.

Justice Court 76 N Main St, Buffalo, WY 82834-1847; 307-684-5720; Fax: 307-684-5146. Hours: 8AM-5PM (MST). *Misdemeanor, Civil Actions Under $3,000, Small Claims.*

Civil Records: Access: Mail, in person. Both court and visitors may perform in person searches. Search fee:

$5.00 per name. Required to search: name, years to search; also helpful: address. Civil cases indexed by defendant, plaintiff. Civil records on computer since 1995; prior records on index cards.

Criminal Records: Access: Mail, in person. Both court and visitors may perform in person searches. Search fee: $5.00 per name. Required to search: name, years to search, DOB; also helpful: SSN. Criminal records on computer since 05/90, card index back 5 years.

General Information: No sex cases released. SASE required. Turnaround time 1 week. Copy fee: $.50 per page. Certification fee: No certification fee. Fee payee: Justice of the Peace. Personal checks accepted. Prepayment is required.

Laramie County

1st Judicial District Court 309 W 20th St, Suite 3205, PO Box 787, Cheyenne, WY 82001; 307-633-4270; Fax: 307-633-4277. Hours: 8AM-5PM (MST). *Felony, Civil Actions Over $7,000, Probate.*

http://webgate.co.laramie.wy.us/dc/dc.html

Civil Records: Access: Phone, fax, mail, in person. Both court and visitors may perform in person searches. Search fee: $5.00 per name. Required to search: name. Civil cases indexed by defendant, plaintiff. Civil records on card index to 1890; on computer back to 1984.

Criminal Records: Access: Phone, fax, mail, in person. Both court and visitors may perform in person searches. Search fee: $5.00 per name. Required to search: name. Criminal records on card index to 1890; on computer back to 1984.

General Information: Public Access terminal is available. No juvenile or paternity records released. SASE required. Turnaround time 2 days. Fax notes: No fee to fax results. Fax available for 800 numbers only. Copy fee: $1.00 for first page, $.50 each add'l. Certification fee: $.50. Fee payee: Laramie County Clerk of District Court. Business checks accepted. Prepayment is required.

Laramie County Circuit Court 309 W 20th St Rm 2300, Cheyenne, WY 82001; 307-633-4298; Fax: 307-633-4392. Hours: 8AM-5PM (MST). *Misdemeanor, Civil Actions Under $7,000, Eviction, Small Claims.*

Civil Records: Access: Fax, mail, in person. Both court and visitors may perform in person searches. Search fee: $5.00 per name. Required to search: name, years to search; also helpful: address. Civil cases indexed by defendant, plaintiff. Civil records on computer from 1988, card index from late 1977.

Criminal Records: Access: Fax, mail, in person. Both court and visitors may perform in person searches. Search fee: $5.00 per name. Required to search: name, years to search; also helpful: address. Criminal records on computer from 1988, card index from late 1977.

General Information: Public Access terminal is available. SASE required. Turnaround time 48 hours. Fax notes: Fee to fax results is $5.00 per document. Copy fee: $1.00 per page. Certification fee: $.50. Fee payee: Laramie County Circuit Court. Business checks accepted. In-state checks only. Prepayment is required.

Lincoln County

3rd Judicial District Court PO Drawer 510, Kemmerer, WY 83101; 307-877-9056; Fax: 307-877-6263. Hours: 8AM-5PM (MST). *Felony, Civil Actions Over $7,000, Probate.*

Civil Records: Access: Phone, fax, mail, in person. Both court and visitors may perform in person searches. Search fee: $5.00 per name. Required to search: name; also helpful: years to search, address. Civil cases indexed by defendant. Civil records on card index from early 1916.

Criminal Records: Access: Phone, fax, mail, in person. Both court and visitors may perform in person

searches. Search fee: $5.00 per name. Required to search: name; also helpful: years to search, address, DOB, SSN. Criminal records on card index from 1916.

General Information: No juvenile, sexual or PD records released. Turnaround time same day. Fax notes: $5.00 per document. Copy fee: $1.00 for first page, $.50 each add'l. Certification fee: $2.50. Fee payee: 3rd Judicial District Court. Personal checks accepted.

Lincoln Circuit Court PO Box 949, Kemmerer, WY 83101; 307-877-4431; Fax: 307-877-4936. Hours: 8AM-5PM (MST). *Misdemeanor, Civil Actions Under $7,000, Eviction, Small Claims.*

Civil Records: Access: Mail, in person. Both court and visitors may perform in person searches. Search fee: $5.00 per name. Required to search: name, years to search. Civil cases indexed by defendant, plaintiff. Civil records on computer from 1/90, on card index from 1984, prior data in archives. All requests must be in writing.

Criminal Records: Access: Mail, in person. Both court and visitors may perform in person searches. Search fee: $5.00 per name. Required to search: name, years to search, DOB; also helpful: SSN. Criminal records on computer from 10/90, card index from 1984, prior in archives. All requests must be in writing.

General Information: No sexual or PD records released. SASE requested. Turnaround time same day. Fax notes: $3.00 per document. Copy fee: $.50 per page. Certification fee: $3.00. Fee payee: Lincoln County Court. Business checks accepted. Out of state checks not accepted. Prepayment is required.

Natrona County

7th Judicial District Court Clerk of District Court, PO Box 2510, Casper, WY 82602; 307-235-9243; Fax: 307-235-9493. Hours: 8AM-5PM (MST). *Felony, Civil Actions Over $7,000, Probate.*

Civil Records: Access: Phone, fax, mail, in person. Both court and visitors may perform in person searches. No search fee. Required to search: name, years to search; also helpful: address. Civil cases indexed by defendant, plaintiff. Civil records on computer, microfiche from 1891.

Criminal Records: Access: Phone, fax, mail, in person. Both court and visitors may perform in person searches. No search fee. Required to search: name, years to search; also helpful: address, DOB, SSN. Criminal records on computer, microfiche from 1891.

General Information: No adoption, juvenile, paternity, mental health records released. SASE required. Turnaround time 5 days. Fax notes: $.30 per page. Copy fee: $1.00 for first page, $.50 each add'l. Certification fee: $.50. Fee payee: Clerk of District Court. Business checks accepted. Prepayment is required.

Natrona Circuit Court PO Box 1339, Casper, WY 82602; 307-235-9266; Fax: 307-235-9331. Hours: 8AM-5PM (MST). *Misdemeanor, Civil Actions Under $7,000, Eviction, Small Claims.*

Note: All search requests must be in writing.

Civil Records: Access: Phone, fax, mail, in person. Only the court performs in person searches; visitors may not. Search fee: $5.00 per name. Required to search: name, years to search; also helpful: address. Civil cases indexed by defendant, plaintiff. Civil records on computer from 1994, on microfiche from 1891.

Criminal Records: Access: Phone, fax, mail, in person. Only the court performs in person searches; visitors may not. Search fee: $5.00 per name. Required to search: name, years to search; also helpful: address, DOB, SSN. Criminal records on computer from 1989, microfiche from 1891.

General Information: No sexual, abuse records released. SASE required. Turnaround time 2 days. Fax notes: No fee to fax results. Fax available for 800

numbers only. Copy fee: $1.00 for first page, $.50 each add'l. Fee payee: Natrona Circuit Court. Personal checks accepted. Prepayment is required.

Niobrara County

8th Judicial District Court Clerk of District Court, PO Box 1318, Lusk, WY 82225; 307-334-2736; Fax: 307-334-2703. Hours: 8AM-Noon, 1-4PM (MST). *Felony, Civil Actions Over $3,000, Probate.*

Civil Records: Access: In person only. Visitors must perform in person searches for themselves. No search fee. Required to search: name, years to search; also helpful: address. Civil cases indexed by defendant, plaintiff. Civil records on card index from early 1900.

Criminal Records: Access: Phone, fax, mail, in person. Both court and visitors may perform in person searches. No search fee. Required to search: name, years to search; also helpful: address, DOB, SSN. Criminal records on card index from early 1900.

General Information: No juvenile or adoption related released, no PD released. SASE required. Turnaround time 2 days. Copy fee: $1.00 for first page, $.50 each add'l. Certification fee: $.50. Fee payee: Niobrara Clerk of District Court. Personal checks accepted. Prepayment is required.

Justice Court PO Box 209, Lusk, WY 82225; 307-334-3845; Fax: 307-334-3846. Hours: 9AM-Noon, 1-5PM (MST). *Misdemeanor, Civil Actions Under $3,000, Small Claims.*

Civil Records: Access: Mail, in person. Both court and visitors may perform in person searches. Search fee: $5.00 per name. Required to search: name, years to search; also helpful: address. Civil cases indexed by plaintiff. Civil records on index cards.

Criminal Records: Access: Fax, mail, in person. Both court and visitors may perform in person searches. Search fee: $5.00 per name. Required to search: name, years to search, DOB, SSN, signed release; also helpful: address. Criminal records on computer from 1988, prior archived.

General Information: No juvenile data released. SASE required. Turnaround time 2 days. Fax notes: $.50 per page. Copy fee: $.50 per page. Certification fee: $3.00. Fee payee: Niobrara Justice Court. Personal checks accepted. Prepayment is required.

Park County

5th Judicial District Court Clerk of District Court, PO Box 1960, Cody, WY 82414; 307-527-8690; Fax: 307-527-8687. Hours: 8AM-5PM (MST). *Felony, Civil Actions Over $7,000, Probate.*

Civil Records: Access: Phone, fax, mail, in person. Both court and visitors may perform in person searches. Search fee: $5.00 per name. Required to search: name, years to search; also helpful: address. Civil cases indexed by defendant, plaintiff. Civil records on computer from 1989, card index back to 1911.

Criminal Records: Access: Phone, fax, mail, in person. Both court and visitors may perform in person searches. Search fee: $5.00 per name. Required to search: name, years to search; also helpful: address, DOB, SSN. Criminal records on computer from 1989, card index back to 1911.

General Information: Public Access terminal is available. No juvenile, adoptions or PD released. SASE preferred. Turnaround time same day. Fax notes: $1.00 per page. Copy fee: $1.00 for first page, $.50 each add'l. Fee payee: Clerk of District Court. Personal checks accepted. Prepayment is required.

Circuit Court - Cody 1002 Sheridan Ave., Cody, WY 82414; 307-527-8590; Fax: 307-527-8596. Hours: 8AM-5PM (MST). *Misdemeanor, Civil Actions Under $7,000, Eviction, Small Claims.*

Note: On January 2, 1995 this court changed status from a Justice Court to a County Court.

Civil Records: Access: Mail, in person. Only the court performs in person searches; visitors may not. Search fee: $5.00 per name. Required to search: name, years to search; also helpful: address. Civil cases indexed by defendant, plaintiff. Civil records on computer since 8/95; limited records available prior to 8/95.

Criminal Records: Access: Mail, in person. Only the court performs in person searches; visitors may not. Search fee: $5.00 per name. Required to search: name, years to search; also helpful: address, DOB, SSN. Criminal records on computer since 1990; limited records available prior to 1990.

General Information: No sexual or confidential data released. SASE required. Turnaround time 5 days. Copy fee: $.50 first 10 pages then $.10 thereafter. Certification fee: No certification fee. Fee payee: Park County Circuit Court. Business checks accepted. Prepayment is required.

Circuit Court - Powell 109 W. 14th, Powell, WY 82435; 307-754-8890; Fax: 307-754-8896. Hours: 8AM-Noon, 1-5PM (MST). *Misdemeanor, Civil Actions Under $7,000, Eviction, Small Claims.*

Civil Records: Access: Mail, in person. Only the court performs in person searches; visitors may not. Search fee: $5.00 per name. Required to search: name, years to search. Civil cases indexed by defendant, plaintiff. Civil records on computer from 1995; prior records very poor.

Criminal Records: Access: Mail, in person. Only the court performs in person searches; visitors may not. Search fee: $5.00 per name. Required to search: name, years to search, DOB. Criminal records on computer from 1991; prior records very poor.

General Information: No sexual, confidential records released. SSE required. Turnaround time 1 week. Copy fee: $.50 per page. Certification fee: No certification fee. Fee payee: Park County Circuit Court. Personal checks accepted. Prepayment is required.

Platte County

8th Judicial District Court PO Box 158, Wheatland, WY 82201; 307-322-3857; Fax: 307-322-5402. Hours: 8AM-5PM (MST). *Felony, Civil Actions Over $3,000, Probate.*

Civil Records: Access: Mail, fax, in person. Both court and visitors may perform in person searches. Search fee: $5.00 per name. Required to search: name, years to search; also helpful: address. Civil cases indexed by defendant. Civil records on card file index last 15 yrs, then to archives.

Criminal Records: Access: Mail, fax, in person. Both court and visitors may perform in person searches. Search fee: $5.00 per name. Required to search: name, years to search; also helpful: address, DOB, SSN. Criminal records on card file index last 15 yrs, then to archives.

General Information: No juvenile data released. SASE required. Turnaround time same day. Copy fee: $1.00 for first page, $.50 each add'l. Certification fee: $.50. Fee payee: Clerk of the Court. Personal checks accepted. Prepayment is required.

Justice Court PO Box 306, Wheatland, WY 82201; 307-322-3441; Fax: 307-322-5402. Hours: 8AM-5PM (MST). *Misdemeanor, Civil Actions Under $3,000, Small Claims.*

Civil Records: Access: Mail, in person. Only the court performs in person searches; visitors may not. Search fee: $5.00 per name. Required to search: name, years to search; also helpful: address. Civil cases indexed by defendant. Civil records on computer since 11/95; on card index since 1976.

Criminal Records: Access: Mail, in person. Only the court performs in person searches; visitors may not. Search fee: $5.00 per name. Required to search: name, years to search; also helpful: address, DOB, SSN.

Criminal records on computer from 11/92, card index from 1976.

General Information: No juvenile data released. SASE required. Turnaround time 2 days. Copy fee: $1.00 for first page, $.50 each add'l. Certification fee: No certification fee. Fee payee: Platte County Justice Court. Business checks accepted. Prepayment is required.

Sheridan County

4th Judicial District Court 224 S. Main, Suite B-11, Sheridan, WY 82801; 307-674-2960; Fax: 307-674-2909. Hours: 8AM-5PM (MST). *Felony, Civil Actions Over $7,000, Probate.*

Civil Records: Access: Phone, mail, fax, in person. Both court and visitors may perform in person searches. Search fee: $5.00 per name. Required to search: name, years to search. Civil cases indexed by defendant, plaintiff. Civil records archived from 1800s.

Criminal Records: Access: Phone, mail, fax, in person. Both court and visitors may perform in person searches. Search fee: $5.00 per name. Required to search: name, years to search, DOB, SSN. Criminal records archived from 1800s.

General Information: No sex related, juvenile or adoption cases released except by judges permission. SASE required. Turnaround time 1 week. Fax notes: Fee to fax results is $5.00 per document. Copy fee: $1.00 for first page, $.25 each add'l. Certification fee: $.50. Fee payee: Clerk of District Court. Personal checks accepted. Prepayment is required.

Circuit Court 224 S. Main, Suite B-7, Sheridan, WY 82801; 307-674-2940; Fax: 307-674-2944. Hours: 8AM-5PM (MST). *Misdemeanor, Civil Actions Under $7,000, Eviction, Small Claims.*

Civil Records: Access: Mail, in person. Only the court performs in person searches; visitors may not. Search fee: $5.00 per name. Required to search: name, years to search; also helpful: address. Civil cases indexed by defendant, plaintiff. Civil records on cards from 1983.

Criminal Records: Access: Mail, in person. Only the court performs in person searches; visitors may not. Search fee: $5.00 per name. Required to search: name, years to search; also helpful: address, DOB, SSN. Criminal records on computer from 1989, on cards from 1983.

General Information: Identity of victims not released in sexual assault cases. SASE required. Turnaround time 2-3 days. Copy fee: $1.00 for first page, $.50 each add'l. Certification fee: $1.00 per page. Fee payee: Sheridan County Court. Personal checks accepted. Prepayment is required.

Sublette County

9th Judicial District Court PO Box 764, Pinedale, WY 82941-0764; 307-367-4376; Fax: 307-367-6474. Hours: 8AM-5PM (MST). *Felony, Civil Actions Over $7,000, Probate.*

Civil Records: Access: Phone, fax, mail, in person. Both court and visitors may perform in person searches. No search fee. Required to search: name; also helpful: years to search, address. Civil cases indexed by defendant, plaintiff. Civil records on card file from 1923.

Criminal Records: Access: Phone, fax, mail, in person. Both court and visitors may perform in person searches. No search fee. Required to search: name, years to search; also helpful: address, DOB, SSN. Criminal records on card file from 1923.

General Information: No PD or juvenile records released. SASE required. Turnaround time same day. Fax notes: $3.00 for first page, $1.00 each add'l. Copy fee: $1.00 for first page, $.50 each add'l. Certification fee: No certification fee. Fee payee: Clerk of District Court. Personal checks accepted.

Sublette Circuit Court PO Box 1796, Pinedale, WY 82941; 307-367-2556; Fax: 307-367-2658. Hours: 8AM-5PM (MST). *Misdemeanor, Civil Actions Under $7,000, Eviction, Small Claims.*

Civil Records: Access: Mail, in person. Only the court performs in person searches; visitors may not. Search fee: $5.00 per name. Required to search: name, years to search; also helpful: address. Civil cases indexed by defendant. Civil records go back 10 years; 8 years back on computer.

Criminal Records: Access: Mail, in person. Only the court performs in person searches; visitors may not. Search fee: $5.00 per name. Required to search: name, years to search, DOB; also helpful: address, SSN. Criminal records go back 10 years; 8 years back on computer.

General Information: SASE not required. Turnaround time 1 week. Copy fee: $1.00 for first page, $.50 each add'l. Certification fee: No certification fee. Fee payee: Circuit Court of Sublette County. Only cashiers checks and money orders accepted. In-state checks only. Prepayment is required.

Sweetwater County

3rd Judicial District Court PO Box 430, Green River, WY 82935; 307-872-6440; Fax: 307-872-6439. Hours: 9AM-5PM (MST). *Felony, Civil Actions Over $7,000, Probate.*

Civil Records: Access: Phone, fax, mail, in person. Both court and visitors may perform in person searches. No search fee. Required to search: name, years to search. Civil cases indexed by defendant, plaintiff. Civil records on computer from 1985, on microfiche from 1960, archived from late 1800.

Criminal Records: Access: Phone, fax, mail, in person. Both court and visitors may perform in person searches. Search fee: $5.00. Required to search: name, years to search. Criminal records on computer from 1985, on microfiche from 1960, archived from late 1800.

General Information: Public Access terminal is available. No PD, juvenile, or adoption records released. SASE required. Turnaround time same day. Fax notes: $1.00 for first page, $.50 each add'l. Copy fee: $1.00 for first page, $.50 each add'l. Certification fee: First free, add'l documents are $.50. Fee payee: Clerk of District Court. Business checks accepted. Prepayment is required.

Green River Circuit Court PO Drawer 1720, Green River, WY 82935; 307-872-6460; Fax: 307-872-6375. Hours: 8AM-5PM (MST). *Misdemeanor, Civil Actions Under $7,000, Eviction, Small Claims.*

Civil Records: Access: Mail, in person. Both court and visitors may perform in person searches. Search fee: $5.00 per name. Required to search: name, years to search. Civil cases indexed by defendant, plaintiff. Civil records on computer from 1994, in card file from 1978-1994, archived prior to 1978.

Criminal Records: Access: Mail, in person. Both court and visitors may perform in person searches. Search fee: $5.00 per name. Required to search: name, years to search, DOB; also helpful: SSN. Criminal Records computerized since 1990; card file from 1978 to 1990.

General Information: No sealed, sexual assault records released. Turnaround time same day. Copy fee: $.50 per page. Certification fee: No certification fee. Fee payee: Sweetwater County Circuit Court. Business checks accepted. In-state checks only. Prepayment is required.

Sweetwater Circuit Court PO Box 2028, Rock Springs, WY 82902; 307-352-6817; Fax: 307-352-6758. Hours: 8AM-5PM (MST). *Misdemeanor, Civil Actions Under $7,000, Eviction, Small Claims.*

Civil Records: Access: Fax, mail, in person. Only the court performs in person searches; visitors may not.

Search fee: $5.00 per name. Fee includes copy fees. Required to search: name, years to search; also helpful: address. Civil cases indexed by defendant, plaintiff. Civil records on computer from 1995, prior on microfiche, archived to 1981.

Criminal Records: Access: Fax, mail, in person. Only the court performs in person searches; visitors may not. Search fee: $5.00 per name. Fee includes copy fees. Required to search: name, years to search; also helpful: address, DOB, SSN. Criminal records on computer from 1989, prior on microfiche, archived to 1981.

General Information: No sexual assault, sealed records released. SASE required. Turnaround time same day. Fax notes: No fee to fax results. No copy fee. Certification fee: No certification fee. Fee payee: Sweetwater Circuit Court. Personal checks accepted. Prepayment is required.

Teton County

9th Judicial District Court PO Box 4460, Jackson, WY 83001; 307-733-2533; Fax: 307-734-1562. Hours: 8AM-5PM (MST). *Felony, Civil Actions Over $3,000, Probate.*

Note: E-mail record search requests are accepted at clerk-of-district-court@tetonwyo.org.

Civil Records: Access: Phone, fax, mail, in person. Both court and visitors may perform in person searches. No search fee. Required to search: name, years to search; also helpful: address. Civil cases indexed by defendant, plaintiff. Civil records on computer since 1990, card index back to 1920s.

Criminal Records: Access: Phone, fax, mail, in person. Both court and visitors may perform in person searches. No search fee. Required to search: name, years to search; also helpful: address, DOB, SSN. Criminal records on computer since 1990, card index back to 1920s.

General Information: No juvenile or adoption records released. SASE required. Turnaround time 2 days. Copy fee: $1.00 for first page, $.50 each add'l. Certification fee: $.50. Fee payee: Clerk of District Court. Personal checks accepted. Prepayment required.

Justice Court PO Box 2906, Jackson, WY 83001; 307-733-7713; Fax: 307-733-8694. Hours: 8AM-5PM (MST). *Misdemeanor, Civil Actions Under $3,000, Small Claims.*

Civil Records: Access: Mail, in person. Only the court performs in person searches; visitors may not. Search fee: $5.00 per name. Required to search: name, years to search. Civil cases indexed by defendant, plaintiff. Civil records on docket books back to 1979. Actual files 5 years.

Criminal Records: Access: Mail, in person. Only the court performs in person searches; visitors may not. Search fee: $5.00 per name. Required to search: name, years to search, DOB. Criminal records citations on computer from 1991. No citation record older than 5 years. On docket books and files back to 1979.

General Information: No juvenile, sexual or PD released. SASE requested. Turnaround time 3-4 days (longer for pre-1992 criminal records). Copy fee: $1.00 for first page, $.50 each add'l. Certification fee: No certification fee. Fee payee: Teton County Justice Court. Personal checks accepted. Prepayment is required.

Uinta County

3rd Judicial District Court PO Drawer 1906, Evanston, WY 82931; 307-783-0320/0401; Fax: 307-783-0400. Hours: 8AM-5PM (MST). *Felony, Civil Actions Over $7,000, Probate.*

www.uintacounty.com

Civil Records: Access: Phone, fax, mail, in person. Both court and visitors may perform in person searches. Search fee: $5.00 per name. Required to search: name, years to search; also helpful: address. Civil cases indexed by defendant, plaintiff. Civil records on microfiche from the late 1800s.

Criminal Records: Access: Phone, fax, mail, in person. Both court and visitors may perform in person searches. Search fee: $5.00 per name. Required to search: name, years to search; also helpful: address, DOB, SSN. Criminal records on microfiche since 1938.

General Information: Signed release necessary on confidential cases. SASE required. Turnaround time 1 day. Fax notes: Fee to fax results is $1.00 per page. Copy fee: $.25 per page; $.50 if civil. First page is always double price. Certification fee: $.50 per seal. Fee payee: Clerk of District Court. Personal checks accepted. Will bill copy & fax fees.

Uinta Circuit Court 225 9th St, 2nd Fl, Evanston, WY 82931; 307-789-2471; Fax: 307-789-5062. Hours: 8AM-5PM (MST). *Misdemeanor, Civil Actions Under $7,000, Eviction, Small Claims.*

Civil Records: Access: Mail, in person. Only the court performs in person searches; visitors may not. Search fee: $5.00 per name. Required to search: name, years to search; also helpful: address. Civil cases indexed by defendant. Civil records on computer from 1994, prior on card index.

Criminal Records: Access: Mail, in person. Only the court performs in person searches; visitors may not. Search fee: $5.00 per name. Required to search: name, years to search; also helpful: address, DOB, SSN. Criminal records on computer since 1989, prior on index cards.

General Information: No juvenile records released. SASE requested. Turnaround time 1 week. Copy fee: $1.00 for first page, $.50 each add'l. Certification fee: No certification fee. Fee payee: Uinta County Court. Only cashiers checks and money orders accepted. Out of state checks not accepted. Prepayment is required.

Washakie County

5th Judicial District Court PO Box 862, Worland, WY 82401; 307-347-4821; Fax: 307-347-4325. Hours: 8AM-5PM (MST). *Felony, Civil Actions Over $3,000, Probate.*

Civil Records: Access: Phone, fax, mail, in person. Both court and visitors may perform in person searches. Search fee: $5.00 per name. Required to search: name; also helpful: years to search, address. Civil cases indexed by defendant. Civil records on computer from 1985, prior on file index.

Criminal Records: Access: Phone, fax, mail, in person. Both court and visitors may perform in person searches. Search fee: $5.00 per name. Required to search: name; also helpful: years to search, address, DOB, SSN. Criminal records on computer from 1985, prior on file index.

General Information: No juvenile, sexual or PD released. SASE required. Turnaround time same day when possible. Fax notes: $1.00 per page. Copy fee:

$1.00 for first page, $.50 each add'l. Certification fee: $.50. Fee payee: Clerk of Court. Personal checks accepted. Prepayment is required.

Justice Court PO Box 927, Worland, WY 82401; 307-347-2702; Fax: 307-347-4325. Hours: 8AM-5PM (MST). *Misdemeanor, Civil Actions Under $3,000, Small Claims.*

Civil Records: Access: Mail, fax, in person. Search fee: $5.00 per name. Required to search: name, years to search. Civil cases indexed by defendant. Civil records on computer since 1988, on card index from late 1970, prior archived.

Criminal Records: Access: Mail, fax, in person. Both court and visitors may perform in person searches. Search fee: $5.00 per name. Required to search: name, years to search, DOB; also helpful: SSN. Criminal records on computer since 1988, on card index from late 1970, prior archived.

General Information: No juvenile or PD released; criminal only. SASE not required. Turnaround time same day. Copy fee: $.25 per document. Certification fee: No certification fee. Fee payee: Justice Court. Personal checks accepted. Prepayment is required.

Weston County

6th Judicial District Court 1 W Main, Newcastle, WY 82701; 307-746-4778; Fax: 307-746-4778. Hours: 8AM-5PM (MST). *Felony, Civil Actions Over $3,000, Probate.*

Civil Records: Access: Phone, fax, mail, in person. Both court and visitors may perform in person searches. No search fee. Required to search: name; also helpful: years to search, address. Civil cases indexed by defendant, plaintiff. Civil records on card index from 1800s; computerized back to 1999.

Criminal Records: Access: Phone, fax, mail, in person. Both court and visitors may perform in person searches. No search fee. Required to search: name; also helpful: years to search, address, DOB, SSN. Criminal records on card index from 1800s; computerized back to 1999.

General Information: No juvenile, sexual or PD released. SASE required. Turnaround time same day. Fax notes: Fee to fax results is $2.00 per document. Copy fee: $1.00 for first page, $.50 each add'l. Certification fee: $.50. Fee payee: Clerk of District Court. Personal checks accepted. Prepayment required.

Justice Court 6 W Warwick, Newcastle, WY 82701; 307-746-3547; Fax: 307-746-3558. Hours: 8:30AM-4:30PM (MST). *Misdemeanor, Civil Actions Under $3,000, Small Claims.*

Civil Records: Access: Mail, fax, in person. Only the court performs in person searches; visitors may not. Search fee: $5.00. Required to search: name, years to search; also helpful: address. Civil cases indexed by defendant. Civil records in files and on computer since.

Criminal Records: Access: Fax, mail, in person. Only the court performs in person searches; visitors may not. Search fee: $5.00. Required to search: name, years to search, offense, date of offense; also helpful: address, DOB, SSN. Criminal records in files and on computer since.

General Information: Turnaround time is minimum 1 day. Fax notes: No fee to fax results. Copy fee: $1.00 first page; $.50 each add'l. Certification fee: $1.00. Fee payee: Justice Court. Business checks accepted.

Wyoming Recording Offices

ORGANIZATION   23 counties, 23 recording offices. The recording officer is County Clerk. The entire state is in the Mountain Time Zone (MST).

REAL ESTATE RECORDS   County Clerks will not perform real estate searches. Copy fees are usually $1.00 per page, and certification fees are usually $2.00 per document. The Assessor maintains property tax records.

UCC RECORDS   Since 07/1/2001, all filings have been centralized at the state. Prior, financing statements were usually filed with the County Clerk and accounts receivable and farm products require dula filing at the state level as well. All recording offices will perform UCC searches. Use search request form UCC-11. Searches fees are usually $10.00 per debtor name. Copy fees vary.

TAX LIEN RECORDS   Federal tax liens on personal property of businesses are filed with the Secretary of State. Other federal and all state tax liens are filed with the County Clerk. Most counties will perform tax lien searches. Search fees are usually $10.00 per name.

Albany County

County Clerk, 525 Grand Ave. Room 202, Laramie, WY 82070. County Clerk, R/E and UCC Recording 307-721-2547 UCC Recording: 307-721-2541; Fax 307-721-2544.
Will search UCC records. Will not search real estate records. **Other Phone Numbers:** Assessor 307-721-2511; Treasurer 307-721-2502; Appraiser/Auditor 307-721-2511; Elections 307-721-2546; Vital Records 307-777-7591.

Big Horn County

County Clerk, P.O. Box 31, Basin, WY 82410. County Clerk, R/E and UCC Recording 307-568-2357; Fax 307-568-9375. www.state.wy.us
Will search UCC records. Will not search real estate records. **Other Phone Numbers:** Assessor 307-568-2547; Treasurer 307-568-2578; Elections 307-568-2357; Vital Records 307-568-2357.

Campbell County

County Clerk, P.O. Box 3010, Gillette, WY 82717-3010. 307-682-7285; Fax 307-687-6455.
Will search UCC records. UCC search includes tax liens. Will not search real estate records. **Other Phone Numbers:** Assessor 307-682-7266.

Carbon County

County Clerk, 415 West Pine, P.O. Box 6, Courthouse, Rawlins, WY 82301. 307-328-2679 R/E Recording: 307-328-2677 UCC Recording: 307-328-2667; Fax 307-328-2690.
Will search UCC records. Will not search real estate records. **Other Phone Numbers:** Assessor 307-328-2637; Treasurer 307-328-2662; Elections 307-328-2650; Vital Records 307-328-2670.

Converse County

County Clerk, P.O. Drawer 990, Douglas, WY 82633-0990. 307-358-2244; Fax 307-358-4065.
Will search UCC records. Will not search real estate records. **Other Phone Numbers:** Assessor 307-358-2741; Treasurer 307-358-3120; Elections 307-358-2244.

Crook County

County Clerk, P.O. Box 37, Sundance, WY 82729. 307-283-1323; Fax 307-283-1091.
Will search UCC records. Will not search real estate records. **Other Phone Numbers:** Assessor 307-283-2054; Treasurer 307-283-1244.

Fremont County

County Clerk, 450 N. 2nd Street, Courthouse - Room 220, Lander, WY 82520. 307-332-2405; Fax 307-332-1132.
Will search UCC records. **Other Phone Numbers:** Assessor 307-332-1188; Treasurer 307-322-1105.

Goshen County

County Clerk, P.O. Box 160, Torrington, WY 82240. County Clerk, R/E and UCC Recording 307-532-4051; Fax 307-532-7375. www.state.wy.us
Will search UCC records. Will not search real estate records. **Other Phone Numbers:** Assessor 307-532-2349; Treasurer 307-532-5151; Elections 307-532-4051.

Hot Springs County

County Clerk, 415 Arapahoe Street, Courthouse, Thermopolis, WY 82443-2783. 307-864-3515; Fax 307-864-5116.
Will search UCC records. Will not search real estate records. **Other Phone Numbers:** Assessor 307-864-3414; Treasurer 307-864-3616.

Johnson County

County Clerk, 76 North Main Street, Buffalo, WY 82834. 307-684-7272; Fax 307-684-2708.
Will search UCC records. Will not search real estate records. **Other Phone Numbers:** Assessor 307-684-7392; Treasurer 307-684-7302.

Laramie County

County Clerk, P.O. Box 608, Cheyenne, WY 82003. 307-633-4351; Fax 307-633-4240.
Will search UCC records. Will not search real estate records. **Other Phone Numbers:** Assessor 307-638-4307; Treasurer 307-638-4225.

Lincoln County

County Clerk, P.O. Box 670, Kemmerer, WY 83101-0670. 307-877-9056; Fax 307-877-3101.
Will search UCC records. Will not search real estate records. **Other Phone Numbers:** Assessor 307-877-9056.

Natrona County

County Clerk, P.O. Box 863, Casper, WY 82602. 307-235-9206; Fax 307-235-9367.
Will search UCC records. Will not search real estate records. **Other Phone Numbers:** Assessor 307-235-9444; Treasurer 307-235-9370.

Niobrara County

County Clerk, P.O. Box 420, Lusk, WY 82225. County Clerk, R/E and UCC Recording 307-334-2211; Fax 307-334-3013.
Will search UCC records. Will not search real estate records. **Other Phone Numbers:** Assessor 307-334-3201; Treasurer 307-334-2432; Elections 307-334-2211; Vital Records 307-334-2211.

Park County

County Clerk, Courthouse, 1002 Sheridan Ave., Cody, WY 82414. 307-527-8600; Fax 307-527-8626.
Will search UCC records. Will not search real estate records. **Other Phone Numbers:** Assessor 307-587-2204 x212; Treasurer 307-527-7163.

Platte County

County Clerk, P.O. Drawer 728, Wheatland, WY 82201. 307-322-2315 R/E Recording: 307-322-1306; Fax 307-322-2245.
Will search UCC records. Will not search real estate records. **Other Phone Numbers:** Assessor 307-322-2858; Treasurer 307-322-2092; Elections 307-322-1307.

Sheridan County

County Clerk, 224 South Main Street, Suite B-2, Sheridan, WY 82801-9998. 307-674-2500; Fax 307-674-2529.
Will search UCC records. Will not search real estate records. **Other Phone Numbers:** Assessor 307-674-2535; Treasurer 307-674-6522.

Sublette County

County Clerk, P.O. Box 250, Pinedale, WY 82941-0250. County Clerk, R/E and UCC Recording 307-367-4372; Fax 307-367-6396.
Will search UCC records. Will not search real estate records. **Other Phone Numbers:** Assessor 307-367-4374; Treasurer 307-367-4373; Elections 307-367-4372.

Sweetwater County

County Clerk, P.O. Box 730, Green River, WY 82935. County Clerk, R/E and UCC Recording 307-872-6409 UCC Recording: 307-872-6407; Fax 307-872-6337. http://www.co.sweet.wy.us/clerk
Will search UCC records. Will not search real estate records. **Other Phone Numbers:** Assessor 307-872-6416; Treasurer 307-872-6389; Appraiser/Auditor 307-872-6400.

Teton County

County Clerk, P.O. Box 1727, Jackson, WY 83001. 307-733-4433 R/E Recording: 307-733-4430; Fax 307-739-8681. http://www.tetonwyo.org/clerk/

Will search UCC records. Will not search real estate records. **Online Access:** Real Estate, Liens, Recordings. Online access to the clerks database of scanned images is available free at http://www.tetonwyo.org/clerk/query. Search for complete documents back to 7/1996; partial documents back to 4/1991. **Other Phone Numbers:** Assessor 307-733-4960; Treasurer 307-733-4770; Elections 307-733-7733; Vital Records 307-777-7591.

Uinta County

County Clerk, P.O. Box 810, Evanston, WY 82931. 307-783-0308 R/E Recording: 307-783-0304; Fax 307-783-0511.

Will search UCC records. UCC search includes tax liens. Will not search real estate records. **Other Phone Numbers:** Assessor 307-789-1780 x338; Treasurer 307-783-0333; Elections 307-783-0423; Vital Records 307-777-7591.

Washakie County

County Clerk, Box 260, Worland, WY 82401-0260. 307-347-3131; Fax 307-347-9366.

Will search UCC records. UCC search includes tax liens if requested. Will not search real estate records. **Other Phone Numbers:** Assessor 307-347-2831.

Weston County

County Clerk, One West Main, Newcastle, WY 82701. 307-746-4744; Fax 307-746-9505.

Will search UCC records. UCC search includes tax liens. Will not search real estate records. **Other Phone Numbers:** Assessor 307-746-4633.

Wyoming County Locator

You will usually be able to find the city name in the City/County Cross Reference below. In that case, it is a simple matter to determine the county from the cross reference. However, only the official US Postal Service city names are included in this index. There are an additional 40,000 place names that people use in their addresses. Therefore, we have also included a ZIP/City Cross Reference immediately following the City/County Cross Reference.

If you know the ZIP Code but the city name does not appear in the City/County Cross Reference index, look up the ZIP Code in the ZIP/City Cross Reference, find the city name, then look up the city name in the City/County Cross Reference. For example, you want to know the county for an address of Menands, NY 12204. There is no "Menands" in the City/County Cross Reference. The ZIP/City Cross Reference shows that ZIP Codes 12201-12288 are for the city of Albany. Looking back in the City/County Cross Reference, Albany is in Albany County.

City/County Cross Reference

AFTON Lincoln
ALADDIN Crook
ALBIN Laramie
ALCOVA Natrona
ALPINE Lincoln
ALVA Crook
ARAPAHOE Fremont
ARMINTO Natrona
ARVADA (82831) Sheridan(40),
  Campbell(31), Johnson(29)
AUBURN Lincoln
BAGGS Carbon
BAIROIL Sweetwater
BANNER (82832) Sheridan(82),
  Johnson(18)
BASIN Big Horn
BEDFORD Lincoln
BEULAH Crook
BIG HORN Sheridan
BIG PINEY Sublette
BILL Converse
BONDURANT Sublette
BOSLER Albany
BOULDER Sublette
BUFFALO Johnson
BUFORD Albany
BURLINGTON (82411) Washakie(73), Big
  Horn(28)
BURNS Laramie
BYRON Big Horn
CARLILE Crook
CARPENTER Laramie
CASPER Carbon
CASPER Natrona
CENTENNIAL Albany
CHEYENNE Laramie
CHUGWATER (82210) Platte(85),
  Goshen(15)
CLEARMONT Sheridan
CODY Park
COKEVILLE Lincoln
CORA Sublette
COWLEY Big Horn
CROWHEART (82512) Sweetwater(75),
  Fremont(25)
DANIEL Sublette
DAYTON Sheridan
DEAVER (82421) Big Horn(83), Park(17)
DEVILS TOWER Crook

DIAMONDVILLE Lincoln
DIXON Carbon
DOUGLAS Converse
DUBOIS Fremont
EDGERTON Natrona
ELK MOUNTAIN Carbon
EMBLEM Big Horn
ENCAMPMENT Carbon
ETNA (83118) Lincoln(96), Sweetwater(4)
EVANSTON Uinta
EVANSVILLE Natrona
FAIRVIEW Lincoln
FARSON Sweetwater
FE WARREN AFB Laramie
FORT BRIDGER Uinta
FORT LARAMIE Goshen
FORT WASHAKIE Fremont
FOUR CORNERS Weston
FRANNIE Park
FREEDOM Lincoln
FRONTIER Lincoln
GARRETT Albany
GILLETTE Campbell
GLENDO (82213) Platte(98), Converse(2)
GLENROCK Converse
GRANGER Sweetwater
GRANITE CANON Laramie
GREEN RIVER Sweetwater
GREYBULL Big Horn
GROVER Lincoln
GUERNSEY Platte
HAMILTON DOME Hot Springs
HANNA Carbon
HARTVILLE Platte
HAWK SPRINGS Goshen
HILAND Natrona
HILLSDALE Laramie
HORSE CREEK Laramie
HUDSON Fremont
HULETT Crook
HUNTLEY Goshen
HYATTVILLE Big Horn
IRON MOUNTAIN Laramie
JACKSON Teton
JAY EM Goshen
JEFFREY CITY Fremont
JELM Albany
KAYCEE (82639) Johnson(94), Natrona(7)
KEELINE Niobrara

KELLY Teton
KEMMERER Lincoln
KINNEAR Fremont
KIRBY Hot Springs
LA BARGE Lincoln
LAGRANGE Goshen
LANCE CREEK Niobrara
LANDER Fremont
LARAMIE Albany
LEITER Sheridan
LINCH Johnson
LINGLE Goshen
LITTLE AMERICA Sweetwater
LONETREE Uinta
LOST SPRINGS (82224) Converse(80),
  Niobrara(20)
LOVELL Big Horn
LUSK Niobrara
LYMAN Uinta
LYSITE Fremont
MANDERSON (82432) Park(78), Big
  Horn(22)
MANVILLE Niobrara
MC FADDEN Carbon
MC KINNON Sweetwater
MEDICINE BOW (82329) Carbon(67),
  Albany(33)
MEETEETSE Park
MERIDEN Laramie
MIDWEST Natrona
MILLS Natrona
MOORCROFT (82721) Crook(56),
  Campbell(44)
MOOSE Teton
MORAN Teton
MOUNTAIN VIEW Uinta
NATRONA Natrona
NEWCASTLE Weston
NODE Niobrara
OPAL Lincoln
OSAGE Weston
OSHOTO (82724) Crook(78), Campbell(22)
OTTO (82434) Washakie(67), Big Horn(33)
PARKMAN Sheridan
PAVILLION Fremont
PINE BLUFFS Laramie
PINEDALE Sublette
POINT OF ROCKS Sweetwater
POWDER RIVER Natrona

POWELL Park
RALSTON Park
RANCHESTER Sheridan
RAWLINS Carbon
RECLUSE Campbell
RELIANCE Sweetwater
RIVERTON Fremont
ROBERTSON Uinta
ROCK RIVER (82083) Albany(50),
  Carbon(50)
ROCK SPRINGS Sweetwater
ROZET Campbell
SADDLESTRING Johnson
SAINT STEPHENS Fremont
SARATOGA Carbon
SAVERY Carbon
SHAWNEE Converse
SHELL Big Horn
SHERIDAN Sheridan
SHOSHONI Fremont
SINCLAIR Carbon
SMOOT Lincoln
STORY Sheridan
SUNDANCE (82729) Crook(97), Weston(3)
SUPERIOR Sweetwater
TEN SLEEP Washakie
TETON VILLAGE Teton
THAYNE (83127) Lincoln(77),
  Sweetwater(23)
THERMOPOLIS Hot Springs
TIE SIDING Albany
TORRINGTON Goshen
UPTON (82730) Weston(90), Crook(10)
VAN TASSELL Niobrara
VETERAN Goshen
WALCOTT Carbon
WAMSUTTER Sweetwater
WAPITI Park
WESTON (82731) Campbell(96), Crook(4)
WHEATLAND (82201) Platte(98),
  Albany(2)
WILSON Teton
WOLF Sheridan
WORLAND Washakie
WRIGHT Campbell
WYARNO Sheridan
YELLOWSTONE NATIONAL PARK Park
YODER Goshen

ZIP/City Cross Reference

82001-82003	CHEYENNE	82059-82059	GRANITE CANON	82190-82190	YELLOWSTONE	82219-82219	JAY EM
82005-82005	FE WARREN AFB	82060-82060	HILLSDALE		NATIONAL PARK	82221-82221	LAGRANGE
82006-82010	CHEYENNE	82061-82061	HORSE CREEK	82201-82201	WHEATLAND	82222-82222	LANCE CREEK
82050-82050	ALBIN	82063-82063	JELM	82210-82210	CHUGWATER	82223-82223	LINGLE
82051-82051	BOSLER	82070-82073	LARAMIE	82212-82212	FORT LARAMIE	82224-82224	LOST SPRINGS
82052-82052	BUFORD	82081-82081	MERIDEN	82213-82213	GLENDO	82225-82225	LUSK
82053-82053	BURNS	82082-82082	PINE BLUFFS	82214-82214	GUERNSEY	82227-82227	MANVILLE
82054-82054	CARPENTER	82083-82083	ROCK RIVER	82215-82215	HARTVILLE	82229-82229	SHAWNEE
82055-82055	CENTENNIAL	82084-82084	TIE SIDING	82217-82217	HAWK SPRINGS	82240-82240	TORRINGTON
82058-82058	GARRETT			82218-82218	HUNTLEY	82242-82242	VAN TASSELL

82243-82243	VETERAN	82442-82442	TEN SLEEP	82715-82715	FOUR CORNERS	82936-82936	LONETREE
82244-82244	YODER	82443-82443	THERMOPOLIS	82716-82718	GILLETTE	82937-82937	LYMAN
82301-82301	RAWLINS	82450-82450	WAPITI	82720-82720	HULETT	82938-82938	MC KINNON
82310-82310	JEFFREY CITY	82501-82501	RIVERTON	82721-82721	MOORCROFT	82939-82939	MOUNTAIN VIEW
82321-82321	BAGGS	82510-82510	ARAPAHOE	82723-82723	OSAGE	82941-82941	PINEDALE
82322-82322	BAIROIL	82512-82512	CROWHEART	82725-82725	RECLUSE	82942-82942	POINT OF ROCKS
82323-82323	DIXON	82513-82513	DUBOIS	82727-82727	ROZET	82943-82943	RELIANCE
82324-82324	ELK MOUNTAIN	82514-82514	FORT WASHAKIE	82729-82729	SUNDANCE	82944-82944	ROBERTSON
82325-82325	ENCAMPMENT	82515-82515	HUDSON	82730-82730	UPTON	82945-82945	SUPERIOR
82327-82327	HANNA	82516-82516	KINNEAR	82731-82731	WESTON	83001-83002	JACKSON
82329-82329	MEDICINE BOW	82520-82520	LANDER	82732-82732	WRIGHT	83011-83011	KELLY
82331-82331	SARATOGA	82523-82523	PAVILLION	82801-82801	SHERIDAN	83012-83012	MOOSE
82332-82332	SAVERY	82524-82524	SAINT STEPHENS	82831-82831	ARVADA	83013-83013	MORAN
82334-82334	SINCLAIR	82601-82615	CASPER	82832-82832	BANNER	83014-83014	WILSON
82335-82335	WALCOTT	82620-82620	ALCOVA	82833-82833	BIG HORN	83025-83025	TETON VILLAGE
82336-82336	WAMSUTTER	82630-82630	ARMINTO	82834-82834	BUFFALO	83101-83101	KEMMERER
82401-82401	WORLAND	82631-82631	BILL	82835-82835	CLEARMONT	83110-83110	AFTON
82410-82410	BASIN	82633-82633	DOUGLAS	82836-82836	DAYTON	83111-83111	AUBURN
82411-82411	BURLINGTON	82635-82635	EDGERTON	82837-82837	LEITER	83112-83112	BEDFORD
82412-82412	BYRON	82636-82636	EVANSVILLE	82838-82838	PARKMAN	83113-83113	BIG PINEY
82414-82414	CODY	82637-82637	GLENROCK	82839-82839	RANCHESTER	83114-83114	COKEVILLE
82420-82420	COWLEY	82638-82638	HILAND	82840-82840	SADDLESTRING	83115-83115	DANIEL
82421-82421	DEAVER	82639-82639	KAYCEE	82842-82842	STORY	83116-83116	DIAMONDVILLE
82422-82422	EMBLEM	82640-82640	LINCH	82844-82844	WOLF	83118-83118	ETNA
82423-82423	FRANNIE	82642-82642	LYSITE	82845-82845	WYARNO	83119-83119	FAIRVIEW
82426-82426	GREYBULL	82643-82643	MIDWEST	82901-82902	ROCK SPRINGS	83120-83120	FREEDOM
82427-82427	HAMILTON DOME	82644-82644	MILLS	82922-82922	BONDURANT	83121-83121	FRONTIER
82428-82428	HYATTVILLE	82646-82646	NATRONA	82923-82923	BOULDER	83122-83122	GROVER
82430-82430	KIRBY	82648-82648	POWDER RIVER	82925-82925	CORA	83123-83123	LA BARGE
82431-82431	LOVELL	82649-82649	SHOSHONI	82926-82926	ROCK SPRINGS	83124-83124	OPAL
82432-82432	MANDERSON	82701-82701	NEWCASTLE	82929-82929	LITTLE AMERICA	83126-83126	SMOOT
82433-82433	MEETEETSE	82710-82710	ALADDIN	82930-82931	EVANSTON	83127-83127	THAYNE
82434-82434	OTTO	82711-82711	ALVA	82932-82932	FARSON	83128-83128	ALPINE
82435-82435	POWELL	82712-82712	BEULAH	82933-82933	FORT BRIDGER	83422-83422	DRIGGS
82440-82440	RALSTON	82713-82713	CARLILE	82934-82934	GRANGER		
82441-82441	SHELL	82714-82714	DEVILS TOWER	82935-82935	GREEN RIVER		

Additional Titles and Information

The 2002 MVR Book

ISBN # 1-879792-65-6   Pub. 1/02   Pages 320   Price $19.95

Description: The national reference detailing — in practical terms — the privacy restrictions, access procedures, regulations, and database systems of all state-held driver and vehicle records. For all states.

The 2002 MVR Decoder Digest

ISBN # 1-879792-66-4   Pub 1/02   Pages 336   Price $19.95

Description: The companion to *The MVR Book*. Translates the codes and abbreviations of violations and licensing categories that appear on motor vehicle records. For all states.

The Public Record Research System – CD-ROM

Updated Semi-annually, License fee of $119.00 includes one update.

Description: In-depth reference to over 26,000 sources of public records and public information. Extensive profiles of federal agencies, county recorder offices, state and county courts, state agencies, accredited post-secondary institutions, occupational licensing and business registration agencies, Public Record Retrieval members. Also includes a place name — county — ZIP Code cross reference. Extremely thorough.

The Public Record Research System – WEB (PRRS-Web)

Updated weekly, Annual subscription fee of $119.00.

Same comprehensive data as the CD-ROM conveniently available on the Internet.

Free demo and registration available at www.publicrecordsources.com.

BRB Publications, Inc.

PO Box 27869
Tempe, AZ 85285-7869
Phone: 800-929-3811
Fax: 1-800-929-4981

To order or for more information visit www.brbpub.com.

Notes:

Notes: